S0-CFU-284

Internal Revenue Code

Income Taxes §§ 1-860G

As of November 12, 2010

Volume 1

CCH Editorial Staff Publication

This publication is designed to provide accurate and authoritative information in regard to the subject matter covered. It is sold with the understanding that the publisher is not engaged in rendering legal, accounting, or other professional service. If legal advice or other expert assistance is required, the services of a competent professional person should be sought.

ISBN 978-0-8080-2485-9 (Set)
ISBN 978-0-8080-2477-4 (Volume 1)
ISBN 978-0-8080-2481-1 (Volume 2)

4025 W. Peterson Ave.
Chicago, IL 60646-6085
1 800 248 3248
www.CCHGroup.com

Printed in the United States of America

About This Edition

This edition of the Internal Revenue Code reflects all of the tax law changes to date. These include changes made by an Act to clarify the health care provided by the Secretary of Veterans Affairs that constitutes minimum essential coverage (P.L. 111-173), the Preservation of Access to Care for Medicare Beneficiaries and Pension Relief Act of 2010 (P.L. 111-192), the Airport and Airway Extension Act of 2010, Part II (P.L. 111-197), the Homebuyer Assistance and Improvement Act of 2010 (P.L. 111-198), the Dodd-Frank Wall Street Reform and Consumer Protection Act (P.L. 111-203), the Airline Safety and Federal Aviation Administration Extension Act of 2010 (P.L. 111-216), an Act to modernize the air traffic control system, improve the safety, reliability, and availability of transportation by air in the United States, provide for modernization of the air traffic control system, reauthorize the Federal Aviation Administration, and for other purposes (P.L. 111-226), the Firearms Excise Tax Improvement Act of 2010 (P.L. 111-237), the Creating Small Business Jobs Act of 2010 (P.L. 111-240), and the Airport and Airway Extension Act of 2010, Part III (P.L. 111-249).

Reproduced here is the complete Internal Revenue Code dealing with income, estate, gift, employment and excise taxes, along with the procedural and administrative provisions. Current texts of the statutes are presented, and a history of each tax Code section (or subsection, if appropriate) is provided in the amendment notes. The amendment notes specifically identify the changes made by prior Acts and serve as a means of reconstructing the former text of a Code section or subsection if reference to prior law is required.

The topical index located at the end of both volumes reflects all of the matters covered in this edition.

This publication is compiled from the 2010 CCH STANDARD FEDERAL TAX REPORTER.

November 2010

Table of Contents

Page

VOLUME ONE

VOLUME TWO

TAX RATES

TAX RATE SCHEDULES FOR 2010

SCHEDULE X: Single Individuals

Taxable Income Over	But Not Over	Pay	+	% on Excess	of the amount over—
$ 0—	$ 8,375	$ 0		10 %	$ 0
8,375—	34,000	837.50		15	8,375
34,000—	82,400	4,681.25		25	34,000
82,400—	171,850	16,781.25		28	82,400
171,850—	373,650	41,827.25		33	171,850
373,650—	. . . .	108,421.25		35	373,650

Example: Bob White, a single individual, has income of $70,000 in 2010. He has no dependents and claims a standard deduction because he lacks sufficient itemized deductions. His taxable income is $60,650 ($70,000 less $5,700 standard deduction less $3,650 personal exemption). His tax is $11,343.75 ($4,681.25 plus $6,662.25 (25% of the $26,650 excess of taxable income over $34,000)).

SCHEDULE Y-1: Married Individuals Filing Jointly and Surviving Spouses

Taxable Income Over	But Not Over	Pay	+	% on Excess	of the amount over—
$ 0—	$ 16,750	$ 0		10 %	$ 0
16,750—	68,000	1,675		15	16,750
68,000—	137,300	9,362.50		25	68,000
137,300—	209,250	26,687.50		28	137,300
209,250—	373,650	46,833.50		33	209,250
373,650—	. . . .	101,085.50		35	373,650

Example: Brenda and Steve Jones have a combined income of $136,000 in 2010. They have two dependent children and itemized deductions totalling $16,000. They file a joint return. Their taxable income is $105,400 ($136,000 less $16,000 itemized deductions less $14,600 for four personal exemptions). Their tax is $18,712.50 ($9,362.50 plus $9,350 (25% of the $37,400 excess of taxable income over $68,000)).

SCHEDULE Y-2: Married Individuals Filing Separate Returns

Taxable Income Over	But Not Over	Pay	+ % on Excess	of the amount over—
$ 0—	$ 8,375	$ 0	10 %	$ 0
8,375—	34,000	837.50	15	8,375
34,000—	68,650	4,681.25	25	34,000
68,650—	104,625	13,343.75	28	68,650
104,625—	186,825	23,416.75	33	104,625
186,825—	....	50,542.75	35	186,825

SCHEDULE Z: Heads of Households

Taxable Income Over	But Not Over	Pay	+ % on Excess	of the amount over—
$ 0—	$ 11,950	$ 0	10 %	$ 0
11,950—	45,550	1,195	15	11,950
45,550—	117,650	6,235	25	45,550
117,650—	190,550	24,260	28	117,650
190,550—	373,650	44,672	33	190,550
373,650—	....	105,095	35	373,650

INCOME TAX RATE SCHEDULE FOR USE BY ESTATES AND NONGRANTOR TRUSTS

Taxable Income Over	But Not Over	Pay	+ % on Excess	of the amount over—
$ 0—	$ 2,300	$ 0	15 %	$ 0
2,300—	5,350	345	25	2,300
5,350—	8,200	1,107.50	28	5,350
8,200—	11,200	1,905.50	33	8,200
11,200—	....	2,895.50	35	11,200

CORPORATION INCOME TAX RATES FOR 2010

Corporations

Taxable Income Over	But Not Over	Pay	+	% on Excess	of the amount over—
$ 0—	$ 50,000	$ 0		15 %	$ 0
50,000—	75,000	7,500		25	50,000
75,000—	100,000	13,750		34	75,000
100,000—	335,000	22,250		39	100,000
335,000—	10,000,000	113,900		34	335,000
10,000,000—	15,000,000	3,400,000		35	10,000,000
15,000,000—	18,333,333	5,150,000		38	15,000,000
18,333,333—	....			35	0

Personal Service Corporations

Taxable income of certain personal service corporations is taxed at a flat rate of 35%.

Controlled Group of Corporations

A controlled group of corporations is subject to the same rates as those listed above as though the group was one corporation.

Personal Holding Companies

In addition to the regular corporate income taxes, a special tax is imposed on any personal holding company. The additional tax is 15% of undistributed personal holding company income.

Regulated Investment Companies

The regular corporate tax rates apply to a company's taxable income. In the case of regulated investment companies, the corporate tax rates apply to investment company taxable income.

Accumulated Earnings Tax

A tax (payable in addition to the regular tax payable by a corporation) is imposed at the rate of 15% on accumulated taxable income exceeding the $250,000 minimum accumulated earnings credit ($150,000 for personal service corporations engaged in the field of health, law, engineering, architecture, accounting, actuarial science, performing arts, or consulting).

Foreign Corporations

The U.S. source income of a foreign corporation that is not effectively connected with a U.S. trade or business is taxed at a flat 30-percent rate or lower treaty rate. Domestic corporate rates apply to the income of a foreign corporation that is effectively connected with a U.S. trade or business.

Real Estate Investment Trusts

A real estate investment trust that distributes at least 90 percent of its taxable income for the tax year is taxed at the same rates that apply to regular corporations.

ESTATE AND GIFT TAXES

Legislative Changes

The Economic Growth and Tax Relief Reconciliation Act of 2001 (P.L. 107-16) (EGTRRA) made dramatic changes to the estate, gift, and generation-skipping transfer (GST) taxes. Effective for estates of decedents dying after December 31, 2009, the estate and GST taxes were repealed, but the gift tax remained effective, at a maximum tax rate of 35%. However, under the "sunset" provision in EGTRRA, the law reverts to pre-2001 Act law in 2011, absent congressional action to the contrary. Thus, under current law for decedents dying or gifts made after December 31, 2010, the applicable exclusion amount is $1 million, and the GST tax exemption amount is $1 million, adjusted for inflation in 2011. In addition, the basic rate structure that applied to decedents dying and gifts made prior to January 1, 2002, will again apply to decedents dying and gifts made after December 31, 2010.

Although several proposals addressing the transfer tax system have been floated, as we go to press, Congress has not yet taken definitive action.

Computation of Taxes

Estate Taxes. The estate tax was repealed with respect to estates of decedents dying after December 31, 2009, but before January 1, 2011. Estate taxes for decedents dying after 1976 are computed by applying the unified transfer tax rate schedule to the aggregate of cumulative lifetime transfers and transfers at death and subtracting the gift taxes payable on the lifetime transfers. Under current law, changes made by the 2001 Act to the estate tax are set to expire in 2011. Unless Congress acts to the contrary, the estates of decedents dying after December 31, 2010, will be subject to a maximum tax rate of 55 % and $1 million applicable exclusion amount.

Gift Taxes. Taxable gifts made after December 31, 2009, but before January 1, 2011, are subject to a maximum tax rate of 35% and exclusion amount of $1 million. Gift taxes for gifts made after 1976 are computed by applying the unified transfer tax rate schedule to cumulative lifetime taxable transfers and subtracting the taxes paid for prior taxable periods. There is an annual exclusion of $13,000 per donee for gifts made in 2010 and 2011 with an annual maximum of $26,000 per donee applicable to spouses who utilize gift-splitting (these amounts are indexed for inflation).

Generation-Skipping Transfer Taxes. Like the estate tax, the tax on generation-skipping transfers was repealed for 2010. Under current law, GST taxes for transfers made after December 31, 2010, are computed by multiplying the taxable amount of a taxable distribution, taxable termination, or direct skip by the applicable rate. The applicable rate is the product of the maximum federal estate tax rate of 55% and the inclusion ratio with respect to the transfer.

Applicable Credit Amount

For estates of decedents dying, and gifts made before January 1, 2002, and after December 31, 2010, the applicable credit amount (called the unified credit before 1998) applies to both estate and gift taxes. The applicable credit amount was subtracted from the taxpayer's estate or gift tax liability. Under EGTRRA, the estate tax applicable exclusion amount was gradually increased to $3.5 million in 2009, before full repeal in 2010. However, unlike the estate tax applicable exclusion amount, the gift tax applicable exclusion amount (after being increased to $1 million for gifts made after 2001) was not be gradually increased in the years leading up to estate tax repeal.

Under current law, the estate and GST taxes were repealed for decedents dying after December 31, 2009. However, in order to comply with the Congressional Budget Act of 1974, EGTRRA provides that all provisions of, and amendments made by, EGTRRA will not apply to estates of decedents dying, gifts made, or generation-skipping transfers after December 31, 2010. Thus, unless Congress acts, the Internal Revenue Code will, thereafter, be applied and administered as if the changes to the transfer taxes made by EGTRRA had not been enacted, and the estate and gift tax applicable exclusion amounts will be reunified at $1 million.

Estate Tax Applicable Credit Amount

Year	*Applicable Credit Amount*	*Applicable Exclusion Amount*
1987 through 1997	$192,800	$600,000
1998	202,050	625,000
1999	211,300	650,000
2000 and 2001	220,550	675,000
2002 and 2003	345,800	1,000,000
2004 and 2005	555,800	1,500,000
2006 through 2008	780,800	2,000,000
2009	1,455,800	3,500,000
2010	Estate Tax Repealed	
2011[1]	345,800	1,000,000

Gift Tax Applicable Credit Amount

Year	*Applicable Credit Amount*	*Applicable Exclusion Amount*
1987 through 1997	$192,800	$600,000
1998	202,050	625,000
1999	211,300	650,000
2000 and 2001	220,550	675,000
2001 through 2009	345,800	1,000,000
2010[2]	330,800	1,000,000
2011[3]	345,800	1,000,000

Unified Transfer Tax Rate Schedule

The unified rate schedule, with adjustments noted at the bottom of the schedule that reflect the phased-in reduction of the maximum transfer tax rates, is to apply to estates of decedents dying, and gifts made, after 1983.[4]

---

[1] Under the sunset provisions of the 2001 Act, the applicable credit amount and applicable exclusion amount for estate and gift taxes are to remain at $345,800 and $1,000,000 indefinitely, and the GST exemption amount will be $1,000,000, indexed for inflation.

[2] The gift tax applicable credit amount drops to $330,800 in 2010 (even though the applicable exclusion amount stays the same, at $1,000,000) because the maximum gift tax rate that applies to transfers made after December 31, 2009, is 35%.

[3] See footnote 1.

[4] Under EGTRRA, the estate and generation-skipping transfer taxes are repealed for decedents dying after and generation-skipping transfers made after December 31, 2009, but before January 1, 2011. The gift tax has not been repealed.

Column A	Column B	Column C	Column D
Taxable amount over	Taxable amount not over	Tax on amount in column A	Rate of tax on excess over amount in column A
			Percent
$ 0	$ 10,000	$ 0	18
10,000	20,000	1,800	20
20,000	40,000	3,800	22
40,000	60,000	8,200	24
60,000	80,000	13,000	26
80,000	100,000	18,200	28
100,000	150,000	23,800	30
150,000	250,000	38,800	32
250,000	500,000	70,800	34
500,000	750,000	155,800	37
750,000	1,000,000	248,300	39
1,000,000	1,250,000	345,800	41
1,250,000	1,500,000	448,300	43
1,500,000	2,000,000	555,800	45
2,000,000	2,500,000	780,800	49
2,500,000	3,000,000	1,025,800	53
3,000,000	....	1,290,800	55

Reductions in Maximum Rates. For decedents dying after December 31, 2001, and before January 1, 2011, certain reductions in the rates were made. For 2002, the 53% and 55% tax brackets were replaced with a 50% maximum tax bracket. In addition, the five-percent surtax that applied to transfers in excess of $10 million was repealed for estates of decedents dying and gifts made after December 31, 2001. For 2003, the maximum tax bracket was 49%. For 2004, the maximum tax bracket was 48%. For 2005, the maximum tax bracket was 47%. For 2006, the maximum tax bracket was 46%. For 2007, 2008, and 2009, the maximum tax bracket was 45%. In 2010, the estate tax repeal became effective. However, in 2010, the gift tax remained in effect, with a maximum rate of 35% for taxable amounts over $500,000; the applicable exclusion amount was $1 million.

Surtax Reinstated. Under current law, the five-percent surtax that applied to estates and taxable gifts larger than $10 million and up to $17,184,000 prior to 2002 will be reinstated for estates of decedents dying and taxable gifts made after December 31, 2010.

Nonresident Aliens

For the estates of decedents dying after November 10, 1988, estate and gift tax rates presently applicable to U.S. citizens are applicable to the estates of nonresident aliens. For the applicable rates, see the section above. With the repeal of the estate tax, the estate tax as it applies to nonresident aliens was also repealed, effective for the estates of decedents dying after December 31, 2009, but before January 1, 2011.

Where permitted by treaty, the estate of a nonresident alien is allowed the unified credit available to a U.S. citizen multiplied by the percentage of the decedent's gross estate situated in the United States. In other cases, a unified credit of $13,000 is allowed. The estate of a resident of a U.S. possession is entitled to a unified credit equal to the greater of (1) $13,000, or (2) $46,800 multiplied by the percentage of the decedent's gross estate situated in the United States.

Credit for State Death Taxes

Under current law, the table below is used to calculate the amount of the credit available for state death taxes paid with respect to property included in a decedent's gross estate for decedents dying before January 1, 2005, and after December 31, 2010. Prior to the effective date of the repeal of this credit, the credit was reduced in three stepped percentages (noted on the following page), beginning with decedents dying in 2002.

State Death Tax Credit Table

Adjusted Taxable Estate[1] At least	But less than	Credit =	+ %	Of Excess Over
$ 0	$ 40,000	$ 0	0	$ 0
40,000	90,000	0	0.8	40,000
90,000	140,000	400	1.6	90,000
140,000	240,000	1,200	2.4	140,000
240,000	440,000	3,600	3.2	240,000
440,000	640,000	10,000	4.0	440,000
640,000	840,000	18,000	4.8	640,000
840,000	1,040,000	27,600	5.6	840,000
1,040,000	1,540,000	38,800	6.4	1,040,000
1,540,000	2,040,000	70,800	7.2	1,540,000
2,040,000	2,540,000	106,800	8.0	2,040,000
2,540,000	3,040,000	146,800	8.8	2,540,000
3,040,000	3,540,000	190,800	9.6	3,040,000
3,540,000	4,040,000	238,800	10.4	3,540,000
4,040,000	5,040,000	290,800	11.2	4,040,000
5,040,000	6,040,000	402,800	12.0	5,040,000
6,040,000	7,040,000	522,800	12.8	6,040,000
7,040,000	8,040,000	650,800	13.6	7,040,000
8,040,000	9,040,000	786,800	14.4	8,040,000
9,040,000	10,040,000	930,800	15.2	9,040,000
10,040,000	....	1,082,800	16.0	10,040,000

[1] The adjusted taxable estate is the taxable estate reduced by $60,000.

The amount of the credit for state death taxes, as computed with reference to the above table, was reduced by the following percentages:

Decedent Dying In	*Reduction %*
2002	25
2003	50
2004	75

For the estates of decedents dying after December 31, 2004, and before January 1, 2011, the state death tax credit was replaced with a deduction from the gross estate for state death taxes actually paid. Assuming no legislative activity to the contrary, the state death tax deduction will be eliminated and the state tax credit will be restored for the estates of decedents dying after December 31, 2010.

OTHER TAXES

Self-Employment (SECA) Taxes

A tax of 15.3% is imposed on net earnings from self-employment. For both 2010 and 2011, this rate consists of a 12.4% component for old-age, survivors, and disability insurance (OASDI) and a 2.9% component for medicare. The OASDI rate (12.4%) applies to net earnings within the OASDI earnings base, which is $106,800 for 2010 and 2011. There is no limit on the amount of earnings subject to the 2.9% medicare portion of the tax.

Social Security (FICA) Taxes

Social Security, Hospital Insurance. For the calendar years 2010 and 2011, a combined tax rate of 7.65% (6.2% for old-age, survivors, and disability insurance (OASDI) and 1.45% for hospital insurance (medicare)) is imposed on both employer and employee. The OASDI rate (6.2%) applies to wages within the OASDI wage base, which is $106,800 for 2010 and 2011. All wages are subject to the 1.45% medicare rate.

Medicare Payments. Medicare Part B premiums ($110.50 per month for 2010 and $115.40 for 2011) qualify as deductible medical expenses.

Unemployment Compensation. A tax rate of 6.2% is imposed on the first $7,000 of wages paid to a covered employee by an employer who employs one or more persons in covered employment in each of 20 days in a year, each day being in a different week, or who has a payroll for covered employment of at least $1,500 in a calendar quarter in the current or preceding calendar year. Because employers are allowed credits against the 6.2% FUTA rate through participation in state unemployment insurance laws, the net FUTA rate actually paid by most employers is 0.8%, except when credit reductions are in effect in a state. For wages paid in 2010 and and the first six months of 2011, the FUTA rate remains at 6.2%; a previously scheduled reduction of 0.2% has been postponed until the second half of 2011.

Railroad Retirement Tax. For 2010 and 2011, a tier I tax rate of 7.65% (consisting of a medicare portion (1.45%) and an OASDI portion (6.2%)) applies to employers and employees. The OASDI portion (6.2%) is imposed on annual compensation within a compensation base of $106,800 for 2010 and 2011. There is no limit on the amount of earnings subject to the 1.45% medicare portion of the tax. For 2010, a tier II tax of 3.9% for employees and 12.1% for employers is imposed on annual compensation within a compensation base of $79,200. As we go to press, the 2011 tier II tax rates have not been published.

Excise Taxes

FUELS

Gasoline (Code Sec. 4081)

Gasoline (per gallon) . . . 18.4 ¢

Diesel fuel and kerosene (Code Secs. 4041 and 4081)

Diesel fuel (except if used on a farm for farming purposes) (per gallon) . . . 24.4 ¢

Diesel fuel for use in trains (per gallon) . . . 0.1 ¢

Diesel-water fuel emulsions . . . 19.8 ¢

Kerosene (except if used in a farm for farming purposes) (per gallon) . . . 24.4 ¢

Special fuels (Code Secs. 4041 and 4042)

Special motor fuel (per gallon) . . . 18.4 ¢

Alcohol sold but not used as fuel (per gallon) (ethanol) . . . 45¢

Alcohol sold, but not used as, fuel (per gallon) (methanol) . . . 60¢ credit, if at least 190 proof

Alcohol sold but not used as fuel, if benefited from the small ethanol producers credit (per gallon) . . . 55¢

Alcohol sold but not used as fuel (per gallon) (ethanol) . . . 33.33¢

Alcohol sold but not used as fuel (per gallon) (methanol) . . . 45¢ credit, if at least 150, but less than 190 proof

Alcohol sold but not used as fuel, if benefited from the small ethanol producers credit (per gallon) . . . 43.33¢

Cellulosic biofuel that is not alcohol (per gallon) . . . $1.01 credit

Cellulosic biofuel that is alcohol (other than ethanol) (per gallon) . . . 41¢ credit

B-100 (100 percent biodiesel) (per gallon) . . . 24.4¢

Biodiesel and biodiesel mixtures (per gallon) . . . $1.00 credit until 2010

Agri-biodiesel (per gallon) . . . $1.00 credit until 2010

Agri-biodiesel if benefited from the small agri-biodiesel producer credit (per gallon) . . . $1.10 credit until 2010

Renewable diesel and renewable diesel mixtures (per gallon) . . . $1.00 credit until 2010

Alternative fuel (as defined in Code Sec. 6426(d)(2)) (per gallon) . . . 50¢ credit until 2010, except for liquefied hydrogen

Any liquid fuel derived from coal (including peat) through the Fischer-Tropsch process (per gallon) . . . 24.4 ¢

Liquefied petroleum gas . . . 18.3 ¢

Liquid fuel derived from biomass (per gallon) . . . 24.4 ¢

Liquid gas derived from biomass (per gallon) . . . 18.4 ¢

Liquefied natural gas (per gallon) . . . 24.3 ¢

Qualified ethanol produced from coal (per gallon) . . . 18.4¢

Qualified methanol produced from coal (per gallon) . . . 18.4¢

Partially exempt ethanol produced from natural gas (per gallon) . . . 11.4 ¢

Partially exempt methanol produced from natural gas (per gallon) . . . 9.25 ¢

Compressed natural gas (per energy equivalent of a gallon of gasoline) . . . 18.3 ¢

Inland waterways fuel use tax (per gallon) . . . 20.1 ¢

Aviation fuels (Code Sec. 4081)

Kerosene used in commercial aviation (when removed from a refinery or terminal directly into the fuel tank of an aircraft) (per gallon) . . . 4.4 ¢

Kerosene used in noncommercial aviation (when removed from a refinery or terminal directly into the fuel tank of an aircraft) (per gallon) . . . . . 21.9 ¢
Noncommercial aviation gasoline (per gallon) . . . . . 19.4 ¢
Crude oil (Code Sec. 4611)
Crude oil (per barrel) . . . . . 8¢

HEAVY TRUCKS, TRAILERS

Trucks and trailers (Code Sec. 4051)
Truck chassis or body (suitable for use with a vehicle in excess of 33,000 lbs. gross vehicle weight) . . . . . 12% of retail price
Trailer and semitrailer chassis or body (suitable for use with a trailer or semitrailer in excess of 26,000 lbs. gross vehicle weight) . . . . . 12% of retail price
Parts and accessories installed on taxable vehicles within six months after being placed in service (when cost of parts or accessories exceeds $1,000) . . . . . 12% of retail price

HIGHWAY-TYPE TIRES

Tires for highway vehicles (Code Sec. 4071)
Tires with load capacity over 3,500 lbs. . . . . . 9.45¢ for each 10 pounds of tire load capacity in excess of 3,500 pounds
Biasply tires . . . . . 4.725¢ for each 10 pounds of tire load capacity in excess of 3,500 pounds
Super single tires . . . . . 4.725¢ for each 10 pounds of tire load capacity in excess of 3,500 pounds

GAS GUZZLER TAX

Fuel economy rating (Code Sec. 4064)
Mileage ratings per gallon of at least 22.5 . . . . . $ 0
Mileage ratings per gallon of at least 21.5 but less than 22.5 1,000
Mileage ratings per gallon of at least 20.5 but less than 21.5 1,300
Mileage ratings per gallon of at least 19.5 but less than 20.5 1,700
Mileage ratings per gallon of at least 18.5 but less than 19.5 2,100
Mileage ratings per gallon of at least 17.5 but less than 18.5 2,600
Mileage ratings per gallon of at least 16.5 but less than 17.5 3,000
Mileage ratings per gallon of at least 15.5 but less than 16.5 3,700
Mileage ratings per gallon of at least 14.5 but less than 15.5 4,500
Mileage ratings per gallon of at least 13.5 but less than 14.5 5,400
Mileage ratings per gallon of at least 12.5 but less than 13.5 6,400
Mileage ratings per gallon of less than 12.5 7,700

FACILITIES AND SERVICES

Communications (Code Sec. 4251)
Local telephone and teletypewriter service . . . . . 3% of amount paid
Transportation of persons by air (Code Secs. 4261(a) and 4261(c))
Domestic passenger tickets: from 1/1/2010 through 12/31/2010 . . . . . 7.5% of amount paid plus $3.70 per each flight segment (excepting segments to or from rural airports) ($8.10 per departure from Alaska or Hawaii)

International passenger tickets (per person): from 1/1/2010 through 12/31/2010 . . . . . $16.10 for each arrival and departure
Transportation of property by air (Code Sec. 4271)
Air freight waybill . . . . . 6.25% of amount paid
Transportation by water (Code Secs. 4461, 4462, and 4471)
Persons $3.00
Port use tax on imports (harbor maintenance tax) . . . . . 0.125% of cargo value

ALCOHOL TAXES

Distilled spirits (Code Sec. 5001)
Distilled spirits (per gallon) $13.50
Beer (Code Sec. 5051)
Beer (per barrel—31 gallons or less) . . . . . $18.00, generally
First 60,000 barrels removed during calendar year by U.S. brewer producing not more than 2 million barrels during year (per barrel) $7.00
Wines (Code Sec. 5041)
Not more than 14 percent alcohol (per gallon) $1.07
More than 14 to 21 percent alcohol (per gallon) $1.57
More than 21 to 24 percent alcohol (per gallon) $3.15
More than 24 percent alcohol (per proof gallon) $13.50
Artificially carbonated wines (per gallon) $3.30
Champagne and other sparkling wines (per gallon) $3.40
Hard cider derived from apples containing at least ½ of 1% and less than 7% alcohol (per gallon) $0.226

TOBACCO TAXES (effective April 1, 2009)

Cigars (Code Sec. 5701(a))
Cigars weighing not more than 3 lbs. (per thousand) $50.33
Cigars weighing more than 3 lbs. . . . . . 52.75% of sale price, not to exceed 40.26 cents per cigar
Cigarettes (Code Sec. 5701(b))
Cigarettes weighing not more than 3 lbs. (per thousand) . . . . . $50.33 (over $1 per pack)
Cigarettes weighing more than 3 lbs. (per thousand) $105.69
Cigarette papers and tubes (Code Secs. 5701(c) and 5701(d))
Cigarette papers (per fifty) . . . . . 3.15¢
Cigarette tubes (per fifty) . . . . . 6.30¢
Tobacco products (Code Secs. 5701(e), 5701(f) and 5701(g))
Snuff (per pound) $1.51
Chewing tobacco (per pound) . . . . . 50.33¢
Pipe tobacco (per pound) . . . . . $2.8311 cents
Roll-your-own tobacco (per pound) $24.78

WAGERING TAXES

Certain wagers (Code Sec. 4401)
State authorized wagers placed with bookmakers and lottery operators . . . . . 0.25% of wager amount
Unauthorized wagers placed with bookmakers and lottery operators . . . . . 2% of wager amount
Occupational taxes (Code Sec. 4411)
License fee on state authorized persons accepting wagers (per year, per person) $50
License fee on unauthorized persons accepting wagers (per year, per person) $500

HIGHWAY MOTOR VEHICLE TAX

Use tax (Code Sec. 4481)
Vehicles of less than 55,000 lbs. . . . . . No tax
Vehicles of 55,000 lbs.—75,000 lbs. . . . . . $100 per year + $22 for each 1,000 lbs. (or fraction thereof) over 55,000 lbs.
Vehicles over 75,000 lbs. . . . . . $550 per year

FIREARMS

Transfer taxes (Code Secs. 5811 and 5845(e))	
Generally (per transfer)	$200
Certain concealable weapons (per transfer)	$5
Occupational taxes (Code Sec. 5801)	
Importer	$1,000 per year
Manufacturers	$1,000 per year
Small importers and manufacturers (gross receipts under $500,000 per year)	$500 per year
Dealers	$500 per year
Regular firearms and ammunition (Code Sec. 4181)	
Pistols and revolvers	10% of sales price
Firearms other than pistols and revolvers	11% of sales price
Ammunition (shells and cartridges)	11% of sales price

RECREATIONAL EQUIPMENT

Sporting goods (Code Sec. 4161)	
Sport fishing equipment	10% of sales price
Fishing tackle boxes	3% of sales price
Electric outboard motors	3% of sales price
Bows with a peak draw weight of at least 30 lbs	11% of sales price
Arrow shafts from 1/1/2010 through 12/31/2011	45¢ per shaft
Quivers, broadheads and points	11% of sales price

ELECTIVE COSMETIC MEDICAL PROCEDURES

Tanning services (Code Sec. 5000B)	
Indoor tanning services	10% of amount paid, starting July 1, 2010

ENVIRONMENTAL TAXES

Oils and chemicals (Code Secs. 4611, 4661, 4681, and 4682)	
Crude oil (per barrel)	8¢
Chemicals	Various rates
Ozone-depleting chemicals	Various rates

FOREIGN INSURANCE POLICIES

Foreign insurance policies (Code Sec. 4371)	
Casualty insurance and indemnity, fidelity and surety bonds (per dollar of premium paid)	4¢
Life insurance, sickness and accident policies, and annuity contracts (per dollar of premium paid)	1¢
Reinsurance of taxable contracts above (per dollar of premium paid)	1¢

VACCINES

Vaccines tax (Code Sec. 4131)	
Any vaccine containing diptheria toxoid, tetanus toxoid, pertussis bacteria, extracted or partial cell bacteria, specific pertussis antigens, or polio virus	75¢ per dose
Any vaccine against measles, mumps, rubella, hepatitis A, hepatitis B, chicken pox, rotavirus gastroenteritis, or the human papillomavirus	75¢ per dose
Any conjugate vaccine against streptococcus pneumoniae	75¢ per dose
Any trivalent vaccine against influenza	75¢ per dose
Any HIB vaccine	75¢ per dose
Any meningococcal vaccine	75¢ per dose

COAL

Black Lung Disability Trust Fund taxes (Code Sec. 4121)	
From underground mines (per ton sold)	$1.10, not to exceed 4.4% of selling price
From surface mines (per ton sold)	55¢, not to exceed 4.4% of selling price

2011 AMOUNTS FOR INFLATION-ADJUSTED TAX ITEMS

The 2011 inflation-adjusted amounts applicable to estate, gift, and generation-skipping transfer taxes are listed below. Rev. Proc. 2010-40, I.R.B. 2010-46, which sets forth the amounts, applies to any of the following transactions or events occurring in calendar year 2011.

Personal Exemption; Standard Deduction

Rev. Proc. 2010-40 does not provide adjustments to several items that affect most individual returns, among them the personal exemption and the standard deduction. It is possible that Congress may act to preserve some of the tax benefits scheduled to expire at the end of 2010.

Special Use Valuation

If an estate of a decedent who dies in 2011 (assuming the estate tax is not repealed) elects to use the Code Sec. 2032A special use valuation method for qualified real property, the aggregate decrease in the property's value may not exceed $1,020,000.

Annual Exclusion for Gifts

The Code Sec. 2503(b) annual gift tax exclusion is $13,000 for 2011. In addition, the first $136,000 of gifts (other than gifts of future interests in property) to a noncitizen spouse in 2011 are not included in the year's total amount of taxable gifts under Code Sec. 2503 and Code Sec. 2523(i)(2).

Attorney Fee Awards

The attorney-fee award limitation under Code Sec. 7430 is $180 per hour for fees incurred in 2011.

Sunset of the 2001 & 2003 Tax Relief Acts

On May 26, 2001, Congress passed the Economic Growth and Tax Relief Reconciliation Act of 2001 (EGTRRA). The Act included cuts in marginal income tax rates, marriage penalty relief, the phase-out and ultimate repeal of the estate tax, along with numerous other tax cuts and incentives. Many of these provisions included phase-in rules and prospective effective dates. In addition, each provision in EGTRRA was subject to a sunset provision. Specifically, Act Section 901 of EGTRRA provides:

SEC. 901. SUNSET OF PROVISIONS OF ACT.

(a) In General.—*All provisions of, and amendments made by, this Act shall not apply—*

(1) to taxable, plan, or limitation years beginning after December 31, 2010, or

(2) in the case of title V, to estates of decedents dying, gifts made, or generation skipping transfers, after December 31, 2010.

(b) Application of Certain Laws.—*The Internal Revenue Code of 1986 and the Employee Retirement Income Security Act of 1974 shall be applied and administered to years, estates, gifts, and transfers described in subsection (a) as if the provisions and amendments described in subsection (a) had never been enacted.*

The Committee Report (S. Rep. No. 107-30) explained that the sunset provision was necessary to comply with Section 313 of the Congressional Budget Act of 1974 (2 U.S.C. 644). Section 313, which was permanently incorporated into the Budget Act in 1990, is commonly referred to as the "Byrd rule" and was named after its principal sponsor, Senator Robert C. Byrd.

The Byrd rule generally permits Senators to raise a point of order on the Senate floor against "extraneous" provisions contained in a reconciliation bill. If the point of order is sustained by the presiding officer (and not overturned if the ruling is appealed by any Senator), the offending provision is stricken unless 3/5 of the Senate membership vote to waive the rule with respect to that provision (i.e., 60 Senators if no seats are vacant).

One of the six types of extraneous provisions is a provision that would increase net outlays or decrease revenues for a fiscal year beyond those covered by the reconciliation measure. The sunset language in EGTRRA prevented any provision in the Act from violating this particular rule and becoming subject to a "point of order."

On May 28, 2003, the Jobs and Growth Tax Relief Reconciliation Act of 2003 (JGTRRA) was signed into law. JGTRRA accelerated many of the tax cuts set in motion under EGTRRA. However, like EGTRRA, the provisions contained in JGTRRA were subject to sunset rules. In fact, JGTRRA contained two sunset rules.

Provisions in Title I of JGTRRA are generally subject to the sunset in EGTRRA and will not apply to tax years beginning after December 31, 2010. Provisions in Title III of JGTRRA are subject to a separate sunset under which such provisions will not apply to tax years beginning after December 31, 2008.

Specifically, Act Section 107 of JGTRRA provides:

SEC. 107. APPLICATION OF EGTRRA SUNSET TO THIS TITLE.

Each amendment made by this title [Title I] shall be subject to title IX of the Economic Growth and Tax Relief Reconciliation Act of 2001 to the same extent and in the same manner as the provision of such Act to which such amendment relates.

Specifically, Act Section 303 of JGTRRA provides:

SEC. 303. SUNSET OF TITLE.

All provisions of, and amendments made by, this title [Title III] shall not apply to taxable years beginning after December 31, 2010, and the Internal Revenue Code of 1986 shall be applied and administered to such years as if such provisions and amendments had never been enacted.

The Tax Increase Prevention and Reconciliation Act of 2005 (TIPRA), which was signed into law on May 17, 2006, extended the sunset date applicable to JGTRRA, Title III. Pursuant to TIPRA, the provisions and amendments of Title III of JGTRRA will not apply to tax years beginning after December 31, 2010. Specifically, Act Sec. 102 of TIPRA states:

SEC. 102. CAPITAL GAINS AND DIVIDENDS RATES.

Section 303 of the Jobs and Growth Tax Relief Reconciliation Act of 2003 is amended by striking "December 31, 2008" and inserting "December 31, 2010".

For all in EGTRRA and JGTRRA that is subject to sunset at the end of 2010, it is also important to remember that, in the decade since EGTRRA and JGTRRA were passed, many of those provisions have been made permanent or extended by other legislation. A number of provisions in EGTRRA and JGTRRA were scheduled to expire even before the sunset. Most of these have been extended by other legislation, some of the provisions, such as AMT relief and the above-the-line deduction for tuition and fees, joined the list of the regularly expiring provisions that Congress deals with every year.

Provisions from EGTRRA involving contribution and benefit limits for IRAs, defined contribution plans, and defined benefit plans; catch-up contributions; roll-over provisions; deemed IRA provisions; qualified retirement planning services; the start-up credit; the saver's credit; ESOP rules; and top-heavy rules were all permanently extended by the Pension Protection Act of 2006. Provisions from the EGTRRA involving qualified tuition and 529 plans were also permanently extended by the Pension Protection Act of 2006. The EGTRRA exclusion for restitution payments to victims of Nazi persecution has been made permanent by other legislation. The sunset of enhancements to the adoption credit and the exclusion for employer-provided adoption assistance is now scheduled for 2012 rather than 2011, thanks to a provision in the 2010 health care reform legislation. Other provisions, such as those involving extended filing deadlines for Presidentially-declared disasters, have also been made obsolete by subsequent legislation.

However, for the provisions not extended or made permanent by other legislation, the EGTRRA and JGTRRA sunsets are scheduled to occur at the end of 2010 absent congressional action. Although numerous options have been expressed on how to deal with the sunset provisions and the tax provisions impacted, there is no agreement in Congress on a path going forward.

The language of the sunset provision states that the sunset will be applied as if EGTRRA and JGTRRA were never enacted. How this will work in practice raises a number of issues *and creates an added level of complexity within the Internal Revenue Code. This publication includes several features to more clearly identify those provisions of the Code impacted by these sunsets. Caution lines highlight each provision impacted by the EGTRRA and/or JGTRRA sunsets. The amendment notes following each provision also provide the history of the amendments made by EGTRRA and JGTRRA, as well as any amendments made by other legislation, and the text of the sunset language.*

The language of the sunset provision states that the sunset will be applied as if EGTRRA and JGTRRA were never enacted. How this will work in practice raises a number of issues and creates an added level of complexity within the Internal Revenue Code. This publication includes several features to more clearly identify those provisions of the Code impacted by these sunsets. Caution lines highlight each provision impacted by the EGTRRA and/or JGTRRA sunsets. The amendment notes following each provision also provide the history of the amendments made by EGTRRA and JGTRRA, as well as any amendments made by other legislation and the text of the sunset language.

TABLE OF CONTENTS

UNITED STATES CODE

TITLE 26—INTERNAL REVENUE CODE

SUBTITLE A—INCOME TAXES

Chapter 1—Normal Taxes and Surtaxes

SUBCHAPTER A. DETERMINATION OF TAX LIABILITY

PART I—TAX ON INDIVIDUALS

PART II—TAX ON CORPORATIONS

PART III—CHANGES IN RATES DURING A TAXABLE YEAR

PART IV—CREDITS AGAINST TAX

Subpart A—Nonrefundable Personal Credits

Subpart B—Other Credits

Subpart C—Refundable Credits

Subpart D—Business Related Credits

Subpart E—Rules for Computing Investment Credit

Subpart F—Rules for Computing Work Opportunity Credit

Subpart G—Credit Against Regular Tax for Prior Year Minimum Tax Liability

Subpart H—Nonrefundable Credit to Holders of Certain Bonds

Subpart I—Qualified Tax Credit Bonds

Subpart J—Build America Bonds

PART V—TAX SURCHARGE—[REPEALED]

PART VI—ALTERNATIVE MINIMUM TAX

PART VII—ENVIRONMENTAL TAX

PART VIII—SUPPLEMENTAL MEDICARE PREMIUM—[REPEALED]

SUBCHAPTER B. COMPUTATION OF TAXABLE INCOME

PART I—DEFINITION OF GROSS INCOME, ADJUSTED GROSS INCOME, TAXABLE INCOME, ETC.

PART II—ITEMS SPECIFICALLY INCLUDED IN GROSS INCOME

PART III—ITEMS SPECIFICALLY EXCLUDED FROM GROSS INCOME

Part X—Terminal Railroad Corporations and Their Shareholders

Part XI—Special Rules Relating to Corporate Preference Items

SUBCHAPTER C. CORPORATE DISTRIBUTIONS AND ADJUSTMENTS

Part I—Distributions by Corporations

Subpart A—Effects on Recipients

Subpart B—Effects on Corporation

Subpart C—Definitions; Constructive Ownership of Stock

PART II—CORPORATE LIQUIDATIONS

Subpart A—Effects on Recipients

Subpart B—Effects on Corporation

Subpart C—Collapsible Corporations—[Repealed]

Subpart D—Definition and Special Rule

PART III—CORPORATE ORGANIZATIONS AND REORGANIZATIONS

Subpart A—Corporate Organizations

Subpart B—Effects on Shareholders and Security Holders

Subpart C—Effects on Corporations

Subpart D—Special Rule; Definitions

PART IV—INSOLVENCY REORGANIZATIONS—[REPEALED]

PART V—CARRYOVERS

PART VI—TREATMENT OF CERTAIN CORPORATE INTERESTS AS STOCK OR INDEBTEDNESS

PART VII—MISCELLANEOUS CORPORATE PROVISIONS—[REPEALED]

SUBCHAPTER D. DEFERRED COMPENSATION, ETC.

PART I—PENSION, PROFIT-SHARING, STOCK BONUS PLANS, ETC.

Subpart A—General Rule

PART II—INCOME IN RESPECT OF DECEDENTS

SUBCHAPTER K. PARTNERS AND PARTNERSHIPS

PART I—DETERMINATION OF TAX LIABILITY

PART II—CONTRIBUTIONS, DISTRIBUTIONS, AND TRANSFERS

Subpart A—Contributions to a Partnership

Subpart B—Distributions by a Partnership

Subpart C—Transfers of Interests in a Partnership

Subpart D—Provisions Common to Other Subparts

PART III—DEFINITIONS

PART IV—SPECIAL RULES FOR ELECTING LARGE PARTNERSHIPS

SUBCHAPTER L. INSURANCE COMPANIES

PART I—LIFE INSURANCE COMPANIES

Subpart A—Tax Imposed

Subpart B—Life Insurance Gross Income

Subpart C—Life Insurance Deductions

Subpart D—Accounting, Allocation, and Foreign Provisions

Subpart E—Definitions and Special Rules

PART II—OTHER INSURANCE COMPANIES

PART III—PROVISIONS OF GENERAL APPLICATION

SUBCHAPTER M. REGULATED INVESTMENT COMPANIES AND REAL ESTATE INVESTMENT TRUSTS

PART I—REGULATED INVESTMENT COMPANIES

PART II—REAL ESTATE INVESTMENT TRUSTS

PART III—PROVISIONS WHICH APPLY TO BOTH REGULATED INVESTMENT COMPANIES AND REAL ESTATE INVESTMENT TRUSTS

PART IV—REAL ESTATE MORTGAGE INVESTMENT CONDUITS

PART V—FINANCIAL ASSET SECURITIZATION INVESTMENT TRUSTS—[REPEALED]

SUBCHAPTER N. TAX BASED ON INCOME FROM SOURCES WITHIN OR WITHOUT THE UNITED STATES

PART I—SOURCE RULES AND OTHER GENERAL RULES RELATING TO FOREIGN INCOME

PART II—NONRESIDENT ALIENS AND FOREIGN CORPORATIONS

Subpart A—Nonresident Alien Individuals

Subpart B—Foreign Corporations

Subpart C—Tax on Gross Transportation Income

Subpart D—Miscellaneous Provisions

Part III—Income From Sources Without the United States

Subpart A—Foreign Tax Credit

Subpart B—Earned Income of Citizens or Residents of United States

Subpart C—Taxation of Foreign Sales Corporations—[Repealed]

Subpart D—Possessions of the United States

Subpart E—Qualifying Foreign Trade Income—[Repealed]

Subpart F—Controlled Foreign Corporations

Subpart G—Export Trade Corporations

Subpart H—Income of Certain Nonresident United States Citizens Subject to Foreign Community Property Laws—[Repealed]

Subpart I—Admissibility of Documentation Maintained in Foreign Countries

Subpart J—Foreign Currency Transactions

PART V—SPECIAL RULES FOR BONDS AND OTHER DEBT INSTRUMENTS

Subpart A—Original Issue Discount

Subpart B—Market Discount on Bonds

Subpart C—Discount on Short-Term Obligations

Subpart D—Miscellaneous Provisions

PART VI—TREATMENT OF CERTAIN PASSIVE FOREIGN INVESTMENT COMPANIES

Subpart A—Interest on Tax Deferral

Subpart B—Treatment of Qualified Electing Funds

Subpart C—Election of Mark to Market for Marketable Stock

Subpart D—General Provisions

SUBCHAPTER Q. READJUSTMENT OF TAX BETWEEN YEARS AND SPECIAL LIMITATIONS

PART I—INCOME AVERAGING

PART II—MITIGATION OF EFFECT OF LIMITATIONS AND OTHER PROVISIONS

PART III—INVOLUNTARY LIQUIDATION AND REPLACEMENT OF LIFO INVENTORIES—[REPEALED]

PART IV—WAR LOSS RECOVERIES—[REPEALED]

PART V—CLAIM OF RIGHT

PART VI—MAXIMUM RATE ON PERSONAL SERVICE INCOME—[REPEALED]

PART VII—RECOVERIES OF FOREIGN EXPROPRIATION LOSSES

SUBCHAPTER R. ELECTION TO DETERMINE CORPORATE TAX ON CERTAIN INTERNATIONAL SHIPPING ACTIVITIES USING PER TON RATE

SUBCHAPTER S. TAX TREATMENT OF S CORPORATIONS AND THEIR SHAREHOLDERS

PART I—IN GENERAL

PART II—TAX TREATMENT OF SHAREHOLDERS

PART III—SPECIAL RULES

PART IV—DEFINITIONS; MISCELLANEOUS

SUBCHAPTER T. COOPERATIVES AND THEIR PATRONS

PART I—TAX TREATMENT OF COOPERATIVES

PART II—TAX TREATMENT BY PATRONS OF PATRONAGE DIVIDENDS AND PER-UNIT RETAIN ALLOCATIONS

PART III—DEFINITIONS; SPECIAL RULES

SUBCHAPTER U. DESIGNATION AND TREATMENT OF EMPOWERMENT ZONES, ENTERPRISE COMMUNITIES, AND RURAL DEVELOPMENT INVESTMENT AREAS

PART I—DESIGNATION

PART II—TAX-EXEMPT FACILITY BONDS FOR EMPOWERMENT ZONES AND ENTERPRISE COMMUNITIES

PART III—ADDITIONAL INCENTIVES FOR EMPOWERMENT ZONES

Subpart A—Empowerment Zone Employment Credit

Chapter 2A—Unearned Income Medicare Contribution

Chapter 3—Withholding of Tax on Nonresident Aliens and Foreign Corporations

SUBCHAPTER A. NONRESIDENT ALIENS AND FOREIGN CORPORATIONS

SUBCHAPTER B. APPLICATION OF WITHHOLDING PROVISIONS

Chapter 4—Taxes To Enforce Reporting on Certain Foreign Accounts

Chapter 4—Rules Applicable to Recovery of Excessive Profits on Government Contracts—[Repealed]

Chapter 5—Tax on Transfers to Avoid Income Tax—[Repealed]

Chapter 6—Consolidated Returns

SUBCHAPTER A. RETURNS AND PAYMENT OF TAX

SUBCHAPTER B. RELATED RULES

PART I—IN GENERAL

PART II—CERTAIN CONTROLLED CORPORATIONS

SUBTITLE B—ESTATE AND GIFT TAXES

Chapter 11—Estate Tax

SUBCHAPTER A. ESTATES OF CITIZENS OR RESIDENTS

PART I—TAX IMPOSED

PART II—CREDITS AGAINST TAX

PART III—GROSS ESTATE

PART IV—TAXABLE ESTATE

SUBCHAPTER B. ESTATES OF NONRESIDENTS NOT CITIZENS

SUBCHAPTER C. MISCELLANEOUS

Chapter 12—Gift Tax

SUBCHAPTER A. DETERMINATION OF TAX LIABILITY

SUBCHAPTER B. TRANSFERS

SUBCHAPTER C. DEDUCTIONS

Chapter 13—Tax on Generation-Skipping Transfers

SUBCHAPTER A. TAX IMPOSED

SUBCHAPTER B. GENERATION-SKIPPING TRANSFERS

SUBCHAPTER C. TAXABLE AMOUNT

SUBCHAPTER D. GST EXEMPTION

SUBCHAPTER E. APPLICABLE RATE; INCLUSION RATIO

SUBCHAPTER F. OTHER DEFINITIONS AND SPECIAL RULES

SUBCHAPTER G. ADMINISTRATION

Chapter 14—Special Valuation Rules

Chapter 15—Gifts and Bequests From Expatriates

SUBTITLE C—EMPLOYMENT TAXES

Chapter 21—Federal Insurance Contributions Act

SUBCHAPTER A. TAX ON EMPLOYEES

SUBCHAPTER B. TAX ON EMPLOYERS

SUBCHAPTER C. GENERAL PROVISIONS

Chapter 22—Railroad Retirement Tax Act

SUBCHAPTER A. TAX ON EMPLOYEES

SUBCHAPTER B. TAX ON EMPLOYEE REPRESENTATIVES

SUBCHAPTER C. TAX ON EMPLOYERS

SUBCHAPTER D. GENERAL PROVISIONS

SUBCHAPTER E. TIER 2 TAX RATE DETERMINATION

Chapter 23—Federal Unemployment Tax Act

Chapter 23A—Railroad Unemployment Repayment Tax

Chapter 24—Collection of Income Tax at Source on Wages

SUBCHAPTER A. WITHHOLDING FROM WAGES

SUBCHAPTER B. WITHHOLDING FROM INTEREST AND DIVIDENDS—[REPEALED]

Chapter 25—General Provisions Relating to Employment Taxes

SUBTITLE D—MISCELLANEOUS EXCISE TAXES

Chapter 31—Retail Excise Taxes

SUBCHAPTER A—LUXURY PASSENGER AUTOMOBILES

SUBCHAPTER B—SPECIAL FUELS

SUBCHAPTER C—HEAVY TRUCKS AND TRAILERS

Chapter 32—Manufacturers Excise Taxes

SUBCHAPTER A. AUTOMOTIVE AND RELATED ITEMS

PART I—GAS GUZZLERS

PART II—TIRES

SUBCHAPTER C. TRANSPORTATION BY AIR

PART I—PERSONS

PART II—PROPERTY

PART III—SPECIAL PROVISIONS APPLICABLE TO TAXES ON TRANSPORTATION BY AIR

SUBCHAPTER D. SAFE DEPOSIT BOXES—[REPEALED]

SUBCHAPTER E. SPECIAL PROVISIONS APPLICABLE TO SERVICES AND FACILITIES TAXES

Chapter 34—Policies Issued By Foreign Insurers

SUBCHAPTER B. INSURED AND SELF-INSURED HEALTH PLANS

Chapter 35—Taxes on Wagering

SUBCHAPTER A. TAX ON WAGERS

SUBCHAPTER B. OCCUPATIONAL TAX

SUBCHAPTER C. MISCELLANEOUS PROVISIONS

Chapter 36—Certain Other Excise Taxes

SUBCHAPTER A. HARBOR MAINTENANCE TAX

SUBCHAPTER B. TRANSPORTATION BY WATER

Chapter 49—Cosmetic Services

SUBTITLE E—ALCOHOL, TOBACCO, AND CERTAIN OTHER EXCISE TAXES

Chapter 51—Distilled Spirits, Wines, and Beer

SUBCHAPTER A. GALLONAGE AND OCCUPATIONAL TAXES

PART I—GALLONAGE TAXES

Subpart A—Distilled Spirits

Subpart B—Rectification—[Repealed]

Subpart C—Wines

Subpart D—Beer

Subpart E—General Provisions

PART II—MISCELLANEOUS PROVISIONS

Subpart A—Manufacturers of Stills

Subpart B—Nonbeverage Domestic Drawback Claimants

Subpart C—Recordkeeping by dealers

SUBCHAPTER E. GENERAL PROVISIONS RELATING TO DISTILLED SPIRITS

PART I—RETURN OF MATERIALS USED IN THE MANUFACTURE OR RECOVERY OF DISTILLED SPIRITS

PART II—REGULATION OF TRAFFIC IN CONTAINERS OF DISTILLED SPIRITS

PART III—MISCELLANEOUS PROVISIONS

SUBCHAPTER F. BONDED AND TAXPAID WINE PREMISES

PART I—ESTABLISHMENT

PART II—OPERATIONS

PART III—CELLAR TREATMENT AND CLASSIFICATION OF WINE

PART IV—GENERAL

SUBCHAPTER G. BREWERIES

PART I—ESTABLISHMENT

Chapter 55—Structured Settlement Factoring Transactions

SUBTITLE F—PROCEDURE AND ADMINISTRATION

Chapter 61—Information and Returns

SUBCHAPTER A. RETURNS AND RECORDS

PART I—RECORDS, STATEMENTS, AND SPECIAL RETURNS

PART II—TAX RETURNS OR STATEMENTS

Subpart A—General Requirement

Subpart B—Income Tax Returns

Subpart C—Estate and Gift Tax Returns

Subpart D—Miscellaneous Provisions

PART III—INFORMATION RETURNS

Subpart A—Information Concerning Persons Subject to Special Provisions

Subpart B—Information Concerning Transactions With Other Persons

Subpart C—Information Regarding Wages Paid Employees

Subpart D—Information Regarding Health Insurance Coverage

Subpart D—Information Concerning Private Foundations—[Repealed]

Subpart E—Registration of and Information Concerning Pension, Etc., Plans

Subpart F—Information Concerning Tax Return Preparers

PART IV—SIGNING AND VERIFYING OF RETURNS AND OTHER DOCUMENTS

SUBCHAPTER B. DEFICIENCY PROCEDURES IN THE CASE OF INCOME, ESTATE, GIFT, AND CERTAIN EXCISE TAXES

SUBCHAPTER C. TAX TREATMENT OF PARTNERSHIP ITEMS

SUBCHAPTER D. TREATMENT OF ELECTING LARGE PARTNERSHIPS

PART I—TREATMENT OF PARTNERSHIP ITEMS AND ADJUSTMENTS

PART II—PARTNERSHIP LEVEL ADJUSTMENTS

Subpart A—Adjustments by Secretary

Subpart B—Claims for Adjustments by Partnership

PART III—DEFINITIONS AND SPECIAL RULES

Chapter 64—Collection

SUBCHAPTER A. GENERAL PROVISIONS

SUBCHAPTER B. RECEIPT OF PAYMENT

Chapter 66—Limitations

SUBCHAPTER A. LIMITATIONS ON ASSESSMENT AND COLLECTION

SUBCHAPTER B. LIMITATIONS ON CREDIT OR REFUND

SUBCHAPTER C. MITIGATION OF EFFECT OF PERIOD OF LIMITATIONS

SUBCHAPTER D. PERIODS OF LIMITATION IN JUDICIAL PROCEEDINGS

Chapter 67—Interest

SUBCHAPTER A. INTEREST ON UNDERPAYMENTS

SUBCHAPTER B. INTEREST ON OVERPAYMENTS

SUBCHAPTER C. DETERMINATION OF INTEREST RATE; COMPOUNDING OF INTEREST

SUBCHAPTER D. NOTICE REQUIREMENTS

Chapter 68—Additions to the Tax, Additional Amounts, and Assessable Penalties

SUBCHAPTER A. ADDITIONS TO THE TAX AND ADDITIONAL AMOUNTS

PART I—GENERAL PROVISIONS

PART II—FAILURE TO COMPLY WITH CERTAIN INFORMATION REPORTING REQUIREMENTS

SUBCHAPTER C. PROCEDURAL REQUIREMENTS

Chapter 69—General Provisions Relating to Stamps

Chapter 70—Jeopardy, Receiverships, Etc.

SUBCHAPTER A. JEOPARDY

PART I—TERMINATION OF TAXABLE YEAR

PART II—JEOPARDY ASSESSMENTS

PART III—SPECIAL RULES WITH RESPECT TO CERTAIN CASH

SUBCHAPTER B. RECEIVERSHIPS, ETC.

Chapter 71—Transferees and Fiduciaries

Chapter 72—Licensing and Registration

SUBCHAPTER A. LICENSING

SUBCHAPTER B. REGISTRATION

Chapter 73—Bonds

Chapter 74—Closing Agreements and Compromises

Chapter 75—Crimes, Other Offenses, and Forfeitures

SUBCHAPTER A. CRIMES

PART I—GENERAL PROVISIONS

PART II—PENALTIES APPLICABLE TO CERTAIN TAXES

SUBCHAPTER B. OTHER OFFENSES

SUBCHAPTER C. FORFEITURES

PART I—PROPERTY SUBJECT TO FORFEITURE

PART II—PROVISIONS COMMON TO FORFEITURES

SUBCHAPTER D. MISCELLANEOUS PENALTY AND FORFEITURE PROVISIONS

Chapter 76—Judicial Proceedings

SUBCHAPTER A. CIVIL ACTIONS BY THE UNITED STATES

SUBCHAPTER B. PROCEEDINGS BY TAXPAYERS AND THIRD PARTIES

SUBCHAPTER C. THE TAX COURT

PART I—ORGANIZATION AND JURISDICTION

PART II—PROCEDURE

PART III—MISCELLANEOUS PROVISIONS

PART IV—DECLARATORY JUDGMENTS

SUBCHAPTER D. COURT REVIEW OF TAX COURT DECISIONS

SUBCHAPTER E. BURDEN OF PROOF

Chapter 77—Miscellaneous Provisions

Chapter 78—Discovery of Liability and Enforcement of Title

SUBCHAPTER A. EXAMINATION AND INSPECTION

SUBCHAPTER B. GENERAL POWERS AND DUTIES

SUBCHAPTER C. SUPERVISION OF OPERATIONS OF CERTAIN MANUFACTURERS—[REPEALED]

SUBCHAPTER D. POSSESSIONS

Chapter 79—Definitions

Chapter 80—General Rules

SUBCHAPTER A. APPLICATION OF INTERNAL REVENUE LAWS

SUBCHAPTER B. EFFECTIVE DATE AND RELATED PROVISIONS

SUBCHAPTER C. PROVISIONS AFFECTING MORE THAN ONE SUBTITLE

SUBTITLE G—THE JOINT COMMITTEE ON TAXATION

Chapter 91—Organization and Membership of the Joint Committee

Chapter 92—Powers and Duties of the Joint Committee

SUBTITLE H—FINANCING OF PRESIDENTIAL ELECTION CAMPAIGNS

Chapter 95—Presidential Election Campaign Fund

PART IV—OTHER PROVISIONS

SUBCHAPTER C. HEALTH BENEFITS OF CERTAIN MINERS

PART I—INDIVIDUAL EMPLOYER PLANS

PART II—1992 UMWA BENEFIT PLAN

SUBCHAPTER D. OTHER PROVISIONS

SUBTITLE K—GROUP HEALTH PLAN REQUIREMENTS

Chapter 100—Group Health Plan Requirements

SUBCHAPTER A. REQUIREMENTS RELATING TO PORTABILITY, ACCESS, AND RENEWABILITY

SUBCHAPTER B. OTHER REQUIREMENTS

SUBCHAPTER C. GENERAL PROVISIONS

INTERNAL REVENUE TITLE

Subtitle A—Income Taxes

CHAPTER 1—NORMAL TAXES AND SURTAXES

Subchapter A—Determination of Tax Liability

PART I—TAX ON INDIVIDUALS

[Sec. 1]

SEC. 1. TAX IMPOSED.

[Sec. 1(a)]

(a) MARRIED INDIVIDUALS FILING JOINT RETURNS AND SURVIVING SPOUSES.—There is hereby imposed on the taxable income of—

(1) every married individual (as defined in section 7703) who makes a single return jointly with his spouse under section 6013, and

(2) every surviving spouse (as defined in section 2(a)),

a tax determined in accordance with the following table:

If taxable income is:	The tax is:
Not over $36,900	15% of taxable income.
Over $36,900 but not over $89,150	$5,535, plus 28% of the excess over $36,900.
Over $89,150 but not over $140,000	$20,165, plus 31% of the excess over $89,150.
Over $140,000 but not over $250,000	$35,928.50, plus 36% of the excess over $140,000.
Over $250,000	$75,528.50, plus 39.6% of the excess over $250,000.

Amendments

• 1993, Omnibus Budget Reconciliation Act of 1993 (P.L. 103-66)

P.L. 103-66, §13201(a):

Amended Code Sec. 1(a). **Effective** for tax years beginning after 12-31-92. For a special rule, see Act Sec. 13201(d) following Code Sec. 1(f). Prior to amendment, Code Sec. 1(a) read as follows:

(a) MARRIED INDIVIDUALS FILING JOINT RETURNS AND SURVIVING SPOUSES.—There is hereby imposed on the taxable income of—

(1) every married individual (as defined in section 7703) who makes a single return jointly with his spouse under section 6013, and

(2) every surviving spouse (as defined in section 2(a)),

a tax determined in accordance with the following table:

If taxable income is:	The tax is:
Not over $32,450	15% of taxable income.
Over $32,450 but not over $78,400	$4,867.50, plus 28% of the excess over $32,450.
Over $78,400	$17,733.50, plus 31% of the excess over $78,400.

P.L. 103-66, §13202(a)(1):

Amended Code Sec. 1(a) (as amended by Act Sec. 13201) by striking the last item in the table contained therein and inserting new items. **Effective** for tax years beginning after 12-31-92. For a special rule, see Act Sec. 13201(d) following Code Sec. 1(f). Prior to amendment, the last item in the table in Code Sec. 1(a) read as follows:

If taxable income is:	The tax is:
Over $140,000	$35,928.50, plus 36% of the excess over $140,000.

• 1990, Omnibus Budget Reconciliation Act of 1990 (P.L. 101-508)

P.L. 101-508, §11101(a):

Amended Code Sec. 1(a). **Effective** for tax years beginning after 12-31-90. Prior to amendment, Code Sec. 1(a) read as follows:

(a) MARRIED INDIVIDUALS FILING JOINT RETURNS AND SURVIVING SPOUSES.—There is hereby imposed on the taxable income of—

(1) every married individual (as defined in section 7703) who makes a single return jointly with his spouse under section 6013, and

(2) every surviving spouse (as defined in section 2(a)),

a tax determined in accordance with the following table:

If taxable income is:	The tax is:
Not over $29,750	15% of taxable income.
Over $29,750	$4,462.50, plus 28% of the excess over $29,750.

[Sec. 1(b)]

(b) HEADS OF HOUSEHOLDS.—There is hereby imposed on the taxable income of every head of a household (as defined in section 2(b)) a tax determined in accordance with the following table:

If taxable income is:	The tax is:
Not over $29,600	15% of taxable income.
Over $29,600 but not over $76,400	$4,440, plus 28% of the excess over $29,600.
Over $76,400 but not over $127,500	$17,544, plus 31% of the excess over $76,400.
Over $127,500 but not over $250,000	$33,385, plus 36% of the excess over $127,500.
Over $250,000	$77,485, plus 39.6% of the excess over $250,000.

Amendments

• 1993, Omnibus Budget Reconciliation Act of 1993 (P.L. 103-66)

P.L. 103-66, §13201(a):

Amended Code Sec. 1(b). **Effective** for tax years beginning after 12-31-92. For a special rule, see Act Sec. 13201(d) following Code Sec. 1(f). Prior to amendment, Code Sec. 1(b) read as follows:

(b) HEADS OF HOUSEHOLDS.—There is hereby imposed on the taxable income of every head of a household (as defined in section 2(b)) a tax determined in accordance with the following table:

If taxable income is:	The tax is:
Not over $26,050	15% of taxable income.
Over $26,050 but not over $67,200	$3,907.50, plus 28% of the excess over $26,500.
Over $67,200	$15,429.50, plus 31% of the excess over $67,200.

P.L. 103-66, §13202(a)(2):

Amended Code Sec. 1(b) (as amended by Act Sec. 13201) by striking the last item in the table contained therein and inserting new items. **Effective** for tax years beginning after 12-31-92. For a special rule, see Act Sec. 13201(d) following Code Sec. 1(f). Prior to amendment, the last item in the table in Code Sec. 1(b) read as follows:

If taxable income is:	The tax is:
Over $127,500	$33,385, plus 36% of the excess over $127,500.

• 1990, Omnibus Budget Reconciliation Act of 1990 (P.L. 101-508)

P.L. 101-508, §11101(a):

Amended Code Sec. 1(b). **Effective** for tax years beginning after 12-31-90. Prior to amendment, Code Sec. 1(b) read as follows:

(b) HEADS OF HOUSEHOLDS.—There is hereby imposed on the taxable income of every head of a household (as defined in section 2(b)) a tax determined in accordance with the following table:

If taxable income is:	The tax is:
Not over $23,900	15% of taxable income.
Over $23,900	$3,585, plus 28% of the excess over $23,900.

[Sec. 1(c)]

(c) UNMARRIED INDIVIDUALS (OTHER THAN SURVIVING SPOUSES AND HEADS OF HOUSEHOLDS).—There is hereby imposed on the taxable income of every individual (other than a surviving spouse as defined in section 2(a) or the head of a household as defined in section 2(b)) who is not a married individual (as defined in section 7703) a tax determined in accordance with the following table:

If taxable income is:	The tax is:
Not over $22,100	15% of taxable income.
Over $22,100 but not over $53,500	$3,315, plus 28% of the excess over $22,100.
Over $53,500 but not over $115,000	$12,107, plus 31% of the excess over $53,500.
Over $115,000 but not over $250,000	$31,172, plus 36% of the excess over $115,000.
Over $250,000	$79,772, plus 39.6% of the excess over $250,000.

Amendments

• 1993, Omnibus Budget Reconciliation Act of 1993 (P.L. 103-66)

P.L. 103-66, §13201(a):

Amended Code Sec. 1(c). **Effective** for tax years beginning after 12-31-92. For a special rule, see Act Sec. 13201(d) following Code Sec. 1(f). Prior to amendment, Code Sec. 1(c) read as follows:

(c) UNMARRIED INDIVIDUALS (OTHER THAN SURVIVING SPOUSES AND HEADS OF HOUSEHOLDS).—There is hereby imposed on the taxable income of every individual (other than a surviving spouse as defined in section 2(a) or the head of a household as defined in section 2(b)) who is not a married individual (as defined in section 7703) a tax determined in accordance with the following table:

If taxable income is:	The tax is:
Not over $19,450	15% of taxable income.
Over $19,450 but not over $47,050	$2,917.50, plus 28% of the excess over $19,450.
Over $47,050	$10,645.50, plus 31% of the excess over $47,050.

P.L. 103-66, §13202(a)(3):

Amended Code Sec. 1(c) (as amended by Act Sec. 13201) by striking the last item in the table contained therein and inserting new items. **Effective** for tax years beginning after 12-31-92. For a special rule, see Act Sec. 13201(d) following Code Sec. 1(f). Prior to amendment, the last item in the table in Code Sec. 1(c) read as follows:

If taxable income is:	The tax is:
Over $115,000	$31,172, plus 36% of the excess over $115,000.

• **1990, Omnibus Budget Reconciliation Act of 1990 (P.L. 101-508)**

P.L. 101-508, §11101(a):

Amended Code Sec. 1(c). **Effective** for tax years beginning after 12-31-90. Prior to amendment, Code Sec. 1(c) read as follows:

(c) UNMARRIED INDIVIDUALS (OTHER THAN SURVIVING SPOUSES AND HEADS OF HOUSEHOLDS).—There is hereby imposed on the taxable income of every individual (other than a surviving spouse as defined in section 2(a) or the head of a household as defined in section 2(b)) who is not a married individual (as defined in section 7703) a tax determined in accordance with the following table:

If taxable income is:	The tax is:
Not over $17,850 .	15% of taxable income.
Over $17,850 . . .	$2,677.50, plus 28% of the excess over $17,850.

[Sec. 1(d)]

(d) MARRIED INDIVIDUALS FILING SEPARATE RETURNS.—There is hereby imposed on the taxable income of every married individual (as defined in section 7703) who does not make a single return jointly with his spouse under section 6013, a tax determined in accordance with the following table:

If taxable income is:	The tax is:
Not over $18,450	15% of taxable income.
Over $18,450 but not over $44,575	$2,767.50, plus 28% of the excess over $18,450.
Over $44,575 but not over $70,000	$10,082.50, plus 31% of the excess over $44,575.
Over $70,000 but not over $125,000	$17,964.25, plus 36% of the excess over $70,000.
Over $125,000	$37,764.25, plus 39.6% of the excess over $125,000.

Amendments

• **1993, Omnibus Budget Reconciliation Act of 1993 (P.L. 103-66)**

P.L. 103-66, §13201(a):

Amended Code Sec. 1(d). **Effective** for tax years beginning after 12-31-92. For a special rule, see Act Sec. 13201(d) following Code Sec. 1(f). Prior to amendment, Code Sec. 1(d) read as follows:

(d) MARRIED INDIVIDUALS FILING SEPARATE RETURNS.—There is hereby imposed on the taxable income of every married individual (as defined in section 7703) who does not make a single return jointly with his spouse under section 6013, a tax determined in accordance with the following table:

If taxable income is:	The tax is:
Not over $16,225 .	15% of taxable income.
Over $16,225 but not over $39,200 .	$2,433.75, plus 28% of the excess over $16,225.
Over $39,200 . . .	$8,866.75, plus 31% of the excess over $39,200.

P.L. 103-66, §13202(a)(4):

Amended Code Sec. 1(d) (as amended by Act Sec. 13201) by striking the last item in the table contained therein and inserting new items. **Effective** for tax years beginning after 12-31-92. For a special rule, see Act Sec. 13201(d) following Code Sec. 1(f). Prior to amendment, the last item in the table in Code Sec. 1(d) read as follows:

If taxable income is:	The tax is:
Over $70,000 . . .	$17,964.25, plus 36% of the excess over $70,000.

• **1990, Omnibus Budget Reconciliation Act of 1990 (P.L. 101-508)**

P.L. 101-508, §11101(a):

Amended Code Sec. 1(d). **Effective** for tax years beginning after 12-31-90. Prior to amendment, Code Sec. 1(d) read as follows:

(d) MARRIED INDIVIDUALS FILING SEPARATE RETURNS.—There is hereby imposed on the taxable income of every married individual (as defined in section 7703) who does not make a single return jointly with his spouse under section 6013, a tax determined in accordance with the following table:

If taxable income is:	The tax is:
Not over $14,875 .	15% of taxable income.
Over $14,875 . . .	$2,231.25, plus 28% of the excess over $14,875.

[Sec. 1(e)]

(e) ESTATES AND TRUSTS.—There is hereby imposed on the taxable income of—

(1) every estate, and

(2) every trust,

taxable under this subsection a tax determined in accordance with the following table:

If taxable income is:	The tax is:
Not over $1,500	15% of taxable income.
Over $1,500 but not over $3,500	$225, plus 28% of the excess over $1,500.
Over $3,500 but not over $5,500	$785, plus 31% of the excess over $3,500.
Over $5,500 but not over $7,500	$1,405, plus 36% of the excess over $5,500.
Over $7,500	$2,125, plus 39.6% of the excess over $7,500.

Amendments

• **1993, Omnibus Budget Reconciliation Act of 1993 (P.L. 103-66)**

P.L. 103-66, §13201(a):

Amended Code Sec. 1(e). **Effective** for tax years beginning after 12-31-92. For a special rule, see Act Sec. 13201(d) following Code Sec. 1(f). Prior to amendment, Code Sec. 1(e) read as follows:

(e) ESTATES AND TRUSTS.—There is hereby imposed on the taxable income of—

(1) every estate, and

(2) every trust,

taxable under this subsection a tax determined in accordance with the following table:

If taxable income is:	The tax is:
Not over $3,300 .	15% of taxable income.
Over $3,300 but not over $9,900	$495, plus 28% of the excess over $3,300.
Over $9,900	$2,343, plus 31% of the excess over $9,900.

P.L. 103-66, §13202(a)(5):

Amended Code Sec. 1(e) (as amended by Act Sec. 13201) by striking the last item in the table contained therein and inserting new items. **Effective** for tax years beginning after 12-31-92. For a special rule, see Act Sec. 13201(d) following Code Sec. 1(f). Prior to amendment, the last item in the table in Code Sec. 1(e) read as follows:

If taxable income is:	The tax is:
Over $5,500	$1,405, plus 36% of the excess over $5,500.

• 1990, Omnibus Budget Reconciliation Act of 1990 (P.L. 101-508)

P.L. 101-508, §11101(a):

Amended Code Sec. 1(e). **Effective** for tax years beginning after 12-31-90. Prior to amendment, Code Sec. 1(e) read as follows:

(e) ESTATES AND TRUSTS.—There is hereby imposed on the taxable income of—

(1) every estate, and

(2) every trust,

taxable under this subsection a tax determined in accordance with the following table:

If taxable income is:	The tax is:
Not over $5,000 .	15% of taxable income.
Over $5,000	$750, plus 28% of the excess over $5,000.

»»→ Caution: The heading for Code Sec. 1(f), below, is subject to the sunset provision of the Economic Growth and Tax Relief Reconciliation Act of 2001 (P.L. 107-16), §901. Absent Congressional action, the changes made to this provision by P.L. 107-16, or that take effect as if included in P.L. 107-16, do not apply after December 31, 2010. For more information about the sunset provision, see page XXI of the Preface to this publication and P.L. 107-16, §901, in the amendment notes. See the amendments notes for a history of amendments to this section and the effective date of each change.

[Sec. 1(f)]

(f) PHASEOUT OF MARRIAGE PENALTY IN 15-PERCENT BRACKET; ADJUSTMENTS IN TAX TABLES SO THAT INFLATION WILL NOT RESULT IN TAX INCREASES.—

(1) IN GENERAL.—Not later than December 15 of 1993, and each subsequent calendar year, the Secretary shall prescribe tables which shall apply in lieu of the tables contained in subsections (a), (b), (c), (d), and (e) with respect to taxable years beginning in the succeeding calendar year.

(2) METHOD OF PRESCRIBING TABLES.—The table which under paragraph (1) is to apply in lieu of the table contained in subsection (a), (b), (c), (d), or (e), as the case may be, with respect to taxable years beginning in any calendar year shall be prescribed—

»»→ Caution: Code Sec. 1(f)(2)(A), below, is subject to the sunset provision of the Economic Growth and Tax Relief Reconciliation Act of 2001 (P.L. 107-16), §901. Absent Congressional action, the changes made to this provision by P.L. 107-16, or that take effect as if included in P.L. 107-16, do not apply after December 31, 2010. For more information about the sunset provision, see page XXI of the Preface to this publication and P.L. 107-16, §901, in the amendment notes. See the amendments notes for a history of amendments to this section and the effective date of each change.

(A) except as provided in paragraph (8), by increasing the minimum and maximum dollar amounts for each rate bracket for which a tax is imposed under such table by the cost-of-living adjustment for such calendar year,

(B) by not changing the rate applicable to any rate bracket as adjusted under subparagraph (A), and

(C) by adjusting the amounts setting forth the tax to the extent necessary to reflect the adjustments in the rate brackets.

(3) COST-OF-LIVING ADJUSTMENT.—For purposes of paragraph (2), the cost-of-living adjustment for any calendar year is the percentage (if any) by which—

(A) the CPI for the preceding calendar year, exceeds

(B) the CPI for calendar year 1992.

(4) CPI FOR ANY CALENDAR YEAR.—For purposes of paragraph (3), the CPI for any calendar year is the average of the Consumer Price Index as of the close of the 12-month period ending on August 31 of such calendar year.

(5) CONSUMER PRICE INDEX.—For purposes of paragraph (4), the term "Consumer Price Index" means the last Consumer Price Index for all-urban consumers published by the Department of Labor. For purposes of the preceding sentence, the revision of the Consumer Price Index which is most consistent with the Consumer Price Index for calendar year 1986 shall be used.

(6) ROUNDING.—

(A) IN GENERAL.—If any increase determined under paragraph (2)(A), section 63(c)(4), section 68(b)(2) or section 151(d)(4) is not a multiple of $50, such increase shall be rounded to the next lowest multiple of $50.

»»→ Caution: Code Sec. 1(f)(6)(B), below, is subject to the sunset provision of the Economic Growth and Tax Relief Reconciliation Act of 2001 (P.L. 107-16), §901. Absent Congressional action, the changes made to this provision by P.L. 107-16, or that take effect as if included in P.L. 107-16, do not apply after December 31, 2010. For more information about the sunset provision, see page XXI of the Preface to this publication and P.L. 107-16, §901, in the amendment notes. See the amendments notes for a history of amendments to this section and the effective date of each change.

(B) TABLE FOR MARRIED INDIVIDUALS FILING SEPARATELY.—In the case of a married individual filing a separate return, subparagraph (A) (other than with respect to sections 63(c)(4) and 151(d)(4)(A)) shall be applied by substituting "$25" for "$50" each place it appears.

(7) SPECIAL RULE FOR CERTAIN BRACKETS.—

(A) CALENDAR YEAR 1994.—In prescribing the tables under paragraph (1) which apply with respect to taxable years beginning in calendar year 1994, the Secretary shall make no adjustment to the dollar amounts at which the 36 percent rate bracket begins or at which the 39.6 percent rate begins under any table contained in subsection (a), (b), (c), (d), or (e).

(B) LATER CALENDAR YEARS.—In prescribing tables under paragraph (1) which apply with respect to taxable years beginning in a calendar year after 1994, the cost-of-living adjustment used in making adjustments to the dollar amounts referred to in subparagraph (A) shall be determined under paragraph (3) by substituting "1993" for "1992".

»»→ Caution: Code Sec. 1(f)(8), below, was added by P.L. 107-16 and amended by P.L. 108-27 and P.L. 108-311, and is subject to the sunset provisions of the Economic Growth and Tax Relief Reconciliation Act of 2001 (P.L. 107-16), §901 and the Jobs and Growth Tax Relief Reconciliation Act of 2003 (P.L. 108-27), §303. Absent Congressional action, the changes made to this provision by P.L. 107-16, and P.L. 108-27, or that take effect as if included in P.L. 107-16, and P.L. 108-27, do not apply after December 31, 2010. For more information about the sunset provisions, see page XXI of the Preface to this publication and P.L. 107-16, §901, P.L. 108-27, §303, and P.L. 108-311, §105, in the amendment notes. See the amendments notes for a history of amendments to this section and the effective date of each change.

(8) ELIMINATION OF MARRIAGE PENALTY IN 15-PERCENT BRACKET.—With respect to taxable years beginning after December 31, 2003, in prescribing the tables under paragraph (1)—

(A) the maximum taxable income in the 15-percent rate bracket in the table contained in subsection (a) (and the minimum taxable income in the next higher taxable income bracket in such table) shall be 200 percent of the maximum taxable income in the 15-percent rate bracket in the table contained in subsection (c) (after any other adjustment under this subsection), and

(B) the comparable taxable income amounts in the table contained in subsection (d) shall be 1/2 of the amounts determined under subparagraph (A).

Amendments

• 2004, Working Families Tax Relief Act of 2004 (P.L. 108-311)

P.L. 108-311, §101(c):

Amended Code Sec. 1(f)(8). **Effective** for tax years beginning after 12-31-2003. Prior to amendment, Code Sec. 1(f)(8) read as follows:

(8) PHASEOUT OF MARRIAGE PENALTY IN 15-PERCENT BRACKET.—

(A) IN GENERAL.—With respect to taxable years beginning after December 31, 2002, in prescribing the tables under paragraph (1)—

(i) the maximum taxable income in the 15-percent rate bracket in the table contained in subsection (a) (and the minimum taxable income in the next higher taxable income bracket in such table) shall be the applicable percentage of the maximum taxable income in the 15-percent rate bracket in the table contained in subsection (c) (after any other adjustment under this subsection), and

(ii) the comparable taxable income amounts in the table contained in subsection (d) shall be 1/2 of the amounts determined under clause (i).

(B) APPLICABLE PERCENTAGE.—For purposes of subparagraph (A), the applicable percentage shall be determined in accordance with the following table:

For taxable years beginning in calendar year—	*The applicable percentage is—*
2003 and 2004	200
2005	180
2006	187
2007	193
2008 and thereafter	200.

(C) ROUNDING.—If any amount determined under subparagraph (A)(i) is not a multiple of $50, such amount shall be rounded to the next lowest multiple of $50.

P.L. 108-311, §105, provides:

SEC. 105. APPLICATION OF EGTRRA SUNSET TO THIS TITLE.

Each amendment made by this title shall be subject to title IX of the Economic Growth and Tax Relief Reconciliation Act of 2001 to the same extent and in the same manner as the provision of such Act to which such amendment relates.

• 2003, Jobs and Growth Tax Relief Reconciliation Act of 2003 (P.L. 108-27)

P.L. 108-27, §102(a):

Amended the table contained in Code Sec. 1(f)(8)(B) by inserting a new item before the item relating to 2005. **Effective** for tax years beginning after 12-31-2002.

P.L. 108-27, §102(b)(1):

Amended Code Sec. 1(f)(8)(A) by striking "2004" and inserting "2002". **Effective** for tax years beginning after 12-31-2002.

P.L. 108-27, §107, provides:

SEC. 107. APPLICATION OF EGTRRA SUNSET TO THIS TITLE.

Each amendment made by this title shall be subject to title IX of the Economic Growth and Tax Relief Reconciliation Act of 2001 to the same extent and in the same manner as the provision of such Act to which such amendment relates.

• 2001, Economic Growth and Tax Relief Reconciliation Act of 2001 (P.L. 107-16)

P.L. 107-16, §301(c)(1):

Amended Code Sec. 1(f)(6)(B) by striking "(other than with" and all that follows through "shall be applied" and inserting "(other than with respect to sections 63(c)(4) and 151(d)(4)(A)) shall be applied". **Effective** for tax years beginning after 12-31-2002 [**effective** date changed by P.L. 108-27, §103(b).—CCH]. Prior to amendment, Code Sec. 1(f)(6)(B) read as follows:

(B) TABLE FOR MARRIED INDIVIDUALS FILING SEPARATELY.—In the case of a married individual filing a separate return, subparagraph (A) (other than with respect to subsection (c)(4) of section 63 (as it applies to subsections (c)(5)(A) and (f) of such section) and section 151(d)(4)(A)) shall be applied by substituting "$25" for "$50" each place it appears.

P.L. 107-16, §302(a):

Amended Code Sec. 1(f) by adding at the end a new paragraph (8). **Effective** for tax years beginning after 12-31-2002 [**effective** date changed by P.L. 108-27, §102(c).—CCH].

P.L. 107-16, §302(b)(1):

Amended Code Sec. 1(f)(2)(A) by inserting "except as provided in paragraph (8)," before "by increasing". **Effective** for tax years beginning after 12-31-2002 [**effective** date changed by P.L. 108-27, §102(c).—CCH].

P.L. 107-16, §302(b)(2):

Amended the heading for Code Sec. 1(f) by inserting "PHASEOUT OF MARRIAGE PENALTY IN 15-PERCENT BRACKET;" before "ADJUSTMENTS". **Effective** for tax years beginning after 12-31-2002 [**effective** date changed by P.L. 108-27, §102(c).—CCH].

P.L. 107-16, §901(a)-(b), provides:

SEC. 901. SUNSET OF PROVISIONS OF ACT.

(a) IN GENERAL.—All provisions of, and amendments made by, this Act shall not apply—

(1) to taxable, plan, or limitation years beginning after December 31, 2010, or

(2) in the case of title V, to estates of decedents dying, gifts made, or generation skipping transfers, after December 31, 2010.

(b) APPLICATION OF CERTAIN LAWS.—The Internal Revenue Code of 1986 and the Employee Retirement Income Security Act of 1974 shall be applied and administered to years, estates, gifts, and transfers described in subsection (a) as if the provisions and amendments described in subsection (a) had never been enacted.

• 1993, Omnibus Budget Reconciliation Act of 1993 (P.L. 103-66)

P.L. 103-66, §13201(b)(3)(A)(i)-(ii):

Amended Code Sec. 1(f) by striking "1990" in paragraph (1) and inserting "1993", and by striking "1989" in paragraph (3)(B) and inserting "1992". **Effective** for tax years beginning after 12-31-92. For a special rule, see Act Sec. 13201(d), below.

P.L. 103-66, §13201(b)(3)(B):

Amended Code Sec. 1(f) by adding at the end thereof new paragraph (7). **Effective** for tax years beginning after 12-31-92. For a special rule, see Act Sec. 13201(d), below

P.L. 103-66, §13201(d), provides:

(d) ELECTION TO PAY ADDITIONAL 1993 TAXES IN INSTALLMENTS.—

(1) IN GENERAL.—At the election of the taxpayer, the additional 1993 taxes may be paid in 3 equal installments.

(2) DATES FOR PAYING INSTALLMENTS.—In the case of any tax payable in installments by reason of paragraph (1)—

(A) the first installment shall be paid on or before the due date for the taxpayer's taxable year beginning in calendar year 1993,

(B) the second installment shall be paid on or before the date 1 year after the date determined under subparagraph (A), and

(C) the third installment shall be paid on or before the date 2 years after the date determined under subparagraph (A).

For purposes of the preceding sentence, the term "due date" means the date prescribed for filing the taxpayer's return determined without regard to extensions.

(3) EXTENSION WITHOUT INTEREST.—For purposes of section 6601 of the Internal Revenue Code of 1986, the date prescribed for the payment of any tax payable in installments under paragraph (1) shall be determined with regard to the extension under paragraph (1).

(4) ADDITIONAL 1993 TAXES.—

(A) IN GENERAL.—For purposes of this subsection, the term "additional 1993 taxes" means the excess of—

(i) the taxpayer's net chapter 1 liability as shown on the taxpayer's return for taxpayer's taxable year beginning in calendar year 1993, over

(ii) the amount which would have been the taxpayer's net chapter 1 liability for such taxable year if such liability had been determined using the rates which would have been in effect under section 1 of the Internal Revenue Code of 1986 for taxable years beginning in calendar year 1993 but for the amendments made by this section and section 13202 and such liability had otherwise been determined on the basis of the amounts shown on the taxpayer's return.

(B) NET CHAPTER 1 LIABILITY.—For purposes of subparagraph (A), the term "net chapter 1 liability" means the liability for tax under chapter 1 of the Internal Revenue Code of 1986 determined—

(i) after the application of any credit against such tax other than the credits under sections 31 and 34, and

(ii) before crediting any payment of estimated tax for the taxable year.

(5) ACCELERATION OF PAYMENTS.—If the taxpayer does not pay any installment under this section on or before the date prescribed for its payment or if the Secretary of the Treasury or his delegate believes that the collection of any amount payable in installments under this section is in jeopardy, the Secretary shall immediately terminate the extension under paragraph (1) and the whole of the unpaid tax shall be paid on notice and demand from the Secretary.

(6) ELECTION ON RETURN.—An election under paragraph (1) shall be made on the taxpayer's return for the taxpayer's taxable year beginning in calendar year 1993.

(7) EXCEPTION FOR ESTATES AND TRUSTS.—This subsection shall not apply in the case of an estate or trust.

• 1990, Omnibus Budget Reconciliation Act of 1990 (P.L. 101-508)

P.L. 101-508, §11101(b)(2):

Amended Code Sec. 1(f)(6)(A) by striking "subsection (g)(4)," after "under paragraph (2)(A),". **Effective** for tax years beginning after 12-31-90.

P.L. 101-508, §11101(d)(1)(A)(i):

Amended Code Sec. 1(f)(1) by striking "1988" and inserting "1990". **Effective** for tax years beginning after 12-31-90.

P.L. 101-508, §11101(d)(1)(A)(ii):

Amended Code Sec. 1(f)(3)(B) by striking "1987" and inserting "1989". **Effective** for tax years beginning after 12-31-90.

P.L. 101-508, §11103(c):

Amended Code Sec. 1(f)(6)(A) by inserting "section 68(b)(2)" after "section 63(c)(4),". **Effective** for tax years beginning after 12-31-90.

P.L. 101-508, § 11104(b)(1):

Amended Code Sec. 1(f)(6)(A) by striking "section 151(d)(3)" and inserting "section 151(d)(4)". **Effective** for tax years beginning after 12-31-90.

P.L. 101-508, § 11104(b)(2):

Amended Code Sec. 1(f)(6)(B) by striking "section 151(d)(3)" and inserting "section 151(d)(4)(A)". **Effective** for tax years beginning after 12-31-90.

• 1989, Omnibus Budget Reconciliation Act of 1989 (P.L. 101-239)

P.L. 101-239, § 7831(a):

Amended Code Sec. 1(f)(6)(B) by striking "(other than with respect to section 63(c)(4))" and inserting "(other than with respect to subsection (c)(4) of section 63 (as it applies to subsections (c)(5)(A) and (f) of such section) and section 151(d)(3))". **Effective** as if included in the provision of P.L. 99-514 to which it relates.

[Sec. 1(g)—Stricken]

Amendments

• 1990, Omnibus Budget Reconciliation Act of 1990 (P.L. 101-508)

P.L. 101-508, § 11101(b)(1):

Amended Code Sec. 1 by striking out subsection (g). **Effective** for tax years beginning after 12-31-90. Prior to amendment, Code Sec. 1(g) read as follows:

(g) PHASEOUT OF 15-PERCENT RATE AND PERSONAL EXEMPTIONS.—

(1) IN GENERAL.—The amount of tax imposed by this section (determined without regard to this subsection) shall be increased by 5 percent of the excess (if any) of—

(A) taxable income, over

(B) the applicable dollar amount.

(2) LIMITATION.—The increase determined under paragraph (1) with respect to any taxpayer for any taxable year shall not exceed the sum of—

(A) 13 percent of the maximum amount of taxable income to which the 15-percent rate applies under the table contained in subsection (a), (b), (c), or (e) (whichever applies), and

(B) 28 percent of the deductions for personal exemptions allowable to the taxpayer for the taxable year under section 151.

In the case of any individual taxable under subsection (d), subparagraph (A) shall apply as if such individual were taxable under subsection (a) and subparagraph (B) shall be applied as if a deduction for a personal exemption were allowable under section 151 to such individual for such individual's spouse.

(3) APPLICABLE DOLLAR AMOUNT.—For purposes of paragraph (1), the applicable dollar amount shall be determined under the following table:

In the case of a taxpayer to which the following subsection of this section applies:	The applicable dollar amount is:
Subsection (a)	$71,900
Subsection (b)	61,650
Subsection (c)	43,150
Subsection (d)	35,950
Subsection (e)	13,000.

(4) ADJUSTMENT FOR INFLATION.—In the case of any taxable year beginning in a calendar year after 1988, each dollar amount contained in paragraph (3) shall be increased by an amount equal to—

(A) such dollar amount, multiplied by

(B) the cost-of-living adjustment determined under subsection (f)(3) for the calendar year in which the taxable year begins.

• 1988, Technical and Miscellaneous Revenue Act of 1988 (P.L. 100-647)

P.L. 100-647, § 1001(a)(3):

Amended Code Sec. 1(g)(2) by inserting before the period at the end thereof "and subparagraph (B) shall be applied as if a deduction for a personal exemption were allowable under section 151 to such individual for such individual's spouse.". **Effective** as if included in the provision of P.L. 99-514 to which it relates.

[Sec. 1(g)]

(g) CERTAIN UNEARNED INCOME OF CHILDREN TAXED AS IF PARENT'S INCOME.—

(1) IN GENERAL.—In the case of any child to whom this subsection applies, the tax imposed by this section shall be equal to the greater of—

(A) the tax imposed by this section without regard to this subsection, or

(B) the sum of—

(i) the tax which would be imposed by this section if the taxable income of such child for the taxable year were reduced by the net unearned income of such child, plus

(ii) such child's share of the allocable parental tax.

(2) CHILD TO WHOM SUBSECTION APPLIES.— This subsection shall apply to any child for any taxable year if—

(A) such child—

(i) has not attained age 18 before the close of the taxable year, or

(ii)(I) has attained age 18 before the close of the taxable year and meets the age requirements of section 152(c)(3) (determined without regard to subparagraph (B) thereof), and

(II) whose earned income (as defined in section 911(d)(2)) for such taxable year does not exceed one-half of the amount of the individual's support (within the meaning of section 152(c)(1)(D) after the application of section 152(f)(5) (without regard to subparagraph (A) thereof)) for such taxable year,

(B) either parent of such child is alive at the close of the taxable year, and

(C) such child does not file a joint return for the taxable year.

(3) ALLOCABLE PARENTAL TAX.—For purposes of this subsection—

(A) IN GENERAL.—The term "allocable parental tax" means the excess of—

(i) the tax which would be imposed by this section on the parent's taxable income if such income included the net unearned income of all children of the parent to whom this subsection applies, over

(ii) the tax imposed by this section on the parent without regard to this subsection.

For purposes of clause (i), net unearned income of all children of the parent shall not be taken into account in computing any exclusion, deduction, or credit of the parent.

(B) CHILD'S SHARE.—A child's share of any allocable parental tax of a parent shall be equal to an amount which bears the same ratio to the total allocable parental tax as the child's net unearned income bears to the aggregate net unearned income of all children of such parent to whom this subsection applies.

(C) SPECIAL RULE WHERE PARENT HAS DIFFERENT TAXABLE YEAR.—Except as provided in regulations, if the parent does not have the same taxable year as the child, the allocable parental tax shall be determined on the basis of the taxable year of the parent ending in the child's taxable year.

(4) NET UNEARNED INCOME.—For purposes of this subsection—

(A) IN GENERAL.—The term "net unearned income" means the excess of—

(i) the portion of the adjusted gross income for the taxable year which is not attributable to earned income (as defined in section 911(d)(2)), over

(ii) the sum of—

(I) the amount in effect for the taxable year under section 63(c)(5)(A) (relating to limitation on standard deduction in the case of certain dependents), plus

(II) The greater of the amount described in subclause (I) or, if the child itemizes his deductions for the taxable year, the amount of the itemized deductions allowed by this chapter for the taxable year which are directly connected with the production of the portion of adjusted gross income referred to in clause (i).

(B) LIMITATION BASED ON TAXABLE INCOME.—The amount of the net unearned income for any taxable year shall not exceed the individual's taxable income for such taxable year.

(C) TREATMENT OF DISTRIBUTIONS FROM QUALIFIED DISABILITY TRUSTS.—For purposes of this subsection, in the case of any child who is a beneficiary of a qualified disability trust (as defined in section 642(b)(2)(C)(ii)), any amount included in the income of such child under sections 652 and 662 during a taxable year shall be considered earned income of such child for such taxable year.

(5) SPECIAL RULES FOR DETERMINING PARENT TO WHOM SUBSECTION APPLIES.—For purposes of this subsection, the parent whose taxable income shall be taken into account shall be—

(A) in the case of parents who are not married (within the meaning of section 7703), the custodial parent (within the meaning of section 152(e)) of the child, and

(B) in the case of married individuals filing separately, the individual with the greater taxable income.

(6) PROVIDING OF PARENT'S TIN.—The parent of any child to whom this subsection applies for any taxable year shall provide the TIN of such parent to such child and such child shall include such TIN on the child's return of tax imposed by this section for such taxable year.

(7) ELECTION TO CLAIM CERTAIN UNEARNED INCOME OF CHILD ON PARENT'S RETURN.—

(A) IN GENERAL.—If—

(i) any child to whom this subsection applies has gross income for the taxable year only from interest and dividends (including Alaska Permanent Fund dividends),

(ii) such gross income is more than the amount described in paragraph (4)(A)(ii)(I) and less than 10 times the amount so described,

(iii) no estimated tax payments for such year are made in the name and TIN of such child, and no amount has been deducted and withheld under section 3406, and

(iv) the parent of such child (as determined under paragraph (5)) elects the application of subparagraph (B),

such child shall be treated (other than [for] purposes of this paragraph) as having no gross income for such year and shall not be required to file a return under section 6012.

(B) INCOME INCLUDED ON PARENT'S RETURN.—In the case of a parent making the election under this paragraph—

(i) the gross income of each child to whom such election applies (to the extent the gross income of such child exceeds twice the amount described in paragraph (4)(A)(ii)(I)) shall be included in such parent's gross income for the taxable year,

(ii) the tax imposed by this section for such year with respect to such parent shall be the amount equal to the sum of—

(I) the amount determined under this section after the application of clause (i), plus

»»→ Caution: Code Sec. 1(g)(7)(B)(ii)(II), below, is subject to the sunset provision of the Economic Growth and Tax Relief Reconciliation Act of 2001 (P.L. 107-16), §901. Absent Congressional action, the changes made to this provision by P.L. 107-16, or that take effect as if included in P.L. 107-16, do not apply after December 31, 2010. For more information about the sunset provision, see page XXI of the Preface to this publication and P.L. 107-16, §901, in the amendment notes. See the amendments notes for a history of amendments to this section and the effective date of each change.

(II) for each such child, 10 percent of the lesser of the amount described in paragraph (4)(A)(ii)(I) or the excess of the gross income of such child over the amount so described, and

(iii) any interest which is an item of tax preference under section 57(a)(5) of the child shall be treated as an item of tax preference of such parent (and not of such child).

(C) REGULATIONS.—The Secretary shall prescribe such regulations as may be necessary or appropriate to carry out the purposes of this paragraph.

Amendments

• 2007, Small Business and Work Opportunity Tax Act of 2007 (P.L. 110-28)

P.L. 110-28, §8241(a):

Amended Code Sec. 1(g)(2)(A). **Effective** for tax years beginning after 5-25-2007. Prior to amendment, Code Sec. 1(g)(2)(A) read as follows:

(A) such child has not attained age 18 before the close of the taxable year,

P.L. 110-28, §8241(b):

Amended Code Sec. 1(g) by striking "MINOR" preceding "CHILDREN" in the heading thereof. **Effective** for tax years beginning after 5-25-2007.

• 2006, Tax Increase Prevention and Reconciliation Act of 2005 (P.L. 109-222)

P.L. 109-222, §510(a):

Amended Code Sec. 1(g)(2)(A) by striking "age 14" and inserting "age 18". **Effective** for tax years beginning after 12-31-2005.

P.L. 109-222, §510(b):

Amended Code Sec. 1(g)(4) by adding at the end a new subparagraph (C). **Effective** for tax years beginning after 12-31-2005.

P.L. 109-222, §510(c):

Amended Code Sec. 1(g)(2) by striking "and" at the end of subparagraph (A), by striking the period at the end of subparagraph (B) and inserting ", and", and by inserting after subparagraph (B) a new subparagraph (C). **Effective** for tax years beginning after 12-31-2005.

• 2004, Working Families Tax Relief Act of 2004 (P.L. 108-311)

P.L. 108-311, §408(a)(1):

Amended Code Sec. 1(g)(7)(B)(ii)(II) by striking "10 per-cent." and inserting "10 percent". **Effective** 10-4-2004.

• 2001, Economic Growth and Tax Relief Reconciliation Act of 2001 (P.L. 107-16)

P.L. 107-16, §101(c)(1):

Amended Code Sec. 1(g)(7)(B)(ii)(II) by striking "15 percent" and inserting "10 percent.". **Effective** for tax years beginning after 12-31-2000.

P.L. 107-16, §901(a)-(b), provides:

SEC. 901. SUNSET OF PROVISIONS OF ACT.

(a) IN GENERAL.—All provisions of, and amendments made by, this Act shall not apply—

(1) to taxable, plan, or limitation years beginning after December 31, 2010, or

(2) in the case of title V, to estates of decedents dying, gifts made, or generation skipping transfers, after December 31, 2010.

(b) APPLICATION OF CERTAIN LAWS.—The Internal Revenue Code of 1986 and the Employee Retirement Income Security Act of 1974 shall be applied and administered to years, estates, gifts, and transfers described in subsection (a) as if the provisions and amendments described in subsection (a) had never been enacted.

• 1998, IRS Restructuring and Reform Act of 1998 (P.L. 105-206)

P.L. 105-206, §6007(f)(1):

Amended Code Sec. 1(g)(3) by striking subparagraph (C) and by redesignating subparagraph (D) as subparagraph (C). **Effective** as if included in P.L. 105-34 to which it relates [**effective** for sales or exchanges after 8-5-97.—CCH]. Prior to being stricken, Code Sec. 1(g)(3)(C) read as follows:

(C) COORDINATION WITH SECTION 644.—If tax is imposed under section 644(a)(1) with respect to the sale or exchange of any property of which the parent was the transferor, for purposes of applying subparagraph (A) to the taxable year of the parent in which such sale or exchange occurs—

(i) taxable income of the parent shall be increased by the amount treated as included in gross income under section 644(a)(2)(A)(i), and

(ii) the amount described in subparagraph (A)(ii) shall be increased by the amount of the excess referred to in section 644(a)(2)(A).

• 1996, Small Business Job Protection Act of 1996 (P.L. 104-188)

P.L. 104-188, §1704(m)(1):

Amended Code Sec. 1(g)(7)(A)(ii). **Effective** for tax years beginning after 12-31-95. Prior to amendment, Code Sec. 1(g)(7)(A)(ii) read as follows:

(ii) such gross income is more than $500 and less than $5,000,

P.L. 104-188, §1704(m)(2)(A)-(B):

Amended Code Sec. 1(g)(7)(B) by striking "$1,000" in clause (i) and inserting "twice the amount described in paragraph (4)(A)(ii)(I)", and by amending subclause (II) of clause (ii). **Effective** for tax years beginning after 12-31-95. Prior to amendment, Code Sec. 1(g)(7)(B)(ii)(II) read as follows:

(II) for each such child, the lesser of $75 or 15 percent of the excess of the gross income of such child over $500, and

• 1990, Omnibus Budget Reconciliation Act of 1990 (P.L. 101-508)

P.L. 101-508, §11101(d)(2):

Amended Code Sec. 1 by striking out subsection (h) and redesignating subsection (i) as subsection (g). **Effective** for tax years beginning after 12-31-90. Prior to amendment, Code Sec. 1(h) read as follows:

(h) TAX SCHEDULES FOR TAXABLE YEARS BEGINNING IN 1987.—In the case of any taxable year beginning in 1987—

(1) subsection (g) shall not apply, and2) the following tables shall apply in lieu of the tables set forth in subsections (a), (b), (c), (d), and (e):

(A) MARRIED INDIVIDUALS FILING RETURNS AND SURVIVING SPOUSES.—The table to apply for purposes of subsection (a) is as follows:

If taxable income is:	*The tax is:*
Not over $3,000 .	11% of taxable income.

Over $3,000 but not over $28,000 . . .	$330, plus 15% of the excess over $3,000.
Over $28,000 but not over $45,000 .	$4,080, plus 28% of the excess over $28,000.
Over $45,000 but not over $90,000 .	$8,840, plus 35% of the excess over $45,000.
Over $90,000 . . .	$24,590, plus 38.5% of the excess over $90,000.

(B) HEADS OF HOUSEHOLDS.—The table to apply for purposes of subsection (b) is as follows:

If taxable income is:	*The tax is:*
Not over $2,500 .	11% of taxable income.
Over $2,500 but not over $23,000 . . .	$275, plus 15% of the excess over $2,500.
Over $23,000 but not over $38,000 .	$3,350, plus 28% of the excess over $23,000.
Over $38,000 but not over $80,000 .	$7,550, plus 35% of the excess over $38,000.
Over $80,000 . . .	$22,250, plus 38.5% of the excess over $80,000.

(C) UNMARRIED INDIVIDUALS OTHER THAN SURVIVING SPOUSES AND HEADS OF HOUSEHOLDS.—The table to apply for purposes of subsection (c) is as follows:

If taxable income is:	*The tax is:*
Not over $1,800 .	11% of taxable income.
Over $1,800 but not over $16,800 . . .	$198, plus 15% of the excess over $1,800.
Over $16,800 but not over $27,000 .	$2,448, plus 28% of the excess over $16,800.
Over $27,000 but not over $54,000 .	$5,304, plus 35% of the excess over $27,000.
Over $54,000 . . .	$14,754, plus 38.5% of the excess over $54,000.

(D) MARRIED INDIVIDUALS FILING SEPARATE RETURNS.—The table to apply for purposes of subsection (d) is as follows:

If taxable income is:	*The tax is:*
Not over $1,500 .	11% of taxable income.
Over $1,500 but not over $14,000 . . .	$165, plus 15% of the excess over $1,500.
Over $14,000 but not over $22,500 .	$2,040, plus 28% of the excess over $14,000.
Over $22,500 but not over $45,000 .	$4,420, plus 35% of the excess over $22,500.
Over $45,000 . . .	$12,295, plus 38.5% of the excess over $45,000.

(E) ESTATES AND TRUSTS.—The table to apply for purposes of subsection (e) is as follows:

If taxable income is:	*The tax is:*
Not over $500 . .	11% of taxable income.
Over $500 but not over $4,700 . . .	$55, plus 15% of the excess over $500.
Over $4,700 but not over $7,550	$685, plus 28% of the excess over $4,700.
Over $7,550 but not over $15,150 . . .	$1,483, plus 35% of the excess over $7,500 [$7,550].
Over $15,150 . . .	$4,143, plus 38.5% of the excess over $15,150.

• 1989, Omnibus Budget Reconciliation Act of 1989 (P.L. 101-239)

P.L. 101-239, §7811(j)(1):

Amended Code Sec. 1(i)(3) by redesignating subparagraph (C) as added by §1014(e)(7) of P.L. 100-647 as subparagraph (D). **Effective** as if included in the provision of P.L. 100-647 to which it relates.

P.L. 101-239, §7816(b):

Amended Code Sec. 1(i)(7)(A) by inserting "(other than [for] purposes of this paragraph)" after "shall be treated". **Effective** as if included in the provision of P.L. 100-647 to which it relates.

• 1988, Technical and Miscellaneous Revenue Act of 1988 (P.L. 100-647)

P.L. 100-647, §1014(e)(1):

Amended Code Sec. 1(i)(3) by adding at the end thereof new subparagraph (C). **Effective** as if included in the provision of P.L. 99-514 to which it relates.

P.L. 100-647, §1014(e)(2):

Amended Code Sec. 1(i)(3)(A) by striking out "any deduction or credit" and inserting in lieu thereof "any exclusion, deduction, or credit". **Effective** as if included in the provision of P.L. 99-514 to which it relates.

P.L. 100-647, §1014(e)(3)(A)-(D):

Amended Code Sec. 1(i)(4)(A) by striking out "gross income for the taxable year which is not earned income" in clause (i) and inserting in lieu thereof "adjusted gross income for the taxable year which is not attributable to earned income", by striking out "his deduction" in clause (ii)(II) and inserting in lieu thereof "his deductions", by striking out "the deductions allowed" in clause (ii)(II) and inserting in lieu thereof "the itemized deductions allowed", and by striking out "gross income" in clause (ii)(II) and inserting in lieu thereof "adjusted gross income". **Effective** as if included in the provision of P.L. 99-514 to which it relates.

P.L. 100-647, §1014(e)(6):

Amended Code Sec. 1(i)(5)(A) by striking out "custodial parent" and inserting in lieu thereof "custodial parent (within the meaning of section 152(e))". **Effective** as if included in the provision of P.L. 99-514 to which it relates.

P.L. 100-647, §1014(e)(7):

Amended Code Sec. 1(i)(3) by adding at the end thereof new subparagraph (C)[(D)]. **Effective** as if included in the provision of P.L. 99-514 to which it relates.

P.L. 100-647, §6006(a):

Amended Code Sec. 1(i) by adding at the end thereof new paragraph (7). **Effective** for tax years beginning after 12-31-88.

[Sec. 1(h)]

(h) MAXIMUM CAPITAL GAINS RATE.—

(1) IN GENERAL.—If a taxpayer has a net capital gain for any taxable year, the tax imposed by this section for such taxable year shall not exceed the sum of—

(A) a tax computed at the rates and in the same manner as if this subsection had not been enacted on the greater of—

(i) taxable income reduced by the net capital gain, or

(ii) the lesser of—

Caution: Code Sec. 1(h)(1)(A)(ii)(I), below, is subject to the sunset provision of the Economic Growth and Tax Relief Reconciliation Act of 2001 (P.L. 107-16), §901. Absent Congressional action, the changes made to this provision by P.L. 107-16, or that take effect as if included in P.L. 107-16, do not apply after December 31, 2010. For more information about the sunset provision, see page XXI of the Preface to this publication and P.L. 107-16, §901, in the amendment notes. See the amendments notes for a history of amendments to this section and the effective date of each change.

(I) the amount of taxable income taxed at a rate below 25 percent; or

(II) taxable income reduced by the adjusted net capital gain;

Caution: Code Sec. 1(h)(1)(B), below, is subject to the sunset provision of the Jobs and Growth Tax Relief Reconciliation Act of 2003 (P.L. 108-27), §303. Absent Congressional action, the changes made to this provision by P.L. 108-27, or that take effect as if included in P.L. 108-27, do not apply after December 31, 2010. For more information about the sunset provision, see page XXI of the Preface to this publication and P.L. 108-27, §303, in the amendment notes. See the amendments notes for a history of amendments to this section and the effective date of each change.

(B) 5 percent (0 percent in the case of taxable years beginning after 2007) of so much of the adjusted net capital gain (or, if less, taxable income) as does not exceed the excess (if any) of—

Caution: Code Sec. 1(h)(1)(B)(i), below, is subject to the sunset provision of the Economic Growth and Tax Relief Reconciliation Act of 2001 (P.L. 107-16), §901. Absent Congressional action, the changes made to this provision by P.L. 107-16, or that take effect as if included in P.L. 107-16, do not apply after December 31, 2010. For more information about the sunset provision, see page XXI of the Preface to this publication and P.L. 107-16, §901, in the amendment notes. See the amendments notes for a history of amendments to this section and the effective date of each change.

(i) the amount of taxable income which would (without regard to this paragraph) be taxed at a rate below 25 percent, over

(ii) the taxable income reduced by the adjusted net capital gain;

Caution: Code Sec. 1(h)(1)(C), below, is subject to the sunset provision of the Jobs and Growth Tax Relief Reconciliation Act of 2003 (P.L. 108-27), §303. Absent Congressional action, the changes made to this provision by P.L. 108-27, or that take effect as if included in P.L. 108-27, do not apply after December 31, 2010. For more information about the sunset provision, see page XXI of the Preface to this publication and P.L. 108-27, §303, in the amendment notes. See the amendments notes for a history of amendments to this section and the effective date of each change.

(C) 15 percent of the adjusted net capital gain (or, if less, taxable income) in excess of the amount on which a tax is determined under subparagraph (B);

(D) 25 percent of the excess (if any) of—

(i) the unrecaptured section 1250 gain (or, if less, the net capital gain (determined without regard to paragraph (11))), over

(ii) the excess (if any) of—

(I) the sum of the amount on which tax is determined under subparagraph (A) plus the net capital gain, over

(II) taxable income; and

(E) 28 percent of the amount of taxable income in excess of the sum of the amounts on which tax is determined under the preceding subparagraphs of this paragraph.

(2) NET CAPITAL GAIN TAKEN INTO ACCOUNT AS INVESTMENT INCOME.—For purposes of this subsection, the net capital gain for any taxable year shall be reduced (but not below zero) by the amount which the taxpayer takes into account as investment income under section 163(d)(4)(B)(iii).

Caution: Code Sec. 1(h)(3), below, is subject to the sunset provision of the Jobs and Growth Tax Relief Reconciliation Act of 2003 (P.L. 108-27), §303. Absent Congressional action, the changes made to this provision by P.L. 108-27, or that take effect as if included in P.L. 108-27, do not apply after December 31, 2010. For more information about the sunset provision, see page XXI of the Preface to this publication and P.L. 108-27, §303, in the amendment notes. See the amendments notes for a history of amendments to this section and the effective date of each change.

(3) ADJUSTED NET CAPITAL GAIN.—For purposes of this subsection, the term "adjusted net capital gain" means the sum of—

(A) net capital gain (determined without regard to paragraph (11)) reduced (but not below zero) by the sum of—

(i) unrecaptured section 1250 gain, and

(ii) 28-percent rate gain, plus

(B) qualified dividend income (as defined in paragraph (11)).

(4) 28-PERCENT RATE GAIN.—For purposes of this subsection, the term "28-percent rate gain" means the excess (if any) of—

(A) the sum of—

(i) collectibles gain; and

(ii) section 1202 gain, over

(B) the sum of—

(i) collectibles loss;

(ii) the net short-term capital loss, and

(iii) the amount of long-term capital loss carried under section 1212(b)(1)(B) to the taxable year.

(5) COLLECTIBLES GAIN AND LOSS.—For purposes of this subsection—

(A) IN GENERAL.—The terms "collectibles gain" and "collectibles loss" mean gain or loss (respectively) from the sale or exchange of a collectible (as defined in section 408(m) without regard to paragraph (3) thereof) which is a capital asset held for more than 1 year but only to the extent such gain is taken into account in computing gross income and such loss is taken into account in computing taxable income.

(B) PARTNERSHIPS, ETC.—For purposes of subparagraph (A), any gain from the sale of an interest in a partnership, S corporation, or trust which is attributable to unrealized appreciation in the value of collectibles shall be treated as gain from the sale or exchange of a collectible. Rules similar to the rules of section 751 shall apply for purposes of the preceding sentence.

(6) UNRECAPTURED SECTION 1250 GAIN.—For purposes of this subsection—

(A) IN GENERAL.—The term "unrecaptured section 1250 gain" means the excess (if any) of—

(i) the amount of long-term capital gain (not otherwise treated as ordinary income) which would be treated as ordinary income if section 1250(b)(1) included all depreciation and the applicable percentage under section 1250(a) were 100 percent, over

(ii) the excess (if any) of—

(I) the amount described in paragraph (4)(B); over

(II) the amount described in paragraph (4)(A).

(B) LIMITATION WITH RESPECT TO SECTION 1231 PROPERTY.—The amount described in subparagraph (A)(i) from sales, exchanges, and conversions described in section 1231(a)(3)(A) for any taxable year shall not exceed the net section 1231 gain (as defined in section 1231(c)(3)) for such year.

(7) SECTION 1202 GAIN.—For purposes of this subsection, the term "section 1202 gain" means the excess of—

(A) the gain which would be excluded from gross income under section 1202 but for the percentage limitation in section 1202(a), over

(B) the gain excluded from gross income under section 1202.

(8) COORDINATION WITH RECAPTURE OF NET ORDINARY LOSSES UNDER SECTION 1231.—If any amount is treated as ordinary income under section 1231(c), such amount shall be allocated among the separate categories of net section 1231 gain (as defined in section 1231(c)(3)) in such manner as the Secretary may by forms or regulations prescribe.

(9) REGULATIONS.—The Secretary may prescribe such regulations as are appropriate (including regulations requiring reporting) to apply this subsection in the case of sales and exchanges by pass-thru entities and of interests in such entities.

(10) PASS-THRU ENTITY DEFINED.—For purposes of this subsection, the term "pass-thru entity" means—

(A) a regulated investment company;

(B) a real estate investment trust;

(C) an S corporation;

(D) a partnership;

(E) an estate or trust;

(F) a common trust fund; and

(G) a qualified electing fund (as defined in section 1295).

»»→ Caution: Code Sec. 1(h)(11), below, was added by P.L. 108-27 and amended by P.L. 108-311, and is subject to the sunset provision of the Jobs and Growth Tax Relief Reconciliation Act of 2003 (P.L. 108-27), §303. Absent Congressional action, the changes made to this provision by P.L. 108-27, or that take effect as if included in P.L. 108-27, do not apply after December 31, 2010. For more information about the sunset provision, see page XXI of the Preface to this publication and P.L. 108-27, §303, in the amendment notes. See the amendments notes for a history of amendments to this section and the effective date of each change.

(11) DIVIDENDS TAXED AS NET CAPITAL GAIN.—

(A) IN GENERAL.—For purposes of this subsection, the term "net capital gain" means net capital gain (determined without regard to this paragraph) increased by qualified dividend income.

(B) QUALIFIED DIVIDEND INCOME.—For purposes of this paragraph—

(i) IN GENERAL.—The term "qualified dividend income" means dividends received during the taxable year from—

(I) domestic corporations, and

(II) qualified foreign corporations.

(ii) CERTAIN DIVIDENDS EXCLUDED.—Such term shall not include—

(I) any dividend from a corporation which for the taxable year of the corporation in which the distribution is made, or the preceding taxable year, is a corporation exempt from tax under section 501 or 521,

(II) any amount allowed as a deduction under section 591 (relating to deduction for dividends paid by mutual savings banks, etc.), and

(III) any dividend described in section 404(k).

(iii) COORDINATION WITH SECTION 246(c).—Such term shall not include any dividend on any share of stock—

(I) with respect to which the holding period requirements of section 246(c) are not met (determined by substituting in section 246(c) "60 days" for "45 days" each place it appears and by substituting "121-day period" for "91-day period"), or

(II) to the extent that the taxpayer is under an obligation (whether pursuant to a short sale or otherwise) to make related payments with respect to positions in substantially similar or related property.

(C) QUALIFIED FOREIGN CORPORATIONS.—

(i) IN GENERAL.—Except as otherwise provided in this paragraph, the term "qualified foreign corporation" means any foreign corporation if—

(I) such corporation is incorporated in a possession of the United States, or

(II) such corporation is eligible for benefits of a comprehensive income tax treaty with the United States which the Secretary determines is satisfactory for purposes of this paragraph and which includes an exchange of information program.

(ii) DIVIDENDS ON STOCK READILY TRADABLE ON UNITED STATES SECURITIES MARKET.—A foreign corporation not otherwise treated as a qualified foreign corporation under clause (i) shall be so treated with respect to any dividend paid by such corporation if the stock with respect to which such dividend is paid is readily tradable on an established securities market in the United States.

(iii) EXCLUSION OF DIVIDENDS OF CERTAIN FOREIGN CORPORATIONS.—Such term shall not include any foreign corporation which for the taxable year of the corporation in which the dividend was paid, or the preceding taxable year, is a passive foreign investment company (as defined in section 1297).

(iv) COORDINATION WITH FOREIGN TAX CREDIT LIMITATION.—Rules similar to the rules of section 904(b)(2)(B) shall apply with respect to the dividend rate differential under this paragraph.

(D) SPECIAL RULES.—

(i) AMOUNTS TAKEN INTO ACCOUNT AS INVESTMENT INCOME.—Qualified dividend income shall not include any amount which the taxpayer takes into account as investment income under section 163(d)(4)(B).

(ii) EXTRAORDINARY DIVIDENDS.—If a taxpayer to whom this section applies receives, with respect to any share of stock, qualified dividend income from 1 or more dividends which are extraordinary dividends (within the meaning of section 1059(c)), any loss on the sale or exchange of such share shall, to the extent of such dividends, be treated as long-term capital loss.

(iii) TREATMENT OF DIVIDENDS FROM REGULATED INVESTMENT COMPANIES AND REAL ESTATE INVESTMENT TRUSTS.—A dividend received from a regulated investment company or a real estate investment trust shall be subject to the limitations prescribed in sections 854 and 857.

»»→ Caution: Code Sec. 1(h)(13), below, was stricken by P.L. 107-16, and is subject to the sunset provision of the Economic Growth and Tax Relief Reconciliation Act of 2001 (P.L. 107-16), §901. Absent Congressional action, the changes made to this provision by P.L. 107-16, or that take effect as if included in P.L. 107-16, do not apply after December 31, 2010. For more information about the sunset provision, see page XXI of the Preface to this publication and P.L. 107-16, §901, in the amendment notes. See the amendments notes for a history of amendments to this section and the effective date of each change.

(13) [Stricken.]

Amendments

• 2004, American Jobs Creation Act of 2004 (P.L. 108-357)

P.L. 108-357, §413(c)(1)(A):

Amended Code Sec. 1(h)(10) by inserting "and" at the end of subparagraph (F), by striking subparagraph (G), and by redesignating subparagraph (H) as subparagraph (G). **Effective** for tax years of foreign corporations beginning after 12-31-2004, and for tax years of United States shareholders with or within which such tax years of foreign corporations end. Prior to being stricken, Code Sec. 1(h)(10)(G) read as follows:

(G) a foreign investment company which is described in section 1246(b)(1) and for which an election is in effect under section 1247; and

P.L. 108-357, §413(c)(1)(B):

Amended Code Sec. 1(h)(11)(C)(iii) by striking "a foreign personal holding company (as defined in section 552), a foreign investment company (as defined in section 1246(b)), or" immediately preceding "a passive foreign investment company". **Effective** for tax years of foreign corporations beginning after 12-31-2004, and for tax years of United States shareholders with or within which such tax years of foreign corporations end.

• 2004, Working Families Tax Relief Act of 2004 (P.L. 108-311)

P.L. 108-311, §402(a)(1):

Amended Code Sec. 1(h)(1)(D)(i) by inserting "(determined without regard to paragraph (11))" after "net capital gain". **Effective** as if included in section 302 of the Jobs and Growth Tax Relief Reconciliation Act of 2003 (P.L. 108-27) [**effective** generally for tax years beginning after 12-31-2002.—CCH].

P.L. 108-311, §402(a)(2)(A)-(C):

Amended Code Sec. 1(h)(11)(B)(iii)(I) by striking "section 246(c)(1)" and inserting "section 246(c)", by striking "120-day period" and inserting "121-day period", and by striking "90-day period" and inserting "91-day period". **Effective** as if included in section 302 of the Jobs and Growth Tax Relief Reconciliation Act of 2003 (P.L. 108-27) [**effective** generally for tax years beginning after 12-31-2002.—CCH].

P.L. 108-311, §402(a)(3):

Amended Code Sec. 1(h)(11)(D)(ii) by striking "an individual" and inserting "a taxpayer to whom this section applies". **Effective** as if included in section 302 of the Jobs and Growth Tax Relief Reconciliation Act of 2003 (P.L. 108-27) [**effective** generally for tax years beginning after 12-31-2002.—CCH].

P.L. 108-311, §408(a)(2)(A)-(B):

Amended Code Sec. 1(h)(6)(A)(ii) by striking "(5)(B)" in subclause (I) and inserting "(4)(B)", and by striking "(5)(A)" in subclause (II) and inserting "(4)(A)". **Effective** 10-4-2004.

• 2003, Jobs and Growth Tax Relief Reconciliation Act of 2003 (P.L. 108-27)

P.L. 108-27, §301(a)(1):

Amended Code Sec. 1(h)(1)(B) by striking "10 percent" and inserting "5 percent (0 percent in the case of taxable years beginning after 2007)". **Effective** for tax years ending on or after 5-6-2003. For a transition rule, see Act Sec. 301(c), below.

P.L. 108-27, §301(a)(2)(A):

Amended Code Sec. 1(h)(1)(C) by striking "20 percent" and inserting "15 percent". **Effective** for tax years ending on or after 5-6-2003. For a transition rule, see Act Sec. 301(c), below.

P.L. 108-27, §301(b)(1)(A)-(C):

Amended Code Sec. 1(h) by striking paragraphs (2) and (9), by redesignating paragraphs (3) through (8) as paragraphs (2) through (7), respectively, and by redesignating paragraphs (10), (11), and (12) as paragraphs (8), (9), and (10), respectively. **Effective** for tax years ending on or after 5-6-2003. For a transition rule, see Act Sec. 301(c), below. Prior to being stricken, Code Sec. 1(h)(2) and (9) read as follows:

(2) REDUCED CAPITAL GAIN RATES FOR QUALIFIED 5-YEAR GAIN.—

(A) REDUCTION IN 10-PERCENT RATE.— In the case of any taxable year beginning after December 31, 2000, the rate under paragraph (1)(B) shall be 8 percent with respect to so much of the amount to which the 10-percent rate would otherwise apply as does not exceed qualified 5-year gain, and 10 percent with respect to the remainder of such amount.

(B) REDUCTION IN 20-PERCENT RATE.— The rate under paragraph (1)(C) shall be 18 percent with respect to so much of the amount to which the 20-percent rate would otherwise apply as does not exceed the lesser of—

(i) the excess of qualified 5-year gain over the amount of such gain taken into account under subparagraph (A) of this paragraph; or

(ii) the amount of qualified 5-year gain (determined by taking into account only property the holding period for which begins after December 31, 2000),

and 20 percent with respect to the remainder of such amount. For purposes of determining under the preceding sentence whether the holding period of property begins after December 31, 2000, the holding period of property acquired pursuant to the exercise of an option (or other right or obligation to acquire property) shall include the period such option (or other right or obligation) was held.

* * *

(9) QUALIFIED 5-YEAR GAIN.—For purposes of this subsection, the term "qualified 5-year gain" means the aggregate long-term capital gain from property held for more than 5 years. The determination under the preceding sentence shall be made without regard to collectibles gain, gain described in paragraph (7)(A)(i), and section 1202 gain.

P.L. 108-27, §301(c), provides:

(c) TRANSITIONAL RULES FOR TAXABLE YEARS WHICH INCLUDE MAY 6, 2003.—For purposes of applying section 1(h) of the Internal Revenue Code of 1986 in the case of a taxable year which includes May 6, 2003—

(1) The amount of tax determined under subparagraph (B) of section 1(h)(1) of such Code shall be the sum of—

(A) 5 percent of the lesser of—

(i) the net capital gain determined by taking into account only gain or loss properly taken into account for the portion of the taxable year on or after May 6, 2003 (determined without regard to collectibles gain or loss, gain described in section 1(h)(6)(A)(i) of such Code, and section 1202 gain), or

(ii) the amount on which a tax is determined under such subparagraph (without regard to this subsection),

(B) 8 percent of the lesser of—

(i) the qualified 5-year gain (as defined in section 1(h)(9) of the Internal Revenue Code of 1986, as in effect on the day before the date of the enactment of this Act) properly taken into account for the portion of the taxable year before May 6, 2003, or

(ii) the excess (if any) of—

(I) the amount on which a tax is determined under such subparagraph (without regard to this subsection), over

(II) the amount on which a tax is determined under subparagraph (A), plus

(C) 10 percent of the excess (if any) of—

(i) the amount on which a tax is determined under such subparagraph (without regard to this subsection), over

(ii) the sum of the amounts on which a tax is determined under subparagraphs (A) and (B).

(2) The amount of tax determined under subparagraph (C) of section (1)(h)(1) of such Code shall be the sum of—

(A) 15 percent of the lesser of—

(i) the excess (if any) of the amount of net capital gain determined under subparagraph (A)(i) of paragraph (1) of this subsection over the amount on which a tax is determined under subparagraph (A) of paragraph (1) of this subsection, or

(ii) the amount on which a tax is determined under such subparagraph (C) (without regard to this subsection), plus

(B) 20 percent of the excess (if any) of—

(i) the amount on which a tax is determined under such subparagraph (C) (without regard to this subsection), over

(ii) the amount on which a tax is determined under subparagraph (A) of this paragraph.

(3) For purposes of applying section 55(b)(3) of such Code, rules similar to the rules of paragraphs (1) and (2) of this subsection shall apply.

(4) In applying this subsection with respect to any passthru entity, the determination of when gains and losses are properly taken into account shall be made at the entity level.

(5) For purposes of applying section 1(h)(11) of such Code, as added by section 302 of this Act, to this subsection, dividends which are qualified dividend income shall be treated as gain properly taken into account for the portion of the taxable year on or after May 6, 2003.

(6) Terms used in this subsection which are also used in section 1(h) of such Code shall have the respective meanings that such terms have in such section.

P.L. 108-27, §302(a):

Amended Code Sec. 1(h), as amended by Act Sec. 301, by adding at the end a new paragraph (11). For the **effective** date, see Act Sec. 302(f), as amended by P.L. 108-311, §402(a)(6), below.

P.L. 108-27, §302(e)(1):

Amended Code Sec. 1(h)(3), as redesignated by Act Sec. 301. For the **effective** date, see Act Sec. 302(f), as amended by P.L. 108-311, §402(a)(6), below. Prior to amendment, but after redesignation, Code Sec. 1(h)(3) read as follows:

(3) ADJUSTED NET CAPITAL GAIN.—For purposes of this subsection, the term "adjusted net capital gain" means net capital gain reduced (but not below zero) by the sum of—

(A) unrecaptured section 1250 gain; and

(B) 28-percent rate gain.

P.L. 108-27, §302(f), as amended by P.L. 108-311, §402(a)(6), provides:

(f) EFFECTIVE DATE.—

(1) IN GENERAL.—Except as provided in paragraph (2), the amendments made by this section shall apply to taxable years beginning after December 31, 2002.

(2) PASS-THRU ENTITIES.—In the case of a pass-thru entity described in subparagraph (A), (B), (C), (D), (E), or (F) of section 1(h)(10) of the Internal Revenue Code of 1986, as amended by this Act, the amendments made by this section shall apply to taxable years ending after December 31, 2002; except that dividends received by such an entity on or before such date shall not be treated as qualified dividend income (as defined in section 1(h)(11)(B) of such Code, as added by this Act).

P.L. 108-27, §303, as amended by P.L. 109-222, §102, provides:

SEC. 303. SUNSET OF TITLE.

All provisions of, and amendments made by, this title shall not apply to taxable years beginning after December 31, 2010, and the Internal Revenue Code of 1986 shall be applied and administered to such years as if such provisions and amendments had never been enacted.

• 2001, Economic Growth and Tax Relief Reconciliation Act of 2001 (P.L. 107-16)

P.L. 107-16, §101(c)(2)(A)-(B):

Amended Code Sec. 1(h) by striking "28 percent" both places it appears in paragraphs (1)(A)(ii)(I) and (1)(B)(i) and inserting "25 percent", and by striking paragraph (13). **Effective** for tax years beginning after 12-31-2000. Prior to being stricken, Code Sec. 1(h)(13) read as follows:

(13) SPECIAL RULES.—

(A) DETERMINATION OF 28-PERCENT RATE GAIN.—In applying paragraph (5)—

(i) the amount determined under subparagraph (A) of paragraph (5) shall include long-term capital gain (not otherwise described in such subparagraph)—

(I) which is properly taken into account for the portion of the taxable year before May 7, 1997; or

(II) from property held not more than 18 months which is properly taken into account for the portion of the taxable year after July 28, 1997, and before January 1, 1998;

(ii) the amount determined under subparagraph (B) of paragraph (5) shall include long-term capital loss (not otherwise described in such subparagraph)—

(I) which is properly taken into account for the portion of the taxable year before May 7, 1997; or

(II) from property held not more than 18 months which is properly taken into account for the portion of the taxable year after July 28, 1997, and before January 1, 1998; and

(iii) subparagraph (B) of paragraph (5) (as in effect immediately before the enactment of this clause) shall apply to amounts properly taken into account before January 1, 1998.

(B) DETERMINATION OF UNRECAPTURED SECTION 1250 GAIN.—The amount determined under paragraph (7)(A)(i) shall not include gain—

(i) which is properly taken into account for the portion of the taxable year before May 7, 1997; or

(ii) from property held not more than 18 months which is properly taken into account for the portion of the taxable year after July 28, 1997, and before January 1, 1998.

(C) SPECIAL RULES FOR PASS-THRU ENTITIES.—In applying this paragraph with respect to any pass-thru entity, the determination of when gains and loss are properly taken into account shall be made at the entity level.

(D) CHARITABLE REMAINDER TRUSTS.—Subparagraphs (A) and (B)(ii) shall not apply to any capital gain distribution made by a trust described in section 664.

P.L. 107-16, §901(a)-(b), provides:

SEC. 901. SUNSET OF PROVISIONS OF ACT.

(a) IN GENERAL.—All provisions of, and amendments made by, this Act shall not apply—

(1) to taxable, plan, or limitation years beginning after December 31, 2010, or

(2) in the case of title V, to estates of decedents dying, gifts made, or generation skipping transfers, after December 31, 2010.

(b) APPLICATION OF CERTAIN LAWS.—The Internal Revenue Code of 1986 and the Employee Retirement Income Security Act of 1974 shall be applied and administered to years, estates, gifts, and transfers described in subsection (a) as if the provisions and amendments described in subsection (a) had never been enacted.

• 2000, Community Renewal Tax Relief Act of 2000 (P.L. 106-554)

P.L. 106-554, §117(b)(1):

Amended Code Sec. 1(h)(8) by striking "means" and all that follows and inserting new text. **Effective** for stock acquired after 12-21-2000. Prior to amendment, Code Sec. 1(h)(8) read as follows:

(8) SECTION 1202 GAIN.—For purposes of this subsection, the term "section 1202 gain" means an amount equal to the gain excluded from gross income under section 1202(a).

• 1998, Tax and Trade Relief Extension Act of 1998 (P.L. 105-277)

P.L. 105-277, §4002(i)(1):

Amended Code Sec. 1(h)(13)(B) by striking "paragraph (7)(A)" and inserting "paragraph (7)(A)(i)". **Effective** as if included in the provision of P.L. 105-206 to which it relates [**effective** for tax years ending after 12-31-97.—CCH]. For special rules, see Act Secs. 4002(i)(2)(A)-(D) and 4003(b), below.

P.L. 105-277, §4002(i)(3):

Amended Code Sec. 1(h)(13) by adding at the end a new subparagraph (D). **Effective** as if included in the provision of P.L. 105-206 to which it relates [**effective** for tax years ending after 12-31-97.—CCH]. For special rules, see Act Secs. 4002(i)(2)(A)-(D) and 4003(b), below.

P.L. 105-277, §4002(i)(2)(A)-(D), provides:

(2)(A) Subparagraphs (A)(i)(II), (A)(ii)(II), and (B)(ii) of section 1(h)(13) of the 1986 Code shall not apply to any distribution after December 31, 1997, by a regulated investment company or a real estate investment trust with respect to—

(i) gains and losses recognized directly by such company or trust, and

(ii) amounts properly taken into account by such company or trust by reason of holding (directly or indirectly) an interest in another such company or trust to the extent that such subparagraphs did not apply to such other company or trust with respect to such amounts.

(B) Subparagraph (A) shall not apply to any distribution which is treated under section 852(b)(7) or 857(b)(8) of the 1986 Code as received on December 31, 1997.

(C) For purposes of subparagraph (A), any amount which is includible in gross income of its shareholders under section 852(b)(3)(D) or 857(b)(3)(D) of the 1986 Code after December 31, 1997, shall be treated as distributed after such date.

(D)(i) For purposes of subparagraph (A), in the case of a qualified partnership with respect to which a regulated investment company meets the holding requirement of clause (iii)—

(I) the subparagraphs referred to in subparagraph (A) shall not apply to gains and losses recognized directly by such partnership for purposes of determining such company's distributive share of such gains and losses, and

(II) such company's distributive share of such gains and losses (as so determined) shall be treated as recognized directly by such company.

The preceding sentence shall apply only if the qualified partnership provides the company with written documentation of such distributive share as so determined.

(ii) For purposes of clause (i), the term "qualified partnership" means, with respect to a regulated investment company, any partnership if—

(I) the partnership is an investment company registered under the Investment Company Act of 1940,

(II) the regulated investment company is permitted to invest in such partnership by reason of section 12(d)(1)(E) of such Act or an exemptive order of the Securities and Exchange Commission under such section, and

(III) the regulated investment company and the partnership have the same taxable year.

(iii) A regulated investment company meets the holding requirement of this clause with respect to a qualified partnership if (as of January 1, 1998)—

(I) the value of the interests of the regulated investment company in such partnership is 35 percent or more of the value of such company's total assets, or

(II) the value of the interests of the regulated investment company in such partnership and all other qualified partnerships is 90 percent or more of the value of such company's total assets.

P.L. 105-277, §4003(b), as amended by P.L. 106-554, §312(b), provides:

(b) PROVISION RELATED TO SECTION 311 OF 1997 ACT.—In the case of any capital gain distribution made after 1997 by a trust to which section 664 of the 1986 Code applies with respect to amounts properly taken into account by such trust during 1997, paragraphs (5)(A)(i)(I), (5)(A)(ii)(I), (7)(A)(i)(II), and (13)(A) of section 1(h) of the 1986 Code (as in effect for taxable years ending on December 31, 1997) shall not apply.

• 1998, IRS Restructuring and Reform Act of 1998 (P.L. 105-206)

P.L. 105-206, §5001(a)(1):

Amended Code Sec. 1(h)(5). **Effective** for tax years ending after 12-31-97. Prior to amendment, Code Sec. 1(h)(5) read as follows:

(5) 28-PERCENT RATE GAIN.—For purposes of this subsection—

(A) IN GENERAL.—The term "28-percent rate gain" means the excess (if any) of—

(i) the sum of—

(I) the aggregate long-term capital gain from property held for more than 1 year but not more than 18 months;

(II) collectibles gain; and

(III) section 1202 gain, over

(ii) the sum of—

(I) the aggregate long-term capital loss (not described in subclause (IV)) from property referred to in clause (i)(I);

(II) collectibles loss;

(III) the net short-term capital loss; and

(IV) the amount of long-term capital loss carried under section 1212(b)(1)(B) to the taxable year.

(B) SPECIAL RULES.—

(i) SHORT SALE GAINS AND HOLDING PERIODS.—Rules similar to the rules of section 1233(b) shall apply where the substantially identical property has been held more than 1 year but not more than 18 months; except that, for purposes of such rules—

(I) section 1233(b)(1) shall be applied by substituting "18 months" for "1 year" each place it appears; and

(II) the holding period of such property shall be treated as being 1 year on the day before the earlier of the date of the closing of the short sale or the date such property is disposed of.

(ii) LONG-TERM LOSSES.—Section 1233(d) shall be applied separately by substituting "18 months" for "1 year" each place it appears.

(iii) OPTIONS.—A rule similar to the rule of section 1092(f) shall apply where the stock was held for more than 18 months.

(iv) SECTION 1256 CONTRACTS.— Amounts treated as long-term capital gain or loss under section 1256(a)(3) shall be treated as attributable to property held for more than 18 months.

P.L. 105-206, §5001(a)(2):

Amended Code Sec. 1(h)(6)(A) by striking "18 months" and inserting "1 year". **Effective** for tax years ending after 12-31-97.

P.L. 105-206, §5001(a)(3):

Amended Code Sec. 1(h)(7)(A)(i) and (ii). **Effective** for tax years ending after 12-31-97. Prior to amendment, Code Sec. 1(h)(7)(A)(i)-(ii) read as follows:

(i) the amount of long-term capital gain (not otherwise treated as ordinary income) which would be treated as ordinary income if—

(I) section 1250(b)(1) included all depreciation and the applicable percentage under section 1250(a) were 100 percent, and

(II) only gain from property held for more than 18 months were taken into account, over

(ii) the excess (if any) of—

(I) the amount described in paragraph (5)(A)(ii), over

(II) the amount described in paragraph (5)(A)(i).

P.L. 105-206, §5001(a)(4):

Amended so much of paragraph (13) of Code Sec. 1(h) as precedes subparagraph (C). **Effective** for tax years ending after 12-31-97. Prior to amendment, so much of Code Sec. 1(h)(13) as preceded subparagraph (C) read as follows:

(13) SPECIAL RULES FOR PERIODS DURING 1997.—

(A) DETERMINATION OF 28-PERCENT RATE GAIN.—In applying paragraph (5)—

(i) the amount determined under subclause (I) of paragraph (5)(A)(i) shall include long-term capital gain (not otherwise described in paragraph (5)(A)(i)) which is properly taken into account for the portion of the taxable year before May 7, 1997;

(ii) the amounts determined under subclause (I) of paragraph (5)(A)(ii) shall include long-term capital loss (not otherwise described in paragraph (5)(A)(ii)) which is properly taken into account for the portion of the taxable year before May 7, 1997; and

(iii) clauses (i)(I) and (ii)(I) of paragraph (5)(A) shall be applied by not taking into account any gain and loss on property held for more than 1 year but not more than 18 months which is properly taken into account for the portion of the taxable year after May 6, 1997, and before July 29, 1997.

(B) OTHER SPECIAL RULES.—

(i) DETERMINATION OF UNRECAPTURED SECTION 1250 GAIN NOT TO INCLUDE PRE-MAY 7, 1997 GAIN.—The amount determined under paragraph (7)(A)(i) shall not include gain properly taken into account for the portion of the taxable year before May 7, 1997.

(ii) OTHER TRANSITIONAL RULES FOR 18-MONTH HOLDING PERIOD.—Paragraphs (6)(A) and (7)(A)(i)(II) shall be applied by substituting "1 year" for "18 months" with respect to gain properly taken into account for the portion of the taxable year after May 6, 1997, and before July 29, 1997.

P.L. 105-206, §6005(d)(1):

Amended Code Sec. 1(h). **Effective** as if included in the provision of P.L. 105-34 to which it relates [**effective** for tax years ending after 5-6-97.—CCH]. Prior to amendment, Code Sec. 1(h) read as follows:

(h) MAXIMUM CAPITAL GAINS RATE.—

(1) IN GENERAL.—If a taxpayer has a net capital gain for any taxable year, the tax imposed by this section for such taxable year shall not exceed the sum of—

(A) a tax computed at the rates and in the same manner as if this subsection had not been enacted on the greater of—

(i) taxable income reduced by the net capital gain, or

(ii) the lesser of—

(I) the amount of taxable income taxed at a rate below 28 percent, or

(II) taxable income reduced by the adjusted net capital gain, plus

(B) 25 percent of the excess (if any) of—

(i) the unrecaptured section 1250 gain (or, if less, the net capital gain), over

(ii) the excess (if any) of—

(I) the sum of the amount on which tax is determined under subparagraph (A) plus the net capital gain, over

(II) taxable income, plus

(C) 28 percent of the amount of taxable income in excess of the sum of—

(i) the adjusted net capital gain, plus

(ii) the sum of the amounts on which tax is determined under subparagraphs (A) and (B), plus

(D) 10 percent of so much of the taxpayer's adjusted net capital gain (or, if less, taxable income) as does not exceed the excess (if any) of—

(i) the amount of taxable income which would (without regard to this paragraph) be taxed at a rate below 28 percent, over

(ii) the taxable income reduced by the adjusted net capital gain, plus

(E) 20 percent of the taxpayer's adjusted net capital gain (or, if less, taxable income) in excess of the amount on which a tax is determined under subparagraph (D).

(2) REDUCED CAPITAL GAIN RATES FOR QUALIFIED 5-YEAR GAIN.—

(A) REDUCTION IN 10-PERCENT RATE.—In the case of any taxable year beginning after December 31, 2000, the rate under paragraph (1)(D) shall be 8 percent with respect to so much of the amount to which the 10-percent rate would otherwise apply as does not exceed qualified 5-year gain, and 10 percent with respect to the remainder of such amount.

(B) REDUCTION IN 20-PERCENT RATE.—The rate under paragraph (1)(E) shall be 18 percent with respect to so much of the amount to which the 20-percent rate would otherwise apply as does not exceed the lesser of—

(i) the excess of qualified 5-year gain over the amount of such gain taken into account under subparagraph (A) of this paragraph, or

(ii) the amount of qualified 5-year gain (determined by taking into account only property the holding period for which begins after December 31, 2000), and 20 percent with respect to the remainder of such amount. For purposes of determining under the preceding sentence whether the holding period of property begins after December 31, 2000, the holding period of property acquired pursuant to the exercise of an option (or other right or obligation to acquire property) shall include the period such option (or other right or obligation) was held.

(3) NET CAPITAL GAIN TAKEN INTO ACCOUNT AS INVESTMENT INCOME.—For purposes of this subsection, the net capital gain for any taxable year shall be reduced (but not below zero) by the amount which the taxpayer takes into account as investment income under section 163(d)(4)(B)(iii).

(4) ADJUSTED NET CAPITAL GAIN.—For purposes of this subsection, the term "adjusted net capital gain" means net capital gain determined without regard to—

(A) collectibles gain,

(B) unrecaptured section 1250 gain,

(C) section 1202 gain, and

(D) mid-term gain.

(5) COLLECTIBLES GAIN.—For purposes of this subsection—

(A) IN GENERAL.—The term "collectibles gain" means gain from the sale or exchange of a collectible (as defined in section 408(m) without regard to paragraph (3) thereof) which is a capital asset held for more than 1 year but only to the extent such gain is taken into account in computing gross income.

(B) PARTNERSHIPS, ETC.—For purposes of subparagraph (A), any gain from the sale of an interest in a partnership, S corporation, or trust which is attributable to unrealized appreciation in the value of collectibles shall be treated as gain from the sale or exchange of a collectible. Rules similar to the rules of section 751 shall apply for purposes of the preceding sentence.

(6) UNRECAPTURED SECTION 1250 GAIN.—For purposes of this subsection—

(A) IN GENERAL.—The term "unrecaptured section 1250 gain" means the amount of long-term capital gain which would be treated as ordinary income if—

(i) section 1250(b)(1) included all depreciation and the applicable percentage under section 1250(a) were 100 percent, and

(ii) in the case of gain properly taken into account after July 28, 1997, only gain from section 1250 property held for more than 18 months were taken into account.

(B) LIMITATION WITH RESPECT TO SECTION 1231 PROPERTY.—The amount of unrecaptured section 1250 gain from sales, exchanges, and conversions described in section 1231(a)(3)(A) for any taxable year shall not exceed the excess of the net section 1231 gain (as defined in section 1231(c)(3)) for such year over the amount treated as ordinary income under section 1231(c)(1) for such year.

(C) PRE-MAY 7, 1997, GAIN.—In the case of a taxable year which includes May 7, 1997, subparagraph (A) shall be applied by taking into account only the gain properly taken into account for the portion of the taxable year after May 6, 1997.

(7) SECTION 1202 GAIN.—For purposes of this subsection, the term "section 1202 gain" means an amount equal to the gain excluded from gross income under section 1202(a).

(8) MID-TERM GAIN.—For purposes of this subsection, the term "mid-term gain" means the amount which would be adjusted net capital gain for the taxable year if—

(A) adjusted net capital gain were determined by taking into account only the gain or loss properly taken into account after July 28, 1997, from property held for more than 1 year but not more than 18 months, and

(B) paragraph (3) and section 1212 did not apply.

(9) QUALIFIED 5-YEAR GAIN.—For purposes of this subsection, the term "qualified 5-year gain" means the amount of long-term capital gain which would be computed for the taxable year if only gains from the sale or exchange of property held by the taxpayer for more than 5 years were taken into account. The determination under the preceding sentence shall be made without regard to collectibles gain, unrecaptured section 1250 gain (determined without regard to subparagraph (B) of paragraph (6)), section 1202 gain, or mid-term gain.

(10) PRE-EFFECTIVE DATE GAIN.—

(A) IN GENERAL.—In the case of a taxable year which includes May 7, 1997, gains and losses properly taken into account for the portion of the taxable year before May 7, 1997, shall be taken into account in determining mid-term gain as if such gains and losses were described in paragraph (8)(A).

(B) SPECIAL RULES FOR PASS-THRU ENTITIES.—In applying subparagraph (A) with respect to any pass-thru entity, the determination of when gains and loss are properly taken into account shall be made at the entity level.

(C) PASS-THRU ENTITY DEFINED.—For purposes of subparagraph (B), the term "pass-thru entity" means—

(i) a regulated investment company,

(ii) a real estate investment trust,

(iii) an S corporation,

(iv) a partnership,

(v) an estate or trust, and

(vi) a common trust fund.

(11) TREATMENT OF PASS-THRU ENTITIES.—The Secretary may prescribe such regulations as are appropriate (including regulations requiring reporting) to apply this subsection in the case of sales and exchanges by pass-thru entities (as defined in paragraph (10)(C)) and of interests in such entities.

• 1997, Taxpayer Relief Act of 1997 (P.L. 105-34)

P.L. 105-34, §311(a):

Amended Code Sec. 1(h). **Effective**, generally, for tax years ending after 5-6-97. For a special rule, see Act Sec. 311(e), below. Prior to amendment, Code Sec. 1(h) read as follows:

(h) MAXIMUM CAPITAL GAINS RATE.—If a taxpayer has a net capital gain for any taxable year, then the tax imposed by this section shall not exceed the sum of—

(1) a tax computed at the rates and in the same manner as if this subsection had not been enacted on the greater of—

(A) taxable income reduced by the amount of the net capital gain, or

(B) the amount of taxable income taxed at a rate below 28 percent, plus

(2) a tax of 28 percent of the amount of taxable income in excess of the amount determined under paragraph (1).

For purposes of the preceding sentence, the net capital gain for any taxable year shall be reduced (but not below zero) by the amount which the taxpayer elects to take into account as investment income for the taxable year under section 163(d)(4)(B)(iii).

P.L. 105-34, §311(e), as amended by P.L. 106-554, §314(c) and P.L. 107-147, §414(a), provides:

(e) ELECTION TO RECOGNIZE GAIN ON ASSETS HELD ON JANUARY 1, 2001.—For purposes of the Internal Revenue Code of 1986—

(1) IN GENERAL.—A taxpayer other than a corporation may elect to treat—

(A) any readily tradable stock (which is a capital asset) held by such taxpayer on January 1, 2001, and not sold before the next business day after such date, as having been sold on such next business day for an amount equal to its closing market price on such next business day (and as having been reacquired on such next business day for an amount equal to such closing market price), and

(B) any other capital asset or property used in the trade or business (as defined in section 1231(b) of the Internal Revenue Code of 1986) held by the taxpayer on January 1, 2001, as having been sold on such date for an amount equal to its fair market value on such date (and as having been reacquired on such date for an amount equal to such fair market value).

(2) TREATMENT OF GAIN OR LOSS.—

(A) Any gain resulting from an election under paragraph (1) shall be treated as received or accrued on the date the asset is treated as sold under paragraph (1) and shall be included in gross income notwithstanding any provision of the Internal Revenue Code of 1986.

(B) Any loss resulting from an election under paragraph (1) shall not be allowed for any taxable year.

(3) ELECTION.—An election under paragraph (1) shall be made in such manner as the Secretary of the Treasury or his delegate may prescribe and shall specify the assets for which such election is made. Such an election, once made with respect to any asset, shall be irrevocable. Such an election shall not apply to any asset which is disposed of (in a transaction in which gain or loss is recognized in whole or in part) before the close of the 1-year period beginning on the date that the asset would have been treated as sold under such election.

(4) READILY TRADABLE STOCK.—For purposes of this subsection, the term "readily tradable stock" means any stock which, as of January 1, 2001, is readily tradable on an established securities market or otherwise.

(5) DISPOSITION OF INTEREST IN PASSIVE ACTIVITY.—Section 469(g)(1)(A) of the Internal Revenue Code of 1986 shall not apply by reason of an election made under paragraph (1).

• 1993, Omnibus Budget Reconciliation Act of 1993 (P.L. 103-66)

P.L. 103-66, §13206(d)(2):

Amended Code Sec. 1(h) by adding at the end thereof a new sentence. **Effective** for tax years beginning after 12-31-92.

• 1990, Omnibus Budget Reconciliation Act of 1990 (P.L. 101-508)

P.L. 101-508, §11101(c):

Amended Code Sec. 1(j). **Effective** for tax years beginning after 12-31-90. Prior to amendment, Code Sec. 1(j) read as follows:

(j) MAXIMUM CAPITAL GAINS RATE.—

(1) IN GENERAL.—If a taxpayer has a net capital gain for any taxable year to which this subsection applies, then the tax imposed by this section shall not exceed the sum of—

(A) a tax computed at the rates and in the same manner as if this subsection had not been enacted on the greater of—

(i) the taxable income reduced by the amount of net capital gain, or

(ii) the amount of taxable income taxed at a rate below 28 percent, plus

(B) a tax of 28 percent of the amount of taxable income in excess of the amount determined under subparagraph (A), plus

(C) the amount of increase determined under subsection (g).

(2) YEARS TO WHICH SUBSECTION APPLIES.—This subsection shall apply to—

(A) any taxable year beginning in 1987, and

(B) any taxable year beginning after 1987 if the highest rate of tax set forth in subsection (a), (b), (c), (d), or (e), (whichever applies) for such taxable year exceeds 28 percent.

P.L. 101-508, §11101(d)(2):

Amended Code Sec. 1 by redesignating subsection (j) as subsection (h). **Effective** for tax years beginning after 12-31-90.

• 1986, Tax Reform Act of 1986 (P.L. 99-514)

P.L. 99-514, §101(a):

Amended Code Sec.1. **Effective** for tax years beginning after 12-31-86. Prior to amendment, Code Sec. 1 read as follows:

SECTION 1. TAX IMPOSED.

(a) MARRIED INDIVIDUALS FILING JOINT RETURNS AND SURVIVING SPOUSES.—There is hereby imposed on the taxable income of every married individual (as defined in section 143) who makes a single return jointly with his spouse under section 6013, and every surviving spouse (as defined in section 2(a)), a tax determined in accordance with the following tables:

(1) FOR TAXABLE YEARS BEGINNING IN 1982.—

If taxable income is:	The tax is:
Not over $3,400	No tax.
Over $3,400 but not over $5,500	12% of the excess over $3,400.
Over $5,500 but not over $7,600	$252, plus 14% of the excess over $5,500.
Over $7,600 but not over $11,900	$546, plus 16% of the excess over $7,600.
Over $11,900 but not over $16,000	$1,234, plus 19% of the excess over $11,900.
Over $16,000 but not over $20,200	$2,013, plus 22% of the excess over $16,000.
Over $20,200 but not over $24,600	$2,937, plus 25% of the excess over $20,200.
Over $24,600 but not over $29,900	$4,037, plus 29% of the excess over $24,600.
Over $29,900 but not over $35,200	$5,574, plus 33% of the excess over $29,900.
Over $35,200 but not over $45,800	$7,323, plus 39% of the excess over $35,200.
Over $45,800 but not over $60,000	$11,457, plus 44% of the excess over $45,800.
Over $60,000 but not over $85,600	$17,705, plus 49% of the excess over $60,000.
Over $85,600	$30,249, plus 50% of the excess over $85,600.

(2) FOR TAXABLE YEARS BEGINNING IN 1983.—

If taxable income is:	The tax is:
Not over $3,400	No tax.
Over $3,400 but not over $5,500	11% of the excess over $3,400.
Over $5,500 but not over $7,600	$231, plus 13% of the excess over $5,500.
Over $7,600 but not over $11,900	$504, plus 15% of the excess over $7,600.

If taxable income is:	The tax is:
Over $11,900 but not over $16,000	$1,149, plus 17% of the excess over $11,900.
Over $16,000 but not over $20,200	$1,846, plus 19% of the excess over $16,000.
Over $20,200 but not over $24,600	$2,644, plus 23% of the excess over $20,200.
Over $24,600 but not over $29,900	$3,656, plus 26% of the excess over $24,600.
Over $29,900 but not over $35,200	$5,034, plus 30% of the excess over $29,900.
Over $35,200 but not over $45,800	$6,624, plus 35% of the excess over $35,200.
Over $45,800 but not over $60,000	$10,334, plus 40% of the excess over $45,800.
Over $60,000 but not over $85,600	$16,014, plus 44% of the excess over $60,000.
Over $85,600 but not over $109,400	$27,278, plus 48% of the excess over $85,600.
Over $109,400	$38,702, plus 50% of the excess over $109,400.

(3) FOR TAXABLE YEARS BEGINNING AFTER 1983.—

If taxable income is:	The tax is:
Not over $3,400	No tax.
Over $3,400 but not over $5,500	11% of the excess over $3,400.
Over $5,500 but not over $7,600	$231, plus 12% of the excess over $5,500.
Over $7,600 but not over $11,900	$483, plus 14% of the excess over $7,600.
Over $11,900 but not over $16,000	$1,085, plus 16% of the excess over $11,900.
Over $16,000 but not over $20,200	$1,741, plus 18% of the excess over $16,000.
Over $20,200 but not over $24,600	$2,497, plus 22% of the excess over $20,200.
Over $24,600 but not over $29,900	$3,465, plus 25% of the excess over $24,600.
Over $29,900 but not over $35,200	$4,790, plus 28% of the excess over $29,900.
Over $35,200 but not over $45,800	$6,274, plus 33% of the excess over $35,200.
Over $45,800 but not over $60,000	$9,772, plus 38% of the excess over $45,800.
Over $60,000 but not over $85,600	$15,168, plus 42% of the excess over $60,000.
Over $85,600 but not over $109,400	$25,920, plus 45% of the excess over $85,600.
Over $109,400 but not over $162,400	$36,630, plus 49% of the excess over $109,400.
Over $162,400	$62,600, plus 50% of the excess over $162,400.

(b) HEADS OF HOUSEHOLDS.—There is hereby imposed on the taxable income of every individual who is the head of a household (as defined in section 2(b)) a tax determined in accordance with the following tables:

(1) FOR TAXABLE YEARS BEGINNING IN 1982.—

If taxable income is:	The tax is:
Not over $2,300	No tax.
Over $2,300 but not over $4,400	12% of the excess over $2,300.
Over $4,400 but not over $6,500	$252, plus 14% of the excess over $4,400.
Over $6,500 but not over $8,700	$546, plus 16% of the excess over $6,500.
Over $8,700 but not over $11,800	$898, plus 20% of the excess over $8,700.
Over $11,800 but not over $15,000	$1,518, plus 22% of the excess over $11,800
Over $15,000 but not over $18,200	$2,222, plus 23% of the excess over $15,000.
Over $18,200 but not over $23,500	$2,958, plus 28% of the excess over $18,200.
Over $23,500 but not over $28,800	$4,442, plus 32% of the excess over $23,500.
Over $28,800 but not over $34,100	$6,138, plus 38% of the excess over $28,800.
Over $34,100 but not over $44,700	$8,152, plus 41% of the excess over $34,100.
Over $44,700 but not over $60,600	$12,498, plus 49% of the excess over $44,700.
Over $60,600	$20,289, plus 50% of the excess over $60,600.

(2) FOR TAXABLE YEARS BEGINNING IN 1983.—

If taxable income is:	The tax is:
Not over $2,300	No tax.
Over $2,300 but not over $4,400	11% of the excess over $2,300.
Over $4,400 but not over $6,500	$231, plus 13% of the excess over $4,400.
Over $6,500 but not over $8,700	$504, plus 15% of the excess over $6,500.
Over $8,700 but not over $11,800	$834, plus 18% of the excess over $8,700.
Over $11,800 but not over $15,000	$1,392, plus 19% of the excess over $11,800.

Over $15,000 but not over $18,200	$2,000, plus 21% of the excess over $15,000.
Over $18,200 but not over $23,500	$2,672, plus 25% of the excess over $18,200.
Over $23,500 but not over $28,800	$3,997, plus 29% of the excess over $23,500.
Over $28,800 but not over $34,100	$5,534, plus 34% of the excess over $28,800.
Over $34,100 but not over $44,700	$7,336, plus 37% of the excess over $34,100.
Over $44,700 but not over $60,600	$11,258, plus 44% of the excess over $44,700.
Over $60,600 but not over $81,800	$18,254, plus 48% of the excess over $60,600.
Over $81,800	$28,430, plus 50% of the excess over $81,800.

(3) FOR TAXABLE YEARS BEGINNING AFTER 1983.—

If taxable income is:	The tax is:
Not over $2,300	No tax.
Over $2,300 but not over $4,400	11% of the excess over $2,300.
Over $4,400 but not over $6,500	$231, plus 12% of the excess over $4,400.
Over $6,500 but not over $8,700	$483, plus 14% of the excess over $6,500.
Over $8,700 but not over $11,800	$791, plus 17% of the excess over $8,700.
Over $11,800 but not over $15,000	$1,318, plus 18% of the excess over $11,800.
Over $15,000 but not over $18,200.	$1,894, plus 20% of the excess over $15,000.
Over $18,200 but not over $23,500	$2,534, plus 24% of the excess over $18,200.
Over $23,500 but not over $28,800	$3,806, plus 28% of the excess over $23,500.
Over $28,800 but not over $34,100	$5,290, plus 32% of the excess over $28,800.
Over $34,100 but not over $44,700	$6,986, plus 35% of the excess over $34,100.
Over $44,700 but not over $60,600	$10,696, plus 42% of the excess over $44,700.
Over $60,600 but not over $81,800	$17,374, plus 45% of the excess over $60,600.
Over $81,800 but not over $108,300	$26,914, plus 48% of the excess over $81,800.
Over $108,300	$39,634, plus 50% of the excess over $108,300.

(c) UNMARRIED INDIVIDUALS (OTHER THAN SURVIVING SPOUSES AND HEADS OF HOUSEHOLDS).—There is hereby imposed on the taxable income of every individual (other than a surviving spouse as defined in section 2(a) or the head of a household as defined in section 2(b)) who is not a married individual (as defined in section 143) a tax determined in accordance with the following tables:

(1) FOR TAXABLE YEARS BEGINNING IN 1982.—

If taxable income is:	The tax is:
Not over $2,300	No tax.
Over $2,300 but not over $3,400	12% of the excess over $2,300.
Over $3,400 but not over $4,400	$132, plus 14% of the excess over $3,400.
Over $4,400 but not over $6,500	$272, plus 16% of the excess over $4,400.
Over $6,500 but not over $8,500	$608, plus 17% of the excess over $6,500.
Over $8,500 but not over $10,800	$948, plus 19% of the excess over $8,500.
Over $10,800 but not over $12,900	$1,385, plus 22% of the excess over $10,800.
Over $12,900 but not over $15,000	$1,847, plus 23% of the excess over $12,900.
Over $15,000 but not over $18,200	$2,330, plus 27% of the excess over $15,000.
Over $18,200 but not over $23,500	$3,194, plus 31% of the excess over $18,200.
Over $23,500 but not over $28,800	$4,837, plus 35% of the excess over $23,500.
Over $28,800 but not over $34,100	$6,692, plus 40% of the excess over $28,800.
Over $34,100 but not over $41,500	$8,812, plus 44% of the excess over $34,100.
Over $41,500	$12,068, plus 50% of the excess over $41,500.

(2) FOR TAXABLE YEARS BEGINNING IN 1983.—

If taxable income is:	The tax is:
Not over $2,300	No tax.
Over $2,300 but not over $3,400	11% of the excess over $2,300.
Over $3,400 but not over $4,400	$121, plus 13% of the excess over $3,400.
Over $4,400 but not over $8,500	$251, plus 15% of the excess over $4,400.
Over $8,500 but not over $10,800	$866, plus 17% of the excess over $8,500.
Over $10,800 but not over $12,900	$1,257, plus 19% of the excess over $10,800.

Over $12,900 but not over $15,000	$1,656, plus 21% of the excess over $12,900.
Over $15,000 but not over $18,200	$2,097, plus 24% of the excess over $15,000.
Over $18,200 but not over $23,500	$2,865, plus 28% of the excess over $18,200.
Over $23,500 but not over $28,800	$4,349, plus 32% of the excess over $23,500.
Over $28,800 but not over $34,100	$6,045, plus 36% of the excess over $28,800.
Over $34,100 but not over $41,500	$7,953, plus 40% of the excess over $34,100.
Over $41,500 but not over $55,300	$10,913 plus 45% of the excess over $41,500.
Over $55,300	$17,123, plus 50% of the excess over $55,300.

(3) FOR TAXABLE YEARS BEGINNING AFTER 1983.—

If taxable income is:	The tax is:
Not over $2,300	No tax.
Over $2,300 but not over $3,400	11% of the excess over $2,300.
Over $3,400 but not over $4,400	$121, plus 12% of the excess over $3,400.
Over $4,400 but not over $6,500	$241, plus 14% of the excess over $4,400.
Over $6,500 but not over $8,500	$535, plus 15% of the excess over $6,500.
Over $8,500 but not over $10,800	$835, plus 16% of the excess over $8,500.
Over $10,800 but not over $12,900	$1,203, plus 18% of the excess over $10,800.
Over $12,900 but not over $15,000	$1,581, plus 20% of the excess over $12,900.
Over $15,000 but not over $18,200	$2,001, plus 23% of the excess over $15,000.
Over $18,200 but not over $23,500	$2,737, plus 26% of the excess over $18,200.
Over $23,500 but not over $28,800	$4,115, plus 30% of the excess over $23,500.
Over $28,800 but not over $34,100	$5,705, plus 34% of the excess over $28,800.
Over $34,100 but not over $41,500	$7,507, plus 38% of the excess over $34,100.
Over $41,500 but not over $55,300	$10,319, plus 42% of the excess over $41,500.
Over $55,300 but not over $81,800	$16,115, plus 48% of the excess over $55,300.
Over $81,800	$28,835, plus 50% of the excess over $81,800.

(d) MARRIED INDIVIDUALS FILING SEPARATE RETURNS.—There is hereby imposed on the taxable income of every married individual (as defined in section 143) who does not make a single return jointly with his spouse under section 6013 a tax determined in accordance with the following tables:

(1) FOR TAXABLE YEARS BEGINNING IN 1982.—

If taxable income is:	The tax is:
Not over $1,700	No tax.
Over $1,700 but not over $2,750	12% of the excess over $1,700.
Over $2,750 but not over $3,800	$126, plus 14% of the excess over $2,750.
Over $3,800 but not over $5,950	$273, plus 16% of the excess over $3,800.
Over $5,950 but not over $8,000	$617, plus 19% of the excess over $5,950.
Over $8,000 but not over $10,100	$1,006.50, plus 22% of the excess over $8,000.
Over $10,100 but not over $12,300	$1,468.50, plus 25% of the excess over $10,100.
Over $12,300 but not over $14,950	$2,018.50, plus 29% of the excess over $12,300.
Over $14,950 but not over $17,600	$2,787, plus 33% of the excess over $14,950.
Over $17,600 but not over $22,900	$3,661.50, plus 39% of the excess over $17,600.
Over $22,900 but not over $30,000	$5,728.50, plus 44% of the excess over $22,900.
Over $30,000 but not over $42,800	$8,852.50, plus 49% of the excess over $30,000.
Over $42,800	$15,124.50, plus 50% of the excess over $42,800.

(2) FOR TAXABLE YEARS BEGINNING IN 1983.—

If taxable income is:	The tax is:
Not over $1,700	No tax.
Over $1,700 but not over $2,750	11% of the excess over $1,700.
Over $2,750 but not over $3,800	$115.50, plus 13% of the excess over $2,750.
Over $3,800 but not over $5,950	$252, plus 15% of the excess over $3,800.
Over $5,950 but not over $8,000	$574.50, plus 17% of the excess over $5,950.

Over $8,000 but not over $10,100	$923, plus 19% of the excess over $8,000.
Over $10,100 but not over $12,300	$1,322, plus 23% of the excess over $10,100.
Over $12,300 but not over $14,950	$1,828, plus 26% of the excess over $12,300.
Over $14,950 but not over $17,600	$2,517, plus 30% of the excess over $14,950.
Over $17,600 but not over $22,900	$3,312, plus 35% of the excess over $17,600.
Over $22,900 but not over $30,000	$5,167, plus 40% of the excess over $22,900.
Over $30,000 but not over $42,800	$8,007, plus 44% of the excess over $30,000.
Over $42,800 but not over $54,700	$13,639, plus 48% of the excess over $42,800.
Over $54,700	$19,351, plus 50% of the excess over $54,700.

(3) FOR TAXABLE YEARS BEGINNING AFTER 1983.—

If taxable income is:	The tax is:
Not over $1,700	No tax.
Over $1,700 but not over $2,750	11% of the excess over $1,700.
Over $2,750 but not over $3,800	$115.50, plus 12% of the excess over $2,750.
Over $3,800 but not over $5,950	$241.50, plus 14% of the excess over $3,800.
Over $5,950 but not over $8,000	$542.50, plus 16% of the excess over $5,950.
Over $8,000 but not over $10,100	$870.50, plus 18% of the excess over $8,000.
Over $10,100 but not over $12,300	$1,248.50, plus 22% of the excess over $10,100.
Over $12,300 but not over $14,950	$1,732.50, plus 25% of the excess over $12,300.
Over $14,950 but not over $17,600	$2,395, plus 28% of the excess over $14,950.
Over $17,600 but not over $22,900	$3,137, plus 33% of the excess over $17,600.
Over $22,900 but not over $30,000	$4,886, plus 38% of the excess over $22,900.
Over $30,000 but not over $42,800	$7,584, plus 42% of the excess over $30,000.
Over $42,800 but not over $54,700	$12,960, plus 45% of the excess over $42,800.
Over $54,700 but not over $81,200	$18,315, plus 49% of the excess over $54,700.
Over $81,200	$31,300, plus 50% of the excess over $81,200.

(e) ESTATES AND TRUSTS.—There is hereby imposed on the taxable income of every estate and trust taxable under this subsection a tax determined in accordance with the following tables:

(1) FOR TAXABLE YEARS BEGINNING IN 1982.—

If taxable income is:	The tax is:
Not over $1,050	12% of taxable income.
Over $1,050 but not over $2,100	$126, plus 14% of the excess over $1,050.
Over $2,100 but not over $4,250	$273, plus 16% of the excess over $2,100.
Over $4,250 but not over $6,300	$617, plus 19% of the excess over $4,250.
Over $6,300 but not over $8,400	$1,006.50, plus 22% of the excess over $6,300.
Over $8,400 but not over $10,600	$1,468.50, plus 25% of the excess over $8,400.
Over $10,600 but not over $13,250	$2,018.50, plus 29% of the excess over $10,600.
Over $13,250 but not over $15,900	$2,787, plus 33% of the excess over $13,250.
Over $15,900 but not over $21,200	$3,661.50, plus 39% of the excess over $15,900.
Over $21,200 but not over $28,300	$5,728.50, plus 44% of the excess over $21,200.
Over $28,300 but not over $41,100	$8,852.50, plus 49% of the excess over $28,300.
Over $41,100	$15,124.50, plus 50% of the excess over $41,100.

(2) FOR TAXABLE YEARS BEGINNING IN 1983.—

If taxable income is:	The tax is:
Not over $1,050	11% of taxable income.
Over $1,050 but not over $2,100	$115.50, plus 13% of the excess over $1,050.
Over $2,100 but not over $4,250	$252, plus 15% of the excess over $2,100.
Over $4,250 but not over $6,300	$574.50, plus 17% of the excess over $4,250.
Over $6,300 but not over $8,400	$923, plus 19% of the excess over $6,300.
Over $8,400 but not over $10,600	$1,322, plus 23% of the excess over $8,400.

Over $10,600 but not over $13,250	$1,828, plus 26% of the excess over $10,600.
Over $13,250 but not over $15,900	$2,517, plus 30% of the excess over $13,250.
Over $15,900 but not over $21,200	$3,312, plus 35% of the excess over $15,900.
Over $21,200 but not over $28,300	$5,167, plus 40% of the excess over $21,200.
Over $28,300 but not over $41,100	$8,007, plus 44% of the excess over $28,300.
Over $41,100 but not over $53,000	$13,639, plus 48% of the excess over $41,100.
Over $53,000	$19,351, plus 50% of the excess over $53,000.

(3) FOR TAXABLE YEARS BEGINNING AFTER 1983.—

If taxable income is:	The tax is:
Not over $1,050	11% of taxable income.
Over $1,050 but not over $2,100	$115.50, plus 12% of the excess over $1,050.
Over $2,100 but not over $4,250	$241.50, plus 14% of the excess over $2,100.
Over $4,250 but not over $6,300	$542.50, plus 16% of the excess over $4,250.
Over $6,300 but not over $8,400	$870.50, plus 18% of the excess over $6,300.
Over $8,400 but not over $10,600	$1,248.50, plus 22% of the excess over $8,400.
Over $10,600 but not over $13,250	$1,732.50, plus 25% of the excess over $10,600.
Over $13,250 but not over $15,900	$2,395, plus 28% of the excess over $13,250.
Over $15,900 but not over $21,200	$3,137, plus 33% of the excess over $15,900.
Over $21,200 but not over $28,300	$4,886, plus 38% of the excess over $21,200.
Over $28,300 but not over $41,100	$7,584, plus 42% of the excess over $28,300.
Over $41,100 but not over $53,000	$12,960, plus 45% of the excess over $41,100.
Over $53,000 but not over $79,500	$18,315, plus 49% of the excess over $53,000.
Over $79,500	$31,300, plus 50% of the excess over $79,500.

(f) ADJUSTMENTS IN TAX TABLES SO THAT INFLATION WILL NOT RESULT IN TAX INCREASES.—

(1) IN GENERAL.—Not later than December 15 of 1984 and each subsequent calendar year, the Secretary shall prescribe tables which shall apply in lieu of the tables contained in paragraph (3) of subsections (a), (b), (c), (d), and (e) with respect to taxable years beginning in the succeeding calendar year.

(2) METHOD OF PRESCRIBING TABLES.—The table which under paragraph (1) is to apply in lieu of the table contained in paragraph (3) of subsection (a), (b), (c), (d), or (e), as the case may be, with respect to taxable years beginning in any calendar year shall be prescribed—

(A) by increasing—

(i) the maximum dollar amount on which no tax is imposed under such table, and

(ii) the minimum and maximum dollar amounts for each rate bracket for which a tax is imposed under such table,

by the cost-of-living adjustment for such calendar year,

(B) by not changing the rate applicable to any rate bracket as adjusted under subparagraph (A)(ii), and

(C) by adjusting the amounts setting forth the tax to the extent necessary to reflect the adjustments in the rate brackets.

If any increase determined under subparagraph (A) is not a multiple of $10, such increase shall be rounded to the nearest multiple of $10 (or if such increase is a multiple of $5, such increase shall be increased to the next highest multiple of $10).

(3) COST-OF-LIVING ADJUSTMENT.—For purposes of paragraph (2), the cost-of-living adjustment for any calendar year is the percentage (if any) by which—

(A) the CPI for the preceding calendar year, exceeds

(B) the CPI for the calendar year 1983.

(4) CPI FOR ANY CALENDAR YEAR.—For purposes of paragraph (3), the CPI for any calendar year is the average of the Consumer Price Index as of the close of the 12-month period ending on September 30 of such calendar year.

(5) CONSUMER PRICE INDEX.—For purposes of paragraph (4), the term "Consumer Price Index" means the last Consumer Price Index for all-urban consumers published by the Department of Labor.

P.L. 99-514, §302(a):

Amended Code Sec. 1 by adding at the end thereof new subsection (j). **Effective** for tax years beginning after 12-31-86.

P.L. 99-514, §302(c), provides:

(c) TRANSITIONAL RULE.—The tax under section 1 of the Internal Revenue Code of 1986 on the long-term capital gain on rights to royalties paid under leases and assignments binding on September 25, 1985, by a limited partnership formed on March 1, 1977, which on October 30, 1979, assigned leases and which assignment was amended on April 27, 1981, shall not exceed 20 percent.

P.L. 99-514, §1411(a):

Amended Code Sec. 1 by inserting after subsection (h) new subsection (i). **Effective** for tax years beginning after 12-31-86.

• 1983, Technical Corrections Act of 1982 (P.L. 97-448)

P.L. 97-448, §101(a)(3), provides:

(3) ELIMINATION OF 50-CENT ROUNDING ERRORS.—If any figure in any table—

(A) which is set forth in section 1 of the Internal Revenue Code of 1954 (as amended by section 101 of the Economic Recovery Tax Act of 1981), and

(B) which applies to married individuals filing separately or to estates and trusts,

differs by not more than 50 cents from the correct amount under the formula used in constructing such table, such figure is hereby corrected to the correct amount.

• 1981, Economic Recovery Tax Act of 1981 (P.L. 97-34)

P.L. 97-34, §101(a):

Amended Code Sec. 1. **Effective** for tax years beginning after 12-31-81. Prior to amendment, Code Sec. 1 read as follows:

SECTION 1. TAX IMPOSED.

(a) MARRIED INDIVIDUALS FILING JOINT RETURNS AND SURVIVING SPOUSES.—There is hereby imposed on the taxable income of—

(1) every married individual (as defined in section 143) who makes a single return jointly with his spouse under section 6013, and

(2) every surviving spouse (as defined in section 2(a)),

a tax determined in accordance with the following table:

If taxable income is:	The tax is:
Not over $3,400	No tax.
Over $3,400 but not over $5,500	14% of excess over $3,400.
Over $5,500 but not over $7,600	$294, plus 16% of excess over $5,500.
Over $7,600 but not over $11,900	$630, plus 18% of excess over $7,600.
Over $11,900 but not over $16,000	$1,404, plus 21% of excess over $11,900.
Over $16,000 but not over $20,200	$2,265, plus 24% of excess over $16,000.
Over $20,200 but not over $24,600	$3,273, plus 28% of excess over $20,200.
Over $24,600 but not over $29,900	$4,505, plus 32% of excess over $24,600.
Over $29,900 but not over $35,200	$6,201, plus 37% of excess over $29,900.
Over $35,200 but not over $45,800	$8,162, plus 43% of excess over $35,200.
Over $45,800 but not over $60,000	$12,720, plus 49% of excess over $45,800.
Over $60,000 but not over $85,600	$19,678, plus 54% of excess over $60,000.
Over $85,600 but not over $109,400	$33,502, plus 59% of excess over $85,600.
Over $109,400 but not over $162,400	$47,544, plus 64% of excess over $109,400.
Over $162,400 but not over $215,400	$81,464, plus 68% of excess over $162,400.
Over $215,400	$117,504, plus 70% of excess over $215,400.

(b) Heads of Households.—There is hereby imposed on the taxable income of every individual who is the head of a household (as defined in section 2(b)) a tax determined in accordance with the following table:

If taxable income is:	The tax is:
Not over $2,300	No tax.
Over $2,300 but not over $4,400	14% of excess over $2,300.
Over $4,400 but not over $6,500	$294, plus 16% of excess over $4,400.
Over $6,500 but not over $8,700	$630, plus 18% of excess over $6,500.
Over $8,700 but not over $11,800	$1,026, plus 22% of excess over $8,700.
Over $11,800 but not over $15,000	$1,708, plus 24% of excess over $11,800.
Over $15,000 but not over $18,200	$2,476, plus 26% of excess over $15,000.
Over $18,200 but not over $23,500	$3,308, plus 31% of excess over $18,200.
Over $23,500 but not over $28,800	$4,951, plus 36% of excess over $23,500.
Over $28,800 but not over $34,100	$6,859, plus 42% of excess over $28,800.
Over $34,100 but not over $44,700	$9,085, plus 46% of excess over $34,100.
Over $44,700 but not over $60,600	$13,961, plus 54% of excess over $44,700.
Over $60,600 but not over $81,800	$22,547, plus 59% of excess over $60,600.
Over $81,800 but not over $108,300	$35,055, plus 63% of excess over $81,800.
Over $108,300 but not over $161,300	$51,750, plus 68% of excess over $108,300.
Over $161,300	$87,790, plus 70% of excess over $161,300.

(c) Unmarried Individuals (Other Than Surviving Spouses and Heads of Households).—There is hereby imposed on the taxable income of every individual (other than a surviving spouse as defined in section 2(a) or the head of a household as defined in section 2(b)) who is not a married individual (as defined in section 143) a tax determined in accordance with the following table:

If taxable income is:	The tax is:
Not over $2,300	No tax.
Over $2,300 but not over $3,400	14% of excess over $2,300.
Over $3,400 but not over $4,400	$154, plus 16% of excess over $3,400.
Over $4,400 but not over $6,500	$314, plus 18% of excess over $4,400.
Over $6,500 but not over $8,500	$692, plus 19% of excess over $6,500.
Over $8,500 but not over $10,800	$1,072, plus 21% of excess over $8,500.
Over $10,800 but not over $12,900	$1,555, plus 24% of excess over $10,800.
Over $12,900 but not over $15,000	$2,059, plus 26% of excess over $12,900.

Over $15,000 but not over $18,200	$2,605, plus 30% of excess over $15,000.
Over $18,200 but not over $23,500	$3,565, plus 34% of excess over $18,200.
Over $23,500 but not over $28,800	$5,367, plus 39% of excess over $23,500.
Over $28,800 but not over $34,100	$7,434, plus 44% of excess over $28,800.
Over $34,100 but not over $41,500	$9,766, plus 49% of excess over $34,100.
Over $41,500 but not over $55,300	$13,392, plus 55% of excess over $41,500.
Over $55,300 but not over $81,800	$20,982, plus 63% of excess over $55,300.
Over $81,800 but not over $108,300	$37,677, plus 68% of excess over $81,800.
Over $108,300	$55,697, plus 70% of excess over $108,300.

(d) MARRIED INDIVIDUALS FILING SEPARATE RETURNS.—There is hereby imposed on the taxable income of every married individual (as defined in section 143) who does not make a single return jointly with his spouse under section 6013 a tax determined in accordance with the following table:

If taxable income is:	The tax is:
Not over $1,700	No tax.
Over $1,700 but not over $2,750	14% of excess over $1,700.
Over $2,750 but not over $3,800	$147, plus 16% of excess over $2,750.
Over $3,800 but not over $5,950	$315, plus 18% of excess over $3,800.
Over $5,950 but not over $8,000	$702, plus 21% of excess over $5,950.
Over $8,000 but not over $10,100	$1,132.50, plus 24% of excess over $8,000.
Over $10,100 but not over $12,300	$1,636.50, plus 28% of excess over $10,100.
Over $12,300 but not over $14,950	$2,252.50, plus 32% of excess over $12,300.
Over $14,950 but not over $17,600	$3,100.50, plus 37% of excess over $14,950.
Over $17,600 but not over $22,900	$4,081, plus 43% of excess over $17,600.
Over $22,900 but not over $30,000	$6,360, plus 49% of excess over $22,900.
Over $30,000 but not over $42,800	$9,839, plus 54% of excess over $30,000.
Over $42,800 but not over $54,700	$16,751, plus 59% of excess over $42,800.
Over $54,700 but not over $81,200	$23,772, plus 64% of excess over $54,700.
Over $81,200 but not over $107,700	$40,732, plus 68% of excess over $81,200.
Over $107,700	$58,752, plus 70% of excess over $107,700.

(e) ESTATES AND TRUSTS.—There is hereby imposed on the taxable income of every estate and trust taxable under this subsection a tax determined in accordance with the following table:

If taxable income is:	The tax is:
Not over $1,050	14% of taxable income.
Over $1,050 but not over $2,100	$147, plus 16% of excess over $1,050.
Over $2,100 but not over $4,250	$315, plus 18% of excess over $2,100.
Over $4,250 but not over $6,300	$702, plus 21% of excess over $4,250.
Over $6,300 but not over $8,400	$1,132.50, plus 24% of excess over $6,300.
Over $8,400 but not over $10,600	$1,636.50, plus 28% of excess over $8,400.
Over $10,600 but not over $13,250	$2,252.50, plus 32% of excess over $10,600.
Over $13,250 but not over $15,900	$3,100.50, plus 37% of excess over $13,250.
Over $15,900 but not over $21,200	$4,081, plus 43% of excess over $15,900.
Over $21,200 but not over $28,300	$6,360, plus 49% of excess over $21,200.
Over $28,300 but not over $41,100	$9,839, plus 54% of excess over $28,300.
Over $41,100 but not over $53,000	$16,751, plus 59% of excess over $41,100.
Over $53,000 but not over $79,500	$23,772, plus 64% of excess over $53,000.
Over $79,500 but not over $106,000	$40,732, plus 68% of excess over $79,500.
Over $106,000	$58,752, plus 70% of excess over $106,000.

P.L. 97-34, § 104(a):

Added Code Sec. 1(f). **Effective** tax years beginning after 12-31-84.

• 1978, Revenue Act of 1978 (P.L. 95-600)

P.L. 95-600, §600, §101(a):

Amended Code Sec. 1. **Effective** for tax years beginning after 12-31-78. Prior to amendment, Code Sec. 1 read as follows:

SECTION 1. TAX IMPOSED.

(a) MARRIED INDIVIDUALS FILING JOINT RETURNS AND SURVIVING SPOUSES.—There is hereby imposed on the taxable income of—

(1) every married individual (as defined in section 143) who makes a single return jointly with his spouse under section 6013, and

(2) every surviving spouse (as defined in section 2(a)),

a tax determined in accordance with the following table:

If taxable income is:	The tax is:
Not over $3,200	No tax.
Over $3,200 but not over $4,200	14% of the excess over $3,200.
Over $4,200 but not over $5,200	$140, plus 15% of excess over $4,200.
Over $5,200 but not over $6,200	$290, plus 16% of excess over $5,200.
Over $6,200 but not over $7,200	$450, plus 17% of excess over $6,200.
Over $7,200 but not over $11,200	$620, plus 19% of excess over $7,200.
Over $11,200 but not over $15,200	$1,380, plus 22% of excess over $11,200.
Over $15,200 but not over $19,200	$2,260, plus 25% of excess over $15,200.
Over $19,200 but not over $23,200	$3,260, plus 28% of excess over $19,200.
Over $23,200 but not over $27,200	$4,380, plus 32% of excess over $23,200.
Over $27,200 but not over $31,200	$5,660, plus 36% of excess over $27,200.
Over $31,200 but not over $35,200	$7,100, plus 39% of excess over $31,200.
Over $35,200 but not over $39,200	$8,660, plus 42% of excess over $35,200.
Over $39,200 but not over $43,200	$10,340, plus 45% of excess over $39,200.
Over $43,200 but not over $47,200	$12,140, plus 48% of excess over $43,200.
Over $47,200 but not over $55,200	$14,060, plus 50% of excess over $47,200.
Over $55,200 but not over $67,200	$18,060, plus 53% of excess over $55,200.
Over $67,200 but not over $79,200	$24,420, plus 55% of excess over $67,200.
Over $79,200 but not over $91,200	$31,020, plus 58% of excess over $79,200.
Over $91,200 but not over $103,200	$37,980, plus 60% of excess over $91,200.
Over $103,200 but not over $123,200	$45,180, plus 62% of excess over $103,200.
Over $123,200 but not over $143,200	$57,580, plus 64% of excess over $123,200.
Over $143,200 but not over $163,200	$70,380, plus 66% of excess over $143,200.
Over $163,200 but not over $183,200	$83,580, plus 68% of excess over $163,200.
Over $183,200 but not over $203,200	$97,180, plus 69% of excess over $183,200.
Over $203,200	$110,980, plus 70% of excess over $203,200.

(b) HEADS OF HOUSEHOLDS.—There is hereby imposed on the taxable income of every individual who is the head of a household (as defined in section 2(b)) a tax determined in accordance with the following table:

If taxable income is:	The tax is:
Not over $2,200	No tax.
Over $2,200 but not over $3,200	14% of the excess over $2,200.
Over $3,200 but not over $4,200	$140, plus 16% of excess over $3,200.
Over $4,200 but not over $6,200	$300, plus 18% of excess over $4,200.
Over $6,200 but not over $8,200	$660, plus 19% of excess over $6,200.
Over $8,200 but not over $10,200	$1,040, plus 22% of excess over $8,200.
Over $10,200 but not over $12,200	$1,480, plus 23% of excess over $10,200.
Over $12,200 but not over $14,200	$1,940, plus 25% of excess over $12,200.
Over $14,200 but not over $16,200	$2,440, plus 27% of excess over $14,200.
Over $16,200 but not over $18,200	$2,980, plus 28% of excess over $16,200.
Over $18,200 but not over $20,200	$3,540, plus 31% of excess over $18,200.
Over $20,200 but not over $22,200	$4,160, plus 32% of excess over $20,200.
Over $22,200 but not over $24,200	$4,800, plus 35% of excess over $22,200.

If taxable income is:	The tax is:
Over $24,200 but not over $26,200	$5,500, plus 36% of excess over $24,200.
Over $26,200 but not over $28,200	$6,220, plus 38% of excess over $26,200.
Over $28,200 but not over $30,200	$6,980, plus 41% of excess over $28,200.
Over $30,200 but not over $34,200	$7,800, plus 42% of excess over $30,200.
Over $34,200 but not over $38,200	$9,480, plus 45% of excess over $34,200.
Over $38,200 but not over $40,200	$11,280, plus 48% of excess over $38,200.
Over $40,200 but not over $42,200	$12,240, plus 51% of excess over $40,200.
Over $42,200 but not over $46,200	$13,260, plus 52% of excess over $42,200.
Over $46,200 but not over $52,200	$15,340, plus 55% of excess over $46,200.
Over $52,200 but not over $54,200	$18,640, plus 56% of excess over $52,200.
Over $54,200 but not over $66,200	$19,760, plus 58% of excess over $54,200.
Over $66,200 but not over $72,200	$26,720, plus 59% of excess over $66,200.
Over $72,200 but not over $78,200	$30,260, plus 61% of excess over $72,200.
Over $78,200 but not over $82,200	$33,920, plus 62% of excess over $78,200.
Over $82,200 but not over $90,200	$36,400, plus 63% of excess over $82,200.
Over $90,200 but not over $102,200	$41,440, plus 64% of excess over $90,200.
Over $102,200 but not over $122,200	$49,120, plus 66% of excess over $102,200.
Over $122,200 but not over $142,200	$62,320, plus 67% of excess over $122,200.
Over $142,200 but not over $162,200	$75,720, plus 68% of excess over $142,200.
Over $162,200 but not over $182,200	$89,320, plus 69% of excess over $162,200.
Over $182,200	$103,120, plus 70% of excess over $182,200.

(c) UNMARRIED INDIVIDUALS (OTHER THAN SURVIVING SPOUSES AND HEADS OF HOUSEHOLDS).—There is hereby imposed on the taxable income of every individual (other than a surviving spouse as defined in section 2(a) or the head of a household as defined in section 2(b)) who is not a married individual (as defined in section 143) a tax determined in accordance with the following table:

If taxable income is:	The tax is:
Not over $2,200	No tax.
Over $2,200 but not over $2,700	14% of the excess over $2,200.
Over $2,700 but not over $3,200	$70, plus 15% of excess over $2,700.
Over $3,200 but not over $3,700	$145, plus 16% of excess over $3,200.
Over $3,700 but not over $4,200	$225, Plus 17% of excess over $3,700.
Over $4,200 but not over $6,200	$310, plus 19% of excess over $4,200.
Over $6,200 but not over $8,200	$690, plus 21% of excess over $6,200.
Over $8,200 but not over $10,200	$1,110, plus 24% of excess over $8,200.
Over $10,200 but not over $12,200	$1,590, plus 25% of excess over $10,200.
Over $12,200 but not over $14,200	$2,090, plus 27% of excess over $12,200.
Over $14,200 but not over $16,200	$2,630, plus 29% of excess over $14,200.
Over $16,200 but not over $18,200	$3,210, plus 31% of excess over $16,200.
Over $18,200 but not over $20,200	$3,830, plus 34% of excess over $18,200.
Over $20,200 but not over $22,200	$4,510, plus 36% of excess over $20,200.
Over $22,200 but not over $24,200	$5,230, plus 38% of excess over $22,200.
Over $24,200 but not over $28,200	$5,990, plus 40% of excess over $24,200.
Over $28,200 but not over $34,200	$7,590, plus 45% of excess over $28,200.
Over $34,200 but not over $40,200	$10,290, plus 50% of excess over $34,200.
Over $40,200 but not over $46,200	$13,290, plus 55% of excess over $40,200.
Over $46,200 but not over $52,200	$16,590, plus 60% of excess over $46,200.
Over $52,200 but not over $62,200	$20,190, plus 62% of excess over $52,200.
Over $62,200 but not over $72,200	$26,390, plus 64% of excess over $62,200.

If taxable income is:	The tax is:
Over $72,200 but not over $82,200	$32,790, plus 66% of excess over $72,200.
Over $82,200 but not over $92,200	$39,390, plus 68% of excess over $82,200.
Over $92,200 but not over $102,200	$46,190, plus 69% of excess over $92,200.
Over $102,200	$53,090, plus 70% of excess over $102,200.

(d) Married Individuals Filing Separate Returns.—There is hereby imposed on the taxable income of every married individual (as defined in section 143) who does not make a single return jointly with his spouse under section 6013 a tax determined in accordance with the following table:

If taxable income is:	The tax is:
Not over $1,600	No tax.
Over $1,600 but not over $2,100	14% of the excess over $1,600.
Over $2,100 but not over $2,600	$70, plus 15% of excess over $2,100.
Over $2,600 but not over $3,100	$145, plus 16% of excess over $2,600.
Over $3,100 but not over $3,600	$225, plus 17% of excess over $3,100.
Over $3,600 but not over $5,600	$310, plus 19% of excess over $3,600.
Over $5,600 but not over $7,600	$690, plus 22% of excess over $5,600.
Over $7,600 but not over $9,600	$1,130, plus 25% of excess over $7,600.
Over $9,600 but not over $11,600	$1,630, plus 28% of excess over $9,600.
Over $11,600 but not over $13,600	$2,190, plus 32% of excess over $11,600.
Over $13,600 but not over $15,600	$2,830, plus 36% of excess over $13,600.
Over $15,600 but not over $17,600	$3,550, plus 39% of excess over $15,600.
Over $17,600 but not over $19,600	$4,330, plus 42% of excess over $17,600.
Over $19,600 but not over $21,600	$5,170, plus 45% of excess over $19,600.
Over $21,600 but not over $23,600	$6,070, plus 48% of excess over $21,600.
Over $23,600 but not over $27,600	$7,030, plus 50% of excess over $23,600.
Over $27,600 but not over $33,600	$9,030, plus 53% of excess over $27,600.
Over $33,600 but not over $39,600	$12,210, plus 55% of excess over $33,600.
Over $39,600 but not over $45,600	$15,510, plus 58% of excess over $39,600.
Over $45,600 but not over $51,600	$18,990, plus 60% of excess over $45,600.
Over $51,600 but not over $61,600	$22,590, plus 62% of excess over $51,600.
Over $61,600 but not over $71,600	$28,790, plus 64% of excess over $61,600.
Over $71,600 but not over $81,600	$35,190, plus 66% of excess over $71,600
Over $81,600 but not over $91,600	$41,790, plus 68% of excess over $81,600.
Over $91,600 but not over $101,600	$48,590, plus 69% of excess over $91,600.
Over $101,600	$55,490, plus 70% of excess over $101,600.

(e) Estates and Trusts.—There is hereby imposed on the taxable income of every estate and trust taxable under this subsection a tax determined in accordance with the following table:

If taxable income is:	The tax is:
Not over $500	14% of the taxable income.
Over $500 but not over $1,000	$70, plus 15% of excess over $500.
Over $1,000 but not over $1,500	$145, plus 16% of excess over $1,000.
Over $1,500 but not over $2,000	$225, plus 17% of excess over $1,500.
Over $2,000 but not over $4,000	$310, plus 19% of excess over $2,000.
Over $4,000 but not over $6,000	$690, Plus 22% of excess over $4,000.
Over $6,000 but not over $8,000	$1,130, plus 25% of excess over $6,000.
Over $8,000 but not over $10,000	$1,630, plus 28% of excess over $8,000.
Over $10,000 but not over $12,000	$2,190, plus 32% of excess over $10,000.
Over $12,000 but not over $14,000	$2,830, plus 36% of excess over $12,000.
Over $14,000 but not over $16,000	$3,550, plus 39% of excess over $14,000.

Over $16,000 but not over $18,000	$4,330, plus 42% of excess over $16,000.
Over $18,000 but not over $20,000	$5,170, plus 45% of excess over $18,000.
Over $20,000 but not over $22,000	$6,070, plus 48% of excess over $20,000.
Over $22,000 but not over $26,000	$7,030, plus 50% of excess over $22,000.
Over $26,000 but not over $32,000	$9,030, plus 53% of excess over $26,000.
Over $32,000 but not over $38,000	$12,210, plus 55% of excess over $32,000.
Over $38,000 but not over $44,000	$15,510, plus 58% of excess over $38,000.
Over $44,000 but not over $50,000	$18,990, plus 60% of excess over $44,000.
Over $50,000 but not over $60,000	$22,590, plus 62% of excess over $50,000.
Over $60,000 but not over $70,000	$28,790, plus 64% of excess over $60,000.
Over $70,000 but not over $80,000	$35,190, plus 66% of excess over $70,000.
Over $80,000 but not over $90,000	$41,790, plus 68% of excess over $80,000
Over $90,000 but not over $100,000	$48,590, plus 69% of excess over $90,000.
Over $100,000	$55,490, plus 70% of excess over $100,000.

• 1977, Tax Reduction and Simplification Act of 1977 (P.L. 95-30)

P.L. 95-30, §101(a):

Amended Code Sec. 1. **Effective** for taxable years beginning after 12-31-76. Prior to amendment, Code Sec. 1 read as follows:

SECTION 1. TAX IMPOSED.

(a) MARRIED INDIVIDUALS FILING JOINT RETURNS AND SURVIVING SPOUSES.—There is hereby imposed on the taxable income of—

(1) every married individual (as defined in section 143) who makes a single return jointly with his spouse under section 6013, and

(2) every surviving spouse (as defined in section 2(a)), a tax determined in accordance with the following table:

If the taxable income is:	The tax is:
Not over $1,000	14% of the taxable income.
Over $1,000 but not over $2,000	$140, plus 15% of excess over $1,000.
Over $2,000 but not over $3,000	$290, plus 16% of excess over $2,000.
Over $3,000 but not over $4,000	$450, plus 17% of excess over $3,000.
Over $4,000 but not over $8,000	$620, plus 19% of excess over $4,000.
Over $8,000 but not over $12,000	$1,380, plus 22% of excess over $8,000.
Over $12,000 but not over $16,000	$2,260, plus 25% of excess over $12,000.
Over $16,000 but not over $20,000	$3,260, plus 28% of excess over $16,000.
Over $20,000 but not over $24,000	$4,380, plus 32% of excess over $20,000.
Over $24,000 but not over $28,000	$5,660, plus 36% of excess over $24,000.
Over $28,000 but not over $32,000	$7,100, plus 39% of excess over $28,000.
Over $32,000 but not over $36,000	$8,660, plus 42% of excess over $32,000.
Over $36,000 but not over $40,000	$10,340, plus 45% of excess over $36,000.
Over $40,000 but not over $44,000	$12,140, plus 48% of excess over $40,000.
Over $44,000 but not over $52,000	$14,060, plus 50% of excess over $44,000.
Over $52,000 but not over $64,000	$18,060, plus 53% of excess over $52,000.
Over $64,000 but not over $76,000	$24,420, plus 55% of excess over $64,000.
Over $76,000 but not over $88,000	$31,020, plus 58% of excess over $76,000.
Over $88,000 but not over $100,000	$37,980, plus 60% of excess over $88,000.
Over $100,000 but not over $120,000	$45,180, plus 62% of excess over $100,000.
Over $120,000 but not over $140,000	$57,580, plus 64% of excess over $120,000.
Over $140,000 but not over $160,000	$70,380, plus 66% of excess over $140,000.
Over $160,000 but not over $180,000	$83,580, plus 68% of excess over $160,000.
Over $180,000 but not over $200,000	$97,180, plus 69% of excess over $180,000.
Over $200,000	$110,980, plus 70% of excess over $200,000.

(b) HEADS OF HOUSEHOLDS.—There is hereby imposed on the taxable income of every individual who is the head of a household (as defined in section 2(b)) a tax determined in accordance with the following table:

If the taxable income is:	The tax is:
Not over $1,000	14% of the taxable income.
Over $1,000 but not over $2,000	$140, plus 16% of excess over $1,000.
Over $2,000 but not over $4,000	$300, plus 18% of excess over $2,000.
Over $4,000 but not over $6,000	$660, plus 19% of excess over $4,000.
Over $6,000 but not over $8,000	$1,040, plus 22% of excess over $6,000.
Over $8,000 but not over $10,000	$1,480, plus 23% of excess over $8,000.
Over $10,000 but not over $12,000	$1,940, plus 25% of excess over $10,000.
Over $12,000 but not over $14,000	$2,440, plus 27% of excess over $12,000.
Over $14,000 but not over $16,000	$2,980, plus 28% of excess over $14,000.
Over $16,000 but not over $18,000	$3,540, plus 31% of excess over $16,000.
Over $18,000 but not over $20,000	$4,160, plus 32% of excess over $18,000.
Over $20,000 but not over $22,000	$4,800, plus 35% of excess over $20,000.
Over $22,000 but not over $24,000	$5,500, plus 36% of excess over $22,000.
Over $24,000 but not over $26,000	$6,220, plus 38% of excess over $24,000.
Over $26,000 but not over $28,000	$6,980, plus 41% of excess over $26,000.
Over $28,000 but not over $32,000	$7,800, plus 42% of excess over $28,000.
Over $32,000 but not over $36,000	$9,480, plus 45% of excess over $32,000.
Over $36,000 but not over $38,000	$11,280, plus 48% of excess over $36,000.
Over $38,000 but not over $40,000	$12,240, plus 51% of excess over $38,000.
Over $40,000 but not over $44,000	$13,260, plus 52% of excess over $40,000.
Over $44,000 but not over $50,000	$15,340, plus 55% of excess over $44,000.
Over $50,000 but not over $52,000	$18,640, plus 56% of excess over $50,000.
Over $52,000 but not over $64,000	$19,760, plus 58% of excess over $52,000.
Over $64,000 but not over $70,000	$26,720, plus 59% of excess over $64,000.
Over $70,000 but not over $76,000	$30,260, plus 61% of excess over $70,000.
Over $76,000 but not over $80,000	$33,920, plus 62% of excess over $76,000.
Over $80,000 but not over $88,000	$36,400, plus 63% of excess over $80,000.
Over $88,000 but not over $100,000	$41,440, plus 64% of excess over $88,000.
Over $100,000 but not over $120,000	$49,120, plus 66% of excess over $100,000.
Over $120,000 but not over $140,000	$62,320, plus 67% of excess over $120,000.
Over $140,000 but not over $160,000	$75,720, plus 68% of excess over $140,000.
Over $160,000 but not over $180,000	$89,320, plus 69% of excess over $160,000.
Over $180,000	$103,120, plus 70% of excess over $180,000.

(c) UNMARRIED INDIVIDUALS (OTHER THAN SURVIVING SPOUSES AND HEADS OF HOUSEHOLDS).—There is hereby imposed on the taxable income of every individual (other than a surviving spouse as defined in section 2(a) or the head of a household as defined in section 2(b)) who is not not a married individual (as defined in section 143) a tax determined in accordance with the following table:

If the taxable income is:	The tax is:
Not over $500	14% of the taxable income.
Over $500 but not over $1,000	$70, plus 15% of excess over $500.
Over $1,000 but not over $1,500	$145, plus 16% of excess over $1,000.
Over $1,500 but not over $2,000	$225, plus 17% of excess over $1,500.
Over $2,000 but not over $4,000	$310, plus 19% of excess over $2,000.
Over $4,000 but not over $6,000	$690, plus 21% of excess over $4,000.
Over $6,000 but not over $8,000	$1,110, plus 24% of excess over $6,000.
Over $8,000 but not over $10,000	$1,590, plus 25% of excess over $8,000.
Over $10,000 but not over $12,000	$2,090, plus 27% of excess over $10,000.

Over $12,000 but not over $14,000	$2,630, plus 29% of excess over $12,000.
Over $14,000 but not over $16,000	$3,210, plus 31% of excess over $14,000.
Over $16,000 but not over $18,000	$3,830, plus 34% of excess over $16,000.
Over $18,000 but not over $20,000	$4,510, plus 36% of excess over $18,000.
Over $20,000 but not over $22,000	$5,230, plus 38% of excess over $20,000.
Over $22,000 but not over $26,000	$5,990, plus 40% of excess over $22,000.
Over $26,000 but not over $32,000	$7,590, plus 45% of excess over $26,000.
Over $32,000 but not over $38,000	$10,290, plus 50% of excess over $32,000.
Over $38,000 but not over $44,000	$13,290, plus 55% of excess over $38,000.
Over $44,000 but not over $50,000	$16,590, plus 60% of excess over $44,000.
Over $50,000 but not over $60,000	$20,190, plus 62% of excess over $50,000.
Over $60,000 but not over $70,000	$26,390, plus 64% of excess over $60,000.
Over $70,000 but not over $80,000	$32,790, plus 66% of excess over $70,000.
Over $80,000 but not over $90,000	$39,390, plus 68% of excess over $80,000.
Over $90,000 but not over $100,000	$46,190, plus 69% of excess over $90,000.
Over $100,000	$53,090, plus 70% of excess over $100,000.

(d) MARRIED INDIVIDUALS FILING SEPARATE RETURNS; ESTATES AND TRUSTS.—There is hereby imposed on the taxable income of every married individual (as defined in section 143) who does not make a single return jointly with his spouse under section 6013, and of every estate and trust taxable under this subsection, a tax determined in accordance with the following table:

If the taxable income is:	**The tax is:**
Not over $500	14% of the taxable income.
Over $500 but not over $1,000	$70, plus 15% of excess over $500.
Over $1,000 but not over $1,500	$145, plus 16% of excess over $1,000.
Over $1,500 but not over $2,000	$225, plus 17% of excess over $1,500.
Over $2,000 but not over $4,000	$310, plus 19% of excess over $2,000.
Over $4,000 but not over $6,000	$690, plus 22% of excess over $4,000.
Over $6,000 but not over $8,000	$1,130, plus 25% of excess over $6,000.
Over $8,000 but not over $10,000	$1,630, plus 28% of excess over $8,000.
Over $10,000 but not over $12,000	$2,190, plus 32% of excess over $10,000.
Over $12,000 but not over $14,000	$2,830, plus 36% of excess over $12,000.
Over $14,000 but not over $16,000	$3,550, plus 39% of excess over $14,000.
Over $16,000 but not over $18,000	$4,330, plus 42% of excess over $16,000.
Over $18,000 but not over $20,000	$5,170, plus 45% of excess over $18,000.
Over $20,000 but not over $22,000	$6,070, plus 48% of excess over $20,000.
Over $22,000 but not over $26,000	$7,030, plus 50% of excess over $22,000.
Over $26,000 but not over $32,000	$9,030, plus 53% of excess over $26,000.
Over $32,000 but not over $38,000	$12,210, plus 55% of excess over $32,000.
Over $38,000 but not over $44,000	$15,510, plus 58% of excess over $38,000.
Over $44,000 but not over $50,000	$18,990, plus 60% of excess over $44,000.
Over $50,000 but not over $60,000	$22,590, plus 62% of excess over $50,000.
Over $60,000 but not over $70,000	$28,790, plus 64% of excess over $60,000.
Over $70,000 but not over $80,000	$35,190, plus 66% of excess over $70,000.
Over $80,000 but not over $90,000	$41,790, plus 68% of excess over $80,000.
Over $90,000 but not over $100,000	$48,590, plus 69% of excess over $90,000.
Over $100,000	$55,490, plus 70% of excess over $100,000.

• 1969, Tax Reform Act of 1969 (P.L. 91-172)

P. L. 91-172, §803(a):

Amended Code Sec. 1. **Effective** for tax years beginning after 12-31-70. Prior to amendment Code Sec. 1 read as follows:

SEC. 1. TAX IMPOSED.

(a) Rates of Tax on Individuals.—

(1) Taxable years beginning in 1964.—In the case of a taxable year beginning on or after January 1, 1964, and

before January 1, 1965, there is hereby imposed on the taxable income of every individual (other than a head of a household to whom subsection (b) applies) a tax determined in accordance with the following table:

If the taxable income is:	The tax is:
Not over $500	16% of the taxable income.
Over $500 but not over $1,000	$80, plus 16.5% of excess over $500.
Over $1,000 but not over $1,500	$162.50, plus 17.5% of excess over $1,000.
Over $1,500 but not over $2,000	$250, plus 18% of excess over $1,500.
Over $2,000 but not over $4,000	$340, plus 20% of excess over $2,000.
Over $4,000 but not over $6,000	$740, plus 23.5% of excess over $4,000.
Over $6,000 but not over $8,000	$1,210, plus 27% of excess over $6,000.
Over $8,000 but not over $10,000	$1,750, plus 30.5% of excess over $8,000.
Over $10,000 but not over $12,000	$2,360, plus 34% of excess over $10,000.
Over $12,000 but not over $14,000	$3,040, plus 37.5% of excess over $12,000.
Over $14,000 but not over $16,000	$3,790, plus 41% of excess over $14,000.
Over $16,000 but not over $18,000	$4,610, plus 44.5% of excess over $16,000.
Over $18,000 but not over $20,000	$5,500, plus 47.5% of excess over $18,000.
Over $20,000 but not over $22,000	$6,450, plus 50.5% of excess over $20,000.
Over $22,000 but not over $26,000	$7,460, plus 53.5% of excess over $22,000.
Over $26,000 but not over $32,000	$9,600, plus 56% of excess over $26,000.
Over $32,000 but not over $38,000	$12,960, plus 58.5% of excess over $32,000.
Over $38,000 but not over $44,000	$16,470, plus 61% of excess over $38,000.
Over $44,000 but not over $50,000	$20,130, plus 63.5% of excess over $44,000.
Over $50,000 but not over $60,000	$23,940, plus 66% of excess over $50,000.
Over $60,000 but not over $70,000	$30,540, plus 68.5% of excess over $60,000.
Over $70,000 but not over $80,000	$37,390, plus 71% of excess over $70,000.
Over $80,000 but not over $90,000	$44,490, plus 73.5% of excess over $80,000.
Over $90,000 but not over $100,000	$51,840, plus 75% of excess over $90,000.
Over $100,000 but not over $200,000	$59,340, plus 76.5% of excess over $100,000.
Over $200,000	$135,840, plus 77% of excess over $200,000.

(2) Taxable years beginning after December 31, 1964.—In the case of a taxable year beginning after December 31, 1964, there is hereby imposed on the taxable income of every individual (other than a head of a household to whom subsection (b) applies) a tax determined in accordance with the following table:

If the taxable income is:	The tax is:
Not over $500	14% of the taxable income.
Over $500 but not over $1,000	$70, plus 15% of excess over $500.
Over $1,000 but not over $1,500	$145, plus 16% of excess over $1,000.
Over $1,500 but not over $2,000	$225, plus 17% of excess over $1,500.
Over $2,000 but not over $4,000	$310, plus 19% of excess over $2,000.
Over $4,000 but not over $6,000	$690, plus 22% of excess over $4,000.
Over $6,000 but not over $8,000	$1,130, plus 25% of excess over $6,000.
Over $8,000 but not over $10,000	$1,630, plus 28% of excess over $8,000.
Over $10,000 but not over $12,000	$2,190, plus 32% of excess over $10,000.
Over $12,000 but not over $14,000	$2,830, plus 36% of excess over $12,000.
Over $14,000 but not over $16,000	$3,550, plus 39% of excess over $14,000.
Over $16,000 but not over $18,000	$4,330, plus 42% of excess over $16,000.
Over $18,000 but not over $20,000	$5,170, plus 45% of excess over $18,000.
Over $20,000 but not over $22,000	$6,070, plus 48% of excess over $20,000.
Over $22,000 but not over $26,000	$7,030, plus 50% of excess over $22,000.

Over $26,000 but not over $32,000	$9,030, plus 53% of excess over $26,000.
Over $32,000 but not over $38,000	$12,210, plus 55% of excess over $32,000.
Over $38,000 but not over $44,000	$15,510, plus 58% of excess over $38,000.
Over $44,000 but not over $50,000	$18,990, plus 60% of excess over $44,000.
Over $50,000 but not over $60,000	$22,590, plus 62% of excess over $50,000.
Over $60,000 but not over $70,000	$28,790, plus 64% of excess over $60,000.
Over $70,000 but not over $80,000	$35,190, plus 66% of excess over $70,000.
Over $80,000 but not over $90,000	$41,790, plus 68% of excess over $80,000.
Over $90,000 but not over $100,000	$48,590, plus 69% of excess over $90,000.
Over $100,000	$55,490, plus 70% of excess over $100,000.

(b) Rates of Tax on Heads of Households.

(1) Rates of tax.—

(A) Taxable years beginning in 1964.—In the case of a taxable year beginning on or after January 1, 1964, and before January 1, 1965, there is hereby imposed on the taxable income of every individual who is the head of a household a tax determined in accordance with the following table:

If the taxable income is:	The tax is:
Not over $1,000	16% of the taxable income.
Over $1,000 but not over $2,000	$160, plus 17.5% of excess over $1,000.
Over $2,000 but not over $4,000	$335, plus 19% of excess over $2,000.
Over $4,000 but not over $6,000	$715, plus 22% of excess over $4,000.
Over $6,000 but not over $8,000	$1,155, plus 23% of excess over $6,000.
Over $8,000 but not over $10,000	$1,615, plus 27% of excess over $8,000.
Over $10,000 but not over $12,000	$2,155, plus 29% of excess over $10,000.
Over $12,000 but not over $14,000	$2,735, plus 32% of excess over $12,000.
Over $14,000 but not over $16,000	$3,375, plus 34% of excess over $14,000.
Over $16,000 but not over $18,000	$4,055, plus 37.5% of excess over $16,000.
Over $18,000 but not over $20,000	$4,805, plus 39% of excess over $18,000.
Over $20,000 but not over $22,000	$5,585, plus 42.5% of excess over $20,000.
Over $22,000 but not over $24,000	$6,435, plus 43.5% of excess over $22,000.
Over $24,000 but not over $26,000	$7,305, plus 45.5% of excess over $24,000.
Over $26,000 but not over $28,000	$8,215, plus 47% of excess over $26,000.
Over $28,000 but not over $32,000	$9,155, plus 48.5% of excess over $28,000.
Over $32,000 but not over $36,000	$11,095, plus 51.5% of excess over $32,000.
Over $36,000 but not over $38,000	$13,155, plus 53% of excess over $36,000.
Over $38,000 but not over $40,000	$14,215, plus 54% of excess over $38,000.
Over $40,000 but not over $44,000	$15,295, plus 56% of excess over $40,000.
Over $44,000 but not over $50,000	$17,535, plus 58.5% of excess over $44,000.
Over $50,000 but not over $52,000	$21,045, plus 59.5% of excess over $50,000.
Over $52,000 but not over $60,000	$22,235, plus 61% of excess over $52,000.
Over $60,000 but not over $64,000	$27,115, plus 62% of excess over $60,000.
Over $64,000 but not over $70,000	$29,595, plus 63.5% of excess over $64,000.
Over $70,000 but not over $76,000	$33,405, plus 65% of excess over $70,000.
Over $76,000 but not over $80,000	$37,305, plus 66% of excess over $76,000.
Over $80,000 but not over $88,000	$39,945, plus 67% of excess over $80,000.
Over $88,000 but not over $90,000	$45,305, plus 69% of excess over $88,000.
Over $90,000 but not over $100,000	$46,685, plus 69.5% of excess over $90,000.
Over $100,000 but not over $120,000	$53,635, plus 71% of excess over $100,000.
Over $120,000 but not over $140,000	$67,835, plus 72.5% of excess over $120,000.

Over $140,000 but not over $160,000	$82,335, plus 74% of excess over $140,000.
Over $160,000 but not over $180,000	$97,135, plus 75% of excess over $160,000.
Over $180,000 but not over $200,000	$112,135, plus 75.5% of excess over $180,000.
Over $200,000	$127,235, plus 77% of excess over $200,000.

(B) Taxable years beginning after December 31, 1964.—In the case of a taxable year beginning after December 31, 1964, there is hereby imposed on the taxable income of every individual who is the head of a household a tax determined in accordance with the following table:

If the taxable income is:	The tax is:
Not over $1,000	14% of the taxable income.
Over $1,000 but not over $2,000	$140, plus 16% of excess over $1,000.
Over $2,000 but not over $4,000	$300, plus 18% of excess over $2,000.
Over $4,000 but not over $6,000	$660, plus 20% of excess over $4,000.
Over $6,000 but not over $8,000	$1,060, plus 22% of excess over $6,000.
Over $8,000 but not over $10,000	$1,500, plus 25% of excess over $8,000.
Over $10,000 but not over $12,000	$2,000, plus 27% of excess over $10,000.
Over $12,000 but not over $14,000	$2,540, plus 31% of excess over $12,000.
Over $14,000 but not over $16,000	$3,160, plus 32% of excess over $14,000.
Over $16,000 but not over $18,000	$3,800, plus 35% of excess over $16,000.
Over $18,000 but not over $20,000	$4,500, plus 36% of excess over $18,000.
Over $20,000 but not over $22,000	$5,220, plus 40% of excess over $20,000.
Over $22,000 but not over $24,000	$6,020, plus 41% of excess over $22,000.
Over $24,000 but not over $26,000	$6,840, plus 43% of excess over $24,000.
Over $26,000 but not over $28,000	$7,700, plus 45% of excess over $26,000.
Over $28,000 but not over $32,000	$8,600, plus 46% of excess over $28,000.
Over $32,000 but not over $36,000	$10,440, plus 48% of excess over $32,000.
Over $36,000 but not over $38,000	$12,360, plus 50% of excess over $36,000.
Over $38,000 but not over $40,000	$13,360, plus 52% of excess over $38,000.
Over $40,000 but not over $44,000	$14,400, plus 53% of excess over $40,000.
Over $44,000 but not over $50,000	$16,520, plus 55% of excess over $44,000.
Over $50,000 but not over $52,000	$19,820, plus 56% of excess over $50,000.
Over $52,000 but not over $64,000	$20,940, plus 58% of excess over $52,000.
Over $64,000 but not over $70,000	$27,900, plus 59% of excess over $64,000.
Over $70,000 but not over $76,000	$31,440, plus 61% of excess over $70,000.
Over $76,000 but not over $80,000	$35,100, plus 62% of excess over $76,000.
Over $80,000 but not over $88,000	$37,580, plus 63% of excess over $80,000.
Over $88,000 but not over $100,000	$42,620, plus 64% of excess over $88,000.
Over $100,000 but not over $120,000	$50,300, plus 66% of excess over $100,000.
Over $120,000 but not over $140,000	$63,500, plus 67% of excess over $120,000.
Over $140,000 but not over $160,000	$76,900, plus 68% of excess over $140,000.
Over $160,000 but not over $180,000	$90,500, plus 69% of excess over $160,000.
Over $180,000	$104,300, plus 70% of excess over $180,000.

(2) Definition of head of household.—For purposes of this subtitle, an individual shall be considered a head of a household if, and only if, such individual is not married at the close of his taxable year, is not a surviving spouse (as defined in section 2(b)), and either—

(A) maintains as his home a household which constitutes for such taxable year the principal place of abode, as a member of such household, of—

(i) a son, stepson, daughter, or stepdaughter of the taxpayer, or a descendant of a son or daughter of the taxpayer, but if such son, stepson, daughter, stepdaughter, or descendant is married at the close of the taxpayer's taxable year, only if the taxpayer is entitled to a deduction for the taxable year for such person under section 151, or

(ii) any other person who is a dependent of the taxpayer, if the taxpayer is entitled to a deduction for the taxable year for such person under section 151, or

(B) maintains a household which constitutes for such taxable year the principal place of abode of the father or mother of the taxpayer, if the taxpayer is entitled to a deduction for the taxable year for such father or mother under section 151.

For purposes of this paragraph and of section 2(b)(1)(B), an individual shall be considered as maintaining a household only if over half of the cost of maintaining the household during the taxable year is furnished by such individual.

(3) Determination of status.—For purposes of this subsection—

(A) a legally adopted child of a person shall be considered a child of such person by blood;

(B) an individual who is legally separated from his spouse under a decree of divorce or of separate maintenance shall not be considered as married;

(C) a taxpayer shall be considered as not married at the close of his taxable year if at any time during the taxable year his spouse is a nonresident alien; and

(D) a taxpayer shall be considered as married at the close of his taxable year if his spouse (other than a spouse described in subparagraph (C)) died during the taxable year.

(4) Limitations.—Notwithstanding paragraph (2), for purposes of this subtitle a taxpayer shall not be considered to be a head of a household—

(A) if at any time during the taxable year he is a nonresident alien; or

(B) by reason of an individual who would not be a dependent for the taxable year but for—

(i) paragraph (9) of section 152(a),

(ii) paragraph (10) of section 152(a), or

(iii) subsection (c) of section 152.

(c) Special Rules.—The tax imposed by subsection (a), and the tax imposed by paragraph (1) of subsection (b), consists of—

(1) a normal tax of 3 percent of the taxable income, and

(2) a surtax equal to (A) the amount determined in accordance with the table in subsection (a) or paragraph (1) of subsection (b), minus (B) the normal tax.

The tax shall in no event exceed 87 percent of the taxable income for the taxable year.

(d) Nonresident Aliens.—In the case of a nonresident alien individual, the tax imposed by subsection (a) shall apply only as provided by section 871 or 877.

(e) Cross Reference.—

For definition of taxable income, see section 63.

• 1966, Foreign Investors Tax Act of 1966 (P.L. 89-809)

P. L. 89-809, §103(a)(2):

Redesignated former Code Sec. 1(d) as (e) and added Code Sec. 1(d). **Effective** 1-1-67.

• 1964, Revenue Act of 1964 (P.L. 88-272)

P. L. 88-272, §§111(a), (b):

Amended Code Secs. 1(a) and 1(b)(1). Prior to amendment, Code Secs. 1(a) and 1(b)(1) read as follows:

(a) Rates of Tax on Individuals.—A tax is hereby imposed for each taxable year on the taxable income of every individual other than a head of a household to whom subsection (b) applies. The amount of the tax shall be determined in accordance with the following table: * * *[Obsolete tax tables are not reproduced.—CCH.]

(b) Rates of Tax on Heads of Households.—

(1) Rates of tax.—A tax is hereby imposed for each taxable year on the taxable income of every individual who is the head of a household. The amount of the tax shall be determined in accordance with the following table: * * *[Obsolete tax tables are not reproduced.—CCH.]

»»→ Caution: Code Sec. 1(i), below, was added by P.L. 107-16 and amended by P.L. 108-27 and P.L. 108-311, and is subject to the sunset provisions of the Economic Growth and Tax Relief Reconciliation Act of 2001 (P.L. 107-16), §901, and the Jobs and Growth Tax Relief Reconciliation Act of 2003 (P.L. 108-27), §303. Absent Congressional action, the changes made to this provision by P.L. 107-16, and P.L. 108-27, or that take effect as if included in P.L. 107-16, and P.L. 108-27, do not apply after December 31, 2010. For more information about the sunset provisions, see page XXI of the Preface to this publication and P.L. 107-16, §901, and P.L. 108-27, §303, in the amendment notes. See the amendments notes for a history of amendments to this section and the effective date of each change.

[Sec. 1(i)]

(i) RATE REDUCTIONS AFTER 2000.—

(1) 10-PERCENT RATE BRACKET.—

(A) IN GENERAL.—In the case of taxable years beginning after December 31, 2000—

(i) the rate of tax under subsections (a), (b), (c), and (d) on taxable income not over the initial bracket amount shall be 10 percent, and

(ii) the 15 percent rate of tax shall apply only to taxable income over the initial bracket amount but not over the maximum dollar amount for the 15-percent rate bracket.

(B) INITIAL BRACKET AMOUNT.—For purposes of this paragraph, the initial bracket amount is—

(i) $14,000 in the case of subsection (a),

(ii) $10,000 in the case of subsection (b), and

(iii) ½ the amount applicable under clause (i) (after adjustment, if any, under subparagraph (C)) in the case of subsections (c) and (d).

(C) INFLATION ADJUSTMENT.—In prescribing the tables under subsection (f) which apply with respect to taxable years beginning in calendar years after 2003—

(i) the cost-of-living adjustment shall be determined under subsection (f)(3) by substituting "2002" for "1992" in subparagraph (B) thereof, and

(ii) the adjustments under clause (i) shall not apply to the amount referred to in subparagraph (B)(iii).

If any amount after adjustment under the preceding sentence is not a multiple of $50, such amount shall be rounded to the next lowest multiple of $50.

(2) REDUCTIONS IN RATES AFTER JUNE 30, 2001.—In the case of taxable years beginning in a calendar year after 2000, the corresponding percentage specified for such calendar year in the following table shall be substituted for the otherwise applicable tax rate in the tables under subsections (a), (b), (c), (d), and (e).

In the case of taxable years beginning during calendar year:	The corresponding percentages shall be substituted for the following percentages: 28%	31%	36%	39.6%
2001	27.5%	30.5%	35.5%	39.1%
2002	27.0%	30.0%	35.0%	38.6%
2003 and thereafter	25.0%	28.0%	33.0%	35.0%

(3) ADJUSTMENT OF TABLES.—The Secretary shall adjust the tables prescribed under subsection (f) to carry out this subsection.

Amendments

• 2008, Economic Stimulus Act of 2008 (P.L. 110-185)

P.L. 110-185, §101(f)(2):

Amended Code Sec. 1(i)(1) by striking subparagraph (D). **Effective** 2-13-2008. Prior to being stricken, Code Sec. 1(i)(1)(D) read as follows:

(D) COORDINATION WITH ACCELERATION OF 10 PERCENT RATE BRACKET BENEFIT FOR 2001.—This paragraph shall not apply to any taxable year to which section 6428 applies.

• 2004, Working Families Tax Relief Act of 2004 (P.L. 108-311)

P.L. 108-311, §101(d)(1):

Amended Code Sec. 1(i)(1)(B)(i) by striking "($12,000 in the case of taxable years beginning after December 31, 2004, and before January 1, 2008)" following "$14,000". **Effective** for tax years beginning after 12-31-2003.

P.L. 108-311, §101(d)(2):

Amended Code Sec. 1(i)(1)(C). **Effective** for tax years beginning after 12-31-2003. Prior to amendment, Code Sec. 1(i)(1)(C) read as follows:

(C) INFLATION ADJUSTMENT.—In prescribing the tables under subsection (f) which apply with respect to taxable years beginning in calendar years after 2000—

(i) except as provided in clause (ii), the Secretary shall make no adjustment to the initial bracket amounts for any taxable year beginning before January 1, 2009,

(ii) there shall be an adjustment under subsection (f) of such amounts which shall apply only to taxable years beginning in 2004, and such adjustment shall be determined under subsection (f)(3) by substituting "2002" for "1992" in subparagraph (B) thereof,

(iii) the cost-of-living adjustment used in making adjustments to the initial bracket amounts for any taxable year beginning after December 31, 2008, shall be determined under subsection (f)(3) by substituting "2007" for "1992" in subparagraph (B) thereof, and

(iv) the adjustments under clauses (ii) and (iii) shall not apply to the amount referred to in subparagraph (B)(iii).

If any amount after adjustment under the preceding sentence is not a multiple of $50, such amount shall be rounded to the next lowest multiple of $50.

P.L. 108-311, §105, provides:

SEC. 105. APPLICATION OF EGTRRA SUNSET TO THIS TITLE.

Each amendment made by this title shall be subject to title IX of the Economic Growth and Tax Relief Reconciliation Act of 2001 to the same extent and in the same manner as the provision of such Act to which such amendment relates.

• 2003, Jobs and Growth Tax Relief Reconciliation Act of 2003 (P.L. 108-27)

P.L. 108-27, §104(a):

Amended Code Sec. 1(i)(1)(B)(i) by striking "($12,000 in the case of taxable years beginning before January 1, 2008)" and inserting "($12,000 in the case of taxable years beginning after December 31, 2004, and before January 1, 2008)". **Effective** for tax years beginning after 12-31-2002. For a special rule, see Act Sec. 104(c)(2), below.

P.L. 108-27, §104(b):

Amended Code Sec. 1(i)(1)(C). **Effective** for tax years beginning after 12-31-2002. For a special rule, see Act Sec. 104(c)(2), below. Prior to amendment, Code Sec. 1(i)(1)(C) read as follows:

(C) INFLATION ADJUSTMENT.—In prescribing the tables under subsection (f) which apply with respect to taxable years beginning in calendar years after 2000—

(i) the Secretary shall make no adjustment to the initial bracket amount for any taxable year beginning before January 1, 2009,

(ii) the cost-of-living adjustment used in making adjustments to the initial bracket amount for any taxable year beginning after December 31, 2008, shall be determined under subsection (f)(3) by substituting "2007" for "1992" in subparagraph (B) thereof, and

(iii) such adjustment shall not apply to the amount referred to in subparagraph (B)(iii).

If any amount after adjustment under the preceding sentence is not a multiple of $50, such amount shall be rounded to the next lowest multiple of $50.

P.L. 108-27, §104(c)(2), provides:

(2) TABLES FOR 2003.—The Secretary of the Treasury shall modify each table which has been prescribed under section 1(f) of the Internal Revenue Code of 1986 for taxable years beginning in 2003 and which relates to the amendment made by subsection (a) to reflect such amendment.

P.L. 108-27, §105(a):

Amended the table contained in Code Sec. 1(i)(2). **Effective** for tax years beginning after 12-31-2002. Prior to amendment, the table contained in Code Sec. 1(i)(2) read as follows:

In the case of taxable years beginning during calendar year:	The corresponding percentages shall be substituted for the following percentages: 28%	31%	36%	39.6%
2001	27.5%	30.5%	35.5%	39.1%
2002 and 2003	27.0%	30.0%	35.0%	38.6%
2004 and 2005	26.0%	29.0%	34.0%	37.6%
2006 and thereafter	25.0%	28.0%	33.0%	35.0%

P.L. 108-27, §107, provides:

SEC. 107. APPLICATION OF EGTRRA SUNSET TO THIS TITLE.

Each amendment made by this title shall be subject to title IX of the Economic Growth and Tax Relief Reconciliation Act of 2001 to the same extent and in the same manner as the provision of such Act to which such amendment relates.

• 2001, Economic Growth and Tax Relief Reconciliation Act of 2001 (P.L. 107-16)

P.L. 107-16, §101(a):

Amended Code Sec. 1 by adding at the end a new subsection (i). **Effective** for tax years beginning after 12-31-2000.

P.L. 107-16, §901(a)-(b), provides:

SEC. 901. SUNSET OF PROVISIONS OF ACT.

(a) IN GENERAL.—All provisions of, and amendments made by, this Act shall not apply—

(1) to taxable, plan, or limitation years beginning after December 31, 2010, or

(2) in the case of title V, to estates of decedents dying, gifts made, or generation skipping transfers, after December 31, 2010.

(b) APPLICATION OF CERTAIN LAWS.—The Internal Revenue Code of 1986 and the Employee Retirement Income Security Act of 1974 shall be applied and administered to years, estates, gifts, and transfers described in subsection (a) as if the provisions and amendments described in subsection (a) had never been enacted.

[Sec. 2]

SEC. 2. DEFINITIONS AND SPECIAL RULES.

[Sec. 2(a)]

(a) DEFINITION OF SURVIVING SPOUSE.—

(1) IN GENERAL.—For purposes of section 1, the term "surviving spouse" means a taxpayer—

(A) whose spouse died during either of his two taxable years immediately preceding the taxable year, and

(B) who maintains as his home a household which constitutes for the taxable year the principal place of abode (as a member of such household) of a dependent (i) who (within the meaning of section 152, determined without regard to subsections (b)(1), (b)(2), and (d)(1)(B) thereof) is a son, stepson, daughter, or stepdaughter of the taxpayer, and (ii) with respect to whom the taxpayer is entitled to a deduction for the taxable year under section 151.

For purposes of this paragraph, an individual shall be considered as maintaining a household only if over half of the cost of maintaining the household during the taxable year is furnished by such individual.

(2) LIMITATIONS.—Notwithstanding paragraph (1), for purposes of section 1 a taxpayer shall not be considered to be a surviving spouse—

(A) if the taxpayer has remarried at any time before the close of the taxable year, or

(B) unless, for the taxpayer's taxable year during which his spouse died, a joint return could have been made under the provisions of section 6013 (without regard to subsection (a)(3) thereof).

(3) SPECIAL RULE WHERE DECEASED SPOUSE WAS IN MISSING STATUS.—If an individual was in a missing status (within the meaning of section 6013(f)(3)) as a result of service in a combat zone (as determined for purposes of section 112) and if such individual remains in such status until the date referred to in subparagraph (A) or (B), then, for purposes of paragraph (1)(A), the date on which such individual died shall be treated as the earlier of the date determined under subparagraph (A) or the date determined under subparagraph (B):

(A) the date on which the determination is made under section 556 of title 37 of the United States Code or under section 5566 of title 5 of such Code (whichever is applicable) that such individual died while in such missing status, or

(B) except in the case of the combat zone designated for purposes of the Vietnam conflict, the date which is 2 years after the date designated under section 112 as the date of termination of combatant activities in that zone.

Amendments

• 2004, Working Families Tax Relief Act of 2004 (P.L. 108-311)

P.L. 108-311, §207(1):

Amended Code Sec. 2(a)(1)(B)(i) by inserting ", determined without regard to subsections (b)(1), (b)(2), and (d)(1)(B) thereof" after "section 152". **Effective** for tax years beginning after 12-31-2004.

• 1999 (P.L. 106-21)

P.L. 106-21, §1(a)(1), (b) and (d)(1), provide:

SECTION 1. AVAILABILITY OF CERTAIN TAX BENEFITS FOR SERVICES AS PART OF OPERATION ALLIED FORCE.

(a) GENERAL RULE.—For purposes of the following provisions of the Internal Revenue Code of 1986, a qualified hazardous duty area shall be treated in the same manner as if it were a combat zone (as determined under section 112 of such Code):

(1) Section 2(a)(3) (relating to special rule where deceased spouse was in missing status).

* * *

(b) QUALIFIED HAZARDOUS DUTY AREA.—For purposes of this section, the term "qualified hazardous duty area" means any area of the Federal Republic of Yugoslavia (Serbia/Montenegro), Albania, the Adriatic Sea, and the northern Ionian Sea (above the 39th parallel) during the period (which includes the date of the enactment of this Act) that any member of the Armed Forces of the United States is entitled to special pay under section 310 of title 37, United States Code (relating to special pay: duty subject to hostile fire or imminent danger) for services performed in such area.

* * *

(d) EFFECTIVE DATES.—

(1) IN GENERAL.—Except as provided in paragraph (2), this section shall take effect on March 24, 1999.

• 1996 (P.L. 104-117)

P.L. 104-117, §1(a)(1), (b) and (e)(1), provide:

SECTION 1. TREATMENT OF CERTAIN INDIVIDUALS PERFORMING SERVICES IN CERTAIN HAZARDOUS DUTY AREAS.

(a) GENERAL RULE.—For purposes of the following provisions of the Internal Revenue Code of 1986, a qualified hazardous duty area shall be treated in the same manner as if it were a combat zone (as determined under section 112 of such Code):

(1) Section 2(a)(3) (relating to special rule where deceased spouse was in missing status).

* * *

(b) QUALIFIED HAZARDOUS DUTY AREA.—For purposes of this section, the term "qualified hazardous duty area" means Bosnia and Herzegovina, Croatia, or Macedonia, if as of the date of the enactment of this section any member of the Armed Forces of the United States is entitled to special pay under section 310 of title 37, United States Code (relating to special pay; duty subject to hostile fire or imminent danger) for services performed in such country. Such term includes any such country only during the period such entitlement is in effect. Solely for purposes of applying section 7508 of the Internal Revenue Code of 1986, in the case of an individual who is performing services as part of Operation Joint Endeavor outside the United States while deployed away from such individual's permanent duty station, the term "qualified hazardous duty area" includes, during the period for which such entitlement is in effect, any area in which such services are performed.

* * *

(e) EFFECTIVE DATE.—

(1) IN GENERAL.—Except as provided in paragraph (2), the provisions of and amendments made by this section shall take effect on November 21, 1995.

• 1986, Tax Reform Act of 1986 (P.L. 99-514)

P.L. 99-514, §1708(a)(1):

Amended Code Sec. 2(a)(3)(B). **Effective** for tax years beginning after 12-31-82. Prior to amendment, Code Sec. 2(a)(3)(B) read as follows:

(B) the date which is—

(i) December 31, 1982, in the case of service in the combat zone designated for purposes of the Vietnam conflict, or

(ii) 2 years after the date designated under section 112 as the date of termination of combatant activities in that zone, in the case of any combat zone other than that referred to in clause (i).

• 1983, Technical Corrections Act of 1982 (P.L. 97-448)

P.L. 97-448, §307(a):

Amended Code Sec. 2(a)(3)(B)(i) by striking out "January 2, 1978" and inserting in lieu thereof "December 31, 1982". **Effective** 1-12-83.

• 1976 (P.L. 94-569)

P.L. 94-569, §3(a):

Amended Code Sec. 2(a)(3)(B). **Effective** 10-20-76. Prior to amendment, Code Sec. 2(a)(3)(B) read as follows:

(B) the date which is 2 years after—

(i) the date of the enactment of this paragraph [January 2, 1975], in the case of service in the combat zone designated for purposes of the Vietnam conflict, or

(ii) the date designated under section 112 as the date of termination of combatant activities in that zone, in the case of any combat zone other than that referred to in clause (i).

• 1974 (P.L. 93-597)

P.L. 93-597, §3(b):

Amended Code Sec. 2(a) by adding paragraph (3). **Effective** with respect to tax years ending on or after 2-28-61.

[Sec. 2(b)]

(b) DEFINITION OF HEAD OF HOUSEHOLD.—

(1) IN GENERAL.—For purposes of this subtitle, an individual shall be considered a head of a household if, and only if, such individual is not married at the close of his taxable year, is not a surviving spouse (as defined in subsection (a)), and either—

(A) maintains as his home a household which constitutes for more than one-half of such taxable year the principal place of abode, as a member of such household, of—

(i) a qualifying child of the individual (as defined in section 152(c), determined without regard to section 152(e)), but not if such child—

(I) is married at the close of the taxpayer's taxable year, and

(II) is not a dependent of such individual by reason of section 152(b)(2) or 152(b)(3), or both, or

(ii) any other person who is a dependent of the taxpayer, if the taxpayer is entitled to a deduction for the taxable year for such person under section 151, or

(B) maintains a household which constitutes for such taxable year the principal place of abode of the father or mother of the taxpayer, if the taxpayer is entitled to a deduction for the taxable year for such father or mother under section 151.

For purposes of this paragraph, an individual shall be considered as maintaining a household only if over half of the cost of maintaining the household during the taxable year is furnished by such individual.

(2) DETERMINATION OF STATUS.—For purposes of this subsection—

(A) an individual who is legally separated from his spouse under a decree of divorce or of separate maintenance shall not be considered as married;

(B) a taxpayer shall be considered as not married at the close of his taxable year if at any time during the taxable year his spouse is a nonresident alien; and

(C) a taxpayer shall be considered as married at the close of his taxable year if his spouse (other than a spouse described in subparagraph (B)) died during the taxable year.

(3) LIMITATIONS.—Notwithstanding paragraph (1), for purposes of this subtitle a taxpayer shall not be considered to be a head of a household—

(A) if at any time during the taxable year he is a nonresident alien; or

(B) by reason of an individual who would not be a dependent for the taxable year but for—

(i) subparagraph (H) of section 152(d)(2), or

(ii) paragraph (3) of section 152(d).

Amendments

• 2005, Gulf Opportunity Zone Act of 2005 (P.L. 109-135)

P.L. 109-135, §412(a):

Amended Code Sec. 2(b)(2)(C) by striking "subparagraph (C)" and inserting "subparagraph (B)". **Effective** 12-21-2005.

• 2004, Working Families Tax Relief Act of 2004 (P.L. 108-311)

P.L. 108-311, §202(a):

Amended Code Sec. 2(b)(1)(A)(i). **Effective** for tax years beginning after 12-31-2004. Prior to amendment, Code Sec. 2(b)(1)(A)(i) read as follows:

(i) a son, stepson, daughter, or stepdaughter of the taxpayer, or a descendant of a son or daughter of the taxpayer, but if such son, stepson, daughter, stepdaughter, or descendant is married at the close of the taxpayer's taxable year, only if the taxpayer is entitled to a deduction for the taxable year for such person under section 151 (or would be so entitled but for paragraph (2) or (4) of section 152(e)), or

P.L. 108-311, §202(b)(1):

Amended Code Sec. 2(b)(2) by striking subparagraph (A) and by redesignating subparagraphs (B), (C), and (D) as subparagraphs (A), (B), and (C), respectively. **Effective** for tax years beginning after 12-31-2004. Prior to being stricken, Code Sec. 2(b)(2)(A) read as follows:

(A) a legally adopted child of a person shall be considered a child of such person by blood;

P.L. 108-311, §202(b)(2):

Amended Code Sec. 2(b)(3)(B)(i)-(ii). **Effective** for tax years beginning after 12-31-2004. Prior to amendment, Code Sec. 2(b)(3)(B)(i)-(ii) read as follows:

(i) paragraph (9) of section 152(a), or

(ii) subsection (c) of section 152.

• 1984, Deficit Reduction Act of 1984 (P.L. 98-369)

P.L. 98-369, §423(c)(2):

Amended Code Sec. 2(b)(1)(A) by striking out "which constitutes for such taxable year" and inserting in lieu thereof "which constitutes for more than one-half of such taxable year", and by striking out "under section 151" in clause (i) and inserting in lieu thereof "under section 151 (or would be so entitled but for paragraph (2) or (4) of section 152(e))". **Effective** for tax years beginning after 12-31-84.

• 1976, Tax Reform Act of 1976 (P.L. 94-455)

P.L. 94-455, §1901(b)(9):

Amended Code Sec. 2(b)(3)(B) by striking out clause (ii); by adding "or" at the end of clause (i), and by redesignating clause (iii) as clause (ii). **Effective** for tax years beginning after 12-31-76. Prior to amendment, Sec. 2(b)(3)(B)(ii) read as follows:

(ii) paragraph (10) of section 152(a), or.

[Sec. 2(c)]

(c) CERTAIN MARRIED INDIVIDUALS LIVING APART.—For purposes of this part, an individual shall be treated as not married at the close of the taxable year if such individual is so treated under the provisions of section 7703(b).

Amendments

• 1986, Tax Reform Act of 1986 (P.L. 99-514)

P.L. 99-514, §1301(j)(10):

Amended Code Sec. 2(c) by striking out "section 143(b)" and inserting in lieu thereof "section 7703(b)". **Effective** for bonds issued after 8-15-86.

• 1976, Tax Reform Act of 1976 (P.L. 94-455)

P.L. 94-455, §1901(a)(1):

Amended Code Sec. 2(c). **Effective** for tax years beginning after 12-31-76. Prior to amendment, subsection (c) read as follows:

(c) CERTAIN MARRIED INDIVIDUALS LIVING APART.—For purposes of this part, an individual who, under section 143(b), is not to be considered as married shall not be considered as married.

[Sec. 2(d)]

(d) NONRESIDENT ALIENS.—In the case of a nonresident alien individual, the taxes imposed by sections 1 and 55 shall apply only as provided by section 871 or 877.

Amendments

• 1988, Technical and Miscellaneous Revenue Act of 1988 (P.L. 100-647)

P.L. 100-647, §1007(g)(13)(A):

Amended Code Sec. 2(d) by striking out "the tax imposed by section 1" and inserting in lieu thereof "the taxes imposed by sections 1 and 55". **Effective** as if included in the provision of P.L. 99-514 to which it relates.

[Sec. 2(e)]

(e) CROSS REFERENCE.—

For definition of taxable income, see section 63.

Amendments

• 1969, Tax Reform Act of 1969 (P.L. 91-172)

P. L. 91-172, §803(b):

Amended Code Sec. 2. Except for Code Sec. 2(c), **effective** for tax years beginning after 12-31-70. Code Sec. 2(c) is **effective** for tax years beginning after 12-31-69. Prior to amendment, Code Sec. 2 read as follows:

SEC. 2. TAX IN CASE OF JOINT RETURN OR RETURN OF SURVIVING SPOUSE.

(a) Rate of Tax.—In the case of a joint return of a husband and wife under section 6013, the tax imposed by section 1 shall be twice the tax which would be imposed if the taxable income were cut in half. For purposes of this subsection, section 3, and section 141, a return of a surviving spouse (as defined in subsection (b)) shall be treated as a joint return of a husband and wife under section 6013.

(b) Definition of Surviving Spouse

(1) In general.—For purposes of subsection (a), the term "surviving spouse" means a taxpayer—

(A) whose spouse died during either of his two taxable years immediately preceding the taxable year, and

(B) who maintains as his home a household which constitutes for the taxable year the principal place of abode (as a member of such household) of a dependent (i) who (within the meaning of section 152) is a son, stepson, daughter, or stepdaughter of the taxpayer, and (ii) with respect to whom the taxpayer is entitled to a deduction for the taxable year under section 151.

(2) Limitations.—Notwithstanding paragraph (1), for purposes of subsection (a) a taxpayer shall not be considered to be a surviving spouse—

(A) if the taxpayer has remarried at any time before the close of the taxable year, or

(B) unless, for the taxpayer's taxable year during which his spouse died, a joint return could have been made under the provisions of section 6013 (without regard to subsection (a)(3) thereof) or under the corresponding provisions of the Internal Revenue Code of 1939.

(c) Certain Married Individuals Living Apart.—For purposes of this part, an individual who, under section 143(b), is not to be considered as married shall not be considered as married."

• 1964, Revenue Act of 1964 (P.L. 88-272)

P. L. 88-272, §112(b):

Amended the second sentence of Code Sec. 2(a) by inserting ", section 3, and section 141" in lieu of "and section 3". **Effective** 1-1-64.

[Sec. 3]

SEC. 3. TAX TABLES FOR INDIVIDUALS.

[Sec. 3(a)]

(a) IMPOSITION OF TAX TABLE TAX.—

(1) IN GENERAL.—In lieu of the tax imposed by section 1, there is hereby imposed for each taxable year on the taxable income of every individual—

(A) who does not itemize his deductions for the taxable year, and

(B) whose taxable income for such taxable year does not exceed the ceiling amount,

a tax determined under tables, applicable to such taxable year, which shall be prescribed by the Secretary and which shall be in such form as he determines appropriate. In the table so prescribed, the amounts of the tax shall be computed on the basis of the rates prescribed by section 1.

(2) CEILING AMOUNT DEFINED.—For purposes of paragraph (1), the term "ceiling amount" means, with respect to any taxpayer, the amount (not less than $20,000) determined by the Secretary for the tax rate category in which such taxpayer falls.

(3) AUTHORITY TO PRESCRIBE TABLES FOR TAXPAYERS WHO ITEMIZE DEDUCTIONS.—The Secretary may provide that this section shall apply also for any taxable year to individuals who itemize their deductions. Any tables prescribed under the preceding sentence shall be on the basis of taxable income.

Amendments

• 1986, Tax Reform Act of 1986 (P.L. 99-514)

P.L. 99-514, §102(b):

Amended Code Sec. 3(a). **Effective** for tax years beginning after 12-31-86. Prior to amendment, Code Sec. 3(a) read as follows:

(a) IMPOSITION OF TAX TABLE TAX.—

(1) IN GENERAL.—In lieu of the tax imposed by section 1, there is hereby imposed for each taxable year on the tax table income of every individual whose tax table income for such year does not exceed the ceiling amount, a tax determined under tables, applicable to such taxable year, which shall be prescribed by the Secretary and which shall be in such form as he determines appropriate. In the tables so prescribed, the amounts of tax shall be computed on the basis of the rates prescribed by section 1.

(2) CEILING AMOUNT DEFINED.—For purposes of paragraph (1), the term "ceiling amount" means, with respect to any taxpayer, the amount (not less than $20,000) determined by the Secretary for the tax rate category in which such taxpayer falls.

(3) CERTAIN TAXPAYERS WITH LARGE NUMBER OF EXEMPTIONS.—The Secretary may exclude from the application of this section taxpayers in any tax rate category having more than the number of exemptions for that category determined by the Secretary.

(4) TAX TABLE INCOME DEFINED.—For purposes of this section, the term "tax table income" means adjusted gross income—

(A) reduced by the sum of—

(i) the excess itemized deductions, and

(ii) the direct charitable deduction, and

(B) increased (in the case of an individual to whom section 63(e) applies) by the unused zero bracket amount.

(5) SECTION MAY BE APPLIED ON THE BASIS OF TAXABLE INCOME.—The Secretary may provide that this section shall be applied for any taxable year on the basis of taxable income in lieu of tax table income.

• 1981, Economic Recovery Tax Act of 1981 (P.L. 97-34)

P.L. 97-34, §101(b)(2)(A), (B), (C):

Amended Code Sec. 3(a) by inserting "and which shall be in such form as he determines appropriate" after "Secretary" in paragraph (1) and by adding at the end thereof paragraph (5). **Effective** 8-13-81.

P.L. 97-34, §121(c)(3):

Amended Code Sec. 3(a)(4)(A). **Effective** for contributions made after 12-31-81, in tax years beginning after such date. Prior to amendment, Code Sec. 3(a)(4)(A) read as follows:

(A) reduced by the excess itemized deductions, and".

[Sec. 3(b)]

(b) SECTION INAPPLICABLE TO CERTAIN INDIVIDUALS.—This section shall not apply to—

(1) an individual making a return under section 443(a)(1) for a period of less than 12 months on account of a change in annual accounting period, and

(2) an estate or trust.

Amendments

• 1986, Tax Reform Act of 1986 (P.L. 99-514)

P.L. 99-514, §141(b)(1):

Amended Code Sec. 3(b) by striking out paragraph (1) and by redesignating paragraphs (2) and (3) as paragraphs (1) and (2), respectively. **Effective** for tax years beginning after 12-31-86. Prior to amendment, Code Sec. 3(b)(1) read as follows:

(1) an individual to whom section 1301 (relating to income averaging) applies for the taxable year,

• 1981, Economic Recovery Tax Act of 1981 (P.L. 97-34)

P.L. 97-34, §101(c)(2)(A):

Amended Code Sec. 3(b)(1). **Effective** for tax years beginning after 12-31-81. Prior to amendment, Code Sec. 3(b)(1) read as follows:

(1) an individual to whom—

(A) section 1301 (relating to income averaging), or

(B) section 1348 (relating to maximum rate on personal service income),

applies for the taxable year,

• 1980, Technical Corrections Act of 1979 (P.L. 96-222)

P.L. 96-222, §108(a)(1)(A):

Amended P.L. 95-615, §202 by redesignating subsection (f) as subsection (g) and by adding a new subsection (f) to provide for the deletion of subparagraph (A) of Code Sec. 3(b)(1). **Effective** as set forth in P.L. 95-615, §209. Prior to amendment, Code Sec. 3(b)(1)(A) read:

(A) section 911 (relating to earned income from sources without the United States),

P.L. 96-222, §108(a)(1)(E):

Amended Code Sec. 3(b)(1) by redesignating subparagraphs (B) and (C) as (A) and (B). **Effective** for tax years beginning after 12-31-78.

• 1978, Revenue Act of 1978 (P.L. 95-600)

P.L. 95-600, §401(b)(1):

Amended Code Sec. 3(b)(1) by deleting subparagraph (B) and redesignating subparagraphs (C) and (D) as (B) and (C).

Effective for tax years beginning after 12-31-78. Prior to deletion, subparagraph (B) read as follows:

(B) section 1201 (relating to alternative capital gains tax),

[Sec. 3(c)]

(c) TAX TREATED AS IMPOSED BY SECTION 1.—For purposes of this title, the tax imposed by this section shall be treated as tax imposed by section 1.

[Sec. 3(d)]

(d) TAXABLE INCOME.—Whenever it is necessary to determine the taxable income of an individual to whom this section applies, the taxable income shall be determined under section 63.

[Sec. 3(e)]

(e) CROSS REFERENCE.—

For computation of tax by Secretary, see section 6014.

Amendments

• 1977, Tax Reduction and Simplification Act of 1977 (P.L. 95-30)

P.L. 95-30, §101(b):

Amended Code Sec. 3. **Effective** for tax years beginning after 12-31-76. Prior to amendment, Code Sec. 3 read as follows:

SEC. 3. TAX TABLES FOR INDIVIDUALS HAVING TAXABLE INCOME OF LESS THAN $20,000.

(a) GENERAL RULE.—In lieu of the tax imposed by section 1, there is hereby imposed for each taxable year on the taxable income of every individual whose taxable income for such year does not exceed $20,000, a tax determined under tables, applicable to such taxable year, which shall be prescribed by the Secretary. In the tables so prescribed, the amounts of tax shall be computed on the basis of the rates prescribed by section 1.

(b) TAX TREATED AS IMPOSED BY SECTION 1.—For purposes of this title, the tax imposed by this section shall be treated as tax imposed by section 1.

• 1976, Tax Reform Act of 1976 (P.L. 94-455)

P.L. 94-455, §501(a):

Amended Code Sec. 3. **Effective** for tax years beginning after 12-31-75. Prior to amendment, such section read as follows:

SEC. 3. OPTIONAL TAX TABLES FOR INDIVIDUALS.

In lieu of the tax imposed by section 1, there is hereby imposed for each taxable year beginning after December 31, 1969, on the taxable income of every individual whose adjusted gross income for such year is less than $10,000 [$15,000 effective for taxable years ending in 1975 or 1976] and who has elected for such year to pay the tax imposed by this section, a tax determined under tables, applicable to such taxable year, which shall be prescribed by the Secretary or his delegate. In the tables so prescribed, the amounts of tax shall be computed on the basis of the taxable income computed by taking the standard deduction and on the basis of the rates prescribed by section 1.

• 1975, Tax Reduction Act of 1975 (P.L. 94-12)

P. L. 94-12, §201(c):

Amended Code Sec. 3 by substituting "$15,000" for "$10,000." **Effective** only for tax years ending in 1975, but P. L. 94-164 extended the effective date to tax years ending in 1976.

• 1969, Tax Reform Act of 1969 (P.L. 91-172)

P. L. 91-172, §803(c):

Amended Code Sec. 3. **Effective** for tax years beginning after 12-31-69. Prior to amendment, Code Sec. 3 (except for the optional tax tables for tax years beginning after 1964 and before 1970, which are not reproduced) read as follows:

SEC. 3. OPTIONAL TAX IF ADJUSTED GROSS INCOME IS LESS THAN $5,000.

(a) Taxable Years Beginning In 1964.—In lieu of the tax imposed by section 1, there is hereby imposed for each taxable year beginning on or after January 1, 1964, and before January 1, 1965, on the taxable income of every individual whose adjusted gross income for such year is less than $5,000 and who has elected for such year to pay the tax imposed by this section, a tax as follows: [optional tax tables for taxable years beginning in 1964 are not reproduced.—CCH.]

(b) Taxable Years Beginning After December 31, 1964.—In lieu of the tax imposed by section 1, there is hereby imposed for each taxable year beginning after December 31, 1964, on the taxable income of every individual whose adjusted gross income for such year is less than $5,000 and who has elected for such year to pay the tax imposed by this section a tax as follows: [optional tax tables for taxable years beginning after 1964 and before 1970 are not reproduced].

• 1964, Revenue Act of 1964 (P.L. 88-272)

P. L. 88-272, §301(a):

Amended Code Sec. 3. **Effective** for tax years beginning after 12-31-63. Prior to amendment, Sec. 3 read as follows:

"Sec. 3. Optional Tax If Adjusted Gross Income Is Less than $5,000.—In lieu of the tax imposed by section 1, there is hereby imposed for each taxable year, on the taxable income of each individual whose adjusted gross income for such year is less than $5,000 and who has elected for such year to pay the tax imposed by this section, the tax shown in the table [tables for years prior to 1969 are not reproduced].

[Sec. 4—Repealed]

Amendments

• 1976, Tax Reform Act of 1976 (P.L. 94-455)

P.L. 94-455, §501(b)(1):

Repealed Code Sec. 4. **Effective** for tax years beginning after 1975. Prior to repeal, Sec. 4 read as follows:

SEC. 4. RULES FOR OPTIONAL TAX.

(a) NUMBER OF EXEMPTIONS.—For purposes of the tables prescribed by the Secretary or his delegate pursuant to section 3, the term "number of exemptions" means the number of exemptions allowed under section 151 as deductions in computing taxable income.

(b) MANNER OF ELECTION.—The election referred to in section 3 shall be made in the manner provided in regulations prescribed by the Secretary or his delegate.

(c) HUSBAND OR WIFE FILING SEPARATE RETURN.—

(1) A husband or wife may not elect to pay the optional tax imposed by section 3 if the tax of the other spouse is determined under section 1 on the basis of taxable income computed without regard to the standard deduction.

(2) Except as otherwise provided in this subsection, in the case of a husband or wife filing a separate return the tax imposed by section 3 shall be the lesser of the tax shown in—

(A) the table prescribed under section 3 applicable in the case of married persons filing separate returns which applies the percentage standard deduction, or

(B) the table prescribed under section 3 applicable in the case of married persons filing separate returns which applies the low income allowance.

(3) The table referred to in paragraph (2)(B) shall not apply in the case of a husband or wife filing a separate return if the tax of the other spouse is determined with regard to the percentage standard deduction; except that an individual described in section 141(d)(2) may elect (under regulations prescribed by the Secretary or his delegate) to

pay the tax shown in the table referred to in paragraph (2)(B) in lieu of the tax shown in the table referred to in paragraph (2)(A). For purposes of this title, an election under the preceding sentence shall be treated as an election made under section 141(d)(2).

(4) For purposes of this subsection, determination of marital status shall be made under section 143.

(d) CERTAIN OTHER TAXPAYERS INELIGIBLE.—Section 3 shall not apply to—

(1) a nonresident alien individual;

(2) a citizen of the United States entitled to the benefits of section 931 (relating to income from sources within possessions of the United States);

(3) an individual making a return under section 443(a)(1) for a period of less than 12 months on account of change in his accounting period;

(4) an estate or trust; or

(5) an individual if the amount of the standard deduction otherwise allowable to such individual is reduced under section 141(e).

(e) TAXABLE INCOME COMPUTED WITH STANDARD DEDUCTION.—Whenever it is necessary to determine the taxable income of a taxpayer who made the election referred to in section 3, the taxable income shall be determined under section 63(b) (relating to definition of taxable income for individuals electing standard deduction).

(f) CROSS REFERENCES.—

(1) For other applicable rules (including rules as to the change of an election under section 3), see section 144.

(2) For disallowance of certain credits against tax, see section 36.

(3) For rule that optional tax is not to apply if individual chooses the benefits of income averaging, see section 1304(b).

(4) For computation of tax by Secretary or his delegate, see section 6014.

[Sec. 5]

SEC. 5. CROSS REFERENCES RELATING TO TAX ON INDIVIDUALS.

[Sec. 5(a)]

(a) OTHER RATES OF TAX ON INDIVIDUALS, ETC.—

(1) For rates of tax on nonresident aliens, see section 871.

(2) For doubling of tax on citizens of certain foreign countries, see section 891.

(3) For rate of withholding in the case of nonresident aliens, see section 1441.

(4) For alternative minimum tax, see section 55.

Amendments

• 1986, Tax Reform Act of 1986 (P.L. 99-514)

P.L. 99-514, §701(e)(4)(A):

Amended Code Sec. 5(a)(4). **Effective** for tax years beginning after 12-31-86. Prior to amendment, Code Sec. 5(a)(4) read as follows:

(4) For minimum tax for taxpayers other than corporations, see section 55.

• 1982, Tax Equity and Fiscal Responsibility Act of 1982 (P.L. 97-248)

P.L. 97-248, §201(d)(4), as amended by P.L. 97-448, §306(a)(1)(A):

Amended Code Sec. 5(a)(4) by striking out "sections 55 and 56" and inserting in lieu thereof "section 55". **Effective** for tax years beginning after 12-31-82.

• 1980, Technical Corrections Act of 1979 (P.L. 96-222)

P.L. 96-222, §104(a)(4)(H)(vii):

Amended Code Sec. 5(a)(4) by changing "section 55" to "sections 55 and 56". **Effective** for tax years beginning after 12-31-79.

• 1978, Revenue Act of 1978 (P.L. 95-600)

P.L. 95-600, §§401(b)(2), 421(e)(1):

Amended Code Sec. 5(a) by deleting subparagraph (3) and by redesignating subparagraphs (4) and (5) as (3) and (4). Further, redesignated subparagraph (4) is amended. **Effective** for tax years beginning after 12-31-78. Prior to amendment, subparagraph (3) read as follows:

"(3) For alternative tax in case of capital gain, see section 1201(b)."

Redesignated subparagraph (4) prior to amendment read as follows:

"(4) For minimum tax for tax preferences, see section 56."

• 1969, Tax Reform Act of 1969 (P.L. 91-172)

P. L. 91-172, §301(b)(2):

Added new paragraph (a)(5). **Effective** 1-1-70.

[Sec. 5(b)]

(b) SPECIAL LIMITATIONS ON TAX.—

(1) For limitation on tax in case of income of members of Armed Forces, astronauts, and victims of certain terrorist attacks on death, see section 692.

(2) For computation of tax where taxpayer restores substantial amount held under claim of right, see section 1341.

Amendments

• 2003, Military Family Tax Relief Act of 2003 (P.L. 108-121)

P.L. 108-121, §110(a)(2)(A):

Amended Code Sec. 5(b)(1) by inserting ", astronauts," after "Forces". **Effective** with respect to any astronaut whose death occurs after 12-31-2002.

• 2002, Victims of Terrorism Tax Relief Act of 2001 (P.L. 107-134)

P.L. 107-134, §101(b)(1):

Amended Code Sec. 5(b)(1) by inserting "and victims of certain terrorist attacks" before "on death". **Effective** for tax years ending before, on, or after September 11, 2001. For a waiver of limitations, see Act Sec. 101(d)(2), below.

P.L. 107-134, §101(d)(2), provides:

(2) WAIVER OF LIMITATIONS.—If refund or credit of any overpayment of tax resulting from the amendments made by this section is prevented at any time before the close of the 1-year period beginning on the date of the enactment of this Act by the operation of any law or rule of law (including res judicata), such refund or credit may nevertheless be made or allowed if claim therefor is filed before the close of such period.

• 1986, Tax Reform Act of 1986 (P.L. 99-514)

P.L. 99-514, §141(b)(2):

Amended Code Sec. 5(b) by striking out paragraph (2) and by redesignating paragraph (3) as paragraph (2). Effec-

tive for tax years beginning after 12-31-86. Prior to amendment, Code Sec. 5(b)(2) read as follows:

(2) For limitation on tax where an individual chooses the benefits of income averaging, see section 1301.

• 1976, Tax Reform Act of 1976 (P.L. 94-455)

P.L. 94-455, §1901(b)(21):

Amended Code Sec. 5(b) by striking out paragraph (1). **Effective** for tax years beginning after 12-31-76. Prior to amendment, it read as follows:

(1) For limitation on tax attributable to sales of oil or gas properties, see section 632.

P.L. 94-455, §1951(c)(3):

Amended Code Sec. 5(b) by striking out paragraph (5) and by redesignating paragraphs (2), (3), and (4), as paragraphs (1), (2), and (3), respectively. **Effective** for taxable years beginning after 12-31-76. Prior to amendment, paragraph (5) read as follows:

(5) For limitation on tax attributable to claims against the United States involving acquisitions of property, see section 1347.

• 1969, Tax Reform Act of 1969 (P.L. 91-172)

P. L. 91-172, §803(d)(6):

Amended Code Secs. 5(b)(1) and 5(b)(5) by striking out "surtax" and inserting in lieu thereof "tax." **Effective** for tax years beginning after 12-31-70.

• 1964, Revenue Act of 1964 (P.L. 88-272)

P. L. 88-272, §232(f)(2):

Amended Code Sec. 5(b). **Effective** for tax years beginning after 12-31-63. Prior to amendment, subsection (b) read as follows:

"(b) Special Limitations on Tax.—

"(1) For limitation on tax attributable to receipt of lump sum under annuity, endowment, or life insurance contract, see section 72(e)(3).

"(2) For limitation on surtax attributable to sales of oil or gas properties, see section 632.

"(3) For limitation on tax in case of income of members of Armed Forces on death, see section 692.

"(4) For limitation on tax with respect to compensation for long-term services, see section 1301.

"(5) For limitation on tax with respect to income from artistic work or inventions, see section 1302.

"(6) For limitation on tax in case of back pay, see section 1303.

"(7) For computation of tax where taxpayer restores substantial amount held under claim of right, see section 1341.

"(8) For limitation on surtax attributable to claims against the United States involving acquisitions of property, see section 1347."

PART II—TAX ON CORPORATIONS

[Sec. 11]

SEC. 11. TAX IMPOSED.

[Sec. 11(a)]

(a) CORPORATIONS IN GENERAL.—A tax is hereby imposed for each taxable year on the taxable income of every corporation.

Amendments

• 1978, Revenue Act of 1978 (P.L. 95-600)

P.L. 95-600, §301(a):

Amended Code Sec. 11(a). **Effective** for tax years beginning after 12-31-78. Prior to amendment, Code Sec. 11(a) read as follows:

(a) CORPORATIONS IN GENERAL.—A tax is hereby imposed for each taxable year on the taxable income of every corporation. The tax shall consist of a normal tax computed under subsection (b) and a surtax computed under subsection (c).

• 1976, Tax Reform Act of 1976 (P.L. 94-455)

P.L. 94-455, §901(a):

Amended and reenacted subsection (a). **Effective** 12-23-75.

• 1964, Revenue Act of 1964 (P.L. 88-272)

P. L. 88-272, §121:

Amended and reenacted subsection (a). **Effective** for tax years beginning after 12-31-63.

[Sec. 11(b)]

(b) AMOUNT OF TAX.—

(1) IN GENERAL.—The amount of the tax imposed by subsection (a) shall be the sum of—

(A) 15 percent of so much of the taxable income as does not exceed $50,000,

(B) 25 percent of so much of the taxable income as exceeds $50,000 but does not exceed $75,000,

(C) 34 percent of so much of the taxable income as exceeds $75,000 but does not exceed $10,000,000, and

(D) 35 percent of so much of the taxable income as exceeds $10,000,000.

In the case of a corporation which has taxable income in excess of $100,000 for any taxable year, the amount of tax determined under the preceding sentence for such taxable year shall be increased by the lesser of (i) 5 percent of such excess, or (ii) $11,750. In the case of a corporation which has taxable income in excess of $15,000,000, the amount of the tax determined under the foregoing provisions of this paragraph shall be increased by an additional amount equal to the lesser of (i) 3 percent of such excess, or (ii) $100,000.

(2) CERTAIN PERSONAL SERVICE CORPORATIONS NOT ELIGIBLE FOR GRADUATED RATES.—Notwithstanding paragraph (1), the amount of the tax imposed by subsection (a) on the taxable income of a qualified personal service corporation (as defined in section 448(d)(2)) shall be equal to 35 percent of the taxable income.

Amendments

• 1993, Omnibus Budget Reconciliation Act of 1993 (P.L. 103-66)

P.L. 103-66, §13221(a)(1)-(3):

Amended Code Sec. 11(b)(1) by striking "and" at the end of subparagraph (B), by striking subparagraph (C) and inserting new subparagraphs (C) and (D), and by adding at the end thereof a new sentence. **Effective** for tax years beginning on or after 1-1-93. Prior to amendment, Code Sec. 11(b)(1)(C) read as follows:

(C) 34 percent of so much of the taxable income as exceeds $75,000.

P.L. 103-66, §13221(b):

Amended Code Sec. 11(b)(2) by striking "34 percent" and inserting "35 percent". **Effective** for tax years beginning on or after 1-1-93.

• 1987, Revenue Act of 1987 (P.L. 100-203)

P.L. 100-203, §10224(a):

Amended Code Sec. 11(b). **Effective** for tax years beginning after 12-31-87. Prior to amendment, Code Sec. 11(b) read as follows:

(b) AMOUNT OF TAX.—The amount of the tax imposed by subsection (a) shall be the sum of—

(1) 15 percent of so much of the taxable income as does not exceed $50,000,

(2) 25 percent of so much of the taxable income as exceeds $50,000 but does not exceed $75,000,

(3) 34 percent of so much of the taxable income as exceeds $75,000.

In the case of a corporation which has taxable income in excess of $100,000 for any taxable year, the amount of tax determined under the preceding sentence for such taxable year shall be increased by the lesser of (A) 5 percent of such excess, or (B) $11,750.

• 1986, Tax Reform Act of 1986 (P.L. 99-514)

P.L. 99-514, §601(a):

Amended Code Sec. 11(b). **Effective** for tax years beginning on or after 7-1-87. See, also, Act Sec. 601(b)(2), below. Prior to amendment, Code Sec. 11(b) read as follows:

(b) AMOUNT OF TAX.—The amount of tax imposed by subsection (a) shall be the sum of—

(1) 15 percent (16 percent for taxable years beginning in 1982) of so much of the taxable income as does not exceed $25,000;

(2) 18 percent (19 percent for taxable years beginning in 1982) of so much of the taxable income as exceeds $25,000 but does not exceed $50,000;

(3) 30 percent of so much of the taxable income as exceeds $50,000 but does not exceed $75,000;

(4) 40 percent of so much of the taxable income as exceeds $75,000 but does not exceed $100,000; plus

(5) 46 percent of so much of the taxable income as exceeds $100,000.

In the case of a corporation with taxable income in excess of $1,000,000 for any taxable year, the amount of tax determined under the preceding sentence for such taxable year shall be increased by the lesser of (A) 5 percent of such excess, or (B) $20,250.

P.L. 99-514, §601(b)(2), provides:

(2) CROSS REFERENCE.—For treatment of taxable years which include July 1, 1987, see section 15 of the Internal Revenue Code of 1986.

P.L. 99-514, §646, as amended by P.L. 100-647, §1006(k), provides:

SEC. 646. CERTAIN ENTITIES NOT TREATED AS CORPORATIONS.

(a) GENERAL RULE.—For purposes of the Internal Revenue Code of 1986, if the entity described in subsection (b) makes an election under subsection (c), such entity shall be treated as a trust to which subpart E of part 1 of subchapter J of chapter 1 of such Code applies.

(b) ENTITY.—An entity is described in this subsection if—

(1) such entity was created in 1906 as a common law trust and is governed by the trust laws of the State of Minnesota,

(2) such entity is exclusively engaged in the leasing of mineral property and activities incidental thereto, and

(3) income interests in such entity are publicly traded as of October 22, 1986 on a national stock exchange.

(c) ELECTION.—

(1) IN GENERAL.—An election under this subsection to have the provisions of this section apply—

(A) shall be made by the board of trustees of the entity before January 1, 1991, and

(B) shall not be valid unless accompanied by an agreement described in paragraph (2).

(2) AGREEMENT.—

(A) IN GENERAL.—The agreement described in this paragraph is a written agreement signed by the board of trustees of the entity which provides that the entity will not acquire any additional property other than property described in subparagraph (B).

(B) PERMISSIBLE ACQUISITIONS.—Property is described in this paragraph if it is—

(i) surface rights to property the acquisition of which—

(I) is necessary to mine mineral rights held on October 22, 1986, and

(II) is required by a written binding agreement between the entity and an unrelated person entered into on or before October 22, 1986,

(ii) surface rights to property which are not described in clause (i) and which—

(I) are acquired in an exchange to which section 1031 applies, and

(II) are necessary to mine mineral rights held on October 22, 1986,

(iii) tangible personal property incidental to the leasing of mineral property and activities incidental thereto, or

(iv) part of any required reserves of the entity.

(3) BEGINNING OF PERIOD FOR WHICH ELECTION IS IN EFFECT.—The period during which an election is in effect under this subsection shall begin on the 1st day of the 1st taxable year beginning after the date of the enactment of this Act and following the taxable year in which the election is made.

(4) MANNER OF ELECTION.—Any election under this subsection shall be made in such manner as the Secretary of the Treasury or his delegate may prescribe.

(d) SPECIAL RULES FOR TAXATION OF TRUST.—

(1) ELECTION TREATED AS A LIQUIDATION.—If an election is made under subsection (c) with respect to any entity—

(A) such entity shall be treated as having been liquidated into a trust immediately before the period described in subsection (c)(3) in a liquidation to which section 333 of the Internal Revenue Code of 1954 (as in effect before the amendments made by this Act) applies, and

(B) for purposes of section 333 of such Code (as so in effect)—

(i) any person holding an income interest in such entity as of such time shall be treated as a qualified electing shareholder, and

(ii) the earnings and profits, and the value of money or stock or securities, of such entity shall be apportioned ratably among persons described in clause (i).

The amendments made by subtitle D of this title and section 1804 of this Act shall not apply to any liquidation under this paragraph.

(2) TERMINATION OF ELECTION.—If an entity ceases to be described in subsection (b) or violates any term of the agreement described in subsection (c)(2), the entity shall, for purposes of the Internal Revenue Code of 1986, be treated as a corporation for the taxable year in which such cessation or violation occurs and for all subsequent taxable years.

(3) TRUST CEASING TO EXIST.—Paragraph (2) shall not apply if the trust ceases to be described in subsection (b) or violates the agreement in subsection (c)(2) because the trust ceases to exist.

(e) SPECIAL RULE FOR PERSONS HOLDING INCOME INTERESTS.—In applying subpart E of part I of subchapter J of chapter 1 of the Internal Revenue Code of 1986 to any entity to which this section applies—

(1) a reversionary interest shall not be taken into account until it comes into possession, and

(2) all items of income, gain, loss, deduction, and credit shall be allocated to persons holding income interests for the period of the allocation.

• 1984, Deficit Reduction Act of 1984 (P.L. 98-369)

P.L. 98-369, §66(a):

Amended Code Sec. 11(b) by adding at the end thereof the flush sentence. **Effective** for tax years beginning after 12-31-83, except that such amendment shall not be treated as a change in a rate of tax for purposes of section 21 of the Internal Revenue Code of 1954.

• 1981, Economic Recovery Tax Act of 1981 (P.L. 97-34)

P.L. 97-34, §231(a):

Amended Code Sec. 11(b) by striking out "17 percent" in paragraph (1) and inserting in lieu thereof "15 percent (16 percent for taxable years beginning in 1982)"; and by striking out "20 percent" in paragraph (2) and inserting in lieu thereof "18 percent (19 percent for taxable years beginning in 1982)". **Effective** for tax years beginning after 12-31-81.

• 1978, Revenue Act of 1978 (P.L. 95-600)

P.L. 95-600, §301(a):

Amended Code Sec. 11(b). **Effective** for tax years beginning after 12-31-78. Prior to amendment, Code Sec. 11(b) read as follows:

(b) NORMAL TAX.—The normal tax is equal to—

(1) in the case of a taxable year ending after December 31, 1978, 22 percent of the taxable income, and

(2) in the case of a taxable year ending after December 31, 1974, and before January 1, 1979, the sum of—

(A) 20 percent of so much of the taxable income as does not exceed $25,000, plus

(B) 22 percent of so much of the taxable income as exceeds $25,000.

• 1977, Tax Reduction and Simplification Act of 1977 (P.L. 95-30)

P.L. 95-30, §201:

Amended subsection (b) by substituting "December 31, 1978" for "December 31, 1977" in paragraph (1) and by substituting "January 1, 1979" for "January 1, 1978" in paragraph (2).

• 1976, Tax Reform Act of 1976 (P.L. 94-455)

P.L. 94-455, §901(a):

Amended subsection (b). **Effective** 12-23-75. Prior to amendment, subsection (b) read as follows:

(b) NORMAL TAX.—

(1) GENERAL RULE.—The normal tax is equal to—

(A) in the case of a taxable year ending after December 31, 1976, 22 percent of the taxable income, and

(B) in the case of a taxable year ending after December 31, 1974, and before January 1, 1977, the sum of—

(i) 20 percent of so much of the taxable income as does not exceed $25,000, plus

(ii) 22 percent of so much of the taxable income as exceeds $25,000.

(2) SIX-MONTH APPLICATION OF GENERAL RULE.—

(A) CALENDAR YEAR TAXPAYERS.—Notwithstanding the provisions of paragraph (1), in the case of a taxpayer who has as his taxable year the calendar year 1976, the normal tax for such taxable year is equal to the sum of—

(i) 21 percent of so much of the taxable income as does not exceed $25,000, plus

(ii) 22 percent of so much of the taxable income as exceeds $25,000.

(B) FISCAL YEAR TAXPAYERS.—Notwithstanding the provisions of paragraph (1), in the case of a taxpayer whose taxable year is not the calendar year, effective on July 1, 1976 paragraph (1) shall cease to apply and the normal tax shall be 22 percent.

• 1975, Revenue Adjustment Act of 1975 (P.L. 94-164)

P.L. 94-164, §4(a):

Amended subsection (b). **Effective** for tax years ending after 12-31-74. Prior to amendment, subsection (b) read:

"(b) Normal Tax.—The normal tax is equal to—

"(1) in the case of a taxable year ending before January 1, 1975, or after December 31, 1975, 22 percent of the taxable income, and

"(2) in the case of a taxable year ending after December 31, 1974, and before January 1, 1976, the sum of—

"(A) 20 percent of so much of the taxable income as does not exceed $25,000, plus

"(B) 22 percent of so much of the taxable income as exceeds $25,000."

• 1975, Tax Reduction Act of 1975 (P.L.94-12)

P.L. 94-12, §303(a):

Amended subsection (b). **Effective** for tax years ending after 12-31-74. Prior to amendment, subsection (b) read:

"(b) Normal Tax.—The normal tax is equal to the following percentage of the taxable income:

"(1) 30 percent, in the case of a taxable year beginning before January 1, 1964, and

"(2) 22 percent, in the case of a taxable year beginning after December 31, 1963."

• 1964, Revenue Act of 1964 (P.L. 88-272)

P.L. 88-272, §121:

Amended subsection (b). **Effective** for tax years beginning after 12-31-63. Prior to amendment, subsection (b) read:

"(b) Normal Tax.—

"(1) Taxable years beginning before July 1, 1964.—In the case of a taxable year beginning before July 1, 1964, the normal tax is equal to 30 percent of the taxable income.

"(2) Taxable years beginning after June 30, 1964.—In the case of a taxable year beginning after June 30, 1964, the normal tax is equal to 25 percent of the taxable income."

• 1963, Tax Rate Extension Act of 1963 (P.L. 88-52)

P.L. 88-52, §2:

Substituted "1964" for "1963" wherever it appeared in Sec. 11(b)(1) and (2).

• 1962, Tax Rate Extension Act of 1962 (P.L. 87-508)

P.L. 87-508, §2:

Substituted "1963" for "1962" wherever it appeared in Sec. 11(b)(1) and (2).

• 1961, Tax Rate Extension Act of 1961 (P.L. 87-72)

P.L. 87-72, §2:

Substituted "1962" for "1961" wherever it appeared in Sec. 11(b)(1) and (2).

• 1960, Public Debt and Tax Rate Extension Act of 1960 (P.L. 86-564)

P.L. 86-564, §201:

Amended 1954 Code Sec. 11(b) by striking out "1960" wherever it appeared, and by substituting "1961".

• 1959, Tax Rate Extension Act of 1959 (P.L.86-75)

P.L. 86-75, §2:

Amended 1954 Code Sec. 11(b) by striking out "1959" wherever it appeared, and by substituting "1960".

• 1958, Tax Rate Extension Act of 1958 (P.L. 85-475)

P.L. 85-475, §2:

Substituted "July 1, 1959" for "July 1, 1958" in Sec. 11(b)(1), and substituted "June 30, 1959" for "June 30, 1958" in Sec. 11(b)(2).

• 1957, Tax Rate Extension Act of 1957 (P.L. 85-12)

P.L. 85-12, §2:

Substituted "July 1, 1958" for "April 1, 1957" in Sec. 11(b)(1), and substituted "June 30, 1958" for "March 31, 1957" in Sec. 11(b)(2).

• 1956, Tax Rate Extension Act of 1956 (P.L. 458, 84th Cong.)

P.L. 458, 84th Cong., 2d Sess., §2:

Substituted "1957" for "1956" wherever it appeared in Sec. 11(b)(1) and (2).

• 1955, Tax Rate Extension Act of 1955 (P.L. 18, 84th Cong.)

P.L. 18, 84th Cong., §2:

Substituted "1956" for "1955" wherever it appeared in Sec. 11(b)(1) and (2).

[Sec. 11(c)]

(c) EXCEPTIONS.—Subsection (a) shall not apply to a corporation subject to a tax imposed by—

(1) section 594 (relating to mutual savings banks conducting life insurance business),

(2) subchapter L (sec. 801 and following, relating to insurance companies), or

(3) subchapter M (sec. 851 and following, relating to regulated investment companies and real estate investment trusts).

Amendments

• 1978, Revenue Act of 1978 (P.L. 95-600)

P.L. 95-600, §301(a):

Amended Code Sec. 11(c). **Effective** for tax years beginning after 12-31-78. Prior to amendment, Code Sec. 11(c) read as follows:

(c) SURTAX.—The surtax is 26 percent of the amount by which the taxable income exceeds the surtax exemption for the taxable year.

• 1976, Tax Reform Act of 1976 (P.L. 94-455)

P.L. 94-455, §901(a):

Amended subsection (c). **Effective** 12-23-75. Prior to amendment, subsection (c) read as follows:

(c) SURTAX.—

(1) GENERAL RULE.—The surtax is 26 percent of the amount by which the taxable income exceeds the surtax exemption for the taxable year.

(2) SPECIAL RULE FOR 1976 FOR CALENDAR YEAR TAXPAYERS.—Notwithstanding the provisions of paragraph (1), in the case of a taxpayer who has as his taxable year the calendar year 1976, the surtax for such taxable year is—

(A) 13 percent of the amount by which the taxable income exceeds the $25,000 surtax exemption (as in effect under subsection (d)(2)) but does not exceed $50,000, plus

(B) 26 percent of the amount by which the taxable income exceeds $50,000.

• 1975, Revenue Adjustment Act of 1975 (P.L. 94-164)

P. L. 94-164, §4(b):

Amended subsection (c). **Effective** for tax years beginning after 12-31-75. Prior to amendment, subsection (c) read:

"(c) Surtax.—The surtax is equal to the following percentage of the amount by which the taxable income exceeds the surtax exemption for the taxable year:

"(1) 22 percent, in the case of a taxable year beginning before January 1, 1964,

"(2) 28 percent, in the case of a taxable year beginning after December 31, 1963, and before January 1, 1965, and

"(3) 26 percent, in the case of a taxable year beginning after December 31, 1964."

• 1964, Revenue Act of 1964 (P.L. 88-272)

P. L. 88-272, §121:

Amended subsection (c). **Effective** with respect to tax years beginning after 12-31-63. Prior to amendment, subsection (c) read:

"(c) Surtax.—The surtax is equal to 22 percent of the amount by which the taxable income (computed without regard to the deduction, if any, provided in section 242 for partially tax-exempt interest) exceeds $25,000."

[Sec. 11(d)]

(d) FOREIGN CORPORATIONS.—In the case of a foreign corporation, the taxes imposed by subsection (a) and section 55 shall apply only as provided by section 882.

Amendments

• 1988, Technical and Miscellaneous Revenue Act of 1988 (P.L. 100-647)

P.L. 100-647, §1007(g)(13)(B):

Amended Code Sec. 11(d) by striking out "the tax imposed by subsection (a)" and inserting in lieu thereof "the taxes imposed by subsection (a) and section 55". **Effective** as if included in the provision of P.L. 99-514 to which it relates.

• 1978, Revenue Act of 1978 (P.L. 95-600)

P.L. 95-600, §301(a):

Amended Code Sec. 11(d). **Effective** for tax years beginning after 12-31-78. Prior to amendment, Code Sec. 11(d)-(f) read as follows:

(d) SURTAX EXEMPTION.—For purposes of this subtitle, the surtax exemption for any taxable year is—

(1) $25,000 in the case of a taxable year ending after December 31, 1978, or

(2) $50,000 in the case of a taxable year ending after December 31, 1974, and before January 1, 1979,

except that, with respect to a corporation to which section 1561 (relating to certain multiple tax benefits in the case of certain controlled corporations) applies for the taxable year, the surtax exemption for the taxable year is the amount determined under such section.

(e) EXCEPTIONS.—Subsection(a) shall not apply to a corporation subject to a tax imposed by—

(1) section 594 (relating to mutual savings banks conducting life insurance business),

(2) subchapter L (sec. 801 and following, relating to insurance companies), or

(3) subchapter M (sec. 851 and following, relating to regulated investment companies and real estate investment trusts).

(f) FOREIGN CORPORATIONS.—In the case of a foreign corporation, the tax imposed by subsection (a) shall apply only as provided by section 882.

• 1977, Tax Reduction and Simplification Act of 1975 (P.L. 95-30)

P.L. 95-30, §201:

Amended subsection (d) by substituting "December 31, 1978" for "December 31, 1977" in paragraph (1) and by substituting "January 1, 1979" for "January 1, 1978" in paragraph (2).

• 1976, Tax Reform Act of 1976 (P.L. 94-455)

P.L. 94-455, §901(a):

Amended subsection (d). **Effective** 12-23-75. Prior to amendment, subsection (d) read as follows:

(d) SURTAX EXEMPTION.—

(1) GENERAL RULE.—For purposes of this subtitle, the surtax exemption for any taxable year is $50,000, except that, with respect to a corporation to which section 1561 or 1564 (relating to surtax exemptions in case of certain controlled corporations) applies for the taxable year, the surtax exemption for the taxable year is the amount determined under such section.

(2) SIX-MONTH APPLICATION OF GENERAL RULE.—Notwithstanding the provisions of paragraph (1)—

(A) CALENDAR YEAR TAXPAYERS.—In the case of a taxpayer who has as his taxable year the calendar year 1976, the provisions of paragraph (1) shall be applied for such taxable year by substituting the amount "$25,000" for the amount "$50,000" appearing therein.

(B) FISCAL YEAR TAXPAYERS.—In the case of a taxpayer whose taxable year is not the calendar year, effective on July 1, 1976, paragraph (1) shall be applied by substituting the amount "$25,000" for the amount "$50,000" appearing therein, and such substitution shall be treated, for purposes of section 21, as a change in a rate of tax.

• 1975, Revenue Adjustment Act of 1975 (P.L. 94-164)

P.L. 94-164, §4(c):

Amended subsection (d). **Effective** for tax years beginning after 12-31-75 and ceasing to apply for tax years beginning after 12-31-76. Prior to amendment, subsection (d) read as follows:

(d) SURTAX EXEMPTION.—For purposes of this subtitle, the surtax exemption for any taxable year is $50,000, except that, with respect to a corporation to which section 1561 or 1564 (relating to surtax exemptions in case of certain controlled corporations) applies for the taxable year, the surtax exemption for the taxable year is the amount determined under such section.

• 1975, Tax Reduction Act of 1975 (P.L. 94-12)

P.L. 94-12, §303(b):

Amended subsection (d). **Effective** only for tax years ending in 1975. Prior to amendment, subsection (d) read as follows:

(d) SURTAX EXEMPTION.—For purposes of this subtitle, the surtax exemption for any taxable year is $25,000, except that, with respect to a corporation to which section 1561 or 1564 (relating to surtax exemptions in case of certain controlled corporations) applies for the taxable year, the surtax exemption for the taxable year is the amount determined under such section.

• 1969, Tax Reform Act of 1969 (P.L. 91-172)

P. L. 91-172, §401(b)(2)(B):

Amended subsection (d) by inserting "or 1564". **Effective** for tax years beginning after 12-31-69.

• 1966, Foreign Investors Tax Act of 1966 (P.L. 89-809)

P. L. 89-809, §104(b)(2)(A), (B):

Amended Code Sec. 11(e) by inserting "or" at the end of paragraph (2), by deleting ", or" at the end of paragraph (3) and inserting a period in place thereof, and by deleting paragraph (4); and added subsection (f). **Effective** 1-1-67.

• 1964, Revenue Act of 1964 (P.L. 88-272)

P. L. 88-272, §121:

Added subsection (d) and amended subsection (e) by changing its designation from subsection (d). **Effective** 1-1-64.

• 1960 (P.L. 86-779)

P. L. 86-779, §10(d):

Amended Code Sec. 11(d)(3) by inserting "and real estate investment trusts" following "regulated investment companies". **Effective** 1-1-61.

[Sec. 12]

SEC. 12. CROSS REFERENCES RELATING TO TAX ON CORPORATIONS.

(1) For tax on the unrelated business income of certain charitable and other corporations exempt from tax under this chapter, see section 511.

(2) For accumulated earnings tax and personal holding company tax, see parts I and II of subchapter G (sec. 531 and following).

(3) For doubling of tax on corporations of certain foreign countries, see section 891.

(4) For alternative tax in case of capital gains, see section 1201(a).

(5) For rate of withholding in case of foreign corporations, see section 1442.

(6) For limitation on benefits of graduated rate schedule provided in section 11(b), see section 1551.

(7) For alternative minimum tax, see section 55.

Amendments

• 1986, Tax Reform Act of 1986 (P.L. 99-514)

P.L. 99-514, §701(e)(4)(B):

Amended Code Sec. 12(7). **Effective** for tax years beginning after 12-31-86. Prior to amendment, Code Sec. 12(7) read as follows:

(7) For minimum tax for tax preferences, see section 56.

• 1984, Deficit Reduction Act of 1984 (P.L. 98-369)

P.L. 98-369, §474(r)(29)(E):

Amended Code Sec. 12 by striking out paragraph (6) and by redesignating paragraphs (7) and (8) as paragraphs (6) and (7), respectively. **Effective** for tax years beginning after 12-31-83, and to carrybacks from such years except that they do not apply with respect to obligations issued before 1-1-84. Prior to amendment, paragraph (6) read as follows:

(6) For withholding of tax on tax-free covenant bonds, see section 1451.

• 1978, Revenue Act of 1978 (P.L. 95-600)

P.L. 95-600, §301(b)(1):

Amended Code Sec. 12(7). **Effective** tax years beginning after 12-31-78. Prior to amendment, paragraph (7) read as follows:

"(7) For limitation on the $50,000 exemption from surtax provided in section 11(c), see section 1551."

• 1975, Tax Reduction Act of 1975 (P.L. 94-12)

P.L. 94-12, §303(c):

Amended Sec. 12 by substituting "$50,000" for $25,000". **Effective** for tax years beginning after 12-31-74.

• 1969, Tax Reform Act of 1969 (P.L. 91-172)

P.L. 91-172, §301(b)(3):

Added new paragraph (8). **Effective** 1-1-70.

• 1964, Revenue Act of 1964 (P.L. 88-272)

P.L. 88-272, §234(b)(4):

Repealed Code Sec. 12(8). **Effective** for tax years beginning after 12-31-63. Prior to repeal, paragraph (8) read as follows:

"(8) For additional tax for corporations filing consolidated returns, see section 1503."

PART III—CHANGES IN RATES DURING A TAXABLE YEAR

[Sec. 15]

SEC. 15. EFFECT OF CHANGES.

[Sec. 15(a)]

(a) GENERAL RULE.—If any rate of tax imposed by this chapter changes, and if the taxable year includes the effective date of the change (unless that date is the first day of the taxable year), then—

(1) tentative taxes shall be computed by applying the rate for the period before the effective date of the change, and the rate for the period on and after such date, to the taxable income for the entire taxable year; and

(2) the tax for such taxable year shall be the sum of that proportion of each tentative tax which the number of days in each period bears to the number of days in the entire taxable year.

[Sec. 15(b)]

(b) REPEAL OF TAX.—For purposes of subsection (a)—

(1) if a tax is repealed, the repeal shall be considered a change of rate; and

(2) the rate for the period after the repeal shall be zero.

[Sec. 15(c)]

(c) EFFECTIVE DATE OF CHANGE.—For purposes of subsections (a) and (b)—

(1) if the rate changes for taxable years "beginning after" or "ending after" a certain date, the following day shall be considered the effective date of the change; and

(2) if a rate changes for taxable years "beginning on or after" a certain date, that date shall be considered the effective date of the change.

[Sec. 15(d)]

(d) SECTION NOT TO APPLY TO INFLATION ADJUSTMENTS.—This section shall not apply to any change in rates under subsection (f) of section 1 (relating to adjustments in tax tables so that inflation will not result in tax increases.)

Amendments

• 1986, Tax Reform Act of 1986 (P.L. 99-514)

P.L. 99-514, §101(b):

Amended Code Sec. 15(d). **Effective** for tax years beginning after 12-31-86. Prior to amendment, Code Sec. 15(d) read as follows:

(d) SECTION NOT TO APPLY TO SECTION 1 RATE CHANGES MADE BY ECONOMIC RECOVERY TAX ACT OF 1981.—This section shall not apply to any change in rates under section 1 attributable to the amendments made by section 101 of the Economic Recovery Tax Act of 1981 or subsection (f) of section 1 (relating to adjustments in tax tables so that inflation will not result in tax increases).

P.L. 99-514, §3(b), provides:

(b) COORDINATION WITH SECTION 15.—

(1) IN GENERAL.—Except as provided in paragraph (2), for purposes of section 15 of the Internal Revenue Code of 1986, no amendment or repeal made by this Act shall be treated as a change in the rate of a tax imposed by chapter 1 of such Code.

(2) EXCEPTION.—Paragraph (1) shall not apply to the amendment made by section 601 (relating to corporate rate reductions).

• 1984, Deficit Reduction Act of 1984 (P.L. 98-369)

P.L. 98-369, §474(b)(1):

Redesignated former Code Sec. 21 as Code Sec. 15. **Effective** for tax years beginning after 12-31-83, and to carrybacks from such years.

• 1981, Economic Recovery Tax Act of 1981 (P.L. 97-34)

P.L. 97-34, §101(d)(3), as amended by P.L. 97-448, §101(a)(1):

Amended Code Sec. 21 by striking out subsections (d), (e), and (f) and inserting in lieu thereof subsection (d). **Effective** for tax years ending after 12-31-81. Prior to amendment, Code Sec. 21(d)-(f) read as follows:

"(d) CHANGE IN SURTAX EXEMPTION.—In applying subsection (a) to a taxable year of a taxpayer which is not a calendar year, the change made by section 303(b) of the Tax Reduction Act of 1975 in the surtax exemption and any change under section 11(d) in the surtax exemption shall be treated as a change in a rate of tax."

"(e) CHANGES MADE BY TAX REDUCTION AND SIMPLIFICATION ACT OF 1977.—In applying subsection (a) to a taxable year of an individual which is not a calendar year, the amendments made by sections 101 and 102 of the Tax Reduction and Simplification Act of 1977 shall not be treated as changes in rate of tax."

"(f) CHANGES MADE BY REVENUE ACT OF 1978.—In applying subsection (a) to a taxable year which is not a calendar year—

"(1) the amendments made by sections 101, 102, and 301 of the Revenue Act of 1978 (and no other amendments made by such Act), and

"(2) the expiration of section 42 (relating to general tax credit), shall be treated as a change in a rate of tax."

• 1978, Revenue Act of 1978 (P.L. 95-600)

P.L. 95-600, §106:

Added Code Sec. 21(f).

• 1977, Tax Reduction and Simplification Act of 1977 (P.L. 95-30)

P.L. 95-30, §101(d)(2)(A):

Repealed Sec. 21(d). **Effective** for tax years beginning after 12-31-76. Former Sec. 21(f) was redesignated as Sec. 21(d). Prior to repeal, Sec. 21(d) read as follows:

"(d) CHANGES MADE BY TAX REFORM ACT OF 1969 IN CASE OF INDIVIDUALS.—In applying subsection (a) to a taxable year of an individuual which is not a calendar year, each change made by the Tax Reform Act of 1969 in part I or in the application of part IV or V of subchapter B for purposes of the determination of taxable income shall be treated as a change in a rate of tax."

P.L. 95-30, §101(d)(2)(A):

Repealed Sec. 21(e). **Effective** for tax years beginning after 12-31-76. Added a new Sec. 21(e). Prior to repeal, Sec. 21(e) read as follows:

"(e) CHANGES MADE BY REVENUE ACT OF 1971.—In applying subsection (a) to a taxable year of an individual which is not a calendar year, each change made by the Revenue Act of 1971 in section 141 (relating to the standard deduction) and section 151 (relating to personal exemptions) shall be treated as a change in a rate of tax."

P.L. 95-30, §101(d)(2)(B):

Redesignated Code Sec. 21(f) as 21(d). **Effective** for tax years beginning after 12-31-76.

P.L. 95-30, §101(d)(2)(C):

Added Code Sec. 21(c). **Effective** for tax years beginning after 12-31-76.

• 1976, Tax Reform Act of 1976 (P.L. 94-455)

P.L. 94-455, §901(c):

Substituted the words that appear after "1975" in subsection (f) above for the words "and the change made by section 3(c) of the Revenue Adjustment Act of 1975 in section 11(d) (relating to corporate surtax exemption) shall be treated as a change in a rate of tax." **Effective** for tax years ending after 12-31-75.

• 1975, Revenue Adjustment Act of 1975 (P.L. 94-164)

P.L. 94-164, §4(d):

Amended subsection (f). **Effective** for tax years beginning after 12-31-75. Prior to amendment, subsection (f) read as follows:

"(f) Increase in Surtax Exemption.—In applying subsection (a) to a taxable year of a taxpayer which is not a calendar year, the change made by section 303(b) of the Tax Reduction Act of 1975 in section 11(d) (relating to corporate surtax exemption) shall be treated as a change in a rate of tax."

• 1975, Tax Reduction Act of 1975 (P.L. 94-12)

P.L. 94-12, §305(b)(2):

Added Code Sec. 21(f). **Effective** 3-29-75.

• 1971, Revenue Act of 1971 (P.L. 92-178)

P.L. 92-178, §205:

Added Code Sec. 21(e).

• 1969, Tax Reform Act of 1969 (P.L. 91-172)

P.L. 91-172, §803(e):

Amended Code Sec. 21(d). Prior to amendment, Code Sec. 21(d) read as follows:

(d) Changes Made by Revenue Act of 1964.—

(1) Individuals.—In applying subsection (a) to the taxable year of an individual beginning in 1963 and ending in 1964—

(A) the rate of tax for the period on and after January 1, 1964, shall be applied to the taxable income determined as if part IV of subchapter B (relating to standard deduction for individuals), as amended by the Revenue Act of 1964, applied to taxable years ending after December 31, 1963, and

(B) section 4 (relating to rules for optional tax), as amended by such Act, shall be applied to taxable years ending after December 31, 1963.

In applying subsection (a) to a taxable year of an individual beginning in 1963 and ending in 1964, or beginning in 1964 and ending in 1965, the change in the tax imposed under section 3 shall be treated as a change in a rate of tax.

(2) Corporations.—In applying subsection (a) to a taxable year of a corporation beginning in 1963 and ending in 1964, if—

(A) the surtax exemption of such corporation for such taxable year is less than $25,000 by reason of the application of section 1561 (relating to surtax exemptions in case of certain controlled corporations), or

(B) an additional tax is imposed on the taxable income of such corporation for such taxable year by section 1562(b) (relating to additional tax in case of component members of controlled groups which elect multiple surtax exemptions),

the change in the surtax exemption, or the imposition of such additional tax, shall be treated as a change in a rate of tax taking effect on January 1, 1964.

• 1964, Revenue Act of 1964 (P.L. 88-272)

P.L. 88-272, §132:

Amended subsection (d). **Effective** with respect to tax years ending after 12-31-63. Prior to amendment, subsection (d) read as follows:

"(d) Taxable Years Beginning Before January 1, 1954, and Ending After December 31, 1953.—In the case of a taxable year beginning before January 1, 1954, and ending after December 31, 1953—

"(1) subsection (a) of this section does not apply; and

"(2) in the application of subsection (j) of section 108 of the Internal Revenue Code of 1939, the provisions of such code referred to in such subsection shall be considered as continuing in effect as if this subtitle had not been enacted."

[Sec. 15(e)]

(e) REFERENCES TO HIGHEST RATE.—If the change referred to in subsection (a) involves a change in the highest rate of tax imposed by section 1 or 11(b), any reference in this chapter to such highest rate (other than in a provision imposing a tax by reference to such rate) shall be treated as a reference to the weighted average of the highest rates before and after the change determined on the basis of the respective portions of the taxable year before the date of the change and on or after the date of the change.

Amendments

• 1988, Technical and Miscellaneous Revenue Act of 1988 (P.L. 100-647)

P.L. 100-647, §1006(a):

Amended Code Sec. 15 by adding at the end thereof new subsection (e). **Effective** as if included in the provision of P.L. 99-514 to which it relates.

»→ Caution: Code Sec. 15(f), below, is subject to the sunset provision of the Economic Growth and Tax Relief Reconciliation Act of 2001 (P.L. 107-16), §901. Absent Congressional action, the changes made to this provision by P.L. 107-16, or that take effect as if included in P.L. 107-16, do not apply after December 31, 2010. For more information about the sunset provision, see page XXI of the Preface to this publication and P.L. 107-16, §901, in the amendment notes. See the amendments notes for a history of amendments to this section and the effective date of each change.

[Sec. 15(f)]

(f) RATE REDUCTIONS ENACTED BY ECONOMIC GROWTH AND TAX RELIEF RECONCILIATION ACT OF 2001.—This section shall not apply to any change in rates under subsection (i) of section 1 (relating to rate reductions after 2000).

Amendments

• 2001, Economic Growth and Tax Relief Reconciliation Act of 2001 (P.L. 107-16)

P.L. 107-16, §101(c)(3):

Amended Code Sec. 15 by adding at the end a new subsection (f). **Effective** for tax years beginning after 12-31-2000.

P.L. 107-16, §901(a)-(b), provides:

SEC. 901. SUNSET OF PROVISIONS OF ACT.

(a) IN GENERAL.—All provisions of, and amendments made by, this Act shall not apply—

(1) to taxable, plan, or limitation years beginning after December 31, 2010, or

(2) in the case of title V, to estates of decedents dying, gifts made, or generation skipping transfers, after December 31, 2010.

(b) APPLICATION OF CERTAIN LAWS.—The Internal Revenue Code of 1986 and the Employee Retirement Income Security Act of 1974 shall be applied and administered to years, estates, gifts, and transfers described in subsection (a) as if the provisions and amendments described in subsection (a) had never been enacted.

PART IV—CREDITS AGAINST TAX

Subpart A—Nonrefundable Personal Credits

[Sec. 21]

SEC. 21. EXPENSES FOR HOUSEHOLD AND DEPENDENT CARE SERVICES NECESSARY FOR GAINFUL EMPLOYMENT.

[Sec. 21(a)]

(a) ALLOWANCE OF CREDIT.—

(1) IN GENERAL.—In the case of an individual for which there are 1 or more qualifying individuals (as defined in subsection (b)(1)) with respect to such individual, there shall be allowed as a credit against the tax imposed by this chapter for the taxable year an amount equal to the applicable percentage of the employment-related expenses (as defined in subsection (b)(2)) paid by such individual during the taxable year.

Caution: Code Sec. 21(a)(2), below, is subject to the sunset provision of the Economic Growth and Tax Relief Reconciliation Act of 2001 (P.L. 107-16), §901. Absent Congressional action, the changes made to this provision by P.L. 107-16, or that take effect as if included in P.L. 107-16, do not apply after December 31, 2010. For more information about the sunset provision, see page XXI of the Preface to this publication and P.L. 107-16, §901, in the amendment notes. See the amendments notes for a history of amendments to this section and the effective date of each change.

(2) APPLICABLE PERCENTAGE DEFINED.—For purposes of paragraph (1), the term "applicable percentage" means 35 percent reduced (but not below 20 percent) by 1 percentage point for each $2,000 (or fraction thereof) by which the taxpayer's adjusted gross income for the taxable year exceeds $15,000.

Amendments

• 2004, Working Families Tax Relief Act of 2004 (P.L. 108-311)

P.L. 108-311, §203(a):

Amended Code Sec. 21(a)(1) by striking "In the case of an individual who maintains a household which includes as a member one or more qualifying individuals (as defined in subsection (b)(1))" and inserting "In the case of an individual for which there are 1 or more qualifying individuals (as defined in subsection (b)(1)) with respect to such individual". **Effective** for tax years beginning after 12-31-2004.

• 2001, Economic Growth and Tax Relief Reconciliation Act of 2001 (P.L. 107-16)

P.L. 107-16, §204(b)(1)-(2):

Amended Code Sec. 21(a)(2) by striking "30 percent" and inserting "35 percent", and by striking "$10,000" and inserting "$15,000". **Effective** for tax years beginning after 12-31-2002.

P.L. 107-16, §901(a)-(b), provides:

SEC. 901. SUNSET OF PROVISIONS OF ACT.

(a) IN GENERAL.—All provisions of, and amendments made by, this Act shall not apply—

(1) to taxable, plan, or limitation years beginning after December 31, 2010, or

(2) in the case of title V, to estates of decedents dying, gifts made, or generation skipping transfers, after December 31, 2010.

(b) APPLICATION OF CERTAIN LAWS.—The Internal Revenue Code of 1986 and the Employee Retirement Income Security Act of 1974 shall be applied and administered to years, estates, gifts, and transfers described in subsection (a) as if the provisions and amendments described in subsection (a) had never been enacted.

[Sec. 21(b)]

(b) DEFINITIONS OF QUALIFYING INDIVIDUAL AND EMPLOYMENT-RELATED EXPENSES.—For purposes of this section—

(1) QUALIFYING INDIVIDUAL.—The term "qualifying individual" means—

(A) a dependent of the taxpayer (as defined in section 152(a)(1)) who has not attained age 13,

(B) a dependent of the taxpayer (as defined in section 152, determined without regard to subsections (b)(1), (b)(2), and (d)(1)(B)) who is physically or mentally incapable of caring for himself or herself and who has the same principal place of abode as the taxpayer for more than one-half of such taxable year, or

(C) the spouse of the taxpayer, if the spouse is physically or mentally incapable of caring for himself or herself and who has the same principal place of abode as the taxpayer for more than one-half of such taxable year.

(2) EMPLOYMENT-RELATED EXPENSES.—

(A) IN GENERAL.—The term "employment-related expenses" means amounts paid for the following expenses, but only if such expenses are incurred to enable the taxpayer to be gainfully employed for any period for which there are 1 or more qualifying individuals with respect to the taxpayer:

(i) expenses for household services, and

(ii) expenses for the care of a qualifying individual.

Such term shall not include any amount paid for services outside the taxpayer's household at a camp where the qualifying individual stays overnight.

(B) EXCEPTION.—Employment-related expenses described in subparagraph (A) which are incurred for services outside the taxpayer's household shall be taken into account only if incurred for the care of—

(i) a qualifying individual described in paragraph (1)(A), or

(ii) a qualifying individual (not described in paragraph (1)(A)) who regularly spends at least 8 hours each day in the taxpayer's household.

(C) DEPENDENT CARE CENTERS.—Employment-related expenses described in subparagraph (A) which are incurred for services provided outside the taxpayer's household by a dependent care center (as defined in subparagraph (D)) shall be taken into account only if—

(i) such center complies with all applicable laws and regulations of a State or unit of local government, and

(ii) the requirements of subparagraph (B) are met.

(D) DEPENDENT CARE CENTER DEFINED.—For purposes of this paragraph, the term "dependent care center" means any facility which—

(i) provides care for more than six individuals (other than individuals who reside at the facility), and

(ii) receives a fee, payment, or grant for providing services for any of the individuals (regardless of whether such facility is operated for profit).

Amendments

• 2005, Gulf Opportunity Zone Act of 2005 (P.L. 109-135)

P.L. 109-135, §404(b):

Amended Code Sec. 21(b)(1)(B) by inserting "(as defined in section 152, determined without regard to subsections (b)(1), (b)(2), and (d)(1)(B))" after "dependent of the taxpayer". **Effective** as if included in the provision of the Working Families Tax Relief Act of 2004 (P.L. 108-311) to which it relates [**effective** for tax years beginning after 12-31-2004.—CCH].

• 2004, Working Families Tax Relief Act of 2004 (P.L. 108-311)

P.L. 108-311, §203(b):

Amended Code Sec. 21(b)(1). **Effective** for tax years beginning after 12-31-2004. Prior to amendment, Code Sec. 21(b)(1) read as follows:

(1) QUALIFYING INDIVIDUAL.—The term "qualifying individual" means—

(A) a dependent of the taxpayer who is under the age of 13 and with respect to whom the taxpayer is entitled to a deduction under section 151(c),

(B) a dependent of the taxpayer who is physically or mentally incapable of caring for himself, or

(C) the spouse of the taxpayer, if he is physically or mentally incapable of caring for himself.

• 1988, Family Support Act of 1988 (P.L. 100-485)

P.L. 100-485, §703(a):

Amended Code Sec. 21(b)(1)(A) by striking "age of 15" and inserting "age of 13". **Effective** for tax years beginning after 12-31-88.

• 1987, Revenue Act of 1987 (P.L. 100-203)

P.L. 100-203, §10101(a):

Amended Code Sec. 21(b)(2)(A) by adding at the end thereof a new sentence. For the **effective** date, see Act Sec. 10101(b), below.

P.L. 100-203, §10101(b), provides:

(b) EFFECTIVE DATE.—

(1) IN GENERAL.—The amendment made by subsection (a) shall apply to expenses paid in taxable years beginning after December 31, 1987.

(2) SPECIAL RULE FOR CAFETERIA PLANS.—For purposes of section 125 of the Internal Revenue Code of 1986, a plan shall not be treated as failing to be a cafeteria plan solely because under the plan a participant elected before January 1, 1988, to receive reimbursement under the plan for dependent care assistance for periods after December 31, 1987, and such assistance included reimbursement for expenses at a camp where the dependent stays overnight [**effective** date changed by P.L. 100-647, §2004(a)].

→ Caution: Code Sec. 21(c)(1)-(2), below, is subject to the sunset provision of the Economic Growth and Tax Relief Reconciliation Act of 2001 (P.L. 107-16), §901. Absent Congressional action, the changes made to this provision by P.L. 107-16, or that take effect as if included in P.L. 107-16, do not apply after December 31, 2010. For more information about the sunset provision, see page XXI of the Preface to this publication and P.L. 107-16, §901, in the amendment notes. See the amendments notes for a history of amendments to this section and the effective date of each change.

[Sec. 21(c)]

(c) DOLLAR LIMIT ON AMOUNT CREDITABLE.—The amount of the employment-related expenses incurred during any taxable year which may be taken into account under subsection (a) shall not exceed—

(1) $3,000 if there is 1 qualifying individual with respect to the taxpayer for such taxable year, or

(2) $6,000 if there are 2 or more qualifying individuals with respect to the taxpayer for such taxable year.

The amount determined under paragraph (1) or (2) (whichever is applicable) shall be reduced by the aggregate amount excludable from gross income under section 129 for the taxable year.

Amendments

• 2001, Economic Growth and Tax Relief Reconciliation Act of 2001 (P.L. 107-16)

P.L. 107-16, §204(a)(1)-(2):

Amended Code Sec. 21(c) by striking "$2,400" in paragraph (1) and inserting "$3,000", and by striking "$4,800" in paragraph (2) and inserting "$6,000". **Effective** for tax years beginning after 12-31-2002.

P.L. 107-16, §901(a)-(b), provides:

SEC. 901. SUNSET OF PROVISIONS OF ACT.

(a) IN GENERAL.—All provisions of, and amendments made by, this Act shall not apply—

(1) to taxable, plan, or limitation years beginning after December 31, 2010, or

(2) in the case of title V, to estates of decedents dying, gifts made, or generation skipping transfers, after December 31, 2010.

(b) APPLICATION OF CERTAIN LAWS.—The Internal Revenue Code of 1986 and the Employee Retirement Income Security Act of 1974 shall be applied and administered to years, estates, gifts, and transfers described in subsection (a) as if the provisions and amendments described in subsection (a) had never been enacted.

• 1988, Family Support Act of 1988 (P.L. 100-485)

P.L. 100-485, §703(b):

Amended Code Sec. 21(c) by adding at the end thereof a new sentence. **Effective** for tax years beginning after 12-31-88.

[Sec. 21(d)]

(d) EARNED INCOME LIMITATION.—

(1) IN GENERAL.—Except as otherwise provided in this subsection, the amount of the employment-related expenses incurred during any taxable year which may be taken into account under subsection (a) shall not exceed—

(A) in the case of an individual who is not married at the close of such year, such individual's earned income for such year, or

(B) in the case of an individual who is married at the close of such year, the lesser of such individual's earned income or the earned income of his spouse for such year.

→ Caution: Code Sec. 21(d)(2), below, is subject to the sunset provision of the Economic Growth and Tax Relief Reconciliation Act of 2001 (P.L. 107-16), §901. Absent Congressional action, the changes made to this provision by P.L. 107-16, or that take effect as if included in P.L. 107-16, do not apply after December 31, 2010. For more information about the sunset provision, see page XXI of the Preface to this publication and P.L. 107-16, §901, in the amendment notes. See the amendments notes for a history of amendments to this section and the effective date of each change.

(2) SPECIAL RULE FOR SPOUSE WHO IS A STUDENT OR INCAPABLE OF CARING FOR HIMSELF.—In the case of a spouse who is a student or a qualified individual described in subsection (b)(1)(C), for purposes of paragraph (1), such spouse shall be deemed for each month during which such spouse is a full-time student at an educational institution, or is such a qualifying individual, to be gainfully employed and to have earned income of not less than—

(A) $250 if subsection (c)(1) applies for the taxable year, or

(B) $500 if subsection (c)(2) applies for the taxable year.

In the case of any husband and wife, this paragraph shall apply with respect to only one spouse for any one month.

Amendments

• 2002, Job Creation and Worker Assistance Act of 2002 (P.L. 107-147)

P.L. 107-147, §418(b)(1)-(2):

Amended Code Sec. 21(d)(2) by striking "$200" and inserting "$250" in subparagraph (A), and by striking "$400" and inserting "$500" in subparagraph (B). **Effective** as if included in the provision of P.L. 107-16 to which it relates [**effective** for tax years beginning after 12-31-2002.—CCH].

• 2001, Economic Growth and Tax Relief Reconciliation Act of 2001 (P.L. 107-16)

P.L. 107-16, §901(a)-(b), provides:

SEC. 901. SUNSET OF PROVISIONS OF ACT.

(a) IN GENERAL.—All provisions of, and amendments made by, this Act shall not apply—

(1) to taxable, plan, or limitation years beginning after December 31, 2010, or

(2) in the case of title V, to estates of decedents dying, gifts made, or generation skipping transfers, after December 31, 2010.

(b) APPLICATION OF CERTAIN LAWS.—The Internal Revenue Code of 1986 and the Employee Retirement Income Security Act of 1974 shall be applied and administered to years, estates, gifts, and transfers described in subsection (a) as if the provisions and amendments described in subsection (a) had never been enacted.

[Sec. 21(e)]

(e) SPECIAL RULES.—For purposes of this section—

(1) PLACE OF ABODE.—An individual shall not be treated as having the same principal place of abode of the taxpayer if at any time during the taxable year of the taxpayer the relationship between the individual and the taxpayer is in violation of local law.

(2) MARRIED COUPLES MUST FILE JOINT RETURN.—If the taxpayer is married at the close of the taxable year, the credit shall be allowed under subsection (a) only if the taxpayer and his spouse file a joint return for the taxable year.

(3) MARITAL STATUS.—An individual legally separated from his spouse under a decree of divorce or of separate maintenance shall not be considered as married.

(4) CERTAIN MARRIED INDIVIDUALS LIVING APART.—If—

(A) an individual who is married and who files a separate return—

(i) maintains as his home a household which constitutes for more than one-half of the taxable year the principal place of abode of a qualifying individual, and

(ii) furnishes over half of the cost of maintaining such household during the taxable year, and

(B) during the last 6 months of such taxable year such individual's spouse is not a member of such household,

such individual shall not be considered as married.

(5) SPECIAL DEPENDENCY TEST IN CASE OF DIVORCED PARENTS, ETC.—If—

(A) section 152(e) applies to any child with respect to any calendar year, and

(B) such child is under the age of 13 or is physically or mentally incapable of caring for himself,

in the case of any taxable year beginning in such calendar year, such child shall be treated as a qualifying individual described in subparagraph (A) or (B) of subsection (b)(1) (whichever is appropriate) with respect to the custodial parent (as defined in section 152(e)(4)(A)), and shall not be treated as a qualifying individual with respect to the noncustodial parent.

(6) PAYMENTS TO RELATED INDIVIDUALS.—No credit shall be allowed under subsection (a) for any amount paid by the taxpayer to an individual—

(A) with respect to whom, for the taxable year, a deduction under section 151(c) (relating to deduction for personal exemptions for dependents) is allowable either to the taxpayer or his spouse, or

(B) who is a child of the taxpayer (within the meaning of section 152(f)(1)) who has not attained the age of 19 at the close of the taxable year.

For purposes of this paragraph, the term "taxable year" means the taxable year of the taxpayer in which the service is performed.

(7) STUDENT.—The term "student" means an individual who during each of 5 calendar months during the taxable year is a full-time student at an educational organization.

(8) EDUCATIONAL ORGANIZATION.—The term "educational organization" means an educational organization described in section 170(b)(1)(A)(ii).

(9) IDENTIFYING INFORMATION REQUIRED WITH RESPECT TO SERVICE PROVIDER.—No credit shall be allowed under subsection (a) for any amount paid to any person unless—

(A) the name, address, and taxpayer identification number of such person are included on the return claiming the credit, or

(B) if such person is an organization described in section 501(c)(3) and exempt from tax under section 501(a), the name and address of such person are included on the return claiming the credit.

In the case of a failure to provide the information required under the preceding sentence, the preceding sentence shall not apply if it is shown that the taxpayer exercised due diligence in attempting to provide the information so required.

(10) IDENTIFYING INFORMATION REQUIRED WITH RESPECT TO QUALIFYING INDIVIDUALS.—No credit shall be allowed under this section with respect to any qualifying individual unless the TIN of such individual is included on the return claiming the credit.

Amendments

• 2007, Tax Technical Corrections Act of 2007 (P.L. 110-172)

P.L. 110-172, §11(a)(1):

Amended Code Sec. 21(e)(5) by striking "section 152(e)(3)(A)" in the flush material after subparagraph (B) and inserting "section 152(e)(4)(A)". **Effective** 12-29-2007.

• 2004, Working Families Tax Relief Act of 2004 (P.L. 108-311)

P.L. 108-311, §203(c):

Amended Code Sec. 21(e)(1). **Effective** for tax years beginning after 12-31-2004. Prior to amendment, Code Sec. 21(e)(1) read as follows:

(1) MAINTAINING HOUSEHOLD.—An individual shall be treated as maintaining a household for any period only if over half the cost of maintaining the household for such period is furnished by such individual (or, if such individual is married during such period, is furnished by such individual and his spouse).

P.L. 108-311, §207(2)(A)-(B):

Amended Code Sec. 21(e)(5) by striking "paragraph (2) or (4) of" immediately preceding "section 152(e)" in subparagraph (A), and by striking "within the meaning of section 152(e)(1)" and inserting "as defined in section 152(e)(3)(A)". **Effective** for tax years beginning after 12-31-2004.

P.L. 108-311, §207(3):

Amended Code Sec. 21(e)(6)(B) by striking "section 151(c)(3)" and inserting "section 152(f)(1)". **Effective** for tax years beginning after 12-31-2004.

• 1996, Small Business Job Protection Act of 1996 (P.L. 104-188)

P.L. 104-188, §1615(b):

Amended Code Sec. 21(e) by adding at the end a new paragraph (10). **Effective**, generally, for returns the due date for which (without regard to extensions) is on or after the 30th day after 8-20-96. For a special rule, see Act Sec. 1615(d)(2), below.

P.L. 104-188, §1615(d)(2), provides:

(2) SPECIAL RULE FOR 1995 AND 1996.—In the case of returns for taxable years beginning in 1995 or 1996, a taxpayer shall not be required by the amendments made by this section to provide a taxpayer identification number for a child who is born after October 31, 1995, in the case of a taxable year beginning in 1995 or November 30, 1996, in the case of a taxable year beginning in 1996.

• 1988, Family Support Act of 1988 (P.L. 100-485)

P.L. 100-485, §703(a):

Amended Code Sec. 21(e)(5)(B) by striking "age of 15" and inserting "age of 13". **Effective** for tax years beginning after 12-31-88.

P.L. 100-485, §703(c)(1):

Amended Code Sec. 21(e) by adding at the end thereof new paragraph (9). **Effective** for tax years beginning after 12-31-88.

[Sec. 21(f)]

(f) REGULATIONS.—The Secretary shall prescribe such regulations as may be necessary to carry out the purposes of this section.

Amendments

• 1986, Tax Reform Act of 1986 (P.L. 99-514)

P.L. 99-514, §104(b)(1)(A):

Amended Code Sec. 21(b)(1)(A) and 21(e)(6)(A) by striking out "section 151(e)" and inserting in lieu thereof "section 151(c)". **Effective** for tax years beginning after 12-31-86.

P.L. 99-514, §104(b)(1)(B):

Amended Code Sec. 21(e)(6)(B) by striking out "section 151(e)(3)" and inserting in lieu thereof "section 151(c)(3)". **Effective** for tax years beginning after 12-31-86.

• 1984, Deficit Reduction Act of 1984 (P.L. 98-369)

P.L. 98-369, §423(c)(4):

Amended Code Sec. 44A(f)(5), prior to its redesignation by Act Sec. 474(c) as (e)(5). **Effective** for tax years beginning after 12-31-84. Prior to amendment it read as follows:

(5) Special Dependency Test in Case of Divorced Parents, etc.—If—

(A) a child (as defined in section 151(e)(3)) who is under the age of 15 or who is physically or mentally incapable of caring for himself receives over half of his support during the calendar year from his parents who are divorced or legally separated under a decree of divorce or separate maintenance or who are separated under a written separation agreement, and

(B) such child is in the custody of one or both of his parents for more than one-half of the calendar year,

in the case of any taxable year beginning in such calendar year such child shall be treated as being a qualifying individual described in subparagraph (A) or (B) of subsection (c)(1), as the case may be, with respect to that parent who has custody for a longer period during such calendar year than the other parent, and shall not be treated as being a qualifying individual with respect to such other parent.

P.L. 98-369, §471(c)(1):

Redesignated the following Code sections of part IV in accordance with the following table. **Effective** for tax years beginning after 12-31-83, and to carrybacks from such years:

Old section number:	New section number:	New subpart designation:
44A	21	A
37	22	A
44C	23	A
41	24	A
33	27	B
44H	28	B
44D	29	B
44F	30	B
31	31	C
43	32	C
32	33	C
39	34	C
45	35	C
44E	40	D
44G	41	D

P.L. 98-369, §474(c):

Amended Code Sec. 21, as redesignated by Act Sec. 471(c)(1), by striking out subsection (b) and by redesignating subsections (c), (d), (e), (f), and (g) as subsections (b), (c), (d), (e), and (f), respectively, by striking out "subsection (c)(1)" in subsection (a) and inserting in lieu thereof "subsection (b)(1)", by striking out "subsection (c)(2)" in subsection (a) and inserting in lieu thereof "subsection (b)(2)", by striking out "subsection (c)(1)(C)" in paragraph (2) of subsection (d) (as redesignated by paragraph (1)) and inserting in lieu thereof "subsection (b)(1)(C)", by striking out "subsection (d)(1)" in subparagraph (A) of subsection (d)(2) (as redesignated by paragraph (1)) and inserting in lieu thereof, "subsection (c)(1)", by striking out "subsection (d)(2)" in subparagraph (B) of subsection (d)(2) (as redesignated by paragraph (1)) and inserting in lieu thereof "subsection (c)(2)". **Effective** for tax years beginning after 12-31-83, and to carrybacks from such years. Prior to amendment, subsection (b) read as follows:

(b) APPLICATION WITH OTHER CREDITS.—The credit allowed by subsection (a) shall not exceed the amount of the tax imposed by this chapter for the taxable year reduced by the sum of the credits allowable under—

(1) section 33 (relating to foreign tax credit),

(2) section 37 (relating to credit for the elderly and the permanently and totally disabled),

(3) section 38 (relating to investment in certain depreciable property),

(4) section 40 (relating to expenses of work incentive programs),

(5) section 41 (relating to contributions to candidates for public office),

(6) section 42 (relating to general tax credit), and

(7) section 44 (relating to purchase of new principal residence).

• 1983, Social Security Amendments of 1983 (P.L. 98-21)

P.L. 98-21, §122(c)(1):

Amended Code Sec. 44A(b)(2) by striking out "relating to credit for the elderly" and inserting in place thereof "relating to credit for the elderly and the permanently and totally disabled'. **Effective** for tax years beginning after 1983.

• 1981, Economic Recovery Tax Act of 1981 (P.L. 97-34)

P.L. 97-34, §124(a):

Amended Code Sec. 44A(a). **Effective** for tax years beginning after 12-31-81. Prior to amendment, Code. Sec. 44A(a) read as follows:

(a) ALLOWANCE OF CREDIT.—In the case of an individual who maintains a household which includes as a member one or more qualifying individuals (as defined in subsection (c)(1)), there shall be allowed as a credit against the tax imposed by this chapter for the taxable year an amount equal to 20 percent of the employment-related expenses (as defined in subsection (c)(2)) paid by such individual during the taxable year.

P.L. 97-34, §124(b)(1):

Amended Code Sec. 44A(d) by striking out "$2,000" and inserting in lieu thereof "$2,400", and by striking out "$4,000" and inserting in lieu thereof "$4,800". **Effective** for tax years beginning after 12-31-81.

P.L. 97-34, §124(b)(2):

Amended Code Sec. 44A(e)(2) by striking out "$166" and inserting in lieu thereof "$200" and by striking out "$333" and inserting in lieu thereof "$400". **Effective** for tax years beginning after 12-31-81.

P.L. 97-34, §124(c):

Amended Code Sec. 44A(c)(2)(B). **Effective** for tax years beginning after 12-31-81. Prior to amendment, Code Sec. 44A(c)(2)(B) read as follows:

(B) EXCEPTION.—Employment-related expenses described in subparagraph (A) which are incurred for services outside the taxpayer's household shall be taken into account only if incurred for the care of a qualifying individual described in paragraph (1)(A).

P.L. 97-34, §124(d):

Amended Code Sec. 44A(c)(2) by adding at the end thereof new subparagraphs (C) and (D). **Effective** for tax years beginning after 12-31-81.

• 1978, Revenue Act of 1978 (P.L. 95-600)

P.L. 95-600, §121(a):

Amended Code Sec. 44A(f)(6). **Effective** for tax years beginning after 12-31-78. Prior to amendment, Code Sec. 44A(f)(6) read as follows:

"(6) PAYMENTS TO RELATED INDIVIDUALS.—

"(A) IN GENERAL.—Except as provided in subparagraph (B), no credit shall be allowed under subsection (a) for any amount paid by the taxpayer to an individual bearing a relationship to the taxpayer described in paragraphs (1) through (8) of section 152(a) (relating to definition of dependent) or to a dependent described in paragraph (9) of such section.

"(B) EXCEPTION.—Subparagraph (A) shall not apply to any amount paid by the taxpayer to an individual with respect to whom, for the taxable year of the taxpayer in which the service is performed, neither the taxpayer nor his spouse is entitled to a deduction under section 151(e) (relating to deduction for personal exemptions for dependents), but only if the service with respect to which such amount is paid constitutes employment within the meaning of section 3121(b)."

• 1976, Tax Reform Act of 1976 (P.L. 94-455)

P.L. 94-455, §504(a)(1):

Added Code Sec. 44A. **Effective** for tax years beginning after 12-31-75.

[Sec. 22]

SEC. 22. CREDIT FOR THE ELDERLY AND THE PERMANENTLY AND TOTALLY DISABLED.

[Sec. 22(a)]

(a) GENERAL RULE.—In the case of a qualified individual, there shall be allowed as a credit against the tax imposed by this chapter for the taxable year an amount equal to 15 percent of such individual's section 22 amount for such taxable year.

[Sec. 22(b)]

(b) QUALIFIED INDIVIDUAL.—For purposes of this section, the term "qualified individual" means any individual—

(1) who has attained age 65 before the close of the taxable year, or

(2) who retired on disability before the close of the taxable year and who, when he retired, was permanently and totally disabled.

[Sec. 22(c)]

(c) SECTION 22 AMOUNT.—For purposes of subsection (a)—

(1) IN GENERAL.—An individual's section 22 amount for the taxable year shall be the applicable initial amount determined under paragraph (2), reduced as provided in paragraph (3) and in subsection (d).

(2) INITIAL AMOUNT.—

(A) IN GENERAL.—Except as provided in subparagraph (B), the initial amount shall be—

(i) $5,000 in the case of a single individual, or a joint return where only one spouse is a qualified individual,

(ii) $7,500 in the case of a joint return where both spouses are qualified individuals, or

(iii) $3,750 in the case of a married individual filing a separate return.

(B) LIMITATION IN CASE OF INDIVIDUALS WHO HAVE NOT ATTAINED AGE 65.—

(i) IN GENERAL.—In the case of a qualified individual who has not attained age 65 before the close of the taxable year, except as provided in clause (ii), the initial amount shall not exceed the disability income for the taxable year.

(ii) SPECIAL RULES IN CASE OF JOINT RETURN.—In the case of a joint return where both spouses are qualified individuals and at least one spouse has not attained age 65 before the close of the taxable year—

(I) if both spouses have not attained age 65 before the close of the taxable year, the initial amount shall not exceed the sum of such spouses' disability income, or

(II) if one spouse has attained age 65 before the close of the taxable year, the initial amount shall not exceed the sum of $5,000 plus the disability income for the taxable year of the spouse who has not attained age 65 before the close of the taxable year.

(iii) DISABILITY INCOME.—For purposes of this subparagraph, the term "disability income" means the aggregate amount includable in the gross income of the individual for the taxable year under section 72 or 105(a) to the extent such amount constitutes wages (or payments in lieu of wages) for the period during which the individual is absent from work on account of permanent and total disability.

(3) REDUCTION.—

(A) IN GENERAL.—The reduction under this paragraph is an amount equal to the sum of the amounts received by the individual (or, in the case of a joint return, by either spouse) as a pension or annuity or as a disability benefit—

(i) which is excluded from gross income and payable under—

(I) title II of the Social Security Act,

(II) the Railroad Retirement Act of 1974, or

(III) a law administered by the Veterans' Administration, or

(ii) which is excluded from gross income under any provision of law not contained in this title.

No reduction shall be made under clause (i)(III) for any amount described in section 104(a)(4).

(B) TREATMENT OF CERTAIN WORKMEN'S COMPENSATION BENEFITS.—For purposes of subparagraph (A), any amount treated as a social security benefit under section 86(d)(3) shall be treated as a disability benefit received under title II of the Social Security Act.

[Sec. 22(d)]

(d) ADJUSTED GROSS INCOME LIMITATION.—If the adjusted gross income of the taxpayer exceeds—

(1) $7,500 in the case of a single individual,

(2) $10,000 in the case of a joint return, or

(3) $5,000 in the case of a married individual filing a separate return,

the section 22 amount shall be reduced by one-half of the excess of the adjusted gross income over $7,500, $10,000, or $5,000, as the case may be.

[Sec. 22(e)]

(e) DEFINITIONS AND SPECIAL RULES.—For purposes of this section—

(1) MARRIED COUPLE MUST FILE JOINT RETURN.—Except in the case of a husband and wife who live apart at all times during the taxable year, if the taxpayer is married at the close of the taxable year, the credit provided by this section shall be allowed only if the taxpayer and his spouse file a joint return for the taxable year.

(2) MARITAL STATUS.—Marital status shall be determined under section 7703.

(3) PERMANENT AND TOTAL DISABILITY DEFINED.—An individual is permanently and totally disabled if he is unable to engage in any substantial gainful activity by reason of any medically determinable physical or mental impairment which can be expected to result in death or which has lasted or can be expected to last for a continuous period of not less than 12 months. An individual shall not be considered to be permanently and totally disabled unless he furnishes proof of the existence thereof in such form and manner, and at such times, as the Secretary may require.

Amendments

• 1986, Tax Reform Act of 1986 (P.L. 99-514)

P.L. 99-514, §1301(j)(8):

Amended Code Sec. 22(e)(2) by striking out "section 143" and inserting in lieu thereof "section 7703". **Effective** for bonds issued after 8-15-86.

[Sec. 22(f)]

(f) NONRESIDENT ALIEN INELIGIBLE FOR CREDIT.—No credit shall be allowed under this section to any nonresident alien.

Amendments

• 1984, Deficit Reduction Act of 1984 (P.L. 98-369)

P.L. 98-369, §471(c)(1):

Redesignated Code Sec. 37 as Code Sec. 22. **Effective** for tax years beginning after 12-31-83, and to carrybacks from such years.

P.L. 98-369, §474(d):

Amended Code Sec. 22, as redesignated by Act Sec. 471(c)(1), by striking out "section 37 amount" each place it appears in the text and inserting in lieu thereof "section 22 amount", by striking out the heading "(c) Section 37 Amount" of subsection (c) and inserting in lieu thereof "(c)

Section 22 Amount.—", and by amending subsection (d). **Effective** for tax years beginning after 12-31-83, and to carrybacks from such years. Prior to amendment, subsection (d) read as follows:

(d) LIMITATIONS.—

(1) Adjusted Gross Income Limitation.—If the adjusted gross income of the taxpayer exceeds—

(A) $7,500 in the case of a single individual,

(B) $10,000 in the case of a joint return, or

(C) $5,000 in the case of a married individual filing a separate return,

the section 37 amount shall be reduced by one half of the excess of the adjusted gross income over $7,500, $10,000, or $5,000, as the case may be.

(2) Limitation Based On Amount of Tax.—The amount of the credit allowed by this section for the taxable year shall not exceed the amount of the tax imposed by this chapter for such taxable year.

• 1983, Social Security Amendments of 1983 (P.L. 98-21)

P.L. 98-21, §122(a):

Amended Code Sec. 37. **Effective** for tax years beginning after 12-31-83. Prior to amendment, Code Sec. 37 read as follows:

SEC. 37. CREDIT FOR THE ELDERLY.

(a) GENERAL RULE—In the case of an individual who has attained age 65 before the close of the taxable year, there shall be allowed as a credit against the tax imposed by this chapter for the taxable year an amount equal to 15 percent of such individual's section 37 amount for such taxable year.

(b) SECTION 37 AMOUNT.—For purposes of subsection (a)—

(1) IN GENERAL.—An individual's section 37 amount for the taxable year is the applicable initial amount determined under paragraph (2), reduced as provided in paragraph (3) and in subsection (c).

(2) INITIAL AMOUNT.—The initial amount is—

(A) $2,500 in the case of a single individual,

(B) $2,500 in the case of a joint return where only one spouse is eligible for the credit under subsection (a),

(C) $3,750 in the case of a joint return where both spouses are eligible for the credit under subsection (a), or

(D) $1,875 in the case of a married individual filing a separate return.

(3) REDUCTION.—The reduction under this paragraph is an amount equal to the sum of the amounts received by the individual (or, in the case of a joint return, by either spouse) as a pension or annuity—

(A) under title II of the Social Security Act,

(B) under the Railroad Retirement Act of 1935 or 1937, or

(C) otherwise excluded from gross income.

No reduction shall be made under this paragraph for any amount excluded from gross income under section 72 (relating to annuities), 101 (relating to life insurance proceeds), 104 (relating to compensation for injuries or sickness), 105 (relating to amounts received under accident and health plans), 120 (relating to amounts received under qualified group legal services plans), 402 (relating to taxability of beneficiary of employees' trust), 403 (relating to taxation of employee annuities), or 405 (relating to qualified bond purchase plans).

(c) LIMITATIONS.

(1) ADJUSTED GROSS INCOME LIMITATION.—If the adjusted gross incoime of the taxpayer exceeds—

(A) $7,500 in the case of a single individual,

(B) $10,000 in the case of a joint return, or

(C) $5,000 in the case of a married individual filing a separate return,

the section 37 amount shall be reduced by one-half of the excess of the adjusted gross income over $7,500, $10,000, or $5,000, as the case may be.

(2) LIMITATION BASED ON AMOUNT OF TAX.—The amount of the credit allowed by this section for the taxable year shall not exceed the amount of the tax imposed by this chapter for such taxable year.

(d) DEFINITIONS AND SPECIAL RULES.—For purposes of this section—

(1) MARRIED COUPLE MUST FILE JOINT RETURN.—Except in the case of a husband and wife who live apart at all times during the taxable year, if the taxpayer is married at the close of the taxable year, the credit provided by this section shall be allowed only if the taxpayer and his spouse file a joint return for the taxable year.

(2) MARITAL STATUS.—Marital status shall be determined under section 143.

(3) JOINT RETURN.—The term "joint return" means the joint return of a husband and wife made under section 6013.

(e) ELECTION OF PRIOR LAW WITH RESPECT TO PUBLIC RETIREMENT SYSTEM INCOME.—

(1) IN GENERAL.—In the case of a taxpayer who has not attained age 65 before the close of the taxable year (other than a married individual whose spouse has attained age 65 before the close of the taxable year), his credit (if any) under this section shall be determined under this subsection.

(2) ONE SPOUSE AGE 65 OR OVER.—In the case of a married individual who has not attained age 65 before the close of the taxable year (and whose gross income includes income described in paragraph (4)(B)) but whose spouse has attained such age, this paragraph shall apply for the taxable year only if both spouses elect, at such time and in such manner as the Secretary shall by regulations prescribe, to have this paragraph apply. If this paragraph applies for the taxable year, the credit (if any) of each spouse under this section shall be determined under this subsection.

(3) COMPUTATION OF CREDIT.—In the case of an individual whose credit under this section for the taxable year is determined under this subsection, there shall be allowed as a credit against the tax imposed by this chapter for the taxable year an amount equal to 15 percent of the amount received by such individual as retirement income (as defined in paragraph (4) and as limited by paragraph (5)).

(4) RETIREMENT INCOME.—For purposes of this subsection, the term "retirement income" means—

(A) in the case of an individual who has attained age 65 before the close of the taxable year, income from—

(i) pensions and annuities (including, in the case of an individual who is, or has been, an employee within the meaning of section 401(c)(1), distributions by a trust described in section 401(a) which is exempt from tax under section 501(a)),

(ii) interest,

(iii) rents,

(iv) dividends,

(v) bonds described in section 405(b)(1) which are received under a qualified bond purchase plan described in section 405(a) or in a distribution from a trust described in section 401(a) which is exempt from tax under section 501(a), or retirement bonds described in section 409, and

(vi) an individual retirement account described in section 408(a) or an individual retirement annuity described in section 408(b); or

(B) in the case of an individual who has not attained age 65 before the close of the taxable year and who performed the services giving rise to the pension or annuity (or is the spouse of the individual who performed the services), income from pensions and annuities under a public retirement system (as defined in paragraph (9)(A)),

to the extent included in gross income without reference to this subsection, but only to the extent such income does not represent compensation for personal services rendered during the taxable year.

(5) LIMITATION ON RETIREMENT INCOME.—For purposes of this subsection, the amount of retirement income shall not exceed $2,500 less—

(A) the reduction provided by subsection (b)(3), and

(B) in the case of any individual who has not attained age 72 before the close of the taxable year—

(i) if such individual has not attained age 62 before the close of the taxable year, any amount of earned income (as defined in paragraph (9)(B)) in excess of $900 received by such individual in the taxable year, or

(ii) if such individual has attained age 62 before the close of the taxable year, the sum of one-half the amount of earned income received by such individual in the taxable year in excess of $1,200 but not in excess of $1,700, and the amount of earned income so received in excess of $1,700.

(6) LIMITATION IN CASE OF MARRIED INDIVIDUALS.—In the case of a joint return, paragraph (5) shall be applied by substituting "$3,750" for "$2,500". The $3,750 provided by the pre-

ceding sentence shall be divided between the spouses in such amounts as may be agreed on by them, except that not more than $2,500 may be assigned to either spouse.

(7) LIMITATION IN THE CASE OF SEPARATE RETURNS.—In the case of a married individual filing a separate return, paragraph (5) shall be applied by substituting "$1,875" for "$2,500".

(8) COMMUNITY PROPERTY LAWS NOT APPLICABLE.—In the case of a joint return, this subsection shall be applied without regard to community property laws.

(9) DEFINITIONS.—For purposes of this subsection—

(A) PUBLIC RETIREMENT SYSTEM DEFINED.—The term "public retirement system" means a pension, annuity, retirement, or similar fund or system established by the United States, a State, a possession of the United States, any political subdivision of any of the foregoing, or the District of Columbia.

(B) EARNED INCOME.—The term "earned income" has the meaning assigned to such term by section 911(d)(2), except that such term does not include any amount received as a pension or annuity.

(f) NONRESIDENT ALIEN INELIGIBLE FOR CREDIT.—No credit shall be allowed under this section to any nonresident alien.

• 1981, Economic Recovery Tax Act of 1981 (P.L. 97-34)

P.L. 97-34, §111(b)(4):

Amended Code Sec. 37(e)(9)(B) by striking out "section 911(b)" and inserting in lieu thereof "section 911(d)(2)". **Effective** for tax years beginning after 12-31-81.

• 1978, Revenue Act of 1978 (P.L. 95-600)

P.L. 95-600, §703(j)(11):

Amended §1901(c)(1) of P.L. 94-455 by striking out paragraph (1). Paragraph (1) of §1901(c)(1) struck out "a Territory" in Code Sec. 37(f) before amendment by P.L. 94-455. **Effective** 10-4-76.

P.L. 95-600, §701(a)(1):

Amended Code Sec. 37(e) by changing paragraph (e)(2). **Effective** for tax years beginning after 12-31-75. Prior to amendment, paragraph (e)(2) read as follows:

"(2) ONE SPOUSE AGE 65 OR OVER.—In the case of a married individual who has not attained age 65 before the close of the taxable year but whose spouse has attained such age, this paragraph shall apply for the taxable year only if both spouses elect, at such time and in such manner as the Secretary shall by regulations prescribe, to have this paragraph apply. If this paragraph applies for the taxable year, the credit (if any) of each spouse under this section shall be determined under this subsection."

P.L. 95-600, §701(a)(2):

Amended Code Sec. 37(e) by changing paragraph (4)(B). **Effective** for tax years beginning after 12-31-75. Prior to amendment, paragraph (4)(B) read as follows:

"(B) in the case of an individual who has not attained age 65 before the close of the taxable year, income from pensions and annuities under a public retirement system (as defined in paragraph (8)(A)),".

P.L. 95-600, §701(a)(3):

Amended Code Sec. 37(e) by changing "paragraph (8)(B)" to "paragraph (9)(B)" in paragraph (5)(B)(i), and by redesignating paragraph (8) as paragraph (9) and by adding a new paragraph (8). **Effective** for tax years beginning after 12-31-77.

• 1977, Tax Reduction and Simplification Act of 1977 (P.L. 95-30)

P.L. 95-30, §403, provides:

SEC. 403. ELECTION OF FORMER RETIREMENT INCOME CREDIT PROVISIONS FOR 1976.

A taxpayer may elect (at such time and in such manner as the Secretary of the Treasury or his delegate shall prescribe) to determine the amount of his credit under section 37 of the Internal Revenue Code of 1954 for his first taxable year beginning in 1976 under the provisions of such section as they existed before the amendment made by section 503 of the Tax Reform Act of 1976.

• 1976, Tax Reform Act of 1976 (P.L. 94-455)

P.L. 94-455, §1901(c)(1):

Amended subsection (f) as it read prior to the amendment by P.L. 94-455, §503(a), by striking out "a Territory." **Effective** for tax years beginning after 12-31-76.

P.L. 94-455, §503(a):

Amended Code Sec. 37. **Effective** for tax years beginning after 12-31-75. Prior to amendment, Code Sec. 37 read as follows:

SEC. 37. RETIREMENT INCOME.

(a) GENERAL RULE.—In the case of an individual who has received earned income before the beginning of the taxable year, there shall be allowed as a credit against the tax imposed by this chapter for the taxable year an amount equal to 17 percent, in the case of a taxable year beginning after December 31, 1964, of the amount received by such individual as retirement income (as defined in subsection (c) and as limited by subsection (d)); but this credit shall not exceed such tax reduced by the credits allowable under section 32(2) (relating to tax withheld at source on tax-free covenant bonds), section 33 (relating to foreign tax credit), and section 35 (relating to partially tax-exempt interest).

(b) INDIVIDUAL WHO HAS RECEIVED EARNED INCOME.—For purposes of subsection (a), an individual shall be considered to have received earned income if he has received, in each of any 10 calendar years before the taxable year, earned income (as defined in subsection (g)) in excess of $600. A widow or widower whose spouse had received such earned income shall be considered to have received earned income.

(c) RETIREMENT INCOME.—For purposes of subsection (a), the term "retirement income" means—

(1) in the case of an individual who has attained the age of 65 before the close of the taxable year, income from—

(A) pensions and annuities (including, in the case of an individual who is, or has been, an employee within the meaning of section 401(c)(1), distributions by a trust described in section 401(a) which is exempt from tax under section 501(a)),

(B) interest,

(C) rents,

(D) dividends,

(E) bonds described in section 405(b)(1) which are received under a qualified bond purchase plan described in section 405(a) or in a distribution from a trust described in section 401(a) which is exempt from tax under section 501(a), or retirement bonds described in section 409, and

(F) an individual retirement account described in section 408(a) or an individual retirement annuity described in section 408(b), or

(2) in the case of an individual who has not attained the age of 65 before the close of the taxable year, income from pensions and annuities under a public retirement system (as defined in subsection (f)),

to the extent included in gross income without reference to this section, but only to the extent such income does not represent compensation for personal services rendered during the taxable year.

(d) LIMITATION ON RETIREMENT INCOME.—For purposes of subsection (a), the amount of retirement income shall not exceed $1,524 less—

(1) in the case of any individual, any amount received by the individual as a pension or annuity—

(A) under title II of the Social Security Act,

(B) under the Railroad Retirement Acts of 1935 or 1937, or

(C) otherwise excluded from gross income, and

(2) in the case of any individual who has not attained age 72 before the close of the taxable year—

(A) if such individual has not attained age 62 before the close of the taxable year, any amount of earned income (as defined in subsection (g)) in excess of $900 received by such individual in the taxable year, or

(B) if such individual has attained age 62 before the close of the taxable year, the sum of (i) one-half the amount of earned income received by such individual in the taxable year in excess of $1,200 but not in excess of $1,700, and (ii) the amount of earned income so received in excess of $1,700.

(e) RULE FOR APPLICATION OF SUBSECTION (d)(1).—Subsection (d)(1) shall not apply to any amount excluded from gross income under section 72 (relating to annuities), 101 (relating to life insurance proceeds), 104 (relating to compensation for injuries or sickness), 105 (relating to amounts received under accident and health plans), 402 (relating to taxability of beneficiary of employees' trust), or 403 (relating to taxation of employee annuities).

(f) PUBLIC RETIREMENT SYSTEM DEFINED.—For purposes of subsection (c) (2), the term "public retirement system" means a pension, annuity, retirement, or similar fund or system established by the United States, a State, a Territory, a possession of the United States, any political subdivision of any of the foregoing, or the District of Columbia.

(g) EARNED INCOME DEFINED.—For purposes of subsections (b) and (d) (2), the term "earned income" has the meaning assigned to such term in section 911 (b), except that such term does not include any amount received as a pension or annuity.

(h) NONRESIDENT ALIEN INELIGIBLE FOR CREDIT.—No credit shall be allowed under subsection (a) to any nonresident alien.

(i) SPECIAL RULES FOR CERTAIN MARRIED COUPLES.

(1) ELECTION.—A husband and wife who make a joint return for the taxable year and both of whom have attained the age of 65 before the close of the taxable year may elect (at such time and in such manner as the Secretary or his delegate by regulations prescribes) to determine the amount of the credit allowed by subsection (a) by applying the provisions of paragraph (2).

(2) SPECIAL RULES.—If an election is made under paragraph (1) for the taxable year, for purposes of subsection (a)—

(A) if either spouse is an individual who has received earned income within the meaning of subsection (b), the other spouse shall be considered to be an individual who has received earned income within the meaning of such subsection; and

(B) subsection (d) shall be considered as providing that the amount of the combined retirement income of both spouses shall not exceed $2,286, less the sum of the amounts specified in paragraphs (1) and (2) of subsection (d) for each spouse.

(j) CROSS REFERENCE.—

For disallowance of credit where tax is computed by Secretary or his delegate, see section 6014(a).

• 1974, Employee Retirement Income Security Act of 1974 (P.L. 93-406)

P.L. 93-406, §2002(g)(1):

Amended Code Sec. 37(c) by deleting "and" at the end of subparagraph (D), adding "retirement bonds described in section 409, and" at the end of subparagraph (E), and adding subparagraph (F). **Effective** 1-1-75.

• 1964, Revenue Act of 1964 (P.L. 88-272)

P.L. 88-272, §201(d)(3):

Amended Code Sec. 37(a) by deleting "section 34 (relating to credit for dividends received by individuals),". **Effective** with respect to dividends received after 12-31-64, in tax years ending after such date.

P.L. 88-272, §113(a):

Amended Sec. 37(a). **Effective** with respect to tax years beginning after 12-31-63. Prior to amendment, Sec. 37(a) read as follows:

"(a) General Rule.—In the case of an individual who has received earned income before the beginning of the taxable year, there shall be allowed as a credit against the tax imposed by this chapter for the taxable year an amount equal to the amount received by such individual as retirement income (as defined in subsection (c) and as limited by subsection (d)), multiplied by the rate provided in section 1 for the first $2,000 of taxable income; but this credit shall not exceed such tax reduced by the credits allowable under section 32(2) (relating to tax withheld at source on tax-free covenant bonds), section 33 (relating to foreign tax credit), section 34 (relating to credit for dividends received by individuals), and section 35 (relating to partially tax-exempt interest)."

P.L. 88-272, §202(a):

Added subsection (i). **Effective** with respect to tax years beginning after 12-31-63.

Amended subsection (j) by redesignating it as (i).

• 1962 (P.L. 87-876)

P.L. 87-876, §1:

Amended Code Sec. 37(d). **Effective** for tax years ending after 10-24-62. Prior to amendment, Sec. 37(d) read as follows:

"(d) Limitation on Retirement Income.—For purposes of subsection (a) the amount of retirement income shall not exceed $1,200 less—

"(1) in the case of any individual, any amount received by the individual as a pension or annuity—

"(A) under title II of the Social Security Act,

"(B) under the Railroad Retirement Acts of 1935 or 1937, or

"(C) otherwise excluded from gross income, and

"(2) in the case of any individual who has not attained the age of 72 before the close of the taxable year, any amount of earned income (as defined in subsection (g))—

"(A) in excess of $900 received by the individual in the taxable year if such individual has not attained the age of 65 before the close of the taxable year, or

"(B) in excess of $1,200 received by the individual in the taxable year if such individual has attained the age of 65 before the close of the taxable year."

• 1962, Self-Employed Individuals Tax Retirement Act of 1962 (P.L. 97-792)

P.L. 87-792, §7:

Amended Code Sec. 37(c)(1) by amending subparagraph (A), striking out "and" at the end of subparagraph (C), striking out "or" at the end of subparagraph (D) and inserting in lieu thereof "and", and adding after subparagraph (D) a new subparagraph (E). **Effective** 1-1-63. Prior to amendment, subparagraph (A) read as follows:

"(A) pension and annuities,"

• 1956 (P.L. 398, 84th Cong.)

P.L. 398, 84th Cong., §[1]:

Amended subsection (d)(2) by lowering the age limitation from "75" to "72" and by the addition of subparagraphs (A) and (B). **Effective** 1-1-56. Prior to the amendment, Code Sec. 37(d)(2) read as follows:

"(2) in the case of any individual who has not attained the age of 75 before the close of the taxable year, any amount of earned income (as defined in subsection (g)) in excess of $900 received by the individual in the taxable year."

• 1955 (P.L. 299, 84th Cong.)

P.L. 299, 84th Cong., §[1]:

Amended subsection (f) by deleting "; except that such term does not include a fund or system established by the United States for members of the Armed Forces of the United States" where it appeared following the words "District of Columbia". **Effective** 1-1-55.

[Sec. 23—Repealed]

Amendments

• 1990, Omnibus Budget Reconciliation Act of 1990 (P.L. 101-508)

P.L. 101-508, §11801(a)(1):

Repealed Code Sec. 23. **Effective** 11-5-90. Prior to repeal, Code Sec. 23 read as follows:

SEC. 23. RESIDENTIAL ENERGY CREDIT.

(a) GENERAL RULE.—In the case of an individual, there shall be allowed as a credit against the tax imposed by this chapter for the taxable year an amount equal to the sum of—

(1) the qualified energy conservation expenditures, plus

(2) the qualified renewable energy source expenditures.

(b) QUALIFIED EXPENDITURES.—For purposes of subsection (a)—

(1) ENERGY CONSERVATION.—In the case of any dwelling unit, the qualified energy conservation expenditures are 15 percent of so much of the energy conservation expenditures made by the taxpayer during the taxable year with respect to such unit as does not exceed $2,000.

(2) RENEWABLE ENERGY SOURCE.—In the case of any dwelling unit, the qualified renewable energy source expenditures are 40 percent of so much of the renewable energy source expenditures made by the taxpayer during the taxable year with respect to such unit as does not exceed $10,000.

(3) PRIOR EXPENDITURES BY TAXPAYER ON SAME RESIDENCE TAKEN INTO ACCOUNT.—If for any prior year a credit was allowed to the taxpayer under this section with respect to any dwelling unit by reason of energy conservation expenditures or renewable energy source expenditures, paragraph (1) or (2) (whichever is appropriate) shall be applied for the taxable year with respect to such dwelling unit by reducing each dollar amount contained in such paragraph by the prior year expenditures taken into account under such paragraph.

(4) MINIMUM DOLLAR AMOUNT.—No credit shall be allowed under this section with respect to any return for any taxable year if the amount which would (but for this paragraph) be allowed with respect to such return is less than $10.

(5) CARRYFORWARDS OF UNUSED CREDIT.—

(A) IN GENERAL.—If the credit allowable under subsection (a) for any taxable year exceeds the limitation imposed by section 26(a) for such taxable year reduced by the sum of the credits allowable under this subpart (other than this section and section 25), such excess shall be carried to the succeeding taxable year and added to the credit allowable under subsection (a) for such succeeding taxable year.

(B) NO CARRYFORWARD TO TAXABLE YEARS BEGINNING AFTER DECEMBER 31, 1987.—No amount may be carried under subparagraph (A) to any taxable year beginning after December 31, 1987.

(c) DEFINITIONS AND SPECIAL RULES.—For purposes of this section—

(1) ENERGY CONSERVATION EXPENDITURES.—The term "energy conservation expenditure" means an expenditure made on or after April 20, 1977, by the taxpayer for insulation or any other energy-conserving component (or for the original installation of such insulation or other component) installed in or on a dwelling unit—

(A) which is located in the United States,

(B) which is used by the taxpayer as his principal residence, and

(C) the construction of which was substantially completed before April 20, 1977.

(2) RENEWABLE ENERGY SOURCE EXPENDITURE.—

(A) IN GENERAL.—The term "renewable energy source expenditure" means an expenditure made on or after April 20, 1977, by the taxpayer for renewable energy source property installed in connection with a dwelling unit—

(i) which is located in the United States, and

(ii) which is used by the taxpayer as his principal residence.

(B) CERTAIN LABOR AND OTHER COSTS INCLUDED.—The term "renewable energy source expenditures" includes—

(i) expenditures for labor costs properly allocable to the onsite preparation, assembly, or original installation of renewable energy source property, and

(ii) expenditures for an onsite well drilled for any geothermal deposit (as defined in section 613(e)(3)), but only if the taxpayer has not elected under section 263(c) to deduct any portion of such expenditures.

(C) SWIMMING POOL, ETC., USED AS STORAGE MEDIUM.—The term "renewable energy source expenditure" does not include any expenditure properly allocable to a swimming pool used as an energy storage medium or to any other energy storage medium which has a primary function other than the function of such storage.

(D) CERTAIN SOLAR PANELS.—No solar panel installed as a roof (or portion thereof) shall fail to be treated as renewable energy source property solely because it constitutes a structural component of the dwelling on which it is installed.

(3) INSULATION.—The term "insulation" means any item—

(A) which is specifically and primarily designed to reduce when installed in or on a dwelling (or water heater) the heat loss or gain of such dwelling (or water heater),

(B) the original use of which begins with the taxpayer,

(C) which can reasonably be expected to remain in operation for at least 3 years, and

(D) which meets the performance and quality standards (if any) which—

(i) have been prescribed by the Secretary by regulations, and

(ii) are in effect at the time of the acquisition of the item.

(4) OTHER ENERGY-CONSERVING COMPONENT.—The term "other energy-conserving component" means any item (other than insulation)—

(A) which is—

(i) a furnace replacement burner designed to achieve a reduction in the amount of fuel consumed as a result of increased combustion efficiency,

(ii) a device for modifying flue openings designed to increase the efficiency of operation of the heating system,

(iii) an electrical or mechanical furnace ignition system, which replaces a gas pilot light,

(iv) a storm or thermal window or door for the exterior of the dwelling,

(v) an automatic energy-saving setback thermostat,

(vi) caulking or weatherstripping of an exterior door or window,

(vii) a meter which displays the cost of energy usage, or

(viii) an item of the kind which the Secretary specifies by regulations as increasing the energy efficiency of the dwelling,

(B) the original use of which begins with the taxpayer,

(C) which can reasonably be expected to remain in operation for at least 3 years, and

(D) which meets the performance and quality standards (if any) which—

(i) have been prescribed by the Secretary by regulations, and

(ii) are in effect at the time of the acquisition of the item.

(5) RENEWABLE ENERGY SOURCE PROPERTY.—The term "renewable energy source property" means property—

(A) which, when installed in connection with a dwelling, transmits or uses—

(i) solar energy, energy derived from the geothermal deposits (as defined in section 613(e)(3)), or any other form of renewable energy which the Secretary specifies by regulations, for the purpose of heating or cooling such dwelling or providing hot water or electricity for use within such dwelling, or

(ii) wind energy for nonbusiness residential purposes,

(B) the original use of which begins with the taxpayer,

(C) which can reasonably be expected to remain in operation for at least 5 years, and

(D) which meet the performance and quality standards (if any) which—

(i) have been prescribed by the Secretary by regulations, and

(ii) are in effect at the time of the acquisition of the property.

(6) REGULATIONS.—

(A) CRITERIA; CERTIFICATION PROCEDURES.—The Secretary shall by regulations—

(i) establish the criteria which are to be used in (I) prescribing performance and quality standards under paragraphs (3), (4), and (5), or (II) specifying any item under paragraph (4)(A)(viii) or any form of renewable energy under paragraph (5)(A)(i), and

(ii) establish a procedure under which a manufacturer of an item may request the Secretary to certify that the item will be treated, for purposes of this section, as insulation, an energy-conserving component, or renewable energy source property.

(B) CONSULTATION.—Performance and quality standards regulations and other regulations shall be prescribed by the Secretary under paragraphs (3), (4), and (5) and under this paragraph only after consultation with the Secretary of Energy, the Secretary of Housing and Urban Development, and other appropriate Federal officers.

(C) ACTION ON REQUESTS.—

(i) IN GENERAL.—The Secretary shall make a final determination with respect to any request filed under subparagraph (A)(ii) for specifying an item under paragraph (4)(A)(viii) or for specifying a form of renewable energy under paragraphs (5)(A)(i) within 1 year after the filing of the request, together with any information required to be filed with such request under subparagraph (A)(ii).

(ii) REPORTS.—Each month the Secretary shall publish a report of any request which has been denied during the preceding month and the reasons for the denial.

(D) EFFECTIVE DATE.—

(i) IN GENERAL.—In the case of any item or energy source specified under paragraph (4)(A)(viii) or (5)(A)(i), the credit allowed by subsection (a) shall apply with respect to expenditures which are made on or after the date on which final notice of such specification is published in the Federal Register.

(ii) EXPENDITURES TAKEN INTO ACCOUNT IN FOLLOWING TAXABLE YEARS.—The Secretary may prescribe by regulations that expenditures made on or after the date referred to in clause (i) and before the close of the taxable year in which such date occurs shall be taken into account in the following taxable year.

(7) WHEN EXPENDITURES MADE; AMOUNT OF EXPENDITURES.—

(A) IN GENERAL.—Except as provided in subparagraph (B), and expenditure with respect to an item shall be treated as made when original installation of the item is completed.

(B) RENEWABLE ENERGY SOURCE EXPENDITURES.—In the case of renewable energy source expenditures in connection with the construction or reconstruction of a dwelling, such expenditures shall be treated as made when the original use of the constructed or reconstructed dwelling by the taxpayer begins.

(C) AMOUNT.—The amount of any expenditure shall be the cost thereof.

(D) ALLOCATION IN CERTAIN CASES.—If less than 80 percent of the use of an item is for nonbusiness residential purposes, only that portion of the expenditures for such item which is properly allocable to use for nonbusiness residential purposes shall be taken into account. For purposes of this subparagraph, use for a swimming pool shall be treated as use which is not for residential purposes.

(8) PRINCIPAL RESIDENCE.—The determination of whether or not a dwelling unit is a taxpayer's principal residence shall be made under principles similar to those applicable to section 1034, except that—

(A) no ownership requirement shall be imposed, and

(B) the period for which a dwelling is treated as the principal residence of the taxpayer shall include the 30-day period ending on the first day on which it would (but for this subparagraph) be treated as his principal residence.

(9) LIMITATIONS ON SECRETARIAL AUTHORITY.—

(A) IN GENERAL.—The Secretary shall not specify any item under paragraph (4)(A)(viii) or any form of renewable energy under paragraph (5)(A)(i) unless the Secretary determines that—

(i) there will be a reduction in oil or natural gas consumption as a result of such specification, and such reduction is sufficient to justify any resulting decrease in Federal revenues,

(ii) such specification will not result in an increased use of any item which is known to be, or reasonably suspected to be, environmentally hazardous or a threat to public health or safety, and

(iii) available Federal subsidies do not make such specification unnecessary or inappropriate (in the light of the most advantageous allocation of economic resources).

(B) FACTORS TAKEN INTO ACCOUNT.—In making any determination under subparagraph (A)(i), the Secretary (after consultation with the Secretary of Energy)—

(i) shall make an estimate of the amount by which the specification will reduce oil and natural gas consumption, and

(ii) shall determine whether such specification compares favorably, on the basis of the reduction in oil and natural gas consumption per dollar of cost to the Federal Government (including revenue loss), with other Federal programs in existence or being proposed.

(C) FACTORS TAKEN INTO ACCOUNT IN MAKING ESTIMATES.—In making any estimate under subparagraph (B)(i), the Secretary shall take into account (among other factors)—

(i) the extent to which the use of any item will be increased as a result of the specification,

(ii) whether sufficient capacity is available to increase production to meet any increase in demand caused by such specification,

(iii) the amount of oil and natural gas used directly or indirectly in the manufacture of such item and other items necessary for its use, and

(iv) the estimated useful life of such item.

(10) PROPERTY FINANCED BY SUBSIDIZED ENERGY FINANCING.—

(A) REDUCTION OF QUALIFIED EXPENDITURES.—For purposes of determining the amount of energy conservation or renewable energy source expenditures made by any individual with respect to any dwelling unit, there shall not be taken into account expenditues which are made from subsidized energy financing.

(B) DOLLAR LIMITS REDUCED.—Paragraph (1) or (2) of subsection (b) (whichever is appropriate) shall be applied with respect to such dwelling unit for any taxable year of such taxpayer by reducing each dollar amount contained in such paragraph (reduced as provided in subsection (b)(3)) by an amount equal to the sum of—

(i) the amount of the expenditures which were made by the taxpayer during such taxable year or any prior taxable year with respect to such dwelling unit and which were not taken into account by reason of subparagraph (A), and

(ii) the amount of any Federal, State, or local grant received by the taxpayer during such taxable year or any prior taxable year which was used to make energy conservation or renewable energy source expenditures with respect to the dwelling unit and which was not included in the gross income of such taxpayer.

(C) SUBSIDIZED ENERGY FINANCING.—For purposes of subparagraph (A), the term "subsidized energy financing" means financing provided under a Federal, State, or local program a principal purpose of which is to provide subsidized financing for projects designed to conserve or produce energy.

(d) SPECIAL RULES.—For purposes of this section—

(1) DOLLAR AMOUNTS IN CASE OF JOINT OCCUPANCY.—In the case of any dwelling unit which is jointly occupied and used during any calendar year as a principal residence by 2 or more individuals—

(A) the amount of the credit allowable under subsection (a) by reason of energy conservation expenditures or by reason of renewable energy source expenditures (as the case may be) made during such calendar year by any of such individuals with respect to such dwelling unit shall be determined by treating all of such individuals as one taxpayer whose taxable year is such calendar year; and

(B) there shall be allowable with respect to such expenditures to each of such individuals, a credit under subsection (a) for the taxable year in which such calendar year ends in an amount which bears the same ratio to the amount determined under subparagraph (A) as the amount of such expenditures made by such individual during such calendar year bears to the aggregate of such expenditures made by all of such individuals during such calendar year.

(2) TENANT-STOCKHOLDER IN COOPERATIVE HOUSING CORPORATION.—In the case of an individual who is a tenant-stockholder (as defined in section 216) in a cooperative housing corporation (as defined in such section), such individual shall be treated as having made his tenant-stockholder's proportionate share (as defined in section 216(b)(3)) of any expenditures of such corporation.

(3) CONDOMINIUMS.—

(A) IN GENERAL.—In the case of an individual who is a member of a condominium management association with respect to a condominium which he owns, such individual shall be treated as having made his proportionate share of any expenditures of such association.

(B) CONDOMINIUM MANAGEMENT ASSOCIATION.—For purposes of this paragraph, the term "condominium management association" means an organization which meets the requirements of paragraph (1) of section 528(c) (other than subparagraph (E) thereof) with respect to a condominium project substantially all of the units of which are used as residences.

(4) JOINT OWNERSHIP OF ENERGY ITEMS.—

(A) IN GENERAL.—Any expenditure otherwise qualifying as an energy conservation expenditure or a renewable energy source expenditure shall not be treated as failing to so qualify merely because such expenditure was made with respect to 2 or more dwelling units.

(B) LIMITS APPLIED SEPARATELY.—In the case of any expenditure described in subparagraph (A), the amount of the credit allowable under subsection (a) shall (subject to paragraph (1)) be computed separately with respect to the amount of the expenditure made by each individual.

(5) 1977 EXPENDITURES ALLOWED FOR 1978.—

(A) NO CREDIT FOR TAXABLE YEARS BEGINNING BEFORE 1978.—No credit shall be allowed under this section for any taxable year beginning before January 1, 1978.

(B) 1977 EXPENDITURES ALLOWED FOR 1978.—In the case of the taxpayer's first taxable year beginning after December 31, 1977, this section shall be applied by taking into account the period beginning April 20, 1977, and ending on the last day of such first taxable year.

(e) BASIS ADJUSTMENTS.—For purposes of this subtitle, if a credit is allowed under this section for any expenditure with respect to any property, the increase in the basis of such property which would (but for this subsection) result from such expenditure shall be reduced by the amount of the credit so allowed.

(f) TERMINATION.—This section shall not apply to expenditures made after December 31, 1985.

P.L. 101-508, §11821(b), provides:

(b) SAVINGS PROVISION.—If—

(1) any provision amended or repealed by this part applied to—

(A) any transaction occurring before the date of the enactment of this Act,

(B) any property acquired before such date of enactment, or

(C) any item of income, loss, deduction, or credit taken into account before such date of enactment, and

(2) the treatment of such transaction, property, or item under such provision would (without regard to the amendments made by this part) affect liability for tax for periods ending after such date of enactment,

nothing in the amendments made by this part shall be construed to affect the treatment of such transaction, property, or item for purposes of determining liability for tax for periods ending after such date of enactment.

• 1984, Deficit Reduction Act of 1984 (P.L. 98-369)

P.L. 98-369, §471(c)(1):

Redesignated former Code 44C as Code Sec. 23. **Effective** for tax years beginning after 12-31-83, and to carrybacks from such years.

P.L. 98-369, §474(e):

Amended Code Sec. 23(b), as redesignated by Act Sec. 471(c)(1), by striking out paragraphs (5) and (6) and inserting in lieu thereof paragraph (5). **Effective** for tax years beginning after 12-31-83, and to carrybacks from such years. Prior to amendment, paragraphs (5) and (6) read as follows:

(5) Application With Other Credits.—The credit allowed by subsection (a) shall not exceed the tax imposed by this chapter for the taxable year, reduced by the sum of the credits allowable under a section of this subpart having a lower number or letter designation than this section, other than credits allowable by sections 31, 39, and 43.

(6) Carryover of Unused Credit.—

(A) In General.—If the credit allowable under subsection (a) for any taxable year exceeds the limitation imposed by paragraph (5) for such taxable year, such excess shall be carried to the succeeding taxable year and added to the credit allowable under subsection (a) for such succeeding taxable year.

(B) No Carryover to Taxable Years Beginning After December 31, 1987.—No amount may be carried under subparagraph (A) to any taxable year beginning after December 31, 1987.

P.L. 98-369, §612(e)(2):

Amended Code Sec. 23(b)(5), as redesignated by Act Sec. 471(c)(1) and amended by Act Sec. 474(e), by striking out "section 25(a)" and inserting in lieu thereof "section 26(a)" and by striking out "(other than this section)" and inserting in lieu thereof "(other than this section and section 25)". **Effective** for interest paid or accrued after 12-31-84, on indebtedness incurred after 12-31-84, and to elections under section 25(c)(2)(A)(ii) of the Internal Revenue Code of 1954 (as added by this Act) for calendar years after 1983.

• 1980, Crude Oil Windfall Profit Tax Act of 1980 (P.L. 96-223)

P.L. 96-223, §201(a):

Redesignated Code Sec. 44C(d)(4) as Code Sec. 44C(d)(5) and added Code Sec. 44C(d)(4).

P.L. 96-223, §201(b)(1):

Added Code Sec. 44C(c)(9).

P.L. 96-223, §201(b)(2):

Amended Code Sec. 44C(c)(6) by adding subparagraphs (C) and (D).

P.L. 96-223, §202(a):

Amended Code Sec. 44C(b)(2). **Effective** for tax years beginning after 12-31-79. Prior to amendment, Code Sec. 44C(b)(2) read:

(2) RENEWABLE ENERGY SOURCE.—In the case of any dwelling unit, the qualified renewable energy source expenditures are the following percentages of the renewable energy source expenditures made by the taxpayer during the taxable year with respect to such unit:

(A) 30 percent of so much of such expenditures as does not exceed $2,000 plus

(B) 20 percent of so much of such expenditures as exceeds $2,000 but does not exceed $10,000.

P.L. 96-223, §202(b):

Amended Code Sec. 44C(c)(5)(A)(i) by striking out "providing hot water" and inserting "providing hot water or electricity". **Effective** for expenditures made after 12-31-79, in tax years ending after such date.

P.L. 96-223, §202(c):

Amended Code Sec. 44C(c)(2)(B). **Effective** for expenditures made after 12-31-79, in tax years ending after such date. Prior to amendment, Code Sec. 44C(c)(2)(B) read:

(B) CERTAIN LABOR COSTS INCLUDED.—The term "renewable energy source expenditure" includes expenditures for labor costs properly allocable to the onsite preparation, assembly, or original installation of renewable energy source property.

P.L. 96-223, §202(d):

Amended Code Sec. 44C(c)(2) by adding subparagraph (D). **Effective** for expenditures made after 12-31-79, in tax years ending after such date.

P.L. 96-223, §203(a)(1):

Amended Code Sec. 44C(c) by adding paragraph (10). **Effective** for tax years beginning after 12-31-80, but only with respect to financing or grants made after such date.

• 1978, Energy Tax Act of 1978 (P.L. 95-618)

P.L. 95-618, §101(a):

Added Code Sec. 44C. **Effective** for tax years ending on or after 4-20-77. This section shall not apply to expenditures made after 12-31-85.

[Sec. 24]

SEC. 24. CHILD TAX CREDIT.

»»→ Caution: Code Sec. 24(a), below, is subject to the sunset provisions of the Economic Growth and Tax Relief Reconciliation Act of 2001 (P.L. 107-16), §901, and the Jobs and Growth Tax Relief Reconciliation Act of 2003 (P.L. 108-27), §303. Absent Congressional action, the changes made to this provision by P.L. 107-16, and P.L. 108-27, or that take effect as if included in P.L. 107-16, and P.L. 108-27, do not apply after December 31, 2010. For more information about the sunset provisions, see page XXI of the Preface to this publication and P.L. 107-16, §901, P.L. 108-27, §303, and P.L. 108-311, §105, in the amendment notes. See the amendments notes for a history of amendments to this section and the effective date of each change.

[Sec. 24(a)]

(a) ALLOWANCE OF CREDIT.—There shall be allowed as a credit against the tax imposed by this chapter for the taxable year with respect to each qualifying child of the taxpayer for which the taxpayer is allowed a deduction under section 151 an amount equal to $1,000.

Amendments

• 2008, Fostering Connections to Success and Increasing Adoptions Act of 2008 (P.L. 110-351)

P.L. 110-351, §501(c)(1):

Amended Code Sec. 24(a) by inserting "for which the taxpayer is allowed a deduction under section 151" after "of the taxpayer". **Effective** for tax years beginning after 12-31-2008.

• 2004, Working Families Tax Relief Act of 2004 (P.L. 108-311)

P.L. 108-311, §101(a):

Amended Code Sec. 24(a). **Effective** for tax years beginning after 12-31-2003. Prior to amendment, Code Sec. 24(a) read as follows:

(a) ALLOWANCE OF CREDIT.—

(1) IN GENERAL.—There shall be allowed as a credit against the tax imposed by this chapter for the taxable year with respect to each qualifying child of the taxpayer an amount equal to the per child amount.

(2) PER CHILD AMOUNT.—For purposes of paragraph (1), the per child amount shall be determined as follows:

In the case of any taxable year beginning in—	*The per child amount is—*
2003 or 2004	$1,000
2005, 2006, 2007, or 2008	700
2009	800
2010 or thereafter	1,000.

P.L. 108-311, §105, provides:

SEC. 105. APPLICATION OF EGTRRA SUNSET TO THIS TITLE.

Each amendment made by this title shall be subject to title IX of the Economic Growth and Tax Relief Reconciliation Act of 2001 to the same extent and in the same manner as the provision of such Act to which such amendment relates.

• 2003, Jobs and Growth Tax Relief Reconciliation Act of 2003 (P.L. 108-27)

P.L. 108-27, §101(a):

Amended the item related to calendar years 2001 through 2004 in the table contained in Code Sec. 24(a)(2). **Effective** for tax years beginning after 12-31-2002. Prior to amendment, the item related to calendar years 2001 through 2004 in the table contained in Code Sec. 24(a)(2) read as follows:

2001, 2002, 2003, or 2004 . . . . $600

P.L. 108-27, §107, provides:

SEC. 107. APPLICATION OF EGTRRA SUNSET TO THIS TITLE.

Each amendment made by this title shall be subject to title IX of the Economic Growth and Tax Relief Reconciliation Act of 2001 to the same extent and in the same manner as the provision of such Act to which such amendment relates.

• 2001, Economic Growth and Tax Relief Reconciliation Act of 2001 (P.L. 107-16)

P.L. 107-16, §201(a):

Amended Code Sec. 24(a). **Effective** for tax years beginning after 12-31-2000. Prior to amendment, Code Sec. 24(a) read as follows:

(a) ALLOWANCE OF CREDIT.—There shall be allowed as a credit against the tax imposed by this chapter for the taxable year with respect to each qualifying child of the taxpayer an amount equal to $500 ($400 in the case of taxable years beginning in 1998).

P.L. 107-16, §901(a)-(b), provides:

SEC. 901. SUNSET OF PROVISIONS OF ACT.

(a) IN GENERAL.—All provisions of, and amendments made by, this Act shall not apply—

(1) to taxable, plan, or limitation years beginning after December 31, 2010, or

(2) in the case of title V, to estates of decedents dying, gifts made, or generation skipping transfers, after December 31, 2010.

(b) APPLICATION OF CERTAIN LAWS.—The Internal Revenue Code of 1986 and the Employee Retirement Income Security Act of 1974 shall be applied and administered to years, estates, gifts, and transfers described in subsection (a) as if the provisions and amendments described in subsection (a) had never been enacted.

»»→ Caution: The headings for Code Sec. 24(b) and Code Sec. 24(b)(1), below, are subject to the sunset provision of the Economic Growth and Tax Relief Reconciliation Act of 2001 (P.L. 107-16), §901. Absent Congressional action, the changes made to this provision by P.L. 107-16, or that take effect as if included in P.L. 107-16, do not apply after December 31, 2010. For more information about the sunset provision, see page XXI of the Preface to this publication and P.L. 107-16, §901, in the amendment notes. See the amendments notes for a history of amendments to this section and the effective date of each change.

[Sec. 24(b)]

(b) LIMITATIONS.—

(1) LIMITATION BASED ON ADJUSTED GROSS INCOME.—The amount of the credit allowable under subsection (a) shall be reduced (but not below zero) by $50 for each $1,000 (or fraction thereof) by which the taxpayer's modified adjusted gross income exceeds the threshold amount. For pur-

poses of the preceding sentence, the term "modified adjusted gross income" means adjusted gross income increased by any amount excluded from gross income under section 911, 931, or 933.

(2) THRESHOLD AMOUNT.—For purposes of paragraph (1), the term "threshold amount" means—

(A) $110,000 in the case of a joint return,

(B) $75,000 in the case of an individual who is not married, and

(C) $55,000 in the case of a married individual filing a separate return.

For purposes of this paragraph, marital status shall be determined under section 7703.

»»→ Caution: Code Sec. 24(b)(3), below, was added and amended by P.L. 107-16 and further amended by P.L. 109-135, and is subject to the sunset provision of the Economic Growth and Tax Relief Reconciliation Act of 2001 (P.L. 107-16), §901. Absent Congressional action, the changes made to this provision by P.L. 107-16, or that take effect as if included in P.L. 107-16, do not apply after December 31, 2010. For more information about the sunset provision, see page XXI of the Preface to this publication and P.L. 107-16, §901, and P.L. 109-135, §402(i)(3)(H), in the amendment notes. See the amendments notes for a history of amendments to this section and the effective date of each change.

(3) LIMITATION BASED ON AMOUNT OF TAX.—In the case of a taxable year to which section 26(a)(2) does not apply, the credit allowed under subsection (a) for any taxable year shall not exceed the excess of—

(A) the sum of the regular tax liability (as defined in section 26(b)) plus the tax imposed by section 55, over

»»→ Caution: Code Sec. 24(b)(3)(B), below, was amended by P.L. 111-5 and P.L. 111-148. For sunset provisions, see P.L. 111-5, §§1004(e), 1142(e), and 1144(d), and P.L. 111-148, §10909(c), in the amendment notes.

(B) the sum of the credits allowable under this subpart (other than this section and sections 25A(i), 25B, 25D, 30, 30B, and 30D) and section 27 for the taxable year.

Amendments

• 2010, Patient Protection and Affordable Care Act (P.L. 111-148)

P.L. 111-148, §10909(b)(2)(A):

Amended Code Sec. 24(b)(3)(B) by striking "23," before "25A(i)". **Effective** for tax years beginning after 12-31-2009.

P.L. 111-148, §10909(c), provides:

(c) APPLICATION AND EXTENSION OF EGTRRA SUNSET.—Notwithstanding section 901 of the Economic Growth and Tax Relief Reconciliation Act of 2001 [P.L. 107-16], such section shall apply to the amendments made by this section and the amendments made by section 202 of such Act by substituting "December 31, 2011" for "December 31, 2010" in subsection (a)(1) thereof.

• 2009, American Recovery and Reinvestment Tax Act of 2009 (P.L. 111-5)

P.L. 111-5, §1004(b)(1):

Amended Code Sec. 24(b)(3)(B) by inserting "25A(i)," after "23,". **Effective** for tax years beginning after 12-31-2008.

P.L. 111-5, §1004(e), provides:

(e) APPLICATION OF EGTRRA SUNSET.—The amendment made by subsection (b)(1) shall be subject to title IX of the Economic Growth and Tax Relief Reconciliation Act of 2001 [P.L. 107-16] in the same manner as the provision of such Act to which such amendment relates.

P.L. 111-5, §1142(b)(1)(A):

Amended Code Sec. 24(b)(3)(B) by inserting "30," after "25D,". **Effective** for vehicles acquired after 2-17-2009. For a transitional rule, see Act Sec. 1142(d) in the amendment notes for Code Sec. 30.

P.L. 111-5, §1142(e), provides:

(e) APPLICATION OF EGTRRA SUNSET.—The amendment made by subsection (b)(1)(A) shall be subject to title IX of the Economic Growth and Tax Relief Reconciliation Act of 2001 [P.L. 107-16] in the same manner as the provision of such Act to which such amendment relates.

P.L. 111-5, §1144(b)(1)(A):

Amended Code Sec. 24(b)(3)(B), as amended by this Act, by inserting "30B," after "30,". **Effective** for tax years beginning after 12-31-2008.

P.L. 111-5, §1144(d), provides:

(d) APPLICATION OF EGTRRA SUNSET.—The amendment made by subsection (b)(1)(A) shall be subject to title IX of the Economic Growth and Tax Relief Reconciliation Act of 2001 [P.L. 107-16] in the same manner as the provision of such Act to which such amendment relates.

• 2008, Energy Improvement and Extension Act of 2008 (P.L. 110-343)

P.L. 110-343, Division B, §106(e)(2)(B):

Amended Code Sec. 24(b)(3)(B) by striking "and 25B" and inserting ", 25B, and 25D". **Effective** for tax years beginning after 12-31-2007.

P.L. 110-343, Division B, §106(f)(3), provides:

(3) APPLICATION OF EGTRRA SUNSET.—The amendments made by subparagraphs (A) and (B) of subsection (e)(2) shall be subject to title IX of the Economic Growth and Tax Relief Reconciliation Act of 2001 [P.L. 107-16] in the same manner as the provisions of such Act to which such amendments relate.

P.L. 110-343, Division B, §205(d)(1)(A):

Amended Code Sec. 24(b)(3)(B), as amended by Act Sec. 106, by striking "and 25D" and inserting "25D, and 30D". **Effective** for tax years beginning after 12-31-2008.

P.L. 110-343, Division B, §205(f), provides:

(f) APPLICATION OF EGTRRA SUNSET.—The amendment made by subsection (d)(1)(A) shall be subject to title IX of the Economic Growth and Tax Relief Reconciliation Act of 2001 [P.L. 107-16] in the same manner as the provision of such Act to which such amendment relates.

• 2006, Pension Protection Act of 2006 (P.L. 109-280)

P.L. 109-280, §811, provides:

SEC. 811. PENSIONS AND INDIVIDUAL RETIREMENT ARRANGEMENT PROVISIONS OF ECONOMIC GROWTH AND TAX RELIEF RECONCILIATION ACT OF 2001 MADE PERMANENT.

Title IX of the Economic Growth and Tax Relief Reconciliation Act of 2001 [P.L. 107-16] shall not apply to the provisions of, and amendments made by, subtitles A through F of title VI [§§601-666]of such Act (relating to pension and individual retirement arrangement provisions).

• 2005, Gulf Opportunity Zone Act of 2005 (P.L. 109-135)

P.L. 109-135, §402(i)(3)(B)(i):

Amended the matter preceding Code Sec. 24(b)(3)(A) by striking "The credit" and inserting "In the case of a taxable year to which section 26(a)(2) does not apply, the credit". **Effective** for tax years beginning after 12-31-2005.

P.L. 109-135, §402(i)(3)(H), provides:

(H) APPLICATION OF EGTRRA SUNSET.—The amendments made by this paragraph (and each part thereof) shall be subject to title IX of the Economic Growth and Tax Relief Reconciliation Act of 2001 in the same manner as the provisions of such Act to which such amendment (or part thereof) relates.

• 2004, Working Families Tax Relief Act of 2004 (P.L. 108-311)

P.L. 108-311, §312(b)(2), provides:

(2) The amendments made by sections 201(b), 202(f), and 618(b) of the Economic Growth and Tax Relief Reconciliation Act of 2001 shall not apply to taxable years beginning during 2004 or 2005.

• 2002, Job Creation and Worker Assistance Act of 2002 (P.L. 107-147)

P.L. 107-147, §601(b)(2), provides:

(2) The amendments made by sections 201(b), 202(f), and 618(b) of the Economic Growth and Tax Relief Reconciliation Act of 2001 shall not apply to taxable years beginning during 2002 and 2003.

• 2001, Economic Growth and Tax Relief Reconciliation Act of 2001 (P.L. 107-16)

P.L. 107-16, §201(b)(1):

Amended Code Sec. 24(b) by adding at the end a new paragraph (3). **Effective** for tax years beginning after 12-31-2001. [But, see P.L. 107-147, §601(b)(2), and P.L. 108-311, §312(b)(2), above.—CCH.]

P.L. 107-16, §201(b)(2)(A):

Amended the heading for Code Sec. 24(b). **Effective** for tax years beginning after 12-31-2001. [But, see P.L. 107-147, §601(b)(2), and P.L. 108-311, §312(b)(2), above.—CCH.] Prior to amendment, the heading for Code Sec. 24(b) read as follows:

LIMITATION BASED ON ADJUSTED GROSS INCOME.—

P.L. 107-16, §201(b)(2)(B):

Amended the heading for Code Sec. 24(b)(1). **Effective** for tax years beginning after 12-31-2001. [But, see P.L. 107-147, §601(b)(2), and P.L. 108-311, §312(b)(2), above.—CCH.] Prior to amendment, the heading for Code Sec. 24(b)(1) read as follows:

IN GENERAL.—

P.L. 107-16, §202(f)(2)(B):

Amended Code Sec. 24(b)(3)(B), as added by Act Sec. 201(b), by striking "this section" and inserting "this section and section 23". **Effective** for tax years beginning after 12-31-2001. [But, see P.L. 107-147, §601(b)(2), and P.L. 108-311, §312(b)(2), above.—CCH.]

P.L. 107-16, §618(b)(2)(A) (as amended by P.L. 107-147, §417(23)(A)):

Amended Code Sec. 24(b)(3)(B), as amended by Act Secs. 201(b) [added by Act Sec. 201(b)(1)] and 202(f), by striking "section 23" and inserting "sections 23 and 25B". **Effective** for tax years beginning after 12-31-2001. [But, see P.L. 107-147, §601(b)(2), and P.L. 108-311, §312(b)(2), above.—CCH.]

P.L. 107-16, §901(a)-(b), provides [but see P.L. 109-280, §811, and P.L. 111-148, §10909(c), above]:

SEC. 901. SUNSET OF PROVISIONS OF ACT.

(a) IN GENERAL.—All provisions of, and amendments made by, this Act shall not apply—

(1) to taxable, plan, or limitation years beginning after December 31, 2010, or

(2) in the case of title V, to estates of decedents dying, gifts made, or generation skipping transfers, after December 31, 2010.

(b) APPLICATION OF CERTAIN LAWS.—The Internal Revenue Code of 1986 and the Employee Retirement Income Security Act of 1974 shall be applied and administered to years, estates, gifts, and transfers described in subsection (a) as if the provisions and amendments described in subsection (a) had never been enacted.

[Sec. 24(c)]

(c) QUALIFYING CHILD.—For purposes of this section—

(1) IN GENERAL.—The term "qualifying child" means a qualifying child of the taxpayer (as defined in section 152(c)) who has not attained age 17.

(2) EXCEPTION FOR CERTAIN NONCITIZENS.—The term "qualifying child" shall not include any individual who would not be a dependent if subparagraph (A) of section 152(b)(3) were applied without regard to all that follows "resident of the United States".

Amendments

• 2004, Working Families Tax Relief Act of 2004 (P.L. 108-311)

P.L. 108-311, §204(a):

Amended Code Sec. 24(c)(1). **Effective** for tax years beginning after 12-31-2004. Prior to amendment, Code Sec. 24(c)(1) read as follows:

(1) IN GENERAL.—The term "qualifying child" means any individual if—

(A) the taxpayer is allowed a deduction under section 151 with respect to such individual for the taxable year,

(B) such individual has not attained the age of 17 as of the close of the calendar year in which the taxable year of the taxpayer begins, and

(C) such individual bears a relationship to the taxpayer described in section 32(c)(3)(B).

P.L. 108-311, §204(b):

Amended Code Sec. 24(c)(2) by striking "the first sentence of section 152(b)(3)" and inserting "subparagraph (A) of section 152(b)(3)". **Effective** for tax years beginning after 12-31-2004.

[Sec. 24(d)]

(d) PORTION OF CREDIT REFUNDABLE.—

»»→ Caution: Code Sec. 24(d)(1), below, was amended by P.L. 109-135. For sunset provision, see P.L. 109-135, §402(i)(3)(H), in the amendment notes.

(1) IN GENERAL.—The aggregate credits allowed to a taxpayer under subpart C shall be increased by the lesser of—

(A) the credit which would be allowed under this section without regard to this subsection and the limitation under section 26(a)(2) or subsection (b)(3), as the case may be, or

(B) the amount by which the aggregate amount of credits allowed by this subpart (determined without regard to this subsection) would increase if the limitation imposed by section 26(a)(2) or subsection (b)(3), as the case may be, were increased by the greater of—

(i) 15 percent of so much of the taxpayer's earned income (within the meaning of section 32) which is taken into account in computing taxable income for the taxable year as exceeds $10,000, or

(ii) in the case of a taxpayer with 3 or more qualifying children, the excess (if any) of—

(I) the taxpayer's social security taxes for the taxable year, over

(II) the credit allowed under section 32 for the taxable year.

The amount of the credit allowed under this subsection shall not be treated as a credit allowed under this subpart and shall reduce the amount of credit otherwise allowable under subsection (a) without regard to section 26(a)(2) or subsection (b)(3), as the case may be. For purposes of subparagraph (B), any amount excluded from gross income by reason of section 112 shall be treated as earned income which is taken into account in computing taxable income for the taxable year.

»»→ Caution: Code Sec. 24(d)(2), below, was stricken by P.L. 107-16, and is subject to the sunset provision of the Economic Growth and Tax Relief Reconciliation Act of 2001 (P.L. 107-16), §901. Absent Congressional action, the changes made to this provision by P.L. 107-16, or that take effect as if included in P.L. 107-16, do not apply after December 31, 2010. For more information about the sunset provision, see page XXI of the Preface to this publication and P.L. 107-16, §901, in the amendment notes. See the amendments notes for a history of amendments to this section and the effective date of each change.

(2) [Stricken.]

»»→ Caution: Former Code Sec. 24(d)(3)-(4), below, was redesignated as Code Sec. 24(d)(2)-(3) by P.L. 107-16, and is subject to the sunset provision of the Economic Growth and Tax Relief Reconciliation Act of 2001 (P.L. 107-16), §901. Absent Congressional action, the changes made to this provision by P.L. 107-16, or that take effect as if included in P.L. 107-16, do not apply after December 31, 2010. For more information about the sunset provision, see page XXI of the Preface to this publication and P.L. 107-16, §901, in the amendment notes. See the amendments notes for a history of amendments to this section and the effective date of each change.

(2) SOCIAL SECURITY TAXES.—For purposes of paragraph (1)—

(A) IN GENERAL.—The term "social security taxes" means, with respect to any taxpayer for any taxable year—

(i) the amount of the taxes imposed by sections 3101 and 3201(a) on amounts received by the taxpayer during the calendar year in which the taxable year begins,

(ii) 50 percent of the taxes imposed by section 1401 on the self-employment income of the taxpayer for the taxable year, and

(iii) 50 percent of the taxes imposed by section 3211(a) on amounts received by the taxpayer during the calendar year in which the taxable year begins.

(B) COORDINATION WITH SPECIAL REFUND OF SOCIAL SECURITY TAXES.—The term "social security taxes" shall not include any taxes to the extent the taxpayer is entitled to a special refund of such taxes under section 6413(c).

(C) SPECIAL RULE.—Any amounts paid pursuant to an agreement under section 3121(l) (relating to agreements entered into by American employers with respect to foreign affiliates) which are equivalent to the taxes referred to in subparagraph (A)(i) shall be treated as taxes referred to in such subparagraph.

(3) INFLATION ADJUSTMENT.—In the case of any taxable year beginning in a calendar year after 2001, the $10,000 amount contained in paragraph (1)(B) shall be increased by an amount equal to—

(A) such dollar amount, multiplied by

(B) the cost-of-living adjustment determined under section 1(f)(3) for the calendar year in which the taxable year begins, determined by substituting "calendar year 2000" for "calendar year 1992" in subparagraph (B) thereof.

Any increase determined under the preceding sentence shall be rounded to the nearest multiple of $50.

(4) SPECIAL RULE FOR 2009 AND 2010.—Notwithstanding paragraph (3), in the case of any taxable year beginning in 2009 or 2010, the dollar amount in effect for such taxable year under paragraph (1)(B)(i) shall be $3,000.

Amendments

• 2009, American Recovery and Reinvestment Tax Act of 2009 (P.L. 111-5)

P.L. 111-5, §1003(a):

Amended Code Sec. 24(d)(4). **Effective** for tax years beginning after 12-31-2008. Prior to amendment, Code Sec. 24(d)(4) read as follows:

(4) SPECIAL RULE FOR 2008.—Notwithstanding paragraph (3), in the case of any taxable year beginning in 2008, the dollar amount in effect for such taxable year under paragraph (1)(B)(i) shall be $8,500.

• 2008, Tax Extenders and Alternative Minimum Tax Relief Act of 2008 (P.L. 110-343)

P.L. 110-343, Division C, §501(a):

Amended Code Sec. 24(d) by adding at the end a new paragraph (4). **Effective** for tax years beginning after 12-31-2007.

• 2007, Tax Technical Corrections Act of 2007 (P.L. 110-172)

P.L. 110-172, §11(c)(1)(A)-(B):

Amended Code Sec. 24(d)(1)(B) by striking "the excess (if any) of" in the matter preceding clause (i) and inserting "the greater of", and by striking "section" in clause (ii)(II) and inserting "section 32". **Effective** as if included in the provision of the Gulf Opportunity Zone Act of 2005 (P.L. 109-135) to which it relates [**effective** for tax years beginning after 12-31-2005.—CCH].

• 2005, Gulf Opportunity Zone Act of 2005 (P.L. 109-135)

P.L. 109-135, §402(i)(3)(B)(ii):

Amended Code Sec. 24(d)(1). **Effective** for tax years beginning after 12-31-2005. Prior to amendment, Code Sec. 24(d)(1) read as follows:

(1) IN GENERAL.—The aggregate credits allowed to a taxpayer under subpart C shall be increased by the lesser of—

(A) the credit which would be allowed under this section without regard to this subsection and the limitation under subsection (b)(3), or

(B) the amount by which the aggregate amount of credits allowed by this subpart (determined without regard to this subsection) would increase if the limitation imposed by subsection (b)(3) were increased by the greater of—

(i) 15 percent of so much of the taxpayer's earned income (within the meaning of section 32) which is taken into account in computing taxable income for the taxable year as exceeds $10,000, or

(ii) in the case of a taxpayer with 3 or more qualifying children, the excess (if any) of—

(I) the taxpayer's social security taxes for the taxable year, over

(II) the credit allowed under section 32 for the taxable year.

The amount of the credit allowed under this subsection shall not be treated as a credit allowed under this subpart and shall reduce the amount of credit otherwise allowable under subsection (a) without regard to subsection (b)(3). For purposes of subparagraph (B), any amount excluded from gross income by reason of section 112 shall be treated as earned income which is taken into account in computing taxable income for the taxable year.

P.L. 109-135, §402(i)(3)(H), provides:

(H) APPLICATION OF EGTRRA SUNSET.—The amendments made by this paragraph (and each part thereof) shall be subject to title IX of the Economic Growth and Tax Relief Reconciliation Act of 2001 in the same manner as the provisions of such Act to which such amendment (or part thereof) relates.

• 2005, Katrina Emergency Tax Relief Act of 2005 (P.L. 109-73)

P.L. 109-73, §406 [repealed by P.L. 109-135, §201(b)(4)(B)], provides:

SEC. 406. SPECIAL RULE FOR DETERMINING EARNED INCOME.

(a) IN GENERAL.—In the case of a qualified individual, if the earned income of the taxpayer for the taxable year which includes August 25, 2005, is less than the earned income of the taxpayer for the preceding taxable year, the credits allowed under sections 24(d) and 32 of the Internal Revenue Code of 1986 may, at the election of the taxpayer, be determined by substituting—

(1) such earned income for the preceding taxable year, for

(2) such earned income for the taxable year which includes August 25, 2005.

(b) QUALIFIED INDIVIDUAL.—For purposes of this section, the term "qualified individual" means any individual whose principal place of abode on August 25, 2005, was located—

(1) in the core disaster area, or

(2) in the Hurricane Katrina disaster area (but outside the core disaster area) and such individual was displaced from such principal place of abode by reason of Hurricane Katrina.

(c) EARNED INCOME.—For purposes of this section, the term "earned income" has the meaning given such term under section 32(c) of such Code.

(d) SPECIAL RULES.—

(1) APPLICATION TO JOINT RETURNS.—For purpose of subsection (a), in the case of a joint return for a taxable year which includes August 25, 2005—

(A) such subsection shall apply if either spouse is a qualified individual, and

(B) the earned income of the taxpayer for the preceding taxable year shall be the sum of the earned income of each spouse for such preceding taxable year.

(2) UNIFORM APPLICATION OF ELECTION.—Any election made under subsection (a) shall apply with respect to both section 24(d) and section 32 of such Code.

(3) ERRORS TREATED AS MATHEMATICAL ERROR.—For purposes of section 6213 of such Code, an incorrect use on a return of earned income pursuant to subsection (a) shall be treated as a mathematical or clerical error.

(4) NO EFFECT ON DETERMINATION OF GROSS INCOME, ETC.—Except as otherwise provided in this section, the Internal Revenue Code of 1986 shall be applied without regard to any substitution under subsection (a).

• 2004, Working Families Tax Relief Act of 2004 (P.L. 108-311)

P.L. 108-311, §102(a):

Amended Code Sec. 24(d)(1)(B)(i) by striking "(10 percent in the case of taxable years beginning before January 1, 2005)" following "15 percent". **Effective** for tax years beginning after 12-31-2003.

P.L. 108-311, §104(a):

Amended Code Sec. 24(d)(1) by adding at the end a new sentence. **Effective** for tax years beginning after 12-31-2003.

P.L. 108-311, §105, provides:

SEC. 105. APPLICATION OF EGTRRA SUNSET TO THIS TITLE.

Each amendment made by this title shall be subject to title IX of the Economic Growth and Tax Relief Reconciliation Act of 2001 to the same extent and in the same manner as the provision of such Act to which such amendment relates.

P.L. 108-311, §312(b)(2), provides:

(2) The amendments made by sections 201(b), 202(f), and 618(b) of the Economic Growth and Tax Relief Reconciliation Act of 2001 shall not apply to taxable years beginning during 2004 or 2005.

• 2002, Job Creation and Worker Assistance Act of 2002 (P.L. 107-147)

P.L. 107-147, §411(b):

Amended Code Sec. 24(d)(1)(B) by striking "amount of credit allowed by this section" and inserting "aggregate amount of credits allowed by this subpart". **Effective** as if included in the provision of P.L. 107-16 to which it relates [**effective** for tax years beginning after 12-31-2000.—CCH].

P.L. 107-147, §601(b)(2), provides:

(2) The amendments made by sections 201(b), 202(f), and 618(b) of the Economic Growth and Tax Relief Reconciliation Act of 2001 shall not apply to taxable years beginning during 2002 and 2003.

• 2001, Railroad Retirement and Survivors' Improvement Act of 2001 (P.L. 107-90)

P.L. 107-90, §204(e)(1), as amended by P.L. 108-311, §408(b)(4):

Amended Code Sec. 24(d)(2)(A)(iii) by striking "section 3211(a)(1)" and inserting "section 3211(a)". **Effective** for calendar years beginning after 12-31-2001.

• 2001, Economic Growth and Tax Relief Reconciliation Act of 2001 (P.L. 107-16)

P.L. 107-16, §201(b)(2)(C)(i)-(ii):

Amended Code Sec. 24(d), as amended by Act Sec. 201(c), by striking "section 26(a)" each place it appears and inserting "subsection (b)(3)", and in paragraph (1)(B) by striking "aggregate amount of credits allowed by this subpart" and inserting "amount of credit allowed by this section". [Note: The second part of this amendment was already made by Act Sec. 201(c)(1), applicable to tax years beginning after 12-31-2000.—CCH.] **Effective** for tax years beginning after 12-31-2001. [But, see P.L. 107-147, §601(b)(2), and P.L. 108-311, §312(b)(2), above.—CCH.]

P.L. 107-16, §201(c)(1):

Amended so much of Code Sec. 24(d) as precedes paragraph (2). **Effective** for tax years beginning after 12-31-2000. Prior to amendment, so much of Code Sec. 24(d) as preceded paragraph (2) read as follows:

(d) ADDITIONAL CREDIT FOR FAMILIES WITH 3 OR MORE CHILDREN.—

(1) IN GENERAL.—In the case of a taxpayer with three or more qualifying children for any taxable year, the aggregate credits allowed under subpart C shall be increased by the lesser of—

(A) the credit which would be allowed under this section without regard to this subsection and the limitation under section 26(a); or

(B) the amount by which the aggregate amount of credits allowed by this subpart (without regard to this subsection) would increase if the limitation imposed by section 26(a) were increased by the excess (if any) of—

(i) the taxpayer's social security taxes for the taxable year, over

(ii) the credit allowed under section 32 (determined without regard to subsection (n)) for the taxable year.

The amount of the credit allowed under this subsection shall not be treated as a credit allowed under this subpart and shall reduce the amount of credit otherwise allowable under subsection (a) without regard to section 26(a).

P.L. 107-16, §201(c)(2):

Amended Code Sec. 24(d) by adding at the end a new paragraph (4). **Effective** for tax years beginning after 12-31-2000.

P.L. 107-16, §201(d)(1)-(2):

Amended Code Sec. 24(d) by striking paragraph (2) and by redesignating paragraphs (3) and (4) as paragraphs (2) and (3), respectively. **Effective** for tax years beginning after 12-31-2000. Prior to being stricken, Code Sec. 24(d)(2) read as follows:

(2) REDUCTION OF CREDIT TO TAXPAYER SUBJECT TO ALTERNATIVE MINIMUM TAX.—For taxable years beginning after December 31, 2001, the credit determined under this subsection for the taxable year shall be reduced by the excess (if any) of—

(A) the amount of tax imposed by section 55 (relating to alternative minimum tax) with respect to such taxpayer for such taxable year, over

(B) the amount of the reduction under section 32(h) with respect to such taxpayer for such taxable year.

P.L. 107-16, §203, provides:

SEC. 203. REFUNDS DISREGARDED IN THE ADMINISTRATION OF FEDERAL PROGRAMS AND FEDERALLY ASSISTED PROGRAMS.

Any payment considered to have been made to any individual by reason of section 24 of the Internal Revenue Code of 1986, as amended by section 201, shall not be taken into account as income and shall not be taken into account as resources for the month of receipt and the following month, for purposes of determining the eligibility of such individual or any other individual for benefits or assistance, or the amount or extent of benefits or assistance, under any Federal program or under any State or local program financed in whole or in part with Federal funds.

P.L. 107-16, §901(a)-(b), provides:

SEC. 901. SUNSET OF PROVISIONS OF ACT.

(a) IN GENERAL.—All provisions of, and amendments made by, this Act shall not apply—

(1) to taxable, plan, or limitation years beginning after December 31, 2010, or

(2) in the case of title V, to estates of decedents dying, gifts made, or generation skipping transfers, after December 31, 2010.

(b) APPLICATION OF CERTAIN LAWS.—The Internal Revenue Code of 1986 and the Employee Retirement Income Security Act of 1974 shall be applied and administered to years, estates, gifts, and transfers described in subsection (a) as if the provisions and amendments described in subsection (a) had never been enacted.

• 1999, Tax Relief Extension Act of 1999 (P.L. 106-170)

P.L. 106-170, §501(b)(1):

Amended Code Sec. 24(d)(2) by striking "1998" and inserting "2001". **Effective** for tax years beginning after 12-31-98.

• 1998, Tax and Trade Relief Extension Act of 1998 (P.L. 105-277)

P.L. 105-277, §2001(b):

Amended Code Sec. 24(d)(2) by striking "The credit" and inserting "For taxable years beginning after December 31, 1998, the credit". **Effective** for tax years beginning after 12-31-97.

• 1998, IRS Restructuring and Reform Act of 1998 (P.L. 105-206)

P.L. 105-206, §6003(a)(1)(A)-(C):

Amended Code Sec. 24(d) by striking paragraphs (3) and (4), by redesignating paragraph (5) as paragraph (3), and by striking paragraphs (1) and (2) and inserting new paragraphs (1) and (2). **Effective** as if included in the provisions of P.L. 105-34 to which it relates [**effective** for tax years beginning after 12-31-97.—CCH]. Prior to amendment, Code Sec. 24(d)(1)-(4) read as follows:

(1) IN GENERAL.—In the case of a taxpayer with 3 or more qualifying children for any taxable year, the amount of the credit allowed under this section shall be equal to the greater of—

(A) the amount of the credit allowed under this section (without regard to this subsection and after application of the limitation under section 26), or

(B) the alternative credit amount determined under paragraph (2).

(2) ALTERNATIVE CREDIT AMOUNT.—For purposes of this subsection, the alternative credit amount is the amount of the credit which would be allowed under this section if the limitation under paragraph (3) were applied in lieu of the limitation under section 26.

(3) LIMITATION.—The limitation under this paragraph for any taxable year is the limitation under section 26 (without regard to this subsection)—

(A) increased by the taxpayer's social security taxes for such taxable year, and

(B) reduced by the sum of—

(i) the credits allowed under this part other than under subpart C or this section, and

(ii) the credit allowed under section 32 without regard to subsection (m) thereof.

(4) UNUSED CREDIT TO BE REFUNDABLE.—If the amount of the credit under paragraph (1)(B) exceeds the amount of the credit under paragraph (1)(A), such excess shall be treated as a credit to which subpart C applies. The rule of section 32(h) shall apply to such excess.

P.L. 105-206, §6003(a)(2):

Amended Code Sec. 24(d)(3), as redesignated by Act Sec. 6003(a)(1)(B), by striking "paragraph (3)" and inserting "paragraph (1)". **Effective** as if included in the provisions of P.L. 105-34 to which it relates [**effective** for tax years beginning after 12-31-97.—CCH].

[Sec. 24(e)]

(e) IDENTIFICATION REQUIREMENT.—No credit shall be allowed under this section to a taxpayer with respect to any qualifying child unless the taxpayer includes the name and taxpayer identification number of such qualifying child on the return of tax for the taxable year.

[Sec. 24(f)]

(f) TAXABLE YEAR MUST BE FULL TAXABLE YEAR.—Except in the case of a taxable year closed by reason of the death of the taxpayer, no credit shall be allowable under this section in the case of a taxable year covering a period of less than 12 months.

Amendments

• 1997, Taxpayer Relief Act of 1997 (P.L. 105-34)

P.L. 105-34, §101(a):

Amended subpart A of part IV of subchapter A of chapter 1 by inserting after Code Sec. 23 a new Code Sec. 24. **Effective** for tax years beginning after 12-31-97.

[Sec. 24—Repealed]

Amendments

• 1986, Tax Reform Act of 1986 (P.L. 99-514)

P.L. 99-514, §112(a):

Repealed Code Sec. 24. **Effective** for tax years beginning after 12-31-86.

Prior to repeal, Code Sec. 24 read as follows:

SEC. 24. CONTRIBUTIONS TO CANDIDATES FOR PUBLIC OFFICE.

[Sec. 24(a)]

(a) GENERAL RULE.—In the case of an individual, there shall be allowed, subject to the limitations of subsection (b), as a credit against the tax imposed by this chapter for the taxable year, an amount equal to one-half of all political contributions and all newsletter fund contributions, payment of which is made by the taxpayer within the taxable year.

Amendments

• 1984, Deficit Reduction Act of 1984 (P.L. 98-369)

P.L. 98-369, §471(c)(1):

Redesignated Code Sec. 41 as Code Sec. 24. **Effective** for tax years beginning after 12-31-83, and to carrybacks from such years.

• 1975 (P.L. 93-625)

P.L. 93-625, §11(a):

Amended Code Sec. 41(a) by adding "and all newsletter fund contributions". **Effective** with respect to any contribution the payment of which is made after 12-31-74, in tax years beginning after such date.

[Sec. 24(b)]

(b) LIMITATIONS.—

(1) MAXIMUM CREDIT.—The credit allowed by subsection (a) for a taxable year shall not exceed $50 ($100 in the case of a joint return under section 6013).

(2) VERIFICATION.—The credit allowed by subsection (a) shall be allowed, with respect to any political contribution or newsletter fund contribution, only if such contribution is verified in such manner as the Secretary shall prescribe by regulations.

Amendments

• 1984, Deficit Reduction Act of 1984 (P.L. 98-369)

P.L. 98-369, §474(f):

Amended Code Sec. 24(b), as redesignated by Act Sec. 482(c)(1), by striking out paragraph (2) and by redesignating paragraph (3) as paragraph (2). **Effective** for tax years beginning after 12-31-83, and to carrybacks from such years. Prior to amendment, paragraph (2) read as follows:

(2) APPLICATION WITH OTHER CREDITS.—The credit allowed by subsection (a) shall not exceed the amount of the tax imposed by this chapter for the taxable year reduced by the sum of the credits allowable under section 33 (relating to foreign tax credit), section 37 (relating to credit for the elderly and the permanently and totally disabled), and section 38 (relating to investment in certain depreciable property).

• 1983, Social Security Amendments of 1983 (P.L. 98-21)

P.L. 98-21, §122(c)(1):

Amended Code Sec. 41(b)(2) by striking out "relating to credit for the elderly" and inserting in place thereof "relating to credit for the elderly and the permanently and totally disabled". **Effective** for tax years beginning after 1983.

• 1978, Revenue Act of 1978 (P.L. 95-600)

P.L. 95-600, §113(c):

Amended Code Sec. 41(b)(1) by striking out "$25" and "$50" and inserting in place thereof "$50" and "$100". **Effective** for contributions made after 12-31-78, in tax years beginning after such date.

• 1976, Tax Reform Act of 1976 (P.L. 94-455)

P.L. 94-455, §503(b)(4):

Substituted "credit for the elderly" for "retirement income" in Code Sec. 41(b)(2). **Effective** for tax years beginning after 12-31-75.

P.L. 94-455, §1901(b)(1)(B):

Amended Code Sec. 41(b)(2) by striking out "section 35 (relating to partially tax-exempt interest),". **Effective** for tax years beginning after 12-31-76.

P.L. 94-455, §1906(b)(13)(A):

Amended 1954 Code by substituting "Secretary" for "Secretary or his delegate" each place it appeared. **Effective** 2-1-78.

• 1975 (P.L.93-625)

P.L. 93-625, §§11(b), 12(a):

Amended Code Sec. 41(b)(1) and (3). **Effective** for any contribution the payment of which is made after 12-31-74, in tax years beginning after such date. Prior to amendment, Code Sec. 41(b)(1) and (3) read as follows:

"(1) MAXIMUM CREDIT.—The credit allowed by subsection (a) for a taxable year shall be limited to $12.50 ($25 in the case of a joint return under section 6013).

* * *

"(3) VERIFICATION.—The credit allowed by subsection (a) shall be allowed, with respect to any political contribution, only if such political contribution is verified in such manner as the Secretary or his delegate shall prescribe by regulations."

[Sec. 24(c)]

(c) DEFINITIONS.—For purposes of this section—

(1) POLITICAL CONTRIBUTION.—The term "political contribution" means a contribution or gift of money to—

(A) an individual who is a candidate for nomination or election to any Federal, State, or local elective public office in any primary, general, or special election, for use by such individual to further his candidacy for nomination or election to such office;

(B) any committee, association, or organization (whether or not incorporated) organized and operated exclusively for the purpose of influencing, or attempting to influence, the nomination or election of one or more individuals who are candidates for nomination or election to any Federal, State, or local elective public office, for use by such committee, association, or organization to further the candidacy of such individual or individuals for nomination or election to such office;

(C) the national committee of a national political party;

(D) the State committee of a national political party as designated by the national committee of such party; or

(E) a local committee of a national political party as designated by the State committee of such party designated under subparagraph (D).

(2) CANDIDATE.—The term "candidate" means, with respect to any Federal, State, or local elective public office, an individual who—

(A) publicly announces before the close of the calendar year following the calendar year in which the contribution or gift is made that he is a candidate for nomination or election to such office; and

(B) meets the qualifications prescribed by law to hold such office.

(3) NATIONAL POLITICAL PARTY.—The term "national political party" means—

(A) in the case of contributions made during a taxable year of the taxpayer in which the electors of President and Vice President are chosen, a political party presenting candidates or electors for such offices on the official election ballot of ten or more States, or

(B) in the case of contributions made during any other taxable year of the taxpayer, a political party which met the qualifications described in subparagraph (A) in the last preceding election of a President and Vice President.

(4) STATE AND LOCAL.—The term "State" means the various States and the District of Columbia; and the term "local" means a political subdivision or part thereof, or two or more political subdivisions or parts thereof, of a State.

(5) NEWSLETTER FUND CONTRIBUTION.—The term "newsletter fund contribution" means a contribution or gift of money to a fund established and maintained by an individual who holds, has been elected to, or is a candidate for nomination or election to, any Federal, State, or local elective public office for use by such individual exclusively for the preparation and circulation of a newsletter.

Amendments

• 1975 (P.L. 93-625)

P.L. 93-625, §11(c), (e):

Amended Code Sec. 41(c) by amending subparagraph (2)(A) and adding paragraph (5). **Effective** for any contribution the payment of which is made after 12-31-74, in tax years beginning after such date. Prior to amendment, subparagraph (2)(A) read as follows:

"(A) has publicly announced that he is a candidate for nomination or election to such office; and".

[Sec. 24(d)]

(d) CROSS REFERENCES.—

(1) For disallowance of credits to estates and trusts, see section 642(a)(2).

(2) For treatment of Indian tribal governments as States (and the political subdivisions of Indian tribal governments as political subdivisions of States), see section 7871.

Amendments

• 1983 (P.L. 97-473)

P.L. 97-473, §202(b)(1):

Amended Code Sec. 41(d). For the **effective** date, see the amendment note for Act Sec. 204, following Code Sec. 7871. Prior to amendment, Code Sec. 41(d) read as follows:

"(d) **Cross References.—**

For disallowance of credits to estates and trusts, see section 642(a)(2)."

• 1976, Tax Reform Act of 1976 (P.L. 94-455)

P.L. 94-455, §1901(b)(1)(H)(ii):

Substituted "642(a)(2)" for "642(a)(3)" in Code Sec. 41(d). **Effective** for tax years beginning after 12-31-76.

• 1971, Revenue Act of 1971 (P.L. 92-178)

P.L. 92-178, §701(a):

Added Code Sec. 41. **Effective** for tax years ending after 12-31-71, but only with respect to political contributions, payment of which is made after such date.

[Sec. 25]

SEC. 25. INTEREST ON CERTAIN HOME MORTGAGES.

[Sec. 25(a)]

(a) ALLOWANCE OF CREDIT.—

(1) IN GENERAL.—There shall be allowed as a credit against the tax imposed by this chapter for the taxable year an amount equal to the product of—

(A) the certificate credit rate, and

(B) the interest paid or accrued by the taxpayer during the taxable year on the remaining principal of the certified indebtedness amount.

(2) LIMITATION WHERE CREDIT RATE EXCEEDS 20 PERCENT.—

(A) IN GENERAL.—If the certificate credit rate exceeds 20 percent, the amount of the credit allowed to the taxpayer under paragraph (1) for any taxable year shall not exceed $2,000.

(B) SPECIAL RULE WHERE 2 OR MORE PERSONS HOLD INTERESTS IN RESIDENCE.—If 2 or more persons hold interests in any residence, the limitation of subparagraph (A) shall be allocated among such persons in proportion to their respective interests in the residence.

[Sec. 25(b)]

(b) CERTIFICATE CREDIT RATE; CERTIFIED INDEBTEDNESS AMOUNT.—For purposes of this section—

(1) CERTIFICATE CREDIT RATE.—The term "certificate credit rate" means the rate of the credit allowable by this section which is specified in the mortgage credit certificate.

(2) CERTIFIED INDEBTEDNESS AMOUNT.—The term "certified indebtedness amount" means the amount of indebtedness which is—

(A) incurred by the taxpayer—

(i) to acquire the principal residence of the taxpayer,

(ii) as a qualified home improvement loan (as defined in section 143(k)(4)) with respect to such residence, or

(iii) as a qualified rehabilitation loan (as defined in section 143(k)(5)) with respect to such residence, and

(B) specified in the mortgage credit certificate.

[Sec. 25(c)]

(c) MORTGAGE CREDIT CERTIFICATE; QUALIFIED MORTGAGE CREDIT CERTIFICATE PROGRAM.—For purposes of this section—

(1) MORTGAGE CREDIT CERTIFICATE.—The term "mortgage credit certificate" means any certificate which—

(A) is issued under a qualified mortgage credit certificate program by the State or political subdivision having the authority to issue a qualified mortgage bond to provide financing on the principal residence of the taxpayer,

(B) is issued to the taxpayer in connection with the acquisition, qualified rehabilitation, or qualified home improvement of the taxpayer's principal residence,

(C) specifies—

(i) the certificate credit rate, and

(ii) the certified indebtedness amount, and

(D) is in such form as the Secretary may prescribe.

(2) QUALIFIED MORTGAGE CREDIT CERTIFICATE PROGRAM.—

(A) IN GENERAL.—The term "qualified mortgage credit certificate program" means any program—

(i) which is established by a State or political subdivision thereof for any calendar year for which it is authorized to issue qualified mortgage bonds,

(ii) under which the issuing authority elects (in such manner and form as the Secretary may prescribe) not to issue an amount of private activity bonds which it may otherwise issue during such calendar year under section 146,

(iii) under which the indebtedness certified by mortgage credit certificates meets the requirements of the following subsections of section 143 (as modified by subparagraph (B) of this paragraph):

(I) subsection (c) (relating to residence requirements),

(II) subsection (d) (relating to 3-year requirement),

(III) subsection (e) (relating to purchase price requirement),

(IV) subsection (f) (relating to income requirements),

(V) subsection (h) (relating to portion of loans required to be placed in targeted areas), and

(VI) paragraph (1) of subsection (i) (relating to other requirements),

(iv) under which no mortgage credit certificate may be issued with respect to any residence any of the financing of which is provided from the proceeds of a qualified mortgage bond or a qualified veterans' mortgage bond.

(v) except to the extent provided in regulations, which is not limited to indebtedness incurred from particular lenders,

(vi) except to the extent provided in regulations, which provides that a mortgage credit certificate is not transferrable, and

(vii) if the issuing authority allocates a block of mortgage credit certificates for use in connection with a particular development, which requires the developer to furnish to the issuing authority and the homebuyer a certificate that the price for the residence is no higher than it would be without the use of a mortgage credit certificate.

Under regulations, rules similar to the rules of subparagraphs (B) and (C) of section 143(a)(2) shall apply to the requirements of this subparagraph.

(B) MODIFICATIONS OF SECTION 143.—Under regulations prescribed by the Secretary, in applying section 143 for purposes of subclauses (II), (IV), AND (V) of subparagraph (A)(iii)—

(i) each qualified mortgage certificate credit program shall be treated as a separate issue,

(ii) the product determined by multiplying—

(I) the certified indebtedness amount of each mortgage credit certificate issued under such program, by

(II) the certificate credit rate specified in such certificate,

shall be treated as proceeds of such issue and the sum of such products shall be treated as the total proceeds of such issue, and

(iii) paragraph (1) of section 143(d) shall be applied by substituting "100 percent" for "95 percent or more".

Clause (iii) shall not apply if the issuing authority submits a plan to the Secretary for administering the 95-percent requirement of section 143(d)(1) and the Secretary is satisfied that such requirement will be met under such plan.

Amendments

• 1988, Technical and Miscellaneous Revenue Act of 1988 (P.L. 100-647)

P.L. 100-647, §1013(a)(25):

Amended Code Sec. 25(c)(2)(A)(ii) by striking out all that follows "an amount of" and inserting in lieu thereof "private activity bonds which it may otherwise issue during such calendar year under section 146,". **Effective** as if included in the provision of P.L. 99-514 to which it relates.

[Sec. 25(d)]

(d) DETERMINATION OF CERTIFICATE CREDIT RATE.—For purposes of this section—

(1) IN GENERAL.—The certificate credit rate specified in any mortgage credit certificate shall not be less than 10 percent or more than 50 percent.

(2) AGGREGATE LIMIT ON CERTIFICATE CREDIT RATES.—

(A) IN GENERAL.—In the case of each qualified mortgage credit certificate program, the sum of the products determined by multiplying—

(i) the certified indebtedness amount of each mortgage credit certificate issued under such program, by

(ii) the certificate credit rate with respect to such certificate,

shall not exceed 25 percent of the nonissued bond amount.

(B) NONISSUED BOND AMOUNT.—For purposes of subparagraph (A), the term "nonissued bond amount" means, with respect to any qualified mortgage credit certificate program, the amount of qualified mortgage bonds which the issuing authority is otherwise authorized to issue and elects not to issue under subsection (c)(2)(A)(ii).

[Sec. 25(e)]

(e) SPECIAL RULES AND DEFINITIONS.—For purposes of this section—

(1) CARRYFORWARD OF UNUSED CREDIT.—

(A) IN GENERAL.—If the credit allowable under subsection (a) for any taxable year exceeds the applicable tax limit for such taxable year, such excess shall be a carryover to each of the 3 succeeding taxable years and, subject to the limitations of subparagraph (B), shall be added to the credit allowable by subsection (a) for such succeeding taxable year.

(B) LIMITATION.—The amount of the unused credit which may be taken into account under subparagraph (A) for any taxable year shall not exceed the amount (if any) by which the applicable tax limit for such taxable year exceeds the sum of—

(i) the credit allowable under subsection (a) for which such taxable year determined without regard to this paragraph, and

(ii) the amounts which, by reason of this paragraph, are carried to such taxable year and are attributable to taxable years before the unused credit year.

»»→ Caution: Code Sec. 25(e)(1)(C), below, was amended by P.L. 107-16, P.L. 109-135, and P.L. 111-148, and is subject to the sunset provision of the Economic Growth and Tax Relief Reconciliation Act of 2001 (P.L. 107-16), §901. Absent Congressional action, the changes made to this provision by P.L. 107-16, or that take effect as if included in P.L. 107-16, do not apply after December 31, 2010. For more information about the sunset provision, see page XXI of the Preface to this publication and P.L. 107-16, §901, P.L. 109-135, §402(i)(3)(H), and P.L. 111-148, §10909(c), in the amendment notes. See the amendments notes for a history of amendments to this section and the effective date of each change.

(C) APPLICABLE TAX LIMIT.—For purposes of this paragraph, the term "applicable tax limit" means—

(i) in the case of a taxable year to which section 26(a)(2) applies, the limitation imposed by section 26(a)(2) for the taxable year reduced by the sum of the credits allowable under this subpart (other than this section and sections 25D, and 1400C), and

(ii) in the case of a taxable year to which section 26(a)(2) does not apply, the limitation imposed by section 26(a)(1) for the taxable year reduced by the sum of the credits allowable under this subpart (other than this section and sections 24, 25A(i), 25B, 25D, 30, 30B, 30D, and 1400C).

(2) INDEBTEDNESS NOT TREATED AS CERTIFIED WHERE CERTAIN REQUIREMENTS NOT IN FACT MET.—Subsection (a) shall not apply to any indebtedness if all the requirements of subsections (c)(1), (d), (e), (f), and (i) of section 143 and clauses (iv), (v), and (vii) of subsection (c)(2)(A), were not in fact met with respect to such indebtedness. Except to the extent provided in regulations, the requirements described in the preceding sentence shall be treated as met if there is a certification, under penalty of perjury, that such requirements are met.

(3) PERIOD FOR WHICH CERTIFICATE IN EFFECT.—

(A) IN GENERAL.—Except as provided in subparagraph (B), a mortgage credit certificate shall be treated as in effect with respect to interest attributable to the period—

(i) beginning on the date such certificate is issued, and

(ii) ending on the earlier of the date on which—

(I) the certificate is revoked by the issuing authority, or

(II) the residence to which such certificate relates ceases to be the principal residence of the individual to whom the certificate relates.

(B) CERTIFICATE INVALID UNLESS INDEBTEDNESS INCURRED WITHIN CERTAIN PERIOD.—A certificate shall not apply to any indebtedness which is incurred after the close of the second calendar year following the calendar year for which the issuing authority made the applicable election under subsection (c)(2)(A)(ii).

(C) NOTICE TO SECRETARY WHEN CERTIFICATE REVOKED.—Any issuing authority which revokes any mortgage credit certificate shall notify the Secretary of such revocation at such time and in such manner as the Secretary shall prescribe by regulations.

(4) REISSUANCE OF MORTGAGE CREDIT CERTIFICATES.—The Secretary may prescribe regulations which allow the administrator of a mortgage credit certificate program to reissue a mortgage credit certificate specifying a certified mortgage indebtedness that replaces the outstanding balance of the certified mortgage indebtedness specified on the original certificate to any taxpayer to whom the original certificate was issued, under such terms and conditions as the Secretary determines are necessary to ensure that the amount of the credit allowable under subsection (a) with respect to such reissued certificate is equal to or less than the amount of credit which would be allowable under subsection (a) with respect to the original certificate for any taxable year ending after such reissuance.

(5) PUBLIC NOTICE THAT CERTIFICATES WILL BE ISSUED.—At least 90 days before any mortgage credit certificate is to be issued after a qualified mortgage credit certificate program, the issuing authority shall provide reasonable public notice of—

(A) the eligibility requirements for such certificate,

(B) the methods by which such certificates are to be issued, and

(C) such other information as the Secretary may require.

(6) INTEREST PAID OR ACCRUED TO RELATED PERSONS.—No credit shall be allowed under subsection (a) for any interest paid or accrued to a person who is a related person to the taxpayer (within the meaning of section 144(a)(3)(A)).

(7) PRINCIPAL RESIDENCE.—The term "principal residence" has the same meaning as when used in section 121.

(8) QUALIFIED REHABILITATION AND HOME IMPROVEMENT.—

(A) QUALIFIED REHABILITATION.—The term "qualified rehabilitation" has the meaning given such term by section 143(k)(5)(B).

(B) QUALIFIED HOME IMPROVEMENT.—The term "qualified home improvement" means an alteration, repair, or improvement described in section 143(k)(4).

(9) QUALIFIED MORTGAGE BOND.—The term "qualified mortgage bond" has the meaning given such term by section 143(a)(1).

(10) MANUFACTURED HOUSING.—For purposes of this section, the term "single family residence" includes any manufactured home which has a minimum of 400 square feet of living space and a minimum width in excesss of 102 inches and which is of a kind customarily used at a fixed location. Nothing in the preceding sentence shall be construed as providing that such a home will be taken into account in making determinations under section 143.

Amendments

• 2010, Patient Protection and Affordable Care Act (P.L. 111-148)

P.L. 111-148, §10909(b)(2)(B):

Amended Code Sec. 25(e)(1)(C) by striking "23," after "other than this section and sections" both places it appears. **Effective** for tax years beginning after 12-31-2009.

P.L. 111-148, §10909(c), provides:

(c) APPLICATION AND EXTENSION OF EGTRRA SUNSET.—Notwithstanding section 901 of the Economic Growth and Tax Relief Reconciliation Act of 2001 [P.L. 107-16], such section shall apply to the amendments made by this section and the amendments made by section 202 of such Act by substituting "December 31, 2011" for "December 31, 2010" in subsection (a)(1) thereof.

• 2009, American Recovery and Reinvestment Tax Act of 2009 (P.L. 111-5)

P.L. 111-5, §1004(b)(2):

Amended Code Sec. 25(e)(1)(C)(ii) by inserting "25A(i)," after "24,". **Effective** for tax years beginning after 12-31-2008.

P.L. 111-5, §1142(b)(1)(B):

Amended Code Sec. 25(e)(1)(C)(ii) by inserting "30," after "25D,". **Effective** for vehicles acquired after 2-17-2009. For a transitional rule, see Act Sec. 1142(d) in the amendment notes for Code Sec. 30.

P.L. 111-5, §1144(b)(1)(B):

Amended Code Sec. 25(e)(1)(C)(ii), as amended by this Act, by inserting "30B," after "30,". **Effective** for tax years beginning after 12-31-2008.

• 2008, Energy Improvement and Extension Act of 2008 (P.L. 110-343)

P.L. 110-343, Division B, §205(d)(1)(B):

Amended Code Sec. 25(e)(1)(C)(ii) by inserting "30D," after "25D,". **Effective** for tax years beginning after 12-31-2008.

• 2006, Pension Protection Act of 2006 (P.L. 109-280)

P.L. 109-280, §811, provides:

SEC. 811. PENSIONS AND INDIVIDUAL RETIREMENT ARRANGEMENT PROVISIONS OF ECONOMIC GROWTH AND TAX RELIEF RECONCILIATION ACT OF 2001 MADE PERMANENT.

Title IX of the Economic Growth and Tax Relief Reconciliation Act of 2001 [P.L. 107-16] shall not apply to the provisions of, and amendments made by, subtitles A through F of title VI [§§601-666]of such Act (relating to pension and individual retirement arrangement provisions).

• 2005, Gulf Opportunity Zone Act of 2005 (P.L. 109-135)

P.L. 109-135, §402(i)(3)(C):

Amended Code Sec. 25(e)(1)(C). **Effective** for tax years beginning after 12-31-2005. Prior to amendment, Code Sec. 25(e)(1)(C) read as follows:

(C) APPLICABLE TAX LIMIT.—For purposes of this paragraph, the term "applicable tax limit" means the limitation imposed by section 26(a) for the taxable year reduced by the sum of the credits allowable under this subpart (this section and sections 23 and 1400C).

P.L. 109-135, §402(i)(3)(H), provides:

(H) APPLICATION OF EGTRRA SUNSET.—The amendments made by this paragraph (and each part thereof) shall be subject to title IX of the Economic Growth and Tax Relief Reconciliation Act of 2001 in the same manner as the provisions of such Act to which such amendment (or part thereof) relates.

P.L. 109-135, §402(i)(4):

Amended Act Sec. 1335(b) of P.L. 109-58 by striking paragraphs (1) through (3) and provided that the Internal Revenue Code of 1986 shall be applied and administered as if the amendments made [by] such paragraphs had never been enacted. **Effective** as if included in the provision of the Energy Policy Act of 2005 (P.L. 109-58) to which it relates. P.L. 109-58, §1335(b)(2) amended Code Sec. 25(e)(1)(C) by striking "this section and sections 23 and 1400C" and inserting "other than this section, section 23, section 25D, and section 1400C". This amendment reinstates the language "this section and sections 23 and 1400C" to Code Sec. 25(e)(1)(C).

• 2005, Energy Tax Incentives Act of 2005 (P.L. 109-58)

P.L. 109-58, §1335(b)(2) [stricken by P.L. 109-135, §402(i)(4)]:

Amended Code Sec. 25(e)(1)(C) by striking "this section and sections 23 and 1400C" and inserting "other than this section, section 23, section 25D, and section 1400C". **Effective** for property placed in service after 12-31-2005, in tax years ending after such date. [Note, this amendment cannot be made to the version of Code Sec. 25(e)(1)(C) as in effect on January 1, 2006.—CCH.]

• 2004, Working Families Tax Relief Act of 2004 (P.L. 108-311)

P.L. 108-311, §312(b)(2), provides:

(2) The amendments made by sections 201(b), 202(f), and 618(b) of the Economic Growth and Tax Relief Reconciliation Act of 2001 shall not apply to taxable years beginning during 2004 or 2005.

• 2002, Job Creation and Worker Assistance Act of 2002 (P.L. 107-147)

P.L. 107-147, §601(b)(2), provides:

(2) The amendments made by sections 201(b), 202(f), and 618(b) of the Economic Growth and Tax Relief Reconciliation Act of 2001 shall not apply to taxable years beginning during 2002 and 2003.

• 2001, Economic Growth and Tax Relief Reconciliation Act of 2001 (P.L. 107-16)

P.L. 107-16, §201(b)(2)(F):

Amended Code Sec. 25(e)(1)(C) by inserting ", 24," after "sections 23". **Effective** for tax years beginning after 12-31-2001. [But, see P.L. 107-147, §601(b)(2), and P.L. 108-311, §312(b)(2), above.—CCH].

P.L. 107-16, §618(b)(2)(B):

Amended Code Sec. 25(e)(1)(C), as amended by Act Sec. 201(b), by inserting "25B," after "24,". **Effective** for tax years beginning after 12-31-2001. [But, see P.L. 107-147, §601(b)(2), and P.L. 108-311, §312(b)(2), above.—CCH].

P.L. 107-16, §901(a)-(b), provides [but see P.L. 109-280, §811, and P.L. 111-148, §10909(c), above]:

SEC. 901. SUNSET OF PROVISIONS OF ACT.

(a) IN GENERAL.—All provisions of, and amendments made by, this Act shall not apply—

(1) to taxable, plan, or limitation years beginning after December 31, 2010, or

(2) in the case of title V, to estates of decedents dying, gifts made, or generation skipping transfers, after December 31, 2010.

(b) APPLICATION OF CERTAIN LAWS.—The Internal Revenue Code of 1986 and the Employee Retirement Income Security Act of 1974 shall be applied and administered to years, estates, gifts, and transfers described in subsection (a) as if the provisions and amendments described in subsection (a) had never been enacted.

• 1998, IRS Restructuring and Reform Act of 1998 (P.L. 105-206)

P.L. 105-206, §6008(d)(7):

Amended Code Sec. 25(e)(1)(C) by striking "section 23" and inserting "sections 23 and 1400C". **Effective** as if included in the provision of P.L. 105-34 to which it relates [**effective** 8-5-97.—CCH].

• 1997, Taxpayer Relief Act of 1997 (P.L. 105-34)

P.L. 105-34, §312(d)(1):

Amended Code Sec. 25(e)(7) by striking "section 1034" and inserting "section 121". **Effective** for sales and exchanges after 5-6-97.

• 1996, Small Business Job Protection Act of 1996 (P.L. 104-188)

P.L. 104-188, §1807(c)(1):

Amended Code Sec. 25(e)(1)(C) by inserting "and section 23" after "this section". **Effective** for tax years beginning after 12-31-96.

[Sec. 25(f)]

(f) REDUCTION IN AGGREGATE AMOUNT OF QUALIFIED MORTGAGE BONDS WHICH MAY BE ISSUED WHERE CERTAIN REQUIREMENTS NOT MET.—

(1) IN GENERAL.—If for any calendar year any mortgage credit certificate program which satisfies procedural requirements with respect to volume limitations prescribed by the Secretary fails to meet the requirements of paragraph (2) of subsection (d), such requirements shall be treated as satisfied with respect to any certified indebtedness of such program, but the applicable State ceiling under subsection (d) of section 146 for the State in which such program operates shall be reduced by 1.25 times the correction amount with respect to such failure. Such reduction shall be applied to such State ceiling for the calendar year following the calendar year in which the Secretary determines the correction amount with respect to such failure.

(2) CORRECTION AMOUNT.—

(A) IN GENERAL.—For purposes of paragraph (1), the term "correction amount" means an amount equal to the excess credit amount divided by 0.25.

(B) EXCESS CREDIT AMOUNT.—

(i) IN GENERAL.—For purposes of subparagraph (A)(ii), the term "excess credit amount" means the excess of—

(I) the credit amount for any mortgage credit certificate program, over

(II) the amount which would have been the credit amount for such program had such program met the requirements of paragraph (2) of subsection (d).

(ii) CREDIT AMOUNT.—For purposes of clause (i), the term "credit amount" means the sum of the products determined under clauses (i) and (ii) of subsection (d)(2)(A).

(3) SPECIAL RULE FOR STATES HAVING CONSTITUTIONAL HOME RULE CITIES.—In the case of a State having one or more constitutional home rule cities (within the meaning of section 146(d)(3)(C)), the reduction in the State ceiling by reason of paragraph (1) shall be allocated to the constitutional home rule city, or to the portion of the State not within such city, whichever caused the reduction.

(4) EXCEPTION WHERE CERTIFICATION PROGRAM.—The provisions of this subsection shall not apply in any case in which there is a certification program which is designed to ensure that the requirements of the section are met and which meets such requirements as the Secretary may by regulations prescribe.

(5) WAIVER.—The Secretary may waive the application of paragraph (1) in any case in which he determines that the failure is due to reasonable cause.

[Sec. 25(g)]

(g) REPORTING REQUIREMENTS.—Each person who makes a loan which is a certified indebtednesss amount under any mortgage credit certificate shall file a report with the Secretary containing—

(1) the name, address, and social security account number of the individual to which the certificate was issued,

(2) the certificate's issuer, date of issue, certified indebtedness amount, and certificate credit rate, and

(3) such other information as the Secretary may require by regulations.

Each person who issues a mortgage credit certificate shall file a report showing such information as the Secretary shall by regulations prescribe. Any such report shall be filed at such time and in such manner as the Secretary may require by regulations.

[Sec. 25(h)]

(h) REGULATIONS; CONTRACTS.—

(1) REGULATIONS.—The Secretary shall prescribe such regulations as may be necessary to carry out the purposes of this section, including regulations which may require recipients of mortgage credit certificates to pay a reasonable processing fee to defray the expenses incurred in administering the program.

(2) CONTRACTS.—The Secretary is authorized to enter into contracts with any person to provide services in connection with the administration of this section.

Amendments

• 1993, Omnibus Budget Reconciliation Act of 1993 (P.L. 103-66)

P.L. 103-66, §13141(b):

Amended Code Sec. 25 by striking subsection (h) and by redesignating subsections (i) and (j) as subsections (h) and (i), respectively. **Effective** for elections for periods after 6-30-92. Prior to repeal, Code Sec. 25(h) read as follows:

(h) TERMINATION.—No election may be made under subsection (c)(2)(A)(ii) for any period after June 30, 1992.

• 1991, Tax Extension Act of 1991 (P.L. 102-227)

P.L. 102-227, §108(b):

Amended Code Sec. 25(h) by striking "December 31, 1991" and inserting "June 30, 1992". **Effective** for elections for periods after 12-31-91.

• 1990, Omnibus Budget Reconciliation Act of 1990 (P.L. 101-508)

P.L. 101-508, §11408(b):

Amended Code Sec. 25(h) by striking "September 30, 1990" and inserting "December 31, 1991". **Effective** for elections for periods after 9-30-90.

• 1989, Omnibus Budget Reconciliation Act of 1989 (P.L. 101-239)

P.L. 101-239, §7104(b):

Amended Code Sec. 25(h) by striking "for any calendar year after 1989" and inserting "for any period after September 30, 1990". **Effective** 12-19-89.

• 1988, Technical and Miscellaneous Revenue Act of 1988 (P.L. 100-647)

P.L. 100-647, §1013(a)(26):

Amended Code Sec. 25(h) by striking out "1987" and inserting in lieu thereof "1988". **Effective** as if included in the provision of P.L. 99-514 to which it relates.

P.L. 100-647, §4005(a)(2):

Amended Code Sec. 25(h) (as amended by Act Sec. 1013(a)(26)) by striking out "1988" and inserting in lieu thereof "1989".

• 1986, Tax Reform Act of 1986 (P.L. 99-514)

P.L. 99-514, §1301(f)(1)(A):

Amended Code Sec. 25(d)(2)(A) by striking out "20 percent" and inserting in lieu thereof "25 percent". **Effective** for nonissued bond amounts elected after 8-15-86.

P.L. 99-514, §1301(f)(1)(B):

Amended Code Sec. 25(f)(2)(A) by striking out "0.20" and inserting in lieu thereof "0.25". **Effective** for nonissued bond amounts elected after 8-15-86.

P.L. 99-514, §1301(f)(2)(A):

Amended Code Sec. 25(b)(2)(A)(ii) by striking out "section 103A(1)(6)" and inserting in lieu thereof "section 143(k)(4)". **Effective** for certificates issued with respect to non-issued bond amounts elected after 8-15-86 [Amended by P.L. 100-647, §1013(b)(2)].

P.L. 99-514, §1301(f)(2)(B):

Amended Code Sec. 25(b)(2)(A)(iii) by striking out "section 103(A)(1)(7)" and inserting in lieu thereof "section 143(k)(5)". **Effective** for certificates issued with respect to non-issued bond amounts elected after 8-15-86 [Amended by P.L. 100-647, §1013(b)(2)].

P.L. 99-514, §1301(f)(2)(C)(i):

Amended Code Sec. 25(c)(2)(A)(iii) and (B) by striking out "section 103A" each place it appears and inserting in lieu thereof "section 143". **Effective** for certificates issued with respect to non-issued bond amounts elected after 8-15-86 [Amended by P.L. 100-647, §1013(b)(2)].

P.L. 99-514, §1301(f)(2)(C)(ii):

Amended Code Sec. 25(c)(2)(A)(ii) by striking out "section 103A" each place it appears and inserting in lieu thereof "section 103". **Effective** for certificates issued with respect to non-issued bond amounts elected after 8-15-86 [Amended by P.L. 100-647, §1013(b)(2)]. Prior to amendment, Code Sec. 25(c)(2)(A)(ii) read as follows:

(ii) under which the issuing authority elects (in such manner and form as the Secretary may prescribe) not to issue an amount of qualified mortgage bonds which it may otherwise issue during such calendar year under section 103A,

P.L. 99-514, §1301(f)(2)(D):

Amended Code Sec. 25(c)(2)(A)(iii) by striking out all the subclauses thereof and inserting in lieu thereof new subclauses (I)—(VI). **Effective** for certificates issued with respect to non-issued bond amounts elected after 8-15-86 [Amended by P.L. 100-647, §1013(b)(2)]. Prior to amendment, Code Sec. 25(c)(2)(A)(iii) read as follows:

(iii) under which the indebtedness certified by mortgage credit certificates meets the requirements of the following subsections of section 103A (as modified by subparagraph (B) of this paragraph):

(I) subsection (d) (relating to residence requirements),

(II) subsection (e) (relating to 3-year requirement),

(III) subsection (f) (relating to purchase price requirement),

(IV) subsection (h) (relating to portion of loans required to be placed in targeted areas), and

(V) subsection (j), other than paragraph (2) thereof (relating to other requirements).

P.L. 99-514, §1301(f)(2)(E):

Amended Code Sec. 25(c)(2)(A) by striking out "section 103A(c)(2)" in the last sentence and inserting in lieu thereof "section 143(a)(2)". **Effective** for certificates issued with respect to non-issued bond amounts elected after 8-15-86 [Amended by P.L. 100-647, §1013(b)(2)].

P.L. 99-514, §1301(f)(2)(F)(i)-(ii):

Amended Code Sec. 25(c)(2)(B) by striking out "subclauses (II) and (IV)" and inserting in lieu thereof "subclauses (II), (IV), and (V)", and by striking out clause (iii) and all that follows and inserting in lieu thereof new clause (iii) and the flush sentence. **Effective** for certificates issued with respect to non-issued bond amounts elected after 8-15-86 [Amended by P.L. 100-647, §1013(b)(2)]. Prior to amendment, Code Sec. 25(c)(2)(B) read as follows:

(B) MODIFICATIONS OF SECTION 103A.—Under regulations prescribed by the Secretary, in applying section 103A for purposes of subclauses (II) and (IV) of subparagraph (A)(iii)—

(i) each qualified mortgage certificate credit program shall be treated as a separate issue,

(ii) the product determined by multiplying—

(I) the certified indebtedness amount of each mortgage credit certificate issued under such program, by

(II) the certificate credit rate specified in such certificate, shall be treated as proceeds of such issue and the sum of such products shall be treated as the total proceeds of such issue, and

(iii) paragraph (1) of section 103A(e) shall be applied by substituting "100 percent" for "90 percent or more".

Clause (iii) shall not apply if the issuing authority submits a plan to the Secretary for administering the 90-percent requirement of section 103A(e)(1) and the Secretary is satisfied that such requirement will be met under such plan.

P.L. 99-514, §1301(f)(2)(G):

Amended Code Sec. 25(d) by striking out paragraph (3). **Effective** for certificates issued with respect to non-issued bond amounts elected after 8-15-86 [Amended by P.L. 100-647, §1013(b)(2)]. Prior to amendment, Code Sec. 25(d)(3) read as follows:

(3) ADDITIONAL LIMIT IN CERTAIN CASES.—In the case of a qualified mortgage credit certificate program in a State which—

(A) has a State ceiling (as defined in section 103A(g)(4)) for the year an election is made that exceeds 20 percent of the average annual aggregate principal amount of mortgages executed during the immediately preceding 3 calendar years for single family owner-occupied residences located within the jurisdiction of such State, or

(B) issued qualified mortgage bonds in an aggregate amount less than $150,000,000 for calendar year 1983,

the certificate credit rate for any mortgage credit certificate shall not exceed 20 percent unless the issuing authority submits a plan to the Secretary to ensure that the weighted average of the certificate credit rates in such mortgage credit certificate program does not exceed 20 percent and the Secretary approves such plan.

P.L. 99-514, §1301(f)(2)(H):

Amended Code Sec. 25(e)(2) by striking out "subsection (d)(1), (e), (f), and (j) of section 103A" and inserting in lieu thereof "subsections (c)(1), (d), (e), (f), and (i) of section 143". **Effective** for certificates issued with respect to non-issued bond amounts elected after 8-15-86 [Amended by P.L. 100-647, §1013(b)(2)].

P.L. 99-514, §1301(f)(2)(I):

Amended Code Sec. 25(e)(6) by striking out "section 103(b)(6)(C)(i)" and inserting in lieu thereof "section 144(a)(3)(A)". **Effective** for certificates issued with respect to non-issued bond amounts elected after 8-15-86 [Amended by P.L. 100-647, §1013(b)(2)].

P.L. 99-514, §1301(f)(2)(J):

Amended Code Sec. 25(e)(8)(A) by striking out "section 103A(1)(7)(B)" and inserting in lieu thereof "section 143(k)(5)(B)". **Effective** for certificates issued with respect to non-issued bond amounts elected after 8-15-86 [Amended by P.L. 100-647, §1013(b)(2)].

P.L. 99-514, §1301(f)(2)(K):

Amended Code Sec. 25(e)(8)(B) by striking out "section 103A(1)(6)" and inserting in lieu thereof "section 143(k)(4)". **Effective** for certificates issued with respect to non-issued bond amounts elected after 8-15-86 [Amended by P.L. 100-647, §1013(b)(2)].

P.L. 99-514, §1301(f)(2)(L):

Amended Code Sec. 25(e)(9) by striking out "section 103A(c)(1)" and inserting in lieu thereof "section 143(a)(1)". **Effective** for certificates issued with respect to non-issued bond amounts elected after 8-15-86 [Amended by P.L. 100-647, §1013(b)(2)].

P.L. 99-514, §1301(f)(2)(M):

Amended Code Sec. 25(e)(10) by striking out "section 103A" and inserting in lieu thereof "section 143". **Effective** for certificates issued with respect to non-issued bond amounts elected after 8-15-86 [Amended by P.L. 100-647, §1013(b)(2)].

P.L. 99-514, §1301(f)(2)(N):

Amended Code Sec. 25(f)(1) by striking out "paragraph (4) of section 103A(g)" and inserting in lieu thereof "subsection (d) of section 146". **Effective** for certificates issued with respect to non-issued bond amounts elected after 8-15-86 [Amended by P.L. 100-647, §1013(b)(2)].

P.L. 99-514, §1301(f)(2)(O):

Amended Code Sec. 25(f)(3) by striking out "section 103A(g)(5)(C)" and inserting in lieu thereof "section 146(d)(3)(C)". **Effective** for certificates issued with respect to non-issued bond amounts elected after 8-15-86 [Amended by P.L. 100-647, §1013(b)(2)].

P.L. 99-514, §1862(a):

Amended Code Sec. 25(c)(2)(A)(iii)(V) by striking out "paragraph (1) of subsection (j)" and inserting in lieu thereof "subsection (j), other than paragraph (2) thereof". **Effective** as if included in the provisions of P.L. 98-369 to which it relates.

P.L. 99-514, §1862(b):

Amended Code Sec. 25(c)(2)(A) by adding at the end thereof a new sentence. **Effective** as if included in the provisions of P.L. 98-369 to which it relates.

P.L. 99-514, §1862(c):

Amended Code Sec. 25(e)(1)(B). **Effective** as if included in the provisions of P.L. 98-369 to which it relates. Prior to amendment, Code Sec. 25(e)(1)(B) read as follows:

(B) LIMITATION.—The amount of the unused credit which may be taken into account under subparagraph (A) for any taxable year shall not exceed the amount by which the applicable tax limit for such taxable year exceeds the sum of the amounts which, by reason of this paragraph, are carried to such taxable year and are attributable to taxable years before the unused credit year.

P.L. 99-514, §1862(d)(1):

Amended Code Sec. 25(a)(1)(B) by striking out "paid or incurred" and inserting in lieu thereof "paid or accrued". **Effective** as if included in the provisions of P.L. 98-369 to which it relates.

P.L. 99-514, §1899A(1):

Amended Code Sec. 25(f)(4) by striking out "insure" and inserting in lieu thereof "ensure". **Effective** 10-22-86.

• 1984, Deficit Reduction Act of 1984 (P.L. 98-369)

P.L. 98-369, §612(a):

Redesignated former Code Sec. 25, as added by Act Sec. 472, as Code Sec. 26 and added new Code Sec. 25. **Effective** for interest paid or accrued after 12-31-84, on indebtedness incurred after 12-31-84, and to elections under section 25(c)(2)(A)(ii) of the Internal Revenue Code of 1954 (as added by this Act) for calendar years after 1983. For rules relating to special elections and transitional rules, see Act Sec. 611(d)(3)-(7), which appears in the amendment notes for Code Sec. 103A(o).

[Sec. 25(i)]

(i) RECAPTURE OF PORTION OF FEDERAL SUBSIDY FROM USE OF MORTGAGE CREDIT CERTIFICATES.—

For provisions increasing the tax imposed by this chapter to recapture a portion of the Federal subsidy from the use of mortgage credit certificates, see section 143(m).

Amendments

• 1993, Omnibus Budget Reconciliation Act of 1993 (P.L. 103-66)

P.L. 103-66, §13141(b):

Amended Code Sec. 25 by redesignating subsection (j) as subsection (i). **Effective** for elections for periods after 6-30-92.

• 1988, Technical and Miscellaneous Revenue Act of 1988 (P.L. 100-647)

P.L. 100-647, §4005(g)(7):

Amended Code Sec. 25 by adding at the end thereof new subsection (j). **Effective**, generally, to bonds issued, and nonissued bond amounts elected, after 12-31-88. For special rules, see Act Sec. 4005(h)(2) and (3), below.

P.L. 100-647, §4005(h)(2) and (3), provide:

(2) SPECIAL RULES RELATING TO CERTAIN REQUIREMENTS AND REFUNDING BONDS.—In the case of a bond issued to refund (or which is part of a series of bonds issued to refund) a bond issued before January 1, 1989—

(A) the amendments made by subsections (b) and (c) shall apply to financing provided after the date of issuance of the refunding issue, and

(B) the amendment made by subsection (f) shall apply to payments (including on loans made before such date of issuance) received on or after such date of issuance.

(3) SUBSECTION (g).—

(A) IN GENERAL.—Except as provided in subparagraph (B), the amendments made by subsection (g) shall apply to financing provided, and mortgage credit certificates issued, after December 31, 1990.

(B) EXCEPTION.—The amendments made by subsection (g) shall not apply to financing provided pursuant to a binding contract (entered into before June 23, 1988) with a homebuilder, lender, or mortgagor if the bonds (the proceeds of which are used to provide such financing) are issued—

(i) before June 23, 1988, or

(ii) before August 1, 1988, pursuant to a written application (made before July 1, 1988) for State bond volume authority.

[Sec. 25A]

SEC. 25A. HOPE AND LIFETIME LEARNING CREDITS.

[Sec. 25A(a)]

(a) ALLOWANCE OF CREDIT.—In the case of an individual, there shall be allowed as a credit against the tax imposed by this chapter for the taxable year the amount equal to the sum of—

(1) the Hope Scholarship Credit, plus

(2) the Lifetime Learning Credit.

Amendments

• 2009, American Recovery and Reinvestment Tax Act of 2009 (P.L. 111-5)

P.L. 111-5, §1004(f), provides:

(f) TREASURY STUDIES REGARDING EDUCATION INCENTIVES.—

(1) STUDY REGARDING COORDINATION WITH NON-TAX STUDENT FINANCIAL ASSISTANCE.—The Secretary of the Treasury and the Secretary of Education, or their delegates, shall—

(A) study how to coordinate the credit allowed under section 25A of the Internal Revenue Code of 1986 with the Federal Pell Grant program under section 401 of the Higher Education Act of 1965 to maximize their effectiveness at promoting college affordability, and

(B) examine ways to expedite the delivery of the tax credit.

(2) STUDY REGARDING INCLUSION OF COMMUNITY SERVICE REQUIREMENTS.—The Secretary of the Treasury and the Secretary of Education, or their delegates, shall study the feasibility of requiring including community service as a condition of taking their tuition and related expenses into account under section 25A of the Internal Revenue Code of 1986.

(3) REPORT.—Not later than 1 year after the date of the enactment of this Act, the Secretary of the Treasury, or the Secretary's delegate, shall report to Congress on the results of the studies conducted under this paragraph.

[Sec. 25A(b)]

(b) HOPE SCHOLARSHIP CREDIT.—

(1) PER STUDENT CREDIT.—In the case of any eligible student for whom an election is in effect under this section for any taxable year, the Hope Scholarship Credit is an amount equal to the sum of—

(A) 100 percent of so much of the qualified tuition and related expenses paid by the taxpayer during the taxable year (for education furnished to the eligible student during any academic period beginning in such taxable year) as does not exceed $1,000, plus

(B) 50 percent of such expenses so paid as exceeds $1,000 but does not exceed the applicable limit.

(2) LIMITATIONS APPLICABLE TO HOPE SCHOLARSHIP CREDIT.—

(A) CREDIT ALLOWED ONLY FOR 2 TAXABLE YEARS.—An election to have this section apply with respect to any eligible student for purposes of the Hope Scholarship Credit under subsection (a)(1) may not be made for any taxable year if such an election (by the taxpayer or any other individual) is in effect with respect to such student for any 2 prior taxable years.

(B) CREDIT ALLOWED FOR YEAR ONLY IF INDIVIDUAL IS AT LEAST 1/2 TIME STUDENT FOR PORTION OF YEAR.—The Hope Scholarship Credit under subsection (a)(1) shall not be allowed for a taxable year with respect to the qualified tuition and related expenses of an individual unless such individual is an eligible student for at least one academic period which begins during such year.

(C) CREDIT ALLOWED ONLY FOR FIRST 2 YEARS OF POSTSECONDARY EDUCATION.—The Hope Scholarship Credit under subsection (a)(1) shall not be allowed for a taxable year with respect to the qualified tuition and related expenses of an eligible student if the student has completed (before the beginning of such taxable year) the first 2 years of postsecondary education at an eligible educational institution.

(D) DENIAL OF CREDIT IF STUDENT CONVICTED OF A FELONY DRUG OFFENSE.—The Hope Scholarship Credit under subsection (a)(1) shall not be allowed for qualified tuition and related expenses for the enrollment or attendance of a student for any academic period if such student has been convicted of a Federal or State felony offense consisting of the possession or distribution of a controlled substance before the end of the taxable year with or within which such period ends.

(3) ELIGIBLE STUDENT.—For purposes of this subsection, the term "eligible student" means, with respect to any academic period, a student who—

(A) meets the requirements of section 484(a)(1) of the Higher Education Act of 1965 (20 U.S.C. 1091(a)(1)), as in effect on the date of the enactment of this section, and

(B) is carrying at least 1/2 the normal full-time work load for the course of study the student is pursuing.

(4) APPLICABLE LIMIT.—For purposes of paragraph (1)(B), the applicable limit for any taxable year is an amount equal to 2 times the dollar amount in effect under paragraph (1)(A) for such taxable year.

[Sec. 25A(c)]

(c) LIFETIME LEARNING CREDIT.—

(1) PER TAXPAYER CREDIT.—The Lifetime Learning Credit for any taxpayer for any taxable year is an amount equal to 20 percent of so much of the qualified tuition and related expenses paid by the taxpayer during the taxable year (for education furnished during any academic period beginning in such taxable year) as does not exceed $10,000 ($5,000 in the case of taxable years beginning before January 1, 2003).

(2) SPECIAL RULES FOR DETERMINING EXPENSES.—

(A) COORDINATION WITH HOPE SCHOLARSHIP.—The qualified tuition and related expenses with respect to an individual who is an eligible student for whom a Hope Scholarship Credit under subsection (a)(1) is allowed for the taxable year shall not be taken into account under this subsection.

(B) EXPENSES ELIGIBLE FOR LIFETIME LEARNING CREDIT.—For purposes of paragraph (1), qualified tuition and related expenses shall include expenses described in subsection (f)(1) with respect to any course of instruction at an eligible educational institution to acquire or improve job skills of the individual.

[Sec. 25A(d)]

(d) LIMITATION BASED ON MODIFIED ADJUSTED GROSS INCOME.—

(1) IN GENERAL.—The amount which would (but for this subsection) be taken into account under subsection (a) for the taxable year shall be reduced (but not below zero) by the amount determined under paragraph (2).

(2) AMOUNT OF REDUCTION.—The amount determined under this paragraph is the amount which bears the same ratio to the amount which would be so taken into account as—

(A) the excess of—

(i) the taxpayer's modified adjusted gross income for such taxable year, over

(ii) $40,000 ($80,000 in the case of a joint return), bears to

(B) $10,000 ($20,000 in the case of a joint return).

(3) MODIFIED ADJUSTED GROSS INCOME.—The term "modified adjusted gross income" means the adjusted gross income of the taxpayer for the taxable year increased by any amount excluded from gross income under section 911, 931, or 933.

»»→ Caution: Code Sec. 25A(e), below, is subject to the sunset provision of the Economic Growth and Tax Relief Reconciliation Act of 2001 (P.L. 107-16), §901. Absent Congressional action, the changes made to this provision by P.L. 107-16, or that take effect as if included in P.L. 107-16, do not apply after December 31, 2010. For more information about the sunset provision, see page XXI of the Preface to this publication and P.L. 107-16, §901, in the amendment notes. See the amendments notes for a history of amendments to this section and the effective date of each change.

[Sec. 25A(e)]

(e) ELECTION NOT TO HAVE SECTION APPLY.—A taxpayer may elect not to have this section apply with respect to the qualified tuition and related expenses of an individual for any taxable year.

Amendments

• 2001, Economic Growth and Tax Relief Reconciliation Act of 2001 (P.L. 107-16)

P.L. 107-16, §401(g)(2)(A):

Amended Code Sec. 25A(e). **Effective** for tax years beginning after 12-31-2001. Prior to amendment, Code Sec. 25A(e) read as follows:

(e) ELECTION TO HAVE SECTION APPLY.—

(1) IN GENERAL.—No credit shall be allowed under subsection (a) for a taxable year with respect to the qualified tuition and related expenses of an individual unless the taxpayer elects to have this section apply with respect to such individual for such year.

(2) COORDINATION WITH EXCLUSIONS.—An election under this subsection shall not take effect with respect to an individual for any taxable year if any portion of any distribution during such taxable year from an education individual retirement account is excluded from gross income under section 530(d)(2).

P.L. 107-16, §901(a)-(b), provides:

SEC. 901. SUNSET OF PROVISIONS OF ACT.

(a) IN GENERAL.—All provisions of, and amendments made by, this Act shall not apply—

(1) to taxable, plan, or limitation years beginning after December 31, 2010, or

(2) in the case of title V, to estates of decedents dying, gifts made, or generation skipping transfers, after December 31, 2010.

(b) APPLICATION OF CERTAIN LAWS.—The Internal Revenue Code of 1986 and the Employee Retirement Income Security Act of 1974 shall be applied and administered to years, estates, gifts, and transfers described in subsection (a) as if the provisions and amendments described in subsection (a) had never been enacted.

[Sec. 25A(f)]

(f) DEFINITIONS.—For purposes of this section—

(1) QUALIFIED TUITION AND RELATED EXPENSES.—

(A) IN GENERAL.—The term "qualified tuition and related expenses" means tuition and fees required for the enrollment or attendance of—

(i) the taxpayer,

(ii) the taxpayer's spouse, or

(iii) any dependent of the taxpayer with respect to whom the taxpayer is allowed a deduction under section 151,

at an eligible educational institution for courses of instruction of such individual at such institution.

(B) EXCEPTION FOR EDUCATION INVOLVING SPORTS, ETC.—Such term does not include expenses with respect to any course or other education involving sports, games, or hobbies, unless such course or other education is part of the individual's degree program.

(C) EXCEPTION FOR NONACADEMIC FEES.—Such term does not include student activity fees, athletic fees, insurance expenses, or other expenses unrelated to an individual's academic course of instruction.

(2) ELIGIBLE EDUCATIONAL INSTITUTION.—The term "eligible educational institution" means an institution—

(A) which is described in section 481 of the Higher Education Act of 1965 (20 U.S.C. 1088), as in effect on the date of the enactment of this section, and

(B) which is eligible to participate in a program under title IV of such Act.

[Sec. 25A(g)]

(g) SPECIAL RULES.—

(1) IDENTIFICATION REQUIREMENT.—No credit shall be allowed under subsection (a) to a taxpayer with respect to the qualified tuition and related expenses of an individual unless the taxpayer includes the name and taxpayer identification number of such individual on the return of tax for the taxable year.

(2) ADJUSTMENT FOR CERTAIN SCHOLARSHIPS, ETC.—The amount of qualified tuition and related expenses otherwise taken into account under subsection (a) with respect to an individual for an academic period shall be reduced (before the application of subsections (b), (c), and (d)) by the

sum of any amounts paid for the benefit of such individual which are allocable to such period as—

(A) a qualified scholarship which is excludable from gross income under section 117,

(B) an educational assistance allowance under chapter 30, 31, 32, 34, or 35 of title 38, United States Code, or under chapter 1606 of title 10, United States Code, and

(C) a payment (other than a gift, bequest, devise, or inheritance within the meaning of section 102(a)) for such individual's educational expenses, or attributable to such individual's enrollment at an eligible educational institution, which is excludable from gross income under any law of the United States.

(3) TREATMENT OF EXPENSES PAID BY DEPENDENT.—If a deduction under section 151 with respect to an individual is allowed to another taxpayer for a taxable year beginning in the calendar year in which such individual's taxable year begins—

(A) no credit shall be allowed under subsection (a) to such individual for such individual's taxable year, and

(B) qualified tuition and related expenses paid by such individual during such individual's taxable year shall be treated for purposes of this section as paid by such other taxpayer.

(4) TREATMENT OF CERTAIN PREPAYMENTS.—If qualified tuition and related expenses are paid by the taxpayer during a taxable year for an academic period which begins during the first 3 months following such taxable year, such academic period shall be treated for purposes of this section as beginning during such taxable year.

(5) DENIAL OF DOUBLE BENEFIT.—No credit shall be allowed under this section for any expense for which a deduction is allowed under any other provision of this chapter.

(6) NO CREDIT FOR MARRIED INDIVIDUALS FILING SEPARATE RETURNS.—If the taxpayer is a married individual (within the meaning of section 7703), this section shall apply only if the taxpayer and the taxpayer's spouse file a joint return for the taxable year.

(7) NONRESIDENT ALIENS.—If the taxpayer is a nonresident alien individual for any portion of the taxable year, this section shall apply only if such individual is treated as a resident alien of the United States for purposes of this chapter by reason of an election under subsection (g) or (h) of section 6013.

[Sec. 25A(h)]

(h) INFLATION ADJUSTMENTS.—

(1) DOLLAR LIMITATION ON AMOUNT OF CREDIT.—

(A) IN GENERAL.—In the case of a taxable year beginning after 2001, each of the $1,000 amounts under subsection (b)(1) shall be increased by an amount equal to—

(i) such dollar amount, multiplied by

(ii) the cost-of-living adjustment determined under section 1(f)(3) for the calendar year in which the taxable year begins, determined by substituting "calendar year 2000" for "calendar year 1992" in subparagraph (B) thereof.

(B) ROUNDING.—If any amount as adjusted under subparagraph (A) is not a multiple of $100, such amount shall be rounded to the next lowest multiple of $100.

(2) INCOME LIMITS.—

(A) IN GENERAL.—In the case of a taxable year beginning after 2001, the $40,000 and $80,000 amounts in subsection (d)(2) shall each be increased by an amount equal to—

(i) such dollar amount, multiplied by

(ii) the cost-of-living adjustment determined under section 1(f)(3) for the calendar year in which the taxable year begins, determined by substituting "calendar year 2000" for "calendar year 1992" in subparagraph (B) thereof.

(B) ROUNDING.—If any amount as adjusted under subparagraph (A) is not a multiple of $1,000, such amount shall be rounded to the next lowest multiple of $1,000.

[Sec. 25A(i)]

(i) AMERICAN OPPORTUNITY TAX CREDIT .—In the case of any taxable year beginning in 2009 or 2010—

(1) INCREASE IN CREDIT .—The Hope Scholarship Credit shall be an amount equal to the sum of—

(A) 100 percent of so much of the qualified tuition and related expenses paid by the taxpayer during the taxable year (for education furnished to the eligible student during any academic period beginning in such taxable year) as does not exceed $2,000, plus

(B) 25 percent of such expenses so paid as exceeds $2,000 but does not exceed $4,000.

(2) CREDIT ALLOWED FOR FIRST 4 YEARS OF POST-SECONDARY EDUCATION .—Subparagraphs (A) and (C) of subsection (b)(2) shall be applied by substituting "4" for "2".

(3) QUALIFIED TUITION AND RELATED EXPENSES TO INCLUDE REQUIRED COURSE MATERIALS .—Subsection (f)(1)(A) shall be applied by substituting "tuition, fees, and course materials" for "tuition and fees".

(4) INCREASE IN AGI LIMITS FOR HOPE SCHOLARSHIP CREDIT .—In lieu of applying subsection (d) with respect to the Hope Scholarship Credit, such credit (determined without regard to this paragraph) shall be reduced (but not below zero) by the amount which bears the same ratio to such credit (as so determined) as—

(A) the excess of—

(i) the taxpayer's modified adjusted gross income (as defined in subsection (d)(3)) for such taxable year, over

(ii) $80,000 ($160,000 in the case of a joint return), bears to

(B) $10,000 ($20,000 in the case of a joint return).

(5) CREDIT ALLOWED AGAINST ALTERNATIVE MINIMUM TAX .—In the case of a taxable year to which section 26(a)(2) does not apply, so much of the credit allowed under subsection (a) as is attributable to the Hope Scholarship Credit shall not exceed the excess of—

(A) the sum of the regular tax liability (as defined in section 26(b)) plus the tax imposed by section 55, over

»»→ Caution: Code Sec. 25A(i)(5)(B), below, was amended by P.L. 111-148. For sunset provision, see P.L. 111-148, §10909(c), in the amendment notes.

(B) the sum of the credits allowable under this subpart (other than this subsection and sections 25D and 30D) and section 27 for the taxable year.

Any reference in this section or section 24, 25, 26, 25B, 904, or 1400C to a credit allowable under this subsection shall be treated as a reference to so much of the credit allowable under subsection (a) as is attributable to the Hope Scholarship Credit.

(6) PORTION OF CREDIT MADE REFUNDABLE .—40 percent of so much of the credit allowed under subsection (a) as is attributable to the Hope Scholarship Credit (determined after application of paragraph (4) and without regard to this paragraph and section 26(a)(2) or paragraph (5), as the case may be) shall be treated as a credit allowable under subpart C (and not allowed under subsection (a)). The preceding sentence shall not apply to any taxpayer for any taxable year if such taxpayer is a child to whom subsection (g) of section 1 applies for such taxable year.

(7) COORDINATION WITH MIDWESTERN DISASTER AREA BENEFITS .—In the case of a taxpayer with respect to whom section 702(a)(1)(B) of the Heartland Disaster Tax Relief Act of 2008 applies for any taxable year, such taxpayer may elect to waive the application of this subsection to such taxpayer for such taxable year.

Amendments

• 2010, Patient Protection and Affordable Care Act (P.L. 111-148)

P.L. 111-148, §10909(b)(2)(C):

Amended Code Sec. 25A(i)(5)(B) by striking "23, 25D," and inserting "25D". **Effective** for tax years beginning after 12-31-2009.

P.L. 111-148, §10909(c), provides:

(c) APPLICATION AND EXTENSION OF EGTRRA SUNSET.—Notwithstanding section 901 of the Economic Growth and Tax Relief Reconciliation Act of 2001 [P.L. 107-16], such section shall apply to the amendments made by this section and the amendments made by section 202 of such Act by substituting "December 31, 2011" for "December 31, 2010" in subsection (a)(1) thereof.

• 2009, American Recovery and Reinvestment Tax Act of 2009 (P.L. 111-5)

P.L. 111-5, §1004(a):

Amended Code Sec. 25A by redesignating subsection (i) as subsection (j) and by inserting after subsection (h) a new subsection (i). **Effective** for tax years beginning after 12-31-2008.

P.L. 111-5, §1004(c), provides:

(c) TREATMENT OF POSSESSIONS.—

(1) PAYMENTS TO POSSESSIONS.—

(A) MIRROR CODE POSSESSION.—The Secretary of the Treasury shall pay to each possession of the United States with a mirror code tax system amounts equal to the loss to that possession by reason of the application of section 25A(i)(6) of the Internal Revenue Code of 1986 (as added by this section) with respect to taxable years beginning in 2009 and 2010. Such amounts shall be determined by the Secretary of the Treasury based on information provided by the government of the respective possession.

(B) OTHER POSSESSIONS.—The Secretary of the Treasury shall pay to each possession of the United States which does not have a mirror code tax system amounts estimated by the Secretary of the Treasury as being equal to the aggregate benefits that would have been provided to residents of such possession by reason of the application of section 25A(i)(6) of such Code (as so added) for taxable years beginning in 2009 and 2010 if a mirror code tax system had been in effect in such possession. The preceding sentence shall not apply with respect to any possession of the United States unless such possession has a plan, which has been approved by the Secretary of the Treasury, under which such possession will promptly distribute such payments to the residents of such possession.

(2) COORDINATION WITH CREDIT ALLOWED AGAINST UNITED STATES INCOME TAXES.—Section 25A(i)(6) of such Code (as added by this section) shall not apply to a bona fide resident of any possession of the United States.

(3) DEFINITIONS AND SPECIAL RULES.—

(A) POSSESSION OF THE UNITED STATES.—For purposes of this subsection, the term "possession of the United States" includes the Commonwealth of Puerto Rico and the Commonwealth of the Northern Mariana Islands.

(B) MIRROR CODE TAX SYSTEM.—For purposes of this subsection, the term "mirror code tax system" means, with respect to any possession of the United States, the income tax system of such possession if the income tax liability of the residents of such possession under such system is determined by reference to the income tax laws of the United States as if such possession were the United States.

(C) TREATMENT OF PAYMENTS.—For purposes of section 1324(b)(2) of title 31, United States Code, the payments under this subsection shall be treated in the same manner as a refund due from the credit allowed under section 25A of the Internal Revenue Code of 1986 by reason of subsection (i)(6) of such section (as added by this section).

P.L. 107-16, §901(a)-(b), provides [but see P.L. 111-148, §10909(c), above]:

SEC. 901. SUNSET OF PROVISIONS OF ACT.

(a) IN GENERAL.—All provisions of, and amendments made by, this Act shall not apply—

(1) to taxable, plan, or limitation years beginning after December 31, 2010, or

(2) in the case of title V, to estates of decedents dying, gifts made, or generation skipping transfers, after December 31, 2010.

(b) APPLICATION OF CERTAIN LAWS.—The Internal Revenue Code of 1986 and the Employee Retirement Income Security Act of 1974 shall be applied and administered to years, estates, gifts, and transfers described in subsection (a) as if the provisions and amendments described in subsection (a) had never been enacted.

[Sec. 25A(j)]

(j) REGULATIONS.—The Secretary may prescribe such regulations as may be necessary or appropriate to carry out this section, including regulations providing for a recapture of the credit allowed under this section in cases where there is a refund in a subsequent taxable year of any amount which was taken into account in determining the amount of such credit.

Amendments

• 2009, American Recovery and Reinvestment Tax Act of 2009 (P.L. 111-5)

P.L. 111-5, §1004(a):

Amended Code Sec. 25A by redesignating subsection (i) as subsection (j). **Effective** for tax years beginning after 12-31-2008.

• 1997, Taxpayer Relief Act of 1997 (P.L. 105-34)

P.L. 105-34, §201(a):

Amended subpart A of part IV of subchapter A of chapter 1 by inserting after Code Sec. 25 a new Code Sec. 25A. **Effective**, generally, for expenses paid after 12-31-97 (in tax years ending after such date), for education furnished in academic periods beginning after such date. For a special rule, see Act Sec. 201(f)(2), below.

P.L. 105-34, §201(f)(2), provides:

(2) LIFETIME LEARNING CREDIT.—Section 25A(a)(2) of the Internal Revenue Code of 1986 shall apply to expenses paid after June 30, 1998 (in taxable years ending after such date), for education furnished in academic periods beginning after such dates.

[Sec. 25B]

SEC. 25B. ELECTIVE DEFERRALS AND IRA CONTRIBUTIONS BY CERTAIN INDIVIDUALS.

[Sec. 25B(a)]

(a) ALLOWANCE OF CREDIT.—In the case of an eligible individual, there shall be allowed as a credit against the tax imposed by this subtitle for the taxable year an amount equal to the applicable percentage of so much of the qualified retirement savings contributions of the eligible individual for the taxable year as do not exceed $2,000.

[Sec. 25B(b)]

(b) APPLICABLE PERCENTAGE.—For purposes of this section—

(1) JOINT RETURNS.—In the case of a joint return, the applicable percentage is—

(A) if the adjusted gross income of the taxpayer is not over $30,000, 50 percent,

(B) if the adjusted gross income of the taxpayer is over $30,000 but not over $32,500, 20 percent,

(C) if the adjusted gross income of the taxpayer is over $32,500 but not over $50,000, 10 percent, and

(D) if the adjusted gross income of the taxpayer is over $50,000, zero percent.

(2) OTHER RETURNS.—In the case of—

(A) a head of household, the applicable percentage shall be determined under paragraph (1) except that such paragraph shall be applied by substituting for each dollar amount therein (as adjusted under paragraph (3)) a dollar amount equal to 75 percent of such dollar amount, and

(B) any taxpayer not described in paragraph (1) or subparagraph (A), the applicable percentage shall be determined under paragraph (1) except that such paragraph shall be applied by substituting for each dollar amount therein (as adjusted under paragraph (3)) a dollar amount equal to 50 percent of such dollar amount.

(3) INFLATION ADJUSTMENT.—In the case of any taxable year beginning in a calendar year after 2006, each of the dollar amount[s]in paragraph (1) shall be increased by an amount equal to—

(A) such dollar amount, multiplied by

(B) the cost-of-living adjustment determined under section 1(f)(3) for the calendar year in which the taxable year begins, determined by substituting "calendar year 2005" for "calendar year 1992" in subparagraph (B) thereof.

Any increase determined under the preceding sentence shall be rounded to the nearest multiple of $500.

Amendments

• 2006, Pension Protection Act of 2006 (P.L. 109-280)

P.L. 109-280, §833(a):

Amended Code Sec. 25B(b). **Effective** for tax years beginning after 2006. Prior to amendment, Code Sec. 25B(b) read as follows:

(b) APPLICABLE PERCENTAGE.—For purposes of this section, the applicable percentage is the percentage determined in accordance with the following table:

Adjusted Gross Income						
Joint return		*Head of a household*		*All other cases*		*Applicable*
Over	*Not over*	*Over*	*Not over*	*Over*	*Not over*	*percentage*
	$30,000		$22,500		$15,000	50
30,000	32,500	22,500	24,375	15,000	16,250	20
32,500	50,000	24,375	37,500	16,250	25,000	10
50,000		37,500		25,000		0

[Sec. 25B(c)]

(c) ELIGIBLE INDIVIDUAL.—For purposes of this section—

(1) IN GENERAL.—The term "eligible individual" means any individual if such individual has attained the age of 18 as of the close of the taxable year.

(2) DEPENDENTS AND FULL-TIME STUDENTS NOT ELIGIBLE.—The term "eligible individual" shall not include—

(A) any individual with respect to whom a deduction under section 151 is allowed to another taxpayer for a taxable year beginning in the calendar year in which such individual's taxable year begins, and

(B) any individual who is a student (as defined in section 152(f)(2)).

Amendments

• 2004, Working Families Tax Relief Act of 2004 (P.L. 108-311)

P.L. 108-311, §207(4):

Amended Code Sec. 25B(c)(2)(B) by striking "151(c)(4)" and inserting "152(f)(2)". **Effective** for tax years beginning after 12-31-2004.

[Sec. 25B(d)]

(d) QUALIFIED RETIREMENT SAVINGS CONTRIBUTIONS.—For purposes of this section—

(1) IN GENERAL.—The term "qualified retirement savings contributions" means, with respect to any taxable year, the sum of—

(A) the amount of the qualified retirement contributions (as defined in section 219(e)) made by the eligible individual,

(B) the amount of—

(i) any elective deferrals (as defined in section 402(g)(3)) of such individual, and

(ii) any elective deferral of compensation by such individual under an eligible deferred compensation plan (as defined in section 457(b)) of an eligible employer described in section 457(e)(1)(A), and

(C) the amount of voluntary employee contributions by such individual to any qualified retirement plan (as defined in section 4974(c)).

(2) REDUCTION FOR CERTAIN DISTRIBUTIONS.—

(A) IN GENERAL.—The qualified retirement savings contributions determined under paragraph (1) shall be reduced (but not below zero) by the aggregate distributions received by the individual during the testing period from any entity of a type to which contributions under paragraph (1) may be made. The preceding sentence shall not apply to the portion of any distribution which is not includible in gross income by reason of a trustee-to-trustee transfer or a rollover distribution.

(B) TESTING PERIOD.—For purposes of subparagraph (A), the testing period, with respect to a taxable year, is the period which includes—

(i) such taxable year,

(ii) the 2 preceding taxable years, and

(iii) the period after such taxable year and before the due date (including extensions) for filing the return of tax for such taxable year.

(C) EXCEPTED DISTRIBUTIONS.—There shall not be taken into account under subparagraph (A)—

(i) any distribution referred to in section 72(p), 401(k)(8), 401(m)(6), 402(g)(2), 404(k), or 408(d)(4), and

(ii) any distribution to which section 408A(d)(3) applies.

(D) TREATMENT OF DISTRIBUTIONS RECEIVED BY SPOUSE OF INDIVIDUAL.—For purposes of determining distributions received by an individual under subparagraph (A) for any taxable year, any distribution received by the spouse of such individual shall be treated as received by such individual if such individual and spouse file a joint return for such taxable year and for the taxable year during which the spouse receives the distribution.

Amendments

• 2006, Pension Protection Act of 2006 (P.L. 109-280)

P.L. 109-280, §811, provides:

SEC. 811. PENSIONS AND INDIVIDUAL RETIREMENT ARRANGEMENT PROVISIONS OF ECONOMIC GROWTH AND TAX RELIEF RECONCILIATION ACT OF 2001 MADE PERMANENT.

Title IX of the Economic Growth and Tax Relief Reconciliation Act of 2001 [P.L. 107-16] shall not apply to the provisions of, and amendments made by, subtitles A through F of title VI [§§601-666]of such Act (relating to pension and individual retirement arrangement provisions).

• 2002, Job Creation and Worker Assistance Act of 2002 (P.L. 107-147)

P.L. 107-147, §411(m):

Amended Code Sec. 25B(d)(2)(A). **Effective** as if included in the provision of P.L. 107-16 to which it relates [**effective** for tax years beginning after 12-31-2001.—CCH]. Prior to amendment, Code Sec. 25B(d)(2)(A) read as follows:

(A) IN GENERAL.—The qualified retirement savings contributions determined under paragraph (1) shall be reduced (but not below zero) by the sum of—

(i) any distribution from a qualified retirement plan (as defined in section 4974(c)), or from an eligible deferred compensation plan (as defined in section 457(b)), received by the individual during the testing period which is includible in gross income, and

(ii) any distribution from a Roth IRA or a Roth account received by the individual during the testing period which is not a qualified rollover contribution (as defined in section 408A(e)) to a Roth IRA or a rollover under section 402(c)(8)(B) to a Roth account.

• 2001, Economic Growth and Tax Relief Reconciliation Act of 2001 (P.L. 107-16)

P.L. 107-16, §901(a)-(b), provides [but see P.L. 109-280, §811, above]:

SEC. 901. SUNSET OF PROVISIONS OF ACT.

(a) IN GENERAL.—All provisions of, and amendments made by, this Act shall not apply—

(1) to taxable, plan, or limitation years beginning after December 31, 2010, or

(2) in the case of title V, to estates of decedents dying, gifts made, or generation skipping transfers, after December 31, 2010.

(b) APPLICATION OF CERTAIN LAWS.—The Internal Revenue Code of 1986 and the Employee Retirement Income Security Act of 1974 shall be applied and administered to years, estates, gifts, and transfers described in subsection (a) as if the provisions and amendments described in subsection (a) had never been enacted.

[Sec. 25B(e)]

(e) ADJUSTED GROSS INCOME.—For purposes of this section, adjusted gross income shall be determined without regard to sections 911, 931, and 933.

[Sec. 25B(f)]

(f) INVESTMENT IN THE CONTRACT.—Notwithstanding any other provision of law, a qualified retirement savings contribution shall not fail to be included in determining the investment in the contract for purposes of section 72 by reason of the credit under this section.

»»→ Caution: Code Sec. 25B(g), below, was amended by P.L. 109-135. For sunset provision, see P.L. 109-135, §402(i)(3)(H), in the amendment notes.

[Sec. 25B(g)]

(g) LIMITATION BASED ON AMOUNT OF TAX.—In the case of a taxable year to which section 26(a)(2) does not apply, the credit allowed under subsection (a) for the taxable year shall not exceed the excess of—

(1) the sum of the regular tax liability (as defined in section 26(b)) plus the tax imposed by section 55, over

»»→ Caution: Code Sec. 25B(g)(2), below, was amended by P.L. 111-148. For sunset provision, see P.L. 111-148, §10909(c), in the amendment notes.

(2) the sum of the credits allowable under this subpart (other than this section and sections 25A(i), 25D, 30, 30B, and 30D) and section 27 for the taxable year.

Amendments

• 2010, Patient Protection and Affordable Care Act (P.L. 111-148)

P.L. 111-148, §10909(b)(2)(D):

Amended Code Sec. 25B(g)(2) by striking "23," before "25A(i)". **Effective** for tax years beginning after 12-31-2009.

P.L. 111-148, §10909(c), provides:

(c) APPLICATION AND EXTENSION OF EGTRRA SUNSET.—Notwithstanding section 901 of the Economic Growth and Tax Relief Reconciliation Act of 2001 [P.L. 107-16], such section shall apply to the amendments made by this section and the amendments made by section 202 of such Act by substituting "December 31, 2011" for "December 31, 2010" in subsection (a)(1) thereof.

• 2009, American Recovery and Reinvestment Tax Act of 2009 (P.L. 111-5)

P.L. 111-5, §1004(b)(4):

Amended Code Sec. 25B(g)(2) by inserting "25A(i)," after "23,". **Effective** for tax years beginning after 12-31-2008.

P.L. 111-5, §1142(b)(1)(C):

Amended Code Sec. 25B(g)(2) by inserting "30," after "25D,". **Effective** for vehicles acquired after 2-17-2009. For a transitional rule, see Act Sec. 1142(d) in the amendment notes for Code Sec. 30.

P.L. 111-5, §1144(b)(1)(C):

Amended Code Sec. 25B(g)(2), as amended by this Act, by inserting "30B," after "30,". **Effective** for tax years beginning after 12-31-2008.

• 2008, Energy Improvement and Extension Act of 2008 (P.L. 110-343)

P.L. 110-343, Division B, §106(e)(2)(C):

Amended Code Sec. 25B(g)(2) by striking "section 23" and inserting "sections 23 and 25D". **Effective** for tax years beginning after 12-31-2007.

P.L. 110-343, Division B, §205(d)(1)(C):

Amended Code Sec. 25B(g)(2), as amended by Act Sec. 106, by striking "and 25D" and inserting ", 25D, and 30D". **Effective** for tax years beginning after 12-31-2008.

• 2006, Pension Protection Act of 2006 (P.L. 109-280)

P.L. 109-280, §811, provides:

SEC. 811. PENSIONS AND INDIVIDUAL RETIREMENT ARRANGEMENT PROVISIONS OF ECONOMIC GROWTH AND TAX RELIEF RECONCILIATION ACT OF 2001 MADE PERMANENT.

Title IX of the Economic Growth and Tax Relief Reconciliation Act of 2001 [P.L. 107-16] shall not apply to the provisions of, and amendments made by, subtitles A through F of title VI [§§601-666]of such Act (relating to pension and individual retirement arrangement provisions).

• 2005, Gulf Opportunity Zone Act of 2005 (P.L. 109-135)

P.L. 109-135, §402(i)(3)(D):

Amended the matter preceding paragraph (1) of Code Sec. 25B(g) by striking "The credit" and inserting "In the case of a taxable year to which section 26(a)(2) does not apply, the credit". **Effective** for tax years beginning after 12-31-2005.

P.L. 109-135, §402(i)(3)(H), provides:

(H) APPLICATION OF EGTRAA SUNSET.—The amendments made by this paragraph (and each part thereof) shall be subject to title IX of the Economic Growth and Tax Relief Reconciliation Act of 2001 in the same manner as the provisions of such Act to which such amendment (or part thereof) relates.

• 2004, Working Families Tax Relief Act of 2004 (P.L. 108-311)

P.L. 108-311, §312(b)(2), provides:

(2) The amendments made by sections 201(b), 202(f), and 618(b) of the Economic Growth and Tax Relief Reconciliation Act of 2001 shall not apply to taxable years beginning during 2004 or 2005.

• 2002, Job Creation and Worker Assistance Act of 2002 (P.L. 107-147)

P.L. 107-147, §601(b)(2), provides:

(2) The amendments made by sections 201(b), 202(f), and 618(b) of the Economic Growth and Tax Relief Reconciliation Act of 2001 shall not apply to taxable years beginning during 2002 and 2003.

• 2001, Economic Growth and Tax Relief Reconciliation Act of 2001 (P.L. 107-16)

P.L. 107-16, §618(b)(1):

Amended Code Sec. 25B, as added by Act Sec. 618(a), by inserting after subsection (f) a new subsection (g). **Effective** for tax years beginning after 12-31-2001. [But, see P.L. 107-147, §601(b)(2), and P.L. 108-311, §312(b)(2), above.—CCH.]

P.L. 107-16, §901(a)-(b), provides [but see P.L. 109-280, §811, and P.L. 111-148, §10909(c), above]:

SEC. 901. SUNSET OF PROVISIONS OF ACT.

(a) IN GENERAL.—All provisions of, and amendments made by, this Act shall not apply—

(1) to taxable, plan, or limitation years beginning after December 31, 2010, or

(2) in the case of title V, to estates of decedents dying, gifts made, or generation skipping transfers, after December 31, 2010.

(b) APPLICATION OF CERTAIN LAWS.—The Internal Revenue Code of 1986 and the Employee Retirement Income Security Act of 1974 shall be applied and administered to years, estates, gifts, and transfers described in subsection (a) as if the provisions and amendments described in subsection (a) had never been enacted.

[Sec. 25B(h)—Stricken]

Amendments

• 2006, Pension Protection Act of 2006 (P.L. 109-280)

P.L. 109-280, §811, provides:

SEC. 811. PENSIONS AND INDIVIDUAL RETIREMENT ARRANGEMENT PROVISIONS OF ECONOMIC GROWTH AND TAX RELIEF RECONCILIATION ACT OF 2001 MADE PERMANENT.

Title IX of the Economic Growth and Tax Relief Reconciliation Act of 2001 [P.L. 107-16] shall not apply to the provisions of, and amendments made by, subtitles A through F of title VI [§§601-666]of such Act (relating to pension and individual retirement arrangement provisions).

P.L. 109-280, §812:

Amended Code Sec. 25B by striking subsection (h). **Effective** 8-17-2006. Prior to being stricken, Code Sec. 25B(h) read as follows:

(h) TERMINATION.—This section shall not apply to taxable years beginning after December 31, 2006.

• 2002, Job Creation and Worker Assistance Act of 2002 (P.L. 107-147)

P.L. 107-147, §417(1):

Amended Code Sec. 25B by redesignating subsection (g) as subsection (h). **Effective** 3-9-2002.

• 2001, Economic Growth and Tax Relief Reconciliation Act of 2001 (P.L. 107-16)

P.L. 107-16, §618(a):

Amended subpart A of part IV of subchapter A of chapter 1 by inserting after Code Sec. 25A a new Code Sec. 25B. **Effective** for tax years beginning after 12-31-2001.

P.L. 107-16, §901(a)-(b), provides [but see P.L. 109-280, §811, above]:

SEC. 901. SUNSET OF PROVISIONS OF ACT.

(a) IN GENERAL.—All provisions of, and amendments made by, this Act shall not apply—

(1) to taxable, plan, or limitation years beginning after December 31, 2010, or

(2) in the case of title V, to estates of decedents dying, gifts made, or generation skipping transfers, after December 31, 2010.

(b) APPLICATION OF CERTAIN LAWS.—The Internal Revenue Code of 1986 and the Employee Retirement Income Security Act of 1974 shall be applied and administered to years, estates, gifts, and transfers described in subsection (a) as if the provisions and amendments described in subsection (a) had never been enacted.

[Sec. 25C]

SEC. 25C. NONBUSINESS ENERGY PROPERTY.

[Sec. 25C(a)]

(a) ALLOWANCE OF CREDIT .—In the case of an individual, there shall be allowed as a credit against the tax imposed by this chapter for the taxable year an amount equal to 30 percent of the sum of—

(1) the amount paid or incurred by the taxpayer during such taxable year for qualified energy efficiency improvements, and

(2) the amount of the residential energy property expenditures paid or incurred by the taxpayer during such taxable year.

Amendments

• 2009, American Recovery and Reinvestment Tax Act of 2009 (P.L. 111-5)

P.L. 111-5, §1121(a):

Amended Code Sec. 25C by striking subsections (a) and (b) and inserting new subsections (a) and (b). **Effective** for tax years beginning after 12-31-2008.

[Sec. 25C(a)—Stricken]

Amendments

• 2009, American Recovery and Reinvestment Tax Act of 2009 (P.L. 111-5)

P.L. 111-5, §1121(a):

Amended Code Sec. 25C by striking subsection (a). **Effective** for tax years beginning after 12-31-2008. Prior to being stricken, Code Sec. 25C(a) read as follows:

(a) ALLOWANCE OF CREDIT.—In the case of an individual, there shall be allowed as a credit against the tax imposed by this chapter for the taxable year an amount equal to the sum of—

(1) 10 percent of the amount paid or incurred by the taxpayer for qualified energy efficiency improvements installed during such taxable year, and

(2) the amount of the residential energy property expenditures paid or incurred by the taxpayer during such taxable year.

[Sec. 25C(b)]

(b) LIMITATION .—The aggregate amount of the credits allowed under this section for taxable years beginning in 2009 and 2010 with respect to any taxpayer shall not exceed $1,500.

Amendments

• 2009, American Recovery and Reinvestment Tax Act of 2009 (P.L. 111-5)

P.L. 111-5, §1121(a):

Amended Code Sec. 25C by striking subsection (b) and inserting a new subsection (b). **Effective** for tax years beginning after 12-31-2008.

[Sec. 25C(b)—Stricken]

Amendments

• 2009, American Recovery and Reinvestment Tax Act of 2009 (P.L. 111-5)

P.L. 111-5, §1121(a):

Amended Code Sec. 25C by striking subsection (b). **Effective** for tax years beginning after 12-31-2008. Prior to being stricken, Code Sec. 25C(b) read as follows:

(b) LIMITATIONS.—

(1) LIFETIME LIMITATION.—The credit allowed under this section with respect to any taxpayer for any taxable year shall not exceed the excess (if any) of $500 over the aggregate credits allowed under this section with respect to such taxpayer for all prior taxable years.

(2) WINDOWS.—In the case of amounts paid or incurred for components described in subsection (c)(2)(B) by any taxpayer for any taxable year, the credit allowed under this section with respect to such amounts for such year shall not exceed the excess (if any) of $200 over the aggregate credits allowed under this section with respect to such amounts for all prior taxable years.

(3) LIMITATION ON RESIDENTIAL ENERGY PROPERTY EXPENDITURES.—The amount of the credit allowed under this section by reason of subsection (a)(2) shall not exceed—

(A) $50 for any advanced main air circulating fan,

(B) $150 for any qualified natural gas, propane, or oil furnace or hot water boiler, and

(C) $300 for any item of energy-efficient building property.

• 2005, Gulf Opportunity Zone Act of 2005 (P.L. 109-135)

P.L. 109-135, §412(b):

Amended Code Sec. 25C(b)(2) by striking "subsection (c)(3)(B)" and inserting "subsection (c)(2)(B)". **Effective** 12-21-2005.

[Sec. 25C(c)]

(c) QUALIFIED ENERGY EFFICIENCY IMPROVEMENTS.—For purposes of this section—

(1) IN GENERAL.—The term "qualified energy efficiency improvements" means any energy efficient building envelope component which meets the prescriptive criteria for such component established by the 2000 International Energy Conservation Code, as such Code (including supplements) is in effect on the date of the enactment of this section (or, in the case of a metal roof with appropriate pigmented coatings, or an asphalt roof with appropriate cooling granules, which meet the Energy Star program requirements), if—

(A) such component is installed in or on a dwelling unit located in the United States and owned and used by the taxpayer as the taxpayer's principal residence (within the meaning of section 121),

(B) the original use of such component commences with the taxpayer, and

(C) such component reasonably can be expected to remain in use for at least 5 years.

(2) BUILDING ENVELOPE COMPONENT.—The term "building envelope component" means—

(A) any insulation material or system which is specifically and primarily designed to reduce the heat loss or gain of a dwelling unit when installed in or on such dwelling unit and meets the prescriptive criteria for such material or system established by the 2009 International Energy Conservation Code, as such Code (including supplements) is in effect on the date of the enactment of the American Recovery and Reinvestment Tax Act of 2009,

(B) exterior windows (including skylights),

(C) exterior doors, and

(D) any metal roof or asphalt roof installed on a dwelling unit, but only if such roof has appropriate pigmented coatings or cooling granules which are specifically and primarily designed to reduce the heat gain of such dwelling unit.

(3) MANUFACTURED HOMES INCLUDED.—The term "dwelling unit" includes a manufactured home which conforms to Federal Manufactured Home Construction and Safety Standards (part 3280 of title 24, Code of Federal Regulations).

(4) QUALIFICATIONS FOR EXTERIOR WINDOWS, DOORS, AND SKYLIGHTS.—Such term shall not include any component described in subparagraph (B) or (C) of paragraph (2) unless such component is equal to or below a U factor of 0.30 and SHGC of 0.30.

Amendments

• 2009, American Recovery and Reinvestment Tax Act of 2009 (P.L. 111-5)

P.L. 111-5, §1121(d)(1):

Amended Code Sec. 25C(c) by adding at the end a new paragraph (4). **Effective** for property placed in service after 2-17-2009.

P.L. 111-5, §1121(d)(2):

Amended Code Sec. 25C(c)(2)(A) by inserting "and meets the prescriptive criteria for such material or system established by the 2009 International Energy Conservation Code, as such Code (including supplements) is in effect on the date of the enactment of the American Recovery and Reinvestment Tax Act of 2009" after "such dwelling unit". **Effective** for property placed in service after 2-17-2009.

• 2008, Energy Improvement and Extension Act of 2008 (P.L. 110-343)

P.L. 110-343, Division B, §302(e)(1):

Amended Code Sec. 25C(c)(1) by inserting ", or an asphalt roof with appropriate cooling granules," before "which meet the Energy Star program requirements". **Effective** for property placed in service after 10-3-2008.

P.L. 110-343, Division B, §302(e)(2)(A)-(B):

Amended Code Sec. 25C(c)(2)(D) by inserting "or asphalt roof" after "metal roof", and by inserting "or cooling granules" after "pigmented coatings". **Effective** for property placed in service after 10-3-2008.

• 2007, Tax Technical Corrections Act of 2007 (P.L. 110-172)

P.L. 110-172, §11(a)(2):

Amended Code Sec. 25C(c)(3) by striking "section 3280" and inserting "part 3280". **Effective** 12-29-2007.

[Sec. 25C(d)]

(d) RESIDENTIAL ENERGY PROPERTY EXPENDITURES.—For purposes of this section—

(1) IN GENERAL.—The term "residential energy property expenditures" means expenditures made by the taxpayer for qualified energy property which is—

(A) installed on or in connection with a dwelling unit located in the United States and owned and used by the taxpayer as the taxpayer's principal residence (within the meaning of section 121), and

(B) originally placed in service by the taxpayer.

Such term includes expenditures for labor costs properly allocable to the onsite preparation, assembly, or original installation of the property.

(2) QUALIFIED ENERGY PROPERTY.—

(A) IN GENERAL.—The term "qualified energy property" means—

(i) energy-efficient building property,

(ii) any qualified natural gas furnace, qualified propane furnace, qualified oil furnace, qualified natural gas hot water boiler, qualified propane hot water boiler, or qualified oil hot water boiler, or

(iii) an advanced main air circulating fan.

(B) PERFORMANCE AND QUALITY STANDARDS.—Property described under subparagraph (A) shall meet the performance and quality standards, and the certification requirements (if any), which—

(i) have been prescribed by the Secretary by regulations (after consultation with the Secretary of Energy or the Administrator of the Environmental Protection Agency, as appropriate), and

(ii) are in effect at the time of the acquisition of the property, or at the time of the completion of the construction, reconstruction, or erection of the property, as the case may be.

(C) REQUIREMENTS AND STANDARDS FOR AIR CONDITIONERS AND HEAT PUMPS.—The standards and requirements prescribed by the Secretary under subparagraph (B) with respect to the energy efficiency ratio (EER) for central air conditioners and electric heat pumps—

(i) shall require measurements to be based on published data which is tested by manufacturers at 95 degrees Fahrenheit, and

(ii) may be based on the certified data of the Air Conditioning and Refrigeration Institute that are prepared in partnership with the Consortium for Energy Efficiency.

(3) ENERGY-EFFICIENT BUILDING PROPERTY.—The term "energy-efficient building property" means—

(A) an electric heat pump water heater which yields an energy factor of at least 2.0 in the standard Department of Energy test procedure,

(B) an electric heat pump which achieves the highest efficiency tier established by the Consortium for Energy Efficiency, as in effect on January 1, 2009.[,]

(C) a central air conditioner which achieves the highest efficiency tier established by the Consortium for Energy Efficiency, as in effect on January 1, 2009,

(D) a natural gas, propane, or oil water heater which has either an energy factor of at least 0.82 or a thermal efficiency of at least 90 percent.[, and]

(E) a stove which uses the burning of biomass fuel to heat a dwelling unit located in the United States and used as a residence by the taxpayer, or to heat water for use in such a dwelling unit, and which has a thermal efficiency rating of at least 75 percent, as measured using a lower heating value.

(4) QUALIFIED NATURAL GAS, PROPANE, AND OIL FURNACES AND HOT WATER BOILERS.—

(A) QUALIFIED NATURAL GAS FURNACE.—The term "qualified natural gas furnace" means any natural gas furnace which achieves an annual fuel utilization efficiency rate of not less than 95.

(B) QUALIFIED NATURAL GAS HOT WATER BOILER.—The term "qualified natural gas hot water boiler" means any natural gas hot water boiler which achieves an annual fuel utilization efficiency rate of not less than 90.

(C) QUALIFIED PROPANE FURNACE.—The term "qualified propane furnace" means any propane furnace which achieves an annual fuel utilization efficiency rate of not less than 95.

(D) QUALIFIED PROPANE HOT WATER BOILER.—The term "qualified propane hot water boiler" means any propane hot water boiler which achieves an annual fuel utilization efficiency rate of not less than 90.

(E) QUALIFIED OIL FURNACES.—The term "qualified oil furnace" means any oil furnace which achieves an annual fuel utilization efficiency rate of not less than 90.

(F) QUALIFIED OIL HOT WATER BOILER.—The term "qualified oil hot water boiler" means any oil hot water boiler which achieves an annual fuel utilization efficiency rate of not less than 90.

(5) ADVANCED MAIN AIR CIRCULATING FAN.—The term "advanced main air circulating fan" means a fan used in a natural gas, propane, or oil furnace and which has an annual electricity use of no more than 2 percent of the total annual energy use of the furnace (as determined in the standard Department of Energy test procedures).

(6) BIOMASS FUEL.—The term "biomass fuel" means any plant-derived fuel available on a renewable or recurring basis, including agricultural crops and trees, wood and wood waste and residues (including wood pellets), plants (including aquatic plants), grasses, residues, and fibers.

Amendments

• 2009, American Recovery and Reinvestment Tax Act of 2009 (P.L. 111-5)

P.L. 111-5, §1121(b)(1):

Amended Code Sec. 25C(d)(3)(B). **Effective** for property placed in service after 2-17-2009. Prior to amendment, Code Sec. 25C(d)(3)(B) read as follows:

(B) an electric heat pump which has a heating seasonal performance factor (HSPF) of at least 9, a seasonal energy efficiency ratio (SEER) of at least 15, and an energy efficiency ratio (EER) of at least 13,

P.L. 111-5, §1121(b)(2):

Amended Code Sec. 25C(d)(3)(C) by striking "2006" and inserting "2009". **Effective** for property placed in service after 2-17-2009.

P.L. 111-5, §1121(b)(3):

Amended Code Sec. 25C(d)(3)(D). **Effective** for property placed in service after 2-17-2009. Prior to amendment, Code Sec. 25C(d)(3)(D) read as follows:

(D) a natural gas, propane, or oil water heater which has an energy factor of at least 0.80 or a thermal efficiency of at least 90 percent, and

P.L. 111-5, §1121(b)(4):

Amended Code Sec. 25C(d)(3)(E) by inserting ", as measured using a lower heating value" after "75 percent". **Effective** for tax years beginning after 12-31-2008.

P.L. 111-5, §1121(c)(1):

Amended Code Sec. 25C(d)(4). **Effective** for property placed in service after 2-17-2009. Prior to amendment, Code Sec. 25C(d)(4) read as follows:

(4) QUALIFIED NATURAL GAS, PROPANE, OR OIL FURNACE OR HOT WATER BOILER.—The term "qualified natural gas, propane, or oil furnace or hot water boiler" means a natural gas, propane, or oil furnace or hot water boiler which achieves an annual fuel utilization efficiency rate of not less than 95.

P.L. 111-5, §1121(c)(2):

Amended Code Sec. 25C(d)(2)(A)(ii). **Effective** for property placed in service after 2-17-2009. Prior to amendment, Code Sec. 25C(d)(2)(A)(ii) read as follows:

(ii) a qualified natural gas, propane, or oil furnace or hot water boiler, or

• 2008, Energy Improvement and Extension Act of 2008 (P.L. 110-343)

P.L. 110-343, Division B, §302(b)(1)(A)-(C):

Amended Code Sec. 25C(d)(3) by striking "and" at the end of subparagraph (D), by striking the period at the end of subparagraph (E) and inserting ", and", and by adding at the end a new subparagraph (F). **Effective** for expenditures made after 12-31-2008.

P.L. 110-343, Division B, §302(b)(2):

Amended Code Sec. 25C(d) by adding at the end a new paragraph (6). **Effective** for expenditures made after 12-31-2008.

P.L. 110-343, Division B, §302(c):

Amended Code Sec. 25C(d)(3)(E) by inserting "or a thermal efficiency of at least 90 percent" after "0.80". **Effective** for expenditures made after 12-31-2008.

P.L. 110-343, Division B, §302(d)(1):

Amended Code Sec. 25C(d)(3), as amended by Act Sec. 302(b)-(c), by striking subparagraph (C) and by redesignating subparagraphs (D), (E), and (F) as subparagraphs (C), (D), and (E), respectively. **Effective** for expenditures made after 12-31-2008. Prior to being stricken, Code Sec. 25C(d)(3)(C) read as follows:

(C) a geothermal heat pump which—

(i) in the case of a closed loop product, has an energy efficiency ratio (EER) of at least 14.1 and a heating coefficient of performance (COP) of at least 3.3,

(ii) in the case of an open loop product, has an energy efficiency ratio (EER) of at least 16.2 and a heating coefficient of performance (COP) of at least 3.6, and

(iii) in the case of a direct expansion (DX) product, has an energy efficiency ratio (EER) of at least 15 and a heating coefficient of performance (COP) of at least 3.5,

P.L. 110-343, Division B, §302(d)(2):

Amended Code Sec. 25C(d)(2)(C). **Effective** for expenditures made after 12-31-2008. Prior to amendment, Code Sec. 25C(d)(2)(C) read as follows:

(C) REQUIREMENTS FOR STANDARDS.—The standards and requirements prescribed by the Secretary under subparagraph (B)—

(i) in the case of the energy efficiency ratio (EER) for central air conditioners and electric heat pumps—

(I) shall require measurements to be based on published data which is tested by manufacturers at 95 degrees Fahrenheit, and

(II) may be based on the certified data of the Air Conditioning and Refrigeration Institute that are prepared in partnership with the Consortium for Energy Efficiency, and

(ii) in the case of geothermal heat pumps—

(I) shall be based on testing under the conditions of ARI/ISO Standard 13256-1 for Water Source Heat Pumps or ARI 870 for Direct Expansion GeoExchange Heat Pumps (DX), as appropriate, and

(II) shall include evidence that water heating services have been provided through a desuperheater or integrated water heating system connected to the storage water heater tank.

[Sec. 25C(e)]

(e) SPECIAL RULES.—For purposes of this section—

(1) APPLICATION OF RULES.—Rules similar to the rules under paragraphs (4), (5), (6), (7), and (8) of section 25D(e) shall apply.

(2) JOINT OWNERSHIP OF ENERGY ITEMS.—

(A) IN GENERAL.—Any expenditure otherwise qualifying as an expenditure under this section shall not be treated as failing to so qualify merely because such expenditure was made with respect to two or more dwelling units.

(B) LIMITS APPLIED SEPARATELY.—In the case of any expenditure described in subparagraph (A), the amount of the credit allowable under subsection (a) shall (subject to paragraph (1)) be computed separately with respect to the amount of the expenditure made for each dwelling unit.

Amendments

• 2009, American Recovery and Reinvestment Tax Act of 2009 (P.L. 111-5)

P.L. 111-5, §1103(b)(2)(A):

Amended Code Sec. 25C(e)(1) by striking "(8), and (9)" and inserting "and (8)". **Effective** for tax years beginning after 12-31-2008.

[Sec. 25C(f)]

(f) BASIS ADJUSTMENTS.—For purposes of this subtitle, if a credit is allowed under this section for any expenditure with respect to any property, the increase in the basis of such property which would (but for this subsection) result from such expenditure shall be reduced by the amount of the credit so allowed.

[Sec. 25C(g)]

(g) TERMINATION.—This section shall not apply with respect to any property placed in service—

(1) after December 31, 2007, and before January 1, 2009, or

(2) after December 31, 2010.

Amendments

• 2009, American Recovery and Reinvestment Tax Act of 2009 (P.L. 111-5)

P.L. 111-5, §1121(e):

Amended Code Sec. 25C(g)(2) by striking "December 31, 2009" and inserting "December 31, 2010". **Effective** for tax years beginning after 12-31-2008.

• 2008, Energy Improvement and Extension Act of 2008 (P.L. 110-343)

P.L. 110-343, Division B, §302(a):

Amended Code Sec. 25C(g) by striking "placed in service after December 31, 2007" and inserting "placed in service—" and new paragraphs (1) and (2). **Effective** for expenditures made after 12-31-2008.

• 2005, Energy Tax Incentives Act of 2005 (P.L. 109-58)

P.L. 109-58, §1333(a):

Amended subpart A of part IV of subchapter A of chapter 1 by inserting after Code Sec. 25B a new Code Sec. 25C. **Effective** for property placed in service after 12-31-2005.

[Sec. 25D]

SEC. 25D. RESIDENTIAL ENERGY EFFICIENT PROPERTY.

[Sec. 25D(a)]

(a) ALLOWANCE OF CREDIT.—In the case of an individual, there shall be allowed as a credit against the tax imposed by this chapter for the taxable year an amount equal to the sum of—

(1) 30 percent of the qualified solar electric property expenditures made by the taxpayer during such year,

(2) 30 percent of the qualified solar water heating property expenditures made by the taxpayer during such year,

(3) 30 percent of the qualified fuel cell property expenditures made by the taxpayer during such year,

(4) 30 percent of the qualified small wind energy property expenditures made by the taxpayer during such year, and

(5) 30 percent of the qualified geothermal heat pump property expenditures made by the taxpayer during such year.

Amendments

• 2008, Energy Improvement and Extension Act of 2008 (P.L. 110-343)

P.L. 110-343, Division B, §106(c)(1):

Amended Code Sec. 25D(a) by striking "and" at the end of paragraph (2), by striking the period at the end of paragraph (3) and inserting ", and", and by adding at the end a new paragraph (4). **Effective** for tax years beginning after 12-31-2007.

P.L. 110-343, Division B, §106(d)(1):

Amended Code Sec. 25D(a), as amended by Act Sec. 106(c), by striking "and" at the end of paragraph (3), by striking the period at the end of paragraph (4) and inserting ", and", and by adding at the end a new paragraph (5). **Effective** for tax years beginning after 12-31-2007.

• 2006, Tax Relief and Health Care Act of 2006 (P.L. 109-432)

P.L. 109-432, Division A, §206(b)(1):

Amended Code Sec. 25D(a)(1) by striking "qualified photovoltaic property expenditures" and inserting "qualified solar electric property expenditures". **Effective** 12-20-2006.

[Sec. 25D(b)]

(b) LIMITATIONS.—

(1) MAXIMUM CREDIT FOR FUEL CELLS.—In the case of any qualified fuel cell property expenditure, the credit allowed under subsection (a) (determined without regard to subsection (c)) for any taxable year shall not exceed $500 with respect to each half kilowatt of capacity of the qualified fuel cell property (as defined in section 48(c)(1)) to which such expenditure relates.

(2) CERTIFICATION OF SOLAR WATER HEATING PROPERTY.—No credit shall be allowed under this section for an item of property described in subsection (d)(1) unless such property is certified for performance by the non-profit Solar Rating Certification Corporation or a comparable entity endorsed by the government of the State in which such property is installed.

Amendments

• 2009, American Recovery and Reinvestment Tax Act of 2009 (P.L. 111-5)

P.L. 111-5, §1122(a)(1):

Amended Code Sec. 25D(b)(1). **Effective** for tax years beginning after 12-31-2008. Prior to amendment, Code Sec. 25D(b)(1) read as follows:

(1) MAXIMUM CREDIT.—The credit allowed under subsection (a) (determined without regard to subsection (c)) for any taxable year shall not exceed—

(A) $2,000 with respect to any qualified solar water heating property expenditures,

(B) $500 with respect to each half kilowatt of capacity of qualified fuel cell property (as defined in section 48(c)(1)) for which qualified fuel cell property expenditures are made,

(C) $500 with respect to each half kilowatt of capacity (not to exceed $4,000) of wind turbines for which qualified small wind energy property expenditures are made, and

(D) $2,000 with respect to any qualified geothermal heat pump property expenditures.

• 2008, Energy Improvement and Extension Act of 2008 (P.L. 110-343)

P.L. 110-343, Division B, §106(b)(1)(A)-(B):

Amended Code Sec. 25D(b)(1), as amended by Act Sec. 106(c)-(d), by striking subparagraph (A), and by redesignating subparagraphs (B) through (E) as subparagraphs (A) through (D), respectively. **Effective** for tax years beginning after 12-31-2008. Prior to being stricken, Code Sec. 25D(b)(1)(A) read as follows:

(A) $2,000 with respect to any qualified solar electric property expenditures,

P.L. 110-343, Division B, §106(c)(2):

Amended Code Sec. 25D(b)(1) by striking "and" at the end of subparagraph (B), by striking the period at the end of subparagraph (C) and inserting ", and", and by adding at the end a new subparagraph (D). **Effective** for tax years beginning after 12-31-2007.

P.L. 110-343, Division B, §106(d)(2):

Amended Code Sec. 25D(b)(1), as amended by Act Sec. 106(c), by striking "and" at the end of subparagraph (C), by striking the period at the end of subparagraph (D) and inserting ", and", and by adding at the end a new subparagraph (E). **Effective** for tax years beginning after 12-31-2007.

• 2006, Tax Relief and Health Care Act of 2006 (P.L. 109-432)

P.L. 109-432, Division A, §206(b)(1):

Amended Code Sec. 25D(b)(1)(A) by striking "qualified photovoltaic property expenditures" and inserting "qualified solar electric property expenditures". **Effective** 12-20-2006.

• 2005, Gulf Opportunity Zone Act of 2005 (P.L. 109-135)

P.L. 109-135, §402(i)(1):

Amended Code Sec. 25D(b)(1) by inserting "(determined without regard to subsection (c))" after "subsection (a)". **Effective** as if included in the provision of the Energy Policy Act of 2005 (P.L. 109-58) to which it relates [**effective** for property placed in service after 12-31-2005, in tax years ending after such date.—CCH].

[Sec. 25D(c)]

(c) LIMITATION BASED ON AMOUNT OF TAX; CARRYFORWARD OF UNUSED CREDIT.—

(1) LIMITATION BASED ON AMOUNT OF TAX .—In the case of a taxable year to which section 26(a)(2) does not apply, the credit allowed under subsection (a) for the taxable year shall not exceed the excess of—

(A) the sum of the regular tax liability (as defined in section 26(b)) plus the tax imposed by section 55, over

(B) the sum of the credits allowable under this subpart (other than this section) and section 27 for the taxable year.

(2) CARRYFORWARD OF UNUSED CREDIT.—

(A) RULE FOR YEARS IN WHICH ALL PERSONAL CREDITS ALLOWED AGAINST REGULAR AND ALTERNATIVE MINIMUM TAX .—In the case of a taxable year to which section 26(a)(2) applies, if the credit allowable under subsection (a) exceeds the limitation imposed by section 26(a)(2) for such taxable year reduced by the sum of the credits allowable under this subpart (other than this section), such excess shall be carried to the succeeding taxable year and added to the credit allowable under subsection (a) for such succeeding taxable year.

(B) RULE FOR OTHER YEARS .—In the case of a taxable year to which section 26(a)(2) does not apply, if the credit allowable under subsection (a) exceeds the limitation imposed by paragraph (1) for such taxable year, such excess shall be carried to the succeeding taxable year and added to the credit allowable under subsection (a) for such succeeding taxable year.

Amendments

• 2008, Energy Improvement and Extension Act of 2008 (P.L. 110-343)

P.L. 110-343, Division B, §106(e)(1):

Amended Code Sec. 25D(c). **Effective** for tax years beginning after 12-31-2007. Prior to amendment, Code Sec. 25D(c) read as follows:

(c) CARRYFORWARD OF UNUSED CREDIT.—

(1) RULE FOR YEARS IN WHICH ALL PERSONAL CREDITS ALLOWED AGAINST REGULAR AND ALTERNATIVE MINIMUM TAX.—In the case of a taxable year to which section 26(a)(2) applies, if the credit allowable under subsection (a) exceeds the limitation imposed by section 26(a)(2) for such taxable year reduced by the sum of the credits allowable under this subpart (other than this section), such excess shall be carried to the succeeding taxable year and added to the credit allowable under subsection (a) for such succeeding taxable year.

(2) RULE FOR OTHER YEARS.—In the case of a taxable year to which section 26(a)(2) does not apply, if the credit allowable under subsection (a) exceeds the limitation imposed by section 26(a)(1) for such taxable year reduced by the sum of the credits allowable under this subpart (other than this section and sections 23, 24, and 25B), such excess shall be carried to the succeeding taxable year and added to the credit allowable under subsection (a) for such succeeding taxable year.

• 2005, Gulf Opportunity Zone Act of 2005 (P.L. 109-135)

P.L. 109-135, §402(i)(3)(E):

Amended Code Sec. 25D(c). **Effective** for tax years beginning after 12-31-2005. Prior to amendment, Code Sec. 25D(c) read as follows:

(c) CARRYFORWARD OF UNUSED CREDIT .—If the credit allowable under subsection (a) exceeds the limitation imposed by section 26(a) for such taxable year reduced by the sum of the credits allowable under this subpart (other than this section), such excess shall be carried to the succeeding taxable year and added to the credit allowable under subsection (a) for such succeeding taxable year.

P.L. 109-135, §402(i)(3)(H), provides:

(H) APPLICATION OF EGTRRA SUNSET.—The amendments made by this paragraph (and each part thereof) shall be subject to title IX of the Economic Growth and Tax Relief Reconciliation Act of 2001 in the same manner as the provisions of such Act to which such amendment (or part thereof) relates.

[Sec. 25D(d)]

(d) DEFINITIONS.—For purposes of this section—

(1) QUALIFIED SOLAR WATER HEATING PROPERTY EXPENDITURE.—The term "qualified solar water heating property expenditure" means an expenditure for property to heat water for use in a dwelling unit located in the United States and used as a residence by the taxpayer if at least half of the energy used by such property for such purpose is derived from the sun.

(2) QUALIFIED SOLAR ELECTRIC PROPERTY EXPENDITURE.—The term "qualified solar electric property expenditure" means an expenditure for property which uses solar energy to generate electricity for use in a dwelling unit located in the United States and used as a residence by the taxpayer.

(3) QUALIFIED FUEL CELL PROPERTY EXPENDITURE.—The term "qualified fuel cell property expenditure" means an expenditure for qualified fuel cell property (as defined in section 48(c)(1)) installed on or in connection with a dwelling unit located in the United States and used as a principal residence (within the meaning of section 121) by the taxpayer.

(4) QUALIFIED SMALL WIND ENERGY PROPERTY EXPENDITURE.—The term "qualified small wind energy property expenditure" means an expenditure for property which uses a wind turbine to generate electricity for use in connection with a dwelling unit located in the United States and used as a residence by the taxpayer.

(5) QUALIFIED GEOTHERMAL HEAT PUMP PROPERTY EXPENDITURE.—

(A) IN GENERAL.—The term "qualified geothermal heat pump property expenditure" means an expenditure for qualified geothermal heat pump property installed on or in connection with a dwelling unit located in the United States and used as a residence by the taxpayer.

(B) QUALIFIED GEOTHERMAL HEAT PUMP PROPERTY.—The term "qualified geothermal heat pump property" means any equipment which—

(i) uses the ground or ground water as a thermal energy source to heat the dwelling unit referred to in subparagraph (A) or as a thermal energy sink to cool such dwelling unit, and

(ii) meets the requirements of the Energy Star program which are in effect at the time that the expenditure for such equipment is made.

Amendments

• 2008, Energy Improvement and Extension Act of 2008 (P.L. 110-343)

P.L. 110-343, Division B, §106(c)(3)(A):

Amended Code Sec. 25D(d) by adding at the end a new paragraph (4). **Effective** for tax years beginning after 12-31-2007.

P.L. 110-343, Division B, §106(d)(3):

Amended Code Sec. 25D(d), as amended by Act Sec. 106(c), by adding at the end a new paragraph (5). **Effective** for tax years beginning after 12-31-2007.

• 2006, Tax Relief and Health Care Act of 2006 (P.L. 109-432)

P.L. 109-432, Division A, §206(b)(2)(A)-(B):

Amended Code Sec. 25D(d)(2) by striking "qualified photovoltaic property expenditure" and inserting "qualified solar electric property expenditure", and in the heading by striking "[Q]UALIFIED PHOTOVOLTAIC PROPERTY EXPENDITURE" and inserting "QUALIFIED SOLAR ELECTRIC PROPERTY EXPENDITURE". **Effective** 12-20-2006.

[Sec. 25D(e)]

(e) SPECIAL RULES.—For purposes of this section—

(1) LABOR COSTS.—Expenditures for labor costs properly allocable to the onsite preparation, assembly, or original installation of the property described in subsection (d) and for piping or wiring to interconnect such property to the dwelling unit shall be taken into account for purposes of this section.

(2) SOLAR PANELS.—No expenditure relating to a solar panel or other property installed as a roof (or portion thereof) shall fail to be treated as property described in paragraph (1) or (2) of subsection (d) solely because it constitutes a structural component of the structure on which it is installed.

(3) SWIMMING POOLS, ETC., USED AS STORAGE MEDIUM.—Expenditures which are properly allocable to a swimming pool, hot tub, or any other energy storage medium which has a function other than the function of such storage shall not be taken into account for purposes of this section.

(4) FUEL CELL EXPENDITURE LIMITATIONS IN CASE OF JOINT OCCUPANCY.—In the case of any dwelling unit with respect to which qualified fuel cell property expenditures are made and which is jointly occupied and used during any calendar year as a residence by two or more individuals, the following rules shall apply:

(A) MAXIMUM EXPENDITURES FOR FUEL CELLS.—The maximum amount of such expenditures which may be taken into account under subsection (a) by all such individuals with respect to such dwelling unit during such calendar year shall be $1,667 in the case of each half kilowatt of capacity of qualified fuel cell property (as defined in section 48(c)(1)) with respect to which such expenditures relate.

(B) ALLOCATION OF EXPENDITURES.—The expenditures allocated to any individual for the taxable year in which such calendar year ends shall be an amount equal to the lesser of—

(i) the amount of expenditures made by such individual with respect to such dwelling during such calendar year, or

(ii) the maximum amount of such expenditures set forth in subparagraph (A) multiplied by a fraction—

(I) the numerator of which is the amount of such expenditures with respect to such dwelling made by such individual during such calendar year, and

(II) the denominator of which is the total expenditures made by all such individuals with respect to such dwelling during such calendar year.

(5) TENANT-STOCKHOLDER IN COOPERATIVE HOUSING CORPORATION.—In the case of an individual who is a tenant-stockholder (as defined in section 216) in a cooperative housing corporation (as defined in such section), such individual shall be treated as having made his tenant-stockholder's proportionate share (as defined in section 216(b)(3)) of any expenditures of such corporation.

(6) CONDOMINIUMS.—

(A) IN GENERAL.—In the case of an individual who is a member of a condominium management association with respect to a condominium which the individual owns, such individual shall be treated as having made the individual's proportionate share of any expenditures of such association.

(B) CONDOMINIUM MANAGEMENT ASSOCIATION.—For purposes of this paragraph, the term "condominium management association" means an organization which meets the requirements of paragraph (1) of section 528(c) (other than subparagraph (E) thereof) with respect to a condominium project substantially all of the units of which are used as residences.

(7) ALLOCATION IN CERTAIN CASES.—If less than 80 percent of the use of an item is for nonbusiness purposes, only that portion of the expenditures for such item which is properly allocable to use for nonbusiness purposes shall be taken into account.

(8) WHEN EXPENDITURE MADE; AMOUNT OF EXPENDITURE.—

(A) IN GENERAL.—Except as provided in subparagraph (B), an expenditure with respect to an item shall be treated as made when the original installation of the item is completed.

(B) EXPENDITURES PART OF BUILDING CONSTRUCTION.—In the case of an expenditure in connection with the construction or reconstruction of a structure, such expenditure shall be treated as made when the original use of the constructed or reconstructed structure by the taxpayer begins.

Amendments

• 2009, American Recovery and Reinvestment Tax Act of 2009 (P.L. 111-5)

P.L. 111-5, §1103(b)(2)(B):

Amended Code Sec. 25D(e) by striking paragraph (9). **Effective** for tax years beginning after 12-31-2008. Prior to being stricken, Code Sec. 25D(e)(9) read as follows:

(9) PROPERTY FINANCED BY SUBSIDIZED ENERGY FINANCING.—For purposes of determining the amount of expenditures made by any individual with respect to any dwelling unit, there shall not be taken into account expenditures which are made from subsidized energy financing (as defined in section 48(a)(4)(C)).

P.L. 111-5, §1122(a)(2)(A)-(B):

Amended Code Sec. 25D(e)(4) by striking all that precedes subparagraph (B) and inserting "(4) FUEL CELL EXPENDITURE LIMITATIONS IN CASE OF JOINT OCCUPANCY.—", introductory text and new subparagraph (A), and by striking subparagraph (C). **Effective** for tax years beginning after 12-31-2008. Prior to amendment, Code Sec. 25D(e)(4) read as follows:

(4) DOLLAR AMOUNTS IN CASE OF JOINT OCCUPANCY.—In the case of any dwelling unit which is jointly occupied and used during any calendar year as a residence by two or more individuals the following rules shall apply:

(A) MAXIMUM EXPENDITURES.—The maximum amount of expenditures which may be taken into account under subsection (a) by all such individuals with respect to such dwelling unit during such calendar year shall be—

(i) $6,667 in the case of any qualified solar water heating property expenditures,

(ii) $1,667 in the case of each half kilowatt of capacity of qualified fuel cell property (as defined in section 48(c)(1)) for which qualified fuel cell property expenditures are made,

(iii) $1,667 in the case of each half kilowatt of capacity (not to exceed $13,333) of wind turbines for which qualified small wind energy property expenditures are made, and

(iv) $6,667 in the case of any qualified geothermal heat pump property expenditures.

(B) ALLOCATION OF EXPENDITURES.—The expenditures allocated to any individual for the taxable year in which such calendar year ends shall be an amount equal to the lesser of—

(i) the amount of expenditures made by such individual with respect to such dwelling during such calendar year, or

(ii) the maximum amount of such expenditures set forth in subparagraph (A) multiplied by a fraction—

(I) the numerator of which is the amount of such expenditures with respect to such dwelling made by such individual during such calendar year, and

(II) the denominator of which is the total expenditures made by all such individuals with respect to such dwelling during such calendar year.

(C) Subparagraphs (A) and (B) shall be applied separately with respect to expenditures described in paragraphs (1), (2), and (3) of subsection (d).

• 2008, Energy Improvement and Extension Act of 2008 (P.L. 110-343)

P.L. 110-343, Division B, §106(b)(2)(A)-(B):

Amended Code Sec. 25D(e)(4)(A), as amended by Act Sec. 106(c)-(d), by striking clause (i), and by redesignating clauses (ii) through (v) as clauses (i) through (iv), respectively. **Effective** for tax years beginning after 12-31-2008. Prior to being stricken, Code Sec. 25D(e)(4)(A)(i) read as follows:

(i) $6,667 in the case of any qualified solar electric property expenditures,

P.L. 110-343, Division B, §106(c)(4):

Amended Code Sec. 25D(e)(4)(A) by striking "and" at the end of clause (ii), by striking the period at the end of clause (iii) and inserting ", and", and by adding at the end a new clause (iv). **Effective** for tax years beginning after 12-31-2007.

P.L. 110-343, Division B, §106(d)(4):

Amended Code Sec. 25D(e)(4)(A), as amended by Act Sec. 106(c), is amended by striking "and" at the end of clause (iii), by striking the period at the end of clause (iv) and inserting ", and", and by adding at the end a new clause (v). **Effective** for tax years beginning after 12-31-2007.

• 2006, Tax Relief and Health Care Act of 2006 (P.L. 109-432)

P.L. 109-432, Division A, §206(b)(1):

Amended Code Sec. 25D(e)(4)(A)(i) by striking "qualified photovoltaic property expenditures" and inserting "qualified solar electric property expenditures". **Effective** 12-20-2006.

• 2005, Gulf Opportunity Zone Act of 2005 (P.L. 109-135)

P.L. 109-135, §402(i)(2):

Amended Code Sec. 25D(e)(4)(A) and (B). **Effective** as if included in the provision of the Energy Policy Act of 2005 (P.L. 109-58) to which it relates [**effective** for property placed in service after 12-31-2005, in tax years ending after such date.—CCH]. Prior to amendment, Code Sec. 25D(e)(4)(A) and (B) read as follows:

(A) The amount of the credit allowable, under subsection (a) by reason of expenditures (as the case may be) made during such calendar year by any of such individuals with respect to such dwelling unit shall be determined by treating all of such individuals as 1 taxpayer whose taxable year is such calendar year.

(B) There shall be allowable, with respect to such expenditures to each of such individuals, a credit under subsection (a) for the taxable year in which such calendar year ends in an amount which bears the same ratio to the amount determined under subparagraph (A) as the amount of such expenditures made by such individual during such calendar year bears to the aggregate of such expenditures made by all of such individuals during such calendar year.

[Sec. 25D(f)]

(f) BASIS ADJUSTMENTS.—For purposes of this subtitle, if a credit is allowed under this section for any expenditure with respect to any property, the increase in the basis of such property which would (but for this subsection) result from such expenditure shall be reduced by the amount of the credit so allowed.

[Sec. 25D(g)]

(g) TERMINATION.—The credit allowed under this section shall not apply to property placed in service after December 31, 2016.

Amendments

• 2008, Energy Improvement and Extension Act of 2008 (P.L. 110-343)

P.L. 110-343, Division B, §106(a):

Amended Code Sec. 25D(g) by striking "December 31, 2008" and inserting "December 31, 2016". **Effective** for tax years beginning after 12-31-2007.

• 2006, Tax Relief and Health Care Act of 2006 (P.L. 109-432)

P.L. 109-432, Division A, §206(a):

Amended Code Sec. 25D(g) by striking "December 31, 2007" and inserting "December 31, 2008". **Effective** 12-20-2006.

• **2005, Energy Tax Incentives Act of 2005 (P.L. 109-58)**

P.L. 109-58, §1335(a):

Amended subpart A of part IV of subchapter A of chapter 1, as amended by this Act, by inserting after Code Sec. 25C a new Code Sec. 25D. **Effective** for property placed in service after 12-31-2005, in tax years ending after such date.

[Sec. 26]

SEC. 26. LIMITATION BASED ON TAX LIABILITY; DEFINITION OF TAX LIABILITY.

[Sec. 26(a)]

(a) LIMITATION BASED ON AMOUNT OF TAX.—

➾➝ ***Caution: Code Sec. 26(a)(1), below, was amended by P.L. 111-148. For sunset provision, see P.L. 111-148, §10909(c), in the amendment notes.***

(1) IN GENERAL.—The aggregate amount of credits allowed by this subpart (other than sections 24, 25A(i), 25B, 25D, 30, 30B, and 30D) for the taxable year shall not exceed the excess (if any) of—

(A) the taxpayer's regular tax liability for the taxable year, over

(B) the tentative minimum tax for the taxable year (determined without regard to the alternative minimum tax foreign tax credit).

For purposes of subparagraph (B), the taxpayer's tentative minimum tax for any taxable year beginning during 1999 shall be treated as being zero.

(2) SPECIAL RULE FOR TAXABLE YEARS 2000 THROUGH 2009.—For purposes of any taxable year beginning during 2000, 2001, 2002, 2003, 2004, 2005, 2006, 2007, 2008, or 2009, the aggregate amount of credits allowed by this subpart for the taxable year shall not exceed the sum of—

(A) the taxpayer's regular tax liability for the taxable year reduced by the foreign tax credit allowable under section 27(a), and

(B) the tax imposed by section 55(a) for the taxable year.

Amendments

• **2010, Patient Protection and Affordable Care Act (P.L. 111-148)**

P.L. 111-148, §10909(b)(2)(E):

Amended Code Sec. 26(a)(1) by striking "23," before "24". **Effective** for tax years beginning after 12-31-2009.

P.L. 111-148, §10909(c), provides:

(c) APPLICATION AND EXTENSION OF EGTRRA SUNSET.—Notwithstanding section 901 of the Economic Growth and Tax Relief Reconciliation Act of 2001 [P.L. 107-16], such section shall apply to the amendments made by this section and the amendments made by section 202 of such Act by substituting "December 31, 2011" for "December 31, 2010" in subsection (a)(1) thereof.

• **2009, American Recovery and Reinvestment Tax Act of 2009 (P.L. 111-5)**

P.L. 111-5, §1004(b)(3):

Amended Code Sec. 26(a)(1) by inserting "25A(i)," after "24,". **Effective** for tax years beginning after 12-31-2008.

P.L. 111-5, §1011(a)(1)-(2):

Amended Code Sec. 26(a)(2) by striking "or 2008" and inserting "2008, or 2009", and by striking "2008" in the heading thereof and inserting "2009". **Effective** for tax years beginning after 12-31-2008.

P.L. 111-5, §1142(b)(1)(D):

Amended Code Sec. 26(a)(1) by inserting "30," after "25D,". **Effective** for vehicles acquired after 2-17-2009. For a transitional rule, see Act Sec. 1142(d) in the amendment notes for Code Sec. 30.

P.L. 111-5, §1144(b)(1)(D):

Amended Code Sec. 26(a)(1), as amended by this Act, by inserting "30B," after "30,". **Effective** for tax years beginning after 12-31-2008.

• **2008, Energy Improvement and Extension Act of 2008 (P.L. 110-343)**

P.L. 110-343, Division B, §106(e)(2)(D):

Amended Code Sec. 26(a)(1) by striking "and 25B" and inserting "25B, and 25D". **Effective** for tax years beginning after 12-31-2007.

P.L. 110-343, Division B, §205(d)(1)(D):

Amended Code Sec. 26(a)(1), as amended by Act Sec. 106, by striking "and 25D" and inserting "25D, and 30D". **Effective** for tax years beginning after 12-31-2008.

• **2008, Tax Extenders and Alternative Minimum Tax Relief Act of 2008 (P.L. 110-343)**

P.L. 110-343, Division C, §101(a)(1)-(2):

Amended Code Sec. 26(a)(2) by striking "or 2007" and inserting "2007, or 2008", and by striking "2007" in the heading thereof and inserting "2008". **Effective** for tax years beginning after 12-31-2007.

• **2007, Tax Increase Prevention Act of 2007 (P.L. 110-166)**

P.L. 110-166, §3(a)(1)-(2):

Amended Code Sec. 26(a)(2) by striking "or 2006" and inserting "2006, or 2007", and by striking "2006" in the heading thereof and inserting "2007". **Effective** for tax years beginning after 12-31-2006.

• **2006, Pension Protection Act of 2006 (P.L. 109-280)**

P.L. 109-280, §811, provides:

SEC. 811. PENSIONS AND INDIVIDUAL RETIREMENT ARRANGEMENT PROVISIONS OF ECONOMIC GROWTH AND TAX RELIEF RECONCILIATION ACT OF 2001 MADE PERMANENT.

Title IX of the Economic Growth and Tax Relief Reconciliation Act of 2001 [P.L. 107-16] shall not apply to the provisions of, and amendments made by, subtitles A through F of title VI [§§601-666]of such Act (relating to pension and individual retirement arrangement provisions).

• **2006, Tax Increase Prevention and Reconciliation Act of 2005 (P.L. 109-222)**

P.L. 109-222, §302(a)(1)-(2):

Amended Code Sec. 26(a)(2) by striking "2005" in the heading thereof and inserting "2006", and by striking "or 2005" and inserting "2005, or 2006". **Effective** for tax years beginning after 12-31-2005.

• **2004, Working Families Tax Relief Act of 2004 (P.L. 108-311)**

P.L. 108-311, §312(a)(1)-(2):

Amended Code Sec. 26(a)(2) by striking "RULE FOR 2000, 2001, 2002, AND 2003.—"and inserting "RULE FOR TAXABLE YEARS 2000 THROUGH 2005.—", and by striking "or 2003" and inserting "2003, 2004, or 2005". **Effective** for tax years beginning after 12-31-2003.

P.L. 108-311, §312(b)(2), provides:

(2) The amendments made by sections 201(b), 202(f), and 618(b) of the Economic Growth and Tax Relief Reconciliation Act of 2001 shall not apply to taxable years beginning during 2004 or 2005.

• 2002, Job Creation and Worker Assistance Act of 2002 (P.L. 107-147)

P.L. 107-147, §601(a)(1)-(2):

Amended Code Sec. 26(a)(2) by striking "RULE FOR 2000 AND 2001.—" and inserting "RULE FOR 2000, 2001, 2002, AND 2003.—", and by striking "during 2000 or 2001," and inserting "during 2000, 2001, 2002, or 2003,". **Effective** for tax years beginning after 12-31-2001.

P.L. 107-147, §601(b)(2), provides:

(2) The amendments made by sections 201(b), 202(f), and 618(b) of the Economic Growth and Tax Relief Reconciliation Act of 2001 shall not apply to taxable years beginning during 2002 and 2003.

• 2001, Economic Growth and Tax Relief Reconciliation Act of 2001 (P.L. 107-16)

P.L. 107-16, §201(b)(2)(D):

Amended Code Sec. 26(a)(1) by inserting "(other than section 24)" after "this subpart". **Effective** for tax years beginning after 12-31-2001. [But, see P.L. 107-147, §601(b)(2), and P.L. 108-311, §312(b)(2), above.—CCH.]

P.L. 107-16, §202(f)(2)(C):

Amended Code Sec. 26(a)(1), as amended by Act Sec. 201(b), by striking "section 24" and inserting "sections 23 and 24". **Effective** for tax years beginning after 12-31-2001. [But, see P.L. 107-147, §601(b)(2), and P.L. 108-311, §312(b)(2), above.—CCH.]

P.L. 107-16, §618(b)(2)(C) (as amended by P.L. 107-147, §618(b)(2)(B)):

Amended Code Sec. 26(a)(1), as amended by Act Secs. 201(b) and 202(f), by striking "and 24" and inserting ", 24, and 25B". **Effective** for tax years beginning after 12-31-2001. [But, see P.L. 107-147, §601(b)(2), and P.L. 108-311, §312(b)(2), above.—CCH.]

P.L. 107-16, §901(a)-(b), provides [but see P.L. 109-280, §811, and P.L. 111-148, §10909(c), above]:

SEC. 901. SUNSET OF PROVISIONS OF ACT.

(a) IN GENERAL.—All provisions of, and amendments made by, this Act shall not apply—

(1) to taxable, plan, or limitation years beginning after December 31, 2010, or

(2) in the case of title V, to estates of decedents dying, gifts made, or generation skipping transfers, after December 31, 2010.

(b) APPLICATION OF CERTAIN LAWS.—The Internal Revenue Code of 1986 and the Employee Retirement Income Security Act of 1974 shall be applied and administered to years, estates, gifts, and transfers described in subsection (a) as if the provisions and amendments described in subsection (a) had never been enacted.

• 1999, Tax Relief Extension Act of 1999

P.L. 106-170, §501(a):

Amended Code Sec. 26(a). **Effective** for tax years beginning after 12-31-98. Prior to amendment, Code Sec. 26(a) read as follows:

(a) LIMITATION BASED ON AMOUNT OF TAX.—The aggregate amount of credits allowed by this subpart for the taxable year shall not exceed the excess (if any) of—

(1) the taxpayer's regular tax liability for the taxable year, over

(2) the tentative minimum tax for the taxable year (determined without regard to the alternative minimum tax foreign tax credit).

For purposes of paragraph (2), the taxpayer's tentative minimum tax for any taxable year beginning during 1998 shall be treated as being zero.

• 1998, Tax and Trade Relief Extension Act of 1998 (P.L. 105-277)

P.L. 105-277, §2001(a):

Amended Code Sec. 26(a) by adding at the end a new flush sentence. **Effective** for tax years beginning after 12-31-97.

[Sec. 26(b)]

(b) REGULAR TAX LIABILITY.—For purposes of this part—

(1) IN GENERAL.—The term "regular tax liability" means the tax imposed by this chapter for the taxable year.

(2) EXCEPTION FOR CERTAIN TAXES.—For purposes of paragraph (1), any tax imposed by any of the following provisions shall not be treated as tax imposed by this chapter:

(A) section 55 (relating to minimum tax),

(B) section 59A (relating to environmental tax),

(C) subsection (m)(5)(B), (q), (t), or (v) of section 72 (relating to additional taxes on certain distributions),

(D) section 143(m) (relating to recapture of proration of Federal subsidy from use of mortgage bonds and mortgage credit certificates),

(E) section 530(d)(4) (relating to additional tax on certain distributions from Coverdell education savings accounts),

(F) section 531 (relating to accumulated earnings tax),

(G) section 541 (relating to personal holding company tax),

(H) section 1351(d)(1) (relating to recoveries of foreign expropriation losses),

(I) section 1374 (relating to tax on certain certain built-in gains of S corporations),

(J) section 1375 (relating to tax imposed when passive investment income of corporation having subchapter C earnings and profits exceeds 25 percent of gross receipts),

(K) subparagraph (A) of section 7518(g)(6) (relating to nonqualified withdrawals from capital construction funds taxed at highest marginal rate),

(L) sections 871(a) and 881 (relating to certain income of nonresident aliens and foreign corporations),

(M) section 860E(e) (relating to taxes with respect to certain residual interests),

(N) section 884 (relating to branch profits tax),

(O) sections 453(l)(3) and 453A(c) (relating to interest on certain deferred tax liabilities),

(P) section 860K (relating to treatment of transfers of high-yield interests to disqualified holders),

(Q) section 220(f)(4) (relating to additional tax on Archer MSA distributions not used for qualified medical expenses),

(R) section 138(c)(2) (relating to penalty for distributions from Medicare Advantage MSA not used for qualified medical expenses if minimum balance not maintained),

(S) sections 106(e)(3)(A)(ii), 223(b)(8)(B)(i)(II), and 408(d)(9)(D)(i)(II) (relating to certain failures to maintain high deductible health plan coverage),

(T) section 170(o)(3)(B) (relating to recapture of certain deductions for fractional gifts),

(U) section 223(f)(4) (relating to additional tax on health savings account distributions not used for qualified medical expenses),

(V) subsections (a)(1)(B)(i) and (b)(4)(A) of section 409A (relating to interest and additional tax with respect to certain deferred compensation),

(W) section 36(f) (relating to recapture of homebuyer credit), and

(X) section 457A(c)(1)(B) (relating to determinability of amounts of compensation).

Amendments

• 2008, Tax Extenders and Alternative Minimum Tax Relief Act of 2008 (P.L. 110-343)

P.L. 110-343, Division C, §801(b):

Amended Code Sec. 26(b)(2), as amended by the Housing Assistance Tax Act of 2008 (P.L. 110-289), by striking "and" at the end of subparagraph (V), by striking the period at the end of subparagraph (W) and inserting ", and", and by adding at the end a new subparagraph (X). **Effective** generally for amounts deferred which are attributable to services performed after 12-31-2008. For a special rule, see Act Sec. 801(d)(2), below.

P.L. 110-343, Division C, §801(d)(2), provides:

(2) APPLICATION TO EXISTING DEFERRALS.—In the case of any amount deferred to which the amendments made by this section do not apply solely by reason of the fact that the amount is attributable to services performed before January 1, 2009, to the extent such amount is not includible in gross income in a taxable year beginning before 2018, such amounts shall be includible in gross income in the later of—

(A) the last taxable year beginning before 2018, or

(B) the taxable year in which there is no substantial risk of forfeiture of the rights to such compensation (determined in the same manner as determined for purposes of section 457A of the Internal Revenue Code of 1986, as added by this section).

• 2008, Housing Assistance Tax Act of 2008 (P.L. 110-289)

P.L. 110-289, §3011(b)(1):

Amended Code Sec. 26(b)(2) by striking "and" at the end of subparagraph (U), by striking the period and inserting ", and" and [at] the end of subparagraph (V), and by inserting after subparagraph (V) a new subparagraph (W). **Effective** for residences purchased on or after 4-9-2008, in tax years ending on or after such date.

• 2007, Tax Technical Corrections Act of 2007 (P.L. 110-172)

P.L. 110-172, §11(a)(3):

Amended Code Sec. 26(b)(2) by redesignating subparagraphs (S) and (T) as subparagraphs (U) and (V), respectively, and by inserting after subparagraph (R) new subparagraphs (S) and (T). **Effective** 12-29-2007.

• 2005, Gulf Opportunity Zone Act of 2005 (P.L. 109-135)

P.L. 109-135, §403(hh)(1):

Amended Code Sec. 26(b)(2) by striking "and" at the end of subparagraph (R), by striking the period at the end of subparagraph (S) and inserting ", and", and by adding at the end a new subparagraph (T). **Effective** as if included in the provision of the American Jobs Creation Act of 2004 (P.L. 108-357) to which it relates [**effective** generally for amounts deferred after 12-31-2004.—CCH].

P.L. 109-135, §412(c):

Amended Code Sec. 26(b)(2)(E) by striking "section 530(d)(3)" and inserting "section 530(d)(4)". **Effective** 12-21-2005.

• 2004, Working Families Tax Relief Act of 2004 (P.L. 108-311)

P.L. 108-311, §401(a)(1):

Amended Code Sec. 26(b)(2) by striking "and" at the end of subparagraph (Q), by striking the period at the end of subparagraph (R) and inserting ", and", and by adding at the end a new subparagraph (S). **Effective** as if included in section 1201 of the Medicare Prescription Drug, Improvement, and Modernization Act of 2003 (P.L. 108-173) [**effective** for tax years beginning after 12-31-2003.—CCH].

P.L. 108-311, §408(a)(5)(A):

Amended Code Sec. 26(b)(2) by striking "Medicare+Choice MSA" and inserting "Medicare Advantage MSA". **Effective** 10-4-2004.

• 2002, Job Creation and Worker Assistance Act of 2002 (P.L. 107-147)

P.L. 107-147, §415(a):

Amended Code Sec. 26(b)(2) by striking "and" at the end of subparagraph (P), by striking the period and inserting ", and" at the end of subparagraph (Q), and by adding at the end a new subparagraph (R). **Effective** as if included in section 4006 of P.L. 105-33 [**effective** for tax years beginning after 12-31-98.—CCH].

• 2001 (P.L. 107-22)

P.L. 107-22, §1(b)(2)(A):

Amended Code Sec. 26(b)(2)(E) by striking "education individual retirement" and inserting "Coverdell education savings". **Effective** 7-26-2001.

• 2000, Community Renewal Tax Relief Act of 2000 (P.L. 106-554)

P.L. 106-554, §202(a)(1):

Amended Code Sec. 26(b)(2)(Q) by striking "medical savings account" and inserting "Archer MSA". **Effective** 12-21-2000.

• 1997, Taxpayer Relief Act of 1997 (P.L. 105-34)

P.L. 105-34, §213(e)(1):

Amended Code Sec. 26(b)(2) by redesignating subparagraphs (E) through (P) as subparagraphs (F) through (Q), respectively, and by inserting after subparagraph (D) a new subparagraph (E). **Effective** for tax years beginning after 12-31-97.

P.L. 105-34, §1602(a)(1):

Amended Code Sec. 26(b)(2) by striking "and" at the end of subparagraph (N), by striking the period at the end of subparagraph (O) and inserting ", and", and by adding at the end a new subparagraph (P). **Effective** as if included in the provisions of P.L. 104-191 to which it relates [**effective** for tax years beginning after 12-31-96.—CCH].

• 1996, Small Business Job Protection Act of 1996 (P.L. 104-188)

P.L. 104-188, §1621(b)(1):

Amended Code Sec. 26(b)(2) by striking "and" at the end of subparagraph (M), striking the period at the end of subparagraph (N) and inserting ", and", and adding at the end a new subparagraph (O). **Effective** 9-1-97.

• 1989, Omnibus Budget Reconciliation Act of 1989 (P.L. 101-239)

P.L. 101-239, §7811(c)(1):

Amended Code Sec. 26(b)(2)(C) and (D). **Effective** as if included in the provision of P.L. 100-647 to which it relates. Prior to amendment, Code Sec. 26(b)(2)(C)-(D) read as follows:

(C) subsection (m)(5)(B), (q), or (v) of section 72 (relating to additional tax on certain distributions),

(D) section 72(t) (relating to 10-percent additional tax on early distributions from qualified retirement plans),

P.L. 101-239, §7811(c)(2):

Amended Code Sec. 26(b)(2) by striking subparagraph (K) and all that follows, and inserting new subparagraphs (K)-(M). **Effective** as if included in the provision of P.L. 100-647 to which it relates. Prior to amendment, Code Sec. 26(b)(2)(K)-(M)[(N)] read as follows:

(K) section 871(a) and 881 (relating to certain income of nonresident aliens and foreign corporations),

(L) section 860E(e) (relating to taxes with respect to certain residual interests), and [,]

(L)[(M)] section 884 (relating to branch profits tax) [, and]

(M)[(N)] section 143(m) (relating to recapture of portion of federal subsidy from use of mortgage bonds and mortgage credit certificates).

P.L. 101-239, §7821(a)(4)(A):

Amended Code Sec. 26(b)(2) by striking "and" at the end of subparagraph (L), by striking the period at the end of subparagraph (M) and inserting ", and", and by adding at the end thereof a new subparagraph (N). **Effective** as if included in the provision of P.L. 100-203 to which it relates.

• 1988, Technical and Miscellaneous Revenue Act of 1988 (P.L. 100-647)

P.L. 100-647, §1006(t)(16)(C):

Amended Code Sec. 26(b)(2) by striking out "and" at the end of subparagraph (J), by striking out the period at the end of subparagraph (K) and inserting in lieu thereof ", and", and by adding at the end thereof new subparagraph (L). **Effective** as if included in the provisions of P.L. 99-514 to which it relates.

P.L. 100-647, §1007(g)(1):

Amended Code Sec. 26(b)(2)(K) by striking out the comma at the end thereof and inserting in lieu thereof ").". **Effective** as if included in the provisions of P.L. 99-514 to which it relates.

P.L. 100-647, §1011A(c)(10)(A)-(B):

Amended Code Sec. 26(b)(2) by striking out ", (o)(2)," in subparagraph (C) after "(m)(5)(B)", and by striking out "408(f) (relating to additional tax on income from certain retirement accounts)" in subparagraph (D) and inserting in lieu thereof "72(t) (relating to 10-percent additional tax on early distributions from qualified retirement plans)". **Effective** as if included in the provisions of P.L. 99-514 to which it relates.

P.L. 100-647, §1012(q)(8):

Amended Code Sec. 26(b)(2) by striking out "and" at the end of subparagraph (J)[K], by striking out the period at the end of subparagraph (K)[L] and inserting in lieu thereof ", and", and by adding at the end thereof new subparagraph (L)[M]. **Effective** as if included in the provisions of P.L. 99-514 to which it relates.

P.L. 100-647, §4005(g)(4):

Amended Code Sec. 26(b)(2) (as amended by title I of this Act) by striking out "and" at the end of subparagraph (K), by striking out the period at the end of subparagaph (L) and inserting in lieu thereof ", and", and by adding at the end thereof new subparagraph (M). **Effective**, generally, to financing provided, and mortgage credit certificates issued, after 12-31-90. For an exception, see Act Sec. 4005(h)(3)(B), below.

P.L. 100-647, §4005(h)(3)(B), provides:

(B) EXCEPTION.—The amendments made by subsection (g) shall not apply to financing provided pursuant to a binding contract (entered into before June 23, 1988) with a homebuilder, lender, or mortgagor if the bonds (the proceeds of which are used to provide such financing) are issued—

(i) before June 23, 1988, or

(ii) before August 1, 1988, pursuant to a written application (made before July 1, 1988) for State bond volume authority.

P.L. 100-647, §5012(b)(2):

Amended Code Sec. 26(b)(2)(C) by striking out "or (q)" and inserting in lieu thereof "(q), or (v)". **Effective**, generally, for contracts entered into on or after 6-21-88. However, for special rules, see Act Sec. 5012(e)(2)-(4), below.

P.L. 100-647, §5012(e)(2)-(4) (as amended by P.L. 101-239, §7815(a)(2)), provides:

(2) SPECIAL RULE WHERE DEATH BENEFIT INCREASES BY MORE THAN $150,000.—If the death benefit under the contract increases by more than $150,000 over the death benefit under the contract in effect on October 20, 1988, the rules of section 7702A(c)(3) of the 1986 Code (as added by this section) shall apply in determining whether such contract is issued on or after June 21, 1988. The preceding sentence shall not apply in the case of a contract which, as of June 21, 1988, required at least 7 level annual premium payments and under which the policyholder makes at least 7 level annual premium payments.

(3) CERTAIN OTHER MATERIAL CHANGES TAKEN INTO ACCOUNT.—A contract entered into before June 21, 1988, shall be treated as entered into after such date if—

(A) on or after June 21, 1988, the death benefit under the contract is increased (or a qualified additional benefit is increased or added) and before June 21, 1988, the owner of the contract did not have a unilateral right under the contract to obtain such increase or addition without providing additional evidence of insurability, or

(B) the contract is converted after June 20, 1988, from a term life insurance contract to a life insurance contract providing coverage other than term life insurance coverage without regard to any right of the owner of the contract to such conversion.

(4) CERTAIN EXCHANGES PERMITTED.—In the case of a modified endowment contract which—

(A) required at least 7 annual level premium payments,

(B) is entered into after June 20, 1988, and before the date of the enactment of this Act, and

(C) is exchanged within 3 months after such date of enactment for a life insurance contract which meets the requirements of section 7702A(b),

the contract which is received in exchange for such contract shall not be treated as a modified endowment contract if the taxpayer elects, notwithstanding section 1035 of the 1986 Code, to recognize gain on such exchange.

[Sec. 26(c)]

(c) TENTATIVE MINIMUM TAX.—For purposes of this part, the term "tentative minimum tax" means the amount determined under section 55(b)(1).

Amendments

• 1986, Tax Reform Act of 1986 (P.L. 99-514)

P.L. 99-514, §261(c):

Amended Code Sec. 26(b)(2) by striking out "and" at the end of subparagraph (G), by striking out the period at the end of subparagraph (H) and inserting in lieu thereof ", and", and by adding at the end thereof new subsection (I). **Effective** for tax years beginning after 12-31-86.

P.L. 99-514, §632(c)(1):

Amended Code Sec. 26(b)(2)(G) by striking out "certain capital gains" and inserting in lieu thereof "certain built-in gains" For the **effective** date, see Act Sec. 633, below.

P.L. 99-514, §633, as amended by P.L. 100-647 §1006(g), provides:

SEC. 633. EFFECTIVE DATES.

(a) GENERAL RULE.—Except as otherwise provided in this section, the amendments made by this subtitle shall apply to—

(1) any distribution in complete liquidation, and any sale or exchange, made by a corporation after July 31, 1986, unless such corporation is completely liquidated before January 1, 1987,

(2) any transaction described in section 338 of the Internal Revenue Code of 1986 for which the acquisition date occurs after December 31, 1986, and

(3) any distribution (not in complete liquidation) made after December 31, 1986.

(b) BUILT-IN GAINS OF S CORPORATIONS.—

(1) IN GENERAL.—The amendments made by section 632 (other than subsection (b) thereof) shall apply to taxable years beginning after December 31, 1986, but only in cases where the return for the taxable year is filed pursuant to an S election made after December 31, 1986.

(2) APPLICATION OF PRIOR LAW.—In the case of any taxable year of an S corporation which begins after December 31, 1986, and to which the amendments made by section 632 (other than subsection (b) thereof) do not apply, paragraph (1) of section 1374(b) of the Internal Revenue Code of 1954 (as in effect on the date before the date of the enactment of this Act) shall be applied as if it read as follows:

"(1) an amount equal to 34 percent of the amount by which the net capital gain of the corporation for the taxable year exceeds $25,000, or".

(c) EXCEPTION FOR CERTAIN PLANS OF LIQUIDATION AND BINDING CONTRACTS.—

(1) IN GENERAL.—The amendments made by this subtitle shall not apply to—

(A) any distribution or sale or exchange made pursuant to a plan of liquidation adopted before August 1, 1986, if the liquidating corporation is completely liquidated before January 1, 1988,

(B) any distribution or sale or exchange made by any corporation if more than 50 percent of the voting stock by value of such corporation is acquired on or after August 1, 1986, pursuant to a written binding contract in effect before such date and if such corporation is completely liquidated before January 1, 1988,

(C) any distribution or sale or exchange made by any corporation if substantially all of the assets of such corporation are sold on or after August 1, 1986, pursuant to 1 or more written binding contracts in effect before such date and if such corporation is completely liquidated before January 1, 1988, or

(D) any transaction described in section 338 of the Internal Revenue Code of 1986 with respect to any target corporation if a qualified stock purchase of such target corporation is made on or after August 1, 1986, pursuant to a written binding contract in effect before such date and the acquisition date (within the meaning of such section 338) is before January 1, 1988.

(2) SPECIAL RULE FOR CERTAIN ACTIONS TAKEN BEFORE NOVEMBER 20, 1985.—For purposes of paragraph (1), transactions shall be treated as pursuant to a plan of liquidation adopted before August 1, 1986, if—

(A) before November 20, 1985—

(i) the board of directors of the liquidating corporation adopted a resolution to solicit shareholder approval for a transaction of a kind described in section 336 or 337, or

(ii) the shareholders or board of directors have approved such a transaction,

(B) before November 20, 1985—

(i) there has been an offer to purchase a majority of the voting stock of the liquidating corporation, or

(ii) the board of directors of the liquidating corporation has adopted a resolution approving an acquisition or recommending the approval of an acquisition to the shareholders, or

(c) before November 20, 1985, a ruling request was submitted to the Secretary of the Treasury or his delegate with respect to a transaction of a kind described in section 336 or 337 of the Internal Revenue Code of 1954 (as in effect before the amendments made by this subtitle).

For purposes of the preceding sentence, any action taken by the board of directors or shareholders of a corporation with respect to any subsidiary of such corporation shall be treated as taken by the board of directors or shareholders of such subsidiary.

(d) TRANSITIONAL RULE FOR CERTAIN SMALL CORPORATIONS.—

(1) IN GENERAL.—In the case of the complete liquidation before January 1, 1989, of a qualified corporation, the amendments made by this subtitle shall not apply to the applicable percentage of each gain or loss which (but for this paragraph) would be recognized by the liquidating corporation by reason of the amendments made by this subtitle. Section 333 of the Internal Revenue Code of 1954 (as in effect on the day before the date of the enactment of this Act) shall continue to apply to any complete liquidation described in the preceding sentence.

(2) PARAGRAPH (1) NOT TO APPLY TO CERTAIN ITEMS.—Paragraph (1) shall not apply to—

(A) any gain or loss which is an ordinary gain or loss (determined without regard to section 1239 of the Internal Revenue Code of 1986).

(B) any gain or loss on a capital asset held for not more than 6 months, and

(C) any gain on an asset acquired by the qualified corporation if—

(i) the basis of such asset in the hands of the qualified corporation is determined (in whole or in part) by reference to the basis of such asset in the hands of the person from whom acquired, and

(ii) a principal purpose for the transfer of such asset to the qualified corporation was to secure the benefits of this subsection.

(3) APPLICABLE PERCENTAGE.—For purposes of this subsection, the term "applicable percentage" means—

(A) 100 percent if the applicable value of the qualified corporation is less than $5,000,000, or

(B) 100 percent reduced by an amount which bears the same ratio to 100 percent as—

(i) the excess of the applicable value of the corporation over $5,000,000, bears to

(ii) $5,000,000.

(4) APPLICABLE VALUE.—For purposes of this subsection, the applicable value is the fair market value of all of the stock of the corporation on the date of the adoption of the plan of complete liquidation (or if greater, on August 1, 1986).

(5) QUALIFIED CORPORATION.—For purposes of this subsection, the term "qualified corporation" means any corporation if—

(A) on August 1, 1986, and at all times thereafter before the corporation is completely liquidated, more than 50 percent (by value) of the stock in such corporation is held by a qualified group, and

(B) the applicable value of such corporation does not exceed $10,000,000.

(6) DEFINITIONS AND SPECIAL RULES.—For purposes of this subsection—

(A) QUALIFIED GROUP.—

(i) IN GENERAL.—Except as provided in clause (ii), the term "qualified group" means any group of 10 or fewer qualified persons who at all times during the 5-year period ending on the date of the adoption of the plan of complete liquidation (or, if shorter, the period during which the corporation or any predecessor was in existence) owned (or was treated as owning under the rules of subparagraph (C)) more than 50 percent (by value) of the stock in such corporation.

(ii) 5-YEAR OWNERSHIP REQUIREMENT NOT TO APPLY IN CERTAIN CASES.—In the case of—

(I) any complete liquidation pursuant to a plan of liquidation adopted before March 31, 1988,

(II) any distribution not in liquidation made before March 31, 1988,

(III) an election to be an S corporation filed before March 31, 1988, or

(IV) a transaction described in section 338 of the Internal Revenue Code of 1986 where the acquisition date (within the meaning of such section 338) is before March 31, 1988,

the term "qualified group" means any group of 10 or fewer qualified persons.

(B) QUALIFIED PERSON.—The term "qualified person" means—

(i) an individual,

(ii) an estate, or

(iii) any trust described in clause (ii) or clause (iii) of section 1361(c)(2)(A) of the Internal Revenue Code of 1986.

(C) ATTRIBUTION RULES.—

(i) IN GENERAL.—Any stock owned by a corporation, trust (other than a trust referred to in subparagraph (B)(iii), or partnership shall be treated as owned proportionately by its shareholders, beneficiaries, or partners, and shall not be treated as owned by such corporation, trust, or partnership. Stock considered to be owned by a person by reason of the application of the preceding sentence shall, for purposes of applying such sentence, be treated as actually owned by such person.

(ii) FAMILY MEMBERS.—Stock owned (or treated as owned) by members of the same family (within the meaning of section 318(a)(1) of the Internal Revenue Code of 1986) shall be treated as owned by 1 person, and shall be treated as owned by such 1 person for any period during which it was owned (or treated as owned) by any such member.

(iii) TREATMENT OF CERTAIN TRUSTS.—Stock owned (or treated as owned) by the estate of any decedent or by any trust referred to in subparagraph (B)(iii) with respect to such decedent shall be treated as owned by 1 person and shall be treated as owned by such 1 person for the period during which it was owned (or treated as owned) by such estate or any such trust or by the decedent.

(D) SPECIAL HOLDING PERIOD RULES.—Any property acquired by reason of the death of an individual shall be treated as owned at all times during which such property was owned (or treated as owned) by the decedent.

(E) CONTROLLED GROUP OF CORPORATIONS.—All members of the same controlled group (as defined in section 267(f)(1) of such Code) shall be treated as 1 corporation for purposes of determining whether any of such corporations met the requirement of paragraph (5)(B) and for purposes of determining the applicable percentage with respect to any of such corporations. For purposes of the preceding sentence, an S corporation shall not be treated as a member of a controlled group unless such corporation was a C corporation for its taxable year which includes August 1, 1986, or it was not described for such taxable year in paragraph (1) or (2) of section 1374(c) of such Code (as in effect on the day before the date of the enactment of this Act).

(7) SECTION 338 TRANSACTIONS.—The provisions of this subsection shall also apply in the case of a transaction described in section 338 of the Internal Revenue Code of 1986 where the acquisition date (within the meaning of such section 338) is before January 1, 1989.

(8) APPLICATION OF SECTION 1374.—Rules similar to the rules of this subsection shall apply for purposes of applying section 1374 of the Internal Revenue Code of 1986 (as amended by section 632) in the case of a qualified corporation makes an election to be an S corporation under section 1362 of such Code before January 1, 1989, without regard to whether such corporation is completely liquidated.

(9) APPLICATION TO NONLIQUIDATING DISTRIBUTIONS.—The provisions of this subsection shall also apply in the case of any distribution (not in complete liquidation) made by a qualified corporation before January 1, 1989, without regard to whether such corporation is completely liquidated.

(e) COMPLETE LIQUIDATION DEFINED.—For purposes of this section, a corporation shall be treated as completely liquidated if all of the assets of such corporation are distributed in complete liquidation, less assets retained to meet claims.

(f) OTHER TRANSITIONAL RULES.—

(1) The amendments made by this subtitle shall not apply to any liquidation of a corporation incorporated under the laws of Pennsylvania on August 3, 1970, if—

(A) the board of directors of such corporation approved a plan of liquidation before January 1, 1986,

(B) an agreement for the sale of a material portion of the assets of such corporation was signed on May 9, 1986 (whether or not the assets are sold in accordance with such agreement), and

(C) the corporation is completely liquidated on or before December 31, 1988.

(2) The amendments made by this subtitle shall not apply to any liquidation (or deemed liquidation under section 338 of the Internal Revenue Code of 1986) of a diversified financial services corporation incorporated under the laws of Delaware on May 9, 1929 (or any direct or indirect subsidiary of such corporation), pursuant to a binding written contract entered into on or before December 31, 1986; but only if the liquidation is completed (or in the case of a section 338 election, the acquisition date occurs) before January 1, 1988.

(3) The amendments made by this subtitle shall not apply to any distribution, or sale, or exchange—

(A) of the assets owned (directly or indirectly) by a testamentary trust established under the will of a decedent dying on June 15, 1956, to its beneficiaries,

(B) made pursuant to a court order in an action filed on January 18, 1984, if such order—

(i) is issued after July 31, 1986, and

(ii) directs the disposition of the assets of such trust and the division of the trust corpus into 3 separate subtrusts.

For purposes of the preceding sentence, an election under section 338(g) of the Internal Revenue Code of 1986 (or an election under section 338(h)(10) of such Code) qualifying as a section 337 liquidation pursuant to regulations prescribed by the Secretary under section 1.338(h)(10)-1T(j) made in connection with a sale or exchange pursuant to a court order described in subparagraph (B) shall be treated as a sale or exchange.

(4)(A) The amendments made by this subtitle shall not apply to any distribution, or sale, or exchange—

(i) if—

(I) an option agreement to sell substantially all of the assets of a selling corporation organized under the laws of Massachusetts on October 20, 1976, is executed before August 1, 1986, the corporation adopts (by approval of its shareholders) a conditional plan of liquidation before August 1, 1986 to become effective upon the exercise of such option agreement (or modification thereto), and the assets are—sold pursuant to the exercise of the option (as originally executed or subsequently modified provided that the purchase price is not thereby increased), or

(II) in the event that the optionee does not acquire substantially all the assets of the corporation, the optionor corporation sells substantially all its assets to another purchaser at a purchase price not greater than that contemplated by such option agreement pursuant to an effective plan of liquidation, and

(ii) the complete liquidation of the corporation occurs within 12 months of the time the plan of liquidation becomes effective, but in no event later than December 31, 1989.

(B) For purposes of subparagraph (A), a distribution, or sale, or exchange, of a distributee corporation (within the meaning of section 337(c)(3) of the Internal Revenue Code of 1986) shall be treated as satisfying the requirements of subparagraph (A) if its subsidiary satisfies the requirements of subparagraph (A).

(C) For purposes of section 56 of the Internal Revenue Code of 1986 (as amended by this Act), any gain or loss not recognized by reason of this paragraph shall not be taken into account in determining the adjusted net book income of the corporation.

(5) In the case of a corporation incorporated under the laws of Wisconsin on April 3, 1948—

(A) a voting trust established not later than December 31, 1987, shall qualify as a trust permitted as a shareholder of an S corporation and shall be treated as only 1 shareholder if the holders of beneficial interests in such voting trust are—

(i) employees or retirees of such corporation, or

(ii) in the case of stock or voting trust certificates acquired from an employee or retiree of such corporation, the spouse, child, or estate of such employee or retiree or a trust created by such employee or retiree which is described in section 1361(c)(2) of the Internal Revenue Code of 1986 (or treated as described in such section by reason of section 1361(d) of such Code), and

(B) the amendment made by section 632 (other than subsection (b) thereof) shall not apply to such corporation if it elects to be an S corporation before January 1, 1989.

(6) The amendments made by this subtitle shall not apply to the liquidation of a corporation incorporated on January 26, 1982, under the laws of the State of Alabama with a principal place of business in Colbert County, Alabama, but

only if such corporation is completely liquidated on or before December 31, 1987.

(7) The amendments made by this subtitle shall not apply to the acquisition by a Delaware bank holding company of all of the assets of an Iowa bank holding company pursuant to a written contract dated December 9, 1981.

(8) The amendments made by this subtitle shall not apply to the liquidation of a corporation incorporated under the laws of Delaware on January 20, 1984, if more than 40 percent of the stock of such corporation was acquired by purchase on June 11, 1986, and there was a tender offer with respect to all additional outstanding shares of such corporation on July 29, 1986, but only if the corporation is completely liquidated on or before December 31, 1987.

(g) TREATMENT OF CERTAIN DISTRIBUTIONS IN RESPONSE TO HOSTILE TENDER OFFER.—

(1) IN GENERAL.—No gain or loss shall be recognized under the Internal Revenue Code of 1986 to a corporation (hereinafter in this subsection referred to as "parent") on a qualified distribution.

(2) QUALIFIED DISTRIBUTION DEFINED.—For purposes of paragraph (1)—

(A) IN GENERAL.—The term "qualified distribution" means a distribution—

(i) by parent of all of the stock of a qualified subsidiary in exchange for stock of parent which was acquired for purposes of such exchange pursuant to a tender offer dated February 16, 1982, and

(ii) pursuant to a contract dated February 13, 1982, and

(iii) which was made not more than 60 days afer the board of directors of parent recommended rejection of an unsolicited tender offer to obtain control of parent.

(B) QUALIFIED SUBSIDIARY.—The term "qualified subsidiary" means a corporation created or organized under the laws of Delaware on September 7, 1976, all of the stock of which was owned by parent immediately before the qualified distribution.

P.L. 99-514, §701(c)(1)(A):

Amended Code Sec. 26(a). For the **effective** date, see Act Sec. 701(f), as amended by P.L. 100-647, §1007(t)(2)-(3), below. Prior to amendment, Code Sec. 26(a) read as follows:

(a) LIMITATION BASED ON AMOUNT OF TAX.—The aggregate amount of credits allowed by this subpart for the taxable year shall not exceed the taxpayer's tax liability for such taxable year.

P.L. 99-514, §701(c)(1)(B)(i)-(v):

Amended Code Sec. 26(b) (as amended by title II) by striking out "this section" in the matter preceding paragraph (1) and inserting in lieu thereof "this part", by striking out "tax liability" in paragraph (1) and inserting in lieu thereof "regular tax liability", by striking out subparagraph (A) of paragraph (2) and inserting in lieu thereof new subparagraph (A) to read as above, by striking out "and" at the end of paragraph (2)(H), by striking out the period at the end of paragraph (2)(I) and inserting in lieu thereof ", and", and adding at the end of paragraph (2) new subparagraph (J), and by striking out "Tax Liability" in the subsection heading and inserting in lieu thereof "Regular Tax Liability". For the **effective** date, see Act Sec. 701(f), as amended by P.L. 100-647, §1007(t)(2)-(3), below. Prior to amendment, Code Sec. 26(b)(2)(A) read as follows:

(A) section 56 (relating to corporate minimum tax),

P.L. 99-514, §701(c)(1)(C):

Amended Code Sec. 26(c). For the **effective** date, see Act Sec. 701(f), as amended by P.L. 100-647, §1007(t)(2)-(3), below. Prior to amendment, Code Sec. 26(c) read as follows:

(c) SIMILAR RULE FOR ALTERNATIVE MINIMUM TAX FOR TAXPAYERS OTHER THAN CORPORATIONS.—

For treatment of tax imposed by section 55 as not imposed by this chapter, see section 55(c).

P.L. 99-514, §701(f), as amended by P.L. 100-647, §1007(t)(2)-(3), provides:

(f) EFFECTIVE DATES.—

(1) IN GENERAL.— Except as otherwise provided in this subsection, the amendments made by this section shall apply to taxable years beginning after December 31, 1986.

(2) ADJUSTMENT OF NET OPERATING LOSS.—

(A) INDIVIDUALS.—In the case of a net operating loss of an individual for a taxable year beginning after December 31, 1982, and before January 1, 1987, for purposes of determining the amount of such loss which may be carried to a taxable year beginning after December 31, 1986, for purposes of the minimum tax, such loss shall be adjusted in the manner provided in section 55(d)(2) of the Internal Revenue Code of 1954 as in effect on the day before the date of the enactment of this Act.

(B) CORPORATIONS.—If the minimum tax of a corporation was deferred under section 56(b) of the Internal Revenue Code of 1954 (as in effect on the day before the date of the enactment of this Act) for any taxable year beginning before January 1, 1987, and the amount of such tax has not been paid for any taxable year beginning before January 1, 1987, the amount of the net operating loss carryovers of such corporation which may be carried to taxable years beginning after December 31, 1986, for purposes of the minimum tax shall be reduced by the amount of tax preferences a tax on which was so deferred.

(3) INSTALLMENT SALES.—Section 56(a)(6) of the Internal Revenue Code of 1986 (as amended by this section) shall not apply to any disposition to which the amendments made by section 811 of this Act (relating to allocation of dealer's indebtedness to installment obligations) do not apply by reason of section 811(c)(2) of this Act.

(4) EXCEPTION FOR CHARITABLE CONTRIBUTIONS BEFORE AUGUST 16, 1986.—Section 57(a)(6) of the Internal Revenue Code of 1986 (as amended by this section) shall not apply to any deduction attributable to contributions made before August 16, 1986.

(5) BOOK INCOME.—

(A) IN GENERAL.—In the case of a corporation to which this paragraph applies, the amount of any increase for any taxable year under section 56(c)(1)(A) of the Internal Revenue Code of 1986 (as added by this section) shall be reduced (but not below zero) by the excess (if any) of—

(i) 50 percent of the excess of taxable income for the 5-taxable year period ending with the taxable year preceding the 1st taxable year to which such section applies over the adjusted net book income for such period, over

(ii) the aggregate amounts taken into account under this paragraph for preceding taxable years.

(B) TAXPAYER TO WHOM PARAGRAPH APPLIES.—This paragraph applies to a taxpayer which was incorporated in Delaware on May 31, 1912.

(C) TERMS.—Any term used in this paragraph which is used in section 56 of such Code (as so added) shall have the same meaning as when used in such section.

(6) CERTAIN PUBLIC UTILITY.—

(A) In the case of investment tax credits described in subparagraph (B) or (C), subsection 38(c)(3)(A)(ii) of the Internal Revenue Code of 1986 shall be applied by substituting "25 percent" for "75 percent", and section 38(c)(3)(B) of the Internal Revenue Code of 1986 shall be applied by substituting "75 percent" for "25 percent".

(B) If, on September 25, 1985, a regulated electric utility owned an undivided interest, within the range of 1,111 and 1,149, in the "maximum dependable capacity, net, megawatts electric" of an electric generating unit located in Illinois or Mississippi for which a binding written contract was in effect on December 31, 1980, then any investment tax credit with respect to such unit shall be described in this subparagraph. The aggregate amount of investment tax credits with respect to the unit in Mississippi allowed solely by reason of being described in this subparagraph shall not exceed $141,000,000.

(C) If, on September 25, 1985, a regulated electric utility owned an undivided interest, within the range of 1,104 and 1,111, in the "maximum dependable capacity, net, megawatts electric" of an electric generating unit located in Louisiana for which a binding written contract was in effect on December 31, 1980, then any investment tax credit of such electric utility shall be described in this subparagraph. The aggregate amount of investment tax credits allowed solely by reason of being described by this subparagraph shall not exceed $20,000,000.

(7) AGREEMENT VESSEL DEPRECIATION ADJUSTMENT.—

(A) For purposes of part VI of subchapter A of chapter 1 of the Internal Revenue Code of 1986, in the case of a qualified taxpayer, alternative minimum taxable income for the taxable year shall be reduced by an amount equal to the agreement vessel depreciation adjustment.

(B) For purposes of this paragraph, the agreement vessel depreciation adjustment shall be an amount equal to the depreciation deduction that would have been allowable for such year under section 167 of such Code with respect to agreement vessels placed in service before January 1, 1987, if the basis of such vessels had not been reduced under section 607 of the Merchant Marine Act of 1936, as amended, and if depreciation with respect to such vessel had been computed using the 25-year straight-line method. The aggregate amount by which basis of a qualified taxpayer is treated as not reduced by reason of this subparagraph shall not exceed $100,000,000.

(C) For purposes of this paragraph, the term "qualified taxpayer" means a parent corporation incorporated in the State of Delaware on December 1, 1972, and engaged in water transportation, and includes any other corporation which is a member of the affiliated group of which the parent corporation is common parent. No taxpayer shall be treated as a qualified corporation for any taxable year beginning after December 31, 1991.

• 1986, Superfund Amendments and Reauthorization Act of 1986 (P.L. 99-499)

P.L. 99-499, §516(b)(1)(A):

Amended Code Sec. 26(b)(2) by redesignating subparagraphs (B) through (J) as subparagraphs (C) through (K), respectively, and by inserting after subparagraph (A) new subparagraph (B). **Effective** for tax years beginning after 12-31-86.

• 1984, Deficit Reduction Act of 1984 (P.L. 98-369)

P.L. 98-369, §472:

Added Code Sec. 25, which was subsequently redesignated as Code Sec. 26. **Effective** for tax years beginning after 12-31-83, and to carrybacks from such years.

P.L. 98-369, §612(a):

Redesignated Code Sec. 25, as added by Act Sec. 472, as Code Sec. 26. **Effective** for interest paid or accrued after 12-31-84, on indebtedness incurred after 12-31-84, and to elections under section 25(c)(2)(A)(ii) of the Internal Revenue Code of 1954 (as added by this Act) for calendar years after 1983. For rules relating to special elections and transitional rules, see Act Sec. 611(d)(3)-(7), which appears in the amendment notes for Code Sec. 103A.

P.L. 98-369, §491(f)(5), provides:

(5) TREATMENT OF TAX IMPOSED UNDER SECTION 409(c).—For purposes of section 26(b) of the Internal Revenue Code of 1954 (as amended by this Act), any tax imposed by section 409(c) of such Code (as in effect before its repeal by this section) shall be treated as a tax imposed by section 408(f) of such Code.

Subpart B—Other Credits

[Sec. 27]

SEC. 27. TAXES OF FOREIGN COUNTRIES AND POSSESSIONS OF THE UNITED STATES; POSSESSION TAX CREDIT.

[Sec. 27(a)]

(a) FOREIGN TAX CREDIT.—The amount of taxes imposed by foreign countries and possessions of the United States shall be allowed as a credit against the tax imposed by this chapter to the extent provided in section 901.

Amendments

• 1984, Deficit Reduction Act of 1984 (P.L. 98-369)

P.L. 98-369, §471(c)(1):

Redesignated Code Sec. 33 as Code Sec. 27. **Effective** for tax years beginninng after 12-31-83, and to carrybacks from such years.

• 1976, Tax Reform Act of 1976 (P.L. 94-455)

P.L. 94-455, §1051(a):

Added "POSSESSION TAX CREDIT" in the heading of Sec. 33, and added "(a) FOREIGN TAX CREDIT.—" at the beginning of the section. **Effective** for tax years beginning after 12-31-75.

[Sec. 27(b)]

(b) SECTION 936 CREDIT.—In the case of a domestic corporation, the amount provided by section 936 (relating to Puerto Rico and possession tax credit) shall be allowed as a credit against the tax imposed by this chapter.

Amendments

• 1976, Tax Reform Act of 1976 (P.L. 94-455)

P.L. 94-455, §1051(a):

Added subsection (b). **Effective** for tax years beginning after 12-31-75.

[Sec. 30]

SEC. 30. CERTAIN PLUG-IN ELECTRIC VEHICLES.

[Sec. 30(a)]

(a) ALLOWANCE OF CREDIT.—There shall be allowed as a credit against the tax imposed by this chapter for the taxable year an amount equal to 10 percent of the cost of any qualified plug-in electric vehicle placed in service by the taxpayer during the taxable year.

[Sec. 30(b)]

(b) PER VEHICLE DOLLAR LIMITATION.—The amount of the credit allowed under subsection (a) with respect to any vehicle shall not exceed $2,500.

[Sec. 30(c)]

(c) APPLICATION WITH OTHER CREDITS.—

(1) BUSINESS CREDIT TREATED AS PART OF GENERAL BUSINESS CREDIT.—So much of the credit which would be allowed under subsection (a) for any taxable year (determined without regard to this subsection) that is attributable to property of a character subject to an allowance for depreciation shall be treated as a credit listed in section 38(b) for such taxable year (and not allowed under subsection (a)).

(2) PERSONAL CREDIT.—

(A) IN GENERAL.—For purposes of this title, the credit allowed under subsection (a) for any taxable year (determined after application of paragraph (1)) shall be treated as a credit allowable under subpart A for such taxable year.

(B) LIMITATION BASED ON AMOUNT OF TAX.—In the case of a taxable year to which section 26(a)(2) does not apply, the credit allowed under subsection (a) for any taxable year (determined after application of paragraph (1)) shall not exceed the excess of—

(i) the sum of the regular tax liability (as defined in section 26(b)) plus the tax imposed by section 55, over

Caution: Code Sec. 30(c)(2)(B)(ii), below, was amended by P.L. 111-148. For sunset provision, see P.L. 111-148, §10909(c), in the amendment notes.

(ii) the sum of the credits allowable under subpart A (other than this section and sections 25D and 30D) and section 27 for the taxable year.

Amendments

• 2010, Patient Protection and Affordable Care Act (P.L. 111-148)

P.L. 111-148, §10909(b)(2)(F):

Amended Code Sec. 30(c)(2)(B)(ii) by striking "23, 25D," and inserting "25D". **Effective** for tax years beginning after 12-31-2009.

P.L. 111-148, §10909(c), provides:

(c) APPLICATION AND EXTENSION OF EGTRRA SUNSET.—Notwithstanding section 901 of the Economic Growth and Tax Relief Reconciliation Act of 2001 [P.L. 107-16], such section shall apply to the amendments made by this section and the amendments made by section 202 of such Act by substituting "December 31, 2011" for "December 31, 2010" in subsection (a)(1) thereof.

• 2001, Economic Growth and Tax Relief Reconciliation Act of 2001 (P.L. 107-16)

P.L. 107-16, §901(a)-(b), provides [but see P.L. 111-148, §10909(c), above]:

SEC. 901. SUNSET OF PROVISIONS OF ACT.

(a) IN GENERAL.—All provisions of, and amendments made by, this Act shall not apply—

(1) to taxable, plan, or limitation years beginning after December 31, 2010, or

(2) in the case of title V, to estates of decedents dying, gifts made, or generation skipping transfers, after December 31, 2010.

(b) APPLICATION OF CERTAIN LAWS.—The Internal Revenue Code of 1986 and the Employee Retirement Income Security Act of 1974 shall be applied and administered to years, estates, gifts, and transfers described in subsection (a) as if the provisions and amendments described in subsection (a) had never been enacted.

[Sec. 30(d)]

(d) QUALIFIED PLUG-IN ELECTRIC VEHICLE.—For purposes of this section—

(1) IN GENERAL.—The term "qualified plug-in electric vehicle" means a specified vehicle—

(A) the original use of which commences with the taxpayer,

(B) which is acquired for use or lease by the taxpayer and not for resale,

(C) which is made by a manufacturer,

(D) which is manufactured primarily for use on public streets, roads, and highways,

(E) which has a gross vehicle weight rating of less than 14,000 pounds, and

(F) which is propelled to a significant extent by an electric motor which draws electricity from a battery which—

(i) has a capacity of not less than 4 kilowatt hours (2.5 kilowatt hours in the case of a vehicle with 2 or 3 wheels), and

(ii) is capable of being recharged from an external source of electricity.

(2) SPECIFIED VEHICLE.—The term "specified vehicle" means any vehicle which—

(A) is a low speed vehicle within the meaning of section 571.3 of title 49, Code of Federal Regulations (as in effect on the date of the enactment of the American Recovery and Reinvestment Tax Act of 2009), or

(B) has 2 or 3 wheels.

(3) MANUFACTURER.—The term "manufacturer" has the meaning given such term in regulations prescribed by the Administrator of the Environmental Protection Agency for purposes of the administration of title II of the Clean Air Act (42 U.S.C. 7521 et seq.).

(4) BATTERY CAPACITY.—The term "capacity" means, with respect to any battery, the quantity of electricity which the battery is capable of storing, expressed in kilowatt hours, as measured from a 100 percent state of charge to a 0 percent state of charge.

[Sec. 30(e)]

(e) SPECIAL RULES.—

(1) BASIS REDUCTION.—For purposes of this subtitle, the basis of any property for which a credit is allowable under subsection (a) shall be reduced by the amount of such credit so allowed.

(2) NO DOUBLE BENEFIT.—The amount of any deduction or other credit allowable under this chapter for a new qualified plug-in electric drive motor vehicle shall be reduced by the amount of credit allowable under subsection (a) for such vehicle.

(3) PROPERTY USED BY TAX-EXEMPT ENTITY.—In the case of a vehicle the use of which is described in paragraph (3) or (4) of section 50(b) and which is not subject to a lease, the person who sold such vehicle to the person or entity using such vehicle shall be treated as the taxpayer that placed such vehicle in service, but only if such person clearly discloses to such person or entity in a document the amount of any credit allowable under subsection (a) with respect to such vehicle (determined without regard to subsection (c)).

(4) PROPERTY USED OUTSIDE UNITED STATES NOT QUALIFIED.—No credit shall be allowable under subsection (a) with respect to any property referred to in section 50(b)(1).

(5) RECAPTURE.—The Secretary shall, by regulations, provide for recapturing the benefit of any credit allowable under subsection (a) with respect to any property which ceases to be property eligible for such credit.

(6) ELECTION NOT TO TAKE CREDIT.—No credit shall be allowed under subsection (a) for any vehicle if the taxpayer elects to not have this section apply to such vehicle.

[Sec. 30(f)]

(f) TERMINATION.—This section shall not apply to any vehicle acquired after December 31, 2011.

Amendments

• 2009, American Recovery and Reinvestment Tax Act of 2009 (P.L. 111-5)

P.L. 111-5, §1142(a):

Amended Code Sec. 30. **Effective** for vehicles acquired after 2-17-2009. For a transitional rule, see Act Sec. 1142(d), below. Prior to amendment, Code Sec. 30 read as follows:

SEC. 30. CREDIT FOR QUALIFIED ELECTRIC VEHICLES.

[Sec. 30(a)]

(a) ALLOWANCE OF CREDIT.—There shall be allowed as a credit against the tax imposed by this chapter for the taxable year an amount equal to 10 percent of the cost of any qualified electric vehicle placed in service by the taxpayer during the taxable year.

[Sec. 30(b)]

(b) LIMITATIONS.—

(1) LIMITATION PER VEHICLE.—The amount of the credit allowed under subsection (a) for any vehicle shall not exceed $4,000.

(2) PHASEOUT.—In the case of any qualified electric vehicle placed in service after December 31, 2005, the credit otherwise allowable under subsection (a) (determined after the application of paragraph (1)) shall be reduced by 75 percent.

(3) APPLICATION WITH OTHER CREDITS.—The credit allowed by subsection (a) for any taxable year shall not exceed the excess (if any) of—

(A) the regular tax for the taxable year reduced by the sum of the credits allowable under subpart A and section 27, over—

(B) the tentative minimum tax for the taxable year.

Amendments

• 2005, Energy Tax Incentives Act of 2005 (P.L. 109-58)

P.L. 109-58, §1322(a)(3)(A):

Amended Code Sec. 30(b)(3)(A) by striking "sections 27 and 29" and inserting "section 27". **Effective** for credits determined under the Internal Revenue Code of 1986 for tax years ending after 12-31-2005.

• 2004, Working Families Tax Relief Act of 2004 (P.L. 108-311)

P.L. 108-311, §318(a):

Amended Code Sec. 30(b)(2). **Effective** for property placed in service after 12-31-2003. Prior to amendment, Code Sec. 30(b)(2) read as follows:

(2) PHASEOUT.—In the case of any qualified electric vehicle placed in service after December 31, 2003, the credit otherwise allowable under subsection (a) (determined after the application of paragraph (1)) shall be reduced by—

(A) 25 percent in the case of property placed in service in calendar year 2004,

(B) 50 percent in the case of property placed in service in calendar year 2005, and

(C) 75 percent in the case of property placed in service in calendar year 2006.

• 2002, Job Creation and Worker Assistance Act of 2002 (P.L. 107-147)

P.L. 107-147, §602(a)(1)(A)-(B):

Amended Code Sec. 30(b)(2) by striking "December 31, 2001," and inserting "December 31, 2003,", and in subparagraphs (A), (B), and (C), by striking "2002", "2003", and "2004", respectively, and inserting "2004", "2005", and "2006", respectively. **Effective** for property placed in service after 12-31-2001.

• 1996, Small Business Job Protection Act of 1996 (P.L. 104-188)

P.L. 104-188, §1205(d)(4):

Amended Code Sec. 30(b)(3)(A) by striking "sections 27, 28, and 29" and inserting "sections 27 and 29". **Effective** for amounts paid or incurred in tax years ending after 6-30-96.

[Sec. 30(c)]

(c) QUALIFIED ELECTRIC VEHICLE.—For purposes of this section—

(1) IN GENERAL.—The term "qualified electric vehicle" means any motor vehicle—

(A) which is powered primarily by an electric motor drawing current from rechargeable batteries, fuel cells, or other portable sources of electrical current,

(B) the original use of which commences with the taxpayer, and

(C) which is acquired for use by the taxpayer and not for resale.

(2) MOTOR VEHICLE.—For purposes of paragraph (1), the term "motor vehicle" means any vehicle which is manufactured primarily for use on public streets, roads, and highways (not including a vehicle operated exclusively on a rail or rails) and which has at least 4 wheels.

[Sec. 30(d)]

(d) SPECIAL RULES.—

(1) BASIS REDUCTION.—The basis of any property for which a credit is allowable under subsection (a) shall be reduced by the amount of such credit (determined without regard to subsection (b)(3)).

(2) RECAPTURE.—The Secretary shall, by regulations, provide for recapturing the benefit of any credit allowable under subsection (a) with respect to any property which ceases to be property eligible for such credit.

(3) PROPERTY USED OUTSIDE UNITED STATES, ETC., NOT QUALIFIED.—No credit shall be allowed under subsection (a) with respect to any property referred to in section 50(b) or with respect to the portion of the cost of any property taken into account under section 179.

(4) ELECTION TO NOT TAKE CREDIT.—No credit shall be allowed under subsection (a) for any vehicle if the taxpayer elects to not have this section apply to such vehicle.

Amendments

• 1996, Small Business Job Protection Act of 1996 (P.L. 104-188)

P.L. 104-188, §1704(j)(4)(A)(i)-(ii):

Amended Code Sec. 30(d) by inserting "(determined without regard to subsection (b)(3))" before the period at the end of paragraph (1), and adding at the end a new paragraph (4). **Effective** 8-20-96.

[Sec. 30(e)]

(e) TERMINATION.—This section shall not apply to any property placed in service after December 31, 2006.

Amendments

• 2002, Job Creation and Worker Assistance Act of 2002 (P.L. 107-147)

P.L. 107-147, §602(a)(2):

Amended Code Sec. 30(e) by striking "December 31, 2004" and inserting "December 31, 2006". **Effective** for property placed in service after 12-31-2001.

• 1992, Energy Policy Act of 1992 (P.L. 102-486)

P.L. 102-486, §1913(b)(1):

Amended subpart B of part IV of subchapter A of chapter 1 by inserting after Code Sec. 29 new Code Sec. 30. **Effective** for property placed in service after 6-30-93.

P.L. 111-5, §1142(d), provides:

(d) TRANSITIONAL RULE.—In the case of a vehicle acquired after the date of the enactment of this Act and before January 1, 2010, no credit shall be allowed under section 30 of the Internal Revenue Code of 1986, as added by this section, if credit is allowable under section 30D of such Code with respect to such vehicle.

[Sec. 30A]

SEC. 30A. PUERTO RICO ECONOMIC ACTIVITY CREDIT.

[Sec. 30A(a)]

(a) ALLOWANCE OF CREDIT.—

(1) IN GENERAL.—Except as otherwise provided in this section, if the conditions of both paragraph (1) and paragraph (2) of subsection (b) are satisfied with respect to a qualified domestic corporation, there shall be allowed as a credit against the tax imposed by this chapter an amount equal to the portion of the tax which is attributable to the taxable income, from sources without the United States, from—

(A) the active conduct of a trade or business within Puerto Rico, or

(B) the sale or exchange of substantially all of the assets used by the taxpayer in the active conduct of such trade or business.

In the case of any taxable year beginning after December 31, 2001, the aggregate amount of taxable income taken into account under the preceding sentence (and in applying subsection (d)) shall not exceed the adjusted base period income of such corporation, as determined in the same manner as under section 936(j).

(2) QUALIFIED DOMESTIC CORPORATION.—For purposes of paragraph (1), the term "qualified domestic corporation" means a domestic corporation—

(A) which is an existing credit claimant with respect to Puerto Rico, and

(B) with respect to which section 936(a)(4)(B) does not apply for the taxable year.

(3) SEPARATE APPLICATION.—For purposes of determining—

(A) whether a taxpayer is an existing credit claimant with respect to Puerto Rico, and

(B) the amount of the credit allowed under this section,

this section (and so much of section 936 as relates to this section) shall be applied separately with respect to Puerto Rico.

[Sec. 30A(b)]

(b) CONDITIONS WHICH MUST BE SATISFIED.—The conditions referred to in subsection (a) are—

(1) 3-YEAR PERIOD.—If 80 percent or more of the gross income of the qualified domestic corporation for the 3-year period immediately preceding the close of the taxable year (or for such part of such period immediately preceding the close of such taxable year as may be applicable) was derived from sources within a possession (determined without regard to section 904(f)).

(2) TRADE OR BUSINESS.—If 75 percent or more of the gross income of the qualified domestic corporation for such period or such part thereof was derived from the active conduct of a trade or business within a possession.

[Sec. 30A(c)]

(c) CREDIT NOT ALLOWED AGAINST CERTAIN TAXES.—The credit provided by subsection (a) shall not be allowed against the tax imposed by—

(1) section 59A (relating to environmental tax),

(2) section 531 (relating to the tax on accumulated earnings),

(3) section 541 (relating to personal holding company tax), or

(4) section 1351 (relating to recoveries of foreign expropriation losses).

[Sec. 30A(d)]

(d) LIMITATIONS ON CREDIT FOR ACTIVE BUSINESS INCOME.—The amount of the credit determined under subsection (a) for any taxable year shall not exceed the sum of the following amounts:

(1) 60 percent of the sum of—

(A) the aggregate amount of the qualified domestic corporation's qualified possession wages for such taxable year, plus

(B) the allocable employee fringe benefit expenses of the qualified domestic corporation for such taxable year.

(2) The sum of—

(A) 15 percent of the depreciation allowances for the taxable year with respect to short-life qualified tangible property,

(B) 40 percent of the depreciation allowances for the taxable year with respect to medium-life qualified tangible property, and

(C) 65 percent of the depreciation allowances for the taxable year with respect to long-life qualified tangible property.

(3) If the qualified domestic corporation does not have an election to use the method described in section 936(h)(5)(C)(ii) (relating to profit split) in effect for the taxable year, the amount of the qualified possession income taxes for the taxable year allocable to nonsheltered income.

[Sec. 30A(e)]

(e) ADMINISTRATIVE PROVISIONS.—For purposes of this title—

(1) the provisions of section 936 (including any applicable election thereunder) shall apply in the same manner as if the credit under this section were a credit under section 936(a)(1)(A) for a domestic corporation to which section 936(a)(4)(A) applies,

(2) the credit under this section shall be treated in the same manner as the credit under section 936, and

(3) a corporation to which this section applies shall be treated in the same manner as if it were a corporation electing the application of section 936.

[Sec. 30A(f)]

(f) DENIAL OF DOUBLE BENEFIT.—Any wages or other expenses taken into account in determining the credit under this section may not be taken into account in determining the credit under section 41.

Amendments

• 2000, Community Renewal Tax Relief Act of 2000 (P.L. 106-554)

P.L. 106-554, §311(a)(2):

Amended Code Sec. 30A by redesignating subsections (f) and (g) as subsections (g) and (h), respectively, and by inserting after subsection (e) a new subsection (f). **Effective** as if included in the provision of P.L. 106-170 to which it relates [**effective** for amounts paid or incurred after 6-30-99.—CCH.].

[Sec. 30A(g)]

(g) DEFINITIONS.—For purposes of this section, any term used in this section which is also used in section 936 shall have the same meaning given such term by section 936.

Amendments

• 2000, Community Renewal Tax Relief Act of 2000 (P.L. 106-554)

P.L. 106-554, §311(a)(2):

Amended Code Sec. 30A by redesignating subsection (f) as subsection (g). **Effective** as if included in the provision of P.L. 106-170 to which it relates [**effective** for amounts paid or incurred after 6-30-99.—CCH.].

[Sec. 30A(h)]

(h) APPLICATION OF SECTION.—This section shall apply to taxable years beginning after December 31, 1995, and before January 1, 2006.

Amendments

• 2000, Community Renewal Tax Relief Act of 2000 (P.L. 106-554)

P.L. 106-554, §311(a)(2):

Amended Code Sec. 30A by redesignating subsection (g) as subsection (h). **Effective** as if included in the provision of P.L. 106-170 to which it relates [**effective** for amounts paid or incurred after 6-30-99.—CCH.].

• 1997, Taxpayer Relief Act of 1997 (P.L. 105-34)

P.L. 105-34, §1601(f)(1)(A):

Amended Code Sec. 30A by changing the heading. **Effective** as if included in the provisions of P.L. 104-188 to which it relates [generally **effective** for tax years beginning after 12-31-95.—CCH]. Prior to amendment, the heading of Code Sec. 30A read as follows:

SEC. 30A. PUERTO RICAN ECONOMIC ACTIVITY CREDIT.

• 1996, Small Business Job Protection Act of 1996 (P.L. 104-188)

P.L. 104-188, §1601(b)(1):

Amended subpart B of part IV of subchapter A of chapter 1 by adding at the end a new Code Sec. 30A. **Effective** for tax years beginning after 12-31-95. For special rules, see Act Sec. 1601(c)(2)-(3), below.

P.L. 104-188, §1601(c)(2)-(3), provides:

(2) SPECIAL RULE FOR QUALIFIED POSSESSION SOURCE INVESTMENT INCOME.—The amendments made by this section shall not apply to qualified possession source investment income received or accrued before July 1, 1996, without regard to the taxable year in which received or accrued.

(3) SPECIAL TRANSITION RULE FOR PAYMENT OF ESTIMATED TAX INSTALLMENT.—In determining the amount of any installment due under section 6655 of the Internal Revenue Code of 1986 after the date of the enactment of this Act and before October 1, 1996, only 1/2 of any increase in tax (for the taxable year for which such installment is made) by reason of the amendments made by subsections (a) and (b) shall be taken into account. Any reduction in such installment by reason of the preceding sentence shall be recaptured by increasing the next required installment for such year by the amount of such reduction.

[Sec. 30B]

SEC. 30B. ALTERNATIVE MOTOR VEHICLE CREDIT.

[Sec. 30B(a)]

(a) ALLOWANCE OF CREDIT.—There shall be allowed as a credit against the tax imposed by this chapter for the taxable year an amount equal to the sum of—

(1) the new qualified fuel cell motor vehicle credit determined under subsection (b),

(2) the new advanced lean burn technology motor vehicle credit determined under subsection (c),

(3) the new qualified hybrid motor vehicle credit determined under subsection (d),

(4) the new qualified alternative fuel motor vehicle credit determined under subsection (e), and

(5) the plug-in conversion credit determined under subsection (i).

Amendments

• 2009, American Recovery and Reinvestment Tax Act of 2009 (P.L. 111-5)

P.L. 111-5, §1143(b):

Amended Code Sec. 30B(a) by striking "and" at the end of paragraph (3), by striking the period at the end of paragraph (4) and inserting ", and", and by adding at the end a new paragraph (5). **Effective** for property placed in service after 2-17-2009.

[Sec. 30B(b)]

(b) NEW QUALIFIED FUEL CELL MOTOR VEHICLE CREDIT.—

(1) IN GENERAL.—For purposes of subsection (a), the new qualified fuel cell motor vehicle credit determined under this subsection with respect to a new qualified fuel cell motor vehicle placed in service by the taxpayer during the taxable year is—

(A) $8,000 ($4,000 in the case of a vehicle placed in service after December 31, 2009), if such vehicle has a gross vehicle weight rating of not more than 8,500 pounds,

(B) $10,000, if such vehicle has a gross vehicle weight rating of more than 8,500 pounds but not more than 14,000 pounds,

(C) $20,000, if such vehicle has a gross vehicle weight rating of more than 14,000 pounds but not more than 26,000 pounds, and

(D) $40,000, if such vehicle has a gross vehicle weight rating of more than 26,000 pounds.

(2) INCREASE FOR FUEL EFFICIENCY.—

(A) IN GENERAL.—The amount determined under paragraph (1)(A) with respect to a new qualified fuel cell motor vehicle which is a passenger automobile or light truck shall be increased by—

(i) $1,000, if such vehicle achieves at least 150 percent but less than 175 percent of the 2002 model year city fuel economy,

(ii) $1,500, if such vehicle achieves at least 175 percent but less than 200 percent of the 2002 model year city fuel economy,

(iii) $2,000, if such vehicle achieves at least 200 percent but less than 225 percent of the 2002 model year city fuel economy,

(iv) $2,500, if such vehicle achieves at least 225 percent but less than 250 percent of the 2002 model year city fuel economy,

(v) $3,000, if such vehicle achieves at least 250 percent but less than 275 percent of the 2002 model year city fuel economy,

(vi) $3,500, if such vehicle achieves at least 275 percent but less than 300 percent of the 2002 model year city fuel economy, and

(vii) $4,000, if such vehicle achieves at least 300 percent of the 2002 model year city fuel economy.

(B) 2002 MODEL YEAR CITY FUEL ECONOMY.—For purposes of subparagraph (A), the 2002 model year city fuel economy with respect to a vehicle shall be determined in accordance with the following tables:

(i) In the case of a passenger automobile:

If vehicle inertia weight class is:	*The 2002 model year city fuel economy is:*
1,500 or 1,750 lbs	45.2 mpg
2,000 lbs	39.6 mpg
2,250 lbs	35.2 mpg
2,500 lbs	31.7 mpg
2,750 lbs	28.8 mpg
3,000 lbs	26.4 mpg
3,500 lbs	22.6 mpg
4,000 lbs	19.8 mpg
4,500 lbs	17.6 mpg
5,000 lbs	15.9 mpg
5,500 lbs	14.4 mpg
6,000 lbs	13.2 mpg
6,500 lbs	12.2 mpg
7,000 to 8,500 lbs	11.3 mpg.

(ii) In the case of a light truck:

If vehicle inertia weight class is:	*The 2002 model year city fuel economy is:*
1,500 or 1,750 lbs	39.4 mpg
2,000 lbs	35.2 mpg
2,250 lbs	31.8 mpg
2,500 lbs	29.0 mpg
2,750 lbs	26.8 mpg
3,000 lbs	24.9 mpg
3,500 lbs	21.8 mpg
4,000 lbs	19.4 mpg
4,500 lbs	17.6 mpg
5,000 lbs	16.1 mpg
5,500 lbs	14.8 mpg
6,000 lbs	13.7 mpg
6,500 lbs	12.8 mpg
7,000 to 8,500 lbs	12.1 mpg.

(C) VEHICLE INERTIA WEIGHT CLASS.—For purposes of subparagraph (B), the term "vehicle inertia weight class" has the same meaning as when defined in regulations prescribed by the Administrator of the Environmental Protection Agency for purposes of the administration of title II of the Clean Air Act (42 U.S.C. 7521 et seq.).

(3) NEW QUALIFIED FUEL CELL MOTOR VEHICLE.—For purposes of this subsection, the term "new qualified fuel cell motor vehicle" means a motor vehicle—

(A) which is propelled by power derived from 1 or more cells which convert chemical energy directly into electricity by combining oxygen with hydrogen fuel which is stored on board the vehicle in any form and may or may not require reformation prior to use,

(B) which, in the case of a passenger automobile or light truck, has received on or after the date of the enactment of this section a certificate that such vehicle meets or exceeds the Bin 5 Tier II emission level established in regulations prescribed by the Administrator of the Environmental Protection Agency under section 202(i) of the Clean Air Act for that make and model year vehicle,

(C) the original use of which commences with the taxpayer,

(D) which is acquired for use or lease by the taxpayer and not for resale, and

(E) which is made by a manufacturer.

[Sec. 30B(c)]

(c) NEW ADVANCED LEAN BURN TECHNOLOGY MOTOR VEHICLE CREDIT.—

(1) IN GENERAL.—For purposes of subsection (a), the new advanced lean burn technology motor vehicle credit determined under this subsection for the taxable year is the credit amount determined under paragraph (2) with respect to a new advanced lean burn technology motor vehicle placed in service by the taxpayer during the taxable year.

(2) CREDIT AMOUNT.—

(A) FUEL ECONOMY.—

(i) IN GENERAL.—The credit amount determined under this paragraph shall be determined in accordance with the following table:

In the case of a vehicle which achieves a fuel economy (expressed as a percentage of the 2002 model year city fuel economy) of—	The credit amount is—
At least 125 percent but less than 150 percent	$400
At least 150 percent but less than 175 percent	$800
At least 175 percent but less than 200 percent	$1,200
At least 200 percent but less than 225 percent	$1,600
At least 225 percent but less than 250 percent	$2,000
At least 250 percent	$2,400.

(ii) 2002 MODEL YEAR CITY FUEL ECONOMY.—For purposes of clause (i), the 2002 model year city fuel economy with respect to a vehicle shall be determined on a gasoline gallon equivalent basis as determined by the Administrator of the Environmental Protection Agency using the tables provided in subsection (b)(2)(B) with respect to such vehicle.

(B) CONSERVATION CREDIT.—The amount determined under subparagraph (A) with respect to a new advanced lean burn technology motor vehicle shall be increased by the conservation credit amount determined in accordance with the following table:

In the case of a vehicle which achieves a lifetime fuel savings (expressed in gallons of gasoline) of—	*The conservation credit amount is—*
At least 1,200 but less than 1,800	$250
At least 1,800 but less than 2,400	$500
At least 2,400 but less than 3,000	$750
At least 3,000	$1,000.

(3) NEW ADVANCED LEAN BURN TECHNOLOGY MOTOR VEHICLE.—For purposes of this subsection, the term "new advanced lean burn technology motor vehicle" means a passenger automobile or a light truck—

(A) with an internal combustion engine which—

(i) is designed to operate primarily using more air than is necessary for complete combustion of the fuel,

(ii) incorporates direct injection,

(iii) achieves at least 125 percent of the 2002 model year city fuel economy,

(iv) for 2004 and later model vehicles, has received a certificate that such vehicle meets or exceeds—

(I) in the case of a vehicle having a gross vehicle weight rating of 6,000 pounds or less, the Bin 5 Tier II emission standard established in regulations prescribed by the Administrator of the Environmental Protection Agency under section 202(i) of the Clean Air Act for that make and model year vehicle, and

(II) in the case of a vehicle having a gross vehicle weight rating of more than 6,000 pounds but not more than 8,500 pounds, the Bin 8 Tier II emission standard which is so established,

(B) the original use of which commences with the taxpayer,

(C) which is acquired for use or lease by the taxpayer and not for resale, and

(D) which is made by a manufacturer.

(4) LIFETIME FUEL SAVINGS.—For purposes of this subsection, the term "lifetime fuel savings" means, in the case of any new advanced lean burn technology motor vehicle, an amount equal to the excess (if any) of—

(A) 120,000 divided by the 2002 model year city fuel economy for the vehicle inertia weight class, over

(B) 120,000 divided by the city fuel economy for such vehicle.

[Sec. 30B(d)]

(d) NEW QUALIFIED HYBRID MOTOR VEHICLE CREDIT.—

(1) IN GENERAL.—For purposes of subsection (a), the new qualified hybrid motor vehicle credit determined under this subsection for the taxable year is the credit amount determined

under paragraph (2) with respect to a new qualified hybrid motor vehicle placed in service by the taxpayer during the taxable year.

(2) CREDIT AMOUNT.—

(A) CREDIT AMOUNT FOR PASSENGER AUTOMOBILES AND LIGHT TRUCKS.—In the case of a new qualified hybrid motor vehicle which is a passenger automobile or light truck and which has a gross vehicle weight rating of not more than 8,500 pounds, the amount determined under this paragraph is the sum of the amounts determined under clauses (i) and (ii).

(i) FUEL ECONOMY.—The amount determined under this clause is the amount which would be determined under subsection (c)(2)(A) if such vehicle were a vehicle referred to in such subsection.

(ii) CONSERVATION CREDIT.—The amount determined under this clause is the amount which would be determined under subsection (c)(2)(B) if such vehicle were a vehicle referred to in such subsection.

(B) CREDIT AMOUNT FOR OTHER MOTOR VEHICLES.—

(i) IN GENERAL.—In the case of any new qualified hybrid motor vehicle to which subparagraph (A) does not apply, the amount determined under this paragraph is the amount equal to the applicable percentage of the qualified incremental hybrid cost of the vehicle as certified under clause (v).

(ii) APPLICABLE PERCENTAGE.—For purposes of clause (i), the applicable percentage is—

(I) 20 percent if the vehicle achieves an increase in city fuel economy relative to a comparable vehicle of at least 30 percent but less than 40 percent,

(II) 30 percent if the vehicle achieves such an increase of at least 40 percent but less than 50 percent, and

(III) 40 percent if the vehicle achieves such an increase of at least 50 percent.

(iii) QUALIFIED INCREMENTAL HYBRID COST.—For purposes of this subparagraph, the qualified incremental hybrid cost of any vehicle is equal to the amount of the excess of the manufacturer's suggested retail price for such vehicle over such price for a comparable vehicle, to the extent such amount does not exceed—

(I) $7,500, if such vehicle has a gross vehicle weight rating of not more than 14,000 pounds,

(II) $15,000, if such vehicle has a gross vehicle weight rating of more than 14,000 pounds but not more than 26,000 pounds, and

(III) $30,000, if such vehicle has a gross vehicle weight rating of more than 26,000 pounds.

(iv) COMPARABLE VEHICLE.—For purposes of this subparagraph, the term "comparable vehicle" means, with respect to any new qualified hybrid motor vehicle, any vehicle which is powered solely by a gasoline or diesel internal combustion engine and which is comparable in weight, size, and use to such vehicle.

(v) CERTIFICATION.—A certification described in clause (i) shall be made by the manufacturer and shall be determined in accordance with guidance prescribed by the Secretary. Such guidance shall specify procedures and methods for calculating fuel economy savings and incremental hybrid costs.

(3) NEW QUALIFIED HYBRID MOTOR VEHICLE.—For purposes of this subsection—

(A) IN GENERAL.—The term "new qualified hybrid motor vehicle" means a motor vehicle—

(i) which draws propulsion energy from onboard sources of stored energy which are both—

(I) an internal combustion or heat engine using consumable fuel, and

(II) a rechargeable energy storage system,

(ii) which, in the case of a vehicle to which paragraph (2)(A) applies, has received a certificate of conformity under the Clean Air Act and meets or exceeds the equivalent qualifying California low emission vehicle standard under section 243(e)(2) of the Clean Air Act for that make and model year, and

(I) in the case of a vehicle having a gross vehicle weight rating of 6,000 pounds or less, the Bin 5 Tier II emission standard established in regulations prescribed by the Administrator of the Environmental Protection Agency under section 202(i) of the Clean Air Act for that make and model year vehicle, and

(II) in the case of a vehicle having a gross vehicle weight rating of more than 6,000 pounds but not more than 8,500 pounds, the Bin 8 Tier II emission standard which is so established,

(iii) which has a maximum available power of at least—

(I) 4 percent in the case of a vehicle to which paragraph (2)(A) applies,

(II) 10 percent in the case of a vehicle which has a gross vehicle weight rating of more than 8,500 pounds and not more than 14,000 pounds, and

(III) 15 percent in the case of a vehicle in excess of 14,000 pounds,

(iv) which, in the case of a vehicle to which paragraph (2)(B) applies, has an internal combustion or heat engine which has received a certificate of conformity under the Clean Air Act as meeting the emission standards set in the regulations prescribed by the Administrator of the Environmental Protection Agency for 2004 through 2007 model year diesel heavy duty engines or ottocycle heavy duty engines, as applicable,

(v) the original use of which commences with the taxpayer,

(vi) which is acquired for use or lease by the taxpayer and not for resale, and

(vii) which is made by a manufacturer.

Such term shall not include any vehicle which is not a passenger automobile or light truck if such vehicle has a gross vehicle weight rating of less than 8,500 pounds.

(B) CONSUMABLE FUEL.—For purposes of subparagraph (A)(i)(I), the term "consumable fuel" means any solid, liquid, or gaseous matter which releases energy when consumed by an auxiliary power unit.

(C) MAXIMUM AVAILABLE POWER.—

(i) CERTAIN PASSENGER AUTOMOBILES AND LIGHT TRUCKS.—In the case of a vehicle to which paragraph (2)(A) applies, the term "maximum available power" means the maximum power available from the rechargeable energy storage system, during a standard 10 second pulse power or equivalent test, divided by such maximum power and the SAE net power of the heat engine.

(ii) OTHER MOTOR VEHICLES.—In the case of a vehicle to which paragraph (2)(B) applies, the term "maximum available power" means the maximum power available from the rechargeable energy storage system, during a standard 10 second pulse power or equivalent test, divided by the vehicle's total traction power. For purposes of the preceding sentence, the term "total traction power" means the sum of the peak power from the rechargeable energy storage system and the heat engine peak power of the vehicle, except that if such storage system is the sole means by which the vehicle can be driven, the total traction power is the peak power of such storage system.

(D) EXCLUSION OF PLUG-IN VEHICLES.—Any vehicle with respect to which a credit is allowable under section 30D (determined without regard to subsection (c) thereof) shall not be taken into account under this section.

Amendments

• 2009, American Recovery and Reinvestment Tax Act of 2009 (P.L. 111-5)

P.L. 111-5, §1141(b)(1):

Amended Code Sec. 30B(d)(3)(D) by striking "subsection (d) thereof" and inserting "subsection (c) thereof". **Effective** for vehicles acquired after 12-31-2009.

• 2008, Energy Improvement and Extension Act of 2008 (P.L. 110-343)

P.L. 110-343, Division B, §205(b):

Amended Code Sec. 30B(d)(3) by adding at the end a new subparagraph (D). **Effective** for tax years beginning after 12-31-2008.

[Sec. 30B(e)]

(e) NEW QUALIFIED ALTERNATIVE FUEL MOTOR VEHICLE CREDIT.—

(1) ALLOWANCE OF CREDIT.—Except as provided in paragraph (5), the new qualified alternative fuel motor vehicle credit determined under this subsection is an amount equal to the applicable percentage of the incremental cost of any new qualified alternative fuel motor vehicle placed in service by the taxpayer during the taxable year.

(2) APPLICABLE PERCENTAGE.—For purposes of paragraph (1), the applicable percentage with respect to any new qualified alternative fuel motor vehicle is—

(A) 50 percent, plus

(B) 30 percent, if such vehicle—

(i) has received a certificate of conformity under the Clean Air Act and meets or exceeds the most stringent standard available for certification under the Clean Air Act for that make and model year vehicle (other than a zero emission standard), or

(ii) has received an order certifying the vehicle as meeting the same requirements as vehicles which may be sold or leased in California and meets or exceeds the most stringent standard available for certification under the State laws of California (enacted in accordance with a waiver granted under section 209(b) of the Clean Air Act) for that make and model year vehicle (other than a zero emission standard).

For purposes of the preceding sentence, in the case of any new qualified alternative fuel motor vehicle which weighs more than 14,000 pounds gross vehicle weight rating, the most stringent standard available shall be such standard available for certification on the date of the enactment of the Energy Tax Incentives Act of 2005.

(3) INCREMENTAL COST.—For purposes of this subsection, the incremental cost of any new qualified alternative fuel motor vehicle is equal to the amount of the excess of the manufacturer's

suggested retail price for such vehicle over such price for a gasoline or diesel fuel motor vehicle of the same model, to the extent such amount does not exceed—

(A) $5,000, if such vehicle has a gross vehicle weight rating of not more than 8,500 pounds,

(B) $10,000, if such vehicle has a gross vehicle weight rating of more than 8,500 pounds but not more than 14,000 pounds,

(C) $25,000, if such vehicle has a gross vehicle weight rating of more than 14,000 pounds but not more than 26,000 pounds, and

(D) $40,000, if such vehicle has a gross vehicle weight rating of more than 26,000 pounds.

(4) NEW QUALIFIED ALTERNATIVE FUEL MOTOR VEHICLE.—For purposes of this subsection—

(A) IN GENERAL.—The term "new qualified alternative fuel motor vehicle" means any motor vehicle—

(i) which is only capable of operating on an alternative fuel,

(ii) the original use of which commences with the taxpayer,

(iii) which is acquired by the taxpayer for use or lease, but not for resale, and

(iv) which is made by a manufacturer.

(B) ALTERNATIVE FUEL.—The term "alternative fuel" means compressed natural gas, liquefied natural gas, liquefied petroleum gas, hydrogen, and any liquid at least 85 percent of the volume of which consists of methanol.

(5) CREDIT FOR MIXED-FUEL VEHICLES.—

(A) IN GENERAL.—In the case of a mixed-fuel vehicle placed in service by the taxpayer during the taxable year, the credit determined under this subsection is an amount equal to—

(i) in the case of a 75/25 mixed-fuel vehicle, 70 percent of the credit which would have been allowed under this subsection if such vehicle was a qualified alternative fuel motor vehicle, and

(ii) in the case of a 90/10 mixed-fuel vehicle, 90 percent of the credit which would have been allowed under this subsection if such vehicle was a qualified alternative fuel motor vehicle.

(B) MIXED-FUEL VEHICLE.—For purposes of this subsection, the term "mixed-fuel vehicle" means any motor vehicle described in subparagraph (C) or (D) of paragraph (3), which—

(i) is certified by the manufacturer as being able to perform efficiently in normal operation on a combination of an alternative fuel and a petroleum-based fuel,

(ii) either—

(I) has received a certificate of conformity under the Clean Air Act, or

(II) has received an order certifying the vehicle as meeting the same requirements as vehicles which may be sold or leased in California and meets or exceeds the low emission vehicle standard under section 88.105-94 of title 40, Code of Federal Regulations, for that make and model year vehicle,

(iii) the original use of which commences with the taxpayer,

(iv) which is acquired by the taxpayer for use or lease, but not for resale, and

(v) which is made by a manufacturer.

(C) 75/25 MIXED-FUEL VEHICLE.—For purposes of this subsection, the term "75/25 mixed-fuel vehicle" means a mixed-fuel vehicle which operates using at least 75 percent alternative fuel and not more than 25 percent petroleum-based fuel.

(D) 90/10 MIXED-FUEL VEHICLE.—For purposes of this subsection, the term "90/10 mixed-fuel vehicle" means a mixed-fuel vehicle which operates using at least 90 percent alternative fuel and not more than 10 percent petroleum-based fuel.

[Sec. 30B(f)]

(f) LIMITATION ON NUMBER OF NEW QUALIFIED HYBRID AND ADVANCED LEAN-BURN TECHNOLOGY VEHICLES ELIGIBLE FOR CREDIT.—

(1) IN GENERAL.—In the case of a qualified vehicle sold during the phaseout period, only the applicable percentage of the credit otherwise allowable under subsection (c) or (d) shall be allowed.

(2) PHASEOUT PERIOD.—For purposes of this subsection, the phaseout period is the period beginning with the second calendar quarter following the calendar quarter which includes the first date on which the number of qualified vehicles manufactured by the manufacturer of the vehicle referred to in paragraph (1) sold for use in the United States after December 31, 2005, is at least 60,000.

(3) APPLICABLE PERCENTAGE.—For purposes of paragraph (1), the applicable percentage is—

(A) 50 percent for the first 2 calendar quarters of the phaseout period,

(B) 25 percent for the 3d and 4th calendar quarters of the phaseout period, and

(C) 0 percent for each calendar quarter thereafter.

(4) CONTROLLED GROUPS.—

(A) IN GENERAL.—For purposes of this subsection, all persons treated as a single employer under subsection (a) or (b) of section 52 or subsection (m) or (o) of section 414 shall be treated as a single manufacturer.

(B) INCLUSION OF FOREIGN CORPORATIONS.—For purposes of subparagraph (A), in applying subsections (a) and (b) of section 52 to this section, section 1563 shall be applied without regard to subsection (b)(2)(C) thereof.

(5) QUALIFIED VEHICLE.—For purposes of this subsection, the term ''qualified vehicle''' means any new qualified hybrid motor vehicle (described in subsection (d)(2)(A)) and any new advanced lean burn technology motor vehicle.

[Sec. 30B(g)]

(g) APPLICATION WITH OTHER CREDITS.—

(1) BUSINESS CREDIT TREATED AS PART OF GENERAL BUSINESS CREDIT.—So much of the credit which would be allowed under subsection (a) for any taxable year (determined without regard to this subsection) that is attributable to property of a character subject to an allowance for depreciation shall be treated as a credit listed in section 38(b) for such taxable year (and not allowed under subsection (a)).

(2) PERSONAL CREDIT.—

(A) IN GENERAL.—For purposes of this title, the credit allowed under subsection (a) for any taxable year (determined after application of paragraph (1)) shall be treated as a credit allowable under subpart A for such taxable year.

(B) LIMITATION BASED ON AMOUNT OF TAX.—In the case of a taxable year to which section 26(a)(2) does not apply, the credit allowed under subsection (a) for any taxable year (determined after application of paragraph (1)) shall not exceed the excess of—

(i) the sum of the regular tax liability (as defined in section 26(b)) plus the tax imposed by section 55, over

Caution: Code Sec. 30B(g)(2)(B)(ii), below, was amended by P.L. 111-148. For sunset provision, see P.L. 111-148, §10909(c), in the amendment notes.

(ii) the sum of the credits allowable under subpart A (other than this section and sections 25D, 30, and 30D) and section 27 for the taxable year.

Amendments

• 2010, Patient Protection and Affordable Care Act (P.L. 111-148)

P.L. 111-148, §10909(b)(2)(G):

Amended Code Sec. 30B(g)(2)(B)(ii) by striking "23," before "25D". **Effective** for tax years beginning after 12-31-2009.

P.L. 111-148, §10909(c), provides:

(c) APPLICATION AND EXTENSION OF EGTRRA SUNSET.—Notwithstanding section 901 of the Economic Growth and Tax Relief Reconciliation Act of 2001 [P.L. 107-16], such section shall apply to the amendments made by this section and the amendments made by section 202 of such Act by substituting ''December 31, 2011'' for ''December 31, 2010'' in subsection (a)(1) thereof.

• 2009, American Recovery and Reinvestment Tax Act of 2009 (P.L. 111-5)

P.L. 111-5, §1144(a):

Amended Code Sec. 30B(g)(2). **Effective** for tax years beginning after 12-31-2008. Prior to amendment, Code Sec. 30B(g)(2) read as follows:

(2) PERSONAL CREDIT.—The credit allowed under subsection (a) (after the application of paragraph (1)) for any taxable year shall not exceed the excess (if any) of—

(A) the regular tax liability (as defined in section 26(b)) reduced by the sum of the credits allowable under subpart A and sections 27 and 30, over

(B) the tentative minimum tax for the taxable year.

• 2005, Gulf Opportunity Zone Act of 2005 (P.L. 109-135)

P.L. 109-135, §412(d):

Amended Code Sec. 30B(g)(2)(A) by striking "regular tax" and inserting "regular tax liability (as defined in section 26(b))". **Effective** 12-21-2005.

• 2001, Economic Growth and Tax Relief Reconciliation Act of 2001 (P.L. 107-16)

P.L. 107-16, §901(a)-(b), provides [but see P.L. 111-148, §10909(c), above]:

SEC. 901. SUNSET OF PROVISIONS OF ACT.

(a) IN GENERAL.—All provisions of, and amendments made by, this Act shall not apply—

(1) to taxable, plan, or limitation years beginning after December 31, 2010, or

(2) in the case of title V, to estates of decedents dying, gifts made, or generation skipping transfers, after December 31, 2010.

(b) APPLICATION OF CERTAIN LAWS.—The Internal Revenue Code of 1986 and the Employee Retirement Income Security Act of 1974 shall be applied and administered to years, estates, gifts, and transfers described in subsection (a) as if the provisions and amendments described in subsection (a) had never been enacted.

[Sec. 30B(h)]

(h) OTHER DEFINITIONS AND SPECIAL RULES.—For purposes of this section—

(1) MOTOR VEHICLE.—The term "motor vehicle" means any vehicle which is manufactured primarily for use on public streets, roads, and highways (not including a vehicle operated exclusively on a rail or rails) and which has at least 4 wheels.

(2) CITY FUEL ECONOMY.—The city fuel economy with respect to any vehicle shall be measured in a manner which is substantially similar to the manner city fuel economy is measured in accordance with procedures under part 600 of subchapter Q of chapter I of title 40, Code of Federal Regulations, as in effect on the date of the enactment of this section.

(3) OTHER TERMS.—The terms "automobile", "passenger automobile", "medium duty passenger vehicle", "light truck", and "manufacturer" have the meanings given such terms in regulations prescribed by the Administrator of the Environmental Protection Agency for purposes of the administration of title II of the Clean Air Act (42 U.S.C. 7521 et seq.).

(4) REDUCTION IN BASIS.—For purposes of this subtitle, the basis of any property for which a credit is allowable under subsection (a) shall be reduced by the amount of such credit so allowed (determined without regard to subsection (g)).

(5) NO DOUBLE BENEFIT.—The amount of any deduction or other credit allowable under this chapter—

(A) for any incremental cost taken into account in computing the amount of the credit determined under subsection (e) shall be reduced by the amount of such credit attributable to such cost, and

(B) with respect to a vehicle described under subsection (b) or (c), shall be reduced by the amount of credit allowed under subsection (a) for such vehicle for the taxable year.

(6) PROPERTY USED BY TAX-EXEMPT ENTITY.—In the case of a vehicle whose use is described in paragraph (3) or (4) of section 50(b) and which is not subject to a lease, the person who sold such vehicle to the person or entity using such vehicle shall be treated as the taxpayer that placed such vehicle in service, but only if such person clearly discloses to such person or entity in a document the amount of any credit allowable under subsection (a) with respect to such vehicle (determined without regard to subsection (g)). For purposes of subsection (g), property to which this paragraph applies shall be treated as of a character subject to an allowance for depreciation.

(7) PROPERTY USED OUTSIDE UNITED STATES, ETC., NOT QUALIFIED.—No credit shall be allowable under subsection (a) with respect to any property referred to in section 50(b)(1) or with respect to the portion of the cost of any property taken into account under section 179.

(8) RECAPTURE.—The Secretary shall, by regulations, provide for recapturing the benefit of any credit allowable under subsection (a) with respect to any property which ceases to be property eligible for such credit (including recapture in the case of a lease period of less than the economic life of a vehicle)., [sic] except that no benefit shall be recaptured if such property ceases to be eligible for such credit by reason of conversion to a qualified plug-in electric drive motor vehicle.

(9) ELECTION TO NOT TAKE CREDIT.—No credit shall be allowed under subsection (a) for any vehicle if the taxpayer elects to not have this section apply to such vehicle.

(10) INTERACTION WITH AIR QUALITY AND MOTOR VEHICLE SAFETY STANDARDS.—Unless otherwise provided in this section, a motor vehicle shall not be considered eligible for a credit under this section unless such vehicle is in compliance with—

(A) the applicable provisions of the Clean Air Act for the applicable make and model year of the vehicle (or applicable air quality provisions of State law in the case of a State which has adopted such provision under a waiver under section 209(b) of the Clean Air Act), and

(B) the motor vehicle safety provisions of sections 30101 through 30169 of title 49, United States Code.

Amendments

• 2009, American Recovery and Reinvestment Tax Act of 2009 (P.L. 111-5)

P.L. 111-5, §1142(b)(2):

Amended Code Sec. 30B(h)(1). **Effective** for vehicles acquired after 2-17-2009. For a transitional rule, see Act Sec. 1142(d) in the amendment notes for Code Sec. 30. Prior to amendment, Code Sec. 30B(h)(1) read as follows:

(1) MOTOR VEHICLE.—The term "motor vehicle" has the meaning given such term by section 30(c)(2).

P.L. 111-5, §1143(c):

Amended Code Sec. 30B(h)(8) by adding at the end ", except that no benefit shall be recaptured if such property ceases to be eligible for such credit by reason of conversion to a qualified plug-in electric drive motor vehicle.". **Effective** for property placed in service after 2-17-2009.

• 2005, Gulf Opportunity Zone Act of 2005 (P.L. 109-135)

P.L. 109-135, §402(j):

Amended Code Sec. 30B(h)(6) by adding at the end "For purposes of subsection (g), property to which this paragraph applies shall be treated as of a character subject to an allowance for depreciation.". **Effective** as if included in the provision of the Energy Policy Act of 2005 (P.L. 109-58) to which it relates [**effective** for property placed in service after 12-31-2005, in tax years ending after such date.—CCH].

[Sec. 30B(i)]

(i) PLUG-IN CONVERSION CREDIT.—

(1) IN GENERAL.—For purposes of subsection (a), the plug-in conversion credit determined under this subsection with respect to any motor vehicle which is converted to a qualified plug-in electric drive motor vehicle is 10 percent of so much of the cost of the [sic] converting such vehicle as does not exceed $40,000.

(2) QUALIFIED PLUG-IN ELECTRIC DRIVE MOTOR VEHICLE.—For purposes of this subsection, the term "qualified plug-in electric drive motor vehicle" means any new qualified plug-in electric drive motor vehicle (as defined in section 30D, determined without regard to whether such vehicle is made by a manufacturer or whether the original use of such vehicle commences with the taxpayer).

(3) CREDIT ALLOWED IN ADDITION TO OTHER CREDITS.—The credit allowed under this subsection shall be allowed with respect to a motor vehicle notwithstanding whether a credit has been allowed with respect to such motor vehicle under this section (other than this subsection) in any preceding taxable year.

(4) TERMINATION.—This subsection shall not apply to conversions made after December 31, 2011.

Amendments

• 2009, American Recovery and Reinvestment Tax Act of 2009 (P.L. 111-5)

P.L. 111-5, §1143(a):

Amended Code Sec. 30B by redesignating subsections (i) and (j) as subsections (j) and (k), respectively, and by inserting after subsection (h) a new subsection (i). **Effective** for property placed in service after 2-17-2009.

[Sec. 30B(j)]

(j) REGULATIONS.—

(1) IN GENERAL.—Except as provided in paragraph (2), the Secretary shall promulgate such regulations as necessary to carry out the provisions of this section.

(2) COORDINATION IN PRESCRIPTION OF CERTAIN REGULATIONS.—The Secretary of the Treasury, in coordination with the Secretary of Transportation and the Administrator of the Environmental Protection Agency, shall prescribe such regulations as necessary to determine whether a motor vehicle meets the requirements to be eligible for a credit under this section.

Amendments

• 2009, American Recovery and Reinvestment Tax Act of 2009 (P.L. 111-5)

P.L. 111-5, §1143(a):

Amended Code Sec. 30B by redesignating subsection (i) as subsection (j). **Effective** for property placed in service after 2-17-2009.

[Sec. 30B(k)]

(k) TERMINATION.—This section shall not apply to any property purchased after—

(1) in the case of a new qualified fuel cell motor vehicle (as described in subsection (b)), December 31, 2014,

(2) in the case of a new advanced lean burn technology motor vehicle (as described in subsection (c)) or a new qualified hybrid motor vehicle (as described in subsection (d)(2)(A)), December 31, 2010,

(3) in the case of a new qualified hybrid motor vehicle (as described in subsection (d)(2)(B)), December 31, 2009, and

(4) in the case of a new qualified alternative fuel vehicle (as described in subsection (e)), December 31, 2010.

Amendments

• 2009, American Recovery and Reinvestment Tax Act of 2009 (P.L. 111-5)

P.L. 111-5, §1143(a):

Amended Code Sec. 30B by redesignating subsection (j) as subsection (k). **Effective** for property placed in service after 2-17-2009.

• 2005, Energy Tax Incentives Act of 2005 (P.L. 109-58)

P.L. 109-58, §1341(a):

Amended subpart B of part IV of subchapter A of chapter 1 by adding at the end a new Code Sec. 30B. **Effective** for property placed in service after 12-31-2005, in tax years ending after such date.

[Sec. 30C]

SEC. 30C. ALTERNATIVE FUEL VEHICLE REFUELING PROPERTY CREDIT.

[Sec. 30C(a)]

(a) CREDIT ALLOWED.—There shall be allowed as a credit against the tax imposed by this chapter for the taxable year an amount equal to 30 percent of the cost of any qualified alternative fuel vehicle refueling property placed in service by the taxpayer during the taxable year.

[Sec. 30C(b)]

(b) LIMITATION.—The credit allowed under subsection (a) with respect to all qualified alternative fuel vehicle refueling property placed in service by the taxpayer during the taxable year at a location shall not exceed—

(1) $30,000 in the case of a property of a character subject to an allowance for depreciation, and

(2) $1,000 in any other case.

Amendments

• 2007, Tax Technical Corrections Act of 2007 (P.L. 110-172)

P.L. 110-172, §6(b)(1):

Amended so much of Code Sec. 30C(b) as precedes paragraph (1). **Effective** as if included in the provision of the Energy Tax Incentives Act of 2005 (P.L. 109-58) to which it relates [**effective** for property placed in service after 12-31-2005, in tax years ending after such date.—CCH]. Prior to amendment, so much of Code Sec. 30C(b) as precedes paragraph (1) read as follows:

(b) LIMITATION.—The credit allowed under subsection (a) with respect to any alternative fuel vehicle refueling property shall not exceed—

[Sec. 30C(c)]

(c) QUALIFIED ALTERNATIVE FUEL VEHICLE REFUELING PROPERTY.—For purposes of this section, the term "qualified alternative fuel vehicle refueling property" has the same meaning as the term "qualified clean-fuel vehicle refueling property" would have under section 179A if—

(1) paragraph (1) of section 179A(d) did not apply to property installed on property which is used as the principal residence (within the meaning of section 121) of the taxpayer, and

(2) only the following were treated as clean-burning fuels for purposes of section 179A(d):

(A) Any fuel at least 85 percent of the volume of which consists of one or more of the following: ethanol, natural gas, compressed natural gas, liquified natural gas, liquefied petroleum gas, or hydrogen.

(B) Any mixture—

(i) which consists of two or more of the following: biodiesel (as defined in section 40A(d)(1)), diesel fuel (as defined in section 4083(a)(3)), or kerosene, and

(ii) at least 20 percent of the volume of which consists of biodiesel (as so defined), determined without regard to any kerosene in such mixture.

(C) Electricity.

Amendments

• 2008, Energy Improvement and Extension Act of 2008 (P.L. 110-343)

P.L. 110-343, Division B, §207(b):

Amended Code Sec. 30C(c)(2) by adding at the end a new subparagraph (C). **Effective** for property placed in service after 10-3-2008, in tax years ending after such date.

• 2007, Tax Technical Corrections Act of 2007 (P.L. 110-172)

P.L. 110-172, §6(b)(2):

Amended Code Sec. 30C(c). **Effective** as if included in the provision of the Energy Tax Incentives Act of 2005 (P.L. 109-58) to which it relates [**effective** for property placed in service after 12-31-2005, in tax years ending after such date.—CCH]. Prior to amendment, Code Sec. 30C(c) read as follows:

(c) QUALIFIED ALTERNATIVE FUEL VEHICLE REFUELING PROPERTY.—

(1) IN GENERAL.—Except as provided in paragraph (2), the term "qualified alternative fuel vehicle refueling property" has the meaning given to such term by section 179A(d), but only with respect to any fuel—

(A) at least 85 percent of the volume of which consists of one or more of the following: ethanol, natural gas, compressed natural gas, liquefied natural gas, liquefied petroleum gas, or hydrogen, or

(B) any mixture of biodiesel (as defined in section 40A(d)(1)) and diesel fuel (as defined in section 4083(a)(3)), determined without regard to any use of kerosene and containing at least 20 percent biodiesel.

(2) RESIDENTIAL PROPERTY.—In the case of any property installed on property which is used as the principal residence (within the meaning of section 121) of the taxpayer, paragraph (1) of section 179A(d) shall not apply.

[Sec. 30C(d)]

(d) APPLICATION WITH OTHER CREDITS.—

(1) BUSINESS CREDIT TREATED AS PART OF GENERAL BUSINESS CREDIT.—So much of the credit which would be allowed under subsection (a) for any taxable year (determined without regard to this subsection) that is attributable to property of a character subject to an allowance for depreciation shall be treated as a credit listed in section 38(b) for such taxable year (and not allowed under subsection (a)).

(2) PERSONAL CREDIT.—The credit allowed under subsection (a) (after the application of paragraph (1)) for any taxable year shall not exceed the excess (if any) of—

(A) the regular tax liability (as defined in section 26(b)) reduced by the sum of the credits allowable under subpart A and section 27, over

(B) the tentative minimum tax for the taxable year.

Amendments

• 2009, American Recovery and Reinvestment Tax Act of 2009 (P.L. 111-5)

P.L. 111-5, §1142(b)(3):

Amended Code Sec. 30C(d)(2)(A) by striking ", 30," after "sections 27". **Effective** for vehicles acquired after 2-17-2009. For a transitional rule, see Act Sec. 1142(d) in the amendment notes for Code Sec. 30.

P.L. 111-5, §1144(b)(2):

Amended Code Sec. 30C(d)(2)(A), as amended by this Act, by striking "sections 27 and 30B" and inserting "section 27". **Effective** for tax years beginning after 12-31-2008.

• 2005, Gulf Opportunity Zone Act of 2005 (P.L. 109-135)

P.L. 109-135, §412(d):

Amended Code Sec. 30C(d)(2)(A) by striking "regular tax" and inserting "regular tax liability (as defined in section 26(b))". **Effective** 12-21-2005.

[Sec. 30C(e)]

(e) SPECIAL RULES.—For purposes of this section—

(1) BASIS REDUCTION.—The basis of any property shall be reduced by the portion of the cost of such property taken into account under subsection (a).

(2) PROPERTY USED BY TAX-EXEMPT ENTITY.—In the case of any qualified alternative fuel vehicle refueling property the use of which is described in paragraph (3) or (4) of section 50(b) and which is not subject to a lease, the person who sold such property to the person or entity using such property shall be treated as the taxpayer that placed such property in service, but only if such person clearly discloses to such person or entity in a document the amount of any credit allowable under subsection (a) with respect to such property (determined without regard to subsection (d)). For purposes of subsection (d), property to which this paragraph applies shall be treated as of a character subject to an allowance for depreciation.

(3) PROPERTY USED OUTSIDE UNITED STATES NOT QUALIFIED.—No credit shall be allowable under subsection (a) with respect to any property referred to in section 50(b)(1) or with respect to the portion of the cost of any property taken into account under section 179.

(4) ELECTION NOT TO TAKE CREDIT.—No credit shall be allowed under subsection (a) for any property if the taxpayer elects not to have this section apply to such property.

(5) RECAPTURE RULES.—Rules similar to the rules of section 179A(e)(4) shall apply.

(6) SPECIAL RULE FOR PROPERTY PLACED IN SERVICE DURING 2009 AND 2010.—In the case of property placed in service in taxable years beginning after December 31, 2008, and before January 1, 2011—

(A) in the case of any such property which does not relate to hydrogen—

(i) subsection (a) shall be applied by substituting "50 percent" for "30 percent",

(ii) subsection (b)(1) shall be applied by substituting "$50,000" for "$30,000", and

(iii) subsection (b)(2) shall be applied by substituting "$2,000" for "$1,000", and

(B) in the case of any such property which relates to hydrogen, subsection (b)(1) shall be applied by substituting "$200,000" for "$30,000".

Amendments

• 2009, American Recovery and Reinvestment Tax Act of 2009 (P.L. 111-5)

P.L. 111-5, §1123(a):

Amended Code Sec. 30C(e) by adding at the end a new paragraph (6). **Effective** for tax years beginning after 12-31-2008.

• 2005, Gulf Opportunity Zone Act of 2005 (P.L. 109-135)

P.L. 109-135, §402(k):

Amended Code Sec. 30C(e)(2) by adding at the end a new sentence. **Effective** as if included in the provision of the Energy Policy Act of 2005 (P.L. 109-58) to which it relates [**effective** for property placed in service after 12-31-2005, in tax years ending after such date.—CCH].

[Sec. 30C(f)]

(f) REGULATIONS.—The Secretary shall prescribe such regulations as necessary to carry out the provisions of this section.

[Sec. 30C(g)]

(g) TERMINATION.—This section shall not apply to any property placed in service—

(1) in the case of property relating to hydrogen, after December 31, 2014, and

(2) in the case of any other property, after December 31, 2010.

Amendments

• 2008, Energy Improvement and Extension Act of 2008 (P.L. 110-343)

P.L. 110-343, Division B, §207(a):

Amended Code Sec. 30C(g)(2) by striking "December 31, 2009" and inserting "December 31, 2010". **Effective** for property placed in service after 10-3-2008, in tax years ending after such date.

• 2005, Energy Tax Incentives Act of 2005 (P.L. 109-58)

P.L. 109-58, §1342(a):

Amended subpart B of part IV of subchapter A of chapter 1, as amended by this Act, by adding at the end a new Code Sec. 30C. **Effective** for property placed in service after 12-31-2005, in tax years ending after such date.

[Sec. 30D]

SEC. 30D. NEW QUALIFIED PLUG-IN ELECTRIC DRIVE MOTOR VEHICLES.

[Sec. 30D(a)]

(a) ALLOWANCE OF CREDIT.—There shall be allowed as a credit against the tax imposed by this chapter for the taxable year an amount equal to the sum of the credit amounts determined under subsection (b) with respect to each new qualified plug-in electric drive motor vehicle placed in service by the taxpayer during the taxable year.

[Sec. 30D(b)]

(b) PER VEHICLE DOLLAR LIMITATION.—

(1) IN GENERAL.—The amount determined under this subsection with respect to any new qualified plug-in electric drive motor vehicle is the sum of the amounts determined under paragraphs (2) and (3) with respect to such vehicle.

(2) BASE AMOUNT.—The amount determined under this paragraph is $2,500.

(3) BATTERY CAPACITY.—In the case of a vehicle which draws propulsion energy from a battery with not less than 5 kilowatt hours of capacity, the amount determined under this paragraph is $417, plus $417 for each kilowatt hour of capacity in excess of 5 kilowatt hours. The amount determined under this paragraph shall not exceed $5,000.

[Sec. 30D(c)]

(c) APPLICATION WITH OTHER CREDITS.—

(1) BUSINESS CREDIT TREATED AS PART OF GENERAL BUSINESS CREDIT.—So much of the credit which would be allowed under subsection (a) for any taxable year (determined without regard to this subsection) that is attributable to property of a character subject to an allowance for depreciation shall be treated as a credit listed in section 38(b) for such taxable year (and not allowed under subsection (a)).

(2) PERSONAL CREDIT.—

(A) IN GENERAL.—For purposes of this title, the credit allowed under subsection (a) for any taxable year (determined after application of paragraph (1)) shall be treated as a credit allowable under subpart A for such taxable year.

(B) LIMITATION BASED ON AMOUNT OF TAX.—In the case of a taxable year to which section 26(a)(2) does not apply, the credit allowed under subsection (a) for any taxable year (determined after application of paragraph (1)) shall not exceed the excess of—

(i) the sum of the regular tax liability (as defined in section 26(b)) plus the tax imposed by section 55, over

Caution: Code Sec. 30D(c)(2)(B)(ii), below, was amended by P.L. 111-148. For sunset provision, see P.L. 111-148, §10909(c), in the amendment notes.

(ii) the sum of the credits allowable under subpart A (other than this section and section 25D) and section 27 for the taxable year.

Amendments

• 2010, Patient Protection and Affordable Care Act (P.L. 111-148)

P.L. 111-148, §10909(b)(2)(H):

Amended Code Sec. 30D(c)(2)(B)(ii) by striking "sections 23 and" and inserting "section". **Effective** for tax years beginning after 12-31-2009.

P.L. 111-148, §10909(c), provides:

(c) APPLICATION AND EXTENSION OF EGTRRA SUNSET.—Notwithstanding section 901 of the Economic Growth and Tax Relief Reconciliation Act of 2001 [P.L. 107-16], such section shall apply to the amendments made by this section and the amendments made by section 202 of such Act by substituting "December 31, 2011" for "December 31, 2010" in subsection (a)(1) thereof.

• 2001, Economic Growth and Tax Relief Reconciliation Act of 2001 (P.L. 107-16)

P.L. 107-16, §901(a)-(b), provides [but see P.L. 111-148, §10909(c), above]:

SEC. 901. SUNSET OF PROVISIONS OF ACT.

(a) IN GENERAL.—All provisions of, and amendments made by, this Act shall not apply—

(1) to taxable, plan, or limitation years beginning after December 31, 2010, or

(2) in the case of title V, to estates of decedents dying, gifts made, or generation skipping transfers, after December 31, 2010.

(b) APPLICATION OF CERTAIN LAWS.—The Internal Revenue Code of 1986 and the Employee Retirement Income Security Act of 1974 shall be applied and administered to years, estates, gifts, and transfers described in subsection (a) as if the provisions and amendments described in subsection (a) had never been enacted.

[Sec. 30D(d)]

(d) NEW QUALIFIED PLUG-IN ELECTRIC DRIVE MOTOR VEHICLE.—For purposes of this section—

(1) IN GENERAL.—The term "new qualified plug-in electric drive motor vehicle" means a motor vehicle—

(A) the original use of which commences with the taxpayer,

(B) which is acquired for use or lease by the taxpayer and not for resale,

(C) which is made by a manufacturer,

(D) which is treated as a motor vehicle for purposes of title II of the Clean Air Act,

(E) which has a gross vehicle weight rating of less than 14,000 pounds, and

(F) which is propelled to a significant extent by an electric motor which draws electricity from a battery which—

(i) has a capacity of not less than 4 kilowatt hours, and

(ii) is capable of being recharged from an external source of electricity.

(2) MOTOR VEHICLE.—The term "motor vehicle" means any vehicle which is manufactured primarily for use on public streets, roads, and highways (not including a vehicle operated exclusively on a rail or rails) and which has at least 4 wheels.

(3) MANUFACTURER.—The term "manufacturer" has the meaning given such term in regulations prescribed by the Administrator of the Environmental Protection Agency for purposes of the administration of title II of the Clean Air Act (42 U.S.C. 7521 et seq.).

(4) BATTERY CAPACITY.—The term "capacity" means, with respect to any battery, the quantity of electricity which the battery is capable of storing, expressed in kilowatt hours, as measured from a 100 percent state of charge to a 0 percent state of charge.

[Sec. 30D(e)]

(e) LIMITATION ON NUMBER OF NEW QUALIFIED PLUG-IN ELECTRIC DRIVE MOTOR VEHICLES ELIGIBLE FOR CREDIT.—

(1) IN GENERAL.—In the case of a new qualified plug-in electric drive motor vehicle sold during the phaseout period, only the applicable percentage of the credit otherwise allowable under subsection (a) shall be allowed.

(2) PHASEOUT PERIOD.—For purposes of this subsection, the phaseout period is the period beginning with the second calendar quarter following the calendar quarter which includes the first date on which the number of new qualified plug-in electric drive motor vehicles manufactured by the manufacturer of the vehicle referred to in paragraph (1) sold for use in the United States after December 31, 2009, is at least 200,000.

(3) APPLICABLE PERCENTAGE.—For purposes of paragraph (1), the applicable percentage is—

(A) 50 percent for the first 2 calendar quarters of the phaseout period,

(B) 25 percent for the 3d [3rd] and 4th calendar quarters of the phaseout period, and

(C) 0 percent for each calendar quarter thereafter.

(4) CONTROLLED GROUPS.—Rules similar to the rules of section 30B(f)(4) shall apply for purposes of this subsection.

[Sec. 30D(f)]

(f) SPECIAL RULES.—

(1) BASIS REDUCTION.—For purposes of this subtitle, the basis of any property for which a credit is allowable under subsection (a) shall be reduced by the amount of such credit so allowed.

(2) NO DOUBLE BENEFIT.—The amount of any deduction or other credit allowable under this chapter for a new qualified plug-in electric drive motor vehicle shall be reduced by the amount of credit allowed under subsection (a) for such vehicle.

(3) PROPERTY USED BY TAX-EXEMPT ENTITY.—In the case of a vehicle the use of which is described in paragraph (3) or (4) of section 50(b) and which is not subject to a lease, the person who sold such vehicle to the person or entity using such vehicle shall be treated as the taxpayer that placed such vehicle in service, but only if such person clearly discloses to such person or entity in a document the amount of any credit allowable under subsection (a) with respect to such vehicle (determined without regard to subsection (c)).

(4) PROPERTY USED OUTSIDE UNITED STATES NOT QUALIFIED.—No credit shall be allowable under subsection (a) with respect to any property referred to in section 50(b)(1).

(5) RECAPTURE.—The Secretary shall, by regulations, provide for recapturing the benefit of any credit allowable under subsection (a) with respect to any property which ceases to be property eligible for such credit.

(6) ELECTION NOT TO TAKE CREDIT.—No credit shall be allowed under subsection (a) for any vehicle if the taxpayer elects to not have this section apply to such vehicle.

(7) INTERACTION WITH AIR QUALITY AND MOTOR VEHICLE SAFETY STANDARDS.—A motor vehicle shall not be considered eligible for a credit under this section unless such vehicle is in compliance with—

(A) the applicable provisions of the Clean Air Act for the applicable make and model year of the vehicle (or applicable air quality provisions of State law in the case of a State which has adopted such provision under a waiver under section 209(b) of the Clean Air Act), and

(B) the motor vehicle safety provisions of sections 30101 through 30169 of title 49, United States Code.

Amendments

• 2009, American Recovery and Reinvestment Tax Act of 2009 (P.L. 111-5)

P.L. 111-5, §1141(a):

Amended Code Sec. 30D. **Effective** for vehicles acquired after 12-31-2009. Prior to amendment, Code Sec. 30D read as follows:

SEC. 30D. NEW QUALIFIED PLUG-IN ELECTRIC DRIVE MOTOR VEHICLES.

[Sec. 30D(a)]

(a) ALLOWANCE OF CREDIT.—

(1) IN GENERAL.—There shall be allowed as a credit against the tax imposed by this chapter for the taxable year an amount equal to the applicable amount with respect to each new qualified plug-in electric drive motor vehicle placed in service by the taxpayer during the taxable year.

(2) APPLICABLE AMOUNT.—For purposes of paragraph (1), the applicable amount is sum of—

(A) $2,500, plus

(B) $417 for each kilowatt hour of traction battery capacity in excess of 4 kilowatt hours.

[Sec. 30D(b)]

(b) LIMITATIONS.—

(1) LIMITATION BASED ON WEIGHT.—The amount of the credit allowed under subsection (a) by reason of subsection (a)(2) shall not exceed—

(A) $7,500, in the case of any new qualified plug-in electric drive motor vehicle with a gross vehicle weight rating of not more than 10,000 pounds,

(B) $10,000, in the case of any new qualified plug-in electric drive motor vehicle with a gross vehicle weight rating of more than 10,000 pounds but not more than 14,000 pounds,

(C) $12,500, in the case of any new qualified plug-in electric drive motor vehicle with a gross vehicle weight rating of more than 14,000 pounds but not more than 26,000 pounds, and

(D) $15,000, in the case of any new qualified plug-in electric drive motor vehicle with a gross vehicle weight rating of more than 26,000 pounds.

(2) LIMITATION ON NUMBER OF PASSENGER VEHICLES AND LIGHT TRUCKS ELIGIBLE FOR CREDIT.—

(A) IN GENERAL.—In the case of a new qualified plug-in electric drive motor vehicle sold during the phaseout period, only the applicable percentage of the credit otherwise allowable under subsection (a) shall be allowed.

(B) PHASEOUT PERIOD.—For purposes of this subsection, the phaseout period is the period beginning with the second calendar quarter following the calendar quarter which includes the first date on which the total number of such new qualified plug-in electric drive motor vehicles sold for use in the United States after December 31, 2008, is at least 250,000.

(C) APPLICABLE PERCENTAGE.—For purposes of subparagraph (A), the applicable percentage is—

(i) 50 percent for the first 2 calendar quarters of the phaseout period,

(ii) 25 percent for the 3d and 4th calendar quarters of the phaseout period, and

(iii) 0 percent for each calendar quarter thereafter.

(D) CONTROLLED GROUPS.—Rules similar to the rules of section 30B(f)(4) shall apply for purposes of this subsection.

[Sec. 30D(c)]

(c) NEW QUALIFIED PLUG-IN ELECTRIC DRIVE MOTOR VEHICLE.—For purposes of this section, the term "new qualified plug-in electric drive motor vehicle" means a motor vehicle—

(1) which draws propulsion using a traction battery with at least 4 kilowatt hours of capacity,

(2) which uses an offboard source of energy to recharge such battery,

(3) which, in the case of a passenger vehicle or light truck which has a gross vehicle weight rating of not more than 8,500 pounds, has received a certificate of conformity under the Clean Air Act and meets or exceeds the equivalent qualifying California low emission vehicle standard under section 243(e)(2) of the Clean Air Act for that make and model year, and

(A) in the case of a vehicle having a gross vehicle weight rating of 6,000 pounds or less, the Bin 5 Tier II emission standard established in regulations prescribed by the Administrator of the Environmental Protection Agency under section 202(i) of the Clean Air Act for that make and model year vehicle, and

(B) in the case of a vehicle having a gross vehicle weight rating of more than 6,000 pounds but not more than 8,500 pounds, the Bin 8 Tier II emission standard which is so established,

(4) the original use of which commences with the taxpayer,

(5) which is acquired for use or lease by the taxpayer and not for resale, and

(6) which is made by a manufacturer.

[Sec. 30D(d)]

(d) APPLICATION WITH OTHER CREDITS.—

(1) BUSINESS CREDIT TREATED AS PART OF GENERAL BUSINESS CREDIT.—So much of the credit which would be allowed under subsection (a) for any taxable year (determined without regard to this subsection) that is attributable to property of a character subject to an allowance for depreciation shall be treated as a credit listed in section 38(b) for such taxable year (and not allowed under subsection (a)).

(2) PERSONAL CREDIT.—

(A) IN GENERAL.—For purposes of this title, the credit allowed under subsection (a) for any taxable year (determined after application of paragraph (1)) shall be treated as a credit allowable under subpart A for such taxable year.

(B) LIMITATION BASED ON AMOUNT OF TAX.—In the case of a taxable year to which section 26(a)(2) does not apply, the credit allowed under subsection (a) for any taxable year (determined after application of paragraph (1)) shall not exceed the excess of—

(i) the sum of the regular tax liability (as defined in section 26(b)) plus the tax imposed by section 55, over

(ii) the sum of the credits allowable under subpart A (other than this section and sections 23 and 25D) and section 27 for the taxable year.

[Sec. 30D(e)]

(e) OTHER DEFINITIONS AND SPECIAL RULES.—For purposes of this section—

(1) MOTOR VEHICLE.—The term "motor vehicle" has the meaning given such term by section 30(c)(2).

(2) OTHER TERMS.—The terms "passenger automobile", "light truck", and "manufacturer" have the meanings given such terms in regulations prescribed by the Administrator of the Environmental Protection Agency for purposes of the administration of title II of the Clean Air Act (42 U.S.C. 7521 et seq.).

(3) TRACTION BATTERY CAPACITY.—Traction battery capacity shall be measured in kilowatt hours from a 100 percent state of charge to a zero percent state of charge.

(4) REDUCTION IN BASIS.—For purposes of this subtitle, the basis of any property for which a credit is allowable under subsection (a) shall be reduced by the amount of such credit so allowed.

(5) NO DOUBLE BENEFIT.—The amount of any deduction or other credit allowable under this chapter for a new qualified plug-in electric drive motor vehicle shall be reduced by the amount of credit allowed under subsection (a) for such vehicle for the taxable year.

(6) PROPERTY USED BY TAX-EXEMPT ENTITY.—In the case of a vehicle the use of which is described in paragraph (3) or (4) of section 50(b) and which is not subject to a lease, the person who sold such vehicle to the person or entity using such vehicle shall be treated as the taxpayer that placed such vehicle in service, but only if such person clearly discloses to such person or entity in a document the amount of any credit allowable under subsection (a) with respect to such vehicle (determined without regard to subsection (b)(2)).

(7) PROPERTY USED OUTSIDE UNITED STATES, ETC., NOT QUALIFIED.—No credit shall be allowable under subsection (a) with respect to any property referred to in section 50(b)(1) or with respect to the portion of the cost of any property taken into account under section 179.

(8) RECAPTURE.—The Secretary shall, by regulations, provide for recapturing the benefit of any credit allowable under subsection (a) with respect to any property which ceases to be property eligible for such credit (including recapture in the case of a lease period of less than the economic life of a vehicle).

(9) ELECTION TO NOT TAKE CREDIT.—No credit shall be allowed under subsection (a) for any vehicle if the taxpayer elects not to have this section apply to such vehicle.

(10) INTERACTION WITH AIR QUALITY AND MOTOR VEHICLE SAFETY STANDARDS.—Unless otherwise provided in this section, a motor vehicle shall not be considered eligible for a credit under this section unless such vehicle is in compliance with—

(A) the applicable provisions of the Clean Air Act for the applicable make and model year of the vehicle (or applicable air quality provisions of State law in the case of a State which has adopted such provision under a waiver under section 209(b) of the Clean Air Act), and

(B) the motor vehicle safety provisions of sections 30101 through 30169 of title 49, United States Code.

[Sec. 30D(f)]

(f) REGULATIONS.—

(1) IN GENERAL.—Except as provided in paragraph (2), the Secretary shall promulgate such regulations as necessary to carry out the provisions of this section.

(2) COORDINATION IN PRESCRIPTION OF CERTAIN REGULATIONS.—The Secretary of the Treasury, in coordination with the Secretary of Transportation and the Administrator of the Environmental Protection Agency, shall prescribe such regulations as necessary to determine whether a motor vehicle meets the requirements to be eligible for a credit under this section.

[Sec. 30D(g)]

(g) TERMINATION.—This section shall not apply to property purchased after December 31, 2014.

Amendments

• 2008, Energy Improvement and Extension Act of 2008 (P.L. 110-343)

P.L. 110-343, Division B, §205(a):

Amended subpart B of part IV of subchapter A of chapter 1 by adding at the end a new Code Sec. 30D. **Effective** for tax years beginning after 12-31-2008.

Subpart C—Refundable Credits

[Sec. 31]

SEC. 31. TAX WITHHELD ON WAGES.

[Sec. 31(a)]

(a) WAGE WITHHOLDING FOR INCOME TAX PURPOSES.—

(1) IN GENERAL.—The amount withheld as tax under chapter 24 shall be allowed to the recipient of the income as a credit against the tax imposed by this subtitle.

(2) YEAR OF CREDIT.—The amount so withheld during any calendar year shall be allowed as a credit for the taxable year beginning in such calendar year. If more than one taxable year begins in a calendar year, such amount shall be allowed as a credit for the last taxable year so beginning.

[Sec. 31(b)]

(b) CREDIT FOR SPECIAL REFUNDS OF SOCIAL SECURITY TAX.—

(1) IN GENERAL.—The Secretary may prescribe regulations providing for the crediting against the tax imposed by this subtitle of the amount determined by the taxpayer or the Secretary to be allowable under section 6413(c) as a special refund of tax imposed on wages. The amount allowed as a credit under such regulations shall, for purposes of this subtitle, be considered an amount withheld at source as tax under section 3402.

(2) YEAR OF CREDIT.—Any amount to which paragraph (1) applies shall be allowed as a credit for the taxable year beginning in the calendar year during which the wages were received. If more than one taxable year begins in the calendar year, such amount shall be allowed as a credit for the last taxable year so beginning.

[Sec. 31(c)]

(c) SPECIAL RULE FOR BACKUP WITHHOLDING.—Any credit allowed by subsection (a) for any amount withheld under section 3406 shall be allowed for the taxable year of the recipient of the income in which the income is received.

Amendments

• 1984, Deficit Reduction Act of 1984 (P.L. 98-369)

P.L. 98-369, §714(j)(2):

Amended paragraph (1) of Code Sec. 31(a) by striking out "under section 3402 as tax on the wages of any individual" and inserting in lieu thereof "as tax under chapter 24". **Effective** as if included in the provision of P.L. 97-248 to which it relates.

• 1983, Interest and Dividend Tax Compliance Act of 1983 (P.L. 98-67)

P.L. 98-67, §104(d)(2):

Added Code Sec. 31(c). **Effective** for payments made after 12-31-83.

P.L. 98-67, §102(a):

Repealed the amendments made to Code Sec. 31 by P.L. 97-248 (as amended by P.L. 97-354 and P.L. 97-448—see below). **Effective** of the close of 6-30-83, as though they had not been enacted. Prior to repeal of these amendments by P.L. 98-67, Code Sec. 31 read as follows:

SEC. 31. TAX WITHHELD ON WAGES, INTEREST, DIVIDENDS, AND PATRONAGE DIVIDENDS.

(a) WAGE WITHHOLDING.—The amount withheld under section 3402 as tax on the wages of any individual shall be allowed to the recipient of the income as a credit against the tax imposed by this subtitle.

(b) WITHHOLDING FROM INTEREST, DIVIDENDS, AND PATRONAGE DIVIDENDS.—The amount withheld under section 3451 as tax on interest, dividends, and patronage dividends shall be allowed to the recipient of the income as a credit against the tax imposed by this subtitle.

(c) CREDIT FOR SPECIAL REFUNDS OF SOCIAL SECURITY TAX.—The Secretary may prescribe regulations providing for the crediting against the tax imposed by this subtitle of the amount determined by the taxpayer or the Secretary to be allowable under section 6413(c) as a special refund of tax imposed on wages. The amount allowed as a credit under such regulations shall, for purposes of this subtitle, be considered an amount withheld at source as tax under section 3402.

(d) YEAR FOR WHICH CREDIT ALLOWED.—

(1) WAGES.—Any credit allowed—

(A) by subsection (a) shall be allowed for the taxable year beginning in the calendar year in which the amount is withheld, or

(B) by subsection (c) shall be allowed for the taxable year beginning in the calendar year in which the wages are received.

For purposes of this paragraph, if more than 1 taxable year begins in a calendar year, such amount shall be allowed as a credit for the last taxable year so beginning.

(2) Interest, dividends, and patronage dividends.—Any credit allowed by subsection (b) shall be allowed for the taxable year of the recipient of the income in which the amount is received.

• 1983, Technical Corrections Act of 1982 (P.L. 97-448)

P.L. 97-448, §306(b)(1)(A):

Amended Code Sec. 31(d), as added by P.L. 97-248. **Effective** as if such amendment had been included in the provision of P.L. 97-248 to which it relates. Prior to amendment, Code Sec. 31(d) read as follows:

"(d) **Year for Which Credit Allowed.**—Any credit allowed by this section shall be allowed for the taxable year beginning in the calendar year in which the amount was withheld (or, in the case of subsection (c), in which the wages were received). If more than 1 taxable year begins in a calendar year, such amount shall be allowed as a credit for the last taxable year so beginning."

P.L. 97-448, §306(b)(1)(B):

Repealed P.L. 97-354, §3(i)(4), which amended Code Sec. 31(d) (as amended by P.L. 97-248, §302). **Effective** as if such amendment had been included in the provision of P.L. 97-248 to which it relates.

• 1982, Subchapter S Revision Act of 1982 (P.L. 37-354)

P.L. 97-354, §3(i)(4):

Amended Code Sec. 31(d), as amended by P.L. 97-248. **Effective** for tax years beginning after 12-31-82. Prior to amendment, it read as follows:

(d) YEAR FOR WHICH CREDIT ALLOWED.—

(1) IN GENERAL.—Except as otherwise provided in paragraph (2), any credit allowed by this section shall be allowed for the taxable year beginning in the calendar year in which the amount was withheld (or, in the case of subsection (c), in which the wages were received). If more than 1 taxable year begins in a calendar year, such amount shall be allowed as a credit for the last taxable year so beginning.

(2) SPECIAL RULE FOR CERTAIN DISTRIBUTIONS OF SUBCHAPTER S CORPORATIONS.—The amount withheld with respect to a distribution by an electing small business corporation (within the meaning of section 1371(b)) which is treated as a distribution of such corporation's undistributed taxable income for the preceding year under section 1375(f)(1) shall be allowed as a credit for the taxable year of the recipient beginning in the calendar year in which the preceding year of the corporation ends.

• 1982, Tax Equity and Fiscal Responsibility Act of 1982 (P.L. 97-248)

P.L. 97-248, §302(a):

Added Code Sec. 31(d) (see historical comment under P.L. 98-67, above). **Effective** for payments of interest, dividends, and patronage dividends paid or credited after 6-30-83.

• 1976, Tax Reform Act of 1976 (P.L. 94-455)

P.L. 94-455, §1906(b)(13)(A), (D):

Amended Code Sec. 31(b)(1) by striking out "or his delegate" after the first "Secretary" and "(or his delegate)" after the second "Secretary." **Effective** 2-1-77.

[Sec. 32]

SEC. 32. EARNED INCOME.

[Sec. 32(a)]

(a) ALLOWANCE OF CREDIT.—

(1) IN GENERAL.—In the case of an eligible individual, there shall be allowed as a credit against the tax imposed by this subtitle for the taxable year an amount equal to the credit percentage of so much of the taxpayer's earned income for the taxable year as does not exceed the earned income amount.

(2) LIMITATION.—The amount of the credit allowable to a taxpayer under paragraph (1) for any taxable year shall not exceed the excess (if any) of—

(A) the credit percentage of the earned income amount, over

»»→ Caution: Code Sec. 32(a)(2)(B), below, is subject to the sunset provision of the Economic Growth and Tax Relief Reconciliation Act of 2001 (P.L. 107-16), §901. Absent Congressional action, the changes made to this provision by P.L. 107-16, or that take effect as if included in P.L. 107-16, do not apply after December 31, 2010. For more information about the sunset provision, see page XXI of the Preface to this publication and P.L. 107-16, §901, in the amendment notes. See the amendments notes for a history of amendments to this section and the effective date of each change.

(B) the phaseout percentage of so much of the adjusted gross income (or, if greater, the earned income) of the taxpayer for the taxable year as exceeds the phaseout amount.

Amendments

• 2001, Economic Growth and Tax Relief Reconciliation Act of 2001 (P.L. 107-16)

P.L. 107-16, §303(d)(1):

Amended Code Sec. 32(a)(2)(B) by striking "modified" before "adjusted gross income". **Effective** for tax years beginning after 12-31-2001.

P.L. 107-16, §901(a)-(b), provides:

SEC. 901. SUNSET OF PROVISIONS OF ACT.

(a) IN GENERAL.—All provisions of, and amendments made by, this Act shall not apply—

(1) to taxable, plan, or limitation years beginning after December 31, 2010, or

(2) in the case of title V, to estates of decedents dying, gifts made, or generation skipping transfers, after December 31, 2010.

(b) APPLICATION OF CERTAIN LAWS.—The Internal Revenue Code of 1986 and the Employee Retirement Income Security Act of 1974 shall be applied and administered to years, estates, gifts, and transfers described in subsection (a) as if the provisions and amendments described in subsection (a) had never been enacted.

• 1996, Personal Responsibility and Work Opportunity Act of 1996 (P.L. 104-193)

P.L. 104-193, §910(a):

Amended Code Sec. 32(a)(2)(B) by striking "adjusted gross income" each place it appears and inserting "modified adjusted gross income". **Effective** for tax years beginning after 12-31-95. For a special rule, see Act Sec. 910(c)(2), below.

P.L. 104-193, §910(c)(2), provides:

(2) ADVANCE PAYMENT INDIVIDUALS.—In the case of any individual who on or before June 26, 1996, has in effect an earned income eligibility certificate for the individual's taxable year beginning in 1996, the amendments made by this section shall apply to taxable years beginning after December 31, 1996.

• 1993, Omnibus Budget Reconciliation Act of 1993 (P.L. 103-66)

P.L. 103-66, §13131(a):

Amended Code Sec. 32 by striking subsection (a) and inserting new subsection (a). **Effective** for tax years beginning after 12-31-93. Prior to amendment, Code Sec. 32(a) read as follows:

(a) ALLOWANCE OF CREDIT.—In the case of an eligible individual, there shall be allowed as a credit against the tax imposed by this subtitle for the taxable year an amount equal to the sum of—

(1) the basic earned income credit, and

(2) the health insurance credit.

• 1990, Omnibus Budget Reconciliation Act of 1990 (P.L. 101-508)

P.L. 101-508, §11111(a):

Amended Code Sec. 32(a). **Effective** for tax years beginning after 12-31-90. Prior to amendment, Code Sec. 32(a) read as follows:

(a) ALLOWANCE OF CREDIT.—In the case of an eligible individual, there is allowed as a credit against the tax imposed by this subtitle for the taxable year an amount equal to 14 percent of so much of the earned income for the taxable year as does not exceed $5,714.

• 1986, Tax Reform Act of 1986 (P.L. 99-514)

P.L. 99-514, §111(a)(1)-(2):

Amended Code Sec. 32(a) by striking out "11 percent" and inserting in lieu thereof "14 percent" and by striking out "$5,000" and inserting in lieu thereof "$5,714". **Effective** for tax years beginning after 12-31-86.

• 1984, Deficit Reduction Act of 1984 (P.L. 98-369)

P.L. 98-369, §471(c)(1):

Redesignated Code Sec. 43 as 32. **Effective** for tax years beginning after 12-31-83, and to carrybacks from such years.

P.L. 98-369, §1042(a):

Amended Code Sec. 32, as redesignated by Act Sec. 471(c)(1), by striking out "10 percent" and inserting in lieu thereof "11 percent". **Effective** for tax years beginning after 1984.

• 1978, Revenue Act of 1978 (P.L. 95-600)

P.L. 95-600, §104(a):

Amended Code Sec. 43(a) by striking out "chapter" and inserting in place thereof "subtitle" and by striking out "$4,000" and inserting in place thereof "$5,000". **Effective** for tax years beginning after 12-31-78.

P.L. 95-600, §103(a):

Amended P.L. 94-12, §209(b) as amended by P.L. 94-455, §401(c)(1)(A), P.L 94-164, §2(f), and P.L. 95-30, §103(b) by striking out, "and before January 1, 1979".

• 1977, Tax Reduction and Simplification Act of 1977 (P.L. 95-30)

P.L. 95-30, §103(b):

Amended P.L. 94-12, §209(b) as amended by P.L. 94-455, §401(c)(1)(A), and P.L. 94-164, §2(f), by striking out "January 1, 1978" and inserting in place thereof "January 1, 1979". **Effective** 5-23-77.

P.L. 95-30, §103(c):

Amended P.L. 94-455, §401(e). **Effective** 5-23-77.

P.L. 94-455, §401(c)(1)(A):

Amended P.L. 94-12, §209(b) as amended by P.L. 94-164, §2(f), by striking out "January 1, 1977" and inserting in place thereof "January 1, 1978." **Effective** as indicated in P.L. 94-455 §401(e), below.

P.L. 94-455, §401(c)(1)(B):

Amended Code Sec. 43(a). **Effective** as indicated in P.L. 94-455, §401(e), below. Before amendment, Code Sec. 43(a) read as follows:

(a) ALLOWANCE OF CREDIT.

(1) GENERAL RULE.—In the case of an eligible individual, there shall be allowed as a credit against the tax imposed by this chapter for the taxable year an amount equal to 10 percent of so much of the earned income for the taxable year as does not exceed $4,000.

(2) APPLICATION OF 6-MONTH RULE.—Notwithstanding the provisions of paragraph (1), the term "5 percent" shall be substituted for the term "10 percent" where it appears in that paragraph.

P.L. 94-455, §401(e), provides:

Amendments made by §401(c) "shall apply to taxable years ending after December 31, 1975, and shall cease to apply to taxable years ending after December 31, 1977."

P.L. 94-455, §402(a):

Amended P.L. 94-164, §2(d) (see below) by striking out "which begins prior to July 1, 1976,". **Effective** 10-4-76.

P.L. 94-455, §402(b):

Amended P.L. 94-164, §2(g). **Effective** 10-4-76, to read as follows:

"(g) Effective Dates.—The amendments made by this section [§2] (other than by subsection (d)) apply to taxable years ending after December 31, 1975, and before January 1, 1978. Subsection (d) applies to taxable years ending after December 31, 1975."

• 1975, Revenue Adjustment Act of 1975 (P.L.94-164)

P.L. 94-164, §2(c):

Amended Code Sec. 43(a). **Effective** as indicated in P.L. 94-164, §2(g), below. Before amendment, such section read as follows:

(a) ALLOWANCE OF CREDIT.—In the case of an eligible individual, there shall be allowed as a credit against the tax imposed by this chapter for the taxable year an amount equal to 10 percent of so much of the earned income for the taxable year as does not exceed $4,000.

P.L. 94-164, §2(d), as amended by P.L. 95-600, §105(f), provides:

(d) Disregard of Refund.—Any refund of Federal income taxes made to any individual by reason of section 43 of the Internal Revenue Code of 1954 (relating to earned income credit), and any payment made by an employer under section 3507 of such Code (relating to advance payment of earned income credit) shall not be taken into account in any year ending before 1980 as income or receipts for purposes of determining the eligibility, for the month in which such refund is made or any month thereafter which begins prior to July 1, 1976, of such individual or any other individual for benefits or assistance, or the amount or extent of benefits or assistance, under any Federal program or under any State or local program financed in whole or in part with Federal funds, but only if such individual (or the family unit of which he is a member) is a recipient of benefits or assistance under such a program for the month before the month in which such refund is made.

P.L. 94-164, §2(f):

Amended P.L. 94-12, §209(b) (relating to the effective date for §204 of that Act) to extend the earned income credit by striking out "January 1, 1976," and inserting in place thereof "January 1, 1977.". **Effective** as indicated in P.L. 94-164, §2(g), below.

P.L. 94-164, §2(g):

Originally provided that amendments made by P.L. 94-164, §2 "apply to taxable years ending after December 31, 1975, and before January 1, 1977."

• 1975, Tax Reduction Act of 1975 (P.L. 94-12)

P.L. 94-12, §204(a):

Added Code Sec. 43(a). **Effective** as indicated in P.L. 94-12, §209(b), below.

P.L. 94-12, §209(b), provides:

§204 applies "to tax years beginning after December 31, 1974, and before January 1, 1976."

[Sec. 32(b)]

(b) PERCENTAGES AND AMOUNTS.—For purposes of subsection (a)—

(1) PERCENTAGES.—The credit percentage and the phaseout percentage shall be determined as follows:

(A) IN GENERAL.—In the case of taxable years beginning after 1995:

In the case of an eligible individual with:	*The credit percentage is:*	*The phaseout percentage is:*
1 qualifying child	34	15.98
2 or more qualifying children	40	21.06
No qualifying children	7.65	7.65

(B) TRANSITIONAL PERCENTAGES FOR 1995.—In the case of taxable years beginning in 1995:

In the case of an eligible individual with:	*The credit percentage is:*	*The phaseout percentage is:*
1 qualifying child	34	15.98
2 or more qualifying children	36	20.22
No qualifying children	7.65	7.65

(C) TRANSITIONAL PERCENTAGES FOR 1994.—In the case of a taxable year beginning in 1994:

In the case of an eligible individual with:	*The credit percentage is:*	*The phaseout percentage is:*
1 qualifying child	26.3	15.98
2 or more qualifying children	30	17.68
No qualifying children	7.65	7.65

»»→ Caution: Code Sec. 32(b)(2), below, is subject to the sunset provision of the Economic Growth and Tax Relief Reconciliation Act of 2001 (P.L. 107-16), §901. Absent Congressional action, the changes made to this provision by P.L. 107-16, or that take effect as if included in P.L. 107-16, do not apply after December 31, 2010. For more information about the sunset provision, see page XXI of the Preface to this publication and P.L. 107-16, §901, in the amendment notes. See the amendments notes for a history of amendments to this section and the effective date of each change.

(2) AMOUNTS.—

(A) IN GENERAL.—Subject to subparagraph (B), the earned income amount and the phaseout amount shall be determined as follows:

In the case of an eligible individual with:	*The earned income amount is:*	*The phaseout amount is:*
1 qualifying child	$6,330	$11,610
2 or more qualifying children	$8,890	$11,610
No qualifying children	$4,220	$ 5,280

(B) JOINT RETURNS.—In the case of a joint return filed by an eligible individual and such individual's spouse, the phaseout amount determined under subparagraph (A) shall be increased by—

(i) $1,000 in the case of taxable years beginning in 2002, 2003, and 2004,

(ii) $2,000 in the case of taxable years beginning in 2005, 2006, and 2007, and

(iii) $3,000 in the case of taxable years beginning after 2007.

(3) SPECIAL RULES FOR 2009 AND 2010.—In the case of any taxable year beginning in 2009 or 2010—

(A) INCREASED CREDIT PERCENTAGE FOR 3 OR MORE QUALIFYING CHILDREN.—In the case of a taxpayer with 3 or more qualifying children, the credit percentage is 45 percent.

(B) REDUCTION OF MARRIAGE PENALTY.—

(i) IN GENERAL.—The dollar amount in effect under paragraph (2)(B) shall be $5,000.

(ii) INFLATION ADJUSTMENT.—In the case of any taxable year beginning in 2010, the $5,000 amount in clause (i) shall be increased by an amount equal to—

(I) such dollar amount, multiplied by

(II) the cost of living adjustment determined under section 1(f)(3) for the calendar year in which the taxable year begins determined by substituting "calendar year 2008" for "calendar year 1992" in subparagraph (B) thereof.

(iii) ROUNDING.—Subparagraph (A) of subsection (j)(2) shall apply after taking into account any increase under clause (ii).

Amendments

• 2009, American Recovery and Reinvestment Tax Act of 2009 (P.L. 111-5)

P.L. 111-5, §1002(a):

Amended Code Sec. 32(b) by adding at the end a new paragraph (3). **Effective** for tax years beginning after 12-31-2008.

• 2005, Katrina Emergency Tax Relief Act of 2005 (P.L. 109-73)

P.L. 109-73, §406 [repealed by P.L. 109-135, §201(b)(4)(B)], provides:

SEC. 406. SPECIAL RULE FOR DETERMINING EARNED INCOME.

(a) IN GENERAL.—In the case of a qualified individual, if the earned income of the taxpayer for the taxable year which includes August 25, 2005, is less than the earned income of the taxpayer for the preceding taxable year, the credits allowed under sections 24(d) and 32 of the Internal Revenue Code of 1986 may, at the election of the taxpayer, be determined by substituting—

(1) such earned income for the preceding taxable year, for

(2) such earned income for the taxable year which includes August 25, 2005.

(b) QUALIFIED INDIVIDUAL.—For purposes of this section, the term "qualified individual" means any individual whose principal place of abode on August 25, 2005, was located—

(1) in the core disaster area, or

(2) in the Hurricane Katrina disaster area (but outside the core disaster area) and such individual was displaced from such principal place of abode by reason of Hurricane Katrina.

(c) EARNED INCOME.—For purposes of this section, the term "earned income" has the meaning given such term under section 32(c) of such Code.

(d) SPECIAL RULES.—

(1) APPLICATION TO JOINT RETURNS.—For purpose of subsection (a), in the case of a joint return for a taxable year which includes August 25, 2005—

(A) such subsection shall apply if either spouse is a qualified individual, and

(B) the earned income of the taxpayer for the preceding taxable year shall be the sum of the earned income of each spouse for such preceding taxable year.

(2) UNIFORM APPLICATION OF ELECTION.—Any election made under subsection (a) shall apply with respect to both section 24(d) and section 32 of such Code.

(3) ERRORS TREATED AS MATHEMATICAL ERROR.—For purposes of section 6213 of such Code, an incorrect use on a return of earned income pursuant to subsection (a) shall be treated as a mathematical or clerical error.

(4) NO EFFECT ON DETERMINATION OF GROSS INCOME, ETC.—Except as otherwise provided in this section, the Internal Revenue Code of 1986 shall be applied without regard to any substitution under subsection (a).

• 2001, Economic Growth and Tax Relief Reconciliation Act of 2001 (P.L. 107-16)

P.L. 107-16, §303(a)(1)(A)-(B):

Amended Code Sec. 32(b)(2). **Effective** for tax years beginning after 12-31-2001. Prior to amendment, Code Sec. 32(b)(2) read as follows:

(2) AMOUNTS.—The earned income amount and the phaseout amount shall be determined as follows:

In the case of an eligible individual with:	*The earned income amount is:*	*The phaseout amount is:*
1 qualifying child	$6,330	$11,610
2 or more qualifying children	$8,890	$11,610
No qualifying children	$4,220	$5,280

P.L. 107-16, §901(a)-(b), provides:

SEC. 901. SUNSET OF PROVISIONS OF ACT.

(a) IN GENERAL.—All provisions of, and amendments made by, this Act shall not apply—

(1) to taxable, plan, or limitation years beginning after December 31, 2010, or

(2) in the case of title V, to estates of decedents dying, gifts made, or generation skipping transfers, after December 31, 2010.

(b) APPLICATION OF CERTAIN LAWS.—The Internal Revenue Code of 1986 and the Employee Retirement Income Security Act of 1974 shall be applied and administered to years, estates, gifts, and transfers described in subsection (a) as if the provisions and amendments described in subsection (a) had never been enacted.

• 1996, Personal Responsibility and Work Opportunity Reconciliation Act of 1996 (P.L. 104-193)

P.L. 104-193, §909(a)(3):

Amended Code Sec. 32(b)(2). **Effective** for tax years beginning after 12-31-95. For a special rule, see Act Sec. 909(c)(2), below. Prior to amendment, Code Sec. 32(b)(2) read as follows:

(2) AMOUNTS.—The earned income amount and the phaseout amount shall be determined as follows:

(A) IN GENERAL.—In the case of taxable years beginning after 1994:

In the case of an eligible individual with:	*The earned income amount is:*	*The phaseout amount is:*
1 qualifying child	$6,000	$11,000
2 or more qualifying children	$8,425	$11,000
No qualifying children	$4,000	$5,000

(B) TRANSITIONAL AMOUNTS.—In the case of a taxable year beginning in 1994:

In the case of an eligible individual with:	*The earned income amount is:*	*The phaseout amount is:*
1 qualifying child	$7,750	$11,000
2 or more qualifying children	$8,425	$11,000
No qualifying children	$4,000	$5,000

P.L. 104-193, §909(c)(2), provides:

(2) ADVANCE PAYMENT INDIVIDUALS.—In the case of any individual who on or before June 26, 1996, has in effect an earned income eligibility certificate for the individual's taxable year beginning in 1996, the amendments made by this section shall apply to taxable years beginning after December 31, 1996.

• 1993, Omnibus Budget Reconciliation Act of 1993 (P.L. 103-66)

P.L. 103-66, §13131(a):

Amended Code Sec. 32 by striking subsection (b) and inserting new subsection (b). **Effective** for tax years beginning after 12-31-93. Prior to amendment, Code Sec. 32(b) read as follows:

(b) COMPUTATION OF CREDIT.—For purposes of this section—

(1) BASIC EARNED INCOME CREDIT.—

(A) IN GENERAL.—The term "basic earned income credit" means an amount equal to the credit percentage of so much of the taxpayer's earned income for the taxable year as does not exceed $5,714.

(B) LIMITATION.—The amount of the basic earned income credit allowable to a taxpayer for any taxable year shall not exceed the excess (if any) of—

(i) the credit percentage of $5,714, over

(ii) the phaseout percentage of so much of the adjusted gross income (or, if greater the earned income) of the taxpayer for the taxable year as exceeds $9,000.

(C) PERCENTAGES.—For purposes of this paragraph—

(i) IN GENERAL.—Except as provided in clause (ii), the percentages shall be determined as follows:

In the case of an eligible individual with:	*The credit percentage is:*	*The phaseout percentage is:*
1 qualifying child	23	16.43
2 or more qualifying children	25	17.86

(ii) TRANSITION PERCENTAGES.—

(I) For taxable years beginning in 1991, the percentages are:

In the case of an eligible individual with:	*The credit percentage is:*	*The phaseout percentage is:*
1 qualifying child	16.7	11.93
2 or more qualifying children	17.3	12.36

(II) For taxable years beginning in 1992, the percentages are:

In the case of an eligible individual with:	*The credit percentage is:*	*The phaseout percentage is:*
1 qualifying child	17.6	12.57
2 or more qualifying children	18.4	13.14

(III) For taxable years beginning in 1993, the percentages are:

In the case of an eligible individual with:	*The credit percentage is:*	*The phaseout percentage is:*
1 qualifying child	18.5	13.21
2 or more qualifying children	19.5	13.93

(D) SUPPLEMENTAL YOUNG CHILD CREDIT.—In the case of a taxpayer with a qualifying child who has not attained age 1 as of the close of the calendar year in which or with which the taxable year of the taxpayer ends—

(i) the credit percentage shall be increased by 5 percentage points, and

(ii) the phaseout percentage shall be increased by 3.57 percentage points.

If the taxpayer elects to take a child into account under this subparagraph, such child shall not be treated as a qualifying individual under section 21.

(2) HEALTH INSURANCE CREDIT.—

(A) IN GENERAL.—The term "health insurance credit" means an amount determined in the same manner as the basic earned income credit except that—

(i) the credit percentage shall be equal to 6 percent, and

(ii) the phaseout percentage shall be equal to 4.285 percent.

(B) LIMITATION BASED ON HEALTH INSURANCE COSTS.—The amount of the health insurance credit determined under subparagraph (A) for any taxable year shall not exceed the amounts paid by the taxpayer during the taxable year for insurance coverage—

(i) which constitutes medical care (within the meaning of section 213(d)(1)(C)), and

(ii) which includes at least 1 qualifying child.

For purposes of this subparagraph, the rules of section 213(d)(6) shall apply.

(C) SUBSIDIZED EXPENSES.—A taxpayer may not take into account under subparagraph (B) any amount to the extent that—

(i) such amount is paid, reimbursed, or subsidized by the Federal Government, a State or local government, or any agency or instrumentality thereof; and

(ii) the payment, reimbursement, or subsidy of such amount is not includible in the gross income of the recipient.

• 1990, Omnibus Budget Reconciliation Act of 1990 (P.L. 101-508)

P.L. 101-508, §11111(a):

Amended Code Sec. 32(b). **Effective** for tax years beginning after 12-31-90. Prior to amendment, Code Sec. 32(b) read as follows:

(b) LIMITATION.—The amount of the credit allowable to a taxpayer under subsection (a) for any taxable year shall not exceed the excess (if any) of—

(1) the maximum credit allowable under subsection (a) to any taxpayer, over

(2) 10 percent of so much of the adjusted gross income (or, if greater, the earned income) of the taxpayer for the taxable year as exceeds $9,000.

In the case of any taxable year beginning in 1987, paragraph (2) shall be applied by substituting "$6,500" for "$9,000."

• 1986, Tax Reform Act of 1986 (P.L. 99-514)

P.L. 99-514, §111(b):

Amended Code Sec. 32(b). **Effective** for tax years beginning after 12-31-86. Prior to amendment, Code Sec. 32(b) read as follows:

(b) LIMITATION.—The amount of the credit allowable to a taxpayer under subsection (a) for any taxable year shall not exceed the excess (if any) of—

(1) $550, over

(2) 12 2/9 percent of so much of the adjusted gross income (or, if greater, the earned income) of the taxpayer for the taxable year as exceeds $6,500.

• 1984, Deficit Reduction Act of 1984 (P.L. 98-369)

P.L. 98-369, §1042(b):

Amended Code Sec. 32(b)(2), as redesignated by Act Sec. 471(c)(1). **Effective** for tax years beginning after 1984.

P.L. 98-369, §1042(d)(1):

Amended Code Sec. 32(b)(1), as redesignated by Code Sec. 471(c)(1), by striking out "$500" and inserting in lieu thereof "$550". **Effective** for tax years beginning after 1984.

• 1978, Revenue Act of 1978 (P.L. 95-600)

P.L. 95-600, §104(b):

Amended Code Sec. 43(b). **Effective** for tax years beginning after 12-31-78. Prior to amendment Code Sec. 43(b) read as follows:

(b) LIMITATION.—The amount of the credit allowable to a taxpayer under subsection (a) for any taxable year shall be reduced (but not below zero) by an amount equal to 10 percent of so much of the adjusted gross income (or, if greater, the earned income) of the taxpayer for the taxable year as exceeds $4,000.

• 1977, Tax Reduction and Simplification Act of 1977 (P.L. 95-30)

P.L. 95-30, §103(b):

Amended P.L. 94-12, §209(b) as amended by P.L. 94-455, §401(c)(1)(A), and P.L. 94-164, §2(f) by striking out "January 1, 1978" and inserting in place thereof "January 1, 1979". **Effective** 5-23-77.

P.L. 95-30, §103(c):

Amended P.L. 94-455, §401(e). **Effective** 5-23-77.

• 1976, Tax Reform Act of 1976 (P.L. 94-455)

P.L. 94-455, §401(c)(1)(A):

Amended P.L. 94-12, §209(b) as amended by P.L. 94-164, §2(f) by striking out "January 1, 1977" and inserting in place thereof "January 1, 1978.". **Effective** as indicated in P.L. 94-455, §401(e), below.

P.L. 94-455, §401(c)(1)(B):

Amended Code Sec. 43(b). **Effective** as indicated in P.L. 94-455, §401(e), below. Prior to amendment Code Sec. 43(b) read as follows:

(b) LIMITATION.

(1) GENERAL RULE.—The amount of the credit allowable to a taxpayer under subsection (a) for any taxable year shall be reduced (but not below zero) by an amount equal to 10 percent of so much of the adjusted gross income (or, if greater, the earned income) of the taxpayer for the taxable year as exceeds $4,000.

(2) APPLICATION OF 6-MONTH RULE.—Notwithstanding the provisions of paragraph (1), the term "5 percent" shall be substituted for the term "10 percent" where it appears in that paragraph.

P.L. 94-455, §401(e), provides:

Amendments made by §401(c) "shall apply to taxable years ending after December 31, 1975, and shall cease to apply to taxable years ending after December 31, 1977."

P.L. 94-455, §402(b):

Amended P.L. 94-164, §2(g) to read as follows:

(g) EFFECTIVE DATES.—The amendments made by this section (other than by subsection (d)) apply to taxable years ending after December 31, 1975, and before January 1, 1978. Subsection (d) applies to taxable years ending after December 31, 1975.

• 1975, Revenue Adjustment Act of 1975 (P.L. 94-164)

P.L. 94-164, §2(c):

Amended Code Sec. 43(b). **Effective** as indicated in P.L. 94-164, §2(g) below. Prior to amendment, such section read as follows:

(b) LIMITATION.—The amount of the credit allowable to a taxpayer under subsection (a) for any taxable year shall be reduced (but not below zero) by an amount equal to 10 percent of so much of the adjusted gross income (or, if greater, the earned income) of the taxpayer for the taxable year as exceeds $4,000.

P.L. 94-164, §2(f):

Amended P.L. 94-12, §209(b) by striking out "January 1, 1976," and inserting in place thereof "January 1, 1977.". **Effective** as indicated in P.L. 94-164, §2(g), below.

P.L. 94-164, §2(g), provides:

Amendments made by P.L. 94-164, §2 "apply to taxable years ending after December 31, 1975, and before January 1, 1977."

• 1975, Tax Reduction Act of 1975 (P.L. 94-12)

P.L. 94-12, §204(a):

Added Code Sec. 43(b). **Effective** as indicated in P.L. 94-12, §209(b), below.

P.L. 94-12, §209(b), provides:

§204 applies "to tax years beginning after December 31, 1974, and before January 1, 1976."

[Sec. 32(c)]

(c) DEFINITIONS AND SPECIAL RULES.—For purposes of this section—

(1) ELIGIBLE INDIVIDUAL.—

(A) IN GENERAL.—The term "eligible individual" means—

(i) any individual who has a qualifying child for the taxable year, or

(ii) any other individual who does not have a qualifying child for the taxable year, if—

(I) such individual's principal place of abode is in the United States for more than one-half of such taxable year,

(II) such individual (or, if the individual is married, either the individual or the individual's spouse) has attained age 25 but not attained age 65 before the close of the taxable year, and

(III) such individual is not a dependent for whom a deduction is allowable under section 151 to another taxpayer for any taxable year beginning in the same calendar year as such taxable year.

For purposes of preceding sentence, marital status shall be determined under section 7703.

(B) QUALIFYING CHILD INELIGIBLE.—If an individual is the qualifying child of a taxpayer for any taxable year of such taxpayer beginning in a calendar year, such individual shall not be treated as an eligible individual for any taxable year of such individual beginning in such calendar year.

(C) EXCEPTION FOR INDIVIDUAL CLAIMING BENEFITS UNDER SECTION 911.—The term "eligible individual" does not include any individual who claims the benefits of section 911 (relating to citizens or residents living abroad) for the taxable year.

(D) LIMITATION ON ELIGIBILITY OF NONRESIDENT ALIENS.—The term "eligible individual" shall not include any individual who is a nonresident alien individual for any portion of the taxable year unless such individual is treated for such taxable year as a resident of the United States for purposes of this chapter by reason of an election under subsection (g) or (h) of section 6013.

(E) IDENTIFICATION NUMBER REQUIREMENT.—No credit shall be allowed under this section to an eligible individual who does not include on the return of tax for the taxable year—

(i) such individual's taxpayer identification number, and

(ii) if the individual is married (within the meaning of section 7703), the taxpayer identification number of such individual's spouse.

(F) INDIVIDUALS WHO DO NOT INCLUDE TIN, ETC., OF ANY QUALIFYING CHILD.—No credit shall be allowed under this section to any eligible individual who has one or more qualifying children if no qualifying child of such individual is taken into account under subsection (b) by reason of paragraph (3)(D).

(2) EARNED INCOME.—

(A) The term "earned income" means—

»»→ Caution: Code Sec. 32(c)(2)(A)(i), below, is subject to the sunset provision of the Economic Growth and Tax Relief Reconciliation Act of 2001 (P.L. 107-16), §901. Absent Congressional action, the changes made to this provision by P.L. 107-16, or that take effect as if included in P.L. 107-16, do not apply after December 31, 2010. For more information about the sunset provision, see page XXI of the Preface to this publication and P.L. 107-16, §901, in the amendment notes. See the amendments notes for a history of amendments to this section and the effective date of each change.

(i) wages, salaries, tips, and other employee compensation, but only if such amounts are includible in gross income for the taxable year, plus

(ii) the amount of the taxpayer's net earnings from self-employment for the taxable year (within the meaning of section 1402(a)), but such net earnings shall be determined with regard to the deduction allowed to the taxpayer by section 164(f).

(B) For purposes of subparagraph (A)—

(i) the earned income of an individual shall be computed without regard to any community property laws,

(ii) no amount received as a pension or annuity shall be taken into account,

(iii) no amount to which section 871(a) applies (relating to income of nonresident alien individuals not connected with United States business) shall be taken into account,

(iv) no amount received for services provided by an individual while the individual is an inmate at a penal institution shall be taken into account,

(v) no amount described in subparagraph (A) received for service performed in work activities as defined in paragraph (4) or (7) of section 407(d) of the Social Security Act to which the taxpayer is assigned under any State program under part A of title IV of such Act shall be taken into account, but only to the extent such amount is subsidized under such State program, and

(vi) a taxpayer may elect to treat amounts excluded from gross income by reason of section 112 as earned income.

(3) QUALIFYING CHILD.—

(A) IN GENERAL.—The term "qualifying child" means a qualifying child of the taxpayer (as defined in section 152(c), determined without regard to paragraph (1)(D) thereof and section 152(e)).

(B) MARRIED INDIVIDUAL.—The term "qualifying child" shall not include an individual who is married as of the close of the taxpayer's taxable year unless the taxpayer is entitled to a deduction under section 151 for such taxable year with respect to such individual (or would be so entitled but for section 152(e)).

(C) PLACE OF ABODE.—For purposes of subparagraph (A), the requirements of section 152(c)(1)(B) shall be met only if the principal place of abode is in the United States.

(D) IDENTIFICATION REQUIREMENTS.—

(i) IN GENERAL.—A qualifying child shall not be taken into account under subsection (b) unless the taxpayer includes the name, age, and TIN of the qualifying child on the return of tax for the taxable year.

(ii) OTHER METHODS.—The Secretary may prescribe other methods for providing the information described in clause (i).

(4) TREATMENT OF MILITARY PERSONNEL STATIONED OUTSIDE THE UNITED STATES.—For purposes of paragraphs (1)(A)(ii)(I) and (3)(C), the principal place of abode of a member of the Armed Forces of the United States shall be treated as in the United States during any period during which such member is stationed outside the United States while serving on extended active duty with the Armed Forces of the United States. For purposes of the preceding sentence, the term "extended active duty" means any period of active duty pursuant to a call or order to such duty for a period in excess of 90 days or for an indefinite period.

»»→ Caution: Code Sec. 32(c)(5), below, was stricken by P.L. 107-16, and is subject to the sunset provision of the Economic Growth and Tax Relief Reconciliation Act of 2001 (P.L. 107-16), §901. Absent Congressional action, the changes made to this provision by P.L. 107-16, or that take effect as if included in P.L. 107-16, do not apply after December 31, 2010. For more information about the sunset provision, see page XXI of the Preface to this publication and P.L. 107-16, §901, in the amendment notes. See the amendments notes for a history of amendments to this section and the effective date of each change.

(5) [Stricken.]

Amendments

• 2008, Heroes Earnings Assistance and Relief Tax Act of 2008 (P.L. 110-245)

P.L. 110-245, §102(a):

Amended Code Sec. 32(c)(2)(B)(vi). **Effective** for tax years ending after 12-31-2007. Prior to amendment, Code Sec. 32(c)(2)(B)(vi) read as follows:

(vi) in the case of any taxable year ending—

(I) after the date of the enactment of this clause, and

(II) before January 1, 2008,

a taxpayer may elect to treat amounts excluded from gross income by reason of section 112 as earned income.

P.L. 110-245, §102(c), provides:

(c) SUNSET NOT APPLICABLE.—Section 105 of the Working Families Tax Relief Act of 2004 [P.L. 108-311] (relating to application of EGTRRA sunset to this title) shall not apply to section 104(b) of such Act.

• 2006, Tax Relief and Health Care Act of 2006 (P.L. 109-432)

P.L. 109-432, Division A, §106(a):

Amended Code Sec. 32(c)(2)(B)(vi)(II) by striking "2007" and inserting "2008". **Effective** for tax years beginning after 12-31-2006.

• 2005, Gulf Opportunity Zone Act of 2005 (P.L. 109-135)

P.L. 109-135, §302(a):

Amended Code Sec. 32(c)(2)(B)(vi)(II) by striking "January 1, 2006" and inserting "January 1, 2007". **Effective** for tax years beginning after 12-31-2005.

• 2004, Working Families Tax Relief Act of 2004 (P.L. 108-311)

P.L. 108-311, §104(b)(1)-(3):

Amended Code Sec. 32(c)(2)(B) by striking "and" at the end of clause (iv), by striking the period at the end of clause (v) and inserting ", and", and by adding at the end a new clause (vi). **Effective** for tax years ending after 10-4-2004.

P.L. 108-311, §105, provides [but see P.L. 110-245, §102(c), above]:

SEC. 105. APPLICATION OF EGTRRA SUNSET TO THIS TITLE.

Each amendment made by this title shall be subject to title IX of the Economic Growth and Tax Relief Reconciliation Act of 2001 to the same extent and in the same manner as the provision of such Act to which such amendment relates.

P.L. 108-311, §205(a):

Amended Code Sec. 32(c)(3). **Effective** for tax years beginning after 12-31-2004. Prior to amendment, Code Sec. 32(c)(3) read as follows:

(3) QUALIFYING CHILD.—

(A) IN GENERAL.—The term "qualifying child" means, with respect to any taxpayer for any taxable year, an individual—

(i) who bears a relationship to the taxpayer described in subparagraph (B),

(ii) who has the same principal place of abode as the taxpayer for more than one-half of such taxable year, and

(iii) who meets the age requirements of subparagraph (C).

(B) RELATIONSHIP TEST.—

(i) IN GENERAL.—An individual bears a relationship to the taxpayer described in this subparagraph if such individual is—

(I) a son, daughter, stepson, or stepdaughter, or a descendant of any such individual,

(II) a brother, sister, stepbrother, or stepsister, or a descendant of any such individual, who the taxpayer cares for as the taxpayer's own child, or

(III) an eligible foster child of the taxpayer.

(ii) MARRIED CHILDREN.—Clause (i) shall not apply to any individual who is married as of the close of the taxpayer's taxable year unless the taxpayer is entitled to a deduction under section 151 for such taxable year with respect to such individual (or would be so entitled but for paragraph (2) or (4) of section 152(e)).

(iii) ELIGIBLE FOSTER CHILD.—For purposes of clause (i), the term "eligible foster child" means an individual not described in subclause (I) or (II) of clause (i) who—

(I) is placed with the taxpayer by an authorized placement agency, and

(II) the taxpayer cares for as the taxpayer's own child.

(iv) ADOPTION.—For purposes of this subparagraph, a child who is legally adopted, or who is placed with the taxpayer by an authorized placement agency for adoption by the taxpayer, shall be treated as a child by blood.

(C) AGE REQUIREMENTS.—An individual meets the requirements of this subparagraph if such individual—

(i) has not attained the age of 19 as of the close of the calendar year in which the taxable year of the taxpayer begins,

(ii) is a student (as defined in section 151(c)(4)) who has not attained the age of 24 as of the close of such calendar year, or

(iii) is permanently and totally disabled (as defined in section 22(e)(3)) at any time during the taxable year.

(D) IDENTIFICATION REQUIREMENTS.—

(i) IN GENERAL.—A qualifying child shall not be taken into account under subsection (b) unless the taxpayer includes the name, age, and TIN of the qualifying child on the return of tax for the taxable year.

(ii) OTHER METHODS.—The Secretary may prescribe other methods for providing the information described in clause (i).

(E) ABODE MUST BE IN THE UNITED STATES.—The requirements of subparagraph (A)(ii) shall be met only if the principal place of abode is in the United States.

P.L. 108-311, §205(b)(1):

Amended Code Sec. 32(c)(1) by striking subparagraph (C) and by redesignating subparagraphs (D), (E), (F), and (G) as subparagraphs (C), (D), (E), and (F), respectively. **Effective** for tax years beginning after 12-31-2004. Prior to being stricken, Code Sec. 32(c)(1)(C) read as follows:

(C) 2 OR MORE CLAIMING QUALIFYING CHILD.—

(i) IN GENERAL.—Except as provided in clause (ii), if (but for this paragraph) an individual may be claimed, and is claimed, as a qualifying child by 2 or more taxpayers for a taxable year beginning in the same calendar year, such individual shall be treated as the qualifying child of the taxpayer who is—

(I) a parent of the individual, or

(II) if subclause (I) does not apply, the taxpayer with the highest adjusted gross income for such taxable year.

(ii) MORE THAN 1 CLAIMING CREDIT.—If the parents claiming the credit with respect to any qualifying child do not file a joint return together, such child shall be treated as the qualifying child of—

(I) the parent with whom the child resided for the longest period of time during the taxable year, or

(II) if the child resides with both parents for the same amount of time during such taxable year, the parent with the highest adjusted gross income.

P.L. 108-311, §205(b)(2):

Amended Code Sec. 32(c)(4) by striking "(3)(E)". and inserting "(3)(C)". **Effective** for tax years beginning after 12-31-2004.

• 2001, Economic Growth and Tax Relief Reconciliation Act of 2001 (P.L. 107-16)

P.L. 107-16, §303(b):

Amended Code Sec. 32(c)(2)(A)(i) by inserting ", but only if such amounts are includible in gross income for the taxable year" after "other employee compensation". **Effective** for tax years beginning after 12-31-2001.

P.L. 107-16, §303(d)(2)(A):

Amended Code Sec. 32(c) by striking paragraph (5). **Effective** for tax years beginning after 12-31-2001. Prior to being stricken, Code Sec. 32(c)(5) read as follows:

(5) MODIFIED ADJUSTED GROSS INCOME.—

(A) IN GENERAL.—The term "modified adjusted gross income" means adjusted gross income determined without regard to the amounts described in subparagraph (B) and increased by the amounts described in subparagraph (C).

(B) CERTAIN AMOUNTS DISREGARDED.—An amount is described in this subparagraph if it is—

(i) the amount of losses from sales or exchanges of capital assets in excess of gains from such sales or exchanges to the extent such amount does not exceed the amount under section 1211(b)(1),

(ii) the net loss from estates and trusts,

(iii) the excess (if any) of amounts described in subsection (i)(2)(C)(ii) over the amounts described in subsection (i)(2)(C)(i) (relating to nonbusiness rents and royalties), or

(iv) 75 percent of the net loss from the carrying on of trades or businesses, computed separately with respect to—

(I) trades or businesses (other than farming) conducted as sole proprietorships,

(II) trades or businesses of farming conducted as sole proprietorships, and

(III) other trades or businesses.

For purposes of clause (iv), there shall not be taken into account items which are attributable to a trade or business which consists of the performance of services by the taxpayer as an employee.

(C) CERTAIN AMOUNTS INCLUDED.—An amount is described in this subparagraph if it is—

(i) interest received or accrued during the taxable year which is exempt from tax imposed by this chapter; or

(ii) amounts received as a pension or annuity, and any distributions or payments received from an individual retirement plan, by the taxpayer during the taxable year to the extent not included in gross income.

Clause (ii) shall not include any amount which is not includible in gross income by reason of a trustee-to-trustee transfer or a rollover distribution.

P.L. 107-16, §303(e)(1):

Amended Code Sec. 32(c)(3)(B)(i). **Effective** for tax years beginning after 12-31-2001. Prior to amendment, Code Sec. 32(c)(3)(B)(i) read as follows:

(i) IN GENERAL.—An individual bears a relationship to the taxpayer described in this subparagraph if such individual is—

(I) a son or daughter of the taxpayer, or a descendant of either,

(II) a stepson or stepdaughter of the taxpayer, or

(III) an eligible foster child of the taxpayer.

P.L. 107-16, §303(e)(2)(A):

Amended Code Sec. 32(c)(3)(B)(iii). **Effective** for tax years beginning after 12-31-2001. Prior to amendment, Code Sec. 32(c)(3)(B)(iii) read as follows:

(iii) ELIGIBLE FOSTER CHILD.—For purposes of clause (i)(III), the term "eligible foster child" means an individual not described in clause (i)(I) or (II) who—

(I) is a brother, sister, stepbrother, or stepsister of the taxpayer (or a descendant of any such relative) or is placed with the taxpayer by an authorized placement agency,

(II) the taxpayer cares for as the taxpayer's own child, and

(III) has the same principal place of abode as the taxpayer for the taxpayer's entire taxable year.

P.L. 107-16, §303(e)(2)(B):

Amended Code Sec. 32(c)(3)(A)(ii) by striking "except as provided in subparagraph (B)(iii)," before "who has the". **Effective** for tax years beginning after 12-31-2001.

P.L. 107-16, §303(f):

Amended Code Sec. 32(c)(1)(C). **Effective** for tax years beginning after 12-31-2001. Prior to amendment, Code Sec. 32(c)(1)(C) read as follows:

(C) 2 OR MORE ELIGIBLE INDIVIDUALS.—If 2 or more individuals would (but for this subparagraph and after application of subparagraph (B)) be treated as eligible individuals with respect to the same qualifying child for taxable years beginning in the same calendar year, only the individual with the highest modified adjusted gross income for such taxable years shall be treated as an eligible individual with respect to such qualifying child.

P.L. 107-16, §303(h):

Amended Code Sec. 32(c)(3)(E) by striking "subparagraphs (A)(ii) and (B)(iii)(II)" and inserting "subparagraph (A)(ii)". **Effective** for tax years beginning after 12-31-2001.

P.L. 107-16, §901(a)-(b), provides:

SEC. 901. SUNSET OF PROVISIONS OF ACT.

(a) IN GENERAL.—All provisions of, and amendments made by, this Act shall not apply—

(1) to taxable, plan, or limitation years beginning after December 31, 2010, or

(2) in the case of title V, to estates of decedents dying, gifts made, or generation skipping transfers, after December 31, 2010.

(b) APPLICATION OF CERTAIN LAWS.—The Internal Revenue Code of 1986 and the Employee Retirement Income Security Act of 1974 shall be applied and administered to years, estates, gifts, and transfers described in subsection (a) as if the provisions and amendments described in subsection (a) had never been enacted.

• 1999, Tax Relief Extension Act of 1999 (P.L. 106-70)

P.L. 106-170, §412(a):

Amended Code Sec. 32(c)(3)(B)(iii) by redesignating subclauses (I) and (II) as subclauses (II) and (III), respectively, and by inserting before subclause (II), as so redesignated, subclause (I). **Effective** for tax years beginning after 12-31-99.

• 1998, IRS Restructuring and Reform Act of 1998 (P.L. 105-206)

P.L. 105-206, §6010(p)(1)(A)-(C):

Amended Code Sec. 32(c)(5) by inserting before the period at the end of subparagraph (A) "and increased by the amounts described in subparagraph (C)", by adding "or" at the end of clause (iii) of subparagraph (B), and by striking all that follows subclause (II) of subparagraph (B)(iv) and inserting a new subclause (III) and a new subparagraph (C) to. **Effective** as if included in the provision of P.L. 105-34 to which it relates [**effective** for tax years beginning after 12-31-97.—CCH]. Prior to amendment, all that followed subclause (II) of Code Sec. 32(c)(5)(B)(iv) read as follows:

(III) other trades or businesses[,]

(v) interest received or accrued during the taxable year which is exempt from tax imposed by this chapter, and

(vi) amounts received as a pension or annuity, and any distributions or payments received from an individual retirement plan, by the taxpayer during the taxable year to the extent not included in gross income.

For purposes of clause (iv), there shall not be taken into account items which are attributable to a trade or business which consists of the performance of services by the taxpayer as an employee. Clause (vi) shall not include any amount which is not includible in gross income by reason of section 402(c), 403(a)(4), 403(b), 408(d)(3), (4), or (5), or 457(e)(10).

P.L. 105-206, §6010(p)(2):

Amended Code Sec. 32(c)(2)(B)(v) by inserting "shall be taken into account" before ", but only". **Effective** as if included in the provision of P.L. 105-34 to which it relates [**effective** for tax years beginning after 12-31-97.—CCH].

P.L. 105-206, §6021(a):

Amended Code Sec. 32(c)(1)(F) by striking "The term `eligible individual' does not include any individual who does not include on the return of tax for the taxable year—" and inserting "No credit shall be allowed under this section to an eligible individual who does not include on the return of tax for the taxable year—". **Effective** as if included in the amendments made by section 451 of P.L. 104-193 [**effective** for returns due after 9-21-96.—CCH].

P.L. 105-206, §6021(b)(1):

Amended Code Sec. 32(c)(3)(D)(i). **Effective** as if included in the amendments made by section 11111 of P.L. 101-508 [**effective** for tax years beginning after 12-31-90.—CCH]. Prior to amendment, Code Sec. 32(c)(3)(D)(i) read as follows:

(i) IN GENERAL.—The requirements of this subparagraph are met if the taxpayer includes the name, age, and TIN of each qualifying child (without regard to this subparagraph) on the return of tax for the taxable year.

P.L. 105-206, §6021(b)(2):

Amended Code Sec. 32(c)(1) by adding at the end a new subparagraph (G). **Effective** as if included in the amendments made by section 11111 of P.L. 101-508 [**effective** for tax years beginning after 12-31-90.—CCH].

P.L. 105-206, §6021(b)(3):

Amended Code Sec. 32(c)(3)(A) by inserting "and" at the end of clause (ii), by striking ", and" at the end of clause (iii) and inserting a period, and by striking clause (iv). **Effective** as if included in the amendments made by section 11111 of P.L. 101-508 [**effective** for tax years beginning after 12-31-90.—CCH]. Prior to being stricken, Code Sec. 32(c)(3)(A)(iv) read as follows:

(iv) with respect to whom the taxpayer meets the identification requirements of subparagraph (D).

• 1997, Taxpayer Relief Act of 1997 (P.L. 105-34)

P.L. 105-34, §312(d)(2):

Amended Code Sec. 32(c)(4) by striking "(as defined in section 1034(h)(3))" after "extended active duty" and by adding at the end a new sentence. **Effective**, generally, for sales and exchanges after 5-6-97.

P.L. 105-34, §1085(b):

Amended Code Sec. 32(c)(5)(B)(iv) by striking "50 percent" and inserting "75 percent". **Effective** for tax years beginning after 12-31-97.

P.L. 105-34, §1085(c):

Amended Code Sec. 32(c)(2)(B) by striking "and" at the end of clause (iii), by striking the period at the end of clause (iv) and inserting ", and", and by adding at the end a new clause (v). **Effective** for tax years beginning after 12-31-97.

P.L. 105-34, §1085(d)(1)-(4):

Amended Code Sec. 32(c)(5)(B) by striking "and" at the end of clause (iii), by striking the period at the end of clause (iv)(III), by inserting after clause (iv)(III) new clauses (v) and (vi), and by adding at the end a new sentence. **Effective** for tax years beginning after 12-31-97.

• 1996, Personal Responsibility and Work Opportunity Reconciliation Act of 1996 (P.L. 104-193)

P.L. 104-193, §451(a):

Amended Code Sec. 32(c)(1) by adding at the end a new subparagraph (F). **Effective** with respect to returns the due date for which (without regard to extensions) is more than 30 days after 8-22-96.

P.L. 104-193, §910(a):

Amended Code Sec. 32(c)(1)(C) by striking "adjusted gross income" each place it appears and inserting "modified adjusted gross income". **Effective** for tax years beginning after 12-31-95. For a special rule, see Act Sec. 910(c)(2), below.

P.L. 104-193, §910(b):

Amended Code Sec. 32(c) by adding at the end a new paragraph (5). **Effective** for tax years beginning after 12-31-95. For a special rule, see Act Sec. 910(c)(2), below.

P.L. 104-193, §910(c)(2), provides:

(2) ADVANCE PAYMENT INDIVIDUALS.—In the case of any individual who on or before June 26, 1996, has in effect an earned income eligibility certificate for the individual's taxable year beginning in 1996, the amendments made by this section shall apply to taxable years beginning after December 31, 1996.

• 1994, Uruguay Round Agreements Act (P.L. 103-465)

P.L. 103-465, §721(a):

Amended Code Sec. 32(c) by adding at the end a new paragraph (4). **Effective** for tax years beginning after 12-31-94.

P.L. 103-465, §722(a):

Amended Code Sec. 32(c)(1) by adding at the end a new subparagraph (E). **Effective** for tax years beginning after 12-31-94.

P.L. 103-465, §723(a):

Amended Code Sec. 32(c)(2)(B) by striking "and" at the end of clause (ii), by striking the period at the end of clause (iii) and inserting ", and", and by adding at the end a new clause (iv). **Effective** for tax years beginning after 12-31-93.

P.L. 103-465, §742(a):

Amended Code Sec. 32(c)(3)(D)(i). **Effective** for returns for tax years beginning after 12-31-94. For exceptions, see Act Sec. 742(c)(2), below. Prior to amendment, Code Sec. 32(c)(3)(D)(i) read as follows:

(i) IN GENERAL.—The requirements of this subparagraph are met if—

(I) the taxpayer includes the name and age of each qualifying child (without regard to this subparagraph) on the return of tax for the taxable year, and

(II) in the case of an individual who has attained the age of 1 year before the close of the taxpayer's taxable year, the taxpayer includes the taxpayer identification number of such individual on such return of tax for such taxable year.

P.L. 103-465, §742(c)(2), provides:

(2) EXCEPTION.—The amendments made by this section shall not apply to—

(A) returns for taxable years beginning in 1995 with respect to individuals who are born after October 31, 1995, and

(B) returns for taxable years beginning in 1996 with respect to individuals who are born after November 30, 1996.

• 1993, Omnibus Budget Reconciliation Act of 1993 (P.L. 103-66)

P.L. 103-66, §13131(b):

Amended Code Sec. 32(c)(1)(A). **Effective** for tax years beginning after 12-31-93. Prior to amendment Code Sec. 32(c)(1)(A) read as follows:

(A) IN GENERAL.—The term "eligible individual" means any individual who has a qualifying child for the taxable year.

P.L. 103-66, §13131(d)(1)(A)-(C):

Amended Code Sec. 32(c)(3)(D)(ii)-(iii) by striking "clause (i) or (ii)" in clause (iii) and inserting "clause (i)", by striking clause (ii), and by redesignating clause (iii) as clause (ii). **Effective** for tax years beginning after 12-31-93. Prior to being stricken, Code Sec. 32(c)(3)(D)(ii) read as follows:

(ii) INSURANCE POLICY NUMBER.—In the case of any taxpayer with respect to which the health insurance credit is allowed under subsection (a)(2), the Secretary may require a taxpayer to include an insurance policy number or other adequate evidence of insurance in addition to any information required to b included in clause (i).

• 1990, Omnibus Budget Reconciliation Act of 1990 (P.L. 101-508)

P.L. 101-508, §11111(a):

Amended Code Sec. 32(c). **Effective** for tax years beginning after 12-31-90. Prior to amendment, Code Sec. 32(c) read as follows:

(c) DEFINITIONS.—For purposes of this section—

(1) ELIGIBLE INDIVIDUAL.—

(A) IN GENERAL.—The term "eligible individual" means an individual who, for the taxable year—

(i) is married (within the meaning of section 7703) and is entitled to a deduction under section 151 for a child (within the meaning of section 151(c)(3)) or would be so entitled but for paragraph (2) or (4) of section 152(e).

(ii) is a surviving spouse (as determined under section 2(a)), or

(iii) is a head of a household (as determined under subsection (b) of section 2 without regard to subparagraphs (A)(ii) and (B) of paragraph (1) of such subsection).

(B) Child must reside with taxpayer in the united states.—An individual shall be treated as satisfying clause (i) of subparagraph (A) only if the child has the same principal place of abode as the individual for more than one-half of the taxable year and such abode is in the United States. An individual shall be treated as satisfying clause (ii) or (iii) of subparagraph (A) only if the household in question is in the United States.

(C) INDIVIDUAL WHO CLAIMS BENEFITS OF SECTION 911 NOT ELIGIBLE INDIVIDUAL.—The term "eligible individual" does not include an individual who, for the taxable year, claims the benefits of section 911 (relating to citizens or residents of the United States living abroad).

(2) EARNED INCOME.—

(A) The term "earned income" means—

(i) wages, salaries, tips and other employee compensation, plus

(ii) the amount of the taxpayer's net earnings from self-employment for the taxable year (within the meaning of section 1402(a)), but such net earnings shall be determined with regard to the deduction allowed to the taxpayer by section 164(f).

(B) For purposes of subparagraph (A)—

(i) the earned income of an individual shall be computed without regard to any community property laws,

(ii) no amount received as a pension or annuity shall be taken into account, and

(iii) no amount to which section 871(a) applies (relating to income of nonresident alien individuals not connected with United States business) shall be taken into account.

• 1986, Tax Reform Act of 1986 (P.L. 99-514)

P.L. 99-514, §104(b)(1)(B):

Amended Code Sec. 32(c)(1)(A)(i) by striking out "section 151(e)(3)" and inserting in lieu thereof "section 151(c)(3)". **Effective** for tax years beginning after 12-31-86.

P.L. 99-514, §1272(d)(4):

Amended Code Sec. 32(c)(1)(C). For the **effective** date as well as special rules, see Act Sec. 1277, as amended by P.L. 100-647, §1012(z)(1)-(2), below. Prior to amendment, Code Sec. 32(c)(1)(C) read as follows:

(C) INDIVIDUAL WHO CLAIMS BENEFITS OF SECTION 911 OR 931 NOT ELIGIBLE INDIVIDUAL.—The term "eligible individual" does not include an individual who, for the taxable year, claims the benefits of—

(i) section 911 (relating to citizens or residents of the United States living abroad), [or]

(ii) section 931 (relating to income from sources within possessions of the United States).

P.L. 99-514, §1277, as amended by P.L. 100-647, §1012(z)(1)-(2), provides:

(a) IN GENERAL.—Except as otherwise provided in this section, the amendments made by this subtitle shall apply to taxable years beginning after December 31, 1986.

(b) SPECIAL RULE FOR GUAM, AMERICAN SAMOA, AND THE NORTHERN MARIANA ISLANDS.—The amendments made by this subtitle shall apply with respect to Guam, American Samoa, or the Northern Mariana Islands (and to residents thereof and corporations created or organized therein) only if (and so long as) an implementing agreement under section 1271 is in effect between the United States and such possession.

(c) SPECIAL RULES FOR THE VIRGIN ISLANDS.—

(1) IN GENERAL.—The amendments made by section 1275(c) shall apply with respect to the Virgin Islands (and residents thereof and corporations created or organized therein) only if (and so long as) an implementing agreement is in effect between the United States and the Virgin Islands with respect to the establishment of rules under which the evasion or avoidance of United States income tax shall not be permitted or facilitated by such possession. Any such implementing agreement shall be executed on behalf of the United States by the Secretary of the Treasury, after consultation with the Secretary of the Interior.

(2) SECTION 1275(b).—

(A) IN GENERAL.—The amendment made by section 1275(b) shall apply with respect to—

(i) any taxable year beginning after December 31, 1986, and

(ii) any pre-1987 open year.

(B) SPECIAL RULES.—In the case of any pre-1987 open year—

(i) the amendment made by section 1275(b) shall not apply to income from sources in the Virgin Islands or income effectively connected with the conduct of a trade or business in the Virgin Islands, and

(ii) the taxpayer shall be allowed a credit—

(I) against any additional tax imposed by subtitle A of the Internal Revenue Code of 1954 (by reason of the amendment made by section 1275(b)) on income not described in clause (i) and from sources in the United States,

(II) for any tax paid to the Virgin Islands before the date of the enactment of this Act and attributable to such income.

For purposes of clause (ii)(II), any tax paid before January 1, 1987, pursuant to a process in effect before August 16, 1986, shall be treated as paid before the date of the enactment of this Act.

(C) PRE-1987 OPEN YEAR.—For purposes of this paragraph, the term "pre-1987 open year" means any taxable year beginning before January 1, 1987, if on the date of the enactment of this Act the assessment of a deficiency of income tax for such taxable year is not barred by any law or rule of law.

(D) EXCEPTION.—In the case of any pre-1987 open year, the amendment made by section 1275(b) shall not apply to any domestic corporation if—

(i) during the fiscal year which ended May 31, 1986, such corporation was actively engaged directly or through a subsidiary in the conduct of a trade or business in the Virgin Islands and such trade or business consists of business related to marine activities, and

(ii) such corporation was incorporated on March 31, 1983, in Delaware.

(E) EXCEPTION FOR CERTAIN TRANSACTIONS.—

(i) IN GENERAL.—In the case of any pre-1987 open year, the amendment made by section 1275(b) shall not apply to any income derived from transactions described in clause (ii) by 1 or more corporations which were formed in Delaware on or about March 6, 1981, and which have owned 1 or more office buildings in St. Thomas, United States Virgin Islands, for at least 5 years before the date of the enactment of this Act.

(ii) DESCRIPTION OF TRANSACTIONS.—The transactions described in this clause are—

(I) the redemptions of limited partnership interests for cash and property described in an agreement (as amended) dated March 12, 1981,

(II) the subsequent disposition of the properties distributed in such redemptions, and

(III) interest earned before January 1, 1987, on bank deposits of proceeds received from such redemptions to the extent such deposits are located in the United States Virgin islands.

(iii) LIMITATION.—The aggregate reduction in tax by reason of this subparagraph shall not exceed $8,312,000. If the taxes which would be payable as the result of the application of the amendment made by section 1275(b) to pre-1987 open years exceeds the limitation of the preceding sentence, such excess shall be treated as attributable to income received in taxable years in reverse chronological order.

(d) REPORT ON IMPLEMENTING AGREEMENTS.—If, during the 1-year period beginning on the date of the enactment of this Act, any implementing agreement described in subsection (b) or (c) is not executed, the Secretary of the Treasury or his delegate shall report to the Committee on Finance of the United States Senate, the Committee on Ways and Means, and the Committee on Interior and Insular Affairs of the House of Representatives with respect to—

(1) the status of such negotiations, and

(2) the reason why such agreement has not been executed.

(e) TREATMENT OF CERTAIN UNITED STATES PERSONS.—Except as otherwise provided in regulations prescribed by the Secretary of the Treasury or his delegate, if a United States person becomes a resident of Guam, American Samoa, or the Northern Mariana Islands, the rules of section 877(c) of the Internal Revenue Code of 1954 shall apply to such person during the 10-year period beginning when such person became such a resident. Notwithstanding subsection (b), the preceding sentence shall apply to dispositions after December 31, 1985, in taxable years ending after such date.

(f) EXEMPTION FROM WITHHOLDING.—Notwithstanding subsection (b), the modification of section 884 of the Internal Revenue Code of 1986 by reason of the amendment to section 881 of such Code by section 1273(b)(1) of this Act shall apply to taxable years beginning after December 31, 1986.

P.L. 99-514, §1301(j)(8):

Amended Code Sec. 32(c) by striking out "section 143" each place it appears and inserting in lieu thereof "section 7703". **Effective** for bonds issued after 8-15-86.

• 1984, Deficit Reduction Act of 1984 (P.L. 98-369)

P.L. 98-369, §423(c)(3):

Amended Code Sec. 43(c)(1), prior to its redesignation as Code Sec. 32(c)(1), by inserting after "section 151(e)(3))" in subparagraph (A)(i) the following: "or would be so entitled but for paragraph (2) or (4) of section 152(e)", and by striking out "the child has the same principal place of abode as the individual" in subparagraph (B) and inserting in lieu thereof "the child has the same principal place of abode as the individual for more than one-half of the taxable year". **Effective** for tax years beginning after 12-31-84.

• 1983, Social Security Amendments of 1983 (P.L. 98-21)

P.L. 98-21, §124(c)(4)(B):

Amended Code Sec. 43(c)(2)(A)(ii) by inserting before the period ", but such net earnings shall be determined with regard to the deduction allowed to the taxpayer by section 164(f)". **Effective** for tax years beginning after 1989.

• 1981, Economic Recovery Tax Act of 1981 (P.L. 97-34)

P.L. 97-34, §111(b)(2):

Amended Code Sec. 43(c)(1)(C)(i) by striking out "relating to income earned by individuals in certain camps outside the United States" and inserting in lieu thereof "relating to citizens or residents of the United States living abroad". **Effective** with respect to tax years beginning after 12-31-81.

P.L. 97-34, §112(b)(3):

Amended Code Sec. 43(c)(1)(C) by striking out "913," in the caption thereof, by striking out clause (ii), and by redesignating clause (iii) as clause (ii). **Effective** with respect to tax years beginning after 12-31-81. Prior to amendment, Code Sec. 43(c)(1)(C)(ii) read: "(ii) section 913 (relating to deduction for certain expenses of living abroad), or"

• 1980, Technical Corrections Act of 1979 (P.L. 96-222)

P.L. 96-222, §101(a)(1):

Amended Code Sec. 43(c)(1)(C). **Effective** for tax years beginning after 12-31-77. Prior to amendment, Code Sec. 43(c)(1)(C) read as follows:

(C) INDIVIDUAL ENTITLED TO EXCLUDE INCOME UNDER SECTION 911 NOT ELIGIBLE INDIVIDUAL.—The term "eligible individual" does not include an individual who, for the taxable year, is entitled to exclude any amount from gross income under section 911 (relating to earned income by employees in certain camps without the United States) or section 931 (relating to income from sources within the possessions of the United States).

• 1978, Revenue Act of 1978 (P.L. 95-600)

P.L. 95-600, §104(d):

Amended Code Sec. 43(c)(2)(B) by striking clause (i) and by redesignating clauses (ii), (iii) and (iv) as clauses (i), (ii) and (iii). **Effective** for tax years beginning after 12-31-78. Prior to be being stricken, clause (i) read:

"(i) except as provided in clause (ii), any amount shall be taken into account only if such amount is includible in the gross income of the taxpayer for the taxable year."

P.L. 95-600, §104(e):

Amended Code Sec. 43(c)(1). **Effective** for tax years beginning after 12-31-78. Prior to amendment, Code Sec. 43(c)(1) read as follows:

"(c) DEFINITIONS.—For purposes of this section—

"(1) ELIGIBLE INDIVIDUAL.—The term `eligible individual' means an individual who, for the taxable year—

"(A) maintains a household (within the meaning of section 44A(f)(1)) in the United States which is the principal place of abode of that individual and—

"(i) a child of that individual if such child meets the requirements of section 151(e)(1)(B) (relating to additional exemptions for dependents), or

"(ii) a child of that individual who is disabled (within the meaning of section 72(m)(7)) and with respect to whom that individual is entitled to claim a deduction under section 151; and

"(B) is not entitled to exclude any amount from gross income under section 911 (relating to earned income from sources without the United States) or section 931 (relating to income from sources within the possessions of the United States)."

• 1978, Tax Treatment Extension Act of 1978 (P.L. 95-615)

P.L. 95-615, 202(f)(5):

Amended Code Sec. 43(c)(1)(B) by changing "relating to earned income from sources without the United States" to "relating to income earned by employees in certain camps."

• 1977, Tax Reduction and Simplification Act of 1977 (P.L. 95-30)

P.L. 95-30, §103(b):

Amended P.L. 94-12, §209(b) as amended by P.L. 94-455, §401(c)(1)(A), and P.L. 94-164, §2(f) by striking out "January 1, 1978" and inserting in place thereof "January 1, 1979". **Effective** 5-23-77.

P.L. 95-30, §103(c):

Amended P.L. 94-455, §401(e) to provide that amendments made by §401(c) of that Act "shall apply to taxable years ending after December 31, 1975, and shall cease to apply to tax years beginning after December 31, 1978". **Effective** 5-23-77.

• 1976, Tax Reform Act of 1976 (P.L. 94-455)

P.L. 94-455, §401(c)(1)(A):

Amended P.L. 94-12, §209(b) as amended by P.L. 94-164, §2(f) by striking out "January 1, 1977" and inserting in place thereof "January 1, 1978.". **Effective** as indicated in P.L. 94-455, §401(e), below.

P.L. 94-455, §401(c)(2):

Amended Code Sec. 43(c)(1)(A). **Effective** as indicated in P.L. 94-455, §401(e), below. Before amendment, Code Sec. 43(c)(1)(A) read as follows:

(A) maintains a household (within the meaning of section 214(b)(3)) in the United States which is the principal place of abode of that individual and of a child of that individual with respect to whom he is entitled to claim a deduction under section 151(e)(1)(B) (relating to additional exemption for dependents), and

P.L. 94-455, §401(e), provides:

Amendments made by §401(c) "shall apply to taxable years ending after December 31, 1975, and shall cease to apply to taxable years ending after December 31, 1977."

P.L. 94-455, §402(b):

Amended P.L. 94-164, §2(g). **Effective** 10-4-76, to read as follows:

(g) Effective Dates.—The amendments made by this section [2] (other than by subsection (d)) apply to taxable years ending after December 31, 1975, and before January 1, 1978. Subsection (d) applies to taxable years ending after December 31, 1975.

• 1975, Revenue Adjustment Act of 1975 (P.L. 94-164)

P.L. 94-164, §2(f):

Amended P.L. 94-12, §209(b). **Effective** as indicated in P.L. 94-164, §2(g), below.

P.L. 94-164, §2(g), provides:

Amendments made by P.L. 94-164, §2 "apply to taxable years ending after December 31, 1975, and before January 1, 1977."

• 1975, Tax Reduction Act of 1975 (P.L. 94-12)

P.L. 94-12, §204(a):

Added Code Sec. 43(c). **Effective** as indicated in P.L. 94-12, §209(b), below.

P.L. 94-12, §209(b), provides:

§204 applies "to tax years beginning after December 31, 1974, and before January 1, 1976."

[Sec. 32(d)]

(d) MARRIED INDIVIDUALS.—In the case of an individual who is married (within the meaning of section 7703), this section shall apply only if a joint return is filed for the taxable year under section 6013.

Amendments

• 1986, Tax Reform Act of 1986 (P.L. 99-514)

P.L. 99-514, §1301(j)(8):

Amended Code Sec. 32(d) by striking out "section 143" each place it appears and inserting in lieu thereof "section 7703". **Effective** for bonds issued after 8-15-86.

• 1975, Tax Reduction Act of 1975 (P.L. 94-12)

P.L. 94-12, §204(a):

Added Code Sec. 43(d). For **effective** date, see the amendment notes under Code Sec. 32(a), formerly Code Sec. 43(a).

[Sec. 32(e)]

(e) TAXABLE YEAR MUST BE FULL TAXABLE YEAR.—Except in the case of a taxable year closed by reason of the death of the taxpayer, no credit shall be allowable under this section in the case of a taxable year covering a period of less than 12 months.

Amendments

• 1975, Tax Reduction Act of 1975 (P.L. 94-12)

P.L. 94-12, §204(a):

Added Code Sec. 43(e). For the **effective** date, see the amendment notes under Code Sec. 32(a), formerly Code Sec. 43(a).

[Sec. 32(f)]

(f) AMOUNT OF CREDIT TO BE DETERMINED UNDER TABLES.—

(1) IN GENERAL.—The amount of the credit allowed by this section shall be determined under tables prescribed by the Secretary.

(2) REQUIREMENTS FOR TABLES.—The tables prescribed under paragraph (1) shall reflect the provisions of subsections (a) and (b) and shall have income brackets of not greater than $50 each—

(A) for earned income between $0 and the amount of earned income at which the credit is phased out under subsection (b), and

»»→ Caution: Code Sec. 32(f)(2)(B), below, is subject to the sunset provision of the Economic Growth and Tax Relief Reconciliation Act of 2001 (P.L. 107-16), §901. Absent Congressional action, the changes made to this provision by P.L. 107-16, or that take effect as if included in P.L. 107-16, do not apply after December 31, 2010. For more information about the sunset provision, see page XXI of the Preface to this publication and P.L. 107-16, §901, in the amendment notes. See the amendments notes for a history of amendments to this section and the effective date of each change.

(B) for adjusted gross income between the dollar amount at which the phaseout begins under subsection (b) and the amount of adjusted gross income at which the credit is phased out under subsection (b).

Amendments

• 2001, Economic Growth and Tax Relief Reconciliation Act of 2001 (P.L. 107-16)

P.L. 107-16, §303(d)(2)(B):

Amended Code Sec. 32(f)(2)(B) by striking "modified" each place it appears. **Effective** for tax years beginning after 12-31-2001. Prior to amendment, Code Sec. 32(f)(2)(B) read as follows:

(B) for modified adjusted gross income between the dollar amount at which the phaseout begins under subsection (b) and the amount of modified adjusted gross income at which the credit is phased out under subsection (b).

P.L. 107-16, §901(a)-(b), provides:

SEC. 901. SUNSET OF PROVISIONS OF ACT.

(a) IN GENERAL.—All provisions of, and amendments made by, this Act shall not apply—

(1) to taxable, plan, or limitation years beginning after December 31, 2010, or

(2) in the case of title V, to estates of decedents dying, gifts made, or generation skipping transfers, after December 31, 2010.

(b) APPLICATION OF CERTAIN LAWS.—The Internal Revenue Code of 1986 and the Employee Retirement Income Security Act of 1974 shall be applied and administered to years, estates, gifts, and transfers described in subsection (a) as if the provisions and amendments described in subsection (a) had never been enacted.

• 1996, Personal Responsibility and Work Opportunity Reconciliation Act of 1996 (P.L. 104-193)

P.L. 104-193, §910(a):

Amended Code Sec. 32(f)(2)(B) by striking "adjusted gross income" each place it appears and inserting "modified adjusted gross income". **Effective** for tax years beginning after 12-31-95. For a special rule, see Act Sec. 910(c)(2), below.

P.L. 104-193, §910(c)(2), provides:

(2) ADVANCE PAYMENT INDIVIDUALS.—In the case of any individual who on or before June 26, 1996, has in effect an earned income eligibility certificate for the individual's taxable year beginning in 1996, the amendments made by this section shall apply to taxable years beginning after December 31, 1996.

• 1986, Tax Reform Act of 1986 (P.L. 99-514)

P.L. 99-514, §111(d)(1):

Amended Code Sec. 32(f)(2) by striking out subparagraphs (A) and (B) and inserting in lieu thereof new subparagraphs (A) and (B). **Effective** for tax years beginning after 12-31-86. Prior to amendment, Code Sec. 32(f)(2)(A)-(B) read as follows:

(A) for earned income between $0 and $11,000, and

(B) for adjusted gross income between $6,500 and $11,000.

• 1984, Deficit Reduction Act of 1984 (P.L. 98-369)

P.L. 98-369, §1042(d)(2):

Amended Code Sec. 32(f)(2)(A) and (B), as redesignated by Act Sec. 471(c)(1). **Effective** for tax years beginning after 12-31-84. Prior to amendment, Code Sec. 32(f)(2)(A) and (B) read as follows:

(A) for earned income between $0 and $10,000, and

(B) for adjusted gross income between $6,000 and $10,000.

• 1978, Revenue Act of 1978 (P.L. 95-600)

P.L. 95-600, §104(c):

Added Code Sec. 43(f). **Effective** for tax years beginning after 12-31-78.

»»→ Caution: Code Sec. 32(g), below, was repealed by P.L. 111-226, applicable to tax years beginning after December 31, 2010.

[Sec. 32(g)]

(g) COORDINATION WITH ADVANCE PAYMENTS OF EARNED INCOME CREDIT.—

(1) RECAPTURE OF EXCESS ADVANCE PAYMENTS.—If any payment is made to the individual by an employer under section 3507 during any calendar year, then the tax imposed by this chapter for

the individual's last taxable year beginning in such calendar year shall be increased by the aggregate amount of such payments.

(2) RECONCILIATION OF PAYMENTS ADVANCED AND CREDIT ALLOWED.—Any increase in tax under paragraph (1) shall not be treated as tax imposed by this chapter for purposes of determining the amount of any credit (other than the credit allowed by subsection (a)) allowable under this part.

Amendments

• 2010, (P.L. 111-226)

P.L. 111-226, §219(a)(2):

Repealed Code Sec. 32(g). **Effective** for tax years beginning after 12-31-2010. Prior to repeal, Code Sec. 32(g) read as follows:

(g) COORDINATION WITH ADVANCE PAYMENTS OF EARNED INCOME CREDIT.—

(1) RECAPTURE OF EXCESS ADVANCE PAYMENTS.—If any payment is made to the individual by an employer under section 3507 during any calendar year, then the tax imposed by this chapter for the individual's last taxable year beginning in such calendar year shall be increased by the aggregate amount of such payments.

(2) RECONCILIATION OF PAYMENTS ADVANCED AND CREDIT ALLOWED.—Any increase in tax under paragraph (1) shall not be treated as tax imposed by this chapter for purposes of determining the amount of any credit (other than the credit allowed by subsection (a)) allowable under this part.

• 2002, Job Creation and Worker Assistance Act of 2002 (P.L. 107-147)

P.L. 107-147, §416(a)(1):

Amended Code Sec. 32(g)(2) by striking "subpart" and inserting "part". **Effective** as if included in section 474 of P.L. 98-369 [generally **effective** for tax years beginning after 12-31-83.—CCH].

• 1980, Technical Corrections Act of 1979 (P.L. 96-222)

P.L. 96-222, §101(a)(2)(E):

Redesignated Code Sec. 43(h) as Sec. 43(g). **Effective** for tax years beginning after 1978.

• 1978, Revenue Act of 1978 (P.L. 95-600)

P.L. 95-600, §105(a):

Added Code Sec. 43(h). **Effective** for tax years beginning after 1978.

»»→ Caution: Code Sec. 32(h), below, was repealed by P.L. 107-16, and is subject to the sunset provision of the Economic Growth and Tax Relief Reconciliation Act of 2001 (P.L. 107-16), §901. Absent Congressional action, the changes made to this provision by P.L. 107-16, or that take effect as if included in P.L. 107-16, do not apply after December 31, 2010. For more information about the sunset provision, see page XXI of the Preface to this publication and P.L. 107-16, §901, in the amendment notes. See the amendments notes for a history of amendments to this section and the effective date of each change.

[Sec. 32(h)—Repealed]

Amendments

• 2001, Economic Growth and Tax Relief Reconciliation Act of 2001 (P.L. 107-16)

P.L. 107-16, §303(c):

Repealed Code Sec. 32(h). **Effective** for tax years beginning after 12-31-2001. Prior to repeal, Code Sec. 32(h) read as follows:

(h) REDUCTION OF CREDIT TO TAXPAYERS SUBJECT TO ALTERNATIVE MINIMUM TAX.—The credit allowed under this section for the taxable year shall be reduced by the amount of tax imposed by section 55 (relating to alternative minimum tax) with respect to such taxpayer for such taxable year.

P.L. 107-16, §901(a)-(b), provides:

SEC. 901. SUNSET OF PROVISIONS OF ACT.

(a) IN GENERAL.—All provisions of, and amendments made by, this Act shall not apply—

(1) to taxable, plan, or limitation years beginning after December 31, 2010, or

(2) in the case of title V, to estates of decedents dying, gifts made, or generation skipping transfers, after December 31, 2010.

(b) APPLICATION OF CERTAIN LAWS.—The Internal Revenue Code of 1986 and the Employee Retirement Income Security Act of 1974 shall be applied and administered to years, estates, gifts, and transfers described in subsection (a) as if the provisions and amendments described in subsection (a) had never been enacted.

• 1988, Technical and Miscellaneous Revenue Act of 1988 (P.L. 100-647)

P.L. 100-647, §1007(g)(12):

Amended Code Sec. 32(h) by striking out "for taxpayers other than corporations" after "alternative minimum tax". **Effective** as if included in the provision of P.L. 99-514 to which it relates.

• 1984, Deficit Reduction Act of 1984 (P.L. 98-369)

P.L. 98-369, §1042(c):

Amended Code Sec. 32, as redesignated by Act Sec. 471(c)(1), by adding subsection (h). **Effective** for tax years beginning after 12-31-84.

[Sec. 32(i)]

(i) DENIAL OF CREDIT FOR INDIVIDUALS HAVING EXCESSIVE INVESTMENT INCOME.—

(1) IN GENERAL.—No credit shall be allowed under subsection (a) for the taxable year if the aggregate amount of disqualified income of the taxpayer for the taxable year exceeds $2,200.

(2) DISQUALIFIED INCOME.—For purposes of paragraph (1), the term "disqualified income" means—

(A) interest or dividends to the extent includible in gross income for the taxable year,

(B) interest received or accrued during the taxable year which is exempt from tax imposed by this chapter,

(C) the excess (if any) of—

(i) gross income from rents or royalties not derived in the ordinary course of a trade or business, over

(ii) the sum of—

(I) the deductions (other than interest) which are clearly and directly allocable to such gross income, plus

(II) interest deductions properly allocable to such gross income,

(D) the capital gain net income (as defined in section 1222) of the taxpayer for such taxable year, and

(E) the excess (if any) of—

(i) the aggregate income from all passive activities for the taxable year (determined without regard to any amount included in earned income under subsection (c)(2) or described in a preceding subparagraph), over

(ii) the aggregate losses from all passive activities for the taxable year (as so determined).

For purposes of subparagraph (E), the term "passive activity" has the meaning given such term by section 469.

Amendments

• 1996, Personal Responsibility and Work Opportunity Reconciliation Act of 1996 (P.L. 104-193)

P.L. 104-193, §909(a)(1):

Amended Code Sec. 32(i)(1) by striking "$2,350" and inserting "$2,200". **Effective** for tax years beginning after 12-31-95. For a special rule, see Act Sec. 909(c)(2), below.

P.L. 104-193, §909(b):

Amended Code Sec. 32(i)(2) by striking "and" at the end of subparagraph (B), by striking the period at the end of subparagraph (C) and inserting a comma, and by adding at the end new subparagraphs (D) and (E). **Effective** for tax years beginning after 12-31-95. For a special rule, see Act Sec. 909(c)(2), below.

P.L. 104-193, §909(c)(2), provides:

(2) ADVANCE PAYMENT INDIVIDUALS.—In the case of any individual who on or before June 26, 1996, has in effect an earned income eligibility certificate for the individual's taxable year beginning in 1996, the amendments made by this section shall apply to taxable years beginning after December 31, 1996.

• 1995, Self-Employed Health Insurance Act (P.L. 104-7)

P.L. 104-7, §4(a):

Amended Code Sec. 32 by redesignating subsections (i) and (j) as subsections (j) and (k), respectively, and by inserting after subsection (h) a new subsection (i). **Effective** for tax years beginning after 12-31-95.

[Sec. 32(j)]

(j) INFLATION ADJUSTMENTS.—

(1) IN GENERAL.—In the case of any taxable year beginning after 1996, each of the dollar amounts in subsections (b)(2) and (i)(1) shall be increased by an amount equal to—

(A) such dollar amount, multiplied by

»»→ Caution: Code Sec. 32(j)(1)(B), below, is subject to the sunset provision of the Economic Growth and Tax Relief Reconciliation Act of 2001 (P.L. 107-16), §901. Absent Congressional action, the changes made to this provision by P.L. 107-16, or that take effect as if included in P.L. 107-16, do not apply after December 31, 2010. For more information about the sunset provision, see page XXI of the Preface to this publication and P.L. 107-16, §901, in the amendment notes. See the amendments notes for a history of amendments to this section and the effective date of each change.

(B) the cost-of-living adjustment determined under section 1(f)(3) for the calendar year in which the taxable year begins, determined—

(i) in the case of amounts in subsections (b)(2)(A) and (i)(1), by substituting "calendar year 1995" for "calendar year 1992" in subparagraph (B) thereof, and

(ii) in the case of the $3,000 amount in subsection (b)(2)(B)(iii), by substituting "calendar year 2007" for "calendar year 1992" in subparagraph (B) of such section 1.

(2) ROUNDING.—

»»→ Caution: Code Sec. 32(j)(2)(A), below, is subject to the sunset provision of the Economic Growth and Tax Relief Reconciliation Act of 2001 (P.L. 107-16), §901. Absent Congressional action, the changes made to this provision by P.L. 107-16, or that take effect as if included in P.L. 107-16, do not apply after December 31, 2010. For more information about the sunset provision, see page XXI of the Preface to this publication and P.L. 107-16, §901, in the amendment notes. See the amendments notes for a history of amendments to this section and the effective date of each change.

(A) IN GENERAL.—If any dollar amount in subsection (b)(2)(A) (after being increased under subparagraph (B) thereof), after being increased under paragraph (1), is not a multiple of $10, such dollar amount shall be rounded to the nearest multiple of $10.

(B) DISQUALIFIED INCOME THRESHOLD AMOUNT.—If the dollar amount in subsection (i)(1), after being increased under paragraph (1), is not a multiple of $50, such amount shall be rounded to the next lowest multiple of $50.

Amendments

• 2001, Economic Growth and Tax Relief Reconciliation Act of 2001 (P.L. 107-16)

P.L. 107-16, §303(a)(2):

Amended Code Sec. 32(j)(1)(B). **Effective** for tax years beginning after 12-31-2001. Prior to amendment, Code Sec. 32(j)(1)(B) read as follows:

(B) the cost-of-living adjustment determined under section 1(f)(3) for the calendar year in which the taxable year begins, determined by substituting "calendar year 1995" for "calendar year 1992" in subparagraph (B) thereof.

P.L. 107-16, §303(a)(3):

Amended Code Sec. 32(j)(2)(A) by striking "subsection (b)(2)" and inserting "subsection (b)(2)(A) (after being increased under subparagraph (B) thereof)". **Effective** for tax years beginning after 12-31-2001.

P.L. 107-16, §901(a)-(b), provides:

SEC. 901. SUNSET OF PROVISIONS OF ACT.

(a) IN GENERAL.—All provisions of, and amendments made by, this Act shall not apply—

(1) to taxable, plan, or limitation years beginning after December 31, 2010, or

(2) in the case of title V, to estates of decedents dying, gifts made, or generation skipping transfers, after December 31, 2010.

(b) APPLICATION OF CERTAIN LAWS.—The Internal Revenue Code of 1986 and the Employee Retirement Income Security Act of 1974 shall be applied and administered to years, estates, gifts, and transfers described in subsection (a) as if the provisions and amendments described in subsection (a) had never been enacted.

• 1996, Personal Responsibility and Work Opportunity Reconciliation Act of 1996 (P.L. 104-193)

P.L. 104-193, §909(a)(2):

Amended Code Sec. 32(j). **Effective** for tax years beginning after 12-31-95. For a special rule, see Act Sec. 909(c)(2), below. Prior to amendment, Code Sec. 32(j) read as follows:

(j) INFLATION ADJUSTMENTS.—

(1) IN GENERAL.—In the case of any taxable year beginning after 1994, each dollar amount contained in subsection (b)(2)(A) shall be increased by an amount equal to—

(A) such dollar amount, multiplied by

(B) the cost-of-living adjustment determined under section 1(f)(3), for the calendar year in which the taxable year begins, by substituting "calendar year 1993" for "calendar year 1992".

(2) ROUNDING.—If any dollar amount after being increased under paragraph (1) is not a multiple of $10, such dollar amount shall be rounded to the nearest multiple of $10 (or, if such dollar amount is a multiple of $5, such dollar amount shall be increased to the next higher multiple of $10).

P.L. 104-193, §909(c)(2), provides:

(2) ADVANCE PAYMENT INDIVIDUALS.—In the case of any individual who on or before June 26, 1996, has in effect an earned income eligibility certificate for the individual's taxable year beginning in 1996, the amendments made by this section shall apply to taxable years beginning after December 31, 1996.

• 1995, Self-Employed Health Insurance Act (P.L. 104-7)

P.L. 104-7, §4(a):

Amended Code Sec. 32 by redesignating subsection (i) as subsection (j). **Effective** for tax years beginning after 12-31-95.

• 1993, Omnibus Budget Reconciliation Act of 1993 (P.L. 103-66)

P.L. 103-66, §13131(c)(1)-(2):

Amended Code Sec. 32(i)(1)-(3) by striking paragraphs (1) and (2) and inserting a new paragraph (1), and by redesignating paragraph (3) as paragraph (2). **Effective** for tax years beginning after 12-31-93. Prior to amendment, Code Sec. 32(i)(1)-(3) read as follows:

(i) INFLATION ADJUSTMENTS.—

(1) IN GENERAL.—In the case of any taxable year beginning after the applicable calendar year, each dollar amount referred to in paragraph (2)(B) shall be increased by an amount equal to—

(A) such dollar amount, multiplied by

(B) the cost-of-living adjustment determined under section 1(f)(3), for the calendar year in which the taxable year begins, by substituting "calendar year 1984" for "calendar year 1989" in subparagraph (B) thereof.

(2) DEFINITIONS, ETC.—For purposes of paragraph (1)—

(A) APPLICABLE CALENDAR YEAR.—The term "applicable calendar year" means—

(i) 1986 in the case of the dollar amount referred to in clause (i) of subparagraph (B), and

(ii) 1987 in the case of the dollar amount referred to in clause (ii) of subparagraph (B).

(B) DOLLAR AMOUNTS.—The dollar amounts referred to in this subparagraph are—

(i) the $5,714 dollar amounts contained in subsection (b)(1), and

(ii) the $9,000 amount contained in subsection (b)(1)(B)(ii).

(3) ROUNDING.—If any dollar amount after being increased under paragraph (1) is not a multiple of $10, such dollar amount shall be rounded to the nearest multiple of $10 (or, if such dollar amount is a multiple of $5, such dollar amount shall be increased to the next higher multiple of $10).

• 1990, Omnibus Budget Reconciliation Act of 1990 (P.L. 101-508)

P.L. 101-508, §11101(d)(1)(B):

Amended Code Sec. 32(i)(1)(B) by striking "1987" and inserting "1989". **Effective** for tax years beginning after 12-31-90.

P.L. 101-508, §11111(e)(1):

Amended Code Sec. 32(i)(2)(A)(i) by striking "or (ii)" after "referred to in clause (i)". **Effective** for tax years beginning after 12-31-90.

P.L. 101-508, §11111(e)(2):

Amended Code Sec. 32(i)(2)(A)(ii) by striking "clause (iii)" and inserting "clause (ii)". **Effective** for tax years beginning after 12-31-90.

P.L. 101-508, §11111(e)(3):

Amended Code Sec. 32(i)(2)(B). Prior to amendment, Code Sec. 32(i)(2)(B) read as follows: **Effective** for tax years beginning after 12-31-90.

(B) DOLLAR AMOUNTS.—The dollar amounts referred to in this subparagraph are—

(i) the $5,714 amount contained in subsection (a),

(ii) the $6,500 amount contained in the last sentence of subsection (b), and

(iii) the $9,000 amount contained in subsection (b)(2).

• 1988, Technical and Miscellaneous Revenue Act of 1988 (P.L. 100-647)

P.L. 100-647, §1001(c):

Amended Code Sec. 32(i)(3). **Effective** as if included in the provision of P.L. 99-514 to which it relates. Prior to amendment, Code Sec. 32(i)(3) read as follows:

(3) ROUNDING.—If any increase determined under paragraph (1) is not a multiple of $10, such increase shall be rounded to the nearest multiple of $10 (or, if such increase is a multiple of $5, such increase shall be increased to the next higher multiple of $10).

• 1986, Tax Reform Act of 1986 (P.L. 99-514)

P.L. 99-514, §111(c):

Amended Code Sec. 32 by adding at the end thereof new subsection (i). **Effective** for tax years beginning after 12-31-86.

[Sec. 32(k)]

(k) RESTRICTIONS ON TAXPAYERS WHO IMPROPERLY CLAIMED CREDIT IN PRIOR YEAR.—

(1) TAXPAYERS MAKING PRIOR FRAUDULENT OR RECKLESS CLAIMS.—

(A) IN GENERAL.—No credit shall be allowed under this section for any taxable year in the disallowance period.

(B) DISALLOWANCE PERIOD.—For purposes of paragraph (1), the disallowance period is—

(i) the period of 10 taxable years after the most recent taxable year for which there was a final determination that the taxpayer's claim of credit under this section was due to fraud, and

(ii) the period of 2 taxable years after the most recent taxable year for which there was a final determination that the taxpayer's claim of credit under this section was due to reckless or intentional disregard of rules and regulations (but not due to fraud).

(2) TAXPAYERS MAKING IMPROPER PRIOR CLAIMS.—In the case of a taxpayer who is denied credit under this section for any taxable year as a result of the deficiency procedures under subchapter B of chapter 63, no credit shall be allowed under this section for any subsequent taxable year unless the taxpayer provides such information as the Secretary may require to demonstrate eligibility for such credit.

Amendments

• 1997, Taxpayer Relief Act of 1997 (P.L. 105-34)

P.L. 105-34, §1085(a)(1):

Amended Code Sec. 32 by redesignating subsections (k) and (l) [and (m) as added by Act Sec. 101(b)] as subsections (l) and (m) [and (n)], respectively, and by inserting after subsection (j) a new subsection (k). **Effective** for tax years beginning after 12-31-96.

[Sec. 32(l)]

(l) COORDINATION WITH CERTAIN MEANS-TESTED PROGRAMS.—For purposes of—

(1) the United States Housing Act of 1937,

(2) title V of the Housing Act of 1949,

(3) section 101 of the Housing and Urban Development Act of 1965,

(4) sections 221(d)(3), 235, and 236 of the National Housing Act, and

(5) the Food and Nutrition Act of 2008,

any refund made to an individual (or the spouse of an individual) by reason of this section, and any payment made to such individual (or such spouse) by an employer under section 3507, shall not be treated as income (and shall not be taken into account in determining resources for the month of its receipt and the following month).

Amendments

• 2008, Food, Conservation, and Energy Act of 2008 (P.L. 110-246)

P.L. 110-246, §4002(b)(1)(B):

Amended Code Sec. 32(l)(5) by striking "Food Stamp Act of 1977" and inserting "Food and Nutrition Act of 2008". **Effective** 10-1-2008.

• 1997, Taxpayer Relief Act of 1997 (P.L. 105-34)

P.L. 105-34, §1085(a)(1):

Amended Code Sec. 32 by redesignating subsection (k) as subsection (l). **Effective** for tax years beginning after 12-31-96.

• 1995, Self-Employed Health Insurance Act (P.L. 104-7)

P.L. 104-7, §4(a):

Amended Code Sec. 32 by redesignating subsection (j) as subsection (k). **Effective** for tax years beginning after 12-31-95.

• 1990, Omnibus Budget Reconciliation Act of 1990 (P.L. 101-508)

P.L. 101-508, §11111(b):

Amended Code Sec. 32 by adding at the end thereof a new subsection (j). **Effective** for tax years beginning after 12-31-90.

P.L. 101-508, §11114 provides:

SEC. 11114. PROGRAM TO INCREASE PUBLIC AWARENESS.

Not later than the first calendar year following the date of the enactment of this subtitle, the Secretary of the Treasury, or the Secretary's delegate, shall establish a taxpayer awareness program to inform the taxpaying public of the availability of the credit for dependent care allowed under section 21 of the Internal Revenue Code of 1986 and the earned income credit and child health insurance under section 32 of such Code. Such public awareness program shall be designed to assure that individuals who may be eligible are informed of the availability of such credit and filing procedures. The Secretary shall use appropriate means of communication to carry out the provisions of this section.

[Sec. 32(m)]

(m) IDENTIFICATION NUMBERS.—Solely for purposes of subsections (c)(1)(E) and (c)(3)(D), a taxpayer identification number means a social security number issued to an individual by the Social Security Administration (other than a social security number issued pursuant to clause (II) (or that portion of clause (III) that relates to clause (II)) of section 205(c)(2)(B)(i) of the Social Security Act).

Amendments

• 2004, Working Families Tax Relief Act of 2004 (P.L. 108-311)

P.L. 108-311, §205(b)(3):

Amended Code Sec. 32(m) by striking "subsections (c)(1)(F)" and inserting "subsections (c)(1)(E)". **Effective** for tax years beginning after 12-31-2004.

• 1997, Taxpayer Relief Act of 1997 (P.L. 105-34)

P.L. 105-34, §1085(a)(1):

Amended Code Sec. 32 by redesignating subsection (l) as subsection (m). **Effective** for tax years beginning after 12-31-96.

• 1996, Personal Responsibility and Work Opportunity Reconciliation Act of 1996 (P.L. 104-193)

P.L. 104-193, §451(b):

Amended Code Sec. 32 by adding at the end a new subsection (l). **Effective** with respect to returns the due date for which (without regard to extensions) is more than 30 days after 8-22-96.

»»→ Caution: Code Sec. 32(n), below, was stricken by P.L. 107-16, and is subject to the sunset provision of the Economic Growth and Tax Relief Reconciliation Act of 2001 (P.L. 107-16), §901. Absent Congressional action, the changes made to this provision by P.L. 107-16, or that take effect as if included in P.L. 107-16, do not apply after December 31, 2010. For more information about the sunset provision, see page XXI of the Preface to this publication and P.L. 107-16, §901, in the amendment notes. See the amendments notes for a history of amendments to this section and the effective date of each change.

[Sec. 32(n)—Stricken]

Amendments

• 2001, Economic Growth and Tax Relief Reconciliation Act of 2001 (P.L. 107-16)

P.L. 107-16, §201(c)(3):

Amended Code Sec. 32 by striking subsection (n). **Effective** for tax years beginning after 12-31-2000. Prior to being stricken, Code Sec. 32(n) read as follows:

(n) SUPPLEMENTAL CHILD CREDIT.—

(1) IN GENERAL.—In the case of a taxpayer with respect to whom a credit is allowed under section 24(a) for the taxable year, the credit otherwise allowable under this section shall be increased by the lesser of—

(A) the excess of—

(i) the credits allowed under subpart A (determined after the application of section 26 and without regard to this subsection), over

(ii) the credits which would be allowed under subpart A after the application of section 26, determined without regard to section 24 and this subsection; or

(B) the excess of—

(i) the sum of the credits allowed under this part (determined without regard to sections 31, 33, and 34 and this subsection), over

(ii) the sum of the regular tax and the Social Security taxes (as defined in section 24(d)).

The credit determined under this subsection shall be allowed without regard to any other provision of this section, including subsection (d).

(2) COORDINATION WITH OTHER CREDITS.—The amount of the credit under this subsection shall reduce the amount of the credits otherwise allowable under subpart A for the taxable year (determined after the application of section 26), but the amount of the credit under this subsection (and such reduction) shall not be taken into account in determining the amount of any other credit allowable under this part.

P.L. 107-16, §901(a)-(b), provides:

SEC. 901. SUNSET OF PROVISIONS OF ACT.

(a) IN GENERAL.—All provisions of, and amendments made by, this Act shall not apply—

(1) to taxable, plan, or limitation years beginning after December 31, 2010, or

(2) in the case of title V, to estates of decedents dying, gifts made, or generation skipping transfers, after December 31, 2010.

(b) APPLICATION OF CERTAIN LAWS.—The Internal Revenue Code of 1986 and the Employee Retirement Income Security Act of 1974 shall be applied and administered to years, estates, gifts, and transfers described in subsection (a) as if the provisions and amendments described in subsection (a) had never been enacted.

• 1998, IRS Restructuring and Reform Act of 1998 (P.L. 105-206)

P.L. 105-206, §6003(b)(1):

Amended Code Sec. 32(m)[(n)]. **Effective** as if included in the provision of P.L. 105-34 to which it relates [**effective** for tax years beginning after 12-31-97.—CCH]. Prior to amendment, Code Sec. 32(m)[(n)] read as follows:

(m) [(n)] SUPPLEMENTAL CHILD CREDIT.—

(1) IN GENERAL.—In the case of a taxpayer with respect to whom a credit is allowed under section 24 for the taxable year, there shall be allowed as a credit under this section an amount equal to the supplemental child credit (if any) determined for such taxpayer for such taxable year under paragraph (2). Such credit shall be in addition to the credit allowed under subsection (a).

(2) SUPPLEMENTAL CHILD CREDIT.—For purposes of this subsection, the supplemental child credit is an amount equal to the excess (if any) of—

(A) the amount determined under section 24(d)(1)(A), over

(B) the amount determined under section 24(d)(1)(B).

The amounts referred to in subparagraphs (A) and (B) shall be determined as if section 24(d) applied to all taxpayers.

(3) COORDINATION WITH SECTION 24.—The amount of the credit under section 24 shall be reduced by the amount of the credit allowed under this subsection.

• 1997, Taxpayer Relief Act of 1997 (P.L. 105-34)

P.L. 105-34, §101(b):

Amended Code Sec. 32 by adding a new subsection (m)[(n)]. **Effective** for tax years beginning after 12-31-97.

[Sec. 33]

SEC. 33. TAX WITHHELD AT SOURCE ON NONRESIDENT ALIENS AND FOREIGN CORPORATIONS.

There shall be allowed as a credit against the tax imposed by this subtitle the amount of tax withheld at source under subchapter A of chapter 3 (relating to withholding of tax on nonresident aliens and on foreign corporations).

Amendments

• 1984, Deficit Reduction Act of 1984 (P.L. 98-369)

P.L. 98-369, §471(c)(1):

Redesignated former Code Sec. 32 as Code Sec. 33. **Effective** for tax years beginning after 12-31-83, and to carrybacks from such years, except that it does not apply to obligations issued before 1-1-84.

P.L. 98-369, §474(j):

Amended Code Sec. 33, as redesignated by Act Sec. 471(c)(1). **Effective** for tax years beginning after 12-31-83, and to carrybacks from such years, except that it does not apply to obligations issued before 1-1-84. Prior to amendment, Code Sec. 33 read as follows:

SEC. 33 TAX WITHHELD AT SOURCE ON NONRESIDENT ALIENS AND FOREIGN CORPORATIONS AND ON TAX-FREE COVENANT BONDS.

There shall be allowed as credits against the tax imposed by this chapter—

(1) the amount of tax withheld at source under subchapter A of chapter 3 (relating to withholding of tax on nonresident aliens and on foreign corporations), and

(2) the amount of tax withheld at source under Subchapter B of chapter 3 (relating to interest on tax-free covenant bonds).

[Sec. 34]

SEC. 34. CERTAIN USES OF GASOLINE AND SPECIAL FUELS.

[Sec. 34(a)]

(a) GENERAL RULE.—There shall be allowed as a credit against the tax imposed by this subtitle for the taxable year an amount equal to the sum of the amounts payable to the taxpayer—

(1) under section 6420 (determined without regard to section 6420(g)),

(2) under section 6421 (determined without regard to section 6421(i)), and

(3) under section 6427 (determined without regard to section 6427(k)).

Amendments

• 2007, Tax Technical Corrections Act of 2007 (P.L. 110-172)

P.L. 110-172, §11(a)(4)(A)-(C):

Amended Code Sec. 34(a) by striking "with respect to gasoline used during the taxable year on a farm for farming purposes" after "under section 6420" in paragraph (1), by striking "with respect to gasoline used during the taxable year: [sic] (A) otherwise than as a fuel in a highway vehicle; [sic] or (B) in vehicles while engaged in furnishing certain public passenger land transportation service" after "under section 6421" in paragraph (2), and by striking "with respect to fuels used for nontaxable purposes or resold during the taxable year" after "under section 6427" in paragraph (3). **Effective** 12-29-2007.

• 1996, Small Business Job Protection Act of 1996 (P.L. 104-188)

P.L. 104-188, §1606(b)(1):

Amended Code Sec. 34(a)(3). **Effective** for vehicles purchased after 8-20-96. Prior to amendment, Code Sec. 34(a)(3) read as follows:

(3) under section 6427—

(A) with respect to fuels used for nontaxable purposes or resold, or

(B) with respect to any qualified diesel-powered highway vehicle purchased (or deemed purchased under section 6427(g)(6)),

during the taxable year (determined without regard to section 6427(k)).

• 1986, Tax Reform Act of 1986 (P.L. 99-514)

P.L. 99-514, §1703(e)(2)(F):

Amended Code Sec. 34(a)(3) by striking out "section 6427(j)" and inserting in lieu thereof "section 6427(k)". **Effective** for gasoline removed (as defined in section 4082 of the Internal Revenue Code of 1986, as amended by Act Sec. 1703) after 12-31-87.

P.L. 99-514, §1877(a):

Amended Code Sec. 34(a)(3). **Effective** as if included in the provision of P.L. 98-369 to which such amendment relates. Prior to amendment, Code Sec. 34(a)(3) read as follows:

(3) under section 6427 with respect to fuels used for nontaxable purposes or resold during the taxable year (determined without regard to section 6427(j)).

• 1984, Deficit Reduction Act of 1984 (P.L. 98-369)

P.L. 98-369, §471(c)(1):

Redesignated Code Sec. 39 as Code Sec. 34. **Effective** for tax years beginning after 12-31-83, and to carrybacks from such years.

P.L. 98-369, §911(d)[c](2)(A):

Amended former Code Sec. 39, prior to its redesignation by Act Sec. 471(c)(1), by striking out "6427(i)" and inserting in lieu thereof "6427(j)" in subsections (a)(4)[3]. **Effective** 8-1-84.

• 1983, Surface Transportation Act of 1982 (P.L. 97-424)

P.L. 97-424, §515(b)(6)(A):

Amended Code Sec. 39(a) by striking out paragraph (3), by redesignating paragraph (4) as paragraph (3), and by inserting "and" at the end of paragraph (2). **Effective** with respect to articles sold after 1-6-83. Prior to amendment, paragraph (3) read as follows:

"(3) under section 6424 with respect to lubricating oil used during the taxable year for certain nontaxable purposes (determined without regard to section 6424(f)), and".

P.L. 97-424, §515(b)(6)(B):

Amended the section heading of Code Sec. 39 by striking out **"SPECIAL FUELS, AND LUBRICATING OIL"**, and inserting **"AND SPECIAL FUELS"**. **Effective** with respect to articles sold after 1-6-83.

• 1980, Crude Oil Windfall Profit Tax of 1980 (P.L. 96-223)

P.L. 96-223, §232(d)(4)(A):

Amended Code Sec. 39(a)(4) by striking out "6427(h)" and inserting "6427(i)". **Effective** 1-1-79.

• 1978, Energy Tax Act of 1978 (P.L. 95-618)

P.L. 95-618, §233(b)(2)(c), (d):

Inserted "for certain nontaxable purposes" in place of "otherwise than in a highway motor vehicle" in Code Sec. 39(a)(3). **Effective** 12-1-78.

• 1978, Surface Transportation Assistance Act of 1978 (P.L. 95-599)

P.L. 95-599, §505(c)(1), (d):

Substituted "6427(h)" for "6427(g)" in Code Sec. 39(a)(4). **Effective** 1-1-79.

• 1976 (P.L. 94-530)

P.L. 94-530, §(c)(1):

Amended Code Sec. 39(a)(4) to substitute "6427(g)" for "6427(f)". **Effective** 10-17-76.

• 1976, Tax Reform Act of 1976 (P.L. 94-455)

P.L. 94-455, §1906(b)(8), (9):

Substituted "6420(g)" for "6420(h)" in subsection (a)(1); and substituted "6424(f)" for "6424(g)" in subsection (a)(3). **Effective** for tax years beginning after 12-31-76.

• 1970 (P.L. 91-258)

P.L. 91-258, §207(c):

Amended subsection (a) by striking out "and" at the end of paragraph (2), by substituting ", and" for the period at the end of paragraph (3), and by adding paragraph (4). **Effective** 7-1-70.

• 1965, Excise Tax Reduction Act of 1965 (P.L. 89-44)

P.L. 89-44, §809(c):

Added Sec. 39. **Effective** 7-1-65.

[Sec. 34(b)]

(b) EXCEPTION.—Credit shall not be allowed under subsection (a) for any amount payable under section 6421 or 6427, if a claim for such amount is timely filed and, under section 6421(i) or 6427(k), is payable under such section.

Amendments

• 1998, IRS Restructuring and Reform Act of 1998 (P.L. 105-206)

P.L. 105-206, §6023(24)(B):

Amended Code Sec. 34(b) by striking "section 6421(j)" and inserting "section 6421(i)". **Effective** 7-22-98.

• 1988, Technical and Miscellaneous Revenue Act of 1988 (P.L. 100-647)

P.L. 100-647, §1017(c)(2):

Amended Code Sec. 34(b) by striking out "section 6421(i) or 6427(j)" and inserting in lieu thereof "section 6421(j) or 6427(k)". **Effective** as if included in the provision of P.L. 99-514 to which it relates.

• 1984, Deficit Reduction Act of 1984 (P.L. 98-369)

P.L. 98-369, §911(d)[c](2)(A):

Amended former Code Sec. 39, prior to its redesignation by Act Sec. 471(c)(1), by striking out "6427(i)" and inserting in lieu thereof "6427(j)" in subsection (b). **Effective** 8-1-84.

• 1983, Surface Transportation Act of 1982 (P.L. 97-424)

P.L. 97-424, §515(b)(6)(B):

Amended Code Sec. 39(b) by striking out "section 6421, 6424, or 6427" and inserting "section 6421 or 6427" and by striking out "section 6421(i), 6424(f), or 6427(i)" and inserting "section 6421(i) or 6427(i)". **Effective** with respect to articles sold after 1-6-83.

• 1980, Crude Oil Windfall Profit Tax of 1980 (P.L. 96-223)

P.L. 96-223, §232(d)(4)(A):

Amended Code Sec. 39(b) by striking out "6427(h)" and inserting "6427(i)". **Effective** 1-1-79.

• 1978, Surface Transportation Assistance Act of 1978 (P.L. 95-599)

P.L. 95-599, §505(c)(1), (d):

Substituted "6427(h)" for "6427(g)" in Code Sec. 39(b). **Effective** 1-1-79.

• 1976 (P.L. 94-530)

P.L. 94-530, §(c)(1):

Amended Code Sec. 39(c) (probably intended to be Sec. 39(b)) to substitute "6427(g)" for "6427(f)". **Effective** 10-17-76.

• 1976, Tax Reform Act of 1976 (P.L. 94-455)

P.L. 94-455, §1901(a)(3):

Amended Code Sec. 39 by striking out subsections (b) and (c) and inserting a new subsection (b). **Effective** for tax years beginning after 12-31-76. Prior to amendment, subsections (b) and (c) read as follows:

(b) TRANSITIONAL RULES.—For purposes of paragraphs (1) and (2) of subsection (a), a taxpayer's first taxable year beginning after June 30, 1965, shall include the period after June 30, 1965, and before the beginning of such first taxable year. For purposes of paragraph (3) of subsection (a), a taxpayer's first taxable year beginning after December 31, 1965, shall include the period after December 31, 1965, and before the beginning of such first taxable year.

(c) EXCEPTION.—Credit shall not be allowed under subsection (a) for any amount payable under section 6421, 6424, or 6427, if a claim for such amount is timely filed, and under section 6421(i), 6424(g), or 6427(f) is payable, under such section.

• 1970 (P.L. 91-258)

P.L. 91-258, §207(c):

Amended Code Sec. 39(c) by substituting "section 6421, 6424, or 6427" for "section 6421 or 6424" and by substituting "section 6421(i), 6424(g), or 6427(f)" for "section 6421(i) or 6424(g)". **Effective** 7-1-70.

• 1965, Excise Tax Reduction Act of 1965 (P.L. 89-44)

P.L. 89-44, §809(c):

Added Sec. 39. **Effective** 7-1-65.

[Sec. 35]

SEC. 35. HEALTH INSURANCE COSTS OF ELIGIBLE INDIVIDUALS.

[Sec. 35(a)]

(a) IN GENERAL.—In the case of an individual, there shall be allowed as a credit against the tax imposed by subtitle A an amount equal to 65 percent (80 percent in the case of eligible coverage months beginning before January 1, 2011) of the amount paid by the taxpayer for coverage of the taxpayer and qualifying family members under qualified health insurance for eligible coverage months beginning in the taxable year.

Amendments

• 2009, TAA Health Coverage Improvement Act of 2009 (P.L. 111-5)

P.L. 111-5, §1899A(a)(1):

Amended Code Sec. 35(a) by inserting "(80 percent in the case of eligible coverage months beginning before January 1, 2011)" after "65 percent". **Effective** for coverage months beginning on or after the first day of the first month beginning 60 days after 2-17-2009.

P.L. 111-5, §1899I, provides:

SEC. 1899I. SURVEY AND REPORT ON ENHANCED HEALTH COVERAGE TAX CREDIT PROGRAM.

(a) SURVEY.—

(1) IN GENERAL.—The Secretary of the Treasury shall conduct a biennial survey of eligible individuals (as defined in section 35(c) of the Internal Revenue Code of 1986) relating to the health coverage tax credit under section 35 of the Internal Revenue Code of 1986 (hereinafter in this section referred to as the "health coverage tax credit").

(2) INFORMATION OBTAINED.—The survey conducted under subsection (a) shall obtain the following information:

(A) HCTC PARTICIPANTS.—In the case of eligible individuals receiving the health coverage tax credit (including individuals participating in the health coverage tax credit program under section 7527 of such Code, hereinafter in this section referred to as the "HCTC program")—

(i) demographic information of such individuals, including income and education levels,

(ii) satisfaction of such individuals with the enrollment process in the HCTC program,

(iii) satisfaction of such individuals with available health coverage options under the credit, including level of premiums, benefits, deductibles, cost-sharing requirements, and the adequacy of provider networks, and

(iv) any other information that the Secretary determines is appropriate.

(B) NON-HCTC PARTICIPANTS.—In the case of eligible individuals not receiving the health coverage tax credit—

(i) demographic information of each individual, including income and education levels,

(ii) whether the individual was aware of the health coverage tax credit or the HCTC program,

(iii) the reasons the individual has not enrolled in the HCTC program, including whether such reasons include the burden of the process of enrollment and the affordability of coverage,

(iv) whether the individual has health insurance coverage, and, if so, the source of such coverage, and

(v) any other information that the Secretary determines is appropriate.

(3) REPORT.—Not later than December 31 of each year in which a survey is conducted under paragraph (1) (beginning in 2010), the Secretary of the Treasury shall report to the Committee on Finance and the Committee on Health, Education, Labor, and Pensions of the Senate and the Committee on Ways and Means, the Committee on Education and Labor, and the Committee on Energy and Commerce of the House of Representatives the findings of the most recent survey conducted under paragraph (1).

(b) REPORT.—Not later than October 1 of each year (beginning in 2010), the Secretary of the Treasury (after consultation with the Secretary of Health and Human Services, and, in the case of the information required under paragraph (7), the Secretary of Labor) shall report to the Committee on Finance and the Committee on Health, Education, Labor, and Pensions of the Senate and the Committee on Ways and Means, the Committee on Education and Labor, and the Committee on Energy and Commerce of the House of Representatives the following information with respect to the most recent taxable year ending before such date:

(1) In each State and nationally—

(A) the total number of eligible individuals (as defined in section 35(c) of the Internal Revenue Code of 1986) and the number of eligible individuals receiving the health coverage tax credit,

(B) the total number of such eligible individuals who receive an advance payment of the health coverage tax credit through the HCTC program,

(C) the average length of the time period of the participation of eligible individuals in the HCTC program, and

(D) the total number of participating eligible individuals in the HCTC program who are enrolled in each category of coverage as described in section 35(e)(1) of such Code,

with respect to each category of eligible individuals described in section 35(c)(1) of such Code.

(2) In each State and nationally, an analysis of—

(A) the range of monthly health insurance premiums, for self-only coverage and for family coverage, for individuals receiving the health coverage tax credit, and

(B) the average and median monthly health insurance premiums, for self-only coverage and for family coverage, for individuals receiving the health coverage tax credit,

with respect to each category of coverage as described in section 35(e)(1) of such Code.

(3) In each State and nationally, an analysis of the following information with respect to the health insurance coverage of individuals receiving the health coverage tax credit who are enrolled in coverage erage described in subparagraphs (B) through (H) of section 35(e)(1) of such Code:

(A) Deductible amounts.

(B) Other out-of-pocket cost-sharing amounts.

(C) A description of any annual or lifetime limits on coverage or any other significant limits on coverage services, or benefits.

The information required under this paragraph shall be reported with respect to each category of coverage described in such subparagraphs.

(4) In each State and nationally, the gender and average age of eligible individuals (as defined in section 35(c) of such Code) who receive the health coverage tax credit, in each category of coverage described in section 35(e)(1) of such Code, with respect to each category of eligible individuals described in such section.

(5) The steps taken by the Secretary of the Treasury to increase the participation rates in the HCTC program among eligible individuals, including outreach and enrollment activities.

(6) The cost of administering the HCTC program by function, including the cost of subcontractors, and recommendations on ways to reduce administrative costs, including recommended statutory changes.

(7) The number of States applying for and receiving national emergency grants under section 173(f) of the Workforce Investment Act of 1998 (29 U.S.C. 2918(f)), the activities funded by such grants on a State-by-State basis, and the time necessary for application approval of such grants.

P.L. 111-5, §1899L, provides:

SEC. 1899L. GAO STUDY AND REPORT.

(a) STUDY.—The Comptroller General of the United States shall conduct a study regarding the health insurance tax credit allowed under section 35 of the Internal Revenue Code of 1986.

(b) REPORT.—Not later than March 1, 2010, the Comptroller General shall submit a report to Congress regarding the results of the study conducted under subsection (a). Such report shall include an analysis of—

(1) the administrative costs—

(A) of the Federal Government with respect to such credit and the advance payment of such credit under section 7527 of such Code, and

(B) of providers of qualified health insurance with respect to providing such insurance to eligible individuals and their qualifying family members,

(2) the health status and relative risk status of eligible individuals and qualifying family members covered under such insurance,

(3) participation in such credit and the advance payment of such credit by eligible individuals and their qualifying family members, including the reasons why such individuals did or did not participate and the effect of the amendments made by this part on such participation, and

(4) the extent to which eligible individuals and their qualifying family members—

(A) obtained health insurance other than qualifying health insurance, or

(B) went without health insurance coverage.

(c) ACCESS TO RECORDS.—For purposes of conducting the study required under this section, the Comptroller General and any of his duly authorized representatives shall have access to, and the right to examine and copy, all documents, records, and other recorded information—

(1) within the possession or control of providers of qualified health insurance, and

(2) determined by the Comptroller General (or any such representative) to be relevant to the study.

The Comptroller General shall not disclose the identity of any provider of qualified health insurance or any eligible individual in making any information obtained under this section available to the public.

(d) DEFINITIONS.—Any term which is defined in section 35 of the Internal Revenue Code of 1986 shall have the same meaning when used in this section.

[Sec. 35(b)]

(b) ELIGIBLE COVERAGE MONTH.—For purposes of this section—

(1) IN GENERAL.—The term "eligible coverage month" means any month if—

(A) as of the first day of such month, the taxpayer—

(i) is an eligible individual,

(ii) is covered by qualified health insurance, the premium for which is paid by the taxpayer,

(iii) does not have other specified coverage, and

(iv) is not imprisoned under Federal, State, or local authority, and

(B) such month begins more than 90 days after the date of the enactment of the Trade Act of 2002.

(2) JOINT RETURNS.—In the case of a joint return, the requirements of paragraph (1)(A) shall be treated as met with respect to any month if at least 1 spouse satisfies such requirements.

[Sec. 35(c)]

(c) ELIGIBLE INDIVIDUAL.—For purposes of this section—

(1) IN GENERAL.—The term "eligible individual" means—

(A) an eligible TAA recipient,

(B) an eligible alternative TAA recipient, and

(C) an eligible PBGC pension recipient.

(2) ELIGIBLE TAA RECIPIENT.—

(A) IN GENERAL.—Except as provided in subparagraph (B), the term "eligible TAA recipient" means, with respect to any month, any individual who is receiving for any day of such month a trade readjustment allowance under chapter 2 of title II of the Trade Act of 1974 or who would be eligible to receive such allowance if section 231 of such Act were applied without regard to subsection (a)(3)(B) of such section. An individual shall continue to be treated as an eligible TAA recipient during the first month that such individual would otherwise cease to be an eligible TAA recipient by reason of the preceding sentence.

(B) SPECIAL RULE.—In the case of any eligible coverage month beginning after the date of the enactment of this paragraph and before January 1, 2011, the term "eligible TAA recipient" means, with respect to any month, any individual who—

(i) is receiving for any day of such month a trade readjustment allowance under chapter 2 of title II of the Trade Act of 1974,

(ii) would be eligible to receive such allowance except that such individual is in a break in training provided under a training program approved under section 236 of such Act that exceeds the period specified in section 233(e) of such Act, but is within the period for receiving such allowances provided under section 233(a) of such Act, or

(iii) is receiving unemployment compensation (as defined in section 85(b)) for any day of such month and who would be eligible to receive such allowance for such month if section 231 of such Act were applied without regard to subsections (a)(3)(B) and (a)(5) thereof.

An individual shall continue to be treated as an eligible TAA recipient during the first month that such individual would otherwise cease to be an eligible TAA recipient by reason of the preceding sentence.

(3) ELIGIBLE ALTERNATIVE TAA RECIPIENT.—The term "eligible alternative TAA recipient" means, with respect to any month, any individual who—

(A) is a worker described in section 246(a)(3)(B) of the Trade Act of 1974 who is participating in the program established under section 246(a)(1) of such Act, and

(B) is receiving a benefit for such month under section 246(a)(2) of such Act.

An individual shall continue to be treated as an eligible alternative TAA recipient during the first month that such individual would otherwise cease to be an eligible alternative TAA recipient by reason of the preceding sentence.

(4) ELIGIBLE PBGC PENSION RECIPIENT.—The term "eligible PBGC pension recipient" means, with respect to any month, any individual who—

(A) has attained age 55 as of the first day of such month, and

(B) is receiving a benefit for such month any portion of which is paid by the Pension Benefit Guaranty Corporation under title IV of the Employee Retirement Income Security Act of 1974.

Amendments

• 2009, TAA Health Coverage Improvement Act of 2009 (P.L. 111-5)

P.L. 111-5, §1899C(a):

Amended Code Sec. 35(c)(2). **Effective** for coverage months beginning after 2-17-2009. Prior to amendment, Code Sec. 35(c)(2) read as follows:

(2) ELIGIBLE TAA RECIPIENT.—The term "eligible TAA recipient" means, with respect to any month, any individual who is receiving for any day of such month a trade readjustment allowance under chapter 2 of title II of the Trade Act of 1974 or who would be eligible to receive such allowance if section 231 of such Act were applied without regard to subsection (a)(3)(B) of such section. An individual shall continue to be treated as an eligible TAA recipient during the first month that such individual would otherwise cease to be an eligible TAA recipient by reason of the preceding sentence.

[Sec. 35(d)]

(d) QUALIFYING FAMILY MEMBER.—For purposes of this section—

(1) IN GENERAL.—The term "qualifying family member" means—

(A) the taxpayer's spouse, and

(B) any dependent of the taxpayer with respect to whom the taxpayer is entitled to a deduction under section 151(c).

Such term does not include any individual who has other specified coverage.

(2) SPECIAL DEPENDENCY TEST IN CASE OF DIVORCED PARENTS, ETC.—If section 152(e) applies to any child with respect to any calendar year, in the case of any taxable year beginning in such calendar year, such child shall be treated as described in paragraph (1)(B) with respect to the custodial parent (as defined in section 152(e)(4)(A)) and not with respect to the noncustodial parent.

Amendments

• 2007, Tax Technical Corrections Act of 2007 (P.L. 110-172)

P.L. 110-172, §11(a)(5)(A)-(B):

Amended Code Sec. 35(d)(2) by striking "paragraph (2) or (4) of" after "If", and by striking "(within the meaning of section 152(e)(1))" and inserting "(as defined in section 152(e)(4)(A))". **Effective** 12-29-2007.

[Sec. 35(e)]

(e) QUALIFIED HEALTH INSURANCE.—For purposes of this section—

(1) IN GENERAL.—The term "qualified health insurance" means any of the following:

(A) Coverage under a COBRA continuation provision (as defined in section 9832(d)(1)).

(B) State-based continuation coverage provided by the State under a State law that requires such coverage.

(C) Coverage offered through a qualified State high risk pool (as defined in section 2744(c)(2) of the Public Health Service Act).

(D) Coverage under a health insurance program offered for State employees.

(E) Coverage under a State-based health insurance program that is comparable to the health insurance program offered for State employees.

(F) Coverage through an arrangement entered into by a State and—

(i) a group health plan (including such a plan which is a multiemployer plan as defined in section 3(37) of the Employee Retirement Income Security Act of 1974),

(ii) an issuer of health insurance coverage,

(iii) an administrator, or

(iv) an employer.

(G) Coverage offered through a State arrangement with a private sector health care coverage purchasing pool.

(H) Coverage under a State-operated health plan that does not receive any Federal financial participation.

(I) Coverage under a group health plan that is available through the employment of the eligible individual's spouse.

(J) In the case of any eligible individual and such individual's qualifying family members, coverage under individual health insurance if the eligible individual was covered under individual health insurance during the entire 30-day period that ends on the date that such individual became separated from the employment which qualified such individual for—

(i) in the case of an eligible TAA recipient, the allowance described in subsection (c)(2),

(ii) in the case of an eligible alternative TAA recipient, the benefit described in subsection (c)(3)(B), or

(iii) in the case of any eligible PBGC pension recipient, the benefit described in subsection (c)(4)(B).

For purposes of this subparagraph, the term 'individual health insurance' means any insurance which constitutes medical care offered to individuals other than in connection with a group health plan and does not include Federal- or State-based health insurance coverage.

(K) In the case of eligible coverage months beginning before January 1, 2011, coverage under an employee benefit plan funded by a voluntary employees' beneficiary association (as defined in section 501(c)(9)) established pursuant to an order of a bankruptcy court, or by agreement with an authorized representative, as provided in section 1114 of title 11, United States Code.

(2) REQUIREMENTS FOR STATE-BASED COVERAGE.—

(A) IN GENERAL.—The term "qualified health insurance" does not include any coverage described in subparagraphs (B) through (H) of paragraph (1) unless the State involved has elected to have such coverage treated as qualified health insurance under this section and such coverage meets the following requirements:

(i) GUARANTEED ISSUE.—Each qualifying individual is guaranteed enrollment if the individual pays the premium for enrollment or provides a qualified health insurance costs credit eligibility certificate described in section 7527 and pays the remainder of such premium.

(ii) NO IMPOSITION OF PREEXISTING CONDITION EXCLUSION.—No pre-existing condition limitations are imposed with respect to any qualifying individual.

(iii) NONDISCRIMINATORY PREMIUM.—The total premium (as determined without regard to any subsidies) with respect to a qualifying individual may not be greater than the total premium (as so determined) for a similarly situated individual who is not a qualifying individual.

(iv) SAME BENEFITS.—Benefits under the coverage are the same as (or substantially similar to) the benefits provided to similarly situated individuals who are not qualifying individuals.

(B) QUALIFYING INDIVIDUAL.—For purposes of this paragraph, the term "qualifying individual" means—

(i) an eligible individual for whom, as of the date on which the individual seeks to enroll in the coverage described in subparagraphs (B) through (H) of paragraph (1), the aggregate of the periods of creditable coverage (as defined in section 9801(c)) is 3 months or longer and who, with respect to any month, meets the requirements of clauses (iii) and (iv) of subsection (b)(1)(A); and

(ii) the qualifying family members of such eligible individual.

(3) EXCEPTION.—The term "qualified health insurance" shall not include—

(A) a flexible spending or similar arrangement, and

(B) any insurance if substantially all of its coverage is of excepted benefits described in section 9832(c).

Amendments

• 2009, TAA Health Coverage Improvement Act of 2009 (P.L. 111-5)

P.L. 111-5, §1899G(a):

Amended Code Sec. 35(e)(1) by adding at the end a new subparagraph (K). **Effective** for coverage months beginning after 2-17-2009.

[Sec. 35(f)]

(f) OTHER SPECIFIED COVERAGE.—For purposes of this section, an individual has other specified coverage for any month if, as of the first day of such month—

(1) SUBSIDIZED COVERAGE.—

(A) IN GENERAL.—Such individual is covered under any insurance which constitutes medical care (except insurance substantially all of the coverage of which is of excepted benefits described in section 9832(c)) under any health plan maintained by any employer (or former employer) of the taxpayer or the taxpayer's spouse and at least 50 percent of the cost of such coverage (determined under section 4980B) is paid or incurred by the employer.

(B) ELIGIBLE ALTERNATIVE TAA RECIPIENTS.—In the case of an eligible alternative TAA recipient, such individual is either—

(i) eligible for coverage under any qualified health insurance (other than insurance described in subparagraph (A), (B), or (F) of subsection (e)(1)) under which at least 50 percent of the cost of coverage (determined under section 4980B(f)(4)) is paid or incurred by an employer (or former employer) of the taxpayer or the taxpayer's spouse, or

(ii) covered under any such qualified health insurance under which any portion of the cost of coverage (as so determined) is paid or incurred by an employer (or former employer) of the taxpayer or the taxpayer's spouse.

(C) TREATMENT OF CAFETERIA PLANS.—For purposes of subparagraphs (A) and (B), the cost of coverage shall be treated as paid or incurred by an employer to the extent the coverage is in lieu of a right to receive cash or other qualified benefits under a cafeteria plan (as defined in section 125(d)).

(2) COVERAGE UNDER MEDICARE, MEDICAID, OR SCHIP.—Such individual—

(A) is entitled to benefits under part A of title XVIII of the Social Security Act or is enrolled under part B of such title, or

(B) is enrolled in the program under title XIX or XXI of such Act (other than under section 1928 of such Act).

(3) CERTAIN OTHER COVERAGE.—Such individual—

(A) is enrolled in a health benefits plan under chapter 89 of title 5, United States Code, or

(B) is entitled to receive benefits under chapter 55 of title 10, United States Code.

[Sec. 35(g)]

(g) SPECIAL RULES.—

(1) COORDINATION WITH ADVANCE PAYMENTS OF CREDIT.—With respect to any taxable year, the amount which would (but for this subsection) be allowed as a credit to the taxpayer under subsection (a) shall be reduced (but not below zero) by the aggregate amount paid on behalf of such taxpayer under section 7527 for months beginning in such taxable year.

(2) COORDINATION WITH OTHER DEDUCTIONS.—Amounts taken into account under subsection (a) shall not be taken into account in determining any deduction allowed under section 162(l) or 213.

(3) MEDICAL AND HEALTH SAVINGS ACCOUNTS.—Amounts distributed from an Archer MSA (as defined in section 220(d)) or from a health savings account (as defined in section 223(d)) shall not be taken into account under subsection (a).

(4) DENIAL OF CREDIT TO DEPENDENTS.—No credit shall be allowed under this section to any individual with respect to whom a deduction under section 151 is allowable to another taxpayer for a taxable year beginning in the calendar year in which such individual's taxable year begins.

(5) BOTH SPOUSES ELIGIBLE INDIVIDUALS.—The spouse of the taxpayer shall not be treated as a qualifying family member for purposes of subsection (a), if—

(A) the taxpayer is married at the close of the taxable year,

(B) the taxpayer and the taxpayer's spouse are both eligible individuals during the taxable year, and

(C) the taxpayer files a separate return for the taxable year.

(6) MARITAL STATUS; CERTAIN MARRIED INDIVIDUALS LIVING APART.—Rules similar to the rules of paragraphs (3) and (4) of section 21(e) shall apply for purposes of this section.

(7) INSURANCE WHICH COVERS OTHER INDIVIDUALS.—For purposes of this section, rules similar to the rules of section 213(d)(6) shall apply with respect to any contract for qualified health insurance under which amounts are payable for coverage of an individual other than the taxpayer and qualifying family members.

(8) TREATMENT OF PAYMENTS.—For purposes of this section—

(A) PAYMENTS BY SECRETARY.—Payments made by the Secretary on behalf of any individual under section 7527 (relating to advance payment of credit for health insurance costs of eligible individuals) shall be treated as having been made by the taxpayer on the first day of the month for which such payment was made.

(B) PAYMENTS BY TAXPAYER.—Payments made by the taxpayer for eligible coverage months shall be treated as having been made by the taxpayer on the first day of the month for which such payment was made.

(9) COBRA PREMIUM ASSISTANCE.—In the case of an assistance eligible individual who receives premium reduction for COBRA continuation coverage under section 3001(a) of title III of division B of the American Recovery and Reinvestment Act of 2009 for any month during the taxable year, such individual shall not be treated as an eligible individual, a certified individual, or a qualifying family member for purposes of this section or section 7527 with respect to such month.

(10) CONTINUED QUALIFICATION OF FAMILY MEMBERS AFTER CERTAIN EVENTS.—In the case of eligible coverage months beginning before January 1, 2011—

(A) MEDICARE ELIGIBILITY.—In the case of any month which would be an eligible coverage month with respect to an eligible individual but for subsection (f)(2)(A), such month shall be treated as an eligible coverage month with respect to such eligible individual solely for purposes of determining the amount of the credit under this section with respect to any qualifying family members of such individual (and any advance payment of such credit under section 7527). This subparagraph shall only apply with respect to the first 24 months after such eligible individual is first entitled to the benefits described in subsection (f)(2)(A).

(B) DIVORCE.—In the case of the finalization of a divorce between an eligible individual and such individual's spouse, such spouse shall be treated as an eligible individual for purposes of this section and section 7527 for a period of 24 months beginning with the date of such finalization, except that the only qualifying family members who may be taken into account with respect to such spouse are those individuals who were qualifying family members immediately before such finalization.

(C) DEATH.—In the case of the death of an eligible individual—

(i) any spouse of such individual (determined at the time of such death) shall be treated as an eligible individual for purposes of this section and section 7527 for a period of 24 months beginning with the date of such death, except that the only qualifying family members who may be taken into account with respect to such spouse are those individuals who were qualifying family members immediately before such death, and

(ii) any individual who was a qualifying family member of the decedent immediately before such death (or, in the case of an individual to whom paragraph (4) applies, the taxpayer to whom the deduction under section 151 is allowable) shall be treated as an eligible individual for purposes of this section and section 7527 for a period of 24 months beginning with the date of such death, except that in determining the amount of such credit only such qualifying family member may be taken into account.

(10)[11] REGULATIONS.—The Secretary may prescribe such regulations and other guidance as may be necessary or appropriate to carry out this section, section 6050T, and section 7527.

Amendments

• 2010, Temporary Extension Act of 2010 (P.L. 111-144)

P.L. 111-144, §3(b)(5)(A):

Amended Code Sec. 35(g)(9) by striking "section 3002(a) of the Health Insurance Assistance for the Unemployed Act of 2009" and inserting "section 3001(a) of title III of division B of the American Recovery and Reinvestment Act of 2009". **Effective** as if included in the provision of section 3001 of division B of the American Recovery and Reinvestment Act of 2009 to which it relates [**effective** for tax years ending after 2-17-2009.—CCH].

• 2009, TAA Health Coverage Improvement Act of 2009 (P.L. 111-5)

P.L. 111-5, §1899E(a):

Amended Code Sec. 35(g) by redesignating paragraph (9) as paragraph (10) and inserting after paragraph (8) a new paragraph (9). **Effective** for months beginning after 12-31-2009.

P.L. 111-5, §3001(a)(14)(A):

Amended Code Sec. 35(g) by redesignating paragraph (9) as paragraph (10) and inserting after paragraph (8) a new paragraph (9). **Effective** for tax years ending after 2-17-2009.

• 2004, Working Families Tax Relief Act of 2004 (P.L. 108-311)

P.L. 108-311, §401(a)(2):

Amended Code Sec. 35(g)(3). **Effective** as if included in section 1201 of the Medicare Prescription Drug, Improvement, and Modernization Act of 2003 (P.L. 108-173) [**effective** for tax years beginning after 12-31-2003.—CCH]. Prior to amendment, Code Sec 35(g)(3) read as follows:

(3) MSA DISTRIBUTIONS.—Amounts distributed from an Archer MSA (as defined in section 220(d)) shall not be taken into account under subsection (a).

• 2002, Trade Act of 2002 (P.L. 107-210)

P.L. 107-210, §201(a):

Amended subpart C of part IV of subchapter A of chapter 1 by redesignating Code Sec. 35 as Code Sec. 36 and inserting after Code Sec. 34 a new Code Sec. 35. **Effective** for tax years beginning after 12-31-2001.

[Sec. 36]

SEC. 36. FIRST-TIME HOMEBUYER CREDIT.

[Sec. 36(a)]

(a) ALLOWANCE OF CREDIT.—In the case of an individual who is a first-time homebuyer of a principal residence in the United States during a taxable year, there shall be allowed as a credit against the tax imposed by this subtitle for such taxable year an amount equal to 10 percent of the purchase price of the residence.

[Sec. 36(b)]

(b) LIMITATIONS.—

(1) DOLLAR LIMITATION.—

(A) IN GENERAL.—Except as otherwise provided in this paragraph, the credit allowed under subsection (a) shall not exceed $8,000.

(B) MARRIED INDIVIDUALS FILING SEPARATELY.—In the case of a married individual filing a separate return, subparagraph (A) shall be applied by substituting "$4,000" for "$8,000".

(C) OTHER INDIVIDUALS.—If two or more individuals who are not married purchase a principal residence, the amount of the credit allowed under subsection (a) shall be allocated among such individuals in such manner as the Secretary may prescribe, except that the total amount of the credits allowed to all such individuals shall not exceed $8,000.

(D) SPECIAL RULE FOR LONG-TIME RESIDENTS OF SAME PRINCIPAL RESIDENCE.—In the case of a taxpayer to whom a credit under subsection (a) is allowed by reason of subsection (c)(6), subparagraphs (A), (B), and (C) shall be applied by substituting "$6,500" for "$8,000" and "$3,250" for "$4,000".

(2) LIMITATION BASED ON MODIFIED ADJUSTED GROSS INCOME.—

(A) IN GENERAL.—The amount allowable as a credit under subsection (a) (determined without regard to this paragraph) for the taxable year shall be reduced (but not below zero) by the amount which bears the same ratio to the amount which is so allowable as—

(i) the excess (if any) of—

(I) the taxpayer's modified adjusted gross income for such taxable year, over

(II) $125,000 ($225,000 in the case of a joint return), bears to

(ii) $20,000.

(B) MODIFIED ADJUSTED GROSS INCOME.—For purposes of subparagraph (A), the term "modified adjusted gross income" means the adjusted gross income of the taxpayer for the taxable year increased by any amount excluded from gross income under section 911, 931, or 933.

(3) LIMITATION BASED ON PURCHASE PRICE.—No credit shall be allowed under subsection (a) for the purchase of any residence if the purchase price of such residence exceeds $800,000.

(4) AGE LIMITATION.—No credit shall be allowed under subsection (a) with respect to the purchase of any residence unless the taxpayer has attained age 18 as of the date of such purchase. In the case of any taxpayer who is married (within the meaning of section 7703), the taxpayer shall be treated as meeting the age requirement of the preceding sentence if the taxpayer or the taxpayer's spouse meets such age requirement.

Amendments

• 2009, Worker, Homeownership, and Business Assistance Act of 2009 (P.L. 111-92)

P.L. 111-92, §11(c)(1):

Amended Code Sec. 36(b)(1) by adding at the end a new subparagraph (D). **Effective** for residences purchased after 11-6-2009.

P.L. 111-92, §11(c)(2):

Amended Code Sec. 36(b)(2)(A)(i)(II) by striking "$75,000 ($150,000" and inserting "$125,000 ($225,000". **Effective** for residences purchased after 11-6-2009.

P.L. 111-92, §11(d):

Amended Code Sec. 36(b) by inserting at the end a new paragraph (3). **Effective** for residences purchased after 11-6-2009.

P.L. 111-92, §12(a)(1):

Amended Code Sec. 36(b), as amended by this Act, by adding at the end a new paragraph (4). **Effective** for purchases after 11-6-2009.

• **2009, American Recovery and Reinvestment Tax Act of 2009 (P.L. 111-5)**

P.L. 111-5, §1006(b)(1):

Amended Code Sec. 36(b) by striking "$7,500" each place it appears and inserting "$8,000". **Effective** for residences purchased after 12-31-2008.

P.L. 111-5, §1006(b)(2):

Amended Code Sec. 36(b)(1)(B) by striking "$3,750" and inserting "$4,000". **Effective** for residences purchased after 12-31-2008.

[Sec. 36(c)]

(c) DEFINITIONS.—For purposes of this section—

(1) FIRST-TIME HOMEBUYER.—The term "first-time homebuyer" means any individual if such individual (and if married, such individual's spouse) had no present ownership interest in a principal residence during the 3-year period ending on the date of the purchase of the principal residence to which this section applies.

(2) PRINCIPAL RESIDENCE.—The term "principal residence" has the same meaning as when used in section 121.

(3) PURCHASE.—

(A) IN GENERAL.—The term "purchase" means any acquisition, but only if—

(i) the property is not acquired from a person related to the person acquiring such property (or, if married, such individual's spouse), and

(ii) the basis of the property in the hands of the person acquiring such property is not determined—

(I) in whole or in part by reference to the adjusted basis of such property in the hands of the person from whom acquired, or

(II) under section 1014(a) (relating to property acquired from a decedent).

(B) CONSTRUCTION.—A residence which is constructed by the taxpayer shall be treated as purchased by the taxpayer on the date the taxpayer first occupies such residence.

(4) PURCHASE PRICE.—The term "purchase price" means the adjusted basis of the principal residence on the date such residence is purchased.

(5) RELATED PERSONS.—A person shall be treated as related to another person if the relationship between such persons would result in the disallowance of losses under section 267 or 707(b) (but, in applying section 267(b) and (c) for purposes of this section, paragraph (4) of section 267(c) shall be treated as providing that the family of an individual shall include only his spouse, ancestors, and lineal descendants).

(6) EXCEPTION FOR LONG-TIME RESIDENTS OF SAME PRINCIPAL RESIDENCE.—In the case of an individual (and, if married, such individual's spouse) who has owned and used the same residence as such individual's principal residence for any 5-consecutive-year period during the 8-year period ending on the date of the purchase of a subsequent principal residence, such individual shall be treated as a first-time homebuyer for purposes of this section with respect to the purchase of such subsequent residence.

Amendments

• **2009, Worker, Homeownership, and Business Assistance Act of 2009 (P.L. 111-92)**

P.L. 111-92, §11(b):

Amended Code Sec. 36(c) by adding at the end a new paragraph (6). **Effective** for residences purchased after 11-6-2009.

P.L. 111-92, §12(c):

Amended Code Sec. 36(c)(3)(A)(i) by inserting "(or, if married, such individual's spouse)" after "person acquiring such property". **Effective** for purchases after 11-6-2009.

[Sec. 36(d)]

(d) EXCEPTIONS.—No credit under subsection (a) shall be allowed to any taxpayer for any taxable year with respect to the purchase of a residence if—

(1) the taxpayer is a nonresident alien,

(2) the taxpayer disposes of such residence (or such residence ceases to be the principal residence of the taxpayer (and, if married, the taxpayer's spouse)) before the close of such taxable year,

(3) a deduction under section 151 with respect to such taxpayer is allowable to another taxpayer for such taxable year, or

(4) the taxpayer fails to attach to the return of tax for such taxable year a properly executed copy of the settlement statement used to complete such purchase.

Amendments

• **2009, Worker, Homeownership, and Business Assistance Act of 2009 (P.L. 111-92)**

P.L. 111-92, §11(g):

Amended Code Sec. 36(d) by striking "or" at the end of paragraph (1), by striking the period at the end of paragraph (2) and inserting ", or", and by adding at the end a new paragraph (3). **Effective** for residences purchased after 11-6-2009.

P.L. 111-92, §12(b):

Amended Code Sec. 36(d), as amended by this Act, by striking "or" at the end of paragraph (2), by striking the period at the end of paragraph (3) and inserting ", or", and by adding at the end a new paragraph (4). **Effective** for returns for tax years ending after 11-6-2009.

• **2009, American Recovery and Reinvestment Tax Act of 2009 (P.L. 111-5)**

P.L. 111-5, §1006(d)(2):

Amended Code Sec. 36(d) by striking paragraph (1). **Effective** for residences purchased after 12-31-2008. Prior to being stricken, Code Sec. 36(d)(1) read as follows:

(1) a credit under section 1400C (relating to first-time homebuyer in the District of Columbia) is allowable to the taxpayer (or the taxpayer's spouse) for such taxable year or any prior taxable year,

P.L. 111-5, §1006(e):

Amended Code Sec. 36(d), as amended by Act Sec. 1006(c)(2) [1006(d)(2)], by striking paragraph (2) and by redesignating paragraphs (3) and (4) as paragraphs (1) and (2), respectively. **Effective** for residences purchased after 12-31-2008. Prior to being stricken, Code Sec. 36(d)(2) read as follows:

(2) the residence is financed by the proceeds of a qualified mortgage issue the interest on which is exempt from tax under section 103,

[Sec. 36(e)]

(e) REPORTING.—If the Secretary requires information reporting under section 6045 by a person described in subsection (e)(2) thereof to verify the eligibility of taxpayers for the credit allowable by this section, the exception provided by section 6045(e) shall not apply.

[Sec. 36(f)]

(f) RECAPTURE OF CREDIT.—

(1) IN GENERAL.—Except as otherwise provided in this subsection, if a credit under subsection (a) is allowed to a taxpayer, the tax imposed by this chapter shall be increased by 6⅔ percent of the amount of such credit for each taxable year in the recapture period.

(2) ACCELERATION OF RECAPTURE.—If a taxpayer disposes of the principal residence with respect to which a credit was allowed under subsection (a) (or such residence ceases to be the principal residence of the taxpayer (and, if married, the taxpayer's spouse)) before the end of the recapture period—

(A) the tax imposed by this chapter for the taxable year of such disposition or cessation shall be increased by the excess of the amount of the credit allowed over the amounts of tax imposed by paragraph (1) for preceding taxable years, and

(B) paragraph (1) shall not apply with respect to such credit for such taxable year or any subsequent taxable year.

(3) LIMITATION BASED ON GAIN.—In the case of the sale of the principal residence to a person who is not related to the taxpayer, the increase in tax determined under paragraph (2) shall not exceed the amount of gain (if any) on such sale. Solely for purposes of the preceding sentence, the adjusted basis of such residence shall be reduced by the amount of the credit allowed under subsection (a) to the extent not previously recaptured under paragraph (1).

(4) EXCEPTIONS.—

(A) DEATH OF TAXPAYER.—Paragraphs (1) and (2) shall not apply to any taxable year ending after the date of the taxpayer's death.

(B) INVOLUNTARY CONVERSION.—Paragraph (2) shall not apply in the case of a residence which is compulsorily or involuntarily converted (within the meaning of section 1033(a)) if the taxpayer acquires a new principal residence during the 2-year period beginning on the date of the disposition or cessation referred to in paragraph (2). Paragraph (2) shall apply to such new principal residence during the recapture period in the same manner as if such new principal residence were the converted residence.

(C) TRANSFERS BETWEEN SPOUSES OR INCIDENT TO DIVORCE.—In the case of a transfer of a residence to which section 1041(a) applies—

(i) paragraph (2) shall not apply to such transfer, and

(ii) in the case of taxable years ending after such transfer, paragraphs (1) and (2) shall apply to the transferee in the same manner as if such transferee were the transferor (and shall not apply to the transferor).

(D) WAIVER OF RECAPTURE FOR PURCHASES IN 2009 AND 2010.—In the case of any credit allowed with respect to the purchase of a principal residence after December 31, 2008—

(i) paragraph (1) shall not apply, and

(ii) paragraph (2) shall apply only if the disposition or cessation described in paragraph (2) with respect to such residence occurs during the 36-month period beginning on the date of the purchase of such residence by the taxpayer.

(E) SPECIAL RULE FOR MEMBERS OF THE ARMED FORCES, ETC.—

(i) IN GENERAL.—In the case of the disposition of a principal residence by an individual (or a cessation referred to in paragraph (2)) after December 31, 2008, in connection with Government orders received by such individual, or such individual's spouse, for qualified official extended duty service—

(I) paragraph (2) and subsection (d)(2) shall not apply to such disposition (or cessation), and

(II) if such residence was acquired before January 1, 2009, paragraph (1) shall not apply to the taxable year in which such disposition (or cessation) occurs or any subsequent taxable year.

(ii) QUALIFIED OFFICIAL EXTENDED DUTY SERVICE.—For purposes of this section, the term "qualified official extended duty service" means service on qualified official extended duty as—

(I) a member of the uniformed services,

(II) a member of the Foreign Service of the United States, or

(III) an employee of the intelligence community.

(iii) DEFINITIONS.—Any term used in this subparagraph which is also used in paragraph (9) of section 121(d) shall have the same meaning as when used in such paragraph.

(5) JOINT RETURNS.—In the case of a credit allowed under subsection (a) with respect to a joint return, half of such credit shall be treated as having been allowed to each individual filing such return for purposes of this subsection.

(6) RETURN REQUIREMENT.—If the tax imposed by this chapter for the taxable year is increased under this subsection, the taxpayer shall, notwithstanding section 6012, be required to file a return with respect to the taxes imposed under this subtitle.

(7) RECAPTURE PERIOD.—For purposes of this subsection, the term "recapture period" means the 15 taxable years beginning with the second taxable year following the taxable year in which the purchase of the principal residence for which a credit is allowed under subsection (a) was made.

Amendments

• 2009, Worker, Homeownership, and Business Assistance Act of 2009 (P.L. 111-92)

P.L. 111-92, §11(a)(2)(A):

Amended Code Sec. 36(f)(4)(D) by striking ", and before December 1, 2009" after "December 31, 2008". **Effective** for residences purchased after 11-30-2009.

P.L. 111-92, §11(a)(2)(B):

Amended the heading of Code Sec. 36(f)(4)(D) by inserting "AND 2010" after "2009". **Effective** for residences purchased after 11-30-2009.

P.L. 111-92, §11(e):

Amended Code Sec. 36(f)(4) by adding at the end a new subparagraph (E). **Effective** for dispositions and cessations after 12-31-2008.

• 2009, American Recovery and Reinvestment Tax Act of 2009 (P.L. 111-5)

P.L. 111-5, §1006(c)(1):

Amended Code Sec. 36(f)(4) by adding at the end a new subparagraph (D). **Effective** for residences purchased after 12-31-2008.

[Sec. 36(g)]

(g) ELECTION TO TREAT PURCHASE IN PRIOR YEAR .—In the case of a purchase of a principal residence after December 31, 2008, a taxpayer may elect to treat such purchase as made on December 31 of the calendar year preceding such purchase for purposes of this section (other than subsections (b)(4), (c), (f)(4)(D), and (h)).

Amendments

• 2009, Worker, Homeownership, and Business Assistance Act of 2009 (P.L. 111-92)

P.L. 111-92, §11(a)(3):

Amended Code Sec. 36(g). **Effective** for residences purchased after 11-30-2009. Prior to amendment, Code Sec. 36(g) read as follows:

(g) ELECTION TO TREAT PURCHASE IN PRIOR YEAR.—In the case of a purchase of a principal residence after December 31, 2008, and before December 1, 2009, a taxpayer may elect to treat such purchase as made on December 31, 2008, for purposes of this section (other than subsections (c) and (f)(4)(D)).

P.L. 111-92, §12(a)(2):

Amended Code Sec. 36(g), as amended by this Act, by inserting "(b)(4)," before "(c)". **Effective** for purchases after 11-6-2009.

• 2009, American Recovery and Reinvestment Tax Act of 2009 (P.L. 111-5)

P.L. 111-5, §1006(a)(2):

Amended Code Sec. 36(g) by striking "July 1, 2009" and inserting "December 1, 2009". **Effective** for residences purchased after 12-31-2008.

P.L. 111-5, §1006(c)(2):

Amended Code Sec. 36(g) by striking "subsection (c)" and inserting "subsections (c) and (f)(4)(D)". **Effective** for residences purchased after 12-31-2008.

[Sec. 36(h)]

(h) APPLICATION OF SECTION.—

(1) IN GENERAL.—This section shall only apply to a principal residence purchased by the taxpayer on or after April 9, 2008, and before May 1, 2010.

(2) EXCEPTION IN CASE OF BINDING CONTRACT.—In the case of any taxpayer who enters into a written binding contract before May 1, 2010, to close on the purchase of a principal residence before July 1, 2010, and who purchases such residence before October 1, 2010, paragraph (1) shall be applied by substituting "October 1, 2010" for "May 1, 2010".

(3) SPECIAL RULE FOR INDIVIDUALS ON QUALIFIED OFFICIAL EXTENDED DUTY OUTSIDE THE UNITED STATES.—In the case of any individual who serves on qualified official extended duty service (as defined in section 121(d)(9)(C)(i)) outside the United States for at least 90 days during the period beginning after December 31, 2008, and ending before May 1, 2010, and, if married, such individual's spouse—

(A) paragraphs (1) and (2) shall each be applied by substituting "May 1, 2011" for "May 1, 2010", and

(B) paragraph (2) shall be applied by substituting "July 1, 2011" for "July 1, 2010", and for "October 1, 2010".

Amendments

• 2010, Homebuyer Assistance and Improvement Act of 2010 (P.L. 111-198)

P.L. 111-198, §2(a):

Amended Code Sec. 36(h)(2) by striking "paragraph (1) shall be applied by substituting 'July 1, 2010'" and inserting "and who purchases such residence before October 1, 2010, paragraph (1) shall be applied by substituting 'October 1, 2010'". **Effective** for residences purchased after 6-30-2010.

P.L. 111-198, §2(b):

Amended Code Sec. 36(h)(3)(B) by inserting ", and for 'October 1, 2010'" after "for 'July 1, 2010'". **Effective** for residences purchased after 6-30-2010.

• 2009, Worker, Homeownership, and Business Assistance Act of 2009 (P.L. 111-92)

P.L. 111-92, §11(a)(1)(A)-(C):

Amended Code Sec. 36(h) by striking "December 1, 2009" and inserting "May 1, 2010", by striking "SECTION.—This section" and inserting "SECTION.—"

"(1) IN GENERAL.—This section",

and by adding at the end a new paragraph (2). **Effective** for residences purchased after 11-30-2009.

P.L. 111-92, §11(f)(1):

Amended Code Sec. 36(h), as amended by Act Sec. 11(a), by adding at the end a new paragraph (3). **Effective** for residences purchased after 11-30-2009.

• 2009, American Recovery and Reinvestment Tax Act of 2009 (P.L. 111-5)

P.L. 111-5, §1006(a)(1):

Amended Code Sec. 36(h) by striking "July 1, 2009" and inserting "December 1, 2009". **Effective** for residences purchased after 12-31-2008.

• 2008, Housing Assistance Tax Act of 2008 (P.L. 110-289)

P.L. 110-289, §3011(a):

Amended subpart C of part IV of subchapter A of chapter 1 by redesignating Code Sec. 36 as Code Sec. 37 and by inserting after Code Sec. 35 a new Code Sec. 36. **Effective** for residences purchased on or after 4-9-2008, in tax years ending on or after such date.

[Sec. 36A]

SEC. 36A. MAKING WORK PAY CREDIT.

[Sec. 36A(a)]

(a) ALLOWANCE OF CREDIT.—In the case of an eligible individual, there shall be allowed as a credit against the tax imposed by this subtitle for the taxable year an amount equal to the lesser of—

(1) 6.2 percent of earned income of the taxpayer, or

(2) $400 ($800 in the case of a joint return).

Amendments

• 2009, American Recovery and Reinvestment Tax Act of 2009 (P.L. 111-5)

P.L. 111-5, §1001(b)-(c) and (f), provides:

(b) TREATMENT OF POSSESSIONS.—

(1) PAYMENTS TO POSSESSIONS.—

(A) MIRROR CODE POSSESSION.—The Secretary of the Treasury shall pay to each possession of the United States with a mirror code tax system amounts equal to the loss to that possession by reason of the amendments made by this section with respect to taxable years beginning in 2009 and 2010. Such amounts shall be determined by the Secretary of the Treasury based on information provided by the government of the respective possession.

(B) OTHER POSSESSIONS.—The Secretary of the Treasury shall pay to each possession of the United States which does not have a mirror code tax system amounts estimated by the Secretary of the Treasury as being equal to the aggregate benefits that would have been provided to residents of such possession by reason of the amendments made by this section for taxable years beginning in 2009 and 2010 if a mirror code tax system had been in effect in such possession. The preceding sentence shall not apply with respect to any possession of the United States unless such possession has a plan, which has been approved by the Secretary of the Treasury, under which such possession will promptly distribute such payments to the residents of such possession.

(2) COORDINATION WITH CREDIT ALLOWED AGAINST UNITED STATES INCOME TAXES.—No credit shall be allowed against United States income taxes for any taxable year under section 36A of the Internal Revenue Code of 1986 (as added by this section) to any person—

(A) to whom a credit is allowed against taxes imposed by the possession by reason of the amendments made by this section for such taxable year, or

(B) who is eligible for a payment under a plan described in paragraph (1)(B) with respect to such taxable year.

(3) DEFINITIONS AND SPECIAL RULES.—

(A) POSSESSION OF THE UNITED STATES.—For purposes of this subsection, the term "possession of the United States" includes the Commonwealth of Puerto Rico and the Commonwealth of the Northern Mariana Islands.

(B) MIRROR CODE TAX SYSTEM.—For purposes of this subsection, the term "mirror code tax system" means, with respect to any possession of the United States, the income tax system of such possession if the income tax liability of the residents of such possession under such system is determined by reference to the income tax laws of the United States as if such possession were the United States.

(C) TREATMENT OF PAYMENTS.—For purposes of section 1324(b)(2) of title 31, United States Code, the payments under this subsection shall be treated in the same manner as a refund due from the credit allowed under section 36A of the Internal Revenue Code of 1986 (as added by this section).

(c) REFUNDS DISREGARDED IN THE ADMINISTRATION OF FEDERAL PROGRAMS AND FEDERALLY ASSISTED PROGRAMS.—Any credit or refund allowed or made to any individual by reason of section 36A of the Internal Revenue Code of 1986 (as added by this section) or by reason of subsection (b) of this section shall not be taken into account as income and shall not be taken into account as resources for the month of receipt and the following 2 months, for purposes of determining the eligibility of such individual or any other individual for benefits or assistance, or the amount or extent of benefits or assistance, under any Federal program or under any State or local program financed in whole or in part with Federal funds.

***

(f) EFFECTIVE DATE.—This section, and the amendments made by this section, shall apply to taxable years beginning after December 31, 2008.

P.L. 111-5, §2201, provides:

SEC. 2201. ECONOMIC RECOVERY PAYMENT TO RECIPIENTS OF SOCIAL SECURITY, SUPPLEMENTAL SECURITY INCOME, RAILROAD RETIREMENT BENEFITS, AND VETERANS DISABILITY COMPENSATION OR PENSION BENEFITS.

(a) AUTHORITY TO MAKE PAYMENTS.—

(1) ELIGIBILITY.—

(A) IN GENERAL.—Subject to paragraph (5)(B), the Secretary of the Treasury shall disburse a $250 payment to each individual who, for any month during the 3-month period ending with the month which ends prior to the month that includes the date of the enactment of this Act, is entitled to a benefit payment described in clause (i), (ii), or (iii) of subparagraph (B) or is eligible for a SSI cash benefit described in subparagraph (C).

(B) BENEFIT PAYMENT DESCRIBED.—For purposes of subparagraph (A):

(i) TITLE II BENEFIT.—A benefit payment described in this clause is a monthly insurance benefit payable (without regard to sections 202(j)(1) and 223(b) of the Social Security Act (42 U.S.C. 402(j)(1), 423(b)) under—

(I) section 202(a) of such Act (42 U.S.C. 402(a));

(II) section 202(b) of such Act (42 U.S.C. 402(b));

(III) section 202(c) of such Act (42 U.S.C. 402(c));

(IV) section 202(d)(1)(B)(ii) of such Act (42 U.S.C. 402(d)(1)(B)(ii));

(V) section 202(e) of such Act (42 U.S.C. 402(e));

(VI) section 202(f) of such Act (42 U.S.C. 402(f));

(VII) section 202(g) of such Act (42 U.S.C. 402(g));

(VIII) section 202(h) of such Act (42 U.S.C. 402(h));

(IX) section 223(a) of such Act (42 U.S.C. 423(a));

(X) section 227 of such Act (42 U.S.C. 427); or

(XI) section 228 of such Act (42 U.S.C. 428).

(ii) RAILROAD RETIREMENT BENEFIT.—A benefit payment described in this clause is a monthly annuity or pension payment payable (without regard to section 5(a)(ii) of the Railroad Retirement Act of 1974 (45 U.S.C. 231d(a)(ii))) under—

(I) section 2(a)(1) of such Act (45 U.S.C. 231a(a)(1));

(II) section 2(c) of such Act (45 U.S.C. 231a(c));

(III) section 2(d)(1)(i) of such Act (45 U.S.C. 231a(d)(1)(i));

(IV) section 2(d)(1)(ii) of such Act (45 U.S.C. 231a(d)(1)(ii));

(V) section 2(d)(1)(iii)(C) of such Act to an adult disabled child (45 U.S.C. 231a(d)(1)(iii)(C));

(VI) section 2(d)(1)(iv) of such Act (45 U.S.C. 231a(d)(1)(iv));

(VII) section 2(d)(1)(v) of such Act (45 U.S.C. 231a(d)(1)(v)); or

(VIII) section 7(b)(2) of such Act (45 U.S.C. 231f(b)(2)) with respect to any of the benefit payments described in clause (i) of this subparagraph.

(iii) VETERANS BENEFIT.—A benefit payment described in this clause is a compensation or pension payment payable under—

(I) section 1110, 1117, 1121, 1131, 1141, or 1151 of title 38, United States Code;

(II) section 1310, 1312, 1313, 1315, 1316, or 1318 of title 38, United States Code;

(III) section 1513, 1521, 1533, 1536, 1537, 1541, 1542, or 1562 of title 38, United States Code; or

(IV) section 1805, 1815, or 1821 of title 38, United States Code, to a veteran, surviving spouse, child, or parent as described in paragraph (2), (3), (4)(A)(ii), or (5) of section 101, title 38, United States Code, who received that benefit during any month within the 3 month period ending with the month which ends prior to the month that includes the date of the enactment of this Act.

(C) SSI CASH BENEFIT DESCRIBED.—A SSI cash benefit described in this subparagraph is a cash benefit payable under section 1611 (other than under subsection (e)(1)(B) of such section) or 1619(a) of the Social Security Act (42 U.S.C. 1382, 1382h).

(2) REQUIREMENT.—A payment shall be made under paragraph (1) only to individuals who reside in 1 of the 50 States, the District of Columbia, Puerto Rico, Guam, the United States Virgin Islands, American Samoa, or the Northern Mariana Islands. For purposes of the preceding sentence, the determination of the individual's residence shall be based on the current address of record under a program specified in paragraph (1).

(3) NO DOUBLE PAYMENTS.—An individual shall be paid only 1 payment under this section, regardless of whether the individual is entitled to, or eligible for, more than 1 benefit or cash payment described in paragraph (1).

(4) LIMITATION.—A payment under this section shall not be made—

(A) in the case of an individual entitled to a benefit specified in paragraph (1)(B)(i) or paragraph (1)(B)(ii)(VIII) if, for the most recent month of such individual's entitlement in the 3-month period described in paragraph (1), such individual's benefit under such paragraph was not payable by reason of subsection (x) or (y) of section 202 the Social Security Act (42 U.S.C. 402) or section 1129A of such Act (42 U.S.C. 1320a-8a);

(B) in the case of an individual entitled to a benefit specified in paragraph (1)(B)(iii) if, for the most recent month of such individual's entitlement in the 3 month period described in paragraph (1), such individual's benefit under such paragraph was not payable, or was reduced, by reason of section 1505, 5313, or 5313B of title 38, United States Code;

(C) in the case of an individual entitled to a benefit specified in paragraph (1)(C) if, for such most recent month, such individual's benefit under such paragraph was not payable by reason of subsection (e)(1)(A) or (e)(4) of section 1611 (42 U.S.C. 1382) or section 1129A of such Act (42 U.S.C. 1320a-8a); or

(D) in the case of any individual whose date of death occurs before the date on which the individual is certified under subsection (b) to receive a payment under this section.

(5) TIMING AND MANNER OF PAYMENTS.—

(A) IN GENERAL.—The Secretary of the Treasury shall commence disbursing payments under this section at the earliest practicable date but in no event later than 120 days after the date of enactment of this Act. The Secretary of the Treasury may disburse any payment electronically to an individual in such manner as if such payment was a benefit payment or cash benefit to such individual under the applicable program described in subparagraph (B) or (C) of paragraph (1).

(B) DEADLINE.—No payments shall be disbursed under this section after December 31, 2010, regardless of any determinations of entitlement to, or eligibility for, such payments made after such date.

(b) IDENTIFICATION OF RECIPIENTS.—The Commissioner of Social Security, the Railroad Retirement Board, and the Secretary of Veterans Affairs shall certify the individuals entitled to receive payments under this section and provide the Secretary of the Treasury with the information needed to disburse such payments. A certification of an individual shall be unaffected by any subsequent determination or redetermination of the individual's entitlement to, or eligibility for, a benefit specified in subparagraph (B) or (C) of subsection (a)(1).

(c) TREATMENT OF PAYMENTS.—

(1) PAYMENT TO BE DISREGARDED FOR PURPOSES OF ALL FEDERAL AND FEDERALLY ASSISTED PROGRAMS.—A payment under subsection (a) shall not be regarded as income and shall not be regarded as a resource for the month of receipt and the following 9 months, for purposes of determining the eligibility of the recipient (or the recipient's spouse or family) for benefits or assistance, or the amount or extent of benefits or assistance, under any Federal program or under any State or local program financed in whole or in part with Federal funds.

(2) PAYMENT NOT CONSIDERED INCOME FOR PURPOSES OF TAXATION.—A payment under subsection (a) shall not be considered as gross income for purposes of the Internal Revenue Code of 1986.

(3) PAYMENTS PROTECTED FROM ASSIGNMENT.—The provisions of sections 207 and 1631(d)(1) of the Social Security Act (42 U.S.C. 407, 1383(d)(1)), section 14(a) of the Railroad Retirement Act of 1974 (45 U.S.C. 231m(a)), and section 5301 of title 38, United States Code, shall apply to any payment made under subsection (a) as if such payment was a benefit payment or cash benefit to such individual under the applicable program described in subparagraph (B) or (C) of subsection (a)(1).

(4) PAYMENTS SUBJECT TO OFFSET.—Notwithstanding paragraph (3), for purposes of section 3716 of title 31, United States Code, any payment made under this section shall not be considered a benefit payment or cash benefit made under the applicable program described in subparagraph (B) or (C) of subsection (a)(1) and all amounts paid shall be subject to offset to collect delinquent debts.

(d) PAYMENT TO REPRESENTATIVE PAYEES AND FIDUCIARIES.—

(1) IN GENERAL.—In any case in which an individual who is entitled to a payment under subsection (a) and whose benefit payment or cash benefit described in paragraph (1) of that subsection is paid to a representative payee or fiduci-

ary, the payment under subsection (a) shall be made to the individual's representative payee or fiduciary and the entire payment shall be used only for the benefit of the individual who is entitled to the payment.

(2) APPLICABILITY.—

(A) PAYMENT ON THE BASIS OF A TITLE II OR SSI BENEFIT.—Section 1129(a)(3) of the Social Security Act (42 U.S.C. 1320a–8(a)(3)) shall apply to any payment made on the basis of an entitlement to a benefit specified in paragraph (1)(B)(i) or (1)(C) of subsection (a) in the same manner as such section applies to a payment under title II or XVI of such Act.

(B) PAYMENT ON THE BASIS OF A RAILROAD RETIREMENT BENEFIT.—Section 13 of the Railroad Retirement Act (45 U.S.C. 231l) shall apply to any payment made on the basis of an entitlement to a benefit specified in paragraph (1)(B)(ii) of subsection (a) in the same manner as such section applies to a payment under such Act.

(C) PAYMENT ON THE BASIS OF A VETERANS BENEFIT.—Sections 5502, 6106, and 6108 of title 38, United States Code, shall apply to any payment made on the basis of an entitlement to a benefit specified in paragraph (1)(B)(iii) of subsection (a) in the same manner as those sections apply to a payment under that title.

(e) APPROPRIATION.—Out of any sums in the Treasury of the United States not otherwise appropriated, the following sums are appropriated for the period of fiscal years 2009 through 2011, to remain available until expended, to carry out this section:

(1) For the Secretary of the Treasury, $131,000,000 for administrative costs incurred in carrying out this section, section 2202, section 36A of the Internal Revenue Code of 1986 (as added by this Act), and other provisions of this Act or the amendments made by this Act relating to the Internal Revenue Code of 1986.

(2) For the Commissioner of Social Security—

(A) such sums as may be necessary for payments to individuals certified by the Commissioner of Social Security as entitled to receive a payment under this section; and

(B) $90,000,000 for the Social Security Administration's Limitation on Administrative Expenses for costs incurred in carrying out this section.

(3) For the Railroad Retirement Board—

(A) such sums as may be necessary for payments to individuals certified by the Railroad Retirement Board as entitled to receive a payment under this section; and

(B) $1,400,000 to the Railroad Retirement Board's Limitation on Administration for administrative costs incurred in carrying out this section.

(4)(A) For the Secretary of Veterans Affairs—

(i) such sums as may be necessary for the Compensation and Pensions account, for payments to individuals certified by the Secretary of Veterans Affairs as entitled to receive a payment under this section; and

(ii) $100,000 for the Information Systems Technology account and $7,100,000 for the General Operating Expenses account for administrative costs incurred in carrying out this section.

(B) The Department of Veterans Affairs Compensation and Pensions account shall hereinafter be available for payments authorized under subsection (a)(1)(A) to individuals entitled to a benefit payment described in subsection (a)(1)(B)(iii).

P.L. 111-5, §2202, provides:

SEC. 2202. SPECIAL CREDIT FOR CERTAIN GOVERNMENT RETIREES.

(a) IN GENERAL.—In the case of an eligible individual, there shall be allowed as a credit against the tax imposed by subtitle A of the Internal Revenue Code of 1986 for the first taxable year beginning in 2009 an amount equal $250 ($500 in the case of a joint return where both spouses are eligible individuals).

(b) ELIGIBLE INDIVIDUAL.—For purposes of this section—

(1) IN GENERAL.—The term "eligible individual" means any individual—

(A) who receives during the first taxable year beginning in 2009 any amount as a pension or annuity for service performed in the employ of the United States or any State, or any instrumentality thereof, which is not considered employment for purposes of chapter 21 of the Internal Revenue Code of 1986, and

(B) who does not receive a payment under section 2201 during such taxable year.

(2) IDENTIFICATION NUMBER REQUIREMENT.— Such term shall not include any individual who does not include on the return of tax for the taxable year—

(A) such individual's social security account number, and

(B) in the case of a joint return, the social security account number of one of the taxpayers on such return.

For purposes of the preceding sentence, the social security account number shall not include a TIN (as defined in section 7701(a)(41) of the Internal Revenue Code of 1986) issued by the Internal Revenue Service. Any omission of a correct social security account number required under this subparagraph shall be treated as a mathematical or clerical error for purposes of applying section 6213(g)(2) of such Code to such omission.

(c) TREATMENT OF CREDIT.—

(1) REFUNDABLE CREDIT.—

(A) IN GENERAL.—The credit allowed by subsection (a) shall be treated as allowed by subpart C of part IV of subchapter A of chapter 1 of the Internal Revenue Code of 1986.

(B) APPROPRIATIONS.—For purposes of section 1324(b)(2) of title 31, United States Code, the credit allowed by subsection (a) shall be treated in the same manner a refund from the credit allowed under section 36A of the Internal Revenue Code of 1986 (as added by this Act).

(2) DEFICIENCY RULES.—For purposes of section 6211(b)(4)(A) of the Internal Revenue Code of 1986, the credit allowable by subsection (a) shall be treated in the same manner as the credit allowable under section 36A of the Internal Revenue Code of 1986 (as added by this Act).

(d) REFUNDS DISREGARDED IN THE ADMINISTRATION OF FEDERAL PROGRAMS AND FEDERALLY ASSISTED PROGRAMS.—Any credit or refund allowed or made to any individual by reason of this section shall not be taken into account as income and shall not be taken into account as resources for the month of receipt and the following 2 months, for purposes of determining the eligibility of such individual or any other individual for benefits or assistance, or the amount or extent of benefits or assistance, under any Federal program or under any State or local program financed in whole or in part with Federal funds.

[Sec. 36A(b)]

(b) LIMITATION BASED ON MODIFIED ADJUSTED GROSS INCOME.—

(1) IN GENERAL.—The amount allowable as a credit under subsection (a) (determined without regard to this paragraph and subsection (c)) for the taxable year shall be reduced (but not below zero) by 2 percent of so much of the taxpayer's modified adjusted gross income as exceeds $75,000 ($150,000 in the case of a joint return).

(2) MODIFIED ADJUSTED GROSS INCOME.—For purposes of subparagraph (A), the term "modified adjusted gross income" means the adjusted gross income of the taxpayer for the taxable year increased by any amount excluded from gross income under section 911, 931, or 933.

[Sec. 36A(c)]

(c) REDUCTION FOR CERTAIN OTHER PAYMENTS.—The credit allowed under subsection (a) for any taxable year shall be reduced by the amount of any payments received by the taxpayer during such taxable year under section 2201, and any credit allowed to the taxpayer under section 2202, of the American Recovery and Reinvestment Tax Act of 2009.

[Sec. 36A(d)]

(d) DEFINITIONS AND SPECIAL RULES.—For purposes of this section—

(1) ELIGIBLE INDIVIDUAL.—

(A) IN GENERAL.—The term "eligible individual" means any individual other than—

(i) any nonresident alien individual,

(ii) any individual with respect to whom a deduction under section 151 is allowable to another taxpayer for a taxable year beginning in the calendar year in which the individual's taxable year begins, and

(iii) an estate or trust.

(B) IDENTIFICATION NUMBER REQUIREMENT.—Such term shall not include any individual who does not include on the return of tax for the taxable year—

(i) such individual's social security account number, and

(ii) in the case of a joint return, the social security account number of one of the taxpayers on such return.

For purposes of the preceding sentence, the social security account number shall not include a TIN issued by the Internal Revenue Service.

(2) EARNED INCOME.—The term "earned income" has the meaning given such term by section 32(c)(2), except that such term shall not include net earnings from self-employment which are not taken into account in computing taxable income. For purposes of the preceding sentence, any amount excluded from gross income by reason of section 112 shall be treated as earned income which is taken into account in computing taxable income for the taxable year.

[Sec. 36A(e)]

(e) TERMINATION.—This section shall not apply to taxable years beginning after December 31, 2010.

Amendments

• **2009, American Recovery and Reinvestment Tax Act of 2009 (P.L. 111-5)**

P.L. 111-5, §1001(a):

Amended subpart C of part IV of subchapter A of chapter 1 by inserting after Code Sec. 36 a new Code Sec. 36A. **Effective** for tax years beginning after 12-31-2008.

»→ Caution: Code Sec. 36B, below, as added by P.L. 111-148, applies to tax years ending after December 31, 2013.

[Sec. 36B]

SEC. 36B. REFUNDABLE CREDIT FOR COVERAGE UNDER A QUALIFIED HEALTH PLAN.

[Sec. 36B(a)]

(a) IN GENERAL.—In the case of an applicable taxpayer, there shall be allowed as a credit against the tax imposed by this subtitle for any taxable year an amount equal to the premium assistance credit amount of the taxpayer for the taxable year.

[Sec. 36B(b)]

(b) PREMIUM ASSISTANCE CREDIT AMOUNT.—For purposes of this section—

(1) IN GENERAL.—The term "premium assistance credit amount" means, with respect to any taxable year, the sum of the premium assistance amounts determined under paragraph (2) with respect to all coverage months of the taxpayer occurring during the taxable year.

(2) PREMIUM ASSISTANCE AMOUNT.—The premium assistance amount determined under this subsection with respect to any coverage month is the amount equal to the lesser of—

(A) the monthly premiums for such month for 1 or more qualified health plans offered in the individual market within a State which cover the taxpayer, the taxpayer's spouse, or any dependent (as defined in section 152) of the taxpayer and which were enrolled in through an Exchange established by the State under [section] 1311 of the Patient Protection and Affordable Care Act, or

(B) the excess (if any) of—

(i) the adjusted monthly premium for such month for the applicable second lowest cost silver plan with respect to the taxpayer, over

(ii) an amount equal to 1/12 of the product of the applicable percentage and the taxpayer's household income for the taxable year.

(3) OTHER TERMS AND RULES RELATING TO PREMIUM ASSISTANCE AMOUNTS.—For purposes of paragraph (2)—

(A) APPLICABLE PERCENTAGE.—

(i) IN GENERAL.—Except as provided in clause (ii), the applicable percentage for any taxable year shall be the percentage such that the applicable percentage for any taxpayer whose household income is within an income tier specified in the following table shall increase, on a sliding scale in a linear manner, from the initial premium percentage to the final premium percentage specified in such table for such income tier:

In the case of household income (expressed as a percent of poverty line) within the following income tier:	The initial premium percentage is—	The final premium percentage is—
Up to 133%	2.0%	2.0%
133% up to 150%	3.0%	4.0%
150% up to 200%	4.0%	6.3%
200% up to 250%	6.3%	8.05%
250% up to 300%	8.05%	9.5%
300% up to 400%	9.5%	9.5%

(ii) INDEXING.—

(I) IN GENERAL.—Subject to subclause (II), in the case of taxable years beginning in any calendar year after 2014, the initial and final applicable percentages under clause (i) (as in effect for the preceding calendar year after application of this clause) shall be adjusted to reflect the excess of the rate of premium growth for the preceding calendar year over the rate of income growth for the preceding calendar year.

(II) ADDITIONAL ADJUSTMENT.—Except as provided in subclause (III), in the case of any calendar year after 2018, the percentages described in subclause (I) shall, in addition to the adjustment under subclause (I), be adjusted to reflect the excess (if any) of the rate of premium growth estimated under subclause (I) for the preceding calendar year over the rate of growth in the consumer price index for the preceding calendar year.

(III) FAILSAFE.—Subclause (II) shall apply for any calendar year only if the aggregate amount of premium tax credits under this section and cost-sharing reductions under section 1402 of the Patient Protection and Affordable Care Act for the preceding calendar year exceeds an amount equal to 0.504 percent of the gross domestic product for the preceding calendar year.

(B) APPLICABLE SECOND LOWEST COST SILVER PLAN.—The applicable second lowest cost silver plan with respect to any applicable taxpayer is the second lowest cost silver plan of the individual market in the rating area in which the taxpayer resides which—

(i) is offered through the same Exchange through which the qualified health plans taken into account under paragraph (2)(A) were offered, and

(ii) provides—

(I) self-only coverage in the case of an applicable taxpayer—

(aa) whose tax for the taxable year is determined under section 1(c) (relating to unmarried individuals other than surviving spouses and heads of households) and who is not allowed a deduction under section 151 for the taxable year with respect to a dependent, or

(bb) who is not described in item (aa) but who purchases only self-only coverage, and

(II) family coverage in the case of any other applicable taxpayer.

If a taxpayer files a joint return and no credit is allowed under this section with respect to 1 of the spouses by reason of subsection (e), the taxpayer shall be treated as described in clause (ii)(I) unless a deduction is allowed under section 151 for the taxable year with respect to a dependent other than either spouse and subsection (e) does not apply to the dependent.

(C) ADJUSTED MONTHLY PREMIUM.—The adjusted monthly premium for an applicable second lowest cost silver plan is the monthly premium which would have been charged (for the rating area with respect to which the premiums under paragraph (2)(A) were determined) for the plan if each individual covered under a qualified health plan taken into account under paragraph (2)(A) were covered by such silver plan and the premium was adjusted only for the age of each such individual in the manner allowed under section 2701 of the Public Health Service Act. In the case of a State participating in the wellness discount demonstration project under section 2705(d) of the Public Health Service Act, the adjusted monthly premium shall be determined without regard to any premium discount or rebate under such project.

(D) ADDITIONAL BENEFITS.—If—

(i) a qualified health plan under section 1302(b)(5) of the Patient Protection and Affordable Care Act offers benefits in addition to the essential health benefits required to be provided by the plan, or

(ii) a State requires a qualified health plan under section 1311(d)(3)(B) of such Act to cover benefits in addition to the essential health benefits required to be provided by the plan,

the portion of the premium for the plan properly allocable (under rules prescribed by the Secretary of Health and Human Services) to such additional benefits shall not be taken into account in determining either the monthly premium or the adjusted monthly premium under paragraph (2).

(E) SPECIAL RULE FOR PEDIATRIC DENTAL COVERAGE.—For purposes of determining the amount of any monthly premium, if an individual enrolls in both a qualified health plan and a plan described in section 1311(d)(2)(B)(ii)(I) of the Patient Protection and Affordable Care Act for any plan year, the portion of the premium for the plan described in such section that (under regulations prescribed by the Secretary) is properly allocable to pediatric dental benefits which are included in the essential health benefits required to be provided by a qualified health plan under section 1302(b)(1)(J) of such Act shall be treated as a premium payable for a qualified health plan.

Amendments

• 2010, Health Care and Education Reconciliation Act of 2010 (P.L. 111-152)

P.L. 111-152, §1001(a)(1)(A)-(B):

Amended Code Sec. 36B, as added by section 1401 of the Patient Protection and Affordable Care Act (P.L. 111-148) and amended by section 10105, in clause (i) of subsection (b)(3)(A), by striking "with respect to any taxpayer" and all that follows up to the end period and inserting "for any taxable year shall be the percentage such that the applicable percentage for any taxpayer whose household income is within an income tier specified in the following table shall increase, on a sliding scale in a linear manner, from the initial premium percentage to the final premium percentage specified in such table for such income tier:" and a new table; and by striking clauses (ii) and (iii) of subsection (b)(3)(A) and inserting a new clause (ii). **Effective** 3-30-2010. Prior to amendment, Code Sec. 36B(b)(3)(A) read as follows:

(A) APPLICABLE PERCENTAGE.—

(i) IN GENERAL.—Except as provided in clause (ii), the applicable percentage with respect to any taxpayer for any taxable year is equal to 2.8 percent, increased by the number of percentage points (not greater than 7) which bears the same ratio to 7 percentage points as—

(I) the taxpayer's household income for the taxable year in excess of 100 percent of the poverty line for a family of the size involved, bears to

(II) an amount equal to 200 percent of the poverty line for a family of the size involved.

(ii) SPECIAL RULE FOR TAXPAYERS UNDER 133 PERCENT OF POVERTY LINE.—If a taxpayer's household income for the taxable year equals or exceeds 100 percent, but not more than 133 percent, of the poverty line for a family of the size involved, the taxpayer's applicable percentage shall be 2 percent.

(iii) INDEXING.—In the case of taxable years beginning in any calendar year after 2014, the Secretary shall adjust the initial and final applicable percentages under clause (i), and the 2 percent under clause (ii), for the calendar year to reflect the excess of the rate of premium growth between the preceding calendar year and 2013 over the rate of income growth for such period.

• 2010, Patient Protection and Affordable Care Act (P.L. 111-148)

P.L. 111-148, §10105(a):

Amended Code Sec. 36B(b)(3)(A)(ii), as added by Act Sec. 1401(a), by striking "is in excess of" and inserting "equals or exceeds". **Effective** 3-23-2010.

[Sec. 36B(c)]

(c) DEFINITION AND RULES RELATING TO APPLICABLE TAXPAYERS, COVERAGE MONTHS, AND QUALIFIED HEALTH PLAN.—For purposes of this section—

(1) APPLICABLE TAXPAYER.—

(A) IN GENERAL.—The term "applicable taxpayer" means, with respect to any taxable year, a taxpayer whose household income for the taxable year equals or exceeds 100 percent but does not exceed 400 percent of an amount equal to the poverty line for a family of the size involved.

(B) SPECIAL RULE FOR CERTAIN INDIVIDUALS LAWFULLY PRESENT IN THE UNITED STATES.—If—

(i) a taxpayer has a household income which is not greater than 100 percent of an amount equal to the poverty line for a family of the size involved, and

(ii) the taxpayer is an alien lawfully present in the United States, but is not eligible for the medicaid program under title XIX of the Social Security Act by reason of such alien status,

the taxpayer shall, for purposes of the credit under this section, be treated as an applicable taxpayer with a household income which is equal to 100 percent of the poverty line for a family of the size involved.

(C) MARRIED COUPLES MUST FILE JOINT RETURN.—If the taxpayer is married (within the meaning of section 7703) at the close of the taxable year, the taxpayer shall be treated as an applicable taxpayer only if the taxpayer and the taxpayer's spouse file a joint return for the taxable year.

(D) DENIAL OF CREDIT TO DEPENDENTS.—No credit shall be allowed under this section to any individual with respect to whom a deduction under section 151 is allowable to another taxpayer for a taxable year beginning in the calendar year in which such individual's taxable year begins.

(2) COVERAGE MONTH.—For purposes of this subsection—

(A) IN GENERAL.—The term "coverage month" means, with respect to an applicable taxpayer, any month if—

(i) as of the first day of such month the taxpayer, the taxpayer's spouse, or any dependent of the taxpayer is covered by a qualified health plan described in subsection (b)(2)(A) that was enrolled in through an Exchange established by the State under section 1311 of the Patient Protection and Affordable Care Act, and

(ii) the premium for coverage under such plan for such month is paid by the taxpayer (or through advance payment of the credit under subsection (a) under section 1412 of the Patient Protection and Affordable Care Act).

(B) EXCEPTION FOR MINIMUM ESSENTIAL COVERAGE.—

(i) IN GENERAL.—The term "coverage month" shall not include any month with respect to an individual if for such month the individual is eligible for minimum essential coverage other than eligibility for coverage described in section 5000A(f)(1)(C) (relating to coverage in the individual market).

(ii) MINIMUM ESSENTIAL COVERAGE.—The term "minimum essential coverage" has the meaning given such term by section 5000A(f).

(C) SPECIAL RULE FOR EMPLOYER-SPONSORED MINIMUM ESSENTIAL COVERAGE.—For purposes of subparagraph (B)—

(i) COVERAGE MUST BE AFFORDABLE.—Except as provided in clause (iii), an employee shall not be treated as eligible for minimum essential coverage if such coverage—

(I) consists of an eligible employer-sponsored plan (as defined in section 5000A(f)(2)), and

(II) the employee's required contribution (within the meaning of section 5000A(e)(1)(B)) with respect to the plan exceeds 9.5 percent of the applicable taxpayer's household income.

This clause shall also apply to an individual who is eligible to enroll in the plan by reason of a relationship the individual bears to the employee.

(ii) COVERAGE MUST PROVIDE MINIMUM VALUE.—Except as provided in clause (iii), an employee shall not be treated as eligible for minimum essential coverage if such coverage consists of an eligible employer-sponsored plan (as defined in section 5000A(f)(2)) and the plan's share of the total allowed costs of benefits provided under the plan is less than 60 percent of such costs.

(iii) EMPLOYEE OR FAMILY MUST NOT BE COVERED UNDER EMPLOYER PLAN.—Clauses (i) and (ii) shall not apply if the employee (or any individual described in the last sentence of clause (i)) is covered under the eligible employer-sponsored plan or the grandfathered health plan.

(iv) INDEXING.—In the case of plan years beginning in any calendar year after 2014, the Secretary shall adjust the 9.5 percent under clause (i)(II) in the same manner as the percentages are adjusted under subsection (b)(3)(A)(ii).

»»→ Caution: Code Sec. 36B(c)(2)(D), below, as added by P.L. 111-148, applies to tax years beginning after December 31, 2013.

(D) EXCEPTION FOR INDIVIDUAL RECEIVING FREE CHOICE VOUCHERS.—The term "coverage month" shall not include any month in which such individual has a free choice voucher provided under section 10108 of the Patient Protection and Affordable Care Act.

(3) DEFINITIONS AND OTHER RULES.—

(A) QUALIFIED HEALTH PLAN.—The term "qualified health plan" has the meaning given such term by section 1301(a) of the Patient Protection and Affordable Care Act, except that such term shall not include a qualified health plan which is a catastrophic plan described in section 1302(e) of such Act.

(B) GRANDFATHERED HEALTH PLAN.—The term "grandfathered health plan" has the meaning given such term by section 1251 of the Patient Protection and Affordable Care Act.

Amendments

• 2010, Health Care and Education Reconciliation Act of 2010 (P.L. 111-152)

P.L. 111-152, §1001(a)(2)(A)-(B):

Amended Code Sec. 36B, as added by section 1401 and amended by section 10105 of the Patient Protection and Affordable Care Act (P.L. 111-148), by striking "9.8 percent" in clauses (i)(II) and (iv) of subsection (c)(2)(C) and inserting "9.5 percent", and by striking "(b)(3)(A)(iii)" in clause (iv) of subsection (c)(2)(C) and inserting "(b)(3)(A)(ii)". **Effective** 3-30-2010.

• 2010, Patient Protection and Affordable Care Act (P.L. 111-148)

P.L. 111-148, §10105(b):

Amended Code Sec. 36B(c)(1)(A), as added by Act Sec. 1401(a), by inserting "equals or" before "exceeds". **Effective** 3-23-2010.

P.L. 111-148, §10105(c):

Amended Code Sec. 36B(c)(2)(C)(iv), as added by Act Sec. 1401(a), by striking "subsection (b)(3)(A)(ii)" and inserting "subsection (b)(3)(A)(iii)". **Effective** 3-23-2010.

P.L. 111-148, §10108(h)(1):

Amended Code Sec. 36B(c)(2), as added by Act Sec. 1401, by adding at the end a new subparagraph (D). **Effective** for tax years beginning after 12-31-2013.

[Sec. 36B(d)]

(d) TERMS RELATING TO INCOME AND FAMILIES.—For purposes of this section—

(1) FAMILY SIZE.—The family size involved with respect to any taxpayer shall be equal to the number of individuals for whom the taxpayer is allowed a deduction under section 151 (relating to allowance of deduction for personal exemptions) for the taxable year.

(2) HOUSEHOLD INCOME.—

(A) HOUSEHOLD INCOME.—The term "household income" means, with respect to any taxpayer, an amount equal to the sum of—

(i) the modified adjusted gross income of the taxpayer, plus

(ii) the aggregate modified adjusted gross incomes of all other individuals who—

(I) were taken into account in determining the taxpayer's family size under paragraph (1), and

(II) were required to file a return of tax imposed by section 1 for the taxable year.

(B) MODIFIED ADJUSTED GROSS INCOME.—The term "modified adjusted gross income" means adjusted gross income increased by—

(i) any amount excluded from gross income under section 911, and

(ii) any amount of interest received or accrued by the taxpayer during the taxable year which is exempt from tax.

(3) POVERTY LINE.—

(A) IN GENERAL.—The term "poverty line" has the meaning given that term in section 2110(c)(5) of the Social Security Act (42 U.S.C. 1397jj(c)(5)).

(B) POVERTY LINE USED.—In the case of any qualified health plan offered through an Exchange for coverage during a taxable year beginning in a calendar year, the poverty line used shall be the most recently published poverty line as of the 1st day of the regular enrollment period for coverage during such calendar year.

Amendments

• 2010, Health Care and Education Reconciliation Act of 2010 (P.L. 111-152)

P.L. 111-152, §1004(a)(1)(A):

Amended Code Sec. 36B(d)(2)(A)(i)-(ii), as added by section 1401 of the Patient Protection and Affordable Care Act (P.L. 111-148), by striking "modified gross" each place it appears and inserting "modified adjusted gross". **Effective** 3-30-2010.

P.L. 111-152, §1004(a)(2)(A):

Amended Code Sec. 36B(d)(2)(B), as added by section 1401 of the Patient Protection and Affordable Care Act (P.L. 111-148). **Effective** 3-30-2010. Prior to amendment, Code Sec. 36B(d)(2)(B) read as follows:

(B) MODIFIED GROSS INCOME.—The term "modified gross income" means gross income—

(i) decreased by the amount of any deduction allowable under paragraph (1), (3), (4), or (10) of section 62(a),

(ii) increased by the amount of interest received or accrued during the taxable year which is exempt from tax imposed by this chapter, and

(iii) determined without regard to sections 911, 931, and 933.

[Sec. 36B(e)]

(e) RULES FOR INDIVIDUALS NOT LAWFULLY PRESENT.—

(1) IN GENERAL.—If 1 or more individuals for whom a taxpayer is allowed a deduction under section 151 (relating to allowance of deduction for personal exemptions) for the taxable year (including the taxpayer or his spouse) are individuals who are not lawfully present—

(A) the aggregate amount of premiums otherwise taken into account under clauses (i) and (ii) of subsection (b)(2)(A) shall be reduced by the portion (if any) of such premiums which is attributable to such individuals, and

(B) for purposes of applying this section, the determination as to what percentage a taxpayer's household income bears to the poverty level for a family of the size involved shall be made under one of the following methods:

(i) A method under which—

(I) the taxpayer's family size is determined by not taking such individuals into account, and

(II) the taxpayer's household income is equal to the product of the taxpayer's household income (determined without regard to this subsection) and a fraction—

(aa) the numerator of which is the poverty line for the taxpayer's family size determined after application of subclause (I), and

(bb) the denominator of which is the poverty line for the taxpayer's family size determined without regard to subclause (I).

(ii) A comparable method reaching the same result as the method under clause (i).

(2) LAWFULLY PRESENT.—For purposes of this section, an individual shall be treated as lawfully present only if the individual is, and is reasonably expected to be for the entire period of enrollment for which the credit under this section is being claimed, a citizen or national of the United States or an alien lawfully present in the United States.

(3) SECRETARIAL AUTHORITY.—The Secretary of Health and Human Services, in consultation with the Secretary, shall prescribe rules setting forth the methods by which calculations of family size and household income are made for purposes of this subsection. Such rules shall be designed to ensure that the least burden is placed on individuals enrolling in qualified health plans through an Exchange and taxpayers eligible for the credit allowable under this section.

[Sec. 36B(f)]

(f) RECONCILIATION OF CREDIT AND ADVANCE CREDIT.—

(1) IN GENERAL.—The amount of the credit allowed under this section for any taxable year shall be reduced (but not below zero) by the amount of any advance payment of such credit under section 1412 of the Patient Protection and Affordable Care Act.

(2) EXCESS ADVANCE PAYMENTS.—

(A) IN GENERAL.—If the advance payments to a taxpayer under section 1412 of the Patient Protection and Affordable Care Act for a taxable year exceed the credit allowed by this section (determined without regard to paragraph (1)), the tax imposed by this chapter for the taxable year shall be increased by the amount of such excess.

(B) LIMITATION ON INCREASE WHERE INCOME LESS THAN 400 PERCENT OF POVERTY LINE.—

(i) IN GENERAL.—In the case of an applicable taxpayer whose household income is less than 400 percent of the poverty line for the size of the family involved for the taxable year, the amount of the increase under subparagraph (A) shall in no event exceed $400 ($250 in the case of a taxpayer whose tax is determined under section 1(c) for the taxable year).

(ii) INDEXING OF AMOUNT.—In the case of any calendar year beginning after 2014, each of the dollar amounts under clause (i) shall be increased by an amount equal to—

(I) such dollar amount, multiplied by

(II) the cost-of-living adjustment determined under section 1(f)(3) for the calendar year, determined by substituting "calendar year 2013" for "calendar year 1992" in subparagraph (B) thereof.

If the amount of any increase under clause (i) is not a multiple of $50, such increase shall be rounded to the next lowest multiple of $50.

(3) INFORMATION REQUIREMENT.—Each Exchange (or any person carrying out 1 or more responsibilities of an Exchange under section 1311(f)(3) or 1321(c) of the Patient Protection and Affordable Care Act) shall provide the following information to the Secretary and to the taxpayer with respect to any health plan provided through the Exchange:

(A) The level of coverage described in section 1302(d) of the Patient Protection and Affordable Care Act and the period such coverage was in effect.

(B) The total premium for the coverage without regard to the credit under this section or cost-sharing reductions under section 1402 of such Act.

(C) The aggregate amount of any advance payment of such credit or reductions under section 1412 of such Act.

(D) The name, address, and TIN of the primary insured and the name and TIN of each other individual obtaining coverage under the policy.

(E) Any information provided to the Exchange, including any change of circumstances, necessary to determine eligibility for, and the amount of, such credit.

(F) Information necessary to determine whether a taxpayer has received excess advance payments.

Amendments

• 2010, Health Care and Education Reconciliation Act of 2010 (P.L. 111-152)

P.L. 111-152, §1004(c):

Amended Code Sec. 36B(f), as added by section 1401(a) of the Patient Protection and Affordable Care Act (P.L. 111-148), by adding at the end a new paragraph (3). **Effective** 3-30-2010.

[Sec. 36B(g)]

(g) REGULATIONS.—The Secretary shall prescribe such regulations as may be necessary to carry out the provisions of this section, including regulations which provide for—

(1) the coordination of the credit allowed under this section with the program for advance payment of the credit under section 1412 of the Patient Protection and Affordable Care Act, and

(2) the application of subsection (f) where the filing status of the taxpayer for a taxable year is different from such status used for determining the advance payment of the credit.

Amendments

• 2010, Patient Protection and Affordable Care Act (P.L. 111-148)

P.L. 111-148, §1401(a):

Amended subpart C of part IV of subchapter A of chapter 1 by inserting after Code Sec. 36A a new Code Sec. 36B. **Effective** for tax years ending after 12-31-2013.

Caution: Former Code Sec. 23 was redesignated as Code Sec. 36C, below, by P.L. 111-148. For sunset provision, see P.L. 111-148, §10909(c), in the amendment notes.

[Sec. 36C]

SEC. 36C. ADOPTION EXPENSES.

[Sec. 36C(a)]

(a) ALLOWANCE OF CREDIT.—

(1) IN GENERAL.—In the case of an individual, there shall be allowed as a credit against the tax imposed by this chapter the amount of the qualified adoption expenses paid or incurred by the taxpayer.

(2) YEAR CREDIT ALLOWED.—The credit under paragraph (1) with respect to any expense shall be allowed—

(A) in the case of any expense paid or incurred before the taxable year in which such adoption becomes final, for the taxable year following the taxable year during which such expense is paid or incurred, and

(B) in the case of an expense paid or incurred during or after the taxable year in which such adoption becomes final, for the taxable year in which such expense is paid or incurred.

Caution: Former Code Sec. 23(a)(3) was amended and redesignated as Code Sec. 36C(a)(3), below, by P.L. 111-148. For sunset provision, see P.L. 111-148, §10909(c), in the amendment notes.

(3) $13,170 CREDIT FOR ADOPTION OF CHILD WITH SPECIAL NEEDS REGARDLESS OF EXPENSES.—In the case of an adoption of a child with special needs which becomes final during a taxable year, the taxpayer shall be treated as having paid during such year qualified adoption expenses with respect to such adoption in an amount equal to the excess (if any) of $13,170 over the aggregate qualified adoption expenses actually paid or incurred by the taxpayer with respect to such adoption during such taxable year and all prior taxable years.

Amendments

• 2010, Patient Protection and Affordable Care Act (P.L. 111-148)

P.L. 111-148, §10909(a)(1)(B)(i)-(ii):

Amended Code Sec. 23(a)(3), in the text by striking "$10,000" and inserting "$13,170", and in the heading by striking "$10,000" and inserting "$13,170". **Effective** for tax years beginning after 12-31-2009.

P.L. 111-148, §10909(b)(1)(A)-(B):

Amended [subpart A of part IV of subchapter A of chapter 1] by redesignating Code Sec. 23, as amended by Act Sec. 10909(a), as Code Sec. 36C, and by moving it before Code Sec. 37 in subpart C of part IV of subchapter A of chapter 1. **Effective** for tax years beginning after 12-31-2009.

P.L. 111-148, §10909(c), provides:

(c) APPLICATION AND EXTENSION OF EGTRRA SUNSET.—Notwithstanding section 901 of the Economic Growth and Tax Relief Reconciliation Act of 2001 [P.L. 107-16], such section shall apply to the amendments made by this section and the amendments made by section 202 of such Act by substituting "December 31, 2011" for "December 31, 2010" in subsection (a)(1) thereof.

• 2002, Job Creation and Worker Assistance Act of 2002 (P.L. 107-147)

P.L. 107-147, §411(c)(1)(A):

Amended Code Sec. 23(a)(1). **Effective** for tax years beginning after 12-31-2002. Prior to amendment, Code Sec. 23(a)(1) read as follows:

(1) IN GENERAL.—In the case of an individual, there shall be allowed as a credit against the tax imposed by this chapter—

(A) in the case of an adoption of a child other than a child with special needs, the amount of the qualified adoption expenses paid or incurred by the taxpayer, and

(B) in the case of an adoption of a child with special needs, $10,000.

[Note: Due to the effective date of the above amendment, the prior law reproduced immediately above never took effect.—CCH.]

P.L. 107-147, §411(c)(1)(B):

Amended Code Sec. 23(a) by adding at the end a new paragraph (3). **Effective** for tax years beginning after 12-31-2002.

P.L. 107-147, §411(c)(1)(C):

Amended Code Sec. 23(a)(2) by striking the last sentence. **Effective** for tax years beginning after 12-31-2001. Prior to being stricken, the last sentence of Code Sec. 23(a)(2) read as follows:

In the case of the adoption of a child with special needs, the credit allowed under paragraph (1) shall be allowed for the taxable year in which the adoption becomes final.

• 2001, Economic Growth and Tax Relief Reconciliation Act of 2001 (P.L. 107-16)

P.L. 107-16, §202(a)(1):

Amended Code Sec. 23(a)(1). **Effective** for tax years beginning after 12-31-2002. Prior to amendment, Code Sec. 23(a)(1) read as follows:

(1) IN GENERAL.—In the case of an individual, there shall be allowed as a credit against the tax imposed by this chapter the amount of the qualified adoption expenses paid or incurred by the taxpayer.

P.L. 107-16, §202(c):

Amended Code Sec. 23(a)(2) by adding at the end a new flush sentence. **Effective** for tax years beginning after 12-31-2001.

P.L. 107-16, §901(a)-(b), provides [but see P.L. 111-148, §10909(c), above]:

SEC. 901. SUNSET OF PROVISIONS OF ACT.

(a) IN GENERAL.—All provisions of, and amendments made by, this Act shall not apply—

(1) to taxable, plan, or limitation years beginning after December 31, 2010, or

(2) in the case of title V, to estates of decedents dying, gifts made, or generation skipping transfers, after December 31, 2010.

(b) APPLICATION OF CERTAIN LAWS.—The Internal Revenue Code of 1986 and the Employee Retirement Income Security Act of 1974 shall be applied and administered to years, estates, gifts, and transfers described in subsection (a) as if the provisions and amendments described in subsection (a) had never been enacted.

• 1997, Taxpayer Relief Act of 1997 (P.L. 105-34)

P.L. 105-34, §1601(h)(2)(A):

Amended Code Sec. 23(a)(2). **Effective** as if included in the provision of P.L. 104-188 to which it relates [**effective** for tax years beginning after 12-31-96.—CCH]. Prior to amendment, Code Sec. 23(a)(2) read as follows:

(2) YEAR CREDIT ALLOWED.—The credit under paragraph (1) with respect to any expense shall be allowed—

(A) for the taxable year following the taxable year during which such expense is paid or incurred, or

(B) in the case of an expense which is paid or incurred during the taxable year in which the adoption becomes final, for such taxable year.

[Sec. 36C(b)]

(b) LIMITATIONS.—

»»→ Caution: Former Code Sec. 23(b)(1) was amended by P.L. 107-16 and P.L. 107-147, and amended and redesignated as Code Sec. 36C(b)(1), below, by P.L. 111-148, and is subject to the sunset provision of the Economic Growth and Tax Relief Reconciliation Act of 2001 (P.L. 107-16), §901. Absent Congressional action, the changes made to this provision by P.L. 107-16, or that take effect as if included in P.L. 107-16, do not apply after December 31, 2010. For more information about the sunset provision, see page XXI of the Preface to this publication and P.L. 107-16, §901, and P.L.111-148, §10909(c), in the amendment notes. See the amendments notes for a history of amendments to this section and the effective date of each change.

(1) DOLLAR LIMITATION.—The aggregate amount of qualified adoption expenses which may be taken into account under subsection (a) for all taxable years with respect to the adoption of a child by the taxpayer shall not exceed $13,170.

»»→ Caution: Former Code Sec. 23(b)(2) was amended by P.L. 107-16 and P.L. 107-147 and redesignated as Code Sec. 36C(b)(2), below, by P.L. 111-148, and is subject to the sunset provision of the Economic Growth and Tax Relief Reconciliation Act of 2001 (P.L. 107-16), §901. Absent Congressional action, the changes made to this provision by P.L. 107-16, or that take effect as if included in P.L. 107-16, do not apply after December 31, 2010. For more information about the sunset provision, see page XXI of the Preface to this publication and P.L. 107-16, §901, and P.L. 111-148, §10909(c), in the amendment notes. See the amendments notes for a history of amendments to this section and the effective date of each change.

(2) INCOME LIMITATION.—

(A) IN GENERAL.—The amount allowable as a credit under subsection (a) for any taxable year (determined without regard to subsection (c)) shall be reduced (but not below zero) by an amount which bears the same ratio to the amount so allowable (determined without regard to this paragraph but with regard to paragraph (1)) as—

(i) the amount (if any) by which the taxpayer's adjusted gross income exceeds $150,000, bears to

(ii) $40,000.

(B) DETERMINATION OF ADJUSTED GROSS INCOME.—For purposes of subparagraph (A), adjusted gross income shall be determined without regard to sections 911, 931, and 933.

(3) DENIAL OF DOUBLE BENEFIT.—

(A) IN GENERAL.—No credit shall be allowed under subsection (a) for any expense for which a deduction or credit is allowed under any other provision of this chapter.

(B) GRANTS.—No credit shall be allowed under subsection (a) for any expense to the extent that funds for such expense are received under any Federal, State, or local program.

»»→ Caution: Former Code Sec. 23(b)(4) was redesignated as Code Sec. 36C(b)(4), below, and stricken by P.L. 111-148. For sunset provision, see P.L. 111-148, §10909(c), in the amendment notes.

(4) [Stricken.]

Amendments

• 2010, Patient Protection and Affordable Care Act (P.L. 111-148)

P.L. 111-148, 10909(a)(1)(A):

Amended Code Sec. 23(b)(1) by striking "$10,000" and inserting "$13,170". **Effective** for tax years beginning after 12-31-2009.

P.L. 111-148, 10909(b)(2)(I)(i):

Amended Code Sec. 36C, as redesignated, by striking paragraph (b)(4). **Effective** for tax years beginning after 12-31-2009. Prior to amendment, Code Sec. 36C(b)(4) read as follows:

(4) LIMITATION BASED ON AMOUNT OF TAX.—In the case of a taxable year to which section 26(a)(2) does not apply, the credit allowed under subsection (a) for any taxable year shall not exceed the excess of—

(A) the sum of the regular tax liability (as defined in section 26(b)) plus the tax imposed by section 55, over

(B) the sum of the credits allowable under this subpart (other than this section and section 25D) and section 27 for the taxable year.

P.L. 111-148, §10909(c), provides:

(c) APPLICATION AND EXTENSION OF EGTRRA SUNSET.—Notwithstanding section 901 of the Economic Growth and Tax

Relief Reconciliation Act of 2001 [P.L. 107-16], such section shall apply to the amendments made by this section and the amendments made by section 202 of such Act by substituting "December 31, 2011" for "December 31, 2010" in subsection (a)(1) thereof.

• 2008, Energy Improvement and Extension Act of 2008 (P.L. 110-343)

P.L. 110-343, Division B, §106(e)(2)(A):

Amended Code Sec. 23(b)(4)(B) by inserting "and section 25D" after "this section". **Effective** for tax years beginning after 12-31-2007.

P.L. 110-343, Division B, §106(f)(3), provides:

(3) APPLICATION OF EGTRRA SUNSET.—The amendments made by subparagraphs (A) and (B) of subsection (e)(2) shall be subject to title IX of the Economic Growth and Tax Relief Reconciliation Act of 2001 [P.L. 107-16] in the same manner as the provisions of such Act to which such amendments relate.

• 2005, Gulf Opportunity Zone Act of 2005 (P.L. 109-135)

P.L. 109-135, §402(i)(3)(A)(i):

Amended the matter preceding Code Sec. 23(b)(4)(A) by striking "The credit" and inserting "In the case of a taxable year to which section 26(a)(2) does not apply, the credit". **Effective** for tax years beginning after 12-31-2005.

P.L. 109-135, §402(i)(3)(H), provides:

(H) APPLICATION OF EGTRRA SUNSET.—The amendments made by this paragraph (and each part thereof) shall be subject to title IX of the Economic Growth and Tax Relief Reconciliation Act of 2001 in the same manner as the provisions of such Act to which such amendment (or part thereof) relates.

• 2004, Working Families Tax Relief Act of 2004 (P.L. 108-311)

P.L. 108-311, §312(b)(2), provides:

(2) The amendments made by sections 201(b), 202(f), and 618(b) of the Economic Growth and Tax Relief Reconciliation Act of 2001 shall not apply to taxable years beginning during 2004 or 2005.

• 2002, Job Creation and Worker Assistance Act of 2002 (P.L. 107-147)

P.L. 107-147, §411(c)(1)(D):

Amended Code Sec. 23(b)(1) by striking "subsection (a)(1)(A)" and inserting "subsection (a)". **Effective** for tax years beginning after 12-31-2001. For a special rule, see Act Sec. 411(c)(1)(F), below.

P.L. 107-147, §411(c)(1)(F), provides:

(F) Expenses paid or incurred during any taxable year beginning before January 1, 2002, may be taken into account in determining the credit under section 23 of the Internal Revenue Code of 1986 only to the extent the aggregate of such expenses does not exceed the applicable limitation under section 23(b)(1) of such Code as in effect on the day before the date of the enactment of the Economic Growth and Tax Relief Reconciliation Act of 2001.

P.L. 107-147, §601(b)(2), provides:

(2) The amendments made by sections 201(b), 202(f), and 618(b) of the Economic Growth and Tax Relief Reconciliation Act of 2001 shall not apply to taxable years beginning during 2002 and 2003.

• 2001, Economic Growth and Tax Relief Reconciliation Act of 2001 (P.L. 107-16)

P.L. 107-16, §202(b)(1)(A)(i)-(iii):

Amended Code Sec. 23(b)(1) by striking "$5,000" and inserting "$10,000", by striking "($6,000, in the case of a child with special needs)" before the period, and by striking "subsection (a)" and inserting "subsection (a)(1)(A)". **Effective** for tax years beginning after 12-31-2001.

P.L. 107-16, §202(b)(2)(A):

Act Sec. 202(b)(2)(A) amended Code Sec. 23(b)(2)(A)(i) by striking "$75,000" and inserting "$150,000". **Effective** for tax years beginning after 12-31-2001.

P.L. 107-16, §202(f)(1):

Act Sec. 202(f)(1) amended Code Sec. 23(b) by adding at the end a new paragraph (4). **Effective** for tax years beginning after 12-31-2001 [but, see P.L. 107-147, §601(b)(2), and P.L. 108-311, §312(b)(2), above.—CCH].

P.L. 107-16, §901(a)-(b), provides [but see P.L. 111-148, §10909(c), above]:

SEC. 901. SUNSET OF PROVISIONS OF ACT.

(a) IN GENERAL.—All provisions of, and amendments made by, this Act shall not apply—

(1) to taxable, plan, or limitation years beginning after December 31, 2010, or

(2) in the case of title V, to estates of decedents dying, gifts made, or generation skipping transfers, after December 31, 2010.

(b) APPLICATION OF CERTAIN LAWS.—The Internal Revenue Code of 1986 and the Employee Retirement Income Security Act of 1974 shall be applied and administered to years, estates, gifts, and transfers described in subsection (a) as if the provisions and amendments described in subsection (a) had never been enacted.

• 1998, IRS Restructuring and Reform Act of 1998 (P.L. 105-206)

P.L. 105-206, §6018(f)(1):

Amended Code Sec. 23(b)(2)(A) by inserting "(determined without regard to subsection (c))" after "for any taxable year". **Effective** as if included in the provision of P.L. 104-188 to which it relates [**effective** for tax years beginning after 12-31-96.—CCH].

• 1997, Taxpayer Relief Act of 1997 (P.L. 105-34)

P.L. 105-34, §1601(h)(2)(B):

Amended Code Sec. 23(b)(2)(B) by striking "determined—" and all that follows and inserting "determined without regard to sections 911, 931, and 933.". **Effective** as if included in the provision of P.L. 104-188 to which it relates [**effective** for tax years beginning after 12-31-96.—CCH]. Prior to amendment, Code Sec. 23(b)(2)(B) read as follows:

(B) DETERMINATION OF ADJUSTED GROSS INCOME.—For purposes of subparagraph (A), adjusted gross income shall be determined—

(i) without regard to sections 911, 931, and 933, and

(ii) after the application of sections 86, 135, 137, 219, and 469.

→ Caution: Former Code Sec. 23(c) was redesignated as Code Sec. 36C(c), below, and stricken by P.L. 111-148. For sunset provision, see P.L. 111-148, §10909(c), in the amendment notes.

[Sec. 36C(c)—Stricken]

Amendments

(c) • 2010, Patient Protection and Affordable Care Act (P.L. 111-148)

P.L. 111-148, §10909(b)(2)(I)(ii):

Amended Code Sec. 36C, as redesignated, by striking subsection (c). **Effective** for tax years beginning after 12-31-2009. Prior to amendment, Code Sec. 36C(c) read as follows:

(c) CARRYFORWARDS OF UNUSED CREDIT.—

(1) RULE FOR YEARS IN WHICH ALL PERSONAL CREDITS ALLOWED AGAINST REGULAR AND ALTERNATIVE MINIMUM TAX.—In the case of a taxable year to which section 26(a)(2) applies, if the credit allowable under subsection (a) for any taxable year exceeds the limitation imposed by section 26(a)(2) for such taxable year reduced by the sum of the credits allowable under this subpart (other than this section and sections 25D and 1400C), such excess shall be carried to the succeeding taxable year and added to the credit allowable under subsection (a) for such taxable year.

(2) RULE FOR OTHER YEARS.—In the case of a taxable year to which section 26(a)(2) does not apply, if the credit allowable under subsection (a) for any taxable year exceeds the limitation imposed by subsection (b)(4) for such taxable year, such excess shall be carried to the succeeding taxable year and

added to the credit allowable under subsection (a) for such taxable year.

(3) LIMITATION.—No credit may be carried forward under this subsection to any taxable year following the fifth taxable year after the taxable year in which the credit arose. For purposes of the preceding sentence, credits shall be treated as used on a first-in first-out basis.

P.L. 111-148, §10909(c), provides:

(c) APPLICATION AND EXTENSION OF EGTRRA SUNSET.—Notwithstanding section 901 of the Economic Growth and Tax Relief Reconciliation Act of 2001 [P.L. 107-16], such section shall apply to the amendments made by this section and the amendments made by section 202 of such Act by substituting "December 31, 2011" for "December 31, 2010" in subsection (a)(1) thereof.

• 2005, Gulf Opportunity Zone Act of 2005 (P.L. 109-135)

P.L. 109-135, §402(i)(3)(A)(ii):

Amended Code Sec. 23(c). **Effective** for tax years beginning after 12-31-2005. Prior to amendment, Code Sec. 23(c) read as follows:

(c) CARRYFORWARDS OF UNUSED CREDIT.—If the credit allowable under subsection (a) for any taxable year exceeds the limitation imposed by subsection (b)(4) for such taxable year, such excess shall be carried to the succeeding taxable year and added to the credit allowable under subsection (a) for such taxable year. No credit may be carried forward under this subsection to any taxable year following the fifth taxable year after the taxable year in which the credit arose. For purposes of the preceding sentence, credits shall be treated as used on a first-in first-out basis.

P.L. 109-135, §402(i)(3)(H), provides:

(H) APPLICATION OF EGTRRA SUNSET.—The amendments made by this paragraph (and each part thereof) shall be subject to title IX of the Economic Growth and Tax Relief Reconciliation Act of 2001 in the same manner as the provisions of such Act to which such amendment (or part thereof) relates.

P.L. 109-135, §402(i)(4):

Amended Act Sec. 1335(b) of P.L. 109-58 by striking paragraphs (1) through (3) and provided that the Internal Revenue Code of 1986 shall be applied and administered as if the amendments made by such paragraphs had never been enacted. **Effective** as if included in the provision of the Energy Policy Act of 2005 (P.L. 109-58) to which it relates. P.L. 109-58, §1335(b)(1), amended Code Sec. 23(c) by striking "this section and section 1400C" and inserting "this section, section 25D, and section 1400C". This amendment reinstates the language "this section and section 1400C" to Code Sec. 23(c).

• 2005, Energy Tax Incentives Act of 2005 (P.L. 109-58)

P.L. 109-58, §1335(b)(1) [stricken by P.L. 109-135, §402(i)(4)]:

Amended Code Sec. 23(c) by striking "this section and section 1400C" and inserting "this section, section 25D, and section 1400C". **Effective** for property placed in service after 12-31-2005, in tax years ending after such date. [Note, this amendment cannot be made to the version of Code Sec. 23(c) as in effect on January 1, 2006.—CCH.]

• 2004, Working Families Tax Relief Act of 2004 (P.L. 108-311)

P.L. 108-311, §312(b)(2), provides:

(2) The amendments made by sections 201(b), 202(f), and 618(b) of the Economic Growth and Tax Relief Reconciliation Act of 2001 shall not apply to taxable years beginning during 2004 or 2005.

• 2002, Job Creation and Worker Assistance Act of 2002 (P.L. 107-147)

P.L. 107-147, §601(b)(2), provides:

(2) The amendments made by sections 201(b), 202(f), and 618(b) of the Economic Growth and Tax Relief Reconciliation Act of 2001 shall not apply to taxable years beginning during 2002 and 2003.

• 2001, Economic Growth and Tax Relief Reconciliation Act of 2001 (P.L. 107-16)

P.L. 107-16, §201(b)(2)(E):

Amended Code Sec. 23(c) by striking "and section 1400C" and inserting "and sections 24 and 1400C". [Note: The amendment made by Act Sec. 202(f)(2)(A)(i)-(ii) deleted the text to which this amendment applied. Thus, essentially it never took effect.—CCH.] **Effective** for tax years beginning after 12-31-2001 [but, see P.L. 107-147, §601(b)(2), and P.L. 108-311, §312(b)(2), above.—CCH].

P.L. 107-16, §202(f)(2)(A)(i)-(ii):

Amended Code Sec. 23(c), as amended by Act Sec. 201(b), by striking "section 26(a)" and inserting "subsection (b)(4)", and by striking "reduced by the sum of the credits allowable under this subpart (other than this section and sections 24 and 1400C)" before ", such excess". **Effective** for tax years beginning after 12-31-2001 [but, see P.L. 107-147, §601(b)(2), and P.L. 108-311, §312(b)(2), above.—CCH].

P.L. 107-16, §901(a)-(b), provides [but see P.L. 111-148, §10909(c), above]:

SEC. 901. SUNSET OF PROVISIONS OF ACT.

(a) IN GENERAL.—All provisions of, and amendments made by, this Act shall not apply—

(1) to taxable, plan, or limitation years beginning after December 31, 2010, or

(2) in the case of title V, to estates of decedents dying, gifts made, or generation skipping transfers, after December 31, 2010.

(b) APPLICATION OF CERTAIN LAWS.—The Internal Revenue Code of 1986 and the Employee Retirement Income Security Act of 1974 shall be applied and administered to years, estates, gifts, and transfers described in subsection (a) as if the provisions and amendments described in subsection (a) had never been enacted.

• 1998, IRS Restructuring and Reform Act of 1998 (P.L. 105-206)

P.L. 105-206, §6008(d)(6):

Amended Code Sec. 23(c) by inserting "and section 1400C" after "other than this section". **Effective** as if included in the provision of P.L. 105-34 to which it relates [**effective** 8-5-97.—CCH].

[Sec. 36C(d)]

(d) DEFINITIONS.—For purposes of this section—

(1) QUALIFIED ADOPTION EXPENSES.—The term "qualified adoption expenses" means reasonable and necessary adoption fees, court costs, attorney fees, and other expenses—

(A) which are directly related to, and the principal purpose of which is for, the legal adoption of an eligible child by the taxpayer,

(B) which are not incurred in violation of State or Federal law or in carrying out any surrogate parenting arrangement,

(C) which are not expenses in connection with the adoption by an individual of a child who is the child of such individual's spouse, and

(D) which are not reimbursed under an employer program or otherwise.

»»→ Caution: Former Code Sec. 23(d)(2) was amended by P.L. 107-16 and redesignated as Code Sec. 36C(d)(2), below, by P.L. 111-148, and is subject to the sunset provision of the Economic Growth and Tax Relief Reconciliation Act of 2001 (P.L. 107-16), §901. Absent Congressional action, the changes made to this provision by P.L. 107-16, or that take effect as if included in P.L. 107-16, do not apply after December 31, 2010. For more information about the sunset provision, see page XXI of the Preface to this publication and P.L. 107-16, §901, and P.L. 111-148, §10909(c), in the amendment notes. See the amendments notes for a history of amendments to this section and the effective date of each change.

(2) ELIGIBLE CHILD.—The term "eligible child" means any individual who—

(A) has not attained age 18, or

(B) is physically or mentally incapable of caring for himself.

(3) CHILD WITH SPECIAL NEEDS.—The term "child with special needs" means any child if—

(A) a State has determined that the child cannot or should not be returned to the home of his parents,

(B) such State has determined that there exists with respect to the child a specific factor or condition (such as his ethnic background, age, or membership in a minority or sibling group, or the presence of factors such as medical conditions or physical, mental, or emotional handicaps) because of which it is reasonable to conclude that such child cannot be placed with adoptive parents without providing adoption assistance, and

(C) such child is a citizen or resident of the United States (as defined in section 217(h)(3)).

Amendments

• 2010, Patient Protection and Affordable Care Act (P.L. 111-148)

P.L. 111-148, §10909(c), provides:

(c) APPLICATION AND EXTENSION OF EGTRRA SUNSET.—Notwithstanding section 901 of the Economic Growth and Tax Relief Reconciliation Act of 2001 [P.L. 107-16], such section shall apply to the amendments made by this section and the amendments made by section 202 of such Act by substituting "December 31, 2011" for "December 31, 2010" in subsection (a)(1) thereof.

• 2001, Economic Growth and Tax Relief Reconciliation Act of 2001 (P.L. 107-16)

P.L. 107-16, §202(d)(1):

Amended Code Sec. 23(d)(2). **Effective** for tax years beginning after 12-31-2001. Prior to amendment, Code Sec. 23(d)(2) read as follows:

(2) ELIGIBLE CHILD.—The term "eligible child" means any individual—

(A) who—

(i) has not attained age 18, or

(ii) is physically or mentally incapable of caring for himself, and

(B) in the case of qualified adoption expenses paid or incurred after December 31, 2001, who is a child with special needs.

P.L. 107-16, §901(a)-(b), provides [but see P.L. 111-148, §10909(c), above]:

SEC. 901. SUNSET OF PROVISIONS OF ACT.

(a) IN GENERAL.—All provisions of, and amendments made by, this Act shall not apply—

(1) to taxable, plan, or limitation years beginning after December 31, 2010, or

(2) in the case of title V, to estates of decedents dying, gifts made, or generation skipping transfers, after December 31, 2010.

(b) APPLICATION OF CERTAIN LAWS.—The Internal Revenue Code of 1986 and the Employee Retirement Income Security Act of 1974 shall be applied and administered to years, estates, gifts, and transfers described in subsection (a) as if the provisions and amendments described in subsection (a) had never been enacted.

[Sec. 36C(e)]

(e) SPECIAL RULES FOR FOREIGN ADOPTIONS.—In the case of an adoption of a child who is not a citizen or resident of the United States (as defined in section 217(h)(3))—

(1) subsection (a) shall not apply to any qualified adoption expense with respect to such adoption unless such adoption becomes final, and

(2) any such expense which is paid or incurred before the taxable year in which such adoption becomes final shall be taken into account under this section as if such expense were paid or incurred during such year.

[Sec. 36C(f)]

(f) FILING REQUIREMENTS.—

(1) MARRIED COUPLES MUST FILE JOINT RETURNS.—Rules similar to the rules of paragraphs (2), (3), and (4) of section 21(e) shall apply for purposes of this section.

(2) TAXPAYER MUST INCLUDE TIN.—

(A) IN GENERAL.—No credit shall be allowed under this section with respect to any eligible child unless the taxpayer includes (if known) the name, age, and TIN of such child on the return of tax for the taxable year.

(B) OTHER METHODS.—The Secretary may, in lieu of the information referred to in subparagraph (A), require other information meeting the purposes of subparagraph (A), including identification of an agent assisting with the adoption.

[Sec. 36C(g)]

(g) BASIS ADJUSTMENTS.—For purposes of this subtitle, if a credit is allowed under this section for any expenditure with respect to any property, the increase in the basis of such property which would (but for this subsection) result from such expenditure shall be reduced by the amount of the credit so allowed.

»»→ Caution: Former Code Sec. 23(h), below, was added by P.L. 107-16, amended by P.L. 107-147 and P.L. 111-148, and redesignated as Code Sec. 36C(h) by P.L. 111-148, and is subject to the sunset provision of the Economic Growth and Tax Relief Reconciliation Act of 2001 (P.L. 107-16), §901. Absent Congressional action, the changes made to this provision by P.L. 107-16, or that take effect as if included in P.L. 107-16, do not apply after December 31, 2010. For more information about the sunset provision, see page XXI of the Preface to this publication and P.L. 107-16, §901, and P.L. 111-148, §10909(c), in the amendment notes. See the amendments notes for a history of amendments to this section and the effective date of each change.

[Sec. 36C(h)]

(h) ADJUSTMENTS FOR INFLATION.—

(1) DOLLAR LIMITATIONS .—In the case of a taxable year beginning after December 31, 2010, each of the dollar amounts in subsections (a)(3) and (b)(1) shall be increased by an amount equal to—

(A) such dollar amount, multiplied by

(B) the cost-of-living adjustment determined under section 1(f)(3) for the calendar year in which the taxable year begins, determined by substituting "calendar year 2009" for "calendar year 1992" in subparagraph (B) thereof.

If any amount as increased under the preceding sentence is not a multiple of $10, such amount shall be rounded to the nearest multiple of $10.

(2) INCOME LIMITATION .—In the case of a taxable year beginning after December 31, 2002, the dollar amount in subsection (b)(2)(A)(i) shall be increased by an amount equal to—

(A) such dollar amount, multiplied by

(B) the cost-of-living adjustment determined under section 1(f)(3) for the calendar year in which the taxable year begins, determined by substituting "calendar year 2001" for "calendar year 1992" in subparagraph (B) thereof.

If any amount as increased under the preceding sentence is not a multiple of $10, such amount shall be rounded to the nearest multiple of $10.

Amendments

• 2010, Patient Protection and Affordable Care Act (P.L. 111-148)

P.L. 111-148, §10909(a)(1)(C):

Amended Code Sec. 23(h). **Effective** for tax years beginning after 12-31-2009. Prior to amendment, Code Sec. 23(h) read as follows:

(h) ADJUSTMENTS FOR INFLATION.—In the case of a taxable year beginning after December 31, 2002, each of the dollar amounts in subsection (a)(3) and paragraphs (1) and (2)(A)(i) of subsection (b) shall be increased by an amount equal to—

(1) such dollar amount, multiplied by

(2) the cost-of-living adjustment determined under section 1(f)(3) for the calendar year in which the taxable year begins, determined by substituting "calendar year 2001" for "calendar year 1992" in subparagraph (B) thereof.

If any amount as increased under the preceding sentence is not a multiple of $10, such amount shall be rounded to the nearest multiple of $10.

P.L. 111-148, §10909(c), provides:

(c) APPLICATION AND EXTENSION OF EGTRRA SUNSET.—Notwithstanding section 901 of the Economic Growth and Tax Relief Reconciliation Act of 2001 {P.L. 107-16], such section shall apply to the amendments made by this section and the amendments made by section 202 of such Act by substituting "December 31, 2011" for "December 31, 2010" in subsection (a)(1) thereof.

• 2002, Job Creation and Worker Assistance Act of 2002 (P.L. 107-147)

P.L. 107-147, §418(a)(1)(A)-(B):

Amended Code Sec. 23(h) by striking "subsection (a)(1)(B)" and inserting "subsection (a)(3)", and by adding at the end a new flush sentence. **Effective** as if included in the provision of P.L. 107-16 to which it relates [**effective** for tax years beginning after 12-31-2001.—CCH].

• 2001, Economic Growth and Tax Relief Reconciliation Act of 2001 (P.L. 107-16)

P.L. 107-16, §202(e)(1):

Amended Code Sec. 23 by redesignating subsection (h) as subsection (i) and by inserting after subsection (g) a new subsection (h). **Effective** for tax years beginning after 12-31-2001.

P.L. 107-16, §901(a)-(b), provides [but see P.L. 111-148, §10909(c), above]:

SEC. 901. SUNSET OF PROVISIONS OF ACT.

(a) IN GENERAL.—All provisions. of, and amendments made by, this Act shall not apply—

(1) to taxable, plan, or limitation years beginning after December 31, 2010, or

(2) in the case of title V, to estates of decedents dying, gifts made, or generation skipping transfers, after December 31, 2010.

(b) APPLICATION OF CERTAIN LAWS.—The Internal Revenue Code of 1986 and the Employee Retirement Income Security Act of 1974 shall be applied and administered to years, estates, gifts, and transfers described in subsection (a) as if the provisions and amendments described in subsection (a) had never been enacted.

[Sec. 36C(i)]

(i) REGULATIONS.—The Secretary shall prescribe such regulations as may be appropriate to carry out this section and section 137, including regulations which treat unmarried individuals who pay or incur qualified adoption expenses with respect to the same child as 1 taxpayer for purposes of applying the dollar amounts in subsections (a)(3) and (b)(1) of this section and in section 137(b)(1).

Amendments

• 2002, Job Creation and Worker Assistance Act of 2002 (P.L. 107-147)

P.L. 107-147, §411(c)(1)(E):

Amended Code Sec. 23(i) by striking "the dollar limitation in subsection (b)(1)" and inserting "the dollar amounts in subsections (a)(3) and (b)(1)". **Effective** for tax years beginning after 12-31-2002.

• 2001, Economic Growth and Tax Relief Reconciliation Act of 2001 (P.L. 107-16)

P.L. 107-16, §202(e)(1):

Amended Code Sec. 23 by redesignating subsection (h) as subsection (i). **Effective** for tax years beginning after 12-31-2001.

P.L. 107-16, §901(a)-(b), provides:

SEC. 901. SUNSET OF PROVISIONS OF ACT.

(a) IN GENERAL.—All provisions of, and amendments made by, this Act shall not apply—

(1) to taxable, plan, or limitation years beginning after December 31, 2010, or

(2) in the case of title V, to estates of decedents dying, gifts made, or generation skipping transfers, after December 31, 2010.

(b) APPLICATION OF CERTAIN LAWS.—The Internal Revenue Code of 1986 and the Employee Retirement Income Security Act of 1974 shall be applied and administered to years, estates, gifts, and transfers described in subsection (a) as if the provisions and amendments described in subsection (a) had never been enacted.

• 1996, Small Business Job Protection Act of 1996 (P.L. 104-188)

P.L. 104-188, §1807(a):

Amended subpart A of part IV of subchapter A of chapter 1 by inserting after Code Sec. 22 a new Code Sec. 23 **Effective** for tax years beginning after 12-31-96.

[Sec. 36—Repealed]

Amendments

• 1977, Tax Reduction and Simplification Act of 1977 (P.L. 95-30)

P.L. 95-30, §101(d)(3):

Repealed Code Sec. 36. **Effective** for tax years beginning after 12-31-76. Prior to repeal, Sec. 36 read as follows:

SEC. 36. CREDITS NOT ALLOWED TO INDIVIDUALS TAKING STANDARD DEDUCTION.

If an individual elects under section 144 to take the standard deduction, the credits provided by section 32 shall not be allowed.

• 1976, Tax Reform Act of 1976 (P.L. 94-455)

P.L. 94-455, §§501(b)(2), 1011(c) (as amended by P.L. 95-30, §302), and 1901(b)(1)(A):

Amended Code Sec. 36 by striking out "PAYING OPTIONAL TAX OR" in the heading; and by striking out "elects to pay the optional tax imposed by section 3, or if he" after "individual". **Effective** for tax years beginning after 12-31-75.

Substituted "sections 32 and" for "sections 32, 33, and" in Code Sec. 36. **Effective** for tax years beginning after 12-31-75. However, P.L. 95-30, §302, changed this effective date to tax years beginning after 12-31-76.

Substituted "section 32" for "sections 32 and 35" in Code Sec. 36. **Effective** for tax years beginning after 12-31-76.

[Sec. 37]

SEC. 37. OVERPAYMENTS OF TAX.

For credit against the tax imposed by this subtitle for overpayments of tax, see section 6401.

Amendments

• 2008, Housing Assistance Tax Act of 2008 (P.L. 110-289)

P.L. 110-289, §3011(a):

Amended subpart C of part IV of subchapter A of chapter 1 by redesignating Code Sec. 36 as Code Sec. 37. **Effective** for residences purchased on or after 4-9-2008, in tax years ending on or after such date.

• 2002, Trade Act of 2002 (P.L. 107-210)

P.L. 107-210, §201(a):

Amended subpart C of part IV of subchapter A of chapter 1 by redesignating Code Sec. 35 as Code Sec. 36. **Effective** for tax years beginning after 12-31-2001.

• 1984, Deficit Reduction Act of 1984 (P.L. 98-369)

P.L. 98-369, §471(c)(1):

Redesignated Code Sec. 45 as Code Sec. 35. **Effective** for tax years beginning after 12-31-83, and to carrybacks from such years.

• 1975, Tax Reduction Act of 1975 (P.L. 94-12)

P.L. 94-12, §§203(a), 204(a), 208(a):

Prior to amendment by P.L. 94-12, Code Sec. 45 was formerly numbered Code Sec. 42. **Effective** 3-29-75.

• 1971, Revenue Act of 1971 (P.L. 92-178)

P.L. 92-178 §601(a):

Redesignated Code Sec. 40 as Code Sec. 42.

• 1965, Excise Reduction Act of 1965 (P.L. 89-44)

P.L. 89-44, §809(c):

Redesignated Code Sec. 39 as Code Sec. 40.

• 1962, Revenue Act of 1962 (P.L. 87-834)

P.L. 87-834, §2:

Redesignated Code Sec. 38 as Code Sec. 39.

Subpart D—Business Related Credits

Sec. 45F.	Employer-provided child care credit.
Sec. 45G.	Railroad track maintenance credit.
Sec. 45H.	Credit for production of low sulfur diesel fuel.
Sec. 45I.	Credit for producing oil and gas from marginal wells.
Sec. 45J.	Credit for production from advanced nuclear power facilities.
Sec. 45K.	Credit for producing fuel from a nonconventional source.
Sec. 45L.	New energy efficient home credit.
Sec. 45M.	Energy efficient appliance credit.
Sec. 45N.	Mine rescue team training credit.
Sec. 45O.	Agricultural chemicals security credit.
Sec. 45P.	Employer wage credit for employees who are active duty members of the uniformed services.
Sec. 45Q.	Credit for carbon dioxide sequestration.
Sec. 45R.	Employee health insurance expenses of small employers.

[Sec. 38]

SEC. 38. GENERAL BUSINESS CREDIT.

[Sec. 38(a)]

(a) ALLOWANCE OF CREDIT.—There shall be allowed as a credit against the tax imposed by this chapter for the taxable year an amount equal to the sum of—

(1) the business credit carryforwards carried to such taxable year,

(2) the amount of the current year business credit, plus

(3) the business credit carrybacks carried to such taxable year.

[Sec. 38(b)]

(b) CURRENT YEAR BUSINESS CREDIT.—For purposes of this subpart, the amount of the current year business credit is the sum of the following credits determined for the taxable year:

(1) the investment credit determined under section 46,

(2) the work opportunity credit determined under section 51(a),

(3) the alcohol fuels credit determined under section 40(a),

(4) the research credit determined under section 41(a),

(5) the low-income housing credit determined under section 42(a),

(6) the enhanced oil recovery credit under section 43(a),

(7) in the case of an eligible small business (as defined in section 44(b)), the disabled access credit determined under section 44(a),

(8) the renewable electricity production credit under section 45(a),

(9) the empowerment zone employment credit determined under section 1396(a),

(10) the Indian employment credit as determined under section 45A(a),

(11) the employer social security credit determined under section 45B(a),

(12) the orphan drug credit determined under section 45C(a),

»»→ Caution: Code Sec. 38(b)(13)-(15), below, is subject to the sunset provision of the Economic Growth and Tax Relief Reconciliation Act of 2001 (P.L. 107-16), §901. Absent Congressional action, the changes made to this provision by P.L. 107-16, or that take effect as if included in P.L. 107-16, do not apply after December 31, 2010. For more information about the sunset provision, see page XXI of the Preface to this publication and P.L. 107-16, §901, in the amendment notes. See the amendments notes for a history of amendments to this section and the effective date of each change.

(13) the new markets tax credit determined under section 45D(a),

(14) in the case of an eligible employer (as defined in section 45E(c)), the small employer pension plan startup cost credit determined under section 45E(a),

(15) the employer-provided child care credit determined under section 45F(a),

(16) the railroad track maintenance credit determined under section 45G(a),

(17) the biodiesel fuels credit determined under section 40A(a),

(18) the low sulfur diesel fuel production credit determined under section 45H(a),

(19) the marginal oil and gas well production credit determined under section 45I(a),

(20) the distilled spirits credit determined under section 5011(a),

(21) the advanced nuclear power facility production credit determined under section 45J(a),

(22) the nonconventional source production credit determined under section 45K(a),

(23) the new energy efficient home credit determined under section 45L(a),

(24) the energy efficient appliance credit determined under section 45M(a),

(25) the portion of the alternative motor vehicle credit to which section 30B(g)(1) applies,

(26) the portion of the alternative fuel vehicle refueling property credit to which section 30C(d)(1) applies,

(27) the Hurricane Katrina housing credit determined under section 1400P(b),

(28) the Hurricane Katrina employee retention credit determined under section 1400R(a),

(29) the Hurricane Rita employee retention credit determined under section 1400R(b),

(30) the Hurricane Wilma employee retention credit determined under section 1400R(c),

(31) the mine rescue team training credit determined under section 45N(a),

(32) in the case of an eligible agricultural business (as defined in section 45O(e)), the agricultural chemicals security credit determined under section 45O(a),

(33) the differential wage payment credit determined under section 45P(a),

(34) the carbon dioxide sequestration credit determined under section 45Q(a)[,]

(35) the portion of the new qualified plug-in electric drive motor vehicle credit to which section 30D(c)(1) applies, plus

(36) the small employer health insurance credit determined under section 45R.

Amendments

• 2010, Patient Protection and Affordable Care Act (P.L. 111-148)

P.L. 111-148, §1421(b):

Amended Code Sec. 38(b) by striking "plus" at the end of paragraph (34), by striking the period at the end of paragraph (35) and inserting ", plus", and by inserting after paragraph (35) a new paragraph (36). **Effective** for amounts paid or incurred in tax years beginning after 12-31-2009 [**effective** date amended by Act Sec. 10105(e)(4).—CCH].

• 2010, Hiring Incentives to Restore Employment Act (P.L. 111-147)

P.L. 111-147, §102, provides:

SEC. 102. BUSINESS CREDIT FOR RETENTION OF CERTAIN NEWLY HIRED INDIVIDUALS IN 2010.

(a) IN GENERAL.—In the case of any taxable year ending after the date of the enactment of this Act, the current year business credit determined under section 38(b) of the Internal Revenue Code of 1986 for such taxable year shall be increased, with respect to each retained worker with respect to which subsection (b)(2) is first satisfied during such taxable year, by the lesser of—

(1) $1,000, or

(2) 6.2 percent of the wages (as defined in section 3401(a)) paid by the taxpayer to such retained worker during the 52 consecutive week period referred to in subsection (b)(2).

(b) RETAINED WORKER.—For purposes of this section, the term "retained worker" means any qualified individual (as defined in section 3111(d)(3) or section 3221(c)(3) of the Internal Revenue Code of 1986)—

(1) who was employed by the taxpayer on any date during the taxable year,

(2) who was so employed by the taxpayer for a period of not less than 52 consecutive weeks, and

(3) whose wages (as defined in section 3401(a)) for such employment during the last 26 weeks of such period equaled at least 80 percent of such wages for the first 26 weeks of such period.

(c) LIMITATION ON CARRYBACKS.—No portion of the unused business credit under section 38 of the Internal Revenue Code of 1986 for any taxable year which is attributable to the increase in the current year business credit under this section may be carried to a taxable year beginning before the date of the enactment of this section.

(d) TREATMENT OF POSSESSIONS.—

(1) PAYMENTS TO POSSESSIONS.—

(A) MIRROR CODE POSSESSIONS.—The Secretary of the Treasury shall pay to each possession of the United States with a mirror code tax system amounts equal to the loss to that possession by reason of the application of this section (other than this subsection). Such amounts shall be determined by the Secretary of the Treasury based on information provided by the government of the respective possession.

(B) OTHER POSSESSIONS.—The Secretary of the Treasury shall pay to each possession of the United States which does not have a mirror code tax system amounts estimated by the Secretary of the Treasury as being equal to the aggregate benefits that would have been provided to residents of such possession by reason of the application of this section (other than this subsection) if a mirror code tax system had been in effect in such possession. The preceding sentence shall not apply with respect to any possession of the United States unless such possession has a plan, which has been approved by the Secretary of the Treasury, under which such possession will promptly distribute such payments to the residents of such possession.

(2) COORDINATION WITH CREDIT ALLOWED AGAINST UNITED STATES INCOME TAXES.—No increase in the credit determined under section 38(b) of the Internal Revenue Code of 1986 against United States income taxes for any taxable year determined under subsection (a) shall be taken into account with respect to any person—

(A) to whom a credit is allowed against taxes imposed by the possession by reason of this section for such taxable year, or

(B) who is eligible for a payment under a plan described in paragraph (1)(B) with respect to such taxable year.

(3) DEFINITIONS AND SPECIAL RULES.—

(A) POSSESSION OF THE UNITED STATES.—For purposes of this subsection, the term "possession of the United States" includes the Commonwealth of Puerto Rico and the Commonwealth of the Northern Mariana Islands.

(B) MIRROR CODE TAX SYSTEM.—For purposes of this subsection, the term "mirror code tax system" means, with respect to any possession of the United States, the income tax system of such possession if the income tax liability of the residents of such possession under such system is determined by reference to the income tax laws of the United States as if such possession were the United States.

(C) TREATMENT OF PAYMENTS.—For purposes of section 1324(b)(2) of title 31, United States Code, rules similar to the rules of section 1001(b)(3)(C) of the American Recovery and Reinvestment Tax Act of 2009 shall apply.

• 2009, American Recovery and Reinvestment Tax Act of 2009 (P.L. 111-5)

P.L. 111-5, §1141(b)(2):

Amended Code Sec. 38(b)(35) by striking "30D(d)(1)" and inserting "30D(c)(1)". **Effective** for vehicles acquired after 12-31-2009.

• 2008, Energy Improvement and Extension Act of 2008 (P.L. 110-343)

P.L. 110-343, Division B, §115(b):

Amended Code Sec. 38(b) by striking "plus" at the end of paragraph (32), by striking the period at the end of paragraph (33) and inserting "plus", and by adding at the end a new paragraph (34). **Effective** for carbon dioxide captured after 10-3-2008.

P.L. 110-343, Division B, §205(c):

Amended Code Sec. 38(b), as amended by this Act, by striking "plus" at the end of paragraph (33), by striking the period at the end of paragraph (34) and inserting "[,] plus", and by adding at the end a new paragraph (35). **Effective** for tax years beginning after 12-31-2008.

• 2008, Heartland, Habitat, Harvest, and Horticulture Act of 2008 (P.L. 110-246)

P.L. 110-246, §15343(b):

Amended Code Sec. 38(b) by striking "plus" at the end of paragraph (30), by striking the period at the end of paragraph (31) and inserting ", plus", and by adding at the end a new paragraph (32). **Effective** for amounts paid or incurred after 5-22-2008.

• 2008, Heroes Earnings Assistance and Relief Tax Act of 2008 (P.L. 110-245)

P.L. 110-245, §111(b):

Amended Code Sec. 38(b) by striking "plus" at the end of paragraph (31), by striking the period at the end of paragraph (32) and inserting ", plus", and by adding at the end a new paragraph (33). **Effective** for amounts paid after 6-17-2008.

• 2007, Tax Technical Corrections Act of 2007 (P.L. 110-172)

P.L. 110-172, §11(a)(6)(A)-(C):

Amended Code Sec. 38(b) by striking "and" each place it appears at the end of any paragraph, by striking "plus" each place it appears at the end of any paragraph, and by inserting "plus" at the end of paragraph (30). [Note: Code Sec. 38(b) does not contain the word "and" at the end of any paragraph. Therefore, the amendment made by Act Sec. 11(a)(6)(A) cannot be made. Moreover, the word "plus" appears only at the end of paragraph (30).—CCH] **Effective** 12-29-2007.

• 2006, Tax Relief and Health Care Act of 2006 (P.L. 109-432)

P.L. 109-432, Division A, §405(b):

Amended Code Sec. 38(b) by striking "and" at the end of paragraph (29), by striking the period at the end of paragraph (30) and inserting ", plus", and by adding at the end a new paragraph (31). **Effective** for tax years beginning after 12-31-2005.

• 2006, Pension Protection Act of 2006 (P.L. 109-280)

P.L. 109-280, §811, provides:

SEC. 811. PENSIONS AND INDIVIDUAL RETIREMENT ARRANGEMENT PROVISIONS OF ECONOMIC GROWTH AND TAX RELIEF RECONCILIATION ACT OF 2001 MADE PERMANENT.

Title IX of the Economic Growth and Tax Relief Reconciliation Act of 2001 [P.L. 107-16] shall not apply to the provisions of, and amendments made by, subtitles A through F of title VI [§§601-666]of such Act (relating to pension and individual retirement arrangement provisions).

• 2005, Gulf Opportunity Zone Act of 2005 (P.L. 109-135)

P.L. 109-135, §103(b)(1):

Amended Code Sec. 38(b) by striking "and" at the end of paragraph (25), by striking the period at the end of paragraph (26) and inserting ", and", and by adding at the end a new paragraph (27). **Effective** 12-21-2005.

P.L. 109-135, §201(b)(1):

Amended Code Sec. 38(b) by striking "and" at the end of paragraph (26), by striking the period at the end of paragraph (27) and inserting a comma, and by adding at the end new paragraphs (28) through (30). **Effective** 12-21-2005.

• 2005, Katrina Emergency Tax Relief Act of 2005 (P.L. 109-73)

P.L. 109-73, §202 [repealed by P.L. 109-135, §201(b)(4)(B)], provides:

SEC. 202. EMPLOYEE RETENTION CREDIT FOR EMPLOYERS AFFECTED BY HURRICANE KATRINA.

(a) IN GENERAL.—In the case of an eligible employer, there shall be allowed as a credit against the tax imposed by chapter 1 of the Internal Revenue Code of 1986 for the taxable year an amount equal to 40 percent of the qualified wages with respect to each eligible employee of such employer for such taxable year. For purposes of the preceding sentence, the amount of qualified wages which may be taken into account with respect to any individual shall not exceed $6,000.

(b) DEFINITIONS.—For purposes of this section—

(1) ELIGIBLE EMPLOYER.—The term "eligible employer" means any employer—

(A) which conducted an active trade or business on August 28, 2005, in a core disaster area, and

(B) with respect to whom the trade or business described in subparagraph (A) is inoperable on any day after August 28, 2005, and before January 1, 2006, as a result of damage sustained by reason of Hurricane Katrina.

(2) ELIGIBLE EMPLOYEE.—The term "eligible employee" means with respect to an eligible employer an employee whose principal place of employment on August 28, 2005, with such eligible employer was in a core disaster area.

(3) QUALIFIED WAGES.—The term "qualified wages" means wages (as defined in section 51(c)(1) of such Code, but without regard to section 3306(b)(2)(B) of such Code) paid or incurred by an eligible employer with respect to an eligible employee on any day after August 28, 2005, and before January 1, 2006, which occurs during the period—

(A) beginning on the date on which the trade or business described in paragraph (1) first became inoperable at the principal place of employment of the employee immediately before Hurricane Katrina, and

(B) ending on the date on which such trade or business has resumed significant operations at such principal place of employment.

Such term shall include wages paid without regard to whether the employee performs no services, performs services at a different place of employment than such principal place of employment, or performs services at such principal place of employment before significant operations have resumed.

(c) CREDIT NOT ALLOWED FOR LARGE BUSINESSES.—The term "eligible employer" shall not include any trade or business for any taxable year if such trade or business employed an average of more than 200 employees on business days during the taxable year.

(d) CERTAIN RULES TO APPLY.—For purposes of this section, rules similar to the rules of sections 51(i)(1), 52, and 280C(a) of such Code shall apply.

(e) EMPLOYEE NOT TAKEN INTO ACCOUNT MORE THAN ONCE.—An employee shall not be treated as an eligible employee for purposes of this section for any period with respect to any employer if such employer is allowed a credit under section 51 of such Code with respect to such employee for such period.

(f) CREDIT TO BE PART OF GENERAL BUSINESS CREDIT.—The credit allowed under this section shall be added to the current year business credit under section 38(b) of such Code and shall be treated as a credit allowed under subpart D of part IV of subchapter A of chapter 1 of such Code.

• 2005, Safe, Accountable, Flexible, Efficient Transportation Equity Act: A Legacy for Users (P.L. 109-59)

P.L. 109-59, §11126(b):

Amended Code Sec. 38(b) by striking "plus" at the end of paragraph (18), by striking the period at the end of paragraph (19) and inserting ", plus", and by adding at the end a new paragraph (20). **Effective** for tax years beginning after 9-30-2005. For a special rule, see Act Sec. 11151(d)(2), below.

P.L. 109-59, §11151(d)(2), provides:

(2) If the Energy Policy Act of 2005 is enacted before the date of the enactment of this Act, for purposes of executing any amendments made by the Energy Policy Act of 2005 to section 38(b) of the Internal Revenue Code of 1986, the amendments made by section 1126(b) of this Act shall be treated as having been executed before such amendments made by the Energy Policy Act of 2005.

• 2005, Energy Tax Incentives Act of 2005 (P.L. 109-58)

P.L. 109-58, §1306(b), as amended by P.L. 109-59, §11151(d)(1):

Amended Code Sec. 38(b), as amended by the Safe, Accountable, Flexible, Efficient Transportation Equity Act: A Legacy for Users, by striking "plus" at the end of paragraph (19), by striking the period at the end of paragraph (20) and inserting ", plus", and by adding at the end a new paragraph (21). **Effective** for production in tax years beginning after 8-8-2005. For a special rule, see P.L. 109-59, Act Sec. 11151(d)(2).

P.L. 109-58, §1322(a)(2):

Amended Code Sec. 38(b), as amended by this Act, by striking "plus" at the end of paragraph (20), by striking the period at the end of paragraph (21) and inserting ", plus", and by adding at the end a new paragraph (22). **Effective** for credits determined under the Internal Revenue Code of 1986 for tax years ending after 12-31-2005.

P.L. 109-58, §1332(b):

Amended Code Sec. 38(b), as amended by this Act, by striking "plus" at the end of paragraph (21), by striking the period at the end of paragraph (22) and inserting ", plus", and by adding at the end a new paragraph (23). **Effective** for qualified new energy efficient homes acquired after 12-31-2005, in tax years ending after such date.

P.L. 109-58, §1334(b):

Amended Code Sec. 38(b), as amended by this Act, by striking "plus" at the end of paragraph (22), by striking the period at the end of paragraph (23) and inserting ", plus", and by adding at the end a new paragraph (24). **Effective** for appliances produced after 12-31-2005.

P.L. 109-58, §1341(b)(1):

Amended Code Sec. 38(b), as amended by this Act, by striking "plus" at the end of paragraph (23), by striking the period at the end of paragraph (24) and inserting ", and", and by adding at the end a new paragraph (25). **Effective** for property placed in service after 12-31-2005, in tax years ending after such date.

P.L. 109-58, §1342(b)(1):

Amended Code Sec. 38(b), as amended by this Act, by striking "plus" at the end of paragraph (24), by striking the period at the end of paragraph (25) and inserting ", and", and by adding at the end a new paragraph (26). **Effective** for property placed in service after 12-31-2005, in tax years ending after such date.

• 2004, American Jobs Creation Act of 2004 (P.L. 108-357)

P.L. 108-357, §245(c)(1):

Amended Code Sec. 38(b) by striking "plus" at the end of paragraph (14), by striking the period at the end of paragraph (15) and inserting ", plus", and by adding at the end a new paragraph (16). **Effective** for tax years beginning after 12-31-2004.

P.L. 108-357, §302(b):

Amended Code Sec. 38(b), as amended by this Act, by striking "plus" at the end of paragraph (15), by striking the period at the end of paragraph (16) and inserting ", plus", and by inserting after paragraph (16) a new paragraph (17). **Effective** for fuel produced, and sold or used, after 12-31-2004, in tax years ending after such date.

P.L. 108-357, §339(b):

Amended Code Sec. 38(b), as amended by this Act, by striking "plus" at the end of paragraph (16), by striking the period at the end of paragraph (17) and inserting ", plus", and by inserting after paragraph (17) a new paragraph (18). **Effective** for expenses paid or incurred after 12-31-2002, in tax years ending after such date.

P.L. 108-357, §341(b):

Amended Code Sec. 38(b), as amended by this Act, by striking "plus" at the end of paragraph (17), by striking the period at the end of paragraph (18) and inserting ", plus", and by inserting after paragraph (18) a new paragraph (19). **Effective** for production in tax years beginning after 12-31-2004.

• 2002, Job Creation and Worker Assistance Act of 2002 (P.L. 107-147)

P.L. 107-147, §411(d)(2):

Amended Code Sec. 38(b)(15) by striking "45F" and inserting "45F(a)". **Effective** as if included in the provision of P.L. 107-16 to which it relates [effective for tax years beginning after 12-31-2001.—CCH].

• 2001, Economic Growth and Tax Relief Reconciliation Act of 2001 (P.L. 107-16)

P.L. 107-16, §205(b)(1):

Amended Code Sec. 38(b), as amended by Act Sec. 619, by striking "plus" at the end of paragraph (13), by striking the period at the end of paragraph (14) and inserting ", plus", and by adding at the end a new paragraph (15). **Effective** for tax years beginning after 12-31-2001.

P.L. 107-16, §619(b):

Amended Code Sec. 38(b) by striking "plus" at the end of paragraph (12), by striking the period at the end of paragraph (13) and inserting ", plus", and by adding at the end a new paragraph (14). **Effective** for costs paid or incurred in tax years beginning after 12-31-2001, with respect to qualified employer plans first effective after such date [**effective** date amended by P.L. 107-147, §411(m)(2)].

P.L. 107-16, §901(a)-(b), provides [but see P.L. 109-280, §811, above]:

SEC. 901. SUNSET OF PROVISIONS OF ACT.

(a) IN GENERAL.—All provisions of, and amendments made by, this Act shall not apply—

(1) to taxable, plan, or limitation years beginning after December 31, 2010, or

(2) in the case of title V, to estates of decedents dying, gifts made, or generation skipping transfers, after December 31, 2010.

(b) APPLICATION OF CERTAIN LAWS.—The Internal Revenue Code of 1986 and the Employee Retirement Income Security Act of 1974 shall be applied and administered to years, estates, gifts, and transfers described in subsection (a) as if the provisions and amendments described in subsection (a) had never been enacted.

• 2000, Community Renewal Tax Relief Act of 2000 (P.L. 106-554)

P.L. 106-554, §121(b)(1):

Amended Code Sec. 38(b) by striking "plus" at the end of paragraph (11), by striking the period at the end of paragraph (12) and inserting ", plus", and by adding at the end a new paragraph (13). **Effective** for investments made after 12-31-2000.

• 1996, Small Business Job Protection Act of 1996 (P.L. 104-188)

P.L. 104-188, §1201(e)(1):

Amended Code Sec. 38(b)(2) by striking "targeted jobs credit" each place it appears and inserting "work opportunity credit". **Effective** for individuals who begin work for the employer after 9-30-96.

P.L. 104-188, §1205(a)(2):

Amended Code Sec. 38(b) by striking "plus" at the end of paragraph (10), striking the period at the end of paragraph (11) and inserting ", plus", and adding at the end a new paragraph (12). **Effective** for amounts paid or incurred in tax years ending after 6-30-96.

• 1993, Omnibus Budget Reconciliation Act of 1993 (P.L. 103-66)

P.L. 103-66, §13302(a)(1):

Amended Code Sec. 38(b) by striking "plus" at the end of paragraph (7), by striking the period at the end of paragraph (8) and inserting ", and", and by adding at the end thereof new paragraph (9). **Effective** 8-10-93.

P.L. 103-66, §13322(a):

Amended Code Sec. 38(b) by striking "plus [and]" at the end of paragraph (8), by striking the period at the end of paragraph (9) and inserting ", plus", and by adding after paragraph (9) new paragraph (10). **Effective** for wages paid or incurred after 12-31-93.

P.L. 103-66, §13443(b)(1):

Amended Code Sec. 38(b) by striking "plus" at the end of paragraph (9), by striking the period at the end of pargraph (10) and inserting ", plus", and by adding at the end new paragraph (11). **Effective** with respect to taxes paid after 12-31-93, with respect to services performed before, on, or after such date (as amended by P.L. 104-188, §1112(a)(2)).

• 1992, Energy Policy Act of 1992 (P.L. 102-486)

P.L. 102-486, §1914(b):

Amended Code Sec. 38(b) by striking "plus" at the end of paragraph (6), by striking the period at the end of paragraph (7) and inserting ", plus", and by adding at the end thereof new paragraph (8). **Effective** for tax years ending after 12-31-92.

• 1990, Omnibus Budget Reconciliation Act of 1990 (P.L. 101-508)

P.L. 101-508, §11511(b)(1):

Amended Code Sec. 38(b) by striking "plus" at the end of paragraph (4), by striking the period at the end of paragraph (5) and inserting ", plus", and by adding at the end thereof new paragraph (6). **Effective** for costs paid or incurred in tax years beginning after 12-31-90.

P.L. 101-508, §11611(b)(1):

Amended Code Sec. 38(b) (as amended by Act Sec. 11511(b)(1)) by striking "plus" at the end of paragraph (5), by striking the period at the end of paragraph (6) and inserting ", plus" and by adding at the end thereof a new paragraph (7). **Effective** for expenditures paid or incurred after 11-5-90.

P.L. 101-508, §11813(b)(2)(A):

Amended Code Sec. 38(b)(1) by striking "section 46(a)" and inserting "section 46". **Effective** for property placed in service after 12-31-90.

[Sec. 38(c)]

(c) LIMITATION BASED ON AMOUNT OF TAX.—

(1) IN GENERAL.—The credit allowed under subsection (a) for any taxable year shall not exceed the excess (if any) of the taxpayer's net income tax over the greater of—

(A) the tentative minimum tax for the taxable year, or

(B) 25 percent of so much of the taxpayer's net regular tax liability as exceeds $25,000.

For purposes of the preceding sentence, the term "net income tax" means the sum of the regular tax liability and the tax imposed by section 55, reduced by the credits allowable under subparts A and B of this part, and the term "net regular tax liability" means the regular tax liability reduced by the sum of the credits allowable under subparts A and B of this part.

(2) EMPOWERMENT ZONE EMPLOYMENT CREDIT MAY OFFSET 25 PERCENT OF MINIMUM TAX.—

(A) IN GENERAL.—In the case of the empowerment zone employment credit credit—

(i) this section and section 39 shall be applied separately with respect to such credit, and

(ii) for purposes of applying paragraph (1) to such credit—

(I) 75 percent of the tentative minimum tax shall be substituted for the tentative minimum tax under subparagraph (A) thereof, and

(II) the limitation under paragraph (1) (as modified by subclause (I)) shall be reduced by the credit allowed under subsection (a) for the taxable year (other than the empowerment zone employment credit, the New York Liberty Zone business employee credit, the eligible small business credits, and the specified credits).

(B) EMPOWERMENT ZONE EMPLOYMENT CREDIT.—For purposes of this paragraph, the term "empowerment zone employment credit" means the portion of the credit under subsection (a) which is attributable to the credit determined under section 1396 (relating to empowerment zone employment credit).

(3) SPECIAL RULES FOR NEW YORK LIBERTY ZONE BUSINESS EMPLOYEE CREDIT.—

(A) IN GENERAL.—In the case of the New York Liberty Zone business employee credit—

(i) this section and section 39 shall be applied separately with respect to such credit, and

(ii) in applying paragraph (1) to such credit—

(I) the tentative minimum tax shall be treated as being zero, and

(II) the limitation under paragraph (1) (as modified by subclause (I)) shall be reduced by the credit allowed under subsection (a) for the taxable year (other than the New York Liberty Zone business employee credit, the eligible small business credits, and the specified credits).

(B) NEW YORK LIBERTY ZONE BUSINESS EMPLOYEE CREDIT.—For purposes of this subsection, the term "New York Liberty Zone business employee credit" means the portion of work opportunity credit under section 51 determined under section 1400L(a).

(4) SPECIAL RULES FOR SPECIFIED CREDITS.—

(A) IN GENERAL.—In the case of specified credits—

(i) this section and section 39 shall be applied separately with respect to such credits, and

(ii) in applying paragraph (1) to such credits—

(I) the tentative minimum tax shall be treated as being zero, and

(II) the limitation under paragraph (1) (as modified by subclause (I)) shall be reduced by the credit allowed under subsection (a) for the taxable year (other than the eligible small business credits and the specified credits),

(B) SPECIFIED CREDITS.—For purposes of this subsection, the term "specified credits" means—

(i) for taxable years beginning after December 31, 2004, the credit determined under section 40,

(ii) the credit determined under section 42 to the extent attributable to buildings placed in service after December 31, 2007,

(iii) the credit determined under section 45 to the extent that such credit is attributable to electricity or refined coal produced—

(I) at a facility which is originally placed in service after the date of the enactment of this paragraph, and

(II) during the 4-year period beginning on the date that such facility was originally placed in service,

(iv) the credit determined under section 45B,

(v) the credit determined under section 45G,

(vi) the credit determined under section 45R,

(vii) the credit determined under section 46 to the extent that such credit is attributable to the energy credit determined under section 48,

(viii) the credit determined under section 46 to the extent that such credit is attributable to the rehabilitation credit under section 47, but only with respect to qualified rehabilitation expenditures properly taken into account for periods after December 31, 2007, and

(ix) the credit determined under section 51.

(5) SPECIAL RULES FOR ELIGIBLE SMALL BUSINESS CREDITS IN 2010.—

(A) IN GENERAL.—In the case of eligible small business credits determined in taxable years beginning in 2010—

(i) this section and section 39 shall be applied separately with respect to such credits, and

(ii) in applying paragraph (1) to such credits—

(I) the tentative minimum tax shall be treated as being zero, and

(II) the limitation under paragraph (1) (as modified by subclause (I)) shall be reduced by the credit allowed under subsection (a) for the taxable year (other than the eligible small business credits).

(B) ELIGIBLE SMALL BUSINESS CREDITS.—For purposes of this subsection, the term "eligible small business credits" means the sum of the credits listed in subsection (b) which are determined for the taxable year with respect to an eligible small business. Such credits shall not be taken into account under paragraph (2), (3), or (4).

(C) ELIGIBLE SMALL BUSINESS.—For purposes of this subsection, the term "eligible small business" means, with respect to any taxable year—

(i) a corporation the stock of which is not publicly traded,

(ii) a partnership, or

(iii) a sole proprietorship,

if the average annual gross receipts of such corporation, partnership, or sole proprietorship for the 3-taxable-year period preceding such taxable year does not exceed $50,000,000. For purposes of applying the test under the preceding sentence, rules similar to the rules of paragraphs (2) and (3) of section 448(c) shall apply.

(D) TREATMENT OF PARTNERS AND S CORPORATION SHAREHOLDERS.—Credits determined with respect to a partnership or S corporation shall not be treated as eligible small business credits by any partner or shareholder unless such partner or shareholder meets the gross receipts test under subparagraph (C) for the taxable year in which such credits are treated as current year business credits.

(6) SPECIAL RULES.—

(A) MARRIED INDIVIDUALS.—In the case of a husband or wife who files a separate return, the amount specified under subparagraph (B) of paragraph (1) shall be $12,500 in lieu of $25,000. This subparagraph shall not apply if the spouse of the taxpayer has no business credit carryforward or carryback to, and has no current year business credit for, the taxable year of such spouse which ends within or with the taxpayer's taxable year.

(B) CONTROLLED GROUPS.—In the case of a controlled group, the $25,000 amount specified under subparagraph (B) of paragraph (1) shall be reduced for each component member of such group by apportioning $25,000 among the component members of such group in such manner as the Secretary shall by regulations prescribe. For purposes of the preceding sentence, the term "controlled group" has the meaning given to such term by section 1563(a).

(C) LIMITATIONS WITH RESPECT TO CERTAIN PERSONS.—In the case of a person described in subparagraph (A) or (B) of section 46(e)(1) (as in effect on the day before the date of the enactment of the Revenue Reconciliation Act of 1990), the $25,000 amount specified under subparagraph (B) of paragraph (1) shall equal such person's ratable share (as determined under section 46(e)(2) (as so in effect)) of such amount.

(D) ESTATES AND TRUSTS.—In the case of an estate or trust, the $25,000 amount specified under subparagraph (B) of paragraph (1) shall be reduced to an amount which bears the same ratio to $25,000 as the portion of the income of the estate or trust which is not allocated to beneficiaries bears to the total income of the estate or trust.

Amendments

• 2010, Creating Small Business Jobs Act of 2010 (P.L. 111-240)

P.L. 111-240, §2013(a):

Amended Code Sec. 38(c) by redesignating paragraph (5) as paragraph (6) and by inserting after paragraph (4) a new paragraph (5). **Effective** for credits determined in tax years beginning after 12-31-2009, and to carrybacks of such credits.

P.L. 111-240, §2013(c)(1):

Amended Code Sec. 38(c)(2)(A)(ii)(II) by inserting "the eligible small business credits," after "the New York Liberty Zone business employee credit,". **Effective** 9-27-2010.

P.L. 111-240, §2013(c)(2):

Amended Code Sec. 38(c)(3)(A)(ii)(II) by inserting ", the eligible small business credits," after "the New York Liberty Zone business employee credit". **Effective** 9-27-2010.

P.L. 111-240, §2013(c)(3):

Amended Code Sec. 38(c)(4)(A)(ii)(II) by inserting "the eligible small business credits and" before "the specified credits". **Effective** 9-27-2010.

• 2010, Patient Protection and Affordable Care Act (P.L. 111-148)

P.L. 111-148, §1421(c):

Amended Code Sec. 38(c)(4)(B) by redesignating clauses (vi), (vii), and (viii) as clauses (vii), (viii), and (ix), respectively, and by inserting after clause (v) a new clause (vi). **Effective** for amounts paid or incurred in tax years beginning after 12-31-2009 [**effective** date amended by Act Sec. 10105(e)(4).—CCH].

• 2008, Energy Improvement and Extension Act of 2008 (P.L. 110-343)

P.L. 110-343, Division B, §103(b)(1):

Amended Code Sec. 38(c)(4)(B), as amended by the Housing Assistance Tax Act of 2008 (P.L. 110-289), by redesignating clause (vi) [clauses (v) and (vi)] as clause[s] (vi) and (vii), respectively, and by inserting after clause (iv) a new clause (v). **Effective** for credits determined under Code Sec. 46 in tax years beginning after 10-3-2008 and to carrybacks of such credits.

P.L. 110-343, Division B, §103(b)(2):

Amended Code Sec. 38(c)(4)(B)(vi), as redesignated by Act Sec. 103(b)(1), by striking "section 47 to the extent attributable to" and inserting "section 46 to the extent that such credit is attributable to the rehabilitation credit under section 47, but only with respect to". **Effective** for credits determined under Code Sec. 46 in tax years beginning after 10-3-2008 and to carrybacks of such credits.

• 2008, Tax Extenders and Alternative Minimum Tax Relief Act of 2008 (P.L. 110-343)

P.L. 110-343, Division C, §316(b)(1)-(2):

Amended Code Sec. 38(c)(4)(B), as amended by this Act, by redesignating clauses (v), (vi), and (vii) as clauses (vi), (vii), and (viii), respectively, and by inserting after clause (iv) a new clause (v). **Effective** for credits determined under Code Sec. 45G in tax years beginning after 12-31-2007, and to carrybacks of such credits.

• 2008, Housing Assistance Tax Act of 2008 (P.L. 110-289)

P.L. 110-289, §3022(b):

Amended Code Sec. 38(c)(4)(B) by redesignating clauses (ii) through (iv) as clauses (iii) through (v) and inserting after clause (i) a new clause (ii). **Effective** for credits determined under section 42 of the Internal Revenue Code of 1986 to the extent attributable to buildings placed in service after 12-31-2007.

P.L. 110-289, §3022(c):

Amended Code Sec. 38(c)(4)(B), as amended by Act Sec. 3022(b), by striking "and" at the end of clause (iv), by redesignating clause (v) as clause (vi), and by inserting after clause (iv) a new clause (v). **Effective** for credits determined under section 47 of the Internal Revenue Code of 1986 to the extent attributable to qualified rehabilitation expenditures properly taken into account for periods after 12-31-2007.

• 2007, Small Business and Work Opportunity Tax Act of 2007 (P.L. 110-28)

P.L. 110-28, §8214(a):

Amended Code Sec. 38(c)(4)(B) by striking "and" at the end of clause (i), by inserting a comma at the end of clause (ii), and by adding at the end new clauses (iii) and (iv). **Effective** for credits determined under Code Secs. 45B and 51 in tax years beginning after 12-31-2006, and to carrybacks of such credits.

• 2005, Gulf Opportunity Zone Act of 2005 (P.L. 109-135)

P.L. 109-135, §412(f)(1):

Amended Code Sec. 38(c)(2)(A)(ii)(II) by striking "or the New York Liberty Zone business employee credit or the specified credits" and inserting ", the New York Liberty Zone business employee credit, and the specified credits". **Effective** 12-21-2005.

P.L. 109-135, §412(f)(2):

Amended Code Sec. 38(c)(3)(A)(ii)(II) by striking "or the specified credits" and inserting "and the specified credits". **Effective** 12-21-2005.

P.L. 109-135, §412(f)(3)(A)-(B):

Amended Code Sec. 38(c)(4)(B) by striking "includes" and inserting "means", and by inserting "and" at the end of clause (i). **Effective** 12-21-2005.

• 2004, American Jobs Creation Act of 2004 (P.L. 108-357)

P.L. 108-357, §711(a):

Amended Code Sec. 38(c) by redesignating paragraph (4) as paragraph (5) and by inserting after paragraph (3) a new paragraph (4). **Effective** for tax years ending after 10-22-2004.

P.L. 108-357, §711(b):

Amended Code Sec. 38(c)(2)(A)(ii)(II) and (3)(A)(ii)(II) by inserting "or the specified credits" after "employee credit". **Effective** for tax years ending after 10-22-2004.

• 2002, Job Creation and Worker Assistance Act of 2002 (P.L. 107-147)

P.L. 107-147, §301(b)(1):

Amended Code Sec. 38(c) by redesignating paragraph (3) as paragraph (4) and by inserting after paragraph (2) a new paragraph (3). **Effective** for tax years ending after 12-31-2001.

P.L. 107-147, §301(b)(2):

Amended Code Sec. 38(c)(2)(A)(ii)(II) by inserting "or the New York Liberty Zone business employee credit" after "employment credit". **Effective** for tax years ending after 12-31-2001.

• 1993, Omnibus Budget Reconciliation Act of 1993 (P.L. 103-66)

P.L. 103-66, §13302(c)(1):

Amended Code Sec. 38(c)(2)-(3) by redesignating paragraph (2) as paragraph (3) and by inserting after paragraph (1) new paragraph (2). **Effective** 8-10-93.

P.L. 103-66, §13311 provides:

SEC. 13311. CREDIT FOR CONTRIBUTIONS TO CERTAIN COMMUNITY DEVELOPMENT CORPORATIONS.

(a) IN GENERAL.—For purposes of section 38 of the Internal Revenue Code of 1986, the current year business credit shall include the credit determined under this section.

(b) DETERMINATION OF CREDIT.—The credit determined under this section for each taxable year in the credit period with respect to any qualified CDC contribution made by the taxpayer is an amount equal to 5 percent of such contribution.

(c) CREDIT PERIOD.—For purposes of this section, the credit period with respect to any qualified CDC contribution is the period of 10 taxable years beginning with the taxable year during which such contribution was made.

(d) QUALIFIED CDC CONTRIBUTION.—For purposes of this section—

(1) IN GENERAL.—The term "qualified CDC contribution" means any transfer of cash—

(A) which is made to a selected community development corporation during the 5-year period beginning on the date such corporation was selected for purposes of this section,

(B) the amount of which is available for use by such corporation for at least 10 years,

(C) which is to be used by such corporation for qualified low-income assistance within its operational area, and

(D) which is designated by such corporation for purposes of this section.

(2) LIMITATIONS ON AMOUNT DESIGNATED.—The aggregate amount of contributions to a selected community development corporation which may be designated by such corporation shall not exceed $2,000,000.

(e) SELECTED COMMUNITY DEVELOPMENT CORPORATIONS.—

(1) IN GENERAL.—For purposes of this section, the term "selected community development corporation" means any corporation—

(A) which is described in section 501(c)(3) of such Code and exempt from tax under section 501(a) of such Code,

(B) the principal purposes of which include promoting employment of, and business opportunities for, low-income individuals who are residents of the operational area, and

(C) which is selected by the Secretary of Housing and Urban Development for purposes of this section.

(2) ONLY 20 CORPORATIONS MAY BE SELECTED.—The Secretary of Housing and Urban Development may select 20 corporations for purposes of this section, subject to the availability of eligible corporations. Such selections may be made only before July 1, 1994. At least 8 of the operational areas of the corporations selected must be rural areas (as defined by section 1393(a)(3) of such Code).

(3) OPERATIONAL AREAS MUST HAVE CERTAIN CHARACTERISTICS.—A corporation may be selected for purposes of this section only if its operational area meets the following criteria:

(A) The area meets the size requirements under section 1392(a)(3).

(B) The unemployment rate (as determined by the appropriate available data) is not less than the national unemployment rate.

(C) The median family income of residents of such area does not exceed 80 percent of the median gross income of residents of the jurisdiction of the local government which includes such area.

(f) QUALIFIED LOW-INCOME ASSISTANCE.—For purposes of this section, the term "qualified low-income assistance" means assistance—

(1) which is designed to provide employment of, and business opportunities for, low-income individuals who are residents of the operational area of the community development corporation, and

(2) which is approved by the Secretary of Housing and Urban Development.

• 1990, Omnibus Budget Reconciliation Act of 1990 (P.L. 101-508)

P.L. 101-508, §11813(b)(2)(B) (amended by P.L. 104-188, §1702(e)(4)):

Amended Code Sec. 38(c) by striking paragraph (2) and by redesignating paragraph (3) as paragraph (2). **Effective** for property placed in service after 12-31-90. Prior to amendment, Code Sec. 38(c)(2) read as follows:

(2) REGULAR INVESTMENT TAX CREDIT MAY OFFSET 25 PERCENT OF MINIMUM TAX.—

(A) IN GENERAL.—In the case of a C corporation, the amount determined under paragraph (1)(A) shall be reduced by the lesser of—

(i) the portion of the regular investment tax credit not used against the normal limitation, or

(ii) 25 percent of the taxpayer's tentative minimum tax for the taxable year.

(B) PORTION OF REGULAR INVESTMENT TAX CREDIT NOT USED AGAINST NORMAL LIMIT.—For purposes of subparagraph (A), the portion of the regular investment tax credit for any taxable year not used against the normal limitation is the excess (if any) of—

(i) the portion of the credit under subsection (a) which is attributable to the application of the regular percentage under section 46, over

(ii) the limitation of paragraph (1) (without regard to this paragraph) reduced by the portion of the credit under subsection (a) which is not so attributable.

(C) LIMITATION.—In no event shall this paragraph permit the allowance of a credit which would result in a net chapter 1 tax less than an amount equal to 10 percent of the amount determined under section 55(b)(1)(A) without regard to the alternative tax net operating loss deduction and without regard to the deduction under section 56(h). For purposes of the preceding sentence, the term "net chapter 1 tax" means the sum of the regular tax liability for the taxable year and the tax imposed by section 55 for the taxable year, reduced by the sum of the credits allowable under this part for the taxable year (other than under section 34).

• 1996, Small Business Job Protection Act of 1996 (P.L. 104-188)

P.L. 104-188, §1702(e)(4):

Amended Code Sec. 38(c)(2)(C), as in effect on the day before the date of the enactment of the Revenue Reconciliation Act of 1990 (P.L. 101-508), by inserting before the period at the end of the first sentence "and without regard to the deduction under section 56(h)". **Effective** as if included in the provision of P.L. 101-508 to which such amendment relates.

• 1990, Omnibus Budget Reconciliation Act of 1990 (P.L. 101-508)

P.L. 101-508, §11813(b)(2)(C)(i)-(ii):

Amended Code Sec. 38(c)(2)(C) (as redesignated by Act Sec. 11813(b)(2)(B)) by inserting "(as in effect on the day before the date of the enactment of the Revenue Reconciliation Act of 1990)" after "46(e)(1)", and by inserting "(as so in effect)" after "46(e)(2)". **Effective** for property placed in service after 12-31-90.

• 1988, Technical and Miscellaneous Revenue Act of 1988 (P.L. 100-647)

P.L. 100-647, §1007(g)(2)(A):

Amended so much of Code Sec. 38(c) as precedes paragraph (4). **Effective** as if included in the provisions of P.L. 99-514 to which it relates. Prior to amendment, so much of Code Sec. 38(c) as precedes paragraph (4) read as follows:

(c) LIMITATION BASED ON AMOUNT OF TAX.—

(1) IN GENERAL.—The credit allowed under subsection (a) for any taxable year shall not exceed the lesser of—

(A) the allowable portion of the taxpayer's net regular tax liability for the taxable year, or

(B) the excess (if any) of the taxpayer's net regular tax liability for the taxable year over the tentative minimum tax for the taxable year.

(2) ALLOWABLE PORTION OF NET REGULAR TAX LIABILITY.—For purposes of this subsection, the allowable portion of the taxpayer's net regular tax liability for the taxable year is the sum of—

(A) so much of the taxpayer's net regular tax liability for the taxable year as does not exceed $25,000, plus

(B) 75 percent of so much of the taxpayer's net regular tax liability for the taxable year as exceeds $25,000.

For purposes of the preceding sentence, the term "net regular tax liability" means the regular tax liability reduced by the sum of the credits allowable under subparts A and B of this part.

(3) REGULAR INVESTMENT TAX CREDIT MAY OFFSET 25 PERCENT OF MINIMUM TAX.—In the case of any C corporation, to the extent the credit under subsection (a) is attributable to the application of the regular percentage under section 46, the limitation of paragraph (1) shall be the greater of—

(A) the lesser of—

(i) the allowable portion of the taxpayer's net regular tax liability for the taxable year, or

(ii) the excess (if any) of the taxpayer's net regular tax liability for the taxable year over 75 percent of the tentative minimum tax for the taxable year, or

(B) 25 percent of the taxpayer's tentative minimum tax for the year.

In no event shall this paragraph permit the allowance of a credit which (in combination with the alternative tax net operating loss deduction and the alternative minimum tax foreign tax credit) would reduce the tax payable under section 55 below an amount equal to 10 percent of the amount which would be determined under section 55(b) without regard to the alternative tax net operating tax deduction and the alternative minimum tax foreign tax credit.

P.L. 100-647, §1007(g)(2)(B)(i)-(ii):

Amended Code Sec. 38(c) by redesignating paragraph (4) as paragraph (3), and by striking out "subparagraphs (A) and (B) of paragraph (1)" each place it appears in such paragraph and inserting in lieu thereof "subparagraph (B) of paragraph (1)". **Effective** as if included in the provision of P.L. 99-514 to which it relates.

[Sec. 38(d)]

(d) ORDERING RULES.—For purposes of any provision of this title where it is necessary to ascertain the extent to which the credits determined under any section referred to in subsection (b) are used in a taxable year or as a carryback or carryforward—

(1) IN GENERAL.—The order in which such credits are used shall be determined on the basis of the order in which they are listed in subsection (b) as of the close of the taxable year in which the credit is used.

(2) COMPONENTS OF INVESTMENT CREDIT.—The order in which the credits listed in section 46 are used shall be determined on the basis of the order in which such credits are listed in section 46 as of the close of the taxable year in which the credit is used.

(3) CREDITS NO LONGER LISTED.—For purposes of this subsection—

(A) the credit allowable by section 40, as in effect on the day before the date of the enactment of the Tax Reform Act of 1984, (relating to expenses of work incentive programs) and the credit allowable by section 41(a), as in effect on the day before the date of the enactment of the Tax Reform Act of 1986, (relating to employee stock ownership credit) shall be treated as referred to in that order after the last paragraph of subsection (b), and

(B) the credit determined under section 46—

(i) to the extent attributable to the employee plan percentage (as defined in section 46(a)(2)(E) as in effect on the day before the date of the enactment of the Tax Reform Act of 1984) shall be treated as a credit listed after paragraph (1) of section 46, and

(ii) to the extent attributable to the regular percentage (as defined in section 46(b)(1) as in effect on the day before the date of the enactment of the Revenue Reconciliation Act of 1990) shall be treated as the first credit listed in section 46.

Amendments

• 1990, Omnibus Budget Reconciliation Act of 1990 (P.L. 101-508)

P.L. 101-508, §11813(b)(2)(D)(i)-(iii):

Amended Code Sec. 38(d) by striking "sections 46(f), 47(a), 196(a), and any other provision" and inserting "any provision", by amending paragraph (2), and by amending subparagraph (B) of paragraph (3). **Effective** for property placed in service after 12-31-90. Prior to amendment, Code Sec. 38(d)(2) and (3)(B) read as follows:

(2) COMPONENTS OF INVESTMENT CREDIT.—The order in which credits attributable to a percentage referred to in section 46(a) are used shall be determined on the basis of the order in which such percentages are listed in section 46(a) as of the close of the taxable year in which the credit is used.

(3) CREDITS NO LONGER LISTED.—For purposes of this subsection—

* * *

(B) the employee plan percentage (as defined in section 46(a)(2)(E), as in effect on the day before the date of the enactment of the Tax Reform Act of 1984) shall be treated as referred to after section 46(a)(2).

• 1988, Technical and Miscellaneous Revenue Act of 1988 (P.L. 100-647)

P.L. 100-647, §1002(e)(8)(A):

Amended Code Sec. 38(d). **Effective** for tax years beginning after 12-31-83, and to carrybacks from such years. Prior to amendment, Code Sec. 38(d) read as follows:

(d) SPECIAL RULES FOR CERTAIN REGULATED COMPANIES.—In the case of any taxpayer to which section 46(f) applies, for purposes of sections 46(f), 47(a), 196(a) and any other provision of this title where it is necessary to ascertain the extent to which the credits determined under section 40(a), 41(a), 42(a), 46(a), or 51(a) are used in a taxable year or as a carryback or carryforward, the order in which such credits are used shall be determined on the basis of the order in which they are listed in subsection (b).

• 1986, Tax Reform Act of 1986 (P.L. 99-514)

P.L. 99-514, §221(a):

Amended Code Sec. 38(c)(1)(B) by striking out "85 percent" and inserting in lieu thereof "75 percent". **Effective** for tax years beginning after 12-31-85.

P.L. 99-514, §231(d)(1):

Amended Code Sec. 38(b), as amended by this Act, by striking out "plus" at the end of paragraph (2), by striking out the period at the end of paragraph (3) and inserting in lieu thereof ", plus", and by adding at the end thereof new paragraph (4). **Effective** for tax years beginning after 12-31-85.

P.L. 99-514, §231(d)(3)(B):

Amended Code Sec. 38(d), as amended by this Act, by inserting "41(a)," after "40(a),". **Effective** for tax years beginning after 12-31-85.

P.L. 99-514, §252(b)(1):

Amended Code Sec. 38(b), as amended by this Act, by striking out "plus" at the end of paragraph (3), by striking out the period at the end of paragraph (4) and inserting in lieu thereof "plus", and by adding at the end thereof new paragraph (5). **Effective** for buildings placed in service after 12-31-86, in tax years ending after such date.

P.L. 99-514, §252(b)(2):

Amended Code Sec. 38(d) by inserting "42(a)," before "46(a)". **Effective** for buildings placed in service after 12-31-86, in tax years ending after such date.

P.L. 99-514, §701(c)(4):

Amended Code Sec. 38(c), as amended by Act Sec. 631(a), by redesignating paragraph (3) as paragraph (4), and by striking out paragraphs (1) and (2) and inserting in lieu thereof new paragraphs (1)-(3). For the **effective** dates, see Act Sec. 701(f), as amended by P.L. 100-647, §1007(f)(2)-(3), below. Prior to amendment, Code Sec. 38(c)(1) and (2) read as follows:

(1) IN GENERAL.—The credit allowed under subsection (a) for any taxable year shall not exceed the sum of—

(A) so much of the taxpayer's net tax liability for the taxable year as does not exceed $25,000, plus

(B) 75 percent of so much of the taxpayer's net tax liability for the taxable year as exceeds $25,000.

(2) NET TAX LIABILITY.—For purposes of paragraph (1), the term "net tax liability" means the tax liability (as defined in section 26(b)), reduced by the sum of the credits allowable under subparts A and B of this part.

P.L. 99-514, §701(f), as amended by P.L. 100-647, §1007(f)(2)-(3), provides:

(f) EFFECTIVE DATES.—

(1) IN GENERAL.—Except as otherwise provided in this subsection, the amendments made by this section shall apply to taxable years beginning after December 31, 1986.

(2) ADJUSTMENT OF NET OPERATING LOSS.—

(A) INDIVIDUALS.—In the case of a net operating loss of an individual for a taxable year beginning after December 31, 1982, and before January 1, 1987, for purposes of determining the amount of such loss which may be carried to a taxable year beginning after December 31, 1986, for purposes of the minimum tax, such loss shall be adjusted in the manner provided in section 55(d)(2) of th Internal Revenue Code of 1954 as in effect on the day before the date of the enactment of this Act.

(B) CORPORATIONS.—If the minimum tax of a corporation was deferred under section 56(b) of the Internal Revenue Code of 1954 (as in effect on the day before the date of the enactment of this Act) for any taxable year beginning before January 1, 1987, and the amount of such tax has not been paid for any taxable year beginning before January 1, 1987, the amount of the net operating loss carryovers of such corporation which may be carried to taxable years beginning after December 31, 1986, for purposes of the minimum tax shall be reduced by the amount of tax preferences a tax on which was so deferred.

(3) INSTALLMENT SALES.—Section 56(a)(6) of the Internal Revenue Code of 1986 (as amended by this section) shall not apply to any disposition to which the amendments made by section 811 of this Act (relating to allocation of dealer's indebtedness to installment obligations) do not apply by reason of section 811(c)(2) of this Act.

(4) EXCEPTION FOR CHARITABLE CONTRIBUTIONS BEFORE AUGUST 16, 1986.—Section 57(a)(6) of the Internal Revenue Code of 1986 (as amended by this section) shall not apply to any deduction attributable to contributions made before August 16, 1986.

(5) BOOK INCOME.—

(A) IN GENERAL.—In the case of a corporation to which this paragraph applies, the amount of any increase for any taxable year under section 56(c)(1)(A) of the Internal Revenue Code of 1986 (as added by this section) shall be reduced (but not below zero) by the excess (if any) of—

(i) 50 percent of the excess of taxable income for the 5-taxable year period ending with the taxable year preceding the 1st taxable year to which such section applies over the adjusted net book income for such period, over

(ii) the aggregate amounts taken into account under this paragraph for preceding taxable years.

(B) TAXPAYER TO WHOM PARAGRAPH APPLIES.—This paragraph applies to a taxpayer which was incorporated in Delaware on May 31, 1912.

(C) TERMS.—Any term used in this paragraph which is used in section 56 of such Code (as so added) shall have the same meaning as when used in such section.

(6) CERTAIN PUBLIC UTILITY [UTILITIES].—

(A) In the case of investment tax credits described in subparagraph (B) or (C), subsection 38(c)(3)(A)(ii) of the Internal Revenue Code of 1986 shall be applied by substituting "25 percent" for "75 percent", and section 38(c)(3)(B) of the Internal Revenue Code of 1986 shall be applied by substituting "75 percent" for "25 percent".

(B) If, on September 25, 1985, a regulated electric utility owned an undivided interest, within the range of 1,111 and 1,149 in the "maximum dependable capacity, net, megawatts electric" of an electric generating unit located in Illinois or Mississippi for which a binding written contract was in effect on December 31, 1980, then any investment tax credit with respect to such unit shall be described in this subparagraph. The aggregate amount of investment tax credits with respect to the unit in Mississippi allowed solely by reason of being described in this subparagraph shall not exceed $141,000,000.

(C) If, on September 25, 1985, a regulated electric utility owned an undivided interest, within the range of 1,104 and 1,111, in the "maximum dependable capacity, net, megawatts electric" of an electric generating unit located in Louisiana for which a binding written contract was in effect on December 31, 1980, then any investment tax credit of such electric utility shall be described in this subparagraph. The aggregate amount of investment tax credits allowed solely by reason of being described by this subparagraph shall not exceed $20,000,000.

(7) AGREEMENT VESSEL DEPRECIATION ADJUSTMENT.—

(A) For purposes of Part VI of subchapter A of chapter 1 of the Internal Revenue Code of 1986, in the case of a qualified taxpayer alternative minimum taxable income for the taxable year shall be reduced by an amount equal to the agreement vessel depreciation adjustment.

(B) For purposes of this paragraph, the agreement vessel depreciation adjustment shall be an amount equal to the depreciation deduction that would have been allowable for such year under section 167 of such Code with respect to agreement vessels placed in service before January 1, 1987, if the basis of such vessels had not been reduced under section 607 of the Merchant Marine Act of 1936, as amended, and if depreciation with respect to such vessel had been computed using the 25-year straight-line method. The aggregate amount by which basis of a qualified taxpayer is treated as not reduced by reason of this subparagraph shall not exceed $100,000,000.

(C) For purposes of this paragraph, the term "qualified taxpayer" means a parent corporation incorporated in the State of Delaware on December 1, 1972, and engaged in water transportation, and includes any other corporation which is a member of the affiliated group of which the parent corporation is the common parent. No taxpayer shall be treated as a qualified corporation for any taxable year beginning after December 31, 1991.

P.L. 99-514, §1171(b)(1):

Amended Code Sec. 38(b) by striking out paragraph (4), by striking out ", plus" at the end of paragraph (3) and inserting in lieu thereof a period, and by inserting "plus" at the end of paragraph (2). **Effective** for compensation paid or accrued after 12-31-86, in tax years ending after such date. However, for an exception, see Act Sec. 1171(c)(2) following Code Sec. 38(d). Prior to amendment, paragraph (4) read as follows:

(4) the employee stock ownership credit determined under section 41(a).

P.L. 99-514, §1171(b)(2)(A)-(B):

Amended Code Sec. 38(d), as amended by Act Sec. 231(d)(3)(B), by striking out "196(a), and 404(i)" and inserting in lieu thereof "and 196(a)" and by striking out "41(a),". **Effective** for compensation paid or accrued after 12-31-86, in tax years ending after such date. However, for an exception, see Act Sec. 1171(c)(2), below.

P.L. 99-514, §1171(c)(2), provides:

(2) Sections 404(i) and 6699 in Continue to Apply to Pre-1987 Credits.—The provisions of sections 404(i) and 6699 of the Internal Revenue Code of 1986 shall continue to apply with respect to credits under section 41 of such Code attributable to compensation paid or accrued before January 1, 1987 (or under section 38 of such Code with respect to qualified investment before January 1, 1983).

• 1984, Deficit Reduction Act of 1984 (P.L. 98-369)

P.L. 98-369, §473:

Added Code Sec. 38. **Effective** for tax years beginning after 12-31-83, and to carrybacks from such years.

P.L. 98-369, §612(e)(1):

Amended Code Sec. 38(c)(2), as added by Act Sec. 473, by striking out "section 25(b)" and inserting in lieu thereof "section 26(b)". **Effective** for interest paid or accrued after 12-31-84, on indebtedness incurred after 12-31-84, and to elections under section 25(c)(2)(A)(ii) of the Internal Revenue Code of 1954 (as added by this Act) for calendar years after 1983.

P.L. 98-369, §474(m)(1):

Repealed former Code Sec. 38. **Effective** for tax years beginning after 12-31-83, and to carrybacks from such years. Prior to amendment, Code Sec. 38 read as follows:

SEC. 38. INVESTMENT IN CERTAIN DEPRECIABLE PROPERTY.

(a) GENERAL RULE.—There shall be allowed, as a credit against the tax imposed by this chapter, the amount determined under subpart B of this part.

(b) REGULATIONS.—The Secretary shall prescribe such regulations as may be necessary to carry out the purposes of this section and subpart B.

• 1962, Revenue Act of 1962 (P.L. 87-834)

P.L. 87-834, §2:

Amended part IV of subchapter A of chapter 1 by redesignating Sec. 38 as Sec. 39 and by inserting after Sec. 37 a new Sec. 38. **Effective** for tax years ending after 12-31-61.

[Sec. 39]

SEC. 39. CARRYBACK AND CARRYFORWARD OF UNUSED CREDITS.

[Sec. 39(a)]

(a) IN GENERAL.—

(1) 1-YEAR CARRYBACK AND 20-YEAR CARRYFORWARD.—If the sum of the business credit carryforwards to the taxable year plus the amount of the current year business credit for the taxable year exceeds the amount of the limitation imposed by subsection (c) of section 38 for such taxable year (hereinafter in this section referred to as the "unused credit year"), such excess (to the extent attributable to the amount of the current year business credit) shall be—

(A) a business credit carryback to the taxable year preceding the unused credit year, and

(B) a business credit carryforward to each of the 20 taxable years following the unused credit year,

and, subject to the limitations imposed by subsections (b) and (c), shall be taken into account under the provisions of section 38(a) in the manner provided in section 38(a).

(2) AMOUNT CARRIED TO EACH YEAR.—

(A) ENTIRE AMOUNT CARRIED TO FIRST YEAR.—The entire amount of the unused credit for an unused credit year shall be carried to the earliest of the 21 taxable years to which (by reason of paragraph (1)) such credit may be carried.

(B) AMOUNT CARRIED TO OTHER 20 YEARS.—The amount of the unused credit for the unused credit year shall be carried to each of the other 20 taxable years to the extent that such unused credit may not be taken into account under section 38(a) for a prior taxable year because of the limitations of subsections (b) and (c).

(3) 5-YEAR CARRYBACK FOR MARGINAL OIL AND GAS WELL PRODUCTION CREDIT.—Notwithstanding subsection (d), in the case of the marginal oil and gas well production credit—

(A) this section shall be applied separately from the business credit (other than the marginal oil and gas well production credit) or the eligible small business credits,

(B) paragraph (1) shall be applied by substituting "each of the 5 taxable years" for "the taxable year" in subparagraph (A) thereof, and

(C) paragraph (2) shall be applied—

(i) by substituting "25 taxable years" for "21 taxable years" in subparagraph (A) thereof, and

(ii) by substituting "24 taxable years" for "20 taxable years" in subparagraph (B) thereof.

(4) 5-YEAR CARRYBACK FOR ELIGIBLE SMALL BUSINESS CREDITS.—

(A) IN GENERAL.—Notwithstanding subsection (d), in the case of eligible small business credits determined in the first taxable year of the taxpayer beginning in 2010—

(i) paragraph (1) shall be applied by substituting "each of the 5 taxable years" for "the taxable year" in subparagraph (A) thereof, and

(ii) paragraph (2) shall be applied—

(I) by substituting "25 taxable years" for "21 taxable years" in subparagraph (A) thereof, and

(II) by substituting "24 taxable years" for "20 taxable years" in subparagraph (B) thereof.

(B) ELIGIBLE SMALL BUSINESS CREDITS.—For purposes of this subsection, the term "eligible small business credits" has the meaning given such term by section 38(c)(5)(B).

Amendments

• 2010, Creating Small Business Jobs Act of 2010 (P.L. 111-240)

P.L. 111-240, §2012(a):

Amended Code Sec. 39(a) by adding at the end a new paragraph (4). **Effective** for credits determined in tax years beginning after 12-31-2009.

P.L. 111-240, §2012(b):

Amended Code Sec. 39(a)(3)(A) by inserting "or the eligible small business credits" after "credit)". **Effective** for credits determined in tax years beginning after 12-31-2009.

• 2005, Gulf Opportunity Zone Act of 2005 (P.L. 109-135)

P.L. 109-135, §412(g)(1):

Amended Code Sec. 39(a)(1)(A) by striking "each of the 1 taxable years" and inserting "the taxable year". **Effective** 12-21-2005.

P.L. 109-135, §412(g)(2):

Amended Code Sec. 39(a)(3)(B). **Effective** 12-21-2005. Prior to amendment, Code Sec. 39(a)(3)(B) read as follows:

(B) paragraph (1) shall be applied by substituting "5 taxable years" for "1 taxable years" in subparagraph (A) thereof, and

• 2004, American Jobs Creation Act of 2004 (P.L. 108-357)

P.L. 108-357, §341(c):

Amended Code Sec. 39(a) by adding at the end a new paragraph (3). **Effective** for production in tax years beginning after 12-31-2004.

• 1997, Taxpayer Relief Act of 1997 (P.L. 105-34)

P.L. 105-34, §1083(a)(1):

Amended Code Sec. 39(a)(1) by striking "3" each place it appears and inserting "1" and by striking "15" each place it appears and inserting "20". **Effective** for credits arising in tax years beginning after 12-31-97.

P.L. 105-34, §1083(a)(2), as amended by P.L. 105-206, §6010(n)(1)-(2):

Amended Code Sec. 39(a)(2) by striking "18" each place it appears and inserting "21" and by striking "17" each place it appears and inserting "20". **Effective** for credits arising in tax years beginning after 12-31-97.

[Sec. 39(b)]

(b) LIMITATION ON CARRYBACKS.—The amount of the unused credit which may be taken into account under section 38(a)(3) for any preceding taxable year shall not exceed the amount by which the limitation imposed by section 38(c) for such taxable year exceeds the sum of—

(1) the amounts determined under paragraphs (1) and (2) of section 38(a) for such taxable year, plus

(2) the amounts which (by reason of this section) are carried back to such taxable year and are attributable to taxable years preceding the unused credit year.

[Sec. 39(c)]

(c) LIMITATION ON CARRYFORWARDS.—The amount of the unused credit which may be taken into account under section 38(a)(1) for any succeeding taxable year shall not exceed the amount by which the limitation imposed by section 38(c) for such taxable year exceeds the sum of the amounts which, by reason of this section, are carried to such taxable year and are attributable to taxable years preceding the unused credit year.

[Sec. 39(d)]

(d) TRANSITIONAL RULE.—No portion of the unused business credit for any taxable year which is attributable to a credit specified in section 38(b) or any portion thereof may be carried back to any taxable year before the first taxable year for which such specified credit or such portion is allowable (without regard to subsection (a)).

Amendments

• 2006, Pension Protection Act of 2006 (P.L. 109-280)

P.L. 109-280, §811, provides:

SEC. 811. PENSIONS AND INDIVIDUAL RETIREMENT ARRANGEMENT PROVISIONS OF ECONOMIC GROWTH AND TAX RELIEF RECONCILIATION ACT OF 2001 MADE PERMANENT.

Title IX of the Economic Growth and Tax Relief Reconciliation Act of 2001 [P.L. 107-16] shall not apply to the provisions of, and amendments made by, subtitles A through F of title VI [§§601-666]of such Act (relating to pension and individual retirement arrangement provisions).

• 2004, American Jobs Creation Act of 2004 (P.L. 108-357)

P.L. 108-357, §245(b)(1):

Amended Code Sec. 39(d). **Effective** with respect to tax years ending after 12-31-2003. Prior to amendment, Code Sec. 39(d) read as follows:

(d) TRANSITIONAL RULES.—

(1) NO CARRYBACK OF ENHANCED OIL RECOVERY CREDIT BEFORE 1991.— No portion of the unused business credit for any taxable year which is attributable to the credit determined under section 43(a) (relating to enhanced oil recovery credit) may be carried to a taxable year beginning before January 1, 1991.

(2) NO CARRYBACK OF SECTION 44 CREDIT BEFORE ENACTMENT.—No portion of the unused business credit for any taxable year which is attributable to the disabled access credit determined under section 44 may be carried to a taxable year ending before the date of the enactment of section 44.

(3) NO CARRYBACK OF RENEWABLE ELECTRICITY PRODUCTION CREDIT BEFORE EFFECTIVE DATE.—No portion of the unused business credit for any taxable year which is attributable to the credit determined under section 45 (relating to electricity produced from certain renewable resources) may be carried back to any taxable year ending before January 1, 1993 (before January 1, 1994, to the extent such credit is attributable to wind as a qualified energy resource).

(4) EMPOWERMENT ZONE EMPLOYMENT CREDIT.—No portion of the unused business credit which is attributable to the credit determined under section 1396 (relating to empowerment zone employment credit) may be carried to any taxable year ending before January 1, 1994.

(5) NO CARRYBACK OF SECTION 45A CREDIT BEFORE ENACTMENT.—No portion of the unused business credit for any taxable year which is attributable to the Indian employment credit determined under section 45A may be carried to a taxable year ending before the date of the enactment of section 45A.

(6) NO CARRYBACK OF SECTION 45B CREDIT BEFORE ENACTMENT.—No portion of the unused business credit for any taxable year which is attributable to the employer social security credit determined under section 45B may be carried back to a taxable year ending before the date of the enactment of section 45B.

(7) NO CARRYBACK OF SECTION 45C CREDIT BEFORE JULY 1, 1996.—No portion of the unused business credit for any taxable year which is attributable to the orphan drug credit determined under section 45C may be carried back to a taxable year ending before July 1, 1996.

(8) NO CARRYBACK OF DC ZONE CREDITS BEFORE EFFECTIVE DATE.—No portion of the unused business credit for any taxable year which is attributable to the credits allowable under subchapter U by reason of section 1400 may be car-

ried back to a taxable year ending before the date of the enactment of section 1400.

(9) NO CARRYBACK OF NEW MARKETS TAX CREDIT BEFORE JANUARY 1, 2001.—No portion of the unused business credit for any taxable year which is attributable to the credit under section 45D may be carried back to a taxable year ending before January 1, 2001.

(10) NO CARRYBACK OF SMALL EMPLOYER PENSION PLAN STARTUP COST CREDIT BEFORE JANUARY 1, 2002.—No portion of the unused business credit for any taxable year which is attributable to the small employer pension plan startup cost credit determined under section 45E may be carried back to a taxable year beginning before January 1, 2002.

• 2001, Economic Growth and Tax Relief Reconciliation Act of 2001 (P.L. 107-16)

P.L. 107-16, §619(c)(1):

Amended Code Sec. 39(d) by adding at the end a new paragraph (10). **Effective** for costs paid or incurred in tax years beginning after 12-31-2001, with respect to qualified employer plans first effective after such date [**effective** date amended by P.L. 107-147, §411(n)(2)].

P.L. 107-16, §901(a)-(b), provides [but see P.L. 109-280, §811, above]:

SEC. 901. SUNSET OF PROVISIONS OF ACT.

(a) IN GENERAL.—All provisions of, and amendments made by, this Act shall not apply—

(1) to taxable, plan, or limitation years beginning after December 31, 2010, or

(2) in the case of title V, to estates of decedents dying, gifts made, or generation skipping transfers, after December 31, 2010.

(b) APPLICATION OF CERTAIN LAWS.—The Internal Revenue Code of 1986 and the Employee Retirement Income Security Act of 1974 shall be applied and administered to years, estates, gifts, and transfers described in subsection (a) as if the provisions and amendments described in subsection (a) had never been enacted.

• 2000, Community Renewal Tax Relief Act of 2000 (P.L. 106-554)

P.L. 106-554, §121(b)(2):

Amended Code Sec. 39(d) by adding at the end a new paragraph (9). **Effective** for investments made after 12-31-2000.

• 1997, Taxpayer Relief Act of 1997 (P.L. 105-34)

P.L. 105-34, §701(b)(1):

Amended Code Sec. 39(d) by adding a new paragraph (8). **Effective** 8-5-97.

• 1996, Small Business Job Protection Act of 1996 (P.L. 104-188)

P.L. 104-188, §1205(c):

Amended Code Sec. 39(d) by adding at the end a new paragraph (7). **Effective** for amounts paid or incurred in tax years ending after 6-30-96.

P.L. 104-188, §1703(n)(1)(A)-(B):

Amended Code Sec. 39(d) by striking "45" in the heading of paragraph (5) and inserting "45A", and striking "45" in the heading of paragraph (6) and inserting "45B". **Effective** as if included in the provision of P.L. 103-66 to which such amendment relates.

• 1993, Omnibus Budget Reconciliation Act of 1993 (P.L. 103-66)

P.L. 103-66, §13302(a)(2):

Amended Code Sec. 39(d) by adding new paragraph (4). **Effective** 8-10-93.

P.L. 103-66, §13322(d):

Amended Code Sec. 39(d) by adding new paragraph (5). **Effective** for wages paid or incurred after 12-31-93.

P.L. 103-66, §13443(b)(2):

Amended Code Sec. 39(d) by adding new paragraph (6). **Effective** with respect to taxes paid after 12-31-93, with respect to services performed before, on, or after such date (as amended by P.L. 104-188, §1112(a)(2)).

• 1992, Energy Policy Act of 1992 (P.L. 102-486)

P.L. 102-486, §1914(c):

Amended Code Sec. 39(d) by redesignating the paragraph added by P.L. 101-508, §11511(b)(2), as paragraph (1), by redesignating the paragraph added by P.L. 101-508, §11611(b)(2), as paragraph (2), and by adding at the end thereof new paragraph (3). **Effective** for tax years ending after 12-31-92.

• 1990, Omnibus Budget Reconciliation Act of 1990 (P.L. 101-508)

P.L. 101-508, §11511(b)(2):

Amended Code Sec. 39(d) by adding at the end thereof new paragraph (5) [(1)]. **Effective** for costs paid or incurred in tax years beginning after 12-31-90.

P.L. 101-508, §11611(b)(2):

Amended Code Sec. 39(d) by adding at the end thereof a new paragraph (5) [(2)]. **Effective** for expenditures paid or incurred after 11-5-90.

P.L. 101-508, §11801(a)(2):

Repealed Code Sec. 39(d)(1), (2), (3), and (4). **Effective** 11-5-90. Prior to repeal, Code Sec. 39(d)(1), (2), (3), and (4) read as follows:

(1) CARRYFORWARDS.—

(A) IN GENERAL.—Any carryforward from an unused credit year under section 46, 50A, 53, 44E, or 44G (as in effect before the enactment of the Tax Reform Act of 1984) which has not expired before the beginning of the first taxable year beginning after December 31, 1983, shall be aggregated with other such carryforwards from such unused credit year and shall be a business credit carryforward to each taxable year beginning after December 31, 1983, which is 1 of the first 15 taxable years after such unused credit year.

(B) AMOUNT CARRIED FORWARD.—The amount carried forward under subparagraph (A) to any taxable year shall be properly reduced for any amount allowable as a credit with respect to such carryforward for any taxable year before the year to which it is being carried.

(2) CARRYBACKS.—In determining the amount allowable as a credit for any taxable year beginning before January 1, 1984, as the result of the carryback of a general business tax credit from a taxable year beginning after December 31, 1983—

(A) paragraph (1) of subsection (b) shall be applied as if it read as follows:

"(1) the sum of the credits allowable for such taxable year under sections 38, 40, 44B, 44E, and 44G (as in effect before enactment of the Tax Reform Act of 1984), plus", and

(B) for purposes of section 38(c) the net tax liability for such taxable year shall be the tax liability (as defined in section 26(b)) reduced by the sum of the credits allowable for such taxable year under sections 33, 37, 41, 44A, 44C, 44D, 44F, and 44H (as so in effect).

(3) SIMILAR RULES FOR RESEARCH CREDIT.—Rules similar to the rules of paragraphs (1) and (2) shall apply to the credit allowable under section 30 (as in effect before the date of the enactment of the Tax Reform Act of 1986) except that—

(A) "December 31, 1985" shall be substituted for "December 31, 1983" each place it appears, and

(B) "January 1, 1986" shall be substituted for "January 1, 1984".

(4) NO CARRYBACK OF LOW-INCOME HOUSING CREDIT BEFORE 1987.—No portion of the unused business credit for any taxable year which is attributable to the credit determined under section 42 (relating to low-income housing credit) may be carried back to a taxable year ending before January 1, 1987.

P.L. 101-508, §11821(b), provides:

(b) SAVINGS PROVISION.—If—

(1) any provision amended or repealed by this part applied to—

(A) any transaction occurring before the date of the enactment of this Act,

(B) any property acquired before such date of enactment, or

(C) any item of income, loss, deduction, or credit taken into account before such date of enactment, and

(2) the treatment of such transaction, property, or item under such provision would (without regard to the amendments made by this part) affect liability for tax for periods ending after such date of enactment,

nothing in the amendments made by this part shall be construed to affect the treatment of such transaction, property, or item for purposes of determining liability for tax for periods ending after such date of enactment.

• 1988, Technical and Miscellaneous Revenue Act of 1988 (P.L. 100-647)

P.L. 100-647, §1002(l)(26):

Amended Code Sec. 39(d) by adding at the end thereof new paragraph (4). **Effective** as if included in the provision of P.L. 99-514 to which it relates.

• 1986, Tax Reform Act of 1986 (P.L. 99-514)

P.L. 99-514, §231(d)(3)(C)(i):

Amended Code Sec. 39(d) by adding at the end thereof new paragraph (3). **Effective** for tax years beginning after 12-31-85.

P.L. 99-514, §1846(1) and (2):

Amended Code Sec. 39(d) by striking out "or 44G" in paragraph (1)(A) and inserting in lieu thereof "or 44G (as in effect before the enactment of the Tax Reform Act of 1984)", and by striking out "as so defined in section 25(b)" in paragraph (2)(B) and inserting in lieu thereof "as defined in section 26(b)". **Effective** as if included in the provision of P.L. 98-369 to which such amendment relates.

• 1984, Deficit Reduction Act of 1984 (P.L. 98-369)

P.L. 98-369, §473:

Added Code Sec. 39. **Effective** for tax years beginning after 12-31-83, and to carrybacks from such years.

[Sec. 40]

SEC. 40. ALCOHOL, etc., USED AS FUEL.

[Sec. 40(a)]

(a) GENERAL RULE.—For purposes of section 38, the alcohol fuels credit determined under this section for the taxable year is an amount equal to the sum of—

(1) the alcohol mixture credit,

(2) the alcohol credit,

(3) in the case of an eligible small ethanol producer, the small ethanol producer credit, plus

(4) the cellulosic biofuel producer credit.

Amendments

• 2008, Heartland, Habitat, Harvest, and Horticulture Act of 2008 (P.L. 110-246)

P.L. 110-246, §15321(a):

Amended Code Sec. 40(a) by striking "plus" at the end of paragraph (1), by striking "plus" at the end of paragraph (2), by striking the period at the end of paragraph (3) and inserting ", plus", and by adding at the end a new paragraph (4). **Effective** for fuel produced after 12-31-2008.

P.L. 110-246, §15321(b)(3)(B):

Amended the heading of Code Sec. 40 by inserting ", etc.," after "Alcohol". **Effective** for fuel produced after 12-31-2008.

• 1990, Omnibus Budget Reconciliation Act of 1990 (P.L. 101-508)

P.L. 101-508, §11502(a):

Amended Code Sec. 40(a) by striking the period at the end of paragraph (2) and inserting ", plus", and by adding at the end thereof new paragraph (3). **Effective** for alcohol produced, and sold or used, in tax years beginning after 12-31-90.

[Sec. 40(b)]

(b) DEFINITION OF ALCOHOL MIXTURE CREDIT, ALCOHOL CREDIT, AND SMALL ETHANOL PRODUCER CREDIT.—For purposes of this section, and except as provided in subsection (h)—

(1) ALCOHOL MIXTURE CREDIT.—

(A) IN GENERAL.—The alcohol mixture credit of any taxpayer for any taxable year is 60 cents for each gallon of alcohol used by the taxpayer in the production of a qualified mixture.

(B) QUALIFIED MIXTURE.—The term "qualified mixture" means a mixture of alcohol and gasoline or of alcohol and a special fuel which—

(i) is sold by the taxpayer producing such mixture to any person for use as a fuel, or

(ii) is used as a fuel by the taxpayer producing such mixture.

(C) SALE OR USE MUST BE IN TRADE OR BUSINESS, ETC.—Alcohol used in the production of a qualified mixture shall be taken into account—

(i) only if the sale or use described in subparagraph (B) is in a trade or business of the taxpayer, and

(ii) for the taxable year in which such sale or use occurs.

(D) CASUAL OFF-FARM PRODUCTION NOT ELIGIBLE.—No credit shall be allowed under this section with respect to any casual off-farm production of a qualified mixture.

(2) ALCOHOL CREDIT.—

(A) IN GENERAL.—The alcohol credit of any taxpayer for any taxable year is 60 cents for each gallon of alcohol which is not in a mixture with gasoline or a special fuel (other than any denaturant) and which during the taxable year—

(i) is used by the taxpayer as a fuel in a trade or business, or

(ii) is sold by the taxpayer at retail to a person and placed in the fuel tank of such person's vehicle.

(B) USER CREDIT NOT TO APPLY TO ALCOHOL SOLD AT RETAIL.—No credit shall be allowed under subparagraph (A)(i) with respect to any alcohol which was sold in a retail sale described in subparagraph (A)(ii).

(3) SMALLER CREDIT FOR LOWER PROOF ALCOHOL.—In the case of any alcohol with a proof which is at least 150 but less than 190, paragraphs (1)(A) and (2)(A) shall be applied by substituting "45 cents" for "60 cents".

(4) SMALL ETHANOL PRODUCER CREDIT.—

(A) IN GENERAL.—The small ethanol producer credit of any eligible small ethanol producer for any taxable year is 10 cents for each gallon of qualified ethanol fuel production of such producer.

(B) QUALIFIED ETHANOL FUEL PRODUCTION.—For purposes of this paragraph, the term "qualified ethanol fuel production" means any alcohol which is ethanol which is produced by an eligible small ethanol producer, and which during the taxable year—

(i) is sold by such producer to another person—

(I) for use by such other person in the production of a qualified mixture in such other person's trade or business (other than casual off-farm production),

(II) for use by such other person as a fuel in a trade or business, or

(III) who sells such ethanol at retail to another person and places such ethanol in the fuel tank of such other person, or

(ii) is used or sold by such producer for any purpose described in clause (i).

(C) LIMITATION.—The qualified ethanol fuel production of any producer for any taxable year shall not exceed 15,000,000 gallons (determined without regard to any qualified cellulosic biofuel production).

(D) ADDITIONAL DISTILLATION EXCLUDED.—The qualified ethanol fuel production of any producer for any taxable year shall not include any alcohol which is purchased by the producer and with respect to which such producer increases the proof of the alcohol by additional distillation.

(5) ADDING OF DENATURANTS NOT TREATED AS MIXTURE.—The adding of any denaturant to alcohol shall not be treated as the production of a mixture.

(6) CELLULOSIC BIOFUEL PRODUCER CREDIT.—

(A) IN GENERAL.—The cellulosic biofuel producer credit of any taxpayer is an amount equal to the applicable amount for each gallon of qualified cellulosic biofuel production.

(B) APPLICABLE AMOUNT.—For purposes of subparagraph (A), the applicable amount means $1.01, except that such amount shall, in the case of cellulosic biofuel which is alcohol, be reduced by the sum of—

(i) the amount of the credit in effect for such alcohol under subsection (b)(1) (without regard to subsection (b)(3)) at the time of the qualified cellulosic biofuel production, plus

(ii) in the case of ethanol, the amount of the credit in effect under subsection (b)(4) at the time of such production.

(C) QUALIFIED CELLULOSIC BIOFUEL PRODUCTION.—For purposes of this section, the term "qualified cellulosic biofuel production" means any cellulosic biofuel which is produced by the taxpayer, and which during the taxable year—

(i) is sold by the taxpayer to another person—

(I) for use by such other person in the production of a qualified cellulosic biofuel mixture in such other person's trade or business (other than casual off-farm production),

(II) for use by such other person as a fuel in a trade or business, or

(III) who sells such cellulosic biofuel at retail to another person and places such cellulosic biofuel in the fuel tank of such other person, or

(ii) is used or sold by the taxpayer for any purpose described in clause (i).

The qualified cellulosic biofuel production of any taxpayer for any taxable year shall not include any alcohol which is purchased by the taxpayer and with respect to which such producer increases the proof of the alcohol by additional distillation.

(D) QUALIFIED CELLULOSIC BIOFUEL MIXTURE.—For purposes of this paragraph, the term "qualified cellulosic biofuel mixture" means a mixture of cellulosic biofuel and gasoline or of cellulosic biofuel and a special fuel which—

(i) is sold by the person producing such mixture to any person for use as a fuel, or

(ii) is used as a fuel by the person producing such mixture.

(E) CELLULOSIC BIOFUEL.—For purposes of this paragraph—

(i) IN GENERAL.—The term "cellulosic biofuel" means any liquid fuel which—

(I) is produced from any lignocellulosic or hemicellulosic matter that is available on a renewable or recurring basis, and

(II) meets the registration requirements for fuels and fuel additives established by the Environmental Protection Agency under section 211 of the Clean Air Act (42 U.S.C. 7545).

(ii) EXCLUSION OF LOW-PROOF ALCOHOL.—Such term shall not include any alcohol with a proof of less than 150. The determination of the proof of any alcohol shall be made without regard to any added denaturants.

(iii) EXCLUSION OF CERTAIN FUELS.—The term "cellulosic biofuel" shall not include any fuel if—

(I) more than 4 percent of such fuel (determined by weight) is any combination of water and sediment,

(II) the ash content of such fuel is more than 1 percent (determined by weight), or

(III) such fuel has an acid number greater than 25.

(F) ALLOCATION OF CELLULOSIC BIOFUEL PRODUCER CREDIT TO PATRONS OF COOPERATIVE.—Rules similar to the rules under subsection (g)(6) shall apply for purposes of this paragraph.

(G) REGISTRATION REQUIREMENT.—No credit shall be determined under this paragraph with respect to any taxpayer unless such taxpayer is registered with the Secretary as a producer of cellulosic biofuel under section 4101.

(H) APPLICATION OF PARAGRAPH.—This paragraph shall apply with respect to qualified cellulosic biofuel production after December 31, 2008, and before January 1, 2013.

Amendments

• 2010, Creating Small Business Jobs Act of 2010 (P.L. 111-240)

P.L. 111-240, §2121(a)(1)-(4):

Amended Code Sec. 40(b)(6)(E)(iii), as added by the Health Care and Education Reconciliation Act of 2010 [P.L. 111-152], by striking "or" at the end of subclause (I), by striking the period at the end of subclause (II) and inserting ", or", by adding at the end a new subclause (III), and by striking "UNPROCESSED" in the heading and inserting "CERTAIN". **Effective** for fuels sold or used on or after 1-1-2010.

• 2010, Health Care and Education Reconciliation Act of 2010 (P.L. 111-152)

P.L. 111-152, §1408(a):

Amended Code Sec. 40(b)(6)(E), by adding at the end a new clause (iii). **Effective** for fuels sold or used on or after 1-1-2010.

• 2008, Heartland, Habitat, Harvest, and Horticulture Act of 2008 (P.L. 110-246)

P.L. 110-246, §15321(b)(1):

Amended Code Sec. 40(b) by adding at the end a new paragraph (6). **Effective** for fuel produced after 12-31-2008.

P.L. 110-246, §15321(e):

Amended Code Sec. 40(b)(4)(C) by inserting "(determined without regard to any qualified cellulosic biofuel production)" after "15,000,000 gallons". **Effective** for fuel produced after 12-31-2008.

• 1990, Omnibus Budget Reconciliation Act of 1990 (P.L. 101-508)

P.L. 101-508, §11502(b):

Amended Code Sec. 40(b) by redesignating paragraph (4) as paragraph (5), by inserting after paragraph (3) new paragraph (4), and by striking "AND ALCOHOL CREDIT" in the heading for such subsection and inserting ", ALCOHOL CREDIT, AND SMALL ETHANOL PRODUCER CREDIT". **Effective** for alcohol produced, and sold or used, in tax years beginning after 12-31-90.

P.L. 101-508, §11502(e)(2):

Amended Code Sec. 40(b) by inserting ", and except as provided in subsection (h)" in the matter preceding paragraph (1). **Effective** for alcohol produced, and sold or used, in tax years beginning after 12-31-90.

[Sec. 40(c)]

(c) COORDINATION WITH EXEMPTION FROM EXCISE TAX.—The amount of the credit determined under this section with respect to any alcohol shall, under regulations prescribed by the Secretary, be properly reduced to take into account any benefit provided with respect to such alcohol solely by reason of the application of section 4041(b)(2), section 6426, or section 6427(e).

Amendments

• 2004, American Jobs Creation Act of 2004 (P.L. 108-357)

P.L. 108-357, §301(c)(1):

Amended Code Sec. 40(c) by striking "subsection (b)(2), (k), or (m) of section 4041, section 4081(c), or section 4091(c)" and inserting "section 4041(b)(2), section 6426, or section 6427(e)". **Effective** for fuel sold or used after 12-31-2004.

• 1987, Revenue Act of 1987 (P.L. 100-203)

P.L. 100-203, §10502(d)(1):

Amended Code Sec. 40(c) by striking out "or section 4081(c)" and inserting in lieu thereof", section 4081(c), or section 4091(c)". **Effective** for sales after 3-31-88.

• 1984, Deficit Reduction Act of 1984 (P.L. 98-369)

P.L. 98-369, §913(b):

Amended Code Sec. 40(c) (as redesignated by Act Sec. 471(c)(1) by striking out "(b)(2) or (k)" and inserting in lieu thereof "(b)(2), (k), or (m)". **Effective** 8-1-84.

[Sec. 40(d)]

(d) DEFINITIONS AND SPECIAL RULES.—For purposes of this section—

(1) ALCOHOL DEFINED.—

(A) IN GENERAL.—The term "alcohol" includes methanol and ethanol but does not include—

(i) alcohol produced from petroleum, natural gas, or coal (including peat), or

(ii) alcohol with a proof of less than 150.

(B) DETERMINATION OF PROOF.—The determination of the proof of any alcohol shall be made without regard to any added denaturants.

(2) SPECIAL FUEL DEFINED.—The term "special fuel" includes any liquid fuel (other than gasoline) which is suitable for use in an internal combustion engine.

(3) MIXTURE OR ALCOHOL NOT USED AS A FUEL, ETC.—

(A) MIXTURES.—If—

(i) any credit was determined under this section with respect to alcohol used in the production of any qualified mixture, and

(ii) any person—

(I) separates the alcohol from the mixture, or

(II) without separation, uses the mixture other than as a fuel,

then there is hereby imposed on such person a tax equal to 60 cents a gallon (45 cents in the case of alcohol with a proof less than 190) for each gallon of alcohol in such mixture.

(B) ALCOHOL.—If—

(i) any credit was determined under this section with respect to the retail sale of any alcohol, and

(ii) any person mixes such alcohol or uses such alcohol other than as a fuel,

then there is hereby imposed on such person a tax equal to 60 cents a gallon (45 cents in the case of alcohol with a proof less than 190) for each gallon of such alcohol.

(C) SMALL ETHANOL PRODUCER CREDIT.—If—

(i) any credit was determined under subsection (a)(3), and

(ii) any person does not use such fuel for a purpose described in subsection (b)(4)(B),

then there is hereby imposed on such person a tax equal to 10 cents a gallon for each gallon of such alcohol.

(D) CELLULOSIC BIOFUEL PRODUCER CREDIT.—If—

(i) any credit is allowed under subsection (a)(4), and

(ii) any person does not use such fuel for a purpose described in subsection (b)(6)(C),

then there is hereby imposed on such person a tax equal to the applicable amount (as defined in subsection (b)(6)(B)) for each gallon of such cellulosic biofuel.

(E) APPLICABLE LAWS.—All provisions of law, including penalties, shall, insofar as applicable and not inconsistent with this section, apply in respect of any tax imposed under subparagraph (A), (B), (C), or (D) as if such tax were imposed by section 4081 and not by this chapter.

(4) VOLUME OF ALCOHOL.—For purposes of determining under subsection (a) the number of gallons of alcohol with respect to which a credit is allowable under subsection (a), the volume of alcohol shall include the volume of any denaturant (including gasoline) which is added under any formulas approved by the Secretary to the extent that such denaturants do not exceed 2 percent of the volume of such alcohol (including denaturants).

(5) PASS-THRU IN THE CASE OF ESTATES AND TRUSTS.—Under regulations prescribed by the Secretary, rules similar to the rules of subsection (d) of section 52 shall apply.

(6) SPECIAL RULE FOR CELLULOSIC BIOFUEL PRODUCER CREDIT.—No cellulosic biofuel producer credit shall be determined under subsection (a) with respect to any cellulosic biofuel unless such cellulosic biofuel is produced in the United States and used as a fuel in the United States. For purposes of this subsection, the term "United States" includes any possession of the United States.

(7) LIMITATION TO ALCOHOL WITH CONNECTION TO THE UNITED STATES.—No credit shall be determined under this section with respect to any alcohol which is produced outside the United States for use as a fuel outside the United States. For purposes of this paragraph, the term "United States" includes any possession of the United States.

Amendments

• 2008, Energy Improvement and Extension Act of 2008 (P.L. 110-343)

P.L. 110-343, Division B, §203(a):

Amended Code Sec. 40(d) by adding at the end a new paragraph (7). **Effective** for claims for credit or payment made on or after 5-15-2008.

• 2008, Heartland, Habitat, Harvest, and Horticulture Act of 2008 (P.L. 110-246)

P.L. 110-246, §15321(c)(1):

Amended Code Sec. 40(d)(3) by redesignating subparagraph (D) as subparagraph (E) and by inserting after subparagraph (C) a new subparagraph (D). **Effective** for fuel produced after 12-31-2008.

P.L. 110-246, §15321(c)(2)(A):

Amended the heading of Code Sec. 40(d)(3)(C) by striking "PRODUCER" and inserting "SMALL ETHANOL PRODUCER". **Effective** for fuel produced after 12-31-2008.

P.L. 110-246, §15321(c)(2)(B):

Amended Code Sec. 40(d)(3)(E), as redesignated by Act Sec. 15321(c)(1), by striking "or (C)" and inserting "(C), or (D)". **Effective** for fuel produced after 12-31-2008.

P.L. 110-246, §15321(d):

Amended Code Sec. 40(d) by adding at the end a new paragraph (6). **Effective** for fuel produced after 12-31-2008.

P.L. 110-246, §15332(a):

Amended Code Sec. 40(d)(4) by striking "5 percent" and inserting "2 percent". **Effective** for fuel sold or used after 12-31-2008.

• 2004, American Jobs Creation Act of 2004 (P.L. 108-357)

P.L. 108-357, §301(c)(2):

Amended Code Sec. 40(d)(4). **Effective** for fuel sold or used after 12-31-2004. Prior to amendment, Code Sec. 40(d)(4) read as follows:

(4) VOLUME OF ALCOHOL.—For purposes of determining—

(A) under subsection (a) the number of gallons of alcohol with respect to which a credit is allowable under subsection (a), or

(B) under section 4041(k) or 4081(c) the percentage of any mixture which consists of alcohol,

the volume of alcohol shall include the volume of any denaturant (including gasoline) which is added under any formulas approved by the Secretary to the extent that such denaturants do not exceed 5 percent of the volume of such alcohol (including denaturants).

• 1990, Omnibus Budget Reconciliation Act of 1990 (P.L. 101-508)

P.L. 101-508, §11502(d)(1):

Amended Code Sec. 40(d)(3) by redesignating subparagraph (C) as subparagraph (D) and by inserting after subparagraph (B) new subparagraph (C). **Effective** for alcohol produced, and sold or used, in tax years beginning after 12-31-90.

P.L. 101-508, §11502(d)(2):

Amended Code Sec. 40(d)(3)(D), as redesignated by Act Sec. 11502(d)(1), by striking "subparagraph (A) or (B)" and inserting "subparagraph (A), (B), or (C)". **Effective** for alcohol produced, and sold or used, in tax years beginning after 12-31-90.

• 1984, Deficit Reduction Act of 1984 (P.L. 98-369)

P.L. 98-369, §912(f):

Amended Code Sec. 40(d)(1)(A)(i), as redesignated, by striking out "coal" and inserting in lieu thereof "coal (including peat)". **Effective** 1-1-85.

[Sec. 40(e)]

(e) TERMINATION.—

(1) IN GENERAL.—This section shall not apply to any sale or use—

(A) for any period after December 31, 2010, or

(B) for any period before January 1, 2011, during which the rates of tax under section 4081(a)(2)(A) are 4.3 cents per gallon.

(2) NO CARRYOVERS TO CERTAIN YEARS AFTER EXPIRATION.—If this section ceases to apply for any period by reason of paragraph (1) or subsection (b)(6)(H), no amount attributable to any sale or use before the first day of such period may be carried under section 39 by reason of this section (treating the amount allowed by reason of this section as the first amount allowed by this subpart) to any taxable year beginning after the 3-taxable-year period beginning with the taxable year in which such first day occurs.

(3) EXCEPTION FOR CELLULOSIC BIOFUEL PRODUCER CREDIT.—Paragraph (1) shall not apply to the portion of the credit allowed under this section by reason of subsection (a)(4).

Amendments

• 2008, Heartland, Habitat, Harvest, and Horticulture Act of 2008 (P.L. 110-246)

P.L. 110-246, §15321(b)(2)(A)-(B):

Amended Code Sec. 40(e) by inserting "or subsection (b)(6)(H)" after "by reason of paragraph (1)" in paragraph (2), and by adding at the end a new paragraph (3). **Effective** for fuel produced after 12-31-2008.

• 2004, American Jobs Creation Act of 2004 (P.L. 108-357)

P.L. 108-357, §301(c)(3)(A)-(B):

Amended Code Sec. 40(e)(1) by striking "2007" in subparagraph (A) and inserting "2010", and by striking "2008" in subparagraph (B) and inserting "2011". **Effective** 10-22-2004.

• 1998, Transportation Equity Act for the 21st Century (P.L. 105-178)

P.L. 105-178, §9003(a)(3)(A)-(B):

Amended Code Sec. 40(e)(1) by striking "December 31, 2000" in subparagraph (A) and inserting "December 31, 2007", and by striking "January 1, 2001" in subparagraph (B) and inserting "January 1, 2008". **Effective** 6-9-98.

• 1996, Small Business Job Protection Act of 1996 (P.L. 104-188)

P.L. 104-188, §1703(j):

Amended Code Sec. 40(e)(1)(B). **Effective** as if included in the provision of P.L. 103-66 to which such amendement relates. Prior to amendment, Code Sec. 40(e)(1)(B) read as follows:

(B) for any period before January 1, 2001, during which the Highway Trust Fund financing rate under section 4081(a)(2) is not in effect.

• 1990, Omnibus Budget Reconciliation Act of 1990 (P.L. 101-508)

P.L. 101-508, §11502(f):

Amended Code Sec. 40(e). **Effective** for alcohol produced, and sold or used, in tax years beginning after 12-31-90. Prior to amendment, Code Sec. 40(e) read as follows:

(e) TERMINATION.—

(1) IN GENERAL.—This section shall not apply to any sale or use after December 31, 1992.

(2) NO CARRYOVERS TO YEARS AFTER 1994.—No amount may be carried under section 39 by reason of this section (treating the amount allowed by reason of this section as the first amount allowed by this subpart) to any taxable year beginning after December 31, 1994.

[Sec. 40(f)]

(f) ELECTION TO HAVE ALCOHOL FUELS CREDIT NOT APPLY.—

(1) IN GENERAL.—A taxpayer may elect to have this section not apply for any taxable year.

(2) TIME FOR MAKING ELECTION.—An election under paragraph (1) for any taxable year may be made (or revoked) at any time before the expiration of the 3-year period beginning on the last date prescribed by law for filing the return for such taxable year (determined without regard to extensions).

(3) MANNER OF MAKING ELECTION.—An election under paragraph (1) (or revocation thereof) shall be made in such manner as the Secretary may by regulations prescribe.

Amendments

• 1984, Deficit Reduction Act of 1984 (P.L. 98-369)

P.L. 98-369, §471(c)(1):

Redesignated former Code Sec. 44E as Code Sec. 40. **Effective** for tax years beginning after 12-31-83, and to carrybacks from such years.

P.L. 98-369, §474(k):

Amended Code Sec. 40, as redesignated by Act Sec. 471(c)(1), by amending subsection (a); by striking out "the credit allowable under this section" in subsection (c) and inserting in lieu thereof "the credit determined under this section", by striking out "credit was allowable" each place it appeared in paragraph (3) of subsection (d) and inserting in lieu thereof "credit was determined", by striking out subsection (e) and redesignating subsection (f) as subsection (e), by amending paragraph (2) of subsection (e) (as redesignated by paragraph (4)), and by adding new subsection (f). **Effective** for tax years beginning after 12-31-83, and to carrybacks from such years. Prior to amendment, subsections (a), (e) and (f)(2) read as follows:

(a) GENERAL RULE.—There shall be allowed as a credit against the tax imposed by this chapter for the taxable year an amount equal to the sum of—

(1) the alcohol mixture credit, plus

(2) the alcohol credit.

* * *

(e) LIMITATION BASED ON AMOUNT OF TAX.—

(1) IN GENERAL.—The amount of the credit allowed by this section for the taxable year shall not exceed the tax imposed by this chapter for the taxable year, reduced by the sum of the credits allowed under a section of this subpart having a lower number designation than this section, other than credits allowable by sections 31, 39, and 43. For purposes of the preceding sentence, the term "tax imposed by this chapter" shall not include any tax treated as not imposed by this chapter under the last sentence of section 53(a).

(2) CARRYOVER OF UNUSED CREDIT.—

(A) IN GENERAL.—If the amount of the credit determined under subsection (a) for any taxable year exceeds the limitation provided by paragraph (1) for such taxable year (hereinafter in this paragraph referred to as the "unused credit year"), such excess shall be an alcohol fuel credit carryover to each of the 15 taxable years following the unused credit year, and shall be added to the amount allowable as credit under subsection (a) for such years. The entire amount of the unused credit for an unused credit year shall be carried to the earliest of the 15 taxable years to which (by reason of the preceding sentence) such credit may be carried, and then to each of the other 14 taxable years to the extent that, because of the limitation contained in subparagraph (B), such unused credit may not be added for a prior taxable year to which such unused credit may be carried.

(B) LIMITATION.—The amount of the unused credit which may be added under subparagraph (A) for any succeeding taxable year shall not exceed the amount by which the limitation provided by paragraph (1) for such succeeding taxable year exceeds the sum of—

(i) the credit allowable under subsection (a) for such taxable year, and

(ii) the amounts which, by reason of this paragraph, are added to the amount allowable for such taxable year and which are attributable to taxable years preceding the unused credit year.

* * *

[f](2) NO CARRYOVERS TO YEARS AFTER 1994.—No amount may be carried under subsection (e)(2) to any taxable year beginning after December 31, 1994.

P.L. 98-369, §912(c):

Amended Code Sec. 40 (as redesignated by Act Sec. 741(c)(1)) by striking out "50 cents" each place it appeared, and inserting in lieu thereof "60 cents", and by striking out "37.5 cents" each place it appeared and inserting in lieu thereof "45 cents". **Effective** 1-1-85.

P.L. 98-369, §474(m)(1):

Repealed former Code Sec. 40. **Effective** for tax years beginning after 12-31-83, and to carrybacks from such years. Prior to repeal, Code Sec. 40 read as follows:

SEC. 40. EXPENSES OF WORK INCENTIVE PROGRAMS.

(a) GENERAL RULE.—There shall be allowed, as a credit against the tax imposed by this chapter, the amount determined under subpart C of this part.

(b) REGULATIONS.—The Secretary shall prescribe such regulations as may be necessary to carry out the purposes of this section and subpart C.

• 1983, Technical Corrections Act of 1982 (P.L. 97-448)

P.L. 97-448, §102(d)(2):

Amended P.L. 97-34, §209(c), to provide that the amendment made by §207(c)(3) shall not apply to any amount that, under the law in effect on 1-11-83, could not be carried to a tax year ending in 1981.

P.L. 97-448, §202(e):

Amended the effective date of Code Sec. 44E(d)(4)(B), as added by P.L. 96-223, §232(b)(1), to be 4-2-80.

• 1983, Surface Transportation Act of 1982 (P.L. 97-424)

P.L. 97-424, §511(b)(2):

Amended Code Sec. 44E(c) by striking out "section 4041(k) or 4081(c)" and inserting "subsection (b)(2) or (k) of section 4041 or section 4081(c)". **Effective** 4-1-83.

P.L. 97-424, §511(d)(3):

Amended Code Sec. 44E by striking out "40 cents" each place it appeared and inserting "50 cents", and by striking out "30 cents" each place it appeared and inserting "37.5 cents". **Effective** 4-1-83.

• 1982, Subchapter S Revision Act of 1982 (P.L. 97-354)

P.L. 97-354, §5(a)(2):

Amended Code Sec. 44E(d)(5). **Effective** for tax years beginning after 12-31-82. Prior to amendment, it read as follows:

"(5) PASS-THROUGH IN THE CASE OF SUBCHAPTER S CORPORATIONS, ETC.—Under regulations prescribed by the Secretary, rules similar to the rules of subsections (d) and (e) of section 52 shall apply."

• 1981, Economic Recovery Tax Act of 1981 (P.L. 97-34)

P.L. 97-34, §207(c)(3):

Amended Code Sec. 44E(e)(2)(A) by striking out "7" each place it appeared and inserting in lieu thereof "15", and by striking out "6" and inserting in lieu thereof "14". **Effective** for unused credit years ending after 9-30-80.

• 1980, Crude Oil Windfall Profit Tax Act of 1980 (P.L. 96-223)

P.L. 96-223, §232(b)(1):

Added Code Sec. 44E. **Effective** for sales or uses after 9-30-80, in tax years ending after such date.

• 1976, Tax Reform Act of 1976 (P.L. 94-455)

P.L. 94-455, §1906(b)(13)(A):

Amended 1954 Code by substituting "Secretary" for "Secretary or his delegate" each place it appeared. **Effective** 2-1-77.

• 1971, Revenue Act of 1971 (P.L. 92-178)

P.L. 92-178, §601(a):

Added new Code Sec. 40 and renumbered former Code Sec. 40 to be new Code Sec. 42. **Effective** for tax years beginning after 12-31-71.

[Sec. 40(g)]

(g) DEFINITIONS AND SPECIAL RULES FOR ELIGIBLE SMALL ETHANOL PRODUCER CREDIT.—For purposes of this section—

(1) ELIGIBLE SMALL ETHANOL PRODUCER.—The term "eligible small ethanol producer" means a person who, at all times during the taxable year, has a productive capacity for alcohol (as defined in subsection (d)(1)(A) without regard to clauses (i) and (ii)) not in excess of 60,000,000 gallons.

(2) AGGREGATION RULE.—For purposes of the 15,000,000 gallon limitation under subsection (b)(4)(C) and the 60,000,000 gallon limitation under paragraph (1), all members of the same controlled group of corporations (within the meaning of section 267(f)) and all persons under common control (within the meaning of section 52(b) but determined by treating an interest of more than 50 percent as a controlling interest) shall be treated as 1 person.

(3) PARTNERSHIP, S CORPORATIONS, AND OTHER PASS-THRU ENTITIES.—In the case of a partnership, trust, S corporation, or other pass-thru entity, the limitations contained in subsection (b)(4)(C) and paragraph (1) shall be applied at the entity level and at the partner or similar level.

(4) ALLOCATION.—For purposes of this subsection, in the case of a facility in which more than 1 person has an interest, productive capacity shall be allocated among such persons in such manner as the Secretary may prescribe.

(5) REGULATIONS.—The Secretary may prescribe such regulations as may be necessary—

(A) to prevent the credit provided for in subsection (a)(3) from directly or indirectly benefiting any person with a direct or indirect productive capacity of more than 60,000,000 gallons of alcohol during the taxable year, or

(B) to prevent any person from directly or indirectly benefiting with respect to more than 15,000,000 gallons during the taxable year.

(6) ALLOCATION OF SMALL ETHANOL PRODUCER CREDIT TO PATRONS OF COOPERATIVE.—

(A) ELECTION TO ALLOCATE.—

(i) IN GENERAL.—In the case of a cooperative organization described in section 1381(a), any portion of the credit determined under subsection (a)(3) for the taxable year may, at the election of the organization, be apportioned pro rata among patrons of the organization on the basis of the quantity or value of business done with or for such patrons for the taxable year.

(ii) FORM AND EFFECT OF ELECTION.—An election under clause (i) for any taxable year shall be made on a timely filed return for such year. Such election, once made, shall be irrevocable for such taxable year. Such election shall not take effect unless the organization designates the apportionment as such in a written notice mailed to its patrons during the payment period described in section 1382(d).

(B) TREATMENT OF ORGANIZATIONS AND PATRONS.—

(i) ORGANIZATIONS.—The amount of the credit not apportioned to patrons pursuant to subparagraph (A) shall be included in the amount determined under subsection (a)(3) for the taxable year of the organization.

(ii) PATRONS.—The amount of the credit apportioned to patrons pursuant to subparagraph (A) shall be included in the amount determined under such subsection for the first taxable year of each patron ending on or after the last day of the payment period (as defined in section 1382(d)) for the taxable year of the organization or, if earlier, for the taxable year of each patron ending on or after the date on which the patron receives notice from the cooperative of the apportionment.

(iii) SPECIAL RULES FOR DECREASE IN CREDITS FOR TAXABLE YEAR.—If the amount of the credit of the organization determined under such subsection for a taxable year is less than the amount of such credit shown on the return of the organization for such year, an amount equal to the excess of—

(I) such reduction, over

(II) the amount not apportioned to such patrons under subparagraph (A) for the taxable year,

shall be treated as an increase in tax imposed by this chapter on the organization. Such increase shall not be treated as tax imposed by this chapter for purposes of determining the amount of any credit under this chapter or for purposes of section 55.

Amendments

• 2005, Energy Tax Incentives Act of 2005 (P.L. 109-58)

P.L. 109-58, §1347(a):

Amended Code Sec. 40(g) by striking "30,000,000" each place it appears and inserting "60,000,000". **Effective** for tax years ending after 8-8-2005.

P.L. 109-58, §1347(b):

Amended Code Sec. 40(g)(6)(A)(ii) by adding at the end a new sentence. **Effective** for tax years ending after 8-8-2005.

• 2004, American Jobs Creation Act of 2004 (P.L. 108-357)

P.L. 108-357, §313(a):

Amended Code Sec. 40(g) by adding at the end a new paragraph (6). **Effective** for tax years ending after 10-22-2004.

• 1990, Omnibus Budget Reconciliation Act of 1990 (P.L. 101-508)

P.L. 101-508, §11502(c):

Amended Code Sec. 40 by adding at the end thereof new subsection (g). **Effective** for alcohol produced, and sold or used, in tax years beginning after 12-31-90.

[Sec. 40(h)]

(h) REDUCED CREDIT FOR ETHANOL BLENDERS.—

(1) IN GENERAL.—In the case of any alcohol mixture credit or alcohol credit with respect to any sale or use of alcohol which is ethanol during calendar years 2001 through 2010—

(A) subsections (b)(1)(A) and (b)(2)(A) shall be applied by substituting "the blender amount" for "60 cents",

(B) subsection (b)(3) shall be applied by substituting "the low-proof blender amount" for "45 cents" and "the blender amount" for "60 cents", and

(C) subparagraphs (A) and (B) of subsection (d)(3) shall be applied by substituting "the blender amount" for "60 cents" and "the low-proof blender amount" for "45 cents".

(2) AMOUNTS.—For purposes of paragraph (1), the blender amount and the low-proof blender amount shall be determined in accordance with the following table:

In the case of any sale or use during calendar year:	*The blender amount is:*	*The low-proof blender amount is:*
2001 or 2002	53 cents	39.26 cents
2003 or 2004	52 cents	38.52 cents
2005, 2006, 2007, or 2008	51 cents	37.78 cents
2009 through 2010	45 cents	33.33 cents.

(3) REDUCTION DELAYED UNTIL ANNUAL PRODUCTION OR IMPORTATION OF 7,500,000,000 GALLONS.—

(A) IN GENERAL.—In the case of any calendar year beginning after 2008, if the Secretary makes a determination described in subparagraph (B) with respect to all preceding calendar years beginning after 2007, the last row in the table in paragraph (2) shall be applied by substituting "51 cents" for "45 cents".

(B) DETERMINATION.—A determination described in this subparagraph with respect to any calendar year is a determination, in consultation with the Administrator of the Environmental Protection Agency, that an amount less than 7,500,000,000 gallons of ethanol (including cellulosic ethanol) has been produced in or imported into the United States in such year.

Amendments

• 2008, Heartland, Habitat, Harvest, and Horticulture Act of 2008 (P.L. 110-246)

P.L. 110-246, §15331(a)(1)(A)-(C):

Amended the table in Code Sec. 40(h)(2) by striking "through 2010" in the first column and inserting ", 2006, 2007, or 2008", by striking the period at the end of the third row, and by adding at the end a new row. **Effective** 5-22-2008.

P.L. 110-246, §15331(a)(2):

Amended Code Sec. 40(h) by adding at the end a new paragraph (3). **Effective** 5-22-2008.

• 2004, American Jobs Creation Act of 2004 (P.L. 108-357)

P.L. 108-357, §301(c)(4)(A)-(B):

Amended Code Sec. 40(h) by striking "2007" in paragraph (1) and inserting "2010", and by striking ", 2006, or 2007" in the table contained in paragraph (2) and inserting "through 2010" **Effective** 10-22-2004.

• 1998, Transportation Equity Act for the 21st Century (P.L. 105-178)

P.L. 105-178, §9003(b)(1):

Amended Code Sec. 40(h). **Effective** 1-1-2001. Prior to amendment, Code Sec. 40(h) read as follows:

(h) REDUCED CREDIT FOR ETHANOL BLENDERS.—In the case of any alcohol mixture credit or alcohol credit with respect to any alcohol which is ethanol—

(1) subsections (b)(1)(A) and (b)(2)(A) shall be applied by substituting "54 cents" for "60 cents";

(2) subsection (b)(3) shall be applied by substituting "40 cents" for "45 cents" and "54 cents" for "60 cents"; and

(3) subparagraphs (A) and (B) of subsection (d)(3) shall be applied by substituting "54 cents" for "60 cents" and "40 cents" for "45 cents".

• 1990, Omnibus Budget Reconciliation Act of 1990 (P.L. 101-508)

P.L. 101-508, §11502(e)(1):

Amended Code Sec. 40 by adding at the end thereof new subsection (h). **Effective** for alcohol produced, and sold or used, in tax years beginning after 12-31-90.

[Sec. 40A]

SEC. 40A. BIODIESEL AND RENEWABLE DIESEL USED AS FUEL.

[Sec. 40A(a)]

(a) GENERAL RULE.—For purposes of section 38, the biodiesel fuels credit determined under this section for the taxable year is an amount equal to the sum of—

(1) the biodiesel mixture credit, plus

(2) the biodiesel credit, plus

(3) in the case of an eligible small agri-biodiesel producer, the small agri-biodiesel producer credit.

Amendments

• **2005, Energy Tax Incentives Act of 2005 (P.L. 109-58)**

P.L. 109-58, §1345(a):

Amended Code Sec. 40A(a). **Effective** for tax years ending after 8-8-2005. Prior to amendment, Code Sec. 40A(a) read as follows:

(a) GENERAL RULE.—For purposes of section 38, the biodiesel fuels credit determined under this section for the taxable year is an amount equal to the sum of—

(1) the biodiesel mixture credit, plus

(2) the biodiesel credit.

P.L. 109-58, §1346(b)(1):

Amended the heading for Code Sec. 40A by inserting "AND RENEWABLE DIESEL" after "BIODIESEL". **Effective** with respect to fuel sold or used after 12-31-2005.

[Sec. 40A(b)]

(b) DEFINITION OF BIODIESEL MIXTURE CREDIT, BIODIESEL CREDIT, AND SMALL AGRI-BIODIESEL PRODUCER CREDIT.—For purposes of this section—

(1) BIODIESEL MIXTURE CREDIT.—

(A) IN GENERAL.—The biodiesel mixture credit of any taxpayer for any taxable year is $1.00 for each gallon of biodiesel used by the taxpayer in the production of a qualified biodiesel mixture.

(B) QUALIFIED BIODIESEL MIXTURE.—The term "qualified biodiesel mixture" means a mixture of biodiesel and diesel fuel (as defined in section 4083(a)(3)), determined without regard to any use of kerosene, which—

(i) is sold by the taxpayer producing such mixture to any person for use as a fuel, or

(ii) is used as a fuel by the taxpayer producing such mixture.

(C) SALE OR USE MUST BE IN TRADE OR BUSINESS, ETC.—Biodiesel used in the production of a qualified biodiesel mixture shall be taken into account—

(i) only if the sale or use described in subparagraph (B) is in a trade or business of the taxpayer, and

(ii) for the taxable year in which such sale or use occurs.

(D) CASUAL OFF-FARM PRODUCTION NOT ELIGIBLE.—No credit shall be allowed under this section with respect to any casual off-farm production of a qualified biodiesel mixture.

(2) BIODIESEL CREDIT.—

(A) IN GENERAL.—The biodiesel credit of any taxpayer for any taxable year is $1.00 for each gallon of biodiesel which is not in a mixture with diesel fuel and which during the taxable year—

(i) is used by the taxpayer as a fuel in a trade or business, or

(ii) is sold by the taxpayer at retail to a person and placed in the fuel tank of such person's vehicle.

(B) USER CREDIT NOT TO APPLY TO BIODIESEL SOLD AT RETAIL.—No credit shall be allowed under subparagraph (A)(i) with respect to any biodiesel which was sold in a retail sale described in subparagraph (A)(ii).

(3) CERTIFICATION FOR BIODIESEL.—No credit shall be allowed under paragraph (1) or (2) of subsection (a) unless the taxpayer obtains a certification (in such form and manner as prescribed by the Secretary) from the producer or importer of the biodiesel which identifies the product produced and the percentage of biodiesel and agri-biodiesel in the product.

(4) SMALL AGRI-BIODIESEL PRODUCER CREDIT.—

(A) IN GENERAL.—The small agri-biodiesel producer credit of any eligible small agri-biodiesel producer for any taxable year is 10 cents for each gallon of qualified agri-biodiesel production of such producer.

(B) QUALIFIED AGRI-BIODIESEL PRODUCTION.—For purposes of this paragraph, the term "qualified agri-biodiesel production" means any agri-biodiesel which is produced by an eligible small agri-biodiesel producer, and which during the taxable year—

(i) is sold by such producer to another person—

(I) for use by such other person in the production of a qualified biodiesel mixture in such other person's trade or business (other than casual off-farm production),

(II) for use by such other person as a fuel in a trade or business, or

(III) who sells such agri-biodiesel at retail to another person and places such agri-biodiesel in the fuel tank of such other person, or

(ii) is used or sold by such producer for any purpose described in clause (i).

(C) LIMITATION.—The qualified agri-biodiesel production of any producer for any taxable year shall not exceed 15,000,000 gallons.

Amendments

• 2008, Energy Improvement and Extension Act of 2008 (P.L. 110-343)

P.L. 110-343, Division B, §202(b)(1):

Amended Code Sec. 40A(b)(1)(A) and (2)(A) by striking "50 cents" and inserting "$1.00". **Effective** for fuel produced, and sold or used, after 12-31-2008.

P.L. 110-343, Division B, §202(b)(3)(A):

Amended Code Sec. 40A(b) by striking paragraph (3) and by redesignating paragraphs (4) and (5) as paragraphs (3) and (4), respectively. **Effective** for fuel produced, and sold or used, after 12-31-2008. Prior to being stricken, Code Sec. 40A(b)(3) read as follows:

(3) CREDIT FOR AGRI-BIODIESEL.—In the case of any biodiesel which is agri-biodiesel, paragraphs (1)(A) and (2)(A) shall be applied by substituting "$1.00" for "50 cents".

• 2005, Gulf Opportunity Zone Act of 2005 (P.L. 109-135)

P.L. 109-135, §412(h):

Amended Code Sec. 40A(b)(5)(B) by striking "(determined without regard to the last sentence of subsection (d)(2))" before "which is produced". **Effective** 12-21-2005.

• 2005, Energy Tax Incentives Act of 2005 (P.L. 109-58)

P.L. 109-58, §1345(b):

Amended Code Sec. 40A(b) by adding at the end a new paragraph (5). **Effective** for tax years ending after 8-8-2005.

P.L. 109-58, §1345(d)(1):

Amended Code Sec. 40A(b)(4) by striking "this section" and inserting "paragraph (1) or (2) of subsection (a)". **Effective** for tax years ending after 8-8-2005.

P.L. 109-58, §1345(d)(2):

Amended the heading of Code Sec. 40A(b) by striking "and Biodiesel Credit" and inserting ", Biodiesel Credit, and Small Agri-biodiesel Producer Credit". **Effective** for tax years ending after 8-8-2005.

[Sec. 40A(c)]

(c) COORDINATION WITH CREDIT AGAINST EXCISE TAX.—The amount of the credit determined under this section with respect to any biodiesel shall be properly reduced to take into account any benefit provided with respect to such biodiesel solely by reason of the application of section 6426 or 6427(e).

[Sec. 40A(d)]

(d) DEFINITIONS AND SPECIAL RULES.—For purposes of this section—

(1) BIODIESEL.—The term "biodiesel" means the monoalkyl esters of long chain fatty acids derived from plant or animal matter which meet—

(A) the registration requirements for fuels and fuel additives established by the Environmental Protection Agency under section 211 of the Clean Air Act (42 U.S.C. 7545), and

(B) the requirements of the American Society of Testing and Materials D6751.

Such term shall not include any liquid with respect to which a credit may be determined under section 40.

(2) AGRI-BIODIESEL.—The term "agri-biodiesel" means biodiesel derived solely from virgin oils, including esters derived from virgin vegetable oils from corn, soybeans, sunflower seeds, cottonseeds, canola, crambe, rapeseeds, safflowers, flaxseeds, rice bran, mustard seeds, and camelina, and from animal fats.

(3) MIXTURE OR BIODIESEL NOT USED AS A FUEL, ETC.—

(A) MIXTURES.—If—

(i) any credit was determined under this section with respect to biodiesel used in the production of any qualified biodiesel mixture, and

(ii) any person—

(I) separates the biodiesel from the mixture, or

(II) without separation, uses the mixture other than as a fuel,

then there is hereby imposed on such person a tax equal to the product of the rate applicable under subsection (b)(1)(A) and the number of gallons of such biodiesel in such mixture.

(B) BIODIESEL.—If—

(i) any credit was determined under this section with respect to the retail sale of any biodiesel, and

(ii) any person mixes such biodiesel or uses such biodiesel other than as a fuel,

then there is hereby imposed on such person a tax equal to the product of the rate applicable under subsection (b)(2)(A) and the number of gallons of such biodiesel.

(C) PRODUCER CREDIT.—If—

(i) any credit was determined under subsection (a)(3), and

(ii) any person does not use such fuel for a purpose described in subsection (b)(4)(B), then there is hereby imposed on such person a tax equal to 10 cents a gallon for each gallon of such agri-biodiesel.

(D) APPLICABLE LAWS.—All provisions of law, including penalties, shall, insofar as applicable and not inconsistent with this section, apply in respect of any tax imposed under subparagraph (A) or (B) as if such tax were imposed by section 4081 and not by this chapter.

(4) PASS-THRU IN THE CASE OF ESTATES AND TRUSTS.—Under regulations prescribed by the Secretary, rules similar to the rules of subsection (d) of section 52 shall apply.

(5) LIMITATION TO BIODIESEL WITH CONNECTION TO THE UNITED STATES.—No credit shall be determined under this section with respect to any biodiesel which is produced outside the United States for use as a fuel outside the United States. For purposes of this paragraph, the term "United States" includes any possession of the United States.

Amendments

• 2008, Energy Improvement and Extension Act of 2008 (P.L. 110-343)

P.L. 110-343, Division B, §202(b)(3)(D):

Amended Code Sec. 40A(d)(3)(C)(ii) by striking "subsection (b)(5)(B)" and inserting "subsection (b)(4)(B)". **Effective** for fuel produced, and sold or used, after 12-31-2008.

P.L. 110-343, Division B, §202(f):

Amended Code Sec. 40A(d)(2) by striking "and mustard seeds" and inserting "mustard seeds, and camelina". **Effective** for fuel produced, and sold or used, after 12-31-2008.

P.L. 110-343, Division B, §203(b):

Amended Code Sec. 40A(d) by adding at the end a new paragraph (5). **Effective** for claims for credit or payment made on or after 5-15-2008.

• 2008, Heartland, Habitat, Harvest, and Horticulture Act of 2008 (P.L. 110-246)

P.L. 110-246, §15321(f)(1):

Amended Code Sec. 40A(d)(1) by adding at the end a new flush sentence. **Effective** for fuel produced after 12-31-2008.

• 2005, Energy Tax Incentives Act of 2005 (P.L. 109-58)

P.L. 109-58, §1345(d)(3):

Amended Code Sec. 40A(d)(3) by redesignating subparagraph (C) as subparagraph (D) and by inserting after subparagraph (B) a new subparagraph (C). **Effective** for tax years ending after 8-8-2005.

[Sec. 40A(e)]

(e) DEFINITIONS AND SPECIAL RULES FOR SMALL AGRI-BIODIESEL PRODUCER CREDIT.—For purposes of this section—

(1) ELIGIBLE SMALL AGRI-BIODIESEL PRODUCER.—The term "eligible small agri-biodiesel producer" means a person who, at all times during the taxable year, has a productive capacity for agri-biodiesel not in excess of 60,000,000 gallons.

(2) AGGREGATION RULE.—For purposes of the 15,000,000 gallon limitation under subsection (b)(4)(C) and the 60,000,000 gallon limitation under paragraph (1), all members of the same controlled group of corporations (within the meaning of section 267(f)) and all persons under common control (within the meaning of section 52(b) but determined by treating an interest of more than 50 percent as a controlling interest) shall be treated as 1 person.

(3) PARTNERSHIP, S CORPORATION, AND OTHER PASS-THRU ENTITIES.—In the case of a partnership, trust, S corporation, or other pass-thru entity, the limitations contained in subsection (b)(4)(C) and paragraph (1) shall be applied at the entity level and at the partner or similar level.

(4) ALLOCATION.—For purposes of this subsection, in the case of a facility in which more than 1 person has an interest, productive capacity shall be allocated among such persons in such manner as the Secretary may prescribe.

(5) REGULATIONS.—The Secretary may prescribe such regulations as may be necessary—

(A) to prevent the credit provided for in subsection (a)(3) from directly or indirectly benefiting any person with a direct or indirect productive capacity of more than 60,000,000 gallons of agri-biodiesel during the taxable year, or

(B) to prevent any person from directly or indirectly benefiting with respect to more than 15,000,000 gallons during the taxable year.

(6) ALLOCATION OF SMALL AGRI-BIODIESEL CREDIT TO PATRONS OF COOPERATIVE.—

(A) ELECTION TO ALLOCATE.—

(i) IN GENERAL.—In the case of a cooperative organization described in section 1381(a), any portion of the credit determined under subsection (a)(3) for the taxable year may, at the election of the organization, be apportioned pro rata among patrons of the organization on the basis of the quantity or value of business done with or for such patrons for the taxable year.

(ii) FORM AND EFFECT OF ELECTION.—An election under clause (i) for any taxable year shall be made on a timely filed return for such year. Such election, once made, shall be irrevocable for such taxable year. Such election shall not take effect unless the organization designates the apportionment as such in a written notice mailed to its patrons during the payment period described in section 1382(d).

(B) TREATMENT OF ORGANIZATIONS AND PATRONS.—

(i) ORGANIZATIONS.—The amount of the credit not apportioned to patrons pursuant to subparagraph (A) shall be included in the amount determined under subsection (a)(3) for the taxable year of the organization.

(ii) PATRONS.—The amount of the credit apportioned to patrons pursuant to subparagraph (A) shall be included in the amount determined under such subsection for the first taxable year of each patron ending on or after the last day of the payment period (as defined in section 1382(d)) for the taxable year of the organization or, if earlier, for the taxable year of each patron ending on or after the date on which the patron receives notice from the cooperative of the apportionment.

(iii) SPECIAL RULES FOR DECREASE IN CREDITS FOR TAXABLE YEAR.—If the amount of the credit of the organization determined under such subsection for a taxable year is less than the amount of such credit shown on the return of the organization for such year, an amount equal to the excess of—

(I) such reduction, over

(II) the amount not apportioned to such patrons under subparagraph (A) for the taxable year, shall be treated as an increase in tax imposed by this chapter on the organization. Such increase shall not be treated as tax imposed by this chapter for purposes of determining the amount of any credit under this chapter or for purposes of section 55.

Amendments

• 2008, Energy Improvement and Extension Act of 2008 (P.L. 110-343)

P.L. 110-343, Division B, §202(b)(3)(C):

Amended Code Sec. 40A(e)(2) and (3) by striking "subsection (b)(5)(C)" and inserting "subsection (b)(4)(C)". **Effective** for fuel produced, and sold or used, after 12-31-2008.

• 2005, Energy Tax Incentives Act of 2005 (P.L. 109-58)

P.L. 109-58, §1345(c):

Amended Code Sec. 40A by redesignating subsection (e) as subsection (f) and by inserting after subsection (d) a new subsection (e). **Effective** for tax years ending after 8-8-2005.

[Sec. 40A(f)]

(f) RENEWABLE DIESEL.—For purposes of this title—

(1) TREATMENT IN THE SAME MANNER AS BIODIESEL.—Except as provided in paragraph (2), renewable diesel shall be treated in the same manner as biodiesel.

(2) EXCEPTION.—Subsection (b)(4) shall not apply with respect to renewable diesel.

(3) RENEWABLE DIESEL DEFINED.—The term "renewable diesel" means liquid fuel derived from biomass which meets—

(A) the registration requirements for fuels and fuel additives established by the Environmental Protection Agency under section 211 of the Clean Air Act (42 U.S.C. 7545), and

(B) the requirements of the American Society of Testing and Materials D975 or D396, or other equivalent standard approved by the Secretary.

Such term shall not include any liquid with respect to which a credit may be determined under section 40. Such term does not include any fuel derived from coprocessing biomass with a feedstock which is not biomass. For purposes of this paragraph, the term "biomass" has the meaning given such term by section 45K(c)(3).

(4) CERTAIN AVIATION FUEL.—

(A) IN GENERAL.—Except as provided in the last 3 sentences of paragraph (3), the term "renewable diesel" shall include fuel derived from biomass which meets the requirements of a Department of Defense specification for military jet fuel or an American Society of Testing and Materials specification for aviation turbine fuel.

(B) APPLICATION OF MIXTURE CREDITS.—In the case of fuel which is treated as renewable diesel solely by reason of subparagraph (A), subsection (b)(1) and section 6426(c) shall be applied with respect to such fuel by treating kerosene as though it were diesel fuel.

Amendments

• 2008, Energy Improvement and Extension Act of 2008 (P.L. 110-343)

P.L. 110-343, Division B, §202(b)(3)(B):

Amended Code Sec. 40A(f)(2). **Effective** for fuel produced, and sold or used, after 12-31-2008. Prior to amendment, Code Sec. 40A(f)(2) read as follows:

(2) EXCEPTIONS.—

(A) RATE OF CREDIT.—Subsections (b)(1)(A) and (b)(2)(A) shall be applied with respect to renewable diesel by substituting "$1.00" for "50 cents".

(B) NONAPPLICATION OF CERTAIN CREDITS.—Subsections (b)(3) and (b)(5) shall not apply with respect to renewable diesel.

P.L. 110-343, Division B, §202(c)(1)-(3):

Amended Code Sec. 40A(f)(3) by striking "diesel fuel" and inserting "liquid fuel", by striking "using a thermal depolymerization process" before "which meets—", and by inserting ", or other equivalent standard approved by the Secretary" after "D396". **Effective** for fuel produced, and sold or used, after 12-31-2008.

P.L. 110-343, Division B, §202(d)(1):

Amended Code Sec. 40A(f)(3) by adding at the end two new sentences. **Effective** for fuel produced, and sold or used, after 10-3-2008.

P.L. 110-343, Division B, §202(d)(2):

Amended Code Sec. 40A(f)(3) by striking "(as defined in section 45K(c)(3))" after "derived from biomass". **Effective** for fuel produced, and sold or used, after 10-3-2008.

P.L. 110-343, Division B, §202(e):

Amended Code Sec. 40A(f) by adding at the end a new paragraph (4). **Effective** for fuel produced, and sold or used, after 12-31-2008.

• 2008, Heartland, Habitat, Harvest, and Horticulture Act of 2008 (P.L. 110-246)

P.L. 110-246, §15321(f)(2):

Amended Code Sec. 40A(f)(3) by adding at the end a new flush sentence. **Effective** for fuel produced after 12-31-2008.

• 2005, Energy Tax Incentives Act of 2005 (P.L. 109-58)

P.L. 109-58, §1346(a):

Amended Code Sec. 40A, as amended by this Act, by redesignating subsection (f) as subsection (g) and by inserting after subsection (e) a new subsection (f). **Effective** with respect to fuel sold or used after 12-31-2005.

[Sec. 40A(g)]

(g) TERMINATION.—This section shall not apply to any sale or use after December 31, 2009.

Amendments

• 2008, Energy Improvement and Extension Act of 2008 (P.L. 110-343)

P.L. 110-343, Division B, §202(a):

Amended Code Sec. 40A(g) by striking "December 31, 2008" and inserting "December 31, 2009". **Effective** for fuel produced, and sold or used, after 12-31-2008.

• 2005, Energy Tax Incentives Act of 2005 (P.L. 109-58)

P.L. 109-58, §1344(a):

Amended Code Sec. 40A(e) by striking "2006" and inserting "2008". **Effective** 8-8-2005.

P.L. 109-58, §1345(c):

Amended Code Sec. 40A by redesignating subsection (e) as subsection (f). **Effective** for tax years ending after 8-8-2005.

P.L. 109-58, §1346(a):

Amended Code Sec. 40A, as amended by this Act, by redesignating subsection (f) as subsection (g). **Effective** with respect to fuel sold or used after 12-31-2005.

• 2004, American Jobs Creation Act of 2004 (P.L. 108-357)

P.L. 108-357, §302(a):

Amended subpart D of part IV of subchapter A of chapter 1 by inserting after Code Sec. 40 a new Code Sec. 40A. **Effective** for fuel produced, and sold or used, after 12-31-2004, in tax years ending after such date.

[Sec. 41]

SEC. 41. CREDIT FOR INCREASING RESEARCH ACTIVITIES.

[Sec. 41(a)]

(a) GENERAL RULE.—For purposes of section 38, the research credit determined under this section for the taxable year shall be an amount equal to the sum of—

(1) 20 percent of the excess (if any) of—

(A) the qualified research expenses for the taxable year, over

(B) the base amount,

(2) 20 percent of the basic research payments determined under subsection (e)(1)(A), and

(3) 20 percent of the amounts paid or incurred by the taxpayer in carrying on any trade or business of the taxpayer during the taxable year (including as contributions) to an energy research consortium for energy research.

Amendments

• 2007, Tax Technical Corrections Act of 2007 (P.L. 110-172)

P.L. 110-172, §6(c)(1):

Amended Code Sec. 41(a)(3) by inserting "for energy research" before the period at the end. **Effective** as if included in the provision of the Energy Tax Incentives Act of 2005 (P.L. 109-58) to which it relates [**effective** for amounts paid or incurred after 8-8-2005, in tax years ending after such date.—CCH].

• 2005, Energy Tax Incentives Act of 2005 (P.L. 109-58)

P.L. 109-58, §1351(a)(1):

Amended Code Sec. 41(a) by striking "and" at the end of paragraph (1), by striking the period at the end of paragraph (2) and inserting ", and", and by adding at the end a new paragraph (3). **Effective** for amounts paid or incurred after 8-8-2005, in tax years ending after such date.

• 1989, Omnibus Budget Reconciliation Act of 1989 (P.L. 101-239)

P.L. 101-239, §7110(b)(2)(A):

Amended Code Sec. 41(a)(1)(B). **Effective** for tax years beginning after 12-31-89. Prior to amendment, Code Sec. 41(a)(1)(B) read as follows:

(B) the base period research expenses, and

[Sec. 41(b)]

(b) QUALIFIED RESEARCH EXPENSES.—For purposes of this section—

(1) QUALIFIED RESEARCH EXPENSES.—The term "qualified research expenses" means the sum of the following amounts which are paid or incurred by the taxpayer during the taxable year in carrying on any trade or business of the taxpayer—

(A) in-house research expenses, and

(B) contract research expenses.

(2) IN-HOUSE RESEARCH EXPENSES.—

(A) IN GENERAL.—The term "in-house research expenses" means—

(i) any wages paid or incurred to an employee for qualified services performed by such employee,

(ii) any amount paid or incurred for supplies used in the conduct of qualified research, and

(iii) under regulations prescribed by the Secretary, any amount paid or incurred to another person for the right to use computers in the conduct of qualified research.

Clause (iii) shall not apply to any amount to the extent that the taxpayer (or any person with whom the taxpayer must aggregate expenditures under subsection (f)(1)) receives or accrues any amount from any other person for the right to use substantially identical personal property.

(B) QUALIFIED SERVICES.—The term "qualified services" means services consisting of—

(i) engaging in qualified research, or

(ii) engaging in the direct supervision or direct support of research activities which constitute qualified research.

If substantially all of the services performed by an individual for the taxpayer during the taxable year consists of services meeting the requirements of clause (i) or (ii), the term "qualified services" means all of the services performed by such individual for the taxpayer during the taxable year.

(C) SUPPLIES.—The term "supplies" means any tangible property other than—

(i) land or improvements to land, and

(ii) property of a character subject to the allowance for depreciation.

(D) WAGES.—

(i) IN GENERAL.—The term "wages" has the meaning given such term by section 3401(a).

(ii) SELF-EMPLOYED INDIVIDUALS AND OWNER-EMPLOYEES.—In the case of an employee (within the meaning of section 401(c)(1)), the term "wages" includes the earned income (as defined in section 401(c)(2)) of such employee.

(iii) EXCLUSION FOR WAGES TO WHICH WORK OPPORTUNITY CREDIT APPLIES.—The term "wages" shall not include any amount taken into account in determining the work opportunity credit under section 51(a).

(3) CONTRACT RESEARCH EXPENSES.—

(A) IN GENERAL.—The term "contract research expenses" means 65 percent of any amount paid or incurred by the taxpayer to any person (other than an employee of the taxpayer) for qualified research.

(B) PREPAID AMOUNTS.—If any contract research expenses paid or incurred during any taxable year are attributable to qualified research to be conducted after the close of such taxable year, such amount shall be treated as paid or incurred during the period during which the qualified research is conducted.

(C) AMOUNTS PAID TO CERTAIN RESEARCH CONSORTIA.—

(i) IN GENERAL.—Subparagraph (A) shall be applied by substituting "75 percent" for "65 percent" with respect to amounts paid or incurred by the taxpayer to a qualified research consortium for qualified research on behalf of the taxpayer and 1 or more unrelated taxpayers. For purposes of the preceding sentence, all persons treated as a single employer under subsection (a) or (b) of section 52 shall be treated as related taxpayers.

(ii) QUALIFIED RESEARCH CONSORTIUM.—The term "qualified research consortium" means any organization which—

(I) is described in section 501(c)(3) or 501(c)(6) and is exempt from tax under section 501(a),

(II) is organized and operated primarily to conduct scientific research, and

(III) is not a private foundation.

(D) AMOUNTS PAID TO ELIGIBLE SMALL BUSINESSES, UNIVERSITIES, AND FEDERAL LABORATORIES.—

(i) IN GENERAL.—In the case of amounts paid by the taxpayer to—

(I) an eligible small business,

(II) an institution of higher education (as defined in section 3304(f)), or

(III) an organization which is a Federal laboratory,

for qualified research which is energy research, subparagraph (A) shall be applied by substituting "100 percent" for "65 percent".

(ii) ELIGIBLE SMALL BUSINESS.—For purposes of this subparagraph, the term "eligible small business" means a small business with respect to which the taxpayer does not own (within the meaning of section 318) 50 percent or more of—

(I) in the case of a corporation, the outstanding stock of the corporation (either by vote or value), and

(II) in the case of a small business which is not a corporation, the capital and profits interests of the small business.

(iii) SMALL BUSINESS.—For purposes of this subparagraph—

(I) IN GENERAL.—The term "small business" means, with respect to any calendar year, any person if the annual average number of employees employed by such person during either of the 2 preceding calendar years was 500 or fewer. For purposes of the preceding sentence, a preceding calendar year may be taken into account only if the person was in existence throughout the year.

(II) STARTUPS, CONTROLLED GROUPS, AND PREDECESSORS.—Rules similar to the rules of subparagraphs (B) and (D) of section 220(c)(4) shall apply for purposes of this clause.

(iv) FEDERAL LABORATORY.—For purposes of this subparagraph, the term "Federal laboratory" has the meaning given such term by section 4(6) of the Stevenson-Wydler Technology Innovation Act of 1980 (15 U.S.C. 3703(6)), as in effect on the date of the enactment of the Energy Tax Incentives Act of 2005.

(4) TRADE OR BUSINESS REQUIREMENT DISREGARDED FOR IN-HOUSE RESEARCH EXPENSES OF CERTAIN STARTUP VENTURES.—In the case of in-house research expenses, a taxpayer shall be treated as meeting the trade or business requirement of paragraph (1) if, at the time such in-house research expenses are paid or incurred, the principal purpose of the taxpayer in making such expenditures is to use the results of the research in the active conduct of a future trade or business—

(A) of the taxpayer, or

(B) of 1 or more other persons who with the taxpayer are treated as a single taxpayer under subsection (f)(1).

Amendments

• 2005, Gulf Opportunity Zone Act of 2005 (P.L. 109-135)

P.L. 109-135, §402(l)(2):

Amended Code Sec. 41(b)(3)(C)(ii) by striking "(other than an energy research consortium)" after "organization". **Effective** as if included in the provision of the Energy Policy Act of 2005 (P.L. 109-58) to which it relates [**effective** for amounts paid or incurred after 8-8-2005, in tax years ending after such date.—CCH].

• 2005, Energy Tax Incentives Act of 2005 (P.L. 109-58)

P.L. 109-58, §1351(a)(3):

Amended Code Sec. 41(b)(3)(C) by inserting "(other than an energy research consortium)" after "organization". **Effective** for amounts paid or incurred after 8-8-2005, in tax years ending after such date.

P.L. 109-58, §1351(b):

Amended Code Sec. 41(b)(3) by adding at the end a new subparagraph (D). **Effective** for amounts paid or incurred after 8-8-2005, in tax years ending after such date.

• 1996, Small Business Job Protection Act of 1996 (P.L. 104-188)

P.L. 104-188, §1201(e)(1):

Amended Code Sec. 41(b)(2)(D)(iii) by striking "targeted jobs credit" each place it appears and inserting "work opportunity credit". **Effective** for individuals who begin work for the employer after 9-30-96.

P.L. 104-188, §1201(e)(4):

Amended Code Sec. 41(b)(2)(D)(iii) by striking "TARGETED JOBS CREDIT" in the heading and inserting "WORK OPPORTUNITY CREDIT". **Effective** for individuals who begin work for the employer after 9-30-96.

P.L. 104-188, §1204(d):

Amended Code Sec. 41(b)(3) by adding at the end a new subparagraph (C). **Effective** for tax years beginning after 6-30-96. For a special rule, see Act Sec. 1204(f)(3), below.

P.L. 104-188, §1204(f)(3), provides:

(3) ESTIMATED TAX.—The amendments made by this section shall not be taken into account under section 6654 or 6655 of the Internal Revenue Code of 1986 (relating to failure to pay estimated tax) in determining the amount of any installment required to be paid for a taxable year beginning in 1997.

• 1989, Omnibus Budget Reconciliation Act of 1989 (P.L. 101-239)

P.L. 101-239, §7110(b)[c]:

Amended Code Sec. 41(b) by adding at the end thereof a new paragraph (4). **Effective** for tax years beginning after 12-31-89.

[Sec. 41(c)]

(c) BASE AMOUNT.—

(1) IN GENERAL.—The term "base amount" means the product of—

(A) the fixed-base percentage, and

(B) the average annual gross receipts of the taxpayer for the 4 taxable years preceding the taxable year for which the credit is being determined (hereinafter in this subsection referred to as the "credit year").

(2) MINIMUM BASE AMOUNT.—In no event shall the base amount be less than 50 percent of the qualified research expenses for the credit year.

(3) FIXED-BASE PERCENTAGE.—

(A) IN GENERAL.—Except as otherwise provided in this paragraph, the fixed-base percentage is the percentage which the aggregate qualified research expenses of the taxpayer for taxable years beginning after December 31, 1983, and before January 1, 1989, is of the aggregate gross receipts of the taxpayer for such taxable years.

(B) START-UP COMPANIES.—

(i) TAXPAYERS TO WHICH SUBPARAGRAPH APPLIES.—The fixed-base percentage shall be determined under this subparagraph if—

(I) the first taxable year in which a taxpayer had both gross receipts and qualified research expenses begins after December 31, 1983, or

(II) there are fewer than 3 taxable years beginning after December 31, 1983, and before January 1, 1989, in which the taxpayer had both gross receipts and qualified research expenses.

(ii) FIXED-BASE PERCENTAGE.—In a case to which this subparagraph applies, the fixed-base percentage is—

(I) 3 percent for each of the taxpayer's 1st 5 taxable years beginning after December 31, 1993, for which the taxpayer has qualified research expenses,

(II) in the case of the taxpayer's 6th such taxable year, 1/6 of the percentage which the aggregate qualified research expenses of the taxpayer for the 4th and 5th such taxable years is of the aggregate gross receipts of the taxpayer for such years,

(III) in the case of the taxpayer's 7th such taxable year, 1/3 of the percentage which the aggregate qualified research expenses of the taxpayer for the 5th and 6th such taxable years is of the aggregate gross receipts of the taxpayer for such years,

(IV) in the case of the taxpayer's 8th such taxable year, 1/2 of the percentage which the aggregate qualified research expenses of the taxpayer for the 5th, 6th, and 7th such taxable years is of the aggregate gross receipts of the taxpayer for such years,

(V) in the case of the taxpayer's 9th such taxable year, 2/3 of the percentage which the aggregate qualified research expenses of the taxpayer for the 5th, 6th, 7th, and 8th such taxable years is of the aggregate gross receipts of the taxpayer for such years,

(VI) in the case of the taxpayer's 10th such taxable year, 5/6 of the percentage which the aggregate qualified research expenses of the taxpayer for the 5th, 6th, 7th, 8th, and 9th such taxable years is of the aggregate gross receipts of the taxpayer for such years, and

(VII) for taxable years thereafter, the percentage which the aggregate qualified research expenses for any 5 taxable years selected by the taxpayer from among the 5th through the 10th such taxable years is of the aggregate gross receipts of the taxpayer for such selected years.

(iii) TREATMENT OF DE MINIMIS AMOUNTS OF GROSS RECEIPTS AND QUALIFIED RESEARCH EXPENSES.—The Secretary may prescribe regulations providing that de minimis amounts of gross receipts and qualified research expenses shall be disregarded under clauses (i) and (ii).

(C) MAXIMUM FIXED-BASE PERCENTAGE.—In no event shall the fixed-base percentage exceed 16 percent.

(D) ROUNDING.—The percentages determined under subparagraphs (A) and (B)(ii) shall be rounded to the nearest 1/100th of 1 percent.

(4) ELECTION OF ALTERNATIVE INCREMENTAL CREDIT.—

(A) IN GENERAL.—At the election of the taxpayer, the credit determined under subsection (a)(1) shall be equal to the sum of—

(i) 3 percent of so much of the qualified research expenses for the taxable year as exceeds 1 percent of the average described in subsection (c)(1)(B) but does not exceed 1.5 percent of such average,

(ii) 4 percent of so much of such expenses as exceeds 1.5 percent of such average but does not exceed 2 percent of such average, and

(iii) 5 percent of so much of such expenses as exceeds 2 percent of such average.

(B) ELECTION.—An election under this paragraph shall apply to the taxable year for which made and all succeeding taxable years unless revoked with the consent of the Secretary.

(5) ELECTION OF ALTERNATIVE SIMPLIFIED CREDIT.—

(A) IN GENERAL.—At the election of the taxpayer, the credit determined under subsection (a)(1) shall be equal to 14 percent (12 percent in the case of taxable years ending before January 1, 2009) of so much of the qualified research expenses for the taxable year as exceeds 50 percent of the average qualified research expenses for the 3 taxable years preceding the taxable year for which the credit is being determined.

(B) SPECIAL RULE IN CASE OF NO QUALIFIED RESEARCH EXPENSES IN ANY OF 3 PRECEDING TAXABLE YEARS.—

(i) TAXPAYERS TO WHICH SUBPARAGRAPH APPLIES.—The credit under this paragraph shall be determined under this subparagraph if the taxpayer has no qualified research expenses in any one of the 3 taxable years preceding the taxable year for which the credit is being determined.

(ii) CREDIT RATE.—The credit determined under this subparagraph shall be equal to 6 percent of the qualified research expenses for the taxable year.

(C) ELECTION.—An election under this paragraph shall apply to the taxable year for which made and all succeeding taxable years unless revoked with the consent of the Secretary. An election under this paragraph may not be made for any taxable year to which an election under paragraph (4) applies.

(6) CONSISTENT TREATMENT OF EXPENSES REQUIRED.—

(A) IN GENERAL.—Notwithstanding whether the period for filing a claim for credit or refund has expired for any taxable year taken into account in determining the fixed-base percentage, the qualified research expenses taken into account in computing such percentage shall be determined on a basis consistent with the determination of qualified research expenses for the credit year.

(B) PREVENTION OF DISTORTIONS.—The Secretary may prescribe regulations to prevent distortions in calculating a taxpayer's qualified research expenses or gross receipts caused by a change in accounting methods used by such taxpayer between the current year and a year taken into account in computing such taxpayer's fixed-base percentage.

(7) GROSS RECEIPTS.—For purposes of this subsection, gross receipts for any taxable year shall be reduced by returns and allowances made during the taxable year. In the case of a foreign corporation, there shall be taken into account only gross receipts which are effectively connected with the conduct of a trade or business within the United States, the Commonwealth of Puerto Rico, or any possession of the United States.

Amendments

• 2008, Tax Extenders and Alternative Minimum Tax Relief Act of 2008 (P.L. 110-343)

P.L. 110-343, Division C, §301(c):

Amended Code Sec. 41(c)(5)(A) by striking "12 percent" and inserting "14 percent (12 percent in the case of taxable years ending before January 1, 2009)". **Effective** for tax years beginning after 12-31-2007.

• 2006, Tax Relief and Health Care Act of 2006 (P.L. 109-432)

P.L. 109-432, Division A, §104(b)(1)(A)-(C):

Amended Code Sec. 41(c)(4)(A) by striking "2.65 percent" and inserting "3 percent", by striking "3.2 percent" and inserting "4 percent", and by striking "3.75 percent" and inserting "5 percent". **Effective** generally for tax years ending after 12-31-2006. For a transitional rule, see Act Sec. 104(b)(3), below.

P.L. 109-432, Division A, §104(b)(3), provides:

(3) TRANSITION RULE.—

(A) IN GENERAL.—In the case of a specified transitional taxable year for which an election under section 41(c)(4) of the Internal Revenue Code of 1986 applies, the credit determined under section 41(a)(1) of such Code shall be equal to the sum of—

(i) the applicable 2006 percentage multiplied by the amount determined under section 41(c)(4)(A) of such Code (as in effect for taxable years ending on December 31, 2006), plus

(ii) the applicable 2007 percentage multiplied by the amount determined under section 41(c)(4)(A) of such Code (as in effect for taxable years ending on January 1, 2007).

(B) DEFINITIONS.—For purposes of subparagraph (A)—

(i) SPECIFIED TRANSITIONAL TAXABLE YEAR.—The term "specified transitional taxable year" means any taxable year which ends after December 31, 2006, and which includes such date.

(ii) APPLICABLE 2006 PERCENTAGE.—The term "applicable 2006 percentage" means the number of days in the specified transitional taxable year before January 1, 2007, divided by the number of days in such taxable year.

(iii) APPLICABLE 2007 PERCENTAGE.—The term "applicable 2007 percentage" means the number of days in the specified transitional taxable year after December 31, 2006, divided by the number of days in such taxable year.

P.L. 109-432, Division A, §104(c)(1):

Amended Code Sec. 41(c) by redesignating paragraphs (5) and (6) as paragraphs (6) and (7), respectively, and by inserting after paragraph (4) a new paragraph (5). **Effective** generally for tax years ending after 12-31-2006. For transitional rules, see Act Sec. 104(c)(2) and (4), below.

P.L. 109-432, Division A, §104(c)(2) and (4), provide:

(2) TRANSITION RULE FOR DEEMED REVOCATION OF ELECTION OF ALTERNATIVE INCREMENTAL CREDIT.—In the case of an election under section 41(c)(4) of the Internal Revenue Code of 1986 which applies to the taxable year which includes January 1, 2007, such election shall be treated as revoked with the consent of the Secretary of the Treasury if the taxpayer makes an election under section 41(c)(5) of such Code (as added by this subsection) for such year.

* * *

(4) TRANSITION RULE FOR NONCALENDAR TAXABLE YEARS.—

(A) IN GENERAL.—In the case of a specified transitional taxable year for which an election under section 41(c)(5) of the Internal Revenue Code of 1986 (as added by this subsection) applies, the credit determined under section 41(a)(1) of such Code shall be equal to the sum of—

(i) the applicable 2006 percentage multiplied by the amount determined under section 41(a)(1) of such Code (as in effect for taxable years ending on December 31, 2006), plus

(ii) the applicable 2007 percentage multiplied by the amount determined under section 41(c)(5) of such Code (as in effect for taxable years ending on January 1, 2007).

(B) DEFINITIONS AND SPECIAL RULES.—For purposes of subparagraph (A)—

(i) DEFINITIONS.—Terms used in this paragraph which are also used in subsection (b)(3) shall have the respective meanings given such terms in such subsection.

(ii) DUAL ELECTIONS PERMITTED.—Elections under paragraphs (4) and (5) of section 41(c) of such Code may both apply for the specified transitional taxable year.

(iii) DEFERRAL OF DEEMED ELECTION REVOCATION.—Any election under section 41(c)(4) of the Internal Revenue Code of 1986 treated as revoked under paragraph (2) shall be treated as revoked for the taxable year after the specified transitional taxable year.

P.L. 109-432, Division A, §123(a), provides:

(a) RESEARCH CREDIT ELECTIONS.—In the case of any taxable year ending after December 31, 2005, and before the date of the enactment of this Act, any election under section 41(c)(4) or section 280C(c)(3)(C) of the Internal Revenue Code of 1986 shall be treated as having been timely made for such taxable year if such election is made not later than the later of April 15, 2007, or such time as the Secretary of the Treasury, or his designee, may specify. Such election shall be made in the manner prescribed by such Secretary or designee.

• 1999, Tax Relief Extension Act of 1999 (P.L. 106-170)

P.L. 106-170, §502(b)(1)(A)-(C):

Amended Code Sec. 41(c)(4)(A) by striking "1.65 percent" and inserting "2.65 percent", by striking "2.2 percent" and inserting "3.2 percent", and by striking "2.75 percent" and inserting "3.75 percent". **Effective** for tax years beginning after 6-30-99. For a special rule, see Act Sec. 502(d), below.

P.L. 106-170, §502(c)(1):

Amended Code Sec. 41(c)(6) by inserting ", the Commonwealth of Puerto Rico, or any possession of the United States" after "United States". **Effective** for amounts paid or incurred after 6-30-99. For a special rule, see Act Sec. 502(d), below.

P.L. 106-170, §502(d), provides:

(d) SPECIAL RULE.—

(1) IN GENERAL.—For purposes of the Internal Revenue Code of 1986, the credit determined under section 41 of such Code which is otherwise allowable under such Code—

(A) shall not be taken into account prior to October 1, 2000, to the extent such credit is attributable to the first suspension period; and

(B) shall not be taken into account prior to October 1, 2001, to the extent such credit is attributable to the second suspension period.

On or after the earliest date that an amount of credit may be taken into account, such amount may be taken into account through the filing of an amended return, an application for expedited refund, an adjustment of estimated taxes, or other means allowed by such Code.

(2) SUSPENSION PERIODS.—For purposes of this subsection—

(A) the first suspension period is the period beginning on July 1, 1999, and ending on September 30, 2000; and

(B) the second suspension period is the period beginning on October 1, 2000, and ending on September 30, 2001.

(3) EXPEDITED REFUNDS.—

(A) IN GENERAL.—If there is an overpayment of tax with respect to a taxable year by reason of paragraph (1), the taxpayer may file an application for a tentative refund of such overpayment. Such application shall be in such manner and form, and contain such information, as the Secretary may prescribe.

(B) DEADLINE FOR APPLICATIONS.—Subparagraph (A) shall apply only to an application filed before the date which is 1 year after the close of the suspension period to which the application relates.

(C) ALLOWANCE OF ADJUSTMENTS.—Not later than 90 days after the date on which an application is filed under this paragraph, the Secretary shall—

(i) review the application;

(ii) determine the amount of the overpayment; and

(iii) apply, credit, or refund such overpayment,

in a manner similar to the manner provided in section 6411(b) of such Code.

(D) CONSOLIDATED RETURNS.—The provisions of section 6411(c) of such Code shall apply to an adjustment under this paragraph in such manner as the Secretary may provide.

(4) CREDIT ATTRIBUTABLE TO SUSPENSION PERIOD.—

(A) IN GENERAL.—For purposes of this subsection, in the case of a taxable year which includes a portion of the suspension period, the amount of credit determined under section 41 of such Code for such taxable year which is attributable to such period is the amount which bears the same ratio to the amount of credit determined under such section 41 for such taxable year as the number of months in the suspension period which are during such taxable year bears to the number of months in such taxable year.

(B) WAIVER OF ESTIMATED TAX PENALTIES.—No addition to tax shall be made under section 6654 or 6655 of such Code for any period before July 1, 1999, with respect to any underpayment of tax imposed by such Code to the extent such underpayment was created or increased by reason of subparagraph (A).

(5) SECRETARY.—For purposes of this subsection, the term "Secretary" means the Secretary of the Treasury (or such Secretary's delegate).

• 1997, Taxpayer Relief Act of 1997 (P.L. 105-34)

P.L. 105-34, §601(b)(1):

Amended Code Sec. 41(c)(4)(B). **Effective** for amounts paid or incurred after 5-31-97. Prior to amendment, Code Sec. 41(c)(4)(B) read as follows:

(B) ELECTION.—An election under this paragraph may be made only for the first taxable year of the taxpayer beginning after June 30, 1996. Such an election shall apply to the taxable year for which made and all succeeding taxable years unless revoked with the consent of the Secretary.

• 1996, Small Business Job Protection Act of 1996 (P.L. 104-188)

P.L. 104-188, §1204(b):

Amended Code Sec. 41(c)(3)(B)(i). **Effective** for tax years ending after 6-30-96. Prior to amendment, Code Sec. 41(c)(3)(B)(i) read as follows:

(i) TAXPAYERS TO WHICH SUBPARAGRAPH APPLIES.—The fixed-base percentage shall be determined under this subparagraph if there are fewer than 3 taxable years beginning after December 31, 1983, and before January 1, 1989, in which the taxpayer had both gross receipts and qualified research expenses.

P.L. 104-188, §1204(c):

Amended Code Sec. 41(c) by redesignating paragraphs (4) and (5) as paragraphs (5) and (6), respectively, and inserting after paragraph (3) a new paragraph (4). **Effective** for tax years beginning after 6-30-96. For a special rule, see Act Sec. 1204(f)(3), below.

P.L. 104-188, §1204(f)(3), provides:

(3) ESTIMATED TAX.—The amendments made by this section shall not be taken into account under section 6654 or 6655 of the Internal Revenue Code of 1986 (relating to failure to pay estimated tax) in determining the amount of any installment required to be paid for a taxable year beginning in 1997.

• 1993, Omnibus Budget Reconciliation Act of 1993 (P.L. 103-66)

P.L. 103-66, §13112(a):

Amended Code Sec. 41(c)(3)(B)(ii). **Effective** for tax years beginning after 12-31-93. Prior to amendment, Code Sec. 41(c)(3)(B)(ii) read as follows:

(ii) FIXED-BASE PERCENTAGE.—In a case to which this subparagraph applies, the fixed-base percentage is 3 percent.

P.L. 103-66, §13112(b)(1):

Amended Code Sec. 41(c)(3)(B)(iii) by striking "clause (i)" and inserting "clauses (i) and (ii)". **Effective** for tax years beginning after 12-31-93.

P.L. 103-66, §13112(b)(2):

Amended Code Sec. 41(c)(3)(D) by striking "subparagraph (A)" and inserting "subparagraphs (A) and (B)(ii)". **Effective** for tax years beginning after 12-31-93.

• 1989, Omnibus Budget Reconciliation Act of 1989 (P.L. 101-239)

P.L. 101-239, §7110(b)(1):

Amended Code Sec. 41(c). **Effective** for tax years beginning after 12-31-89. Prior to amendment, Code Sec. 41(c) read as follows:

(c) BASE PERIOD RESEARCH EXPENSES.—For purposes of this section—

(1) IN GENERAL.—The term "base period research expenses" means the average of the qualified research expenses for each year in the base period.

(2) BASE PERIOD.—

(A) IN GENERAL.—For purposes of this subsection, the term "base period" means the 3 taxable years immediately preceding the taxable year for which the determination is being made (hereinafter in this subsection referred to as the "determination year").

(B) TRANSITIONAL RULES.—Subparagraph (A) shall be applied—

(i) by substituting "first taxable year" for "3 taxable years" in the case of the first determination year ending after June 30, 1981, and

(ii) by substituting "2" for "3" in the case of the second determination year ending after June 30, 1981.

(3) MINIMUM BASE PERIOD RESEARCH EXPENSES.—In no event shall the base period research expenses be less than 50 percent of the qualified research expenses for the determination year.

[Sec. 41(d)]

(d) QUALIFIED RESEARCH DEFINED.—For purposes of this section—

(1) IN GENERAL.—The term "qualified research" means research—

(A) with respect to which expenditures may be treated as expenses under section 174,

(B) which is undertaken for the purpose of discovering information—

(i) which is technological in nature, and

(ii) the application of which is intended to be useful in the development of a new or improved business component of the taxpayer, and

(C) substantially all of the activities of which constitute elements of a process of experimentation for a purpose described in paragraph (3).

Such term does not include any activity described in paragraph (4).

(2) TESTS TO BE APPLIED SEPARATELY TO EACH BUSINESS COMPONENT.—For purposes of this subsection—

(A) IN GENERAL.—Paragraph (1) shall be applied separately with respect to each business component of the taxpayer.

(B) BUSINESS COMPONENT DEFINED.—The term "business component" means any product, process, computer software, technique, formula, or invention which is to be—

(i) held for sale, lease, or license, or

(ii) used by the taxpayer in a trade or business of the taxpayer.

(C) SPECIAL RULE FOR PRODUCTION PROCESSES.—Any plant process, machinery, or technique for commercial production of a business component shall be treated as a separate business component (and not as part of the business component being produced).

(3) PURPOSES FOR WHICH RESEARCH MAY QUALIFY FOR CREDIT.—For purposes of paragraph (1)(C)—

(A) IN GENERAL.—Research shall be treated as conducted for a purpose described in this paragraph if it relates to—

(i) a new or improved function,

(ii) performance, or

(iii) reliability or quality.

(B) CERTAIN PURPOSES NOT QUALIFIED.—Research shall in no event be treated as conducted for a purpose described in this paragraph if it relates to style, taste, cosmetic, or seasonal design factors.

(4) ACTIVITIES FOR WHICH CREDIT NOT ALLOWED.—The term "qualified research" shall not include any of the following:

(A) RESEARCH AFTER COMMERCIAL PRODUCTION.—Any research conducted after the beginning of commercial production of the business component.

(B) ADAPTATION OF EXISTING BUSINESS COMPONENTS.—Any research related to the adaptation of an existing business component to a particular customer's requirement or need.

(C) DUPLICATION OF EXISTING BUSINESS COMPONENT.—Any research related to the reproduction of an existing business component (in whole or in part) from a physical examination of the business component itself or from plans, blueprints, detailed specifications, or publicly available information with respect to such business component.

(D) SURVEYS, STUDIES, ETC.—Any—

(i) efficiency survey,

(ii) activity relating to management function or technique,

(iii) market research, testing, or development (including advertising or promotions),

(iv) routine data collection, or

(v) routine or ordinary testing or inspection for quality control.

(E) COMPUTER SOFTWARE.—Except to the extent provided in regulations, any research with respect to computer software which is developed by (or for the benefit of) the taxpayer primarily for internal use by the taxpayer, other than for use in—

(i) an activity which constitutes qualified research (determined with regard to this subparagraph), or

(ii) a production process with respect to which the requirements of paragraph (1) are met.

(F) FOREIGN RESEARCH.—Any research conducted outside the United States, the Commonwealth of Puerto Rico, or any possession of the United States.

(G) SOCIAL SCIENCES, ETC.—Any research in the social sciences, arts, or humanities.

(H) FUNDED RESEARCH.—Any research to the extent funded by any grant, contract, or otherwise by another person (or governmental entity).

Amendments

• 1999, Tax Relief Extension Act of 1999 (P.L. 106-170)

P.L. 106-170, §502(c)(1):

Amended Code Sec. 41(d)(4)(F) by inserting ", the Commonwealth of Puerto Rico, or any possession of the United States" after "United States". **Effective** for amounts paid or incurred after 6-30-99. For a special rule, see Act Sec. 502(d) under the amendment notes following Code Sec. 41(c).

[Sec. 41(e)]

(e) CREDIT ALLOWABLE WITH RESPECT TO CERTAIN PAYMENTS TO QUALIFIED ORGANIZATIONS FOR BASIC RESEARCH.—For purposes of this section—

(1) IN GENERAL.—In the case of any taxpayer who makes basic research payments for any taxable year—

(A) the amount of basic research payments taken into account under subsection (a)(2) shall be equal to the excess of—

(i) such basic research payments, over

(ii) the qualified organization base period amount, and

(B) that portion of such basic research payments which does not exceed the qualified organization base period amount shall be treated as contract research expenses for purposes of subsection (a)(1).

(2) BASIC RESEARCH PAYMENTS DEFINED.—For purposes of this subsection—

(A) IN GENERAL.—The term "basic research payment" means, with respect to any taxable year, any amount paid in cash during such taxable year by a corporation to any qualified organization for basic research but only if—

(i) such payment is pursuant to a written agreement between such corporation and such qualified organization, and

(ii) such basic research is to be performed by such qualified organization.

(B) EXCEPTION TO REQUIREMENT THAT RESEARCH BE PERFORMED BY THE ORGANIZATION.—In the case of a qualified organization described in subparagraph (C) or (D) of paragraph (6), clause (ii) of subparagraph (A) shall not apply.

(3) QUALIFIED ORGANIZATION BASE PERIOD AMOUNT.—For purposes of this subsection, the term "qualified organization base period amount" means an amount equal to the sum of—

(A) the minimum basic research amount, plus

(B) the maintenance-of-effort amount.

(4) MINIMUM BASIC RESEARCH AMOUNT.—For purposes of this subsection—

(A) IN GENERAL.—The term "minimum basic research amount" means an amount equal to the greater of—

(i) 1 percent of the average of the sum of amounts paid or incurred during the base period for—

(I) any in-house research expenses, and

(II) any contract research expenses, or

(ii) the amounts treated as contract research expenses during the base period by reason of this subsection (as in effect during the base period).

(B) FLOOR AMOUNT.—Except in the case of a taxpayer which was in existence during a taxable year (other than a short taxable year) in the base period, the minimum basic research amount for any base period shall not be less than 50 percent of the basic research payments for the taxable year for which a determination is being made under this subsection.

(5) MAINTENANCE-OF-EFFORT AMOUNT.—For purposes of this subsection—

(A) IN GENERAL.—The term "maintenance-of-effort amount" means, with respect to any taxable year, an amount equal to the excess (if any) of—

(i) an amount equal to—

(I) the average of the nondesignated university contributions paid by the taxpayer during the base period, multiplied by

(II) the cost-of-living adjustment for the calendar year in which such taxable year begins, over

(ii) the amount of nondesignated university contributions paid by the taxpayer during such taxable year.

(B) NONDESIGNATED UNIVERSITY CONTRIBUTIONS.—For purposes of this paragraph, the term "nondesignated university contribution" means any amount paid by a taxpayer to any qualified organization described in paragraph (6)(A)—

(i) for which a deduction was allowable under section 170, and

(ii) which was not taken into account—

(I) in computing the amount of the credit under this section (as in effect during the base period) during any taxable year in the base period, or

(II) as a basic research payment for purposes of this section.

(C) COST-OF-LIVING ADJUSTMENT DEFINED.—

(i) IN GENERAL.—The cost-of-living adjustment for any calendar year is the cost-of-living adjustment for such calendar year determined under section 1(f)(3), by substituting "calendar year 1987" for "calendar year 1992" in subparagraph (B) thereof [of Code Sec. 1(f)(3)].

(ii) SPECIAL RULE WHERE BASE PERIOD ENDS IN A CALENDAR YEAR OTHER THAN 1983 OR 1984.—If the base period of any taxpayer does not end in 1983 or 1984, section 1(f)(3)(B) shall, for purposes of this paragraph, be applied by substituting the calendar year in which such base period ends for 1992. Such substitution shall be in lieu of the substitution under clause (i).

(6) QUALIFIED ORGANIZATION.—For purposes of this subsection, the term "qualified organization" means any of the following organizations:

(A) EDUCATIONAL INSTITUTIONS.—Any educational organization which—

(i) is an institution of higher education (within the meaning of section 3304(f)), and

(ii) is described in section 170(b)(1)(A)(ii).

(B) CERTAIN SCIENTIFIC RESEARCH ORGANIZATIONS.—Any organization not described in subparagraph (A) which—

(i) is described in section 501(c)(3) and is exempt from tax under section 501(a),

(ii) is organized and operated primarily to conduct scientific research, and

(iii) is not a private foundation.

(C) SCIENTIFIC TAX-EXEMPT ORGANIZATIONS.—Any organization which—

(i) is described in—

(I) section 501(c)(3) (other than a private foundation), or

(II) section 501(c)(6),

(ii) is exempt from tax under section 501(a),

(iii) is organized and operated primarily to promote scientific research by qualified organizations described in subparagraph (A) pursuant to written research agreements, and

(iv) currently expends—

(I) substantially all of its funds, or

(II) substantially all of the basic research payments received by it,

for grants to, or contracts for basic research with, an organization described in subparagraph (A).

(D) CERTAIN GRANT ORGANIZATIONS.—Any organization not described in subparagraph (B) or (C) which—

(i) is described in section 501(c)(3) and is exempt from tax under section 501(a) (other than a private foundation),

(ii) is established and maintained by an organization established before July 10, 1981, which meets the requirements of clause (i),

(iii) is organized and operated exclusively for the purpose of making grants to organizations described in subparagraph (A) pursuant to written research agreements for purposes of basic research, and

(iv) makes an election, revocable only with the consent of the Secretary, to be treated as a private foundation for purposes of this title (other than section 4940, relating to excise tax based on investment income).

(7) DEFINITIONS AND SPECIAL RULES.—For purposes of this subsection—

(A) BASIC RESEARCH.—The term "basic research" means any original investigation for the advancement of scientific knowledge not having a specific commercial objective, except that such term shall not include—

(i) basic research conducted outside of the United States, and

(ii) basic research in the social sciences, arts, or humanities.

(B) BASE PERIOD.—The term "base period" means the 3-taxable-year period ending with the taxable year immediately preceding the 1st taxable year of the taxpayer beginning after December 31, 1983.

(C) EXCLUSION FROM INCREMENTAL CREDIT CALCULATION.—For purposes of determining the amount of credit allowable under subsection (a)(1) for any taxable year, the amount of the basic research payments taken into account under subsection (a)(2)—

(i) shall not be treated as qualified research expenses under subsection (a)(1)(A), and

(ii) shall not be included in the computation of base amount under subsection (a)(1)(B).

(D) TRADE OR BUSINESS QUALIFICATION.—For purposes of applying subsection (b)(1) to this subsection, any basic research payments shall be treated as an amount paid in carrying on a trade or business of the taxpayer in the taxable year in which it is paid (without regard to the provisions of subsection (b)(3)(B)).

(E) CERTAIN CORPORATIONS NOT ELIGIBLE.—The term "corporation" shall not include—

(i) an S corporation,

(ii) a personal holding company (as defined in section 542), or

(iii) a service organization (as defined in section 414(m)(3)).

Amendments

• 1993, Omnibus Budget Reconciliation Act of 1993 (P.L. 103-66)

P.L. 103-66, §13201(b)(3)(C):

Amended Code Sec. 41(e)(5)(C) by striking "1989" each place it appears and inserting "1992". **Effective** for tax years beginning after 12-31-92.

• 1990, Omnibus Budget Reconciliation Act of 1990 (P.L. 101-508)

P.L. 101-508, §11101(d)(1)(C)(i)-(iii):

Amended Code Sec. 41(e)(5)(C) by inserting ", by substituting `calendar year 1987' for `calendar year 1989' in subparagraph (B) thereof" before the period at the end of clause (i), by striking "1987" in clause (ii) and inserting "1989", and by adding at the end of clause (ii) a new sentence. **Effective** for tax years beginning after 12-31-90.

• 1989, Omnibus Budget Reconciliation Act of 1989 (P.L. 101-239)

P.L. 101-239, §7110(b)(2)(B):

Amended Code Sec. 41(e)(7)(C)(ii) by striking "base period research expenses" and inserting "base amount". **Effective** for tax years beginning after 12-31-89.

[Sec. 41(f)]

(f) SPECIAL RULES.—For purposes of this section—

(1) AGGREGATION OF EXPENDITURES.—

(A) CONTROLLED GROUP OF CORPORATIONS.—In determining the amount of the credit under this section—

(i) all members of the same controlled group of corporations shall be treated as a single taxpayer, and

(ii) the credit (if any) allowable by this section to each such member shall be its proportionate shares of the qualified research expenses, basic research payments, and amounts paid or incurred to energy research consortiums, [sic] giving rise to the credit.

(B) COMMON CONTROL.—Under regulations prescribed by the Secretary, in determining the amount of the credit under this section—

(i) all trades or businesses (whether or not incorporated) which are under common control shall be treated as a single taxpayer, and

(ii) the credit (if any) allowable by this section to each such person shall be its proportionate shares of the qualified research expenses, basic research payments, and amounts paid or incurred to energy research consortiums, [sic] giving rise to the credit.

The regulations prescribed under this subparagraph shall be based on principles similar to the principles which apply in the case of subparagraph (A).

(2) ALLOCATIONS.—

(A) PASS-THRU IN THE CASE OF ESTATES AND TRUSTS.—Under regulations prescribed by the Secretary, rules similar to the rules of subsection (d) of section 52 shall apply.

(B) ALLOCATION IN THE CASE OF PARTNERSHIPS.—In the case of partnerships, the credit shall be allocated among partners under regulations prescribed by the Secretary.

(3) ADJUSTMENTS FOR CERTAIN ACQUISITIONS, ETC.—Under regulations prescribed by the Secretary—

(A) ACQUISITIONS.—If, after December 31, 1983, a taxpayer acquires the major portion of a trade or business of another person (hereinafter in this paragraph referred to as the "predecessor") or the major portion of a separate unit of a trade or business of a predecessor, then, for purposes of applying this section for any taxable year ending after such acquisition, the amount of qualified research expenses paid or incurred by the taxpayer during periods before such acquisition shall be increased by so much of such expenses paid or incurred by the predecessor with respect to the acquired trade or business as is attributable to the portion of such trade or business or separate unit acquired by the taxpayer, and the gross receipts of the taxpayer for such periods shall be increased by so much of the gross receipts of such predecessor with respect to the acquired trade or business as is attributable to such portion.

(B) DISPOSITIONS.—If, after December 31, 1983—

(i) a taxpayer disposes of the major portion of any trade or business or the major portion of a separate unit of a trade or business in a transaction to which subparagraph (A) applies, and

(ii) the taxpayer furnished the acquiring person such information as is necessary for the application of subparagraph (A),

then, for purposes of applying this section for any taxable year ending after such disposition, the amount of qualified research expenses paid or incurred by the taxpayer during periods before such disposition shall be decreased by so much of such expenses as is attributable to the portion of such trade or business or separate unit disposed of by the taxpayer, and the gross receipts of the taxpayer for such periods shall be decreased by so much of the gross receipts as is attributable to such portion.

(C) CERTAIN REIMBURSEMENTS TAKEN INTO ACCOUNT IN DETERMINING FIXED-BASE PERCENTAGE.—If during any of the 3 taxable years following the taxable year in which a disposition to which subparagraph (B) applies occurs, the disposing taxpayer (or a person with whom the taxpayer is required to aggregate expenditures under paragraph (1)) reimburses the acquiring person (or a person required to so aggregate expenditures with such person) for research on behalf of the taxpayer, then the amount of qualified research expenses of the taxpayer for the taxable years taken into account in computing the fixed-base percentage shall be increased by the lesser of—

(i) the amount of the decrease under subparagraph (B) which is allocable to taxable years so taken into account, or

(ii) the product of the number of taxable years so taken into account, multiplied by the amount of the reimbursement described in this subparagraph.

(4) SHORT TAXABLE YEARS.—In the case of any short taxable year, qualified research expenses and gross receipts shall be annualized in such circumstances and under such methods as the Secretary may prescribe by regulation.

(5) CONTROLLED GROUP OF CORPORATIONS.—The term "controlled group of corporations" has the same meaning given to such term by section 1563(a), except that—

(A) "more than 50 percent" shall be substituted for "at least 80 percent" each place it appears in section 1563(a)(1), and

(B) the determination shall be made without regard to subsections (a)(4) and (e)(3)(C) of section 1563.

(6) ENERGY RESEARCH CONSORTIUM.—

(A) IN GENERAL.—The term "energy research consortium" means any organization—

(i) which is—

(I) described in section 501(c)(3) and is exempt from tax under section 501(a) and is organized and operated primarily to conduct energy research, or

(II) organized and operated primarily to conduct energy research in the public interest (within the meaning of section 501(c)(3)),

(ii) which is not a private foundation,

(iii) to which at least 5 unrelated persons paid or incurred during the calendar year in which the taxable year of the organization begins amounts (including as contributions) to such organization for energy research, and

(iv) to which no single person paid or incurred (including as contributions) during such calendar year an amount equal to more than 50 percent of the total amounts received by such organization during such calendar year for energy research.

(B) TREATMENT OF PERSONS.—All persons treated as a single employer under subsection (a) or (b) of section 52 shall be treated as related persons for purposes of subparagraph (A)(iii) and as a single person for purposes of subparagraph (A)(iv).

(C) FOREIGN RESEARCH.—For purposes of subsection (a)(3), amounts paid or incurred for any energy research conducted outside the United States, the Commonwealth of Puerto Rico, or any possession of the United States shall not be taken into account.

(D) DENIAL OF DOUBLE BENEFIT.—Any amount taken into account under subsection (a)(3) shall not be taken into account under paragraph (1) or (2) of subsection (a).

(E) ENERGY RESEARCH.—The term "energy research" does not include any research which is not qualified research.

Amendments

• 2007, Tax Technical Corrections Act of 2007 (P.L. 110-172)

P.L. 110-172, §6(c)(2):

Amended Code Sec. 41(f)(6) by adding at the end a new subparagraph (E). **Effective** as if included in the provision of the Energy Tax Incentives Act of 2005 (P.L. 109-58) to which it relates [**effective** for amounts paid or incurred after 8-8-2005, in tax years ending after such date.—CCH].

P.L. 110-172, §11(e)(2):

Amended Code Sec. 41(f)(1)(A)(ii) and (B)(ii) by striking "qualified research expenses and basic research payments" and inserting "qualified research expenses, basic research payments, and amounts paid or incurred to energy research consortiums,". **Effective** as if included in the provision of the Energy Tax Incentives Act of 2005 (P.L. 109-58) to which it relates [**effective** for amounts paid or incurred after 8-8-2005, in tax years ending after such date.—CCH].

• 2005, Gulf Opportunity Zone Act of 2005 (P.L. 109-135)

P.L. 109-135, §402(l)(1):

Amended Code Sec. 41(f)(6) by adding at the end new subparagraphs (C) and (D). **Effective** as if included in the provision of the Energy Policy Act of 2005 (P.L. 109-58) to which it relates [**effective** for amounts paid or incurred after 8-8-2005, in tax years ending after such date.—CCH].

• 2005, Energy Tax Incentives Act of 2005 (P.L. 109-58)

P.L. 109-58, §1351(a)(2):

Amended Code Sec. 41(f) by adding at the end a new paragraph (6). **Effective** for amounts paid or incurred after 8-8-2005, in tax years ending after such date.

• 1989, Omnibus Budget Reconciliation Act of 1989 (P.L. 101-239)

P.L. 101-239, §7110(b)(2)(C):

Amended Code Sec. 41(f)(1) by striking "proportionate share of the increase in qualified research expenses" each place it appears and inserting "proportionate shares of the qualified research expenses and basic research payments" **Effective** for tax years beginning after 12-31-89.

P.L. 101-239, §7110(b)(2)(D)(i)-(ii):

Amended Code Sec. 41(f)(3)(A) by striking "June 30, 1980" and inserting "December 31, 1983", and by inserting before the period ", and the gross receipts of the taxpayer for such periods shall be increased by so much of the gross receipts of such predecessor with respect to the acquired trade or business as is attributable to such portion". **Effective** for tax years beginning after 12-31-89.

P.L. 101-239, §7110(b)(2)(E)(i)-(ii):

Amended Code Sec. 41(f)(3)(B) by striking "June 30, 1980" and inserting "December 31, 1983", and by inserting before the period ", and the gross receipts of the taxpayer for such periods shall be decreased by so much of the gross receipts as is attributable to such portion". **Effective** for tax years beginning after 12-31-89.

P.L. 101-239, §7110(b)(2)(F)(i):

Amended Code Sec. 41(f)(3)(C) by striking "for the base period" and all that follows through "described in this subparagraph" and inserting "for the taxable years" through "described in this subparagraph". **Effective** for tax years beginning after 12-31-89. Prior to amendment, Code Sec. 41(f)(3)(C) read as follows:

(C) INCREASE IN BASE PERIOD.—If during any of the 3 taxable years following the taxable year in which a disposition to which subparagraph (B) applies occurs, the disposing taxpayer (or a person with whom the taxpayer is required to aggregate expenditures under paragraph (1)) reimburses the acquiring person (or a person required to so aggregate expenditures with such person) for research on behalf of the taxpayer, then the amount of qualified research expenses of the taxpayer for the base period for such taxable year shall be increased by the lesser of—

(i) the amount of the decrease under subparagraph (B) which is allocable to such base period, or

(ii) the product of the number of years in the base period, multiplied by the amount of the reimbursement described in this subparagraph.

P.L. 101-239, §7110(b)(2)(F)(ii):

Amended the heading of Code Sec. 41(f)(3)(C). **Effective** for tax years beginning after 12-31-89. Prior to amendment, the heading for Code Sec. 41(f)(3)(C) read as follows:

(C) INCREASE IN BASE PERIOD.—

P.L. 101-239, §7110(b)(2)(G):

Amended Code Sec. 41(f)(4) by inserting "and gross receipts" after "qualified research expenses". **Effective** for tax years beginning after 12-31-89.

[Sec. 41(g)]

(g) SPECIAL RULE FOR PASS-THRU OF CREDIT.—In the case of an individual who—

(1) owns an interest in an unincorporated trade or business,

(2) is a partner in a partnership,

(3) is a beneficiary of an estate or trust, or

(4) is a shareholder in an S corporation,

the amount determined under subsection (a) for any taxable year shall not exceed an amount (separately computed with respect to such person's interest in such trade or business or entity) equal to the amount of tax attributable to that portion of a person's taxable income which is allocable or apportionable to the person's interest in such trade or business or entity. If the amount determined under subsection (a) for any taxable year exceeds the limitation of the preceding sentence, such amount may be carried to other taxable years under the rules of section 39; except that the limitation of the preceding sentence shall be taken into account in lieu of the limitation of section 38(c) in applying section 39.

Amendments

• 1988, Technical and Miscellaneous Revenue Act of 1988 (P.L. 100-647)

P.L. 100-647, §1002(h)(1):

Amended Code Sec. 41(g) by adding at the end thereof a new sentence. **Effective** as if included in the provision of P.L. 99-514 to which it relates.

[Sec. 41(h)]

(h) TERMINATION.—

(1) IN GENERAL.—This section shall not apply to any amount paid or incurred—

(A) after June 30, 1995, and before July 1, 1996, or

(B) after December 31, 2009.

(2) TERMINATION OF ALTERNATIVE INCREMENTAL CREDIT.—No election under subsection (c)(4) shall apply to taxable years beginning after December 31, 2008.

(2)[(3)] COMPUTATION FOR TAXABLE YEAR IN WHICH CREDIT TERMINATES.—In the case of any taxable year with respect to which this section applies to a number of days which is less than the total number of days in such taxable year—

(A) the amount determined under subsection (c)(1)(B) with respect to such taxable year shall be the amount which bears the same ratio to such amount (determined without regard to this paragraph) as the number of days in such taxable year to which this section applies bears to the total number of days in such taxable year, and

(B) for purposes of subsection (c)(5), the average qualified research expenses for the preceding 3 taxable years shall be the amount which bears the same ratio to such average qualified research expenses (determined without regard to this paragraph) as the number of days in such taxable year to which this section applies bears to the total number of days in such taxable year.

Amendments

• 2008, Tax Extenders and Alternative Minimum Tax Relief Act of 2008 (P.L. 110-343)

P.L. 110-343, Division C, §301(a)(1):

Amended Code Sec. 41(h)(1)(B) by striking "December 31, 2007" and inserting "December 31, 2009". **Effective** for amounts paid or incurred after 12-31-2007.

P.L. 110-343, Division C, §301(b):

Amended Code Sec. 41(h) by redesignating paragraph (2) as paragraph (3), and by inserting after paragraph (1) a new paragraph (2). **Effective** for tax years beginning after 12-31-2007.

P.L. 110-343, Division C, §301(d):

Amended Code Sec. 41(h)(3) [as redesignated]. **Effective** for tax years beginning after 12-31-2007. Prior to amendment, Code Sec. 41(h)(3) read as follows:

(3) COMPUTATION OF BASE AMOUNT.—In the case of any taxable year with respect to which this section applies to a number of days which is less than the total number of days in such taxable year, the base amount with respect to such

taxable year shall be the amount which bears the same ratio to the base amount for such year (determined without regard to this paragraph) as the number of days in such taxable year to which this section applies bears to the total number of days in such taxable year.

• 2006, Tax Relief and Health Care Act of 2006 (P.L. 109-432)

P.L. 109-432, Division A, §104(a)(1):

Amended Code Sec. 41(h)(1)(B) by striking "2005" and inserting "2007". **Effective** for amounts paid or incurred after 12-31-2005.

• 2004, Working Families Tax Relief Act of 2004 (P.L. 108-311)

P.L. 108-311, §301(a)(1):

Amended Code Sec. 41(h)(1)(B) by striking "June 30, 2004" and inserting "December 31, 2005". **Effective** for amounts paid or incurred after 6-30-2004.

• 1999, Tax Relief Extension Act of 1999 (P.L. 106-170)

P.L. 106-170, §502(a)(1)(A)-(B):

Amended Code Sec. 41(h)(1) by striking "June 30, 1999" and inserting "June 30, 2004", and by striking the material following subparagraph (B). **Effective** for amounts paid or incurred after 6-30-99. For a special rule, see Act Sec. 502(d) under the amendment notes following Code Sec. 41(c). Prior to amendment, the material following subparagraph (B) read as follows:

Notwithstanding the preceding sentence, in the case of a taxpayer making an election under subsection (c)(4) for its first taxable year beginning after June 30, 1996, and before July 1, 1997, this section shall apply to amounts paid or incurred during the 36-month period beginning with the first month of such year. The 36 months referred to in the preceding sentence shall be reduced by the number of full months after June 1996 (and before the first month of such first taxable year) during which the taxpayer paid or incurred any amount which is taken into account in determining the credit under this section.

• 1998, Tax and Trade Relief Extension Act of 1998 (P.L. 105-277)

P.L. 105-277, §1001(a)(1)-(3):

Amended Code Sec. 41(h)(1) by striking "June 30, 1998" and inserting "June 30, 1999", by striking "24-month" and inserting "36-month", and by striking "24 months" and inserting "36 months". **Effective** for amounts paid or incurred after 6-30-98.

• 1997, Taxpayer Relief Act of 1997 (P.L. 105-34)

P.L. 105-34, §601(a)(1)-(2):

Amended Code Sec. 41(h)(1) by striking "May 31, 1997" and inserting "June 30, 1998", and by striking in the last sentence "during the first 11 months of such taxable year." and inserting "during the 24-month period beginning with the first month of such year. The 24 months referred to in the preceding sentence shall be reduced by the number of full months after June 1996 (and before the first month of such first taxable year) during which the taxpayer paid or incurred any amount which is taken into account in determining the credit under this section.". **Effective** for amounts paid or incurred after 5-31-97.

• 1996, Small Business Job Protection Act of 1996 (P.L. 104-188)

P.L. 104-188, §1204(a):

Amended Code Sec. 41(h). **Effective** for tax years ending after 6-30-96. For a special rule, see Act Sec. 1204(f)(3), below. Prior to amendment, Code Sec. 41(h) read as follows:

(h) TERMINATION.—

(1) IN GENERAL.—This section shall not apply to any amount paid or incurred after June 30, 1995.

(2) COMPUTATION OF BASE AMOUNT.—In the case of any taxable year which begins before July 1, 1995, and ends after June 30, 1995, the base amount with respect to such taxable year shall be the amount which bears the same ratio to the base amount for such year (determined without regard to this paragraph) as the number of days in such taxable year before July 1, 1995, bears to the total number of days in such taxable year.

P.L. 104-188, §1204(f)(3), provides:

(3) ESTIMATED TAX.—The amendments made by this section shall not be taken into account under section 6654 or 6655 of the Internal Revenue Code of 1986 (relating to failure to pay estimated tax) in determining the amount of any installment required to be paid for a taxable year beginning in 1997.

• 1993, Omnibus Budget Reconciliation Act of 1993 (P.L. 103-66)

P.L. 103-66, §13111(a)(1)(A) and (B):

Amended Code Sec. 41(h) by striking "June 30, 1992" each place it appears and inserting "June 30, 1995", and by striking "July 1, 1992" each place it appears and inserting "July 1, 1995". **Effective** for tax years ending after 6-30-92.

• 1991, Tax Extension Act of 1991 (P.L. 102-227)

P.L. 102-227, §102(a)(1)-(2):

Amended Code Sec. 41(h) by striking "December 31, 1991" each place it appears and inserting "June 30, 1992", and by striking "January 1, 1992" each place it appears and inserting "July 1, 1992". **Effective** for tax years ending after 12-31-91.

• 1990, Omnibus Budget Reconciliation Act of 1990 (P.L. 101-508)

P.L. 101-508, §11402(a)(1)-(2):

Amended Code Sec. 41(h) by striking "December 31, 1990" each place it appears and inserting "December 31, 1991", and by striking "January 1, 1991" each place it appears and inserting "January 1, 1992". **Effective** for tax years beginning after 12-31-89.

• 1989, Omnibus Budget Reconciliation Act of 1989 (P.L. 101-239)

P.L. 101-239, §7110(a)(1)(A)-(B):

Amended Code Sec. 41(h), as redesignated by Act Sec. 7814(e)(2)(C), by striking "December 31, 1989" each place it appears and inserting "December 31, 1990", and by striking "January 1, 1990" each place it appears and inserting "January 1, 1991". **Effective** 12-19-89.

P.L. 101-239, §7110(b)(2)(H)(i)-(ii):

Amended Code Sec. 41(h)(2), as amended by Act Sec. 7814(e)(2)(C), by striking "BASE PERIOD EXPENSES" in the heading and inserting "BASE AMOUNT", and by striking "any amount for any base period" and all that follows through "such base period" and inserting "the base amount with respect to such taxable year shall be the amount which bears the same ratio to the base amount for such year (determined without regard to this paragraph)". **Effective** for tax years beginning after 12-31-89. Prior to amendment, Code Sec. 41(h)(2) read as follows:

(2) COMPUTATION OF BASE PERIOD EXPENSES.—In the case of any taxable year which begins before January 1, 1990, and ends after December 31, 1989, any amount for any base period with respect to such taxable year shall be the amount which bears the same ratio to such amount for such base period as the number of days in such taxable year before January 1, 1990, bears to the total number of days in such taxable year.

P.L. 101-239, §7814(e)(2)(C):

Amended Code Sec. 41 by striking subsection (h) and redesignating subsection (i) as subsection (h). **Effective** as if included in the provision of P.L. 100-647 to which it relates. Prior to amendment, Code Sec. 41(h) read as follows:

(h) ELECTION TO HAVE RESEARCH CREDIT NOT APPLY.—

(1) IN GENERAL.—A taxpayer may elect to have this section not apply for any taxable year.

(2) TIME FOR MAKING ELECTION.—An election under paragraph (1) for any taxable year may be made (or revoked) at any time before the expiration of the 3-year period beginning on the last day prescribed by law for filing the return for such taxable year (determined without regard to extensions).

(3) MANNER OF MAKING ELECTION.—An election under paragraph (1) (or revocation thereof) shall be made in such manner as the Secretary may by regulations prescribe.

• **1988, Technical and Miscellaneous Revenue Act of 1988 (P.L. 100-647)**

P.L. 100-647, §4008(b)(1):

Amended Code Sec. 41 by inserting after subsection (g) new subsection (h). **Effective** for tax years beginning after 12-31-88.

P.L. 100-647, §4007(a)(1)-(2):

Amended Code Sec. 41(h) (prior to its redesignation by Act Sec. 4008(b)(1)) by striking out "December 31, 1988" each place it appears and inserting in lieu thereof "December 31, 1989", and by striking out "January 1, 1989" each place it appears and inserting in lieu thereof "January 1, 1990". **Effective** 11-10-88.

P.L. 100-647, §4008(b)(1):

Amended Code Sec. 41 by redesignating subsection (h) as subsection (i). **Effective** for tax years beginning after 12-31-88.

• **1986, Tax Reform Act of 1986 (P.L. 99-514)**

P.L. 99-514, §231(a)(1):

Added Code Sec. 30(h), now redesignated as Code Sec. 41. **Effective** for tax years ending after 12-31-85.

P.L. 99-514, §231(b):

Amended Code Sec. 30(d), now redesignated as Code Sec. 41. **Effective** for tax years beginning after 12-31-85. Prior to amendment, Code Sec. 30(d) read as follows:

(d) QUALIFIED RESEARCH.—For purposes of this section the term "qualified research" has the same meaning as the term research or experimental has under section 174, except that such term shall not include—

(1) qualified research conducted outside the United States,

(2) qualified research in the social sciences or humanities, and

(3) qualified research to the extent funded by any grant, contract, or otherwise by another person (or any governmental entity).

P.L. 99-514, §231(c)(1):

Amended Code Sec. 30(a), now redesignated as Code Sec. 41. **Effective** for tax years beginning after 12-31-85. However, for a special rule, see Act Sec. 231(g)(3), below. Prior to amendment, Code Sec. 30(a) read as follows:

(a) GENERAL RULE.—There shall be allowed as a credit against the tax imposed by this chapter for the taxable year an amount equal to 25 percent of the excess (if any) of—

(1) the qualified research expenses for the taxable year, over

(2) the base period research expenses.

P.L. 99-514, §231(c)(2):

Amended Code Sec. 30(e), now redesignated as Code Sec. 41. **Effective** for tax years beginning after 12-31-85. Prior to amendment, Code Sec. 30(e) read as follows:

(e) CREDIT AVAILABLE WITH RESPECT TO CERTAIN BASIC RESEARCH BY COLLEGES, UNIVERSITIES, AND CERTAIN RESEARCH ORGANIZATIONS—

(1) IN GENERAL.—65 percent of any amount paid or incurred by a corporation (as such term is defined in section 170(e)(4)(D)) to any qualified organization for basic research to be performed by such organization shall be treated as contract research expenses. The preceding sentence shall apply only if the amount is paid or incurred pursuant to a written research agreement between the corporation and the qualified organization.

(2) QUALIFIED ORGANIZATION.—For purposes of this subsection, the term "qualified organization" means—

(A) any educational organization which is described in section 170(b)(1)(A)(ii) and which is an institution of higher education (as defined in section 3304(f)), and

(B) any other organization which—

(i) is described in section 501(c)(3) and exempt from tax under section 501(a),

(ii) is organized and operated primarily to conduct scientific research, and

(iii) is not a private foundation.

(3) BASIC RESEARCH.—The term "basic research" means any original investigation for the advancement of scientific knowledge not having a specific commercial objective, except that such term shall not include—

(A) basic research conducted outside the United States, and

(B) basic research in the social sciences or humanities.

(4) SPECIAL RULES FOR GRANTS TO CERTAIN FUNDS.—

(A) IN GENERAL.—For purposes of this subsection, a qualified fund shall be treated as a qualified organization and the requirements of paragraph (1) that the basic research be performed by the qualified organization shall not apply.

(B) QUALIFIED FUND.—For purposes of subparagraph (A), the term "qualified fund" means any organization which—

(i) is described in section 501(c)(3) and exempt from tax under section 501(a) and is not a private foundation,

(ii) is established and maintained by an organization established before July 10, 1981, which meets the requirements of clause (i),

(iii) is organized and operated exclusively for purposes of making grants pursuant to written research agreements to organizations described in paragraph (2)(A) for purposes of basic research, and

(iv) makes an election under this paragraph.

(C) EFFECT OF ELECTION.—

(i) IN GENERAL.—Any organization which makes an election under this paragraph shall be treated as a private foundation for purposes of this title (other than section 4940, relating to excise tax based on investment income).

(ii) ELECTION REVOCABLE ONLY WITH CONSENT.—An election under this paragraph, once made, may be revoked only with the consent of the Secretary.

P.L. 99-514, §231(d)(2):

Transferred Code Sec. 30 to subpart D of part IV of subchapter A of chapter 1, inserted it after section 40, and redesignated it as section 41. **Effective** for tax years beginning after 12-31-85.

P.L. 99-514, §231(d)(3)(C)(ii):

Amended Code Sec. 41(g), as redesignated by Act Sec. 231. **Effective** for tax years beginning after 12-31-85. Prior to amendment, Code Sec. 41(g) read as follows:

(g) LIMITATION BASED ON AMOUNT OF TAX.—

(1) LIABILITY FOR TAX.—

(A) IN GENERAL.—Except as provided in subparagraph (B), the credit allowed by subsection (a) for any taxable year shall not exceed the taxpayer's tax liability for the taxable year (as defined in section 26(b)), reduced by the sum of the credits allowable under subpart A and sections 27, 28, and 29.

(B) SPECIAL RULE FOR PASSTHROUGH OF CREDIT.—In the case of an individual who—

(i) owns an interest in an unincorporated trade or business,

(ii) is a partner in a partnership,

(iii) is a beneficiary of an estate or trust, or

(iv) is a shareholder in an S corporation,

the credit allowed by subsection (a) for any taxable year shall not exceed the lesser of the amount determined under subparagraph (A) for the taxable year or an amount (separately computed with respect to such person's interest in such trade or business or entity) equal to the amount of tax attributable to that portion of a person's taxable income which is allocable or apportionable to the person's interest in such trade or business or entity.

(2) CARRYBACK AND CARRYOVER OF UNUSED CREDIT.—

(A) ALLOWANCE OF CREDIT.—If the amount of the credit determined under this section for any taxable year exceeds the limitation provided by paragraph (1) for such taxable year (hereinafter in this paragraph referred to as the "unused credit year"), such excess shall be—

(i) a research credit carryback to each of the 3 taxable years preceding the unused credit year, and

(ii) a research credit carryover to each of the 15 taxable years following the unused credit year,

and shall be added to the amount allowable as a credit by this section for such years. If any portion of such excess is a carryback to a taxable year beginning before July 1, 1981, this section shall be deemed to have been in effect for such taxable year for purposes of allowing such carryback as a credit under this section. The entire amount of the unused credit for an unused credit year shall be carried to the earliest of the 18 taxable years to which (by reason of clauses (i) and (ii)) such credit may be carried, and then to each of the other 17 taxable years to the extent that, because of the limitation contained in subparagraph (B), such unused credit may not be added for a prior taxable year to which such unused credit may be carried.

(B) LIMITATION.—The amount of the unused credit which may be added under subparagraph (A) for any preceding or succeeding taxable year shall not exceed the amount by which the limitation provided by paragraph (1) for such taxable year exceeds the sum of—

(i) the credit allowable under this section for such taxable year, and

(ii) the amounts which, by reason of this paragraph, are added to the amount allowable for such taxable year and which are attributable to taxable years preceding the unused credit year.

P.L. 99-514, §231(e):

Amended Code Sec. 41(b)(2)(A)(iii), as redesignated by Act Sec. 231. **Effective** for tax years beginning after 12-31-85. Prior to amendment, Code Sec. 41(b)(2)(A)(iii) read as follows:

(iii) any amount paid or incurred to another person for the right to use personal property in the conduct of qualified research.

P.L. 99-514, §231(g)(3), provides:

(3) BASIC RESEARCH.—Section 41(a)(2) of the Internal Revenue Code of 1986 (as added by this section), and the amendments made by subsection (c)(2), shall apply to taxable years beginning after December 31, 1986.

P.L. 99-514, §1847(b)(1):

Amended Code Sec. 30(b)(2)(D), now redesignated as Code Sec. 41, by striking out "New Jobs or Win Credit" in the heading for clause (iii) and inserting in lieu thereof "Targeted Jobs Credit". **Effective** as if included in the provision of P.L. 98-369 to which such amendment relates.

• 1984, Deficit Reduction Act of 1984 (P.L. 98-369)

P.L. 98-369, §471(c)(1):

Redesignated former Code Sec. 44F as Code Sec. 30. **Effective** for tax years beginning after 12-31-83, and to carrybacks from such years.

P.L. 98-369, §474(i)(1):

Amended Code Sec. 30, as redesignated by Act Sec. 471(c)(1), by striking out "in computing the credit under section 40 or 44B" in subsection (b)(2)(D)(iii) and inserting in lieu thereof "in determining the targeted job credit under section 51(a)", and by amending subparagraph (A) of subsection (g)(1). **Effective** for tax years beginning after 12-31-83, and to carrybacks from such years. Prior to amendment, subparagraph (A) of subsection (g)(1) read as follows:

(A) IN GENERAL.—Except as provided in subparagraph (B), the credit allowed by subsection (a) for any taxable year shall not exceed the amount of the tax imposed by this chapter reduced by the sum of the credits allowable under a section of this part having a lower number or letter designation than this section, other than the credits allowable by sections 31, 39, and 43. For purposes of the preceding sentence, the term "tax imposed by this chapter" shall not include any tax treated as not imposed by this chapter under the last sentence of section 53(a).

P.L. 98-369, §474(i)(2), provides:

(2) NEW SECTION 30 TREATED AS CONTINUATION OF OLD SECTION 44F.—For purposes of determining—

(A) whether any excess credit under old section 44F for a taxable year beginning before January 1, 1984, is allowable as a carryover under new section 30, and

(B) the period during which new section 30 is in effect,

new section 30 shall be treated as a continuation of old section 44F (and shall apply only to the extent old section 44F would have applied).

P.L. 98-369, §612(e)(1):

Amended Code Sec. 30(g)(1)(A), as redesignated by Act Sec. 471(c)(1) and amended by Act Sec. 474(i)(1), by striking out "section 25(b)" and inserting in lieu thereof "section 26(b)". **Effective** for interest paid or accrued after 12-31-84, on indebtedness incurred after 12-31-84, and to elections under section 25(c)(2)(A)(ii) of the Internal Revenue Code of 1954 (as added by this Act) for calendar years after 1983.

• 1983, Technical Corrections Act of 1982 (P.L. 97-448)

P.L. 97-448, §102(h)(2):

Amended Code Sec. 44F(b)(2)(A) by adding a new sentence at the end thereof. **Effective** with respect to amounts paid or incurred after 3-31-82.

• 1982, Subchapter S Revision Act of 1982 (P.L. 97-354)

P.L. 97-354, §5(a)(3)(A):

Amended Code Sec. 44F(f)(2)(A). **Effective** for tax years beginning after 12-31-82. Prior to amendment, it read as follows:

"(A) PASSTHROUGH IN THE CASE OF SUBCHAPTER S CORPORATIONS, ETC.—Under regulations prescribed by the Secretary, rules similar to the rules of subsections (d) and (e) of section 52 shall apply."

P.L. 97-354, §5(a)(3)(B):

Amended Code Sec. 44F(g)(1)(B)(iv) by striking out "an electing small business corporation (within the meaning of section 1371(b))" and inserting in lieu thereof "an S corporation". **Effective** for tax years beginning after 12-31-82.

• 1981, Economic Recovery Tax Act of 1981 (P.L. 97-34)

P.L. 97-34, §221(a):

Added Code Sec. 44F. **Effective** for amounts paid or incurred after 6-30-81 [**effective** date changed by P.L. 99-514, §231].

P.L. 97-34, §221(d)(2), as amended by P.L. 99-514, §231(a)(2), provides:

(2) TRANSITIONAL RULE.—

(A) IN GENERAL.—If, with respect to the first taxable year to which the amendments made by this section apply and which ends in 1981 or 1982, the taxpayer may only take into account qualified research expenses paid or incurred during a portion of such taxable year, the amount of the qualified research expenses taken into account for the base period of such taxable year shall be the amount which bears the same ratio to the total qualified research expenses for such base period as the number of months in such portion of such taxable year bears to the total number of months in such taxable year.

(B) DEFINITIONS.—For purposes of the preceding sentence, the terms "qualified research expenses" and "base period" have the meanings given to such terms by section 44F of the Internal Revenue Code of 1954 (as added by this section).

[Sec. 41—Repealed]

Amendments

• 1988, Technical and Miscellaneous Revenue Act of 1988 (P.L. 100-647)

P.L. 100-647, §1011B(l)(3), provides:

(3) If any newspaper corporation described in section 1177(b) of the Reform Act, as amended by this subsection, pays in cash a dividend within 60 days after the date of the enactment of this Act to the corporation's employee stock ownership plans and if a corporate resolution declaring such dividend was adopted before November 30, 1987, and such resolution specifies that such dividend shall be contingent upon passage by the Congress of technical corrections, then such dividend (to the extent the aggregate amount so paid does not exceed $3,500,000) shall be treated as if it had been declared and paid in 1987 for all purposes of the Internal Revenue Code of 1986. **Effective** for compensation paid or accrued after 12-31-86, in tax years ending after such date. However, for an exception, see Act Sec. 1171(c)(2), below.

• 1986, Tax Reform Act of 1986 (P.L. 99-514)

P.L. 99-514, §1171(a):

Repealed Code Sec. 41. **Effective** for compensation paid or accrued after 12-31-86, in tax years ending after such date. However, for an exception, see Act Sec. 1171(c)(2), below. Prior to repeal, Code Sec. 41 read as follows:

SEC. 41. EMPLOYEE STOCK OWNERSHIP CREDIT.

(a) GENERAL RULE.—

(1) AMOUNT OF CREDIT.—In the case of a corporation which elects to have this section apply for the taxable year and which meets the requirements of subsection (c)(1), for purposes of section 38, the amount of the employee stock ownership credit determined under this section for the taxable year is an amount equal to the amount of the credit determined under paragraph (2) for such taxable year.

(2) DETERMINATION OF AMOUNT.—

(A) IN GENERAL.—The amount of the credit determined under this paragraph for the taxable year shall be equal to the lessor of—

(i) the aggregate value of employer securities transferred by the corporation for the taxable year to a tax credit employee stock ownership plan maintained by the corporation, or

(ii) the applicable percentage of the amount of the aggregate compensation (within the meaning of section 415(c)(3)) paid or accrued during the taxable year to all employees under a tax credit employee stock ownership plan.

(B) APPLICABLE PERCENTAGE.—For purposes of applying subparagraph (A)(ii), the applicable percentage shall be determined in accordance with the following table:

For aggregate compensation paid or accrued during a portion of the taxable occuring in calendar year:	*The applicable percentage is:*
1983	0.5
1984	0.5
1985	0.5
1986	0.5
1987	0.5
1988 or thereafter	0.

(b) CERTAIN REGULATED COMPANIES.—No credit attributable to compensation taken into account for the ratemaking purposes involved shall be determined under this section with respect to a taxpayer if—

(1) the taxpayer's cost of service for ratemaking purposes or in its regulated books of account is reduced by reason of any portion of such credit which results from the transfer of employer securities or cash to a tax credit employee stock ownership plan which meets the requirements of section 409;

(2) the base to which the taxpayer's rate of return for ratemaking purposes is applied is reduced by reason of any portion of such credit which results from a transfer described in paragraph (1) to such employee stock ownership plan; or

(3) any portion of the amount of such credit which results from a transfer described in paragraph (1) to such employee stock ownership plan is treated for ratemaking purposes in any way other than as though it had been contributed by the taxpayer's common shareholders.

Under regulations prescribed by the Secretary, rules similar to the rules of paragraphs (4) and (7) of section 46(f) shall apply for purposes of the preceding sentence.

(c) DEFINITIONS AND SPECIAL RULES.—

(1) REQUIREMENTS FOR CORPORATION.—A corporation meets the requirements of this paragraph if it—

(A) establishes a plan—

(i) which meets the requirements of section 409, and

(ii) under which no more than one-third of the employer contributions for the taxable year are allocated to the group of employees consisting of—

(I) officers,

(II) shareholders owning more than 10 percent of the employer's stock (within the meaning of section 415(c)(6)(B)(iv)), or

(III) employees described in section 415(c)(6)(B)(iii), and

(B) agrees, as a condition for the allowance of the credit allowed by this subsection—

(i) to make transfers of employer securities to a tax credit employee stock ownership plan maintained by the corporation having an aggregate value of not more than the applicable percentage for the taxable year (determined under subsection (a)(2)) of the amount of the aggregate compensation (within the meaning of section 415(c)(3)) paid or accrued by the corporation during the taxable year, and

(ii) to make such transfers at the times prescribed in paragraph (2).

(2) TIMES FOR MAKING TRANSFERS.—The transfers required under paragraph (1)(B) shall be made no later than 30 days after the due date (including extensions) for filing the return for the taxable year.

(3) ADJUSTMENTS TO CREDIT.—If the credit determined under this section is reduced by a final determination, the employer may reduce the amount required to be transferred to the tax credit employee stock ownership plan under paragraph (1)(B) for the taxable year in which the final determination occurs or any succeeding taxable year by an amount equal to such reduction to the extent such reduction is not taken into account in any deduction allowed under section 404(i)(2).

(4) CERTAIN CONTRIBUTIONS OF CASH TREATED AS CONTRIBUTIONS OF EMPLOYER SECURITIES.—For purposes of this section, a transfer of cash shall be treated as a transfer of employer securities if the cash is, under the tax credit employee stock ownership plan, used within 30 days to purchase employer securities.

(5) DISALLOWANCE OF DEDUCTION.—Except as provided in section 404(i), no deduction shall be allowed under section 162, 212, or 404 for amounts required to be transferred to a tax credit employee stock ownership plan under this section.

(6) EMPLOYER SECURITIES.—For purposes of this section, the term "employer securities" has the meaning given such term in section 409(1).

(7) VALUE.—For purposes of this section, the term "value" means—

(A) in the case of securities listed on a national exchange, the average of closing prices of such securities for the 20 consecutive trading days immediately preceding the date on which the securities are contributed to the plan, or

(B) in the case of securities not listed on a national exchange, the fair market value as determined in good faith and in accordance with regulations prescribed by the Secretary.

P.L. 99-514, §1171(c)(2), provides:

(2) SECTIONS 404(I) [(i)] AND 6699 TO CONTINUE TO APPLY TO PRE-1987 CREDITS.—The provisions of sections 404(i) and 6699 of the Internal Revenue Code of 1986 shall continue to apply with respect to credits under section 41 of such Code attributable to compensation paid or accrued before January 1, 1987 (or under section 38 of such Code with respect to qualified investment before January 1, 1983).

P.L. 99-514, §1177, as amended by P.L. 100-647, §1011B(l), provides:

SEC. 1177. TRANSITION RULES.

(a) SECTION 1171.—The amendments made by section 1171 shall not apply in the case of a tax credit employee stock ownership plan if—

(1) such plan was favorably approved on September 23, 1983, by employees, and

(2) not later than January 11, 1984, the employer of such employees was 100 percent owned by such plan.

(b) SUBTITLE NOT TO APPLY TO CERTAIN NEWSPAPER.—The amendments made by section 1175 shall not apply to any daily newspaper—

(1) which was first published on December 17, 1855, and which began publication under its current name in 1954, and

(2) which is published in a constitutional home rule city (within the meaning of section 146(d)(3)(C) of the Internal Revenue Code of 1986) which has a population of less than 2,500,000.

• 1984, Deficit Reduction Act of 1984 (P.L. 98-369)

P.L. 98-369, §14:

Amended Code Sec. 44G(a)(2)(B), as in effect prior to its redesignation by Act Sec. 471(c)(1) as Code Sec. 41, by striking out the table contained therein and inserting a new table in lieu thereof. **Effective** for tax years ending after 12-31-83. However, see special rule below. Prior to amendment, the table read as follows:

For aggregate compensation paid or accrued during a portion of the taxable year occuring in calendar year:	*The applicable percentage is:*
1983	0.5
1984	.05
1985	0.75
1986	0.75
1987	0.75
1988 or thereafter	0

P.L. 98-369, §18(b), provides:

(b) Special Rule for Section 14.—The amendment made by section 14 shall not apply in the case of a tax credit employee stock ownership plan if—

(1) such plan was favorably approved on September 23, 1983, by employees, and

(2) not later than January 11, 1984, the employer of such employees was 100 percent owned by such plan.

P.L. 98-369, §471(c)(1):

Redesignated former Code Sec. 44G as Code Sec. 41. **Effective** for tax years beginning after 12-31-83, and to carrybacks from such years.

P.L. 98-369, §474(l):

Amended Code Sec. 41, as redesignated by Act Sec. 471(c)(1) by amending paragraph (1) of subsection (a) and subsection (b), and by striking out "the credit allowed under this section" in subsection (c)(3) and inserting in lieu thereof "the credit determined under this section". **Effective** for tax years beginning after 12-31-83, and to carrybacks from such years. Prior to amendment, subsections (a)(1) and (b) read as follows:

(1) Credit Allowed.—In the case of a corporation which elects to have this section apply for the taxble year and which meets the requirements of subsection (c)(1), there is allowed as a credit against the tax imposed by this chapter for the taxable year an amount equal to the amount of the credit determined under paragraph (2) for such taxable year.

(b) Limitation Based on Amount of Tax.—

(1) Liability For Tax.—

(A) In General.—The credit allowed by subsection (a) for any taxable year shall not exceed an amount equal to the sum of—

(i) so much of the liability for tax for the taxable year as does not exceed $25,000, plus

(ii) 90 percent of so much of the liability for tax for the taxable year as exceeds $25,000.

(B) Liability for Tax Defined.—For purposes of this paragraph the term "liability for tax" means the tax imposed by this chapter for the taxable year, reduced by the sum of the credits allowed under a section of this subpart having a lower number designation than this section, other than credits allowable by sections 31, 39, and 43. For purposes of the preceding sentence, the term "tax imposed by this chapter" shall not include any tax treated as not imposed by this chapter under the last sentence of section 53(a).

(C) Controlled Groups.—In the case of a controlled group of corporations, the $25,000 amount specified in subparagraph (A) shall be reduced for each component member of such group by apportioning $25,000 among the component members of such group in such manner as the Secretary shall by regulations prescribe. For purposes of the preceding sentence, the term "controlled group of corporations" has the meaning assigned to such term by section 1563(a) (determined without regard to subsections (a)(4) and (e)(3)(C) of such section).

(2) Carryback and Carryover of Unused Credit.—

(A) Allowance of Credit.—If the amount of the credit determined under this section for any taxable year exceeds the limitation provided under paragraph (1)(A) for such taxable year (hereinafter in this paragraph referred to as the "unused credit year"), such excess shall be—

(i) an employee stock ownership credit carryback to each of the 3 taxable years preceding the unused credit year, and

(ii) an employee stock ownership credit carryover to each of the 15 taxable years following the unused credit year,

and shall be added to the amount allowable as a credit by this section for such years. If any portion of such excess is a carryback to a taxable year ending before January 1, 1983, this section shall be deemed to have been in effect for such taxable year for purposes of allowing such carryback as a credit under this section. The entire amount of the unused credit for an unused credit year shall be carried to the earliest of the 18 taxable years to which (by reason of clauses (i) and (ii)) such credit may be carried, and then to each of the other 17 taxable years to the extent that, because of the limitation contained in subparagraph (B), such unused credit may not be added for a prior taxable year to which such unused credit may be carried.

(B) Limitation.—The amount of the unused credit which may be added under subparagraph (A) for any preceding or succeeding taxable year shall not exceed the amount by which the limitation provided under para[g]raph (1)(A) for such taxable year exceeds the sum of—

(i) the credit allowable under this section for such taxable year, and

(ii) the amounts which, by reason of this paragraph, are added to the amount allowable for such taxable year and which are attributable to taxable years preceding the unused credit year.

(3) Certain Regulated Companies.—No credit attributable to compensation taken into account for the ratemaking purposes involved shall be allowed under this section to a taxpayer if—

(A) the taxpayer's cost of service for ratemaking purposes or in its regulated books of accounts is reduced by reason of any portion of such credit which results from the transfer of employer securities or cash to a tax credit employee stock ownership plan which meets the requirements of section 409A;

(B) the base to which the taxpayer's rate of return for ratemaking purposes is applied is reduced by reason of any portion of such credit which results from a transfer described in subparagraph (A) to such employee stock ownership plan; or

(C) any portion of the amount of such credit which results from a transfer described in subparagraph (A) to such employee stock ownership plan is treated for ratemaking purposes in any way other than as though it had been contributed by the taxpayer's common shareholders.

Under regulations prescribed by the Sercretary [sic], rules similar to the rules of paragraphs (4) and (7) of section 46(f) shall apply for purposes of the preceding sentence.

P.L. 98-369, §491(e)(2):

Amended former Code Sec. 44G(c)(1)(A)(i) by striking out "section 409A" and inserting in lieu thereof "section 409". **Effective** 1-1-84.

P.L. 98-369, §491(e)(3):

Amended former Code Sec. 44G(c)(6) by striking out "section 409A(1)" and inserting in lieu thereof "section 409(l)". **Effective** 1-1-84.

• 1983, Technical Corrections Act of 1982 (P.L. 97-448)

P.L. 97-448, §103(g)(1):

Amended Code Sec. 44G(b)(3) by striking out "No credit" and inserting in lieu thereof "No credit attributable to compensation taken into account for the ratemaking purposes involved", and by adding the sentence at the end thereof. **Effective** as if such amendment had been included in the provision of P.L. 97-34 to which it relates.

• 1981, Economic Recovery Tax Act of 1981 (P.L. 97-34)

P.L. 97-34, §331(a):

Added Code Sec. 44G. **Effective** for aggregate compensation (within the meaning of Code Sec. 415(c)(3)), paid or accrued after 12-31-82, in tax years ending after such date.

[Sec. 42]

SEC. 42. LOW-INCOME HOUSING CREDIT.

[Sec. 42(a)]

(a) IN GENERAL.—For purposes of section 38, the amount of the low-income housing credit determined under this section for any taxable year in the credit period shall be an amount equal to—

(1) the applicable percentage of

(2) the qualified basis of each qualified low-income building.

[Sec. 42(b)]

(b) APPLICABLE PERCENTAGE: 70 PERCENT PRESENT VALUE CREDIT FOR CERTAIN NEW BUILDINGS; 30 PERCENT PRESENT VALUE CREDIT FOR CERTAIN OTHER BUILDINGS.—

(1) DETERMINATION OF APPLICABLE PERCENTAGE.—For purposes of this section, the term "applicable percentages" means, with respect to any building, the appropriate percentage prescribed by the Secretary for the earlier of—

(i) the month in which such building is placed in service, or

(ii) at the election of the taxpayer—

(I) the month in which the taxpayer and the housing credit agency enter into an agreement with respect to such building (which is binding on such agency, the taxpayer, and all successors in interest) as to the housing credit dollar amount to be allocated to such building, or

(II) in the case of any building to which subsection (h)(4)(B) applies, the month in which the tax-exempt obligations are issued.

A month may be elected under clause (ii) only if the election is made not later than the 5th day after the close of such month. Such an election, once made, shall be irrevocable.

(B) METHOD OF PRESCRIBING PERCENTAGES.—The percentages prescribed by the Secretary for any month shall be percentages which will yield over a 10-year period amounts of credit under subsection (a) which have a present value equal to—

(i) 70 percent of the qualified basis of a new building which is not federally subsidized for the taxable year, and

(ii) 30 percent of the qualified basis of a building not described in clause (i).

(C) METHOD OF DISCOUNTING.—The present value under subparagraph (B) shall be determined—

(i) as of the last day of the 1st year of the 10-year period referred to in subparagraph (B),

(ii) by using a discount rate equal to 72 percent of the average of the annual Federal mid-term rate and the annual Federal long-term rate applicable under section 1274(d)(1) to the month applicable under clause (i) or (ii) of subparagraph (A) and compounded annually, and

(iii) by assuming that the credit allowable under this section for any year is received on the last day of such year.

(2) TEMPORARY MINIMUM CREDIT RATE FOR NON-FEDERALLY SUBSIDIZED NEW BUILDINGS.—In the case of any new building—

(A) which is placed in service by the taxpayer after the date of the enactment of this paragraph and before December 31, 2013, and

(B) which is not federally subsidized for the taxable year,

the applicable percentage shall not be less than 9 percent.

(3) CROSS REFERENCES.—

(A) For treatment of certain rehabilitation expenditures as separate new buildings, see subsection (e).

(B) For determination of applicable percentage for increases in qualified basis after the 1st year of the credit period, see subsection (f)(3).

(C) For authority of housing credit agency to limit applicable percentage and qualified basis which may be taken into account under this section with respect to any building, see subsection (h)(7).

Amendments

• 2008, Housing Assistance Tax Act of 2008 (P.L. 110-289)

P.L. 110-289, §3002(a)(1):

Amended Code Sec. 42(b) by striking paragraph (1), by redesignating paragraph (2) as paragraph (1), and by inserting after paragraph (1), as so redesignated, a new paragraph (2). **Effective** for buildings placed in service after 7-30-2008. Prior to being stricken, Code Sec. 42(b)(1) read as follows:

(1) BUILDING PLACED IN SERVICE DURING 1987.—In the case of any qualified low-income building placed in service by the taxpayer during 1987, the term "applicable percentage" means—

(A) 9 percent for new buildings which are not federally subsidized for the taxable year, or

(B) 4 percent for—

(i) new buildings which are federally subsidized for the taxable year, and

(ii) existing buildings.

P.L. 110-289, §3002(a)(2)(A):

Amended Code Sec. 42(b), as amended by Act Sec. 3002(a)(1), by striking "For purposes of this section—" and all that follows through "means the appropriate" and inserting the following:

(1) DETERMINATION OF APPLICABLE PERCENTAGE.—For purposes of this section, the term "applicable percentage" means, with respect to any building, the appropriate

Effective for buildings placed in service after 7-30-2008. Prior to amendment, "For purposes of this section—" and all that follows through "means the appropriate" read as follows:

For purposes of this section—

(1) BUILDINGS PLACED IN SERVICE AFTER 1987.—

(A) IN GENERAL.—In the case of any qualified low-income building placed in service by the taxpayer after 1987, the term "applicable percentage" means the appropriate

P.L. 110-289, §3002(a)(2)(B):

Amended Code Sec. 42(b)(1)(B)(i), as redesignated by Act Sec. 3002(a)(1), by striking "a building described in paragraph (1)(A)" and inserting "a new building which is not federally subsidized for the taxable year". **Effective** for buildings placed in service after 7-30-2008.

P.L. 110-289, §3002(a)(2)(C):

Amended Code Sec. 42(b)(1)(B)(ii), as redesignated by Act Sec. 3002(a)(1), by striking "a building described in paragraph (1)(B)" and inserting "a building not described in clause (i)." **Effective** for buildings placed in service after 7-30-2008.

• 1990, Omnibus Budget Reconciliation Act of 1990 (P.L. 101-508)

P.L. 101-508, §11701(a)(1)(B):

Amended Code Sec. 42(b)(1) by striking the last sentence. **Effective** as if included in the provision of P.L. 101-239 to which it relates. Prior to amendment, the last sentence read as follows:

A building shall not be treated as described in subparagraph (B) if, at any time during the credit period, moderate rehabilitation assistance is provided with respect to such building under section 8(e)(2) of the United States Housing Act of 1937.

• 1989, Omnibus Budget Reconciliation Act of 1989 (P.L. 101-239)

P.L. 101-239, §7108(c)(2):

Amended Code Sec. 42(b)(3)(C) by striking "subsection (h)(6))" and inserting "subsection (h)(7)". For the **effective** date see Act Sec. 7108(r)[s](1)-(2), below.

P.L. 101-239, §7108(h)(5):

Amended Code Sec. 42(b)(1) by adding at the end a new sentence. For the **effective** date see Act Sec. 7108(r)[s](1)-(2), below.

P.L. 101-239, §7108(r)[s](1)-(2) (as amended by P.L. 104-188, §1702(g)(5)(A)), provides:

(r) EFFECTIVE DATES.—

(1) IN GENERAL.—Except as otherwise provided in this subsection, the amendments made by this section shall apply to determinations under section 42 of the Internal Revenue Code of 1986 with respect to housing credit dollar amounts allocated from State housing credit ceilings for calendar years after 1989.

(2) BUILDINGS NOT SUBJECT TO ALLOCATION LIMITS.—Except as otherwise provided in this subsection, to the extent paragraph (1) of section 42(h) of such Code does not apply to any building by reason of paragraph (4) thereof, the amendments made by this section shall apply to buildings placed in service after December 31, 1989.

• 1988, Technical and Miscellaneous Revenue Act of 1988 (P.L. 100-647)

P.L. 100-647, §1002(l)(1)(A):

Amended Code Sec. 42(b)(2)(A) by striking out "for the month" and all that follows and inserting the new material. **Effective** as if included in the provision of P.L. 99-514 to which it relates. Prior to amendment, Code Sec. 42(b)(2)(A) read as follows:

(A) IN GENERAL.—In the case of any qualified low-income building placed in service by the taxpayer after 1987, the term "applicable percentage" means the appropriate percentage prescribed by the Secretary for the month in which such building is placed in service.

P.L. 100-647, §1002(l)(1)(B):

Amended Code Sec. 42(b)(2)(C)(ii) by striking out "the month in which the building was placed in service" and inserting in lieu thereof "the month applicable under clause (i) or (ii) of subparagraph (A)". **Effective** as if included in the provision of P.L. 99-514 to which it relates.

P.L. 100-647, §1002(l)(9)(B):

Amended Code Sec. 42(b)(3). **Effective** as if included in the provision of P.L. 99-514 to which it relates. Prior to amendment, Code Sec. 42(b)(3) read as follows:

(3) CROSS REFERENCE.—

For treatment of certain rehabilitation expenditures as separate new buildings, see subsection (e).

[Sec. 42(c)]

(c) QUALIFIED BASIS; QUALIFIED LOW-INCOME BUILDING.—For purposes of this section—

(1) QUALIFIED BASIS.—

(A) DETERMINATION.—The qualified basis of any qualified low-income building for any taxable year is an amount equal to—

(i) the applicable fraction (determined as of the close of such taxable year) of

(ii) the eligible basis of such building (determined under subsection (d)(5)).

(B) APPLICABLE FRACTION.—For purposes of subparagraph (A), the term "applicable fraction" means the smaller of the unit fraction or the floor space fraction.

(C) UNIT FRACTION.—For purposes of subparagraph (B), the term "unit fraction" means the fraction—

(i) the numerator of which is the number of low-income units in the building, and

(ii) the denominator of which is the number of residential rental units (whether or not occupied) in such building.

(D) FLOOR SPACE FRACTION.—For purposes of subparagraph (B), the term "floor space fraction" means the fraction—

(i) the numerator of which is the total floor space of the low-income units in such building, and

(ii) the denominator of which is the total floor space of the residential rental units (whether or not occupied) in such building.

(E) QUALIFIED BASIS TO INCLUDE PORTION OF BUILDING USED TO PROVIDE SUPPORTIVE SERVICES FOR HOMELESS.—In the case of a qualified low-income building described in subsection (i)(5)(B)(iii), the qualified basis of such building for any taxable year shall be increased by the lesser of—

(i) so much of the eligible basis of such building as is used throughout the year to provide supportive services designed to assist tenants in locating and retaining permanent housing, or

(ii) 20 percent of the qualified basis of such building (determined without regard to this subparagraph).

(2) QUALIFIED LOW-INCOME BUILDING.—The term "qualified low-income building" means any building—

(A) which is part of a qualified low-income housing project at all times during the period—

(i) beginning on the 1st day in the compliance period on which such building is part of such a project, and

(ii) ending on the last day of the compliance period with respect to such building, and

(B) to which the amendments made by section 201(a) of the Tax Reform Act of 1986 apply.

Amendments

• 2008, Housing Assistance Tax Act of 2008 (P.L. 110-289)

P.L. 110-289, §3004(a):

Amended Code Sec. 42(c)(2) by striking the flush sentence at the end. **Effective** for buildings placed in service after 7-30-2008. Prior to being stricken, the flush sentence at the end of Code Sec. 42(c)(2) read as follows:

Such term does not include any building with respect to which moderate rehabilitation assistance is provided, at any time during the compliance period, under section 8(e)(2) of the United States Housing Act of 1937 (other than assistance under the Stewart B. McKinney Homeless Assistance Act (as in effect on the date of the enactment of this sentence)).

• 2000 (P.L. 106-400)

P.L. 106-400, §2, provides:

SEC. 2. REFERENCES.

Any reference in any law, regulation, document, paper, or other record of the United States to the Stewart B. McKinney Homeless Assistance Act shall be deemed to be a reference to the "McKinney-Vento Homeless Assistance Act".

• 1996, Small Business Job Protection Act of 1996 (P.L. 104-188)

P.L. 104-188, §1704(t)(64):

Amended Code Sec. 42(c)(2) by striking "of 1988" after "Homeless Assistance Act" in the last sentence. **Effective** 8-20-96.

• 1990, Omnibus Budget Reconciliation Act of 1990 (P.L. 101-508)

P.L. 101-508, §11407(b)(5)(A):

Amended Code Sec. 42(c)(2), as added by Act Sec. 11701(a)(1)(A), by inserting before the period "(other than assistance under the Stewart B. McKinney Homeless Assistance Act of 1988 (as in effect on the date of the enactment of this sentence))" For the **effective** date, see Act Sec. 11407(b)(10)(A), below.

P.L. 101-508, §11407(b)(10)(A), provides:

(A) IN GENERAL.—Except as otherwise provided in this paragraph, the amendments made by this subsection shall apply to—

(i) determinations under section 42 of the Internal Revenue Code of 1986 with respect to housing credit dollar amounts allocated from State housing credit ceilings for calendar years after 1990, or

(ii) buildings placed in service after December 31, 1990, to the extent paragraph (1) of section 42(h) of such Code does not apply to any building by reason of paragraph (4) thereof, but only with respect to bonds issued after such date.

P.L. 101-508, §11701(a)(1)(A):

Amended Code Sec. 42(c)(2) by adding at the end thereof a new sentence. **Effective** as if included in the provision of P.L. 101-239 to which it relates.

• 1989, Omnibus Budget Reconciliation Act of 1989 (P.L. 101-239)

P.L. 101-239, §7108(i)(2):

Amended Code Sec. 42(c)(1) by adding at the end thereof a new subparagraph (E). For the **effective** date see Act Sec. 7108(r)[s](1)-(2) following Code Sec. 42(b).

• 1988, Technical and Miscellaneous Revenue Act of 1988 (P.L. 100-647)

P.L. 100-647, §1002(l)(2)(A):

Amended Code Sec. 42(c)(2)(A). **Effective** as if included in the provision of P.L. 99-514 to which it relates. Prior to amendment, Code Sec. 42(c)(2)(A) read as follows:

(A) which at all times during the compliance period with respect to such building is part of a qualified low-income housing project, and

[Sec. 42(d)]

(d) ELIGIBLE BASIS.—For purposes of this section—

(1) NEW BUILDINGS.—The eligible basis of a new building is its adjusted basis as of the close of the 1st taxable year of the credit period.

(2) EXISTING BUILDINGS.—

(A) IN GENERAL.—The eligible basis of an existing building is—

(i) in the case of a building which meets the requirements of subparagraph (B), its adjusted basis as of the close of the 1st taxable year of the credit period, and

(ii) zero in any other case.

(B) REQUIREMENTS.—A building meets the requirements of this subparagraph if—

(i) the building is acquired by purchase (as defined in section 179(d)(2)),

(ii) there is a period of at least 10 years between the date of its acquisition by the taxpayer and the date the building was last placed in service,

(iii) the building was not previously placed in service by the taxpayer or by any person who was a related person with respect to the taxpayer as of the time previously placed in service, and

(iv) except as provided in subsection (f)(5), a credit is allowable under subsection (a) by reason of subsection (e) with respect to the building.

(C) ADJUSTED BASIS.—For purposes of subparagraph (A), the adjusted basis of any building shall not include so much of the basis of such building as is determined by reference to the basis of other property held at any time by the person acquiring the building.

(D) SPECIAL RULES FOR SUBPARAGRAPH (B).—

(i) SPECIAL RULES FOR CERTAIN TRANSFERS.—For purposes of determining under subparagraph (B)(ii) when a building was last placed in service, there shall not be taken into account any placement in service—

(I) in connection with the acquisition of the building in a transaction in which the basis of the building in the hands of the person acquiring it is determined in whole or in part by reference to the adjusted basis of such building in the hands of the person from whom acquired,

(II) by a person whose basis in such building is determined under section 1014(a) (relating to property acquired from a decedent),

(III) by any governmental unit or qualified nonprofit organization (as defined in subsection (h)(5)) if the requirements of subparagraph (B)(ii) are met with respect to the placement in service by such unit or organization and all the income from such property is exempt from Federal income taxation,

(IV) by any person who acquired such building by foreclosure (or by instrument in lieu of foreclosure) of any purchase-money security interest held by such person if the requirements of subparagraph (B)(ii) are met with respect to the placement in service by such person and such building is resold within 12 months after the date such building is placed in service by such person after such foreclosure, or

(V) of a single-family residence by any individual who owned and used such residence for no other purpose than as his principal residence.

(ii) RELATED PERSON.—For purposes of subparagraph (B)(iii), a person (hereinafter in this subclause referred to as the "related person") is related to any person if the related person bears a relationship to such person specified in section 267(b) or 707(b)(1), or the related person and such person are engaged in trades or businesses under common control (within the meaning of subsections (a) and (b) of section 52).

(3) ELIGIBLE BASIS REDUCED WHERE DISPROPORTIONATE STANDARDS FOR UNITS.—

(A) IN GENERAL.—Except as provided in subparagraph (B), the eligible basis of any building shall be reduced by an amount equal to the portion of the adjusted basis of the building which is attributable to residential rental units in the building which are not low-income units and which are above the average quality standard of the low-income units in the building.

(B) EXCEPTION WHERE TAXPAYER ELECTS TO EXCLUDE EXCESS COSTS.—

(i) IN GENERAL.—Subparagraph (A) shall not apply with respect to a residential rental unit in a building which is not a low-income unit if—

(I) the excess described in clause (ii) with respect to such unit is not greater than 15 percent of the cost described in clause (ii)(II), and

(II) the taxpayer elects to exclude from the eligible basis of such building the excess described in clause (ii) with respect to such unit.

(ii) EXCESS.—The excess described in this clause with respect to any unit is the excess of—

(I) the cost of such unit, over

(II) the amount which would be the cost of such unit if the average cost per square foot of low-income units in the building were substituted for the cost per square foot of such unit.

The Secretary may by regulation provide for the determination of the excess under this clause on a basis other than square foot costs.

(4) SPECIAL RULES RELATING TO DETERMINATION OF ADJUSTED BASIS.—For purposes of this subsection—

(A) IN GENERAL.—Except as provided in subparagraphs (B) and (C), the adjusted basis of any building shall be determined without regard to the adjusted basis of any property which is not residential rental property.

(B) BASIS OF PROPERTY IN COMMON AREAS, ETC., INCLUDED.—The adjusted basis of any building shall be determined by taking into account the adjusted basis of property (of a character subject to the allowance for depreciation) used in common areas or provided as comparable amenities to all residential rental units in such building.

(C) INCLUSION OF BASIS OF PROPERTY USED TO PROVIDE SERVICES FOR CERTAIN NONTENANTS.—

(i) IN GENERAL.—The adjusted basis of any building located in a qualified census tract (as defined in paragraph (5)(C)) shall be determined by taking into account the adjusted basis of property (of a character subject to the allowance for depreciation and not otherwise taken into account) used throughout the taxable year in providing any community service facility.

(ii) LIMITATION.—The increase in the adjusted basis of any building which is taken into account by reason of clause (i) shall not exceed the sum of—

(I) 25 percent of so much of the eligible basis of the qualified low-income housing project of which it is a part as does not exceed $15,000,000, plus

(II) 10 percent of so much of the eligible basis of such project as is not taken into account under subclause (I).

For purposes of the preceding sentence, all community service facilities which are part of the same qualified low-income housing project shall be treated as one facility.

(iii) COMMUNITY SERVICE FACILITY.—For purposes of this subparagraph, the term "community service facility" means any facility designed to serve primarily individuals whose income is 60 percent or less of area median income (within the meaning of subsection (g)(1)(B)).

(D) NO REDUCTION FOR DEPRECIATION.—The adjusted basis of any building shall be determined without regard to paragraphs (2) and (3) of section 1016(a).

(5) SPECIAL RULES FOR DETERMINING ELIGIBLE BASIS.—

(A) FEDERAL GRANTS NOT TAKEN INTO ACCOUNT IN DETERMINING ELIGIBLE BASIS.—The eligible basis of a building shall not include any costs financed with the proceeds of a federally funded grant.

(B) INCREASE IN CREDIT FOR BUILDINGS IN HIGH COST AREAS.—

(i) IN GENERAL.—In the case of any building located in a qualified census tract or difficult development area which is designated for purposes of this subparagraph—

(I) in the case of a new building, the eligible basis of such building shall be 130 percent of such basis determined without regard to this subparagraph, and

(II) in the case of an existing building, the rehabilitation expenditures taken into account under subsection (e) shall be 130 percent of such expenditures determined without regard to this subparagraph.

(ii) QUALIFIED CENSUS TRACT.—

(I) IN GENERAL.—The term "qualified census tract" means any census tract which is designated by the Secretary of Housing and Urban Development and, for the most recent year for which census data are available on household income in such tract, either in which 50 percent or more of the households have an income which is less than 60 percent of the area median gross income for such year or which has a poverty rate of at least 25 percent. If the Secretary of Housing and Urban Development determines that sufficient data for any period are not available to apply this clause on the basis of census tracts, such Secretary shall apply this clause for such period on the basis of enumeration districts.

(II) LIMIT ON MSA'S DESIGNATED.—The portion of a metropolitan statistical area which may be designated for purposes of this subparagraph shall not exceed an area having 20 percent of the population of such metropolitan statistical area.

(III) DETERMINATION OF AREAS.—For purposes of this clause, each metropolitan statistical area shall be treated as a separate area and all nonmetropolitan areas in a State shall be treated as 1 area.

(iii) DIFFICULT DEVELOPMENT AREAS.—

(I) IN GENERAL.—The term "difficult development areas" means any area designated by the Secretary of Housing and Urban Development as an area which has high construction, land, or utility costs relative to area median gross income.

(II) LIMIT ON AREAS DESIGNATED.—The portions of metropolitan statistical areas which may be designated for purposes of this subparagraph shall not exceed an aggregate area having 20 percent of the population of such metropolitan statistical areas. A comparable rule shall apply to nonmetropolitan areas.

(iv) SPECIAL RULES AND DEFINITIONS.—For purposes of this subparagraph—

(I) population shall be determined on the basis of the most recent decennial census for which data are available,

(II) area median gross income shall be determined in accordance with subsection (g)(4),

(III) the term "metropolitan statistical area" has the same meaning as when used in section 143(k)(2)(B), and

(IV) the term "nonmetropolitan area" means any county (or portion thereof) which is not within a metropolitan statistical area.

(v) BUILDINGS DESIGNATED BY STATE HOUSING CREDIT AGENCY.—Any building which is designated by the State housing credit agency as requiring the increase in credit under this subparagraph in order for such building to be financially feasible as part of a qualified low-income housing project shall be treated for purposes of this subparagraph as located in a difficult development area which is designated for purposes of this subparagraph. The preceding sentence shall not apply to any building if paragraph (1) of subsection (h) does not apply to any portion of the eligible basis of such building by reason of paragraph (4) of such subsection.

(6) CREDIT ALLOWABLE FOR CERTAIN BUILDINGS ACQUIRED DURING 10-YEAR PERIOD DESCRIBED IN PARAGRAPH (2)(B)(ii).—

(A) IN GENERAL.—Paragraph (2)(B)(ii) shall not apply to any federally- or State-assisted building.

(B) BUILDINGS ACQUIRED FROM INSURED DEPOSITORY INSTITUTIONS IN DEFAULT.—On application by the taxpayer, the Secretary may waive paragraph (2)(B)(ii) with respect to any building acquired from an insured depository institution in default (as defined in section 3 of the Federal Deposit Insurance Act) or from a receiver or conservator of such an institution.

(C) FEDERALLY-OR STATE-ASSISTED BUILDING.—For purposes of this paragraph—

(i) FEDERALLY-ASSISTED BUILDING.—The term "federally-assisted building" means any building which is substantially assisted, financed, or operated under section 8 of the United States Housing Act of 1937, section 221(d)(3), 221(d)(4), or 236 of the National Housing Act, section 515 of the Housing Act of 1949, or any other housing program administered by the Department of Housing and Urban Development or by the Rural Housing Service of the Department of Agriculture.

(ii) STATE-ASSISTED BUILDING.—The term "State-assisted building" means any building which is substantially assisted, financed, or operated under any State law similar in purposes to any of the laws referred to in clause (i).

(7) ACQUISITION OF BUILDING BEFORE END OF PRIOR COMPLIANCE PERIOD.—

(A) IN GENERAL.—Under regulations prescribed by the Secretary, in the case of a building described in subparagraph (B) (or interest therein) which is acquired by the taxpayer—

(i) paragraph (2)(B) shall not apply, but

(ii) the credit allowable by reason of subsection (a) to the taxpayer for any period after such acquisition shall be equal to the amount of credit which would have been allowable under subsection (a) for such period to the prior owner referred to in subparagraph (B) had such owner not disposed of the building.

(B) DESCRIPTION OF BUILDING.—A building is described in this subparagraph if—

(i) a credit was allowed by reason of subsection (a) to any prior owner of such building, and

(ii) the taxpayer acquired such building before the end of the compliance period for such building with respect to such prior owner (determined without regard to any disposition by such prior owner).

Amendments

• 2008, Housing Assistance Tax Act of 2008 (P.L. 110-289)

P.L. 110-289, §3003(a):

Amended Code Sec. 42(d)(5)(C), before redesignation by Act Sec. 3003(g), by adding at the end a new clause (v). **Effective** for buildings placed in service after 7-30-2008.

P.L. 110-289, §3003(c):

Amended Code Sec. 42(d)(4)(C)(ii) by striking "10 percent of the eligible basis of the qualified low-income housing project of which it is a part. For purposes of" and inserting "the sum of—", new subclauses (I) and (II), and the flush phrase "For purposes of". **Effective** for buildings placed in service after 7-30-2008.

P.L. 110-289, §3003(d):

Amended Code Sec. 42(d)(5)(A). **Effective** for buildings placed in service after 7-30-2008. Prior to amendment, Code Sec. 42(d)(5)(A) read as follows:

(A) ELIGIBLE BASIS REDUCED BY FEDERAL GRANTS.—If, during any taxable year of the compliance period, a grant is made with respect to any building or the operation thereof and any portion of such grant is funded with Federal funds (whether or not includible in gross income), the eligible basis of such building for such taxable year and all succeeding taxable years shall be reduced by the portion of such grant which is so funded.

P.L. 110-289, §3003(e)(1)-(3):

Amended Code Sec. 42(d)(2)(D)(iii), before redesignation by Act Sec. 3003(g)(2), by striking all that precedes subclause (II), by redesignating subclause (II) as clause (iii) and moving such clause two ems to the left, and by striking the last sentence thereof. **Effective** for buildings placed in service after 7-30-2008. Prior to amendment, Code Sec. 42(d)(2)(D)(iii) read as follows:

(iii) RELATED PERSON, ETC.—

(I) APPLICATION OF SECTION 179.—For purposes of subparagraph (B)(i), section 179(d) shall be applied by substituting "10 percent" for "50 percent" in section 267(b) and 707(b) and in section 179(d)(7).

(II) RELATED PERSON.—For purposes of subparagraph (B)(iii), a person (hereinafter in this subclause referred to as the "related person") is related to any person if the related person bears a relationship to such person specified in section 267(b) or 707(b)(1), or the related person and such person are engaged in trades or businesses under common control (within the meaning of subsections (a) and (b) of section 52). For purposes of the preceding sentence, in applying section 267(b) or 707(b)(1), "10 percent" shall be substituted for "50 percent".

P.L. 110-289, §3003(f):

Amended Code Sec. 42(d)(6). **Effective** for buildings placed in service after 7-30-2008. Prior to amendment, Code Sec. 42(d)(6) read as follows:

(6) CREDIT ALLOWABLE FOR CERTAIN FEDERALLY-ASSISTED BUILDINGS ACQUIRED DURING 10-YEAR PERIOD DESCRIBED IN PARAGRAPH (2)(B)(ii).—

(A) IN GENERAL.—On application by the taxpayer, the Secretary (after consultation with the appropriate Federal official) may waive paragraph (2)(B)(ii) with respect to any federally-assisted building if the Secretary determines that such waiver is necessary—

(i) to avert an assignment of the mortgage secured by property in the project (of which such building is a part) to the Department of Housing and Urban Development or the Farmers Home Administration, or

(ii) to avert a claim against a Federal mortgage insurance fund (or such Department or Administration) with respect to a mortgage which is so secured.

The preceding sentence shall not apply to any building described in paragraph (7)(B).

(B) FEDERALLY-ASSISTED BUILDING.—For purposes of subparagraph (A), the term "federally-assisted building" means any building which is substantially assisted, financed, or operated under—

(i) section 8 of the United States Housing Act of 1937,

(ii) section 221(d)(3) or 236 of the National Housing Act, or

(iii) section 515 of the Housing Act of 1949,

as such Acts are in effect on the date of the enactment of the Tax Reform Act of 1986.

(C) LOW-INCOME BUILDINGS WHERE MORTGAGE MAY BE PREPAID.—A waiver may be granted under paragraph (A) (without regard to any clause thereof) with respect to a federally-assisted building described in clause (ii) or (iii) of subparagraph (B) if—

(i) the mortgage on such building is eligible for prepayment under subtitle B of the Emergency Low Income Housing Preservation Act of 1987 or under section 502(c) of the Housing Act of 1949 at any time within 1 year after the date of the application for such a waiver,

(ii) the appropriate Federal official certifies to the Secretary that it is reasonable to expect that, if the waiver is not granted, such building will cease complying with its low-income occupancy requirements, and

(iii) the eligibility to prepay such mortgage without the approval of the appropriate Federal official is waived by all persons who are so eligible and such waiver is binding on all successors of such persons.

(D) BUILDINGS ACQUIRED FROM INSURED DEPOSITORY INSTITUTIONS IN DEFAULT.—A waiver may be granted under subparagraph (A) (without regard to any clause thereof) with respect to any building acquired from an insured depository institution in default (as defined in section 3 of the Federal Deposit Insurance Act) or from a receiver or conservator of such an institution.

(E) APPROPRIATE FEDERAL OFFICIAL.—For purposes of subparagraph (A), the term "appropriate Federal official" means—

(i) the Secretary of Housing and Urban Development in the case of any building described in subparagraph (B) by reason of clause (i) or (ii) thereof, and

(ii) the Secretary of Agriculture in the case of any building described in subparagraph (B) by reason of clause (iii) thereof.

P.L. 110-289, §3003(g)(1):

Amended Code Sec. 42(d)(2)(B)(ii) by striking "the later of —" and all that follows and inserting "the date the building was last placed in service,". **Effective** for buildings placed in service after 7-30-2008. Prior to amendment, Code Sec. 42(d)(2)(B)(ii) read as follows:

(ii) there is a period of at least 10 years between the date of its acquisition by the taxpayer and the later of—

(I) the date the building was last placed in service, or

(II) the date of the most recent nonqualified substantial improvement of the building,

P.L. 110-289, §3003(g)(2):

Amended Code Sec. 42(d)(2)(D) by striking clause (i) and by redesignating clauses (ii) and (iii) as clauses (i) and (ii), respectively. **Effective** for buildings placed in service after 7-30-2008. Prior to being stricken, Code Sec. 42(d)(2)(D)(i) read as follows:

(i) NONQUALIFIED SUBSTANTIAL IMPROVEMENT.—For purposes of subparagraph (B)(ii)—

(I) IN GENERAL.—The term "nonqualified substantial improvement" means any substantial improvement if section 167(k) (as in effect on the day before the date of the enactment of the Revenue Reconciliation Act of 1990) was elected with respect to such improvement or section 168 (as in effect on the day before the date of the enactment of the Tax Reform Act of 1986) applied to such improvement.

(II) DATE OF SUBSTANTIAL IMPROVEMENT.—The date of a substantial improvement is the last day of the 24-month period referred to in subclause (III).

(III) SUBSTANTIAL IMPROVEMENT.—The term "substantial improvement" means the improvements added to capital account with respect to the building during any 24-month period, but only if the sum of the amounts added to such account during such period equals or exceeds 25 percent of the adjusted basis of the building (determined without regard to paragraphs (2) and (3) of section 1016(a)) as of the 1st day of such period.

P.L. 110-289, §3003(g)(3):

Amended Code Sec. 42(d)(5) by striking subparagraph (B) and by redesignating subparagraph (C) as subparagraph (B). **Effective** for buildings placed in service after 7-30-2008. Prior to being stricken, Code Sec. 42(d)(5)(B) read as follows:

(B) ELIGIBLE BASIS NOT TO INCLUDE EXPENDITURES WHERE SECTION 167(k) SELECTED.—The eligible basis of any building shall not include any portion of its adjusted basis which is attributable to amounts with respect to which an election is made under section 167(k) (as in effect on the day before the date of the enactment of the Revenue Reconciliation Act of 1990).

P.L. 110-289, §3004(h), provides:

(h) GAO STUDY REGARDING MODIFICATIONS TO LOW-INCOME HOUSING TAX CREDIT.—Not later than December 31, 2012, the Comptroller General of the United States shall submit to Congress a report which analyzes the implementation of the modifications made by this subtitle to the low-income housing tax credit under section 42 of the Internal Revenue Code of 1986. Such report shall include an analysis of the distribution of credit allocations before and after the effective date of such modifications.

• 2004, Working Families Tax Relief Act of 2004 (P.L. 108-311)

P.L. 108-311, §408(a)(3):

Amended Code Sec. 42(d)(2)(D)(iii)(I) by striking "section 179(b)(7)" and inserting "section 179(d)(7)". **Effective** 10-4-2004.

• 2000, Community Renewal Tax Relief Act of 2000 (P.L. 106-554)

P.L. 106-554, §134(a)(1)-(3):

Amended Code Sec. 42(d)(4) by striking "subparagraph (B)" in subparagraph (A) and inserting "subparagraphs (B) and (C)", by redesignating subparagraph (C) as subparagraph (D), and by inserting after subparagraph (B) a new subparagraph (C). **Effective** as noted in Act Sec. 137, below.

P.L. 106-554, §135(b)(1)-(2):

Amended the first sentence of Code Sec. 42(d)(5)(C)(ii)(I) by inserting "either" before "in which 50 percent", and by inserting before the period "or which has a poverty rate of at least 25 percent". **Effective** as noted in Act Sec. 137, below.

P.L. 106-554, §137, provides:

Except as otherwise provided in this subtitle, the amendments made by this subtitle shall apply to—

(1) housing credit dollar amounts allocated after December 31, 2000; and

(2) buildings placed in service after such date to the extent paragraph (1) of section 42(h) of the Internal Revenue Code of 1986 does not apply to any building by reason of paragraph (4) thereof, but only with respect to bonds issued after such date.

• 1990, Omnibus Budget Reconciliation Act of 1990 (P.L. 101-508)

P.L. 101-508, §11407(b)(4):

Amended Code Sec. 42(d)(5)(C)(ii)(I) by adding at the end thereof a new sentence. **Effective** as noted in Act Sec. 11407(b)(10)(A), below.

P.L. 101-508, §11407(b)(10)(A), provides:

(A) IN GENERAL.—Except as otherwise provided in this paragraph, the amendments made by this subsection shall apply to—

(i) determinations under section 42 of the Internal Revenue Code of 1986 with respect to housing credit dollar amounts allocated from State housing credit ceilings for calendar years after 1990, or

(ii) buildings placed in service after December 31, 1990, to the extent paragraph (1) of section 42(h) of such Code does not apply to any building by reason of paragraph (4) thereof, but only with respect to bonds issued after such date.

P.L. 101-508, §11407(b)(8):

Amended Code Sec. 42(d)(2)(D)(ii) by striking "or" at the end of subclause (III), by striking the period at the end of subclause (IV) and inserting ", or", and by adding at the end thereof new subclause (V). **Effective** 11-5-90.

P.L. 101-508, §11407(c), provides:

(c) ELECTION TO ACCELERATE CREDIT INTO 1990.—

(1) IN GENERAL.—At the election of an individual, the credit determined under section 42 of the Internal Revenue Code of 1986 for the taxpayer's first taxable year ending on or after October 25, 1990, shall be 150 percent of the amount which would (but for this paragraph) be so allowable with respect to investments held by such individual on or before October 25, 1990.

(2) REDUCTION IN AGGREGATE CREDIT TO REFLECT INCREASED 1990 CREDIT.—The aggregate credit allowable to any person under section 42 of such Code with respect to any investment for taxable years after the first taxable year referred to in paragraph (1) shall be reduced on a pro rata basis by the amount of the increased credit allowable by reason of paragraph (1) with respect to such first taxable year. The preceding sentence shall not be construed to affect whether any taxable year is part of the credit, compliance, or extended use periods.

(3) ELECTION.—The election under paragraph (1) shall be made at the time and in the manner prescribed by the Secretary of the Treasury or his delegate, and, once made, shall be irrevocable. In the case of a partnership, such election shall be made by the partnership.

P.L. 101-508, §11701(a)(2):

Amended Code Sec. 42(d)(5)(C)(ii)(I) by inserting "which is designated by the Secretary of Housing and Urban Development and, for the most recent year for which census data are available on household income in such tract," after "census tract", and by inserting before the period "for such year". **Effective** as if included in the provision of P.L. 101-239 to which it relates.

P.L. 101-508, §11812(b)(3) (as amended by P.L. 104-188, §1704(t)(53)):

Amended Code Secs. 42(d)(2)(D)(i)(I) and 42(d)(5)(B) [in the text only] by striking "section 167(k)" and inserting "section 167(k) (as in effect on the day before the date of the enactment of the Revenue Reconciliation Act of 1990)". **Effective** for property placed in service after 11-5-90. For exceptions, see Act Sec. 11812(c)(2)-(3) below.

P.L. 101-508, §11812(c)(2)-(3), provides:

(2) EXCEPTION.—The amendments made by this section shall not apply to any property to which section 168 of the Internal Revenue Code of 1986 does not apply by reason of subsection (f)(5) thereof.

(3) EXCEPTION FOR PREVIOUSLY GRANDFATHER EXPENDITURES.—The amendments made by this section shall not apply to rehabilitation expenditures described in section 252(f)(5) of the Tax Reform Act of 1986 (as added by section 1002(l)(31) of the Technical and Miscellaneous Revenue Act of 1988).

• 1989, Omnibus Budget Reconciliation Act of 1989 (P.L. 101-239)

P.L. 101-239, §7108(d)(1):

Amended Code Sec. 42(d)(2)(B) by striking "and" at the end of clause (ii), by striking the period at the end of clause (iii) and inserting ", and", and by adding at the end thereof a new clause (iv). For the **effective** date of the above amendment, see Act Sec. 7108(r)[s](1)-(2) following Code Sec. 42(b).

P.L. 101-239, §7108(f):

Amended Code Sec. 42(d)(6) by redesignating subparagraph (C) as subparagraph (E) and inserting after subparagraph (B) new subparagraphs (C) and (D). **Effective** 12-19-89.

P.L. 101-239, §7108(g):

Amended Code Sec. 42(d)(5) by adding at the end thereof a new subparagraph (D). For the **effective** date, see Act Sec. 7108(r)[s](1)-(2) following Code Sec. 42(b).

P.L. 101-239, §7108(l)(1):

Amended Code Sec. 42(d)(1) by inserting "as of the close of the 1st taxable year of the credit period" before the period. **Effective** as if included in the amendments made by section 252 of P.L. 99-514.

P.L. 101-239, §7108(l)(2):

Amended Code Sec. 42(d)(2)(A) by striking "subparagraph (B)" and all that follows through the end of clause (i) and inserting "subparagraph (B), its adjusted basis as of the close of the 1st taxable year of the credit period, and". **Effective** as if included in the amendments made by section 252 of P.L. 99-514. Prior to amendment, Code Sec. 42(d)(2)(A)(i) read as follows:

(i) in the case of a building which meets the requirements of subparagraph (B), the sum of—

(I) the portion of its adjusted basis attributable to its acquisition cost, plus

(II) amounts chargeable to capital account and incurred by the taxpayer (before the close of the 1st taxable year of the credit period for such building) for property (or additions or improvements to property) of a character subject to the allowance for depreciation, and

P.L. 101-239, §7108(l)(3)(A):

Amended Code Sec. 42(d)(2)(C) by striking "ACQUISITION COST" in the heading and inserting "ADJUSTED BASIS" and by striking "cost" in the text and inserting "adjusted basis". **Effective** as if included in the amendments made by section 252 of P.L. 99-514.

P.L. 101-239, §7108(l)(3)(B):

Amended Code Sec. 42(d)(5), as amended by subsection (g), by striking subparagraph (A), by redesignating subparagraphs (B), (C), and (D) as subparagraphs (A), (B), and (C), respectively, and by amending the paragraph heading. **Effective** as if included in the amendments made by section 252 of P.L. 99-514. Prior to amendment, the heading for Code Sec. 42(d)(5) and Code Sec. 42(d)(5)(A) read as follows:

(5) ELIGIBLE BASIS DETERMINED WHEN BUILDING PLACED IN SERVICE.—

(A) IN GENERAL.—Except as provided in subparagraphs (B) and (C), the eligible basis of any building for the entire compliance period for such building shall be its eligible basis on the date such building is placed in service (increased, in the case of an existing building which meets the requirements of paragraph (2)(B), by the amounts described in paragraph (2)(A)(i)(II)).

P.L. 101-239, §7811(a)(1):

Amended Code Sec. 42(d)(5)(C) by inserting "Section" before "167(k)" in the subparagraph heading. **Effective** as if included in the provision of P.L. 100-647 to which it relates.

P.L. 101-239, §7831(c)(6):

Amended Code Sec. 42(d)(7)(A) by inserting "(or interest therein)" after "a building described in subparagraph (B)". **Effective** as if included in the provision of P.L. 99-514 to which it relates.

P.L. 101-239, §7841(d)(13):

Amended Code Sec. 42(d)(6)(A)(i) by striking "Farmers' Home Administration" and inserting "Farmers Home Administration". **Effective** 12-19-89.

P.L. 101-239, §7841(d)(14):

Amended Code Sec. 42(d)(7)(A)(ii) by striking "sebsection (a)" and inserting "subsection (a)". **Effective** 12-19-89.

• 1988, Technical and Miscellaneous Revenue Act of 1988 (P.L. 100-647)

P.L. 100-647, §1002(l)(3):

Amended Code Sec. 42(d)(2)(D)(ii). **Effective** as if included in the provision of P.L. 99-514 to which it relates. Prior to amendment, Code Sec. 42(d)(2)(D)(ii) read as follows:

(ii) SPECIAL RULE FOR NONTAXABLE EXCHANGES.—For purposes of determining under subparagraph (B)(ii) when a building was last placed in service, there shall not be taken into account any placement in service in connection with the acquisition of the building in a transaction in which the basis of the building in the hands of the person acquiring it is determined in whole or in part by reference to the adjusted basis of such building in the hands of the person from whom acquired.

P.L. 100-647, §1002(l)(4):

Amended Code Sec. 42(d)(3). **Effective** as if included in the provision of P.L. 99-514 to which it relates. Prior to amendment, Code Sec. 42(d)(3) read as follows:

(3) ELIGIBLE BASIS REDUCED WHERE DISPROPORTIONATE STANDARDS FOR UNITS.—The eligible basis of any building shall be reduced by an amount equal to the portion of the adjusted basis of the building which is attributable to residential rental units in the building which are not low-income units and which are above the average quality standard of the low-income units in the building.

P.L. 100-647, §1002(l)(5):

Amended Code Sec. 42(d)(5)(A) by inserting before the period "(increased, in the case of an existing building which meets the requirements of paragraph (2)(B), by the amounts described in paragraph (2)(A)(i)(II))". **Effective** as if included in the provision of P.L. 99-514 to which it relates.

P.L. 100-647, §1002(l)(6)(A):

Amended Code Sec. 42(d)(5) by adding at the end thereof new subparagraph (C). **Effective** as if included in the provision of P.L. 99-514 to which it relates.

P.L. 100-647, §1002(l)(6)(B):

Amended Code Sec. 42(d)(5)(A) by striking out "subparagraph (B)" and inserting in lieu thereof "subparagraphs (B) and (C)". **Effective** as if included in the provision of P.L. 99-514 to which it relates.

P.L. 100-647, §1002(l)(7):

Amended Code Sec. 42(d)(6)(A) by inserting "or" at the end of clause (i), by striking out ", or" at the end of clause (ii) and inserting in lieu thereof a period, and by striking out clause (iii). **Effective** as if included in the provision of P.L. 99-514 to which it relates. Prior to amendment, Code Sec. 42(d)(6)(A)(iii) read as follows:

(iii) to the extent provided in regulations, by reason of other circumstances of financial distress.

P.L. 100-647, §1002(l)(8):

Amended Code Sec. 42(d)(6)(B)(ii) by striking out "of 1934" after "National Housing Act". **Effective** as if included in the provision of P.L. 99-514 to which it relates.

[Sec. 42(e)]

(e) REHABILITATION EXPENDITURES TREATED AS SEPARATE NEW BUILDING.—

(1) IN GENERAL.—Rehabilitation expenditures paid or incurred by the taxpayer with respect to any building shall be treated for purposes of this section as a separate new building.

(2) REHABILITATION EXPENDITURES.—For purposes of paragraph (1)—

(A) IN GENERAL.—The term "rehabilitation expenditures" means amounts chargeable to capital account and incurred for property (or additions or improvements to property) of a character subject to the allowance for depreciation in connection with the rehabilitation of a building.

(B) COST OF ACQUISITION, ETC., NOT INCLUDED.—Such term does not include the cost of acquiring any building (or interest therein) or any amount not permitted to be taken into account under paragraph (3) or (4) of subsection (d).

(3) MINIMUM EXPENDITURES TO QUALIFY.—

(A) IN GENERAL.—Paragraph (1) shall apply to rehabilitation expenditures with respect to any building only if—

(i) the expenditures are allocable to 1 or more low-income units or substantially benefit such units, and

(ii) the amount of such expenditures during any 24-month period meets the requirements of whichever of the following subclauses requires the greater amount of such expenditures:

(I) The requirement of this subclause is met if such amount is not less than 20 percent of the adjusted basis of the building (determined as of the 1st day of such period and without regard to paragraphs (2) and (3) of section 1016(a)).

(II) The requirement of this subclause is met if the qualified basis attributable to such amount, when divided by the low-income units in the building, is $6,000 or more.

(B) EXCEPTION FROM 10 PERCENT REHABILITATION.—In the case of a building acquired by the taxpayer from a governmental unit, at the election of the taxpayer, subparagraph (A)(ii)(I) shall not apply and the credit under this section for such rehabilitation expenditures shall be determined using the percentage applicable under subsection (b)(2)(B)(ii).

(C) DATE OF DETERMINATION.—The determination under subparagraph (A) shall be made as of the close of the 1st taxable year in the credit period with respect to such expenditures.

(D) INFLATION ADJUSTMENT.—In the case of any expenditures which are treated under paragraph (4) as placed in service during any calendar year after 2009, the $6,000 amount in subparagraph (A)(ii)(II) shall be increased by an amount equal to—

(i) such dollar amount, multiplied by

(ii) the cost-of-living adjustment determined under section 1(f)(3) for such calendar year by substituting "calendar year 2008" for "calendar year 1992" in subparagraph (B) thereof.

Any increase under the preceding sentence which is not a multiple of $100 shall be rounded to the nearest multiple of $100.

(4) SPECIAL RULES.—For purposes of applying this section with respect to expenditures which are treated as a separate building by reason of this subsection—

(A) such expenditures shall be treated as placed in service at the close of the 24-month period referred to in paragraph (3)(A), and

(B) the applicable fraction under subsection (c)(1) shall be the applicable fraction for the building (without regard to paragraph (1)) with respect to which the expenditures were incurred.

Nothing in subsection (d)(2) shall prevent a credit from being allowed by reason of this subsection.

(5) NO DOUBLE COUNTING.—Rehabilitation expenditures may, at the election of the taxpayer, be taken into account under this subsection or subsection (d)(2)(A)(i) but not under both such subsections.

(6) REGULATIONS TO APPLY SUBSECTION WITH RESPECT TO GROUP OF UNITS IN BUILDING.—The Secretary may prescribe regulations, consistent with the purposes of this subsection, treating a group of units with respect to which rehabilitation expenditures are incurred as a separate new building.

Amendments

• 2008, Housing Assistance Tax Act of 2008 (P.L. 110-289)

P.L. 110-289, §3003(b)(1)(A)-(B):

Amended Code Sec. 42(e)(3)(A)(ii) by striking "10 percent" in subclause (I) and inserting "20 percent", and by striking "$3,000" in subclause (II) and inserting "$6,000". **Effective** generally for buildings with respect to which housing credit dollar amounts are allocated after 7-30-2008. For a special rule, see Act Sec. 3003(h)(2)(B), below.

P.L. 110-289, §3003(b)(2):

Amended Code Sec. 42(e)(3) by adding at the end a new subparagraph (D). **Effective** generally for buildings with respect to which housing credit dollar amounts are allocated after 7-30-2008. For a special rule, see Act Sec. 3003(h)(2)(B), below.

P.L. 110-289, §3003(h)(2)(B), provides:

(B) BUILDINGS NOT SUBJECT TO ALLOCATION LIMITS.—To the extent paragraph (1) of section 42(h) of the Internal Revenue Code of 1986 does not apply to any building by reason of paragraph (4) thereof, the amendments made by subsection (b) shall apply [to] buildings financed with bonds issued pursuant to allocations made after the date of the enactment of this Act [7-30-2008.—CCH].

• 1989, Omnibus Budget Reconciliation Act of 1989 (P.L. 101-239)

P.L. 101-239, §7108(d)(3):

Amended Code Sec. 42(e)(3) by redesignating subparagraph (B) as subparagraph (C) and by striking so much of such paragraph as precedes newly redesignated subparagraph (C) and inserting new paragraph (3) and subparagraphs (A) and (B). For the **effective** date, see Act Sec. 7108(r)[s](1)-(2) following Code Sec. 42(b). Prior to amendment, so much of Code Sec. 42(e)(3) that preceded subparagraph (B) read as follows:

(3) AVERAGE OF REHABILITATION EXPENDITURES MUST BE $2,000 OR MORE.—

(A) IN GENERAL.—Paragraph (1) shall apply to rehabilitation expenditures with respect to any building only if the qualified basis attributable to such expenditures incurred during any 24-month period, when divided by the low-income units in the building, is $2,000 or more.

P.L. 101-239, §7108(l)(3)(C):

Amended Code Sec. 42(e)(5) by striking "subsection (d)(2)(A)(i)(II)" and inserting "subsection (d)(2)(A)(i)". **Effective** as if included in the amendments made by section 252 of P.L. 99-514.

P.L. 101-239, §7841(d)(15):

Amended Code Sec. 42(e)(2)(A) by striking "captial account" and inserting "capital account". **Effective** 12-19-89.

[Sec. 42(f)]

(f) DEFINITION AND SPECIAL RULES RELATING TO CREDIT PERIOD.—

(1) CREDIT PERIOD DEFINED.—For purposes of this section, the term "credit period" means, with respect to any building, the period of 10 taxable years beginning with—

(A) the taxable year in which the building is placed in service, or

(B) at the election of the taxpayer, the succeeding taxable year,

but only if the building is a qualified low-income building as of the close of the 1st year of such period. The election under subparagraph (B), once made, shall be irrevocable.

(2) SPECIAL RULE FOR 1ST YEAR OF CREDIT PERIOD.—

(A) IN GENERAL.—The credit allowable under subsection (a) with respect to any building for the 1st taxable year of the credit period shall be determined by substituting for the applicable fraction under subsection (c)(1) the fraction—

(i) the numerator of which is the sum of the applicable fractions determined under subsection (c)(1) as of the close of each full month of such year during which such building was in service, and

(ii) the denominator of which is 12.

(B) DISALLOWED 1ST YEAR CREDIT ALLOWED IN 11TH YEAR.—Any reduction by reason of subparagraph (A) in the credit allowable (without regard to subparagraph (A)) for the 1st taxable year of the credit period shall be allowable under subsection (a) for the 1st taxable year following the credit period.

(3) DETERMINATION OF APPLICABLE PERCENTAGE WITH RESPECT TO INCREASES IN QUALIFIED BASIS AFTER 1ST YEAR OF CREDIT PERIOD.—

(A) IN GENERAL.—In the case of any building which was a qualified low-income building as of the close of the 1st year of the credit period, if—

(i) as of the close of any taxable year in the compliance period (after the 1st year of the credit period) the qualified basis of such building exceeds

(ii) the qualified basis of such building as of the close of the 1st year of the credit period,

the applicable percentage which shall apply under subsection (a) for the taxable year to such excess shall be the percentage equal to 2/3 of the applicable percentage which (after the application of subsection (h)) would but for this paragraph apply to such basis.

(B) 1ST YEAR COMPUTATION APPLIES.—A rule similar to the rule of paragraph (2)(A) shall apply to any increase in qualified basis to which subparagraph (A) applies for the 1st year of such increase.

(4) DISPOSITIONS OF PROPERTY.—If a building (or an interest therein) is disposed of during any year for which credit is allowable under subsection (a), such credit shall be allocated between the parties on the basis of the number of days during such year the building (or interest) was held by each. In any case, proper adjustments shall be made in the application of subsection (j).

(5) CREDIT PERIOD FOR EXISTING BUILDINGS NOT TO BEGIN BEFORE REHABILITATION CREDIT ALLOWED.—

(A) IN GENERAL.—The credit period for an existing building shall not begin before the 1st taxable year of the credit period for rehabilitation expenditures with respect to the building.

(B) ACQUISITION CREDIT ALLOWED FOR CERTAIN BUILDINGS NOT ALLOWED A REHABILITATION CREDIT.—

(i) IN GENERAL.—In the case of a building described in clause (ii)—

(I) subsection (d)(2)(B)(iv) shall not apply, and

(II) the credit period for such building shall not begin before the taxable year which would be the 1st taxable year of the credit period for rehabilitation expenditures with respect to the building under the modifications described in clause (ii)(II).

(ii) BUILDING DESCRIBED.—A building is described in this clause if—

(I) a waiver is granted under subsection (d)(6)(C) with respect to the acquisition of the building, and

(II) a credit would be allowed for rehabilitation expenditures with respect to such building if subsection (e)(3)(A)(ii)(I) did not apply and if the dollar amount in effect under subsection (e)(3)(A)(ii)(II) were two-thirds of such amount.

Amendments

• 2008, Housing Assistance Tax Act of 2008 (P.L. 110-289)

P.L. 110-289, §3003(b)(3):

Amended Code Sec. 42(f)(5)(B)(ii)(II) by striking "if subsection (e)(3)(A)(ii)(II)" and all that follows and inserting "if the dollar amount in effect under subsection (e)(3)(A(ii)(II) were two-thirds of such amount.". **Effective** generally for buildings with respect to which housing credit dollar amounts are allocated after 7-30-2008. For a special rule, see Act Sec. 3003(h)(2)(B), below. Prior to amendment, Code Sec. 42(f)(5)(B)(ii)(II) read as follows:

(II) a credit would be allowed for rehabilitation expenditures with respect to such building if subsection (e)(3)(A)(ii)(I) did not apply and if subsection (e)(3)(A)(ii)(II) were applied by substituting "$2,000" for "$3,000".

P.L. 110-289, §3003(h)(2)(B), provides:

(B) BUILDINGS NOT SUBJECT TO ALLOCATION LIMITS.—To the extent paragraph (1) of section 42(h) of the Internal Revenue Code of 1986 does not apply to any building by reason of paragraph (4) thereof, the amendments made by subsection (b) shall apply [to] buildings financed with bonds issued pursuant to allocations made after the date of the enactment of this Act [7-30-2008.—CCH].

• 1989, Omnibus Budget Reconciliation Act of 1989 (P.L. 101-239)

P.L. 101-239, §7108(d)(2):

Amended Code Sec. 42(f) by adding at the end thereof a new paragraph (5). For the **effective** date of the above amendment, see Act Sec. 7108(r)[s](1)-(2) following Code Sec. 42(b).

P.L. 101-239, §7831(c)(4):

Amended Code Sec. 42(f) by adding at the end thereof a new paragraph (4). **Effective** as if included in the provision of P.L. 99-514 to which it relates.

• 1988, Technical and Miscellaneous Revenue Act of 1988 (P.L. 100-647)

P.L. 100-647, §1002(l)(2)(B):

Amended Code Sec. 42(f)(1) by striking out "beginning with" and all that follows and adding the material following "taxable years". **Effective** as if included in the provision of P.L. 99-514 to which it relates. Prior to amendment, Code Sec. 42(f)(1) read as follows:

(1) CREDIT PERIOD DEFINED.—For purposes of this section, the term "credit period" means, with respect to any building, the period of 10 taxable years beginning with the taxa-

ble year in which the building is placed in service or, at the election of the taxpayer, the succeeding taxable year. Such an election, once made, shall be irrevocable.

P.L. 100-647, § 1002(l)(9)(A):

Amended Code Sec. 42(f)(3). **Effective** as if included in the provision of P.L. 99-514 to which it relates. Prior to amendment, Code Sec. 42(f)(3) read as follows:

(3) SPECIAL RULE WHERE INCREASE IN QUALIFIED BASIS AFTER 1ST YEAR OF CREDIT PERIOD.—

(A) CREDIT INCREASED.—If—

(i) as of the close of any taxable year in the compliance period (after the 1st year of the credit period) the qualified basis of any building exceeds

(ii) the qualified basis of such building as of the close of the 1st year of the credit period,

the credit allowable under subsection (a) for the taxable year (determined without regard to this paragraph) shall be increased by an amount equal to the product of such excess and the percentage equal to 2/3 of the applicable percentage for such building.

(B) 1ST YEAR COMPUTATION APPLIES.—A rule similar to the rule of paragraph (2)(A) shall apply to the additional credit allowable by reason of this paragraph for the 1st year in which such additional credit is allowable.

[Sec. 42(g)]

(g) QUALIFIED LOW-INCOME HOUSING PROJECT.—For purposes of this section—

(1) IN GENERAL.—The term "qualified low-income housing project" means any project for residential rental property if the project meets the requirements of subparagraph (A) or (B) whichever is elected by the taxpayer:

(A) 20-50 TEST.—The project meets the requirements of this subparagraph if 20 percent or more of the residential units in such project are both rent-restricted and occupied by individuals whose income is 50 percent or less of area median gross income.

(B) 40-60 TEST.—The project meets the requirements of this subparagraph if 40 percent or more of the residential units in such project are both rent-restricted and occupied by individuals whose income is 60 percent or less of area median gross income.

Any election under this paragraph, once made, shall be irrevocable. For purposes of this paragraph, any property shall not be treated as failing to be residential rental property merely because part of the building in which such property is located is used for purposes other than residential rental purposes.

(2) RENT-RESTRICTED UNITS.—

(A) IN GENERAL.—For purposes of paragraph (1), a residential unit is rent-restricted if the gross rent with respect to such unit does not exceed 30 percent of the imputed income limitation applicable to such unit. For purposes of the preceding sentence, the amount of the income limitation under paragraph (1) applicable for any period shall not be less than such limitation applicable for the earliest period the building (which contains the unit) was included in the determination of whether the project is a qualified low-income housing project.

(B) GROSS RENT.—For purposes of subparagraph (A), gross rent—

(i) does not include any payment under section 8 of the United States Housing Act of 1937 or any comparable rental assistance program (with respect to such unit or occupants thereof),

(ii) includes any utility allowance determined by the Secretary after taking into account such determinations under section 8 of the United States Housing Act of 1937,

(iii) does not include any fee for a supportive service which is paid to the owner of the unit (on the basis of the low-income status of the tenant of the unit) by any governmental program of assistance (or by an organization described in section 501(c)(3) and exempt from tax under section 501(a)) if such program (or organization) provides assistance for rent and the amount of assistance provided for rent is not separable from the amount of assistance provided for supportive services, and

(iv) does not include any rental payment to the owner of the unit to the extent such owner pays an equivalent amount to the Farmers' Home Administration under section 515 of the Housing Act of 1949.

For purposes of clause (iii), the term "supportive service" means any service provided under a planned program of services designed to enable residents of a residential rental property to remain independent and avoid placement in a hospital, nursing home, or intermediate care facility for the mentally or physically handicapped. In the case of a single-room occupancy unit or a building described in subsection (i)(3)(B)(iii), such term includes any service provided to assist tenants in locating and retaining permanent housing.

(C) IMPUTED INCOME LIMITATION APPLICABLE TO UNIT.—For purposes of this paragraph, the imputed income limitation applicable to a unit is the income limitation which would apply under paragraph (1) to individuals occupying the unit if the number of individuals occupying the unit were as follows:

(i) In the case of a unit which does not have a separate bedroom, 1 individual.

(ii) In the case of a unit which has 1 or more separate bedrooms, 1.5 individuals for each separate bedroom.

In the case of a project with respect to which a credit is allowable by reason of this section and for which financing is provided by a bond described in section 142(a)(7), the imputed income limitation shall apply in lieu of the otherwise applicable income limitation for purposes of applying section 142(d)(4)(B)(ii).

(D) TREATMENT OF UNITS OCCUPIED BY INDIVIDUALS WHOSE INCOMES RISE ABOVE LIMIT.—

(i) IN GENERAL.—Except as provided in clause (ii), notwithstanding an increase in the income of the occupants of a low-income unit above the income limitation applicable under paragraph (1), such unit shall continue to be treated as a low-income unit if the income of such occupants initially met such income limitation and such unit continues to be rent-restricted.

(ii) NEXT AVAILABLE UNIT MUST BE RENTED TO LOW-INCOME TENANT IF INCOME RISES ABOVE 140 PERCENT OF INCOME LIMIT.—If the income of the occupants of the unit increases above 140 percent of the income limitation applicable under paragraph (1), clause (i) shall cease to apply to any such unit if any residential rental unit in the building (of a size comparable to, or smaller than, such unit) is occupied by a new resident whose income exceeds such income limitation. In the case of a project described in section 142(d)(4)(B), the preceding sentence shall be applied by substituting "170 percent" for "140 percent" and by substituting "any low-income unit in the building is occupied by a new resident whose income exceeds 40 percent of area median gross income" for "any residential unit in the building (of a size comparable to, or smaller than, such unit) is occupied by a new resident whose income exceeds such income limitation".

(E) UNITS WHERE FEDERAL RENTAL ASSISTANCE IS REDUCED AS TENANT'S INCOME INCREASES.—If the gross rent with respect to a residential unit exceeds the limitation under subparagraph (A) by reason of the fact that the income of the occupants thereof exceeds the income limitation applicable under paragraph (1), such unit shall, nevertheless, be treated as a rent-restricted unit for purposes of paragraph (1) if—

(i) a Federal rental assistance payment described in subparagraph (B)(i) is made with respect to such unit or its occupants, and

(ii) the sum of such payment and the gross rent with respect to such unit does not exceed the sum of the amount of such payment which would be made and the gross rent which would be payable with respect to such unit if—

(I) the income of the occupants thereof did not exceed the income limitation applicable under paragraph (1), and

(II) such units were rent-restricted within the meaning of subparagraph (A).

The preceding sentence shall apply to any unit only if the result described in clause (ii) is required by Federal statute as of the date of the enactment of this subparagraph and as of the date the Federal rental assistance payment is made.

(3) DATE FOR MEETING REQUIREMENTS.—

(A) IN GENERAL.—Except as otherwise provided in this paragraph, a building shall be treated as a qualified low-income building only if the project (of which such building is a part) meets the requirements of paragraph (1) not later than the close of the 1st year of the credit period for such building.

(B) BUILDINGS WHICH RELY ON LATER BUILDINGS FOR QUALIFICATION.—

(i) IN GENERAL.—In determining whether a building (hereinafter in this subparagraph referred to as the "prior building") is a qualified low-income building, the taxpayer may take into account 1 or more additional buildings placed in service during the 12-month period described in subparagraph (A) with respect to the prior building only if the taxpayer elects to apply clause (ii) with respect to each additional building taken into account.

(ii) TREATMENT OF ELECTED BUILDINGS.—In the case of a building which the taxpayer elects to take into account under clause (i), the period under subparagraph (A) for such building shall end at the close of the 12-month period applicable to the prior building.

(iii) DATE PRIOR BUILDING IS TREATED AS PLACED IN SERVICE.—For purposes of determining the credit period and the compliance period for the prior building, the prior building shall be treated for purposes of this section as placed in service on the most recent date any additional building elected by the taxpayer (with respect to such prior building) was placed in service.

(C) SPECIAL RULE.—A building—

(i) other than the 1st building placed in service as part of a project, and

(ii) other than a building which is placed in service during the 12-month period described in subparagraph (A) with respect to a prior building which becomes a qualified low-income building,

shall in no event be treated as a qualified low-income building unless the project is a qualified low-income housing project (without regard to such building) on the date such building is placed in service.

(D) PROJECTS WITH MORE THAN 1 BUILDING MUST BE IDENTIFIED.—For purposes of this section, a project shall be treated as consisting of only 1 building unless, before the close of the 1st calendar year in the project period (as defined in subsection (h)(1)(F)(ii)), each building which is (or will be) part of such project is identified in such form and manner as the Secretary may provide.

(4) CERTAIN RULES MADE APPLICABLE.—Paragraphs (2) (other than subparagraph (A) thereof), (3), (4), (5), (6), and (7) of section 142(d), and section 6652(j), shall apply for purposes of determining whether any project is a qualified low-income housing project and whether any unit is a low-income unit; except that, in applying such provisions for such purposes, the term "gross rent" shall have the meaning given such term by paragraph (2)(B) of this subsection.

(5) ELECTION TO TREAT BUILDING AFTER COMPLIANCE PERIOD AS NOT PART OF A PROJECT.—For purposes of this section, the taxpayer may elect to treat any building as not part of a qualified low-income housing project for any period beginning after the compliance period of such building.

(6) SPECIAL RULE WHERE DE MINIMIS EQUITY CONTRIBUTION.—Property shall not be treated as failing to be residential rental property for purposes of this section merely because the occupant of a residential unit in the project pays (on a voluntary basis) to the lessor a de minimis amount to be held toward the purchase by such occupant of a residential unit in such project if—

(A) all amounts so paid are refunded to the occupant on the cessation of his occupancy of a unit in the project, and

(B) the purchase of the unit is not permitted until after the close of the compliance period with respect to the building in which the unit is located.

Any amount paid to the lessor as described in the preceding sentence shall be included in gross rent under paragraph (2) for purposes of determining whether the unit is rent-restricted.

(7) SCATTERED SITE PROJECTS.—Buildings which would (but for their lack of proximity) be treated as a project for purposes of this section shall be so treated if all of the dwelling units in each of the buildings are rent-restricted (within the meaning of paragraph (2)) residential rental units.

(8) WAIVER OF CERTAIN DE MINIMIS ERRORS AND RECERTIFICATIONS.—On application by the taxpayer, the Secretary may waive—

(A) any recapture under subsection (j) in the case of any de minimis error in complying with paragraph (1), or

(B) any annual recertification of tenant income for purposes of this subsection, if the entire building is occupied by low-income tenants.

(9) CLARIFICATION OF GENERAL PUBLIC USE REQUIREMENT.—A project does not fail to meet the general public use requirement solely because of occupancy restrictions or preferences that favor tenants—

(A) with special needs,

(B) who are members of a specified group under a Federal program or State program or policy that supports housing for such a specified group, or

(C) who are involved in artistic or literary activities.

Amendments

• 2008, Housing Assistance Tax Act of 2008 (P.L. 110-289)

P.L. 110-289, §3004(g):

Amended Code Sec. 42(g) by adding at the end a new paragraph (9). **Effective** for buildings placed in service before, on, or after 7-30-2008.

• 1993, Omnibus Budget Reconciliation Act of 1993 (P.L. 103-66)

P.L. 103-66, §13142(b)(3):

Amended Code Sec. 42(g) by adding at the end thereof new paragraph (8). For the **effective** date of the above amendment, see Act Sec. 13142(b)(6), below.

P.L. 103-66, §13142(b)(6) (as amended by P.L. 104-188, §1703(b)(1)), provides:

(6) EFFECTIVE DATES.—

(A) IN GENERAL.—Except as provided in subparagraphs (B) and (C), the amendments made by this subsection shall apply to—

(i) determinations under section 42 of the Internal Revenue Code of 1986 with respect to housing credit dollar amounts allocated from State housing credit ceilings after June 30, 1992, or

(ii) buildings placed in service after June 30, 1992, to the extent paragraph (1) of section 42(h) of such Code does not apply to any building by reason of paragraph (4) thereof, but only with respect to bonds issued after such date.

(B) FULL-TIME STUDENTS, WAIVER AUTHORITY, AND PROHIBITED DISCRIMINATION.—The amendments made by paragraphs (2), (3), and (4) shall take effect on the date of the enactment of this Act.

(C) HOME ASSISTANCE.—The amendment made by paragraph (2) shall apply to periods after the date of the enactment of this Act.

• 1990, Omnibus Budget Reconciliation Act of 1990 (P.L. 101-508)

P.L. 101-508, §11407(b)(3):

Amended Code Sec. 42(g)(2)(B) by striking "and" at the end of clause (ii), by striking the period at the end of clause (iii) and inserting ", and", and by inserting after clause (iii) new clause (iv). For the **effective** date of the above amendment, see Act Sec. 11407(b)(10)(A), below.

P.L. 101-508, §11407(b)(10)(A), provides:

(A) IN GENERAL.—Except as otherwise provided in this paragraph, the amendments made by this subsection shall apply to—

(i) determinations under section 42 of the Internal Revenue Code of 1986 with respect to housing credit dollar amounts allocated from State housing credit ceilings for calendar years after 1990, or

(ii) buildings placed in service after December 31, 1990, to the extent paragraph (1) of section 42(h) of such Code does not apply to any building by reason of paragraph (4) thereof, but only with respect to bonds issued after such date.

P.L. 101-508, §11701(a)(3)(A):

Amended Code Sec. 42(g)(2)(D)(i) by inserting before the period "and such unit continues to be rent-restricted" **Effec-**

tive as if included in the provision of P.L. 101-239 to which it relates.

P.L. 101-508, §11701(a)(3)(B), provides:

(B) In the case of a building to which (but for this subparagraph) the amendment made by subparagraph (A) does not apply, such amendment shall apply to—

(i) determinations of qualified basis for taxable years beginning after the date of the enactment of this Act, and

(ii) determinations of qualified basis for taxable years beginning on or before such date except that determinations for such taxable years shall be made without regard to any reduction in gross rent after August 3, 1990, for any period before August 4, 1990.

P.L. 101-508, §11701(a)(4):

Amended Code Sec. 42(g)(2)(D)(ii) by adding at the end thereof a new sentence. **Effective** as if included in the provision of P.L. 101-239 to which it relates.

P.L. 101-508, §11701(a)(5)(A):

Amended Code Sec. 42(g)(3)(A) by striking "the 12-month period beginning on the date the building is placed in service" and inserting "the 1st year of the credit period for such building". **Effective** as if included in the provision of P.L. 101-239 to which it relates.

P.L. 101-508, §11701(a)(5)(B), provides:

(B) In the case of a building to which the amendment made by subparagraph (A) does not apply, the period specified in section 42(g)(3)(A) of the Internal Revenue Code of 1986 (as in effect before the amendment made by subparagraph (A)) shall not expire before the close of the taxable year following the taxable year in which the building is placed in service.

• 1989, Omnibus Budget Reconciliation Act of 1989 (P.L. 101-239)

P.L. 101-239, §7108(e)(1)(A):

Amended Code Sec. 42(g)(2) by redesignating subparagraph (C) as subparagraph (E) and by inserting after subparagraph (B) new subparagraphs (C) and (D). For the **effective** date, see Act Sec. 7108(r)[s](1)-(2) following Code Sec. 42(b).

P.L. 101-239, §7108(e)(1)(B):

Amended Code Sec. 42(g)(2)(A) by striking "the income limitation under paragraph (1) applicable to individuals occupying such unit" and inserting "the imputed income limitation applicable to such unit". For the **effective** date, see Act Sec. 7108(r)[s](1)-(2) following Code Sec. 42(b).

P.L. 101-239, §7108(e)(2):

Amended Code Sec. 42(g)(2)(A) by adding at the end thereof a new sentence. For the **effective** date, see Act Sec. 7108(r)[s](1)-(2) following Code Sec. 42(b).

P.L. 101-239, §7108(h)(2)(A)-(C):

Amended Code Sec. 42(g)(2)(B) by striking "and" at the end of clause (i), by striking the period at the end of clause (ii) and inserting ", and" and by adding at the end a new clause (iii) and flush left sentence. For the **effective** date, see Act Sec. 7108(r)[s](1)-(2) following Code Sec. 42(b).

P.L. 101-239, §7108(h)(3):

Amended Code Sec. 42(g) by adding at the end thereof a new paragraph (7). For the **effective** date, see Act Sec. 7108(r)[s](1)-(2) following Code Sec. 42(b).

P.L. 101-239, §7108(m)(3):

Amended Code Sec. 42(g)(3) by adding at the end thereof a new subparagraph (D). For the **effective** date, see Act Sec. 7108(r)[s](1)-(2) following Code Sec. 42(b).

P.L. 101-239, §7108(n)(2):

Amended Code Sec. 42(g)(4) by striking "(other than section 142(d)(4)(B)(iii))" after "such provisions". For the **effective** date, see Act Sec. 7108(r)[s](1)-(2) following Code Sec. 42(b).

• 1988, Technical and Miscellaneous Revenue Act of 1988 (P.L. 100-647)

P.L. 100-647, §1002(l)(10):

Amended Code Sec. 42(g)(2)(B) by striking out "Federal rental assistance" and inserting in lieu thereof "rental assistance". **Effective** as if included in the provision of P.L. 99-514 to which it relates.

P.L. 100-647, §1002(l)(11):

Amended Code Sec. 42(g)(2) by adding at the end thereof new subparagraph (C). **Effective** as if included in the provision of P.L. 99-514 to which it relates.

P.L. 100-647, §1002(l)(12):

Amended Code Sec. 42(g)(3). **Effective** as if included in the provision of P.L. 99-514 to which it relates. Prior to amendment, Code Sec. 42(g)(3) read as follows:

(3) DATE FOR MEETING REQUIREMENTS.—

(A) PROJECTS CONSISTING OF 1 BUILDING.—In the case of a project which does not have any other building in service, such project shall not be treated as meeting the requirements of paragraph (1) unless it meets such requirements not later than the date which is 12 months after the date such project is placed in service.

(B) PROJECTS CONSISTING OF MORE THAN 1 BUILDING.—In the case of a project which has a building in service when a later building is placed in service as part of such project, such project shall not be treated as meeting the requirements of paragraph (1) with respect to such later building unless—

(i) such project meets such requirements without regard to such later building on the date such later building is placed in service, and

(ii) such project meets such requirements with regard to such later building not later than the date which is 12 months after the date such later building is placed in service.

P.L. 100-647, §1002(l)(13):

Amended Code Sec. 42(g)(4) by inserting before the period "; except that, in applying such provisions (other than section 142(d)(4)(B)(iii)) for such purposes, the term `gross rent' shall have the meaning given such term by paragraph (2)(B) of this subsection". **Effective** as if included in the provision of P.L. 99-514 to which it relates.

P.L. 100-647, §1002(l)(32):

Amended Code Sec. 42(g) by adding at the end thereof new paragraph (6). **Effective** as if included in the provision of P.L. 99-514 to which it relates.

[Sec. 42(h)]

(h) LIMITATION ON AGGREGATE CREDIT ALLOWABLE WITH RESPECT TO PROJECTS LOCATED IN A STATE.—

(1) CREDIT MAY NOT EXCEED CREDIT AMOUNT ALLOCATED TO BUILDING.—

(A) IN GENERAL.—The amount of the credit determined under this section for any taxable year with respect to any building shall not exceed the housing credit dollar amount allocated to such building under this subsection.

(B) TIME FOR MAKING ALLOCATION.—Except in the case of an allocation which meets the requirements of subparagraph (C), (D), (E), or (F), an allocation shall be taken into account under subparagraph (A) only if it is made not later than the close of the calendar year in which the building is placed in service.

(C) EXCEPTION WHERE BINDING COMMITMENT.—An allocation meets the requirements of this subparagraph if there is a binding commitment (not later than the close of the calendar year in which the building is placed in service) by the housing credit agency to allocate a specified housing credit dollar amount to such building beginning in a specified later taxable year.

(D) EXCEPTION WHERE INCREASE IN QUALIFIED BASIS.—

(i) IN GENERAL.—An allocation meets the requirements of this subparagraph if such allocation is made not later than the close of the calendar year in which ends the taxable year to which it will 1st apply but only to the extent the amount of such allocation does not exceed the limitation under clause (ii).

(ii) LIMITATION.—The limitation under this clause is the amount of credit allowable under this section (without regard to this subsection) for a taxable year with respect to an increase in the qualified basis of the building equal to the excess of—

(I) the qualified basis of such building as of the close of the 1st taxable year to which such allocation will apply, over

(II) the qualified basis of such building as of the close of the 1st taxable year to which the most recent prior housing credit allocation with respect to such building applied.

(iii) HOUSING CREDIT DOLLAR AMOUNT REDUCED BY FULL ALLOCATION.—Notwithstanding clause (i), the full amount of the allocation shall be taken into account under paragraph (2).

(E) EXCEPTION WHERE 10 PERCENT OF COST INCURRED.—

(i) IN GENERAL.—An allocation meets the requirements of this subparagraph if such allocation is made with respect to a qualified building which is placed in service not later than the close of the second calendar year following the calendar year in which the allocation is made.

(ii) QUALIFIED BUILDING.—For purposes of clause (i), the term "qualified building" means any building which is part of a project if the taxpayer's basis in such project (as of the date which is 1 year after the date that the allocation was made) is more than 10 percent of the taxpayer's reasonably expected basis in such project (as of the close of the second calendar year referred to in clause (i)). Such term does not include any existing building unless a credit is allowable under subsection (e) for rehabilitation expenditures paid or incurred by the taxpayer with respect to such building for a taxable year ending during the second calendar year referred to in clause (i) or the prior taxable year.

(F) ALLOCATION OF CREDIT ON A PROJECT BASIS.—

(i) IN GENERAL.—In the case of a project which includes (or will include) more than 1 building, an allocation meets the requirements of this subparagraph if—

(I) the allocation is made to the project for a calendar year during the project period,

(II) the allocation only applies to buildings placed in service during or after the calendar year for which the allocation is made, and

(III) the portion of such allocation which is allocated to any building in such project is specified not later than the close of the calendar year in which the building is placed in service.

(ii) PROJECT PERIOD.—For purposes of clause (i), the term "project period" means the period—

(I) beginning with the 1st calendar year for which an allocation may be made for the 1st building placed in service as part of such project, and

(II) ending with the calendar year the last building is placed in service as part of such project.

(2) ALLOCATED CREDIT AMOUNT TO APPLY TO ALL TAXABLE YEARS ENDING DURING OR AFTER CREDIT ALLOCATION YEAR.—Any housing credit dollar amount allocated to any building for any calendar year—

(A) shall apply to such building for all taxable years in the compliance period ending during or after such calendar year, and

(B) shall reduce the aggregate housing credit dollar amount of the allocating agency only for such calendar year.

(3) HOUSING CREDIT DOLLAR AMOUNT FOR AGENCIES.—

(A) IN GENERAL.—The aggregate housing credit dollar amount which a housing credit agency may allocate for any calendar year is the portion of the State housing credit ceiling allocated under this paragraph for such calendar year to such agency.

(B) STATE CEILING INITIALLY ALLOCATED TO STATE HOUSING CREDIT AGENCIES.—Except as provided in subparagraphs (D) and (E), the State housing credit ceiling for each calendar year shall be allocated to the housing credit agency of such State. If there is more than 1 housing credit agency of a State, all such agencies shall be treated as a single agency.

(C) STATE HOUSING CREDIT CEILING.—The State housing credit ceiling applicable to any State for any calendar year shall be an amount equal to the sum of—

(i) the unused State housing credit ceiling (if any) of such State for the preceding calendar year,

(ii) the greater of—

(I) $1.75 ($1.50 for 2001) multiplied by the State population, or

(II) $2,000,000,

(iii) the amount of State housing credit ceiling returned in the calendar year, plus

(iv) the amount (if any) allocated under subparagraph (D) to such State by the Secretary.

For purposes of clause (i), the unused State housing credit ceiling for any calendar year is the excess (if any) of the sum of the amounts described in clauses (ii) through (iv) over the aggregate housing credit dollar amount allocated for such year. For purposes of clause (iii), the amount of State housing credit ceiling returned in the calendar year equals the housing credit dollar amount previously allocated within the State to any project which fails to meet the 10 percent test under paragraph (1)(E)(ii) on a date after the close of the calendar year in which the allocation was made or which does not become a qualified low-income housing project within the period required by this section or the terms of the allocation or to any project with respect to which an allocation is cancelled by mutual consent of the housing credit agency and the allocation recipient.

(D) UNUSED HOUSING CREDIT CARRYOVERS ALLOCATED AMONG CERTAIN STATES.—

(i) IN GENERAL.—The unused housing credit carryover of a State for any calendar year shall be assigned to the Secretary for allocation among qualified States for the succeeding calendar year.

(ii) UNUSED HOUSING CREDIT CARRYOVER.—For purposes of this subparagraph, the unused housing credit carryover of a State for any calendar year is the excess (if any) of the unused State housing credit ceiling for such year (as defined in subparagraph (C)(i)) over the excess (if any) of—

(I) the unused State housing credit ceiling for the year preceding such year, over

(II) the aggregate housing credit dollar amount allocated for such year.

(iii) FORMULA FOR ALLOCATION OF UNUSED HOUSING CREDIT CARRYOVERS AMONG QUALIFIED STATES.—The amount allocated under this subparagraph to a qualified State for any calendar year shall be the amount determined by the Secretary to bear the same ratio to the aggregate unused housing credit carryovers of all States for the preceding calendar year as such State's population for the calendar year bears to the population of all qualified States for the calendar year. For purposes of the preceding sentence, population shall be determined in accordance with section 146(j).

(iv) QUALIFIED STATE.—For purposes of this subparagraph, the term "qualified State" means, with respect to a calendar year, any State—

(I) which allocated its entire State housing credit ceiling for the preceding calendar year, and

(II) for which a request is made (not later than May 1 of the calendar year) to receive an allocation under clause (iii).

(E) SPECIAL RULE FOR STATES WITH CONSTITUTIONAL HOME RULE CITIES.—For purposes of this subsection—

(i) IN GENERAL.—The aggregate housing credit dollar amount for any constitutional home rule city for any calendar year shall be an amount which bears the same ratio to the State housing credit ceiling for such calendar year as—

(I) the population of such city, bears to

(II) the population of the entire State.

(ii) COORDINATION WITH OTHER ALLOCATIONS.—In the case of any State which contains 1 or more constitutional home rule cities, for purposes of applying this paragraph with respect to housing credit agencies in such State other than constitutional home rule cities, the State housing credit ceiling for any calendar year shall be reduced by the aggregate housing credit dollar amounts determined for such year for all constitutional home rule cities in such State.

(iii) CONSTITUTIONAL HOME RULE CITY.—For purposes of this paragraph, the term "constitutional home rule city" has the meaning given such term by section 146(d)(3)(C).

(F) STATE MAY PROVIDE FOR DIFFERENT ALLOCATION.—Rules similar to the rules of section 146(e) (other than paragraph (2)(B) thereof) shall apply for purposes of this paragraph.

(G) POPULATION.—For purposes of this paragraph, population shall be determined in accordance with section 146(j).

(H) COST-OF-LIVING ADJUSTMENT.—

(i) IN GENERAL.—In the case of a calendar year after 2002, the $2,000,000 and $1.75 amounts in subparagraph (C) shall each be increased by an amount equal to—

(I) such dollar amount, multiplied by

(II) the cost-of-living adjustment determined under section 1(f)(3) for such calendar year by substituting "calendar year 2001" for "calendar year 1992" in subparagraph (B) thereof.

(ii) ROUNDING.—

(I) In the case of the $2,000,000 amount, any increase under clause (i) which is not a multiple of $5,000 shall be rounded to the next lowest multiple of $5,000.

(II) In the case of the $1.75 amount, any increase under clause (i) which is not a multiple of 5 cents shall be rounded to the next lowest multiple of 5 cents.

(I) INCREASE IN STATE HOUSING CREDIT CEILING FOR 2008 AND 2009.—In the case of calendar years 2008 and 2009—

(i) the dollar amount in effect under subparagraph (C)(ii)(I) for such calendar year (after any increase under subparagraph (H)) shall be increased by $0.20, and

(ii) the dollar amount in effect under subparagraph (C)(ii)(II) for such calendar year (after any increase under subparagraph (H)) shall be increased by an amount equal to 10 percent of such dollar amount (rounded to the next lowest multiple of $5,000).

(4) CREDIT FOR BUILDINGS FINANCED BY TAX-EXEMPT BONDS SUBJECT TO VOLUME CAP NOT TAKEN INTO ACCOUNT.—

(A) IN GENERAL.—Paragraph (1) shall not apply to the portion of any credit allowable under subsection (a) which is attributable to eligible basis financed by any obligation the interest on which is exempt from tax under section 103 if—

(i) such obligation is taken into account under section 146, and

(ii) principal payments on such financing are applied within a reasonable period to redeem obligations the proceeds of which were used to provide such financing or such financing is refunded as described in section 146(i)(6).

(B) SPECIAL RULE WHERE 50 PERCENT OR MORE OF BUILDING IS FINANCED WITH TAX-EXEMPT BONDS SUBJECT TO VOLUME CAP.—For purposes of subparagraph (A), if 50 percent or more of the aggregate basis of any building and the land on which the building is located is financed by an obligation described in subparagraph (A), paragraph (1) shall not apply to any portion of the credit allowable under subsection (a) with respect to such building.

(5) PORTION OF STATE CEILING SET-ASIDE FOR CERTAIN PROJECTS INVOLVING QUALIFIED NONPROFIT ORGANIZATIONS.—

(A) IN GENERAL.—Not more than 90 percent of the State housing credit ceiling for any State for any calendar year shall be allocated to projects other than qualified low-income housing projects described in subparagraphs [sic] (B).

(B) PROJECTS INVOLVING QUALIFIED NONPROFIT ORGANIZATIONS.—For purposes of subparagraph (A), a qualified low-income housing project is described in this subparagraph if a qualified nonprofit organization is to own an interest in the project (directly or through a partnership) and materially participate (within the meaning of section 469(h)[)] in the development and operation of the project throughout the compliance period.

(C) QUALIFIED NONPROFIT ORGANIZATION.—For purposes of this paragraph, the term "qualified nonprofit organization" means any organization if—

(i) such organization is described in paragraph (3) or (4) of section 501(c) and is exempt from tax under section 501(a),

(ii) such organization is determined by the State housing credit agency not to be affiliated with or controlled by a for-profit organization; and

(iii) 1 of the exempt purposes of such organization includes the fostering of low-income housing.

(D) TREATMENT OF CERTAIN SUBSIDIARIES.—

(i) IN GENERAL.—For purposes of this paragraph, a qualified nonprofit organization shall be treated as satisfying the ownership and material participation test of subparagraph (B) if any qualified corporation in which such organization holds stock satisfies such test.

(ii) QUALIFIED CORPORATION.—For purposes of clause (i), the term "qualified corporation" means any corporation if 100 percent of the stock of such corporation is held by 1 or more qualified nonprofit organizations at all times during the period such corporation is in existence.

(E) STATE MAY NOT OVERRIDE SET-ASIDE.—Nothing in subparagraph (F) of paragraph (3) shall be construed to permit a State not to comply with subparagraph (A) of this paragraph.

(6) BUILDINGS ELIGIBLE FOR CREDIT ONLY IF MINIMUM LONG-TERM COMMITMENT TO LOW-INCOME HOUSING.—

(A) IN GENERAL.—No credit shall be allowed by reason of this section with respect to any building for the taxable year unless an extended low-income housing commitment is in effect as of the end of such taxable year.

(B) EXTENDED LOW-INCOME HOUSING COMMITMENT.—For purposes of this paragraph, the term "extended low-income housing commitment" means any agreement between the taxpayer and the housing credit agency—

(i) which requires that the applicable fraction (as defined in subsection (c)(1)) for the building for each taxable year in the extended use period will not be less than the applicable fraction specified in such agreement and which prohibits the actions described in subclauses (I) and (II) of subparagraph (E)(ii),

(ii) which allows individuals who meet the income limitation applicable to the building under subsection (g) (whether prospective, present, or former occupants of the building) the right to enforce in any State court the requirement and prohibitions of clause (i),

(iii) which prohibits the disposition to any person of any portion of the building to which such agreement applies unless all of the building to which such agreement applies is disposed of to such person,

(iv) which prohibits the refusal to lease to a holder of a voucher or certificate of eligibility under section 8 of the United States Housing Act of 1937 because of the status of the prospective tenant as such a holder,

(v) which is binding on all successors of the taxpayer, and

(vi) which, with respect to the property, is recorded pursuant to State law as a restrictive covenant.

(C) ALLOCATION OF CREDIT MAY NOT EXCEED AMOUNT NECESSARY TO SUPPORT COMMITMENT.—

(i) IN GENERAL.—The housing credit dollar amount allocated to any building may not exceed the amount necessary to support the applicable fraction specified in the extended low-income housing commitment for such building, including any increase in such fraction pursuant to the application of subsection (f)(3) if such increase is reflected in an amended low-income housing commitment.

(ii) BUILDINGS FINANCED BY TAX-EXEMPT BONDS.—If paragraph (4) applies to any building the amount of credit allowed in any taxable year may not exceed the amount necessary to support the applicable fraction specified in the extended low-income housing commitment for such building. Such commitment may be amended to increase such fraction.

(D) EXTENDED USE PERIOD.—For purposes of this paragraph, the term "extended use period" means the period—

(i) beginning on the 1st day in the compliance period on which such building is part of a qualified low-income housing project, and

(ii) ending on the later of—

(I) the date specified by such agency in such agreement, or

(II) the date which is 15 years after the close of the compliance period.

(E) EXCEPTIONS IF FORECLOSURE OR IF NO BUYER WILLING TO MAINTAIN LOW-INCOME STATUS.—

(i) IN GENERAL.—The extended use period for any building shall terminate—

(I) on the date the building is acquired by foreclosure (or instrument in lieu of foreclosure) unless the Secretary determines that such acquisition is part of an arrangement with the taxpayer a purpose of which is to terminate such period, or

(II) on the last day of the period specified in subparagraph (I) if the housing credit agency is unable to present during such period a qualified contract for the acquisition of the low-income portion of the building by any person who will continue to operate such portion as a qualified low-income building.

Subclause (II) shall not apply to the extent more stringent requirements are provided in the agreement or in State law.

(ii) EVICTION, ETC. OF EXISTING LOW-INCOME TENANTS NOT PERMITTED.—The termination of an extended use period under clause (i) shall not be construed to permit before the close of the 3-year period following such termination—

(I) the eviction or the termination of tenancy (other than for good cause) of an existing tenant of any low-income unit, or

(II) any increase in the gross rent with respect to such unit not otherwise permitted under this section.

(F) QUALIFIED CONTRACT.—For purposes of subparagraph (E), the term "qualified contract" means a bona fide contract to acquire (within a reasonable period after the contract is entered into) the nonlow-income portion of the building for fair market value and the low-income portion of the building for an amount not less than the applicable fraction (specified in the extended low-income housing commitment) of—

(i) the sum of—

(I) the outstanding indebtedness secured by, or with respect to, the building,

(II) the adjusted investor equity in the building, plus

(III) other capital contributions not reflected in the amounts described in subclause (I) or (II), reduced by

(ii) cash distributions from (or available for distribution from) the project.

The Secretary shall prescribe such regulations as may be necessary or appropriate to carry out this paragraph, including regulations to prevent the manipulation of the amount determined under the preceding sentence.

(G) ADJUSTED INVESTOR EQUITY.—

(i) IN GENERAL.—For purposes of subparagraph (E), the term "adjusted investor equity" means, with respect to any calendar year, the aggregate amount of cash taxpayers invested with respect to the project increased by the amount equal to—

(I) such amount, multiplied by

(II) the cost-of-living adjustment for such calendar year, determined under section 1(f)(3) by substituting the base calendar year for "calendar year 1987".

An amount shall be taken into account as an investment in the project only to the extent there was an obligation to invest such amount as of the beginning of the credit period and to the extent such amount is reflected in the adjusted basis of the project.

(ii) COST-OF-LIVING INCREASES IN EXCESS OF 5 PERCENT NOT TAKEN INTO ACCOUNT.—Under regulations prescribed by the Secretary, if the CPI for any calendar year (as defined in section 1(f)(4)) exceeds the CPI for the preceding calendar year by more than 5 percent, the CPI for the base calendar year shall be increased such that such excess shall never be taken into account under clause (i).

(iii) BASE CALENDAR YEAR.—For purposes of this subparagraph, the term "base calendar year" means the calendar year with or within which the 1st taxable year of the credit period ends.

(H) LOW-INCOME PORTION.— For purposes of this paragraph, the low-income portion of a building is the portion of such building equal to the applicable fraction specified in the extended low-income housing commitment for the building.

(I) PERIOD FOR FINDING BUYER.—The period referred to in this subparagraph is the 1-year period beginning on the date (after the 14th year of the compliance period) the taxpayer submits a written request to the housing credit agency to find a person to acquire the taxpayer's interest in the low-income portion of the building.

(J) EFFECT OF NONCOMPLIANCE.—If, during a taxable year, there is a determination that an extended low-income housing agreement was not in effect as of the beginning of such year, such determination shall not apply to any period before such year and subparagraph (A) shall be applied without regard to such determination if the failure is corrected within 1 year from the date of the determination.

(K) PROJECTS WHICH CONSIST OF MORE THAN 1 BUILDING.—The application of this paragraph to projects which consist of more than 1 building shall be made under regulations prescribed by the Secretary.

(7) SPECIAL RULES.—

(A) BUILDING MUST BE LOCATED WITHIN JURISDICTION OF CREDIT AGENCY.—A housing credit agency may allocate its aggregate housing credit dollar amount only to buildings located in the jurisdiction of the governmental unit of which such agency is a part.

(B) AGENCY ALLOCATIONS IN EXCESS OF LIMIT.—If the aggregate housing credit dollar amounts allocated by a housing credit agency for any calendar year exceed the portion of the State housing credit ceiling allocated to such agency for such calendar year, the housing credit dollar amounts so allocated shall be reduced (to the extent of such excess) for buildings in the reverse of the order in which the allocations of such amounts were made.

(C) CREDIT REDUCED IF ALLOCATED CREDIT DOLLAR AMOUNT IS LESS THAN CREDIT WHICH WOULD BE ALLOWABLE WITHOUT REGARD TO PLACED IN SERVICE CONVENTION, ETC.—

(i) IN GENERAL.—The amount of the credit determined under this section with respect to any building shall not exceed the clause (ii) percentage of the amount of the credit which would (but for this subparagraph) be determined under this section with respect to such building.

(ii) DETERMINATION OF PERCENTAGE.—For purposes of clause (i), the clause (ii) percentage with respect to any building is the percentage which—

(I) the housing credit dollar amount allocated to such building bears to

(II) the credit amount determined in accordance with clause (iii).

(iii) DETERMINATION OF CREDIT AMOUNT.—The credit amount determined in accordance with this clause is the amount of the credit which would (but for this subparagraph) be determined under this section with respect to the building if—

(I) this section were applied without regard to paragraphs (2)(A) and (3)(B) of subsection (f), and

(II) subsection (f)(3)(A) were applied without regard to "the percentage equal to ⅔ of".

(D) HOUSING CREDIT AGENCY TO SPECIFY APPLICABLE PERCENTAGE AND MAXIMUM QUALIFIED BASIS.—In allocating a housing credit dollar amount to any building, the housing credit agency shall specify the applicable percentage and the maximum qualified basis which may be taken into account under this section with respect to such building. The applicable percentage and maximum qualified basis so specified shall not exceed the applicable percentage and qualified basis determined under this section without regard to this subsection.

(8) OTHER DEFINITIONS.—For purposes of this subsection—

(A) HOUSING CREDIT AGENCY.—The term "housing credit agency" means any agency authorized to carry out this subsection.

(B) POSSESSIONS TREATED AS STATES.—The term "State" includes a possession of the United States.

Amendments

• 2008, Housing Assistance Tax Act of 2008 (P.L. 110-289)

P.L. 110-289, §3001:

Amended Code Sec. 42(h)(3) by adding at the end a new subparagraph (I). **Effective** 7-30-2008.

P.L. 110-289, §3004(b):

Amended Code Sec. 42(h)(1)(E)(ii) by striking "(as of the later of the date which is 6 months after the date that the allocation was made or the close of the calendar year in which the allocation is made)" and inserting "(as of the date which is 1 year after the date that the allocation was made)". **Effective** for buildings placed in service after 7-30-2008.

P.L. 110-289, §3007(b):

Amended Code Sec. 42(h)(4)(A)(ii) by inserting "or such financing is refunded as described in section 146(i)(6)" before the period at the end. **Effective** for repayments of loans received after 7-30-2008.

• 2002, Job Creation and Worker Assistance Act of 2002 (P.L. 107-147)

P.L. 107-147, §417(2):

Amended the second sentence of Code Sec. 42(h)(3)(C) by striking "the amounts described in" and all that follows through the period and inserting "the amounts described in clauses (ii) through (iv) over the aggregate housing credit dollar amount allocated for such year." **Effective** 3-9-2002. Prior to amendment, the second sentence of Code Sec. 42(h)(3)(C) read as follows:

For purposes of clause (i), the unused State housing credit ceiling for any calendar year is the excess (if any) of the sum of the amounts described in clauses (i)[(ii)] through (iv) over the aggregate housing credit dollar amount allocated for such year.

• 2000, Community Renewal Tax Relief Act of 2000 (P.L. 106-554)

P.L. 106-554, §131(a):

Amended Code Sec. 42(h)(3)(C)(i)-(ii). **Effective** for calendar years after 2000. Prior to amendment, Code Sec. 42(h)(3)(C)(i)-(ii) read as follows:

(i) $1.25 multiplied by the State population,

(ii) the unused State housing credit ceiling (if any) of such State for the preceding calendar year,

P.L. 106-554, §131(b):

Amended Code Sec. 42(h)(3) by adding at the end a new subparagraph (H). **Effective** for calendar years after 2000.

P.L. 106-554, §131(c)(1)(A)-(B):

Amended Code Sec. 42(h)(3)(C) (as amended by Act Sec. 131(a)) by striking "clause (ii)" in the matter following clause (iv) and inserting "clause (i)", and by striking "clauses (i)" in the matter following clause (iv) and inserting "clauses (ii)". **Effective** for calendar years after 2000.

P.L. 106-554, §131(c)(2)(A)-(B):

Amended Code Sec. 42(h)(3)(D)(ii) by striking "subparagraph (C)(ii)" and inserting "subparagraph (C)(i)", and by striking "clauses (i)" in subclause (II) and inserting "clauses (ii)". **Effective** for calendar years after 2000.

P.L. 106-554, §135(a)(1):

Amended the first sentence of Code Sec. 42(h)(1)(E)(ii) by striking "(as of" the first place it appears and inserting "(as of the later of the date which is 6 months after the date that the allocation was made or". **Effective** as noted in Act Sec. 137, below.

P.L. 106-554, §135(a)(2):

Amended the last sentence of Code Sec. 42(h)(3)(C) by striking "project which" and inserting "project which fails to meet the 10 percent test under paragraph (1)(E)(ii) on a date after the close of the calendar year in which the allocation was made or which". **Effective** as noted in Act Sec. 137, below.

P.L. 106-554, §136(a):

Amended Code Sec. 42(h)(3)(D)(ii) by striking "the excess" and all that follows and inserting new text. **Effective** as noted in Act Sec. 137, below. Prior to amendment, Code Sec. 42(h)(3)(D)(ii) read as follows:

(ii) UNUSED HOUSING CREDIT CARRYOVER.—For purposes of this subparagraph, the unused housing credit carryover of a State for any calendar year is the excess (if any) of the unused State housing credit ceiling for such year (as defined in subparagraph (C)(i)) over the excess (if any) of—

(I) the aggregate housing credit dollar amount allocated for such year, over

(II) the sum of the amounts described in clauses (ii) and (iii) of subparagraph (C).

P.L. 106-554, §136(b):

Amended the second sentence of Code Sec. 42(h)(3)(C) by striking "clauses (i)[(ii)] and (iii)" and inserting "clauses (i)[(ii)]through (iv)". **Effective** as noted in Act Sec. 137, below.

P.L. 106-554, §137, provides:

Except as otherwise provided in this subtitle, the amendments made by this subtitle shall apply to—

(1) housing credit dollar amounts allocated after December 31, 2000; and

(2) buildings placed in service after such date to the extent paragraph (1) of section 42(h) of the Internal Revenue Code of 1986 does not apply to any building by reason of paragraph (4) thereof, but only with respect to bonds issued after such date.

• 1993, Omnibus Budget Reconciliation Act of 1993 (P.L. 103-66)

P.L. 103-66, §13142(b)(4):

Amended Code Sec. 42(h) by redesignating clauses (iv) and (v) as clauses (v) and (vi) and by inserting after clause

(iii) a new clause (iv). For the **effective** date, see Act Sec. 13142(b)(6), below.

P.L. 103-66, §13142(b)(6) (as amended by P.L. 104-188, §1703(b)(1)), provides:

(6) EFFECTIVE DATES.—

(A) IN GENERAL.—Except as provided in subparagraphs (B) and (C), the amendments made by this subsection shall apply to—

(i) determinations under section 42 of the Internal Revenue Code of 1986 with respect to housing credit dollar amounts allocated from State housing credit ceilings after June 30, 1992, or

(ii) buildings placed in service after June 30, 1992, to the extent paragraph (1) of section 42(h) of such Code does not apply to any building by reason of paragraph (4) thereof, but only with respect to bonds issued after such date.

(B) FULL-TIME STUDENTS, WAIVER AUTHORITY, AND PROHIBITED DISCRIMINATION.—The amendments made by paragraphs (2), (3), and (4) shall take effect on the date of the enactment of this Act.

(C) HOME ASSISTANCE.—The amendment made by paragraph (2) shall apply to periods after the date of the enactment of this Act.

• 1990, Omnibus Budget Reconciliation Act of 1990 (P.L. 101-508)

P.L. 101-508, §11407(b)(9)(A)-(C):

Amended Code Sec. 42(h)(5) by inserting "own an interest in the project (directly or through a partnership) and" after "nonprofit organization is to" in subparagraph (B), by striking "and" at the end of clause (i) of subparagraph (C), by redesignating clause (ii) of such subparagraph as clause (iii), by inserting after clause (i) of such subparagraph new clause (ii), and by inserting "ownership and" before "material participation" in subparagraph (D). **Effective** 11-5-90.

P.L. 101-508, §11701(a)(6)(A):

Amended Code Sec. 42(h)(3)(C) by striking "the amount described in clause (i)" in the second sentence and inserting "the sum of the amounts described in clauses (i) and (iii)". **Effective** as if included in the provision of P.L. 101-239 to which it relates.

P.L. 101-508, §11701(a)(6)(B):

Amended Code Sec. 42(h)(3)(D)(ii)(II) by striking "the amount described in clause (i)" and inserting "the sum of the amounts described in clauses (i) and (iii)". **Effective** as if included in the provision of P.L. 101-239 to which it relates.

P.L. 101-508, §11701(a)(7)(A):

Amended Code Sec. 42(h)(6)(B)(i) by inserting before the comma "and which prohibits the actions described in subclauses (I) and (II) of subparagraph (E)(ii)". **Effective** as if included in the provision of P.L. 101-239 to which it relates.

P.L. 101-508, §11701(a)(7)(B):

Amended Code Sec. 42(h)(6)(B)(ii) by striking "requirement" and inserting "requirement and prohibitions". **Effective** as if included in the provision of P.L. 101-239 to which it relates.

P.L. 101-508, §11701(a)(8)(A):

Amended Code Sec. 42(h)(6)(B) by redesignating clauses (iii) and (iv) as clauses (iv) and (v), respectively, and by inserting after clause (ii) new clause (iii). **Effective** as if included in the provision of P.L. 101-239 to which it relates.

P.L. 101-508, §11701(a)(8)(B):

Amended Code Sec. 42(h)(6) by striking subparagraph (J) and by redesignating subparagraphs (K) and (L) as subparagraphs (J) and (K), respectively. **Effective** as if included in the provision of P.L. 101-239 to which it relates. Prior to amendment, Code Sec. 42(h)(6)(J) read as follows:

(J) SALES OF LESS THAN LOW-INCOME PORTION OF BUILDING.—In the case of a sale or exchange of only a portion of the low-income portion of the building, only the same portion (as the portion sold or exchanged) of the amount determined under subparagraph (F) shall be taken into account thereunder.

P.L. 101-508, §11701(a)(8)(C):

Amended Code Sec. 42(h)(6)(E)(ii)(II) by inserting before the period "not otherwise permitted under this section". **Effective** as if included in the provision of P.L. 101-239 to which it relates.

P.L. 101-508, §11701(a)(8)(D):

Amended Code Sec. 42(h)(6)(F) by inserting "the nonlow-income portion of the building for fair market value and" before "the low-income portion". **Effective** as if included in the provision of P.L. 101-239 to which it relates.

P.L. 101-508, §11701(a)(9):

Amended Code Sec. 42(h)(6)(E)(i)(I) by inserting before the comma "unless the Secretary determines that such acquisition is part of an arrangement with the taxpayer a purpose of which is to terminate such period". **Effective** as if included in the provision of P.L. 101-239 to which it relates.

• 1989, Omnibus Budget Reconciliation Act of 1989 (P.L. 101-239)

P.L. 101-239, §7108(b)(1):

Amended Code Sec. 42(h)(3) by redesignating subparagraphs (D), (E) and (F) as subparagraphs (E), (F), and (G), respectively, and by striking subparagraph (C) and inserting new subparagraphs (C)-(D). **Effective** for calendar years after 1989, but clauses (ii), (iii), and (iv) of section 42(h)(3)(C) of such Code shall be applied without regard to allocations for 1989 or any preceding year. Prior to amendment, Code Sec. 42(h)(3)(C) read as follows:

(C) STATE HOUSING CREDIT CEILING.—The State housing credit ceiling applicable to any State for any calendar year shall be an amount equal to $1.25 multiplied by the State population.

P.L. 101-239, §7108(b)(2)(A):

Amended Code Sec. 42(h)(5)(E) by striking "subparagraph (E)" and inserting "subparagraph (F)". **Effective** for calendar years after 1989, but clauses (ii), (iii), and (iv) of section 42(h)(3)(C) of such Code shall be applied without regard to allocations for 1989 or any preceding year.

P.L. 101-239, §7108(b)(2)(B):

Amended Code Sec. 42(h)(6) by striking subparagraph (B) and by redesignating subparagraphs (C), (D), and (E) as subparagraphs (B), (C), and (D), respectively. **Effective** for calendar years after 1989, but clauses (ii), (iii), and (iv) of section 42(h)(3)(C) of such Code shall be applied without regard to allocations for 1989 or any preceding year. Prior to amendment, Code Sec. 42(h)(6)(B) read as follows:

(B) HOUSING CREDIT DOLLAR AMOUNT MAY NOT BE CARRIED OVER, ETC.—

(i) NO CARRYOVER.—The portion of the aggregate housing credit dollar amount of any housing credit agency which is not allocated for any calendar year may not be carried over to any other calendar year.

(ii) [Repealed.]

P.L. 101-239, §7108(c)(1):

Amended Code Sec. 42(h) by redesignating paragraphs (6) and (7) as paragraphs (7) and (8), respectively, and by inserting after paragraph (5) a new paragraph (6). For the **effective** date, see Act Sec. 7108(r)[s](1)-(2) following Code Sec. 42(b).

P.L. 101-239, §7108(j):

Amended Code Sec. 42(h)(4)(B) by striking "70 percent" each place it appears and inserting "50 percent". For the **effective** date, see Act Sec. 7108(r)[s](1)-(2) following Code Sec. 42(b).

P.L. 101-239, §7108(m)(1):

Amended Code Sec. 42(h)(1) by adding at the end thereof a new subparagraph (F). For the **effective** date, see Act Sec. 7108(r)[s](1)-(2) following Code Sec. 42(b).

P.L. 101-239, §7108(m)(2):

Amended Code Sec. 42(h)(1)(B) by striking "or (E)" and inserting "(E), or (F)". For the **effective** date, see Act Sec. 7108(r)[s](1)-(2) following Code Sec. 42(b).

P.L. 101-239, §7811(a)(2):

Amended Code Sec. 42(h)(5)(D)(ii) by striking "clause (ii)" and inserting "clause (i)". **Effective** as if included in the provision of P.L. 100-647 to which it relates.

• 1988, Technical and Miscellaneous Revenue Act of 1988 (P.L. 100-647)

P.L. 100-647, §1002(l)(14)(A):

Amended Code Sec. 42(h)(1). **Effective** as if included in the provision of P.L. 99-514 to which it relates. Prior to amendment, Code Sec. 42(h)(1) read as follows:

(1) CREDIT MAY NOT EXCEED CREDIT AMOUNT ALLOCATED TO BUILDING.—No credit shall be allowed by reason of this section for any taxable year with respect to any building in excess of the housing credit dollar amount allocated to such building under this subsection. An allocation shall be taken into account under the preceding sentence only if it occurs not later than the earlier of—

(A) the 60th day after the close of the taxable year, or

(B) the close of the calendar year in which such taxable year ends.

P.L. 100-647, §1002(l)(14)(B):

Repealed Code Sec. 42(h)(6)(B)(ii). **Effective** as if included in the provision of P.L. 99-514 to which it relates. Prior to repeal, Code Sec. 42(h)(6)(B)(ii) read as follows:

(ii) ALLOCATION MAY NOT BE EARLIER THAN YEAR IN WHICH BUILDING PLACED IN SERVICE.—A housing credit agency may allocate its housing credit dollar amount for any calendar year only to buildings placed in service before the close of such calendar year.

P.L. 100-647, §1002(l)(15):

Amended Code Sec. 42(h)(4)(A) by striking out "financed" and all that follows and inserting the material following "basis". **Effective** as if included in the provision of P.L. 99-514 to which it relates. Prior to amendment, Code Sec. 42(h)(4)(A) read as follows:

(A) IN GENERAL.—Paragraph (1) shall not apply to the portion of any credit allowable under subsection (a) which is attributable to eligible basis financed by any obligation the interest of which is exempt from tax under section 103 and which is taken into account under section 146.

P.L. 100-647, §1002(l)(16):

Amended Code Sec. 42(h)(5) by redesignating subparagraph (D) as subparagraph (E) and by inserting after subparagraph (C) new subparagraph (D). **Effective** as if included in the provision of P.L. 99-514 to which it relates.

P.L. 100-647, §1002(l)(17):

Amended Code Sec. 42(h)(6)(D). **Effective** as if included in the provision of P.L. 99-514 to which it relates. Prior to amendment, Code Sec. 42(h)(6)(D) read as follows:

(D) CREDIT ALLOWABLE DETERMINED WITHOUT REGARD TO AVERAGING CONVENTION, ETC.—For purposes of this subsection, the credit allowable under subsection (a) with respect to any building shall be determined—

(i) without regard to paragraphs (2)(A) and (3)(B) of subsection (f), and

(ii) by applying subsection (f)(3)(A) without regard to "the percentage equal to 2/3 of".

P.L. 100-647, §1002(l)(18):

Amended Code Sec. 42(h)(6) by adding at the end thereof new subparagraph (E). **Effective** as if included in the provision of P.L. 99-514 to which it relates.

P.L. 100-647, §4003(a):

Amended Code Sec. 42(h)(1) by adding at the end thereof new subparagraph (E). **Effective** for amounts allocated in calendar years after 1987.

P.L. 100-647, §4003(b)(1):

Amended Code Sec. 42(h)(1)(B) (as amended by section 1002 of this Act) by striking out "(C) or (D)" and inserting in lieu thereof "(C), (D), or (E)". **Effective** for amounts allocated in calendar years after 1987.

[Sec. 42(i)]

(i) DEFINITIONS AND SPECIAL RULES.—For purposes of this section—

(1) COMPLIANCE PERIOD.—The term "compliance period" means, with respect to any building, the period of 15 taxable years beginning with the 1st taxable year of the credit period with respect thereto.

(2) DETERMINATION OF WHETHER BUILDING IS FEDERALLY SUBSIDIZED.—

(A) IN GENERAL.—Except as otherwise provided in this paragraph, for purposes of subsection (b)(1), a new building shall be treated as federally subsidized for any taxable year if, at any time during such taxable year or any prior taxable year, there is or was outstanding any obligation the interest on which is exempt from tax under section 103 the proceeds of which are or were used (directly or indirectly) with respect to such building or the operation thereof.

(B) ELECTION TO REDUCE ELIGIBLE BASIS BY PROCEEDS OF OBLIGATIONS.—A tax-exempt obligation shall not be taken into account under subparagraph (A) if the taxpayer elects to exclude from the eligible basis of the building for purposes of subsection (d) the proceeds of such obligation.

(C) SPECIAL RULE FOR SUBSIDIZED CONSTRUCTION FINANCING.—Subparagraph (A) shall not apply to any tax-exempt obligation used to provide construction financing for any building if—

(i) such obligation (when issued) identified the building for which the proceeds of such obligation would be used, and

(ii) such obligation is redeemed before such building is placed in service.

(3) LOW-INCOME UNIT.—

(A) IN GENERAL.—The term "low-income unit" means any unit in a building if—

(i) such unit is rent-restricted (as defined in subsection (g)(2)), and

(ii) the individuals occupying such unit meet the income limitation applicable under subsection (g)(1) to the project of which such building is a part.

(B) EXCEPTIONS.—

(i) IN GENERAL.—A unit shall not be treated as a low-income unit unless the unit is suitable for occupancy and used other than on a transient basis.

(ii) SUITABILITY FOR OCCUPANCY.—For purposes of clause (i), the suitability of a unit for occupancy shall be determined under regulations prescribed by the Secretary taking into account local health, safety, and building codes.

(iii) TRANSITIONAL HOUSING FOR HOMELESS.—For purposes of clause (i), a unit shall be considered to be used other than on a transient basis if the unit contains sleeping accommodations and kitchen and bathroom facilities and is located in a building—

(I) which is used exclusively to facilitate the transition of homeless individuals (within the meaning of section 103 of the Stewart B. McKinney Homeless Assistance Act (42 U.S.C. 11302), as in effect on the date of the enactment of this clause) to independent living within 24 months, and

(II) in which a governmental entity or qualified nonprofit organization (as defined in subsection (h)(5)) provides such individuals with temporary housing and supportive services designed to assist such individuals in locating and retaining permanent housing.

(iv) SINGLE-ROOM OCCUPANCY UNITS.—For purposes of clause (i), a single-room occupancy unit shall not be treated as used on a transient basis merely because it is rented on a month-by-month basis.

(C) SPECIAL RULE FOR BUILDINGS HAVING 4 OR FEWER UNITS.—In the case of any building which has 4 or fewer residential rental units, no unit in such building shall be treated as a low-income unit if the units in such building are owned by—

(i) any individual who occupies a residential unit in such building, or

(ii) any person who is related (as defined in subsection (d)(2)(D)(iii)) to such individual.

(D) CERTAIN STUDENTS NOT TO DISQUALIFY UNIT.—A unit shall not fail to be treated as a low-income unit merely because it is occupied—

(i) by an individual who is—

(I) a student and receiving assistance under title IV of the Social Security Act,

(II) a student who was previously under the care and placement responsibility of the State agency responsible for administering a plan under part B or part E of title IV of the Social Security Act, or

(III) enrolled in a job training program receiving assistance under the Job Training Partnership Act or under other similar Federal, State, or local laws, or

(ii) entirely by full-time students if such students are—

(I) single parents and their children and such parents are not dependents (as defined in section 152, determined without regard to subsections (b)(1), (b)(2), and (d)(1)(B) thereof) of another individual and such children are not dependents (as so defined) of another individual other than a parent of such children, or. [sic]

(II) married and file a joint return.

(E) OWNER-OCCUPIED BUILDINGS HAVING 4 OR FEWER UNITS ELIGIBLE FOR CREDIT WHERE DEVELOPMENT PLAN.—

(i) IN GENERAL.—Subparagraph (C) shall not apply to the acquisition or rehabilitation of a building pursuant to a development plan of action sponsored by a State or local government or a qualified nonprofit organization (as defined in subsection (h)(5)(C)).

(ii) LIMITATION ON CREDIT.—In the case of a building to which clause (i) applies, the applicable fraction shall not exceed 80 percent of the unit fraction.

(iii) CERTAIN UNRENTED UNITS TREATED AS OWNER-OCCUPIED.—In the case of a building to which clause (i) applies, any unit which is not rented for 90 days or more shall be treated as occupied by the owner of the building as of the 1st day it is not rented.

(4) NEW BUILDING.—The term "new building" means a building the original use of which begins with the taxpayer.

(5) EXISTING BUILDING.—The term "existing building" means any building which is not a new building.

(6) APPLICATION TO ESTATES AND TRUSTS.—In the case of an estate or trust, the amount of the credit determined under subsection (a) and any increase in tax under subsection (j) shall be apportioned between the estate or trust and the beneficiaries on the basis of the income of the estate or trust allocable to each.

(7) IMPACT OF TENANT'S RIGHT OF 1ST REFUSAL TO ACQUIRE PROPERTY.—

(A) IN GENERAL.—No Federal income tax benefit shall fail to be allowable to the taxpayer with respect to any qualified low-income building merely by reason of a right of 1st refusal held by the tenants (in cooperative form or otherwise) or resident management corporation of such building or by a qualified nonprofit organization (as defined in subsection (h)(5)(C)) or government agency to purchase the property after the close of the compliance period for a price which is not less than the minimum purchase price determined under subparagraph (B).

(B) MINIMUM PURCHASE PRICE.—For purposes of subparagraph (A), the minimum purchase price under this subparagraph is an amount equal to the sum of—

(i) the principal amount of outstanding indebtedness secured by the building (other than indebtedness incurred within the 5-year period ending on the date of the sale to the tenants), and

(ii) all Federal, State, and local taxes attributable to such sale.

Except in the case of Federal income taxes, there shall not be taken into account under clause (ii) any additional tax attributable to the application of clause (ii).

(8) TREATMENT OF RURAL PROJECTS.—For purposes of this section, in the case of any project for residential rental property located in a rural area (as defined in section 520 of the Housing Act of 1949), any income limitation measured by reference to area median gross income shall be measured by reference to the greater of area median gross income or national non-metropolitan median income. The preceding sentence shall not apply with respect to any building if paragraph (1) of section 42(h) does not apply by reason of paragraph (4) thereof to any portion of the credit determined under this section with respect to such building.

(9) COORDINATION WITH LOW-INCOME HOUSING GRANTS.—

(A) REDUCTION IN STATE HOUSING CREDIT CEILING FOR LOW-INCOME HOUSING GRANTS RECEIVED IN 2009.—For purposes of this section, the amounts described in clauses (i) through (iv) of subsection (h)(3)(C) with respect to any State for 2009 shall each be reduced by so much of such amount as is taken into account in determining the amount of any grant to such State under section 1602 of the American Recovery and Reinvestment Tax Act of 2009.

(B) SPECIAL RULE FOR BASIS.—Basis of a qualified low-income building shall not be reduced by the amount of any grant described in subparagraph (A).

Amendments

• 2009, American Recovery and Reinvestment Tax Act of 2009 (P.L. 111-5)

P.L. 111-5, §1404:

Amended Code Sec. 42(i) by adding at the end a new paragraph (9). **Effective** 2-17-2009.

P.L. 111-5, §1602, provides:

SEC. 1602. GRANTS TO STATES FOR LOW-INCOME HOUSING PROJECTS IN LIEU OF LOW-INCOME HOUSING CREDIT ALLOCATIONS FOR 2009.

(a) IN GENERAL.—The Secretary of the Treasury shall make a grant to the housing credit agency of each State in an amount equal to such State's low-income housing grant election amount.

(b) LOW-INCOME HOUSING GRANT ELECTION AMOUNT.—For purposes of this section, the term "lowincome housing grant election amount" means, with respect to any State, such amount as the State may elect which does not exceed 85 percent of the product of—

(1) the sum of—

(A) 100 percent of the State housing credit ceiling for 2009 which is attributable to amounts described in clauses (i) and (iii) of section 42(h)(3)(C) of the Internal Revenue Code of 1986, and

(B) 40 percent of the State housing credit ceiling for 2009 which is attributable to amounts described in clauses (ii) and (iv) of such section, multiplied by

(2) 10.

(c) SUBAWARDS FOR LOW-INCOME BUILDINGS.—

(1) IN GENERAL.—A State housing credit agency receiving a grant under this section shall use such grant to make subawards to finance the construction or acquisition and rehabilitation of qualified low-income buildings. A subaward under this section may be made to finance a qualified low-income building with or without an allocation under section 42 of the Internal Revenue Code of 1986, except that a State housing credit agency may make subawards to finance qualified low-income buildings without an allocation only if it makes a determination that such use will increase the total funds available to the State to build and rehabilitate affordable housing. In complying with such determination requirement, a State housing credit agency shall establish a process in which applicants that are allocated credits are required to demonstrate good faith efforts to obtain investment commitments for such credits before the agency makes such subawards.

(2) SUBAWARDS SUBJECT TO SAME REQUIREMENTS AS LOW-INCOME HOUSING CREDIT ALLOCATIONS.—Any such subaward with respect to any qualified low-income building shall be made in the same manner and shall be subject to the same limitations (including rent, income, and use restrictions on such building) as an allocation of housing credit dollar amount allocated by such State housing credit agency under section 42 of the Internal Revenue Code of 1986, except that such subawards shall not be limited by, or otherwise affect (except as provided in subsection (h)(3)(J) of such section), the State housing credit ceiling applicable to such agency.

(3) COMPLIANCE AND ASSET MANAGEMENT.— The State housing credit agency shall perform asset management functions to ensure compliance with section 42 of the Internal Revenue Code of 1986 and the long-term viability of buildings funded by any subaward under this section. The State housing credit agency may collect reasonable fees from a subaward recipient to cover expenses associated with the performance of its duties under this paragraph. The State housing credit agency may retain an agent or other private contractor to satisfy the requirements of this paragraph.

(4) RECAPTURE.—The State housing credit agency shall impose conditions or restrictions, including a requirement providing for recapture, on any subaward under this section so as to assure that the building with respect to which such subaward is made remains a qualified low-income building during the compliance period. Any such recapture shall be payable to the Secretary of the Treasury for deposit in the general fund of the Treasury and may be enforced by means of liens or such other methods as the Secretary of the Treasury determines appropriate.

(d) RETURN OF UNUSED GRANT FUNDS.—Any grant funds not used to make subawards under this section before January 1, 2011, shall be returned to the Secretary of the Treasury on such date. Any subawards returned to the State housing credit agency on or after such date shall be promptly returned to the Secretary of the Treasury. Any amounts returned to the Secretary of the Treasury under this subsection shall be deposited in the general fund of the Treasury.

(e) DEFINITIONS.—Any term used in this section which is also used in section 42 of the Internal Revenue Code of 1986 shall have the same meaning for purposes of this section as when used in such section 42. Any reference in this section to the Secretary of the Treasury shall be treated as including the Secretary's delegate.

(f) APPROPRIATIONS.—There is hereby appropriated to the Secretary of the Treasury such sums as may be necessary to carry out this section.

• 2008, Housing Assistance Tax Act of 2008 (P.L. 110-289)

P.L. 110-289, §3002(b)(1):

Amended Code Sec. 42(i)(2)(A) by striking ", or any below market Federal loan," following "under section 103". **Effective** for buildings placed in service after 7-30-2008.

P.L. 110-289, §3002(b)(2)(A)(i)-(iii):

Amended Code Sec. 42(i)(2)(B) by striking "BALANCE OF LOAN OR" in the heading, by striking "loan or" in the matter preceding clause (i), and by striking "subsection (d)—" and all that follows and inserting "subsection (d) the proceeds of such obligation.". **Effective** for buildings placed in service after 7-30-2008. Prior to amendment, Code Sec. 42(i)(2)(B) read as follows:

(B) ELECTION TO REDUCE ELIGIBLE BASIS BY BALANCE OF LOAN OR PROCEEDS OF OBLIGATIONS.—A loan or tax-exempt obligation shall not be taken into account under subparagraph (A) if the taxpayer elects to exclude from the eligible basis of the building for purposes of subsection (d)—

(i) in the case of a loan, the principal amount of such loan, and

(ii) in the case of a tax-exempt obligation, the proceeds of such obligation.

P.L. 110-289, §3002(b)(2)(B)(i)-(iii):

Amended Code Sec. 42(i)(2)(C) by striking "or below market Federal loan" following "any tax-exempt obligation" in the matter preceding clause (i), by striking "or loan (when issued or made)" in clause (i) and inserting "(when issued)", by striking "the proceeds of such obligation or loan" in clause (i) and inserting "the proceeds of such obligation", and by striking ", and such loan is repaid," following "such obligation is redeemed" in clause (ii). **Effective** for buildings placed in service after 7-30-2008.

P.L. 110-289, §3002(b)(2)(C):

Amended Code Sec. 42(i)(2) by striking subparagraphs (D) and (E). **Effective** for buildings placed in service after 7-30-2008. Prior to being stricken, Code Sec. 42(i)(2)(D) and (E) read as follows:

(D) BELOW MARKET FEDERAL LOAN.—For purposes of this paragraph, the term "below market Federal loan" means any loan funded in whole or in part with Federal funds if the interest rate payable on such loan is less than the applicable Federal rate in effect under section 1274(d)(1) (as of the date on which the loan was made). Such term shall not include any loan which would be a below market Federal loan solely by reason of assistance provided under section 106, 107, or 108 of the Housing and Community Development Act of 1974 (as in effect on the date of the enactment of this sentence).

(E) BUILDINGS RECEIVING HOME ASSISTANCE OR NATIVE AMERICAN HOUSING ASSISTANCE.—

(i) IN GENERAL.—Assistance provided under the HOME Investment Partnerships Act (as in effect on the date of the enactment of this subparagraph) or the Native American Housing Assistance and Self-Determination Act of 1996 (25 U.S.C. 4101 et seq.) (as in effect on October 1, 1997) with respect to any building shall not be taken into account under subparagraph (D) if 40 percent or more of the residential units in the building are occupied by individuals whose income is 50 percent or less of area median gross income. Subsection (d)(5)(C) shall not apply to any building to which the preceding sentence applies.

(ii) SPECIAL RULE FOR CERTAIN HIGH-COST HOUSING AREAS.—In the case of a building located in a city described in section 142(d)(6), clause (i) shall be applied by substituting "25 percent" for "40 percent."

P.L. 110-289, §3004(e):

Amended Code Sec. 42(i)(3)(D)(i) by striking "or" at the end of subclause (I), by redesignating subclause (II) as subclause (III), and by inserting after subclause (I) a new subclause (II). **Effective** for determinations made after 7-30-2008.

P.L. 110-289, §3004(f):

Amended Code Sec. 42(i) by adding at the end a new paragraph (8). **Effective** for determinations made after 7-30-2008.

• 2007, Mortgage Forgiveness Debt Relief Act of 2007 (P.L. 110-142)

P.L. 110-142, §6(a):

Amended Code Sec. 42(i)(3)(D)(ii)(I). **Effective** for housing credit amounts allocated before, on, or after 12-20-2007, and buildings placed in service before, on, or after 12-20-2007, to the extent Code Sec. 42(h)(1) does not apply to any building by reason of paragraph (4) thereof. Prior to amendment, Code Sec. 42(i)(3)(D)(ii)(I) read as follows:

(I) single parents and their children and such parents and children are not dependents (as defined in section 152, determined without regard to subsections (b)(1), (b)(2), and (d)(1)(B) thereof) of another individual, or

• 2004, Working Families Tax Relief Act of 2004 (P.L. 108-311)

P.L. 108-311, §207(8):

Amended Code Sec. 42(i)(3)(D)(ii)(I) by inserting ", determined without regard to subsections (b)(1), (b)(2), and (d)(1)(B) thereof" after "section 152". **Effective** for tax years beginning after 12-31-2004.

• 2000, Community Renewal Tax Relief Act of 2000 (P.L. 106-554)

P.L. 106-554, §134(b)(1):

Amended Code Sec. 42(i)(2)(E)(i) by inserting "or the Native American Housing Assistance and Self-Determination Act of 1996) (25 U.S.C. 4101 et seq.) (as in effect on October 1, 1997)" after "this subparagraph)". **Effective** as noted in Act Sec. 137, below.

P.L. 106-554, §134(b)(2):

Amended Code Sec. 42(i)(2)(E) by inserting "OR NATIVE AMERICAN HOUSING ASSISTANCE" after "HOME ASSISTANCE" in the subparagraph heading. **Effective** as noted in Act Sec. 137, below.

P.L. 106-554, §137, provides:

Except as otherwise provided in this subtitle, the amendments made by this subtitle shall apply to—

(1) housing credit dollar amounts allocated after December 31, 2000; and

(2) buildings placed in service after such date to the extent paragraph (1) of section 42(h) of the Internal Revenue Code of 1986 does not apply to any building by reason of paragraph (4) thereof, but only with respect to bonds issued after such date.

• 1993, Omnibus Budget Reconciliation Act of 1993 (P.L. 103-66)

P.L. 103-66, §13142(b)(2):

Amended Code Sec. 42(i)(3)(D). For the **effective** date, see Act Sec. 13142(b)(6), below. Prior to amendment, Code Sec. 42(i)(3)(D) read as follows:

(D) CERTAIN STUDENTS NOT TO DISQUALIFY UNIT.—A unit shall not fail to be treated as a low-income unit merely because it is occupied by an individual who is—

(i) a student and receiving assistance under title IV of the Social Security Act, or

(ii) enrolled in a job training program receiving assistance under the Job Training Partnership Act or under other similar Federal, State, or local laws.

P.L. 103-66, §13142(b)(5):

Amended Code Sec. 42(i)(2) by adding at the end thereof new subparagraph (E). For the **effective** date, see Act Sec. 13142(b)(6), below.

P.L. 103-66, §13142(b)(6) (as amended by P.L. 104-188, §1703(b)(1)), provides:

(6) EFFECTIVE DATES.—

(A) IN GENERAL.—Except as provided in subparagraphs (B) and (C), the amendments made by this subsection shall apply to—

(i) determinations under section 42 of the Internal Revenue Code of 1986 with respect to housing credit dollar amounts allocated from State housing credit ceilings after June 30, 1992, or

(ii) buildings placed in service after June 30, 1992, to the extent paragraph (1) of section 42(h) of such Code does not apply to any building by reason of paragraph (4) thereof, but only with respect to bonds issued after such date.

(B) FULL-TIME STUDENTS, WAIVER AUTHORITY, AND PROHIBITED DISCRIMINATION.—The amendments made by paragraphs (2), (3), and (4) shall take effect on the date of the enactment of this Act.

(C) HOME ASSISTANCE.—The amendment made by paragraph (2) shall apply to periods after the date of the enactment of this Act.

• 1990, Omnibus Budget Reconciliation Act of 1990 (P.L. 101-508)

P.L. 101-508, §11407(b)(1):

Amended Code Sec. 42(i)(7), as redesignated by Act. Sec. 11701(a)(10)), by striking "the tenants of such building" and inserting "the tenants (in cooperative form or otherwise) or resident management corporation of such building or by a qualified nonprofit organization (as defined in subsection (h)(5)(C)) or government agency". **Effective** 11-5-90.

P.L. 101-508, §11407(b)(6):

Amended Code Sec. 42(i)(3)(D). **Effective** 11-5-90. Prior to amendment, Code Sec. 42(i)(3)(D) read as follows:

(D) STUDENTS IN GOVERNMENT-SUPPORTED JOB TRAINING PROGRAMS NOT TO DISQUALIFY UNIT.—A unit shall not fail to be treated as a low-income unit merely because it is occupied by an individual who is enrolled in a job training program receiving assistance under the Job Training Partnership Act or under other similar Federal, State or local laws.

P.L. 101-508, §11701(a)(10):

Amended Code Sec. 42(i) by redesignating paragraph (8) as paragraph (7). **Effective** as if included in the provision of P.L. 101-239 to which it relates.

• 1989, Omnibus Budget Reconciliation Act of 1989 (P.L. 101-239)

P.L. 101-239, §7108(h)(1):

Amended Code Sec. 42(i)(3)(B), before amendment by Act Sec. 7108(i)(1), by adding at the end thereof a new sentence. See Act Sec. 7108(i)(1), below. **Effective** as if included in the amendments made by section 252 of P.L. 99-514.

P.L. 101-239, §7108(h)(4):

Amended Code Sec. 42(i)(3), as amended by subtitle H, by adding at the end thereof a new subparagraph (E). For the **effective** date, see Act Sec. 7801(r)[s](1)-(2) following Code Sec. 42(b).

P.L. 101-239, §7108(i)(1):

Amended Code Sec. 42(i)(3)(B). For the **effective** date, see Act Sec. 7801(r)[s](1)-(2) following Code Sec. 42(b). Prior to amendment, Code Sec. 42(i)(3)(B) read as follows:

(B) EXCEPTIONS.—A unit shall not be treated as a low-income unit unless the unit is suitable for occupancy (as determined under regulations prescribed by the Secretary taking into account local health, safety, and building codes) and used other than on a transient basis. For purposes of the preceding sentence, a single-room occupancy unit shall not be treated as used on a transient basis merely because it is rented on a month-by-month basis.

P.L. 101-239, §7108(k):

Amended Code Sec. 42(i)(2)(D) by adding at the end thereof a new sentence. For the **effective** date, see Act Sec. 7801(r)[s](1)-(2) following Code Sec. 42(b).

P.L. 101-239, §7108(q)[r]:

Amended Code Sec. 42(i) by adding at the end thereof a new paragraph (8)[7]. For the **effective** date, see Act Sec. 7801(r)[s](1)-(2) following Code Sec. 42(b).

P.L. 101-239, §7831(c)(1):

Amended Code Sec. 42(i)(3)(B) by inserting "(as determined under regulations prescribed by the Secretary taking into account local health, safety, and building codes)" after "suitable for occupancy". See the amendment note for Act Sec. 7108(i)(1). **Effective** as if included in the provision of P.L. 99-514 to which it relates.

P.L. 101-239, §7831(c)(2):

Amended Code Sec. 42(i)(3) by adding at the end thereof a new subparagraph (D). **Effective** as if included in the provision of P.L. 99-514 to which it relates.

P.L. 101-239, §7831(c)(3):

Amended Code Sec. 42(i) by adding at the end thereof a new paragraph (6). **Effective** as if included in the provision of P.L. 99-514 to which it relates.

• 1988, Technical and Miscellaneous Revenue Act of 1988 (P.L. 100-647)

P.L. 100-647, §1002(l)(19)(A)(i)-(iii):

Amended Code Sec. 42(i)(2)(A) by inserting "or any prior taxable year" after "such taxable year", by striking out "there is outstanding" and inserting in lieu thereof "there is or was outstanding", and by striking out "are used" and inserting in lieu thereof "are or were used". **Effective** as if included in the provision of P.L. 99-514 to which it relates.

P.L. 100-647, §1002(l)(19)(B):

Amended Code Sec. 42(i)(2)(B). **Effective** as if included in the provision of P.L. 99-514 to which it relates. Prior to amendment, Code Sec. 42(i)(2)(B) read as follows:

(B) ELECTION TO REDUCE ELIGIBLE BASIS BY OUTSTANDING BALANCE OF LOAN.—A loan shall not be taken into account under subparagraph (A) if the taxpayer elects to exclude an amount equal to the outstanding balance of such loan from the eligible basis of the building for purposes of subsection (d).

P.L. 100-647, §1002(l)(19)(C):

Amended Code Sec. 42(i)(2) by redesignating subparagraph (C) as subparagraph (D) and inserting after subparagraph (B) new subparagraph (C). **Effective** as if included in the provision of P.L. 99-514 to which it relates.

P.L. 100-647, §1002(l)(19)(D):

Amended Code Sec. 42(i)(2)(D) by striking out "subparagraph (A)" and inserting in lieu thereof "this paragraph". **Effective** as if included in the provision of P.L. 99-514 to which it relates.

[Sec. 42(j)]

(j) RECAPTURE OF CREDIT.—

(1) IN GENERAL.—If—

(A) as of the close of any taxable year in the compliance period, the amount of the qualified basis of any building with respect to the taxpayer is less than

(B) the amount of such basis as of the close of the preceding taxable year,

then the taxpayer's tax under this chapter for the taxable year shall be increased by the credit recapture amount.

(2) CREDIT RECAPTURE AMOUNT.—For purposes of paragraph (1), the credit recapture amount is an amount equal to the sum of—

(A) the aggregate decrease in the credits allowed to the taxpayer under section 38 for all prior taxable years which would have resulted if the accelerated portion of the credit allowable by reason of this section were not allowed for all prior taxable years with respect to the excess of the amount described in paragraph (1)(B) over the amount described in paragraph (1)(A), plus

(B) interest at the overpayment rate established under section 6621 on the amount determined under subparagraph (A) for each prior taxable year for the period beginning on the due date for filing the return for the prior taxable year involved.

No deduction shall be allowed under this chapter for interest described in subparagraph (B).

(3) ACCELERATED PORTION OF CREDIT.—For purposes of paragraph (2), the accelerated portion of the credit for the prior taxable years with respect to any amount of basis is the excess of—

(A) the aggregate credit allowed by reason of this section (without regard to this subsection) for such years with respect to such basis, over

(B) the aggregate credit which would be allowable by reason of this section for such years with respect to such basis if the aggregate credit which would (but for this subsection) have been allowable for the entire compliance period were allowable ratably over 15 years.

(4) SPECIAL RULES.—

(A) TAX BENEFIT RULE.—The tax for the taxable year shall be increased under paragraph (1) only with respect to credits allowed by reason of this section which were used to reduce tax liability. In the case of credits not so used to reduce tax liability, the carryforwards and carrybacks under section 39 shall be appropriately adjusted.

(B) ONLY BASIS FOR WHICH CREDIT ALLOWED TAKEN INTO ACCOUNT.—Qualified basis shall be taken into account under paragraph (1)(B) only to the extent such basis was taken into account in determining the credit under subsection (a) for the preceding taxable year referred to in such paragraph.

(C) NO RECAPTURE OF ADDITIONAL CREDIT ALLOWABLE BY REASON OF SUBSECTION (f)(3).—Paragraph (1) shall apply to a decrease in qualified basis only to the extent such decrease exceeds the amount of qualified basis with respect to which a credit was allowable for the taxable year referred to in paragraph (1)(B) by reason of subsection (f)(3).

(D) NO CREDITS AGAINST TAX.—Any increase in tax under this subsection shall not be treated as a tax imposed by this chapter for purposes of determining the amount of any credit under this chapter.

(E) NO RECAPTURE BY REASON OF CASUALTY LOSS.—The increase in tax under this subsection shall not apply to a reduction in qualified basis by reason of a casualty loss to the extent such loss is restored by reconstruction or replacement within a reasonable period established by the Secretary.

(F) NO RECAPTURE WHERE DE MINIMIS CHANGES IN FLOOR SPACE.—The Secretary may provide that the increase in tax under this subsection shall not apply with respect to any building if—

(i) such increase results from a de minimis change in the floor space fraction under subsection (c)(1), and

(ii) the building is a qualified low-income building after such change.

(5) CERTAIN PARTNERSHIPS TREATED AS THE TAXPAYER.—

(A) IN GENERAL.—For purposes of applying this subsection to a partnership to which this paragraph applies—

(i) such partnership shall be treated as the taxpayer to which the credit allowable under subsection (a) was allowed,

(ii) the amount of such credit allowed shall be treated as the amount which would have been allowed to the partnership were such credit allowable to such partnership,

(iii) paragraph (4)(A) shall not apply, and

(iv) the amount of the increase in tax under this subsection for any taxable year shall be allocated among the partners of such partnership in the same manner as such partnership's taxable income for such year is allocated among such partners.

(B) PARTNERSHIPS TO WHICH PARAGRAPH APPLIES.—This paragraph shall apply to any partnership which has 35 or more partners unless the partnership elects not to have this paragraph apply.

(C) SPECIAL RULES.—

(i) HUSBAND AND WIFE TREATED AS 1 PARTNER.—For purposes of subparagraph (B)(i), a husband and wife (and their estates) shall be treated as 1 partner.

(ii) ELECTION IRREVOCABLE.—Any election under subparagraph (B), once made, shall be irrevocable.

(6) NO RECAPTURE ON DISPOSITION OF BUILDING WHICH CONTINUES IN QUALIFIED USE.—

(A) IN GENERAL.—The increase in tax under this subsection shall not apply solely by reason of the disposition of a building (or an interest therein) if it is reasonably expected that such building will continue to be operated as a qualified low-income building for the remaining compliance period with respect to such building.

(B) STATUTE OF LIMITATIONS.—If a building (or an interest therein) is disposed of during any taxable year and there is any reduction in the qualified basis of such building which results in an increase in tax under this subsection for such taxable or any subsequent taxable year, then—

(i) the statutory period for the assessment of any deficiency with respect to such increase in tax shall not expire before the expiration of 3 years from the date the Secretary is notified by the taxpayer (in such manner as the Secretary may prescribe) of such reduction in qualified basis, and

(ii) such deficiency may be assessed before the expiration of such 3-year period notwithstanding the provisions of any other law or rule of law which would otherwise prevent such assessment.

Amendments

• 2008, Housing Assistance Tax Act of 2008 (P.L. 110-289)

P.L. 110-289, §3004(c):

Amended Code Sec. 42(j)(6). For the **effective** date, see Act Sec. 3004(i)(2), below. Prior to amendment, Code Sec. 42(j)(6) read as follows:

(6) NO RECAPTURE ON DISPOSITION OF BUILDING (OR INTEREST THEREIN) WHERE BOND POSTED.—In the case of a disposition of a building or an interest therein the taxpayer shall be discharged from liability for any additional tax under this subsection by reason of such disposition if—

(A) the taxpayer furnishes to the Secretary a bond in an amount satisfactory to the Secretary and for the period required by the Secretary, and

(B) it is reasonably expected that such building will continue to be operated as a qualified low-income building for the remaining compliance period with respect to such building.

P.L. 110-289, §3004(i)(2), provides:

(2) REPEAL OF BONDING REQUIREMENT ON DISPOSITION OF BUILDING.—The amendment made by subsection (c) shall apply to—

(A) interests in buildings disposed [of] after the date of the enactment of this Act [7-30-2008.—CCH], and

(B) interests in buildings disposed of on or before such date if—

(i) it is reasonably expected that such building will continue to be operated as a qualified low-income building (within the meaning of section 42 of the Internal Revenue Code of 1986) for the remaining compliance period (within the meaning of such section) with respect to such building, and

(ii) the taxpayer elects the application of this subparagraph with respect to such disposition.

• 1998, IRS Restructuring and Reform Act of 1998 (P.L. 105-206)

P.L. 105-206, §6004(g)(5):

Amended Code Sec. 42(j)(4)(D) by striking "subpart A, B, D, or G of this part" and inserting "this chapter". **Effective** as if included in the provision of P.L. 105-34 to which it relates [**effective** for obligations issued after 12-31-97.—CCH].

• 1988, Technical and Miscellaneous Revenue Act of 1988 (P.L. 100-647)

P.L. 100-647, §1002(l)(20):

Amended Code Sec. 42(j)(4) by adding at the end thereof new subparagraph (F). **Effective** as if included in the provision of P.L. 99-514 to which it relates.

P.L. 100-647, §1002(l)(21):

Amended Code Sec. 42(j)(5)(B)(i). **Effective** as if included in the provision of P.L. 99-514 to which it relates. Prior to amendment, Code Sec. 42(j)(5)(B)(i) read as follows:

(i) which has 35 or more partners each of whom is a natural person or an estate, and

P.L. 100-647, §1002(l)(22)(A)-(B):

Amended Code Sec. 42(j)(6) by inserting "(OR INTEREST THEREIN)" after "BUILDING" in the heading, and by inserting "or an interest therein" after "disposition of a building" in the text. **Effective** as if included in the provision of P.L. 99-514 to which it relates.

P.L. 100-647, §1007(g)(3)(B):

Amended Code Sec. 42(j)(4)(D) by striking out "or D" and inserting in lieu thereof "D, or G". **Effective** as if included in the provision of P.L. 99-514 to which it relates.

P.L. 100-647, §4004(a):

Amended Code Sec. 42(j)(5)(B) (as amended by title I of this Act). **Effective** as if included in the amendments made by section 252 of P.L. 99-514. See, also, Act Sec. 4004(b)(2), below. Prior to amendment (but after amendment by Act Sec. 1002(l)(21)), Code Sec. 42(j)(5)(B) read as follows:

(B) PARTNERSHIPS TO WHICH PARAGRAPH APPLIES.—This paragraph shall apply to any partnership—

(i) more than 1/2 the capital interests, and more than 1/2 the profit interests, in which are owned by a group of 35 or more partners each of whom is a natural person or an estate, and

(ii) which elects the application of this paragraph.

P.L. 100-647, §4004(b)(2), provides:

(2) PERIOD FOR ELECTION.—The period for electing not to have section 42(j)(5) of the 1986 Code apply to any partnership shall not expire before the date which is 6 months after the date of the enactment of this Act.

[Sec. 42(k)]

(k) APPLICATION OF AT-RISK RULES.—For purposes of this section—

(1) IN GENERAL.—Except as otherwise provided in this subsection, rules similar to the rules of section 49(a)(1) (other than subparagraphs (D)(ii)(II) and (D)(iv)(I) thereof), section 49(a)(2), and section 49(b)(1) shall apply in determining the qualified basis of any building in the same manner as such sections apply in determining the credit base of property.

(2) SPECIAL RULES FOR DETERMINING QUALIFIED PERSON.—For purposes of paragraph (1)—

(A) IN GENERAL.—If the requirements of subparagraphs (B), (C), and (D) are met with respect to any financing borrowed from a qualified nonprofit organization (as defined in subsection (h)(5)), the determination of whether such financing is qualified commercial financing with respect to any qualified low-income building shall be made without regard to whether such organization—

(i) is actively and regularly engaged in the business of lending money, or

(ii) is a person described in section 49(a)(1)(D)(iv)(II).

(B) FINANCING SECURED BY PROPERTY.—The requirements of this subparagraph are met with respect to any financing if such financing is secured by the qualified low-income building, except that this subparagraph shall not apply in the case of a federally assisted building described in subsection (d)(6)(B) if—

(i) a security interest in such building is not permitted by a Federal agency holding or insuring the mortgage secured by such building, and

(ii) the proceeds from the financing (if any) are applied to acquire or improve such building.

(C) PORTION OF BUILDING ATTRIBUTABLE TO FINANCING.—The requirements of this subparagraph are met with respect to any financing for any taxable year in the compliance period if, as of the close of such taxable year, not more than 60 percent of the eligible basis of the qualified low-income building is attributable to such financing (reduced by the principal and interest of any governmental financing which is part of a wrap-around mortgage involving such financing).

(D) REPAYMENT OF PRINCIPAL AND INTEREST.—The requirements of this subparagraph are met with respect to any financing if such financing is fully repaid on or before the earliest of—

(i) the date on which such financing matures,

(ii) the 90th day after the close of the compliance period with respect to the qualified low-income building, or

(iii) the date of its refinancing or the sale of the building to which such financing relates.

In the case of a qualified nonprofit organization which is not described in section 49(a)(1)(D)(iv)(II) with respect to a building, clause (ii) of this subparagraph shall be applied as if the date described therein were the 90th day after the earlier of the date the building ceases to be a qualified low-income building or the date which is 15 years after the close of a compliance period with respect thereto.

(3) PRESENT VALUE OF FINANCING.—If the rate of interest on any financing described in paragraph (2)(A) is less than the rate which is 1 percentage point below the applicable Federal rate as of the time such financing is incurred, then the qualified basis (to which such financing relates) of the qualified low-income building shall be the present value of the amount of such financing, using as the discount rate such applicable Federal rate. For purposes of the preceding sentence, the rate of interest on any financing shall be determined by treating interest to the extent of governmental subsidies as not payable.

(4) FAILURE TO FULLY REPAY.—

(A) IN GENERAL.—To the extent that the requirements of paragraph (2)(D) are not met, then the taxpayer's tax under this chapter for the taxable year in which such failure occurs shall be increased by an amount equal to the applicable portion of the credit under this section with respect to such building, increased by an amount of interest for the period—

(i) beginning with the due date for the filing of the return of tax imposed by chapter 1 for the 1st taxable year for which such credit was allowable, and

(ii) ending with the due date for the taxable year in which such failure occurs,

determined by using the underpayment rate and method under section 6621.

(B) APPLICABLE PORTION.—For purposes of subparagraph (A), the term "applicable portion" means the aggregate decrease in the credits allowed to a taxpayer under section 38 for all prior taxable years which would have resulted if the eligible basis of the building were reduced by the amount of financing which does not meet requirements of paragraph (2)(D).

(C) CERTAIN RULES TO APPLY.—Rules similar to the rules of subparagraphs (A) and (D) of subsection (j)(4) shall apply for purposes of this subsection.

Amendments

• 1990, Omnibus Budget Reconciliation Act of 1990 (P.L. 101-508)

P.L. 101-508, §11813(b)(3)(A)(i)-(iii):

Amended Code Sec. 42(k)(1) by striking "46(c)(8)" and inserting "49(a)(1)", by striking "46(c)(9)" and inserting "49(a)(2)", and by striking "47(d)(1)" and inserting "49(b)(1)". **Effective** for property placed in service after 12-31-90. For exceptions, see Act Sec. 11813(c)(2), below.

P.L. 101-508, §11813(b)(3)(B):

Amended Code Sec. 42(k) by striking "46(c)(8)(D)(iv)(II)" in paragraphs (2)(A)(ii) and (2)(D) and inserting "49(a)(1)(D)(iv)(II)". **Effective** for property placed in service after 12-31-90. For exceptions, see Act Sec. 11813(c)(2), below.

P.L. 101-508, §11813(c)(2), provides:

(2) EXCEPTIONS.—The amendments made by this section shall not apply to—

(A) any transition property (as defined in section 49(e) of the Internal Revenue Code of 1986 (as in effect on the day before the date of the enactment of this Act),

(B) any property with respect to which qualified progress expenditures were previously taken into account under section 46(d) of such Code (as so in effect), and

(C) any property described in section 46(b)(2)(C) of such Code (as so in effect).

• 1989, Omnibus Budget Reconciliation Act of 1989 (P.L. 101-239)

P.L. 101-239, §7108(o)[p]:

Amended Code Sec. 42(k)(2)(D) by adding at the end thereof a new sentence. For the **effective** date, see Act Sec. 7801(r)[s](1)-(2) following Code Sec. 42(b).

• 1988, Technical and Miscellaneous Revenue Act of 1988 (P.L. 100-647)

P.L. 100-647, §1002(l)(23):

Amended the last sentence in Code Sec. 42(k)(2)(B) by inserting new text after "building,". The above amendment is **effective** as if included in the provision of P.L. 99-514 to which it relates. Prior to amendment, the last sentence of Code Sec. 42(k)(2)(B) read as follows:

(B) FINANCING SECURED BY PROPERTY.—The requirements of this subparagraph are met with respect to any financing if such financing is secured by the qualified low-income building.

[Sec. 42(l)]

(l) CERTIFICATIONS AND OTHER REPORTS TO SECRETARY.—

(1) CERTIFICATION WITH RESPECT TO 1ST YEAR OF CREDIT PERIOD.—Following the close of the 1st taxable year in the credit period with respect to any qualified low-income building, the taxpayer

shall certify to the Secretary (at such time and in such form and in such manner as the Secretary prescribes)—

(A) the taxable year, and calendar year, in which such building was placed in service,

(B) the adjusted basis and eligible basis of such building as of the close of the 1st year of the credit period,

(C) the maximum applicable percentage and qualified basis permitted to be taken into account by the appropriate housing credit agency under subsection (h),

(D) the election made under subsection (g) with respect to the qualified low-income housing project of which such building is a part, and

(E) such other information as the Secretary may require.

In the case of a failure to make the certification required by the preceding sentence on the date prescribed therefor, unless it is shown that such failure is due to reasonable cause and not to willful neglect, no credit shall be allowable by reason of subsection (a) with respect to such building for any taxable year ending before such certification is made.

(2) ANNUAL REPORTS TO THE SECRETARY.—The Secretary may require taxpayers to submit an information return (at such time and in such form and manner as the Secretary prescribes) for each taxable year setting forth—

(A) the qualified basis for the taxable year of each qualified low-income building of the taxpayer,

(B) the information described in paragraph (1)(C) for the taxable year, and

(C) such other information as the Secretary may require.

The penalty under section 6652(j) shall apply to any failure to submit the return required by the Secretary under the preceding sentence on the date prescribed therefor.

(3) ANNUAL REPORTS FROM HOUSING CREDIT AGENCIES.—Each agency which allocates any housing credit amount to any building for any calendar year shall submit to the Secretary (at such time and in such manner as the Secretary shall prescribe) an annual report specifying—

(A) the amount of housing credit amount allocated to each building for such year, and

(B) sufficient information to identify each such building and the taxpayer with respect thereto, and

(C) such other information as the Secretary may require.

The penalty under section 6652(j) shall apply to any failure to submit the report required by the preceding sentence on the date prescribed therefor.

Amendments

• 1989, Omnibus Budget Reconciliation Act of 1989 (P.L. 101-239)

P.L. 101-239, §7108(p)[q](1)(2):

Amended Code Sec. 42(l)(1) by striking "Not later than the 90th day following" and inserting "Following", and by inserting "at such time and" before "in such form". **Effective** for tax years ending on or after 12-31-89.

• 1988, Technical and Miscellaneous Revenue Act of 1988 (P.L. 100-647)

P.L. 100-647, §1002(l)(24)(A):

Amended Code Sec. 42(l) by redesignating paragraph (2) as paragraph (3) and by inserting after paragraph (1) new paragraph (2). **Effective** as if included in the provision of P.L. 99-514 to which it relates.

P.L. 100-647, §1002(l)(24)(B):

Amended the subsection heading for Code Sec. 42(l). **Effective** as if included in the provision of P.L. 99-514 to which it relates. Prior to amendment, the subsection heading for Code Sec. 42(l) read as follows:

(l) CERTIFICATIONS TO SECRETARY.—

[Sec. 42(m)]

(m) RESPONSIBILITIES OF HOUSING CREDIT AGENCIES.—

(1) PLANS FOR ALLOCATION OF CREDIT AMONG PROJECTS.—

(A) IN GENERAL.—Notwithstanding any other provision of this section, the housing credit dollar amount with respect to any building shall be zero unless—

(i) such amount was allocated pursuant to a qualified allocation plan of the housing credit agency which is approved by the governmental unit (in accordance with rules similar to the rules of section 147(f)(2) (other than subparagraph (B)(ii) thereof)) of which such agency is a part,

(ii) such agency notifies the chief executive officer (or the equivalent) of the local jurisdiction within which the building is located of such project and provides such individual a reasonable opportunity to comment on the project,

(iii) a comprehensive market study of the housing needs of low-income individuals in the area to be served by the project is conducted before the credit allocation is made and at the developer's expense by a disinterested party who is approved by such agency, and

(iv) a written explanation is available to the general public for any allocation of a housing credit dollar amount which is not made in accordance with established priorities and selection criteria of the housing credit agency.

(B) QUALIFIED ALLOCATION PLAN.—For purposes of this paragraph, the term "qualified allocation plan" means any plan—

(i) which sets forth selection criteria to be used to determine housing priorities of the housing credit agency which are appropriate to local conditions,

(ii) which also gives preference in allocating housing credit dollar amounts among selected projects to—

(I) projects serving the lowest income tenants,

(II) projects obligated to serve qualified tenants for the longest periods,

(III) projects which are located in qualified census tracts (as defined in subsection (d)(5)(C)) and the development of which contributes to a concerted community revitalization plan, and

(iii) which provides a procedure that the agency (or an agent or other private contractor of such agency) will follow in monitoring for noncompliance with the provisions of this section and in notifying the Internal Revenue Service of such noncompliance which such agency becomes aware of and in monitoring for noncompliance with habitability standards through regular site visits.

(C) CERTAIN SELECTION CRITERIA MUST BE USED.—The selection criteria set forth in a qualified allocation plan must include—

(i) project location,

(ii) housing needs characteristics,

(iii) project characteristics, including whether the project includes the use of existing housing as part of a community revitalization plan,

(iv) sponsor characteristics,

(v) tenant populations with special housing needs,

(vi) public housing waiting lists,

(vii) tenant populations of individuals with children,

(viii) projects intended for eventual tenant ownership,

(ix) the energy efficiency of the project, and

(x) the historic nature of the project.

(D) APPLICATION TO BOND FINANCED PROJECTS.—Subsection (h)(4) shall not apply to any project unless the project satisfies the requirements for allocation of a housing credit dollar amount under the qualified allocation plan applicable to the area in which the project is located.

(2) CREDIT ALLOCATED TO BUILDING NOT TO EXCEED AMOUNT NECESSARY TO ASSURE PROJECT FEASIBILITY.—

(A) IN GENERAL.—The housing credit dollar amount allocated to a project shall not exceed the amount the housing credit agency determines is necessary for the financial feasibility of the project and its viability as a qualified low-income housing project throughout the credit period.

(B) AGENCY EVALUATION.—In making the determination under subparagraph (A), the housing credit agency shall consider—

(i) the sources and uses of funds and the total financing planned for the project,

(ii) any proceeds or receipts expected to be generated by reason of tax benefits,

(iii) the percentage of the housing credit dollar amount used for project costs other than the cost of intermediaries, and

(iv) the reasonableness of the developmental and operational costs of the project.

Clause (iii) shall not be applied so as to impede the development of projects in hard-to-develop areas. Such a determination shall not be construed to be a representation or warranty as to the feasibility or viability of the project.

(C) DETERMINATION MADE WHEN CREDIT AMOUNT APPLIED FOR AND WHEN BUILDING PLACED IN SERVICE.—

(i) IN GENERAL.—A determination under subparagraph (A) shall be made as of each of the following times:

(I) The application for the housing credit dollar amount.

(II) The allocation of the housing credit dollar amount.

(III) The date the building is placed in service.

(ii) CERTIFICATION AS TO AMOUNT OF OTHER SUBSIDIES.—Prior to each determination under clause (i), the taxpayer shall certify to the housing credit agency the full extent of all Federal, State, and local subsidies which apply (or which the taxpayer expects to apply) with respect to the building.

(D) APPLICATION TO BOND FINANCED PROJECTS.—Subsection (h)(4) shall not apply to any project unless the governmental unit which issued the bonds (or on behalf of which the bonds were issued) makes a determination under rules similar to the rules of subparagraphs (A) and (B).

Amendments

• 2008, Housing Assistance Tax Act of 2008 (P.L. 110-289)

P.L. 110-289, §3004(d):

Amended Code Sec. 42(m)(1)(C) by striking "and" at the end of clause (vii), by striking the period at the end of clause (viii) and inserting a comma, and by adding at the end new clauses (ix) and (x). **Effective** for allocations made after 12-31-2008.

• 2002, Job Creation and Worker Assistance Act of 2002 (P.L. 107-147)

P.L. 107-147, §417(3):

Amended Code Sec. 42(m)(1)(B)(ii) by striking the second [first]"and" at the end of subclause (II) and by inserting "and" at the end of subclause (III). **Effective** 3-9-2002.

• 2000, Community Renewal Tax Relief Act of 2000 (P.L. 106-554)

P.L. 106-554, §132(a)(1)-(2):

Amended Code Sec. 42(m)(1)(C) by inserting ", including whether the project includes the use of existing housing as part of a community revitalization plan" before the comma at the end of clause (iii), and by striking clauses (v), (vi), and (vii) and inserting new clauses (v)-(viii). **Effective** as noted in Act Sec. 137, below. Prior to amendment, Code Sec. 42(m)(1)(C)(v)-(vii) read as follows:

(v) participation of local tax-exempt organizations,

(vi) tenant populations with special housing needs, and

(vii) public housing waiting lists.

P.L. 106-554, §132(b):

Amended Code Sec. 42(m)(1)(B)(ii) by striking "and" at the end of subclause (I), by adding "and" at the end of subclause (II), and by inserting after subclause (II) a new subclause (III). **Effective** as noted in Act Sec. 137, below.

P.L. 106-554, §133(a):

Amended Code Sec. 42(m)(1)(A) by striking "and" at the end of clause (i), by striking the period at the end of clause (ii) and inserting a comma, and by adding at the end new clauses (iii) and (iv). **Effective** as noted in Act Sec. 137, below.

P.L. 106-554, §133(b):

Amended Code Sec. 42(m)(1)(B)(iii) by inserting before the period "and in monitoring for noncompliance with habitability standards through regular site visits". **Effective** as noted in Act Sec. 137, below.

P.L. 106-554, §137, provides:

Except as otherwise provided in this subtitle, the amendments made by this subtitle shall apply to—

(1) housing credit dollar amounts allocated after December 31, 2000; and

(2) buildings placed in service after such date to the extent paragraph (1) of section 42(h) of the Internal Revenue Code of 1986 does not apply to any building by reason of paragraph (4) thereof, but only with respect to bonds issued after such date.

• 1993, Omnibus Budget Reconciliation Act of 1993 (P.L. 103-66)

P.L. 103-66, §13142(b)(1)(A)-(C):

Amended Code Sec. 42(m)(2)(B) by striking "and" at the end of clause (ii), by striking the period at the end of clause (iii) and inserting ", and", and by inserting after clause (iii) new clause (iv). For the **effective** date, see Act Sec. 13142(b)(6), below.

P.L. 103-66, §13142(b)(6), provides:

(6) EFFECTIVE DATES.—

(A) IN GENERAL.—Except as provided in subparagraphs (B) and (C), the amendments made by this subsection shall apply to—

(i) determinations under section 42 of the Internal Revenue Code of 1986 with respect to housing credit dollar amounts allocated from State housing credit ceilings after June 30, 1992, or

(ii) buildings placed in service after June 30, 1992, to the extent paragraph (1) of section 42(h) of such Code does not apply to any building by reason of paragraph (4) thereof, but only with respect to bonds issued after such date.

(B) WAIVER AUTHORITY AND PROHIBITED DISCRIMINATION.—The amendments made by paragraphs (3) and (4) shall take effect on the date of the enactment of this Act.

(C) HOME ASSISTANCE.—The amendment made by paragraph (2) shall apply to periods after the date of the enactment of this Act.

• 1990, Omnibus Budget Reconciliation Act of 1990 (P.L. 101-508)

P.L. 101-508, §11407(b)(2):

Amended Code Sec. 42(m)(1)(B)(iv). **Effective** 1-1-92 for buildings placed in service before, on, or after such date. Prior to amendment, Code Sec. 42(m)(1)(B)(iv) read as follows:

(iv) which provides a procedure that the agency will follow in notifying the Internal Revenue Service of noncompliance with the provisions of this section which such agency becomes aware of.

P.L. 101-508, §11407(b)(7)(A):

Amended Code Sec. 42(m)(2)(B) by striking "and" at the end of clause (i), by striking the period at the end of clause (ii) and inserting ", and", and by adding at the end thereof new clause (iii) and the last sentence. For the **effective** date, see Act Sec. 11407(b)(10)(A), below.

P.L. 101-508, §11407(b)(7)(B):

Amended Code Sec. 42(m)(1)(B) by striking clause (ii) and by redesignating clauses (iii) and (iv) as clauses (ii) and (iii), respectively. For the **effective** date, see Act Sec. 11407(b)(10)(A), below. Prior to amendment, Code Sec. 42(m)(1)(B)(ii) read as follows:

(ii) which gives the highest priority to those projects as to which the highest percentage of the housing credit dollar amount is to be used for project costs other than the cost of intermediaries unless granting such priority would impede the development of projects in hard-to-develop areas,

P.L. 101-508, §11407(b)(10)(A), provides:

(A) IN GENERAL.—Except as otherwise provided in this paragraph, the amendments made by this subsection shall apply to—

(i) determinations under section 42 of the Internal Revenue Code of 1986 with respect to housing credit dollar amounts allocated from State housing credit ceilings for calendar years after 1990, or

(ii) buildings placed in service after December 31, 1990, to the extent paragraph (1) of section 42(h) of such Code does not apply to any building by reason of paragraph (4) thereof, but only with respect to bonds issued after such date.

• 1989, Omnibus Budget Reconciliation Act of 1989 (P.L. 101-239)

P.L. 101-239, §7108(o):

Amended Code Sec. 42 by redesignating subsection (m) and (n) as subsections (n) and (o), respectively, and by inserting after subsection (l) a new subsection (m). For the **effective** date of the above amendment see Act Sec. 7108(r)[s](1)-(2) following Code Sec. 42(b). For a special rule, see Act Sec. 7801(r)[s](6) below.

P.L. 101-239, §7108(r)[s](6), provides:

(6) CERTAIN RULES WHICH APPLY TO BONDS.—Paragraphs (1)(D) and (2)(D) of section 42(m) of such Code, as added by this section, shall apply to obligations issued after December 31, 1989.

[Sec. 42(n)]

(n) REGULATIONS.—The Secretary shall prescribe such regulations as may be necessary or appropriate to carry out the purposes of this section, including regulations—

(1) dealing with—

(A) projects which include more than 1 building or only a portion of a building,

(B) buildings which are placed in service in portions,

(2) providing for the application of this section to short taxable years,

(3) preventing the avoidance of the rules of this section, and

(4) providing the opportunity for housing credit agencies to correct administrative errors and omissions with respect to allocations and record keeping within a reasonable period after their discovery, taking into account the availability of regulations and other administrative guidance from the Secretary.

Amendments

• 1989, Omnibus Budget Reconciliation Act of 1989 (P.L. 101-239)

P.L. 101-239, §7108(o):

Amended Code Sec. 42 by redesignating subsection (m) as subsection (n). For the **effective** date, see Act Sec. 7108(r)[s](1)-(2) following Code Sec. 42(b).

P.L. 101-239, §7831(c)(5):

Amended Code Sec. 42(m), before redesignation by Act Sec. 7108(o), by striking "and" at the end of paragraph (2), by striking the period at the end of paragraph (3) and inserting, "and", and by adding at the end thereof a new paragraph (4). **Effective** as if included in the provision of P.L. 99-514 to which it relates.

• 1986, Tax Reform Act of 1986 (P.L. 99-514)

P.L. 99-514, §252(a):

Amended subpart D of part IV of subchapter A of chapter 1, as amended by this Act, by adding at the end thereof new Code Sec. 42. **Effective** for buildings placed in service after 12-31-86, in tax years ending after such date. However, for a special rule and for transitional rules, see Act Sec. 252(e)(2) and (f), below.

P.L. 99-514, §252(e)(2), provides:

(2) SPECIAL RULE FOR REHABILITATION EXPENDITURES.—Subsection (e) of section 42 of the Internal Revenue Code of 1986 (as added by this section) shall apply for purposes of paragraph (1).

P.L. 99-514, §252(f), as amended by P.L. 100-647, §1002(l)(28)-(31), provides:

(f) TRANSITIONAL RULES.—

(1) LIMITATION TO NON-ACRS BUILDINGS NOT TO APPLY TO CERTAIN BUILDINGS, ETC.—

(A) IN GENERAL.—In the case of a building which is part of a project described in subparagraph (B)—

(i) section 42(c)(2)(B) of the Internal Revenue Code of 1986 (as added by this section) shall not apply,

(ii) such building shall be treated as not federally subsidized for purposes of section 42(b)(1)(A) of such Code,

(iii) the eligible basis of such building shall be treated, for purposes of section 42(h)(4)(A) of such Code, as if it were financed by an obligation the interest on which is exempt from tax under section 103 of such Code and which is taken into account under section 146 of such Code, and

(iv) the amendments made by section 803 shall not apply.

(B) PROJECT DESCRIBED.—A project is described in this subparagraph if—

(i) an urban development action grant application with respect to such project was submitted on September 13, 1984,

(ii) a zoning commission map amendment related to such project was granted on July 17, 1985, and

(iii) the number assigned to such project by the Federal Housing Administration is 023-36602.

(C) ADDITIONAL UNITS ELIGIBLE FOR CREDIT.—In the case of a building to which subparagraph (A) applies and which is part of a project which meets the requirements of subparagraph (D), for each low-income unit in such building which is occupied by individuals whose income is 30 percent or less of area median gross income, one additional unit (not otherwise a low-income unit) in such building shall be treated as a low-income unit for purposes of such section 42.

(D) PROJECT DESCRIBED.—A project is described in this subparagraph if—

(i) rents charged for units in such project are restricted by State regulations,

(ii) the annual cash flow of such project is restricted by State law,

(iii) the project is located on land owned by or ground leased from a public housing authority,

(iv) construction of such project begins on or before December 31, 1986, and units within such project are placed in service on or before June 1, 1990, and

(v) for a 20-year period, 20 percent or more of the residential units in such project are occupied by individuals whose income is 50 percent or less of area median gross income.

(E) MAXIMUM ADDITIONAL CREDIT.—The maximum present value of additional credits under section 42 of such Code by reason of subparagraph (C) shall not exceed 25 percent of the eligible basis of the building.

(2) ADDITIONAL ALLOCATION OF HOUSING CREDIT CEILING.—

(A) IN GENERAL.—There is hereby allocated to each housing credit agency described in subparagraph (B) an additional housing credit dollar amount determined in accordance with the following table:

For calendar year:	*The additional allocation is:*
1987	$3,900,000
1988	$7,600,000
1989	$1,300,000

(B) HOUSING CREDIT AGENCIES DESCRIBED.—The housing credit agencies described in this subparagraph are:

(i) A corporate governmental agency constituted as a public benefit corporation and established in 1971 under the provisions of Article XII of the Private Housing Finance Law of the State.

(ii) A city department established on December 20, 1979, pursuant to chapter XVIII of a municipal code of such city for the purpose of supervising and coordinating the formation and execution of projects and programs affecting housing within such city.

(iii) The State housing finance agency referred to in subparagraph (C), but only with respect to projects described in subparagraph (C).

(C) PROJECT DESCRIBED.—A project is described in this subparagraph if such project is a qualified low-income housing project which—

(i) receives financing from a State housing finance agency from the proceeds of bonds issued pursuant to chapter 708 of the Acts of 1966 of such State pursuant to loan commitments from such agency made between May 8, 1984, and July 8, 1986, and

(ii) is subject to subsidy commitments issued pursuant to a program established under chapter 574 of the Acts of 1983 of such State having award dates from such agency between May 31, 1984, and June 11, 1985.

(D) SPECIAL RULES.—

(i) Any building—

(I) which is allocated any housing credit dollar amount by a housing credit agency described in clause (iii) of subparagraph (B), and

(II) which is placed in service after June 30, 1986, and before January 1, 1987,

shall be treated for purposes of the amendments made by this section as placed in service on January 1, 1987.

(ii) Section 42(c)(2)(B) of the Internal Revenue Code of 1986 shall not apply to any building which is allocated any housing credit dollar amount by any agency described in subparagraph (B).

(E) ALL UNITS TREATED AS LOW INCOME UNITS IN CERTAIN CASES.—In the case of any building—

(i) which is allocated any housing credit dollar amount by any agency described in subparagraph (B), and

(ii) which after the application of subparagraph (D)(ii) is a qualified low-income building at all times during any taxable year, such building shall be treated as described in section 42(b)(1)(B) of such Code and having an applicable fraction for such year of 1. The preceding sentence shall apply to any building only to the extent of the portion of the additional housing credit dollar amount (allocated to such agency under subparagraph (A)) allocated to such building.

(3) CERTAIN PROJECTS PLACED IN SERVICE BEFORE 1987.—

(A) IN GENERAL.—In the case of a building which is part of a project described in subparagraph (B)—

(i) section 42(c)(2)(B) of such Code shall not apply,

(ii) such building shall be treated as placed in service during the first calendar year after 1986 and before 1990 in which such building is a qualified low-income building (determined after the application of clause (i)), and

(iii) for purposes of section 42(h) of such Code, such building shall be treated as having allocated to it a housing credit dollar amount equal to the dollar amount appearing in the clause of subparagraph (B) in which such building is described.

(B) PROJECT DESCRIBED.—A project is described in this subparagraph if the code number assigned to such project by the Farmers' Home Administration appears in the following table:

The code number is:	*The housing credit dollar amount is:*
(i) 49284553664	$16,000
(ii) 4927742022446	$22,000
(iii) 49270742276087	$64,000
(iv) 490270742387293	$48,000
(v) 4927074218234	$32,000
(vi) 49270742274019	$36,000
(vii) 51460742345074	$53,000

(C) DETERMINATION OF ADJUSTED BASIS.—The adjusted basis of any building to which this paragraph applies for purposes of section 42 of such Code shall be its adjusted basis as of the close of the taxable year ending before the first taxable year of the credit period for such building.

(D) CERTAIN RULES TO APPLY.—Rules similar to the rules of subparagraph (E) of paragraph (2) shall apply for purposes of this paragraph.

(4) DEFINITIONS.—For purposes of this subsection, terms used in such subsection which are also used in section 42 of the Internal Revenue Code of 1986 (as added by this section) shall have the meanings given such terms by such section 42.

(5) TRANSITIONAL RULE.—In the case of any rehabilitation expenditures incurred with respect to units located in the neighborhood strategy area within the community development block grant program in Ft. Wayne, Indiana—

(A) the amendments made by this section shall not apply, and

(B) paragraph (1) of section 167(k) of the Internal Revenue Code of 1986, shall be applied as if it did not contain the phrase "and before January 1, 1987".

The number of units to which the preceding sentence applies shall not exceed 150.

• 1986, Omnibus Budget Reconciliation Act of 1986 (P.L. 99-509)

P.L. 99-509, §8072(a):

Amended Code Sec. 42(k)(1), as added by P.L. 99-514, by striking out "subparagraph (D)(iv)(I)" and inserting in lieu thereof "subparagraphs (D)(ii)(II) and (D)(iv)(I)". **Effective** as if included in the amendment made by section 252(a) of P.L. 99-514.

• 1975, Revenue Adjustment Act of 1975 (P.L. 94-164)

P.L. 94-164, §3(b), as amended by P.L. 94-455, §401(a) and P.L. 95-30, §103(c):

Pursuant to §3(b), as amended (see below), Code Sec. 42 expired with respect to tax years ending after 1978. Prior to its expiration, it read as follows:

SEC. 42. GENERAL TAX CREDIT.

(a) ALLOWANCE OF CREDIT.—In the case of an individual, there shall be allowed as a credit against the tax imposed by section 1, or against the tax imposed in lieu of the tax imposed by section 1, for the taxable year an amount equal to the greater of—

(1) 2 percent of so much of the taxpayer's taxable income for the taxable year (reduced by the zero bracket amount) as does not exceed $9,000; or

(2) $35 multiplied by each exemption for which the taxpayer is entitled to a deduction for the taxable year under section 151.

(b) APPLICATION WITH OTHER CREDITS.—The credit allowed by subsection (a) shall not exceed the amount of the tax imposed by section 1, or the amount of the tax imposed in lieu of the tax imposed by section 1, for the taxable year. In determining the credits allowed under—

(1) section 33 (relating to foreign tax credit),

(2) section 37 (relating to credit for the elderly),

(3) section 38 (relating to investment in certain depreciable property),

(4) section 40 (relating to expenses of work incentive programs), and

(5) section 41 (relating to contributions to candidates for public office),

the tax imposed by this chapter shall (before any other reductions) be reduced by the credit allowed by this section.

(c) SPECIAL RULE FOR MARRIED INDIVIDUALS FILING SEPARATE RETURNS.—

(1) IN GENERAL.—In the case of a married individual who files a separate return for the taxable year, the amount of the credit allowable under subsection (a) for the taxable year shall be the amount determined under paragraph (2) of subsection (a).

(2) MARITAL STATUS.—For purposes of this subsection, the determination of marital status shall be made under section 143.

(d) CERTAIN PERSONS NOT ELIGIBLE.—This section shall not apply to any estate or trust, nor shall it apply to any nonresident alien individual.

(e) INCOME TAX TABLES TO REFLECT CREDIT.—The tables prescribed by the Secretary under section 3 shall reflect the credit allowed by this section.

• 1977, Tax Reduction and Simplification Act of 1977 (P.L. 95-30)

P.L. 95-30, §101(c)(1):

Amended Code Sec. 42(a). **Effective** for tax years beginning after 12-31-76. Prior to amendment, Code Sec. 42(a) read as follows:

(a) ALLOWANCE OF CREDIT.—In the case of an individual, there shall be allowed as a credit against the tax imposed by this chapter for the taxable year an amount equal to the greater of—

(1) 2 percent of so much of the taxpayer's taxable income for the taxable year as does not exceed $9,000; or

(2) $35 multiplied by each exemption for which the taxpayer is entitled to a deduction for the taxable year under subsection (b) or (e) of section 151.

P.L. 95-30, §101(c)(2), (b):

Added Code Sec. 42(e). **Effective** for tax years beginning after 12-31-78, (as amended by P.L. 95-30, §103(a), and P.L. 94-455, §94-455, §401(a)).

P.L. 95-30, §101(c)(3):

Amended Code Sec. 42(c). **Effective** for tax years beginning after 12-31-76. Prior to amendment, Code Sec. 42(c) read as follows:

(c) SPECIAL RULE FOR MARRIED INDIVIDUALS FILING SEPARATE RETURNS.—

(1) IN GENERAL.—Notwithstanding subsection (a), in the case of a married individual who files a separate return for the taxable year, the amount of the credit allowable under subsection (a) for the taxable year shall be equal to either—

(A) the amount determined under paragraph (1) subsection (a); or

(B) if this subparagraph applies to the individual for the taxable year, the amount determined under paragraph (2) of subsection (a).

For purposes of the preceding sentence, paragraph (1) of subsection (a) shall be applied by substituting "$4,500" for "$9,000".

(2) APPLICATION OF PARAGRAPH (1)(B)—Subparagraph (B) of paragraph (1) shall apply to any taxpayer for any taxable year if—

(A) such taxpayer elects to have such subparagraph apply for such taxable year, and

(B) the spouse of such taxpayer elects to have such subparagraph apply for any taxable year corresponding, for purposes of section 142(a), to the taxable year of the taxpayer.

Any such election shall be made at such time, and in such manner, as the Secretary shall by regulations prescribe.

(3) MARITAL STATUS.—For purposes of this subsection, the determination of marital status shall be made under section 143.

P.L. 95-30, § 101(c)(4):

Amended Code Sec. 42(b) by substituting "by section 1, or the amount of the tax imposed in lieu of the tax imposed by section 1" for "by this chapter". **Effective** for tax years beginning after 12-31-76.

P.L. 95-30, § 103(a):

Amended P.L. 94-164, § 3(b) (effective date), as amended by P.L. 94-455, § 401(a), to provide that the general tax credit would apply to tax years ending after 12-31-75, and would cease to apply to tax years ending after 12-31-78.

P.L. 95-30, § 103(c):

Amended P.L. 94-455, § 401(e) (effective date) to provide that the general tax credit would apply to tax years ending after 12-31-75, and would cease to apply to tax years ending after 12-31-78.

• 1976, Tax Reform Act of 1976 (P.L. 94-455)

P.L. 94-455, § 401(a):

Amended the heading and subsection (a) of section 42. **Effective** for tax years ending after 12-31-75, and shall cease to apply to tax years ending after 12-31-77. Prior to amendment, Code Sec. 42(a) read as follows:

SEC. 42. TAXABLE INCOME CREDIT.

(a) ALLOWANCE OF CREDIT.—

(1) IN GENERAL.—In the case of an individual, there shall be allowed as a credit against the tax imposed by this chapter for the taxable year an amount equal to the greater of—

(A) 2 percent of so much of the taxpayer's taxable income for the taxable year as does not exceed $9,000; or

(B) $35 multiplied by each exemption for which the taxpayer is entitled to a deduction for the taxable year under subsection (b) or (e) of section 151.

(2) APPLICATION OF SIX-MONTH RULE.—Notwithstanding the provisions of paragraph (1) of this subsection, the percentage "1 percent" shall be substituted for "2 percent" in subparagraph (A) of such paragraph, and the amount "$17.50" shall be substituted for the amount "$35" in subparagraph (B) of such paragraph.

P.L. 94-455, § 401(e):

Amended section 3(b) (effective date) of P.L. 94-164 (see below) by substituting "December 31, 1977" for "December 31, 1976."

P.L. 94-455, § 401(a)(1):

Amended P.L. 94-164, § 3(b), by delaying the termination date of § 3(a) of such law, which added Code Sec. 42(d), until tax years ending after 12-31-77.

P.L. 94-455, § 401(a)(2)(B):

Amended paragraph (1) of Code Sec. 42(c). **Effective** for tax years ending after 12-31-75, and shall cease to apply to tax years ending after 12-31-77. Prior to amendment, paragraph (1) read as follows:

(1) IN GENERAL.—Notwithstanding subsection (a), in the case of a married individual who files a separate return for the taxable year, the amount of the credit allowable under subsection (a) for the taxable year shall be equal to either—

(A) the amount determined under paragraph (1)(A) of subsection (a); or

(B) if this subparagraph applies to the individual for the taxable year, the amount determined under paragraph (1)(B) of subsection (a).

For purposes of the preceding sentence, paragraph (1) of subsection (a) shall be applied by substituting "$4,500" for "$9,000".

P.L. 94-455, § 503(b)(4):

Substituted "credit for the elderly" for "retirement income" in Code Sec. 42(b)(2). **Effective** for tax years beginning after 12-31-75.

• 1975, Revenue Adjustment Act of 1975 (P.L. 94-164)

P.L. 94-164, § 3(a), (b):

Amended subsection (a). **Effective** for tax years ending after 12-31-75, and ceasing to apply for tax years ending after 12-31-76. Prior to amendment, subsection (a) read as follows:

(a) GENERAL RULE.—In the case of an individual, there shall be allowed as a credit against the tax imposed by this chapter for the taxable year $30, multiplied by each exemption for which the taxpayer is entitled for the taxable year under subsection (b) or (e) of section 151.

P.L. 94-164, § 3(a), (b):

Amended subsection (b). **Effective** for tax years ending after 12-31-75, and ceasing to apply for tax years ending after 12-31-78 (as amended by P.L. 95-30 § 103(a), and P.L. 94-455, § 401(a)). Prior to amendment, subsection (b) read as follows:

(b) APPLICATION WITH OTHER CREDITS.—The credit allowed by subsection (a) shall not exceed the amount of the tax imposed by this chapter for the taxable year. In determining the credits allowed under—

(1) section 33 (relating to foreign tax credit),

(2) section 37 (relating to retirement income),

(3) section 38 (relating to investment in certain depreciable property),

(4) section 40 (relating to expenses of work incentive programs), and

(5) section 41 (relating to contributions to candidates for public office),

the tax imposed by this chapter shall (before any other reductions) be reduced by the credit allowed by this section.

P.L. 94-164, § 3(a), (b):

Added Code Sec. 42(c). **Effective** for tax years ending after 12-31-75, and ceasing to apply for tax years ending after 12-31-78 (as amended by P.L. 95-30 § 103(a), and P.L. 94-455, § 94-455, § 401(a)).

P.L. 94-164, § 3(a):

Added Code Sec. 42(d). **Effective** for tax years ending after 12-31-75 and ceasing to apply for tax years ending after 12-31-78.

• 1975, Tax Reduction Act of 1975 (P.L. 94-12)

P.L. 94-12, § 203(a):

Added Code Sec. 42(a) and (b) in place of former Code Sec. 42 (now Code Sec. 45). **Effective** only for tax years ending in 1975.

[Sec. 42(o)—Stricken]

Amendments

• 1993, Omnibus Budget Reconciliation Act of 1993 (P.L. 103-66)

P.L. 103-66, § 13142(a)(1):

Amended Code Sec. 42 by striking subsection (o). **Effective** for periods ending after 6-30-92. Prior to being stricken, Code Sec. 42(o) read as follows:

(o) TERMINATION.—

(1) IN GENERAL.—Except as provided in paragraph (2)—

(A) clause (i) of subsection (h)(3)(C) shall not apply to any amount allocated after June 30, 1992, and

(B) subsection (h)(4) shall not apply to any building placed in service after June 30, 1992.

(2) EXCEPTION FOR BONDS-FINANCED BUILDINGS IN PROGRESS.—For purposes of paragraph (1)(B), a building shall be treated as placed in service before July 1, 1992 if—

(A) the bonds with respect to such building are issued before July 1, 1992,

(B) the taxpayer's basis in the project (of which the building is a part) as of June 30, 1992, is more than 10 percent of the taxpayer's reasonably expected basis in such project as of June 30, 1994, and

(C) such building is placed in service before July 1, 1994.

• 1991, Tax Extension Act of 1991 (P.L. 102-227)

P.L. 102-227, §107(a)(1)(A)-(C):

Amended Code Sec. 42(o)(1) by striking ", for any calendar year after 1991" after "paragraph (2)", by inserting before the comma at the end of subparagraph (A) "to any amount allocated after June 30, 1992", and by striking "1991" in subparagraph (B) and inserting "June 30, 1992". **Effective** for calendar years after 1991.

P.L. 102-227, §107(a)(2)(A)-(D):

Amended Code Sec. 42(o)(2) by striking "1992" each place it appears and inserting "July 1, 1992", by striking "December 31, 1991" in subparagraph (B) and inserting "June 30, 1992", by striking "December 31, 1993" in subparagraph (B) and inserting "June 30, 1994", and by striking "January 1, 1994" in subparagraph (C) and inserting "July 1, 1994". **Effective** for calendar years after 1991.

• 1990, Omnibus Budget Reconciliation Act of 1990 (P.L. 101-508)

P.L. 101-508, §11407(a)(1):

Amended Code Sec. 42(o) by striking "1990" each place it appears in paragraph (1) and inserting "1991", and by striking paragraph (2) and inserting new paragraph (2). **Effective** calendar years after 1989. Prior to amendment, Code Sec. 42(o)(2) read as follows:

(2) EXCEPTION FOR BOND-FINANCED BUILDINGS IN PROGRESS.—For purposes of paragraph (1)(B), a building shall be treated as placed in service before 1990 if—

(A) the bonds with respect to such building are issued before 1990,

(B) such building is constructed, reconstructed, or rehabilitated by the taxpayer,

(C) more than 10 percent of the reasonably anticipated cost of such construction, reconstruction, or rehabilitation has been incurred as of January 1, 1990, and some of such cost is incurred on or after such date, and

(D) such building is placed in service before January 1, 1992.

• 1989, Omnibus Budget Reconciliation Act of 1989 (P.L. 101-239)

P.L. 101-239, §7108(a)(1):

Amended Code Sec. 42(n)[o]. For the **effective** date, see Act Sec. 7108(r)[s](1)-(2) following Code Sec. 42(b). Prior to amendment, Code Sec. 42(n) read as follows:

(n) TERMINATION.—The State housing credit ceiling under subsection (h) shall be zero for any calendar year after 1989 and subsection (h)(4) shall not apply to any building placed in service after 1989.

P.L. 101-239, §7108(o):

Amended Code Sec. 42 by redesignating subsection (n) as subsection (o). For the **effective** date, see Act Sec. 7108(r)[s](1)-(2) following Code Sec. 42(b).

• 1988, Technical and Miscellaneous Revenue Act of 1988 (P.L. 100-647)

P.L. 100-647, §1002(l)(25):

Amended Code Sec. 42(n)(1) by inserting ", and, except for any building described in paragraph (2)(B), subsection (h)(4) shall not apply to any building placed in service after 1989" before the period at the end thereof. **Effective** as if included in the provision of P.L. 99-514 to which it relates.

P.L. 100-647, §4003(b)(3):

Amended Code Sec. 42(n) (as amended by this Act). **Effective** for amounts allocated in calendar years after 1987. Prior to amendment (but after amendment by Act Sec. 1002(l)(25)), Code Sec. 42(n) read as follows:

(n) TERMINATION.—

(1) IN GENERAL.—Except as provided in paragraph (2), the State housing credit ceiling under subsection (h) shall be zero for any calendar year after 1989, and, except for any building described in paragraph (2)(B), subsection (h)(4) shall not apply to any building placed in service after 1989.

(2) CARRYOVER OF 1989 LIMIT FOR CERTAIN PROJECTS IN PROGRESS.—

(A) IN GENERAL.—The aggregate housing credit amount of any agency for 1989 which is not allocated for 1989 shall be treated for purposes of applying this section to any building described in subparagraph (B) as the housing credit amount of such agency for 1990.

(B) DESCRIPTION.—A building is described in this subparagraph if—

(i) such building is constructed, reconstructed, or rehabilitated by the taxpayer,

(ii) more than 10 percent of the reasonably anticipated cost of such construction, reconstruction, or rehabilitation has been incurred as of January 1, 1989, and

(iii) such building is placed in service before January 1, 1991.

(C) CERTAIN RULE NOT TO APPLY.—Subsection (h)(6)(B)(i) shall not apply for purposes of this paragraph.

[Sec. 43]

SEC. 43. ENHANCED OIL RECOVERY CREDIT.

[Sec. 43(a)]

(a) GENERAL RULE.—For purposes of section 38, the enhanced oil recovery credit for any taxable year is an amount equal to 15 percent of the taxpayer's qualified enhanced oil recovery costs for such taxable year.

[Sec. 43(b)]

(b) PHASE-OUT OF CREDIT AS CRUDE OIL PRICES INCREASE.—

(1) IN GENERAL.—The amount of the credit determined under subsection (a) for any taxable year shall be reduced by an amount which bears the same ratio to the amount of such credit (determined without regard to this paragraph) as—

(A) the amount by which the reference price for the calendar year preceding the calendar year in which the taxable year begins exceeds $28, bears to

(B) $6.

(2) REFERENCE PRICE.—For purposes of this subsection, the term "reference price" means, with respect to any calendar year, the reference price determined for such calendar year under section 45K(d)(2)(C).

(3) INFLATION ADJUSTMENT.—

(A) IN GENERAL.—In the case of any taxable year beginning in a calendar year after 1991, there shall be substituted for the $28 amount under paragraph (1)(A) an amount equal to the product of—

(i) $28, multiplied by

(ii) the inflation adjustment factor for such calendar year.

(B) INFLATION ADJUSTMENT FACTOR.—The term "inflation adjustment factor" means, with respect to any calendar year, a fraction the numerator of which is the GNP implicit price deflator for the preceding calendar year and the denominator of which is the GNP implicit price deflator for 1990. For purposes of the preceding sentence, the term "GNP implicit price deflator" means the first revision of the implicit price deflator for the gross national product as computed and published by the Secretary of Commerce. Not later than April 1 of any calendar year, the Secretary shall publish the inflation adjustment factor for the preceding calendar year.

Amendments

• 2005, Energy Tax Incentives Act of 2005 (P.L. 109-58)

P.L. 109-58, §1322(a)(3)(B):

Amended Code Sec. 43(b)(2) by striking "section 29(d)(2)(C)" and inserting "section 45K(d)(2)(C)". **Effective** for credits determined under the Internal Revenue Code of 1986 for tax years ending after 12-31-2005.

[Sec. 43(c)]

(c) QUALIFIED ENHANCED OIL RECOVERY COSTS.—For purposes of this section—

(1) IN GENERAL.—The term "qualified enhanced oil recovery costs" means any of the following:

(A) Any amount paid or incurred during the taxable year for tangible property—

(i) which is an integral part of a qualified enhanced oil recovery project, and

(ii) with respect to which depreciation (or amortization in lieu of depreciation) is allowable under this chapter.

(B) Any intangible drilling and development costs—

(i) which are paid or incurred in connection with a qualified enhanced oil recovery project, and

(ii) with respect to which the taxpayer may make an election under section 263(c) for the taxable year.

(C) Any qualified tertiary injectant expenses (as defined in section 193(b)) which are paid or incurred in connection with a qualified enhanced oil recovery project and for which a deduction is allowable for the taxable year.

(D) Any amount which is paid or incurred during the taxable year to construct a gas treatment plant which—

(i) is located in the area of the United States (within the meaning of section 638(1)) lying north of 64 degrees North latitude,

(ii) prepares Alaska natural gas for transportation through a pipeline with a capacity of at least 2,000,000,000,000 Btu of natural gas per day, and

(iii) produces carbon dioxide which is injected into hydrocarbon-bearing geological formations.

(2) QUALIFIED ENHANCED OIL RECOVERY PROJECT.—For purposes of this subsection—

(A) IN GENERAL.—The term "qualified enhanced oil recovery project" means any project—

(i) which involves the application (in accordance with sound engineering principles) of 1 or more tertiary recovery methods (as defined in section 193(b)(3)) which can reasonably be expected to result in more than an insignificant increase in the amount of crude oil which will ultimately be recovered,

(ii) which is located within the United States (within the meaning of section 638(1)), and

(iii) with respect to which the first injection of liquids, gases, or other matter commences after December 31, 1990.

(B) CERTIFICATION.—A project shall not be treated as a qualified enhanced oil recovery project unless the operator submits to the Secretary (at such times and in such manner as the Secretary provides) a certification from a petroleum engineer that the project meets (and continues to meet) the requirements of subparagraph (A).

(3) AT-RISK LIMITATION.—For purposes of determining qualified enhanced oil recovery costs, rules similar to the rules of section 49(a)(1), section 49(a)(2), and section 49(b) shall apply.

(4) SPECIAL RULE FOR CERTAIN GAS DISPLACEMENT PROJECTS.—For purposes of this section, immiscible nonhydrocarbon gas displacement shall be treated as a tertiary recovery method under section 193(b)(3).

(5) ALASKA NATURAL GAS.—For purposes of paragraph (1)(D)—

(A) IN GENERAL.—The term "Alaska natural gas" means natural gas entering the Alaska natural gas pipeline (as defined in section 168(i)(16) (determined without regard to subparagraph (B) thereof)) which is produced from a well—

(i) located in the area of the State of Alaska lying north of 64 degrees North latitude, determined by excluding the area of the Alaska National Wildlife Refuge (including the continental shelf thereof within the meaning of section 638(1)), and

(ii) pursuant to the applicable State and Federal pollution prevention, control, and permit requirements from such area (including the continental shelf thereof within the meaning of section 638(1)).

(B) NATURAL GAS.—The term "natural gas" has the meaning given such term by section 613A(e)(2).

Amendments

• 2005, Gulf Opportunity Zone Act of 2005 (P.L. 109-135)

P.L. 109-135, §412(i):

Amended Code Sec. 43(c)(5). **Effective** 12-21-2005. Prior to amendment, Code Sec. 43(c)(5) read as follows:

(5) ALASKA NATURAL GAS.—For purposes of paragraph (1)(D)—

(1) IN GENERAL.—The term "Alaska natural gas" means natural gas entering the Alaska natural gas pipeline (as defined in section 168(i)(16) (determined without regard to subparagraph (B) thereof)) which is produced from a well—

(A) located in the area of the State of Alaska lying north of 64 degrees North latitude, determined by excluding the area of the Alaska National Wildlife Refuge (including the continental shelf thereof within the meaning of section 638(1)), and

(B) pursuant to the applicable State and Federal pollution prevention, control, and permit requirements from such area (including the continental shelf thereof within the meaning of section 638(1)).

(2) NATURAL GAS.—The term "natural gas" has the meaning given such term by section 613A(e)(2).

• 2004, American Jobs Creation Act of 2004 (P.L. 108-357)

P.L. 108-357, §707(a):

Amended Code Sec. 43(c)(1) by adding at the end a new subparagraph (D). **Effective** for costs paid or incurred in tax years beginning after 12-31-2004.

P.L. 108-357, §707(b):

Amended Code Sec. 43(c) by adding at the end a new paragraph (5). **Effective** for costs paid or incurred in tax years beginning after 12-31-2004.

• 2000, Community Renewal Tax Relief Act of 2000 (P.L. 106-554)

P.L. 106-554, §317(a)(1)-(2):

Amended Code Sec. 43(c)(1)(C) by inserting "(as defined in section 193(b))" after "expenses", and by striking "under section 193" following "is allowable". **Effective** as if included in section 11511 of P.L. 101-508 [**effective** for costs paid or incurred in tax years beginning after 12-31-90.—CCH].

[Sec. 43(d)]

(d) OTHER RULES.—

(1) DISALLOWANCE OF DEDUCTION.—Any deduction allowable under this chapter for any costs taken into account in computing the amount of the credit determined under subsection (a) shall be reduced by the amount of such credit attributable to such costs.

(2) BASIS ADJUSTMENTS.—For purposes of this subtitle, if a credit is determined under this section for any expenditure with respect to any property, the increase in the basis of such property which would (but for this subsection) result from such expenditure shall be reduced by the amount of the credit so allowed.

[Sec. 43(e)]

(e) ELECTION TO HAVE CREDIT NOT APPLY.—

(1) IN GENERAL.—A taxpayer may elect to have this section not apply for any taxable year.

(2) TIME FOR MAKING ELECTION.—An election under paragraph (1) for any taxable year may be made (or revoked) at any time before the expiration of the 3-year period beginning on the last date prescribed by law for filing the return for such taxable year (determined without regard to extensions).

(3) MANNER OF MAKING ELECTION.—An election under paragraph (1) (or revocation thereof) shall be made in such manner as the Secretary may by regulations prescribe.

Amendments

• 1990, Omnibus Budget Reconciliation Act of 1990 (P.L. 101-508)

P.L. 101-508, §11511(a):

Amended subpart D of part IV of subchapter A of Chapter 1 by adding at the end thereof a new Code Sec. 43. **Effective**, generally, for costs paid or incurred in tax years beginning after 12-31-90. For a special rule, see Act Sec. 11511(d)(2), below.

P.L. 101-508, §11511(d)(2), provides:

(2) SPECIAL RULE FOR SIGNIFICANT EXPANSION OF PROJECTS.—For purposes of section 43(c)(2)(A)(iii) of the Internal Revenue Code of 1986 (as added by subsection (a)), any significant expansion after December 31, 1990, of a project begun before January 1, 1991, shall be treated as a project with respect to which the first injection commences after December 31, 1990.

[Sec. 44]

SEC. 44. EXPENDITURES TO PROVIDE ACCESS TO DISABLED INDIVIDUALS.

[Sec. 44(a)]

(a) GENERAL RULE.—For purposes of section 38, in the case of an eligible small business, the amount of the disabled access credit determined under this section for any taxable year shall be an amount equal to 50 percent of so much of the eligible access expenditures for the taxable year as exceed $250 but do not exceed $10,250.

[Sec. 44(b)]

(b) ELIGIBLE SMALL BUSINESS.—For purposes of this section, the term "eligible small business" means any person if—

(1) either—

(A) the gross receipts of such person for the preceding taxable year did not exceed $1,000,000, or

(B) in the case of a person to which subparagraph (A) does not apply, such person employed not more than 30 full-time employees during the preceding taxable year, and

(2) such person elects the application of this section for the taxable year.

For purposes of paragraph (1)(B), an employee shall be considered full-time if such employee is employed at least 30 hours per week for 20 or more calendar weeks in the taxable year.

[Sec. 44(c)]

(c) ELIGIBLE ACCESS EXPENDITURES.—For purposes of this section—

(1) IN GENERAL.—The term "eligible access expenditures" means amounts paid or incurred by an eligible small business for the purpose of enabling such eligible small business to comply with applicable requirements under the Americans With Disabilities Act of 1990 (as in effect on the date of the enactment of this section).

(2) CERTAIN EXPENDITURES INCLUDED.—The term "eligible access expenditures" includes amounts paid or incurred—

(A) for the purpose of removing architectural, communication, physical, or transportation barriers which prevent a business from being accessible to, or usable by, individuals with disabilities,

(B) to provide qualified interpreters or other effective methods of making aurally delivered materials available to individuals with hearing impairments,

(C) to provide qualified readers, taped texts, and other effective methods of making visually delivered materials available to individuals with visual impairments,

(D) to acquire or modify equipment or devices for individuals with disabilities, or

(E) to provide other similar services, modifications, materials, or equipment.

(3) EXPENDITURES MUST BE REASONABLE.—Amounts paid or incurred for the purposes described in paragraph (2) shall include only expenditures which are reasonable and shall not include expenditures which are unnecessary to accomplish such purposes.

(4) EXPENSES IN CONNECTION WITH NEW CONSTRUCTION ARE NOT ELIGIBLE.—The term "eligible access expenditures" shall not include amounts described in paragraph (2)(A) which are paid or incurred in connection with any facility first placed in service after the date of the enactment of this section.

(5) EXPENDITURES MUST MEET STANDARDS.—The term "eligible access expenditures" shall not include any amount unless the taxpayer establishes, to the satisfaction of the Secretary, that the resulting removal of any barrier (or the provision of any services, modifications, materials, or equipment) meets the standards promulgated by the Secretary with the concurrence of the Architectural and Transportation Barriers Compliance Board and set forth in regulations prescribed by the Secretary.

[Sec. 44(d)]

(d) DEFINITION OF DISABILITY; SPECIAL RULES.—For purposes of this section—

(1) DISABILITY.—The term "disability" has the same meaning as when used in the Americans With Disabilities Act of 1990 (as in effect on the date of the enactment of this section).

(2) CONTROLLED GROUPS.—

(A) IN GENERAL.—All members of the same controlled group of corporations (within the meaning of section 52(a)) and all persons under common control (within the meaning of section 52(b)) shall be treated as 1 person for purposes of this section.

(B) DOLLAR LIMITATION.—The Secretary shall apportion the dollar limitation under subsection (a) among the members of any group described in subparagraph (A) in such manner as the Secretary shall by regulations prescribe.

(3) PARTNERSHIPS AND S CORPORATIONS.—In the case of a partnership, the limitation under subsection (a) shall apply with respect to the partnership and each partner. A similar rule shall apply in the case of an S corporation and its shareholders.

(4) SHORT YEARS.—The Secretary shall prescribe such adjustments as may be appropriate for purposes of paragraph (1) of subsection (b) if the preceding taxable year is a taxable year of less than 12 months.

(5) GROSS RECEIPTS.—Gross receipts for any taxable year shall be reduced by returns and allowances made during such year.

(6) TREATMENT OF PREDECESSORS.—The reference to any person in paragraph (1) of subsection (b) shall be treated as including a reference to any predecessor.

(7) DENIAL OF DOUBLE BENEFIT.—In the case of the amount of the credit determined under this section—

(A) no deduction or credit shall be allowed for such amount under any other provision of this chapter, and

(B) no increase in the adjusted basis of any property shall result from such amount.

[Sec. 44(e)]

(e) REGULATIONS.—The Secretary shall prescribe regulations necessary to carry out the purposes of this section.

Amendments

• 1990, Omnibus Budget Reconciliation Act of 1990 (P.L. 101-508)

P.L. 101-508, §11611(a):

Amended subpart D of part IV of subchapter A of chapter 1 (as amended by subtitle E) by adding at the end thereof a new section 44. **Effective** for expenditures paid or incurred after the date of the enactment of this Act.

[Sec. 44—Repealed]

Amendments

• 1984, Deficit Reduction Act of 1984 (P.L. 98-369)

P.L. 98-369, §474(m)(1):

Repealed Code Sec. 44. **Effective** for tax years beginning after 12-31-83, and to carrybacks from such years. Prior to repeal, Code Sec. 44 read as follows:

SEC. 44. PURCHASE OF NEW PRINCIPAL RESIDENCE.

(a) GENERAL RULE.—In the case of an individual there is allowed, as a credit against the tax imposed by this chapter for the taxable year, an amount equal to 5 percent of the purchase price of a new principal residence purchased or constructed by the taxpayer.

(b) LIMITATIONS.—

(1) MAXIMUM CREDIT.—The credit allowed under subsection (a) may not exceed $2,000.

(2) LIMITATION TO ONE RESIDENCE.—The credit under this section shall be allowed with respect to only one residence of the taxpayer.

(3) MARRIED INDIVIDUALS.—In the case of a husband and wife who file a joint return under section 6013, the amount specified under paragraph (1) shall apply to the joint return. In the case of a married individual filing a separate return, paragraph (1) shall be applied by substituting "$1,000" for "$2,000".

(4) CERTAIN OTHER TAXPAYERS.—In the case of individuals to whom paragraph (3) does not apply who together purchase the same new principal residence for use as their principal residence, the amount of the credit allowed under subsection (a) shall be allocated among such individuals as prescribed by the Secretary, but the sum of the amounts allowed to such individuals shall not exceed $2,000 with respect to that residence.

(5) APPLICATION WITH OTHER CREDITS.—The credit allowed by subsection (a) shall not exceed the amount of the tax imposed by this chapter for the taxable year, reduced by the sum of the credits allowable under sections 33, 37, 38, 40, 41, and 42.

(c) DEFINITIONS.—For purposes of this section—

(1) NEW PRINCIPAL RESIDENCE.—The term "new principal residence" means a principal residence (within the meaning of section 1034), the original use of which commences with the taxpayer, and includes, without being limited to, a single family structure, a residential unit in a condominium or cooperative housing project, and a mobile home.

(2) PURCHASE PRICE.—The term "purchase price" means the adjusted basis of the new principal residence on the date of the acquisition thereof.

(3) PURCHASE.—The term "purchase" means any acquisition of property, but only if—

(A) the property is not acquired from a person whose relationship to the person acquiring it would result in the disallowance of losses under section 267 or 707(b) (but, in applying section 267(b) and (c) for purposes of this section, paragraph (4) of section 267(c) shall be treated as providing that the family of an individual shall include only his spouse, ancestors, and lineal descendants), and

(B) the basis of the property in the hands of the person acquiring it is not determined—

(i) in whole or in part by reference to the adjusted basis of such property in the hands of the person from whom acquired, or

(ii) under section 1014(a) (relating to property acquired from a decedent).

(d) RECAPTURE FOR CERTAIN DISPOSITIONS.—

(1) IN GENERAL.—Except as provided in paragraphs (2) and (3), if the taxpayer disposes of property with respect to the purchase of which a credit was allowed under subsection (a) at any time within 36 months after the date on which he acquired it (or, in the case of construction by the taxpayer, on the day on which he first occupied it) as his principal residence, then the tax imposed under this chapter for the taxable year in which terminates the replacement period under paragraph (2) with respect to the disposition is increased by an amount equal to the amount allowed as a credit for the purchase of such property.

(2) ACQUISITION OF NEW RESIDENCE.—If, in connection with a disposition described in paragraph (1) and within the applicable period prescribed in section 1034, the taxpayer purchases or constructs a new principal residence, then the provisions of paragraph (1) shall not apply and the tax imposed by this chapter for the taxable year following the taxable year during which disposition occurs is increased by an amount which bears the same ratio to the amount allowed as a credit for the purchase of the old residence as (A) the adjusted sales price of the old residence (within the meaning of section 1034), reduced (but not below zero) by the taxpayer's cost of purchasing the new residence (within the meaning of such section) bears to (B) the adjusted sales price of the old residence.

(3) DEATH OF OWNER; CASUALTY LOSS; INVOLUNTARY CONVERSION; ETC.—The provisions of paragraph (1) do not apply to—

(A) a disposition of a residence made on account of the death of any individual having a legal or equitable interest therein occurring during the 36 month period to which reference is made under such paragraph,

(B) a disposition of the old residence if it is substantially or completely destroyed by a casualty described in section 165(c)(3) or compulsorily and involuntarily converted (within the meaning of section 1033(a)), or

(C) a disposition pursuant to a settlement in a divorce or legal separation proceeding where the other spouse retains the residence as principal residence.

(e) PROPERTY TO WHICH SECTION APPLIES.—

(1) IN GENERAL.—The provisions of this section apply to a new principal residence—

(A) the construction of which began before March 26, 1975,

(B) which is acquired and occupied by the taxpayer after March 12, 1975, and before January 1, 1977, and

(C) if not constructed by the taxpayer, which was acquired by the taxpayer under a binding contract entered into by the taxpayer before January 1, 1976.

(2) SELF-CONSTRUCTED PROPERTY BEGUN BEFORE MARCH 13, 1975.—In the case of property the construction of which was begun by the taxpayer before March 13, 1975, only that

portion of the basis of such property properly allocable to construction after March 12, 1975, shall be taken into account in determining the amount of the credit allowable under subsection (a).

(3) BINDING CONTRACT.—For purposes of this subsection, a contract for the purchase of a residence which is conditioned upon the purchaser's obtaining a loan for the purchase of the residence (including conditions as to the amount or interest rate of such loan) is not considered nonbinding on account of that condition.

(4) CERTIFICATION MUST BE ATTACHED TO RETURN.—This section does not apply to any residence (other than a residence constructed by the taxpayer) unless there is attached to the return of tax on which the credit is claimed a written certification (which may be in any form) signed by the seller of such residence that—

(A) construction of the residence began before March 26, 1975, and

(B) the purchase price of the residence is the lowest price at which the residence was offered for sale after February 28, 1975.

For purposes of this paragraph, a written certification filed by a taxpayer is sufficient whether or not it is on a form prescribed by the Secretary so long as such certification is signed by the seller and contains the information required under this paragraph.

• 1976, Tax Reform Act of 1976 (P.L. 94-455)

P.L. 94-455, §1906(b)(13)(A):

Amended 1954 Code by substituting "Secretary" for "Secretary or his delegate" each place it appeared. **Effective** 2-1-77.

• 1975, Emergency Compensation and Special Unemployment Assistance Extension Act of 1975 (P.L. 94-45)

P.L. 94-45:

Amended Code Sec. 44(e)(4). **Effective** as noted therein. Prior to amendment Code Sec. 44(e)(4) read as follows:

(4) Certification Must Be Attached to Return.—This section shall not apply to any residence (other than a residence constructed by the taxpayer) unless there is attached to the return of tax on which the credit is claimed a certification by the seller, in accordance with the regulations prescribed by the Secretary or his delegate, that the purchase price is the lowest price at which the residence was ever offered for sale.

• 1975, Tax Reduction Act of 1975 (P.L. 94-12)

P.L. 94-12, §208(a):

Added Code Sec. 44. **Effective** as noted in Code Sec. 44(e).

P.L. 94-12, §208(b)-(c), as amended by P.L. 94-45, provides:

(b) Suits to Recover Amounts of Price Increases.—If—

(1) any person certifies under section 44(e)(4) of the Internal Revenue Code of 1954 that the price for which a residence was sold is the lowest price at which the residence was ever offered for sale after February 28, 1975, and

(2) the price for which the residence was sold exceeded the lowest price at which the residence was ever offered for sale after February 28, 1975.

such person shall be liable to the purchaser of such residence in an amount equal to three times the amount of such excess. The United States district courts shall have jurisdiction of suits to recover such amounts without regard to any other provision of law. In any suit brought under this subsection in which judgment is entered for the purchaser, he shall also be entitled to recover a reasonable attorney's fee.

(c) Denial of Deduction.—Notwithstanding the provisions of section 162 or 212 of the Internal Revenue Code of 1954, no deduction shall be allowed in computing taxable income for two-thirds of any amount paid or incurred on a judgment entered against any person in a suit brought under subsection (b).

[Sec. 44B—Repealed]

Amendments

• 1984, Deficit Reduction Act of 1984 (P.L. 98-369)

P.L. 98-369, §474(m)(1):

Repealed Code Sec. 44B. **Effective** for tax years beginning after 12-31-83, and to carrybacks from such years. Prior to repeal, Code Sec. 44B read as follows:

SEC. 44B. CREDIT FOR EMPLOYMENT OF CERTAIN NEW EMPLOYEES.

(a) GENERAL RULE.—At the election of the taxpayer, there shall be allowed, as a credit against the tax imposed by this chapter, the amount determined under subpart D of this part.

(b) REGULATIONS.—The Secretary shall prescribe such regulations as may be necessary to carry out the purposes of this section and subpart D.

(c) ELECTION.—

(1) TIME FOR MAKING ELECTION.—An election under subsection (a) for any taxable year may be made (or revoked) at any time before the expiration of the 3-year period beginning on the last date prescribed by law for filing the return for such taxable year (determined without regard to extensions).

(2) MANNER OF MAKING ELECTION.—Any election under subsection (a) (or revocation thereof) shall be made in such manner as the Secretary may by regulations prescribe.

• 1980, Technical Corrections Act of 1979 (P.L. 96-222)

P.L. 96-222, §103(a)(6)(G)(i):

Amended Code Sec. 44B(a) by striking out "at the taxpayer" and inserting "of the taxpayer". **Effective** for amounts paid or incurred after 12-31-78, in tax years ending after such date.

P.L. 96-222, §103(a)(6)(G)(ii):

Amended Code Sec. 44B(c)(2) by striking out "may be" and inserting "may by". **Effective** for amounts paid or incurred after 12-31-78, in tax years ending after such date.

• 1978, Revenue Act of 1978 (P.L. 95-600)

P.L. 95-600, §321(b)(1) as amended by P.L. 96-222, §301(a)(6)(B):

Amended Code Sec. 44B. **Effective**, originally, to amounts paid or incurred after 1978, in tax years ending after such date, but P.L. 96-222, §301(a)(6)(B) made the amendments applicable to tax years beginning after 1976. Prior to amendment Code Sec. 44B read as follows:

"(a) GENERAL RULE.—There shall be allowed as a credit against the tax imposed by this chapter the amount determined under subpart D of this part.

"(b) REGULATIONS.—The Secretary shall prescribe such regulations as may be necessary to carry out the purposes of this section and subpart D."

• 1977, Tax Reduction and Simplification Act of 1975 (P.L. 95-30)

P.L. 95-30, §202(a):

Added Code Sec. 44B. **Effective** for tax years beginning after 12-31-76, and for credit carrybacks from such years.

[Sec. 45]

SEC. 45. ELECTRICITY PRODUCED FROM CERTAIN RENEWABLE RESOURCES, etc. [sic]

[Sec. 45(a)]

(a) GENERAL RULE.—For purposes of section 38, the renewable electricity production credit for any taxable year is an amount equal to the product of—

(1) 1.5 cents, multiplied by
(2) the kilowatt hours of electricity—
(A) produced by the taxpayer—
(i) from qualified energy resources, and
(ii) at a qualified facility during the 10-year period beginning on the date the facility was originally placed in service, and
(B) sold by the taxpayer to an unrelated person during the taxable year.

Amendments

• 2004, American Jobs Creation Act of 2004 (P.L. 108-357)

P.L. 108-357, §710(b)(3)(B):

Amended the heading of Code Sec. 45 by inserting before the period at the end ", etc". **Effective** generally for electricity produced and sold after 10-22-2004, in tax years ending after such date.

[Sec. 45(b)]

(b) LIMITATIONS AND ADJUSTMENTS.—

(1) PHASEOUT OF CREDIT.—The amount of the credit determined under subsection (a) shall be reduced by an amount which bears the same ratio to the amount of the credit (determined without regard to this paragraph) as—

(A) the amount by which the reference price for the calendar year in which the sale occurs exceeds 8 cents, bears to

(B) 3 cents.

(2) CREDIT AND PHASEOUT ADJUSTMENT BASED ON INFLATION.—The 1.5 cent amount in subsection (a), the 8 cent amount in paragraph (1), the $4.375 amount in subsection (e)(8)(A), the $3 amount in subsection (e)(8)(D)(ii)(I), and in subsection (e)(8)(B)(i) the reference price of fuel used as a feedstock (within the meaning of subsection (c)(7)(A)) in 2002 shall each be adjusted by multiplying such amount by the inflation adjustment factor for the calendar year in which the sale occurs. If any amount as increased under the preceding sentence is not a multiple of 0.1 cent, such amount shall be rounded to the nearest multiple of 0.1 cent.

(3) CREDIT REDUCED FOR GRANTS, TAX-EXEMPT BONDS, SUBSIDIZED ENERGY FINANCING, AND OTHER CREDITS.—The amount of the credit determined under subsection (a) with respect to any project for any taxable year (determined after the application of paragraphs (1) and (2)) shall be reduced by the amount which is the product of the amount so determined for such year and the lesser of ½ or a fraction—

(A) the numerator of which is the sum, for the taxable year and all prior taxable years, of—

(i) grants provided by the United States, a State, or a political subdivision of a State for use in connection with the project,

(ii) proceeds of an issue of State or local government obligations used to provide financing for the project the interest on which is exempt from tax under section 103,

(iii) the aggregate amount of subsidized energy financing provided (directly or indirectly) under a Federal, State, or local program provided in connection with the project, and

(iv) the amount of any other credit allowable with respect to any property which is part of the project, and

(B) the denominator of which is the aggregate amount of additions to the capital account for the project for the taxable year and all prior taxable years.

The amounts under the preceding sentence for any taxable year shall be determined as of the close of the taxable year. This paragraph shall not apply with respect to any facility described in subsection (d)(2)(A)(ii).

(4) CREDIT RATE AND PERIOD FOR ELECTRICITY PRODUCED AND SOLD FROM CERTAIN FACILITIES.—

(A) CREDIT RATE.—In the case of electricity produced and sold in any calendar year after 2003 at any qualified facility described in paragraph (3), (5), (6), (7), (9), or (11) of subsection (d), the amount in effect under subsection (a)(1) for such calendar year (determined before the application of the last sentence of paragraph (2) of this subsection) shall be reduced by one-half.

(B) CREDIT PERIOD.—

(i) IN GENERAL.—Except as provided in clause (ii) or clause (iii), in the case of any facility described in paragraph (3), (4), (5), (6), or (7) of subsection (d), the 5-year period beginning on the date the facility was originally placed in service shall be substituted for the 10-year period in subsection (a)(2)(A)(ii).

(ii) CERTAIN OPEN-LOOP BIOMASS FACILITIES.—In the case of any facility described in subsection (d)(3)(A)(ii) placed in service before the date of the enactment of this paragraph, the 5-year period beginning on January 1, 2005, shall be substituted for the 10-year period in subsection (a)(2)(A)(ii).

(iii) TERMINATION.—Clause (i) shall not apply to any facility placed in service after the date of the enactment of this clause.

Amendments

• 2008, Energy Improvement and Extension Act of 2008 (P.L. 110-343)

P.L. 110-343, Division B, §102(d):

Amended Code Sec. 45(b)(4)(A) by striking "or (9)" and inserting "(9), or (11)". **Effective** for electricity produced and sold after 10-3-2008, in tax years ending after such date.

P.L. 110-343, Division B, §108(b)(2):

Amended Code Sec. 45(b)(2) by inserting "the $3 amount in subsection (e)(8)(D)(ii)(I)," after "subsection (e)(8)(A),". **Effective** for fuel produced and sold after 9-30-2008.

• 2005, Energy Tax Incentives Act of 2005 (P.L. 109-58)

P.L. 109-58, §1301(b)(1)-(2):

Amended Code Sec. 45(b)(4)(B) by inserting "or clause (iii)" after "clause (ii)" in clause (i), and by adding at the end a new clause (iii). **Effective** 8-8-2005.

P.L. 109-58, §1301(c)(2):

Amended Code Sec. 45(b)(4)(A) by striking "or (7)" and inserting "(7), or (9)". **Effective** 8-8-2005.

P.L. 109-58, §1301(f)(1):

Amended Code Sec. 45(b)(4)(B)(ii) by striking "the date of the enactment of this Act" and inserting "January 1, 2005,". **Effective** as if included in the amendments made by section 710 of P.L. 108-357 [**effective** generally for electricity produced and sold after 12-31-2004, in tax years ending after such date.—CCH].

• 2004, American Jobs Creation Act of 2004 (P.L. 108-357)

P.L. 108-357, §710(b)(3)(C):

Amended Code Sec. 45(b)(2) by striking "The 1.5 cent amount" and all that follows through "paragraph (1)" and inserting "The 1.5 cent amount in subsection (a), the 8 cent amount in paragraph (1), the $4.375 amount in subsection (e)(8)(A), and in subsection (e)(8)(B)(i) the reference price of fuel used as a feedstock (within the meaning of subsection (c)(7)(A)) in 2002". **Effective** generally for electricity produced and sold after 10-22-2004, in tax years ending after such date. For a special rule, see Act Sec. 710(g)(4), below. Prior to amendment, Code Sec. 45(b)(2) read as follows:

(2) CREDIT AND PHASEOUT ADJUSTMENT BASED ON INFLATION.—The 1.5 cent amount in subsection (a) and the 8 cent amount in paragraph (1) shall each be adjusted by multiplying such amount by the inflation adjustment factor for the calendar year in which the sale occurs. If any amount as increased under the preceding sentence is not a multiple of 0.1 cent, such amount shall be rounded to the nearest multiple of 0.1 cent.

P.L. 108-357, §710(c):

Amended Code Sec. 45(b) by adding at the end a new paragraph (4). **Effective** for electricity produced and sold after 12-31-2004, in tax years ending after such date. For a special rule, see Act Sec. 710(g)(4), below.

P.L. 108-357, §710(f)(1)-(2):

Amended Code Sec. 45(b)(3) by inserting "the lesser of 1/2 or" before "a fraction" in the matter preceding subparagraph (A), and by adding at the end a new sentence. **Effective** generally for electricity produced and sold after 10-22-2004, in tax years ending after such date. For special rules, see Act Sec. 710(g)(2) and (4), below.

P.L. 108-357, §710(g)(2), provides:

(2) CERTAIN BIOMASS FACILITIES.—With respect to any facility described in section 45(d)(3)(A)(ii) of the Internal Revenue Code of 1986, as added by subsection (b)(1), which is placed in service before the date of the enactment of this Act, the amendments made by this section shall apply to electricity produced and sold after December 31, 2004, in taxable years ending after such date.

P.L. 108-357, §710(g)(4), as amended by P.L. 109-58, §1301(f)(6), provides:

(4) NONAPPLICATION OF AMENDMENTS TO PREEFFECTIVE DATE POULTRY WASTE FACILITIES.—The amendments made by this section shall not apply with respect to any poultry waste facility (within the meaning of section 45(c)(3)(C), as in effect on the day before the date of the enactment of this Act) placed in service before January 1, 2005.

[Sec. 45(c)]

(c) RESOURCES.—For purposes of this section:

(1) IN GENERAL.—The term "qualified energy resources" means—

(A) wind,

(B) closed-loop biomass,

(C) open-loop biomass,

(D) geothermal energy,

(E) solar energy,

(F) small irrigation power,

(G) municipal solid waste,

(H) qualified hydropower production, and

(I) marine and hydrokinetic renewable energy.

(2) CLOSED-LOOP BIOMASS.—The term "closed-loop biomass" means any organic material from a plant which is planted exclusively for purposes of being used at a qualified facility to produce electricity.

(3) OPEN-LOOP BIOMASS.—

(A) IN GENERAL.—The term "open-loop biomass" means—

(i) any agricultural livestock waste nutrients, or

(ii) any solid, nonhazardous, cellulosic waste material or any lignin material which is derived from—

(I) any of the following forest related resources: mill and harvesting residues, precommercial thinnings, slash, and brush,

(II) solid wood waste materials, including waste pallets, crates, dunnage, manufacturing and construction wood wastes (other than pressure-treated, chemically-treated, or painted wood wastes), and landscape or right-of-way tree trimmings, but not including municipal solid waste, gas derived from the biodegradation of solid waste, or paper which is commonly recycled, or

(III) agriculture sources, including orchard tree crops, vineyard, grain, legumes, sugar, and other crop by-products or residues.

Such term shall not include closed-loop biomass or biomass burned in conjunction with fossil fuel (cofiring) beyond such fossil fuel required for startup and flame stabilization.

(B) AGRICULTURAL LIVESTOCK WASTE NUTRIENTS.—

(i) IN GENERAL.—The term "agricultural livestock waste nutrients" means agricultural livestock manure and litter, including wood shavings, straw, rice hulls, and other bedding material for the disposition of manure.

(ii) AGRICULTURAL LIVESTOCK.—The term "agricultural livestock" includes bovine, swine, poultry, and sheep.

(4) GEOTHERMAL ENERGY.—The term "geothermal energy" means energy derived from a geothermal deposit (within the meaning of section 613(e)(2)).

(5) SMALL IRRIGATION POWER.—The term "small irrigation power" means power—

(A) generated without any dam or impoundment of water through an irrigation system canal or ditch, and

(B) the nameplate capacity rating of which is not less than 150 kilowatts but is less than 5 megawatts.

(6) MUNICIPAL SOLID WASTE.—The term "municipal solid waste" has the meaning given the term "solid waste" under section 2(27) of the Solid Waste Disposal Act (42 U.S.C. 6903).

(7) REFINED COAL.—

(A) IN GENERAL.—The term "refined coal" means a fuel—

(i) which—

(I) is a liquid, gaseous, or solid fuel produced from coal (including lignite) or high carbon fly ash, including such fuel used as a feedstock,

(II) is sold by the taxpayer with the reasonable expectation that it will be used for purpose of producing steam, and

(III) is certified by the taxpayer as resulting (when used in the production of steam) in a qualified emission reduction.

(ii) which is steel industry fuel.

(B) QUALIFIED EMISSION REDUCTION.—The term "qualified emission reduction" means a reduction of at least 20 percent of the emissions of nitrogen oxide and at least 40 percent of the emissions of either sulfur dioxide or mercury released when burning the refined coal (excluding any dilution caused by materials combined or added during the production process), as compared to the emissions released when burning the feedstock coal or comparable coal predominantly available in the marketplace as of January 1, 2003.

(C) STEEL INDUSTRY FUEL.—

(i) IN GENERAL.—The term "steel industry fuel" means a fuel which—

(I) is produced through a process of liquifying coal waste sludge and distributing it on coal, and

(II) is used as a feedstock for the manufacture of coke.

(ii) COAL WASTE SLUDGE.—The term "coal waste sludge"' means the tar decanter sludge and related byproducts of the coking process, including such materials that have been stored in ground, in tanks and in lagoons, that have been treated as hazardous wastes under applicable Federal environmental rules absent liquefaction and processing with coal into a feedstock for the manufacture of coke.

(8) QUALIFIED HYDROPOWER PRODUCTION.—

(A) IN GENERAL.—The term "qualified hydropower production" means—

(i) in the case of any hydroelectric dam which was placed in service on or before the date of the enactment of this paragraph, the incremental hydropower production for the taxable year, and

(ii) in the case of any nonhydroelectric dam described in subparagraph (C), the hydropower production from the facility for the taxable year.

(B) DETERMINATION OF INCREMENTAL HYDROPOWER PRODUCTION.—

(i) IN GENERAL.—For purposes of subparagraph (A), incremental hydropower production for any taxable year shall be equal to the percentage of average annual hydropower production at the facility attributable to the efficiency improvements or additions of capacity placed in service after the date of the enactment of this paragraph, determined by using the same water flow information used to determine an historic average annual hydropower production baseline for such facility. Such percentage and baseline shall be certified by the Federal Energy Regulatory Commission.

(ii) OPERATIONAL CHANGES DISREGARDED.—For purposes of clause (i), the determination of incremental hydropower production shall not be based on any operational changes at such facility not directly associated with the efficiency improvements or additions of capacity.

(C) NONHYDROELECTRIC DAM.—For purposes of subparagraph (A), a facility is described in this subparagraph if—

(i) the hydroelectric project installed on the nonhydroelectric dam is licensed by the Federal Energy Regulatory Commission and meets all other applicable environmental, licensing, and regulatory requirements,

(ii) the nonhydroelectric dam was placed in service before the date of the enactment of this paragraph and operated for flood control, navigation, or water supply purposes and did not produce hydroelectric power on the date of the enactment of this paragraph, and

(iii) the hydroelectric project is operated so that the water surface elevation at any given location and time that would have occurred in the absence of the hydroelectric project is maintained, subject to any license requirements imposed under applicable law that change the water surface elevation for the purpose of improving environmental quality of the affected waterway.

The Secretary, in consultation with the Federal Energy Regulatory Commission, shall certify if a hydroelectric project licensed at a nonhydroelectric dam meets the criteria in clause (iii). Nothing in this section shall affect the standards under which the Federal Energy Regulatory Commission issues licenses for and regulates hydropower projects under part I of the Federal Power Act.

(9) INDIAN COAL.—

(A) IN GENERAL.—The term "Indian coal" means coal which is produced from coal reserves which, on June 14, 2005—

(i) were owned by an Indian tribe, or

(ii) were held in trust by the United States for the benefit of an Indian tribe or its members.

(B) INDIAN TRIBE.—For purposes of this paragraph, the term "Indian tribe" has the meaning given such term by section 7871(c)(3)(E)(ii).

(10) MARINE AND HYDROKINETIC RENEWABLE ENERGY.—

(A) IN GENERAL.—The term "marine and hydrokinetic renewable energy" means energy derived from—

(i) waves, tides, and currents in oceans, estuaries, and tidal areas,

(ii) free flowing water in rivers, lakes, and streams,

(iii) free flowing water in an irrigation system, canal, or other man-made channel, including projects that utilize nonmechanical structures to accelerate the flow of water for electric power production purposes, or

(iv) differentials in ocean temperature (ocean thermal energy conversion).

(B) EXCEPTIONS.—Such term shall not include any energy which is derived from any source which utilizes a dam, diversionary structure (except as provided in subparagraph (A)(iii)), or impoundment for electric power production purposes.

Amendments

• 2008, Energy Improvement and Extension Act of 2008 (P.L. 110-343)

P.L. 110-343, Division B, §101(b)(1)(A)-(C):

Amended Code Sec. 45(c)(7)(A)(i), as amended by Act Sec. 108, by striking subclause (IV), by adding "and" at the end of subclause (II), and by striking ", and" at the end of subclause (III) and inserting a period. **Effective** for coal produced and sold from facilities placed in service after 12-31-2008. Prior to being stricken, Code Sec. 45(c)(7)(A)(i)(IV) read as follows:

(IV) is produced in such a manner as to result in an increase of at least 50 percent in the market value of the refined coal (excluding any increase caused by materials combined or added during the production process), as compared to the value of the feedstock coal, or

P.L. 110-343, Division B, §101(b)(2):

Amended Code Sec. 45(c)(7)(B) by inserting "at least 40 percent of the emissions of" after "nitrogen oxide and". **Effective** for coal produced and sold from facilities placed in service after 12-31-2008.

P.L. 110-343, Division B, §101(e):

Amended Code Sec. 45(c)(8)(C). **Effective** for property originally placed in service after 12-31-2008. Prior to amendment, Code Sec. 45(c)(8)(C) read as follows:

(C) NONHYDROELECTRIC DAM.—For purposes of subparagraph (A), a facility is described in this subparagraph if—

(i) the facility is licensed by the Federal Energy Regulatory Commission and meets all other applicable environmental, licensing, and regulatory requirements,

(ii) the facility was placed in service before the date of the enactment of this paragraph and did not produce hydroelectric power on the date of the enactment of this paragraph, and

(iii) turbines or other generating devices are to be added to the facility after such date to produce hydroelectric power, but only if there is not any enlargement of the diversion structure, or construction or enlargement of a bypass channel, or the impoundment or any withholding of any additional water from the natural stream channel.

P.L. 110-343, Division B, §102(a):

Amended Code Sec. 45(c)(1) by striking "and" at the end of subparagraph (G), by striking the period at the end of subparagraph (H) and inserting ", and", and by adding at the end a new subparagraph (I). **Effective** for electricity produced and sold after 10-3-2008, in tax years ending after such date.

P.L. 110-343, Division B, §102(b):

Amended Code Sec. 45(c) by adding at the end a new paragraph (10). **Effective** for electricity produced and sold after 10-3-2008, in tax years ending after such date.

P.L. 110-343, Division B, §108(a)(1):

Amended Code Sec. 45(c)(7)(A), as amended by this Act. **Effective** for fuel produced and sold after 9-30-2008. Prior to amendment, Code Sec. 45(c)(7)(A) read as follows:

(A) IN GENERAL.—The term "refined coal" means a fuel which—

(i) is a liquid, gaseous, or solid fuel produced from coal (including lignite) or high carbon fly ash, including such fuel used as a feedstock,

(ii) is sold by the taxpayer with the reasonable expectation that it will be used for purpose of producing steam,

(iii) is certified by the taxpayer as resulting (when used in the production of steam) in a qualified emission reduction, and

(iv) is produced in such a manner as to result in an increase of at least 50 percent in the market value of the refined coal (excluding any increase caused by materials combined or added during the production process), as compared to the value of the feedstock coal.

P.L. 110-343, Division B, §108(a)(2):

Amended Code Sec. 45(c)(7) by adding at the end a new subparagraph (C). **Effective** for fuel produced and sold after 9-30-2008.

• 2007, Tax Technical Corrections Act of 2007 (P.L. 110-172)

P.L. 110-172, §7(b)(1):

Amended Code Sec. 45(c)(3)(A)(ii) by striking "which is segregated from other waste material and" after "lignin material". **Effective** as if included in the provision of the American Jobs Creation Act of 2004 (P.L. 108-357) to which it relates [**effective** generally for electricity produced and sold after 10-22-2004, in tax years ending after such date. For special rules, see P.L. 108-357, §710(g)(2) and (4), in the amendment notes below.—CCH].

• 2005, Gulf Opportunity Zone Act of 2005 (P.L. 109-135)

P.L. 109-135, §402(b):

Amended Code Sec. 45(c)(3)(A)(ii) by striking "nonhazardous lignin waste material" and inserting "lignin material". **Effective** as if included in the provision of the Energy Policy Act of 2005 (P.L. 109-58) to which it relates [**effective**, generally, for electricity produced and sold after 10-22-2004, in tax years ending after such date.—CCH].

P.L. 109-135, §403(t):

Amended Code Sec. 45(c)(7)(A)(i) by striking "synthetic" before "fuel produced". **Effective** as if included in the provision of the American Jobs Creation Act of 2004 (P.L. 108-357) to which it relates [**effective** for electricity produced and sold after 10-22-2004, in tax years ending after such date, generally.—CCH].

• 2005, Energy Tax Incentives Act of 2005 (P.L. 109-58)

P.L. 109-58, §1301(c)(1):

Amended Code Sec. 45(c)(1) by striking "and" at the end of subparagraph (F), by striking the period at the end of subparagraph (G) and inserting ", and", and by adding at the end a new subparagraph (H). **Effective** 8-8-2005.

P.L. 109-58, §1301(c)(3):

Amended Code Sec. 45(c) by adding at the end a new paragraph (8). **Effective** 8-8-2005.

P.L. 109-58, §1301(d)(2):

Amended Code Sec. 45(c), as amended by this Act, by adding at the end a new paragraph (9). **Effective** 8-8-2005.

P.L. 109-58, §1301(d)(4):

Amended the heading for Code Sec. 45(c) by striking "QUALIFIED ENERGY RESOURCES AND REFINED COAL" and inserting "RESOURCES". **Effective** 8-8-2005.

P.L. 109-58, §1301(f)(2):

Amended Code Sec. 45(c)(3)(A)(ii) by inserting "or any nonhazardous lignin waste material" after "cellulosic waste material". **Effective** as if included in the amendments made by section 710 of P.L. 108-357 [**effective** generally for electricity produced and sold after 10-22-2004, in tax years ending after such date.—CCH].

• 2004, American Jobs Creation Act of 2004 (P.L. 108-357)

P.L. 108-357, §710(a):

Amended Code Sec. 45(c). **Effective** generally for electricity produced and sold after 10-22-2004, in tax years ending after such date. For special rules, see Act Sec. 710(g)(2) and (4), below. Prior to amendment, Code Sec. 45(c) read as follows:

(c) DEFINITIONS.—For purposes of this section—

(1) QUALIFIED ENERGY RESOURCES.—The term "qualified energy resources" means—

(A) wind,

(B) closed-loop biomass, and

(C) poultry waste.

(2) CLOSED-LOOP BIOMASS.—The term "closed-loop biomass" means any organic material from a plant which is planted exclusively for purposes of being used at a qualified facility to produce electricity.

(3) QUALIFIED FACILITY.—

(A) WIND FACILITY.—In the case of a facility using wind to produce electricity, the term "qualified facility" means any facility owned by the taxpayer which is originally placed in service after December 31, 1993, and before January 1, 2006.

(B) CLOSED-LOOP BIOMASS FACILITY.—In the case of a facility using closed-loop biomass to produce electricity, the term "qualified facility" means any facility owned by the taxpayer which is originally placed in service after December 31, 1992, and before January 1, 2006.

(C) POULTRY WASTE FACILITY.—In the case of a facility using poultry waste to produce electricity, the term "qualified facility" means any facility of the taxpayer which is originally placed in service after December 31, 1999, and before January 1, 2006.

(4) POULTRY WASTE.—The term "poultry waste" means poultry manure and litter, including wood shavings, straw, rice hulls, and other bedding material for the disposition of manure.

P.L. 108-357, §710(g)(2), provides:

(2) CERTAIN BIOMASS FACILITIES.—With respect to any facility described in section 45(d)(3)(A)(ii) of the Internal Revenue Code of 1986, as added by subsection (b)(1), which is placed in service before the date of the enactment of this Act, the amendments made by this section shall apply to electricity produced and sold after December 31, 2004, in taxable years ending after such date.

P.L. 108-357, §710(g)(4), as amended by P.L. 109-58, §1301(f)(6), provides:

(4) NONAPPLICATION OF AMENDMENTS TO PREEFFECTIVE DATE POULTRY WASTE FACILITIES.—The amendments made by this section shall not apply with respect to any poultry waste facility (within the meaning of section 45(c)(3)(C), as in effect on the day before the date of the enactment of this Act) placed in service before January 1, 2005.

• 2004, Working Families Tax Relief Act of 2004 (P.L. 108-311)

P.L. 108-311, §313(a):

Amended Code Sec. 45(c)(3)(A)-(C) by striking "January 1, 2004" and inserting "January 1, 2006". **Effective** for facilities placed in service after 12-31-2003.

• 2002, Job Creation and Worker Assistance Act of 2002 (P.L. 107-147)

P.L. 107-147, §603(a):

Amended Code Sec. 45(c)(3)(A)-(C) by striking "2002" and inserting "2004". **Effective** for facilities placed in service after 12-31-2001.

• 1999, Tax Relief Extension Act of 1999 (P.L. 106-170)

P.L. 106-170, §507(a):

Amended Code Sec. 45(c)(3). **Effective** 12-17-99. Prior to amendment, Code Sec. 45(c)(3) read as follows:

(3) QUALIFIED FACILITY.—The term "qualified facility" means any facility owned by the taxpayer which is originally placed in service after December 31, 1993 (December 31, 1992, in the case of a facility using closed-loop biomass to produce electricity), and before July 1, 1999.

P.L. 106-170, §507(b)(1):

Amended Code Sec. 45(c)(1) by striking "and" at the end of subparagraph (A), by striking the period at the end of subparagraph (B) and inserting ", and", and by adding at the end a new subparagraph (C). **Effective** 12-17-99.

P.L. 106-170, §507(b)(2):

Amended Code Sec. 45(c) by adding at the end a new paragraph (4). **Effective** 12-17-99.

[Sec. 45(d)]

(d) QUALIFIED FACILITIES.—For purposes of this section:

(1) WIND FACILITY.—In the case of a facility using wind to produce electricity, the term "qualified facility" means any facility owned by the taxpayer which is originally placed in service after December 31, 1993, and before January 1, 2013. Such term shall not include any facility with respect to which any qualified small wind energy property expenditure (as defined in subsection (d)(4) of section 25D) is taken into account in determining the credit under such section.

(2) CLOSED-LOOP BIOMASS FACILITY.—

(A) IN GENERAL.—In the case of a facility using closed-loop biomass to produce electricity, the term "qualified facility" means any facility—

(i) owned by the taxpayer which is originally placed in service after December 31, 1992, and before January 1, 2014, or

(ii) owned by the taxpayer which before January 1, 2014, is originally placed in service and modified to use closed-loop biomass to co-fire with coal, with other biomass, or with both, but only if the modification is approved under the Biomass Power for Rural Development Programs or is part of a pilot project of the Commodity Credit Corporation as described in 65 Fed. Reg. 63052.

(B) EXPANSION OF FACILITY.—Such term shall include a new unit placed in service after the date of the enactment of this subparagraph in connection with a facility described in subparagraph (A)(i), but only to the extent of the increased amount of electricity produced at the facility by reason of such new unit.

(C) SPECIAL RULES.—In the case of a qualified facility described in subparagraph (A)(ii)—

(i) the 10-year period referred to in subsection (a) shall be treated as beginning no earlier than the date of the enactment of this clause, and

(ii) if the owner of such facility is not the producer of the electricity, the person eligible for the credit allowable under subsection (a) shall be the lessee or the operator of such facility.

(3) OPEN-LOOP BIOMASS FACILITIES.—

(A) IN GENERAL.—In the case of a facility using open-loop biomass to produce electricity, the term "qualified facility" means any facility owned by the taxpayer which—

(i) in the case of a facility using agricultural livestock waste nutrients—

(I) is originally placed in service after the date of the enactment of this subclause and before January 1, 2014, and

(II) the nameplate capacity rating of which is not less than 150 kilowatts, and

(ii) in the case of any other facility, is originally placed in service before January 1, 2014.

(B) EXPANSION OF FACILITY.—Such term shall include a new unit placed in service after the date of the enactment of this subparagraph in connection with a facility described in subparagraph (A), but only to the extent of the increased amount of electricity produced at the facility by reason of such new unit.

(C) CREDIT ELIGIBILITY.—In the case of any facility described in subparagraph (A), if the owner of such facility is not the producer of the electricity, the person eligible for the credit allowable under subsection (a) shall be the lessee or the operator of such facility.

(4) GEOTHERMAL OR SOLAR ENERGY FACILITY.—In the case of a facility using geothermal or solar energy to produce electricity, the term "qualified facility" means any facility owned by the taxpayer which is originally placed in service after the date of the enactment of this paragraph and before January 1, 2014 (January 1, 2006, in the case of a facility using solar energy). Such term shall not include any property described in section 48(a)(3) the basis of which is taken into account by the taxpayer for purposes of determining the energy credit under section 48.

(5) SMALL IRRIGATION POWER FACILITY.—In the case of a facility using small irrigation power to produce electricity, the term "qualified facility" means any facility owned by the taxpayer which is originally placed in service after the date of the enactment of this paragraph and before October 3, 2008.

(6) LANDFILL GAS FACILITIES.—In the case of a facility producing electricity from gas derived from the biodegradation of municipal solid waste, the term "qualified facility" means any facility owned by the taxpayer which is originally placed in service after the date of the enactment of this paragraph and before January 1, 2014.

(7) TRASH FACILITIES.—In the case of a facility (other than a facility described in paragraph (6)) which uses municipal solid waste to produce electricity, the term "qualified facility" means any facility owned by the taxpayer which is originally placed in service after the date of the enactment of this paragraph and before January 1, 2014. Such term shall include a new unit placed in service in connection with a facility placed in service on or before the date of the enactment of this paragraph, but only to the extent of the increased amount of electricity produced at the facility by reason of such new unit.

(8) REFINED COAL PRODUCTION FACILITY.—In the case of a facility that produces refined coal, the term "refined coal production facility" means—

(A) with respect to a facility producing steel industry fuel, any facility (or any modification to a facility) which is placed in service before January 1, 2010, and

(B) with respect to any other facility producing refined coal, any facility placed in service after the date of the enactment of the American Jobs Creation Act of 2004 and before January 1, 2010.

(9) QUALIFIED HYDROPOWER FACILITY.—In the case of a facility producing qualified hydroelectric production described in subsection (c)(8), the term "qualified facility" means—

(A) in the case of any facility producing incremental hydropower production, such facility but only to the extent of its incremental hydropower production attributable to efficiency improvements or additions to capacity described in subsection (c)(8)(B) placed in service after the date of the enactment of this paragraph and before January 1, 2014, and

(B) any other facility placed in service after the date of the enactment of this paragraph and before January 1, 2014.

(C) CREDIT PERIOD.—In the case of a qualified facility described in subparagraph (A), the 10-year period referred to in subsection (a) shall be treated as beginning on the date the efficiency improvements or additions to capacity are placed in service.

(10) INDIAN COAL PRODUCTION FACILITY.—In the case of a facility that produces Indian coal, the term "Indian coal production facility" means a facility which is placed in service before January 1, 2009.

(11) MARINE AND HYDROKINETIC RENEWABLE ENERGY FACILITIES.—In the case of a facility producing electricity from marine and hydrokinetic renewable energy, the term "qualified facility" means any facility owned by the taxpayer—

(A) which has a nameplate capacity rating of at least 150 kilowatts, and

(B) which is originally placed in service on or after the date of the enactment of this paragraph and before January 1, 2014.

Amendments

• 2009, American Recovery and Reinvestment Tax Act of 2009 (P.L. 111-5)

P.L. 111-5, §1101(a)(1)-(3):

Amended Code Sec. 45(d) by striking "2010" in paragraph (1) and inserting "2013", by striking "2011" each place it appears in paragraphs (2), (3), (4), (6), (7) and (9) and inserting "2014", and by striking "2012" in paragraph (11)(B) and inserting "2014". **Effective** for property placed in service after 2-17-2009.

P.L. 111-5, §1101(b):

Amended Code Sec. 45(d)(5) by striking "and before" and all that follows and inserting "and before October 3, 2008.". **Effective** as if included in section 102 of the Energy Improvement and Extension Act of 2008 (P.L. 110-343) [**effective** for electricity produced and sold after 10-3-2008, in tax years ending after such date.—CCH]. Prior to being stricken, "and before" and all that followed read as follows:

and before January 1, 2011.

• 2008, Energy Improvement and Extension Act of 2008 (P.L. 110-343)

P.L. 110-343, Division B, §101(a)(1):

Amended Code Sec. 45(d)(1) and (8) by striking "January 1, 2009" and inserting "January 1, 2010". **Effective** for property originally placed in service after 12-31-2008.

P.L. 110-343, Division B, §101(a)(2)(A)-(G):

Amended Code Sec. 45(d) by striking "January 1, 2009" and inserting "January 1, 2011" in clauses (i) and (ii) of paragraph (2)(A), clauses (i)(I) and (ii) of paragraph (3)(A), paragraphs (4), (5), (6), and (7), and subparagraphs (A) and (B) of paragraph (9). **Effective** for property originally placed in service after 12-31-2008.

P.L. 110-343, Division B, §101(c)(1)-(2):

Amended Code Sec. 45(d)(7) by striking "facility which burns" and inserting "facility (other than a facility described in paragraph (6)) which uses", and by striking "COMBUSTION" following "TRASH" in the heading. **Effective** for electricity produced and sold after 10-3-2008.

P.L. 110-343, Division B, §101(d)(1):

Amended Code Sec. 45(d)(3) by redesignating subparagraph (B) as subparagraph (C) and by inserting after subparagraph (A) a new subparagraph (B). **Effective** for property placed in service after 10-3-2008.

P.L. 110-343, Division B, §101(d)(2):

Amended Code Sec. 45(d)(2) by redesignating subparagraph (B) as subparagraph (C) and inserting after subparagraph (A) a new subparagraph (B). **Effective** for property placed in service after 10-3-2008.

P.L. 110-343, Division B, §102(c):

Amended Code Sec. 45(d) by adding at the end a new paragraph (11). **Effective** for electricity produced and sold after 10-3-2008, in tax years ending after such date.

P.L. 110-343, Division B, §102(e):

Amended Code Sec. 45(d)(5), as amended by Act Sec. 101, by striking "January 1, 2012" and inserting "the date of the enactment of paragraph (11)". **Effective** for electricity produced and sold after 10-3-2008, in tax years ending after such date. [This amendment cannot be made because the text "January 1, 2012" does not exist. —CCH.]

P.L. 110-343, Division B, §106(c)(3)(B):

Amended Code Sec. 45(d)(1) by adding at the end a new sentence. **Effective** for tax years beginning after 12-31-2007.

P.L. 110-343, Division B, §108(c):

Amended Code Sec. 45(d)(8), as amended by this Act. **Effective** for fuel produced and sold after 9-30-2008. Prior to amendment, Code Sec. 45(d)(8) read as follows:

(8) REFINED COAL PRODUCTION FACILITY.—In the case of a facility that produces refined coal, the term "refined coal production facility" means a facility which is placed in service after the date of the enactment of this paragraph and before January 1, 2010.

• 2007, Tax Technical Corrections Act of 2007 (P.L. 110-172)

P.L. 110-172, §7(b)(2):

Amended Code Sec. 45(d)(2)(B) by inserting "and" at the end of clause (i), by striking clause (ii), and by redesignating clause (iii) as clause (ii). **Effective** as if included in the provision of the American Jobs Creation Act of 2004 (P.L. 108-357) to which it relates [**effective** generally for electricity produced and sold after 10-22-2004, in tax years ending after such date. For special rules, see P.L. 108-357, §710(g)(2) and (4), in the amendment notes below.—CCH]. Prior to being stricken, Code Sec. 45(d)(2)(B)(ii) read as follows:

(ii) the amount of the credit determined under subsection (a) with respect to the facility shall be an amount equal to the amount determined without regard to this clause multiplied by the ratio of the thermal content of the closed-loop biomass used in such facility to the thermal content of all fuels used in such facility, and

• 2006, Tax Relief and Health Care Act of 2006 (P.L. 109-432)

P.L. 109-432, Division A, §201:

Amended Code Sec. 45(d) by striking "January 1, 2008" each place it appears and inserting "January 1, 2009". **Effective** 12-20-2006.

• 2005, Gulf Opportunity Zone Act of 2005 (P.L. 109-135)

P.L. 109-135, §412(j)(1)-(2):

Amended Code Sec. 45(d) by striking "The term" and inserting "In the case of a facility that produces refined coal, the term" in paragraph (8), and by striking "The term" and inserting "In the case of a facility that produces Indian coal, the term" in paragraph (10). **Effective** 12-21-2005.

• 2005, Energy Tax Incentives Act of 2005 (P.L. 109-58)

P.L. 109-58, §1301(a)(1)-(2):

Amended Code Sec. 45(d) by striking "January 1, 2006" each place it appears in paragraphs (1), (2), (3), (5), (6), and (7) and inserting "January 1, 2008", and by striking "January 1, 2006" in paragraph (4) and inserting "January 1, 2008 (January 1, 2006, in the case of a facility using solar energy)". **Effective** 8-8-2005.

P.L. 109-58, §1301(c)(4):

Amended Code Sec. 45(d) by adding at the end a new paragraph (9). **Effective** 8-8-2005.

P.L. 109-58, §1301(d)(3):

Amended Code Sec. 45(d), as amended by this Act, by adding at the end a new paragraph (10). **Effective** 8-8-2005.

P.L. 109-58, §1301(e):

Amended Code Sec. 45(d)(7) by adding at the end a new sentence. **Effective** as if included in the amendments made by section 710 of P.L. 108-357 [**effective** generally for electricity produced and sold after 10-22-2004, in tax years ending after such date.—CCH].

• 2004, American Jobs Creation Act of 2004 (P.L. 108-357)

P.L. 108-357, §710(b)(1):

Amended Code Sec. 45 by redesignating subsection (d) as subsection (e) and by inserting after subsection (c) a new subsection (d). **Effective** generally for electricity produced and sold after 10-22-2004, in tax years ending after such date. For special rules, see Act Sec. 710(g)(2) and (4), below.

P.L. 108-357, §710(g)(2), provides:

(2) CERTAIN BIOMASS FACILITIES.—With respect to any facility described in section 45(d)(3)(A)(ii) of the Internal Revenue Code of 1986, as added by subsection (b)(1), which is placed in service before the date of the enactment of this Act, the amendments made by this section shall apply to electricity produced and sold after December 31, 2004, in taxable years ending after such date.

P.L. 108-357, §710(g)(4), as amended by P.L. 109-58, §1301(f)(6), provides:

(4) NONAPPLICATION OF AMENDMENTS TO PREEFFECTIVE DATE POULTRY WASTE FACILITIES.—The amendments made by this section shall not apply with respect to any poultry waste facility (within the meaning of section 45(c)(3)(C), as in effect on the day before the date of the enactment of this Act) placed in service before January 1, 2005.

[Sec. 45(e)]

(e) DEFINITIONS AND SPECIAL RULES.—For purposes of this section—

(1) ONLY PRODUCTION IN THE UNITED STATES TAKEN INTO ACCOUNT.—Sales shall be taken into account under this section only with respect to electricity the production of which is within—

(A) the United States (within the meaning of section 638(1)), or

(B) a possession of the United States (within the meaning of section 638(2)).

(2) COMPUTATION OF INFLATION ADJUSTMENT FACTOR AND REFERENCE PRICE.—

(A) IN GENERAL.—The Secretary shall, not later than April 1 of each calendar year, determine and publish in the Federal Register the inflation adjustment factor and the reference price for such calendar year in accordance with this paragraph.

(B) INFLATION ADJUSTMENT FACTOR.—The term "inflation adjustment factor" means, with respect to a calendar year, a fraction the numerator of which is the GDP implicit price deflator for the preceding calendar year and the denominator of which is the GDP implicit price deflator for the calendar year 1992. The term "GDP implicit price deflator" means the most recent revision of the implicit price deflator for the gross domestic product as computed and published by the Department of Commerce before March 15 of the calendar year.

(C) REFERENCE PRICE.—The term "reference price" means, with respect to a calendar year, the Secretary's determination of the annual average contract price per kilowatt hour of electricity generated from the same qualified energy resource and sold in the previous year in the United States. For purposes of the preceding sentence, only contracts entered into after December 31, 1989, shall be taken into account.

(3) PRODUCTION ATTRIBUTABLE TO THE TAXPAYER.—In the case of a facility in which more than 1 person has an ownership interest, except to the extent provided in regulations prescribed by the Secretary, production from the facility shall be allocated among such persons in proportion to their respective ownership interests in the gross sales from such facility.

(4) RELATED PERSONS.—Persons shall be treated as related to each other if such persons would be treated as a single employer under the regulations prescribed under section 52(b). In the case of a corporation which is a member of an affiliated group of corporations filing a consolidated return, such corporation shall be treated as selling electricity to an unrelated person if such electricity is sold to such a person by another member of such group.

(5) PASS-THRU IN THE CASE OF ESTATES AND TRUSTS.—Under regulations prescribed by the Secretary, rules similar to the rules of subsection (d) of section 52 shall apply.

(6) [Stricken.]

(7) CREDIT NOT TO APPLY TO ELECTRICITY SOLD TO UTILITIES UNDER CERTAIN CONTRACTS.—

(A) IN GENERAL.—The credit determined under subsection (a) shall not apply to electricity—

(i) produced at a qualified facility described in subsection (d)(1) which is originally placed in service after June 30, 1999, and

(ii) sold to a utility pursuant to a contract originally entered into before January 1, 1987 (whether or not amended or restated after that date).

(B) EXCEPTION.—Subparagraph (A) shall not apply if—

(i) the prices for energy and capacity from such facility are established pursuant to an amendment to the contract referred to in subparagraph (A)(ii),

(ii) such amendment provides that the prices set forth in the contract which exceed avoided cost prices determined at the time of delivery shall apply only to annual quantities of electricity (prorated for partial years) which do not exceed the greater of—

(I) the average annual quantity of electricity sold to the utility under the contract during calendar years 1994, 1995, 1996, 1997, and 1998, or

(II) the estimate of the annual electricity production set forth in the contract, or, if there is no such estimate, the greatest annual quantity of electricity sold to the utility under the contract in any of the calendar years 1996, 1997, or 1998, and

(iii) such amendment provides that energy and capacity in excess of the limitation in clause (ii) may be—

(I) sold to the utility only at prices that do not exceed avoided cost prices determined at the time of delivery, or

(II) sold to a third party subject to a mutually agreed upon advance notice to the utility.

For purposes of this subparagraph, avoided cost prices shall be determined as provided for in 18 CFR 292.304(d)(1) or any successor regulation.

(8) REFINED COAL PRODUCTION FACILITIES.—

(A) DETERMINATION OF CREDIT AMOUNT.—In the case of a producer of refined coal, the credit determined under this section (without regard to this paragraph) for any taxable year shall be increased by an amount equal to $4.375 per ton of qualified refined coal—

(i) produced by the taxpayer at a refined coal production facility during the 10-year period beginning on the date the facility was originally placed in service, and

(ii) sold by the taxpayer—

(I) to an unrelated person, and

(II) during such 10-year period and such taxable year.

(B) PHASEOUT OF CREDIT.—The amount of the increase determined under subparagraph (A) shall be reduced by an amount which bears the same ratio to the amount of the increase (determined without regard to this subparagraph) as—

(i) the amount by which the reference price of fuel used as a feedstock (within the meaning of subsection (c)(7)(A)) for the calendar year in which the sale occurs exceeds an amount equal to 1.7 multiplied by the reference price for such fuel in 2002, bears to

(ii) $8.75.

(C) APPLICATION OF RULES.—Rules similar to the rules of the subsection (b)(3) and paragraphs (1) through (5) of this subsection shall apply for purposes of determining the amount of any increase under this paragraph.

(D) SPECIAL RULE FOR STEEL INDUSTRY FUEL.—

(i) IN GENERAL.—In the case of a taxpayer who produces steel industry fuel—

(I) this paragraph shall be applied separately with respect to steel industry fuel and other refined coal, and

(II) in applying this paragraph to steel industry fuel, the modifications in clause (ii) shall apply.

(ii) MODIFICATIONS.—

(I) CREDIT AMOUNT.—Subparagraph (A) shall be applied by substituting "$2 per barrel-of-oil equivalent" for "$4.375 per ton".

(II) CREDIT PERIOD.—In lieu of the 10-year period referred to in clauses (i) and (ii)(II) of subparagraph (A), the credit period shall be the period beginning on the later of the date such facility was originally placed in service, the date the modifications described in clause (iii) were placed in service, or October 1, 2008, and ending on the later of December 31, 2009, or the date which is 1 year after the date such facility or the modifications described in clause (iii) were placed in service.

(III) NO PHASEOUT.—Subparagraph (B) shall not apply.

(iii) MODIFICATIONS.—The modifications described in this clause are modifications to an existing facility which allow such facility to produce steel industry fuel.

(iv) BARREL-OF-OIL EQUIVALENT.—For purposes of this subparagraph, a barrel-of-oil equivalent is the amount of steel industry fuel that has a Btu content of 5,800,000 Btus.

(9) COORDINATION WITH CREDIT FOR PRODUCING FUEL FROM A NONCONVENTIONAL SOURCE.—

(A) IN GENERAL.—The term "qualified facility" shall not include any facility which produces electricity from gas derived from the biodegradation of municipal solid waste if such biodegradation occurred in a facility (within the meaning of section 45K) the production from which is allowed as a credit under section 45K for the taxable year or any prior taxable year.

(B) REFINED COAL FACILITIES.—

(i) IN GENERAL.—The term "refined coal production facility" shall not include any facility the production from which is allowed as a credit under section 45K for the taxable year or any prior taxable year (or under section 29, as in effect on the day before the date of enactment of the Energy Tax Incentives Act of 2005, for any prior taxable year).

(ii) EXCEPTION FOR STEEL INDUSTRY COAL.—In the case of a facility producing steel industry fuel, clause (i) shall not apply to so much of the refined coal produced at such facility as is steel industry fuel.

(10) INDIAN COAL PRODUCTION FACILITIES.—

(A) DETERMINATION OF CREDIT AMOUNT.—In the case of a producer of Indian coal, the credit determined under this section (without regard to this paragraph) for any taxable year shall be increased by an amount equal to the applicable dollar amount per ton of Indian coal—

(i) produced by the taxpayer at an Indian coal production facility during the 7-year period beginning on January 1, 2006, and

(ii) sold by the taxpayer—

(I) to an unrelated person, and

(II) during such 7-year period and such taxable year.

(B) APPLICABLE DOLLAR AMOUNT.—

(i) IN GENERAL.—The term "applicable dollar amount" for any taxable year beginning in a calendar year means—

(I) $1.50 in the case of calendar years 2006 through 2009, and

(II) $2.00 in the case of calendar years beginning after 2009.

(ii) INFLATION ADJUSTMENT.—In the case of any calendar year after 2006, each of the dollar amounts under clause (i) shall be equal to the product of such dollar amount and the inflation adjustment factor determined under paragraph (2)(B) for the calendar year, except that such paragraph shall be applied by substituting "2005" for "1992".

(C) APPLICATION OF RULES.—Rules similar to the rules of the subsection (b)(3) and paragraphs (1), (3), (4), and (5) of this subsection shall apply for purposes of determining the amount of any increase under this paragraph.

(D) TREATMENT AS SPECIFIED CREDIT.—The increase in the credit determined under subsection (a) by reason of this paragraph with respect to any facility shall be treated as a specified credit for purposes of section 38(c)(4)(A) during the 4-year period beginning on the later of January 1, 2006, or the date on which such facility is placed in service by the taxpayer.

(11) ALLOCATION OF CREDIT TO PATRONS OF AGRICULTURAL COOPERATIVE.—

(A) ELECTION TO ALLOCATE.—

(i) IN GENERAL.—In the case of an eligible cooperative organization, any portion of the credit determined under subsection (a) for the taxable year may, at the election of the organization, be apportioned among patrons of the organization on the basis of the amount of business done by the patrons during the taxable year.

(ii) FORM AND EFFECT OF ELECTION.—An election under clause (i) for any taxable year shall be made on a timely filed return for such year. Such election, once made, shall be irrevocable for such taxable year. Such election shall not take effect unless the organization designates the apportionment as such in a written notice mailed to its patrons during the payment period described in section 1382(d).

(B) TREATMENT OF ORGANIZATIONS AND PATRONS.—The amount of the credit apportioned to any patrons under subparagraph (A)—

(i) shall not be included in the amount determined under subsection (a) with respect to the organization for the taxable year, and

(ii) shall be included in the amount determined under subsection (a) for the first taxable year of each patron ending on or after the last day of the payment period (as defined in section 1382(d)) for the taxable year of the organization or, if earlier, for the taxable year of each patron ending on or after the date on which the patron receives notice from the cooperative of the apportionment.

(C) SPECIAL RULES FOR DECREASE IN CREDITS FOR TAXABLE YEAR.—If the amount of the credit of a cooperative organization determined under subsection (a) for a taxable year is less than the amount of such credit shown on the return of the cooperative organization for such year, an amount equal to the excess of—

(i) such reduction, over

(ii) the amount not apportioned to such patrons under subparagraph (A) for the taxable year,

shall be treated as an increase in tax imposed by this chapter on the organization. Such increase shall not be treated as tax imposed by this chapter for purposes of determining the amount of any credit under this chapter.

(D) ELIGIBLE COOPERATIVE DEFINED.—For purposes of this section the term "eligible cooperative" means a cooperative organization described in section 1381(a) which is owned more than 50 percent by agricultural producers or by entities owned by agricultural producers. For this purpose an entity owned by an agricultural producer is one that is more than 50 percent owned by agricultural producers.

Amendments

• 2008, Energy Improvement and Extension Act of 2008 (P.L. 110-343)

P.L. 110-343, Division B, §108(b)(1):

Amended Code Sec. 45(e)(8) by adding at the end a new subparagraph (D). **Effective** for fuel produced and sold after 9-30-2008.

P.L. 110-343, Division B, §108(d)(1)(A)-(B):

Amended Code Sec. 45(e)(9)(B) by striking "The term" and inserting "(i) IN GENERAL.—The term", and by adding at the end a new clause (ii). **Effective** for fuel produced and sold after 9-30-2008.

• 2007, Tax Technical Corrections Act of 2007 (P.L. 110-172)

P.L. 110-172, §9(a):

Amended Code Sec. 45(e)(7)(A)(i) by striking "placed in service by the taxpayer" and inserting "originally placed in service". **Effective** as if included in the provision of the Tax Relief Extension Act of 1999 (P.L. 106-170) to which it relates [**effective** 12-17-1999.—CCH].

• 2005, Energy Tax Incentives Act of 2005 (P.L. 109-58)

P.L. 109-58, §1301(d)(1):

Amended Code Sec. 45(e) by adding at the end a new paragraph (10). **Effective** 8-8-2005.

P.L. 109-58, §1301(f)(3):

Amended Code Sec. 45(e) by striking paragraph (6). **Effective** as if included in the amendments made by section 710 of P.L. 108-357 [**effective** generally for electricity produced and sold after 10-22-2004, in tax years ending after such date.—CCH]. Prior to being stricken, Code Sec. 45(e)(6) read as follows:

(6) CREDIT ELIGIBILITY IN THE CASE OF GOVERNMENT-OWNED FACILITIES USING POULTRY WASTE.—In the case of a facility using poultry waste to produce electricity and owned by a governmental unit, the person eligible for the credit under subsection (a) is the lessee or the operator of such facility.

P.L. 109-58, §1301(f)(4)(A):

Amended Code Sec. 45(e)(9). **Effective** as if included in the amendments made by section 710 of P.L. 108-357 [**effective** generally for electricity produced and sold after 10-22-2004, in tax years ending after such date.—CCH]. Prior to amendment, Code Sec. 45(e)(9) read as follows:

(9) COORDINATION WITH CREDIT FOR PRODUCING FUEL FROM A NONCONVENTIONAL SOURCE.—The term "qualified facility" shall not include any facility the production from which is allowed as a credit under section 29 for the taxable year or any prior taxable year.

P.L. 109-58, §1301(f)(4)(B):

Amended Code Sec. 45(e)(8)(C) by striking "and (9)" after "through (5)". **Effective** as if included in the amendments made by section 710 of P.L. 108-357 [**effective** generally for electricity produced and sold after 10-22-2004, in tax years ending after such date.—CCH].

P.L. 109-58, §1302(a):

Amended Code Sec. 45(e), as amended by this Act, by adding at the end a new paragraph (11). **Effective** for tax years of cooperative organizations ending after 8-8-2005.

P.L. 109-58, §1322(a)(3)(C)(i)-(ii):

Amended Code Sec. 45(e)(9), as added [amended] by this Act, by striking "section 29" each place it appears and inserting "section 45K", and by inserting "(or under section 29, as in effect on the day before the date of enactment of the Energy Tax Incentives Act of 2005, for any prior taxable year)" before the period at the end thereof. **Effective** for credits determined under the Internal Revenue Code of 1986 for tax years ending after 12-31-2005.

• 2004, American Jobs Creation Act of 2004 (P.L. 108-357)

P.L. 108-357, §710(b)(1):

Amended Code Sec. 45 by redesignating subsection (d) as subsection (e). **Effective** generally for electricity produced and sold after 10-22-2004, in tax years ending after such date. For special rules, see Act Sec. 710(g)(2) and (4), below.

P.L. 108-357, §710(b)(2):

Amended Code Sec. 45(e), as so redesignated, by adding at the end a new paragraph (8). **Effective** for refined coal produced and sold after 10-22-2004. For special rules, see Act Sec. 710(g)(2) and (4), below.

P.L. 108-357, §710(b)(3)(A):

Amended Code Sec. 45(e), as so redesignated, by striking "subsection (c)(3)(A)" in paragraph (7)(A)(i) and inserting "subsection (d)(1)". **Effective** generally for electricity produced and sold after 10-22-2004, in tax years ending after such date. For special rules, see Act Sec. 710(g)(2) and (4), below.

P.L. 108-357, §710(d):

Amended Code Sec. 45(e), as redesignated and amended by this section, by inserting after paragraph (8) a new paragraph (9). **Effective** generally for electricity produced and sold after 10-22-2004, in tax years ending after such date. For special rules, see Act Sec. 710(g)(2) and (4), below.

P.L. 108-357, §710(g)(2), provides:

(2) CERTAIN BIOMASS FACILITIES.—With respect to any facility described in section 45(d)(3)(A)(ii) of the Internal Revenue Code of 1986, as added by subsection (b)(1), which is placed in service before the date of the enactment of this Act, the amendments made by this section shall apply to electricity produced and sold after December 31, 2004, in taxable years ending after such date.

P.L. 108-357, §710(g)(4), as amended by P.L. 109-58, §1301(f)(6), provides:

(4) NONAPPLICATION OF AMENDMENTS TO PREEFFECTIVE DATE POULTRY WASTE FACILITIES.—The amendments made by this section shall not apply with respect to any poultry waste facility (within the meaning of section 45(c)(3)(C), as in effect on the day before the date of the enactment of this Act) placed in service before January 1, 2005.

• 2000, Community Renewal Tax Relief Act of 2000 (P.L. 106-554)

P.L. 106-554, §319(1):

Amended Code Sec. 45(d)(7)(A)(i) by striking "paragraph (3)(A)" and inserting "subsection (c)(3)(A)". **Effective** 12-21-2000.

• 1999, Tax Relief Extension Act of 1999 (P.L. 106-170)

P.L. 106-170, §507(c):

Amended Code Sec. 45(d) by adding at the end new paragraphs (6) and (7). **Effective** 12-17-99.

• 1992, Energy Policy Act of 1992 (P.L. 102-386)

P.L. 102-486, §1914(a):

Amended subpart D of part IV of subchapter A of chapter 1 by adding at the end thereof new Code Sec. 45. **Effective** for tax years ending after 12-31-92.

[Sec. 45A]

SEC. 45A. INDIAN EMPLOYMENT CREDIT.

[Sec. 45A(a)]

(a) AMOUNT OF CREDIT.—For purposes of section 38, the amount of the Indian employment credit determined under this section with respect to any employer for any taxable year is an amount equal to 20 percent of the excess (if any) of—

(1) the sum of—

(A) the qualified wages paid or incurred during such taxable year, plus

(B) qualified employee health insurance costs paid or incurred during such taxable year, over

(2) the sum of the qualified wages and qualified employee health insurance costs (determined as if this section were in effect) which were paid or incurred by the employer (or any predecessor) during calendar year 1993.

[Sec. 45A(b)]

(b) QUALIFIED WAGES; QUALIFIED EMPLOYEE HEALTH INSURANCE COSTS.—For purposes of this section—

(1) QUALIFIED WAGES.—

(A) IN GENERAL.—The term "qualified wages" means any wages paid or incurred by an employer for services performed by an employee while such employee is a qualified employee.

(B) COORDINATION WITH WORK OPPORTUNITY CREDIT.—The term "qualified wages" shall not include wages attributable to service rendered during the 1-year period beginning with the day the individual begins work for the employer if any portion of such wages is taken into account in determining the credit under section 51.

(2) QUALIFIED EMPLOYEE HEALTH INSURANCE COSTS.—

(A) IN GENERAL.—The term "qualified employee health insurance costs" means any amount paid or incurred by an employer for health insurance to the extent such amount is attributable to coverage provided to any employee while such employee is a qualified employee.

(B) EXCEPTION FOR AMOUNTS PAID UNDER SALARY REDUCTION ARRANGEMENTS.—No amount paid or incurred for health insurance pursuant to a salary reduction arrangement shall be taken into account under subparagraph (A).

(3) LIMITATION.—The aggregate amount of qualified wages and qualified employee health insurance costs taken into account with respect to any employee for any taxable year (and for the base period under subsection (a)(2)) shall not exceed $20,000.

Amendments

• 1998, IRS Restructuring and Reform Act of 1998 (P.L. 105-206)

P.L. 105-206, §6023(1):

Amended the heading for subparagraph (B) of Code Sec. 45A(b)(1) by striking "TARGETED JOBS CREDIT" and inserting "WORK OPPORTUNITY CREDIT". **Effective** 7-22-98.

• 1996, Small Business Job Protection Act of 1996 (P.L. 104-188)

P.L. 104-188, §1201(e)(1):

Amended Code Sec. 45A(b)(1)(B) by striking "targeted jobs credit" each place it appears and inserting "work opportunity credit". **Effective** for individuals who begin work for the employer after 9-30-96.

[Sec. 45A(c)]

(c) QUALIFIED EMPLOYEE.—For purposes of this section—

(1) IN GENERAL.—Except as otherwise provided in this subsection, the term "qualified employee" means, with respect to any period, any employee of an employer if—

(A) the employee is an enrolled member of an Indian tribe or the spouse of an enrolled member of an Indian tribe,

(B) substantially all of the services performed during such period by such employee for such employer are performed within an Indian reservation, and

(C) the principal place of abode of such employee while performing such services is on or near the reservation in which the services are performed.

(2) INDIVIDUALS RECEIVING WAGES IN EXCESS OF $30,000 NOT ELIGIBLE.—An employee shall not be treated as a qualified employee for any taxable year of the employer if the total amount of the wages paid or incurred by such employer to such employee during such taxable year (whether or not for services within an Indian reservation) exceeds the amount determined at an annual rate of $30,000.

(3) INFLATION ADJUSTMENT.—The Secretary shall adjust the $30,000 amount under paragraph (2) for years beginning after 1994 at the same time and in the same manner as under section 415(d), except that the base period taken into account for purposes of such adjustment shall be the calendar quarter beginning October 1, 1993.

(4) EMPLOYMENT MUST BE TRADE OR BUSINESS EMPLOYMENT.—An employee shall be treated as a qualified employee for any taxable year of the employer only if more than 50 percent of the wages paid or incurred by the employer to such employee during such taxable year are for services performed in a trade or business of the employer. Any determination as to whether the preceding sentence applies with respect to any employee for any taxable year shall be made without regard to subsection (e)(2).

(5) CERTAIN EMPLOYEES NOT ELIGIBLE.—The term "qualified employee" shall not include—

(A) any individual described in subparagraph (A), (B), or (C) of section 51(i)(1),

(B) any 5-percent owner (as defined in section 416(i)(1)(B)), and

(C) any individual if the services performed by such individual for the employer involve the conduct of class I, II, or III gaming as defined in section 4 of the Indian Gaming Regulatory Act (25 U.S.C. 2703), or are performed in a building housing such gaming activity.

(6) INDIAN TRIBE DEFINED.—The term "Indian tribe" means any Indian tribe, band, nation, pueblo, or other organized group or community, including any Alaska Native village, or regional or village corporation, as defined in, or established pursuant to, the Alaska Native Claims Settlement Act (43 U.S.C. 1601 et seq.) which is recognized as eligible for the special programs and services provided by the United States to Indians because of their status as Indians.

(7) INDIAN RESERVATION DEFINED.—The term "Indian reservation" has the meaning given such term by section 168(j)(6).

Amendments

• 2006, Pension Protection Act of 2006 (P.L. 109-280)

P.L. 109-280, §811, provides:

SEC. 811. PENSIONS AND INDIVIDUAL RETIREMENT ARRANGEMENT PROVISIONS OF ECONOMIC GROWTH AND TAX RELIEF RECONCILIATION ACT OF 2001 MADE PERMANENT.

Title IX of the Economic Growth and Tax Relief Reconciliation Act of 2001 [P.L. 107-16] shall not apply to the provisions of, and amendments made by, subtitles A through F of title VI [§§601-666]of such Act (relating to pension and individual retirement arrangement provisions).

• 2004, Working Families Tax Relief Act of 2004 (P.L. 108-311)

P.L. 108-311, §404(b)(1):

Amended Code Sec. 45A(c)(3) by inserting ", except that the base period taken into account for purposes of such adjustment shall be the calendar quarter beginning October 1, 1993" before the period at the end. **Effective** as if included in the provision of the Economic Growth and Tax Relief Reconciliation Act of 2001 (P.L. 107-16) to which it relates [**effective** for years beginning after 12-31-2001.—CCH].

• 2001, Economic Growth and Tax Relief Reconciliation Act of 2001 (P.L. 107-16)

P.L. 107-16, §901(a)-(b), provides [but see P.L. 109-280, §811, above]:

SEC. 901. SUNSET OF PROVISIONS OF ACT.

(a) IN GENERAL.—All provisions of, and amendments made by, this Act shall not apply—

(1) to taxable, plan, or limitation years beginning after December 31, 2010, or

(2) in the case of title V, to estates of decedents dying, gifts made, or generation skipping transfers, after December 31, 2010.

(b) APPLICATION OF CERTAIN LAWS.—The Internal Revenue Code of 1986 and the Employee Retirement Income Security Act of 1974 shall be applied and administered to years, estates, gifts, and transfers described in subsection (a) as if the provisions and amendments described in subsection (a) had never been enacted.

[Sec. 45A(d)]

(d) EARLY TERMINATION OF EMPLOYMENT BY EMPLOYER.—

(1) IN GENERAL.—If the employment of any employee is terminated by the taxpayer before the day 1 year after the day on which such employee began work for the employer—

(A) no wages (or qualified employee health insurance costs) with respect to such employee shall be taken into account under subsection (a) for the taxable year in which such employment is terminated, and

(B) the tax under this chapter for the taxable year in which such employment is terminated shall be increased by the aggregate credits (if any) allowed under section 38(a) for prior taxable years by reason of wages (or qualified employee health insurance costs) taken into account with respect to such employee.

(2) CARRYBACKS AND CARRYOVERS ADJUSTED.—In the case of any termination of employment to which paragraph (1) applies, the carrybacks and carryovers under section 39 shall be properly adjusted.

(3) SUBSECTION NOT TO APPLY IN CERTAIN CASES.—

(A) IN GENERAL.—Paragraph (1) shall not apply to—

(i) a termination of employment of an employee who voluntarily leaves the employment of the taxpayer,

(ii) a termination of employment of an individual who before the close of the period referred to in paragraph (1) becomes disabled to perform the services of such employment unless such disability is removed before the close of such period and the taxpayer fails to offer reemployment to such individual, or

(iii) a termination of employment of an individual if it is determined under the applicable State unemployment compensation law that the termination was due to the misconduct of such individual.

(B) CHANGES IN FORM OF BUSINESS.—For purposes of paragraph (1), the employment relationship between the taxpayer and an employee shall not be treated as terminated—

(i) by a transaction to which section 381(a) applies if the employee continues to be employed by the acquiring corporation, or

(ii) by reason of a mere change in the form of conducting the trade or business of the taxpayer if the employee continues to be employed in such trade or business and the taxpayer retains a substantial interest in such trade or business.

(4) SPECIAL RULE.—Any increase in tax under paragraph (1) shall not be treated as a tax imposed by this chapter for purposes of—

(A) determining the amount of any credit allowable under this chapter, and

(B) determining the amount of the tax imposed by section 55.

[Sec. 45A(e)]

(e) OTHER DEFINITIONS AND SPECIAL RULES.—For purposes of this section—

(1) WAGES.—The term "wages" has the same meaning given to such term in section 51.

(2) CONTROLLED GROUPS.—

(A) All employers treated as a single employer under section (a) or (b) of section 52 shall be treated as a single employer for purposes of this section.

(B) The credit (if any) determined under this section with respect to each such employer shall be its proportionate share of the wages and qualified employee health insurance costs giving rise to such credit.

(3) CERTAIN OTHER RULES MADE APPLICABLE.—Rules similar to the rules of section 51(k) and subsections (c), (d), and (e) of section 52 shall apply.

(4) COORDINATION WITH NONREVENUE LAWS.—Any reference in this section to a provision not contained in this title shall be treated for purposes of this section as a reference to such provision as in effect on the date of the enactment of this paragraph.

(5) SPECIAL RULE FOR SHORT TAXABLE YEARS.—For any taxable year having less than 12 months, the amount determined under subsection (a)(2) shall be multiplied by a fraction, the numerator of which is the number of days in the taxable year and the denominator of which is 365.

[Sec. 45A(f)]

(f) TERMINATION.—This section shall not apply to taxable years beginning after December 31, 2009.

Amendments

• 2008, Tax Extenders and Alternative Minimum Tax Relief Act of 2008 (P.L. 110-343)

P.L. 110-343, Division C, §314(a):

Amended Code Sec. 45A(f) by striking "December 31, 2007" and inserting "December 31, 2009". **Effective** for tax years beginning after 12-31-2007.

• 2006, Tax Relief and Health Care Act of 2006 (P.L. 109-432)

P.L. 109-432, Division A, §111(a):

Amended Code Sec. 45A(f) by striking "2005" and inserting "2007". **Effective** for tax years beginning after 12-31-2005.

• 2004, Working Families Tax Relief Act of 2004 (P.L. 108-311)

P.L. 108-311, §315:

Amended Code Sec. 45A(f) by striking "December 31, 2004" and inserting "December 31, 2005". **Effective** 10-4-2004.

• 2002, Job Creation and Worker Assistance Act of 2002 (P.L. 107-147)

P.L. 107-147, §613(a):

Amended Code Sec. 45A(f) by striking "December 31, 2003" and inserting "December 31, 2004". **Effective** 3-9-2002.

• 1993, Omnibus Budget Reconciliation Act of 1993 (P.L. 103-66)

P.L. 103-66, §13322(b):

Amended Subpart D of part IV of subchapter A of chapter 1 by adding at the end thereof new Code Sec. 45A. **Effective** for wages paid or incurred after 12-31-93.

[Sec. 45B]

SEC. 45B. CREDIT FOR PORTION OF EMPLOYER SOCIAL SECURITY TAXES PAID WITH RESPECT TO EMPLOYEE CASH TIPS.

[Sec. 45B(a)]

(a) GENERAL RULE.—For purposes of section 38, the employer social security credit determined under this section for the taxable year is an amount equal to the excess employer social security tax paid or incurred by the taxpayer during the taxable year.

[Sec. 45B(b)]

(b) EXCESS EMPLOYER SOCIAL SECURITY TAX.—For purposes of this section—

(1) IN GENERAL.—The term "excess employer social security tax" means any tax paid by an employer under section 3111 with respect to tips received by an employee during any month, to the extent such tips—

(A) are deemed to have been paid by the employer to the employee pursuant to section 3121(q) (without regard to whether such tips are reported under section 6053), and

(B) exceed the amount by which the wages (excluding tips) paid by the employer to the employee during such month are less than the total amount which would be payable (with respect to such employment) at the minimum wage rate applicable to such individual under section 6(a)(1) of the Fair Labor Standards Act of 1938 (as in effect on January 1, 2007, and determined without regard to section 3(m) of such Act).

(2) ONLY TIPS RECEIVED FOR FOOD OR BEVERAGES TAKEN INTO ACCOUNT.—In applying paragraph (1), there shall be taken into account only tips received from customers in connection with the providing, delivering, or serving of food or beverages for consumption if the tipping of employees delivering or serving food or beverages by customers is customary.

Amendments

• 2007, Small Business and Work Opportunity Tax Act of 2007 (P.L. 110-28)

P.L. 110-28, §8213(a):

Amended Code Sec. 45B(b)(1)(B) by inserting "as in effect on January 1, 2007, and" before "determined without regard to". **Effective** for tips received for services performed after 12-31-2006.

• 1996, Small Business Job Protection Act of 1996 (P.L. 104-188)

P.L. 104-188, §1112(a)(1):

Amended Code Sec. 45B(b)(1)(A) by inserting "(without regard to whether such tips are reported under section 6053)" after "section 3121(q)". **Effective** as if included in the amendments made by, and the provisions of, section 13443 of P.L. 103-66.

P.L. 104-188, §1112(b)(1):

Amended Code Sec. 45B(b)(2). **Effective** for tips received for services performed after 12-31-96. Prior to amendment, Code Sec. 45B(b)(2) read as follows:

(2) ONLY TIPS RECEIVED AT FOOD AND BEVERAGE ESTABLISHMENTS TAKEN INTO ACCOUNT.—In applying paragraph (1), there shall be taken into account only tips received from customers in connection with the provision of food or beverages for consumption on the premises of an establishment with respect to which the tipping of employees serving food or beverages by customers is customary.

[Sec. 45B(c)]

(c) DENIAL OF DOUBLE BENEFIT.—No deduction shall be allowed under this chapter for any amount taken into account in determining the credit under this section.

[Sec. 45B(d)]

(d) ELECTION NOT TO CLAIM CREDIT.—This section shall not apply to a taxpayer for any taxable year if such taxpayer elects to have this section not apply for such taxable year.

Amendments

• 1993, Omnibus Budget Reconciliation Act of 1993 (P.L. 103-66)

P.L. 103-66, §13443(a):

Amended Subpart D of part IV of subchapter A of chapter 1 by adding at the end thereof new Code Sec. 45B. **Effective** with respect to taxes paid after 12-31-93, with respect to services performed before, on, or after such date (as amended by P.L. 104-188, §1112(a)(2)).

[Sec. 45C]

SEC. 45C. CLINICAL TESTING EXPENSES FOR CERTAIN DRUGS FOR RARE DISEASES OR CONDITIONS.

[Sec. 45C(a)]

(a) GENERAL RULE.—For purposes of section 38, the credit determined under this section for the taxable year is an amount equal to 50 percent of the qualified clinical testing expenses for the taxable year.

Amendments

• 1996, Small Business Job Protection Act of 1996 (P.L. 104-188)

P.L. 104-188, §1205(a)(1):

Transferred Code Sec. 28 to subpart D of part IV of subchapter A of chapter 1, inserted it after Code Sec. 45B, and redesignated it as Code Sec. 45C. **Effective** for amounts paid or incurred in tax years ending after 6-30-96.

P.L. 104-188, §1205(d)(1):

Amended Code Sec. 45C(a), as redesignated by Act Sec. 1205(a)(1), by striking "There shall be allowed as a credit against the tax imposed by this chapter for the taxable year" and inserting "For purposes of section 38, the credit determined under this section for the taxable year is". **Effective** for amounts paid or incurred in tax years ending after 6-30-96.

[Sec. 45C(b)]

(b) QUALIFIED CLINICAL TESTING EXPENSES.—For purposes of this section—

(1) QUALIFIED CLINICAL TESTING EXPENSES.—

(A) IN GENERAL.—Except as otherwise provided in this paragraph, the term "qualified clinical testing expenses" means the amounts which are paid or incurred by the taxpayer during the taxable year which would be described in subsection (b) of section 41 if such subsection were applied with the modifications set forth in subparagraph (B).

(B) MODIFICATIONS.—For purposes of subparagraph (A), subsection (b) of section 41 shall be applied—

(i) by substituting "clinical testing" for "qualified research" each place it appears in paragraphs (2) and (3) of such subsection, and

(ii) by substituting "100 percent" for "65 percent" in paragraph (3)(A) of such subsection.

(C) EXCLUSION FOR AMOUNTS FUNDED BY GRANTS, ETC.—The term "qualified clinical testing expenses" shall not include any amount to the extent such amount is funded by any grant, contract, or otherwise by another person (or any governmental entity).

(D) SPECIAL RULE.—For purposes of this paragraph, section 41 shall be deemed to remain in effect for periods after June 30, 1995, and before July 1, 1996, and periods after December 31, 2009.

(2) CLINICAL TESTING.—

(A) IN GENERAL.—The term "clinical testing" means any human clinical testing—

(i) which is carried out under an exemption for a drug being tested for a rare disease or condition under section 505(i) of the Federal Food, Drug, and Cosmetic Act (or regulations issued under such section),

(ii) which occurs—

(I) after the date such drug is designated under section 526 of such Act, and

(II) before the date on which an application with respect to such drug is approved under section 505(b) of such Act or, if the drug is a biological product, before the date on which a license for such drug is issued under section 351 of the Public Health Service Act; and

(iii) which is conducted by or on behalf of the taxpayer to whom the designation under such section 526 applies.

(B) TESTING MUST BE RELATED TO USE FOR RARE DISEASE OR CONDITION.—Human clinical testing shall be taken into account under subparagraph (A) only to the extent such testing is related to the use of a drug for the rare disease or condition for which it was designated under section 526 of the Federal Food, Drug, and Cosmetic Act.

Amendments

• 2008, Tax Extenders and Alternative Minimum Tax Relief Act of 2008 (P.L. 110-343)

P.L. 110-343, Division C, §301(a)(2):

Amended Code Sec. 45C(b)(1)(D) by striking "after December 31, 2007" and inserting "after December 31, 2009". **Effective** for amounts paid or incurred after 12-31-2007.

• 2006, Tax Relief and Health Care Act of 2006 (P.L. 109-432)

P.L. 109-432, Division A, §104(a)(2):

Amended Code Sec. 45C(b)(1)(D) by striking "2005" and inserting "2007". **Effective** for amounts paid or incurred after 12-31-2005.

• 2004, Working Families Tax Relief Act of 2004 (P.L. 108-311)

P.L. 108-311, §301(a)(2):

Amended Code Sec. 45C(b)(1)(D) by striking "June 30, 2004" and inserting "December 31, 2005". **Effective** for amounts paid or incurred after 6-30-2004.

• 1999, Tax Relief Extension Act of 1999 (P.L. 106-170)

P.L. 106-170, §502(a)(2):

Amended Code Sec. 45C(b)(1)(D) by striking "June 30, 1999" and inserting "June 30, 2004". **Effective** for amounts paid or incurred after 6-30-99.

• 1998, Tax and Trade Relief Extension Act of 1998 (P.L. 105-277)

P.L. 105-277, §1001(b):

Amended Code Sec. 45C(b)(1)(D) by striking "June 30, 1998" and inserting "June 30, 1999". **Effective** for amounts paid or incurred after 6-30-98.

• 1997, FDA Modernization Act of 1997 (P.L. 105-115)

P.L. 105-115, §125(b)(2)(O):

Amended Code Sec. 45C(b)(2)(A)(ii)(II) by striking "or 507" after "505(b)". **Effective** 11-21-97.

• 1997, Taxpayer Relief Act of 1997 (P.L. 105-34)

P.L. 105-34, §601(b)(2):

Amended Code Sec. 45C(b)(1)[(D)] by striking "May 31, 1997" and inserting "June 30, 1998". **Effective** for amounts paid or incurred after 5-31-97.

• 1996, Small Business Job Protection Act of 1996 (P.L. 104-188)

P.L. 104-188, §1204(e):

Amended Code Sec. 28(b)(1)(D) [before redesignation as Code Sec. 45C by Act Sec. 1205(a)(1)] by inserting ", and before July 1, 1996, and periods after May 31, 1997" after "June 30, 1995". **Effective** for tax years ending after 6-30-96. For a special rule, see Act Sec. 1204(f)(3), below.

P.L. 104-188, §1204(f)(3), provides:

(3) ESTIMATED TAX.—The amendments made by this section shall not be taken into account under section 6654 or 6655 of the Internal Revenue Code of 1986 (relating to failure to pay estimated tax) in determining the amount of any installment required to be paid for a taxable year beginning in 1997.

• 1993, Omnibus Budget Reconciliation Act of 1993 (P.L. 103-66)

P.L. 103-66, §13111(a)(2):

Amended Code Sec. 28(b)(1)(D) by striking "June 30, 1992" and inserting "June 30, 1995". **Effective** for tax years ending after 6-30-92.

• 1991, Tax Extension Act of 1991 (P.L. 102-227)

P.L. 102-227, §102(b):

Amended Code Sec. 28(b)(1)(D) by striking "December 31, 1991" and inserting "June 30, 1992". **Effective** for tax years beginning after 12-31-91.

• 1990, Omnibus Budget Reconciliation Act of 1990 (P.L. 101-508)

P.L. 101-508, §11402(b)(2):

Amended Code Sec. 28(b)(1)(D) by striking "December 31, 1990" and inserting "December 31, 1991". **Effective** for tax years beginning after 12-31-89.

• 1989, Omnibus Budget Reconciliation Act of 1989 (P.L. 101-239)

P.L. 101-239, §7110(a)(3):

Amended Code Sec. 28(b)(1)(D) by striking "December 31, 1989" and inserting "December 31, 1990". **Effective** 12-19-89.

• 1988, Technical and Miscellaneous Revenue Act of 1988 (P.L. 100-647)

P.L. 100-647, §1018(q)(1):

Amended Code Sec. 28(b)(2)(A)(ii)(II). **Effective** as if included in the provision of P.L. 99-514 to which it relates. Prior to amendment, Code Sec. 28(b)(2)(A)(ii)(II) read as follows:

(II) before the date on which an application with respect to such drug is approved under section 505(b) of such Act or, if the drug is a biological product, before the date on which a license for such drug is issued under section 351 of the Public Health Services Act, and

P.L. 100-647, §4008(c)(1):

Amended Code Sec. 28(b)(1) by striking out "1988" and inserting in lieu thereof "1989". **Effective** for tax years beginning after 12-31-88.

[Sec. 45C(c)]

(c) COORDINATION WITH CREDIT FOR INCREASING RESEARCH EXPENDITURES.—

(1) IN GENERAL.—Except as provided in paragraph (2), any qualified clinical testing expenses for a taxable year to which an election under this section applies shall not be taken into account for purposes of determining the credit allowable under section 41 for such taxable year.

(2) EXPENSES INCLUDED IN DETERMINING BASE PERIOD RESEARCH EXPENSES.—Any qualified clinical testing expenses for any taxable year which are qualified research expenses (within the meaning of section 41(b)) shall be taken into account in determining base period research expenses for purposes of applying section 41 to subsequent taxable years.

[Sec. 45C(d)]

(d) DEFINITION AND SPECIAL RULES.—

(1) RARE DISEASE OR CONDITION.—For purposes of this section, the term "rare disease or condition" means any disease or condition which—

(A) affects less than 200,000 persons in the United States, or

(B) affects more than 200,000 persons in the United States but for which there is no reasonable expectation that the cost of developing and making available in the United States a drug for such disease or condition will be recovered from sales in the United States of such drug.

Determinations under the preceding sentence with respect to any drug shall be made on the basis of the facts and circumstances as of the date such drug is designated under section 526 of the Federal Food, Drug, and Cosmetic Act.

(2) SPECIAL LIMITATIONS ON FOREIGN TESTING.—

(A) IN GENERAL.—No credit shall be allowed under this section with respect to any clinical testing conducted outside the United States unless—

(i) such testing is conducted outside the United States because there is an insufficient testing population in the United States, and

(ii) such testing is conducted by a United States person or by any other person who is not related to the taxpayer to whom the designation under section 526 of the Federal Food, Drug, and Cosmetic Act applies.

(B) SPECIAL LIMITATION FOR CORPORATIONS TO WHICH SECTION 936 APPLIES.—No credit shall be allowed under this section with respect to any clinical testing conducted by a corporation to which an election under section 936 applies.

(3) CERTAIN RULES MADE APPLICABLE.—Rules similar to the rules of paragraphs (1) and (2) of section 41(f) shall apply for purposes of this section.

(4) ELECTION.—This section shall apply to any taxpayer for any taxable year only if such taxpayer elects (at such time and in such manner as the Secretary may by regulations prescribe) to have this section apply for such taxable year.

Amendments

• 1996, Small Business Job Protection Act of 1996 (P.L. 104-188)

P.L. 104-188, §1205(d)(2):

Amended Code Sec. 45C(d), as redesignated from Code Sec. 28 by Act Sec. 1205(a)(1), by striking paragraph (2) and by redesignating paragraphs (3), (4), and (5) as paragraphs (2), (3), and (4). **Effective** for amounts paid or incurred in tax years ending after 6-30-96. Prior to amendment, Code Sec. 45C(d)(2) read as follows:

(2) LIMITATION BASED ON AMOUNT OF TAX.—The credit allowed by this section for any taxable year shall not exceed the excess (if any) of—

(A) the regular tax (reduced by the sum of the credits allowable under subpart A and section 27), over

(B) the tentative minimum tax for the taxable year.

• 1986, Tax Reform Act of 1986 (P.L. 99-514)

P.L. 99-514, §231(d)(3)(A)(i):

Amended Code Sec. 28(b) and (c) by striking out "section 30" each place it appears and inserting in lieu thereof "section 41". **Effective** for tax years beginning after 12-31-85.

P.L. 99-514, §231(d)(3)(A)(ii):

Amended Code Sec. 28(c)(2) by striking out "section 30(b)" and inserting in lieu thereof "section 41(b)". **Effective** for tax years beginning after 12-31-85.

P.L. 99-514, §231(d)(3)(A)(iii):

Amended Code Sec. 28(d)(4) by striking out "section 30(f)" and inserting in lieu thereof "section 41(f)". **Effective** for tax years beginning after 12-31-85.

P.L. 99-514, §231(d)(3)(A)(iv):

Amended Code Sec. 28(b)(1)(D) by striking out "1985" and inserting in lieu thereof "1988". **Effective** for tax years beginning after 12-31-85.

P.L. 99-514, §232:

Amended Code Sec. 28 by striking out "1987" in subsection (e) and inserting in lieu thereof "1990". **Effective** 10-22-86.

P.L. 99-514, §701(c)(2):

Amended Code Sec. 28(d)(2). **Effective** for tax years beginning after 12-31-86. Prior to amendment, Code Sec. 28(d)(2) read as follows:

(2) LIMITATION BASED ON AMOUNT OF TAX.—The credit allowed by this section for any taxable year shall not exceed the taxpayer's tax liability for the taxable year (as defined in section 26(b)), reduced by the sum of the credits allowable under subpart A, and section 27.

P.L. 99-514, §1275(c)(4):

Amended Code Sec. 28(d)(3)(B). For the **effective** date as well as special rules, see Act Sec. 1277, as amended by P.L. 100-647, §1012(e)(1)-(2), below. Prior to amendment, Code Sec. 28(d)(3)(B) read as follows:

(B) SPECIAL LIMITATION FOR CORPORATIONS TO WHICH SECTION 934(b) OR 936 APPLIES.—No credit shall be allowed under this section with respect to any clinical testing conducted by a corporation to which section 934(b) applies or to which an election under section 936 applies.

P.L. 99-514, §1277, as amended by P.L. 100-647, §1012(e)(1)-(2), provides:

SEC. 1277. EFFECTIVE DATE.

(a) IN GENERAL.—Except as otherwise provided in this section, the amendments made by this subtitle shall apply to taxable years beginning after December 31, 1986.

(b) SPECIAL RULE FOR GUAM, AMERICAN SAMOA, AND THE NORTHERN MARIANA ISLANDS.—The amendments made by this subtitle shall apply with respect to Guam, American Samoa, or the Northern Mariana Islands (and to residents thereof and corporations created or organized therein) only if (and so long as) an implementing agreement under section 1271 is in effect between the United States and such possession.

(c) SPECIAL RULES FOR THE VIRGIN ISLANDS.—

(1) IN GENERAL.—The amendments made by section 1275(c) shall apply with respect to the Virgin Islands (and residents thereof and corporations created or organized therein) only if (and so long as) an implementing agreement is in effect between the United States and the Virgin Islands with respect to the establishment of rules under which the evasion or avoidance of United States income tax shall not be permitted or facilitated by such possession. Any such implementing agreement shall be executed on behalf of the United States by the Secretary of the Treasury, after consultation with the Secretary of the Interior.

(2) SECTION 1275(b).—

(A) IN GENERAL.—The amendment made by section 1275(b) shall apply with respect to—

(i) any taxable year beginning after December 31, 1986, and

(ii) any pre-1987 open year.

(B) SPECIAL RULES.—In the case of any pre-1987 open year—

(i) the amendment made by section 1275(b) shall not apply to income from sources in the Virgin Islands or income effectively connected with the conduct of a trade or business in the Virgin Islands, and

(ii) the taxpayer shall be allowed a credit—

(I) against any additional tax imposed by subtitle A of the Internal Revenue Code of 1954 (by reason of the amendment made by section 1275(b)) on income not described in clause (i) and from sources in the United States,

(II) for any tax paid to the Virgin Islands before the date of the enactment of this Act and attributable to such income.

For purposes of clause (ii)(II), any tax paid before January 1, 1987, pursuant to a process in effect before August 16, 1986, shall be treated as paid before the date of the enactment of this Act.

(C) PRE-1987 OPEN YEAR.—For purposes of this paragraph, the term "pre-1987 open year" means any taxable year beginning before January 1, 1987, if on the date of the enactment of this Act the assessment of a deficiency of income tax for such taxable year is not barred by any law or rule of law.

(D) EXCEPTION.—In the case of any pre-1987 open year, the amendment made by section 1275(b) shall not apply to any domestic corporation if—

(i) during the fiscal year which ended May 31, 1986, such corporation was actively engaged directly or through a subsidiary in the conduct of a trade or business in the Virgin Islands and such trade or business consists of business related to marine activities, and

(ii) such corporation was incorporated on March 31, 1983, in Delaware.

(E) EXCEPTION FOR CERTAIN TRANSACTIONS.—

(i) IN GENERAL.—In the case of any pre-1987 open year, the amendment made by section 1275(b) shall not apply to any income derived from transactions described in clause (ii) by 1 or more corporations which were formed in Delaware on or about March 6, 1981, and which have owned 1 or more office buildings in St. Thomas, United States Virgin Islands, for at least 5 years before the date of the enactment of this Act.

(ii) DESCRIPTION OF TRANSACTIONS.—The transactions described in this clause are—

(I) the redemptions of limited partnership interests for cash and property described in an agreement (as amended) dated March 12, 1981,

(II) the subsequent disposition of the properties distributed in such redemptions, and

(III) interest earned before January 1, 1987, on bank deposits of proceeds received from such redemptions to the extent such deposits are located in the United States Virgin Islands.

(iii) LIMITATION.—The aggregate reduction in tax by reason of this subparagraph shall not exceed $8,312,000. If the taxes which would be payable as the result of the application of the amendment made by section 1275(b) to pre-1987 open years exceeds the limitation of the preceding sentence, such excess shall be treated as attributable to income received in taxable years in reverse chronological order.

(d) REPORT ON IMPLEMENTING AGREEMENTS.—If, during the 1-year period beginning on the date of the enactment of this Act, any implementing agreement described in subsection (b) or (c) is not executed, the Secretary of the Treasury or his delegate shall report to the Committee on Finance of the United States Senate, the Committee on Ways and Means, and the Committee on Interior and Insular Affairs of the House of Representatives with respect to—

(1) the status of such negotiations, and

(2) the reason why such agreement has not been executed.

(e) TREATMENT OF CERTAIN UNITED STATES PERSONS.—Except as otherwise provided in regulations prescribed by the Secretary of the Treasury or his delegate, if a United States person becomes a resident of Guam, American Samoa, or the Northern Mariana Islands, the rules of section 877(c) of the Internal Revenue Code of 1954 shall apply to such person during the 10-year period beginning when such person became such a resident. Notwithstanding subsection (b), the preceding sentence shall apply to dispositions after December 31, 1985, in taxable years ending after such date.

(f) EXEMPTION FROM WITHHOLDING.—Notwithstanding subsection (b), the modification of section 884 of the Internal Revenue Code of 1986 by reason of the amendment to section 881 of such Code by section 1273(b)(1) of this Act shall apply to taxable years beginning after December 31, 1986.

P.L. 99-514, §1879(b)(1)(A) and (B):

Amended Code Sec. 28(b)(2)(A)(ii) by striking out "the date of such drug" in subclause (I) and inserting in lieu thereof "the date such drug", and by striking out "of such Act" in subclause (II) and inserting in lieu thereof "of such Act or, if the drug is a biological product, before the date on which a license for such drug is issued under section 351 of the Public Health Services Act". **Effective** for amounts paid or incurred after 12-31-82, in tax years ending after such date.

P.L. 99-514, §1879(b)(2):

Amended Code Sec. 28(d)(1). **Effective** for amounts paid or incurred after 12-31-82, in tax years ending after such date. Prior to amendment, Code Sec. 28(d)(1) read as follows:

(1) RARE DISEASE OR CONDITION.—For purposes of this section, the term "rare disease or condition" means any disease or condition which occurs so infrequently in the United States that there is no reasonable expectation that the cost of developing and making available in the United States a drug for such disease or condition will be recovered from sales in the United States of such drug. Determinations under the preceding sentence with respect to any drug shall be made on the basis of the facts and circumstances as of the date such drug is designated under section 526 of the Federal Food, Drug, and Cosmetic Act.

• 1984, Deficit Reduction Act of 1984 (P.L. 98-369)

P.L. 98-369, §471(c)(1):

Redesignated former Code Sec. 44H as Code Sec. 28. **Effective** for tax years beginning after 12-31-83, and to carrybacks from such years.

P.L. 98-369, §474(g)(1):

Amended Code Sec. 28, as redesignated by Act Sec. 471(c)(1), by striking out "section 44F" each place it appears and inserting in lieu thereof "section 30", by striking out "section 44F(b)" in subsection (c)(2) and inserting in lieu thereof "section 30(b)," and by striking out "section 44F(f)" in subsection (d)(4) and inserting in lieu thereof "section 30(f)". **Effective** for tax years beginning after 12-31-83, and to carrybacks from such years.

P.L. 98-369, §474(g)(2):

Amended Code Sec. 28, as redesignated by Act Sec. 471(c)(1), by changing paragraph (2) of section (d). **Effective** to tax years beginning after 12-31-83, and to carrybacks from such years. Prior to amendment, section 28(d)(2) read as follows:

(2) LIMITATION BASED ON AMOUNT OF TAX.—The credit allowed by this section for any taxable year shall not exceed the amount of the tax imposed by this chapter for the taxable year reduced by the sum of the credits allowable under a section of this subpart having a lower number or letter designation than this section, other than the credits allowable by sections 31, 39, and 43. For purposes of the preceding sentence, the term "tax imposed by this chapter" shall not include any tax treated as not imposed by this chapter under the last sentence of section 53(a).

P.L. 98-369, §612(e)(1):

Amended section 28(d)(2), as amended by Act Secs. 471(c)(1) and 474(g)(2), by striking out "section 25(b)" and inserting in lieu thereof "section 26(b)". **Effective** for interest paid or accrued after 12-31-84, on indebtedness incurred after 12-31-84, and to elections under section 25(c)(2)(A)(ii) of the Internal Revenue Code of 1954 (as added by this Act) for calendar years after 1983.

• 1983, Orphan Drug Act of 1982 (P.L. 97-414)

P.L. 97-414, §4(a):

Added Code Sec. 44H. **Effective** for amounts paid or incurred after 12-31-82.

P.L. 97-414, §5, as amended by P.L. 98-551, §4(b), provides:

Sec. 5. (a) The Secretary may make grants to and enter into contracts with public and private entities and individuals to assist in defraying the cost of qualified clinical testing expenses incurred in connection with the development of drugs for rare diseases and conditions.

(b) For purposes of subsection (a):

(1) The term "qualified clinical testing" means any human clinical testing—

(A) which is carried out under an exemption for a drug for a rare disease or condition under section 505(i) of the Federal Food, Drug, and Cosmetic Act (or regulations issued under such section),

(B) which occurs—

(i) after the date such drug is designated under section 526 of such Act, and

(ii) before the date on which an application with respect to such drug is submitted under section 505(b) of such Act.

(2) The term "rare disease or condition" means any disease or condition which (A) affects less than 200,000 persons in the United States or (B) affects more than 200,000 in the United States and for which there is no reasonable expectation that the cost of developing and making available in the United States a drug for such disease or condition will be recovered from sales in the United States of such drug. Determinations under the preceding sentence with respect to any drug shall be made on the basis of the facts and circumstances as of the date the request for designation of the drug under this subsection is made.

[Sec. 45C(e)—Stricken]

Amendments

• 1997, Taxpayer Relief Act of 1997 (P.L. 105-34)

P.L. 105-34, §604(a):

Amended Code Sec. 45C by striking subsection (e). **Effective** for amoounts paid or incurred after 5-31-97. Prior to being stricken, Code Sec. 45C(e) read as follows:

(e) TERMINATION.—This section shall not apply to any amount paid or incurred—

(1) after December 31, 1994, and before July 1, 1996, or

(2) after May 31, 1997.

• 1996, Small Business Job Protection Act of 1996 (P.L. 104-188)

P.L. 104-188, §1205(b):

Amended Code Sec. 45C(e), as redesignated by Act Sec. 1205(a)(1). Act Sec. 1205(a)(1) redesignated Code Sec. 28 as Code Sec. 45C. **Effective** for amounts paid or incurred in tax years ending after 6-30-96. Prior to amendment, Code Sec. 45C(e) read as follows:

(e) TERMINATION.—This section shall not apply to any amount paid or incurred after December 31, 1994.

• 1993, Omnibus Budget Reconciliation Act of 1993 (P.L. 103-66)

P.L. 103-66, §13111(b):

Amended Code Sec. 28(e) by striking "June 30, 1992" and inserting "December 31, 1994." **Effective** for tax years ending after 6-30-92.

• 1991, Tax Extension Act of 1991 (P.L. 102-227)

P.L. 102-227, §111(a):

Amended Code Sec. 28(e) by striking "December 31, 1991" and inserting "June 30, 1992". **Effective** for tax years ending after 12-31-91.

• 1990, Omnibus Budget Reconciliation Act of 1990 (P.L. 101-508)

P.L. 101-508, §11411:

Amended Code Sec. 28(e) by striking "December 31, 1990" and inserting "December 31, 1991". **Effective** 11-5-90.

[Sec. 45D]

SEC. 45D. NEW MARKETS TAX CREDIT.

[Sec. 45D(a)]

(a) ALLOWANCE OF CREDIT.—

(1) IN GENERAL.—For purposes of section 38, in the case of a taxpayer who holds a qualified equity investment on a credit allowance date of such investment which occurs during the taxable year, the new markets tax credit determined under this section for such taxable year is an amount equal to the applicable percentage of the amount paid to the qualified community development entity for such investment at its original issue.

(2) APPLICABLE PERCENTAGE.—For purposes of paragraph (1), the applicable percentage is—

(A) 5 percent with respect to the first 3 credit allowance dates, and

(B) 6 percent with respect to the remainder of the credit allowance dates.

(3) CREDIT ALLOWANCE DATE.—For purposes of paragraph (1), the term "credit allowance date" means, with respect to any qualified equity investment—

(A) the date on which such investment is initially made, and

(B) each of the 6 anniversary dates of such date thereafter.

[Sec. 45D(b)]

(b) QUALIFIED EQUITY INVESTMENT.—For purposes of this section—

(1) IN GENERAL.—The term "qualified equity investment" means any equity investment in a qualified community development entity if—

(A) such investment is acquired by the taxpayer at its original issue (directly or through an underwriter) solely in exchange for cash,

(B) substantially all of such cash is used by the qualified community development entity to make qualified low-income community investments, and

(C) such investment is designated for purposes of this section by the qualified community development entity.

Such term shall not include any equity investment issued by a qualified community development entity more than 5 years after the date that such entity receives an allocation under subsection (f). Any allocation not used within such 5-year period may be reallocated by the Secretary under subsection (f).

(2) LIMITATION.—The maximum amount of equity investments issued by a qualified community development entity which may be designated under paragraph (1)(C) by such entity shall not exceed the portion of the limitation amount allocated under subsection (f) to such entity.

(3) SAFE HARBOR FOR DETERMINING USE OF CASH.—The requirement of paragraph (1)(B) shall be treated as met if at least 85 percent of the aggregate gross assets of the qualified community development entity are invested in qualified low-income community investments.

(4) TREATMENT OF SUBSEQUENT PURCHASERS.—The term "qualified equity investment" includes any equity investment which would (but for paragraph (1)(A)) be a qualified equity investment in the hands of the taxpayer if such investment was a qualified equity investment in the hands of a prior holder.

(5) REDEMPTIONS.—A rule similar to the rule of section 1202(c)(3) shall apply for purposes of this subsection.

(6) EQUITY INVESTMENT.—The term "equity investment" means—

(A) any stock (other than nonqualified preferred stock as defined in section 351(g)(2)) in an entity which is a corporation, and

(B) any capital interest in an entity which is a partnership.

[Sec. 45D(c)]

(c) QUALIFIED COMMUNITY DEVELOPMENT ENTITY.—For purposes of this section—

(1) IN GENERAL.—The term "qualified community development entity" means any domestic corporation or partnership if—

(A) the primary mission of the entity is serving, or providing investment capital for, low-income communities or low-income persons,

(B) the entity maintains accountability to residents of low-income communities through their representation on any governing board of the entity or on any advisory board to the entity, and

(C) the entity is certified by the Secretary for purposes of this section as being a qualified community development entity.

(2) SPECIAL RULES FOR CERTAIN ORGANIZATIONS.—The requirements of paragraph (1) shall be treated as met by—

(A) any specialized small business investment company (as defined in section 1044(c)(3)), and

(B) any community development financial institution (as defined in section 103 of the Community Development Banking and Financial Institutions Act of 1994 (12 U.S.C. 4702)).

[Sec. 45D(d)]

(d) QUALIFIED LOW-INCOME COMMUNITY INVESTMENTS.—For purposes of this section—

(1) IN GENERAL.—The term "qualified low-income community investment" means—

(A) any capital or equity investment in, or loan to, any qualified active low-income community business,

(B) the purchase from another community development entity of any loan made by such entity which is a qualified low-income community investment,

(C) financial counseling and other services specified in regulations prescribed by the Secretary to businesses located in, and residents of, low-income communities, and

(D) any equity investment in, or loan to, any qualified community development entity.

(2) QUALIFIED ACTIVE LOW-INCOME COMMUNITY BUSINESS.—

(A) IN GENERAL.—For purposes of paragraph (1), the term "qualified active low-income community business" means, with respect to any taxable year, any corporation (including a nonprofit corporation) or partnership if for such year—

(i) at least 50 percent of the total gross income of such entity is derived from the active conduct of a qualified business within any low-income community,

(ii) a substantial portion of the use of the tangible property of such entity (whether owned or leased) is within any low-income community,

(iii) a substantial portion of the services performed for such entity by its employees are performed in any low-income community,

(iv) less than 5 percent of the average of the aggregate unadjusted bases of the property of such entity is attributable to collectibles (as defined in section 408(m)(2)) other than collectibles that are held primarily for sale to customers in the ordinary course of such business, and

(v) less than 5 percent of the average of the aggregate unadjusted bases of the property of such entity is attributable to nonqualified financial property (as defined in section 1397C(e)).

(B) PROPRIETORSHIP.—Such term shall include any business carried on by an individual as a proprietor if such business would meet the requirements of subparagraph (A) were it incorporated.

(C) PORTIONS OF BUSINESS MAY BE QUALIFIED ACTIVE LOW-INCOME COMMUNITY BUSINESS.—The term "qualified active low-income community business" includes any trades or businesses which would qualify as a qualified active low-income community business if such trades or businesses were separately incorporated.

(3) QUALIFIED BUSINESS.—For purposes of this subsection, the term "qualified business" has the meaning given to such term by section 1397C(d); except that—

(A) in lieu of applying paragraph (2)(B) thereof, the rental to others of real property located in any low-income community shall be treated as a qualified business if there are substantial improvements located on such property, and

(B) paragraph (3) thereof shall not apply.

[Sec. 45D(e)]

(e) LOW-INCOME COMMUNITY.—For purposes of this section—

(1) IN GENERAL.—The term "low-income community" means any population census tract if—

(A) the poverty rate for such tract is at least 20 percent, or

(B)(i) in the case of a tract not located within a metropolitan area, the median family income for such tract does not exceed 80 percent of statewide median family income, or

(ii) in the case of a tract located within a metropolitan area, the median family income for such tract does not exceed 80 percent of the greater of statewide median family income or the metropolitan area median family income.

Subparagraph (B) shall be applied using possessionwide median family income in the case of census tracts located within a possession of the United States.

(2) TARGETED POPULATIONS.—The Secretary shall prescribe regulations under which 1 or more targeted populations (within the meaning of section 103(20) of the Riegle Community Development and Regulatory Improvement Act of 1994 (12 U.S.C. 4702(20))) may be treated as low-income communities. Such regulations shall include procedures for determining which entities are qualified active low-income community businesses with respect to such populations.

(3) AREAS NOT WITHIN CENSUS TRACTS.—In the case of an area which is not tracted for population census tracts, the equivalent county divisions (as defined by the Bureau of the Census for purposes of defining poverty areas) shall be used for purposes of determining poverty rates and median family income.

(4) TRACTS WITH LOW POPULATION.—A population census tract with a population of less than 2,000 shall be treated as a low-income community for purposes of this section if such tract—

(A) is within an empowerment zone the designation of which is in effect under section 1391, and

(B) is contiguous to 1 or more low-income communities (determined without regard to this paragraph).

(5) MODIFICATION OF INCOME REQUIREMENT FOR CENSUS TRACTS WITHIN HIGH MIGRATION RURAL COUNTIES.—

(A) IN GENERAL.—In the case of a population census tract located within a high migration rural county, paragraph (1)(B)(i) shall be applied by substituting "85 percent" for "80 percent".

(B) HIGH MIGRATION RURAL COUNTY.—For purposes of this paragraph, the term "high migration rural county" means any county which, during the 20-year period ending with the year in which the most recent census was conducted, has a net out-migration of inhabitants from the county of at least 10 percent of the population of the county at the beginning of such period.

Amendments

• 2004, American Jobs Creation Act of 2004 (P.L. 108-357)

P.L. 108-357, §221(a):

Amended Code Sec. 45D(e)(2). **Effective** for designations made by the Secretary of the Treasury after 10-22-2004. Prior to amendment, Code Sec. 45D(e)(2) read as follows:

(2) TARGETED AREAS.—The Secretary may designate any area within any census tract as a low-income community if—

(A) the boundary of such area is continuous,

(B) the area would satisfy the requirements of paragraph (1) if it were a census tract, and

(C) an inadequate access to investment capital exists in such area.

P.L. 108-357, §221(b):

Amended Code Sec. 45D(e) by adding at the end a new paragraph (4). **Effective** for investments made after 10-22-2004.

P.L. 108-357, §223(a):

Amended Code Sec. 45D(e), as amended by this Act, by inserting after paragraph (4) a new paragraph (5). **Effective** as if included in the amendment made by section 121(a) of the Community Renewal Tax Relief Act of 2000 (P.L. 106-554) [**effective** for investments made after 12-31-2000.—CCH].

[Sec. 45D(f)]

(f) NATIONAL LIMITATION ON AMOUNT OF INVESTMENTS DESIGNATED.—

(1) IN GENERAL.—There is a new markets tax credit limitation for each calendar year. Such limitation is—

(A) $1,000,000,000 for 2001,

(B) $1,500,000,000 for 2002 and 2003,

(C) $2,000,000,000 for 2004 and 2005,

(D) $3,500,000,000 for 2006 and 2007,

(E) $5,000,000,000 for 2008, and

(F) $5,000,000,000 for 2009.

(2) ALLOCATION OF LIMITATION.—The limitation under paragraph (1) shall be allocated by the Secretary among qualified community development entities selected by the Secretary. In making allocations under the preceding sentence, the Secretary shall give priority to any entity—

(A) with a record of having successfully provided capital or technical assistance to disadvantaged businesses or communities, or

(B) which intends to satisfy the requirement under subsection (b)(1)(B) by making qualified low-income community investments in 1 or more businesses in which persons unrelated to such entity (within the meaning of section 267(b) or 707(b)(1)) hold the majority equity interest.

(3) CARRYOVER OF UNUSED LIMITATION.—If the new markets tax credit limitation for any calendar year exceeds the aggregate amount allocated under paragraph (2) for such year, such limitation for the succeeding calendar year shall be increased by the amount of such excess. No amount may be carried under the preceding sentence to any calendar year after 2014.

Amendments

• 2009, American Recovery and Reinvestment Tax Act of 2009 (P.L. 111-5)

P.L. 111-5, §1403(a)(1)-(3):

Amended Code Sec. 45D(f)(1) by striking "and" at the end of subparagraph (C), by striking ", 2007, 2008, and 2009." in subparagraph (D), and inserting "and 2007,", and by adding at the end new subparagraphs (E)-(F). **Effective** 2-17-2009.

P.L. 111-5, §1403(b), provides:

(b) SPECIAL RULE FOR ALLOCATION OF INCREASED 2008 LIMITATION.—The amount of the increase in the new markets tax credit limitation for calendar year 2008 by reason of the amendments made by subsection (a) shall be allocated in accordance with section 45D(f)(2) of the Internal Revenue Code of 1986 to qualified community development entities (as defined in section 45D(c) of such Code) which—

(1) submitted an allocation application with respect to calendar year 2008, and

(2)(A) did not receive an allocation for such calendar year, or

(B) received an allocation for such calendar year in an amount less than the amount requested in the allocation application.

• 2008, Tax Extenders and Alternative Minimum Tax Relief Act of 2008 (P.L. 110-343)

P.L. 110-343, Division C, §302:

Amended Code Sec. 45D(f)(1)(D) by striking "and 2008" and inserting "2008, and 2009". **Effective** 10-3-2008.

• 2006, Tax Relief and Health Care Act of 2006 (P.L. 109-432)

P.L. 109-432, Division A, §102(a):

Amended Code Sec. 45D(f)(1)(D) by striking "and 2007" and inserting ", 2007, and 2008". **Effective** 12-20-2006.

[Sec. 45D(g)]

(g) RECAPTURE OF CREDIT IN CERTAIN CASES.—

(1) IN GENERAL.—If, at any time during the 7-year period beginning on the date of the original issue of a qualified equity investment in a qualified community development entity, there is a recapture event with respect to such investment, then the tax imposed by this chapter for the taxable year in which such event occurs shall be increased by the credit recapture amount.

(2) CREDIT RECAPTURE AMOUNT.—For purposes of paragraph (1), the credit recapture amount is an amount equal to the sum of—

(A) the aggregate decrease in the credits allowed to the taxpayer under section 38 for all prior taxable years which would have resulted if no credit had been determined under this section with respect to such investment, plus

(B) interest at the underpayment rate established under section 6621 on the amount determined under subparagraph (A) for each prior taxable year for the period beginning on the due date for filing the return for the prior taxable year involved.

No deduction shall be allowed under this chapter for interest described in subparagraph (B).

(3) RECAPTURE EVENT.—For purposes of paragraph (1), there is a recapture event with respect to an equity investment in a qualified community development entity if—

(A) such entity ceases to be a qualified community development entity,

(B) the proceeds of the investment cease to be used as required of subsection (b)(1)(B), or

(C) such investment is redeemed by such entity.

(4) SPECIAL RULES.—

(A) TAX BENEFIT RULE.—The tax for the taxable year shall be increased under paragraph (1) only with respect to credits allowed by reason of this section which were used to reduce tax liability. In the case of credits not so used to reduce tax liability, the carryforwards and carrybacks under section 39 shall be appropriately adjusted.

(B) NO CREDITS AGAINST TAX.—Any increase in tax under this subsection shall not be treated as a tax imposed by this chapter for purposes of determining the amount of any credit under this chapter or for purposes of section 55.

[Sec. 45D(h)]

(h) BASIS REDUCTION.—The basis of any qualified equity investment shall be reduced by the amount of any credit determined under this section with respect to such investment. This subsection shall not apply for purposes of sections 1202, 1400B, and 1400F.

[Sec. 45D(i)]

(i) REGULATIONS.—The Secretary shall prescribe such regulations as may be appropriate to carry out this section, including regulations—

(1) which limit the credit for investments which are directly or indirectly subsidized by other Federal tax benefits (including the credit under section 42 and the exclusion from gross income under section 103),

(2) which prevent the abuse of the purposes of this section,

(3) which provide rules for determining whether the requirement of subsection (b)(1)(B) is treated as met,

(4) which impose appropriate reporting requirements,

(5) which apply the provisions of this section to newly formed entities, and

(6) which ensure that non-metropolitan counties receive a proportional allocation of qualified equity investments.

Amendments

• 2006, Tax Relief and Health Care Act of 2006 (P.L. 109-432)

P.L. 109-432, Division A, §102(b):

Amended Code Sec. 45D(i) by striking "and" at the end of paragraph (4), by striking the period at the end of paragraph (5) and inserting ", and", and by adding at the end a new paragraph (6). **Effective** 12-20-2006.

• 2000, Community Renewal Tax Relief Act of 2000 (P.L. 106-554)

P.L. 106-554, §121(a):

Amended subpart D of part IV of subchapter A of chapter 1 by adding at the end a new Code Sec. 45D. **Effective** for investments made after 12-31-2000.

P.L. 106-554, §121(f)-(g), provides:

(f) GUIDANCE ON ALLOCATION OF NATIONAL LIMITATION.—Not later than 120 days after the date of the enactment of this Act, the Secretary of the Treasury or the Secretary's delegate shall issue guidance which specifies—

(1) how entities shall apply for an allocation under section 45D(f)(2) of the Internal Revenue Code of 1986, as added by this section;

(2) the competitive procedure through which such allocations are made; and

(3) the actions that such Secretary or delegate shall take to ensure that such allocations are properly made to appropriate entities.

(g) AUDIT AND REPORT.—Not later than January 31 of 2004, 2007, and 2010, the Comptroller General of the United States shall, pursuant to an audit of the new markets tax credit program established under section 45D of the Internal Revenue Code of 1986 (as added by subsection (a)), report to Congress on such program, including all qualified community development entities that receive an allocation under the new markets credit under such section.

[Sec. 45E]

SEC. 45E. SMALL EMPLOYER PENSION PLAN STARTUP COSTS.

[Sec. 45E(a)]

(a) GENERAL RULE.—For purposes of section 38, in the case of an eligible employer, the small employer pension plan startup cost credit determined under this section for any taxable year is an amount equal to 50 percent of the qualified startup costs paid or incurred by the taxpayer during the taxable year.

[Sec. 45E(b)]

(b) DOLLAR LIMITATION.—The amount of the credit determined under this section for any taxable year shall not exceed—

(1) $500 for the first credit year and each of the 2 taxable years immediately following the first credit year, and

(2) zero for any other taxable year.

[Sec. 45E(c)]

(c) ELIGIBLE EMPLOYER.—For purposes of this section—

(1) IN GENERAL.—The term "eligible employer" has the meaning given such term by section 408(p)(2)(C)(i).

(2) REQUIREMENT FOR NEW QUALIFIED EMPLOYER PLANS.—Such term shall not include an employer if, during the 3-taxable year period immediately preceding the 1st taxable year for which the credit under this section is otherwise allowable for a qualified employer plan of the employer, the employer or any member of any controlled group including the employer (or any predecessor of either) established or maintained a qualified employer plan with respect to which contributions were made, or benefits were accrued, for substantially the same employees as are in the qualified employer plan.

[Sec. 45E(d)]

(d) OTHER DEFINITIONS.—For purposes of this section—

(1) QUALIFIED STARTUP COSTS.—

(A) IN GENERAL.—The term "qualified startup costs" means any ordinary and necessary expenses of an eligible employer which are paid or incurred in connection with—

(i) the establishment or administration of an eligible employer plan, or

(ii) the retirement-related education of employees with respect to such plan.

(B) PLAN MUST HAVE AT LEAST 1 PARTICIPANT.—Such term shall not include any expense in connection with a plan that does not have at least 1 employee eligible to participate who is not a highly compensated employee.

(2) ELIGIBLE EMPLOYER PLAN.—The term "eligible employer plan" means a qualified employer plan within the meaning of section 4972(d).

(3) FIRST CREDIT YEAR.—The term "first credit year" means—

(A) the taxable year which includes the date that the eligible employer plan to which such costs relate becomes effective, or

(B) at the election of the eligible employer, the taxable year preceding the taxable year referred to in subparagraph (A).

[Sec. 45E(e)]

(e) SPECIAL RULES.—For purposes of this section—

(1) AGGREGATION RULES.—All persons treated as a single employer under subsection (a) or (b) of section 52, or subsection (m) or (o) of section 414, shall be treated as one person. All eligible employer plans shall be treated as 1 eligible employer plan.

(2) DISALLOWANCE OF DEDUCTION.—No deduction shall be allowed for that portion of the qualified startup costs paid or incurred for the taxable year which is equal to the credit determined under subsection (a).

(3) ELECTION NOT TO CLAIM CREDIT.—This section shall not apply to a taxpayer for any taxable year if such taxpayer elects to have this section not apply for such taxable year.

Amendments

• 2006, Pension Protection Act of 2006 (P.L. 109-280)

P.L. 109-280, §811, provides:

SEC. 811. PENSIONS AND INDIVIDUAL RETIREMENT ARRANGEMENT PROVISIONS OF ECONOMIC GROWTH AND TAX RELIEF RECONCILIATION ACT OF 2001 MADE PERMANENT.

Title IX of the Economic Growth and Tax Relief Reconciliation Act of 2001 [P.L. 107-16] shall not apply to the provisions of, and amendments made by, subtitles A through F of title VI [§§601-666]of such Act (relating to pension and individual retirement arrangement provisions).

• 2002, Job Creation and Worker Assistance Act of 2002 (P.L. 107-147)

P.L. 107-147, §411(n)(1):

Amended Code Sec. 45E(e)(1) by striking "(n)" and inserting "(m)". **Effective** as if included in the provision of P.L. 107-16 to which it relates [**effective** for costs paid or incurred in tax years beginning after 12-31-2001, with respect to qualified employer plans first effective after such date.—CCH].

• 2001, Economic Growth and Tax Relief Reconciliation Act of 2001 (P.L. 107-16)

P.L. 107-16, §619(a):

Amended subpart D of part IV of subchapter A of chapter 1 by adding at the end a new Code Sec. 45E. **Effective** for costs paid or incurred in tax years beginning after 12-31-2001, with respect to qualified employer plans first effective after such date [**effective** date changed by P.L. 107-147, §411(m)(2).—CCH].

P.L. 107-16, §901(a)-(b), provides [but see P.L. 109-280, §811, above]:

SEC. 901. SUNSET OF PROVISIONS OF ACT.

(a) IN GENERAL.—All provisions of, and amendments made by, this Act shall not apply—

(1) to taxable, plan, or limitation years beginning after December 31, 2010, or

(2) in the case of title V, to estates of decedents dying, gifts made, or generation skipping transfers, after December 31, 2010.

(b) APPLICATION OF CERTAIN LAWS.—The Internal Revenue Code of 1986 and the Employee Retirement Income Security Act of 1974 shall be applied and administered to years, estates, gifts, and transfers described in subsection (a) as if the provisions and amendments described in subsection (a) had never been enacted.

»»→ Caution: Code Sec. 45F, below, is subject to the sunset provision of the Economic Growth and Tax Relief Reconciliation Act of 2001 (P.L. 107-16), §901. Absent Congressional action, the changes made to this provision by P.L. 107-16, or that take effect as if included in P.L. 107-16, do not apply after December 31, 2010. For more information about the sunset provision, see page XXI of the Preface to this publication and P.L. 107-16, §901, in the amendment notes. See the amendments notes for a history of amendments to this section and the effective date of each change.

[Sec. 45F]

SEC. 45F. EMPLOYER-PROVIDED CHILD CARE CREDIT.

[Sec. 45F(a)]

(a) IN GENERAL.—For purposes of section 38, the employer-provided child care credit determined under this section for the taxable year is an amount equal to the sum of—

(1) 25 percent of the qualified child care expenditures, and

(2) 10 percent of the qualified child care resource and referral expenditures,

of the taxpayer for such taxable year.

[Sec. 45F(b)]

(b) DOLLAR LIMITATION.—The credit allowable under subsection (a) for any taxable year shall not exceed $150,000.

[Sec. 45F(c)]

(c) DEFINITIONS.—For purposes of this section—

(1) QUALIFIED CHILD CARE EXPENDITURE.—

(A) IN GENERAL.—The term "qualified child care expenditure" means any amount paid or incurred—

(i) to acquire, construct, rehabilitate, or expand property—

(I) which is to be used as part of a qualified child care facility of the taxpayer,

(II) with respect to which a deduction for depreciation (or amortization in lieu of depreciation) is allowable, and

(III) which does not constitute part of the principal residence (within the meaning of section 121) of the taxpayer or any employee of the taxpayer,

(ii) for the operating costs of a qualified child care facility of the taxpayer, including costs related to the training of employees, to scholarship programs, and to the providing of increased compensation to employees with higher levels of child care training, or

(iii) under a contract with a qualified child care facility to provide child care services to employees of the taxpayer.

(B) FAIR MARKET VALUE.—The term "qualified child care expenditures" shall not include expenses in excess of the fair market value of such care.

(2) QUALIFIED CHILD CARE FACILITY.—

(A) IN GENERAL.—The term "qualified child care facility" means a facility—

(i) the principal use of which is to provide child care assistance, and

(ii) which meets the requirements of all applicable laws and regulations of the State or local government in which it is located, including the licensing of the facility as a child care facility.

Clause (i) shall not apply to a facility which is the principal residence (within the meaning of section 121) of the operator of the facility.

(B) SPECIAL RULES WITH RESPECT TO A TAXPAYER.—A facility shall not be treated as a qualified child care facility with respect to a taxpayer unless—

(i) enrollment in the facility is open to employees of the taxpayer during the taxable year,

(ii) if the facility is the principal trade or business of the taxpayer, at least 30 percent of the enrollees of such facility are dependents of employees of the taxpayer, and

(iii) the use of such facility (or the eligibility to use such facility) does not discriminate in favor of employees of the taxpayer who are highly compensated employees (within the meaning of section 414(q)).

(3) QUALIFIED CHILD CARE RESOURCE AND REFERRAL EXPENDITURE.—

(A) IN GENERAL.—The term "qualified child care resource and referral expenditure" means any amount paid or incurred under a contract to provide child care resource and referral services to an employee of the taxpayer.

(B) NONDISCRIMINATION.—The services shall not be treated as qualified unless the provision of such services (or the eligibility to use such services) does not discriminate in favor of employees of the taxpayer who are highly compensated employees (within the meaning of section 414(q)).

[Sec. 45F(d)]

(d) RECAPTURE OF ACQUISITION AND CONSTRUCTION CREDIT.—

(1) IN GENERAL.—If, as of the close of any taxable year, there is a recapture event with respect to any qualified child care facility of the taxpayer, then the tax of the taxpayer under this chapter for such taxable year shall be increased by an amount equal to the product of—

(A) the applicable recapture percentage, and

(B) the aggregate decrease in the credits allowed under section 38 for all prior taxable years which would have resulted if the qualified child care expenditures of the taxpayer described in subsection (c)(1)(A) with respect to such facility had been zero.

(2) APPLICABLE RECAPTURE PERCENTAGE.—

(A) IN GENERAL.—For purposes of this subsection, the applicable recapture percentage shall be determined from the following table:

If the recapture event occurs in:	*The applicable recapture percentage is:*
Years 1-3	100
Year 4	85
Year 5	70
Year 6	55
Year 7	40
Year 8	25
Years 9 and 10	10
Years 11 and thereafter	0.

(B) YEARS.—For purposes of subparagraph (A), year 1 shall begin on the first day of the taxable year in which the qualified child care facility is placed in service by the taxpayer.

(3) RECAPTURE EVENT DEFINED.—For purposes of this subsection, the term "recapture event" means—

(A) CESSATION OF OPERATION.—The cessation of the operation of the facility as a qualified child care facility.

(B) CHANGE IN OWNERSHIP.—

(i) IN GENERAL.—Except as provided in clause (ii), the disposition of a taxpayer's interest in a qualified child care facility with respect to which the credit described in subsection (a) was allowable.

(ii) AGREEMENT TO ASSUME RECAPTURE LIABILITY.—Clause (i) shall not apply if the person acquiring such interest in the facility agrees in writing to assume the recapture liability of the person disposing of such interest in effect immediately before such disposition. In the event of such an assumption, the person acquiring the interest in the facility shall be treated as the taxpayer for purposes of assessing any recapture liability (computed as if there had been no change in ownership).

(4) SPECIAL RULES.—

(A) TAX BENEFIT RULE.—The tax for the taxable year shall be increased under paragraph (1) only with respect to credits allowed by reason of this section which were used to reduce tax liability. In the case of credits not so used to reduce tax liability, the carryforwards and carrybacks under section 39 shall be appropriately adjusted.

(B) NO CREDITS AGAINST TAX.—Any increase in tax under this subsection shall not be treated as a tax imposed by this chapter for purposes of determining the amount of any credit under this chapter or for purposes of section 55.

(C) NO RECAPTURE BY REASON OF CASUALTY LOSS.—The increase in tax under this subsection shall not apply to a cessation of operation of the facility as a qualified child care facility by reason of a casualty loss to the extent such loss is restored by reconstruction or replacement within a reasonable period established by the Secretary.

Amendments

• 2002, Job Creation and Worker Assistance Act of 2002 (P.L. 107-147)

P.L. 107-147, §411(d)(1):

Amended Code Sec. 45F(d)(4)(B) by striking "subpart A, B, or D of this part" and inserting "this chapter or for purposes of section 55". **Effective** as if included in the provision of P.L. 107-16 to which it relates [**effective** for tax years beginning after 12-31-2001.—CCH].

[Sec. 45F(e)]

(e) SPECIAL RULES.—For purposes of this section—

(1) AGGREGATION RULES.—All persons which are treated as a single employer under subsections (a) and (b) of section 52 shall be treated as a single taxpayer.

(2) PASS-THRU IN THE CASE OF ESTATES AND TRUSTS.—Under regulations prescribed by the Secretary, rules similar to the rules of subsection (d) of section 52 shall apply.

(3) ALLOCATION IN THE CASE OF PARTNERSHIPS.—In the case of partnerships, the credit shall be allocated among partners under regulations prescribed by the Secretary.

[Sec. 45F(f)]

(f) NO DOUBLE BENEFIT.—

(1) REDUCTION IN BASIS.—For purposes of this subtitle—

(A) IN GENERAL.—If a credit is determined under this section with respect to any property by reason of expenditures described in subsection (c)(1)(A), the basis of such property shall be reduced by the amount of the credit so determined.

(B) CERTAIN DISPOSITIONS.—If, during any taxable year, there is a recapture amount determined with respect to any property the basis of which was reduced under subparagraph (A), the basis of such property (immediately before the event resulting in such recapture) shall be increased by an amount equal to such recapture amount. For purposes of the preceding sentence, the term "recapture amount" means any increase in tax (or adjustment in carrybacks or carryovers) determined under subsection (d).

(2) OTHER DEDUCTIONS AND CREDITS.—No deduction or credit shall be allowed under any other provision of this chapter with respect to the amount of the credit determined under this section.

Amendments

• 2001, Economic Growth and Tax Relief Reconciliation Act of 2001 (P.L. 107-16)

P.L. 107-16, §205(a):

Amended subpart D of part IV of subchapter A of chapter 1, as amended by Act Sec. 619, by adding at the end a new Code Sec. 45F. **Effective** for tax years beginning after 12-31-2001.

P.L. 107-16, §901(a)-(b), provides:

SEC. 901. SUNSET OF PROVISIONS OF ACT.

(a) IN GENERAL.—All provisions of, and amendments made by, this Act shall not apply—

(1) to taxable, plan, or limitation years beginning after December 31, 2010, or

(2) in the case of title V, to estates of decedents dying, gifts made, or generation skipping transfers, after December 31, 2010.

(b) APPLICATION OF CERTAIN LAWS.—The Internal Revenue Code of 1986 and the Employee Retirement Income Security Act of 1974 shall be applied and administered to years, estates, gifts, and transfers described in subsection (a) as if the provisions and amendments described in subsection (a) had never been enacted.

[Sec. 45G]

SEC. 45G. RAILROAD TRACK MAINTENANCE CREDIT.

[Sec. 45G(a)]

(a) GENERAL RULE.—For purposes of section 38, the railroad track maintenance credit determined under this section for the taxable year is an amount equal to 50 percent of the qualified railroad track maintenance expenditures paid or incurred by an eligible taxpayer during the taxable year.

[Sec. 45G(b)]

(b) LIMITATION.—

(1) IN GENERAL.—The credit allowed under subsection (a) for any taxable year shall not exceed the product of—

(A) $3,500, multiplied by

(B) the sum of—

(i) the number of miles of railroad track owned or leased by the eligible taxpayer as of the close of the taxable year, and

(ii) the number of miles of railroad track assigned for purposes of this subsection to the eligible taxpayer by a Class II or Class III railroad which owns or leases such railroad track as of the close of the taxable year.

(2) ASSIGNMENTS.—With respect to any assignment of a mile of railroad track under paragraph (1)(B)(ii)—

(A) such assignment may be made only once per taxable year of the Class II or Class III railroad and shall be treated as made as of the close of such taxable year,

(B) such mile may not be taken into account under this section by such railroad for such taxable year, and

(C) such assignment shall be taken into account for the taxable year of the assignee which includes the date that such assignment is treated as effective.

Amendments

• 2005, Gulf Opportunity Zone Act of 2005 (P.L. 109-135)

P.L. 109-135, §403(f)(1):

Amended Code Sec. 45G(b). **Effective** as if included in the provision of the American Jobs Creation Act of 2004 (P.L. 108-357) to which it relates [**effective** for tax years beginning after 12-31-2004.—CCH]. Prior to amendment, Code Sec. 45G(b) read as follows:

(b) LIMITATION.—The credit allowed under subsection (a) for any taxable year shall not exceed the product of—

(1) $3,500, and

(2) the number of miles of railroad track owned or leased by the eligible taxpayer as of the close of the taxable year. A mile of railroad track may be taken into account by a person other than the owner only if such mile is assigned to such person by the owner for purposes of this subsection. Any mile which is so assigned may not be taken into account by the owner for purposes of this subsection.

[Sec. 45G(c)]

(c) ELIGIBLE TAXPAYER.—For purposes of this section, the term "eligible taxpayer" means—

(1) any Class II or Class III railroad, and

(2) any person who transports property using the rail facilities of a Class II or Class III railroad or who furnishes railroad-related property or services to a Class II or Class III railroad, but only with respect to miles of railroad track assigned to such person by such Class II or Class III railroad for purposes of subsection (b).

Amendments

• 2005, Gulf Opportunity Zone Act of 2005 (P.L. 109-135)

P.L. 109-135, §403(f)(2):

Amended Code Sec. 45G(c)(2). **Effective** as if included in the provision of the American Jobs Creation Act of 2004 (P.L. 108-357) to which it relates [**effective** for tax years beginning after 12-31-2004.—CCH]. Prior to amendment, Code Sec. 45G(c)(2) read as follows:

(2) any person who transports property using the rail facilities of a person described in paragraph (1) or who furnishes railroad-related property or services to such a person.

[Sec. 45G(d)]

(d) QUALIFIED RAILROAD TRACK MAINTENANCE EXPENDITURES.—For purposes of this section, the term "qualified railroad track maintenance expenditures" means gross expenditures (whether or not otherwise chargeable to capital account) for maintaining railroad track (including roadbed, bridges, and related track structures) owned or leased as of January 1, 2005, by a Class II or Class III railroad (determined without regard to any consideration for such expenditures given by the Class II or Class III railroad which made the assignment of such track).

Amendments

• 2006, Tax Relief and Health Care Act of 2006 (P.L. 109-432)

P.L. 109-432, Division A, §423(a)(1)-(2):

Amended Code Sec. 45G(d) by inserting "gross" after "means", and by inserting "(determined without regard to any consideration for such expenditures given by the Class II or Class III railroad which made the assignment of such track)" after "Class II or Class III railroad". **Effective** as if included in the amendment made by section 245(a) of the American Jobs Creation Act of 2004 (P.L. 108-357) [**effective** for tax years beginning after 12-31-2004.—CCH].

[Sec. 45G(e)]

(e) OTHER DEFINITIONS AND SPECIAL RULES.—

(1) CLASS II OR CLASS III RAILROAD.—For purposes of this section, the terms "Class II railroad" and "Class III railroad" have the respective meanings given such terms by the Surface Transportation Board.

(2) CONTROLLED GROUPS.—Rules similar to the rules of paragraph (1) of section 41(f) shall apply for purposes of this section.

(3) BASIS ADJUSTMENT.—For purposes of this subtitle, if a credit is allowed under this section with respect to any railroad track, the basis of such track shall be reduced by the amount of the credit so allowed.

[Sec. 45G(f)]

(f) APPLICATION OF SECTION.—This section shall apply to qualified railroad track maintenance expenditures paid or incurred during taxable years beginning after December 31, 2004, and before January 1, 2010.

Amendments

• 2008, Tax Extenders and Alternative Minimum Tax Relief Act of 2008 (P.L. 110-343)

P.L. 110-343, Division C, §316(a):

Amended Code Sec. 45G(f) by striking "January 1, 2008" and inserting "January 1, 2010". **Effective** for expenditures paid or incurred during tax years beginning after 12-31-2007.

• 2004, American Jobs Creation Act of 2004 (P.L. 108-357)

P.L. 108-357, §245(a):

Amended subpart D of part IV of subchapter A of chapter 1 by adding at the end a new Code Sec. 45G. **Effective** for tax years beginning after 12-31-2004.

[Sec. 45H]

SEC. 45H. CREDIT FOR PRODUCTION OF LOW SULFUR DIESEL FUEL.

[Sec. 45H(a)]

(a) IN GENERAL.—For purposes of section 38, the amount of the low sulfur diesel fuel production credit determined under this section with respect to any facility of a small business refiner is an amount equal to 5 cents for each gallon of low sulfur diesel fuel produced during the taxable year by such small business refiner at such facility.

[Sec. 45H(b)]

(b) MAXIMUM CREDIT.—

(1) IN GENERAL.—The aggregate credit determined under subsection (a) for any taxable year with respect to any facility shall not exceed—

(A) 25 percent of the qualified costs incurred by the small business refiner with respect to such facility, reduced by

(B) the aggregate credits determined under this section for all prior taxable years with respect to such facility.

(2) REDUCED PERCENTAGE.—In the case of a small business refiner with average daily domestic refinery runs for the 1-year period ending on December 31, 2002, in excess of 155,000 barrels, the number of percentage points described in paragraph (1) shall be reduced (not below zero) by the product of such number (before the application of this paragraph) and the ratio of such excess to 50,000 barrels.

Amendments

• 2007, Tax Technical Corrections Act of 2007 (P.L. 110-172)

P.L. 110-172, §7(a)(3)(A):

Amended subsection (b)(1)(A) of Code Sec. 45H (as amended by Act Sec. 7(a)(1)) by striking "qualified capital costs" and inserting "qualified costs". **Effective** as if included in the provision of the American Jobs Creation Act of 2004 (P.L. 108-357) to which it relates [**effective** for expenses paid or incurred after 12-31-2002, in tax years ending after such date.—CCH].

[Sec. 45H(c)]

(c) DEFINITIONS AND SPECIAL RULE.—For purposes of this section—

(1) SMALL BUSINESS REFINER.—The term "small business refiner" means, with respect to any taxable year, a refiner of crude oil—

(A) with respect to which not more than 1,500 individuals are engaged in the refinery operations of the business on any day during such taxable year, and

(B) the average daily domestic refinery run or average retained production of which for all facilities of the taxpayer for the 1-year period ending on December 31, 2002, did not exceed 205,000 barrels.

(2) QUALIFIED COSTS.—The term "qualified costs" means, with respect to any facility, those costs paid or incurred during the applicable period for compliance with the applicable EPA regulations with respect to such facility, including expenditures for the construction of new process operation units or the dismantling and reconstruction of existing process units to be used in the production of low sulfur diesel fuel, associated adjacent or offsite equipment (including tankage, catalyst, and power supply), engineering, construction period interest, and sitework.

(3) APPLICABLE EPA REGULATIONS.—The term "applicable EPA regulations" means the Highway Diesel Fuel Sulfur Control Requirements of the Environmental Protection Agency.

(4) APPLICABLE PERIOD.—The term "applicable period" means, with respect to any facility, the period beginning on January 1, 2003, and ending on the earlier of the date which is 1 year after the date on which the taxpayer must comply with the applicable EPA regulations with respect to such facility or December 31, 2009.

(5) LOW SULFUR DIESEL FUEL.—The term "low sulfur diesel fuel" means diesel fuel with a sulfur content of 15 parts per million or less.

Amendments

• 2007, Tax Technical Corrections Act of 2007 (P.L. 110-172)

P.L. 110-172, §7(a)(3)(A):

Amended subsection (c)(2) of Code Sec. 45H (as amended by Act Sec. 7(a)(1)) by striking "qualified capital costs" and inserting "qualified costs". **Effective** as if included in the provision of the American Jobs Creation Act of 2004 (P.L. 108-357) to which it relates [**effective** for expenses paid or incurred after 12-31-2002, in tax years ending after such date.—CCH].

P.L. 110-172, §7(a)(3)(B):

Amended the heading of Code Sec. 45H(c)(2) by striking "CAPITAL" before "COSTS". **Effective** as if included in the provision of the American Jobs Creation Act of 2004 (P.L. 108-357) to which it relates [**effective** for expenses paid or incurred after 12-31-2002, in tax years ending after such date.—CCH].

[Sec. 45H(d)—Stricken]

Amendments

• 2007, Tax Technical Corrections Act of 2007 (P.L. 110-172)

P.L. 110-172, §7(a)(1)(A):

Amended Code Sec. 45H by striking subsection (d) and by redesignating subsections (e), (f), and (g) as subsections (d), (e), and (f), respectively. **Effective** as if included in the provision of the American Jobs Creation Act of 2004 (P.L. 108-357) to which it relates [**effective** for expenses paid or incurred after 12-31-2002, in tax years ending after such date.—CCH]. Prior to being stricken, Code Sec. 45H(d) read as follows:

(d) REDUCTION IN BASIS.—For purposes of this subtitle, if a credit is determined under this section for any expenditure with respect to any property, the increase in basis of such property which would (but for this subsection) result from such expenditure shall be reduced by the amount of the credit so determined.

[Sec. 45H(d)]

(d) SPECIAL RULE FOR DETERMINATION OF REFINERY RUNS.—For purposes this section and section 179B(b), in the calculation of average daily domestic refinery run or retained production, only refineries which on April 1, 2003, were refineries of the refiner or a related person (within the meaning of section 613A(d)(3)), shall be taken into account.

Amendments

• 2007, Tax Technical Corrections Act of 2007 (P.L. 110-172)

P.L. 110-172, §7(a)(1)(A):

Amended Code Sec. 45H by redesignating subsection (e) as subsection (d). **Effective** as if included in the provision of the American Jobs Creation Act of 2004 (P.L. 108-357) to which it relates [**effective** for expenses paid or incurred after 12-31-2002, in tax years ending after such date.—CCH].

[Sec. 45H(e)]

(e) CERTIFICATION.—

(1) REQUIRED.—No credit shall be allowed unless, not later than the date which is 30 months after the first day of the first taxable year in which the low sulfur diesel fuel production credit is determined with respect to a facility, the small business refiner obtains certification from the Secretary, after consultation with the Administrator of the Environmental Protection Agency, that the taxpayer's qualified costs with respect to such facility will result in compliance with the applicable EPA regulations.

(2) CONTENTS OF APPLICATION.—An application for certification shall include relevant information regarding unit capacities and operating characteristics sufficient for the Secretary, after consultation with the Administrator of the Environmental Protection Agency, to determine that such qualified costs are necessary for compliance with the applicable EPA regulations.

(3) REVIEW PERIOD.—Any application shall be reviewed and notice of certification, if applicable, shall be made within 60 days of receipt of such application. In the event the Secretary does not notify the taxpayer of the results of such certification within such period, the taxpayer may presume the certification to be issued until so notified.

(4) STATUTE OF LIMITATIONS.—With respect to the credit allowed under this section—

(A) the statutory period for the assessment of any deficiency attributable to such credit shall not expire before the end of the 3-year period ending on the date that the review period described in paragraph (3) ends with respect to the taxpayer, and

(B) such deficiency may be assessed before the expiration of such 3-year period notwithstanding the provisions of any other law or rule of law which would otherwise prevent such assessment.

Amendments

• 2007, Tax Technical Corrections Act of 2007 (P.L. 110-172)

P.L. 110-172, §7(a)(1)(A):

Amended Code Sec. 45H by redesignating subsection (f) as subsection (e). **Effective** as if included in the provision of the American Jobs Creation Act of 2004 (P.L. 108-357) to which it relates [**effective** for expenses paid or incurred after 12-31-2002, in tax years ending after such date.—CCH].

P.L. 110-172, §7(a)(3)(A):

Amended subsection (e)(1) and (2) of Code Sec. 45H (as amended by Act Sec. 7(a)(1)) by striking "qualified capital costs" and inserting "qualified costs". **Effective** as if included in the provision of the American Jobs Creation Act of 2004 (P.L. 108-357) to which it relates [**effective** for expenses paid or incurred after 12-31-2002, in tax years ending after such date.—CCH].

[Sec. 45H(f)]

(f) COOPERATIVE ORGANIZATIONS.—

(1) APPORTIONMENT OF CREDIT.—

(A) IN GENERAL.—In the case of a cooperative organization described in section 1381(a), any portion of the credit determined under subsection (a) for the taxable year may, at the election of the organization, be apportioned among patrons eligible to share in patronage dividends on the basis of the quantity or value of business done with or for such patrons for the taxable year.

(B) FORM AND EFFECT OF ELECTION.—An election under subparagraph (A) for any taxable year shall be made on a timely filed return for such year. Such election, once made, shall be irrevocable for such taxable year.

(2) TREATMENT OF ORGANIZATIONS AND PATRONS.—

(A) ORGANIZATIONS.—The amount of the credit not apportioned to patrons pursuant to paragraph (1) shall be included in the amount determined under subsection (a) for the taxable year of the organization.

(B) PATRONS.—The amount of the credit apportioned to patrons pursuant to paragraph (1) shall be included in the amount determined under subsection (a) for the first taxable year of each patron ending on or after the last day of the payment period (as defined in section 1382(d)) for the taxable year of the organization or, if earlier, for the taxable year of each patron ending on or after the date on which the patron receives notice from the cooperative of the apportionment.

(3) SPECIAL RULE.—If the amount of a credit which has been apportioned to any patron under this subsection is decreased for any reason—

(A) such amount shall not increase the tax imposed on such patron, and

(B) the tax imposed by this chapter on such organization shall be increased by such amount.

The increase under subparagraph (B) shall not be treated as tax imposed by this chapter for purposes of determining the amount of any credit under this chapter or for purposes of section 55.

Amendments

• 2007, Tax Technical Corrections Act of 2007 (P.L. 110-172)

P.L. 110-172, §7(a)(1)(A):

Amended Code Sec. 45H by redesignating subsection (g) as subsection (f). **Effective** as if included in the provision of the American Jobs Creation Act of 2004 (P.L. 108-357) to which it relates [**effective** for expenses paid or incurred after 12-31-2002, in tax years ending after such date.—CCH].

• 2004, American Jobs Creation Act of 2004 (P.L. 108-357)

P.L. 108-357, §339(a):

Amended subpart D of part IV of subchapter A of chapter 1, as amended by this Act, by inserting after Code Sec. 45G a new Code Sec. 45H. **Effective** for expenses paid or incurred after 12-31-2002, in tax years ending after such date.

[Sec. 45H(g)]

(g) ELECTION TO NOT TAKE CREDIT.—No credit shall be determined under subsection (a) for the taxable year if the taxpayer elects not to have subsection (a) apply to such taxable year.

Amendments

• 2007, Tax Technical Corrections Act of 2007 (P.L. 110-172)

P.L. 110-172, §7(a)(2)(A):

Amended Code Sec. 45H, as amended by Act Sec. 7(a)(1), by adding at the end a new subsection (g). **Effective** as if included in the provision of the American Jobs Creation Act of 2004 (P.L. 108-357) to which it relates [**effective** for expenses paid or incurred after 12-31-2002, in tax years ending after such date.—CCH].

[Sec. 45I]

SEC. 45I. CREDIT FOR PRODUCING OIL AND GAS FROM MARGINAL WELLS.

[Sec. 45I(a)]

(a) GENERAL RULE.—For purposes of section 38, the marginal well production credit for any taxable year is an amount equal to the product of—

(1) the credit amount, and

(2) the qualified crude oil production and the qualified natural gas production which is attributable to the taxpayer.

Amendments

• 2005, Gulf Opportunity Zone Act of 2005 (P.L. 109-135)

P.L. 109-135, §412(k):

Amended Code Sec. 45I(a)(2) by striking "qualified credit oil production" and inserting "qualified crude oil production". **Effective** 12-21-2005.

[Sec. 45I(b)]

(b) CREDIT AMOUNT.—For purposes of this section—

(1) IN GENERAL.—The credit amount is—

(A) $3 per barrel of qualified crude oil production, and

(B) 50 cents per 1,000 cubic feet of qualified natural gas production.

(2) REDUCTION AS OIL AND GAS PRICES INCREASE.—

(A) IN GENERAL.—The $3 and 50 cents amounts under paragraph (1) shall each be reduced (but not below zero) by an amount which bears the same ratio to such amount (determined without regard to this paragraph) as—

(i) the excess (if any) of the applicable reference price over $15 ($1.67 for qualified natural gas production), bears to

(ii) $3 ($0.33 for qualified natural gas production).

The applicable reference price for a taxable year is the reference price of the calendar year preceding the calendar year in which the taxable year begins.

(B) INFLATION ADJUSTMENT.—In the case of any taxable year beginning in a calendar year after 2005, each of the dollar amounts contained in subparagraph (A) shall be increased to an amount equal to such dollar amount multiplied by the inflation adjustment factor for such calendar year (determined under section 43(b)(3)(B) by substituting "2004" for "1990").

(C) REFERENCE PRICE.—For purposes of this paragraph, the term "reference price" means, with respect to any calendar year—

(i) in the case of qualified crude oil production, the reference price determined under section 45K(d)(2)(C), and

(ii) in the case of qualified natural gas production, the Secretary's estimate of the annual average wellhead price per 1,000 cubic feet for all domestic natural gas.

Amendments

• 2005, Energy Tax Incentives Act of 2005 (P.L. 109-58)

P.L. 109-58, §1322(a)(3)(B):

Amended Code Sec. 45I(b)(2)(C)(i) by striking "section 29(d)(2)(C)" and inserting "section 45K(d)(2)(C)". **Effective** for credits determined under the Internal Revenue Code of 1986 for tax years ending after 12-31-2005.

[Sec. 45I(c)]

(c) QUALIFIED CRUDE OIL AND NATURAL GAS PRODUCTION.—For purposes of this section—

(1) IN GENERAL.—The terms "qualified crude oil production" and "qualified natural gas production" mean domestic crude oil or natural gas which is produced from a qualified marginal well.

(2) LIMITATION ON AMOUNT OF PRODUCTION WHICH MAY QUALIFY.—

(A) IN GENERAL.—Crude oil or natural gas produced during any taxable year from any well shall not be treated as qualified crude oil production or qualified natural gas production to the extent production from the well during the taxable year exceeds 1,095 barrels or barrel-of-oil equivalents (as defined in section 45K(d)(5)).

(B) PROPORTIONATE REDUCTIONS.—

(i) SHORT TAXABLE YEARS.—In the case of a short taxable year, the limitations under this paragraph shall be proportionately reduced to reflect the ratio which the number of days in such taxable year bears to 365.

(ii) WELLS NOT IN PRODUCTION ENTIRE YEAR.—In the case of a well which is not capable of production during each day of a taxable year, the limitations under this paragraph applicable to the well shall be proportionately reduced to reflect the ratio which the number of days of production bears to the total number of days in the taxable year.

(3) DEFINITIONS.—

(A) QUALIFIED MARGINAL WELL.—The term "qualified marginal well" means a domestic well—

(i) the production from which during the taxable year is treated as marginal production under section 613A(c)(6), or

(ii) which, during the taxable year—

(I) has average daily production of not more than 25 barrel-of-oil equivalents (as so defined), and

(II) produces water at a rate not less than 95 percent of total well effluent.

(B) CRUDE OIL, ETC.—The terms "crude oil", "natural gas", "domestic", and "barrel" have the meanings given such terms by section 613A(e).

Amendments

• 2005, Energy Tax Incentives Act of 2005 (P.L. 109-58)

P.L. 109-58, §1322(a)(3)(D)(i):

Amended Code Sec. 45I(c)(2)(A) by striking "section 29(d)(5))" and inserting "section 45K(d)(5))". **Effective** for credits determined under the Internal Revenue Code of 1986 for tax years ending after 12-31-2005.

[Sec. 45I(d)]

(d) OTHER RULES.—

(1) PRODUCTION ATTRIBUTABLE TO THE TAXPAYER.—In the case of a qualified marginal well in which there is more than one owner of operating interests in the well and the crude oil or natural gas production exceeds the limitation under subsection (c)(2), qualifying crude oil production or qualifying natural gas production attributable to the taxpayer shall be determined on the basis of the ratio which taxpayer's revenue interest in the production bears to the aggregate of the revenue interests of all operating interest owners in the production.

(2) OPERATING INTEREST REQUIRED.—Any credit under this section may be claimed only on production which is attributable to the holder of an operating interest.

(3) PRODUCTION FROM NONCONVENTIONAL SOURCES EXCLUDED.—In the case of production from a qualified marginal well which is eligible for the credit allowed under section 45K for the taxable year, no credit shall be allowable under this section unless the taxpayer elects not to claim the credit under section 45K with respect to the well.

Amendments

• 2005, Energy Tax Incentives Act of 2005 (P.L. 109-58)

P.L. 109-58, §1322(a)(3)(D)(ii):

Amended Code Sec. 45I(d)(3) by striking "section 29" both places it appears and inserting "section 45K". **Effective** for credits determined under the Internal Revenue Code of 1986 for tax years ending after 12-31-2005.

• 2004, American Jobs Creation Act of 2004 (P.L. 108-357)

P.L. 108-357, §341(a):

Amended subpart D of part IV of subchapter A of chapter 1, as amended by this Act, by inserting after Code Sec. 45H a new Code Sec. 45I. **Effective** for production in tax years beginning after 12-31-2004.

[Sec. 45J]

SEC. 45J. CREDIT FOR PRODUCTION FROM ADVANCED NUCLEAR POWER FACILITIES.

[Sec. 45J(a)]

(a) GENERAL RULE.—For purposes of section 38, the advanced nuclear power facility production credit of any taxpayer for any taxable year is equal to the product of—

(1) 1.8 cents, multiplied by

(2) the kilowatt hours of electricity—

(A) produced by the taxpayer at an advanced nuclear power facility during the 8-year period beginning on the date the facility was originally placed in service, and

(B) sold by the taxpayer to an unrelated person during the taxable year.

[Sec. 45J(b)]

(b) NATIONAL LIMITATION.—

(1) IN GENERAL.—The amount of credit which would (but for this subsection and subsection (c)) be allowed with respect to any facility for any taxable year shall not exceed the amount which bears the same ratio to such amount of credit as—

(A) the national megawatt capacity limitation allocated to the facility, bears to

(B) the total megawatt nameplate capacity of such facility.

(2) AMOUNT OF NATIONAL LIMITATION.—The aggregate amount of national megawatt capacity limitation allocated by the Secretary under paragraph (3) shall not exceed 6,000 megawatts.

(3) ALLOCATION OF LIMITATION.—The Secretary shall allocate the national megawatt capacity limitation in such manner as the Secretary may prescribe.

(4) REGULATIONS.—Not later than 6 months after the date of the enactment of this section, the Secretary shall prescribe such regulations as may be necessary or appropriate to carry out the purposes of this subsection. Such regulations shall provide a certification process under which the Secretary, after consultation with the Secretary of Energy, shall approve and allocate the national megawatt capacity limitation.

Amendments

• 2007, Tax Technical Corrections Act of 2007 (P.L. 110-172)

P.L. 110-172, §6(a):

Amended Code Sec. 45J(b)(2). **Effective** as if included in the provision of the Energy Tax Incentives Act of 2005 (P.L. 109-58) to which it relates [**effective** for production in tax years beginning after 8-8-2005.—CCH]. Prior to amendment, Code Sec. 45J(b)(2) read as follows:

(2) AMOUNT OF NATIONAL LIMITATION.—The national megawatt capacity limitation shall be 6,000 megawatts.

[Sec. 45J(c)]

(c) OTHER LIMITATIONS.—

(1) ANNUAL LIMITATION.—The amount of the credit allowable under subsection (a) (after the application of subsection (b)) for any taxable year with respect to any facility shall not exceed an amount which bears the same ratio to $125,000,000 as—

(A) the national megawatt capacity limitation allocated under subsection (b) to the facility, bears to

(B) 1,000.

(2) PHASEOUT OF CREDIT.—

(A) IN GENERAL.—The amount of the credit determined under subsection (a) shall be reduced by an amount which bears the same ratio to the amount of the credit (determined without regard to this paragraph) as—

(i) the amount by which the reference price (as defined in section 45(e)(2)(C)) for the calendar year in which the sale occurs exceeds 8 cents, bears to

(ii) 3 cents.

(B) PHASEOUT ADJUSTMENT BASED ON INFLATION.—The 8 cent amount in subparagraph (A) shall be adjusted by multiplying such amount by the inflation adjustment factor (as defined in section 45(e)(2)(B)) for the calendar year in which the sale occurs. If any amount as increased under the preceding sentence is not a multiple of 0.1 cent, such amount shall be rounded to the nearest multiple of 0.1 cent.

Amendments

• 2005, Gulf Opportunity Zone Act of 2005 (P.L. 109-135)

P.L. 109-135, §402(d)(1):

Amended Code Sec. 45J(c)(2). **Effective** as if included in the provision of the Energy Policy Act of 2005 (P.L. 109-58) to which it relates [**effective** for production in tax years beginning after 8-8-2005.—CCH]. Prior to amendment, Code Sec. 45J(c)(2) read as follows:

(2) OTHER LIMITATIONS.—Rules similar to the rules of section 45(b)(1) shall apply for purposes of this section.

[Sec. 45J(d)]

(d) ADVANCED NUCLEAR POWER FACILITY.—For purposes of this section—

(1) IN GENERAL.—The term "advanced nuclear power facility" means any advanced nuclear facility—

(A) which is owned by the taxpayer and which uses nuclear energy to produce electricity, and

(B) which is placed in service after the date of the enactment of this paragraph and before January 1, 2021.

(2) ADVANCED NUCLEAR FACILITY.—For purposes of paragraph (1), the term "advanced nuclear facility" means any nuclear facility the reactor design for which is approved after December 31, 1993, by the Nuclear Regulatory Commission (and such design or a substantially similar design of comparable capacity was not approved on or before such date).

[Sec. 45J(e)]

(e) OTHER RULES TO APPLY.—Rules similar to the rules of paragraphs (1), (3), (4), and (5) of section 45(e) shall apply for purposes of this section.

Amendments

• 2005, Gulf Opportunity Zone Act of 2005 (P.L. 109-135)

P.L. 109-135, §402(d)(2):

Amended Code Sec. 45J(e) by striking "(2)," following "paragraphs (1),". **Effective** as if included in the provision of the Energy Policy Act of 2005 (P.L. 109-58) to which it relates [**effective** for production in tax years beginning after 8-8-2005.—CCH].

• 2005, Energy Tax Incentives Act of 2005 (P.L. 109-58)

P.L. 109-58, §1306(a):

Amended subpart D of part IV of subchapter A of chapter 1 by adding after Code Sec. 45I a new Code Sec. 45J. **Effective** for production in tax years beginning after 8-8-2005.

[Sec. 45K]

SEC. 45K. CREDIT FOR PRODUCING FUEL FROM A NONCONVENTIONAL SOURCE.

[Sec. 45K(a)]

(a) ALLOWANCE OF CREDIT.—For purposes of section 38, the nonconventional source production credit determined under this section for the taxable year is an amount equal to—

(1) $3, multiplied by

(2) the barrel-of-oil equivalent of qualified fuels—

(A) sold by the taxpayer to an unrelated person during the taxable year, and

(B) the production of which is attributable to the taxpayer.

Amendments

• 2005, Gulf Opportunity Zone Act of 2005 (P.L. 109-135)

P.L. 109-135, §402(g):

Amended Code Sec. 45K(a) by striking "if the taxpayer elects to have this section apply," following "For purposes of section 38,". **Effective** as if included in the provision of the Energy Policy Act of 2005 (P.L. 109-58) to which it relates [**effective** for credits determined under the Internal Revenue Code of 1986 for tax years ending after 12-31-2005.—CCH].

• 2005, Energy Tax Incentives Act of 2005 (P.L. 109-58)

P.L. 109-58, §1322(a)(3)(E):

Amended Code Sec. 45K(a), as redesignated by Act Sec. 1322(a)(1), by striking "There shall be allowed as a credit against the tax imposed by this chapter for the taxable year" and inserting "For purposes of section 38, if the taxpayer elects to have this section apply, the nonconventional source production credit determined under this section for the taxable year is". **Effective** for credits determined under the Internal Revenue Code of 1986 for tax years ending after 12-31-2005.

[Sec. 45K(b)]

(b) LIMITATIONS AND ADJUSTMENTS.—

(1) PHASEOUT OF CREDIT.—The amount of the credit allowable under subsection (a) shall be reduced by an amount which bears the same ratio to the amount of the credit (determined without regard to this paragraph) as—

(A) the amount by which the reference price for the calendar year in which the sale occurs exceeds $23.50, bears to

(B) $6.

(2) CREDIT AND PHASEOUT ADJUSTMENT BASED ON INFLATION.—The $3 amount in subsection (a) and the $23.50 and $6 amounts in paragraph (1) shall each be adjusted by multiplying such

amount by the inflation adjustment factor for the calendar year in which the sale occurs. In the case of gas from a tight formation, the $3 amount in subsection (a) shall not be adjusted.

(3) CREDIT REDUCED FOR GRANTS, TAX-EXEMPT BONDS, AND SUBSIDIZED ENERGY FINANCING.—

(A) IN GENERAL.—The amount of the credit allowable under subsection (a) with respect to any project for any taxable year (determined after the application of paragraphs (1) and (2)) shall be reduced by the amount which is the product of the amount so determined for such year and a fraction—

(i) the numerator of which is the sum, for the taxable year and all prior taxable years, of—

(I) grants provided by the United States, a State, or a political subdivision of a State for use in connection with the project,

(II) proceeds of any issue of State or local government obligations used to provide financing for the project the interest on which is exempt from tax under section 103, and

(III) the aggregate amount of subsidized energy financing (within the meaning of section 48(a)(4)(C)) provided in connection with the project, and

(ii) the denominator of which is the aggregate amount of additions to the capital account for the project for the taxable year and all prior taxable years.

(B) AMOUNTS DETERMINED AT CLOSE OF YEAR.—The amounts under subparagraph (A) for any taxable year shall be determined as of the close of the taxable year.

(4) CREDIT REDUCED FOR ENERGY CREDIT.—The amount allowable as a credit under subsection (a) with respect to any project for any taxable year (determined after the application of paragraphs (1), (2), and (3)) shall be reduced by the excess of—

(A) the aggregate amount allowed under section 38 for the taxable year or any prior taxable year by reason of the energy percentage with respect to property used in the project, over

(B) the aggregate amount recaptured with respect to the amount described in subparagraph (A)—

(i) under section 49(b) or 50(a) for the taxable year or any prior taxable year, or

(ii) under this paragraph for any prior taxable year.

The amount recaptured under section 49(b) or 50(a) with respect to any property shall be appropriately reduced to take into account any reduction in the credit allowed by this section by reason of the preceding sentence.

(5) CREDIT REDUCED FOR ENHANCED OIL RECOVERY CREDIT.—The amount allowable as a credit under subsection (a) with respect to any project for any taxable year (determined after application of paragraphs (1), (2), (3), and (4)) shall be reduced by the excess (if any) of—

(A) the aggregate amount allowed under section 38 for the taxable year and any prior taxable year by reason of any enhanced oil recovery credit determined under section 43 with respect to such project, over

(B) the aggregate amount recaptured with respect to the amount described in subparagraph (A) under this paragraph for any prior taxable year.

Amendments

• 2005, Energy Tax Incentives Act of 2005 (P.L. 109-58)

P.L. 109-58, §1322(a)(3)(F):

Amended Code Sec. 45K(b), as redesignated by Act Sec. 1322(a)(1), by striking paragraph (6). **Effective** for credits determined under the Internal Revenue Code of 1986 for tax years ending after 12-31-2005. Prior to being stricken, Code Sec. 45K(b)(6) read as follows:

(6) APPLICATION WITH OTHER CREDITS.—The credit allowed by subsection (a) for any taxable year shall not exceed the excess (if any) of—

(A) the regular tax for the taxable year reduced by the sum of the credits allowable under subpart A and section 27, over

(B) the tentative minimum tax for the taxable year.

• 1996, Small Business Job Protection Act of 1996 (P.L. 104-188)

P.L. 104-188, §1205(d)(3):

Amended Code Sec. 29(b)(6)(A) by striking "sections 27 and 28" and inserting "section 27". **Effective** for amounts paid or incurred in tax years ending after 6-30-96.

• 1990, Omnibus Budget Reconciliation Act of 1990 (P.L. 101-508)

P.L. 101-508, §11501(c)(1):

Amended Code Sec. 29(b) by redesignating paragraph (5) as paragraph (6) and by inserting after paragraph (4) new paragraph (5). **Effective** for tax years beginning after 12-31-90.

P.L. 101-508, §11813(b)(1)(A):

Amended Code Sec. 29(b)(3)(A)(i)(III) by striking "section 48(l)(11)(C)" and inserting "section 48(a)(4)(C)". **Effective** for property placed in service after 12-31-90. For exceptions, see Act Sec. 11813(c)(2), below.

P.L. 101-508, §11813(b)(1)(B):

Amended Code Sec. 29(b)(4) by striking "section 47" each place it appears and inserting "section 49(b) or 50(a)". **Effective** for property placed in service after 12-31-90. For exceptions, see Act Sec. 11813(c)(2), below.

P.L. 101-508, §11813(c)(2), provides:

(2) EXCEPTIONS.—The amendments made by this section shall not apply to—

(A) any transition property (as defined in section 49(e) of the Internal Revenue Code of 1986 (as in effect on the day before the date of the enactment of this Act),

(B) any property with respect to which qualified progress expenditures were previously taken into account under section 46(d) of such Code (as so in effect), and

(C) any property described in section 46(b)(2)(C) of such Code (as so in effect).

[Sec. 45K(c)]

(c) DEFINITION OF QUALIFIED FUELS.—For purposes of this section—

(1) IN GENERAL.—The term "qualified fuels" means—

(A) oil produced from shale and tar sands,

(B) gas produced from—

(i) geopressured brine, Devonian shale, coal seams, or a tight formation, or

(ii) biomass, and

(C) liquid, gaseous, or solid synthetic fuels produced from coal (including lignite), including such fuels when used as feedstocks.

(2) GAS FROM GEOPRESSURED BRINE, ETC.—

(A) IN GENERAL.—Except as provided in subparagraph (B), the determination of whether any gas is produced from geopressured brine, Devonian shale, coal seams, or a tight formation shall be made in accordance with section 503 of the Natural Gas Policy Act of 1978 (as in effect before the repeal of such section).

(B) SPECIAL RULES FOR GAS FROM TIGHT FORMATIONS.—The term "gas produced from a tight formation" shall only include gas from a tight formation—

(i) which, as of April 20, 1977, was committed or dedicated to interstate commerce (as defined in section 2(18) of the Natural Gas Policy Act of 1978, as in effect on the date of the enactment of this clause), or

(ii) which is produced from a well drilled after such date of enactment.

(3) BIOMASS.—The term "biomass" means any organic material other than—

(A) oil and natural gas (or any product thereof), and

(B) coal (including lignite) or any product thereof.

Amendments

• 2005, Energy Tax Incentives Act of 2005 (P.L. 109-58)

P.L. 109-58, §1322(b)(1)(A):

Amended Code Sec. 29(c)(2)(A), before redesignation as Code Sec. 45K by Act Sec. 1322(a), by inserting "(as in effect before the repeal of such section)" after "1978". **Effective** 8-8-2005.

• 1990, Omnibus Budget Reconciliation Act of 1990 (P.L. 101-508)

P.L. 101-508, §11501(b)(1):

Amended Code Sec. 29(c)(2)(B). **Effective** for gas produced after 12-31-90. Prior to amendment, Code Sec. 29(c)(2)(B) read as follows:

(B) SPECIAL RULES FOR GAS FROM TIGHT FORMATIONS.—The term "gas produced from a tight formation" shall only include—

(i) gas the price of which is regulated by the United States, and

(ii) gas for which the maximum lawful price applicable under the Natural Gas Policy Act of 1978 is at least 150 percent of the then applicable price under section 103 of such Act.

P.L. 101-508, §11813(b)(1)(C):

Amended Code Sec. 29(c)(3). **Effective** for property placed in service after 12-31-90. For exceptions, see Act Sec. 11813(c)(2), below. Prior to amendment, Code Sec. 29(c)(3) read as follows:

(3) BIOMASS.—The term "biomass" means any organic material which is an alternate substance (as defined in section 48(l)(3)(B)) other than coal (including lignite) or any product of such coal.

P.L. 101-508, §11813(c)(2), provides:

(2) EXCEPTIONS.—The amendments made by this section shall not apply to—

(A) any transition property (as defined in section 49(e) of the Internal Revenue Code of 1986 (as in effect on the day before the date of the enactment of this Act),

(B) any property with respect to which qualified progress expenditures were previously taken into account under section 46(d) of such Code (as so in effect), and

(C) any property described in section 46(b)(2)(C) of such Code (as so in effect).

P.L. 101-508, §11816(a):

Amended Code Sec. 29(c)(1) by inserting "and" at the end of subparagraph (B), by striking the comma at the end of subparagraph (C) and inserting a period, and by striking subparagraphs (D) and (E). **Effective** 11-5-90. Prior to amendment, Code Sec. 29(c)(1)(D) and (E) read as follows:

(D) qualifying processed wood fuels, and

(E) steam produced from solid agricultural byproducts (not including timber byproducts).

P.L. 101-508, §11816(b)(1):

Amended Code Sec. 29(c) by striking paragraphs (4) and (5). **Effective** 11-5-90. Prior to amendment, Code Sec. 29(c)(4) and (5) read as follows:

(4) QUALIFYING PROCESSED WOOD FUEL.—

(A) IN GENERAL.—The term "qualifying processed wood fuel" means any processed solid wood fuel (other than charcoal, fireplace products, or a product used for ornamental or recreational purposes) which has a Btu content per unit of volume or weight, determined without regard to any nonwood elements, which is at least 40 percent greater per unit of volume or weight than the Btu content of the wood from which it is produced (determined immediately before the processing).

(B) ELECTION.—A taxpayer shall elect, at such time and in such manner as the Secretary by regulations may prescribe, as to whether Btu content per unit shall be determined for purposes of this paragraph on a volume or weight basis. Any such election—

(i) shall apply to all production from a facility; and

(ii) shall be effective for the taxable year with respect to which it is made and for all subsequent taxable years and, once made, may be revoked only with the consent of the Secretary.

(5) AGRICULTURAL BYPRODUCT STEAM.—Steam produced from solid agricultural byproducts which is used by the taxpayer in his trade or business shall be treated as having been sold by the taxpayer to an unrelated person on the date on which it is used.

P.L. 101-508, §11821(b), provides:

(b) SAVINGS PROVISION.—If—

(1) any provision amended or repealed by this part applied to—

(A) any transaction occurring before the date of the enactment of this Act,

(B) any property acquired before such date of enactment, or

(C) any item of income, loss, deduction, or credit taken into account before such date of enactment, and

(2) the treatment of such transaction, property, or item under such provision would (without regard to the amendments made by this part) affect liability for tax for periods ending after such date of enactment,

nothing in the amendments made by this part shall be construed to affect the treatment of such transaction, property, or item for purposes of determining liability for tax for periods ending after such date of enactment.

[Sec. 45K(d)]

(d) OTHER DEFINITIONS AND SPECIAL RULES.—For purposes of this section—

(1) ONLY PRODUCTION WITHIN THE UNITED STATES TAKEN INTO ACCOUNT.—Sales shall be taken into account under this section only with respect to qualified fuels the production of which is within—

(A) the United States (within the meaning of section 638(1)), or

(B) a possession of the United States (within the meaning of section 638(2)).

(2) COMPUTATION OF INFLATION ADJUSTMENT FACTOR AND REFERENCE PRICE.—

(A) IN GENERAL.—The Secretary shall, not later than April 1 of each calendar year, determine and publish in the Federal Register the inflation adjustment factor and the reference price for the preceding calendar year in accordance with this paragraph.

(B) INFLATION ADJUSTMENT FACTOR.—The term "inflation adjustment factor" means, with respect to a calendar year, a fraction the numerator of which is the GNP implicit price deflator for the calendar year and the denominator of which is the GNP implicit price deflator for calendar year 1979. The term "GNP implicit price deflator" means the first revision of the implicit price deflator for the gross national product as computed and published by the Department of Commerce.

(C) REFERENCE PRICE.—The term "reference price" means with respect to a calendar year the Secretary's estimate of the annual average wellhead price per barrel for all domestic crude oil the price of which is not subject to regulation by the United States.

(3) PRODUCTION ATTRIBUTABLE TO THE TAXPAYER.—In the case of a property or facility in which more than 1 person has an interest, except to the extent provided in regulations prescribed by the Secretary, production from the property or facility (as the case may be) shall be allocated among such persons in proportion to their respective interests in the gross sales from such property or facility.

(4) GAS FROM GEOPRESSURED BRINE, DEVONIAN SHALE, COAL SEAMS, OR A TIGHT FORMATION.—The amount of the credit allowable under subsection (a) shall be determined without regard to any production attributable to a property from which gas from Devonian shale, coal seams, geopressured brine, or a tight formation was produced in marketable quantities before January 1, 1980.

(5) BARREL-OF-OIL EQUIVALENT.—The term "barrel-of-oil equivalent" with respect to any fuel means that amount of such fuel which has a Btu content of 5.8 million; except that in the case of qualified fuels described in subparagraph (C) of subsection (c)(1), the Btu content shall be determined without regard to any material from a source not described in such subparagraph.

(6) BARREL DEFINED.—The term "barrel" means 42 United States gallons.

(7) RELATED PERSONS.—Persons shall be treated as related to each other if such persons would be treated as a single employer under the regulations prescribed under section 52(b). In the case of a corporation which is a member of an affiliated group of corporations filing a consolidated return, such corporation shall be treated as selling qualified fuels to an unrelated person if such fuels are sold to such a person by another member of such group.

(8) PASS-THRU IN THE CASE OF ESTATES AND TRUSTS.—Under regulations prescribed by the Secretary, rules similar to the rules of subsection (d) of section 52 shall apply.

Amendments

• **1990, Omnibus Budget Reconciliation Act of 1990 (P.L. 101-508)**

P.L. 101-508, §11816(b)(2):

Amended Code Sec. 29(d)(4). **Effective** 11-5-90. Prior to amendment, Code Sec. 29(d)(4) read as follows:

(4) SPECIAL RULES APPLICABLE TO GAS FROM GEOPRESSURED BRINE, DEVONIAN SHALE, COAL SEAMS, OR A TIGHT FORMATION.—

(A) CREDIT ALLOWED ONLY FOR NEW PRODUCTION.—The amount of the credit allowable under subsection (a) shall be determined without regard to any production attributable to a property from which gas from Devonian shale, coal seams, geopressured brine, or a tight formation was produced in marketable quantities before January 1, 1980.

(B) REFERENCE PRICE AND APPLICATION OF PHASEOUT FOR DEVONIAN SHALE.—

(i) REFERENCE PRICE FOR DEVONIAN SHALE.—For purposes of this section, the term "reference price" for gas from Devonian shale sold during calendar years 1980, 1981, and 1982 shall be the average wellhead price per thousand cubic feet for such year of high cost natural gas (as defined in section 107(c)(2), (3), and (4) of the Natural Gas Policy Act of 1978 and determined under section 503 of that Act) as estimated by the Secretary after consultation with the Federal Energy Regulatory Commission.

(ii) DIFFERENT PHASEOUT TO APPLY FOR 1980, 1981, AND 1982.—For purposes of applying paragraphs (1) and (2) of subsection (b) with respect to sales during calendar years 1980, 1981, and 1982 of gas from Devonian shale, "$4.05" shall be substituted for "$23.50" and "$1.03" shall be substituted for "$6.00."

P.L. 101-508, §11816(b)(3):

Amended Code Sec. 29(d) by striking paragraph (5) and redesignating the following paragraphs accordingly. **Effective** 11-5-90. Prior to amendment, Code Sec. 29(d)(5) read as follows:

(5) PHASEOUT DOES NOT APPLY FOR FIRST 3 YEARS OF PRODUCTION FROM FACILITY PRODUCING QUALIFYING PROCESSED WOOD OR

STEAM FROM SOLID AGRICULTURAL BYPRODUCTS.—In the case of a facility for the production of—

(A) qualifying processed wood fuel, or

(B) steam from solid agricultural byproducts,

paragraph (1) of subsection (b) shall not apply with respect to the amount of the credit allowable under subsection (a) for fuels sold during the 3-year period beginning on the date the facility is placed in service.

P.L. 101-508, §11816(b)(4):

Amended Code Sec. 29(d)(5) (as redesignated by Act Sec. 11816(b)(3)) by striking "subparagraph (C), (D), or (E)" and inserting "subparagraph (C)." **Effective** 11-5-90.

P.L. 101-508, §11821(b), provides:

(b) SAVINGS PROVISION.—If—

(1) any provision amended or repealed by this part applied to—

(A) any transaction occurring before the date of the enactment of this Act,

(B) any property acquired before such date of enactment, or

(C) any item of income, loss, deduction, or credit taken into account before such date of enactment, and

(2) the treatment of such transaction, property, or item under such provision would (without regard to the amendments made by this part) affect liability for tax for periods ending after such date of enactment,

nothing in the amendments made by this part shall be construed to affect the treatment of such transaction, property, or item for purposes of determining liability for tax for periods ending after such date of enactment.

[Sec. 45K(e)]

(e) APPLICATION OF SECTION.—This section shall apply with respect to qualified fuels—

(1) which are—

(A) produced from a well drilled after December 31, 1979, and before January 1, 1993, or

(B) produced in a facility placed in service after December 31, 1979, and before January 1, 1993, and

(2) which are sold before January 1, 2003.

Amendments

• 2005, Energy Tax Incentives Act of 2005 (P.L. 109-58)

P.L. 109-58, §1322(b)(1)(B):

Amended Code Sec. 29(c)(2)(A) [Code Sec. 29], before redesignation as Code Sec. 45K by Act Sec. 1322(a) and as amended by Act Sec. 1321, by striking subsection (e) and redesignating subsections (f), (g), and (h) as subsections (e), (f), and (g), respectively. **Effective** 8-8-2005. Prior to being stricken, Code Sec. 29(e) read as follows:

(e) APPLICATION WITH THE NATURAL GAS POLICY ACT OF 1978.—

(1) NO CREDIT IF SECTION 107 OF THE NATURAL GAS POLICY ACT OF 1978 IS UTILIZED.—Subsection (a) shall apply with respect to any natural gas described in subsection (c)(1)(B)(i) which is sold during the taxable year only if such natural gas is sold at a lawful price which is determined without regard to the provisions of section 107 of the Natural Gas Policy Act of 1978 and subtitle B of title I of such Act.

(2) TREATMENT OF THIS SECTION.—For purposes of section 107(d) of the Natural Gas Policy Act of 1978, this section shall not be treated as allowing any credit, exemption, deduction, or comparable adjustment applicable to the computation of any Federal tax.

• 1990, Omnibus Budget Reconciliation Act of 1990 (P.L. 101-508)

P.L. 101-508, §11501(a)(1)-(2):

Amended Code Sec. 29(f)(1) by striking "1991" in clauses (i) and (ii) of subparagraph (A) and inserting "1993", and by striking "2001" in subparagraph (B) and inserting "2003". **Effective** 11-5-90.

P.L. 101-508, §11816(b)(5):

Amended Code Sec. 29(f). **Effective** 11-5-90. Prior to amendment, subsection (f) (as amended by Act Sec. 11501(a)(1)-(2)) read as follows:

(f) APPLICATION OF SECTION.—

(1) IN GENERAL.—Except as provided in paragraph (2), this section shall apply with respect to qualified fuels—

(A) which are—

(i) produced from a well drilled after December 31, 1979, and before January 1, 1993, or

(ii) produced in a facility placed in service after December 31, 1979, and before January 1, 1993, and

(B) which are sold after December 31, 1979, and before January 1, 2003.

(2) SPECIAL RULES APPLICABLE TO QUALIFIED PROCESSED WOOD AND SOLID AGRICULTURAL BYPRODUCT STEAM.—

(A) CREDIT ALLOWED ONLY FOR CERTAIN PRODUCTION.—In the case of qualifying processed wood fuel and steam from solid agricultural byproducts, this section shall apply only with respect to—

(i) qualifying processed wood fuel produced in facilities placed in service after December 31, 1979, and before January 1, 1982, which is sold before the later of—

(I) October 1, 1983, or

(II) the date which is 3 years after the date on which the facility is placed in service; and

(ii) steam produced in facilities placed in service after December 31, 1979, from solid agricultural byproducts which is sold before January 1, 1985.

(B) EXPANDED PRODUCTION OF STEAM TREATED AS NEW FACILITY PRODUCTION.—For purposes of this subsection and subsection (d)(5), in the case of a facility for the production of steam from solid agricultural byproducts which was placed in service before January 1, 1980, any production of steam attributable to an expansion of the capacity of the facility to produce such steam through placing additional or replacement equipment in service after December 31, 1979, shall be treated as if it were produced by a facility placed in service on the date on which such equipment is placed in service.

P.L. 101-508, §11821(b), provides:

(b) SAVINGS PROVISION.—If—

(1) any provision amended or repealed by this part applied to—

(A) any transaction occuring before the date of the enactment of this Act,

(B) any property acquired before such date of enactment, or

(C) any item of income, loss, deduction, or credit taken into account before such date of enactment, and

(2) the treatment of such transaction, property, or item under such provision would (without regard to the amendments made by this part) affect liability for tax for periods ending after such date of enactment,

nothing in the amendments made by this part shall be construed to affect the treatment of such transaction, property, or item for purposes of determining liability for tax for periods ending after such date of enactment.

• 1988, Technical and Miscellaneous Revenue Act of 1988 (P.L. 100-647)

P.L. 100-647, §6302:

Amended Code Sec. 29(f)(1)(A)(i) and (ii) by striking out "January 1, 1990" and inserting in lieu thereof "January 1, 1991". **Effective** 11-10-88.

• **1986, Tax Reform Act of 1986 (P.L. 99-514)**

P.L. 99-514, §701(c)(3):

Amended Code Sec. 29(b)(5). **Effective** for tax years beginning after 12-31-86. Prior to amendment, Code Sec. 29(b)(5) read as follows:

(5) APPLICATION WITH OTHER CREDITS.—The credit allowed by subsection (a) for a taxable year shall not exceed the taxpayer's tax liability for the taxable year (as defined in section 26(b)), reduced by the sum of the credits allowable under subpart A and sections 27 and 28.

P.L. 99-514, §1879(c)(1):

Amended Code Sec. 29(d)(8) by adding a new sentence at the end thereof. **Effective** as if included in the amendments made by P.L. 96-223, §231.

• **1984, Deficit Reduction Act of 1984 (P.L. 98-369)**

P.L. 98-369, §471(c)(1):

Redesignated former Code Sec. 44D as Code Sec. 29. **Effective** for tax years beginning after 12-31-83, and to carrybacks from such years.

P.L. 98-369, §474(h):

Amended Code Sec. 29(b)(5), as redesignated by Act Sec. 471(c)(1). **Effective** for tax years beginning after 12-31-83, and to carrybacks from such years. Prior to amendment, Code Sec. 29(b)(5) read as follows:

(5) APPLICATION WITH OTHER CREDITS.—The credit allowed by subsection (a) for a taxable year shall not exceed the tax imposed by this chapter for such taxable year, reduced by the sum of the credits allowable under a section of this subpart having a lower number or letter designation than this section, other than the credits allowable by sections 31, 39, and 43. For purposes of the preceding sentence, the term "tax imposed by this chapter" shall not include any tax treated as not imposed by this chapter under the last sentence of section 53(a).

P.L. 98-369, §612(e)(1):

Amended Code Sec. 29(b)(5), as redesignated by Act Sec. 471(c)(1) and amended by Act Sec. 475(h), by striking out "section 25(b)" and inserting in lieu thereof "section 26(b)". **Effective** for interest paid or accrued after 12-31-84, on indebtedness incurred after 12-31-84, and to elections under section 25(c)(2)(A)(ii) of the Internal Revenue Code of 1954 (as added by this Act) for calendar years after 1983.

P.L. 98-369, §722(d)(1):

Amended Code Sec. 29(b)(1)(A), as redesignated by Act Sec. 471(c)(1), by striking out "in which the taxable year begins" and inserting in lieu thereof "in which the sale occurs". **Effective** for tax years ending after 12-31-79.

P.L. 98-369, §722(d)(2):

Amended Code Sec. 29(b)(2), as redesignated by Act Sec. 471(c)(1), by striking out "in which a taxable year begins" and inserting in lieu thereof "in which the sale occurs". **Effective** for tax years ending after 12-31-79.

• **1983, Technical Corrections Act of 1982 (P.L. 97-448)**

P.L. 97-448, §202(a):

Amended Code Sec. 44D(f) by striking out "December 3, 1979" each place it appeared and inserting in lieu thereof "December 31, 1979". **Effective** as if it had been included in the provision of P.L. 96-223 to which it relates.

• **1982, Subchapter S Revision Act of 1982 (P.L. 37-354)**

P.L. 97-354, §5(a)(1):

Amended Code Sec. 44D(d)(9). **Effective** for tax years beginning after 12-31-82. Prior to amendment, it read as follows:

(9) PASSTHROUGH IN THE CASE OF SUBCHAPTER S CORPORATIONS, ETC.—Under regulations prescribed by the Secretary, rules similar to the rules of subsections (d) and (e) of section 52 shall apply.

• **1981, Economic Recovery Tax Act of 1981 (P.L. 97-34)**

P.L. 97-34, §611(a):

Amended Code Sec. 44D(e). **Effective** for tax years beginning after 12-31-79. Prior to amendment, Code Sec. 44D(e) read as follows:

(e) CREDIT NOT ALLOWABLE IF TAXPAYER MAKES ELECTION UNDER NATURAL GAS POLICY ACT OF 1978.—If the taxpayer makes an election under section 107(d) of the Natural Gas Policy Act of 1978 to have subsections (a) and (b) of section 107 of that Act, and subtitle B of title I of that Act, apply with respect to gas described in subsection (c)(1)(B)(i) produced from any well on a property, then the credit allowable by subsection (a) shall not be allowed with respect to any gas produced on that property.

• **1980, Crude Oil Windfall Profit Tax Act of 1980 (P.L. 96-223)**

P.L. 96-223, §231(a):

Added Code Sec. 44D. **Effective** for tax years ending after 12-31-79.

[Sec. 45K(f)]

(f) EXTENSION FOR CERTAIN FACILITIES.—

(1) IN GENERAL.—In the case of a facility for producing qualified fuels described in subparagraph (B)(ii) or (C) of subsection (c)(1)—

(A) for purposes of subsection (e)(1)(B), such facility shall be treated as being placed in service before January 1, 1993, if such facility is placed in service before July 1, 1998, pursuant to a binding written contract in effect before January 1, 1997, and

(B) if such facility is originally placed in service after December 31, 1992, paragraph (2) of subsection (e) shall be applied with respect to such facility by substituting "January 1, 2008" for "January 1, 2003".

(2) SPECIAL RULE.—Paragraph (1) shall not apply to any facility which produces coke or coke gas unless the original use of the facility commences with the taxpayer.

Amendments

• **2005, Energy Tax Incentives Act of 2005 (P.L. 109-58)**

P.L. 109-58, §1322(b)(1)(B):

Amended Code Sec. 29(c)(2)(A) [Code Sec. 29], before redesignation as Code Sec. 45K by Act Sec. 1322(a) and as amended by Act Sec. 1321, by redesignating subsection (g) as subsection (f). **Effective** 8-8-2005.

P.L. 109-58, §1322(b)(2)(A)-(B):

Amended Code Sec. 29(g)(1), before redesignation by Act Sec. 1322(a) and Act Sec. 1322(b)(1), by striking "subsection (f)(1)(B)" and inserting "subsection (e)(1)(B)" in subparagraph (A), and by striking "subsection (f)" and inserting "subsection (e)" in subparagraph (B). **Effective** 8-8-2005.

• **1996, Small Business Job Protection Act of 1996 (P.L. 104-188)**

P.L. 104-188, §1207(a):

Amended Code Sec. 29(g)(1)(A) by striking "January 1, 1997" and inserting "July 1, 1998" and by striking "January 1, 1996" and inserting "January 1, 1997". **Effective** 8-20-96.

• **1992, Energy Policy Act of 1992 (P.L. 102-486)**

P.L. 102-486, §1918:

Amended Code Sec. 29 by adding at the end thereof new subsection (g). **Effective** 10-24-92.

[Sec. 45K(g)]

(g) EXTENSION FOR FACILITIES PRODUCING COKE OR COKE GAS.—Notwithstanding subsection (e)—

(1) IN GENERAL.—In the case of a facility for producing coke or coke gas (other than from petroleum based products) which was placed in service before January 1, 1993, or after June 30, 1998, and before January 1, 2010, this section shall apply with respect to coke and coke gas produced in such facility and sold during the period—

(A) beginning on the later of January 1, 2006, or the date that such facility is placed in service, and

(B) ending on the date which is 4 years after the date such period began.

(2) SPECIAL RULES.—In determining the amount of credit allowable under this section solely by reason of this subsection—

(A) DAILY LIMIT.—The amount of qualified fuels sold during any taxable year which may be taken into account by reason of this subsection with respect to any facility shall not exceed an average barrel-of-oil equivalent of 4,000 barrels per day. Days before the date the facility is placed in service shall not be taken into account in determining such average.

(B) EXTENSION PERIOD TO COMMENCE WITH UNADJUSTED CREDIT AMOUNT.—For purposes of applying subsection (b)(2) to the $3 amount in subsection (a), in the case of fuels sold after 2005, subsection (d)(2)(B) shall be applied by substituting "2004" for "1979".

(C) DENIAL OF DOUBLE BENEFIT.—This subsection shall not apply to any facility producing qualified fuels for which a credit was allowed under this section for the taxable year or any preceding taxable year by reason of subsection (f).

(D) NONAPPLICATION OF PHASEOUT.—Subsection (b)(1) shall not apply.

(E) COORDINATION WITH SECTION 45.—No credit shall be allowed with respect to any qualified fuel which is steel industry fuel (as defined in section 45(c)(7)) if a credit is allowed to the taxpayer for such fuel under section 45.

Amendments

• 2008, Energy Improvement and Extension Act of 2008 (P.L. 110-343)

P.L. 110-343, Division B, §108(d)(2):

Amended Code Sec. 45K(g)(2) by adding at the end a new subparagraph (E). **Effective** for fuel produced and sold after 9-30-2008.

• 2006, Tax Relief and Health Care Act of 2006 (P.L. 109-432)

P.L. 109-432, Division A, §211(a):

Amended Code Sec. 45K(g)(2) by adding at the end a new subparagraph (D). **Effective** as if included in section 1321 of the Energy Policy Act of 2005 (P.L. 109-58) [**effective** for fuel produced and sold after 12-31-2005, in tax years ending after such date.—CCH].

P.L. 109-432, Division A, §211(b):

Amended Code Sec. 45K(g)(1) by inserting "(other than from petroleum based products)" after "coke or coke gas". **Effective** as if included in section 1321 of the Energy Policy Act of 2005 (P.L. 109-58) [**effective** for fuel produced and sold after 12-31-2005, in tax years ending after such date.—CCH].

• 2005, Gulf Opportunity Zone Act of 2005 (P.L. 109-135)

P.L. 109-135, §412(l)(1)-(2):

Amended Code Sec. 45K(g) by striking "subsection (f)" and inserting "subsection (e)" in the matter preceding paragraph (1), and by striking "subsection (g)" and inserting "subsection (f)" in paragraph (2)(C). **Effective** 12-21-2005.

• 2005, Energy Tax Incentives Act of 2005 (P.L. 109-58)

P.L. 109-58, §1321(a):

Amended Code Sec. 29 by adding at the end a new subsection (h). **Effective** for fuel produced and sold after 12-31-2005, in tax years ending after such date.

P.L. 109-58, §1322(a)(1):

Amended the Internal Revenue Code of 1986 by redesignating Code Sec. 29 as Code Sec. 45K and by moving Code Sec. 45K (as so redesignated) from subpart B of part IV of subchapter A of chapter 1 to the end of subpart D of part IV of subchapter A of chapter 1. **Effective** for credits determined under the Internal Revenue Code of 1986 for tax years ending after 12-31-2005.

P.L. 109-58, §1322(b)(1)(B):

Amended Code Sec. 29(c)(2)(A) [Code Sec. 29], before redesignation by Act Sec. 1322(a) and as amended by Act Sec. 1321, by redesignating subsection (h) as subsection (g). **Effective** 8-8-2005.

[Sec. 45L]

SEC. 45L. NEW ENERGY EFFICIENT HOME CREDIT.

[Sec. 45L(a)]

(a) ALLOWANCE OF CREDIT.—

(1) IN GENERAL.—For purposes of section 38, in the case of an eligible contractor, the new energy efficient home credit for the taxable year is the applicable amount for each qualified new energy efficient home which is—

(A) constructed by the eligible contractor, and

(B) acquired by a person from such eligible contractor for use as a residence during the taxable year.

(2) APPLICABLE AMOUNT.—For purposes of paragraph (1), the applicable amount is an amount equal to—

(A) in the case of a dwelling unit described in paragraph (1) or (2) of subsection (c), $2,000, and

(B) in the case of a dwelling unit described in paragraph (3) of subsection (c), $1,000.

[Sec. 45L(b)]

(b) DEFINITIONS.—For purposes of this section—

(1) ELIGIBLE CONTRACTOR.—The term "eligible contractor" means—

(A) the person who constructed the qualified new energy efficient home, or

(B) in the case of a qualified new energy efficient home which is a manufactured home, the manufactured home producer of such home.

(2) QUALIFIED NEW ENERGY EFFICIENT HOME.—The term "qualified new energy efficient home" means a dwelling unit—

(A) located in the United States,

(B) the construction of which is substantially completed after the date of the enactment of this section, and

(C) which meets the energy saving requirements of subsection (c).

(3) CONSTRUCTION.—The term "construction" includes substantial reconstruction and rehabilitation.

(4) ACQUIRE.—The term "acquire" includes purchase.

[Sec. 45L(c)]

(c) ENERGY SAVING REQUIREMENTS.—A dwelling unit meets the energy saving requirements of this subsection if such unit is—

(1) certified—

(A) to have a level of annual heating and cooling energy consumption which is at least 50 percent below the annual level of heating and cooling energy consumption of a comparable dwelling unit—

(i) which is constructed in accordance with the standards of chapter 4 of the 2003 International Energy Conservation Code, as such Code (including supplements) is in effect on the date of the enactment of this section, and

(ii) for which the heating and cooling equipment efficiencies correspond to the minimum allowed under the regulations established by the Department of Energy pursuant to the National Appliance Energy Conservation Act of 1987 and in effect at the time of completion of construction, and

(B) to have building envelope component improvements account for at least 1/5 of such 50 percent,

(2) a manufactured home which conforms to Federal Manufactured Home Construction and Safety Standards (part 3280 of title 24, Code of Federal Regulations) and which meets the requirements of paragraph (1), or

(3) a manufactured home which conforms to Federal Manufactured Home Construction and Safety Standards (part 3280 of title 24, Code of Federal Regulations) and which—

(A) meets the requirements of paragraph (1) applied by substituting "30 percent" for "50 percent" both places it appears therein and by substituting "1/3" for "1/5" in subparagraph (B) thereof, or

(B) meets the requirements established by the Administrator of the Environmental Protection Agency under the Energy Star Labeled Homes program.

Amendments

• 2007, Tax Technical Corrections Act of 2007 (P.L. 110-172)

P.L. 110-172, §11(a)(7):

Amended Code Sec. 45L(c)(2) and (3) by striking "section 3280" and inserting "part 3280". **Effective** 12-29-2007.

[Sec. 45L(d)]

(d) CERTIFICATION.—

(1) METHOD OF CERTIFICATION.—A certification described in subsection (c) shall be made in accordance with guidance prescribed by the Secretary, after consultation with the Secretary of Energy. Such guidance shall specify procedures and methods for calculating energy and cost savings.

(2) FORM.—Any certification described in subsection (c) shall be made in writing in a manner which specifies in readily verifiable fashion the energy efficient building envelope components and energy efficient heating or cooling equipment installed and their respective rated energy efficiency performance.

[Sec. 45L(e)]

(e) BASIS ADJUSTMENT.—For purposes of this subtitle, if a credit is allowed under this section in connection with any expenditure for any property, the increase in the basis of such property which would (but for this subsection) result from such expenditure shall be reduced by the amount of the credit so determined.

[Sec. 45L(f)]

(f) COORDINATION WITH INVESTMENT CREDIT.—For purposes of this section, expenditures taken into account under section 47 or 48(a) shall not be taken into account under this section.

[Sec. 45L(g)]

(g) TERMINATION.—This section shall not apply to any qualified new energy efficient home acquired after December 31, 2009.

Amendments

• 2008, Energy Improvement and Extension Act of 2008 (P.L. 110-343)

P.L. 110-343, Division B, §304:

Amended Code Sec. 45L(g) by striking "December 31, 2008" and inserting "December 31, 2009". **Effective** 10-3-2008.

• 2006, Tax Relief and Health Care Act of 2006 (P.L. 109-432)

P.L. 109-432, Division A, §205:

Amended Code Sec. 45L(g) by striking "December 31, 2007" and inserting "December 31, 2008". **Effective** 12-20-2006.

• 2005, Energy Tax Incentives Act of 2005 (P.L. 109-58)

P.L. 109-58, §1332(a):

Amended subpart D of part IV of subchapter A of chapter 1, as amended by this Act, by adding at the end a new Code Sec. 45L. **Effective** for qualified new energy efficient homes acquired after 12-31-2005, in tax years ending after such date.

[Sec. 45M]

SEC. 45M. ENERGY EFFICIENT APPLIANCE CREDIT.

[Sec. 45M(a)]

(a) GENERAL RULE.—

(1) IN GENERAL.—For purposes of section 38, the energy efficient appliance credit determined under this section for any taxable year is an amount equal to the sum of the credit amounts determined under paragraph (2) for each type of qualified energy efficient appliance produced by the taxpayer during the calendar year ending with or within the taxable year.

(2) CREDIT AMOUNTS.—The credit amount determined for any type of qualified energy efficient appliance is—

(A) the applicable amount determined under subsection (b) with respect to such type, multiplied by

(B) the eligible production for such type.

[Sec. 45M(b)]

(b) APPLICABLE AMOUNT.—For purposes of subsection (a)—

(1) DISHWASHERS.—The applicable amount is—

(A) $45 in the case of a dishwasher which is manufactured in calendar year 2008 or 2009 and which uses no more than 324 kilowatt hours per year and 5.8 gallons per cycle, and

(B) $75 in the case of a dishwasher which is manufactured in calendar year 2008, 2009, or 2010 and which uses no more than 307 kilowatt hours per year and 5.0 gallons per cycle (5.5 gallons per cycle for dishwashers designed for greater than 12 place settings).

(2) CLOTHES WASHERS.—The applicable amount is—

(A) $75 in the case of a residential top-loading clothes washer manufactured in calendar year 2008 which meets or exceeds a 1.72 modified energy factor and does not exceed a 8.0 water consumption factor,

(B) $125 in the case of a residential top-loading clothes washer manufactured in calendar year 2008 or 2009 which meets or exceeds a 1.8 modified energy factor and does not exceed a 7.5 water consumption factor,

(C) $150 in the case of a residential or commercial clothes washer manufactured in calendar year 2008, 2009, or 2010 which meets or exceeds 2.0 modified energy factor and does not exceed a 6.0 water consumption factor, and

(D) $250 in the case of a residential or commercial clothes washer manufactured in calendar year 2008, 2009, or 2010 which meets or exceeds 2.2 modified energy factor and does not exceed a 4.5 water consumption factor.

(3) REFRIGERATORS.—The applicable amount is—

(A) $50 in the case of a refrigerator which is manufactured in calendar year 2008, and consumes at least 20 percent but not more than 22.9 percent less kilowatt hours per year than the 2001 energy conservation standards,

(B) $75 in the case of a refrigerator which is manufactured in calendar year 2008 or 2009, and consumes at least 23 percent but no more than 24.9 percent less kilowatt hours per year than the 2001 energy conservation standards,

(C) $100 in the case of a refrigerator which is manufactured in calendar year 2008, 2009, or 2010, and consumes at least 25 percent but not more than 29.9 percent less kilowatt hours per year than the 2001 energy conservation standards, and

(D) $200 in the case of a refrigerator manufactured in calendar year 2008, 2009, or 2010 and which consumes at least 30 percent less energy than the 2001 energy conservation standards.

Amendments

• 2008, Energy Improvement and Extension Act of 2008 (P.L. 110-343)

P.L. 110-343, Division B, §305(a):

Amended Code Sec. 45M(b). **Effective** for appliances produced after 12-31-2007. Prior to amendment, Code Sec. 45M(b) read as follows:

(b) APPLICABLE AMOUNT.—

(1) IN GENERAL.—For purposes of subsection (a)—

(A) DISHWASHERS.—The applicable amount is the energy savings amount in the case of a dishwasher which—

(i) is manufactured in calendar year 2006 or 2007, and

(ii) meets the requirements of the Energy Star program which are in effect for dishwashers in 2007.

(B) CLOTHES WASHERS.—The applicable amount is $100 in the case of a clothes washer which—

(i) is manufactured in calendar year 2006 or 2007, and

(ii) meets the requirements of the Energy Star program which are in effect for clothes washers in 2007.

(C) REFRIGERATORS.—

(i) 15 PERCENT SAVINGS.—The applicable amount is $75 in the case of a refrigerator which—

(I) is manufactured in calendar year 2006, and

(II) consumes at least 15 percent but not more than 20 percent less kilowatt hours per year than the 2001 energy conservation standards.

(ii) 20 PERCENT SAVINGS.—The applicable amount is $125 in the case of a refrigerator which—

(I) is manufactured in calendar year 2006 or 2007, and

(II) consumes at least 20 percent but not more than 25 percent less kilowatt hours per year than the 2001 energy conservation standards.

(iii) 25 PERCENT SAVINGS.—The applicable amount is $175 in the case of a refrigerator which—

(I) is manufactured in calendar year 2006 or 2007, and

(II) consumes at least 25 percent less kilowatt hours per year than the 2001 energy conservation standards.

(2) ENERGY SAVINGS AMOUNT.—For purposes of paragraph (1)(A)—

(A) IN GENERAL.—The energy savings amount is the lesser of—

(i) the product of—

(I) $3, and

(II) 100 multiplied by the energy savings percentage, or

(ii) $100.

(B) ENERGY SAVINGS PERCENTAGE.—For purposes of subparagraph (A), the energy savings percentage is the ratio of—

(i) the EF required by the Energy Star program for dishwashers in 2007 minus the EF required by the Energy Star program for dishwashers in 2005, to

(ii) the EF required by the Energy Star program for dishwashers in 2007.

[Sec. 45M(c)]

(c) ELIGIBLE PRODUCTION.—The eligible production in a calendar year with respect to each type of energy efficient appliance is the excess of—

(1) the number of appliances of such type which are produced by the taxpayer in the United States during such calendar year, over

(2) the average number of appliances of such type which were produced by the taxpayer (or any predecessor) in the United States during the preceding 2-calendar year period.

Amendments

• 2008, Energy Improvement and Extension Act of 2008 (P.L. 110-343)

P.L. 110-343, Division B, §305(b)(1)(A)-(D):

Amended Code Sec. 45M(c) by striking paragraph (2), by striking "(1) IN GENERAL" and all that follows through "the eligible" and inserting "The eligible", by moving the text of such subsection in line with the subsection heading, and by redesignating subparagraphs (A) and (B) as paragraphs (1) and (2), respectively, and by moving such paragraphs 2 ems to the left. **Effective** for appliances produced after 12-31-2007. Prior to amendment, Code Sec. 45M(c) read as follows:

(c) ELIGIBLE PRODUCTION.—

(1) IN GENERAL.—Except as provided in paragraphs [sic](2), the eligible production in a calendar year with respect to each type of energy efficient appliance is the excess of—

(A) the number of appliances of such type which are produced by the taxpayer in the United States during such calendar year, over

(B) the average number of appliances of such type which were produced by the taxpayer (or any predecessor) in the United States during the preceding 3-calendar year period.

(2) SPECIAL RULE FOR REFRIGERATORS.—The eligible production in a calendar year with respect to each type of refrigerator described in subsection (b)(1)(C) is the excess of—

(A) the number of appliances of such type which are produced by the taxpayer in the United States during such calendar year, over

(B) 110 percent of the average number of appliances of such type which were produced by the taxpayer (or any predecessor) in the United States during the preceding 3-calendar year period.

P.L. 110-343, Division B, §305(b)(2):

Amended Code Sec. 45M(c)(2), as amended by Act Sec. 305(b)(1), by striking "3-calendar year" and inserting "2-calendar year". **Effective** for appliances produced after 12-31-2007.

[Sec. 45M(d)]

(d) TYPES OF ENERGY EFFICIENT APPLIANCE.—For purposes of this section, the types of energy efficient appliances are—

(1) dishwashers described in subsection (b)(1),

(2) clothes washers described in subsection (b)(2), and

(3) refrigerators described in subsection (b)(3).

Amendments

• 2008, Energy Improvement and Extension Act of 2008 (P.L. 110-343)

P.L. 110-343, Division B, §305(c):

Amended Code Sec. 45M(d). **Effective** for appliances produced after 12-31-2007. Prior to amendment, Code Sec. 45M(d) read as follows:

(d) TYPES OF ENERGY EFFICIENT APPLIANCE.—For purposes of this section, the types of energy efficient appliances are—

(1) dishwashers described in subsection (b)(1)(A),

(2) clothes washers described in subsection (b)(1)(B),

(3) refrigerators described in subsection (b)(1)(C)(i),

(4) refrigerators described in subsection (b)(1)(C)(ii), and

(5) refrigerators described in subsection (b)(1)(C)(iii).

[Sec. 45M(e)]

(e) LIMITATIONS.—

(1) AGGREGATE CREDIT AMOUNT ALLOWED.—The aggregate amount of credit allowed under subsection (a) with respect to a taxpayer for any taxable year shall not exceed $75,000,000 reduced by the amount of the credit allowed under subsection (a) to the taxpayer (or any predecessor) for all prior taxable years beginning after December 31, 2007.

(2) AMOUNT ALLOWED FOR CERTAIN REFRIGERATORS AND CLOTHES WASHERS.—Refrigerators described in subsection (b)(3)(D) and clothes washers described in subsection (b)(2)(D) shall not be taken into account under paragraph (1).

(3) LIMITATION BASED ON GROSS RECEIPTS.—The credit allowed under subsection (a) with respect to a taxpayer for the taxable year shall not exceed an amount equal to 2 percent of the average annual gross receipts of the taxpayer for the 3 taxable years preceding the taxable year in which the credit is determined.

(4) GROSS RECEIPTS.—For purposes of this subsection, the rules of paragraphs (2) and (3) of section 448(c) shall apply.

Amendments

• 2008, Energy Improvement and Extension Act of 2008 (P.L. 110-343)

P.L. 110-343, Division B, §305(d)(1):

Amended Code Sec. 45M(e)(1). **Effective** for appliances produced after 12-31-2007. Prior to amendment, Code Sec. 45M(e)(1) read as follows:

(1) AGGREGATE CREDIT AMOUNT ALLOWED.—The aggregate amount of credit allowed under subsection (a) with respect to a taxpayer for any taxable year shall not exceed $75,000,000 reduced by the amount of the credit allowed under subsection (a) to the taxpayer (or any predecessor) for all prior taxable years.

P.L. 110-343, Division B, §305(d)(2):

Amended Code Sec. 45M(e)(2). **Effective** for appliances produced after 12-31-2007. Prior to amendment, Code Sec. 45M(e)(2) read as follows:

(2) AMOUNT ALLOWED FOR 15 PERCENT SAVINGS REFRIGERATORS.—In the case of refrigerators described in subsection (b)(1)(C)(i), the aggregate amount of the credit allowed under subsection (a) with respect to a taxpayer for any taxable year shall not exceed $20,000,000.

[Sec. 45M(f)]

(f) DEFINITIONS.—For purposes of this section—

(1) QUALIFIED ENERGY EFFICIENT APPLIANCE.—The term "qualified energy efficient appliance" means—

(A) any dishwasher described in subsection (b)(1),

(B) any clothes washer described in subsection (b)(2), and

(C) any refrigerator described in subsection (b)(3).

(2) DISHWASHER.—The term "dishwasher" means a residential dishwasher subject to the energy conservation standards established by the Department of Energy.

(3) CLOTHES WASHER.—The term "clothes washer" means a residential model clothes washer, including a commercial residential style coin operated washer.

(4) TOP-LOADING CLOTHES WASHER.—The term "top-loading clothes washer" means a clothes washer which has the clothes container compartment access located on the top of the machine and which operates on a vertical axis.

(5) REFRIGERATOR.—The term "refrigerator" means a residential model automatic defrost refrigerator-freezer which has an internal volume of at least 16.5 cubic feet.

(6) MODIFIED ENERGY FACTOR.—The term "modified energy factor" means the modified energy factor established by the Department of Energy for compliance with the Federal energy conservation standard.

(7) PRODUCED.—The term "produced" includes manufactured.

(8) 2001 ENERGY CONSERVATION STANDARD.—The term "2001 energy conservation standard" means the energy conservation standards promulgated by the Department of Energy and effective July 1, 2001.

(9) GALLONS PER CYCLE.—The term "gallons per cycle" means, with respect to a dishwasher, the amount of water, expressed in gallons, required to complete a normal cycle of a dishwasher.

(10) WATER CONSUMPTION FACTOR.—The term "water consumption factor" means, with respect to a clothes washer, the quotient of the total weighted per-cycle water consumption divided by the cubic foot (or liter) capacity of the clothes washer.

Amendments

• 2008, Energy Improvement and Extension Act of 2008 (P.L. 110-343)

P.L. 110-343, Division B, §305(e)(1):

Amended Code Sec. 45M(f)(1). **Effective** for appliances produced after 12-31-2007. Prior to amendment, Code Sec. 45M(f)(1) read as follows:

(1) QUALIFIED ENERGY EFFICIENT APPLIANCE.—The term "qualified energy efficient appliance" means—

(A) any dishwasher described in subsection (b)(1)(A),

(B) any clothes washer described in subsection (b)(1)(B), and

(C) any refrigerator described in subsection (b)(1)(C).

P.L. 110-343, Division B, §305(e)(2):

Amended Code Sec. 45M(f)(3) by inserting "commercial" before "residential" the second place it appears. **Effective** for appliances produced after 12-31-2007.

P.L. 110-343, Division B, §305(e)(3):

Amended Code Sec. 45M(f) by redesignating paragraphs (4), (5), (6), and (7) as paragraphs (5), (6), (7), and (8), respectively, and by inserting after paragraph (3) a new paragraph (4). **Effective** for appliances produced after 12-31-2007.

P.L. 110-343, Division B, §305(e)(4):

Amended Code Sec. 45M(f)(6), as redesignated by Act Sec. 305(e)(3). **Effective** for appliances produced after 12-31-2007. Prior to amendment, Code Sec. 45M(f)(6) read as follows:

(6) EF.—The term "EF" means the energy factor established by the Department of Energy for compliance with the Federal energy conservation standards.

P.L. 110-343, Division B, §305(e)(5):

Amended Code Sec. 45M(f), as amended by Act Sec. 305(e)(3), by adding at the end new paragraphs (9)-(10). **Effective** for appliances produced after 12-31-2007.

[Sec. 45M(g)]

(g) SPECIAL RULES.—For purposes of this section—

(1) IN GENERAL.—Rules similar to the rules of subsections (c), (d), and (e) of section 52 shall apply.

(2) CONTROLLED GROUP.—

(A) IN GENERAL.—All persons treated as a single employer under subsection (a) or (b) of section 52 or subsection (m) or (o) of section 414 shall be treated as a single producer.

(B) INCLUSION OF FOREIGN CORPORATIONS.—For purposes of subparagraph (A), in applying subsections (a) and (b) of section 52 to this section, section 1563 shall be applied without regard to subsection (b)(2)(C) thereof.

(3) VERIFICATION.—No amount shall be allowed as a credit under subsection (a) with respect to which the taxpayer has not submitted such information or certification as the Secretary, in consultation with the Secretary of Energy, determines necessary.

Amendments

• 2005, Energy Tax Incentives Act of 2005 (P.L. 109-58)

P.L. 109-58, §1334(a):

Amended subpart D of part IV of subchapter A of chapter 1, as amended by this Act, by adding at the end a new Code Sec. 45M. **Effective** for appliances produced after 12-31-2005.

[Sec. 45N]

SEC. 45N. MINE RESCUE TEAM TRAINING CREDIT.

[Sec. 45N(a)]

(a) AMOUNT OF CREDIT.—For purposes of section 38, the mine rescue team training credit determined under this section with respect to each qualified mine rescue team employee of an eligible employer for any taxable year is an amount equal to the lesser of—

(1) 20 percent of the amount paid or incurred by the taxpayer during the taxable year with respect to the training program costs of such qualified mine rescue team employee (including wages of such employee while attending such program), or

(2) $10,000.

[Sec. 45N(b)]

(b) QUALIFIED MINE RESCUE TEAM EMPLOYEE.—For purposes of this section, the term "qualified mine rescue team employee" means with respect to any taxable year any full-time employee of the taxpayer who is—

(1) a miner eligible for more than 6 months of such taxable year to serve as a mine rescue team member as a result of completing, at a minimum, an initial 20-hour course of instruction as prescribed by the Mine Safety and Health Administration's Office of Educational Policy and Development, or

(2) a miner eligible for more than 6 months of such taxable year to serve as a mine rescue team member by virtue of receiving at least 40 hours of refresher training in such instruction.

[Sec. 45N(c)]

(c) ELIGIBLE EMPLOYER.—For purposes of this section, the term "eligible employer" means any taxpayer which employs individuals as miners in underground mines in the United States.

[Sec. 45N(d)]

(d) WAGES.—For purposes of this section, the term "wages" has the meaning given to such term by subsection (b) of section 3306 (determined without regard to any dollar limitation contained in such section).

[Sec. 45N(e)]

(e) TERMINATION.—This section shall not apply to taxable years beginning after December 31, 2009.

Amendments

• 2008, Tax Extenders and Alternative Minimum Tax Relief Act of 2008 (P.L. 110-343)

P.L. 110-343, Division C, §310:

Amended Code Sec. 45N(e) by striking "December 31, 2008" and inserting "December 31, 2009". **Effective** 10-3-2008.

• 2006, Tax Relief and Health Care Act of 2006 (P.L. 109-432)

P.L. 109-432, Division A, §405(a):

Amended subpart D of part IV of subchapter A of chapter 1 by adding at the end a new Code Sec. 45N. **Effective** for tax years beginning after 12-31-2005.

[Sec. 45O]

SEC. 45O. AGRICULTURAL CHEMICALS SECURITY CREDIT.

[Sec. 45O(a)]

(a) IN GENERAL.—For purposes of section 38, in the case of an eligible agricultural business, the agricultural chemicals security credit determined under this section for the taxable year is 30 percent of the qualified security expenditures for the taxable year.

[Sec. 45O(b)]

(b) FACILITY LIMITATION.—The amount of the credit determined under subsection (a) with respect to any facility for any taxable year shall not exceed—

(1) $100,000, reduced by

(2) the aggregate amount of credits determined under subsection (a) with respect to such facility for the 5 prior taxable years.

[Sec. 45O(c)]

(c) ANNUAL LIMITATION.—The amount of the credit determined under subsection (a) with respect to any taxpayer for any taxable year shall not exceed $2,000,000.

[Sec. 45O(d)]

(d) QUALIFIED CHEMICAL SECURITY EXPENDITURE.—For purposes of this section, the term "qualified chemical security expenditure" means, with respect to any eligible agricultural business for any taxable year, any amount paid or incurred by such business during such taxable year for—

(1) employee security training and background checks,

(2) limitation and prevention of access to controls of specified agricultural chemicals stored at the facility,

(3) tagging, locking tank valves, and chemical additives to prevent the theft of specified agricultural chemicals or to render such chemicals unfit for illegal use,

(4) protection of the perimeter of specified agricultural chemicals,

(5) installation of security lighting, cameras, recording equipment, and intrusion detection sensors,

(6) implementation of measures to increase computer or computer network security,

(7) conducting a security vulnerability assessment,

(8) implementing a site security plan, and

(9) such other measures for the protection of specified agricultural chemicals as the Secretary may identify in regulation.

Amounts described in the preceding sentence shall be taken into account only to the extent that such amounts are paid or incurred for the purpose of protecting specified agricultural chemicals.

[Sec. 45O(e)]

(e) ELIGIBLE AGRICULTURAL BUSINESS.—For purposes of this section, the term "eligible agricultural business" means any person in the trade or business of—

(1) selling agricultural products, including specified agricultural chemicals, at retail predominantly to farmers and ranchers, or

(2) manufacturing, formulating, distributing, or aerially applying specified agricultural chemicals.

[Sec. 45O(f)]

(f) SPECIFIED AGRICULTURAL CHEMICAL.—For purposes of this section, the term "specified agricultural chemical" means—

(1) any fertilizer commonly used in agricultural operations which is listed under—

(A) section 302(a)(2) of the Emergency Planning and Community Right-to-Know Act of 1986,

(B) section 101 of part 172 of title 49, Code of Federal Regulations, or

(C) part 126, 127, or 154 of title 33, Code of Federal Regulations, and

(2) any pesticide (as defined in section 2(u) of the Federal Insecticide, Fungicide, and Rodenticide Act), including all active and inert ingredients thereof, which is customarily used on crops grown for food, feed, or fiber.

[Sec. 45O(g)]

(g) CONTROLLED GROUPS.—Rules similar to the rules of paragraphs (1) and (2) of section 41(f) shall apply for purposes of this section.

[Sec. 45O(h)]

(h) REGULATIONS.—The Secretary may prescribe such regulations as may be necessary or appropriate to carry out the purposes of this section, including regulations which—

(1) provide for the proper treatment of amounts which are paid or incurred for [the] purpose of protecting any specified agricultural chemical and for other purposes, and

(2) provide for the treatment of related properties as one facility for purposes of subsection (b).

[Sec. 45O(i)]

(i) TERMINATION.—This section shall not apply to any amount paid or incurred after December 31, 2012.

Amendments

• 2008, Heartland, Habitat, Harvest, and Horticulture Act of 2008 (P.L. 110-246)

P.L. 110-246, §15343(a):

Amended subpart D of part IV of subchapter A of chapter 1 by adding at the end a new Code Sec. 45O. **Effective** for amounts paid or incurred after 5-22-2008.

[Sec. 45P]

SEC. 45P. EMPLOYER WAGE CREDIT FOR EMPLOYEES WHO ARE ACTIVE DUTY MEMBERS OF THE UNIFORMED SERVICES.

[Sec. 45P(a)]

(a) GENERAL RULE.—For purposes of section 38, in the case of an eligible small business employer, the differential wage payment credit for any taxable year is an amount equal to 20 percent of the sum of the eligible differential wage payments for each of the qualified employees of the taxpayer during such taxable year.

[Sec. 45P(b)]

(b) DEFINITIONS.—For purposes of this section—

(1) ELIGIBLE DIFFERENTIAL WAGE PAYMENTS.—The term "eligible differential wage payments" means, with respect to each qualified employee, so much of the differential wage payments (as defined in section 3401(h)(2)) paid to such employee for the taxable year as does not exceed $20,000.

(2) QUALIFIED EMPLOYEE.—The term "qualified employee" means a person who has been an employee of the taxpayer for the 91-day period immediately preceding the period for which any differential wage payment is made.

(3) ELIGIBLE SMALL BUSINESS EMPLOYER.—

(A) IN GENERAL.—The term "eligible small business employer" means, with respect to any taxable year, any employer which—

(i) employed an average of less than 50 employees on business days during such taxable year, and

(ii) under a written plan of the employer, provides eligible differential wage payments to every qualified employee of the employer.

(B) CONTROLLED GROUPS.—For purposes of subparagraph (A), all persons treated as a single employer under subsection (b), (c), (m), or (o) of section 414 shall be treated as a single employer.

[Sec. 45P(c)]

(c) COORDINATION WITH OTHER CREDITS.—The amount of credit otherwise allowable under this chapter with respect to compensation paid to any employee shall be reduced by the credit determined under this section with respect to such employee.

[Sec. 45P(d)]

(d) DISALLOWANCE FOR FAILURE TO COMPLY WITH EMPLOYMENT OR REEMPLOYMENT RIGHTS OF MEMBERS OF THE RESERVE COMPONENTS OF THE ARMED FORCES OF THE UNITED STATES.—No credit shall be allowed under subsection (a) to a taxpayer for—

(1) any taxable year, beginning after the date of the enactment of this section, in which the taxpayer is under a final order, judgment, or other process issued or required by a district court

of the United States under section 4323 of title 38 of the United States Code with respect to a violation of chapter 43 of such title, and

(2) the 2 succeeding taxable years.

[Sec. 45P(e)]

(e) CERTAIN RULES TO APPLY.—For purposes of this section, rules similar to the rules of subsections (c), (d), and (e) of section 52 shall apply.

[Sec. 45P(f)]

(f) TERMINATION.—This section shall not apply to any payments made after December 31, 2009.

Amendments

• 2008, Heroes Earnings Assistance and Relief Tax Act of 2008 (P.L. 110-245)

P.L. 110-245, §111(a):

Amended subpart D of part IV of subchapter A of chapter 1 by adding at the end a new Code Sec. 45P. **Effective** for amounts paid after 6-17-2008.

[Sec. 45Q]

SEC. 45Q. CREDIT FOR CARBON DIOXIDE SEQUESTRATION.

[Sec. 45Q(a)]

(a) GENERAL RULE.—For purposes of section 38, the carbon dioxide sequestration credit for any taxable year is an amount equal to the sum of—

(1) $20 per metric ton of qualified carbon dioxide which is—

(A) captured by the taxpayer at a qualified facility, and

(B) disposed of by the taxpayer in secure geological storage and not used by the taxpayer as described in paragraph (2)(B), and

(2) $10 per metric ton of qualified carbon dioxide which is—

(A) captured by the taxpayer at a qualified facility,

(B) used by the taxpayer as a tertiary injectant in a qualified enhanced oil or natural gas recovery project, and

(C) disposed of by the taxpayer in secure geological storage.

Amendments

• 2009, American Recovery and Reinvestment Tax Act of 2009 (P.L. 111-5)

P.L. 111-5, §1131(a):

Amended Code Sec. 45Q(a)(2) by striking "and" at the end of subparagraph (A), by striking the period at the end of subparagraph (B) and inserting ", and", and by adding at the end a new subparagraph (C). **Effective** for carbon dioxide captured after 2-17-2009.

P.L. 111-5, §1131(b)(2):

Amended Code Sec. 45Q(a)(1)(B) by inserting "and not used by the taxpayer as described in paragraph (2)(B)" after "storage". **Effective** for carbon dioxide captured after 2-17-2009.

[Sec. 45Q(b)]

(b) QUALIFIED CARBON DIOXIDE.—For purposes of this section—

(1) IN GENERAL.—The term "qualified carbon dioxide" means carbon dioxide captured from an industrial source which—

(A) would otherwise be released into the atmosphere as industrial emission of greenhouse gas, and

(B) is measured at the source of capture and verified at the point of disposal or injection.

(2) RECYCLED CARBON DIOXIDE.—The term "qualified carbon dioxide" includes the initial deposit of captured carbon dioxide used as a tertiary injectant. Such term does not include carbon dioxide that is re-captured, recycled, and re-injected as part of the enhanced oil and natural gas recovery process.

[Sec. 45Q(c)]

(c) QUALIFIED FACILITY.—For purposes of this section, the term "qualified facility" means any industrial facility—

(1) which is owned by the taxpayer,

(2) at which carbon capture equipment is placed in service, and

(3) which captures not less than 500,000 metric tons of carbon dioxide during the taxable year.

[Sec. 45Q(d)]

(d) SPECIAL RULES AND OTHER DEFINITIONS.—For purposes of this section—

(1) ONLY CARBON DIOXIDE CAPTURED AND DISPOSED OF OR USED WITHIN THE UNITED STATES TAKEN INTO ACCOUNT.—The credit under this section shall apply only with respect to qualified carbon dioxide the capture and disposal or use of which is within—

(A) the United States (within the meaning of section 638(1)), or

(B) a possession of the United States (within the meaning of section 638(2)).

(2) SECURE GEOLOGICAL STORAGE.—The Secretary, in consultation with the Administrator of the Environmental Protection Agency[,] the Secretary of Energy, and the Secretary of the Interior, [sic], shall establish regulations for determining adequate security measures for the geological storage of carbon dioxide under paragraph (1)(B) or (2)(C) of subsection (a) such that the carbon dioxide does not escape into the atmosphere. Such term shall include storage at deep saline formations, oil and gas reservoirs, and unminable coal seams under such conditions as the Secretary may determine under such regulations.

(3) TERTIARY INJECTANT.—The term "tertiary injectant" has the same meaning as when used within section 193(b)(1).

(4) QUALIFIED ENHANCED OIL OR NATURAL GAS RECOVERY PROJECT.—The term "qualified enhanced oil or natural gas recovery project" has the meaning given the term "qualified enhanced oil recovery project" by section 43(c)(2), by substituting "crude oil or natural gas" for "crude oil" in subparagraph (A)(i) thereof.

(5) CREDIT ATTRIBUTABLE TO TAXPAYER.—Any credit under this section shall be attributable to the person that captures and physically or contractually ensures the disposal of or the use as a tertiary injectant of the qualified carbon dioxide, except to the extent provided in regulations prescribed by the Secretary.

(6) RECAPTURE.—The Secretary shall, by regulations, provide for recapturing the benefit of any credit allowable under subsection (a) with respect to any qualified carbon dioxide which ceases to be captured, disposed of, or used as a tertiary injectant in a manner consistent with the requirements of this section.

(7) INFLATION ADJUSTMENT.—In the case of any taxable year beginning in a calendar year after 2009, there shall be substituted for each dollar amount contained in subsection (a) an amount equal to the product of—

(A) such dollar amount, multiplied by

(B) the inflation adjustment factor for such calendar year determined under section 43(b)(3)(B) for such calendar year, determined by substituting "2008" for "1990".

Amendments

• 2009, American Recovery and Reinvestment Tax Act of 2009 (P.L. 111-5)

P.L. 111-5, §1131(b)(1)(A)-(C):

Amended Code Sec. 45Q(d)(2) by striking "subsection (a)(1)(B)" and inserting "paragraph (1)(B) or (2)(C) of subsection (a)", by striking "and unminable coal seams" and inserting ", oil and gas reservoirs, and unminable coal seams", and by inserting "the Secretary of Energy, and the Secretary of the Interior," after "Environmental Protection Agency". **Effective** for carbon dioxide captured after 2-17-2009.

[Sec. 45Q(e)]

(e) APPLICATION OF SECTION.—The credit under this section shall apply with respect to qualified carbon dioxide before the end of the calendar year in which the Secretary, in consultation with the Administrator of the Environmental Protection Agency, certifies that 75,000,000 metric tons of qualified carbon dioxide have been taken into account in accordance with subsection (a).

Amendments

• 2009, American Recovery and Reinvestment Tax Act of 2009 (P.L. 111-5)

P.L. 111-5, §1131(b)(3):

Amended Code Sec. 45Q(e) by striking "captured and disposed of or used as a tertiary injectant" and inserting "taken into account in accordance with subsection (a)". **Effective** for carbon dioxide captured after 2-17-2009.

• 2008, Energy Improvement and Extension Act of 2008 (P.L. 110-343)

P.L. 110-343, Division B, §115(a):

Amended subpart D of part IV of subchapter A of chapter 1 by adding a the end a new Code Sec. 45Q. **Effective** for carbon dioxide captured after 10-3-2008.

[Sec. 45R]

SEC. 45R. EMPLOYEE HEALTH INSURANCE EXPENSES OF SMALL EMPLOYERS.

[Sec. 45R(a)]

(a) GENERAL RULE.—For purposes of section 38, in the case of an eligible small employer, the small employer health insurance credit determined under this section for any taxable year in the credit period is the amount determined under subsection (b).

[Sec. 45R(b)]

(b) HEALTH INSURANCE CREDIT AMOUNT.—Subject to subsection (c), the amount determined under this subsection with respect to any eligible small employer is equal to 50 percent (35 percent in the case of a tax-exempt eligible small employer) of the lesser of—

(1) the aggregate amount of nonelective contributions the employer made on behalf of its employees during the taxable year under the arrangement described in subsection (d)(4) for premiums for qualified health plans offered by the employer to its employees through an Exchange, or

(2) the aggregate amount of nonelective contributions which the employer would have made during the taxable year under the arrangement if each employee taken into account under paragraph (1) had enrolled in a qualified health plan which had a premium equal to the average

premium (as determined by the Secretary of Health and Human Services) for the small group market in the rating area in which the employee enrolls for coverage.

[Sec. 45R(c)]

(c) PHASEOUT OF CREDIT AMOUNT BASED ON NUMBER OF EMPLOYEES AND AVERAGE WAGES.—The amount of the credit determined under subsection (b) without regard to this subsection shall be reduced (but not below zero) by the sum of the following amounts:

(1) Such amount multiplied by a fraction the numerator of which is the total number of full-time equivalent employees of the employer in excess of 10 and the denominator of which is 15.

(2) Such amount multiplied by a fraction the numerator of which is the average annual wages of the employer in excess of the dollar amount in effect under subsection (d)(3)(B) and the denominator of which is such dollar amount.

[Sec. 45R(d)]

(d) ELIGIBLE SMALL EMPLOYER.—For purposes of this section—

(1) IN GENERAL.—The term "eligible small employer" means, with respect to any taxable year, an employer—

(A) which has no more than 25 full-time equivalent employees for the taxable year,

(B) the average annual wages of which do not exceed an amount equal to twice the dollar amount in effect under paragraph (3)(B) for the taxable year, and

(C) which has in effect an arrangement described in paragraph (4).

(2) FULL-TIME EQUIVALENT EMPLOYEES.—

(A) IN GENERAL.—The term "full-time equivalent employees" means a number of employees equal to the number determined by dividing—

(i) the total number of hours of service for which wages were paid by the employer to employees during the taxable year, by

(ii) 2,080.

Such number shall be rounded to the next lowest whole number if not otherwise a whole number.

(B) EXCESS HOURS NOT COUNTED.—If an employee works in excess of 2,080 hours of service during any taxable year, such excess shall not be taken into account under subparagraph (A).

(C) HOURS OF SERVICE.—The Secretary, in consultation with the Secretary of Labor, shall prescribe such regulations, rules, and guidance as may be necessary to determine the hours of service of an employee, including rules for the application of this paragraph to employees who are not compensated on an hourly basis.

(3) AVERAGE ANNUAL WAGES.—

(A) IN GENERAL.—The average annual wages of an eligible small employer for any taxable year is the amount determined by dividing—

(i) the aggregate amount of wages which were paid by the employer to employees during the taxable year, by

(ii) the number of full-time equivalent employees of the employee determined under paragraph (2) for the taxable year.

Such amount shall be rounded to the next lowest multiple of $1,000 if not otherwise such a multiple.

(B) DOLLAR AMOUNT.—For purposes of paragraph (1)(B) and subsection (c)(2)—

(i) 2010, 2011, 2012, AND 2013.—The dollar amount in effect under this paragraph for taxable years beginning in 2010, 2011, 2012, or 2013 is $25,000.

(ii) SUBSEQUENT YEARS.—In the case of a taxable year beginning in a calendar year after 2013, the dollar amount in effect under this paragraph shall be equal to $25,000, multiplied by the cost-of-living adjustment under section 1(f)(3) for the calendar year, determined by substituting "calendar year 2012" for "calendar year 1992" in subparagraph (B) thereof.

(4) CONTRIBUTION ARRANGEMENT.—An arrangement is described in this paragraph if it requires an eligible small employer to make a nonelective contribution on behalf of each employee who enrolls in a qualified health plan offered to employees by the employer through an exchange in an amount equal to a uniform percentage (not less than 50 percent) of the premium cost of the qualified health plan.

(5) SEASONAL WORKER HOURS AND WAGES NOT COUNTED.—For purposes of this subsection—

(A) IN GENERAL.—The number of hours of service worked by, and wages paid to, a seasonal worker of an employer shall not be taken into account in determining the full-time equivalent employees and average annual wages of the employer unless the worker works for the employer on more than 120 days during the taxable year.

(B) DEFINITION OF SEASONAL WORKER.—The term "seasonal worker" means a worker who performs labor or services on a seasonal basis as defined by the Secretary of Labor, including workers covered by section 500.20(s)(1) of title 29, Code of Federal Regulations and retail workers employed exclusively during holiday seasons.

Amendments

• 2010, Patient Protection and Affordable Care Act (P.L. 111-148)

P.L. 111-148, §10105(e)(1):

Amended Code Sec. 45R(d)(3)(B), as added by Act Sec. 1421(a). **Effective** as if included in the enactment of Act Sec. 1421 [**effective** for amounts paid or incurred in tax years beginning after 12-31-2009 [**effective** date amended by Act Sec. 10105(e)(4).—CCH]]. Prior to amendment, Code Sec, 45R(d)(3)(B) read as follows:

(B) DOLLAR AMOUNT.—For purposes of paragraph (1)(B)—

(i) 2011, 2012, AND 2013.—The dollar amount in effect under this paragraph for taxable years beginning in 2011, 2012, or 2013 is $20,000.

(ii) SUBSEQUENT YEARS.—In the case of a taxable year beginning in a calendar year after 2013, the dollar amount in effect under this paragraph shall be equal to $20,000, multiplied by the cost-of-living adjustment determined under section 1(f)(3) for the calendar year, determined by substituting "calendar year 2012" for "calendar year 1992" in subparagraph (B) thereof.

[Sec. 45R(e)]

(e) OTHER RULES AND DEFINITIONS.—For purposes of this section—

(1) EMPLOYEE.—

(A) CERTAIN EMPLOYEES EXCLUDED.—The term "employee" shall not include—

(i) an employee within the meaning of section 401(c)(1),

(ii) any 2-percent shareholder (as defined in section 1372(b)) of an eligible small business which is an S corporation,

(iii) any 5-percent owner (as defined in section 416(i)(1)(B)(i)) of an eligible small business, or

(iv) any individual who bears any of the relationships described in subparagraphs (A) through (G) of section 152(d)(2) to, or is a dependent described in section 152(d)(2)(H) of, an individual described in clause (i), (ii), or (iii).

(B) LEASED EMPLOYEES.—The term "employee" shall include a leased employee within the meaning of section 414(n).

(2) CREDIT PERIOD.—The term "credit period" means, with respect to any eligible small employer, the 2-consecutive-taxable year period beginning with the 1st taxable year in which the employer (or any predecessor) offers 1 or more qualified health plans to its employees through an Exchange.

(3) NONELECTIVE CONTRIBUTION.—The term "nonelective contribution" means an employer contribution other than an employer contribution pursuant to a salary reduction arrangement.

(4) WAGES.—The term "wages" has the meaning given such term by section 3121(a) (determined without regard to any dollar limitation contained in such section).

(5) AGGREGATION AND OTHER RULES MADE APPLICABLE.—

(A) AGGREGATION RULES.—All employers treated as a single employer under subsection (b), (c), (m), or (o) of section 414 shall be treated as a single employer for purposes of this section.

(B) OTHER RULES.—Rules similar to the rules of subsections (c), (d), and (e) of section 52 shall apply.

[Sec. 45R(f)]

(f) CREDIT MADE AVAILABLE TO TAX-EXEMPT ELIGIBLE SMALL EMPLOYERS.—

(1) IN GENERAL.—In the case of a tax-exempt eligible small employer, there shall be treated as a credit allowable under subpart C (and not allowable under this subpart) the lesser of—

(A) the amount of the credit determined under this section with respect to such employer, or

(B) the amount of the payroll taxes of the employer during the calendar year in which the taxable year begins.

(2) TAX-EXEMPT ELIGIBLE SMALL EMPLOYER.—For purposes of this section, the term "tax-exempt eligible small employer" means an eligible small employer which is any organization described in section 501(c) which is exempt from taxation under section 501(a).

(3) PAYROLL TAXES.—For purposes of this subsection—

(A) IN GENERAL.—The term "payroll taxes" means—

(i) amounts required to be withheld from the employees of the tax-exempt eligible small employer under section 3401(a),

(ii) amounts required to be withheld from such employees under section 3101(b), and

(iii) amounts of the taxes imposed on the tax-exempt eligible small employer under section 3111(b).

(B) SPECIAL RULE.—A rule similar to the rule of section 24(d)(2)(C) shall apply for purposes of subparagraph (A).

[Sec. 45R(g)]

(g) APPLICATION OF SECTION FOR CALENDAR YEARS 2010, 2011, 2012, AND 2013.—In the case of any taxable year beginning in 2010, 2011, 2012, or 2013, the following modifications to this section shall apply in determining the amount of the credit under subsection (a):

(1) NO CREDIT PERIOD REQUIRED.—The credit shall be determined without regard to whether the taxable year is in a credit period and for purposes of applying this section to taxable years beginning after 2013, no credit period shall be treated as beginning with a taxable year beginning before 2014.

(2) AMOUNT OF CREDIT.—The amount of the credit determined under subsection (b) shall be determined—

(A) by substituting "35 percent (25 percent in the case of a tax-exempt eligible small employer)" for "50 percent (35 percent in the case of a tax-exempt eligible small employer)",

(B) by reference to an eligible small employer's nonelective contributions for premiums paid for health insurance coverage (within the meaning of section 9832(b)(1)) of an employee, and

(C) by substituting for the average premium determined under subsection (b)(2) the amount the Secretary of Health and Human Services determines is the average premium for the small group market in the State in which the employer is offering health insurance coverage (or for such area within the State as is specified by the Secretary).

(3) CONTRIBUTION ARRANGEMENT.—An arrangement shall not fail to meet the requirements of subsection (d)(4) solely because it provides for the offering of insurance outside of an Exchange.

Amendments

• 2010, Patient Protection and Affordable Care Act (P.L. 111-148)

P.L. 111-148, §10105(e)(2):

Amended Code Sec. 45R(g), as added by Act Sec. 1421(a), by striking "2011" both places it appears and inserting "2010, 2011". **Effective** as if included in the enactment of Act Sec. 1421 [**effective** for amounts paid or incurred in tax years beginning after 12-31-2009 [**effective** date amended by Act Sec. 10105(e)(4).—CCH]].

[Sec. 45R(h)]

(h) INSURANCE DEFINITIONS.—Any term used in this section which is also used in the Public Health Service Act or subtitle A of title I of the Patient Protection and Affordable Care Act shall have the meaning given such term by such Act or subtitle.

[Sec. 45R(i)]

(i) REGULATIONS.—The Secretary shall prescribe such regulations as may be necessary to carry out the provisions of this section, including regulations to prevent the avoidance of the 2-year limit on the credit period through the use of successor entities and the avoidance of the limitations under subsection (c) through the use of multiple entities.

Amendments

• 2010, Patient Protection and Affordable Care Act (P.L. 111-148)

P.L. 111-148, §1421(a):

Amended subpart D of part IV of subchapter A of chapter 1 by inserting after Code Sec. 45Q a new Code Sec. 45R. **Effective** for amounts paid or incurred in tax years beginning after 12-31-2009 [**effective** date amended by Act Sec. 10105(e)(4).—CCH].

Subpart E—Rules for Computing Investment Credit

[Sec. 46]

SEC. 46. AMOUNT OF CREDIT.

For purposes of section 38, the amount of the investment credit determined under this section for any taxable year shall be the sum of—

(1) the rehabilitation credit,

(2) the energy credit,

(3) the qualifying advanced coal project credit,

(4) the qualifying gasification project credit[,]

(5) the qualifying advanced energy project credit, and

(6) the qualifying therapeutic discovery project credit.

Amendments

• 2010, Patient Protection and Affordable Care Act (P.L. 111-148)

P.L. 111-148, §9023(b)(1)-(3):

Amended Code Sec. 46 by adding a comma at the end of paragraph (2), by striking the period at the end of paragraph (5) and inserting ", and" and by adding at the end a new paragraph (6). **Effective** for amounts paid or incurred after 12-31-2008, in tax years beginning after such date.

• 2009, American Recovery and Reinvestment Tax Act of 2009 (P.L. 111-5)

P.L. 111-5, §1302(a):

Amended Code Sec. 46 by striking "and" at the end of paragraph (3), by striking the period at the end of paragraph (4), and by adding at the end a new paragraph (5). **Effective** for periods after 2-17-2009, under rules similar to the rules of Code Sec. 48(m) (as in effect on the day before the date of the enactment of the Revenue Reconciliation Act of 1990).

• 2005, Energy Tax Incentives Act of 2005 (P.L. 109-58)

P.L. 109-58, §1307(a):

Amended Code Sec. 46 by striking "and" at the end of paragraph (1), by striking the period at the end of paragraph (2), and by adding at the end new paragraphs (3) and (4). **Effective** for periods after 8-8-2005, under rules similar to the rules of Code Sec. 48(m) (as in effect on the day before the date of the enactment of P.L. 101-508 [11-4-90.—CCH]).

• 2004, American Jobs Creation Act of 2004 (P.L. 108-357)

P.L. 108-357, §322(d)(1)(A)-(C):

Amended Code Sec. 46 by adding "and" at the end of paragraph (1), by striking ", and" at the end of paragraph (2) and inserting a period, and by striking paragraph (3). **Effective** with respect to expenditures paid or incurred after 10-22-2004. Prior to being stricken, Code Sec. 46(3) read as follows:

(3) the reforestation credit.

• 1990, Omnibus Budget Reconciliation Act of 1990 (P.L. 101-508)

P.L. 101-508, §11406:

Amended Code Sec. 46(b)(2)(A) by striking "Sept. 30, 1990" in clauses (viii) [(VIII)] and (ix) [(IX)] of the table contained therein and inserting "Dec. 31, 1991". **Effective** 11-5-90.

P.L. 101-508, §11813(a):

Amended Code Sec. 46. **Effective,** generally, to property placed in service after 12-31-90. For exceptions, see Act Sec. 11813(c)(2), below.

P.L. 101-508, §11813(c)(2), provides:

(2) EXCEPTIONS.—The amendments made by this section shall not apply to—

(A) any transition property (as defined in section 49(e) of the Internal Revenue Code of 1986 (as in effect on the day before the date of the enactment of this Act),

(B) any property with respect to which qualified progress expenditures were previously taken into account under section 46(d) of such Code (as so in effect), and

(C) any property described in section 46(b)(2)(C) of such Code (as so in effect)

Prior to amendment, Code Sec. 46 read as follows:

SEC. 46. AMOUNT OF CREDIT.

[Sec. 46(a)]

(a) AMOUNT OF INVESTMENT CREDIT.—For purposes of section 38, the amount of the investment credit determined under this section for any taxable year shall be an amount equal to the sum of the following percentages of the qualified investment (as determined under subsections (c) and (d)):

(1) the regular percentage,

(2) in the case of energy property, the energy percentage, and

(3) in the case of that portion of the basis of any property which is attributable to qualified rehabilitation expenditures, the rehabilitation percentage.

Amendments

• 1984, Deficit Reduction Act of 1984 (P.L. 98-369)

P.L. 98-369, §474(o)(1):

Amended Code Sec. 46(a). **Effective** for tax years beginning after 12-31-83, and to carrybacks from such years, but shall not be construed as reducing the amount of any credit allowable for qualified investment in taxable years beginning before 1-1-84. Prior to amendment, but after the amendment made by Act Sec. 713(c)(1)(C), Code Sec. 46(a) read as follows:

(a) GENERAL RULE.—

(1) FIRST-IN-FIRST-OUT RULE.—The amount of the credit allowed by section 38 for the taxable year shall be an amount equal to the sum of—

(A) the investment credit carryovers carried to such taxable year,

(B) the amount of the credit determined under paragraph (2) for such taxable year, plus

(C) the investment credit carrybacks carried to such taxable year.

(2) AMOUNT OF CREDIT.—

(A) IN GENERAL.—The amount of the credit determined under this paragraph for the taxable year shall be an amount equal to the sum of the following percentage of the qualified investment (as determined under subsections (c) and (d)):

(i) the regular percentage,

(ii) in the case of energy property, the energy percentage,

(iii) the employee plan percentage, and

(iv) in the case of that portion of the basis of any property which is attributable to qualified rehabilitation expenditures, the rehabilitation percentage.

(B) REGULAR PERCENTAGE.—For purposes of this paragraph, the regular percentage is 10 percent.

(C) ENERGY PERCENTAGE.—For purposes of this paragraph—

(i) IN GENERAL.—The energy percentage shall be determined in accordance with the following table:

Column A—Description In the case of:	Column B—Percentage The energy percentage is:	Column C—Period For the period: Beginning on:	And ending on
I. General Rule.—Property not described in any of the following provisions of this column	10 percent	Oct. 1, 1978	Dec. 31, 1982.
II. Solar, Wind, or Geothermal Property.—Property described in section 48(l)(2)(A)(ii) or 48(l)(3)(A)(viii)	A. 10 percent	Oct. 1, 1978	Dec. 31, 1979.
	B. 15 percent	Jan. 1, 1980	Dec. 31, 1985.

Column A—Description	Column B—Percentage	Column C—Period	
In the case of:	The energy percentage is:	For the period:	
		Beginning on:	And ending on
III. Ocean Thermal Property.—Property described in section 48(l)(3)(A)(ix)	15 percent	Jan. 1, 1980	Dec. 31, 1985.
IV. Qualified Hydroelectric Generating Property.—Property described in section 48(l)(2)(A)(vii)	11 percent	Jan. 1, 1980	Dec. 31, 1985.
V. Qualified Intercity Buses.—Property described in section 48(l)(2)(A)(ix)	10 percent	Jan. 1, 1980	Dec. 31, 1985.
VI. Biomass Property.—Property described in section 48(l)(15)	10 percent	Oct. 1, 1978	Dec. 31, 1985.
VII. Chlor-Alkali Electrolytic Cells.—Property described in section 48(l)(5)(M)	10 percent	Jan. 1, 1980	Dec. 31, 1982.

(ii) PERIODS FOR WHICH PERCENTAGE NOT SPECIFIED.—In the case of any energy property, the energy percentage shall be zero for any period for which an energy percentage is not specified for such property under clause (i) (as modified by clauses (iii) and (iv)).

(iii) LONGER PERIOD FOR CERTAIN LONG-TERM PROJECTS.—For the purpose of applying the energy percentage contained in subclause (I) of clause (i) with respect to property which is a part of a project with a normal construction period of 2 years or more (within the meaning of section 46(d)(2)(A)(i)), "December 31, 1990" shall be substituted for "December 31, 1982" if—

(I) before January 1, 1983, all engineering studies in connection with the commencement of the construction of the project have been completed and all environmental and construction permits required under Federal, State, or local law in connection with the commencement of the construction of the project have been applied for, and

(II) before January 1, 1986, the taxpayer has entered into binding contracts for the acquisition, construction, reconstruction, or erection of equipment specially designed for the project and the aggregate cost to the taxpayer of that equipment is at least 50 percent of the reasonably estimated cost for all such equipment which is to be placed in service as part of the project upon its completion.

(iv) LONGER PERIOD FOR CERTAIN HYDROELECTRIC GENERATING PROPERTY.—If an application has been docketed by the Federal Energy Regulatory Commission before January 1, 1986, with respect to the installation of any qualified hydroelectric generating property, for purposes of applying the energy percentage contained in subclause (IV) of clause (i) with respect to such property, "December 31, 1988" shall be substituted for "December 31, 1985."

(D) SPECIAL RULE FOR CERTAIN ENERGY PROPERTY.—For purposes of this paragraph, the regular percentage shall not apply to any energy property which, but for section 48(l)(1), would not be section 38 property. In the case of any qualified hydroelectric generating property which is a fish passageway, the preceding sentence shall not apply to any period after 1979 for which the energy percentage for such property is greater than zero.

(E) EMPLOYEE PLAN PERCENTAGE.—For purposes of this paragraph, the employee plan percentage is—

(i) with respect to the period beginning on January 21, 1975, and ending on December 31, 1982, 1 percent,

(ii) with respect to the period beginning on January 1, 1977, and ending on December 31, 1982, an additional percentage (not in excess of 1/2 of 1 percent) which results in an amount equal to the amount determined under section 48(n)(1)(B), and

(iii) with respect to any period beginning after December 31, 1982, zero.

This subparagraph shall apply to a corporation only if it meets the requirements of section 409A and only if it elects (at such time, in such form, and in such manner as the Secretary prescribes) to have this subparagraph apply.

(F) Rehabilitation Percentage.—For purposes of this paragraph—

(i) In General.—

In the case of qualified rehabilitation expenditures with respect to a:	The rehabilitation percentage is:
30-year building	15
40-year building	20
Certified historic structure	25

(ii) Regular and Energy Percentages Not to Apply.—The regular percentage and the energy percentage shall not apply to that portion of the basis of any property which is attributable to qualified rehabilitation expenditures.

(iii) Definitions.—

(I) 30-Year Building.—The term "30-year building" means a qualified rehabilitated building other than a 40-year building and other than a certified historic structure.

(II) 40-Year Building.—The term "40-year building" means a qualified rehabilitated building (other than a certified historic structure) which would meet the requirements of section 48(g)(1)(B) if "40" were substituted for "30" each place it appears in subparagraph (B) thereof.

(III) Certified Historic Structure.—The term "certified historic structure" means a qualified rehabilitated building which meets the requirements of section 48(g)(3).

(3) Limitation Based on Amount of Tax.—Notwithstanding paragraph (1), the credit allowed by section 38 for the taxable year shall not exceed—

(A) so much of the liability for tax for the taxable year as does not exceed $25,000, plus

(B) 85 percent of so much of the liability for tax for the taxable year as exceeds $25,000.

(4) Liability for Tax.—For purposes of paragraph (3), the liability for tax for the taxable year shall be the tax imposed by this chapter for such year, reduced by the sum of the credits allowable under—

(A) section 33 (relating to foreign tax credit), and

(B) section 37 (relating to credit for the elderly and the permanently and totally disabled).

For purposes of this paragraph, any tax imposed for the taxable year by section 56 (relating to corporate minimum tax), section 72(m)(5)(B) (relating to 10 percent tax on premature distributions to key-employees), section 72(q)(1) (relating to 5-percent tax on premature distributions under annuity contracts), section 402(e) (relating to tax on lump sum distributions), section 408(f) (relating to additional tax on income from certain retirement accounts), section 531 (relating to accumulated earnings tax), section 541 (relating to personal holding company tax), or section 1374 (relating to tax on certain capital gains of S corporations), and any additional tax imposed for the taxable year by section 1351(d)(1) (relating to recoveries of foreign expropriation losses), shall not be considered tax imposed by this chapter for such year.

(5) Married Individuals.—In the case of a husband or wife who files a separate return, the amount specified under subparagraphs (A) and (B) of paragraph (3) shall be $12,500 in lieu of $25,000. This paragraph shall not apply if the spouse of the taxpayer has no qualified investment for, and no unused credit carryback or carryover to, the taxable year of such spouse which ends within or with the taxpayer's taxable year.

(6) Controlled Groups.—In the case of a controlled group, the $25,000 amount specified under paragraph (3) shall be reduced for each component member of such group by apportioning $25,000 among the component members of such group in such manner as the Secretary shall by regulations prescribe. For purposes of the preceding sentence, the term "controlled group" has the meaning asssigned to such term by section 1563(a).

(7) Special Rules in the Case of Energy Property.—Under regulations prescribed by the Secretary—

(A) In General.—This subsection and subsection (b) shall be applied separately—

(i) first with respect to so much of the credit allowed by section 38 as is not attributable to the energy percentage, and

(ii) second with respect to so much of the credit allowed by section 38 as is attributable to the application of the energy percentage to energy property.

(B) Rules of Application for Energy Property.—In applying this subsection and subsection (b) for taxable years ending after September 30, 1978, with respect to so much of the credit allowed by section 38 as is described in subparagraph (A)(ii)—

(i) paragraph (3)(B) shall be applied by substituting "100 percent" for "85 percent," and

(ii) the liability for tax shall be the amount determined under paragraph (4) reduced by so much of the credit allowed by section 38 as is described in subparagraph (A)(i).

P.L. 98-369, §713(c)(1)(C):

Amended Code Sec. 46(a)(4) by striking out "tax on premature distributions to owner-employees" and inserting in lieu thereof "tax on premature distributions to key employees". **Effective** as if included in the provision of P.L. 97-248 to which it relates.

• 1983, Social Security Amendments of 1983 (P.L. 98-21)

P.L. 98-21, §122(c)(1):

Amended Code Sec. 46(a)(4)(B), by striking out "relating to credit for the elderly" and inserting in place thereof "relating to credit for the elderly and the permanently and totally disabled". **Effective** for tax years beginning after 1983.

• 1983, Surface Transportation Act of 1982 (P.L. 97-424)

P.L. 97-424, §546(b):

Amended Code Sec. 46(a)(2)(C)(i) by adding in the table new subsection VII. **Effective** 1-6-83.

• 1983, Technical Corrections Act of 1982 (P.L. 97-448)

P.L. 97-448, §102(f)(5)(A):

Amended Code Sec. 46(a)(2)(F)(iii)(II) by striking out "any building" and inserting in lieu thereof "a qualified rehabilitated building". **Effective** as if it had been included in the provision of P.L. 97-34 to which it relates.

P.L. 97-448, §102(f)(5)(B):

Amended Code Sec. 46(a)(2)(F)(iii)(III) by striking out "has the meaning given to such term by section 48(g)(3)" and inserting in lieu thereof "means a qualified rehabilitated building which meets the requirements of section 48(g)(3)". **Effective** as if it had been included in the provision of P.L. 97-34 to which it relates.

P.L. 97-448, §202(f):

Amended Code Sec. 46(a)(2)(C)(iii)(I). **Effective** as if it had been included in the provision of P.L. 96-223 to which it relates. Prior to amendment, Code Sec. 46(a)(2)(C)(iii)(I) read as follows:

"(I) before January 1, 1983, the taxpayer has completed all engineering studies in connection with the commencement of the construction of the project, and has applied for all environmental and construction permits required under Federal, State, or local law in connection with the commencement of the construction of the project, and"

P.L. 97-448, §306(a)(1)(A):

Amended P.L. 97-248, §201 by redesignating the second subsection (c) as subsection (d).

• 1982, Subchapter S Revision Act of 1982 (P.L. 97-354)

P.L. 97-354, §5(a)(4):

Amended Code Sec. 46(a)(4) by striking out in the second sentence "section 1378 (relating to tax on certain capital gains of subchapter S corporations)," and inserting in lieu thereof "section 1374 (relating to tax on certain capital gains of S corporations),". **Effective** for tax years beginning after 12-31-82.

• 1982, Tax Equity and Fiscal Responsibility Act of 1982 (P.L. 97-248)

P.L. 97-248, §201(c)[d](8)(A):

Amended Code Sec. 46(a)(4) by striking out "(relating to minimum tax for tax preferences)" and inserting in lieu thereof "(relating to corporate minimum tax)". **Effective** for tax years beginning after 12-31-82.

P.L. 97-248, §205(b)(1):

Amended Code Sec. 46(a)(3)(B). **Effective** for tax years beginning after 12-31-82. Prior to amendment, it read as follows:

"(B) the following percentage of so much of the liability for tax for the taxable year as exceeds $25,000:

If the taxable year ends in:	The percentage is:
1979	60
1980	70
1981	80
1982 or thereafter	90"

P.L. 97-248, §205(b)(2)(A):

Amended Code Sec. 46(a) by striking out paragraphs (7) and (8) and by redesignating paragraph (9) as paragraph (7). **Effective** for tax years beginning after 12-31-82. Prior to amendment, paragraphs (7) and (8) read as follows:

"(7) ALTERNATIVE LIMITATION IN THE CASE OF CERTAIN UTILITIES.—

(A) In general.—If, for the taxable year ending in 1979—

(i) the amount of the qualified investment of the taxpayer which is attributable to public utility property is 25 percent or more of his aggregate qualified investment, and

(ii) the application of this paragraph results in a percentage higher than 60 percent,

then subparagraph (B) of paragraph (3) of this subsection shall be applied by substituting for `60 percent' the taxpayer's applicable percentage for such year.

(B) APPLICABLE PERCENTAGE.—The applicable percentage for any taxpayer for any taxable year ending in 1979 is—

(i) 50 percent, plus

(ii) that portion of 20 percent which the taxpayer's amount of qualified investment which is public utility property bears to his aggregate qualified investment.

If the proportion referred to in clause (ii) is 75 percent or more, the applicable percentage of the taxpayer for the year shall be 70 percent.

(C) Public utility property defined.—For purposes of this paragraph, the term `public utility property' has the meaning given to such term by the first sentence of subsection (c)(3)(B).

(8) Alternative limitation in the case of certain railroads and airlines.—

(A) In general.—If, for a taxable year ending in 1979 or 1980—

(i) the amount of the qualified investment of the taxpayer which is attributable to railroad property or to airline property, as the case may be, is 25 percent or more of his aggregate qualified investment, and

(ii) the application of this paragraph results in a percentage higher than 60 percent (70 percent in the case of a taxable year ending in 1980),

then subparagraph (B) of paragraph (3) of this subsection shall be applied by substituting for `60 percent' (`70 percent' in the case of a taxable year ending in 1980) the taxpayer's applicable percentage for such year.

(B) Applicable percentage.—The applicable percentage of any taxpayer for any taxable year under this paragraph is—

(i) 50 percent, plus

(ii) that portion of the tentative percentage for the taxable year which the taxpayer's amount of qualified investment which is railroad property or airline property (as the case may be) bears to his aggregate qualified investment.

If the proportion referred to in clause (ii) is 75 percent or more, the applicable percentage of the taxpayer for the taxable year shall be 90 percent (80 percent in the case of a taxable year ending in 1980).

(C) Tentative percentage.—For purposes of subparagraph (B), the tentative percentage shall be determined under the following table:

If the taxable year ends in:	The tentative percentage is:
1979	40
1980	30

(D) Railroad property defined.—For purposes of this paragraph, the term `railroad property' means section 38 property used by the taxpayer directly in connection with the trade or business carried on by the taxpayer of operating a railroad (including a railroad switching or terminal company).

(E) Airline property defined.—For purposes of this paragraph, the term `airline property' means section 38 property used by the taxpayer directly in connection with the trade or business carried on by the taxpayer of the furnishing or sale of transportation as a common carrier by air subject to the jurisdiction of the Civil Aeronautics Board or the Federal Aviation Administration."

P.L. 97-248, §205(b)(2)(B):

Amended Code Sec. 46(a)(7)(B)(i) as redesignated. **Effective** for tax years beginning after 12-31-82. Prior to amendment, it read as follows:

"(i) paragraph (3)(B) shall be applied by substituting `100 percent' for the percentage determined under the table contained in such paragraph,"

P.L. 97-248, §205(b)(2)(C):

Amended Code Sec. 46(a)(7)(B) as redesignated by striking clause (ii) and by redesignating clause (iii) as clause (ii). **Effective** for tax years beginning after 12-31-82. Prior to amendment, clause (ii) read as follows:

"(ii) paragraphs (7) and (8) shall not apply, and"

P.L. 97-248, §265(b)(2)(A)(i):

Amended Code Sec. 46(a)(4) by inserting "section 72(q)(1) (relating to 5-percent tax on premature distributions under annuity contracts)," after "owner-employees)". **Effective** for distributions after 12-31-82.

• 1981, Economic Recovery Tax Act of 1981 (P.L. 97-34)

P.L. 97-34, §212(a)(1):

Amended Code Sec. 46(a)(2)(A) by striking out "and" at the end of clause (ii); by striking out the period at the end of clause (iii) and inserting in lieu thereof "and"; and by adding at the end thereof new clause (iv). **Effective** for expenditures incurred after 12-31-81, in tax years ending after such date.

P.L. 97-34, §212(e)(2), as amended by P.L. 97-448, §102(f)(1), provides:

(2) TRANSITIONAL RULE.—The amendments made by this section shall not apply with respect to any rehabilitation of a building if—

(A) the physical work on such rehabilitation began before January 1, 1982, and

(B) such building does not meet the requirements of paragraph (1) of section 48(g) of the Internal Revenue Code of 1954 (as amended by this Act).

P.L. 97-34, §212(a)(2):

Amended Code Sec. 46(a)(2) by adding at the end thereof new subparagraph (F). **Effective** for expenditures incurred after 12-31-81, in tax years ending after such date. See the historical comment for P.L. 97-34, §212(e)(1), above, for a transitional rule.

P.L. 97-34, §332(a):

Amended Code Sec. 46(a)(2)(E) by striking out "December 31, 1983" in clauses (i) and (ii) and inserting "December 31, 1982", by striking out "and" at the end of clause (i), by striking out the period at the end of clause (ii) and inserting ", and", and by adding clause (iii). **Effective** 8-13-81.

• 1980, Crude Oil Windfall Profit Tax of 1980 (P.L. 96-223)

P.L. 96-223, §221(a):

Amended Code Sec. 46(a)(2)(C). **Effective** 4-3-80. Prior to amendment, Code Sec. 46(a)(2)(C) read:

(C) ENERGY PERCENTAGE.—For purposes of this paragraph, the energy percentage is—

(i) 10 percent with respect to the period beginning on October 1, 1978, and ending on December 31, 1982, or

(ii) zero with respect to any other period.

P.L. 96-223, §222(e)(2):

Amended Code Sec. 46(a)(2)(D) by adding a new last sentence. **Effective** for periods after 12-31-79 under rules similar to the rules of Code Sec. 48(m).

P.L. 96-223, §223(b)(1):

Amended Code Sec. 46(a)(9) by inserting at the end of clause (A)(i) "and", by striking out "(other than solar or wind energy property), and" and inserting a period at the end of clause (A)(ii), by striking out clause (iii) in subparagraph (A), by striking out "OTHER THAN SOLAR OR WIND ENERGY PROPERTY" in the heading of subparagraph (B), and by striking out subparagraph (C). **Effective** for qualified investments for tax years beginning after 12-31-79. Prior to amendment, Code Sec. 46(a)(9)(A)(iii) and (C) read:

(iii) then with respect to so much of the credit allowed by section 38 as is attributable to the application of the energy percentage to solar or wind energy property.

* * *

(C) REFUNDABLE CREDIT FOR SOLAR OR WIND ENERGY PROPERTY.—In the case of so much of the credit allowed by section 38 as is described in subparagraph (A)(iii)—

(i) paragraph (3) shall not apply, and

(ii) for purposes of this title (other than section 38, this subpart, and chapter 63), such credit shall be treated as if it were allowed by section 39 and not by section 38.

• 1980, Technical Corrections Act of 1979 (P.L. 96-222)

P.L. 96-222, §4.

Amended P.L. 95-600 by inserting the following new paragraph after section 3: "For purposes of applying the amendments made by this Act to sections 46 and 48 of the Internal Revenue Code of 1954, the Energy Tax Act of 1978 [P.L. 95-618] shall be deemed to have been enacted immediately before this Act."

P.L. 96-222, §101(a)(7)(B):

Amended Act Sec. 141 of P.L. 95-600 by revising paragraph (g) which relates to the effective dates for amendments concerning tax credit employee stock ownership plans. For the **effective** date, see the amendment note at §101(a)(7)(B), P.L. 96-222, following the text of Code Sec. 409A(n).

P.L. 96-222, §101(a)(7)(L)(iii)(I) and (v)(I):

Amended Code Sec. 46(a)(2)(A)(iii) and (E) by striking out "ESOP" and inserting "employee plan" and by striking out in the heading of paragraph 46(a)(2)(E) "ESOP" and inserting "EMPLOYEE PLAN". **E ffective** for tax years beginning after 12-31-78.

P.L. 96-222, §101(a)(7)(M)(i):

Amended Code Sec. 46(a)(2)(E) by adding "and ending on" before "December 31, 1983" each place it appears. **Effective** for qualified investment for tax years beginning after 12-31-80.

P.L. 96-222, §103(a)(2)(B)(i):

Amended Code Sec. 46(a) by redesignating paragraph (10) as paragraph (9). **Effective** for tax years ending after 12-31-78.

P.L. 96-222, §103(a)(2)(B)(ii):

Amended Code Sec. 46(a)(9)(B)(i), as redesignated. **Effective** for tax years ending after 12-31-79. Prior to amendment, Code Sec. 46(a)(9)(B)(i) read as follows:

"(i) paragraph (3)(C) shall be applied by substituting `100 percent' for `50 percent',".

P.L. 96-222, §103(a)(2)(B)(iii):

Amended Code Sec. 46(a)(9)(B)(ii), as redesignated, by striking out "(7), (8), and (9)" and inserting "(7) and (8)". **Effective** for tax years ending after 12-31-78.

• 1978, Energy Tax Act of 1978 (P.L. 95-618)

P.L. 95-618, §301(a)(1):

Amended Code Sec. 46(a)(2). See under P.L. 95-600, §311(c) for prior law.

• 1978, Revenue Act of 1978 (P.L. 95-600)

P.L. 95-600, §311(a):

Amended Code Sec. 46(a)(2)(B). **Effective** 11-6-78. Before amendment, Code Sec. 46(a)(2) read:

"(2) AMOUNT OF CREDIT FOR CURRENT TAXABLE YEAR.—

(A) 10 PERCENT CREDIT.—Except as otherwise provided in subparagraph (B), in the case of a property described in subparagraph (D), the amount of the credit determined under this paragraph for the taxable year shall be an amount equal to 10 percent of the qualified investment (as determined under subsections (c) and (d)).

(B) ADDITIONAL CREDIT.—In the case of a corporation which elects (at such time, in such form, and in such manner as the Secretary prescribes) to have the provisions of this subparagraph apply, the amount of the credit determined under this paragraph shall be an amount equal to—

(i) 11 percent of the qualified investment (as determined under subsections (c) and (d)), plus

(ii) an additional percent (not in excess of one-half percent) of the qualified investment (as determined under such subsections) equal in amount to the amount determined under section 301(e) of the Tax Reduction Act of 1975.

An election may not be made to have the provisions of this subparagraph apply unless the corporation meets the requirements of section 301(d) of the Tax Reduction Act of 1975.

(C) 7 PERCENT CREDIT.—In the case of property not described in subparagraph (D), the amount of credit determined under this paragraph for the taxable year shall be an amount equal to 7 percent of the qualified investment (as determined under subsections (c) and (d)).

(D) TRANSITIONAL RULES.—The provisions of subparagraphs (A) and (B) shall apply only to—

(i) property to which subsection (d) does not apply, the construction, reconstruction, or erection of which is completed by the taxpayer after January 21, 1975, but only to the extent of the basis thereof attributable to the construction, reconstruction, or erection after January 21, 1975, and before January 1, 1981,

(ii) property to which subsection (d) does not apply, acquired by the taxpayer after January 21, 1975, and before January 1, 1981, and placed in service by the taxpayer before January 1, 1981, and

(iii) property to which subsection (d) applies, but only to the extent of the qualified investment (as determined under subsections (c) and (d)) with respect to qualified progress expenditures made after January 21, 1975, and before January 1, 1981.

For purposes of applying clause (ii) of subparagraph (B), the date `December 31, 1976,' shall be substituted for the date `January 21, 1975,' each place it appears in this subparagraph."

P.L. 95-600, §141(e):

Amended Code Sec. 46(a)(2)(E) by striking out "and ending on December 31, 1980," each place it appears and inserting in place thereof "[and ending on] December 31, 1983". **Effective** for qualified investment for tax years beginning after 12-31-78. For the text of such section before the above amendment, see the amendment note for §141(f)(2), below.

P.L. 95-600, §141(f)(2):

Amended Code Sec. 46(a)(2)(E) by striking out "section 301(e) of the Tax Reduction Act of 1975" and inserting in place thereof "section 48(n)(1)(B)" and by striking out "section 301(d) of the Tax Reduction Act of 1975" and inserting in place thereof "section 409A". **Effective** for qualified investment for tax years beginning after 12-31-78. Before amendment by Act secs. 141(e) and (f)(2), but after amendment by P.L. 95-618, §301, such Code section read:

"(E) ESOP PERCENTAGE.—For purposes of this paragraph, the ESOP percentage is—

(i) with respect to the period beginning on January 21, 1975, and ending on December 31, 1980, 1 percent, and

(ii) with respect to the period beginning on January 1, 1977, and ending on December 31, 1980, an additional percentage (not in excess of 1/2 of 1 percent) which results in an amount equal to the amount determined under section 301(e) of the Tax Reduction Act of 1975.

This subparagraph shall apply to a corporation only if it meets the requirements of section 301(d) of the Tax Reduction Act of 1975 and only if it elects (at such time, in such form, and in such manner as the Secretary prescribes) to have this subparagraph apply."

P.L. 95-600, §312(a):

Amended Code Sec. 46(a)(3). **Effective** for tax years ending after 12-31-78. Before amendment, such Code section read:

"(3) LIMITATION BASED ON AMOUNT OF TAX.—Notwithstanding paragraph (1), the credit allowed by section 38 for the taxable year shall not exceed—

(A) so much of the liability for tax for the taxable year as does not exceed $25,000, plus

(B) for taxable years ending on or before the last day of the suspension period (as defined in section 48(j)), 25 percent of so much of the liability for tax for the taxable year as exceeds $25,000, or

(C) for taxable years ending after the last day of such suspension period, 50 percent of so much of the liability for tax for the taxable year as exceeds $25,000.

In applying subparagraph (C) to a taxable year beginning on or before the last day of such suspension period and ending after the last day of such suspension period, the percent referred to in such subparagraph shall be the sum of 25 percent plus the percent which bears the same ratio to 25 percent as the number of days in such year after the last day of the suspension period bears to the total number of days in such year. The amount otherwise determined under this paragraph shall be reduced (but not below zero) by the credit which would have been allowable under paragraph (1) for such taxable year with respect to suspension period property but for the application of section 48(h)(1)."

P.L. 95-600, §312(b)(1):

Amended Code Sec. 46(a)(7). **Effective** for tax years ending after 12-31-78. Before amendment, such section read:

"(7) ALTERNATIVE LIMITATION IN THE CASE OF CERTAIN UTILITIES.—

(A) IN GENERAL.—If, for a taxable year ending after calendar year 1974 and before calendar year 1981, the amount of the qualified investment of the taxpayer which is attributable to public utility property is 25 percent or more of his aggregate qualified investment, then subparagraph (C) of paragraph (3) of this subsection shall be applied by substituting for 50 percent his applicable percentage for such year.

(B) APPLICABLE PERCENTAGE.—The applicable percentage of any taxpayer for any taxable year is—

(i) 50 percent, plus

(ii) that portion of the tentative percentage for the taxable year which the taxpayer's amount of qualified investment which is public utility property bears to his aggregate qualified investment.

If the proportion referred to in clause (ii) is 75 percent or more, the applicable percentage of the taxpayer for the year shall be 50 percent plus the tentative percentage for such year.

(C) TENTATIVE PERCENTAGE.—For purposes of subparagraph (B), the tentative percentage shall be determined under the following table:

If the taxable year ends in:	The tentative percentage is:
1975 or 1976	50
1977	40
1978	30
1979	20
1980	10

(D) PUBLIC UTILITY PROPERTY DEFINED.—For purposes of this paragraph, the term "public utility property" has the meaning given to such term by the first sentence of subsection (c)(3)(B)."

P.L. 95-600, §312(b)(2):

Amended Code Sec. 46(a) by striking out former paragraphs (8) and (9), and adding a new paragraph (8). **Effective** for tax years ending after 12-31-78. Before repeal, Code Secs. 46(a)(8) and (9) read:

"(8) ALTERNATIVE LIMITATION IN THE CASE OF CERTAIN RAILROADS.—

(A) IN GENERAL.—If, for a taxable year ending after calendar year 1976, and before calendar year 1983, the amount of the qualified investment of the taxpayer which is attributable to railroad property is 25 percent or more of his aggregate qualified investment, then subparagraph (C) of paragraph (3) of this subsection shall be applied by substituting for 50 percent his applicable percentage for such year.

(B) APPLICABLE PERCENTAGE.—The applicable percentage of any taxpayer for any taxable year under this paragraph is—

(i) 50 percent, plus

(ii) that portion of the tentative percentage for the taxable year which the taxpayer's amount of qualified investment which is railroad property bears to his aggregate qualified investment.

If the proportion referred to in clause (ii) is 75 percent or more, the applicable percentage of the taxpayer for the year shall be 50 percent plus the tentative percentage for such year.

(C) TENTATIVE PERCENTAGE.—For purposes of subparagraph (b), the tentative percentage shall be determined under the following table:

If the taxable year ends in:	The tentative percentage is:
1977 or 1978	50
1979	40
1980	30
1981	20
1982	10

(D) RAILROAD PROPERTY DEFINED.—For purposes of this paragraph, the term "railroad property" means section 38 property used by the taxpayer directly in connection with the trade or business carried on by the taxpayer of operating a railroad (including a railroad switching or terminal company)."

"(9) ALTERNATIVE LIMITATION IN THE CASE OF CERTAIN AIRLINES.—

(A) IN GENERAL.—If, for a taxable year ending after calendar year 1976 and before calendar year 1983, the amount of the qualified investment of the taxpayer which is attributable to airline property is 25 percent or more of his aggregate qualified investment, then subparagraph (C) of paragraph (3) of this subsection shall be applied by substituting for 50 percent his applicable percentage for such year.

(B) APPLICABLE PERCENTAGE.—The applicable percentage of any taxpayer for any taxable year under this paragraph is—

(i) 50 percent, plus

(ii) that portion of the tentative percentage for the taxable year which the taxpayer's amount of qualified investment which is airline property bears to his aggregate qualified investment.

If the proportion referred to in clause (ii) is 75 percent or more, the applicable percentage of the taxpayer for the year shall be 50 percent plus the tentative percentage for such year.

(C) TENTATIVE PERCENTAGE.—For purposes of subparagraph (B), the tentative percentage shall be determined under the following table:

If the taxable year ends in:	The tentative percentage is:
1977 or 1978	50
1979	40
1980	30
1981	20
1982	10

(D) AIRLINE PROPERTY DEFINED.—For purposes of this paragraph, the term "airline property" means section 38 property used by the taxpayer directly in connection with the trade or business carried on by the taxpayer of the furnishing or sale of transportation as a common carrier by air subject to the jurisdiction of the Civil Aeronautics Board or the Federal Aviation Administration."

• 1978, Energy Tax Act of 1978 (P.L. 95-618)

P.L. 95-618, §301(c)(1):

Added Code Sec. 46(a)(10). **Effective** 11-10-78.

• 1976, Tax Reform Act of 1976 (P.L. 94-455)

P.L. 94-455, §503(b)(4)

Substituted "credit for the elderly" for "retirement income" in Code Sec. 46(a)(3)(C). **Effective** for tax years beginning after 12-31-75.

P.L. 94-455, §802(a)(1) and (2):

Amended Code Sec. 46(a) by redesignating paragraphs (2) through (6) as (3) through (7), respectively, and by amending subsection (a)(1). **Effective** for tax years beginning after 12-31-75. Prior to the amendment, subsection (a)(1) read as follows:

(a) DETERMINATION OF AMOUNT.—

(1) GENERAL RULE.—

(A) TEN PERCENT CREDIT.—Except as otherwise provided in this paragraph, in the case of a property described in subparagraph (D), the amount of the credit allowed by section 38 for the taxable year shall be an amount equal to 10 percent of the qualified investment (as determined under subsections (c) and (d)).

(B) ELEVEN PERCENT CREDIT.—Except as otherwise provided in this paragraph, in the case of a corporation which elects to have the provisions of this subparagraph apply, the amount of the credit allowed by section 38 for the taxable year with respect to property described in subparagraph (D) shall be an amount equal to 11 percent of the qualified investment (as determined under subsections (c) and (d)). An election may not be made to have the provisions of this subparagraph apply for the taxable year unless the corporation meets the requirements of section 301(d) of the Tax Reduction Act of 1975. An election by a corporation to have the provisions of this subparagraph apply shall be made at such time, in such form, and in such manner as the Secretary or his delegate may prescribe.

(C) SEVEN PERCENT CREDIT.—Except as otherwise provided in this paragraph, the amount of credit allowed by section 38 for the taxable year shall be an amount equal to 7 percent of the qualified investment (as determined under subsections (c) and (d)).

(D) TRANSITIONAL RULES.—The provisions of subparagraphs (A) and (B) shall apply only to—

(i) property to which subsection (d) does not apply, the construction, reconstruction, or erection of which is completed by the taxpayer after January 21, 1975, but only to the extent of the basis thereof attributable to the construction, reconstruction, or erection after January 21, 1975, and before January 1, 1977,

(ii) property to which subsection (d) does not apply, acquired by the taxpayer after January 21, 1975, and before January 1, 1977, and placed in service by the taxpayer before January 1, 1977, and

(iii) property to which subsection (d) applies, but only to the extent of the qualified investment (as determined under subsections (c) and (d)) with respect to qualified progress expenditures made after January 21, 1975, and before January 1, 1977.

P.L. 94-455, §802(b)(1):

Substituted "paragraph 3" for "paragraph 2" in paragraphs (4), (5), (6), and (7) of Code Sec. 46(a) (as redesignated by §802(a)). **Effective** for tax years beginning after 12-31-75.

P.L. 94-455, §1701(b):

Added a new paragraph (8) to Code Sec. 46(a). **Effective** 10-4-76.

P.L. 94-455, §1703:

Added a new paragraph (9) to Code Sec. 46(a). **Effective** 10-4-76.

P.L. 94-455, §1901(a)(4)(A)

Substituted "§408(f)" for "§408(e)" in the second sentence of Code Sec. 46(a)(4) as redesignated by this Act. **Effective** for tax years beginning after 12-31-76.

P.L. 94-455, §1901(b)(1)(C), as amended by P. L. 95-600, §703(j)(9):

Amended Code Sec. 46(a)(4) by striking out subparagraph (B), by inserting "and" at the end of subparagraph (A), and by redesignating subparagraph (C) as subparagraph (B). **Effective** for tax years beginning after 12-31-76. Prior to the amendment, former subparagraph (B) read as follows:

"(B) section 35 (relating to partially tax-exempt interest), and."

P.L. 94-455, §1906(b)(13)(A):

Amended 1954 Code by substituting "Secretary" for "Secretary or his delegate" each place it appeared. **Effective** 2-1-77.

P.L. 94-455, §803(c):

Amended §301(d) of P.L. 94-12 (see below) as follows:

(1) by adding at the end of paragraph (3) the following sentence: "For purposes of this paragraph, the amount of compensation paid to a participant for a year is the amount of such participant's compensation within the meaning of section 415(c)(3) of such Code for such year.",

(2) by striking out paragraph (6) and inserting in lieu thereof the following:

"(6) On making a claim for credit, adjustment, or refund under section 38 of the Internal Revenue Code of 1954, the employer states in such claim that it agrees, as a condition of receiving any such credit, adjustment, or refund—

"(A) in the case of a taxable year beginning before January 1, 1977, to transfer employer securities forthwith to the plan having an aggregate value at the time of the claim of 1 percent of the amount of the qualified investment (as determined under section 46(c) and (d) of such Code) of the taxpayer for the taxable year, and

"(B) in the case of a taxable year beginning after December 31, 1976—

"(i) to transfer employer securities to the plan having an aggregate value at the time of the claim of 1 percent of the amount of the qualified investment (as determined under section 46(c) and (d) of such Code) of the employer for the taxable year,

"(ii) except as provided in clause (iii), to effect the transfer not later than 30 days after the time (including extensions) for filing its income tax return for a taxable year, and

"(iii) in the case of an employer whose credit (as determined under section 46(a)(2)(B) of such Code) for a taxable year beginning after December 31, 1976, exceeds the limitations of paragraph (3) of section 46(a) of such Code—

"(I) to effect that portion of the transfer allocable to investment credit carrybacks of such excess credit at the time required under clause (ii) for the unused credit year (within the meaning of section 46(b) of such Code), and

"(II) to effect that portion of the transfer allocable to investment credit carryovers of such excess credit at the time required under clause (ii) for the taxable year to which such portion is carried over.

"For purposes of meeting the requirements of this paragraph, a transfer of cash shall be treated as a transfer of employer securities if the cash is, under the plan, used to purchase employer securities.",

(3) by deleting paragraph (8) and inserting in lieu thereof the following:

"(8)(A) Except as provided in subparagraph (B)(iii), if the amount of the credit determined under section 46(a)(2)(B) of the Internal Revenue Code of 1954 is recaptured or redetermined in accordance with the provisions of such Code, the amounts transferred to the plan under this subsection and subsection (e) and allocated under the plan shall remain in the plan or in participant accounts, as the case may be, and continue to be allocated in accordance with the plan.

"(B) If the amount of the credit determined under section 46(a)(2)(B) of the Internal Revenue Code of 1954 is recaptured in accordance with the provisions of such Code—

"(i) the employer may reduce the amount required to be transferred to the plan under paragraph (6) of this subsection, or under paragraph (3) of subsection (e), for the current taxable year or any succeeding taxable years by the portion of the amount so recaptured which is attributable to the contribution to such plan,

"(ii) notwithstanding the provisions of paragraph (12), the employer may deduct such portion, subject to the limitations of section 404 of such Code (relating to deductions for contributions to an employees' trust or plan), or

"(iii) if the requirements of subsection (f)(1) are met, the employer may withdraw from the plan an amount not in excess of such portion.

"(C) If the amount of the credit claimed by an employer for a prior taxable year under section 38 of the Internal Revenue Code of 1954 is reduced because of a redetermination which becomes final during the taxable year, and the employer transferred amounts to a plan which were taken into account for purposes of this subsection for that prior taxable year, then—

"(i) the employer may reduce the amount it is required to transfer to the plan under paragraph (6) of this subsection, or under paragraph (3) of subsection (e), for the taxable year or any succeeding taxable year by the portion of the amount of such reduction in the credit or increase in tax which is attributable to the contribution to such plan, or

"(ii) notwithstanding the provisions of paragraph (12), the employer may deduct such portion subject to the limitations of section 404 of such Code.",

(4) by striking out "in control of the employer (within the meaning of section 368(c) of the Internal Revenue Code of 1954)" in paragraph (9)(A) and inserting in lieu thereof "a member of a controlled group of corporations which includes the employer (within the meaning of section 1563(a) of the Internal Revenue Code of 1954, determined without regard to section 1563(a)(4) and (e)(3)(C) of such Code)", and

(5) by adding at the end thereof the following new paragraphs:

"(13)(A) As reimbursement for the expense of establishing the plan, the employer may withhold from amounts due the plan for the taxable year for which the plan is established, or the plan may pay, so much of the amounts paid or incurred in connection with the establishment of the plan as does not exceed the sum of 10 percent of the first $100,000 that the employer is required to transfer to the plan for that taxable year under paragraph (6) (including any amounts transferred under subsection (e)(3)) and 5 percent of any amount in excess of the first $100,000 of such amount.

"(B) As reimbursement for the expense of administering the plan, the employer may withhold from amounts due the plan, or the plan may pay, so much of the amounts paid or incurred during the taxable year as expenses of administering the plan as does not exceed the smaller of—

"(i) the sum of 10 percent of the first $100,000 and 5 percent of any amount in excess of $100,000 of the income from dividends paid to the plan with respect to stock of the employer during the plan year ending with or within the employer's taxable year, or

"(ii) $100,000,

"(14) The return of a contribution made by an employer to an employee stock ownership plan designed to satisfy the requirements of this subsection or subsection (e) (or a provision for such a return) does not fail to satisfy the requirements of this subsection, subsection (e), section 401(a) of the Internal Revenue Code of 1954, or section 403(c)(1) of the Employee Retirement Income Security Act of 1974 if—

"(A) the contribution is conditioned under the plan upon determination by the Secretary of the Treasury that such plan meets the applicable requirements of this subsection, subsection (e), or section 401(a) of such Code,

"(B) the application for such a determination is filed with the Secretary not later than 90 days after the date on which the credit under section 38 is allowed, and

"(C) the contribution is returned within one year after the date on which the Secretary issues notice to the employer that such plan does not satisfy the requirements of this subsection, subsection (e), or section 401(a) of such Code."

P.L. 94-455, §803(d):

Added the following new subsections to section 301 of P.L. 94-12 (see below):

"(e) PLAN REQUIREMENTS FOR TAXPAYERS ELECTING ADDITIONAL ONE-HALF PERCENT CREDIT.—

"(1) GENERAL RULE.—For purposes of clause (ii) of section 46(a)(2)(B) of the Internal Revenue Code of 1954, the amount determined under this subsection for a taxable year is an amount equal to the sum of the matching employee contributions for the taxable year which meet the requirements of this subsection.

"(2) ELECTION; BASIC PLAN REQUIREMENTS.—No amount shall be determined under this subsection for the taxable year unless the corporation elects to have this subsection apply for that year. A corporation may not elect to have the provisions of this subsection apply for a taxable year unless the corporation meets the requirements of subsection (d) and the requirements of this subsection.

"(3) EMPLOYER CONTRIBUTION.—On making a claim for credit, adjustment, or refund under section 38 of the Internal Revenue Code of 1954, the employer shall state in such claim that the employer agrees, as a condition of receiving any such credit, adjustment, or refund attributable to the provisions of section 46(a)(2)(B)(ii) of such Code, to transfer at the time described in subsection (d)(6)(B) employer securities (as defined in subsection (d)(9)(A)) to the plan having an aggregate value at the time of the transfer of not more than one-half of one percent of the amount of the qualified investment (as determined under subsections (c) and (d) of section 46 of such Code) of the taxpayer for the taxable year. For purposes of meeting the requirements of this paragraph, a transfer of cash shall be treated as a transfer of employer securities if the cash is, under the plan, used to purchase employer securities.

"(4) REQUIREMENTS RELATING TO MATCHING EMPLOYEE CONTRIBUTIONS.—

"(A) An amount contributed by an employee under a plan described in subsection (d) for the taxable year may not be treated as a matching employee contribution for that taxable year under this subsection unless—

"(i) each employee who participates in the plan described in subsection (d) is entitled to make such a contribution,

"(ii) the contribution is designated by the employee as a contribution intended to be used for matching employer amounts transferred under paragraph (3) to a plan which meets the requirements of this subsection, and

"(iii) the contribution is in the form of an amount paid in cash to the employer or plan administrator not later than 24 months after the close of the taxable year in which the portion of the credit allowed by section 38 of such Code (and determined under clause (ii) of section 46(a)(2)(B) of such Code which the contribution is to match) is allowed, and is invested forthwith in employer securities (as defined in subsection (d)(9)(A)).

"(B) The sum of the amounts of matching employee contributions taken into account for purposes of this subsection for any taxable year may not exceed the value (at the time of transfer) of the employer securities transferred to the plan in accordance with the requirements of paragraph (3) for the year for which the employee contributions are designated as matching contributions.

"(C) The employer may not make participation in the plan a condition of employment and the plan may not require matching employee contributions as a condition of participation in the plan.

"(D) Employee contributions under the plan must meet the requirements of section 401(a)(4) of such Code (relating to contributions).

"(5) A plan must provide for allocation of all employer securities transferred to it or purchased by it under this subsection to the account of each participant (who was a participant at any time during the plan year, whether or not he is a participant at the close of the plan year) as of the close of the plan year in an amount equal to his matching employee contributions for the year. Matching employee contributions and amounts so allocated shall be deemed to be allocated under subsection (d)(3).

"(f) RECAPTURE.—

"(1) GENERAL RULE.—Amounts transferred to a plan under subsection (d)(6) or (e)(3) may be withdrawn from the plan by the employer if the plan provides that while subject to recapture—

"(A) amounts so transferred with respect to a taxable year are segregated from other plan assets, and

"(B) separate accounts are maintained for participants on whose behalf amounts so transferred have been allocated for a taxable year.

"(2) COORDINATION WITH OTHER LAW.—Notwithstanding any other law or rule of law, an amount withdrawn by the employer will neither fail to be considered to be nonforfeitable nor fail to be for the exclusive benefit of participants or their beneficiaries merely because of the withdrawal from the plan of—

"(A) amounts described in paragraph (1), or

"(B) employer amounts transferred under subsection (e)(3) to the plan which are not matched by matching employee contributions or which are in excess of the limitations of section 415 of such Code,

nor will the withdrawal of any such amount be considered to violate the provisions of section 403(c)(1) of the Employee Retirement Income Security Act of 1974."

P.L. 94-455, §803(e):

Amended §301(d) of P.L. 94-12 (see below) as follows:

(1) The heading of section 301(d) of the Tax Reduction Act of 1975 is amended by striking out "11-PERCENT" and inserting in lieu thereof "ADDITIONAL".

(2) Section 301(d) of the Tax Reduction Act of 1975 is amended by—

(A) striking out "A corporation" in paragraph (1) and inserting in lieu thereof "Except as expressly provided in subsections (e) and (f), a corporation",

(B) inserting "or subsection (e)(3)" in paragraph (7)(A) immediately after "(6)",

(C) striking out "this subsection" in paragraph (10) and substituting in lieu thereof "this subsection and subsections (e) and (f)", and

(D) striking out "this subsection" each time it appears in paragraph (11) and substituting in lieu thereof "this subsection or subsection (e) or (f)".

• 1975, Tax Reduction Act of 1975 (P.L. 94-12)

P.L. 94-12, §301(a):

Amended Code Sec. 46(a)(1). **Effective** 3-29-75. Prior to amendment, Code Sec. 46(a)(1) read as follows:

"(1) GENERAL RULE.—The amount of the credit allowed by section 38 for the taxable year shall be equal to 7 percent of the qualified investment (as defined in subsection (c))."

P. L. 94-12, §301(b)(2):

Amended Code Sec. 46(a) by adding new paragraph (6). **Effective** for tax years ending after 12-31-74.

P. L. 94-12, §301(d), provides:

"(d) PLAN REQUIREMENTS FOR TAXPAYERS ELECTING PERCENT CREDIT.—In order to meet the requirements of this subsection—

"(1) A corporation (hereinafter in this subsection referred to as the `employer') must establish an employee stock ownership plan (described in paragraph (2)) which is funded by transfers of employer securities in accordance with the provisions of paragraph (6) and which meets all other requirements of this subsection.

"(2) The plan referred to in paragraph (1) must be a defined contribution plan established in writing which—

"(A) is a stock bonus plan, a stock bonus and a money purchase pension plan, or a profit-sharing plan,

"(B) is designed to invest primarily in employer securities, and

"(C) meets such other requirements (similar to requirements applicable to employee stock ownership plans as defined in section 4975(e)(7) of the Internal Revenue Code of

1954) as the Secretary of the Treasury or his delegate may prescribe.

"(3) The plan must provide for the allocation of all employer securities transferred to it or purchased by it (because of the requirements of section 46(a)(1)(B) of the Internal Revenue Code of 1954) to the account of each participant (who was a participant at any time during the plan year, whether or not he is a participant at the close of the plan year) as of the close of each plan year in an amount which bears substantially the same proportion to the amount of all such securities allocated to all participants in the plan for that plan year as the amount of compensation paid to such participant (disregarding any compensation in excess of the first $100,000 per year) bears to the compensation paid to all such participants during that year (disregarding any compensation in excess of the first $100,000 with respect to any participant). Notwithstanding the first sentence of this paragraph, the allocation to participants' accounts may be extended over whatever period may be necessary to comply with the requirements of section 415 of the Internal Revenue Code of 1954.

"(4) The plan must provide that each participant has a nonforfeitable right to any stock allocated to his account under paragraph (3), and that no stock allocated to a participant's account may be distributed from that account before the end of the eighty-fourth month beginning after the month in which the stock is allocated to the account except in the case of separation from the service, death, or disability.

"(5) The plan must provide that each participant is entitled to direct the plan as to the manner in which any employer securities allocated to the account of the participant are to be voted.

"(6) On making a claim for credit, adjustment, or refund under section 38 of the Internal Revenue Code of 1954, the employer states in such claim that it agrees, as a condition of receiving any such credit, adjustment, or refund, to transfer employer securities forthwith to the plan having an aggregate value at the time of the claim of 1 percent of the amount of the qualified investment (as determined under section 46(c) and (d) of such Code) of the taxpayer for the taxable year. For purposes of meeting the requirements of this paragraph, a transfer of cash shall be treated as a transfer of employer securities if the cash is, under the plan, used to purchase employer securities.

"(7) Notwithstanding any other provision of law to the contrary, if the plan does not meet the requirements of section 401 of the Internal Revenue Code of 1954—

"(A) stock transferred under paragraph (6) and allocated to the account of any participant under paragraph (3) and dividends thereon shall not be considered income of the participant or his beneficiary under the Internal Revenue Code of 1954 until actually distributed or made available to the participant or his beneficiary and, at such time, shall be taxable under section 72 of such Code (treating the participant or his beneficiary as having a basis of zero in the contract),

"(B) no amount shall be allocated to any participant in excess of the amount which might be allocated if the plan met the requirements of section 401 of such Code, and

"(C) the plan must meet the requirements of sections 410 and 415 of such Code.

"(8) If the amount of the credit determined under section 46(a)(1)(B) of the Internal Revenue Code of 1954, is recaptured in accordance with the provisions of such Code, the amounts transferred to the plan under this subsection and allocated under the plan shall remain in the plan or in participant accounts, as the case may be and continue to be allocated in accordance with the original plan agreement.

"(9) For purposes of this subsection, the term—

"(A) `employer securities' means common stock issued by the employer or a corporation which is in control of the employer (within the meaning of section 368(c) of the Internal Revenue Code of 1954) with voting power and dividend rights no less favorable than the voting power and dividend rights of other common stock issued by the employer or such controlling corporation, or securities issued by the employer or such controlling corporation, convertible into such stock, and

"(B) `value' means the average of closing prices of the employer's securities, as reported by a national exchange on which securities are listed, for the 20 consecutive trading days immediately preceding the date of transfer or allocation of such securities or, in the case of securities not listed on a national exchange, the fair market value as determined in good faith and in accordance with regulations issued by the Secretary of the Treasury or his delegate.

"(10) The Secretary of the Treasury or his delegate shall prescribe such regulations and require such reports as may be necessary to carry out the provisions of this subsection.

"(11) If the employer fails to meet any requirement imposed under this subsection or under any obligation undertaken to comply with the requirement of this subsection, he is liable to the United States for a civil penalty of an amount equal to the amount involved in such failure. The preceding sentence shall not apply if the taxpayer corrects such failure (as determined by the Secretary of the Treasury or his delegate) within 90 days after notice thereof. For purposes of this paragraph, the term `amount involved' means an amount determined by the Secretary or his delegate, but not in excess of 1 percent of the qualified investment of the taxpayer for the taxable year under section 46(a)(1)(B) and not less than the product of one-half of one percent of such amount multiplied by the number of months (or parts thereof) during which such failure continues. The amount of such penalty may be collected by the Secretary of the Treasury in the same manner in which a deficiency in the payment of Federal income tax may be collected.

"(12) Notwithstanding any provision of the Internal Revenue Code of 1954 to the contrary, no deductions shall be allowed under section 162, 212, or 404 of such Code for amounts transferred to an employee stock ownership plan and taken into account under this subsection."

• 1974, Employee Retirement Income Security Act of 1974 (P.L. 93-406)

P.L. 93-406, §2001(g)(2)(B):

Added "section 72(m)(5)(B) (relating to 10 percent tax on premature distributions to owner-employees)," to the last sentence of Code Sec. 46(a)(3). **Effective** for distributions made in taxable years beginning after 12-31-75.

P.L. 93-406, §2002(g)(2):

Added "section 408(e) (relating to additional tax on income from certain retirement accounts)," to the last sentence of Code Sec. 46(a)(3). **Effective** 1-1-75.

P.L. 93-406, §2005(c)(4):

Added "section 402(e) (relating to tax on lump sum distributions)," to the last sentence of Code Sec. 46(a)(3). **Effective** for distributions or payments made after 12-31-73 in taxable years beginning after that date. Prior to amendment, the last sentence of Code Sec. 46(a)(3) read as follows:

"For purposes of this paragraph, any tax imposed for the taxable year by section 56 (relating to minimum tax for tax preferences), section 531 (relating to accumulated earnings tax), section 541 (relating to personal holding company tax), or section 1378 (relating to tax on certain capital gains of subchapter S corporations) and any additional tax imposed for the taxable year by section 1351(d)(1) (relating to recoveries of foreign expropriation losses), shall not be considered tax imposed by this chapter for such year."

• 1969, Tax Reform Act of 1969 (P.L. 91-172)

P.L. 91-172, §301(b)(4):

Amended the second sentence of Code Sec. 46(a)(3) by adding the phrase "section 56 (relating to minimum tax for tax preferences)." **Effective** for tax years ending on or after 12-31-69.

P.L. 91-172, §401(e)(1):

Amended Sec. 46(a)(5). **Effective** for tax years ending on or after 12-31-70. Prior to amendment Sec. 46(a)(5) read as follows:

"(5) Affiliated groups.—In the case of an affiliated group, the $25,000 amount specified under subparagraphs (A) and (B) of paragraph (2) shall be reduced for each member of the group by apportioning $25,000 among the members of such group in such manner as the Secretary or his delegate shall by regulations prescribe. For purposes of the preceding sentence, the term "affiliated group" has the meaning assigned to such term by section 1504(a), except that all corporations shall be treated as includible corporations (without any exclusion under section 1504(b))."

• 1966 (P.L. 89-800)

P.L. 89-800, §3(a):

Amended Code Sec. 46(a)(2). **Effective** for tax years ending after 10-9-66. Prior to amendment, Sec. 46(a)(2) read as follows:

"(2) Limitation based on amount of tax.—Notwithstanding paragraph (1), the credit allowed by section 38 for the taxable year shall not exceed—

"(A) so much of the liability for tax for the taxable year as does not exceed $25,000, plus

"(B) 25 percent of so much of the liability for tax for the taxable year as exceeds $25,000."

• 1966 (P.L. 89-389)

P.L. 89-389, §2(b):

Amended Code Sec. 46(a)(3) by substituting ", section 541 (relating to personal holding company tax), or section 1378 (relating to tax on certain capital gains of subchapter S corporations)" for "or by section 541 (relating to personal holding company tax)". **Effective** with respect to tax years of electing small business corporations beginning after 4-14-66, but not with respect to sales or exchanges occurring before 2-24-66.

• 1966 (P.L. 89-384)

P.L. 89-384, §1(c):

Amended Code Sec. 46(a)(3) by inserting ", and any additional tax imposed for the taxable year by section 1351(d)(1) (relating to recoveries of foreign expropriation losses)," immediately after "personal holding company tax)". **Effective** with respect to amounts received after 12-31-64, in respect of foreign expropriation losses sustained after 12-31-58.

• 1964, Revenue Act of 1964 (P.L. 88-272)

P.L. 88-272, §201(d)(4):

Amended Code Sec. 46(a)(3) by deleting subparagraph (3)(B) and relettering old subparagraphs (C) and (D) as (B) and (C). **Effective** with respect to dividends received after 12-31-64, in taxable years ending after such date. Prior to deletion, Sec. 46(a)(3)(B) read as follows: "(B) section 34 (relating to dividends received by individuals),".

[Sec. 46(b)]

(b) DETERMINATION OF PERCENTAGES.—For purposes of subsection (a)—

(1) REGULAR PERCENTAGE.—The regular percentage is 10 percent.

(2) ENERGY PERCENTAGE.—

(A) IN GENERAL.—The energy percentage shall be determined in accordance with the following table:

Column A—Description	Column B—Percentage	Column C—Period	
In the case of:	The energy percentage is:	For the period:	
		Beginning on:	And ending on:
(I) General Rule.—Property not described in any of the following provisions of this column.	10 percent	Oct. 1, 1978	Dec. 31, 1982
(II) Solar Wind, or Geothermal Property.—Property described in section 48(l)(2)(A)(ii) or 48(l)(3)(A)(viii).	A. 10 percent	Oct. 1, 1978	Dec. 31, 1979
	B. 15 percent	Jan. 1, 1980	Dec. 31, 1985
(III) Ocean Thermal Property.—Property described in section 48(l)(3)(A)(ix).	15 percent	Jan. 1, 1980	Dec. 31, 1985
(IV) Qualified Hydroelectric Generating Property.—Property described in section 48(l)(2)(A)(vii).	11 percent	Jan. 1, 1980	Dec. 31, 1985
(V) Qualified Intercity Buses.—Property described in section 48(l)(2)(A)(ix).	10 percent	Jan. 1, 1980	Dec. 31, 1985
(VI) Biomass Property.—Property described in section 48(l)(15).	10 percent	Oct. 1, 1978	Dec. 31, 1985
(VII) Clor-Alkali Electrolytic Cells.—Property described in section 48(l)(5)(M).	10 percent	Jan. 1, 1980	Dec. 31, 1982
(VIII) Solar Energy Property.—Property described in section 48(l)(4) (other than wind energy property).	A. 15 percent	Jan. 1, 1986	Dec. 31, 1986
	B. 12 percent	Jan. 1, 1987	Dec. 31, 1987
	C. 10 percent	Jan. 1, 1988	Sept. 30, 1990
(IX) Geothermal Property.—Property described in section 48(l)(3)(A)(viii).	A. 15 percent	Jan. 1, 1986	Dec. 31, 1986
	B. 10 percent	Jan. 1, 1987	Sept. 30, 1990
(X) Ocean Thermal Property.—Property described in section 48(l)(3)(A)(ix).	15 percent	Jan. 1, 1986	Sept. 30, 1990
(XI) Biomass Property.—Property described in section 48(l)(15).	A. 15 percent	Jan. 1, 1986	Dec. 31, 1986
	B. 10 percent	Jan. 1, 1987	Dec. 31, 1987

(B) PERIODS FOR WHICH PERCENTAGE NOT SPECIFIED.—In the case of any energy property, the energy percentage shall be zero for any period for which an energy percentage is not specified for such property under subparagraph (A) (as modified by subparagraphs (C) and (D)).

(C) LONGER PERIOD FOR CERTAIN LONG-TERM PROJECTS.—For the purpose of applying the energy percentage contained in clause (i) of subparagraph (A) with respect to property which is part of a project with a normal construction period of 2 years or more (within the meaning of subsection (d)(2)(A)(i)), "December 31, 1990" shall be substituted for "December 31, 1982" if—

(i) before January 1, 1983, all engineering studies in connection with the commencement of the construction of the project have been completed and all environmental and construction permits required under Federal, State, or local law in connection with the commencement of the construction of the project have been applied for, and

(ii) before January 1, 1986, the taxpayer has entered into binding contracts for the acquisition, construction, reconstruction, or erection of equipment specially designed for the project and the aggregate cost to the taxpayer of that equipment is at least 50 percent of the reasonably estimated cost for all such equipment which is to be placed in service as part of the project upon its completion.

(D) LONGER PERIOD FOR CERTAIN HYDROELECTRIC GENERATING PROPERTY.—If an application has been docketed by the Federal Energy Regulatory Commission before January 1, 1986, with respect to the installation of any qualified hydro[e]lectric generating property, for purposes of applying the energy percentage contained in clause (iv) of subparagraph (A) with respect to such property, "December 31, 1988" shall be substituted for "December 31, 1985".

(E) CERTAIN RULES MADE APPLICABLE.—Rules similar to the rules of subsections (c) and (d) of section 49 shall apply to any credit allowable by reason of subparagraph (C) or (D).

(3) SPECIAL RULE FOR CERTAIN ENERGY PROPERTY.—The regular percentage shall not apply to any energy property which, but for section 48(l)(1), would not be section 38 property. In the case of any qualified hydroelectric generating property which is a fish passageway, the preceding sentence shall not apply to any period after 1979 for which the energy percentage for such property is greater than zero.

(4) REHABILITATION PERCENTAGE.—

(A) IN GENERAL.—The term "rehabilitation percentage" means—

(i) 10 percent in the case of qualified rehabilitation expenditures with respect to a qualified rehabilitated building other than a certified historic structure, and

(ii) 20 percent in the case of such expenditure with respect to a certified historic structure.

(B) REGULAR AND ENERGY PERCENTAGES NOT TO APPLY.—The regular percentage and the energy percentages shall not apply to that portion of the basis of any property which is attributable to qualified rehabilitation expenditures.

Amendments

• 1989, Omnibus Budget Reconciliation Act of 1989 (P.L. 101-239)

P.L. 101-239, §7106:

Amended the table contained in Code Sec. 46(b)(2)(A) by striking "Dec. 31, 1989" in clauses (viii), (ix), and (x) and inserting "Sept. 30, 1990". **Effective** 12-19-89.

• 1988, Technical and Miscellaneous Revenue Act of 1988 (P.L. 100-647)

P.L. 100-647, §4006, amended by P.L. 101-239, §7814(d):

Amended the table under Code Sec. 46(b)(2)(A) by striking out "Dec. 31, 1988" and inserting in lieu thereof "Dec. 31, 1989" in the item relating to the 10 percent credit in clause (viii), the item relating to the 10 percent credit in clause (ix), and clause (x). **Effective** 11-10-88.

• 1986, Tax Reform Act of 1986 (P.L. 99-514)

P.L. 99-514, §251(a):

Amended Code Sec. 46(b)(4). **Effective,** generally, for property placed in service after 12-31-86 in tax years ending after such date. Prior to amendment, Code Sec. 46(b)(4) read as follows:

(4) REHABILITATION PERCENTAGE.—

(A) IN GENERAL.—

In the case of qualified rehabilitation expenditures with respect to a:	*The rehabilitation percentage is:*
30-year building	15
40-year building	20
Certified historic structure	25

(B) REGULAR AND ENERGY PERCENTAGES NOT TO APPLY.—The regular percentages and the energy percentages shall not apply to that portion of the basis of any property which is attributable to qualified rehabilitation expenditures.

(C) DEFINITIONS.—For purpose of this paragraph—

(i) 30-YEAR BUILDING.—The term "30-year building" means a qualified rehabilitated building other than a 40-year building and other than a certified historic structure.

(ii) 40-YEAR BUILDING.—The term "40-year building" means a qualified rehabilitated building (other than a certified historic structure) which would meet the requirements of section 48(g)(1)(B) if "40" were substituted for "30" each place it appears in subparagraph (B) thereof.

(iii) CERTIFIED HISTORIC STRUCTURE.—The term "certified historic structure" means a qualified rehabilitated building which meets the requirements of section 48(g)(3).

P.L. 99-514, §421(a):

Amended Code Sec. 46(b)(2)(A) by adding at the end thereof new items (viii)-(xi). **Effective** for periods beginning after 12-31-85, under rules similar to rules under section 48(m).

P.L. 99-514, §421(b):

Added Code Sec. 46(b)(2)(E). **Effective** for periods beginning after 12-31-85, under rules similar to rules under section 48(m).

P.L. 99-514, §1847(b)(11):

Amended Code Sec. 46(b)(2)(A) by striking out "48(l)(3)(A)(vii)" in the table contained in such subparagraph and inserting in lieu thereof "48(l)(3)(A)(viii)". **Effective** as if included in the provision of P.L. 98-369 to which such amendment relates.

• 1984, Deficit Reduction Act of 1984 (P.L. 98-369)

P.L. 98-369, §474(o)(1):

Amended Code Sec. 46(b). **Effective** for tax years beginning after 12-31-83, and to carrybacks from such years, but shall not be construed as reducing the amount of any credit allowable for qualified investment in taxable years beginning before 1-1-84. Prior to amendment, Code Sec. 46(b) read as follows:

(b) CARRYBACK AND CARRYOVER OF UNUSED CREDITS.—

(1) IN GENERAL.—If the sum of the amount of the investment credit carryovers to the taxable year under subsection (a)(1)(A) plus the amount determined under subsection (a)(1)(B) for the taxable year exceeds the amount of the limitation imposed by subsection (a)(3) for such taxable year (hereinafter in this subsection referred to as the "unused credit year"), such excess attributable to the amount determined under subsection (a)(1)(B) shall be—

(A) an investment credit carryback to each of the 3 taxable years preceding the unused credit year, and

(B) an investment credit carryover to each of the 7 taxable years following the unused credit year,

and, subject to the limitations imposed by paragraphs (2) and (3), shall be taken into account under the provisions of subsection (a)(1) in the manner provided in such subsection. The entire amount of the unused credit for an unused credit year shall be carried to the earliest of the 10 taxable years to which (by reason of subparagraphs (A) and (B)) such credit may be carried and then to each of the other 9 taxable years to the extent, because of the limitations imposed by paragraphs (2) and (3), such unused credit may not be taken into account under subsection (a)(1) for a prior taxable year to which such unused credit may be carried. In the case of an unused credit for an unused credit year ending before January 1, 1971, which is an investment credit carryover to a taxable year beginning after December 31, 1970 (determined without regard to this sentence), this paragraph shall be applied—

(C) by substituting "10 taxable years" for "7 taxable years" in subparagraph (B), and by substituting "13 taxable years" for "10 taxable years," and "12 taxable years" for "9 taxable years" in the preceding sentence, and

(D) by carrying such an investment credit carryover to a later taxable year (than the taxable year to which it would, but for this subparagraph, be carried) to which it may be carried if, because of the amendments made by section 802(b)(2) of the Tax Reform Act of 1976, carrying such carryover to the taxable year to which it would, but for this subparagraph, be carried would cause a portion of an unused credit from an unused credit year ending after December 31, 1970 to expire.

In the case of an unused credit for an unused credit year ending after December 31, 1973, this paragraph shall be applied by substituting "15" for "7" in subparagraph (B), and by substituting "18" for "10", and "17" for "9" in the second sentence.

(2) LIMITATION ON CARRYBACKS.—The amount of the unused credit which may be taken into account under subsection (a)(1) for any preceding taxable year shall not exceed the amount by which the limitation imposed by subsection (a)(3) for such taxable year exceeds the sum of—

(A) the amounts determined under subparagraphs (A) and (B) of subsection (a)(1) for such taxable year, plus

(B) the amounts which (by reason of this subsection) are carried back to such taxable year and are attributable to taxable years preceding the unused credit year.

(3) LIMITATION ON CARRYOVERS.—The amount of the unused credit which may be taken into account under subsection (a)(1)(A) for any succeeding taxable year shall not exceed the amount by which the limitation imposed by subsection (a)(3) for such taxable year exceeds the sum of the amounts which, by reason of this subsection, are carried to such taxable year and are attributable to taxable years preceding the unused credit year.

• 1983, Technical Corrections Act of 1982 (P.L. 97-448)

P.L. 97-448, §102(d)(2):

Amended P.L. 97-34, §209(c), to provide that the amendment made by §207, below, does not apply to any amount that, under the law in effect on 1-11-83, could not be carried to a tax year ending in 1981.

• 1981, Economic Recovery Tax Act of 1981 (P.L. 97-34)

P.L. 97-34, §207(c)(1):

Amended Code Sec. 46(b)(1) by adding the last sentence at the end thereof. **Effective** for unused credit years ending after 12-31-73.

• 1976, Tax Reform Act of 1976 (P.L. 94-455)

P.L. 94-455, §802(b)(2):

Amended Code Sec. 46(b). **Effective** for tax years beginning after 12-31-75. Prior to the amendment, Code Sec. 46(b) read as follows:

(b) CARRYBACK AND CARRYOVER OF UNUSED CREDITS.—

(1) ALLOWANCE OF CREDIT.—If the amount of the credit determined under subsection (a)(1) for any taxable year exceeds the limitation provided by subsection (a)(2) for such taxable year (hereinafter in this subsection referred to as "unused credit year"), such excess shall be—

(A) an investment credit carryback to each of the 3 taxable years preceding the unused credit year, and

(B) an investment credit carryover to each of the 7 taxable years following the unused credit year,

and shall be added to the amount allowable as a credit by section 38 for such years, except that such excess may be a carryback only to a taxable year ending after December 31, 1961. The entire amount of the unused credit for an unused credit year shall be carried to the earliest of the 10 taxable years to which (by reason of subparagraphs (A) and (B)) such credit may be carried, and then to each of the other 9 taxable years to the extent that, because of the limitation contained in paragraph (2), such unused credit may not be added for a prior taxable year to which such unused credit may be carried. In the case of an unused credit for an unused credit year ending before January 1, 1971, which is an investment credit carryover to a taxable year beginning after December 31, 1970 (determined without regard to this sentence), this paragraph shall be applied by substituting "10 taxable years" for "7 taxable years" in subparagraph (B) and by substituting "13 taxable years" for "10 taxable years" and "12 taxable years" for "9 taxable years" in the preceding sentence.

(2) LIMITATION.—The amount of the unused credit which may be added under paragraph (1) for any preceding or succeeding taxable year shall not exceed the amount by which the limitation provided by subsection (a)(2) for such taxable year exceeds the sum of—

(A) the credit allowable under subsection (a)(1) for such taxable year, and

(B) the amounts which, by reason of this subsection, are added to the amount allowable for such taxable year and attributable to taxable years preceding the unused credit year.

(3) SPECIAL RULES FOR CARRYOVERS FROM PRE-1971 UNUSED CREDIT YEARS.—The extent to which an investment credit carryover from an unused credit year ending before January 1, 1971, may be added under paragraph (1) for a taxable year beginning after December 31, 1970, shall be determined without regard to paragraph (2)(A). In determining the excess under paragraph (1) for any taxable year beginning after December 31, 1970, the limitation provided by subsection (a)(2) for such taxable year shall be reduced by the investment credit carryovers from such unused credit years (to the extent such unused credit may not be added for a prior taxable year).

(4) TAXABLE YEAR BEGINNING BEFORE JANUARY 1, 1962.—For purposes of determining the amount of an investment credit carryback that may be added under paragraph (1) for a taxable year beginning before January 1, 1962, and ending after December 31, 1961, the amount of the limitation provided by subsection (a)(2) is the amount which bears the same ratio to such limitation as the number of days in such year after December 31, 1961, bears to the total number of days in such year.

(5) CERTAIN TAXABLE YEARS ENDING IN 1969, 1970, OR 1971.—The amount which may be added under this subsection for any taxable year beginning after December 31, 1968, and ending after April 18, 1969, and before January 1, 1972, shall not exceed 20 percent of the higher of—

(A) the aggregate of the investment credit carrybacks and investment credit carryovers to the taxable year, or

(B) the highest amount computed under subparagraph (A) for any preceding taxable year which began after December 31, 1968, and ended after April 18, 1969.

In the case of a taxable year ending after August 15, 1971, and before January 1, 1972, the percentage contained in the preceding sentence shall be increased by 6 percentage points for each month (or portion thereof) in the taxable year after August 15, 1971.

(6) ADDITIONAL 3-YEAR CARRYOVER PERIOD IN CERTAIN CASES.—Any portion of an investment credit carryback or carryover to any taxable year beginning after December 31, 1968, and ending after April 18, 1969, and before January 1, 1971, which—

(A) may be added under this subsection under the limitation provided by paragraph (2), and

(B) may not be added under the limitation provided by paragraph (5), shall be an investment credit carryover to each of the 3 taxable years following the 7th taxable year after the unused credit year, and shall (subject to the provisions of paragraphs (1), (2), and (5)) be added to the amount allowable as a credit by section 38 for such years.

• 1971, Revenue Act of 1971 (P.L. 92-178)

P.L. 92-178, §106(a):

Added paragraph (3) to Code Sec. 46(b). **Effective** for tax years beginning after 12-31-70.

P.L. 92-178, §106(b):

Added the last sentence in Code Sec. 46(b)(1). **Effective** for tax years beginning after 12-31-70.

P.L. 92-178, §106(c)(1):

Amended Code Sec. 46(b)(5). **Effective** for tax years ending after 8-15-71. Prior to amendment, Code Sec. 46(b)(5) read as follows:

"(5) Taxable years beginning after December 31, 1968, and ending after April 18, 1969.—The amount which may be added under this subsection for any taxable year beginning after December 31, 1968, and ending after April 18, 1969, shall not exceed 20 percent of the higher of—

"(A) the aggregate of the investment credit carrybacks and investment credit carryovers to the taxable year, or

"(B) the highest amount computed under subparagraph (A) for any preceding taxable year which began after December 31, 1968, and ended after April 18, 1969."

P.L. 92-178, §106(c)(2):

Amended Code Sec. 46(b)(6). **Effective** for tax years beginning after 12-31-70. Prior to amendment, Code Sec. 46(b)(6) read as follows:

"(6) Additional 3-year carryover period in certain cases.—Any portion of an investment credit carryback or carryover to any taxable year beginning after December 31, 1968, and ending after April 18, 1969, which—

"(A) may be added under this subsection under the limitation provided by paragraph (2), and

"(B) may not be added under the limitation provided by paragraph (5),

shall be an investment credit carryover to each of the 3 taxable years following the last taxable year for which such portion may be added under paragraph (1), and shall (subject to the provisions of paragraphs (1), (2), and (5)) be added to the amount allowable as a credit by section 38 for such years."

• 1969, Tax Reform Act of 1969 (P.L. 91-172)

P.L. 91-172, §703(b):

Added Code Secs. 46(b)(5) and 46(b)(6).

• 1967 (P.L. 90-225)

P.L. 90-225, §2(a):

Repealed Code Sec. 46(b)(3). **Effective** with respect to investment credit carrybacks attributable to net operating loss carrybacks from tax years ending after 7-31-67. Prior to repeal, Code Sec. 46(b)(3) read as follows:

"(3) Effect of net operating loss carryback.—To the extent that the excess described in paragraph (1) arises by reason of a net operating loss carryback, subparagraph (A) of paragraph (1) shall not apply."

• 1966 (P.L. 89-800)

P.L. 89-800, §3(b):

Amended Code Sec. 46(b)(1)(B) by substituting "7 taxable years" for "5 taxable years" and amended the last sentence of Code Sec. 46(b)(1) by substituting "10 taxable years" for "8 taxable years" and "other 9 taxable years" for "other 7 taxable years". **Effective** only if the fifth taxable year following the unused credit year ends after 12-31-66.

[Sec. 46(c)]

(c) QUALIFIED INVESTMENT.—

(1) IN GENERAL.—For purposes of this subpart, the term "qualified investment" means, with respect to any taxable year, the aggregate of—

(A) the applicable percentage of the basis of each new section 38 property (as defined in section 48(b)) placed in service by the taxpayer during such taxable year, plus

(B) the applicable percentage of the cost of each used section 38 property (as defined in section 48(c)(1)) placed in service by the taxpayer during such taxable year.

(2) APPLICABLE PERCENTAGE IN CERTAIN CASES.—Except as provided in paragraphs (3), (6), and (7), the applicable percentage for purposes of paragraph (1), for any property shall be determined under the following table:

If the useful life is—	*The applicable percentage is—*
3 years or more but less than 5 years	33⅓
5 years or more but less than 7 years	66⅔
7 years or more	100

For purposes of this subpart, the useful life of any property shall be the useful life used in computing the allowance for depreciation under section 167 for the taxable year in which the property is placed in service.

(3) PUBLIC UTILITY PROPERTY.—

(A) To the extent that the credit allowed by section 38 with respect to any public utility property is determined at the rate of 7 percent, in the case of any property which is public utility property, the amount of the qualified investment shall be 4/7 of the amount determined under paragraph (1). The preceding sentence shall not apply for purposes of applying the energy percentage.

(B) For purposes of subparagraph (A), the term "public utility property" means property used predominantly in the trade or business of the furnishing or sale of—

(i) electrical energy, water, or sewage disposal services,

(ii) gas through a local distribution system, or

(iii) telephone service, telegraph service by means of domestic telegraph operations (as defined in section 222(a)(5) of the Communications Act of 1934, as amended; 47 U.S.C. 222(a)(5)), or other communication services (other than international telegraph service),

if the rates for such furnishing or sale, as the case may be, have been established or approved by a State or political subdivision thereof, by an agency or instrumentality of the United States, or by a public service or public utility commission or other similar body of any State or political subdivision thereof. Such term also means communication property of the type used by persons engaged in providing telephone or microwave communication services to which clause (iii) applies, if such property is used predominantly for communication purposes.

(C) In the case of any interest in a submarine cable circuit used to furnish telegraph service between the United States and a point outside the United States of a taxpayer engaged in furnishing international telegraph service (if the rates for such furnishing have been established or approved by a governmental unit, agency, instrumentality, commission, or similar body described in subparagraph (B)), the qualified investment shall not exceed the qualified investment attributable to so much of the interest of the taxpayer in the circuit as does not exceed 50 percent of all interests in the circuit.

(4) COORDINATION WITH SUBSECTION (d).—The amount which would (but for this paragraph) be treated as qualified investment under this subsection with respect to any property shall be reduced (but not below zero) by any amount treated by the taxpayer or a predecessor of the taxpayer (or, in the case of a sale and leaseback described in section 47(a)(3)(C), by the lessee) as qualified investment with respect to such property under subsection (d), to the extent the amount so treated has not been required to be recaptured by reason of section 47(a)(3).

(5) APPLICABLE PERCENTAGE IN THE CASE OF CERTAIN POLLUTION CONTROL FACILITIES.—

(A) IN GENERAL.—Notwithstanding paragraph (2), in the case of property—

(i) with respect to which an election under section 169 applies, and

(ii) the useful life of which (determined without regard to section 169) is not less than 5 years,

100 percent shall be the applicable percentage for purposes of applying paragraph (1) with respect to so much of the adjusted basis of the property as (after the application of section 169(f)) constitutes the amortizable basis for purposes of section 169.

(B) SPECIAL RULE WHERE PROPERTY IS FINANCED BY PRIVATE ACTIVITY BONDS.—To the extent that any property is financed by the proceeds of a private activity bond (within the meaning of section 141) the interest on which is exempt from tax under section 103, subparagraph (A) shall be applied by substituting "50 percent" for "100 percent." This subparagraph shall not apply for purposes of applying the energy percentage.

(6) SPECIAL RULE FOR COMMUTER HIGHWAY VEHICLES.—

(A) IN GENERAL.—Notwithstanding paragraph (2) or (3), in the case of a commuter highway vehicle the useful life of which is 3 years or more, or which is recovery property (within the meaning of section 168), the applicable percentage for purposes of paragraph (1) shall be 100 percent.

(B) DEFINITION OF COMMUTER HIGHWAY VEHICLE.—For purposes of subparagraph (A), the term "commuter highway vehicle" means a highway vehicle—

(i) the seating capacity of which is at least 8 adults (not including the driver),

(ii) at least 80 percent of the mileage use of which can reasonably be expected to be (I) for purposes of transporting the taxpayer's employees between their residences and their place of employment, and (II) on trips during which the number of employees transported for such purposes is at least one-half of the adult seating capacity of such vehicle (not including the driver),

(iii) which is acquired by the taxpayer on or after the date of the enactment of the Energy Tax Act of 1978, and placed in service by the taxpayer before January 1, 1986, and

(iv) with respect to which the taxpayer makes an election under this paragraph on his return for the taxable year in which such vehicle is placed in service.

(7) APPLICABLE PERCENTAGE FOR PROPERTY TO WHICH SECTION 168 APPLIES.—Notwithstanding paragraph (2), the applicable percentage for purposes of paragraph (1) shall be—

(A) in the case of property to which section 168 applies other than 3-year property (within the meaning of section 168(e)), 100 percent, and

(B) in the case of 3-year property (within the meaning of section 168(e)), 60 percent.

For purposes of subparagraph (A), RRB replacement property (within the meaning of section 168 (f)(3)(B) (as in effect on the day before the date of enactment of the Tax Reform Act of 1986) shall be treated as property which is not 3-year property.

(8) CERTAIN NONRECOURSE FINANCING EXCLUDED FROM CREDIT BASE.—

(A) LIMITATION.—The credit base of any property to which this paragraph applies shall be reduced by the nonqualified nonrecourse financing with respect to such property (as of the close of the taxable year in which placed in service).

(B) PROPERTY TO WHICH PARAGRAPH APPLIES.—This paragraph applies to any property which—

(i) is placed in service during the taxable year by a taxpayer described in section 465(a)(1), and

(ii) is used in connection with an activity with respect to which any loss is subject to limitation under section 465.

(C) CREDIT BASE DEFINED.—For purposes of this paragraph, the term "credit base" means—

(i) in the case of new section 38 property, the basis of the property, or

(ii) in the case of used section 38 property, the cost of such property.

(D) NONQUALIFIED NONRECOURSE FINANCING.—

(i) IN GENERAL.—For purposes of this paragraph and paragraph (9), the term "nonqualified nonrecourse financing" means any nonrecourse financing which is not qualified commercial financing.

(ii) QUALIFIED COMMERCIAL FINANCING.—For purposes of this paragraph, the term "qualified commercial financing" means any financing with respect to any property if—

(I) such property is acquired by the taxpayer from a person who is not a related person,

(II) the amount of the nonrecourse financing with respect to such property does not exceed 80 percent of the credit base of such property, and

(III) such financing is borrowed from a qualified person or represents a loan from any Federal, State, or local government or instrumentality thereof, or is guaranteed by any Federal, State, or local government.

Such term shall not include any convertible debt.

(iii) NONRECOURSE FINANCING.—For purposes of this subparagraph, the term "nonrecourse financing" includes—

(I) any amount with respect to which the taxpayer is protected against loss through guarantees, stop-loss agreements, or other similar arrangements, and

(II) except to the extent provided in regulations, any amount borrowed from a person who has an interest (other than as a creditor) in the activity in which the property is used or from a related person to a person (other than the taxpayer) having such an interest.

In the case of amounts borrowed by a corporation from a shareholder, subclause (II) shall not apply to an interest as a shareholder.

(iv) QUALIFIED PERSON.—For purposes of this paragraph, the term "qualified person" means any person which is actively and regularly engaged in the business of lending money and which is not—

(I) a related person with respect to the taxpayer,

(II) a person from which the taxpayer acquired the property (or a related person to such person), or

(III) a person who receives a fee with respect to the taxpayer's investment in the property (or a related person to such person).

(v) RELATED PERSON.—For purposes of this subparagraph, the term "related person" has the meaning given such term by section 465(b)(3)(C). Except as otherwise provided in regulations prescribed by the Secretary, the determination of whether a person is a related person shall be made as of the close of the taxable year in which the property is placed in service.

(E) APPLICATION TO PARTNERSHIPS AND S CORPORATIONS.—For purposes of this paragraph and paragraph (9)—

(i) IN GENERAL.—Except as otherwise provided in this subparagraph, in the case of any partnership or S corporation, the determination of whether a partner's or shareholder's allocable share of any financing is nonqualified nonrecourse financing shall be made at the partner or shareholder level.

(ii) SPECIAL RULE FOR CERTAIN RECOURSE FINANCING OF S CORPORATION.—A shareholder of an S corporation shall be treated as liable for his allocable share of any financing provided by a qualified person to such corporation if—

(I) such financing is recourse financing (determined at the corporate level), and

(II) such financing is provided with respect to qualified business property of such corporation.

(iii) QUALIFIED BUSINESS PROPERTY.—For purposes of clause (ii), the term "qualified business property" means any property if—

(I) such property is used by the corporation in the active conduct of a trade or business,

(II) during the entire 12-month period ending on the last day of the taxable year, such corporation had at least 3 full-time employees who were not owner-employees (as defined in section 465(c)(7)(E)(i)) and substantially all the services of whom were services directly related to such trade or business, and

(III) during the entire 12-month period ending on the last day of such taxable year, such corporation had at least 1 full-time employee substantially all of the services of whom were in the active management of the trade or business.

Such term shall not include any master sound recording or other tangible or intangible asset associated with literary, artistic, or musical properties.

(iv) DETERMINATION OF ALLOCABLE SHARE.—The determination of any partner's or shareholder's allocable share of any financing shall be made in the same manner as the credit allowable by section 38 with respect to such property.

(F) SPECIAL RULE FOR CERTAIN ENERGY PROPERTY.—

(i) IN GENERAL.—Subparagraph (A) shall not apply with respect to qualified energy property.

(ii) QUALIFIED ENERGY PROPERTY.—The term "qualified energy property" means energy property to which (but for this subparagraph) subparagraph (A) applies and—

(I) which is described in clause (iii),

(II) with respect to which the energy percentage determined under subsection (b)(2) at the time such property is placed in service is greater than zero,

(III) as of the close of the taxable year in which the property is placed in service, not more than 75 percent of the basis of such property is attributable to nonqualified nonrecourse financing, and

(IV) with respect to which any nonqualified nonrecourse financing in connection with such property consists of a level payment loan.

For purposes of subclause (II), the energy percentage for property described in clause (iii)(V) shall be treated as being greater than zero during any period the energy percentage for property described in section 48(l)(14) is greater than zero.

(iii) PROPERTY TO WHICH THIS SUBPARAGRAPH APPLIES.—Energy property is described in this clause if such property is—

(I) described in clause (ii), (iv), or (vii) or [of] section 48(l)(2)[A],

(II) described in section 48(l)(15),

(III) described in section 48(l)(3)(A)(iii) (but only to the extent such property is used for converting an alternate substance into alcohol for fuel purposes),

(IV) described in clause (i) of section 48(l)(2)(A) (but only to the extent such property is also described in section 48(l)(3)(A)(viii) or (ix)), or

(V) property comprising a system for using the same energy source for the sequential generation of electrical power, mechanical shaft power, or both, in combination with steam, heat, or other forms of useful energy.

(iv) LEVEL PAYMENT LOAN DEFINED.—The term "level payment loan" means a loan in which each installment is substantially equal, a portion of each installment is attributable to the repayment of principal, and that portion is increased commensurate with decreases in the portion of the payment attributable to interest.

(9) SUBSEQUENT DECREASES IN NONQUALIFIED NONRECOURSE FINANCING WITH RESPECT TO THE PROPERTY.—

(A) IN GENERAL.—If, at the close of a taxable year following the taxable year in which the property was placed in service, there is a net decrease in the amount of nonqualified nonrecourse financing with respect to such property, such net decrease shall be taken into account as an increase in the credit base for such property in accordance with subparagraph (C).

(B) CERTAIN TRANSACTIONS NOT TAKEN INTO ACCOUNT.—For purposes of this paragraph, nonqualified nonrecourse financing shall not be treated as decreased through the surrender or other use of property financed by nonqualified nonrecourse financing.

(C) MANNER IN WHICH TAKEN INTO ACCOUNT.—

(i) CREDIT DETERMINED BY REFERENCE TO TAXABLE YEAR PROPERTY PLACED IN SERVICE.—For purposes of determining the amount of credit allowable under section 38 and the amount of credit subject to the early disposition or cessation rules under section 47, any increase in a taxpayer's credit base for any property by reason of this paragraph shall be taken into account as if it were property placed in service by the taxpayer in the taxable year in which the property referred to in subparagraph (A) was first placed in service.

(ii) CREDIT ALLOWED FOR YEAR OF DECREASE IN NONQUALIFIED NONRECOURSE FINANCING.—Any credit allowable under this subpart for any increase in qualified investment by reason of this paragraph shall be treated as earned during the taxable year of the decrease in the amount of nonqualified nonrecourse financing.

Amendments

• 1988, Technical and Miscellaneous Revenue Act of 1988 (P.L. 100-647)

P.L. 100-647, §1002(a)(17)(A)-(D):

Amended Code Sec. 46(c)(7) by striking out "recovery property" and inserting in lieu thereof "property to which section 168 applies", by striking out "168(c)" each place it appears and inserting in lieu thereof "168(e)", by striking out "168(f)(3)(B)" and inserting in lieu thereof "168(f)(3)(B) (as in effect on the day before the date of enactment of the Tax Reform Act of 1986)", and by striking out "RECOVERY PROPERTY" in the paragraph heading and inserting in lieu thereof "PROPERTY TO WHICH SECTION 168 APPLIES". **Effective** as if included in the provision of P.L. 99-514 to which it relates.

P.L. 100-647, §1013(a)(44)(A)-(B):

Amended Code Sec. 46(c)(5)(B) by striking out "industrial development bonds" in the heading and inserting in lieu thereof "private activity bonds", and by striking "an industrial development bond (within the meaning of section 103(b)(2))" and inserting in lieu thereof "a private activity bond (within the meaning of section 141)". **Effective** as if included in the provision of P.L. 99-514 to which it relates.

• 1986, Tax Reform Act of 1986 (P.L. 99-514)

P.L. 99-514, §201(d)(7)(B):

Amended Code Sec. 46(c)(8)(D)(v) by striking out "section 168(e)(4)" and inserting in lieu thereof "section 465(b)(3)(C)". **Effective,** generally, for property placed in service after 12-31-86, in tax years ending after such date. For transitional rules, see Act Secs. 203-204 and 251 following Code Sec. 168.

P.L. 99-514, §1844(a):

Amended Code Sec. 46(c)(8)(D)(v) by striking out "clause (i)" and inserting in lieu thereof "this subparagraph". **Effective** as if included in the provision of P.L. 98-369 to which it relates.

P.L. 99-514, §1844(b)(3):

Amended Code Sec. 46(c)(9)(A) by striking out "additional qualified investment in" and inserting in lieu thereof "an increase in the credit base for". **Effective** as if included in the provision of P.L. 98-369 to which it relates.

P.L. 99-514, §1844(b)(5):

Amended Code Sec. 46(c)(9)(C)(i) by striking out "any increase in a taxpayer's qualified investment" and all that follows down through the period at the end thereof and inserting in lieu thereof "any increase in a taxpayer's credit base for any property by reason of this paragraph shall be taken into account as if it were property placed in service by the taxpayer in the taxable year in which the property referred to in subparagraph (A) was first placed in service." **Effective** as if included in the provision of P.L. 98-369 to which it relates. Prior to amendment, Code Sec. 46(c)(9)(C)(i) read as follows:

(i) CREDIT DETERMINED BY REFERENCE TO TAXABLE YEAR PROPERTY PLACED IN SERVICE.—For purposes of determining the amount of credit allowable under section 38 and the amount of credit subject to the early disposition or cessation rules under section 47, any increase in a taxpayer's qualified investment in property by reason of this paragraph shall be deemed to be additional qualified investment made by the taxpayer in the year in which the property referred to in subparagraph (A) was first placed in service.

• 1984, Deficit Reduction Act of 1984 (P.L. 98-369)

P.L. 98-369, §16(a):

Repealed P.L. 97-34, §302(c)(3), which struck out "clause (i), (ii), or (iii) of subparagraph (A) or subparagraph (B) of section 128(c)(2)" in Code Sec. 46(c)(8) and inserted in lieu thereof "subparagraph (A) or (B) of section 128(c)(1)". **Effective** as if the amendment by P.L. 97-34 had not been enacted.

P.L. 98-369, §113(b)(2)(B):

Amended Code Sec. 46(c)(7)(A) by inserting "recovery" before "property" the first place it appears. **Effective** as if included in P.L. 97-34, §§201 and 211(a)(1) and (f)(1).

P.L. 98-369, §431(a):

Amended so much of Code Sec. 46(c)(8) as preceded paragraph (F). **Effective** for property placed in service after 7-18-84, in tax years ending after such date but does not apply to any property to which the amendments made by P.L. 97-34, §211(f) do not apply. Prior to amendment, it read as follows:

(8) Limitation to Amount at Risk.—

(A) In General.—In the case of new or used section 38 property which—

(i) is placed in service during the taxable year by a taxpayer described in section 465(a)(1), and

(ii) is used in connection with an activity with respect to which any loss is subject to limitation under section 465,

the basis of such property for purposes of paragraph (1) shall not exceed the amount the taxpayer is at risk with respect to such property as of the close of such taxable year.

(B) Amount at Risk.—

(i) In General.—Except as provided in clause (ii), the term "at risk" has the same meaning given such term by section 465(b) (without regard to paragraph (5) thereof).

(ii) Certain Financing.—In the case of a taxpayer who at all times is at risk (determined without regard to this clause) in an amount equal to at least 20 percent of the basis (determined under section 168(d)(1)(A)(i)) of property described in subparagraph (A) and who acquired such property from a person who is not a related person, such taxpayer shall for purposes of this paragraph be considered at risk with respect to any amount borrowed in connection with such property (other than convertible debt) to the extent that such amount—

(I) is borrowed from a qualified person, or

(II) represents a loan from any Federal, State, or local government or instrumentality therof, or is a guaranteed by, any Federal, State, or local government.

(C) Special Rule for Partnerships and Subchapter S Corporations.—In the case of any partnership or S corporation, any amount treated as at risk under subparagraph (B)(ii) shall be allocated among the partners or shareholders (and treated as an amount at risk with respect to such persons) in the same manner as the credit allowable by section 38.

(D) Qualified Person.—For purposes of this paragraph, the term "qualified person" means any person—

(i) which—

(I) is an institution described in clause (i), (ii), or (iii) of subparagraph (A) or subparagraph (B) of subsection 128(c)(2) or an insurance company to which subchapter L applies, or

(II) is a pension trust qualified under section 401(a) or a person not described in subclause (I) and which is actively and regularly engaged in the business of lending money,

(ii) which is not a related person with respect to the taxpayer,

(iii) which is not a person who receives a fee with respect to the taxpayer's investment in property described in subparagraph (A) or a related person to such person, and

(iv) which is not a person from which the taxpayer acquired the property described in subparagraph (A) or a related person to such person."

(E) Related Person.—For purposes of this paragraph, the term "related person" has the same meaning as such term is used in section 168(e)(4), except that in applying section 168(e)(4)(D)(i) in the case of a person described in subparagraph (D)(i)(II) of this paragraph, sections 267(b) and 707(b)(1) shall be applied by substituting "0 percent" for "50 percent".

P.L. 98-369, §431(b)(1):

Amended Code Sec. 46(c)(9). **Effective** for property placed in service after 7-18-84, in tax years ending after such date but does not apply to any property to which the amendments made by P.L. 97-34, §211(f) do not apply. Prior to amendment, it read as follows:

(9) Subsequent Increases in the Taxpayer's Amount at Risk with Respect to the Property.—

(A) In General.—If, at the close of a taxable year subsequent to the year in which property was placed in service, the amount which the taxpayer has at risk with respect to such property has increased (as determined under subparagraph (B)), such increase shall be taken into account as additional qualified investment in such property in accordance with subparagraph (C).

(B) Increases to Be Taken Into Account.—For purposes of subparagraphs (A) and (C), the amount which a taxpayer has at risk with respect to the property shall be treated as increased by the sum of the cash and the fair market value of property (other than property with respect to which the taxpayer is not at risk) used during the taxable year to reduce the principal sum of any amount with respect to which the taxpayer is not at risk.

(C) Manner in Which Taken Into Account.—For purposes of determining the amount of credit allowed under section 38 and the amount of credit subject to the early disposition rules under section 47, an increase in a taxpayer's qualified investment in property (determined under subparagraph (B)) shall be deemed to be additional qualified investment made by the taxpayer in the year in which the property referred to in subparagraph (A) was first placed in service. However, the credit determined by taking into account the increase in qualified investment under this paragraph shall be considered a credit earned in the taxable year of such increase.

P.L. 98-369, §431(d)(1):

Amended Code Sec. 46(c)(8)(F)(i). **Effective** for property placed in service after 7-18-84, in tax years ending after such date; except that it shall not apply to any property to which the amendments made by section 211(f) of P.L. 97-34 do not apply. At the election of the taxpayer, the amendments made by this section shall apply as if included in the amendments made by section 211(f) of P.L. 97-34. Any election made under the preceding sentence shall apply to all property of the taxpayer to which the amendments made by such section 211(f) apply and shall be made at such time and in such manner as the Secretary of the Treasury or his delegate may by regulations prescribe. Prior to amendment, it read as follows:

(i) In General.—The provisions of subparagraph (A) shall not apply to amounts borrowed with respect to qualified energy property (other than amounts described in subparagraph (B)).

P.L. 98-369, §431(d)(2):

Amended Code Sec. 46(c)(8)(F)(ii)(III). **Effective** for property placed in service after 7-18-84, in tax years ending after such date; except that it shall not apply to any property to which the amendments made by section 211(f) of P.L. 97-34 do not apply. At the election of the taxpayer, the amendments made by this section shall apply as if included in the amendments made by section 211(f) of P.L. 97-34. Any election made under the preceding sentence shall apply to all property of the taxpayer to which the amendments made by such section 211(f) apply and shall be made at such time and in such manner as the Secretary of the Treasury or his delegate may by regulations prescribe. Prior to amendment, it read as follows:

(III) with respect to which the taxpayer, as of the close of the taxable year in which the property is placed in service, is at risk (within the meaning of section 465(b) without regard to paragraph (5) thereof) in an amount equal to at least 25 percent of the basis of the property, and

P.L. 98-369, §431(d)(3):

Amended Code Sec. 46(c)(8)(F)(ii)(IV) by striking out "nonrecourse financing (other than financing described in section 46(c)(8)(B)(ii))" and inserting in lieu thereof "nonqualified nonrecourse financing". **Effective** for property placed in service after 7-18-84, in tax years ending after such date; except that it shall not apply to any property to which the amendments made by section 211(f) of P.L. 97-34 do not apply. At the election of the taxpayer, the amendments made by this section shall apply as if included in the amendments made by section 211(f) of P.L. 97-34. Any election made under the preceding sentence shall apply to all property of the taxpayer to which the amendments made by such section 211(f) apply and shall be made at such time and in such manner as the Secretary of the Treasury or his delegate may by regulations prescribe.

P.L. 98-369, §474(o)(2):

Amended Code Sec. 46(c)(8)(F)(ii)(II) by striking out "section 46(a)(2)(C)" and inserting in lieu thereof "subsection (b)(2)". **Effective** for tax years beginning after 12-31-83, and to carrybacks from such years, but shall not be construed as reducing the amount of any credit allowable for qualified investment in taxable years beginning before 1-1-84.

• 1983, Technical Corrections Act of 1982 (P.L. 97-448)

P.L. 97-448, §102(e)(1):

Amended Code Sec. 46(c)(7) by striking out subparagraph (A) and inserting in lieu thereof the following: "(A) in the case of property other than 3-year property (within the meaning of section 168(c)), 100 percent, and", and by striking out "shall be treated as 5-year property" in the last sentence and inserting in lieu thereof "shall be treated as property which is not 3-year property". **Effective** as if it had been included in the provision of P.L. 97-34 to which it relates. Prior to amendment, Code Sec. 46(c)(7)(A) read as follows:

"(A) in the case of 15-year public utility, 10-year, or 5-year property (within the meaning of section 168(c)), 100 percent, and"

• 1982, Subchapter S Revision Act of 1982 (P.L. 97-354)

P.L. 97-354, §5(a)(5):

Amended Code Sec. 46(c)(8)(C) by striking out "electing small business corporation (within the meaning of section 1371(b))" and inserting in lieu thereof "S corporation". **Effective** for tax years beginning after 12-31-82.

• 1981, Economic Recovery Tax Act of 1981 (P.L. 97-34)

P.L. 97-34, §211(a)(1):

Added Code Sec. 46(c)(7). **Effective** for property placed in service after 12-31-80.

P.L. 97-34, §211(e)(1):

Amended Code Sec. 46(c)(2) by revising the heading and so much of the paragraph as precedes the table. **Effective** for property placed in service after 12-31-80. Prior to amendment, Code Sec. 46(c)(2) read as follows:

(2) APPLICABLE PERCENTAGE.—For purposes of paragraph (1), the applicable percentage for any property shall be determined under the following table:

P.L. 97-34, §211(e)(2):

Amended Code Sec. 46(c)(6)(A). **Effective** for property placed in service after 12-31-80. Prior to amendment, Code Sec. 46(c)(6)(A) read as follows:

(A) IN GENERAL.—Notwithstanding paragraph (2), in the case of a commuter highway vehicle the useful life of which is 3 years or more, the applicable percentage for purposes of paragraph (1) shall be 100 percent.

P.L. 97-34, §211(f)(1):

Added Code Sec. 46(c)(8) and (9). **Effective** for property placed in service after 2-18-81, unless acquired pursuant to a contract binding on or before that date. Also, see Act Sec. 211(i)(5), below.

P.L. 97-34, §211(i)(5), provides:

(5) AT RISK RULES.—

(A) IN GENERAL.—The amendment made by subsection (f) shall not apply to—

(i) property placed in service by the taxpayer on or before February 18, 1981, and

(ii) property placed in service by the taxpayer after February 18, 1981, where such property is acquired by the taxpayer pursuant to a binding contract entered into on or before that date.

(B) BINDING CONTRACT.—For purposes of subparagraph (A)(ii), property acquired pursuant to a binding contract shall, under regulations prescribed by the Secretary, include property acquired in a manner so that it would have qualified as pretermination property under section 49(b) (as in effect before its repeal by the Revenue Act of 1978).

P.L. 97-34, §302(c)(3) [repealed by P.L. 98-369, §16(a)]:

Amended Code Sec. 46(c)(8), as added by Act Sec. 211(f)(1), by striking out in subparagraph (D)(i)(I) "clause (i), (ii), or (iii) of subparagraph (A) or subparagraph (B) of section 128(c)(2)" and inserting "subparagraph (A) or (B) of section 128(c)(1)". **Effective** for tax years beginning after 12-31-84.

• 1980, Technical Corrections Act of 1979 (P.L. 96-222)

P.L. 96-222, §103(a)(3):

Amended Code Sec. 46(c)(5) by adding a new sentence at the end of the paragraph. **Effective** as indicated in P.L. 95-600, Act Sec. 313(b), below.

• 1978, Revenue Act of 1978 (P.L. 95-600)

P.L. 95-600, §311(c)(1):

Amended Code Sec. 46(c)(3)(A), as amended by P.L. 95-618, §301(a)(2)(A), by inserting "To the extent that the credit allowed by section 38 with respect to any public utility property is determined at the rate of 7 percent" in place of "For the period beginning on January 1, 1981,". **Effective** 11-10-78. [Note: Congress apparently intended for the amendment made by P.L. 95-618, §301(a)(2)(A) to precede this change.] For the text of Code Sec. 46(c)(3)(A) before the above amendment, but after the amendment made by P.L. 95-618, §301(a)(2)(A), see the amendment note for the latter law.

P.L. 95-600, §313(a):

Amended Code Sec. 46(c)(5). **Effective** as indicated in Act Sec. 313(b), below. Before amendment, such code section read:

"(5) APPLICABLE PERCENTAGE IN THE CASE OF CERTAIN POLLUTION CONTROL FACILITIES.—Notwithstanding subsection (c)(2), in the case of property—

"(A) with respect to which an election under section 169 applies, and

"(B) the useful life of which (determined without regard to section 169) is not less than 5 years,

50 percent shall be the applicable percentage for purposes of applying paragraph (1) with respect to so much of the adjusted basis of the property as (after the application of section 169(f)) constitutes the amortizable basis for purposes of section 169."

P.L. 95-600, §313(b), provides:

"(b) EFFECTIVE DATE.—The amendment made by subsection (a) shall apply to—

"(1) property acquired by the taxpayer after December 31, 1978, and

"(2) property the construction, reconstruction, or erection of which was completed by the taxpayer after December 31, 1978 (but only to the extent of the basis thereof attributable to construction, reconstruction, or erection after such date)."

• 1978, Energy Tax Act of 1978 (P.L. 95-618)

P.L. 95-618, §301(a)(2)(A):

Amended Code Sec. 46(c)(3)(A) to read as follows. **Effective** 11-10-78.

"(A) For the period beginning on January 1, 1981, in the case of any property which is public utility property, the amount of the qualified investment shall be 4/7 of the amount determined under paragraph (1). The preceding sentence shall not apply for purposes of applying the energy percentage."

[Note: Congress apparently intended for such amendment to be made before amendments made by P.L. 95-600, §311(c)(1). See the amendment note for such law.] Before amendment, Code Sec. 46(c)(3)(A) read:

"(A) To the extent that subsection (a)(2)(C) applies to property which is public utility property, the amount of the qualified investment shall be 4/7 of the amount determined under paragraph (1)."

P.L. 95-618, §241(a):

Added Code Sec. 46(c)(6). **Effective** 11-10-78.

• 1976, Tax Reform Act of 1976 (P.L. 94-455)

P.L. 94-455, §802(b)(3):

Substituted "subsection (a)(2)(C)" for "subsection (a)(1)(C)" in subparagraph (A) of Code Sec. 46(c)(3). **Effective** for tax years beginning after 12-31-75.

P.L. 94-455, §1901(a)(4)(B):

Deleted ", sec." after "47 U.S.C." in clause (iii) of Code Sec. 46(c)(3)(B). **Effective** for tax years beginning after 12-31-76.

P.L. 94-455, §2112(a)(2):

Added a new paragraph (5) to Code Sec. 46(c). **Effective** for property acquired by the taxpayer after 12-31-76, and to property the construction, reconstruction, or erection of which was completed by the taxpayer after 12-31-76, (but only to the extent of the basis thereof attributable to construction, reconstruction, or erection after such date), in tax years beginning after such date.

• 1975, Tax Reduction Act of 1975 (P.L. 94-12)

P.L. 94-12, §301(b)(1):

Amended Code Sec. 46(c)(3)(A). **Effective** for property in service after 1-21-75 in tax years ending after that date. Prior to amendment Code Sec. 46(c)(3)(A) read as follows:

"(A) In the case of section 38 property which is public utility property, the amount of the qualified investment shall be 4/7 of the amount determined under paragraph (1)."

P.L. 94-12, §302(b)(1):

Amended Code Sec. 46(c) by adding new paragraph (4). **Effective** for tax years ending after 12-31-74.

• 1971, Revenue Act of 1971 (P.L. 92-178)

P.L. 92-178, §§102(a)(1), 102(b):

Amended Code Sec. 46(c)(2). **Effective** for property described in Code Sec. 50. Prior to amendment, Code Sec. 46(c)(2) read as follows:

"(2) Applicable percentage.—For purposes of paragraph (1), the applicable percentage for any property shall be determined under the following table:

If the useful life is—	The applicable percentage is—
4 years or more but less than 6 years	33 1/3
6 years or more but less than 8 years	66 2/3
8 years or more	100

For purposes of this paragraph, the useful life of any property shall be determined as of the time such property is placed in service by the taxpayer."

P.L. 92-178, §105(a):

Amended Code Sec. 46(c)(3)(A) by substituting "4/7" for "3/7". **Effective** for property described in Code Sec. 50.

P.L. 92-178, §105(b):

Amended Code Sec. 46(c)(3)(B) and added Code Sec. 46(c)(3)(C). **Effective** for property described in Code Sec. 50. Prior to amendment, Code Sec. 46(c)(3)(B) read as follows:

"(B) for purposes of subparagraph (A), the term 'public utility property' means property used predominantly in the trade or business of the furnishing or sale of—

"(i) electrical energy, water, or sewage disposal services,

"(ii) gas through a local distribution system,

"(iii) telephone service, or

"(iv) telegraph service by means of domestic telegraph operations (as defined in section 222(a)(5) of the Communications Act of 1934, as amended; 47 U. S. C., Sec. 222(a)(5))

if the rates for such furnishing or sale, as the case may be, have been established or approved by a State or political sudivision thereof, by an agency or instrumentality of the United States, or by a public service or public utility commission or other similar body of any State or political subdivision thereof."

P.L. 92-178, §107(a):

Repealed Code Sec. 46(c)(4). **Effective** for casualties and thefts occurring after 8-15-71. Prior to repeal, Code Sec. 46(c)(4) read as follows:

"(4) Certain replacement property.—For purposes of paragraph (a), if section 38 property is placed in service by the taxpayer to replace property which was—

"(A) destroyed or damaged by fire, storm, shipwreck, or other casualty, or

"(B) stolen,

the basis of such section 38 property (in the case of new section 38 property), or the cost of such section 38 property (in the case of used section 38 property), which (but for this paragraph) would be taken into account under paragraph (1) shall be reduced by an amount equal to the amount received by the taxpayer as compensation, by insurance or otherwise, for the property so destroyed, damaged, or stolen, or to the adjusted basis of such property, whichever is the lesser. No reduction in basis or cost shall be made under the preceding sentence in any case in which the reduction in qualified investment attributable to the substitution required by section 47(a)(1) with respect to the property so destroyed, damaged, or stolen (determined without regard to section 47(a)(4)) is greater than the reduction described in the preceding sentence."

P.L. 92-178, §102(d)(2), provides:

"(2) In redetermining qualified investment for purposes of section 47(a) of the Internal Revenue Code of 1954 in the case of any property which ceases to be section 38 property with respect to the taxpayer after August 15, 1971, or which becomes public utility property after such date, section 46(c)(2) of such Code shall be applied as amended by subsection (a) [i. e., §102(a) of P.L. 92-178]."

[Sec. 46(d)]

(d) QUALIFIED PROGRESS EXPENDITURES.—

(1) INCREASE IN QUALIFIED INVESTMENT.—

(A) IN GENERAL.—In the case of any taxpayer who has made an election under paragraph (6), the amount of the qualified investment of such taxpayer for the taxable year (determined under subsection (c) without regard to this subsection) shall be increased by an amount equal to the aggregate of the applicable percentage of each qualified progress expenditure for the taxable year with respect to progress expenditure property.

(B) APPLICABLE PERCENTAGE.—

(i) RECOVERY PROPERTY.—For purposes of subparagraph (A), the applicable percentage for property to which section 168 applies shall be determined under subsection (c)(7) based on a reasonable expectation of what the character of the property will be when it is placed in service.

(ii) NONRECOVERY PROPERTY.—For purposes of subparagraph (A), the applicable percentage for property to which section 168 does not apply shall be determined under subsection (c)(2) based on a reasonable expectation of what the useful life of the property will be when it is placed in service.

(iii) APPLICATION ON BASIS OF FACTS KNOWN.—Clauses (i) and (ii) shall be applied on the basis of the facts known at the close of the taxable year of the taxpayer in which the expenditure is made.

(2) PROGRESS EXPENDITURE PROPERTY DEFINED.—

(A) IN GENERAL.—For purposes of this subsection, the term "progress expenditure property" means any property which is being constructed by or for the taxpayer and which—

(i) has a normal construction period of two years or more, and

(ii) it is reasonable to believe will be new section 38 property in the hands of the taxpayer when it is placed in service.

Clauses (i) and (ii) of the preceding sentence shall be applied on the basis of facts known at the close of the taxable year of the taxpayer in which construction begins (or, if later, at the close of the first taxable year to which an election under this subsection applies).

(B) NORMAL CONSTRUCTION PERIOD.—For purposes of subparagraph (A), the term "normal construction period" means the period reasonably expected to be required for the construction of the property—

(i) beginning with the date on which physical work on the construction begins (or, if later, the first day of the first taxable year to which an election under this subsection applies), and

(ii) ending on the date on which it is expected that the property will be available for placing in service.

(3) QUALIFIED PROGRESS EXPENDITURES DEFINED.—For purposes of this subsection—

(A) SELF-CONSTRUCTED PROPERTY.—In the case of any self-constructed property, the term "qualified progress expenditures" means the amount which, for purposes of this subpart, is, properly chargeable (during such taxable year) to capital account with respect to such property.

(B) NON-SELF-CONSTRUCTED PROPERTY.—In the case of non-self-constructed property, the term "qualified progress expenditures" means the lesser of—

(i) the amount paid during the taxable year to another person for the construction of such property, or

(ii) the amount which represents that proportion of the overall cost to the taxpayer of the construction by such other person which is properly attributable to that portion of such construction which is completed during such taxable year.

(4) SPECIAL RULES FOR APPLYING PARAGRAPH (3).—For purposes of paragraph (3)—

(A) COMPONENT PARTS, ETC.—Property which is to be a component part of, or is otherwise to be included in, any progress expenditure property shall be taken into account—

(i) at a time not earlier than the time at which it becomes irrevocably devoted to use in the progress expenditure property, and

(ii) as if (at the time referred to in clause (i)) the taxpayer had expended an amount equal to that portion of the cost to the taxpayer of such component or other property which, for purposes of this subpart, is properly chargeable (during such taxable year) to capital account with respect to such property.

(B) CERTAIN BORROWINGS DISREGARDED.—Any amount borrowed directly or indirectly by the taxpayer from the person constructing the property for him shall not be treated as an amount expended for such construction.

(C) CERTAIN UNUSED EXPENDITURES CARRIED OVER.—In the case of non-self-constructed property, if for the taxable year—

(i) the amount under clause (i) of paragraph (3)(B) exceeds the amount under clause (ii) of paragraph (3)(B), then the amount of such excess shall be taken into account under such clause (i) for the succeeding taxable year, or

(ii) the amount under clause (ii) of paragraph (3)(B) exceeds the amount under clause (i) of paragraph (3)(B), then the amount of such excess shall be taken into account under such clause (ii) for the succeeding taxable year.

(D) DETERMINATION OF PERCENTAGE OF COMPLETION.—In the case of non-self-constructed property, the determination under paragraph (3)(B)(ii) of the proportion of the overall cost to the taxpayer of the construction of any property which is properly attributable to construction completed during any taxable year shall be made, under regulations prescribed by the Secretary, on the basis of engineering or architectural estimates or on the basis of cost accounting records. Unless the taxpayer establishes otherwise by clear and convincing evidence, the construction shall be deemed to be completed not more rapidly than ratably over the normal construction period.

(E) NO QUALIFIED PROGRESS EXPENDITURES FOR CERTAIN PRIOR PERIODS.—In the case of any property, no qualified progress expenditures shall be taken into account under this subsection for any period before January 22, 1975 (or, if later, before the first day of the first taxable year to which an election under this subsection applies).

(F) NO QUALIFIED PROGRESS EXPENDITURES FOR PROPERTY FOR YEAR IT IS PLACED IN SERVICE, ETC.—In the case of any property, no qualified progress expenditures shall be taken into account under this subsection for the earlier of—

(i) the taxable year in which the property is placed in service, or

(ii) the first taxable year for which recapture is required under section 47(a)(3) with respect to such property,

or for any taxable year thereafter.

(5) OTHER DEFINITIONS.—For purposes of this subsection—

(A) SELF-CONSTRUCTED PROPERTY.—The term "self-constructed property" means property more than half of the construction expenditures for which it is reasonable to believe will be made directly by the taxpayer.

(B) NON-SELF-CONSTRUCTED PROPERTY.—The term "non-self-constructed property" means property which is not self-constructed property.

(C) CONSTRUCTION, ETC.—The term "construction" includes reconstruction and erection, and the term "constructed" includes reconstructed and erected.

(D) ONLY CONSTRUCTION OF SECTION 38 PROPERTY TO BE TAKEN INTO ACCOUNT.—Construction shall be taken into account only if, for purposes of this subpart, expenditures therefor are properly chargeable to capital account with respect to the property.

(6) ELECTION.—An election under this subsection may be made at such time and in such manner as the Secretary may by regulations prescribe. Such an election shall apply to the taxable year for which made and to all subsequent taxable years. Such an election, once made, may not be revoked except with the consent of the Secretary.

(7) TRANSITIONAL RULES.—The qualified investment taken into account under this subsection for any taxable year beginning before January 1, 1980, with respect to any property shall be (in lieu of the full amount) an amount equal to the sum of—

(A) the applicable percentage of the full amount determined under the following table:

For a taxable year beginning in:	The applicable percentage is:
1974 or 1975	20
1976	40
1977	60
1978	80
1979	100;

plus

(B) in the case of any property to which this subsection applied for one or more preceding taxable years, 20 percent of the full amount for each such preceding taxable year.

For purposes of this paragraph, the term "full amount", when used with respect to any property for any taxable year, means the amount of the qualified investment for such property for such year determined under this subsection without regard to this paragraph.

Amendments

• 1988, Technical and Miscellaneous Revenue Act of 1988 (P.L. 100-647)

P.L. 100-647, §1002(a)(25)(A)-(B):

Amended Code Sec. 46(d)(1)(B) by striking out "recovery property (within the meaning of section 168)" in clause (i) and inserting in lieu thereof "property to which section 168 applies", and by striking out "which is not recovery property (within the meaning of section 168)" in clause (ii) and inserting in lieu thereof "to which section 168 does not apply". **Effective** as if included in the provision of P.L. 99-514 to which it relates.

• 1981, Economic Recovery Tax Act of 1981 (P.L. 97-34)

P.L. 97-34, §211(b)(1):

Amended Code Sec. 46(d)(1). **Effective** for progress expenditures made after 12-31-80. Prior to amendment, Code Sec. 46(d)(1) read as follows:

(1) IN GENERAL.—In the case of any taxpayer who has made an election under paragraph (6), the amount of his qualified investment for the taxable year (determined under subsection (c) without regard to this subsection) shall be increased by an amount equal to his aggregate qualified progress expenditures for the taxable year with respect to progress expenditure property.

P.L. 97-34, §211(b)(2);

Amended Code Sec. 46(d)(2)(A)(ii) by striking out "having a useful life of 7 years or more" after "section 38 property". **Effective** for progress expenditures made after 12-3-80.

• 1976, Tax Reform Act of 1976 (P.L. 94-455)

P.L. 94-455, §1906(b)(13)(A):

Amended 1954 Code by substituting "Secretary" for "Secretary or his delegate" each place it appeared. **Effective** 2-1-77.

• 1975, Tax Reduction Act of 1975 (P.L. 94-12)

P.L. 94-12, §302(a):

Added Code Sec. 46(d). **Effective** for tax years ending after 1974.

[Sec. 46(e)]

(e) LIMITATIONS WITH RESPECT TO CERTAIN PERSONS.—

(1) IN GENERAL.—In the case of—

(A) an organization to which section 593 applies, and

(B) a regulated investment company or a real estate investment trust subject to taxation under subchapter M (sec. 851 and following),

the qualified investment shall equal such person's ratable share of such qualified investment.

(2) RATABLE SHARE.—For purposes of paragraph (1), the ratable share of any person for any taxable year of qualified investment shall be—

(A) in the case of an organization referred to in paragraph (1)(A), 50 percent thereof, and

(B) in the case of a regulated investment company or a real estate investment trust, the ratio (i) the numerator of which is its taxable income and (ii) the denominator of which is its taxable income computed without regard to the deduction for dividends paid provided by section 852(b)(2)(D) or 857(b)(2)(B), as the case may be.

For purposes of subparagraph (B) of the preceding sentence, the term "taxable income" means in the case of a regulated investment company its investment company taxable income (within the meaning of section 852(b)(2)), and in the case of a real estate investment trust its real estate investment trust taxable income (within the meaning of section 857(b)(2)) determined without regard to any deduction for capital gains dividends (as defined in section 857(b)(3)(C)) and by excluding any net capital gain.

(3) NONCORPORATE LESSORS.—A credit shall be allowed by section 38 to a person which is not a corporation with respect to property of which such person is the lessor only if—

(A) the property subject to the lease has been manufactured or produced by the lessor, or

(B) the term of the lease (taking into account options to renew) is less than 50 percent of the useful life of the property, and for the period consisting of the first 12 months after the date on which the property is transferred to the lessee the sum of the deductions with respect to such property which are allowable to the lessor solely by reason of section 162 (other than rents and reimbursed amounts with respect to such property) exceeds 15 percent of the rental income produced by such property.

In the case of property of which a partnership is the lessor, the credit otherwise allowable under section 38 with respect to such property to any partner which is a corporation shall be allowed notwithstanding the first sentence of this paragraph. For purposes of this paragraph, an S corporation shall be treated as a person which is not a corporation. This paragraph shall not apply with respect to any property which is treated as section 38 property by reason of section 48(a)(1)(E). For purposes of subparagraph (B), in the case of any property to which section 168 applies, the useful life shall be the class life for such property (as defined in section 168(i)(1)).

(4) SPECIAL RULES WHERE SECTION 593 ORGANIZATION IS LESSEE.—

(A) IN GENERAL.—For purposes of paragraph (1)(A), if an organization described in section 593 is the lessee of any section 38 property, the lessor of such property shall be treated as an organization described in section 593 with respect to such property.

(B) EXCEPTION FOR SHORT-TERM LEASES.—This paragraph shall not apply to any property by reason of use under a lease with a term of less than 6 months (determined under section 168(i)(3)).

(C) ELECTION NOT TO HAVE SUBPARAGRAPH (A) APPLY.—Subparagraph (A) shall not apply for any taxable year to an organization described in section 593 if such organization elects to compute for such year and all subsequent taxable years the amount of the deduction for a reasonable addition to a reserve for bad debts on the basis of actual experience. Any such election shall apply to any successor organization engaged in substantially similar activities and, once made, shall be irrevocable. Notwithstanding the preceding provisions of this subparagraph, any such election shall terminate effective with respect to the 1st taxable year of the organization making such election which begins after 1986 and during which such organization (or any successor organization) was not at any time the lessee under any lease of regular investment tax credit property. For purposes of the preceding sentence, the term "regular investment tax credit property" means any section 38 property if the regular percentage applied to such property and the amount of qualified investment with respect to such property would have been reduced under paragraph (1) but for an election under this subparagraph.

(D) SPECIAL RULES FOR PARTNERSHIPS, ETC.—For purposes of paragraph (1)(A), rules similar to the rules of paragraphs (5) and (6) of section 168(h) shall apply.

(E) EXCEPTION FOR QUALIFIED REHABILITATED BUILDINGS LEASED TO SECTION 593 ORGANIZATIONS.—Subparagraph (A) shall not apply to qualified investment attributable to qualified rehabilitation expenditures for any portion of a building if such portion of the building would not be tax-exempt use property (as defined in section 168(h) if the section 593 organization were a tax-exempt entity (as defined in section 168(h)(2)).

Amendments

• 1988, Technical and Miscellaneous Revenue Act of 1988 (P.L. 100-647)

P.L. 100-647, §1002(a)(4)(A)-(D):

Amended Code Sec. 46(e)(4) by striking out "168(j)(6)" in subparagraph (B) and inserting in lieu thereof "168(i)(3)," by striking out "paragraphs (8) and (9) of section 168(j)" in subparagraph (D) and inserting in lieu thereof "paragraphs (5) and (6) of section 168(h)", by striking out "168(j)" in subparagraph (E) and inserting in lieu thereof "168(h)", and by striking out "168(j)(4)" in subparagraph (E) and inserting in lieu thereof "168(h)(2)". **Effective** as if included in the provision of P.L. 99-514 to which it relates.

P.L. 100-647, §102(a)(15)(A)-(C):

Amended the last sentence of Code Sec. 46(e)(3) by striking out "recovery property (within the meaning of section 168)" and inserting in lieu thereof "property to which section 168 applies", by striking out "present class life" and inserting in lieu thereof "class life", and by striking out "168(g)(2)" and inserting in lieu thereof "168(i)(1)". **Effective** as if included in the provision of P.L. 99-514 to which it relates.

P.L. 100-647, §1009(a)(1):

Amended Code Sec. 46(e)(4)(C) by adding at the end thereof two new sentences. **Effective** as if included in the provision of P.L. 99-514 to which it relates.

• 1986, Tax Reform Act of 1986 (P.L. 99-514)

P.L. 99-514, §1802(a)(6):

Amended Code Sec. 46(e)(4) by adding at the end thereof new subparagraph (D). **Effective** as if included in the provision of P.L. 98-369 to which it relates.

P.L. 99-514, §1802(a)(8):

Amended Code Sec. 46(e)(4) by adding at the end thereof new subparagraph (E). **Effective** as if included in the provision of P.L. 98-369 to which it relates.

• 1984, Deficit Reduction Act of 1984 (P.L. 98-369)

P.L. 98-369, §31(f):

Amended Code Sec. 46(e) by adding a new paragraph (4) at the end thereof. **Effective** for property placed in service by the taxpayer after 11-5-83, in tax years ending after such date and to property placed in service by the taxpayer on or before 11-5-83, if the use by the tax-exempt entity is pursuant to a lease entered into after 11-5-83. For special rules, see Act Sec. 31(g) in the amendment notes for Code Sec. 168(j).

P.L. 98-369, §474(o)(3)(A):

Amended Code Sec. 46(e)(1) by striking out "and the $25,000 amount specified under subparagraphs (A) and (B) of subsection (a)(3)", and by striking out "such items" and inserting in lieu thereof "such qualified investment". **Effective** for tax years beginning after 12-31-83, and to carrybacks from such years, but shall not be construed as reducing the amount of any credit allowable for qualified investment in tax years beginning before 1-1-84.

P.L. 98-369, §474(o)(3)(B):

Amended Code Sec. 46(e)(2) by striking out "the items described therein" and inserting in lieu thereof "qualified investment". **Effective** for tax years beginning after 12-31-83, and to carrybacks from such years, but shall not be construed as reducing the amount of any credit allowable for qualified investment in tax years beginning before 1-1-84.

• 1982, Subchapter S Revision Act of 1982 (P.L. 97-354)

P.L. 97-354, §5(a)(6):

Amended Code Sec. 46(e)(3) by striking out "an electing small business corporation (as defined in section 1371)" and inserting in lieu thereof "an S corporation". **Effective** for tax years beginning after 12-31-82.

• 1981, Economic Recovery Tax Act of 1981 (P.L. 97-34)

P.L. 97-34, §211(d):

Amended Code Sec. 46(e)(3) by adding the last sentence at the end thereof. **Effective** for leases entered into after 6-25-81.

• 1980, Technical Corrections Act of 1979 (P.L. 96-222)

P.L. 96-222, §103(a)(4)(A):

Amended Code Sec. 46(e)(3) by adding a new sentence at the end of the paragraph. **Effective** for tax years ending after 10-31-78.

• 1978, Revenue Act of 1978 (P.L. 95-600)

P.L. 95-600, §316(b)(1), (c):

Amended Code Sec. 46(e)(1). **Effective** for tax years ending after 10-31-78. Prior to amendment such section read:

"(1) IN GENERAL.—In the case of—

(A) an organization to which section 593 applies,

(B) a regulated investment company or a real estate investment trust subject to taxation under subchapter M (sec. 851 and following), and

(C) a cooperative organization described in section 1381(a),

the qualified investment and the $25,000 amount specified under subparagraphs (A) and (B) of subsection (a)(3) shall equal such person's ratable share of such items."

P.L. 95-600, §316(b)(2), (c):

Amended Code Sec. 46(e)(2). **Effective** for tax years ending after 10-31-78. Prior to amendment such section read:

"(2) RATABLE SHARE.—For purposes of paragraph (1), the ratable share of any person for any taxable year of the items described therein shall be—

(A) in the case of an organization referred to in paragraph (1)(A), 50 percent thereof,

(B) in the case of a regulated investment company or a real estate investment trust, the ratio (i) the numerator of which is its taxable income and (ii) the denominator of which is its taxable income computed without regard to the deduction for dividends paid provided by section 852(b)(2)(D) or 857(b)(2)(B), as the case may be, and

(C) in the case of a cooperative organization, the ratio (i) the numerator of which is its taxable income and (ii) the denominator of which is its taxable income increased by amounts to which section 1382(b) or (c) applies and similar amounts the tax treatment of which is determined without regard to subchapter T (sec. 1381 and following).

For purposes of subparagraph (B) of the preceding sentence, the term "taxable income" means in the case of a regulated investment company its investment company taxable income (within the meaning of section 852(b)(2)), and in the case of a real estate investment trust its real estate investment trust taxable income (within the meaning of section 857(b)(2)) determined without regard to any deduction for capital gains dividends (as defined in section 857(b)(3)(C)) and by excluding any net capital gain."

• 1976, Tax Reform Act of 1976 (P.L. 94-455)

P.L. 94-455, §802(b)(4):

Substituted "subsection (a)(3)" for "subsection (a)(2)" in paragraph (1) of Code Sec. 46(e). **Effective** for tax years beginning after 12-31-75.

P.L. 94-455, §1607(b)(1)(B):

Amended Code Sec. 46(e)(2) by substituting "857(b)(2)(B)" for "857(b)(2)(C)" in subparagraph (B); and by inserting "determined without regard to any deduction for capital gains dividends (as defined in section 857(b)(3)(C)) and by excluding any net capital gain" immediately before the period at the end of the last sentence. **Effective** for tax years ending after 10-4-76, except that in the case of a taxpayer which has a net operating loss (as defined in Code Sec. 172(c)) for any tax year ending after 10-4-76, for which the provisions of part II of subchapter M of chapter 1 of subtitle A of the Code apply to such taxpayer, such loss shall not be a net operating loss carryback under Code Sec. 172 to any tax year ending on or before 10-4-76.

• 1975, Tax Reduction Act of 1975 (P.L. 94-12)

P.L. 94-12, §302(a):

Redesignated Sec. 46(d) as 46(e).

• 1971, Revenue Act of 1971 (P.L. 92-178)

P.L. 92-178, §108(a):

Added paragraph (3) to Code Sec. 46(d). **Effective** for leases entered into after 9-22-71.

[Sec. 46(f)]

(f) LIMITATION IN CASE OF CERTAIN REGULATED COMPANIES.—

(1) GENERAL RULE.—Except as otherwise provided in this subsection, no credit determined under subsection (a) shall be allowed by section 38 with respect to any property described in section 50 (as in effect before its repeal by the Revenue Act of 1978) which is public utility property (as defined in paragraph (5)) of the taxpayer—

(A) COST OF SERVICE REDUCTION.—If the taxpayer's cost of service for ratemaking purposes is reduced by reason of any portion of the credit determined under subsection (a) and allowable by section 38 (determined without regard to this subsection); or

(B) RATE BASE REDUCTION.—If the base to which the taxpayer's rate of return for ratemaking purposes is applied is reduced by reason of any portion of the credit determined under subsection (a) and allowable by section 38 (determined without regard to this subsection).

Subparagraph (B) shall not apply if the reduction in the rate base is restored not less rapidly than ratably. If the taxpayer makes an election under this sentence within 90 days after the date of the enactment of this paragraph in the manner prescribed by the Secretary, the immediately preceding sentence shall not apply to property described in paragraph (5)(B) if any agency or instrumentality of the United States having jurisdiction for ratemaking purposes with respect to such taxpayer's trade or business referred to in paragraph (5)(B) determines that the natural domestic supply of the product furnished by the taxpayer in the course of such trade or business is insufficient to meet the present and future requirements of the domestic economy.

(2) SPECIAL RULE FOR RATABLE FLOW-THROUGH.—If the taxpayer makes an election under this paragraph within 90 days after the date of the enactment of this paragraph in the manner prescribed by the Secretary, paragraph (1) shall not apply, but no credit determined under subsection (a) shall be allowed by section 38 with respect to any property described in section 50 (as in effect before its repeal by the Revenue Act of 1978) which is public utility property (as defined in paragraph (5)) of the taxpayer—

(A) COST OF SERVICE REDUCTION.—If the taxpayer's cost of service for ratemaking purposes or in its regulated books of account is reduced by more than a ratable portion of the credit determined under subsection (a) and allowable by section 38 (determined without regard to this subsection), or

(B) RATE BASE REDUCTION.—If the base to which the taxpayer's rate of return for ratemaking purposes is applied is reduced by reason of any portion of the credit determined under subsection (a) and allowable by section 38 (determined without regard to this subsection).

(3) SPECIAL RULE FOR IMMEDIATE FLOW-THROUGH IN CERTAIN CASES.—In the case of property to which section 167(l)(2)(C) applies, if the taxpayer makes an election under this paragraph within 90 days after the date of the enactment of this paragraph in the manner prescribed by the Secretary, paragraphs (1) and (2) shall not apply to such property.

(4) LIMITATION.—

(A) IN GENERAL.—The requirements of paragraphs (1), (2), and (9) regarding cost of service and rate base adjustments shall not be applied to public utility property of the taxpayer to disallow the credit with respect to such property before the first final determination which is inconsistent with paragraph (1), (2), or (9) (as the case may be) is put into effect with respect to public utility property (to which this subsection applies) of the taxpayer. Thereupon, paragraph (1), (2), or (9) shall apply to disallow the credit with respect to public utility property (to which this subsection applies) placed in service by the taxpayer—

(i) before the date that the first final determination, or a subsequent determination, which is inconsistent with paragraph (1), (2), or (9) (as the case may be) is put into effect, and

(ii) on or after the date that a determination referred to in clause (i) is put into effect and before the date that a subsequent determination thereafter which is consistent with paragraph (1), (2), or (9) (as the case may be) is put into effect.

(B) DETERMINATIONS.—For purposes of this paragraph, a determination is a determination made with respect to public utility property (to which this subsection applies) by a governmental unit, agency, instrumentality, or commission or similar body described in subsection (c)(3)(B) which determines the effect of the credit determined under subsection (a) and allowed by section 38 (determined without regard to this subsection)—

(i) on the taxpayer's cost of service or rate base for ratemaking purposes, or

(ii) in the case of a taxpayer which made an election under paragraph (2) or the election described in paragraph (9), on the taxpayer's cost of service for ratemaking purposes or in its regulated books of account or rate base for ratemaking purposes.

(C) SPECIAL RULES.—For purposes of this paragraph—

(i) a determination is final if all rights to appeal or to request a review, a rehearing, or a redetermination, have been exhausted or have lapsed,

(ii) the first final determination is the first final determination made after the date of the enactment of this subsection, and

(iii) a subsequent determination is a determination subsequent to a final determination.

(5) PUBLIC UTILITY PROPERTY.—For purposes of this subsection, the term "public utility property" means—

(A) property which is public utility property within the meaning of subsection (c)(3)B), and

(B) property used predominantly in the trade or business of the furnishing or sale of (i) steam through a local distribution system or (ii) the transportation of gas or steam by pipeline, if the rates for such furnishing or sale are established or approved by a governmental unit, agency, instrumentality, or commission described in subsection (c)(3)(B).

(6) RATABLE PORTION.—For purposes of determining ratable restorations to base under paragraph (1) and for purposes of determining ratable portions under paragraph (2)(A), the period of time used in computing depreciation expense for purposes of reflecting operating results in the taxpayer's regulated books of account shall be used.

(7) REORGANIZATIONS, ASSETS ACQUISITIONS, ETC.—If by reason of a corporate reorganization, by reason of any other acquisition of the assets of one taxpayer by another taxpayer, by reason of the fact that any trade or business of the taxpayer is subject to ratemaking by more than one body, or by reason of other circumstances, the application of any provisions of this subsection to any public utility property does not carry out the purposes of this subsection, the Secretary shall provide by regulations for the application of such provisions in a manner consistent with the purposes of this subsection.

(8) PROHIBITION OF IMMEDIATE FLOWTHROUGH.—An election made under paragraph (3) shall apply only to the amount of the credit determined under subsection (a) and allowable under section 38 with respect to public utility property (within the meaning of the first sentence of subsection (c)(3)(B)) determined as if the Tax Reduction Act of 1975, the Tax Reform Act of 1976, the Energy Act of 1978, and the Revenue Act of 1978 had not been enacted. Any taxpayer who had timely made an election under paragraph (3) may, at his own option and without regard to any requirement imposed by an agency described in subsection (c)(3)(B), elect within 90 days after the date of the enactment of the Tax Reduction Act of 1975 (in such manner as the Secretary shall prescribe) to have the provisions of paragraph (3) apply with respect to the amount of the credit determined under subsection (a) and allowable under section 38 with respect to such property which is in excess of the amount determined under the preceding sentence. If such taxpayer does not make such an election, paragraph (1) or (2) (whichever paragraph is applicable without regard to this paragraph) shall apply to such excess credit, except that if neither paragraph (1) nor (2) is applicable (without regard to this paragraph), paragraph (1) shall apply unless the taxpayer elects (in such manner as the Secretary shall prescribe) within 90 days after the date of the enactment of the Tax Reduction Act of 1975 to have the provisions of paragraph (2) apply. The provisions of this paragraph shall not be applied to disallow such excess credit before the first final determination which is inconsistent with such requirements is made, determined in the same manner as under paragraph (4).

(10) USE OF INCONSISTENT ESTIMATES AND PROJECTIONS, ETC., FOR PURPOSES OF PARAGRAPHS (1) AND (2).—

(A) IN GENERAL.—One way in which the requirements of paragraph (1) or (2) are not met is if the taxpayer, for ratemaking purposes, uses a procedure or adjustment which is inconsistent with the requirements of paragraph (1) or paragraph (2), as the case may be.

(B) USE OF INCONSISTENT ESTIMATES AND PROJECTIONS.—The procedures and adjustments which are to be treated as inconsistent for purposes of subparagraph (A) shall include any procedure or adjustment for ratemaking purposes which uses an estimate or projection of the taxpayer's qualified investment for purposes of the credit allowable by section 38 unless such estimate or projection is consistent with the estimates and projections of property which are used, for ratemaking purposes, with respect to the taxpayer's depreciation expense and rate base.

(C) REGULATORY AUTHORITY.—The Secretary may by regulations prescribe procedures and adjustments (in addition to those specified in subparagraph (B)) which are to be treated as inconsistent for purposes of subparagraph (A).

Amendments

• 1986, Tax Reform Act of 1986 (P.L. 99-514)

P.L. 99-514, §211(b), provides:

(b) NORMALIZATION RULES.—If, for any taxable year beginning after December 31, 1985, the requirements of paragraph (1) or (2) of section 46(f) of the Internal Revenue Code of 1986 are not met with respect to public utility property to which the regular percentage applied for purposes of determining the amount of the investment tax credit—

(1) all credits for open taxable years as of the time of the final determination referred to in section 46(f)(4)(A) of such Code shall be recaptured, and

(2) if the amount of the taxpayer's unamortized credits (or the credits not previously restored to rate base) with respect to such property (whether or not for open years) exceeds the amount referred to in paragraph (1), the taxpayer's tax for the taxable year shall be increased by the amount of such excess.

If any portion of the excess described in paragraph (2) is attributable to a credit which is allowable as a carryover to a taxable year beginning after December 31, 1985, in lieu of applying paragraph (2) with respect to such portion, the amount of such carryover shall be reduced by the amount of such portion. Rules similar to the rules of this subsection shall apply in the case of any property with respect to which the requirements of section 46(f)(9) of such Code are met.

P.L. 99-514, §1848(a):

Repealed Code Sec. 46(f)(9). **Effective** as if included in the provision of P.L. 98-369 to which it relates. Prior to repeal, Code Sec. 46(f)(9) read as follows:

(9) SPECIAL RULE FOR ADDITIONAL CREDIT.—If the taxpayer makes an election under subparagraph (E) of subsection (a)(2), for a taxable year beginning after December 31, 1975, then, notwithstanding the prior paragraphs of this subsection, no credit shall be allowed by section 38 in excess of the amount which would be allowed without regard to the provisions of subparagraph (E) of subsection (a)(2) if—

(A) the taxpayer's cost of service for ratemaking purposes or in its regulated books of account is reduced by reason of any portion of such credit which results from the transfer of employer securities or cash to a tax credit employee stock ownership plan which meets the requirements of section 409A;

(B) the base to which the taxpayer's rate of return for ratemaking purposes is applied is reduced by reason of any portion of such credit which results from a transfer described in subparagraph (A) to such employee stock ownership plan; or

(C) any portion of the amount of such credit which results from a transfer described in subparagraph (A) to such employee stock ownership plan is treated for ratemaking purposes in any way other than as though it had been contributed by the taxpayer's common shareholders.

• 1984, Deficit Reduction Act of 1984 (P.L. 98-369)

P.L. 98-369, §474(o)(4)(A):

Amended Code Sec. 46(f)(1) and (2) by striking out "no credit shall be allowed by section 38" and inserting in lieu thereof "no credit determined under subsection (a) shall be allowed by section 38". **Effective** for tax years beginning after 12-31-83, and to carrybacks from such years, but shall not be construed as reducing the amount of any credit allowable for qualified investment in tax years beginning before 1-1-84.

P.L. 98-369, §474(o)(4)(B):

Amended Code Sec. 46(f)(1) and (2) by striking out "the credit allowable by section 38" each place it appeared and inserting in lieu thereof "the credit determined under subsection (a) and allowable by section 38". **Effective** for tax years beginning after 12-31-83, and to carrybacks from such years, but shall not be construed as reducing the amount of any credit allowable for qualified investment in tax years beginning before 1-1-84.

P.L. 98-369, §474(o)(4)(C):

Amended Code Sec. 46(f)(4)(B) by striking out "the credit allowed by section 38" and inserting in lieu thereof "the credit determined under subsection (a) and allowed by section 38". **Effective** for tax years beginning after 12-31-83, and to carrybacks from such years, but shall not be construed as reducing the amount of any credit allowable for qualified investment in tax years beginning before 1-1-84.

P.L. 98-369, §474(o)(5)(A)-(B):

Amended Code Sec. 46(f)(8) by striking out "the credit allowable under section 38" each place it appeared and inserting in lieu thereof "the credit determined under subsection (a) and allowable under section 38", and by striking out "(within the meaning of subsection (a)(7)(C))" and inserting in lieu thereof "(within the meaning of the first sentence of subsection (c)(3)(B))". **Effective** for tax years beginning after 12-31-83, and to carrybacks from such years, but shall not be construed as reducing the amount of any credit allowable for qualified investment in tax years beginning before 1-1-84.

• 1983, Surface Transportation Act of 1982 (P.L. 97-424)

P.L. 97-424, §541(b):

Added Code Sec. 46(f)(10). **Effective** for tax years beginning after 12-31-79, except that the following special rules are provided in Act Sec. 541(c)(2)-(5):

(2) SPECIAL RULE FOR PERIODS BEGINNING BEFORE MARCH 1, 1980.—

(A) IN GENERAL.—Subject to the provisions of paragraphs (3) and (4), notwithstanding the provisions of sections 167(l) and 46(f) of the Internal Revenue Code of 1954 and of any regulations prescribed by the Secretary of the Treasury (or his delegate) under such sections, the use for ratemaking purposes or for reflecting operating results in the taxpayer's regulated books of account, for any period before March 1, 1980, of—

(i) any estimates or projections relating to the amounts of the taxpayer's tax expense, depreciation expense, deferred tax reserve, credit allowable under section 38 of such code, or rate base, or

(ii) any adjustments to the taxpayer's rate of return,

shall not be treated as inconsistent with the requirements of subparagraph (G) of such section 167(l)(3) nor inconsistent with the requirements of paragraph (1) or (2) of such section 46(f), where such estimates or projections, or such rate of return adjustments, were included in a qualified order.

(B) QUALIFIED ORDER DEFINED.—For purposes of this subsection, the term "qualified order" means an order—

(i) by a public utility commission which was entered before March 13, 1980,

(ii) which used the estimates, projections, or rate of return adjustments referred to in subparagraph (A) to determine the amount of the rates to be collected by the taxpayer or the amount of a refund with respect to rates previously collected, and

(iii) which ordered such rates to be collected or refunds to be made (whether or not such order actually was implemented or enforced).

(3) LIMITATIONS ON APPLICATION OF PARAGRAPH (2).—

(A) PARAGRAPH (2) NOT TO APPLY TO AMOUNTS ACTUALLY FLOWED THROUGH.—Paragraph (2) shall not apply to the amount of any—

(i) rate reduction, or

(ii) refund,

which was actually made pursuant to a qualified order.

(B) TAXPAYER MUST ENTER INTO CLOSING AGREEMENT BEFORE PARAGRAPH (2) APPLIES.—Paragraph (2) shall not apply to any taxpayer unless, before the later of—

(i) July 1, 1983, or

(ii) 6 months after the refunds or rate reductions are actually made pursuant to a qualified order,

the taxpayer enters into a closing agreement (within the meaning of section 7121 of the Internal Revenue Code of 1954) which provides for the payment by the taxpayer of the amount of which paragraph (2) does not apply by reason of subparagraph (A).

(4) SPECIAL RULES RELATING TO PAYMENT OF REFUNDS OR INTERESTBY THE UNITED STATES OR THE TAXPAYER.—

(A) REFUND DEFINED.—For purposes of this subsection, the term "refund" shall include any credit allowed by the taxpayer under a qualified order but shall not include interest payable with respect to any refund (or credit) under such order.

(B) NO INTEREST PAYABLE BY UNITED STATES.—No interest shall be payable under section 6611 of the Internal Revenue Code of 1954 on any overpayment of tax which is attributable to the application of paragraph (2).

(C) PAYMENTS MAY BE MADE IN TWO EQUAL INSTALLMENTS.—

(i) IN GENERAL.—The taxpayer may make any payment required by reason of paragraph (3) in 2 equal installments, the first installment being due on the last date on which a taxpayer may enter into a closing agreement under paragraph (3)(B), and the second payment being due 1 year after the last date for the first payment.

(ii) INTEREST PAYMENTS.—For purposes of section 6601 of such Code, the last date prescribed for payment with respect to any payment required by reason of paragraph (3) shall be the last due date on which such payment is due under clause (i).

(5) NO INFERENCE.—The application of subparagraph (G) of section 167(l)(3) of the Internal Revenue Code of 1954, and the application of paragraphs (1) and (2) of section 46(f) of such Code, to taxable years beginning before January 1, 1980, shall be determined without any inference drawn from the amendments made by subsections (a) and (b) of this section or from the rules contained in paragraphs (2), (3), and (4). Nothing in the preceding sentence shall be construed to limit the relief provided by paragraphs (2), (3), and (4).

• 1981, Economic Recovery Tax Act of 1981 (P.L. 97-34)

P.L. 97-34, §209(d)(2), provides:

(2) TRANSITIONAL RULE FOR REQUIREMENTS OF SECTION 46(f).—If, by the terms of the applicable rate order last entered before the date of the enactment of this Act by a regulatory commission having appropriate jurisdiction, a regulated public utility would (but for this provision) fail to meet the requirements of paragraph (1) or (2) of section 46(f) of the Internal Revenue Code of 1954 with respect to property for an accounting period ending after December 31, 1980, such regulated public utility shall not fail to meet such requirements if, by the terms of its first rate order determining cost of service with respect to such property which becomes effective after the date of the enactment of this Act and on or before January 1, 1983, such regulated public utility meets such requirements. This provision shall not apply to any rate order which, under the rules in effect before the date of the enactment of this Act, was inconsistent with the requirements of paragraph (1) or (2) of section 46(f) of such Code (whichever would have been applicable).

• 1980, Technical Corrections Act of 1979 (P.L. 96-222)

P.L. 96-222, §101(a)(7)(A):

Amended Code Sec. 46(f)(9)(A) by changing "an employee stock ownership plan which meets the requirements of section 301(d) of the Tax Reduction Act of 1975" to "a tax credit employee stock ownership plan which meets the requirements of section 409A". Amended Code Sec. 46(f)(9) by changing "subparagraph (B) of subsection (a)(2)" each place it appears to "subparagraph (E) of subsection (a)(2)". **Effective** for stock acquired after 12-31-79.

P.L. 96-222, §107(a)(3)(A):

Amended Code Sec. 46(f)(8) by changing "subsection (a)(7)(D)" to "subsection (a)(7)(C)". **Effective** 11-10-78.

• 1978, Revenue Act of 1978 (P.L. 95-600)

P.L. 95-600, §312(c)(2), as amended by P.L. 96-222, §103(a)(2)(A):

Amended paragraphs (1) and (2) of Code Sec. 46(f), by striking out "described in section 50" and inserting in lieu thereof "described in section 50 (as in effect before its repeal by the Revenue Act of 1978).". **Effective** for tax years ending after 12-31-78.

P.L. 95-600, §311(c)(2):

Amended in first sentence of Code Sec. 46(f)(8), by inserting "the Energy Tax Act of 1978, and the Revenue Act of

1978" in place of "and the Energy Tax Act of 1978". **Effective** 11-7-78. [Note: Congress apparently intended the above amendment to apply after the amendment made by P.L. 95-618, §301(a)(2)(B), see the amendment note after such law section, below.] Prior to the above amendment, but after amendments made by P.L. 95-618, Sec. 301(a)(2)(B), and P.L. 95-600, Sec. 703(a)(1), the first sentence of such code section read:

"An election made under paragraph (3) shall apply only to the amount of the credit allowable under section 38 with respect to public utility property (within the meaning of subsection (a)(7)(D)) determined as if the Tax Reduction Act of 1975, the Tax Reform Act of 1976, and the Energy Tax Act of 1978 had not been enacted."

• 1978, Energy Tax Act of 1978 (P.L. 95-618)

P.L. 95-618, §301(a)(2)(B):

Amended the first sentence of Code Sec. 46(f)(8), by inserting ", the Tax Reform Act of 1976, and the Energy Tax Act of 1978" in place of "and the Tax Reform Act of 1976". **Effective** 11-10-78. [Note: Congress apparently intended the above amendment to apply after the amendment made by P.L. 95-600, Sec. 703(a)(1), but before the amendment made by P.L. 95-600, Sec. 311(c)(2).] Before the above amendments, but after the amendment made by P.L. 95-600, Sec. 703(a)(1), the first sentence of such code section read:

"An election made under paragraph (3) shall apply only to the amount of the credit allowable under section 38 with respect to public utility property (within the meaning of subsection (a)(7)(D)) determined as if the Tax Reduction Act of 1975 and the Tax Reform Act of 1976 had not been enacted."

P.L. 95-600, §§703(a)(1), (r):

Amended the first sentence of Code Sec. 46(f)(8), by inserting "subsection (a)(7)(D)" in place of "subsection (a)(6)(D)". **Effective** 10-4-76.

• 1976, Tax Reform Act of 1976 (P.L. 94-455)

P.L. 94-455, §802(b)(5):

Amended Code Sec. 46(f)(8) by adding "and the Tax Reform Act of 1976" after "1975" in the first sentence. **Effective** for tax years beginning after 12-31-75.

P.L. 94-455, §803(a):

Added a new paragraph (9) to Code Sec. 46(f). **Effective** for tax years beginning after 12-31-75.

P.L. 94-455, §803(b)(1):

Amended paragraph (4) of Code Sec. 46(f) by substituting "paragraphs (1), (2), and (9)" for "paragraphs (1) and (2)" in subparagraph (A); by substituting "paragraph (1), (2), or (9)" for "paragraph (1) or (2)" each place it appears in subparagraph (A); and by substituting "paragraph (2) or the election described in paragraph (9)," for "paragraph (2)," in subparagraph (B)(ii). **Effective** for tax years beginning after 12-31-75.

P.L. 94-455, §1906(b)(13)(A):

Amended 1954 Code by substituting "Secretary" for "Secretary or his delegate" each place it appeared. **Effective** 2-1-77.

• 1975, Tax Reduction Act of 1975 (P.L. 94-12)

P.L. 94-12, §§301(b)(3), 302(a):

Redesignated as Sec. 46(f) by P. L. 94-12, §302(a). Sec. 46(f)(8) added by Sec. 301(b)(3). **Effective** for tax years ending after 12-31-74.

• 1971, Revenue Act of 1971 (P.L. 92-178)

P.L. 92-178, §105(c):

Added Code Sec. 46(e). **Effective** for property described in Code Sec. 50.

P.L. 92-178, §101(c), provides:

Taxpayers who are subject to the provisions of Code Sec. 46(f) are not covered by Sec. 101(c) of the Revenue Act of 1971 or by Sec. 203(e) of the Revenue Act of 1964.—CCH.

"(c) Accounting for Investment Credit in Certain Financial Reports and Reports to Federal Agencies.—

"(1) In general.—It was the intent of the Congress in enacting, in the Revenue Act of 1962, the investment credit allowed by section 38 of the Internal Revenue Code of 1954, and it is the intent of the Congress in restoring that credit in this Act, to provide an incentive for modernization and growth of private industry. Accordingly, notwithstanding any other provision of law, on and after the date of the enactment of this Act—

"(A) no taxpayer shall be required to use, for purposes of financial reports subject to the jurisdiction of any Federal agency or reports made to any Federal agency, any particular method of accounting for the credit allowed by such section 38,

"(B) a taxpayer shall disclose, in any such report, the method of accounting for such credit used by him for purposes of such report, and

"(C) a taxpayer shall use the same method of accounting for such credit in all such reports made by him, unless the Secretary of the Treasury or his delegate consents to a change to another method.

"(2) Exceptions.—Paragraph (1) shall not apply to taxpayers who are subject to the provisions of section 46(e) of the Internal Revenue Code of 1954 (as added by section 105(c) of this Act) or to section 203(e) of the Revenue Act of 1964 (as modified by section 105(e) of this Act) [see below]."

• 1971, Revenue Act of 1971 (P. L. 92-178):

P.L. 92-178, §105(e), provides:

"(e) Application of Section 203(e) of Revenue Act of 1964.—Section 203(e) of the Revenue Act of 1964 [see below] shall not apply to public utility property to which section 46(e) of the Internal Revenue Code of 1954 (as added by subsection (c)) applies."

• 1964, Revenue Act of 1964 (P.L. 88-272)

P.L. 88-272, §203(e), provides:

"(e) Treatment of Investment Credit by Federal Regulatory Agencies.—It was the intent of the Congress in providing an investment credit under section 38 of the Internal Revenue Code of 1954, and it is the intent of the Congress in repealing the reduction in basis required by section 48(g) of such Code, to provide an incentive for modernization and growth of private industry (including that portion thereof which is regulated). Accordingly, Congress does not intend that any agency or instrumentality of the United States having jurisdiction with respect to a taxpayer shall, without the consent of the taxpayer, use—

"(1) in the case of public utility property (as defined in section 46(c)(3)(B) of the Internal Revenue Code of 1954), more than a proportionate part (determined with reference to the average useful life of the property with respect to which the credit was allowed) of the credit against tax allowed for any taxable year by section 38 of such Code, or

"(2) in the case of any other property, any credit against tax allowed by section 38 of such Code,

to reduce such taxpayer's Federal income taxes for the purpose of establishing the cost of service of the taxpayer or to accomplish a similar result by any other method."

[Sec. 46(g)]

(g) 50 PERCENT CREDIT IN THE CASE OF CERTAIN VESSELS.—

(1) IN GENERAL.—In the case of a qualified withdrawal out of the untaxed portion of a capital gain account or out of an ordinary income account in a capital construction fund established under section 607 of the Merchant Marine Act, 1936 (46 U.S.C. 1177), for—

(A) the acquisition, construction, or reconstruction of a qualified vessel, or

(B) the acquisition, construction, or reconstruction of barges or containers which are part of the complement of a qualified vessel and to which subsection (f)(1)(B) of such section 607 applies,

for purposes of section 38 there shall be deemed to have been made (at the time of such withdrawal) a qualified investment (within the meaning of subsection (c)) or qualified progress expenditures (within the meaning of subsection (d)), whichever is appropriate, with respect to property which is section 38 property.

(2) AMOUNT OF CREDIT.—For purposes of paragraph (1), the amount of the qualified investment shall be 50 percent of the applicable percentage of the qualified withdrawal referred to in paragraph (1), or the amount of the qualified progress expenditures shall be 50 percent of such withdrawal, as the case may be. For purposes of determining the amount of the credit allowable by reason of this subsection for any taxable year, the limitation of section 38(c) shall be

determined without regard to subsection (d)(1)(A) of such section 607.

(3) COORDINATION WITH SECTION 38.—The amount of the credit allowable by reason of this subsection with respect to any property shall be the minimum amount allowable under section 38 with respect to such property. If, without regard to this subsection, a greater amount is allowable under section 38 with respect to such property, then such greater amount shall apply and this subsection shall not apply.

(4) COORDINATION WITH SECTION 47.—Section 47 shall be applied—

(A) to any property to which this subsection applies, and

(B) to the payment (out of the untaxed portion of a capital gain account or out of the ordinary income account of a capital construction fund established under section 607 of the Merchant Marine Act, 1936) of the principal of any indebtedness incurred in connection with property with respect to which a credit was allowed under section 38.

For purposes of section 47, any payment described in subparagraph (B) of the preceding sentence shall be treated as a disposition occurring less than 3 years after the property was placed in service; but, in the case of a credit allowable without regard to this subsection, the aggregate amount which may be recaptured by reason of this sentence shall not exceed 50 percent of such credit.

(5) DEFINITIONS.—Any term used in section 607 of the Merchant Marine Act, 1936, shall have the same meaning when used in this subsection.

(6) NO INFERENCE.—Nothing in this subsection shall be construed to infer that any property described in this subsection is or is not section 38 property, and any determination of such issue shall be made as if this subsection had not been enacted.

Amendments

• 1984, Deficit Reduction Act of 1984 (P.L. 98-369)

P.L. 98-369, §474(o)(6):

Amended Code Sec. 46(g)(2) by striking out "the limitation of subsection (a)(3)" and inserting in lieu thereof "the limitation of section 38(c)". **Effective** for tax years beginning after 12-31-83, and to carrybacks from such years, but shall not be construed as reducing the amount of any credit allowable for qualified investment in tax years beginning before 1-1-84.

• 1978, Revenue Act of 1978 (P.L. 95-600)

P.L. 95-600, §703(a)(2), (r):

Amended Code Sec. 46(g)(5) by striking out "Merchant Marine Act, 1970" and inserting in place thereof "Merchant Marine Act, 1936". **Effective** 10-4-76.

• 1976, Tax Reform Act of 1976 (P.L. 94-455)

P.L. 94-455, §805(a):

Added Code Sec. 46(g). **Effective** for tax years beginning after 12-31-75 in the case of property placed in service after such date. Section 46(g)(4) is **effective** for tax years beginning after 12-31-75.

[Sec. 46(h)]

(h) SPECIAL RULES FOR COOPERATIVES.—In the case of a cooperative organization described in section 1381(a)—

(1) that portion of the credit determined under subsection (a) and allowable to the organization under section 38 which the organization cannot use for the taxable year to which the qualified investment is attributable because of the limitation contained in section 38(c) shall be allocated to the patrons of the organization,

(2) section 47 (relating to certain dispositions, etc., of section 38 property) shall be applied as if any allocated portion of the credit had been retained by the organization, and

(3) the rules necessary to carry out the purposes of this subsection shall be determined under regulations prescribed by the Secretary.

Amendments

• 1984, Deficit Reduction Act of 1984 (P.L. 98-369)

P.L. 98-369, §474(o)(7):

Amended Code Sec. 46(h)(1) by striking out "the credit allowable to the organization under section 38" and inserting in lieu thereof "the credit determined under subsection (a) and allowable to the organization under section 38", and by striking out "the limitation contained in subsection (a)(3)" and inserting in lieu thereof "the limitation contained in section 38(c)". **Effective** for tax years beginning after 12-31-83, and to carrybacks from such years, but shall not be construed as reducing the amount of any credit allowable for qualified investment in tax years beginning before 1-1-84.

• 1978, Revenue Act of 1978 (P.L. 95-600)

P.L. 95-600, §316(a), (c):

Added Code Sec. 46(h). **Effective** for tax years ending after 10-31-78.

[Sec. 47]

SEC. 47. REHABILITATION CREDIT.

[Sec. 47(a)]

(a) GENERAL RULE.—For purposes of section 46, the rehabilitation credit for any taxable year is the sum of—

(1) 10 percent of the qualified rehabilitation expenditures with respect to any qualified rehabilitated building other than a certified historic structure, and

(2) 20 percent of the qualified rehabilitation expenditures with respect to any certified historic structure.

[Sec. 47(b)]

(b) WHEN EXPENDITURES TAKEN INTO ACCOUNT.—

(1) IN GENERAL.—Qualified rehabilitation expenditures with respect to any qualified rehabilitated building shall be taken into account for the taxable year in which such qualified rehabilitated building is placed in service.

(2) COORDINATION WITH SUBSECTION (d).—The amount which would (but for this paragraph) be taken into account under paragraph (1) with respect to any qualified rehabilitated building shall be reduced (but not below zero) by any amount of qualified rehabilitation expenditures taken into account under subsection (d) by the taxpayer or a predecessor of the taxpayer (or, in the case of a sale and leaseback described in section 50(a)(2)(C), by the lessee), to the extent any amount so taken into account has not been required to be recaptured under section 50(a).

Amendments

• 1990, Omnibus Budget Reconciliation Act of 1990 (P.L. 101-508)

P.L. 101-508, §11801(c)(8)(A):

Amended Code Sec. 47(b) by inserting "or" at the end of paragraph (1), by striking out ", or" at the end of paragraph (2) and inserting a period, and by striking paragraph (3). **Effective**, generally, on the date of the enactment of this Act. For exceptions, see Act Sec. 11821(b), below. Prior to being stricken, Code Sec. 47(b)(3) read as follows:

(3) a transfer to which subsection (c) of section 374 (relating to exchanges under the final system plan for ConRail) applies.

P.L. 101-508, §11821(b), provides:

(b) SAVINGS PROVISION.—If—

(1) any provision amended or repealed by this part applied to—

(A) any transaction occurring before the date of the enactment of this Act,

(B) any property acquired before such date of enactment, or

(C) any item of income, loss, deduction, or credit taken into account before such date of enactment, and

(2) the treatment of such transaction, property, or item under such provision would (without regard to the amendments made by this part) affect liability for tax for periods ending after such date of enactment,

nothing in the amendments made by this part shall be construed to affect the treatment of such transaction, property, or item for purposes of determining liability for tax for periods ending after such date of enactment.

[Sec. 47(c)]

(c) DEFINITIONS.—For purposes of this section—

(1) QUALIFIED REHABILITATED BUILDING.—

(A) IN GENERAL.—The term "qualified rehabilitated building" means any building (and its structural components) if—

(i) such building has been substantially rehabilitated,

(ii) such building was placed in service before the beginning of the rehabilitation,

(iii) in the case of any building other than a certified historic structure, in the rehabilitation process—

(I) 50 percent or more of the existing external walls of such building are retained in place as external walls,

(II) 75 percent or more of the existing external walls of such building are retained in place as internal or external walls, and

(III) 75 percent or more of the existing internal structural framework of such building is retained in place, and

(iv) depreciation (or amortization in lieu of depreciation) is allowable with respect to such building.

(B) BUILDING MUST BE FIRST PLACED IN SERVICE BEFORE 1936.—In the case of a building other than a certified historic structure, a building shall not be a qualified rehabilitated building unless the building was first placed in service before 1936.

(C) SUBSTANTIALLY REHABILITATED DEFINED.—

(i) IN GENERAL.—For purposes of subparagraph (A)(i), a building shall be treated as having been substantially rehabilitated only if the qualified rehabilitation expenditures during the 24-month period selected by the taxpayer (at the time and in the manner prescribed by regulation) and ending with or within the taxable year exceed the greater of—

(I) the adjusted basis of such building (and its structural components), or

(II) $5,000.

The adjusted basis of the building (and its structural components) shall be determined as of the beginning of the 1st day of such 24-month period, or of the holding period of the building, whichever is later. For purposes of the preceding sentence, the determination of the beginning of the holding period shall be made without regard to any reconstruction by the taxpayer in connection with the rehabilitation.

(ii) SPECIAL RULE FOR PHASED REHABILITATION.—In the case of any rehabilitation which may reasonably be expected to be completed in phases set forth in architectural plans and specifications completed before the rehabilitation begins, clause (i) shall be applied by substituting "60-month period" for "24-month period".

(iii) LESSEES.—The Secretary shall prescribe by regulation rules for applying this subparagraph to lessees.

(D) RECONSTRUCTION.—Rehabilitation includes reconstruction.

(2) QUALIFIED REHABILITATION EXPENDITURE DEFINED.—

(A) IN GENERAL.—The term "qualified rehabilitation expenditure" means any amount properly chargeable to capital account—

(i) for property for which depreciation is allowable under section 168 and which is—

(I) nonresidential real property,

(II) residential rental property,

(III) real property which has a class life of more than 12.5 years, or

(IV) an addition or improvement to property described in subclause (I), (II), or (III), and

(ii) in connection with the rehabilitation of a qualified rehabilitated building.

(B) CERTAIN EXPENDITURES NOT INCLUDED.—The term "qualified rehabilitation expenditure" does not include—

(i) STRAIGHT LINE DEPRECIATION MUST BE USED.—Any expenditure with respect to which the taxpayer does not use the straight line method over a recovery period determined under subsection (c) or (g) of section 168. The preceding sentence shall not apply to any expenditure to the extent the alternative depreciation system of section 168(g) applies to such expenditure by reason of subparagraph (B) or (C) of section 168(g)(1).

(ii) COST OF ACQUISITION.—The cost of acquiring any building or interest therein.

(iii) ENLARGEMENTS.—Any expenditure attributable to the enlargement of an existing building.

(iv) CERTIFIED HISTORIC STRUCTURE, ETC.—Any expenditure attributable to the rehabilitation of a certified historic structure or a building in a registered historic district, unless the rehabilitation is a certified rehabilitation (within the meaning of subparagraph (C)). The preceding sentence shall not apply to a building in a registered historic district if—

(I) such building was not a certified historic structure,

(II) the Secretary of the Interior certified to the Secretary that such building is not of historic significance to the district, and

(III) if the certification referred to in subclause (II) occurs after the beginning of the rehabilitation of such building, the taxpayer certifies to the Secretary that, at the beginning of such rehabilitation, he in good faith was not aware of the requirements of subclause (II).

(v) TAX-EXEMPT USE PROPERTY.—

(I) IN GENERAL.—Any expenditure in connection with the rehabilitation of a building which is allocable to the portion of such property which is (or may reasonably be expected to be) tax-exempt use property (within the meaning of section 168(h), except that "50 percent" shall be substituted for "35 percent" in paragraph (1)(B)(iii) thereof).

(II) CLAUSE NOT TO APPLY FOR PURPOSES OF PARAGRAPH (1)(C).—This clause shall not apply for purposes of determining under paragraph (1)(C) whether a building has been substantially rehabilitated.

(vi) EXPENDITURES OF LESSEE.—Any expenditure of a lessee of a building if, on the date the rehabilitation is completed, the remaining term of the lease (determined without regard to any renewal periods) is less than the recovery period determined under section 168(c).

(C) CERTIFIED REHABILITATION.—For purposes of subparagraph (B), the term "certified rehabilitation" means any rehabilitation of a certified historic structure which the Secretary of the Interior has certified to the Secretary as being consistent with the historic character of such property or the district in which such property is located.

(D) NONRESIDENTIAL REAL PROPERTY; RESIDENTIAL RENTAL PROPERTY; CLASS LIFE.—For purposes of subparagraph (A), the terms "nonresidential real property," "residential rental property," and "class life" have the respective meanings given such terms by section 168.

(3) CERTIFIED HISTORIC STRUCTURE DEFINED.—

(A) IN GENERAL.—The term "certified historic structure" means any building (and its structural components) which—

(i) is listed in the National Register, or

(ii) is located in a registered historic district and is certified by the Secretary of the Interior to the Secretary as being of historic significance to the district.

(B) REGISTERED HISTORIC DISTRICT.—The term "registered historic district" means—

(i) any district listed in the National Register, and

(ii) any district—

(I) which is designated under a statute of the appropriate State or local government, if such statute is certified by the Secretary of the Interior to the Secretary as containing criteria which will substantially achieve the purpose of preserving and rehabilitating buildings of historic significance to the district, and

(II) which is certified by the Secretary of the Interior to the Secretary as meeting substantially all of the requirements for the listing of districts in the National Register.

Amendments

• 2008, Housing Assistance Tax Act of 2008 (P.L. 110-289)

P.L. 110-289, §3025(a):

Amended Code Sec. 47(c)(2)(B)(v)(I) by striking "section 168(h)" and inserting "section 168(h), except that '50 percent' shall be substituted for '35 percent' in paragraph (1)(B)(iii) thereof". **Effective** for expenditures properly taken into account for periods after 12-31-2007.

[Sec. 47(d)]

(d) PROGRESS EXPENDITURES.—

(1) IN GENERAL.—In the case of any building to which this subsection applies, except as provided in paragraph (3)—

(A) if such building is self-rehabilitated property, any qualified rehabilitation expenditure with respect to such building shall be taken into account for the taxable year for which such expenditure is properly chargeable to capital account with respect to such building, and

(B) if such building is not self-rehabilitated property, any qualified rehabilitation expenditure with respect to such building shall be taken into account for the taxable year in which paid.

(2) PROPERTY TO WHICH SUBSECTION APPLIES.—

(A) IN GENERAL.—This subsection shall apply to any building which is being rehabilitated by or for the taxpayer if—

(i) the normal rehabilitation period for such building is 2 years or more, and

(ii) it is reasonable to expect that such building will be a qualified rehabilitated building in the hands of the taxpayer when it is placed in service.

Clauses (i) and (ii) shall be applied on the basis of facts known as of the close of the taxable year of the taxpayer in which the rehabilitation begins (or, if later, at the close of the first taxable year to which an election under this subsection applies).

(B) NORMAL REHABILITATION PERIOD.—For purposes of subparagraph (A), the term "normal rehabilitation period" means the period reasonably expected to be required for the rehabilitation of the building—

(i) beginning with the date on which physical work on the rehabilitation begins (or, if later, the first day of the first taxable year to which an election under this subsection applies), and

(ii) ending on the date on which it is expected that the property will be available for placing in service.

(3) SPECIAL RULES FOR APPLYING PARAGRAPH (1).—For purposes of paragraph (1)—

(A) COMPONENT PARTS, ETC.—Property which is to be a component part of, or is otherwise to be included in, any building to which this subsection applies shall be taken into account—

(i) at a time not earlier than the time at which it becomes irrevocably devoted to use in the building, and

(ii) as if (at the time referred to in clause (i)) the taxpayer had expended an amount equal to that portion of the cost to the taxpayer of such component or other property which, for purposes of this subpart, is properly chargeable (during such taxable year) to capital account with respect to such building.

(B) CERTAIN BORROWING DISREGARDED.—Any amount borrowed directly or indirectly by the taxpayer from the person rehabilitating the property for him shall not be treated as an amount expended for such rehabilitation.

(C) LIMITATION FOR BUILDINGS WHICH ARE NOT SELF-REHABILITATED—

(i) IN GENERAL.—In the case of a building which is not self-rehabilitated, the amount taken into account under paragraph (1)(B) for any taxable year shall not exceed the amount which represents the portion of the overall cost to the taxpayer of the rehabilitation which is properly attributable to the portion of the rehabilitation which is completed during such taxable year.

(ii) CARRY-OVER OF CERTAIN AMOUNTS.—In the case of a building which is not a self-rehabilitated building, if for the taxable year—

(I) the amount which (but for clause (i)) would have been taken into account under paragraph (1)(B) exceeds the limitation of clause (i), then the amount of such excess shall be taken into account under paragraph (1)(B) for the succeeding taxable year, or

(II) the limitation of clause (i) exceeds the amount taken into account under paragraph (1)(B), then the amount of such excess shall increase the limitation of clause (i) for the succeeding taxable year.

(D) DETERMINATION OF PERCENTAGE OF COMPLETION.—The determination under subparagraph (C)(i) of the portion of the overall cost to the taxpayer of the rehabilitation which is properly attributable to rehabilitation completed during any taxable year shall be made, under regulations prescribed by the Secretary, on the basis of engineering or architectural estimates or on the basis of cost accounting records. Unless the taxpayer establishes otherwise by clear and convincing evidence, the rehabilitation shall be deemed to be completed not more rapidly than ratably over the normal rehabilitation period.

(E) NO PROGRESS EXPENDITURES FOR CERTAIN PRIOR PERIODS.—No qualified rehabilitation expenditures shall be taken into account under this subsection for any period before the first day of the first taxable year to which an election under this subsection applies.

(F) NO PROGRESS EXPENDITURES FOR PROPERTY FOR YEAR IT IS PLACED IN SERVICE, ETC.—In the case of any building, no qualified rehabilitation expenditures shall be taken into account under this subsection for the earlier of—

(i) the taxable year in which the building is placed in service, or

(ii) the first taxable year for which recapture is required under section 50(a)(2) with respect to such property,

or for any taxable year thereafter.

(4) SELF-REHABILITATED BUILDING.—For purposes of this subsection, the term "self-rehabilitated building" means any building if it is reasonable to believe that more than half of the qualified rehabilitation expenditures for such building will be made directly by the taxpayer.

(5) ELECTION.—This subsection shall apply to any taxpayer only if such taxpayer has made an election under this paragraph. Such an election shall apply to the taxable year for which made and all subsequent taxable years. Such an election, once made, may be revoked only with the consent of the Secretary.

Amendments

• 1990, Omnibus Budget Reconciliation Act of 1990 (P.L. 101-508)

P.L. 101-508, §11813(a):

Amended Code Sec. 47. **Effective** for property placed in service after 12-31-90. For exceptions, see Act Sec. 11813(c)(2), below.

P.L. 101-508, §11813(c)(2), provides:

(2) EXCEPTIONS.—The amendments made by this section shall not apply to—

(A) any transition property (as defined in section 49(e) of the Internal Revenue Code of 1986[)] (as in effect on the day before the date of the enactment of this Act),

(B) any property with respect to which qualified progress expenditures were previously taken into account under section 46(d) of such Code (as so in effect), and

(C) any property described in section 46(b)(2)(C) of [sic] Code (as so in effect).

Prior to amendment, Code Sec. 47 read as follows:

SEC. 47. CERTAIN DISPOSITIONS, ETC., OF SECTION 38 PROPERTY.

[Sec. 47(a)]

(a) GENERAL RULE.—Under regulations prescribed by the Secretary—

(1) EARLY DISPOSITION, ETC.—If during any taxable year any property is disposed of, or otherwise ceases to be section 38 property with respect to the taxpayer, before the close of the useful life which was taken into account in computing the credit under section 38, then the tax under this chapter for such taxable year shall be increased by an amount equal to the aggregate decrease in the credits allowed under section 38 for all prior taxable years which would have resulted solely from substituting, in determining qualified investment, for such useful life the period beginning with the time such property was placed in service by the taxpayer and ending with the time such property ceased to be section 38 property.

(2) PROPERTY BECOMES PUBLIC UTILITY PROPERTY.—If during any taxable year any property taken into account in determining qualified investment becomes public utility property (within the meaning of section 46(c)(3)(B)), then the tax under this chapter for such taxable year shall be increased by an amount equal to the aggregate decrease in the credits allowed under section 38 for all prior taxable years which would have resulted solely from treating the property, for purposes of determining qualified investment, as public utility property (after giving due regard to the period before such change in use). If the application of this paragraph to any property is followed by the application of paragraph (1) to such property, proper adjustment shall be made in applying paragraph (1).

(3) PROPERTY CEASES TO BE PROGRESS EXPENDITURE PROPERTY.—

(A) IN GENERAL.—If during any taxable year any property taken into account in determining qualified investment under section 46(d) ceases (by reason of sale or other disposition, cancellation or abandonment of contract, or otherwise) to be, with respect to the taxpayer, property which, when placed in service, will be new section 38 property, then the tax under this chapter for such taxable year shall be increased by an amount equal to the aggregate decrease in the credits allowed under section 38 for all prior taxable years which would have resulted solely from reducing to zero the qualified investment taken into account with respect to such property.

(B) CERTAIN EXCESS CREDIT RECAPTURED.—Any amount which would have been applied as a reduction of the qualified investment in property by reason of paragraph (4) of section 46(c) but for the fact that a reduction under such paragraph cannot reduce qualified investment below zero shall be treated as an amount required to be recaptured under subparagraph (A) for the taxable year in which the property is placed in service.

(C) CERTAIN SALES AND LEASEBACKS.—Under regulations prescribed by the Secretary, a sale by, and leaseback to, a taxpayer who, when the property is placed in service, will be a lessee to whom section 48(d) applies shall not be treated as a cessation described in subparagraph (A) to the extent that the qualified investment which will be passed through to the lessee under section 48(d) with respect to such property is not less than the qualified progress expenditures properly taken into account by the lessee with respect to such property.

(D) COORDINATION WITH PARAGRAPHS (1) AND (5).—If, after property is placed in service, there is a disposition or other cessation described in paragraph (1), or a disposition, cessation, or change in expected use described in paragraph (5), then paragraph (1) or (5), as the case may be, shall be applied as if any credit, which was allowable by reason of section 46(d) and which has not been required to be recaptured before such disposition, cessation, or change in use were allowable for the taxable year the property was placed in service.

(4) SPECIAL RULES FOR COMMUTER HIGHWAY VEHICLES.—

(A) USEFUL LIFE.—For purposes of this subsection, 3 years shall be treated as the useful life which was taken into account in computing the credit under section 38 with respect to any commuter highway vehicle (as defined in section 46(c)(6)(B)).

(B) CHANGE IN USE.—If less than 80 percent of the mileage use of any commuter highway vehicle by the taxpayer during that portion of any taxable year which is within the first 36 months of the operation of such vehicle by the taxpayer meets the requirements of section 46(c)(6)(B), then the tax under this chapter for such taxable year shall be increased by an amount equal to the aggregate decrease in the credits allowed under section 38 for all prior taxable years which would have resulted solely from treating such vehicle, for purposes of determining qualified investment, as not being a commuter highway vehicle. If the application of this subparagraph to any property is followed by the application of paragraph (1) to such property, proper adjustment shall be made in applying paragraph (1).

(5) SPECIAL RULES FOR RECOVERY PROPERTY.—

(A) GENERAL RULE.—If, during any taxable year, section 38 recovery property is disposed of, or otherwise ceases to be section 38 property with respect to the taxpayer before the close of the recapture period, then, except as provided in subparagraph (D), the tax under this chapter for such taxable year shall be increased by the recapture percentage of the aggregate decrease in the credits allowed under section 38 for all prior taxable years which would have resulted solely from reducing to zero the qualified investment taken into account with respect to such property.

(B) RECAPTURE PERCENTAGE.—For purposes of subparagraph (A), the recapture percentage shall be determined in accordance with the following table:

If the recovery property ceases to be section 38 property within—	The recapture percentage is: For property other than 3-year property	For 3-year property The recapture percentage is:
One full year after placed in service	100	100
One full year after the close of the period described in clause (i)	80	66
One full year after the close of the period described in clause (ii)	60	33
One full year after the close of the period described in clause (iii)	40	0
One full year after the close of the period described in clause (iv)	20	0

(C) PROPERTY CEASES TO BE PROGRESS EXPENDITURE PROPERTY.—If, during any taxable year, any recovery property taken into account in determining qualified investment under section 46(d)(1) ceases to be progress expenditure property (as determined under paragraph (3)) or becomes, with respect to the taxpayer, recovery property of a character other than that expected in determining the applicable percentage under section 46(d)(1)(B)(i), then the tax under this chapter for such taxable year shall be adjusted in accordance with regulations prescribed by the Secretary.

(D) LIMITATION.—The tax for the taxable year shall be increased under subparagraph (A) only with respect to the credits allowed under section 38 which were used to reduce tax liability. In the case of credits not so used to reduce tax liability, the carrybacks and carryovers under section 39 shall be appropriately adjusted.

(E) DEFINITIONS AND SPECIAL RULES.—

(i) SECTION 38 RECOVERY PROPERTY.—For purposes of this paragraph, the term "section 38 recovery property" means any section 38 property which is recovery property (within the meaning of section 168).

(ii) RECAPTURE PERIOD.—For purposes of this paragraph, the term "recapture period" means, with respect to any recovery property, the period consisting of the first full year after the property is placed in service and the 4 succeeding full years (the 2 succeeding full years in the case of 3-year property).

(iii) CLASSIFICATION OF PROPERTY.—For purposes of this paragraph, property shall be classified as provided in section 168(e).

(iv) PARAGRAPH (1) NOT TO APPLY.—Paragraph (1) shall not apply with respect to any recovery property.

(v) TREATMENT AS RECOVERY PROPERTY.—Any reference in this paragraph to recovery property shall be treated as including a reference to any property to which section 168 (as amended by the Tax Reform Act of 1986) applies.

(6) CARRYBACKS AND CARRYOVERS ADJUSTED.—In the case of any cessation described in paragraph (1), (3), or (5) or any change in use described in paragraph (2) or (4), the carrybacks and carryovers under section 39 shall be adjusted by reason of such cessation (or change in use).

(7) AIRCRAFT USED OUTSIDE THE UNITED STATES AFTER APRIL 18, 1969.—

(A) GENERAL RULE.—Any aircraft which was new section 38 property for the taxable year in which it was placed in service and which is used outside the United States under a qualifying lease or leases shall be treated as not ceasing to be section 38 property by reason of such use until such aircraft has been so used for a period or periods exceeding 3½ years in total. For purposes of the preceding sentence, the registration of such aircraft under the laws of a foreign country shall be treated as use outside the United States.

(B) COMPUTATION OF QUALIFIED INVESTMENT.—If an aircraft described in subparagraph (A) is disposed of or otherwise ceases to be section 38 property, the increase under paragraph (1) and the adjustment under paragraph (6) shall not be greater than the increase or adjustment which would result if the qualified investment of such aircraft were based upon a useful life equal to the lesser of (i) the actual useful life of such aircraft with respect to the taxpayer, or, (ii) twice the number of full calendar months during which such aircraft was registered by the Administrator of the Federal Aviation Agency and was used in the United States, operated to and from the United States, or operated under contract with the United States. For purposes of the preceding sentence, an aircraft shall be treated as used in the United States for any calendar month beginning after such aircraft was placed in service, if such month is included in a taxable year ending before January 1, 1971, for which such aircraft was section 38 property (determined without regard to this paragraph).

(C) QUALIFYING LEASE DEFINED.—For purposes of subparagraph (A), the term "qualifying lease" means a lease from an air carrier (as defined in section 101 of the Federal Aviation Act of 1958, as amended (49 U. S. C. 1301)) which complies with the provisions of the Federal Aviation Act of 1958, as amended, and the rules and regulations promulgated by the Secretary of Transportation thereunder, but only if such lease was executed after April 18, 1969.

(8) MOTION PICTURE FILMS AND VIDEO TAPES.—

(A) DISPOSITION WHERE DEPRECIATION EXCEEDS 90 PERCENT OF BASIS OR COST.—A qualified film (within the meaning of section 48(k)(1)(B)) which has an applicable percentage determined under section 48(k)(3) shall cease to be section 38 property with respect to the taxpayer at the close of the first day on which the aggregate amount allowable as a deduction under section 167 equals or exceeds 90 percent of the basis or cost of such film (adjusted for any partial dispositions).

(B) OTHER DISPOSITIONS.—In the case of a disposition of the exclusive right to display a qualified film which has an applicable percentage determined under section 48(k)(3) in one or more mediums of publication or exhibition in one or more specifically defined geographical areas over the remaining initial period of commercial exploitation of the film or tape in such geographical areas, the taxpayer shall be considered to have disposed of all or part of such film or tape and shall recompute the credit earned on all of his basis or cost or on that part of the basis or cost properly allocable to that part of the film or tape disposed of. In the case of an affiliated group of corporations, a transfer within the affiliated group shall not be treated as a disposition until there is a transfer outside the group. For purposes of the preceding sentence, the term "affiliated group" has the meaning given to such term by section 1504 (determined as if section 1504(b) did not include paragraph (3) thereof). For purposes of this paragraph, section 1504(a) shall be applied by substituting "50 percent" for "80 percent" each place it appears.

(9) AIRCRAFT LEASED TO FOREIGN PERSONS OR ENTITIES.—

(A) IN GENERAL.—Any aircraft which was new section 38 property for the taxable year in which it was placed in service and which is used by any foreign person or entity (as defined in section 168(h)(2)) under a qualified lease (as defined in paragraph (7)(C)) entered into before January 1, 1990, shall not be treated as ceasing to be section 38 property by reason of such use until such aircraft has been so used for a period or periods exceeding 3 years in total.

(B) RECAPTURE PERIOD EXTENDED.—For purposes of paragraphs (1) and (5)(B) of this subsection, any period during which there was use described in subparagraph (A) of an aircraft shall be disregarded.

Amendments

• 1988, Technical and Miscellaneous Revenue Act of 1988 (P.L. 100-647)

P.L. 100-647, §1002(a)(26)(A):

Amended Code Sec. 47(a)(5)(E) by adding at the end thereof a new clause (v). **Effective** as if included in the provision of P.L. 99-514 to which it relates.

P.L. 100-647, §1002(a)(26)(B):

Amended Code Sec. 47(a)(5)(D) by striking out the last sentence. **Effective** as if included in the provision of P.L. 99-514 to which it relates. Prior to amendment, the last sentence of Code Sec. 47(a)(5)(D) read as follows:

If, prior to a disposition to which this subsection applies, any portion of any credit is not allowable with respect to any property by reason of section 168(i)(3), such portion shall be treated (for purposes of this subparagraph) as not having been used to reduce tax liability.

P.L. 100-647, §1002(a)(26)(C):

Amended Code Sec. 47(a)(5)(E)(iii) by striking out "section 168(c)" and inserting in lieu thereof "section 168(e)". **Effective** as if included in the provision of P.L. 99-514 to which it relates.

P.L. 100-647, §1002(a)(27):

Amended Code Sec. 47(a)(9)(A) by striking out "section 168(j)(4)(C)" and inserting in lieu thereof "section 168(h)(2)". **Effective** as if included in the provision of P.L. 99-514 to which it relates.

• 1986, Tax Reform Act of 1986 (P.L. 99-514)

P.L. 99-514, §1802(a)(5)(A):

Amended Code Sec. 47(a) by adding at the end thereof new paragraph (9). **Effective** as if included in the provision of P.L. 98-369 to which such amendment relates.

• 1985 (P.L. 99-121)

P.L. 99-121, §103(b)(6):

Amended Code Sec. 47(a)(5) by striking out "For 15-year, 10-year, and 5-year property" in the table contained in subparagraph (B) and inserting in lieu thereof "For property other than 3-year property". **Effective** as if included in the amendments made by P.L. 98-369, §111.

• 1984, Civil Aeronautics Board Sunset Act of 1984 (P.L. 98-443)

P.L. 98-443, §9(p):

Amended Code Sec. 47(a)(7)(C) by striking out "Civil Aeronautics Board" and inserting in lieu thereof "Secretary of Transportation". **Effective** 1-1-85.

• 1984, Deficit Reduction Act of 1984 (P.L. 98-369)

P.L. 98-369, §474(o)(8):

Amended Code Sec. 47(a)(5)(D) and (6) by striking out "under section 46(b)" and inserting in lieu thereof "under section 39". **Effective** for tax years beginning after 12-31-83, and to carrybacks from such years.

P.L. 98-369, §1067(b), provides:

(b) Special Rule for Subsection (a).—The amount of any recapture under section 47 of the Internal Revenue Code of 1954 with respect to the credit allowed under section 38 of such Code with respect to progress expenditures (within the meaning of section 46(d) of such Code) shall apply only to the percentage of the cost basis of the coal gasification facility to which the amendment made by subsection (a) applies.

• 1982, Tax Equity and Fiscal Responsibility Act of 1982 (P.L. 97-248)

P.L. 97-248, §208(a)(2)(B):

Amended Code Sec. 47(a)(5)(D) by adding the last sentence at the end thereof. **Effective** for agreements entered into after 7-1-82, or to property placed in service after 7-1-82. However, it does not apply, generally, to transitional safe harbor lease property.

• 1981, Economic Recovery Tax Act of 1981 (P.L. 97-34)

P.L. 97-34, §211(g)(1):

Amended Code Sec. 47(a) by redesignating paragraphs (5), (6), and (7) as paragraphs (6), (7), and (8), respectively, and by inserting after paragraph (4) new paragraph (5). **Effective** for property placed in service after 12-31-80.

P.L. 97-34, §211(g)(2)(A):

Amended Code Sec. 47(a)(3)(D). **Effective** for property placed in service after 12-31-80. Prior to amendment, Code Sec. 47(a)(3)(D) read as follows:

(D) COORDINATION WITH PARAGRAPH (1).—If, after property is placed in service, there is a disposition or other cessation described in paragraph (1), paragraph (1) shall be applied as if any credit which was allowable by reason of section 46(d) and which has not been required to be recaptured before such cessation were allowable for the taxable year the property was placed in service.

P.L. 97-34, §211(g)(2)(B), (C):

Amended Code Sec. 47(a)(6) as redesignated by P.L. 97-34, §211(g)(1), by striking out "paragraph (1) or (3)" and inserting in lieu thereof "paragraph (1), (3), or (5)," and amended Code Sec. 47(a)(7)(B) as redesignated by that section by striking out "paragraph (5)" and inserting in lieu thereof "paragraph (6)". **Effective** for property placed in service after 12-31-80.

• 1978, Energy Tax Act of 1978 (P.L. 95-618)

P.L. 95-618, §241(b)(1):

Redesignated former Code Sec. 47(a)(4) as (a)(5) and inserted a new (a)(4). **Effective** 11-10-78. Former section 47(a)(4), before redesignation, read:

"(4) CARRYBACKS AND CARRYOVERS ADJUSTED.—In the case of any cessation described in paragraph (1) or (3) or any change in use described in paragraph (2), the carrybacks and carryovers under section 46(b) shall be adjusted by reason of such cessation (or change in use)."

P.L. 95-618, §241(b)(2):

Amended Code Sec. 47(a)(5), as redesignated by Act Sec. 241(b)(1), by striking out "paragraph (2)" and inserting in place thereof "paragraph (2) or (4)". **Effective** 11-10-78.

P.L. 95-618, §241(b)(3):

Amended Code Sec. 47(a)(6)(B) by striking out "paragraph (4)" and inserting in place thereof "paragraph (5)". **Effective** 11-10-78.

• 1976, Tax Reform Act of 1976 (P.L. 94-455)

P.L. 94-455, §804(b):

Added a new paragraph (7) to Code Sec. 47(a). **Effective** for tax years beginning after 12-31-74. At the election of the taxpayer, made within 1 year after 10-4-76, in such manner as the Secretary of the Treasury or his delegate may by regulations prescribe, the amendment shall also apply to property which is property described in Code Sec. 50(a) and which is placed in service in tax years beginning before 1-1-75.

P.L. 94-455, §1906(b)(13)(A):

Amended 1954 Code by substituting "Secretary" for "Secretary or his delegate" each place it appeared. **Effective** 2-1-77.

• 1975, Tax Reduction Act of 1975 (P.L. 94-12)

P.L. 94-12, §302(b)(2)(A);

Amended Sec. 47(a) by redesignating paragraph (3) as paragraph (4) and by adding new paragraph (3). **Effective** for tax years ending after 12-31-74.

P.L. 94-12, §302(c)(1):

Amended Sec. 47(a)(4) [as renumbered] by substituting "paragraph (1) or (3)" for "paragraph (1)". **Effective** for tax years ending after 12-31-74.

P.L. 94-12, §302(2):

Amended Sec. 47(a)(5) [See amendment note for P.L. 92-178, Act Sec. 107(b)(1), below.] and (6)(B) by substituting "paragraph (4)" for "paragraph (3)". **Effective** for tax years ending after 12-31-74.

In redetermining qualified investment for purposes of section 47(a) in the case of any property which ceases to be section 38 property with respect to the taxpayer after 8-15-71, or which becomes public utility property after such date, Code Sec. 46(c)(2) shall be applied. See the amendatory notes following Code Sec. 46(c).—CCH.

• 1971, Revenue Act of 1971 (P.L. 92-178)

P.L. 92-178, §102(c):

Amended Code Sec. 47(a)(6)(A) by substituting "3½ years" for "4 years" in the first sentence. **Effective** for leases executed after 4-18-69.

P.L. 92-178, §107(a)(1):

Repealed Code Sec. 47(a)(4). **Effective** for casualties and thefts occurring after 8-15-71. Prior to repeal, Code Sec. 47(a)(4) read as follows:

"(4) Property destroyed by casualty, etc.—No increase shall be made under paragraph (1) and no adjustment shall be made under paragraph (3) in any case in which—

"(A) any property is disposed of, or otherwise ceases to be section 38 property with respect to the taxpayer, on account of its destruction or damage by fire, storm, shipwreck, or other casualty, or by reason of its theft,

"(B) section 38 property is placed in service by the taxpayer to replace the property described in subparagraph (A), and

"(C) the reduction in basis or cost of such section 38 property described in the first sentence of section 46(c)(4) is equal to or greater than the reduction in qualified investment which (but for this paragraph) would be made by reason of the substitution required by paragraph (1) with respect to the property described in subparagraph (A).

"Subparagraphs (B) and (C) shall not apply with respect to any casualty or theft occurring after April 18, 1969."

P.L. 92-178, §107(b)(1):

Repealed Code Sec. 47(a)(5). However, such repeal is not applicable if replacement property described in subparagraph (B) of said section is not property described in Code Sec. 50. Before repeal, Code Sec. 47(a)(5) read:

"(5) CERTAIN PROPERTY REPLACED AFTER APRIL 18, 1969.—In any case in which—

(A) section 38 property is disposed of, and

(B) property which would be section 38 property but for section 49 is placed in service by the taxpayer to replace the property disposed of,

the increase under paragraph (1) and the adjustment under paragraph (4) shall not be greater than the increase or adjustment which would result if the qualified investment of the property described in subparagraph (B) (determined as if such property were section 38 property) were substituted for the qualified investment of the property disposed of (as determined under paragraph (1)). Except in the case of a disposition by reason of a casualty or theft occurring before April 19, 1969, the preceding sentence shall apply only if the section 38 property disposed of is replaced within 6 months after the date of such disposition."

• 1971 (P.L. 91-676)

P.L. 91-676, §1:

Amended Code Sec. 47(a) by adding subparagraph (6).

• 1969, Tax Reform Act of 1969 (P.L. 91-172)

P.L. 91-172, §703(c)(1):

Amended Code Sec. 47(a)(4) by adding the last sentence.

P.L. 91-172, §703(c)(2):

Added Code Sec. 47(a)(5).

[Sec. 47(b)]

(b) SECTION NOT TO APPLY IN CERTAIN CASES.—Subsection (a) shall not apply to—

(1) a transfer by reason of death,

(2) a transaction to which section 381(a) applies, or

(3) a transfer to which subsection (c) of section 374 (relating to exchanges under the final system plan for ConRail) applies.

For purposes of subsection (a), property shall not be treated as ceasing to be section 38 property with respect to the taxpayer by reason of a mere change in the form of conducting the trade or business so long as the property is retained in such trade or business as section 38 property and the taxpayer retains a substantial interest in such trade or business.

Amendments

• 1978, Revenue Act of 1978 (P.L. 95-600)

P.L. 95-600, §317(a), (b):

Amended Code Sec. 47(b). **Effective** for tax years ending after 3-31-76. Before amendment, such section read:

"(b) SECTION NOT TO APPLY IN CERTAIN CASES.—Subsection (a) shall not apply to—

(1) a transfer by reason of death, or

(2) a transaction to which section 381(a) applies.

For purposes of subsection (a), property shall not be treated as ceasing to be section 38 property with respect to the taxpayer by reason of a mere change in the form of conducting the trade or business so long as the property is retained in such trade or business as section 38 property and the taxpayer retains a substantial interest in such trade or business."

• 1962, Revenue Act of 1962 (P.L. 87-834)

P.L. 87-834, §2(b), (h):

Added Code Sec. 47(b). **Effective** for tax years ending after 12-31-61.

[Sec. 47(c)]

(c) SPECIAL RULE.—Any increase in tax under subsection (a) shall not be treated as tax imposed by this chapter for purposes of determining the amount of any credit allowable under subpart A, B, D, or G.

Amendments

• 1988, Technical and Miscellaneous Revenue Act of 1988 (P.L. 100-647)

P.L. 100-647, §1007(g)(3)(A):

Amended Code Sec. 47(c) by striking out "or D" and inserting in lieu thereof "D, or G". **Effective** as if included in the provision of P.L. 99-514 to which it relates.

• 1984, Deficit Reduction Act of 1984 (P.L. 98-369)

P.L. 98-369, §474(o)(9):

Amended Code Sec. 47(c) by striking out "subpart A" and inserting in lieu thereof "subpart A, B, or D". **Effective** for tax years beginning after 12-31-83, and to carryback from such years.

[Sec. 47(d)]

(d) INCREASES IN NONQUALIFIED NONRECOURSE FINANCING.—

(1) IN GENERAL.—If, as of the close of the taxable year, there is a net increase with respect to the taxpayer in the amount of nonqualified nonrecourse financing (within the meaning of section 46(c)(8)) with respect to any property to which section 46(c)(8) applied, then the tax under this chapter for such taxable year shall be increased by an amount equal to the aggregate decrease in credits allowed under section 38 for all prior taxable years which would have resulted from reducing the credit base (as defined in section 46(c)(8)(C)) taken into account with respect to such property by the amount of such net increase. For purposes of determining the amount of credit subject to the early disposition or cessation rules of subsection (a), the net increase in the amount of the nonqualified nonrecourse financing with respect to the property shall be treated as reducing the property's credit base (and correspondingly reducing the

qualified investment in the property) in the year in which the property was first placed in service.

(2) TRANSFERS OF DEBT MORE THAN 1 YEAR AFTER INITIAL BORROWING NOT TREATED AS INCREASING NONQUALIFIED NONRECOURSE FINANCING.—For purposes of paragraph (1), the amount of nonqualified nonrecourse financing (within the meaning of section 46(c)(8)(D)) with respect to the taxpayer shall not be treated as increased by reason of a transfer of (or agreement to transfer) any evidence of an indebtedness if such transfer occurs (or such agreement is entered into) more than 1 year after the date such indebtedness was incurred.

(3) SPECIAL RULES FOR CERTAIN ENERGY PROPERTY.—

(A) IN GENERAL.—In the case of the second taxable year following the taxable year in which any qualified energy property (within the meaning of section 46(c)(8)(F)) is placed in service by the taxpayer and any succeeding taxable year, the taxpayer, for purposes of paragraph (1), shall be treated as increasing the amount of nonqualified nonrecourse financing (within the meaning of section 46(c)(8)) with respect to such property for such taxable year in an amount equal to the credit recapture amount (if any).

(B) CREDIT RECAPTURE AMOUNT.—For purposes of this paragraph, the term "credit recapture amount" means an amount equal to the excess (if any) of—

(i) the total amount of principal to be paid as of the close of any taxable year under a nonrecourse level payment loan (as defined in section 46(c)(8)(F)(iv)) with respect to such property, over

(ii) the sum of—

(I) the amount of principal actually paid as of the close of such taxable year, plus

(II) the sum of the credit recapture amounts with respect to such property for all preceding taxable years.

(C) SPECIAL RULES FOR DETERMINING PRINCIPAL TO BE PAID.—For purposes of subparagraph (b)(i), in determining the amount of the principal to be paid under a level payment loan, such determination shall be made as if such loan was to be fully repaid by the end of a period equal to the earlier of—

(i) the class life (as defined in section 168(i)(1)) of the property or, if the property has no class life, a similar period determined by the Secretary, or

(ii) the period at the end of which full repayment is to occur under the terms of the loan.

(D) SPECIAL RULE FOR CERTAIN CUMULATIVE DEFICIENCIES.—If the excess of—

(i) the amount of the total scheduled principal payments under a loan described in subparagraph (B)(i) as of the close of the taxable year, over

(ii) the total principal actually paid under such loan as of the close of such taxable year,

is equal to or greater than the amount of such total scheduled payments for the 5-taxable year period ending with such taxable year, then, notwithstanding subparagraph (B), the credit recapture amount for such taxable year shall be equal to the principal remaining to be paid as of the close of such taxable year over the sum of the credit recapture amounts with respect to such property for all preceding taxable years.

(E) SPECIAL RULE FOR CERTAIN DISPOSITIONS.—

(i) IN GENERAL.—If any property which is held by the taxpayer and to which this paragraph applies is disposed of by the taxpayer, then for purposes of paragraph (1) and notwithstanding subparagraph (B), the credit recapture amount for the taxpayer shall be an amount equal to the unpaid principal on the loan described in subparagraph (B)(i) as of the date of disposition reduced by the sum of the credit recapture amounts with respect to such property for all preceding taxable years;

(ii) ASSUMPTIONS, ETC.—Any amount of the loan described in subparagraph (B)(i) which is assumed or taken subject to by any person shall be treated for purposes of clause (i) as not reducing unpaid principal with respect to such loan.

(G) ADDITIONAL INTEREST.—In the case of any increase in tax under paragraph (1) by reason of the application of this paragraph, there shall be added to such tax interest on such tax (determined at the underpayment rate established under section 6621) as if the increase in tax under paragraph (1) was for the taxable year in which the property was placed in service.

Amendments

• 1988, Technical and Miscellaneous Revenue Act of 1988 (P.L. 100-647)

P.L. 100-647, §1002(a)(18):

Amended Code Sec. 47(d)(1) by striking out "section 48(c)(8)(C)" and inserting in lieu thereof "section 46(c)(8)(C)". **Effective** as if included in the provision of P.L. 99-514 to which it relates.

P.L. 100-647, §1002(a)(28)(A)-(B):

Amended Code Sec. 47(d)(3)(C)(i) by striking out "present class life (as defined in section 168(g)(2))" and inserting in lieu thereof "class life (as defined in section 168(i)(1))"; and by striking out "no present class life" and inserting in lieu thereof "no class life". **Effective** as if included in the provision of P.L. 99-514 to which it relates.

• 1986, Tax Reform Act of 1986 (P.L. 99-514)

P.L. 99-514, §1511(c)(2):

Amended Code Sec. 47(d)(3)(G) by striking out "determined under section 6621" and inserting in lieu thereof "determined at the underpayment rate established under section 6621". **Effective** for purposes of determining interest for periods after 12-31-86.

P.L. 99-514, §1844(b)(1)(A)-(B):

Amended Code Sec. 47(d)(1) by striking out "reducing the qualified investment" and inserting in lieu thereof "reducing the credit base (as defined in section 48(c)(8)(C))", and by adding at the end thereof a new sentence. **Effective** as if included in the provision of P.L. 98-369 to which such amendment relates.

P.L. 99-514, §1844(b)(2):

Repealed Code Sec. 47(d)(3)(F). **Effective** as if included in the provision of P.L. 98-369 to which such amendment relates. Prior to repeal, Code Sec. 47(d)(3)(F) read as follows:

(F) APPLICATION WITH SUBSECTION (a).—The amount of any increase in tax under subsection (a) with repsect to any property to which this paragraph applies shall be determined by reducing the qualified investment with respect to such property by the aggregate credit recapture amounts for all taxable years under this paragraph.

P.L. 99-514, §1844(b)(4):

Amended Code Sec. 47(d)(3)(E)(i) by inserting "reduced the sum of the credit recapture amounts with respect to such property for all preceding taxable years" before the semicolon at the end thereof. **Effective** as if included in the provision of P.L. 98-369 to which such amendment relates.

• 1984, Deficit Reduction Act of 1984 (P.L. 98-369)

P.L. 98-369, §431(b)(2):

Amended so much of Code Sec. 47(d) as preceded paragraph (3). **Effective** for property placed in service after 7-18-84, in tax years ending after such date but does not apply to any property to which the amendments made by P.L. 97-34, §211(f) do not apply. See Act Sec. 421(d)(2)-(4) in the notes following former Code Sec. 47(e) for an exception. Prior to amendment, it read as follows:

(d) Property Ceasing to Be at Risk.—

(1) In General.—If the taxpayer ceases to any extent to be at risk (within the meaning of section 46(c)(8)(B)) with respect to any amount in connection with section 38 property, then the tax under this chapter for such taxable year shall be increased by an amount equal to the aggregate decrease in credits allowed under section 38 for all prior taxable years which would have resulted from substituting, in determining qualified investment, the amount determined under section 46(c)(8) with respect to such property if, on the date the property was placed in service, the taxpayer had not been at risk with respect to the amount he ceased to be at risk to.

(2) Certain Transfers Not Treated as Ceasing To Be at Risk.—If, after the 12-month period after the date on which a taxpayer borrows an amount from a qualified person (within the meaning of section 46(c)(8)(D)) with respect to which such taxpayer is considered at risk under section 46(c)(8)(B), the qualified person transfers or agrees to transfer any evidence of such indebtedness to a person who is not a qualified person, then, for purposes of paragraph (1), the taxpayer shall not be treated as ceasing to be at risk with respect to such amount.

P.L. 98-369, §431(d)(4):

Amended Code Sec. 47(d)(3)(A) by striking out "ceasing to be at risk" and inserting in lieu thereof "increasing the amount of nonqualified nonrecourse financing (within the meaning of section 46(c)(8))". **Effective** for property placed in service after 7-18-84, in tax years ending after such date, except that such amendments shall not apply to any property to which the amendments made by section 211(f) of P.L. 97-34 do not apply. However, Act Sec. 431(e)(2) provides the following exception:

(2) Amendments May Be Elected Retroactively.—At the election of the taxpayer, the amendments made by this section shall apply as if included in the amendments made by section 211(f) of of the Economic Recovery Tax Act of 1981. Any election made under the preceding sentence shall apply to all property of the taxpayer to which the amendments made by such section 211(f) apply and shall be made at such time and in such manner as the Secretary of the Treasury or his delegate may by regulations prescribe.

P.L. 98-369, §431(d)(5):

Amended Code Sec. 47(d)(3)(B)(i) by striking out "other than a loan described in section 46(c)(8)(B)(ii)". **Effective** for property placed in service after 7-18-84, in tax years ending after such date, except that such amendments shall not apply to any property to which the amendments made by section 211(f) of P.L. 97-34 do not apply. However, Act Sec. 431(e)(2) provides the following exception:

(2) Amendments May Be Elected Retroactively.—At the election of the taxpayer, the amendments made by this section shall apply as if included in the amendments made by section 211(f) of of the Economic Recovery Tax Act of 1981. Any election made under the preceding sentence shall apply to all property of the taxpayer to which the amendments made by such section 211(f) apply and shall be made at such time and in such manner as the Secretary of the Treasury or his delegate may by regulations prescribe.

• 1982, Technical Corrections Act of 1982 (P.L. 97-448)

P.L. 97-448, §102(e)(3)(A):

Amended Code Sec. 47(d)(2) by striking out "section 48(c)(8)(D)" and inserting in lieu thereof "section 46(c)(8)(D)", and by striking out "section 48(c)(8)(B)" and inserting in lieu thereof "section 46(c)(8)(B)". **Effective** as if such amendment had been included in the provision of P.L. 97-34 to which it relates.

P.L. 97-448, §102(e)(3)(B):

Amended Code Sec. 47(d)(3)(A) by striking out "section 46(c)(8)(E)" and inserting in lieu thereof "section 46(c)(8)(F)". **Effective** as if such amendment had been included in the provision of P.L. 97-34 to which it relates.

• 1981, Economic Recovery Tax Act of 1981 (P.L. 97-34)

P.L. 97-34, §211(f)(2):

Added Code Sec. 47(d). **Effective** for property placed in service after 2-18-81, unless acquired pursuant to a contract binding on or before that date.

P.L. 97-34, §211(i)(5), provides:

(5) AT RISK RULES.—

(A) IN GENERAL.—The amendment made by subsection (f) shall not apply to—

(i) property placed in service by the taxpayer on or before February 18, 1981, and

(ii) property placed in service by the taxpayer after February 18, 1981, where such property is acquired by the taxpayer pursuant to a binding contract entered into on or before that date.

(B) BINDING CONTRACT.—For purposes of subparagraph (A)(ii), property acquired pursuant to a binding contract shall, under regulations prescribed by the Secretary, include property acquired in a manner so that it would have qualified as pretermination property under section 49(b) (as in effect before its repeal by the Revenue Act of 1978).

[Sec. 47(e)]

(e) TRANSFERS BETWEEN SPOUSES OR INCIDENT TO DIVORCE.—In the case of any transfer described in subsection (a) of section 1041—

(1) subsection (a) of this section shall not apply, and

(2) the same tax treatment under this section with respect to the transferred property shall apply to the transferee as would have applied to the transferor.

Amendments

• 1984, Deficit Reduction Act of 1984 (P.L. 98-369)

P.L. 98-369, §421(b)(7):

Added Code Sec. 47(e). **Effective** for transfers after 7-18-84, in tax years ending after such date. For exceptions, see Act Sec. 421(d)(2)-(4) below:

P.L. 98-369, §421(d)(2)-(4), provides:

(2) Election to have Amendments Apply to Transfers After 1983.—If both spouses or former spouses make an election under this paragraph, the amendments made by this section shall apply to all transfers made by such spouses (or former spouses) after December 31, 1983.

(3) Exception for Transfers Pursuant to Existing Decrees.—Except in the case of an election under paragraph (2), the amendments made by this section shall not apply to transfers under any instrument in effect on or before the date of the enactment of this Act unless both spouses (or former spouses) elect to have such amendments apply to transfers under such instrument.

(4) Election.—Any election under paragraph (2) or (3) shall be made in such manner, at such time, and subject to such conditions, as the Secretary of the Treasury or his delegate may by regulations prescribe.

[Sec. 48]

SEC. 48. ENERGY CREDIT.

[Sec. 48(a)]

(a) ENERGY CREDIT.—

(1) IN GENERAL.—For purposes of section 46, except as provided in paragraphs (1)(B), (2)(B), (3)(B), and (4)(B) of subsection (c), the energy credit for any taxable year is the energy percentage of the basis of each energy property placed in service during such taxable year.

(2) ENERGY PERCENTAGE.—

(A) IN GENERAL.—The energy percentage is—

(i) 30 percent in the case of—

(I) qualified fuel cell property,

(II) energy property described in paragraph (3)(A)(i) but only with respect to periods ending before January 1, 2017,

(III) energy property described in paragraph (3)(A)(ii), and

(IV) qualified small wind energy property, and

(ii) in the case of any energy property to which clause (i) does not apply, 10 percent.

(B) COORDINATION WITH REHABILITATION CREDIT.—The energy percentage shall not apply to that portion of the basis of any property which is attributable to qualified rehabilitation expenditures.

(3) ENERGY PROPERTY.—For purposes of this subpart, the term "energy property" means any property—

(A) which is—

(i) equipment which uses solar energy to generate electricity, to heat or cool (or provide hot water for use in) a structure, or to provide solar process heat, excepting property used to generate energy for the purposes of heating a swimming pool,

(ii) equipment which uses solar energy to illuminate the inside of a structure using fiber-optic distributed sunlight but only with respect to periods ending before January 1, 2017,

(iii) equipment used to produce, distribute, or use energy derived from a geothermal deposit (within the meaning of section 613(e)(2)), but only, in the case of electricity generated by geothermal power, up to (but not including) the electrical transmission stage,

(iv) qualified fuel cell property or qualified microturbine property,

(v) combined heat and power system property,

(vi) qualified small wind energy property, or

(vii) equipment which uses the ground or ground water as a thermal energy source to heat a structure or as a thermal energy sink to cool a structure, but only with respect to periods ending before January 1, 2017,

(B)(i) the construction, reconstruction, or erection of which is completed by the taxpayer, or

(ii) which is acquired by the taxpayer if the original use of such property commences with the taxpayer,

(C) with respect to which depreciation (or amortization in lieu of depreciation) is allowable, and

(D) which meets the performance and quality standards (if any) which—

(i) have been prescribed by the Secretary by regulations (after consultation with the Secretary of Energy), and

(ii) are in effect at the time of the acquisition of the property.

Such term shall not include any property which is part of a facility the production from which is allowed as a credit under section 45 for the taxable year or any prior taxable year.

(4) SPECIAL RULE FOR PROPERTY FINANCED BY SUBSIDIZED ENERGY FINANCING OR INDUSTRIAL DEVELOPMENT BONDS.—

(A) REDUCTION OF BASIS.—For purposes of applying the energy percentage to any property, if such property is financed in whole or in part by—

(i) subsidized energy financing, or

(ii) the proceeds of a private activity bond (within the meaning of section 141) the interest on which is exempt from tax under section 103,

the amount taken into account as the basis of such property shall not exceed the amount which (but for this subparagraph) would be so taken into account multiplied by the fraction determined under subparagraph (B).

(B) DETERMINATION OF FRACTION.—For purposes of subparagraph (A), the fraction determined under this subparagraph is 1 reduced by a fraction—

(i) the numerator of which is that portion of the basis of the property which is allocable to such financing or proceeds, and

(ii) the denominator of which is the basis of the property.

(C) SUBSIDIZED ENERGY FINANCING.—For purposes of subparagraph (A), the term "subsidized energy financing" means financing provided under a Federal, State, or local program a principal purpose of which is to provide subsidized financing for projects designed to conserve or produce energy.

(D) TERMINATION.—This paragraph shall not apply to periods after December 31, 2008, under rules similar to the rules of section 48(m) (as in effect on the day before the date of the enactment of the Revenue Reconciliation Act of 1990).

(5) ELECTION TO TREAT QUALIFIED FACILITIES AS ENERGY PROPERTY.—

(A) IN GENERAL.—In the case of any qualified property which is part of a qualified investment credit facility—

(i) such property shall be treated as energy property for purposes of this section, and

(ii) the energy percentage with respect to such property shall be 30 percent.

(B) DENIAL OF PRODUCTION CREDIT.—No credit shall be allowed under section 45 for any taxable year with respect to any qualified investment credit facility.

(C) QUALIFIED INVESTMENT CREDIT FACILITY.—For purposes of this paragraph, the term "qualified investment credit facility" means any of the following facilities if no credit has been allowed under section 45 with respect to such facility and the taxpayer makes an irrevocable election to have this paragraph apply to such facility:

(i) WIND FACILITIES.—Any qualified facility (within the meaning of section 45) described in paragraph (1) of section 45(d) if such facility is placed in service in 2009, 2010, 2011, or 2012.

(ii) OTHER FACILITIES.—Any qualified facility (within the meaning of section 45) described in paragraph (2), (3), (4), (6), (7), (9), or (11) of section 45(d) if such facility is placed in service in 2009, 2010, 2011, 2012, or 2013.

(D) QUALIFIED PROPERTY.—For purposes of this paragraph, the term "qualified property" means property—

(i) which is—

(I) tangible personal property, or

(II) other tangible property (not including a building or its structural components), but only if such property is used as an integral part of the qualified investment credit facility, and

(ii) with respect to which depreciation (or amortization in lieu of depreciation) is allowable.

Amendments

• 2009, American Recovery and Reinvestment Tax Act of 2009 (P.L. 111-5)

P.L. 111-5, §1102(a):

Amended Code Sec. 48(a) by adding at the end a new paragraph (5). **Effective** for facilities placed in service after 12-31-2008.

P.L. 111-5, §1103(b)(1):

Amended Code Sec. 48(a)(4) by adding at the end a new subparagraph (D). **Effective** for periods after 12-31-2008, under rules similar to the rules of Code Sec. 48(m) (as in effect on the day before the date of the enactment of the Revenue Reconciliation Act of 1990 [10-30-90]).

• 2008, Energy Improvement and Extension Act of 2008 (P.L. 110-343)

P.L. 110-343, Division B, §103(a)(1):

Amended Code Sec. 48(a)(2)(A)(i)(II) and (3)(A)(ii) by striking "January 1, 2009" and inserting "January 1, 2017". **Effective** 10-3-2008.

P.L. 110-343, Division B, §103(c)(1):

Amended Code Sec. 48(a)(3)(A) by striking "or" at the end of clause (iii), by inserting "or" at the end of clause (iv), and by adding at the end a new clause (v). **Effective** for periods after 10-3-2008, in tax years ending after such date, under rules similar to the rules of Code Sec. 48(m) (as in effect on the day before the date of the enactment of the Revenue Reconciliation Act of 1990 (P.L. 101-508)).

P.L. 110-343, Division B, §103(c)(3):

Amended Code Sec. 48(a)(1) by striking "paragraphs (1)(B) and (2)(B)" and inserting "paragraphs (1)(B), (2)(B), and (3)(B)". **Effective** for periods after 10-3-2008, in tax years ending after such date, under rules similar to the rules of Code Sec. 48(m) (as in effect on the day before the date of the enactment of the Revenue Reconciliation Act of 1990 (P.L. 101-508)).

P.L. 110-343, Division B, §103(e)(1):

Amended Code Sec. 48(a)(3) by striking the second sentence thereof. **Effective** for periods after 2-13-2008, in tax years ending after such date, under rules similar to the rules of Code Sec. 48(m) (as in effect on the day before the date of the enactment of the Revenue Reconciliation Act of 1990 (P.L. 101-508)). Prior to being stricken, the second sentence of Code Sec. 48(a)(3) read as follows:

The term "energy property" shall not include any property which is public utility property (as defined in section 46(f)(5) as in effect on the day before the date of the enactment of the Revenue Reconciliation Act of 1990).

P.L. 110-343, Division B, §104(a):

Amended Code Sec. 48(a)(3)(A), as amended by Act Sec. 103, by striking "or" at the end of clause (iv), by adding "or" at the end of clause (v), and by inserting after clause (v) a new clause (vi). **Effective** for periods after 10-3-2008, in tax years ending after such date, under rules similar to the rules of Code Sec. 48(m) (as in effect on the day before the date of the enactment of the Revenue Reconciliation Act of 1990 (P.L. 101-508)).

P.L. 110-343, Division B, §104(b):

Amended Code Sec. 48(a)(2)(A)(i) by striking "and" at the end of subclause (II) and by inserting after subclause (III) a new subclause (IV). **Effective** for periods after 10-3-2008, in tax years ending after such date, under rules similar to the rules of Code Sec. 48(m) (as in effect on the day before the date of the enactment of the Revenue Reconciliation Act of 1990 (P.L. 101-508)).

P.L. 110-343, Division B, §104(d):

Amended Code Sec. 48(a)(1), as amended by Act Sec. 103, by striking "paragraphs (1)(B), (2)(B), and (3)(B)" and inserting "paragraphs (1)(B), (2)(B), (3)(B), and (4)(B)". **Effective** for periods after 10-3-2008, in tax years ending after such date, under rules similar to the rules of Code Sec. 48(m) (as in effect on the day before the date of the enactment of the Revenue Reconciliation Act of 1990 (P.L. 101-508)).

P.L. 110-343, Division B, §105(a):

Amended Code Sec. 48(a)(3)(A), as amended by this Act, by striking "or" at the end of clause (v), by inserting "or" at the end of clause (vi), and by adding at the end a new clause (vii). **Effective** for periods after 10-3-2008, in tax years ending after such date, under rules similar to the rules of Code Sec. 48(m) (as in effect on the day before the date of the enactment of the Revenue Reconciliation Act of 1990 (P.L. 101-508)).

• 2006, Tax Relief and Health Care Act of 2006 (P.L. 109-432)

P.L. 109-432, Division A, §207(1):

Amended Code Sec. 48[(a)] by striking "January 1, 2008" both places it appears and inserting "January 1, 2009". **Effective** 12-20-2006.

• 2005, Gulf Opportunity Zone Act of 2005 (P.L. 109-135)

P.L. 109-135, §412(m):

Amended Code Sec. 48(a)(1), as amended by Act Sec. 1336 of P.L. 109-58, by striking "paragraph (1)(B) or (2)(B) of subsection (d)" and inserting "paragraphs (1)(B) and (2)(B) of subsection (c)". **Effective** 12-21-2005.

P.L. 109-135, §412(n)(1)-(2):

Amended Code Sec. 48(a)(3)(A) by redesignating clause (iii), as added by P.L. 109-58, §1336, as clause (iv) and by moving such clause to the end of such subparagraph, and by striking "or" at the end of clause (ii). **Effective** 12-21-2005.

• 2005, Energy Tax Incentives Act of 2005 (P.L. 109-58)

P.L. 109-58, §1336(a):

Amended Code Sec. 48(a)(3)(A) by striking "or" at the end of clause (i), by adding "or" at the end of clause (ii), and by inserting after clause (ii) a new clause (iii). **Effective** for periods after 12-31-2005, in tax years ending after such date, under rules similar to the rules of Code Sec. 48(m) (as in effect on the day before the date of the enactment of P.L. 101-508 [11-4-90.—CCH]).

P.L. 109-58, §1336(c):

Amended Code Sec. 48(a)(2)(A). **Effective** for periods after 12-31-2005, in tax years ending after such date, under rules similar to the rules of Code Sec. 48(m) (as in effect on the day before the date of the enactment of P.L. 101-508 [11-4-90.—CCH]). Prior to amendment, Code Sec. 48(a)(2)(A) read as follows:

(A) IN GENERAL.—The energy percentage is 10 percent.

P.L. 109-58, §1336(d):

Amended Code Sec. 48(a)(1) by inserting "except as provided in paragraph (1)(B) or (2)(B) of subsection (d)," before "the energy credit". **Effective** for periods after 12-31-2005, in tax years ending after such date, under rules similar to the rules of Code Sec. 48(m) (as in effect on the day before the date of the enactment of P.L. 101-508 [11-4-90.—CCH]).

P.L. 109-58, §1337(a):

Amended Code Sec. 48(a)(2)(A), as amended by this Act. **Effective** for periods after 12-31-2005, in tax years ending after such date, under rules similar to the rules of Code Sec. 48(m) (as in effect on the day before the date of the enactment of P.L. 101-508 [11-4-90.—CCH]). Prior to amendment, Code Sec. 48(a)(2)(A) read as follows:

(A) IN GENERAL.—The energy percentage is—

(i) in the case of qualified fuel cell property, 30 percent, and

(ii) in the case of any other energy property, 10 percent.

P.L. 109-58, §1337(b):

Amended Code Sec. 48(a)(3)(A) by striking "or" at the end of clause (i), by redesignating clause (ii) as clause (iii), and by inserting after clause (i) a new clause (ii). [Note: Act Sec. 1336(a) already struck "or" at the end of clause (i). Therefore, this amendment cannot be made. —CCH.] **Effective** for periods after 12-31-2005, in tax years ending after such date, under rules similar to the rules of Code Sec. 48(m) (as in effect on the day before the date of the enactment of P.L. 101-508 [11-4-90.—CCH]).

P.L. 109-58, §1337(c):

Amended Code Sec. 48(a)(3)(A)(i) by inserting "excepting property used to generate energy for the purposes of heating a swimming pool," after "solar process heat,". **Effective** for periods after 12-31-2005, in tax years ending after such date, under rules similar to the rules of Code Sec. 48(m) (as in effect on the date before the date of the enactment of P.L. 101-508 [11-4-90.—CCH]).

• 2004, American Jobs Creation Act of 2004 (P.L. 108-357)

P.L. 108-357, §322(d)(2)(A)(iii):

Amended Code Sec. 48 by redesignating paragraph (5) of subsection (a) as subsection (b). **Effective** with respect to expenditures paid or incurred after 10-22-2004.

P.L. 108-357, §322(d)(2)(B):

Amended Code Sec. 48 by striking "; REFORESTATION CREDIT" following "ENERGY CREDIT" in the heading. **Effective** with respect to expenditures paid or incurred after 10-22-2004.

P.L. 108-357, §710(e):

Amended Code Sec. 48(a)(3) by adding at the end a new sentence. **Effective** generally for electricity produced and sold after 10-22-2004, in tax years ending after such date.

• 1992, Energy Policy Act of 1992 (P.L. 102-486)

P.L. 102-486, §1916(a)(1)-(3):

Amended Code Sec. 48(a)(2) by striking "Except as provided in subparagraph (B), the" in subparagraph (A) and inserting "The", by striking subparagraph (B), and by redesignating subparagraph (C) as subparagraph (B). **Effective** 6-30-92. Prior to amendment, Code Sec. 48(a)(2)(B) read as follows:

(B) TERMINATION.—Effective with respect to periods after June 30, 1992, the energy percentage is zero. For purposes of the preceding sentence, rules similar to the rules of section 48(m) (as in effect on the day before the date of the enactment of the Revenue Reconciliation Act of 1990) shall apply.

• 1991, Tax Extension Act of 1991 (P.L. 102-227)

P.L. 102-227, §106:

Amended Code Sec. 48(a)(2)(B) by striking "December 31, 1991" and inserting "June 30, 1992". **Effective** 12-11-91.

[Sec. 48(b)]

(b) CERTAIN PROGRESS EXPENDITURE RULES MADE APPLICABLE.—Rules similar to the rules of subsections (c)(4) and (d) of section 46 (as in effect on the day before the date of the enactment of the Revenue Reconciliation Act of 1990) shall apply for purposes of subsection (a).

Amendments

• 2004, American Jobs Creation Act of 2004 (P.L. 108-357)

P.L. 108-357, §322(d)(2)(A)(i)-(iii):

Amended Code Sec. 48 by striking subsection (b), by striking "this subsection" in paragraph (5) of subsection (a) and inserting "subsection (a)", and by redesignating such paragraph (5) as subsection (b). **Effective** with respect to expenditures paid or incurred after 10-22-2004.

[Sec. 48(b)—Stricken]

Amendments

• 2004, American Jobs Creation Act of 2004 (P.L. 108-357)

P.L. 108-357, §322(d)(2)(A)(i):

Amended Code Sec. 48 by striking subsection (b). **Effective** with respect to expenditures paid or incurred after 10-22-2004. Prior to being stricken, Code Sec. 48(b) read as follows:

(b) REFORESTATION CREDIT.—

(1) IN GENERAL.—For purposes of section 46, the reforestation credit for any taxable year is 10 percent of the portion of the amortizable basis of any qualified timber property which was acquired during such taxable year and which is taken into account under section 194 (after the application of section 194(b)(1)).

(2) DEFINITIONS.—For purposes of this subpart, the terms "amortizable basis" and "qualified timber property" have the respective meanings given to such terms by section 194.

• 1990, Omnibus Budget Reconciliation Act of 1990 (P.L. 101-508)

P.L. 101-508, §11813(a):

Amended Code Sec. 48. **Effective,** generally, to property placed in service after 12-31-90. For exceptions, see Act Sec. 11813(c)(2), below.

P.L. 101-508, §11813(c)(2), provides:

(2) EXCEPTIONS.—The amendments made by this section shall not apply to—

(A) any transition property (as defined in section 49(e) of the Internal Revenue Code of 1986[)] (as in effect on the day before the date of the enactment of this Act),

(B) any property with respect to which qualified progress expenditures were previously taken into account under section 46(d) of such Code (as so in effect), and

(C) any property described in section 46(b)(2)(C) of such Code (as so in effect).

Prior to amendment, Code Sec. 48 read as follows:

SEC. 48. DEFINITIONS; SPECIAL RULES.

[Sec. 48(a)]

(a) SECTION 38 PROPERTY.—

(1) IN GENERAL.—Except as provided in this subsection, the term "section 38 property" means—

(A) tangible personal property (other than an air conditioning or heating unit), or

(B) other tangible property (not including a building and its structural components) but only if such property—

(i) is used as an integral part of manufacturing, production, or extraction or of furnishing transportation, communications, electrical energy, gas, water, or sewage disposal services, or

(ii) constitutes a research facility used in connection with any of the activities referred to in clause (i), or

(iii) constitutes a facility used in connection with any of the activities referred to in clause (i) for the bulk storage of fungible commodities (including commodities in a liquid or gaseous state), or

(C) elevators and escalators, but only if—

(i) the construction, reconstruction, or erection of the elevator or escalator is completed by the taxpayer after June 30, 1963, or

(ii) the elevator or escalator is acquired after June 30, 1963, and the original use of such elevator or escalator commences with the taxpayer and commences after such date, or

(D) single purpose agricultural or horticultural structures; or

(E) in the case of a qualified rehabilitated building, that portion of the basis which is attributable to qualified rehabilitation expenditures (within the meaning of subsection (g)), or

(F) in the case of qualified timber property (within the meaning of section 194(c)(1)), that portion of the basis of such property constituting the amortizable basis acquired during the taxable year (other than that portion of such amortizable basis attributable to property which otherwise qualifies as section 38 property) and taken into account under section 194 (after the application of section 194(b)(1)), or

(G) a storage facility (not including a building and its structural components) used in connection with the distribution of petroleum or any primary product of petroleum.

Such term includes only property to which section 168 applies without regard to any useful life and any other property with respect to which depreciation (or amortization in lieu of depreciation) is allowable and having a useful life (determined as of the time such property is placed in service) of 3 years or more. The preceding sentence shall not apply to property described in subparagraph (F) and, for purposes of this subpart, the useful life of such property shall be treated as its normal growing period.

(2) PROPERTY USED OUTSIDE THE UNITED STATES.—

(A) IN GENERAL.—Except as provided in subparagraph (B), the term "section 38 property" does not include property which is used predominantly outside the United States.

(B) EXCEPTIONS.—Subparagraph (A) shall not apply to—

(i) any aircraft which is registered by the Administrator of the Federal Aviation Agency and which is operated to and from the United States or is operated under contract with the United States;

(ii) rolling stock which is used within and without the United States and which is—

(I) of a domestic railroad corporation providing transportation subject to subchapter I of chapter 105 of title 49, or

(II) of a United States person (other than a corporation described in subclause (I)) but only if the rolling stock is not leased to one or more foreign persons for periods aggregating more than 12 months in any 24-month period;

(iii) any vessel documented under the laws of the United States which is operated in the foreign or domestic commerce of the United States;

(iv) any motor vehicle of a United States person (as defined in section 7701(a)(30)) which is operated to and from the United States;

(v) any container of a United States person which is used in the transportation of property to and from the United States;

(vi) any property (other than a vessel or an aircraft) of a United States person which is used for the purpose of exploring for, developing, removing, or transporting resources from the outer Continental Shelf (within the meaning of section 2 of the Outer Continental Shelf Lands Act, as amended and supplemented; (43 U.S.C. 1331));

(vii) any property which is owned by a domestic corporation (other than a corporation which has an election in effect under section 936) or by a United States citizen (other than a citizen entitled to the benefits of section 931 or 933) and which is used predominantly in a possession of the United States by such a corporation or such a citizen, or by a corporation created or organized in, or under the law of, a possession of the United States;

(viii) any communications satellite (as defined in section 103(3) of the Communications Satellite Act of 1962, 47 U. S. C. 702(3)), or any interest therein, of a United States person;

(ix) any cable, or any interest therein, of a domestic corporation engaged in furnishing telephone service to which section 46(c)(3)(B)(iii) applies (or of a wholly owned domestic subsidiary of such a corporation), if such cable is part of a submarine cable system which constitutes part of a communication link exclusively between the United States and one or more foreign countries;

(x) any property (other than a vessel or an aircraft) of a United States person which is used in international or territorial waters within the northern portion of the Western Hemisphere for the purpose of exploring for, developing, removing, or transporting resources from ocean waters or deposits under such waters; and

(xi) any property described in subsection (l)(3)(A)(ix) which is owned by a United States person and which is used in international or territorial waters to generate energy for use in the United States.

For purposes of clause (x), the term "northern portion of the Western Hemisphere" means the area lying west of the 30th meridian west of Greenwich, east of the international dateline, and north of the Equator, but not including any foreign country which is a country of South America.

(3) PROPERTY USED FOR LODGING.—Property which is used predominantly to furnish lodging or in connection with the furnishing of lodging shall not be treated as section 38 property. The preceding sentence shall not apply to—

(A) nonlodging commercial facilities which are available to persons not using the lodging facilities on the same basis as they are available to persons using the lodging facilities,

(B) property used by a hotel or motel in connection with the trade or business of furnishing lodging where the predominant portion of the accommodations is used by transients,

(C) coin-operated vending machines and coin-operated washing machines and dryers, and

(D) a certified historic structure to the extent of that portion of the basis which is attributable to qualified rehabilitation expenditures.

(4) PROPERTY USED BY CERTAIN TAX-EXEMPT ORGANIZATIONS.—Property used by an organization (other than a cooperative described in section 521) which is exempt from the tax imposed by this chapter shall be treated as section 38 property only if such property is used predominantly in an unrelated trade or business the income of which is subject to tax under section 511. If the property is debt-financed property (as defined in section 514(b)), the basis or cost of such property for purposes of computing qualified investment under section 46(c) shall include only that percentage of the basis or cost which is the same percentage as is used under section 514(a), for the year the property is placed in service, in computing the amount of gross income to be taken into account during such taxable year with respect to such property. If any qualified rehabilitated building is used by the tax-exempt organization pursuant to a lease, this paragraph shall not apply to that portion of the basis of such building which is attributable to qualified rehabilitation expenditures.

(5) PROPERTY USED BY GOVERNMENTAL UNITS OR FOREIGN PERSONS OR ENTITIES.—

(A) IN GENERAL.—Property used—

(i) by the United States, any State or political subdivision thereof, any possession of the United States, or any agency or instrumentality of any of the foregoing, or

(ii) by any foreign person or entity (as defined in section 168(h)(2)(C)), but only with respect to property to which section 168(h)(2)(A)(iii) applies (determined after the application of section 168(h)(2)(B)),

shall not be treated as section 38 property.

(B) EXCEPTION FOR SHORT-TERM LEASES.—

(i) IN GENERAL.—This paragraph and paragraph (4) shall not apply to any property by reason of use under a lease with a term of less than 6 months (determined under section 168(i)(3)).

(ii) EXCEPTION FOR CERTAIN OIL DRILLING PROPERTY AND CERTAIN CONTAINERS.—For purposes of this paragraph and paragraph (4), clause (i) shall be applied by substituting the lease term limitation in section 168(h)(1)(C)(ii) for the lease term limitation in clause (i) in the case of property which is leased to a foreign person or entity and—

(I) which is used in offshore drilling for oil and gas (including drilling vessels, barges, platforms, and drilling equipment) and support vessels with respect to such property, or

(II) which is a container described in section 48(a)(2)(B)(v) (without regard to whether such container is used outside the United States) or container chassis or trailer but only if such container, chassis, or trailer has a present class life of not more than 6 years.

(C) EXCEPTION FOR QUALIFIED REHABILITATED BUILDINGS LEASED TO GOVERNMENTS, ETC.—If any qualified rehabilitated building is leased to a governmental unit (or a foreign person or entity), this paragraph shall not apply to that portion of the basis of such building which is attributable to qualified rehabilitation expenditures.

(D) SPECIAL RULES FOR PARTNERSHIPS, ETC.—For purposes of this paragraph and paragraph (4), rules similar to the rules of paragraphs (5) and (6) of section 168(h) shall apply.

(E) CROSS REFERENCE.—

For provision providing special rules for the application of this paragraph and paragraph (4), see section 168(h).

(6) LIVESTOCK.—Livestock (other than horses) acquired by the taxpayer shall be treated as section 38 property, except that if substantially identical livestock is sold or otherwise disposed of by the taxpayer during the one-year period beginning 6 months before the date of such acquisition and if section 47(a) (relating to certain dispositions, etc., of section 38 property) does not apply to such sale or other disposition, then, unless such sale or other disposition constitutes an involuntary conversion (within the meaning of section 1033), the cost of the livestock acquired shall, for purposes of this subpart, be reduced by an amount equal to the amount realized on such sale or other disposition. Horses shall not be treated as section 38 property.

(7) PROPERTY COMPLETED ABROAD OR PREDOMINANTLY OF FOREIGNORIGIN.—

(A) IN GENERAL.—Property shall not be treated as section 38 property if—

(i) such property was completed outside the United States, or

(ii) less than 50 percent of the basis of such property is attributable to value added within the United States.

For purposes of this subparagraph, the term "United States" includes the Commonwealth of Puerto Rico and the possessions of the United States.

(B) PERIOD OF APPLICATION OF PARAGRAPH.—Except as provided in subparagraph (D), subparagraph (A) shall apply only with respect to property described in section 50 (as in effect before its repeal by the Revenue Act of 1978)—

(i) the construction, reconstruction, or erection of which by the taxpayer is begun after August 15, 1971, and on or before the date of termination of Proclamation 4074, or

(ii) which is acquired pursuant to an order placed on or before the date of termination of Proclamation 4074, unless acquired pursuant to an order which the taxpayer establishes was placed before August 16, 1971.

(C) PRESIDENT MAY EXEMPT ARTICLES.—If the President of the United States shall at any time determine that the application of subparagraph (A) to any article or class of articles is not in the public interest, he may by Executive order specify that subparagraph (A) shall not apply to such article or class of articles. Subparagraph (A) shall not apply to an article or class of articles for the period specified in such Executive order. Any period specified under the preceding sentence shall not apply to property ordered before (or to property the construction, reconstruction, or erection of which began before) the date of the Executive order specifying such period, except that, if the President determines it to be in the public interest, such period shall apply to property ordered (or property the construction, reconstruction, or erection of which began) after a date (before the date of the Executive order) specified in the Executive order.

(D) COUNTRIES MAINTAINING TRADE RESTRICTIONS OR ENGAGING IN DISCRIMINATORY ACTS.—If, on or after the date of the termination of Proclamation 4074, the President determines that a foreign country—

(i) maintains nontariff trade restrictions, including variable import fees, which substantially burden United States commerce in a manner inconsistent with provisions of trade agreements, or

(ii) engages in discriminatory or other acts (including tolerance of international cartels) or policies unjustifiably restricting United States commerce,

he may provide by Executive order for the application of subparagraph (A) to any article or class of articles manufactured or produced in such foreign country for such period as may be provided by Executive order.

(8) [Stricken.]

(9) [Repealed.]

(10) BOILERS FUELED BY OIL OR GAS.—

(A) IN GENERAL.—The term "section 38 property" does not include any boiler primarily fueled by petroleum or petroleum products (including natural gas) unless the use of coal is precluded by Federal air pollution regulations (or by State air pollution regulations in effect on October 1, 1978) or unless the use of such boiler will be an exempt use within the meaning of subparagraph (B). For purposes of the preceding sentence, the term "petroleum or petroleum products" does not include petroleum coke or petroleum pitch.

(B) EXEMPT USE DEFINED.—For purposes of subparagraph (A), the term "exempt use" means—

(i) use in an apartment, hotel, motel, or other residential facility,

(ii) use in a vehicle, aircraft, or vessel, or in transportation by pipeline,

(iii) use on a farm for farming purposes (within the meaning of section 6420(c)),

(iv) use in—

(I) a shopping center,

(II) an office building,

(III) a wholesale or retail establishment,

(IV) any other facility which is not an integral part of manufacturing, processing, or mining, or

(V) any facility for the production of electric power having a heat rate of less than 9,500 Btu's per kilowatt hour and which is capable of converting to synthetic fuels (as certified by the Secretary),

(v) use in the exploration for, or the development, extraction, transmission, or storage of, crude oil, natural gas, or natural gas liquids, and

(vi) use in Hawaii.

Except as provided in clauses (iv) (V) and (vi) of the preceding sentence, the term "exempt use" does not include use of a boiler which is public utility property (within the meaning of section 46(f)(5)).

Amendments

• 1990, Omnibus Budget Reconciliation Act of 1990 (P.L. 101-508)

P.L. 101-508, §11801(c)(6)(A):

Amended Code Sec. 48(a) by striking paragraph (8). **Effective**, generally, 11-5-91. For exceptions, see Act Sec. 11821(b), below. Prior to being stricken, Code Sec. 48(a)(8) read as follows:

(8) AMORTIZED PROPERTY.—Any property with respect to which an election under section 167(k), 184, or 188 applies shall not be treated as section 38 property.

P.L. 101-508, §11821(b), provides:

(b) SAVINGS PROVISION.—If—

(1) any provision amended or repealed by this part applied to—

(A) any transaction occurring before the date of the enactment of this Act,

(B) any property acquired before such date of enactment, or

(C) any item of income, loss, deduction, or credit taken into account before such date of enactment, and

(2) the treatment of such transaction, property, or item under such provision would (without regard to the amendments made by this part) affect liability for tax for periods ending after such date of enactment,

nothing in the amendments made by this part shall be construed to affect the treatment of such transaction, property, or item for purposes of determining liability for tax for periods ending after such date of enactment.

• 1988, Technical and Miscellaneous Revenue Act of 1988 (P.L. 100-647)

P.L. 100-647, §1002(a)(14)(A)-(G):

Amended Code Sec. 48(a)(5) by striking out "168(j)(4)(C)" and inserting in lieu thereof "168(h)(2)(C)", by striking out "168(j)(4)(A)(iii)" and inserting in lieu thereof "168(h)(2)(A)(iii)", by striking out "168(j)(4)(B)" and inserting in lieu thereof "168(h)(2)(B)", by striking out "168(j)(6)" and inserting in lieu thereof "168(i)(3)", by striking out "168(j)(3)(C)(ii)" and inserting in lieu thereof "168(h)(1)(C)(ii)", by striking out "paragraphs (8) and (9) of section 168(j)" and inserting in lieu thereof "paragraphs (5) and (6) of section 168(h)", and by striking out subparagraph (E) and inserting new subparagraph (E). **Effective** as if included in the provision of P.L. 99-514 to which it relates. Prior to amendment, Code Sec. 48(a)(5)(E) read as follows:

(E) CROSS REFERENCE.—

For provisions providing special rules for the application of this paragraph and paragraph (4), see section 168(j).

P.L. 100-647, §1002(a)(29):

Amended Code Sec. 48(a)(1) by striking out "recovery property (within the meaning of section 168)" in the material following subparagraph (G) and inserting in lieu thereof "property to which section 168 applies". **Effective** as if included in the provision of P.L. 99-514 to which it relates.

• 1986, Tax Reform Act of 1986 (P.L. 99-514)

P.L. 99-514, §1272(d)(5):

Amended Code Sec. 48(a)(2)(B)(vii) by striking out "932," after "931". For the **effective** date of the above amendment, see Act Sec. 1277, below.

P.L. 99-514, §1275(c)(5):

Amended Code Sec. 48(a)(2)(B)(vii) by striking out "or which is entitled to the benefits of section 934(b)" after "section 936" and by striking out ", 933, or 934(c)" and inserting in lieu thereof "or 933". For the **effective** date of the above amendment as well as special rules, see Act Sec. 1277, below.

P.L. 99-514, §1277, as amended by P.L. 100-647 §1012(z)(2), provides:

(a) IN GENERAL.—Except as otherwise provided in this section, the amendments made by this subtitle shall apply to taxable years beginning after December 31, 1986.

(b) SPECIAL RULE FOR GUAM, AMERICAN SAMOA, AND THE NORTHERN MARIANA ISLANDS.—The amendments made by this subtitle shall apply with respect to Guam, American Samoa, or the Northern Mariana Islands (and to residents thereof and corporations created or organized therein) only if (and so long as) an implementing agreement under section 1271 is in effect between the United States and such possession.

(c) SPECIAL RULES FOR THE VIRGIN ISLANDS.—

(1) IN GENERAL.—The amendments made by section 1275(c) shall apply with respect to the Virgin Islands (and residents thereof and corporations created or organized therein) only if (and so long as) an implementing agreement is in effect between the United States and the Virgin Islands with respect to the establishment of rules under which the evasion or avoidance of United States income tax shall not be permitted or facilitated by such possession. Any such implementing agreement shall be executed on behalf of the United States by the Secretary of the Treasury, after consultation with the Secretary of the Interior.

(2) SECTION 1275(b).—

(A) IN GENERAL.—The amendment made by section 1275(b) shall apply with respect to—

(i) any taxable year beginning after December 31, 1986, and

(ii) any pre-1987 open year.

(B) SPECIAL RULES.—In the case of any pre-1987 open year—

(i) the amendment made by section 1275(b) shall not apply to income from sources in the Virgin Islands or income effectively connected with the conduct of a trade or business in the Virgin Islands, and

(ii) the taxpayer shall be allowed a credit—

(I) against any additional tax imposed by subtitle A of the Internal Revenue Code of 1954 (by reason of the amendment made by section 1275(b)) on income not described in clause (i),

(II) for any tax paid to the Virgin Islands before the date of the enactment of this Act and attributable to such income.

For purposes of clause (ii)(II), any tax paid before January 1, 1987, pursuant to a process in effect before August 16, 1986, shall be treated as paid before the date of the enactment of this Act.

(C) PRE-1987 OPEN YEAR.—For purposes of this paragraph, the term "pre-1987 open year" means any taxable year beginning before January 1, 1987, if on the date of the enactment of this Act the assessment of a deficiency of income tax for such taxable year is not barred by any law or rule of law.

(D) EXCEPTION.—In the case of any pre-1987 open year, the amendment made by section 1275(b) shall not apply to any domestic corporation if—

(i) during the fiscal year which ended May 31, 1986, such corporation was actively engaged directly or through a subsidiary in the conduct of a trade or business in the Virgin Islands and such trade or business consists of business related to marine activities, and

(ii) such corporation was incorporated on March 31, 1983, in Delaware.

(E) EXCEPTION FOR CERTAIN TRANSACTIONS.—

(i) IN GENERAL.—In the case of any pre-1987 open year, the amendment made by section 1275(b) shall not apply to any income derived from transactions described in clause (ii) by 1 or more corporations which were formed in Delaware on or about March 6, 1981, and which have owned 1 or more office buildings in St. Thomas, United States Virgin Islands, for at least 5 years before the date of the enactment of this Act.

(ii) DESCRIPTION OF TRANSACTIONS.—The transactions described in this clause are—

(I) the redemptions of limited partnership interests for cash and property described in an agreement (as amended) dated March 12, 1981,

(II) the subsequent disposition of the properties distributed in such redemptions, and

(III) interests earned before January 1, 1987, on bank deposits of proceeds received from such redemptions to the extent such deposits are located in the United States Virgin Islands.

(iii) LIMITATION.—The aggregate reduction in tax by reason of this subparagraph shall not exceed $8,312,000. If the taxes which would be payable as the result of the application of the amendment made by section 1275(b) to pre-1987 open years exceeds the limitation of the preceding sentence, such excess shall be treated as attributable to income received in taxable years in reverse chronological order.

(d) REPORT ON IMPLEMENTING AGREEMENTS.—If, during the 1-year period beginning on the date of the enactment of this Act, any implementing agreement described in subsection (b) or (c) is not executed, the Secretary of the Treasury or his delegate shall report to the Committee on Finance of the United States Senate, the Committee on Ways and Means, and the Committee on Interior and Insular Affairs of the House of Representatives with respect to—

(1) the status of such negotiations, and

(2) the reason why such agreement has not been executed.

(e) TREATMENT OF CERTAIN UNITED STATES PERSONS.—Except as otherwise provided in regulations prescribed by the Secretary of the Treasury or his delegate, if a United States person becomes a resident of Guam, American Samoa, or the Northern Mariana Islands, the rules of section 877(c) of the Internal Revenue Code of 1954 shall apply to such person during the 10-year period beginning when such person became such a resident. Notwithstanding subsection (b), the preceding sentence shall apply to dispositions after December 31, 1985, in taxable years ending after such date.

(f) EXEMPTION FROM WITHHOLDING.—Notwithstanding subsection (b), the modification of section 884 of the Internal Revenue Code of 1986 by reason of the amendment to section 881 of such Code by section 1273(b)(1) of this Act shall apply to taxable years beginning after December 31, 1986.

P.L. 99-514, §1802(a)(4)(C):

Amended Code Sec. 48(a)(5) by redesignating subparagraph (D) as subparagraph (E) and by inserting after subparagraph (C) new subparagraph (D). **Effective** as if included in the provision of P.L. 98-369 to which such amendment relates.

P.L. 99-514, §1802(a)(5)(B):

Repealed Code Sec. 48(a)(5)(B)(iii). **Effective** as if included in the provision of P.L. 98-369 to which such amendment relates. Prior to repeal, Code Sec. 48(a)(5)(B)(iii) read as follows:

(iii) EXCEPTION FOR CERTAIN AIRCRAFT.—

(I) IN GENERAL.—In the case of any aircraft used under a qualifying lease (as defined in section 47(a)(7)(C)) and which is leased to a foreign person or entity before January 1, 1990, clause (i) shall be applied by substituting "3 years" for "6 months".

(II) RECAPTURE PERIOD EXTENDED.—For purposes of applying subparagraph (B) of section 47(a)(5) and paragraph (1) of section 47(a), there shall not be taken into account any period of a lease to which subclause (I) applies.

P.L. 99-514, §1802(a)(9)(A)(i)-(ii):

Amended Code Sec. 48(a)(4) by striking out "514(c)" and inserting in lieu thereof "514(b)", and by striking out "514(b)" and inserting in lieu thereof "514(a)". **Effective** as if included in the provision of P.L. 98-369 to which such amendment relates.

• 1984, Deficit Reduction Act of 1984 (P.L. 98-369)

P.L. 98-369, §31(b):

Amended Code Sec. 48(a)(5). **Effective** for property placed in service by the taxpayer after 5-23-83, in tax years ending after such date and to property placed in service by the taxpayer on or before 5-23-83, if the use by the tax-exempt entity is pursuant to a lease entered into after 5-23-83. Special rules appear in Act Sec. 31(g), which appears in the notes following Code Sec. 168(j). Prior to amendment, Sec. 48(a)(5) read as follows:

(5) Property Used by Governmental Units.—Property used by the United States, any State or political subdivision thereof, any international organization, or any agency or instrumentality of any of the foregoing shall not be treated as section 38 property. For purposes of the preceding sentence, the International Telecommunications Satellite Consortium, the International Maritime Satellite Organization, and any successor organization of such Consortium or Organization shall not be treated as an international organization. If any qualified rehabilitated building is used by the governmental unit pursuant to a lease, this paragraph shall not apply to that portion of the basis of such building which is attributable to qualified rehabilitation expenditures.

• 1982, Technical Corrections Act of 1982 (P.L. 97-448)

P.L. 97-448, §102(e)(2)(A):

Amended Code Sec. 48(a)(1)(G) by inserting "(not including a building and its structural components)" after "storage facility". **Effective** as if it had been included in the provision of P.L. 97-34 to which it relates.

• 1981, Economic Recovery Tax Act of 1981 (P.L. 97-34)

P.L. 97-34, §211(a)(2):

Repealed Code Sec. 48(a)(9). **Effective** for property placed in service after 12-31-80. Prior to repeal, Code Sec. 48(a)(9) read as follows:

(9) RAILROAD TRACK.—In the case of a railroad (including a railroad switching or terminal company) which uses the retirement-replacement method of accounting for depreciation of its railroad track, the term "section 38 property" includes replacement track material, if—

(A) the replacement is made pursuant to a scheduled program for replacement,

(B) the replacement is made pursuant to observations by maintenance-of-way personnel of specific track material needing replacement,

(C) the replacement is made pursuant to the detection by a rail-test car of specific track material needing replacement, or

(D) the replacement is made as a result of a casualty.

Replacements made as a result of a casualty shall be section 38 property only to the extent that, in the case of each casualty, the qualified investment with respect to the replacement track material exceeds $50,000. For purposes of this paragraph, the term "track material" includes ties, rail, other track material, and ballast.

P.L. 97-34, §211(c):

Amended Code Sec. 48(a)(1) by striking out the period at the end of subparagraph (F) and inserting in lieu thereof ", or"; and by inserting immediately after subparagraph (F) new subparagraph (G). **Effective** for periods after 12-31-80, under rules similar to those under Code Sec. 48(m).

P.L. 97-34, §211(e)(4):

Amended the second sentence of Code Sec. 48(a)(1) by striking out "includes only property" and inserting in lieu thereof "includes only recovery property (within the meaning of section 168 without regard to any useful life) and any other property." **Effective** for property placed in service after 12-31-80.

P.L. 97-34, §211(h):

Amended Code Sec. 48(a)(2)(B)(ii). **Effective** for tax years beginning after 12-31-80. Prior to amendment, Code Sec. 48(a)(2)(B)(ii) read as follows:

(ii) rolling stock, of a domestic railroad corporation providing transportation subject to subchapter I of chapter 105 of title 49, which is used within and without the United States;

P.L. 97-34, §212(c):

Amended Code Sec. 48(a)(3) by striking out "and" at the end of subparagraph (B); by striking out the period at the end of subparagraph (C) and inserting in lieu thereof ", and"; and by adding at the end thereof new subparagraph (D). **Effective** for expenditures incurred after 12-31-81, in tax years ending after such date.

P.L. 97-34, §212(e)(2), as amended by P.L. 97-448, §102(f)(1), provides:

(2) TRANSITIONAL RULE.—The amendments made by this section shall not apply with respect to any rehabilitation of a building if—

(A) the physical work on such rehabilitation began before January 1, 1982, and

(B) such building does not meet the requirements of paragraph (1) of section 48(g) of the Internal Revenue Code of 1954 (as amended by this Act).

P.L. 97-34, §212(d)(2)(A):

Amended Code Sec. 48(a)(8) by striking out "188, or 191" and inserting in lieu thereof "or 188". **Effective** for expenditures incurred after 12-31-81, in tax years ending after such date. But see the transitional rule following P.L. 97-34, §212(c), above.

P.L. 97-34, §214(a):

Amended Code Sec. 48(a)(4) by adding the last sentence at the end thereof. **Effective** for uses after 7-29-80, in tax years ending after such date.

P.L. 97-34, §214(b):

Amended Code Sec. 48(a)(5) by adding the last sentence at the end thereof. **Effective** for uses after 7-29-80, in tax years ending after such date.

• 1980, Miscellaneous Revenue Act of 1980 (P.L. 96-605)

P.L. 96-605, §109(a)

Amended Code Sec. 48(a)(5). **Effective** for tax years beginning after 12-31-79. Prior to amendment, Code Sec. 48(a)(5) read as follows:

"(5) PROPERTY USED BY GOVERNMENTAL UNITS.—Property used by the United States, any State or political subdivision thereof, any international organization (other than the International Telecommunications Satellite Consortium or any successor organization), or any agency or instrumentality of any of the foregoing shall not be treated as section 38 property."

• 1980, Recreational Boating Safety and Facilities Improvement Act of 1980 (P.L. 96-451)

P.L. 96-451, §302(a)(1)-(3):

Amended Code Sec. 48(a)(1) by striking out the period at the end of subparagraph (E) and inserting ", or"; by inserting after subparagraph (E) subparagraph (F); and by adding the last sentence at the end thereof. **Effective** for additions to capital account made after 12-31-79. (Note: An earlier Code Section 194 was added by P.L. 96-364, enacted on 9-26-80.)

• 1980, Crude Oil Windfall Profit Tax Act of 1980 (P.L. 96-223)

P.L. 96-223, §222(i)(2):

Amended Code Sec. 48(a)(2)(B) by striking out "and" at the end of clause (ix), by striking out the period at the end of clause (x) and inserting ", and", and by adding clause (xi). **Effective** for periods after 12-31-79, under rules similar to the rules of Code Sec. 48(m).

P.L. 96-223, §223(a)(1), as amended by P.L. 97-448, §202(c):

Amended Code Sec. 48(a)(10)(A) by adding a new last sentence. **Effective** for periods after 12-31-79, under rules similar to the rules of Code Sec. 48(m).

• 1979, Technical Corrections Act of 1979 (P.L. 96-222)

P.L. 96-222, §103(a)(2)(A):

Amended P.L. 95-600, §312(c)(2). **Effective** for tax years ending after 12-31-78.

Paragraphs (1) and (2) of section 46(f) and subparagraph (B) of section 48(a)(7) are each amended by striking out "described in section 50" and inserting in lieu thereof "described in section 50 (as in effect before its repeal by the Revenue Act of 1978)".

P.L. 96-222, §108(c)(6):

Amended Code Sec. 48(a)(10)(B) by changing "section 46(f)(51)" to "section 46(f)(5)". **Effective** as provided in P.L. 95-618, §301(d)(4), below.

• 1978, Energy Tax Act of 1978 (P.L. 95-618)

P.L. 95-618, §301(d)(1):

Amended Code Sec. 48(a)(1)(A). Effective as provided in Act Sec. 301(d)(4), below. Before amendment, such section read:

"(A) tangible personal property, or"

P.L. 95-618, §301(d)(2):

Added Code Sec. 48(a)(10). **Effective** as provided in Act Sec. 301(d)(4), below.

P.L. 95-618, §301(d)(4), provides:

"(4) EFFECTIVE DATE.—

(A) IN GENERAL.—The amendments made by this subsection shall apply to property which is placed in service after September 30, 1978.

(B) BINDING CONTRACTS.—The amendments made by this subsection shall not apply to property which is constructed, reconstructed, erected, or acquired pursuant to a contract which, on October 1, 1978, and at all times thereafter, was binding on the taxpayer."

• 1978, Revenue Act of 1978 (P.L. 95-600)

P.L. 95-600, §314(a), (c):

Amended Code Sec. 48(a)(1) by striking out the period at the end of subparagraph (C) and inserting in place thereof ", or" and by adding subparagraph (D). **Effective** for tax years ending after 8-15-71.

P.L. 95-600, §315(a), (d):

Amended Code. Sec. 48(a)(1) by striking out the period at the end of subparagraph (D) and inserting in place thereof "; or" and adding subparagraph (E). **Effective** for tax years ending after 10-31-78.

P.L. 95-600, §312(c)(3):

Amended Code Sec. 48(a)(7)(A) by striking out "(other than pre-termination property)". **Effective** for tax years ending after 12-31-78, Prior to amendment, such section read:

"(A) IN GENERAL.—Property (other than pre-termination property) shall not be treated as section 38 property if—

(i) such property was completed outside the United States, or

(ii) less than 50 percent of the basis of such property is attributable to value added within the United States.

For purposes of this subparagraph, the term "United States" includes the Commonwealth of Puerto Rico and the possessions of the United States."

P.L. 95-600, §312(c)(2):

Amended Code Sec. 48(a)(7)(B) by striking out "described in section 50". **Effective** for tax years ending after 12-31-78. Prior to amendment, such section read:

"(B) PERIOD OF APPLICATION OF PARAGRAPH.—Except as provided in subparagraph (D), subparagraph (A) shall apply only with respect to property described in section 50—

(i) the construction, reconstruction, or erection of which by the taxpayer is begun after August 15, 1971, and on or before the date of termination of Proclamation 4074, or

(ii) which is acquired pursuant to an order placed on or before the date of termination of Proclamation 4074, unless acquired pursuant to an order which the taxpayer establishes was placed before August 16, 1971."

P.L. 95-600, §315(c):

Amended Code Sec. 48(a)(8). **Effective** for property placed in service after 10-31-78, for tax years ending after such date. Before amendment, such section read:

"(8) AMORTIZED PROPERTY.—Any property with respect to which an election under section 167(k), 184, or 188 applies shall not be treated as section 38 property."

• 1978 (P.L. 95-473)

P.L. 95-473, §2(a)(2)(A):

Amended Code Section 48(a)(2)(B)(ii) by striking out "subject to part I of the Interstate Commerce Act" and substituting "providing transportation subject to subchapter I of chapter 105 of title 49". **Effective** 10-17-78.

• 1976, Tax Reform Act of 1976 (P.L. 94-455)

P.L. 94-455, §1051(h)(1):

Substituted "which has an election in effect under section 936 or which is entitled to the benefits of section 934(b)" for "entitled to the benefits of section 931 or 934(b)" in Code Sec. 48(a)(2)(B)(vii). **Effective** for tax years beginning after 12-31-75.

P.L. 94-455, §1901(a)(5)(A),(B):

Substituted "(43 U.S.C. 1331)" for "43 U.S.C. sec. 1331" in Code Sec. 48(a)(2)(B)(vi) and deleted ",sec." after "47 U.S.C." in Code Sec. 48(a)(2)(B)(viii). **Effective** for tax years beginning after 12-31-76.

P.L. 94-455, §1901(b)(11)(A):

Amended Code Sec. 48(a)(8) by striking out "187,". **Effective** for tax years beginning after 12-31-76.

P.L. 94-455, §2112(a)(1):

Deleted "169," and the last sentence in Code Sec. 48(a)(8). **Effective** for (A) property acquired by the taxpayer after 12-31-76, and (B) property the construction, reconstruction, or erection of which was completed by the taxpayer after 12-31-76 (but only to the extent of the basis thereof attributable to construction, reconstruction, or erection after such date), in taxable years beginning after such date. Prior to deletion, the sentence read as follows:

"In the case of any property to which section 169 applies, the preceding sentence shall apply only to so much of the adjusted basis of the property as (after the application of section 169(f)) constitutes the amortizable basis for purposes of section 169."

• 1975, Tax Reduction Act of 1975 (P.L. 94-12)

P.L. 94-12, §604(a):

Amended Code Sec. 48(a)(2) by adding "within the northern portion of the Western Hemisphere" in clause (x) and by adding the last sentence at the end of such subsection.

P.L. 94-12, §604(b), provides:

"(b) Effective Date.—

"(1) In general.—The amendments made by subsection (a) shall apply to property, the construction, reconstruction, or erection of which was completed after March 18, 1975, or the acquisition of which by the taxpayer occurred after such date.

"(2) Binding contract.—The amendments made by subsection (a) shall not apply to property constructed, reconstructed, erected, or acquired pursuant to a contract which was on April 1, 1974, and at all times thereafter, binding on the taxpayer.

"(3) Certain lease-back transactions, etc.—Where a person who is a party to a binding contract described in paragraph (2) transfers rights in such contract (or in the property to which such contract relates) to another person but a party to such contract retains a right to use the property under a lease with such other person, then to the extent of the transferred rights such other person shall, for purposes of paragraph (2), succeed to the position of the transferor with respect to such binding contract and such property. The preceding sentence shall apply, in any case in which the lessor does not make an election under section 48(d) of the Internal Revenue Code of 1954, only if a party to such contract retains a right to use the property under a long-term lease."

• 1971, Revenue Act of 1971 (P.L. 92-178)

P.L. 92-178, §102(a)(2):

Substituted "3 years" for "4 years" in the second sentence of Code Sec. 48(a)(1). **Effective** for property described in Code Sec. 50.

P.L. 92-178, §103:

Added paragraph (7). **Effective** as noted in that paragraph.

P.L. 92-178, §104(a)(1):

Effective for property described in Code Sec. 50. Substituted clauses (ii) and (iii) in Code Sec. 48(a)(1)(B) for the following:

"(ii) constitutes a research or storage facility used in connection with any of the activities referred to in clause (i), or"

P.L. 92-178, §104(b):

Amended Code Sec. 48(a)(3) by deleting "and" at the end of subparagraph (A), substituting ", and" for a period at the end of subparagraph (B), and adding subparagraph (C). **Effective** for property described in Code Sec. 50.

P.L. 92-178, §104(c)(1):

Added "(other than the International Telecommunications Satellite Consortium or any successor organization)" in Code Sec. 48(a)(5). **Effective** for tax years ending after 12-31-61

P.L. 92-178, § 104(c)(2):.

Amended Code Sec. 48(a)(2)(B) by deleting "and" at the end of clause (vi), substituting a semicolon for a period at the end of clause (vii), and adding clause (viii). **Effective** for tax years ending after 12-31-61.

P.L. 92-178, §104(c)(3):

Added clause (ix) in Code Sec. 48(a)(2)(B). **Effective** for property described in Code Sec. 50.

P.L. 92-178, §104(d):

Added clause (x) in Code Sec. 48(a)(2)(B). **Effective** for property described in Code Sec. 50.

P.L. 92-178, §104(e)

Substituted paragraph (6) in Code Sec. 48(a) for the following:

"(6) Livestock.—Livestock shall not be treated as section 38 property." **Effective** for property described in Code Sec. 50.

P.L. 92-178, §104(f)(1):

Added paragraph (8) in Code Sec. 48(a). **Effective** for property described in Code Sec. 50.

P.L. 92-178, §104(g):

Added paragraph (9) in Code Sec. 48(a). **Effective** for tax years ending after 12-31-61.

• 1969, Tax Reform Act of 1969 (P.L. 91-172)

P.L. 91-172, §121(d)(2)(A):

Amended Code Sec. 48(a)(4) by adding the last sentence. **Effective** for tax years beginning after 12-31-69.

• 1967 (P.L. 90-26)

P.L. 90-26, §3:

Amended Code Sec. 48(a)(2)(B)(i) by adding at the end thereof "or is operated under contract with the United States". **Effective** for tax years ending after 3-9-67.

• 1966, Foreign Investors Tax Act of 1966

P.L. 89-809, §201(a):

Amended Code Sec. 48(a)(2)(B) by striking out "and" at the end of clause (v), by substituting "; and" for the period at the end of clause (vi), and by adding a new clause (vii). **Effective** for tax years ending after 12-31-65, but only with respect to property placed in service after that date. In applying section 46(b) (relating to carryback and carryover of unused credits), the amount of any investment credit carryback to any tax year ending on or before 12-31-65, shall be determined without regard to these amendments.

• 1964, Revenue Act of 1964 (P.L. 88-272)

P.L. 88-272, §203(c):

Amended Code Sec. 48(a) by adding subparagraph (C) in paragraph (1). **Effective** for tax years ending after 6-30-63.

[Sec. 48(b)]

(b) NEW SECTION 38 PROPERTY.—For purposes of this subpart—

(1) IN GENERAL.—The term "new section 38 property" means section 38 property the original use of which commences with the taxpayer. Such term includes any section 38 property the reconstruction of which is completed by the taxpayer, but only with respect to that portion of the basis which is properly attributable to such reconstruction.

(2) SPECIAL RULE FOR SALE-LEASEBACKS.—For purposes of the first sentence of paragraph (1), in the case of any section 38 property which—

(A) is originally placed in service by a person, and

(B) is sold and leased back by such person, or is leased to such person, within 3 months after the date such property was originally placed in service,

such property shall be treated as originally placed in service not earlier than the date on which such property is used under the leaseback (or lease) referred to in subparagraph (B). The preceding sentence shall not apply to any property if the lessee and lessor of such property make an election under this sentence. Such an election, once made, may be revoked only with the consent of the Secretary.

(3) SPECIAL RULE FOR ENERGY PROPERTY.—The principles of paragraph (2) shall be applicable in determining whether the original use of property commences with the taxpayer for purposes of section 48(1)(2)(B)(ii).

Amendments

• 1986, Tax Reform Act of 1986 (P.L. 99-514)

P.L. 99-514, §1809(e)(1):

Amended Code Sec. 48(b)(1) by adding at the end thereof a new sentence. **Effective** as if included in the provision of P.L. 98-369 to which such amendment relates.

P.L. 99-514, §1809(e)(2)(A)-(D):

Amended Code Sec. 48(b)(2) by striking out "paragraph (1)" and inserting in lieu thereof "the first sentence of paragraph (1)", by striking out "used under the lease" and inserting in lieu thereof "used under the leaseback (or lease) referred to in subparagraph (B)", by adding at the end thereof a [2] new sentence[s] to read as above, and by striking out "3 months of" in subparagraph (B) and inserting in lieu thereof "3 months after". **Effective** as if included in the provision of P.L. 98-369 to which such amendment relates.

• 1984, Deficit Reduction Act of 1984 (P.L. 98-369)

P.L. 98-369, §114(a):

Amended Code Sec. 48(b). **Effective** for property originally placed in service after 4-11-84 (determined without regard to such amendment). Prior to amendment, Code Sec. 48(b) read as follows:

(b) New Section 38 Property.—For purposes of this subpart, the term "new section 38 property" means section 38 property—

(1) the construction, reconstruction, or erection of which is completed by the taxpayer after December 31, 1961, or

(2) acquired after December 31, 1961, if the original use of such property commences with the taxpayer and commences after such date.

In applying section 46(c)(1)(A) in the case of property described in paragraph (1), there shall be taken into account only that portion of the basis which is properly attributable to construction, reconstruction, or erection after December 31, 1961. For purposes of determining whether section 38 property subject to a lease is new section 38 property, such property shall be treated as originally placed in service not earlier than the date such property is used under the lease but only if such property is leased within 3 months after such property is placed in service.

• 1982, Tax Equity and Fiscal Responsibility Act of 1982 (P.L. 97-248)

P.L. 97-248, §209(c):

Amended Code Sec. 48(b) by adding the last sentence at the end thereof. **Effective** for agreements entered into after 12-31-83.

[Sec. 48(c)]

(c) USED SECTION 38 PROPERTY.—

(1) IN GENERAL.—For purposes of this subpart, the term "used section 38 property" means section 38 property acquired by purchase after December 31, 1961, which is not new section 38 property. Property shall not be treated as "used section 38 property" if, after its acquisition by the taxpayer, it is used by a person who used such property before such acquisition (or by a person who bears a relationship described in section 179(d)(2)(A) or (B) to a person who used such property before such acquisition).

(2) DOLLAR LIMITATION.—

(A) IN GENERAL.—The cost of used section 38 property taken into account under section 46(c)(1)(B) for any taxable year shall not exceed $125,000 ($150,000 for taxable years beginning after 1987). If such cost exceeds $125,000 (or $150,000 as the case may be), the taxpayer shall select (at such time and in such manner as the Secretary shall by regulations prescribe) the items to be taken into account, but only to the extent of an aggregate cost of $125,000 (or $150,000). Such a selection, once made, may be changed only in the manner, and to the extent, provided by such regulations.

(B) MARRIED INDIVIDUALS.—In the case of a husband or wife who files a separate return, the limitation under subparagraph (A) shall be $62,500 ($75,000 for taxable years beginning after 1987). This subparagraph shall not apply if the spouse of the taxpayer has no used section 38 property which may be taken into account as qualified investment for the taxable year of such spouse which ends within or with the taxpayer's taxable year.

(C) CONTROLLED GROUPS.—In the case of a controlled group, the amount specified under subparagraph (A) shall be reduced for each component member of the group by apportioning such amount among the component members of such group in accordance with their respective amounts of used section 38 property which may be taken into account.

(D) PARTNERSHIPS AND S CORPORATIONS.—In the case of a partnership, the limitation contained in subparagraph (A) shall apply with respect to the partnership and with respect to each partner. A similar rule shall apply in the case of an S corporation and its shareholders.

(3) DEFINITIONS.—For purposes of this subsection—

(A) PURCHASE.—The term "purchase" has the meaning assigned to such term by section 179(d)(2).

(B) COST.—The cost of used section 38 property does not include so much of the basis of such property as is determined by reference to the adjusted basis of other property held at any time by the person acquiring such property. If property is disposed of (other than by reason of its destruction or damage by fire, storm, shipwreck, or other casualty, or its theft) and used section 38 property similar or related in service or use is acquired as a replacement therefor in a transaction to which the preceding sentence does not apply, the cost of the used section 38 property acquired shall be its basis reduced by the adjusted basis of the property replaced. The cost of used section 38 property shall not be reduced with respect to the adjusted basis of any property disposed of if, by reason of section 47, such disposition involved an increase of tax or a reduction of the unused credit carrybacks or carryovers described in section 39.

(C) CONTROLLED GROUP.—The term "controlled group" has the meaning assigned to such term by section 1563(a), except that the phrase "more that 50 percent" shall be substituted for the phrase "at least 80 percent" each place it appears in section 1563(a)(1).

Amendments

• 1984, Deficit Reduction Act of 1984 (P.L. 98-369)

P.L. 98-369, §11(a):

Amended Code Sec. 48(c)(2)(A) by striking out "$150,000 ($125,000 for taxable years beginning in 1981, 1982, 1983, or 1984)" and inserting in lieu thereof "$125,000 ($150,000 for taxable years beginning after 1987)" and by striking out "$150,000 (or $125,000)" each place it appeared and inserting in lieu thereof "$125,000 (or $150,000"). **Effective** for tax years ending after 12-31-83.

P.L. 98-369, §11(b):

Amended Code Sec. 48(c)(2)(B) by striking out "$75,000 ($62,500 for taxable years beginning in 1981, 1982, 1983, or 1984)" and inserting in lieu thereof "$62,500 ($75,000 for taxable years beginning after 1987)". **Effective** for tax years ending after 12-31-83.

P.L. 98-369, §474(o)(10):

Amended Code Sec. 48(c)(3)(B) by striking out "section 46(b)" and inserting in lieu thereof "section 39". **Effective** for tax years beginning after 12-31-83, and to carryback from such years, but shall not be construed as reducing the amount of any credit allowable for qualified investment in tax years beginning before 1-1-84.

• 1982, Subchapter S Revision Act of 1982 (P.L. 97-354)

P.L. 97-354, §3(d):

Amended Code Sec. 48(c)(2)(D) (1) by adding at the end thereof the following new sentence: "A similar rule shall apply in the case of an S corporation and its shareholders.", (2) and by striking out "PARTNERSHIPS" in the subparagraph heading and inserting in lieu thereof "PARTNERSHIPS AND S CORPORATIONS". **E ffective** for tax years beginning after 12-31-82.

• 1981, Economic Recovery Tax Act of 1981 (P.L. 97-34)

P.L. 97-34, §213(a), as amended by P.L. 97-448, §102(g):

Amended Code Sec. 48(c)(2)(A), (B), and (C). **Effective** for tax years beginning after 12-31-80. Prior to amendment, Code Sec. 48(c)(2)(A), (B), and (C) read as follows:

(2) DOLLAR LIMITATION.—

(A) IN GENERAL.—The cost of used section 38 property taken into account under section 46(c)(1)(B) for any taxable year shall not exceed $100,000. If such cost exceeds $100,000, the taxpayer shall select (at such time and in such manner as the Secretary shall by regulations prescribe) the items to be taken into account, but only to the extent of an aggregate cost of $100,000. Such a selection, once made, may be changed only in the manner, and to the extent, provided by such regulations.

(B) MARRIED INDIVIDUALS.—In the case of a husband or wife who files a separate return, the limitation under subparagraph (A) shall be $50,000 in lieu of $100,000. This subparagraph shall not apply if the spouse of the taxpayer has no used section 38 property which may be taken into account as qualified investment for the taxable year of such spouse which ends within or with the taxpayer's taxable year.

(C) CONTROLLED GROUPS.—In the case of a controlled group, the $100,000 amount specified under subparagraph (A) shall be reduced for each component member of the group by apportioning $100,000 among the component members of such group in accordance with their respective amounts of used section 38 property which may be taken into account.

• 1978, Revenue Act of 1978 (P.L. 95-600)

P.L. 95-600, §311(b):

Amended P.L. 94-12, §301(c)(2) by striking out "and before January 1, 1981". **Effective** 11-6-78.

• 1976, Tax Reform Act of 1976 (P.L. 94-455)

P.L. 94-455, §1906(b)(13)(A):

Amended 1954 Code by substituting "Secretary" for "Secretary or his delegate" each place it appeared. **Effective** 2-1-77.

• 1975, Tax Reduction Act of 1975 (P.L. 94-12)

P.L. 94-12, §301(c):

Amended Sec. 48(c)(2) by substituting "$100,000" for "$50,000" each place the latter appeared and by substituting "$50,000" for "$25,000". **Effective** only for tax years beginning after 12-31-74, and before 1-1-81 [**effective** date changed by P.L. 94-455, §801].

• 1969, Tax Reform Act of 1969 (P.L. 91-172)

P.L. 91-172, §401(e)(2):

Amended Sec. 48(c)(2)(C). **Effective** for tax years ending on or after 12-31-70. Prior to amendment, Sec. 48(c)(2)(C) read as follows:

(C) Affiliated groups.—In the case of an affiliated group, the $50,000 amount specified under subparagraph (A) shall be reduced for each member of the group by apportioning $50,000 among the members of such group in accordance with their respective amounts of used section 38 property which may be taken into account.

P.L. 91-172, §401(e)(3):

Amended Sec. 48(c)(3)(C). **Effective** for tax years ending on or after 12-31-70. Prior to amendment, Sec. 48(c)(3)(C) read as follows:

(C) Affiliated group.—The term "affiliated group" has the meaning assigned to such term by section 1504(a), except that—

(i) the phrase "more than 50 percent" shall be substituted for the phrase "at least 80 percent" each place it appears in section 1504(a), and

(ii) all corporations shall be treated as includible corporations (without any exclusion under section 1504(b)).

[Sec. 48(d)]

(d) CERTAIN LEASED PROPERTY.—

(1) GENERAL RULE.—A person (other than a person referred to in section 46(e)(1)) who is a lessor of property may (at such time, in such manner, and subject to such conditions as are provided by regulations prescribed by the Secretary) elect with respect to any new section 38 property (other than property described in paragraph (4)) to treat the lessee as having acquired such property for an amount equal to—

(A) except as provided in subparagraph (B), the fair market value of such property, or

(B) if the property is leased by a corporation which is a component member of a controlled group (within the meaning of section 38(c)(3)(B)) to another corporation which is a component member of the same controlled group, the basis of such property to the lessor.

(2) SPECIAL RULE FOR CERTAIN SHORT TERM LEASES.—

(A) IN GENERAL.—A person (other than a person referred to in section 46(e)(1)) who is a lessor of property described in paragraph (4) may (at such time, in such manner, and subject to such conditions as are provided by regulations prescribed by the Secretary) elect with respect to such property to treat the lessee as having acquired a portion of such property for the amount determined under subparagraph (B).

(B) DETERMINATION OF LESSEE'S INVESTMENT.—The amount for which a lessee of property described in paragraph (4) shall be treated as having acquired a portion of such property is an amount equal to a fraction, the numerator of which is the term of the lease and the denominator of which is the class life of the property leased (determined under section 167(m)), of the amount for which the lessee would be treated as having acquired the property under paragraph (1).

(C) DETERMINATION OF LESSOR'S QUALIFIED INVESTMENT.—The qualified investment of a lessor of property described in paragraph (4) in any such property with respect to which he has made an election under this paragraph is an amount equal to his qualified investment in such property (as determined under section 46(c)) multiplied by a fraction equal to the excess of one over the fraction used under subparagraph (B) to determine the lessee's investment in such property.

(3) LIMITATIONS.—The elections provided by paragraphs (1) and (2) may be made with respect to property which would be new section 38 property if acquired by the lessee. For purposes of the preceding sentence and section 46(c), the useful life of property in the hands of the lessee is the useful life of such property in the hands of the lessor. If a lessor makes the election provided by paragraph (1) with respect to any property, the lessee shall be treated for all purposes of this subpart as having acquired such property. If a lessor makes the election provided by paragraph (2) with respect to any property, the lessee shall be treated for all purposes of this subpart as having acquired a fractional portion of such property equal to the fraction determined under paragraph (2)(B) with respect to such property.

(4) PROPERTY TO WHICH PARAGRAPH (2) APPLIES.—Paragraph (2) shall apply only to property which—

(A) is new section 38 property,

(B) has a class life (determined under section 167(m)) in excess of 14 years,

(C) is leased for a period which is less than 80 percent of its class life, and

(D) is not leased subject to a net lease (within the meaning of section 57(c)(1)(B) (as in effect on the day before the date of the enactment of the Tax Reform Act of 1986)).

(5) COORDINATION WITH BASIS ADJUSTMENT.—In the case of any property with respect to which an election is made under this subsection—

(A) subsection (q) (other than paragraph (4)) shall not apply with respect to such property,

(B) the lessee of such property shall include ratably in gross income over the shortest recovery period which could be applicable under section 168 with respect to such property an amount equal to 50 percent of the amount of the credit allowable under section 38 to the lessee with respect to such property, and

(C) in the case of a disposition of such property to which section 47 applies, this paragraph shall be applied in accordance with regulations prescribed by the Secretary.

(6) COORDINATION WITH AT-RISK RULES.—

(A) EXTENSION OF AT-RISK RULES TO CERTAIN LESSORS.—

(i) IN GENERAL.—If—

(I) a lessor makes an election under this subsection with respect to any at-risk property leased to an at-risk lessee, and

(II) but for this clause, section 46(c)(8) would not apply to such property in the hands of the lessor,

section 46(c)(8) shall apply to the lessor with respect to such property.

(ii) EXCEPTIONS.—Clause (i) shall not apply—

(I) if the lessor manufactured or produced the property,

(II) if the property has a readily ascertainable fair market value, or

(III) in circumstances which the Secretary determines by regulations to be circumstances where the application of clause (i) is not necessary to carry out the purposes of section 46(c)(8).

(B) REQUIREMENT THAT LESSOR BE AT RISK.—In the case of any property which, in the hands of the lessor, is property to which section 46(c)(8) applies, the amount of the credit allowable to the lessee under section 38 with respect to such property by reason of an election under this subsection shall at no time exceed the credit which would have been allowable to the lessor with respect to such property (determined without regard to section 46(e)(3) if—

(i) the lessor's basis in such property were equal to the lessee acquisition amount, and

(ii) no election had been made under this subsection.

(C) LESSEE SUBJECT TO AT-RISK LIMITATIONS.—

(i) IN GENERAL.—In the case of any lease where—

(I) the lessee is an at-risk lessee,

(II) the property is at-risk property, and

(III) the at-risk percentage is less than the required percentage,

any credit allowable under section 38 to the lessee by reason of an election under this subsection (hereinafter in this paragraph referred to as the "total credit") shall be allowable only as provided in subparagraph (D).

(ii) AT-RISK PERCENTAGE.—For purposes of this paragraph, the term "at-risk percentage" means the percentage obtained by dividing—

(I) the present value (as of the time the lease is entered into) of the aggregate lease at-risk payments, by

(II) the lessee acquisition amount.

For purposes of subclause (I), the present value shall be determined by using a discount rate equal to the underpayment rate in effect under section 6621 as of the time the lease is entered into.

(iii) REQUIRED PERCENTAGE.—For purposes of clause (i)(III), the term "required percentage" means the sum of—

(I) 2 times the sum of the percentages applicable to the property under section 46(a), plus

(II) 10 percent.

In the case of 3-year property, such term means 60 percent of the required percentage determined under the preceding sentence.

(iv) LESSEE ACQUISITION AMOUNT.—For purposes of this paragraph, the term "lessee acquisition amount" means the amount for which the lessee is treated as having acquired the property by reason of an election under this subsection.

(v) LEASE AT-RISK PAYMENT.—For purposes of this paragraph, the term "lease at-risk payment" means any rental payment—

(I) which the lessee is required to make under the lease in all events, and

(II) with respect to which the lessee is not protected against loss through nonrecourse financing, guarantees, stop-loss agreements, or other similar arrangements.

(D) YEAR FOR WHICH CREDIT ALLOWABLE.—

(i) IN GENERAL.—Except as provided in clause (ii), in any case to which subparagraph (C)(i) applies, the portion of the total credit allowable for any taxable year shall be an amount which bears the same ratio to such total credit as—

(I) the aggregate rental payments made by the lessee under the lease during such taxable year, bears to

(II) the lessee acquisition amount.

(ii) REMAINING AMOUNT ALLOWABLE FOR YEAR IN WHICH AGGREGATE RENTAL PAYMENTS EXCEED REQUIRED PERCENTAGE OF ACQUISITION AMOUNT.—The total credit (to the extent not allowable for a preceding taxable year) shall be allowable for the first taxable year as of the close of which the aggregate rental payments made by the lessee under the lease equal or exceed the required percentage (as defined in subparagraph (C)(iii)) of the lessee acquisition amount.

(E) DEFINITION OF AT-RISK LESSEE AND AT-RISK PROPERTY.—For purposes of this paragraph—

(i) AT-RISK LESSEE.—The term "at-risk lessee" means any lessee who is a taxpayer described in section 465(a)(1).

(ii) AT-RISK PROPERTY.—The term "at-risk property" means any property used by an at-risk lessee in connection with an activity with respect to which any loss is subject to limitation under section 465.

(F) SPECIAL RULES FOR SUBPARAGRAPHS(c) AND(d).—

(i) SUBPARAGRAPHS(c) AND(d) APPLY IN LIEU OF OTHER AT-RISK RULES.—In the case of any election under this subsection, paragraphs (8) and (9) of section 46(c) and subsection (d) of section 47 shall only apply with respect to the lessor.

(ii) APPLICATION TO PARTNERSHIPS AND S CORPORATIONS.—For purposes of subparagraphs (C) and (D), rules similar to the rules of subparagraph (E) of section 46(c)(8) shall apply.

(iii) SUBSEQUENT REDUCTIONS IN AT-RISK AMOUNT.—Under regulations prescribed by the Secretary, the principles of subsection (d) of section 47 shall apply for purposes of subparagraphs (C) and (D).

(G) REGULATIONS.—The Secretary shall prescribe such regulations as may be necessary to carry out the purposes of this paragraph, including regulations—

(i) providing for such adjustments as may be appropriate where expenses connected with the lease are borne by the lessor, and

(ii) providing the extent to which contingencies in the lease will be disregarded.

Amendments

• 1986, Tax Reform Act of 1986 (P.L. 99-514)

P.L. 99-514, §701(e)(4)(c):

Amended Code Sec. 48(d)(4)(D) by striking out "section 57(c)(1)(B)" and inserting in lieu thereof "section 57(c)(1)(B) (as in effect on the day before the date of the enactment of the Tax Reform Act of 1986)". **Effective**, generally, for tax years beginning after 12-31-86. However, for exceptions, see the amendment notes following Code Sec. 56.

P.L. 99-514, §1511(c)(3):

Amended Code Sec. 48(d)(6)(C)(ii) by striking out "the rate" in the last sentence and inserting in lieu thereof "the underpayment rate". **Effective** for purposes of determining interest for periods after 12-31-86.

• 1984, Deficit Reduction Act of 1984 (P.L. 98-369)

P.L. 98-369, §474(o)(11):

Amended Code Sec. 48(d)(1)(B) by striking out "section 46(a)(6)" and inserting in lieu thereof "section 38(c)(3)(B)". **Effective** for tax years beginning after 12-31-83, and to carryback from such years, but shall not be construed as reducing the amount of any credit allowable for qualified investment in tax years beginning before 1-1-84.

P.L. 98-369, §431(c):

Amended Code Sec. 48(d) by adding paragraph (6). **Effective** for property placed in service after 7-18-84, in tax years ending after such date; except that such amendments shall not apply to any property to which the amendments made by section 211(f) of P.L. 97-34 do not apply. However, at the election of the taxpayer, the amendment applied by this section shall apply as if included in the amendments made by section 211(f) of P.L. 97-34. Any election made under the preceding sentence shall apply to all property of the taxpayer to which the amendments made by such section 211(f) apply and shall be made at such time and in such manner as the Secretary of the Treasury or his delegate may by regulations prescribe.

• 1982, Tax Equity and Fiscal Responsibility Act of 1982 (P.L. 97-248)

P.L. 97-248, §205(a)(4):

Amended Code Sec. 48(d) by adding at the end thereof new paragraph (5). **Effective** for periods after 12-31-82, under rules similar to the rules of Code Sec. 48(m) except that the amendments do not apply to any property that—

(i) is constructed, reconstructed, erected, or acquired pursuant to a contract which was entered into after 8-13-81, and was, on 7-1-82, and at all times thereafter, binding on the taxpayer,

(ii) is placed in service after 12-31-82, and before 1-1-86,

(iii) with respect to which an election under section 168(f)(8)(A) of such Code is not in effect at any time, and

(iv) is not described in section 167(1)(3)(A) of such Code.

P.L. 97-248, §205(c)(1)(C)-(E), provides the following special rules:

(C) Special rule for integrated manufacturing facilities.—

(i) In general.—In the case of any integrated manufacturing facility, the requirements of clause (i) of subparagraph (B) shall be treated as met if—

(I) the on-site construction of the facility began before July 1, 1982, and

(II) during the period beginning after August 13, 1981, and ending on July 1, 1982, the taxpayer constructed (or entered into binding contracts for the construction of) more than 20 percent of the cost of such facility.

(ii) Integrated manufacturing facility.—For purposes of clause (i) the term "integrated manufacturing facility" means 1 or more facilities—

(I) located on a single site,

(II) for the manufacture of 1 or more manufactured products from raw materials by the application of 2 or more integrated manufacturing processes.

(D) Special rule for historic structures.—In the case of any certified historic structure (as defined in section 48(g)(3) of the Internal Revenue Code of 1954), clause (i) of subparagraph (B) shall be applied by substituting "December 31, 1980" for "August 13, 1981."

(E) Certain projects with respect to historic structures.—In the case of any certified historic structure (as so defined), the requirements of clause (i) of subparagraph (B) shall be treated as met with respect to such property—

(i) if the rehabilitation begins after December 31, 1980, and before July 1, 1982, or

(ii) if—

(I) before July 1, 1982, a public offering with respect to interests in such property was registered with the Securities and Exchange Commission,

(II) before such date an application with respect to such property was filed under section 8 of the United States Housing Act of 1937, and

(III) such property is placed in service before July 1, 1984.

• 1978, Revenue Act of 1978, (95-600)

P.L. 95-600, §703(a)(3):

Amended Code Sec. 48(d)(1)(B) by striking out "section 46(a)(5)" and inserting in place thereof "section 46(a)(6)". **Effective** 10-4-76.

P.L. 95-600, §703(a)(4):

Amended Code Sec. 48(d)(4)(D) by striking out "section 57(c)(2)" and inserting in place thereof "section 57(c)(1)(B)". **Effective** 10-4-76.

• 1976, Tax Reform Act of 1976 (P.L. 94-455)

P.L. 94-455, §1906(b)(13)(A):

Amended 1954 Code by substituting "Secretary" for "Secretary or his delegate" each place it appeared. **Effective** 2-1-77.

• 1975, Tax Reduction Act of 1975 (P.L. 94-12)

P.L. 94-12, §302(c)(3):

Amended Sec. 48(d)(1) and (2) by substituting "section 46(e)(1)" for "section 46(d)(1)". **Effective** for tax years ending after 12-31-74.

• 1971 Revenue Act of 1971 (P.L. 92-178)

P.L. 92-178, §108(c):

Amended Code Sec. 48(d). **Effective** for leases entered into after 11-8-71. Prior to amendment, Code Sec. 48(d) read as follows:

"(d) Certain Leased Property.—A person (other than a person referred to in section 46(d)(1)) who is a lessor of property may (at such time, in such manner, and subject to such conditions as are provided by regulations prescribed by the Secretary or his delegate) elect with respect to any new section 38 property to treat the lessee as having acquired such property for an amount equal to—

"(1) except as provided in paragraph (2), the fair market value of such property, or

"(2) if such property is leased by a corporation which is a component member of a controlled group (within the meaning of section 46(a)(5)) to another corporation which is a component member of the same controlled group, the basis of such property to the lessor.

The election provided by the preceding sentence may be made only with respect to property which would be new section 38 property if acquired by the lessee. For purposes of the preceding sentence and section 46(c), the useful life of property in the hands of the lessee is the useful life of such property in the hands of the lessor. If a lessor makes the election provided by this subsection with respect to any property, the lessee shall be treated for all purposes of this subpart as having acquired such property. In the case of suspension period property which is leased and is property of a kind which the lessor ordinarily leases to one lessee for a substantial portion of the useful life of the property, the lessor of the property shall be deemed to have elected to treat the first such lessee as having acquired such property for purposes of applying the last sentence of section 46(a)(2). In the case of section 38 property which (i) is leased after October 9, 1966 (other than pursuant to a binding contract to lease entered into before October 10, 1966), (ii) is not suspension period property with respect to the lessor but is suspension period property if acquired by the lessee, and (iii) is property of the same kind which the lessor ordinarily sold to customers before October 10, 1966, or ordinarily leased before such date and made an election under this subsection, the lessor of such property shall be deemed to have made an election under this subsection with respect to such property."

P.L. 92-178, §108(b):

Amended Code Sec. 48(d) (see immediately above) by substituting "section 46(d)(1)" for "section 46(d)". **Effective** for leases entered into after 9-22-71.

• 1969, Tax Reform Act of 1969 (P.L. 91-172)

P.L. 91-172, §401(e)(4):

Amended Sec. 48(d)(2). **Effective** for tax years ending on or after 12-31-70. Prior to amendment, Sec. 48(d)(2) read as follows:

(2) if such property is leased by a corporation which is a member of an affiliated group (within the meaning of section 46(a)(5)) to another corporation which is a member of the same affiliated group, the basis of such property to the lessor.

• 1966 (P.L. 89-800)

P.L. 89-800, §1(b):

Amended Code Sec. 48(d) by adding the last two sentences. **Effective** for tax years ending after 10-9-66.

• 1964, Revenue Act of 1964 (P.L. 88-272)

P.L. 88-272, §203(a)(3)(A):

Repealed last sentence of subsection (d), which read as follows: "If a lessor makes the election provided by this subsection with respect to any property, then, under regulations prescribed by the Secretary or his delegate, subsection (g) shall not apply with respect to such property and the deductions otherwise allowable under section 162 to the lessee for amounts paid to the lessor under the lease shall be adjusted in a manner consistent with the provisions of subsection (g)." For property placed in service after 12-31-63, repeal **effective** with respect to tax years ending after such date. For property placed in service before 1-1-64, repeal **effective** with respect to tax years beginning after 12-31-63.

P.L. 88-272, §203(b):

Amended paragraphs (1) and (2). **Effective** with respect to property possession of which is transferred to a lessee on or after 2-26-64, the date of enactment of the Act. Prior to amendment, paragraphs (1) and (2) read as follows:

"(1) if such property was constructed by the lessor (or by a corporation which controls or is controlled by the lessor within the meaning of section 368(c)), the fair market value of such property, or

"(2) if paragraph (1) does not apply, the basis of such property to the lessor."

[Sec. 48(e)—Repealed]

Amendments

• 1982, Subchapter S Revision Act of 1982 (P.L. 97-354)

P.L. 97-354, §5(a)(7):

Repealed Code Sec. 48(e). **Effective** for tax years beginning after 12-31-82. Prior to repeal, Code Sec. 48(e) read as follows:

(e) SUBCHAPTER S CORPORATIONS.—In the case of an electing small business corporation (as defined in section 1371)—

(1) the qualified investment for each taxable year shall be apportioned pro rata among the persons who are shareholders of such corporation on the last day of such taxable year; and

(2) any person to whom any investment has been apportioned under paragraph (1) shall be treated (for purposes of this subpart) as the taxpayer with respect to such investment, and such investment shall not (by reason of such apportionment) lose its character as an investment in new section 38 property or used section 38 property, as the case may be.

[Sec. 48(f)]

(f) ESTATES AND TRUSTS.—In the case of an estate or trust—

(1) the qualified investment for any taxable year shall be apportioned between the estate or trust and the beneficiaries on the basis of the income of the estate or trust allocable to each, and

(2) any beneficiary to whom any investment has been apportioned under paragraph (1) shall be treated (for purposes of this subpart) as the taxpayer with respect to such investment, and such investment shall not (by reason of such apportionment) lose its character as an investment in new section 38 property or used section 38 property, as the case may be.

Amendments

• 1984, Deficit Reduction Act of 1984 (P.L. 98-369)

P.L. 98-369, §474(o)(12):

Amended Code Sec. 48(f) by adding "and" at the end of paragraph (1), striking out ", and" at the end of paragraph (2) and inserting in lieu thereof a period, and by striking out paragraph (3). **Effective** for tax years beginning after 12-31-83, and to carryback from such years, but shall not be construed as reducing the amount of any credit allowable for qualified investment in tax years beginning before 1-1-84. Prior to being stricken, paragraph (3) read as follows:

(3) the $25,000 amount specified under subparagraphs (A) and (B) of section 46(a)(3) applicable to such estate or trust shall be reduced to an amount which bears the same ratio to $25,000 as the amount of the qualified investment allocated to the estate or trust under paragraph (1) bears to the entire amount of the qualified investment.

• 1976, Tax Reform Act of 1976 (P.L. 94-455)

P.L. 94-455, §802(b)(6):

Substituted "section 46(a)(3)" for "section 46(a)(2)" in Code Sec. 48(f). **Effective** for tax years beginning after 12-31-75.

[Sec. 48(g)]

(g) SPECIAL RULES FOR QUALIFIED REHABILITATED BUILDINGS.—For purposes of this subpart—

(1) QUALIFIED REHABILITATED BUILDING.—For purposes of this subsection—

(A) IN GENERAL.—The term "qualified rehabilitated building" means any building (and its structural components) if—

(i) such building has been substantially rehabilitated,

(ii) such building was placed in service before the beginning of the rehabilitation, and

(iii) in the case of any building other than a certified historic structure, in the rehabilitation process—

(I) 50 percent or more of the existing external walls of such building are retained in place as external walls,

(II) 75 percent or more of the existing external walls of such building are retained in place as internal or external walls, and

(III) 75 percent or more of the existing internal structural framework of such building is retained in place.

(B) BUILDING MUST BE FIRST PLACED IN SERVICE BEFORE 1936.—In the case of a building other than a certified historic structure, a building shall not be a qualified rehabilitated building unless the building was first placed in service before 1936.

(C) SUBSTANTIALLY REHABILITATED DEFINED.—

(i) IN GENERAL.—For purposes of subparagraph (A)(i), a building shall be treated as having been substantially rehabilitated only if the qualified rehabilitation expenditures during the 24-month period selected by the taxpayer (at the time and in the manner prescribed by regulations) and ending with or within the taxable year exceed the greater of—

(I) the adjusted basis of such building (and its structural components), or

(II) $5,000.

The adjusted basis of the building (and its structural components) shall be determined as of the beginning of the 1st day of such 24-month period, or of the holding period of the building, whichever is later. For purposes of the preceding sentence, the determination of the beginning of the holding period shall be made without regard to any reconstruction by the taxpayer in connection with the rehabilitation.

(ii) SPECIAL RULE FOR PHASED REHABILITATION.—In the case of any rehabilitation which may reasonably be expected to be completed in phases set forth in architectural plans and specifications completed before the rehabilitation begins, clause (i) shall be applied by substituting "60-month period" for "24-month period".

(iii) LESSEES.—The Secretary shall prescribe by regulation rules for applying this subparagraph to lessees.

(D) RECONSTRUCTION.—Rehabilitation includes reconstruction.

(2) QUALIFIED REHABILITATION EXPENDITURE DEFINED.—For purposes of this section—

(A) IN GENERAL.—The term "qualified rehabilitation expenditure" means any amount properly chargeable to capital account—

(i) for property for which depreciation is allowable under section 168 and which is—

(I) nonresidential real property,

(II) residential rental property,

(III) real property which has a class life of more than 12.5 years, or

(IV) an addition or improvement to property or housing described in subclause (I), (II), or (III), and

(ii) in connection with the rehabilitation of a qualified rehabilitated building.

(B) CERTAIN EXPENDITURES NOT INCLUDED.—The term "qualified rehabilitation expenditure" does not include—

(i) STRAIGHT LINE DEPRECIATION MUST BE USED.—Any expenditure with respect to which the taxpayer does not use the straight line method over a recovery period determined under subsection (c) or (g) of section 168. The preceding sentence shall not apply to any expenditure to the extent the alternative depreciation system of section 168(g) applies to such expenditure by reason of subparagraph (B) or (C) of section 168(g)(1).

(ii) COST OF ACQUISITION.—The cost of acquiring any building or interest therein.

(iii) ENLARGEMENTS.—Any expenditure attributable to the enlargement of an existing building.

(iv) CERTIFIED HISTORIC STRUCTURE, ETC.—Any expenditure attributable to the rehabilitation of a certified historic structure or a building in a registered historic district, unless the rehabilitation is a certified rehabilitation (within the meaning of subparagraph (C)). The preceding sentence shall not apply to a building in a registered historic district if—

(I) such building was not a certified historic structure.

(II) the Secretary of the Interior certified to the Secretary that such building is not of historic significance to the district, and

(III) if the certification referred to in subclause (II) occurs after the beginning of the rehabilitation of such building, the taxpayer certifies to the Secretary that, at the beginning of such rehabilitation, he in good faith was not aware of the requirement of subclause (II).

(v) TAX-EXEMPT USE PROPERTY.—

(I) IN GENERAL.—Any expenditure in connection with the rehabilitation of a building which is allocable to that portion of such building which is (or may reasonably be expected to be) tax-exempt use property (within the meaning of section 168(h)).

(II) CLAUSE NOT TO APPLY FOR PURPOSES OF PARAGRAPH (1)(C).—This clause shall not apply for purposes of determining under paragraph (1)(C) whether a building has been substantially rehabilitated.

(vi) EXPENDITURES OF LESSEE.—Any expenditure of a lessee of a building if, on the date the rehabilitation is completed, the remaining term of the lease (determined without regard to any renewal periods) is less than the recovery period determined under section 168(c).

(C) CERTIFIED REHABILITATION.—For purposes of subparagraph (B), the term "certified rehabilitation" means any rehabilitation of a certified historic structure which the Secretary of the Interior has certified to the Secretary as being consistent with the historic character of such property or the district in which such property is located.

(D) NONRESIDENTIAL REAL PROPERTY; RESIDENTIAL RENTAL PROPERTY; CLASS LIFE.—For purposes of subparagraph (A), the terms "nonresidential real property," "residential rental property," and "class life" have the respective meanings given such terms by section 168.

(3) CERTIFIED HISTORIC STRUCTURE DEFINED.—For purposes of this subsection—

(A) IN GENERAL.—The term "certified historic structure" means any building (and its structural components) which—

(i) is listed in the National Register, or

(ii) is located in a registered historic district and is certified by the Secretary of the Interior to the Secretary as being of historic significance to the district.

(B) REGISTERED HISTORIC DISTRICT.—The term "registered historic district" means—

(i) any district listed in the National Register, and

(ii) any district—

(I) which is designated under a statute of the appropriate State or local government, if such statute is certified by the Secretary of the Interior to the Secretary as containing criteria which will substantially achieve the purpose of preserving and rehabilitating buildings of historic significance to the district, and

(II) which is certified by the Secretary of the Interior to the Secretary as meeting substantially all of the requirements for the listing of districts in the National Register.

(4) PROPERTY TREATED AS NEW SECTION 38 PROPERTY.—Property which is treated as section 38 property by reason of subsection (a)(1)(E) shall be treated as new section 38 property.

Amendments

• 1986, Tax Reform Act of 1986 (P.L. 99-514)

P.L. 99-514, §251(b):

Amended Code Sec. 48(g). **Effective** for property placed in service after 12-31-86, in tax years ending after such date. However, for transitional rules, see Act Sec. 251(d)(2)-(7), following Code Sec. 168. Prior to amendment, Code Sec. 48(g) read as follows:

(g) SPECIAL RULES FOR QUALIFIED REHABILITATED BUILDINGS.—For purposes of this subpart—

(1) QUALIFIED REHABILITATED BUILDING DEFINED—

(A) IN GENERAL.—The term "qualified rehabilitated building" means any building (and its structural components)—

(i) which has been substantially rehabilitated,

(ii) which was placed in service before the beginning of the rehabilitation, and

(iii) 75 percent or more of the existing external walls of which are retained in place as external walls in the rehabilitation process.

(B) 30 YEARS MUST HAVE ELAPSED SINCE CONSTRUCTION.—In the case of a building other than a certified historic structure, a building shall not be a qualified rehabilitated building unless there is a period of at least 30 years between the date the physical work on the rehabilitation began and the date the building was first placed in service.

(C) SUBSTANTIALLY REHABILITATED DEFINED.—

(i) IN GENERAL.—For purposes of subparagraph (A)(i), a building shall be treated as having been substantially rehabilitated only if the qualified rehabilitation expenditures during the 24-month period selected by the taxpayer (at the time and in the manner prescribed by regulations) and ending with or within the taxable year exceed the greater of—

(I) the adjusted basis of such building (and its structural components), or

(II) $5,000.

The adjusted basis of the building (and its structural components) shall be determined as of the beginning of the first day of such 24-month period, or of the holding period of the building (within the meaning of section 1250(e)), whichever is later. For purposes of the preceding sentence, the determination of the beginning of the holding period shall be made without regard to any reconstruction by the taxpayer in connection with the rehabilitation.

(ii) SPECIAL RULE FOR PHASED REHABILITATION.—In the case of any rehabilitation which may reasonably be expected to be completed in phases set forth in architectural plans and specifications completed before the rehabilitation begins, clause (i) shall be applied by substituting "60-month period" for "24-month period".

(iii) LESSEES.—The Secretary shall prescribe by regulation rules for applying this provision to lessees.

(D) RECONSTRUCTION.—Rehabilitation includes reconstruction.

(E) ALTERNATIVE TEST FOR DEFINITION OF QUALIFIED REHABILITATED BUILDING.—The requirement in clause (iii) of subparagraph (A) shall be deemed to be satisfied if in the rehabilitation process—

(i) 50 percent or more of the existing external walls of the building are retained in place as external walls,

(ii) 75 percent or more of the existing external walls of such building are retained in place as internal or external walls, and

(iii) 75 percent or more of the existing internal structural framework of such building is retained in place.

(2) QUALIFIED REHABILITATION EXPENDITURE DEFINED.—

(A) IN GENERAL.—The term "qualified rehabilitation expenditure" means any amount properly chargeable to capital account which is incurred after December 31, 1981—

(i) for real property (or additions or improvements to real property) which have a recovery period (within the meaning of section 168) of 19 (15 years in the case of low-income housing) years, and

(ii) in connection with the rehabilitation of a qualified rehabilitated building.

(B) CERTAIN EXPENDITURES NOT INCLUDED.—The term "qualified rehabilitation expenditure" does not include—

(i) ACCELERATED METHODS OF DEPRECIATION MAY NOT BE USED.—Any expenditures with respect to which an election has not been made under section 168(b)(3) (to use the straight-line method of depreciation). The preceding sentence shall not apply to any expenditure to the extent subsection (f)(12) or (j) of section 168 applies to such expenditure.

(ii) COST OF ACQUISITION.—The cost of acquiring any building or interest therein.

(iii) ENLARGEMENTS.—Any expenditure attributable to the enlargement of an existing building.

(iv) CERTIFIED HISTORIC STRUCTURE, ETC.—Any expenditure attributable to the rehabilitation of a certified historic structure or a building in a registered historic district, unless the rehabilitation is a certified rehabilitation (within the meaning of subparagraph (C)). The preceding sentence shall not apply to a building in a registered historic district if—

(I) such building was not a certified historic structure,

(II) the Secretary of the Interior certified to the Secretary that such building is not of historic significance to the district, and

(III) if the certification referred to in subclause (II) occurs after the beginning of the rehabilitation of such building, the taxpayer certifies to the Secretary that, at the beginning of such rehabilitation, he in good faith was not aware of the requirements of subclause (II).

(v) EXPENDITURES OF LESSEE.—Any expenditure of a lessee of a building if, on the date the rehabilitation is completed, the remaining term of the lease (determined without regard to any renewal periods) is less than 19 years (15 years in the case of low-income housing).

(vi) TAX-EXEMPT USE PROPERTY.—

(I) IN GENERAL.—Any expenditure in connection with the rehabilitation of a building which is allocable to that portion of such building which is (or may reasonably be expected to be) tax-exempt use property (within the meaning of section 168(j)).

(II) CLAUSE NOT TO APPLY FOR PURPOSES OF PARAGRAPH (1)(C).—This clause shall not apply for purposes of determining under paragraph (1)(C) whether a building has been substantially rehabilitated.

(C) CERTIFIED REHABILITATION.—For purposes of subparagraph (B), the term "certified rehabilitation" means any rehabilitation of a certified historic structure which the Secretary of the Interior has certified to the Secretary as being consistent with the historic character of such property or the district in which such property is located.

(D) LOW-INCOME HOUSING.—For purposes of subparagraph (B), the term "low-income housing" has the meaning given such term by section 168(c)(2)(F).

(3) CERTIFIED HISTORIC STRUCTURE DEFINED.—

(A) IN GENERAL.—The term "certified historic structure" means any building (and its structural components) which—

(i) is listed in the National Register, or

(ii) is located in a registered historic district and is certified by the Secretary of the Interior to the Secretary as being of historic significance to the district.

(B) REGISTERED HISTORIC DISTRICT.—The term "registered historic district" means—

(i) any district listed in the National Register, and

(ii) any district—

(I) which is designated under a statute of the appropriate State or local government, if such statute is certified by the Secretary of the Interior to the Secretary as containing criteria which will substantially achieve the purpose of preserving and rehabilitating buildings of historic significance to the district, and

(II) which is certified by the Secretary of the Interior to the Secretary as meeting substantially all of the requirements for the listing of districts in the National Register.

(4) PROPERTY TREATED AS NEW SECTION 38 PROPERTY.—Property which is treated as section 38 property by reason of subsection (a)(1)(E) shall be treated as new section 38 property.

P.L. 99-514, §1802(a)(9)(B):

Amended Code Sec. 48(g)(2)(B)(vi)(I) by striking out "section 168(j)(3)" and inserting in lieu thereof "section 168(j)". **Effective** as if included in the provision of P.L. 98-369 to which it relates.

• 1985 (P.L. 99-121)

P.L. 99-121, §103(b)(5):

Amended Code Sec. 48(g)(2) by striking out "18" in subparagraphs (A)(i) and (B)(v) thereof and inserting in lieu thereof "19". **Effective** with respect to property placed in service by the taxpayer after 5-8-85. However, for an exception and special rule, see Act Sec. 105(b)(2) and (5), below.

P.L. 99-121, §105(b)(2), provides:

(2) EXCEPTION.—The amendments made by section 103 shall not apply to property placed in service by the taxpayer before January 1, 1987, if—

(A) the taxpayer or a qualified person entered into a binding contract to purchase or construct such property before May 9, 1985, or

(B) construction of such property was commenced by or for the taxpayer or a qualified person before May 9, 1985.

For purposes of this paragraph, the term "qualified person" means any person whose rights in such a contract or such property are transferred to the taxpayer, but only if such property is not placed in service before such rights are transferred to the taxpayer.

P.L. 99-121, §105(b)(5), provides:

(5) SPECIAL RULE FOR LEASING OF QUALIFIED REHABILITATED BUILDINGS.—The amendment made by paragraph (5) of section 103(b) to section 48(g)(2)(B)(v) of the Internal Revenue Code of 1954 shall not apply to leases entered into before May 22, 1985, but only if the lessee signed the lease before May 17, 1985.

• 1984, Deficit Reduction Act of 1984 (P.L. 98-369)

P.L. 98-369, §31(c)(1):

Amended Code Sec. 48(g)(2)(B) by adding at the end thereof new clause (vi). **Effective** for property placed in service by the taxpayer after 5-23-83, in tax years ending after such date and to property placed in service by the taxpayer on or before 5-23-83, if the use by the tax-exempt entity is pursuant to a lease entered into after 5-23-83.

P.L. 98-369, §31(c)(2):

Amended Code Sec. 48(g)(2)(B)(i) by adding at the end a new sentence. **Effective**, to the extent it relates to Code Sec. 168(f)(12), as if it had been included in the amendments made by §216(a) of P.L. 97-248. For special rules, see Act Sec. 31(g) in the amendment notes for Code Sec. 168(j).

P.L. 98-369, §111(e)(8):

Amended Code Sec. 48(g)(2) by striking out "property" each place it appears in subparagraph (A)(i) and inserting in lieu thereof "real property", by striking out "15" in subparagraph (A)(i) and inserting in lieu thereof "18 (15 years in the case of low-income housing)", by striking out "15 years" in subparagraph (B)(v) and inserting in lieu thereof "18 years (15 years in the case of low-income housing)", and by adding new subparagraph (D) at the end thereof. **Effective** for property placed in service by the taxpayer after 3-15-84. For an exception, see Act Sec. 111(g)[f](2)-(4) in the amendment notes following Code Sec. 168(b).

P.L. 98-369, §1043(a):

Amended Code Sec. 48(g)(1) by adding at the end thereof new subparagraph (E). **Effective** for expenditures incurred after 12-31-83, in tax years ending after such date.

• 1983, Technical Corrections Act of 1982 (P.L. 97-448)

P.L. 97-448, §102(f)(2):

Amended Code Sec. 48(g)(1)(C)(i) by striking out "the 24-month period ending on the last day of the taxable year" and inserting in lieu thereof "the 24-month period selected by the taxpayer (at the time and in the manner prescribed by regulations) and ending with or within the taxable year". **Effective** as if it had been included in the provision of P.L. 97-34 to which it relates.

P.L. 97-448, §102(f)(3):

Amended Code Sec. 48(g)(5)(A) by striking out "a credit is allowed under this section" and inserting in lieu thereof "a credit is determined under section 46(a)(2)", and by striking out "the credit so allowed" and inserting in lieu thereof "the credit so determined". **Effective** as if it had been included in the provision of P.L. 97-34 to which it relates.

P.L. 97-448, §102(f)(6):

Amended Code Sec. 48(g)(1)(C)(i) by striking out "property" the first 2 places it appears and inserting in lieu thereof "building (and its structural components)", by striking out "property" the third place it appears and inserting in lieu thereof "building", and by adding the sentence at the end thereof. **Effective** as if it had been included in the provision of P.L. 97-34 to which it relates.

• 1982, Tax Equity and Fiscal Responsibility Act of 1982 (P.L. 97-248)

P.L. 97-248, §205(a)(5)(A):

Amended Code Sec. 48(g) by striking out paragraph (5). **Effective** for periods after 12-31-82, under rules similar to the rules of Code Sec. 48(m). However, see amendment notes for P.L. 97-248, under Code Sec. 48(d) for an exception. Prior to amendment, Code Sec. 48(g)(5) read as follows:

"(5) Adjustment to basis.—

(A) In general.—For purposes of this subtitle, if a credit is determined under section 46(a)(2) for any qualified rehabilitation expenditure in connection with a qualified rehabilitated building other than a certified historic structure, the increase in basis of such property which would (but for this paragraph) result from such expenditure shall be reduced by the amount of the credit so determined.

(B) Certain dispositions.—If during any taxable year there is a recapture amount determined with respect to any qualified rehabilitated building the basis of which was reduced under subparagraph (A), the basis of such building (immediately before the event resulting in such recapture) shall be increased by an amount equal to such recapture amount. For purposes of the preceding sentence, the term `recapture amount' means any increase in tax (or adjustment in carrybacks or carryovers) determined under section 47(a)(5)."

• 1981, Economic Recovery Tax Act of 1981 (P.L. 97-34)

P.L. 97-34, §212(b):

Amended Code Sec. 48(g). **Effective** for expenditures incurred after 12-31-81, in tax years ending after such date. Prior to amendment, Code Sec. 48(g) read as follows:

(g) SPECIAL RULES FOR QUALIFIED REHABILITATED BUILDINGS.—For purposes of this subpart—

(1) QUALIFIED REHABILITATED BUILDING DEFINED.—

(A) IN GENERAL.—The term "qualified rehabilitated building" means any building (and its structural components)—

(i) which has been rehabilitated,

(ii) which was placed in service before the beginning of the rehabilitation, and

(iii) 75 percent or more of the existing external walls of which are retained in place as external walls in the rehabilitation process.

(B) 20 YEARS MUST HAVE ELAPSED SINCE CONSTRUCTION OR PRIOR REHABILITATION.—A building shall not be a qualified rehabilitated building unless there is a period of at least 20 years between—

(i) the date the physical work on this rehabilitation of the building began, and

(ii) the later of—

(I) the date such building was first placed in service, or

(II) the date such building was placed in service in connection with a prior rehabilitation with respect to which a credit was allowed by reason of subsection (a)(1)(E).

(C) MAJOR PORTION TREATED AS SEPARATE BUILDING IN CERTAIN CASES.—Where there is a separate rehabilitation of a major portion of a building, such major portion shall be treated as a separate building.

(D) REHABILITATION INCLUDES RECONSTRUCTION.—Rehabilitation includes reconstruction.

(2) QUALIFIED REHABILITATION EXPENDITURE DEFINED.—

(A) IN GENERAL.—The term "qualified rehabilitation expenditure" means any amount properly chargeable to capital account which is incurred after October 31, 1978—

(i) for property (or additions or improvements to property) with a useful life of 5 years or more, and

(ii) in connection with the rehabilitation of a qualified rehabilitated building.

(B) CERTAIN EXPENDITURES NOT INCLUDED.—The term "qualified rehabilitation expenditure" does not include—

(i) PROPERTY OTHERWISE SECTION 38 PROPERTY.—Any expenditure for property which constitutes section 38 property (determined without regard to subsections (a)(1)(E) and (l)).

(ii) COST OF ACQUISITION.—The cost of acquiring any building or any interest therein.

(iii) ENLARGEMENTS.—Any expenditure attributable to the enlargement of the existing building.

(iv) CERTIFIED HISTORIC STRUCTURES.—Any expenditure attributable to the rehabilitation of a certified historic structure (within the meaning of section 191(d)(1)), unless the rehabilitation is a certified rehabilitation (within the meaning of section 191(d)(4)).

(3) PROPERTY TREATED AS NEW SECTION 38 PROPERTY.—Property which is treated as section 38 property by reason of subsection (a)(1)(E) shall be treated as new section 38 property.

P.L. 97-34, §212(e)(2), as amended by P.L. 97-448, §102(f)(1), provides the following transitional rule:

(2) TRANSITIONAL RULE.—The amendments made by this section shall not apply with respect to any rehabilitation of a building if—

(A) the physical work on such rehabilitation began before January 1, 1982, and

(B) such building does not meet the requirements of paragraph (1) of section 48(g) of the Internal Revenue Code of 1954 (as amended by this Act).

• 1980, Technical Corrections Act of 1979 (P.L. 96-222)

P.L. 96-222, §103(a)(4)(B):

Amended Code Sec. 48(g)(2)(B)(i) by striking out "subsection (a)(1)(E)" and inserting "subsections (a)(1)(E) and (l)". **Effective** for tax years ending after 10-31-78.

• 1978, Revenue Act of 1978 (P.L. 95-600)

P.L. 95-600, §315(b), (d):

Added new Code Sec. 48(g). **Effective** for tax years ending after 10-31-78.

• 1964, Revenue Act of 1964 (P.L. 88-272)

P.L. 88-272, §203(a)(1):

Repealed Sec. 48(g). For property placed in service after 12-31-63, **effective** for taxable years ending after such date; for property placed in service before 1-1-64, **effective** for tax years beginning after 12-31-63. Prior to repeal Code Sec. 48(g) read as follows:

"(g) Adjustments to Basis of Property.—

"(1) In general.—The basis of any section 38 property shall be reduced, for purposes of this subtitle other than this subpart, by an amount equal to 7 percent of the qualified investment as determined under section 46(c) with respect to such property.

"(2) Certain dispositions, etc.—If the tax under this chapter is increased for any taxable year under paragraph (1) or (2) of section 47(a) or an adjustment in carrybacks or carryovers is made under paragraph (3) of such section, the basis of the property described in such paragraph (1) or (2), as the case may be (immediately before the event on account of which such paragraph (1), (2), or (3) applies), shall be increased by an amount equal to the portion of such increase and the portion of such adjustment attributable to such property."

[Sec. 48(h)—Repealed]

Amendments

• 1978, Revenue Act of 1978 (P.L. 95-600)

P.L. 95-600, §312(c)(1), (d):

Repealed Code Sec. 48(h). **Effective** for tax years ending after 12-31-78. Prior to repeal, Code Sec. 48(h) read as follows:

(h) SUSPENSION OF INVESTMENT CREDIT.—For purposes of this subpart—

(1) GENERAL RULE.—Section 38 property which is suspension period property shall not be treated as new or used section 38 property.

(2) SUSPENSION PERIOD PROPERTY DEFINED.—Except as otherwise provided in this subsection and subsection (i), the term "suspension period property" means section 38 property—

(A) the physical construction, reconstruction, or erection of which (i) is begun during the suspension period, or (ii) is begun, pursuant to an order placed during such period, before May 24, 1967, or

(B) which (i) is acquired by the taxpayer during the suspension period, or (ii) is acquired by the taxpayer, pursuant to an order placed during such period, before May 24, 1967.

In applying subparagraph (A) to any section 38 property, there shall be taken into account only that portion of the basis which is properly attributable to construction, reconstruction, or erection before May 24, 1967.

(3) BINDING CONTRACTS.—To the extent that any property is constructed, reconstructed, erected, or acquired pursuant to a contract which was, on October 9, 1966, and at all times thereafter, binding on the taxpayer, such property shall not be deemed to be suspension period property.

(4) EQUIPPED BUILDING RULE.—If—

(A) pursuant to a plan of the taxpayer in existence on October 9, 1966 (which plan was not substantially modified at any time after such date and before the taxpayer placed the equipped building in service), the taxpayer has constructed, reconstructed, erected, or acquired a building and the machinery and equipment necessary to the planned use of the building by the taxpayer, and

(B) more than 50 percent of the aggregate adjusted basis of all the property of a character subject to the allowance for depreciation making up such building as so equipped is attributable to either property the construction, reconstruction, or erection of which was begun by the taxpayer before October 10, 1966, or property the acquisition of which by the taxpayer occurred before such date,

then all section 38 property comprising such building as so equipped (and any incidental section 38 property adjacent to such building which is necessary to the planned use of the building) shall be treated as section 38 property which is not suspension period property. For purposes of subparagraph (B) of the preceding sentence, the rules of paragraphs (3) and (6) shall be applied. For purposes of this paragraph, a special purpose structure shall be treated as a building.

(5) PLANT FACILITY RULE.—

(A) GENERAL RULE.—If—

(i) pursuant to a plan of the taxpayer in existence on October 9, 1966 (which plan was not substantially modified at any time after such date and before the taxpayer placed the plant facility in service), the taxpayer has constructed, reconstructed or erected a plant facility, and either

(ii) the construction, reconstruction, or erection of such plant facility was commenced by the taxpayer before October 10, 1966, or

(iii) more than 50 percent of the aggregate adjusted basis of all the property of a character subject to the allowance for depreciation making up such plant facility is attributable to either property the construction, reconstruction, or erection of which was begun by the taxpayer before October 10,

1966, or property the acquisition of which by the taxpayer occurred before such date,

then all section 38 property comprising such plant facility shall be treated as section 38 property which is not suspension period property. For purposes of clause (iii) of the preceding sentence, the rules of paragraphs (3) and (6) shall be applied.

(B) PLANT FACILITY DEFINED.—For purposes of this paragraph, the term "plant facility" means a facility which does not include any building (or of which buildings constitute an insignificant portion) and which is—

(i) a self-contained, single operating unit or processing operation,

(ii) located on a single site, and

(iii) identified, on October 9, 1966, in the purchasing and internal financial plans of the taxpayer as a single unitary project.

(C) SPECIAL RULE.—For purposes of this subsection, if—

(i) a certificate of convenience and necessity has been issued before October 10, 1966, by a Federal regulatory agency with respect to two or more plant facilities which are included under a single plan of the taxpayer to construct, reconstruct or erect such plant facilities, and

(ii) more than 50 percent of the aggregate adjusted basis of all the property of a character subject to the allowance for depreciation making up such plant facilities is attributable to either property the construction, reconstruction, or erection of which was begun by the taxpayer before October 10, 1966, or property the acquisition of which by the taxpayer occurred before such date,

such plant facilities shall be treated as a single plant facility.

(D) COMMENCEMENT OF CONSTRUCTION.—For purposes of subparagraph (A)(ii), the construction, reconstruction, or erection of a plant facility shall not be considered to have commenced until construction, reconstruction, or erection has commenced at the site of such plant facility. The preceding sentence shall not apply if the site of such plant facility is not located on land.

(6) MACHINERY OR EQUIPMENT RULE.—Any piece of machinery or equipment—

(A) more than 50 percent of the parts and components of which (determined on the basis of cost) were held by the taxpayer on October 9, 1966, or are acquired by the taxpayer pursuant to a binding contract which was in effect on such date, for inclusion or use in such piece of machinery or equipment, and

(B) the cost of the parts and components of which is not an insignificant portion of the total cost,

shall be treated as property which is not suspension period property.

(7) CERTAIN LEASE-BACK TRANSACTIONS, ETC.—Where a person who is a party to a binding contract described in paragraph (3) transfers rights in such contract (or in the property to which such contract relates) to another person but a party to such contract retains a right to use the property under a lease with such other person, then to the extent of the transferred rights such other person shall, for purposes of paragraph (3), succeed to the position of the transferor with respect to such binding contract and such property. The preceding sentence shall apply, in any case in which the lessor does not make an election under subsection (d), only if a party to such contract retains a right to use the property under a long-term lease.

(8) CERTAIN LEASE AND CONTRACT OBLIGATIONS.—Where, pursuant to a binding lease or contract to lease in effect on October 9, 1966, a lessor or lessee is obligated to construct, reconstruct, erect, or acquire property specified in such lease or contract, any property so constructed, reconstructed, erected, or acquired by the lessor or lessee which is section 38 property shall be treated as property which is not suspension period property. In the case of any project which includes property other than the property to be leased to such lessee, the preceding sentence shall be applied, in the case of the lessor, to such other property only if the binding leases and contracts with all lessees in effect on October 9, 1966, cover real property constituting 25 percent or more of the project (determined on the basis of rental value). For purposes of the preceding sentences of this paragraph, in the case of any project where one or more vendor-vendee relationships exist, such vendors and vendees shall be treated as lessors and lessees. Where, pursuant to a binding contract in effect on October 9, 1966, (i) the taxpayer is required to construct, reconstruct, erect, or acquire property specified in the contract, to be used to produce one or more products, and (ii) the other party is required to take substantially all of the products to be produced over a substantial portion of the expected useful life of the property, then such property shall be treated as property which is not suspension period property. Clause (ii) of the preceding sentence shall not apply if a political subdivision of a State is the other party to the contract and is required by the contract to make substantial expenditures which benefit the taxpayer.

(9) CERTAIN TRANSFERS TO BE DISREGARDED.—

(A) If property or rights under a contract are transferred in—

(i) a transfer by reason of death, or

(ii) a transaction as a result of which the basis of the property in the hands of the transferee is determined by reference to its basis in the hands of the transferor by reason of the application of section 332, 351, 361, 371(a), 374(a), 721, or 731,

and such property (or the property acquired under such contract) would not be treated as suspension period property in the hands of the decedent or the transferor, such property shall not be treated as suspension period property in the hands of the transferee.

(B) If—

(i) property or rights under a contract are acquired in a transaction to which section 334(b)(2) applies,

(ii) the stock of the distributing corporation was acquired before October 10, 1966, or pursuant to a binding contract in effect October 9, 1966, and

(iii) such property (or the property acquired under such contract) would not be treated as suspension period property in the hands of the distributing corporation,

such property shall not be treated as suspension period property in the hands of the distributee.

(10) PROPERTY ACQUIRED FROM AFFILIATED CORPORATION.—For purposes of this subsection, in the case of property acquired by a corporation which is a member of an affiliated group from another member of the same group—

(A) such corporation shall be treated as having acquired such property on the date on which it was acquired by such other member,

(B) such corporation shall be treated as having entered into a binding contract for the construction, reconstruction, or erection, or acquisition of such property on the date on which such other member entered into a contract for the construction, reconstruction, erection, or acquisition of such property, and

(C) such corporation shall be treated as having commenced the construction, reconstruction, or erection of such property on the date on which such other member commenced such construction, reconstruction, or erection.

For purposes of the preceding sentence, the term "affiliated group" has the meaning assigned to it by section 1504(a), except that all corporations shall be treated as includible corporations (without any exclusion under section 1504(b)).

(11) CERTAIN TANGIBLE PROPERTY CONSTRUCTED DURING SUSPENSION PERIOD AND LEASED NEW THEREAFTER.—Tangible personal property constructed or reconstructed by a person shall not be suspension period property if—

(A) such person leases such property after the close of the suspension period and the original use of such property commences after the close of such period,

(B) such construction or reconstruction, and such lease transaction, was not pursuant to an order placed during the suspension period, and

(C) an election is made under subsection (d) with respect to such property which satisfies the requirements of such subsection.

(12) WATER AND AIR POLLUTION CONTROL FACILITIES.—

(A) IN GENERAL.—Any water pollution control facility or air pollution control facility shall be treated as property which is not suspension period property.

(B) WATER POLLUTION CONTROL FACILITY.—For purposes of subparagraph (A), the term "water pollution control facility" means any section 38 property which—

(i) is used primarily to control water pollution by removing, altering, or disposing of wastes, including the necessary intercepting sewers, outfall sewers, pumping, power, and other equipment, and their appurtenances, and

(ii) is certified by the State water pollution control agency (as defined in section 13(a) of the Federal Water Pollution Control Act) as being in conformity with the State program or requirements for control of water pollution and is certified by the Secretary of Interior as being in compliance with the applicable regulations of Federal agencies and the general policies of the United States for cooperation with the States in the prevention and abatement of water pollution under the Federal Water Pollution Control Act.

(C) AIR POLLUTION CONTROL FACILITY.—For purposes of subparagraph (A), the term "air pollution control facility" means any section 38 property which—

(i) is used primarily to control atmospheric pollution or contamination by removing, altering, or disposing of atmospheric pollutants or contaminants; and

(ii) is certified by the State air pollution control agency (as defined in section 302(b) of the Clean Air Act) as being in conformity with the State program or requirements for control of air pollution and is certified by the Secretary of Health, Education, and Welfare as being in compliance with the applicable regulations of Federal agencies and the general policies of the United States for cooperation with the States in the prevention and abatement of air pollution under the Clean Air Act.

(D) STANDARDS FOR FACILITY.—Subparagraph (A) shall apply in the case of any facility only if the taxpayer constructs, reconstructs, erects, or acquires such facility in furtherance of Federal, State, or local standards for the control of water pollution or atmospheric pollution or contaminants.

(13) CERTAIN REPLACEMENT PROPERTY.—Section 38 property constructed, reconstructed, erected, or acquired by the taxpayer shall be treated as property which is not suspension period property to the extent such property is placed in service to replace property which was—

(A) destroyed or damaged by fire, storm, shipwreck, or other casualty, or

(B) stolen,

but only to the extent the basis (in the case of new section 38 property) or cost (in the case of used section 38 property) of such section 38 property does not exceed the adjusted basis of the property destroyed, damaged, or stolen.

• 1967 (P.L. 90-26)

P.L. 90-26, §2(a):

Amended subparagraphs (A) and (B) of Code Sec. 48(h)(2). **Effective** for tax years ending after 3-9-67. Prior to amendment, these subparagraphs read as follows:

"(A) the physical construction, reconstruction, or erection of which begins either during the suspension period or pursuant to an order placed during such period, or

"(B) which is acquired by the taxpayer either during the suspension period or pursuant to an order placed during such period."

[Sec. 48(i)—Repealed]

Amendments

• 1978, Revenue Act of 1978 (P.L. 95-600)

P.L. 95-600, §312(c)(1), (d):

Repealed Code Sec. 48(i). **Effective** for tax years ending after 12-31-78. Prior to repeal, Code Sec. 48(i) read as follows:

(i) EXEMPTION FROM SUSPENSION OF $20,000 OF INVESTMENT.—

(1) IN GENERAL.—In the case of property acquired by the taxpayer by purchase for use in his trade or business which would (but for this subsection) be suspension period property, the taxpayer may select items to which this subsection applies, to the extent of an aggregate cost, for the suspension period, of $20,000. Any item so selected shall be treated as property which is not suspension period property for purposes of this subpart (other than for purposes of paragraphs (4), (5), (6), (7), (8), (9), and (10) of subsection (h)).

(2) APPLICABLE RULES.—Under regulations prescribed by the Secretary, rules similar to the rules provided by paragraphs (2) and (3) of subsection (c) shall be applied for purposes of this subsection. Subsection (d) shall not apply with respect to any item to which this subsection applies.

• 1976, Tax Reform Act of 1976 (P.L. 94-455)

P.L. 94-455, §1906(b)(13)(A):

Amended 1954 Code by substituting "Secretary" for "Secretary or his delegate" each place it appeared. **Effective** 2-1-77.

[Sec. 48(j)—Repealed]

Amendments

• 1978, Revenue Act of 1978 (P.L. 95-600)

P.L. 95-600, §312(c)(1), (d):

Repealed Code Sec. 48(j). **Effective** for tax years ending after 12-31-78. Prior to repeal, Code Sec. 48(j) read as follows:

(j) SUSPENSION PERIOD.—For purposes of this subpart, the term "suspension period" means the period beginning on October 10, 1966, and ending on March 9, 1967.

• 1967 (P.L. 90-26)

P.L. 90-26, §1:

Amended Code Sec. 48(j) by substituting "March 9, 1967" for "December 31, 1967". **Effective** for tax years ending after 3-9-67.

• 1966 (P.L. 89-800)

P.L. 89-800, §1(a):

Redesignated Code Sec. 48(h) as Sec. 48(k) and added new Secs. 48(h), (i), and (j). **Effective** for tax years ending after 10-9-66.

[Sec. 48(k)]

(k) MOVIE AND TELEVISION FILMS.—

(1) ENTITLEMENT TO CREDIT.—

(A) IN GENERAL.—A credit shall be allowable under section 38 to a taxpayer with respect to any motion picture film or video tape—

(i) only if such film or tape is new section 38 property (determined without regard to useful life) which is a qualified film, and

(ii) only to the extent that the taxpayer has an ownership interest in such film or tape.

(B) QUALIFIED FILM DEFINED.—For purposes of this subsection, the term "qualified film" means any motion picture film or video tape created primarily for use as public entertainment or for educational purposes. Such term does not include any film or tape the market for which is primarily topical or is otherwise essentially transitory in nature.

(C) OWNERSHIP INTEREST.—For purposes of this subsection, a person's "ownership interest" in a qualified film shall be determined on the basis of his proportionate share of any loss which may be incurred with respect to the production costs of such film.

(2) APPLICABLE PERCENTAGE TO BE 66 2/3.—Except as provided in paragraph (3), the applicable percentage under section 46(c)(2) for any qualified film shall be 66 2/3 percent.

(3) ELECTION OF 90-PERCENT RULE.—

(A) IN GENERAL.—If the taxpayer makes an election under this paragraph, the applicable percentage under section 46(c)(2) shall be determined as if the useful life of the film would have expired at the close of the first taxable year by the close of which the aggregate amount allowable as a deduction under section 167 would equal or exceed 90 percent of the basis of the film.

(B) MAKING OF ELECTION.—An election under this paragraph shall be made at such time and in such manner as the Secretary may by regulations prescribe. Such an election shall apply for the taxable year for which it is made and for all subsequent taxable years and may be revoked only with the consent of the Secretary.

(C) WHO MAY ELECT.—If for any prior taxable year paragraph (2) of this subsection applied to the taxpayer or any related business entity, or if for the taxable year paragraph (2) applies to any related business entity, an election under this paragraph may be made by the taxpayer only with the consent of the Secretary.

(D) RELATED BUSINESS ENTITY.—Two or more corporations, partnerships, trusts, estates, proprietorships, or other entities shall be treated as related business entities if 50 percent or more of the beneficial interest in each of such entities is owned by the same or related persons (taking into account only persons who own at least 10 percent of such beneficial interest). For purposes of this subparagraph, a person is a related person to another person if—

(i) such persons are component members of a controlled group of corporations (within the meaning of section 1563(a), except that section 1563(b)(2) shall not apply and except that "more than 50 percent" shall be substituted for "at least 80 percent" each place it appears in section 1563(a)), or

(ii) the relationship between such persons would result in a disallowance of losses under section 267 or 707(b), except that for these purposes a family of an individual includes only his spouse and minor children.

For purposes of this subparagraph, the term "beneficial interest" means voting stock in the case of a corporation, profits interest or capital interest in the case of a partnership, or beneficial interest in the case of a trust or estate.

(4) PREDOMINANT USE TEST OR AT-RISK RULES; QUALIFIED INVESTMENT.—In the case of any qualified film—

(A) section 48(a)(2), section 46(c)(8), or section 46(c)(9) shall not apply, and

(B) in determining qualified investment under section 46(c)(1), there shall be used (in lieu of the basis of the property) an amount equal to the qualified United States production costs (as defined in paragraph (5)).

(5) QUALIFIED UNITED STATES PRODUCTION COSTS.—

(A) IN GENERAL.—For purposes of this subsection, the term "qualified United States production costs" means with respect to any film—

(i) direct production costs allocable to the United States, plus

(ii) if 80 percent or more of the direct production costs are allocable to the United States, all other production costs other than direct production costs allocable outside the United States.

(B) PRODUCTION COSTS.—For purposes of this subsection, the term "production costs" includes—

(i) a reasonable allocation of general overhead costs,

(ii) compensation (other than participations described in clause (vi)) for services performed by actors, production personnel, directors, and producers,

(iii) costs of "first" distribution of prints,

(iv) the cost of the screen rights and other material being filmed,

(v) "residuals" payable under contracts with labor organizations, and

(vi) participations payable as compensation to actors, production personnel, directors, and producers.

Participations on all qualified films placed in service by a taxpayer during a taxable year shall be taken into account under clause (vi) only to the extent of the lesser of 25 percent of each such participation or 12½ percent of the aggregate qualified United States production costs (other than costs described in clauses (v) and (vi) of this subparagraph) for such films, but taking into account for both the 25 percent limit and 12½ percent limit no more than $1,000,000 in participations for any one individual with respect to any one film. For purposes of this subparagraph (other than clauses (v) and (vi) and the preceding sentence), costs shall be taken into account only if they are capitalized.

(C) DIRECT PRODUCTION COSTS.—For purposes of this paragraph, the term "direct production costs" does not include items referred to in clause (i), (iv), (v), or (vi) of subparagraph (B). The term also does not include advertising and promotional costs and such other costs as may be provided in regulations prescribed by the Secretary.

(D) ALLOCATION OF DIRECT PRODUCTION COSTS.—For purposes of this paragraph—

(i) Compensation for services performed shall be allocated to the country in which the services are performed, except that payments to United States persons for services performed outside the United States shall be allocated to the United States. For purposes of the preceding sentence, payments to an S corporation or a partnership shall be considered payments to a United States person only to the extent that such payments are included in the gross income of a United States person other than an S corporation or partnership.

(ii) Amounts for equipment and supplies shall be allocated to the country in which, with respect to the production of the film, the predominant use occurs.

(iii) All other items shall be allocated under regulations prescribed by the Secretary which are consistent with the allocation principle set forth in clause (ii).

(6) UNITED STATES.—For purposes of this subsection, the term "United States" includes the possessions of the United States.

Amendments

• 1984, Deficit Reduction Act of 1984 (P.L. 98-369)

P.L. 98-369, §113(b)(3):

Amended Code Sec. 48(k)(4) by inserting ", section 46(c)(8), or section 46(c)(9)" after "section 48(a)(2)" in subparagraph (A), by inserting "or at-risk rules" after "test" in the heading thereof, and by striking out "issued" and inserting in lieu thereof "used". **Effective** as if included in the amendments made by P.L. 97-34 §§201 and 211(a)(1) and (f)(1).

P.L. 98-369, §721(x)(1):

Amended Code Sec. 48(k)(5)(D)(i) by striking out "electing small business corporation" and inserting in lieu thereof "S corporation". **Effective** as if included in P.L. 97-354.

• 1982, Subchapter S Revision Act of 1982 (P.L. 97-354)

P.L. 97-354, §5(a)(8):

Amended the second sentence of Code Sec. 48(k)(5)(D)(i) by striking out "an electing small business corporation (within the meaning of section 1371)" and inserting in lieu thereof "an S corporation". **Effective** for tax years beginning after 12-31-82.

• 1976, Tax Reform Act of 1976 (P.L. 94-455)

P.L. 94-455, §804(a):

Amended Code Sec. 48 by redesignating subsection (k) as subsection (l) and by inserting new subsection (k). **Effective** for tax years beginning after 12-31-74. But see Sec. 804(e), below.

P.L. 94-455, §804(c), (d) and (e), provide:

(c) ALTERNATIVE METHODS OF COMPUTING CREDIT FOR PAST PERIODS.

(1) GENERAL RULE FOR DETERMINING USEFUL LIFE, PREDOMINANT FOREIGN USE, ETC.—In the case of a qualified film (within the meaning of section 48(k)(1)(B) of the Internal Revenue Code of 1954) placed in service in a taxable year beginning before January 1, 1975, with respect to which neither an election under paragraph (2) of this subsection or an election under subsection (e)(2) applies—

(A) the applicable percentage under section 46(c)(2) of such Code shall be determined as if the useful life of the film would have expired at the close of the first taxable year by the close of which the aggregate amount allowable as a deduction under section 167 of such Code would equal or exceed 90 percent of the basis of such property (adjusted for any partial dispositions),

(B) for purposes of section 46(c)(1) of such Code, the basis of the property shall be determined by taking into account the total production costs (within the meaning of section 48(k)(5)(B) of such Code),

(C) for purposes of section 48(a)(2) of such Code, such film shall be considered to be used predominantly outside the United States in the first taxable year for which 50 percent or more of the gross revenues received or accrued during the taxable year from showing the film were received or accrued from showing the film outside the United States, and

(D) section 47(a)(7) of such Code shall apply.

(2) ELECTION OF 40-PERCENT METHOD.—

(A) IN GENERAL.—A taxpayer may elect to have this paragraph apply to all qualified films placed in service during taxable years beginning before January 1, 1975 (other than films to which an election under subsection (e)(2) of this section applies).

(B) EFFECT OF ELECTION.—If the taxpayer makes an election under this paragraph, then section 48(k) of the Internal Revenue Code of 1954 shall apply to all qualified films described in subparagraph (A) with the following modifications:

(i) subparagraph (B) of paragraph (4) shall not apply, but in determining qualified investment under section 46(c)(1) of such Code, there shall be used (in lieu of the basis of such property) an amount equal to 40 percent of the aggregate production costs (within the meaning of paragraph (5)(B) of such section 48(k)),

(ii) paragraph (2) shall be applied by substituting "100 percent" for "66⅔ percent", and

(iii) paragraph (3) and paragraph (5) (other than subparagraph (B)) shall not apply.

(C) RULES RELATING TO ELECTIONS.—An election under this paragraph shall be made not later than the day which is 6 months after the date of the enactment of this Act and shall be made in such manner as the Secretary of the Treasury or his delegate shall by regulations prescribe. Such an election may be revoked only with the consent of the Secretary of the Treasury or his delegate.

(D) THE TAXPAYER MUST CONSENT TO JOIN IN CERTAIN PROCEEDINGS.—No election may be made under this paragraph or subsection (e)(2) by any taxpayer unless he consents, under regulations prescribed by the Secretary of the Treasury or his delegate, to treat the determination of the investment credit allowable on each film subject to an election as a separate cause of action, and to join in any judicial proceeding for determining the person entitled to, and the amount of, the credit allowable under section 38 of the Internal Revenue Code of 1954 with respect to any film covered by such election.

(3) ELECTION TO HAVE CREDIT DETERMINED IN ACCORDANCE WITH PREVIOUS LITIGATION.—

(A) IN GENERAL.—A taxpayer described in subparagraph (B) may elect to have this paragraph apply to all films (whether or not qualified) placed in service in taxable years beginning before January 1, 1975, and with respect to which an election under subsection (e)(2) is not made.

(B) WHO MAY ELECT.—A taxpayer may make an election under this paragraph if he has filed an action in any court of competent jurisdiction, before January 1, 1976, for a determination of such taxpayer's rights to the allowance of a credit against tax under section 38 of the Internal Revenue Code of 1954 for any taxable year beginning before January 1, 1975, with respect to any film.

(C) EFFECT OF ELECTION.—If the taxpayer makes an election under this paragraph—

(i) paragraphs (1) and (2) of this subsection, and subsection (d) shall not apply to any film placed in service by the taxpayer, and

(ii) subsection 48(k) of the Internal Revenue Code of 1954 shall not apply to any film placed in service by the taxpayer in any taxable year beginning before January 1, 1975, and with respect to which an election under subsection (e)(2) is not made,

and the right of the taxpayer to the allowance of a credit against tax under section 38 of such Code with respect to any film placed in service in any taxable year beginning before January 1, 1975, and as to which an election under subsection (e)(2) is not made, shall be determined as though this section (other than this paragraph) has not been enacted.

(D) RULES RELATING TO ELECTIONS.—An election under this paragraph shall be made not later than the day which is 90 days after the date of the enactment of this Act, by filing a notification of such election with the national office of the Internal Revenue Service. Such an election, once made, shall be irrevocable.

(d) ENTITLEMENT TO CREDIT.—Paragraph (1) of section 48(k) of the Internal Revenue Code of 1954 (relating to entitlement to credit) shall apply to any motion picture film or video tape placed in service in any taxable year beginning before January 1, 1975.

(e) EFFECTIVE DATES.—

(1) IN GENERAL.—The amendments made by subsections (a) [above] and (b) [see historical note for P.L. 94-455 under Code Sec. 47(a)] shall apply to taxable years beginning after December 31, 1974.

(2) ELECTION MAY ALSO APPLY TO PROPERTY DESCRIBED IN SECTION 50(a).—At the election of the taxpayer, made within 1 year after the date of the enactment of this Act [October 4, 1976] in such manner as the Secretary of the Treasury or his delegate may by regulations prescribe, the amendments made by subsections (a) and (b) shall also apply to property which is property described in section 50(a) of the Internal Revenue Code of 1954 and which is placed in service in taxable years beginning before January 1, 1975.

[Sec. 48(l)]

(l) ENERGY PROPERTY.—For purposes of this subpart—

(1) TREATMENT AS SECTION 38 PROPERTY.—For any period for which the energy percentage determined under section 46(b)(2) for any energy property is greater than zero—

(A) such energy property shall be treated as meeting the requirements of paragraph (1) of subsection (a), and

(B) paragraph (3) of subsection (a) shall not apply to such property.

(2) ENERGY PROPERTY DEFINED.—The term "energy property" means property—

(A) which is—

(i) alternative energy property,

(ii) solar or wind energy property,

(iii) specially defined energy property,

(iv) recycling equipment,

(v) shale oil equipment,

(vi) equipment for producing natural gas from geopressured brine,

(vii) qualified hydroelectric generating property,

(viii) cogeneration equipment, or

(ix) qualified intercity buses,

(B)(i) the construction, reconstruction, or erection of which is completed by the taxpayer after September 30, 1978, or

(ii) which is acquired after September 30, 1978, if the original use of such property commences with the taxpayer and commences after such date, and

(C) with respect to which depreciation (or amortization in lieu of depreciation) is allowable, and which has a useful life (determined as of the time such property is placed in service) of 3 years or more or to which section 168 applies.

(3) ALTERNATIVE ENERGY PROPERTY.—

(A) IN GENERAL.—The term "alternative energy property" means—

(i) a boiler the primary fuel for which will be an alternate substance,

(ii) a burner (including necessary on-site equipment to bring the alternate substance to the burner) for a combustor other than a boiler if the primary fuel for such burner will be an alternate substance,

(iii) equipment for converting an alternate substance into a synthetic liquid, gaseous, or solid fuel,

(iv) equipment designed to modify existing equipment which uses oil or natural gas as a fuel or as feedstock so that such equipment will use either a substance other than oil and natural gas, or oil mixed with a substance other than oil and natural gas (where such other substance will provide not less than 25 percent of the fuel or feedstock),

(v) equipment to convert—

(I) coal (including lignite), or any nonmarketable substance derived therefrom, into a substitute for a petroleum or natural gas derived feedstock for the manufacture of chemicals or other products, or

(II) coal (including lignite), or any substance derived therefrom, into methanol, ammonia, or a hydroprocessed coal liquid or solid,

(vi) pollution control equipment required (by Federal, State, or local regulations) to be installed on or in connection with equipment described in clause (i), (ii), (iii), (iv), or (v),

(vii) equipment used for the unloading, transfer, storage, reclaiming from storage, and preparation (including, but not limited to, washing, crushing, drying, and weighing) at the point of use of an alternate substance for use in equipment described in clause (i), (ii), (iii), (iv), (v), or (vi),

(viii) equipment used to produce, distribute, or use energy derived from a geothermal deposit (within the meaning of section 613(e)(3)), but only, in the case of electricity generated by geothermal power, up to (but not including) the electrical transmission stage, and

(ix) equipment, placed in service at either of 2 locations designated by the Secretary after consultation with the Secretary of Energy, which converts ocean thermal energy to usable energy.

The equipment described in clause (vii) includes equipment used for the storage of fuel derived from garbage at the site at which such fuel was produced from garbage.

(B) ALTERNATE SUBSTANCE.—The term "alternate substance" means any substance other than—

(i) oil and natural gas, and

(ii) any product of oil and natural gas.

(C) SPECIAL RULE FOR CERTAIN POLLUTION CONTROL EQUIPMENT.—The term "pollution control equipment" does not include any equipment which—

(i) is installed on or in connection with property which, as of October 1, 1978, was using coal (including lignite), and

(ii) was required to be installed by Federal, State, or local regulations in effect on such date.

For purposes of the preceding sentence, in the case of property which is alternative energy property solely by reason of the amendments made by section 222(b) of the Crude Oil Windfall Profit Tax Act of 1980, "January 1, 1980" shall be substituted for "October 1, 1978".

(4) SOLAR OR WIND ENERGY PROPERTY.—The term "solar or wind energy property" means any equipment which uses solar or wind energy—

(A) to generate electricity,

(B) to heat or cool (or provide hot water for use in) a structure, or

(C) to provide solar process heat.

(5) SPECIALLY DEFINED ENERGY PROPERTY.—The term "specially defined energy property" means—

(A) a recuperator,

(B) a heat wheel,

(C) a regenerator,

(D) a heat exchanger,

(E) a waste heat boiler,

(F) a heat pipe,

(G) an automatic energy control system,

(H) a turbulator,

(I) a preheater,

(J) a combustible gas recovery system,

(K) an economizer,

(L) modifications to alumina electrolytic cells,

(M) modifications to chlor-alkali electrolytic cells, or

(N) any other property of a kind specified by the Secretary by regulations,

the principal purpose of which is reducing the amount of energy consumed in any existing industrial or commercial process and which is installed in connection with an existing industrial or commercial facility. The Secretary shall not specify any property under subparagraph (N) unless he determines that such specification meets the requirements of paragraph (9) of section 23(c) for specification of items under section 23(c)(4)(A)(viii).

(6) RECYCLING EQUIPMENT.—

(A) IN GENERAL.—The term "recycling equipment" means any equipment which is used exclusively—

(i) to sort and prepare solid waste for recycling, or

(ii) in the recycling of solid waste.

(B) CERTAIN EQUIPMENT NOT INCLUDED.—The term "recycling equipment" does not include—

(i) any equipment used in a process after the first marketable product is produced, or

(ii) in the case of recycling iron or steel, any equipment used to reduce the waste to a molten state and in any process thereafter.

(C) 10 PERCENT VIRGIN MATERIAL ALLOWED.—Any equipment used in the recycling of material which includes some virgin materials shall not be treated as failing to meet the exclusive use requirements of subparagraph (A) if the amount of such virgin materials is 10 percent or less.

(D) CERTAIN EQUIPMENT INCLUDED.—The term "recycling equipment" includes any equipment which is used in the conversion of solid waste into a fuel or into useful energy such as steam, electricity, or hot water.

(7) SHALE OIL EQUIPMENT.—The term "shale oil equipment" means equipment for producing or extracting oil from oil-bearing shale rock; but does not include equipment for hydrogenation, refining, or other process subsequent to retorting.

(8) EQUIPMENT FOR PRODUCING NATURAL GAS FROM GEOPRESSURED BRINE.— The term "equipment for producing natural gas from geopressured brine" means equipment which is used exclusively to extract natural gas described in section 613A(b)(3)(C)(i).

(9) EQUIPMENT MUST MEET CERTAIN STANDARDS TO QUALIFY.—Equipment qualifies under paragraph (3), (4), (5), (6), (7), or (8) only if it meets the performance and quality standards (if any) which—

(A) have been prescribed by the Secretary by regulations (after consultation with the Secretary of Energy), and

(B) are in effect at the time of the acquisition of the property.

(10) EXISTING.—For purposes of this subsection, the term "existing" means—

(A) when used in connection with a facility, 50 percent or more of the basis of such facility is attributable to construction, reconstruction, or erection before October 1, 1978, or

(B) when used in connection with an industrial or commercial process, such process was carried on in the facility as of October 1, 1978.

(11) SPECIAL RULE FOR PROPERTY FINANCED BY SUBSIDIZED ENERGY FINANCING OR INDUSTRIAL DEVELOPMENT BONDS.—

(A) REDUCTION OF QUALIFIED INVESTMENT.—For purposes of applying the energy percentage to any property, if such property is financed in whole or in part by—

(i) subsidized energy financing, or

(ii) the proceeds of a private activity bond (within the meaning of section 141) the interest on which is exempt from tax under section 103,

the amount taken into account as qualified investment shall not exceed the amount which (but for this subparagraph) would be the qualified investment multiplied by the fraction determined under subparagraph (B).

(B) DETERMINATION OF FRACTION.—For purposes of subparagraph (A), the fraction determined under this subparagraph is 1 reduced by a fraction—

(i) the numerator of which is that portion of the qualified investment in the property which is allocable to such financing or proceeds, and

(ii) the denominator of which is the qualified investment in the property.

(C) SUBSIDIZED ENERGY FINANCING.—For purposes of subparagraph (A), the term "subsidized energy financing" means financing provided under a Federal, State, or local program a principal purpose of which is to provide subsidized financing for projects designed to conserve or produce energy.

(12) INDUSTRIAL INCLUDES AGRICULTURAL.—The term "industrial" includes agricultural.

(13) QUALIFIED HYDROELECTRIC GENERATING PROPERTY.—

(A) IN GENERAL.—The term "qualified hydroelectric generating property" means property installed at a qualified hydroelectric site which is—

(i) equipment for increased capacity to generate electricity by water (up to, but not including, the electrical transmission stage), and

(ii) structures for housing such generating equipment, fish passageways, and dam rehabilitation property, required by reason of the installation of equipment described in clause (i).

(B) QUALIFIED HYDROELECTRIC SITE.—The term "qualified hydroelectric site" means any site—

(i) at which—

(I) there is a dam the construction of which was completed before October 18, 1979, and which was not significantly enlarged after such date, or

(II) electricity is to be generated without any dam or other impoundment of water, and

(ii) the installed capacity of which is less than 125 megawatts.

(C) LIMITATION ON CREDIT WHEN INSTALLED CAPACITY EXCEEDS 25 MEGAWATTS.—For purposes of applying the energy percentage to any qualified hydroelectric generating property placed in service in connection with a site the installed capacity of which exceeds 25 megawatts, the amount taken into account as qualified investment shall not exceed the amount which (but for this subparagraph) would be the qualified investment multiplied by a fraction—

(i) the numerator of which is 25 reduced by 1 for each whole megawatt by which such installed capacity exceeds 100 megawatts, and

(ii) the denominator of which is the number of megawatts of such installed capacity but not in excess of 100.

(D) DAM REHABILITATION PROPERTY.—For purposes of this paragraph, the term "dam rehabilitation property" means any amount properly chargeable to capital account for property (or additions or improvements to property) in connection with the rehabilitation of a dam.

(E) INSTALLED CAPACITY.—The term "installed capacity" means, with respect to any site, the installed capacity of all electrical generating equipment placed in service at such site. Such term includes the capacity of equipment installed during the 3 taxable years following the taxable year in which the equipment is placed in service.

(14) COGENERATION EQUIPMENT.—

(A) IN GENERAL.—The term "cogeneration equipment" means property which is an integral part of a system for using the same fuel to produce both qualified energy and electricity at an industrial or commercial facility at which, as of January 1, 1980, electricity or qualified energy was produced.

(B) ONLY COGENERATION INCREASES TAKEN INTO ACCOUNT.—The term "cogeneration equipment" includes property only to the extent that such property increases the capacity of the system to produce qualified energy or electricity, whichever is the secondary energy product of the system.

(C) LIMITATION ON USE OF OIL OR GAS.—The term "cogeneration equipment" does not include any property which is part of a system if—

(i) such system uses oil or natural gas (or a product of oil or natural gas) as a fuel for any purpose other than—

(I) start-up,

(II) flame control, or

(III) back-up, or

(ii) more than 20 percent (determined on a Btu basis) of the fuel for such system for any taxable year consists of oil or natural gas (or a product of oil or natural gas).

(D) QUALIFIED ENERGY.—The term "qualified energy" means steam, heat, or other forms of useful energy (other than electric energy) to be used for industrial, commercial, or space-heating purposes (other than in the production of electricity).

(E) INDUSTRIAL INCLUDES PURIFICATION AND DESALINIZATION OF WATER.—The term "industrial" includes the purification of water and the desalinization of water.

(15) BIOMASS PROPERTY.—

(A) IN GENERAL.—The term "biomass property" means—

(i) any property described in clause (i), (ii), or (iii) of paragraph (3)(A), as modified by the last sentence of paragraph (3)(A) and by subparagraph (B) of this paragraph, and

(ii) any equipment described in so much of clause (vi) or (vii) of paragraph (3)(A) as relates to property described in clause (i) of this subparagraph.

(B) MODIFICATIONS.—For purposes of subparagraph (A)—

(i) the term "alternate substance" has the meaning given to such term by paragraph (3)(B), except that such term does not include any inorganic substance and does not include coal (including lignite) or any product of such coal, and

(ii) clause (iii) of paragraph (3)(A) shall be applied by substituting "a qualified fuel" for "a synthetic liquid, gaseous, or solid fuel."

(C) QUALIFIED FUEL.—For purposes of subparagraph (B), the term "qualified fuel" means—

(i) any synthetic solid fuel, and

(ii) alcohol for fuel purposes if the primary source of energy for the facility producing the alcohol is not oil or natural gas or a product of oil or natural gas.

(16) QUALIFIED INTERCITY BUSES.—

(A) IN GENERAL.—Paragraph (2)(A)(ix) shall apply only with respect to the qualified investment in qualified intercity buses of a taxpayer—

(i) which is a common carrier regulated by the Interstate Commerce Commission or an appropriate State agency (as determined by the Secretary), and

(ii) which is engaged in the trade or business of furnishing intercity passenger transportation or intercity charter service by bus.

(B) QUALIFIED INTERCITY BUS.—The term "qualified intercity bus" means an automobile bus—

(i) the chassis of which is an automobile bus chassis and the body of which is an automobile bus body,

(ii) which has—

(I) a seating capacity of more than 35 passengers (in addition to the driver), and

(II) 1 or more baggage compartments, separated from the passenger area, with a capacity of at least 200 cubic feet, and

(iii) which is used predominantly by the taxpayer in the trade or business of furnishing intercity passenger transportation or intercity charter service.

(C) OPERATING CAPACITY MUST INCREASE.—Under regulations prescribed by the Secretary—

(i) IN GENERAL.—The amount of qualified investment taken into account under paragraph (2)(A)(ix) for any taxable year shall not exceed the amount of the qualified investment which is attributable to an increase in the taxpayer's total operating seating capacity for the taxable year over such capacity as of the close of the preceding taxable year.

(ii) SPECIAL RULES.—The regulations prescribed under this subparagraph—

(I) shall provide that only buses used predominantly on a full-time basis in the trade or business of furnishing intercity passenger or intercity charter service shall be taken into account in determining the taxpayer's total operating seating capacity, and

(II) shall provide rules treating related taxpayers as 1 person.

(17) EXCLUSION FOR PUBLIC UTILITY PROPERTY.—The terms "alternative energy property", "biomass property", "solar or wind energy property," "recycling equipment", and "cogeneration property" do not include property which is public utility property (within the meaning of 46(f)(5)).

Amendments

• 1988, Technical and Miscellaneous Revenue Act of 1988 (P.L. 100-647)

P.L. 100-647, §1002(a)(30):

Amended Code Sec. 48(l)(2)(C) by striking out "which is recovery property (within the meaning of section 168)" and inserting in lieu thereof "to which section 168 applies". **Effective** as if included in the provision of P.L. 99-514 to which it relates.

P.L. 100-647, §1013(a)(41):

Amended Code Sec. 48(l)(11)(A)(ii) by striking out "an industrial development bond (within the meaning of section 103(b)(2))" and inserting in lieu thereof "a private activity bond (within the meaning of section 141)". **Effective** as if included in the provision of P.L. 99-514 to which it relates.

• 1986, Tax Reform Act of 1986 (P.L. 99-514)

P.L. 99-514, §1847(b)(6)(A)-(B):

Amended Code Sec. 48(l)(5) by striking out "section 44C(c)" and inserting in lieu thereof "section 23(c)", and by striking out "section 44C(c)(4)(A)(viii)"and inserting in lieu thereof "section 23(c)(4)(A)(viii)". **Effective** as if included in the provision of P.L. 98-369 to which it relates.

• 1984, Deficit Reduction Act of 1984 (P.L. 98-369)

P.L. 98-369, §474(o)(13):

Amended Code Sec. 48(l)(1) by striking out "section 46(a)(2)(C)" and inserting in lieu thereof "section 46(b)(2)". **Effective** for tax years beginning after 12-31-83, and to carrybacks from such years, but shall not be construed as reducing the amount of any credit allowable for qualified investment in tax years beginning before 1-1-84.

P.L. 98-369, §735(c)(1):

Amended Code Sec. 48(l)(16)(B)(i). **Effective** as if included in the provision of the Highway Revenue Act of 1982 to which such amendment relates. Prior to amendment, it read as follows:

(i) the chassis and body of which is exempt under section 4063(a)(6) from the tax imposed by section 4061(a),

• 1983, Surface Transportation Act of 1982 (P.L. 97-424)

P.L. 97-424, §546(a):

Amended Code Sec. 48(l)(5) by striking out "or" at the end of subparagraph (L), by redesignating subparagraph (M) as subparagraph (N), by inserting a new subparagraph (M) and by striking out "(M)" in the second sentence and inserting "(N)". **Effective** 1-6-83.

• 1982, Miscellaneous Revenue Act of 1982 (P.L. 97-362)

P.L. 97-362, §104(a):

Amended Code Sec. 48(l)(7) by striking out "but does not" and all that follows, and inserting in lieu thereof "; except that such term does not include equipment for hydrogenation, refining, or other process subsequent to retorting other than hydrogenation or other process which is applied in the vicinity of the property from which the shale was extracted and which is applied to bring the shale oil to a grade and quality suitable for transportation to and processing in a refinery." **Effective** for periods beginning after 12-31-80, and before 1-1-83, under rules similar to the rules of Code Sec. 48(m).

• 1981, Economic Recovery Tax Act of 1981 (P.L. 97-34)

P.L. 97-34, §211(e)(3):

Amended Code Sec. 48(l)(2)(C) by inserting "or which is recovery property (within the meaning of section 168)" before the period at the end thereof. **Effective** for property placed in service after 12-31-80.

• 1980, Crude Oil Windfall Profit Tax Act of 1980 (P.L. 96-223)

P.L. 96-223, §221(b)(1):

Amended Code Sec. 48(l)(1). **Effective** 4-3-80. Prior to amendment Code Sec. 48 (l)(1) read:

(1) Treatment as Section 38 property.—For the period beginning on October 1, 1978, and ending on December 31, 1982—

(A) any energy property shall be treated as meeting the requirement of paragraph (1) of subsection (a), and

(B) paragraph (3) of subsection (a) shall not apply to any energy property.

P.L. 96-223, §221(b)(2):

Amended Code Sec. 48(l)(11), as amended by §223(c)(1), by striking out "5 percent" and inserting "one-half of the energy percentage determined under section 46(a)(2)(C)". **Effective** 4-3-80.

P.L. 96-223, §222(a):

Amended Code Sec. 48(l)(2)(A) by striking "or" at the end of clause (v) and by adding clauses (vii), (viii) and (ix). **Effective** for periods after 12-31-79, under rules similar to the rules of Code Sec. 48(m).

P.L. 96-223, §222(b):

Amended Code Sec. 48(l)(3)(A) by striking out "(other than coke or coke gas" at the end of clause (iii), by amending clause (v) to read as above, by striking out "and" at the end of clause (vii), by striking out the period at the end of clause (viii) and inserting ", and", and by adding clause (ix). **Effective** for periods after 12-31-79, under rules similar to the rules of section 48(m) of the Code. Prior to amendment clause (v) read:

(v) equipment which uses coal (including lignite) as a feedstock for the manufacture of chemicals or other products (other than coke or coke gas).

P.L. 96-223, §222(c):

Amended Code Sec. 48(l)(4) by striking out "or" at the end of subparagraph (A), by inserting ", or" at the end of subparagraph (B), and by adding subparagraph (C). **Effective** for periods after 12-31-79, under rules similar to rules of Code Sec. 48(m).

P.L. 96-223, §222(d)(1):

Amended Code Sec. 48(l)(5) by striking out "or" at the end of subparagraph (K), by redesignating subparagraph (L) as (M), and by adding a new subparagraph (L). **Effective** for periods after 9-30-78, under rules similar to the rules of Code Sec. 48(m).

P.L. 96-223, §222(d)(2):

Amended Code Sec. 48(1)(5) by adding a new last sentence. **Effective** for periods after 12-31-79, under rules similar to the rules of Code Sec. 48(m).

P.L. 96-223, §222(e)(1):

Added Code Sec. 48(1)(13). **Effective** for periods after 12-31-79, under rules similar to the rules of Code Sec. 48(m).

P.L. 96-223, §222(f):

Added Code Sec. 48(1)(14). **Effective** for periods after 12-31-79, under rules similar to the rules of Code Sec. 48(m).

P.L. 96-223, §222(g)(1):

Added Code Sec. 48(1)(15). **Effective** for periods after 12-31-79, under rules similar to the rules of Code Sec. 48(m).

P.L. 96-223, §222(g)(2):

Amended Code Sec. 48(1)(3)(A) by adding to the end a new sentence. **Effective** for periods after 12-31-79, under rules similar to the rules of Code Sec. 48(m).

P.L. 96-223, §222(h):

Added Code Sec. 48(1)(16). **Effective** for periods after 12-31-79, under rules similar to the rules of Code Sec. 48(m).

P.L. 96-223, §222(i)(1)(A):

Amended Code Sec. 48(1)(3) by striking out subparagraph (B) and redesignating subparagraphs (C) and (D) as (B) and (C), respectively. **Effective** for periods after 12-31-79, under rules similar to the rules of Code Sec. 48(m). Prior to amendment former subparagraph (B) read:

(B) EXCLUSION FOR PUBLIC UTILITY PROPERTY.—The terms "alternative energy property", "solar or wind energy property", and "recycling equipment" do not include property which is public utility property (within the meaning of section 46(f)(5)).

P.L. 96-223, §222(i)(1)(B):

Added Code Sec. 48(1)(17). **Effective** for periods after 12-31-79, under rules similar to the rules of Code Sec. 48(m).

P.L. 96-223, §222(i)(3):

Amended Code Sec. 48(1)(3)(C) as redesignated by Act Sec. 222(i)(1)(A) by adding at the end a new sentence. **Effective** for periods after 12-31-79, under rules similar to the rules of Code Sec. 48(m).

P.L. 96-223, §223(c)(1):

Amended Code Sec. 48(1)(11), as amended by Act Sec. 221(b)(2). For the **effective** dates, see P.L. 96-223, §223(c)(2), below. Prior to amendment by Act Secs. 223(c)(1) and 221(b)(2), Code Sec. 48(1)(11) read:

(11) SPECIAL RULE FOR PROPERTY FINANCED BY INDUSTRIAL DEVELOPMENT BONDS.—In the case of property which is financed in whole or in part by the proceeds of an industrial development bond (within the meaning of section 103(b)(2)) the interest on which is exempt from tax under section 103, the energy percentage shall be 5 percent.

P.L. 96-223, §223(c)(2), provides:

(2) EFFECTIVE DATES.—

(A) IN GENERAL.—Except as provided in subparagraph (B), the amendment made by paragraph (1) shall apply to periods after December 31, 1982, under rules similar to the rules of section 48(m) of the Internal Revenue Code of 1954.

(B) EARLIER APPLICATION FOR CERTAIN PROPERTY.—In the case of property which is—

(i) qualified hydroelectric generating property (described in section 48(l)(2)(A)(vii) of such Code),

(ii) cogeneration equipment (described in section 48(l)(2)(A)(viii) of such Code),

(iii) qualified intercity buses (described in section 48(l)(2)(A)(ix) of such Code),

(iv) ocean thermal property (described in section 48(l)(3)(A)(ix) of such Code), or

(v) expanded energy credit property,

the amendment made by paragraph (1) shall apply to periods after December 31, 1979, under rules similar to the rules of section 48(m) of the Internal Revenue Code of 1954.

(C) EXPANDED ENERGY CREDIT PROPERTY.—For purposes of subparagraph (B), the term "expanded energy credit property" means—

(i) property to which section 48(l)(3)(A) of such Code applies because of the amendments made by paragraphs (1) and (2) of section 222(b),

(ii) property described in section 48(l)(4)(C) of such Code (relating to solar process heat),

(iii) property described in section 48(l)(5)(L) of such Code (relating to alumina electrolytic cells), and

(iv) property described in the last sentence of section 48(l)(3)(A) of such Code (relating to storage equipment for refuse-derived fuel).

(D) FINANCING TAKEN INTO ACCOUNT.—For the purpose of applying the provisions of section 48(l)(11) of such Code in the case of property financed in whole or in part by subsidized energy financing (within the meaning of section 48(l)(11)(C) of such Code), no financing made before January 1, 1980, shall be taken into account. The preceding sentence shall not apply to financing provided from the proceeds of any tax-exempt industrial development bond (within the meaning of section 103(b)(2) of such Code).

• 1978, Energy Tax Act of 1978 (P.L. 95-618)

P.L. 95-618, §301(b):

Redesignated former Code Sec. 48(l) as Code Sec. 48(n). **Effective** 11-10-78, and added new Code Sec. 48(l).

[Sec. 48(m)]

(m) APPLICATION OF CERTAIN TRANSITIONAL RULES.—Where the application of any provision of subsection (l) of this section or subsection (b) or (c)(3) of section 46 is expressed in terms of a period, such provision shall apply only to—

(1) property to which section 46(d) does not apply, the construction, reconstruction, or erection of which is completed by the taxpayer on or after the first day of such period, but only to the extent of the basis thereof attributable to the construction, reconstruction, or erection during such period,

(2) property to which section 46(d) does not apply, acquired by the taxpayer during such period and placed in service by the taxpayer during such period, and

(3) property to which section 46(d) applies, but only to the extent of the qualified investment (as determined under subsections (c) and (d) of section 46) with respect to qualified progress expenditures made during such period.

Amendments

• 1984, Deficit Reduction Act of 1984 (P.L. 98-369)

P.L. 98-369, §474(o)(14):

Amended Code Sec. 48(m) by striking out "subsection (a)(2)" and inserting in lieu thereof "subsection (b)". **Effective** for tax years beginning after 12-31-83, and to carrybacks from such years, but shall not be construed as reducing the amount of any credit allowable for qualified investment in tax years beginning before 1-1-84.

• 1978, Energy Tax Act of 1978 (P.L. 95-618)

P.L. 95-618, §301(b):

Added Code Sec. 48(m). **Effective** 11-10-78.

[Sec. 48(n)—Repealed]

Amendments

• 1984, Deficit Reduction Act of 1984 (P.L. 98-369)

P.L. 98-369, §474(o)(15):

Repealed Code Sec. 48(n), except that paragraph (4) shall continue to apply in the case of any recapture under Code section 47(f) of a credit allowable for a taxable year beginning before 1-1-84. **Effective** for tax years beginning after 12-31-83, and to carrybacks from such years, but shall not be construed as reducing the amount of any credit allowable for qualified investment in tax years beginning before 1-1-84. Prior to repeal, Code Sec. 48(n) read as follows:

(n) REQUIREMENTS FOR ALLOWANCE OF EMPLOYEE PLAN PERCENTAGE—

(1) IN GENERAL.—

(A) BASIC EMPLOYEE PLAN PERCENTAGE.—The basic employee plan percentage shall not apply to any taxpayer for any taxable year unless the taxpayer on his return for such taxable year agrees, as a condition for the allowance of such percentage—

(i) to make transfers of employer securities to a tax credit employee stock ownership plan maintained by the taxpayer having an aggregate value which does not exceed 1 percent of the amount of the qualified investment (as determined under subsections (c) and (d) of section 46) for the taxable year, and

(ii) to make such transfers at the times prescribed in subparagraph (C).

(B) MATCHING EMPLOYEE PLAN PERCENTAGE.—The matching employee plan percentage shall not apply to any taxpayer for any taxable year unless the basic employee plan percentage applies to such taxpayer for such taxable year, and the taxpayer on his return for such taxable year agrees, as a condition for the allowance of the matching employee plan percentage—

(i) to make transfers of employer securities to a tax credit employee stock ownership plan maintained by the employer having an aggregate value equal to the lesser of—

(I) the sum of the qualified matching employee contributions made to such plan for the taxable year, or

(II) one-half of 1 percent of the amount of the qualified investment (as determined under subsections (c) and (d) of section 46) for the taxable year, and

(ii) to make such transfers at the times prescribed in subparagraph (C).

(C) TIMES FOR MAKING TRANSFERS.—The aggregate of the transfers required under subparagraphs (A) and (B) shall be made—

(i) to the extent allocable to that portion of the employee plan credit allowed for the taxable year or allowed as a carryback to a preceding taxable year, not later than 30 days after the due date (including extensions) for filing the return for the taxable year, or

(ii) to the extent allocable to that portion of the employee plan credit which is allowed as a carryover in a succeeding taxable year, not later than 30 days after the due date (including extensions) for filing the return for such succeeding taxable year.

The Secretary may by regulations provide that transfers may be made later than the times prescribed in the preceding sentence where the amount of any credit or carryover or carryback for any taxable year exceeds the amount shown on the return for the taxable year including where such excess is attributable to qualified matching employee contributions made after the close of the taxable year.

(D) ORDERING RULES.—For purposes of subparagraph (C), the portion of the employee plan credit allowed for the current year or as a carryover or carryback shall be determined—

(i) first by treating the credit or carryover or carryback as attributable to the regular percentage,

(ii) second by treating the portion (not allocated under clause (i)) of such credit or carryover or carryback as attributable to the basic employee plan percentage, and

(iii) finally by treating the portion (not allocated under clause (i) or (ii)) as attributable to the matching employee plan percentage.

(2) QUALIFIED MATCHING EMPLOYEE CONTRIBUTION DEFINED.—

(A) IN GENERAL.—For purposes of this subsection, the term "qualified matching employee contribution" means, with respect to any taxable year, any contribution made by an employee to an a tax credit employee stock ownership plan maintained by the taxpayer if—

(i) each employee who is entitled to an allocation of employer securities transferred to the tax credit employee stock ownership plan under paragraph (1)(A) is entitled to make such a contribution,

(ii) the contribution is designated by the employee as a contribution intended to be taken into account under this subparagraph for the taxable year,

(iii) the contribution is paid in cash to the employer or plan administrator not later than 24 months after the close of the taxable year, and is invested forthwith in employer securities, and

(iv) the tax credit employee stock ownership plan meets the requirements of subparagraph (B).

(B) PLAN REQUIREMENTS.—For purposes of subparagraph (A), a tax credit employee stock ownership plan meets the requirements of this subparagraph if—

(i) participation in the tax credit employee stock ownership plan is not required as a condition of employment and the tax credit employee stock ownership plan does not require matching employee contributions as a condition of participation in the tax credit employee stock ownership plan, and

(ii) the tax credit employee stock ownership plan provides for allocation of all employer securities transferred to it or purchased by it (because of the requirements of paragraph (1)(B)) to the account of each participant in an amount equal to such participant's matching employee contributions for the year.

(3) CERTAIN CONTRIBUTIONS OF CASH TREATED AS CONTRIBUTIONS OF EMPLOYER SECURITIES.—For purposes of this subsection, a transfer of cash shall be treated as a transfer of employer securities if the cash is, under the tax credit employee stock ownership plan, used within 30 days to purchase employer securities.

(4) ADJUSTMENTS IF EMPLOYEE PLAN CREDIT RECAPTURED.—If any portion of the employee plan credit is recaptured under section 47 or the employee plan credit is reduced by a final determination—

(A) the employer may reduce the amount required to be transferred to the tax credit employee stock ownership plan under paragraph (1) for the current taxable year or any succeeding taxable year by an amount equal to such portion (or reduction), or

(B) notwithstanding the provisions of paragraph (5) and to the extent not taken into account under subparagraph (A), the employer may deduct an amount equal to such portion (or reduction), subject to the limitations of section 404.

(5) DISALLOWANCE OF DEDUCTION.—No deduction shall be allowed under section 162, 212, or 404 for amounts required to be transferred to a tax credit employee stock ownership plan under this subsection.

(6) DEFINITIONS.—For purposes of this subsection—

(A) EMPLOYER SECURITIES.—The term "employer securities" has the meaning given to such term by section 409A(l).

(B) VALUE.—The term "value" means—

(i) in the case of securities listed on a national exchange, the average of closing prices of such securities for the 20 consecutive trading days immediately preceding the date on which the securities are contributed to the plan, or

(ii) in the case of securities not listed on a national exchange, the fair market value as determined in good faith and in accordance with regulations prescribed by the Secretary.

• 1981, Economic Recovery Tax Act of 1981 (P.L. 97-34)

P.L. 97-34, §332(b):

Amended Code Sec. 48(n)(1)(A)(i) by striking out "equal to" and inserting "which does not exceed". **Effective** for qualified investments made after 12-31-81.

• 1980, Miscellaneous Revenue Act of 1980 (P.L. 96-605)

P.L. 96-605, §223(a):

Amended Code Sec. 48(n)(6)(B)(i) by striking out "the due date for filing the return for the taxable year (determined with regard to extensions)" and inserting in lieu thereof "the date on which the securities are contributed to the plan". **Effective** with respect to tax years beginning after 12-31-80.

• 1980, Technical Corrections Act of 1979 (P.L. 96-222)

P.L. 96-222, §101(a)(7)(B):

Amended Act Sec. 141 of P.L. 95-600 by revising paragraph (g). For the **effective** dates, see the amendment note for §101(a)(7)(B), P.L. 96-222, following the text of Code Sec. 409A(n).

P.L. 96-222, §101(a)(7)(G):

Amended Code Sec. 48(n)(1)(B)(i). For **effective** date, see the amendment note at §101(a)(7)(B), P.L. 96-222, following the text of Code Sec. 409A(n). Prior to amendment, Code Sec. 48(n)(1)(B)(i) read as follows:

(i) to make transfers of employer securities to an ESOP maintained by the taxpayer having an aggregate value equal to the sum of the qualified matching employee contributions made to such ESOP for the taxable year, and

P.L. 96-222, §101(a)(7)(H):

Amended Code Sec. 48(n)(1)(C) by inserting at the end of the last sentence "(including where such excess is attributable to qualified matching employee contributions made after the close of the taxable year)". For the **effective** date and special election, see the amendment note at §101(a)(7)(B), P.L. 96-222, following the text of Code Sec. 409A(n).

P.L. 96-222, §101(a)(7)(L)(i)(I), (II), (III) and (IV):

Amended Code Sec. 48(n)(1)(A)(i), (2) and (5) by striking out "an ESOP" each place it appeared and inserting "a tax credit employee stock ownership plan". **Effective** for tax years beginning after 12-31-78.

P.L. 96-222, §101(a)(7)(L)(ii)(III), (IV), (V) and (VI):

Amended Code Sec. 48(n)(1)(B)(i) (as amended by §101(a)(7)(L)(i)), (2), (3) and (4)(A) by striking out "ESOP" each place it appeared and inserting "tax credit employee stock ownership plan". **Effective** for tax years beginning after 12-31-78.

P.L. 96-222, §101(a)(7)(L)(iii)(II):

Amended Code Sec. 48(n) (as amended by §101(a)(7)(L)(i) and (ii)) by striking out "ESOP" each place it appeared and inserting "employee plan". **Effective** for tax years beginning after 12-31-78.

P.L. 96-222, §101(a)(7)(L)(v)(II), (III) and (IV):

Amended the subsection heading of 48(n) by striking out "ESOP" and inserting "EMPLOYEE PLAN" and the subparagraph headings of 48(n)(1)(A) and (B) and the paragraph heading for 48(n)(4) by striking out "ESOP" and inserting "EMPLOYEE PLAN". **E ffective** for tax years beginning after 12-31-78.

P.L. 96-222, §101(a)(7)(M)(ii):

Amended Code Sec. 48(n)(2) by adding "and" at the end of clause (i), by deleting clause (ii), and by redesignating clause (iii) as clause (ii). **Effective** for qualified investment for tax years beginning after 12-31-78. Prior to deletion, clause (ii) read as follows:

(ii) employee contributions under the ESOP meet the requirements of section 401(a)(4), and

• 1978, Revenue Act of 1978 (P.L. 95-600)

P.L. 95-600, §141(b), (g)(1):

Redesignated Code Sec. 48(n), formerly Code Sec. 48(l) before redesignation by P.L. 95-618, §301(b), as Code Sec. 48(p) and added new Code Sec. 48(n). **Effective** for qualified investment for tax years beginning after 12-31-78.

• 1978, Energy Tax Act of 1978 (P.L. 95-618)

P.L. 95-618, §301(b):

Redesignated former Code Sec. 48(l) as Code Sec. 48(n). **Effective** 11-10-78.

[Sec. 48(o)]

(o) CERTAIN CREDITS DEFINED.—For purposes of this title—

(1) REGULAR INVESTMENT CREDIT.—The term "regular investment credit" means that portion of the credit allowable by section 38 which is attributable to the regular percentage.

(2) ENERGY INVESTMENT CREDIT.—The term "energy investment credit" means that portion of the credit allowable by section 38 which is attributable to the energy percentage.

(3) REHABILITATION INVESTMENT CREDIT.—The term "rehabilitation investment credit" means that portion of the credit allowable by section 38 which is attributable to the rehabilitation percentage.

Amendments

• 1984, Deficit Reduction Act of 1984 (P.L. 98-369)

P.L. 98-369, §474(o)(16):

Amended Code Sec. 48(o) by striking out paragraphs (3), (4), (5), (6), and (7) and by redesignating paragraph (8) as paragraph (3). **Effective** for tax years beginning after 12-31-83, and to carrybacks from such years, but shall not be construed as reducing the amount of any credit allowable for qualified investment in tax years beginning before 1-1-84. Prior to amendment, Code Sec. 48(o)(3)-(8) read as follows:

(3) Employee Plan Credit.—The term "employee plan credit" means the sum of—

(A) the basic employee plan credit, and

(B) the matching employee plan credit.

(4) Basic Employee Plan Credit.—The term "basic employee plan credit" means that portion of the credit allowable by section 38 which is attributable to the basic employee plan percentage.

(5) Matching Employee Plan Credit.—The term "matching employee plan credit" means that portion of the credit allowable by section 38 which is attributable to the matching employee plan percentage.

(6) Basic Employee Plan Percentage.—The term "basic employee plan percentage" means the 1-percent employee plan percentage set forth in section 46(a)(2)(E)(i).

(7) Matching Employee Plan Percentage.—The term "matching employee plan percentage" means the additional employee plan percentage (not to exceed 1/2 of 1 percent) set forth in section 46(a)(2)(E)(ii).

(8) Rehabilitation Investment Credit.—The term "rehabilitation investment credit" means that portion of the credit allowable by section 38 which is attributable to the rehabilitation percentage.

• 1981, Economic Recovery Tax Act of 1981 (P.L. 97-34)

P.L. 97-34, §212(a)(3):

Amended Code Sec. 48(o) by adding at the end thereof new paragraph (8). **Effective** for expenditures incurred after 12-31-81, in tax years ending after such date.

P.L. 97-34, §212(e)(2), as amended by P.L. 97-448, §102(f)(1), provides:

(2) TRANSITIONAL RULE.—The amendments made by this section shall not apply with respect to any rehabilitation of a building if—

(A) the physical work on such rehabilitation began before January 1, 1982, and

(B) such building does not meet the requirements of paragraph (1) of section 48(g) of the Internal Revenue Code of 1954 (as amended by this Act).

• 1980, Technical Corrections Act of 1979 (P.L. 96-222)

P.L. 96-222, §101(a)(7)(B):

Amended Act Sec. 141 of P.L. 95-600 by revising paragraph (g) which relates to the effective dates for the amendments concerning tax credit employee stock ownership plans. For **effective** dates, see the amendment note for §101(a)(7)(B), P.L. 96-222, following the text of Code Sec. 409A(n).

P.L. 96-222, §101(a)(7)(L)(iii)(III), (v)(IV) and (V):

Amended Code Sec. 48(o) by striking out "ESOP" each place it appeared and inserting "employee plan"; amended the paragraph headings of Code Sec. 48(o)(4), (5), (6) and (7) by striking out "ESOP" and inserting "EMPLOYEE PLAN"; and amended the paragraph heading of Code Sec. 48(o)(3) by striking out "ESOP" and inserting "EMPLOYEE PLAN". **Effective** for tax years beginning after 12-31-78.

P.L. 96-222, §101(a)(7)(M)(iii):

Amended Code Sec. 48(o)(5) (as amended by §101(a)(7)(L)) by adding "percentage" after "attributable to the matching employee plan". **Effective** for qualified investment for tax years beginning after 12-31-78.

• 1978, Revenue Act of 1978 (P.L. 95-600)

P.L. 95-600, §141(b):

Added Code Sec. 48(o). **Effective** for qualified investment for tax years beginning after 12-31-78.

[Sec. 48(p)]

(p) SINGLE PURPOSE AGRICULTURAL OR HORTICULTURAL STRUCTURE DEFINED.—For purposes of this section—

(1) IN GENERAL.—The term "single purpose agricultural or horticultural structure" means—

(A) a single purpose livestock structure, and

(B) a single purpose horticultural structure.

(2) SINGLE PURPOSE LIVESTOCK STRUCTURE.—The term "single purpose livestock structure" means any enclosure or structure specifically designed, constructed, and used—

(A) for housing, raising, and feeding a particular type of livestock and their produce, and

(B) for housing the equipment (including any replacements) necessary for the housing, raising, and feeding referred to in subparagraph (A).

(3) SINGLE PURPOSE HORTICULTURAL STRUCTURE.—The term "single purpose horticultural structure" means—

(A) a greenhouse specifically designed, constructed, and used for the commercial production of plants, and

(B) a structure specifically designed, constructed and used for the commercial production of mushrooms.

(4) STRUCTURES WHICH INCLUDE WORK SPACE.—An enclosure or structure which provides work space shall be treated as a single purpose agricultural or horticultural structure only if such work space is solely for—

(A) the stocking, caring for, or collecting of livestock or plants (as the case may be) or their produce,

(B) the maintenance of the enclosure or structure, and

(C) the maintenance or replacement of the equipment or stock enclosed or housed therein.

(5) SPECIAL RULE FOR APPLYING SECTION 47.—For purposes of section 47, any single purpose agricultural or horticultural structure shall be treated as meeting the requirements of this subsection for any period during which such structure is held for the use under which it qualified under this subsection.

(6) LIVESTOCK.—The term "livestock" includes poultry.

Amendments

• 1978, Revenue Act of 1978 (P.L. 95-600)

P.L. 95-600, §314(b), (c):

Redesignated Code Sec. 48(p) (formerly Code Sec. 48(l) and Code Sec. 48(n) before redesignation by P.L. 95-618, Sec. 301(b), and P.L. 95-600, Sec. 141(b), (g), respectively), as Code Sec. 48(q) and added new Code Sec. 48(p). **Effective** for tax years ending after 8-15-71. [Note: Congress apparently intended to make the above amendments in the order reflected despite effective date discrepancies.]

P.L. 95-600, §141(b):

Redesignated Code Sec. 48(n) (formerly Code Sec. 48(l) before redesignation by P.L. 95-618, Sec. 301(b)), as Code Sec. 48(p). **Effective** for qualified investment for tax years beginning after 12-31-78. [Note: Congress apparently intended to make this amendment after the change made by P.L. 95-618, Sec. 301(b), and before the amendment made by P.L. 95-600, Sec. 314(b), above, despite effective date discrepancies.]

[Sec. 48(q)]

(q) BASIS ADJUSTMENT TO SECTION 38 PROPERTY.—

(1) IN GENERAL.—For purposes of this subtitle, if a credit is determined under section 46(a) with respect to section 38 property, the basis of such property shall be reduced by 50 percent of the amount of the credit so determined.

(2) CERTAIN DISPOSITIONS.—If during any taxable year there is a recapture amount determined with respect to any section 38 property the basis of which was reduced under paragraph (1), the basis of such property (immediately before the event resulting in such recapture) shall be increased by an amount equal to 50 percent of such recapture amount. For purposes of the preceding sentence, the term "recapture amount" means any increase in tax (or adjustment in carrybacks or carryovers) determined under section 47.

(3) SPECIAL RULE FOR QUALIFIED REHABILITATED BUILDINGS.—In the case of any credit determined under section 46(a) for any qualified rehabilitation expenditure in connection with a qualified rehabilitated building, paragraphs (1) and (2) of this subsection and paragraph (5) of subsection (d) shall be applied without regard to the phrase "50 percent of".

(4) ELECTION OF REDUCED CREDIT IN LIEU OF BASIS ADJUSTMENT FOR REGULAR PERCENTAGE.—

(A) IN GENERAL.—If the taxpayer elects to have this paragraph apply with respect to any recovery property—

(i) paragraphs (1) and (2) shall not apply to so much of the credit determined under section 46(a) with respect to such property as is attributable to the regular percentage set forth in section 46(b)(1); and

(ii) the amount of the credit allowable under section 38 with respect to such property shall be determined under subparagraph (B).

(B) REDUCTION IN CREDIT.—In the case of any recovery property to which an election under subparagraph (A) applies—

(i) solely for the purposes of applying the regular percentage, the applicable percentage under subsection (c) or (d) of section 46 shall be deemed to be 100 percent, and

(ii) notwithstanding section 46(b)(1), the regular percentage shall be—

(I) 8 percent in the case of recovery property other than 3-year property, or

(II) 4 percent in the case of recovery property which is 3-year property.

For purposes of the preceding sentence, RRB replacement property (within the meaning of section 168(f)(3)(B)) shall be treated as property which is not 3-year property.

(C) TIME AND MANNER OF MAKING ELECTION.—

(i) IN GENERAL.—An election under this subsection with respect to any property shall be made on the taxpayer's return of the tax imposed by this chapter for the taxpayer's taxable year in which such property is placed in service (or in the case of property to which an election under section 46(d) applies, for the first taxable year for which qualified progress expenditures were taken into account with respect to such property).

(ii) REVOCABLE ONLY WITH CONSENT.—An election under this subsection with respect to any property, once made, may be revoked only with the consent of the Secretary.

(5) RECAPTURE OF REDUCTIONS.—

(A) IN GENERAL.—For purposes of sections 1245 and 1250, any reduction under this subsection shall be treated as a deduction allowed for depreciation.

(B) SPECIAL RULE FOR SECTION 1250.—For purposes of section 1250(b), the determination of what would have been the depreciation adjustments under the straight line method shall be made as if there had been no reduction under this section.

(6) ADJUSTMENT IN BASIS OF INTEREST IN PARTNERSHIP OR S CORPORATION.—The adjusted basis of—

(A) a partner's interest in a partnership, and

(B) stock in an S corporation,

shall be appropriately adjusted to take into account adjustments made under this subsection in the basis of property held by the partnership or S corporation (as the case may be).

(7) SPECIAL RULE FOR QUALIFIED FILMS.—If a credit is allowed under section 38 with respect to any qualified film (within the meaning of subsection (k)(1)(B)) then, in lieu of any reduction under paragraph (1)—

(A) to the extent that the credit is determined with respect to any amount described in clause (v) or (vi) of subsection (k)(5)(B), any deduction allowable under this chapter with respect to such amount shall be reduced by 50 percent of the amount of the credit so determined, and

(B) the basis of the taxpayer's ownership interest (within the meaning of subsection (k)(1)(C)) shall be reduced by the excess of—

(i) 50 percent of the amount of the credit determined under subsection (k), over

(ii) the amount of the reduction under subparagraph (A).

Amendments

• 1986, Tax Reform Act of 1986 (P.L. 99-514)

P.L. 99-514, §251(c):

Amended Code Sec. 48(q)(3) by striking out "other than a certified historic structure" following "rehabilitated building". **Effective** for property placed in service after 12-31-86, in tax years ending after such date. However, for transitional rules, see Act Sec. 251(d)(2)-(6), following Code Sec. 46.

P.L. 99-514, §1809(d)(2):

Amended Code Sec. 48(q) by redesignating paragraph (6)[7] as paragraph (7). **Effective** as if included in the provision of P.L. 98-369 to which it relates.

• 1984, Deficit Reduction Act of 1984 (P.L. 98-369)

P.L. 98-369, §113(b)(4):

Amended Code Sec. 48(q) by adding new paragraph (6)[7]. **Effective** as if included in the amendments made by P.L. 97-248, §205(a)(1).

P.L. 98-369, §474(o)(17):

Amended Code Sec. 48(q) by striking out "section 46(a)(2)" each place it appeared and inserting in lieu thereof "section 46(a)", and by striking out "section 46(a)(2)(B)" each place it appeared and inserting in lieu thereof "section 46(b)(1)". **Effective** for tax years beginning after 12-31-83, and to carrybacks from such years, but shall not be construed as reducing the amount of any credit allowable for qualified investment in tax years beginning before 1-1-84.

P.L. 98-369, §712(b):

Amended Code Sec. 48(q) by adding at the end thereof new paragraph (6). **Effective** as if included in the provision of P.L. 97-248 to which it relates.

• 1983, Technical Corrections Act of 1982 (P.L. 97-448)

P.L. 97-448, §306(a)(3):

Amended Code Sec. 48(q)(3) by striking out "paragraphs (1) and (2)" and inserting in lieu thereof "paragraphs (1) and (2) of this subsection and paragraph (5) of subsection (d)". **Effective** as if it had been included in the provision of P.L. 97-248 to which it relates.

• 1982, Tax Equity and Fiscal Responsibility Act of 1982 (P.L. 97-248)

P.L. 97-248, §205(a)(1):

Amended Code Sec. 48 by redesignating subsection (q) as subsection (r) and by inserting after subsection (p) new subsection (q). For **effective** date and special rules, see amendment notes for P.L. 97-248 under Code Sec. 48(d).

[Sec. 48(r)]

(r) CERTAIN SECTION 501(d) ORGANIZATIONS.—

(1) IN GENERAL.—In the case of eligible section 501(d) organizations—

(A) any business engaged in by such organization for the common benefit of its members and the taxable income from which is included in the gross income of its members shall be treated as an unrelated business for purposes of paragraph (4) of subsection (a),

(B) The qualified investment for each taxable year with respect to such business shall be apportioned pro rata among such members in the same manner as the taxable income of such organization, and

(C) any individual to whom any investment has been apportioned under subparagraph (B) shall be treated for purposes of this subpart (other than section 47) as the taxpayer with respect to such investment, and such investment shall not (by reason of such apportionment) lose its character as an investment in new section 38 property or used section 38 property, as the case may be.

(2) LIMITATION ON USED SECTION 38 PROPERTY APPLIED AT ORGANIZATION LEVEL.—The limitation under subparagraph (A) of subsection (c)(2) shall apply with respect to the section 501(d) organization.

(3) RECAPTURE.—For purposes of applying section 47 to any property for which credit was allowed under section 38 by reason of this subsection—

(A) the section 501(d) organization shall be treated as the taxpayer to which the credit under section 38 was allowed,

(B) the amount of such credit allowed with respect to the property shall be treated as the amount which would have been allowed to the section 501(d) organization were such credit allowable to such organization,

(C) subparagraph (D) of section 47(a)(5) shall not apply, and

(D) the amount of the increase in tax under section 47 for any taxable year with respect to property to which this subsection applies shall be allocated pro rata among the members of such organization in the same manner as such organization's taxable income for such year is allocated among such members.

(4) NO INVESTMENT CREDIT ALLOWED TO MEMBER IF MEMBER CLAIMS OTHER INVESTMENT CREDIT.—

No credit shall be allowed to an individual by reason of this subsection if such individual claims a credit under section 38 without regard to this subsection. The amount of the credit not allowed by reason of the preceding sentence shall not be allowed to any other person.

(5) ELIGIBLE SECTION 501(d) ORGANIZATION.—For purposes of this subsection, the term "eligible section 501(d) organization" means any organization—

(A) which elects to be treated as an organization described in section 501(d) and which is exempt from tax under section 501(a), and

(B) which does not provide a substantially higher standard of living for any person or persons than it does for the majority of the members of the community.

Amendments

• 1986, Tax Reform Act of 1986 (P.L. 99-514)

P.L. 99-514, §1879(j)(1):

Amended Code Sec. 48 by redesignating subsection (r) as subsection (s) and by inserting after subsection (q) new subsection (r). **Effective** for periods after 12-31-78 (under rules similar to the rules of section 48(m) of the Internal Revenue Code of 1954), in tax years ending after such date. However, see Act Sec. 1879(j)(3) for a special rule, below.

P.L. 99-514, §1879(j)(3), provides:

(3) Special Rule.—If refund or credit of any overpayment of tax resulting from the application of this subsection is prevented at any time before the close of the date which is 1 year after the date of the enactment of this Act by operation of any law or rule of law (including res judicata), refund or credit of such overpayment (to the extent attributable to the application of the amendments made by this subsection) may, nevertheless, be made or allowed if claim therefor is filed before the close of such 1-year period.

[Sec. 48(s)]

(s) SPECIAL RULES RELATING TO SOUND RECORDINGS.—

(1) IN GENERAL.—For purposes of this title, in the case of any sound recording, the original use of which commences with the taxpayer, the taxpayer may elect to treat such recording as recovery property which is 3-year property to the extent that the taxpayer has an ownership interest in such recording.

(2) FAILURE TO MAKE ELECTION.—If a taxpayer does not make an election under paragraph (1) with respect to any sound recording—

(A) no credit shall be allowed under section 38 with respect to such recording, and

(B) such recording shall not be treated as recovery property.

(3) PREDOMINANT USE TEST AND AT RISK RULES NOT TO APPLY; QUALIFIED INVESTMENT.—In the case of any sound recording—

(A) sections 46(c)(8), 46(c)(9), and 48(a)(2) shall not apply, and

(B) in determining the qualified investment under section 46(c)(1), there shall be used (in lieu of the basis of the property) an amount equal to the production costs which are allocable to the United States (as determined under rules similar to the rules of section 48(k)(5)(D)).

(4) OWNERSHIP INTEREST.—For purposes of determining the credit allowable under section 38, the ownership interest of any person in a sound recording shall be determined on the basis of his proportionate share of any loss which may be incurred with respect to the production costs of such sound recording.

(5) SOUND RECORDING.—For purposes of this subsection, the term "sound recording" means works which result from the fixation of a series of musical, spoken, or other sounds, regardless of the nature of the material objects (such as discs, tapes, or other phonorecordings) in which such sounds are embodied.

(6) PRODUCTION COSTS.—

(A) IN GENERAL.—For purposes of this subsection, the term "production costs" includes—

(i) a reasonable allocation of general overhead costs,

(ii) compensation for services performed by song writers, artists, production personnel, directors, producers, and similar personnel,

(iii) costs of "first" distribution of records or tapes, and

(iv) the cost of the material being recorded.

(B) CERTAIN COSTS NOT TAKEN INTO ACCOUNT.—Except as provided in subparagraph (C), the term "production costs" shall not include—

(i) "residuals" payable under contracts with labor organizations, or

(ii) participations or royalties payable as compensation to song writers, artists, production personnel, directors, producers, and similar personnel, or

(iii) any other contingent amounts.

(C) CERTAIN CONTINGENT AMOUNTS TAKEN INTO ACCOUNT.—In the case of any amount which is described in subparagraph (B) and which is incurred in the taxable year in which the sound recording is placed in service or the next taxable year—

(i) subparagraph (B) shall not apply, and

(ii) for purposes of sections 38 and 168, the taxpayer shall be treated as having placed in service in each such taxable year 3-year recovery property with a basis equal to the amount so incurred in such taxable year.

(7) ELECTION MADE SEPARATELY.—An election under paragraph (1) shall be made separately with respect to each sound recording and must be made by all persons having an ownership interest in such recording.

(8) UNITED STATES.—For purposes of this subsection, the term "United States" includes the possessions of the United States.

(9) TERMINATION.—This subsection shall not apply to any property placed in service after December 31, 1985, unless such property is transition property (as defined in section 49(e)(1)).

Amendments

• 1988, Technical and Miscellaneous Revenue Act of 1988 (P.L. 100-647)

P.L. 100-647, §1002(a)(16)(A):

Amended Code Sec. 48(s) by adding at the end thereof new paragraph (9).

• 1986, Tax Reform Act of 1986 (P.L. 99-514)

P.L. 99-514, §803(b)(2)(B):

Amended paragraph (5) of Code Sec. 48(r) (subsequently redesignated as subsection (s) by Act Sec. 1879(j)(1)). For the **effective** date as well as special rules, see Act Sec. 803(d), below. Prior to amendment, Code Sec. 48(r)(5) read as follows:

(5) SOUND RECORDING.—For purposes of this subsection, the term "sound recording" means any sound recording described in section 280(c)(2).

P.L. 99-514, §803(d), as amended by P.L. 100-647, §1008(b)(7), and P.L. 101-239, §7831(d)(1), provides:

(d) EFFECTIVE DATE.—

(1) IN GENERAL.—Except as provided in this subsection, the amendments made by this section shall apply to costs incurred after December 31, 1986, in taxable years ending after such date.

(2) SPECIAL RULE FOR INVENTORY PROPERTY.—In the case of any property which is inventory in the hands of the taxpayer—

(A) IN GENERAL.—The amendments made by this section shall apply to taxable years beginning after December 31, 1986.

(B) CHANGE IN METHOD OF ACCOUNTING.—If the taxpayer is required by the amendments made by this section to change its method of accounting with respect to such property for any taxable year—

(i) such change shall be treated as initiated by the taxpayer,

(ii) such change shall be treated as made with the consent of the Secretary, and

(iii) the period for taking into account the adjustments under section 481 by reason of such change shall not exceed 4 years.

(3) SPECIAL RULE FOR SELF-CONSTRUCTED PROPERTY.—The amendments made by this section shall not apply to any property which is produced by the taxpayer for use by the taxpayer if substantial construction had occurred before March 1, 1986.

(4) TRANSITIONAL RULE FOR CAPITALIZATION OF INTEREST AND TAXES.—

(A) TRANSITION PROPERTY EXEMPTED FROM INTEREST CAPITALIZATION.—Section 263A of the Internal Revenue Code of 1986 (as added by this section) and the amendment made by subsection (b)(1) shall not apply to interest costs which are allocable to any property—

(i) to which the amendments made by section 201 do not apply by reason of sections 204(a)(1)(D) and (E) and 204(a)(5)(A), and

(ii) to which the amendments made by section 251 do not apply by reason of section 251(d)(3)(M).

(B) INTEREST AND TAXES.—Section 263A of such Code shall not apply to property described in the matter following subparagraph (B) of section 207(e)(2) of the Tax Equity and Fiscal Responsibility Act of 1982 to the extent it would require the capitalization of interest and taxes paid or incurred in connection with such property which are not required to be capitalized under section 189 of such Code (as in effect before the amendment made by subsection (b)(1)).

(5) TRANSITION RULE CONCERNING CAPITALIZATION OF INVENTORY RULES.—In the case of a corporation which on the date of the enactment of this Act was a member of an affiliated group of corporations (within the meaning of section 1504(a) of the Internal Revenue Code of 1986), the parent of which—

(A) was incorporated in California on April 15, 1925,

(B) adopted LIFO accounting as of the close of the taxable year ended December 31, 1950, and

(C) was, on May 22, 1986, merged into a Delaware corporation incorporated on March 12, 1986,

the amendments made by this section shall apply under a cut-off method whereby the uniform capitalization rules are applied only in costing layers of inventory acquired during taxable years beginning on or after January 1, 1987.

(6) TREATMENT OF CERTAIN REHABILITATION PROJECT.—The amendments made by this section shall not apply to interest and taxes paid or incurred with respect to the rehabilitation and conversion of a certified historic building which was formerly a factory into an apartment project with 155 units, 39 units of which are for low-income families, if the project was approved for annual interest assistance on June 10, 1986, by the housing authority of the State in which the project is located.

(7) SPECIAL RULE FOR CASUALTY LOSSES.—Section 263A(d)(2) of the Internal Revenue Code of 1986 (as added by this section) shall apply to expenses incurred on or after the date of the enactment of this Act.

P.L. 99-514, §1879(j)(1):

Redesignated subsection (r) as (s). **Effective** for periods after 12-31-78 (under rules similar to the rules of section 48(m) of the Internal Revenue Code of 1954), in tax years ending after such date. However, see Act Sec. 1879(j)(3) following Code Sec. 48(r) for a special rule.

• 1984, Deficit Reduction Act of 1984 (P.L. 98-369)

P.L. 98-369, §113(a)(1):

Amended Code Sec. 48 by redesignating subsection (r) as subsection (s) and by inserting after subsection (q) new subsection (r). **Effective** for property placed in service after 3-15-84, in tax years ending after such date.

P.L. 98-369, §474(o)(18):

Amended Code Sec. 48(r), redesignated as (s) by Act Sec. 113(a), by striking out "section 381(c)(23)" and inserting in lieu thereof "section 381(c)(26)". **Effective** for tax years beginning after 12-31-83, and to carrybacks from such years, but shall not be construed as reducing the amount of any credit allowable for qualified investment in tax years beginning before 1-1-84.

[Sec. 48(t)]

(t) CROSS REFERENCE.—

For application of this subpart to certain acquiring corporations, see section 381(c)(26).

Amendments

• 1988, Technical and Miscellaneous Revenue Act of 1988 (P.L. 100-647)

P.L. 100-647, §1002(a)(20):

Amended Code Sec. 48 by redesignating subsection (s)[t] as subsection (t). **Effective** as if included in the provision of P.L. 99-514 to which it relates.

• 1984, Deficit Reduction Act of 1984 (P.L. 98-369)

P.L. 98-369, §113(a)(1):

Amended Code Sec. 48 by redesignating subsection (r) as (s). **Effective** for property placed in service after 3-15-84, in tax years ending after such date.

• 1982, Tax Equity and Fiscal Responsibility Act of 1982 (P.L. 97-248)

P.L. 97-248, §205(a)(1):

Redesignated subsection (q) as (r). For **effective** date, see Code Sec. 48(d).

• 1980, Technical Corrections Act of 1979 (P.L. 96-222)

P.L. 96-222, §101(a)(7)(B):

Amended Act Sec. 141 of P.L. 95-600 by revising paragraph (g). For the **effective** dates, see the amendment note for §101(a)(7)(B), P.L. 96-222, following the text of Code Sec. 409A(n).

• 1978, Revenue Act of 1978 (P.L. 95-600)

P.L. 95-600, §314(b), (c):

Redesignated Code Sec. 48(p), as Code Sec. 48(q). **Effective** for tax years ending after 8-15-71.

P.L. 95-600, §141(b), (g)(1):

Redesignated Code Sec. 48(n) as Code Sec. 48(p). **Effective** for qualified investment for tax years beginning after 12-31-78.

• 1978, Energy Tax Act of 1978 (P.L. 95-618)

P.L. 95-618, §301(b):

Redesignated Code Sec. 48(l) as Code Sec. 48(n). **Effective** 11-10-78. [Note: Congress apparently intended the amendments made by this Act Sec. to precede changes made by P.L. 95-600, Secs. 141(b) and 314(b), despite effective date discrepancies.]

• 1976, Tax Reform Act of 1976 (P.L. 94-455)

P.L. 94-455, §804(a):

Redesignated Code Sec. 48(k) as Code Sec. 48(l) and inserted a new Code Sec. 48(k). For **effective** date, see note under new Code Sec. 48(k).

• 1966 (P.L. 89-800)

P.L. 89-800, §1(a):

Redesignated Code Sec. 48(h) as Sec. 48(k). **Effective** for tax years ending after 10-9-66.

• 1962, Revenue Act of 1962 (P.L. 87-834)

P.L. 87-834, §2:

Added Code Secs. 46, 47 and 48. **Effective** for tax years ending after 12-31-61.

[Sec. 48(c)]

(c) DEFINITIONS.—For purposes of this section—

(1) QUALIFIED FUEL CELL PROPERTY.—

(A) IN GENERAL.—The term "qualified fuel cell property" means a fuel cell power plant which—

(i) has a nameplate capacity of at least 0.5 kilowatt of electricity using an electrochemical process, and

(ii) has an electricity-only generation efficiency greater than 30 percent.

(B) LIMITATION.—In the case of qualified fuel cell property placed in service during the taxable year, the credit otherwise determined under subsection (a) for such year with respect to such property shall not exceed an amount equal to $1,500 for each 0.5 kilowatt of capacity of such property.

(C) FUEL CELL POWER PLANT.—The term "fuel cell power plant" means an integrated system comprised of a fuel cell stack assembly and associated balance of plant components which converts a fuel into electricity using electrochemical means.

(D) TERMINATION.—The term "qualified fuel cell property" shall not include any property for any period after December 31, 2016.

(2) QUALIFIED MICROTURBINE PROPERTY.—

(A) IN GENERAL.—The term "qualified microturbine property" means a stationary microturbine power plant which—

(i) has a nameplate capacity of less than 2,000 kilowatts, and

(ii) has an electricity-only generation efficiency of not less than 26 percent at International Standard Organization conditions.

(B) LIMITATION.—In the case of qualified microturbine property placed in service during the taxable year, the credit otherwise determined under subsection (a) for such year with respect to such property shall not exceed an amount equal [to] $200 for each kilowatt of capacity of such property.

(C) STATIONARY MICROTURBINE POWER PLANT.—The term "stationary microturbine power plant" means an integrated system comprised of a gas turbine engine, a combustor, a recuperator or regenerator, a generator or alternator, and associated balance of plant components which converts a fuel into electricity and thermal energy. Such term also includes all secondary components located between the existing infrastructure for fuel delivery and the existing infrastructure for power distribution, including equipment and controls for meeting relevant power standards, such as voltage, frequency, and power factors.

(D) TERMINATION.—The term "qualified microturbine property" shall not include any property for any period after December 31, 2016.

(3) COMBINED HEAT AND POWER SYSTEM PROPERTY.—

(A) COMBINED HEAT AND POWER SYSTEM PROPERTY.—The term "combined heat and power system property" means property comprising a system—

(i) which uses the same energy source for the simultaneous or sequential generation of electrical power, mechanical shaft power, or both, in combination with the generation of steam or other forms of useful thermal energy (including heating and cooling applications),

(ii) which produces—

(I) at least 20 percent of its total useful energy in the form of thermal energy which is not used to produce electrical or mechanical power (or combination thereof), and

(II) at least 20 percent of its total useful energy in the form of electrical or mechanical power (or combination thereof),

(iii) the energy efficiency percentage of which exceeds 60 percent, and

(iv) which is placed in service before January 1, 2017.

(B) LIMITATION.—

(i) IN GENERAL.—In the case of combined heat and power system property with an electrical capacity in excess of the applicable capacity placed in service during the taxable year, the credit under subsection (a)(1) (determined without regard to this paragraph) for such year shall be equal to the amount which bears the same ratio to such credit as the applicable capacity bears to the capacity of such property.

(ii) APPLICABLE CAPACITY.—For purposes of clause (i), the term "applicable capacity" means 15 megawatts or a mechanical energy capacity of more than 20,000 horsepower or an equivalent combination of electrical and mechanical energy capacities.

(iii) MAXIMUM CAPACITY.—The term "combined heat and power system property" shall not include any property comprising a system if such system has a capacity in excess of 50 megawatts or a mechanical energy capacity in excess of 67,000 horsepower or an equivalent combination of electrical and mechanical energy capacities.

(C) SPECIAL RULES.—

(i) ENERGY EFFICIENCY PERCENTAGE.—For purposes of this paragraph, the energy efficiency percentage of a system is the fraction—

(I) the numerator of which is the total useful electrical, thermal, and mechanical power produced by the system at normal operating rates, and expected to be consumed in its normal application, and

(II) the denominator of which is the lower heating value of the fuel sources for the system.

(ii) DETERMINATIONS MADE ON BTU BASIS.—The energy efficiency percentage and the percentages under subparagraph (A)(ii) shall be determined on a Btu basis.

(iii) INPUT AND OUTPUT PROPERTY NOT INCLUDED.—The term "combined heat and power system property" does not include property used to transport the energy source to the facility or to distribute energy produced by the facility.

(D) SYSTEMS USING BIOMASS.—If a system is designed to use biomass (within the meaning of paragraphs (2) and (3) of section 45(c) without regard to the last sentence of paragraph (3)(A)) for at least 90 percent of the energy source—

(i) subparagraph (A)(iii) shall not apply, but

(ii) the amount of credit determined under subsection (a) with respect to such system shall not exceed the amount which bears the same ratio to such amount of credit (determined without regard to this subparagraph) as the energy efficiency percentage of such system bears to 60 percent.

(4) QUALIFIED SMALL WIND ENERGY PROPERTY.—

(A) IN GENERAL.—The term "qualified small wind energy property" means property which uses a qualifying small wind turbine to generate electricity.

(B) QUALIFYING SMALL WIND TURBINE.—The term "qualifying small wind turbine" means a wind turbine which has a nameplate capacity of not more than 100 kilowatts.

(C) TERMINATION.—The term "qualified small wind energy property" shall not include any property for any period after December 31, 2016.

Amendments

• 2009, American Recovery and Reinvestment Tax Act of 2009 (P.L. 111-5)

P.L. 111-5, §1103(a):

Amended Code Sec. 48(c)(4) by striking subparagraph (B) and by redesignating subparagraphs (C) and (D) as subparagraphs (B) and (C). **Effective** for periods after 12-31-2008, under rules similar to the rules of Code Sec. 48(m) (as in effect on the day before the date of the enactment of the Revenue Reconciliation Act of 1990 [10-30-90]). Prior to being stricken, Code Sec. 48(c)(4)(B) read as follows:

(B) LIMITATION.—In the case of qualified small wind energy property placed in service during the taxable year, the credit otherwise determined under subsection (a)(1) for such year with respect to all such property of the taxpayer shall not exceed $4,000.

• 2008, Energy Improvement and Extension Act of 2008 (P.L. 110-343)

P.L. 110-343, Division B, §103(a)(2):

Amended Code Sec. 48(c)(1)(E) by striking "December 31, 2008" and inserting "December 31, 2016". **Effective** 10-3-2008.

P.L. 110-343, Division B, §103(a)(3):

Amended Code Sec. 48(c)(2)(E) by striking "December 31, 2008" and inserting "December 31, 2016". **Effective** 10-3-2008.

P.L. 110-343, Division B, §103(c)(2)(A)-(B):

Amended Code Sec. 48(c) by striking "QUALIFIED FUEL CELL PROPERTY; QUALIFIED MICROTURBINE PROPERTY" in the heading and inserting "DEFINITIONS", and by adding at the end a new paragraph (3). **Effective** for periods after 10-3-2008, in tax years ending after such date, under rules similar to the rules of Code Sec. 48(m) (as in effect on the day before the date of the enactment of the Revenue Reconciliation Act of 1990 (P.L. 101-508)).

P.L. 110-343, Division B, §103(d):

Amended Code Sec. 48(c)(1)(B) by striking "$500" and inserting "$1,500". **Effective** for periods after 10-3-2008, in tax years ending after such date, under rules similar to the rules of Code Sec. 48(m) (as in effect on the day before the date of the enactment of the Revenue Reconciliation Act of 1990 (P.L. 101-508)).

P.L. 110-343, Division B, §103(e)(2)(A):

Amended Code Sec. 48(c)(1) by striking subparagraph (D) and redesignating subparagraph (E) as subparagraph (D). **Effective** for periods after 2-13-2008, in tax years ending after such date, under rules similar to the rules of Code Sec. 48(m) (as in effect on the day before the date of the enactment of the Revenue Reconciliation Act of 1990 (P.L. 101-508)). Prior to being stricken, Code Sec. 48(c)(1)(D) read as follows:

(D) SPECIAL RULE.—The first sentence of the matter in subsection (a)(3) which follows subparagraph (D) thereof shall not apply to qualified fuel cell property which is used predominantly in the trade or business of the furnishing or sale of telephone service, telegraph service by means of domestic telegraph operations, or other telegraph services (other than international telegraph services).

P.L. 110-343, Division B, §103(e)(2)(B):

Amended Code Sec. 48(c)(2) by striking subparagraph (D) and redesignating subparagraph (E) as subparagraph (D). **Effective** for periods after 2-13-2008, in tax years ending after such date, under rules similar to the rules of Code Sec. 48(m) (as in effect on the day before the date of the enactment of the Revenue Reconciliation Act of 1990 (P.L. 101-508)). Prior to being stricken, Code Sec. 48(c)(2)(D) read as follows:

(D) SPECIAL RULE.—The first sentence of the matter in subsection (a)(3) which follows subparagraph (D) thereof shall not apply to qualified microturbine property which is used predominantly in the trade or business of the furnishing or sale of telephone service, telegraph service by means of domestic telegraph operations, or other telegraph services (other than international telegraph services).

P.L. 110-343, Division B, §104(c):

Amended Code Sec. 48(c), as amended by Act Sec. 103, by adding at the end a new paragraph (4). **Effective** for periods after 10-3-2008, in tax years ending after such date, under rules similar to the rules of Code Sec. 48(m) (as in effect on the day before the date of the enactment of the Revenue Reconciliation Act of 1990 (P.L. 101-508)).

• 2007, Tax Technical Corrections Act of 2007 (P.L. 110-172)

P.L. 110-172, §11(a)(8):

Amended Code Sec. 48(c) by striking "subsection" in the text preceding paragraph (1) and inserting "section". **Effective** 12-29-2007.

P.L. 110-172, §11(a)(9):

Amended Code Sec. 48(c)(1)(B) and (2)(B) by striking "paragraph (1)" and inserting "subsection (a)". **Effective** 12-29-2007.

• 2006, Tax Relief and Health Care Act of 2006 (P.L. 109-432)

P.L. 109-432, Division A, §207(2):

Amended Code Sec. 48[(c)] by striking "December 31, 2007" both places it appears and inserting "December 31, 2008". **Effective** 12-20-2006.

• 2005, Energy Tax Incentives Act of 2005 (P.L. 109-58)

P.L. 109-58, §1336(b):

Amended Code Sec. 48 by adding at the end a new subsection (c). **Effective** for periods after 12–31–2005, in tax years ending after such date, under rules similar to the rules of Code Sec. 48(m) (as in effect on the day before the date of the enactment of P.L. 101-508 [11-4-90.—CCH]).

[Sec. 48(d)]

(d) COORDINATION WITH DEPARTMENT OF TREASURY GRANTS.—In the case of any property with respect to which the Secretary makes a grant under section 1603 of the American Recovery and Reinvestment Tax Act of 2009—

(1) DENIAL OF PRODUCTION AND INVESTMENT CREDITS.—No credit shall be determined under this section or section 45 with respect to such property for the taxable year in which such grant is made or any subsequent taxable year.

(2) RECAPTURE OF CREDITS FOR PROGRESS EXPENDITURES MADE BEFORE GRANT.—If a credit was determined under this section with respect to such property for any taxable year ending before such grant is made—

(A) the tax imposed under subtitle A on the taxpayer for the taxable year in which such grant is made shall be increased by so much of such credit as was allowed under section 38,

(B) the general business carryforwards under section 39 shall be adjusted so as to recapture the portion of such credit which was not so allowed, and

(C) the amount of such grant shall be determined without regard to any reduction in the basis of such property by reason of such credit.

(3) TREATMENT OF GRANTS.—Any such grant shall—

(A) not be includible in the gross income of the taxpayer, but

(B) shall be taken into account in determining the basis of the property to which such grant relates, except that the basis of such property shall be reduced under section 50(c) in the same manner as a credit allowed under subsection (a).

Amendments

• 2009, American Recovery and Reinvestment Tax Act of 2009 (P.L. 111-5)

P.L. 111-5, §1104:

Amended Code Sec. 48 by adding at the end a new subsection (d). **Effective** 2-17-2009.

P.L. 111-5, §1603, provides:

SEC. 1603. GRANTS FOR SPECIFIED ENERGY PROPERTY IN LIEU OF TAX CREDITS.

(a) IN GENERAL.—Upon application, the Secretary of the Treasury shall, subject to the requirements of this section, provide a grant to each person who places in service specified energy property to reimburse such person for a portion of the expense of such property as provided in subsection (b). No grant shall be made under this section with respect to any property unless such property—

(1) is placed in service during 2009 or 2010, or

(2) is placed in service after 2010 and before the credit termination date with respect to such property, but only if the construction of such property began during 2009 or 2010.

(b) GRANT AMOUNT.—

(1) IN GENERAL.—The amount of the grant under subsection (a) with respect to any specified energy property shall be the applicable percentage of the basis of such property.

(2) APPLICABLE PERCENTAGE.—For purposes of paragraph (1), the term "applicable percentage" means—

(A) 30 percent in the case of any property described in paragraphs (1) through (4) of subsection (d), and

(B) 10 percent in the case of any other property.

(3) DOLLAR LIMITATIONS.—In the case of property described in paragraph (2), (6), or (7) of subsection (d), the amount of any grant under this section with respect to such property shall not exceed the limitation described in section 48(c)(1)(B), 48(c)(2)(B), or 48(c)(3)(B) of the Internal Revenue Code of 1986, respectively, with respect to such property.

(c) TIME FOR PAYMENT OF GRANT.—The Secretary of the Treasury shall make payment of any grant under subsection (a) during the 60-day period beginning on the later of—

(1) the date of the application for such grant, or

(2) the date the specified energy property for which the grant is being made is placed in service.

(d) SPECIFIED ENERGY PROPERTY.—For purposes of this section, the term "specified energy property" means any of the following:

(1) QUALIFIED FACILITIES.—Any qualified property (as defined in section 48(a)(5)(D) of the Internal Revenue Code of 1986) which is part of a qualified facility (within the meaning of section 45 of such Code) described in paragraph (1), (2), (3), (4), (6), (7), (9), or (11) of section 45(d) of such Code.

(2) QUALIFIED FUEL CELL PROPERTY.—Any qualified fuel cell property (as defined in section 48(c)(1) of such Code).

(3) SOLAR PROPERTY.—Any property described in clause (i) or (ii) of section 48(a)(3)(A) of such Code.

(4) QUALIFIED SMALL WIND ENERGY PROPERTY.—Any qualified small wind energy property (as defined in section 48(c)(4) of such Code).

(5) GEOTHERMAL PROPERTY.—Any property described in clause (iii) of section 48(a)(3)(A) of such Code.

(6) QUALIFIED MICROTURBINE PROPERTY.— Any qualified microturbine property (as defined in section 48(c)(2) of such Code).

(7) COMBINED HEAT AND POWER SYSTEM PROPERTY.—Any combined heat and power system property (as defined in section 48(c)(3) of such Code).

(8) GEOTHERMAL HEAT PUMP PROPERTY.—Any property described in clause (vii) of section 48(a)(3)(A) of such Code.

Such term shall not include any property unless depreciation (or amortization in lieu of depreciation) is allowable with respect to such property.

(e) CREDIT TERMINATION DATE.—For purposes of this section, the term "credit termination date" means—

(1) in the case of any specified energy property which is part of a facility described in paragraph (1) of section 45(d) of the Internal Revenue Code of 1986, January 1, 2013,

(2) in the case of any specified energy property which is part of a facility described in paragraph (2), (3), (4), (6), (7), (9), or (11) of section 45(d) of such Code, January 1, 2014, and

(3) in the case of any specified energy property described in section 48 of such Code, January 1, 2017.

In the case of any property which is described in paragraph (3) and also in another paragraph of this subsection, paragraph (3) shall apply with respect to such property.

(f) APPLICATION OF CERTAIN RULES.—In making grants under this section, the Secretary of the Treasury shall apply rules similar to the rules of section 50 of the Internal Revenue Code of 1986. In applying such rules, if the property is disposed of, or otherwise ceases to be specified energy property, the Secretary of the Treasury shall provide for the recapture of the appropriate percentage of the grant amount in such manner as the Secretary of the Treasury determines appropriate.

(g) EXCEPTION FOR CERTAIN NON-TAXPAYERS.—The Secretary of the Treasury shall not make any grant under this section to—

(1) any Federal, State, or local government (or any political subdivision, agency, or instrumentality thereof),

(2) any organization described in section 501(c) of the Internal Revenue Code of 1986 and exempt from tax under section 501(a) of such Code,

(3) any entity referred to in paragraph (4) of section 54(j) of such Code, or

(4) any partnership or other pass-thru entity any partner (or other holder of an equity or profits interest) of which is described in paragraph (1), (2) or (3).

(h) DEFINITIONS.—Terms used in this section which are also used in section 45 or 48 of the Internal Revenue Code of 1986 shall have the same meaning for purposes of this section as when used in such section 45 or 48. Any reference in this section to the Secretary of the Treasury shall be treated as including the Secretary's delegate.

(i) APPROPRIATIONS.—There is hereby appropriated to the Secretary of the Treasury such sums as may be necessary to carry out this section.

(j) TERMINATION.—The Secretary of the Treasury shall not make any grant to any person under this section unless the application of such person for such grant is received before October 1, 2011.

[Sec. 48A]

SEC. 48A. QUALIFYING ADVANCED COAL PROJECT CREDIT.

[Sec. 48A(a)]

(a) IN GENERAL.—For purposes of section 46, the qualifying advanced coal project credit for any taxable year is an amount equal to—

(1) 20 percent of the qualified investment for such taxable year in the case of projects described in subsection (d)(3)(B)(i),

(2) 15 percent of the qualified investment for such taxable year in the case of projects described in subsection (d)(3)(B)(ii), and

(3) 30 percent of the qualified investment for such taxable year in the case of projects described in clause (iii) of subsection (d)(3)(B).

Amendments

• 2008, Energy Improvement and Extension Act of 2008 (P.L. 110-343)

P.L. 110-343, Division B, §111(a):

Amended Code Sec. 48A(a) by striking "and" at the end of paragraph (1), by striking the period at the end of paragraph (2) and inserting ", and", and by adding at the end a new paragraph (3). **Effective** for credits the application for which is submitted during the period described in Code Sec. 48A(d)(2)(A)(ii) and which are allocated or reallocated after 10-3-2008.

[Sec. 48A(b)]

(b) QUALIFIED INVESTMENT.—

(1) IN GENERAL.—For purposes of subsection (a), the qualified investment for any taxable year is the basis of eligible property placed in service by the taxpayer during such taxable year which is part of a qualifying advanced coal project—

(A)(i) the construction, reconstruction, or erection of which is completed by the taxpayer, or

(ii) which is acquired by the taxpayer if the original use of such property commences with the taxpayer, and

(B) with respect to which depreciation (or amortization in lieu of depreciation) is allowable.

(2) SPECIAL RULE FOR CERTAIN SUBSIDIZED PROPERTY.—Rules similar to section 48(a)(4) (without regard to subparagraph (D) thereof) shall apply for purposes of this section.

(3) CERTAIN QUALIFIED PROGRESS EXPENDITURES RULES MADE APPLICABLE.—Rules similar to the rules of subsections (c)(4) and (d) of section 46 (as in effect on the day before the enactment of the Revenue Reconciliation Act of 1990) shall apply for purposes of this section.

Amendments

• 2009, American Recovery and Reinvestment Tax Act of 2009 (P.L. 111-5)

P.L. 111-5, §1103(b)(2)(C):

Amended Code Sec. 48A(b)(2) by inserting "(without regard to subparagraph (D) thereof)" after "section 48(a)(4)". **Effective** for periods after 12-31-2008, under rules similar to the rules of Code Sec. 48(m) (as in effect on the day before the date of the enactment of the Revenue Reconciliation Act of 1990 [10-30-1990]).

[Sec. 48A(c)]

(c) DEFINITIONS.—For purposes of this section—

(1) QUALIFYING ADVANCED COAL PROJECT.—The term "qualifying advanced coal project" means a project which meets the requirements of subsection (e).

(2) ADVANCED COAL-BASED GENERATION TECHNOLOGY.—The term "advanced coal-based generation technology" means a technology which meets the requirements of subsection (f).

(3) ELIGIBLE PROPERTY.—The term "eligible property" means—

(A) in the case of any qualifying advanced coal project using an integrated gasification combined cycle, any property which is a part of such project and is necessary for the gasification of coal, including any coal handling and gas separation equipment, and

(B) in the case of any other qualifying advanced coal project, any property which is a part of such project.

(4) COAL.—The term "coal" means anthracite, bituminous coal, subbituminous coal, lignite, and peat.

(5) GREENHOUSE GAS CAPTURE CAPABILITY.—The term "greenhouse gas capture capability" means an integrated gasification combined cycle technology facility capable of adding compo-

nents which can capture, separate on a long-term basis, isolate, remove, and sequester greenhouse gases which result from the generation of electricity.

(6) ELECTRIC GENERATION UNIT.—The term "electric generation unit" means any facility at least 50 percent of the total annual net output of which is electrical power, including an otherwise eligible facility which is used in an industrial application.

(7) INTEGRATED GASIFICATION COMBINED CYCLE.—The term "integrated gasification combined cycle" means an electric generation unit which produces electricity by converting coal to synthesis gas which is used to fuel a combined-cycle plant which produces electricity from both a combustion turbine (including a combustion turbine/fuel cell hybrid) and a steam turbine.

[Sec. 48A(d)]

(d) QUALIFYING ADVANCED COAL PROJECT PROGRAM.—

(1) ESTABLISHMENT.—Not later than 180 days after the date of enactment of this section, the Secretary, in consultation with the Secretary of Energy, shall establish a qualifying advanced coal project program for the deployment of advanced coal-based generation technologies.

(2) CERTIFICATION.—

(A) APPLICATION PERIOD.—Each applicant for certification under this paragraph shall submit an application meeting the requirements of subparagraph (B). An applicant may only submit an application—

(i) for an allocation from the dollar amount specified in clause (i) or (ii) of paragraph (3)(B) during the 3-year period beginning on the date the Secretary establishes the program under paragraph (1), and

(ii) for an allocation from the dollar amount specified in paragraph (3)(B)(iii) during the 3-year period beginning at the earlier of the termination of the period described in clause (i) or the date prescribed by the Secretary.

(B) REQUIREMENTS FOR APPLICATIONS FOR CERTIFICATION.—An application under subparagraph (A) shall contain such information as the Secretary may require in order to make a determination to accept or reject an application for certification as meeting the requirements under subsection (e)(1). Any information contained in the application shall be protected as provided in section 552(b)(4) of title 5, United States Code.

(C) TIME TO ACT UPON APPLICATIONS FOR CERTIFICATION.—The Secretary shall issue a determination as to whether an applicant has met the requirements under subsection (e)(1) within 60 days following the date of submittal of the application for certification.

(D) TIME TO MEET CRITERIA FOR CERTIFICATION.—Each applicant for certification shall have 2 years from the date of acceptance by the Secretary of the application during which to provide to the Secretary evidence that the criteria set forth in subsection (e)(2) have been met.

(E) PERIOD OF ISSUANCE.—An applicant which receives a certification shall have 5 years from the date of issuance of the certification in order to place the project in service and if such project is not placed in service by that time period then the certification shall no longer be valid.

(3) AGGREGATE CREDITS.—

(A) IN GENERAL.—The aggregate credits allowed under subsection (a) for projects certified by the Secretary under paragraph (2) may not exceed $2,550,000,000.

(B) PARTICULAR PROJECTS.—Of the dollar amount in subparagraph (A), the Secretary is authorized to certify—

(i) $800,000,000 for integrated gasification combined cycle projects the application for which is submitted during the period described in paragraph (2)(A)(i),

(ii) $500,000,000 for projects which use other advanced coal-based generation technologies the application for which is submitted during the period described in paragraph (2)(A)(i), and

(iii) $1,250,000,000 for advanced coal-based generation technology projects the application for which is submitted during the period described in paragraph (2)(A)(ii).

(4) REVIEW AND REDISTRIBUTION.—

(A) REVIEW.—Not later than 6 years after the date of enactment of this section, the Secretary shall review the credits allocated under this section as of the date which is 6 years after the date of enactment of this section.

(B) REDISTRIBUTION.—The Secretary may reallocate credits available under clauses (i) and (ii) of paragraph (3)(B) if the Secretary determines that—

(i) there is an insufficient quantity of qualifying applications for certification pending at the time of the review, or

(ii) any certification made pursuant to paragraph (2) has been revoked pursuant to paragraph (2)(D) because the project subject to the certification has been delayed as a result of third party opposition or litigation to the proposed project.

(C) REALLOCATION.—If the Secretary determines that credits under clause (i) or (ii) of paragraph (3)(B) are available for reallocation pursuant to the requirements set forth in paragraph (2), the Secretary is authorized to conduct an additional program for applications for certification.

(5) DISCLOSURE OF ALLOCATIONS.—The Secretary shall, upon making a certification under this subsection or section 48B(d), publicly disclose the identity of the applicant and the amount of the credit certified with respect to such applicant.

Amendments

• 2008, Energy Improvement and Extension Act of 2008 (P.L. 110-343)

P.L. 110-343, Division B, §111(b):

Amended Code Sec. 48A(d)(3)(A) by striking "$1,300,000,000" and inserting "$2,550,000,000". **Effective** for credits the application for which is submitted during the period described in Code Sec. 48A(d)(2)(A)(ii) and which are allocated or reallocated after 10-3-2008.

P.L. 110-343, Division B, §111(c)(1):

Amended Code Sec. 48A(d)(3)(B). **Effective** for credits the application for which is submitted during the period described in Code Sec. 48A(d)(2)(A)(ii) and which are allocated or reallocated after 10-3-2008. Prior to amendment, Code Sec. 48A(d)(3)(B) read as follows:

(B) PARTICULAR PROJECTS.—Of the dollar amount in subparagraph (A), the Secretary is authorized to certify—

(i) $800,000,000 for integrated gasification combined cycle projects, and

(ii) $500,000,000 for projects which use other advanced coal-based generation technologies.

P.L. 110-343, Division B, §111(c)(2):

Amended Code Sec. 48A(d)(2)(A). **Effective** for credits the application for which is submitted during the period described in Code Sec. 48A(d)(2)(A)(ii) and which are allocated or reallocated after 10-3-2008. Prior to amendment, Code Sec. 48A(d)(2)(A) read as follows:

(A) APPLICATION PERIOD.—Each applicant for certification under this paragraph shall submit an application meeting the requirements of subparagraph (B). An applicant may only submit an application during the 3-year period beginning on the date the Secretary establishes the program under paragraph (1).

P.L. 110-343, Division B, §111(d):

Amended Code Sec. 48A(d) by adding at the end a new paragraph (5). **Effective** for certifications made after 10-3-2008.

• 2007, Tax Technical Corrections Act of 2007 (P.L. 110-172)

P.L. 110-172, §11(a)(10):

Amended Code Sec. 48A(d)(4)(B)(ii) by striking "subsection" both places it appears before "paragraph". **Effective** 12-29-2007.

[Sec. 48A(e)]

(e) QUALIFYING ADVANCED COAL PROJECTS.—

(1) REQUIREMENTS.—For purposes of subsection (c)(1), a project shall be considered a qualifying advanced coal project that the Secretary may certify under subsection (d)(2) if the Secretary determines that, at a minimum—

(A) the project uses an advanced coal-based generation technology—

(i) to power a new electric generation unit; or

(ii) to retrofit or repower an existing electric generation unit (including an existing natural gas-fired combined cycle unit);

(B) the fuel input for the project, when completed, is at least 75 percent coal;

(C) the project, consisting of one or more electric generation units at one site, will have a total nameplate generating capacity of at least 400 megawatts;

(D) the applicant provides evidence that a majority of the output of the project is reasonably expected to be acquired or utilized;

(E) the applicant provides evidence of ownership or control of a site of sufficient size to allow the proposed project to be constructed and to operate on a long-term basis;

(F) the project will be located in the United States; and

(G) in the case of any project the application for which is submitted during the period described in subsection (d)(2)(A)(ii), the project includes equipment which separates and sequesters at least 65 percent (70 percent in the case of an application for reallocated credits under subsection (d)(4)) of such project's total carbon dioxide emissions.

(2) REQUIREMENTS FOR CERTIFICATION.—For the purpose of subsection (d)(2)(D), a project shall be eligible for certification only if the Secretary determines that—

(A) the applicant for certification has received all Federal and State environmental authorizations or reviews necessary to commence construction of the project; and

(B) the applicant for certification, except in the case of a retrofit or repower of an existing electric generation unit, has purchased or entered into a binding contract for the purchase of the main steam turbine or turbines for the project, except that such contract may be contingent upon receipt of a certification under subsection (d)(2).

(3) PRIORITY FOR CERTAIN PROJECTS.—In determining which qualifying advanced coal projects to certify under subsection (d)(2), the Secretary shall—

(A) certify capacity, in accordance with the procedures set forth in subsection (d), in relatively equal amounts to—

(i) projects using bituminous coal as a primary feedstock,

(ii) projects using subbituminous coal as a primary feedstock, and

(iii) projects using lignite as a primary feedstock,

(B) give high priority to projects which include, as determined by the Secretary—

(i) greenhouse gas capture capability,

(ii) increased by-product utilization,

(iii) applicant participants who have a research partnership with an eligible educational institution (as defined in section 529(e)(5)), and

(iv) other benefits, and

(C) give highest priority to projects with the greatest separation and sequestration percentage of total carbon dioxide emissions.

Amendments

• 2008, Energy Improvement and Extension Act of 2008 (P.L. 110-343)

P.L. 110-343, Division B, §111(c)(3)(A):

Amended Code Sec. 48A(e)(1) by striking "and" at the end of subparagraph (E), by striking the period at the end of subparagraph (F) and inserting "; and", and by adding at the end a new subparagraph (G). **Effective** for credits the application for which is submitted during the period described in Code Sec. 48A(d)(2)(A)(ii) and which are allocated or reallocated after 10-3-2008.

P.L. 110-343, Division B, §111(c)(3)(B):

Amended Code Sec. 48A(e)(3) by striking "and" at the end of subparagraph (A)(iii), by striking the period at the end of subparagraph (B)(iii) and inserting ", and", and by adding at the end a new subparagraph (C). **Effective** for credits the application for which is submitted during the period described in Code Sec. 48A(d)(2)(A)(ii) and which are allocated or reallocated after 10-3-2008.

P.L. 110-343, Division B, §111(c)(4)(A)-(C):

Amended Code Sec. 48A(e)(3)(B), as amended by Act Sec. 111(c)(3)(B), by striking "and" at the end of clause (ii), by redesignating clause (iii) as clause (iv), and by inserting after clause (ii) a new clause (iii). **Effective** for credits the application for which is submitted during the period described in Code Sec. 48A(d)(2)(A)(ii) and which are allocated or reallocated after 10-3-2008.

P.L. 110-343, Division B, §111(c)(5):

Amended Code Sec. 48A(e)(3) by striking "INTEGRATED GASIFICATION COMBINED CYCLE" in the heading and inserting "CERTAIN". **Effective** as if included in the amendment made by §1307(b) of the Energy Tax Incentives Act of 2005 [**effective** for periods after 8-8-2005, under rules similar to the rules of Code Sec. 48(m) (as in effect on the day before the date of the enactment of the Energy Tax Incentives Act of 2005 (P.L. 110-508).—CCH].

[Sec. 48A(f)]

(f) ADVANCED COAL-BASED GENERATION TECHNOLOGY.—

(1) IN GENERAL.—For the purpose of this section, an electric generation unit uses advanced coal-based generation technology if—

(A) the unit—

(i) uses integrated gasification combined cycle technology, or

(ii) except as provided in paragraph (3), has a design net heat rate of 8530 Btu/kWh (40 percent efficiency), and

(B) the unit is designed to meet the performance requirements in the following table:

Performance characteristic:	Design level for project:
SO_2 (percent removal)	99 percent
NO_x (emissions)	0.07 lbs/MMBTU
PM* (emissions)	0.015 lbs/MMBTU
Hg (percent removal)	90 percent

For purposes of the performance requirement specified for the removal of SO_2 in the table contained in subparagraph (B), the SO_2 removal design level in the case of a unit designed for the use of feedstock substantially all of which is subbituminous coal shall be 99 percent SO_2 removal or the achievement of an emission level of 0.04 pounds or less of SO_2 per million Btu, determined on a 30-day average.

(2) DESIGN NET HEAT RATE.—For purposes of this subsection, design net heat rate with respect to an electric generation unit shall—

(A) be measured in Btu per kilowatt hour (higher heating value),

(B) be based on the design annual heat input to the unit and the rated net electrical power, fuels, and chemicals output of the unit (determined without regard to the cogeneration of steam by the unit),

(C) be adjusted for the heat content of the design coal to be used by the unit—

(i) if the heat content is less than 13,500 Btu per pound, but greater than 7,000 Btu per pound, according to the following formula: design net heat rate = unit net heat rate × [1-[((13,500-design coal heat content, Btu per pound)/1,000)* 0.013]], and

(ii) if the heat content is less than or equal to 7,000 Btu per pound, according to the following formula: design net heat rate = unit net heat rate × [1-[((13,500–design coal heat content, Btu per pound)/1,000)* 0.018]], and

(D) be corrected for the site reference conditions of—

(i) elevation above sea level of 500 feet,

(ii) air pressure of 14.4 pounds per square inch absolute,

(iii) temperature, dry bulb of 63°F,

(iv) temperature, wet bulb of 54°F, and

(v) relative humidity of 55 percent.

(3) EXISTING UNITS.—In the case of any electric generation unit in existence on the date of the enactment of this section, such unit uses advanced coal-based generation technology if, in lieu of the requirements under paragraph (1)(A)(ii), such unit achieves a minimum efficiency of 35 percent and an overall thermal design efficiency improvement, compared to the efficiency of the unit as operated, of not less than—

(A) 7 percentage points for coal of more than 9,000 Btu,

(B) 6 percentage points for coal of 7,000 to 9,000 Btu, or

(C) 4 percentage points for coal of less than 7,000 Btu.

Amendments

• 2006, Tax Relief and Health Care Act of 2006 (P.L. 109-432)

P.L. 109-432, Division A, §203(a):

Amended Code Sec. 48A(f)(1) by adding at the end a new flush sentence. **Effective** with respect to applications for certification under Code Sec. 48A(d)(2) submitted after 10-2-2006.

[Sec. 48A(g)]

(g) APPLICABILITY.—No use of technology (or level of emission reduction solely by reason of the use of the technology), and no achievement of any emission reduction by the demonstration of any technology or performance level, by or at one or more facilities with respect to which a credit is allowed under this section, shall be considered to indicate that the technology or performance level is—

(1) adequately demonstrated for purposes of section 111 of the Clean Air Act (42 U.S.C. 7411);

(2) achievable for purposes of section 169 of that Act (42 U.S.C. 7479); or

(3) achievable in practice for purposes of section 171 of such Act (42 U.S.C. 7501).

Amendments

• 2005, Energy Tax Incentives Act of 2005 (P.L. 109-58)

P.L. 109-58, §1307(b):

Amended subpart E of part IV of subchapter A of chapter 1 by inserting after Code Sec. 48 new Code Secs. 48A-48B. **Effective** for periods after 8-8-2005, under rules similar to the rules of Code Sec. 48(m) (as in effect on the day before the date of enactment of P.L. 101-508 [11-4-90.—CCH].

[Sec. 48A(h)]

(h) COMPETITIVE CERTIFICATION AWARDS MODIFICATION AUTHORITY.—In implementing this section or section 48B, the Secretary is directed to modify the terms of any competitive certification award and any associated closing agreement where such modification—

(1) is consistent with the objectives of such section,

(2) is requested by the recipient of the competitive certification award, and

(3) involves moving the project site to improve the potential to capture and sequester carbon dioxide emissions, reduce costs of transporting feedstock, and serve a broader customer base,

unless the Secretary determines that the dollar amount of tax credits available to the taxpayer under such section would increase as a result of the modification or such modification would result in such project not being originally certified. In considering any such modification, the Secretary shall consult with other relevant Federal agencies, including the Department of Energy.

Amendments

• 2008, Heartland, Habitat, Harvest, and Horticulture Act of 2008 (P.L. 110-246)

P.L. 110-246, §15346(a):

Amended Code Sec. 48A by adding at the end a new subsection (h). **Effective** 5-22-2008 and is applicable to all competitive certification awards entered into under section 48A or 48B of the Internal Revenue Code of 1986, whether such awards were issued before, on, or after 5-22-2008.

[Sec. 48A(i)]

(i) RECAPTURE OF CREDIT FOR FAILURE TO SEQUESTER.—The Secretary shall provide for recapturing the benefit of any credit allowable under subsection (a) with respect to any project which fails to attain or maintain the separation and sequestration requirements of subsection (e)(1)(G).

Amendments

• 2008, Energy Improvement and Extension Act of 2008 (P.L. 110-343)

P.L. 110-343, Division B, §111(c)(3)(C):

Amended Code Sec. 48A by adding at the end a new subsection (i). **Effective** for credits the application for which is submitted during the period described in Code Sec. 48A(d)(2)(A)(ii) and which are allocated or reallocated after 10-3-2008.

[Sec. 48B]

SEC. 48B. QUALIFYING GASIFICATION PROJECT CREDIT.

[Sec. 48B(a)]

(a) IN GENERAL.—For purposes of section 46, the qualifying gasification project credit for any taxable year is an amount equal to 20 percent (30 percent in the case of credits allocated under subsection (d)(1)(B)) of the qualified investment for such taxable year.

Amendments

• 2008, Energy Improvement and Extension Act of 2008 (P.L. 110-343)

P.L. 110-343, Division B, §112(a):

Amended Code Sec. 48B(a) by inserting "(30 percent in the case of credits allocated under subsection (d)(1)(B))" after "20 percent". **Effective** for credits described in Code Sec. 48B(d)(1)(B) which are allocated or reallocated after 10-3-2008.

[Sec. 48B(b)]

(b) QUALIFIED INVESTMENT.—

(1) IN GENERAL.—For purposes of subsection (a), the qualified investment for any taxable year is the basis of eligible property placed in service by the taxpayer during such taxable year which is part of a qualifying gasification project—

(A)(i) the construction, reconstruction, or erection of which is completed by the taxpayer, or

(ii) which is acquired by the taxpayer if the original use of such property commences with the taxpayer, and

(B) with respect to which depreciation (or amortization in lieu of depreciation) is allowable.

(2) SPECIAL RULE FOR CERTAIN SUBSIDIZED PROPERTY.—Rules similar to section 48(a)(4) (without regard to subparagraph (D) thereof) shall apply for purposes of this section.

(3) CERTAIN QUALIFIED PROGRESS EXPENDITURES RULES MADE APPLICABLE.—Rules similar to the rules of subsections (c)(4) and (d) of section 46 (as in effect on the day before the enactment of the Revenue Reconciliation Act of 1990) shall apply for purposes of this section.

Amendments

• 2009, American Recovery and Reinvestment Tax Act of 2009 (P.L. 111-5)

P.L. 111-5, §1103(b)(2)(D):

Amended Code Sec. 48B(b)(2) by inserting "(without regard to subparagraph (D) thereof)" after "section 48(a)(4)". **Effective** for periods after 12-31-2008, under rules similar to the rules of Code Sec. 48(m) (as in effect on the day before the enactment of the Revenue Reconciliation Act of 1990 [10-30-90]).

[Sec. 48B(c)]

(c) DEFINITIONS.—For purposes of this section—

(1) QUALIFYING GASIFICATION PROJECT.—The term "qualifying gasification project" means any project which—

(A) employs gasification technology,

(B) will be carried out by an eligible entity, and

(C) any portion of the qualified investment of which is certified under the qualifying gasification program as eligible for credit under this section in an amount (not to exceed $650,000,000) determined by the Secretary.

(2) GASIFICATION TECHNOLOGY.—The term "gasification technology" means any process which converts a solid or liquid product from coal, petroleum residue, biomass, or other materials which are recovered for their energy or feedstock value into a synthesis gas composed primarily of carbon monoxide and hydrogen for direct use or subsequent chemical or physical conversion.

(3) ELIGIBLE PROPERTY.—The term "eligible property" means any property which is a part of a qualifying gasification project and is necessary for the gasification technology of such project.

(4) BIOMASS.—

(A) IN GENERAL.—The term "biomass" means any—

(i) agricultural or plant waste,

(ii) byproduct of wood or paper mill operations, including lignin in spent pulping liquors, and

(iii) other products of forestry maintenance.

(B) EXCLUSION.—The term "biomass" does not include paper which is commonly recycled.

(5) CARBON CAPTURE CAPABILITY.—The term "carbon capture capability" means a gasification plant design which is determined by the Secretary to reflect reasonable consideration for, and be capable of, accommodating the equipment likely to be necessary to capture carbon dioxide from the gaseous stream, for later use or sequestration, which would otherwise be emitted in the flue gas from a project which uses a nonrenewable fuel.

(6) COAL.—The term "coal" means anthracite, bituminous coal, subbituminous coal, lignite, and peat.

(7) ELIGIBLE ENTITY.—The term "eligible entity" means any person whose application for certification is principally intended for use in a domestic project which employs domestic gasification applications related to—

(A) chemicals,

(B) fertilizers,

(C) glass,

(D) steel,

(E) petroleum residues,

(F) forest products,

(G) agriculture, including feedlots and dairy operations, and

(H) transportation grade liquid fuels.

(8) PETROLEUM RESIDUE.—The term "petroleum residue" means the carbonized product of high-boiling hydrocarbon fractions obtained in petroleum processing.

Amendments

• 2008, Energy Improvement and Extension Act of 2008 (P.L. 110-343)

P.L. 110-343, Division B, §112(e):

Amended Code Sec. 48B(c)(7) by striking "and" at the end of subparagraph (F), by striking the period at the end of subparagraph (G) and inserting ", and", and by adding at the end a new subparagraph (H). **Effective** for credits described in Code Sec. 48B(d)(1)(B) which are allocated or reallocated after 10-3-2008.

[Sec. 48B(d)]

(d) QUALIFYING GASIFICATION PROJECT PROGRAM.—

(1) IN GENERAL.—Not later than 180 days after the date of the enactment of this section, the Secretary, in consultation with the Secretary of Energy, shall establish a qualifying gasification project program to consider and award certifications for qualified investment eligible for credits under this section to qualifying gasification project sponsors under this section. The total amounts of credit that may be allocated under the program shall not exceed—

(A) $350,000,000, plus

(B) $250,000,000 for qualifying gasification projects that include equipment which separates and sequesters at least 75 percent of such project's total carbon dioxide emissions.

(2) PERIOD OF ISSUANCE.—A certificate of eligibility under paragraph (1) may be issued only during the 10-fiscal year period beginning on October 1, 2005.

(3) SELECTION CRITERIA.—The Secretary shall not make a competitive certification award for qualified investment for credit eligibility under this section unless the recipient has documented to the satisfaction of the Secretary that—

(A) the award recipient is financially viable without the receipt of additional Federal funding associated with the proposed project,

(B) the recipient will provide sufficient information to the Secretary for the Secretary to ensure that the qualified investment is spent efficiently and effectively,

(C) a market exists for the products of the proposed project as evidenced by contracts or written statements of intent from potential customers,

(D) the fuels identified with respect to the gasification technology for such project will comprise at least 90 percent of the fuels required by the project for the production of chemical feedstocks, liquid transportation fuels, or coproduction of electricity,

(E) the award recipient's project team is competent in the construction and operation of the gasification technology proposed, with preference given to those recipients with experience which demonstrates successful and reliable operations of the technology on domestic fuels so identified, and

(F) the award recipient has met other criteria established and published by the Secretary.

(4) SELECTION PRIORITIES.—In determining which qualifying gasification projects to certify under this section, the Secretary shall—

(A) give highest priority to projects with the greatest separation and sequestration percentage of total carbon dioxide emissions, and

(B) give high priority to applicant participants who have a research partnership with an eligible educational institution (as defined in section 529(e)(5)).

Amendments

• 2008, Energy Improvement and Extension Act of 2008 (P.L. 110-343)

P.L. 110-343, Division B, §112(b):

Amended Code Sec. 48B(d)(1) by striking "shall not exceed $350,000,000" and all that follows and inserting "shall not exceed—"and new subparagraphs (A)-(B). **Effective** for credits described in Code Sec. 48B(d)(1)(B) which are allocated or reallocated after 10-3-2008. Prior to amendment, Code Sec. 48B(d)(1) read as follows:

(1) IN GENERAL.—Not later than 180 days after the date of the enactment of this section, the Secretary, in consultation with the Secretary of Energy, shall establish a qualifying gasification project program to consider and award certifica-

tions for qualified investment eligible for credits under this section to qualifying gasification project sponsors under this section. The total amounts of credit that may be allocated under the program shall not exceed $350,000,000 under rules similar to the rules of section 48A(d)(4).

P.L. 110-343, Division B, §112(d):

Amended Code Sec. 48B(d) by adding at the end a new paragraph (4). **Effective** for credits described in Code Sec. 48B(d)(1)(B) which are allocated or reallocated after 10-3-2008.

[Sec. 48B(e)]

(e) DENIAL OF DOUBLE BENEFIT.—A credit shall not be allowed under this section for any qualified investment for which a credit is allowed under section 48A.

Amendments

• 2005, Energy Tax Incentives Act of 2005 (P.L. 109-58)

P.L. 109-58, §1307(b):

Amended subpart E of part IV of subchapter A of chapter 1 by inserting after Code Sec. 48 new Code Secs. 48A-48B. **Effective** for periods after 8-8-2005, under rules similar to the rules of Code Sec. 48(m) (as in effect on the day before the date of enactment of P.L. 101-508 [11-4-90.—CCH]).

[Sec. 48B(f)]

(f) RECAPTURE OF CREDIT FOR FAILURE TO SEQUESTER.—The Secretary shall provide for recapturing the benefit of any credit allowable under subsection (a) with respect to any project which fails to attain or maintain the separation and sequestration requirements for such project under subsection (d)(1).

Amendments

• 2008, Energy Improvement and Extension Act of 2008 (P.L. 110-343)

P.L. 110-343, Division B, §112(c):

Amended Code Sec. 48B by adding at the end a new subsection (f). **Effective** for credits described in Code Sec. 48B(d)(1)(B) which are allocated or reallocated after 10-3-2008.

[Sec. 48C]

SEC. 48C. QUALIFYING ADVANCED ENERGY PROJECT CREDIT.

[Sec. 48C(a)]

(a) IN GENERAL.—For purposes of section 46, the qualifying advanced energy project credit for any taxable year is an amount equal to 30 percent of the qualified investment for such taxable year with respect to any qualifying advanced energy project of the taxpayer.

[Sec. 48C(b)]

(b) QUALIFIED INVESTMENT.—

(1) IN GENERAL.—For purposes of subsection (a), the qualified investment for any taxable year is the basis of eligible property placed in service by the taxpayer during such taxable year which is part of a qualifying advanced energy project.

(2) CERTAIN QUALIFIED PROGRESS EXPENDITURES RULES MADE APPLICABLE.—Rules similar to the rules of subsections (c)(4) and (d) of section 46 (as in effect on the day before the enactment of the Revenue Reconciliation Act of 1990) shall apply for purposes of this section.

(3) LIMITATION.—The amount which is treated for all taxable years with respect to any qualifying advanced energy project shall not exceed the amount designated by the Secretary as eligible for the credit under this section.

[Sec. 48C(c)]

(c) DEFINITIONS.—

(1) QUALIFYING ADVANCED ENERGY PROJECT.—

(A) IN GENERAL.—The term "qualifying advanced energy project" means a project—

(i) which re-equips, expands, or establishes a manufacturing facility for the production of—

(I) property designed to be used to produce energy from the sun, wind, geothermal deposits (within the meaning of section 613(e)(2)), or other renewable resources,

(II) fuel cells, microturbines, or an energy storage system for use with electric or hybrid-electric motor vehicles,

(III) electric grids to support the transmission of intermittent sources of renewable energy, including storage of such energy,

(IV) property designed to capture and sequester carbon dioxide emissions,

(V) property designed to refine or blend renewable fuels or to produce energy conservation technologies (including energy-conserving lighting technologies and smart grid technologies),

(VI) new qualified plug-in electric drive motor vehicles (as defined by section 30D), qualified plug-in electric vehicles (as defined by section 30(d)), or components which are designed specifically for use with such vehicles, including electric motors, generators, and power control units, or

(VII) other advanced energy property designed to reduce greenhouse gas emissions as may be determined by the Secretary, and

(ii) any portion of the qualified investment of which is certified by the Secretary under subsection (d) as eligible for a credit under this section.

(B) EXCEPTION.—Such term shall not include any portion of a project for the production of any property which is used in the refining or blending of any transportation fuel (other than renewable fuels).

(2) ELIGIBLE PROPERTY.—The term "eligible property" means any property—

(A) which is necessary for the production of property described in paragraph (1)(A)(i),

(B) which is—

(i) tangible personal property, or

(ii) other tangible property (not including a building or its structural components), but only if such property is used as an integral part of the qualified investment credit facility, and

(C) with respect to which depreciation (or amortization in lieu of depreciation) is allowable.

[Sec. 48C(d)]

(d) QUALIFYING ADVANCED ENERGY PROJECT PROGRAM.—

(1) ESTABLISHMENT.—

(A) IN GENERAL.—Not later than 180 days after the date of enactment of this section, the Secretary, in consultation with the Secretary of Energy, shall establish a qualifying advanced energy project program to consider and award certifications for qualified investments eligible for credits under this section to qualifying advanced energy project sponsors.

(B) LIMITATION.—The total amount of credits that may be allocated under the program shall not exceed $2,300,000,000.

(2) CERTIFICATION.—

(A) APPLICATION PERIOD.—Each applicant for certification under this paragraph shall submit an application containing such information as the Secretary may require during the 2-year period beginning on the date the Secretary establishes the program under paragraph (1).

(B) TIME TO MEET CRITERIA FOR CERTIFICATION.—Each applicant for certification shall have 1 year from the date of acceptance by the Secretary of the application during which to provide to the Secretary evidence that the requirements of the certification have been met.

(C) PERIOD OF ISSUANCE.—An applicant which receives a certification shall have 3 years from the date of issuance of the certification in order to place the project in service and if such project is not placed in service by that time period, then the certification shall no longer be valid.

(3) SELECTION CRITERIA.—In determining which qualifying advanced energy projects to certify under this section, the Secretary—

(A) shall take into consideration only those projects where there is a reasonable expectation of commercial viability, and

(B) shall take into consideration which projects—

(i) will provide the greatest domestic job creation (both direct and indirect) during the credit period,

(ii) will provide the greatest net impact in avoiding or reducing air pollutants or anthropogenic emissions of greenhouse gases,

(iii) have the greatest potential for technological innovation and commercial deployment,

(iv) have the lowest levelized cost of generated or stored energy, or of measured reduction in energy consumption or greenhouse gas emission (based on costs of the full supply chain), and

(v) have the shortest project time from certification to completion.

(4) REVIEW AND REDISTRIBUTION.—

(A) REVIEW.—Not later than 4 years after the date of enactment of this section, the Secretary shall review the credits allocated under this section as of such date.

(B) REDISTRIBUTION.—The Secretary may reallocate credits awarded under this section if the Secretary determines that—

(i) there is an insufficient quantity of qualifying applications for certification pending at the time of the review, or

(ii) any certification made pursuant to paragraph (2) has been revoked pursuant to paragraph (2)(B) because the project subject to the certification has been delayed as a result of third party opposition or litigation to the proposed project.

(C) REALLOCATION.—If the Secretary determines that credits under this section are available for reallocation pursuant to the requirements set forth in paragraph (2), the Secretary is authorized to conduct an additional program for applications for certification.

(5) DISCLOSURE OF ALLOCATIONS.—The Secretary shall, upon making a certification under this subsection, publicly disclose the identity of the applicant and the amount of the credit with respect to such applicant.

[Sec. 48C(e)]

(e) DENIAL OF DOUBLE BENEFIT.—A credit shall not be allowed under this section for any qualified investment for which a credit is allowed under section 48, 48A, or 48B.

Amendments

• 2009, American Recovery and Reinvestment Tax Act of 2009 (P.L. 111-5)

P.L. 111-5, §1302(b):

Amended subpart E of part IV of subchapter A of chapter 1 by inserting after Code Sec. 48B a new Code Sec. 48C. **Effective** for periods after the date of the enactment of this Act, under rules similar to the rules of Code Sec. 48(m) (as in effect on the day before the date of the enactment of the Revenue Reconciliation Act of 1990 [10-30-90]).

[Sec. 48D]

SEC. 48D. QUALIFYING THERAPEUTIC DISCOVERY PROJECT CREDIT.

[Sec. 48D(a)]

(a) IN GENERAL.—For purposes of section 46, the qualifying therapeutic discovery project credit for any taxable year is an amount equal to 50 percent of the qualified investment for such taxable year with respect to any qualifying therapeutic discovery project of an eligible taxpayer.

[Sec. 48D(b)]

(b) QUALIFIED INVESTMENT.—

(1) IN GENERAL.—For purposes of subsection (a), the qualified investment for any taxable year is the aggregate amount of the costs paid or incurred in such taxable year for expenses necessary for and directly related to the conduct of a qualifying therapeutic discovery project.

(2) LIMITATION.—The amount which is treated as qualified investment for all taxable years with respect to any qualifying therapeutic discovery project shall not exceed the amount certified by the Secretary as eligible for the credit under this section.

(3) EXCLUSIONS.—The qualified investment for any taxable year with respect to any qualifying therapeutic discovery project shall not take into account any cost—

(A) for remuneration for an employee described in section 162(m)(3),

(B) for interest expenses,

(C) for facility maintenance expenses,

(D) which is identified as a service cost under section 1.263A-1(e)(4) of title 26, Code of Federal Regulations, or

(E) for any other expense as determined by the Secretary as appropriate to carry out the purposes of this section.

(4) CERTAIN PROGRESS EXPENDITURE RULES MADE APPLICABLE.—In the case of costs described in paragraph (1) that are paid for property of a character subject to an allowance for depreciation, rules similar to the rules of subsections (c)(4) and (d) of section 46 (as in effect on the day before the date of the enactment of the Revenue Reconciliation Act of 1990) shall apply for purposes of this section.

(5) APPLICATION OF SUBSECTION.—An investment shall be considered a qualified investment under this subsection only if such investment is made in a taxable year beginning in 2009 or 2010.

[Sec. 48D(c)]

(c) DEFINITIONS.—

(1) QUALIFYING THERAPEUTIC DISCOVERY PROJECT.—The term "qualifying therapeutic discovery project" means a project which is designed—

(A) to treat or prevent diseases or conditions by conducting pre-clinical activities, clinical trials, and clinical studies, or carrying out research protocols, for the purpose of securing approval of a product under section 505(b) of the Federal Food, Drug, and Cosmetic Act or section 351(a) of the Public Health Service Act,

(B) to diagnose diseases or conditions or to determine molecular factors related to diseases or conditions by developing molecular diagnostics to guide therapeutic decisions, or

(C) to develop a product, process, or technology to further the delivery or administration of therapeutics.

(2) ELIGIBLE TAXPAYER.—

(A) IN GENERAL.—The term "eligible taxpayer" means a taxpayer which employs not more than 250 employees in all businesses of the taxpayer at the time of the submission of the application under subsection (d)(2).

(B) AGGREGATION RULES.—All persons treated as a single employer under subsection (a) or (b) of section 52, or subsection (m) or (o) of section 414, shall be so treated for purposes of this paragraph.

(3) FACILITY MAINTENANCE EXPENSES.—The term "facility maintenance expenses" means costs paid or incurred to maintain a facility, including—

(A) mortgage or rent payments,

(B) insurance payments,

(C) utility and maintenance costs, and

(D) costs of employment of maintenance personnel.

[Sec. 48D(d)]

(d) QUALIFYING THERAPEUTIC DISCOVERY PROJECT PROGRAM.—

(1) ESTABLISHMENT.—

(A) IN GENERAL.—Not later than 60 days after the date of the enactment of this section, the Secretary, in consultation with the Secretary of Health and Human Services, shall establish a qualifying therapeutic discovery project program to consider and award certifications for qualified investments eligible for credits under this section to qualifying therapeutic discovery project sponsors.

(B) LIMITATION.—The total amount of credits that may be allocated under the program shall not exceed $1,000,000,000 for the 2-year period beginning with 2009.

(2) CERTIFICATION.—

(A) APPLICATION PERIOD.—Each applicant for certification under this paragraph shall submit an application containing such information as the Secretary may require during the period beginning on the date the Secretary establishes the program under paragraph (1).

(B) TIME FOR REVIEW OF APPLICATIONS.—The Secretary shall take action to approve or deny any application under subparagraph (A) within 30 days of the submission of such application.

(C) MULTI-YEAR APPLICATIONS.—An application for certification under subparagraph (A) may include a request for an allocation of credits for more than 1 of the years described in paragraph (1)(B).

(3) SELECTION CRITERIA.—In determining the qualifying therapeutic discovery projects with respect to which qualified investments may be certified under this section, the Secretary—

(A) shall take into consideration only those projects that show reasonable potential—

(i) to result in new therapies—

(I) to treat areas of unmet medical need, or

(II) to prevent, detect, or treat chronic or acute diseases and conditions,

(ii) to reduce long-term health care costs in the United States, or

(iii) to significantly advance the goal of curing cancer within the 30-year period beginning on the date the Secretary establishes the program under paragraph (1), and

(B) shall take into consideration which projects have the greatest potential—

(i) to create and sustain (directly or indirectly) high quality, high-paying jobs in the United States, and

(ii) to advance United States competitiveness in the fields of life, biological, and medical sciences.

(4) DISCLOSURE OF ALLOCATIONS.—The Secretary shall, upon making a certification under this subsection, publicly disclose the identity of the applicant and the amount of the credit with respect to such applicant.

[Sec. 48D(e)]

(e) SPECIAL RULES.—

(1) BASIS ADJUSTMENT.—For purposes of this subtitle, if a credit is allowed under this section for an expenditure related to property of a character subject to an allowance for depreciation, the basis of such property shall be reduced by the amount of such credit.

(2) DENIAL OF DOUBLE BENEFIT.—

(A) BONUS DEPRECIATION.—A credit shall not be allowed under this section for any investment for which bonus depreciation is allowed under section 168(k), 1400L(b)(1), or 1400N(d)(1).

(B) DEDUCTIONS.—No deduction under this subtitle shall be allowed for the portion of the expenses otherwise allowable as a deduction taken into account in determining the credit under this section for the taxable year which is equal to the amount of the credit determined for such taxable year under subsection (a) attributable to such portion. This subparagraph shall not apply to expenses related to property of a character subject to an allowance for depreciation the basis of which is reduced under paragraph (1), or which are described in section 280C(g).

(C) CREDIT FOR RESEARCH ACTIVITIES.—

(i) IN GENERAL.—Except as provided in clause (ii), any expenses taken into account under this section for a taxable year shall not be taken into account for purposes of determining the credit allowable under section 41 or 45C for such taxable year.

(ii) EXPENSES INCLUDED IN DETERMINING BASE PERIOD RESEARCH EXPENSES.—Any expenses for any taxable year which are qualified research expenses (within the meaning of section 41(b)) shall be taken into account in determining base period research expenses for purposes of applying section 41 to subsequent taxable years.

[Sec. 48D(f)]

(f) COORDINATION WITH DEPARTMENT OF TREASURY GRANTS.—In the case of any investment with respect to which the Secretary makes a grant under section 9023(e) of the Patient Protection and Affordable Care Act of 2009 [sic]—

(1) DENIAL OF CREDIT.—No credit shall be determined under this section with respect to such investment for the taxable year in which such grant is made or any subsequent taxable year.

(2) RECAPTURE OF CREDITS FOR PROGRESS EXPENDITURES MADE BEFORE GRANT.—If a credit was determined under this section with respect to such investment for any taxable year ending before such grant is made—

(A) the tax imposed under subtitle A on the taxpayer for the taxable year in which such grant is made shall be increased by so much of such credit as was allowed under section 38,

(B) the general business carryforwards under section 39 shall be adjusted so as to recapture the portion of such credit which was not so allowed, and

(C) the amount of such grant shall be determined without regard to any reduction in the basis of any property of a character subject to an allowance for depreciation by reason of such credit.

(3) TREATMENT OF GRANTS.—Any such grant shall not be includible in the gross income of the taxpayer.

Amendments

• 2010, Patient Protection and Affordable Care Act (P.L. 111-148)

P.L. 111-148, §9023(a):

Amended subpart E of part IV of subchapter A of chapter 1 by inserting after Code Sec. 48C a new Code Sec. 48D. **Effective** for amounts paid or incurred after 12-31-2008, in tax years beginning after such date.

[Sec. 49]

SEC. 49. AT-RISK RULES.

[Sec. 49(a)]

(a) GENERAL RULE.—

(1) CERTAIN NONRECOURSE FINANCING EXCLUDED FROM CREDIT BASE.—

(A) LIMITATION.—The credit base of any property to which this paragraph applies shall be reduced by the nonqualified nonrecourse financing with respect to such credit base (as of the close of the taxable year in which placed in service).

(B) PROPERTY TO WHICH PARAGRAPH APPLIES.—This paragraph applies to any property which—

(i) is placed in service during the taxable year by a taxpayer described in section 465(a)(1), and

(ii) is used in connection with an activity with respect to which any loss is subject to limitation under section 465.

(C) CREDIT BASE DEFINED.—For purposes of this paragraph, the term "credit base" means—

(i) the portion of the basis of any qualified rehabilitated building attributable to qualified rehabilitation expenditures,

(ii) the basis of any energy property,

(iii) the basis of any property which is part of a qualifying advanced coal project under section 48A,

(iv) the basis of any property which is part of a qualifying gasification project under section 48B,

(v) the basis of any property which is part of a qualifying advanced energy project under section 48C, and

(vi) the basis of any property to which paragraph (1) of section 48D(e) applies which is part of a qualifying therapeutic discovery project under such section 48D.

(D) NONQUALIFIED NONRECOURSE FINANCING.—

(i) IN GENERAL.—For purposes of this paragraph and paragraph (2), the term "nonqualified nonrecourse financing" means any nonrecourse financing which is not qualified commercial financing.

(ii) QUALIFIED COMMERCIAL FINANCING.—For purposes of this paragraph, the term "qualified commercial financing" means any financing with respect to any property if—

(I) such property is acquired by the taxpayer from a person who is not a related person,

(II) the amount of the nonrecourse financing with respect to such property does not exceed 80 percent of the credit base of such property, and

(III) such financing is borrowed from a qualified person or represents a loan from any Federal, State, or local government or instrumentality thereof, or is guaranteed by any Federal, State, or local government.

Such term shall not include any convertible debt.

(iii) NONRECOURSE FINANCING.—For purposes of this subparagraph, the term "nonrecourse financing" includes—

(I) any amount with respect to which the taxpayer is protected against loss through guarantees, stop-loss agreements, or other similar arrangements, and

(II) except to the extent provided in regulations, any amount borrowed from a person who has an interest (other than as a creditor) in the activity in which the property is used or from a related person to a person (other than the taxpayer) having such an interest.

In the case of amounts borrowed by a corporation from a shareholder, subclause (II) shall not apply to an interest as a shareholder.

(iv) QUALIFIED PERSON.—For purposes of this paragraph, the term "qualified person" means any person which is actively and regularly engaged in the business of lending money and which is not—

(I) a related person with respect to the taxpayer,

(II) a person from which the taxpayer acquired the property (or a related person to such person), or

(III) a person who receives a fee with respect to the taxpayer's investment in the property (or a related person to such person).

(v) RELATED PERSON.—For purposes of this subparagraph, the term "related person" has the meaning given such term by section 465(b)(3)(C). Except as otherwise provided in regulations prescribed by the Secretary, the determination of whether a person is a related person shall be made as of the close of the taxable year in which the property is placed in service.

(E) APPLICATION TO PARTNERSHIPS AND S CORPORATIONS.—For purposes of this paragraph and paragraph (2)—

(i) IN GENERAL.—Except as otherwise provided in this subparagraph, in the case of any partnership or S corporation, the determination of whether a partner's or shareholder's allocable share of any financing is nonqualified nonrecourse financing shall be made at the partner or shareholder level.

(ii) SPECIAL RULE FOR CERTAIN RECOURSE FINANCING OF S CORPORATION.—A shareholder of an S corporation shall be treated as liable for his allocable share of any financing provided by a qualified person to such corporation if—

(I) such financing is recourse financing (determined at the corporate level), and

(II) such financing is provided with respect to qualified business property of such corporation.

(iii) QUALIFIED BUSINESS PROPERTY.—For purposes of clause (ii), the term "qualified business property" means any property if—

(I) such property is used by the corporation in the active conduct of a trade or business,

(II) during the entire 12-month period ending on the last day of the taxable year, such corporation had at least 3 full-time employees who were not owner-employees (as defined in section 465(c)(7)(E)(i)) and substantially all the services of whom were services directly related to such trade or business, and

(III) during the entire 12-month period ending on the last day of such taxable year, such corporation had at least 1 full-time employee substantially all of the services of whom were in the active management of the trade or business.

(iv) DETERMINATION OF ALLOCABLE SHARE.—The determination of any partner's or shareholder's allocable share of any financing shall be made in the same manner as the credit allowable by section 38 with respect to such property.

(F) SPECIAL RULES FOR ENERGY PROPERTY.—Rules similar to the rules of subparagraph (F) of section 46(c)(8) (as in effect on the day before the date of the enactment of the Revenue Reconciliation Act of 1990) shall apply for purposes of this paragraph.

(2) SUBSEQUENT DECREASES IN NONQUALIFIED NONRECOURSE FINANCING WITH RESPECT TO THE PROPERTY.—

(A) IN GENERAL.—If, at the close of a taxable year following the taxable year in which the property was placed in service, there is a net decrease in the amount of nonqualified nonrecourse financing with respect to such property, such net decrease shall be taken into account as an increase in the credit base for such property in accordance with subparagraph (C).

(B) CERTAIN TRANSACTIONS NOT TAKEN INTO ACCOUNT.—For purposes of this paragraph, nonqualified nonrecourse financing shall not be treated as decreased through the surrender or other use of property financed by nonqualified nonrecourse financing.

(C) MANNER IN WHICH TAKEN INTO ACCOUNT.—

(i) CREDIT DETERMINED BY REFERENCE TO TAXABLE YEAR PROPERTY PLACED IN SERVICE.—For purposes of determining the amount of credit allowable under section 38 and the amount of credit subject to the early disposition or cessation rules under section 50(a), any increase in a taxpayer's credit base for any property by reason of this paragraph shall be taken into account as if it were property placed in service by the taxpayer in the taxable year in which the property referred to in subparagraph (A) was first placed in service.

(ii) CREDIT ALLOWED FOR YEAR OF DECREASE IN NONQUALIFIED NONRECOURSE FINANCING.—Any credit allowable under this subpart for any increase in qualified investment by reason of this paragraph shall be treated as earned during the taxable year of the decrease in the amount of nonqualified nonrecourse financing.

Amendments

• 2010, Patient Protection and Affordable Care Act (P.L. 111-148)

P.L. 111-148, §9023(c)(1)(A)-(C):

Amended Code Sec. 49(a)(1)(C) by striking "and" at the end of clause (iv), by striking the period at the end of clause (v) and inserting ", and", and by adding at the end a new clause (vi). **Effective** for amounts paid or incurred after 12-31-2008, in tax years beginning after such date.

• 2009, American Recovery and Reinvestment Tax Act of 2009 (P.L. 111-5)

P.L. 111-5, §1302(c)(1):

Amended Code Sec. 49(a)(1)(C) by striking "and" at the end of clause (iii), by striking the period at the end of clause (iv) and inserting ", and", and by adding after clause (iv) a new clause (v). **Effective** for periods after 2-17-2009, under rules similar to the rules of Code Sec. 48(m) (as in effect on the day before the date of the enactment of the Revenue Reconciliation Act of 1990 [10-30-90]).

• 2005, Energy Tax Incentives Act of 2005 (P.L. 109-58)

P.L. 109-58, §1307(c)(1):

Amended Code Sec. 49(a)(1)(C) by striking "and" at the end of clause (ii), by striking clause (iii), and by adding after clause (ii) new clauses (iii)-(iv). **Effective** for periods after 8-8-2005, under rules similar to the rules of Code Sec. 48(m) (as in effect on the day before the date of enactment of P.L. 101-508 [11-4-90.—CCH]). Prior to being stricken, Code Sec. 49(a)(1)(C)(iii) read as follows:

(iii) the amortizable basis of any qualified timber property.

[Sec. 49(b)]

(b) INCREASES IN NONQUALIFIED NONRECOURSE FINANCING.—

(1) IN GENERAL.—If, as of the close of the taxable year, there is a net increase with respect to the taxpayer in the amount of nonqualified nonrecourse financing (within the meaning of subsection (a)(1)) with respect to any property to which subsection (a)(1) applied, then the tax under this chapter for such taxable year shall be increased by an amount equal to the aggregate decrease in credits allowed under section 38 for all prior taxable years which would have resulted from reducing the credit base (as defined in subsection (a)(1)(C)) taken into account with respect to such property by the amount of such net increase. For purposes of determining the amount of credit subject to the early disposition or cessation rules of section 50(a), the net increase in the amount of the nonqualified nonrecourse financing with respect to the property shall be treated as reducing the property's credit base in the year in which the property was first placed in service.

(2) TRANSFERS OF DEBT MORE THAN 1 YEAR AFTER INITIAL BORROWING NOT TREATED AS INCREASING NONQUALIFIED NONRECOURSE FINANCING.—For purposes of paragraph (1), the amount of nonqualified nonrecourse financing (within the meaning of subsection (a)(1)(D)) with respect to the taxpayer shall not be treated as increased by reason of a transfer of (or agreement to transfer) any evidence of any indebtedness if such transfer occurs (or such agreement is entered into) more than 1 year after the date such indebtedness was incurred.

(3) SPECIAL RULES FOR CERTAIN ENERGY PROPERTY.—Rules similar to the rules of section 47(d)(3) (as in effect on the day before the date of the enactment of the Revenue Reconciliation Act of 1990) shall apply for purposes of this subsection.

(4) SPECIAL RULE.—Any increase in tax under paragraph (1) shall not be treated as tax imposed by this chapter for purposes of determining the amount of any credit allowable under this chapter.

Amendments

• 1998, IRS Restructuring and Reform Act of 1998 (P.L. 105-206)

P.L. 105-206, §6004(g)(6):

Amended Code Sec. 49(b)(4) by striking "subpart A, B, D, or G" and inserting "this chapter". **Effective** as if included in the provision of P.L. 105-34 to which it relates [**effective** for obligations issued after 12-31-97.—CCH].

• 1990, Omnibus Budget Reconcilliation Act of 1990 (P.L. 101-508)

P.L. 101-508, §11813(a):

Amended Code Sec. 49. **Effective**, generally, for property placed in service after 12-31-90. However, for exceptions see Act Sec. 11813(c)(2) below.

P.L. 101-508, §11813(c)(2), provides:

(2) EXCEPTIONS.—The amendments made by this section shall not apply to—

(A) any transition property (as defined in section 49(c) of the Internal Revenue Code of 1986 (as in effect on the day before the date of the enactment of this Act),

(B) any property with respect to which qualified progress expenditures were previously taken into account under section 46(d) of such Code (as so in effect), and

(C) any property described in section 46(b)(2)(C) of such Code (as so in effect).

Prior to amendment, Code Sec. 49 read as follows:

SEC. 49. TERMINATION OF REGULAR PERCENTAGE.

[Sec. 49(a)]

(a) GENERAL RULE.—For purposes of determining the amount of the investment tax credit determined under section 46, the regular percentage shall not apply to any property placed in service after December 31, 1985.

[Sec. 49(b)]

(b) EXCEPTIONS.—Subject to the provisions of subsections (c) and (d), subsection (a) shall not apply to the following:

(1) TRANSITION PROPERTY.—Property which is transition property (within the meaning of subsection (e)).

(2) QUALIFIED PROGRESS EXPENDITURE FOR PERIODS BEFORE JANUARY 1, 1986.—In the case of any taxpayer who has made an election under section 46(d)(6), the portion of the adjusted basis of any progress expenditure property attributable to qualified progress expenditures for periods before January 1, 1986.

(3) QUALIFIED TIMBER PROPERTY.—The portion of the adjusted basis of qualified timber property which is treated as section 38 property under section 48(a)(1)(F).

[Sec. 49(c)]

(c) 35-PERCENT REDUCTION IN CREDIT FOR TAXABLE YEARS AFTER 1986.—

(1) REDUCTION IN CURRENT YEAR INVESTMENT CREDIT.—Any portion of the current year business credit under section 38(b) for any taxable year beginning after June 30, 1987, which is attributable to the regular investment credit shall be reduced by 35 percent.

(2) UNEXPIRED CARRYFORWARDS TO 1ST TAXABLE YEAR BEGINNING AFTER JUNE 30, 1987.—Any portion of the business credit carryforward under section 38(a)(1) attributable to the regular investment credit which has not expired as of the close of the taxable year preceding the 1st taxable year of the taxpayer beginning after June 30, 1987, shall be reduced by 35 percent.

(3) SPECIAL RULE FOR TAXABLE YEARS BEGINNING BEFORE AND ENDING AFTER JULY 1, 1987.—In the case of any taxable year beginning before and ending after July 1, 1987—

(A) any portion of the current year business credit under section 38(b) for such taxable year, or

(B) any portion of the business credit carryforward under section 38(a)(1) to such year,

which is attributable to the regular investment credit shall be reduced by the applicable percentage.

(4) TREATMENT OF DISALLOWED CREDIT.—

(A) IN GENERAL.—The amount of the reduction of the regular investment credit under paragraphs (1) and (2) shall not be allowed as a credit for any taxable year.

(B) NO CARRYBACK FOR YEARS STRADDLING JULY 1, 1987; GROSS UP OF CARRYFORWARDS.—In any case to which paragraph (3) applies—

(i) the amount of the reduction under paragraph (3) may not be carried back to any taxable year, but

(ii) there shall be added to the carryforwards from the taxable year (before applying paragraph (2)) an amount equal to the amount which bears the same ratio to the carryforwards from such taxable year (determined without regard to this clause) as—

(I) the applicable percentage, bears to

(II) 1 minus the applicable percentage.

(5) DEFINITIONS AND SPECIAL RULES.—For purposes of this subsection—

(A) APPLICABLE PERCENTAGE.—The term "applicable percentage" means, with respect to a taxable year beginning before and ending after July 1, 1987, the percentage which bears the same ratio to 35 percent as—

(i) the number of months in such taxable year after June 30, 1987, bears to

(ii) the number of months in such taxable year.

(B) REGULAR INVESTMENT CREDIT.—

(i) IN GENERAL.—The term "regular investment credit" means the credit determined under section 46(a) to the extent attributable to the regular percentage.

(ii) EXCEPTION FOR TIMBER PROPERTY.—The term "regular investment credit" shall not include any portion of the regular investment credit which is attributable to section 38 property described in section 48(a)(1)(F).

(C) [Repealed.]

Amendments

• 1988, Technical and Miscellaneous Revenue Act of 1988 (P.L. 100-647)

P.L. 100-647, §1002(e)(2):

Amended Code Sec. 49(c)(4)(B). **Effective** as if included in the provision of P.L. 99-514 to which it relates. Prior to amendment, Code Sec. 49(c)(4)(B) read as follows:

(B) NO CARRYBACK FOR YEAR STRADDLING JULY 1, 1987; GROSS UP OF CARRYFORWARDS.—The amount of the reduction of the regular investment credit under paragraph (3)—

(i) may not be carried back to any taxable year, but

(ii) shall be added to the carryforwards from the taxable year before applying paragraph (2).

P.L. 100-647, §1002(e)(3):

Amended Code Sec. 49(c)(5)(B)(i). **Effective** as if included in the provision of P.L. 99-514 to which it relates. Prior to amendment, Code Sec. 49(c)(5)(B)(i) read as follows:

(i) IN GENERAL.—The term "regular investment credit" has the meaning given such term by section 48(o).

P.L. 100-647, §1002(e)(8)(B):

Repealed Code Sec. 49(c)(5)(C). **Effective** for tax years beginning after 12-31-83, and to carrybacks from such years. Prior to repeal, Code Sec. 49(c)(5)(C) read as follows:

(C) PORTION OF CREDITS ATTRIBUTABLE TO REGULAR INVESTMENT CREDIT.—The portion of any current year business credit or business credit carryforward which is attributable to the regular investment credit shall be determined on the basis that the regular investment credit is used first.

[Sec. 49(d)]

(d) FULL BASIS ADJUSTMENT.—

(1) IN GENERAL.—In the case of periods after December 31, 1985, with respect to so much of the credit determined under section 46(a) with respect to transition property as is attributable to the regular investment credit (as defined in subsection (c)(5)(B))—

(A) paragraphs (1), (2), and (7) of section 48(q) and section 48(d)(5) shall be applied by substituting "100 percent" for "50 percent" each place it appears, and

(B) sections 48(q)(4) and 196(d) shall not apply.

(2) SPECIAL RULE FOR QUALIFIED PROGRESS EXPENDITURES.—If the taxpayer made an election under section 48(q)(4) with respect to any qualified progress expenditures for periods before January 1, 1986—

(A) paragraph (1) shall not apply to the portion of the adjusted basis attributable to such expenditures, and

(B) such election shall not apply to such expenditures for periods after December 31, 1985.

Amendments

• 1988, Technical and Miscellaneous Revenue Act of 1988 (P.L. 100-647)

P.L. 100-647, §1002(e)(1):

Amended Code Sec. 49(d)(1). **Effective** as if included in the provision of P.L. 99-514 to which it relates. Prior to amendment, Code Sec. 49(d)(1) read as follows:

(1) IN GENERAL.—In the case of periods after December 31, 1985, section 48(q) (relating to basis adjustment to section 38 property) shall be applied with respect to transaction [transition] property—

(A) by substituting "100 percent" for "50 percent" in paragraph (1), and

(B) without regard to paragraph (4) thereof (relating to election of reduced credit in lieu of basis adjustment).

[Sec. 49(e)]

(e) TRANSITION PROPERTY.—For purposes of this section—

(1) TRANSITION PROPERTY.—The term "transition property" means any property placed in service after December 31, 1985, and to which the amendments made by section 201 of the Tax Reform Act of 1986 do not apply, except that in making such determination—

(A) section 203(a)(1)(A) of such Act shall be applied by substituting "1985" for "1986",

(B) sections 203(b)(1) and 204(a)(3) of such Act shall be applied by substituting "December 31, 1985" for "March 1, 1986",

(C) in the case of transition property with a class life of less than 7 years—

(i) section 203(b)(2) of such Act shall apply, and

(ii) in the case of property with a class life—

(I) of less than 5 years, the applicable date shall be July 1, 1986, and

(II) at least 5 years, but less than 7 years, the applicable date shall be January 1, 1987, and

(D) section 203(b)(3) shall be applied by substituting "1986" for "1987".

(2) TREATMENT OF PROGRESS EXPENDITURES.—No progress expenditures for periods after December 31, 1985, with respect to any property shall be taken into account for purposes of applying the regular percentage unless it is reasonable to expect that such property will be transition property when placed in service. If any progress expenditures are taken into account by reason of the preceding sentence and subsequently there is not a reasonable expectation that such property would be transition property when placed in service, the credits attributable to progress expenditures with respect to such property shall be recaptured under section 47.

Amendments

• 1986, Tax Reform Act of 1986 (P.L. 99-514)

P.L. 99-514, §211(a):

Amended subpart E of part IV of subchapter A of chapter 1 by adding new section 49. **Effective** for property placed in service after 12-31-85, in tax years ending after such date. However, for exceptions, see Act Sec. 211(d) and (e)(2)-(4), below and Act Sec. 211(b) following Code Sec. 46(f).

P.L. 99-514, §§211(d)-(e), 212 and 213, as amended by P.L. 100-647, §1002(e)-(g), provide:

(d) EXCEPTION FOR CERTAIN AIRCRAFT USED IN ALASKA.—

(1) The amendments made by subsection (a) shall not apply to property originally placed in service after December 29, 1982, and before August 1, 1985, by a corporation incorporated in Alaska on May 21, 1953, and used by it—

(A) in part, for the transportation of mail for the United States Postal Service in the State of Alaska, and

(B) in part, to provide air service in the State of Alaska on routes which had previously been served by an air carrier that received compensation from the Civil Aeronautics Board for providing service.

(2) In the case of property described in subparagraph (A)—

(A) such property shall be treated as recovery property described in section 208(d)(5) of the Tax Equity and Fiscal Responsibility Act of 1982 ("TEFRA");

(B) "48 months" shall be substituted for "3 months" each place it appears in applying—

(i) section 48(b)(2)(B) of the Code, and

(ii) section 168(f)(8)(D) of the Code (as in effect after the amendments made by the Technical Corrections Act of 1982 but before the amendments made by TEFRA); and

(C) the limitation of section 168(f)(8)(D)(ii)(III) (as then in effect) shall be read by substituting "the lessee's original cost basis.", for "the adjusted basis of the lessee at the time of the lease.".

(3) The aggregate amount of property to which this paragraph shall apply shall not exceed $60,000,000.

(e) EFFECTIVE DATE.—

(1) IN GENERAL.—Except as provided in this subsection, the amendments made by this section shall apply to property placed in service after December 31, 1985, in taxable years ending after such date. Section 49(c) of the Internal Revenue Code of 1986 (as added by subsection (a)) shall apply to taxable years ending after June 30, 1987, and to amounts carried to such taxable years.

(2) EXCEPTIONS FOR CERTAIN FILMS.—For purposes of determining whether any property is transition property within the meaning of section 49(e) of the Internal Revenue Code of 1986—

(A) in the case of any motion picture or television film, construction shall be treated as including production for purposes of section 203(b)(1) of this Act, and written contemporary evidence of an agreement (in accordance with industry practice) shall be treated as a written binding contract for such purposes,

(B) in the case of any television film, a license agreement or agreement for production services between a television network and a producer shall be treated as a binding contract for purposes of section 203(b)(1)(A) of this Act, and

(C) a motion picture film shall be treated as described in section 203(b)(1)(A) of this Act if—

(i) funds were raised pursuant to a public offering before September 26, 1985, for the production of such film,

(ii) 40 percent of the funds raised pursuant to such public offering are being spent on films the production of which commenced before such date, and

(iii) all of the films funded by such public offering are required to be distributed pursuant to distribution agreements entered into before September 26, 1985.

(3) NORMALIZATION RULES.—The provisions of subsection (b) shall apply to any violation of the normalization requirements under paragrapgh (1) or (2) of section 46(f) of the Internal Revenue Code of 1986 occurring in taxable years ending after December 31, 1985.

(4) ADDITIONAL EXCEPTIONS.—

(A) Subsections (c) and (d) of section 49 of the Internal Revenue Code of 1986 shall not apply to any continuous caster facility for slabs and blooms which is subject to a lease and which is part of a project the second phase of which is a continuous slab caster which was placed in service before December 31, 1985.

(B) For purposes of determining whether an automobile manufacturing facility (including equipment and incidental appurtenances) is transition property within the meaning of section 49(e), property with respect to which the Board of Directors of an automobile manufacturer formally approved the plan for the project on January 7, 1985 shall be treated as transition property and subsections (c) and (d) of section 49 of such Code shall not apply to such property, but only with respect to $70,000,000 of regular investment tax credits.

(C) Any solid waste disposal facility which will process and incinerate solid waste of one or more public or private entities including Dakota County, Minnesota, and with respect to which a bond carryforward from 1985 was elected in an amount equal to $12,500,000 shall be treated as transition property within the meaning of section 49(e) of the Internal Revenue Code of 1986.

(D) For purposes of section 49 of such Code, the following property shall be treated as transition property:

(i) 2 catamarans built by a shipbuilder incorporated in the State of Washington in 1964, the contracts for which were signed on April 22, 1986 and November 12, 1985, and 1 barge built by such shipbuilder the contract for which was signed on August 7, 1985.

(ii) 2 large passenger ocean-going United States flag cruise ships with a passenger rated capacity of up to 250 which are built by the shipbuilder described in clause (i), which are the first such ships built in the United States since 1952, and which were designed at the request of a Pacific Coast cruise line pursuant to a contract entered into in October 1985. This clause shall apply only to that portion of the cost of each ship which does not exceed $40,000,000.

(iii) Property placed in service during 1986 by Satellite Industries, Inc., with headquarters in Minneapolis, Minnesota, to the extent that the cost of such property does not exceed $1,950,000.

(E) Subsections (c) and (d) of section 49 of such Code shall not apply to property described in section 204(a)(4) of this Act.

SEC. 212. EFFECTIVE 15-YEAR CARRYBACK OF EXISTING CARRYFORWARDS OF STEEL COMPANIES.

(a) GENERAL RULE.—If a qualified corporation makes an election under this section for its 1st taxable year beginning after December 31, 1986, with respect to any portion of its existing carryforwards, the amount determined under subsection (b) shall be treated as a payment against the tax imposed by chapter 1 of the Internal Revenue Code of 1986 made by such corporation on the last day prescribed by law (without regard to extensions) for filing its return of tax under chapter 1 of such Code for such 1st taxable year.

(b) AMOUNT.—For purposes of subsection (a), the amount determined under this subsection shall be the lesser of—

(1) 50 percent of the portion of the corporation's existing carryforwards to which the election under subsection (a) applies, or

(2) the corporation's net tax liability for the carryback period.

(c) CORPORATION MAKING ELECTION MAY NOT USE SAME AMOUNTS UNDER SECTION 38.—In the case of a qualified corporation which makes an election under subsection (a), the portion of such corporation's existing carryforwards to which such an election applies shall not be taken into account under section 38 of the Internal Revenue Code of 1986 for any taxable year beginning after December 31, 1986.

(d) NET TAX LIABILITY FOR CARRYBACK PERIOD.—For purposes of this section—

(1) IN GENERAL.—A corporation's net tax liability for the carryback period is the aggregate of such corporation's net tax liability for taxable years in the carryback period.

(2) NET TAX LIABILITY.—The term "net tax liability" means, with respect to any taxable year, the amount of the tax imposed by chapter 1 of the Internal Revenue Code of 1954 for such taxable year, reduced by the sum of the credits allowable under part IV of subchapter A of such chapter 1 (other than section 34 thereof). For purposes of the preceding sentence, any tax treated as not imposed by chapter 1 of such Code under section 26(b)(2) of such Code shall not be treated as tax imposed by such chapter 1.

(3) CARRYBACK PERIOD.—The term "carryback period" means the period—

(A) which begins with the corporation's 15th taxable year preceding the 1st taxable year from which there is an unused credit included in such corporation's existing carryforwards (but in no event shall such period begin before the corporation's 1st taxable year ending after December 31, 1961), and

(B) which ends with the corporation's last taxable year beginning before January 1, 1986.

(e) NO RECOMPUTATION OF MINIMUM TAX, ETC.—Nothing in this section shall be construed to affect—

(1) the amount of the tax imposed by section 56 of the Internal Revenue Code of 1986, or

(2) the amount of any credit allowable under such Code, for any taxable year in the carryback period.

(f) REINVESTMENT REQUIREMENT.—

(1) IN GENERAL.—Any amount determined under this section must be committed to reinvestment in, and modernization of the steel industry through investment in modern plant and equipment, research and development, and other appropriate projects, such as working capital for steel operations and programs for the retraining of steel workers.

(2) SPECIAL RULE.—In the case of the LTV Corporation, in lieu of the requirements of paragraph (1)—

(A) such corporation shall place such refund in a separate account; and

(B) amounts in such separate account—

(i) shall only be used by the corporation—

(I) to purchase an insurance policy which provides that, in the event the corporation becomes involved in a title 11 or similar case (as defined in section 368(a)(3)(A) of the Internal Revenue Code of 1954), the insurer will provide life and health insurance coverage during the 1-year period beginning on the date when the corporation receives the refund to any individual with respect to whom the corporation would (but for such involvement) have been obligated to provide such coverage the coverage provided by the insurer will be identical to the coverage which the corporation would (but for such involvement) have been obligated to provide, and provides that the payment of insurance premiums will not be required during such 1-year period to keep such policy in force, or

(II) directly in connection with the trade or business of the corporation in the manufacture or production of steel; and

(ii) shall be used (or obligated) for purposes described in clause (i) not later than 3 months after the corporation receives the refund.

(3) In the case of a qualified corporation, no offset to any refund under this section may be made by reason of any tax imposed by section 4971 of the Internal Revenue Code of 1986 (or any interest or penalty attributable to any such tax), and the date on which any such refund is to be paid shall be determined without regard to such corporation's status under title 11, United States Code.

(g) DEFINITIONS.—For purposes of this section—

(1) QUALIFIED CORPORATION.—

(A) IN GENERAL.—The term "qualified corporation" means any corporation which is described in section 806(b) of the Steel Import Stabilization Act and a company which was unincorporated on February 11, 1983, in Michigan.

(B) CERTAIN PREDECESSORS INCLUDED.—In the case of any qualified corporation which has carryforward attributable to a predecessor corporation described in such section 806(b), the qualified corporation and the predecessor corporation shall be treated as 1 corporation for purposes of subsections (d) and (e).

(2) EXISTING CARRYFORWARDS.—The term "existing carryforward" means the aggregate of the amounts which—

(A) are unused business credit carryforwards to the taxpayer's 1st taxable year beginning after December 31, 1986 (determined without regard to the limitations of section 38(c) and any reduction under section 49 of the Internal Revenue Code of 1986), and

(B) are attributable to the amount of the regular investment credit determined for periods before January 1, 1986, under section 46(a)(1) of such Code (relating to regular percentage), or any corresponding provision of prior law, determined on the basis that the regular investment credit was used first.

(3) SPECIAL RULE FOR RESTRUCTURING.—In the case of any corporation, any restructuring shall not limit, increase, or otherwise affect the benefits which would have been available under this section but for such restructuring.

(h) TENTATIVE REFUNDS.—Rules similar to the rules of section 6425 of the Internal Revenue Code of 1986 shall apply to any overpayment resulting from the application of this section.

SEC. 213. EFFECTIVE 15-YEAR CARRYBACK OF EXISTING CARRYFORWARDS OF QUALIFIED FARMERS.

(a) GENERAL RULE.—If a taxpayer who is a qualified farmer makes an election under this section for its 1st taxable year beginning after December 31, 1986, with respect to any portion of its existing carryforwards, the amount determined under subsection (b) shall be treated as a payment against the tax imposed by chapter 1 of the Internal Revenue Code of 1986 made by such taxpayer on the last day prescribed by law (without regard to extensions) for filing its return of tax under chapter 1 of such Code for such 1st taxable year.

(b) AMOUNT.—For purposes of subsection (a), the amount determined under this subsection shall be equal to the smallest of—

(1) 50 percent of the portion of the taxpayer's existing carryforwards to which the election under subsection (a) applies,

(2) the taxpayer's net tax liability for the carryback period (within the meaning of section 212(d) of this Act), or

(3) $750.

(c) TAXPAYER MAKING ELECTION MAY NOT USE SAME AMOUNTS UNDER SECTION 38.—In the case of a qualified farmer who makes an election under subsection (a), the portion of such farmer's existing carryforwards to which such an election applies shall not be taken into account under section 38 of the Internal Revenue Code of 1986 for any taxable year beginning after December 31, 1986.

(d) NO RECOMPUTATION OF MINIMUM TAX, ETC.—Nothing in this section shall be construed to affect—

(1) the amount of the tax imposed by section 56 of the Internal Revenue Code of 1954, or

(2) the amount of any credit allowable under such Code, for any taxable year in the carryback period (within the meaning of section 212(d)(3) of this Act).

(e) DEFINITIONS AND SPECIAL RULES.—For purposes of this section—

(1) QUALIFIED FARMER.—The term "qualified farmer" means any taxpayer who, during the 3-taxable year period preceding the taxable year for which an election is made under subsection (a), derived 50 percent or more of the taxpayer's gross income from the trade or business of farming.

(2) EXISTING CARRYFORWARD.—The term "existing carryforward" means the aggregate of the amounts which—

(A) are unused business credit carryforwards to the taxpayer's 1st taxable year beginning after December 31, 1986 (determined without regard to the limitations of section 38(c) of the Internal Revenue Code of 1986), and

(B) are attributable to the amount of the investment credit determined for periods before January 1, 1986, under section 46(a) of such Code (or any corresponding provision of prior law) with respect to section 38 property which was used by the taxpayer in the trade or business of farming, determined on the basis that such credit was used first.

(3) FARMING.—The term "farming" has the meaning given such term by section 2032A(e)(4) and (5) of such Code.

• 1978, Revenue Act of 1978 (P.L. 95-600)

P.L. 95-600, §312(c)(1), (d):

Repealed Code Sec. 49. **Effective** for tax years after 12-31-78. Prior to repeal, Code Sec. 49 read as follows:

SEC. 49. TERMINATION FOR PERIOD BEGINNING APRIL 19, 1969, AND ENDING DURING 1971.

(a) GENERAL RULE.—For purposes of this subpart, the term "section 38 property" does not include property—

(1) the physical construction, reconstruction, or erection of which is begun after April 18, 1969, or

(2) which is acquired by the taxpayer after April 18, 1969,

other than pretermination property.

This subsection shall not apply to property described in section 50.

(b) PRETERMINATION PROPERTY.—For purposes of this subpart—

(1) BINDING CONTRACTS.—Any property shall be treated as pretermination property to the extent that such property is constructed, reconstructed, erected, or acquired pursuant to a contract which was, on April 18, 1969, and at all times thereafter, binding on the taxpayer.

(2) EQUIPPED BUILDING RULE.—If—

(A) pursuant to a plan of the taxpayer in existence on April 18, 1969 (which plan was not substantially modified at any time after such date and before the taxpayer placed the equipped building in service), the taxpayer has constructed, reconstructed, erected, or acquired a building and the machinery and equipment necessary to the planned use of the building by the taxpayer, and

(B) more than 50 percent of the aggregate adjusted basis of all the property of a character subject to the allowance for depreciation making up such building as so equipped is attributable to either property the construction, reconstruction, or erection of which was begun by the taxpayer before April 19, 1969, or property the acquisition of which by the taxpayer occurred before such date,

then all property comprising such building as so equipped (and any incidental property adjacent to such building which is necessary to the planned use of the building) shall be pretermination property. For purposes of subparagraph (B) of the preceding sentence, the rules of paragraphs (1) and (4) shall be applied. For purposes of this paragraph, a special purpose structure shall be treated as a building.

(3) PLANT FACILITY RULE.—

(A) GENERAL RULE.—If—

(i) pursuant to a plan of the taxpayer in existence on April 18, 1969 (which plan was not substantially modified at any time after such date and before the taxpayer placed the plant facility in service), the taxpayer has constructed, reconstructed, or erected a plant facility, and either

(ii) the construction, reconstruction, or erection of such plant facility was commenced by the taxpayer before April 19, 1969, or

(iii) more than 50 percent of the aggregate adjusted basis of all the property of a character subject to the allowance for depreciation making up such plant facility is attributable to either property the construction, reconstruction, or erection of which was begun by the taxpayer before April 19, 1969, or property the acquisition of which by the taxpayer occurred before such date,

then all property comprising such plant facility shall be pretermination property. For purposes of clause (iii) of the preceding sentence, the rules of paragraphs (1) and (4) shall be applied.

(B) PLANT FACILITY DEFINED.—For purposes of this paragraph, the term "plant facility" means a facility which does not include any building (or of which buildings constitute an insignificant portion) and which is—

(i) a self-contained, single operating unit or processing operation,

(ii) located on a single site, and

(iii) identified, on April 18, 1969, in the purchasing and internal financial plans of the taxpayer as a single unitary project.

(C) SPECIAL RULE.—For purposes of this subsection, if—

(i) a certificate of convenience and necessity has been issued before April 19, 1969, by a Federal regulatory agency with respect to two or more plant facilities which are included under a single plan of the taxpayer to construct, reconstruct, or erect such plant facilities, and

(ii) more than 50 percent of the aggregate adjusted basis of all the property of a character subject to the allowance for depreciation making up such plant facilities is attributable to either property the construction, reconstruction, or erection of which was begun by the taxpayer before April 19, 1969, or property the acquisition of which by the taxpayer occurred before such date,

such plant facilities shall be treated as a single plant facility.

(D) COMMENCEMENT OF CONSTRUCTION.—For purposes of subparagraph (A)(ii), the construction, reconstruction, or erection of a plant facility shall not be considered to have commenced until construction, reconstruction, or erection has commenced at the site of such plant facility. The preceding sentence shall not apply if the site of such plant facility is not located on land.

(4) MACHINERY OR EQUIPMENT RULE.—Any piece of machinery or equipment—

(A) more than 50 percent of the parts and components of which (determined on the basis of cost) were held by the taxpayer on April 18, 1969, or are acquired by the taxpayer pursuant to a binding contract which was in effect on such date, for inclusion or use in such piece of machinery or equipment, and

(B) the cost of the parts and components of which is not an insignificant portion of the total cost,

shall be treated as property which is pretermination property.

(5) CERTAIN LEASEBACK TRANSACTIONS, ETC.—

(A) Where a person who is a party to a binding contract described in paragraph (1) transfers rights in such contract (or in the property to which such contract relates) to another person but a party to such contract retains a right to use the property under a lease with such other person, then to the extent of the transferred rights such other person shall, for purposes of paragraph (1), succeed to the position of the transferor with respect to such binding contract and such property. In any case in which the lessor does not make an election under section 48(d)—

(i) the preceding sentence shall apply only if a party to the contract retains the right to use the property under a lease for a term of at least 1 year; and

(ii) if such use is retained (other than under a longterm lease), the lessor shall be deemed for the purposes of section 47 as having made a disposition of the property at such time as the lessee loses the right to use the property.

For purposes of clause (ii), if the lessee transfers the lease in a transfer described in paragraph (7), the lessee shall be considered as having the right to use of the property so long as the transferee has such use.

(B) For purposes of subparagraph (A)—

(i) a person who holds property (or rights in property) which is pretermination property by reason of the application of paragraph (4) shall, with respect to such property, be treated as a party to a binding contract described in paragraph (1), and

(ii) a corporation which is a member of the same affiliated group (as defined in paragraph (8)) as the transferor described in subparagraph (A) and which simultaneously with the transfer of property to another person acquires a right to use such property under a lease with such other person shall be treated as the transferor and as a party to the contract.

(6) CERTAIN LEASE AND CONTRACT OBLIGATIONS.—

(A) Where, pursuant to a binding lease or contract to lease in effect on April 18, 1969, a lessor or lessee is obligated to construct, reconstruct, erect, or acquire property specified in such lease or contract or in a related document filed before April 19, 1969, with a Federal regulatory agency, or property the specifications of which are readily ascertainable from the terms of such lease or contract or from such related document, any property so constructed, reconstructed, erected, or acquired by the lessor or lessee shall be pretermination property. In the case of any project which includes property other than the property to be leased to such lessee, the preceding sentence shall be applied, in the case of the lessor, to such other property only if the binding leases and contracts with all lessees in effect on April 18, 1969, cover real property constituting 25 percent or more of the project (determined on the basis of rental value). For purposes of the preceding sentences of this paragraph, in the case of any project where one or more vendorvendee relationships exist, such vendors and vendees shall be treated as lessors and lessees.

(B) Where, in order to perform a binding contract or contracts in effect on April 18, 1969, (i) the taxpayer is required to construct, reconstruct, erect, or acquire property specified in any order of a Federal regulatory agency for which application was filed before April 19, 1969, (ii) the property is to be used to transport one or more products under such contract or contracts, and (iii) one or more parties to the contract or contracts are required to take or to provide more than 50 percent of the products to be transported over a substantial portion of the expected useful life of the property, then such property shall be pretermination property.

(C) Where, in order to perform a binding contract in effect on April 18, 1969, the taxpayer is required to construct, reconstruct, erect, or acquire property specified in the contract to be used to produce one or more products and (unless the other party to the contract is a State or a political subdivision of a State which is required by the contract to make substantial expenditures which benefit the taxpayer) the other party to the contract is required to take substantially all of the products to be produced over a substantial portion of the expected useful life of the property, then such property shall be pretermination property. For purposes of applying the preceding sentence in the case of a contract for the extraction of minerals, property shall be treated as specified in the contract if (i) the specifications for such property are readily ascertainable from the location and characteristics of the mineral properties specified in such contract from which the minerals are to be extracted; (ii) such property is necessary for and is to be used solely in the extraction of minerals under such contract; (iii) the physical construction, reconstruction, or erection of such property is begun by the taxpayer before April 19, 1970, such property is acquired by the taxpayer before April 19, 1970, or such property is constructed, reconstructed, erected, or acquired pursuant to a contract which was, on April 18, 1970, and at all times thereafter, binding on the taxpayer; (iv) such property is placed in service on or before December 31, 1972; (v) such contract is a fixed price contract (except for provisions for price changes under which the loss of the credit allowed by section 38 would not result in a price change); and (vi) such property is not placed in service to replace other property used in extracting minerals under such contract.

(7) CERTAIN TRANSFERS TO BE DISREGARDED.—

(A) If property or rights under a contract are transferred in—

(i) a transfer by reason of death,

(ii) a transaction as a result of which the basis of the property in the hands of the transferee is determined by reference to its basis in the hands of the transferor by reason of the application of section 332, 351, 361, 371(a), 374(a), 721, or 731, or

(iii) a sale of substantially all of the assets of the transferor pursuant to the terms of a contract, which was on April 18, 1969, and at all times thereafter, binding on the transferee,

and such property (or the property acquired under such contract) would be treated as pre-termination property in the hands of the decedent or the transferor, such property shall be treated as pre-termination property in the hands of the transferee.

(B) If—

(i) property or rights under a contract are acquired in a transaction to which section 334(b)(2) applies,

(ii) the stock of the distributing corporation was acquired before April 19, 1969, or pursuant to a binding contract in effect April 18, 1969, and

(iii) such property (or the property acquired under such contract) would be treated as pre-termination property in the hands of the distributing corporation,

such property shall be treated as pre-termination property in the hands of the distributee.

(8) PROPERTY ACQUIRED FROM AFFILIATED CORPORATION.—In the case of property acquired by a corporation which is a member of an affiliated group from another member of the same group—

(A) such corporation shall be treated as having acquired such property on the date on which it was acquired by such other member,

(B) such corporation shall be treated as having entered into a binding contract for the construction, reconstruction, erection, or acquisition of such property on the date on which such other member entered into a contract for the construction, reconstruction, erection, or acquisition of such property, and

(C) such corporation shall be treated as having commenced the construction, reconstruction, or erection of such property on the date on which such other member commenced such construction, reconstruction, or erection.

For purposes of this subsection and subsection (c), a contract between two corporations which are members of the same affiliated group shall not be treated as a binding contract as between such corporations, unless, at all times after June 30, 1969, and prior to the completion of performance of such contract, such corporations are not members of the same affiliated group. For purposes of the preceding sentences, the term "affiliated group" has the meaning assigned to it by section 1504(a), except that all corporations shall be treated as includible corporations (without any exclusion under section 1504(b)).

(9) BARGES FOR OCEAN-GOING VESSELS.—Barges specifically designed and constructed, reconstructed, erected, or acquired for use with ocean-going vessels which are designed to carry barges and which are pre-termination property, but not in excess of—

(A) the number to be used with such vessels specified in applications for mortgage or construction loan insurance filed with the Secretary of Commerce on or before April 18, 1969, under title XI of the Merchant Marine Act, 1936, or

(B) if subparagraph (A) does not apply and if more than 50 percent of the barges which the taxpayer establishes as necessary to the initial planned use of such vessels are pre-termination property (determined without regard to this paragraph), the number which the taxpayer establishes as so necessary,

together with the machinery and equipment to be installed on such barges and necessary for their planned use, shall be treated as pre-termination property.

(10) CERTAIN NEW-DESIGN PRODUCTS.—Where—

(A) on April 18, 1969, the taxpayer had undertaken a project to produce a product of a new design pursuant to binding contracts in effect on such date which—

(i) were fixed-price contracts (except for provisions requiring or permitting price changes resulting from changes in rates of pay or costs of materials), and

(ii) covered more than 50 percent of the entire production of such design to be delivered by the taxpayer before January 1, 1973, and

(B) on or before April 18, 1969, more than 50 percent of the aggregate adjusted basis of all property of a character subject to the allowance for depreciation required to carry out such binding contracts was property the construction, reconstruction, or erection of which had been begun by the taxpayer, or had been acquired by the taxpayer (or was under a binding contract for such construction, reconstruction, erection, or acquisition),

then all tangible personal property placed in service by the taxpayer before January 1, 1972, which is required to carry out such binding contracts shall be deemed to be pre-termination property. For purposes of subparagraph (B) of the preceding sentence, jigs, dies, templates, and similar items which can be used only for the manufacture or assembly of the production under the project and which were described in written engineering and internal financial plans of the taxpayer in existence on April 18, 1969, shall be treated as property which on such date was under a binding contract for construction.

(c) LEASED PROPERTY.—In the case of property which is leased after April 18, 1969 (other than pursuant to a binding contract to lease entered into before April 19, 1969), which is section 38 property with respect to the lessor but is property which would not be section 38 property because of the application of subsection (a) if acquired by the lessee, and which is property of the same kind which the lessor ordinarily sold to customers before April 19, 1969, or ordinarily leased before such date and made an election under section 48(d), such property shall not be section 38 property with respect to either the lessor or the lessee.

• 1971, Revenue Act of 1971 (P.L. 92-178)

P.L. 92-178, §101(b)(1)-(4):

Added the last sentence in Code Sec. 49(a) and substituted the above Sec. 49 heading for the following: "SEC. 49. TERMINATION OF CREDIT." For **effective** date, see Code Sec. 50. Substituted the word "subpart" for "section" in the first sentence of Code Sec. 49(b). Repealed Code Sec. 49(d). **Effective** 12-10-71. Prior to repeal, Code Sec. 49(d) read as follows:

(d) Property Placed in Service After 1975.—For purposes of this subpart, the term "section 38 property" does not include any property placed in service after December 31, 1975.

• 1969, Tax Reform Act of 1969 (P.L. 91-172)

P.L. 91-172, §703(a):

Added Code Sec. 49. **Effective** 12-31-69.

[Sec. 50]

SEC. 50. OTHER SPECIAL RULES.

[Sec. 50(a)]

(a) RECAPTURE IN CASE OF DISPOSITIONS, ETC.—Under regulations prescribed by the Secretary—

(1) EARLY DISPOSITION, ETC.—

(A) GENERAL RULE.—If, during any taxable year, investment credit property is disposed of, or otherwise ceases to be investment credit property with respect to the taxpayer, before the close of the recapture period, then the tax under this chapter for such taxable year shall be increased by the recapture percentage of the aggregate decrease in the credits allowed under section 38 for all prior taxable years which would have resulted solely from reducing to zero any credit determined under this subpart with respect to such property.

(B) RECAPTURE PERCENTAGE.—For purposes of subparagraph (A), the recapture percentage shall be determined in accordance with the following table:

If the property ceases to be investment credit property within—	*The recapture percentage is:*
(i) One full year after placed in service	100
(ii) One full year after the close of the period described in clause (i)	80
(iii) One full year after the close of the period described in clause (ii)	60
(iv) One full year after the close of the period described in clause (iii)	40
(v) One full year after the close of the period described in clause (iv)	20

(2) PROPERTY CEASES TO QUALIFY FOR PROGRESS EXPENDITURES.—

(A) IN GENERAL.—If during any taxable year any building to which section 47(d) applied ceases (by reason of sale or other disposition, cancellation or abandonment of contract, or otherwise) to be, with respect to the taxpayer, property which, when placed in service, will be a qualified rehabilitated building, then the tax under this chapter for such taxable year shall be increased by an amount equal to the aggregate decrease in the credits allowed under section 38 for all prior taxable years which would have resulted solely from reducing to zero the credit determined under this subpart with respect to such building.

(B) CERTAIN EXCESS CREDIT RECAPTURED.—Any amount which would have been applied as a reduction under paragraph (2) of section 47(b) but for the fact that a reduction under such paragraph cannot reduce the amount taken into account under section 47(b)(1) below zero shall be treated as an amount required to be recaptured under subparagraph (A) for the taxable year during which the building is placed in service.

(C) CERTAIN SALES AND LEASEBACKS.—Under regulations prescribed by the Secretary, a sale by, and leaseback to, a taxpayer who, when the property is placed in service, will be a lessee to whom the rules referred to in subsection (d)(5) apply shall not be treated as a cessation described in subparagraph (A) to the extent that the amount which will be passed through to the lessee under such rules with respect to such property is not less than the qualified rehabilitation expenditures properly taken into account by the lessee under section 47(d) with respect to such property.

(D) COORDINATION WITH PARAGRAPH (1).—If, after property is placed in service, there is a disposition or other cessation described in paragraph (1), then paragraph (1) shall be applied as if any credit which was allowable by reason of section 47(d) and which has not been required to be recaptured before such disposition, cessation, or change in use were allowable for the taxable year the property was placed in service.

(E) SPECIAL RULES.—Rules similar to the rules of this paragraph shall apply in cases where qualified progress expenditures were taken into account under the rules referred to in section 48(b).

(3) CARRYBACKS AND CARRYOVERS ADJUSTED.—In the case of any cessation described in paragraph (1) or (2), the carrybacks and carryovers under section 39 shall be adjusted by reason of such cessation.

(4) SUBSECTION NOT TO APPLY IN CERTAIN CASES.—Paragraphs (1) and (2) shall not apply to—

(A) a transfer by reason of death, or

(B) a transaction to which section 381(a) applies.

For purposes of this subsection, property shall not be treated as ceasing to be investment credit property with respect to the taxpayer by reason of a mere change in the form of conducting the trade or business so long as the property is retained in such trade or business as investment credit property and the taxpayer retains a substantial interest in such trade or business.

(5) DEFINITIONS AND SPECIAL RULES.—

(A) INVESTMENT CREDIT PROPERTY.—For purposes of this subsection, the term "investment credit property" means any property eligible for a credit determined under this subpart.

(B) TRANSFER BETWEEN SPOUSES OR INCIDENT TO DIVORCE.—In the case of any transfer described in subsection (a) of section 1041—

(i) the foregoing provisions of this subsection shall not apply, and

(ii) the same tax treatment under this subsection with respect to the transferred property shall apply to the transferee as would have applied to the transferor.

(C) SPECIAL RULE.—Any increase in tax under paragraph (1) or (2) shall not be treated as tax imposed by this chapter for purposes of determining the amount of any credit allowable under this chapter.

Amendments

• 2005, Gulf Opportunity Zone Act of 2005 (P.L. 109-135)

P.L. 109-135, §412(o):

Amended Code Sec. 50(a)(2)(E) by striking "section 48(a)(5)" and inserting "section 48(b)". **Effective** 12-21-2005.

• 1998, IRS Restructuring and Reform Act of 1998 (P.L. 105-206)

P.L. 105-206, §6004(g)(7):

Amended Code Sec. 50(a)(5)(C) by striking "subpart A, B, D, or G" and inserting "this chapter". **Effective** as if included in the provision of P.L. 105-34 to which it relates [**effective** for obligations issued after 12-31-97.—CCH].

• 1996, Small Business Job Protection Act of 1996 (P.L. 104-188)

P.L. 104-188, §1702(h)(11):

Amended Code Sec. 50(a)(2)(E) by striking "section 48(a)(5)(A)" and inserting "section 48(a)(5)". **Effective** as if included in the provision of P.L. 101-508 to which it relates.

P.L. 104-188, §1704(t)(29):

Amended Code Sec. 50(a)(2)(C) by striking "subsection (c)(4)" and inserting "subsection (d)(5)". **Effective** 8-20-96.

[Sec. 50(b)]

(b) CERTAIN PROPERTY NOT ELIGIBLE.—No credit shall be determined under this subpart with respect to—

(1) PROPERTY USED OUTSIDE UNITED STATES.—

(A) IN GENERAL.—Except as provided in subparagraph (B), no credit shall be determined under this subpart with respect to any property which is used predominantly outside the United States.

(B) EXCEPTIONS.—Subparagraph (A) shall not apply to any property described in section 168(g)(4).

(2) PROPERTY USED FOR LODGING.—No credit shall be determined under this subpart with respect to any property which is used predominantly to furnish lodging or in connection with the furnishing of lodging. The preceding sentence shall not apply to—

(A) nonlodging commercial facilities which are available to persons not using the lodging facilities on the same basis as they are available to persons using the lodging facilities;

(B) property used by a hotel or motel in connection with the trade or business of furnishing lodging where the predominant portion of the accommodations is used by transients;

(C) a certified historic structure to the extent of that portion of the basis which is attributable to qualified rehabilitation expenditures; and

(D) any energy property.

(3) PROPERTY USED BY CERTAIN TAX-EXEMPT ORGANIZATION.—No credit shall be determined under this subpart with respect to any property used by an organization (other than a cooperative described in section 521) which is exempt from the tax imposed by this chapter unless such property is used predominantly in an unrelated trade or business the income of which is subject to tax under section 511. If the property is debt-financed property (as defined in section 514(b)), the amount taken into account for purposes of determining the amount of the credit under this subpart with respect to such property shall be that percentage of the amount (which but for this paragraph would be so taken into account) which is the same percentage as is used under section 514(a), for the year the property is placed in service, in computing the amount of gross income to be taken into account during such taxable year with respect to such property. If any qualified rehabilitated building is used by the tax-exempt organization pursuant to a lease, this paragraph shall not apply for purposes of determining the amount of the rehabilitation credit.

(4) PROPERTY USED BY GOVERNMENTAL UNITS OR FOREIGN PERSONS OR ENTITIES.—

(A) IN GENERAL.—No credit shall be determined under this subpart with respect to any property used—

(i) by the United States, any State or political subdivision thereof, any possession of the United States, or any agency or instrumentality of any of the foregoing, or

(ii) by any foreign person or entity (as defined in section 168(h)(2)(C)), but only with respect to property to which section 168(h)(2)(A)(iii) applies (determined after the application of section 168(h)(2)(B)).

(B) EXCEPTION FOR SHORT-TERM LEASES.—This paragraph and paragraph (3) shall not apply to any property by reason of use under a lease with a term of less than 6 months (determined under section 168(i)(3)).

(C) EXCEPTION FOR QUALIFIED REHABILITATED BUILDINGS LEASED TO GOVERNMENTS, ETC.—If any qualified rehabilitated building is leased to a governmental unit (or a foreign person or entity) this paragraph shall not apply for purposes of determining the rehabilitation credit with respect to such building.

(D) SPECIAL RULES FOR PARTNERSHIPS, ETC.—For purposes of this paragraph and paragraph (3), rules similar to the rules of paragraphs (5) and (6) of section 168(h) shall apply.

(E) CROSS REFERENCE.—

For special rules for the application of this paragraph and paragraph (3), see section 168(h).

[Sec. 50(c)]

(c) BASIS ADJUSTMENT TO INVESTMENT CREDIT PROPERTY.—

(1) IN GENERAL.—For purposes of this subtitle, if a credit is determined under this subpart with respect to any property, the basis of such property shall be reduced by the amount of the credit so determined.

(2) CERTAIN DISPOSITIONS.—If during any taxable year there is a recapture amount determined with respect to any property the basis of which was reduced under paragraph (1), the basis of such property (immediately before the event resulting in such recapture) shall be increased by an amount equal to such recapture amount. For purposes of the preceding sentence, the term "recapture amount" means any increase in tax (or adjustment in carrybacks or carryovers) determined under subsection (a).

(3) SPECIAL RULE.—In the case of any energy credit—

(A) only 50 percent of such credit shall be taken into account under paragraph (1), and

(B) only 50 percent of any recapture amount attributable to such credit shall be taken into account under paragraph (2).

(4) RECAPTURE OF REDUCTIONS.—

(A) IN GENERAL.—For purposes of sections 1245 and 1250, any reduction under this subsection shall be treated as a deduction allowed for depreciation.

(B) SPECIAL RULE FOR SECTION 1250.—For purposes of section 1250(b), the determination of what would have been the depreciation adjustments under the straight line method shall be made as if there had been no reduction under this section.

(5) ADJUSTMENT IN BASIS OF INTEREST IN PARTNERSHIP OR S CORPORATION.—The adjusted basis of—

(A) a partner's interest in a partnership, and

(B) stock in an S corporation,

shall be appropriately adjusted to take into account adjustments made under this subsection in the basis of property held by the partnership or S corporation (as the case may be).

Amendments

• 2004, American Jobs Creation Act of 2004 (P.L. 108-357)

P.L. 108-357, §322(d)(2)(D):

Amended Code Sec. 50(c)(3) by striking "or reforestation credit" following "energy credit". **Effective** with respect to expenditures paid or incurred after 10-22-2004.

[Sec. 50(d)]

(d) CERTAIN RULES MADE APPLICABLE.—For purposes of this subpart, rules similar to the rules of the following provisions (as in effect on the day before the date of the enactment of the Revenue Reconciliation Act of 1990) shall apply:

(1) Section 46(e) (relating to limitations with respect to certain persons).

(2) Section 46(f) (relating to limitation in case of certain regulated companies).

(3) Section 46(h) (relating to special rules for cooperatives).

(4) Paragraphs (2) and (3) of section 48(b) (relating to special rule for sale-leasebacks).

(5) Section 48(d) (relating to certain leased property).

(6) Section 48(f) (relating to certain estates and trusts).

(7) Section 48(r) (relating to certain 501(d) organizations).

Paragraphs (1)(A), (2)(A), and (4) of the section 46(e) referred to in paragraph (1) of this subsection shall not apply to any taxable year beginning after December 31, 1995.

Amendments

• 1996, Small Business Job Protection Act of 1996 (P.L. 104-188)

P.L. 104-188, §1616(b)(1):

Amended Code Sec. 50(d) by adding at the end a new sentence. **Effective** for tax years beginning after 12-31-95.

• 1990, Omnibus Budget Reconcilliation Act of 1990 (P.L. 101-508)

P.L. 101-508, §11813(a):

Added Code Sec. 50. **Effective**, generally, for property placed in service after 12-31-90. However, for exceptions see Act Sec. 11813(c)(2) below.

P.L. 101-508, §11813(c)(2), provides:

(2) EXCEPTIONS.—The amendments made by this section shall not apply to—

(A) any transition property (as defined in section 49(e) of the Internal Revenue Code of 1986 (as in effect on the day before the date of the enactment of this Act),

(B) any property with respect to which qualified progress expenditures were previously taken into account under section 46(d) of such Code (as so in effect), and

(C) any property described in section 46(b)(2)(C) of such Code (as so in effect).

[Sec. 50—Repealed]

Amendments

• 1978, Revenue Act of 1978 (P.L. 95-600)

P.L. 95-600, §312(c)(1), (d):

Repealed Code Sec. 50. **Effective** for tax years ending after 12-31-78. Prior to repeal, Code Sec. 50 read as follows:

SEC. 50. RESTORATION OF CREDIT.

(a) GENERAL RULE.—Section 49(a) (relating to termination of credit) shall not apply to property—

(1) the construction, reconstruction, or erection of which—

(A) is completed by the taxpayer after August 15, 1971, or

(B) is begun by the taxpayer after March 31, 1971, or

(2) which is acquired by the taxpayer—

(A) after August 15, 1971, or

(B) after March 31, 1971, and before August 16, 1971, pursuant to an order which the taxpayer establishes was placed after March 31, 1971.

(b) TRANSITIONAL RULE.—In applying section 46(c)(1)(A) in the case of property described in subsection (a)(1)(A) the construction, reconstruction, or erection of which is begun before April 1, 1971, there shall be taken into account only that portion of the basis which is properly attributable to construction, reconstruction, or erection after August 15, 1971. This subsection shall not apply to pretermination property (within the meaning of section 49(b)).

• 1971, Revenue Act of 1971 (P.L. 92-178)

P.L. 92-178, §101(a):

Added Code Sec. 50(b). **Effective** as noted in that section.

Subpart C—Rules for Computing Credit for Expenses of Work Incentive Programs—[Repealed]

[Sec. 50A—Repealed]

Amendments

• 1984, Deficit Reduction Act of 1984 (P.L. 98-369)

P.L. 98-369, §474(m)(2):

Repealed Code Sec. 50A. **Effective** for tax years beginning after 12-31-83, and to carrybacks from such years. Prior to repeal, Code Sec. 50A read as follows:

SEC. 50A. AMOUNT OF CREDIT.

[Sec. 50A(a)]

(a) DETERMINATION OF AMOUNT.—

(1) GENERAL RULE.—The amount of the credit allowed by section 40 for the taxable year shall be equal to the sum of—

(A) 50 percent of the first-year work incentive program expenses, and

(B) 25 percent of the second-year work incentive program expenses.

(2) LIMITATION BASED ON AMOUNT OF TAX.—Notwithstanding paragraph (1), the amount of the credit allowed by section 40 for the taxable year shall not exceed the liability for tax for the taxable year.

(3) LIABILITY FOR TAX.—For purposes of paragraph (2), the liability for tax for the taxable year shall be the tax imposed by this chapter for such year, reduced by the sum of the credits allowable under—

(A) section 33 (relating to foreign tax credit),

(B) section 37 (relating to credit for the elderly),

(C) section 38 (relating to investment in certain depreciable property), and

(D) section 41 (relating to contributions to candidates for public office).

For purposes of this paragraph, any tax imposed for the taxable year by section 56 (relating to minimum tax for tax preferences), section 72(m)(5)(B) (relating to 10 percent tax on premature distributions to owneremployees), section 72(q)(1) (relating to 5-percent tax on premature distributions under annuity contracts), section 402(e) (relating to tax on lump sum distributions), section 408(f) (relating to additional tax on income from certain retirement accounts), section 531 (relating to accumulated earnings tax), section 541 (relating to personal holding company tax), or section 1374 (relating to tax on certain capital gains of S corporations), and any additional tax imposed for the taxable year by section 1351(d)(1) (relating to recoveries of foreign expropriation losses), shall not be considered tax imposed by this chapter for such year.

(4) LIMITATION WITH RESPECT TO NONBUSINESS ELIGIBLE EMPLOYEES.—

(A) IN GENERAL.—In the case of any work incentive program expenses paid or incurred by the taxpayer during the taxable year to eligible employees whose services are not performed in connection with a trade or business of the taxpayer—

(i) paragraph (1)(A) shall be applied by substituting "35 percent" for "50 percent",

(ii) subparagraph (B) of paragraph (1) shall not apply, and

(iii) the aggregate amount of such work incentive program expenses which may be taken into account under paragraph (1) for such taxable year may not exceed $12,000.

(B) DEPENDENT CARE CREDIT MAY NOT BE CLAIMED.—No credit shall be allowed under section 44A with respect to any amounts paid or incurred by the taxpayer with respect to which the taxpayer is allowed a credit under section 40.

(C) MARRIED INDIVIDUALS.—In the case of a husband or wife who files a separate return, subparagraph (A) shall be applied by substituting "$6,000" for "$12,000". The preceding sentence shall not apply if the spouse of the taxpayer has no work incentive program expenses described in such subparagraph for the taxable year.

Amendments

• 1982, Subchapter S Revision Act of 1982 (P.L. 97-354)

P.L. 97-354, §5(a)(9):

Amended Code Sec. 50A(a)(3) by striking out "section 1378 (relating to tax on certain capital gains of subchapter S corporations)," and inserting in lieu thereof "section 1374 (relating to tax on certain capital gains of S corporations),". **Effective** for tax years beginning after 12-31-82.

• 1982, Tax Equity and Fiscal Responsibility Act of 1982 (P.L. 97-248)

P.L. 97-248, §265(b)(2)(A)(ii):

Amended Code Sec. 50A(a)(3) by inserting "section 72(q)(1) (relating to 5-percent tax on premature distributions under annuity contracts)," after "owner-employees),". **Effective** for distributions after 12-31-82.

• 1980, Technical Corrections Act of 1979 (P.L. 96-222)

P.L. 96-222, §103(a)(7)(A):

Amended Act Sec. 322(f)(1) of the Revenue Act of 1978 by adding at the end the following new sentence:

For purposes of applying section 50A(a)(2) of the Internal Revenue Code of 1954 with respect to a taxable year beginning before January 1, 1979, the rules of sections 50A(a)(4), 50A(a)(5), and 50B(e)(3) of such Code (as in effect on the day before the date of the enactment of this Act) shall apply. **Effective** as provided in P.L. 95-600, Act Sec. 322(f), below.

P.L. 96-222, §103(a)(7)(B)(i) and (ii):

Amended Act Sec. 322(f)(2)(B) by striking out "September 27, 1978," and inserting "September 26, 1978, for purposes of applying the amendments made by this section," and by striking out "January 1, 1979" and inserting "January 1, 1979, and any wages paid or incurred after December 31, 1978, with respect to such individual shall be considered to be attributable to services rendered after that date.".

P.L. 96-222, §103(a)(7)(D)(i):

Amended Code Sec. 50A(a)(4)(C) by striking out "$6,000 and" and inserting "$6,000 for".

• 1980 (P.L. 96-178)

P.L. 96-178, §6(c):

Amended Code Sec. 50A(a)(4)(C) by substituting "$6,000 for" for "$6,000 and".

• Revenue Act of 1978 (P.L. 95-600)

P.L. 95-600, §322(a), (b):

Amended Code Sec. 50A(a). **Effective** as provided in Act Sec. 322(f), below. Prior to amendment, Code Sec. 50A(a) read as follows:

(a) DETERMINATION OF AMOUNT.—

(1) GENERAL RULE.—The amount of the credit allowed by section 40 for the taxable year shall be equal to 20 percent of the work incentive program expenses (as defined in section 50B(a)).

(2) LIMITATION BASED ON AMOUNT OF TAX.—Notwithstanding paragraph (1), the credit allowed by section 40 for the taxable year shall not exceed—

(A) so much of the liability for tax for the taxable year as does not exceed $50,000, plus

(B) 50 percent of so much of the liability for tax for the taxable year as exceeds $50,000.

The preceding sentence shall not apply to so much of the credit allowed by section 40 as is attributable to Federal welfare recipient employment incentive expenses described in subsection (a)(6)(B).

(3) LIABILITY FOR TAX.—For purposes of paragraph (2), the liability for tax for the taxable year shall be the tax imposed by this chapter for such year, reduced by the sum of the credits allowable under—

(A) section 33 (relating to foreign tax credit),

(B) section 37 (relating to credit for the elderly),

(C) section 38 (relating to investment in certain depreciable property), and

(D) section 41 (relating to contributions to candidates for public office).

For purposes of this paragraph, any tax imposed for the taxable year by section 56 (relating to minimum tax for tax preferences), section 72(m)(5)(B) (relating to 10 percent tax on premature distributions to owner-employees), section 402(e) (relating to tax on lump sum distributions), section 408(f) (relating to additional tax on income from certain retirement accounts), section 531 (relating to accumulated earnings tax), section 541 (relating to personal holding company tax), or section 1378 (relating to tax on certain capital gains of subchapter S corporations), and any additional tax imposed for the taxable year by section 1351(d)(1) (relating to recoveries of foreign expropriation losses), shall not be considered tax imposed by this chapter for such year.

(4) MARRIED INDIVIDUALS.—In the case of a husband or wife who files a separate return, the amount specified under subparagraphs (A) and (B) of paragraph (2) shall be $25,000 in lieu of $50,000. This paragraph shall not apply if the spouse of the taxpayer has no work incentive program expenses for, and no unused credit carryback or carryover to, the taxable year of such spouse which ends within or with the taxpayer's taxable year.

(5) CONTROLLED GROUPS.—In the case of a controlled group, the $50,000 amount specified under paragraph (2) shall be reduced for each component member of such group by apportioning $50,000 among the component members of such group in such manner as the Secretary shall by regulations prescribe. For purposes of the preceding sentence, the term "controlled group" has the meaning assigned to such term by section 1563(a).

(6) LIMITATION WITH RESPECT TO CERTAIN ELIGIBLE EMPLOYEES.—

(A) NONBUSINESS ELIGIBLE EMPLOYEES.—Notwithstanding paragraph (1), the credit allowed by section 40 with respect to Federal welfare recipient employment incentive expenses paid or incurred by the taxpayer during the taxable year to an eligible employee whose services are not performed in connection with a trade or business of the taxpayer shall not exceed $1,000.

(B) CHILD DAY CARE SERVICES ELIGIBLE EMPLOYEES.—Notwithstanding paragraph (1), the credit allowed by section 40 with respect to Federal welfare recipient employment incentive expenses paid or incurred by the taxpayer during the taxable year to an eligible employee whose services are performed in connection with a child day care services program, conducted by the taxpayer, shall not exceed $1,000.

P.L. 95-600, §322(f) as amended by P.L. 96-178, §6(a), (b), provides:

(f) EFFECTIVE DATE.—

(1) IN GENERAL.—Except as otherwise provided in this subsection, the amendments made by this section shall apply to work incentive program expenses paid or incurred after December 31, 1978, in taxable years ending after such date; except that so much of the amendment made by subsection (a) as affects section 50A(a)(2) of the Internal Revenue Code of 1954 shall apply to taxable years beginning after December 31, 1978. For purposes of applying section 50A(a)(2) of the Internal Revenue Code of 1954 with respect to a taxable year beginning before January 1, 1979, the rules of sections 50A(a)(4), 50A(a)(5), and 50B(e)(3) of such Code (as in effect on the day before the date of the enactment (January 2, 1980) of this Act shall apply.

(2) SPECIAL RULES FOR CERTAIN ELIGIBLE EMPLOYEES.—

(A) ELIGIBLE EMPLOYEES HIRED BEFORE SEPTEMBER 27, 1978.—In the case of any eligible employee (as defined in section 50B(h)) hired before September 27, 1978, no credit shall be allowed under section 40 with respect to second-year work incentive program expenses (as defined in section 50B(a)) attributable to service performed by such employee.

(B) ELIGIBLE EMPLOYEES HIRED AFTER SEPTEMBER 26, 1978.—In the case of any eligible employee (as defined in section 50B(h)) hired after September 26, 1978, for purposes of applying the amendments made by this section, such individual shall be treated for purposes of the credit allowed by section 40 as having first begun work for the taxpayer not earlier than January 1, 1979, and any wages paid or incurred after December 31, 1978, with respect to such individual shall be considered to be attributable to services rendered after that date.

• 1976, Tax Reform Act of 1976 (P.L. 94-455)

P.L. 94-455, §503(b)(4),:

Substituted "credit for the elderly" for "retirement income" in Code Sec. 50A(a)(3)(C). **Effective** for tax years beginning after 12-31-75.

P.L. 94-455, §1901(a)(6):

Substituted "section 408(f)" for "section 408(e)" in the second sentence of Code Sec. 50A(a)(3). **Effective** for tax years beginning after 12-31-76.

P.L. 94-455, §1901(b)(1)(D):

Amended Code Sec. 50A(a)(3) by striking out subparagraph B and redesignating subparagraphs (C), (D), and (E), as subparagraphs (B), (C), and (D), respectively. **Effective** for tax years beginning after 12-31-76. Prior to amendment, subparagraph (B) read as follows:

"(B) section 35 (relating to partially tax-exempt interest)."

P.L. 94-455, §1906(b)(13)(A):

Amended 1954 Code by substituting "Secretary" for "Secretary or his delegate" each place it appeared. **Effective** 2-1-77.

P.L. 94-455, §2107(a)(1)-(3):

Amended Code Sec. 50A(a) by substituting "$50,000" for "$25,000" each place it appeared in paragraph (2); by substituting "$25,000" for "$12,500" and "$50,000" for "$25,000" in paragraph (4); and by substituting "$50,000" for "$25,000" each place it appeared in paragraph (5). **Effective** 10-4-76.

• 1976 (P.L. 94-401)

P.L. 94-401, §4(a):

Amended Sec. 50A(a) by adding at the end of paragraph (2) a new sentence and by amending paragraph (6). **Effective** for Federal welfare recipient employment incentive expenses paid or incurred by the taxpayer to an eligible employee taxpayer hired after 9-7-76 for services in connection with a child day care services program of the taxpayer. Prior to amendment, Code Sec. 50A(a)(6) read as follows:

"(6) Limitation With Respect to Nonbusiness Eligible Employees.—Notwithstanding paragraph (1), the credit allowed by section 40 with respect to Federal welfare recipient employment incentive expenses paid or incurred by the taxpayer during the taxable year to an eligible employee whose services are not performed in connection with a trade or business of the taxpayer shall not exceed $1,000."

• 1975, Tax Reduction Act of 1975 (P.L. 94-12)

P.L. 94-12, §401(a)(1):

Amended Sec. 50A(a) by adding paragraph (6). **Effective** for expenses paid or incurred for eligible employees hired after 3-29-75.

• 1974, Employee Retirement Income Security Act of 1974 (P.L. 93-406)

P.L. 93-406, §2001(g)(2)(B):

Amended the second sentence of Code Sec. 50A(a)(3) by adding "section 72(m)(5)(B) (relating to 10 percent tax on premature distributions to owner-employees),". **Effective** for distributions made in tax years beginning after 12-31-75.

P.L. 93-406, §2001(g)(2):

Amended the second sentence of Code Sec. 50A(a)(3) by adding "section 408(e) (relating to additional tax on income from certain retirement accounts),". **Effective** 1-1-75.

P.L. 93-406, §2005(c)(4):

Amended the second sentence of Code Sec. 50A(a)(3) by adding "section 402(e) (relating to tax on lump sum distributions),". **Effective** for distributions or payments made after 12-31-73, in tax years beginning after that date. Prior to amendment, the second sentence of Code Sec. 50A(a)(3) read as follows:

"For purposes of this paragraph, any tax imposed for the taxable year by section 56 (relating to minimum tax for tax preferences), section 531 (relating to accumulated earnings tax), section 541 (relating to personal holding company tax), or section 1378 (relating to tax on certain capital gains of subchapter S corporations), and any additional tax imposed for the taxable year by section 1351(d)(1) (relating to recoveries of foreign expropriation losses), shall not be considered tax imposed by this chapter for such year."

• 1971, Revenue Act of 1971 (P.L. 92-178)

P.L. 92-178, §601(b):

Added Code Sec. 50A(a). **Effective** for tax years beginning after 12-31-71.

[Sec. 50A(b)]

(b) CARRYBACK AND CARRYOVER OF UNUSED CREDIT.—

(1) ALLOWANCE OF CREDIT.—If the amount of the credit determined under subsection (a)(1) for any taxable year exceeds the limitation provided by subsection (a)(2) for such taxable year (hereinafter in this subsection referred to as "unused credit year"), such excess shall be—

(A) a work incentive program credit carryback to each of the 3 taxable years preceding the unused credit year, and

(B) a work incentive program credit carryover to each of the 7 taxable years following the unused credit year,

and shall be added to the amount allowable as a credit by section 40 for such years, except that such excess may be a carryback only to a taxable year beginning after December 31, 1971. The entire amount of the unused credit for an unused credit year shall be carried to the earliest of the 10 taxable years to which (by reason of subparagraphs (A) and (B)) such credit may be carried, and then to each of the other 9 taxable years to the extent that, because of the limitation contained in paragraph (2), such unused credit may not be added for a prior taxable year to which such unused credit may be carried. In the case of an unused credit for an unused credit year ending after December 31, 1973, this paragraph shall be applied by substituting "15" for "7" in subparagraph (B), and by substituting "18" for "10", and "17" for "9" in the second sentence.

(2) LIMITATION.—The amount of the unused credit which may be added under paragraph (1) for any preceding or succeeding taxable year shall not exceed the amount by which the limitation provided by subsection (a)(2) for such taxable year exceeds the sum of—

(A) the credit allowable under subsection (a)(1) for such taxable year, and

(B) the amounts which, by reason of this subsection, are added to the amount allowable for such taxable year and attributable to taxable years preceding the unused credit year.

Amendments

• 1981, Economic Recovery Tax Act of 1981 (P.L. 97-34)

P.L. 97-34, §207(c)(1):

Amended Code Sec. 50A(b)(1) by adding the last sentence at the end thereof. **Effective** for unused credit years ending after 12-31-73.

• 1971, Revenue Act of 1971 (P.L. 92-178)

P.L. 92-178, §601(b):

Added Code Sec. 50A(b). **Effective** tax years beginning after 12-31-71.

[Sec. 50A(c)]

Amendments

• 1978, Revenue Act of 1978 (P.L. 95-600)

P.L. 95-600, §322(c), (f):

Repealed Code Sec. 50A(c). **Effective** for work incentive program expenses paid or incurred after 12-31-78, in tax years ending after such date. Prior to repeal, Code Sec. 50A(c) read as follows:

(c) EARLY TERMINATION OF EMPLOYMENT BY EMPLOYER, ETC.—

(1) GENERAL RULE.—Under regulations prescribed by the Secretary—

(A) WORK INCENTIVE PROGRAM EXPENSES.—If the employment of any employee with respect to whom work incentive program expenses are taken into account under subsection (a) is terminated by the taxpayer at any time during the first 90 days of such employment (whether or not consecutive) or before the close of the 90th calendar day after the day in which such employee completes 90 days of employment with the taxpayer, the tax under this chapter for the taxable year in which such employment is terminated shall be increased by an amount (determined under such regulations) equal to the credits allowed under section 40 for such taxable year and all prior taxable years attributable to work incentive program expenses paid or incurred with respect to such employee.

(B) CARRYBACKS AND CARRYOVERS ADJUSTED.—In the case of any termination of employment to which subparagraph (A) applies, the carrybacks and carryovers under subsection (b) shall be properly adjusted.

(2) SUBSECTION NOT TO APPLY IN CERTAIN CASES.—

(A) IN GENERAL.—Paragraph (1) shall not apply to—

(i) a termination of employment of an employee who voluntarily leaves the employment of the taxpayer,

(ii) a termination of employment of an individual who, before the close of the period referred to in paragraph (1)(A), becomes disabled to perform the services of such employment, unless such disability is removed before the close of such period and the taxpayer fails to offer reemployment to such individual,

(iii) a termination of employment of an individual, if it is determined under the applicable State unemployment compensation law that the termination was due to the misconduct of such individual,

(iv) a termination of employment of an individual with respect to whom Federal welfare recipient employment incentive expenses (as described in section 50B(a)(2)) are taken into account under subsection (a), or

(v) a termination of employment of an individual due to a substantial reduction in the trade or business operations of the taxpayer.

(B) CHANGE IN FORM OF BUSINESS, ETC.—For purposes of paragraph (1), the employment relationship between the taxpayer and an employee shall not be treated as terminated—

(i) by a transaction to which section 381(a) applies, if the employee continues to be employed by the acquiring corporation, or

(ii) by reason of a mere change in the form of conducting the trade or business of the taxpayer, if the employee continues to be employed in such trade or business and the taxpayer retains a substantial interest in such trade or business.

(3) SPECIAL RULE.—Any increase in tax under paragraph (1) shall not be treated as tax imposed by this chapter for purposes of determining the amount of any credit allowable under subpart A.

• 1976, Tax Reform Act of 1976 (P.L. 94-455)

P.L. 94-455, §1906(b)(13)(A):

Amended 1954 Code by substituting "Secretary" for "Secretary or his delegate" each place it appeared. **Effective** 2-1-77.

P.L. 94-455, §2107(b):

Substituted "90 days" for "12 months" each place it appeared; substituted "90th calendar day" for "12th calendar month"; and substituted "day" for "calendar month" in subparagraph A of Code Sec. 50A(c)(1). **Effective** 10-4-76.

P.L. 94-455, §2107(c):

Amended subparagraph (A) of Code Sec. 50A(c)(2) by striking out "or" at the end of clause (iii); by substituting a comma and "or" for the period at the end of clause (iv); and by adding at the end thereof a new clause (v). **Effective** 10-4-76.

• 1975, Tax Reduction Act of 1975 (P.L. 94-12)

P.L. 94-12, §401(a)(2):

Added clause (iv) to Code Sec. 50A(c)(2)(A). **Effective** for expenses paid or incurred for eligible employees hired after 3-29-75.

• 1971, Revenue Act of 1971 (P.L. 92-178)

P.L. 92-178, §601(b):

Added Code Sec. 50A(c). **Effective** for tax years beginning after 12-31-71.

[Sec. 50A(d)—Repealed]

Amendments

• 1978, Revenue Act of 1978 (P.L. 95-600)

P.L. 95-600, §322(c), (f):

Repealed Code Sec. 50A(d). **Effective** for work incentive program expenses paid or incurred after 12-31-78, in tax years ending after such date. Prior to repeal, Code Sec. 50A(d) read as follows:

(d) FAILURE TO PAY COMPARABLE WAGES.—

(1) GENERAL RULE.—Under regulations prescribed by the Secretary, if during the period described in subsection (c)(1)(A), the taxpayer pays wages (as defined in section 50B(b)) to an employee with respect to whom work incentive program expenses are taken into account under subsection (a) which are less than the wages paid to other employees who perform comparable services, the tax under this chapter for the taxable year in which such wages are so paid shall be increased by an amount (determined under such regulations) equal to the credits allowed under section 40 for such taxable year and all prior taxable years attributable to work incentive program expenses paid or incurred with respect to such employee, and the carrybacks and carryovers under subsection (b) shall be properly adjusted.

(2) SPECIAL RULE.—Any increase in tax under paragraph (1) shall not be treated as tax imposed by this chapter for purposes of determining the amount of any credit allowable under subpart A.

• 1976, Tax Reform Act of 1976 (P.L. 94-455)

P.L. 94-455, §1906(b)(13)(A):

Amended 1954 Code by substituting "Secretary" for "Secretary or his delegate" each place it appeared. **Effective** 2-1-77.

• 1971, Revenue Act of 1971 (P.L. 92-178)

P. L. 92-178, §601(b):

Added Code Sec. 50A(d). **Effective** for tax years beginning after 12-31-71.

[Sec. 50B—Repealed]

Amendments

• 1984, Deficit Reduction Act of 1984 (P.L. 98-369)

P.L. 98-369, §474(m)(2):

Repealed Code Sec. 50B. **Effective** for tax years beginning after 12-31-83, and to carrybacks from such years. Prior to repeal, Code Sec. 50B read as follows:

SEC. 50B. DEFINITIONS; SPECIAL RULES.

[Sec. 50B(a)]

(a) WORK INCENTIVE PROGRAM EXPENSES.—For purposes of this subpart—

(1) IN GENERAL.—The term "work incentive program expenses" means the amount of wages paid or incurred by the taxpayer for services rendered by eligible employees.

(2) FIRST-YEAR WORK INCENTIVE PROGRAM EXPENSES.—The term "first-year work incentive program expenses" means, with respect to any eligible employee, work incentive program expenses attributable to service rendered during the one-year period which begins on the day the eligible employee begins work for the taxpayer.

(3) SECOND-YEAR WORK INCENTIVE PROGRAM EXPENSES.—The term "second-year work incentive program expenses" means, with respect to any eligible employee, work incentive program expenses attributable to service rendered during the one-year period which begins on the day after the last day of the one-year period described in paragraph (2).

(4) LIMITATION ON AMOUNT OF WORK INCENTIVE PROGRAM EXPENSES.—The amount of the work incentive program expenses taken into account with respect to any eligible employee for any one-year period described in paragraph (2) or (3) (as the case may be) shall not exceed $6,000.

(5) TERMINATION.—The term "work incentive program expenses" shall not include any amount paid or incurred in any taxable year beginning after December 31, 1981.

Amendments

• 1981, Economic Recovery Tax Act of 1981 (P.L. 97-34)

P.L. 97-34, §261(b)(2)(B)(i);

Amended Code Sec. 50B(a) by adding at the end thereof new paragraph (5). **Effective** as noted in P.L. 97-34, §261(g), in the amendment notes following Code Sec. 51(c).

• 1978, Revenue Act of 1978 (P.L. 95-600)

P.L. 95-600, §322(d)(1), (f):

Amended Code Sec. 50B(a). **Effective** for work incentive program expenses paid or incurred after 12-31-78, in tax years ending after such date. [Note: for special rules regarding certain eligible employees, see P.L. 95-600, §322(f)(2), reflected in the amendment notes following Code Sec. 50(A)(a).] Prior to amendment, Code Sec. 50B(a) read as follows:

(a) WORK INCENTIVE PROGRAM EXPENSES.—

(1) IN GENERAL.—For purposes of this subpart, the term "work incentive program expenses" means the sum of—

(A) the amount of wages paid or incurred by the taxpayer for services rendered during the first 12 months of employment (whether or not consecutive) of employees who are certified by the Secretary of Labor as—

(i) having been placed in employment under a work incentive program established under section 432(b)(1) of the Social Security Act, and

(ii) not having displaced any individual from employment, plus

(B) the amount of Federal welfare recipient employment incentive expenses paid or incurred by the taxpayer for services rendered during the first 12 months of employment (whether or not consecutive).

(2) DEFINITIONS.—For purposes of this section, the term "Federal welfare recipient employment incentive expenses" means the amount of wages paid or incurred by the taxpayer for services rendered to the taxpayer by an eligible employee—

(A) before January 1, 1980, or

(B) in the case of an eligible employee whose services are performed in connection with a child day care services program of the taxpayer, before January 1, 1979.

(3) EXCLUSION.—No item taken into account under paragraph (1)(A) shall be taken into account under paragraph (1)(B). No item taken into account under paragraph (1)(B) shall be taken into account under paragraph 1(A).

Note: The text of Code Sec. 50B(a), immediately above, reads as amended by P.L. 96-178, §3(a)(3). The amendment by P.L. 96-178 substituted "January 1, 1979" for "October 1, 1978" in Code Sec. 50B(a)(2)(B).

• 1977 (P.L. 95-171)

P.L. 95-171, §1(e):

Amended Code Sec. 50B(a)(2) by substituting "October 1, 1978" for "October 1, 1977". **Effective** 10-1-77.

• 1976, Tax Reform Act of 1976 (P.L. 94-455)

P.L. 94-455, §2107(d), (e):

Substituted "before January 1, 1980" for "before July 1, 1976" in paragraph (2) of Code Sec. 50B(a); and substituted "for services rendered during the first 12 months of employment (whether or not consecutive)" for "during the taxable year" in subparagraph (b) of Code Sec. 50B(a)(1). **Effective** 10-4-76.

• 1976 (P.L. 94-401)

P.L. 94-401, §4(b):

Amended Code Sec. 50B(a)(2). **Effective** for Federal welfare recipient employment incentive expenses paid or incurred by the taxpayer to an eligible employee taxpayer hired after 9-7-76 for services in connection with a child day care services program of the taxpayer. Prior to amendment, Code Sec. 50B(a)(2) read as follows:

"(2) Definition.—For purposes of this section, the term `Federal welfare recipient employment incentive expenses' means the amount of wages paid or incurred by the taxpayer for services rendered to the taxpayer before July 1, 1976, by an eligible employee."

• 1975, Tax Reduction Act of 1975 (P.L. 94-12)

P.L. 94-12, §401(a)(3):

Amended Code Sec. 50B(a). Prior to amendment, this section read as follows:

"(a) Work Incentive Program Expenses.—For purposes of this subpart, the term `work incentive program expenses' means the wages paid or incurred by the taxpayer for services rendered during the first 12 months of employment (whether or not consecutive) of employees who are certified by the Secretary of Labor as—

"(1) having been placed in employment under a work incentive program established under section 432(b)(1) of the Social Security Act, and

"(2) not having displaced any individual from employment."

• 1971, Revenue Act of 1971 (P.L. 92-178)

P.L. 92-178, §601(b):

Added Code Sec. 50B(a). **Effective** for tax years beginning after 12-31-71.

[Sec. 50B(b)]

(b) WAGES.—For purposes of subsection (a), the term "wages" means only cash remuneration (including amounts deducted and withheld).

Amendments

• 1971, Revenue Act of 1971 (P.L. 92-178)

P.L. 92-178, §601(b):

Added Code Sec. 50B(b). **Effective** for tax years beginning after 12-31-71.

[Sec. 50B(c)]

(c) LIMITATIONS.—

(1) REIMBURSED EXPENSES.—No item shall be taken into account under subsection (a) to the extent that the taxpayer is reimbursed for such item.

(2) GEOGRAPHICAL LIMITATION.—No item shall be taken into account under subsection (a) with respect to any expense paid or incurred by the taxpayer with respect to employment outside the United States.

(3) INELIGIBLE INDIVIDUALS.—No item shall be taken into account under subsection (a) with respect to an individual who—

(A) bears any of the relationships described in paragraphs (1) through (8) of section 152(a) to the taxpayer, or, if the taxpayer is a corporation, to an individual who owns, directly or indirectly, more than 50 percent in value of the outstanding stock of the corporation (determined with the application of section 267(c)),

(B) if the taxpayer is an estate or trust, is a grantor, beneficiary, or fiduciary of the estate or trust, or is an individual who bears any of the relationships described in paragraphs (1) through (8) of section 152(a) to a grantor, beneficiary, or fiduciary of the estate or trust, or

(C) is a dependent (described in section 152(a)(9)) of the taxpayer, or, if the taxpayer is a corporation, of an individual described in subparagraph (A), or, if the taxpayer is an estate or trust, of a grantor, beneficiary, or fiduciary of the estate or trust.

Amendments

• 1978, Revenue Act of 1978 (P.L. 95-600)

P.L. 95-600, §322(d)(2), (f):

Repealed Code Sec. 50B(c)(1) and (4) and redesignated former paragraphs (c)(2), (3) and (5) as paragraphs (c)(1), (2) and (3), respectively. **Effective** for work incentive program expenses paid or incurred after 12-31-78, in tax years ending after such date. Prior to repeal, Code Sec. 50B(c)(1) and (4) read:

"(1) TRADE OR BUSINESS EXPENSES.—No item shall be taken into account under subsection (a)(1)(A) unless such item is incurred in a trade or business of the taxpayer."

* * *

"(4) MAXIMUM PERIOD OF TRAINING OR INSTRUCTION.—No item with respect to any employee shall be taken into account under subsection (a)(1)(A) after the end of the 24-month period beginning with the date of initial employment of such employee by the taxpayer."

• 1975, Tax Reduction Act of 1975 (P.L. 94-12)

P.L. 94-12, §401(a)(4):

Amended Code Sec. 50B(c)(1) and (4) by substituting "subsection (a)(1)(A)" for "subsection (a)." **Effective** for expenses paid or incurred for eligible employees hired after 3-29-75.

• 1971, Revenue Act of 1971 (P.L. 92-178)

P.L. 92-178, §601(b):

Added Code Sec. 50B(c). **Effective** for taxable years beginning after 12-31-71.

[Sec. 50B(d)]

(d) SUBCHAPTER S CORPORATIONS.—In case of an electing small business corporation (as defined in section 1371)—

(1) the work incentive program expenses for each taxable year shall be apportioned pro rata among the persons who are shareholders of such corporation on the last day of such taxable year, and

(2) any person to whom any expenses have been apportioned under paragraph (1) shall be treated (for purposes of this subpart) as the taxpayer with respect to such expenses.

Amendments

• 1982, Subchapter S Revision Act of 1982 (P.L. 97-354)

P.L. 97-354, §5(a)(10):

Repealed Code Sec. 50B(d). **Effective** for tax years beginning after 1982.

• 1971, Revenue Act of 1971 (P.L. 92-178)

P.L. 92-178, §601(b):

Added Code Sec. 50B(d). **Effective** for tax years beginning after 12-31-71.

[Sec. 50B(e)]

(e) ESTATES AND TRUSTS.—In the case of an estate or trust—

(1) the work incentive program expenses for any taxable year shall be apportioned between the estate or trust and the beneficiaries on the basis of the income of the estate or trust allocable to each, and

(2) any beneficiary to whom any expenses have been apportioned under paragraph (1) shall be treated (for purposes of this subpart) as the taxpayer with respect to such expenses.

Amendments

• 1978, Revenue Act of 1978 (P.L. 95-600)

P.L. 95-600, §322(d)(3), (f):

Amended Code Sec. 50B(e). **Effective** for work incentive program expenses paid or incurred after 12-31-78, in tax years ending after such date. Prior to amendment, Code Sec. 50B(e) read as follows:

(e) ESTATES AND TRUSTS.—In the case of an estate or trust—

(1) the work incentive program expenses for any taxable year shall be apportioned between the estate or trust and the beneficiaries on the basis of the income of the estate or trust allocable to each,

(2) any beneficiary to whom any expenses have been apportioned under paragraph (1) shall be treated (for purposes of this subpart) as the taxpayer with respect to such expenses, and

(3) the $50,000 amount specified under subparagraphs (A) and (B) of section 50A(a)(2) applicable to such estate or trust shall be reduced to an amount which bears the same ratio to $50,000 as the amount of the expenses allocated to the trust under paragraph (1) bears to the entire amount of such expenses.

• 1976, Tax Reform Act of 1976 (P.L. 94-455)

P.L. 94-455, §2107(a)(4):

Substituted "$50,000" for $25,000 in Code Sec. 50B(e)(3). **Effective** 10-4-76.

• 1971, Revenue Act of 1971 (P.L. 92-178)

P.L. 92-178, §601(b):

Added Code Sec. 50B(e). **Effective** for tax years beginning after 12-31-71.

[Sec. 50B(f)]

(f) LIMITATIONS WITH RESPECT TO CERTAIN PERSONS.—In the case of—

(1) an organization to which section 593 applies,

(2) a regulated investment company or a real estate investment trust subject to taxation under subchapter M (section 851 and following), and

(3) a cooperative organization described in section 1381(a),

rules similar to the rules provided in subsections (e) and (h) of section 46 shall apply under regulations prescribed by the Secretary.

Amendments

• 1980, Technical Corrections Act of 1979 (P.L. 96-222)

P.L. 96-222, §103(a)(5):

Amended Code Sec. 50B(f)(3) by striking out "section 46(e)" and inserting "subsections (e) and (h) of section 46". **Effective** for tax years ending after 10-31-78.

• 1976, Tax Reform Act of 1976 (P.L. 94-455)

P.L. 94-455, §1906(b)(13)(A):

Amended 1954 Code by substituting "Secretary" for "Secretary or his delegate" each place it appeared. **Effective** 2-1-77.

• 1975, Tax Reduction Act of 1975 (P.L. 94-12)

P.L. 94-12, §302(c)(4):

Substituted "section 46(e)" for "section 46(d)" in Code Sec. 50B(f). **Effective** for tax years ending after 12-31-74.

• 1971, Revenue Act of 1971 (P.L. 92-178)

P.L. 92-178, §601(b):

Added Code Sec. 50B(f). **Effective** for tax years beginning after 12-31-71.

[Sec. 50B(g)]

(g) SPECIAL RULES FOR CONTROLLED GROUPS.—

(1) CONTROLLED GROUP OF CORPORATIONS.—For purposes of this subpart, all employees of all corporations which are members of the same controlled group of corporations shall be treated as employed by a single employer. In any such case, the credit (if any) allowable by section 40 to each such member shall be its proportionate share of the work incen-

tive program expenses giving rise to such credit. For purposes of this subsection, the term "controlled group of corporations" has the meaning given to such term by section 1563(a), except that—

(A) "more than 50 percent" shall be substituted for "at least 80 percent" each place it appears in section 1563(a)(1), and

(B) the determination shall be made without regard to subsections (a)(4) and (e)(3)(C) of section 1563.

(2) EMPLOYEES OF PARTNERSHIPS, PROPRIETORSHIPS, ETC., WHICH ARE UNDER COMMON CONTROL.—For purposes of this subpart, under regulations prescribed by the Secretary—

(A) all employees of trades or business (whether or not incorporated) which are under common control shall be treated as employed by a single employer, and

(B) the credit (if any) allowable by section 40 with respect to each trade or business shall be its proportionate share of the work incentive program expenses giving rise to such credit.

The regulations prescribed under this paragraph shall be based on principles similar to the principles which apply in the case of paragraph (1).

Amendments

• 1980, Technical Corrections Act of 1979 (P.L. 96-222)

P.L. 96-222, §103(a)(7)(D)(ii):

Amended Code Sec. 50B(g)(2)(B) by striking out "giving to such credit" and inserting "giving rise to such credit". **Effective** for work incentive program expenses paid or incurred after 12-31-78, in tax years ending after such date.

• 1980 (P.L. 96-178)

P.L. 96-178, §6(c)(2):

Amended Code Sec. 50B(g)(2)(B) by adding "rise" after "giving." **Effective** 1-1-79.

• 1978, Revenue Act of 1978 (P.L. 95-600)

P.L. 95-600, §322(d)(4), (f):

Redesignated Code Sec. 50B(g) and (h) as subsections (h) and (i), respectively, and added new subsection (g). **Effective** for work incentive program expenses paid or incurred after 12-31-78, in tax years ending after such date.

[Sec. 50B(h)]

(h) ELIGIBLE EMPLOYEE.—

(1) ELIGIBLE EMPLOYEE.—For purposes of this subpart the term "eligible employee" means an individual—

(A) who has been certified (of for whom a written request for certification has been made) on or before the day the individual began work for the taxpayer by the Secretary of Labor or by the appropriate agency of State or local government as—

(i) being eligible for financial assistance under part A of title IV of the Social Security Act and as having continually received such financial assistance during the 90-day period which immediately precedes the date on which such individual is hired by the employer, or

(ii) having been placed in employment under a work incentive program established under section 432(b)(1) of the Social Security Act,

(B) who has been employed by the taxpayer for a period in excess of 30 consecutive days on a substantially fulltime basis (except as provided in subsection (i)),

(C) who has not displaced any other individual from employment by the taxpayer, and

(D) who is not a migrant worker.

The term "eligible employee" includes an employee of the taxpayer whose services are not performed in connection with a trade or business of the taxpayer.

(2) MIGRANT WORKER.—For purposes of paragraph (1), the term "migrant worker" means an individual who is employed for services for which the customary period of employment by one employer is less than 30 days if the nature of such services requires that such individual travel from place to place over a short period of time.

Amendments

• 1989, Omnibus Budget Reconcilliation Act of 1989 (P.L. 101-239)

P.L. 101-239, §7644(a):

Amended so much of subparagraph (A) of section 50B(h)(1) of the Internal Revenue Code of 1954 (as in effect for tax years beginning before 1-1-82) as precedes clause (i). **Effective** for purposes of credits first claimed after 3-11-87. Prior to amendment, so much of Code Sec. 50B(h)(1)(A) as preceded clause (i) read as follows:

(A) who has been certified by the Secretary of Labor or by the appropriate agency of State or local government as—

• 1980, Adoption Assistance and Child Welfare Act of 1980 (P.L. 96-272)

P.L. 96-272, §208(b)(2) and (3)(A):

Added "(except as provided in subsection (i))" following "basis" in Code Sec. 50B(h)(1)(B. **Effective** for tax years beginning after 1979.

• 1980, Technical Corrections Act of 1979 (P.L. 96-222)

P.L. 96-222, §103(a)(7)(D)(iii):

Amended Code Sec. 50B(h)(1)(A) by striking out "9-day" and inserting "90-day". **Effective** for work incentive program expenses paid or incurred after 12-31-78, in tax years ending after such date.

• 1980 (P.L. 96-178)

P.L. 96-178, §6(c)(3):

Amended Code Sec. 50B(h)(1)(A)(i) by substituting "90-day period" for "9-day period".

• 1978, Revenue Act of 1978 (P.L. 95-600)

P.L. 95-600, §322(d)(4), (5), (f):

Amended Code Sec. 50B(h)(1) (as redesignated by Act Sec. 322(d)(4), below). **Effective** for work incentive program expenses paid or incurred after 12-31-78, in tax years ending after such date. [Note: For special rules concerning certain eligible employees, see P.L. 95-600, §322(f)(2) reflected in the amendment notes after Code Sec. 50A(a).]

P.L. 95-600, §322(d)(4), (f):

Redesignated former Code Sec. 50B(g) as subsection (h). **Effective** for work incentive program expenses paid or incurred after 12-31-78, in tax years ending after such date. Prior to redesignation, such code section read:

"(g) ELIGIBLE EMPLOYEE.—

"(1) ELIGIBLE EMPLOYEE.—For purposes of subsection (a)(1)(B), the term `eligible employee' means an individual—

"(A) who has been certified by the Secretary of Labor or by the appropriate agency of State or local government as being eligible for financial assistance under part A of title IV of the Social Security Act and as having continuously received such financial assistance during the 90 day period which immediately precedes the date on which such individual is hired by the taxpayer,

"(B) who has been employed by the taxpayer for a period in excess of 30 consecutive days on a substantially full-time basis,

"(C) who has not displaced any other individual from employment by the taxpayer, and

"(D) who is not a migrant worker.

The term `eligible employee' includes an employee of the taxpayer whose services are not performed in connection with a trade or business of the taxpayer.

"(2) MIGRANT WORKER.—For purposes of paragraph (1), the term `migrant worker' means an individual who is employed for services for which the customary period of employment by one employer is less than 30 days if the nature of such services requires that such individual travel from place to place over a short period of time."

• 1976, Tax Reform Act of 1976 (P.L. 94-455)

P.L. 94-455, §2107(f):

Added "Secretary of Labor or by" after "certified by" in subparagraph (A) of Code Sec. 50B(g)(1). **Effective** 10-4-76.

• 1975, Tax Reduction Act of 1975 (P.L. 94-12)

P.L. 94-12, §401(a)(5):

Redesignated Code Sec. 50B(g) as (h) and added a new subsection (g). **Effective** for expenses paid or incurred for eligible employees hired after 3-29-75.

• 1971, Revenue Act of 1971 (P.L. 92-178)

P.L. 92-178, §601(b):

Added Code Sec. 50B(g). **Effective** for tax years beginning after 12-31-71.

[Sec. 50B(i)]

(i) SPECIAL RULES WITH RESPECT TO EMPLOYMENT OF DAY CARE WORKERS.—

(1) ELIGIBLE EMPLOYEE.—An individual who would be an "eligible employee" (as that term is defined for purposes of this section) except for the fact that such individual's employment is not on a substantially fulltime basis, shall be deemed to be an eligible employee as so defined, if such employee's employment is related to the provision of child day care services and is performed on either a fulltime or parttime basis.

(2) ALTERNATIVE COMPUTATION WITH RESPECT TO CHILD DAY CARE SERVICES ELIGIBLE EMPLOYEES PAID FROM FUNDS MADE AVAILABLE UNDER TITLE XX OF THE SOCIAL SECURITY ACT.—The amount of the credit allowed a taxpayer under section 40, as determined under section 50A and the preceding provisions of this section, with respect to work incentive program expenses paid or incurred by him with respect to an eligible employee whose services are perfomed in connection with a child day care services program conducted by the taxpayer, and with respect to whom the taxpayer is reimbursed (in whole or in part) from funds made available pursuant to section 2007 of the Social Security Act, at the option of the taxpayer shall be equal to 100 percent of the unreimbursed wages paid or incurred by the taxpayer with respect to such employee, but not more than the amount of the limitation in paragraph (4).

(3) UNREIMBURSED WAGES.—For purposes of this subsection, the term "unreimbursed wages" means work incentive program expenses for which the taxpayer was not reimbursed under section 2007 of the Social Security Act or under any other grant or program.

(4) LIMITATION.—The amount of the credit, as determined under paragraph (2), with respect to any employee shall not exceed the lesser of—

(A) an amount equal to $6,000 minus the amount of the funds reimbursed to the taxpayer with respect to such employee from funds made available pursuant to section 2007 of the Social Security Act; or

(B) with respect to work incentive program expenses attributable to service rendered—

(i) during the oneyear period which begins on the day such employee begins work for the taxpayer, an amount equal to the lesser of—

(I) $3,000, or

(II) 50 percent of the sum of the amount of the unreimbursed wages of such employee and the amount reimbursed to the taxpayer with respect to such employee from funds made available pursuant to section 2007 of the Social Security Act; or

(ii) during the oneyear period which begins on the day after the last day of the oneyear period described in clause (i), an amount equal to the lesser of—

(I) $1,500, or

(II) 25 percent of the sum of the amount of the unreimbursed wages of such employee and the amount reimbursed to the taxpayer with respect to such employee from funds made available pursuant to section 2007 of the Social Security Act.

Amendments

• 1980, Adoption Assistance and Child Welfare Act of 1980 (P.L. 96-272)

P.L. 96-272, §208(b)(1) and (3)(A):

Amended Code Sec. 50B(i). **Effective** for tax years beginning after 1979. Prior to amendment, Code Sec. 50B(i) read:

(i) SPECIAL RULES WITH RESPECT TO EMPLOYMENT OF DAY CARE WORKERS.—

(1) ELIGIBLE EMPLOYEE.—An individual who would be an "eligible employee" (as that term is defined for purposes of this section) except for the fact that such individual's employment is not on a substantially full-time basis, shall be deemed to be an eligible employee as so defined, if such employee's employment consists of services performed in connection with a child day care program of the taxpayer, on either a full-time or part-time basis.

(2) ALTERNATIVE LIMITATION WITH RESPECT TO CHILD DAY CARE SERVICES ELIGIBLE EMPLOYEES.—The amount of the credit allowed a taxpayer under the preceding provisions of this section with respect to work incentive program expenses paid or incurred by him with respect to an eligible employee whose services are performed in connection with a child day care services program conducted by the taxpayer shall, at the election of the taxpayer, be determined by including (in computing the amount of such expenses so paid or incurred by him) any amount with respect to such employee for which he was reimbursed from funds made available pursuant to section 3(c) of Public Law 94-401 or section 2007 of title XX of the Social Security Act, except that, if the total amount of such credit, as so computed, plus such amount reimbursed to him under such sections, exceeds the lesser of $6,000 or 100 percent of the total expenses paid or incurred by him with respect to such employee, the amount of such credit shall be reduced (but not below zero) so as to provide that such total does not exceed the lesser of $6,000 or 100 percent of the total expenses paid or incurred by him with respect to such employee.

• 1980 (P.L. 96-178)

P.L. 96-178, §3(a)(1) and (2):

Added Code Sec. 50B(i). **Effective** with respect to tax years beginning after 12-31-78, and before 1-1-80.

[Sec. 50B(j)]

(j) CROSS REFERENCE.—

For application of this subpart to certain acquiring corporations, see section 381(c)(24).

Amendments

• 1980 (P.L. 96-178)

P.L. 96-178, §3(a)(1):

Redesignated subsection (i) as subsection (j). **Effective** with respect to tax years beginning after 12-31-78, and before 1-1-80.

• 1978, Revenue Act of 1978 (P.L. 95-600)

P.L. 95-600, §322(d)(4), (f):

Redesignated former Code Sec. 50B(h) as subsection (i). **Effective** for work incentive program expenses paid or incurred after 12-31-78, in tax years ending after such date.

• 1975, Tax Reduction Act of 1975 (P.L. 94-12)

P.L. 94-12, §401(a)(5):

Redesignated Code Sec. 50B(g) as (h) and added a new subsection (g). **Effective** for expenses paid or incurred for eligible employees hired after 3-29-75.

• 1971, Revenue Act of 1971 (P.L. 92-178)

P.L. 92-178, §601(b):

Added Code Sec. 50B(h) when it was designated Code Sec. 50B(g). **Effective** for tax years beginning after 12-31-71.

Subpart F—Rules for Computing Work Opportunity Credit

[Sec. 51]

SEC. 51. AMOUNT OF CREDIT.

[Sec. 51(a)]

(a) DETERMINATION OF AMOUNT.—For purposes of section 38, the amount of the work opportunity credit determined under this section for the taxable year shall be equal to 40 percent of the qualified first-year wages for such year.

Amendments

• **1997, Taxpayer Relief Act of 1997 (P.L. 105-34)**

P.L. 105-34, §603(d)(1):

Amended Code Sec. 51(a) by striking "35 percent" and inserting "40 percent". **Effective** for individuals who begin work for the employer after 9-30-97.

• **1996, Small Business Job Protection Act of 1996 (P.L. 104-188)**

P.L. 104-188, §1201(a):

Amended Code Sec. 51(a) by striking "40 percent" and inserting "35 percent". **Effective** for individuals who begin work for the employer after 9-30-96.

P.L. 104-188, §1201(e)(1):

Amended Code Sec. 51(a) by striking "targeted jobs credit" each place it appears and inserting "work opportunity credit". **Effective** for individuals who begin work for the employer after 9-30-96.

[Sec. 51(b)]

(b) QUALIFIED WAGES DEFINED.—For purposes of this subpart—

(1) IN GENERAL.—The term "qualified wages" means the wages paid or incurred by the employer during the taxable year to individuals who are members of a targeted group.

(2) QUALIFIED FIRST-YEAR WAGES.—The term "qualified first-year wages" means, with respect to any individual, qualified wages attributable to service rendered during the 1-year period beginning with the day the individual begins work for the employer.

(3) LIMITATION ON WAGES PER YEAR TAKEN INTO ACCOUNT.—The amount of the qualified first-year wages which may be taken into account with respect to any individual shall not exceed $6,000 per year ($12,000 per year in the case of any individual who is a qualified veteran by reason of subsection (d)(3)(A)(ii)).

Amendments

• **2007, Small Business and Work Opportunity Tax Act of 2007 (P.L. 110-28)**

P.L. 110-28, §8211(d)(2)(A)-(B):

Amended Code Sec. 51(b)(3) by inserting "($12,000 per year in the case of any individual who is a qualified veteran by reason of subsection (d)(3)(A)(ii))" before the period at the end, and by striking "ONLY FIRST $6,000 OF" in the heading and inserting "LIMITATION ON". **Effective** for individuals who begin work for the employer after 5-25-2007.

[Sec. 51(c)]

(c) WAGES DEFINED.—For purposes of this subpart—

(1) IN GENERAL.—Except as otherwise provided in this subsection and subsection (h)(2), the term "wages" has the meaning given to such term by subsection (b) of section 3306 (determined without regard to any dollar limitation contained in such section).

(2) ON-THE-JOB TRAINING AND WORK SUPPLEMENTATION PAYMENTS.—

(A) EXCLUSION FOR EMPLOYERS RECEIVING ON-THE-JOB TRAINING PAYMENTS.—The term "wages" shall not include any amounts paid or incurred by an employer for any period to any individual for whom the employer receives federally funded payments for on-the-job training of such individual for such period.

(B) REDUCTION FOR WORK SUPPLEMENTATION PAYMENTS TO EMPLOYERS.—The amount of wages which would (but for this subparagraph) be qualified wages under this section for an employer with respect to an individual for a taxable year shall be reduced by an amount equal to the amount of the payments made to such employer (however utilized by such employer) with respect to such individual for such taxable year under a program established under section 482(e) of the Social Security Act.

(3) PAYMENTS FOR SERVICES DURING LABOR DISPUTES.—If—

(A) the principal place of employment of an individual with the employer is at a plant or facility, and

(B) there is a strike or lockout involving employees at such plant or facility.

the term "wages" shall not include any amount paid or incurred by the employer to such individual for services which are the same as, or substantially similar to, those services performed by employees participating in, or affected by, the strike or lockout during the period of such strike or lockout.

(4) TERMINATION.—The term "wages" shall not include any amount paid or incurred to an individual who begins work for the employer—

(A) after December 31, 1994, and before October 1, 1996, or

(B) after August 31, 2011.

(5) COORDINATION WITH PAYROLL TAX FORGIVENESS.—The term "wages" shall not include any amount paid or incurred to a qualified individual (as defined in section 3111(d)(3)) during the 1-year period beginning on the hiring date of such individual by a qualified employer (as defined in section 3111(d)) unless such qualified employer makes an election not to have section 3111(d) apply.

Amendments

• 2010, Hiring Incentives to Restore Employment Act (P.L. 111-147)

P.L. 111-147, §101(b):

Amended Code Sec. 51(c) by adding at the end a new paragraph (5). **Effective** for wages paid after 3-18-2010.

• 2007, Small Business and Work Opportunity Tax Act of 2007 (P.L. 110-28)

P.L. 110-28, §8211(a):

Amended Code Sec. 51(c)(4)(B) by striking "December 31, 2007" and inserting "August 31, 2011". **Effective** for individuals who begin work for the employer after 5-25-2007.

• 2006, Tax Relief and Health Care Act of 2006 (P.L. 109-432)

P.L. 109-432, Division A, §105(a):

Amended Code Sec. 51(c)(4)(B) by striking "2005" and inserting "2007". **Effective** for individuals who begin work for the employer after 12-31-2005.

• 2004, Working Families Tax Relief Act of 2004 (P.L. 108-311)

P.L. 108-311, §303(a)(1):

Amended Code Sec. 51(c)(4) by striking "December 31, 2003" and inserting "December 31, 2005". **Effective** for individuals who begin work for the employer after 12-31-2003.

• 2002, Job Creation and Worker Assistance Act of 2002 (P.L. 107-147)

P.L. 107-147, §604(a):

Amended Code Sec. 51(c)(4)(B) by striking "2001" and inserting "2003". **Effective** for individuals who began work for the employer after 12-31-2001.

• 1999, Tax Relief Extension Act of 1999 (P.L. 106-170)

P.L. 106-170, §505(a):

Amended Code Sec. 51(c)(4)(B) by striking "June 30, 1999" and inserting "December 31, 2001". **Effective** for individuals who begin work for the employer after 6-30-99.

• 1998, Tax and Trade Relief Extension Act of 1998 (P.L. 105-277)

P.L. 105-277, §1002(a):

Amended Code Sec. 51(c)(4)(B) by striking "June 30, 1998" and inserting "June 30, 1999". **Effective** for individuals who begin work for the employer after 6-30-98.

• 1997, Taxpayer Relief Act of 1997 (P.L. 105-34)

P.L. 105-34, §603(a):

Amended Code Sec. 51(c)(4)(B) by striking "September 30, 1997" and inserting "June 30, 1998". **Effective** for individuals who begin work for the employer after 9-30-97.

• 1996, Small Business Job Protection Act of 1996 (P.L. 104-188)

P.L. 104-188, §1201(d):

Amended Code Sec. 51(c)(4). **Effective** for individuals who begin work for the employer after 9-30-96. Prior to amendment, Code Sec. 51(c)(4) read as follows:

(4) TERMINATION.—The term "wages" shall not include any amount paid or incurred to an individual who begins work for the employer after December 31, 1994.

P.L. 104-188, §1201(f):

Amended Code Sec. 51(c)(1) by striking ",subsection (d)(8)(D)," after "this subsection". **Effective** for individuals who begin work for the employer after 9-30-96.

• 1993, Omnibus Budget Reconcilliation Act of 1993 (P.L. 103-66)

P.L. 103-66, §13102(a):

Amended Code Sec. 51(c)(4) by striking "June 30, 1992" and inserting "December 31, 1994". **Effective** for individuals who begin work for the employer after 6-30-92.

• 1991, Tax Extension Act of 1991 (P.L. 102-227)

P.L. 102-227, §105(a):

Amended Code Sec. 51(c)(4) by striking "December 31, 1991" and inserting "June 30, 1992". **Effective** for individuals who begin work for the employer after 12-31-91.

• 1990, Omnibus Budget Reconcilliation Act of 1990 (P.L. 101-508)

P.L. 101-508, §11405(a):

Amended Code Sec. 51(c)(4) by striking "September 30, 1990" and inserting "December 31, 1991". **Effective** for individuals who begin work for the employer after 9-30-90.

• 1989, Omnibus Budget Reconcilliation Act of 1989 (P.L. 101-239)

P.L. 101-239, §7103(a):

Amended Code Sec. 51(c)(4) by striking "December 31, 1989" and inserting "September 30, 1990". **Effective** 12-19-89.

• 1988, Technical and Miscellaneous Revenue Act of 1988 (P.L. 100-647)

P.L. 100-647, §4010(a):

Amended Code Sec. 51(c)(4) by striking out "December 31, 1988" and inserting in lieu thereof "December 31, 1989". **Effective** 11-10-98.

• 1988, Family Support Act of 1988 (P.L. 100-485)

P.L. 100-485, §202(c)(6):

Amended Code Sec. 51(c)(2)(B) by striking out "section 414" and inserting "section 482(e)". **Effective** 10-1-90. For special rules, see Act Sec. 204(c) below.

P.L. 100-485, §204(b), provides:

(b) SPECIAL RULES.—(1)(A) If any State makes the changes in its State plan approved under section 402 of the Social Security Act that are required in order to carry out the amendments made by this title and formally notifies the Secretary of Health and Human Services of its desire to become subject to such amendments as of the first day of any calendar quarter beginning on or after the date on which the proposed regulations of the Secretary of Health and Human Services are published under section 203(a) (or, if earlier, the date on which such regulations are required to be published under such section) and before October 1, 1990, such amendments shall become effective with respect to that State as of such first day.

(B) In the case of any State in which the amendments made by this title become effective (in accordance with subparagraph (A)) with respect to any quarter of a fiscal year beginning before October 1, 1990, the limitation applicable to the State for the fiscal year under section 403(k)(2) of the Social Security Act (as added by section 201(c)(1) of this Act) shall be an amount that bears the same ratio to such limitation (as otherwise determined with respect to the State for the fiscal year) as the number of quarters in the fiscal year throughout which such amendments apply to the State bears to 4.

• 1987, Revenue Act of 1987 (P.L. 100-203)

P.L. 100-203, §10601(a):

Amended Code Sec. 51(c) by redesignating paragraph (3) as paragraph (4) and inserting after paragraph (2) new paragraph (3). **Effective** for amounts paid or incurred on or after 1-1-87, for services rendered on or after such date.

[Sec. 51(d)]

(d) MEMBERS OF TARGETED GROUPS.—For purposes of this subpart—

(1) IN GENERAL.—An individual is a member of a targeted group if such individual is—

(A) a qualified IV-A recipient,

(B) a qualified veteran,

(C) a qualified ex-felon,

(D) a designated community resident,

(E) a vocational rehabilitation referral,

(F) a qualified summer youth employee,

(G) a qualified supplemental nutrition assistance program benefits recipient,

(H) a qualified SSI recipient, or

(I) a long-term family assistance recipient.

(2) QUALIFIED IV-A RECIPIENT.—

(A) IN GENERAL.—The term "qualified IV-A recipient" means any individual who is certified by the designated local agency as being a member of a family receiving assistance under a IV-A program for any 9 months during the 18-month period ending on the hiring date.

(B) IV-A PROGRAM.—For purposes of this paragraph, the term "IV-A program" means any program providing assistance under a State program funded under part A of title IV of the Social Security Act and any successor of such program.

(3) QUALIFIED VETERAN.—

(A) IN GENERAL.—The term "qualified veteran" means any veteran who is certified by the designated local agency as—

(i) being a member of a family receiving assistance under a supplemental nutrition assistance program under the Food and Nutrition Act of 2008 for at least a 3-month period ending during the 12-month period ending on the hiring date, or

(ii) entitled to compensation for a service-connected disability, and—

(I) having a hiring date which is not more that [sic] 1 year after having been discharged or released from active duty in the Armed Forces of the United States, or

(II) having aggregate periods of unemployment during the 1-year period ending on the hiring date which equal or exceed 6 months.

(B) VETERAN.—For purposes of subparagraph (A), the term "veteran" means any individual who is certified by the designated local agency as—

(i)(I) having served on active duty (other than active duty for training) in the Armed Forces of the United States for a period of more than 180 days, or

(II) having been discharged or released from active duty in the Armed Forces of the United States for a service-connected disability, and

(ii) not having any day during the 60-day period ending on the hiring date which was a day of extended active duty in the Armed Forces of the United States.

For purposes of clause (ii), the term "extended active duty" means a period of more than 90 days during which the individual was on active duty (other than active duty for training).

(C) OTHER DEFINITIONS.—For purposes of subparagraph (A), the terms "compensation" and "service-connected" have the meanings given such terms under section 101 of title 38, United States Code.

(4) QUALIFIED EX-FELON.—The term "qualified ex-felon" means any individual who is certified by the designated local agency—

(A) as having been convicted of a felony under any statute of the United States or any State, and

(B) as having a hiring date which is not more than 1 year after the last date on which such individual was so convicted or was released from prison.

(5) DESIGNATED COMMUNITY RESIDENTS.—

(A) IN GENERAL.—The term "designated community resident" means any individual who is certified by the designated local agency—

(i) as having attained age 18 but not age 40 on the hiring date, and

(ii) as having his principal place of abode within an empowerment zone, enterprise community, renewal community, or rural renewal county.

(B) INDIVIDUAL MUST CONTINUE TO RESIDE IN ZONE, COMMUNITY, OR COUNTY.—In the case of a designated community resident, the term "qualified wages" shall not include wages paid or incurred for services performed while the individual's principal place of abode is outside an empowerment zone, enterprise community, renewal community, or rural renewal county.

(C) RURAL RENEWAL COUNTY.—For purposes of this paragraph, the term "rural renewal county" means any county which—

(i) is outside a metropolitan statistical area (defined as such by the Office of Management and Budget), and

(ii) during the 5-year periods 1990 through 1994 and 1995 through 1999 had a net population loss.

(6) VOCATIONAL REHABILITATION REFERRAL.—The term "vocational rehabilitation referral" means any individual who is certified by the designated local agency as—

(A) having a physical or mental disability which, for such individual, constitutes or results in a substantial handicap to employment, and

(B) having been referred to the employer upon completion of (or while receiving) rehabilitative services pursuant to—

(i) an individualized written plan for employment under a State plan for vocational rehabilitation services approved under the Rehabilitation Act of 1973,

(ii) a program of vocational rehabilitation carried out under chapter 31 of title 38, United States Code, or

(iii) an individual work plan developed and implemented by an employment network pursuant to subsection (g) of section 1148 of the Social Security Act with respect to which the requirements of such subsection are met.

(7) QUALIFIED SUMMER YOUTH EMPLOYEE.—

(A) IN GENERAL.—The term "qualified summer youth employee" means any individual—

(i) who performs services for the employer between May 1 and September 15,

(ii) who is certified by the designated local agency as having attained age 16 but not 18 on the hiring date (or if later, on May 1 of the calendar year involved),

(iii) who has not been an employee of the employer during any period prior to the 90-day period described in subparagraph (B)(i), and

(iv) who is certified by the designated local agency as having his principal place of abode within an empowerment zone, enterprise community, or renewal community.

(B) SPECIAL RULES FOR DETERMINING AMOUNT OF CREDIT.—For purposes of applying this subpart to wages paid or incurred to any qualified summer youth employee—

(i) subsection (b)(2) shall be applied by substituting "any 90-day period between May 1 and September 15" for "the 1-year period beginning with the day the individual begins work for the employer", and

(ii) subsection (b)(3) shall be applied by substituting "$3,000" for "$6,000".

The preceding sentence shall not apply to an individual who, with respect to the same employer, is certified as a member of another targeted group after such individual has been a qualified summer youth employee.

(C) YOUTH MUST CONTINUE TO RESIDE IN ZONE OR COMMUNITY.—Paragraph (5)(B) shall apply for purposes of subparagraph (A)(iv).

(8) QUALIFIED SUPPLEMENTAL NUTRITION ASSISTANCE PROGRAM BENEFITS RECIPIENT.—

(A) IN GENERAL.—The term "qualified supplemental nutrition assistance program benefits recipient" means any individual who is certified by the designated local agency—

(i) as having attained age 18 but not age 40 on the hiring date, and

(ii) as being a member of a family—

(I) receiving assistance under a supplemental nutrition assistance program under the Food and Nutrition Act of 2008 for the 6-month period ending on the hiring date, or

(II) receiving such assistance for at least 3 months of the 5-month period ending on the hiring date, in the case of a member of a family who ceases to be eligible for such assistance under section 6(o) of the Food and Nutrition Act of 2008.

(B) PARTICIPATION INFORMATION.—Notwithstanding any other provision of law, the Secretary of the Treasury and the Secretary of Agriculture shall enter into an agreement to provide information to designated local agencies with respect to participation in the supplemental nutrition assistance program.

(9) QUALIFIED SSI RECIPIENT.—The term "qualified SSI recipient" means any individual who is certified by the designated local agency as receiving supplemental security income benefits under title XVI of the Social Security Act (including supplemental security income benefits of the type described in section 1616 of such Act or section 212 of Public Law 93-66) for any month ending within the 60-day period ending on the hiring date.

(10) LONG-TERM FAMILY ASSISTANCE RECIPIENT.—The term "long-term family assistance recipient" means any individual who is certified by the designated local agency—

(A) as being a member of a family receiving assistance under a IV-A program (as defined in paragraph (2)(B)) for at least the 18-month period ending on the hiring date,

(B)(i) as being a member of a family receiving such assistance for 18 months beginning after August 5, 1997, and

(ii) as having a hiring date which is not more than 2 years after the end of the earliest such 18-month period, or

(C)(i) as being a member of a family which ceased to be eligible for such assistance by reason of any limitation imposed by Federal or State law on the maximum period such assistance is payable to a family, and

(ii) as having a hiring date which is not more than 2 years after the date of such cessation.

(11) HIRING DATE.—The term "hiring date" means the day the individual is hired by the employer.

(12) DESIGNATED LOCAL AGENCY.—The term "designated local agency" means a State employment security agency established in accordance with the Act of June 6, 1933, as amended (29 U.S.C. 49-49n).

(13) SPECIAL RULES FOR CERTIFICATIONS.—

(A) IN GENERAL.—An individual shall not be treated as a member of a targeted group unless—

(i) on or before the day on which such individual begins work for the employer, the employer has received a certification from a designated local agency that such individual is a member of a targeted group, or

(ii)(I) on or before the day the individual is offered employment with the employer, a pre-screening notice is completed by the employer with respect to such individual, and

(II) not later than the 28th day after the individual begins work for the employer, the employer submits such notice, signed by the employer and the individual under penalties of perjury, to the designated local agency as part of a written request for such a certification from such agency.

For purposes of this paragraph, the term "pre-screening notice" means a document (in such form as the Secretary shall prescribe) which contains information provided by the individual on the basis of which the employer believes that the individual is a member of a targeted group.

(B) INCORRECT CERTIFICATIONS.—If—

(i) an individual has been certified by a designated local agency as a member of a targeted group, and

(ii) such certification is incorrect because it was based on false information provided by such individual,

the certification shall be revoked and wages paid by the employer after the date on which notice of revocation is received by the employer shall not be treated as qualified wages.

(C) EXPLANATION OF DENIAL OF REQUEST.—If a designated local agency denies a request for certification of membership in a targeted group, such agency shall provide to the person making such request a written explanation of the reasons for such denial.

(14) CREDIT ALLOWED FOR UNEMPLOYED VETERANS AND DISCONNECTED YOUTH HIRED IN 2009 OR 2010.—

(A) IN GENERAL.—Any unemployed veteran or disconnected youth who begins work for the employer during 2009 or 2010 shall be treated as a member of a targeted group for purposes of this subpart.

(B) DEFINITIONS.—For purposes of this paragraph—

(i) UNEMPLOYED VETERAN.—The term "unemployed veteran" means any veteran (as defined in paragraph (3)(B), determined without regard to clause (ii) thereof) who is certified by the designated local agency as—

(I) having been discharged or released from active duty in the Armed Forces at any time during the 5-year period ending on the hiring date, and

(II) being in receipt of unemployment compensation under State or Federal law for not less than 4 weeks during the 1-year period ending on the hiring date.

(ii) DISCONNECTED YOUTH.—The term "disconnected youth" means any individual who is certified by the designated local agency—

(I) as having attained age 16 but not age 25 on the hiring date,

(II) as not regularly attending any secondary, technical, or post-secondary school during the 6-month period preceding the hiring date,

(III) as not regularly employed during such 6-month period, and

(IV) as not readily employable by reason of lacking a sufficient number of basic skills.

Amendments

• 2009, American Recovery and Reinvestment Tax Act of 2009 (P.L. 111-5)

P.L. 111-5, §1221(a):

Amended Code Sec. 51(d) by adding at the end a new paragraph (14). **Effective** for individuals who begin work for the employer after 12-31-2008.

• 2008, Food, Conservation, and Energy Act of 2008 (P.L. 110-246)

P.L. 110-246, §4002(b)(1)(A)-(B) and (D):

Amended Code Sec. 51(d) by striking "food stamp program" each place it appears and inserting "supplemental nutrition assistance program"; by striking "Food Stamp Act of 1977" each place it appears and inserting "Food and Nutrition Act of 2008"; by striking "food stamp" each place it appears and inserting "supplemental nutrition assistance program benefits". **Effective** 10-1-2008.

• 2007, Small Business and Work Opportunity Tax Act of 2007 (P.L. 110-28)

P.L. 110-28, §8211(b)(1):

Amended Code Sec. 51(d)(5). **Effective** for individuals who begin work for the employer after 5-25-2007. Prior to amendment, Code Sec. 51(d)(5) read as follows:

(5) HIGH-RISK YOUTH.—

(A) IN GENERAL.—The term "high-risk youth" means any individual who is certified by the designated local agency—

(i) as having attained age 18 but not age 25 on the hiring date, and

(ii) as having his principal place of abode within an empowerment zone, enterprise community, or renewal community.

(B) YOUTH MUST CONTINUE TO RESIDE IN ZONE OR COMMUNITY.—In the case of a high-risk youth, the term "qualified wages" shall not include wages paid or incurred for services performed while such youth's principal place of abode is outside an empowerment zone, enterprise community, or renewal community.

P.L. 110-28, §8211(b)(2):

Amended Code Sec. 51(d)(1)(D). **Effective** for individuals who begin work for the employer after 5-25-2007. Prior to amendment, Code Sec. 51(d)(1)(D) read as follows:

(D) a high-risk youth,

P.L. 110-28, §8211(c):

Amended Code Sec. 51(d)(6)(B) by striking "or" at the end of clause (i), by striking the period at the end of clause (ii) and inserting ", or", and by adding at the end a new clause (iii). **Effective** for individuals who begin work for the employer after 5-25-2007.

P.L. 110-28, §8211(d)(1)(A):

Amended Code Sec. 51(d)(3)(A) by striking "agency as being a member of a family" and all that follows and inserting "agency as—" and new clauses (i)-(ii). **Effective** for individuals who begin work for the employer after 5-25-2007. Prior to amendment, Code Sec. 51(d)(3)(A) read as follows:

(A) IN GENERAL.—The term "qualified veteran" means any veteran who is certified by the designated local agency as being a member of a family receiving assistance under a food stamp program under the Food Stamp Act of 1977 for at least a 3-month period ending during the 12-month period ending on the hiring date.

P.L. 110-28, §8211(d)(1)(B):

Amended Code Sec. 51(d)(3) by adding at the end a new subparagraph (C). **Effective** for individuals who begin work for the employer after 5-25-2007.

• 2006, Tax Relief and Health Care Act of 2006 (P.L. 109-432)

P.L. 109-432, Division A, §105(b):

Amended Code Sec. 51(d)(4) by adding "and" at the end of subparagraph (A), by striking ", and" at the end of subparagraph (B) and inserting a period, and by striking all that follows subparagraph (B). **Effective** for individuals who begin work for the employer after 12-31-2006. Prior to being stricken, all that follows Code Sec. 51(d)(4)(B) read as follows:

(C) as being a member of a family which had an income during the 6 months immediately preceding the earlier of the month in which such income determination occurs or the month in which the hiring date occurs, which, on an annual basis, would be 70 percent or less of the Bureau of Labor Statistics lower living standard.

Any determination under subparagraph (C) shall be valid for the 45-day period beginning on the date such determination is made.

P.L. 109-432, Division A, §105(c):

Amended Code Sec. 51(d)(8)(A)(i) by striking "25" and inserting "40". **Effective** for individuals who begin work for the employer after 12-31-2006.

P.L. 109-432, Division A, §105(d):

Amended Code Sec. 51(d)(12)(A)(ii)(II) by striking "21st day" and inserting "28th day". **Effective** for individuals who begin work for the employer after 12-31-2006.

P.L. 109-432, Division A, §105(e)(1):

Amended Code Sec. 51(d)(1) by striking "or" at the end of subparagraph (G), by striking the period at the end of subparagraph (H) and inserting ", or", and by adding at the end a new subparagraph (I). **Effective** for individuals who begin work for the employer after 12-31-2006.

P.L. 109-432, Division A, §105(e)(2):

Amended Code Sec. 51(d) by redesignating paragraphs (10) through (12) as paragraphs (11) through (13), respectively, and by inserting after paragraph (9) a new paragraph (10). **Effective** for individuals who begin work for the employer after 12-31-2006.

• 2005, Katrina Emergency Tax Relief Act of 2005 (P.L. 109-73)

P.L. 109-73, §201 [as amended by P.L. 110-343, Division C, §319(a)], provides:

SEC. 201. WORK OPPORTUNITY TAX CREDIT FOR HURRICANE KATRINA EMPLOYEES.

(a) IN GENERAL.—For purposes of section 51 of the Internal Revenue Code of 1986, a Hurricane Katrina employee shall be treated as a member of a targeted group.

(b) HURRICANE KATRINA EMPLOYEE.—For purposes of this section, the term "Hurricane Katrina employee" means—

(1) any individual who on August 28, 2005, had a principal place of abode in the core disaster area and who is hired during the 4-year period beginning on such date for a position the principal place of employment of which is located in the core disaster area, and

(2) any individual who on such date had a principal place of abode in the core disaster area, who is displaced from such abode by reason of Hurricane Katrina, and who is hired during the period beginning on such date and ending on December 31, 2005.

(c) REASONABLE IDENTIFICATION ACCEPTABLE.—In lieu of the certification requirement under subparagraph (A) of section 51(d)(12) of such Code, an individual may provide to the employer reasonable evidence that the individual is a Hurricane Katrina employee, and subparagraph (B) of such section shall be applied as if such evidence were a certification described in such subparagraph.

(d) SPECIAL RULES FOR DETERMINING CREDIT.— For purposes of applying subpart F of part IV of subchapter A of chapter 1 of such Code to wages paid or incurred to any Hurricane Katrina employee—

(1) section 51(c)(4) of such Code shall not apply, and

(2) section 51(i)(2) of such Code shall not apply with respect to the first hire of such employee as a Hurricane Katrina employee, unless such employee was an employee of the employer on August 28, 2005.

• 2000, Community Renewal Tax Relief Act of 2000 (P.L. 106-554)

P.L. 106-554, §102(a):

Amended Code Sec. 51(d)(5)(A)(ii) and (B) by striking "empowerment zone or enterprise community" and inserting "empowerment zone, enterprise community, or renewal community". **Effective** for individuals who begin work for the employer after 12-31-2001.

P.L. 106-554, §102(b):

Amended Code Sec. 51(d)(7)(A)(iv) by striking "empowerment zone or enterprise community" and inserting "empowerment zone, enterprise community, or renewal community". **Effective** for individuals who begin work for the employer after 12-31-2001.

P.L. 106-554, §102(c):

Amended Code Sec. 51(d)(5)(B) and (7)(C) by inserting "OR COMMUNITY" in the heading after "ZONE". **Effective** for individuals who begin work for the employer after 12-31-2001.

P.L. 106-554, §316(a)(1)-(2):

Amended Code Sec. 51(d)(2)(B) by striking "plan approved" and inserting "program funded", and by striking "(relating to assistance for needy families with minor children)" following "Social Security Act". **Effective** as if included in the provision of P.L. 104-188 to which it relates [**effective** for individuals who begin work for the employer after 9-30-96.—CCH].

• 1998, Tax and Trade Relief Extension Act of 1998 (P.L. 105-277)

P.L. 105-277, §4006(c)(1):

Amended Code Sec. 51(d)(6)(B)(i) by striking "rehabilitation plan" and inserting "plan for employment". **Effective** 10-21-98. However, for a special rule, see Act Sec. 4006(c)(1), below.

P.L. 105-277, §4006(c)(1), provides:

(c) CLERICAL AMENDMENTS.—

(1) Clause (i) of section 51(d)(6)(B) of the 1986 Code is amended by striking "rehabilitation plan" and inserting "plan for employment". The reference to "plan for employment" in such clause shall be treated as including a reference to the rehabilitation plan referred to in such clause as in effect before the amendment made by the preceding sentence.

• 1997, Taxpayer Relief Act of 1997 (P.L. 105-34)

P.L. 105-34, §603(b)(1):

Amended Code Sec. 51(d)(2)(A) by striking all that follows "a IV-A program" and inserting "for any 9 months during the 18-month period ending on the hiring date.". **Effective** for individuals who begin work for the employer after 9-30-97.

P.L. 105-34, §603(b)(2):

Amended Code Sec. 51(d)(3)(A). **Effective** for individuals who begin work for the employer after 9-30-97. Prior to amendment, Code Sec. 51(d)(3)(A) read as follows:

(A) IN GENERAL.—The term "qualified veteran" means any veteran who is certified by the designated local agency as being—

(i) a member of a family receiving assistance under a IV-A program (as defined in paragraph (2)(B)) for at least a 9-month period ending during the 12-month period ending on the hiring date, or

(ii) a member of a family receiving assistance under a food stamp program under the Food Stamp Act of 1977 for at least a 3-month period ending during the 12-month period ending on the hiring date.

P.L. 105-34, §603(c)(1):

Amended Code Sec. 51(d)(1) by striking "or" at the end of subparagraph (F), by striking the period at the end of subparagraph (G) and inserting ", or", and by adding a new subparagraph (H). **Effective** for individuals who begin work for the employer after 9-30-97.

P.L. 105-34, §603(c)(2):

Amended Code Sec. 51(d) by redesignating paragraphs (9), (10), and (11) as paragraphs (10), (11), and (12), respectively, and by inserting after paragraph (8) a new paragraph (9). **Effective** for individuals who begin work for the employer after 9-30-97.

• 1997, Balanced Budget Act of 1997 (P.L. 105-33)

P.L. 105-33, §5514(a)(1):

Struck the change made by P.L. 104-193, which amended Code Sec. 51(d)(9) by striking all that followed "agency as" and inserted "being eligible for financial assistance under part A of title IV of the Social Security Act and as having continually received such financial assistance during the 90-day period which immediately precedes the date on which such individual is hired by the employer". Thus, the amendment to Code Sec. 51(d)(9) by P.L. 104-193 never took effect. **Effective** 7-1-97.

• 1996, Personal Responsibility and Work Opportunity Reconciliation Act of 1996 (P.L. 104-193)

P.L. 104-193, §110(l)(1):

Amended Code Sec. 51(d)(9) by striking all that follows "agency as" and inserting "being eligible for financial assistance under part A of title IV of the Social Security Act and as having continually received such financial assistance during the 90-day period which immediately precedes the date on which such individual is hired by the employer". **Effective** 7-1-97. Prior to amendment, Code Sec. 51(d)(9) read as follows:

(9) ELIGIBLE WORK INCENTIVE EMPLOYEES.—The term "eligible work incentive employee" means an individual who has been certified by the designated local agency as—

(A) being eligible for financial assistance under part A of title IV of the Social Security Act and as having continually received such financial assistance during the 90-day period which immediately precedes the date on which such individual is hired by the employer, or

(B) having been placed in employment under a work incentive program established under section 432(b)(1) or 445 of the Social Security Act.

• 1996, Small Business Job Protection Act of 1996 (P.L. 104-188)

P.L. 104-188, §1201(b):

Amended Code Sec. 51(d). **Effective** for individuals who begin work for the employer after 9-30-96. Prior to amendment, Code Sec. 51(d) read as follows:

(d) MEMBERS OF TARGETED GROUPS.—For purposes of this subpart—

(1) IN GENERAL.—An individual is a member of a targeted group if such individual is—

(A) a vocational rehabilitation referral,

(B) an economically disadvantaged youth,

(C) an economically disadvantaged Vietnam-era veteran,

(D) an SSI recipient,

(E) a general assistance recipient,

(F) a youth participating in a cooperative education program,

(G) an economically disadvantaged ex-convict,

(H) an eligible work incentive employee,

(I) an involuntarily terminated CETA employee, or

(J) a qualified summer youth employee.

(2) VOCATIONAL REHABILITATION REFERRAL.—The term "vocational rehabilitation referral" means any individual who is certified by the designated local agency as—

(A) having a physical or mental disability which, for such individual, constitutes or results in a substantial handicap to employment, and

(B) having been referred to the employer upon completion of (or while receiving) rehabilitative services pursuant to—

(i) an individualized written rehabilitation plan under a State plan for vocational rehabilitation services approved under the Rehabilitation Act of 1973, or

(ii) a program of vocational rehabilitation carried out under chapter 31 of title 38, United States Code.

(3) ECONOMICALLY DISADVANTAGED YOUTH.—

(A) IN GENERAL.—The term "economically disadvantaged youth" means any individual who is certified by the designated local agency as—

(i) meeting the age requirements of subparagraph (B), and

(ii) being a member of an economically disadvantaged family (as determined under paragraph (11)).

(B) AGE REQUIREMENTS.—An individual meets the age requirements of this subpararaph if such individual has attained age 18 but not age 23 on the hiring date.

(4) VIETNAM VETERAN WHO IS A MEMBER OF AN ECONOMICALLY DISADVANTAGED FAMILY.—The term "Vietnam veteran who is a member of an economically disadvantaged family" means any individual who is certified by the designated local agency as—

(A)(i) having served on active duty (other than active duty for training) in the Armed Forces of the United States for a period of more than 180 days, any part of which occurred after August 4, 1964, and before May 8, 1975, or

(ii) having been discharged or released from active duty in the Armed Forces of the United States for a service-connected disability if any part of such active duty was performed after August 4, 1964, and before May 8, 1975,

(B) not having any day during the preemployment period which was a day of extended active duty in the Armed Forces of the United States and

(C) being a member of an economically disadvantaged family (determined under paragraph (11)).

For purposes of subparagraph (B), the term "extended active duty" means a period of more than 90 days during which the individual was on active duty (other than active duty for training).

(5) SSI RECIPIENTS.—The term "SSI recipient" means any individual who is certified by the designated local agency as receiving supplemental security income benefits under title XVI of the Social Security Act (including supplemental security income benefits of the type described in section 1616 of such Act or section 212 of Public Law 93-66) for any month ending in the pre-employment period.

(6) GENERAL ASSISTANCE RECIPIENTS.—

(A) IN GENERAL.—The term "general assistance recipient" means any individual who is certified by the designated local agency as receiving assistance under a qualified general assistance program for any period of not less than 30 days ending within the preemployment period.

(B) QUALIFIED GENERAL ASSISTANCE PROGRAM.—The term "qualified general assistance program" means any program of a State or a political subdivision of a State—

(i) which provides general assistance or similar assistance which—

(I) is based on need, and

(II) consists of money payments or voucher or scrip, and

(ii) which is designated by the Secretary (after consultation with the Secretary of Health and Human Services) as meeting the requirements of clause (i).

(7) ECONOMICALLY DISADVANTAGED EX-CONVICT.—The term "economically disadvantaged ex-convict" means any individual who is certified by the designated local agency—

(A) as having been convicted of a felony under any statute of the United States or any State,

(B) as being a member of an economically disadvantaged family (as determined under paragraph (11)), and

(C) as having a hiring date which is not more than 5 years after the last date on which such individual was so convicted or was released from prison.

(8) YOUTH PARTICIPATING IN A QUALIFIED COOPERATIVE EDUCATION PROGRAM.—

(A) IN GENERAL.—The term "youth participating in a qualified cooperative education program" means any individual who is certified by the school participating in the program as—

(i) having attained age 16 and not having attained age 20,

(ii) not having graduated from a high school or vocational school,

(iii) being enrolled in and actively pursuing a qualified cooperative education program, and

(iv) being a member of an economically disadvantaged family (as determined under paragraph (11)).

(B) QUALIFIED COOPERATIVE EDUCATION PROGRAM DEFINED.—The term "qualified cooperative education program" means a program of vocational education for individuals who (through written cooperative arrangements between a qualified school and 1 or more employers) receive instruction (including required academic instruction) by alternation of study and school with a job in any occupational field (but only if these 2 experiences are planned by the school and employer so that each contributes to the student's education and employability).

(C) QUALIFIED SCHOOL DEFINED.—The term "qualified school" means—

(i) a specialized high school used exclusively or principally for the provision of vocational education to individuals who are available for study in preparation for entering the labor market,

(ii) the department of a high school exclusively or principally used for providing vocational education to persons who are available for study in preparation for entering the labor market, or

(iii) a technical or vocational school used exclusively or principally for the provision of vocational education to persons who have completed or left high school and who are available for study in preparation for entering the labor market.

A school which is not a public school shall be treated as a qualified school only if it is exempt from tax under section 501(a).

(D) WAGES.—In the case of remuneration attributable to services performed while the individual meets the requirements of clauses (i), (ii), and (iii) of subparagraph (A), wages, and unemployment insurance wages, shall be determined without regard to section 3306(c)(10)(C).

(9) ELIGIBLE WORK INCENTIVE EMPLOYEES.—The term "eligible work incentive employee" means an individual who has been certified by the designated local agency as—

(A) being eligible for financial assistance under part A of title IV of the Social Security Act and as having continually received such financial assistance during the 90-day period which immediately precedes the date on which such individual is hired by the employer, or

(B) having been placed in employment under a work incentive program established under section 432(b)(1) or 445 of the Social Security Act.

(10) INVOLUNTARILY TERMINATED CETA EMPLOYEE.—The term "involuntarily terminated CETA employee" means an individual who is certified by the designated local agency as having been involuntarily terminated after December 31, 1980, from employment financed in whole or in part under a program under part D of title II or title VI of the Comprehensive Employment and Training Act. This paragraph shall not apply to any individual who begins work for the employer after December 31, 1982.

(11) MEMBERS OF ECONOMICALLY DISADVANTAGED FAMILIES.—An individual is a member of an economically disadvantaged family if the designated local agency determines that such individual was a member of a family which had an income during the 6 months immediately preceding the earlier of the month in which such determination occurs or the month in which the hiring date occurs, which, on an annual basis, would be 70 percent or less of the Bureau of Labor Statistics lower living standard. Any such determination shall be valid for the 45-day period beginning on the date such determination is made. Any such determination with respect to an individual who is a qualified summer youth employee or youth participating in a qualified cooperative education program with respect to any employer shall also apply for purposes of determining whether such individual is a member of another targeted group with respect to such employer.

(12) QUALIFIED SUMMER YOUTH EMPLOYEE.—

(A) IN GENERAL.—The term "qualified summer youth employee" means an individual—

(i) who performs services for the employer between May 1 and September 15,

(ii) who is certified by the designated local agency as having attained age 16 but not 18 on the hiring date (or if later, on May 1 of the calendar year involved),

(iii) who has not been an employee of the employer during any period prior to the 90-day period described in subparagraph (B)(iii), and

(iv) who is certified by the designated local agency as being a member of an economically disadvantaged family (as determined under paragraph (11)).

(B) SPECIAL RULES FOR DETERMINING AMOUNT OF CREDIT.—For purposes of applying this subpart to wages paid or incurred to any qualified summer youth employee—

(i) subsection (b)(2) shall be applied by substituting "any 90-day period between May 1 and September 15" for "the 1-year period beginning with the day the individual begins work for the employer", and

(ii) subsection (b)(3) shall be applied by substituting "$3,000" for "$6,000".

(C) SPECIAL RULE FOR CONTINUED EMPLOYMENT FOR SAME EMPLOYER.—In the case of an individual who, with respect to the same employer, is certified as a member of another targeted group after such individual has been a qualified summer youth employee, paragraph (14) shall be applied by substituting "certified" for "hired by the employer".

(13) PREEMPLOYMENT PERIOD.—The term "preemployment period" means the 60-day period ending on the hiring date.

(14) HIRING DATE.—The term "hiring date" means the day the individual is hired by the employer.

(15) DESIGNATED LOCAL AGENCY.—The term "designated local agency" means a State employment security agency established in accordance with the Act of June 6, 1933, as amended (29 U.S.C. 49-49n).

(16) SPECIAL RULES FOR CERTIFICATIONS.—

(A) IN GENERAL.—An individual shall not be treated as a member of a targeted group unless, on or before the day on which such individual begins work for the employer, the employer—

(i) has received a certification from a designated local agency that such individual is a member of a targeted group, or

(ii) has requested in writing such certification from the designated local agency.

For purposes of the preceding sentence, if on or before the day on which such individual begins work for the employer, such individual has received from a designated local agency (or other agency or organization designated pursuant to a written agreement with such designated local agency) a written preliminary determination that such individual is a member of a targeted group, then "the fifth day" shall be substituted for "the day" in such sentence.

(B) INCORRECT CERTIFICATIONS.—If—

(i) an individual has been certified as a member of a targeted group, and

(ii) such certification is incorrect because it was based on false information provided by such individual,

the certification shall be revoked and wages paid by the employer after the date on which notice of revocation is received by the employer shall not be treated as qualified wages.

(C) EMPLOYER REQUEST MUST SPECIFY POTENTIAL BASIS FOR ELIGIBILITY.—In any request for a certification of an individual as a member of a targeted group, the employer shall—

(i) specify each subparagraph (but not more than 2) of paragraph (1) by reason of which the employer believes that such individual is such a member, and

(ii) certify that a good faith effort was made to determine that such individual is such a member.

• 1989, Omnibus Budget Reconcilliation Act of 1989 (P.L. 101-239)

P.L. 101-239, §7103(c)(1):

Amended Code Sec. 51(d)(16) by adding at the end a new subparagraph (C). **Effective** for individuals who begin work for the employer after 12-31-89.

• 1988, Technical and Miscellaneous Revenue Act of 1988 (P.L. 100-647)

P.L. 100-647, §1017(a):

Amended Code Sec. 51(d)(12)(B)(i) by striking out "subsection (a)(1)" and inserting in lieu thereof "subsection (a)". **Effective** as if included in the provision of P.L. 99-514 to which it relates.

P.L. 100-647, §4010(c)(1):

Amended Code Sec. 51(d)(3)(B) by striking out "age 25" and inserting in lieu thereof "age 23". **Effective** for individuals who begin work for the employer after 12-31-88.

P.L. 100-647, §4010(d)(1):

Amended Code Sec. 51(d)(12)(B) by striking out clause (i) and by redesignating clauses (ii) and (iii) as clauses (i) and (ii). **Effective** for individuals who begin work for the employer after 12-31-88. Prior to amendment, Code Sec. 51(d)(12)(B)(i) read as follows:

(i) subsection (a) shall be applied by substituting "85 percent" for "40 percent",

• 1986, Tax Reform Act of 1986 (P.L. 99-514)

P.L. 99-514, §1701(b)(2)(B)(i)-(iii):

Amended Code Sec. 51(d)(12)(B) by striking out "50 percent" and inserting in lieu thereof "40 percent" in clause (i), by striking out clause (ii) and redesignating clauses (iii) and (iv) as clauses (ii) and (iii), respectively, and by striking out "subsection (b)(4)" and inserting in lieu thereof "subsection (b)(3)" in clause (iii) (as redesignated). **Effective** for individuals who begin work for the employer after 12-31-85. Prior to amendment, Code Sec. 51(d)(12)(B)(ii) read as follows:

(ii) subsections (a)(2) and (b)(3) shall not apply,

• 1984, Deficit Reduction Act of 1984 (P.L. 98-369)

P.L. 98-369, §712(n):

Amended Code Sec. 51(d)(11) by adding a new sentence at the end. **Effective** as if included in the provision of P.L. 97-248 to which it relates.

P.L. 98-369, §1041(c)(2):

Amended Code Sec. 51(d)(16)(A) by adding the last sentence. **Effective** for individuals who begin work for the employer after 7-18-84.

P.L. 98-369, §1041(c)(3):

Amended Code Sec. 51(d)(12)(A)(ii) by striking out "(as defined in paragraph (14))" and inserting in lieu thereof "(or if later, on May 1 of the calendar year involved)". **Effective** for individuals who begin work for the employer after 12-31-84.

P.L. 98-369, §2663(j)(5)(A):

Amended Code Sec. 51(d)(6)(B)(ii) by striking out "Health, Education, and Welfare" and inserting in lieu thereof "Health and Human Services". **Effective** 7-18-84, but shall not be construed as changing or affecting any right, liability, status, or interpretation which existed (under the provisions of law involved) before that date.

• 1983, Technical Corrections Act of 1982 (P.L. 97-448)

P.L. 97-448, §102(l)(1):

Amended Code Sec. 51(d)(8)(D) by striking out "subparagraph (A)" and inserting "clauses (i), (ii), and (iii) of subparagraph (A)". **Effective** as if it had been included in the provision of P.L. 97-34 to which it relates.

P.L. 97-448, §102(l)(3):

Amended Code Sec. 51(d)(9)(B) by striking out "section 432(b)(1)" and inserting in lieu thereof "section 432(b)(1) or 445". **Effective** as if it had been included in the provision of the P.L. 97-34 to which it relates.

P.L. 97-448, §102(l)(4):

Amended Code Sec. 51(d)(11) by striking out "the month in which such determination occurs" and inserting in lieu thereof "the earlier of the month in which such determination occurs or the month in which the hiring date occurs". **Effective** for certifications made after 7-18-84 with respect to individuals beginning work for an employer after 5-11-82.

• 1982, Tax Equity and Fiscal Responsibility Act of 1982 (P.L. 97-248)

P.L. 97-248, §233(b)(1)-(5):

Amended Code Sec. 51(d) by striking out [in (1)] "or" at the end of subparagraph (H); by striking out the period at the end of subparagraph (I) and inserting in lieu thereof ", or"; by inserting after subparagraph (I) new subparagraph (J); by redesignating paragraphs (12), (13), (14), and (15) as paragraphs (13), (14), (15), and (16), respectively; and by inserting after paragraph (11) new paragraph (12). **Effective** for amounts paid or incurred after 4-30-83, to individuals beginning work for the employer after such date.

P.L. 97-248, §233(c):

Amended Code Sec. 51(d)(10) by adding the last sentence **Effective** 9-3-82.

P.L. 97-248, §233(d):

Amended Code Sec. 51(d)(6)(B)(i)(II) by inserting before the comma "or voucher or scrip". **Effective** for amounts paid or incurred after 7-1-82, to individuals beginning work for the employer after such date.

P.L. 97-248, §233(f):

Amended Code Sec. 51(d)(15)(A), as in effect before the amendments made by this Act, by striking out "before the day", which followed "targeted group unless," and inserting in lieu thereof "on or before the day". **Effective** for individuals who begin work for the taxpayer after 5-11-82.

• 1981, Economic Recovery Tax Act of 1981 (P.L. 97-34)

P.L. 97-34, §261(b)(1):

Amended Code Sec. 51(d)(1) by striking out "or" at the end of subparagraph (F); by striking out the period at the end of subparagraph (G) and inserting in lieu thereof a comma; and by adding at the end thereof new subparagraphs (H) and (I). **Effective** as noted in P.L. 97-34, §261(g), in the amendment notes following Code Sec. 51(c).

P.L. 97-34, §261(b)(2)(A):

Amended Code Sec. 51(d) by redesignating paragraphs (9), (10), (11), and (12) as paragraphs (11), (12), (13), and (14), respectively, and by inserting after paragraph (8) new paragraphs (9) and (10). **Effective** as noted in P.L. 97-34, §261(g), in the amendment notes following Code Sec. 51(c).

P.L. 97-34, §261(b)(2)(B)(iii):

Amended Code Sec. 51(d)(3)(A)(ii), (4)(C), and (7)(B) by striking out "paragraph (9)" and inserting in lieu thereof "paragraph (11)". **Effective** as noted in P.L. 97-34, §261(g), in the amendment notes following Code Sec. 51(c).

P.L. 97-34, §261(b)(3):

Amended Code Sec. 51(d)(4) by inserting "and" at the end of subparagraph (B), by striking out ", and" at the end of subparagraph (C) and inserting in lieu thereof a period; and by striking out subparagraph (D). **Effective** as noted in P.L. 97-34, §261(g), in the amendment notes following Code Sec. 51(c). Prior to amendment, Code Sec. 51(d)(4)(D) read as follows:

(D) not having attained the age of 35 on the hiring date.

P.L. 97-34, §261(b)(4):

Amended Code Sec. 51(d)(8)(A) by striking out "and" at the end of clause (ii), by striking out the period at the end of clause (iii) and inserting in lieu thereof ", and"; and by adding at the end thereof new clause (iv). **Effective** as noted in P.L. 97-34, §261(g), in the amendment notes following Code Sec. 51(c).

P.L. 97-34, §261(c)(1):

Amended Code Sec. 51(d) by adding at the end thereof new paragraph (15). **Effective** as noted in P.L. 97-34, §261(g), in the amendment notes following Code Sec. 51(c).

P.L. 97-34, §261(c)(2):

Amended Code Sec. 51(d)(11) as redesignated. **Effective** as noted in P.L. 97-34, §261(g), in the amendment notes following Code Sec. 51(c). Prior to amendment and prior to redesignation, Code Sec. 51(d)(11) read as follows:

(9) MEMBERS OF ECONOMICALLY DISADVANTAGED FAMILIES.—An individual is a member of an economically disadvantaged family if the designated local agency determines that such individual was a member of a family which had an income during the 6 months immediately preceding the month in which the hiring date occurs, which, on an annual basis would be less than 70 percent of the Bureau of Labor Statistic's lower living standard.

P.L. 97-34, §261(f)(1)(A):

Amended Code Sec. 51(d)(14) as redesignated. **Effective** 10-12-81. Prior to amendment, and prior to redesignation, Code Sec. 51(d)(14) read:

(12) DESIGNATED LOCAL AGENCY.—The term "designated local agency" means the agency for any locality designated jointly by the Secretary and the Secretary of Labor to perform certification of employees for employers in that locality.

P.L. 97-34, §261(f)(2), as amended by P.L. 97-248, §233(e), P.L. 98-369, §1041(b), P.L. 99-514, §1701(d), P.L. 100-647, §4010(b), and P.L. 101-239, §7103(b), provides:

(2) AUTHORIZATION OF APPROPRIATIONS.—There is authorized to be appropriated for fiscal year 1982 the sum of $30,000,000, and for fiscal years 1983, 1984, 1985, 1986, 1987, 1988, 1989, and 1990 such sums as may be necessary, to carry out the functions described by the amendments made by paragraph (1), except that, of the amounts appropriated pursuant to this paragraph—

(A) $5,000,000 shall be used to test whether individuals certified as members of targeted groups under section 51 of such Code are eligible for such certification (including the use of statistical sampling techniques), and

(B) the remainder shall be distributed under performance standards prescribed by the Secretary of Labor.

The Secretary of Labor shall each calendar year beginning with calendar year 1983 report to the Committee on Ways and Means of the House of Representatives and to the Committee on Finance of the Senate with respect to the results of the testing conducted under subparagraph (A) during the preceding calendar year.

• 1980, Technical Corrections Act of 1979 (P.L. 96-222)

P.L. 96-222, §103(a)(6)(E)(i):

Amended Code Sec. 51(d)(8)(D). **Effective**, generally, for amounts paid or incurred after 12-31-78, in tax years ending after such date. Prior to amendment, Code Sec. 51(d)(8)(D) read as follows:

(D) INDIVIDUAL MUST BE CURRENTLY PURSUING PROGRAM.—Wages shall be taken into account with respect to a qualified cooperative education program only if the wages are attributable to services performed while the individual meets the requirements of subparagraph (A).

P.L. 96-222, §103(a)(6)(F):

Amended Code Sec. 51(d)(8)(A)(i) by striking out "age 19" and inserting "age 20". **Effective** with respect to wages paid or incurred on or after 11-27-79, in tax years ending on or after such date.

P.L. 96-222, §103(a)(6)(G)(iv):

Amended Code Sec. 51(d)(1)(E) by striking out "or", **Effective**, generally, for amounts paid or incurred after 12-31-78, in tax years ending after such date.

P.L. 96-222, §103(a)(6)(G)(v):

Amended Code Sec. 51(d)(4)(A)(i) by striking out "active day" and inserting "active duty". **Effective**, generally, for amounts paid or incurred after 12-31-78, in tax years ending after such date.

P.L. 96-222, §103(a)(6)(G)(vi):

Amended Code Sec. 51(d)(4)(B) by striking out "premployment" and inserting "preemployment". **Effective**, generally, for amounts paid or incurred after 12-31-78, in tax years ending after such date.

P.L. 96-222, §103(a)(6)(G)(vii):

Amended Code Sec. 51(d)(5) by striking out "pre-employment" and inserting "preemployment". **Effective**, generally, for amounts paid or incurred after 12-31-78, in tax years ending after such date.

P.L. 96-222, §103(a)(6)(G)(viii):

Amended Code Sec. 51(d)(12) by striking out "employer" and inserting "employers". **Effective**, generally, for amounts paid or incurred after 12-31-78, in tax years ending after such date.

[Sec. 51(e)—Repealed]

Amendments

• 1981, Economic Recovery Tax Act of 1981 (P.L. 97-34)

P.L. 97-34, §261(e)(1):

Repealed Code Sec. 51(e). **Effective** for tax years beginning after 12-31-81. Prior to repeal, Code Sec. 51(e) read as follows:

(e) QUALIFIED FIRST-YEAR WAGES CANNOT EXCEED 30 PERCENT OF FUTA WAGES FOR ALL EMPLOYEES.—The amount of the qualified first-year wages which may be taken into account under subsection (a)(1) for any taxable year shall not exceed 30 percent of the aggregate unemployment insurance wages paid by the employer during the calendar year ending in such taxable year. For purposes of the preceding sentence, except as provided in subsection (h)(1), the term "unemployment insurance wages" has the meaning given to the term "wages" by section 3306(b).

• 1980, Technical Corrections Act of 1979 (P.L. 96-222)

P.L. 96-222, §103(a)(6)(G)(ix):

Amended the last sentence of Code Sec. 51(e) by inserting "except as provided in subsection (h)(1)," after "the preceding sentence,". **Effective**, generally, for amounts paid or incurred after 12-31-78, in tax years ending after such date.

[Sec. 51(e)]

(e) CREDIT FOR SECOND-YEAR WAGES FOR EMPLOYMENT OF LONG-TERM FAMILY ASSISTANCE RECIPIENTS.—

(1) IN GENERAL.—With respect to the employment of a long-term family assistance recipient—

(A) the amount of the work opportunity credit determined under this section for the taxable year shall include 50 percent of the qualified second-year wages for such year, and

(B) in lieu of applying subsection (b)(3), the amount of the qualified first-year wages, and the amount of qualified second-year wages, which may be taken into account with respect to such a recipient shall not exceed $10,000 per year.

(2) QUALIFIED SECOND-YEAR WAGES.—For purposes of this subsection, the term "qualified second-year wages" means qualified wages—

(A) which are paid to a long-term family assistance recipient, and

(B) which are attributable to service rendered during the 1-year period beginning on the day after the last day of the 1-year period with respect to such recipient determined under subsection (b)(2).

(3) SPECIAL RULES FOR AGRICULTURAL AND RAILWAY LABOR.—If such recipient is an employee to whom subparagraph (A) or (B) of subsection (h)(1) applies, rules similar to the rules of such subparagraphs shall apply except that—

(A) such subparagraph (A) shall be applied by substituting "$10,000" for "$6,000", and

(B) such subparagraph (B) shall be applied by substituting "$833.33" for "$500".

Amendments

• 2006, Tax Relief and Health Care Act of 2006 (P.L. 109-432)

P.L. 109-432, Division A, §105(e)(3):

Amended Code Sec. 51 by inserting after subsection (d) a new subsection (e). **Effective** for individuals who begin work for the employer after 12-31-2006.

[Sec. 51(f)]

(f) REMUNERATION MUST BE FOR TRADE OR BUSINESS EMPLOYMENT.—

(1) IN GENERAL.—For purposes of this subpart, remuneration paid by an employer to an employee during any taxable year shall be taken into account only if more than one-half of the remuneration so paid is for services performed in a trade or business of the employer.

(2) SPECIAL RULE FOR CERTAIN DETERMINATION.—Any determination as to whether paragraph (1), or subparagraph (A) or (B) of subsection (h)(1), applies with respect to any employee for any taxable year shall be made without regard to subsections (a) and (b) of section 52.

Amendments

• 1981, Economic Recovery Tax Act of 1981 (P.L. 97-34)

P.L. 97-34, §261(e)(2):

Amended Code Sec. 51(f) by striking out paragraph (3) and by striking out "any year" in paragraphs (1) and (2) and inserting in lieu thereof "any taxable year". **Effective** for tax years beginning after 12-31-81. Prior to repeal, Code Sec. 51(f)(3) read as follows:

(3) YEAR DEFINED.—For purposes of this subsection and subsection (h), the term "year" means the taxable year; except that, for purposes of applying so much of such subsections as relates to subsection (e), such term means the calendar year.

[Sec. 51(g)]

(g) UNITED STATES EMPLOYMENT SERVICE TO NOTIFY EMPLOYERS OF AVAILABILITY OF CREDIT.—The United States Employment Service, in consultation with the Internal Revenue Service, shall take such steps as may be necessary or appropriate to keep employers apprised of the availability of the work opportunity credit determined under this subpart.

Amendments

• 1996, Small Business Job Protection Act of 1996 (P.L. 104-188)

P.L. 104-188, §1201(e)(1):

Amended Code Sec. 51(g) by striking "targeted jobs credit" each place it appears and inserting "work opportunity credit". **Effective** for individuals who begin work for the employer after 9-30-96.

• 1984, Deficit Reduction Act of 1984 (P.L. 98-369)

P.L. 98-369, §474(p)(2):

Amended Code Sec. 51(g) by striking out "the credit provided by section 44B" and inserting in lieu thereof "the targeted jobs credit determined under this subpart". **Effective** for tax years beginning after 12-31-83, and to carrybacks from such years.

• 1981, Economic Recovery Tax Act of 1981 (P.L. 97-34)

P.L. 97-34, §261(f)(1)(B):

Amended Code Sec. 51(g) by striking out "Secretary of Labor" each place it appeared in the heading and text and inserting in lieu thereof "United States Employment Service". See the historical comment for P.L. 97-34, §261(f)(2) regarding authorization of appropriations. **Effective** 10-12-81.

[Sec. 51(h)]

(h) SPECIAL RULES FOR AGRICULTURAL LABOR AND RAILWAY LABOR.—For purposes of this subpart—

(1) UNEMPLOYMENT INSURANCE WAGES.—

(A) AGRICULTURAL LABOR.—If the services performed by any employee for an employer during more than one-half of any pay period (within the meaning of section 3306(d)) taken into account with respect to any year constitute agricultural labor (within the meaning of section 3306(k)), the term "unemployment insurance wages" means, with respect to the remuneration paid by the employer to such employee for such year, an amount equal to so much of such remuneration as constitutes "wages" within the meaning of section 3121(a), except that the contribution and benefit base for each calendar year shall be deemed to be $6,000.

(B) RAILWAY LABOR.—If more than one-half of remuneration paid by an employer to an employee during any year is remuneration for service described in section 3306(c)(9), the term "unemployment insurance wages" means, with respect to such employee for such year, an amount equal to so much of the remuneration paid to such employee during such year which would be subject to contributions under section 8(a) of the Railroad Unemployment Insurance Act (45 U.S.C. 358(a)) if the maximum amount subject to such contributions were $500 per month.

(2) WAGES.—In any case to which subparagraph (A) or (B) of paragraph (1) applies, the term "wages" means unemployment insurance wages (determined without regard to any dollar limitation).

[Sec. 51(i)]

(i) CERTAIN INDIVIDUALS INELIGIBLE.—

(1) RELATED INDIVIDUALS.—No wages shall be taken into account under subsection (a) with respect to an individual who—

(A) bears any of the relationships described in subparagraphs (A) through (G) of section 152(d)(2) to the taxpayer, or, if the taxpayer is a corporation, to an individual who owns, directly or indirectly, more than 50 percent in value of the outstanding stock of the corporation, or, if the taxpayer is an entity other than a corporation, to any individual who owns, directly or indirectly, more than 50 percent of the capital and profits interests in the entity (determined with the application of section 267(c)),

(B) if the taxpayer is an estate or trust, is a grantor, beneficiary, or fiduciary of the estate or trust, or is an individual who bears any of the relationships described in subparagraphs (A) through (G) of section 152(d)(2) to a grantor, beneficiary, or fiduciary of the estate or trust, or

(C) is a dependent (described in section 152(d)(2)(H)) of the taxpayer, or, if the taxpayer is a corporation, of an individual described in subparagraph (A), or, if the taxpayer is an estate or trust, of a grantor, beneficiary, or fiduciary of the estate or trust.

(2) NONQUALIFYING REHIRES.—No wages shall be taken into account under subsection (a) with respect to any individual if, prior to the hiring date of such individual, such individual had been employed by the employer at any time.

(3) INDIVIDUALS NOT MEETING MINIMUM EMPLOYMENT PERIODS.—

(A) REDUCTION OF CREDIT FOR INDIVIDUALS PERFORMING FEWER THAN 400 HOURS OF SERVICE.—In the case of an individual who has performed at least 120 hours, but less than 400 hours, of service for the employer, subsection (a) shall be applied by substituting "25 percent" for "40 percent".

(B) DENIAL OF CREDIT FOR INDIVIDUALS PERFORMING FEWER THAN 120 HOURS OF SERVICE.—No wages shall be taken into account under subsection (a) with respect to any individual unless such individual has performed at least 120 hours of service for the employer.

Amendments

• 2004, Working Families Tax Relief Act of 2004 (P.L. 108-311)

P.L. 108-311, §207(5)(A):

Amended Code Sec. 51(i)(1)(A) and (B) by striking "paragraphs (1) through (8) of section 152(a)" both places it appears and inserting "subparagraphs (A) through (G) of section 152(d)(2)". **Effective** for tax years beginning after 12-31-2004.

P.L. 108-311, §207(5)(B):

Amended Code Sec. 51(i)(1)(C) by striking "152(a)(9)" and inserting "152(d)(2)(H)". **Effective** for tax years beginning after 12-31-2004.

• 1999, Tax Relief Extension Act of 1999 (P.L. 106-170)

P.L. 106-170, §505(b):

Amended Code Sec. 51(i)(2) by striking "during which he was not a member of a targeted group" following "at any time". **Effective** for individuals who begin work for the employer after 6-30-99.

• 1997, Taxpayer Relief Act of 1997 (P.L. 105-34)

P.L. 105-34, §603(d)(2):

Amended Code Sec. 51(i)(3). **Effective** for individuals who begin work for the employer after 9-30-97. Prior to amendment, Code Sec. 51(i)(3) read as follows:

(3) INDIVIDUALS NOT MEETING MINIMUM EMPLOYMENT PERIOD.—No wages shall be taken into account under subsection (a) with respect to any individual unless such individual either—

(A) is employed by the employer at least 180 days (20 days in the case of a qualified summer youth employee), or

(B) has completed at least 400 hours (120 hours in the case of a qualified summer youth employee) of services performed for the employer.

• 1996, Small Business Job Protection Act of 1996 (P.L. 104-188)

P.L. 104-188, §1201(c):

Amended Code Sec. 51(i)(3). **Effective** for individuals who begin work for the employer after 9-30-96. Prior to amendment, Code Sec. 51(i)(3) read as follows:

(3) INDIVIDUALS NOT MEETING MINIMUM EMPLOYMENT PERIOD.—No wages shall be taken into account under subsection (a) with respect to any individual unless such individual either—

(A) is employed by the employer at least 90 days (14 days in the case of an individual described in subsection (d)(12)), or

(B) has completed at least 120 hours (20 hours in the case of an individual described in subsection (d)(12)) of services performed for the employer.

• 1993, Omnibus Budget Reconcilliation Act of 1993 (P.L. 103-66)

P.L. 103-66, §13302(d):

Amended Code Sec. 51(i)(1)(A) by inserting ", or, if the taxpayer is an entity other than a corporation, to any individual who owns, directly or indirectly, more than 50 percent of the capital and profits interests in the entity," after "of the corporation". **Effective** 8-10-96.

• 1986, Tax Reform Act of 1986 (P.L. 99-514)

P.L. 99-514, §1701(c):

Amended Code Sec. 51(i) by adding at the end thereof new paragraph (3). **Effective** for individuals who begin work for the employer after 12-31-85.

• 1981, Economic Recovery Tax Act of 1981 (P.L. 97-34)

P.L. 97-34, §261(d):

Amended Code Sec. 51 by adding at the end thereof new subsection (i). **Effective** as noted in P.L. 97-34, §261(g), in the amendment notes following Code Sec. 51(c).

[Sec. 51(j)]

(j) ELECTION TO HAVE WORK OPPORTUNITY CREDIT NOT APPLY.—

(1) IN GENERAL.—A taxpayer may elect to have this section not apply for any taxable year.

(2) TIME FOR MAKING ELECTION.—An election under paragraph (1) for any taxable year may be made (or revoked) at any time before the expiration of the 3-year period beginning on the last date prescribed by law for filing the return for such taxable year (determined without regard to extensions).

(3) MANNER OF MAKING ELECTION.—An election under paragraph (1) (or revocation thereof) shall be made in such manner as the Secretary may by regulations prescribe.

Amendments

• 1996, Small Business Job Protection Act of 1996 (P.L. 104-188)

P.L. 104-188, §1201(e)(5):

Amended Code Sec. 51(j) by striking "TARGETED JOBS CREDIT" in the heading and inserting "WORK OPPORTUNITY CREDIT". **E ffective** for individuals who begin work for the employer after 9-30-96.

• 1984, Deficit Reduction Act of 1984 (P.L. 98-369)

P.L. 98-369, §474(p)(3):

Amended Code Sec. 51 by adding at the end thereof new subsection (j). **Effective** for tax years beginning after 12-31-83, and to carrybacks from such years.

[Sec. 51(k)]

(k) TREATMENT OF SUCCESSOR EMPLOYERS; TREATMENT OF EMPLOYEES PERFORMING SERVICES FOR OTHER PERSONS.—

(1) TREATMENT OF SUCCESSOR EMPLOYERS.—Under regulations prescribed by the Secretary, in the case of a successor employer referred to in section 3306(b)(1), the determination of the amount of the credit under this section with respect to wages paid by such successor employer shall be made in the same manner as if such wages were paid by the predecessor employer referred to in such section.

(2) TREATMENT OF EMPLOYEES PERFORMING SERVICES FOR OTHER PERSONS.—No credit shall be determined under this section with respect to remuneration paid by an employer to an employee for services performed by such employee for another person unless the amount reasonably expected to be received by the employer for such services from such other person exceeds the remuneration paid by the employer to such employee for such services.

Amendments

• 1986, Tax Reform Act of 1986 (P.L. 99-514)

P.L. 99-514, §1878(f)(1):

Amended Code Sec. 51 by redesignating subsection (j)[k] as subsection (k). **Effective** as if included in the provision of P.L. 98-369 to which such amendment relates.

• 1984, Deficit Reduction Act of 1984 (P.L. 98-369)

P.L. 98-369, §1041(c)(1):

Amended Code Sec. 51 by adding at the end thereof new subsection (j)[k]. **Effective** for individuals who begin work for the employer after 7-18-84.

• 1978, Revenue Act of 1978 (P.L. 95-600)

P.L. 95-600, §321(a):

Amended Code Sec. 51. **Effective**, generally, for amounts paid or incurred after 12-31-78, in tax years ending after such date. For special rules, see Act Sec. 321(d), below. Prior to amendment, Code Sec. 51 read as follows:

SEC. 51. AMOUNT OF CREDIT.

(a) DETERMINATION OF AMOUNT.—The amount of the credit allowable by section 44B shall be—

(1) for a taxable year beginning in 1977, an amount equal to 50 percent of the excess of the aggregate unemployment

insurance wages paid during 1977 over 102 percent of the aggregate unemployment insurance wages paid during 1976, and

(2) for a taxable year beginning in 1978, an amount equal to 50 percent of the excess of the aggregate unemployment insurance wages paid during 1978 over 102 percent of the aggregate unemployment insurance wages paid during 1977.

(b) MINIMUM PRECEDING YEAR WAGES.—For purposes of determining the amount of the credit under subsection (a) with respect to 1977 or 1978, 102 percent of the amount of the aggregate unemployment insurance wages paid during the preceding calendar year shall be deemed to be not less than 50 percent of the amount of such wages paid during 1977 or 1978, as the case may be.

(c) TOTAL WAGES MUST INCREASE.—The amount of the credit allowable by section 44B for any taxable year shall not exceed the amount which would be determined for such year under subsection (a) (without regard to subsection (b)) if—

(1) the aggregate amounts taken into account as unemployment insurance wages were determined without any dollar limitation, and

(2) "105 percent" were substituted for "102 percent" in the appropriate paragraph of subsection (a).

(d) $100,000 PER YEAR LIMITATION ON CREDIT.—Except as provided in subsection (e), the amount of the credit determined under this subpart for any employer (and the amount of the credit allowable by section 44B to any taxpayer) with respect to any calendar year shall not exceed $100,000.

(e) ADDITIONAL 10 PERCENT CREDIT FOR VOCATIONAL REHABILITATION REFERRALS.—

(1) IN GENERAL.—The amount of the credit allowable by section 44B for any taxable year beginning in 1977 or 1978 (determined without regard to this subsection) shall be increased by an amount equal to 10 percent of the unemployment insurance wages paid by the employer to vocational rehabilitation referrals during the calendar year in which such taxable year begins.

(2) ONLY FIRST YEAR TAKEN INTO ACCOUNT.—For purposes of this subsection, unemployment insurance wages may be taken into account with respect to any individual—

(A) only to the extent attributable to services rendered during the 1-year period beginning with his first payment of wages by the employer after the beginning of such individual's rehabilitation plan, and

(B) only if such first payment occurs after December 31, 1976.

(3) ONLY FIRST $4,200 OF WAGES TAKEN INTO ACCOUNT FOR ANY INDIVIDUAL.—For purposes of this subsection, the unemployment insurance wages paid during 1978 which are taken into account with respect to any individual shall not exceed $4,200 reduced by the amount of unemployment insurance wages paid by the employer to such individual during 1977.

(4) 20-PERCENT LIMITATION.—The amount of the credit allowable by reason of this subsection for any taxable year shall not exceed one-fifth of the credit determined for such year under this section without regard to this subsection and subsection (d).

(f) DEFINITIONS—For purposes of this subpart—

(1) UNEMPLOYMENT INSURANCE WAGES.—Except as otherwise provided in this subpart, the term "unemployment insurance wages" has the meaning given to the term "wages" by section 3306(b), except that, in the case of amounts paid during 1978, "$4,200" shall be substituted for "$6,000" each place it appears in section 3306(b).

(2) AGRICULTURAL LABOR.—If the services performed by any employee for an employer during more than one-half of any pay period (within the meaning of section 3306(d)) taken into account with respect to any calendar year constitute agricultural labor (within the meaning of section 3306(k)), the term "unemployment insurance wages" means, with respect to the remuneration paid by the employer to such employee for such year, an amount equal to so much of such remuneration as constitutes "wages" within the meaning of section 3121(a), except that the contribution and benefit base for each calendar year shall be deemed to be $4,200.

(3) RAILWAY LABOR.—If more than one-half of the remuneration paid by an employer to an employee during the calendar year is remuneration for service described in section 3306(c)(9), the term "unemployment insurance wages" means, with respect to such employee for such year, an amount equal to 7/8 of so much of the remuneration paid to such employee during such year as is subject to contributions under section 8(a) of the Railroad Unemployment Insurance Act (45 U.S.C. 358(a)).

(4) VOCATIONAL REHABILITATION REFERRAL.—The term "vocational rehabilitation referral" means any individual who—

(A) has a physical or mental disability which, for such individual, constitutes or results in a substantial handicap to employment, and

(B) has been referred to the employer upon completion of (or while receiving) rehabilitative services pursuant to—

(i) an individualized written rehabilitation plan under a State plan for vocational rehabilitation services approved under the Rehabilitation Act of 1973, or

(ii) a program of vocational rehabilitation carried out under chapter 31 of title 38, United States Code.

(g) RULES FOR APPLICATION OF SECTION.—For purposes of this subpart—

(1) REMUNERATION MUST BE FOR TRADE OR BUSINESS EMPLOYMENT WITHIN UNITED STATES.—Remuneration paid by an employer to an employee during any calendar year shall be taken into account only if more than onehalf of the remuneration so paid is for services performed in the United States in a trade or business of the employer.

(2) SPECIAL RULE FOR CERTAIN DETERMINATIONS.—Any determination as to whether paragraph (1) of this subsection, or paragraph (2) or (3) of subsection (f), applies with respect to any employee for any calendar year shall be made without regard to subsections (a) and (b) of section 52.

P.L. 95-600, §321(d), as amended by P.L. 96-222, §103(a)(6)(B)-(D), provides:

"(d) EFFECTIVE DATE.—

"(1) IN GENERAL.—Except as otherwise provided in this subsection, the amendments made by this section shall apply to amounts paid or incurred after December 31, 1978, in taxable years ending after such date.

"(2) SPECIAL RULES FOR NEWLY TARGETED GROUPS.—

"(A) INDIVIDUAL MUST BE HIRED AFTER SEPTEMBER 26, 1978.—In the case of a member of a newly targeted group for purposes of applying the amendments made by this section—

"(i) such individual shall be taken into account for purposes of the credit allowable by section 44B of the Internal Revenue Code of 1954 only if such individual is first hired by the employer after September 26, 1978, and

"(ii) such individual shall be treated for purposes of such credit as having first begun work for the employer not earlier than January 1, 1979.

"(B) MEMBER OF NEWLY TARGETED GROUP DEFINED.—For purposes of subparagraph (A), an individual is a member of a newly targeted group if—

"(i) such individual meets the requirements of subparagraph (A), (C) (D), (E), (F), or (G) of section 51(d)(1) of such Code, and

"(ii) in the case of an individual meeting the requirements of subparagraph (A) of such section 51(d)(1), a credit was not claimed for such individual by the taxpayer for a taxable year beginning before January 1, 1979.

"(3) TRANSITIONAL RULE.—In the case of a taxable year which begins in 1978 and ends after December 31, 1978, the amount of the credit determined under section 51 of the Internal Revenue Code of 1954 shall be the sum of—

"(A) the amount of the credit which would be so determined without regard to the amendments made by this section, plus

"(B) the amount which would be so determined by reason of the amendments made by this section.

"(4) SUBSECTION(c)(2).—The amendments made by subsection (c)(2) shall apply to taxable years beginning after December 31, 1978.

"(5) SUBSECTION (b).—The amendments made by subsection (b) shall apply to taxable years beginning after December 31, 1976."

• 1977, Tax Reduction and Simplification Act of 1977 (P.L. 95-30)

P.L. 95-30, §202(b):

Added Code Sec. 51. **Effective** for tax years beginning after 12-31-76, and for credit carrybacks from such years.

[Sec. 51A—Repealed]

Amendments

• 2006, Tax Relief and Health Care Act of 2006 (P.L. 109-432)

P.L. 109-432, Division A, §105(e)(4)(A):

Repealed Code Sec. 51A. **Effective** for individuals who begin work for the employer after 12-31-2006. Prior to repeal, Code Sec. 51A read as follows:

SEC. 51A. TEMPORARY INCENTIVES FOR EMPLOYING LONG-TERM FAMILY ASSISTANCE RECIPIENTS.

[Sec. 51A(a)]

(a) DETERMINATION OF AMOUNT.—For purposes of section 38, the amount of the welfare-to-work credit determined under this section for the taxable year shall be equal to—

(1) 35 percent of the qualified first-year wages for such year, and

(2) 50 percent of the qualified second-year wages for such year.

[Sec. 51A(b)]

(b) QUALIFIED WAGES DEFINED.—For purposes of this section—

(1) IN GENERAL.—The term "qualified wages" means the wages paid or incurred by the employer during the taxable year to individuals who are long-term family assistance recipients.

(2) QUALIFIED FIRST-YEAR WAGES.—The term "qualified first-year wages" means, with respect to any individual, qualified wages attributable to service rendered during the 1-year period beginning with the day the individual begins work for the employer.

(3) QUALIFIED SECOND-YEAR WAGES.—The term "qualified second-year wages" means, with respect to any individual, qualified wages attributable to service rendered during the 1-year period beginning on the day after the last day of the 1-year period with respect to such individual determined under paragraph (2).

(4) ONLY FIRST $10,000 OF WAGES PER YEAR TAKEN INTO ACCOUNT.—The amount of the qualified first-year wages, and the amount of qualified second-year wages, which may be taken into account with respect to any individual shall not exceed $10,000 per year.

(5) WAGES.—

(A) IN GENERAL.—The term "wages" has the meaning given such term by section 51(c), without regard to paragraph (4) thereof.

(B) CERTAIN AMOUNTS TREATED AS WAGES.—The term "wages" includes amounts paid or incurred by the employer which are excludable from such recipient's gross income under—

(i) section 105 (relating to amounts received under accident and health plans),

(ii) section 106 (relating to contributions by employer to accident and health plans),

(iii) section 127 (relating to educational assistance programs), but only to the extent paid or incurred to a person not related to the employer, or

(iv) section 129 (relating to dependent care assistance programs).

The amount treated as wages by clause (i) or (ii) for any period shall be based on the reasonable cost of coverage for the period, but shall not exceed the applicable premium for the period under section 4980B(f)(4).

(C) SPECIAL RULES FOR AGRICULTURAL AND RAILWAY LABOR.—If such recipient is an employee to whom subparagraph (A) or (B) of section 51(h)(1) applies, rules similar to the rules of such subparagraphs shall apply except that—

(i) such subparagraph (A) shall be applied by substituting "$10,000" for "$6,000", and

(ii) such subparagraph (B) shall be applied by substituting "$833.33" for "$500".

Amendments

• 2001, Economic Growth and Tax Relief Reconciliation Act of 2001 (P.L. 107-16)

P.L. 107-16, §411(c):

Amended Code Sec. 51A(b)(5)(B)(iii) by striking "or would be so excludable but for section 127(d)" after "educational assistance programs)". **Effective** with respect to expenses relating to courses beginning after 12-31-2001.

P.L. 107-16, §901(a)-(b), provides:

SEC. 901. SUNSET OF PROVISIONS OF ACT.

(a) IN GENERAL.—All provisions of, and amendments made by, this Act shall not apply—

(1) to taxable, plan, or limitation years beginning after December 31, 2010, or

(2) in the case of title V, to estates of decedents dying, gifts made, or generation skipping transfers, after December 31, 2010.

(b) APPLICATION OF CERTAIN LAWS.—The Internal Revenue Code of 1986 and the Employee Retirement Income Security Act of 1974 shall be applied and administered to years, estates, gifts, and transfers described in subsection (a) as if the provisions and amendments described in subsection (a) had never been enacted.

[Sec. 51A(c)]

(c) LONG-TERM FAMILY ASSISTANCE RECIPIENTS.—For purposes of this section—

(1) IN GENERAL.—The term "long-term family assistance recipient" means any individual who is certified by the designated local agency (as defined in section 51(d)(11))—

(A) as being a member of a family receiving assistance under a IV-A program (as defined in section 51(d)(2)(B)) for at least the 18-month period ending on the hiring date,

(B)(i) as being a member of a family receiving such assistance for 18 months beginning after the date of the enactment of this section, and

(ii) as having a hiring date which is not more than 2 years after the end of the earliest such 18-month period, or

(C)(i) as being a member of a family which ceased to be eligible after the date of the enactment of this section for such assistance by reason of any limitation imposed by Federal or State law on the maximum period such assistance is payable to a family, and

(ii) as having a hiring date which is not more than 2 years after the date of such cessation.

(2) HIRING DATE.—The term "hiring date" has the meaning given such term by section 51(d).

Amendments

• 2002, Job Creation and Worker Assistance Act of 2002 (P.L. 107-147)

P.L. 107-147, §417(4):

Amended Code Sec. 51A(c)(1) by striking "51(d)(10)" and inserting "51(d)(11)". **Effective** 3-9-2002.

[Sec. 51A(d)]

(d) CERTAIN RULES TO APPLY.—

(1) IN GENERAL.—Rules similar to the rules of section 52, and subsections (d)(11), (f), (g), (i) (as in effect on the day before the date of the enactment of the Taxpayer Relief Act of 1997), (j), and (k) of section 51, shall apply for purposes of this section.

(2) CREDIT TO BE PART OF GENERAL BUSINESS CREDIT, ETC.—References to section 51 in section 38(b), 280C(a), and 1396(c)(3) shall be treated as including references to this section.

[Sec. 51A(e)]

(e) COORDINATION WITH WORK OPPORTUNITY CREDIT.—If a credit is allowed under this section to an employer with respect to an individual for any taxable year, then for purposes of applying section 51 to such employer, such individual shall not be treated as a member of a targeted group for such taxable year.

[Sec. 51A(f)]

(f) TERMINATION.—This section shall not apply to individuals who begin work for the employer after December 31, 2007.

Amendments

• 2006, Tax Relief and Health Care Act of 2006 (P.L. 109-432)

P.L. 109-432, Division A, §105(a):

Amended Code Sec. 51A(f) by striking "2005" and inserting "2007". **Effective** for individuals who begin work for the employer after 12-31-2005.

• 2004, Working Families Tax Relief Act of 2004 (P.L. 108-311)

P.L. 108-311, §303(a)(2):

Amended Code Sec. 51A(f) by striking "December 31, 2003" and inserting "December 31, 2005". **Effective** for individuals who begin work for the employer after 12-31-2003.

• 2002, Job Creation and Worker Assistance Act of 2002 (P.L. 107-147)

P.L. 107-147, §605(a):

Amended Code Sec. 51A(f) by striking "2001" and inserting "2003". **Effective** for individuals who began work for the employer after 12-31-2001.

• 1999, Tax Relief Extension Act of 1999 (P.L. 106-170)

P.L. 106-170, §505(a):

Amended Code Sec. 51A(f) by striking "June 30, 1999" and inserting "December 31, 2001". **Effective** for individuals who begin work for the employer after 6-30-99.

• 1998, Tax and Trade Relief Extension Act of 1998 (P.L. 105-277)

P.L. 105-277, §1003:

Amended Code Sec. 51A(f) by striking "April 30, 1999" and inserting "June 30, 1999". **Effective** 10-21-98.

• 1997, Taxpayer Relief Act of 1997 (P.L. 105-34)

P.L. 105-34, §801(a):

Amended subpart F of part IV of subchapter A of chapter 1 by inserting after Code Sec. 51 a new Code Sec. 51A. **Effective** for individuals who begin work for the employer after 12-31-97.

[Sec. 52]

SEC. 52. SPECIAL RULES.

[Sec. 52(a)]

(a) CONTROLLED GROUP OF CORPORATIONS.—For purposes of this subpart, all employees of all corporations which are members of the same controlled group of corporations shall be treated as employed by a single employer. In any such case, the credit (if any) determined under section 51(a) with respect to each such member shall be its proportionate share of the wages giving rise to such credit. For purposes of this subsection, the term "controlled group of corporations" has the meaning given to such term by section 1563(a), except that—

(1) "more than 50 percent" shall be substituted for "at least 80 percent" each place it appears in section 1563(a)(1), and

(2) the determination shall be made without regard to subsections (a)(4) and (e)(3)(C) of section 1563.

[Sec. 52(b)]

(b) EMPLOYEES OF PARTNERSHIPS, PROPRIETORSHIPS, ETC., WHICH ARE UNDER COMMON CONTROL.—For purposes of this subpart, under regulations prescribed by the Secretary—

(1) all employees of trades or business (whether or not incorporated) which are under common control shall be treated as employed by a single employer, and

(2) the credit (if any) determined under section 51(a) with respect to each trade or business shall be its proportionate share of the wages giving rise to such credit.

The regulations prescribed under this subsection shall be based on principles similar to the principles which apply in the case of subsection (a).

[Sec. 52(c)]

(c) TAX-EXEMPT ORGANIZATIONS.—No credit shall be allowed under section 38 for any work opportunity credit determined under this subpart to any organization (other than a cooperative described in section 521) which is exempt from income tax under this chapter.

Amendments

• 1997, Taxpayer Relief Act of 1997 (P.L. 105-34)

P.L. 105-34, §1601(b):

Amended Code Sec. 52(c) by striking "targeted jobs credit" and inserting "work opportunity credit". **Effective** as if included in the provision of P.L. 104-188 to which it relates [**effective** for individuals who begin to work for the employer after 9-30-96.—CCH].

[Sec. 52(d)]

(d) ESTATES AND TRUSTS.—In the case of an estate or trust—

(1) the amount of the credit determined under this subpart for any taxable year shall be apportioned between the estate or trust and the beneficiaries on the basis of the income of the estate or trust allocable to each, and

(2) any beneficiary to whom any amount has been apportioned under paragraph (1) shall be allowed, subject to section 38(c), a credit under section 38(a) for such amount.

[Sec. 52(e)]

(e) LIMITATIONS WITH RESPECT TO CERTAIN PERSONS.—Under regulations prescribed by the Secretary, in the case of—

(1) a regulated investment company or a real estate investment trust subject to taxation under subchapter M (section 851 and following), and

(2) a cooperative organization described in section 1381(a),

rules similar to the rules provided in subsections (e) and (h) of section 46 (as in effect on the day before the date of the enactment of the Revenue Reconciliation Act of 1990) shall apply in determining the amount of the credit under this subpart.

Amendments

• 1996, Small Business Job Protection Act of 1996 (P.L. 104-188)

P.L. 104-188, §1616(b)(2):

Amended Code Sec. 52(e) by striking paragraph (1) and redesignating paragraphs (2) and (3) as paragraphs (1) and (2), respectively. **Effective** for tax years beginning after 12-31-95. Prior to amendment, Code Sec. 52(e)(1) read as follows:

(1) an organization to which section 593 (relating to reserves for losses on loans) applies,

• 1990, Omnibus Budget Reconcilliation Act of 1990 (P.L. 101-508)

P.L. 101-508, §11813(b)(4):

Amended Code Sec. 52(e) by striking "section 46" and inserting "section 46 (as in effect on the day before the date of the enactment of the Revenue Reconciliation Act of 1990)". **Effective**, generally, for property placed in service after 12-31-90. However, for exceptions, see Act Sec. 11813(c)(2) below.

P.L. 101-508, §11813(c)(2), provides:

(2) EXCEPTIONS.—The amendments made by this section shall not apply to—

(A) any transition property (as defined in section 49(e) of the Internal Revenue Code of 1986) (as in effect on the day before the date of the enactment of this Act),

(B) any property with respect to which qualified progress expenditures were previously taken into account under section 46(d) of such Code (as so in effect), and

(C) any property described in section 46(b)(2)(C) of such Code (as so in effect).

• 1984, Deficit Reduction Act of 1984 (P.L. 98-369)

P.L. 98-369, §474(p)(4):

Amended Code Sec. 52(a) by striking out "the credit (if any) allowable by section 44B to each such member" and inserting in lieu thereof "the credit (if any) determined under section 51(a) with respect to each such member". **Effective** for tax years beginning after 12-31-83, and to carrybacks from such years.

P.L. 98-369, §474(p)(5):

Amended Code Sec. 52(b) by striking out "the credit (if any) allowable by section 44B" and inserting in lieu thereof "the credit (if any) determined under section 51(a)". **Effective** for tax years beginning after 12-31-83, and to carrybacks from such years.

P.L. 98-369, §474(p)(6):

Amended Code Sec. 52(c) by striking out "credit shall be allowed under section 44B" and inserting in lieu thereof "credit shall be allowed under section 38 for any targeted jobs credit determined under this subpart". **Effective** for tax years beginning after 12-31-83, and to carrybacks from such years.

P.L. 98-369, §474(p)(7):

Amended Code Sec. 52(d)(2) by striking out ", subject to section 53, a credit under section 44B" and inserting in lieu thereof ", subject to section 38(c), a credit under section 38(a)". **Effective** for tax years beginning after 12-31-83, and to carrybacks from such years.

• 1982, Subchapter S Revision Act of 1982 (P.L. 97-354)

P.L. 97-354, §5(a)(11):

Amended Code Sec. 52 by striking out subsection (d) and by redesignating subsections (e) and (f) as subsections (d) and (e), respectively. **Effective** for tax years beginning after 12-31-82. Prior to being stricken, Code Sec. 52(d) read as follows:

(d) SUBCHAPTER S CORPORATIONS.—In the case of an electing small business corporation (as defined in section 1371)—

(1) the amount of the credit determined under this subpart for any taxable year shall [be] apportioned pro rata among the persons who are shareholders of such corporation on the last day of such taxable year, and

(2) any person to whom an amount is apportioned under paragraph (1) shall be allowed, subject to section 53, a credit under section 44B for such amount.

• 1980, Technical Corrections Act of 1979 (P.L. 96-222)

P.L. 96-222, §103(a)(5):

Amended Code Sec. 52(f)(3) and 52(h) by striking out "section 46(e)" and inserting "subsections (e) and (h) of section 46". **Effective** for tax years ending after 10-31-78.

• 1978, Revenue Act of 1978 (P.L. 95-600)

P.L. 95-600, §321(c)(1), (d):

Amended Code Sec. 52. **Effective** for amounts paid or incurred after 12-31-78, in tax years ending after such date. [Note: for special rules concerning newly targeted groups and a transitional rule, see P.L. 95-600, Sec. 321(d), reflected in the amendment notes after Code Sec. 51.—CCH.] Prior to amendment, Code Sec. 52 read as follows:

SEC. 52. SPECIAL RULES.

(a) CONTROLLED GROUP OF CORPORATIONS.—For purposes of this subpart, all employees of all corporations which are members of the same controlled group of corporations shall be treated as employed by a single employer. In any such case, the credit (if any) allowable by section 44B to each such member shall be its proportionate contribution to the increase in unemployment insurance wages giving rise to such credit. For purposes of this subsection, the term "controlled group of corporations" has the meaning given to such term by section 1563(a), except that—

(1) "more than 50 percent" shall be substituted for "at least 80 percent" each place it appears in section 1563(a)(1), and

(2) the determination shall be made without regard to subsections (a)(4) and (e)(3)(C) of section 1563.

(b) EMPLOYEES OF PARTNERSHIPS, PROPRIETORSHIPS, ETC., WHICH ARE UNDER COMMON CONTROL.—For purposes of this subpart, under regulations prescribed by the Secretary—

(1) all employees of trades or business (whether or not incorporated) which are under common control shall be treated as employed by a single employer, and

(2) the credit (if any) allowable by section 44B with respect to each trade or business shall be its proportionate contribution to the increase in unemployment insurance wages giving rise to such credit.

The regulations prescribed under this subsection shall be based on principles similar to the principles which apply in the case of subsection (a).

(c) ADJUSTMENTS FOR CERTAIN ACQUISITIONS, ETC.—Under regulations prescribed by the Secretary—

(1) ACQUISITIONS.—If, after December 31, 1975, an employer acquires the major portion of a trade or business of another person (hereinafter in this paragraph referred to as the "predecessor") or the major portion of a separate unit of a trade or business of a predecessor, then, for purposes of applying this subpart for any calendar year ending after such acquisition, the amount of unemployment insurance wages deemed paid by the employer during periods before such acquisition shall be increased by so much of such wages paid by the predecessor with respect to the acquired

trade or business as is attributable to the portion of such trade or business acquired by the employer.

(2) DISPOSITIONS.—If, after December 31, 1975—

(A) an employer disposes of the major portion of any trade or business of the employer or the major portion of a separate unit of a trade or business of the employer in a transaction to which paragraph (1) applies, and

(B) the employer furnishes the acquiring person such information as is necessary for the application of paragraph (1),

then, for purposes of applying this subpart for any calendar year ending after such disposition, the amount of unemployment insurance wages deemed paid by the employer during periods before such disposition shall be decreased by so much of such wages as is attributable to such trade or business or separate unit.

(d) TAX-EXEMPT ORGANIZATIONS.—No credit shall be allowed under section 44B to any organization (other than a cooperative described in section 521) which is exempt from income tax under this chapter.

(e) CHANGE IN STATUS FROM SELF-EMPLOYED TO EMPLOYEE.—If—

(1) during 1976 or 1977 an individual has net earnings from self-employment (as defined in section 1402 (a)) which are attributable to a trade or business, and

(2) for any portion of the succeeding calendar year such individual is an employee of such trade or business,

then, for purposes of determining the credit allowable for a taxable year beginning in such succeeding calendar year, the employer's aggregate unemployment insurance wages for 1976 or 1977, as the case may be, shall be increased by an amount equal to so much of the net earnings referred to in paragraph (1) as does not exceed $4,200.

(f) SUBCHAPTER S CORPORATIONS.—In the case of an electing small business corporation (as defined in section 1371)—

(1) the amount of the credit determined under this subpart for any taxable year shall be apportioned pro rata among the persons who are shareholders of such corporation on the last day of such taxable year, and

(2) any person to whom an amount is apportioned under paragraph (1) shall be allowed, subject to section 53, a credit under section 44B for such amount.

(g) ESTATES AND TRUSTS.—In the case of an estate or trust—

(1) the amount of the credit determined under this subpart for any taxable year shall be apportioned between the estate or trust and the beneficiaries on the basis of the income of the estate or trust allocable to each,

(2) any beneficiary to whom any amount has been apportioned under paragraph (1) shall be allowed, subject to section 53, a credit under section 44B for such amount, and

(3) the $100,000 amount specified in section 51(d) applicable to such estate or trust shall be reduced to an amount which bears the same ratio to $100,000 as the portion of the credit allocable to the estate or trust under paragraph (1) bears to the entire amount of such credit.

(h) LIMITATIONS WITH RESPECT TO CERTAIN PERSONS.—Under regulations prescribed by the Secretary, in the case of—

(1) an organization to which section 593 (relating to reserves for losses on loans) applies,

(2) a regulated investment company or a real estate investment trust subject to taxation under subchapter M (section 851 and following), and

(3) a cooperative organization described in section 1381(a),

rules similar to the rules provided in subsections (e) and (h) of section 46 shall apply in determining the amount of the credit under this subpart.

(i) $50,000 LIMITATION IN THE CASE OF MARRIED INDIVIDUALS FILING SEPARATE RETURNS.—In the case of a husband or wife who files a separate return, the limitation under section 51(d) shall be $50,000 in lieu of $100,000. This subsection shall not apply if the spouse of the taxpayer has no interest in a trade or business for the taxable year of such spouse which ends within or with the taxpayer's taxable year.

(j) CERTAIN SHORT TAXABLE YEARS.—If the employer has more than one taxable year beginning in 1977 or 1978, the credit under this subpart shall be determined for the employer's last taxable year beginning in 1977 or 1978, as the case may be.

• 1977, Tax Reduction and Simplification Act of 1977 (P.L. 95-30)

P.L. 95-30, §202(b):

Added Code Sec. 52. **Effective** for tax years beginning after 12-31-76, and for credit carrybacks from such years.

Subpart G—Credit Against Regular Tax for Prior Year Minimum Tax Liability

[Sec. 53]

SEC. 53. CREDIT FOR PRIOR YEAR MINIMUM TAX LIABILITY.

[Sec. 53(a)]

(a) ALLOWANCE OF CREDIT.—There shall be allowed as a credit against the tax imposed by this chapter for any taxable year an amount equal to the minimum tax credit for such taxable year.

[Sec. 53(b)]

(b) MINIMUM TAX CREDIT.—For purposes of subsection (a), the minimum tax credit for any taxable year is the excess (if any) of—

(1) the adjusted net minimum tax imposed for all prior taxable years beginning after 1986, over

(2) the amount allowable as a credit under subsection (a) for such prior taxable years.

[Sec. 53(c)]

(c) LIMITATION.—The credit allowable under subsection (a) for any taxable year shall not exceed the excess (if any) of—

(1) The regular tax liability of the taxpayer for such taxable year reduced by the sum of the credits allowable under subparts A, B, D, E, and F of this part, over

(2) the tentative minimum tax for the taxable year.

[Sec. 53(d)]

(d) DEFINITIONS.—For purposes of this section—

(1) NET MINIMUM TAX.—

(A) IN GENERAL.—The term "net minimum tax" means the tax imposed by section 55.

(B) CREDIT NOT ALLOWED FOR EXCLUSION PREFERENCES.—

(i) ADJUSTED NET MINIMUM TAX.—The adjusted net minimum tax for any taxable year is—

(I) the amount of the net minimum tax for such taxable year, reduced by

(II) the amount which would be the net minimum tax for such taxable year if the only adjustments and items of tax preference taken into account were those specified in clause (ii).

(ii) SPECIFIED ITEMS.—The following are specified in this clause—

(I) the adjustments provided for in subsection (b)(1) of section 56, and

(II) the items of tax preference described in paragraphs (1), (5), and (7) of section 57(a).

(iii) CREDIT ALLOWABLE FOR EXCLUSION PREFERENCES OF CORPORATIONS.—In the case of a corporation—

(I) the preceding provisions of this subparagraph shall not apply, and

(II) the adjusted net minimum tax for any taxable year is the amount of the net minimum tax for such year.

(2) TENTATIVE MINIMUM TAX.—The term "tentative minimum tax" has the meaning given to such term by section 55(b).

Amendments

• 2009, American Recovery and Reinvestment Tax Act of 2009 (P.L. 111-5)

P.L. 111-5, §1142(b)(4)(A):

Amended Code Sec. 53(d)(1)(B) by striking clause (iii) and redesignating clause (iv) as clause (iii). **Effective** for vehicles acquired after 2-17-2009. For a transitional rule, see Act Sec. 1142(d) in the amendment notes for Code Sec. 30. Prior to being stricken, Code Sec. 53(d)(1)(B)(iii) read as follows:

(iii) SPECIAL RULE.—The adjusted net minimum tax for the taxable year shall be increased by the amount of the credit not allowed under section 30 solely by reason of the application of section 30(b)(3)(B).

P.L. 111-5, §1142(b)(4)(B):

Amended clause (II) of Code Sec. 53(d)(1)(B)(iii), as redesignated by Act Sec. 1142(b)(4)(A), by striking "increased in the manner provided in clause (iii)" after "such year". **Effective** for vehicles acquired after 2-17-2009. For a transitional rule, see Act Sec. 1142(d) in the amendment notes for Code Sec. 30.

• 2005, Energy Tax Incentives Act of 2005 (P.L. 109-58)

P.L. 109-58, §1322(a)(3)(G):

Amended Code Sec. 53(d)(1)(B)(iii) by striking "under section 29" and all that follows through "or not allowed". **Effective** for credits determined under the Internal Revenue Code of 1986 for tax years ending after 12-31-2005. Prior to amendment, Code Sec. 53(d)(1)(B)(iii) read as follows:

(iii) SPECIAL RULE.—The adjusted net minimum tax for the taxable year shall be increased by the amount of the credit not allowed under section 29 (relating to credit for producing fuel from a nonconventional source) solely by reason of the application of section 29(b)(6)(B) or not allowed under section 30 solely by reason of the application of section 30(b)(3)(B).

• 2004, American Jobs Creation Act of 2004 (P.L. 108-357)

P.L. 108-357, §421(a)(2):

Amended Code Sec. 53(d)(1)(B)(i)(II) by striking "and if section 59(a)(2) did not apply" before the period at the end. **Effective** for tax years beginning after 12-31-2004.

• 1996, Small Business Job Protection Act of 1996 (P.L. 104-188)

P.L. 104-188, §1205(d)(5)(A)-(B):

Amended Code Sec. 53(d)(1)(B) by striking "or not allowed under section 28 solely by reason of the application of section 28(d)(2)(B)," after "29(b)(6)(B)" in clause (iii), and by striking "or not allowed under section 28 solely by reason of the application of section 28(d)(2)(B)" before the period in clause (iv)(II) [as it read prior to the amendment by Act Sec. 1704(j)(1)]. **Effective** for amounts paid or incurred in tax years ending after 6-30-96. [Note: for the text of the law as amended by Act Sec. 1205(d)(5)(B), see the prior law for Code Sec. 53(d)(1)(B)(iv)(II) in the amendment note directly below.—CCH.].

P.L. 104-188, §1704(j)(1):

Amended Code Sec. 53(d)(1)(B)(iv)(II). **Effective** for tax years beginning after 12-31-90. Prior to amendment, Code Sec. 53(d)(1)(B)(iv)(II) read as follows:

(II) the adjusted net minimum tax for any taxable year is the amount of the net minimum tax for such year increased by the amount of any credit not allowed under section 29 solely by reason of the application of section 29(b)(5)(B).

• 1993, Omnibus Budget Reconcilliation Act of 1993 (P.L. 103-66)

P.L. 103-66, §13113(b)(2):

Amended Code Sec. 53(d)(1)(B)(ii)(II) by striking "and (6)" and inserting "(6), and (8)". **Effective** for stock issued after 8-10-93.

P.L. 103-66, §13171(c):

Amended Code Sec. 53(d)(1)(B)(ii)(II) (as amended by Act Sec. 13113(b)(2)) by striking "(5), (6), and (8)" and inserting "(5), and (7)". **Effective** for contributions made after 6-30-92, except that in the case of any contribution of capital gain property which is not tangible personal property, such amendments shall apply only if the contribution is made after 12-31-92.

• 1992, Energy Policy Act of 1992 (P.L. 102-486)

P.L. 102-486, §1913(b)(2)(C)(i):

Amended Code Sec. 53(d)(1)(B)(iii) by striking "section 29(b)(5)(B) or" and inserting "section 29(b)(6)(B),". **Effective** for tax years beginning after 12-31-90 (as amended by P.L. 104-188, §1702(e)(5)).

P.L. 102-486, §1913(b)(2)(C)(ii):

Amended Code Sec. 53(d)(1)(B)(iii) by inserting ", or not allowed under section 30 solely by reason of the application of section 30(b)(3)(B)" before the period. **Effective** for property placed in service after 6-30-93.

• 1989, Omnibus Budget Reconcilliation Act of 1989 (P.L. 101-239)

P.L. 101-239, §7612(a)(1):

Amended Code Sec. 53(d)(1)(B) by adding at the end thereof a new clause (iv). **Effective** for purposes of determining the adjusted net minimum tax for tax years beginning after 12-31-89.

P.L. 101-239, §7612(a)(2)(A)-(B):

Amended Code Sec. 53(d)(1)(B) by striking "subsections (b)(1) and (c)(3)" and inserting "subsection (b)(1)" after "provided for in" in clause (ii), and by striking the last sentence. **Effective** for purposes of determining the adjusted net minimum tax for tax years beginning after 12-31-89. Prior to amendment, the last sentence of Code Sec. 53(d)(1)(B) read as follows:

In the case of taxable years beginning after 1989, the adjustments provided in section 56(g) shall be treated as specified in this clause to the extent attributable to items which are excluded from gross income for any taxable year for purposes of the regular tax, or are not deductible for any taxable year under the adjusted current earnings method of section 56(g).

P.L. 101-239, §7612(b)(1):

Amended Code Sec. 53(d)(1)(B)(iii) and (iv) by inserting "or not allowed under section 28 solely by reason of the application of section 28(d)(2)(B)" after "section 29(d)(5)(B)". **Effective** for purposes of determining the amount of the minimum tax credit for tax years beginning after 12-31-89; except that, for such purposes, section 53(b)(1) of the Internal Revenue Code of 1986 shall be applied as if such amendment had been in effect for all prior tax years.

P.L. 101-239, §7811(d)(2):

Amended Code Sec. 53(d)(1)(B)(i)(II) by inserting "and if section 59(a)(2) did not apply" before the period at the end thereof. **Effective** as if included in the provision of P.L. 100-647 to which it relates.

• 1988, Technical and Miscellaneous Revenue Act of 1988 (P.L. 100-647)

P.L. 100-647, §1007(g)(4):

Amended Code Sec. 53(d)(1)(B) by striking out "earning and profits" in the last sentence and inserting in lieu thereof "current earnings". **Effective** as if included in the provision of P.L. 99-514 to which it relates.

P.L. 100-647, §6304(a):

Amended Code Sec. 53(d)(1)(B) by adding at the end thereof new clause (iii). **Effective** as if included in the amendments made by section 701 of P.L. 99-514.

• 1986, Tax Reform Act of 1986 (P.L. 99-514)

P.L. 99-514, §701(b):

Amended part IV of subchapter A of chapter 1 by adding at the end thereof new subpart G (Code Sec. 53). **Effective**, generally, for tax years beginning after 12-31-86. However, for exceptions, see Act Sec. 701(f)(2)-(7) following the amendment notes for Code Sec. 56.

• 1984, Deficit Reduction Act of 1984 (P.L. 98-369)

P.L. 98-369, §713(c)(1)(C):

Amended Code Sec. 53(a) by striking out "tax on premature distributions to owner-employees" and inserting in lieu thereof "tax on premature distributions to key employees". **Effective** as if included in the provision of P.L. 97-248 to which it relates.

P.L. 98-369, §474(p)(8):

Repealed Code Sec. 53. **Effective** for tax years beginning after 12-31-83, and to carrybacks from such years. Prior to repeal, but after the amendment to subsection (a) by Act Sec. 713(c)(1)(C), Code Sec. 53 read as follows:

SEC. 53. LIMITATION BASED ON AMOUNT OF TAX.

[Sec. 53(a)]

(a) GENERAL RULE.—Notwithstanding section 51, the amount of the credit allowed by section 44B for the taxable year shall not exceed 90 percent of the excess of the tax imposed by this chapter for the taxable year over the sum of the credits allowable under—

(1) section 33 (relating to foreign tax credit),

(2) section 37 (relating to credit for the elderly and the permanently and totally disabled),

(3) section 38 (relating to investment in certain depreciable property),

(4) section 40 (relating to expenses of work incentive programs),

(5) section 41 (relating to contributions to candidates for public office),

(6) section 42 (relating to general tax credit), and

(7) section 44A (relating to expenses for household and dependent care services necessary for gainful employment).

For purposes of this subsection, any tax imposed for the taxable year by section 56 (relating to corporate minimum tax), section 72(m)(5)(B) (relating to 10 percent tax on premature distributions to key employees), section 72(q)(1) (relating to 5-percent tax on premature distributions under annuity contracts), section 408(f) (relating to additional tax on income from certain retirement accounts), section 402(e) (relating to tax on lump-sum distributions), section 531 (relating to accumulated earnings tax), section 541 (relating to personal holding company tax), or section 1374 (relating to tax on certain capital gains of S corporations), and any additional tax imposed for the taxable year by section 1351(d)(1) (relating to recoveries of foreign expropriation losses), shall not be considered tax imposed by this chapter for such year.

Amendments

• 1983, Social Security Amendments of 1983 (P.L. 98-21)

P.L. 98-21, §122(c)(1):

Amended Code Sec. 53(a)(2) by striking out "relating to credit for the elderly" and inserting in place thereof "relating to credit for the elderly and the permanently and totally disabled". **Effective** for tax years beginning after 1983.

• 1983, Technical Corrections Act of 1982 (P.L. 97-448)

P.L. 97-448, §306(a)(1)(A):

Amended section 201 of P.L. 97-248 by redesignating the second subsection (c) as subsection (d).

• 1982, Subchapter S Revision Act of 1982 (P.L. 97-354)

P.L. 97-354, §5(a)(12):

Amended the second sentence of Code Sec. 53(a) by striking out "section 1378 (relating to tax on certain capital gains of subchapter S corporations)," and inserting in lieu thereof "section 1374 (relating to tax on certain capital gains of S corporations),". **Effective** for tax years beginning after 12-31-82.

• 1982, Tax Equity and Fiscal Responsibility Act of 1982 (P.L. 97-248)

P.L. 97-248, §201(d)(8)(A):

Amended Code Sec. 53(a) by striking out "(relating to minimum tax for tax preferences)" and inserting in lieu thereof "(relating to corporate minimum tax)". **Effective** for tax years beginning after 12-31-82.

P.L. 97-248, §265(b)(2)(A)(iii):

Amended Code Sec. 53(a) by inserting "section 72(q)(1) (relating to 5-percent tax on premature distributions under annuity contracts)," after "owner-employees)". **Effective** for distributions after 12-31-82.

• 1978, Revenue Act of 1978 (P.L. 95-600)

P.L. 95-600, §321(c)(2)(A), (d):

Amended Code Sec. 53(a) by striking out "the amount of the tax imposed by this chapter for the taxable year, reduced by" and inserting in place thereof "90 percent of the excess of the tax imposed by this chapter for the taxable year over the sum of". **Effective** for tax years beginning after 12-31-78. Prior to amendment, Code Sec. 53(a) read:

(a) GENERAL RULE.—Notwithstanding section 51, the amount of the credit allowed by section 44B for the taxable year shall not exceed the amount of the tax imposed by this chapter for the taxable year, reduced by the sum of the credits allowable under—

(1) section 33 (relating to foreign tax credit),

(2) section 37 (relating to credit for the elderly),

(3) section 38 (relating to investment in certain depreciable property),

(4) section 40 (relating to expenses of work incentive programs),

(5) section 41 (relating to contributions to candidates for public office),

(6) section 42 (relating to general tax credit), and

(7) section 44A (relating to expenses for household and dependent care services necessary for gainful employment).

For purposes of this subsection, any tax imposed for the taxable year by section 56 (relating to minimum tax for tax preferences), section 72(m)(5)(B) (relating to 10 percent tax on premature distributions to owneremployees), section 408(f) (relating to additional tax on income from certain retirement accounts), section 402(e) (relating to tax on lump-sum distributions), section 531 (relating to accumulated earnings tax), section 541 (relating to personal holding company tax), or section 1378 (relating to tax on certain capital gains of subchapter S corporations), and any additional tax imposed for the taxable year by section 1351(d)(1) (relating to recoveries of foreign expropriation losses), shall not be considered tax imposed by this chapter for such year.

• 1977, Tax Reduction and Simplification Act of 1977 (P.L. 95-30)

P.L. 95-30, §202(b):

Added Code Sec. 53(a). **Effective** for tax years beginning after 12-31-76, and for credit carrybacks from such years.

[Sec. 53(b)]

Amendments

• 1978, Revenue Act of 1978 (P.L. 95-600)

P.L. 95-600, §321(c)(2)(B), (d):

Repealed Code Sec. 53(b). **Effective** for tax years beginning after 12-31-78. Prior to repeal, Code Sec. 53(b) read as follows:

(b) SPECIAL RULE FOR PASS-THRU OF CREDIT.—In the case of a partner in a partnership, a beneficiary of an estate or trust, and a shareholder in a subchapter S corporation, the limitation provided by subsection (a) for the taxable year shall not exceed a limitation separately computed with respect to such person's interest in such entity by taking an amount which bears the same relationship to such limitation as—

(1) that portion of the person's taxable income which is allocable or apportionable to the person's interest in such entity, bears to

(2) the person's taxable income for such year reduced by his zero bracket amount (determined under section 63(d)), if any.

• 1977, Tax Reduction and Simplification Act of 1977 (P.L. 95-30)

P.L. 95-30, §202(b):

Added Code Sec. 53(b). **Effective** for tax years beginning after 12-31-76, and for credit carrybacks from such years.

[Sec. 53(b)—Repealed]

(b) CARRYBACK AND CARRYOVER OF UNUSED CREDIT.—

(1) ALLOWANCE OF CREDIT.—If the amount of the credit determined under section 51 for any taxable year exceeds the limitation provided by subsection (a) for such taxable year (hereinafter in this subsection referred to as the "unused credit year"), such excess shall be—

(A) a new employee credit carryback to each of the 3 taxable years preceding the unused credit year, and

(B) a new employee credit carryover to each of the 15 taxable years following the unused credit year,

and shall be added to the amount allowable as a credit by section 44B for such years. If any portion of such excess is a carryback to a taxable year beginning before January 1, 1977, section 44B shall be deemed to have been in effect for such taxable year for purposes of allowing such carryback as a credit under such section. The entire amount of the unused credit for an unused credit year shall be carried to the earliest of the 18 taxable years to which (by reason of subparagraphs (A) and (B)) such credit may be carried, and then to each of the other 17 taxable years to the extent that, because of the limitation contained in paragraph (2), such unused credit may not be added for a prior taxable year to which such unused credit may be carried.

(2) LIMITATION.—The amount of the unused credit which may be added under paragraph (1) for any preceding or succeeding taxable year shall not exceed the amount by which the limitation provided by subsection (a) for such taxable year exceeds the sum of—

(A) the credit allowable under section 44B for such taxable year, and

(B) the amounts which, by reason of this subsection, are added to the amount allowable for such taxable year and which are attributable to taxable years preceding the unused credit year.

Amendments

• 1983, Technical Corrections Act of 1982 (P.L. 97-448)

P.L. 97-448, §102(d)(2):

Added subsection (c)(3) to section 209 of P.L. 97-34 to read as under the amendment note for P.L. 97-34, §207(c)(2).

P.L. 97-448, §102(d)(3):

Amended paragraph (2) of section 207(c) of the Economic Recovery Tax Act of 1981, P.L. 97-34 (relating to new employee credit) by striking out "section 53(c)" and inserting in lieu thereof "section 53(b)".

• 1981, Economic Recovery Tax Act of 1981 (P.L. 97-34)

P.L. 97-34, §207(c)(2):

Amended Code Sec. 53(b)(1) by striking out "7" in subparagraph (B) and inserting in lieu thereof "15"; by striking out "10" and inserting in lieu thereof "18"; and by striking out "9" and inserting in lieu thereof "17". **Effective** for unused credit years beginning after 12-31-76.

(3) Carryover must have been alive in 1981.—The amendments made by subsections (a), (b), and (c) of section 207 shall not apply to any amount which, under the law in effect on the day before the date of the enactment of this Act, could not be carried to a taxable year ending in 1981.

• 1978, Revenue Act of 1978 (P.L. 95-600)

P.L. 95-600, §321(c)(2)(B), (d):

Redesignated Code Sec. 53(c) as subsection (b). **Effective** for tax years beginning after 12-31-78.

• 1977, Tax Reduction and Simplification Act of 1977 (P.L. 95-30)

P.L. 95-30, §202(b):

Added Code Sec. 53. **Effective** for tax years beginning after 12-31-76, and for credit carrybacks from such years.

[Sec. 53(e)]

(e) SPECIAL RULE FOR INDIVIDUALS WITH LONG-TERM UNUSED CREDITS.—

(1) IN GENERAL.—If an individual has a long-term unused minimum tax credit for any taxable year beginning before January 1, 2013, the amount determined under subsection (c) for such taxable year shall not be less than the AMT refundable credit amount for such taxable year.

(2) AMT REFUNDABLE CREDIT AMOUNT.—For purposes of paragraph (1), the term "AMT refundable credit amount" means, with respect to any taxable year, the amount (not in excess of the long-term unused minimum tax credit for such taxable year) equal to the greater of—

(A) 50 percent of the long-term unused minimum tax credit for such taxable year, or

(B) the amount (if any) of the AMT refundable credit amount determined under this paragraph for the taxpayer's preceding taxable year (determined without regard to subsection (f)(2)).

(3) LONG-TERM UNUSED MINIMUM TAX CREDIT.—

(A) IN GENERAL.—For purposes of this subsection, the term "long-term unused minimum tax credit" means, with respect to any taxable year, the portion of the minimum tax credit determined under subsection (b) attributable to the adjusted net minimum tax for taxable years before the 3rd taxable year immediately preceding such taxable year.

(B) FIRST-IN, FIRST-OUT ORDERING RULE.—For purposes of subparagraph (A), credits shall be treated as allowed under subsection (a) on a first-in, first-out basis.

(4) CREDIT REFUNDABLE.—For purposes of this title (other than this section), the credit allowed by reason of this subsection shall be treated as if it were allowed under subpart C.

Amendments

• 2008, Tax Extenders and Alternative Minimum Tax Relief Act of 2008 (P.L. 110-343)

P.L. 110-343, Division C, §103(a):

Amended Code Sec. 53(e)(2). **Effective** for tax years beginning after 12-31-2007. Prior to amendment, Code Sec. 53(e)(2) read as follows:

(2) AMT REFUNDABLE CREDIT AMOUNT.—For purposes of paragraph (1)—

(A) IN GENERAL.—The term "AMT refundable credit amount" means, with respect to any taxable year, the amount (not in excess of the long-term unused minimum tax credit for such taxable year) equal to the greater of—

(i) $5,000,

(ii) 20 percent of the long-term unused minimum tax credit for such taxable year, or

(iii) the amount (if any) of the AMT refundable credit amount determined under this paragraph for the taxpayer's preceding taxable year (as determined before any reduction under subparagraph (B)).

(B) PHASEOUT OF AMT REFUNDABLE CREDIT AMOUNT.—

(i) IN GENERAL.—In the case of an individual whose adjusted gross income for any taxable year exceeds the threshold amount (within the meaning of section 151(d)(3)(C)), the AMT refundable credit amount determined under subparagraph (A) for such taxable year shall be reduced by the applicable percentage (within the meaning of section 151(d)(3)(B)).

(ii) ADJUSTED GROSS INCOME.—For purposes of clause (i), adjusted gross income shall be determined without regard to sections 911, 931, and 933.

• 2007, Tax Technical Corrections Act of 2007 (P.L. 110-172)

P.L. 110-172, §2(a):

Amended Code Sec. 53(e)(2)(A). **Effective** as if included in the provision of the Tax Relief and Health Care Act of 2006 (P.L. 109-432) to which it relates [**effective** for tax years beginning after 12-20-2006.—CCH]. Prior to amendment, Code Sec. 53(e)(2)(A) read as follows:

(A) IN GENERAL.—The term "AMT refundable credit amount" means, with respect to any taxable year, the amount equal to the greater of—

(i) the lesser of—

(I) $5,000, or

(II) the amount of long-term unused minimum tax credit for such taxable year, or

(ii) 20 percent of the amount of such credit.

• 2006, Tax Relief and Health Care Act of 2006 (P.L. 109-432)

P.L. 109-432, Division A, §402(a):

Amended Code Sec. 53 by adding at the end a new subsection (e). **Effective** for tax years beginning after 12-20-2006.

[Sec. 53(f)]

(f) TREATMENT OF CERTAIN UNDERPAYMENTS, INTEREST, AND PENALTIES ATTRIBUTABLE TO THE TREATMENT OF INCENTIVE STOCK OPTIONS.—

(1) ABATEMENT.—Any underpayment of tax outstanding on the date of the enactment of this subsection which is attributable to the application of section 56(b)(3) for any taxable year ending before January 1, 2008, and any interest or penalty with respect to such underpayment which is outstanding on such date of enactment, is hereby abated. The amount determined under subsection (b)(1) shall not include any tax abated under the preceding sentence.

(2) INCREASE IN CREDIT FOR CERTAIN INTEREST AND PENALTIES ALREADY PAID.—The AMT refundable credit amount, and the minimum tax credit determined under subsection (b), for the taxpayer's first 2 taxable years beginning after December 31, 2007, shall each be increased by 50 percent of the aggregate amount of the interest and penalties which were paid by the taxpayer before the date of the enactment of this subsection and which would (but for such payment) have been abated under paragraph (1).

Amendments

• 2008, Tax Extenders and Alternative Minimum Tax Relief Act of 2008 (P.L. 110-343)

P.L. 110-343, Division C, §103(b):

Amended Code Sec. 53 by adding at the end a new subsection (f). **Effective** 10-3-2008.

Subpart H—Nonrefundable Credit to Holders of Certain Bonds

[Sec. 54]

SEC. 54. CREDIT TO HOLDERS OF CLEAN RENEWABLE ENERGY BONDS.

[Sec. 54(a)]

(a) ALLOWANCE OF CREDIT.—If a taxpayer holds a clean renewable energy bond on one or more credit allowance dates of the bond occurring during any taxable year, there shall be allowed as a credit against the tax imposed by this chapter for the taxable year an amount equal to the sum of the credits determined under subsection (b) with respect to such dates.

[Sec. 54(b)]

(b) AMOUNT OF CREDIT.—

(1) IN GENERAL.—The amount of the credit determined under this subsection with respect to any credit allowance date for a clean renewable energy bond is 25 percent of the annual credit determined with respect to such bond.

(2) ANNUAL CREDIT.—The annual credit determined with respect to any clean renewable energy bond is the product of—

(A) the credit rate determined by the Secretary under paragraph (3) for the day on which such bond was sold, multiplied by

(B) the outstanding face amount of the bond.

(3) DETERMINATION.—For purposes of paragraph (2), with respect to any clean renewable energy bond, the Secretary shall determine daily or cause to be determined daily a credit rate which shall apply to the first day on which there is a binding, written contract for the sale or exchange of the bond. The credit rate for any day is the credit rate which the Secretary or the Secretary's designee estimates will permit the issuance of clean renewable energy bonds with a specified maturity or redemption date without discount and without interest cost to the qualified issuer.

(4) CREDIT ALLOWANCE DATE.—For purposes of this section, the term "credit allowance date" means—

(A) March 15,

(B) June 15,

(C) September 15, and

(D) December 15.

Such term also includes the last day on which the bond is outstanding.

(5) SPECIAL RULE FOR ISSUANCE AND REDEMPTION.—In the case of a bond which is issued during the 3-month period ending on a credit allowance date, the amount of the credit determined under this subsection with respect to such credit allowance date shall be a ratable portion of the credit otherwise determined based on the portion of the 3-month period during which the bond is outstanding. A similar rule shall apply when the bond is redeemed or matures.

[Sec. 54(c)]

(c) LIMITATION BASED ON AMOUNT OF TAX.—The credit allowed under subsection (a) for any taxable year shall not exceed the excess of—

(1) the sum of the regular tax liability (as defined in section 26(b)) plus the tax imposed by section 55, over

(2) the sum of the credits allowable under this part (other than subparts C, I, and J, section 1400N(l), and this section).

Amendments

• 2009, American Recovery and Reinvestment Tax Act of 2009 (P.L. 111-5)

P.L. 111-5, §1531(c)(3):

Amended Code Sec. 54(c)(2) by striking "and I" and inserting ", I, and J". **Effective** for obligations issued after 2-17-2009.

• 2008, Heartland, Habitat, Harvest, and Horticulture Act of 2008 (P.L. 110-246)

P.L. 110-246, §15316(c)(1):

Amended Code Sec. 54(c)(2) by striking "subpart C" and inserting "subparts C and I". **Effective** for obligations issued after 5-22-2008.

• 2005, Gulf Opportunity Zone Act of 2005 (P.L. 109-135)

P.L. 109-135, §101(b)(1):

Amended Code Sec. 54(c)(2) by inserting ", section 1400N(l)," after "subpart C". **Effective** for tax years ending on or after 8-28-2005.

[Sec. 54(d)]

(d) CLEAN RENEWABLE ENERGY BOND.—For purposes of this section—

(1) IN GENERAL.—The term "clean renewable energy bond" means any bond issued as part of an issue if—

(A) the bond is issued by a qualified issuer pursuant to an allocation by the Secretary to such issuer of a portion of the national clean renewable energy bond limitation under subsection (f)(2),

(B) 95 percent or more of the proceeds of such issue are to be used for capital expenditures incurred by qualified borrowers for one or more qualified projects,

(C) the qualified issuer designates such bond for purposes of this section and the bond is in registered form, and

(D) the issue meets the requirements of subsection (h).

(2) QUALIFIED PROJECT; SPECIAL USE RULES.—

(A) IN GENERAL.—The term "qualified project" means any qualified facility (as determined under section 45(d) without regard to paragraph (10) and to any placed in service date) owned by a qualified borrower.

(B) REFINANCING RULES.—For purposes of paragraph (1)(B), a qualified project may be refinanced with proceeds of a clean renewable energy bond only if the indebtedness being refinanced (including any obligation directly or indirectly refinanced by such indebtedness) was originally incurred by a qualified borrower after the date of the enactment of this section.

(C) REIMBURSEMENT.—For purposes of paragraph (1)(B), a clean renewable energy bond may be issued to reimburse a qualified borrower for amounts paid after the date of the enactment of this section with respect to a qualified project, but only if—

(i) prior to the payment of the original expenditure, the qualified borrower declared its intent to reimburse such expenditure with the proceeds of a clean renewable energy bond,

(ii) not later than 60 days after payment of the original expenditure, the qualified issuer adopts an official intent to reimburse the original expenditure with such proceeds, and

(iii) the reimbursement is made not later than 18 months after the date the original expenditure is paid.

(D) TREATMENT OF CHANGES IN USE.—For purposes of paragraph (1)(B), the proceeds of an issue shall not be treated as used for a qualified project to the extent that a qualified borrower or qualified issuer takes any action within its control which causes such proceeds not to be used for a qualified project. The Secretary shall prescribe regulations specifying remedial actions that may be taken (including conditions to taking such remedial actions) to prevent an action described in the preceding sentence from causing a bond to fail to be a clean renewable energy bond.

[Sec. 54(e)]

(e) MATURITY LIMITATIONS.—

(1) DURATION OF TERM.—A bond shall not be treated as a clean renewable energy bond if the maturity of such bond exceeds the maximum term determined by the Secretary under paragraph (2) with respect to such bond.

(2) MAXIMUM TERM.—During each calendar month, the Secretary shall determine the maximum term permitted under this paragraph for bonds issued during the following calendar month. Such maximum term shall be the term which the Secretary estimates will result in the present value of the obligation to repay the principal on the bond being equal to 50 percent of the face amount of such bond. Such present value shall be determined without regard to the requirements of subsection (l)(6) and using as a discount rate the average annual interest rate of tax-exempt obligations having a term of 10 years or more which are issued during the month. If the term as so determined is not a multiple of a whole year, such term shall be rounded to the next highest whole year.

[Sec. 54(f)]

(f) LIMITATION ON AMOUNT OF BONDS DESIGNATED.—

(1) NATIONAL LIMITATION.—There is a national clean renewable energy bond limitation of $1,200,000,000.

(2) ALLOCATION BY SECRETARY.—The Secretary shall allocate the amount described in paragraph (1) among qualified projects in such manner as the Secretary determines appropriate, except that the Secretary may not allocate more than $750,000,000 of the national clean renewable energy bond limitation to finance qualified projects of qualified borrowers which are governmental bodies.

Amendments

• 2006, Tax Relief and Health Care Act of 2006 (P.L. 109-432)

P.L. 109-432, Division A, §202(a)(1):

Amended Code Sec. 54(f)(1) by striking "$800,000,000" and inserting "$1,200,000,000". **Effective** for bonds issued after 12-31-2006.

P.L. 109-432, Division A, §202(a)(2):

Amended Code Sec. 54(f)(2) by striking "$500,000,000" and inserting "$750,000,000". **Effective** for allocations or reallocations after 12-31-2006.

[Sec. 54(g)]

(g) CREDIT INCLUDED IN GROSS INCOME.—Gross income includes the amount of the credit allowed to the taxpayer under this section (determined without regard to subsection (c)) and the amount so included shall be treated as interest income.

[Sec. 54(h)]

(h) SPECIAL RULES RELATING TO EXPENDITURES.—

(1) IN GENERAL.—An issue shall be treated as meeting the requirements of this subsection if, as of the date of issuance, the qualified issuer reasonably expects—

(A) at least 95 percent of the proceeds of such issue are to be spent for one or more qualified projects within the 5-year period beginning on the date of issuance of the clean energy bond,

(B) a binding commitment with a third party to spend at least 10 percent of the proceeds of such issue will be incurred within the 6-month period beginning on the date of issuance of the clean energy bond or, in the case of a clean energy bond the proceeds of which are to be loaned to two or more qualified borrowers, such binding commitment will be incurred within the 6-month period beginning on the date of the loan of such proceeds to a qualified borrower, and

(C) such projects will be completed with due diligence and the proceeds of such issue will be spent with due diligence.

(2) EXTENSION OF PERIOD.—Upon submission of a request prior to the expiration of the period described in paragraph (1)(A), the Secretary may extend such period if the qualified issuer establishes that the failure to satisfy the 5-year requirement is due to reasonable cause and the related projects will continue to proceed with due diligence.

(3) FAILURE TO SPEND REQUIRED AMOUNT OF BOND PROCEEDS WITHIN 5 YEARS.—To the extent that less than 95 percent of the proceeds of such issue are expended by the close of the 5-year period beginning on the date of issuance (or if an extension has been obtained under paragraph (2), by the close of the extended period), the qualified issuer shall redeem all of the nonqualified bonds within 90 days after the end of such period. For purposes of this paragraph, the amount of the nonqualified bonds required to be redeemed shall be determined in the same manner as under section 142.

[Sec. 54(i)]

(i) SPECIAL RULES RELATING TO ARBITRAGE.—A bond which is part of an issue shall not be treated as a clean renewable energy bond unless, with respect to the issue of which the bond is a part, the qualified issuer satisfies the arbitrage requirements of section 148 with respect to proceeds of the issue.

[Sec. 54(j)]

(j) COOPERATIVE ELECTRIC COMPANY; QUALIFIED ENERGY TAX CREDIT BOND LENDER; GOVERNMENTAL BODY; QUALIFIED BORROWER.—For purposes of this section—

(1) COOPERATIVE ELECTRIC COMPANY.—The term "cooperative electric company" means a mutual or cooperative electric company described in section 501(c)(12) or section 1381(a)(2)(C), or a not-for-profit electric utility which has received a loan or loan guarantee under the Rural Electrification Act.

(2) CLEAN RENEWABLE ENERGY BOND LENDER.—The term "clean renewable energy bond lender" means a lender which is a cooperative which is owned by, or has outstanding loans to, 100 or more cooperative electric companies and is in existence on February 1, 2002, and shall include any affiliated entity which is controlled by such lender.

(3) GOVERNMENTAL BODY.—The term "governmental body" means any State, territory, possession of the United States, the District of Columbia, Indian tribal government, and any political subdivision thereof.

(4) QUALIFIED ISSUER.—The term "qualified issuer" means—

(A) a clean renewable energy bond lender,

(B) a cooperative electric company, or

(C) a governmental body.

(5) QUALIFIED BORROWER.—The term "qualified borrower" means—

(A) a mutual or cooperative electric company described in section 501(c)(12) or 1381(a)(2)(C), or

(B) a governmental body.

[Sec. 54(k)]

(k) SPECIAL RULES RELATING TO POOL BONDS.—No portion of a pooled financing bond may be allocable to any loan unless the borrower has entered into a written loan commitment for such portion prior to the issue date of such issue.

[Sec. 54(l)]

(l) OTHER DEFINITIONS AND SPECIAL RULES.—For purposes of this section—

(1) BOND.—The term "bond" includes any obligation.

(2) POOLED FINANCING BOND.—The term "pooled financing bond" shall have the meaning given such term by section 149(f)(6)(A).

(3) PARTNERSHIP; S CORPORATION; AND OTHER PASS-THRU ENTITIES.—

(A) IN GENERAL.—Under regulations prescribed by the Secretary, in the case of a partnership, trust, S corporation, or other pass-thru entity, rules similar to the rules of section 41(g) shall apply with respect to the credit allowable under subsection (a).

(B) NO BASIS ADJUSTMENT.—In the case of a bond held by a partnership or an S corporation, rules similar to the rules under section 1397E(l) shall apply.

(4) RATABLE PRINCIPAL AMORTIZATION REQUIRED.—A bond shall not be treated as a clean renewable energy bond unless it is part of an issue which provides for an equal amount of principal to be paid by the qualified issuer during each calendar year that the issue is outstanding.

(5) REPORTING.—Issuers of clean renewable energy bonds shall submit reports similar to the reports required under section 149(e).

Amendments

• 2009, American Recovery and Reinvestment Tax Act of 2009 (P.L. 111-5)

P.L. 111-5, §1541(b)(1):

Amended Code Sec. 54(l) by striking paragraph (4) and by redesignating paragraphs (5) and (6) as paragraphs (4) and (5), respectively. **Effective** for tax years ending after 2-17-2009. Prior to being stricken, Code Sec. 54(l)(4) read as follows:

(4) BONDS HELD BY REGULATED INVESTMENT COMPANIES.—If any clean renewable energy bond is held by a regulated investment company, the credit determined under subsection (a) shall be allowed to shareholders of such company under procedures prescribed by the Secretary.

• 2006, Tax Relief and Health Care Act of 2006 (P.L. 109-432)

P.L. 109-432, Division A, §107(b)(2):

Amended Code Sec. 54(l)(3)(B) by striking "section 1397E(i)" and inserting "section 1397E(l)". **Effective** for obligations issued after 12-20-2006 pursuant to allocations of the national zone academy bond limitation for calendar years after 2005.

• 2006, Tax Increase Prevention and Reconciliation Act of 2005 (P.L. 109-222)

P.L. 109-222, §508(d)(3):

Amended Code Sec. 54(l)(2) by striking "section 149(f)(4)(A)" and inserting "section 149(f)(6)(A)". **Effective** for bonds issued after 5-17-2006.

• 2005, Gulf Opportunity Zone Act of 2005 (P.L. 109-135)

P.L. 109-135, §402(c)(1):

Amended Code Sec. 54(l) by striking paragraph (5), and by redesignating paragraphs (6) and (7) as paragraphs (5) and (6), respectively. **Effective** as if included in the provision of the Energy Policy Act of 2005 (P.L. 109-58) to which it relates [**effective** for bonds issued after 12-31-2005.—CCH]. Prior to being stricken, Code Sec. 54(l)(5) read as follows:

(5) TREATMENT FOR ESTIMATED TAX PURPOSES.—Solely for purposes of sections 6654 and 6655, the credit allowed by this section (determined without regard to subsection (c)) to a taxpayer by reason of holding a clean renewable energy bond on a credit allowance date shall be treated as if it were a payment of estimated tax made by the taxpayer on such date.

[Sec. 54(m)]

(m) TERMINATION.—This section shall not apply with respect to any bond issued after December 31, 2009.

Amendments

• 2008, Energy Improvement and Extension Act of 2008 (P.L. 110-343)

P.L. 110-343, Division B, §107(c):

Amended Code Sec. 54(m) by striking "December 31, 2008" and inserting "December 31, 2009". **Effective** for obligations issued after 10-3-2008.

• 2006, Tax Relief and Health Care Act of 2006 (P.L. 109-432)

P.L. 109-432, Division A, §202(a)(3):

Amended Code Sec. 54(m) by striking "December 31, 2007" and inserting "December 31, 2008". **Effective** for bonds issued after 12-31-2006.

• 2005, Energy Tax Incentives Act of 2005 (P.L. 109-58)

P.L. 109-58, §1303(a):

Amended part IV of subchapter A of chapter 1 by adding at the end a new subpart H (Code Sec. 54). **Effective** for bonds issued after 12-31-2005.

P.L. 109-58, §1303(d), provides:

(d) ISSUANCE OF REGULATIONS.—The Secretary of Treasury shall issue regulations required under section 54 of the Internal Revenue Code of 1986 (as added by this section) not later than 120 days after the date of the enactment of this Act.

Subpart I—Qualified Tax Credit Bonds

[Sec. 54A]

SEC. 54A. CREDIT TO HOLDERS OF QUALIFIED TAX CREDIT BONDS.

[Sec. 54A(a)]

(a) ALLOWANCE OF CREDIT.—If a taxpayer holds a qualified tax credit bond on one or more credit allowance dates of the bond during any taxable year, there shall be allowed as a credit against the tax imposed by this chapter for the taxable year an amount equal to the sum of the credits determined under subsection (b) with respect to such dates.

[Sec. 54A(b)]

(b) AMOUNT OF CREDIT.—

(1) IN GENERAL.—The amount of the credit determined under this subsection with respect to any credit allowance date for a qualified tax credit bond is 25 percent of the annual credit determined with respect to such bond.

(2) ANNUAL CREDIT.—The annual credit determined with respect to any qualified tax credit bond is the product of—

(A) the applicable credit rate, multiplied by

(B) the outstanding face amount of the bond.

(3) APPLICABLE CREDIT RATE.—For purposes of paragraph (2), the applicable credit rate is the rate which the Secretary estimates will permit the issuance of qualified tax credit bonds with a specified maturity or redemption date without discount and without interest cost to the qualified issuer. The applicable credit rate with respect to any qualified tax credit bond shall be determined as of the first day on which there is a binding, written contract for the sale or exchange of the bond.

(4) SPECIAL RULE FOR ISSUANCE AND REDEMPTION.—In the case of a bond which is issued during the 3-month period ending on a credit allowance date, the amount of the credit determined under this subsection with respect to such credit allowance date shall be a ratable portion of the credit otherwise determined based on the portion of the 3-month period during which the bond is outstanding. A similar rule shall apply when the bond is redeemed or matures.

[Sec. 54A(c)]

(c) LIMITATION BASED ON AMOUNT OF TAX.—

(1) IN GENERAL.—The credit allowed under subsection (a) for any taxable year shall not exceed the excess of—

(A) the sum of the regular tax liability (as defined in section 26(b)) plus the tax imposed by section 55, over

(B) the sum of the credits allowable under this part (other than subparts C and J and this subpart).

(2) CARRYOVER OF UNUSED CREDIT.—If the credit allowable under subsection (a) exceeds the limitation imposed by paragraph (1) for such taxable year, such excess shall be carried to the succeeding taxable year and added to the credit allowable under subsection (a) for such taxable year (determined before the application of paragraph (1) for such succeeding taxable year).

Amendments

• 2009, American Recovery and Reinvestment Tax Act of 2009 (P.L. 111-5)

P.L. 111-5, §1531(c)(2):

Amended Code Sec. 54A(c)(1)(B) by striking "subpart C" and inserting "subparts C and J". **Effective** for obligations issued after 2-17-2009.

[Sec. 54A(d)]

(d) QUALIFIED TAX CREDIT BOND.—For purposes of this section—

(1) QUALIFIED TAX CREDIT BOND.—The term "qualified tax credit bond" means—

(A) a qualified forestry conservation bond,

(B) a new clean renewable energy bond,

(C) a qualified energy conservation bond,

(D) a qualified zone academy bond, or

(E) a qualified school construction bond,

which is part of an issue that meets requirements of paragraphs (2), (3), (4), (5), and (6).

(2) SPECIAL RULES RELATING TO EXPENDITURES.—

(A) IN GENERAL.—An issue shall be treated as meeting the requirements of this paragraph if, as of the date of issuance, the issuer reasonably expects—

(i) 100 percent or more of the available project proceeds to be spent for 1 or more qualified purposes within the 3-year period beginning on such date of issuance, and

(ii) a binding commitment with a third party to spend at least 10 percent of such available project proceeds will be incurred within the 6-month period beginning on such date of issuance.

(B) FAILURE TO SPEND REQUIRED AMOUNT OF BOND PROCEEDS WITHIN 3 YEARS.—

(i) IN GENERAL.—To the extent that less than 100 percent of the available project proceeds of the issue are expended by the close of the expenditure period for 1 or more qualified purposes, the issuer shall redeem all of the nonqualified bonds within 90 days after the end of such period. For purposes of this paragraph, the amount of the nonqualified bonds required to be redeemed shall be determined in the same manner as under section 142.

(ii) EXPENDITURE PERIOD.—For purposes of this subpart, the term "expenditure period" means, with respect to any issue, the 3-year period beginning on the date of issuance. Such term shall include any extension of such period under clause (iii).

(iii) EXTENSION OF PERIOD.—Upon submission of a request prior to the expiration of the expenditure period (determined without regard to any extension under this clause), the Secretary may extend such period if the issuer establishes that the failure to expend the proceeds within the original expenditure period is due to reasonable cause and the expenditures for qualified purposes will continue to proceed with due diligence.

(C) QUALIFIED PURPOSE.—For purposes of this paragraph, the term "qualified purpose" means—

(i) in the case of a qualified forestry conservation bond, a purpose specified in section 54B(e),

(ii) in the case of a new clean renewable energy bond, a purpose specified in section 54C(a)(1),

(iii) in the case of a qualified energy conservation bond, a purpose specified in section 54D(a)(1),

(iv) in the case of a qualified zone academy bond, a purpose specified in section 54E(a)(1), and

(v) in the case of a qualified school construction bond, a purpose specified in section 54F(a)(1).

(D) REIMBURSEMENT.—For purposes of this subtitle, available project proceeds of an issue shall be treated as spent for a qualified purpose if such proceeds are used to reimburse the issuer for amounts paid for a qualified purpose after the date that the Secretary makes an allocation of bond limitation with respect to such issue, but only if—

(i) prior to the payment of the original expenditure, the issuer declared its intent to reimburse such expenditure with the proceeds of a qualified tax credit bond,

(ii) not later than 60 days after payment of the original expenditure, the issuer adopts an official intent to reimburse the original expenditure with such proceeds, and

(iii) the reimbursement is made not later than 18 months after the date the original expenditure is paid.

(3) REPORTING.—An issue shall be treated as meeting the requirements of this paragraph if the issuer of qualified tax credit bonds submits reports similar to the reports required under section 149(e).

(4) SPECIAL RULES RELATING TO ARBITRAGE.—

(A) IN GENERAL.—An issue shall be treated as meeting the requirements of this paragraph if the issuer satisfies the requirements of section 148 with respect to the proceeds of the issue.

(B) SPECIAL RULE FOR INVESTMENTS DURING EXPENDITURE PERIOD.—An issue shall not be treated as failing to meet the requirements of subparagraph (A) by reason of any investment of available project proceeds during the expenditure period.

(C) SPECIAL RULE FOR RESERVE FUNDS.—An issue shall not be treated as failing to meet the requirements of subparagraph (A) by reason of any fund which is expected to be used to repay such issue if—

(i) such fund is funded at a rate not more rapid than equal annual installments,

(ii) such fund is funded in a manner reasonably expected to result in an amount not greater than an amount necessary to repay the issue, and

(iii) the yield on such fund is not greater than the discount rate determined under paragraph (5)(B) with respect to the issue.

(5) MATURITY LIMITATION.—

(A) IN GENERAL.—An issue shall be treated as meeting the requirements of this paragraph if the maturity of any bond which is part of such issue does not exceed the maximum term determined by the Secretary under subparagraph (B).

(B) MAXIMUM TERM.—During each calendar month, the Secretary shall determine the maximum term permitted under this paragraph for bonds issued during the following calendar month. Such maximum term shall be the term which the Secretary estimates will result in the present value of the obligation to repay the principal on the bond being equal to 50 percent of the face amount of such bond. Such present value shall be determined using as a discount rate the average annual interest rate of tax-exempt obligations having a term of 10 years or more which are issued during the month. If the term as so determined is not a multiple of a whole year, such term shall be rounded to the next highest whole year.

(6) PROHIBITION ON FINANCIAL CONFLICTS OF INTEREST.—An issue shall be treated as meeting the requirements of this paragraph if the issuer certifies that—

(A) applicable State and local law requirements governing conflicts of interest are satisfied with respect to such issue, and

(B) if the Secretary prescribes additional conflicts of interest rules governing the appropriate Members of Congress, Federal, State, and local officials, and their spouses, such additional rules are satisfied with respect to such issue.

Amendments

• 2009, American Recovery and Reinvestment Tax Act of 2009 (P.L. 111-5)

P.L. 111-5, §1521(b)(1):

Amended Code Sec. 54A(d)(1) by striking "or" at the end of subparagraph (C), by inserting "or" at the end of subparagraph (D), and by inserting after subparagraph (D) a new subparagraph (E). **Effective** for obligations issued after 2-17-2009.

P.L. 111-5, §1521(b)(2):

Amended Code Sec. 54A(d)(2)(C) by striking "and" at the end of clause (iii), by striking the period at the end clause (iv) and inserting ", and", and by adding at the end a new clause (v). **Effective** for obligations issued after 2-17-2009.

• 2008, Energy Improvement and Extension Act of 2008 (P.L. 110-343)

P.L. 110-343, Division B, §107(b)(1):

Amended Code Sec. 54A(d)(1). **Effective** for obligations issued after 10-3-2008. Prior to amendment, Code Sec. 54A(d)(1) read as follows:

(1) QUALIFIED TAX CREDIT BOND.—The term "qualified tax credit bond" means a qualified forestry conservation bond which is part of an issue that meets the requirements of paragraphs (2), (3), (4), (5), and (6).

P.L. 110-343, Division B, §107(b)(2):

Amended Code Sec. 54A(d)(2)(C). **Effective** for obligations issued after 10-3-2008. Prior to amendment, Code Sec. 54A(d)(2)(C) read as follows:

(C) QUALIFIED PURPOSE.—For purposes of this paragraph, the term "qualified purpose" means a purpose specified in section 54B(e).

P.L. 110-343, Division B, §301(b)(1):

Amended Code Sec. 54A(d)(1), as amended by this Act. **Effective** for obligations issued after 10-3-2008. Prior to amendment, Code Sec. 54A(d)(1) read as follows:

(1) QUALIFIED TAX CREDIT BOND.—The term "qualified tax credit bond" means—

(A) a qualified forestry conservation bond, or

(B) a new clean renewable energy bond,

which is part of an issue that meets requirements of paragraphs (2), (3), (4), (5), and (6).

P.L. 110-343, Division B, §301(b)(2):

Amended Code Sec. 54A(d)(2)(C), as amended by this Act. **Effective** for obligations issued after 10-3-2008. Prior to amendment, Code Sec. 54A(d)(2)(C) read as follows:

(C) QUALIFIED PURPOSE.—For purposes of this paragraph, the term "qualified purpose" means—

(i) in the case of a qualified forestry conservation bond, a purpose specified in section 54B(e), and

(ii) in the case of a new clean renewable energy bond, a purpose specified in section 54C(a)(1).

• 2008, Tax Extenders and Alternative Minimum Tax Relief Act of 2008 (P.L. 110-343)

P.L. 110-343, Division C, §313(b)(1):

Amended Code Sec. 54A(d)(1), as amended by this Act, by striking "or" at the end of subparagraph (B), by inserting "or" at the end of subparagraph (C), and by inserting after subparagraph (C) a new subparagraph (D). **Effective** for obligations issued after 10-3-2008.

P.L. 110-343, Division C, §313(b)(2):

Amended Code Sec. 54A(d)(2)(C), as amended by this Act, by striking "and" at the end of clause (ii), by striking the period at the end of clause (iii) and inserting ", and", and by adding at the end a new clause (iv). **Effective** for obligations issued after 10-3-2008.

[Sec. 54A(e)]

(e) OTHER DEFINITIONS.—For purposes of this subchapter—

(1) CREDIT ALLOWANCE DATE.—The term "credit allowance date" means—

(A) March 15,

(B) June 15,

(C) September 15, and

(D) December 15.

Such term includes the last day on which the bond is outstanding.

(2) BOND.—The term "bond" includes any obligation.

(3) STATE.—The term "State" includes the District of Columbia and any possession of the United States.

(4) AVAILABLE PROJECT PROCEEDS.—The term "available project proceeds" means—

(A) the excess of—

(i) the proceeds from the sale of an issue, over

(ii) the issuance costs financed by the issue (to the extent that such costs do not exceed 2 percent of such proceeds), and

(B) the proceeds from any investment of the excess described in subparagraph (A).

[Sec. 54A(f)]

(f) CREDIT TREATED AS INTEREST.—For purposes of this subtitle, the credit determined under subsection (a) shall be treated as interest which is includible in gross income.

[Sec. 54A(g)]

(g) S CORPORATIONS AND PARTNERSHIPS.—In the case of a tax credit bond held by an S corporation or partnership, the allocation of the credit allowed by this section to the shareholders of such corporation or partners of such partnership shall be treated as a distribution.

[Sec. 54A(h)]

(h) BONDS HELD BY REAL ESTATE INVESTMENT TRUSTS.—If any qualified tax credit bond is held by a real estate investment trust, the credit determined under subsection (a) shall be allowed to beneficiaries of such trust (and any gross income included under subsection (f) with respect to such credit shall be distributed to such beneficiaries) under procedures prescribed by the Secretary.

Amendments

• 2009, American Recovery and Reinvestment Tax Act of 2009 (P.L. 111-5)

P.L. 111-5, §1541(b)(2):

Amended Code Sec. 54A(h). **Effective** for tax years ending after 2-17-2009. Prior to amendment, Code Sec. 54A(h) read as follows:

(h) BONDS HELD BY REGULATED INVESTMENT COMPANIES AND REAL ESTATE INVESTMENT TRUSTS.—If any qualified tax credit bond is held by a regulated investment company or a real estate investment trust, the credit determined under subsection (a) shall be allowed to shareholders of such company or beneficiaries of such trust (and any gross income included under subsection (f) with respect to such credit shall be treated as distributed to such shareholders or beneficiaries) under procedures prescribed by the Secretary.

[Sec. 54A(i)]

(i) CREDITS MAY BE STRIPPED.—Under regulations prescribed by the Secretary—

(1) IN GENERAL.—There may be a separation (including at issuance) of the ownership of a qualified tax credit bond and the entitlement to the credit under this section with respect to such bond. In case of any such separation, the credit under this section shall be allowed to the person who on the credit allowance date holds the instrument evidencing the entitlement to the credit and not to the holder of the bond.

(2) CERTAIN RULES TO APPLY.—In the case of a separation described in paragraph (1), the rules of section 1286 shall apply to the qualified tax credit bond as if it were a stripped bond and to the credit under this section as if it were a stripped coupon.

Amendments

• 2008, Heartland, Habitat, Harvest, and Horticulture Act of 2008 (P.L. 110-246)

P.L. 110-246, §15316(a):

Amended part IV of subchapter A of chapter 1 by adding at the end a new subpart I (Code Secs. 54A-54B). **Effective** for obligations issued after 5-22-2008.

[Sec. 54B]

SEC. 54B. QUALIFIED FORESTRY CONSERVATION BONDS.

[Sec. 54B(a)]

(a) QUALIFIED FORESTRY CONSERVATION BOND.—For purposes of this subchapter, the term "qualified forestry conservation bond" means any bond issued as part of an issue if—

(1) 100 percent of the available project proceeds of such issue are to be used for one or more qualified forestry conservation purposes,

(2) the bond is issued by a qualified issuer, and

(3) the issuer designates such bond for purposes of this section.

[Sec. 54B(b)]

(b) LIMITATION ON AMOUNT OF BONDS DESIGNATED.—The maximum aggregate face amount of bonds which may be designated under subsection (a) by any issuer shall not exceed the limitation amount allocated to such issuer under subsection (d).

[Sec. 54B(c)]

(c) NATIONAL LIMITATION ON AMOUNT OF BONDS DESIGNATED.—There is a national qualified forestry conservation bond limitation of $500,000,000.

[Sec. 54B(d)]

(d) ALLOCATIONS.—

(1) IN GENERAL.—The Secretary shall make allocations of the amount of the national qualified forestry conservation bond limitation described in subsection (c) among qualified forestry conservation purposes in such manner as the Secretary determines appropriate so as to ensure that all of such limitation is allocated before the date which is 24 months after the date of the enactment of this section.

(2) SOLICITATION OF APPLICATIONS.—The Secretary shall solicit applications for allocations of the national qualified forestry conservation bond limitation described in subsection (c) not later than 90 days after the date of the enactment of this section.

[Sec. 54B(e)]

(e) QUALIFIED FORESTRY CONSERVATION PURPOSE.—For purposes of this section, the term "qualified forestry conservation purpose" means the acquisition by a State or any political subdivision or instrumentality thereof or a 501(c)(3) organization (as defined in section 150(a)(4)) from an unrelated person of forest and forest land that meets the following qualifications:

(1) Some portion of the land acquired must be adjacent to United States Forest Service Land.

(2) At least half of the land acquired must be transferred to the United States Forest Service at no net cost to the United States and not more than half of the land acquired may either remain with or be conveyed to a State.

(3) All of the land must be subject to a native fish habitat conservation plan approved by the United States Fish and Wildlife Service.

(4) The amount of acreage acquired must be at least 40,000 acres.

[Sec. 54B(f)]

(f) QUALIFIED ISSUER.—For purposes of this section, the term "qualified issuer" means a State or any political subdivision or instrumentality thereof or a 501(c)(3) organization (as defined in section 150(a)(4)).

[Sec. 54B(g)]

(g) SPECIAL ARBITRAGE RULE.—In the case of any qualified forestry conservation bond issued as part of an issue, section 54A(d)(4)(C) shall be applied to such issue without regard to clause (i).

[Sec. 54B(h)]

(h) ELECTION TO TREAT 50 PERCENT OF BOND ALLOCATION AS PAYMENT OF TAX.—

(1) IN GENERAL.—If—

(A) a qualified issuer receives an allocation of any portion of the national qualified forestry conservation bond limitation described in subsection (c), and

(B) the qualified issuer elects the application of this subsection with respect to such allocation,

then the qualified issuer (without regard to whether the issuer is subject to tax under this chapter) shall be treated as having made a payment against the tax imposed by this chapter, for the taxable year preceding the taxable year in which the allocation is received, in an amount equal to 50 percent of the amount of such allocation.

(2) TREATMENT OF DEEMED PAYMENT.—

(A) IN GENERAL.—Notwithstanding any other provision of this title, the Secretary shall not use the payment of tax described in paragraph (1) as an offset or credit against any tax liability of the qualified issuer but shall refund such payment to such issuer.

(B) NO INTEREST.—Except as provided in paragraph (3)(A), the payment described in paragraph (1) shall not be taken into account in determining any amount of interest under this title.

(3) REQUIREMENT FOR, AND EFFECT OF, ELECTION.—

(A) REQUIREMENT.—No election under this subsection shall take effect unless the qualified issuer certifies to the Secretary that any payment of tax refunded to the issuer under this subsection will be used exclusively for 1 or more qualified forestry conservation purposes. If the qualified issuer fails to use any portion of such payment for such purpose, the issuer shall be liable to the United States in an amount equal to such portion, plus interest at the overpayment rate under section 6621 for the period from the date such portion was refunded to the date such amount is paid. Any such amount shall be assessed and collected in the same manner as tax imposed by this chapter, except that subchapter B of chapter 63 (relating to deficiency procedures) shall not apply in respect of such assessment or collection.

(B) EFFECT OF ELECTION ON ALLOCATION.—If a qualified issuer makes the election under this subsection with respect to any allocation—

(i) the issuer may issue no bonds pursuant to the allocation, and

(ii) the Secretary may not reallocate such allocation for any other purpose.

Amendments

• 2008, Heartland, Habitat, Harvest, and Horticulture Act of 2008 (P.L. 110-246)

P.L. 110-246, §15316(a):

Amended part IV of subchapter A of chapter 1 by adding at the end a new subpart I (Code Secs. 54A-54B). **Effective** for obligations issued after 5-22-2008.

[Sec. 54C]

SEC. 54C. NEW CLEAN RENEWABLE ENERGY BONDS.

[Sec. 54C(a)]

(a) NEW CLEAN RENEWABLE ENERGY BOND.—For purposes of this subpart, the term "new clean renewable energy bond" means any bond issued as part of an issue if—

(1) 100 percent of the available project proceeds of such issue are to be used for capital expenditures incurred by governmental bodies, public power providers, or cooperative electric companies for one or more qualified renewable energy facilities,

(2) the bond is issued by a qualified issuer, and

(3) the issuer designates such bond for purposes of this section.

[Sec. 54C(b)]

(b) REDUCED CREDIT AMOUNT.—The annual credit determined under section 54A(b) with respect to any new clean renewable energy bond shall be 70 percent of the amount so determined without regard to this subsection.

[Sec. 54C(c)]

(c) LIMITATION ON AMOUNT OF BONDS DESIGNATED.—

(1) IN GENERAL.—The maximum aggregate face amount of bonds which may be designated under subsection (a) by any issuer shall not exceed the limitation amount allocated under this subsection to such issuer.

(2) National limitation on amount of bonds designated.—There is a national new clean renewable energy bond limitation of $800,000,000 which shall be allocated by the Secretary as provided in paragraph (3), except that—

(A) not more than 33⅓ percent thereof may be allocated to qualified projects of public power providers,

(B) not more than 33⅓ percent thereof may be allocated to qualified projects of governmental bodies, and

(C) not more than 33⅓ percent thereof may be allocated to qualified projects of cooperative electric companies.

(3) Method of allocation.—

(A) Allocation among public power providers.—After the Secretary determines the qualified projects of public power providers which are appropriate for receiving an allocation of the national new clean renewable energy bond limitation, the Secretary shall, to the maximum extent practicable, make allocations among such projects in such manner that the amount allocated to each such project bears the same ratio to the cost of such project as the limitation under paragraph (2)(A) bears to the cost of all such projects.

(B) Allocation among governmental bodies and cooperative electric companies.—The Secretary shall make allocations of the amount of the national new clean renewable energy bond limitation described in paragraphs (2)(B) and (2)(C) among qualified projects of governmental bodies and cooperative electric companies, respectively, in such manner as the Secretary determines appropriate.

(4) Additional limitation.—The national new clean renewable energy bond limitation shall be increased by $1,600,000,000. Such increase shall be allocated by the Secretary consistent with the rules of paragraphs (2) and (3).

Amendments

• 2009, American Recovery and Reinvestment Tax Act of 2009 (P.L. 111-5)

P.L. 111-5, §1111:

Amended Code Sec. 54C(c) by adding at the end a new paragraph (4). **Effective** 2-17-2009.

[Sec. 54C(d)]

(d) Definitions.—For purposes of this section—

(1) Qualified renewable energy facility.—The term "qualified renewable energy facility" means a qualified facility (as determined under section 45(d) without regard to paragraphs (8) and (10) thereof and to any placed in service date) owned by a public power provider, a governmental body, or a cooperative electric company.

(2) Public power provider.—The term "public power provider" means a State utility with a service obligation, as such terms are defined in section 217 of the Federal Power Act (as in effect on the date of the enactment of this paragraph).

(3) Governmental body.—The term "governmental body" means any State or Indian tribal government, or any political subdivision thereof.

(4) Cooperative electric company.—The term "cooperative electric company" means a mutual or cooperative electric company described in section 501(c)(12) or section 1381(a)(2)(C).

(5) Clean renewable energy bond lender.—The term "clean renewable energy bond lender" means a lender which is a cooperative which is owned by, or has outstanding loans to, 100 or more cooperative electric companies and is in existence on February 1, 2002, and shall include any affiliated entity which is controlled by such lender.

(6) Qualified issuer.—The term "qualified issuer" means a public power provider, a cooperative electric company, a governmental body, a clean renewable energy bond lender, or a not-for-profit electric utility which has received a loan or loan guarantee under the Rural Electrification Act.

Amendments

• 2008, Energy Improvement and Extension Act of 2008 (P.L. 110-343)

P.L. 110-343, Division B, §107(a):

Amended subpart I of part IV of subchapter A of chapter 1 by adding at the end a new Code Sec. 54C. **Effective** for obligations issued after 10-3-2008.

[Sec. 54D]

SEC. 54D. QUALIFIED ENERGY CONSERVATION BONDS.

[Sec. 54D(a)]

(a) Qualified Energy Conservation Bond.—For purposes of this subchapter, the term "qualified energy conservation bond" means any bond issued as part of an issue if—

(1) 100 percent of the available project proceeds of such issue are to be used for one or more qualified conservation purposes,

(2) the bond is issued by a State or local government, and

(3) the issuer designates such bond for purposes of this section.

[Sec. 54D(b)]

(b) REDUCED CREDIT AMOUNT.—The annual credit determined under section 54A(b) with respect to any qualified energy conservation bond shall be 70 percent of the amount so determined without regard to this subsection.

[Sec. 54D(c)]

(c) LIMITATION ON AMOUNT OF BONDS DESIGNATED.—The maximum aggregate face amount of bonds which may be designated under subsection (a) by any issuer shall not exceed the limitation amount allocated to such issuer under subsection (e).

[Sec. 54D(d)]

(d) NATIONAL LIMITATION ON AMOUNT OF BONDS DESIGNATED.—There is a national qualified energy conservation bond limitation of $3,200,000,000.

Amendments

• 2009, American Recovery and Reinvestment Tax Act of 2009 (P.L. 111-5)

P.L. 111-5, §1112(a):

Amended Code Sec. 54D(d) by striking "$800,000,000" and inserting "$3,200,000,000". **Effective** 2-17-2009.

[Sec. 54D(e)]

(e) ALLOCATIONS.—

(1) IN GENERAL.—The limitation applicable under subsection (d) shall be allocated by the Secretary among the States in proportion to the population of the States.

(2) ALLOCATIONS TO LARGEST LOCAL GOVERNMENTS.—

(A) IN GENERAL.—In the case of any State in which there is a large local government, each such local government shall be allocated a portion of such State's allocation which bears the same ratio to the State's allocation (determined without regard to this subparagraph) as the population of such large local government bears to the population of such State.

(B) ALLOCATION OF UNUSED LIMITATION TO STATE.—The amount allocated under this subsection to a large local government may be reallocated by such local government to the State in which such local government is located.

(C) LARGE LOCAL GOVERNMENT.—For purposes of this section, the term "large local government" means any municipality or county if such municipality or county has a population of 100,000 or more.

(3) ALLOCATION TO ISSUERS; RESTRICTION ON PRIVATE ACTIVITY BONDS.—Any allocation under this subsection to a State or large local government shall be allocated by such State or large local government to issuers within the State in a manner that results in not less than 70 percent of the allocation to such State or large local government being used to designate bonds which are not private activity bonds.

(4) SPECIAL RULES FOR BONDS TO IMPLEMENT GREEN COMMUNITY PROGRAMS.—In the case of any bond issued for the purpose of providing loans, grants, or other repayment mechanisms for capital expenditures to implement green community programs, such bond shall not be treated as a private activity bond for purposes of paragraph (3).

Amendments

• 2009, American Recovery and Reinvestment Tax Act of 2009 (P.L. 111-5)

P.L. 111-5, §1112(b)(2):

Amended Code Sec. 54D(e) by adding at the end a new paragraph (4). **Effective** 2-17-2009.

[Sec. 54D(f)]

(f) QUALIFIED CONSERVATION PURPOSE.—For purposes of this section—

(1) IN GENERAL.—The term "qualified conservation purpose" means any of the following:

(A) Capital expenditures incurred for purposes of—

(i) reducing energy consumption in publicly-owned buildings by at least 20 percent,

(ii) implementing green community programs (including the use of loans, grants, or other repayment mechanisms to implement such programs),

(iii) rural development involving the production of electricity from renewable energy resources, or

(iv) any qualified facility (as determined under section 45(d) without regard to paragraphs (8) and (10) thereof and without regard to any placed in service date).

(B) Expenditures with respect to research facilities, and research grants, to support research in—

(i) development of cellulosic ethanol or other nonfossil fuels,

(ii) technologies for the capture and sequestration of carbon dioxide produced through the use of fossil fuels,

(iii) increasing the efficiency of existing technologies for producing nonfossil fuels,

(iv) automobile battery technologies and other technologies to reduce fossil fuel consumption in transportation, or

(v) technologies to reduce energy use in buildings.

(C) Mass commuting facilities and related facilities that reduce the consumption of energy, including expenditures to reduce pollution from vehicles used for mass commuting.

(D) Demonstration projects designed to promote the commercialization of—

(i) green building technology,

(ii) conversion of agricultural waste for use in the production of fuel or otherwise,

(iii) advanced battery manufacturing technologies,

(iv) technologies to reduce peak use of electricity, or

(v) technologies for the capture and sequestration of carbon dioxide emitted from combusting fossil fuels in order to produce electricity.

(E) Public education campaigns to promote energy efficiency.

(2) SPECIAL RULES FOR PRIVATE ACTIVITY BONDS.—For purposes of this section, in the case of any private activity bond, the term "qualified conservation purposes" shall not include any expenditure which is not a capital expenditure.

Amendments

• 2009, American Recovery and Reinvestment Tax Act of 2009 (P.L. 111-5)

P.L. 111-5, §1112(b)(1):

Amended Code Sec. 54D(f)(1)(A)(ii) by inserting "(including the use of loans, grants, or other repayment mechanisms to implement such programs)" after "green community programs". **Effective** 2-17-2009.

[Sec. 54D(g)]

(g) POPULATION.—

(1) IN GENERAL.—The population of any State or local government shall be determined for purposes of this section as provided in section 146(j) for the calendar year which includes the date of the enactment of this section.

(2) SPECIAL RULE FOR COUNTIES.—In determining the population of any county for purposes of this section, any population of such county which is taken into account in determining the population of any municipality which is a large local government shall not be taken into account in determining the population of such county.

[Sec. 54D(h)]

(h) APPLICATION TO INDIAN TRIBAL GOVERNMENTS.—An Indian tribal government shall be treated for purposes of this section in the same manner as a large local government, except that—

(1) an Indian tribal government shall be treated for purposes of subsection (e) as located within a State to the extent of so much of the population of such government as resides within such State, and

(2) any bond issued by an Indian tribal government shall be treated as a qualified energy conservation bond only if issued as part of an issue the available project proceeds of which are used for purposes for which such Indian tribal government could issue bonds to which section 103(a) applies.

Amendments

• 2008, Energy Improvement and Extension Act of 2008 (P.L. 110-343)

P.L. 110-343, Division B, §301(a):

Amended subpart I of part IV of subchapter A of chapter 1, as amended by Act Sec. 107, by adding at the end a new Code Sec. 54D. **Effective** for obligations issued after 10-3-2008.

[Sec. 54E]

SEC. 54E. QUALIFIED ZONE ACADEMY BONDS.

[Sec. 54E(a)]

(a) QUALIFIED ZONE ACADEMY BONDS.—For purposes of this subchapter, the term "qualified zone academy bond" means any bond issued as part of an issue if—

(1) 100 percent of the available project proceeds of such issue are to be used for a qualified purpose with respect to a qualified zone academy established by an eligible local education agency,

(2) the bond is issued by a State or local government within the jurisdiction of which such academy is located, and

(3) the issuer—

(A) designates such bond for purposes of this section,

(B) certifies that it has written assurances that the private business contribution requirement of subsection (b) will be met with respect to such academy, and

(C) certifies that it has the written approval of the eligible local education agency for such bond issuance.

[Sec. 54E(b)]

(b) PRIVATE BUSINESS CONTRIBUTION REQUIREMENT.—For purposes of subsection (a), the private business contribution requirement of this subsection is met with respect to any issue if the eligible local education agency that established the qualified zone academy has written commitments from private entities to make qualified contributions having a present value (as of the date of issuance of the issue) of not less than 10 percent of the proceeds of the issue.

[Sec. 54E(c)]

(c) LIMITATION ON AMOUNT OF BONDS DESIGNATED.—

(1) NATIONAL LIMITATION.—There is a national zone academy bond limitation for each calendar year. Such limitation is $400,000,000 for 2008 and $1,400,000,000 for 2009 and 2010, and, except as provided in paragraph (4), zero thereafter.

(2) ALLOCATION OF LIMITATION.—The national zone academy bond limitation for a calendar year shall be allocated by the Secretary among the States on the basis of their respective populations of individuals below the poverty line (as defined by the Office of Management and Budget). The limitation amount allocated to a State under the preceding sentence shall be allocated by the State education agency to qualified zone academies within such State.

(3) DESIGNATION SUBJECT TO LIMITATION AMOUNT.—The maximum aggregate face amount of bonds issued during any calendar year which may be designated under subsection (a) with respect to any qualified zone academy shall not exceed the limitation amount allocated to such academy under paragraph (2) for such calendar year.

(4) CARRYOVER OF UNUSED LIMITATION.—

(A) IN GENERAL.—If for any calendar year—

(i) the limitation amount for any State, exceeds

(ii) the amount of bonds issued during such year which are designated under subsection (a) with respect to qualified zone academies within such State,

the limitation amount for such State for the following calendar year shall be increased by the amount of such excess.

(B) LIMITATION ON CARRYOVER.—Any carryforward of a limitation amount may be carried only to the first 2 years following the unused limitation year. For purposes of the preceding sentence, a limitation amount shall be treated as used on a first-in first-out basis.

(C) COORDINATION WITH SECTION 1397E.—Any carryover determined under section 1397E(e)(4) (relating to carryover of unused limitation) with respect to any State to calendar year 2008 or 2009 shall be treated for purposes of this section as a carryover with respect to such State for such calendar year under subparagraph (A), and the limitation of subparagraph (B) shall apply to such carryover taking into account the calendar years to which such carryover relates.

Amendments

• 2009, American Recovery and Reinvestment Tax Act of 2009 (P.L. 111-5)

P.L. 111-5, §1522(a):

Amended Code Sec. 54E(c)(1) by striking "and 2009" and inserting "and $1,400,000,000 for 2009 and 2010". **Effective** for obligations issued after 12-31-2008.

[Sec. 54E(d)]

(d) DEFINITIONS.—For purposes of this section—

(1) QUALIFIED ZONE ACADEMY.—The term "qualified zone academy" means any public school (or academic program within a public school) which is established by and operated under the supervision of an eligible local education agency to provide education or training below the postsecondary level if—

(A) such public school or program (as the case may be) is designed in cooperation with business to enhance the academic curriculum, increase graduation and employment rates, and better prepare students for the rigors of college and the increasingly complex workforce,

(B) students in such public school or program (as the case may be) will be subject to the same academic standards and assessments as other students educated by the eligible local education agency,

(C) the comprehensive education plan of such public school or program is approved by the eligible local education agency, and

(D)(i) such public school is located in an empowerment zone or enterprise community (including any such zone or community designated after the date of the enactment of this section), or

(ii) there is a reasonable expectation (as of the date of issuance of the bonds) that at least 35 percent of the students attending such school or participating in such program (as the case may be) will be eligible for free or reduced-cost lunches under the school lunch program established under the National School Lunch Act.

(2) ELIGIBLE LOCAL EDUCATION AGENCY.—For purposes of this section, the term "eligible local education agency" means any local educational agency as defined in section 9101 of the Elementary and Secondary Education Act of 1965.

(3) QUALIFIED PURPOSE.—The term "qualified purpose" means, with respect to any qualified zone academy—

(A) rehabilitating or repairing the public school facility in which the academy is established,

(B) providing equipment for use at such academy,

(C) developing course materials for education to be provided at such academy, and

(D) training teachers and other school personnel in such academy.

(4) QUALIFIED CONTRIBUTIONS.—The term "qualified contribution" means any contribution (of a type and quality acceptable to the eligible local education agency) of—

(A) equipment for use in the qualified zone academy (including state-of-the-art technology and vocational equipment),

(B) technical assistance in developing curriculum or in training teachers in order to promote appropriate market driven technology in the classroom,

(C) services of employees as volunteer mentors,

(D) internships, field trips, or other educational opportunities outside the academy for students, or

(E) any other property or service specified by the eligible local education agency.

Amendments

• 2008, Tax Extenders and Alternative Minimum Tax Relief Act of 2008 (P.L. 110-343)

P.L. 110-343, Division C, §313(a):

Amended subpart I of part IV of subchapter A of chapter 1 by adding at the end a new Code Sec. 54E. **Effective** for obligations issued after 10-3-2008.

[Sec. 54F]

SEC. 54F. QUALIFIED SCHOOL CONSTRUCTION BONDS.

[Sec. 54F(a)]

(a) QUALIFIED SCHOOL CONSTRUCTION BOND.— For purposes of this subchapter, the term "qualified school construction bond" means any bond issued as part of an issue if—

(1) 100 percent of the available project proceeds of such issue are to be used for the construction, rehabilitation, or repair of a public school facility or for the acquisition of land on which such a facility is to be constructed with part of the proceeds of such issue,

(2) the bond is issued by a State or local government within the jurisdiction of which such school is located, and

(3) the issuer designates such bond for purposes of this section.

[Sec. 54F(b)]

(b) LIMITATION ON AMOUNT OF BONDS DESIGNATED.—The maximum aggregate face amount of bonds issued during any calendar year which may be designated under subsection (a) by any issuer shall not exceed the limitation amount allocated under subsection (d) for such calendar year to such issuer.

[Sec. 54F(c)]

(c) NATIONAL LIMITATION ON AMOUNT OF BONDS DESIGNATED.—There is a national qualified school construction bond limitation for each calendar year. Such limitation is—

(1) $11,000,000,000 for 2009,

(2) $11,000,000,000 for 2010, and

(3) except as provided in subsection (e), zero after 2010.

[Sec. 54F(d)]

(d) ALLOCATION OF LIMITATION.—

(1) ALLOCATION AMONG STATES.—Except as provided in paragraph (2)(C), the limitation applicable under subsection (c) for any calendar year shall be allocated by the Secretary among the States in proportion to the respective amounts each such State is eligible to receive under section 1124 of the Elementary and Secondary Education Act of 1965 (20 U.S.C. 6333) for the most recent fiscal year ending before such calendar year. The limitation amount allocated to a State under the preceding sentence shall be allocated by the State education agency (or such other agency as is authorized under State law to make such allocation) to issuers within such State.

(2) 40 PERCENT OF LIMITATION ALLOCATED AMONG LARGEST SCHOOL DISTRICTS.—

(A) IN GENERAL.—40 percent of the limitation applicable under subsection (c) for any calendar year shall be allocated under subparagraph (B) by the Secretary among local educational agencies which are large local educational agencies for such year.

(B) ALLOCATION FORMULA.—The amount to be allocated under subparagraph (A) for any calendar year shall be allocated among large local educational agencies in proportion to the respective amounts each such agency received under section 1124 of the Elementary and Secondary Education Act of 1965 (20 U.S.C. 6333) for the most recent fiscal year ending before such calendar year.

(C) REDUCTION IN STATE ALLOCATION.—The allocation to any State under paragraph (1) shall be reduced by the aggregate amount of the allocations under this paragraph to large local educational agencies within such State.

(D) ALLOCATION OF UNUSED LIMITATION TO STATE.—The amount allocated under this paragraph to a large local educational agency for any calendar year may be reallocated by such agency to the State in which such agency is located for such calendar year. Any amount reallocated to a State under the preceding sentence may be allocated as provided in paragraph (1).

(E) LARGE LOCAL EDUCATIONAL AGENCY.—For purposes of this paragraph, the term "large local educational agency" means, with respect to a calendar year, any local educational agency if such agency is—

(i) among the 100 local educational agencies with the largest numbers of children aged 5 through 17 from families living below the poverty level, as determined by the Secretary using the most recent data available from the Department of Commerce that are satisfactory to the Secretary, or

(ii) 1 of not more than 25 local educational agencies (other than those described in clause (i)) that the Secretary of Education determines (based on the most recent data available satisfactory to the Secretary) are in particular need of assistance, based on a low level of resources for school construction, a high level of enrollment growth, or such other factors as the Secretary deems appropriate.

(3) ALLOCATIONS TO CERTAIN POSSESSIONS.—The amount to be allocated under paragraph (1) to any possession of the United States other than Puerto Rico shall be the amount which would have been allocated if all allocations under paragraph (1) were made on the basis of respective populations of individuals below the poverty line (as defined by the Office of Management and Budget). In making other allocations, the amount to be allocated under paragraph (1) shall be reduced by the aggregate amount allocated under this paragraph to possessions of the United States.

(4) ALLOCATIONS FOR INDIAN SCHOOLS.—In addition to the amounts otherwise allocated under this subsection, $200,000,000 for calendar year 2009, and $200,000,000 for calendar year 2010, shall be allocated by the Secretary of the Interior for purposes of the construction, rehabilitation, and repair of schools funded by the Bureau of Indian Affairs. In the case of amounts allocated under the preceding sentence, Indian tribal governments (as defined in section 7701(a)(40)) shall be treated as qualified issuers for purposes of this subchapter.

Amendments

• 2010, Hiring Incentives to Restore Employment Act (P.L. 111-147)

P.L. 111-147, §301(b)(1):

Amended the second sentence of Code Sec. 54F(d)(1) by striking "by the State" and inserting "by the State education agency (or such other agency as is authorized under State law to make such allocation)". **Effective** as if included in section 1521 of the American Recovery and Reinvestment Tax Act of 2009 [**effective** for obligations issued after 2-17-2009.—CCH].

[Sec. 54F(e)]

(e) CARRYOVER OF UNUSED LIMITATION.—If for any calendar year—

(1) the amount allocated under subsection (d) to any State, exceeds

(2) the amount of bonds issued during such year which are designated under subsection (a) pursuant to such allocation,

the limitation amount under such subsection for such State for the following calendar year shall be increased by the amount of such excess. A similar rule shall apply to the amounts allocated under paragraphs (2) and (4) of subsection (d).

Amendments

• 2010, Hiring Incentives to Restore Employment Act (P.L. 111-147)

P.L. 111-147, §301(b)(2):

Amended the second sentence of Code Sec. 54F(e) by striking "subsection (d)(4)" and inserting "paragraphs (2) and (4) of subsection (d)". **Effective** as if included in section 1521 of the American Recovery and Reinvestment Tax Act of 2009 [**effective** for obligations issued after 2-17-2009.—CCH].

• 2009, American Recovery and Reinvestment Tax Act of 2009 (P.L. 111-5)

P.L. 111-5, §1521(a):

Amended subpart I of part IV of subchapter A of chapter 1 by adding at the end a new Code Sec. 54F. **Effective** for obligations issued after 2-17-2009.

Subpart J—Build America Bonds

[Sec. 54AA]

SEC. 54AA. BUILD AMERICA BONDS.

[Sec. 54AA(a)]

(a) IN GENERAL.—If a taxpayer holds a build America bond on one or more interest payment dates of the bond during any taxable year, there shall be allowed as a credit against the tax imposed by this chapter for the taxable year an amount equal to the sum of the credits determined under subsection (b) with respect to such dates.

[Sec. 54AA(b)]

(b) AMOUNT OF CREDIT.—The amount of the credit determined under this subsection with respect to any interest payment date for a build America bond is 35 percent of the amount of interest payable by the issuer with respect to such date.

[Sec. 54AA(c)]

(c) LIMITATION BASED ON AMOUNT OF TAX.—

(1) IN GENERAL.—The credit allowed under subsection (a) for any taxable year shall not exceed the excess of—

(A) the sum of the regular tax liability (as defined in section 26(b)) plus the tax imposed by section 55, over

(B) the sum of the credits allowable under this part (other than subpart C and this subpart).

(2) CARRYOVER OF UNUSED CREDIT.—If the credit allowable under subsection (a) exceeds the limitation imposed by paragraph (1) for such taxable year, such excess shall be carried to the succeeding taxable year and added to the credit allowable under subsection (a) for such taxable year (determined before the application of paragraph (1) for such succeeding taxable year).

[Sec. 54AA(d)]

(d) BUILD AMERICA BOND.—

(1) IN GENERAL.—For purposes of this section, the term "build America bond" means any obligation (other than a private activity bond) if—

(A) the interest on such obligation would (but for this section) be excludable from gross income under section 103,

(B) such obligation is issued before January 1, 2011, and

(C) the issuer makes an irrevocable election to have this section apply.

(2) APPLICABLE RULES.—For purposes of applying paragraph (1)—

(A) for purposes of section 149(b), a build America bond shall not be treated as federally guaranteed by reason of the credit allowed under subsection (a) or section 6431,

(B) for purposes of section 148, the yield on a build America bond shall be determined without regard to the credit allowed under subsection (a), and

(C) a bond shall not be treated as a build America bond if the issue price has more than a de minimis amount (determined under rules similar to the rules of section 1273(a)(3)) of premium over the stated principal amount of the bond.

[Sec. 54AA(e)]

(e) INTEREST PAYMENT DATE.—For purposes of this section, the term "interest payment date" means any date on which the holder of record of the build America bond is entitled to a payment of interest under such bond.

[Sec. 54AA(f)]

(f) SPECIAL RULES.—

(1) INTEREST ON BUILD AMERICA BONDS INCLUDIBLE IN GROSS INCOME FOR FEDERAL INCOME TAX PURPOSES.—For purposes of this title, interest on any build America bond shall be includible in gross income.

(2) APPLICATION OF CERTAIN RULES.—Rules similar to the rules of subsections (f), (g), (h), and (i) of section 54A shall apply for purposes of the credit allowed under subsection (a).

[Sec. 54AA(g)]

(g) SPECIAL RULE FOR QUALIFIED BONDS ISSUED BEFORE 2011.—In the case of a qualified bond issued before January 1, 2011—

(1) ISSUER ALLOWED REFUNDABLE CREDIT.—In lieu of any credit allowed under this section with respect to such bond, the issuer of such bond shall be allowed a credit as provided in section 6431.

(2) QUALIFIED BOND.—For purposes of this subsection, the term "qualified bond" means any build America bond issued as part of an issue if—

(A) 100 percent of the excess of—

(i) the available project proceeds (as defined in section 54A) of such issue, over

(ii) the amounts in a reasonably required reserve (within the meaning of section 150(a)(3)) with respect to such issue,

are to be used for capital expenditures, and

(B) the issuer makes an irrevocable election to have this subsection apply.

[Sec. 54AA(h)]

(h) REGULATIONS.—The Secretary may prescribe such regulations and other guidance as may be necessary or appropriate to carry out this section and section 6431.

Amendments

• 2009, American Recovery and Reinvestment Tax Act of 2009 (P.L. 111-5)

P.L. 111-5, §1531(a):

Amended part IV of subchapter A of chapter 1 by adding at the end a new subpart J (Code Sec. 54AA). **Effective** for obligations issued after 2-17-2009.

P.L. 111-5, §1531(d), provides:

(d) TRANSITIONAL COORDINATION WITH STATE LAW.—Except as otherwise provided by a State after the date of the enactment of this Act, the interest on any build America bond (as defined in section 54AA of the Internal Revenue Code of 1986, as added by this section) and the amount of any credit determined under such section with respect to such bond shall be treated for purposes of the income tax laws of such State as being exempt from Federal income tax.

PART VI—ALTERNATIVE MINIMUM TAX

[Sec. 55]

SEC. 55. ALTERNATIVE MINIMUM TAX IMPOSED.

[Sec. 55(a)]

(a) GENERAL RULE.—There is hereby imposed (in addition to any other tax imposed by this subtitle) a tax equal to the excess (if any) of—

(1) the tentative minimum tax for the taxable year, over

(2) the regular tax for the taxable year.

[Sec. 55(b)]

(b) TENTATIVE MINIMUM TAX.—For purposes of this part—

(1) AMOUNT OF TENTATIVE TAX.—

(A) NONCORPORATE TAXPAYERS.—

(i) IN GENERAL.—In the case of a taxpayer other than a corporation, the tentative minimum tax for the taxable year is the sum of—

(I) 26 percent of so much of the taxable excess as does not exceed $175,000, plus

(II) 28 percent of so much of the taxable excess as exceeds $175,000.

The amount determined under the preceding sentence shall be reduced by the alternative minimum tax foreign tax credit for the taxable year.

(ii) TAXABLE EXCESS.—For purposes of this subsection, the term "taxable excess" means so much of the alternative minimum taxable income for the taxable year as exceeds the exemption amount.

(iii) MARRIED INDIVIDUAL FILING SEPARATE RETURN.—In the case of a married individual filing a separate return, clause (i) shall be applied by substituting "$87,500" for "$175,000" each place it appears. For purposes of the preceding sentence, marital status shall be determined under section 7703.

(B) CORPORATIONS.—In the case of a corporation, the tentative minimum tax for the taxable year is—

(i) 20 percent of so much of the alternative minimum taxable income for the taxable year as exceeds the exemption amount, reduced by

(ii) the alternative minimum tax foreign tax credit for the taxable year.

(2) ALTERNATIVE MINIMUM TAXABLE INCOME.—The term "alternative minimum taxable income" means the taxable income of the taxpayer for the taxable year—

(A) determined with the adjustments provided in section 56 and section 58, and

(B) increased by the amount of the items of tax preference described in section 57.

If a taxpayer is subject to the regular tax, such taxpayer shall be subject to the tax imposed by this section (and, if the regular tax is determined by reference to an amount other than taxable income, such amount shall be treated as the taxable income of such taxpayer for purposes of the preceding sentence).

Caution: Code Sec. 55(b)(3), below, is subject to the sunset provision of the Jobs and Growth Tax Relief Reconciliation Act of 2003 (P.L. 108-27), §303. Absent Congressional action, the changes made to this provision by P.L. 108-27, or that take effect as if included in P.L. 108-27, do not apply after December 31, 2010. For more information about the sunset provision, see page XXI of the Preface to this publication and P.L. 108-27, §303, in the amendment notes. See the amendments notes for a history of amendments to this section and the effective date of each change.

(3) MAXIMUM RATE OF TAX ON NET CAPITAL GAIN OF NONCORPORATE TAXPAYERS.—The amount determined under the first sentence of paragraph (1)(A)(i) shall not exceed the sum of—

(A) the amount determined under such first sentence computed at the rates and in the same manner as if this paragraph had not been enacted on the taxable excess reduced by the lesser of—

(i) the net capital gain; or

(ii) the sum of—

(I) the adjusted net capital gain, plus

(II) the unrecaptured section 1250 gain, plus

(B) 5 percent (0 percent in the case of taxable years beginning after 2007) of so much of the adjusted net capital gain (or, if less, taxable excess) as does not exceed an amount equal to the excess described in section 1(h)(1)(B), plus

(C) 15 percent of the adjusted net capital gain (or, if less, taxable excess) in excess of the amount on which tax is determined under subparagraph (B), plus

(D) 25 percent of the amount of taxable excess in excess of the sum of the amounts on which tax is determined under the preceding subparagraphs of this paragraph.

Terms used in this paragraph which are also used in section 1(h) shall have the respective meanings given such terms by section 1(h) but computed with the adjustments under this part.

(4) MAXIMUM RATE OF TAX ON QUALIFIED TIMBER GAIN OF CORPORATIONS.—In the case of any taxable year to which section 1201(b) applies, the amount determined under clause (i) of subparagraph (B) shall not exceed the sum of—

(A) 20 percent of so much of the taxable excess (if any) as exceeds the qualified timber gain (or, if less, the net capital gain), plus

(B) 15 percent of the taxable excess in excess of the amount on which a tax is determined under subparagraph (A).

Any term used in this paragraph which is also used in section 1201 shall have the meaning given such term by such section, except to the extent such term is subject to adjustment under this part.

Amendments

• 2008, Heartland, Habitat, Harvest, and Horticulture Act of 2008 (P.L. 110-246)

P.L. 110-246, §15311(b):

Amended Code Sec. 55(b) by adding at the end a new paragraph (4). **Effective** for tax years ending after 5-22-2008.

• 2004, Working Families Tax Relief Act of 2004 (P.L. 108-311)

P.L. 108-311, §406(d):

Amended Code Sec. 55(b)(3)(B) by striking "the amount on which a tax is determined under" and inserting "an amount equal to the excess described in". **Effective** as if included in the provision of the Taxpayer Relief Act of 1997 (P.L. 105-34) to which it relates [**effective** for tax years ending after 5-6-1997.—CCH].

• 2003, Jobs and Growth Tax Relief Reconciliation Act of 2003 (P.L. 108-27)

P.L. 108-27, §301(a)(1):

Amended Code Sec. 55(b)(3)(B) by striking "10 percent" and inserting "5 percent (0 percent in the case of taxable years beginning after 2007)". **Effective** for tax years ending on or after 5-6-2003. For a transitional rule, see Act Sec. 301(c), below.

P.L. 108-27, §301(a)(2)(B):

Amended Code Sec. 55(b)(3)(C) by striking "20 percent" and inserting "15 percent". **Effective** for tax years ending on or after 5-6-2003. For a transitional rule, see Act Sec. 301(c), below.

P.L. 108-27, §301(b)(2):

Amended Code Sec. 55(b)(3) by striking "In the case of taxable years beginning after December 31, 2000, rules similar to the rules of section 1(h)(2) shall apply for purposes of subparagraphs (B) and (C)." before "Terms used in this paragraph which are also used in section 1(h) shall have the same respective meanings given such terms by section 1(h) but computed with the adjustments of this part.". **Effective** for tax years ending on or after 5-6-2003. For a transitional rule, see Act Sec. 301(c), below.

P.L. 108-27, §301(c), provides:

(c) TRANSITIONAL RULES FOR TAXABLE YEARS WHICH INCLUDE MAY 6, 2003.—For purposes of applying section 1(h) of the

Internal Revenue Code of 1986 in the case of a taxable year which includes May 6, 2003—

(1) The amount of tax determined under subparagraph (B) of section 1(h)(1) of such Code shall be the sum of—

(A) 5 percent of the lesser of—

(i) the net capital gain determined by taking into account only gain or loss properly taken into account for the portion of the taxable year on or after May 6, 2003 (determined without regard to collectibles gain or loss, gain described in section 1(h)(6)(A)(i) of such Code, and section 1202 gain), or

(ii) the amount on which a tax is determined under such subparagraph (without regard to this subsection),

(B) 8 percent of the lesser of—

(i) the qualified 5-year gain (as defined in section 1(h)(9) of the Internal Revenue Code of 1986, as in effect on the day before the date of the enactment of this Act) properly taken into account for the portion of the taxable year before May 6, 2003, or

(ii) the excess (if any) of—

(I) the amount on which a tax is determined under such subparagraph (without regard to this subsection), over

(II) the amount on which a tax is determined under subparagraph (A), plus

(C) 10 percent of the excess (if any) of—

(i) the amount on which a tax is determined under such subparagraph (without regard to this subsection), over

(ii) the sum of the amounts on which a tax is determined under subparagraphs (A) and (B).

(2) The amount of tax determined under subparagraph (C) of section (1)(h)(1) of such Code shall be the sum of—

(A) 15 percent of the lesser of—

(i) the excess (if any) of the amount of net capital gain determined under subparagraph (A)(i) of paragraph (1) of this subsection over the amount on which a tax is determined under subparagraph (A) of paragraph (1) of this subsection, or

(ii) the amount on which a tax is determined under such subparagraph (C) (without regard to this subsection), plus

(B) 20 percent of the excess (if any) of—

(i) the amount on which a tax is determined under such subparagraph (C) (without regard to this subsection), over

(ii) the amount on which a tax is determined under subparagraph (A) of this paragraph.

(3) For purposes of applying section 55(b)(3) of such Code, rules similar to the rules of paragraphs (1) and (2) of this subsection shall apply.

(4) In applying this subsection with respect to any pass-thru entity, the determination of when gains and losses are properly taken into account shall be made at the entity level.

(5) For purposes of applying section 1(h)(11) of such Code, as added by section 302 of this Act, to this subsection, dividends which are qualified dividend income shall be treated as gain properly taken into account for the portion of the taxable year on or after May 6, 2003.

(6) Terms used in this subsection which are also used in section 1(h) of such Code shall have the respective meanings that such terms have in such section.

P.L. 108-27, §303, as amended by P.L. 109-222, §102, provides:

SEC. 303. SUNSET OF TITLE.

All provisions of, and amendments made by, this title shall not apply to taxable years beginning after December 31, 2010, and the Internal Revenue Code of 1986 shall be applied and administered to such years as if such provisions and amendments had never been enacted.

• 1998, IRS Restructuring and Reform Act of 1998 (P.L. 105-206)

P.L. 105-206, §6005(d)(2):

Amended Code Sec. 55(b)(3). **Effective** as if included in the provision of P.L. 105-34 to which it relates [**effective** for tax years ending after 5-6-97.—CCH]. Prior to amendment, Code Sec. 55(b)(3) read as follows:

(3) MAXIMUM RATE OF TAX ON NET CAPITAL GAIN OF NONCORPORATE TAXPAYERS.—The amount determined under the first sentence of paragraph (1)(A)(i) shall not exceed the sum of—

(A) the amount determined under such first sentence computed at the rates and in the same manner as if this paragraph had not been enacted on the taxable excess reduced by the lesser of—

(i) the net capital gain, or

(ii) the sum of—

(I) the adjusted net capital gain, plus

(II) the unrecaptured section 1250 gain, plus

(B) 25 percent of the lesser of—

(i) the unrecaptured section 1250 gain, or

(ii) the amount of taxable excess in excess of the sum of—

(I) the adjusted net capital gain, plus

(II) the amount on which a tax is determined under subparagraph (A), plus

(C) 10 percent of so much of the taxpayer's adjusted net capital gain (or, if less, taxable excess) as does not exceed the amount on which a tax is determined under section 1(h)(1)(D), plus

(D) 20 percent of the taxpayer's adjusted net capital gain (or, if less, taxable excess) in excess of the amount on which tax is determined under subparagraph (C).

In the case of taxable years beginning after December 31, 2000, rules similar to the rules of section 1(h)(2) shall apply for purposes of subparagraphs (C) and (D). Terms used in this paragraph which are also used in section 1(h) shall have the respective meanings given such terms by section 1(h).

• 1997, Taxpayer Relief Act of 1997 (P.L. 105-34)

P.L. 105-34, §311(b)(1):

Amended Code Sec. 55(b) by adding a new paragraph (3). **Effective** for tax years ending after 5-6-97.

P.L. 105-34, §311(b)(2)(A):

Amended Code Sec. 55(b)(1)(A)(ii) by striking "clause (i)" and inserting "this subsection". **Effective** for tax years ending after 5-6-97.

• 1993, Omnibus Budget Reconciliation Act of 1993 (P.L. 103-66)

P.L. 103-66, §13203(a):

Amended Code Sec. 55(b)(1). **Effective** for tax years beginning after 12-31-92. Prior to amendment, Code Sec. 55(b)(1) read as follows:

(b) TENTATIVE MINIMUM TAX.—For purposes of this part—

(1) IN GENERAL.—The tentative minimum tax for the taxable year is—

(A) 20 percent (24 percent in the case of a taxpayer other than a corporation) of so much of the alternative minimum taxable income for the taxable year as exceeds the exemption amount, reduced by

(B) the alternative minimum tax foreign tax credit for the taxable year.

• 1990, Omnibus Budget Reconciliation Act of 1990 (P.L. 101-508)

P.L. 101-508, §11102(a):

Amended Code Sec. 55(b)(1)(A) by striking "21 percent" and inserting "24 percent". **Effective** for years beginning after 12-31-90.

• 1988, Technical and Miscellaneous Revenue Act of 1988 (P.L. 100-647)

P.L. 100-647, §1007(a)(2):

Amended Code Sec. 55(b)(2) by adding at the end thereof a new sentence. **Effective** as if included in the provision of P.L. 99-514 to which it relates.

[Sec. 55(c)]

(c) REGULAR TAX.—

(1) IN GENERAL.—For purposes of this section, the term "regular tax" means the regular tax liability for the taxable year (as defined in section 26(b)) reduced by the foreign tax credit allowable under section 27(a), the section 936 credit allowable under section 27(b), and the

Puerto Rico economic activity credit under section 30A. Such term shall not include any increase in tax under section 45(e)(11)(C), 49(b) or 50(a) or subsection (j) or (k) of section 42.

(2) COORDINATION WITH INCOME AVERAGING FOR FARMERS AND FISHERMEN.—Solely for purposes of this section, section 1301 (relating to averaging of farm and fishing income) shall not apply in computing the regular tax liability.

(3) CROSS REFERENCES.—

For provisions providing that certain credits are not allowable against the tax imposed by this section, see sections 26(a), 30C(d)(2), and 38(c).

Amendments

• 2009, American Recovery and Reinvestment Tax Act of 2009 (P.L. 111-5)

P.L. 111-5, §1142(b)(5):

Amended Code Sec. 55(c)(3) by striking "30(b)(3)," following "sections 26(a),". **Effective** for vehicles acquired after 2-17-2009. For a transitional rule, see Act Sec. 1142(d) in the amendment notes following Code Sec. 30.

P.L. 111-5, §1144(b)(3):

Amended Code Sec. 55(c)(3) by striking "30B(g)(2)," before "30C(d)(2)". **Effective** for tax years beginning after 12-31-2008.

• 2005, Gulf Opportunity Zone Act of 2005 (P.L. 109-135)

P.L. 109-135, §403(h):

Amended Code Sec. 55(c)(2) by striking "regular tax" and inserting "regular tax liability". **Effective** as if included in the provision of the American Jobs Creation Act of 2004 (P.L. 108-357) to which it relates [**effective** for tax years beginning after 12-31-2003.—CCH].

P.L. 109-135, §412(p)(1):

Amended Code Sec. 55(c)(3) by inserting "30B(g)(2), 30C(d)(2)," after "30(b)(3)". **Effective** 12-21-2005.

P.L. 109-135, §412(p)(2):

Repealed the amendment made by §1341(b)(3) of the Energy Policy Act of 2005 (P.L. 109-58). P.L. 109-58, §1341(b)(3), amended Code Sec. 55(c)(2) by inserting "30B(g)(2)," after "30(b)(2),". **Effective** 12-21-2005.

P.L. 109-135, §412(p)(3):

Repealed the amendment made by §1342(b)(3) of the Energy Policy Act of 2005 (P.L. 109-58). P.L. 109-58, §1342(b)(3), amended Code Sec. 55(c)(2) by inserting "30C(d)(2)," after "30B(g)(2),". **Effective** 12-21-2005.

• 2005, Energy Tax Incentives Act of 2005 (P.L. 109-58)

P.L. 109-58, §1302(b):

Amended the last sentence of Code Sec. 55(c)(1), by inserting "45(e)(11)(C)," after "section" [and before "49(b)"]. **Effective** for tax years of cooperative organizations ending after 8-8-2005.

P.L. 109-58, §1322(a)(3)(H):

Amended Code Sec. 55(c)(3) by striking "29(b)(6)," following "sections 26(a),". **Effective** for credits determined under the Internal Revenue Code of 1986 for tax years ending after 12-31-2005.

P.L. 109-58, §1341(b)(3) [repealed by P.L. 109-135, §412(p)(2)]:

Amended Code Sec. 55(c)(2), as amended by this Act, by inserting "30B(g)(2)," after "30(b)(2),". **Effective** for property placed in service after 12-31-2005, in tax years ending after such date.

P.L. 109-58, §1342(b)(3) [repealed by P.L. 109-135, §412(p)(3)]:

Amended Code Sec. 55(c)(2), as amended by this Act, by inserting "30C(d)(2)," after "30B(g)(2),". **Effective** for property placed in service after 12-31-2005, in tax years ending after such date.

• 2004, American Jobs Creation Act of 2004 (P.L. 108-357)

P.L. 108-357, §314(a):

Amended Code Sec. 55(c) by redesignating paragraph (2) as paragraph (3) and by inserting after paragraph (1) a new paragraph (2). **Effective** for tax years beginning after 12-31-2003.

• 1997, Taxpayer Relief Act of 1997 (P.L. 105-34)

P.L. 105-34, §1601(f)(1)(C):

Amended Code Sec. 55(c)(1) by striking "Puerto Rican" and inserting "Puerto Rico". **Effective** as if included in the provision of P.L. 104-188 to which it relates [generally **effective** for tax years beginning after 12-31-95.—CCH].

• 1996, Small Business Job Protection Act of 1996 (P.L. 104-188)

P.L. 104-188, §1205(d)(6):

Amended Code Sec. 55(c)(2) by striking "28(d)(2)," after "26(a),". **Effective** for amounts paid or incurred in tax years ending after 6-30-96.

P.L. 104-188, §1401(b)(3):

Amended Code Sec. 55(c)(1) by striking "shall not include any tax imposed by section 402(d) and" after "Such terms". **Effective**, generally, for tax years beginning after 12-31-99. For a special transitional rule, see Act Sec. 1401(c)(2) in the amendment notes following Code Sec. 402(d).

P.L. 104-188, §1601(b)(2)(A):

Amended Code Sec. 55(c)(1) by striking "and the section 936 credit allowable under section 27(b)" and inserting ", the section 936 credit allowable under section 27(b), and the Puerto Rican economic activity credit under section 30A". **Effective** for tax years beginning after 12-31-95. For special rules, see Act Sec. 1601(c)(2)-(3), below.

P.L. 104-188, §1601(c)(2)-(3), provides:

(2) SPECIAL RULE FOR QUALIFIED POSSESSION SOURCE INVESTMENT INCOME.—The amendments made by this section shall not apply to qualified possession source investment income received or accrued before July 1, 1996, without regard to the taxable year in which received or accrued.

(3) SPECIAL TRANSITION RULE FOR PAYMENT OF ESTIMATED TAX INSTALLMENT.—In determining the amount of any installment due under section 6655 of the Internal Revenue Code of 1986 after the date of the enactment of this Act and before October 1, 1996, only 1/2 of any increase in tax (for the taxable year for which such installment is made) by reason of the amendments made by subsections (a) and (b) shall be taken into account. Any reduction in such installment by reason of the preceding sentence shall be recaptured by increasing the next required installment for such year by the amount of such reduction.

• 1992, Energy Policy Act of 1992 (P.L. 102-486)

P.L. 102-486, §1913(b)(2)(D):

Amended Code Sec. 55(c)(2) by striking "29(b)(5)," and inserting "29(b)(6), 30(b)(3),". **Effective** for property placed in service after 6-30-93.

• 1992, Unemployment Compensation Amendments of 1992 (P.L. 102-318)

P.L. 102-318, §521(b)(1):

Amended Code Sec. 55(c)(1) by striking "section 402(e)" and inserting "section 402(d)". **Effective** for distributions after 12-31-92.

• 1990, Omnibus Budget Reconciliation Act of 1990 (P.L. 101-508)

P.L. 101-508, §11813(b)(5):

Amended Code Sec. 55(c)(1) by striking "section 47" and inserting "section 49(b) or 50(a)". **Effective**, generally, for property placed in service after 12-31-90. However, for exceptions, see Act Sec. 11813(c)(2) below.

P.L. 101-508, §11813(c)(2), provides:

(2) EXCEPTIONS.—The amendments made by this section shall not apply to—

(A) any transition property (as defined in section 49(e) of the Internal Revenue Code of 1986 (as in effect on the day before the date of the enactment of this Act),

(B) any property with respect to which qualified progress expenditures were previously taken into account under section 46(d) of such Code (as so in effect), and

(C) any property described in section 46(b)(2)(C) of such Code (as so in effect).

• **1988, Technical and Miscellaneous Revenue Act of 1988 (P.L. 100-647)**

P.L. 100-647, §1002(l)(28):

Amended Code Sec. 55(c)(1) by striking out "section 42(j)" and inserting in lieu thereof "subsection (j) or (k) of section 42". **Effective** as if included in the provision of P.L. 99-514 to which it relates.

P.L. 100-647, §1007(a)(1):

Amended Code Sec. 55(c)(1) by inserting "and the section 936 credit allowable under section 27(b)" before the period at the end of the first sentence. **Effective** as if included in the provision of P.L. 99-514 to which it relates.

»» Caution: Code Sec. 55(d), below, was amended by P.L. 107-16, P.L. 108-27, and P.L. 108-311, and is subject to the sunset provisions of the Economic Growth and Tax Relief Reconciliation Act of 2001 (P.L. 107-16), §901, and the Jobs and Growth Tax Relief Reconciliation Act of 2003 (P.L. 108-27), §303. Absent Congressional action, the changes made to this provision by P.L. 107-16, and P.L. 108-27, or that take effect as if included in P.L. 107-16, and P.L. 108-27, do not apply after December 31, 2010. For more information about the sunset provisions, see page XXI of the Preface to this publication and P.L. 107-16, §901, P.L. 108-27, §303, and P.L. 108-311, §105, in the amendment notes. See the amendments notes for a history of amendments to this section and the effective date of each change.

[Sec. 55(d)]

(d) EXEMPTION AMOUNT.—For purposes of this section—

(1) EXEMPTION AMOUNT FOR TAXPAYERS OTHER THAN CORPORATIONS.—In the case of a taxpayer other than a corporation, the term "exemption amount" means—

(A) $45,000 ($70,950 in the case of taxable years beginning in 2009) in the case of—

(i) a joint return, or

(ii) a surviving spouse,

(B) $33,750 ($46,700 in the case of taxable years beginning in 2009) in the case of an individual who—

(i) is not a married individual, and

(ii) is not a surviving spouse,

(C) 50 percent of the dollar amount applicable under paragraph (1)(A) in the case of a married individual who files a separate return, and

(D) $22,500 in the case of an estate or trust.

For purposes of this paragraph, the term "surviving spouse" has the meaning given to such term by section 2(a), and marital status shall be determined under section 7703.

(2) CORPORATIONS.—In the case of a corporation, the term "exemption amount" means $40,000.

(3) PHASE-OUT OF EXEMPTION AMOUNT.—The exemption amount of any taxpayers shall be reduced (but not below zero) by an amount equal to 25 percent of the amount by which the alternative minimum taxable income of the taxpayer exceeds—

(A) $150,000 in the case of a taxpayer described in paragraph (1)(A) or (2),

(B) $112,500 in the case of a taxpayer described in paragraph (1)(B), and

(C) $75,000 in the case of a taxpayer described in subparagraph (C) or (D) of paragraph (1).

In the case of a taxpayer described in paragraph (1)(C), alternative minimum taxable income shall be increased by the lesser of (i) 25 percent of the excess of alternative minimum taxable income (determined without regard to this sentence) over the minimum amount of such income (as so determined) for which the exemption amount under paragraph (1)(C) is zero, or (ii) such exemption amount (determined without regard to this paragraph).

Amendments

• **2009, American Recovery and Reinvestment Tax Act of 2009 (P.L. 111-5)**

P.L. 111-5, §1012(a)(1)-(2):

Amended Code Sec. 55(d)(1) by striking "($69,950 in the case of taxable years beginning in 2008)" in subparagraph (A) and inserting "($70,950 in the case of taxable years beginning in 2009)", and by striking "($46,200 in the case of taxable years beginning in 2008)" in subparagraph (B) and inserting "($46,700 in the case of taxable years beginning in 2009)". **Effective** for tax years beginning after 12-31-2008.

• **2008, Tax Extenders and Alternative Minimum Tax Relief Act of 2008 (P.L. 110-343)**

P.L. 110-343, Division C, §102(a)(1)-(2):

Amended Code Sec. 55(d)(1) by striking "($66,250 in the case of taxable years beginning in 2007)" in subparagraph (A) and inserting "($69,950 in the case of taxable years beginning in 2008)", and by striking "($44,350 in the case of taxable years beginning in 2007)" in subparagraph (B) and inserting "($46,200 in the case of taxable years beginning in 2008)". **Effective** for tax years beginning after 12-31-2007.

• 2007, Tax Increase Prevention Act of 2007 (P.L. 110-166)

P.L. 110-166, §2(a)(1)-(2):

Amended Code Sec. 55(d)(1) by striking "($62,550 in the case of taxable years beginning in 2006)" in subparagraph (A) and inserting "($66,250 in the case of taxable years beginning in 2007)", and by striking "($42,500 in the case of taxable years beginning in 2006)" in subparagraph (B) and inserting "($44,350 in the case of taxable years beginning in 2007)". **Effective** for tax years beginning after 12-31-2006.

• 2006, Tax Increase Prevention and Reconciliation Act of 2005 (P.L. 109-222)

P.L. 109-222, §301(a)(1)-(2):

Amended Code Sec. 55(d)(1) by striking "$58,000" and all that follows through "2005" in subparagraph (A) and inserting "$62,550 in the case of taxable years beginning in 2006", and by striking "$40,250" and all that follows through "2005" in subparagraph (B) and inserting "$42,500 in the case of taxable years beginning in 2006". **Effective** for tax years beginning after 12-31-2005. Prior to amendment, Code Sec. 55(d)(1)(A)-(B) read as follows:

(A) $45,000 ($58,000 in the case of taxable years beginning in 2003, 2004, and 2005) in the case of—

(i) a joint return, or

(ii) a surviving spouse,

(B) $33,750 ($40,250 in the case of taxable years beginning in 2003, 2004, and 2005) in the case of an individual who—

(i) is not a married individual, and

(ii) is not a surviving spouse,

• 2004, Working Families Tax Relief Act of 2004 (P.L. 108-311)

P.L. 108-311, §103(a):

Amended Code Sec. 55(d)(1)(A)-(B) by striking "2003 and 2004" and inserting "2003, 2004, and 2005". **Effective** for tax years beginning after 12-31-2004.

P.L. 108-311, §105, provides:

SEC. 105. APPLICATION OF EGTRRA SUNSET TO THIS TITLE.

Each amendment made by this title shall be subject to title IX of the Economic Growth and Tax Relief Reconciliation Act of 2001 to the same extent and in the same manner as the provision of such Act to which such amendment relates.

• 2003, Jobs and Growth Tax Relief Reconciliation Act of 2003 (P.L. 108-27)

P.L. 108-27, §106(a)(1):

Amended Code Sec. 55(d)(1)(A) by striking "$49,000 in the case of taxable years beginning in 2001, 2002, 2003, and 2004" and inserting "$58,000 in the case of taxable years beginning in 2003 and 2004". **Effective** for tax years beginning after 12-31-2002.

P.L. 108-27, §106(a)(2):

Amended Code Sec. 55(d)(1)(B) by striking "$35,750 in the case of taxable years beginning in 2001, 2002, 2003, and 2004" and inserting "$40,250 in the case of taxable years beginning in 2003 and 2004". **Effective** for tax years beginning after 12-31-2002.

P.L. 108-27, §107, provides:

SEC. 107. APPLICATION OF EGTRRA SUNSET TO THIS TITLE.

Each amendment made by this title shall be subject to title IX of the Economic Growth and Tax Relief Reconciliation Act of 2001 to the same extent and in the same manner as the provision of such Act to which such amendment relates.

• 2001, Economic Growth and Tax Relief Reconciliation Act of 2001 (P.L. 107-16)

P.L. 107-16, §701(a)(1):

Amended Code Sec. 55(d)(1)(A) by striking "$45,000" and inserting "$45,000 ($49,000 in the case of taxable years beginning in 2001, 2002, 2003, and 2004)". **Effective** for tax years beginning after 12-31-2000.

P.L. 107-16, §701(a)(2):

Amended Code Sec. 55(d)(1)(B) by striking "$33,750" and inserting "$33,750 ($35,750 in the case of taxable years beginning in 2001, 2002, 2003, and 2004)". **Effective** for tax years beginning after 12-31-2000.

P.L. 107-16, §701(b)(1):

Amended Code Sec. 55(d)(1) by striking "and" at the end of subparagraph (B), by striking subparagraph (C), and by inserting after subparagraph (B) new subparagraphs (C) and (D). **Effective** for tax years beginning after 12-31-2000. Prior to being stricken, Code Sec. 55(d)(1)(C) read as follows:

(C) $22,500 in the case of—

(i) a married individual who files a separate return, or

(ii) an estate or trust.

P.L. 107-16, §701(b)(2):

Amended Code Sec. 55(d)(3)(C) by striking "paragraph (1)(C)" and inserting "subparagraph (C) or (D) of paragraph (1)". **Effective** for tax years beginning after 12-31-2000.

P.L. 107-16, §701(b)(3)(A)-(B):

Amended the last sentence of Code Sec. 55(d)(3) by striking "paragraph (1)(C)(i)" and inserting "paragraph (1)(C)"; and by striking "$165,000 or (ii) $22,500" and inserting "the minimum amount of such income (as so determined) for which the exemption amount under paragraph (1)(C) is zero, or (ii) such exemption amount (determined without regard to this paragraph)". **Effective** for tax years beginning after 12-31-2000.

P.L. 107-16, §901(a)-(b), provides:

SEC. 901. SUNSET OF PROVISIONS OF ACT.

(a) IN GENERAL.—All provisions of, and amendments made by, this Act shall not apply—

(1) to taxable, plan, or limitation years beginning after December 31, 2010, or

(2) in the case of title V, to estates of decedents dying, gifts made, or generation skipping transfers, after December 31, 2010.

(b) APPLICATION OF CERTAIN LAWS.—The Internal Revenue Code of 1986 and the Employee Retirement Income Security Act of 1974 shall be applied and administered to years, estates, gifts, and transfers described in subsection (a) as if the provisions and amendments described in subsection (a) had never been enacted.

• 1993, Omnibus Budget Reconciliation Act of 1993 (P.L. 103-66)

P.L. 103-66, §13203(b)(1)-(3):

Amended Code Sec. 55(d)(1)(A)-(C) by striking "$40,000" in subparagraph (A) and inserting "$45,000", by striking "$30,000" in subparagraph (B) and inserting "$33,750", and by striking "$20,000" in subparagraph (C) and inserting "$22,500". **Effective** for tax years beginning after 12-31-92.

P.L. 103-66, §13203(c)(1):

Amended Code Sec. 55(d)(3) by striking "$155,000 or (ii) $20,000" in the last sentence and inserting "$165,000 or (ii) $22,500". **Effective** for tax years beginning after 12-31-92.

• 1988, Technical and Miscellaneous Revenue Act of 1988 (P.L. 100-647)

P.L. 100-647, §1007(a)(3):

Amended Code Sec. 55(d)(3) by adding at the end thereof a new sentence. **Effective** for tax years ending after the date of the enactment of this Act.

• 1986, Tax Reform Act of 1986 (P.L. 99-514)

P.L. 99-514, §252(c):

Amended Code Sec. 55(c)(1), as amended by section 701 of this Act, by inserting "or section 42(j)" after "section 47". **Effective** for buildings placed in service after 12-31-86, in tax years ending after such date. However, for a special rule and for transitional rules, see Act Sec. 252(e)(2) and (f) following Code Sec. 42.

P.L. 99-514, §701(a):

Amended Code Sec. 55. **Effective**, generally, for tax years beginning after 12-31-86. However, for special rules, see Act Sec. 701(f)(2)-(7) following Code Sec. 56. Prior to amendment Code Sec. 55 read as follows:

SEC. 55. ALTERNATIVE MINIMUM TAX FOR TAXPAYERS OTHER THAN CORPORATIONS.

(a) TAX IMPOSED.—In the case of a taxpayer other than a corporation, there is imposed (in addition to any other tax imposed by this subtitle) a tax equal to the excess (if any) of—

(1) an amount equal to 20 percent of so much of the alternative minimum taxable income as exceeds the exemption amount, over

(2) the regular tax for the taxable year.

(b) ALTERNATIVE MINIMUM TAXABLE INCOME.—For purposes of this title, the term "alternative minimum taxable income" means the adjusted gross income (determined without regard to the deduction allowed by section 172) of the taxpayer for the taxable year—

(1) reduced by the sum of—

(A) the alternative tax net operating loss deduction, plus

(B) the alternative tax itemized deductions, plus

(C) any amount included in income under section 87 or 667, and

(2) increased by the amount of items of tax preference.

(c) CREDITS.—

(1) IN GENERAL.—For purposes of determining any credit allowable under subpart A, B, or D of part IV of this subchapter (other than the foreign tax credit allowed under section 27(a))—

(A) the tax imposed by this section shall not be treated as a tax imposed by this chapter, and

(B) the amount of the foreign tax credit allowed by section 27(a) shall be determined without regard to this section.

(2) FOREIGN TAX CREDIT ALLOWED AGAINST ALTERNATIVE MINIMUM TAX.—

(A) DETERMINATION OF FOREIGN TAX CREDIT.—The total amount of the foreign tax credit which can be taken against the tax imposed by subsection (a) shall be determined under subpart A of part III of subchapter N (section 901 and following).

(B) INCREASE IN AMOUNT OF FOREIGN TAXES TAKEN INTO ACCOUNT.—For purposes of the determination provided by subparagraph (A), the amount of the taxes paid or accrued to foreign countries or possessions of the United States during the taxable year shall be increased by an amount equal to the lesser of—

(i) the foreign tax credit allowable under section 27(a) in computing the regular tax for the taxable year, or

(ii) the tax imposed by subsection (a).

(C) SECTION 904(a) LIMITATION.—For purposes of the determination provided by subparagraph (A), the limitation of section 904(a) shall be an amount equal to the same proportion of the sum of the tax imposed by subsection (a) against which such credit is taken and the regular tax as—

(i) the taxpayer's alternative minimum taxable income from sources without the United States (but not in excess of the taxpayer's entire alternative minimum taxable income), bears to

(ii) his entire alternative minimum taxable income.

For such purpose, the amount of the limitation of section 904(a) shall not exceed the tax imposed by subsection (a).

(D) DEFINITION OF ALTERNATIVE MINIMUM TAXABLE INCOME FROM SOURCES WITHOUT THE UNITED STATES.—For purposes of subparagraph (C), the term "alternative minimum taxable income from sources without the United States" means adjusted gross income from sources without the United States, adjusted as provided in paragraphs (1) and (2) of subsection (b) (taking into account in such adjustment only items described in such paragraphs which are properly attributable to items of gross income from sources without the United States).

(E) SPECIAL RULE FOR APPLYING SECTION 904(c).—In determining the amount of foreign taxes paid or accrued during the taxable year which may be deemed to be paid or accrued in a preceding or succeeding taxable year under section 904(c)—

(i) the limitation of section 904(a) shall be deemed to be the amount of foreign tax credit allowable under section 27(a) in computing the regular tax for the taxable year increased by the amount of the limitation determined under subparagraph (C), and

(ii) any increase under subparagraph (B) shall be taken into account.

(3) CARRYOVER AND CARRYBACK OF CERTAIN CREDITS.—In the case of any taxable year for which a tax is imposed by this section, for purposes of determining the amount of any carryover or carryback to any other taxable year of any credit allowable under section 23, 25, 30, or 38, the amount of the limitation under section 26, 30(g), or 38(c) (as the case may be) shall be deemed to be—

(A) the amount of such credit allowable for such taxable year (determined without regard to this paragraph), reduced (but not below zero) by

(B) the amount of the tax imposed by this section for the taxable year, reduced by—

(i) the amount of the credit allowable under section 27(a),

(ii) in the case of the limitation under section 30(g), the amount of such tax taken into account under this subparagraph with respect to the limitations under section 26, and

(iii) in the case of the limitation under section 38(c), the amount of such tax taken into account under this subparagraph with respect to limitations under sections 26 and 30(g).

(d) ALTERNATIVE TAX NET OPERATING LOSS DEDUCTION DEFINED.—For purposes of this section—

(1) IN GENERAL.—The term "alternative tax net operating loss deduction" means the net operating loss deduction allowable for the taxable year under section 172, except that in determining the amount of such deduction—

(A) in the case of taxable years beginning after December 31, 1982, section 172(b)(2) shall be applied by substituting "alternative minimum taxable income" for "taxable income" each place it appears, and

(B) the net operating loss (within the meaning of section 172(c)) for any loss year shall be adjusted as provided in paragraph (2).

(2) ADJUSTMENTS TO NET OPERATING LOSS COMPUTATION.—

(A) POST-1982 LOSS YEARS.—In the case of a loss year beginning after December 31, 1982, the net operating loss for such year under section 172(c) shall—

(i) be reduced by the amount of the items of tax preference arising in such year which are taken into account in computing the net operating loss, and

(ii) be computed by taking into account only itemized deductions which are alternative tax itemized deductions for the taxable year and which are otherwise described in section 172(c).

(B) PRE-1983 YEARS.—In the case of loss years beginning before January 1, 1983, the amount of the net operating loss which may be carried over to taxable years beginning after December 31, 1982, for purposes of paragraph (1), shall be equal to the amount which may be carried from the loss year to the first taxable year of the taxpayer beginning after December 31, 1982.

(e) ALTERNATIVE TAX ITEMIZED DEDUCTIONS.—For purposes of this section—

(1) IN GENERAL.—The term "alternative tax itemized deductions" means an amount equal to the sum of any amount allowable as a deduction for the taxable year (other than a deduction allowable in computing adjusted gross income) under—

(A) section 165(a) for losses described in subsection (c)(3) or (d) of section 165,

(B) section 170 (relating to charitable deductions),

(C) section 213 (relating to medical deductions),

(D) this chapter for qualified interest, or

(E) section 691(c) (relating to deduction for estate tax).

(2) AMOUNTS WHICH MAY BE CARRIED OVER.—No amount shall be taken into account under paragraph (1) to the extent such amount may be carried to another taxable year for purposes of the regular tax.

(3) QUALIFIED INTEREST.—The term "qualified interest" means the sum of—

(A) any qualified housing interest, and

(B) any amount allowed as a deduction for interest (other than qualified housing interest) to the extent such amount does not exceed the qualified net investment income of the taxpayer for the taxable year.

(4) QUALIFIED HOUSING INTEREST.—

(A) IN GENERAL.—The term "qualified housing interest" means interest which is paid or accrued during the taxable year on indebtedness which is incurred in acquiring, constructing, or substantially rehabilitating any property which—

(i) is the principal residence (within the meaning of section 1034) of the taxpayer at the time such interest accrues or is paid, or

(ii) is a qualified dwelling used by the taxpayer (or any member of his family within the meaning of section 267(c)(4)) during the taxable year.

(B) QUALIFIED DWELLING.—The term "qualified dwelling" means any—

(i) house,

(ii) apartment,

(iii) condominium, or

(iv) mobile home not used on a transient basis (within the meaning of section 7701(a)(19)(C)(v)),

including all structures or other property appurtenant thereto.

(C) SPECIAL RULE FOR INDEBTEDNESS INCURRED BEFORE JULY 1, 1982.—The term "qualified housing interest" includes interest paid or accrued on indebtedness which—

(i) was incurred by the taxpayer before July 1, 1982, and

(ii) is secured by property which, at the time such indebtedness was incurred, was—

(I) the principal residence (within the meaning of section 1034) of the taxpayer, or

(II) a qualified dwelling used by the taxpayer (or any member of his family (within the meaning of section 267(c)(4))).

(5) QUALIFIED NET INVESTMENT INCOME.—For purposes of this subsection—

(A) IN GENERAL.—The term "qualified net investment income" means the excess of—

(i) qualified investment income, over

(ii) qualified investment expenses.

(B) QUALIFIED INVESTMENT INCOME.—The term "qualified investment income" means the sum of—

(i) investment income (within the meaning of section 163(d)(3)(B) other than clause (ii) thereof),

(ii) any capital gain net income attributable to the disposition of property held for investment, and

(iii) the amount of items of tax preference described in paragraph (1) of section 57(a).

(C) QUALIFIED INVESTMENT EXPENSES.—The term "qualified investment expenses" means the deductions directly connected with the production of qualified investment income to the extent that—

(i) such deductions are allowable in computing adjusted gross income, and

(ii) such deductions are not items of tax preference.

(6) SPECIAL RULES FOR ESTATES AND TRUSTS.—

(A) IN GENERAL.—In the case of an estate or trust, the alternative tax itemized deduction for any taxable year includes the deductions allowable under sections 642(c), 651(a), and 661(a).

(B) DETERMINATION OF ADJUSTED GROSS INCOME.—The adjusted gross income of an estate or trust shall be computed in the same manner as in the case of an individual, except that the deductions for costs paid or incurred in connection with the administration of the estate or trust shall be treated as allowable in arriving at adjusted gross income.

(7) LIMITATION ON MEDICAL DEDUCTION.—In applying subparagraph (C) of paragraph (1), the amount allowable as a deduction under section 213 shall be determined by substituting "10 percent" for "5 percent" in section 213(a).

(8) TREATMENT OF INTEREST IN LIMITED PARTNERSHIPS AND SUBCHAPTER S CORPORATIONS.—

(A) CERTAIN INTEREST TREATED AS NOT ALLOWABLE IN COMPUTING ADJUSTED GROSS INCOME.—Any amount allowable as a deduction for interest in indebtedness incurred or continued to purchase or carry a limited business interest shall be treated as not allowable in computing adjusted gross income.

(B) INCOME AND LOSSES TAKEN INTO ACCOUNT IN COMPUTING QUALIFIED NET INVESTMENT INCOME.—Any income or loss derived from a limited business interest shall be taken into account in computing qualified net investment income.

(C) LIMITED BUSINESS INTEREST.—The term "limited business interest" means an interest—

(i) as a limited partner in a partnership, or

(ii) as a shareholder in an S corporation if the taxpayer does not actively participate in the management of such corporation.

(f) OTHER DEFINITIONS.—For purposes of this section—

(1) EXEMPTION AMOUNT.—The term "exemption amount" means—

(A) $40,000 in the case of—

(i) a joint return, or

(ii) a surviving spouse (as defined in section 2(a)),

(B) $30,000 in the case of an individual who—

(i) is not a married individual (as defined in section 143), and

(ii) is not a surviving spouse (as so defined), and

(C) $20,000 in the case of—

(i) a married individual (as so defined) who files a separate return, or

(ii) an estate or trust.

(2) REGULAR TAX.—The term "regular tax" means the taxes imposed by this chapter for the taxable year (computed without regard to this section and without regard to the taxes imposed by sections 47(a), 72(m)(5)(B), 72(q), 402(e), 408(f), and 667(b)) reduced by the sum of the credits allowable under subparts A, B, and D of part IV of this subchapter. For purposes of this paragraph, the amount of the credits allowable under such subpart shall be determined without regard to this section.

P.L. 99-514, §1847(a)(1):

Amended Code Sec. 55(c)(3)(A) by striking out "of such limitation" and inserting in lieu thereof "of such credit allowable". **Effective** as if included in the provision of P.L. 98-369 to which such amendment relates.

P.L. 99-514, §1847(a)(2):

Amended Code Sec. 55(c)(2)(E)(i). **Effective** with respect to tax years beginning after 12-31-82. Prior to amendment, Code Sec. 55(c)(2)(E)(i) read as follows:

(i) the limitation of section 904(a) shall be increased by the amount of the limitation determined under subparagraph (C), and

• 1984, Deficit Reduction Act of 1984 (P.L. 98-369)

P.L. 98-369, §474(q)(1):

Amended Code Sec. 55(c)(1) by striking out "subpart A of Part IV" each place it appeared and inserting in lieu thereof "subpart A, B, or D of part IV", and by striking out "section 33(a)" each place it appeared and inserting in lieu thereof "section 27(a)". **Effective** for tax years beginning after 12-31-83, and to carrybacks from such years.

P.L. 98-369, §474(q)(2):

Amended Code Sec. 55(c)(2)(B)(i) by striking out "section 33(a)" and inserting in lieu thereof "section 27(a)". **Effective** for tax years beginning after 12-31-83, and to carrybacks from such years.

P.L. 98-369, §474(q)(3):

Amended Code Sec. 55(c)(3). **Effective** for tax years beginning after 12-31-83, and to carrybacks from such years. Prior to amendment, Code Sec. 55(c)(3) read as follows:

(3) Carryover and Carryback of Certain Credits.—

(A) In General.—In the case of any taxable year in which a tax is imposed by this section, for purposes of determining the amount of any carryback or carryover of any applicable credit to any other taxable year, the amount of the applicable credit limitation for such taxable year shall be deemed to be—

(i) the amount of the applicable credit allowable for such taxable year (determined without regard to this paragraph), reduced (but not below zero) by

(ii) the amount of the tax imposed by this section for the taxable year, reduced by—

(I) the amount of the credit allowable under section 33(a), and

(II) the amount of such tax taken into account under this clause with respect to any applicable credit having a lower number or letter designation.

(B) Applicable Credits, Etc.—For purposes of this paragraph—

(i) Applicable Credit.—The term "applicable credit" means any credit allowable under section 38, 40, 44B, 44C, 44E, or 44F.

(ii) Applicable Credit Limitation.—The term "applicable credit limitation" means, with respect to any applicable credit, the limitation under section 46(a)(3), 53(a), 44C(b)(5), 44E(e)(1), 44F(g)(1), or 50A(a)(2), whichever is appropriate.

P.L. 98-369, §474(q)(4):

Amended Code Sec. 55(f)(2) by striking out "allowable under subpart A of part IV of this subchapter (other than under sections 31, 39, and 43)" and inserting in lieu thereof "allowable under subparts A, B, and D of part IV of this subchapter." **Effective** for tax years beginning after 12-31-83, and to carrybacks from such years.

P.L. 98-369, §491(d)(1):

Amended Code Sec. 55(f)(2) by striking "409(c)". **Effective** for obligations issued after 12-31-83.

P.L. 98-369, §612(e)(3):

Amended Code Sec. 55(c)(3) by striking out "25" each place it appears and inserting in lieu thereof "26", and by striking out "section 23, 30, or 38" and inserting in lieu thereof "section 23, 25, 30, or 38". **Effective** for interest paid or accrued after 1984, on indebtedness incurred after 1984 and to Code Sec. 25(c)(2)(A)(ii) elections for calendar years after 1983.

P.L. 98-369, §711(a)(1):

Amended Code Sec. 55(f)(2) by striking out "sections 72(m)(5)(B)" and inserting in lieu thereof "sections 47(a), 72(m)(5)(B)". **Effective** as if included in the provision of P.L. 97-248 to which it relates.

P.L. 98-369, §711(a)(5):

Amended Code Sec. 55(b)(1)(C) by striking out "section 667" and inserting in lieu thereof "section 87 or 667". **Effective** as if included in the provision of P.L. 97-248 to which it relates.

• 1983, Technical Corrections Act of 1982 (P.L. 97-448)

P.L. 97-448, §101(aa):

Amended clause (ii) of section 102(b)(1)(B) of P.L. 97-34 by striking out "qualified net capital gain" and inserting "qualified net capital gain (or, if lesser, the alternative minimum taxable income within the meaning of section 55(b)(1) of such Code)". For amended section 102(b)(1)(B)(ii), see the amendment note below for P.L. 97-34, § 102(b).

P.L. 97-448, §103(g)(2)(E):

Amended Code Sec. 55(c)(4) by striking out "44G(b)(1),". **Effective** as if it had been included in the provision of P.L. 97-34 to which it relates. For amended Code Sec. 55(a)(4), see the amendment note below for P.L. 97-248, §201(a).

P.L. 97-448, §305(c):

Amended the last sentence of Code Sec. 55(b)(1) as in effect on the day before the date of the enactment of the Tax Equity and Fiscal Responsibility Act of 1982, by striking out "subparagraph (A)" and inserting in lieu thereof "subparagraph (A) (and in determining the sum of itemized deductions for purposes of subparagraph (C)(i))". **Effective** as if included in the amendments made by Act Sec. 421 of P.L. 95-600. For amended Code Sec. 55(b)(1), see the amendment note below for P.L. 97-248, §201(a).

P.L. 97-448, §306(a)(1)(C):

Amended Code Sec. 55(d)(2)(B) by striking out "subparagraph (A)" and inserting in lieu thereof "paragraph (1)". **Effective** as if it had been included in the provision of P.L. 97-248 to which it relates.

• 1982, Tax Equity and Fiscal Responsibility Act of 1982 (P.L. 97-248)

P.L. 97-248, §201(a):

Amended Code Sec. 55. **Effective** for tax years beginning after 12-31-82. Prior to amendment, Code Sec. 55 read as follows:

(a) ALTERNATIVE MINIMUM TAX IMPOSED.—In the case of a taxpayer other than a corporation, if—

(1) an amount equal to the sum of—

(A) 10 percent of so much of the alternative minimum taxable income as exceeds $20,000 but does not exceed $60,000 plus

(B) 20 percent of so much of the alternative minimum taxable income as exceeds $60,000, exceeds

(2) the regular tax for the taxable year, then there is imposed (in addition to all other taxes imposed by this title) a tax equal to the amount of such excess.

(b) DEFINITIONS.—For purposes of this section—

(1) ALTERNATIVE MINIMUM TAXABLE INCOME.—The term "alternative minimum taxable income" means gross income—

(A) reduced by the sum of the deductions allowed for the taxable year,

(B) reduced by the sum of any amounts included in income under section 86 or 667, and

(C) increased by an amount equal to the sum of the tax preference items for—

(i) adjusted itemized deductions (within the meaning of section 57(a)(1)), and

(ii) capital gains (within the meaning of section 57(a)(9)).

For purposes of subparagraph (A) (and in determining the sum of itemized deductions for purposes of subparagraph (C)(i)), a deduction shall not be taken into account to the extent such deduction may be carried to another taxable year.

(2) REGULAR TAX.—The term "regular tax" means the taxes imposed by this chapter for the taxable year (computed without regard to this section and without regard to the taxes imposed by sections 72(m)(5)(B), 402(e), 408(f), 409(c), and 667(b)) reduced by the sum of the credits allowable under subpart A of part IV of this subchapter (other than under sections 31, 39 and 43). For purposes of this paragraph, the amount of the credits allowable under such subpart shall be determined without regard to this section.

(3) TREATMENT OF ZERO BRACKET AMOUNT.—In the case of an individual who does not itemize his itemized deductions, the zero bracket amount shall be treated as a deduction allowed.

(c) CREDITS.—

(1) IN GENERAL.—For purposes of—

(A) determining the amount of any credit allowable under subpart A of part IV of this subchapter (other than the foreign tax credit allowable under section 33(a)) against the tax imposed by subsection (a), the tax imposed by subsection (a) shall be treated as a tax imposed by this chapter only to the extent of the amount which would be determined under subsection (a)(1) if the alternative minimum taxable income was reduced by the sum of—

(i) the net capital gain, and

(ii) the adjusted itemized deductions, and

(B) determining the amount of any such credit (including the credit allowable under section 33(a)) against the tax imposed by this chapter (other than the tax imposed by this section) for the current taxable year, this section shall be disregarded.

(2) RULES FOR DETERMINING AMOUNT OF CREDIT ALLOWABLE.—For purposes of determining the amount of any credit under subpart A of part IV of this subchapter (other than the credits imposed by sections 31, 39, and 43) which can be taken against the tax imposed by subsection (a)—

(A) the amount of such credit shall be increased by an amount equal to the lesser of—

(i) the amount of such credit allowable in computing the regular tax for the current taxable year, or

(ii) the excess of—

(I) the amount of the tax imposed by subsection (a), over

(II) the sum of the amounts determined under this subparagraph with respect to credits allowed under a section of such subpart having a higher number designation than such credit (other than the credits allowable by sections 31, 39, and 43), and

(B) in the case of any credit under section 38, 40, or 44B, such credit shall be reduced, under regulations prescribed by the Secretary, by that portion of such credit which is not attributable to an active trade or business of the taxpayer.

(3) FOREIGN TAX CREDIT ALLOWED AGAINST ALTERNATIVE MINIMUM TAX.

(A) DETERMINATION OF FOREIGN TAX CREDIT.—The total amount of the foreign tax credit which can be taken against the tax imposed by subsection (a) shall be determined under subpart A of part III of subchapter N (sec. 901 and following).

(B) SECTION 904(a) LIMITATION.—For purposes of the determination provided by subparagraph (A), the limitation of section 904(a) shall be an amount equal to the same proportion of the sum of the tax imposed by subsection (a) against which such credit is taken and the regular tax (excluding the tax imposed by section 56) as—

(i) the taxpayer's alternative minimum taxable income from sources without the United States (but not in excess of the taxpayer's entire alternative minimum taxable income), bears to

(ii) his entire alternative minimum taxable income.

For such purpose, the amount of the limitation of section 904(a) shall not exceed the tax imposed by subsection (a).

(C) DEFINITION OF ALTERNATIVE MINIMUM TAXABLE INCOME FROM SOURCES WITHOUT THE UNITED STATES.—For purposes of subparagraph (B), the term `alternative minimum taxable income from sources without the United States' means the items of gross income from sources without the United States adjusted as provided in subparagraph[s](A), (B), and (C) of section 55(b)(1) (taking into account in such adjustment only items described in such subparagraphs which are properly attributable to items of gross income from sources without the United States).

(D) SPECIAL RULE FOR APPLYING SECTION 904(c).—In determining the amount of foreign taxes paid or accrued during the taxable year which may be deemed to be paid or accrued in a preceding or succeeding taxable year under section 904(c)—

(i) the limitation of section 904(a) shall be increased by the amount of the limitation determined under subparagraph (B), and

(ii) any increase under paragraph (2)(A) shall be taken into account.

(4) CARRYOVER AND CARRYBACK OF CERTAIN CREDITS.—

(A) IN GENERAL.—For purposes of determining the amount of any carryover or carryback to any other taxable year of any credit allowable under subpart A of part IV of this subchapter (other than section 33), the amount of the limitation under section 44F(g)(1), 44E(e)(1), 44C(b)(1) and (2), 53(b), 50A(a)(2), or 46(a)(3) (to the extent such limitation does not exceed the amount of the credit allowable in computing the regular tax for the current taxable year) shall be increased for the current taxable year by the amount determined under subparagraph (A) of paragraph (1) of this subsection, and decreased by—

(i) the sum of the credits allowed under a section having a lower number designation than the section allowing such credit (other than the credits allowable by sections 31, 33, 39, and 43) against the tax imposed by subsection (a), and

(ii) the amount determined with respect to such credit under paragraph (2)(B) for the current taxable year.

(B) AMOUNT OF CREDIT.—Any increase under paragraph (2)(A) shall be taken into account in determining the amount of any carryover or carryback from the current taxable year."

• 1981, Economic Recovery Tax Act of 1981 (P.L. 97-34)

P.L. 97-34, §101(d)(1):

Amended Code Sec. 55(a)(1) by striking out all that followed "$60,000" in subparagraph (B) and inserting in lieu thereof, "exceeds", and by striking out subparagraph (C). **Effective** for tax years beginning after 12-31-81. Prior to amendment, Code Sec. 55(a)(1)(B) and (C) read:

(B) 20 percent of so much of the alternative minimum taxable income as exceeds $60,000 but does not exceed $100,000, plus

(C) 25 percent of so much of the alternative minimum taxable income as exceeds $100,000, exceeds

P.L. 97-34, §102(b), provides:

(b) APPLICATION WITH ALTERNATIVE MINIMUM TAX.—

(1) IN GENERAL.—If subsection (a) applies to any taxpayer for any taxable year, then the amount determined under section 55(a)(1) of the Internal Revenue Code of 1954 for such taxable year shall be equal to the lesser of—

(A) the amount determined under such section 55(a)(1) determined without regard to this subection, or

(B) the sum of—

(i) the amount which would be determined under such section 55(a)(1) if the alternative minimum taxable income was the excess of—

(I) the alternative minimum taxable income (within the meaning of section 55(b)(1) of such Code) of the taxpayer, over

(II) the qualified net capital gain of the taxpayer, and

(ii) 20 percent of the qualified net capital gain (or, if lesser, the alternative minimum taxable income within the meaning of section 55(b)(1) of such Code).

(2) NO CREDITS ALLOWABLE.—For purposes of section 55(c) of such Code, no credit allowable under subpart A of part IV of subchapter A of chapter 1 of such Code (other than section 33(a) of such Code) shall be allowable against the amount described in paragraph (1)(B)(ii).

P.L. 97-34, §221(b)(1)(A), as amended by P.L. 99-514, §231(a)(2):

Amended Code Sec. 55(c)(4)(A) by striking out "section 44E(e)(1)" and inserting in lieu thereof "section 44F(g)(1), 44E(e)(1)". **Effective** for amounts paid or incurred after 6-30-81. See the historical comment for P.L. 97-34, §221(d)(2), following Code Sec. 44F(a), for a transitional rule.

P.L. 97-34, §331(d)(1)(A):

Amended Code Sec. 55(c)(4)(A) by inserting "44G(b)(1)," before "53(b)". **Effective** for tax years ending after 12-31-82.

• 1980 (P.L. 96-603)

P.L. 96-603, §4(a)(1):

Amended Code Sec. 55(c)(1). **Effective** for tax years beginning after 1979. Prior to amendment, Code Sec. 55(c)(1) provided:

"(1) CREDITS OTHER THAN FOREIGN TAX CREDIT NOT ALLOWABLE, ETC.—For purposes of determining the amount of any credit allowable under subpart A of part IV of this subchapter (other than the foreign tax credit allowed under section 33(a))—

"(A) the tax imposed by this section shall not be treated as a tax imposed by this chapter, and

"(B) the amount of the foreign tax credit allowed under section 33(a) shall be determined without regard to this section.".

P.L. 96-603, §4(a)(2):

Amended Code Sec. 55(c) by redesignating paragraphs (2) and (3) as paragraphs (3) and (4), respectively and by adding a new paragraph (2). **Effective** for tax years beginning after 1979.

P.L. 96-603, §4(a)(3):

Amended Code Sec. 55(c)(4), as redesignated. **Effective** for tax years beginning after 1979. Prior to amendment, Code Sec. 55(c)(4) provided:

"(4) CARRYOVER AND CARRYBACK OF CERTAIN CREDITS.—In any taxable year in which a tax is imposed by this section (referred to as the current taxable year)—

"(A) EMPLOYMENT CREDIT.—For purposes of determining under section 53(c) the amount of any jobs credit carryback or carryover to any other taxable year, the amount of the limitation under section 53(b) for the current taxable year shall be deemed to be—

"(i) the amount of the credit allowable under section 44B for the current taxable year without regard to this subparagraph, reduced by

"(ii) the amount equal to the lesser of (I) the amount of the credit allowable under section 44B for the current taxable year without regard to this subparagraph, or (II) the net tax imposed by this section for the current taxable year.

"(B) WORK INCENTIVE PROGRAM CREDIT.—For purposes of determining under section 50(A)(b) the amount of any work incentive program credit carryback or carryover to any other taxable year, the amount of the limitation under section 50A(a)(2) for the current taxable year shall be deemed to be—

"(i) the amount of the credit allowable under section 40 for the current taxable year without regard to this subparagraph, reduced by

"(ii) the amount equal to the lesser of (I) the amount of the credit allowable under section 40 for the current taxable year without regard to this subparagraph, or, (II) the net tax imposed by this section for the current taxable year reduced by the amount of reduction described in clause (ii) of subparagraph (A).

"(C) INVESTMENT CREDIT.—For purposes of determining under section 46(b) the amount of any investment credit carryback or carryover to any other taxable year, the amount of the limitation under section 46(a)(3) for the current taxable year shall be deemed to be

"(i) the amount of the credit allowable under section 38 for the current taxable year without regard to this subparagraph, reduced by

"(ii) the amount equal to the lesser of (I) the amount of the credit allowable under section 38 for the current taxable year without regard to this subparagraph, or (II) the net tax imposed by this section for the current taxable year reduced by the sum of the amounts of reduction described in clause (ii) of subparagraphs (A) and (B).

"(D) NET TAX IMPOSED BY THIS SECTION.—For purposes of this paragraph, the term 'net tax imposed by this section' means the tax imposed by this section reduced by the foreign tax credit allowed under section 33(a), as modified by paragraph (2).

In determining any carryover under subsection 44C(b)(6), a rule similar to the rule set forth in subparagraph (A) shall be treated as inserted in this paragraph before subparagraph (A), and the applications of subparagraphs (A), (B), and (C) shall be adjusted accordingly. In determining any carryover under section 44E(e)(2), a rule similar to the rule set forth in subparagraph (A) shall be treated as inserted in this paragraph before subparagraph (A), and the applications of subparagraphs (A), (B), and (C) shall be adjusted accordingly."

P.L. 96-603, §4(b)(1):

Amended Code Sec. 55(b)(2) by striking out "credit allowable under section 33" and inserting in lieu thereof "credits allowable under such subpart". **Effective** for tax years beginning after 1979.

P.L. 96-603, §4(b)(2):

Amended Code Sec. 55(c)(3) by striking out subparagraph (B) and redesignating subparagraphs (C), (D), and (E) as subparagraphs (B), (C), and (D), respectively. **Effective** for tax years beginning after 1979. Prior to amendment, Code Sec. 55(c)(3)(B) provided:

"(B) INCREASE IN AMOUNT OF FOREIGN TAXES TAKEN INTO ACCOUNT.—For purposes of the determination provided by subparagraph (A), the amount of taxes paid or accrued to foreign countries or possessions of the United States during the taxable year shall be increased by an amount equal to the lesser of—

"(i) the foreign tax credit allowable under section 33(a) in computing the regular tax for the taxable year, or

"(ii) the tax imposed by subsection (a).".

Amended Code Sec. 55(c)(3)(C) and (D)(i), as redesignated, by striking out "subparagraph (C)" and inserting in lieu thereof "subparagraph (B)", effective for taxable years beginning after 1979.

Amended Code Sec. 55(c)(3)(D)(ii), as so redesignated, effective for taxable years beginning after 1979. Prior to amendment, Code Sec. 55(c)(3)(D)(ii) provided:

"(ii) any increase under subparagraph (B) shall be taken into account.".

• 1980, Crude Oil Windfall Profit Tax Act of 1980 (P.L. 96-223)

P.L. 96-223, §232(b)(2)(A):

Amended Code Sec. 55(c)(3) by adding the last sentence. **Effective** for uses or sales after 9-30-80, in tax years ending after such date.

P.L. 96-223, §232(c)(2):

Amended Code Sec. 55(b)(1)(B) by striking out "section 667" and inserting "section 86 or 667". For the **effective** date, see P.L. 96-223, §232(c)(1), following Code Sec. 86.

• 1980, Technical Corrections Act of 1979 (P.L. 96-222)

P.L. 96-222, §104(a)(4)(A):

Amended Code Sec. 55(b)(1) by adding the last sentence. **Effective** for tax years beginning after 12-31-78.

P.L. 96-222, §104(a)(4)(B):

Amended Code Sec. 55(c)(1) and (2). **Effective** tax years beginning after 12-31-78. Prior to amendment, Code Sec. 55(c)(1) and (2) read as follows:

(1) CREDITS OTHER THAN THE FOREIGN TAX CREDIT NOT ALLOWABLE.—For purposes of determining the amount of any credit allowable under subpart A of part IV of this subchapter (other than the foreign tax credit allowed under section 33(a)), the tax imposed by this section shall not be treated as a tax imposed by this chapter.

(2) FOREIGN TAX CREDIT ALLOWED AGAINST ALTERNATIVE MINIMUM TAX.—The total amount of the foreign tax credit which can be taken against the tax imposed by subsection (a) shall be determined under section 901 and sections 903 through 908. For purposes of this determination—

(A) the amount of taxes paid or accrued to foreign countries or possessions of the United States in the taxable year shall be deemed to include an amount equal to the lesser of (i) the foreign tax credit allowed under section 33(a) in computing the regular tax for the taxable year, or (ii) the tax imposed under subsection (a);

(B) the limitation of section 904(a) shall be an amount equal to the same proportion of the sum of the tax imposed by this section against which such credit is taken and the regular tax (excluding the tax imposed by section 56) which the taxpayer's alternative minimum taxable income from sources without the United States (but not in excess of the taxpayer's entire alternative minimum taxable income) bears to his entire alternative minimum taxable income for the same taxable year. For purposes of the preceding sentence, the entire alternative minimum taxable income shall be reduced by an amount equal to the zero bracket amount;

(C) the term "alternative minimum taxable income from sources without United States" means the excess of the items of gross income from sources without the United States over that portion of the deductions taken into account in computing alternative minimum taxable income which are deducted from those items of gross income in computing taxable income from sources without the United States; for purposes of this subparagraph, and except as provided in section 904, gross and taxable income from sources without the United States shall be determined under part I of subchapter N of chapter 1; and

(D) the amount of foreign taxes paid during the taxable year which may be deemed to be paid in a preceding or succeeding year under section 904(c), the limitation of section 904(a) shall be increased by the lesser of (i) the amount described in subparagraph (B) or (ii) the tax imposed under subsection (a).

P.L. 96-222, §104(a)(4)(C):

Amended Code Sec. 55(b)(2) by adding the last sentence. **Effective** for tax years beginning after 12-31-78.

P.L. 96-222, §104(a)(4)(D):

Amended Code Sec. 55(b) by adding paragraph (3). **Effective** for tax years beginning after 12-31-78.

P.L. 96-222, §104(a)(4)(G):

Amended Code Sec. 55(c)(3) by adding the last sentence. **Effective** for tax years beginning after 12-31-79.

P.L. 96-222, §104(a)(4)(H)(i):

Amended Code Sec. 55(a) by deleting all that followed paragraph (1) and inserting that which follows paragraph (1). **Effective** for tax years beginning after 12-31-78.

P.L. 96-222, §104(a)(4)(H)(ii):

Amended Code Sec. 55(c)(3)(A) by changing "section 53(c)" to "section 53(b)'. **Effective** for tax years beginning after 12-31-78.

P.L. 96-222, §104(a)(4)(H)(viii):

Amended Code Sec. 55(b) by adding "409(c)," after "408(f)". **Effective** for tax years beginning after 12-31-78.

• 1978, Revenue Act of 1978 (P.L. 95-600)

P.L. 95-600, §421(a), (g):

Added Code Sec. 55. **Effective** for tax years beginning after 12-31-78.

[Sec. 55(e)]

(e) EXEMPTION FOR SMALL CORPORATIONS.—

(1) IN GENERAL.—

(A) $7,500,000 GROSS RECEIPTS TEST.—The tentative minimum tax of a corporation shall be zero for any taxable year if the corporation's average annual gross receipts for all 3-taxable-year periods ending before such taxable year does not exceed $7,500,000. For purposes of the preceding sentence, only taxable years beginning after December 31, 1993, shall be taken into account.

(B) $5,000,000 GROSS RECEIPTS TEST FOR FIRST 3-YEAR PERIOD.—Subparagraph (A) shall be applied by substituting "$5,000,000" for "$7,500,000" for the first 3-taxable-year period (or portion thereof) of the corporation which is taken into account under subparagraph (A).

(C) FIRST TAXABLE YEAR CORPORATION IN EXISTENCE.—If such taxable year is the first taxable year that such corporation is in existence, the tentative minimum tax of such corporation for such year shall be zero.

(D) SPECIAL RULES.—For purposes of this paragraph, the rules of paragraphs (2) and (3) of section 448(c) shall apply.

(2) PROSPECTIVE APPLICATION OF MINIMUM TAX IF SMALL CORPORATION CEASES TO BE SMALL.—In the case of a corporation whose tentative minimum tax is zero for any prior taxable year by reason of paragraph (1), the application of this part for taxable years beginning with the first taxable year such corporation ceases to be described in paragraph (1) shall be determined with the following modifications:

(A) Section 56(a)(1) (relating to depreciation) and section 56(a)(5) (relating to pollution control facilities) shall apply only to property placed in service on or after the change date.

(B) Section 56(a)(2) (relating to mining exploration and development costs) shall apply only to costs paid or incurred on or after the change date.

(C) Section 56(a)(3) (relating to treatment of long-term contracts) shall apply only to contracts entered into on or after the change date.

(D) Section 56(a)(4) (relating to alternative net operating loss deduction) shall apply in the same manner as if, in section 56(d)(2), the change date were substituted for "January 1, 1987" and the day before the change date were substituted for "December 31, 1986" each place it appears.

(E) Section 56(g)(2)(B) (relating to limitation on allowance of negative adjustments based on adjusted current earnings) shall apply only to prior taxable years beginning on or after the change date.

(F) Section 56(g)(4)(A) (relating to adjustment for depreciation to adjusted current earnings) shall not apply.

(G) Subparagraphs (D) and (F) of section 56(g)(4) (relating to other earnings and profits adjustments and depletion) shall apply in the same manner as if the day before the change date were substituted for "December 31, 1989" each place it appears therein.

(3) EXCEPTION.—The modifications in paragraph (2) shall not apply to—

(A) any item acquired by the corporation in a transaction to which section 381 applies, and

(B) any property the basis of which in the hands of the corporation is determined by reference to the basis of the property in the hands of the transferor, if such item or property was subject to any provision referred to in paragraph (2) while held by the transferor.

(4) CHANGE DATE.—For purposes of paragraph (2), the change date is the first day of the first taxable year for which the taxpayer ceases to be described in paragraph (1).

(5) LIMITATION ON USE OF CREDIT FOR PRIOR YEAR MINIMUM TAX LIABILITY.—In the case of a taxpayer whose tentative minimum tax for any taxable year is zero by reason of paragraph (1), section 53(c) shall be applied for such year by reducing the amount otherwise taken into account under section 53(c)(1) by 25 percent of so much of such amount as exceeds $25,000. Rules similar to the rules of section 38(c)(6)(B) shall apply for purposes of the preceding sentence.

Amendments

• 2010, Creating Small Business Jobs Act of 2010 (P.L. 111-240)

P.L. 111-240, §2013(b):

Amended Code Sec. 55(e)(5) by striking "38(c)(3)(B)" and inserting "38(c)(6)(B)". **Effective** 9-27-2010.

• 1998, IRS Restructuring and Reform Act of 1998 (P.L. 105-206)

P.L. 105-206, §6006(a):

Amended Code Sec. 55(e)(1). **Effective** as if included in the provision of P.L. 105-34 to which it relates [**effective** for tax years beginning after 12-31-97.—CCH]. Prior to amendment, Code Sec. 55(e)(1) read as as follows:

(1) IN GENERAL.—The tentative minimum tax of a corporation shall be zero for any taxable year if—

(A) such corporation met the $5,000,000 gross receipts test of section 448(c) for its first taxable year beginning after December 31, 1996, and

(B) such corporation would meet such test for the taxable year and all prior taxable years beginning after such first taxable year if such test were applied by substituting "$7,500,000" for "$5,000,000".

• 1997, Taxpayer Relief Act of 1997 (P.L. 105-34)

P.L. 105-34, §401(a):

Amended Code Sec. 55 by adding at the end a new subsection (e). **Effective** for tax years beginning after 12-31-97.

• 1984, Deficit Reduction Act of 1984 (P.L. 98-369)

P.L. 98-369, §711(a)(4):

Amended Code Sec. 55(e)(8)(B). **Effective** as if included in the provision of P.L. 97-248 to which it relates. Prior to amendment, it read as follows:

(B) Income Treated as Qualified Investment Income.—Any income derived from a limited business interest shall be treated as qualified investment income.

• 1983, Technical Corrections Act of 1982 (P.L. 97-448)

P.L. 97-448, §306(a)(1)(B):

Amended Code Sec. 55(e)(5)(B)(ii) by striking out "net capital gain" and inserting in lieu thereof "capital gain net income". **Effective** if included in the provision of P.L. 97-248 to which it relates.

• 1982, Subchapter S Revision Act of 1982 (P.L. 37-354)

P.L. 97-354, §5(a)(13):

Amended Code Sec. 55(e)(8)(C)(ii) by striking out "an electing small business corporation (as defined in section 1371(b))" and inserting in lieu thereof "an S corporation". **Effective** for tax years beginning after 12-31-82.

[Sec. 56]

SEC. 56. ADJUSTMENTS IN COMPUTING ALTERNATIVE MINIMUM TAXABLE INCOME.

[Sec. 56(a)]

(a) ADJUSTMENTS APPLICABLE TO ALL TAXPAYERS.—In determining the amount of the alternative minimum taxable income for any taxable year the following treatment shall apply (in lieu of the treatment applicable for purposes of computing the regular tax):

(1) DEPRECIATION.—

(A) IN GENERAL.—

(i) PROPERTY OTHER THAN CERTAIN PERSONAL PROPERTY.—Except as provided in clause (ii), the depreciation deduction allowable under section 167 with respect to any tangible property placed in service after December 31, 1986, shall be determined under the alternative system of section 168(g). In the case of property placed in service after December 31, 1998, the preceding sentence shall not apply but clause (ii) shall continue to apply.

(ii) 150-PERCENT DECLINING BALANCE METHOD FOR CERTAIN PROPERTY.—The method of depreciation used shall be—

(I) the 150 percent declining balance method,

(II) switching to the straight line method for the 1st taxable year for which using the straight line method with respect to the adjusted basis as of the beginning of the year will yield a higher allowance.

The preceding sentence shall not apply to any section 1250 property (as defined in section 1250(c)) (and the straight line method shall be used for such section 1250 property) or to any other property if the depreciation deduction determined under section 168 with respect to such other property for purposes of the regular tax is determined by using the straight line method.

(B) EXCEPTION FOR CERTAIN PROPERTY.—This paragraph shall not apply to property described in paragraph (1), (2), (3), or (4) of section 168(f), or in section 168(e)(3)(C)(iv).

(C) COORDINATION WITH TRANSITIONAL RULES.—

(i) IN GENERAL.—This paragraph shall not apply to property placed in service after December 31, 1986, to which the amendments made by section 201 of the Tax Reform Act of 1986 do not apply by reason of section 203, 204, or 251(d) of such Act.

(ii) TREATMENT OF CERTAIN PROPERTY PLACED IN SERVICE BEFORE 1987.—This paragraph shall apply to any property to which the amendments made by section 201 of the Tax Reform Act of 1986 apply by reason of an election under section 203(a)(1)(B) of such Act without regard to the requirement of subparagraph (A) that the property be placed in service after December 31, 1986.

(D) NORMALIZATION RULES.—With respect to public utility property described in section 168(i)(10), the Secretary shall prescribe the requirements of a normalization method of accounting for this section.

(2) MINING EXPLORATION AND DEVELOPMENT COSTS.—

(A) IN GENERAL.—With respect to each mine or other natural deposit (other than an oil, gas, or geothermal well) of the taxpayer, the amount allowable as a deduction under section 616(a) or 617(a) (determined without regard to section 291(b)) in computing the regular tax for costs paid or incurred after December 31, 1986, shall be capitalized and amortized ratably over the 10-year period beginning with the taxable year in which the expenditures were made.

(B) LOSS ALLOWED.—If a loss is sustained with respect to any property described in subparagraph (A), a deduction shall be allowed for the expenditures described in subparagraph (A) for the taxable year in which such loss is sustained in an amount equal to the lesser of—

(i) the amount allowable under section 165(a) for the expenditures if they had remained capitalized, or

(ii) the amount of such expenditures which have not previously been amortized under subparagraph (A).

(3) TREATMENT OF CERTAIN LONG-TERM CONTRACTS.—In the case of any long-term contract entered into by the taxpayer on or after March 1, 1986, the taxable income from such contract shall be determined under the percentage of completion method of accounting (as modified by section 460(b)). For purposes of the preceding sentence, in the case of a contract described in section 460(e)(1), the percentage of the contract completed shall be determined under section 460(b)(1) by using the simplified procedures for allocation of costs prescribed under section 460(b)(3). The first sentence of this paragraph shall not apply to any home construction contract (as defined in section 460(e)(6)).

(4) ALTERNATIVE TAX NET OPERATING LOSS DEDUCTION.—The alternative tax net operating loss deduction shall be allowed in lieu of the net operating loss deduction allowed under section 172.

(5) POLLUTION CONTROL FACILITIES.—In the case of any certified pollution control facility placed in service after December 31, 1986, the deduction allowable under section 169 (without regard to section 291) shall be determined under the alternative system of section 168(g). In the case of such a facility placed in service after December 31, 1998, such deduction shall be determined under section 168 using the straight line method.

(6) ADJUSTED BASIS.—The adjusted basis of any property to which paragraph (1) or (5) applies (or with respect to which there are any expenditures to which paragraph (2) or subsection (b)(2) applies) shall be determined on the basis of the treatment prescribed in paragraph (1), (2), or (5), or subsection (b)(2), whichever applies.

(7) SECTION 87 NOT APPLICABLE.—Section 87 (relating to alcohol fuel credit) shall not apply.

Amendments

• 2005, Energy Tax Incentives Act of 2005 (P.L. 109-58)

P.L. 109-58, §1326(d):

Amended Code Sec. 56(a)(1)(B) by inserting ", or in section 168(e)(3)(C)(iv)" before the period. **Effective** for property placed in service after 4-11-2005. For an exception, see Act Sec. 1326(e)(2), below.

P.L. 109-58, §1326(e)(2), provides:

(2) EXCEPTION.—The amendments made by this section shall not apply to any property with respect to which the taxpayer or a related party has entered into a binding contract for the construction thereof on or before April 11, 2005, or, in the case of self-constructed property, has started construction on or before such date.

• 2002, Job Creation and Worker Assistance Act of 2002 (P.L. 107-147)

P.L. 107-147, §417(5):

Amended the flush sentence at the end of Code Sec. 56(a)(1)(A)(ii) by striking "such 1250" and inserting "such section 1250". **Effective** 3-9-2002.

• 2000, Community Renewal Tax Relief Act of 2000 (P.L. 106-554)

P.L. 106-554, §314(d):

Amended Code Sec. 56(a)(1)(A) by inserting before "or to any other property" in the flush sentence at the end of clause (ii) the following: "(and the straight line method shall be used for such 1250 property)". **Effective** as if included in the provision of P.L. 105-34 to which it relates **[effective** 8-5-97.—CCH].

• Tax and Trade Relief Extension Act of 1998 (P.L. 105-277)

P.L. 105-277, §4006(c)(2):

Amended Code Sec. 56(a)(3) by striking "section 460(b)(2)" and inserting "section 460(b)(1)" and by striking "section 460(b)(4)" and inserting "section 460(b)(3)". **Effective** 10-21-98

• 1997, Taxpayer Relief Act of 1997 (P.L. 105-34)

P.L. 105-34, §402(a):

Amended Code Sec. 56(a)(1)(A)(i) by adding a new sentence. **Effective** 8-9-97.

P.L. 105-34, §402(b):

Amended Code Sec. 56(a)(5) by adding a new sentence. **Effective** 8-9-97.

P.L. 105-34, §403(a):

Amended Code Sec. 56(a) by striking paragraph (6) and by redesignating paragraphs (7) and (8) as paragraphs (6) and (7), respectively. **Effective** for dispositions in tax years beginning after 12-31-87. For a special rule, see Act Sec. 403(b)(2), below. Prior to being stricken, Code Sec. 56(a)(6) read as follows:

(6) INSTALLMENT SALES OF CERTAIN PROPERTY.—In the case of any disposition after March 1, 1986, of any property described in section 1221(1), income from such disposition shall be determined without regard to the installment method under section 453. This paragraph shall not apply to any disposition with respect to which an election is in effect under section 453(l)(2)(B).

P.L. 105-34, §403(b)(2), provides:

(2) SPECIAL RULE FOR 1987.—In the case of taxable years beginning in 1987, the last sentence of section 56(a)(6) of the Internal Revenue Code of 1986 (as in effect for such taxable years) shall be applied by inserting "or in the case of a taxpayer using the cash receipts and disbursements method of accounting, any disposition described in section 453C(e)(1)(B)(ii)" after "section 453C(e)(4)".

• 1990, Omnibus Budget Reconciliation Act of 1990 (P.L. 101-508)

P.L. 101-508, §11812(b)(4):

Amended Code Sec. 56(a)(1)(D) by striking "section 167(l)(3)(A)" and inserting "section 168(i)(10)". **Effective**, generally, for property placed in service after 11-5-90. However, for exceptions, see Act Sec. 11812(c)(2) and (3), below.

P.L. 101-508, §11812(c)(2)-(3), provides:

(2) EXCEPTION.—The amendments made by this section shall not apply to any property to which section 168 of the Internal Revenue Code of 1986 does not apply by reason of subsection (f)(5) thereof.

(3) EXCEPTION FOR PREVIOUSLY GRANDFATHER EXPENDITURES.—The amendments made by this section shall not apply to rehabilitation expenditures described in section 252(f)(5) of the Tax Reform Act of 1986 (as added by section 1002(l)(31) of the Technical and Miscellaneous Revenue Act of 1988).

• 1989, Omnibus Budget Reconciliation Act of 1989 (P.L. 101-239)

P.L. 101-239, §7612(c)(1):

Amended Code Sec. 56(a)(3) by striking "with respect to which the requirement of clauses (i) and (ii) of section 460(e)(1)(B) are met" after "460(e)(6))". **Effective** for contracts entered into in tax years beginning after 9-30-90.

P.L. 101-239, §7815(e)(2)(B):

Amended Code Sec. 56(a)(3) by striking "The preceding sentence shall not" and inserting "The first sentence of this paragraph shall not". **Effective** if included in the provision of P.L. 100-647 to which it relates.

P.L. 101-239, §7821(a)(5), provides:

(5) In the case of taxable years beginning in 1987, the reference to section 453 contained in section 56(a)(6) of the Internal Revenue Code of 1986 shall be treated as including a reference to section 453A.

• 1988, Technical and Miscellaneous Revenue Act of 1988 (P.L. 100-647)

P.L. 100-647, §1002(a)(12):

Amended Code Sec. 56(a)(1)(C)(i) by striking out "do not apply" and inserting in lieu thereof "do not apply by reason of section 203, 204, or 251(d) of such Act". **Effective** as if included in the provision of P.L. 99-514 to which it relates.

P.L. 100-647, §1007(b)(1):

Amended Code Sec. 56(a)(3) by adding at the end thereof a new sentence. **Effective** as if included in the provision of P.L. 99-514 to which it relates.

P.L. 100-647, §1007(b)(15):

Amended Code Sec. 56(a)(1)(A)(i) by striking out "real" in the heading and inserting in lieu thereof "personal". **Effective** as if included in the provision of P.L. 99-514 to which it relates.

P.L. 100-647, §1007(b)(19):

Amended Code Sec. 56(a) by adding at the end thereof new paragraph (8). **Effective** as if included in the provision of P.L. 99-514 to which it relates.

P.L. 100-647, §5041(b)(4):

Amended Code Sec. 56(a)(3) by adding at the end thereof a new sentence. **Effective**, generally, for contracts entered into on or after 6-21-88. For special rules, see Act Sec. 5041(e)(1)(B)-(C), below.

P.L. 100-647, §5041(e)(1)(B)-(C), provides:

(B) BINDING BIDS.—The amendments made by subsections (a), (b), and (c) shall not apply to any contract resulting from the acceptance of a bid made before June 21, 1988. The preceding sentence shall apply only if the bid could not have been revoked or altered at any time on or after June 21, 1988.

(C) SPECIAL RULE FOR CERTAIN SHIP CONTRACTS.—The amendments made by subsections (a), (b), and (c) shall not apply in the case of a qualified ship contract (as defined in section 10203(b)(2)(B) of the Revenue Act of 1987).

• 1987, Revenue Act of 1987 (P.L. 100-203)

P.L. 100-203, §10202(d):

Amended Code Sec. 56(a)(6). For the **effective** date, see Act Sec. 10202(e), as amended by P.L. 100-647, §2004(d)(4), below. Prior to amendment Code Sec. 56(a)(6) read as follows:

(6) INSTALLMENT SALES OF CERTAIN PROPERTY.—In the case of any—

(A) disposition after March 1, 1986, of property described in section 1221(1), or

(B) other disposition if an obligation arising from such disposition would be an applicable installment obligation (as defined in section 453C(e)) to which section 453C applies,

income from such disposition shall be determined without regard to the installment method under section 453 or 453A and all payments to be received for the disposition shall be deemed received in the taxable year of the disposition. This paragraph shall not apply to any disposition with respect to which an election is in effect under section 453C(e)(4).

P.L. 100-203, §10202(e), as amended by P.L. 100-647, §2004(d)(4), provides:

(e) EFFECTIVE DATES.—

(1) IN GENERAL.—Except as provided in this subsection, the amendments made by this section shall apply to dispositions in taxable years beginning after December 31, 1987.

(2) SPECIAL RULES FOR DEALERS.—

(A) IN GENERAL.—In the case of dealer dispositions (within the meaning of section 453A of the Internal Revenue Code of 1986), the amendments made by subsections (a) and (b) shall apply to installment obligations arising from dispositions after December 31, 1987.

(B) SPECIAL RULES FOR OBLIGATIONS ARISING FROM DEALER DISPOSITIONS AFTER FEBRUARY 28, 1986, AND BEFORE JANUARY 1, 1988.—

(i) IN GENERAL.—In the case of an applicable installment obligation arising from a disposition described in subclause (I) or (II) of section 453C(e)(1)(A)(i) of the Internal Revenue Code of 1986 (as in effect before the amendments made by this section) before January 1, 1988, the amendments made by subsections (a) and (b) shall apply to taxable years beginning after December 31, 1987.

(ii) CHANGE IN METHOD OF ACCOUNTING.—In the case of any taxpayer who is required by clause (i) to change its method of accounting for any taxable year with respect to obligations described in clause (i)—

(I) such change shall be treated as initiated by the taxpayer,

(II) such change shall be treated as made with the consent of the Secretary of the Treasury or his delegate, and

(III) the net amount of adjustments required by section 481 of the Internal Revenue Code of 1986 shall be taken into account over a period not longer than 4 taxable years.

(C) CERTAIN RULES MADE APPLICABLE.—For purposes of this paragraph, rules similar to the rules of paragraphs (4) and (5) of section 812(c) of the Tax Reform Act of 1986 (as added by the Technical and Miscellaneous Revenue Act of 1988) shall apply.

(3) SPECIAL RULE FOR NONDEALERS.—

(A) ELECTION.—A taxpayer may elect, at such time and in such manner as the Secretary of the Treasury or his delegates may prescribe, to have the amendments made by subsections (a) and (c) apply to taxable years ending after December 31, 1986, with respect to dispositions and pledges occurring after August 16, 1986.

(B) PLEDGING RULES.—Except as provided in subparagraph (A)—

(i) IN GENERAL.—Section 453A(d) of the Internal Revenue Code of 1986 shall apply to any installment obligation which is pledged to secure any secured indebtedness (within the meaning of section 453A(d)(4) of such Code) after December 17, 1987, in taxable years ending after such date.

(ii) COORDINATION WITH SECTION 453C.—For purposes of section 453C of such Code (as in effect before its repeal), the face amount of any obligation to which section 453A(d) of such Code applies shall be reduced by the amount treated as payments on such obligation under section 453A(d) of such Code and the amount of any indebtedness secured by it shall not be taken into account.

(4) MINIMUM TAX.—The amendment made by subsection (d) shall apply to dispositions in taxable years beginning after December 31, 1986.

(5) COORDINATION WITH TAX REFORM ACT OF 1986.—The amendments made by this section shall not apply to any installment obligation or to any taxpayer during any period to the extent the amendment made by section 811 of the Tax Reform Act of 1986 do not apply to such obligation or during such period.

[Sec. 56(b)]

(b) ADJUSTMENTS APPLICABLE TO INDIVIDUALS.—In determining the amount of the alternative minimum taxable income of any taxpayer (other than a corporation), the following treatment shall apply (in lieu of the treatment applicable for purposes of computing the regular tax):

(1) LIMITATION ON DEDUCTIONS.—

(A) IN GENERAL.—No deduction shall be allowed—

(i) for any miscellaneous itemized deduction (as defined in section 67(b)), or

(ii) for any taxes described in paragraph (1), (2), or (3) of section 164(a) or clause (ii) of section 164(b)(5)(A).

Clause (ii) shall not apply to any amount allowable in computing adjusted gross income.

Caution: Code Sec. 56(b)(1)(B), below, prior to amendment by P.L. 111-148, applies to tax years beginning on or before December 31, 2012.

(B) MEDICAL EXPENSES.—In determining the amount allowable as a deduction under section 213, subsection (a) of section 213 shall be applied by substituting "10 percent" for "7.5 percent".

Caution: Code Sec. 56(b)(1)(B), below, as amended by P.L. 111-148, applies to tax years beginning after December 31, 2012.

(B) MEDICAL EXPENSES.—In determining the amount allowable as a deduction under section 213, subsection (a) of section 213 shall be applied without regard to subsection (f) of such section.

(C) INTEREST.—In determining the amount allowable as a deduction for interest, subsections (d) and (h) of section 163 shall apply, except that—

(i) in lieu of the exception under section 163(h)(2)(D), the term "personal interest" shall not include any qualified housing interest (as defined in subsection (e)),

(ii) sections 163(d)(6) and 163(h)(5) (relating to phase-ins) shall not apply,

(iii) interest on any specified private activity bond (and any amount treated as interest on a specified private activity bond under section 57(a)(5)(B)) and any deduction referred to in section 57(a)(5)(A), shall be treated as includible in gross income (or as deductible) for purposes of applying section 163(d),

(iv) in lieu of the exception under section 163(d)(3)(B)(i), the term "investment interest" shall not include any qualified housing interest (as defined in subsection (e)), and

(v) the adjustments of this section and sections 57 and 58 shall apply in determining net investment income under section 163(d).

(D) TREATMENT OF CERTAIN RECOVERIES.—No recovery of any tax to which subparagraph (A)(ii) applied shall be included in gross income for purposes of determining alternative minimum taxable income.

(E) STANDARD DEDUCTION AND DEDUCTION FOR PERSONAL EXEMPTIONS NOT ALLOWED.—The standard deduction under section 63(c), the deduction for personal exemptions under section 151, and the deduction under section 642(b) shall not be allowed. The preceding sentence shall not apply to so much of the standard deduction as is determined under subparagraphs (D) and (E) of section 63(c)(1).

(F) SECTION 68 NOT APPLICABLE.—Section 68 shall not apply.

(2) CIRCULATION AND RESEARCH AND EXPERIMENTAL EXPENDITURES.—

(A) IN GENERAL.—The amount allowable as a deduction under section 173 or 174(a) in computing the regular tax for amounts paid or incurred after December 31, 1986, shall be capitalized and—

(i) in the case of circulation expenditures described in section 173, shall be amortized ratably over the 3-year period beginning with the taxable year in which the expenditures were made, or

(ii) in the case of research and experimental expenditures described in section 174(a), shall be amortized ratably over the 10-year period beginning with the taxable year in which the expenditures were made.

(B) LOSS ALLOWED.—If a loss is sustained with respect to any property described in subparagraph (A), a deduction shall be allowed for the expenditures described in subparagraph (A) for the taxable year in which such loss is sustained in an amount equal to the lesser of—

(i) the amount allowable under section 165(a) for the expenditures if they had remained capitalized, or

(ii) the amount of such expenditures which have not previously been amortized under subparagraph (A).

(C) SPECIAL RULE FOR PERSONAL HOLDING COMPANIES.—In the case of circulation expenditures described in section 173, the adjustments provided in this paragraph shall apply also to a personal holding company (as defined in section 542).

(D) EXCEPTION FOR CERTAIN RESEARCH AND EXPERIMENTAL EXPENDITURES.—If the taxpayer materially participates (within the meaning of section 469(h)) in an activity, this paragraph shall not apply to any amount allowable as deduction under section 174(a) for expenditures paid or incurred in connection with such activity.

(3) TREATMENT OF INCENTIVE STOCK OPTIONS.—Section 421 shall not apply to the transfer of stock acquired pursuant to the exercise of an incentive stock option (as defined in section 422). Section 422(c)(2) shall apply in any case where the disposition and the inclusion for purposes of this part are within the same taxable year and such section shall not apply in any other case. The adjusted basis of any stock so acquired shall be determined on the basis of the treatment prescribed by this paragraph.

Amendments

• 2010, Patient Protection and Affordable Care Act (P.L. 111-148)

P.L. 111-148, §9013(c):

Amended Code Sec. 56(b)(1)(B) by striking "by substituting '10 percent' for '7.5 percent'" and inserting "without regard to subsection (f) of such section". **Effective** for tax years beginning after 12-31-2012.

• 2009, American Recovery and Reinvestment Tax Act of 2009 (P.L. 111-5)

P.L. 111-5, §1008(d):

Amended the last sentence of Code Sec. 56(b)(1)(E) by striking "section 63(c)(1)(D)" and inserting "subparagraphs (D) and (E) of section 63(c)(1)". **Effective** for purchases on or after 2-17-2009 in tax years ending after such date.

• 2008, Tax Extenders and Alternative Minimum Tax Relief Act of 2008 (P.L. 110-343)

P.L. 110-343, Division C, §706(b)(3):

Amended Code Sec. 56(b)(1)(E) by adding at the end a new sentence. **Effective** for disasters declared in tax years beginning after 12-31-2007.

P.L. 110-343, Division C, §712, provides:

SEC. 712. COORDINATION WITH HEARTLAND DISASTER RELIEF.

The amendments made by this subtitle, other than the amendments made by sections 706(a)(2), 710, and 711, shall not apply to any disaster described in section 702(c)[b](1)(A), or to any expenditure or loss resulting from such disaster.

• 2005, Gulf Opportunity Zone Act of 2005 (P.L. 109-135)

P.L. 109-135, §403(r)(2):

Amended Code Sec. 56(b)(1)(A)(ii) by inserting "or clause (ii) of section 164(b)(5)(A)" before the period at the end. **Effective** as if included in the provision of the American Jobs Creation Act of 2004 (P.L. 108-357) to which it relates [**effective** for tax years beginning after 12-31-2003.—CCH].

• 1990, Omnibus Budget Reconciliation Act of 1990 (P.L. 101-508)

P.L. 101-508, §11103(b):

Amended Code Sec. 56(b)(1) by adding at the end thereof a new subparagraph (F). **Effective** for tax years beginning after 12-31-90.

P.L. 101-508, §11801(c)(9)(G) (as amended by P.L. 104-188, §1702(h)(12)):

Amended Code Sec. 56(b)(3) by striking "section 422A" and inserting "section 422" and by striking "Section 422A(c)(2)" and inserting "Section 422(c)(2)". **Effective** 11-5-90.

• 1989, Omnibus Budget Reconciliation Act of 1989 (P.L. 101-239)

P.L. 101-239, §7612(d)(1):

Amended Code Sec. 56(b)(2) by adding at the end thereof a new subparagraph (D). **Effective** for tax years beginning after 12-31-90.

P.L. 101-239, §7811(d)(3)(A)-(B):

Amended Code Sec. 56(b)(3) by inserting "Section 422A(c)(2) shall apply in any case where the disposition and the inclusion for purposes of this part are within the same taxable year and such section shall not apply in any other case." after the first sentence, and by striking "the preceding sentence" and inserting "this paragraph". **Effective** as if included in the provision of P.L. 100-647 to which it relates.

• 1988, Technical and Miscellaneous Revenue Act of 1988 (P.L. 100-647)

P.L. 100-647, §1007(b)(2):

Amended Code Sec. 56(b)(1)(E). **Effective** as if included in the provision of P.L. 99-514 to which it relates. Prior to amendment, Code Sec. 56(b)(1)(E) read as follows:

(E) STANDARD DEDUCTION NOT ALLOWED.—The standard deduction provided in section 63(c) shall not be allowed.

P.L. 100-647, §1007(b)(3):

Amended Code Sec. 56(b)(1)(C) by striking out "and" at the end of clause (ii), by striking out the period at the end of clause (iii) and inserting in lieu thereof a comma, and by adding at the end thereof new clauses (iv)-(v). **Effective** as if included in the provision of P.L. 99-514 to which it relates.

P.L. 100-647, §1007(b)(4)(A)-(B):

Amended Code Sec. 56(b)(1)(C)(iii) by striking out "specified activity bond" and inserting in lieu thereof "specified private activity bond", and by striking out "section 56(a)(5)(B)" and inserting in lieu thereof "section 57(a)(5)(B)". **Effective** as if included in the provision of P.L. 99-514 to which it relates.

P.L. 100-647, §1007(b)(14)(A):

Amended Code Sec. 56(b) by adding at the end thereof new paragraph (3). **Effective** with respect to options exercised after 12-31-87.

P.L. 100-647, §1007(b)(16):

Amended Code Sec. 56(b)(1) by striking out "itemized" before "DEDUCTIONS" in the paragraph heading. **Effective** as if included in the provision of P.L. 99-514 to which it relates.

P.L. 100-647, §2004(b)(2):

Amended Code Sec. 56(b)(1)(C)(ii) by striking out "163(h)(6)" and inserting in lieu thereof "163(h)(5)". **Effective** as if included in the provision of P.L. 100-203 to which it relates.

[Sec. 56(c)]

(c) ADJUSTMENTS APPLICABLE TO CORPORATIONS.—In determining the amount of the alternative minimum taxable income of a corporation, the following treatment shall apply:

(1) ADJUSTMENT FOR ADJUSTED CURRENT EARNINGS.—Alternative minimum taxable income shall be adjusted as provided in subsection (g).

(2) MERCHANT MARINE CAPITAL CONSTRUCTION FUNDS.—In the case of a capital construction fund established under chapter 535 of title 46, United States Code—

(A) subparagraphs (A), (B), and (C) of section 7518(c)(1) (and the corresponding provisions of such chapter 535) shall not apply to—

(i) any amount deposited in such fund after after December 31, 1986, or

(ii) any earnings (including gains and losses) after December 31, 1986, on amounts in such fund, and

(B) no reduction in basis shall be made under section 7518(f) (or the corresponding provisions of such chapter 535) with respect to the withdrawal from the fund of any amount to which subparagraph (A) applies.

For purposes of this paragraph, any withdrawal of deposits or earnings from the fund shall be treated as allocable first to deposits made before (and earnings received or accrued before) January 1, 1987.

(3) SPECIAL DEDUCTION FOR CERTAIN ORGANIZATIONS NOT ALLOWED.—The deduction determined under section 833(b) shall not be allowed.

Amendments

•2006 (P.L. 109-304)

P.L. 109-304, §17(e)(1)(A)-(B):

Amended Code Sec. 56(c)(2) by striking "section 607 of the Merchant Marine Act, 1936 (46 U.S.C. 1177)" and substituting "chapter 535 of title 46, United States Code"; and by striking "such section 607" and substituting "such chapter 535" in subparagraphs (A) and (B). **Effective** 10-6-2006.

• 1990, Omnibus Budget Reconciliation Act of 1990 (P.L. 101-508)

P.L. 101-508, §11801(c)(2)(A):

Amended Code Sec. 56(c)(1). **Effective** 11-5-90. Prior to amendment, Code Sec. 56(c)(1) read as follows:

(1) ADJUSTMENT FOR BOOK INCOME OR ADJUSTED CURRENT EARNINGS.—

(A) BOOK INCOME ADJUSTMENT.—For taxable years beginning in 1987, 1988, and 1989, alternative minimum taxable income shall be adjusted as provided under subsection (f).

(B) ADJUSTED CURRENT EARNINGS.—For taxable years beginning after 1989, alternative minimum taxable income shall be adjusted as provided under subsection (g).

P.L. 101-508, §11821(b), provides:

(b) SAVINGS PROVISION.—If—

(1) any provision amended or repealed by this part applied to—

(A) any transaction occurring before the date of the enactment of this Act,

(B) any property acquired before such date of enactment, or

(C) any item of income, loss, deduction, or credit taken into account before such date of enactment, and

(2) the treatment of such transaction, property, or item under such provision would (without regard to the amendments made by this part) affect liability for tax for periods ending after such date of enactment,

nothing in the amendments made by this part shall be construed to affect the treatment of such transaction, property, or item for purposes of determining liability for tax for periods ending after such date of enactment.

• 1988, Technical and Miscellaneous Revenue Act of 1988 (P.L. 100-647)

P.L. 100-647, §1007(b)(13)(A)-(B):

Amended Code Sec. 56(c)(1) by striking out "ADJUSTED EARNINGS AND PROFITS" in the paragraph heading and inserting in lieu thereof "ADJUSTED CURRENT EARNINGS", and by striking out "Adjusted earnings and profits" in the heading of subparagraph (B) and inserting in lieu thereof "Adjusted current earnings". **Effective** as if included in the provision of P.L. 99-514 to which it relates.

[Sec. 56(d)]

(d) ALTERNATIVE TAX NET OPERATING LOSS DEDUCTION DEFINED.—

(1) IN GENERAL.—For purposes of subsection (a)(4), the term "alternative tax net operating loss deduction" means the net operating loss deduction allowable for the taxable year under section 172, except that—

(A) the amount of such deduction shall not exceed the sum of—

(i) the lesser of—

(I) the amount of such deduction attributable to net operating losses (other than the deduction described in clause (ii)(I)), or

(II) 90 percent of alternative minimum taxable income determined without regard to such deduction and the deduction under section 199, plus

(ii) the lesser of—

(I) the amount of such deduction attributable to an applicable net operating loss with respect to which an election is made under section 172(b)(1)(H), or

(II) alternative minimum taxable income determined without regard to such deduction and the deduction under section 199 reduced by the amount determined under clause (i), and

(B) in determining the amount of such deduction—

(i) the net operating loss (within the meaning of section 172(c)) for any loss year shall be adjusted as provided in paragraph (2), and

(ii) appropriate adjustments in the application of section 172(b)(2) shall be made to take into account the limitation of subparagraph (A).

(2) ADJUSTMENTS TO NET OPERATING LOSS COMPUTATION.—

(A) POST-1986 LOSS YEARS.—In the case of a loss year beginning after December 31, 1986, the net operating loss for such year under section 172(c) shall—

(i) be determined with the adjustments provided in this section and section 58, and

(ii) be reduced by the items of tax preference determined under section 57 for such year.

An item of tax preference shall be taken into account under clause (ii) only to the extent such item increased the amount of the net operating loss for the taxable year under section 172(c).

(B) PRE-1987 YEARS.—In the case of loss years beginning before January 1, 1987, the amount of the net operating loss which may be carried over to taxable years beginning after December 31, 1986, for purposes of paragraph (2), shall be equal to the amount which may be carried from the loss year to the first taxable year of the taxpayer beginning after December 31, 1986.

(3) NET OPERATING LOSS ATTRIBUTABLE TO FEDERALLY DECLARED DISASTERS.—In the case of a taxpayer which has a qualified disaster loss (as defined by section 172(b)(1)(J)) for the taxable year, paragraph (1) shall be applied by increasing the amount determined under subparagraph (A)(ii)(I) thereof by the sum of the carrybacks and carryovers of such loss.

Amendments

• 2009, Worker, Homeownership, and Business Assistance Act of 2009 (P.L. 111-92)

P.L. 111-92, §13(b):

Amended Code Sec. 56(d)(1)(A)(ii)(I). **Effective** generally for tax years ending after 12-31-2002. For a transitional rule, see Act Sec. 13(e)(4), below. For an exception, see Act Sec. 13(f), below. Prior to amendment, Code Sec. 56(d)(1)(A)(ii)(I) read as follows:

(I) the amount of such deduction attributable to the sum of carrybacks of net operating losses from taxable years ending during 2001 or 2002 and carryovers of net operating losses to taxable years ending during 2001 and 2002, or

P.L. 111-92, §13(e)(4), provides:

(4) TRANSITIONAL RULE.—In the case of any net operating loss (or, in the case of a life insurance company, any loss from operations) for a taxable year ending before the date of the enactment of this Act—

(A) any election made under section 172(b)(3) or 810(b)(3) of the Internal Revenue Code of 1986 with respect to such loss may (notwithstanding such section) be revoked before the due date (including extension of time) for filing the return for the taxpayer's last taxable year beginning in 2009, and

(B) any application under section 6411(a) of such Code with respect to such loss shall be treated as timely filed if filed before such due date.

P.L. 111-92, §13(f), provides:

(f) EXCEPTION FOR TARP RECIPIENTS.—The amendments made by this section shall not apply to—

(1) any taxpayer if—

(A) the Federal Government acquired before the date of the enactment of this Act an equity interest in the taxpayer pursuant to the Emergency Economic Stabilization Act of 2008,

(B) the Federal Government acquired before such date of enactment any warrant (or other right) to acquire any equity interest with respect to the taxpayer pursuant to the Emergency Economic Stabilization Act of 2008, or

(C) such taxpayer receives after such date of enactment funds from the Federal Government in exchange for an interest described in subparagraph (A) or (B) pursuant to a program established under title I of division A of the Emergency Economic Stabilization Act of 2008 (unless such taxpayer is a financial institution (as defined in section 3 of such Act) and the funds are received pursuant to a program established by the Secretary of the Treasury for the stated purpose of increasing the availability of credit to small businesses using funding made available under such Act), or

(2) the Federal National Mortgage Association and the Federal Home Loan Mortgage Corporation, and

(3) any taxpayer which at any time in 2008 or 2009 was or is a member of the same affiliated group (as defined in section 1504 of the Internal Revenue Code of 1986, determined without regard to subsection (b) thereof) as a taxpayer described in paragraph (1) or (2).

• 2008, Tax Extenders and Alternative Minimum Tax Relief Act of 2008 (P.L. 110-343)

P.L. 110-343, Division C, §708(c):

Amended Code Sec. 56(d) by adding at the end a new paragraph (3). **Effective** for losses arising in tax years beginning after 12-31-2007, in connection with disasters declared after such date.

P.L. 110-343, Division C, §712, provides:

SEC. 712. COORDINATION WITH HEARTLAND DISASTER RELIEF.

The amendments made by this subtitle, other than the amendments made by sections 706(a)(2), 710, and 711, shall not apply to any disaster described in section 702(c)[b](1)(A), or to any expenditure or loss resulting from such disaster.

• 2005, Gulf Opportunity Zone Act of 2005 (P.L. 109-135)

P.L. 109-135, §403(a)(14):

Amended Code Sec. 56(d)(1)(A)(i)(II) and (ii)(II) by striking "such deduction" and inserting "such deduction and the deduction under section 199". **Effective** as if included in the provision of the American Jobs Creation Act of 2004 (P.L. 108-357) to which it relates [**effective** for tax years beginning after 12-31-2004.—CCH].

• 2004, Working Families Tax Relief Act of 2004 (P.L. 108-311)

P.L. 108-311, §403(b)(4)(A):

Amended Code Sec. 56(d)(1)(A)(i)(I) by striking "attributable to carryovers" following "(other than the deduction". **Effective** as if included in the provision of the Job Creation and Worker Assistance Act of 2002 (P.L. 107-147) to which it relates [**effective** for tax years after 12-31-90.—CCH].

P.L. 108-311, §403(b)(4)(B)(i)-(ii):

Amended Code Sec. 56(d)(1)(A)(ii)(I) by striking "for taxable years" and inserting "from taxable years", and by striking "carryforwards" and inserting "carryovers". **Effective** as if included in the provision of the Job Creation and Worker Assistance Act of 2002 (P.L. 107-147) to which it relates [**effective** for tax years after 12-31-90.—CCH].

• 2002, Job Creation and Worker Assistance Act of 2002 (P.L. 107-147)

P.L. 107-147, §102(c)(1):

Amended Code Sec. 56(d)(1)(A). **Effective** for tax years after 12-31-90 [**effective** date changed by P.L. 108-311, §403(b)(3).—CCH]. Prior to amendment, Code Sec. 56(d)(1)(A) read as follows.

(A) the amount of such deduction shall not exceed 90 percent of alternate minimum taxable income determined without regard to such deduction, and

• 1996, Small Business Job Protection Act of 1996 (P.L. 104-188)

P.L. 104-188, §1702(e)(1)(A):

Amended Code Sec. 56(d)(1)(B)(ii). **Effective** as if included in the provision of P.L. 101-508 to which it relates. Prior to amendment, Code Sec. 56(d)(1)(B)(ii) read as follows:

(ii) in the case of taxable years beginning after December 31, 1986, section 172(b)(2) shall be applied by substituting "90 percent of alternative minimum taxable income determined without regard to the alternative tax net operating loss deduction" for "taxable income" each place it appears.

• 1992, Energy Policy Act of 1992 (P.L. 102-486)

P.L. 102-486, §1915(c)(2):

Amended Code Sec. 56(d)(1)(A). **Effective** for tax years beginning after 12-31-92. Prior to amendment, Code Sec. 56(d)(1)(A) read as follows:

(A) the amount of such deduction shall not exceed the excess (if any) of—

(i) 90 percent of alternative minimum taxable income determined without regard to such deduction and the deduction under subsection (h), over

(ii) the deduction under subsection (h), and

• 1990, Omnibus Budget Reconciliation Act of 1990 (P.L. 101-508)

P.L. 101-508, §11531(b)(1):

Amended Code Sec. 56(d)(1)(A). **Effective** for tax years beginning after 12-31-90. Prior to amendment, Code Sec. 56(d)(1)(A) read as follows:

(A) the amount of such deduction shall not exceed 90 percent of alternative minimum taxable income determined without regard to such deduction, and

• 1988, Technical and Miscellaneous Revenue Act of 1988 (P.L. 100-647)

P.L. 100-647, §1007(d)(5)(A)-(B):

Amended Code Sec. 56(d)(2)(A) by striking out "(other than subsection (a)(6) thereof)" after "57 for such year", and by adding at the end thereof a new sentence. **Effective** as if included in the provision of P.L. 99-514 to which it relates.

[Sec. 56(e)]

(e) QUALIFIED HOUSING INTEREST.—For purposes of this part—

(1) IN GENERAL.—The term "qualified housing interest" means interest which is qualified residence interest (as defined in section 163(h)(3)) and is paid or accrued during the taxable year on indebtedness which is incurred in acquiring, constructing, or substantially improving any property which—

(A) is the principal residence (within the meaning of section 121) of the taxpayer at the time such interest accrues, or

(B) is a qualified dwelling which is a qualified residence (within the meaning of section 163(h)(4)).

Such term also includes interest on any indebtedness resulting from the refinancing of indebtedness meeting the requirements of the preceding sentence; but only to the extent that the amount of the indebtedness resulting from such refinancing does not exceed the amount of the refinanced indebtedness immediately before the refinancing.

(2) QUALIFIED DWELLING.—The term "qualified dwelling" means any—

(A) house,

(B) apartment,

(C) condominium, or

(D) mobile home not used on a transient basis (within the meaning of section 7701(a)(19)(C)(v)),

including all structures or other property appurtenant thereto.

(3) SPECIAL RULE FOR INDEBTEDNESS INCURRED BEFORE JULY 1, 1982.—The term "qualified housing interest" includes interest which is qualified residence interest (as defined in section 163(h)(3)) and is paid or accrued on indebtedness which—

(A) was incurred by the taxpayer before July 1, 1982, and

(B) is secured by property which, at the time such indebtedness was incurred, was—

(i) the principal residence (within the meaning of section 121) of the taxpayer, or

(ii) a qualified dwelling used by the taxpayer (or any member of his family (within the meaning of section 267(c)(4))).

Amendments

• 1997, Taxpayer Relief Act of 1997 (P.L. 105-34)

P.L. 105-34, §312(d)(1):

Amended Code Sec. 56(e)(1)(A) and (3)(B)(i) by striking "section 1034" and inserting "section 121". **Effective** for sales and exchanges after 5-6-97.

• 1988, Technical and Miscellaneous Revenue Act of 1988 (P.L. 100-647)

P.L. 100-647, §1007(b)(6)(A)(i)-(ii):

Amended Code Sec. 56(e)(1) by striking out "interest which is" and inserting in lieu thereof "interest which is qualified residence interest (as defined in section 163(h)(3)) and is", and by striking out "section 163(h)(3)" in subparagraph (B) and inserting in lieu thereof "section 163(h)(4)". **Effective** as if included in the provision of P.L. 99-514 to which it relates.

P.L. 100-647, §1007(b)(6)(B):

Amended Code Sec. 56(e)(3) by striking out "interest paid or accrued" and inserting in lieu thereof "interest which is qualified residence interest (as defined in section 163(h)(3)) and is paid or accrued". **Effective** as if included in the provision of P.L. 99-514 to which it relates.

P.L. 100-647, §2004(b)(3)(A)-(B):

Amended Code Sec. 56(e)(1) by striking out "substantially rehabilitating" and inserting in lieu thereof "substantially improving", and by striking out "or is paid" after "interest accrues" in subparagraph (A). **Effective** as if included in the provision of P.L. 100-203 to which it relates.

[Sec. 56(f)—Repealed]

Amendments

• 1990, Omnibus Budget Reconciliation Act of 1990 (P.L. 101-508)

P.L. 101-508, §11801(a)(3):

Repealed Code Sec. 56(f). **Effective**, generally, on 11-5-90. Prior to repeal, Code Sec. 56(f) read as follows:

(f) ADJUSTMENTS FOR BOOK INCOME OF CORPORATIONS.—

(1) IN GENERAL.—The alternative minimum taxable income of any corporation for any taxable year beginning in 1987, 1988, or 1989 shall be increased by 50 percent of the amount (if any) by which—

(A) the adjusted net book income of the corporation, exceeds

(B) the alternative minimum taxable income for the taxable year (determined without regard to this subsection and the alternative tax net operating loss deduction).

(2) ADJUSTED NET BOOK INCOME.—For purposes of this subsection—

(A) IN GENERAL.—The term "adjusted net book income" means the net income or loss of the taxpayer set forth on the taxpayer's applicable financial statement, adjusted as provided in this paragraph.

(B) ADJUSTMENTS FOR CERTAIN TAXES.—The amount determined under subparagraph (A) shall be appropriately adjusted to disregard any Federal income taxes, or income, war profits, or excess profits taxes imposed by any foreign country or possession of the United States, which are directly or indirectly taken into account on the taxpayer's applicable financial statement. The preceding sentence shall not apply to any such taxes (otherwise eligible for the credit provided by section 901 without regard to section 901(j)) imposed by a foreign country or possession of the United States if the taxpayer does not choose to take, to any extent, the benefits of section 901. No adjustment shall be made under this subparagraph for the tax imposed by section 59A.

(C) SPECIAL RULES FOR RELATED CORPORATIONS.—

(i) CONSOLIDATED RETURNS.—If the taxpayer files a consolidated return for any taxable year, adjusted net book income for such taxable year shall take into account items on the taxpayer's applicable financial statement which are properly allocable to members of such group included on such return.

(ii) TREATMENT OF DIVIDENDS.—In the case of any corporation which is not included on a consolidated return with the taxpayer, adjusted net book income shall take into account the earnings of such other corporation only to the extent of the sum of the dividends received from such other corporation and other amounts required to be included in gross income under this chapter in respect of the earnings of such other corporation.

(D) STATEMENTS COVERING DIFFERENT PERIODS.—Appropriate adjustments shall be made in adjusted net book income in any case in which an applicable financial statement covers a period other than the taxable year.

(E) SPECIAL RULE FOR COOPERATIVES.—In the case of a cooperative to which section 1381 applies, the amount determined under subparagraph (A) shall be reduced by the amounts referred to in section 1382(b) (relating to patronage dividends and per-unit retain allocations) to the extent such amounts were not otherwise taken into account in determining adjusted net book income.

(F) TREATMENT OF TAXES ON DIVIDENDS FROM 936 CORPORATIONS.—

(i) IN GENERAL.—For purposes of determining the alternative minimum tax foreign tax credit, 50 percent of any withholding tax or income tax paid to a possession of the United States with respect to dividends received from a corporation eligible for the credit provided by section 936 shall be treated as a tax paid to a foreign country by the corporation receiving the dividend.

(ii) LIMITATION.—If the aggregate amount of the dividends referred to in clause (i) for any taxable year exceeds the excess referred to in paragraph (1), the amount treated as a tax paid to a foreign country under clause (i) shall not exceed the amount which would be so treated without regard to this clause multiplied by a fraction—

(I) the numerator of which is the excess referred to in paragraph (1), and

(II) the denominator of which is the aggregate amount of such dividends.

(iii) TREATMENT OF TAXES IMPOSED ON 936 CORPORATION.—For purposes of this subparagraph, taxes paid by any corporation eligible for the credit provided by section 936 to a possession of the United States shall be treated as a withholding tax paid with respect to any dividend paid by such corporation to the extent such taxes would be treated as paid by the corporation receiving the dividend under rules similar to the rules of section 902 (and the amount of any such dividend shall be increased by the amount so treated).

(G) RULES FOR ALASKA NATIVE CORPORATIONS.—The amount determined under subparagraph (A) shall be appropriately adjusted to allow:

(i) cost recovery and depletion attributable to property the basis of which is determined under section 21(c) of the Alaska Native Claims Settlement Act (43 U.S.C. 1620(c)), and

(ii) deductions for amounts payable made pursuant to section 7(i) or section 7(j) of such Act (43 U.S.C. 1606(i) and 1606(j)) only at such time as the deductions are allowed for tax purposes.

(H) SPECIAL RULES FOR LIFE INSURANCE COMPANIES.—

(i) POLICYHOLDER DIVIDENDS OF MUTUAL COMPANIES.—In determining the adjusted net book income of any mutual life insurance company, a reduction shall be allowed for policyholder dividends with respect to any taxable year only to the extent such dividends exceed the differential earnings amount determined for such taxable year under section 809.

(ii) OTHER ADJUSTMENTS.—To the extent provided by the Secretary, such additional adjustments shall be made as may be necessary to make the calculation of adjusted net book income in the case of any life insurance company consistent with the calculation of adjusted net book income generally.

(I) EXCLUSION OF CERTAIN INCOME FROM TRANSFER OF STOCK FOR DEBT.—In determining adjusted net book income, there shall not be taken into account any income resulting from the transfer of stock by the corporation issuing such stock to a creditor in satisfaction of its indebtedness. The preceding sentence shall apply only in the case of a debtor in a title 11 case (as defined in section 108(d)(2)) or to the extent the debtor is insolvent (as defined in section 108(d)(3)).

(J) SECRETARIAL AUTHORITY TO ADJUST ITEMS.—Under regulations, adjusted net book income shall be properly adjusted to prevent the omission or duplication of any item.

(3) APPLICABLE FINANCIAL STATEMENT.—For purposes of this subsection—

(A) IN GENERAL.—The term "applicable financial statement" means, with respect to any taxable year, any statement covering such taxable year—

(i) which is required to be filed with the Securities and Exchange Commission,

(ii) which is a certified audited income statement to be used for the purposes of a statement or report—

(I) for credit purposes,

(II) to shareholders, or

(III) for any other substantial nontax purpose,

(iii) which is an income statement for a substantial nontax purpose required to be provided to—

(I) the Federal Government or any agency thereof,

(II) a State government or any agency thereof, or

(III) a political subdivision of a State or any agency thereof, or

(iv) which is an income statement to be used for the purposes of a statement or report—

(I) for credit purposes,

(II) to shareholders, or

(III) for any other substantial nontax purpose.

(B) EARNINGS AND PROFITS USED IN CERTAIN CASES.—If—

(i) a taxpayer has no applicable financial statement, or

(ii) a taxpayer has only a statement described in subparagraph (A)(iv) and the taxpayer elects the application of this subparagraph,

the net income or loss set forth on the taxpayer's applicable financial statement shall, for purposes of this subsection, be treated as being equal to the taxpayer's earnings and profits for the taxable year (without diminution by reason of distributions during the tax year). Such election, once made, shall remain in effect for any taxable year for which the taxpayer is described in this subparagraph unless revoked with the consent of the Secretary.

(C) SPECIAL RULE WHERE MORE THAN 1 STATEMENT.—For purposes of subparagraph (A), if a taxpayer has a statement described in more than 1 clause or subclause, the applicable financial statement shall be the statement described in the clause or subclause with the lowest number designation. If the taxpayer has 2 or more statements described in the clause (or subclause) with the lowest number designation, the applicable financial statement shall be the one of such statements specified in regulations.

(4) EXCEPTION FOR CERTAIN CORPORATIONS.—This subsection shall not apply to any S corporation, regulated investment company, real estate investment trust, or REMIC.

P.L. 101-508, §11821(b), provides:

(b) SAVINGS PROVISION.—If—

(1) any provision amended or repealed by this part applied to—

(A) any transaction occurring before the date of the enactment of this Act,

(B) any property acquired before such date of enactment, or

(C) any item of income, loss, deduction, or credit taken into account before such date of enactment, and

(2) the treatment of such transaction, property, or item under such provision would (without regard to the amend-

Sec. 56(f)—Repealed

ments made by this part) affect liability for tax for periods ending after such date of enactment,

nothing in the amendments made by this part shall be construed to affect the treatment of such transaction, property, or item for purposes of determining liability for tax for periods ending after such date of enactment.

• 1988, Technical and Miscellaneous Revenue Act of 1988 (P.L. 100-647)

P.L. 100-647, §1007(b)(7):

Amended Code Sec. 56(f)(2)(B) by striking out "any such taxes" in the last sentence and inserting in lieu thereof "any such taxes (otherwise eligible for the credit provided by section 901 without regard to section 901(j))". **Effective** as if included in the provision of P.L. 99-514 to which it relates.

P.L. 100-647, §1007(b)(8):

Amended Code Sec. 56(f)(3)(A)(iii) by striking out "an income statement" and inserting in lieu thereof "an income statement for a substantial nontax purpose". **Effective** as if included in the provision of P.L. 99-514 to which it relates.

P.L. 100-647, §1007(b)(9):

Amended Code Sec. 56(f)(3)(B) by striking out "paragraph (3)(A)" and inserting in lieu thereof "this subsection". **Effective** as if included in the provision of P.L. 99-514 to which it relates.

P.L. 100-647, §1007(b)(10):

Amended Code Sec. 56(f)(3)(C) by adding at the end thereof a new sentence. **Effective** as if included in the provision of P.L. 99-514 to which it relates.

P.L. 100-647, §1007(b)(11)(A):

Amended Code Sec. 56(f)(2)(F). **Effective** as if included in the provision of P.L. 99-514 to which it relates. Prior to amendment, Code Sec. 56(f)(2)(F) read as follows:

(F) TREATMENT OF DIVIDENDS FROM 936 CORPORATIONS.—

(i) IN GENERAL.—In determining the amount of adjusted net book income, any dividend received from a corporation eligible for the credit provided by section 936 shall be increased by the amount of any withholding tax paid to a possession of the United States with respect to such dividend.

(ii) TREATMENT AS FOREIGN TAXES.—

(I) IN GENERAL.—50 percent of any withholding tax paid to a possession of the United States with respect to dividends referred to in clause (i) (to the extent such dividends do not exceed the excess referred to in paragraph (1), determined without regard to clause (i)) shall, for purposes of this part, be treated as a tax paid by the corporation receiving the dividend to a foreign country.

(II) TREATMENT OF TAXES IMPOSED ON 936 CORPORATION.—For purposes of this subparagraph, taxes paid by any corporation eligible for the credit provided by section 936 to a possession of the United States, shall be treated as a withholding tax paid with respect to any dividend paid by such corporation to the extent such taxes would be treated as paid by the corporation receiving the dividend under rules similar to the rules of section 902.

P.L. 100-647, §2001(c)(3)(A):

Amended Code Sec. 56(f)(2)(B) by adding at the end thereof the following new sentence: "No adjustment shall be made under this subparagraph for the tax imposed by section 59A.". **Effective** as if included in the provision of P.L. 99-499 to which it relates.

P.L. 100-647, §6303(a):

Amended Code Sec. 56(f)(2) by redesignating subparagraph (I) as subparagraph (J) and by inserting after subparagraph (H) new subparagraph (I). **Effective** for tax years beginning after 12-31-86.

• 1987, Revenue Act of 1987 (P.L. 100-203)

P.L. 100-203, §10243(a):

Amended Code Sec. 56(f)(2) by redesignating subparagraph (H) as subparagraph (I) and by inserting after subparagraph (G) new subparagraph (H). **Effective** for tax years beginning after 12-31-87.

[Sec. 56(g)]

(g) ADJUSTMENTS BASED ON ADJUSTED CURRENT EARNINGS.—

(1) IN GENERAL.—The alternative minimum taxable income of any corporation for any taxable year shall be increased by 75 percent of the excess (if any) of—

(A) the adjusted current earnings of the corporation, over

(B) the alternative minimum taxable income (determined without regard to this subsection and the alternative tax net operating loss deduction).

(2) ALLOWANCE OF NEGATIVE ADJUSTMENTS.—

(A) IN GENERAL.—The alternative minimum taxable income for any corporation of any taxable year shall be reduced by 75 percent of the excess (if any) of—

(i) the amount referred to in subparagraph (B) of paragraph (1), over

(ii) the amount referred to in subparagraph (A) of paragraph (1).

(B) LIMITATION.—The reduction under subparagraph (A) for any taxable year shall not exceed the excess (if any) of—

(i) the aggregate increases in alternative minimum taxable income under paragraph (1) for prior taxable years, over

(ii) the aggregate reductions under subparagraph (A) of this paragraph for prior taxable years.

(3) ADJUSTED CURRENT EARNINGS.—For purposes of this subsection, the term "adjusted current earnings" means the alternative minimum taxable income for the taxable year—

(A) determined with the adjustments provided in paragraph (4), and

(B) determined without regard to this subsection and the alternative tax net operating loss deduction.

(4) ADJUSTMENTS.—In determining adjusted current earnings, the following adjustments shall apply:

(A) DEPRECIATION.—

(i) PROPERTY PLACED IN SERVICE AFTER 1989.—The depreciation deduction with respect to any property placed in service in a taxable year beginning after 1989 shall be determined under the alternative system of section 168(g). The preceding sentence shall not apply to any property placed in service after December 31, 1993, and the depreciation deduction with respect to such property shall be determined under the rules of subsection (a)(1)(A).

(ii) PROPERTY TO WHICH NEW ACRS SYSTEM APPLIES.—In the case of any property to which the amendments made by section 201 of the Tax Reform Act of 1986 apply and which is placed in service in a taxable year beginning before 1990, the depreciation deduction shall be determined—

(I) by taking into account the adjusted basis of such property (as determined for purposes of computing alternative minimum taxable income) as of the close of the last taxable year beginning before January 1, 1990, and

(II) by using the straight-line method over the remainder of the recovery period applicable to such property under the alternative system of section 168(g).

(iii) PROPERTY TO WHICH ORIGINAL ACRS SYSTEM APPLIES.—In the case of any property to which section 168 (as in effect on the day before the date of the enactment of the Tax Reform Act of 1986 and without regard to subsection (d)(1)(A)(ii) thereof) applies and which is placed in service in a taxable year beginning before 1990, the depreciation deduction shall be determined—

(I) by taking into account the adjusted basis of such property (as determined for purposes of computing the regular tax) as of the close of the last taxable year beginning before January 1, 1990, and

(II) by using the straight line method over the remainder of the recovery period which would apply to such property under the alternative system of section 168(g).

(iv) PROPERTY PLACED IN SERVICE BEFORE 1981.—In the case of any property not described in clause (i), (ii), or (iii), the amount allowable as depreciation or amortization with respect to such property shall be determined in the same manner as for purposes of computing taxable income.

(v) SPECIAL RULE FOR CERTAIN PROPERTY.—In the case of any property described in paragraph (1), (2), (3), or (4) of section 168(f), the amount of depreciation allowable for purposes of the regular tax shall be treated as the amount allowable under the alternative system of section 168(g).

(B) INCLUSION OF ITEMS INCLUDED FOR PURPOSES OF COMPUTING EARNINGS AND PROFITS.—

(i) IN GENERAL.—In the case of any amount which is excluded from gross income for purposes of computing alternative minimum taxable income but is taken into account in determining the amount of earnings and profits—

(I) such amount shall be included in income in the same manner as if such amount were includible in gross income for purposes of computing alternative minimum taxable income, and

(II) the amount of such income shall be reduced by any deduction which would have been allowable in computing alternative minimum taxable income if such amount were includible in gross income.

The preceding sentence shall not apply in the case of any amount excluded from gross income under section 108 (or the corresponding provisions of prior law) or under section 139A or 1357. In the case of any insurance company taxable under section 831(b), this clause shall not apply to any amount not described in section 834(b).

(ii) INCLUSION OF BUILDUP IN LIFE INSURANCE CONTRACTS.—In the case of any life insurance contract—

(I) the income on such contract (as determined under section 7702(g)) for any taxable year shall be treated as includible in gross income for such year, and

(II) there shall be allowed as a deduction that portion of any premium which is attributable to insurance coverage.

(iii) TAX EXEMPT INTEREST ON CERTAIN HOUSING BONDS.—Clause (i) shall not apply in the case of any interest on a bond to which section 57(a)(5)(C)(iii) applies.

(iv) TAX EXEMPT INTEREST ON BONDS ISSUED IN 2009 AND 2010.—

(I) IN GENERAL.—Clause (i) shall not apply in the case of any interest on a bond issued after December 31, 2008, and before January 1, 2011.

(II) TREATMENT OF REFUNDING BONDS.—For purposes of subclause (I), a refunding bond (whether a current or advance refunding) shall be treated as issued on the date of the issuance of the refunded bond (or in the case of a series of refundings, the original bond).

(III) EXCEPTION FOR CERTAIN REFUNDING BONDS.—Subclause (II) shall not apply to any refunding bond which is issued to refund any bond which was issued after December 31, 2003, and before January 1, 2009.

(C) DISALLOWANCE OF ITEMS NOT DEDUCTIBLE IN COMPUTING EARNINGS AND PROFITS.—

(i) IN GENERAL.—A deduction shall not be allowed for any item if such item would not be deductible for any taxable year for purposes of computing earnings and profits.

(ii) SPECIAL RULE FOR CERTAIN DIVIDENDS.—

(I) IN GENERAL.—Clause (i) shall not apply to any deduction allowable under section 243 or 245 for any dividend which is a 100-percent dividend or which is received from a 20-percent owned corporation (as defined in section 243(c)(2)), but only to the extent such dividend is attributable to income of the paying corporation which is subject to tax under this chapter (determined after the application of sections 30A, 936 (including subsections (a)(4), (i), and (j) thereof) and 921 (as in effect before its repeal by the FSC Repeal and Extraterritorial Income Exclusion Act of 2000)).

(II) 100-PERCENT DIVIDEND.—For purposes of subclause (I), the term "100 percent dividend" means any dividend if the percentage used for purposes of determining the amount allowable as a deduction under section 243 or 245 with respect to such dividend is 100 percent.

(iii) TREATMENT OF TAXES ON DIVIDENDS FROM 936 CORPORATIONS.—

(I) IN GENERAL.—For purposes of determining the alternative minimum foreign tax credit, 75 percent of any withholding or income tax paid to a possession of the United States with respect to dividends received from a corporation eligible for the credit provided by section 936 shall be treated as a tax paid to a foreign country by the corporation receiving the dividend.

(II) LIMITATION.—If the aggregate amount of the dividends referred to in subclause (I) for any taxable year exceeds the excess referred to in paragraph (1), the amount treated as tax paid to a foreign country under subclause (I) shall not exceed the amount which would be so treated without regard to this subclause multiplied by a fraction the numerator of which is the excess referred to in paragraph (1) and the denominator of which is the aggregate amount of such dividends.

(III) TREATMENT OF TAXES IMPOSED ON 936 CORPORATION.—For purposes of this clause, taxes paid by any corporation eligible for the credit provided by section 936 to a possession of the United States shall be treated as a withholding tax paid with respect to any dividend paid by such corporation to the extent such taxes would be treated as paid by the corporation receiving the dividend under rules similar to the rules of section 902 (and the amount of any such dividend shall be increased by the amount so treated).

(IV) SEPARATE APPLICATION OF FOREIGN TAX CREDIT LIMITATIONS.—In determining the alternative minimum foreign tax credit, section 904(d) shall be applied as if dividends from a corporation eligible for the credit provided by section 936 were a separate category of income referred to in a subparagraph of section 904(d)(1).

(V) COORDINATION WITH LIMITATION ON 936 CREDIT.—Any reference in this clause to a dividend received from a corporation eligible for the credit provided by section 936 shall be treated as a reference to the portion of any such dividend for which the dividends received deduction is disallowed under clause (i) after the application of clause (ii)(I).

(VI) APPLICATION TO SECTION 30A CORPORATIONS.—References in this clause to section 936 shall be treated as including references to section 30A.

(iv) SPECIAL RULE FOR CERTAIN DIVIDENDS RECEIVED BY CERTAIN COOPERATIVES.—In the case of an organization to which part I of subchapter T (relating to tax treatment of cooperatives) applies which is engaged in the marketing of agricultural or horticultural products, clause (i) shall not apply to any amount allowable as a deduction under section 245(c).

(v) DEDUCTION FOR DOMESTIC PRODUCTION.—Clause (i) shall not apply to any amount allowable as a deduction under section 199.

(vi) SPECIAL RULE FOR CERTAIN DISTRIBUTIONS FROM CONTROLLED FOREIGN CORPORATIONS.—Clause (i) shall not apply to any deduction allowable under section 965.

(D) CERTAIN OTHER EARNINGS AND PROFITS ADJUSTMENTS.—

(i) INTANGIBLE DRILLING COSTS.—The adjustments provided in section 312(n)(2)(A) shall apply in the case of amounts paid or incurred in taxable years beginning after December 31, 1989. In the case of a taxpayer other than an integrated oil company (as defined in section 291(b)(4)), in the case of any oil or gas well, this clause shall not apply in the case of amounts paid or incurred in taxable years beginning after December 31, 1992.

(ii) CERTAIN AMORTIZATION PROVISIONS NOT TO APPLY.—Sections 173 and 248 shall not apply to expenditures paid or incurred in taxable years beginning after December 31, 1989.

(iii) LIFO INVENTORY ADJUSTMENTS.—The adjustments provided in section 312(n)(4) shall apply, but only with respect to taxable years beginning after December 31, 1989.

(iv) INSTALLMENT SALES.—In the case of any installment sale in a taxable year beginning after December 31, 1989, adjusted current earnings shall be computed as if the corporation did not use the installment method. The preceding sentence shall not apply to the applicable percentage (as determined under section 453A) of the gain from any installment sale with respect to which section 453A(a)(1) applies.

(E) DISALLOWANCE OF LOSS ON EXCHANGE OF DEBT POOLS.—No loss shall be recognized on the exchange of any pool of debt obligations for another pool of debt obligations having substantially the same effective interest rates and maturities.

(F) DEPLETION.—

(i) IN GENERAL.—The allowance for depletion with respect to any property placed in service in a taxable year beginning after December 31, 1989, shall be cost depletion determined under section 611.

(ii) EXCEPTION FOR INDEPENDENT OIL AND GAS PRODUCERS AND ROYALTY OWNERS.—In the case of any taxable year beginning after December 31, 1992, clause (i) (and subparagraph (C)(i)) shall not apply to any deduction for depletion computed in accordance with section 613A(c).

(G) TREATMENT OF CERTAIN OWNERSHIP CHANGES.—If—

(i) there is an ownership change (within the meaning of section 382) in a taxable year beginning after 1989 with respect to any corporation, and

(ii) there is a net unrealized built-in loss (within the meaning of section 382(h)) with respect to such corporation,

then the adjusted basis of each asset of such corporation (immediately after the ownership change) shall be its proportionate share (determined on the basis of respective fair market values) of the fair market value of the assets of such corporation (determined under section 382(h)) immediately before the ownership change.

(H) ADJUSTED BASIS.—The adjusted basis of any property with respect to which an adjustment under this paragraph applies shall be determined by applying the treatment prescribed in this paragraph.

(I) TREATMENT OF CHARITABLE CONTRIBUTIONS.—Notwithstanding subparagraphs (B) and (C), no adjustment related to the earnings and profits effects of any charitable contribution shall be made in computing adjusted current earnings.

(5) OTHER DEFINITIONS.—For purposes of paragraph (4)—

(A) EARNINGS AND PROFITS.—The term "earnings and profits" means earnings and profits computed for purposes of subchapter C.

(B) TREATMENT OF ALTERNATIVE MINIMUM TAXABLE INCOME.—The treatment of any item for purposes of computing alternative minimum taxable income shall be determined without regard to this subsection.

(6) EXCEPTION FOR CERTAIN CORPORATIONS.—This subsection shall not apply to any S corporation, regulated investment company, real estate investment trust, or REMIC.

Amendments

• 2009, American Recovery and Reinvestment Tax Act of 2009 (P.L. 111-5)

P.L. 111-5, §1503(b):

Amended Code Sec. 56(g)(4)(B) by adding at the end a new clause (iv). **Effective** for obligations issued after 12-31-2008.

• 2008, Housing Assistance Tax Act of 2008 (P.L. 110-289)

P.L. 110-289, §3022(a)(2):

Amended Code Sec. 56(g)(4)(B) by adding at the end a new clause (iii). **Effective** for bonds issued after 7-30-2008.

• 2007, Tax Technical Corrections Act of 2007 (P.L. 110-172)

P.L. 110-172, §11(g)(1):

Amended Code Sec. 56(g)(4)(C)(ii)(I) by striking "921" and inserting "921 (as in effect before its repeal by the FSC Repeal and Extraterritorial Income Exclusion Act of 2000)". **Effective** 12-29-2007.

P.L. 110-172, §11(g)(2):

Amended Code Sec. 54(g)(4)(C)(iv) [56(g)(4)(C)(iv)] by striking "a cooperative described in section 927(a)(4)" and inserting "an organization to which part I of subchapter T (relating to tax treatment of cooperatives) applies which is engaged in the marketing of agricultural or horticultural products". **Effective** 12-29-2007.

• 2004, American Jobs Creation Act of 2004 (P.L. 108-357)

P.L. 108-357, §101(b)(4):

Amended Code Sec. 56(g)(4)(B)(i) by striking "114 or" after "law) or under" in the second sentence. **Effective** for transactions after 12-31-2004. For transitional and special rules, see Act Sec. 101(d)-(f), below.

P.L. 108-357, §101(d)-(f), provides:

(d) TRANSITIONAL RULE FOR 2005 AND 2006.—

(1) IN GENERAL.—In the case of transactions during 2005 or 2006, the amount includible in gross income by reason of the amendments made by this section shall not exceed the applicable percentage of the amount which would have been so included but for this subsection.

(2) APPLICABLE PERCENTAGE.—For purposes of paragraph (1), the applicable percentage shall be as follows:

(A) For 2005, the applicable percentage shall be 20 percent.

(B) For 2006, the applicable percentage shall be 40 percent.

(e) REVOCATION OF ELECTION TO BE TREATED AS DOMESTIC CORPORATION.—If, during the 1-year period beginning on the date of the enactment of this Act, a corporation for which an election is in effect under section 943(e) of the Internal Revenue Code of 1986 revokes such election, no gain or loss shall be recognized with respect to property treated as transferred under clause (ii) of section 943(e)(4)(B) of such Code to the extent such property—

(1) was treated as transferred under clause (i) thereof, or

(2) was acquired during a taxable year to which such election applies and before May 1, 2003, in the ordinary course of its trade or business.

The Secretary of the Treasury (or such Secretary's delegate) may prescribe such regulations as may be necessary to prevent the abuse of the purposes of this subsection.

[**Note:** Act Sec. 101(f) of P.L. 108-357, below, was stricken by P.L. 109-222, §513(b), applicable to tax years beginning after 5-17-2006.—CCH.]

(f) BINDING CONTRACTS.—The amendments made by this section shall not apply to any transaction in the ordinary course of a trade or business which occurs pursuant to a binding contract—

(1) which is between the taxpayer and a person who is not a related person (as defined in section 943(b)(3) of such Code, as in effect on the day before the date of the enactment of this Act), and

(2) which is in effect on September 17, 2003, and at all times thereafter.

For purposes of this subsection, a binding contract shall include a purchase option, renewal option, or replacement option which is included in such contract and which is enforceable against the seller or lessor.

P.L. 108-357, §102(b):

Amended Code Sec. 56(g)(4)(C) by adding at the end a new clause (v). **Effective** for tax years beginning after 12-31-2004.

P.L. 108-357, §248(b)(1):

Amended the second sentence of Code Sec. 56(g)(4)(B)(i), as amended by this Act, by inserting "or 1357" after "section 139A". **Effective** for tax years beginning after 10-22-2004.

P.L. 108-357, §422(b):

Amended Code Sec. 56(g)(4)(C) by inserting after clause (v) a new clause (vi). **Effective** for tax years ending on or after 10-22-2004.

P.L. 108-357, §835(b)(1):

Amended Code Sec. 56(g)(6) by striking "REMIC, or FASIT" and inserting "or REMIC". For the **effective** date, see Act Sec. 835(c), below.

P.L. 108-357, §835(c), provides:

(c) EFFECTIVE DATE.—

(1) IN GENERAL.—Except as provided in paragraph (2), the amendments made by this section shall take effect on January 1, 2005.

(2) EXCEPTION FOR EXISTING FASITS.—Paragraph (1) shall not apply to any FASIT in existence on the date of the enactment of this Act [10-22-2004.—CCH] to the extent that regular interests issued by the FASIT before such date continue to remain outstanding in accordance with the original terms of issuance.

• 2003, Medicare Prescription Drug, Improvement, and Modernization Act of 2003 (P.L. 108-173)

P.L. 108-173, §1202(b):

Amended Code Sec. 56(g)(4)(B) by inserting "or 139A" after "section 114". **Effective** for tax years ending after 12-8-2003.

• 2000, FSC Repeal and Extraterritorial Income Exclusion Act of 2000 (P.L. 106-519)

P.L. 106-519, §4(1):

Amended the second sentence of Code Sec. 56(g)(4)(B)(i) by inserting before the period "or under section 114". **Effective** generally for transactions after 9-30-2000. For special rules, see Act Sec. 5(b)-(d) in the amendment notes following Code Sec. 921.

• 1997, Taxpayer Relief Act of 1997 (P.L. 105-34)

P.L. 105-34, §1212(a):

Amended Code Sec. 56(g)(4)(B)(i) by adding at the end a new sentence. **Effective** for tax years beginning after 12-31-97.

• 1996, Small Business Job Protection Act of 1996 (P.L. 104-188)

P.L. 104-188, §1601(b)(2)(B)(i)-(ii):

Amended Code Sec. 56(g)(4)(C)(ii)(I) by inserting "30A," before "936", and by striking "and (i)" and inserting ", (i), and (j)". **Effective** for tax years beginning after 12-31-95. For special rules, see Act Sec. 1601(c)(2)-(3), below.

P.L. 104-188, §1601(b)(2)(C):

Amended Code Sec. 56(g)(4)(C)(iii) by adding at the end a new subclause (VI). **Effective** for tax years beginning after 12-31-95. For special rules, see Act Sec. 1601(c)(2)-(3), below.

P.L. 104-188, §1601(c)(2)-(3), provides:

(2) SPECIAL RULE FOR QUALIFIED POSSESSION SOURCE INVESTMENT INCOME.—The amendments made by this section shall not apply to qualified possession source investment income received or accrued before July 1, 1996, without regard to the taxable year in which received or accrued.

(3) SPECIAL TRANSITION RULE FOR PAYMENT OF ESTIMATED TAX INSTALLMENT.—In determining the amount of any installment due under section 6655 of the Internal Revenue Code of 1986 after the date of the enactment of this Act and before October 1, 1996, only 1/2 of any increase in tax (for the taxable year for which such installment is made) by reason of the amendments made by subsections (a) and (b) shall be taken into account. Any reduction in such installment by reason of the preceding sentence shall be recaptured by increasing the next required installment for such year by the amount of such reduction.

P.L. 104-188, §1621(b)(2):

Amended Code Sec. 56(g)(6) by striking "or REMIC" and inserting "REMIC, or FASIT". **Effective** 9-1-97.

P.L. 104-188, §1702(e)(1)(B), provides:

(B) For purposes of applying sections 56(g)(1) and 56(g)(3) of the Internal Revenue Code of 1986 with respect to taxable years beginning in 1991 and 1992, the references in such sections to the alternative tax net operating loss deduction shall be treated as including a reference to the deduction under section 56(h) of such Code as in effect before the amendments made by section 1915 of the Energy Policy Act of 1992.

P.L. 104-188, §1702(c)(1):

Amended Code Sec. 56(g)(4) by redesignating subparagraphs (I) and (J) as subparagraphs (H) and (I), respectively. **Effective** as if included in the provision of P.L. 101-508 to which it relates.

P.L. 104-188, §1702(g)(4):

Amended Code Sec. 56(g)(4)(D)(iii) by inserting ", but only with respect to taxable years beginning after December 31, 1989" before the period at the end thereof. **Effective** as if included in the provision of P.L. 101-508 to which it relates.

P.L. 104-188, §1704(t)(1):

Amended Code Sec. 56(g)(4)(C)(ii)(II) by striking "of the subclause" and inserting "of subclause". **Effective** 8-20-96.

• 1993, Omnibus Budget Reconciliation Act of 1993 (P.L. 103-66)

P.L. 103-66, §13115(a):

Amended Code Sec. 56(g)(4)(A)(i) by adding at the end thereof a new sentence. **Effective** for property placed in service after 12-31-93. However, for exceptions, see Act Sec. 13115(b)(2), below.

P.L. 103-66, §13115(b)(2), provides:

(2) COORDINATION WITH TRANSITIONAL RULES.—The amendments made by this section shall not apply to any property to which paragraph (1) of section 56(a) of the Internal Revenue Code of 1986 does not apply by reason of subparagraph (C)(i) thereof.

P.L. 103-66, §13171(b):

Amended Code Sec. 56(g)(4) by adding at the end thereof a new subparagraph (J). **Effective** for contributions made after 6-30-92, except that in the case of any contribution of capital gain property which is not tangible personal property, such amendments shall apply only if the contribution is made after 12-31-92.

P.L. 103-66, §13227(c)(1):

Amended Code Sec. 56(g)(4)(C)(ii)(I) by striking "sections 936 and 921" and inserting "sections 936 (including subsections (a)(4) and (i) thereof) and 921". **Effective** for tax years beginning after 12-31-93.

P.L. 103-66, §13227(c)(2):

Amended Code Sec. 56(g)(4)(C)(iii) by adding new clauses (IV) and (V). **Effective** for tax years beginning after 12-31-93.

• 1992, Energy Policy Act of 1992 (P.L. 102-486)

P.L. 102-486, §1915(a)(2):

Amended Code Sec. 56(g)(4)(F). **Effective** for tax years beginning after 12-31-92. Prior to amendment, Code Sec. 56(g)(4)(F) read as follows:

(F) DEPLETION.—The allowance for depletion with respect to any property placed in service in a taxable year beginning after 1989 shall be cost depletion determined under section 611.

P.L. 102-486, §1915(b)(2):

Amended Code Sec. 56(g)(4)(D)(i) by adding at the end thereof a new sentence. **Effective** for tax years beginning after 12-31-92.

• 1990, Omnibus Budget Reconciliation Act of 1990 (P.L. 101-508)

P.L. 101-508, §11301(b):

Amended Code Sec. 56(g)(4) by striking subparagraph (F) and redesignating subparagraphs (G) and (H) as subparagraphs (F) and (G), respectively. For the **effective** date, see Act Sec. 11301(d)(2), below. Prior to amendment, Code Sec. 56(g)(4)(F) read as follows:

(F) ACQUISITION EXPENSES OF LIFE INSURANCE COMPANIES.—Acquisition expenses of life insurance companies shall be capitalized and amortized in accordance with the treatment generally required under generally accepted accounting principles as if this subparagraph applied to all taxable years.

P.L. 101-508, §11301(d)(2), provides:

(2) SUBSECTION (b).—

(A) IN GENERAL.—The amendment made by subsection (b) shall apply to taxable years beginning on or after September 30, 1990, except that, in the case of a small insurance company, such amendment shall apply to taxable years beginning after December 31, 1989. For purposes of this paragraph, the term "small insurance company" means any insurance company which meets the requirements of section 806(a)(3) of the Internal Revenue Code of 1986; except that paragraph (2) of section 806(c) of such Code shall not apply.

(B) SPECIAL RULES FOR YEAR WHICH INCLUDES SEPTEMBER 30, 1990.—In the case of any taxable year which includes September 30, 1990, the amount of acquisition expenses which is required to be capitalized under section 56(g)(4)(F) of the Internal Revenue Code of 1986 (as in effect before the amendment made by subsection (b)) by a company which is not a small insurance company shall be the amount which bears the same ratio to the amount which (but for this subparagraph) would be so required to be capitalized as the number of days in such taxable year before September 30, 1990, bears to the total number of days in such taxable year. A similar reduction shall be made in the amount amortized for such taxable year under such section 56(g)(4)(F).

P.L. 101-508, §11704(a)(1):

Amended Code Sec. 56(g)(4)(D)(ii) by striking "year" and inserting "years". **Effective** 11-5-90.

P.L. 101-508, §11801(c)(2)(B), as amended by P.L. 104-188, §1704(t)(48):

Amended Code Sec. 56(g)(1) and (2) by striking "beginning after 1989" after "any taxable year" the first time it appears. **Effective**, generally, on 11-5-90.

P.L. 101-508, §11801(c)(2)(C):

Amended Code Sec. 56(g)(4)(C)(iii). **Effective**, generally, on 11-5-90. Prior to amendment, Code Sec. 56(g)(4)(C)(iii) read as follows:

(iii) SPECIAL RULE FOR DIVIDENDS FROM SECTION 936 COMPANIES.—In the case of any dividend received from a corporation eligible for the credit provided by section 936, rules similar to the rules of subparagraph (F) of subsection (f)(1) shall apply, except that "75 percent" shall be substituted for "50 percent" in clause (i) thereof.

P.L. 101-508, §11821(b), provides:

(b) SAVINGS PROVISION.—If—

(1) any provision amended or repealed by this part applied to—

(A) any transactions occurring before the date of the enactment of this Act,

(B) any property acquired before such date of enactment, or

(C) any item of income, loss, deduction, or credit taken into account before such date of enactment, and

(2) the treatment of such transaction, property, or item under such provision would (without regard to the amendments made by this part) affect liability for tax for periods ending after such date of enactment,

nothing in the amendments made by this part shall be construed to affect the treatment of such transaction, property, or item for purposes of determining liability for tax for periods ending after such date of enactment.

• 1989, Omnibus Budget Reconciliation Act of 1989 (P.L. 101-239)

P.L. 101-239, §7205(b):

Amended Code Sec. 56(g)(4)(H) by striking clause (ii) and all that follows and inserting a new clause (ii) and flush left sentence. **Effective**, generally, for ownership changes and acquisitions after 10-2-89, in tax years ending after such date. However, for special rules, see Act Sec. 7205(c)(2)-(4), below. Prior to amendment, Code Sec. 56(g)(4)(H)(ii) and all that followed read as follows:

(ii)(I) the aggregate adjusted bases of the assets of such corporation (immediately after the change), exceed

(II) the value of the stock of such corporation (as determined for purposes of section 382), properly adjusted for liabilities and other relevant items,

then the adjusted basis of each asset of such corporation (as of such time) shall be its proportionate share (determined on the basis of respective fair market values) of the amount referred to in clause (ii)(II).

P.L. 101-239, §7205(c)(2)-(4), provides:

(2) BINDING CONTRACT.—The amendments made by this section shall not apply to any ownership change or acquisition pursuant to a written binding contract in effect on October 2, 1989, and at all times thereafter before such change or acquisition.

(3) BANKRUPTCY PROCEEDINGS.—In the case of a reorganization described in section 368(a)(1)(G) of the Internal Revenue Code of 1986, or an exchange of debt for stock in a title 11 or similar case (as defined in section 368(a)(3) of such Code), the amendments made by this section shall not apply to any ownership change resulting from such a reorganization or proceeding if a petition in such case was filed with the court before October 3, 1989.

(4) SUBSIDIARIES OF BANKRUPT PARENT.—The amendments made by this section shall not apply to any built-in loss of a corporation which is a member (on October 2, 1989) of an affiliated group the common parent of which (on such date) was subject to title 11 or similar case (as defined in section 368(a)(3) of such Code). The preceding sentence shall apply only if the ownership change or acquisition is pursuant to the plan approved in such proceeding and is before the date 2 years after the date on which the petition which commenced such proceeding was filed.

P.L. 101-239, §7611(a)(1)(A):

Amended Code Sec. 56(g)(4)(A)(i). **Effective** for tax years beginning after 12-31-89. Prior to amendment, Code Sec. 56(g)(4)(A)(i) read as follows:

(i) PROPERTY PLACED IN SERVICE AFTER 1989.—The depreciation deduction with respect to any property placed in service in a taxable year beginning after 1989 shall be determined under whichever of the following methods yields deductions with a smaller present value:

(I) The alternative system of section 168(g), or

(II) The method used for book purposes.

P.L. 101-239, §7611(a)(1)(B):

Amended Code Sec. 56(g)(4)(A) by striking clauses (v) and (vi) and by redesignating clause (vii) as clause (v). **Effective** for tax years beginning after 12-31-89. Prior to amendment, Code Sec. 56(g)(4)(A)(v)-(vi) read as follows:

(v) SLOWER METHOD USED IF USED FOR BOOK PURPOSES.—In the case of any property to which clause (ii), (iii), or (iv) applies, if the depreciation method used for book purposes yields deductions for taxable years beginning after 1989 with a smaller present value than the method which would otherwise be used under such clause, the method used for book purposes shall be used in lieu of the method which would otherwise be used under such clause.

(vi) ELECTION TO HAVE CUMULATIVE LIMITATION.—

(I) IN GENERAL.—In the case of any property placed in service during a taxable year to which an election under this clause applies, in lieu of applying clause (i), the depreciation deduction for such property for any taxable year shall be the lesser of the accumulated 168(g) depreciation or the accumulated book depreciation; reduced by the aggregate amount of the depreciation deductions determined under this subclause with respect to such property for prior taxable years.

(II) ACCUMULATED 168(g) DEPRECIATION.—For purposes of this clause, the term "accumulated section 168(g) depreciation" means the aggregate amount of the depreciation deductions determined under the alternative system of section 168(g) with respect to the property for all periods before the close of the taxable year.

(III) ACCUMULATED BOOK DEPRECIATION.—For purposes of this clause, the term "accumulated book depreciation" means the aggregate amount of the depreciation deductions determined under the method used for book purposes with respect to the property for all periods before the close of the taxable year.

(IV) ELECTION.—The taxpayer may make an election under this clause for any taxable year beginning after 1989. Such an election, once made with respect to any such taxable year, shall apply to all property placed in service during such taxable year, and shall be irrevocable.

(V) SIMILAR RULES FOR PROPERTY DESCRIBED IN CLAUSE (i), (iii), OR (iv).—Rules similar to the rules of the preceding provisions of this clause shall also apply in the case of property to which clause (ii), (iii), or (iv) applies.

P.L. 101-239, §7611(a)(2):

Amended Code Sec. 56(g)(4)(A)(iii) by inserting "and which is placed in service in a taxable year beginning before 1990" after "thereof) applies". **Effective** for tax years beginning after 12-31-89.

P.L. 101-239, §7611(b):

Amended Code Sec. 56(g)(4)(D). **Effective** for tax years beginning after 12-31-89. Prior to amendment, Code Sec. 56(g)(4)(D) read as follows:

(D) CERTAIN OTHER EARNINGS AND PROFITS ADJUSTMENTS.—

(i) IN GENERAL.—The adjustments provided in section 312(n) shall apply, except that—

(I) paragraphs (1), (2), and (3) shall apply only to amounts paid or incurred in taxable years beginning after December 31, 1989,

(II) paragraph (4) shall apply only to taxable years beginning after December 31, 1989,

(III) paragraph (5) shall apply only to installment sales in taxable years beginning after December 31, 1989, and

(IV) paragraphs (6), (7), and (8) shall not apply.

(ii) SPECIAL RULE FOR INTANGIBLE DRILLING COSTS AND MINERAL EXPLORATION AND DEVELOPMENT COSTS.—If—

(I) the present value of the deductions provided under subparagraph (A)(ii) or (B)(ii) of section 312(n)(2) with respect to amounts paid or incurred in taxable years beginning after December 31, 1989, exceeds

(II) the present value of the deductions for such amounts under the method used for book purposes,

such amounts shall be deductible under the method used for book purposes in lieu of that provided in such subparagraph.

P.L. 101-239, §7611(c):

Amended Code Sec. 56(g)(4)(G). **Effective** for tax years beginning after 12-31-89. Prior to amendment, Code Sec. 56(g)(4)(G) read as follows:

(G) DEPLETION.—The allowances for depletion with respect to any property placed in service in a taxable year beginning after 1989, shall be determined under whichever of the following methods yields deductions with a smaller present value:

(i) cost depletion determined under section 611, or

(ii) the method used for book purposes.

P.L. 101-239, §7611(d):

Amended Code Sec. 56(g)(4)(C)(ii). **Effective** for tax years beginning after 12-31-89. Prior to amendment, Code Sec. 56(g)(4)(C)(ii) read as follows:

(ii) SPECIAL RULE FOR 100-PERCENT DIVIDENDS.—Clause (i) shall not apply to any deduction allowable under section 243 or 245 for a 100-percent dividend—

(I) if the corporation receiving such dividend and the corporation paying such dividend could not be members of the same affiliated group under section 1504 by reason of section 1504(b),

(II) but only to the extent such dividend is attributable to income of the paying corporation which is subject to tax under this chapter (determined after the application of sections 936 and 921).

For purposes of the preceding sentence, the term "100 percent dividend" means any dividend if the percentage used for purposes of determining the amount allowable as a deduction under section 243 or 245 with respect to such dividend is 100 percent.

P.L. 101-239, §7611(e):

Amended Code Sec. 56(g)(4)(C) by adding at the end thereof a new clause (iv). **Effective** for tax years beginning after 12-31-89.

P.L. 101-239, §7611(f)(1):

Amended Code Sec. 56(g)(4)(H)(i) by striking "after the date of the enactment of the Tax Reform Act of 1986" and inserting "in a taxable year beginning after 1989". **Effective** for tax years beginning after 12-31-89.

P.L. 101-239, §7611(f)(2):

Amended Code Sec. 56(g)(4)(B)(i) by adding at the end thereof a new sentence. **Effective** for tax years beginning after 12-31-89.

P.L. 101-239, §7611(f)(3):

Repealed Code Sec. 56(g)(4)(B)(iii). **Effective** for tax years beginning after 12-31-89. Prior to repeal, Code Sec. 56(g)(4)(B)(iii) read as follows:

(iii) INCLUSION OF INCOME ON ANNUITY CONTRACT.—In the case of any annuity contract, the income on such contract (as determined under section 72(u)(2)) shall be treated as includible in gross income for such year. The preceding sentence shall not apply to any annuity contract which is held under a plan described in section 403(a) or which is described in section 72(u)(3)(C).

P.L. 101-239, §7611(f)(4):

Amended Code Sec. 56(g)(5) by striking subparagraphs (A) and (C) and by redesignating subparagraphs (B) and (D) as subparagraphs (A) and (B), respectively. **Effective** for tax years beginning after 12-31-89. Prior to amendment, Code Sec. 56(g)(5)(A) and (C) read as follows:

(A) BOOK PURPOSES.—The term "book purposes" means the treatment for purposes of preparing the applicable financial statement referred to in subsection (f).

* * *

(C) PRESENT VALUE.—Present value shall be determined as of the time the property is placed in service (or, if later, as of the beginning of the first taxable year beginning after 1989) and under regulations prescribed by the Secretary.

P.L. 101-239, §7611(g)(3), provides:

(3) REGULATIONS ON EARNINGS AND PROFITS RULES.—Not later than March 15, 1991, the Secretary of the Treasury or his delegate shall prescribe initial regulations providing guidance as to which items of income are included in adjusted current earnings under section 56(g)(4)(B)(i) of the Internal Revenue Code of 1986 and which items of deduction are disallowed under section 56(g)(4)(C) of such Code.

P.L. 101-239, §7815(e)(4):

Amended Code Sec. 56(g)(4)(D)(i), prior to amendment by Act Sec. 7611(b), by adding "and" at the end of subclause (III) and by striking subclauses (IV) and (V) and by adding a new subclause (IV). **Effective** as if included in the provision of P.L. 100-647 to which it relates. Prior to amendment, Code Sec. 56(g)(4)(D)(i)(IV)-(V) read as follows:

(IV) paragraph (6) shall apply only to contracts entered into on or after March 1, 1986, and

(V) paragraphs (7) and (8) shall not apply.

• 1988, Technical and Miscellaneous Revenue Act of 1988 (P.L. 100-647)

P.L. 100-647, §1007(b)(11)(B):

Amended Code Sec. 56(g)(4)(C)(iii) by striking out "clause (ii)(I)" and inserting in lieu thereof "clause (i)". **Effective** as if included in the provision of P.L. 99-514 to which it relates.

P.L. 100-647, §1007(b)(12):

Amended Code Sec. 56(g)(4)(B)(iii) by adding at the end thereof a new sentence. **Effective** as if included in the provision of P.L. 99-514 to which it relates.

P.L. 100-647, §1007(b)(17):

Amended Code Sec. 56(g)(4)(A) by adding at the end thereof new clauses (vi)-(vii). **Effective** as if included in the provision of P.L. 99-514 to which it relates.

P.L. 100-647, §1007(b)(18):

Amended Code Sec. 56(g)(4) by adding at the end thereof new subparagraph (I). **Effective** as if included in the provision of P.L. 99-514 to which it relates.

P.L. 100-647, §6079(a)(1):

Amended the last sentence of Code Sec. 56(g)(4)(B)(iii). **Effective** as if included in the amendments made by section 701 of P.L. 99-514. Prior to amendment, the last sentence of Code Sec. 56(g)(4)(B)(iii) read as follows:

The preceding sentence shall not apply to any annuity contract held under a plan described in section 403(a).

• 1986, Tax Reform Act of 1986 (P.L. 99-514)

P.L. 99-514, §701(a):

Amended Code Sec. 56. **Effective**, generally, for tax years beginning after 12-31-86. For exceptions, see Act Sec. 701(f)(2)-(7), below. Prior to amendment, Code Sec. 56 read as follows:

SEC. 56. CORPORATE MINIMUM TAX.

[Sec. 56(a)]

(a) GENERAL RULE.—In addition to the other taxes imposed by this chapter, there is hereby imposed for each taxable year, with respect to the income of every corporation, a tax equal to 15 percent of the amount by which the sum of the items of tax preference exceeds the greater of—

(1) $10,000, or

(2) the regular tax deduction for the taxable year (as determined under subsection (c)).

Amendments

• 1983, Technical Corrections Act of 1982 (P.L. 97-448)

P.L. 97-448, §306(a)(1)(A):

Amended section 201 on P.L. 97-248 by redesignating the second subsection (c) as subsection (d).

• 1982, Tax Equity and Fiscal Responsibility Act of 1982 (P.L. 97-248)

P.L. 97-248, §201(d)(1)(A):

Amended Code Sec. 56(a) by striking out "person" each place it appeared and inserting in lieu thereof "corporation." **Effective** for tax years beginning after 12-31-82.

• 1976 (P.L. 94-568)

P.L. 94-568, §3(a):

Amended the effective date provision of Sec. 301(g)(2) of the Tax Reform Act of 1976 (see below), to read as follows:

(2) TAX CARRYOVER.

(A) IN GENERAL.—Except as provided in subparagraph (B), the amount of any tax carryover under section 56(c) of the Internal Revenue Code of 1954 from a taxable year beginning before January 1, 1976, shall not be allowed as a tax carryover for any taxable year beginning after December 31, 1975.

(B) Except as provided by paragraph (4) and in section 56(e) of the Internal Revenue Code of 1954, in the case of a corporation which is not an electing small business corporation (as defined in section 1371(b) of such Code) or a personal holding company (as defined in section 524 of such Code), the amount of any tax carryover under section 56(c) of such Code from a taxable year beginning before July 1, 1976, shall not be allowed as a tax carryover for any taxable year beginning after June 30, 1976. **Effective** 10-4-76.

• 1976, Tax Reform Act of 1976 (P.L. 94-455)

P.L. 94-455, §301(a):

Amended Code Sec. 56(a). For the **effective** date, see Act Sec. 301(g), below. Prior to amendment Code Sec. 56(a) read as follows:

(a) IN GENERAL.—In addition to the other taxes imposed by this chapter, there is hereby imposed for each taxable year, with respect to the income of every person, a tax equal to 10 percent of the amount (if any) by which—

(1) the sum of the items of tax preference in excess of $30,000, is greater than

(2) the sum of—

(A) the taxes imposed by this chapter for the taxable year (computed without regard to this part and without regard to the taxes imposed by sections 72(m)(5)(B), 402(e), 408(f), 531 and 541) reduced by the sum of the credits allowable under—

(i) section 33 (relating to foreign tax credit),

(ii) section 37 (relating to retirement income),

(iii) section 38 (relating to investment credit),

(iv) section 40 (relating to expenses of work incentive program),

(v) section 41 (relating to contributions to candidates for public office),

(vi) section 42 (relating to credit for personal exemptions), and

(vii) section 44 (relating to credit for purchase of new principal residence); and

(B) the tax carryovers to the taxable year.

P.L. 94-455, §301(f), provides:

(f) SECTION 21 NOT TO APPLY.—For purposes of section 21 of the Internal Revenue Code of 1954, the amendments made by this section shall not be treated as a change in a rate of tax.

P.L. 94-455, §301(g), provides:

(g) EFFECTIVE DATE.—

(1) IN GENERAL.—Except as provided by paragraph (4), the amendments made by this section shall apply to items of tax preference for taxable years beginning after December 31, 1975.

(2) [For amended text, see P.L. 94-568, above.] TAX CARRYOVER.—Except as provided in paragraph (4) and in section 56(e) of the Internal Revenue Code of 1954, the amount of any tax carryover under section 56(c) of such Code from a taxable year beginning before January 1, 1976, shall not be allowed as a tax carryover for any taxable year beginning after December 31, 1975.

(3) SPECIAL RULE FOR TAXABLE YEAR 1976 IN THE CASE OF A CORPORATION.—Notwithstanding any provision of the Internal Revenue Code of 1954 to the contrary, in the case of a corporation which is not an electing small business corporation or a personal holding company the tax imposed by section 56 of such Code for taxable years beginning in 1976, is an amount equal to the sum of—

(A) the amount of the tax which would have been imposed for such taxable year under such section as such section was in effect on the day before the date of the enactment of the Tax Reform Act of 1976, and

(B) one-half of the amount by which the amount of the tax which would be imposed for such taxable year under such section as amended by the Tax Reform Act of 1976 (but for this paragraph) exceeds the amount determined under subparagraph (A).

(4) CERTAIN FINANCIAL INSTITUTIONS.—In the case of a taxpayer which is a financial institution to which section 585 or 593 of the Internal Revenue Code of 1954 applies, the amendments made by this section shall apply only to taxable years beginning after December 31, 1977, and paragraph (2) shall be applied by substituting "January 1, 1978" for "January 1, 1976" and by substituting "December 31, 1977" for "December 31, 1975".

For amendments made by earlier Acts, see amendment note under Code Sec. 46(c).

[Sec. 56(b)]

(b) DEFERRAL OF TAX LIABILITY IN CASE OF CERTAIN NET OPERATING LOSSES.—

(1) IN GENERAL.—If for any taxable year a corporation—

(A) has a net operating loss any portion of which (under section 172) remains as a net operating loss carryover to a succeeding taxable year, and

(B) has items of tax preference in excess of $10,000,

then an amount equal to the lesser of the tax imposed by subsection (a) or 15 percent of the amount of the net operating loss carryover described in subparagraph (A) shall be treated as tax liability not imposed for the taxable year, but as imposed for the succeeding taxable year or years pursuant to paragraph (2).

(2) YEAR OF LIABILITY.—In any taxable year in which any portion of the net operating loss carryover attributable to the excess described in paragraph (1)(B) reduces taxable income, the amount of tax liability described in paragraph (1) shall be treated as tax liability imposed in such taxable year in an amount equal to 15 percent of such reduction.

(3) PRIORITY OF APPLICATION.—For purposes of paragraph (2), if any portion of the net operating loss carryover described in paragraph (1)(A) is not attributable to the excess described in paragraph (1)(B), such portion shall be considered as being applied in reducing taxable income before such other portion.

Amendments

• 1982, Tax Equity and Fiscal Responsibility Act of 1982 (P.L. 97-248)

P.L. 97-248, §201(d)(1)(A) (as amended by P.L. 97-448, §306(a)(1)(A)):

Amended Code Sec. 56(b) by striking out "person" and inserting in lieu thereof "corporation". **Effective** for tax years beginning after 12-31-82.

• 1976, Tax Reform Act of 1976 (P.L. 94-455)

P.L. 94-455, §301(b):

Amended Code Sec. 56(b) by substituting "$10,000" for "$30,000" in paragraph (1)(B); and by substituting "15 percent" for "10 percent" in paragraphs (1) and (2).

P.L. 94-455, §301(f), provides:

(f) SECTION 21 NOT TO APPLY.—For purposes of section 21 of the Internal Revenue Code of 1954, the amendments made by this section shall not be treated as a change in a rate of tax.

For **effective** date, see Act Sec. 301(g), above.

For amendments made by earlier Acts, see amendment note under Code Sec. 56(c).

[Sec. 56(c)]

(c) REGULAR TAX DEDUCTION DEFINED.—For purposes of this section, the term "regular tax deduction" means an amount equal to the taxes imposed by this chapter for the taxable year (computed without regard to this part and without regard to the taxes imposed by sections 531 and 541), reduced by the sum of the credits allowable under subparts A, B, and D of part IV. For purposes of the preceding sentence, the amount of the credit determined under section 38 for any taxable year shall be determined without regard to the employee stock ownership credit determined under section 41.

Amendments

• 1986, Tax Reform Act of 1986 (P.L. 99-514)

P.L. 99-514, §1171(b)(3):

Amended Code Sec. 56(c) by striking out the last sentence. **Effective** for compensation paid or accrued after 12-31-86, in tax years ending after such date. Prior to amendment, the last sentence of Code Sec. 56(c) read as follows:

For purposes of the preceding sentence, the amount of the credit determined under section 38 for any taxable year shall be determined without regard to the employee stock ownership credit determined under section 41.

• 1984, Deficit Reduction Act of 1984 (P.L. 98-369)

P.L. 98-369, §474(r)(1)(A):

Amended Code Sec. 56(c) by striking out "subpart A of part IV other than sections 39 and 44G" and inserting in lieu thereof "subparts A, B, and D of part IV", and by amending the last sentence. **Effective** for tax years beginning after 12-31-83, and to carrybacks from such years. Prior to amendment, the last sentence read as follows:

For purposes of the preceding sentence, the amount of the credit allowable under section 38 shall be determined without regard to the employee plan percentage set forth in section 46(a)(2)(E).

• 1982, Tax Equity and Fiscal Responsibility Act of 1982 (P.L. 97-248)

P.L. 97-248, §201(d)(1)(B) (as amended by P.L. 97-448, §306(a)(1)(A)):

Amended Code Sec. 56 by striking out "one-half (or in the case of a corporation, an amount equal to)" in subsection (c). **Effective** for tax years beginning after 12-31-82. But see Act Sec. 201(d)(2) for a special rule.

P.L. 97-248, §201(d)(1)(C) (amended by P.L. 97-448, §306(a)(1)(A)):

Amended Code Sec. 56 by striking out "sections 72(m)(5)(B), 402(e), 408(f), 531, and 541" in subsection (c) and inserting in lieu thereof "sections 531 and 541". **Effective** for tax years beginning after 12-31-82. But see Act Sec. 201(d)(2) for a special rule.

P.L. 97-248, §201(d)(1)(D) (amended by P.L. 97-448, §306(a)(1)(A)):

Amended Code Sec. 56 by striking out "31, 39, 43, and 44G" in subsection (c) and inserting in lieu thereof "39 and 44G." **Effective** for tax years beginning after 12-31-82. But see Act Sec. 201(d)(2) for a special rule.

P.L. 97-248, §201(d)(1)(E) (amended by P.L. 97-448, §306(a)(1)(A)):

Amended Code Sec. 56 by striking out the section heading **"IMPOSITION OF TAX"** and inserting a new heading. **Effective** for tax years beginning after 12-31-82.

P.L. 97-248, §201(d)(2), provides:

Special rule for pre-1983 section 56(b) tax deferrals.—The amendments made by subsection (c)(1) of this section to section 56(b) of the Internal Revenue Code of 1954 shall not apply to any net operating loss carryover from any taxable year beginning before January 1, 1983, which is attributable to any excess described in section 56(b)(1)(B) of such Code for such taxable year.

• 1981, Economic Recovery Tax Act of 1981 (P.L. 97-34)

P.L. 97-34, §331(c)(2):

Amended Code Sec. 56(c) by striking out "and 43" and inserting "43, and 44G". **Effective** for tax years ending after 12-31-82.

• 1980, Technical Corrections Act of 1979 (P.L. 96-222)

P.L. 96-222, §101(a)(7)(B)

Amended Act Sec. 141 of P.L. 95-600 by revising paragraph (g) which relates to the effective dates for amendments concerning tax credit employee stock ownership plans. For **effective** dates, see the amendment note at §101(a)(7)(B), P.L. 96-222, following the text of Code Sec. 409A(n) and also below.

P.L. 96-222, §101(a)(6)(B), provides:

(6) RETROACTIVE APPLICATION OF AMENDMENT MADE BY SUBSECTION (d).—In determining the regular tax deduction under section 56(c) of the Internal Revenue Code of 1954 for any taxable year beginning before January 1, 1979, the amount of the credit allowable under section 38 of such Code shall be determined without regard to section 46(a)(2)(B) of such Code (as in effect before the enactment of the Energy Tax Act of 1978).

P.L. 96-222, §101(a)(7)(L)(iii)(IV):

Amended Code Sec. 56(c) by striking out "ESOP" and inserting "employee plan" before "percentage set forth in section 46(a)(2)(E),". **Effective** for tax years beginning after 12-31-78.

• 1978, Energy Tax Act of 1978 (P.L. 95-618)

P.L. 95-618, §101(b)(2):

Amended Code Sec. 56(c) by striking out all language after "the sum of the" and inserting in lieu thereof "credits allowable under subpart A of part IV other than sections 31,

39, and 43." **Effective** for tax years ending on or after 4-20-77. Before amendment, Code Sec. 56(c) read as follows:

"(c) REGULAR TAX DEDUCTION DEFINED.—For purposes of this section the term `regular tax deduction' means an amount equal to one-half of (or in the case of a corporation, an amount equal to) the taxes imposed by this chapter for the taxable year (computed without regard to this part and without regard to the taxes imposed by sections 72(m)(5)(B), 402(e), 408(f), 531, and 541), reduced by the sum of the credits allowable under—

(1) section 33 (relating to foreign tax credit),

(2) section 37 (relating to credit for the elderly),

(3) section 38 (relating to investment credit),

(4) section 40 (relating to expenses of work incentive program),

(5) section 41 (relating to contributions to candidates for public office),

(6) section 42 (relating to general tax credit),

(7) section 44 (relating to purchase of new principal residence),

(8) section 44A (relating to expenses for household and dependent care services necessary for gainful employment), and

(9) section 44B (relating to credit for employment of certain new employees)."

• 1978, Revenue Act of 1978 (P.L. 95-600)

P.L. 95-600, §141(d):

Amended Code Sec. 56(c) by adding the last sentence. **Effective** as indicated in P.L. 95-600, §141(g).

P.L. 95-600, §141(g), provides:

(g) EFFECTIVE DATES.—

(1) IN GENERAL.—The amendments made by this section (other than by subsection (f)(3)) shall apply with respect to qualified investment for taxable years beginning after December 31, 1978. The amendment made by subsection (f)(7) shall apply to years beginning after December 31, 1978.

(2) RETROACTIVE APPLICATION OF AMENDMENT MADE BY SUBSECTION (d).—In determining the regular tax deduction under section 6 of the Internal Revenue Code of 1954 for any taxable year beginning before January 1, 1979, the amount of the credit allowable under section 38 shall be determined without regard to section 46(a)(2)(B) of such Code (as in effect before the enactment of the Energy Tax Act of 1978).

• 1977, Tax Reduction and Simplification Act of 1977 (P.L. 95-30)

P.L. 95-30, §202(d)(2)(A):

Amended Code Sec. 56(c) by deleting "and" at the end of paragraph (7), adding ", and" for the period at the end of paragraph (8), and adding new paragraph (9). **Effective** for tax years beginning after 12-31-76.

• 1976, Tax Reform Act of 1976 (P.L. 94-455)

P.L. 94-455, §301(b)(2):

Amended Code Sec. 56(c). For the **effective** date, see Act Sec. 301(g), above. Prior to amendment, Code Sec. 56(c) read as follows:

(c) TAX CARRYOVERS.—If for any taxable year—

(1) the taxes imposed by this chapter (computed without regard to this part and without regard to the taxes imposed by sections 72(m)(5)(B), 402(e), 408(f), 531 and 541) reduced by the sum of the credits allowable under—

(A) section 33 (relating to foreign tax credit),

(B) section 37 (relating to retirement income),

(C) section 38 (relating to investment credit),

(D) section 40 (relating to expenses of work incentive program),

(E) section 41 (relating to contributions to candidates for public office),

(F) section 42 (relating to credit for personal exemptions), and

(G) section 44 (relating to credit for purchase of new principal residence), exceed

(2) the sum of the items of tax preference in excess of $30,000,

then the excess of the taxes described in paragraph (1) over the sum described in paragraph (2) shall be a tax carryover to each of the 7 taxable years following such year. The entire amount of the excess for a taxable year shall be carried to the first of such 7 taxable years, and then to each of the other such taxable years to the extent that such excess is not used to reduce the amount subject to tax under subsection (a) for a prior taxable year to which [such]excess may be carried.

P.L. 94-455, §301(f), provides:

(f) SECTION 21 NOT TO APPLY.—For purposes of section 21 of the Internal Revenue Code of 1954, the amendments made by this section shall not be treated as a change in a rate of tax.

• 1975, Tax Reduction Act of 1975 (P.L. 94-12)

P.L. 94-12, §203(b)(2)-(3):

Amended Code Sec. 56(a)(2) by deleting "and" at the end of clause (iv), by substituting ", and" for "; and" at the end of clause (v), and by adding clauses (vi) and (vii).

P.L. 94-12, §208(d)(2)-(3):

Amended Code Sec. 56(c)(1) by deleting "and" at the end of subparagraph (D), by deleting "exceed" at the end of subparagraph (E) and by adding clauses (F) and (G).

For **effective** dates see Code Secs. 42 and 44.

• 1974, Employee Retirement Income Security Act of 1974 (P.L. 93-406)

P.L. 93-406, §2001(g)(2)(D):

Amended Code Sec. 56(a)(2)(A) and Code Sec. 56(c)(1) by adding "72(m)(5)(B)". **Effective** for distributions made in tax years beginning after 1975.

P.L. 93-406, §2002(g)(4):

Amended Code Sec. 56(a)(2)(A) and Code Sec. 56(c)(1) by adding "408(f)". **Effective** 1-1-75.

P.L. 93-406, §2005(c)(7):

Amended Code Sec. 56(a)(2)(A) and Code Sec. 56(c)(1) by adding "402(e)". **Effective** for distributions or payments made after 1973.

• 1971, Revenue Act of 1971 (P.L. 92-178)

P.L. 92-178, §601(c)(4):

Amended Code Sec. 56(a)(2) by deleting "and" at the end of clause (ii), substituting a comma for ", and" at the end of clause (iii) of P. L. 92-178 and adding clauses (iv) and (v). **Effective** for tax years ending after 12-31-71.

P.L. 92-178, §601(c)(5):

Amended Code Sec. 56(c)(1) by deleting "and" at the end of subparagraph (B), deleting "exceed" at the end of subparagraph (C), and adding subparagraphs (D) and (E). **Effective** for tax years ending after 12-31-71.

• 1970, Excise, Estate, and Gift Tax Adjustment Act of 1970 (P.L. 91-614)

P.L. 91-614, §501(a):

Amended Code Sec. 56 by adding Code Sec. 56(c) and by substituting paragraph (2) of Code Sec. 56(a) for the following:

(2) the taxes imposed by this chapter for the taxable year (computed without regard to this part and without regard to the taxes imposed by sections 531 and 541) reduced by the sum of the credits allowable under—

(A) section 33 (relating to foreign tax credit),

(B) section 37 (relating to retirement income), and

(C) section 38 (relating to investment credit).

P.L. 91-614, §501(b), provides:

"(b) Effective Date.—The amendments made by subsection (a) shall apply to taxable years ending after December 31, 1969. In the case of a taxable year beginning in 1969 and ending in 1970, the excess referred to in section 56(c) of the Internal Revenue Code of 1954 (as added by subsection (a)) shall be an amount equal to the excess determined under such section (without regard to this sentence) multiplied by a fraction—

(1) the numerator of which is the number of days in the taxable year occurring after December 31, 1969, and

(2) the denominator of which is the number of days in the entire taxable year.

P.L. 91-172, §301(a):

Added new Code section 56. **Effective** 1-1-70. In case of a taxable year beginning in 1969 and ending in 1970, the tax imposed by Code Sec. 56 shall be an amount equal to the tax imposed by such section (determined without regard to this sentence) multiplied by a fraction—

(1) the numerator of which is the number of days in the taxable year occurring after December 31, 1969, and

(2) the denominator of which is the number of days in the entire taxable year.

[Sec. 56(d)]

(d) REGULAR TAX DEDUCTION ADJUSTMENT FOR TIMBER.—In the case of a corporation, the regular tax deduction (as determined under subsection (c)) shall be reduced by an amount equal to the lesser of—

(1) one-third of the amount determined under subsection (c) without regard to this subsection, or

(2) the preference reduction for timber determined under section 57(a)(9)(C).

Amendments

• 1976, Tax Reform Act of 1976 (P.L. 94-455)

P.L. 94-455, §301(c)(4)(B):

Added Code Sec. 56(d). For **effective** date, see Act Sec. 301(g), above.

P.L. 94-455, §301(f), provides:

(f) SECTION 21 NOT TO APPLY.—For purposes of section 21 of the Internal Revenue Code of 1954, the amendments made by this section shall not be treated as a change in a rate of tax.

[Sec. 56(e)]

(e) TAX CARRYOVER FOR TIMBER.—

(1) IN GENERAL.—In the case of a corporation, if for any taxable year, including a taxable year beginning before January 1, 1976—

(A) the taxes imposed by this chapter (computed without regard to this part and without regard to the tax imposed by section 531) which, under regulations prescribed by the Secretary, are attributable to income from timber, reduced by the sum of the credits allowable under—

(i) section 27 (relating to foreign tax credit), and

(ii) section 38 (relating to general business credit), exceed,

(B) the items of tax preference (as determined under section 57),

then the excess of the taxes described in subparagraph (A) over the items of tax preference shall be a tax carryover to each of the 7 taxable years following such year. The entire amount of the excess shall be carried to the first of such 7 taxable years, and then to each of the other such taxable years to the extent that such excess is not used to reduce the amount subject to tax under subsection (a) for a prior taxable year to which such excess may be carried.

(2) LIMITATION.—The amount of any carryover under paragraph (1) which may be deducted in a taxable year shall be limited to—

(A) the excess of—

(i) the amount of timber preference income for the taxable year (as defined in section 57(e)), over

(ii) the amount determined under section 57(a)(9)(C) for the taxable year,

(B) reduced by the excess of—

(i) the regular tax deduction for the taxable year (as determined under subsection (c) without regard to this subsection), over

(ii) the amount determined under subsection (d) for the taxable year.

Amendments

• 1984, Deficit Reduction Act of 1984 (P.L. 98-369)

P.L. 98-369, §474(r)(1)(B):

Amended Code Sec. 56(e)(1)(A) by striking out clauses (i), (ii), (iii), and (iv) and inserting in lieu thereof clauses (i) and (ii). **Effective** for tax years beginning after 12-31-83, and to carrybacks from such years. Prior to amendment, clauses (i), (ii), (iii), and (iv) read as follows:

(i) section 33 (relating to foreign tax credit),

(ii) section 38 (relating to investment credit),

(iii) section 40 (relating to expenses of work incentive programs, and

(iv) section 44B (relating to credit for employment of certain new employees), exceed

• 1977, Tax Reduction and Simplification Act of 1977 (P.L. 95-30)

P.L. 95-30, §202(d)(2)(B):

Amended Code Sec. 56(e)(1) by deleting "and" at the end of clause (ii), deleting "exceed" and adding "and" at the end of clause (iii), and adding new clause (iv). **Effective** for tax years beginning after 12-31-76.

• 1976, Tax Reform Act of 1976 (P.L. 94-455)

P.L. 94-455, §301(c)(4)(B):

Added Code Sec. 56(e). For **effective** date, see Act Sec. 301(g), above.

P.L. 94-455, §301(f), provides:

(f) SECTION 21 NOT TO APPLY.—For purposes of section 21 of the Internal Revenue Code of 1954, the amendments made by this section shall not be treated as a change in a rate of tax.

• 1986, Tax Reform Act of 1986 (P.L. 99-514)

P.L. 99-514, §701(f)(2)-(7), as amended by P.L. 100-647 §1007(f)(2)-(3), provides:

(2) ADJUSTMENT OF NET OPERATING LOSS.—

(A) INDIVIDUALS.—In the case of a net operating loss of an individual for a taxable year beginning after December 31, 1982, and before January 1, 1987, for purposes of determining the amount of such loss which may be carried to a taxable year beginning after December 31, 1986, for purposes of the minimum tax, such loss shall be adjusted in the manner provided in section 55(d)(2) of the Internal Revenue Code of 1954 as in effect on the day before the date of the enactment of this Act.

(B) CORPORATIONS.—If the minimum tax of a corporation was deferred under section 56(b) of the Internal Revenue Code of 1954 (as in effect on the day before the date of the enactment of this Act) for any taxable year beginning before January 1, 1987, and the amount of such tax has not been paid for any taxable year beginning before January 1, 1987, the amount of the net operating loss carryovers of such corporation which may be carried to taxable years beginning after December 31, 1986, for purposes of the minimum tax shall be reduced by the amount of tax preferences a tax on which was so deferred.

(3) INSTALLMENT SALES.—Section 56(a)(6) of the Internal Revenue Code of 1986 (as amended by this section) shall not apply to any disposition to which the amendments made by section 811 of this Act (relating to allocation of dealer's indebtedness to installment obligations) do not apply by reason of section 811(c)(2) of this Act.

(4) EXCEPTION FOR CHARITABLE CONTRIBUTIONS BEFORE AUGUST 16, 1986.—Section 57(a)(6) of the Internal Revenue Code of 1986 (as amended by this section) shall not apply to any deduction attributable to contributions made before August 16, 1986.

(5) BOOK INCOME.—

(A) IN GENERAL.—In the case of a corporation to which this paragraph applies, the amount of any increase for any taxable year under section 56(c)(1)(A) of the Internal Revenue Code of 1986 (as added by this section) shall be reduced (but not below zero) by the excess (if any) of—

(i) 50 percent of the excess of taxable income for the 5-taxable year period ending with the taxable year preceding the 1st taxable year to which such section applies over the adjusted net book income for such period, over

(ii) the aggregate amounts taken into account under this paragraph for preceding taxable years.

(B) TAXPAYER TO WHOM PARAGRAPH APPLIES.—This paragraph applies to a taxpayer which was incorporated in Delaware on May 31, 1912.

(C) TERMS.—Any term used in this paragraph which is used in section 56 of such Code (as so added) shall have the same meaning as when used in such section.

(6) CERTAIN PUBLIC UTILITY.—

(A) In the case of investment tax credits described in subparagraph (B) or (C), subsection 38(c)(3)(A)(ii) of the Internal Revenue Code of 1986 shall be applied by substituting "25 percent" for "75 percent", and section 38(c)(3)(B) of the Internal Revenue Code of 1986 shall be applied by substituting "75 percent" for "25 percent".

(B) If, on September 25, 1985, a regulated electric utility owned an undivided interest, within the range of 1,111 and 1,149, in the "maximum dependable capacity, net, megawatts electric" of an electric generating unit located in Illinois or Mississippi for which a binding written contract was in effect on December 31, 1980, then any investment tax credit with respect to such unit shall be described in this subparagraph. The aggregate amount of investment tax credits with respect to the unit in Mississippi allowed solely by reason of being described in this subparagraph shall not exceed $141,000,000.

(C) If, on September 25, 1985, a regulated electric utility owned an undivided interest, within the range of 1,104 and 1,111, in the "maximum dependable capacity, net, magawatts electric" of an electric generating unit located in Louisiana for which a binding written contract was in effect on December 31, 1980, then any investment tax credit of such electric utility shall be described in this subparagraph. The aggregate amount of investment tax credits allowed solely by reason of being described by this subparagraph shall not exceed $20,000,000.

(7) AGREEMENT VESSEL DEPRECIATION ADJUSTMENT.—

(A) For purposes of part VI of subchapter A of chapter 1 of the Internal Revenue Code of 1986, in the case of a qualified taxpayer, alternative minimum taxable income for the taxable year shall be reduced by an amount equal to the agreement vessel depreciation adjustment.

(B) For purposes of this paragraph, the agreement vessel depreciation adjustment shall be an amount equal to the depreciation deduction that would have been allowable for such year under section 167 of such Code with respect to agreement vessels placed in service before January 1, 1987, if the basis of such vessels had not been reduced under section 607 of the Merchant Marine Act of 1936, as amended, and if depreciation with respect to such vessel had been computed using the 25-year straight-line method. The aggregate amount by which basis of a qualified taxpayer is treated as not reduced by reason of this subparagraph shall not exceed $100,000,000.

(C) For purposes of this paragraph, the term "qualified taxpayer" means a parent corporation incorporated in the State of Delaware on December 1, 1972, and engaged in water transportation, and includes any other corporation which is a member of the affiliated group of which the parent corporation is the common parent. No taxpayer shall be treated as a qualified corporation for any taxable year beginning after December 31, 1991.

[Sec. 56(h)—Stricken]

Amendments

• 1992, Energy Policy Act of 1992 (P.L. 102-486)

P.L. 102-486, §1915(c)(1):

Amended Code Sec. 56 by striking subsection (h). **Effective** for tax years beginning after 12-31-92. Prior to amendment, Code Sec. 56(h) read as follows:

(h) ADJUSTMENT BASED ON ENERGY PREFERENCES.—

(1) IN GENERAL.—In computing the alternative minimum taxable income of any taxpayer other than an integrated oil company for any taxable year beginning after 1990, there shall be allowed as a deduction an amount equal to the lesser of—

(A) the alternative tax energy preference deduction, or

(B) 40 percent of alternative minimum taxable income.

(2) PHASE-OUT OF DEDUCTION AS OIL PRICES INCREASE.—The amount of the deduction under paragraph (1) (determined without regard to this paragraph) shall be reduced (but not below zero) by the amount which bears the same ratio to such amount as—

(A) the excess of the reference price of crude oil for the calendar year preceding the calendar year in which the taxable year begins over $28, bears to

(B) $6.

For purposes of this paragraph, the reference price for any calendar year shall be determined under section 29(d)(2)(C) and the $28 amount under subparagraph (A) shall be adjusted at the same time and in the same manner as under section 43(b)(3).

(3) ALTERNATIVE TAX ENERGY PREFERENCE DEDUCTION.—For purposes of paragraph (1), the term "alternative tax energy preference deduction" means an amount equal to the sum of—

(A) in the case of the intangible drilling cost preference, an amount equal to the sum of—

(i) 75 percent of the portion of the intangible drilling cost preference attributable to qualified exploratory costs, plus

(ii) 15 percent of the excess (if any) of—

(I) the intangible drilling cost preference, over

(II) the portion of the intangible drilling cost preference attributable to qualified exploratory costs, plus

(B) 50 percent of the marginal production depletion preference.

(4) INTANGIBLE DRILLING COST PREFERENCE.—For purposes of this subsection—

(A) IN GENERAL.—The term "intangible drilling cost preference" means the amount by which alternative minimum taxable income would be reduced if it were computed without regard to section 57(a)(2) and subsection (g)(4)(D)(i).

(B) PORTION ATTRIBUTABLE TO QUALIFIED EXPLORATORY COSTS.—For purposes of subparagraph (A), the portion of the intangible drilling cost preference attributable to qualified exploratory costs is an amount which bears the same ratio to the intangible drilling cost preference as—

(i) the qualified exploratory costs of the taxpayer for the taxable year, bear to

(ii) the total intangible drilling and development costs with respect to which the taxpayer may make an election under section 263(c) for the taxable year.

(5) MARGINAL PRODUCTION DEPLETION PREFERENCE.—For purposes of this subsection, the term "marginal production depletion preference" means the amount by which alternative minimum taxable income would be reduced if it were computed as if section 57(a)(1) and subsection (g)(4)(G) did not apply to any allowance for depletion determined under section 613A(c)(6).

(6) QUALIFIED EXPLORATORY COSTS.—For purposes of this subsection—

(A) IN GENERAL.—The term "qualified exploratory costs" means intangible drilling and development costs of a taxpayer other than an integrated oil company which—

(i) the taxpayer may elect to deduct as expenses under section 263(c), and

(ii) are paid or incurred in connection with the drilling of an exploratory well located in the United States (within the meaning of section 638(1)).

(B) EXPLORATORY WELL.—The term "exploratory well" means any of the following oil or gas wells:

(i) An oil or gas well which is completed (or if not completed, with respect to which drilling operations cease) before the completion of any other well which—

(I) is located within 1.25 miles from the well, and

(II) is capable of production in commercial quantities.

(ii) An oil or gas well which is not described in clause (i) but which has a total depth which is at least 800 feet below the deepest completion depth of any well within 1.25 miles which is capable of production in commercial quantities.

(iii) An oil or gas well capable of production in commercial quantities which is not described in clause (i) or (ii) but which is completed into a new reservoir, except that this clause shall not apply to a gas well if the gas is produced (or to be produced) from Devonian shale, coal seams, or a tight formation (determined in a manner similar to the manner under section 29(c)(2)).

A well shall not be treated as an exploratory well unless the operator submits to the Secretary (at such time and in such manner as the Secretary may provide) a certification from a petroleum engineer that the well is described in one of the preceding clauses.

(C) CERTAIN COSTS NOT INCLUDED.—The term "qualified exploratory costs" shall not include any cost paid or incurred—

(i) in constructing, acquiring, transporting, erecting, or installing an offshore platform, or

(ii) with respect to the drilling of a well from an offshore platform unless it is the first well which penetrates a reservoir.

(D) INTEGRATED OIL COMPANY.—For purposes of this paragraph, the term "integrated oil company" means, with respect to any taxable year, any producer of crude oil to whom subsection (c) of section 613A does not apply by reason of paragraph (2) or (4) of section 613A(d).

(7) SPECIAL RULES.—

(A) ALTERNATIVE MINIMUM TAXABLE INCOME.—For purposes of paragraphs (1)(B), (4)(A), and (5), alternative minimum taxable income shall be determined without regard to the deduction allowable under this subsection and the alternative tax net operating loss deduction under subsection (a)(4).

(B) GEOTHERMAL DEPOSITS.—For purposes of this subsection, intangible drilling and development costs shall not include costs with respect to wells drilled for any geothermal deposits (as defined in section 613(e)(3)).

(8) REGULATIONS.—The Secretary may by regulation provide for appropriate adjustments in computing alternative minimum taxable income or adjusted current earnings for any taxable year following a taxable year for which a deduction was allowed under this subsection to ensure that no double benefit is allowed by reason of such deduction.

• 1990, Omnibus Budget Reconciliation Act of 1990 (P.L. 101-508)

P.L. 101-508, §11531(a):

Amended Code Sec. 56 by adding at the end thereof new subsection (h). **Effective** for tax years beginning after 12-31-90.

[Sec. 57]

SEC. 57. ITEMS OF TAX PREFERENCE.

[Sec. 57(a)]

(a) GENERAL RULE.—For purposes of this part, the items of tax preference determined under this section are—

(1) DEPLETION.—With respect to each property (as defined in section 614), the excess of the deduction for depletion allowable under section 611 for the taxable year over the adjusted basis of the property at the end of the taxable year (determined without regard to the depletion deduction for the taxable year). Effective with respect to taxable years beginning after December 31, 1992, this paragraph shall not apply to any deduction for depletion computed in accordance with section 613A(c).

(2) INTANGIBLE DRILLING COSTS.—

(A) IN GENERAL.—With respect to all oil, gas, and geothermal properties of the taxpayer, the amount (if any) by which the amount of the excess intangible drilling costs arising in the taxable year is greater than 65 percent of the net income of the taxpayer from oil, gas, and geothermal properties for the taxable year.

(B) EXCESS INTANGIBLE DRILLING COSTS.—For purposes of subparagraph (A), the amount of the excess intangible drilling costs arising in the taxable year is the excess of—

(i) the intangible drilling and development costs paid or incurred in connection with oil, gas, and geothermal wells (other than costs incurred in drilling a nonproductive well) allowable under section 263(c) or 291(b) for the taxable year, over

(ii) the amount which would have been allowable for the taxable year if such costs had been capitalized and straight line recovery of intangibles (as defined in subsection (b)) had been used with respect to such costs.

(C) NET INCOME FROM OIL, GAS, AND GEOTHERMAL PROPERTIES.—For purposes of subparagraph (A), the amount of the net income of the taxpayer from oil, gas, and geothermal properties for the taxable year is the excess of—

(i) the aggregate amount of gross income (within the meaning of section 613(a)) from all oil, gas, and geothermal properties of the taxpayer received or accrued by the taxpayer during the taxable year, over

(ii) the amount of any deductions allocable to such properties reduced by the excess described in subparagraph (B) for such taxable year.

(D) PARAGRAPH APPLIED SEPARATELY WITH RESPECT TO GEOTHERMAL PROPERTIES AND OIL AND GAS PROPERTIES.—This paragraph shall be applied separately with respect to—

(i) all oil and gas properties which are not described in clause (ii), and

(ii) all properties which are geothermal deposits (as defined in section 613(e)(2)).

(E) EXCEPTION FOR INDEPENDENT PRODUCERS.—In the case of any oil or gas well—

(i) IN GENERAL.—In the case of any taxable year beginning after December 31, 1992, this paragraph shall not apply to any taxpayer which is not an integrated oil company (as defined in section 291(b)(4)).

(ii) LIMITATION ON BENEFIT.—The reduction in alternative minimum taxable income by reason of clause (i) for any taxable year shall not exceed 40 percent (30 percent in case of taxable years beginning in 1993) of the alternative minimum taxable income for such year determined without regard to clause (i) and the alternative tax net operating loss deduction under section 56(a)(4).

(3) [Repealed.]

(4) [Stricken.]

(5) TAX-EXEMPT INTEREST.—

(A) IN GENERAL.—Interest on specified private activity bonds reduced by any deduction (not allowable in computing the regular tax) which would have been allowable if such interest were includible in gross income.

(B) TREATMENT OF EXEMPT-INTEREST DIVIDENDS.—Under regulations prescribed by the Secretary, any exempt-interest dividend (as defined in section 852(b)(5)(A)) shall be treated as interest on a specified private activity bond to the extent of its proportionate share of the interest on such bonds received by the company paying such dividend.

(C) SPECIFIED PRIVATE ACTIVITY BONDS.—

(i) IN GENERAL.—For purposes of this part, the term "specified private activity bond" means any private activity bond (as defined in section 141) which is issued after August 7, 1986, and the interest on which is not includible in gross income under section 103.

(ii) EXCEPTION FOR QUALIFIED 501(c)(3) BONDS.—For purposes of clause (i), the term "private activity bond" shall not include any qualified 501(c)(3) bond (as defined in section 145).

(iii) EXCEPTION FOR CERTAIN HOUSING BONDS.—For purposes of clause (i), the term "private activity bond" shall not include any bond issued after the date of the enactment of this clause if such bond is—

(I) an exempt facility bond issued as part of an issue 95 percent or more of the net proceeds of which are to be used to provide qualified residential rental projects (as defined in section 142(d)),

(II) a qualified mortgage bond (as defined in section 143(a)), or

(III) a qualified veterans' mortgage bond (as defined in section 143(b)).

The preceding sentence shall not apply to any refunding bond unless such preceding sentence applied to the refunded bond (or in the case of a series of refundings, the original bond).

(iv) EXCEPTION FOR REFUNDINGS.—For purposes of clause (i), the term "private activity bond" shall not include any refunding bond (whether a current or advance refunding) if the refunded bond (or in the case of a series of refundings, the original bond) was issued before August 8, 1986.

(v) CERTAIN BONDS ISSUED BEFORE SEPTEMBER 1, 1986.—For purposes of this subparagraph, a bond issued before September 1, 1986, shall be treated as issued before August 8, 1986, unless such bond would be a private activity bond if—

(I) paragraphs (1) and (2) of section 141(b) were applied by substituting "25 percent" for "10 percent" each place it appears,

(II) paragraphs (3), (4), and (5) of section 141(b) did not apply, and

(III) subparagraph (B) of section 141(c)(1) did not apply.

(vi) EXCEPTION FOR BONDS ISSUED IN 2009 AND 2010.—

(I) IN GENERAL.—For purposes of clause (i), the term "private activity bond" shall not include any bond issued after December 31, 2008, and before January 1, 2011.

(II) TREATMENT OF REFUNDING BONDS.—For purposes of subclause (I), a refunding bond (whether a current or advance refunding) shall be treated as issued on the date of the issuance of the refunded bond (or in the case of a series of refundings, the original bond).

(III) EXCEPTION FOR CERTAIN REFUNDING BONDS.—Subclause (II) shall not apply to any refunding bond which is issued to refund any bond which was issued after December 31, 2003, and before January 1, 2009.

(6) ACCELERATED DEPRECIATION OR AMORTIZATION ON CERTAIN PROPERTY PLACED IN SERVICE BEFORE JANUARY 1, 1987.—The amounts which would be treated as items of tax preference with respect to the taxpayer under paragraphs (2), (3), (4), and (12) of this subsection (as in effect on the day before the date of the enactment of the Tax Reform Act of 1986). The preceding sentence shall not apply to any property to which section 56(a)(1) or (5) applies.

➻ Caution: Code Sec. 57(a)(7), below, is subject to the sunset provision of the Jobs and Growth Tax Relief Reconciliation Act of 2003 (P.L. 108-27), §303. Absent Congressional action, the changes made to this provision by P.L. 108-27, or that take effect as if included in P.L. 108-27, do not apply after December 31, 2010. For more information about the sunset provision, see page XXI of the Preface to this publication and P.L. 108-27, §303, in the amendment notes. See the amendments notes for a history of amendments to this section and the effective date of each change.

(7) EXCLUSION FOR GAINS ON SALE OF CERTAIN SMALL BUSINESS STOCK.—An amount equal to 7 percent of the amount excluded from gross income for the taxable year under section 1202.

Amendments

• 2009, American Recovery and Reinvestment Tax Act of 2009 (P.L. 111-5)

P.L. 111-5, §1503(a):

Amended Code Sec. 57(a)(5)(C) by adding at the end a new clause (vi). **Effective** for obligations issued after 12-31-2008.

• 2008, Housing Assistance Tax Act of 2008 (P.L. 110-289)

P.L. 110-289, §3022(a)(1):

Amended Code Sec. 57(a)(5)(C) by redesignating clauses (iii) and (iv) as clauses (iv) and (v), respectively, and by inserting after clause (ii) a new clause (iii). **Effective** for bonds issued after 7-30-2008.

• 2003, Jobs and Growth Tax Relief Reconciliation Act of 2003 (P.L. 108-27)

P.L. 108-27, §301(b)(3)(A)-(B):

Amended Code Sec. 57(a)(7) by striking "42 percent" the first place it appears and inserting "7 percent", and by striking the last sentence. **Effective** for dispositions on or after 5-6-2003. Prior to amendment, the last sentence of Code Sec. 57(a)(7) read as follows:

In the case of stock the holding period of which begins after December 31, 2000 (determined with the application of the last sentence of section 1(h)(2)(B)), the preceding sentence shall be applied by substituting "28 percent" for "42 percent".

P.L. 108-27, §303, as amended by P.L. 109-222, §102, provides:

SEC. 303. SUNSET OF TITLE.

All provisions of, and amendments made by, this title shall not apply to taxable years beginning after December 31, 2010, and the Internal Revenue Code of 1986 shall be applied and administered to such years as if such provisions and amendments had never been enacted.

• 1998, IRS Restructuring and Reform Act of 1998 (P.L. 105-206)

P.L. 105-206, §6005(d)(3):

Amended Code Sec. 57(a)(7) by adding at the end a new sentence. **Effective** as if included in the provision of P.L. 105-34 to which it relates [**effective** for tax years ending after 5-6-97.—CCH].

• 1997, Taxpayer Relief Act of 1997 (P.L. 105-34)

P.L. 105-34, §311(b)(2)(B):

Amended Code Sec. 57(a)(7) by striking "one-half" and inserting "42 percent". **Effective** for tax years ending after 5-6-97.

• 1996, Small Business Job Protection Act of 1996 (P.L. 104-188)

P.L. 104-188, §1616(b)(3):

Amended Code Sec. 57(a) by striking paragraph (4). **Effective** for tax years beginning after 12-31-95. Prior to being stricken, Code Sec. 57(a)(4) read as follows:

(4) RESERVES FOR LOSSES ON BAD DEBTS OF FINANCIAL INSTITUTIONS.—In the case of a financial institution to which section 593 applies, the amount by which the deduction allowable for the taxable year for a reasonable addition to a reserve for bad debts exceeds the amount that would have been allowable had the institution maintained its bad debt reserve for all taxable years on the basis of actual experience.

• 1993, Omnibus Budget Reconciliation Act of 1993 (P.L. 103-66)

P.L. 103-66, §13113(b)(1):

Amended Code Sec. 57(a) by adding at the end thereof new paragraph (8). **Effective** for stock issued after 8-10-93.

P.L. 103-66, §13171(a):

Amended Code Sec. 57(a)(6)-(8) by striking paragraph (6) and redesignating paragraphs (7) and (8) as paragraphs (6) and (7). **Effective** for contributions made after 6-30-92, except that in the case of any contribution of capital gain property which is not tangible personal property, such amendment applies only if the contribution is made after 12-31-92. Prior to being stricken, Code Sec. 57(a)(6) read as follows:

(6) APPRECIATED PROPERTY CHARITABLE DEDUCTION.—

(A) IN GENERAL.—The amount by which the deduction allowable under section 170 or 642(c) would be reduced if all capital gain property were taken into account at its adjusted basis.

(B) CAPITAL GAIN PROPERTY.—For purposes of subparagraph (A), the term "capital gain property" has the meaning given to such term by section 170(b)(1)(C)(iv). Such term shall not include any property to which an election under section 170(b)(1)(C)(iii) applies. In the case of any taxable year beginning in 1991, such term shall not include any tangible personal property. In the case of a contribution made before July 1, 1992, in a taxable year beginning in 1992, such term shall not include any tangible personal property.

• 1992, Energy Policy Act of 1992 (P.L. 102-486)

P.L. 102-486, §1915(a)(1):

Amended Code Sec. 57(a)(1) by adding at the end thereof a new sentence. **Effective** for tax years beginning after 12-31-92.

P.L. 102-486, §1915(b)(1):

Amended Code Sec. 57(a)(2) by adding at the end thereof new subparagraph (E). **Effective** for tax years beginning after 12-31-92.

• 1991, Tax Extension Act of 1991 (P.L. 102-227)

P.L. 102-227, §112:

Amended Code Sec. 57(a)(6)(B) by adding at the end thereof a new sentence. **Effective** 12-11-91.

• 1990, Omnibus Budget Reconciliation Act of 1990 (P.L. 101-508)

P.L. 101-508, §11344:

Amended Code Sec. 57(a)(6)(B) by adding at the end thereof a new sentence. **Effective** 11-5-90.

P.L. 101-508, §11801(c)(12)(A):

Amended Code Sec. 57(a)(4) by striking "585 or" after "to which section". **Effective** on 11-5-90.

P.L. 101-508, §11815(b)(3):

Amended Code Sec. 57(a)(2)(D)(ii) by striking "section 613(e)(3)" and inserting "section 613(e)(2)". **Effective** on 11-5-90.

P.L. 101-508, §11821(b), provides:

(b) SAVINGS PROVISION.—If—

(1) any provision amended or repealed by this part applied to—

(A) any transaction occurring before the date of the enactment of this Act,

(B) any property acquired before such date of enactment, or

(C) any item of income, loss, deduction, or credit taken into account before such date of enactment, and

(2) the treatment of such transaction, property, or item under such provision would (without regard to the amendments made by this part) affect liability for tax for periods ending after such date of enactment,

nothing in the amendments made by this part shall be construed to affect the treatment of such transaction, property, or item for purposes of determining liability for tax for periods ending after such date of enactment.

• 1988, Technical and Miscellaneous Revenue Act of 1988 (P.L. 100-647)

P.L. 100-647, §1007(b)(14)(B):

Repealed Code Sec. 57(a)(3). **Effective** with repect to options exercised after 12-31-87. Prior to repeal, Code Sec. 57(a)(3) read as follows:

(3) INCENTIVE STOCK OPTIONS.—

(A) IN GENERAL.—With respect to the transfer of a share of stock pursuant to the exercise of an incentive stock option (as defined in section 422A), the amount by which the fair market value of the share at the time of exercise exceeds the option price. For purposes of this paragraph, the fair market value of a share of stock shall be determined without regard to any restriction other than a restriction which, by its terms, will never lapse.

(B) BASIS ADJUSTMENT.—In determining the amount of gain or loss recognized for purposes of this part on any disposition of a share of stock acquired pursuant to an exercise (in a taxable year beginning after December 31, 1986) of an incentive stock option, the basis of such stock shall be increased by the amount of the excess referred to in subparagraph (A).

P.L. 100-647, §1007(c)(1):

Amended Code Sec. 57(a)(5)(C)(iii) by inserting "(whether a current or advance refunding)" after "any refunding bond". **Effective** as if included in the provision of P.L. 99-514 to which it relates.

P.L. 100-647, §1007(c)(2):

Amended Code Sec. 57(a)(5)(C)(i). **Effective** as if included in the provision of P.L. 99-514 to which it relates. Prior to amendment, Code Sec. 57(a)(5)(C)(i) read as follows:

(i) IN GENERAL.— For purposes of this part, the term "specified private activity bonds" means any private activity bond (as defined in section 141) issued after August 7, 1986.

P.L. 100-647, §1007(c)(3):

Amended Code Sec. 57(a)(6)(A) by inserting "or 642(c)" after "section 170". **Effective** as if included in the provision of P.L. 99-514 to which it relates.

[Sec. 57(b)]

(b) STRAIGHT LINE RECOVERY OF INTANGIBLES DEFINED.—For purposes of paragraph (2) of subsection (a)—

(1) IN GENERAL.—The term "straight line recovery of intangibles", when used with respect to intangible drilling and development costs for any well, means (except in the case of an election under paragraph (2)) ratable amortization of such costs over the 120-month period beginning with the month in which production from such well begins.

(2) ELECTION.—If the taxpayer elects with respect to the intangible drilling and development costs for any well, the term "straight line recovery of intangibles" means any method which would be permitted for purposes of determining cost depletion with respect to such well and which is selected by the taxpayer for purposes of subsection (a)(2).

Amendments

• 1986, Tax Reform Act of 1986 (P.L. 99-514)

P.L. 99-514, §701(a):

Amended Code Sec. 57. **Effective** for tax years beginning after 12-31-86. For exceptions, see Act Sec. 701(f)(2)-(7) following Code Sec. 56. Prior to amendment, Code Sec. 57 read as follows:

SEC. 57. ITEMS OF TAX PREFERENCE.

[Sec. 57(a)]

(a) IN GENERAL.—For purposes of this part, the items of tax preference are—

(1) EXCLUSION OF DIVIDENDS.—Any amount excluded from gross income for the taxable year under section 116.

(2) ACCELERATED DEPRECIATION ON REAL PROPERTY.—With respect to each section 1250 property (as defined in section 1250(c)), the amount by which the deduction allowable for the taxable year for exhaustion, wear and tear, obsolescence, or amortization exceeds the depreciation deduction which would have been allowable for the taxable year had the taxpayer depreciated the property under the straight line method for each taxable year of its useful life (determined without regard to section 167(k)) for which the taxpayer has held the property.

(3) ACCELERATED DEPRECIATION ON LEASED PERSONAL PROPERTY.—With respect to each item of section 1245 property (as defined in section 1245(a)(3)) which is subject to a lease, the amount by which—

(A) the deduction allowable for the taxable year for depreciation or amortization, exceeds

(B) the deduction which would have been allowable for the taxable year had the taxpayer depreciated the property under the straight-line method for each taxable year of its useful life for which the taxpayer has held the property.

For purposes of subparagraph (B), useful life shall be determined as if section 167(m)(1) (relating to asset depreciation range) did not include the last sentence thereof.

(4) AMORTIZATION OF CERTIFIED POLLUTION CONTROL FACILITIES.—With respect to each certified pollution control facility for which an election is in effect under section 169, the amount by which the deduction allowable for the taxable year under such section exceeds the depreciation deduction which would otherwise be allowable under section 167.

(5) MINING EXPLORATION AND DEVELOPMENT COSTS.—With respect to each mine or other natural deposit (other than an oil or gas well) of the taxpayer, an amount equal to the excess of—

(A) the amount allowable as a deduction under section 616(a) or 617, over

(B) the amount which would have been allowable if the expenditures had been capitalized and amortized ratably over the 10-year period beginning with the taxable year in which such expenditures were made.

(6) CIRCULATION AND RESEARCH AND EXPERIMENTAL EXPENDITURES.—An amount equal to the excess of—

(A) the amount allowable as a deduction under section 173 or 174(a) for the taxable year, over

(B) the amount which would have been allowable for the taxable year with respect to expenditures paid or incurred during such taxable year if—

(i) the circulation expenditures described in section 173 had been capitalized and amortized ratably over the 3-year period beginning with the taxable year in which such expenditures were made, or

(ii) the research and experimental expenditures described in section 174 had been capitalized and amortized ratably over the 10-year period beginning with the taxable year in which such expenditures were made.

(7) RESERVES FOR LOSSES ON BAD DEBTS OF FINANCIAL INSTITUTIONS.—In the case of a financial institution to which section 585 or 593 applies, the amount by which the deduction allowable for the taxable year for a reasonable addition to a reserve for bad debts exceeds the amount that would have been allowable had the institution maintained its bad debt reserve for all taxable years on the basis of actual experience.

(8) DEPLETION.—With respect to each property (as defined in section 614), the excess of the deduction for depletion allowable under section 611 for the taxable year over the adjusted basis of the property at the end of the taxable year (determined without regard to the depletion deduction for the taxable year).

(9) CAPITAL GAINS.—

(A) INDIVIDUALS.—In the case of a taxpayer other than a corporation, an amount equal to the net capital gain deduction for the taxable year determined under section 1202.

(B) CORPORATIONS.—In the case of a corporation having a net capital gain for the taxable year, an amount equal to the product obtained by multiplying the net capital gain by a fraction the numerator of which is the highest rate of tax specified in section 11(b), minus the alternative tax rate under section 1201(a), for the taxable year, and the denominator of which is the highest rate of tax specified in section 11(b) for the taxable year. In the case of a corporation to which section 1201(a) does not apply, the amount under this subparagraph shall be determined under regulations prescribed by the Secretary in a manner consistent with the preceding sentence.

(C) PREFERENCE REDUCTION FOR TIMBER.—In the case of a corporation, the amount of the tax preference under subparagraph (B) shall be reduced (but not below zero) by the sum of—

(i) one-third of the corporation's timber preference income (as defined in subsection (e)), plus

(ii) $20,000,

but in no event shall this reduction exceed the amount of timber preference income.

(D) PRINCIPAL RESIDENCE.—For purposes of subparagraph (A), gain from the sale or exchange of a principal residence (within the meaning of section 1034) shall not be taken into account.

(E) SPECIAL RULE FOR CERTAIN INSOLVENT TAXPAYERS.—

(i) IN GENERAL.—The amount of the tax preference under subparagraph (A) shall be reduced (but not below zero) by the excess (if any) of—

(I) the applicable percentage of gain from any farm insolvency transaction, over

(II) the applicable percentage of any loss from any farm insolvency transaction which offsets such gain.

(ii) REDUCTION LIMITED TO AMOUNT OF INSOLVENCY.—The amount of the reduction determined under clause (i) shall not exceed the amount by which the taxpayer is insolvent immediately before the transaction (reduced by any portion of such amount previously taken into account under this clause).

(iii) FARM INSOLVENCY TRANSACTION.—For purposes of this subparagraph, the term "farm insolvency transaction" means—

(I) the transfer by a farmer of farmland to a creditor in cancellation of indebtedness or

(II) the sale or exchange by the farmer of property described in subclause (I) under the threat of foreclosure,

but only if the farmer is insolvent immediately before such transaction.

(iv) INSOLVENT.—For purposes of this subparagraph, the term "insolvent" means the excess of liabilities over the fair market value of assets.

(v) APPLICABLE PERCENTAGE.—For purposes of this subparagraph, the term "applicable percentage" means that percentage of net capital gain with respect to which a deduction is allowed under section 1202(a).

(vi) FARMLAND.—For purposes of this subparagraph, the term "farmland" means any land used or held for use in the trade or business of farming (within the meaning of section 2032A(e)(5)).

(vii) FARMER.—For purposes of this subparagraph, the term "farmer" means any taxpayer if 50 percent or more of the average annual gross income of the taxpayer for the 3 preceding taxable years is attributable to the trade or business of farming (within the meaning of section 2032A(e)(5)).

(10) INCENTIVE STOCK OPTIONS.—With respect to the transfer of a share of stock pursuant to the exercise of an incentive stock option (as defined in section 422A), the amount by which the fair market value of the share at the time of exercise exceeds the option price. For purposes of this paragraph, the fair market value of a share of stock shall be determined without regard to any restriction other than a restriction which, by its terms, will never lapse.

(11) INTANGIBLE DRILLING COSTS.—

(A) IN GENERAL.—With respect to all oil, gas, and geothermal properties of the taxpayer, the amount (if any) by which the amount of the excess intangible drilling costs arising in the taxable year is greater than the amount of the net income of the taxpayer from oil, gas, and geothermal properties for the taxable year.

(B) EXCESS INTANGIBLE DRILLING COSTS.—For purposes of subparagraph (A), the amount of the excess intangible drilling costs arising in the taxable year is the excess of—

(i) the intangible drilling and development costs described in section 263(c) paid or incurred in connection with oil, gas, and geothermal wells (other than costs incurred in drilling a nonproductive well) allowable under this chapter for the taxable year, over

(ii) the amount which would have been allowable for the taxable year if such costs had been capitalized and straight line recovery of intangibles (as defined in subsection (d)) had been used with respect to such costs.

(C) NET INCOME FROM OIL, GAS, AND GEOTHERMAL PROPERTIES.—For purposes of subparagraph (A), the amount of the net income of the taxpayer from oil, gas, and geothermal properties for the taxable year is the excess of—

(i) the aggregate amount of gross income (within the meaning of section 613(a)) from all oil, gas, and geothermal properties of the taxpayer received or accrued by the taxpayer during the taxable year, over

(ii) the amount of any deductions allocable to such properties reduced by the excess described in subparagraph (B) for such taxable year.

(D) PARAGRAPH APPLIED SEPARATELY WITH RESPECT TO GEOTHERMAL PROPERTIES AND OIL AND GAS PROPERTIES.—This paragraph shall be applied separately with respect to—

(i) all oil and gas properties which are not described in clause (ii), and

(ii) all properties which are geothermal deposits (as defined in section 613(e)(3)).

(12) ACCELERATED COST RECOVERY DEDUCTION.—

(A) IN GENERAL.—With respect to each recovery property (other than 19-year real property and low-income housing) which is subject to a lease, the amount (if any) by which the deduction allowed under section 168(a) for the taxable year exceeds the deduction which would have been allowable for the taxable year had the property been depreciated using the straight-line method (with a half-year convention and without regard to salvage value) and a recovery period determined in accordance with the following table:

In the case of:	The recovery period is:
3-year property	5 years.
5-year property	8 years.
10-year property	15 years.
15-year public utility property	22 years.

(B) 19-YEAR REAL PROPERTY AND LOW-INCOME HOUSING.—With respect to each recovery property which is 19-year real property or low-income housing, the amount (if any) by which the deduction allowed under section 168(a) (or, in the case of property described in section 167(k), under section 167) for the taxable year exceeds the deduction which would have been allowable for the taxable year had the property been depreciated using a straight-line method (without regard to salvage value) over a recovery period of—

(i) 19 years in the case of 19-year real property, and

(ii) 15 years in the case of low-income housing property.

(C) SUBPARAGRAPHS(a) AND(b) INAPPLICABLE WHERE LONGER RECOVERY PERIODS APPLY.—If, pursuant to section 168(b)(3) or 168(f)(2), the recovery period for any property is longer than the recovery period for such property set forth in subparagraph (A) or (B), subparagraph (A) or (B) (as the case may be) shall not apply to such property.

(D) PARAGRAPHS (2) AND (3) SHALL NOT APPLY.—Paragraphs (2) and (3) shall not apply to recovery property.

(E) DEFINITIONS.—For purposes of this paragraph, the terms "3-year property", "5-year property", "10-year property", "15-year public utility property", "19-year real property", "low-income housing", and "recovery property", shall have the same meanings given such terms under section 168.

Paragraphs (1), (3), (5), (6), (11), and (12)(A) shall not apply to a corporation other than a personal holding company (as defined in section 542).

Amendments

• 1986, Tax Reform Act of 1986 (P.L. 99-514)

P.L. 99-514, §1809(a)(3):

Amended Code Sec. 57(a)(12)(B) by striking out so much of such subparagraph as precedes clause (i) thereof and inserting the new material. **Effective** as if included in the provision of P.L. 98-369 to which it relates. Prior to amendment, Code Sec. 57(a)(12)(B) read as follows:

(B) 19-YEAR REAL PROPERTY AND LOW-INCOME HOUSING.—With respect to each recovery property which is 19-year real property or low-income housing, the amount (if any) by which the deduction allowed under section 168(a) [(or, in the case of property described in section 167(k), under section 167)] for the taxable year exceeds the deduction which would have been allowable for a taxable year had the property been depreciated using a straight-line method (without regard to salvage value) over a recovery period of—

(i) 19 years in the case of 19-year real property, and

(ii) 15 years in the case of low-income housing property.

• 1986, Consolidated Omnibus Budget Reconciliation Act of 1985 (P.L. 99-272)

P.L. 99-272, §13208(a):

Amended Code Sec. 57(a)(9) by adding at the end thereof new subparagraph (E). **Effective** for transfers or sales or exchanges made after 12-31-81, in tax years ending after such date. For a special rule, see P.L. 99-272, §13208(c), below.

P.L. 99-272, §13208(c), as added by P.L. 99-514, §1896, provides:

(c) STATUTE OF LIMITATIONS.—If refund or credit of any overpayment of tax resulting from the application of the amendment made by subsection (a) is prevented at any time before the close of the date which is 1 year after the date of the enactment of this Act, by the operation of any law or rule of law (including res judicata), refund or credit of such overpayment (to the extent attributable to the application of such amendment) may, nevertheless, be made or allowed if claim therefor is filed on or before the close of such 1-year period.

• 1985 (P.L. 99-121)

P.L. 99-121, §103(b)(1)(B):

Amended Code Sec. 57(a)(12) by striking out "18-year real property" each place it appeared in the text and headings thereof and inserting in lieu thereof "19-year real property". **Effective** with respect to property placed in service by the taxpayer after 5-8-85. For an exception, see Act Sec. 105(b)(2), below.

P.L. 99-121, §103(b)(7):

Amended Code Sec. 57(a)(12)(B)(i) by striking out "18 years" and inserting in lieu thereof "19 years". **Effective** with respect to property placed in service by the taxpayer after 5-8-85. For an exception, see Act Sec. 105(b)(2), below.

P.L. 99-121, §105(b)(2), provides:

(2) EXCEPTION.—The amendments made by section 103 shall not apply to property placed in service by the taxpayer before January 1, 1987, if—

(A) the taxpayer or a qualified person entered into a binding contract to purchase or construct such property before May 9, 1985, or

(B) construction of such property was commenced by or for the taxpayer or a qualified person before May 9, 1985.

For purposes of this paragraph, the term "qualified person" means any person whose rights in such a contract or such property are transferred to the taxpayer, but only if such property is not placed in service before such rights are transferred to the taxpayer.

• 1984, Deficit Reduction Act of 1984 (P.L. 98-369)

P.L. 98-369, §16(b):

Amended Code Sec. 57(a)(1). **Effective** for taxable years ending after 12-31-83. Prior to amendment, Code Sec. 57(a)(1) read as follows:

(1) Exclusion of Interest and Dividends.—Any amount excluded from gross income for the taxable year under section 116 or 128.

P.L. 98-369, §111(e)(5):

Amended Code Sec. 57(a)(12)(A) by striking out "15-year real property" and inserting in lieu thereof "18-year real property and low-income housing". **Effective**, generally, for property placed in service by the taxpayer after 3-15-84. For special rules, see Act Sec. 111(g)(2)-(4), following Code Sec. 168(b).

P.L. 98-369, §111(e)(6):

Amended Code Sec. 57(a)(12)(B). **Effective**, generally, for property placed in service by the taxpayer after 3-15-84. For special rules, see Act Sec. 111(g)(2)-(4), following Code Sec. 168(b). Prior to amendment by Act Sec. 111(e)(6), but after amendment by Act Sec. 722(a)(1), it read as follows:

(B) 15-Year Real Property.—With respect to each recovery property which is 15-year real property, the amount (if any) by which the deduction allowed under section 168(a) (or, in the case of property described in section 167(k), under section 167) for the taxble year exceeds the deduction which would have been allowable for the taxable year had the property been depreciated using a 15-year period and the straight-line method (without regard to salvage value).

P.L. 98-369, §111(e)(7):

Amended Code Sec. 57(a)(12)(E) by striking out "`15-year real property'" and inserting in lieu thereof "`18-year real property', `low-income housing',". **Effective**, generally, for property placed in service by the taxpayer after 3-15-84. For special rules, see Act Sec. 111(g)(2)-(4) following Code Sec. 168(b).

P.L. 98-369, §555(a)(2):

Amended Code Sec. 57(a)(10) by adding the sentence at the end thereof. **Effective** for options exercised after 3-20-84. In the case of an option issued after 3-20-84, pursuant to a plan adopted or corporate action taken by the board of directors of the grantor corporation before 5-13-84, the preceding sentence shall be applied by substituting "12-31-84" for "3-20-84".

P.L. 98-369, §711(a)(3)(A):

Amended Code Sec. 57(a)(6)(B). **Effective** as if included in the provision of P.L. 97-248 to which it relates. Prior to amendment, Code Sec. 57(a)(6)(B) read as follows:

(B) the amount which would have been allowable for the taxable year if the circulation expenditures described in section 173 or the research and experimental expenditures described in section 174 had been capitalized and amortized ratably over the 10-year period beginining with the taxable year in which such expenditures were made.

P.L. 98-369, §722(a)(1)(A)-(B):

Amended Code Sec. 57(a)(12) by striking out "(or, in the case of property described in section 167(k), under section 167)" in subparagraph (A), and inserting "(or, in the case of property described in section 167(k), under section 167)" after "section 168(a)" in subparagraph (B) [as amended by Act Sec. 111(e)(6)]. [A technical correction apparently will be needed to rectify the unintentional omission.—CCH.] **Effective** as if included in the provision of P.L. 97-448 to which it relates.

• 1983, Technical Corrections Act of 1982 (P.L. 97-448)

P.L. 97-448, §102(b)(1)(A):

Amended the next to the last sentence of Code Sec. 57(a) by striking out "and (12)" and inserting in lieu thereof "and (12)(A)". **Effective** as if included in the amendment made by P.L. 97-34, §205(b), but not applicable to tax years beginning after 12-31-82.

P.L. 97-448, §102(b)(3):

Amended Code Sec. 57(a)(12) by redesignating subparagraphs (C) and (D) as subparagraphs (D) and (E), respectively, and by inserting after subparagraph (B) the new subparagraph (C). **Effective** as if it had been included in the provision of P.L. 97-34 to which it relates.

P.L. 97-448, §102(b)(4):

Amended Code Sec. 57(a)(12)(A) by striking out "under section 168(a)" and inserting in lieu thereof "under section 168(a) (or, in the case of property described in section 167(k), under section 167)". **Effective** as if such amendment had been included in the provision of P.L. 97-34 to which it relates.

P.L. 97-448, §102(f)(1):

Amended subparagraph (B) of section 212(e)(2) of P.L. 97-34 under the amendment note for P.L. 97-34, §212(e)(2).

• 1982, Subchapter S Revision Act of 1982 (P.L. 97-354)

P.L. 97-354, §5(a)(14):

Amended the last sentence of Code Sec. 57(a) by striking out "an electing small business corporation (as defined in section 1371(b)) and". **Effective** for tax years beginning after 12-31-82.

• 1982, Tax Equity and Fiscal Responsibility Act of 1982 (P.L. 97-248)

P.L. 97-248, §201(b)(1)(A):

Amended Code Sec. 57(a) by striking out paragraph (1) and inserting in lieu thereof new paragraph (1). **Effective** for tax years beginning after 12-31-82. Prior to amendment, Code Sec. 57(a)(1) read as follows:

"(1) Adjusted itemized deductions.—In the case of an individual, an amount equal to the adjusted itemized deductions for the taxable year (as determined under subsection (b))."

P.L. 97-248, §201(b)(1)(B):

Amended Code Sec. 57(a) by striking out paragraphs (5) and (6) and inserting in lieu thereof new paragraphs (5) and (6). **Effective** for to tax years beginning after 12-31-82. Prior to amendment, Code Sec. 57(a)(5) and (6) read as follows:

(5) Amortization of railroad rolling stock.—With respect to each unit of railroad rolling stock for which an election is in effect under section 184, the amount by which the deduction allowable for the taxable year under such section exceeds the depreciation deduction which would otherwise be allowable under section 167.

(6) Stock options.—With respect to the transfer of a share of stock pursuant to the exercise of a qualified stock option (as defined in section 422(b)) or a restricted stock option (as defined in section 424(b)), the amount by which the fair market value of the share at the time of exercise exceeds the option price.

P.L. 97-248, §201(b)(1)(C):

Amended Code Sec. 57(a) by striking out paragraph (10) and inserting in lieu thereof new paragraph (10). **Effective** for tax years beginning after 12-31-82. Prior to amendment, paragraph (10) read as follows:

"(10) Amortization of child care facilities.—With respect to each item of section 188 property for which an election is in effect under section 188, the amount by which the deduction allowable for the taxable year under such section exceeds the depreciation deduction which would otherwise be allowable under section 167."

P.L. 97-248, §201(b)(2)(A):

Amended the next to last sentence of Code Sec. 57(a) by striking out "(3), (11), and (12)" and inserting in lieu thereof "(1), (3), (5), (6), (11), and (12)(A)". **Effective** for tax years beginning after 12-31-82.

P.L. 97-248, §201(b)(2)(B):

Amended Code Sec. 57(a) by striking out the last sentence. **Effective** for tax years beginning after 12-31-82. Prior to amendment, the last sentence read as follows:

"For purposes of section 56, in the case of a taxpayer other than a corporation, the adjusted itemized deductions described in paragraph (1) and capital gains described in paragraph (9) shall not be treated as items of tax preference.".

• 1981, Economic Recovery Tax Act of 1981 (P.L. 97-34)

P.L. 97-34, §205(a):

Amended Code Sec. 57(a) by inserting immediately after paragraph (11) new paragraph (12). **Effective** for property placed in service after 12-31-80, in tax years ending after such date.

P.L. 97-34, §205(b):

Amended Code Sec. 57(a) by striking out "and (11)" in the next to the last sentence and inserting in lieu thereof ", (11), and (12)(A)". **Effective** for property placed in service after 12-31-80, in tax years ending after such date.

P.L. 97-34, §212(d)(2)(B):

Amended Code Sec. 57(a)(2) by striking out "or 191". **Effective** for expenditures incurred after 12-31-81, in tax years ending after such date.

P.L. 97-34, §212(e)(2), provides:

(2) TRANSITIONAL RULE.—The amendments made by this section shall not apply with respect to any rehabilitation of a building if—

(A) the physical work on such rehabilitation began before January 1, 1982, and

(B) such building does not meet the requirements of paragraph (1) of section 48(g) of the Internal Revenue Code of 1954 (as amended by this Act).

• 1978, Revenue Act of 1978 (P.L. 95-600)

P.L. 95-600, §701(b)(1)(A), (b)(5):

Inserted "In the case of an individual, an amount" in place of "An amount" in Code Sec. 57(a)(1). **Effective** as if included in the amendments made by P.L. 94-455, Sec. 301.

P.L. 95-600, §701(f)(3)(D), (f)(8):

Inserted "or 191" after "167(k)" in Code Sec. 57(a)(2). **Effective** for additions to capital account made after 6-14-76, and before 6-15-81.

P.L. 95-600, §402(b):

Amended Code Sec. 57(a)(9)(A). **Effective** for tax years ending after 10-31-78. Prior to amendment, such section read:

"(A) Individuals.—In the case of a taxpayer other than a corporation, an amount equal to one-half of the net capital gain for the taxable year."

P.L. 95-600, §301(b)(2), (c):

Inserted "the highest rate of tax specified in section 11(b)" in place of "the sum of the normal tax rate and the surtax rate under section 11", each place it appeared in Code Sec. 57(a)(9)(B). **Effective** for tax years beginning after 12-31-78.

P.L. 95-600, §421(b)(1), (g):

Added Code Sec. 57(a)(9)(D). **Effective** for sales and exchanges made after 7-26-78, in tax years ending after such date.

P.L. 95-600, §421(b)(2), (g):

Amended Code Sec. 57(a) by striking out the last sentence (as amended by Act Sec. 701(b)(1)), below, and inserting the last two sentences. **Effective** for tax years beginning after 12-31-78.

P.L. 95-600, §701(b)(1), (5):

Inserted "Paragraphs (3) and" in place of "Paragraphs (1), (3), and" in the last sentence of Code Sec. 57(a). **Effective** as if included in the amendments made by P.L. 94-455, §301. Prior to amendment, the last sentence read:

"Paragraphs (1), (3), and (11) shall not apply to a corporation."

• 1978, Energy Tax Act of 1978 (P.L. 95-618)

P.L. 95-618, §402(b), (c)(1):

Amended Code Sec. 57(a)(11). **Effective** for wells commenced on or after 10-1-78, in tax years ending on or after such date. Prior to amendment, such section read:

"(11) INTANGIBLE DRILLING COSTS.—

(A) IN GENERAL.—With respect to all oil and gas properties of the taxpayer, the amount (if any) by which the amount of the excess intangible drilling costs arising in the taxable year is greater than the amount of the net income of the taxpayer from oil and gas properties for the taxable year.

(B) EXCESS INTANGIBLE DRILLING COSTS.—For purposes of subparagraph (A), the amount of the excess intangible drilling costs arising in the taxable year is the excess of—

(i) the intangible drilling and development costs described in section 263(c) paid or incurred in connection with oil and gas wells (other than costs incurred in drilling a nonproductive well) allowable under this chapter for the taxable year, over

(ii) the amount which would have been allowable for the taxable year if such costs had been capitalized and straight line recovery of intangibles (as defined in subsection (d)) had been used with respect to such costs.

(C) NET INCOME FROM OIL AND GAS PROPERTIES.—For purposes of subparagraph (A), the amount of the net income of the taxpayer from oil and gas properties for the taxable year is the excess of—

(i) the aggregate amount of gross income (within the meaning of section 613(a)) from all oil and gas properties of the taxpayer received or accrued by the taxpayer during the taxable year, over

(ii) the amount of any deductions allocable to such properties reduced by the excess described in subparagraph (B) for such taxable year."

• 1977, Tax Reduction and Simplification Act of 1977 (P.L. 95-30)

P.L. 95-30, §101(d)(5):

Amended paragraph 1 of Sec. 57(a) by striking out "excess" in the heading and text and inserting in lieu thereof "adjusted,". **Effective** for tax years beginning after 12-31-76.

P.L. 95-30, §308, as amended by P.L. 95-618, §401, and P.L. 95-600, §422:

Amended Code Sec. 57(a)(11). **Effective** for tax years beginning after 12-31-76. Prior to amendment, Code Sec. 57(a)(11) read as follows:

(11) INTANGIBLE DRILLING COSTS.—The excess of the intangible drilling and development costs described in section 263(c) paid or incurred in connection with oil and gas wells

(other than costs incurred in drilling a nonproductive well) allowable under this chapter for the taxable year over the amount which would have been allowable for the taxable year if such costs had been capitalized and straight line recovery of intangibles (as defined in subsection (d)) had been used with respect to such costs.

• 1976, Tax Reform Act of 1976 (P.L. 94-455)

P.L. 94-455, §301(c)(1)(A):

Amended paragraph (1) of Code Sec. 57(a). For **effective** date, see §301(g), below. Prior to amendment paragraph (1) read as follows:

(1) EXCESS INVESTMENT INTEREST.—The amount of the excess investment interest for the taxable year (as determined under subsection (b)).

P.L. 94-455, §301(c)(1)(B):

P.L. 94-455, §301(c)(1)(B) amended Code Sec. 57(a) by striking out the matter following paragraph (10) and inserting in lieu thereof paragraph (11). For **effective** date, see §301(g), below. Prior to amendment the deleted matter read as follows:

Paragraph (1) shall apply only to taxable years beginning before January 1, 1972. Paragraphs (1) and (3) shall not apply to a corporation other than an electing small business corporation (as defined in section 1371(b)) and a personal holding company (as defined in section 542).

P.L. 94-455, §301(c)(1)(C):

Amended paragraph (3) of Code Sec. 57(a). For **effective** date, see §301(g), below. Prior to amendment, paragraph (3) read as follows:

(3) ACCELERATED DEPRECIATION ON PERSONAL PROPERTY SUBJECT TO A NET LEASE.—With respect to each item of section 1245 property (as defined in section 1245(a)(3)) which is the subject of a net lease, the amount by which the deduction allowable for the taxable year for exhaustion, wear and tear, obsolescence, or amortization exceeds the depreciation deduction which would have been allowable for the taxable year had the taxpayer depreciated the property under the straight line method for each taxable year of its useful life for which the taxpayer has held the property.

P.L. 94-455, §301(c)(4)(A):

P.L. 94-455, §301(c)(4)(A) added a new subparagraph (C) to Code Sec. 57(a)(9). For **effective** date, see §301(g), below.

P.L. 94-455, §301(f), provides:

(f) SECTION 21 NOT TO APPLY.—For purposes of section 21 of the Internal Revenue Code of 1954, the amendments made by this section shall not be treated as a change in a rate of tax.

P.L. 94-455, §301(g), provides:

(g) EFFECTIVE DATE.—

(1) IN GENERAL.—Except as provided by paragraph (4), the amendments made by this section shall apply to items of tax preference for taxable years beginning after December 31, 1975.

(2) TAX CARRYOVER.—Except as provided in paragraph (4) and in section 56(e) of the Internal Revenue Code of 1954, the amount of any tax carryover under section 56(c) of such Code from a taxable year beginning before January 1, 1976, shall not be allowed as a tax carryover for any taxable year beginning after December 31, 1975.

(3) SPECIAL RULE FOR TAXABLE YEAR 1976 IN THE CASE OF A CORPORATION.—Notwithstanding any provision of the Internal Revenue Code of 1954 to the contrary, in the case of a corporation which is not an electing small business corporation or a personal holding company the tax imposed by section 56 of such Code for taxable years beginning in 1976, is an amount equal to the sum of—

(A) the amount of the tax which would have been imposed for such taxable year under such section as such section was in effect on the day before the date of the enactment of the Tax Reform Act of 1976, and

(B) one-half of the amount by which the amount of the tax which would be imposed for such taxable year under such section as amended by the Tax Reform Act of 1976 (but for this paragraph) exceeds the amount determined under subparagraph (A).

(4) CERTAIN FINANCIAL INSTITUTIONS.—In the case of a taxpayer which is a financial institution to which section 585 or 593 of the Internal Revenue Code of 1954 applies, the amendments made by this section shall apply only to taxable years beginning after December 31, 1977, and paragraph (2) shall be applied by substituting "January 1, 1978" for "January 1, 1976" and by substituting "December 31, 1977" for "December 31, 1975".

P.L. 94-455, §1901(b)(33)(A)-(B):

Substituted "the net capital gain" for "the amount by which the net long-term capital gain exceeds the net short-term capital loss" in Code Sec. 57(a)(9)(A); and substituted "In the case of a corporation having a net capital gain for the taxable year, an amount equal to the product obtained by multiplying the net capital gain" for "In the case of a corporation, if the net long-term capital gain exceeds the net short-term capital loss for the taxable year, an amount equal to the product obtained by multiplying such excess" in the first sentence of Code Sec. 57(a)(9)(B). **Effective** for tax years beginning after 12-31-76.

• 1971, Revenue Act of 1971 (P.L. 92-178)

P.L. 92-178, §303(b):

Added Code Sec. 57(a)(10). **Effective** for tax years ending after 12-31-71.

[Sec. 57(b)]

(b) APPLICATION WITH SECTION 291.—

(1) IN GENERAL.—

(A) POLLUTION CONTROL FACILITIES; BAD DEBT RESERVES.—In the case of any item of tax preference of a corporation described in paragraph (4) or (7) of subsection (a), only 59⅚ percent of the amount of such item of tax preference (determined without regard to this subsection) shall be taken into account as an item of tax preference.

(B) IRON ORE AND COAL.—In the case of any item of tax preference of a corporation described in paragraph (8) of subsection (a) (but only to the extent such item is allocable to a deduction for depletion for iron ore and coal, including lignite), only 71.6 percent of the amount of such item of tax preference (determined without regard to this subsection) shall be taken into account as an item of tax preference.

(2) CERTAIN CAPITAL GAINS.—In determining the net capital gain of any corporation for purposes of paragraph (9)(B) of subsection (a), there shall be taken into account only 59⅚ percent of any gain from the sale or exchange of section 1250 property which is equal to 80 percent of the excess determined under section 291(a)(1) with respect to such property.

Amendments

• 1986, Tax Reform Act of 1986 (P.L. 99-514)

P.L. 99-514, §1804(k)(3)(C):

Amended Code Sec. 57(b)(1)(B). **Effective** as if included in the provision of P.L. 98-369 to which it relates. Prior to amendment, Code Sec. 57(b)(1)(B) read as follows:

(B) IRON ORE AND COAL.—In the case of any item of tax preference of a corporation described in paragraph (8) of subsection (a) (but only to the extent such item is allocable to a deduction for depletion for iron ore and coal (including lignite)),

only 71.6 percent of the amount of such item of tax preference (determined without regard to this subsection) shall be taken into account as an item of tax preference.

P.L. 99-514, §1804(k)(3)(D):

Amended Code Sec. 57(b)(2) by striking out "85 percent" and inserting in lieu thereof "80 percent". **Effective** as if included in the provision of P.L. 98-369 to which it relates.

• 1984, Deficit Reduction Act of 1984 (P.L. 98-369)

P.L. 98-369, §68(c)(1):

Amended Code Sec. 57(b)(1). **Effective** for tax years beginning after 12-31-84. Prior to amendment, Code Sec. 57(b)(1) read as follows:

(1) In General.—In the case of any item of tax preference of a corporation described in—

(A) paragraph (4) or (7) of subsection (a), or

(B) paragraph (8) of subsection (a) (but only to the extent such item is allocable to a deduction for depletion for iron ore and coal (including lignite)),

only 71.6 percent of the amount of such item of tax preference (determined without regard to this subsection) shall be taken into account as an item of tax preference.

P.L. 98-369, §68(c)(2):

Amended Code Sec. 57(b) by striking out "71.6 percent" and inserting in lieu thereof "59⁵/₆ percent". **Effective** for tax years beginning after 12-31-84.

• 1982, Subchapter S Revision Act of 1982 (P.L. 97-354)

P.L. 97-354, §5(a)(15):

Amended Code Sec. 57(b) by striking out "an applicable corporation" in paragraph (1) and inserting in lieu thereof "a corporation", by striking out "applicable corporation" in paragraph (2) and inserting in lieu thereof "corporation", and by striking out paragraph (3). **Effective** for tax years beginning after 12-31-82. Prior to being stricken, paragraph (3) read as follows:

(3) APPLICABLE CORPORATION DEFINED.—For purposes of this subsection, the term `applicable corporation' has the meaning given such term by section 291(e)(2)."

• 1982, Tax Equity and Fiscal Responsibility Act of 1982 (P.L. 97-248)

P.L. 97-248, §204(b):

Amended Code Sec. 57(b). **Effective** for tax years ending after 12-31-82, with respect to items of tax preference described in section 57(b) of such Code to which section 291 of such Code applies; except that in the case of an item described in section 291(a)(2) of such Code, it shall apply to tax years beginning after 12-31-83. Prior to amendment, Code Sec. 57(b) read as follows:

(b) Adjusted Itemized Deductions.—

(1) In general.—For purposes of paragraph (1) of subsection (a), the amount of the adjusted itemized deductions for any taxable year is the amount by which the sum of the itemized deductions (as defined in section 63(f) without regard to paragraph (3) thereof) other than—

(A) the deduction for State and local, and foreign, taxes provided by section 164(a),

(B) the deduction for medical, dental, etc., expenses provided by section 213,

(C) the deduction for casualty losses described in section 165(c)(3), and

(D) the deduction allowable under section 691(c),

exceeds 60 percent of the taxpayer's adjusted gross income reduced by the items in subparagraphs (A) through (D) for the taxable year.

(2) Special rules for estates and trusts.—

(A) In general.—In the case of an estate or trust, for purposes of paragraph (1) of subsection (a), the amount of the adjusted itemized deductions for any taxable year is the amount by which the sum of the deductions for the taxable year other than—

(i) the deductions allowable in arriving at adjusted gross income,

(ii) the deduction for personal exemption provided by section 642(b),

(iii) the deduction for casualty losses described in section 165(c)(3),

(iv) the deductions allowable under section 651(a), 661(a), or 691(c),

(v) the deduction for State and local, and foreign, taxes provided by section 164(a), and

(vi) the deductions allowable to a trust under section 642(c) to the extent that a corresponding amount is included in the gross income of the beneficiary under section 662(a)(1) for the taxable year of the beneficiary with which or within which the taxable year of the trust ends,

exceeds 60 percent of the adjusted gross income reduced by the items in clauses (iii) through (vi) for the taxable year.

(B) Determination of adjusted gross income.—For purposes of this paragraph, the adjusted gross income of an estate or trust shall be computed in the same manner as in the case of an individual, except that—

(i) the deductions for costs paid or incurred in connection with the administration of the estate or trust, and

(ii) to the extent provided in subparagraph (C), the deductions under section 642(c),

shall be treated as allowable in arriving at adjusted gross income.

(C) Treatment of certain charitable contributions.—For purposes of this paragraph, the following deductions under section 642(c) (relating to deductions for amounts paid or permanently set aside for charitable purposes) shall be treated as deductions allowable in arriving at adjusted gross income:

(i) deductions allowable to an estate,

(ii) deductions allowable to a trust all of the unexpired interests in which are devoted to one or more of the purposes described in section 170(c) (determined without regard to section 170(c)(2)(A)),

(iii) deductions allowable to a trust which is a pooled income fund within the meaning of section 642(c)(5),

(iv) deductions allowable to a trust—

(I) all the income interests in which are devoted to one or more of the purposes described in section 170(c) (determined without regard to section 170(c)(2)(A)),

(II) all of the interests (other than income interests) in which are held by a corporation, and

(III) the grantor of which is a corporation.

(v) deductions allowable to a trust which are attributable to transfers to the trust before January 1, 1977, and

(vi) deductions allowable to a trust, all of the income interest of which is devoted solely to one or more of the purposes described in section 170(c)(2)(B), which are attributable to transfers pursuant to a will or pursuant to an inter vivos trust in which the grantor had the power to revoke at the date of his death.

• 1981, Economic Recovery Tax Act of 1981 (P.L. 97-34)

P.L. 97-34, §121(c)(1):

Amended Code Sec. 57(b)(1) by inserting "without regard to paragraph (3) thereof" after "section 63(f)". **Effective** for contributions made after 12-31-81, in tax years beginning after such date.

• 1980 (P.L. 96-596)

P.L. 96-596, §3(a):

Amended Code Sec. 57(b)(2)(C) by redesignating clauses (iv) and (v) as clauses (v) and (vi), respectively, and by inserting after clause (iii) new clause (iv). **Effective** for tax years beginning after 12-31-75.

• 1980, Technical Corrections Act of 1979 (P.L. 96-222)

P.L. 96-222, §104(a)(4)(E):

Amended Code Sec. 57(b) by adding, "and foreign," after "State and local" in paragraphs (1)(A) and (2)(A)(v). **Effective** for tax years beginning after 12-31-78.

P.L. 96-222, §104(a)(4)(F):

Amended Code Sec. 57(b)(2)(A) by changing "clauses (i) through (vi)" to "clauses (iii) through (vi)". **Effective** for tax years beginning after 12-31-78.

P.L. 96-222, §107(a)(1)(A):

Amended Code Sec. 57(b)(2)(C) by changing "section 170(c)(2)(B)" to "section 170(c) (determined without regard to section 170(c)(2)(A))". **Effective** as if included in the amendments made by P.L. 94-455, §301.

• 1978, Revenue Act of 1978 (P.L. 95-600)

P.L. 95-600, §421(b)(3), (g):

Amended Code Sec. 57(b)(1). **Effective** for tax years beginning after 12-31-78. Prior to amendment, but after the amendments made by Act Sec. 701(b)(4), such section read:

(b) ADJUSTED ITEMIZED DEDUCTIONS.—

(1) IN GENERAL.—For purposes of paragraph (1) of subsection (a), the amount of the adjusted itemized deductions for any taxable year is the amount by which the sum of the deductions for the taxable year other than—

(A) deductions allowable in arriving at adjusted gross income,

(B) the deduction for personal exemptions provided by section 151,

(C) the deduction for medical, dental, etc., expenses provided by section 213,

(D) the deduction for casualty losses described in section 165(c)(3), and

(E) the deduction allowable under section 691(c),

exceeds 60 percent (but does not exceed 100 percent) of the taxpayer's adjusted gross income for the taxable year."

P.L. 95-600, §421(b)(4), (g):

Amended Code Sec. 57(b)(2)(A). **Effective** for tax years beginning after 12-31-78. Prior to amendment, but after the amendment made by Act Sec. 701(b)(3), such section read:

(2) SPECIAL RULES FOR ESTATES AND TRUSTS.—

(A) IN GENERAL.—In the case of an estate or trust, for purposes of paragraph (1) of subsection (a), the amount of the adjusted itemized deductions for any taxable year is the amount by which the sum of the deductions for the taxable year other than—

(i) the deductions allowable in arriving at adjusted gross income,

(ii) the deduction for personal exemption provided by section 642(b),

(iii) the deduction for casualty losses described in section 165(c)(3),

(iv) the deductions allowable under section 651(a), 661(a), or 691(c), and

(v) the deductions allowable to a trust under section 642(c) to the extent that a corresponding amount is included in the gross income of the beneficiary under section 662(a)(1) for the taxable year of the beneficiary with which or within which the taxable year of the trust ends,

exceeds 60 percent (but does not exceed 100 percent) of the adjusted gross income of the estate or trust for the taxable year.

P.L. 95-600, §701(b)(3), (5):

Amended Code Sec. 57(b)(2). **Effective** as if such amendments were included in amendments made by P.L. 94-455, §301. Prior to amendment, such section read:

(2) SPECIAL RULE FOR TRUSTS AND ESTATES.—In the case of a trust or estate, any deduction allowed or allowable for the taxable year—

(A) under section 642(c) (but only to the extent that the amount of the deduction allowable under such section is included in the income of the beneficiary under section 662(a)(1) for the taxable year of the beneficiary with which or within which the taxable year of the trust ends);

(B) under section 642(d), 642(e), 642(f), 651(a), 661(a), or 691; or

(C) for costs paid or incurred in connection with the administration of the trust or estate;

shall, for purposes of paragraph (1), be treated as a deduction allowable in arriving at an adjusted gross income."

P.L. 95-600, §701(b)(4), (5):

Added Code Sec. 57(b)(1)(E). **Effective** as if such amendment was included in the amendments made by P.L. 94-455, §301.

• 1977, Tax Reduction and Simplification Act of 1977 (P.L. 95-30)

P.L. 95-30, §101(d)(5):

Amended the heading of Sec 57(b) and so much of paragraph (1) of Sec. 57(b) as precedes subparagraph (A) by striking out "excess" and inserting in lieu there of "adjusted,", and amended paragraph (1) of Sec. 57(b) by striking out subparagraph (B) and by redesignating subparagraphs (C) through (E) as subparagraphs (B) through (D). **Effective** for tax years beginning after 12-31-76. Prior to being deleted, subparagraph (B) of paragraph (1) of Sec. 57(b) read as follows:

(B) the standard deduction provided by section 141,"

• 1976, Tax Reform Act of 1976 (P.L. 94-455)

P.L. 94-455, §301(c)(2):

Amended Code Sec. 57(b). For **effective** date, see Act Sec. 301(g) under Code Sec. 57. Prior to amendment, Code Sec. 57(b) read as follows:

(b) EXCESS INVESTMENT INTEREST.—

(1) IN GENERAL.—For purposes of paragraph (1) of subsection (a), the excess investment interest for any taxable year is the amount by which the investment interest expense for the taxable year exceeds the sum of—

(A) the net investment income for the taxable year, and

(B) the amount (if any) by which the deductions allowable under sections 162, 163, 164(a)(1) or (2), and 212 attributable to property of the taxpayer subject to a net lease exceeds the gross rental income produced by such property for the taxable year.

(2) DEFINITIONS.—For purposes of this subsection—

(A) NET INVESTMENT INCOME.—The term "net investment income" means the excess of investment income over investment expenses.

(B) INVESTMENT INCOME.—The term "investment income" means—

(i) the gross income from interest, dividends, rents, and royalties,

(ii) the net short-term capital gain attributable to the disposition of property held for investment, and

(iii) amounts treated under sections 1245 and 1250 as gain from the sale or exchange of property which is neither a capital asset nor property described in section 1231,

but only to the extent such income, gain and amounts are not derived from the conduct of a trade or business.

(C) INVESTMENT EXPENSES.—The term "investment expenses" means the deductions allowable under sections 162, 164(a)(1) or (2), 166, 167, 171, 212, 243, 244, 245, or 611 directly connected with the production of investment income. For purposes of this subparagraph, the deduction allowable under section 167 with respect to any property may be treated as the amount which would have been allowable had the taxpayer depreciated the property under the straight line method for each taxable year of its useful life for which the taxpayer has held the property, and the deduction allowable under section 611 with respect to any property may be treated as the amount which would have been allowable had the taxpayer determined the deduction under section 611 without regard to section 613 for each taxable year for which the taxpayer has held the property.

(D) INVESTMENT INTEREST EXPENSE.—The term "investment interest expense" means interest paid or accrued on indebtedness incurred or continued to purchase or carry property held for investment. For purposes of the preceding sentence, interest paid or accrued on indebtedness incurred or continued in the construction of property to be used in a trade or business shall not be treated as an investment interest expense.

(3) PROPERTY SUBJECT TO NET LEASE.—For purposes of this subsection, property which is subject to a net lease entered into after October 9, 1969, shall be treated as property held for investment and not as property used in a trade or business.

P.L. 94-455, §301(f), provides:

(f) SECTION 21 NOT TO APPLY.—For purposes of section 21 of the Internal Revenue Code of 1954 the amendments made by this section shall not be treated as a change in a rate of tax.

• 1971, Revenue Act of 1971 (P.L. 92-178)

P.L. 92-178, §304(b)(1):

Amended Code Sec. 57(b)(1). **Effective** for tax years beginning after 12-31-69. Prior to amendment, such section read as follows:

(1) IN GENERAL.—For purposes of paragraph (1) of subsection (a), the excess investment interest for any taxable year is the amount by which the investment interest expenses for the taxable year exceed the net investment income for the taxable year.

P.L. 92-178, §304(d):

Added "162" in the first sentence of Code Sec. 57(b)(2)(C). **Effective** for tax years beginning after 12-31-69.

[Sec. 57(c)]

(c) NET LEASES.—

(1) IN GENERAL.—For purposes of this section, property shall be considered to be subject to a net lease for a taxable year if—

(A) for such taxable year the sum of the deductions of the lessor with respect to such property which are allowable solely by reason of section 162 (other than rents and reimbursed amounts with respect to such property) is less than 15 percent of the rental income produced by such property, or

(B) the lessor is either guaranteed a specified return or is guaranteed in whole or in part against loss of income.

(2) MULTIPLE LEASES OF SINGLE PARCEL OF REAL PROPERTY.—If a parcel of real property of the taxpayer is leased under two or more leases, paragraph (1)(A) shall, at the election of the taxpayer, be applied by treating all leased portions of such property as subject to a single lease.

(3) ELIMINATION OF 15-PERCENT TEST AFTER 5 YEARS IN CASE OF REAL PROPERTY.—At the election of the taxpayer, paragraph (1)(A) shall not apply with respect to real property of the taxpayer which has been in use for more than 5 years.

(4) ELECTIONS.—An election under paragraph (2) or (3) shall be made at such time and in such manner as the Secretary prescribes by regulations.

Amendments

• 1971, Revenue Act of 1971 (P.L. 92-178)

P. L. 92-178, §304(a):

Amended Code Sec. 57(c). **Effective** for tax years beginning after 12-31-69. Prior to amendment, Code Sec. 57(c) read as follows:

(c) Net Leases.—For purposes of this section, property shall be considered to be subject to a net lease for a taxable year if—

(1) for such taxable year the sum of the deductions with respect to such property which are allowable solely by reason of section 162 is less than 15 percent of the rental income produced by such property, or

(2) the lessor is either guaranteed a specified return or is guaranteed in whole or in part against loss of income.

• 1969, Tax Reform Act of 1969 (P.L. 91-172)

P. L. 91-172, §301(a):

Added Sec. 57(c). **Effective** 1-1-70.

[Sec. 57(d)]

(d) STRAIGHT LINE RECOVERY OF INTANGIBLES DEFINED.—For purposes of paragraph (11) of subsection (a)—

(1) IN GENERAL.—The term "straight line recovery of intangibles," when used with respect to intangible drilling and development costs for any well, means (except in the case of an election under paragraph (2)) ratable amortization of such costs over the 120-month period beginning with the month in which production from such well begins.

(2) ELECTION.—If the taxpayer elects, at such time and in such manner as the Secretary may by regulations prescribe, with respect to the intangible drilling and development costs for any well, the term "straight line recovery of intangibles" means any method which would be permitted for purposes of determining cost depletion with respect to such well and which is selected by the taxpayer for purposes of subsection (a)(11).

Amendments

• 1976, Tax Reform Act of 1976 (P.L. 94-455)

P.L. 94-455, §301(c)(3):

Added Code Sec. 57(d). For **effective** date, Act Sec 301(g) under Code Sec. 57.

P.L. 94-455, §301(f), provides:

(f) SECTION 21 NOT TO APPLY.—For purposes of section 21 of the Internal Revenue Code of 1954, the amendments made by this section shall not be treated as a change in a rate of tax.

[Sec. 57(e)]

(e) TIMBER PREFERENCE INCOME DEFINED.—For purposes of this part, the term "timber preference income" means the sum of—

(1) the gains referred to in section 631(a) and section 631(b),

(2) long-term capital gains on timber, and

(3) gains on the sale of timber included in paragraph 1231(b)(1),

multiplied by the fraction determined in paragraph 57(a)(9)(B).

Amendments

• 1976, Tax Reform Act of 1976 (P.L. 94-455)

P.L. 94-455, §301(c)(4)(C):

Added Code Sec. 57(e). For **effective** date, see Act Sec. 301(g) under Code Sec. 57.

P.L. 94-455, §301(f), provides:

(f) SECTION 21 NOT TO APPLY.—For purposes of section 21 of the Internal Revenue Code of 1954, the amendments made by this section shall not be treated as a change in a rate of tax.

[Sec. 58]

SEC. 58. DENIAL OF CERTAIN LOSSES.

[Sec. 58(a)]

(a) DENIAL OF FARM LOSS.—

(1) IN GENERAL.—For purposes of computing the amount of the alternative minimum taxable income for any taxable year of a taxpayer other than a corporation—

(A) DISALLOWANCE OF FARM LOSS.—No loss of the taxpayer for such taxable year from any tax shelter farm activity shall be allowed.

(B) DEDUCTION IN SUCCEEDING TAXABLE YEAR.—Any loss from a tax shelter farm activity disallowed under subparagraph (A) shall be treated as a deduction allocable to such activity in the 1st succeeding taxable year.

(2) TAX SHELTER FARM ACTIVITY.—For purposes of this subsection, the term "tax shelter farm activity" means—

(A) any farming syndicate as defined in section 464(c) and

(B) any other activity consisting of farming which is a passive activity (within the meaning of section 469(c)).

(3) APPLICATION TO PERSONAL SERVICE CORPORATIONS.—For purposes of paragraph (1), a personal service corporation (within the meaning of section 469(j)(2)) shall be treated as a taxpayer other than a corporation.

(4) DETERMINATION OF LOSS.—In determining the amount of the loss from any tax shelter farm activity, the adjustments of sections 56 and 57 shall apply.

Amendments

• 1988, Technical and Miscellaneous Revenue Act of 1988 (P.L. 100-647)

P.L. 100-647, §1007(d)(1)(A)-(B):

Amended Code Sec. 58(a)(2) by striking out "(as modified by section 461(i)(4)(A))" after "section 464(c)", and by striking out "section 469(d), without regard to paragraph (1)(B) thereof" and inserting in lieu thereof "section 469(c)". **Effective** as if included in the provision of P.L. 99-514 to which it relates.

P.L. 100-647, §1007(d)(2):

Amended Code Sec. 58(a)(3) by striking out "section 469(g)(1)(C)" and inserting in lieu thereof "section 469(j)(2)". **Effective** as if included in the provision of P.L. 99-514 to which it relates.

P.L. 100-647, §1007(d)(3):

Amended Code Sec. 58(a) by adding at the end thereof new paragraph (4). **Effective** as if included in the provision of P.L. 99-514 to which it relates.

[Sec. 58(b)]

(b) DISALLOWANCE OF PASSIVE ACTIVITY LOSS.—In computing the alternative minimum taxable income of the taxpayer for any taxable year, section 469 shall apply, except that in applying section 469—

(1) the adjustments of sections 56 and 57 shall apply,

(2) the provisions of section 469(m) (relating to phase-in of disallowance) shall not apply, and

(3) in lieu of applying section 469(j)(7), the passive activity loss of a taxpayer shall be computed without regard to qualified housing interest (as defined in section 56(e)).

Amendments

• 1988, Technical and Miscellaneous Revenue Act of 1988 (P.L. 100-647)

P.L. 100-647, §1007(d)(4):

Amended Code Sec. 58(b) by striking out paragraphs (1)-(3) and inserting in lieu thereof new paragraphs (1)-(3). **Effective** as if included in the provision of P.L. 99-514 to which it relates. Prior to amendment, Code Sec. 58(b)(1)-(3) read as follows:

(1) the adjustments of section 56 shall apply,

(2) any deduction to the extent such deduction is an item of tax preference under section 57(a) shall not be taken into account, and

(3) the provisions of section 469(m) (relating to phase-in of disallowance) shall not apply.

• 1987, Revenue Act of 1987 (P.L. 100-203)

P.L. 100-203, §10212(b):

Amended Code Sec. 58(b)(3) by striking out "469(l)" and inserting in lieu thereof "469(m)". **Effective** as if included in the amendments made by P.L. 99-514, §501.

[Sec. 58(c)]

(c) SPECIAL RULES.—For purposes of this section—

(1) SPECIAL RULE FOR INSOLVENT TAXPAYERS.—

(A) IN GENERAL.—The amount of losses to which subsection (a) or (b) applies shall be reduced by the amount (if any) by which the taxpayer is insolvent as of the close of the taxable year.

(B) INSOLVENT.—For purposes of this paragraph, the term "insolvent" means the excess of liabilities over the fair market value of assets.

(2) LOSS ALLOWED FOR YEAR OF DISPOSITION OF FARM SHELTER ACTIVITY.—If the taxpayer disposes of his entire interest in any tax shelter farm activity during any taxable year, the amount of the loss attributable to such activity (determined after carryovers under subsection (a)(1)(B)) shall (to the extent otherwise allowable) be allowed for such taxable year in computing alternative minimum taxable income and not treated as a loss from a tax shelter farm activity.

Amendments

• 1986, Tax Reform Act of 1986 (P.L. 99-514)

P.L. 99-514, §701(a):

Amended Code Sec. 58. **Effective**, generally, for tax years beginning after 12-31-86. For exceptions, see Act Sec. 701(f)(2)-(7) following Code Sec. 56. Prior to amendment it read as follows:

SEC. 58. RULES FOR APPLICATION OF THIS PART.

[Sec. 58(a)—Stricken]

Amendments

• 1983, Technical Corrections Act of 1982 (P.L. 97-448)

P.L. 97-448, §306(a)(1)(A):

Amended section 201 of P.L. 97-34 by redesignating the second subsection (c) as subsection (d). **Effective** for tax years beginning after 12-31-82.

• 1982, Tax Equity and Fiscal Responsibility Act of 1982 (P.L. 97-248)

P.L. 97-248, §201(d)(3)(A):

Struck out Code Sec. 58(a). **Effective** for tax years beginning after 12-31-82. Prior to amendment subsection (a) read as follows:

(a) Married Individuals Filing Separate Returns.—In the case of a married individual who files a separate return for the taxable year, section 56 shall be applied by substituting $5,000 for $10,000 each place it appears. In the case of a married individual who files a separate return for the taxable year, the amount determined under paragraph (1) of section 55(a) shall be an amount equal to one-half of the amount which would be determined under such paragraph if the amount of the individual's alternative minimum taxable income were multiplied by 2.

• 1978, Revenue Act of 1978 (P.L. 95-600)

P.L. 95-600, §421(c)(1), (g):

Amended Code Sec. 58(a) by adding the last sentence. **Effective** for tax years beginning after 12-31-78.

• 1976, Tax Reform Act of 1976 (P.L. 94-455)

P.L. 94-455, §301(d)(1):

Amended Code Sec. 58(a). For the **effective** date, see Act Sec. 301(g), below. Prior to amendment, Code Sec. 58(a) read as follows:

(a) HUSBAND AND WIFE.—In the case of a husband or wife who files a separate return for the taxable year, the $30,000 amount specified in section 56 shall be $15,000.

P.L. 94-455, §301(f), provides:

(f) SECTION 21 NOT TO APPLY.—For purposes of section 21 of the Internal Revenue Code of 1954, the amendments made by this section shall not be treated as a change in a rate of tax.

P.L. 94-455, §301(g), provides:

(g) EFFECTIVE DATE.

(1) IN GENERAL.—Except as provided by paragraph (4), the amendments made by this section shall apply to items of tax preference for taxable years beginning after December 31, 1975.

(2) TAX CARRYOVER.—Except as provided in paragraph (4) and in section 56(e) of the Internal Revenue Code of 1954, the amount of any tax carryover under section 56(c) of such Code from a taxable year beginning before January 1, 1976,

shall not be allowed as a tax carryover for any taxable year beginning after December 31, 1975.

(3) SPECIAL RULE FOR TAXABLE YEAR 1976 IN THE CASE OF A CORPORATION.—Notwithstanding any provision of the Internal Revenue Code of 1954 to the contrary, in the case of a corporation which is not an electing small business corporation or a personal holding company the tax imposed by section 56 of such Code for taxable years beginning in 1976, is an amount equal to the sum of—

(A) the amount of the tax which would have been imposed for such taxable year under such section as such section was in effect on the day before the date of the enactment of the Tax Reform Act of 1976, and

(B) one-half of the amount by which the amount of the tax which would be imposed for such taxable year under such section as amended by the Tax Reform Act of 1976 (but for this paragraph) exceeds the amount determined under subparagraph (A).

(4) CERTAIN FINANCIAL INSTITUTIONS.—In the case of a taxpayer which is a financial institution to which section 585 or 593 of the Internal Revenue Code of 1954 applies, the amendments made by this section shall apply only to taxable years beginning after December 31, 1977, and paragraph (2) shall be applied by substituting "January 1, 1978" for "January 1, 1976" and by substituting "December 31, 1977" for "December 31, 1975".

• 1969, Tax Reform Act of 1969 (P.L. 91-172)

P.L. 91-172, §301(a):

Added Code Sec. 58(a). **Effective** 1-1-70.

[Sec. 58(b)]

(b) MEMBERS OF CONTROLLED GROUPS.—In the case of a controlled group of corporations (as defined in section 1563(a)), the $10,000 amount specified in section 56 shall be divided among the component members of such group in proportion to their respective regular tax deductions (within the meaning of section 56(c)) for the taxable year.

Amendments

• 1978, Revenue Act of 1978 (P.L. 95-600)

P.L. 95-600, §701(b)(2), (5):

Amended Code Sec. 58(b). **Effective** as if such amendment were included in amendments made by P.L. 94-455, §301. Prior to amendment, Code Sec. 58(b) read:

"(b) MEMBERS OF CONTROLLED GROUPS.—In the case of a controlled group of corporations (as defined in section 1563(a)), the $10,000 amount specified in section 56 shall be divided equally among the component members of such group unless all component members consent (at such time and in such manner as the Secretary prescribes by regulations) to an apportionment plan providing for an unequal allocation of such amount."

• 1976, Tax Reform Act of 1976 (P.L. 94-455)

P.L. 94-455, §301(d)(2):

Substituted "$10,000" for "$30,000" in Code Sec. 58(b). For **effective** date, see Act Sec. 301(g) in the amendments for Code Sec. 58(a), above.

P.L. 94-455, §301(f), provides:

(f) SECTION 21 NOT TO APPLY.—For purposes of section 21 of the Internal Revenue Code of 1954, the amendments made by this section shall not be treated as a change in a rate of tax.

P.L. 94-455, §1906(b)(13)(A):

Amended 1954 Code by substituting "Secretary" for "Secretary or his delegate" each place it appeared. **Effective** 2-1-77.

• 1969, Tax Reform Act of 1969 (P.L. 91-172)

P.L. 91-172, §301(a):

Added Code Sec. 58(b). **Effective** 1-1-70.

[Sec. 58(c)]

(c) ESTATES AND TRUSTS.—In the case of an estate or trust, the items of tax preference (and any itemzed deductions) for any taxable year shall be apportioned between the estate or trust and the beneficiaries in accordance with regulations prescribed by the Secretary.

Amendments

• 1986, Tax Reform Act of 1986 (P.L. 99-514)

P.L. 99-514, §1875(a):

Amended Code Sec. 58(c) by striking out "of tax preference" and inserting in lieu thereof "of tax preference (and any itemized deductions)". **Effective** as if included in the provision of P.L. 98-369 to which it relates.

• 1983, Technical Corrections Act of 1982 (P.L. 97-448)

P.L. 97-448, §306(a)(1)(A):

Amended section 201 of P.L. 97-248 by redesignating the second subsection (c) as subsection (d). **Effective** for tax years beginning after 12-31-82.

• 1982, Tax Equity and Fiscal Responsibility Act of 1982 (P.L. 97-248)

P.L. 97-248, §201(d)(3)(B):

Amended Code Sec. 58 by striking out subsection (c) and inserting a new subsection (c). **Effective** for tax years beginning after 12-31-82. Prior to amendment, subsection (c) read as follows:

(c) Estates and Trusts.—In the case of an estate or trust—

(1) the sum of the items of tax preference for any taxable year of the estate or trust shall be apportioned between the estate or trust and the beneficiaries in accordance with regulations prescribed by the Secretary,

(2) the $10,000 amount specified in section 56 applicable to such estate or trust shall be reduced to an amount which bears the same ratio to $10,000 as the portion of the sum of the items of tax preference allocated to the estate or trust under paragraph (1) bears to such sum, and

(3) the liability for the tax imposed by section 55(a) shall be determined as in the case of a married individual filing separately.

• 1980, Technical Corrections Act of 1979 (P.L. 96-222)

P.L. 96-222, §107(a)(1)(C):

Amended Code Sec. 58(c)(1) by striking out "on the basis of the income of the estate or trust allocable to each" and inserting "in accordance with regulations prescribed by the Secretary". **Effective** for tax years beginning after 12-31-78.

• 1978, Revenue Act of 1978 (P.L. 95-600)

P.L. 95-600, §421(c)(2), (g):

Amended Code Sec. 58(c). **Effective** for tax years beginning after 12-31-78. Prior to amendment, Code Sec. 58(c) read as follows:

(c) ESTATES AND TRUSTS.—In the case of an estate or trust—

(1) the sum of the items of tax preference for any taxable year of the estate or trust shall be apportioned between the estate or trust and the beneficiaries on the basis of the income of the estate or trust allocable to each, and

(2) the $10,000 amount specified in section 56 applicable to such estate or trust shall be reduced to an amount which bears the same ratio to $10,000 as the portion of the sum of the items of tax preference allocated to the estate or trust under paragraph (1) bears to such sum.

• 1976, Tax Reform Act of 1976 (P.L. 94-455)

P.L. 94-455, §301(d)(2):

Substituted "$10,000" for "$30,000" each place it appears in Code Sec. 58(c)(2). For **effective** date, see Act Sec. 301(g) in the amendments for Code Sec. 58(a), above.

P.L. 94-455, §301(f), provides:

(f) SECTION 21 NOT TO APPLY.—For purposes of section 21 of the Internal Revenue Code of 1954, the amendments made by this section shall not be treated as a change in a rate of tax.

• 1969, Tax Reform Act of 1969 (P.L. 91-172)

P.L. 91-172, §301(a):

Added Code Sec. 58(c). **Effective** 1-1-70.

[Sec. 58(d)]

(d) CERTAIN CAPITAL GAINS OF S CORPORATIONS.—If for a taxable year of an S corporation a tax is imposed on the income of such corporation under section 1374, such corporation shall be subject to the tax imposed by section 56, but computed only with reference to the item of tax preference set forth in section 57(a)(9)(B) to the extent attributable to gains subject to the tax imposed by section 1374.

Amendments

• 1982, Subchapter S Revision Act of 1982 (P.L. 97-354)

P.L. 97-354, §5(a)(16):

Amended Code Sec. 58(d). **Effective** for tax years beginning after 12-31-82. Prior to amendment, it read as follows:

"(d) ELECTING SMALL BUSINESS CORPORATIONS AND THEIR SHAREHOLDERS.—

(1) IN GENERAL.—Except as provided in paragraph (2), the items of tax preference of an electing small business corporation (as defined in section 1371(b)) for each taxable year of the corporation shall be treated as items of tax preference of the shareholders of such corporation, and, except as provided in paragraph (2), shall not be treated as items of tax preference of such corporation. The sum of the items so treated shall be apportioned pro rata among such shareholders in a manner consistent with section 1374(c)(1). For purposes of this paragraph, this part shall be treated as applying to such corporation.

(2) CERTAIN CAPITAL GAINS.—If for a taxable year of an electing small business corporation a tax is imposed on the income of such corporation under section 1378, such corporation shall be subject to the tax imposed by section 56, but computed only with reference to the item of tax preference set forth in section 57(a)(9)(B) to the extent attributable to gains subject to the tax imposed by section 1378."

• 1976, Tax Reform Act of 1976 (P.L. 94-455)

P.L. 94-455, §1901(b)(40):

Deleted the words ", notwithstanding the provision of section 1371(b)(1)," in Code Sec. 58(d)(2). **Effective** for tax years beginning after 12-31-76.

• 1969, Tax Reform Act of 1969 (P.L. 91-172)

P.L. 91-172, §301(a):

Added Code Sec. 58(d). **Effective** 1-1-70.

[Sec. 58(e)]

(e) PARTICIPANTS IN A COMMON TRUST FUND.—The items of tax preference of a common trust fund (as defined in section 584(a)) for each taxable year of the fund shall be treated as items of tax preference of the participants of such fund and shall be apportioned pro rata among such participants. For purposes of this subsection, this part shall be treated as applying to such fund.

Amendments

• 1969, Tax Reform Act of 1969 (P.L. 91-172)

P.L. 91-172, §301(a):

Added Code Sec. 58(e). **Effective** 1-1-70.

[Sec. 58(f)]

(f) REGULATED INVESTMENT COMPANIES, ETC.—In the case of a regulated investment company to which part I of subchapter M applies or a real estate investment trust to which part II of subchapter M applies—

(1) the item of tax preference set forth in section 57(a)(9) shall not be treated as an item of tax preference of such company or such trust for each taxable year to the extent that such item is attributable to amounts taken into account as income by the shareholders of such company under section 852(b)(3), or by the shareholders or holders of beneficial interests of such trust under section 857(b)(3), and

(2) the items of tax preference of such company or such trust for each taxable year (other than the item of tax preference set forth in section 57(a)(9) and, in the case of a real estate investment trust, the items of tax preference set forth in paragraphs (2) and (12)(B) of section 57(a)) shall be treated as items of tax preference of the shareholders of such company, or the shareholders or holders of beneficial interests of such trust (and not as items of tax preference of such company or such trust), in the same proportion that the dividends (other than capital gain dividends) paid to each such shareholder, or holder of beneficial interest, bears to the taxable income of such company or such trust determined without regard to the deduction for dividends paid.

Amendments

• 1969, Tax Reform Act of 1969 (P.L. 91-172)

P.L. 91-172, §301(a):

Added Code Sec. 58(f). **Effective** 1-1-70.

[Sec. 58(g)]

(g) TAX PREFERENCES ATTRIBUTABLE TO FOREIGN SOURCES.—

(1) IN GENERAL.—For purposes of section 56, the items of tax preference set forth in section 57(a) (other than in paragraph (9) of such section) which are attributable to sources within any foreign country or possession of the United States shall be taken into account only to the extent that such items reduce the tax imposed by this chapter (other than the tax imposed by section 56) on income derived from sources within the United States. For purposes of the preceding sentence, items of tax preference shall be treated as reducing the tax imposed by this chapter before items which are not items of tax preference.

(2) CAPITAL GAINS.—For purposes of section 56, the items of tax preference set forth in section 57(a)(9) which are attributable to sources within any foreign country or possession of the United States shall not be taken into account if preferential treatment is not accorded gain from the sale or exchange of capital assets (or property treated as capital assets).

For purposes of this paragraph, preferential treatment is accorded such items which are attributable to a foreign country or possession of the United States if such country or possession imposes no significant amount of tax with respect to such items; except that, for purposes of subparagraph (B), preferential treatment shall be deemed not to be accorded to capital gain recognized on the receipt of property (other than money) in exchange for stock of a corporation which is engaged in the active conduct of a trade or business within one or more foreign countries or possessions if (i) such exchange is described in section 332, 351, 354, 355, 356, or 361, (ii) such exchange is made in the foreign country or possession in which such corporation's business is primarily carried on, (iii) such exchange is not subject to tax by such foreign country or possession because it is regarded under the laws of such country or possession as a transaction in which gain or loss is either not realized or not recognized, and (iv) such gain, if it had been realized and recognized under the laws of such country or possession, would not have been accorded preferential treatment and would have been subject to tax at a rate of at least 28 percent (30 percent if the exchange occurs before January 1, 1979). For purposes of computing the minimum tax, if any, which may be payable on a subsequent transaction involving any property received upon the exchange of stock described in the preceding sentence, the property received shall be treated as having the same basis in the taxpayer's hands immediately after such exchange as such stock had immediately before such exchange.

Amendments

• 1983, Technical Corrections Act of 1982 (P.L. 97-448)

P.L. 97-448, §102(b)(2):

Amended Code Sec. 58(f)(2) by striking out "the item of tax preference set forth in section 57(a)(2)" and inserting in lieu thereof "the items of tax preference set forth in paragraphs (2) and (12)(B) of section 57(a)". **Effective** as if it had been included in the provision of P.L. 97-34 to which it relates.

P.L. 97-448, §306(a)(1)(A):

Amended section 201 of P.L. 97-248 by redesignating the second subsection (c) as subsection (d).

• 1982, Tax Equity and Fiscal Responsibility Act of 1982 (P.L. 97-248)

P.L. 97-248, §201(d)(3)(C):

Amended Code Sec. 58(g) by striking out "paragraphs (6) and" in paragraph (1) and inserting in lieu thereof "paragraph"; and by inserting the language preceding the last two sentences in place of the following:

"(2) Capital gains and stock options.—For purposes of section 56, the items of tax preference set forth in paragraphs (6) and (9) of section 57(a) which are attributable to sources within any foreign country or possession of the United States shall not be taken into account if, under the tax laws of such country or possession—

(A) in the case of the item set forth in paragraph (6) of section 57(a), preferential treatment is not accorded transfers of shares of stock pursuant to stock options described in such paragraph, and

(B) in the case of the item set forth in paragraph (9) of section 57(a), preferential treatment is not accorded gain from the sale or exchange of capital assets (or property treated as capital assets)." **Effective** for tax years beginning after 12-31-82.

• 1978, Revenue Act of 1978 (P.L. 95-600)

P. L. 95-600, §423(a), (b):

Amended Code Sec. 58(g)(2). **Effective** 11-6-78. Prior to amendment, Code Sec. 58(g)(2) read:

"(2) CAPITAL GAINS AND STOCK OPTIONS.—For purposes of section 56, the items of tax preference set forth in paragraphs (6) and (9) of section 57(a) which are attributable to sources within any foreign country or possession of the United States shall not be taken into account if, under the tax laws of such country or possession—

"(A) in the case of the item set forth in paragraph (6) of section 57(a), preferential treatment is not accorded transfers of shares of stock pursuant to stock options described in such paragraph, and

"(B) in the case of the item set forth in paragraph (9) of section 57(a), preferential treatment is not accorded gain from the sale or exchange of capital assets (or property treated as capital assets).

"For purposes of this paragraph, preferential treatment is accorded such items which are attributable to a foreign country or possession of the United States if such country or possession imposes no significant amount of tax with respect to such items."

• 1971, Revenue Act of 1971 (P.L. 92-178)

P.L. 92-178, §308(a):

Added the last sentence in Code Sec. 58(g). **Effective** for tax years beginning after 12-31-69.

• 1969, Tax Reform Act of 1969 (P.L. 91-172)

P.L. 91-172, §301(a):

Added Sec. 58(g). **Effective** 1-1-70.

[Sec. 58(h)]

(h) REGULATIONS TO INCLUDE TAX BENEFIT RULE.—The Secretary shall prescribe regulations under which items of tax preference shall be properly adjusted where the tax treatment giving rise to such items will not result in the reduction of the taxpayer's tax under this subtitle for any taxable years.

Amendments

• 1989, Omnibus Budget Reconciliation Act of 1989 (P.L. 101-239)

P.L. 101-239, §7811(d)(1)(B), provides:

(B) The repeal of section 58(h) of the Internal Revenue Code of 1954 by the Tax Reform Act of 1986 shall be effective only with respect to items of tax preference arising in taxable years beginning after December 31, 1986.

• 1976, Tax Reform Act of 1976 (P.L. 94-455)

P.L. 94-455, §301(d)(3):

Added Code Sec. 58(h). For **effective** date, see Act Sec. 301(g) in the amendments for Code Sec. 58(a), above.

P.L. 94-455, §301(f), provides:

(f) SECTION 21 NOT TO APPLY.—For purposes of section 21 of the Internal Revenue Code of 1954, the amendments made by this section shall not be treated as a change in a rate of tax.

[Sec. 58(i)]

(i) OPTIONAL 10-YEAR WRITEOFF OF CERTAIN TAX PREFERENCES—

(1) IN GENERAL.—For purposes of this title, in the case of an individual, any qualified expenditure to which an election under this paragraph applies shall be allowed as a deduction ratably over the 10-year period (3-year period in the case of circulation expenditures described in section 173) beginning with the taxable year in which such expenditure was made.

(2) QUALIFIED EXPENDITURE—For purposes of this subsection, the term "qualified expenditure" means any amount which, but for an election under this subsection, would have been allowable as a deduction for the taxable year in which paid or incurred under—

(A) section 173 (relating to circulation expenditures),

(B) section 174(a) (relating to research and experimental expenditures),

(C) section 263(c) (relating to intangible drilling and development expenditures),

(D) section 616(a) (relating to development expenditures), or

(E) section 617 (relating to deduction of certain mining exploration expenditures).

(3) OTHER SECTIONS NOT APPLICABLE.—Except as provided in this subsection, no deduction shall be allowed under any other section for any qualifed expenditure to which an election under this subsection applies.

(4) SPECIAL ELECTION FOR INTANGIBLE DRILLING AND DEVELOPMENT COSTS NOT ALLOCABLE TO LIMITED BUSINESS INTEREST.—

(A) IN GENERAL.—In the case of any nonlimited partnership intangible drilling costs (with respect to wells located in the United States) to which an election under this paragraph applies—

(i) the applicable percentage of such costs (adjusted as provided in section 48(q)) shall be allowed as a deduction for the taxable year in which paid or incurred and for each of the 4 succeeding taxable years, and

(ii) such costs shall be treated, for purposes of determining the amount of the credit allowable under section 38 for the taxable year in which paid or incurred, as qualified investment (within the meaning of subsections (c) and (d) of section 46) with respect to property placed in service during such year.

(B) APPLICABLE PERCENTAGE.—For purposes of subparagraph (A), the term "applicable percentage" means the percentage determined in accordance with the following table:

Taxable Year:	*Applicable percentage:*
1	15
2	22
3	21
4	21
5	21

(C) NONLIMITED INTANGIBLE DRILLING COSTS.—For purposes of this paragraph, the term "nonlimited intangible drilling costs" means any qualified expenditure described in paragraph (2)(C) of an individual which is not allocable to a limited business interest (as defined in section 55(e)(8)(C)) of such individual.

(5) ELECTION.—

(A) IN GENERAL.—An election may be made under this subsection with respect to any qualified expenditure.

(B) REVOCABLE ONLY WITH CONSENT.—An election under this subsection with respect to any qualified expenditure may be revoked only with the consent of the Secretary.

(C) TIME AND MANNER.—An election under this subsection shall be made at such time and in such manner as the Secretary shall by regulations prescribe.

(D) PARTNERS AND SHAREHOLDERS OF S CORPORATIONS.—In the case of a partnership, any election under this subsection shall be made separately by each partner with respect to the partner's allocable share of any qualified expenditure. A similar rule shall apply in the case of an S corporation and its shareholders.

(6) DISPOSITIONS.—

(A) OIL, GAS, AND GEOTHERMAL PROPERTY.—In the case of any disposition of any oil, gas, or geothermal property to which section 1254 applies (determined without regard to this section)—

(i) any deduction under paragraph (1) or (4)(A) with respect to costs which are allocable to such property shall, for purposes of section 1254, be treated as a deduction allowable under section 263(c), and

(ii) in the case of any credit allowable under section 38 by reason of paragraph (4)(B) which is allocable to such property, such disposition shall, for purposes of section 47, be treated as a disposition of section 38 recovery property which is not 3-year property.

(B) APPLICATION OF SECTION 617(d).—In the case of any disposition of mining property to which section 617(d) applies (determined without regard to this subsection), any amount allowable as a deduction under paragraph (1) which is allocable to such property shall, for purposes of section 617(d), be treated as a deduction allowable under section 617(a).

(7) AMOUNTS TO WHICH ELECTION APPLY NOT TREATED AS TAX PREFERENCE.—Any qualified expenditure to which an election under paragraph (1) or (4) applies shall not be treated as an item of tax preference under section 57(a).

Amendments

• 1984, Deficit Reduction Act of 1984 (P.L. 98-369)

P.L. 98-369, §711(a)(2):

Amended Code Sec. 58(i)(4)(A) by inserting "(with respect to wells located in the United States)" after "intangible drilling costs". **Effective** as if included in the provision of P.L. 97-248 to which it relates.

P.L. 98-369, §711(a)(3)(B):

Amended Code Sec. 58(i)(1) by striking out "10-year period" and inserting in lieu thereof "10-year period (3-year period in the case of circulation expenditures described in section 173)". **Effective** as if included in the provision of P.L. 97-248 to which it relates.

• 1982, Subchapter S Revision Act of 1982 (P.L. 97-354)

P.L. 97-354, §3(c)(1):

Amended Code Sec. 58(i)(4)(C). **Effective** for tax years beginning after 12-31-82. Prior to amendment, it read as follows:

"(C) NONLIMITED PARTNERSHIP INTANGIBLE DRILLING COSTS.—For purposes of this paragraph, the term `nonlimited partnership intangible drilling costs' means any qualified expenditure described in paragraph (2)(C) of an individual which is not allocable to such individual's interest as a limited partner in a limited partnership."

P.L. 97-354, §3(c)(2):

Amended Code Sec. 58(i)(5)(D) by adding at the end thereof "A similar rule shall apply in the case of an S corporation and its shareholders.", and by striking out "PARTNERS" in the subparagraph heading and inserting in lieu thereof "PARTNERS AND SHAREHOLDERS OF S CORPORATIONS". **Effective** for tax years beginning after 12-31-82.

P.L. 97-354, §3(c)(3):

Amended the paragraph heading for paragraph (4) of Code Sec. 58(i) by striking out "INTEREST AS LIMITED PARTNER" and inserting in lieu thereof "LIMITED BUSINESS INTEREST". **Effective** for tax years beginning after 12-31-82.

• 1982, Tax Equity and Fiscal Responsibility Act of 1982 (P.L. 97-248)

P.L. 97-248, §201(c)(1):

Added Code Sec. 58(i). **Effective** for tax years beginning after 12-31-82.

• 1978, Revenue Act of 1978 (P.L. 95-600)

P.L. 95-600, §421(c)(3), (g):

Repealed Code Sec. 58(i). **Effective** for tax years beginning after 12-31-78. Prior to repeal, Code Sec. 58(i) read as follows:

"(i) CORPORATION DEFINED.—Except as provided in subsection (d)(2), for purposes of this part, the term "corporation" does not include an electing small business corporation (as defined in section 1371(b)) or a personal holding company (as defined in section 542)."

• 1976, Tax Reform Act of 1976 (P.L. 94-455)

P.L. 94-455, §301(d)(3):

Added Code Sec. 58(i). For **effective** date, see Act Sec. 301(g) in the amendments for Code Sec. 58(a), above.

P.L. 94-455, §301(f), provides:

(f) SECTION 21 NOT TO APPLY.—For purposes of section 21 of the Internal Revenue Code of 1954, the amendments made by this section shall not be treated as a change in a rate of tax.

[Sec. 59]

SEC. 59. OTHER DEFINITIONS AND SPECIAL RULES.

[Sec. 59(a)]

(a) ALTERNATIVE MINIMUM TAX FOREIGN TAX CREDIT.—For purposes of this part—

(1) IN GENERAL.—The alternative minimum tax foreign tax credit for any taxable year shall be the credit which would be determined under section 27(a) for such taxable year if—

(A) the pre-credit tentative minimum tax were the tax against which such credit was taken for purposes of section 904 for the taxable year and all prior taxable years beginning after December 31, 1986,

(B) section 904 were applied on the basis of alternative minimum taxable income instead of taxable income, and

(C) the determination of whether any income is high-taxed income for purposes of section 904(d)(2) were made on the basis of the applicable rate specified in subparagraph (A)(i) or (B)(i) of section 55(b)(1) (whichever applies) in lieu of the highest rate of tax specified in section 1 or 11 (whichever applies).

(2) PRE-CREDIT TENTATIVE MINIMUM TAX.—For purposes of this subsection, the term "pre-credit tentative minimum tax" means—

(A) in the case of a taxpayer other than a corporation, the amount determined under the first sentence of section 55(b)(1)(A)(i), or

(B) in the case of a corporation, the amount determined under section 55(b)(1)(B)(i).

(3) ELECTION TO USE SIMPLIFIED SECTION 904 LIMITATION.—

(A) IN GENERAL.—In determining the alternative minimum tax foreign tax credit for any taxable year to which an election under this paragraph applies—

(i) subparagraph (B) of paragraph (1) shall not apply, and

(ii) the limitation of section 904 shall be based on the proportion which—

(I) the taxpayer's taxable income (as determined for purposes of the regular tax) from sources without the United States (but not in excess of the taxpayer's entire alternative minimum taxable income), bears to

(II) the taxpayer's entire alternative minimum taxable income for the taxable year.

(B) ELECTION.—

(i) IN GENERAL.—An election under this paragraph may be made only for the taxpayer's first taxable year which begins after December 31, 1997, and for which the taxpayer claims an alternative minimum tax foreign tax credit.

(ii) ELECTION REVOCABLE ONLY WITH CONSENT.—An election under this paragraph, once made, shall apply to the taxable year for which made and all subsequent taxable years unless revoked with the consent of the Secretary.

Amendments

• 2004, American Jobs Creation Act of 2004 (P.L. 108-357)

P.L. 108-357, §421(a)(1):

Amended Code Sec. 59(a) by striking paragraph (2) and by redesignating paragraphs (3) and (4) as paragraphs (2) and (3), respectively. **Effective** for tax years beginning after 12-31-2004. Prior to being stricken, Code Sec. 59(a)(2) read as follows:

(2) LIMITATION TO 90 PERCENT OF TAX.—

(A) IN GENERAL.—The alternative minimum tax foreign tax credit for any taxable year shall not exceed the excess (if any) of—

(i) the pre-credit tentative minimum tax for the taxable year, over

(ii) 10 percent of the amount which would be the pre-credit tentative minimum tax without regard to the alternative tax net operating loss deduction and section 57(a)(2)(E).

(B) CARRYBACK AND CARRYFORWARD.—If the alternative minimum tax foreign tax credit exceeds the amount determined under subparagraph (A), such excess shall, for purposes of this part, be treated as an amount to which section 904(c) applies.

• 1998, IRS Restructuring and Reform Act of 1998 (P.L. 105-206)

P.L. 105-206, §6011(a):

Amended Code Sec. 59(a) by redesignating paragraph (3), as added by Act Sec. 1103 of P.L. 105-34, as paragraph (4). **Effective** as if included in the provision of P.L. 105-34 to which it relates [**effective** for tax years beginning after 12-31-97.—CCH].

• 1997, Taxpayer Relief Act of 1997 (P.L. 105-34)

P.L. 105-34, §1057(a):

Amended Code Sec. 59(a)(2) by striking subparagraph (C). **Effective** for tax years beginning after 8-5-97. Prior to being stricken, Code Sec. 59(a)(2)(C) read as follows:

(C) EXCEPTION.—Subparagraph (A) shall not apply to any domestic corporation if—

(i) more than 50 percent of the stock of such domestic corporation (by vote and value) is owned by United States persons who are not members of an affiliated group (as defined in section 1504 of such Code) which includes such corporation,

(ii) all of the activities of such corporation are conducted in 1 foreign country with which the United States has an income tax treaty in effect and such treaty provides for the exchange of information between such foreign country and the United States,

(iii) all of the current earnings and profits of such corporation are distributed at least annually (other than current earnings and profits retained for normal maintenance or capital replacements or improvements of an existing business), and

(iv) all of such distributions by such corporation to United States persons are used by such persons in a trade or business conducted in the United States.

P.L. 105-34, §1103(a):

Amended Code Sec. 59(a) by adding at the end a new paragraph (3)[(4)]. **Effective** for tax years beginning after 12-31-97.

• 1996, Small Business Job Protection Act of 1996 (P.L. 104-188)

P.L. 104-188, §1703(e)(1)-(4):

Amended Code Sec. 59(a) by striking "the amount determined under section 55(b)(1)(A)" in paragraph[s] (1)(A) and (2)(A)(i) and inserting "the pre-credit tentative minimum tax", by striking "specified in section 55(b)(1)(A)" in paragraph (1)(C) and inserting "specified in subparagraph (A)(i) or (B)(i) of section 55(b)(1) (whichever applies)", by striking "which would be determined under section 55(b)(1)(A)" in paragraph (2)(A)(ii) and inserting "which would be the pre-credit tentative minimum tax", and by adding at the end thereof a new paragraph (3). **Effective** as if included in the provision of P.L. 103-66 to which it relates.

• 1992, Energy Policy Act of 1992 (P.L.102-486)

P.L. 102-486, §1915(c)(3):

Amended Code Sec. 59(a)(2)(A)(ii) by striking "and the alternative tax energy preference deduction under section 56(h)" and inserting "and section 57(a)(2)(E)". **Effective** for tax years beginning after 12-31-92.

• 1990, Omnibus Budget Reconciliation Act of 1990 (P.L. 101-508)

P.L. 101-508, §11531(b)(2):

Amended Code Sec. 59(a)(2)(A)(ii) by inserting "and the alternative tax energy preference deduction under section 56(h)" after "deduction". **Effective** for tax years beginning after 12-31-90.

P.L. 101-508, §11801(c)(2)(D):

Amended Code Sec. 59(a)(1) by inserting "and" at the end of subparagraph (B), by striking subparagraph (C), and by redesignating subparagraph (D) as subparagraph (C). **Effective** 11-5-90. Prior to repeal, Code Sec. 59(a)(1)(C) read as follows:

(C) for purposes of section 904, any increase in alternative minimum taxable income by reason of section 56(c)(1)(A) (relating to adjustment for book income) shall have the same proportionate source (and character) as alternative minimum taxable income determined without regard to such increase, and

P.L. 101-508, §11821(b), provides:

(b) SAVINGS PROVISION.—If—

(1) any provision amended or repealed by this part applied to—

(A) any transaction occurring before the date of the enactment of this Act,

(B) any property acquired before such date of enactment, or

(C) any item of income, loss, deduction, or credit taken into account before such date of enactment, and

(2) the treatment of such transaction, property, or item under such provision would (without regard to the amendments made by this part) affect liability for tax for periods ending after such date of enactment,

nothing in the amendments made by this part shall be construed to affect the treatment of such transaction, property, or item for purposes of determining liability for tax for periods ending after such date of enactment.

• 1989, Omnibus Budget Reconciliation Act of 1989 (P.L. 101-239)

P.L. 101-239, §7612(e)(1):

Amended Code Sec. 59(a)(2) by adding at the end thereof a new subparagraph (C). **Effective** for tax years beginning after 3-31-90. For a special rule, see Act Sec. 7612(e)(2)(B), below.

P.L. 101-239, §7612(e)(2)(B), provides:

(B) Special rule for year which includes march 31, 1990.—In the case of any taxable year (of a corporation described in subparagraph (C) of section 59(a)(2) of the Internal Revenue Code of 1986 (as added by paragraph (1))) which begins after December 31, 1989, and includes March 31, 1990, the amount determined under clause (ii) of section 59(a)(2)(A) of such Code shall be an amount which bears the same ratio to the amount which would have been determined under such clause without regard to this subparagraph as the number of days in such taxable year on or before March 31, 1990, bears to the total number of days in such taxable year.

• 1988, Technical and Miscellaneous Revenue Act of 1988 (P.L. 100-647)

P.L. 100-647, §1007(e)(3):

Amended Code Sec. 59(a)(1) by striking out "and" at the end of subparagraph (B), by striking out the period at the end of subparagraph (C) and inserting in lieu thereof ", and", and by adding at the end thereof new subparagraph (D). **Effective** as if included in the provision of P.L. 99-514 to which it relates.

[Sec. 59(b)]

(b) MINIMUM TAX NOT TO APPLY TO INCOME ELIGIBLE FOR CREDITS UNDER SECTION 30A OR 936.—In the case of any corporation for which a credit is allowable for the taxable year under section 30A or 936, alternative minimum taxable income shall not include any income with respect to which a credit is determined under section 30A or 936.

Amendments

• 1998, IRS Restructuring and Reform Act of 1998 (P.L. 105-206)

P.L. 105-206, §6023(2):

Amended the heading for subsection (b) of Code Sec. 59 by striking "SECTION 936 CREDIT" and inserting "CREDITS UNDER SECTION 30A OR 936". **E ffective** 7-22-98.

• 1996, Small Business Job Protection Act of 1996 (P.L. 104-188)

P.L. 104-188, §1601(b)(2)(D):

Amended Code Sec. 59(b) by striking "section 936," and all that follows and inserting "section 30A or 936, alternative minimum taxable income shall not include any income with respect to which a credit is determined under section 30A or 936.". **Effective** for tax years beginning after 12-31-95. For special rules, see Act Sec. 1601(c)(2)-(3), below. Prior to amendment, Code Sec. 59(b) read as follows:

(b) MINIMUM TAX NOT TO APPLY TO INCOME ELIGIBLE FOR SECTION 936 CREDIT.—In the case of any corporation for which a credit is allowable for the taxable year under section 936, alternative minimum taxable income shall not include any amount with respect to which the requirements of subparagraph (A) or (B) of section 936(a)(1) are met.

P.L. 104-188, §1601(c)(2)-(3), provides:

(2) SPECIAL RULE FOR QUALIFIED POSSESSION SOURCE INVESTMENT INCOME.—The amendments made by this section shall not apply to qualified possession source investment income received or accrued before July 1, 1996, without regard to the taxable year in which received or accrued.

(3) SPECIAL TRANSITION RULE FOR PAYMENT OF ESTIMATED TAX INSTALLMENT.—In determining the amount of any installment due under section 6655 of the Internal Revenue Code of 1986 after the date of the enactment of this Act and before October 1, 1996, only ½ of any increase in tax (for the taxable year for which such installment is made) by reason of the amendments made by subsections (a) and (b) shall be taken into account. Any reduction in such installment by reason of the preceding sentence shall be recaptured by increasing the next required installment for such year by the amount of such reduction.

[Sec. 59(c)]

(c) TREATMENT OF ESTATES AND TRUSTS.—In the case of any estate or trust, the alternative minimum taxable income of such estate or trust and any beneficiary thereof shall be determined by applying part I of subchapter J with the adjustments provided in this part.

[Sec. 59(d)]

(d) APPORTIONMENT OF DIFFERENTLY TREATED ITEMS IN CASE OF CERTAIN ENTITIES.—

(1) IN GENERAL.—The differently treated items for the taxable year shall be apportioned (in accordance with regulations prescribed by the Secretary)—

(A) REGULATED INVESTMENT COMPANIES AND REAL ESTATE INVESTMENT TRUSTS.—In the case of a regulated investment company to which part I of subchapter M applies or a real estate investment company to which part II of subchapter M applies, between such company or trust and shareholders and holders of beneficial interest in such company or trust.

(B) COMMON TRUST FUNDS.—In the case of a common trust fund (as defined in section 584(a)), pro rata among the participants of such fund.

(2) DIFFERENTLY TREATED ITEMS.—For purposes of this section, the term "differently treated item" means any item of tax preference or any other item which is treated differently for purposes of this part than for purposes of computing the regular tax.

[Sec. 59(e)]

(e) OPTIONAL 10-YEAR WRITEOFF OF CERTAIN TAX PREFERENCES.—

(1) IN GENERAL.—For purposes of this title, any qualified expenditure to which an election under this paragraph applies shall be allowed as a deduction ratably over the 10-year period (3-year period in the case of circulation expenditures described in section 173) beginning with the taxable year in which such expenditure was made (or, in the case of a qualified expenditure described in paragraph (2)(C), over the 60-month period beginning with the month in which such expenditure was paid or incurred).

(2) QUALIFIED EXPENDITURE.—For purposes of this subsection, the term "qualified expenditure" means any amount which, but for an election under this subsection, would have been allowable as a deduction (determined without regard to section 291) for the taxable year in which paid or incurred under,

(A) section 173 (relating to circulation expenditures),

(B) section 174(a) (relating to research and experimental expenditures),

(C) section 263(c) (relating to intangible drilling and development expenditures),

(D) section 616(a) (relating to development expenditures), or

(E) section 617(a) (relating to mining exploration expenditures).

(3) OTHER SECTIONS NOT APPLICABLE.—Except as provided in this subsection, no deduction shall be allowed under any other section for any qualified expenditure to which an election under this subsection applies.

(4) ELECTION.—

(A) IN GENERAL.—An election may be made under paragraph (1) with respect to any portion of any qualified expenditure.

(B) REVOCABLE ONLY WITH CONSENT.—Any election under this subsection may be revoked only with the consent of the Secretary.

(C) PARTNERS AND SHAREHOLDERS OF S CORPORATIONS.—In the case of a partnership, any election under paragraph (1) shall be made separately by each partner with respect to the partner's allocable share of any qualified expenditure. A similar rule shall apply in the case of an S corporation and its shareholders.

(5) DISPOSITIONS.—

(A) APPLICATION OF SECTION 1254.—In the case of any disposition of property to which section 1254 applies (determined without regard to this section), any deduction under paragraph (1) with respect to amounts which are allocable to such property shall, for purposes of section 1254, be treated as a deduction allowable under section 263(c), 616(a), or 617(a), whichever is appropriate.

(B) APPLICATION OF SECTION 617(d).—In the case of any disposition of mining property to which section 617(d) applies (determined without regard to this subsection), any deduction under paragraph (1) with respect to amounts which are allocable to such property shall, for purposes of section 617(d), be treated as a deduction allowable under section 617(a).

(6) AMOUNTS TO WHICH ELECTION APPLY NOT TREATED AS TAX PREFERENCE.—Any portion of any qualified expenditure to which an election under paragraph (1) applies shall not be treated as an item of tax preference under section 57(a) and section 56 shall not apply to such expenditure.

Amendments

• 1989, Omnibus Budget Reconciliation Act of 1989 (P.L. 101-239)

P.L. 101-239, §7611(f)(5)(B):

Amended Code Sec. 59(e)(1) by inserting "(or, in the case of a qualified expenditure described in paragraph (2)(C), over the 60-month period beginning with the month in which such expenditure was paid or incurred)" before the period at the end thereof. **Effective** for costs paid or incurred in tax years beginning after 12-31-89.

• 1988, Technical and Miscellaneous Revenue Act of 1988 (P.L. 100-647)

P.L. 100-647, §1007(e)(1):

Amended Code Sec. 59(e)(2) by striking out "would have been allowable as a deduction" and inserting in lieu thereof "would have been allowable as a deduction (determined without regard to section 291)". **Effective** as if included in the provision of P.L. 99-514 to which it relates.

[Sec. 59(f)]

(f) COORDINATION WITH SECTION 291.—Except as otherwise provided in this part, section 291 (relating to cutback of corporate preferences) shall apply before the application of this part.

[Sec. 59(g)]

(g) TAX BENEFIT RULE.—The Secretary may prescribe regulations under which differently treated items shall be properly adjusted where the tax treatment giving rise to such items will not result in the reduction of the taxpayer's regular tax for the taxable year for which item is taken into account or for any other taxable year.

Amendments

• 1989, Omnibus Budget Reconciliation Act of 1989 (P.L. 101-239)

P.L. 101-239, §7811(d)(1)(A):

Amended Code Sec. 59(g) by striking "for any taxable year" and inserting "for the taxable year for which the item is taken into account or for any other taxable year". **Effective** as if included in the provision of P.L. 100-647 to which it relates.

[Sec. 59(h)]

(h) COORDINATION WITH CERTAIN LIMITATIONS.—The limitations of sections 704(d), 465, and 1366(d) (and such other provisions as may be specified in regulations) shall be applied for purposes of computing the alternative minimum taxable income of the taxpayer for the taxable year with the adjustments of sections 56, 57, and 58.

Amendments

• 1988, Technical and Miscellaneous Revenue Act of 1988 (P.L. 100-647)

P.L. 100-647, §1007(e)(2):

Amended Code Sec. 59(h) by striking out "taxable year" and all that follows and inserting in lieu thereof "taxable year with the adjustments of sections 56, 57, and 58." **Effective** as if included in the provisions of P.L. 99-514 to which it relates. Prior to amendment, Code Sec. 59(h) read as follows:

(h) COORDINATION WITH CERTAIN LIMITATIONS.—The limitations of sections 704(d), 465, and 1366(d) (and such other provisions as may be specified in regulations) shall be applied for purposes of computing the alternative minimum taxable income of the taxpayer for the taxable year—

(1) with the adjustments of section 56, and

(2) by not taking into account any deduction to the extent such deduction is an item of tax preference under section 57(a).

[Sec. 59(i)]

(i) SPECIAL RULE FOR AMOUNTS TREATED AS TAX PREFERENCE.—For purposes of this subtitle (other than this part), any amount shall not fail to be treated as wholly exempt from tax imposed by this subtitle solely by reason of being included in alternative minimum taxable income.

Amendments

• 1989, Omnibus Budget Reconciliation Act of 1989 (P.L. 101-239)

P.L. 101-239, §7611(f)(6)(A)-(B):

Amended Code Sec. 59(i) by striking "interest shall" and inserting "any amount shall", and by striking "INTEREST" in the subsection heading and inserting "AMOUNTS". **E ffective** for tax years beginning after 12-31-89.

• 1988, Technical and Miscellaneous Revenue Act of 1988 (P.L. 100-647)

P.L. 100-647, §1007(e)(4)(A)-(B):

Amended Code Sec. 59(i) by striking out "of this subtitle" and inserting in lieu thereof "of this subtitle (other than this part)", and by striking out "by this title" and inserting in lieu thereof "by this subtitle". **Effective** as if included in the provision of P.L. 99-514 to which it relates.

• 1986, Tax Reform Act of 1986 (P.L. 99-514)

P.L. 99-514, §701(a):

Added new Code Sec. 59. **Effective**, generally, for tax years beginning after 12-31-86. However, for exceptions, see Act Sec. 701(f)(2)-(7) following Code Sec. 56.

[Sec. 59(j)]

(j) TREATMENT OF UNEARNED INCOME OF MINOR CHILDREN.—

(1) IN GENERAL.—In the case of a child to whom section 1(g) applies, the exemption amount for purposes of section 55 shall not exceed the sum of—

(A) such child's earned income (as defined in section 911(d)(2)) for the taxable year, plus

(B) $5,000.

(2) INFLATION ADJUSTMENT.—In the case of any taxable year beginning in a calendar year after 1998, the dollar amount in paragraph (1)(B) shall be increased by an amount equal to the product of—

(A) such dollar amount, and

(B) the cost-of-living adjustment determined under section 1(f)(3) for the calendar year in which the taxable year begins, determined by substituting "1997" for "1992" in subparagraph (B) thereof.

If any increase determined under the preceding sentence is not a multiple of $50, such increase shall be rounded to the nearest multiple of $50.

Amendments

• 1997, Taxpayer Relief Act of 1997 (P.L. 105-34)

P.L. 105-34, §1201(b)(1):

Amended Code Sec. 59(j). **Effective** for tax years beginning after 12-31-97. Prior to amendment, Code Sec. 59(j) read as follows:

(j) TREATMENT OF UNEARNED INCOME OF MINOR CHILDREN.—

(1) LIMITATION ON EXEMPTION AMOUNT.—In the case of a child to whom section 1(g) applies, the exemption amount for purposes of section 55 shall not exceed the sum of—

(A) such child's earned income (as defined in section 911(d)(2)) for the taxable year, plus

(B) twice the amount in effect for the taxable year under section 63(c)(5)(A) (or, if greater, the child's share of the unused parental minimum tax exemption).

(2) LIMITATION BASED ON PARENTAL MINIMUM TAX.—

(A) IN GENERAL.—In the case of a child to whom section 1(g) applies, the amount of the tax imposed by section 55 shall not exceed such child's share of the allocable parental minimum tax.

(B) ALLOCABLE PARENTAL MINIMUM TAX.—For purposes of this paragraph, the term "allocable parental minimum tax" means the excess of—

(i) the tax which would be imposed by section 55 on the parent if—

(I) the amount of the parent's tentative minimum tax were increased by the aggregate of the tentative minimum taxes of all children of the parent to whom section 1(g) applies and

(II) the amount of the parent's regular tax were increased by the aggregate of the regular taxes of all children of the parent to whom section 1(g) applies, over

(ii) the tax imposed by section 55 on the parent without regard to this subparagraph.

(C) CHILD SHARE.—A child's share of any allocable parental minimum tax shall be determined under rules similar to the rules of section 1(g)(3)(B).

(D) OTHER RULES MADE APPLICABLE.—For purposes of this paragraph, rules similar to the rules of paragraphs (3)(D), (5), and (6) of section 1(g) shall apply.

(3) UNUSED PARENTAL MINIMUM TAX EXEMPTION.—

(A) IN GENERAL.—For purposes of this subsection, the term "unused parental minimum tax exemption" means the excess (if any) of—

(i) the exemption amount applicable to the parent under section 55(d), over

(ii) the parent's alternative minimum taxable income.

(B) CERTAIN RULES MADE APPLICABLE.—A child's share of any unused parental minimum tax exemption shall be determined under rules similar to the rules of section 1(g)(3)(B), and rules similar to the rules of paragraphs (3)(D) and (5) of section 1(g) shall apply for purposes of this paragraph.

• 1996, Small Business Job Protection Act of 1996 (P.L. 104-188)

P.L. 104-188, §1702(a)(1):

Amended Code Sec. 59(j)(3)(B) by striking "section 1(i)(3)(B)" and inserting "section 1(g)(3)(B)". **Effective** as if included in the provision of P.L. 101-508 to which such amendment relates.

P.L. 104-188, §1704(m)(3):

Amended Code Sec. 59(j)(1)(B) by striking "$1,000" and inserting "twice the amount in effect for the taxable year under section 63(c)(5)(A)". **Effective** for tax years beginning after 12-31-95.

• 1990, Omnibus Budget Reconciliation Act of 1990 (P.L. 101-508)

P.L. 101-508, §11101(d)(3)(A)(B):

Amended Code Sec. 59(j) by striking "section 1(i)" each place it appears and inserting "section 1(g)" and by striking "section 1(i)(3)(B)" in paragraph (2)(C) and inserting "section 1(g)(3)(B)". **Effective** for tax years beginning after 12-31-90.

P.L. 101-508, §11702(d)(1):

Amended Code Sec. (59)(j)(1)(B) by inserting "(or, if greater, the child's share of the unused parental minimum tax exemption)" before the period at the end thereof. **Effective** as if included in the provision of P.L. 100-647 to which it relates.

P.L. 101-508, §11702(d)(2):

Amended Code Sec. 59(j) by adding a new paragraph (3). **Effective** as if included in the provision of P.L. 100-647 to which it relates.

P.L. 101-508, §11702(d)(3):

Amended Code Sec. 59(j)(2)(D) by striking "paragraphs (5) and (6) " and inserting "paragraphs (3)(D), (5), and (6)". **Effective** as if included in the provision of P.L. 100-647 to which it relates.

• 1989, Omnibus Budget Reconciliation Act of 1989 (P.L. 101-239)

P.L. 101-239, §7811(j)(7):

Amended Code Sec. 59(j)(2)(D) by striking "OTHERS" and inserting "OTHER" in the subparagraph heading. **Effective** as if included in the provision of P.L. 100-647 to which it relates.

• 1988, Technical and Miscellaneous Revenue Act of 1988 (P.L. 100-647)

P.L. 100-647, §1014(e)(5)(A):

Amended Code Sec. 59 by adding at the end thereof new subsection (j). **Effective** for tax years beginning after 12-31-88.

PART VII—ENVIRONMENTAL TAX

[Sec. 59A]

SEC. 59A. ENVIRONMENTAL TAX.

[Sec. 59A(a)]

(a) IMPOSITION OF TAX.—In the case of a corporation, there is hereby imposed (in addition to any other tax imposed by this subtitle) a tax equal to 0.12 percent of the excess of—

(1) the modified alternative minimum taxable income of such corporation for the taxable year, over

(2) $2,000,000.

[Sec. 59A(b)]

(b) MODIFIED ALTERNATIVE MINIMUM TAXABLE INCOME.—For purposes of this section, the term "modified alternative minimum taxable income" means alternative minimum taxable income (as defined in section 55(b)(2)) but determined without regard to—

(1) the alternative tax net operating loss deduction (as defined in section 56(d)), and

(2) the deduction allowed under 164(a)(5).

Amendments

• 1992, Energy Policy Act of 1992 (P.L.102-486)

P.L. 102-486, §1915(c)(4):

Amended Code Sec. 59A(b)(1) by striking "or the alternative tax energy preference deduction under section 56(h)" after "section 56(d))". **Effective** for tax years beginning after 12-31-92.

• 1990, Omnibus Budget Reconciliation Act of 1990 (P.L. 101-508)

P.L. 101-508, §11531(b)(3):

Amended Code Sec. 59A(b)(1) by inserting "or the alternative tax energy preference deduction under section 56(h)" before ", and". **Effective** for tax years beginning after 12-31-90.

P.L. 101-508, §11801(c)(2)(E):

Amended Code Sec. 59A(b)(2) by striking "(and the last sentence of section 56(f)(2)(B))" after "section 164(a)(5)". **Effective** 11-5-90.

P.L. 101-508, §11821(b), provides:

(b) SAVINGS PROVISION.—If—

(1) any provision amended or repealed by this part applied to—

(A) any transaction occurring before the date of the enactment of this Act,

(B) any property acquired before such date of enactment, or

(C) any item of income, loss, deduction, or credit taken into account before such date of enactment, and

(2) the treatment of such transaction, property, or item under such provision would (without regard to the amendments made by this part) affect liability for tax for periods ending after such date of enactment,

nothing in the amendments made by this part shall be construed to affect the treatment of such transaction, property, or item for purposes of determining liability for tax for periods ending after such date of enactment.

• 1988, Technical and Miscellaneous Revenue Act of 1988 (P.L. 100-647)

P.L. 100-647, §2001(c)(3)(B):

Amended Code Sec. 59A(b)(2) by inserting "(and the last sentence of section 56(f)(2)(B))" before the period at the end thereof. **Effective** as if included in the provision of P.L. 99-499 to which it relates.

[Sec. 59A(c)]

(c) EXCEPTION FOR RIC'S AND REIT'S.—The tax imposed by subsection (a) shall not apply to—

(1) a regulated investment company to which part I of subchapter M applies, and

(2) a real estate investment trust to which part II of subchapter M applies.

Amendments

• 1988, Technical and Miscellaneous Revenue Act of 1988 (P.L. 100-647)

P.L. 100-647, §2001(c)(1):

Amended Code Sec. 59A by inserting after subsection (b) new subsection (c). **Effective** as if included in the provision of P.L. 99-499 to which it relates.

[Sec. 59A(d)]

(d) SPECIAL RULES.—

(1) SHORT TAXABLE YEARS.—The application of this section to taxable years of less than 12 months shall be in accordance with regulations prescribed by the Secretary.

(2) SECTION 15 NOT TO APPLY.—Section 15 shall not apply to the tax imposed by this section.

Amendments

• 1988, Technical and Miscellaneous Revenue Act of 1988 (P.L. 100-647)

P.L. 100-647, §2001(c)(1):

Amended Code Sec. 59A by redesignating subsection (c) as subsection (d). **Effective** as if included in the provision of P.L. 99-499 to which it relates.

[Sec. 59A(e)]

(e) APPLICATION OF TAX.—

(1) IN GENERAL.—The tax imposed by this section shall apply to taxable years beginning after December 31, 1986, and before January 1, 1996.

(2) EARLIER TERMINATION.—The tax imposed by this section shall not apply to taxable years—

(A) beginning during a calendar year during which no tax is imposed under section 4611(a) by reason of paragraph (2) of section 4611(e), and

(B) beginning after the calendar year which includes the termination date under paragraph (3) of section 4611(e).

Amendments

• 1990, Omnibus Budget Reconciliation Act of 1990 (P.L. 101-508)

P.L. 101-508, §11231(a)(1)(A):

Amended Code Sec. 59A(e)(1) by striking "January 1, 1992" and inserting "January 1, 1996". **Effective** 11-5-90.

• 1986, Superfund Amendments and Reauthorization Act of 1986 (P.L. 99-499)

P.L. 99-499, §516(a):

Amended Subchapter A of chapter 1 by adding at the end thereof new part VII. **Effective** for tax years beginning after 12-31-86.

PART VIII—SUPPLEMENTAL MEDICARE PREMIUM—[Repealed]

[Sec. 59B—Repealed]

Amendments

• 1989, Medicare Catastrophic Coverage Repeal Act of 1989 (P.L. 101-234)

P.L. 101-234, §102(a):

Repeals Section 111 of the Medicare Catastrophic Coverage Act of 1988 (P.L. 100-360), and the provisions of law amended by such sections are restored or revived as if such sections had not been enacted. **Effective** for tax years beginning after 12-31-88. Therefore, Part VIII—Supplemental Medicare Premium of subchapter A of chapter 1 (Code Sec. 59B) is repealed. Prior to repeal, Part VIII read as follows:

PART VIII—SUPPLEMENTAL MEDICARE PREMIUM

SEC. 59B. SUPPLEMENTAL MEDICARE PREMIUM.

(a) IMPOSITION OF PREMIUM.—In the case of an individual to whom this section applies, there is hereby imposed (in addition to any other amount imposed by this subtitle) for each taxable year a supplemental premium equal to the annual premium for such year determined under subsection (c).

(b) INDIVIDUALS SUBJECT TO PREMIUM.—This section shall apply to an individual for any taxable year if—

(1) such individual is a medicare-eligible individual for more than 6 full months beginning in the taxable year, and

(2) such individual's adjusted income tax liability for the taxable year equals or exceeds $150.

(c) DETERMINATION OF AMOUNT OF SUPPLEMENTAL PREMIUM.—For purposes of this section—

(1) IN GENERAL.—Except as otherwise provided in this subsection, the annual premium determined under this subsection with respect to any individual for any taxable year shall be equal to the product of—

(A) the supplemental premium rate determined under subsection (d) or (e) (whichever applies) for the taxable year, multiplied by

(B) the amount determined by dividing—

(i) the individual's adjusted income tax liability for the taxable year, by

(ii) $150.

(2) LIMITATION ON ANNUAL PREMIUM.—

(A) YEARS BEFORE 1994.—In the case of any taxable year beginning before 1994, the annual premium determined under this subsection with respect to any individual shall not exceed the limitation determined under the following table:

In the case of taxable years beginning in:	*The limitation is:*
1989	$800
1990	850
1991	900
1992	950
1993	1,050

(B) YEARS AFTER 1993.—In the case of any taxable year beginning in a calendar year after 1993, the annual premium determined under this subsection with respect to any individual shall not exceed—

(i) the limitation which would be in effect under this paragraph for taxable years beginning in the preceding calendar year without regard to the last sentence of this subparagraph, increased by

(ii) the percentage (if any) by which—

(I) the medicare-part B value for the 2nd preceding calendar year, exceeds

(II) such value for the 3rd preceding calendar year.

If the limitation determined under the preceding sentence is not a multiple of $50, such limitation shall be rounded to the nearest multiple of $50.

(C) MEDICARE-PART B VALUE.—

(i) IN GENERAL.—For purposes of subparagraph (B), the term "medicare-part B value" means, with respect to any calendar year, an amount equal to the excess of—

(I) the average per capita part B outlays for the year, over

(II) 12 times the monthly premium for months in such calendar year established under section 1839 of such Act (without regard to subsections (b), (f), (g)(4), and (g)(5) thereof).

(ii) AVERAGE PER CAPITA PART B OUTLAYS.—For purposes of clause (i), the term "average per capita part B outlays" means, with respect to a calendar year—

(I) the outlays under part B of title XVIII of the Social Security Act for the year, divided by

(II) the average number of individuals covered under such part during the year.

(iii) SPECIAL RULE FOR COVERED OUTPATIENT DRUGS.—In applying the limitation under subparagraph (B) with respect to taxable years beginning in any calendar year before 1998, for purposes of this subparagraph—

(I) the term "outlays" does not include outlays for covered outpatient drugs (as defined in section 1861(t)(2) of the Social Security Act), and

(II) the monthly premium shall be computed under clause (i)(II) excluding premiums under section 1839(g) of such Act attributable to the prescription drug monthly premium.

(3) TABLES.—The annual premium shall be determined under tables which shall be prescribed by the Secretary. Such tables shall be based on the foregoing provisions of this subsection; except that such tables may have adjusted income tax liability brackets of less than $150.

(d) DETERMINATION OF SUPPLEMENTAL PREMIUM RATE FOR YEARS BEFORE 1994.—In the case of any taxable year beginning before 1994, the supplemental premium rate determined under this subsection shall be the sum of the catastrophic coverage premium rate and the prescription drug premium rate determined under the following table:

In the case of any taxable year beginning in:	*The catastrophic coverage premium rate is:*	*The prescription drug premium rate is:*
1989 . .	$22.50 . .	0
1990 . .	$27.14 . .	$10.36
1991 . .	$30.17 . .	8.83
1992 . .	$30.55 . .	9.95
1993 . .	$29.55 . .	12.45.

[Sec. 59B(e)]

(e) SUPPLEMENTAL PREMIUM RATE FOR YEARS AFTER 1993.—

(1) IN GENERAL.—In the case of any taxable year beginning in a calendar year after 1993, except as provided in paragraph (2), the supplemental premium rate determined under this subsection shall be the sum of—

(A) the catastrophic coverage premium rate (which would be in effect under this section for taxable years beginning in the preceding calendar year if paragraph (2) did not apply to any preceding calendar year) adjusted by the percentage determined under paragraph (3) for the calendar year in which the taxable year begins, and

(B) the prescription drug premium rate (which would be in effect under this section for taxable years beginning in the preceding calendar year if paragraph (2) did not apply to any preceding calendar year) adjusted by the percentage determined under paragraph (4) for the calendar year in which the taxable year begins.

(2) SUPPLEMENTAL PREMIUM RATE CANNOT GO DOWN, AND CANNOT GO UP BY MORE THAN $1.50.—

(A) IN GENERAL.—In no event shall the supplemental premium rate determined under this subsection for any taxable year beginning in a calendar year after 1993—

(i) be less than, or

(ii) exceed by more than $1.50,

the supplemental premium rate in effect under this section for taxable years beginning in the preceding calendar year.

(B) DETERMINATION OF COMPONENT RATES WHERE SUBPARAGRAPH (A) APPLIES.—If subparagraph (A) affects the supplemental premium rate determined under this subsection for taxable years beginning in any calendar year, the supplemental premium rate determined after the application of subparagraph (A) shall be allocated between the catastrophic coverage premium rate and the prescription drug premium rate on the basis of the respective amounts of such rates without regard to the application of subparagraph (A).

(3) PERCENTAGE ADJUSTMENT FOR CATASTROPHIC COVERAGE PREMIUM RATE.—

(A) IN GENERAL.—The percentage determined under this paragraph for any calendar year shall be the sum of—

(i) the outlay-premium percentage, and

(ii) the reserve account percentage.

For purposes of the preceding sentence, negative percentages shall be taken into account as negatives.

(B) OUTLAY-PREMIUM PERCENTAGE.—

(i) IN GENERAL.—Except as otherwise provided in this subparagraph, the outlay-premium percentage for any calendar year is—

(I) the percentage by which the per capita catastrophic outlays in the 2nd preceding calendar year exceed such outlays in the 3rd preceding calendar year, reduced (including below zero) by

(II) the percentage by which the per capita catastrophic coverage premium liability for the 2nd preceding calendar year exceeds such liability for the 3rd preceding calendar year (determined as if the catastrophic coverage premium rate for the 2nd preceding calendar year were the same as the rate in effect for the 3rd preceding calendar year).

If there is no excess described in subclause (I) or (II), such subclause shall be applied by substituting "is less than" for "exceeds" and the percentage determined with such substitution shall be taken into account as a negative percentage.

(ii) ADJUSTMENT FOR MORE RECENT INCREASES IN COST-OF-LIVING.—If—

(I) the percentage increase in the CPI for the 12-month period ending with May of the preceding calendar year, exceeds (or is less than)

(II) such increase for the 12-month period ending with May of the 2nd preceding calendar year,

by at least 1 percentage point, the percentage determined under clause (i) for the calendar year shall be adjusted up (or down, respectively) by 1/2 of the amount by which such excess (or shortage, respectively) exceeds 1 percent.

(C) RESERVE ACCOUNT PERCENTAGE.—

(i) IN GENERAL.—The reserve account percentage for any calendar year is the percentage which the rate change determined under clause (ii) is of the catastrophic coverage premium rate which would be in effect under this section for taxable years beginning in the preceding calendar year if paragraph (2) did not apply to any preceding calendar year. If there is an excess determined under clause (iii), the percentage determined under the preceding sentence shall be taken into account as a negative percentage.

(ii) DETERMINATION OF RATE CHANGE.—The rate change determined under this clause for any calendar year is the adjustment in the catastrophic coverage premium rate (otherwise in effect for taxable years beginning in the 2nd preceding calendar year) which the Secretary determines would have resulted in an aggregate increase (or decrease) in the premiums imposed by this section for such taxable years equal to 63 percent of the shortfall or excess determined under clause (iii) for the calendar year.

(iii) DETERMINATION OF SHORTFALL OR EXCESS.—The shortfall (or excess) determined under this clause for any calendar year is the amount by which—

(I) 20 percent of the outlays during the 2nd preceding calendar year from the Medicare Catastrophic Coverage Account created under section 1841B of the Social Security Act, exceeds (or is less than)

(II) the balance in such Account as of the close of such 2nd preceding calendar year (determined by taking into account previous premium increases by reason of the reserve account percentage under this subsection or by reason of section 1839(g)(2) of the Social Security Act but not credited to the Account).

(D) DEFINITIONS.—For purposes of this paragraph—

(i) PER CAPITA CATASTROPHIC OUTLAYS.—The term "per capita catastrophic outlays" means, with respect to any calendar year, the amount (as determined by the Secretary of Health and Human Services) equal to—

(I) the outlays during such year from the Medicare Catastrophic Coverage Account created under section 1841B of the Social Security Act, divided by

(II) the average number of individuals entitled to receive benefits under part A of title XVIII of the Social Security Act during such calendar year.

(ii) PER CAPITAL CATASTROPHIC COVERAGE PREMIUM LIABILITY.—The term "per capita catastrophic coverage premium liability" means, with respect to any calendar year, the amount (as determined by the Secretary) equal to—

(I) the aggregate premiums imposed by this section for taxable years beginning in such calendar year to the extent attributable to the catastrophic coverage premium rate, divided by

(II) the number of individuals who had premium liability under this section for such taxable years.

(iii) PERCENTAGE INCREASE IN CPI.—The percentage increase in the CPI for any 12-month period shall be the percentage by which the Consumer Price Index (as defined in section 1(f)(5)) for the last month of such period exceeds such Index for the last month of the preceding 12-month period.

(4) PERCENTAGE ADJUSTMENT FOR PRESCRIPTION DRUG PREMIUM RATE.—The percentage determined under this paragraph for any calendar year shall be determined under rules similar to the rules of paragraph (3); except that—

(A) in determining the prescription drug premium rate for any calendar year before 1998, the following percentages shall be substituted for 20 percent in paragraph (3)(C)(iii)(I):

In the case of calendar year:	*The percentage is:*
1994	75
1995	50
1996	25
1997	25;

(B) no adjustment by reason of the outlay-premium percentage shall be made for any calendar year before 1998,

(C) any reference to the Medicare Catastrophic Coverage Account shall be treated as a reference to the Federal Catastrophic Drug Insurance Trust Fund, and

(D) any reference to the catastrophic coverage premium rate shall be treated as a reference to the prescription drug premium rate.

(f) DEFINITIONS AND SPECIAL RULES.—

(1) MEDICARE-ELIGIBLE INDIVIDUAL.—For purposes of this section—

(A) IN GENERAL.—Except as otherwise provided in this paragraph, the term "medicare-eligible individual" means, with respect to any month, any individual who is entitled to (or, on application without the payment of an additional premium, would be entitled to) benefits under part A of title XVIII of the Social Security Act for such month.

(B) EXCEPTIONS.—The term "medicare-eligible individual" shall not include for any month—

(i) any individual who is entitled to benefits under part A of title XVIII of the Social Security Act for such month solely by reason of the payment of a premium under section 1818 of such Act, or

(ii) any qualified nonresident.

(2) SPECIAL RULES FOR JOINT RETURNS.—In the case of a joint return—

(A) WHERE PREMIUM APPLIES TO BOTH SPOUSES.—If both spouses meet the requirements of subsection (b)(1) for the taxable year—

(i) such spouses shall be treated as 1 individual for purposes of applying this section, except that

(ii) the limitation of subsection (c)(2) shall be twice the amount which would otherwise apply.

(B) WHERE PREMIUM APPLIES TO ONLY 1 SPOUSE.—If only 1 spouse meets the requirements of subsection (b)(1) for the taxable year—

(i) this section shall be applied separately with respect to such spouse, and

(ii) the adjusted income tax liability of such spouse shall be determined under paragraph (4)—

(I) by taking into account one-half of the income tax liability determined with respect to the joint return, and

(II) by taking into account under clause (ii) of paragraph (4)(C) only amounts attributable to such spouse.

(3) SEPARATE RETURNS BY MARRIED INDIVIDUALS.—If an individual is married as of the close of the taxable year (within the meaning of section 7703) but does not file a joint return for the taxable year and such individual does not live apart from his spouse at all times during the taxable year—

(A) the limitation of subsection (c)(2) shall be twice the amount which would otherwise apply if both the individual and the spouse of the individual meet the requirement of subsection (b)(1) with respect to the calendar year in which the taxable year begins (determined without regard to subparagraph (B) of this paragraph),

(B) if such individual does not otherwise meet the requirements of subsection (b)(1), such individual shall be treated as meeting the requirements of subsection (b)(1) for the taxable year if the spouse of such individual meets such requirements with respect to the calendar year in which the taxable year begins, and

(C) in applying subparagraph (C) of paragraph (4)—

(i) the dollar limitation of clause (i) thereof shall be ½ of the amount which applies to a joint return where both spouses meet the requirements of subsection (b)(1), and

(ii) the individual shall be deemed to receive social security benefits during the taxable year in an amount not less than ½ of the aggregate social security benefits received by such individual and his spouse during the taxable year.

(4) ADJUSTED INCOME TAX LIABILITY.—For purposes of this section—

(A) IN GENERAL.—The term "adjusted income tax liability" means an amount equal to the income tax liability, reduced by the excess (if any) of—

(i) 15 percent of the governmental retiree exclusion amount (if any) determined under subparagraph (C) for the taxable year, over

(ii) the amount of the credit allowable under section 22 for the taxable year.

(B) INCOME TAX LIABILITY.—The term "income tax liability" means—

(i) the tax imposed by this chapter (determined without regard to this section), reduced by

(ii) the credits allowed under part IV of this subchapter (other than under sections 31, 33, and 34).

(C) GOVERNMENTAL RETIREE EXCLUSION AMOUNT.—The governmental retiree exclusion amount for any taxable year is the lesser of—

(i) $6,000 ($9,000 in the case of a joint return where both spouses meet the requirements of subsection (b)(1) for the taxable year), or

(ii) the amount which is received as an annuity (whether for a period certain or during 1 or more lives) under a governmental plan (as defined in the 1st sentence of section 414(d)) and which is includible in gross income under section 72 for the taxable year.

The amount determined under the preceding sentence shall be reduced by the social security benefits (as defined in section 86(d)) received during the taxable year.

(D) INDEXING.—In the case of any taxable year beginning in a calendar year after 1989, subparagraph (C)(i) shall be applied by substituting for each dollar amount contained in such subparagraph an amount equal to—

Sec. 59B—Repealed

(i) the dollar amount which would be in effect under subparagraph (C)(i) for taxable years beginning in the preceding calendar year without regard to the last sentence of this subparagraph, increased by

(ii) the cost-of-living adjustment determined under section 215(i) of the Social Security Act for the calendar year in which the taxable year begins.

Any amount determined under the preceding sentence shall be rounded to the nearest multiple of $50.

(5) QUALIFIED NONRESIDENT.—

(A) IN GENERAL.—For purposes of paragraph (1), the term "qualified nonresident" means, with respect to any month during the taxable year, any individual if—

(i) such individual is not furnished during such taxable year or any of the 4 preceding taxable years any service for which a claim for payment is made under part A of title XVIII of the Social Security Act.

(ii) such individual is not entitled to benefits under part B of title XVIII of the Social Security Act at any time during such taxable year or any of the 4 preceding taxable years, and

(iii) such individual is present in a foreign country or countries for at least 330 full days during—

(I) the 12-month period ending at the close of the taxable year, and

(II) each of the 4 consecutive preceding 12-month periods.

(B) SPECIAL RULE FOR INDIVIDUALS WHO DIE DURING THE TAXABLE YEAR.—An individual who dies during the taxable year shall be treated as meeting the requirement of subparagraph (A)(iii)(I) if such individual is present in a foreign country or countries for at least a number of full days equal to 90 percent of the days during such taxable year before the date of death.

(6) COORDINATION WITH OTHER PROVISIONS.—

(A) NOT TREATED AS MEDICAL EXPENSE.—For purposes of section 213, the supplemental premium imposed by this section for any taxable year shall not be treated as an expense paid for medical care.

(B) NOT TREATED AS TAX FOR CERTAIN PURPOSES.—The supplemental premium imposed by this section shall not be treated as a tax imposed by this chapter for purposes of determining—

(i) the amount of any credit allowable under this chapter, or

(ii) the amount of the minimum tax imposed by section 55.

(C) TREATED AS TAX FOR SUBTITLE F.—For purposes of subtitle F, the supplemental premium imposed by this section shall be treated as if it were a tax imposed by section 1.

(D) SECTION 15 NOT TO APPLY.—Section 15 shall not apply to the supplemental premium imposed by this section.

(7) SECTION NOT TO AFFECT LIABILITY TO POSSESSIONS, ETC.—This section shall not apply for purposes of determining liability to any possession of the United States. For purposes of sections 932 and 7654, the supplemental premium imposed by this section shall not be treated as a tax imposed by this chapter.

(8) SHORT TAXABLE YEARS.—In the case of a taxable year of less than 12 months, this section shall be applied under regulations prescribed by the Secretary.

• 1988, Medicare Catastrophic Coverage Act of 1988 (P.L. 100-360)

P.L. 100-360, §111(a):

Amended subchapter A of chapter 1 by adding at the end thereof new Part VIII. **Effective**, generally, for tax years beginning after 12-31-88. However, see Act Sec. 111(e)(2) and (d), below.

P.L. 100-360, §111(e)(2), provides:

(2) WAIVER OF ESTIMATED TAX REQUIREMENT FOR YEARS BEGINNING IN 1989.—In the case of a taxable year beginning in 1989, the premium imposed by section 59B of the Internal Revenue Code of 1986 (as added by this section) shall not be treated as a tax for purposes of applying section 6654 of such Code.

P.L. 100-360, §111(d) further provides:

(d) ANNOUNCEMENT OF SUPPLEMENTAL PREMIUM RATE.—In the case of calendar year 1993 or any calendar year thereafter—

(1) not later than July 1 of such calendar year, the Secretary of the Treasury or his delegate shall make an announcement of the estimated supplemental premium rate under section 59B of the Internal Revenue Code of 1986 for taxable years beginning in the following calendar year, and

(2) not later than October 1 of such calendar year, the Secretary of the Treasury or his delegate shall make an announcement of the actual supplemental premium rate under such section for such taxable years.

Subchapter B—Computation of Taxable Income

PART I—DEFINITION OF GROSS INCOME, ADJUSTED GROSS INCOME, TAXABLE INCOME, ETC.

[Sec. 61]

SEC. 61. GROSS INCOME DEFINED.

[Sec. 61(a)]

(a) GENERAL DEFINITION.—Except as otherwise provided in this subtitle, gross income means all income from whatever source derived, including (but not limited to) the following items:

(1) Compensation for services, including fees, commissions, fringe benefits, and similar items;

(2) Gross income derived from business;

(3) Gains derived from dealings in property;

(4) Interest;

(5) Rents;

(6) Royalties;

(7) Dividends;

(8) Alimony and separate maintenance payments;

(9) Annuities;

(10) Income from life insurance and endowment contracts;

(11) Pensions;

(12) Income from discharge of indebtedness;

(13) Distributive share of partnership gross income;

(14) Income in respect of a decedent; and

(15) Income from an interest in an estate or trust.

Amendments

• 2009, Supplemental Appropriations Act, 2009 (P.L. 111-32)

P.L. 111-32, §1302(h)(2), provides:

(2) FOR PURPOSES OF TAXATION.—A voucher issued under the program or any payment made for such a voucher pursuant to subsection (a)(3) shall not be considered as gross income of the purchaser of a vehicle for purposes of the Internal Revenue Code of 1986.

• 2007 (P.L. 110-141)

P.L. 110-141, §1, provides:

SECTION 1. EXCLUSION FROM INCOME FOR PAYMENTS FROM THE HOKIE SPIRIT MEMORIAL FUND.

For purposes of the Internal Revenue Code of 1986, gross income shall not include any amount received from the Virginia Polytechnic Institute & State University, out of amounts transferred from the Hokie Spirit Memorial Fund established by the Virginia Tech Foundation, an organization organized and operated as described in section 501(c)(3) of the Internal Revenue Code of 1986, if such amount is paid on account of the tragic event on April 16, 2007, at such university.

• 2006, Tax Relief and Health Care Act of 2006 (P.L. 109-432)

P.L. 109-432, Division C, §403(c) and (d)(2), provide:

(c) TAX INCENTIVE FOR SALE OF EXISTING MINERAL AND GEOTHERMAL RIGHTS TO TAX-EXEMPT ENTITIES.—

(1) EXCLUSION.—For purposes of the Internal Revenue Code of 1986, gross income shall not include 25 percent of the qualifying gain from a conservation sale of a qualifying mineral or geothermal interest.

(2) QUALIFYING GAIN.—For purposes of this subsection, the term "qualifying gain" means any gain which would be recognized as long-term capital gain under such Code.

(3) CONSERVATION SALE.—For purposes of this subsection, the term "conservation sale" means a sale which meets the following requirements:

(A) TRANSFEREE IS AN ELIGIBLE ENTITY.—The transferee of the qualifying mineral or geothermal interest is an eligible entity.

(B) QUALIFYING LETTER OF INTENT REQUIRED.—At the time of the sale, such transferee provides the taxpayer with a qualifying letter of intent.

(C) NONAPPLICATION TO CERTAIN SALES.—The sale is not made pursuant to an order of condemnation or eminent domain.

(4) QUALIFYING MINERAL OR GEOTHERMAL INTEREST.—For purposes of this subsection—

(A) IN GENERAL.—The term "qualifying mineral or geothermal interest" means an interest in any mineral or geothermal deposit located on eligible Federal land which constitutes a taxpayer's entire interest in such deposit.

(B) ENTIRE INTEREST.—For purposes of subparagraph (A)—

(i) an interest in any mineral or geothermal deposit is not a taxpayer's entire interest if such interest in such mineral or geothermal deposit was divided in order to avoid the requirements of such subparagraph or section 170(f)(3)(A) of such Code, and

(ii) a taxpayer's entire interest in such deposit does not fail to satisfy such subparagraph solely because the taxpayer has retained an interest in other deposits, even if the other deposits are contiguous with such certain deposit and were acquired by the taxpayer along with such certain deposit in a single conveyance.

(5) OTHER DEFINITIONS.—For purposes of this subsection—

(A) ELIGIBLE ENTITY.—The term "eligible entity" means—

(i) a governmental unit referred to in section 170(c)(1) of such Code, or an agency or department thereof operated primarily for 1 or more of the conservation purposes specified in clause (i), (ii), or (iii) of section 170(h)(4)(A) of such Code, or

(ii) an entity which is—

(I) described in section 170(b)(1)(A)(vi) or section 170(h)(3)(B) of such Code, and

(II) organized and at all times operated primarily for 1 or more of the conservation purposes specified in clause (i), (ii), or (iii) of section 170(h)(4)(A) of such Code.

(B) QUALIFYING LETTER OF INTENT.—The term "qualifying letter of intent" means a written letter of intent which includes the following statement: "The transferee's intent is that this acquisition will serve 1 or more of the conservation purposes specified in clause (i), (ii), or (iii) of section 170(h)(4)(A) of the Internal Revenue Code of 1986, that the transferee's use of the deposits so acquired will be consistent with section 170(h)(5) of such Code, and that the use of the deposits will continue to be consistent with such section, even if ownership or possession of such deposits is subsequently transferred to another person.".

(6) TAX ON SUBSEQUENT TRANSFERS.—

(A) IN GENERAL.—A tax is hereby imposed on any subsequent transfer by an eligible entity of ownership or possession, whether by sale, exchange, or lease, of an interest acquired directly or indirectly in—

(i) a conservation sale described in paragraph (1), or

(ii) a transfer described in clause (i), (ii), or (iii) of subparagraph (D).

(B) AMOUNT OF TAX.—The amount of tax imposed by subparagraph (A) on any transfer shall be equal to the sum of—

(i) 20 percent of the fair market value (determined at the time of the transfer) of the interest the ownership or possession of which is transferred, plus

(ii) the product of—

(I) the highest rate of tax specified in section 11 of such Code, times

(II) any gain or income realized by the transferor as a result of the transfer.

(C) LIABILITY.—The tax imposed by subparagraph (A) shall be paid by the transferor.

(D) RELIEF FROM LIABILITY.—The person (otherwise liable for any tax imposed by subparagraph (A)) shall be relieved of liability for the tax imposed by subparagraph (A) with respect to any transfer if—

(i) the transferee is an eligible entity which provides such person, at the time of transfer, a qualifying letter of intent,

(ii) in any case where the transferee is not an eligible entity, it is established to the satisfaction of the Secretary of the Treasury, that the transfer of ownership or possession, as the case may be, will be consistent with section 170(h)(5) of such Code, and the transferee provides such person, at the time of transfer, a qualifying letter of intent, or

(iii) tax has previously been paid under this paragraph as a result of a prior transfer of ownership or possession of the same interest.

(E) ADMINISTRATIVE PROVISIONS.—For purposes of subtitle F of such Code, the taxes imposed by this paragraph shall be treated as excise taxes with respect to which the deficiency procedures of such subtitle apply.

(7) REPORTING.—The Secretary of the Treasury may require such reporting as may be necessary or appropriate to further the purpose under this subsection that any conservation use be in perpetuity.

(d) EFFECTIVE DATES.—

* * *

(2) TAX INCENTIVE.—Subsection (c) shall apply to sales occurring on or after the date of the enactment of this Act.

• 2005, Katrina Emergency Tax Relief Act of 2005 (P.L. 109-73)

P.L. 109-73, §304 [but see P.L. 110-343, Division C, §702, in the amendment notes for Code Sec. 1400N(a)], provides:

SEC. 304. MILEAGE REIMBURSEMENTS TO CHARITABLE VOLUNTEERS EXCLUDED FROM GROSS INCOME.

(a) IN GENERAL.—For purposes of the Internal Revenue Code of 1986, gross income of an individual for taxable years ending on or after August 25, 2005, does not include amounts received, from an organization described in section 170(c) of such Code, as reimbursement of operating expenses with respect to use of a passenger automobile for the benefit of such organization in connection with providing relief relating to Hurricane Katrina during the period beginning on August 25, 2005, and ending on December 31, 2006. The preceding sentence shall apply only to the extent that the expenses which are reimbursed would be deductible under chapter 1 of such Code if section 274(d) of such Code were applied—

(1) by using the standard business mileage rate in effect under section 162(a) at the time of such use, and

(2) as if the individual were an employee of an organization not described in section 170(c) of such Code.

(b) APPLICATION TO VOLUNTEER SERVICES ONLY.— Subsection (a) shall not apply with respect to any expenses relating to the performance of services for compensation.

(c) NO DOUBLE BENEFIT.—No deduction or credit shall be allowed under any other provision of such Code with respect to the expenses excludable from gross income under subsection (a).

P.L. 109-73, §401 [but see P.L. 110-343, Division C, §702, in the amendment notes for Code Sec. 1400N(a)], provides:

SEC. 401. EXCLUSIONS OF CERTAIN CANCELLATIONS OF INDEBTEDNESS BY REASON OF HURRICANE KATRINA.

(a) IN GENERAL.—For purposes of the Internal Revenue Code of 1986, gross income shall not include any amount which (but for this section) would be includible in gross income by reason of the discharge (in whole or in part) of indebtedness of a natural person described in subsection (b) by an applicable entity (as defined in section 6050P(c)(1) of such Code).

(b) PERSONS DESCRIBED.—A natural person is described in this subsection if the principal place of abode of such person on August 25, 2005, was located—

(1) in the core disaster area, or

(2) in the Hurricane Katrina disaster area (but outside the core disaster area) and such person suffered economic loss by reason of Hurricane Katrina.

(c) EXCEPTIONS.—

(1) BUSINESS INDEBTEDNESS.—Subsection (a) shall not apply to any indebtedness incurred in connection with a trade or business.

(2) REAL PROPERTY OUTSIDE CORE DISASTER AREA.—Subsection (a) shall not apply to any discharge of indebtedness to the extent that real property constituting security for such indebtedness is located outside of the Hurricane Katrina disaster area.

(d) DENIAL OF DOUBLE BENEFIT.—For purposes of the Internal Revenue Code of 1986, the amount excluded from gross income under subsection (a) shall be treated in the same manner as an amount excluded under section 108(a) of such Code.

(e) EFFECTIVE DATE.—This section shall apply to discharges made on or after August 25, 2005, and before January 1, 2007.

• 2002, Victims of Terrorism Tax Relief Act of 2001 (P.L. 107-134)

P.L. 107-134, §105, provides:

SEC. 105. EXCLUSION OF CERTAIN CANCELLATIONS OF INDEBTEDNESS.

(a) IN GENERAL.—For purposes of the Internal Revenue Code of 1986—

(1) gross income shall not include any amount which (but for this section) would be includible in gross income by reason of the discharge (in whole or in part) of indebtedness of any taxpayer if the discharge is by reason of the death of an individual incurred as the result of the terrorist attacks against the United States on September 11, 2001, or as the result of illness incurred as a result of an attack involving anthrax occurring on or after September 11, 2001, and before January 1, 2002; and

(2) return requirements under section 6050P of such Code shall not apply to any discharge described in paragraph (1).

(b) EFFECTIVE DATE.—This section shall apply to discharges made on or after September 11, 2001, and before January 1, 2002.

• 1984, Deficit Reduction Act of 1984 (P.L. 98-369)

P.L. 98-369, §531(c):

Amended Code Sec. 61(a) by striking out "commissions, and similar items" and inserting in lieu thereof "commissions, fringe benefits, and similar items". **Effective** 1-1-85.

P.L. 98-369, §531(h), as amended by P.L. 99-272, §13207(d), provides:

(h) Moratorium on Issuance of Regulations Relating to Faculty Housing.—

(1) In General.—Any regulation providing for the inclusion in gross income under section 61 of the Internal Revenue Code of 1954 of the excess (if any) of the fair market value of qualified campus lodging over the greater of—

(A) the operating costs paid or incurred in furnishing such lodging, or

(B) the rent received for such lodging, shall not be issued before January 1, 1986.

(2) Qualified Campus Lodging.—For purposes of this subsection, the term "qualified campus lodging" means lodging which is—

(A) located on (or in close proximity to) a campus of an educational institution (described in section 170(b)(1)(A)(ii) of the Internal Revenue Code of 1954), and

(B) provided by such institution to an employee of such institution, or to a spouse or dependent (within the meaning of section 152 of such Code) of such employee.

(3) Application of Subsection.—This subsection shall apply with respect to lodging furnished after December 31, 1983, and before January 1, 1986.

P.L. 98-369, §1026, provides:

SEC. 1026. NO GAIN RECOGNIZED FROM NET GIFTS MADE BEFORE MARCH 4, 1981.

(a) In General.—In the case of any transfer of property subject to gift tax made before March 4, 1981, for purposes of subtitle A of the Internal Revenue Code of 1954, gross income of the donor shall not include any amount attributable to the donee's payment of (or agreement to pay) any gift tax imposed with respect to such gift.

(b) Gift Tax Defined.—For purposes of subsection (a), the term "gift tax" means—

(1) the tax imposed by chapter 12 of such Code, and

(2) any tax imposed by a State (or the District of Columbia) on transfers by gifts.

(c) Statute of Limitations.—If refund or credit of any overpayment of tax resulting from subsection (a) is prevented on the date of the enactment of this Act (or at any time within 1 year after such date) by the operation of any law or rule of law (including res judicata), refund or credit of such overpayment (to the extent attributable to subsection (a)) may nevertheless be made or allowed if claim therefor is filed within 1 year after the date of the enactment of this Act.

P.L. 95-427, §1, as amended by P.L. 97-34, §801, and P.L. 96-167, §1, provides:

SEC. 1. FRINGE BENEFIT REGULATIONS.

(a) In General.—No fringe benefit regulation shall be issued—

(1) in final form on or after May 1, 1978, and on or before December 31, 1983, or

(2) in proposed or final form on or after May 1, 1978, if such regulation has an effective date on or before December 31, 1983.

(b) Definition of Fringe Benefit Regulation.—For purposes of subsection (a), the term "fringe benefit regulation" means a regulation providing for the inclusion of any fringe benefit in gross income by reason of section 61 of the Internal Revenue Code of 1954.

[Sec. 61(b)]

(b) Cross References.—

For items specifically included in gross income, see part II (sec. 71 and following). For items specifically excluded from gross income, see part III (sec. 101 and following).

[Sec. 62]

SEC. 62. ADJUSTED GROSS INCOME DEFINED.

[Sec. 62(a)]

(a) General Rule.—For purposes of this subtitle, the term "adjusted gross income" means, in the case of an individual, gross income minus the following deductions:

(1) Trade and business deductions.—The deductions allowed by this chapter (other than by part VII of this subchapter) which are attributable to a trade or business carried on by the taxpayer, if such trade or business does not consist of the performance of services by the taxpayer as an employee.

(2) Certain trade and business deductions of employees.—

(A) Reimbursed expenses of employees.—The deductions allowed by part VI (section 161 and following) which consist of expenses paid or incurred by the taxpayer, in connection with the performance by him of services as an employee, under a reimbursement or other expense allowance arrangement with his employer. The fact that the reimbursement may be provided by a third party shall not be determinative of whether or not the preceding sentence applies.

(B) Certain expenses of performing artists.—The deductions allowed by section 162 which consist of expenses paid or incurred by a qualified performing artist in connection with the performances by him of services in the performing arts as an employee.

(C) Certain expenses of officials.—The deductions allowed by section 162 which consist of expenses paid or incurred with respect to services performed by an official as an employee of a State or a political subdivision thereof in a position compensated in whole or in part on a fee basis.

(D) Certain expenses of elementary and secondary school teachers.—In the case of taxable years beginning during 2002, 2003, 2004, 2005, 2006, 2007, 2008, or 2009, the deductions allowed by section 162 which consist of expenses, not in excess of $250, paid or incurred by an eligible educator in connection with books, supplies (other than nonathletic supplies for courses of instruction in health or physical education), computer equipment (including related software and services) and other equipment, and supplementary materials used by the eligible educator in the classroom.

(E) Certain expenses of members of reserve components of the armed forces of the united states.—The deductions allowed by section 162 which consist of expenses, determined at a rate not in excess of the rates for travel expenses (including per diem in lieu of subsistence) authorized for employees of agencies under subchapter I of chapter 57 of title 5, United States Code, paid or incurred by the taxpayer in connection with the performance of services by such taxpayer as a member of a reserve component of the Armed Forces of the United States for any period during which such individual is more than 100 miles away from home in connection with such services.

(3) Losses from sale or exchange of property.—The deductions allowed by part VI (sec. 161 and following) as losses from the sale or exchange of property.

(4) Deductions attributable to rents and royalties.—The deductions allowed by part VI (sec. 161 and following), by section 212 (relating to expenses for production of income), and by

section 611 (relating to depletion) which are attributable to property held for the production of rents or royalties.

(5) CERTAIN DEDUCTIONS OF LIFE TENANTS AND INCOME BENEFICIARIES OF PROPERTY.—In the case of a life tenant of property, or an income beneficiary of property held in trust, or an heir, legatee, or devisee of an estate, the deduction for depreciation allowed by section 167 and the deduction allowed by section 611.

(6) PENSION, PROFIT-SHARING AND ANNUITY PLANS OF SELF-EMPLOYED INDIVIDUALS.—In the case of an individual who is an employee within the meaning of section 401(c)(1), the deduction allowed by section 404.

(7) RETIREMENT SAVINGS.—The deduction allowed by section 219 (relating to deduction for certain retirement savings).

(8) [Repealed.]

(9) PENALTIES FORFEITED BECAUSE OF PREMATURE WITHDRAWAL OF FUNDS FROM TIME SAVINGS ACCOUNTS OR DEPOSITS.—The deductions allowed by section 165 for losses incurred in any transaction entered into for profit, though not connected with a trade or business to the extent that such losses include amounts forfeited to a bank, mutual savings bank, savings and loan association, building and loan association, cooperative bank or homestead association as a penalty for premature withdrawal of funds from a time savings account, certificate of deposit, or similar class of deposit.

(10) ALIMONY.—The deduction allowed by section 215.

(11) REFORESTATION EXPENSES.—The deduction allowed by section 194.

(12) CERTAIN REQUIRED REPAYMENTS OF SUPPLEMENTAL UNEMPLOYMENT COMPENSATION BENEFITS.—The deduction allowed by section 165 for the repayment to a trust described in paragraph (9) or (17) of section 501(c) of supplemental unemployment compensation benefits received from such trust if such repayment is required because of the receipt of trade readjustment allowances under section 231 or 232 of the Trade Act of 1974 (19 U.S.C. 2291 and 2292).

(13) JURY DUTY PAY REMITTED TO EMPLOYER.—Any deduction allowable under this chapter by reason of an individual remitting any portion of any jury pay to such individual's employer in exchange for payment by the employer of compensation for the period such individual was performing jury duty. For purposes of the preceding sentence, the term "jury pay" means any payment received by the individual for the discharge of jury duty.

(14) DEDUCTION FOR CLEAN-FUEL VEHICLES AND CERTAIN REFUELING PROPERTY.—The deduction allowed by section 179A.

(15) MOVING EXPENSES.—The deduction allowed by section 217.

(16) ARCHER MSAS.—The deduction allowed by section 220.

(17) INTEREST ON EDUCATION LOANS.—The deduction allowed by section 221.

➤➤➤ Caution: Code Sec. 62(a)(18), below, is subject to the sunset provision of the Economic Growth and Tax Relief Reconciliation Act of 2001 (P.L. 107-16), §901. Absent Congressional action, the changes made to this provision by P.L. 107-16, or that take effect as if included in P.L. 107-16, do not apply after December 31, 2010. For more information about the sunset provision, see page XXI of the Preface to this publication and P.L. 107-16, §901, in the amendment notes. See the amendments notes for a history of amendments to this section and the effective date of each change.

(18) HIGHER EDUCATION EXPENSES.—The deduction allowed by section 222.

(19) HEALTH SAVINGS ACCOUNTS.—The deduction allowed by section 223.

(20) COSTS INVOLVING DISCRIMINATION SUITS, ETC.—Any deduction allowable under this chapter for attorney fees and court costs paid by, or on behalf of, the taxpayer in connection with any action involving a claim of unlawful discrimination (as defined in subsection (e)) or a claim of a violation of subchapter III of chapter 37 of title 31, United States Code or a claim made under section 1862(b)(3)(A) of the Social Security Act (42 U.S.C. 1395y(b)(3)(A)). The preceding sentence shall not apply to any deduction in excess of the amount includible in the taxpayer's gross income for the taxable year on account of a judgment or settlement (whether by suit or agreement and whether as lump sum or periodic payments) resulting from such claim.

(21) ATTORNEYS FEES RELATING TO AWARDS TO WHISTLEBLOWERS.—Any deduction allowable under this chapter for attorney fees and court costs paid by, or on behalf of, the taxpayer in connection with any award under section 7623(b) (relating to awards to whistleblowers). The preceding sentence shall not apply to any deduction in excess of the amount includible in the taxpayer's gross income for the taxable year on account of such award.

Nothing in this section shall permit the same item to be deducted more than once.

Amendments

• 2008, Tax Extenders and Alternative Minimum Tax Relief Act of 2008 (P.L. 110-343)

P.L. 110-343, Division C, §203(a):

Amended Code Sec. 62(a)(2)(D) by striking "or 2007" and inserting "2007, 2008, or 2009". **Effective** for tax years beginning after 12-31-2007.

• 2006, Tax Relief and Health Care Act of 2006 (P.L. 109-432)

P.L. 109-432, Division A, §108(a):

Amended Code Sec. 62(a)(2)(D) by striking "or 2005" and inserting "2005, 2006, or 2007". **Effective** for tax years beginning after 12-31-2005.

P.L. 109-432, Division A, §406(a)(3):

Amended Code Sec. 62(a) by inserting after paragraph (20) a new paragraph (21). **Effective** for information provided on or after 12-20-2006.

• 2005, Gulf Opportunity Zone Act of 2005 (P.L. 109-135)

P.L. 109-135, §412(q)(1)(A)-(B):

Amended Code Sec. 62(a) by redesignating paragraph (19), as added by P.L. 108-357, §703, as paragraph (20), and by moving such paragraph after paragraph (19) (relating to health savings accounts). **Effective** 12-21-2005.

• 2004, American Jobs Creation Act of 2004 (P.L. 108-357)

P.L. 108-357, §703(a):

Amended Code Sec. 62(a) by inserting after paragraph (18)[(19)]a new paragraph (19)[(20)]. **Effective** for fees and costs paid after 10-22-2004 with respect to any judgment or settlement occurring after such date.

• 2004, Working Families Tax Relief Act of 2004 (P.L. 108-311)

P.L. 108-311, §307(a):

Amended Code Sec. 62(a)(2)(D) by striking "or 2003" and inserting ", 2003, 2004, or 2005". **Effective** for expenses paid or incurred in tax years beginning after 12-31-2003.

• 2003, Medicare Prescription Drug, Improvement, and Modernization Act of 2003 (P.L. 108-173)

P.L. 108-173, §1201(b):

Amended Code Sec. 62(a) by inserting after paragraph (18) a new paragraph (19). **Effective** for tax years beginning after 12-31-2003.

• 2003, Military Family Tax Relief Act of 2003 (P.L. 108-121)

P.L. 108-121, §109(b):

Amended Code Sec. 62(a)(2) by adding at the end a new subparagraph (E). **Effective** for amounts paid or incurred in tax years beginning after 12-31-2002.

• 2002, Job Creation and Worker Assistance Act of 2002 (P.L. 107-147)

P.L. 107-147, §406(a):

Amended Code Sec. 62(a)(2) by adding at the end a new subparagraph (D). **Effective** for tax years beginning after 12-31-2001.

• 2001, Economic Growth and Tax Relief Reconciliation Act of 2001 (P.L. 107-16)

P.L. 107-16, §431(b):

Amended Code Sec. 62(a) by inserting after paragraph (17) a new paragraph (18). **Effective** for payments made in tax years beginning after 12-31-2001.

P.L. 107-16, §901(a)-(b), provides:

SEC. 901. SUNSET OF PROVISIONS OF ACT.

(a) IN GENERAL.—All provisions of, and amendments made by, this Act shall not apply—

(1) to taxable, plan, or limitation years beginning after December 31, 2010, or

(2) in the case of title V, to estates of decedents dying, gifts made, or generation skipping transfers, after December 31, 2010.

(b) APPLICATION OF CERTAIN LAWS.—The Internal Revenue Code of 1986 and the Employee Retirement Income Security Act of 1974 shall be applied and administered to years, estates, gifts, and transfers described in subsection (a) as if the provisions and amendments described in subsection (a) had never been enacted.

• 2000, Community Renewal Tax Relief Act of 2000 (P.L. 106-554)

P.L. 106-554, §202(b)(1):

Amended Code Sec. 62(a)(16). **Effective** on 12-21-2000. Prior to amendment, Code Sec. 62(a)(16) read as follows:

(16) MEDICAL SAVINGS ACCOUNTS.—The deduction allowed by section 220.

• 1997, Taxpayer Relief Act of 1997 (P.L. 105-34)

P.L. 105-34, §202(b):

Amended Code Sec. 62(a) by inserting after paragraph (16) a new paragraph (17). **Effective** for any qualified education loan (as defined in Code Sec. 221(e)(1), as added by Act. Sec. 202) incurred on, before, or after 8-5-97, but only with respect to (1) any loan interest payment due and paid after 12-31-97, and (2) the portion of the 60-month period referred to in Code Sec. 221(d) (as added by Act Sec. 202) after 12-31-97.

P.L. 105-34, §975(a):

Amended Code Sec. 62(a)(2) by adding at the end a new subparagraph (C). **Effective** for expenses paid or incurred in tax years beginning after 12-31-86.

• 1996, Health Insurance Portability and Accountability Act of 1996 (P.L. 104-191)

P.L. 104-191, §301(b):

Amended Code Sec. 62(a) by inserting after paragraph (15) a new paragraph (16). **Effective** for tax years beginning after 12-31-96.

• 1996, Small Business Job Protection Act (P.L. 104-188)

P.L. 104-188, §1401(b)(4):

Repealed Code Sec. 62(a)(8). **Effective**, generally, for tax years beginning after 12-31-99. For a special transition rule, see Act Sec. 1401(c)(2) in the amendment notes following Code Sec. 402(d). Prior to repeal, Code Sec. 62(a)(8) read as follows:

(8) CERTAIN PORTION OF LUMP-SUM DISTRIBUTIONS FROM PENSION PLANS TAXED UNDER SECTION 402(d).—The deduction allowed by section 402(d)(3).

• 1993, Omnibus Budget Reconciliation Act of 1993 (P.L. 103-66)

P.L. 103-66, §13213(c)(1):

Amended Code Sec. 62(a) by adding at the end thereof paragraph (15). **Effective** for expenses incurred after 12-31-93.

• 1992, Energy Policy Act of 1992 (P.L. 102-486)

P.L. 102-486, §1913(a)(2):

Amended Code Sec. 62(a) by inserting after paragraph (13) new paragraph (14). **Effective** for property placed in service after 6-30-93.

• 1992, Unemployment Compensation Amendments of 1992 (P.L. 102-318)

P.L. 102-318, §521(b)(2):

Amended Code Sec. 62(a)(8) by striking "402(e)" in the text and heading and inserting "402(d)". **Effective** for distributions after 12-31-92.

• 1990, Omnibus Budget Reconciliation Act of 1990 (P.L. 101-508)

P.L. 101-508, §11802(e)(1):

Amended Code Sec. 62(a)(13). **Effective** 11-5-90. Prior to amendment, Code Sec. 62(a)(13) read as follows:

(13) JURY DUTY PAY REMITTED TO EMPLOYER.—The deduction allowed by section 220.

P.L. 101-508, §11821(b), provides:

(b) SAVINGS PROVISION.—If—

(1) any provision amended or repealed by this part applied to—

(A) any transaction occurring before the date of the enactment of this Act,

(B) any property acquired before such date of enactment, or

(C) any item of income, loss, deduction, or credit taken into account before such date of enactment, and

(2) the treatment of such transaction, property, or item under such provision would (without regard to the amendments made by this part) affect liability for tax for periods ending after such date of enactment,

nothing in the amendments made by this part shall be construed to affect the treatment of such transaction, property, or item for purposes of determining liability for tax for periods ending after such date of enactment.

• 1988, Technical and Miscellaneous Revenue Act of 1988 (P.L. 100-647)

P.L. 100-647, §1001(b)(3)(A):

Amended Code Sec. 62(a)(2)(A) by adding at the end thereof a new sentence. **Effective** as if included in the provision of P.L. 99-514 to which it relates.

P.L. 100-647, §6007(b):

Amended Code Sec. 62(a) by inserting after paragraph (12) a new paragraph (13). **Effective** as if included in the amendments made by Act Sec. 132 of P.L. 99-514.

• 1986, Tax Reform Act of 1986 (P.L. 99-514)

P.L. 99-514, §131(b)(1):

Amended Code Sec. 62 by striking out paragraph (16). **Effective** for tax years beginning after 12-31-86. Prior to amendment, Code Sec. 62(16) read as follows:

(16) DEDUCTION FOR TWO-EARNER MARRIED COUPLES.—The deduction allowed by section 221.

P.L. 99-514, §132(b)(1):

Amended Code Sec. 62(2). **Effective** for tax years beginning after 12-31-86. Prior to amendment, Code Sec. 62(2) read as follows:

(2) TRADE AND BUSINESS DEDUCTIONS OF EMPLOYEES.—

(A) REIMBURSED EXPENSES.—The deductions allowed by part VI (sec. 161 and following) which consist of expenses paid or incurred by the taxpayer, in connection with the performance by him of services as an employee, under a reimbursement or other expense allowance arrangement with his employer.

(B) EXPENSES FOR TRAVEL AWAY FROM HOME.—The deductions allowed by part VI (sec. 161 and following) which consist of expenses of travel, meals and lodging while away from home, paid or incurred by the taxpayer in connection with the performance by him of services as an employee.

(C) TRANSPORTATION EXPENSES.—The deductions allowed by part VI (sec. 161 and following) which consist of expenses of transportation paid or incurred by the taxpayer in connection with the performance by him of services as an employee.

(D) OUTSIDE SALESMEN.—The deductions allowed by part VI (sec. 161 and following) which are attributable to a trade or business carried on by the taxpayer, if such trade or business consists of the performance of services by the taxpayer as an employee and if such trade or business is to solicit, away from the employer's place of business, business for the employer.

P.L. 99-514, §132(b)(2)(A)-(B):

Amended Code Sec. 62 by striking out "For purposes of this subtitle" and inserting in lieu thereof "(a) General Rule.—For purposes of this subtitle", and by adding at the end thereof new subsection (b). **Effective** for tax years beginning after 12-31-86.

P.L. 99-514, §132(c):

Amended Code Sec. 62(a) (as amended by subsection (b)) by striking out paragraph (8). **Effective** for tax years beginning after 12-31-86. Prior to amendment, paragraph (8) read as follows:

(8) MOVING EXPENSE DEDUCTION.—The deduction allowed by section 217.

P.L. 99-514, §301(b)(1):

Amended Code Sec. 62(a), as amended by Act Sec. 132, by striking out paragraph (3) and redesignating paragraphs (4), (5), (6), (7), (10), (11), (12), (13), (14), and (15) as paragraphs (3) through (12), respectively. **Effective** for tax years beginning after 12-31-86. Prior to amendment, Code Sec. 62(a)(3) read as follows:

(3) LONG-TERM CAPITAL GAINS.—The deduction allowed by section 1202.

P.L. 99-514, §1875(c)(3):

Amended Code Sec. 62(7) by striking out "to the extent attributable to contributions made on behalf of such individual". **Effective** as if included in the amendments made by P.L. 97-248, §238. Prior to amendment, Code Sec. 62(7) read as follows:

(7) PENSION, PROFIT-SHARING AND ANNUITY PLANS OF SELF-EMPLOYED INDIVIDUALS.—In the case of an individual who is an employee within the meaning of section 401(c)(1), the deduction allowed by section 404 to the extent attributable to contributions made on behalf of such individual.

• 1984, Deficit Reduction Act of 1984 (P.L. 98-369)

P.L. 98-369, §491(d)(2)(A)-(B):

Amended Code Sec. 62(7) by striking out "the deductions allowed by section 404 and section 405(c)" and inserting in lieu thereof "the deduction allowed by section 404", and by striking out "ANNUITY, AND BOND PURCHASE" in the heading and inserting in lieu thereof "AND ANNUITY". **Effective** for obligations issued after 12-31-83.

• 1982, Subchapter S Revision Act of 1982 (P.L. 37-354)

P.L. 97-354, §5(a)(17):

Repealed Code Sec. 62(9). **Effective** for years beginning on or after 1-1-84.

• 1981, Economic Recovery Tax Act of 1981 (P.L. 97-34)

P.L. 97-34, §103(b):

Amended Code Sec. 62, as amended by P.L. 97-34, §112(b)(2), by inserting after paragraph (15) new paragraph (16). **Effective** for tax years beginning after 12-31-81.

P.L. 97-34, §112(b)(2):

Amended Code Sec. 62 by striking out paragraph (14) and redesignating paragraphs (15) and (16) as paragraphs (14) and (15), respectively. **Effective** with respect to tax years beginning after 12-31-81. Prior to amendment, former paragraph (14) read as follows:

(14) DEDUCTION FOR CERTAIN EXPENSES OF LIVING ABROAD.—The deduction allowed by section 913.

P.L. 97-34, §311(h)(1):

Amended Code Sec. 62(10) by striking out "and the deduction allowed by section 220 (relating to retirement savings for certain married individuals)". **Effective** for tax years beginning after 12-31-81. The transitional rule provides that, for purposes of the 1954 Code, any amount allowed as a deduction under section 220 of the Code (as in effect before its repeal by P.L. 97-34) shall be treated as if it were allowed by Code Sec. 219.

• 1980, (P.L. 96-608)

P.L. 96-608, §3(a):

Amended Code Sec. 62 by adding paragraph (16). **Effective** with respect to repayments made in tax years beginning after 12-38-80.

• 1980, Recreational Boating Safety and Facilities Improvement Act of 1980 (P.L. 96-451)

P.L. 96-451, §301(b):

Amended Code Sec. 62 by inserting after paragraph (14) "(15) REFORESTATION EXPENSES.—The deduction allowed by section 194.". **Effective** with respect to additions to capital accounts made after 12-31-79. [Note: An earlier Code Section 194 was enacted by P.L. 96-364, enacted on 9-26-80.—CCH.]

• 1978, Tax Treatment Extension Act of 1978 (P.L. 95-615)

P.L. 95-615, §§203(b), 209:

Added Code Sec. 62(14). **Effective** as provided in Act Sec. 209, below.

P.L. 95-615, §209, provides:

ACT SEC. 209. EFFECTIVE DATES.

(a) GENERAL RULE.—Except as provided in subsections (b) and (c) the amendments made by this title shall apply to taxable years beginning after December 31, 1977.

* * *

(c) ELECTION OF PRIOR LAW.

(1) A taxpayer may elect not to have the amendments made by this title apply with respect to any taxable year beginning after December 31, 1977, and before January 1, 1979.

(2) An election under this subsection shall be filed with a taxpayer's timely filed return for the first taxable year beginning after December 31, 1977.

• 1976, Tax Reform Act of 1976 (P.L. 94-455)

P.L. 94-455, §502(a):

Added a new paragraph (13) to Code Sec. 62. **Effective** for tax years beginning after 12-31-76.

P.L. 94-455, §1501(b)(1):

Amended Code Sec. 62(10) by inserting before the period the following: "and the deduction allowed by section 220 (relating to retirement savings for certain married individuals)." **Effective** for tax years beginning after 12-31-76.

P.L. 94-455, §1901(a)(8)-(9):

Amended Code Sec. 62 by redesignating paragraph (11), as added by P.L. 93-483, as paragraph (12), and amended Code Sec. 62(12), as redesignated above, by striking out the comma after "business." **Effective** for tax years beginning after 12-31-76.

• 1974 (P.L. 93-483)

P. L. 93-483, §6:

Amended Code Sec. 62 by adding paragraph (12). [P. L. 93-483 actually designated the new paragraph as paragraph (11)—presumably overlooking the fact that a paragraph (11) had been previously added by P. L. 93-406.—CCH.] **Effective** for tax years beginning after 12-31-72.

• 1974, Employee Retirement Income Security Act of 1974 (P.L. 93-406)

P. L. 93-406, §2002(a)(2):

Added subparagraph (10). **Effective** for tax years beginning after 12-31-74.

P. L. 93-406, §2005(c)(9):

Amended Code Sec. 62 by adding subparagraph (11). **Effective** for payments made after 1973, in tax years beginning after 1973.

• 1969, Tax Reform Act of 1969 (P.L. 91-172)

P. L. 91-172, §531(b):

Added Code Sec. 62(9). **Effective** for tax years of electing small business corporations beginning after 12-31-70.

• 1964, Revenue Act of 1964 (P.L. 88-272)

P. L. 88-272, §213(b):

Amended Code Sec. 62 by adding new paragraph (8). **Effective** 1-1-64.

• 1962, Self-Employed Individuals Tax Retirement Act of 1962 (P.L. 87-792)

P. L. 87-792, §7:

Amended Code Sec. 62 by adding new paragraph (7). **Effective** 1-1-63.

[Sec. 62(b)]

(b) QUALIFIED PERFORMING ARTIST.—

(1) IN GENERAL.—For purposes of subsection (a)(2)(B), the term "qualified performing artist" means, with respect to any taxable year, any individual if—

(A) such individual performed services in the performing arts as an employee during the taxable year for at least 2 employers,

(B) the aggregate amount allowable as a deduction under section 162 in connection with the performance of such services exceeds 10 percent of such individual's gross income attributable to the performance of such services, and

(C) the adjusted gross income of such individual for the taxable year (determined without regard to subsection (a)(2)(B)) does not exceed $16,000.

(2) NOMINAL EMPLOYER NOT TAKEN INTO ACCOUNT.—An individual shall not be treated as performing services in the performing arts as an employee for any employer during any taxable year unless the amount received by such individual from such employer for the performance of such services during the taxable year equals or exceeds $200.

(3) SPECIAL RULES FOR MARRIED COUPLES.—

(A) IN GENERAL.—Except in the case of a husband and wife who lived apart at all times during the taxable year, if the taxpayer is married at the close of the taxable year, subsection (a)(2)(B) shall apply only if the taxpayer and his spouse file a joint return for the taxable year.

(B) APPLICATION OF PARAGRAPH (1).—In the case of a joint return—

(i) paragraph (1) (other than subparagraph (C) thereof) shall be applied separately with respect to each spouse, but

(ii) paragraph (1)(C) shall be applied with respect to their combined adjusted gross income.

(C) DETERMINATION OF MARITAL STATUS.—For purposes of this subsection, marital status shall be determined under section 7703(a).

(D) JOINT RETURN.—For purposes of this subsection, the term "joint return" means the joint return of a husband and wife made under section 6013.

Amendments

• 1986, Tax Reform Act of 1986 (P.L. 99-514)

P.L. 99-514, §132(b)(2)(A)-(B):

Amended Code Sec. 62 by striking out "For purposes of this subtitle" and inserting in lieu thereof "(a) General Rule.—For purposes of this subtitle", and by adding at the end thereof new subsection (b). **Effective** for tax years beginning after 12-31-86.

[Sec. 62(c)]

(c) CERTAIN ARRANGEMENTS NOT TREATED AS REIMBURSEMENT ARRANGEMENTS.—For purposes of subsection (a)(2)(A), an arrangement shall in no event be treated as a reimbursement or other expense allowance arrangement if—

(1) such arrangement does not require the employee to substantiate the expenses covered by the arrangement to the person providing the reimbursement, or

(2) such arrangement provides the employee the right to retain any amount in excess of the substantiated expenses covered under the arrangement.

The substantiation requirements of the preceding sentence shall not apply to any expense to the extent that substantiation is not required under section 274(d) for such expense by reason of the regulations prescribed under the 2nd sentence thereof.

Amendments

• 1988, Family Support Act of 1988 (P.L. 100-485)

P.L. 100-485, §702(a):

Amended Code Sec. 62 by adding at the end thereof new subsection (c). **Effective** to tax years beginning after 12-31-88.

[Sec. 62(d)]

(d) DEFINITION; SPECIAL RULES.—

(1) ELIGIBLE EDUCATOR.—

(A) IN GENERAL.—For purposes of subsection (a)(2)(D), the term "eligible educator" means, with respect to any taxable year, an individual who is a kindergarten through grade 12 teacher, instructor, counselor, principal, or aide in a school for at least 900 hours during a school year.

(B) SCHOOL.—The term "school" means any school which provides elementary education or secondary education (kindergarten through grade 12), as determined under State law.

(2) COORDINATION WITH EXCLUSIONS.—A deduction shall be allowed under subsection (a)(2)(D) for expenses only to the extent the amount of such expenses exceeds the amount excludable under section 135, 529(c)(1), or 530(d)(2) for the taxable year.

Amendments

• 2002, Job Creation and Worker Assistance Act of 2002 (P.L. 107-147)

P.L. 107-147, §406(b):

Amended Code Sec. 62 by adding at the end a new subsection (d). **Effective** for tax years beginning after 12-31-2001.

[Sec. 62(e)]

(e) UNLAWFUL DISCRIMINATION DEFINED.—For purposes of subsection (a)(20), the term "unlawful discrimination" means an act that is unlawful under any of the following:

(1) Section 302 of the Civil Rights Act of 1991 (2 U.S.C. 1202).

(2) Section 201, 202, 203, 204, 205, 206, or 207 of the Congressional Accountability Act of 1995 (2 U.S.C. 1311, 1312, 1313, 1314, 1315, 1316, or 1317).

(3) The National Labor Relations Act (29 U.S.C. 151 et seq.).

(4) The Fair Labor Standards Act of 1938 (29 U.S.C. 201 et seq.).

(5) Section 4 or 15 of the Age Discrimination in Employment Act of 1967 (29 U.S.C. 623 or 633a).

(6) Section 501 or 504 of the Rehabilitation Act of 1973 (29 U.S.C. 791 or 794).

(7) Section 510 of the Employee Retirement Income Security Act of 1974 (29 U.S.C. 1140).

(8) Title IX of the Education Amendments of 1972 (20 U.S.C. 1681 et seq.).

(9) The Employee Polygraph Protection Act of 1988 (29 U.S.C. 2001 et seq.).

(10) The Worker Adjustment and Retraining Notification Act (29 U.S.C. 2102 et seq.).

(11) Section 105 of the Family and Medical Leave Act of 1993 (29 U.S.C. 2615).

(12) Chapter 43 of title 38, United States Code (relating to employment and reemployment rights of members of the uniformed services).

(13) Section 1977, 1979, or 1980 of the Revised Statutes (42 U.S.C. 1981, 1983, or 1985).

(14) Section 703, 704, or 717 of the Civil Rights Act of 1964 (42 U.S.C. 2000e-2, 2000e-3, or 2000e-16).

(15) Section 804, 805, 806, 808, or 818 of the Fair Housing Act (42 U.S.C. 3604, 3605, 3606, 3608, or 3617).

(16) Section 102, 202, 302, or 503 of the Americans with Disabilities Act of 1990 (42 U.S.C. 12112, 12132, 12182, or 12203).

(17) Any provision of Federal law (popularly known as whistleblower protection provisions) prohibiting the discharge of an employee, the discrimination against an employee, or any other form of retaliation or reprisal against an employee for asserting rights or taking other actions permitted under Federal law.

(18) Any provision of Federal, State, or local law, or common law claims permitted under Federal, State, or local law—

(i) providing for the enforcement of civil rights, or

(ii) regulating any aspect of the employment relationship, including claims for wages, compensation, or benefits, or prohibiting the discharge of an employee, the discrimination against an employee, or any other form of retaliation or reprisal against an employee for asserting rights or taking other actions permitted by law.

Amendments

• 2005, Gulf Opportunity Zone Act of 2005 (P.L. 109-135)

P.L. 109-135, §412(q)(2):

Amended Code Sec. 62(e) by striking "subsection (a)(19)" and inserting "subsection (a)(20)". **Effective** 12-21-2005.

• 2004, American Jobs Creation Act of 2004 (P.L. 108-357)

P.L. 108-357, §703(b):

Amended Code Sec. 62 by adding at the end a new subsection (e). **Effective** for fees and costs paid after 10-22-2004 with respect to any judgment or settlement occurring after such date.

[Sec. 63]

SEC. 63. TAXABLE INCOME DEFINED.

[Sec. 63(a)]

(a) IN GENERAL.—Except as provided in subsection (b), for purposes of this subtitle, the term "taxable income" means gross income minus the deductions allowed by this chapter (other than the standard deduction).

[Sec. 63(b)]

(b) INDIVIDUALS WHO DO NOT ITEMIZE THEIR DEDUCTIONS.—In the case of an individual who does not elect to itemize his deductions for the taxable year, for purposes of this subtitle, the term "taxable income" means adjusted gross income, minus—

(1) the standard deduction, and

(2) the deduction for personal exemptions provided in section 151.

[Sec. 63(c)]

(c) STANDARD DEDUCTION.—For purposes of this subtitle—

(1) IN GENERAL.—Except as otherwise provided in this subsection, the term "standard deduction" means the sum of—

(A) the basic standard deduction,

(B) the additional standard deduction,

(C) in the case of any taxable year beginning in 2008 or 2009, the real property tax deduction,

(D) the disaster loss deduction, and

(E) the motor vehicle sales tax deduction.

»»→ Caution: Code Sec. 63(c)(2), below, was amended by P.L. 107-16, P.L. 107-147, and P.L. 108-311, and is subject to the sunset provision of the Economic Growth and Tax Relief Reconciliation Act of 2001 (P.L. 107-16), §901. Absent Congressional action, the changes made to this provision by P.L. 107-16, or that take effect as if included in P.L. 107-16, do not apply after December 31, 2010. For more information about the sunset provision, see page XXI of the Preface to this publication and P.L. 107-16, §901, P.L. 107-16, §901, and P.L. 108-311, §105, in the amendment notes. See the amendments notes for a history of amendments to this section and the effective date of each change.

(2) BASIC STANDARD DEDUCTION.—For purposes of paragraph (1), the basic standard deduction is—

(A) 200 percent of the dollar amount in effect under subparagraph (C) for the taxable year in the case of—

(i) a joint return, or

(ii) a surviving spouse (as defined in section 2(a)),

(B) $4,400 in the case of a head of household (as defined in section 2(b)), or

(C) $3,000 in any other case.

(3) ADDITIONAL STANDARD DEDUCTION FOR AGED AND BLIND.—For purposes of paragraph (1), the additional standard deduction is the sum of each additional amount to which the taxpayer is entitled under subsection (f).

»»→ Caution: Code Sec. 63(c)(4), below, was amended by P.L. 107-16, P.L. 107-147, and P.L. 108-311, and is subject to the sunset provision of the Economic Growth and Tax Relief Reconciliation Act of 2001 (P.L. 107-16), §901. Absent Congressional action, the changes made to this provision by P.L. 107-16, or that take effect as if included in P.L. 107-16, do not apply after December 31, 2010. For more information about the sunset provision, see page XXI of the Preface to this publication and P.L. 107-16, §901, and P.L. 108-311, §105, in the amendment notes. See the amendments notes for a history of amendments to this section and the effective date of each change.

(4) ADJUSTMENTS FOR INFLATION.—In the case of any taxable year beginning in a calendar year after 1988, each dollar amount contained in paragraph (2)(B), (2)(C), or (5) or subsection (f) shall be increased by an amount equal to—

(A) such dollar amount, multiplied by

(B) the cost-of-living adjustment determined under section 1(f)(3) for the calendar year in which the taxable year begins, by substituting for "calendar year 1992" in subparagraph (B) thereof—

(i) "calendar year 1987" in the case of the dollar amounts contained in paragraph (2)(B), (2)(C), or (5)(A) or subsection (f), and

(ii) "calendar year 1997" in the case of the dollar amount contained in paragraph (5)(B).

(5) LIMITATION ON BASIC STANDARD DEDUCTION IN THE CASE OF CERTAIN DEPENDENTS.—In the case of an individual with respect to whom a deduction under section 151 is allowable to another taxpayer for a taxable year beginning in the calendar year in which the individual's taxable year begins, the basic standard deduction applicable to such individual for such individual's taxable year shall not exceed the greater of—

(A) $500, or

(B) the sum of $250 and such individual's earned income.

(6) CERTAIN INDIVIDUALS, ETC., NOT ELIGIBLE FOR STANDARD DEDUCTION.—In the case of—

(A) a married individual filing a separate return where either spouse itemizes deductions,

(B) a nonresident alien individual,

(C) an individual making a return under section 443(a)(1) for a period of less than 12 months on account of a change in his annual accounting period, or

(D) an estate or trust, common trust fund, or partnership,

the standard deduction shall be zero.

(7) REAL PROPERTY TAX DEDUCTION.—For purposes of paragraph (1), the real property tax deduction is the lesser of—

(A) the amount allowable as a deduction under this chapter for State and local taxes described in section 164(a)(1), or

(B) $500 ($1,000 in the case of a joint return).

Any taxes taken into account under section 62(a) shall not be taken into account under this paragraph.

»»→ Caution: Code Sec. 63(c)(7), below, was stricken by P.L. 108-311, and is subject to the sunset provision of the Economic Growth and Tax Relief Reconciliation Act of 2001 (P.L. 107-16), §901. Absent Congressional action, the changes made to this provision by P.L. 107-16, or that take effect as if included in P.L. 107-16, do not apply after December 31, 2010. For more information about the sunset provision, see page XXI of the Preface to this publication and P.L. 107-16, §901, and P.L. 108-311, §105, in the amendment notes. See the amendments notes for a history of amendments to this section and the effective date of each change.

(7) APPLICABLE PERCENTAGE.—For purposes of paragraph (2), the applicable percentage shall be determined in accordance with the following table:

For taxable years beginning in calendar year—	*The applicable percentage is—*
2003 and 2004	200
2005	174
2006	184
2007	187
2008	190
2009 and thereafter	200.

(8) DISASTER LOSS DEDUCTION.—For the purposes of paragraph (1), the term "disaster loss deduction" means the net disaster loss (as defined in section 165(h)(3)(B)).

(9) MOTOR VEHICLE SALES TAX DEDUCTION.—For purposes of paragraph (1), the term "motor vehicle sales tax deduction" means the amount allowable as a deduction under section 164(a)(6). Such term shall not include any amount taken into account under section 62(a).

Amendments

• 2009, American Recovery and Reinvestment Tax Act of 2009 (P.L. 111-5)

P.L. 111-5, §1008(c)(1):

Amended Code Sec. 63(c)(1) by striking "and" at the end of subparagraph (C), by striking the period at the end of subparagraph (D) and inserting ", and", and by adding at the end a new subparagraph (E). **Effective** for purchases on or after 2-17-2009 in tax years ending after such date.

P.L. 111-5, §1008(c)(2):

Amended Code Sec. 63(c) by adding at the end a new paragraph (9). **Effective** for purchases on or after 2-17-2009 in tax years ending after such date.

• 2008, Tax Extenders and Alternative Minimum Tax Relief Act of 2008 (P.L. 110-343)

P.L. 110-343, Division C, §204(a):

Amended Code Sec. 63(c)(1)(C), as added by the Housing Assistance Tax Act of 2008 (P.L. 110-289), by inserting "or 2009" after "2008". **Effective** for tax years beginning after 12-31-2008.

P.L. 110-343, Division C, §706(b)(1):

Amended Code Sec. 63(c)(1), as amended by the Housing Assistance Tax Act of 2008 (P.L. 110-289), by striking "and" at the end of subparagraph (B), by striking the period at the end of subparagraph (C) and inserting ", and", and by adding at the end a new subparagraph (D). **Effective** for disasters declared in tax years beginning after 12-31-2007.

P.L. 110-343, Division C, §706(b)(2):

Amended Code Sec. 63(c), as amended by the Housing Assistance Tax Act of 2008 (P.L. 110-289), by adding at the end a new paragraph (8). **Effective** for disasters declared in tax years beginning after 12-31-2007.

P.L. 110-343, Division C, §712, provides:

SEC. 712. COORDINATION WITH HEARTLAND DISASTER RELIEF.

The amendments made by this subtitle, other than the amendments made by sections 706(a)(2), 710, and 711, shall not apply to any disaster described in section 702(c)[b](1)(A), or to any expenditure or loss resulting from such disaster.

• 2008, Housing Assistance Tax Act of 2008 (P.L. 110-289)

P.L. 110-289, §3012(a):

Amended Code Sec. 63(c)(1) by striking "and" at the end of subparagraph (A), by striking the period at the end of subparagraph (B) and inserting ", and", and by adding at the end a new subparagraph (C). **Effective** for tax years beginning after 12-31-2007.

P.L. 110-289, §3012(b):

Amended Code Sec. 63(c) by adding at the end a new paragraph (7). **Effective** for tax years beginning after 12-31-2007.

• 2004, Working Families Tax Relief Act of 2004 (P.L. 108-311)

P.L. 108-311, §101(b)(1):

Amended Code Sec. 63(c)(2). **Effective** for tax years beginning after 12-31-2003. Prior to amendment, Code Sec. 63(c)(2) read as follows:

(2) BASIC STANDARD DEDUCTION.—For purposes of paragraph (1), the basic standard deduction is—

(A) the applicable percentage of the dollar amount in effect under subparagraph (D) for the taxable year in the case of—

(i) a joint return, or

(ii) a surviving spouse (as defined in section 2(a)),

(B) $4,400 in the case of a head of household (as defined in section 2(b)),

(C) one-half of the amount in effect under subparagraph (A) in the case of a married individual filing a separate return, or

(D) $3,000 in any other case.

If any amount determined under subparagraph (A) is not a multiple of $50, such amount shall be rounded to the next lowest multiple of $50.

P.L. 108-311, §101(b)(2)(A):

Amended Code Sec. 63(c)(4) by striking "(2)(D)" each place it occurs and inserting "(2)(C)". **Effective** for tax years beginning after 12-31-2003.

P.L. 108-311, §101(b)(2)(B):

Amended Code Sec. 63(c) by striking paragraph (7). **Effective** for tax years beginning after 12-31-2003. Prior to being stricken, Code Sec. 63(c)(7) read as follows:

(7) APPLICABLE PERCENTAGE.—For purposes of paragraph (2), the applicable percentage shall be determined in accordance with the following table:

For taxable years beginning in calendar year—	*The applicable percentage is—*
2003 and 2004	200
2005	174
2006	184
2007	187
2008	190
2009 and thereafter	200.

P.L. 108-311, §105, provides:

SEC. 105. APPLICATION OF EGTRRA SUNSET TO THIS TITLE.

Each amendment made by this title shall be subject to title IX of the Economic Growth and Tax Relief Reconciliation Act of 2001 to the same extent and in the same manner as the provision of such Act to which such amendment relates.

• 2003, Jobs and Growth Tax Relief Reconciliation Act of 2003 (P.L. 108-27)

P.L. 108-27, §103(a):

Amended the table contained in Code Sec. 63(c)(7) by inserting a new item before the item relating to 2005. **Effective** for tax years beginning after 12-31-2002.

P.L. 108-27, §107, provides:

SEC. 107. APPLICATION OF EGTRRA SUNSET TO THIS TITLE.

Each amendment made by this title shall be subject to title IX of the Economic Growth and Tax Relief Reconciliation Act of 2001 to the same extent and in the same manner as the provision of such Act to which such amendment relates.

• 2002, Job Creation and Worker Assistance Act of 2002 (P.L. 107-147)

P.L. 107-147, §411(e)(1)(A)-(E):

Amended Code Sec. 63(c)(2) by striking "subparagraph (C)" and inserting "subparagraph (D)" in subparagraph (A), by striking "or" at the end of subparagraph (B), by redesignating subparagraph (C) as subparagraph (D), by inserting after subparagraph (B) a new subparagraph (C), and by inserting a new flush sentence at the end. **Effective** as if included in the provision of P.L. 107-16 to which it relates [applicable to tax years beginning after 12-31-2002.—CCH].

P.L. 107-147, §411(e)(2)(A):

Amended Code Sec. 63(c)(4) by striking "paragraph (2) or (5)" and inserting "paragraph (2)(B), (2)(D), or (5)". **Effective** as if included in the provision of P.L. 107-16 to which it relates [applicable to tax years beginning after 12-31-2002.—CCH].

P.L. 107-147, §411(e)(2)(B):

Amended Code Sec. 63(c)(4)(B)(i) by striking "paragraph (2)" and inserting "paragraph (2)(B), (2)(D),". **Effective** as if included in the provision of P.L. 107-16 to which it relates [applicable to tax years beginning after 12-31-2002.—CCH].

P.L. 107-147, §411(e)(2)(C):

Amended Code Sec. 63(c)(4) by striking the flush sentence at the end. **Effective** as if included in the provision of P.L. 107-16 to which it relates [applicable to tax years beginning after 12-31-2002.—CCH]. Prior to being stricken, the flush sentence at the end of Code Sec. 63(c)(4) read as follows:

The preceding sentence shall not apply to the amount referred to in paragraph (2)(A).

• 2001, Economic Growth and Tax Relief Reconciliation Act of 2001 (P.L. 107-16)

P.L. 107-16, §301(a)(1)-(4):

Amended Code Sec. 63(c)(2) by striking "$5,000" in subparagraph (A) and inserting "the applicable percentage of the dollar amount in effect under subparagraph (C) for the taxable year"; by adding "or" at the end of subparagraph (B); by striking "in the case of" and all that follows in subparagraph (C) and inserting "in any other case."; and by striking subparagraph (D). **Effective** for tax years beginning after 12-31-2002 [**effective** date changed by P.L. 108-27, §103(b).—CCH]. Prior to amendment, Code Sec. 63(c)(2)(C) and (D) read as follows:

(C) $3,000 in the case of an individual who is not married and who is not a surviving spouse or head of household, or

(D) $2,500 in the case of a married individual filing a separate return.

P.L. 107-16, §301(b):

Amended Code Sec. 63(c) by adding at the end a new paragraph (7). **Effective** for tax years beginning after 12-31-2002 [**effective** date changed by P.L. 108-27, §103(b).—CCH].

P.L. 107-16, §301(c)(2):

Amended Code Sec. 63(c)(4) by adding at the end a new flush sentence. **Effective** for tax years beginning after 12-31-2002 [**effective** date changed by P.L. 108-27, §103(b).—CCH].

P.L. 107-16, §901(a)-(b), provides:

SEC. 901. SUNSET OF PROVISIONS OF ACT.

(a) IN GENERAL.—All provisions of, and amendments made by, this Act shall not apply—

(1) to taxable, plan, or limitation years beginning after December 31, 2010, or

(2) in the case of title V, to estates of decedents dying, gifts made, or generation skipping transfers, after December 31, 2010.

(b) APPLICATION OF CERTAIN LAWS.—The Internal Revenue Code of 1986 and the Employee Retirement Income Security Act of 1974 shall be applied and administered to years, estates, gifts, and transfers described in subsection (a) as if the provisions and amendments described in subsection (a) had never been enacted.

• 1997, Taxpayer Relief Act of 1997 (P.L. 105-34)

P.L. 105-34, §1201(a)(1):

Amended Code Sec. 63(c)(5) by striking "shall not exceed" and all that follows and inserting "shall not exceed the greater of —(A) $500, or (B) the sum of $250 and such individual's earned income.". **Effective** for tax years beginning after 12-31-97. Prior to amendment, Code Sec. 63(c)(5) read as follows:

(5) LIMITATION ON BASIC STANDARD DEDUCTION IN THE CASE OF CERTAIN DEPENDENTS.—In the case of an individual with respect to whom a deduction under section 151 is allowable to another taxpayer for a taxable year beginning in the calendar year in which the individual's taxable year begins, the basic standard deduction applicable to such individual for such individual's taxable year shall not exceed the greater of—

(A) $500, or

(B) such individual's earned income.

P.L. 105-34, §1201(a)(2)(A)-(B):

Amended Code Sec. 63(c)(4) by striking "(5)(A)" in the material preceding subparagraph (A) and inserting "(5)", and by striking "by substituting" and all that follows in subparagraph (B) and inserting "by substituting for 'calendar year 1992' in subparagraph (B) thereof—" and clauses (i) and (ii). **Effective** for tax years beginning after 12-31-97. Prior to amendment, Code Sec. 63(c)(4)(B) read as follows:

(B) the cost-of-living adjustment determined under section 1(f)(3) for the calendar year in which the taxable year begins, by substituting "calendar year 1987" for "calendar year 1992" in subparagraph (B) thereof.

• 1993, Omnibus Budget Reconciliation Act of 1993 (P.L. 103-66)

P.L. 103-66, §13201(b)(3)(D):

Amended Code Sec. 63(c)(4)(B) by striking "1989" and inserting "1992". **Effective** for tax years beginning after 12-31-92.

• 1990, Omnibus Budget Reconciliation Act of 1990 (P.L. 101-508)

P.L. 101-508, §11101(d)(1)(D):

Amended Code Sec. 63(c)(4)(B) by inserting ", by substituting 'calendar year 1987' for 'calendar year 1989' in subparagraph (B) thereof" before the period at the end. **Effective** for tax years beginning after 12-31-90.

• 1988, Technical and Miscellaneous Revenue Act of 1988 (P.L. 100-647)

P.L. 100-647, §1001(b)(1)(A)-(B):

Amended Code Sec. 63(c)(5) by striking out "the standard deduction applicable" and inserting in lieu thereof "the basic standard deduction applicable", and by striking out "STANDARD DEDUCTION" in the paragraph heading and inserting in lieu thereof "BASIC STANDARD DEDUCTION". **Effective** as if included in the provision of P.L. 99-514 to which it relates.

[Sec. 63(d)]

(d) ITEMIZED DEDUCTIONS.—For purposes of this subtitle, the term "itemized deductions" means the deductions allowable under this chapter other than—

(1) the deductions allowable in arriving at adjusted gross income, and

(2) the deduction for personal exemptions provided by section 151.

[Sec. 63(e)]

(e) ELECTION TO ITEMIZE.—

(1) IN GENERAL.—Unless an individual makes an election under this subsection for the taxable year, no itemized deduction shall be allowed for the taxable year. For purposes of this subtitle, the determination of whether a deduction is allowable under this chapter shall be made without regard to the preceding sentence.

(2) TIME AND MANNER OF ELECTION.—Any election under this subsection shall be made on the taxpayer's return, and the Secretary shall prescribe the manner of signifying such election on the return.

(3) CHANGE OF ELECTION.—Under regulations prescribed by the Secretary, a change of election with respect to itemized deductions for any taxable year may be made after the filing of the return for such year. If the spouse of the taxpayer filed a separate return for any taxable year corresponding to the taxable year of the taxpayer, the change shall not be allowed unless, in accordance with such regulations—

(A) the spouse makes a change of election with respect to itemized deductions, for the taxable year covered in such separate return, consistent with the change of treatment sought by the taxpayer, and

(B) the taxpayer and his spouse consent in writing to the assessment (within such period as may be agreed on with the Secretary) of any deficiency, to the extent attributable to such change of election, even though at the time of the filing of such consent the assessment of such deficiency would otherwise be prevented by the operation of any law or rule of law.

This paragraph shall not apply if the tax liability of the taxpayer's spouse for the taxable year corresponding to the taxable year of the taxpayer has been compromised under section 7122.

[Sec. 63(f)]

(f) AGED OR BLIND ADDITIONAL AMOUNTS.—

(1) ADDITIONAL AMOUNTS FOR THE AGED.—The taxpayer shall be entitled to an additional amount of $600—

(A) for himself if he has attained age 65 before the close of his taxable year, and

(B) for the spouse of the taxpayer if the spouse has attained age 65 before the close of the taxable year and an additional exemption is allowable to the taxpayer for such spouse under section 151(b).

(2) ADDITIONAL AMOUNT FOR BLIND.—The taxpayer shall be entitled to an additional amount of $600—

(A) for himself if he is blind at the close of the taxable year, and

(B) for the spouse of the taxpayer if the spouse is blind as of the close of the taxable year and an additional exemption is allowable to the taxpayer for such spouse under section 151(b).

For purposes of subparagraph (B), if the spouse dies during the taxable year the determination of whether such spouse is blind shall be made as of the time of such death.

(3) HIGHER AMOUNT FOR CERTAIN UNMARRIED INDIVIDUALS.—In the case of an individual who is not married and is not a surviving spouse, paragraphs (1) and (2) shall be applied by substituting "$750" for "$600".

(4) BLINDNESS DEFINED.—For purposes of this subsection, an individual is blind only if his central visual acuity does not exceed 20/200 in the better eye with correcting lenses, or if his visual acuity is greater than 20/200 but is accompanied by a limitation in the fields of vision such that the widest diameter of the visual field subtends an angle no greater than 20 degrees.

[Sec. 63(g)]

(g) MARITAL STATUS.—For purposes of this section, marital status shall be determined under section 7703.

Amendments

• 1986, Tax Reform Act of 1986 (P.L. 99-514)

P.L. 99-514, §102(a):

Amended Code Sec. 63. **Effective** for tax years beginning after 12-31-86. Prior to amendment, Code Sec. 63 read as follows:

SEC. 63. TAXABLE INCOME DEFINED.

[Sec. 63(a)]

(a) CORPORATIONS.—For purposes of this subtitle, in the case of a corporation, the term "taxable income" means gross income minus the deductions allowed by this chapter.

[Sec. 63(b)]

(b) INDIVIDUALS.—For purposes of this subtitle, in the case of an individual, the term "taxable income" means adjusted gross income—

(1) reduced by the sum of—

(A) the excess itemized deductions,

(B) the deductions for personal exemptions provided by section 151, and

(C) the direct charitable deduction, and

(2) increased (in the case of an individual for whom an unused zero bracket amount computation is provided by subsection (e)) by the unused zero bracket amount (if any).

Amendments

• 1981, Economic Recovery Tax Act of 1981 (P.L. 97-34)

P.L. 97-34, §121(b)(1):

Amended Code Sec. 63(b)(1) by striking out "and" at the end of subparagraph (A) and by inserting after subparagraph (B) "(C) the direct charitable deduction, and". **Effective** for contributions made after 12-31-81, in tax years beginning after such date.

[Sec. 63(c)]

(c) EXCESS ITEMIZED DEDUCTIONS.—For purposes of this subtitle, the term "excess itemized deductions" means the excess (if any) of—

(1) the itemized deductions, over

(2) the zero bracket amount.

[Sec. 63(d)]

(d) ZERO BRACKET AMOUNT.—For purposes of this subtitle, the term "zero bracket amount" means—

(1) in the case of an individual to whom subsection (a), (b), (c), or (d) of section 1 applies, the maximum amount of taxable income on which no tax is imposed by the applicable subsection of section 1, or

(2) zero in any other case.

Amendments

• 1981, Economic Recovery Tax Act of 1981 (P.L. 97-34)

P.L. 97-34, §104(b):

Amended Code Sec. 63(d). **Effective** for tax years beginning after 12-31-84.

• 1978, Revenue Act of 1978 (P.L. 95-600)

P.L. 95-600, §§101(b)(1), (2), (3), (f)(1):

Amended Code Sec. 63(d). **Effective** for tax years beginning after 12-31-78. Prior to amendment, Code Sec. 63(d) read as follows:

(d) ZERO BRACKET AMOUNT.—For purposes of this subtitle, the term "zero bracket amount" means—

(1) $3,200 in the case of—

(A) a joint return under section 6013, or

(B) a surviving spouse (as defined in section 2(a)),

(2) $2,200 in the case of an individual who is not married and who is not a surviving spouse (as so defined),

(3) $1,600 in the case of a married individual filing a separate return, or

(4) zero in any other case.

[Sec. 63(e)]

(e) UNUSED ZERO BRACKET AMOUNT.—

(1) INDIVIDUALS FOR WHOM COMPUTATION MUST BE MADE.—A computation for the taxable year shall be made under this subsection for the following individuals:

(A) a married individual filing a separate return where either spouse itemizes deductions,

(B) a nonresident alien individual,

(C) a citizen of the United States entitled to the benefits of section 931 (relating to income from sources within possessions of the United States), and

(D) an individual with respect to whom a deduction under section 151(e) is allowable to another taxpayer for a taxable year beginning in the calendar year in which the individual's taxable year begins.

(2) COMPUTATION.—For purposes of this subtitle, an individual's unused zero bracket amount for the taxable year is an amount equal to the excess (if any) of—

(A) the zero bracket amount, over

(B) the itemized deductions.

In the case of an individual referred to in paragraph (1)(D), if such individual's earned income (as defined in section 911(d)(2)) exceeds the itemized deductions, such earned income shall be substituted for the itemized deductions in subparagraph (B).

Amendments

• **1981, Economic Recovery Tax Act of 1981 (P.L. 97-34)**

P.L. 97-34, §111(b)(4):

Amended Code Sec. 63(e)(2) by striking out "section 911(b)" and inserting in lieu thereof "section 911(d)(2)". **Effective** for tax years beginning after 12-31-81.

[Sec. 63(f)]

(f) ITEMIZED DEDUCTIONS.—For purposes of this subtitle, the term "itemized deductions" means the deductions allowable by this chapter other than—

(1) the deductions allowable in arriving at adjusted gross income,

(2) the deductions for personal exemptions provided by section 151, and

(3) the direct charitable deduction.

Amendments

• **1981, Economic Recovery Tax Act of 1981 (P.L. 97-34)**

P.L. 97-34, §121(c)(2):

Amended Code Sec. 63(f) by striking out "and" at the end of paragraph (1); by striking out the period at the end of paragraph (2) and inserting in lieu thereof ", and "; and by adding at the end thereof new paragraph (3). **Effective** for contributions made after 12-31-81, in tax years beginning after such date.

[Sec. 63(g)]

(g) ELECTION TO ITEMIZE.—

(1) IN GENERAL.—Unless an individual makes an election under this subsection for the taxable year, no itemized deduction shall be allowed for the taxable year. For purposes of this subtitle, the determination of whether a deduction is allowable under this chapter shall be made without regard to the preceding sentence.

(2) WHO MAY ELECT.—Except as provided in paragraph (3), an individual may make an election under this subsection for the taxable year only if such individual's itemized deductions exceed the zero bracket amount.

(3) CERTAIN INDIVIDUALS TREATED AS ELECTING TO ITEMIZE.—An individual who has an unused zero bracket amount (as determined under subsection (e)(2)) shall be treated as having made an election under this subsection for the taxable year.

(4) TIME AND MANNER OF ELECTION.—Any election under this subsection shall be made on the taxpayer's return, and the Secretary shall prescribe the manner of signifying such election on the return.

(5) CHANGE OF TREATMENT.—Under regulations prescribed by the Secretary, a change of treatment with respect to the zero bracket amount and itemized deductions for any taxable year may be made after the filing of the return for such year. If the spouse of the taxpayer filed a separate return for any taxable year corresponding to the taxable year of the taxpayer, the change shall not be allowed unless, in accordance with such regulations—

(A) the spouse makes a change of treatment with respect to the zero bracket amount and itemized deductions, for the taxable year covered in such separate return, consistent with the change of treatment sought by the taxpayer, and

(B) the taxpayer and his spouse consent in writing to the assessment, within such period as may be agreed on with the Secretary, of any deficiency, to the extent attributable to such change of treatment, even though at the time of the filing of such consent the assessment of such deficiency would otherwise be prevented by the operation of any law or rule of law.

This paragraph shall not apply if the tax liability of the taxpayer's spouse, for the taxable year corresponding to the taxable year of the taxpayer, has been compromised under section 7122.

[Sec. 63(h)]

(h) MARITAL STATUS.—For purposes of this section marital status shall be determined under section 143.

Amendments

• **1977, Tax Reduction and Simplification Act of 1977 (P.L. 95-30)**

P.L. 95-30, §102(a):

Amended Code Sec. 63. **Effective** for tax years beginning after 12-31-76. Prior to amendment, Code Sec. 63 read as follows:

SEC. 63. TAXABLE INCOME DEFINED.

(a) GENERAL RULE.—Except as provided in subsection (b), for purposes of this subtitle the term "taxable income" means gross income, minus the deductions allowed by this chapter, other than the standard deduction allowed by part IV (sec. 141 and following).

(b) INDIVIDUALS ELECTING STANDARD DEDUCTION.—In the case of an individual electing under section 144 to use the standard deduction provided in part IV (sec. 141 and following), for purposes of this subtitle the term "taxable income" means adjusted gross income, minus—

(1) such standard deduction, and

(2) the deductions for personal exemptions provided in section 151.

[Sec. 63(i)]

(i) DIRECT CHARITABLE DEDUCTION.—For purposes of this section, the term "direct charitable deduction" means that portion of the amount allowable under section 170(a) which is taken as a direct charitable deduction for the taxable year under section 170(i).

Amendments

• **1981, Economic Recovery Tax Act of 1981 (P.L. 97-34)**

P.L. 97-34, §121(b)(2):

Added Code Sec. 63(i). **Effective** for contributions made after 12-31-81, in tax years beginning after such date.

• **1986, Tax Reform Act of 1986 (P.L. 99-514)**

P.L. 99-514, §1272(d)(6):

Amended Code Sec. 63(c)(6), as amended by title I of this Act, by striking out subparagraph (C) and by redesignating subparagraphs (D) and (E) as subparagraphs (C) and (D), respectively. **Effective** for tax years beginning after 12-31-86. For a special rule, see Act Sec. 1277(b), below. Prior to amendment, Code Sec. 63(c)(6)(C) read as follows:

(C) a citizen of the United States entitled to the benefits of section 931 (relating to income from sources within possessions of the United States),

P.L. 99-514, §1277(b), provides:

(b) SPECIAL RULE FOR GUAM, AMERICAN SAMOA, AND THE NORTHERN MARIANA ISLANDS.—The amendments made by this subtitle shall apply with respect to Guam, American Samoa, or the Northern Mariana Islands (and to residents thereof and corporations created or organized therein) only if (and so long as) an implementing agreement under section 1271 is in effect between the United States and such possession.

[Sec. 63(h)—Repealed]

Amendments

• **1990, Omnibus Budget Reconciliation Act of 1990 (P.L. 101-508)**

P.L. 101-508, §11801(a)(4):

Repealed Code Sec. 63(h). **Effective** 11-5-90. Prior to repeal, Code Sec. 63(h) read as follows:

(h) TRANSITIONAL RULE FOR TAXABLE YEARS BEGINNING IN 1987.—In the case of any taxable year beginning in 1987, paragraph (2) of subsection (c) shall be applied—

(1) by substituting "$3,760" for "$5,000",

(2) by substituting "$2,540" for "$4,400",

(3) by substituting "$2,540" for "$3,000", and

(4) by substituting "$1,880" for "$2,500".

The preceding sentence shall not apply if the taxpayer is entitled to an additional amount determined under subsection (f) (relating to additional amount for aged and blind) for the taxable year.

P.L. 101-508, §11821(b), provides:

(b) SAVINGS PROVISION.—If—

(1) any provision amended or repealed by this part applied to—

(A) any transaction occurring before the date of the enactment of this Act,

(B) any property acquired before such date of enactment, or

(C) any item of income, loss, deduction, or credit taken into account before such date of enactment, and

(2) the treatment of such transaction, property, or item under such provision would (without regard to the amendments made by this part) affect liability for tax for periods ending after such date of enactment,

nothing in the amendments made by this part shall be construed to affect the treatment of such transaction, property, or item for purposes of determining liability for tax for periods ending after such date of enactment.

[Sec. 64]

SEC. 64. ORDINARY INCOME DEFINED.

For purposes of this subtitle, the term "ordinary income" includes any gain from the sale or exchange of property which is neither a capital asset nor property described in section 1231(b). Any gain from the sale or exchange of property which is treated or considered, under other provisions of this subtitle, as "ordinary income" shall be treated as gain from the sale or exchange of property which is neither a capital asset nor property described in section 1231(b).

Amendments

• 1976, Tax Reform Act of 1976 (P.L. 94-455)

P.L. 94-455, §1901(a)(10), (d):

Added Code Sec. 64. **Effective** for tax years beginning after 12-31-76.

[Sec. 65]

SEC. 65. ORDINARY LOSS DEFINED.

For purposes of this subtitle, the term "ordinary loss" includes any loss from the sale or exchange of property which is not a capital asset. Any loss from the sale or exchange of property which is treated or considered, under other provisions of this subtitle, as "ordinary loss" shall be treated as loss from the sale or exchange of property which is not a capital asset.

Amendments

• 1976, Tax Reform Act of 1976 (P.L. 94-455)

P.L. 94-455, §1901(a)(11), (d):

Added Code Sec. 65. **Effective** for tax years beginning after 12-31-76.

[Sec. 66]

SEC. 66. TREATMENT OF COMMUNITY INCOME.

[Sec. 66(a)]

(a) TREATMENT OF COMMUNITY INCOME WHERE SPOUSES LIVE APART.—If—

(1) 2 individuals are married to each other at any time during a calendar year;

(2) such individuals—

(A) live apart at all times during the calendar year, and

(B) do not file a joint return under section 6013 with each other for a taxable year beginning or ending in the calendar year;

(3) one or both of such individuals have earned income for the calendar year which is community income; and

(4) no portion of such earned income is transferred (directly or indirectly) between such individuals before the close of the calendar year,

then, for purposes of this title, any community income of such individuals for the calendar year shall be treated in accordance with the rules provided by section 879(a).

Amendments

• 1980, Miscellaneous Revenue Act of 1980 (P.L. 96-605)

P.L. 96-605, §101(a):

Added Code Sec. 66(a). **Effective** for calendar years beginning 12-31-80.

[Sec. 66(b)]

(b) SECRETARY MAY DISREGARD COMMUNITY PROPERTY LAWS WHERE SPOUSE NOT NOTIFIED OF COMMUNITY INCOME.—The Secretary may disallow the benefits of any community property law to any taxpayer with respect to any income if such taxpayer acted as if solely entitled to such income and failed to notify the taxpayer's spouse before the due date (including extensions) for filing the return for the taxable year in which the income was derived of the nature and amount of such income.

Amendments

• 1980, Miscellaneous Revenue Act of 1980 (P.L. 96-605)

P.L. 96-605, §101(a):

Added Code Sec. 66(b). **Effective** for calendar years beginning 12-31-80.

[Sec. 66(c)]

(c) SPOUSE RELIEVED OF LIABILITY IN CERTAIN OTHER CASES.—Under regulations prescribed by the Secretary, if—

(1) an individual does not file a joint return for any taxable year,

(2) such individual does not include in gross income for such taxable year an item of community income properly includible therein which, in accordance with the rules contained in section 879(a), would be treated as the income of the other spouse,

(3) the individual establishes that he or she did not know of, and had no reason to know of, such item of community income, and

(4) taking into account all facts and circumstances, it is inequitable to include such item of community income in such individual's gross income,

then, for purposes of this title, such item of community income shall be included in the gross income of the other spouse (and not in the gross income of the individual). Under procedures prescribed by the Secretary, if, taking into account all the facts and circumstances, it is inequitable to hold the individual liable for any unpaid tax or any deficiency (or any portion of either) attributable to any item for which relief is not available under the preceding sentence, the Secretary may relieve such individual of such liability.

Amendments

• 1998, IRS Restructuring and Reform Act of 1998 (P.L. 105-206)

P.L. 105-206, §3201(b):

Amended Code Sec. 66(c) by adding at the end a new sentence. **Effective**, generally, for any liability for tax arising after 7-22-98, and any liability for tax arising on or before such date but remaining unpaid as of such date. However, for an exception, see Act Sec. 3201(g)(2), below.

P.L. 105-206, §3201(g)(2), provides:

(2) 2-YEAR PERIOD.—The 2-year period under subsection (b)(1)(E) or (c)(3)(B) of section 6015 of the Internal Revenue Code of 1986 shall not expire before the date which is 2 years after the date of the first collection activity after the date of the enactment of this Act.

[Sec. 66(d)]

(d) DEFINITIONS.—For purposes of this section—

(1) EARNED INCOME.—The term "earned income" has the meaning given to such term by section 911(d)(2).

(2) COMMUNITY INCOME.—The term "community income" means income which, under applicable community property laws, is treated as community income.

(3) COMMUNITY PROPERTY LAWS.—The term "community property laws" means the community property laws of a State, a foreign country, or a possession of the United States.

Amendments

• 1989, Omnibus Budget Reconciliation Act of 1989 (P.L. 101-239)

P.L. 101-239, §7841(d)(8):

Amended Code Sec. 66(d)(1) by striking "section 911(b)" and inserting "section 911(d)(2)". **Effective** 12-19-89.

• 1984, Deficit Reduction Act of 1984 (P.L. 98-369)

P.L. 98-369, §424(b)(1):

Amended Code Sec. 66 by redesignating subsection (b) as subsection (d) and by inserting after subsection (a) new subsections (b) and (c). For the **effective** date, see Act Sec. 424(c), below.

P.L. 98-369, §424(b)(2)(A):

Amended the section heading of Code Sec. 66 by striking out "Where Spouses Live Apart" at the end. For the **effective** date, see Act Sec. 424(c), below.

P.L. 98-369, §424(b)(2)(B):

Amended the subsection heading of Code Sec. 66(a) by striking out "General Rule" and inserting in lieu thereof "Treatment of Community Income Where Spouses Live Apart". For the **effective** date, see Act Sec. 424(c), below.

P.L. 98-369, §424(c), as amended by P.L. 100-647, §6004, provides:

(c) EFFECTIVE DATES.—

(1) IN GENERAL.—Except as provided in paragraph (2), the amendments made by subsections (a) and (b) shall apply to all taxable years to which the Internal Revenue Code of 1954 applies. Corresponding provisions shall be deemed to be included in the Internal Revenue Code of 1939 and shall apply to all taxable years to which such Code applies.

(2) AUTHORITY TO DISREGARD COMMUNITY PROPERTY LAWS.—Subsection (b) of section 66 of the Internal Revenue Code of 1954, as added by subsection (b), shall apply to taxable years beginning after December 31, 1984.

(3) TRANSITIONAL RULE.—If—

(A) a joint return under section 6013 of the Internal Revenue Code of 1954 was filed before January 1, 1985,

(B) on such return there is an understatement (as defined in section 6661(b)(2)(A) of such Code) which is attributable to disallowed deductions attributable to activities of one spouse,

(C) the amount of such disallowed deductions exceeds the taxable income shown on such return,

(D) without regard to any determination before October 21, 1988, the other spouse establishes that in signing the return he or she did not know, and had no reason to know, that there was such an understatement, and

(E) the marriage between such spouses terminated and immediately after such termination the net worth of the other spouse was less than $10,000

notwithstanding any law or rule of law (including res judicata), the other spouse shall be relieved of liability for tax (including, interest, penalties, and other amounts) for such taxable year to the extent such liability is attributable to such understatement, and, to the extent the liability so attributable has been collected from such other spouse, it shall be refunded or credited to such other spouse. No credit or refund shall be made under the preceding sentence unless claim therefor has been submitted to the Secretary of the Treasury or his delegate before the date 1 year after the date of the enactment of this paragraph, and no interest on such credit or refund shall be allowed for any period before such date of enactment.

[Sec. 67]

SEC. 67. 2-PERCENT FLOOR ON MISCELLANEOUS ITEMIZED DEDUCTIONS.

[Sec. 67(a)]

(a) GENERAL RULE.—In the case of an individual, the miscellaneous itemized deductions for any taxable year shall be allowed only to the extent that the aggregate of such deductions exceeds 2 percent of adjusted gross income.

[Sec. 67(b)]

(b) MISCELLANEOUS ITEMIZED DEDUCTIONS.—For purposes of this section, the term "miscellaneous itemized deductions" means the itemized deductions other than—

(1) the deduction under section 163 (relating to interest),

(2) the deduction under section 164 (relating to taxes),

(3) the deduction under section 165(a) for casualty or theft losses described in paragraph (2) or (3) of section 165(c) or for losses described in section 165(d),

(4) the deductions under section 170 (relating to charitable, etc., contributions and gifts) and section 642(c) (relating to deduction for amounts paid or permanently set aside for a charitable purpose),

(5) the deduction under section 213 (relating to medical, dental, etc., expenses),

(6) any deduction allowable for impairment-related work expenses,

(7) the deduction under section 691(c) (relating to deduction for estate tax in case of income in respect of the decedent),

(8) any deduction allowable in connection with personal property used in a short sale,

(9) the deduction under section 1341 (relating to computation of tax where taxpayer restores substantial amount held under claim of right),

(10) the deduction under section 72(b)(3) (relating to deduction where annuity payments cease before investment recovered),

(11) the deduction under section 171 (relating to deduction for amortizable bond premium), and

(12) the deduction under section 216 (relating to deductions in connection with cooperative housing corporations).

Amendments

• 1998, Tax and Trade Relief Extension Act of 1998 (P.L. 105-277)

P.L. 105-277, §4004(b)(1):

Amended Code Sec. 67(b)(3) by striking "for losses described in subsection (c)(3) or (d) of section 165" and inserting "for casualty or theft losses described in paragraph (2) or (3) of section 165(c) or for losses described in section 165(d)". **Effective** for tax years beginning after 12-31-86.

• 1993, Omnibus Budget Reconciliation Act of 1993 (P.L. 103-66)

P.L. 103-66, §13213(c)(2):

Amended Code Sec. 67(b) by striking paragraph (6) and redesignating paragraphs (7) through (13) as paragraphs (6) through (12). **Effective** for expenses incurred after 12-31-93. Prior to amendment, Code Sec. 67(b)(6) read as follows:

(6) the deduction under section 217 (relating to moving expenses).

• 1988, Technical and Miscellaneous Revenue Act of 1988 (P.L. 100-647)

P.L. 100-647, §1001(f)(2)(A)-(B):

Amended Code Sec. 67(b)(4) by striking out "deduction" and inserting in lieu thereof "deductions", and by inserting before the comma at the end thereof "and section 642(c) (relating to deduction for amounts paid or permanently set aside for a charitable purpose)". **Effective** as if included in the provision of P.L. 99-514 to which it relates.

[Sec. 67(c)]

(c) DISALLOWANCE OF INDIRECT DEDUCTION THROUGH PASS-THRU ENTITY.—

(1) IN GENERAL.—The Secretary shall prescribe regulations which prohibit the indirect deduction through pass-thru entities of amounts which are not allowable as a deduction if paid or incurred directly by an individual and which contain such reporting requirements as may be necessary to carry out the purposes of this subsection.

(2) TREATMENT OF PUBLICLY OFFERED REGULATED INVESTMENT COMPANIES.—

(A) IN GENERAL.—Paragraph (1) shall not apply with respect to any publicly offered regulated investment company.

(B) PUBLICLY OFFERED REGULATED INVESTMENT COMPANIES.—For purposes of this subsection—

(i) IN GENERAL.—The term "publicly offered regulated investment company" means a regulated investment company the shares of which are—

(I) continuously offered pursuant to a public offering (within the meaning of section 4 of the Securities Act of 1933, as amended (15 U.S.C. 77a to 77aa)),

(II) regularly traded on an established securities market, or

(III) held by or for no fewer than 500 persons at all times during the taxable year.

(ii) SECRETARY MAY REDUCE 500 PERSON REQUIREMENT.—The Secretary may by regulation decrease the minimum shareholder requirement of clause (i)(III) in the case of regulated investment companies which experience a loss of shareholders through net redemptions of their shares.

(3) TREATMENT OF CERTAIN OTHER ENTITIES.—Paragraph (1) shall not apply—

(A) with respect to cooperatives and real estate investment trusts, and

(B) except as provided in regulations, with respect to estates and trusts.

Amendments

• 1989, Omnibus Budget Reconciliation Act of 1989 (P.L. 101-239)

P.L. 101-239, §7814(f):

Amended Code Sec. 67(c) by striking paragraph (4). **Effective** as if included in the provision of P.L. 100-647 to which it relates. Prior to amendment, Code Sec. 67(c)(4) read as follows:

(4) TERMINATION.—This subsection shall not apply to any taxable year beginning after December 31, 1989.

• 1988, Technical and Miscellaneous Revenue Act of 1988 (P.L. 100-647)

P.L. 100-647, §1001(f)(4):

Amended Code Sec. 67(c) by striking out the last sentence and inserting in lieu thereof a new last sentence. **Effective** as if included in the provision of P.L. 99-514 to which it relates. Prior to amendment, the last sentence of Code Sec. 67(c) read as follows:

The preceding sentence shall not apply with respect to estates, trusts, cooperatives, and real estate investment trusts.

P.L. 100-647, §4011(a):

Amended Code Sec. 67(c). **Effective** for tax years beginning after 12-31-87. Prior to amendment, Code Sec. 67(c) read as follows:

(c) DISALLOWANCE OF INDIRECT DEDUCTION THROUGH PASS-THRU ENTITY.—The Secretary shall prescribe regulations which prohibit the indirect deduction through pass-thru entities of amounts which are not allowable as a deduction if paid or incurred directly by an individual and which contain such reporting requirements as may be necessary to carry out the purposes of this subsection. The preceding sentence shall not apply—

(1) with respect to cooperatives and real estate investment trusts, and

(2) except as provided in regulations, with respect to estates and trusts.

• 1987, Revenue Act of 1987 (P.L. 100-203)

P.L. 100-203, §10104(a), provides:

(a) 1-YEAR DELAY IN TREATMENT OF PUBLICLY OFFERED REGULATED INVESTMENT COMPANIES UNDER 2-PERCENT FLOOR.—

(1) GENERAL RULE.—Section 67(c) of the Internal Revenue Code of 1986 to the extent it relates to indirect deductions through a publicly offered regulated investment company shall apply only to taxable years beginning after December 31, 1987.

(2) PUBLICLY OFFERED REGULATED INVESTMENT COMPANY DEFINED.—For purposes of this subsection—

(A) IN GENERAL.—The term "publicly offered regulated investment company" means a regulated investment company the shares of which are—

(i) continuously offered pursuant to a public offering (within the meaning of section 4 of the Securities Act of 1933, as amended (15 U.S.C. 77a to 77aa)),

(ii) regularly traded on an established securities market, or

(iii) held by or for no fewer than 500 persons at all times during the taxable year.

(B) SECRETARY MAY REDUCE 500 PERSON REQUIREMENT.—The Secretary of the Treasury or his delegate may by regulation decrease the minimum shareholder requirement of subparagraph (A)(iii) in the case of regulated investment companies which experience a loss of shareholders through net redemptions of their shares.

[Sec. 67(d)]

(d) IMPAIRMENT-RELATED WORK EXPENSES.—For purposes of this section, the term "impairment-related work expenses" means expenses—

(1) of a handicapped individual (as defined in section 190(b)(3)) for attendant care services at the individual's place of employment and other expenses in connection with such place of employment which are necessary for such individual to be able to work, and

(2) with respect to which a deduction is allowable under section 162 (determined without regard to this section).

[Sec. 67(e)]

(e) DETERMINATION OF ADJUSTED GROSS INCOME IN CASE OF ESTATES AND TRUSTS.—For purposes of this section, the adjusted gross income of an estate or trust shall be computed in the same manner as in the case of an individual, except that—

(1) the deductions for costs which are paid or incurred in connection with the administration of the estate or trust and which would not have been incurred if the property were not held in such trust or estate, and

(2) the deductions allowable under sections 642(b), 651, and 661,

shall be treated as allowable in arriving at adjusted gross income. Under regulations, appropriate adjustments shall be made in the application of part I of subchapter J of this chapter to take into account the provisions of this section.

Amendments

• 1988, Technical and Miscellaneous Revenue Act of 1988 (P.L. 100-647)

P.L. 100-647, §1001(f)(3):

Amended Code Sec. 67(e). **Effective** as if included in the provision of P.L. 99-514 to which it relates. Prior to amendment, Code Sec. 67(e) read as follows:

(e) DETERMINATION OF ADJUSTED GROSS INCOME IN CASE OF ESTATES AND TRUSTS.—For purposes of this section, the adjusted gross income of an estate or trust shall be computed in the same manner as in the case of an individual, except that the deductions for costs which are paid or incurred in connection with the administration of the estate or trust and would not have been incurred if the property were not held in such trust or estate shall be treated as allowable in arriving at adjusted gross income.

• 1986, Tax Reform Act of 1986 (P.L. 99-514)

P.L. 99-514, §132(a):

Amended part I of subchapter B of chapter 1 by adding at the end thereof new Code Sec. 67. **Effective** for tax years beginning after 12-31-86.

[Sec. 67(f)]

(f) COORDINATION WITH OTHER LIMITATION.—This section shall be applied before the application of the dollar limitation of the second sentence of section 162(a) (relating to trade or business expenses).

Amendments

• 2000, Community Renewal Tax Relief Act of 2000 (P.L. 106-554)

P.L. 106-554, §319(2):

Amended Code Sec. 67(f) by striking "the last sentence" and inserting "the second sentence". **Effective** 12-21-2000.

• 1988, Technical and Miscellaneous Revenue Act of 1988 (P.L. 100-647)

P.L. 100-647, §1001(f)(1):

Amended Code Sec. 67 by adding at the end thereof new subsection (f). **Effective** as if included in the provision of P.L. 99-514 to which it relates.

[Sec. 68]

SEC. 68. OVERALL LIMITATION ON ITEMIZED DEDUCTIONS.

[Sec. 68(a)]

(a) GENERAL RULE.—In the case of an individual whose adjusted gross income exceeds the applicable amount, the amount of the itemized deductions otherwise allowable for the taxable year shall be reduced by the lesser of—

(1) 3 percent of the excess of adjusted gross income over the applicable amount, or

(2) 80 percent of the amount of the itemized deductions otherwise allowable for such taxable year.

[Sec. 68(b)]

(b) APPLICABLE AMOUNT.—

(1) IN GENERAL.—For purposes of this section, the term "applicable amount" means $100,000 ($50,000 in the case of a separate return by a married individual within the meaning of section 7703).

(2) INFLATION ADJUSTMENTS.—In the case of any taxable year beginning in a calendar year after 1991, each dollar amount contained in paragraph (1) shall be increased by an amount equal to—

(A) such dollar amount, multiplied by

(B) the cost-of-living adjustment determined under section 1(f)(3) for the calendar year in which the taxable year begins, by substituting "calendar year 1990" for "calendar year 1992" in subparagraph (B) thereof.

Amendments

• 1993, Omnibus Budget Reconciliation Act of 1993 (P.L. 103-66)

P.L. 103-66, §13201(b)(3)(E):

Amended Code Sec. 68(b)(2)(B) by striking "1989" and inserting "1992". **Effective** for tax years beginning after 12-31-92.

[Sec. 68(c)]

(c) EXCEPTION FOR CERTAIN ITEMIZED DEDUCTIONS.—For purposes of this section, the term "itemized deductions" does not include—

(1) the deduction under section 213 (relating to medical, etc. expenses),

(2) any deduction for investment interest (as defined in section 163(d)), and

(3) the deduction under section 165(a) for casualty or theft losses described in paragraph (2) or (3) of section 165(c) or for losses described in section 165(d).

Amendments

• 1998, Tax and Trade Relief Extension Act of 1998 (P.L. 105-277)

P.L. 105-277, §4004(b)(2):

Amended Code Sec. 68(c)(3) by striking "for losses described in subsection (c)(3) or (d) of section 165" and inserting "for casualty or theft losses described in paragraph (2) or (3) of section 165(c) or for losses described in section 165(d)". **Effective** for tax years beginning after 12-31-90.

[Sec. 68(d)]

(d) COORDINATION WITH OTHER LIMITATIONS.—This section shall be applied after the application of any other limitation on the allowance of any itemized deduction.

[Sec. 68(e)]

(e) EXCEPTION FOR ESTATES AND TRUSTS.—This section shall not apply to any estate or trust.

»»→ Caution: Code Sec. 68(f), below, is subject to the sunset provision of the Economic Growth and Tax Relief Reconciliation Act of 2001 (P.L. 107-16), §901. Absent Congressional action, the changes made to this provision by P.L. 107-16, or that take effect as if included in P.L. 107-16, do not apply after December 31, 2010. For more information about the sunset provision, see page XXI of the Preface to this publication and P.L. 107-16, §901, in the amendment notes. See the amendments notes for a history of amendments to this section and the effective date of each change.

[Sec. 68(f)]

(f) PHASEOUT OF LIMITATION.—

(1) IN GENERAL.—In the case of taxable years beginning after December 31, 2005, and before January 1, 2010, the reduction under subsection (a) shall be equal to the applicable fraction of the amount which would (but for this subsection) be the amount of such reduction.

(2) APPLICABLE FRACTION.—For purposes of paragraph (1), the applicable fraction shall be determined in accordance with the following table:

For taxable years beginning in calendar year—	*The applicable fraction is—*
2006 and 2007	2/3
2008 and 2009	1/3.

Amendments

• 2001, Economic Growth and Tax Relief Reconciliation Act of 2001 (P.L. 107-16)

P.L. 107-16, §103(a):

Amended Code Sec. 68 by adding at the end a new subsection (f). **Effective** for tax years beginning after 12-31-2005.

P.L. 107-16, §901(a)-(b), provides:

SEC. 901. SUNSET OF PROVISIONS OF ACT.

(a) IN GENERAL.—All provisions of, and amendments made by, this Act shall not apply—

(1) to taxable, plan, or limitation years beginning after December 31, 2010, or

(2) in the case of title V, to estates of decedents dying, gifts made, or generation skipping transfers, after December 31, 2010.

(b) APPLICATION OF CERTAIN LAWS.—The Internal Revenue Code of 1986 and the Employee Retirement Income Security Act of 1974 shall be applied and administered to years, estates, gifts, and transfers described in subsection (a) as if the provisions and amendments described in subsection (a) had never been enacted.

[Sec. 68(f)—Repealed]

Amendments

• 1993, Omnibus Budget Reconciliation Act of 1993 (P.L. 103-66)

P.L. 103-66, §13204:

Repealed Code Sec. 68(f). **Effective** 8-10-93. Prior to repeal, Code Sec. 68(f) read as follows:

(f) TERMINATION.—This section shall not apply to any taxable year beginning after December 31, 1995.

• 1990, Omnibus Budget Reconciliation Act of 1990 (P.L. 101-508)

P.L. 101-508, §11103(a):

Amended part I of subchapter B of chapter 1 by adding at the end thereof a new Code Sec. 68. **Effective** for tax years beginning after 12-31-90.

»»→ Caution: Code Sec. 68(g), below, is subject to the sunset provision of the Economic Growth and Tax Relief Reconciliation Act of 2001 (P.L. 107-16), §901. Absent Congressional action, the changes made to this provision by P.L. 107-16, or that take effect as if included in P.L. 107-16, do not apply after December 31, 2010. For more information about the sunset provision, see page XXI of the Preface to this publication and P.L. 107-16, §901, in the amendment notes. See the amendments notes for a history of amendments to this section and the effective date of each change.

[Sec. 68(g)]

(g) TERMINATION.—This section shall not apply to any taxable year beginning after December 31, 2009.

Amendments

• 2001, Economic Growth and Tax Relief Reconciliation Act of 2001 (P.L. 107-16)

P.L. 107-16, §103(a):

Amended Code Sec. 68 by adding at the end a new subsection (g). **Effective** for tax years beginning after 12-31-2005.

P.L. 107-16, §901(a)-(b), provides:

SEC. 901. SUNSET OF PROVISIONS OF ACT.

(a) IN GENERAL.—All provisions of, and amendments made by, this Act shall not apply—

(1) to taxable, plan, or limitation years beginning after December 31, 2010, or

(2) in the case of title V, to estates of decedents dying, gifts made, or generation skipping transfers, after December 31, 2010.

(b) APPLICATION OF CERTAIN LAWS.—The Internal Revenue Code of 1986 and the Employee Retirement Income Security Act of 1974 shall be applied and administered to years, estates, gifts, and transfers described in subsection (a) as if the provisions and amendments described in subsection (a) had never been enacted.

PART II—ITEMS SPECIFICALLY INCLUDED IN GROSS INCOME

[Sec. 71]

SEC. 71. ALIMONY AND SEPARATE MAINTENANCE PAYMENTS.

[Sec. 71(a)]

(a) GENERAL RULE.—Gross income includes amounts received as alimony or separate maintenance payments.

[Sec. 71(b)]

(b) ALIMONY OR SEPARATE MAINTENANCE PAYMENTS DEFINED.—For purposes of this section—

(1) IN GENERAL.—The term "alimony or separate maintenance payment" means any payment in cash if—

(A) such payment is received by (or on behalf of) a spouse under a divorce or separation instrument,

(B) the divorce or separation instrument does not designate such payment as a payment which is not includible in gross income under this section and not allowable as a deduction under section 215,

(C) in the case of an individual legally separated from his spouse under a decree of divorce or of separate maintenance, the payee spouse and the payor spouse are not members of the same household at the time such payment is made, and

(D) there is no liability to make any such payment for any period after the death of the payee spouse and there is no liability to make any payment (in cash or property) as a substitute for such payments after the death of the payee spouse.

(2) DIVORCE OR SEPARATION INSTRUMENT.—The term "divorce or separation instrument" means—

(A) a decree of divorce or separate maintenance or a written instrument incident to such a decree,

(B) a written separation agreement, or

(C) a decree (not described in subparagraph (A)) requiring a spouse to make payments for the support or maintenance of the other spouse.

[Sec. 71(c)]

(c) PAYMENTS TO SUPPORT CHILDREN.—

(1) IN GENERAL.—Subsection (a) shall not apply to that part of any payment which the terms of the divorce or separation instrument fix (in terms of an amount of money or a part of the payment) as a sum which is payable for the support of children of the payor spouse.

(2) TREATMENT OF CERTAIN REDUCTIONS RELATED TO CONTINGENCIES INVOLVING CHILD.—For purposes of paragraph (1), if any amount specified in the instrument will be reduced—

(A) on the happening of a contingency specified in the instrument relating to a child (such as attaining a specified age, marrying, dying, leaving school, or a similar contingency), or

(B) at a time which can clearly be associated with a contingency of a kind specified in subparagraph (A),

an amount equal to the amount of such reduction will be treated as an amount fixed as payable for the support of children of the payor spouse.

(3) SPECIAL RULE WHERE PAYMENT IS LESS THAN AMOUNT SPECIFIED IN INSTRUMENT.—For purposes of this subsection, if any payment is less than the amount specified in the instrument, then so much of such payment as does not exceed the sum payable for support shall be considered a payment for such support.

[Sec. 71(d)]

(d) SPOUSE.—For purposes of this section, the term "spouse" includes a former spouse.

[Sec. 71(e)]

(e) EXCEPTION FOR JOINT RETURNS.—This section and section 215 shall not apply if the spouses make a joint return with each other.

[Sec. 71(f)]

(f) RECOMPUTATION WHERE EXCESS FRONT-LOADING OF ALIMONY PAYMENTS.—

(1) IN GENERAL.—If there are excess alimony payments—

(A) the payor spouse shall include the amount of such excess payments in gross income for the payor spouse's taxable year beginning in the 3rd post-separation year, and

(B) the payee spouse shall be allowed a deduction in computing adjusted gross income for the amount of such excess payments for the payee's taxable year beginning in the 3rd post-separation year.

(2) EXCESS ALIMONY PAYMENTS.—For purposes of this subsection, the term "excess alimony payments" mean the sum of—

(A) the excess payments for the 1st post-separation year, and

(B) the excess payments for the 2nd post-separation year.

(3) EXCESS PAYMENTS FOR 1ST POST-SEPARATION YEAR.—For purposes of this subsection, the amount of the excess payments for the 1st post-separation year is the excess (if any) of—

(A) the amount of the alimony or separate maintenance payments paid by the payor spouse during the 1st post-separation year, over

(B) the sum of—

(i) the average of—

(I) the alimony or separate maintenance payments paid by the payor spouse during the 2nd post-separation year, reduced by the excess payments for the 2nd post-separation year, and

(II) the alimony or separate maintenance payments paid by the payor spouse during the 3rd post-separation year, plus

(ii) $15,000.

(4) EXCESS PAYMENTS FOR 2ND POST-SEPARATION YEAR.—For purposes of this subsection, the amount of the excess payments for the 2nd post-separation year is the excess (if any) of—

(A) the amount of the alimony or separate maintenance payments paid by the payor spouse during the 2nd post-separation year, over

(B) the sum of—

(i) the amount of the alimony or separate maintenance payments paid by the payor spouse during the 3rd post-separation year, plus

(ii) $15,000.

(5) EXCEPTIONS.—

(A) WHERE PAYMENT CEASES BY REASON OF DEATH OR REMARRIAGE.—Paragraph (1) shall not apply if—

(i) either spouse dies before the close of the 3rd post-separation year, or the payee spouse remarries before the close of the 3rd post-separation year, and

(ii) the alimony or separate maintenance payments cease by reason of such death or remarriage.

(B) SUPPORT PAYMENTS.—For purposes of this subsection, the term "alimony or separate maintenance payment" shall not include any payment received under a decree described in subsection (b)(2)(C).

(C) FLUCTUATING PAYMENTS NOT WITHIN CONTROL OF PAYOR SPOUSE.—For purposes of this subsection, the term "alimony or separate maintenance payment" shall not include any payment to the extent it is made pursuant to a continuing liability (over a period of not less than 3 years) to pay a fixed portion or portions of the income from a business or property or from compensation for employment or self-employment.

(6) POST-SEPARATION YEARS.—For purposes of this subsection, the term "1st post-separation years" means the 1st calendar year in which the payor spouse paid to the payee spouse alimony or separate maintenance payments to which this section applies. The 2nd and 3rd post-separation years shall be the 1st and 2nd succeeding calendar years, respectively.

[Sec. 71(g)]

(g) CROSS REFERENCES.—

(1) For deduction of alimony or separate maintenance payments, see section 215.

(2) For taxable status of income of an estate or trust in the case of divorce, etc., see section 682.

Amendments

• 1986, Tax Reform Act of 1986 (P.L. 99-514)

P.L. 99-514, §1843(a):

Amended Code Sec. 71 by adding at the end thereof new subsection (g). **Effective** as if included in the provision of P.L. 98-369 to which it relates.

P.L. 99-514, §1843(b):

Amended Code Sec. 71(b)(1)(D) by striking out "(and the divorce or separation instrument states that there is no such liability)". **Effective** as if included in the provision of P.L. 98-369 to which it relates. Prior to amendment Code Sec. 71(b)(1)(D) read as follows:

(D) there is no liability to make any such payment for any period after the death of the payee spouse and there is no liability to make any payment (in cash or property) as a substitute for such payments after the death of the payee spouse (and the divorce or separation instrument states that there is no such liability).

P.L. 99-514, §1843(c)(1):

Amended Code Sec. 71(f). For the **effective** date, see Act Sec. 1843(c)(2)-(3), below. Prior to amendment, Code Sec. 71(f) read as follows:

(f) SPECIAL RULES TO PREVENT EXCESS FRONT-LOADING OF ALIMONY PAYMENTS.—

(1) REQUIREMENT THAT PAYMENTS BE FOR MORE THAN 6 YEARS.—Alimony or separate maintenance payments (in excess of $10,000 during any calendar year) paid by the payor spouse to the payee spouse shall not be treated as alimony or separate maintenance payments unless such payments are to be made by the payor spouse to the payee spouse in each of the 6 post-separation years (not taking into account any termination contingent on the death of either spouse or the remarriage of the payee spouse).

(2) RECOMPUTATION WHERE PAYMENTS DECREASE BY MORE THAN $10,000.—If there is an excess amount determined under paragraph (3) for any computation year—

(A) the payor spouse shall include such excess amount in gross income for the payor spouse's taxable year beginning in the computation year, and

(B) the payee spouse shall be allowed a deduction in computing adjusted gross income for such excess amount for the payee spouse's taxable year beginning in the computation year.

(3) DETERMINATION OF EXCESS AMOUNT.—The excess amount determined under this paragraph for any computation year is the sum of—

(A) the excess (if any) of—

(i) the amount of alimony or separate maintenance payments paid by the payor spouse during the immediately preceding post-separation year, over

(ii) the amount of the alimony or separate maintenance payments paid by the payor spouse during the computation year increased by $10,000, plus

(B) a like excess for each of the other preceding post-separation years.

In determining the amount of the alimony or separate maintenance payments paid by the payor spouse during any preceding post-separation year, the aount paid during such year shall be reduced by any excess previously determined in respect of such year under this paragraph.

(4) DEFINITIONS.—For purposes of this subsection—

(A) POST-SEPARATION YEAR.—The term "post-separation year" means any calendar year in the 6 calendar year period beginning with the first calendar year in which the payor spouse paid to the payee spouse alimony or separate maintenance payments to which this section applies.

(B) COMPUTATION YEAR.—The term "computation year" means the post-separation year for which the excess under paragraph (3) is being determined.

(5) EXCEPTIONS.—

(A) WHERE PAYMENTS CEASE BY REASON OF DEATH OR REMARRIAGE.—Paragraph (2) shall not apply to any post-separation year (and subsequent post-separation years) if—

(i) either spouse dies before the close of such post-separation year or the payee spouse remarries before the close of such post-separation year, and

(ii) the alimony or separate maintenance payments cease by reason of such death or remarriage.

(B) SUPPORT PAYMENTS.—For purposes of this subsection, the term "alimony or separate maintenance payment" shall not include any payment received under a decree described in subsection (b)(2)(C).

(C) FLUCTUATING PAYMENTS NOT WITHIN CONTROL OF PAYOR SPOUSE.—For purposes of this subsection, the term "alimony or separate maintenance payment" shall not include any payment to the extent it is made pursuant to a continuing liability (over a period of not less than 6 years) to pay a fixed portion of the income from a business or property or from compensation for employment or self-employment.

P.L. 99-514, §1843(c)(2)-(3), provides:

(2) EFFECTIVE DATES.—

(A) IN GENERAL.—The amendment made by paragraph (1) shall apply with respect to divorce or separation instruments (as defined in section 71(b)(2)) of the Internal Revenue Code of 1986) executed after December 31, 1986.

(B) MODIFICATIONS OF INSTRUMENTS EXECUTED BEFORE JANUARY 1, 1987.—The amendments made by paragraph (1) shall also apply to any divorce or separation instrument (as so defined) executed before January 1, 1987, but modified on or after such date if the modification expressly provides that the amendments made by paragraph (1) shall apply to such modification.

(3) TRANSITIONAL RULE.—In the case of any instrument to which the amendment made by paragraph (1) does not apply, paragraph (2) of section 71(f) of the Internal Revenue Code of 1954 (as in effect on the day before the date of the enactment of this Act) shall apply only with respect to the first 3 post-separation years.

P.L. 99-514, §1843(d):

Amended Code Sec. 71(c)(2)(B) by striking out "specified in paragraph (1)" and inserting in lieu thereof "specified in subparagraph (A)". **Effective** as if included in the provision of P.L. 98-369 to which it relates.

• 1984, Deficit Reduction Act of 1984 (P.L. 98-369)

P.L. 98-369, §422(a):

Amended Code Sec. 71. **Effective** for divorce or separation instruments (as defined in section 71(b)(2) of the Internal Revenue Code of 1954, as amended by this section) executed after 12-31-84. Also **effective** for any divorce or separation instrument (as so defined) executed before 1-1-85, but modified on or after such date if the modification expressly provides that the amendments made by this section shall apply to such modification. Prior to amendment, Code Sec. 71 read as follows:

(a) General Rule.—

(1) Decree of Divorce or Separate Maintenance.—If a wife is divorced or legally separated from her husband under a decree of divorce or of separate maintenance, the wife's gross income includes periodic payments (whether or not made at regular intervals) received after such decree in discharge of (or attributable to property transferred, in trust or otherwise, in discharge of) a legal obligation which, because of the marital or family relationship, is imposed on or incurred by the husband under the decree or under a written instrument incident to such divorce or separation.

(2) Written Separation Agreement.—If a wife is separated from her husband and there is a written separation agreement executed after the date of the enactment of this title, the wife's gross income includes periodic payments (whether or not made at regular intervals) received after such agreement is executed which are made under such agreement and because of the marital or family relationship (or which are attributable to property transferred, in trust or otherwise, under such agreement and because of such relationship). This paragraph shall not apply if the husband and wife make a single return jointly.

(3) Decree for Support.—If a wife is separated from her husband, the wife's gross income includes periodic payments (whether or not made at regular intervals) received by her after the date of the enactment of this title from her husband under a decree entered after March 1, 1954, requiring the husband to make the payments for her support or maintenance. This paragraph shall not apply if the husband and wife make a single return jointly.

(b) Payments to Support Minor Children.—Subsection (a) shall not apply to that part of any payment which the terms of the decree, instrument, or agreement fix, in terms of an amount of money or a part of the payment, as a sum which is payable for the support of minor children of the husband. For purposes of the preceding sentence, if any payment is less than the amount specified in the decree, instrument, or agreement, then so much of such payment as does not exceed the sum payable for support shall be considered a payment for such support.

(c) Principal Sum Paid in Installments.—

(1) General Rule.—For purposes of subsection (a), installment payments discharging a part of an obligation the principal sum of which is, either in terms of money or property, specified in the decree, instrument, or agreement shall not be treated as periodic payments.

(2) Where Period for Payment Is More Than 10 Years.—If, by the terms of the decree, instrument, or agreement, the principal sum referred to in paragraph (1) is to be paid or may be paid over a period ending more than 10 years from the date of such decree, instrument, or agreement, then (notwithstanding paragraph (1)) the installment payments shall be treated as periodic payments for purposes of subsection (a), but (in the case of any one taxable year of the wife) only to the extent of 10 percent of the principal sum. For purposes of the preceding sentence, the part of any principal sum which is allocable to a period after the taxable year of the wife in which it is received shall be treated as an installment payment for the taxable year in which it is received.

(d) Rule for Husband in Case of Transferred Property.—The husband's gross income does not include amounts received which, under subsection (a), are (1) includible in the gross income of the wife, and (2) attributable to transferred property.

(e) Cross References.—

(1) For definitions of "husband" and "wife", see section 7701(a)(17).

(2) For deduction by husband of periodic payments not attributable to transferred property, see section 215.

(3) For taxable status of income of an estate or trust in case of divorce, etc., see section 682.

[Sec. 72]

SEC. 72. ANNUITIES; CERTAIN PROCEEDS OF ENDOWMENT AND LIFE INSURANCE CONTRACTS.

»»→ Caution: Code Sec. 72(a), below, prior to amendment by P.L. 111-240, applies to amounts received in tax years beginning on or before December 31, 2010.

[Sec. 72(a)]

(a) GENERAL RULE FOR ANNUITIES.—Except as otherwise provided in this chapter, gross income includes any amount received as an annuity (whether for a period certain or during one or more lives) under an annuity, endowment, or life insurance contract.

»»→ Caution: Code Sec. 72(a), below, as amended by P.L. 111-240, applies to amounts received in tax years beginning after December 31, 2010.

[Sec. 72(a)]

(a) GENERAL RULE FOR ANNUITIES.—

(1) INCOME INCLUSION.—Except as otherwise provided in this chapter, gross income includes any amount received as an annuity (whether for a period certain or during one or more lives) under an annuity, endowment, or life insurance contract.

(2) PARTIAL ANNUITIZATION.—If any amount is received as an annuity for a period of 10 years or more or during one or more lives under any portion of an annuity, endowment, or life insurance contract—

(A) such portion shall be treated as a separate contract for purposes of this section,

(B) for purposes of applying subsections (b), (c), and (e), the investment in the contract shall be allocated pro rata between each portion of the contract from which amounts are received as an annuity and the portion of the contract from which amounts are not received as an annuity, and

(C) a separate annuity starting date under subsection (c)(4) shall be determined with respect to each portion of the contract from which amounts are received as an annuity.

Amendments

• 2010, Creating Small Business Jobs Act of 2010 (P.L. 111-240)

P.L. 111-240, §2113(a):

Amended Code Sec. 72(a). **Effective** for amounts received in tax years beginning after 12-31-2010. Prior to amendment, Code Sec. 72(a) read as follows:

(a) GENERAL RULE FOR ANNUITIES.—Except as otherwise provided in this chapter, gross income includes any amount received as an annuity (whether for a period certain or during one or more lives) under an annuity, endowment, or life insurance contract.

[Sec. 72(b)]

(b) EXCLUSION RATIO.—

(1) IN GENERAL.—Gross income does not include that part of any amount received as an annuity under an annuity, endowment, or life insurance contract which bears the same ratio to such amount as the investment in the contract (as of the annuity starting date) bears to the expected return under the contract (as of such date).

(2) EXCLUSION LIMITED TO INVESTMENT.—The portion of any amount received as an annuity which is excluded from gross income under paragraph (1) shall not exceed the unrecovered investment in the contract immediately before the receipt of such amount.

(3) DEDUCTION WHERE ANNUITY PAYMENTS CEASE BEFORE ENTIRE INVESTMENT RECOVERED.—

(A) IN GENERAL.—If—

(i) after the annuity starting date, payments as an annuity under the contract cease by reason of the death of an annuitant, and

(ii) as of the date of such cessation, there is unrecovered investment in the contract,

the amount of such unrecovered investment (in excess of any amount specified in subsection (e)(5) which was not included in gross income) shall be allowed as a deduction to the annuitant for his last taxable year.

(B) PAYMENTS TO OTHER PERSONS.—In the case of any contract which provides for payments meeting the requirements of subparagraphs (B) and (C) of subsection (c)(2), the deduction under subparagraph (A) shall be allowed to the person entitled to such payments for the taxable year in which such payments are received.

(C) NET OPERATING LOSS DEDUCTIONS PROVIDED.—For purposes of section 172, a deduction allowed under this paragraph shall be treated as if it were attributable to a trade or business of the taxpayer.

(4) UNRECOVERED INVESTMENT.—For purposes of this subsection, the unrecovered investment in the contract as of any date is—

(A) the investment in the contract (determined without regard to subsection (c)(2)) as of the annuity starting date, reduced by

(B) the aggregate amount received under the contract on or after such annuity starting date and before the date as of which the determination is being made, to the extent such amount was excludable from gross income under this subtitle.

Amendments

• 1996, Small Business Job Protection Act of 1996 (P.L. 104-188)

P.L. 104-188, §1704(l)(1):

Amended Code Sec. 72(b)(4)(A) by inserting "(determined without regard to subsection (c)(2))" after "contract". **Effective** as if included in the amendments made by section 1122(c) of P.L. 99-514.

• 1986, Tax Reform Act of 1986 (P.L. 99-514)

P.L. 99-514, §1122(c)(2):

Amended Code Sec. 72(b). For the **effective** date, as well as special rules, see Act Sec. 1122(h)(1)-(7) following Code Sec. 72(e). Prior to amendment, Code Sec. 72(b) read as follows:

(b) EXCLUSION RATIO.—Gross income does not include that part of any amount received as an annuity under an annuity, endowment, or life insurance contract which bears the same ratio to such amount as the investment in the contract (as of the annuity starting date) bears to the expected return under the contract (as of such date). This subsection shall not apply to any amount to which subsection (d)(1) (relating to certain employee annuities) applies.

[Sec. 72(c)]

(c) DEFINITIONS.—

(1) INVESTMENT IN THE CONTRACT.—For purposes of subsection (b), the investment in the contract as of the annuity starting date is—

(A) the aggregate amount of premiums or other consideration paid for the contract, minus

(B) the aggregate amount received under the contract before such date, to the extent that such amount was excludable from gross income under this subtitle or prior income tax laws.

(2) ADJUSTMENT IN INVESTMENT WHERE THERE IS REFUND FEATURE.—If—

(A) the expected return under the contract depends in whole or in part on the life expectancy of one or more individuals;

(B) the contract provides for payments to be made to a beneficiary (or to the estate of an annuitant) on or after the death of the annuitant or annuitants; and

(C) such payments are in the nature of a refund of the consideration paid,

then the value (computed without discount for interest) of such payments on the annuity starting date shall be subtracted from the amount determined under paragraph (1). Such value shall be computed in accordance with actuarial tables prescribed by the Secretary. For purposes of this paragraph and of subsection (e)(2)(A), the term "refund of the consideration paid" includes amounts payable after the death of an annuitant by reason of a provision in the contract for a life annuity with minimum period of payments certain, but (if part of the consideration was contributed by an employer) does not include that part of any payment to a beneficiary (or to the estate of the annuitant) which is not attributable to the consideration paid by the employee for the contract as determined under paragraph (1)(A).

(3) EXPECTED RETURN.—For purposes of subsection (b), the expected return under the contract shall be determined as follows:

(A) LIFE EXPECTANCY.—If the expected return under the contract, for the period on and after the annuity starting date, depends in whole or in part on the life expectancy of one or more individuals, the expected return shall be computed with reference to actuarial tables prescribed by the Secretary.

(B) INSTALLMENT PAYMENTS.—If subparagraph (A) does not apply, the expected return is the aggregate of the amounts receivable under the contract as an annuity.

(4) ANNUITY STARTING DATE.—For purposes of this section, the annuity starting date in the case of any contract is the first day of the first period for which an amount is received as an annuity under the contract; except that if such date was before January 1, 1954, then the annuity starting date is January 1, 1954.

Amendments

• 1976, Tax Reform Act of 1976 (P.L. 94-455)

P.L. 94-455, §1906(b)(13)(A):

Amended 1954 Code by substituting "Secretary" for "Secretary or his delegate" each place it appeared. **Effective** 2-1-77.

[Sec. 72(d)]

(d) SPECIAL RULES FOR QUALIFIED EMPLOYER RETIREMENT PLANS.—

(1) SIMPLIFIED METHOD OF TAXING ANNUITY PAYMENTS.—

(A) IN GENERAL.—In the case of any amount received as an annuity under a qualified employer retirement plan—

(i) subsection (b) shall not apply, and

(ii) the investment in the contract shall be recovered as provided in this paragraph.

(B) METHOD OF RECOVERING INVESTMENT IN CONTRACT.—

(i) IN GENERAL.—Gross income shall not include so much of any monthly annuity payment under a qualified employer retirement plan as does not exceed the amount obtained by dividing—

(I) the investment in the contract (as of the annuity starting date), by

(II) the number of anticipated payments determined under the table contained in clause (iii) (or, in the case of a contract to which subsection (c)(3)(B) applies, the number of monthly annuity payments under such contract).

(ii) CERTAIN RULES MADE APPLICABLE.—Rules similar to the rules of paragraphs (2) and (3) of subsection (b) shall apply for purposes of this paragraph.

(iii) NUMBER OF ANTICIPATED PAYMENTS.—If the annuity is payable over the life of a single individual, the number of anticipated payments shall be determined as follows:

If the age of the annuitant on the annuity starting date is:	*The number of anticipated payments is:*
Not more than 55	360
More than 55 but not more than 60	310
More than 60 but not more than 65	260
More than 65 but not more than 70	210
More than 70	160

(iv) NUMBER OF ANTICIPATED PAYMENTS WHERE MORE THAN ONE LIFE.—If the annuity is payable over the lives of more than 1 individual, the number of anticipated payments shall be determined as follows:

If the combined ages of annuitants are:	*The number is:*
Not more than 110	410
More than 110 but not more than 120	360
More than 120 but not more than 130	310
More than 130 but not more than 140	260
More than 140	210

(C) ADJUSTMENT FOR REFUND FEATURE NOT APPLICABLE.—For purposes of this paragraph, investment in the contract shall be determined under subsection (c)(1) without regard to subsection (c)(2).

(D) SPECIAL RULE WHERE LUMP SUM PAID IN CONNECTION WITH COMMENCEMENT OF ANNUITY PAYMENTS.—If, in connection with the commencement of annuity payments under any qualified employer retirement plan, the taxpayer receives a lump-sum payment—

(i) such payment shall be taxable under subsection (e) as if received before the annuity starting date, and

(ii) the investment in the contract for purposes of this paragraph shall be determined as if such payment had been so received.

(E) EXCEPTION.—This paragraph shall not apply in any case where the primary annuitant has attained age 75 on the annuity starting date unless there are fewer than 5 years of guaranteed payments under the annuity.

(F) ADJUSTMENT WHERE ANNUITY PAYMENTS NOT ON MONTHLY BASIS.—In any case where the annuity payments are not made on a monthly basis, appropriate adjustments in the application of this paragraph shall be made to take into account the period on the basis of which such payments are made.

(G) QUALIFIED EMPLOYER RETIREMENT PLAN.—For purposes of this paragraph, the term "qualified employer retirement plan" means any plan or contract described in paragraph (1), (2), or (3) of section 4974(c).

(2) TREATMENT OF EMPLOYEE CONTRIBUTIONS UNDER DEFINED CONTRIBUTION PLANS.—For purposes of this section, employee contributions (and any income allocable thereto) under a defined contribution plan may be treated as a separate contract.

Amendments

• 1997, Taxpayer Relief Act of 1997 (P.L. 105-34)

P.L. 105-34, §1075(a):

Amended Code Sec. 72(d)(1)(B) by adding new clause (iv). **Effective** for annuity starting dates beginning after 12-31-97.

P.L. 105-34, §1075(b)(1)-(2):

Amended Code Sec. 72(d)(1)(B)(iii) by inserting the text after the heading and before the table, and by striking "primary" in the table. **Effective** for annuity starting dates beginning after 12-31-97.

• 1996, Small Business Job Protection Act of 1996 (P.L. 104-188)

P.L. 104-188, §1403(a):

Amended Code Sec. 72(d). **Effective** for cases where the annuity starting date is after the 90th day after 8-20-96. Prior to amendment, Code Sec. 72(d) read as follows:

(d) TREATMENT OF EMPLOYEE CONTRIBUTIONS UNDER DEFINED CONTRIBUTION PLANS AS SEPARATE CONTRACTS.—For purposes of this section, employee contributions (and any income allocable thereto) under a defined contribution plan may be treated as a separate contract.

• 1988, Technical and Miscellaneous Revenue Act of 1988 (P.L. 100-647)

P.L. 100-647, §1011A(b)(2)(A):

Amended Code Sec. 72 by adding after subsection (c) new subsection (d). **Effective** as if included in the provision of P.L. 99-514 to which it relates.

• 1986, Tax Reform Act of 1986 (P.L. 99-514)

P.L. 99-514, §1122(c)(1):

Repealed Code Sec. 72(d). For the **effective** date, as well as special rules, see Act Sec. 1122(h)(1)-(7) following Code Sec. 72(e). Prior to repeal, Code Sec. 72(d) read as follows:

(d) EMPLOYEES' ANNUITIES.—

(1) EMPLOYEE'S CONTRIBUTIONS RECOVERABLE IN 3 YEARS.—WHERE—

(A) part of the consideration for an annuity, endowment, or life insurance contract is contributed by the employer, and

(B) during the 3-year period beginning on the date on which an amount is first received under the contract as an annuity, the aggregate amount receivable by the employee under the terms of the contract is equal to or greater than the consideration for the contract contributed by the employee,

then all amounts received as an annuity under the contract shall be excluded from gross income until there has been so excluded an amount equal to the consideration for the contract contributed by the employee. Thereafter all amounts so received under the contract shall be included in gross income.

(2) SPECIAL RULES FOR APPLICATION OF PARAGRAPH (1).—For purposes of paragraph (1)—

(A) if the employee died before any amount was received as an annuity under the contract, the words "receivable by the employee" shall be read as "receivable by a beneficiary of the employee"; and

(B) any contribution made with respect to the contract while the employee is an employee within the meaning of section 401(c)(1) which is not allowed as a deduction under section 404 shall be treated as consideration for the contract contributed by the employee.

(3) CROSS REFERENCE.—

For certain rules for determining whether amounts contributed by employer are includible in the gross income of the employee, see part I of subchapter D (sec. 401 and following, relating to pension, profit-sharing, and stock bonus plans, etc.).

• 1976, Tax Reform Act of 1976 (P.L. 94-455)

P.L. 94-455, §1901(a)(12), (d):

Amended Code Sec. 72(d)(1) by striking out "(whether or not before January 1, 1954)" and by striking out "(under this paragraph and prior income tax laws)". **Effective** for tax years beginning after 12-31-76.

• 1962, Self-Employed Individuals Tax Retirement Act of 1962 (P.L. 87-792)

P.L. 87-792, §4:

Amended Code Sec. 72(d)(2). **Effective** 1-1-63. Prior to amendment, Code Sec. 72(d)(2) read as follows:

(2) Special Rules for Application of Paragraph (1).—For purposes of paragraph (1), if the employee died before any amount was received as an annuity under the contract, the words "receivable by the employee" shall be read as "receivable by a beneficiary of the employee".

[Sec. 72(e)]

(e) AMOUNTS NOT RECEIVED AS ANNUITIES.—

(1) APPLICATION OF SUBSECTION.—

(A) IN GENERAL.—This subsection shall apply to any amount which—

(i) is received under an annuity, endowment, or life insurance contract, and

(ii) is not received as an annuity, if no provision of this subtitle (other than this subsection) applies with respect to such amount.

(B) DIVIDENDS.—For purposes of this section, any amount received which is in the nature of a dividend or similar distribution shall be treated as an amount not received as an annuity.

(2) GENERAL RULE.—Any amount to which this subsection applies—

(A) if received on or after the annuity starting date, shall be included in gross income, or

(B) if received before the annuity starting date—

(i) shall be included in gross income to the extent allocable to income on the contract, and

(ii) shall not be included in gross income to the extent allocable to the investment in the contract.

(3) ALLOCATION OF AMOUNTS TO INCOME AND INVESTMENT.—For purposes of paragraph (2)(B)—

(A) ALLOCATION TO INCOME.—Any amount to which this subsection applies shall be treated as allocable to income on the contract to the extent that such amount does not exceed the excess (if any) of—

(i) the cash value of the contract (determined without regard to any surrender charge) immediately before the amount is received, over

(ii) the investment in the contract at such time.

(B) ALLOCATION TO INVESTMENT.—Any amount to which this subsection applies shall be treated as allocable to investment in the contract to the extent that such amount is not allocated to income under subparagraph (A).

(4) SPECIAL RULES FOR APPLICATION OF PARAGRAPH (2)(B).—For purposes of paragraph (2)(B)—

(A) LOANS TREATED AS DISTRIBUTIONS.—If, during any taxable year, an individual—

(i) receives (directly or indirectly) any amount as a loan under any contract to which this subsection applies, or

(ii) assigns or pledges (or agrees to assign or pledge) any portion of the value of any such contract,

such amount or portion shall be treated as received under the contract as an amount not received as an annuity. The preceding sentence shall not apply for purposes of determining investment in the contract, except that the investment in the contract shall be increased by any amount included in gross income by reason of the amount treated as received under the preceding sentence.

(B) TREATMENT OF POLICYHOLDER DIVIDENDS.—Any amount described in paragraph (1)(B) shall not be included in gross income under paragraph (2)(B)(i) to the extent such amount is retained by the insurer as a premium or other consideration paid for the contract.

(C) TREATMENT OF TRANSFERS WITHOUT ADEQUATE CONSIDERATION.—

(i) IN GENERAL.—If an individual who holds an annuity contract transfers it without full and adequate consideration, such individual shall be treated as receiving an amount equal to the excess of—

(I) the cash surrender value of such contract at the time of transfer, over

(II) the investment in such contract at such time,

under the contract as an amount not received as an annuity.

(ii) EXCEPTION FOR CERTAIN TRANSFERS BETWEEN SPOUSES OR FORMER SPOUSES.—Clause (i) shall not apply to any transfer to which section 1041(a) (relating to transfers of property between spouses or incident to divorce) applies.

(iii) ADJUSTMENT TO INVESTMENT IN CONTRACT OF TRANSFEREE.—If under clause (i) an amount is included in the gross income of the transferor of an annuity contract, the investment in the contract of the transferee in such contract shall be increased by the amount so included.

(5) RETENTION OF EXISTING RULES IN CERTAIN CASES.—

(A) IN GENERAL.—In any case to which this paragraph applies—

(i) paragraphs (2)(B) and (4)(A) shall not apply, and

(ii) if paragraph (2)(A) does not apply,

the amount shall be included in gross income, but only to the extent it exceeds the investment in the contract.

(B) EXISTING CONTRACTS.—This paragraph shall apply to contracts entered into before August 14, 1982. Any amount allocable to investment in the contract after August 13, 1982, shall be treated as from a contract entered into after such date.

(C) CERTAIN LIFE INSURANCE AND ENDOWMENT CONTRACTS.—Except as provided in paragraph (10) and except to the extent prescribed by the Secretary by regulations, this paragraph shall apply to any amount not received as an annuity which is received under a life insurance or endowment contract.

(D) CONTRACTS UNDER QUALIFIED PLANS.—Except as provided in paragraph (8), this paragraph shall apply to any amount received—

(i) from a trust described in section 401(a) which is exempt from tax under section 501(a),

(ii) from a contract—

(I) purchased by a trust described in clause (i),

(II) purchased as part of a plan described in section 403(a),

(III) described in section 403(b), or

(IV) provided for employees of a life insurance company under a plan described in section 818(a)(3), or

(iii) from an individual retirement account or an individual retirement annuity.

Any dividend described in section 404(k) which is received by a participant or beneficiary shall, for purposes of this subparagraph, be treated as paid under a separate contract to which clause (ii)(I) applies.

(E) FULL REFUNDS, SURRENDERS, REDEMPTIONS, AND MATURITIES.—This paragraph shall apply to—

(i) any amount received, whether in a single sum or otherwise, under a contract in full discharge of the obligation under the contract which is in the nature of a refund of the consideration paid for the contract, and

(ii) any amount received under a contract on its complete surrender, redemption, or maturity.

In the case of any amount to which the preceding sentence applies, the rule of paragraph (2)(A) shall not apply.

(6) INVESTMENT IN THE CONTRACT.—For purposes of this subsection, the investment in the contract as of any date is—

(A) the aggregate amount of premiums or other consideration paid for the contract before such date, minus

(B) the aggregate amount received under the contract before such date, to the extent that such amount was excludable from gross income under this subtitle or prior income tax laws.

(7) [Repealed.]

(8) EXTENSION OF PARAGRAPH (2)(B) TO QUALIFIED PLANS.—

(A) IN GENERAL.—Notwithstanding any other provision of this subsection, in the case of any amount received before the annuity starting date from a trust or contract described in paragraph (5)(D), paragraph (2)(B) shall apply to such amounts.

(B) ALLOCATION OF AMOUNT RECEIVED.—For purposes of paragraph (2)(B), the amount allocated to the investment in the contract shall be the portion of the amount described in subparagraph (A) which bears the same ratio to such amount as the investment in the contract bears to the account balance. The determination under the preceding sentence shall be made as of the time of the distribution or at such other time as the Secretary may prescribe.

(C) TREATMENT OF FORFEITABLE RIGHTS.—If an employee does not have a nonforfeitable right to any amount under any trust or contract to which subparagraph (A) applies, such amount shall not be treated as part of the account balance.

(D) INVESTMENT IN THE CONTRACT BEFORE 1987.—In the case of a plan which on May 5, 1986, permitted withdrawal of any employee contributions before separation from service, subparagraph (A) shall apply only to the extent that amounts received before the annuity starting date (when increased by amounts previously received under the contract after December 31, 1986) exceed the investment in the contract as of December 31, 1986.

(9) EXTENSION OF PARAGRAPH (2)(B) TO QUALIFIED TUITION PROGRAMS AND COVERDELL EDUCATION SAVINGS ACCOUNTS.—Notwithstanding any other provision of this subsection, paragraph (2)(B) shall apply to amounts received under a qualified tuition program (as defined in section 529(b)) or under a Coverdell education savings account (as defined in section 530(b)). The rule of paragraph (8)(B) shall apply for purposes of this paragraph.

(10) TREATMENT OF MODIFIED ENDOWMENT CONTRACTS.—

(A) IN GENERAL.—Notwithstanding paragraph (5)(C), in the case of any modified endowment contract (as defined in section 7702A)—

(i) paragraphs (2)(B) and (4)(A) shall apply, and

(ii) in applying paragraph (4)(A), "any person" shall be substituted for "an individual".

(B) TREATMENT OF CERTAIN BURIAL CONTRACTS.—Notwithstanding subparagraph (A), paragraph (4)(A) shall not apply to any assignment (or pledge) of a modified endowment contract if such assignment (or pledge) is solely to cover the payment of expenses referred to in section 7702(e)(2)(C)(iii) and if the maximum death benefit under such contract does not exceed $25,000.

(11) SPECIAL RULES FOR CERTAIN COMBINATION CONTRACTS PROVIDING LONG-TERM CARE INSURANCE.—Notwithstanding paragraphs (2), (5)(C), and (10), in the case of any charge against the cash value of an annuity contract or the cash surrender value of a life insurance contract made as payment for coverage under a qualified long-term care insurance contract which is part of or a rider on such annuity or life insurance contract—

(A) the investment in the contract shall be reduced (but not below zero) by such charge, and

(B) such charge shall not be includible in gross income.

(12) ANTI-ABUSE RULES.—

(A) IN GENERAL.—For purposes of determining the amount includible in gross income under this subsection—

(i) all modified endowment contracts issued by the same company to the same policyholder during any calendar year shall be treated as 1 modified endowment contract, and

(ii) all annuity contracts issued by the same company to the same policyholder during any calendar year shall be treated as 1 annuity contract.

The preceding sentence shall not apply to any contract described in paragraph (5)(D).

(B) REGULATORY AUTHORITY.—The Secretary may by regulations prescribe such additional rules as may be necessary or appropriate to prevent avoidance of the purposes of this subsection through serial purchases of contracts or otherwise.

Amendments

• 2006, Pension Protection Act of 2006 (P.L. 109-280)

P.L. 109-280, §844(a):

Amended Code Sec. 72(e) by redesignating paragraph (11) as paragraph (12) and by inserting after paragraph (10) a new paragraph (11). **Effective** for contracts issued after 12-31-1996, but only with respect to tax years beginning after 12-31-2009.

P.L. 109-280, §1304(a), provides:

(a) PERMANENT EXTENSION OF MODIFICATIONS.—Section 901 of the Economic Growth and Tax Relief Reconciliation Act of 2001 [P.L. 107-16] (relating to sunset provisions) shall not apply to section 402 of such Act (relating to modifications to qualified tuition programs).

• 2001 (P.L. 107-22)

P.L. 107-22, §1(b)(1)(A):

Amended Code Sec. 72(e)(9) by striking "an education individual retirement" and inserting "a Coverdell education savings". **Effective** 7-26-2001.

P.L. 107-22, §1(b)(3)(A), as amended by P.L. 108-311, §408(b)(3):

Amended the heading for Code Sec. 72(e)(9) by striking "EDUCATIONAL INDIVIDUAL RETIREMENT" and inserting "COVERDELIEDUCATION SAVINGS". **Effective** 7-26-2001.

• 2001, Economic Growth and Tax Relief Reconciliation Act of 2001 (P.L. 107-16)

P.L. 107-16, §402(a)(4)(A):

Amended Code Sec. 72(e)(9) by striking "qualified State tuition" each place it appears and inserting "qualified tuition". **Effective** for tax years beginning after 12-31-2001.

P.L. 107-16, §402(a)(4)(B):

Amended the heading for Code Sec. 72(e)(9) by striking "QUALIFIED STATE TUITION" and inserting "QUALIFIED TUITION". **Effective** for tax years beginning after 12-31-2001.

P.L. 107-16, §901(a)-(b), provides [but see P.L. 109-280, §1304(a), above]:

SEC. 901. SUNSET OF PROVISIONS OF ACT.

(a) IN GENERAL.—All provisions of, and amendments made by, this Act shall not apply—

(1) to taxable, plan, or limitation years beginning after December 31, 2010, or

(2) in the case of title V, to estates of decedents dying, gifts made, or generation skipping transfers, after December 31, 2010.

(b) APPLICATION OF CERTAIN LAWS.—The Internal Revenue Code of 1986 and the Employee Retirement Income Security Act of 1974 shall be applied and administered to years, estates, gifts, and transfers described in subsection (a) as if the provisions and amendments described in subsection (a) had never been enacted.

• 1998, IRS Restructuring and Reform Act of 1998 (P.L. 105-206)

P.L. 105-206, §6004(d)(3)(B):

Amended Code Sec. 72(e) by inserting after paragraph (8) a new paragraph (9). **Effective** as if included in the provision of P.L. 105-34 to which it relates [**effective** for tax years beginning after 12-31-97.—CCH].

• 1989, Omnibus Budget Reconciliation Act of 1989 (P.L. 101-239)

P.L. 101-239, §7815(a)(3):

Amended Code Sec. 72(e)(11)(A) by adding at the end thereof a new sentence. **Effective** as if included in the provision of P.L. 100-647 to which it relates.

P.L. 101-239, §7815(a)(5):

Amended Code Sec. 72(e)(11)(A) by striking "12-month period" and inserting "calendar year". **Effective** as if included in the provision of P.L. 100-647 to which it relates.

• 1988, Technical and Miscellaneous Revenue Act of 1988 (P.L. 100-647)

P.L. 100-647, §1011A(b)(2)(B):

Amended Code Sec. 72(e) by striking out paragraph (9). **Effective** as if included in the provision of P.L. 99-514 to which it relates. Prior to amendment, Code Sec. 72(e)(9) read as follows:

(9) TREATMENT OF EMPLOYEE CONTRIBUTIONS AS SEPARATE CONTRACT.—Any employee contributions (and any income allocable thereto) under a defined contribution plan shall be treated as a separate contract for purposes of this subsection.

P.L. 100-647, §1011A(b)(9)(A):

Repealed Code Sec. 72(e)(7). **Effective** as if included in the provision of P.L. 99-514 to which it relates. Prior to repeal, Code Sec. 72(e)(7) read as follows:

(7) SPECIAL RULES FOR PLANS WHERE SUBSTANTIALLY ALL CONTRIBUTIONS ARE EMPLOYEE CONTRIBUTIONS.—

(A) IN GENERAL.—In the case of any plan or contract to which this paragraph applies, subparagraph (D) of paragraph (5) shall not apply to any amount received from such plan or contract.

(B) PLANS OR CONTRACTS TO WHICH THIS PARAGRAPH APPLIES.—This paragraph shall apply to any plan or contract—

(i) which is described in clause (i) or subclause (I), (II), or (III) of clause (ii) of paragraph (5)(D), and

(ii) with respect to which 85 percent or more of the total contributions during a representative period are derived from employee contributions.

For purposes of clause (ii), deductible employee contributions (as defined in subsection (o)(5)(A)) shall not be taken into account.

(C) SPECIAL RULE FOR CERTAIN FEDERAL PLANS.—If the Federal Government or an instrumentality thereof maintains more than 1 plan, subparagraph (B) shall be applied by aggregating all such plans which are actively administered by the Federal Government or such instrumentality.

P.L. 100-647, §1011A(b)(9)(B):

Amended Code Sec. 72(e)(5)(D) by striking out "paragraphs (7) and (8)" and inserting in lieu thereof "paragraph (8)". **Effective** as if included in the provision of P.L. 99-514 to which it relates.

P.L. 100-647, §1011A(b)(9)(C):

Amended Code Sec. 72(e)(8)(A) by striking out "(other than paragraph (7))" after "of this subsection". **Effective** as if included in the provision of P.L. 99-514 to which it relates.

P.L. 100-647, §5012(a)(1):

Amended Code Sec. 72(e) by adding at the end thereof a new paragraph (10). For the **effective** date, see Act Sec. 5012(e), below.

P.L. 100-647, §5012(a)(2):

Amended Code Sec. 72(e)(5)(C) by striking out "Except to the extent" and inserting in lieu thereof "Except as provided in paragraph (10) and except to the extent". For the **effective** date, see Act Sec. 5012(e), below.

P.L. 100-647, §5012(d)(1):

Amended Code Sec. 72(e)(4)(A) by adding at the end thereof a new sentence. For the **effective** date, see Act Sec. 5012(e), below.

P.L. 100-647, §5012(d)(2):

Amended Code Sec. 72(e) by adding at the end thereof a new paragraph (11). For the **effective** date, see Act Sec. 5012(e), below.

P.L. 100-647, §5012(e), amended by P.L. 101-239, §7815(a)(2), provides:

(e) EFFECTIVE DATES.—

(1) IN GENERAL.—Except as otherwise provided in this subsection, the amendments made by this section shall apply to contracts entered into on or after June 21, 1988.

(2) SPECIAL RULE WHERE DEATH BENEFIT INCREASES BY MORE THAN $150,000.—If the death benefit under the contract increases by more than $150,000 over the death benefit under the contract in effect on October 20, 1988, the rules of section 7702A(c)(3) of the 1986 Code (as added by this section) shall apply in determining whether such contract is issued on or after June 21, 1988. The preceding sentence shall not apply in the case of a contract which, as of June 21, 1988, required at least 7 level annual premium payments and under which the policyholder makes at least 7 level annual premium payments.

(3) CERTAIN OTHER MATERIAL CHANGES TAKEN INTO ACCOUNT.—A contract entered into before June 21, 1988, shall be treated as entered into after such date if—

(A) on or after June 21, 1988, the death benefit under the contract is increased (or a qualified additional benefit is increased or added) and before June 21, 1988, the owner of the contract did not have a unilateral right under the contract to obtain such increase or addition without providing additional evidence of insurability, or

(B) the contract is converted after June 20, 1988, from a term life insurance contract to a life insurance contract providing coverage other than term life insurance coverage without regard to any right of the owner of the contract to such conversion.

(4) CERTAIN EXCHANGES PERMITTED.—In the case of a modified endowment contract which—

(A) required at least 7 annual level premium payments,

(B) is entered into after June 20, 1988, and before the date of the enactment of this Act, and

(C) is exchanged within 3 months after such date of enactment for a life insurance contract which meets the requirements of section 7702A(b),

the contract which is received in exchange for such contract shall not be treated as a modified endowment contract if the taxpayer elects, notwithstanding section 1035 of the 1986 Code, to recognize gain on such exchange.

(5) SPECIAL RULE FOR ANNUITY CONTRACTS.—In the case of annuity contracts, the amendments made by subsection (d) shall apply to contracts entered into after October 21, 1988.

• 1986, Tax Reform Act of 1986 (P.L. 99-514)

P.L. 99-514, §1122(c)(3)(A):

Amended Code Sec. 72(e) by adding at the end thereof new paragraphs (8) and (9). For the **effective** date, as well as special rules, see Act Sec. 1122(h)(1)-(7), below.

P.L. 99-514, §1122(c)(3)(B):

Amended Code Sec. 72(e)(5)(D) by striking out "paragraph (7)" and inserting in lieu thereof "paragraphs (7) and (8)". For the **effective** date, as well as special rules, see Act Sec. 1122(h)(1)-(7), below.

P.L. 99-514, §1122(h)(1)-(7), as amended by P.L. 100-647, §1011A(b)(13)-(15), provides:

(h) Effective Dates.—

(1) IN GENERAL.—Except as otherwise provided in this subsection, the amendments made by this section shall apply to amounts distributed after December 31, 1986, in taxable years ending after such date.

(2) SUBSECTION(c).—

(A) SUBSECTION(c)(1).—The amendment made by subsection (c)(1) shall apply to individuals whose annuity starting date is after July 1, 1986.

(B) SUBSECTION(c)(2).—The amendment made by subsection (c)(2) shall apply to individuals whose annuity starting date is after December 31, 1986, except that section 72(b)(3) of the Internal Revenue Code of 1986 (as added by such subsection) shall apply to individuals whose annuity starting date is after July 1, 1986.

(C) SPECIAL RULE FOR AMOUNTS NOT RECEIVED AS ANNUITIES.—In the case of any plan not described in section 72(e)(8)(D) of the Internal Revenue Code of 1986 (as added by subsection (c)(3)), the amendments made by subsection (c)(3) shall apply to amounts received after July 1, 1986.

(3) SPECIAL RULE FOR INDIVIDUALS WHO ATTAINED AGE 50 BEFORE JANUARY 1, 1986.—

(A) IN GENERAL.—In the case of a lump sum distribution to which this paragraph applies—

(i) the existing capital gains provisions shall continue to apply, and

(ii) the requirement of subparagraph (B) of section 402(e)(4) of the Internal Revenue Code of 1986 (as amended by subsection (a)) that the distribution be received after attaining age 59½ shall not apply.

(B) COMPUTATION OF TAX.—If subparagraph (A) applies to any lump sum distribution of any taxpayer for any taxable year, the tax imposed by section 1 of the Internal Revenue Code of 1986 on such taxpayer for such taxable year shall be equal to the sum of—

(i) the tax imposed by such section 1 on the taxable income of the taxpayer (reduced by the portion of such lump sum distribution to which clause (ii) applies), plus

(ii) 20 percent of the portion of such lump sum distribution to which the existing capital gains provisions continue to apply by reason of this paragraph.

(C) LUMP SUM DISTRIBUTIONS TO WHICH PARAGRAPH APPLIES.—This paragraph shall apply to any lump sum distribution if—

(i) such lump sum distribution is received by an employee who has attained age 50 before January 1, 1986, or by an individual, estate, or trust with respect to such an employee and

(ii) the taxpayer makes an election under this paragraph.

Not more than 1 election may be made under this paragraph with respect to an employee. An election under this subparagraph shall be treated as an election under section 402(e)(4)(B) of such Code for purposes of such Code.

(4) 5-YEAR PHASE-OUT OF CAPITAL GAINS TREATMENT.—

(A) Notwithstanding the amendment made by subsection (b), if the taxpayer elects the application of this paragraph with respect to any distribution after December 31, 1986, and before January 1, 1992, the phase-out percentage of the amount which would have been treated, without regard to this subparagraph, as long-term capital gain under the existing capital gains provisions shall be treated as long-term capital gain.

(B) For purposes of this paragraph—

In the case of distributions during calendar year:	*The phase-out percentage is:*
1987	100
1988	95
1989	75
1990	50
1991	25

(C) No more than 1 election may be made under this paragraph with respect to an employee. An election under this paragraph shall be treated as an election under section

402(e)(4)(B) of the Internal Revenue Code of 1986 for purposes of such Code.

(5) ELECTION OF 10-YEAR AVERAGING.—An employee who has attained age 50 before January 1, 1986, and elects the application of paragraph (3) or section 402(e)(1) of the Internal Revenue Code of 1986 (as amended by this Act) may elect to have such section applied by substituting "10 times" for "5 times" and "1/10" for "1/5" in subparagraph (B) thereof. For purposes of the preceding sentence, section 402(e)(1) of such Code shall be applied by using the rate of tax in effect under section 1 of the Internal Revenue Code of 1954 for taxable years beginning during 1986 and by including in gross income the zero bracket amount in effect under section 63(d) of such Code for such years. This paragraph shall also apply to an individual, estate, or trust which receives a distribution with respect to an employee described in this paragraph.

(6) EXISTING CAPITAL GAIN PROVISIONS.—For purposes of paragraphs (3) and (4), the term "existing capital gains provisions" means the provisions of paragraph (2) of section 402(a) of the Internal Revenue Code of 1954 (as in effect on the day before the date of the enactment of this Act) and paragraph (2) of section 403(a) of such Code (as so in effect).

(7) SUBSECTION(d).—The amendments made by subsection (d) shall apply to taxable years beginning after December 31, 1985.

(8) FROZEN DEPOSITS.—The amendments made by subsection (e)(2) shall apply to amounts transferred to an employee before, on, or after the date of the enactment of this Act, except that in the case of an amount transferred on or before such date, the 60-day period referred to in section 402(a)(5)(C) of the Internal Revenue Code of 1986 shall not expire before the 60th day after the date of the enactment of this Act.

P.L. 99-514, §1826(b)(3):

Amended Code Sec. 72(e)(4) by adding at the end thereof new subparagraph (C). **Effective** for contracts issued after the date which is 6 months after 10-22-86, in tax years ending after such date.

P.L. 99-514, §1852(c)(1)(A)-(C):

Amended Code Sec. 72(e)(7)(B) by striking out "any trust or contract" and inserting in lieu thereof "any plan or contract", by striking out "85 percent of" and inserting in lieu thereof "85 percent or more of", and by adding at the end thereof a new sentence. **Effective** as if included in the provision of P.L. 98-369 to which it relates.

P.L. 99-514, §1854(b)(1):

Amended Code Sec. 72(e)(5) by adding at the end of subparagraph (D) a new flush sentence. **Not effective** for dividends paid before 1-1-86, if the taxpayer treated such dividends in a manner inconsistent with such amendments on a return filed with the Secretary before 10-22-86.

• 1984, Deficit Reduction Act of 1984 (P.L. 98-369)

P.L. 98-369, §211(b)(1):

Amended Code Sec. 72(e)(5)(D)(i)(IV) by striking out "section 805(d)(3)" and inserting in lieu thereof "section 818(a)(3)". **Effective** for tax years beginning after 12-31-83.

P.L. 98-369, §523(a):

Amended Code Sec. 72(e) by adding at the end thereof new paragraph (7). **Effective** for any amount received or loan made after 10-16-84.

P.L. 98-369, §523(b)(1):

Amended Code Sec. 72(e)(5)(D) by striking out "This" and inserting in lieu thereof "Except as provided in paragraph (7), this". **Effective** for any amount received or loan made after 10-16-84.

• 1982, Tax Equity and Fiscal Responsibility Act of 1982 (P.L. 97-248)

P.L. 97-248, §265(a):

Amended Code Sec. 72(e). **Effective** 8-13-82. Prior to amendment, it read as follows:

(e) AMOUNTS NOT RECEIVED AS ANNUITIES.—

(1) GENERAL RULE.—If any amount is received under an annuity, endowment, or life insurance contract, if such amount is not received as an annuity, and if no other provision of this subtitle applies, then such amount—

(A) if received on or after the annuity starting date, shall be included in gross income; or

(B) if subparagraph (A) does not apply, shall be included in gross income, but only to the extent that it (when added to amounts previously received under the contract which were excludable from gross income under this subtitle or prior income tax laws) exceeds the aggregate premiums or other consideration paid.

For purposes of this section, any amount received which is in the nature of a dividend or similar distribution shall be treated as an amount not received as an annuity.

(2) SPECIAL RULES FOR APPLICATION OF PARAGRAPH (1).—For purposes of paragraph (1), the following shall be treated as amounts not received as an annuity:

(A) any amount received, whether in a single sum or otherwise, under a contract in full discharge of the obligation under the contract which is in the nature of a refund of the consideration paid for the contract; and

(B) any amount received under a contract on its surrender, redemption, or maturity.

In the case of any amount to which the preceding sentence applies, the rule of paragraph (1)(B) shall apply (and the rule of paragraph (1)(A) shall not apply).

• 1964, Revenue Act of 1964 (P.L. 88-272)

P. L. 88-272, §232(b):

Repealed Sec. 72(e)(3), **Effective** 1-1-64. Prior to amendment, 72(e)(3) read as follows:

(3) Limit on tax attributable to receipt of lump sum.—If a lump sum is received under an annuity, endowment, or life insurance contract, and the part which is includible in gross income is determined under paragraph (1), then the tax attributable to the inclusion of such part in gross income for the taxable year shall not be greater than the aggregate of the taxes attributable to such part had it been included in the gross income of the taxpayer ratably over the taxable year in which received and the preceding 2 taxable years.

[Sec. 72(f)]

(f) SPECIAL RULES FOR COMPUTING EMPLOYEES' CONTRIBUTIONS.—In computing, for purposes of subsection (c)(1)(A), the aggregate amount of premiums or other consideration paid for the contract, and for purposes of subsection (e)(6), the aggregate premiums or other consideration paid, amounts contributed by the employer shall be included, but only to the extent that—

(1) such amounts were includible in the gross income of the employee under this subtitle or prior income tax laws; or

(2) if such amounts had been paid directly to the employee at the time they were contributed, they would not have been includible in the gross income of the employee under the law applicable at the time of such contribution.

Paragraph (2) shall not apply to amounts which were contributed by the employer after December 31, 1962, and which would not have been includible in the gross income of the employee by reason of the application of section 911 if such amounts had been paid directly to the employee at the time of contribution. The preceding sentence shall not apply to amounts which were contributed by the employer, as determined under regulations prescribed by the Secretary, to provide pension or annuity credits, to the extent such credits are attributable to services performed before January 1, 1963, and are provided pursuant to pension or annuity plan provisions in existence on March 12, 1962, and on that date applicable to such services, or to the extent such credits are attributable to services performed as a foreign missionary (within the meaning of section 403(b)(2)(D)(iii), as in effect before the enactment of the Economic Growth and Tax Relief Reconciliation Act of 2001).

Amendments

• 2006, Pension Protection Act of 2006 (P.L. 109-280)

P.L. 109-280, §811, provides:

SEC. 811. PENSIONS AND INDIVIDUAL RETIREMENT ARRANGEMENT PROVISIONS OF ECONOMIC GROWTH AND TAX RELIEF RECONCILIATION ACT OF 2001 MADE PERMANENT.

Title IX of the Economic Growth and Tax Relief Reconciliation Act of 2001 [P.L. 107-16] shall not apply to the provisions of, and amendments made by, subtitles A through F of title VI [§§601-666]of such Act (relating to pension and individual retirement arrangement provisions).

• 2004, Working Families Tax Relief Act of 2004 (P.L. 108-311)

P.L. 108-311, §408(a)(4):

Amended Code Sec. 72(f) by striking "Economic Growth and Tax Relief Reconciliation Act of 2001" and inserting "Economic Growth and Tax Relief Reconciliation Act of 2001)". **Effective** 10-4-2004.

• 2001, Economic Growth and Tax Relief Reconciliation Act of 2001 (P.L. 107-16)

P.L. 107-16, §632(a)(3)(A):

Amended Code Sec. 72(f) by striking "section 403(b)(2)(D)(iii))" and inserting "section 403(b)(2)(D)(iii), as in effect before the enactment of the Economic Growth and Tax Relief Reconciliation Act of 2001[)]". **Effective** for years beginning after 12-31-2001.

P.L. 107-16, §901(a)-(b), provides [but see P.L. 109-280, §811, above]:

SEC. 901. SUNSET OF PROVISIONS OF ACT.

(a) IN GENERAL.—All provisions of, and amendments made by, this Act shall not apply—

(1) to taxable, plan, or limitation years beginning after December 31, 2010, or

(2) in the case of title V, to estates of decedents dying, gifts made, or generation skipping transfers, after December 31, 2010.

(b) APPLICATION OF CERTAIN LAWS.—The Internal Revenue Code of 1986 and the Employee Retirement Income Security Act of 1974 shall be applied and administered to years, estates, gifts, and transfers described in subsection (a) as if the provisions and amendments described in subsection (a) had never been enacted.

• 1996, Small Business Job Protection Act of 1996 (P.L. 104-188)

P.L. 104-188, §1463(a):

Amended Code Sec. 72(f) by inserting ", or to the extent such credits are attributable to services performed as a foreign missionary (within the meaning of section 403(b)(2)(D)(iii))" before the last period in the last sentence. **Effective** for tax years beginning after 12-31-96.

• 1988, Technical and Miscellaneous Revenue Act of 1988 (P.L. 100-647)

P.L. 100-647, §1011A(b)(1)(A):

Amended Code Sec. 72(f) by striking out "for purposes of subsections (d)(1) and (e)(7), the consideration for the contract contributed by the employee," following "paid for the contract". **Effective** as if included in the provision of P.L. 99-514 to which it relates.

• 1986, Tax Reform Act of 1986 (P.L. 99-514)

P.L. 99-514, §1852(c)(3)(A) and (B):

Amended Code Sec. 72(f) by striking out "subsection (d)(1)" and inserting in lieu thereof "subsections (d)(1) and (e)(7)", and by striking out "subsection (e)(1)(B)" and inserting in lieu thereof "subsection (e)(6)". **Effective** as if included in the provision of P.L. 98-369 to which it relates.

• 1976, Tax Reform Act of 1976 (P.L. 94-455)

P.L. 94-455, §1906(b)(13)(A):

Amended 1954 Code by substituting "Secretary" for "Secretary or his delegate" each place it appeared. **Effective** 2-1-77.

• 1962, Revenue Act of 1962 (P.L. 87-834)

P.L. 87-834, §11(b):

Amended Code Sec. 72(f) by adding the last two sentences. **Effective** for tax years ending after 12-31-62.

[Sec. 72(g)]

(g) RULES FOR TRANSFEREE WHERE TRANSFER WAS FOR VALUE.—Where any contract (or any interest therein) is transferred (by assignment or otherwise) for a valuable consideration, to the extent that the contract (or interest therein) does not, in the hands of the transferee, have a basis which is determined by reference to the basis in the hands of the transferor, then—

(1) for purposes of this section, only the actual value of such consideration, plus the amount of the premiums and other consideration paid by the transferee after the transfer, shall be taken into account in computing the aggregate amount of the premiums or other consideration paid for the contract;

(2) for purposes of subsection (c) (1) (B), there shall be taken into account only the aggregate amount received under the contract by the transferee before the annuity starting date, to the extent that such amount was excludable from gross income under this subtitle or prior income tax laws; and

(3) the annuity starting date is January 1, 1954, or the first day of the first period for which the transferee received an amount under the contract as an annuity, whichever is the later.

For purposes of this subsection, the term "transferee" includes a beneficiary of, or the estate of, the transferee.

[Sec. 72(h)]

(h) OPTION TO RECEIVE ANNUITY IN LIEU OF LUMP SUM.—If—

(1) a contract provides for payment of a lump sum in full discharge of an obligation under the contract, subject to an option to receive an annuity in lieu of such lump sum;

(2) the option is exercised within 60 days after the day on which such lump sum first became payable; and

(3) part or all of such lump sum would (but for this subsection) be includible in gross income by reason of subsection (e) (1),

then, for purposes of this subtitle, no part of such lump sum shall be considered as includible in gross income at the time such lump sum first became payable.

[Sec. 72(i)—Repealed]

Amendments

• 1976, Tax Reform Act of 1976 (P.L. 94-455)

P.L. 94-455, §1951(b)(1)(A):

Repealed Sec. 72(i). **Effective** 12-31-76. Prior to amendment, Code Sec. 72(i) read as follows:

(i) JOINT AND SURVIVOR ANNUITIES WHERE FIRST ANNUITANT DIED IN 1951, 1952, OR 1953.—Where an annuitant died after December 31, 1950, and before January 1, 1954, and the basis of a surviving annuitant's interest in the joint and survivor annuity contract was determinable under section 113(a)(5) of the Internal Revenue Code of 1939, then—

(1) subsection (d) shall not apply with respect to such contract;

(2) for purposes of this section, the aggregate amount of premiums or other consideration paid for the contract is the basis of the contract determined under such section 113(a)(5);

(3) for purposes of subsection (c)(1)(B), there shall be taken into account only the aggregate amount received by the surviving annuitant under the contract before the annuity starting date, to the extent that such amount was excludable from gross income under this subtitle or prior income tax laws; and

(4) the annuity starting date is January 1, 1954, or the first day of the first period for which the surviving annuitant received an amount under the contract as an annuity, whichever is the later.

P.L. 94-455, §1951(b)(1)(B), provides:

(B) SAVINGS PROVISION.—Notwithstanding subparagraph (A), if the provisions of section 72(i) applied to amounts received in taxable years beginning before January 1, 1977, under an annuity contract, then amounts received under such contract on or after such date shall be treated as if such provisions were not repealed.

[Sec. 72(j)]

(j) INTEREST.—Notwithstanding any other provision of this section, if any amount is held under an agreement to pay interest thereon, the interest payments shall be included in gross income.

[Sec. 72(k)—Repealed]

Amendments

• 1984, Deficit Reduction Act of 1984 (P.L. 98-369)

P.L. 98-369, §421(b)(1):

Repealed Code Sec. 72(k). **Effective** for transfers after 7-18-84, in tax years ending after such date. Prior to repeal, it read as follows:

(k) Payments in Discharge of Alimony.—

(1) In General.—This section shall not apply to so much of any payment under an annuity, endowment, or life insurance contract (or any interest therein) as is includible in the gross income of the wife under section 71 or section 682 (relating to income of an estate or trust in case of divorce, etc.).

(2) Cross Reference.—

For definition of "wife", see section 7701(a)(17).

P.L. 98-369, §421(d)(2)-(4), provides:

(2) Election to Have Amendments Apply to Transfers After 1983.—If both spouses or former spouses make an election under this paragraph, the amendments made by this section shall apply to all transfers made by such spouses (or former spouses) after December 31, 1983.

(3) Exception for Transfers Pursuant to Existing Decrees.—Except in the case of an election under paragraph (2), the amendments made by this section shall not apply to transfers under any instrument in effect on or before the date of the enactment of this Act unless both spouses (or former spouses) elect to have such amendments apply to transfers under such instrument.

(4) Election.—Any election under paragraph (2) or (3) shall be made in such manner, at such time, and subject to such conditions, as the Secretary of the Treasury or his delegate may by regulations prescribe.

[Sec. 72(l)]

(l) FACE-AMOUNT CERTIFICATES.—For purposes of this section, the term "endowment contract" includes a face-amount certificate, as defined in section 2(a)(15) of the Investment Company Act of 1940 (15 U. S. C., sec. 80a-2), issued after December 31, 1954.

[Sec. 72(m)]

(m) SPECIAL RULES APPLICABLE TO EMPLOYEE ANNUITIES AND DISTRIBUTIONS UNDER EMPLOYEE PLANS.—

(1) [Repealed.]

(2) COMPUTATION OF CONSIDERATION PAID BY THE EMPLOYEE.—In computing—

(A) the aggregate amount of premiums or other consideration paid for the contract for purposes of subsection (c)(1)(A) (relating to the investment in the contract), and

(B) the aggregate premiums or other consideration paid for purposes of subsection (e)(6) (relating to certain amounts not received as an annuity),

any amount allowed as a deduction with respect to the contract under section 404 which was paid while the employee was an employee within the meaning of section 401(c)(1) shall be treated as consideration contributed by the employer, and there shall not be taken into account any portion of the premiums or other consideration for the contract paid while the employee was an owner-employee which is properly allocable (as determined under regulations prescribed by the Secretary) to the cost of life, accident, health, or other insurance.

(3) LIFE INSURANCE CONTRACTS.—

(A) This paragraph shall apply to any life insurance contract—

(i) purchased as a part of a plan described in section 403(a), or

(ii) purchased by a trust described in section 401(a) which is exempt from tax under section 501(a) if the proceeds of such contract are payable directly or indirectly to a participant in such trust or to a beneficiary of such participant.

(B) Any contribution to a plan described in subparagraph (A)(i) or a trust described in subparagraph (A)(ii) which is allowed as a deduction under section 404, and any income of a trust described in subparagraph (A)(ii), which is determined in accordance with regulations prescribed by the Secretary to have been applied to purchase the life insurance protection under a contract described in subparagraph (A), is includible in the gross income of the participant for the taxable year when so applied.

(C) In the case of the death of an individual insured under a contract described in subparagraph (A), an amount equal to the cash surrender value of the contract immediately before the death of the insured shall be treated as a payment under such plan or a distribution by such trust, and the excess of the amount payable by reason of the death of the insured over such cash surrender value shall not be includible in gross income under this section and shall be treated as provided in section 101.

(4) [Repealed.]

(5) PENALTIES APPLICABLE TO CERTAIN AMOUNTS RECEIVED BY 5-PERCENT OWNERS.—

(A) This paragraph applies to amounts which are received from a qualified trust described in section 401(a) or under a plan described in section 403(a) at any time by an individual who is, or has been, a 5-percent owner, or by a successor of such an individual, but only to the extent such amounts are determined, under regulations prescribed by the Secretary, to exceed the benefits provided for such individual under the plan formula.

(B) If a person receives an amount to which this paragraph applies, his tax under this chapter for the taxable year in which such amount is received shall be increased by an amount equal to 10 percent of the portion of the amount so received which is includible in his gross income for such taxable year.

(C) For purposes of this paragraph, the term "5-percent owner" means any individual who, at any time during the 5 plan years preceding the plan year ending in the taxable year in which the amount is received, is a 5-percent owner (as defined in section 416(i)(1)(B)).

(6) OWNER-EMPLOYEE DEFINED.—For purposes of this subsection, the term "owner-employee" has the meaning assigned to it by section 401(c)(3) and includes an individual for whose benefit an individual retirement account or annuity described in section 408(a) or (b) is maintained. For purposes of the preceding sentence, the term "owner-employee" shall include an employee within the meaning of section 401(c)(1).

(7) MEANING OF DISABLED.—For purposes of this section, an individual shall be considered to be disabled if he is unable to engage in any substantial gainful activity by reason of any medically determinable physical or mental impairment which can be expected to result in death or to be of long-continued and indefinite duration. An individual shall not be considered to be disabled unless he furnishes proof of the existence thereof in such form and manner as the Secretary may require.

(8) [Repealed.]

(9) [Repealed.]

(10) DETERMINATION OF INVESTMENT IN THE CONTRACT IN THE CASE OF QUALIFIED DOMESTIC RELATIONS ORDERS.—Under regulations prescribed by the Secretary, in the case of a distribution or payment made to an alternate payee who is the spouse or former spouse of the participant pursuant to a qualified domestic relations order (as defined in section 414(p)), the investment in the contract as of the date prescribed in such regulations shall be allocated on a pro rata basis between the present value of such distribution or payment and the present value of all other benefits payable with respect to the participant to which such order relates.

Amendments

• 1996, Small Business Job Protection Act of 1996 (P.L. 104-188)

P.L. 104-188, §1704(t)(2):

Amended Code Sec. 72(m)(2) by inserting "and" at the end of subparagraph (A), by striking subparagraph (B), and by redesignating subparagraph (C) as subparagraph (B). **Effective** 8-20-96. Prior to amendment, Code Sec. 72(m)(2)(B) read as follows:

(B) the consideration for the contract contributed by the employee for purposes of subsection (d)(1) (relating to employee's contributions recoverable in 3 years) and subsection (e)(7) (relating to plans where substantially all contributions are employee contributions), and

• 1986, Tax Reform Act of 1986 (P.L. 99-514)

P.L. 99-514, §1123(d)(1):

Amended Code Sec. 72(m)(5)(A). For the **effective** date, see Act Sec. 1123(e), below. Prior to amendment, Code Sec. 72(m)(5)(A) read as follows:

(A) This subparagraph shall apply—

(i) to amounts which—

(I) are received from a qualified trust described in section 401(a) or under a plan described in section 403(a), and

(II) are received by a 5-percent owner before such owner attains the age of 59½ years, for any reason other than such owner becoming disabled (within the meaning of paragraph (7) of this section), and

(ii) to amounts which are received from a qualified trust described in section 401(a) or under a plan described in section 403(a) at any time by a 5-percent owner, or by the successor of such owner, but only to the extent that such amounts are determined (under regulations prescribed by the Secretary) to exceed the benefits provided for such individual under the plan formula.

Clause (i) shall not apply to any amount received by an individual in his capacity as a policyholder of an annuity, endowment, or life insurance contract which is in the nature of a dividend or similar distribution and clause (i) shall not apply to amounts attributable to benefits accrued before January 1, 1985.

P.L. 99-514, §1123(e), as amended by P.L. 100-647, §1011A(c)(12), provides:

(e) EFFECTIVE DATE.—

(1) IN GENERAL.—Except as otherwise provided in this subsection, the amendments made by this section shall apply to taxable years beginning after December 31, 1986.

(2) SUBSECTION(c).—The amendments made by subsection (c) shall apply to taxable years beginning after December 31, 1988.

(3) EXCEPTION WHERE DISTRIBUTION COMMENCES.—The amendments made by this section shall not apply to distri-

butions to any employee from a plan maintained by any employer if—

(A) as of March 1, 1986, the employee separated from service with the employer,

(B) as of March 1, 1986, the accrued benefit of the employee was in pay status pursuant to a written election providing a specific schedule for the distribution of the entire accrued benefit of the employee, and

(C) such distribution is made pursuant to such written election.

(4) TRANSITION RULE.—The amendments made by this section shall not apply with respect to any benefits with respect to which a designation is in effect under section 242(b)(2) of the Tax Equity and Fiscal Responsibility Act of 1982.

(5) SPECIAL RULE FOR DISTRIBUTIONS UNDER AN ANNUITY CONTRACT.—The amendments made by paragraphs (1), (2), and (3) of subsection (b) shall not apply to any distribution under an annuity contract if—

(A) as of March 1, 1986, payments were being made under such contract pursuant to a written election providing a specific schedule for the distribution of the taxpayer's interest in such contract, and

(B) such distribution is made pursuant to such written election.

P.L. 99-514, §1852(a)(2)(A):

Amended Code Sec. 72(m)(5)(A). **Effective** as if included in the provision of P.L. 98-369 to which it relates. Prior to amendment, Code Sec. 72(m)(5)(A) read as follows:

(A) This paragraph shall apply—

(i) to amounts (other than any amount received by an individual in his capacity as a policyholder of an annuity, endowment, or life insurance contract which is in the nature of a dividend or similar distribution) which are received from a qualified trust described in section 401(a) or under a plan described in section 403(a) and which are received by an individual, who is, or has been, a 5-percent owner, before such individual attains the age of 59½ years, for any reason other than the individual's becoming disabled (within the meaning of paragraph (7) of this subsection), but only to the extent that such amounts are attributable to contributions paid on behalf of such individual (other than contributions made by him as a 5-percent owner) while he was a 5-percent owner, and

(ii) to amounts which are received from a qualified trust described in section 401(a) or under a plan described in section 403(a) at any time by an individual who is, or has been, a 5-percent owner, or by the successor of such individual, but only to the extent that such amounts are determined, under regulations prescribed by the Secretary, to exceed the benefits provided for such individual under the plan formula.

P.L. 99-514, §1852(a)(2)(B):

Amended Code Sec. 72(m)(5)(C). **Effective** as if included in the provision of P.L. 98-369 to which it relates. Prior to amendment, Code Sec. 72(m)(5)(C) read as follows:

(C) For purposes of this paragraph, the term "5-percent owner" have [has] the same meaning as when used in section 416.

P.L. 99-514, §1852(a)(2)(C):

Amended Code Sec. 72(m)(5) by striking out "OWNER-EMPLOYEES" in the paragraph heading and inserting in lieu thereof "5-PERCENT OWNERS". **Effective** as if included in the provision of P.L. 98-369 to which it relates.

P.L. 99-514, §1852(c)(4)(A) and (B):

Amended Code Sec. 72(m)(2) by striking out "3 years)" in subparagraph (B) and inserting in lieu thereof "3 years) and subsection (e)(7) (relating to plans where substantially all contributions are employee contributions)", and by striking out "subsection (e)(1)(B)" in subparagraph (C) and inserting in lieu thereof "subsection (e)(6)". **Effective** as if included in the provision of P.L. 98-369 to which it relates.

P.L. 99-514, §1898(c)(1)(B):

Amended Code Sec. 72(m)(10) by inserting "who is the spouse or former spouse of the participant" after "alternate payee". **Effective** for payments made after the date of the enactment of this Act.

• 1984, Retirement Equity Act of 1984 (P.L. 98-397)

P.L. 98-397, §204(c)(2):

Added Code Sec. 72(m)(10). **Effective** 1-1-85. However, in the case of a domestic relations order entered before such date, the plan administrator shall treat such order as a qualified domestic relations order if such administrator is paying benefits pursuant to such order on such date, and may treat any other such order entered before such date as a qualified domestic relations order even if such order does not meet the requirements of such amendments. For other special rules, see the notes for P.L. 98-397 following Code Sec. 401(a).

• 1984, Deficit Reduction Act of 1984 (P.L. 98-369)

P.L. 98-369, §521(d):

Amended Code Sec. 72(m)(5) [as amended by this Act] (1) by striking out "key employee" each place it appears in subparagraph (A) [and the subsection heading] and inserting in lieu thereof "5-percent owner", (2) by striking out "in a top-heavy plan" in clause (i) of subparagraph (A), and (3) by striking out "the terms `key employee' and `top-heavy plan'" in subparagraph (C) and inserting in lieu thereof "the term `5-percent owner'". **Effective** for years beginning after 12-31-84.

P.L. 98-369, §713(c)(1)(A):

Amended Code Sec. 72(m)(5)(A)(i) by striking out "as an owner-employee" and inserting in lieu thereof "as a key employee". **Effective** as if included in the provision of P.L. 97-248 to which it relates.

P.L. 98-369, §713(c)(1)(B):

Amended the paragraph heading of Code Sec. 72(m)(5) by striking out "OWNER-EMPLOYEES" and inserting in lieu thereof "KEY EMPLOYEES". **Effective** as if included in the provision of P.L. 97-248 to which it relates.

P.L. 98-369, §713(d)(1):

Repealed Code Sec. 72(m)(9). **Effective** for contributions made in tax years beginning after 12-31-83. Prior to amendment, it read as follows:

(9) Return of Excess Contributions Before Due Date of Return.—

(A) In General.—If an excess contribution is distributed in a qualified distribution—

(i) such distribution of such excess contribution shall not be included in gross income, and

(ii) this section (other than this paragraph) shall be applied as if such excess contribution and such distribution had not been made.

(B) Excess Contribution.—For purposes of this paragraph, the term "excess contribution" means any contribution to a qualified trust described in section 401(a) or under a plan described in section 403(a) or 405(a) made on behalf of an employee (within the meaning of section 401(c)) for any taxable year to the extent such contribution exceeds the amount allowable as a deduction under section 404(a).

(C) Qualified Distribution.—The term "qualified distribution" means any distribution of an excess contribution which meets requirements similar to the requirements of subparagraphs (A), (B), and (C) of section 408(d)(4). In the case of such distribution, the rules of the last sentence of section 408(d)(4) shall apply.

• 1983, Technical Corrections Act of 1982 (P.L. 97-448)

P.L. 97-448, §103(d)(3):

Amended paragraph (1) of section 312(f) of P.L. 97-34 by striking out "plans which include employees within the meaning of section 401(c)(1) with respect to". For the amended **effective** date, see below.

P.L. 97-448, §306(a)(11):

Added paragraph (3) to section 236(c) of P.L. 97-248 to read as below under the amendment note for P.L. 97-248, §236(b)(1).

• 1982, Tax Equity and Fiscal Responsibility Act of 1982 (P.L. 97-248)

P.L. 97-248, §236(b)(1):

Amended Code Sec. 72 by striking out paragraphs (m)(4) and (m)(8). **Effective** for loans, assignments, and pledges made after 8-13-82. For purposes of the preceding sentence, the outstanding balance of any loan which is renegotiated, extended, renewed, or revised after such date shall be treated as an amount received as a loan on the date of such renegotiation, extension, renewal, or revision. Prior to amendment, Code Sec. 72(m)(4) and (m)(8) read as follows:

"(4) Amounts constructively received.—

(A) Assignments or pledges.—If during any taxable year an owner-employee assigns (or agrees to assign) or pledges (or agrees to pledge) any portion of his interest in a trust described in section 401(a) which is exempt from tax under section 501(a), an individual retirement account described in section 408(a), an individual retirement annuity described in section 408(b) or any portion of the value of a contract purchased as part of a plan described in section 403(a), such portion shall be treated as having been received by such owner-employee as a distribution from such trust or as an amount received under the contract.

(B) Loans on contracts.—If during any taxable year, an owner-employee receives, directly or indirectly, any amount from any insurance company as a loan under a contract purchased by a trust described in section 401(a) which is exempt from tax under section 501(a) or purchased as part of a plan described in section 403(a), and issued by such insurance company, such amount shall be treated as an amount received under the contract."

* * *

"(8) Loans to owner-employees.—If, during any taxable year, an owner-employee receives, directly or indirectly, any amount as a loan from a trust described in section 401(a) which is exempt from tax under section 501(a), such amount shall be treated as having been received by such owner-employee as a distribution from such trust."

P.L. 97-248, §236(c)(2), as amended by P.L. 98-369, §§554 and 713(b)(2) and (3), provides:

(2) Exception for certain loans used to repay outstanding obligations.—

(A) In general.—Any qualified refunding loan shall not be treated as a distribution by reason of the amendments made by this section to the extent such loan is repaid before August 14, 1983.

(B) Qualified refunding loan.—For purposes of subparagraph (A), the term "qualified refunding loan" means any loan made after August 13, 1982, and before August 14, 1983, to the extent such loan is used to make a required principal payment.

(C) Required principal payment.—For purposes of subparagraph (B), the term "required principal payment" means any principal repayment on a loan under the plan which was outstanding on August 13, 1982, if such repayment is required to be made after August 13, 1982, and before August 14, 1983 or if such loan was payable on demand.

(D) SPECIAL RULE FOR NON-KEY EMPLOYEES.—In the case of a non-key employee (within the meaning of section 416(i)(2) of the Internal Revenue Code of 1954), this paragraph shall be applied by substituting "January 1, 1985" for "August 14, 1983" each place it appears.

(3) Treatment of certain renegotiations.—If—

(A) the taxpayer after August 13, 1982, and before September 4, 1982, borrows money from a government plan (as defined in section 219(e)(4) of the Internal Revenue Code of 1954),

(B) under the applicable State law, such loan requires the renegotiation of all outstanding prior loans made to the taxpayer under such plan, and

(C) the renegotiation described in subparagraph (B) does not change the interest rate on, or extend the duration of, any such outstanding prior loan,

then the renegotiation described in subparagraph (B) shall not be treated as a renegotiation, extension, renewal, or revision for purposes of paragraph (1). If the renegotiation described in subparagraph (B) does not meet the requirements of subparagraph (C) solely because it extends the duration of any such outstanding prior loan, the requirements of subparagraph (C) shall be treated as met with respect to such renegotiation if, before April 1, 1983, such extension is eliminated.

P.L. 97-248, §237(d)(1):

Amended Code Sec. 72(m)(5) by striking out "an owner-employee" the first place it appeared and inserting in lieu thereof "a key employee"; by striking out "while he was an owner-employee" and inserting in lieu thereof "while he was a key employee in a top-heavy plan"; and by striking out "an owner-employee" in clause (ii) and inserting in lieu thereof "a key employee". **Effective** for tax years beginning after 12-31-83.

P.L. 97-248, §237(d)(2):

Amended Code Sec. 72(m)(5) by adding new subparagraph (C) at the end thereof. **Effective** for tax years beginning after 12-31-83.

P.L. 97-248, §237(d)(3):

Amended paragraph (6) of Code Sec. 72(m) by striking out "except in applying paragraph (5)," before "include an employee". **Effective** for years beginning after 12-31-83.

• 1981, Economic Recovery Tax Act of 1981 (P.L. 97-34)

P.L. 97-34, §312(d)(1):

Amended Code Sec. 72(m)(6) by adding at the end a new sentence. **Effective** for tax years beginning after 12-31-81. Also see the transitional rule below.

P.L. 97-34, §312(d)(2):

Added Code Sec. 72(m)(8). **Effective** for tax years beginning after 12-31-81. The transitional rule provides that the amendments made by P.L. 97-34, Act Sec. 312(d), shall not apply to any loan from a plan to a self-employed individual who is an employee within the meaning of Code Sec. 401(c)(1) which is outstanding on 12-31-81. For purposes of the preceding sentence, any loan which is renegotiated, extended, renewed, or revised after such date shall be treated as a new loan.

P.L. 97-34, §312(e)(1):

Added Code Sec. 72(m)(9). **Effective** for tax years beginning after 12-31-81.

• 1976, Tax Reform Act of 1976 (P.L. 94-455)

P.L. 94-455, §1901(a)(13):

Substituted "an individual retirement account" for "an individual retirement amount" in Code Sec. 72(m)(4)(A). **Effective** for tax years beginning after 12-31-76.

P.L. 94-455, §1906(b)(13)(A):

Amended 1954 Code by substituting "Secretary" for "Secretary or his delegate" each place it appeared. **Effective** 2-1-77.

• 1974, Employee Retirement Income Security Act of 1974 (P.L. 93-406)

P.L. 93-406, §2001(e)(5):

Repealed clause (iii) of Code Sec. 72(m)(5)(A). **Effective** for contributions made in tax years beginning after 1975. Prior to amendment, Code Sec. 72(m)(5)(A)(iii) read as follows:

(iii) to amounts which are received, by an individual who is, or has been, an owner-employee, by reason of the distribution under the provisions of section 401(e)(2)(E) of his entire interest in all qualified trusts described in section 401(a) and in all plans described in section 403(a).

P.L. 93-406, §2001(g)(1):)

Amended Code Sec. 72(m)(5)(B). **Effective** for distributions made in tax years beginning after 1975. Prior to amendment, Code Sec. 72(m)(5)(B) read as follows:

"(B)(i) If the aggregate of the amounts to which this paragraph applies received by any person in his taxable year equals or exceeds $2,500, the increase in his tax for the taxable year in which such amounts are received and attributable to such amounts shall not be less than 110 percent of the aggregate increase in taxes, for the taxable year and the 4 immediately preceding taxable years, which would have resulted if such amounts had been included in such person's gross income ratably over such taxable years.

"(ii) If deductions have been allowed under section 404 for contributions paid on behalf of the individual while he is an owner-employee for a number of prior taxable years less than 4, clause (i) shall be applied by taking into account a number of taxable years immediately preceding the taxable year in which the amount was so received equal to such lesser number."

P.L. 93-406, §2001(g)(2)(A):

Repealed Code Sec. 72(m)(5)(C), (D) and (E). **Effective** for tax years beginning after 1975. Prior to amendment Code Sec. 72(m)(5)(C), (D) and (E) read as follows:

(C) If subparagraph (B) does not apply to a person for the taxable year, the increase in tax of such person for the taxable year attributable to the amounts to which this paragraph applies shall be 110 percent of such increase (computed without regard to this subparagraph).

(D) Subparagraph (a)(ii) of this paragraph shall not apply to any amount to which section 402(a)(2) or 403(a)(2) applies.

(E) For special rules for computation of taxable income for taxable years to which this paragraph applies, see subsection (n)(3).

P.L. 93-406, §2001(h)(2):

Repealed Code Sec. 72(m)(1). **Effective** for tax years ending after 9-2-74. Prior to amendment Code Sec. 72(m)(1) read as follows:

(1) CERTAIN AMOUNTS RECEIVED BEFORE ANNUITY STARTING DATE.—Any amounts received under an annuity, endowment, or life insurance contract before the annuity starting date which are not received as an annuity (within the meaning of subsection (e)(2)) shall be included in the recipient's gross income for the taxable year in which received to the extent that—

(A) such amounts, plus all amounts theretofore received under the contract includible in gross income under this paragraph, do not exceed

(B) the aggregate premiums or other consideration paid for the contract while the employee was an owner-employee which were allowed as deductions under section 404 for the taxable year and all prior taxable years.

Any such amounts so received which are not includible in gross income under this paragraph shall be subject to the provisions of subsection (e).

P.L. 93-406, §2001(h)(3):

Amended Code Sec. 72(m)(5)(A)(i) by substituting "(other than contributions made by him as an owner-employee)" for "(whether or not paid by him)" and adding the word "and" at the end thereof. **Effective** for tax years ending after 9-2-74.

P.L. 93-406, §2002(g)(10)(A):

Amended Code Sec. 72(m)(4)(A) by adding ", an individual retirement amount described in section 408(a), an individual retirement annuity described in section 408(b)" after "section 501(a)". **Effective** 1-1-75.

P.L. 93-406, §2002(g)(10)(B):

Amended Code Sec. 72(m)(6). **Effective** 1-1-75. Prior to amendment, Code Sec. 72(m)(6) read as follows:

"(6) Owner-employee defined.—For purposes of this subsection, the term `owner-employee' has the meaning assigned to it by section 401(c)(3)."

• 1965, Social Security Amendments of 1965 (P.L. 89-97)

P.L. 89-97, §106(d):

Amended Code Sec. 72(m)(5)(A)(i) by substituting "paragraph (7) of this subsection" for "section 213(g)(3)" and added Code Sec. 72(m)(7). **Effective** for tax years beginning after 1966.

• 1962, Self-Employed Individuals Tax Retirement Act of 1962 (P.L. 87-792)

P.L. 87-792, §4:

Added Code Sec. 72(m). **Effective** 1-1-63.

[Sec. 72(n)]

(n) ANNUITIES UNDER RETIRED SERVICEMAN'S FAMILY PROTECTION PLAN OR SURVIVOR BENEFIT PLAN.—Subsection (b) shall not apply in the case of amounts received after December 31, 1965, as an annuity under chapter 73 of title 10 of the United States Code, but all such amounts shall be excluded from gross income until there has been so excluded (under section 122(b)(1) or this section, including amounts excluded before January 1, 1966) an amount equal to the consideration for the contract (as defined by section 122(b)(2)), plus any amount treated pursuant to section 101(b)(2)(D) (as in effect on the day before the date of the enactment of the Small Business Job Protection Act of 1996) as additional consideration paid by the employee. Thereafter all amounts so received shall be included in gross income.

Amendments

• 1998, IRS Restructuring and Reform Act of 1998 (P.L. 105-206)

P.L. 105-206, §6023(3):

Amended Code Sec. 72(n) by inserting "(as in effect on the day before the date of the enactment of the Small Business Job Protection Act of 1996)" after "section 101(b)(2)(D)". **Effective** 7-22-98.

• 1988, Technical and Miscellaneous Revenue Act of 1988 (P.L. 100-647)

P.L. 100-647, §1011A(b)(1)(B):

Amended Code Sec. 72(n) by striking out "Subsections (b) and (d)" and inserting in lieu thereof "Subsection (b)". **Effective** as if included in the provision of P.L. 99-514 to which it relates.

• 1974, Employee Retirement Income Security Act of 1974 (P.L. 93-406)

P.L. 93-406, §2005(c)(3):

Repealed former Sec. 72(n) (see below) and redesignated Code Sec. 72(o) as Code Sec. 72(n). **Effective** for tax years ending on or after 9-21-72.

P.L. 93-406, §2008(b)(2):

Added "or Survivor Benefit Plan" in the heading of the above section. **Effective** for tax years ending on or after 9-21-72.

P.L. 93-406, §2005(c)(3):

Repealed Code Sec. 72(n). **Effective** for distributions or payments made after 12-31-73, in tax years beginning after such date. Prior to repeal, Code Sec. 72(n) read as follows:

"(n) Treatment of Total Distributions.—

"(1) Application of subsection.—

"(A) General rule.—This subsection shall apply to amounts—

"(i) distributed to a distributee, in the case of an employees' trust described in section 401(a) which is exempt from tax under section 501(a), or

"(ii) paid to a payee, in the case of an annuity plan described in section 403(a),

if the total distributions or amounts payable to the distributee or payee with respect to an employee (including an individual who is an employee within the meaning of section 401(c)(1)) are paid to the distributee or payee within one taxable year of the distributee or payee, but only to the extent that section 402(a)(2) or 403(a)(2)(A) does not apply to such amounts.

"(B) Distributions to which applicable.—This subsection shall apply only to distributions or amounts paid—

"(i) on account of the employee's death,

"(ii) with respect to an individual who is an employee without regard to section 401(c)(1), on account of his separation from the service, "(iii) with respect to an employee within the meaning of section 401(c)(1), after he has attained the age of 59½ years, or

"(iv) with respect to an employee within the meaning of section 401(c)(1), after he has become disabled (within the meaning of subsection (m)(7)).

"(C) Minimum period of service.—This subsection shall apply to amounts distributed or paid to an employee from or under a plan only if he has been a participant in the plan for 5 or more taxable years prior to the taxable year in which such amounts are distributed or paid.

"(D) Amounts subject to penalty.—This subsection shall not apply to amounts described in clauses (ii) and (iii) of subparagraph (A) of subsection (m)(5) (but, in the case of amounts described in clause (ii) of such subparagraph, only to the extent that subsection (m)(5) applies to such amounts).

"(2) Limitation of tax.—In any case to which this subsection applies, the tax attributable to the amounts to which this subsection applies for the taxable year in which such amounts are received shall not exceed whichever of the following is the greater:

"(A) 5 times the increase in tax which would result from the inclusion in gross income of the recipient of 20 percent of so much of the amount so received as is includible in gross income, or

"(B) 5 times the increase in tax which would result if the taxable income of the recipient for such taxable year equaled 20 percent of the amount of the taxable income of the recipient for such taxable year determined under paragraph (3)(A).

"(3) Determination of taxable income.—Notwithstanding section 63 (relating to definition of taxable income), for purposes only of computing the tax under this chapter attributable to amounts to which this subsection or subsection (m)(5) applies and which are includible in gross income—

"(A) the taxable income of the recipient for the taxable year of receipt shall be treated as being not less than the amount by which (i) the aggregate of such amounts so includible in gross income exceeds (ii) the amount of the deductions allowed for such taxable year under section 151 (relating to deductions for personal exemptions); and

"(B) in making ratable inclusion computations under paragraph (5)(B) of subsection (m), the taxable income of the recipient for each taxable year involved in such ratable inclusion shall be treated as being not less than the amount required by such paragraph (5)(B) to be treated as includible in gross income for such taxable year.

In any case in which the preceding sentence results in an increase in taxable income for any taxable year, the resulting increase in the taxes imposed by section 1 or 3 for such taxable year shall not be reduced by any credit under part IV of subchapter A (other than sections 31 and 39 thereof) which, but for this sentence, would be allowable.

"(4) Special rule for employees without regard to section 401(c)(1).—In the case of amounts to which this subsection applies which are distributed or paid with respect to an individual who is an employee without regard to section 401(c)(1), paragraph (2) shall be applied with the following modifications:

"(A) `7 times' shall be substituted for `5 times', and `14²/₇ percent' shall be substituted for `20 percent'.

"(B) Any amount which is received during the taxable year by the employee as compensation (other than as deferred compensation within the meaning of section 404) for personal services performed for the employer in respect of whom the amounts distributed or paid are received shall not be taken into account.

"(C) No portion of the total distributions or amounts payable (of which the amounts distributed or paid are a part) to which section 402(a)(2) or 403(a)(2)(A) applies shall be taken into account.

Subparagraph (B) shall not apply if the employee has not attained the age of 59½ years, unless he has died or become disabled (within the meaning of subsection (m)(7))."

• 1969, Tax Reform Act of 1969 (P.L. 91-172)

P.L. 91-172, §515(b)(1):

Amended Code Sec. 72(n)(1). **Effective** for tax years ending after 12-31-69. Prior to amendment, Code Sec. 72(n)(1) read as follows:

"(n) Treatment of Certain Distributions With Respect to Contributions by Self-Employed Individuals.—

(1) Application of subsection.—

(A) Distributions by employees' trust.—Subject to the provisions of subparagraph (C), this subsection shall apply to amounts distributed to a distributee, in the case of an employees' trust described in section 401(a) which is exempt from tax under section 501(a), if the total distributions payable to the distributee with respect to an employee are paid to the distributee within one taxable year of the distributee—

(i) on account of the employee's death,

(ii) after the employee has attained the age of 59½ years, or

(iii) after the employee has become disabled (within the meaning of subsection (m)(7)).

(B) Annuity plans.—Subject to the provisions of subparagraph (C), this subsection shall apply to amounts paid to a payee, in the case of an annuity plan described in section 403(a), if the total amounts payable to the payee with respect to an employee are paid to the payee within one taxable year of the payee—

(i) on account of the employee's death,

(ii) after the employee has attained the age of 59½ years, or

(iii) after the employee has become disabled (within the meaning of subsection (m)(7)).

(C) Limitations and exceptions.—This subsection shall apply—

(i) only with respect to so much of any distribution or payment to which (without regard to this subparagraph) subparagraph (A) or (B) applies as is attributable to contributions made on behalf of an employee while he was an employee within the meaning of section 401(c)(1), and

(ii) if the recipient is the employee on whose behalf such contributions were made, only if contributions which were allowed as a deduction under section 404 have been made on behalf of such employee while he was an employee within the meaning of section 401(c)(1) for 5 or more taxable years prior to the taxable year in which the total distributions payable or total amounts payable, as the case may be, are paid.

This subsection shall not apply to amounts described in clauses (ii) and (iii) of subparagraph (A) of subsection (m)(5) (but, in the case of amounts described in clause (ii) of such subparagraph, only to the extent that subsection (m)(5) applies to such amounts)."

P.L. 91-172, §515(b)(2):

Amended Code Sec. 72(n) by adding section (n)(4) at the end of 72(n). **Effective** for tax years ending after 12-31-69.

• 1965, Social Security Amendments of 1965 (P.L. 89-97)

P.L. 89-97, §106(d):

Amended Code Sec. 72(n)(1)(A)(iii) and (B)(iii) by substituting "subsection (m)(7)" for "section 213(g)(3)". **Effective** for tax years beginning after 1966.

• 1965, Excise Reduction Act of 1965 (P.L. 89-44)

P.L. 89-44, §809(d)(2):

Amended the last sentence of Code Sec. 72(n)(3) by substituting "sections 31 and 39" for "section 31".

• 1962, Self-Employed Individuals Tax Retirement Act of 1962 (P.L. 87-792)

P.L. 87-792, §4:

Added Code Sec. 72(n).

[Sec. 72(o)]

(o) SPECIAL RULES FOR DISTRIBUTIONS FROM QUALIFIED PLANS TO WHICH EMPLOYEE MADE DEDUCTIBLE CONTRIBUTIONS.—

(1) TREATMENT OF CONTRIBUTIONS.—For purposes of this section and sections 402 and 403, notwithstanding section 414(h), any deductible employee contribution made to a qualified employer plan or government plan shall be treated as an amount contributed by the employer which is not includible in the gross income of the employee.

(2) [Repealed.]

(3) AMOUNTS CONSTRUCTIVELY RECEIVED.—

(A) IN GENERAL.—For purposes of this subsection, rules similar to the rules provided by subsection (p) (other than the exception contained in paragraph (2) thereof) shall apply.

(B) PURCHASE OF LIFE INSURANCE.—To the extent any amount of accumulated deductible employee contributions of an employee are applied to the purchase of life insurance contracts, such amount shall be treated as distributed to the employee in the year so applied.

(4) SPECIAL RULE FOR TREATMENT OF ROLLOVER AMOUNTS.—For purposes of sections 402(c), 403(a)(4), 403(b)(8), 408(d)(3), and 457(e)(16), the Secretary shall prescribe regulations providing for such allocations of amounts attributable to accumulated deductible employee contributions, and for such other rules, as may be necessary to insure that such accumulated deductible employee contributions do not become eligible for additional tax benefits (or freed from limitations) through the use of rollovers.

(5) DEFINITIONS AND SPECIAL RULES.—For purposes of this subsection—

(A) DEDUCTIBLE EMPLOYEE CONTRIBUTIONS.—The term "deductible employee contributions" means any qualified voluntary employee contribution (as defined in section 219(e)(2)) made after December 31, 1981, in a taxable year beginning after such date and made for a taxable year beginning before January 1, 1987, and allowable as a deduction under section 219(a) for such taxable year.

(B) ACCUMULATED DEDUCTIBLE EMPLOYEE CONTRIBUTIONS.—The term "accumulated deductible employee contributions" means the deductible employee contributions—

(i) increased by the amount of income and gain allocable to such contributions, and

(ii) reduced by the sum of the amount of loss and expense allocable to such contributions and the amounts distributed with respect to the employee which are attributable to such contributions (or income or gain allocable to such contributions).

(C) QUALIFIED EMPLOYER PLAN.—The term "qualified employer plan" has the meaning given to such term by subsection (p)(3)(A)(i).

(D) GOVERNMENT PLAN.—The term "government plan" has the meaning given such term by subsection (p)(3)(B).

(6) ORDERING RULES.—Unless the plan specifies otherwise, any distribution from such plan shall not be treated as being made from the accumulated deductible employee contributions until all other amounts to the credit of the employee have been distributed.

Amendments

• 2006, Pension Protection Act of 2006 (P.L. 109-280)

P.L. 109-280, §811, provides:

SEC. 811. PENSIONS AND INDIVIDUAL RETIREMENT ARRANGEMENT PROVISIONS OF ECONOMIC GROWTH AND TAX RELIEF RECONCILIATION ACT OF 2001 MADE PERMANENT.

Title IX of the Economic Growth and Tax Relief Reconciliation Act of 2001 [P.L. 107-16] shall not apply to the provisions of, and amendments made by, subtitles A through F of title VI [§§601-666]of such Act (relating to pension and individual retirement arrangement provisions).

• 2001, Economic Growth and Tax Relief Reconciliation Act of 2001 (P.L. 107-16)

P.L. 107-16, §641(e)(1):

Amended Code Sec. 72(o)(4) by striking "and 408(d)(3)" and inserting "403(b)(8), 408(d)(3), and 457(e)(16)". **Effective**, generally, for distributions after 12-31-2001. For a special rule, see Act Sec. 641(f)(3), below.

P.L. 107-16, §641(f)(3), provides:

(3) SPECIAL RULE.—Notwithstanding any other provision of law, subsections (h)(3) and (h)(5) of section 1122 of the Tax Reform Act of 1986 shall not apply to any distribution from an eligible retirement plan (as defined in clause (iii) or (iv) of section 402(c)(8)(B) of the Internal Revenue Code of 1986) on behalf of an individual if there was a rollover to such plan on behalf of such individual which is permitted solely by reason of any amendment made by this section.

P.L. 107-16, §901(a)-(b), provides [but see P.L. 109-280, §811, above]:

SEC. 901. SUNSET OF PROVISIONS OF ACT.

(a) IN GENERAL.—All provisions of, and amendments made by, this Act shall not apply—

(1) to taxable, plan, or limitation years beginning after December 31, 2010, or

(2) in the case of title V, to estates of decedents dying, gifts made, or generation skipping transfers, after December 31, 2010.

(b) APPLICATION OF CERTAIN LAWS.—The Internal Revenue Code of 1986 and the Employee Retirement Income Security Act of 1974 shall be applied and administered to years, estates, gifts, and transfers described in subsection (a) as if the provisions and amendments described in subsection (a) had never been enacted.

• 1992, Unemployment Compensation Amendments of 1992 (P.L. 102-318)

P.L. 102-318, §521(b)(3):

Amended Code Sec. 72(o)(4) by striking "sections 402(a)(5), 402(a)(7)" and inserting "sections 402(c)". **Effective** for distributions after 12-31-92.

• 1988, Technical and Miscellaneous Revenue Act of 1988 (P.L. 100-647)

P.L. 100-647, §1011A(c)(8):

Repealed Code Sec. 72(o)(2). **Effective** as if included in the provision of P.L. 99-514 to which it relates. Prior to repeal, Code Sec. 72(o)(2) read as follows:

(2) ADDDITIONAL TAX IF AMOUNT RECEIVED BEFORE AGE $59^1/_2$.—If—

(A) any accumulated deductible employee contributions are received from a qualified employer plan or government plan,

(B) such amount is received by the employee before the employee attains the age of $59^1/_2$, and

(C) such amount is not attributable to such employee's becoming disabled (within the meaning of subsection (m)(7)),

then the employee's tax under this chapter for the taxable year in which such amount is received shall be increased by an amount equal to 10 percent of the amount so received to the extent that such amount is includible in gross income. For purposes of this title, any tax imposed by this paragraph shall be treated as a tax imposed by subsection (m)(5)(B).

• 1986, Tax Reform Act of 1986 (P.L. 99-514)

P.L. 99-514, §1101(b)(2)(C)(i)-(iii):

Amended Code Sec. 72(o)(5) by inserting "and made for a taxable year beginning before January 1, 1987," after "date" in subparagraph (A), by striking out "section 219(e)(3)" in subparagraph (C) and inserting in lieu thereof "subsection (p)(3)(A)(i)", and by striking out "section 219(e)(4)" in subparagraph (D) and inserting in lieu thereof "subsection (p)(3)(B)". **Effective** for contributions for tax years beginning after 12-31-86.

• 1984, Deficit Reduction Act of 1984 (P.L. 98-369)

P.L. 98-369, §491(d)(3):

Amended Code Sec. 72(o)(1) by striking out "402, 403, and 405" and inserting in lieu thereof "402 and 403". **Effective** for obligations issued after 12-31-83.

P.L. 98-369, §491(d)(4):

Amended Code Sec. 72(o)(4) by striking out "408(d)(3), and 409(b)(3)(C)" and inserting in lieu thereof "and 408(d)(3)". **Effective** for obligations issued after 12-31-83.

P.L. 98-369, §713(b)(1)(A):

Amended Code Sec. 72(o)(3)(A) by striking out "subsection (p)" and inserting in lieu thereof "subsection (p) (other than the exception contained in paragraph (2) thereof)". **Effective** as if included in the provision of P.L. 97-248 to which it relates.

• 1983, Technical Corrections Act of 1982 (P.L. 97-448)

P.L. 97-448, §103(c)(6):

Amended Code Sec. 72(o)(2)(A) by striking out "to which the employee made one or more deductible employee contributions". **Effective** as if it had been included in the provision of P.L. 97-34 to which it relates.

• 1982, Tax Equity and Fiscal Responsibility Act of 1982 (P.L. 97-248)

P.L. 97-248, §236(b)(2):

Amended Code Sec. 72(o)(3)(A) by striking out "subsection (m)(4) and (8)" and inserting in lieu thereof "subsection (p)". **Effective** for loans, assignments, and pledges made after 8-13-82. See, however, amendment notes for Code Sec. 72(m), P.L. 97-248, Act Sec. 236(c)(2) and (3).

• 1981, Economic Recovery Tax Act of 1981 (P.L. 97-34)

P.L. 97-34, §311(b)(1):

Added Code Sec. 72(o). **Effective** for tax years beginning after 12-31-81. The transitional rule provides that, for purposes of the 1954 Code, any amount allowed as a deduction under section 220 of the Code (as in effect before its repeal by P.L. 97-34) shall be treated as if it were allowed by section 219 of the Code.

[Sec. 72(p)]

(p) LOANS TREATED AS DISTRIBUTIONS.—For purposes of this section—

(1) TREATMENT AS DISTRIBUTIONS.—

(A) LOANS.—If during any taxable year a participant or beneficiary receives (directly or indirectly) any amount as a loan from a qualified employer plan, such amount shall be treated as having been received by such individual as a distribution under such plan.

(B) ASSIGNMENTS OR PLEDGES.—If during any taxable year a participant or beneficiary assigns (or agrees to assign) or pledges (or agrees to pledge) any portion of his interest in a qualified employer plan, such portion shall be treated as having been received by such individual as a loan from such plan.

(2) EXCEPTION FOR CERTAIN LOANS.—

(A) GENERAL RULE.—Paragraph (1) shall not apply to any loan to the extent that such loan (when added to the outstanding balance of all other loans from such plan whether made on, before, or after August 13, 1982), does not exceed the lesser of—

(i) $50,000, reduced by the excess (if any) of—

(I) the highest outstanding balance of loans from the plan during the 1-year period ending on the day before the date on which such loan was made, over

(II) the outstanding balance of loans from the plan on the date on which such loan was made, or

(ii) the greater of (I) one-half of the present value of the nonforfeitable accrued benefit of the employee under the plan, or (II) $10,000.

For purposes of clause (ii), the present value of the nonforfeitable accrued benefit shall be determined without regard to any accumulated deductible employee contributions (as defined in subsection (o)(5)(B)).

(B) REQUIREMENT THAT LOAN BE REPAYABLE WITHIN 5 YEARS.—

(i) IN GENERAL.—Subparagraph (A) shall not apply to any loan unless such loan, by its terms, is required to be repaid within 5 years.

(ii) EXCEPTION FOR HOME LOANS.—Clause (i) shall not apply to any loan used to acquire any dwelling unit which within a reasonable time is to be used (determined at the time the loan is made) as the principal residence of the participant.

(C) REQUIREMENT OF LEVEL AMORTIZATION.—Except as provided in regulations, this paragraph shall not apply to any loan unless substantially level amortization of such loan (with payments not less frequently than quarterly) is required over the term of the loan.

(D) RELATED EMPLOYERS AND RELATED PLANS.—For purposes of this paragraph—

(i) the rules of subsections (b), (c), and (m) of section 414 shall apply, and

(ii) all plans of an employer (determined after the application of such subsections) shall be treated as 1 plan.

(3) DENIAL OF INTEREST DEDUCTIONS IN CERTAIN CASES.—

(A) IN GENERAL.—No deduction otherwise allowable under this chapter shall be allowed under this chapter for any interest paid or accrued on any loan to which paragraph (1) does not apply by reason of paragraph (2) during the period described in subparagraph (B).

(B) PERIOD TO WHICH SUBPARAGRAPH (A) APPLIES.—For purposes of subparagraph (A), the period described in this subparagraph is the period—

(i) on or after the 1st day on which the individual to whom the loan is made is a key employee (as defined in section 416(i)), or

(ii) such loan is secured by amounts attributable to elective deferrals described in subparagraph (A) or (C) of section 402(g)(3).

(4) QUALIFIED EMPLOYER PLAN, ETC.—For purposes of this subsection—

(A) QUALIFIED EMPLOYER PLAN.—

(i) IN GENERAL.—The term "qualified employer plan" means—

(I) a plan described in section 401(a) which includes a trust exempt from tax under section 501(a),

(II) an annuity plan described in section 403(a), and

(III) a plan under which amounts are contributed by an individual's employer for an annuity contract described in section 403(b).

(ii) SPECIAL RULE.—The term "qualified employer plan" shall include any plan which was (or was determined to be) a qualified employer plan or a government plan.

(B) GOVERNMENT PLAN.—The term "government plan" means any plan, whether or not qualified, established and maintained for its employees by the United States, by a State or political subdivision thereof, or by an agency or instrumentality of any of the foregoing.

(5) SPECIAL RULES FOR LOANS, ETC., FROM CERTAIN CONTRACTS.—For purposes of this subsection, any amount received as a loan under a contract purchased under a qualified employer plan (and any assignment or pledge with respect to such a contract) shall be treated as a loan under such employer plan.

Amendments

• 2005, Katrina Emergency Tax Relief Act of 2005 (P.L. 109-73)

P.L. 109-73, §103 [repealed by P.L. 109-135, §201(b)(4)(A)], provides:

SEC. 103. LOANS FROM QUALIFIED PLANS FOR RELIEF RELATING TO HURRICANE KATRINA.

(a) INCREASE IN LIMIT ON LOANS NOT TREATED AS DISTRIBUTIONS.—In the case of any loan from a qualified employer plan (as defined under section 72(p)(4) of the Internal Revenue Code of 1986) to a qualified individual made after the date of enactment of this Act and before January 1, 2007—

(1) clause (i) of section 72(p)(2)(A) of such Code shall be applied by substituting "$100,000" for "$50,000", and

(2) clause (ii) of such section shall be applied by substituting "the present value of the nonforfeitable accrued benefit of the employee under the plan" for "one-half of the present value of the nonforfeitable accrued benefit of the employee under the plan".

(b) DELAY OF REPAYMENT.—In the case of a qualified individual with an outstanding loan on or after August 25, 2005, from a qualified employer plan (as defined in section 72(p)(4) of such Code)—

(1) if the due date pursuant to subparagraph (B) or (C) of section 72(p)(2) of such Code for any repayment with respect to such loan occurs during the period beginning on August 25, 2005, and ending on December 31, 2006, such due date shall be delayed for 1 year,

(2) any subsequent repayments with respect to any such loan shall be appropriately adjusted to reflect the delay in the due date under paragraph (1) and any interest accruing during such delay, and

(3) in determining the 5-year period and the term of a loan under subparagraph (B) or (C) of section 72(p)(2) of such Code, the period described in paragraph (1) shall be disregarded.

(c) QUALIFIED INDIVIDUAL.—For purposes of this section, the term "qualified individual" means an individual whose principal place of abode on August 28, 2005, is located in the Hurricane Katrina disaster area and who has sustained an economic loss by reason of Hurricane Katrina.

• 1996, Small Business Job Protection Act of 1996 (P.L. 104-188)

P.L. 104-188, §1704(t)(77):

Amended Code Sec. 72(p)(4)(A)(ii). **Effective** 8-20-96. Prior to amendment, Code Sec. 72(p)(4)(A)(ii) read as follows:

(ii) SPECIAL RULES.—The term "qualified employer plan"—

(I) shall include any plan which was (or was determined to be) a qualified employer plan or a government plan, but

(II) shall not include a plan described in subsection (e)(7).

• 1988, Technical and Miscellaneous Revenue Act of 1988 (P.L. 100-647)

P.L. 100-647, §1011A(h)(1):

Amended Code Sec. 72(p)(3)(A) by inserting "to which paragraph (1) does not apply by reason of paragraph (2) during the period" after "loan". **Effective** as if included in the provision of P.L. 99-514 to which it relates.

P.L. 100-647, §1011A(h)(2):

Amended Code Sec. 72(p)(3)(B). **Effective** as if included in the provision of P.L. 99-514 to which it relates. Prior to amendment, Code Sec. 72(p)(3)(B) read as follows:

(B) LOANS TO WHICH SUBPARAGRAPH (A) APPLIES.—For purposes of subparagraph (A), a loan is described in this subparagraph—

(i) if paragraph (1) does not apply to such loan by reason of paragraph (2), and

(ii) if—

(I) such loan is made to a key employee (as defined in section 416(i)), or

(II) such loan is secured by amounts attributable to elective 401(k) or 403(b) deferrals (as defined in section 402(g)(3)).

• 1986, Tax Reform Act of 1986 (P.L. 99-514)

P.L. 99-514, §1101(b)(2)(B):

Amended Code Sec. 72(p)(3). **Effective** for contributions for tax years beginning after 12-31-86. Prior to amendment, Code Sec. 72(p)(3) read as follows:

(3) QUALIFIED EMPLOYER PLAN, ETC.—For purposes of this subsection, the term "qualified employer plan" means any plan which was (or was determined to be) a qualified employer plan (as defined in section 219(e)(3) other than a plan described in subsection (e)(7). For purposes of this subsection, such term includes any government plan (as defined in section 219(e)(4)).

P.L. 99-514, §1134(a):

Amended Code Sec. 72(p)(2)(A)(i). **Effective** for loans made, renewed, renegotiated, modified, or extended after 12-31-86. Prior to amendment, Code Sec. 72(p)(2)(A)(i) read as follows:

(i) $50,000, or

P.L. 99-514, §1134(b):

Amended Code Sec. 72(p)(2) by redesignating subparagraph (C) as subparagraph (D) and inserting after subparagraph (B) new subparagraph (C). **Effective** for loans made, renewed, renegotiated, modified, or extended after 12-31-86.

P.L. 99-514, §1134(c):

Amended Code Sec. 72(p) by redesignating paragraphs (3) and (4) as paragraphs (4) and (5), respectively and by inserting after paragraph (2) new paragraph (3). **Effective** for loans made, renewed, renegotiated, modified, or extended after 12-31-86.

P.L. 99-514, §1134(d):

Amended Code Sec. 72(p)(2)(B)(ii). **Effective** for loans made, renewed, renegotiated, modified, or extended after 12-31-86. Prior to amendment, Code Sec. 72(p)(2)(B)(ii) read as follows:

(ii) EXCEPTION FOR HOME LOANS.—Clause (i) shall not apply to any loan used to acquire, construct, reconstruct, or substantially rehabilitate any dwelling unit which within a reasonable time is to be used (determined at the time the loan is made) as a principal residence of the participant or a member of the family (within the meaning of section 267(c)(4)) of the participant.

• 1984, Deficit Reduction Act of 1984 (P.L. 98-369)

P.L. 98-369, §523(b)(2):

Amended Code Sec. 72(p)(3) by inserting "other than a plan described in subsection (e)(7)" after "section 219(e)(3)". **Effective** for any amount received or loan made after 10-16-84.

P.L. 98-369, §713(b)(1)(B):

Amended Code Sec. 72(p)(2)(A) by adding at the end thereof a new sentence. **Effective** as if included in the provision of P.L. 97-248 to which it relates.

P.L. 98-369, §713(b)(4):

Amended Code Sec. 72(p)(2)(A)(ii). **Effective** as if included in the provision of P.L. 97-248 to which it relates. Prior to amendment, Code Sec. 72(p)(2)(A)(ii) read as follows:

(ii) 1/2 of the present value of the nonforfeitable accrued benefit of the employee under the plan (but not less than $10,000).

• 1983, Technical Corrections Act of 1982 (P.L. 97-448)

P.L. 97-448, §103(c)(3)(B)(i):

Amended Code Sec. 72(p)(3) by striking out "without regard to subparagraph (D) thereof". **Effective** as if the matter struck out had never been included in such paragraph.

• 1982, Tax Equity and Fiscal Responsibility Act of 1982 (P.L. 97-248)

P.L. 97-248, §236(a):

Amended Code Sec. 72 by redesignating subsection (p) as subsection (q) and by inserting after subsection (o) new subsection (p). **Effective** for loans, assignments, and pledges made after 8-13-82. But see P.L. 97-248, Act section 236(c)(2) and (3) in amendment notes for Code Sec. 72(m).

[Sec. 72(q)]

(q) 10-PERCENT PENALTY FOR PREMATURE DISTRIBUTIONS FROM ANNUITY CONTRACTS.—

(1) IMPOSITION OF PENALTY.—If any taxpayer receives any amount under an annuity contract, the taxpayer's tax under this chapter for the taxable year in which such amount is received shall be increased by an amount equal to 10 percent of the portion of such amount which is includible in gross income.

(2) SUBSECTION NOT TO APPLY TO CERTAIN DISTRIBUTIONS.—Paragraph (1) shall not apply to any distribution—

(A) made on or after the date on which the taxpayer attains age 59 1/2,

(B) made on or after the death of the holder (or, where the holder is not an individual, the death of the primary annuitant (as defined in subsection (s)(6)(B))),

(C) attributable to the taxpayer's becoming disabled within the meaning of subsection (m)(7),

(D) which is a part of a series of substantially equal periodic payments (not less frequently than annually) made for the life (or life expectancy) of the taxpayer or the joint lives (or joint life expectancies) of such taxpayer and his designated beneficiary,

(E) from a plan, contract, account, trust, or annuity described in subsection (e)(5)(D),

(F) allocable to investment in the contract before August 14, 1982,

(G) under a qualified funding asset (within the meaning of section 130(d), but without regard to whether there is a qualified assignment),

(H) to which subsection (t) applies (without regard to paragraph (2) thereof),

(I) under an immediate annuity contract (within the meaning of section 72(u)(4)), or

(J) which is purchased by an employer upon the termination of a plan described in section 401(a) or 403(a) and which is held by the employer until such time as the employee separates from service.

(3) CHANGE IN SUBSTANTIALLY EQUAL PAYMENTS.—If—

(A) paragraph (1) does not apply to a distribution by reason of paragraph (2)(D), and

(B) the series of payments under such paragraph are subsequently modified (other than by reason of death or disability)—

(i) before the close of the 5-year period beginning on the date of the first payment and after the taxpayer attains age 59 1/2, or

(ii) before the taxpayer attains age 59 1/2,

the taxpayer's tax for the 1st taxable year in which such modification occurs shall be increased by an amount, determined under regulations, equal to the tax which (but for paragraph (2)(D)) would have been imposed, plus interest for the deferral period (within the meaning of subsection (t)(4)(B)).

Amendments

• 1989, Omnibus Budget Reconciliation Act of 1989 (P.L. 101-239)

P.L. 101-239, §7811(m)(4):

Amended Code Sec. 72(q)(2)(B) by striking "subsection (s)(6)(B))" and inserting "subsection (s)(6)(B)))". **Effective** as if included in the provision of P.L. 100-647 to which it relates.

• 1988, Technical and Miscellaneous Revenue Act of 1988 (P.L. 100-647)

P.L. 100-647, §1011A(b)(9)(D):

Amended Code Sec. 72(q)(2)(E) by striking out "(determined without regard to subsection (e)(7))" after "subsection (e)(5)(D)". **Effective** as if included in the provision of P.L. 99-514 to which it relates.

P.L. 100-647, §1011A(c)(4):

Amended Code Sec. 72(q)(2)(D) and (G) by striking out the period at the end thereof and inserting in lieu thereof a comma. **Effective** as if included in the provision of P.L. 99-514 to which it relates.

P.L. 100-647, §1011A(c)(5):

Amended Code Sec. 72(q)(3)(B) by striking out "employee" each place it appears and inserting in lieu thereof "taxpayer". **Effective** as if included in the provision of P.L. 99-514 to which it relates.

P.L. 100-647, §1011A(c)(6):

Amended Code Sec. 72(q)(2) by inserting after subparagraph (G) new subparagraph (H). **Effective** as if included in the provision of P.L. 99-514 to which it relates.

P.L. 100-647, §1011A(c)(7):

Amended Code Sec. 72(q)(2)(D) by inserting "designated" before "beneficiary". **Effective** as if included in the provision of P.L. 99-514 to which it relates.

P.L. 100-647, §1018(t)(1)(B):

Amended Code Sec. 72(q)(2)(B) by striking out the last parenthesis. **Effective** as if included in the provision of P.L. 99-514 to which it relates.

P.L. 100-647, §1018(u)(8):

Amended Code Sec. 72(q)(2) by striking out the period at the end of subparagraph (D) and inserting in lieu thereof a comma. **Effective** as if included in the provision of P.L. 99-514 to which it relates.

• 1986, Tax Reform Act of 1986 (P.L. 99-514)

P.L. 99-514, §1123(b)(1)(A)-(B):

Amended Code Sec. 72(q) by striking out "5 percent" in paragraph (1) thereof and inserting in lieu thereof "10 percent", and by striking out "5-Percent" in the heading thereof and inserting in lieu thereof "10-Percent". For the **effective** date, see Act Sec. 1123(e), reproduced under the amendment notes for Code Sec. 72(m).

P.L. 99-514, §1123(b)(2):

Amended Code Sec. 72(q)(2)(D). For the **effective** date, see Act Sec. 1123(e), reproduced under the amendment notes for Code Sec. 72(m). Prior to amendment, Code Sec. 72(q)(2)(D) read as follows:

(D) which is one of a series of substantially equal periodic payments made for the life of a taxpayer or over a period extending for at least 60 months after the annuity starting date,

P.L. 99-514, §1123(b)(3):

Amended Code Sec. 72(q) by adding at the end thereof new paragraph (3). For the **effective** date, see Act Sec. 1123(e), reproduced under the amendment notes for Code Sec. 72(m).

P.L. 99-514, §1123(b)(3)[4]:

Amended Code Sec. 72(q)(2) by striking out "This subsection" and inserting in lieu thereof "Paragraph (1)". For the **effective** date, see Act Sec. 1123(e), reproduced under the amendment notes for Code Sec. 72(m).

P.L. 99-514, §1123(b)(4)[5]:

Amended Code Sec. 72(q)(2) by striking out "or" at the end of subparagraph (G)[F], by striking out the period at the end of subparagraph (H)[G], and by adding at the end thereof new subparagraphs (I)[H] and (J)[I]. For the **effective** date, see Act Sec. 1123(e), reproduced under the amendment notes for Code Sec. 72(m).

P.L. 99-514, §1826(c):

Amended Code Sec. 72(q)(2)(B). **Effective** for distributions commencing after the date 6 months after 10-22-86. Prior to amendment, Code Sec. 72(q)(2)(B) read as follows:

(B) made to a beneficiary (or to the estate of an annuitant) on or after the death of an annuitant,

P.L. 99-514, §1826(d):

Amended Code Sec. 72(q)(2) by striking out "or" at the end of subparagraph (E), by striking out the period at the end of subparagraph (F) and inserting in lieu thereof ", or", and by adding at the end thereof new subparagraph (G). **Effective** as if included in the provision of P.L. 98-369 to which it relates.

P.L. 99-514, §1852(c)(2):

Amended Code Sec. 72(q)(2)(E) by striking out "subsection (e)(5)(D)" and inserting in lieu thereof "subsection (e)(5)(D) (determined without regard to subsection (e)(7))". **Effective** as if included in the provision of P.L. 98-369 to which it relates.

• 1984, Deficit Reduction Act of 1984 (P.L. 98-369)

P.L. 98-369, §222(a):

Amended Code Sec. 72(q)(1). **Effective** for contracts issued after the day which is 6 months after 7-18-84, in tax years ending after such date. For a transitional rule, see Act Sec. 222(c)(2), following Code Sec. 72(s). Prior to amendment, Code Sec. 72(q)(1) read as follows:

(1) IMPOSITION OF PENALTY.—

(A) IN GENERAL.—If any taxpayer receives any amount under an annuity contract, the taxpayer's tax under this chapter for the taxable year in which such amount is received shall be increased by an amount equal to 5 percent of the portion of such amount includible in gross income which is properly allocable to any investment in the annuity contract made during the 10-year period ending on the date such amount was received by the taxpayer.

(B) ALLOCATION ON FIRST-IN, FIRST-OUT BASIS.—For purposes of subparagraph (A), the amount includible in gross income shall be allocated to the earliest investment in the contract with respect to which amounts have not been previously fully allocated under this paragraph.

• 1982, Tax Equity and Fiscal Responsibility Act of 1982 (P.L. 97-248)

P.L. 97-248, §265(b)(1):

Amended Code Sec. 72 by redesignating subsection (q) (as redesignated by Act Sec. 236(a)) as subsection (r) and by adding after subsection (p) new subsection (q). **Effective** for distributions after 12-31-82.

[Sec. 72(r)]

(r) CERTAIN RAILROAD RETIREMENT BENEFITS TREATED AS RECEIVED UNDER EMPLOYER PLANS.—

(1) IN GENERAL.—Notwithstanding any other provision of law, any benefit provided under the Railroad Retirement Act of 1974 (other than a tier 1 railroad retirement benefit) shall be treated for purposes of this title as a benefit provided under an employer plan which meets the requirements of section 401(a).

(2) TIER 2 TAXES TREATED AS CONTRIBUTIONS.—

(A) IN GENERAL.—For purposes of paragraph (1)—

(i) the tier 2 portion of the tax imposed by section 3201 (relating to tax on employees) shall be treated as an employee contribution,

(ii) the tier 2 portion of the tax imposed by section 3211 (relating to tax on employee representatives) shall be treated as an employee contribution, and

(iii) the tier 2 portion of the tax imposed by section 3221 (relating to tax on employers) shall be treated as an employer contribution.

(B) TIER 2 PORTION.—For purposes of subparagraph (A)—

(i) AFTER 1984.—With respect to compensation paid after 1984, the tier 2 portion shall be the taxes imposed by sections 3201(b), 3211(b), and 3221(b).

(ii) AFTER SEPTEMBER 30, 1981, AND BEFORE 1985.—With respect to compensation paid before 1985 for services rendered after September 30, 1981, the tier 2 portion shall be—

(I) so much of the tax imposed by section 3201 as is determined at the 2 percent rate, and

(II) so much of the taxes imposed by sections 3211 and 3221 as is determined at the 11.75 percent rate.

With respect to compensation paid for services rendered after December 31, 1983, and before 1985, subclause (I) shall be applied by substituting "2.75 percent" for "2 percent", and subclause (II) shall be applied by substituting "12.75 percent" for "11.75 percent".

(iii) BEFORE OCTOBER 1, 1981.—With respect to compensation paid for services rendered during any period before October 1, 1981, the tier 2 portion shall be the excess (if any) of—

(I) the tax imposed for such period by section 3201, 3211, or 3221, as the case may be (other than any tax imposed with respect to man-hours), over

(II) the tax which would have been imposed by such section for such period had the rates of the comparable taxes imposed by chapter 21 for such period applied under such section.

(C) CONTRIBUTIONS NOT ALLOCABLE TO SUPPLEMENTAL ANNUITY OR WINDFALL BENEFITS.—For purposes of paragraph (1), no amount treated as an employee contribution under this paragraph shall be allocated to—

(i) any supplemental annuity paid under section 2(b) of the Railroad Retirement Act of 1974, or

(ii) any benefit paid under section 3(h), 4(e), or 4(h) of such Act.

(3) TIER 1 RAILROAD RETIREMENT BENEFIT.—For purposes of paragraph (1), the term "tier 1 railroad retirement benefit" has the meaning given such term by section 86(d)(4).

Amendments

• 2001, Railroad Retirement and Survivors' Improvement Act of 2001 (P.L. 107-90)

P.L. 107-90, §204(e)(2):

Amended Code Sec. 72(r)(2)(B)(i) by striking "3211(a)(2)" and inserting "3211(b)". **Effective** for calendar years beginning after 12-31-2001.

• 1983, Railroad Retirement Solvency Act of 1983 (P.L. 98-76)

P.L. 98-76, §224(a):

Redesignated former Code Sec. 72(r) to be new Code Sec. 72(s) and adopted new Code Sec. 72(r). **Effective**:

(1) IN GENERAL.—Except as provided in paragraph (2), the amendments made by section 224 shall apply to benefits received after December 31, 1983, in taxable years ending after such date.

(2) TREATMENT OF CERTAIN LUMP-SUM PAYMENTS RECEIVED AFTER DECEMBER 31, 1983.—The amendments made by section 224 shall not apply to any portion of a lump-sum payment received after December 31, 1983, if the generally applicable payment date for such portion was before January 1, 1984.

(3) NO FRESH START.—For purposes of determining whether any benefit received after December 31, 1983, is includible in gross income by reason of section 72(r) of the Internal Revenue Code of 1954, as added by this Act, the amendments made by section 224 [shall] be treated as having been in effect during all periods before 1984.

P.L. 98-76, §224(c), as amended by P.L. 100-203, §9034 and P.L. 101-239, §10102, provides:

(c) SECTION 72(r) REVENUE INCREASE TRANSFERRED TO CERTAIN RAILROAD ACCOUNTS.—

(1) IN GENERAL.—

(A) TRANSFERS TO RAILROAD RETIREMENT ACCOUNT.—There are hereby appropriated to the Railroad Retirement Account amounts (other than amounts described in subparagraph (B)) equivalent to the aggregate increase in tax liabilities under chapter 1 of the Internal Revenue Code of 1954 which is attributable to the application of section 72(r) of the Internal Revenue Code of 1954 (as added by this Act) with respect to benefits received before October 1, 1990.

(B) REVENUE INCREASES ATTRIBUTABLE TO WINDFALL BENEFITS RECEIVED AFTER SEPTEMBER 30, 1988, TRANSFERRED TO DUAL BENEFITS PAYMENTS ACCOUNT.—There are hereby appropriated to the Dual Benefits Payments Account amounts equivalent to the aggregate increase in tax liabilities under chapter 1 of such Code which is attributable to the application of section 72(r) of such Code (as added by this Act) with respect to windfall benefits received after September 30, 1988.

(C) WINDFALL BENEFITS DEFINED.—For purposes of this paragraph, the term "windfall benefits" means any benefit paid under section 3(h), 4(e), or 4(h) of the Railroad Retirement Act of 1974.

(2) TRANSFERS.—The amounts appropriated by paragraph (1) shall be transferred from time to time (but not less frequently than quarterly) from the general fund of the Treasury on the basis of estimates made by the Secretary of the Treasury of the amounts referred to in paragraph (1). Any such quarterly payment shall be made on the first day of such quarter and shall take into account benefits estimated to be received during such quarter. Proper adjustments shall be made in the amounts subsequently transferred to the extent prior estimates were in excess of or less than the amounts required to be transferred.

(3) REVENUE INCREASES FROM TAX ON SUPPLEMENTAL ANNUITIES NOT INCLUDED.—Paragraph (1) shall not apply to tax liabilities attributable to supplemental annuities paid under section 2(b) of the Railroad Retirement Act of 1974.

[Sec. 72(s)]

(s) REQUIRED DISTRIBUTIONS WHERE HOLDER DIES BEFORE ENTIRE INTEREST IS DISTRIBUTED.—

(1) IN GENERAL.—A contract shall not be treated as an annuity contract for purposes of this title unless it provides that—

(A) if any holder of such contract dies on or after the annuity starting date and before the entire interest in such contract has been distributed, the remaining portion of such interest will be distributed at least as rapidly as under the method of distributions being used as of the date of his death, and

(B) if any holder of such contract dies before the annuity starting date, the entire interest in such contract will be distributed within 5 years after the death of such holder.

(2) EXCEPTION FOR CERTAIN AMOUNTS PAYABLE OVER LIFE OF BENEFICIARY.—If—

(A) any portion of the holder's interest is payable to (or for the benefit of) a designated beneficiary,

(B) such portion will be distributed (in accordance with regulations) over the life of such designated beneficiary (or over a period not extending beyond the life expectancy of such beneficiary), and

(C) such distributions begin not later than 1 year after the date of the holder's death or such later date as the Secretary may by regulations prescribe,

then for purposes of paragraph (1), the portion referred to in subparagraph (A) shall be treated as distributed on the day on which such distributions begin.

(3) SPECIAL RULE WHERE SURVIVING SPOUSE BENEFICIARY.—If the designated beneficiary referred to in paragraph (2)(A) is the surviving spouse of the holder of the contract, paragraphs (1) and (2) shall be applied by treating such spouse as the holder of such contract.

(4) DESIGNATED BENEFICIARY.—For purposes of this subsection, the term "designated beneficiary" means any individual designated a beneficiary by the holder of the contract.

(5) EXCEPTION FOR CERTAIN ANNUITY CONTRACTS.—This subsection shall not apply to any annuity contract—

(A) which is provided—

(i) under a plan described in section 401(a) which includes a trust exempt from tax under section 501, or

(ii) under a plan described in section 403(a),

(B) which is described in section 403(b),

(C) which is an individual retirement annuity or provided under an individual retirement account or annuity, or

(D) which is a qualified funding asset (as defined in section 130(d), but without regard to whether there is a qualified assignment).

(6) SPECIAL RULE WHERE HOLDER IS CORPORATION OR OTHER NON-INDIVIDUAL.—

(A) IN GENERAL.—For purposes of this subsection, if the holder of the contract is not an individual, the primary annuitant shall be treated as the holder of the contract.

(B) PRIMARY ANNUITANT.—For purposes of subparagraph (A), the term "primary annuitant" means the individual, the events in the life of whom are of primary importance in affecting the timing or amount of the payout under the contract.

(7) TREATMENT OF CHANGES IN PRIMARY ANNUITANT WHERE HOLDER OF CONTRACT IS NOT AN INDIVIDUAL.—For purposes of this subsection, in the case of a holder of an annuity contract which is not an individual, if there is a change in a primary annuitant (as defined in paragraph (6)(B)), such change shall be treated as the death of the holder.

Amendments

• 1988, Technical and Miscellaneous Revenue Act of 1988 (P.L. 100-647)

P.L. 100-647, §1018(k)(1):

Amended Code Sec. 72(s)(5) by striking out "or" at the end of subparagraph (B), by striking the period at the end of subparagraph (C) and inserting in lieu thereof ", or", and by adding at the end thereof new subparagraph (D). **Effective** as if included in the provision of P.L. 99-514 to which it relates.

P.L. 100-647, §1018(k)(2):

Amended Code Sec. 72(s)(5) by striking out "ANNUITY CONTRACTS WHICH ARE PART OF QUALIFIED PLANS" in the heading and inserting in lieu thereof "CERTAIN ANNUITY CONTRACTS". **Effective** as if included in the provision of P.L. 99-514 to which it relates.

P.L. 100-647, §1018(t)(1)(A):

Amended Code Sec. 72(s)(7) by striking out "primary annuity" and inserting in lieu thereof "primary annuitant". **Effective** as if included in the provision of P.L. 99-514 to which it relates.

• 1986, Tax Reform Act of 1986 (P.L. 99-514)

P.L. 99-514, §1826(a):

Amended Code Sec. 72(s) by adding at the end thereof new paragraph (5). **Effective** as if included in the provision of P.L. 98-369 to which it relates.

P.L. 99-514, §1826(b)(1):

Amended Code Sec. 72(s) by adding at the end thereof new paragraphs (6) and (7). **Effective** for contracts issued after the date which is 6 months after 10-22-86 in tax years ending after such date.

P.L. 99-514, §1826(b)(2):

Amended Code Sec. 72(s)(1) by striking out "the holder of such contract" each place it appears and inserting in lieu thereof "any holder of such contract". **Effective** for contracts issued after the date which is 6 months after 10-22-86 in tax years ending after such date.

• 1984, Deficit Reduction Act of 1984 (P.L. 98-369)

P.L. 98-369, §222(b):

Amended Code Sec. 72 by redesignating subsection (s) as subsection (t) and by inserting after subsection (r) new subsection (s). **Effective** for contracts issued after the day which is 6 months after 7-18-84, in tax years ending after such date. For a transitional rule, see Act Sec. 222(c)(2), below.

P.L. 98-369, §222(c)(2), provides:

(2) Transitional Rules for Contracts Issued Before Effective Date.—In the case of any contract (other than a single premium contract) which is issued on or before the day which is 6 months after the date of the enactment of this Act, for purposes of section 72(q)(1)(A) of the Internal Revenue Code of 1954 (as in effect on the day before the date of the enactment of this Act), any investment in such contract which is made during any calendar year shall be treated as having been made on January 1 of such calendar year.

[Sec. 72(t)]

(t) 10-PERCENT ADDITIONAL TAX ON EARLY DISTRIBUTIONS FROM QUALIFIED RETIREMENT PLANS.—

(1) IMPOSITION OF ADDITIONAL TAX.—If any taxpayer receives any amount from a qualified retirement plan (as defined in section 4974(c)), the taxpayer's tax under this chapter for the taxable year in which such amount is received shall be increased by an amount equal to 10 percent of the portion of such amount which is includible in gross income.

(2) SUBSECTION NOT TO APPLY TO CERTAIN DISTRIBUTIONS.—Except as provided in paragraphs (3) and (4), paragraph (1) shall not apply to any of the following distributions:

(A) IN GENERAL.—Distributions which are—

(i) made on or after the date on which the employee attains age 59½,

(ii) made to a beneficiary (or to the estate of the employee) on or after the death of the employee,

(iii) attributable to the employee's being disabled within the meaning of subsection (m)(7),

(iv) part of a series of substantially equal periodic payments (not less frequently than annually) made for the life (or life expectancy) of the employee or the joint lives (or joint life expectancies) of such employee and his designated beneficiary,

(v) made to an employee after separation from service after attainment of age 55,

(vi) dividends paid with respect to stock of a corporation which are described in section 404(k), or

(vii) made on account of a levy under section 6331 on the qualified retirement plan.

(B) MEDICAL EXPENSES.—Distributions made to the employee (other than distributions described in subparagraph (A), (C) or (D)) to the extent such distributions do not exceed the amount allowable as a deduction under section 213 to the employee for amounts paid during the taxable year for medical care (determined without regard to whether the employee itemizes deductions for such taxable year).

(C) PAYMENTS TO ALTERNATE PAYEES PURSUANT TO QUALIFIED DOMESTIC RELATIONS ORDERS.—Any distribution to an alternate payee pursuant to a qualified domestic relations order (within the meaning of section 414(p)(1)).

(D) DISTRIBUTIONS TO UNEMPLOYED INDIVIDUALS FOR HEALTH INSURANCE PREMIUMS.—

(i) IN GENERAL.—Distributions from an individual retirement plan to an individual after separation from employment—

(I) if such individual has received unemployment compensation for 12 consecutive weeks under any Federal or State unemployment compensation law by reason of such separation,

(II) if such distributions are made during any taxable year during which such unemployment compensation is paid or the succeeding taxable year, and

(III) to the extent such distributions do not exceed the amount paid during the taxable year for insurance described in section 213(d)(1)(D) with respect to the individual and the individual's spouse and dependents (as defined in section 152, determined without regard to subsections (b)(1), (b)(2), and (d)(1)(B) thereof).

(ii) DISTRIBUTIONS AFTER REEMPLOYMENT.—Clause (i) shall not apply to any distribution made after the individual has been employed for at least 60 days after the separation from employment to which clause (i) applies.

(iii) SELF-EMPLOYED INDIVIDUALS.—To the extent provided in regulations, a self-employed individual shall be treated as meeting the requirements of clause (i)(I) if, under Federal or State law, the individual would have received unemployment compensation but for the fact the individual was self-employed.

(E) DISTRIBUTIONS FROM INDIVIDUAL RETIREMENT PLANS FOR HIGHER EDUCATION EXPENSES.—Distributions to an individual from an individual retirement plan to the extent such distributions do not exceed the qualified higher education expenses (as defined in paragraph (7)) of the taxpayer for the taxable year. Distributions shall not be taken into account under the preceding sentence if such distributions are described in subparagraph (A), (C), or (D) or to the extent paragraph (1) does not apply to such distributions by reason of subparagraph (B).

(F) DISTRIBUTIONS FROM CERTAIN PLANS FOR FIRST HOME PURCHASES.—Distributions to an individual from an individual retirement plan which are qualified first-time homebuyer distributions (as defined in paragraph (8)). Distributions shall not be taken into account under the preceding sentence if such distributions are described in subparagraph (A), (C), (D), or (E) or to the extent paragraph (1) does not apply to such distributions by reason of subparagraph (B).

(G) DISTRIBUTIONS FROM RETIREMENT PLANS TO INDIVIDUALS CALLED TO ACTIVE DUTY.—

(i) IN GENERAL.—Any qualified reservist distribution.

(ii) AMOUNT DISTRIBUTED MAY BE REPAID.—Any individual who receives a qualified reservist distribution may, at any time during the 2-year period beginning on the day after the end of the active duty period, make one or more contributions to an individual retirement plan of such individual in an aggregate amount not to exceed the amount of such distribution. The dollar limitations otherwise applicable to contributions to individual retirement plans shall not apply to any contribution made pursuant to the preceding sentence. No deduction shall be allowed for any contribution pursuant to this clause.

(iii) QUALIFIED RESERVIST DISTRIBUTION.—For purposes of this subparagraph, the term "qualified reservist distribution" means any distribution to an individual if—

(I) such distribution is from an individual retirement plan, or from amounts attributable to employer contributions made pursuant to elective deferrals described in subparagraph (A) or (C) of section 402(g)(3) or section 501(c)(18)(D)(iii),

(II) such individual was (by reason of being a member of a reserve component (as defined in section 101 of title 37, United States Code)) ordered or called to active duty for a period in excess of 179 days or for an indefinite period, and

(III) such distribution is made during the period beginning on the date of such order or call and ending at the close of the active duty period.

(iv) APPLICATION OF SUBPARAGRAPH.—This subparagraph applies to individuals ordered or called to active duty after September 11, 2001. In no event shall the 2-year period referred to in clause (ii) end before the date which is 2 years after the date of the enactment of this subparagraph.

(3) LIMITATIONS.—

(A) CERTAIN EXCEPTIONS NOT TO APPLY TO INDIVIDUAL RETIREMENT PLANS.—Subparagraphs (A)(v) and (C) of paragraph (2) shall not apply to distributions from an individual retirement plan.

(B) PERIODIC PAYMENTS UNDER QUALIFIED PLANS MUST BEGIN AFTER SEPARATION.—Paragraph (2)(A)(iv) shall not apply to any amount paid from a trust described in section 401(a) which is exempt from tax under section 501(a) or from a contract described in section 72(e)(5)(D)(ii) unless the series of payments begins after the employee separates from service.

(4) CHANGE IN SUBSTANTIALLY EQUAL PAYMENTS.—

(A) IN GENERAL.—If—

(i) paragraph (1) does not apply to a distribution by reason of paragraph (2)(A)(iv), and

(ii) the series of payments under such paragraph are subsequently modified (other than by reason of death or disability)—

(I) before the close of the 5-year period beginning with the date of the first payment and after the employee attains age 59½, or

(II) before the employee attains age 59½,

the taxpayer's tax for the 1st taxable year in which such modification occurs shall be increased by an amount, determined under regulations, equal to the tax which (but for paragraph (2)(A)(iv)) would have been imposed, plus interest for the deferral period.

(B) DEFERRAL PERIOD.—For purposes of this paragraph, the term "deferral period" means the period beginning with the taxable year in which (without regard to paragraph (2)(A)(iv)) the distribution would have been includible in gross income and ending with the taxable year in which the modification described in subparagraph (A) occurs.

(5) EMPLOYEE.—For purposes of this subsection, the term "employee" includes any participant, and in the case of an individual retirement plan, the individual for whose benefit such plan was established.

(6) SPECIAL RULES FOR SIMPLE RETIREMENT ACCOUNTS.—In the case of any amount received from a simple retirement account (within the meaning of section 408(p)) during the 2-year period beginning on the date such individual first participated in any qualified salary reduction arrangement maintained by the individual's employer under section 408(p)(2), paragraph (1) shall be applied by substituting "25 percent" for "10 percent".

(7) QUALIFIED HIGHER EDUCATION EXPENSES.—For purposes of paragraph (2)(E)—

(A) IN GENERAL.—The term "qualified higher education expenses" means qualified higher education expenses (as defined in section 529(e)(3)) for education furnished to—

(i) the taxpayer,

(ii) the taxpayer's spouse, or

(iii) any child (as defined in section 152(f)(1)) or grandchild of the taxpayer or the taxpayer's spouse, at an eligible educational institution (as defined in section 529(e)(5)).

(B) COORDINATION WITH OTHER BENEFITS.—The amount of qualified higher education expenses for any taxable year shall be reduced as provided in section 25A(g)(2).

(8) QUALIFIED FIRST-TIME HOMEBUYER DISTRIBUTIONS.—For purposes of paragraph (2)(F)—

(A) IN GENERAL.—The term "qualified first-time homebuyer distribution" means any payment or distribution received by an individual to the extent such payment or distribution is used by the individual before the close of the 120th day after the day on which such payment or distribution is received to pay qualified acquisition costs with respect to a principal residence of a first-time homebuyer who is such individual, the spouse of such individual, or any child, grandchild, or ancestor of such individual or the individual's spouse.

(B) LIFETIME DOLLAR LIMITATION.—The aggregate amount of payments or distributions received by an individual which may be treated as qualified first-time homebuyer distributions for any taxable year shall not exceed the excess (if any) of—

(i) $10,000, over

(ii) the aggregate amounts treated as qualified first-time homebuyer distributions with respect to such individual for all prior taxable years.

(C) QUALIFIED ACQUISITION COSTS.—For purposes of this paragraph, the term "qualified acquisition costs" means the costs of acquiring, constructing, or reconstructing a residence. Such term includes any usual or reasonable settlement, financing, or other closing costs.

(D) FIRST-TIME HOMEBUYER; OTHER DEFINITIONS.—For purposes of this paragraph—

(i) FIRST-TIME HOMEBUYER.—The term "first-time homebuyer" means any individual if—

(I) such individual (and if married, such individual's spouse) had no present ownership interest in a principal residence during the 2-year period ending on the date of acquisition of the principal residence to which this paragraph applies, and

(II) subsection (h) or (k) of section 1034 (as in effect on the day before the date of the enactment of this paragraph) did not suspend the running of any period of time specified in section 1034 (as so in effect) with respect to such individual on the day before the date the distribution is applied pursuant to subparagraph (A).

(ii) PRINCIPAL RESIDENCE.—The term "principal residence" has the same meaning as when used in section 121.

(iii) DATE OF ACQUISITION.—The term "date of acquisition" means the date—

(I) on which a binding contract to acquire the principal residence to which subparagraph (A) applies is entered into, or

(II) on which construction or reconstruction of such a principal residence is commenced.

(E) SPECIAL RULE WHERE DELAY IN ACQUISITION.—If any distribution from any individual retirement plan fails to meet the requirements of subparagraph (A) solely by reason of a delay or cancellation of the purchase or construction of the residence, the amount of the distribution may be contributed to an individual retirement plan as provided in section 408(d)(3)(A)(i) (determined by substituting "120th day" for "60th day" in such section), except that—

(i) section 408(d)(3)(B) shall not be applied to such contribution, and

(ii) such amount shall not be taken into account in determining whether section 408(d)(3)(B) applies to any other amount.

(9) SPECIAL RULE FOR ROLLOVERS TO SECTION 457 PLANS.—For purposes of this subsection, a distribution from an eligible deferred compensation plan (as defined in section 457(b)) of an eligible employer described in section 457(e)(1)(A) shall be treated as a distribution from a qualified retirement plan described in 4974(c)(1) to the extent that such distribution is attributable to an amount transferred to an eligible deferred compensation plan from a qualified retirement plan (as defined in section 4974(c)).

(10) DISTRIBUTIONS TO QUALIFIED PUBLIC SAFETY EMPLOYEES IN GOVERNMENTAL PLANS.—

(A) IN GENERAL.—In the case of a distribution to a qualified public safety employee from a governmental plan (within the meaning of section 414(d)) which is a defined benefit plan, paragraph (2)(A)(v) shall be applied by substituting "age 50" for "age 55".

(B) QUALIFIED PUBLIC SAFETY EMPLOYEE.—For purposes of this paragraph, the term "qualified public safety employee" means any employee of a State or political subdivision of a State who provides police protection, firefighting services, or emergency medical services for any area within the jurisdiction of such State or political subdivision.

Amendments

• 2008, Worker, Retiree, and Employer Recovery Act of 2008 (P.L. 110-458)

P.L. 110-458, §108(e):

Amended the first sentence of Code Sec. 72(t)(2)(G)(iv) [prior to amendment by P.L. 110-245] by inserting "on or" before "before". **Effective** as if included in the provision of the 2006 Act to which the amendment relates [**effective** for distributions after 9-11-2001.—CCH].

• 2008, Heroes Earnings Assistance and Relief Tax Act of 2008 (P.L. 110-245)

P.L. 110-245, §107(a):

Amended Code Sec. 72(t)(2)(G)(iv) by striking ", and before December 31, 2007" following "September 11, 2001". **Effective** for individuals ordered or called to active duty on or after 12-31-2007.

• 2006, Pension Protection Act of 2006 (P.L. 109-280)

P.L. 109-280, §811, provides:

SEC. 811. PENSIONS AND INDIVIDUAL RETIREMENT ARRANGEMENT PROVISIONS OF ECONOMIC GROWTH AND TAX RELIEF RECONCILIATION ACT OF 2001 MADE PERMANENT.

Title IX of the Economic Growth and Tax Relief Reconciliation Act of 2001 [P.L. 107-16] shall not apply to the provisions of, and amendments made by, subtitles A through F of title VI [§§601-666]of such Act (relating to pension and individual retirement arrangement provisions).

P.L. 109-280, §827(a):

Amended Code Sec. 72(t)(2) by adding at the end a new subparagraph (G). **Effective** for distributions after 9-11-2001. For a waiver of limitations, see Act Sec. 827(c)(2), below.

P.L. 109-280, §827(c)(2), provides:

(2) WAIVER OF LIMITATIONS.—If refund or credit of any overpayment of tax resulting from the amendments made by this section is prevented at any time before the close of the 1-year period beginning on the date of the enactment of this Act by the operation of any law or rule of law (including res judicata), such refund or credit may nevertheless be made or allowed if claim therefor is filed before the close of such period.

P.L. 109-280, §828(a):

Amended Code Sec. 72(t) by adding at the end a new paragraph (10). **Effective** for distributions after 8-17-2006.

• 2005, Katrina Emergency Tax Relief Act of 2005 (P.L. 109-73)

P.L. 109-73, §101 [repealed by P.L. 109-135, §201(b)(4)(A)], provides:

SEC. 101. TAX-FAVORED WITHDRAWALS FROM RETIREMENT PLANS FOR RELIEF RELATING TO HURRICANE KATRINA.

(a) IN GENERAL.—Section 72(t) of the Internal Revenue Code of 1986 shall not apply to any qualified Hurricane Katrina distribution.

(b) AGGREGATE DOLLAR LIMITATION.—

(1) IN GENERAL.—For purposes of this section, the aggregate amount of distributions received by an individual which may be treated as qualified Hurricane Katrina distributions for any taxable year shall not exceed the excess (if any) of—

(A) $100,000, over

(B) the aggregate amounts treated as qualified Hurricane Katrina distributions received by such individual for all prior taxable years.

(2) TREATMENT OF PLAN DISTRIBUTIONS.—If a distribution to an individual would (without regard to paragraph (1)) be a qualified Hurricane Katrina distribution, a plan shall not be treated as violating any requirement of the Internal Revenue Code of 1986 merely because the plan treats such distribution as a qualified Hurricane Katrina distribution, unless the aggregate amount of such distributions from all plans maintained by the employer (and any member of any controlled group which includes the employer) to such individual exceeds $100,000.

(3) CONTROLLED GROUP.—For purposes of paragraph (2), the term "controlled group" means any group treated as a single employer under sub-section (b), (c), (m), or (o) of section 414 of such Code.

(c) AMOUNT DISTRIBUTED MAY BE REPAID.—

(1) IN GENERAL.—Any individual who receives a qualified Hurricane Katrina distribution may, at any time during the 3-year period beginning on the day after the date on which such distribution was received, make one or more contributions in an aggregate amount not to exceed the amount of such distribution to an eligible retirement plan of which such individual is a beneficiary and to which a rollover contribution of such distribution could be made under section 402(c), 403(a)(4), 403(b)(8), 408(d)(3), or 457(e)(16) of such Code, as the case may be.

(2) TREATMENT OF REPAYMENTS OF DISTRIBUTIONS FROM ELIGIBLE RETIREMENT PLANS OTHER THAN IRAS.—For purposes of such Code, if a contribution is made pursuant to paragraph (1) with respect to a qualified Hurricane Katrina distribution from an eligible retirement plan other than an individual retirement plan, then the taxpayer shall, to the extent of the amount of the contribution, be treated as having received the qualified Hurricane Katrina distribution in an eligible rollover distribution (as defined in section 402(c)(4) of such Code) and as having transferred the amount to the eligible retirement plan in a direct trustee to trustee transfer within 60 days of the distribution.

(3) TREATMENT OF REPAYMENTS FOR DISTRIBUTIONS FROM IRAS.—For purposes of such Code, if a contribution is made pursuant to paragraph (1) with respect to a qualified Hurricane Katrina distribution from an individual retirement plan (as defined by section 7701(a)(37) of such Code), then, to the extent of the amount of the contribution, the qualified Hurricane Katrina distribution shall be treated as a distribution described in section 408(d)(3) of such Code and as having been transferred to the eligible retirement plan in a direct trustee to trustee transfer within 60 days of the distribution.

(d) DEFINITIONS.—For purposes of this section—

(1) QUALIFIED HURRICANE KATRINA DISTRIBUTION.—Except as provided in subsection (b), the term "qualified Hurricane Katrina distribution" means any distribution from an eligible retirement plan made on or after August 25, 2005, and before January 1, 2007, to an individual whose principal place of abode on August 28, 2005, is located in the Hurricane Katrina disaster area and who has sustained an economic loss by reason of Hurricane Katrina.

(2) ELIGIBLE RETIREMENT PLAN.—The term "eligible retirement plan" shall have the meaning given such term by section 402(c)(8)(B) of such Code.

(e) INCOME INCLUSION SPREAD OVER 3 YEAR PERIOD FOR QUALIFIED HURRICANE KATRINA DISTRIBUTIONS.—

(1) IN GENERAL.—In the case of any qualified Hurricane Katrina distribution, unless the taxpayer elects not to have this subsection apply for any taxable year, any amount required to be included in gross income for such taxable year shall be so included ratably over the 3-taxable year period beginning with such taxable year.

(2) SPECIAL RULE.—For purposes of paragraph (1), rules similar to the rules of subparagraph (E) of section 408A(d)(3) of such Code shall apply.

(f) SPECIAL RULES.—

(1) EXEMPTION OF DISTRIBUTIONS FROM TRUSTEE TO TRUSTEE TRANSFER AND WITHHOLDING RULES.—For purposes of sections 401(a)(31), 402(f), and 3405 of such Code, qualified Hurricane Katrina distributions shall not be treated as eligible rollover distributions.

(2) QUALIFIED HURRICANE KATRINA DISTRIBUTIONS TREATED AS MEETING PLAN DISTRIBUTION REQUIREMENTS.—For purposes of such Code, a qualified Hurricane Katrina distribution shall be treated as meeting the requirements of sections 401(k)(2)(B)(i), 403(b)(7)(A)(ii), 403(b)(11), and 457(d)(1)(A) of such Code.

P.L. 109-73, §102 [repealed by P.L. 109-135, §201(b)(4)(A)], provides:

SEC. 102. RECONTRIBUTIONS OF WITHDRAWALS FOR HOME PURCHASES CANCELLED DUE TO HURRICANE KATRINA.

(a) RECONTRIBUTIONS.—

(1) IN GENERAL.—Any individual who received a qualified distribution may, during the period beginning on August 25, 2005, and ending on February 28, 2006, make one or more contributions in an aggregate amount not to exceed the amount of such qualified distribution to an eligible retirement plan (as defined in section 402(c)(8)(B) of the Internal Revenue Code of 1986) of which such individual is a beneficiary and to which a rollover contribution of such distribution could be made under section 402(c), 403(a)(4), 403(b)(8), or 408(d)(3) of such Code, as the case may be.

(2) TREATMENT OF REPAYMENTS.—Rules similar to the rules of paragraphs (2) and (3) of section 101(c) of this Act shall apply for purposes of this section.

(b) QUALIFIED DISTRIBUTION DEFINED.—For purposes of this section, the term "qualified distribution" means any distribution—

(1) described in section 401(k)(2)(B)(i)(IV), 403(b)(7)(A)(ii) (but only to the extent such distribution relates to financial hardship), 403(b)(11)(B), or 72(t)(2)(F) of such Code,

(2) received after February 28, 2005, and before August 29, 2005, and

(3) which was to be used to purchase or construct a principal residence in the Hurricane Katrina disaster area, but which was not so purchased or constructed on account of Hurricane Katrina.

• 2004, Working Families Tax Relief Act of 2004 (P.L. 108-311)

P.L. 108-311, §207(6):

Amended Code Sec. 72(t)(2)(D)(i)(III) by inserting ", determined without regard to subsections (b)(1), (b)(2), and (d)(1)(B) thereof" after "section 152". **Effective** for tax years beginning after 12-31-2004.

P.L. 108-311, §207(7):

Amended Code Sec. 72(t)(7)(A)(iii) by striking "151(c)(3)" and inserting "152(f)(1)". **Effective** for tax years beginning after 12-31-2004.

• 2001, Economic Growth and Tax Relief Reconciliation Act of 2001 (P.L. 107-16)

P.L. 107-16, §641(a)(2)(C):

Amended Code Sec. 72(t) by adding at the end a new paragraph (9) to read as above. **Effective**, generally, for distributions after 12-31-2001. For a special rule, see Act Sec. 641(f)(3), in the amendment notes following Code Sec. 72(o).

P.L. 107-16, §901(a)-(b), provides [but see P.L. 109-280, §811, above]:

SEC. 901. SUNSET OF PROVISIONS OF ACT.

(a) IN GENERAL.—All provisions of, and amendments made by, this Act shall not apply—

(1) to taxable, plan, or limitation years beginning after December 31, 2010, or

(2) in the case of title V, to estates of decedents dying, gifts made, or generation skipping transfers, after December 31, 2010.

(b) APPLICATION OF CERTAIN LAWS.—The Internal Revenue Code of 1986 and the Employee Retirement Income Security Act of 1974 shall be applied and administered to years, estates, gifts, and transfers described in subsection (a) as if the provisions and amendments described in subsection (a) had never been enacted.

• 1998, IRS Restructuring and Reform Act of 1998 (P.L. 105-206)

P.L. 105-206, §3436(a):

Amended Code Sec. 72(t)(2)(A) by striking "or" at the end of clauses (iv) and (v), by striking the period at the end of clause (vi) and inserting ", or", and by adding at the end a new clause (vii). **Effective** for distributions after 12-31-99.

P.L. 105-206, §6005(c)(1)(A)-(B):

Amended Code Sec. 72(t)(8)(E) by striking "120 days" and inserting "120th day", and by striking "60 days" and inserting "60th day". **Effective** as if included in the provision of P.L. 105-34 to which it relates [**effective** for distributions in tax years beginning after 12-31-97.—CCH].

P.L. 105-206, §6023(4):

Amended Code Sec. 72(t)(3)(A) by striking "(A)(v)," and inserting "(A)(v)". **Effective** 7-22-98.

• 1997, Taxpayer Relief Act of 1997 (P.L. 105-34)

P.L. 105-34, §203(a):

Amended Code Sec. 72(t)(2) by adding at the end a new subparagraph (E). **Effective** for distributions after 12-31-97, with respect to expenses paid after such date (in tax years ending after such date), for education furnished in academic periods beginning after such date.

P.L. 105-34, §203(b):

Amended Code Sec. 72(t) by adding at the end a new paragraph (7). **Effective** for distributions after 12-31-97, with respect to expenses paid after such date (in tax years ending after such date), for education furnished in academic periods beginning after such date.

P.L. 105-34, §303(a):

Amended Code Sec. 72(t)(2) (as amended by Act Sec. 203) by adding a new subparagraph (F). **Effective** for payments and distributions in tax years beginning after 12-31-97.

P.L. 105-34, §303(b):

Amended Code Sec. 72(t) (as amended by Act Sec. 203) by adding a new paragraph (8). **Effective** for payments and distributions in tax years beginning after 12-31-97.

• 1996, Health Insurance Portability and Accountability Act of 1996 (P.L. 104-191)

P.L. 104-191, §361(a):

Amended Code Sec. 72(t)(3)(A) by striking "(B)," after "(A)(v),". **Effective** for distributions after 12-31-96.

P.L. 104-191, §361(b):

Amended Code Sec. 72(t)(2) by adding at the end a new subparagraph (D). **Effective** for distributions after 12-31-96.

P.L. 104-191, §361(c):

Amended Code Sec. 72(t)(2)(B) by striking "or (C)" and inserting ", (C), or (D)". **Effective** for distributions after 12-31-96.

• 1996, Small Business Job Protection Act of 1996 (P.L. 104-188)

P.L. 104-188, §1421(b)(4)(A):

Amended Code Sec. 72(t) by adding at the end a new paragraph (6). **Effective** for tax years beginning after 12-31-96.

• 1990, Omnibus Budget Reconciliation Act of 1990 (P.L. 101-508)

P.L. 101-508, §11802(a):

Amended Code Sec. 72(t) by striking subparagraph (C) of paragraph (2), by redesignating subparagraph (D) as subparagraph (C), and in paragraph (3)(A) by striking "(C), and (D)" and inserting "and (C)". **Effective** 11-5-90. Prior to repeal, Code Sec. 72(t)(2)(C) read as follows:

(C) EXCEPTIONS FOR DISTRIBUTIONS FROM EMPLOYEE STOCK OWNERSHIP PLANS.—Any distribution made before January 1, 1990, to an employee from an employee stock ownership plan (as defined in section 4975(e)(7)) or a tax credit employee stock ownership plan (as defined in section 409) if—

(i) such distribution is attributable to assets which have been invested in employer securities (within the meaning of section 409(l)) at all times during the 5-plan-year period preceding the plan year in which the distribution is made, and

(ii) at all times during such period the requirements of sections 401(a)(28) and 409 (as in effect at such times) are met with respect to such employer securities.

P.L. 101-508, §11821(b)(1)-(2), provides:

(b) SAVINGS PROVISION.—If—

(1) any provision amended or repealed by this part applied to—

(A) any transaction occurring before the date of the enactment of this Act,

(B) any property acquired before such date of enactment, or

(C) any item of income, loss, deduction, or credit taken into account before such date of enactment, and

(2) the treatment of such transaction, property, or item under such provision would (without regard to the amend-

ments made by this part) affect liability for tax for periods ending after such date of enactment,

nothing in the amendments made by this part shall be construed to affect the treatment of such transaction, property, or item for purposes of determining liability for tax for periods ending after such date of enactment.

• 1988, Technical and Miscellaneous Revenue Act of 1988 (P.L. 100-647)

P.L. 100-647, §1011A(c)(1):

Amended Code Sec. 72(t)(2)(A) by striking out "on account of early retirement under the plan" after "separation from service" in clause (v). **Effective** as if included in the provision of P.L. 99-514 to which it relates.

P.L. 100-647, §1011A(c)(2):

Amended Code Sec. 72(t)(2)(C). **Effective** as if included in the provision of P.L. 99-514 to which it relates. Prior to amendment, Code Sec. 72(t)(2)(C) read as follows:

(C) CERTAIN PLANS.—

(i) IN GENERAL.—Except as provided in clause (ii), any distribution made before January 1, 1990, to an employee from an employee stock ownership plan defined in section 4975(e)(7) to the extent that, on average, a majority of assets in the plan have been invested in employer securities (as defined in section 409(l)) for the 5-plan-year period preceding the plan year in which the distribution is made.

(ii) BENEFITS DISTRIBUTED MUST BE INVESTED IN EMPLOYER SECURITIES FOR 5 YEARS.—Clause (i) shall not apply to any distribution which is attributable to assets which have not been invested in employer securities at all times during the period referred to in clause (i).

P.L. 100-647, §1011A(c)(3):

Amended Code Sec. 72(t)(3)(A) by striking out "and (C)" and inserting in lieu thereof "(C), and (D)". **Effective** as if included in the provision of P.L. 99-514 to which it relates.

P.L. 100-647, §1011A(c)(7):

Amended Code Sec. 72(t)(2)(A)(iv) by inserting "designated" before "beneficiary". **Effective** as if included in the provision of P.L. 99-514 to which it relates.

P.L. 100-647, §1011A(c)(13), provides:

(13) Section 72(t) of the 1986 Code shall apply to any distribution without regard to whether such distribution is made without the consent of the participant pursuant to section 411(a)(11) or section 417(e) of the 1986 Code.

• 1986, Tax Reform Act of 1986 (P.L. 99-514)

P.L. 99-514, §1123(a):

Amended Code Sec. 72 by redesignating subsection (t) as subsection (u) and inserting after subsection (s) new subsection (t) to read as above. For the **effective** date, see Act Sec. 1123(e), reproduced under the amendment notes for Code Sec. 72(m).

[Sec. 72(u)]

(u) TREATMENT OF ANNUITY CONTRACTS NOT HELD BY NATURAL PERSONS.—

(1) IN GENERAL.—If any annuity contract is held by a person who is not a natural person—

(A) such contract shall not be treated as an annuity contract for purposes of this subtitle (other than subchapter L) and

(B) the income on the contract for any taxable year of the policyholder shall be treated as ordinary income received or accrued by the owner during such taxable year.

For purposes of this paragraph, holding by a trust or other entity as an agent for a natural person shall not be taken into account.

(2) INCOME ON THE CONTRACT.—

(A) IN GENERAL.—For purposes of paragraph (1), the term "income on the contract" means, with respect to any taxable year of the policyholder, the excess of—

(i) the sum of the net surrender value of the contract as of the close of the taxable year plus all distributions under the contract received during the taxable year or any prior taxable year, reduced by

(ii) the sum of the amount of net premiums under the contract for the taxable year and prior taxable years and amounts includible in gross income for prior taxable years with respect to such contract under this subsection.

Where necessary to prevent the avoidance of this subsection, the Secretary may substitute "fair market value of the contract" for "net surrender value of the contract" each place it appears in the preceding sentence.

(B) NET PREMIUMS.—For purposes of this paragraph, the term "net premiums" means the amount of premiums paid under the contract reduced by any policyholder dividends.

(3) EXCEPTIONS.—This subsection shall not apply to any annuity contract which—

(A) is acquired by the estate of a decedent by reason of the death of the decedent,

(B) is held under a plan described in section 401(a) or 403(a), under a program described in section 403(b), or under an individual retirement plan,

(C) is a qualified funding asset (as defined in section 130(d), but without regard to whether there is a qualified assignment),

(D) is purchased by an employer upon the termination of a plan described in section 401(a) or 403(a) and which is held by the employer until all amounts under such contract are distributed to the employee for whom such contract was purchased or the employee's beneficiary, or

(E) is an immediate annuity.

(4) IMMEDIATE ANNUITY.—For purposes of this subsection, the term "immediate annuity" means an annuity—

(A) which is purchased with a single premium or annuity consideration,

(B) the annuity starting date (as defined in subsection (c)(4)) of which commences no later than 1 year from the date of the purchase of the annuity, and

(C) which provides for a series of substantially equal periodic payments (to be made not less frequently than annually) during the annuity period.

Amendments

• 1988, Technical and Miscellaneous Revenue Act of 1988 (P.L. 100-647)

P.L. 100-647, §1011A(i)(1):

Amended Code Sec. 72(u)(1)(A) by inserting "(other than subchapter L)" after "subtitle". **Effective** as if included in the provision of P.L. 99-514 to which it relates.

P.L. 100-647, §1011A(i)(2):

Amended Code Sec. 72(u)(3)(D) by striking out "until such time as the employee separates from service" and inserting in lieu thereof "until all amounts under such contract are distributed to the employee for whom such contract was purchased or the employee's beneficiary". **Effective** as if included in the provision of P.L. 99-514 to which it relates.

P.L. 100-647, §1011A(i)(3):

Amended Code Sec. 72(u)(3) by striking out "which" at the beginning of subparagraphs (D) and (E). **Effective** as if included in the provision of P.L. 99-514 to which it relates.

P.L. 100-647, §1011A(i)(4):

Amended Code Sec. 72(u)(4) by striking out "and" at the end of subparagraph (A), by striking out the period at the end of subparagraph (B) and inserting in lieu thereof ", and", and by adding at the end thereof new subparagraph (C). **Effective** as if included in the provision of P.L. 99-514 to which it relates.

• 1986, Tax Reform Act of 1986 (P.L. 99-514)

P.L. 99-514, §1135(a):

Amended Code Sec. 72, as amended by Act Sec. 12[1]23, by redesignating subsection (u) as subsection (v) and by inserting after subsection (t) new subsection (u). **Effective** for contributions to annuity contracts after 2-28-86.

[Sec. 72(v)]

(v) 10-PERCENT ADDITIONAL TAX FOR TAXABLE DISTRIBUTIONS FROM MODIFIED ENDOWMENT CONTRACTS.—

(1) IMPOSITION OF ADDITIONAL TAX.—If any taxpayer receives any amount under a modified endowment contract (as defined in section 7702A), the taxpayer's tax under this chapter for the taxable year in which such amount is received shall be increased by an amount equal to 10 percent of the portion of such amount which is includible in gross income.

(2) SUBSECTION NOT TO APPLY TO CERTAIN DISTRIBUTIONS.—Paragraph (1) shall not apply to any distribution—

(A) made on or after the date on which the taxpayer attains age 59½,

(B) which is attributable to the taxpayer's becoming disabled (within the meaning of subsection (m)(7)), or

(C) which is part of a series of substantially equal periodic payments (not less frequently than annually) made for the life (or life expectancy) of the taxpayer or the joint lives (or joint life expectancies) of such taxpayer and his beneficiary.

Amendments

• 1988, Technical and Miscellaneous Revenue Act of 1988 (P.L. 100-647)

P.L. 100-647, §5012(b)(1):

Amended Code Sec. 72 by redesignating subsection (v) as subsection (w) and by inserting a new subsection (v).

[Sec. 72(w)]

(w) APPLICATION OF BASIS RULES TO NONRESIDENT ALIENS.—

(1) IN GENERAL.—Notwithstanding any other provision of this section, for purposes of determining the portion of any distribution which is includible in gross income of a distributee who is a citizen or resident of the United States, the investment in the contract shall not include any applicable nontaxable contributions or applicable nontaxable earnings.

(2) APPLICABLE NONTAXABLE CONTRIBUTION.—For purposes of this subsection, the term "applicable nontaxable contribution" means any employer or employee contribution—

(A) which was made with respect to compensation—

(i) for labor or personal services performed by an employee who, at the time the labor or services were performed, was a nonresident alien for purposes of the laws of the United States in effect at such time, and

(ii) which is treated as from sources without the United States, and

(B) which was not subject to income tax (and would have been subject to income tax if paid as cash compensation when the services were rendered) under the laws of the United States or any foreign country.

(3) APPLICABLE NONTAXABLE EARNINGS.—For purposes of this subsection, the term "applicable nontaxable earnings" means earnings—

(A) which are paid or accrued with respect to any employer or employee contribution which was made with respect to compensation for labor or personal services performed by an employee,

(B) with respect to which the employee was at the time the earnings were paid or accrued a nonresident alien for purposes of the laws of the United States, and

(C) which were not subject to income tax under the laws of the United States or any foreign country.

(4) REGULATIONS.—The Secretary shall prescribe such regulations as may be necessary to carry out the provisions of this subsection, including regulations treating contributions and earnings as not subject to tax under the laws of any foreign country where appropriate to carry out the purposes of this subsection.

Amendments

• 2004, American Jobs Creation Act of 2004 (P.L. 108-357)

P.L. 108-357, §906(a):

Amended Code Sec. 72 by redesignating subsection (w) as subsection (x) and by inserting after subsection (v) a new subsection (w). **Effective** for distributions on or after 10-22-2004.

[Sec. 72(x)]

(x) CROSS REFERENCE.—

For limitation on adjustments to basis of annuity contracts sold, see section 1021.

Amendments

• 2004, American Jobs Creation Act of 2004 (P.L. 108-357)

P.L. 108-357, §906(a):

Amended Code Sec. 72 by redesignating subsection (w) as subsection (x). **Effective** for distributions on or after 10-22-2004.

• 1988, Technical and Miscellaneous Revenue Act of 1988 (P.L. 100-647)

P.L. 100-647, §5012(b)(1):

Amended Code Sec. 72 by redesignating subsection (v) as subsection (w). For the **effective** date, see Code Sec. 5012(e) below.

P.L. 100-647, §5012(e), as amended by P.L. 101-239, §7815(a)(2), provides:

(c) EFFECTIVE DATES.—

(1) IN GENERAL—Except as otherwise provided in this subsection, the amendments made by this section shall apply to contracts entered into on or after June 21, 1988.

(2) SPECIAL RULE WHERE DEATH BENEFIT INCREASES BY MORE THAN $150,000.—If the death benefit under the contract increases by more than $150,000 over the death benefit under the contract in effect on October 20, 1988, the rules of section 7702A(c)(3) of the 1986 Code (as added by this section) shall apply in determining whether such contract is issued on or after June 21, 1988. The preceding sentence shall not apply in the case of a contract which, as of June 21, 1988, required at least 7 level annual premium payments and under which the policyholder makes at least 7 level annual premium payments.

(3) CERTAIN OTHER MATERIAL CHANGES TAKEN INTO ACCOUNT.—A contract entered into before June 21, 1988, shall be treated as entered into after such date if—

(A) on or after June 21, 1988, the death benefit under the contract is increased (or a qualified additional benefit is increased or added) and before June 21, 1988, the owner of the contract did not have a unilateral right under the contract to obtain such increase or addition without providing additional evidence of insurability, or

(B) the contract is converted after June 20, 1988, from a term life insurance contract to a life insurance contract providing coverage other than term life insurance coverage without regard to any right of the owner of the contract to such conversion.

(4) CERTAIN EXCHANGES PERMITTED.—In the case of a modified endowment contract which—

(A) required at least 7 annual level premium payments,

(B) is entered into after June 20, 1988, and before the date of the enactment of this Act, and

(C) is exchanged within 3 months after such date of enactment for a life insurance contract which meets the requirements of section 7702A(b),

the contract which is received in exchange for such contract shall not be treated as a modified endowment contract if the taxpayer elects, notwithstanding section 1035 of the 1986 Code, to recognize gain on such exchange.

(5) SPECIAL RULE FOR ANNUITY CONTRACTS.—In the case of annuity contracts, the amendments made by subsection (d) shall apply to contracts entered into after October 21, 1988.

• 1986, Tax Reform Act of 1986 (P.L. 99-514)

P.L. 99-514, §1123(a):

Amended Code Sec. 72 by redesignating subsection (t) as subsection (u). For the **effective** date, see Act Sec. 1123(e), reproduced under the amendment notes for Code Sec. 72(m).

P.L. 99-514, §1135(a):

Amended Code Sec. 72, as amended by Act Sec. 1223 [1123], by redesignating subsection (u) as subsection (v). **Effective** for contributions to annuity contracts after 2-28-86.

• 1984, Deficit Reduction Act of 1984 (P.L. 98-369)

P.L. 98-369, §222(b):

Redesignated former Code Sec. 72(s) as Code Sec. 72(t). **Effective** for contracts issued after the day which is 6 months after 7-18-84, in tax years ending after such date.

• 1983, Railroad Retirement Solvency Act of 1983 (P.L. 98-76)

P.L. 98-76, §224(a):

Redesignated former Code Sec. 72(r) as Code Sec. 72(s). **Effective** for benefits received after 1983 in tax years ending after 1983.

• 1982, Tax Equity and Fiscal Responsibility Act of 1982 (P.L. 97-248)

P.L. 97-248, §236(a):

Redesignated Code Sec. 72(p) as Code Sec. 72(q). **Effective** for loans, assignments, and pledges made after 8-13-82.

P.L. 97-248, §265(b)(1):

Redesignated Code Sec. 72(q) as Code Sec. 72(r). **Effective** for distributions after 12-31-82.

• 1981, Economic Recovery Tax Act of 1981 (P.L. 97-34)

P.L. 97-34, §311(b)(1):

Redesignated Code Sec. 72(o) as Code Sec. 72(p). **Effective** 1-1-82.

• 1974, Employee Retirement Income Security Act of 1974 (P.L. 93-406)

P.L. 93-406, §2005(c)(3):

Redesignated Code Sec. 72(p) as Code Sec. 72(o).

• 1966 (P.L. 89-365)

P.L. 89-365, §[1]:

Redesignated Code Sec. 72(o) as Code Sec. 72(p).

• 1962, Self-Employed Individuals Tax Retirement Act of 1962 (P.L. 87-792)

P.L. 87-792, §4:

Redesignated Code Sec. 72(m) as Code Sec. 72(o). **Effective** 1-1-63.

[Sec. 73]

SEC. 73. SERVICES OF CHILD.

[Sec. 73(a)]

(a) TREATMENT OF AMOUNTS RECEIVED.—Amounts received in respect of the services of a child shall be included in his gross income and not in the gross income of the parent, even though such amounts are not received by the child.

[Sec. 73(b)]

(b) TREATMENT OF EXPENDITURES.—All expenditures by the parent or the child attributable to amounts which are includible in the gross income of the child (and not of the parent) solely by reason of subsection (a) shall be treated as paid or incurred by the child.

[Sec. 73(c)]

(c) PARENT DEFINED.—For purposes of this section, the term "parent" includes an individual who is entitled to the services of a child by reason of having parental rights and duties in respect of the child.

[Sec. 73(d)]

(d) CROSS REFERENCE.—

For assessment of tax against parent in certain cases, see section 6201(c).

[Sec. 74]

SEC. 74. PRIZES AND AWARDS.

[Sec. 74(a)]

(a) GENERAL RULE.—Except as otherwise provided in this section or in section 117 (relating to qualified scholarships), gross income includes amounts received as prizes and awards.

[Sec. 74(b)]

(b) EXCEPTION FOR CERTAIN PRIZES AND AWARDS TRANSFERRED TO CHARITIES.—Gross income does not include amounts received as prizes and awards made primarily in recognition of religious, charitable, scientific, educational, artistic, literary, or civic achievement, but only if—

(1) the recipient was selected without any action on his part to enter the contest or proceeding;

(2) the recipient is not required to render substantial future services as a condition to receiving the prize or award; and

(3) the prize or award is transferred by the payor to a governmental unit or organization described in paragraph (1) or (2) of section 170(c) pursuant to a designation made by the recipient.

[Sec. 74(c)]

(c) EXCEPTIONS FOR CERTAIN EMPLOYEE ACHIEVEMENT AWARDS.—

(1) IN GENERAL.—Gross income shall not include the value of an employee achievement award (as defined in section 274(j)) received by the taxpayer if the cost to the employer of the employee achievement award does not exceed the amount allowable as a deduction to the employer for the cost of the employee achievement award.

(2) EXCESS DEDUCTION AWARD.—If the cost to the employer of the employee achievement award received by the taxpayer exceeds the amount allowable as a deduction to the employer, then gross income includes the greater of—

(A) an amount equal to the portion of the cost to the employer of the award that is not allowable as a deduction to the employer (but not in excess of the value of the award), or

(B) the amount by which the value of the award exceeds the amount allowable as a deduction to the employer.

The remaining portion of the value of such award shall not be included in the gross income of the recipient.

(3) TREATMENT OF TAX-EXEMPT EMPLOYERS.—In the case of an employer exempt from taxation under this subtitle, any reference in this subsection to the amount allowable as a deduction to the employer shall be treated as a reference to the amount which would be allowable as a deduction to the employer if the employer were not exempt from taxation under this subtitle.

(4) CROSS REFERENCE.—

For provisions excluding certain de minimis fringes from gross income, see section 132(e).

Amendments

• 1986, Tax Reform Act of 1986 (P.L. 99-514)

P.L. 99-514, §122 (a)(1)(A)-(D):

Amended Code Sec. 74 by striking out "Except as provided in subsection (b) and" in subsection (a) and inserting in lieu thereof "Except as otherwise provided in this section or", by striking out "EXCEPTION" in the heading for subsection (b) and inserting in lieu thereof "EXCEPTION FOR CERTAIN PRIZES AND AWARDS TRANSFERRED TO CHARITIES", by striking out "and" at the end of subsection (b)(1), by striking out the period at the end of subsection (b)(2) and inserting in lieu thereof "; and", and by adding after subsection (b)(2) new paragraph (3), and by adding new subsection (c). **Effective** for prizes and awards granted after 12-31-86.

P.L. 99-514, §123(b)(1):

Amended Code Sec. 74(a) by striking out "(relating to scholarship and fellowship grants)" and inserting in lieu thereof "(relating to qualified scholarships)". **Effective** for tax years beginning after 12-31-86, but only in the case of scholarships and fellowships granted after 8-16-86.

[Sec. 75]

SEC. 75. DEALERS IN TAX-EXEMPT SECURITIES.

[Sec. 75(a)]

(a) ADJUSTMENT FOR BOND PREMIUM.—In computing the gross income of a taxpayer who holds during the taxable year a municipal bond (as defined in subsection (b) (1)) primarily for sale to customers in the ordinary course of his trade or business—

(1) if the gross income of the taxpayer from such trade or business is computed by the use of inventories and his inventories are valued on any basis other than cost, the cost of securities sold (as defined in subsection (b) (2)) during such year shall be reduced by an amount equal to the amortizable bond premium which would be disallowed as a deduction for such year by section 171(a)(2) (relating to deduction for amortizable bond premium) if the definition in section 171(d) of the term "bond" did not exclude such municipal bond; or

(2) if the gross income of the taxpayer from such trade or business is computed without the use of inventories, or by use of inventories valued at cost, and the municipal bond is sold or otherwise disposed of during such year, the adjusted basis (computed without regard to this paragraph) of the municipal bond shall be reduced by the amount of the adjustment which would be required under section 1016(a)(5) (relating to adjustment to basis for amortizable bond premium) if the definition in section 171(d) of the term "bond" did not exclude such municipal bond.

Notwithstanding the provisions of paragraph (1), no reduction to the cost of securities sold during the taxable year shall be made in respect of any obligation described in subsection (b)(1)(A)(ii) which is held by the taxpayer at the close of the taxable year; but in the taxable year in which any such obligation is sold or otherwise disposed of, if such obligation is a municipal bond (as defined in subsection (b)(1)), the cost of securities sold during such year shall be reduced by an amount equal to the adjustment described in paragraph (2), without regard to the fact that the taxpayer values his inventories on any basis other than cost.

Amendments

• 1958, Technical Amendments Act of 1958 (P.L. 85-866)

P.L. 85-866, §2(a)(2), (3):

Struck out "short term" as it preceded "municipal bond" each place the latter phrase appears in Sec. 75(a), and added the last sentence in Sec. 75(a). **Effective** for tax years ending after 12-31-57, but only for obligations acquired after that date.

[Sec. 75(b)]

(b) DEFINITIONS.—For purposes of subsection (a)—

(1) The term "municipal bond" means any obligation issued by a government or political subdivision thereof if the interest on such obligation is excludable from gross income; but such term does not include such an obligation if—

(A)(i) it is sold or otherwise disposed of by the taxpayer within 30 days after the date of its acquisition by him, or

(ii) its earliest maturity or call date is a date more than 5 years from the date on which it was acquired by the taxpayer; and

(B) when it is sold or otherwise disposed of by the taxpayer—

(i) in the case of a sale, the amount realized, or

(ii) in the case of any other disposition, its fair market value at the time of such disposition,

is higher than its adjusted basis (computed without regard to this section and section 1016(a)(6)).

Determinations under subparagraph (B) shall be exclusive of interest.

(2) The term "cost of securities sold" means the amount ascertained by subtracting the inventory value of the closing inventory of a taxable year from the sum of—

(A) the inventory value of the opening inventory for such year, and

(B) the cost of securities and other property purchased during such year which would properly be included in the inventory of the taxpayer if on hand at the close of the taxable year.

Amendments

• 1958, Technical Amendments Act of 1958 (P.L. 85-866)

P.L. 85-866, § 2(a)(1):

Amended Code Sec. 75(b)(1). **Effective** for obligations acquired after 12-31-57. Prior to amendment, Code Sec. 75(b)(1) read as follows:

(b) Definitions.—For purposes of subsection (a)—

(1) The term "short-term municipal bond" means any obligation issued by a government or political subdivision thereof if the interest on such obligation is excludable from gross income; but such term does not include such an obligation if—

(A) it is sold or otherwise disposed of by the taxpayer within 30 days after the date of its acquisition by him, or

(B) its earliest maturity or call date is a date more than 5 years from the date on which it was acquired by the taxpayer.

[Sec. 77]

SEC. 77. COMMODITY CREDIT LOANS.

[Sec. 77(a)]

(a) ELECTION TO INCLUDE LOANS IN INCOME.—Amounts received as loans from the Commodity Credit Corporation shall, at the election of the taxpayer, be considered as income and shall be included in gross income for the taxable year in which received.

[Sec. 77(b)]

(b) EFFECT OF ELECTION ON ADJUSTMENTS FOR SUBSEQUENT YEARS.—If a taxpayer exercises the election provided for in subsection (a) for any taxable year, then the method of computing income so adopted shall be adhered to with respect to all subsequent taxable years unless with the approval of the Secretary a change to a different method is authorized.

Amendments

• 1976, Tax Reform Act of 1976 (P.L. 94-455)

P.L. 94-455, § 1906(b)(13)(A):

Amended 1954 Code by substituting "Secretary" for "Secretary or his delegate" each place it appeared. **Effective** 2-1-77.

[Sec. 78]

SEC. 78. DIVIDENDS RECEIVED FROM CERTAIN FOREIGN CORPORATIONS BY DOMESTIC CORPORATIONS CHOOSING FOREIGN TAX CREDIT.

If a domestic corporation chooses to have the benefits of subpart A of part III of subchapter N (relating to foreign tax credit) for any taxable year, an amount equal to the taxes deemed to be paid by such corporation under section 902(a) (relating to credit for corporate stockholder in foreign corporation) or under section 960(a)(1) (relating to taxes paid by foreign corporation) for such taxable year shall be treated for purposes of this title (other than section 245) as a dividend received by such domestic corporation from the foreign corporation.

Amendments

• 1976, Tax Reform Act of 1976 (P.L. 94-455)

P.L. 94-455, § 1033(b)(1):

Substituted "section 902(a)" for "section 902(a)(1)"; and substituted "section 960(a)(1)" for "section 960(a)(1)(C)" in Code Sec. 78. For the **effective** date, see Act Sec. 1033(c), below.

P.L. 94-455, § 1033(c) (as amended by P.L. 99-514, 32), provides:

(c) Effective Dates.—The amendments made by this section (amending this section and sections 78, 535, 545, and 960 of this title) shall apply—

"(1) in respect of any distribution received by a domestic corporation after December 31, 1977, and

"(2) in respect of any distribution received by a domestic corporation before January 1, 1978, in a taxable year of such corporation beginning after December 31, 1975, but only to the extent that such distribution is made out of the accumulated profits of a foreign corporation for a taxable year (of such foreign corporation) beginning after December 31, 1975.

For purposes of paragraph (2), a distribution made by a foreign corporation out of its profits which are attributable to a distribution received from a foreign corporation to which section 902(b) of the Internal Revenue Code of 1986 [formerly I.R.C. 1954]applies shall be treated as made out of the accumulated profits of a foreign corporation for a taxable year beginning before January 1, 1976, to the extent that such distribution was paid out of the accumulated profits of such foreign corporation for a taxable year beginning before January 1, 1976."

• 1962, Revenue Act of 1962 (P.L. 87-834)

P.L. 87-834, § 9(b):

Added Code Sec. 78. **Effective** for distributions received after 12-31-64, and to distributions received in tax years beginning after 12-31-62 to the extent attributable to accumulated profits of foreign corporations for tax years beginning after 12-31-62.

[Sec. 79]

SEC. 79. GROUP-TERM LIFE INSURANCE PURCHASED FOR EMPLOYEES.

[Sec. 79(a)]

(a) GENERAL RULE.—There shall be included in the gross income of an employee for the taxable year an amount equal to the cost of group-term life insurance on his life provided for part or all of such year under a policy (or policies) carried directly or indirectly by his employer (or employers); but only to the extent that such cost exceeds the sum of—

(1) the cost of $50,000 of such insurance, and

(2) the amount (if any) paid by the employee toward the purchase of such insurance.

[Sec. 79(b)]

(b) EXCEPTIONS.—Subsection (a) shall not apply to—

(1) the cost of group-term life insurance on the life of an individual which is provided under a policy carried directly or indirectly by an employer after such individual has terminated his employment with such employer and is disabled (within the meaning of section 72(m)(7)),

(2) the cost of any portion of the group-term life insurance on the life of an employee provided during part or all of the taxable year of the employee under which—

(A) the employer is directly or indirectly the beneficiary, or

(B) a person described in section 170(c) is the sole beneficiary,

for the entire period during such taxable year for which the employee receives such insurance, and

(3) the cost of any group-term life insurance which is provided under a contract to which section 72(m)(3) applies.

Amendments

• 1984, Deficit Reduction Act of 1984 (P.L. 98-369)

P.L. 98-369, §223(a)(2):

Amended Code Sec. 79(b)(1). **Effective** for tax years beginning after 12-31-83. For special rules, see Act Sec. 223(d)(2), below. Prior to amendment, it read as follows:

(1) the cost of group-term life insurance on the life of an individual which is provided under a policy carried directly or indirectly by an employer after such individual has terminated his employment with such employer and either has reached the retirement age with respect to such employer or is disabled (within the meaning of section 72(m)(7)),

P.L. 98-369, §223(d)(2), as amended by P.L. 99-514, §1827(b)(1)-(3), provides:

(2) Inclusion of Former Employees in the Case of Existing Group-Term Insurance Plans.—

(A) In General.—The amendments made by subsection (a) shall not apply—

(i) to any group-term life insurance plan of the employer in existence on January 1, 1984, or

(ii) to any group-term life insurance plan of the employer (or a successor employer) which is a comparable successor to a plan described in clause (i),

but only with respect to an individual who attained age 55 on or before January 1, 1984, and was employed by such employer (or a predecessor employer) at any time during 1983. Such amendments also shall not apply to any employee who retired from employment on or before January 1, 1984, and who, when he retired, was covered by the plan (or a predecessor plan).

(B) Special Rule in the Case of Discriminatory Group-Term Life Insurance Plan.—In the case of any plan which, after December 31, 1986, is a discriminatory group-term life insurance plan (as defined in section 79(d) of the Internal Revenue Code of 1954), subparagraph (A) shall not apply in the case of any individual retiring under such plan after December 31, 1986.

(C) Benefits to Certain Retired Individuals Not Taken Into Account for Purposes of Determining Whether Plan Is Discriminatory.—For purposes of determining whether a plan described in subparagraph (A) meets the requirements of section 79(d) of the Internal Revenue Code of 1954 with respect to group-term life insurance for former employees, coverage provided to employees who retired on or before December 31, 1986 may, at the employer's election, be disregarded.

(D) Comparable Successor Plans.—For purposes of subparagraph (A), a plan shall not fail to be treated as a comparable successor to a plan described in subparagraph (A)(i) with respect to any employee whose benefits do not increase or decrease under the successor plan.

• 1965, Social Security Amendments of 1965 (P.L. 89-97)

P.L. 89-97, §106(d):

Amended Sec. 79(b)(1) by substituting "section 72(m)(7)," for "paragraph (3) of section 213(g), determined without regard to paragraph (4) thereof)". **Effective** for tax years beginning after 12-31-66.

[Sec. 79(c)]

(c) DETERMINATION OF COST OF INSURANCE.—For purposes of this section and section 6052, the cost of group-term insurance on the life of an employee provided during any period shall be determined on the basis of uniform premiums (computed on the basis of 5-year age brackets) prescribed by regulations by the Secretary.

Amendments

• 1988, Technical and Miscellaneous Revenue Act of 1988 (P.L. 100-647)

P.L. 100-647, §5013(a):

Amended Code Sec. 79(c) by striking out the last sentence. **Effective** for tax years beginning after 12-31-88. Prior to amendment, the last sentence of Code Sec. 79(c) read as follows:

In the case of an employee who has attained age 64, the cost prescribed shall not exceed the cost with respect to such individual if he were age 63.

• 1964, Revenue Act of 1964 (P.L. 88-272)

P.L. 88-272, §204(a)(1):

Added section 79. **Effective** for group-term life insurance provided after 12-31-63, in tax years ending after such date. In applying Code Sec. 79(b) to a tax year beginning before 5-1-64, if paragraph (2)(B) of such section applies with respect to an employee for the period beginning 5-1-64, and ending with the close of his first tax year ending after 4-30-64, such paragraph (2)(B) shall be treated as applying with respect to such employee for the period beginning 1-1-64, and ending 4-30-64.

[Sec. 79(d)]

(d) NONDISCRIMINATION REQUIREMENTS.—

(1) IN GENERAL.—In the case of a discriminatory group-term life insurance plan—

(A) subsection (a)(1) shall not apply with respect to any key employee, and

(B) the cost of group-term life insurance on the life of any key employee shall be the greater of—

(i) such cost determined without regard to subsection (c), or

(ii) such cost determined with regard to subsection (c).

(2) DISCRIMINATORY GROUP-TERM LIFE INSURANCE PLAN.—For purposes of this subsection, the term "discriminatory group-term life insurance plan" means any plan of an employer for providing group-term life insurance unless—

(A) the plan does not discriminate in favor of key employees as to eligibility to participate, and

(B) the type and amount of benefits available under the plan do not discriminate in favor of participants who are key employees.

(3) NONDISCRIMINATORY ELIGIBILITY CLASSIFICATION.—

(A) IN GENERAL.—A plan does not meet requirements of subparagraph (A) of paragraph (2) unless—

(i) such plan benefits 70 percent or more of all employees of the employer,

(ii) at least 85 percent of all employees who are participants under the plan are not key employees,

(iii) such plan benefits such employees as qualify under a classification set up by the employer and found by the Secretary not to be discriminatory in favor of key employees, or

(iv) in the case of a plan which is part of a cafeteria plan, the requirements of section 125 are met.

(B) EXCLUSION OF CERTAIN EMPLOYEES.—For purposes of subparagraph (A), there may be excluded from consideration—

(i) employees who have not completed 3 years of service;

(ii) part-time or seasonal employees;

(iii) employees not included in the plan who are included in a unit of employees covered by an agreement between employee representatives and one or more employers which the Secretary finds to be a collective bargaining agreement, if the benefits provided under the plan were the subject of good faith bargaining between such employee representatives and such employer or employers; and

(iv) employees who are nonresident aliens and who receive no earned income (within the meaning of section 911(d)(2)) from the employer which constitutes income from sources within the United States (within the meaning of section 861(a)(3)).

(4) NONDISCRIMINATORY BENEFITS.—A plan does not meet the requirements of paragraph (2)(B) unless all benefits available to participants who are key employees are available to all other participants.

(5) SPECIAL RULE.—A plan shall not fail to meet the requirements of paragraph (2)(B) merely because the amount of life insurance on behalf of the employees under the plan bears a uniform relationship to the total compensation or the basic or regular rate of compensation of such employees.

(6) KEY EMPLOYEE DEFINED.—For purposes of this subsection, the term "key employee" has the meaning given to such term by paragraph (1) of section 416(i). Such term also includes any former employee if such employee when he retired or separated from service was a key employee.

(7) EXEMPTION FOR CHURCH PLANS.—

(A) IN GENERAL.—This subsection shall not apply to a church plan maintained for church employees.

(B) DEFINITIONS.—For purposes of subparagraph (A), the terms "church plan" and "church employee" have the meaning given such terms by paragraphs (1) and (3)(B) of section 414(e), respectively, except that—

(i) section 414(e) shall be applied by substituting "section 501(c)(3)" for "section 501" each place it appears, and

(ii) the term "church employee" shall not include an employee of—

(I) an organization described in section 170(b)(1)(A)(ii) above the secondary school level (other than a school for religious training),

(II) an organization described in section 170(b)(1)(A)(iii), and

(III) an organization described in section 501(c)(3), the basis of the exemption for which is substantially similar to the basis for exemption of an organization described in subclause (II).

(8) TREATMENT OF FORMER EMPLOYEES.—To the extent provided in regulations, this subsection shall be applied separately with respect to former employees.

Amendments

• 1990, Omnibus Budget Reconciliation Act of 1990 (P.L. 101-508)

P.L. 101-508, §11703(e)(1):

Amended Code Sec. 79(d)(6) by striking "any retired employee" and inserting "any former employee". **Effective** for employees separating from service after the date of enactment of this Act.

• 1989 (P.L. 101-140)

P.L. 101-140, §203(a)(1), provides:

Code Sec. 79(d), as amended by Section 1151(c)(1) of the Tax Reform Act of 1986 (P.L. 99-514), shall be applied as if the amendment made by such section had not been enacted. Code Sec. 79(d) as amended by Act Sec. 1151(c)(1) of P.L. 99-514 read as follows:

(d) NONDISCRIMINATION REQUIREMENTS.—In the case of a group-term life insurance plan which is a discriminatory employee benefit plan, subsection (a)(1) shall apply only to the extent provided in section 89.

P.L. 101-140, §203(b)(1)(A):

Amended Code Sec. 79(d)(7) (as in effect on the date before the enactment of the Tax Reform Act of 1986). **Effective** as if included in Sec. 1151 of P.L. 99-514. Prior to amendment, Code Sec. 79(d)(7) (as in effect on the date before the enactment of the Tax Reform Act of 1986) read as follows:

(7) CERTAIN CONTROLLED GROUPS, ETC.—All employees who are treated as employed by a single employer under subsection (b), (c), or (m) of section 414 shall be treated as employed by a single employer for purposes of this section.

• 1989 (P.L. 101-136)

P.L. 101-136, §528, provides:

No monies appropriated by this Act may be used to implement or enforce section 1151 of the Tax Reform Act of 1986 or the amendments made by such section.

• 1986, Tax Reform Act of 1986 (P.L. 99-514)

P.L. 99-514, §1151(c)(1):

Amended Code Sec. 79(d). **Effective** for years beginning after the later of 12-31-87, or the earlier of the date which is 3 months after the date on which the Secretary of the Treasury or his delegate issues such regulations as are necessary to carry out the provisions of section 89 of the Internal Revenue Code of 1986 (as added by this section), or 12-31-88. However, for special rules, see Act Sec. 1151(k)(2)-(5), below.

P.L. 99-514, §1151(k)(2)-(5), provides:

(2) SPECIAL RULE FOR COLLECTIVE BARGAINING PLAN.—In the case of a plan maintained pursuant to 1 or more collective bargaining agreements between employee representatives and 1 or more employers ratified before March 1, 1986, the amendments made by this section shall not apply to employees covered by such an agreement in years beginning before the earlier of—

(A) the date on which the last of such collective bargaining agreements terminates (determined without regard to any extension thereof after February 28, 1986), or

(B) January 1, 1991.

A plan shall not be required to take into account employees to which the preceding sentence applies for purposes of applying section 89 of the Internal Revenue Code of 1986 (as added by this section) to employees to which the preceding sentence does not apply for any year preceding the year described in the preceding sentence.

(3) EXCEPTION FOR CERTAIN GROUP-TERM INSURANCE PLANS.—In the case of a plan described in section 223(d)(2) of the Tax Reform Act of 1984, such plan shall be treated as meeting the requirements of section 89 of the Internal Revenue Code of 1986 (as added by this section) with respect to individuals described in section 223(d)(2) of such Act. An employer may elect to disregard such individuals in applying section 89 of such Code (as so added) to other employees of the employer.

(4) SPECIAL RULE FOR CHURCH PLANS.—In the case of a church plan (within the meaning of section 414(e)(3) of the Internal Revenue Code of 1986) maintaining an insured accident and health plan, the amendments made by this section shall apply to years beginning after December 31, 1988.

(5) CAFETERIA PLANS.—The amendments made by subsection (d)(2) shall apply to taxable years beginning after December 31, 1983.

P.L. 99-514, §1827(a)(1):

Amended Code Sec. 79(d)(1)(B). **Effective** for tax years ending after the date of the enactment of this Act. Prior to amendment, Code Sec. 79(d)(1)(B) read as follows:

(B) the cost of group-term life insurance on the life of any key employee shall be determined without regard to subsection (c).

P.L. 99-514, §1827(c)(1) and (2):

Amended Code Sec. 79(d)(6) by striking out all that follows "section 416(i)" and inserting in lieu thereof a period, and by adding at the end thereof a new sentence. **Effective** as if included in the provision of P.L. 98-369 to which it relates. Prior to amendment, Code Sec. 79(d)(6) read as follows:

(6) KEY EMPLOYEE DEFINED.—For purposes of this subsection, the term "key employee" has the meaning given to such term by paragraph (1) of section 416(i), except that subparagraph (A)(iv) of such paragraph shall be applied by not taking into account employees described in paragraph (3)(B) who are not participants in the plan.

P.L. 99-514, §1827(d):

Amended Code Sec. 79(d) by adding at the end thereof new paragraph (8). **Effective** as if included in the provision of P.L. 98-369 to which it relates.

• 1984, Deficit Reduction Act of 1984 (P.L. 98-369)

P.L. 98-369, §223(b):

Amended Code Sec. 79(d)(1). **Effective** for tax years beginning after 12-31-83. Prior to amendment, it read as follows:

(1) In General.—In the case of a discriminatory group-term life insurance plan, paragraph (1) of subsection (a) shall not apply with respect to any key employee.

• 1982, Tax Equity and Fiscal Responsibility Act of 1982 (P.L. 97-248)

P.L. 97-248, §244(a):

Added Code Sec. 79(d). **Effective** for tax years beginning after 12-31-83.

[Sec. 79(e)]

(e) EMPLOYEE INCLUDES FORMER EMPLOYEE.—For purposes of this section, the term "employee" includes a former employee.

Amendments

• 1984, Deficit Reduction Act of 1984 (P.L. 98-369)

P.L. 98-369, §223(a)(1):

Amended Code Sec. 79 by adding new subsection (e) at the end thereof. **Effective** for tax years beginning after 12-31-83. For special rules, see Act Sec. 223(d)(2) in the notes following Code Sec. 79(b).

[Sec. 80]

SEC. 80. RESTORATION OF VALUE OF CERTAIN SECURITIES.

[Sec. 80(a)]

(a) GENERAL RULE.—In the case of a domestic corporation subject to the tax imposed by section 11 or 801, if the value of any security (as defined in section 165(g)(2))—

(1) which became worthless by reason of the expropriation, intervention, seizure, or similar taking by the government of any foreign country, any political subdivision thereof, or any agency or instrumentality of the foregoing of property to which such security was related, and

(2) which was taken into account as a loss from the sale or exchange of a capital asset or with respect to which a deduction for a loss was allowed under section 165,

is restored in whole or in part during any taxable year by reason of any recovery of money or other property in respect of the property to which such security was related, the value so restored (to the extent that, when added to the value so restored during prior taxable years, it does not exceed the amount of the loss described in paragraph (2)) shall, except as provided in subsection (b), be included in gross income for the taxable year in which such restoration occurs.

Amendments

• 1984, Deficit Reduction Act of 1984 (P.L. 98-369)

P.L. 98-369, §211(b)(2):

Amended Code Sec. 80(a) by striking out "802" and inserting in lieu thereof "801". **Effective** for tax years beginning after 12-31-83.

• 1966 (P.L. 89-384)

P.L. 89-384, §1(b):

Added Code Sec. 80(a). **Effective** for tax years beginning after 12-31-65, but only with respect to losses described in Code Sec. 80(a)(2) sustained after 12-31-58.

[Sec. 80(b)]

(b) REDUCTION FOR FAILURE TO RECEIVE TAX BENEFIT.—The amount otherwise includible in gross income under subsection (a) in respect of any security shall be reduced by an amount equal to the amount (if any) of the loss described in subsection (a)(2) which did not result in a reduction of the taxpayer's tax under this subtitle for any taxable year, determined under regulations prescribed by the Secretary.

Amendments

• 1976, Tax Reform Act of 1976 (P.L. 94-455)

P.L. 94-455, §1906(b)(13)(A):

Amended 1954 Code by substituting "Secretary" for "Secretary or his delegate" each place it appeared. **Effective** 2-1-77.

• 1966 (P.L. 89-384)

P.L. 89-384, §1(b):

Added Code Sec. 80(b). **Effective** for tax years beginning after 12-31-65, but only with respect to losses described in Code Sec. 80(a)(2) sustained after 12-31-58.

[Sec. 80(c)]

(c) CHARACTER OF INCOME.—For purposes of this subtitle—

(1) Except as provided in paragraph (2), the amount included in gross income under this section shall be treated as ordinary income.

(2) If the loss described in subsection (a)(2) was taken into account as a loss from the sale or exchange of a capital asset, the amount included in gross income under this section shall be treated as long-term capital gain.

Amendments

• 1976, Tax Reform Act of 1976 (P.L. 94-455)

P.L. 94-455, §1901(b)(3)(K):

Substituted "ordinary income" for "gain from the sale or exchange of property which is neither a capital asset nor property described in section 1231" in Code Sec. 80(c)(1). **Effective** for tax years beginning after 12-31-76.

• 1966 (P.L. 89-384)

P.L. 89-384, §1(b):

Added Code Sec. 80(c). **Effective** for tax years beginning after 12-31-65, but only with respect to losses described in Code Sec. 80(a)(2) sustained after 12-31-58.

[Sec. 80(d)]

(d) TREATMENT UNDER FOREIGN EXPROPRIATION LOSS RECOVERY PROVISION.—This section shall not apply to any recovery of a foreign expropriation loss to which section 1351 applies.

Amendments

• 1966 (P.L. 89-384)

P.L. 89-384, §1(b):

Added Code Sec. 80(d). **Effective** for tax years beginning after 12-31-65, but only with respect to losses described in Code Sec. 80(a)(2) sustained after 12-31-58.

[Sec. 81—Repealed]

Amendments

• 1987, Revenue Act of 1987 (P.L. 100-203)

P.L. 100-203, §10201(b)(1):

Repealed Code Sec. 81. For the **effective** date, see Act Sec. 10201(c), below. Prior to repeal, Code Sec. 81 read as follows:

SEC. 81. INCREASES IN VACATION PAY SUSPENSE ACCOUNT.

There shall be included in gross income for the taxable year the amount of any increase in any suspense account for such taxable year required by paragraph (2)(B) of section 463(c) (relating to accrual of vacation pay).

P.L. 100-203, §10201(c), provides as follows:

(c) EFFECTIVE DATE.—

(1) IN GENERAL.—The amendments made by this section shall apply to taxable years beginning after December 31, 1987.

(2) CHANGE IN METHOD OF ACCOUNTING.—In the case of any taxpayer who elected to have section 463 of the Internal Revenue Code of 1986 apply for such taxpayer's last taxable year beginning before January 1, 1988, and who is required to change his method of accounting by reason of the amendments made by this section—

(A) such change shall be treated as initiated by the taxpayer,

(B) such change shall be treated as having been made with the consent of the Secretary, and

(C) the net amount of adjustments required by section 481 of such Code to be taken into account by the taxpayer—

(i) shall be reduced by the balance in the suspense account under section 463(c) of such Code as of the close of such last taxable year, and

(ii) shall be taken into account over the 4-taxable year period beginning with the taxable year following such last taxable year as follows:

In the case of the:	*The percentage taken into account is:*
1st year	25
2nd year	5
3rd year	35
4th year	35

Notwithstanding subparagraph (C)(ii), if the period the adjustments are required to be taken into account under section 481 of such Code is less than 4 years, such adjustments shall be taken into account ratably over such shorter period.

• 1986, Tax Reform Act of 1986 (P.L. 99-514)

P.L. 99-514, §805(c)(1)(A):

Amended Code Sec. 81. **Effective**, generally, for tax years beginning after 12-31-86. However, for a special rule, see Act Sec. 805(d)(2), below. Prior to amendment, Code Sec. 81 read as follows:

SEC. 81. CERTAIN INCREASES IN SUSPENSE ACCOUNTS.

There shall be included in gross income for the taxable year for which an increase is required—

(1) CERTAIN DEALERS' RESERVES.—The amount of any increase in the suspense account required by paragraph (4)(B)(ii) of section 166(f) (relating to certain debt obligations guaranteed by dealers).

(2) VACATION PAY.—The amount of any increase in the suspense account required by paragraph (2)(B) of section 463(c) (relating to accrual of vacation pay).

P.L. 99-514, §805(d)(2), provides:

(2) CHANGE IN METHOD OF ACCOUNTING.—In the case of any taxpayer who maintained a reserve for bad debts for such taxpayer's last taxable year begining before January 1, 1987, and who is required by the amendments made by this section to change its method of accounting for any taxable year—

(A) such change shall be treated as initiated by the taxpayer,

(B) such change shall be treated as made with the consent of the Secretary, and

(C) the net amount of adjustments required by section 481 of the Internal Revenue Code of 1986 to be taken into account by the taxpayer shall—

(i) in the case of a taxpayer maintaining a reserve under section 166(f), be reduced by the balance in the suspense account under section 166(f)(4) of such Code as of the close of such last taxable year, and

(ii) be taken into account ratably in each of the first 4 taxable years beginning after December 31, 1986.

• 1976, Tax Reform Act of 1976 (P.L. 94-455)

P.L. 94-455, §605(b), (c):

Substituted "section 166(f)" for "section 166(g)" in Code Sec. 81(1). **Effective** for guarantees made after 12-31-75, in tax years beginning after such date.

• 1975 (P.L. 93-625)

P.L. 93-625, §4(c):

Amended Code Sec. 81. **Effective** for tax years beginning after 12-31-73. However, if the taxpayer maintained an account for vacation pay under section 97 of P.L. 85-866, as amended, for his last taxable year ending before 1-1-73, the amendments made by P. L. 93-625 would apply to tax years ending after 12-31-72. Prior to amendment, Code Sec. 81 read as follows:

"SEC. 81. INCREASES IN SUSPENSE ACCOUNT UNDER SECTION 166(g).

"The amount of any increase in the suspense account required by paragraph (4)(B)(ii) of section 166(g) (relating to certain debt obligations guaranteed by dealers) shall be included in gross income for the taxable year for which such increase is required."

• 1966 (P.L. 89-722)

P.L. 89-722, §[1(b)]:

Added new Code Sec. 81. **Effective**, generally, for tax years ending after 10-21-65. See, however, the amendment note for Code Sec. 166(g) for exceptions to this effective date.

[Sec. 82]

SEC. 82. REIMBURSEMENT FOR EXPENSES OF MOVING.

Except as provided in section 132(a)(6), there shall be included in gross income (as compensation for services) any amount received or accrued, directly or indirectly, by an individual as a payment for or reimbursement of expenses of moving from one residence to another residence which is attributable to employment or self-employment.

Amendments

• 1993, Omnibus Budget Reconciliation Act of 1993 (P.L. 103-66)

P.L. 103-66, §13213(d)(3)(A):

Amended Code Sec. 82 by striking "There shall" and inserting "Except as provided in section 132(a)(6), there shall". **Effective** for reimbursements or other payments in respect of expenses incurred after such date.

• 1969, Tax Reform Act of 1969 (P.L. 91-172)

P.L. 91-172, §231(b):

Added Sec. 82. **Effective** for tax years beginning after 12-31-69, except that it shall not apply (at the election of the taxpayer made at such time and manner as the Secretary of the Treasury or his delegate prescribes) with respect to moving expenses paid or incurred before 1-1-71 [changed from 7-1-70 by P.L. 91-684]in connection with the commencement of work by the taxpayer as an employee at a new principal place of work of which the taxpayer had been notified by his employer on or before 12-19-69.

[Sec. 83]

SEC. 83. PROPERTY TRANSFERRED IN CONNECTION WITH PERFORMANCE OF SERVICES.

[Sec. 83(a)]

(a) GENERAL RULE.—If, in connection with the performance of services, property is transferred to any person other than the person for whom such services are performed, the excess of—

(1) the fair market value of such property (determined without regard to any restriction other than a restriction which by its terms will never lapse) at the first time the rights of the person having the beneficial interest in such property are transferable or are not subject to a substantial risk of forfeiture, whichever occurs earlier, over

(2) the amount (if any) paid for such property,

shall be included in the gross income of the person who performed such services in the first taxable year in which the rights of the person having the beneficial interest in such property are transferable or are not subject to a substantial risk of forfeiture, whichever is applicable. The preceding sentence shall not apply if such person sells or otherwise disposes of such property in an arm's length transaction before his rights in such property become transferable or not subject to a substantial risk of forfeiture.

[Sec. 83(b)]

(b) ELECTION TO INCLUDE IN GROSS INCOME IN YEAR OF TRANSFER.—

(1) IN GENERAL.—Any person who performs services in connection with which property is transferred to any person may elect to include in his gross income, for the taxable year in which such property is transferred, the excess of—

(A) the fair market value of such property at the time of transfer (determined without regard to any restriction other than a restriction which by its terms will never lapse), over

(B) the amount (if any) paid for such property.

If such election is made, subsection (a) shall not apply with respect to the transfer of such property, and if such property is subsequently forfeited, no deduction shall be allowed in respect of such forfeiture.

(2) ELECTION.—An election under paragraph (1) with respect to any transfer of property shall be made in such manner as the Secretary prescribes and shall be made not later than 30 days after the date of such transfer. Such election may not be revoked except with the consent of the Secretary.

Amendments

• 1976, Tax Reform Act of 1976 (P.L. 94-455)

P.L. 94-455, §1901(a)(15):

Amended Code Sec. 83(b)(2) by striking out "(or, if later, 30 days after the date of the enactment of the Tax Reform Act of 1969)." **Effective** for tax years beginning after 12-31-76.

P. L. 94-455, §1906(b)(13)(A):

Amended 1954 Code by substituting "Secretary" for "Secretary or his delegate" each place it appeared. **Effective** 2-1-77.

[Sec. 83(c)]

(c) SPECIAL RULES.—For purposes of this section—

(1) SUBSTANTIAL RISK OF FORFEITURE.—The rights of a person in property are subject to a substantial risk of forfeiture if such person's rights to full enjoyment of such property are conditioned upon the future performance of substantial services by any individual.

(2) TRANSFERABILITY OF PROPERTY.—The rights of a person in property are transferable only if the rights in such property of any transferee are not subject to a substantial risk of forfeiture.

(3) SALES WHICH MAY GIVE RISE TO SUIT UNDER SECTION 16(b) OF THE SECURITIES EXCHANGE ACT OF 1934.—So long as the sale of property at a profit could subject a person to suit under SECTION 16(b) of the Securities Exchange Act of 1934, such person's rights in such property are—

(A) subject to a substantial risk of forfeiture, and

(B) not transferable.

(4) For purposes of determining an individual's basis in property transferred in connection with the performance of services, rules similar to the rules of section 72(w) shall apply.

Amendments

• 2004, American Jobs Creation Act of 2004 (P.L. 108-357)

P.L. 108-357, §906(b):

Amended Code Sec. 83(c) by adding after paragraph (3) a new paragraph (4). **Effective** for distributions on or after 10-22-2004.

• 1986, Tax Reform Act of 1986 (P.L. 99-514)

P.L. 99-514, §1879(p), provides:

(p) AMENDMENT RELATED TO SECTION 252 OF THE ECONOMIC RECOVERY TAX ACT OF 1981.—

(1) Notwithstanding subsection (c) of section 252 of the Economic Recovery Tax Act of 1981, the amendment made by subsection (a) of such section 252 (and the provisions of subsection (b) of such section 252) shall apply to any transfer of stock to any person if—

(A) such transfer occurred in November or December of 1973 and was pursuant to the exercise of an option granted in November or December of 1971,

(B) in December 1973 the corporation granting the option was acquired by another corporation in a transaction qualifying as a reorganization under section 368 of the Internal Revenue Code of 1954,

(C) the fair market value (as of July 1, 1974) of the stock received by such person in the reorganization in exchange for the stock transferred to him pursuant to the exercise of such option was less than 50 percent of the fair market value of the stock so received (as of December 4, 1973),

(D) in 1975 or 1976 such person sold substantially all of the stock received in such reorganization, and

(E) such person makes an election under this section at such time and in such manner as the Secretary of the Treasury or his delegate shall prescribe.

(2) Limitation on Amount of Benefit.—Subsection (a) shall not apply to transfers with respect to any employee to the extent that the application of subsection (a) with respect to such employee would (but for this subsection) result in a reduction in liability for income tax with respect to such employee for all taxable years in excess of $100,000 (determined without regard to any interest).

(3) Statute of Limitations.—

(A) Overpayments.—If refund or credit of any overpayment of tax resulting from the application of subsection (a) is prevented on the date of the enactment of this Act (or at any time within 6 months after such date of enactment) by the operation of any law or rule of law, refund or credit of such overpayment (to the extent attributable to the application of subsection (a)) may, nevertheless, be made or allowed if claim therefor is filed before the close of such 6-month period.

(B) Deficiencies.—If the assessment of any deficiency of tax resulting from the application of subsection (a) is prevented on the date of the enactment of this Act (or at any time within 6 months after such date of enactment) by the operation of any law or rule of law, assessment of such deficiency (to the extent attributable to the application of subsection (a)) may, nevertheless, be made within such 6-month period.

• 1983, Technical Corrections Act of 1982 (P.L. 97-448)

P.L. 97-448, §102(k)(1):

Amended Code Sec. 83(c)(3) by striking out "Securities and Exchange Act of 1934" each place it appeared and inserting in lieu thereof "Securities Exchange Act of 1934". **Effective** as if it had been included in the provision of P.L. 97-34 to which it relates.

P.L. 97-448, §102(k)(2):

Amended section 252 of P.L. 97-34 (relating to effective date) by striking out "taxable years ending after December 31, 1981" and inserting "transfers after December 31, 1981". For the amended **effective** date, see the amendment note, below, for P.L. 97-34, §252(a).

• 1981, Economic Recovery Tax Act of 1981 (P.L. 97-34)

P.L. 97-34, §252(a):

Amended Code Sec. 83(c) by adding at the end thereof new paragraph (3). **Effective** for transfers after 12-31-81. For a special rule related to P.L. 97-34, §252(a), see amendment note for P.L. 99-514, §1879(p).

P.L. 97-34, §252(b), provides:

(b) SPECIAL RULE FOR CERTAIN ACCOUNTING RULES.—For purposes of section 83 of the Internal Revenue Code of 1954, property is subject to substantial risk of forfeiture and is not transferable so long as such property is subject to a restriction on transfer to comply with the "Pooling-of-Interests Accounting" rules set forth in Accounting Series Release Numbered 130 ((10/5/72) 37 FR 20937; 17 CFR 211.130) and Accounting Series Release Numbered 135 ((1/18/73) 38 FR 1734; 17 CFR 211.135).

[Sec. 83(d)]

(d) CERTAIN RESTRICTIONS WHICH WILL NEVER LAPSE.—

(1) VALUATION.—In the case of property subject to a restriction which by its terms will never lapse, and which allows the transferee to sell such property only at a price determined under a formula, the price so determined shall be deemed to be the fair market value of the property unless established to the contrary by the Secretary, and the burden of proof shall be on the Secretary with respect to such value.

(2) CANCELLATION.—If, in the case of property subject to a restriction which by its terms will never lapse, the restriction is cancelled, then, unless the taxpayer establishes—

(A) that such cancellation was not compensatory, and

(B) that the person, if any, who would be allowed a deduction if the cancellation were treated as compensatory, will treat the transaction as not compensatory, as evidenced in such manner as the Secretary shall prescribe by regulations,

the excess of the fair market value of the property (computed without regard to the restrictions) at the time of cancellation over the sum of—

(C) the fair market value of such property (computed by taking the restriction into account) immediately before the cancellation, and

(D) the amount, if any, paid for the cancellation,

shall be treated as compensation for the taxable year in which such cancellation occurs.

Amendments

• 1976, Tax Reform Act of 1976 (P.L. 94-455)

P.L. 94-455, §1906(b)(13)(A):

Amended 1954 Code by substituting "Secretary" for "Secretary or his delegate" each place it appeared. **Effective** 2-1-77.

[Sec. 83(e)]

(e) APPLICABILITY OF SECTION.—This section shall not apply to—

(1) a transaction to which section 421 applies,

(2) a transfer to or from a trust described in section 401(a) or a transfer under an annuity plan which meets the requirements of section 404(a)(2),

(3) the transfer of an option without a readily ascertainable fair market value,

(4) the transfer of property pursuant to the exercise of an option with a readily ascertainable fair market value at the date of grant, or

(5) group-term life insurance to which section 79 applies.

Amendments

• 1986, Tax Reform Act of 1986 (P.L. 99-514)

P.L. 99-514, §1827(e):

Amended Code Sec. 83(e)(5) by striking out "the cost of" following "(5)". **Effective** as if included in the provision of P.L. 98-369 to which it relates.

• 1984, Deficit Reduction Act of 1984 (P.L. 98-369)

P.L. 98-369, §223(c):

Amended Code Sec. 83(e) by striking out "or" at the end of paragraph (3), by striking out the period at the end of paragraph (4) and inserting in lieu thereof ", or", and by adding at the end thereof new paragraph (5). **Effective** for tax years beginning after 12-31-83. For special rules, see Act Sec. 556, below, and Act Sec. 223(d)(2) following Code Sec. 79(b).

P.L. 98-369, §556, provides:

SEC. 556. TIME FOR MAKING CERTAIN SECTION 83(b) ELECTIONS.

In the case of any transfer of property in connection with the performance of services on or before November 18, 1982, the election permitted by section 83(b) of the Internal Revenue Code of 1954 may be made, notwithstanding paragraph (2) of such section 83(b), with the income tax return for any taxable year ending after July 18, 1984, and beginning before the date of the enactment of the Tax Reform Act of 1986 if—

(1) the amount paid for such property was not less than its fair market value at the time of transfer (determined without regard to any restriction other than a restriction which by its terms will never lapse), and

(2) the election is consented to by the person transferring such property.

The election shall contain that information required by the Secretary of the Treasury or his delegate for elections permitted by such section 83(b). The period for assessing any tax attributable to a transfer of property which is the subject of an election made pursuant to this section shall not expire before the date which is 3 years after the date such election was made.

[Sec. 83(f)]

(f) HOLDING PERIOD.—In determining the period for which the taxpayer has held property to which subsection (a) applies, there shall be included only the period beginning at the first time his rights in such property are transferable or are not subject to a substantial risk of forfeiture, whichever occurs earlier.

[Sec. 83(g)]

(g) CERTAIN EXCHANGES.—If property to which subsection (a) applies is exchanged for property subject to restrictions and conditions substantially similar to those to which the property given in such exchange was subject, and if section 354, 355, 356, or 1036 (or so much of section 1031 as relates to section 1036) applied to such exchange, or if such exchange was pursuant to the exercise of a conversion privilege—

(1) such exchange shall be disregarded for purposes of subsection (a), and

(2) the property received shall be treated as property to which subsection (a) applies.

[Sec. 83(h)]

(h) DEDUCTION BY EMPLOYER.—In the case of a transfer of property to which this section applies or a cancellation of a restriction described in subsection (d), there shall be allowed as a deduction under section 162, to the person for whom were performed the services in connection with which such property was transferred, an amount equal to the amount included under subsection (a), (b), or (d)(2) in the gross income of the person who performed such services. Such deduction shall be allowed for the taxable year of such person in which or with which ends the taxable year in which such amount is included in the gross income of the person who performed such services.

Amendments

• 1969, Tax Reform Act of 1969 (P.L. 91-172)

P.L. 91-172, §321(a):

Added Code Sec. 83. **Effective** for tax years ending after 6-30-69.

[Sec. 83(i)—Repealed]

Amendments

• 1990, Omnibus Budget Reconciliation Act of 1990 (P.L. 101-508)

P.L. 101-508, §11801(a)(5):

Repealed Code Sec. 83(i). **Effective** 11-5-90. Prior to repeal, Code Sec. 83(i) read as follows:

(i) TRANSITION RULES.—This section shall apply to property transferred after June 30, 1969, except that this section shall not apply to property transferred—

(1) pursuant to a binding written contract entered into before April 22, 1969,

(2) upon the exercise of an option granted before April 22, 1969,

(3) before May 1, 1970, pursuant to a written plan adopted and approved before July 1, 1969,

(4) before January 1, 1973, upon the exercise of an option granted pursuant to a binding written contract entered into before April 22, 1969, between a corporation and the transferor requiring the transferor to grant options to employees of such corporation (or a subsidiary of such corporation) to purchase a determinable number of shares of stock of such corporation, but only if the transferee was an employee of such corporation (or a subsidiary of such corporation) on or before April 22, 1969, or

(5) in exchange for (or pursuant to the exercise of a conversion privilege contained in) property transferred before July 1, 1969, or for property to which this section does not apply (by reason of paragraphs (1), (2), (3), or (4)), if section 354, 355, 356, or 1036 (or so much of section 1031 as relates to section 1036) applies, or if gain or loss is not otherwise required to be recognized upon the exercise of such conversion privilege, and if the property received in such exchange is subject to restrictions and conditions substantially similar to those to which the property given in such exchange was subject.

P.L. 101-508, §11821(b)(1)-(2), provides:

(b) SAVINGS PROVISION.—If—

(1) any provision amended or repealed by this part applied to—

(A) any transaction occurring before the date of the enactment of this Act,

(B) any property acquired before such date of enactment, or

(C) any item of income, loss, deduction, or credit taken into account before such date of enactment, and

(2) the treatment of such transaction, property, or item under such provision would (without regard to the amendments made by this part) affect liability for tax for periods ending after such date of enactment,

nothing in the amendments made by this part shall be construed to affect the treatment of such transaction, property, or item for purposes of determining liability for tax for periods ending after such date of enactment.

[Sec. 84]

SEC. 84. TRANSFER OF APPRECIATED PROPERTY TO POLITICAL ORGANIZATION.

[Sec. 84(a)]

(a) GENERAL RULE.—If—

(1) any person transfers property to a political organization, and

(2) the fair market value of such property exceeds its adjusted basis,

then for purposes of this chapter the transferor shall be treated as having sold such property to the political organization on the date of the transfer, and the transferor shall be treated as having realized an amount equal to the fair market value of such property on such date.

[Sec. 84(b)]

(b) BASIS OF PROPERTY.—In the case of a transfer of property to a political organization to which subsection (a) applies, the basis of such property in the hands of the political organization shall be the same as it would be in the hands of the transferor, increased by the amount of gain recognized to the transferor by reason of such transfer.

[Sec. 84(c)]

(c) POLITICAL ORGANIZATION DEFINED.—For purposes of this section, the term "political organization" has the meaning given to such term by section 527(e)(1).

Amendments

• 1975 (P.L. 93-625)

P.L. 93-625, §13(a):

Added Code Sec. 84. **Effective** for transfers made after 5-7-74, in tax years ending after such date.

P.L. 93-625, §13(c), provides:

(c) Nonrecognition of Gain or Loss Where Organization Sold Contributed Property Before August 2, 1973.—In the case of the sale or exchange before August 2, 1973, by an organization described in section 527(e)(1) of the Internal Revenue Code of 1954 of property which such organization acquired by contribution (within the meaning of section 271(b)(2) of such Code), no gain or loss shall be recognized by such organization.

[Sec. 85]

SEC. 85. UNEMPLOYMENT COMPENSATION.

[Sec. 85(a)]

(a) GENERAL RULE.—In the case of an individual, gross income includes unemployment compensation.

[Sec. 85(b)]

(b) UNEMPLOYMENT COMPENSATION DEFINED.—For purposes of this section, the term "unemployment compensation" means any amount received under a law of the United States or of a State which is in the nature of unemployment compensation.

Amendments

• 1986, Tax Reform Act of 1986 (P.L. 99-514)

P.L. 99-514, §121:

Amended Code Sec. 85. **Effective** for amounts received after 12-31-86, in tax years ending after such date. Prior to amendment, Code Sec. 85 read as follows:

SEC. 85. UNEMPLOYMENT COMPENSATION.

(a) IN GENERAL.—If the sum for the taxable year of the adjusted gross income of the taxpayer (determined without regard to this section, section 86, and section 221) and the unemployment compensation exceeds the base amount, gross income for the taxable year includes unemployment compensation in an amount equal to the lesser of—

(1) one-half of the amount of the excess of such sum over the base amount, or

(2) the amount of the unemployment compensation.

(b) BASE AMOUNT DEFINED.—For purposes of this section, the term "base amount" means—

(1) except as provided in paragraphs (2) and (3), $12,000,

(2) $18,000, in the case of a joint return under section 6013, or

(3) zero, in the case of a taxpayer who—

(A) is married at the close of the taxable year (within the meaning of section 143) but does not file a joint return for such year, and

(B) does not live apart from his spouse at all times during the taxable year.

(c) UNEMPLOYMENT COMPENSATION DEFINED.—For purposes of this section, the term "unemployment compensation" means any amount received under a law of the United States or of a State which is in the nature of unemployment compensation.

• 1984, Deficit Reduction Act of 1984 (P.L. 98-369)

P.L. 98-369, §1075(b), provides:

(b) WAIVER OF STATUTE OF LIMITATIONS.—If credit or refund of any overpayment of tax resulting from the amendment made by subsection (a) is barred on the date of the enactment of this Act or at any time during the 1-year period beginning on the date of the enactment of this Act by the operation of any law or rule of law (including res judicata), refund or credit of such overpayment (to the extent attributable to the amendment made by subsection (a)) may, nevertheless, be made or allowed if claim therefor is filed before the close of such 1-year period.

• 1983, Social Security Amendments of 1983 (P.L. 98-21)

P.L. 98-21, §121(f)(1):

Amended Code Sec. 85(a) by striking out "this section," and inserting in place thereof "this section, section 86,". **Effective**, generally, for benefits received after 1983 in tax years ending after 1983 as provided in Act Sec. 121(g).

P.L. 98-21, §122(c)(2):

Amended Code Sec. 85(a) by striking out ", section 105(d),". **Effective**, generally, for tax years beginning after 1983 as provided in Act Sec. 122(d).

• 1982, Tax Equity and Fiscal Responsibility Act of 1982 (P.L. 97-248)

P.L. 97-248, §611(a):

Amended Code Sec. 85(b) by striking out "$20,000" and inserting in lieu thereof "$12,000"; and by striking out "$25,000" and inserting in lieu thereof "$18,000". **Effective** as noted in Act Sec. 611(b), below:

P.L. 97-248, §611(b), provides:

(b) Effective Dates.—

(1) Compensation paid after 1981.—The amendments made by this section shall apply to payments of unemployment compensation made after December 31, 1981, in taxable years ending after such date.

(2) No addition to tax for underpayment of estimated tax attributable to application of amendments to compensation paid in 1982.—No, addition to tax shall be made under section 6654 of the Internal Revenue Code of 1954 with respect to any underpayment to the extent such underpayment is attributable to unemployment compensation which is received during 1982 and which (but for the amendments made by subsection (a)) would not be includable in gross income.

(3) Special rule for fiscal year taxpayers.—In the case of a taxable year (other than a calendar year) which includes January 1, 1982—

(A) the amendments made by this section shall be applied by taking into account the entire amount of unemployment compensation received during such taxable year, but

(B) the increase in gross income for such taxable year as a result of such amendments shall not exceed the amount of unemployment compensation paid after December 31, 1981.

(4) Unemployment compensation defined.—For purposes of this subsection, the term "unemployment compensation" has the meaning given to such term by section 85(c) of the Internal Revenue Code of 1954.

• 1981, Economic Recovery Tax Act of 1981 (P.L. 97-34)

P.L. 97-34, §103(c)(1):

Amended Code Sec. 85(a) by striking out "and without regard to section 105(d)" and inserting in lieu thereof, "section 105(d), and section 221". **Effective** for tax years beginning after 12-31-81.

• 1978, Revenue Act of 1978 (P.L. 95-600)

P.L. 95-600, §112(a), (d) (as amended by P.L. 98-369, §1075(a)):

Added Code Sec. 85. **Effective** for payments of unemployment compensation made after 12-31-78, in tax years ending after such date; except that such amendments shall not apply to payments made for weeks of unemployment ending before 12-1-78. For a special rule see P.L. 98-369, Act Sec. 1075(b), below.

[Sec. 85(c)]

(c) SPECIAL RULE FOR 2009.—In the case of any taxable year beginning in 2009, gross income shall not include so much of the unemployment compensation received by an individual as does not exceed $2,400.

Amendments

• 2009, American Recovery and Reinvestment Tax Act of 2009 (P.L. 111-5)

P.L. 111-5, §1007(a):

Amended Code Sec. 85 by adding at the end a new subsection (c). **Effective** for tax years beginning after 12-31-2008.

[Sec. 86]

SEC. 86. SOCIAL SECURITY AND TIER 1 RAILROAD RETIREMENT BENEFITS.

[Sec. 86(a)]

(a) IN GENERAL.—

(1) IN GENERAL.—Except as provided in paragraph (2), gross income for the taxable year of any taxpayer described in subsection (b) (notwithstanding section 207 of the Social Security Act) includes social security benefits in an amount equal to the lesser of—

(A) one-half of the social security benefits received during the taxable year, or

(B) one-half of the excess described in subsection (b)(1).

(2) ADDITIONAL AMOUNT.—In the case of a taxpayer with respect to whom the amount determined under subsection (b)(1)(A) exceeds the adjusted base amount, the amount included in gross income under this section shall be equal to the lesser of—

(A) the sum of—

(i) 85 percent of such excess, plus

(ii) the lesser of the amount determined under paragraph (1) or an amount equal to one-half of the difference between the adjusted base amount and the base amount of the taxpayer, or

(B) 85 percent of the social security benefits received during the taxable year.

Amendments

• 1993, Omnibus Budget Reconciliation Act of 1993 (P.L. 103-66)

P.L. 103-66, §13215(a)(1):

Amended Code Sec. 86(a) by adding at the end thereof new paragraph (2). **Effective** for tax years beginning after 12-31-93.

P.L. 103-66, §13215(a)(2)(A)-(B):

Amended Code Sec. 86(a) by striking "Gross" and inserting "(1) In general.—Except as provided in paragraph (2), gross", and by redesignating paragraphs (1) and (2) as subparagraphs (A) and (B), respectively. **Effective** for tax years beginning after 12-31-93.

[Sec. 86(b)]

(b) TAXPAYERS TO WHOM SUBSECTION (a) APPLIES.—

(1) IN GENERAL.—A taxpayer is described in this subsection if—

(A) the sum of—

(i) the modified adjusted gross income of the taxpayer for the taxable year, plus

(ii) one-half of the social security benefits received during the taxable year, exceeds

(B) the base amount.

(2) MODIFIED ADJUSTED GROSS INCOME.—For purposes of this subsection, the term "modified adjusted gross income" means adjusted gross income—

→→→ Caution: Code Sec. 86(b)(2)(A), below, is subject to the sunset provision of the Economic Growth and Tax Relief Reconciliation Act of 2001 (P.L. 107-16), §901. Absent Congressional action, the changes made to this provision by P.L. 107-16, or that take effect as if included in P.L. 107-16, do not apply after December 31, 2010. For more information about the sunset provision, see page XXI of the Preface to this publication and P.L. 107-16, §901, in the amendment notes. See the amendments notes for a history of amendments to this section and the effective date of each change.

(A) determined without regard to this section and sections 135, 137, 199, 221, 222, 911, 931, and 933, and

(B) increased by the amount of interest received or accrued by the taxpayer during the taxable year which is exempt from tax.

Amendments

• 2004, American Jobs Creation Act of 2004 (P.L. 108-357)

P.L. 108-357, §102(d)(1):

Amended Code Sec. 86(b)(2)(A) by inserting "199," before "221". **Effective** for tax years beginning after 12-31-2004.

• 2001, Economic Growth and Tax Relief Reconciliation Act of 2001 (P.L. 107-16)

P.L. 107-16, §431(c)(1):

Amended Code Sec. 86(b)(2) by inserting "222," after "221,". **Effective** for payments made in tax years beginning after 12-31-2001.

P.L. 107-16, §901(a)-(b), provides:

SEC. 901. SUNSET OF PROVISIONS OF ACT.

(a) IN GENERAL.—All provisions of, and amendments made by, this Act shall not apply—

(1) to taxable, plan, or limitation years beginning after December 31, 2010, or

(2) in the case of title V, to estates of decedents dying, gifts made, or generation skipping transfers, after December 31, 2010.

(b) APPLICATION OF CERTAIN LAWS.—The Internal Revenue Code of 1986 and the Employee Retirement Income Security Act of 1974 shall be applied and administered to years, estates, gifts, and transfers described in subsection (a) as if the provisions and amendments described in subsection (a) had never been enacted.

• 1998, Tax and Trade Relief Extension Act of 1998 (P.L. 105-227)

P.L. 105-277, §4003(a)(2)(B):

Amended Code Sec. 86(b)(2)(A) by inserting "221," after "137,". **Effective** as if included in the provision of P.L. 105-34 to which it relates [generally **effective** for interest payments due and paid after 12-31-97, on any qualified education loan.—CCH].

• 1996, Small Business Job Protection Act of 1996 (P.L. 104-188)

P.L. 104-188, §1704(t)(3):

Amended Code Sec. 86(b)(2) by striking "adusted" and inserting "adjusted". **Effective** 8-20-96.

P.L. 104-188, §1807(c)(2):

Amended Code Sec. 86(b)(2)(A) by inserting "137," before "911". **Effective** for tax years beginning after 12-31-96.

• 1988, Technical and Miscellaneous Revenue Act of 1988 (P.L. 100-647)

P.L. 100-647, §6009(c)(1):

Amended Code Sec. 86(b)(2)(A) by inserting "135," before "911". **Effective** for tax years beginning after 12-31-89.

[Sec. 86(c)]

(c) BASE AMOUNT AND ADJUSTED BASE AMOUNT.—For purposes of this section—

(1) BASE AMOUNT.—The term "base amount" means—

(A) except as otherwise provided in this paragraph, $25,000,

(B) $32,000 in the case of a joint return, and

(C) zero in the case of a taxpayer who—

(i) is married as of the close of the taxable year (within the meaning of section 7703) but does not file a joint return for such year, and

(ii) does not live apart from his spouse at all times during the taxable year.

(2) ADJUSTED BASE AMOUNT.—The term "adjusted base amount" means—

(A) except as otherwise provided in this paragraph, $34,000,

(B) $44,000 in the case of a joint return, and

(C) zero in the case of a taxpayer described in paragraph (1)(C).

Amendments

• 1993, Omnibus Budget Reconciliation Act of 1993 (P.L. 103-66)

P.L. 103-66, §13215(b):

Amended Code Sec. 86(c). **Effective** for tax years beginning after 12-31-93. Prior to amendment, Code Sec. 86(c) read as follows:

(c) BASE AMOUNT.—For purposes of this section, the term "base amount" means—

(1) except as otherwise provided in this subsection, $25,000,

(2) $32,000, in the case of a joint return, and

(3) zero, in the case of a taxpayer who—

(A) is married at the close of the taxable year (within the meaning of section 7703) but does not file a joint return for such year, and

(B) does not live apart from his spouse at all times during the taxable year.

[Sec. 86(d)]

(d) SOCIAL SECURITY BENEFIT.—

(1) IN GENERAL.—For purposes of this section, the term "social security benefit" means any amount received by the taxpayer by reason of entitlement to—

(A) a monthly benefit under title II of the Social Security Act, or

(B) a tier 1 railroad retirement benefit.

(2) ADJUSTMENT FOR REPAYMENTS DURING YEAR.—

(A) IN GENERAL.—For purposes of this section, the amount of social security benefits received during any taxable year shall be reduced by any repayment made by the taxpayer during the taxable year of a social security benefit previously received by the taxpayer (whether or not such benefit was received during the taxable year).

(B) DENIAL OF DEDUCTION.—If (but for this subparagraph) any portion of the repayments referred to in subparagraph (A) would have been allowable as a deduction for the taxable year under section 165, such portion shall be allowable as a deduction only to the extent it exceeds the social security benefits received by the taxpayer during the taxable year (and not repaid during such taxable year).

(3) WORKMEN'S COMPENSATION BENEFITS SUBSTITUTED FOR SOCIAL SECURITY BENEFITS.—For purposes of this section, if, by reason of section 224 of the Social Security Act (or by reason of section 3(a)(1) of the Railroad Retirement Act of 1974), any social security benefit is reduced by reason of the receipt of a benefit under a workmen's compensation act, the term "social security benefit" includes that portion of such benefit received under the workmen's compensation act which equals such reduction.

(4) TIER 1 RAILROAD RETIREMENT BENEFIT.—For purposes of paragraph (1), the term "tier 1 railroad retirement benefit" means—

(A) the amount of the annuity under the Railroad Retirement Act of 1974 equal to the amount of the benefit to which the taxpayer would have been entitled under the Social Security Act if all of the service after December 31, 1936, of the employee (on whose employment record the annuity is being paid) had been included in the term "employment" as defined in the Social Security Act, and

(B) a monthly annuity amount under section 3(f)(3) of the Railroad Retirement Act of 1974.

(5) EFFECT OF EARLY DELIVERY OF BENEFIT CHECKS.—For purposes of subsection (a), in any case where section 708 of the Social Security Act causes social security benefit checks to be delivered before the end of the calendar month for which they are issued, the benefits involved shall be deemed to have been received in the succeeding calendar month.

Amendments

• 1994, Social Security Independence and Program Improvements Act of 1994 (P.L. 103-296)

P.L. 103-296, §309(d):

Amended Code Sec. 86(d)(1) by striking the last sentence. **Effective** for benefits received after 12-31-95, in tax years ending after such date. Prior to amendment, the last sentence of Code Sec. 86(d)(1) read as follows:

For purposes of the preceding sentence, the amount received by any taxpayer shall be determined as if the Social Security Act did not contain section 203(i) thereof.

[Sec. 86(e)]

(e) LIMITATION ON AMOUNT INCLUDED WHERE TAXPAYER RECEIVES LUMP-SUM PAYMENT.—

(1) LIMITATION.—If—

(A) any portion of a lump-sum payment of social security benefits received during the taxable year is attributable to prior taxable years, and

(B) the taxpayer makes an election under this subsection for the taxable year,

then the amount included in gross income under this section for the taxable year by reason of the receipt of such portion shall not exceed the sum of the increases in gross income under this chapter for prior taxable years which would result solely from taking into account such portion in the taxable years to which it is attributable.

(2) SPECIAL RULES.—

(A) YEAR TO WHICH BENEFIT ATTRIBUTABLE.—For purposes of this subsection, a social security benefit is attributable to a taxable year if the generally applicable payment date for such benefit occurred during such taxable year.

(B) ELECTION.—An election under this subsection shall be made at such time and in such manner as the Secretary shall by regulations prescribe. Such election, once made, may be revoked only with the consent of the Secretary.

[Sec. 86(f)]

(f) TREATMENT AS PENSION OR ANNUITY FOR CERTAIN PURPOSES.—For purposes of—

(1) section 22(c)(3)(A) (relating to reduction for amounts received as pension or annuity),

(2) section 32(c)(2) (defining earned income),

(3) section 219(f)(1) (defining compensation), and

(4) section 911(b)(1) (defining foreign earned income), any social security benefit shall be treated as an amount received as a pension or annuity.

Amendments

• 1988, Technical and Miscellaneous Revenue Act of 1988 (P.L. 100-647)

P.L. 100-647, §1001(e):

Amended Code Sec. 86(f) by inserting "and" at the end of paragraph (3), by striking out paragraph (4), and redesignating paragraph (5) as paragraph (4). **Effective** as if included in the provision of P.L. 99-514 to which it relates. Prior to amendment, Code Sec. 86(f)(4) read as follows:

(4) Section 221(b)(2) (defining earned income), and

• 1986, Tax Reform Act of 1986 (P.L. 99-514)

P.L. 99-514, §131(b)(2):

Amended Code Sec. 86(b)(2)(A) by striking out "sections 221," and inserting in lieu thereof "sections". **Effective** for tax years beginning after 12-31-86.

P.L. 99-514 §1301(j)(8):

Amended Code Sec. 86(c)(3) by striking out "section 143" and inserting in lieu thereof "section 7703". **Effective**, generally, for bonds issued after 8-15-86. However, for transitional rules, see Act Sec. 1311-1318 following Code Sec. 103.

P.L. 99-514, §1847(b)(2):

Amended Code Sec. 86(f)(1) by striking out "section 37(c)(3)(A)" and inserting in lieu thereof "section 22(c)(3)(A)". **Effective** as if included in the provision of P.L. 98-369 to which it relates.

• 1986, Consolidated Omnibus Budget Reconciliation Act of 1985 (P.L. 99-272)

P.L. 99-272, §13204(a):

Amended Code Sec. 86(d)(4). **Effective** for any monthly benefit for which the generally applicable payment date is after 12-31-85. Prior to amendment, Code Sec. 86(d)(4) read as follows:

(4) TIER 1 RAILROAD RETIREMENT BENEFIT.—For purposes of paragraph (1), the term "tier 1 railroad retirement benefit" means a monthly benefit under section 3(a), 3(f)(3), 4(a), or 4(f) of the Railroad Retirement Act of 1974.

P.L. 99-272, §12111(b):

Amended Code Sec. 86(d) by adding at the end thereof new paragraph (5). **Effective** for benefit checks issued for months ending after the date of enactment of this Act.

• 1984, Deficit Reduction Act of 1984 (P.L. 98-369)

P.L. 98-369, §474(r)(2):

Amended Code Sec. 86(f)(1), prior to amendment by Act Sec. 2661(o)(1), by striking out "section 43(c)(2)" and inserting in lieu thereof "section 32(c)(2)". **Effective** for tax years beginning after 12-31-83, and to carrybacks from such years.

P.L. 98-369, §2661(o)(1):

Amended Code Sec. 86(f), as amended by Act Sec. 474(r)(2), by redesignating paragraphs (1), (2), (3) and (4) as (2), (3), (4) and (5), respectively and by inserting new paragraph (1). **Effective** as if it had been included in the enactment of P.L. 98-21.

• 1983, Railroad Retirement Solvency Act of 1983 (P.L. 98-76)

P.L. 98-76, §224(d):

Amended Code Sec. 86(d)(4) by adding "3(f)(3)," after "section 3(a),". **Effective** for benefits received after 1983 in tax years ending after 1983.

• 1983, Social Security Amendments of 1983 (P.L. 98-21)

P.L. 98-21, §121(a):

Added Code Sec. 86. **Effective**, generally, for benefits received after 1983 in tax years ending after 1983, as provided in Act Sec. 121(g), below.

P.L. 98-21, §121(g), provides:

(g) EFFECTIVE DATES.—

(1) IN GENERAL.—Except as provided in paragraph (2), the amendments made by this section shall apply to benefits received after December 31, 1983, in taxable years ending after such date.

(2) TREATMENT OF CERTAIN LUMP-SUM PAYMENTS RECEIVED AFTER DECEMBER 31, 1983.—The amendments made by this section shall not apply to any portion of a lump-sum payment of social security benefits (as defined in section 86(d) of the Internal Revenue Code of 1954) received after December 31, 1983, if the generally applicable payment date for such portion was before January 1, 1984.

P.L. 98-21, §335(b)(2)(A):

Amended Code Sec. 86(a) by inserting "(notwithstanding section 207 of the Social Security Act)" before "includes". **Effective** 4-20-83 for benefits received after 1983 in tax years ending after 1983.

[Sec. 87]

SEC. 87. ALCOHOL AND BIODIESEL FUELS CREDITS.

Gross income includes—

(1) the amount of the alcohol fuel credit determined with respect to the taxpayer for the taxable year under section 40(a), and

(2) the biodiesel fuels credit determined with respect to the taxpayer for the taxable year under section 40A(a).

Amendments

• 2004, American Jobs Creation Act of 2004 (P.L. 108-357)

P.L. 108-357, §302(c)(1)(A):

Amended Code Sec. 87. **Effective** for fuel produced, and sold or used, after 12-31-2004, in tax years ending after such date. Prior to amendment, Code Sec. 87 read as follows:

SEC. 87. ALCOHOL FUEL CREDIT.

Gross income includes the amount of the alcohol fuel credit determined with respect to the taxpayer for the taxable year under section 40(a).

Amendments

• 1984, Deficit Reduction Act of 1984 (P.L. 98-369)

P.L. 98-369, §474(r)(3):

Amended Code Sec. 87. **Effective** for tax years beginning after 12-31-83, and to carrybacks from such years. Prior to amendment, Code Sec. 87 read as follows:

SEC. 87. ALCOHOL FUEL CREDIT.

Gross income includes an amount equal to the amount of the credit allowable to the taxpayer under section 44E for the taxable year (determined without regard to subsection (e) thereof).

• 1983, Social Security Amendments of 1983 (P.L. 98-21)

P.L. 98-21, §121(a):

Redesignated Code Sec. 86 as Code Sec. 87. **Effective**, generally, for tax years ending after 1983.

• 1980, Crude Oil Windfall Profit Tax Act of 1980 (P.L. 96-223)

P.L. 96-223, §232(c)(1):

Added Code Sec. 86. **Effective** for sales and uses after 9-30-80, in tax years ending after such date.

[Sec. 88]

SEC. 88. CERTAIN AMOUNTS WITH RESPECT TO NUCLEAR DECOMMISSIONING COSTS.

In the case of any taxpayer who is required to include the amount of any nuclear decommissioning costs in the taxpayer's cost of service for ratemaking purposes, there shall be includible in the gross income of such taxpayer the amount so included for any taxable year.

Amendments

• 1986, Tax Reform Act of 1986 (P.L. 99-514)

P.L. 99-514, §1807(a)(4)(E)(vii):

Amended Code Sec. 88 by striking out "of ratemaking purposes" and inserting in lieu thereof "for ratemaking purposes". **Effective** as if included in the provision of P.L. 98-369 to which it relates.

• 1984, Deficit Reduction Act of 1984 (P.L. 98-369)

P.L. 98-369, §91(f)(1):

Act Sec. 91(f)(1) added Code Sec. 88. **Effective** for amounts with respect to which a deduction would be allowable under chapter 1 of the Internal Revenue Code of 1954 (determined without regard to such amendments) after—

(A) in the case of amounts to which section 461(h) of such Code (as added by such amendments) applies, 7-18-84, and

(B) in the case of amounts to which section 461(i) of such Code (as so added) applies, after 3-31-84.

For special rules, see Act Sec. 91(g)(i) following Code Sec. 461(h).

[Sec. 89—Repealed]

Amendments

• 1989 (P.L. 101-140)

P.L. 101-140, §202(a):

Repealed Code Sec. 89. **Effective** as if included in section 1151 of the Tax Reform Act of 1986 (P.L. 99-514) [P.L. 99-514, §1151, added Code Sec. 89. Therefore, Code Sec. 89 never took effect.—CCH]. Prior to repeal, Code Sec. 89 read as follows:

SEC. 89. BENEFITS PROVIDED UNDER CERTAIN EMPLOYEE BENEFIT PLANS.

[Sec. 89(a)]

(a) BENEFITS UNDER DISCRIMINATORY PLANS.—

(1) IN GENERAL.—Notwithstanding any provision of part III of this subchapter, gross income of a highly compensated employee who is a participant in a discriminatory employee benefit plan during any testing year shall include an amount equal to such employee's excess benefit under such plan for such testing year.

(2) YEAR OF INCLUSION.—

(A) IN GENERAL.—Except as provided in subparagraph (B), any amount included in gross income under paragraph (1) shall be taken into account for the taxable year of the employee with or within which the testing year ends.

(B) ELECTION TO DELAY INCLUSION FOR 1 YEAR.—If an employer maintaining a plan with a testing year ending after September 30 and on or before December 31 of a calendar year elects the application of this subparagraph—

(i) amounts included in gross income under paragraph (1) with respect to employees of such employer shall be taken into account for the taxable year of the employee following the taxable year determined under subparagraph (A), but

(ii) any deduction of the employer which is attributable to such amounts shall be allowable for the taxable year with or within which the testing year following the testing year in which the excess benefits occurred ends.

Amendments

• 1988, Technical and Miscellaneous Revenue Act of 1988 (P.L. 100-647)

P.L. 100-647, §1011B(a)(1):

Amended Code Sec. 89(a)(2). **Effective** as if included in the provision of P.L. 99-514 to which it relates. For special transitional provisions applicable to Code Sec. 89, see Act Sec. 3021(c), in the Amendment Notes following Code Sec. 89(m). Prior to amendment, Code Sec. 89(a)(2) read as follows:

(2) YEAR OF INCLUSION.—Any amount included in gross income under paragraph (1) shall be taken into account for the taxable year of the employee with or within which the plan year ends.

P.L. 100-647, §3021(a)(1)(A):

Amended Code Sec. 89, as amended by title I, by striking out "plan year" each place it appears and inserting in lieu thereof "testing year". **Effective** as if included in the provision of P.L. 99-514 to which it relates. For special transitional provisions applicable to Code Sec. 89, see Act Sec. 3021(c), in the Amendment Notes following Code Sec. 89(m).

[Sec. 89(b)]

(b) EXCESS BENEFIT.—For purposes of this section—

(1) IN GENERAL.—The excess benefit of any highly compensated employee is the excess of such employee's employer-provided benefit under the plan over the highest permitted benefit.

(2) HIGHEST PERMITTED BENEFIT.—For purposes of paragraph (1), the highest permitted benefit under any plan shall be determined by reducing the nontaxable benefits of highly compensated employees (beginning with the employees with the greatest nontaxable benefits) until such plan would not be treated as a discriminatory employee benefit plan if such reduced benefits were taken into account.

(3) PLANS OF SAME TYPE.—In computing the excess benefit with respect to any benefit, there shall be taken into account all plans of the employer of the same type.

(4) NONTAXABLE BENEFITS.—For purposes of this subsection, the term "nontaxable benefit" means any benefit provided under a plan to which this section applies which (without regard to subsection (a)(1)) is excludable from gross income under this chapter. Such term includes any group-term life insurance the cost of which is includible in gross income under section 79.

Amendments

• 1988, Technical and Miscellaneous Revenue Act of 1988 (P.L. 100-647)

P.L. 100-647, §1011B(a)(2):

Amended Code Sec. 89(b)(4) by adding at the end thereof a new sentence. **Effective** as if included in the provision of P.L. 99-514 to which it relates. For special transitional provisions applicable to Code Sec. 89, see Act Sec. 3021(c), in the Amendment Notes following Code Sec. 89(m).

[Sec. 89(c)]

(c) DISCRIMINATORY EMPLOYEE BENEFIT PLAN.—For purposes of this section, the term "discriminatory employee benefit plan" means any statutory employee benefit plan unless such plan meets the—

(1) eligibility requirements of subsection (d), and

(2) benefit requirements of subsection (e).

[Sec. 89(d)]

(d) ELIGIBILITY REQUIREMENTS.—

(1) IN GENERAL.—A plan meets the eligibility requirements of this subsection for any testing year if—

(A) at least 90 percent of all employees who are not highly compensated employees—

(i) are eligible to participate in such plan (or in any other plan of the employer of the same type), and

(ii) would (if they participated) have available under such plans an employer-provided benefit which is at least 50 percent of the largest employer-provided benefit available under all such plans of the employer to any highly compensated employee,

(B) at least 50 percent of the employees eligible to participate in such plan are not highly compensated employees, and

(C) such plan does not contain any provision relating to eligibility to participate which (by its terms or otherwise) discriminates in favor of highly compensated employees.

(2) ALTERNATIVE ELIGIBILITY PERCENTAGE TEST.—A plan shall be treated as meeting the requirements of paragraph (1)(B) if—

(A) the percentage determined by dividing the number of highly compensated employees eligible to participate in the plan by the total number of highly compensated employees, does not exceed

(B) the percentage similarly determined with respect to employees who are not highly compensated employees.

Amendments

• 1988, Technical and Miscellaneous Revenue Act of 1988 (P.L. 100-647)

P.L. 100-647, §3021(a)(1)(A):

Amended Code Sec. 89, as amended by title I, by striking out "plan year" each place it appears and inserting in lieu thereof "testing year". **Effective** as if included in the provision of P.L. 99-514 to which it relates. For special transitional provisions applicable to Code Sec. 89, see Act Sec. 3021(c), in the Amendment Notes following Code Sec. 89(m).

[Sec. 89(e)]

(e) BENEFIT REQUIREMENTS.—

(1) IN GENERAL.—A plan meets the benefit requirements of this subsection for any testing year if the average employer-provided benefit received by employees other than highly compensated employees under all plans of the employer of the same type is at least 75 percent of the average employer-provided benefit received by highly compensated employees under all plans of the employer of the same type.

(2) AVERAGE EMPLOYER-PROVIDED BENEFIT.—For purposes of this subsection, the term "average employer-provided benefit" means, with respect to highly compensated employees, an amount equal to—

(A) the aggregate employer-provided benefits received by highly compensated employees under all plans of the type being tested, divided by

(B) the number of highly compensated employees (whether or not covered under such plans).

The average employer-provided benefit with respect to employees other than highly compensated employees shall be determined in the same manner as the average employer-provided benefit for highly compensated employees.

Amendments

• 1988, Technical and Miscellaneous Revenue Act of 1988 (P.L. 100-647)

P.L. 100-647, §3021(a)(1)(A):

Amended Code Sec. 89, as amended by title I, by striking out "plan year" each place it appears and inserting in lieu thereof "testing year". **Effective** as if included in the provision of P.L. 99-514 to which it relates. For special transitional provisions applicable to Code Sec. 89, see Act Sec. 3021(c), in the Amendment Notes following Code Sec. 89(m).

[Sec. 89(f)]

(f) SPECIAL RULE WHERE HEALTH OR GROUP-TERM PLAN MEETS 80-PERCENT COVERAGE TEST.—If at least 80 percent of the employees who are not highly compensated employees are covered under a health plan or group-term life insurance plan during the testing year, such plan shall be treated as meeting the requirements of subsections (d) and (e) for such year. The preceding sentence shall not apply if the plan does not meet the requirements of subsection (d)(1)(C) (relating to nondiscriminatory provisions).

Amendments

• 1988, Technical and Miscellaneous Revenue Act of 1988 (P.L. 100-647)

P.L. 100-647, §3021(a)(1)(A):

Amended Code Sec. 89, as amended by title I, by striking out "plan year" each place it appears and inserting in lieu thereof "testing year". **Effective** as if included in the provision of P.L. 99-514 to which it relates. For special transitional provisions applicable to Code Sec. 89, see Act Sec. 3021(c), in the Amendment Notes following Code Sec. 89(m).

P.L. 100-647, §6070 [Repealed by P.L. 101-140, §203(a)(7)], provides a special definition of part-time employee for purposes of Code Sec. 89(f):

For purposes of section 89(f) of the 1986 Code, in the case of a plan maintained by an employer which employs fewer than 10 employees on a normal working day during a plan year, section 89(h)(1)(B) of such Code shall be applied—

(1) by substituting "35 hours" for "17½ hours" in the case of a plan year beginning in 1989, and

(2) by substituting "25 hours" for "17½ hours" in the case of plan years beginning in 1990.

All persons treated as 1 employer for purposes of subsection (b), (c), (m), (n), or (o) section 414 of the 1986 Code shall be treated as 1 employer for purposes of the preceding sentence.

[Sec. 89(g)]

(g) OPERATING RULES.—

(1) AGGREGATION OF COMPARABLE HEALTH PLANS.—In the case of health plans maintained by an employer—

(A) IN GENERAL.—An employer may treat a group of comparable plans as 1 plan for purposes of applying subsections (d)(1)(B), (d)(2) and (f).

(B) COMPARABLE PLANS.—For purposes of subparagraph (A), a group of comparable plans is any group (selected by the employer) of plans of the same type if the smallest employer-provided benefit available to any participant in any such plan is at least 95 percent of the largest employer-provided benefit available to any participant in any such plan.

(C) EMPLOYEES COVERED BY MORE THAN 1 PLAN.—The Secretary may provide that 2 or more plans providing benefits to the same participant shall be treated as 1 plan for purposes of applying subections (d)(1)(B), (d)(2), and (f).

(D) SPECIAL RULES FOR APPLYING SUBSECTION (f).—

(i) IN GENERAL.—For purposes of applying subsection (f)—

(I) except as provided in clause (ii), subparagraph (B) shall be applied by substituting "90 percent" for "95 percent", and

(II) a group of plans of the same type shall be treated as comparable plans if the requirements of subparagraph (E) are met.

(ii) ELECTION TO USE LOWER PERCENTAGE IN DETERMINING COMPARABILITY.—If an election by the employer under this clause applies for the testing year—

(I) subclause (I) of clause (i) shall not apply,

(II) for purposes of applying subsection (f), subparagraph (B) of this paragraph shall be applied by substituting "80 percent" for "95 percent", and

(III) subsection (f) shall be applied with respect to all health plans maintained by the employer by substituting "90 percent" for "80 percent".

(E) PLANS TREATED AS COMPARABLE IF EMPLOYEE COST DIFFERENCE IS $100 OR LESS.—

(i) IN GENERAL.—A group of plans of the same type shall be treated as comparable with respect to a group of employees if—

(I) such plans are available to all employees in the group on the same terms, and

(II) the difference in annual cost to employees between the plans with the lowest and highest annual employee cost is not greater than $100.

(ii) COORDINATION WITH SUBPARAGRAPH (B).—A plan not in the group of plans described in clause (i) shall be treated as part of such group if, under subparagraph (B) (without regard to clause (iii) of this subparagraph), such plan is comparable to the plan in such group with the largest employer-provided benefit.

(iii) OTHER PLANS PROVIDING COMPARABLE BENEFITS.—A plan not in the group of plans described in clause (i) shall be treated as part of such group with respect to an employee if—

(I) in the case of an employee who is not a highly compensated employee, such employee is eligible to participate in the plan in such group with the largest employer-provided benefit (without regard to clause (ii)),

(II) in the case of an employee who is not a highly compensated employee, the annual cost to such employee under such plan is not lower than the lowest cost permitted within such group, and

(III) the employer-provided benefit under such plan is less than the employer-provided benefit under the plan in such group with the largest such benefit (without regard to clause (ii)).

(iv) SEPARATE APPLICATION OF REQUIREMENTS.—If an employer elects the application of paragraph (2)(A)(ii), the amount under clause (i) shall be allocated among plans covering spouses and dependents and plans covering employees in such manner as the employer specifies.

(v) COST-OF-LIVING ADJUSTMENT.—In the case of testing years beginning after 1989, the $100 amount under clause (i) shall be increased by the percentage (if any) by which—

(I) the CPI for the calendar year preceding the year in which the testing year begins, exceeds

(II) the CPI for 1988.

For purposes of this clause, the CPI for any calendar year shall be determined under section 1(f).

(2) SPECIAL RULES FOR APPLYING BENEFIT REQUIREMENTS TO HEALTH PLANS.—

(A) ELECTION.—For purposes of determining whether the requirements of subsection (e) or (f) are met with respect to health plans, the employer may elect—

(i) to disregard any employee if such employee and his spouse and dependents (if any) are covered by a health plan providing core benefits maintained by another employer, and

(ii) to apply subsection (e) or (f) separately with respect to coverage of spouses or dependents by such plans and to take into account with respect to such coverage only employees with a spouse or dependents who are not covered by a health plan providing core benefits maintained by another employer.

The provisions of the preceding sentence shall not apply for purposes of applying subsection (f) unless the requirements of subsection (f) would be met if such subsection were applied without regard to the preceding sentence and on the basis of eligibility to participate rather than coverage.

(B) SWORN STATEMENTS.—Any employer who elects the application of subparagraph (A) shall obtain and maintain, in such manner as the Secretary may prescribe, adequate sworn statements to demonstrate whether individuals have—

(i) a spouse or dependents,

(ii) core health benefits under a plan of another employer, and

(iii) the health coverage (if any) received by the employee from the employer.

The Secretary shall provide a method for meeting the requirements of this subparagraph through the use of valid sampling techniques. No statement shall be required under clause (ii) with respect to any individual eligible for coverage at no cost under a health plan which provides core health benefits and with respect to whom the employee does not elect any core health coverage from the employer.

(C) PRESUMPTION WHERE NO STATEMENT.—In the absence of a statement described in subparagraph (B)—

(i) an employee who is not a highly compensated employee shall be treated—

(I) as not covered by another plan of another employer providing core benefits, and

(II) as having a spouse and dependents not covered by another plan of another employer providing core benefits, and

(ii) a highly compensated employee shall be treated—

(I) as covered by another plan of another employer providing core benefits, and

(II) as not having a spouse or dependents.

(D) Certain individuals may not be disregarded.—In the case of a highly compensated employee who receives employer-provided benefits under all health plans of the employer which are more than 133⅓ percent of the average employer-provided benefit under such plans for employees other than highly compensated employees, the employer may not disregard such employee, or his spouse or dependents for purposes of clause (i) or (ii) of subparagraph (A). The Secretary shall make such adjustments as are necessary in applying the rules of the preceding sentence to subsection (f).

(E) SPECIAL RULE.—No employee who is not a highly compensated employee may be disregarded under subparagraph (A)(i) with respect to any health plan of the employer unless under such plan such employee is entitled, when the coverage under the other health plan referred to in subparagraph (A)(i) ceases, to elect coverage under the plan of the employer (whether or not an election is otherwise available). Such election is to be on the same terms as if such employee was making such election during a subsequent open season. Rules similar to the rules of the preceding sentences of this subparagraph shall apply in the case of an employee treated as not having a spouse or dependents or having a spouse or dependents covered by a health plan of another employer providing core benefits.

(3) EMPLOYER-PROVIDED BENEFIT.—For purposes of this section—

(A) IN GENERAL.—Except as provided in subsection (k), an employee's employer-provided benefit under any statutory employee benefit plan is—

(i) in the case of any health or group-term life insurance plan, the value of the coverage, or

(ii) in the case of any other plan, the value of the benefits, provided during the testing year to or on behalf of such employee to the extent attributable to contributions made by the employer.

(B) SPECIAL RULE FOR HEALTH PLANS.—The value of the coverage provided by any health plan shall be determined under procedures prescribed by the Secretary which shall—

(i) set forth the values of various standard types of coverage involving a representative group, and

(ii) provide for adjustments to take into account the specific coverage and group involved.

(C) SPECIAL RULE FOR GROUP-TERM LIFE PLANS.—

(i) IN GENERAL.—Except as provided in clause (ii), in determining the value of coverage under a group-term life insurance plan, the amount taken into account for any employee shall be based on the cost of the insurance determined under section 79(c) for an employee who is age 40.

(ii) EXCESS BENEFIT.—For purposes of subsection (b), the excess benefit with respect to coverage under a group-term life insurance plan shall be equal to the greater of—

(I) the cost of such excess benefit (expressed as dollars of coverage) determined without regard to section 79(c), or

(II) such cost determined with regard to section 79(c).

(D) SALARY REDUCTIONS.—

(i) IN GENERAL.—Except for purposes of subsections (d)(1)(A)(ii) and (j)(5), any salary reduction shall be treated as an employer-provided benefit.

(ii) SPECIAL RULE FOR SUBSECTION(d)(1)(a)[(A)](ii).—Notwithstanding clause (i), any salary reduction under a cafeteria plan (within the meaning of section 125) shall [be] treated as an employer-provided benefit for purposes of subsection (d)(1)(A)(ii) if—

(I) the percentage of employees who are not highly compensated employees eligible to participate in the plan is not greater than the percentage of highly compensated employees so eligible,

(II) all employees eligible to participate in the plan are eligible under the same terms and conditions, and

(III) no highly compensated employee eligible under the plan is eligible to participate in any other plan maintained by the employer for any benefit of the same type unless the benefit is available on the same terms and conditions to every employee who is not a highly compensated employee eligible to participate in the plan.

(iii) REGULATIONS.—Notwithstanding clause (i) or (ii), the Secretary may by regulations provide that any salary reduction shall or shall not be treated as an employer-provided benefit to prevent avoidance of the purposes of this section.

(E) SPECIAL RULE FOR MULTIEMPLOYER PLANS.—

(i) IN GENERAL.—Except as provided in regulations and clause (ii), an employer may treat the contribution such employer makes to a multiemployer plan on behalf of an employee as the employer-provided benefit of such employee under such plan.

(ii) ADJUSTMENT.—If—

(I) the allocation of plan benefits between highly compensated employees and other employees under a multiemployer plan (or within either of such groups) varies materially from the allocation of employer contributions to such plan, or

(II) the employer contributions relate to benefits of different types,

the employer-provided benefit determined under clause (i) shall be appropriately adjusted to take into account such material variation or such employer contribution.

(iii) EXCEPTION FOR PROFESSIONALS.—This subparagraph shall not apply to any employer maintaining a multiemployer plan if such employer makes contributions to such plan on behalf of any individual performing services in the field of health, law, engineering, architecture, accounting, actuarial science, financial services, or consulting or in such other field as the Secretary may prescribe.

(4) ELECTION TO TEST PLANS OF DIFFERENT TYPES TOGETHER.—

(A) IN GENERAL.—Except as provided in subparagraph (B), the employer may elect to treat all plans of the types specified in such election as plans of the same type for purposes of applying subsection (e).

(B) EXCEPTION FOR HEALTH PLANS.—Subparagraph (A) shall not apply for purposes of determining whether any health plan meets the requirements of subsection (e); except that benefits provided under health plans which meet such requirements may be taken into account in determining whether plans of other types meet the requirements of subsection (e).

(5) SEPARATE LINE OF BUSINESS EXCEPTION.—If, under section 414(r), an employer is treated as operating separate lines of business for a year, the employer may apply the preceding provisions of this section separately with respect to employees in each such separate line of business. The preceding sentence shall not apply to any plan unless such plan is available to a group of employees as qualify under a classification set up by the employer and found by the Secretary not to be discriminatory in favor of highly compensated employees. In applying section 414(r)(7) for purposes of this section, an operating unit shall be treated as in a separate geographic area from another unit if such units are all at least 35 miles apart.

(6) TIME FOR TESTING.—

(A) IN GENERAL.—Except as otherwise provided in this paragraph, the determination of whether any plan is a discriminatory employee benefit plan for any testing year shall be made on the basis of the facts as of the testing day.

(B) ADJUSTMENT WHERE BENEFIT OF HIGHLY COMPENSATED EMPLOYEE CHANGES.—If the employer-provided benefit (actually provided or made available) of a highly compensated employee changes during the testing year by reason of any change in the terms of the plan or the making of an election by such employee, the amount taken into account as such employee's employer-provided benefit shall be adjusted to take into account such change and the portion of the testing year during which the changed benefit is provided (or made available).

(C) TREATMENT OF NON-HIGHLY COMPENSATED EMPLOYEES WHERE CHANGE IN PLAN.—Rules similar to the rules of subparagraph (B) shall apply in the case of employees who are not highly compensated employees and who are affected by any change in the terms of the plan, except that the determination of such employees' employer-provided benefits (actually provided or made available) shall be determined as of the date after such change selected by the employer and permitted under regulations prescribed by the Secretary.

(D) TESTING DAY.—For purposes of this paragraph, the term "testing day" means—

(i) the day designated in the plan as the testing day for purposes of this paragraph, or

(ii) if there is no day so designated, the last day of the testing year.

(E) LIMITATIONS.—

(i) DESIGNATION MUST BE CONSISTENT FOR ALL PLANS OF SAME TYPE.—No day may be designated under subparagraph (D)(i) with respect to any plan unless the same day is so designated with respect to all other plans of the employer of the same type.

(ii) DESIGNATION BINDING.—Any designation under subparagraph (D)(i) shall apply to the testing year for which made and all subsequent years unless revoked with the consent of the Secretary.

(F) SPECIAL RULE FOR MULTIPLE EMPLOYER PLAN.—In the case of a multiemployer plan or any other plan maintained by more than 1 employer, each employer may, subject to such rules as the Secretary may prescribe, elect its own testing year under paragraph (13) of subsection (j) and its own testing date under this paragraph.

(7) SAMPLING.—For purposes of determining whether a plan is a discriminatory employee benefit plan (but not for purposes of identifying the highly compensated employees who have a discriminatory excess or the amount of any such excess), determinations under this section may be made on the basis of a statistically valid random sample. The preceding sentence shall apply only if—

(A) the sampling is conducted by an independent person in a manner not inconsistent with regulations prescribed by the Secretary, and

(B) the statistical method and sample size result in a 95 percent probability that the results will have a margin of error not greater than 3 percent.

Amendments

• 1988, Technical and Miscellaneous Revenue Act of 1988 (P.L. 100-647)

P.L. 100-647, §1011B(a)(3):

Amended Code Sec. 89(g)(1) by adding at the end thereof new subparagraph (C). **Effective** as if included in the amendments of section 1151 of P.L. 99-514.

P.L. 100-647, §1011B(a)(4):

Amended Code Sec. 89(g)(2)(B) by adding at the end thereof a new sentence. **Effective** as if included in the amendments of section 1151 of P.L. 99-514.

P.L. 100-647, §1011B(a)(5):

Amended Code Sec. 89(g)(2)(D) by striking out "under such plan" and inserting in lieu thereof "under such plans". **Effective** as if included in the amendments of section 1151 of P.L. 99-514.

P.L. 100-647, §1011B(a)(6):

Amended Code Sec. 89(g) by striking out paragraph (6). **Effective** as if included in the amendments of section 1151 of P.L. 99-514. Prior to amendment, Code Sec. 89(g)(6) read as follows:

(6) SPECIAL RULE FOR APPLYING ELIGIBILITY REQUIREMENTS AND 80-PERCENT TEST TO HEALTH PLANS.—For purposes of determining whether the requirements of subsection (d)(1)(A)(ii) or of subsection (f) are met with respect to health plans, the employer may elect—

(A) to apply this section separately with respect to coverage of spouses and dependents by such plans, and

(B) to take into account with respect to such coverage only those employees with a spouse or dependent (determined under rules similar to the rules of paragraphs (2)(B) and (C)).

P.L. 100-647, §3021(a)(1)(A):

Amended Code Sec. 89, as amended by title I, by striking out "plan year" each place it appears and inserting in lieu thereof "testing year". **Effective** as if included in the amendments of section 1151 of P.L. 99-514.

P.L. 100-647, §3021(a)(2)(A):

Amended Code Sec. 89(g) by adding at the end thereof a new paragraph (6). **Effective** as if included in the amendments of section 1151 of P.L. 99-514.

P.L. 100-647, §3021(a)(3):

Amended Code Sec. 89(g) by adding at the end thereof a new paragraph (7). **Effective** as if included in the amendments of section 1151 of P.L. 99-514.

P.L. 100-647, §3021(a)(4):

Amended Code Sec. 89(g)(3) by adding at the end thereof a new subparagraph (E). **Effective** as if included in the amendments of section 1151 of P.L. 99-514.

P.L. 100-647, §3021(a)(6):

Amended Code Sec. 89(g)(1), as amended by section 1011B(a)(3), by adding at the end thereof new subparagraphs (D) and (E). **Effective** as if included in the amendments of section 1151 of P.L. 99-514.

P.L. 100-647, §3021(a)(7)(A)(i)-(ii):

Amended Code Sec. 89(g)(2)(A) by striking out "subsection (e)" each place it appears and inserting in lieu thereof "subsection (e) or (f)" and by adding at the end thereof a new sentence. **Effective** as if included in the amendments of section 1151 of P.L. 99-514.

P.L. 100-647, §3021(a)(7)(B):

Amended Code Sec. 89(g)(2)(D) by adding at the end thereof a new sentence. **Effective** as if included in the amendments of section 1151 of P.L. 99-514.

P.L. 100-647, §3021(a)(8)(A)-(B):

Amended Code Sec. 89(g)(2) by adding at the end thereof a new subparagraph (E) to read as above and by striking out "and" at the end of subparagraph (B)(i), by striking out the period at the end of subparagraph (B)(ii) and inserting in lieu thereof ", and" and by adding at the end thereof a new clause (iii). **Effective** for testing years beginning after 12-31-89.

P.L. 100-647, §3021(a)(11):

Amended Code Sec. 89(g)(3)(D). **Effective** as if included in the amendments made by section 1151 of P.L. 99-514. Prior to amendment, Code Sec. 89(g)(3)(D) read as follows:

(D) SALARY REDUCTIONS.—Except for purposes of subsections (d)(1)(A)(ii) and (j)(5), any salary reduction shall be treated as an employer-provided benefit.

P.L. 100-647, §3021(b)(2)(B):

Amended Code Sec. 89(g)(5) by adding at the end thereof a new sentence. **Effective** for years beginning after 12-31-86. For special transitional provisions applicable to Code Sec. 89, see Act Sec. 3021(c), in the Amendment Notes following Code Sec. 89(m).

[Sec. 89(h)]

(h) EXCLUDED EMPLOYEES.—

(1) IN GENERAL.—The following employees shall be excluded from consideration under this section:

(A) Employees who have not completed 1 year of service (or in the case of core benefits under a health plan, 6 months of service). An employee shall be excluded from consideration until the 1st day of the 1st month (or 1st day of a period of less than 31 days specified by the plan) beginning after completion of the period of service required under the preceding sentence.

(B) Employees who normally work less than 17½ hours per week.

(C) Employees who normally work during not more than 6 months during any year.

(D) Employees who have not attained age 21.

(E) Employees who are included in a unit of employees covered by an agreement which the Secretary finds to be a collective bargaining agreement between employee representatives and 1 or more employers if there is evidence that the type of benefits provided under the plan was the subject of good faith bargaining between the employee representatives and such employer or employers.

(F) Employees who are nonresident aliens and who receive no earned income (within the meaning of section 911(d)(2)) from the employer which constitutes income from sources within the United States (within the meaning of section 861(a)(3)).

(G) Employees who are students if—

(i) such students are performing services described in section 3121(b)(10), and

(ii) core health coverage is made available to such students by such employer.

Subparagraphs (A), (B), (C), and (D) shall be applied by substituting a shorter period of service, smaller number of hours or months, or lower age specified in the plan for the period of service, number of hours or months, or age (as the case may be) specified in such subparagraph.

(2) CERTAIN EXCLUSIONS NOT TO APPLY IF EXCLUDED EMPLOYEES COVERED.—Except to the extent provided in regulations, employees shall not be excluded from consideration under any subparagraph of paragraph (1) (other than subparagraph (F)) unless no employee described in such subparagraph (determined with regard to the last sentence of paragraph (1)) is eligible under the plan.

(3) EXCLUSION MUST APPLY TO ALL PLANS.—

(A) IN GENERAL.—An exclusion shall apply under any subparagraph of paragraph (1) (other than subparagraph (F) thereof) only if the exclusion applies to all statutory employee benefit plans of the employer of the same type. In the case of a cafeteria plan, all benefits under the cafeteria plan shall be treated as provided under plans of the same type.

(B) EXCEPTION.—Subparagraph (A) shall not apply to any difference in waiting periods for core and noncore benefits provided by health plans.

(4) EXCEPTION FOR SEPARATE LINE OF BUSINESS.—If any line of business is treated separately under subsection (g)(5), then paragraphs (2) and (3) shall be applied separately to such line of business.

(5) REQUIREMENTS MAY BE MET SEPARATELY WITH RESPECT TO EXCLUDED GROUP.—Notwithstanding paragraphs (2) and (3), if employees do not meet minimum age or service requirements described in paragraph (1) (without regard to the last sentence thereof) and are covered under a plan of the employer which meets the requirements of this section separately with respect to such employees, such employees may be excluded from consideration in determining whether any plan of the employer meets the requirements of this section.

(6) SPECIAL RULE FOR MULTIEMPLOYER PLAN.—Except as provided in regulations, any multiemployer plan shall not be taken into account in applying subparagraph (A), (B), (C), or (D) of paragraph (1) with respect to other plans of the employer. For purposes of this paragraph, a rule similar to the rule of subsection (g)(3)(E)(iii) shall apply.

Amendments

• 1988, Technical and Miscellaneous Revenue Act of 1988 (P.L. 100-647)

P.L. 100-647, §1011B(a)(7):

Amended Code Sec. 89(h)(1)(A) by inserting "(or 1st day of a period of less than 31 days specified by the plan)" after "month". **Effective** as if included in the provision of P.L. 99-514 to which it relates.

P.L. 100-647, §1011B(a)(28):

Amended Code Sec. 89(h)(4) by striking out "subsection (h)(5)" and inserting in lieu thereof "subsection (g)(5)". **Effective** as if included in the provision of P.L. 99-514 to which it relates.

P.L. 100-647, §3021(a)(5)(A):

Amended Code Sec. 89(h) by adding at the end thereof a new paragraph (6). **Effective** as if included in the amendments made by section 1151 of P.L. 99-514. For special transitional provisions appicable to Code Sec. 89, see Act Sec. 3021(c), in the Amendment Notes of Code Sec. 89(m).

P.L. 100-647, §3021(a)(5)(B):

Amended Code Sec. 89(h)(1) by adding after subparagraph (F) a new subparagraph (G). **Effective** as if included in the amendments made by section 1151 of P.L. 99-514. For special transitional provisions applicable to Code Sec. 89, see Act Sec. 3021(c), in the Amendment Notes following Code Sec. 89(m).

[Sec. 89(i)]

(i) STATUTORY EMPLOYEE BENEFIT PLAN.—For purposes of this section—

(1) IN GENERAL.—The term "statutory employee benefit plan" means—

(A) an accident or health plan (within the meaning of section 105(e)), and

(B) any plan of an employer for providing group-term life insurance (within the meaning of section 79).

(2) EMPLOYER MAY ELECT TO TREAT OTHER PLANS AS STATUTORY EMPLOYEE BENEFIT PLAN.—An employer may elect to treat any of the following plans as statutory employee benefit plans:

(A) A qualified group legal services plan (within the meaning of section 120(b)).

(B) An educational assistance program (within the meaning of section 127(b)).

(C) A dependent care assistance program (within the meaning of section 129(d)).

An election under this paragraph with respect to any plan shall apply with respect to all plans of the same type as such plan.

(3) PLANS OF THE SAME TYPE.—2 or more plans shall be treated as of the same type if such plans are described in the same subparagraph of paragraph (1) or (2).

(4) CHURCH PLANS.—The term "statutory employee benefit plan" shall not include a plan maintained by a church for church employees. For purposes of this paragraph, the term "church" has the meaning given such term by section 3121(w)(3)(A), including a qualified church-controlled organization (as defined in section 3121(w)(3)(B)).

Amendments

• 1988, Technical and Miscellaneous Revenue Act of 1988 (P.L. 100-647)

P.L. 100-647, §6051(a):

Amended Code Sec. 89(i) by adding at the end thereof a new paragraph (4). **Effective** as if included in the amendments made by section 1151 of P.L. 99-514. For special transitional provisions applicable to Code Sec. 89, see Act Sec. 3021(c), in the Amendment Notes of Code Sec. 89(m).

[Sec. 89(j)]

(j) OTHER DEFINITIONS AND SPECIAL RULES.—For purposes of this section—

(1) HIGHLY COMPENSATED EMPLOYEE.—The term "highly compensated employee" has the meaning given such term by section 414(q).

(2) HEALTH PLAN.—The term "health plan" means any plan described in paragraph (1)(A) of subsection (i).

(3) TREATMENT OF FORMER EMPLOYEES.—Except to the extent provided in regulations, this section shall be applied separately to former employees under requirements similar to the requirements that apply to employees.

(4) GROUP-TERM LIFE INSURANCE PLANS.—

(A) IN GENERAL.—Any group-term life insurance plan shall not be treated as 2 or more separate plans merely because the amount of life insurance under the plan on behalf of employees bears a uniform relationship to the compensation of such employees.

(B) LIMITATION ON COMPENSATION.—For purposes of subparagraph (A), compensation in excess of the amount applicable under section 401(a)(17) shall not be taken into account.

(C) LIMITATION.—This paragraph shall not apply to any plan if such plan is combined with plans of other types pursuant to an election under subsection (g)(4).

(D) COMPENSATION.—For purposes of applying this paragraph—

(i) IN GENERAL.—Compensation shall be determined on any basis determined by the employer which does not discriminate in favor of highly compensated employees.

(ii) SPECIAL RULES FOR 1989 AND 1990.—In the case of testing years beginning in 1989 or 1990, the employer may elect to treat base compensation as compensation.

(5) SPECIAL RULE FOR EMPLOYEES WORKING LESS THAN 30 HOURS PER WEEK.—Any health plan shall not fail to meet the requirements of this section merely because the employer-provided benefit is proportionately reduced for employees who normally work less than 30 hours per week.

(6) TREATMENT OF SELF-EMPLOYED INDIVIDUALS.—In the case of a statutory employee benefit plan—

(A) TREATMENT AS EMPLOYEE, ETC.—The term "employee" includes any self-employed individual (as defined in section 401(c)(1)), and the term "compensation" includes such individual's earned income (as defined in section 401(c)(2)).

(B) EMPLOYER.—An individual who owns the entire interest in an unincorporated trade or business shall be treated as his own employer. A partnership shall be treated as the employer of each partner who is treated as an employee under subparagraph (A).

(7) CERTAIN PLANS TREATED AS MEETING OTHER NONDISCRIMINATION REQUIREMENTS.—If an employer makes an election under subsection (i)(2) to have this section apply to any plan and such plan meets the requirements of this section, such plan shall be treated as meeting any other nondiscrimination requirement imposed on such plan (other than any requirement under section 120(c)(3), 127(b)(3), or 129(d)(4)).

(8) SPECIAL RULES FOR CERTAIN DISPOSITIONS OR ACQUISITIONS.—

(A) IN GENERAL.—If a person becomes, or ceases to be, a member of a group described in subsection (b), (c), (m), or (o) of section 414, then the requirements of this section shall be treated as having been met during the transition period with respect to any plan covering employees of such person or any other member of such group if—

(i) such requirements were met immediately before each such change, and

(ii) either—

(I) the coverage under such plan is not significantly changed during the transition period (other than by reason of the change in members in such group), or

(II) such plan meets such other requirements as the Secretary may prescribe by regulation.

(B) TRANSITION PERIOD.—For purposes of subparagraph (A), the term "transition period" means the period—

(i) beginning on the date of the change in members of a group, and

(ii) ending on the last day of the 1st plan year beginning after the date of such change.

(9) COORDINATION WITH MEDICARE, ETC.—If a plan may be coordinated with health benefits provided under any Federal, State, or foreign law or under any other health plan covering the employee or family member of the employee, such plan shall not fail to meet the requirements of this section with respect to health benefits merely because the amount of such benefits provided to any employee or family member of any employee are coordinated in a manner which does not discriminate in favor of highly compensated employees.

(10) DISABILITY BENEFITS.—

(A) IN GENERAL.—If a plan may be coordinated with disability benefits provided under any Federal, State, or foreign law or under any other plan covering the employee, such plan shall not fail to meet the requirements of this section with respect to disability benefits merely because the amount of such benefits provided to an employee are coordinated in a manner which does not discriminate in favor of highly compensated employees.

(B) CERTAIN DISABILITY PLANS EXEMPT FROM NONDISCRIMINATION RULES.—Subsection (a) shall not apply to any disability coverage other than disability coverage the benefits of which are excludable from gross income under section 105(b) or (c).

(11) SEPARATE APPLICATION IN THE CASE OF OPTIONS.—Except as provided in subsection (g)(1), each option or different benefit shall be treated as a separate plan.

(12) EMPLOYERS WITH ONLY HIGHLY COMPENSATED EMPLOYEES.—The requirements of subsections (d) and (e) shall not apply to any statutory employee benefit plan for any year for which the only employees of the employer maintaining the plan are highly compensated employees.

(13) TESTING YEAR.—The term "testing year" means—

(A) any 12-month period beginning with the calendar month designated in the plan for purposes of this section, or

(B) if there is no such designation, the calendar year.

No period may be designated under subparagraph (A) unless the same period is designated with respect to all other plans of the employer of the same type. Any designation under subparagraph (A) may be changed only with the consent of the Secretary.

Amendments

• 1988, Technical and Miscellaneous Revenue Act of 1988 (P.L. 100-647)

P.L. 100-647, §1011B(a)(8):

Amended Code Sec. 89(j) by adding at the end thereof new paragraph (12). **Effective** as if included in the provision of P.L. 99-514 to which it relates.

P.L. 100-647, §1011B(a)(21):

Amended Code Sec. 89(j)(6) by striking out "described in subparagraph (A), (B), or (C) of subsection (i)(2)" after "statutory employee benefit plan". **Effective** as if included in the provision of P.L. 99-514 to which it relates.

P.L. 100-647, §3021(a)(1)(B):

Amended Code Sec. 89(j) by adding at the end thereof a new paragraph (13). **Effective** as if included in the amendments made by section 1151 of P.L. 99-514.

P.L. 100-647, §3021(a)(9):

Amended Code Sec. 89(j)(11) by striking out "Each option" and inserting in lieu thereof "Except as provided in subsection (g)(1), each option". **Effective** as if included in the amendments made by section 1151 of P.L. 99-514.

P.L. 100-647, §3021(a)(12):

Amended Code Sec. 89(j)(5) by striking out the last sentence thereof. **Effective** as if included in the amendments made by section 1151 of P.L. 99-514. Prior to amendment, the last sentence of Code Sec. 89(j)(5) read as follows:

The preceding sentence shall apply only where the average work week of the employees who are not higly compensated employees is 30 hours or more.

P.L. 100-647, §3021(a)(13)(A):

Amended Code Sec. 89(j)(8)(A)(ii). **Effective** as if included in the amendments made by section 1151 of P.L. 99-514. Prior to amendment, Code Sec. 89(j)(8)(A)(ii) read as follows:

(ii) the coverage under such plan is not significantly changed during the transition period (other than by reason of the change in members of a group).

P.L. 100-647, §3021(b)(3)(A):

Amended Code Sec. 89(j)(4) by adding at the end thereof a new subparagraph (D). **Effective** for years beginning after 12-31-86.

P.L. 100-647, §3021(b)(3)(B):

Amended Code Sec. 89(j)(4)(A) by striking out "(within the meaning of section 414(s))" after "compensation". **Effective** for years beginning after 12-31-86.

For special transitional provisions applicable to Code Sec. 89, see Act Sec. 3021(c), in the Amendment Notes following Code Sec. 89(m).

[Sec. 89(k)]

(k) REQUIREMENT THAT PLAN BE IN WRITING, ETC.—

(1) IN GENERAL.—Notwithstanding any provision of part III of this subchapter, gross income of an employee shall include an amount equal to such employee's employer-provided benefit for the taxable year under an employee benefit plan to which this subsection applies unless, except to the extent provided in regulations—

(A) such plan is in writing,

(B) the employee's rights under such plan are legally enforceable,

(C) employees are provided reasonable notification of benefits available in the plan,

(D) such plan is maintained for the exclusive benefit of employees, and

(E) such plan was established with the intention of being maintained for an indefinite period of time.

Such inclusion shall be coordinated (under regulations prescribed by the Secretary) with any inclusion under subsection (a) with respect to such plan. In the case of a statutory employee benefit plan described in subsection (i)(1)(B), any amount required to be included in gross income under this subsection shall be included in the gross income of the beneficiary.

(2) PLANS TO WHICH SUBSECTION APPLIES.—This subsection shall apply to—

(A) any statutory employee benefit plan,

(B) a qualified tuition reduction program (within the meaning of section 117(d)),

(C) a cafeteria plan (within the meaning of section 125),

(D) a fringe benefit program providing no-additional-cost services, qualified employee discounts, or employer-operated eating facilities which are excludable from gross income under section 132, and

(E) a plan to which section 505 applies.

(3) SPECIAL RULE FOR DETERMINING INCLUSION.—For purposes of paragraph (1), an employee's employer-provided benefit shall be the value of the benefits provided to the employee.

(4) PLANS TO WHICH CONTRIBUTIONS ARE MADE BY MORE THAN 1 EMPLOYER.—For purposes of paragraph (1)(D), in the case of a plan to which contributions are made by more than 1 employer, each employer shall be treated as employing employees of all other employers.

(5) LOSS OF EXEMPTION FOR CERTAIN PLANS.—If a plan described in paragraph (2)(E) fails to meet the requirements of paragraph (1), the organization which is part of such plan shall not be exempt from tax under section 501(a).

Amendments

• 1988, Technical and Miscellaneous Revenue Act of 1988 (P.L. 100-647)

P.L. 100-647, §1011B(a)(9):

Amended Code Sec. 89(k) by adding at the end thereof new paragraph (5). **Effective** as if included in the provision of P.L. 99-514 to which it relates.

P.L. 100-647, §1011B(a)(29):

Amended Code Sec. 89(k)(1) by striking out the last sentence and inserting in lieu thereof two new sentences to read as above. **Effective** as if included in the provision of P.L. 99-514 to which it relates. Prior to amendment, the last sentence of Code Sec. 89(k)(1) read as follows:

Such inclusion shall be in lieu of any inclusion under subsection (a) with respect to such plan.

For special transitional provisions applicable to Code Sec. 89, see Act Sec. 3021(c), in the Amendment Notes following Code Sec. 89(m).

[Sec. 89(l)]

(l) REPORTING REQUIREMENTS.—

(1) IN GENERAL.—If an employee of an employer maintaining a plan is required to include any amount in gross income under this section for any testing year ending with or within a calendar year, the employer shall separately include such amount on the statement which the employer is required to provide the employee under section 6051(a) (and any statement required to be furnished under section 6051(d)).

(2) PENALTY.—For penalty for failing to report, see section 6652(k).

Amendments

• 1988, Technical and Miscellaneous Revenue Act of 1988 (P.L. 100-647)

P.L. 100-647, §1011B(a)(34):

Amended Code Sec. 89(l)(2) by striking out "6652(l)" and inserting in lieu thereof "6652(k)". **Effective** as if included in the provision of P.L. 99-514 to which it relates.

P.L. 100-647, §3021(a)(1)(A):

Amended Code Sec. 89, as amended by title I, by striking out "plan year" each place it appears and inserting in lieu thereof "testing year". **Effective** as if included in the provision of P.L. 99-514 to which it relates.

For special transitional provisions applicable to Code Sec. 89, see Act Sec. 3021(c), in the Amendment Notes following Code Sec. 89(m).

[Sec. 89(m)]

(m) REGULATIONS.—The Secretary shall prescribe such regulations as may be necessary or appropriate to carry out the purposes of this section, including regulations providing for appropriate adjustments in case of individuals not employees of the employer throughout the testing year.

Amendments

• 1989 (P.L. 101-136)

P.L. 101-136, §528, provides:

SEC. 528. No monies appropriated by this Act may be used to implement or enforce section 1151 of the Tax Reform Act of 1986 or the amendments made by such section.

• 1988, Technical and Miscellaneous Revenue Act of 1988 (P.L. 100-647)

P.L. 100-647, §3021(a)(1)(A):

Amended Code Sec. 89, as amended by title I, by striking out "plan year" each place it appears and inserting in lieu thereof "testing year". **Effective** as if included in the provision of P.L. 99-514 to which it relates.

P.L. 100-647, §3021(c) [Repealed by P.L. 101-140, §203(a)(7)], provides special transitional rules for purposes of Code Sec. 89.:

(c) TRANSITIONAL PROVISIONS FOR PURPOSES OF SECTION 89.—

(1) TEMPORARY VALUATION RULES.—In the case of testing years beginning before the later of January 1, 1991, or the date 1 year after the Secretary of the Treasury or his delegate first issues such valuation rules as are necessary to apply the provisions of section 89 of the 1986 Code to health plans (or if later the effective date of such rules)—

(A) Section 89(g)(3)(B) of the 1986 Code shall not apply.

(B)(i) Except as provided in clause (ii), the value of coverage under a health plan for purposes of section 89 of the 1986 Code shall be determined in substantially the same manner as costs under a health plan are determined under section 4980B(f)(4) of the 1986 Code.

(ii) For purposes of determining whether an employer meets the requirements of subsections (d), (e), and (f) of section 89 of the 1986 Code, value under clause (i) may be determined under any other reasonable method selected by the employer.

(2) FORMER EMPLOYEES.—The amendments made by section 1151 of the Reform Act shall not apply to former employees who separated from service with the employer before January 1, 1989 (and were not reemployed on or after such date), and such former employees shall not be taken into account in determining whether the requirements of section 89 of the 1986 Code are met with respect to other former employees. The preceding sentence shall not apply to the extent that—

(A) the value of employer-provided benefits provided to any such former employee exceeds the value of such benefits which were provided under the terms of the plan as in effect on December 31, 1988, or

(B) the employer-provided benefits provided to such former employees are modified so as to discriminate in favor of such former employees who are highly compensated employees.

Any excess value under the preceding sentence shall be determined without regard to any increase required by Federal law, regulation or rule or any increase which is the same for employees separating on or before December 31, 1988, and employees separating after such date and which does not discriminate in favor of highly compensated employees who separated from service after December 31, 1988.

(3) WRITTEN PLAN REQUIREMENT.—The requirements of section 89(k)(1)(A) of the 1986 Code shall be treated as met with respect to any testing year beginning in 1989, if—

(A) the plan is in writing before the close of such year,

(B) the employees had reasonable notice of the plan's essential features on or before the beginning of such year, and

(C) the provisions of the written plan apply for the entire year.

(4) RULES TO BE PRESCRIBED BEFORE NOVEMBER 15, 1988.—Not later than November 15, 1988, the Secretary of the Treasury

or his delegate shall issue such rules as may be necessary to carry out the provisions of section 89 of the 1986 Code.

• 1986, Tax Reform Act of 1986 (P.L. 99-514)

P.L. 99-514, §1151(a):

Amended part II of subchapter B of chapter 1 by adding at the end thereof new Code Sec. 89. For the **effective** date, see Act Sec. 1151(k) below.

P.L. 99-514, §1151(k), as amended by P.L. 100-647, §1011B(25)-(26), provides:

(k) EFFECTIVE DATES.—

(1) IN GENERAL.—The amendments made by this section shall apply to years beginning after the later of—

(A) December 31, 1987, or

(B) the earlier of—

(i) the date which is 3 months after the date on which the Secretary of the Treasury or his delegate issues such regulations as are necessary to carry out the provisions of section 89 of the Internal Revenue Code of 1986 (as added by this section), or

(ii) December 31, 1988

Notwithstanding the preceding sentence, the amendments made by subsections (e)(1) and (i)(3)(C) shall, to the extent they relate to sections 106, 162(i)(2), and 162(k) of the Internal Revenue Code of 1986, apply to years beginning after 1986.

(2) SPECIAL RULE FOR COLLECTIVE BARGAINING PLAN.—In the case of a plan maintained pursuant to 1 or more collective bargaining agreements between employee representatives and 1 or more employers ratified before March 1, 1986, the amendments made by this section shall not apply to employees covered by such an agreement in years beginning before the earlier of—

(A) the date on which the last of such collective bargaining agreements terminates (determined without regard to any extension thereof after February 28, 1986), or

(B) January 1, 1991.

A plan shall not be required to take into account employees to which the preceding sentence applies for purposes of applying section 89 of the Internal Revenue Code of 1986 (as added by this section) to employees to which the preceding sentence does not apply for any year preceding the year described in the preceding sentence.

(3) EXCEPTION FOR CERTAIN GROUP-TERM INSURANCE PLANS.—In the case of a plan described in section 223(d)(2) of the Tax Reform Act of 1984, such plan shall be treated as meeting the requirements of section 89 of the Internal Revenue Code of 1986 (as added by this section) with respect to individuals described in section 223(d)(2) of such Act. An employer may elect to disregard such individuals in applying section 89 of such Code (as so added) to other employees of the employer.

* * *

(6) CERTAIN PLANS MAINTAINED BY EDUCATIONAL INSTITUTIONS.—If an educational organization described in section 170(b)(1)(A)(ii) of the Internal Revenue Code of 1986 makes an election under this paragraph with respect to a plan described in section 125(c)(2)(C) of such Code, the amendments made by this section shall apply with respect to such plan for plan years beginning after the date of the enactment of this Act.

[Sec. 90]

SEC. 90. ILLEGAL FEDERAL IRRIGATION SUBSIDIES.

[Sec. 90(a)]

(a) GENERAL RULE.—Gross income shall include an amount equal to any illegal Federal irrigation subsidy received by the taxpayer during the taxable year.

[Sec. 90(b)]

(b) ILLEGAL FEDERAL IRRIGATION SUBSIDY.—For purposes of this section—

(1) IN GENERAL.—The term "illegal federal irrigation subsidy" means the excess (if any) of—

(A) the amount required to be paid for any Federal irrigation water delivered to the taxpayer during the taxpayer year, over

(B) the amount paid for such water.

(2) FEDERAL IRRIGATION WATER.—The term "Federal irrigation water" means any water made available for agricultural purposes from the operation of any reclamation or irrigation project referred to in paragraph (8) of section 202 of the Reclamation Reform Act of 1982.

[Sec. 90(c)]

(c) DENIAL OF DEDUCTION.—No deduction shall be allowed under this subtitle by reason of any inclusion in gross income under subsection (a).

Amendments

• 1987, Revenue Act of 1987 (P.L. 100-203)

P.L. 100-203, §10611(a):

Amended part II of subchapter B of chapter 1 by adding at the end thereof new Code Sec. 90. **Effective** for water delivered to the taxpayer in months beginning after 12-22-87.

PART III—ITEMS SPECIFICALLY EXCLUDED FROM GROSS INCOME

[Sec. 101]

SEC. 101. CERTAIN DEATH BENEFITS.

[Sec. 101(a)]

(a) PROCEEDS OF LIFE INSURANCE CONTRACTS PAYABLE BY REASON OF DEATH.—

(1) GENERAL RULE.—Except as otherwise provided in paragraph (2), subsection (d), subsection (f), and subsection (j), gross income does not include amounts received (whether in a single sum or otherwise) under a life insurance contract, if such amounts are paid by reason of the death of the insured.

(2) TRANSFER FOR VALUABLE CONSIDERATION.—In the case of a transfer for a valuable consideration, by assignment or otherwise, of a life insurance contract or any interest therein, the amount excluded from gross income by paragraph (1) shall not exceed an amount equal to the sum of the actual value of such consideration and the premiums and other amounts subsequently paid by the transferee. The preceding sentence shall not apply in the case of such a transfer—

(A) if such contract or interest therein has a basis for determining gain or loss in the hands of a transferee determined in whole or in part by reference to such basis of such contract or interest therein in the hands of the transferor, or

(B) if such transfer is to the insured, to a partner of the insured, to a partnership in which the insured is a partner, or to a corporation in which the insured is a shareholder or officer.

The term "other amounts" in the first sentence of this paragraph includes interest paid or accrued by the transferee on indebtedness with respect to such contract or any interest therein if such interest paid or accrued is not allowable as a deduction by reason of section 264(a)(4).

Amendments

• 2006, Pension Protection Act of 2006 (P.L. 109-280)

P.L. 109-280, §863(c)(1):

Amended Code Sec. 101(a)(1) by striking "and subsection (f)" and inserting "subsection (f), and subsection (j)". **Effective** for life insurance contracts issued after the date of the enactment of this Act, except for a contract issued after such date pursuant to an exchange described in Code Sec. 1035 for a contract issued on or prior to that date. For purposes of the preceding sentence, any material increase in the death benefit or other material change shall cause the contract to be treated as a new contract except that, in the case of a master contract (within the meaning of Code Sec. 264(f)(4)(E)), the addition of covered lives shall be treated as a new contract only with respect to such additional covered lives.

• 1997, Taxpayer Relief Act of 1997 (P.L. 105-34)

P.L. 105-34, §1084(b)(2) (as amended by P.L. 105-206, §6010(o)(3)(B)):

Amended Code Sec. 101(a)(2) by adding at the end a new flush sentence. For the **effective** date, see Act Sec. 1084(d), below.

P.L. 105-34, §1084(d), provides:

(d) EFFECTIVE DATE.—The amendments made by this section shall apply to contracts issued after June 8, 1997, in taxable years ending after such date. For purposes of the preceding sentence, any material increase in the death benefit or other material change in the contract shall be treated as a new contract except that, in the case of a master contract (within the meaning of section 264(f)(4)(E) of the Internal Revenue Code of 1986), the addition of covered lives shall be treated as a new contract only with respect to such additional covered lives. For purposes of this subsection, an increase in the death benefit under a policy or contract issued in connection with a lapse described in section 501(d)(2) of the Health Insurance Portability and Accountability Act of 1996 shall not be treated as a new contract.

• 1982, Tax Equity and Fiscal Responsibility Act of 1982 (P.L. 97-248)

P.L. 97-248, §266(b):

Amended Code Sec. 101(a)(1) by striking out "and in subsection (d)" and inserting in lieu thereof ", subsection (d), and subsection (f)". **Effective** for contracts entered into before 1-1-85 [**effective** date amended by P.L. 98-369, §221(h)(1).—CCH].

P.L. 97-248, §266(c)(2)-(3), as amended by P.L. 97-448, §306(a)(13), provides:

(2) Special rule for contracts entered into before January 1, 1983.—Any contract entered into before January 1, 1983, which meets the requirements of section 101(f) of the Internal Revenue Code of 1954 on the date which is 1 year after the date of the enactment of this Act shall be treated as meeting the requirements of such section for any period before the date on which such contract meets such requirements. Any death benefits paid under a flexible premium life insurance contract (within the meaning of section 101(f)(3)(A) of such Code before the date which is 1 year after such date of enactment shall be excluded from gross income.

(3) Special rule for certain contracts.—Any contract entered into before January 1, 1983, shall be treated as meeting the requirements of subparagraph (A) of section 101(f)(1) of such Code if such contract would meet such requirements if section 101(f)(2)(C) of such Code were applied by substituting "3 percent" for "4 percent".

[Sec. 101(b)—Repealed]

Amendments

• 1996, Small Business Job Protection Act of 1996 (P.L. 104-188)

P.L. 104-188, §1402(a):

Repealed Code Sec. 101(b). **Effective** with respect to decedents dying after 8-20-96. Prior to repeal, Code Sec. 101(b) read as follows:

(b) EMPLOYEES' DEATH BENEFITS.—

(1) GENERAL RULE.—Gross income does not include amounts received (whether in a single sum or otherwise) by the beneficiaries or the estate of an employee, if such amounts are paid by or on behalf of an employer and are paid by reason of the death of the employee.

(2) SPECIAL RULES FOR PARAGRAPH (1).—

(A) $5,000 LIMITATION.—The aggregate amounts excludable under paragraph (1) with respect to the death of any employee shall not exceed $5,000.

(B) NONFORFEITABLE RIGHTS.—Paragraph (1) shall not apply to amounts with respect to which the employee possessed, immediately before his death, a nonforfeitable right to receive the amounts while living. This subparagraph shall not apply to a lump sum distribution (as defined in section 402(e)(4))—

(i) by a stock bonus, pension, or profit-sharing trust described in section 401(a) which is exempt from tax under section 501(a),

(ii) under an annuity contract under a plan described in section 403(a), or

(iii) under an annuity contract purchased by an employer which is an organization referred to in section 170(b)(1)(A)(ii) or (vi) or which is a religious organization (other than a trust) and which is exempt from tax under section 501(a), but only with respect to that portion of such total distributions payable which bears the same ratio to the amount of such total distributions payable which is (without regard to this subsection) includible in gross income, as the amounts contributed by the employer for such annuity contract which are excludable from gross income under section 403(b) bear to the total amounts contributed by the employer for such annuity contract.

(C) JOINT AND SURVIVOR ANNUITIES.—Paragraph (1) shall not apply to amounts received by a surviving annuitant under a joint and survivor's annuity contract after the first day of the first period for which an amount was received as an annuity by the employee (or would have been received if the employee had lived).

(D) OTHER ANNUITIES.—In the case of any amount to which section 72 (relating to annuities, etc.) applies, the amount which is excludable under paragraph (1) (as modified by the preceding subparagraphs of this paragraph) shall be determined by reference to the value of such amount as of the day on which the employee died. Any amount so excludable under paragraph (1) shall, for purposes of section 72, be treated as additional consideration paid by the employee. Paragraph (1) shall not apply in the case of an annuity under chapter 73 of title 10 of the United States Code if the member or former member of the uniformed services by reason of whose death such annuity is payable died after attaining retirement age.

(3) TREATMENT OF SELF-EMPLOYED INDIVIDUALS.—For purposes of this subsection—

(A) SELF-EMPLOYED INDIVIDUAL NOT CONSIDERED EMPLOYEE.—Except as provided in subparagraph (B), the term "employee" does not include a self-employed individual described in section 401(c)(1).

(B) SPECIAL RULE FOR CERTAIN DISTRIBUTIONS.—In the case of any amount paid or distributed—

(i) by a trust described in section 401(a) which is exempt from tax under section 501(a), or

(ii) under a plan described in section 403(a),

the term "employee" includes a self-employed individual described in section 401(c)(1).

• 1984, Deficit Reduction Act of 1984 (P.L. 98-369)

P.L. 98-369, §713(e):

Amended Code Sec. 101(b)(3)(B). **Effective** as if included in the provision of P.L. 97-248 to which it relates. Prior to amendment, it read as follows:

(B) Special Rule for Certain Lump Sum Distributions.—In the case of any lump sum distribution described in the second sentence of paragraph (2)(B), the term "employee" includes a self-employed individual described in section 401(c)(1).

• 1982, Subchapter S Revision Act of 1982 (P.L. 97-354)

P.L. 97-354, §6(b)(2), provides:

"(2) ALLOWANCE OF EXCLUSION OF DEATH BENEFIT.—Notwithstanding section 241(b) of the Tax Equity and Fiscal Responsibility Act of 1982, in the case of amounts received under a plan of an S corporation, the amendment made by section 239 of such Act shall apply with respect to decedents dying after December 31, 1982."

• 1982, Tax Equity and Fiscal Responsibility Act of 1982 (P.L. 97-248)

P.L. 97-248, §239:

Amended Code Sec. 101(b)(3). **Effective** with respect to decedents dying after 12-31-83. Prior to amendment, Code Sec. 101(b)(3) read:

"(3) Self-employed individual not considered an employee.—For purposes of this subsection, the term `employee' does not include an individual who is an employee within the meaning of section 401(c)(1) (relating to self-employed individuals)."

• 1974, Employee Retirement Income Security Act of 1974 (P.L. 93-406)

P.L. 93-406, §2005(c)(15):

Amended Code Sec. 101(b)(2)(B) by substituting "a lump sum distribution (as defined in section 402(e)(4)" for "total distributions payable (as defined in section 402(a)(3)) which are paid to a distributee within one taxable year of the distributee by reason of the employee's death". **Effective** for distributions or payments made after 1973, in tax years beginning after 1973.

P.L. 93-406, §2008(b)(3):

Amended Code Sec. 101(b)(2)(D) by substituting "if the member or former member of the uniformed services by reason of whose death such annuity is payable" for "if the individual who made the election under such chapter." **Effective** with respect to individuals dying on or after 9-21-72.

• 1969, Tax Reform Act of 1969 (P.L. 91-172)

P.L. 91-172, §101(j)(1):

Amended Code Sec. 101(b)(2)(B)(iii) by substituting "section 170(b)(1)(A)(ii) or (vi) or which is a religious organization (other than a trust)" for "section 503(b)(1), (2), or (3)." **Effective** 1-1-70.

• 1966 (P.L. 89-365)

P.L. 89-365, §[1]:

Amended Code Sec. 101(b)(2)(D) by adding the last sentence. **Effective** with respect to individuals making an election under chapter 73 of title 10 of the United States Code who die after 12-31-65.

• 1962, Self-Employed Individuals Tax Retirement Act of 1962 (P.L. 87-792)

P.L. 87-792, §7:

Amended Code Sec. 101(b)(2)(B)(ii), and added at the end of Sec. 101(b) a new paragraph (3). **Effective** 1-1-63. Prior to amendment, Sec. 101(b)(2)(B)(ii) read as follows:

"(ii) under an annuity contract under a plan which meets the requirements of paragraphs (3), (4), (5), and (6) of section 401(a), or"

• 1958, Technical Amendments Act of 1958 (P.L. 85-866)

P.L. 85-866, §23(d):

Amended Sec. 101(b)(2)(B). **Effective** 1-1-58. Prior to amendment, Sec. 101(b)(2)(B) read as follows:

"(B) Nonforfeitable Rights.—Paragraph (1) shall not apply to amounts with respect to which the employee possessed, immediately before his death, a nonforfeitable right to receive the amounts while living (other than total distributions payable, as defined in section 402(a)(3), which are paid to a distributee, by a stock bonus, pension, or profit-sharing trust described in section 401(a) which is exempt from tax under section 501(a), or under an annuity contract under a plan which meets the requirements of paragraphs (3), (4), (5), and (6) of section 401(a), within one taxable year of the distributee by reason of the employee's death)."

[Sec. 101(c)]

(c) INTEREST.—If any amount excluded from gross income by subsection (a) is held under an agreement to pay interest thereon, the interest payments shall be included in gross income.

Amendments

• 1996, Small Business Job Protection Act of 1996 (P.L. 104-188)

P.L. 104-188, §1402(b)(1):

Amended Code Sec. 101(c) by striking "subsection (a) or (b)" and inserting "subsection (a)". **Effective** with respect to decedents dying after 8-20-96.

[Sec. 101(d)]

(d) PAYMENT OF LIFE INSURANCE PROCEEDS AT A DATE LATER THAN DEATH.—

(1) GENERAL RULE.—The amounts held by an insurer with respect to any beneficiary shall be prorated (in accordance with such regulations as may be prescribed by the Secretary) over the period or periods with respect to which such payments are to be made. There shall be excluded from the gross income of such beneficiary in the taxable year received any amount determined by such proration. Gross income includes, to the extent not excluded by the preceding sentence, amounts received under agreements to which this subsection applies.

(2) AMOUNT HELD BY AN INSURER.—An amount held by an insurer with respect to any beneficiary shall mean an amount to which subsection (a) applies which is—

(A) held by any insurer under an agreement provided for in the life insurance contract, whether as an option or otherwise, to pay such amount on a date or dates later than the death of the insured, and

(B) is equal to the value of such agreement to such beneficiary

(i) as of the date of death of the insured (as if any option exercised under the life insurance contract were exercised at such time), and

(ii) as discounted on the basis of the interest rate used by the insurer in calculating payments under the agreement and mortality tables prescribed by the Secretary.

(3) APPLICATION OF SUBSECTION.—This subsection shall not apply to any amount to which subsection (c) is applicable.

Amendments

• 1986, Tax Reform Act of 1986 (P.L. 99-514)

P.L. 99-514, §1001(a):

Amended the second sentence of Code Sec. 101(d)(1). **Effective** for amounts received with respect to deaths occurring after 10-22-86, in tax years ending after such date. Prior to amendment, the second sentence of Code Sec. 101(d)(1) read as follows:

There shall be excluded from the gross income of such beneficiary in the taxable year received—

(A) any amount determined by such proration, and

(B) in the case of the surviving spouse of the insured, that portion of the excess of the amounts received under one or more agreements specified in paragraph (2)(A) (whether or not payment of any part of such amounts is guaranteed by the insurer) over the amount determined in subparagraph (A) of this paragraph which is not greater than $1,000 with respect to any insured.

P.L. 99-514, §1001(b):

Amended Code Sec. 101(d)(2)(B)(ii). **Effective** for amounts received with respect to deaths occurring after 10-22-86, in tax years ending after such date. Prior to amendment, Code Sec. 101(d)(2)(B)(ii) read as follows:

(ii) as discounted on the basis of the interest rate and mortality tables used by the insurer in calculating payments under the agreement.

P.L. 99-514, §1001(c):

Amended Code Sec. 101(d) by striking out paragraph (3) and by redesignating paragraph (4) as paragraph (3). **Effective** for amounts received with respect to deaths occurring after 10-22-86, in tax years ending after such date. Prior to amendment, Code Sec. 101(d)(3) read as follows:

(3) SURVIVING SPOUSE.—For purposes of this subsection, the term "surviving spouse" means the spouse of the insured as of the date of death, including a spouse legally separated but not under a decree of absolute divorce.

• 1976, Tax Reform Act of 1976 (P.L. 94-455)

P.L. 94-455, §1906(b)(13)(A):

Amended 1954 Code by substituting "Secretary" for "Secretary or his delegate" each place it appeared. **Effective** 2-1-77.

[Sec. 101(e)—Repealed]

Amendments

• 1984, Deficit Reduction Act of 1984 (P.L. 98-369)

P.L. 98-369, §421(b)(2):

Repealed Code Sec. 101(e). **Effective** for transfers after 7-18-84, in tax years ending after such date. Prior to repeal, it read as follows:

(e) Alimony, etc., Payments.—

(1) In general.—This section shall not apply to so much of any payment as is includible in the gross income of the wife under section 71 (relating to alimony) or section 682 (relating to income of an estate or trust in case of divorce, etc.).

(2) Cross reference.—

For definition of "wife" see section 7701 (a) (17).

P.L. 98-369, §421(d)(2)-(4), provides:

(2) Election to Have Amendments Apply to Transfers After 1983.—If both spouses or former spouses make an election under this paragraph, the amendments made by this section shall apply to all transfers made by such spouses (or former spouses) after December 31, 1983.

(3) Exception for Transfers Pursuant to Existing Decrees.—Except in the case of an election under paragraph (2), the amendments made by this section shall not apply to transfers under any instrument in effect on or before the date of the enactment of this Act unless both spouses (or former spouses) elect to have such amendments apply to transfers under such instrument.

(4) Election.—Any election under paragraph (2) or (3) shall be made in such manner, at such time, and subject to such conditions, as the Secretary of the Treasury or his delegate may by regulations prescribe.

[Sec. 101(f)]

(f) PROCEEDS OF FLEXIBLE PREMIUM CONTRACTS ISSUED BEFORE JANUARY 1, 1985 PAYABLE BY REASON OF DEATH.—

(1) IN GENERAL.—Any amount paid by reason of the death of the insured under a flexible premium life insurance contract issued before January 1, 1985 shall be excluded from gross income only if—

(A) under such contract—

(i) the sum of the premiums paid under such contract does not at any time exceed the guidelines premium limitation as of such time, and

(ii) any amount payable by reason of the death of the insured (determined without regard to any qualified additional benefit) is not at any time less than the applicable percentage of the cash value of such contract at such time, or

(B) by the terms of such contract, the cash value of such contract may not at any time exceed the net single premium with respect to the amount payable by reason of the death of the insured (determined without regard to any qualified additional benefit) at such time.

(2) GUIDELINE PREMIUM LIMITATION.—For purposes of this subsection—

(A) GUIDELINE PREMIUM LIMITATION.—The term "guideline premium limitation" means, as of any date, the greater of—

(i) the guideline single premium, or

(ii) the sum of the guideline level premiums to such date.

(B) GUIDELINE SINGLE PREMIUM.—The term "guideline single premium" means the premium at issue with respect to future benefits under the contract (without regard to any qualified additional benefit), and with respect to any charges for qualified additional benefits, at the time of a determination under subparagraph (A) or (E) and which is based on—

(i) the mortality and other charges guaranteed under the contract, and

(ii) interest at the greater of an annual effective rate of 6 percent or the minimum rate or rates guaranteed upon isssue of the contract.

(C) GUIDELINE LEVEL PREMIUM.—The term "guideline level premium" means the level annual amount, payable over the longest period permitted under the contract (but ending not less than 20 years from date of issue or not later than age 95, if earlier), computed on the same basis as the guideline single premium, except that subparagraph (B)(ii) shall be applied by substituting "4 percent" for "6 percent".

(D) COMPUTATIONAL RULES.—In computing the guideline single premium or guideline level premium under subparagraph (B) or (C)—

(i) the excess of the amount payable by reason of the death of the insured (determined without regard to any qualified additional benefit) over the cash value of the contract shall be deemed to be not greater than such excess at the time the contract was issued,

(ii) the maturity date shall be the latest maturity date permitted under the contract, but not less than 20 years after the date of issue or (if earlier) age 95, and

(iii) the amount of any endowment benefit (or sum of endowment benefits) shall be deemed not to exceed the least amount payable by reason of the death of the insured (determined without regard to any qualified additional benefit) at any time under the contract.

(E) ADJUSTMENTS.—The guideline single premium and guideline level premium shall be adjusted in the event of a change in the future benefits or any qualified additional benefit under the contract which was not reflected in any guideline single premiums or guideline level premium previously determined.

(3) OTHER DEFINITIONS AND SPECIAL RULES.—For purposes of this subsection—

(A) FLEXIBLE PREMIUM LIFE INSURANCE CONTRACT.—The terms "flexible premium life insurance contract" and "contract" mean a life insurance contract (including any qualified additional benefits) which provides for the payment of one or more premiums which are not fixed by the insurer as to both timing and amount. Such terms do not include that portion of any contract which is treated under State law as providing any annuity benefits other than as a settlement option.

(B) PREMIUMS PAID.—The term "premiums paid" means the premiums paid under the contract less any amounts (other than amounts includible in gross income) to which section 72(e) applies. If, in order to comply with the requirements of paragraph (1)(A), any portion of any premium paid during any contract year is returned by the insurance company (with interest) within 60 days after the end of a contract year—

(i) the amount so returned (excluding interest) shall be deemed to reduce the sum of the premiums paid under the contract during such year, and

(ii) notwithstanding the provisions of section 72(e), the amount of any interest so returned shall be includible in the gross income of the recipient.

(C) APPLICABLE PERCENTAGE.—The term "applicable percentage" means—

(i) 140 percent in the case of an insured with an attained age at the beginning of the contract year of 40 or less, and

(ii) in the case of an insured with an attained age of more than 40 as of the beginning of the contract year, 140 percent reduced (but not below 105 percent) by one percent for each year in excess of 40.

(D) CASH VALUE.—The cash value of any contract shall be determined without regard to any deduction for any surrender charge or policy loan.

(E) QUALIFIED ADDITIONAL BENEFITS.—The term "qualified additional benefits" means any—

(i) guaranteed insurability,

(ii) accidental death benefit,

(iii) family term coverage, or

(iv) waiver of premium.

(F) PREMIUM PAYMENTS NOT DISQUALIFYING CONTRACT.—The payment of a premium which would result in the sum of the premiums paid exceeding the guideline premium limitation shall be disregarded for purposes of paragraph (1)(A)(i) if the amount of such premium does not exceed the amount necessary to prevent the termination of the contract without cash value on or before the end of the contract year.

(G) NET SINGLE PREMIUM.—In computing the net single premium under paragraph (1)(B)—

(i) the mortality basis shall be that guaranteed under the contract (determined by reference to the most recent mortality table allowed under all State laws on the date of issuance),

(ii) interest shall be based on the greater of—

(I) an annual effective rate of 4 percent (3 percent for contracts issued before July 1, 1983), or

(II) the miminum rate or rates guaranteed upon issue of the contract, and

(iii) the computational rules of paragraph (2)(D) shall apply, except that the maturity date referred to in clause (ii) thereof shall not be earlier than age 95.

(H) CORRECTION OF ERRORS.—If the taxpayer establishes to the satisfaction of the Secretary that—

(i) the requirements described in paragraph (1) for any contract year was not satisfied due to reasonable error, and

(ii) reasonable steps are being taken to remedy the error,

the Secretary may waive the failure to satisfy such requirements.

(l) REGULATIONS.—The Secretary shall prescribe such regulations as may be necessary or appropriate to carry out the purposes of this subsection.

Amendments

• 1984, Deficit Reduction Act of 1984 (P.L. 98-369)

P.L. 98-369, §221(b)(2)(A):

Amended Code Sec. 101(f)(1) by striking out "flexible premium life insurance contract" and inserting in lieu thereof "flexible premium life insurance contract issued before January 1, 1985". **Effective** 1-1-84. For a transitional rule see P.L. 98-369, §221(b)(3), below.

P.L. 98-369, §221(b)(2)(B):

Amended the subsection heading of Code Sec. 101(f) by striking out "Flexible Premium Contracts" and inserting in lieu thereof "Flexible Premium Contracts Issued Before January 1, 1985". **Effective** 1-1-84. For a transitional rule see P.L. 98-369, §221(b)(3), below.

P.L. 98-369, §221(b)(3), as added by P.L. 99-514, §1825(d), provides:

(3) Transitional Rule.—Any flexible premium contract issued during 1984 which meets the requirements of section 7702 of the Internal Revenue Code of 1954 (as added by this section) shall be treated as meeting the requirements of section 101(f) of such Code.

• 1982, Tax Equity and Fiscal Responsibility Act of 1982 (P.L. 97-248)

P.L. 97-248, §266(a) (as amended by P.L. 98-369, §221(b)(1)):

Amended Code Sec. 101 by adding at the end thereof new subsection (f). **Effective** for contracts entered into before 1-1-85 [**effective** date changed by P.L. 98-369]. For an exception, see amendment note for P.L. 97-248, Act Sec. 266(c)(2), (3), under Code Sec. 101(a).

• 1976, Tax Reform Act of 1976 (P.L. 94-455)

P.L. 94-455, §1901(a)(16):

Repealed Code Sec. 101(f). **Effective** with respect to tax years beginning after 12-31-76. Prior to repeal, Code Sec. 101(f) read as follows:

(f) Effective Date of Section.—This section shall apply only to amounts received by reason of the death of an insured or an employee occurring after the date of enactment of this title. Section 22(b)(1) of the Internal Revenue Code of 1939 shall apply to amounts received by reason of the death of an insured or an employee occurring on or before such date.

[Sec. 101(g)]

(g) TREATMENT OF CERTAIN ACCELERATED DEATH BENEFITS.—

(1) IN GENERAL.—For purposes of this section, the following amounts shall be treated as an amount paid by reason of the death of an insured:

(A) Any amount received under a life insurance contract on the life of an insured who is a terminally ill individual.

(B) Any amount received under a life insurance contract on the life of an insured who is a chronically ill individual.

(2) TREATMENT OF VIATICAL SETTLEMENTS.—

(A) IN GENERAL.—If any portion of the death benefit under a life insurance contract on the life of an insured described in paragraph (1) is sold or assigned to a viatical settlement provider, the amount paid for the sale or assignment of such portion shall be treated as an amount paid under the life insurance contract by reason of the death of such insured.

(B) VIATICAL SETTLEMENT PROVIDER.—

(i) IN GENERAL.—The term "viatical settlement provider" means any person regularly engaged in the trade or business of purchasing, or taking assignments of, life insurance contracts on the lives of insureds described in paragraph (1) if—

(I) such person is licensed for such purposes (with respect to insureds described in the same subparagraph of paragraph (1) as the insured) in the State in which the insured resides, or

(II) in the case of an insured who resides in a State not requiring the licensing of such persons for such purposes with respect to such insured, such person meets the requirements of clause (ii) or (iii), whichever applies to such insured.

(ii) TERMINALLY ILL INSUREDS.—A person meets the requirements of this clause with respect to an insured who is a terminally ill individual if such person—

(I) meets the requirements of sections 8 and 9 of the Viatical Settlements Model Act of the National Association of Insurance Commissioners, and

(II) meets the requirements of the Model Regulations of the National Association of Insurance Commissioners (relating to standards for evaluation of reasonable payments) in determining amounts paid by such person in connection with such purchases or assignments.

(iii) CHRONICALLY ILL INSUREDS.—A person meets the requirements of this clause with respect to an insured who is a chronically ill individual if such person—

(I) meets requirements similar to the requirements referred to in clause (ii)(I), and

(II) meets the standards (if any) of the National Association of Insurance Commissioners for evaluating the reasonableness of amounts paid by such person in connection with such purchases or assignments with respect to chronically ill individuals.

(3) SPECIAL RULES FOR CHRONICALLY ILL INSUREDS.—In the case of an insured who is a chronically ill individual—

(A) IN GENERAL.—Paragraphs (1) and (2) shall not apply to any payment received for any period unless—

(i) such payment is for costs incurred by the payee (not compensated for by insurance or otherwise) for qualified long-term care services provided for the insured for such period, and

(ii) the terms of the contract giving rise to such payment satisfy—

(I) the requirements of section 7702B(b)(1)(B), and

(II) the requirements (if any) applicable under subparagraph (B).

For purposes of the preceding sentence, the rule of section 7702B(b)(2)(B) shall apply.

(B) OTHER REQUIREMENTS.—The requirements applicable under this subparagraph are—

(i) those requirements of section 7702B(g) and section 4980C which the Secretary specifies as applying to such a purchase, assignment, or other arrangement,

(ii) standards adopted by the National Association of Insurance Commissioners which specifically apply to chronically ill individuals (and, if such standards are adopted, the analogous requirements specified under clause (i) shall cease to apply), and

(iii) standards adopted by the State in which the policyholder resides (and if such standards are adopted, the analogous requirements specified under clause (i) and (subject to section 4980C(f)) standards under clause (ii), shall cease to apply).

(C) PER DIEM PAYMENTS.—A payment shall not fail to be described in subparagraph (A) by reason of being made on a per diem or other periodic basis without regard to the expenses incurred during the period to which the payment relates.

(D) LIMITATION ON EXCLUSION FOR PERIODIC PAYMENTS.—For limitation on amount of periodic payments which are treated as described in paragraph (1), see section 7702B(d).

(4) DEFINITIONS.—For purposes of this subsection—

(A) TERMINALLY ILL INDIVIDUAL.—The term "terminally ill individual" means an individual who has been certified by a physician as having an illness or physical condition which can reasonably be expected to result in death in 24 months or less after the date of the certification.

(B) CHRONICALLY ILL INDIVIDUAL.—The term "chronically ill individual" has the meaning given such term by section 7702B(c)(2); except that such term shall not include a terminally ill individual.

(C) QUALIFIED LONG-TERM CARE SERVICES.—The term "qualified long-term care services" has the meaning given such term by section 7702B(c).

(D) PHYSICIAN.—The term "physician" has the meaning given to such term by section 1861(r)(1) of the Social Security Act (42 U.S.C. 1395x(r)(1)).

(5) EXCEPTION FOR BUSINESS-RELATED POLICIES.—This subsection shall not apply in the case of any amount paid to any taxpayer other than the insured if such taxpayer has an insurable interest with respect to the life of the insured by reason of the insured being a director, officer, or employee of the taxpayer or by reason of the insured being financially interested in any trade or business carried on by the taxpayer.

Amendments

• 1996, Health Insurance Portability and Accountability Act of 1996 (P.L. 104-191)

P.L. 104-191, §331(a):

Amended Code Sec. 101 by adding at the end a new subsection (g). **Effective** for amounts received after 12-31-96.

[Sec. 101(h)]

(h) SURVIVOR BENEFITS ATTRIBUTABLE TO SERVICE BY A PUBLIC SAFETY OFFICER WHO IS KILLED IN THE LINE OF DUTY.—

(1) IN GENERAL.—Gross income shall not include any amount paid as a survivor annuity on account of the death of a public safety officer (as such term is defined in section 1204 of the Omnibus Crime Control and Safe Streets Act of 1968) killed in the line of duty—

(A) if such annuity is provided, under a governmental plan which meets the requirements of section 401(a), to the spouse (or a former spouse) of the public safety officer or to a child of such officer; and

(B) to the extent such annuity is attributable to such officer's service as a public safety officer.

(2) EXCEPTIONS.—Paragraph (1) shall not apply with respect to the death of any public safety officer if, as determined in accordance with the provisions of the Omnibus Crime Control and Safe Streets Act of 1968—

(A) the death was caused by the intentional misconduct of the officer or by such officer's intention to bring about such officer's death;

(B) the officer was voluntarily intoxicated (as defined in section 1204 of such Act) at the time of death;

(C) the officer was performing such officer's duties in a grossly negligent manner at the time of death; or

(D) the payment is to an individual whose actions were a substantial contributing factor to the death of the officer.

Amendments

• 1997, Taxpayer Relief Act of 1997 (P.L. 105-34)

P.L. 105-34, §1528(a):

Amended Code Sec. 101 by adding a new subsection (h). **Effective** for amounts received in tax years beginning after 12-31-96, with respect to individuals dying after such date, and to amounts received in tax years beginning after 12-31-2001, with respect to individuals dying on or before 12-31-96. [**effective** date amended by P.L. 107-15, §2.]

[Sec. 101(i)]

(i) CERTAIN EMPLOYEE DEATH BENEFITS PAYABLE BY REASON OF DEATH OF CERTAIN TERRORIST VICTIMS OR ASTRONAUTS.—

(1) IN GENERAL.—Gross income does not include amounts (whether in a single sum or otherwise) paid by an employer by reason of the death of an employee who is a specified terrorist victim (as defined in section 692(d)(4)).

(2) LIMITATION.—

(A) IN GENERAL.—Subject to such rules as the Secretary may prescribe, paragraph (1) shall not apply to amounts which would have been payable after death if the individual had died other than as a specified terrorist victim (as so defined).

(B) EXCEPTION.—Subparagraph (A) shall not apply to incidental death benefits paid from a plan described in section 401(a) and exempt from tax under section 501(a).

(3) TREATMENT OF SELF-EMPLOYED INDIVIDUALS.—For purposes of paragraph (1), the term "employee" includes a self-employed individual (as defined in section 401(c)(1)).

(4) RELIEF WITH RESPECT TO ASTRONAUTS.—The provisions of this subsection shall apply to any astronaut whose death occurs in the line of duty.

Amendments

• 2003, Military Family Tax Relief Act of 2003 (P.L. 108-121)

P.L. 108-121, §110(b)(1):

Amended Code Sec. 101(i) by adding at the end a new paragraph (4). **Effective** for amounts paid after 12-31-2002, with respect to deaths occurring after such date.

P.L. 108-121, §110(b)(2):

Amended the heading for Code Sec. 101(i) by inserting "OR ASTRONAUTS" after "VICTIMS". **Effective** for amounts paid after 12-31-2002, with respect to deaths occurring after such date.

• 2002, Victims of Terrorism Tax Relief Act of 2001 (P.L. 107-134)

P.L. 107-134, §102(a):

Amended Code Sec. 101 by adding at the end a new subsection (i). **Effective** for tax years ending before, on, or after 9-11-2001. For a waiver of limitations, see Act Sec. 102(b)(2), below.

P.L. 107-134, §102(b)(2), provides:

(2) WAIVER OF LIMITATIONS.—If refund or credit of any overpayment of tax resulting from the amendments made by this section is prevented at any time before the close of the 1-year period beginning on the date of the enactment of this Act by the operation of any law or rule of law (including res judicata), such refund or credit may nevertheless be made or allowed if claim therefor is filed before the close of such period.

[Sec. 101(j)]

(j) TREATMENT OF CERTAIN EMPLOYER-OWNED LIFE INSURANCE CONTRACTS.—

(1) GENERAL RULE.—In the case of an employer-owned life insurance contract, the amount excluded from gross income of an applicable policyholder by reason of paragraph (1) of subsection (a) shall not exceed an amount equal to the sum of the premiums and other amounts paid by the policyholder for the contract.

(2) EXCEPTIONS.—In the case of an employer-owned life insurance contract with respect to which the notice and consent requirements of paragraph (4) are met, paragraph (1) shall not apply to any of the following:

(A) EXCEPTIONS BASED ON INSURED'S STATUS.—Any amount received by reason of the death of an insured who, with respect to an applicable policyholder—

(i) was an employee at any time during the 12-month period before the insured's death, or

(ii) is, at the time the contract is issued—

(I) a director,

(II) a highly compensated employee within the meaning of section 414(q) (without regard to paragraph (1)(B)(ii) thereof), or

(III) a highly compensated individual within the meaning of section 105(h)(5), except that "35 percent" shall be substituted for "25 percent" in subparagraph (C) thereof.

(B) EXCEPTION FOR AMOUNTS PAID TO INSURED'S HEIRS.—Any amount received by reason of the death of an insured to the extent—

(i) the amount is paid to a member of the family (within the meaning of section 267(c)(4)) of the insured, any individual who is the designated beneficiary of the insured under the contract (other than the applicable policyholder), a trust established for the benefit of any such member of the family or designated beneficiary, or the estate of the insured, or

(ii) the amount is used to purchase an equity (or capital or profits) interest in the applicable policyholder from any person described in clause (i).

(3) EMPLOYER-OWNED LIFE INSURANCE CONTRACT.—

(A) IN GENERAL.—For purposes of this subsection, the term "employer-owned life insurance contract" means a life insurance contract which—

(i) is owned by a person engaged in a trade or business and under which such person (or a related person described in subparagraph (B)(ii)) is directly or indirectly a beneficiary under the contract, and

(ii) covers the life of an insured who is an employee with respect to the trade or business of the applicable policyholder on the date the contract is issued.

For purposes of the preceding sentence, if coverage for each insured under a master contract is treated as a separate contract for purposes of sections 817(h), 7702, and 7702A, coverage for each such insured shall be treated as a separate contract.

(B) APPLICABLE POLICYHOLDER.—For purposes of this subsection—

(i) IN GENERAL.—The term "applicable policyholder" means, with respect to any employer-owned life insurance contract, the person described in subparagraph (A)(i) which owns the contract.

(ii) RELATED PERSONS.—The term "applicable policyholder" includes any person which—

(I) bears a relationship to the person described in clause (i) which is specified in section 267(b) or 707(b)(1), or

(II) is engaged in trades or businesses with such person which are under common control (within the meaning of subsection (a) or (b) of section 52).

(4) NOTICE AND CONSENT REQUIREMENTS.—The notice and consent requirements of this paragraph are met if, before the issuance of the contract, the employee—

(A) is notified in writing that the applicable policyholder intends to insure the employee's life and the maximum face amount for which the employee could be insured at the time the contract was issued,

(B) provides written consent to being insured under the contract and that such coverage may continue after the insured terminates employment, and

(C) is informed in writing that an applicable policyholder will be a beneficiary of any proceeds payable upon the death of the employee.

(5) DEFINITIONS.—For purposes of this subsection—

(A) EMPLOYEE.—The term "employee" includes an officer, director, and highly compensated employee (within the meaning of section 414(q)).

(B) INSURED.—The term "insured" means, with respect to an employer-owned life insurance contract, an individual covered by the contract who is a United States citizen or resident. In the case of a contract covering the joint lives of 2 individuals, references to an insured include both of the individuals.

Amendments

• 2006, Pension Protection Act of 2006 (P.L. 109-280)

P.L. 109-280, §863(a):

Amended Code Sec. 101 by adding at the end a new subsection (j). **Effective** for life insurance contracts issued after the date of the enactment of this Act, except for a contract issued after such date pursuant to an exchange described in Code Sec. 1035 for a contract issued on or prior to that date. For purposes of the preceding sentence, any material increase in the death benefit or other material change shall cause the contract to be treated as a new contract except that, in the case of a master contract (within the meaning of Code Sec. 264(f)(4)(E)), the addition of covered lives shall be treated as a new contract only with respect to such additional covered lives.

[Sec. 102]

SEC. 102. GIFTS AND INHERITANCES.

[Sec. 102(a)]

(a) GENERAL RULE.—Gross income does not include the value of property acquired by gift, bequest, devise, or inheritance.

[Sec. 102(b)]

(b) INCOME.—Subsection (a) shall not exclude from gross income—

(1) the income from any property referred to in subsection (a); or

(2) where the gift, bequest, devise, or inheritance is of income from property, the amount of such income.

Where, under the terms of the gift, bequest, devise, or inheritance, the payment, crediting, or distribution thereof is to be made at intervals, then, to the extent that it is paid or credited or to be distributed out of income from property, it shall be treated for purposes of paragraph (2) as a gift, bequest, devise, or inheritance of income from property. Any amount included in the gross income of a beneficiary under subchapter J shall be treated for purposes of paragraph (2) as a gift, bequest, devise, or inheritance of income from property.

[Sec. 102(c)]

(c) EMPLOYEE GIFTS.—

(1) IN GENERAL.— Subsection (a) shall not exclude from gross income any amount transferred by or for an employer to, or for the benefit of, an employee.

(2) CROSS REFERENCES.—

For provisions excluding certain employee achievement awards from gross income, see section 74(c).

For provisions excluding certain de minimis fringes from gross income, see section 132(e).

Amendments

• 1986, Tax Reform Act of 1986 (P.L. 99-514)

P.L. 99-514, §122(b):

Amended Code Sec. 102 by adding at the end thereof new subsection (c). **Effective** for prizes and awards granted after 12-31-86.

[Sec. 103]

SEC. 103. INTEREST ON STATE AND LOCAL BONDS.

[Sec. 103(a)]

(a) EXCLUSION.—Except as provided in subsection (b), gross income does not include interest on any State or local bond.

[Sec. 103(b)]

(b) EXCEPTIONS.—Subsection (a) shall not apply to—

(1) PRIVATE ACTIVITY BOND WHICH IS NOT A QUALIFIED BOND.—Any private activity bond which is not a qualified bond (within the meaning of section 141).

(2) ARBITRAGE BOND.—Any arbitrage bond (within the meaning of section 148).

(3) BOND NOT IN REGISTERED FORM, ETC.—Any bond unless such bond meets the applicable requirements of section 149.

[Sec. 103(c)]

(c) DEFINITIONS.—For purposes of this section and part IV—

(1) STATE OR LOCAL BOND.—The term "State or local bond" means an obligation of a state or political subdivision thereof.

(2) STATE.—The term "State" includes the District of Columbia and any possession of the United States.

Amendments

• 1998, IRS Restructuring and Reform Act of 1998 (P.L. 105-206)

P.L. 105-206, §3105, provides:

SEC. 3105. ADMINISTRATIVE APPEAL OF ADVERSE INTERNAL REVENUE SERVICE DETERMINATION OF TAX-EXEMPT STATUS OF BOND ISSUE.

The Internal Revenue Service shall amend its administrative procedures to provide that if, upon examination, the Internal Revenue Service proposes to an issuer that interest on previously issued obligations of such issuer is not excludable from gross income under section 103(a) of the Internal Revenue Code of 1986, the issuer of such obligations shall have an administrative appeal of right to a senior officer of the Internal Revenue Service Office of Appeals.

• 1988, Technical and Miscellaneous Revenue Act of 1988 (P.L. 100-647)

P.L. 100-647, §1013(c)(11)(E), provides:

(E) A refunding bond issued before July 1, 1987, shall be treated as meeting the requirement of subparagraph (A) of section 1313(c)(1) of the Reform Act if such bond met the requirement of such subparagraph as in effect before the amendments made by this paragraph.

P.L. 100-647, §1013(c)(12)(A):

Amended Code Sec. 103(b)(6)(N) by redesignating clauses (ii) and (iii) as clauses (iii) and (iv), respectively, and by striking out clause (i) and inserting in lieu thereof new clauses (i) and (ii). **Effective** as if included in the provision of P.L. 99-514 to which it relates. Prior to amendment, clause (i) read as follows:

(i) IN GENERAL.—This paragraph shall not apply to any obligation issued after December 31, 1986 (including any obligations issued to refund an obligation issued on or before such date).

P.L. 100-647, §1013(a)(34)(A):

Amended Code Sec. 103(c)(7) of the Internal Revenue Code of 1954 (as in effect on the day before the date of the enactment of P.L. 99-514) by striking out "necessary" and inserting in lieu thereof "necessary". **Effective** for obligations sold after 5-2-78, and to which Treasury Reg. §1.103-13 (1979) was provided to apply.

• **1986, Tax Reform Act of 1986 (P.L. 99-514)**

P.L. 99-514, §1301(a):

Amended Code Sec. 103. **Effective** for bonds issued after 8-15-86. See, however, the special rules provided in Act Secs. 1312-1317, below. Prior to amendment, Code Sec. 103 read as follows:

SEC. 103. INTEREST ON CERTAIN GOVERNMENTAL OBLIGATIONS.

[Sec. 103(a)]

(a) GENERAL RULE.—Gross income does not include interest on—

(1) the obligations of a State, a Territory, or a possession of the United States, or any political subdivision of any of the foregoing, or of the District of Columbia; and

(2) qualified scholarship funding bonds.

Amendments

• **1976, Tax Reform Act of 1976 (P.L. 94-455)**

P.L. 94-455, §1901(a):

Amended Code Sec. 103(a) by adding "and" at the end of paragraph (1), by striking out paragraphs (2) and (3), and by renumbering paragraph (4) as paragraph (2). **Effective** for tax years beginning after 12-31-76. Prior to repeal, paragraphs (2) and (3) read as follows:

(2) the obligations of the United States;

(3) the obligations of a corporation organized under Act of Congress, if such corporation is an instrumentality of the United States and if under the respective Acts authorizing the issue of the obligations the interest is wholly exempt from the taxes imposed by this subtitle; or

P.L. 94-455, §2105(a):

Amended Code Sec. 103(a) by striking out "or" at the end of paragraph (2), inserting "; or" in place of the period at the end of paragraph (3), and adding a new paragraph (4). **Effective** with respect to obligations issued on or after 10-4-76.

[Sec. 103(b)]

(b) INDUSTRIAL DEVELOPMENT BONDS.—

(1) SUBSECTION (a)(1) OR (2) NOT TO APPLY.—Except as otherwise provided in this subsection, any industrial development bond shall be treated as an obligation not described in subsection (a)(1) or (2).

(2) INDUSTRIAL DEVELOPMENT BOND.—For purposes of this section, the term "industrial development bond" means any obligation—

(A) which is issued as part of an issue all or a major portion of the proceeds of which are to be used directly or indirectly in any trade or business carried on by any person who is not an exempt person (within the meaning of paragraph (3)), and

(B) the payment of the principal or interest on which (under the terms of such obligation or any underlying arrangement) is, in whole or in major part—

(i) secured by any interest in property used or to be used in a trade or business or in payments in respect of such property, or

(ii) to be derived from payments in respect of property, or borrowed money, used or to be used in a trade or business.

(3) EXEMPT PERSON.—For purposes of paragraph (2)(A), the term "exempt person" means—

(A) a governmental unit, or

(B) an organization described in section 501(c)(3) and exempt from tax under section 501(a) (but only with respect to a trade or business carried on by such organization which is not an unrelated trade or business, determined by applying section 513(a) to such organization).

(4) CERTAIN EXEMPT ACTIVITIES.—Paragraph (1) shall not apply to any obligation which is issued as part of an issue substantially all of the proceeds of which are to be used to provide—

(A) projects for residential rental property if at all times during the qualified project period—

(i) 15 percent or more in the case of targeted area projects, or

(ii) 20 percent or more in the case of any other project,

of the units in each project are to be occupied by individuals of low or moderate income,

(B) sports facilities,

(C) convention or trade show facilities,

(D) airports, docks, wharves, mass commuting facilities, parking facilities, or storage or training facilities directly related to any of the foregoing,

(E) sewage or solid waste disposal facilities or facilities for the local furnishing of electric energy or gas,

(F) air or water pollution control facilities,

(G) facilities for the furnishing of water for any purpose if—

(i) the water is or will be made available to members of the general public (including electric utility, industrial, agricultural, or commercial users), and

(ii) either the facilities are operated by a governmental unit or the rates for the furnishing or sale of the water have been established or approved by a State or political subdivision thereof, by an agency or instrumentality of the United States, or by a public service or public utility commission or other similar body of any State or political subdivision thereof,

(H) qualified hydroelectric generating facilities,

(I) qualified mass commuting vehicles, or

(J) local district heating or cooling facilities.

For purposes of subparagraph (E), the local furnishing of electric energy or gas from a facility shall include furnishing solely within the area consisting of a city and 1 contiguous county. For purposes of subparagraph (A), any property shall not be treated as failing to be residential rental property merely because part of the building in which such property is located is used for purposes other than residential rental purposes.

(5) INDUSTRIAL PARKS.—Paragraph (1) shall not apply to any obligation issued as part of an issue substantially all of the proceeds of which are to be used for the acquisition or development of land as the site for an industrial park. For purposes of the preceding sentence, the term "development of land" includes the provision of water, sewage, drainage, or similar facilities, or of transportation, power, or communication facilities, which are incidental to use of the site as an industrial park, but, except with respect to such facilities, does not include the provision of structures or buildings.

(6) EXEMPTION FOR CERTAIN SMALL ISSUES.—

(A) IN GENERAL.—Paragraph (1) shall not apply to any obligation issued as part of an issue the aggregate authorized face amount of which is $1,000,000 or less and substantially all of the proceeds of which are to be used (i) for the acquisition, construction, reconstruction, or improvement of land or property of a character subject to the allowance for depreciation, or (ii) to redeem part or all of a prior issue which was issued for purposes described in clause (i) or this clause.

(B) CERTAIN PRIOR ISSUES TAKEN INTO ACCOUNT.—If—

(i) the proceeds of two or more issues of obligations (whether or not the issuer of each such issue is the same) are or will be used primarily with respect to facilities located in the same incorporated municipality or located in the same county (but not in any incorporated municipality),

(ii) the principal user of such facilities is or will be the same person or two or more related persons, and

(iii) but for this subparagraph, subparagraph (A) would apply to each such issue,

then, for purposes of subparagraph (A), in determining the aggregate face amount of any later issue there shall be taken into account the face amount of obligations issued under all prior such issues and outstanding at the time of such later issue (not including as outstanding any obligation which is to be redeemed from the proceeds of the later issue).

(C) RELATED PERSONS.—For purposes of this paragraph and paragraph (13), a person is a related person to another person if—

(i) the relationship between such persons would result in a disallowance of losses under section 267 or 707(b), or

(ii) such persons are members of the same controlled group of corporations (as defined in section 1563(a), except that "more than 50 percent" shall be substituted for "at least 80 percent" each place it appears therein).

(D) $10,000,000 LIMIT IN CERTAIN CASES.—At the election of the issuer, made at such time and in such manner as the Secretary shall by regulations prescribe, with respect to any issue this paragraph shall be applied—

(i) by substituting "$10,000,000" for "$1,000,000" in subparagraph (A), and

(ii) in determining the aggregate face amount of such issue, by taking into account not only the amount described in subparagraph (B), but also the aggregate amount of capital expenditures with respect to facilities described in subparagraph (E) paid or incurred during the 6-year period beginning 3 years before the date of such issue and ending 3 years after such date (and financed otherwise than out of the proceeds of outstanding issues to which subparagraph (A) applied), as if the aggregate amount of such capital expenditures constituted the face amount of a prior outstanding issue described in subparagraph (B).

(E) FACILITIES TAKEN INTO ACCOUNT.—For purposes of subparagraph (D)(ii), the facilities described in this subparagraph are facilities—

(i) located in the same incorporated municipality or located in the same county (but not in any incorporated municipality), and

(ii) the principal user of which is or will be the same person or two or more related persons.

For purposes of clause (i), the determination of whether or not facilities are located in the same governmental unit shall be made as of the date of issue of the issue in question.

(F) CERTAIN CAPITAL EXPENDITURES NOT TAKEN INTO ACCOUNT.—For purposes of subparagraph (D)(ii), any capital expenditure—

(i) to replace property destroyed or damaged by fire, storm, or other casualty, to the extent of the fair market value of the property replaced,

(ii) required by a change made after the date of issue of the issue in question in a Federal or State law or local ordinance of general application or required by a change made after such date in rules and regulations of general application issued under such a law or ordinance,

(iii) required by circumstances which could not be reasonably foreseen on such date of issue or arising out of a mistake of law or fact (but the aggregate amount of expenditures not taken into account under this clause with respect to any issue shall not exceed $1,000,000), or

(iv) described in clause (i) or (ii) of section 30(b)(2)(A) for which a deduction was allowed under section 174(a),

shall not be taken into account.

(G) LIMITATION ON LOSS OF TAX EXEMPTION.—In applying subparagraph (D)(ii) with respect to capital expenditures made after the date of any issue, no obligation issued as a part of such issue shall be treated as an obligation not described in subsection (a)(1) by reason of any such expenditure for any period before the date on which such expenditure is paid or incurred.

(H) CERTAIN REFINANCING ISSUES.—In the case of any issue described in subparagraph (A)(ii), an election may be made under subparagraph (D) only if all of the prior issues being redeemed are issues to which subparagraph (A) applies. In applying subparagraph (D)(ii) with respect to such a refinancing issue, capital expenditures shall be taken into account only for purposes of determining whether the prior issues being redeemed qualified (and would have continued to qualify) under subparagraph (A).

(I) AGGREGATE AMOUNT OF CAPITAL EXPENDITURES WHERE THERE IS URBAN DEVELOPMENT ACTION GRANT.—In the case of any issue substantially all of the proceeds of which are to be used to provide facilities with respect to which an urban development action grant has been made under section 119 of the Housing and Community Development Act of 1974, capital expenditures of not to exceed $10,000,000 shall not be taken into account for purposes of applying subparagraph (D)(ii).

(J) ISSUES FOR RESIDENTIAL PURPOSES.—This paragraph shall not apply to any obligation which is issued as a part of an issue a significant portion of the proceeds of which are to be used directly or indirectly to provide residential real property for family units.

(K) LIMITATIONS ON TREATMENT OF OBLIGATIONS AS PART OF THE SAME ISSUE.—For purposes of this paragraph, separate lots of obligations which (but for this subparagraph) would be treated as part of the same issue shall be treated as separate issues unless the proceeds of such lots are to be used with respect to 2 or more facilities—

(i) which are located in more than 1 State, or

(ii) which have, or will have, as the same principal user the same person or related persons.

(L) FRANCHISES.—For purposes of subparagraph (K), a person (other than a governmental unit) shall be considered a principal user of a facility if such person (or a group of related persons which includes such person)—

(i) guarantees, arranges, participates in, or assists with the issuance (or pays any portion of the cost of issuance) of any obligation the proceeds of which are to be used to finance or refinance such facility, and

(ii) provides any property, or any franchise, trademark, or trade name (within the meaning of section 1253), which is to be used in connection with such facility.

(M) PARAGRAPH NOT TO APPLY IF OBLIGATIONS ISSUED WITH CERTAIN OTHER TAX-EXEMPT OBLIGATIONS.—This paragraph shall not apply to any obligation which is issued as part of an issue (other than an issue to which subparagraph (D) applies) if the interest on any other obligation which is part of such issue is excluded from gross income under any provision of law other than this paragraph.

(N) TERMINATION DATES.—

(i) IN GENERAL.—Except as provided in clause (ii), this paragraph shall not apply to any obligation issued after December 31, 1986.

(ii) CERTAIN REFUNDINGS.—This paragraph shall apply to any obligation (or series of obligations) issued to refund an obligation issued on or before December 31, 1986, if—

(I) the average maturity date of the issue of which the refunding obligation is a part is not later than the average maturity date of the obligations to be refunded by such issue,

(II) the amount of the refunding obligation does not exceed the outstanding amount of the refunded obligation, and

(III) the proceeds of the refunding obligation are used to redeem the refunded obligation not later than 90 days after the date of the issuance of the refunding obligation.

For purposes of subclause (i), average maturity shall be determined in accordance with subsection (b)(14)(B)(i).

(iii) OBLIGATIONS USED TO FINANCE MANUFACTURING FACILITIES.—In the case of any obligation which is part of an issue substantially all of the proceeds of which are to be used to provide a manufacturing facility, clause (i) shall be applied by substituting "1988" for "1986".

(iv) MANUFACTURING FACILITY.—For purposes of this subparagraph, the term "manufacturing facility" means any facility which is used in the manufacturing or production of tangible personal property (including the processing resulting in a change in the condition of such property).

(O) RESTRICTIONS ON FINANCING CERTAIN FACILITIES.—This paragraph shall not apply to an issue if—

(i) more than 25 percent of the proceeds of the issue are used to provide a facility the primary purpose of which is one of the following: retail food and beverage services, automobile sales or service, or the provision of recreation or entertainment; or

(ii) any portion of the proceeds of the issue is to be used to provide the following: any private or commercial golf course, country club, massage parlor, tennis club, skating facility (including roller skating, skateboard, and ice skating), racquet sports facility (including any handball or racquetball court), hot tub facility, suntan facility, or racetrack.

(P) AGGREGATION OF ISSUES WITH RESPECT TO SINGLE PROJECT.—For purposes of this paragraph, 2 or more issues part or all of which are to be used with respect to a single building, an enclosed shopping mall, or a strip of offices, stores, or warehouses using substantial common facilities shall be treated as 1 issue (and any person who is a principal user with respect to any of such issues shall be treated as a principal user with respect to the aggregated issue).

(7) [Repealed.]

(8) QUALIFIED HYDROELECTRIC GENERATING FACILITIES.—For purposes of this section—

(A) QUALIFIED HYDROELECTRIC GENERATING FACILITY.—The term "qualified hydroelectric generating facility" means any qualified hydroelectric generating property which is owned by a State, political subdivision thereof, or agency or instrumentality of any of the foregoing.

(B) QUALIFIED HYDROELECTRIC GENERATING PROPERTY.—

(i) IN GENERAL.—Except as provided in clause (ii), the term "qualified hydroelectric generating property" has the meaning given to such term by section 48(l)(13).

(ii) DAM MUST BE OWNED BY GOVERNMENTAL BODY.—The term "qualified hydroelectric generating property" does not include any property installed at the site of any dam described in section 48(l)(13)(B)(i)(I) unless such dam was owned by one or more governmental bodies described in subparagraph (A) on October 18, 1979, and at all times thereafter until the obligations are no longer outstanding.

(C) LIMITATION.—Paragraph (4)(H) of this subsection shall not apply to any issue of obligations (otherwise qualifying under paragraph (4)(H)) if the portion of the proceeds of such issue which is used to provide qualified hydroelectric generating facilities exceeds (by more than an insubstantial amount) the product of—

(i) the eligible cost of the facilities being provided in whole or in part from the proceeds of the issue, and

(ii) the installed capacity fraction.

(D) INSTALLED CAPACITY FRACTION.—The term "installed capacity fraction" means the fraction—

(i) the numerator of which is 25, reduced by 1 for each megawatt by which the installed capacity exceeds 100 megawatts, and

(ii) the denominator of which is the number of megawatts of the installed capacity (but not in excess of 100).

For purposes of the preceding sentence, the term "installed capacity" has the meaning given to such term by section 48(l)(13)(E).

(E) ELIGIBLE COST.—

(i) IN GENERAL.—The eligible cost of any facilities is that portion of the total cost of such facilities which is reasonably expected—

(I) to be the cost to the governmental body described in subparagraph (A), and

(II) to be attributable to periods after October 18, 1979, and before 1986 (determined under rules similar to the rules of section 48(m)).

(ii) LONGER PERIOD FOR CERTAIN HYDROELECTRIC GENERATING PROPERTY.—If an application has been docketed by the Federal Energy Regulatory Commission before January 1, 1986, with respect to the installation of any qualified hydroelectric generating property, clause (i)(II) shall be applied with respect to such property by substituting "1989" for "1986".

(F) CERTAIN PRIOR ISSUES TAKEN INTO ACCOUNT.—If the proceeds of 2 or more issues (whether or not the issuer of each issue is the same) are or will be used to finance the same facilities, then, for purposes of subparagraph (C), in determining the amount of the proceeds of any later issue used to finance such facilities, there shall be taken into account the proceeds used to finance such facilities of all prior such issues which are outstanding at the time of such later issue (not including as outstanding any obligation which is to be redeemed from the proceeds of the later issue).

(9) QUALIFIED MASS COMMUTING VEHICLES.—

(A) IN GENERAL.—For purposes of paragraph (4)(I), the term "qualified mass commuting vehicle" means any bus, subway car, rail car, ferry, or similar equipment—

(i) which is leased to a mass transit system wholly owned by 1 or more governmental units (or agencies or instrumentalities thereof), and

(ii) which is used by such system in providing mass commuting services (or, in the case of a ferry, mass transportation services).

(B) TERMINATION.—Paragraph (4)(I) shall not apply to any obligation issued after December 31, 1984.

(10) LOCAL DISTRICT HEATING OR COOLING FACILITY.—For purposes of this section—

(A) IN GENERAL.—The term "local district heating or cooling facility" means property used as an integral part of a local district heating or cooling system.

(B) LOCAL DISTRICT HEATING OR COOLING SYSTEM.—

(i) IN GENERAL.—The term "local district heating or cooling system" means any local system consisting of a pipeline or network (which may be connected to a heating or cooling source) providing hot water, chilled water, or steam to 2 or more users for—

(I) residential, commercial, or industrial heating or cooling, or

(II) process steam.

(ii) LOCAL SYSTEM.—For purposes of this subparagraph, a local system includes facilities furnishing heating and cooling to an area consisting of a city and one contiguous county.

(11) [Repealed.]

(12) PROJECTS FOR RESIDENTIAL RENTAL PROPERTY.—For purposes of paragraph (4)(A)—

(A) TARGETED AREA PROJECT.—The term "targeted area project" means—

(i) a project located in a qualified census tract (within the meaning of section 103A(k)(2)), or

(ii) an area of chronic economic distress (within the meaning of section 103A(k)(3)).

(B) QUALIFIED PROJECT PERIOD.—The term "qualified project period" means the period beginning on the first day on which 10 percent of the units in the project are occupied and ending on the later of—

(i) the date which is 10 years after the date on which 50 percent of the units in the project are occupied,

(ii) the date which is a qualified number of days after the date on which any of the units in the project are occupied, or

(iii) the date on which any assistance provided with respect to the project under section 8 of the United States Housing Act of 1937 terminates.

For purposes of clause (ii), the term "qualified number" means, with respect to an obligation described in paragraph (4)(A), 50 percent of the number of days which comprise the term of the obligation with the longest maturity.

(C) INDIVIDUALS OF LOW AND MODERATE INCOME.—Individuals of low and moderate income shall be determined by the Secretary in a manner consistent with determinations of lower income families under section 8 of the United States Housing Act of 1937 (or if such program is terminated, under such program as in effect immediately before such termination), except that the percentage of median gross income which qualifies as low or moderate income shall be 80 percent.

(13) EXCEPTION.—Paragraphs (4), (5), and (6) shall not apply with respect to any obligation for any period during which it is held by a person who is a substantial user of the facilities or a related person. For purposes of this paragraph—

(A) a partnership and each of its partners (and their spouses and minor children) shall be treated as related persons, and

(B) an S corporation and each of its shareholders (and their spouses and minor children) shall be treated as related persons.

(14) MATURITY MAY NOT EXCEED 120 PERCENT OF ECONOMIC LIFE.—

(A) GENERAL RULE.—Paragraphs (4), (5), and (6) shall not apply to any obligation issued as part of an issue if—

(i) the average maturity of the obligations which are part of such issue, exceeds

(ii) 120 percent of the average reasonably expected economic life of the facilities being financed with the proceeds of such issue.

(B) DETERMINATION OF AVERAGES.—For purposes of subparagraph (A)—

(i) the average maturity of any issue shall be determined by taking into account the respective issue prices of the obligations which are issued as part of such issue, and

(ii) the average reasonably expected economic life of the facilities being financed with any issue shall be determined by taking into account the respective cost of such facilities.

(C) SPECIAL RULES.—

(i) DETERMINATION OF ECONOMIC LIFE.—For purposes of this paragraph, the reasonably expected economic life of any facility shall be determined as of the later of—

(I) the date on which the obligations are issued, or

(II) the date on which the facility is placed in service (or expected to be placed in service).

(ii) TREATMENT OF LAND.—

(I) LAND NOT TAKEN INTO ACCOUNT.—Except as provided in subclause (II), land shall not be taken into account under subparagraph (A)(ii)

(II) ISSUES WHERE 25 PERCENT OR MORE OF PROCEEDS USED TO FINANCE LAND.—If 25 percent or more of the proceeds of any issue is used to finance land, such land shall be taken into account under subparagraph (A)(ii) and shall be treated as having an economic life of 50 years.

(15) AGGREGATE LIMIT PER TAXPAYER FOR SMALL ISSUE EXCEPTION.—

(A) IN GENERAL.—Paragraph (6) of this subsection shall not apply to any issue if the aggregate authorized face amount of such issue allocated to any test-period beneficiary (when increased by the outstanding tax-exempt IDB's of such beneficiary) exceeds $40,000,000.

(B) OUTSTANDING TAX-EXEMPT IDB'S OF ANY PERSON.—For purposes of applying subparagraph (A) with respect to any issue, the outstanding tax-exempt IDB's of any person who is a test-period beneficiary with respect to such issue is the aggregate face amount of all industrial development bonds the interest on which is exempt from tax under subsection (a)—

(i) which are allocated to such beneficiary, and

(ii) which are outstanding at the time of such later issue (not including as outstanding any obligation which is to be redeemed from the proceeds of the later issue).

(C) ALLOCATION OF FACE AMOUNT OF AN ISSUE.—

(i) IN GENERAL.—Except as otherwise provided in regulations, the portion of the face amount of an issue allocated to any test-period beneficiary of a facility financed by the proceeds of such issue (other than an owner of such facility) is an amount which bears the same relationship to the entire face amount of such issue as the portion of such facility used by such beneficiary bears to the entire facility.

(ii) OWNERS.—Except as otherwise provided in regulations, the portion of the face amount of an issue allocated to any test-period beneficiary who is an owner of a facility financed by the proceeds of such issue is an amount which bears the same relationship to the entire face amount of such issue as the portion of such facility owned by such beneficiary bears to the entire facility.

(D) TEST-PERIOD BENEFICIARY.—For purposes of this paragraph, except as provided in regulations, the term "test-period beneficiary" means any person who was an owner or a principal user of facilities being financed by the issue at any time during the 3-year period beginning on the later of—

(i) the date such facilities were placed in service, or

(ii) the date of the issue.

(E) TREATMENT OF RELATED PERSONS.—For purposes of this paragraph, all persons who are related (within the meaning of paragraph (6)(C)) to each other shall be treated as one person.

(16) LIMITATION ON USE FOR LAND ACQUISITION.—

(A) IN GENERAL.—Paragraphs (4), (5), and (6) shall not apply with respect to any obligation issued as part of an issue if—

(i) any portion of the proceeds of such issue are to be used (directly or indirectly) for the acquisition of land (or an interest therein) to be used for farming purposes, or

(ii) 25 percent or more of the proceeds of such issue are to be used (directly or indirectly) for the acquisition of land not described in clause (i) (or an interest therein).

In the case of an obligation described in paragraph (5) (relating to industrial parks), clause (ii) shall be applied by substituting "50 percent" for "25 percent".

(B) EXCEPTION FOR FIRST-TIME FARMERS.—

(i) IN GENERAL.—If the requirements of clause (ii) are met with respect to any land, subparagraph (A) shall not apply to such land, and paragraph (17) shall not apply to property located thereon or to property to be acquired within 1 year to be used in farming, but only to the extent of expenditures (financed with the proceeds of the issue) not in excess of $250,000.

(ii) ACQUISITION BY FIRST-TIME FARMERS.—The requirements of this clause are met with respect to any land if—

(I) such land is to be used for farming purposes, and

(II) such land is to be acquired by an individual who is a first-time farmer, who will be the principal user of such land, and who will materially and substantially participate on the farm of which such land is a part in the operation of such farm.

(iii) FIRST-TIME FARMER.—For purposes of this subparagraph, the term "first-time farmer" means any individual if such individual has not at any time had any direct or indirect ownership interest in substantial farmland in the operation of which such individual materially participated. For purposes of this subparagraph, any ownership or material participation by an individual's spouse or minor child shall be treated as ownership and material participation by the individual.

(iv) FARM.—For purposes of this subparagraph, the term "farm" has the meaning given such term by section 6420(c)(2).

(v) SUBSTANTIAL FARMLAND.—The term "substantial farmland" means any parcel of land unless—

(I) such parcel is smaller than 15 percent of the median size of a farm in the county in which such parcel is located, and

(II) the fair market value of the land does not at any time while held by the individual exceed $125,000.

(C) EXCEPTION FOR CERTAIN LAND ACQUIRED FOR ENVIRONMENTAL PURPOSES.—Any land, acquired by a public agency in connection with an airport, mass transit, or port development project which consists of facilities described in paragraph (4)(D) shall not be taken into account under subparagraph (A) if—

(i) such land is acquired for a noise abatement, wetland preservation, future use, or other public purpose, and

(ii) there is not other significant use of such land.

(17) ACQUISITION OF EXISTING PROPERTY NOT PERMITTED.—

(A) IN GENERAL.—Paragraphs (4), (5), and (6) shall not apply to any obligation issued as part of an issue if any portion of the proceeds of such issue is to be used for the acquisition of any property (or an interest therein) unless the first use of such property is pursuant to such acquisition.

(B) EXCEPTION FOR CERTAIN REHABILITATIONS.—Subparagraph (A) shall not apply with respect to any building (and the equipment therefor) if—

(i) the rehabilitation expenditures with respect to such building equals or exceeds

(ii) 15 percent of the portion of the cost of acquiring such building (and equipment) financed with the proceeds of the issue.

A rule similar to the rule of the preceding sentence shall apply in the case of facilities other than a building except that clause (ii) shall be applied by substituting "100 percent" for "15 percent".

(C) REHABILITATION EXPENDITURES.—For purposes of this paragraph—

(i) IN GENERAL.—Except as provided in this subparagraph, the term "rehabilitation expenditures" means any amount properly chargeable to capital account which is incurred by the person acquiring the building for property (or additions or improvements to property) in connection with the rehabilitation of a building. In the case of an integrated operation contained in a building before its acquisition, such term includes rehabilitating existing equipment in such building or replacing it with equipment having substantially the same function. For purposes of this clause, any amount incurred by a successor to the person acquiring the building or by the seller under a sales contract with such person shall be treated as incurred by such person.

(ii) CERTAIN EXPENDITURES NOT INCLUDED.—The term "rehabilitation expenditures" does not include any expenditure described in section 48(g)(2)(B) (other than clause (i) thereof).

(iii) PERIOD DURING WHICH EXPENDITURES MUST BE INCURRED.—The term "rehabilitation expenditures" shall not include any amount which is incurred after the date 2 years after the later of—

(I) the date on which the building was acquired, or

(II) the date on which the obligation was issued.

(D) SPECIAL RULE FOR CERTAIN PROJECTS.—In the case of a project involving 2 or more buildings, this paragraph shall be applied on a project basis.

(18) NO PORTION OF BONDS MAY BE ISSUED FOR SKYBOXES, AIRPLANES, GAMBLING ESTABLISHMENTS, ETC.—Paragraphs (4), (5), and (6) shall not apply to any obligation issued as part of an issue if any portion of the proceeds of such issue is to be used to provide any airplane, skybox, or other private luxury box, any health club facility, any facility primarily used for gambling, or any store the principal business of which is the sale of alcoholic beverages for consumption off premises.

Amendments

• 1986, Tax Reform Act of 1986 (P.L. 99-514)

P.L. 99-514, §1866, as amended by P.L. 100-647, §1018(m), provides:

ACT SEC. 1866. TRANSITIONAL RULE FOR LIMIT ON SMALL ISSUE EXCEPTION.

The amendment made by section 623 of the Tax Reform Act of 1984 shall not apply to any obligation (or series of obligations) issued to refund another tax-exempt IDB to which the amendment made by such section 623 did not apply if—

(1) the average maturity of the issue of which the refunding obligation is a part does not exceed the average maturity of the obligations to be refunded by such issue,

(2) the amount of the refunding obligation does not exceed the amount of the refunded obligation, and

(3) the proceeds of the refunding obligation are used to redeem the refunded obligation not later than 90 days after the date of the issuance of the refunding obligation.

For purposes of the preceding sentence, the term "tax-exempt IDB" means any industrial development bond (as defined in section 103(b) of the Internal Revenue Code of 1954) the interest on which is exempt from tax under section 103(a) of such Code. For purposes of paragraph (1), average maturity shall be determined in accordance with subsection (b)(14)(B)(i) of such Code.

• 1986, Consolidated Omnibus Budget Reconciliation Act of 1985 (P.L. 99-272)

P.L. 99-272, §13209(e):

Repealed Code Sec. 103(b)(11). **Effective** 4-7-86. Prior to repeal, Code Sec. 103(b)(11) read as follows:

(11) POLLUTION CONTROL FACILITIES ACQUIRED BY REGIONAL POLLUTION CONTROL AUTHORITIES.—

(A) IN GENERAL.—For purposes of subparagraph (F) of paragraph (4), an obligation shall be treated as described in such subparagraph if it is part of an issue substantially all of the proceeds of which are used by a qualified regional pollution control authority to acquire existing air or water pollution control facilities which the authority itself will operate in order to maintain or improve the control of pollutants.

(B) RESTRICTIONS.—Subparagraph (A) shall apply only if—

(i) the amount paid, directly or indirectly, for the facilities does not exceed their fair market value,

(ii) the fees or charges imposed, directly or indirectly, on the seller for any use of the facilities after the sale are not less than the amounts that would be charged if the facilities were financed with obligations the interest on which is not exempt from tax, and

(iii) no person other than the qualified regional pollution control authority is considered after the sale as the owner of the facilities for purposes of Federal income taxes.

(C) QUALIFIED REGIONAL POLLUTION CONTROL AUTHORITY DEFINED.—For purposes of this paragraph, the term "qualified regional pollution control authority" means an authority which—

(i) is a political subdivision created by State law to control air or water pollution,

(ii) has within its jurisdictional boundaries all or part of at least 2 counties (or equivalent political subdivisions), and

(iii) operates air or water pollution control facilities.

P.L. 99-272, §13209(a)-(d), provides:

SEC. 13209. TREATMENT OF CERTAIN POLLUTION CONTROL BONDS.

(a) GENERAL RULE.—For purposes of subparagraph (F) of section 103(b)(4) of the Internal Revenue Code of 1954 (relating to pollution control facilities), any obligation issued after December 31, 1985, shall be treated as described in such subparagraph if it is part of an issue substantially all of the proceeds of which are used by a qualified regional pollution control authority to acquire existing air or water pollution control facilities which the authority itself will operate in order to maintain or improve control of pollutants. The provisions of section 103(b)(17) of such Code (relating to prohibition on acquisition of existing property not permitted) shall not apply to any obligation described in the preceding sentence.

(b) $200,000,000 LIMITATION.—The aggregate amount of obligations to which subsection (a) applies shall not exceed $200,000,000, except that the amount of such obligations issued during calendar year 1986 to which subsection (a) applies shall not exceed $100,000,000.

(c) RESTRICTIONS.—Subsection (a) shall apply only if—

(1) the amount paid (directly or indirectly) for the facilities does not exceed their fair market value,

(2) the fees or charges imposed (directly or indirectly) on any seller for the use of any facilities after the sale are not less than the amounts charged for the use of such facilities to persons other than the seller,

(3) the original use of the facilities acquired with the proceeds of such obligations commenced before September 3, 1982, and

(4) no person other than the qualified regional pollution control authority is considered after the sale as the owner of the facilities for purposes of Federal income taxes.

(d) QUALIFIED REGIONAL POLLUTION CONTROL AUTHORITY DEFINED.—For purposes of this section, the term "qualified regional pollution control authority" means an authority which—

(1) is a political subdivision created by State law to control air or water pollution,

(2) has within its jurisdictional boundaries all or part of at least 2 counties (or equivalent political subdivision),

(3) operates air or water pollution control facilities, and

(4) was created on September 1, 1969.

• 1984, Deficit Reduction Act of 1984 (P.L. 98-369)

P.L. 98-369, §474(r)(4):

Amended Code Sec. 103(b)(6)(F)(iv) by striking out "section 44F(b)(2)(A)" and inserting in lieu thereof "section 30(b)(2)(A)". **Effective** for tax years beginning after 12-31-83, and to carrybacks from such years.

P.L. 98-369, §623:

Added Code Sec. 103(b)(15). **Effective** for obligations issued after 12-31-83. Special rules and exceptions appear below, following Act Sec. 630. For a special rule relating to P.L. 98-369, §623, see amendment note for P.L. 99-514, §1866.

P.L. 98-369, §627(a)-(c):

Added Code Sec. 103(b)(16)-(18). **Effective** for obligations issued after 12-31-83, except that if

(1) there was an inducement resolution (or other comparable preliminary approval) for an issue before June 19, 1984, by any issuing authority, and

(2) such issues are issued before January 1, 1985,

the amendments made by subsections (a) and (b) of section 627 (except to the extent such amendments relate to farm land), and in the case of a race track, the amendment made by section 627(c), will not apply. Other special rules and exceptions follow Act Sec. 630, below.

P.L. 98-369, §628(c):

Amended Code Sec. 103(b)(6) by adding subparagraph (P). **Effective** for obligations issued after 12-31-83.

P.L. 98-369, §628(d):

Amended Code Sec. 103(b)(13) by adding the last sentence thereof. **Effective** for obligations issued after 12-31-83.

P.L. 98-369, §628(e):

Amended Code Sec. 103(b)(4) by adding the last sentence. **Effective** for obligations issued after 12-31-83.

P.L. 98-369, §628(g):

Amended Code Sec. 103(b) by repealing paragraph (7). **Effective** for refunding obligations issued after 7-18-84, except that if substantially all the proceeds of the refunded issue were used to provide airports or docks, such amendment shall only apply to refunding obligations issued after 12-31-84. In the case of any refunding obligation with respect to the Alabama State Docks Department or the Dade County Florida Airport, the preceding sentence shall be applied by substituting "December 31, 1985" for "December 31, 1984". Prior to its repeal, paragraph (7) read as follows:

(7) Advance Refund of Qualified Public Facilities.—

(A) In General.—Paragraph (1) shall not apply to a refunding issue if substantially all the proceeds of the refunded issue were used to provide a qualified public facility.

(B) Qualified Public Facility Defined.—For purposes of subparagraph (A), the term qualified public facility means facilities described in subparagraph (C) or (D) of paragraph (4) which are generally available to the general public.

P.L. 98-369, §630:

Amended Code Sec. 103(b)(6)(N). **Effective** for obligations issued after 12-31-83. Special rules are reproduced below. Prior to amendment, Code Sec. 103(b)(6)(N) read as follows:

(N) Paragraph Not to Apply to Obligations Issued After December 31, 1986.—This paragraph shall not apply to any obligation issued after December 31, 1986 (including any obligation issued to refund an obligation issued on or before such date).

P.L. 98-369, §§613, 625, 628(f), 629, 631(c)(3), (5) and (d)-(f), 632, 643-645, 647 and 648, as amended by P.L. 99-514, provide the following special rules and exceptions applicable to Code Sec. 103:

Sec. 613 Advance Refunding of Certain Veterans' Mortgage Bonds Permitted.

(a) IN GENERAL.—Notwithstanding section 103A(n) of the Internal Revenue Code of 1954, an issuer of applicable mortgage bonds may issue advance refunding bonds with respect to such applicable mortgage bonds.

(b) LIMITATION ON AMOUNT OF ADVANCED REFUNDING.—

(1) IN GENERAL.—The amount of advanced refunding bonds which may be issued under subsection (a) shall not exceed the lesser of—

(A) $300,000,000, or

(B) the excess of—

(i) the projected aggregate payments of principal on the applicable mortgage bonds during the 15-fiscal year period beginning with fiscal year 1984, over

(ii) the projected aggregate payments during such period of principal on mortgages financed by the applicable mortgage bonds.

(2) ASSUMPTIONS USED IN MAKING PROJECTION.—The computation under paragraph (1)(B) shall be made by using the following percentages of the prepayment experience of the Federal Housing Administration in the State or region in which the issuer of the advance refunding bonds is located:

Fiscal Year:	Percentage:
1984	15
1985	20
1986	25
1987 and thereafter	30.

(c) DEFINITIONS.—For purposes of this section—

(1) APPLICABLE MORTGAGE BONDS.—The term "applicable mortgage bonds" means any qualified veterans' mortgage bonds issued as part of an issue—

(A) which was outstanding on December 31, 1981,

(B) with respect to which the excess determined under subsection (b)(1)(B) exceeds 12 percent of the aggregate principal amount of such bonds outstanding on July 1, 1983,

(C) with respect to which the amount of the average annual prepayments during fiscal years 1981, 1982, and 1983 was less than 2 percent of the average of the loan balances as of the beginning of each of such fiscal years, and

(D) with, for fiscal year 1983, had a prepayment experience rate that did not exceed 20 percent of the prepayment experience rate of the Federal Housing Administration in the State or region in which the issuer is located.

(2) QUALIFIED VETERANS' MORTGAGE BONDS.— The term "qualified veterans' mortgage bonds" has the meaning given to such term by section 103(A)(c)(3) of the Internal Revenue Code of 1954.

(3) FISCAL YEAR.—The term "fiscal year" means the fiscal year of the State.

Sec. 625. Student Loan Bonds.

(a) Arbitrage Regulations.—

(1) In General.—The Secretary shall prescribe regulations which specify the circumstances under which a qualified student loan bond shall be treated as an arbitrage bond for purposes of section 103 of the Internal Revenue Code of 1954. Such regulations may provide that—

(A) paragraphs (4) and (5) of section 103(c) of such Code shall not apply, and

(B) rules similar to section 103(c)(6) shall apply,

to qualified student loan bonds.

(2) Definitions.—For purposes of this subsection—

(A) Qualified Student Loan Bond.—The term "qualified student loan bond" has the meaning given to such term by section 103(o)(3) of the Internal Revenue Code of 1954 (as amended by this Act).

(B) Arbitrage Bond.—The term "arbitrage bond" has the meaning given to such term by section 103(c)(2).

(3) Effective Date.—

(A) In General.—Except as otherwise provided in this paragraph, any regulations prescribed by the Secretary under paragraph (1) shall apply to obligations issued after the qualified date.

(B) Qualified Date.—

(i) In General.—For purposes of this paragraph, the term "qualified date" means the earlier of—

(I) the date on which the Higher Education Act of 1965 expires, or

(II) the date, after the date of enactment of this Act, on which the Higher Education Act of 1965 is reauthorized.

(ii) Publication of Regulations.—Notwithstanding clause (i), the qualified date shall not be a date which is prior to the date that is 6 months after the date on which the regulations prescribed under paragraph (1) are published in the Federal Register.

(C) Refunding Obligations.—Regulations prescribed by the Secretary under paragraph (1) shall not apply to any obligation (or series of refunding obligations) issued exclusively to refund any qualified student loan bond which was issued before the qualified date, except that the requirements of subparagraphs (A) and (B) of section 626(b)(4) of this Act must be met with respect to such refunding.

(D) Fulfillment of Commitments.—Regulations prescribed by the Secretary under paragraph (1) shall not apply to any obligations which are needed to fulfill written commitments to acquire or finance student loans which are originated after June 30, 1984, and before the qualified date, but only if—

(i) such commitments are binding on the qualified date, and

(ii) the amount of such commitments is consistent with practices of the issuer which were in effect on March 15, 1984, with respect to establishing secondary markets for student loans.

(b) Arbitrage Limitation on Student Loan Bonds Which Are Not Qualified Student Loan Bonds.—Under regulations prescribed by the Secretary of the Treasury or his delegate, any student loan bond (other than a qualified student loan bond) issued after December 31, 1985, shall be treated as an obligation not described in subsection (a)(1) or (2) of section 103 of the Internal Revenue Code of 1954 unless the issue of which such obligation is a part meets requirements similar to those of sections 103(c)(6) and 103A(i) of such Code.

(c) Issuance of Student Loan Bonds Which Are Not Tax-Exempt.—Any issuer who may issue obligations described in section 103(a) of the Internal Revenue Code of 1954 may elect to issue student loan bonds which are not described in such section 103(a) of such Code without prejudice to—

(1) the status of any other obligations issued, or to be issued, by such issuer as obligations described in section 103(a) of such Code, or

(2) the status of the issuer as an organization exempt from taxation under such Code.

(d) Federal Executive Branch Jurisdiction Over Tax-Exempt Status.—For purposes of Federal law, any determination by the executive branch of the Federal Government of whether interest on any obligation is exempt from taxation under the Internal Revenue Code of 1954 shall be exclusively within the jurisdiction of the Department of the Treasury.

(e) Study on Tax Exempt Student Loan Bonds.—

(1) In General.—The Comptroller General of the United States and the Director of the Congressional Budget Office, shall conduct studies of—

(A) the appropriate role of tax-exempt bonds which are issued in connection with the guaranteed student loan program and the PLUS program established under the Higher Education Act of 1965, and

(B) the appropriate arbitrage rules for such bonds.

(2) Report.—The Comptroller General of the United States and the Director of the Congressional Budget Office, shall submit to the Committee on Finance and the Committee on Labor and Human Resources of the Senate and the Committee on Ways and Means and the Committee on Education and Labor of the House of Representatives reports on the studies conducted under paragraph (1) by no later than 9 months after the date of enactment of this Act.

Sec. 628. Miscellaneous Industrial Development Bond Provisions.

* * *

(f) Public Approval Requirement in the Case of Public Airport.—If—

(1) the proceeds of any issue are to be used to finance a facility or facilities located on a public airport, and

(2) the governmental unit issuing such obligations is the owner or operator of such airport,

such governmental unit shall be deemed to be the only governmental unit having jurisdiction over such airport for purposes of subsection (k) of section 103 of the Internal Revenue Code of 1954 (relating to public approval for industrial development bonds).

* * *

(h) Small Issue Limit in Case of Certain Urban Development Action Grants.—In the case of any obligation issued on December 11, 1981, section 103(b)(6)(I) of the Internal Revenue Code of 1954 shall be applied by substituting "$15,000,000" for "$10,000,000" if—

(1) such obligation is part of an issue,

(2) substantially all of the proceeds of such issue are used to provide facilities with respect to which an urban development action grant under section 119 of the Housing and Community Development Act of 1974 was preliminarily approved by the Secretary of Housing and Urban Development on January 10, 1980, and

(3) the Secretary of Housing and Urban Development determines, at the time such grant is approved, that the amount of such grant will equal or exceed 5 percent of the total capital expenditures incurred with respect to such facilities.

Sec. 629. Certain Public Utilities Treated as Exempted Persons Under Section 103(b); Special Rules for Certain Railroads.

(a) Certain Public Utilities.—For purposes of applying section 103(b)(3) of the Internal Revenue Code with respect to—

(1) any obligations issued after the date of enactment of this Act, and

(2) any obligations issued after December 31, 1969, which were treated as obligations described in section 103(a) of such Code on the day on which such obligations were issued,

the term "exempt person" shall include a regulated public utility having any customer service area within a State served by a public power authority which was required as a condition of a Federal Power Commission license specified by an Act of Congress enacted prior to the enactment of section 107 of the Revenue and Expenditure Control Act of 1968 (Public Law 90-364) to contract to sell power to one such utility and which is authorized by State law to sell power to other such utilities, but only with respect to the purchase by any such utility and resale to its customers of any output of any electrical generation facility or any portion thereof or any use of any electrical transmission facility or any portion thereof financed by such power authority and owned by it or by such State, and provided that by agreement between such power authority and any such utility there shall be no markup in the resale price charged by such utility of that component of the resale price which represents the price paid by such utility for such output or use.

(b) Certain Railroads.—Section 103(b)(1) of the Internal Revenue Code of 1954 shall not apply to any obligation which is described in section 103(b)(6)(A) of such Code if—

(1) substantially all of the proceeds of such obligation are used to acquire railroad track and right-of-way from a railroad involved in a title 11 or similar proceeding (within the meaning of section 368(a)(3)(A) of such Code), and

(2) the Federal Railroad Administration provides joint financing for such acquisitions.

(c) Special Rules for Subsection (a).—

(1) Obligations Subject to Cap.—Any obligation described in subsection (a) shall be treated as a private activity bond for purposes of section 103(n) of the Internal Revenue Code of 1954.

(2) Limitation on Amount of Obligations to Which Subsection (a)(1) Applies.—The aggregate amount of obligations to which subsection (a)(1) applies shall not exceed $625,000,000.

(3) Limitation on Purposes.—Subsection (a)(1) shall only apply to obligations issued as part of an issue substantially all the proceeds of which are used to provide 1 or more of the following:

(A) Cable facilities.

(B) Small hydroelectric facilities.

(C) The acquisition of an interest in an electrical generating facility.

Sec. 631. Effective Dates.

* * *

(c) Other Provisions Relating to Tax-Exempt Bonds.—

* * *

(3) Exceptions.—

(A) Construction or Binding Agreement.—The amendments (and provisions) referred to in paragraph (1) shall not apply to obligations with respect to facilities—

[Caution: P.L. 98-369, §631(c)(3)(A)(i)-(ii), as amended by P.L. 99-514, §1872(a)(2)(B), is effective with respect to obligations issued after 3-28-85.]

(i) the original use of which commences with the taxpayer and the construction, reconstruction, or rehabilitation of which began before October 19, 1983, or

(ii) with respect to which a binding contract to incur significant expenditures was entered into before October 19, 1983.

(i) the original use of which commences with the taxpayer and the construction, reconstruction, or rehabilitation of which began before October 19, 1983, and was completed on or after such date,

(ii) the original use of which commences with the taxpayer and with respect to which a binding contract to incur significant expenditures for construction, reconstruction, or rehabilitation was entered into before October 19, 1983, and some of such expenditures are incurred on or after such date, or

(iii) acquired after October 19, 1983, pursuant to a binding contract entered into on or before such date.

(B) Facilities.—Subparagraph (C) of subsection (b)(2) shall apply for purposes of subparagraph (A) of this paragraph.

(C) Exception.—Subparagraph (A) shall not apply with respect to the amendment made by section 628(e) and the provisions of section 628(f) and 629(b).

* * *

(5) Special Rule for Health Club Facilities.—In the case of any health club facility, with respect to the amendment made by section 627(c)—

(A) paragraph (1) shall be applied by substituting "April 12, 1984" for "December 31, 1983", and

(B) paragraph (3) shall be applied by substituting "April 13, 1984" for "October 19, 1983" each place it appears.

(d) Provisions of This Subtitle Not To Apply to Certain Property.—The amendments made by this subtitle shall not apply to any property (and shall not apply to obligations issued to finance such property) if such property is described in any of the following paragraphs:

(1) Any property described in paragraph (5), (6), or (7) of section 31(g) of this Act.

(2) Any property described in paragraph (4), (8), or (17) of section 31(g) of this Act but only if the obligation is issued before January 1, 1985, and only if before June 19, 1984, the issuer had evidenced an intent to issue obligations exempt from taxation under the Internal Revenue Code of 1954 in connection with such property.

(3) Any property described in paragraph (3) of section 216(b) of the Tax Equity and Fiscal Responsibility Act of 1982.

(4) Any solid waste disposal facility described in section 103(b)(4)(E) of the Internal Revenue Code of 1954 if—

(A) a State public authority created pursuant to State legislation which took effect on June 18, 1973, took formal action before October 19, 1983, to commit development funds for such facility,

(B) such authority issues obligations for any such facility before January 1, 1987, and

(C) expenditures have been made for the development of any such facility before October 19, 1983.

(5) Any solid waste disposal facility described in section 103(b)(4)(E) of the Internal Revenue Code of 1954 if—

(A) a city government, by resolutions adopted on April 10, 1980, and December 27, 1982, took formal action to authorize the submission of a proposal for a feasibility study for such facility and to authorize the presentation to the Department of the Army (U.S. Army Missile Command) of a proposed agreement to jointly pursue construction and operation of such facility,

(B) such city government (or a public authority on its behalf) issues obligations for such facility before January 1, 1988, and

(C) expenditures have been made for the development of such facility before October 19, 1983. Notwithstanding the foregoing provisions of this subsection, the amendments made by section 624 (relating to arbitrage) shall apply to obligations issued to finance property described in paragraph (5).

(e) Determination of Significant Expenditure.—

(1) In General.—For purposes of this section, the term "significant expenditures" means expenditures which equal or exceed the lesser of—

(A) $15,000,000, or

(B) 20 percent of the estimated cost of the facilities.

(2) Certain Grants Treated as Expenditures.—For purposes of paragraph (1), the amount of any UDAG grant preliminarily approved on May 5, 1981, or April 4, 1983, shall be treated as an expenditure with respect to the facility for which such grant was so approved.

(f) Exception for Certain Other Amendments.—If—

(1) there was an inducement resolution (or other comparable preliminary approval) for an issue before June 19, 1984, by any issuing authority, and

(2) such issue is issued before January 1, 1985, the following amendments shall not apply:

(A) the amendments made by section 623,

(B) the amendments made by subsections (a) and (b) of section 627 (except to the extent such amendments relate to farm land),

(C) in the case of a race track, the amendment made by section 627(c), and

(D) the amendments made by section 628(c).

Sec. 632. Miscellaneous Exceptions and Special Rules.

(a) Exception From Provisions Other Than Arbitrage and Federal Guarantees.—Notwithstanding any other provision of this subtitle, the amendments made by this subtitle (other than by section 622 (relating to Federal guarantees) and section 624 (relating to arbitrage)) shall not apply to the following obligations:

* * *

(2) Obligations issued to finance a redevelopment program on 9 city blocks adjacent to a transit station but only if such program was approved on October 25, 1983.

(3) Obligations issued pursuant to an inducement resolution adopted on August 8, 1978, for a redevelopment plan for which a redevelopment trust fund was established on September 7, 1977.

(4) Obligations issued to finance a UDAG project which was preliminarily approved on December 29, 1982, and which received final approval on May 3, 1984.

(5) Obligations issued to finance a parking garage pursuant to an inducement resolution adopted on March 9, 1984, in connection with a project for which a UDAG grant application was made on January 31, 1984.

(6) Obligations which—

(A) are issued to finance a downtown development project with respect to which an urban development action grant is made but only if such grant—

(i) was preliminarily approved on November 3, 1983, and

(ii) received final approval before June 1, 1984, and

(B) are issued in connection with inducement resolutions that were adopted on December 21, 1982, July 5, 1983, and March 1, 1983.

But only to the extent the aggregate face amount of such obligations does not exceed $34,000,000.

(7) Obligations with respect to which an inducement resolution was adopted on March 5, 1984, for the purpose of acquiring existing airport facilities at more than 12 locations in 1 State but—

(A) only if the Civil Aeronautics Board certifies that such transaction would reduce the amount of Federal subsidies provided under section 419 of the Airline Deregulation Act of 1978, and

(B) only to the extent the aggregate face amount of such obligations does not exceed $25,000,000.

(8) Obligations described in subsection (b).

(b) Certain Parking Facility Bonds.—For purposes of the Internal Revenue Code of 1954, any obligation issued with respect to a parking facility approved by an agency of a county government on December 1, 1982, as part of an urban revitalization plan shall be treated as an obligation described in section 103(b)(4)(D) of such Code.

(c) Exception to Certain Bond Limitations.—The amendments made by section 621 (relating to the limitations on amount of private activity bonds) and section 626(a) (relating to the prohibition on acquiring existing facilities) shall not apply to obligations issued before January 1, 1987, in connection with the Claymont, Delaware regeneration plant of the Delaware Economic Development Authority, but only to the extent the aggregate face amount of such obligation does not exceed $30,000,000.

(d) Certain Obligations Treated as Not Federally Guaranteed.—For purposes of section 103(h) of the Internal Revenue Code of 1954, obligations (including refunding obligations) shall not be treated as federally guaranteed if—

(A) such obligations are issued with respect to any facility, and

(B) any obligation was issued on June 3, 1982 in the principal amount of $11,312,125 for the purpose of financing the development, study, or related costs incurred with respect to such facility.

The amendment made by section 626 shall not apply to any obligations described in the preceding sentence.

(e) Certain Expenditures Treated as Significant Expenditures.—For purposes of this title, expenditures of $850,000 incurred with respect to any project involving $15,000,000 shall be treated as significant expenditures if such expenditures were incurred pursuant to an agreement entered into on July 13, 1982, relating to the discharge of industrial waste after January 1, 1986.

(f) Certain Ordinances Treated as Inducement Resolutions.—For purposes of this title, any ordinance passed on May 3, 1982, with respect to a planned development district shall be treated as an inducement resolution with respect to obligations issued in 1984 in connection with a mall project for such district.

(g) Delayed Effective Date With Respect to Certain IDBS.—

(1) FERC Projects.—Notwithstanding any other provision of this title, any amendments made by this title (other than the amendments to section 103(c) of the Internal Revenue Code of 1954) which, but for this paragraph, would apply to industrial development bonds issued after December 31,

1984, shall not apply to any of the following obligations issued before January 1, 1986:

(A) obligations issued with respect to Federal Energy Regulatory Commission project 4657, but only to the extent the aggregate face amount of such obligations does not exceed $12,900,000;

(B) obligations issued with respect to Federal Energy Regulatory Commission project 2853, but only to the extent the aggregate face amount of such obligations does not exceed $28,600,000; or

(C) obligations issued with respect to Federal Energy Regulatory Commission project 4700, but only to the extent the aggregate face amount of such obligations does not exceed $3,850,000.

(2) Park Central New Town in Town Project.—Notwithstanding any other provision of this title, any amendments made by this title (other than the amendments to section 103(c) of the Internal Revenue Code of 1954) which, but for this paragraph, would apply to industrial development bonds issued after December 31, 1984, shall not apply to any obligation issued before January 1, 1988, with respect to Park Central New Town In Town Project located in Port Arthur, Texas, but only to the extent the aggregate face amount of such obligations does not exceed $80,000,000.

Sec. 643. Tax-exempt Status of Obligations of Certain Educational Organizations.

(a) In General.—For purposes of section 103 of the Internal Revenue Code of 1954, a qualified educational organization shall be treated as a State governmental unit, but only with respect to a trade or business carried on by such organization which is not an unrelated trade or business (determined by applying section 513(a) of such Code to such organization).

(b) Qualified Educational Organization.—For purposes of subsection (a), the term "qualified educational organization" means a college or university created on February 22, 1855, by specific act of the legislature of the State within which such college or university is located.

(c) Effective Date.—This section shall apply to obligations issued after December 31, 1953.

Sec. 644. Local Furnishing of Electricity or Gas.

(a) General Rule.—For the purposes of section 103(b)(4)(E), facilities for the local furnishing of electric energy also shall include a facility that is part of a system providing service to the general populace (i) if at least 97 percent (measured both by total number of metered customers and by their annual consumption on a kilowatt hour basis) of the retail customers of such system are located in two contiguous counties, and (ii) if the remainder of such customers are located in a portion of a third contiguous county which portion is located on a peninsula not directly connected by land to the rest of the county of which it is a part.

(b) Election to Allocate to 1984 One-Half of State Limit for 1985, 1986, and 1987.—Solely for purposes of issuing obligations described in subsection (a), the issuing authorities of a State may elect (at such time and in such manner as the Secretary of the Treasury shall by regulations prescribe) to use in 1984 one-half of the amount which would have been the State limit for the calendar years 1985, 1986, and 1987.

Sec. 645. Local Furnishing Where Facility Initially Authorized by Federal Government.

For the purpose of section 103(b)(4)(E), facilities for the local furnishing of electric energy also shall include a facility that is part of a system providing service to the general populace—

(i) if the facility was initially authorized by the Federal Government in 1962;

(ii) if the facility receives financing of at least 25 percent by an exempt person;

(iii) if the electric energy generated by the facility is purchased by an electric cooperative qualified as a rural electric borrower under 7 U.S.C. section 901 et seq. and;

(iv) if the facility is located in a noncontiguous State.

Sec. 647. Special Rule for Possessions and District of Columbia.

Notwithstanding any other provision of law, in the case of obligations issued before July 1, 1987—

(1) the Virgin Islands and American Samoa shall have authority to issue industrial development bonds (within the meaning of section 103(b)(2) of the Internal Revenue Code of 1954), and

(2) the District of Columbia housing finance agency shall have the authority to issue obligations described in section 103(b)(4)(A) of such Code and to issue mortgage subsidy bonds (as defined in section 103A of such Code).

Sec. 648. Special Arbitrage Rule.

Securities or obligations are not described in section 103(c)(2)(A) or (B) of the Internal Revenue Code of 1954 and are not subject to yield restrictions to the extent that on the date of issue of a bond issue which is payable from the investment earnings on such securities or obligations—

(1) such securities or obligations are held in a fund which, except to the extent of the investment earnings on such securities or obligations, cannot be used, under State constitutional or statutory restrictions continuously in effect since October 9, 1969, to pay debt service on the bond issue or to finance the facilities that are to be financed with the proceeds of the bonds,

(2) the fund has received no substantial discretionary contributions after October 9, 1969,

(3) the issuer (A) had a practice of issuing bonds secured by the investment earnings of the fund during the period commencing January 1, 1960, and ending on October 9, 1969, and (B) has had a continuous practice of issuing bonds secured by the investment earnings of the fund at least once during each 5-year period beginning on October 9, 1969, and

(4) the amount of securities or obligations benefitting from this rule cannot exceed the principal amount of bonds (to which such securities or other obligations would, but for this rule, be allocated) which could be issued under applicable laws restricting the amount of bonds that can be issued (but not restrictions on the purposes for which bonds can be issued) in effect on October 9, 1969, as applied to the facts on the day of issue.

P.L. 98-369, §712(h):

Amended P.L. 97-248, §217(e) by adding the following:

For purposes of applying section 168(f)(8)(D)(v) of the Internal Revenue Code of 1954, the amendments made by subsection (c) [relating to Code Sec. 103(b)(9)(A), below] shall apply to agreements entered into after the date of the enactment of this Act.

• 1982, Tax Equity and Fiscal Responsibility Act of 1982 (P.L. 97-248)

P.L. 97-248, §214(a):

Amended Code Sec. 103(b)(6) by adding at the end thereof new subparagraphs (K) and (L). **Effective** for obligations issued after 9-3-82.

P.L. 97-248, §214(b):

Amended Code Sec. 103(b)(6), as amended by Act Sec. 214(a) by adding at the end thereof new subparagraph (M). **Effective** for obligations issued after 9-3-82.

P.L. 97-248, §214(c):

Amended Code Sec. 103(b)(6), as amended by Act Sec. 214(a) and (b) by adding at the end thereof new subparagraph (N). **Effective** 9-3-82.

P.L. 97-248, §214(d)(1)(3):

Amended Code Sec. 103(b)(6)(F) by striking out "or" at the end of clause (ii), by adding "or" at the end of clause (iii), and by adding at the end thereof new clause (iv). **Effective** for expenditures made after 9-3-82.

P.L. 97-248, §214(e):

Amended Code Sec. 103(b)(6) by adding at the end thereof new subparagraph (O). **Effective** for obligations issued after 12-31-82.

P.L. 97-248, §215(b)(2):

Amended Code Sec. 103(b)(2) by striking out "For purposes of this subsection" and inserting in lieu thereof "For purposes of this section". **Effective** for obligations issued after 12-31-82 (including any obligations issued to refund an obligation issued prior to such date).

P.L. 97-248, §217(a)(1)(3):

Amended Code Sec. 103(b)(4) by striking out "or" at the end of subparagraph (H), by striking out the period at the end of subparagraph (I) and inserting in lieu thereof ", or", and by inserting after subparagraph (I) new subparagraph (J). **Effective** for obligations issued after 9-3-82.

P.L. 97-248, §217(a)(2)(B):

Amended Code Sec. 103(b) by redesignating paragraph (10) as paragraph (13) and by adding after paragraph (9) new paragraph (10). **Effective** for obligations issued after 9-3-82.

P.L. 97-248, §217(a)(3):

Amended Code Sec. 103(b)(6)(C) by striking out "paragraph (7)" and inserting in lieu thereof "paragraph (13)". **Effective** for obligations issued after 9-3-82.

P.L. 97-248, §217(b):

Amended Code Sec. 103(b)(4) by striking out "electric energy from" in the last sentence and inserting in lieu thereof "electric energy or gas from". **Effective** for obligations issued after 9-3-82.

P.L. 97-248, §217(c):

Amended Code Sec. 103(b)(9)(A) by inserting "ferry," after "rail car"; and by inserting after "mass commuting services" in clause (ii) the phrase "(or, in the case of a ferry, mass transportation services)". **Effective** for obligations issued after 9-3-82.

P.L. 97-248, §217(d):

Amended Code Sec. 103(b) by inserting after paragraph (10) as added by Act Sec. 217(a) new paragraph (11). **Effective** for obligations issued after 9-3-82.

P.L. 97-248, §218, provides:

SEC. 218 TREATMENT OF CERTAIN REFUNDING OBLIGATIONS.

(a) General rule.—Paragraph (1) of section 103(b) of the Internal Revenue Code of 1954 shall not apply to any qualified refunding obligation issued by a qualified issuer after the date of the enactment of this Act.

(b) Qualified refunding obligation.—For purposes of subsection (a), a qualified refunding obligation is any obligation issued as part of an issue if—

(1) substantially all of the proceeds of such issue are used to defease refunded bonds which were issued under a pooled security arrangement pursuant to a bond resolution which was adopted in 1974 and under which at least 20 facilities have been financed before 1978, and

(2) each refunded bond is to be retired within 6 months after the first date on which there is no premium for early retirement of such bond.

(c) Qualified issuer.—For purposes of subsection (a), a qualified issuer is a political subdivision created by a State in 1932 which is engaged primarily in promoting economic development.

P.L. 97-248, §219:

Amended Code Sec. 103(b) by adding new paragraph (14) at the end thereof. **Effective** for obligations issued after 12-31-82.

P.L. 97-248, §221(a):

Amended Code Sec. 103(b)(4)(A). **Effective** for obligations issued after 9-3-82, except that they do not apply with respect to any obligation to which the amendments made by section 1103 of the Mortgage Subsidy Bond Tax Act of 1980 do not apply by reason of section 1104 of such Act. Prior to amendment, it read as follows:

"(A) projects for residential rental property if each obligation issued pursuant to the issue is in registered form and if—

(i) 15 percent or more in the case of targeted area projects, or

(ii) 20 percent or more in the case of any other project,

of the units in each project are to be occupied by individuals of low or moderate income (within the meaning of section 167(k)(3)(B)),"

P.L. 97-248, §221(b):

Amended Code Sec. 103(b) by inserting after paragraph (11) new paragraph (12). **Effective** for obligations issued after 9-3-82, except that they do not apply with respect to any obligation to which the amendments made by section 1103 of the Mortgage Subsidy Bond Tax Act of 1980 do not apply by reason of section 1104 of such Act.

P.L. 97-248, §221(c)(1):

Amended Code Sec. 103(b)(4) by striking out the second sentence, which read as follows:

"For purposes of subparagraph (A), the term `targeted area project' means a project located in a qualified census tract (within the meaning of section 103A(k)(2) or an area of economic distress (within the meaning of section 103A(k)(3))". **Effective** for obligations issued after September 3, 1982 except not applicable with respect to any obligation to which the amendments made by section 1103 of the Mortgage Subsidy Bond Tax Act of 1980 do not apply by reason of section 1104 of such Act.

P.L. 97-248, §310(c)(1):

Amended Code Sec. 103(b)(4)(A) [as amended by Act Sec. 221(a)]by striking out "if each obligation issued pursuant to the issue is in registered form and", which preceded "and if —". **Effective** for obligations issued after 12-31-82.

• 1981, Economic Recovery Tax Act of 1981 (P.L. 97-34)

P.L. 97-34, §811(a):

Amended Code Sec. 103(b)(4) by striking out "or" at the end of subparagraph (G); by striking out the period at the end of subparagraph (H) and inserting in lieu thereof ", or"; and by inserting after subparagraph (H) new subparagraph (I). **Effective** for obligations issued after 8-13-81.

P.L. 97-34, §811(b):

Amended Code Sec. 103(b) by redesignating paragraph (9) as paragraph (10) and by inserting after paragraph (8) new paragraph (9). **Effective** for obligations issued after 8-13-81.

• 1980, Omnibus Reconciliation Act of 1980 (P.L. 96-499)

P.L. 96-499, §1103(a):

Amended Code Sec. 103(b)(4)(A). For the **effective** date of this amendment, see the historical note under former Code Sec. 103A(n). Prior to amendment Code Sec. 103(b)(4)(A) provided:

"(A) residential real property for family units"

P.L. 96-499, §1103(b):

Amended Code Sec. 103(b)(4) by inserting a sentence before the last sentence. For the **effective** date of this amendment, see the historical comment under former Code Sec. 103A(n).

P.L. 96-499, §1103(c).

Amended Code Sec. 103(b)(6) by adding new subparagraph (J). For the **effective** date of this provision, see the historical note under former Code Sec. 103A(n).

• 1980, Crude Oil Windfall Profit Tax Act of 1980 (P.L. 96-223)

P.L. 96-223, §242(a)(1):

Amended Code Sec. 103(b)(4) by striking out "or" at the end of subparagraph (F), by striking out the period at the end of subparagraph (G) and inserting ", or", and by adding subparagraph (H). **Effective** with respect to obligations issued after 10-18-79.

P.L. 96-223, §242(a)(2):

Redesignated Code Sec. 103(b)(8) as Code Sec. 103(b)(9) and added Code Sec. 103(b)(8). **Effective** with respect to obligations issued after 10-18-79.

P.L. 96-223, §242(b), provides:

(b) APPLICATION OF SECTION 103(b)(4)(H) TO CERTAIN FACILITIES.—

(1) IN GENERAL.—For purposes of section 103(b)(4)(H) of the Internal Revenue Code of 1954 (relating to qualified hydroelectric generating facilities), in the case of a hydroelectric generating facility described in paragraph (2)—

(A) the facility shall be treated as a qualified hydroelectric generating facility (as defined in section 103(b)(8)(A) of such Code) without regard to clause (ii) of section 48(l)(13)(B) of such Code (relating to maximum generating capacity), and

(B) the fraction referred to in subparagraph (C) of section 103(b)(8) of such Code shall be deemed to be 1.

(2) FACILITIES TO WHICH PARAGRAPH (1) APPLIES.—A facility is described in this paragraph if—

(A) it would be a qualified hydroelectric generating facility (as defined in section 103(b)(8)(A) of such Code) if clause (ii) of section 48(l)(13)(B) did not apply,

(B) it constitutes an expansion of generating capacity at an existing hydroelectric generating facility,

(C) such facility is located at 1 of 2 dams located in the same county where—

(i) the rated capacity of the hydroelectric generating facilities at each such dam on October 18, 1979, was more than 750 megawatts,

(ii) the construction of the first such dam began in 1956, power at such first dam was first generated in 1959, and full power production at such first dam began in 1961, and

(iii) the construction of the second such dam began in 1959, power at such second dam was first generated in 1963, and full power production at such second dam began in 1964,

(D) acquisition or construction of the existing facility referred to in subparagraph (B) was financed with the proceeds of an obligation described in section 103(a)(1) of such Code,

(E) the existing facility is owned and operated by a State, political subdivision of a State, or agency or instrumentality of any of the foregoing,

(F) no more than 60 percent of the electric power and energy produced by such existing facility and of the qualified hydroelectric generating facility is to be sold to anyone other than an exempt person (within the meaning of section 103(b)(3) of such Code), and

(G) the agency of the State in which the facility is located which has jurisdiction over water rights had granted, before October 18, 1979, a water right under which expanded power and energy generating capacity for the facility was contemplated.

The provisions of P.L. 96-223, §242(b) are applicable with respect to obligations issued after October 18, 1979.

P.L. 96-223, §243(a), provides:

(a) CERTAIN STATE OBLIGATIONS FOR RENEWABLE ENERGY PROPERTY.—

(1) IN GENERAL.—Paragraph (1) of subsection (b) of section 103 of the Internal Revenue Code of 1954 shall not apply to any obligation issued as part of an issue substantially all of the proceeds of which are to be used to provide renewable energy property, if—

(A) the obligations are general obligations of a State,

(B) the authority for the issuance of the obligations requires that taxes be levied in sufficient amount to provide for the payment of principal and interest on such obligations,

(C) the amount of such obligations, when added to the sum of the amounts of all such obligations previously issued by the State which are outstanding, does not exceed the smaller of—

(i) $500,000,000 or

(ii) one-half of 1 percent of the value of all property in the State,

(D) such obligations are issued pursuant to a program to provide financing for small scale energy projects which was established by a State the legislature of which, before October 18, 1979, approved a constitutional amendment to provide for such a program, and

(E) such obligations meet the requirements of paragraph (1) of section 103(h) of the Internal Revenue Code of 1954.

(2) RENEWABLE ENERGY PROPERTY.—For purposes of this subsection, the term "renewable energy property" means property used to produce energy (including heat, electricity, and substitute fuels) from renewable energy sources (including wind, solar, and geothermal energy, waste heat, biomass, and water).

The provisions of P.L. 96-223, §243(a) are applicable with respect to obligations issued after April 3, 1980.

• 1978, Revenue Act of 1978 (P.L. 95-600)

P.L. 95-600, §331(a):

Substituted "$10,000,000" for "$5,000,000" in the heading and in the text of Code Sec. 103(b)(6)(D). **Effective** for obligations issued after 12-31-78, in tax years ending after such date, and for capital expenditures made after 12-31-78, with respect to obligations issued before 1-1-79.

P.L. 95-600, §331(b):

Added new subparagraph (I) in Code Sec. 103(b)(6). **Effective** for obligations issued after 9-30-79, in tax years ending after such date, and for capital expenditures made after 9-30-79, with respect to obligations issued after that date.

P.L. 95-600, §332(a):

Added the last sentence of Code Sec. 103(b)(4). **Effective** for tax years ending after 4-30-68, but only with respect to obligations issued after such date.

P.L. 95-600, §333(a):

Amended Code Sec. 103(b)(4)(G). **Effective** for obligations issued after 11-6-78 in tax years ending after such date. Prior to amendment, Code Sec. 103(b)(4)(G) read as follows:

(G) facilities for the furnishing of water, if available on reasonable demand to members of the general public.

P.L. 95-600, §334(a):

Redesignated paragraph (7) of Code Sec. 103(b) as paragraph (8) and inserted after paragraph (6) a new paragraph (7). **Effective** for obligations issued after 11-6-78.

P.L. 95-600, §334(b):

Amended paragraph (8) of Code Sec. 103(b) (as redesignated by Act Sec. 334(a)). **Effective** for obligations issued after 11-6-78. Prior to amendment, Code Sec. 103(b)(8) read as follows:

(8) Exception.—Paragraphs (4), (5), and (6) shall not apply with respect to any obligation for any period during which it is held by a person who is a substantial user of the facilities or a related person.

P.L. 95-600, §703(j)(1)(A):

Amended the heading of Code Sec. 103(b)(1). **Effective** 10-4-76.

• 1976, Tax Reform Act of 1976 (P.L. 94-455)

P. L. 94-455, §1901(a)(17):

Repealed Code Sec. 103(b), redesignated former Code Sec. 103(c) as Code Sec. 103(b), and added "or (2)" after "(a)(1)" in redesignated Code Sec. 103(b)(1). **Effective** for tax years beginning after 12-31-76. Prior to repeal, Code Sec. 103(b) read as follows:

(b) EXCEPTION.—Subsection (a)(2) shall not apply to interest on obligations of the United States issued after September 1, 1917 (other than postal savings certificates of deposit, to the extent they represent deposits made before March 1, 1941), unless under the respective Acts authorizing the issuance thereof such interest is wholly exempt from the taxes imposed by this subtitle.

P.L. 94-455, §1906(b)(13)(A):

Amended 1954 Code by substituting "Secretary" for "Secretary or his delegate" each place it appeared. **Effective** 2-1-77.

• 1971, Revenue Act of 1971 (P.L. 92-178)

P.L. 92-178, §315(a):

Amended Code Sec. 103(c)(4) by substituting "or gas" for ", gas, or water, or" in subparagraph (E), adding ", or" at the end of subparagraph (F), and adding new subparagraph (G). **Effective** for obligations issued after 1-1-69.

P.L. 92-178, §315(b):

Amended Code Sec. 103(c)(6)(F) by substituting "$1,000,000" for "$250,000" in clause (iii). **Effective** for expenditures incurred after 12-10-71.

• 1968, Renegotiation Amendments Act of 1968 (P.L. 90-634)

P.L. 90-634, §401(a):

Added subparagraphs (D) through (H) to Code Sec. 103(c)(6). **Effective** for obligations issued after 10-24-68.

P.L. 90-364, §107(a):

Added Code Sec. 103(c) and relettered former Code Sec. 103(c) as Code Sec. 103(d). The **effective** date of the amendment is prescribed by P.L. 90-364, §107(b), as follows:

"(b) Effective Date.—

"(1) In general.—Except as provided by paragraph (2), the amendment made by subsection (a) shall apply to taxable years ending after April 30, 1968, but only with respect to obligations issued after such date.

"(2) Transitional provisions.—Section 103(c)(1) of the Internal Revenue Code of 1954, as amended by subsection (a), shall not apply with respect to any obligation issued before January 1, 1969, if before May 1, 1968—

"(A) the issuance of the obligation (or the project in connection with which the proceeds of the obligations are to be used) was authorized or approved by the governing body of the governmental unit issuing the obligation or by the voters of such governmental unit;

"(B) in connection with the issuance of such obligation or with the use of the proceeds to be derived from the sale of such obligation or the property to be acquired or improved with such proceeds, a governmental unit has made a significant financial commitment;

"(C) any person (other than a governmental unit) who will use the proceeds to be derived from the sale of such obligation or the property to be acquired or improved with such proceeds has expended (or has entered into a binding contract to expend) for purposes which are related to the use of such proceeds or property, an amount equal to or in excess of 20 percent of such proceeds; or

"(D) in the case of an obligation issued in conjunction with a project where financial assistance will be provided by a governmental agency concerned with economic development, such agency has approved the project or an application for financial assistance is pending."

[Sec. 103(c)]

(c) ARBITRAGE.—

(1) SUBSECTION (a)(1) OR (2) NOT TO APPLY TO ARBITRAGE BONDS.—Except as provided in this subsection, any arbitrage bond shall be treated as an obligation not described in subsection (a)(1) or (2).

(2) ARBITRAGE BOND.—For purposes of this subsection, the term "arbitrage bond" means any obligation which is issued as part of an issue all or a major portion of the proceeds of which are reasonably expected to be used directly or indirectly—

(A) to acquire securities (within the meaning of section 165(g)(2)(A) or (B)) or obligations (other than obligations described in subsection (a)(1) or (2)) which may be reasonably expected at the time of issuance of such issue, to produce a yield over the term of the issue which is materially higher (taking into account any discount or premium) than the yield on obligations of such issue, or

(B) to replace funds which were used directly or indirectly to acquire securities or obligations described in subparagraph (A).

(3) EXCEPTION.—Paragraph (1) shall not apply to any obligation—

(A) which is issued as part of an issue substantially all of the proceeds of which are reasonably expected to be used to provide permanent financing for real property used or to be used for residential purposes for the personnel of an educational organization described in section 170(b)(1)(A)(ii) which grants baccalaureate or higher degrees, or to replace funds which were so used, and

(B) the yield on which over the term of the issue is not reasonably expected, at the time of issuance of such issue, to be substantially lower than the yield on obligations acquired or to be acquired in providing such financing.

This paragraph shall not apply with respect to any obligation for any period during which it is held by a person who is a substantial user of property financed by the proceeds of the issue of which such obligation is a part, or by a member of the family (within the meaning of section 318(a)(1)) of any such person.

(4) SPECIAL RULES.—For purposes of paragraph (1), an obligation shall not be treated as an arbitrage bond solely by reason of the fact that—

(A) the proceeds of the issue of which such obligation is a part may be invested for a temporary period in securities or other obligations until such proceeds are needed for the purpose for which such issue was issued, or

(B) an amount of the proceeds of the issue of which such obligation is a part may be invested in securities or other obligations which are part of a reasonably required reserve or replacement fund.

The amount referred to in subparagraph (B) shall not exceed 15 percent of the proceeds of the issue of which such obligation is a part unless the issuer establishes that a higher amount is necessary.

(5) STUDENT LOAN INCENTIVE PAYMENTS.—Payments made by the Commissioner of Education pursuant to section 438 of the Higher Education Act of 1965 are not to be taken into account, for purposes of paragraph (2)(A), in determining yields on student loan notes.

(6) INVESTMENTS IN NONPURPOSE OBLIGATIONS.—

(A) IN GENERAL.—For purposes of this title, any obligation which is part of an issue of industrial development bonds which does not meet the requirements of subparagraphs (C) and (D) shall be treated as an obligation which is not described in subsection (a).

(B) EXCEPTIONS.—Subparagraph (A) shall not apply to any obligation described in subsection (b)(4)(A) or to any housing program obligation under section 11(b) of the Housing Act of 1937.

(C) LIMITATION ON INVESTMENT IN NONPURPOSE OBLIGATIONS.—

(i) IN GENERAL.—An issue meets the requirements of this subparagraph only if—

(I) at no time during any bond year, the amount invested in nonpurpose obligations with a yield higher than the yield on the issue exceeds 150 percent of the debt service on the issue for the bond year, and

(II) the aggregate amount invested as provided in subclause (I) is promptly and appropriately reduced as the amount of outstanding obligations of the issue is reduced.

(ii) EXCEPTION FOR TEMPORARY PERIODS.—Clause (i) shall not apply to—

(I) proceeds of the issue invested for an initial temporary period until such proceeds are needed for the governmental purpose of the issue, and

(II) temporary investment periods related to debt service.

(iii) DEBT SERVICE DEFINED.—For purposes of this subparagraph, the debt service on the issue for any bond year is the scheduled amount of interest and amortization of principal payable for such year with respect to such issue. For purposes of the preceding sentence, there shall not be taken into account amounts scheduled with respect to any bond which has been retired before the beginning of the bond year.

(iv) NO DISPOSITION IN CASE OF LOSS.—This subparagraph shall not require the sale or disposition of any investment if such sale or disposition would result in a loss which exceeds the amount which would be paid to the United States (but for such sale or disposition) at the time of such sale or disposition.

(D) REBATE TO UNITED STATES.—An issue shall be treated as meeting the requirements of this subparagraph only if an amount equal to the sum of—

(i) the excess of—

(I) the aggregate amount earned on all nonpurpose obligations (other than investments attributable to an excess described in this clause), over

(II) the amount which would have been earned if all nonpurpose obligations were invested at a rate equal to the yield on the issue, plus

(ii) any income attributable to the excess described in clause (i),

is paid to the United States by the issuer in accordance with the requirements of subparagraph (E).

(E) DUE DATE OF PAYMENTS UNDER SUBPARAGRAPH (D).—The amount which is required to be paid to the United States by the issuer shall be paid in installments which are made at least once every 5 years. Each installment shall be in an amount which insures that 90 percent of the amount described in subparagraph (D) with respect to the issue at the time payment of such installment is required will have been paid to the United States. The last installment shall be made no later than 30 days after the day on which the last obligation of the issue is redeemed and shall be in an amount sufficient to pay the remaining balance of the amount described in subparagraph (D) with respect to such issue.

(F) SPECIAL RULES FOR APPLYING SUBPARAGRAPH(d).—

(i) IN GENERAL.—In determining the aggregate amount earned on nonpurpose obligations for purposes of subparagraph (D)—

(I) any gain or loss on the disposition of a nonpurpose obligation shall be taken into account, and

(II) unless the issuer otherwise elects, any amount earned on a bona fide debt service fund shall not be taken into account if the gross earnings on such fund for the bond year is less than $100,000.

(ii) TEMPORARY INVESTMENTS.—Under regulations prescribed by the Secretary, an issue shall, for purposes of this paragraph, be treated as meeting the requirements of subparagraph (D) if the gross proceeds of such issue are expended for the governmental purpose for which the bond was issued by no later than the day which is 6 months after the date of issuance of such issue. Gross proceeds which are held in a bona fide debt service fund shall not be considered gross proceeds for purposes of this clause only.

(G) EXEMPTION FROM GROSS INCOME OF SUM REBATED.—Gross income does not include the sum described in subparagraph (D). Notwithstanding any other provision of this title, no deduction shall be allowed for any amount paid to the United States under subparagraph (D).

(H) DEFINITIONS.—For purposes of this paragraph—

(i) NONPURPOSE OBLIGATIONS.—The term "nonpurpose obligation" means any security (within the meaning of subparagraph (A) or (B) of section 165(g)(2)) or any obligation not described in subsection (a) which—

(I) is acquired with the gross proceeds of an issue, and

(II) is not acquired in order to carry out the governmental purpose of the issue.

(ii) GROSS PROCEEDS.—The gross proceeds of an issue include—

(I) amounts received (including repayments of principal) as a result of investing the original proceeds of the issue, and

(II) amounts used to pay debt service on the issue.

(iii) YIELD.—The yield on the issue shall be determined on the basis of the issue price (within the meaning of section 1273 or 1274).

(7) REGULATIONS.—The Secretary shall prescribe such regulations as may be necessary to carry out the purposes of this subsection.

Amendments

• 1986, Tax Reform Act of 1986 (P.L. 99-514)

P.L. 99-514, §1867(b), provides:

(b) The amendment made by section 624 of the Tax Reform Act of 1984 shall not apply to obligations issued with respect to the Downtown Muskogee Revitalization Project for which a UDAG grant was preliminarily approved on May 5, 1981, if—

(1) such obligation is issued before January 1, 1986, or

(2) such obligation is issued after such date to provide additional financing for such project except that the aggregate amount of obligations to which this subsection applies shall not exceed $10,000,000.

• 1984, Deficit Reduction Act of 1984 (P.L. 98-369)

P.L. 98-369, §624(a):

Amended Code Sec. 103(c) by redesignating paragraph (6) as paragraph (7) and by inserting after paragraph (5) new paragraph (6). **Effective** with respect to bonds issued after 12-31-84 but do not apply to obligations issued for the Essex County New Jersey Resource Recovery Project authorized by the Port Authority of New York and New Jersey on 11-10-83, as part of an agreement approved by Essex County, New Jersey, on 7-7-81, and approved by the State of New Jersey on 12-31-81. The aggregate face amount of bonds to which this paragraph applies shall not exceed $350,000,000.

P.L. 98-369, §624(b)(2):

Amended Code Sec. 103(c) by striking out "Bonds" in the heading. **Effective** with respect to bonds issued after 12-31-84 but do not apply to obligations issued for the Essex County New Jersey Resource Recovery Project authorized by the Port Authority of New York and New Jersey on 11-10-83, as part of an agreement approved by Essex County, New Jersey, on 7-7-81, and approved by the State of New Jersey on 12-31-81. The aggregate face amount of bonds to which this paragraph applies shall not exceed $350,000,000. Prior to amendment, the heading read as follows:

(c) Arbitrage Bonds.—

P.L. 98-369, §624(b)(3):

Amended Code Sec. 103(c)(1) by inserting "to arbitrage bonds" in the heading. **Effective** with respect to bonds issued after 12-31-84 but do not apply to obligations issued for the Essex County New Jersey Resource Recovery Project authorized by the Port Authority of New York and New Jersey on 11-10-83, as part of an agreement approved by Essex County, New Jersey, on 7-7-81, and approved by the State of New Jersey on 12-31-81. The aggregate face amount of bonds to which this paragraph applies shall not exceed $350,000,000.

• 1978, Revenue Act of 1978 (P.L. 95-600)

P.L. 95-600, §703(j)(1)(B):

Amended Code Sec. 103(c)(1) by striking out "(a)(1) or (4)" each place it appeared (including the paragraph heading) and inserting in lieu thereof "(a)(1) or (2)". **Effective** 10-4-76.

P.L. 95-600, §703(j)(1)(C):

Amended Code Sec. 103(c)(2) by striking out "subsection (a)(1) or (2) or (4)" and inserting in lieu thereof "subsection (a)(1) or (2)". **Effective** 10-4-76.

P.L. 95-600, §703(j)(1)(D):

Amended Code Sec. 103(c)(5) by striking out "subsection (d)(2)(A)" and inserting in lieu thereof "paragraph (2)(A)". **Effective** 10-4-76.

P.L. 95-600, §703(q)(1):

Amended Code Sec. 103(c)(5) by substituting "section 438 of the Higher Education Act of 1965" for "section 2 of the Emergency Insured Student Loan Act of 1969". **Effective** for payments made by the Commissioner of Education after 1976.

• 1976, Tax Reform Act of 1976 (P.L. 94-455)

P.L. 94-455, §1901(a)(17):

Redesignated Code Sec. 103(d) as Code Sec. 103(c) and added "or (2)" after "(a)(1)" in Code Sec. 103(c)(2)(A). **Effective** for tax years beginning after 12-31-76.

P.L. 94-455, §1901(b):

Amended paragraph (3)(A) to substitute "educational organization described in section 170(b)(1)(A)(ii)" for "educational institution (within the meaning of section 151(e)(4))". **Effective** for tax years beginning after 12-31-76.

P.L. 94-455, §1906(b)(13)(A):

Amended 1954 Code by substituting "Secretary" for "Secretary or his delegate" each place it appeared. **Effective** 2-1-77.

P.L. 94-455, §2105(c)(1):

Redesignated paragraph (5) as paragraph (6) and inserted a new paragraph (5). **Effective** with respect to obligations issued on or after 10-4-76.

P.L. 94-455, §2105(c)(2):

Inserted "(a)(1) or (4)" in place of "(a)(1)" in paragraph (1) and added "or (4)" after "(a)(1) or (2)" in paragraph (2). **Effective** with respect to obligations issued on or after 10-4-76.

• 1969, Tax Reform Act of 1969 (P.L. 91-172)

P.L. 91-172, §601(a):

Added Code Sec. 103(d). **Effective** with respect to obligations issued after 10-9-69.

[Sec. 103(d)]

(d) CERTAIN IRRIGATION DAMS.—A dam for the furnishing of water for irrigation purposes which has a subordinate use in connection with the generation of electric energy by water shall be treated as meeting the requirements of subsection (b)(4)(G) if—

(1) substantially all of the stored water is contractually available for release from such dam for irrigation purposes, and

(2) the water so released is available on reasonable demand to members of the general public.

Amendments

• 1978, Revenue Act of 1978 (P.L. 95-600)

P.L. 95-600, §703(j)(1)(E):

Amended Code Sec. 103(d) by striking out "subsection (c)(4)(G)" and inserting in lieu thereof "subsection (b)(4)(G)". **Effective** 10-4-76.

• 1976, Tax Reform Act of 1976 (P.L. 94-455)

P.L. 94-455, §1901(a)(17):

Amended Code Sec. 103 by relettering subsection (d) as subsection (c). **Effective** for tax years beginning after 12-31-76.

• 1975, Revenue Adjustment Act of 1975 (P.L. 94-164)

P.L. 94-164, §7(a):

Amended Code Sec. 103 by redesignating subsection (e) as subsection (f) and by inserting new subsection (e). **Effective** with respect to obligations issued after 12-23-75.

[Sec. 103(e)]

(e) QUALIFIED SCHOLARSHIP FUNDING BONDS.—For purposes of subsection (a), the term "qualified scholarship funding bonds" means obligations issued by a corporation which—

(1) is a corporation not for profit established and operated exclusively for the purpose of acquiring student loan notes incurred under the Higher Education Act of 1965, and

(2) is organized at the request of the State or one or more political subdivisions thereof or is requested to exercise such power by one or more political subdivisions and required by its corporate charter and bylaws, or required by State law, to devote any income (after payment of expenses, debt service, and the creation of reserves for the same) to the purchase of additional student loan notes or to pay over any income to the State or a political subdivision thereof.

Amendments

• 1976, Tax Reform Act of 1976 (P.L. 94-455)

P.L. 94-455, §1901(a)(17):

Relettered Code Sec. 103(f) as Code Sec. 103(e). **Effective** for tax years beginning after 12-31-76.

P.L. 94-455, §2105(b):

Added Code Sec. 103(f) and relettered former Code Sec. 103(f) as Code Sec. 103(g). **Effective** with respect to obligations issued on or after 10-4-76.

[Sec. 103(f)]

(f) CERTAIN FEDERALLY GUARANTEED OBLIGATIONS.—Any obligation the payment of interest or principal (or both) of which is guaranteed in whole or in part under title I of the New York City Loan Guarantee Act of 1978 shall, with respect to interest accrued during the period for which such guarantee is in effect, be treated as an obligation not described in subsection (a).

Amendments

• 1978, New York City Loan Guarantee Act of 1978 (P.L. 95-339)

P.L. 95-339, §201(a):

Redesignated former subsection (f) as (g) and added new subsection (f). **Effective** for tax years ending after 8-8-78.

[Sec. 103(g)]

(g) QUALIFIED STEAM-GENERATING OR ALCOHOL-PRODUCING FACILITIES.—

(1) IN GENERAL.—For purposes of subsection (b)(4)(E), the term "solid waste disposal facility" includes—

(A) a qualified steam-generating facility, and

(B) a qualified alcohol-producing facility.

(2) QUALIFIED STEAM-GENERATING FACILITY DEFINED.—For purposes of paragraph (1), the term "qualified steam-generating facility" means a steam-generating facility for which—

(A) more than half of the fuel (determined on a Btu basis) is solid waste or fuel derived from solid waste, and

(B) substantially all of the solid waste derived fuel is produced at a facility which is—

(i) located at or adjacent to the site for such steam-generating facility, and

(ii) owned and operated by the person who owns and operates the steam-generating facility.

(3) QUALIFIED ALCOHOL-PRODUCING FACILITY.—For purposes of paragraph (1), the term "qualified alcohol-producing facility" means a facility—

(A) the primary product of which is alcohol,

(B) more than half of the feedstock for which is solid waste or a feedstock derived from solid waste, and

(C) substantially all of the solid waste derived feedstock for which is produced at a facility which is—

(i) located at or adjacent to the site for such alcohol-producing facility, and

(ii) owned and operated by the person who owns and operates the alcohol-producing facility.

(4) SPECIAL LOCATION RULE IN CASE OF STEAM-GENERATING FACILITY.—A facility for producing solid waste derived fuel shall be treated as a facility which meets the requirements of clauses (i) and (ii) of paragraph (2)(B) if—

(A) such facility and the steam-generating facility are owned and operated by or for a State or the same political subdivision or subdivisions of a State, and

(B) substantially all of the solid waste used in producing the solid waste derived fuel at the facility producing such fuel is collected from the area in which the steam-generating facility is located.

Amendments

• 1980, Crude Oil Windfall Profit Tax Act of 1980 (P.L. 96-223)

P.L. 96-223, §241(a):

Added Code Sec. 103(g). **Effective** with respect to obligations issued after 10-18-79.

P.L. 96-223, §241(b)-(c), provides:

(b) CERTAIN SOLID WASTE AND ENERGY-PRODUCING FACILITIES.—

(1) GENERAL RULE.—For purposes of section 103 of the Internal Revenue Code of 1954, any obligation issued by an authority for 2 or more political subdivisions of a State which is part of an issue substantially all of the proceeds of which are to be used to provide solid waste-energy producing facilities shall be treated as an obligation of a political subdivision of a State which meets the requirements of section 103(b)(4)(E) of such Code (relating to solid waste disposal, etc., facilities). Nothing in the preceding sentence shall be construed to override the limitations of section 103(c) of such Code (relating to arbitrage bonds).

(2) SOLID WASTE-ENERGY PRODUCING FACILITIES.—For purposes of paragraph (1), the term "solid waste-energy producing facilities" means any solid waste disposal facility and any facility for the production of steam and electrical energy if—

(A) substantially all of the fuel for the facility producing steam and electrical energy is derived from solid waste from such solid waste disposal facility,

(B) both such solid waste disposal facility and the facility producing steam and electrical energy are owned and operated by the authority referred to in paragraph (1), and

(C) all of the electrical energy and steam produced by the facility for producing steam and electricity which is not used by such facility is sold, for purposes other than resale, to an agency or instrumentality of the United States.

(3) SOLID WASTE DISPOSAL FACILITY.—For purposes of paragraph (2), the term "solid waste disposal facility" means any solid waste disposal facility within the meaning of section 103(b)(4)(E) of the Internal Revenue Code of 1954 (determined without regard to section 103(g) of such Code).

(4) OBLIGATIONS MUST BE IN REGISTERED FORM.—This subsection shall not apply to any obligation which is not issued in registered form.

(c) SPECIAL RULE FOR CERTAIN ALCOHOL-PRODUCING FACILITIES.—

(1) IN GENERAL.—Subparagraph (C) of section 103(g)(3) of the Internal Revenue Code of 1954 (as added by subsection (a)) shall not apply to any facility for the production of alcohol from solid waste if—

(A) substantially all of the solid waste derived feedstock for such facility is produced at a facility which—

(i) went into full production in 1977,

(ii) is located within the limits of a city, and

(iii) is located in the same metropolitan area as the alcohol-producing facility, and

(B) before March 1, 1980, there were negotiations between a governmental body and an organization described in section 501(c)(3) of the Internal Revenue Code of 1954 with respect to the utilization of a special process for the production of alcohol at such alcohol-producing facility.

(2) LIMITATION.—The aggregate amount of obligations which may be issued by reason of paragraph (1) with respect to any project shall not exceed $30,000,000.

(3) TERMINATION.—This subsection shall not apply to obligations issued after December 31, 1985.

The provisions of P.L. 96-223, §241(b) and (c) are applicable with respect to obligations issued after October 18, 1979.

[Sec. 103(h)]

(h) OBLIGATION MUST NOT BE GUARANTEED, ETC.—

(1) IN GENERAL.—An obligation shall not be treated as an obligation described in subsection (a) if such obligation is federally guaranteed.

(2) FEDERALLY GUARANTEED DEFINED.—For purposes of paragraph (1), an obligation is federally guaranteed if—

(A) the payment of principal or interest with respect to such obligation is guaranteed (in whole or in part) by the United States (or any agency or instrumentality thereof),

(B) such obligation is issued as part of an issue and a significant portion of the proceeds of such issue are to be—

(i) used in making loans the payment of principal or interest with respect to which are to be guaranteed (in whole or in part) by the United States (or any agency or instrumentality thereof), or

(ii) invested (directly or indirectly) in federally insured deposits or accounts, or

(C) the payment of principal or interest on such obligation is otherwise indirectly guaranteed (in whole or in part) by the United States (or an agency or instrumentality thereof).

(3) EXCEPTIONS.—

(A) CERTAIN INSURANCE PROGRAMS.—An obligation shall not be treated as federally guaranteed by reason of—

(i) any guarantee by the Federal Housing Administration, the Veterans' Administration, the Federal National Mortgage Association, the Federal Home Loan Mortgage Corporation, or the Government National Mortgage Association,

(ii) any guarantee of student loans and any guarantee by the Student Loan Marketing Association to finance student loans,

(iii) any guarantee by the Small Business Administration with respect to qualified contracts for pollution control facilities (within the meaning of section 404(a) of the Small Business Investment Act of 1958, as in effect on the date of the enactment of the Tax Reform Act of 1984) if—

(I) the Administrator of the Small Business Administration charges a fee for making such guarantee, and

(II) the amount of such fee equals or exceeds 1 percent of the amount guaranteed, or

(iv) any guarantee by the Bonneville Power Authority pursuant to the Northwest Power Act (16 U.S.C. 839d) as in effect on the date of the enactment of the Tax Reform Act of 1984 with respect to any obligation issued before July 1, 1989.

(B) DEBT SERVICE, ETC.—Paragraph (1) shall not apply to—

(i) proceeds of the issue invested for an initial temporary period until such proceeds are needed for the purpose for which such issue was issued,

(ii) investments of a bona fide debt service fund,

(iii) investments of a reserve which meet the requirements of subsection (c)(4)(B),

(iv) investments in obligations issued by the United States Treasury, or

(v) other investments permitted under regulations.

(C) EXCEPTION FOR HOUSING PROGRAMS.—

(i) IN GENERAL.—Except as provided in clause (ii), paragraph (1) shall not apply to—

(I) an obligation described in subsection (b)(4)(A) or a housing program obligation under section 11(b) of the United States Housing Act of 1937,

(II) a qualified mortgage bond (as defined in section 103A(c)(1)), or

(III) a qualified veterans' mortgage bond (as defined in section 103A(c)(3)).

(ii) EXCEPTION NOT TO APPLY WHERE OBLIGATION INVESTED IN FEDERALLY INSURED DEPOSITS OR ACCOUNTS.—Clause (i) shall not apply to any obligation which is federally guaranteed within the meaning of paragraph (2)(B)(ii).

(D) LOANS TO, OR GUARANTEES BY, FINANCIAL INSTITUTIONS.—Except as provided in paragraph (2)(B)(ii), an obligation which is issued as part of an issue shall not be treated as federally guaranteed merely by reason of the fact that the proceeds of such issue are used in making loans to a financial institution or there is a guarantee by a financial institution.

(4) DEFINITIONS.—For purposes of this subsection—

(A) TREATMENT OF CERTAIN ENTITIES WITH AUTHORITY TO BORROW FROM UNITED STATES.—To the extent provided in regulations prescribed by the Secretary, any entity with statutory authority to borrow from the United States shall be treated as an instrumentality of the United States. Except in the case of a private activity bond (as defined in subsection (n)(7)), nothing in the preceding sentence shall be construed as treating the District of Columbia or any possession of the United States as an instrumentality of the United States.

(B) FEDERALLY INSURED DEPOSIT OR ACCOUNT.—The term "federally insured deposit or account" means any deposit or account in a financial institution to the extent such deposit or account is insured under Federal law by the Federal Deposit Insurance Corporation, the Federal Savings and Loan Insurance Corporation, the National Credit Union Administration, or any similar federally chartered corporation.

(5) CERTAIN OBLIGATIONS SUBSIDIZED UNDER ENERGY PROGRAM.—

(A) IN GENERAL.—An obligation to which this paragraph applies shall be treated as an obligation not described in subsection (a) if the payment of the principal or interest with respect to such obligation is to be made (in whole or in part) under a program of a State, or a political subdivision of a State the principal purpose of which is to encourage the production or conservation of energy.

(B) OBLIGATIONS TO WHICH PARAGRAPH APPLIES.—This paragraph shall apply to any obligations to which paragraph (1) of subsection (b) does not apply by reason of—

(i) subsection (b)(4)(H) (relating to qualified hydroelectric generating facilities), or

(ii) subsection (g) (relating to qualified steam-generating or alcohol-producing facilities).

Amendments

• 1984, Deficit Reduction Act of 1984 (P.L. 98-369)

P.L. 98-369, §622:

Amended Code Sec. 103(h). **Effective** for obligations issued after 12-31-83, except that Code Sec. 103(h)(2)(B)(ii) applies to obligations issued after 4-14-83, except that such clause shall not apply to any obligation issued pursuant to a binding contract in effect on 3-4-83. See, also the exceptions following Act Sec. 630, in the notes following Code Sec. 103(b). Prior to amendment, Code Sec. 103(h) read as follows:

(h) Certain Obligations Must Not Be Guaranteed or Subsidized Under an Energy Program.—

(1) In General.—An obligation to which this subsection applies shall be treated as an obligation not described in subsection (a) if—

(A) the payment of principal or interest with respect to such obligation is guaranteed (in whole or in part) by the United States under a program a principal purpose of which is to encourage the production or conservation of energy, or

(B) the payment of the principal or interest with respect to such obligation is to be made (in whole or in part) with funds provided under such a program of the United States, a State, or a political subdivision of a State.

(2) Obligations to Which This Subsection Applies.—This subsection shall apply to any obligations to which paragraph (1) of subsection (b) does not apply by reason of—

(A) subsection (b)(4)(H) (relating to qualified hydroelectric generating facilities), or

(B) subsection (g) (relating to qualified steam-generating or alcohol-producing facilities).

• 1982, Tax Equity and Fiscal Responsibility Act of 1982 (P.L. 97-248)

P.L. 97-248, §310(c)(2)(A):

Amended Code Sec. 103(h)(1) by striking out subparagraph (A) and by redesignating subparagraphs (B) and (C) as subparagraphs (A) and (B), respectively. **Effective** for obligations issued after 12-31-82. Prior to amendment subparagraph (A) read as follows:

"(A) such obligation is not issued in registered form,"

P.L. 97-248, §310(c)(2)(B):

Amended the heading for subsection (h) of Code Sec. 103 by striking out "MUST BE IN REGISTERED FORM AND NOT" and inserting in lieu thereof "MUST NOT BE". **Effective** for obligations issued after 12-31-82.

• 1980, Crude Oil Windfall Profit Tax Act of 1980 (P.L. 96-223)

P.L. 96-223, §244(a):

Added Code Sec. 103(h). **Effective** for obligations issued after 10-18-79.

[Sec. 103(i)]

(i) OBLIGATIONS OF CERTAIN VOLUNTEER FIRE DEPARTMENTS.—

(1) IN GENERAL.—An obligation of a volunteer fire department shall be treated as an obligation of a political subdivision of a State if—

(A) such department is a qualified volunteer fire department with respect to an area within the jurisdiction of such political subdivision, and

(B) such obligation is issued as part of an issue substantially all of the proceeds of which are to be used for the acquisition, construction, reconstruction, or improvement of a firehouse or firetruck used or to be used by such department.

(2) QUALIFIED VOLUNTEER FIRE DEPARTMENT.—For purposes of this subsection, the term "qualified volunteer fire department" means, with respect to a political subdivision of a State, any organization—

(A) which is organized and operated to provide firefighting or emergency medical services for persons in an area (within the jurisdiction of such political subdivision) which is not provided with any other firefighting services,

(B) which is required (by written agreement) by the political subdivision to furnish firefighting services in such area.

[Sec. 103(j)]

(j) OBLIGATIONS MUST BE IN REGISTERED FORM TO BE TAX-EXEMPT.—

(1) IN GENERAL.—Nothing in subsection (a) or in any other provision of law shall be construed to provide an exemption from Federal income tax for interest on any registration-required obligation unless the obligation is in registered form.

(2) REGISTRATION-REQUIRED OBLIGATION.—The term "registration-required obligation" means any obligation other than an obligation which—

(A) is not of a type offered to the public,

(B) has a maturity (at issue) of not more than 1 year, or

(C) is described in section 163(f)(2)(B).

(3) SPECIAL RULES.—

(A) BOOK ENTRIES PERMITTED.—For purposes of paragraph (1), a book entry obligation shall be treated as in registered form if the right to the principal of, and stated interest on, such obligation may be transferred only through a book entry consistent with regulations prescribed by the Secretary.

(B) NOMINEES.—The Secretary shall prescribe such regulations as may be necessary to carry out the purpose of paragraph (1) where there is a nominee or chain of nominees.

Amendments

• 1982, Tax Equity and Fiscal Responsibility Act of 1982 (P.L. 97-248)

P.L. 97-248, §310(b)(1):

Amended Code Sec. 103 by redesignating subsection (j) as subsection (k) and by inserting after subsection (i) new subsection (j). **Effective** for obligations issued after 12-31-82, except that the amendments made by Act Sec. 310(b)(1) shall not apply to any obligations issued after 12-31-82, on the exercise of a warrant or the conversion of a convertible obligation if such warrant or obligation was offered or sold outside the United States without registration under the Securities Act of 1933 and was issued before 8-10-82. A rule similar to the rule of the preceding sentence shall also apply in the case of any regulations issued under section 163(f)(2)(C) of the Internal Revenue Code of 1954 (as added by this section) except that the date on which such regulations take effect shall be substituted for "August 10, 1982".

P.L. 97-248, §310(d)(4), as added by P.L. 97-448, §306(b)(2), provides:

(4) EFFECTIVE DATE FOR TAX-EXEMPT OBLIGATIONS.—In the case of obligations the interest on which is exempt from tax (determined without regard to the amendments made by this section)—

(A) under section 103 of the Internal Revenue Code of 1954, or

(B) under any other provision of law (without regard to the identity of the holder),

the amendments made by this section shall apply only to obligations issued after June 30, 1983. The preceding sentence shall not apply in the case of any obligation which under the Internal Revenue Code of 1954 (as in effect on the day before the date of the enactment of the Tax Equity and Fiscal Responsibility Act of 1982) was required to be in registered form.

[Sec. 103(k)]

(k) PUBLIC APPROVAL FOR INDUSTRIAL DEVELOPMENT BONDS.—

(1) IN GENERAL.—Notwithstanding subsection (b), an industrial development bond shall be treated as an obligation not described in subsection (a) unless the requirements of paragraph (2) of this subsection are satisfied.

(2) PUBLIC APPROVAL REQUIREMENT.—

(A) IN GENERAL.—An obligation shall satisfy the requirements of this paragraph if such obligation is issued as a part of an issue which has been approved by—

(i) the governmental unit—

(I) which issued such obligation, or

(II) on behalf of which such obligation was issued, and

(ii) each governmental unit having jurisdiction over the area in which any facility, with respect to which financing is to be provided from the proceeds of such issue, is located (except that if more than 1 governmental unit within a State has jurisdiction over the entire area within such State in which such facility is located, only 1 such unit need approve such issue).

(B) APPROVAL BY A GOVERNMENTAL UNIT.—For purposes of subparagraph (A), an issue shall be treated as having been approved by any governmental unit if such issue is approved—

(i) by the applicable elected representative of such governmental unit after a public hearing following reasonable public notice, or

(ii) by voter referendum of such governmental unit.

(C) SPECIAL RULES FOR APPROVAL OF FACILITY.—If there has been public approval under subparagraph (A) of the plan of financing a facility, such approval shall constitute approval under subparagraph (A) for any issue—

(i) which is issued pursuant to such plan within 3 years after the date of the first issue pursuant to the approval, and

(ii) all or substantially all of the proceeds of which are to be used to finance such facility or to refund previous financing under such plan.

(D) REFUNDING OBLIGATIONS.—No approval under subparagraph (A) shall be necessary with respect to any obligation which is issued to refund an obligation approved under subparagraph (A) (or treated as approved under subparagraph (C)) unless the maturity date of such obligation is later than the maturity date of the obligation to be refunded.

(E) APPLICABLE ELECTED REPRESENTATIVE.—For purposes of this paragraph—

(i) IN GENERAL.—The term "applicable elected representative" means with respect to any governmental unit—

(I) an elected legislative body of such unit, or

(II) the chief elected executive officer, the chief elected State legal officer of the executive branch, or any other elected official of such unit designated for purposes of this paragraph by such chief elected executive officer or by State law.

(ii) NO APPLICABLE ELECTED REPRESENTATIVE.—If (but for this clause) a governmental unit has no applicable elected representative, the applicable elected representative for purposes of clause (i) shall be the applicable elected representative of the governmental unit—

(I) which is the next higher governmental unit with such a representative, and

(II) from which the authority of the governmental unit with no such representative is derived.

Amendments

• 1982, Tax Equity and Fiscal Responsibility Act of 1982 (P.L. 97-248)

P.L. 97-248, §215(a):

Amended Code Sec. 103 by redesignating subsection (k) as subsection (l) and by inserting after subsection (j) new subsection (k). **Effective** for obligations issued after 12-31-82, other than obligations issued solely to refund any obligation that was issued prior to 7-1-82, and that has a maturity not exceeding 3 years.

[Sec. 103(l)]

(l) INFORMATION REPORTING REQUIREMENTS FOR CERTAIN BONDS.—

(1) IN GENERAL.—Notwithstanding subsection (b), any industrial development bond or any other obligation which is issued as part of an issue all or a major portion of the proceeds of which are to be used directly or indirectly—

(A) to finance loans to individuals for educational expenses, or

(B) by an organization described in section 501(c)(3) which is exempt from taxation by reason of section 501(a),

shall be treated as an obligation not described in paragraph (1) or (2) of subsection (a) unless such bond satisfies the requirements of paragraph (2).

(2) INFORMATION REPORTING REQUIREMENT.—An obligation satisfies the requirement of this paragraph if the issuer submits to the Secretary, not later than the 15th day of the 2nd calendar month after the close of the calendar quarter in which the obligation is issued, a statement concerning the issue of which the obligation is a part which contains—

(A) the name and address of the issuer,

(B) the date of issue, the amount of lendable proceeds of the issue, and the stated interest rate, term, and face amount of each obligation which is part of the issue,

(C) where required, the name of the applicable elected representative who approved the issue, or a description of the voter referendum by which the issue was approved,

(D) the name, address, and employer identification number of—

(i) each initial principal user of any facilities provided with the proceeds of the issue,

(ii) the common parent of any affiliated group of corporations (within the meaning of section 1504(a)) of which such initial principal user is a member, and

(iii) if the issue is treated as a separate issue under subsection (b)(6)(K), any person treated as a principal user under subsection (b)(6)(L),

(E) a description of any property to be financed from the proceeds of the issue, and

(F) if such obligation is a private activity bond (as defined in subsection (n)(7)), such information as the Secretary may require for purposes of determining whether the requirements of subsection (n) are met with respect to such obligation.

(3) EXTENSION OF TIME.—The Secretary may grant an extension of time for the filing of any statement required under paragraph (2) if there is reasonable cause for the failure to file such statement in a timely fashion.

Amendments

• 1982, Tax Equity and Fiscal Responsibility Act of 1982 (P.L. 97-248)

P.L. 97-248, §215(b)(1):

Amended Code Sec. 103 by redesignating subsection (l) as subsection (m) and by adding at the end thereof new subsection (l). **Effective** for obligations issued after 12-31-82 (including any obligations issued to refund an obligation issued prior to such date).

[Sec. 103(m)]

(m) OBLIGATIONS EXEMPT OTHER THAN UNDER THIS TITLE.—

(1) PRIOR EXEMPTIONS.—For purposes of this title, notwithstanding any provisions of this section or section 103A any obligation the interest on which is exempt from taxation under this title under any provision of law which is in effect on the date of the enactment of this subsection (other than a provision of this title) shall be treated as an obligation described in subsection (a). In the case of an obligation issued after December 31, 1983, such obligation shall not be treated as described in this paragraph unless the appropriate requirements of subsections (b), (c), (h), (j), (k), (l), (n) and (o) of this section and section 103A are met with respect to such obligation. For purposes of applying such requirements, a possession of the United States shall be treated as a State; except that clause (ii) of subsection (n)(4)(A) shall not apply.

(2) NO OTHER INTEREST TO BE EXEMPT EXCEPT AS PROVIDED BY THIS TITLE.—Notwithstanding any other provision of law, no interest on any obligation shall be exempt from taxation under this title unless such interest—

(A) is on an obligation described in paragraph (1), or

(B) is exempt from tax under this title without regard to any provision of law which is not contained in this title and which is not contained in a revenue Act.

(3) EXCEPTIONS.—The following obligations shall be treated as obligations described in paragraph (1) (without regard to the second sentence thereof):

(A) Any obligation issued pursuant to the Northwest Power Act (16 U.S.C. 839d) as in effect on the date of the enactment of the Tax Reform Act of 1984.

(B) Any obligation issued pursuant to section 608(a)(6)(A) of Public Law 97-468.

(C) Any obligation issued before June 19, 1984, under section 11(b) of the United States Housing Act of 1937.

Amendments

• 1984, Deficit Reduction Act of 1984 (P.L. 98-369)

P.L. 98-369, §628(a)(1):

Amended Code Sec. 103(m)(1) by adding the last sentence thereof. **Effective** for obligations issued after 12-31-83. Special rules appear after Act Sec. 630, in the notes for former Code Sec. 103(b).

P.L. 98-369, §628(a)(2):

Amended Code Sec. 103(m)(2)(B). **Effective** for obligations issued after 12-31-83. Special rules appear after Act Sec. 630, in the notes for former Code Sec. 103(b). Prior to amendment, it read as follows:

(B) is exempt from taxation under any provision of this title.

P.L. 98-369, §628(a)(3):

Added Code Sec. 103(m)(3). **Effective** for obligations issued after 12-31-83. Special rules appear after Act Sec. 630, in the notes for former Code Sec. 103(b).

[Sec. 103(n)]

(n) LIMITATION ON AGGREGATE AMOUNT OF PRIVATE ACTIVITY BONDS ISSUED DURING ANY CALENDAR YEAR.—

(1) IN GENERAL.—A private activity bond issued as part of an issue shall be treated as an obligation not described in subsection (a) if the aggregate amount of private activity bonds issued pursuant to such issue, when added to the aggregate amount of private activity bonds previously issued by the issuing authority during the calendar year, exceeds such authority's private activity bond limit for such calendar year.

(2) PRIVATE ACTIVITY BOND LIMIT FOR STATE AGENCIES.—For purposes of this subsection—

(A) IN GENERAL.—The private activity bond limit for any agency of the State authorized to issue private activity bonds for any calendar year shall be 50 percent of the State ceiling for such calendar year.

(B) SPECIAL RULE WHERE STATE HAS MORE THAN 1 AGENCY.—If more than 1 agency of the State is authorized to issue private activity bonds, all such agencies shall be treated as a single agency.

(3) PRIVATE ACTIVITY BOND LIMIT FOR OTHER ISSUERS.—For purposes of this subsection—

(A) IN GENERAL.—The private activity bond limit for any issuing authority (other than a State agency) for any calendar year shall be an amount which bears the same ratio to 50 percent of the State ceiling for such calendar year as—

(i) the population of the jurisdiction of such issuing authority, bears to

(ii) the population for the entire State.

(B) OVERLAPPING JURISDICTIONS.—For purposes of subparagraph (A)(i), the rules of section 103A(g)(3)(B) shall apply.

(4) STATE CEILING.—For purposes of this subsection—

(A) IN GENERAL.—The State ceiling applicable to any State for any calendar year shall be the greater of

(i) an amount equal to $150 multiplied by the State's population, or

(ii) $200,000,000.

(B) PHASE IN OF LIMITATION WHERE AMOUNT OF 1983 PRIVATE ACTIVITY BONDS EXCEEDS THE CEILING.—

(i) IN GENERAL.—In the case of any State which has an excess bond amount for 1983, the State ceiling for calendar year 1984 shall be the sum of the State ceiling determined under subparagraph (A) plus 50 percent of the excess bond amount for 1983.

(ii) EXCESS BOND AMOUNT FOR 1983.—For purposes of clause (i), the excess bond amount for 1983 in any State is the excess (if any) of—

(I) the aggregate amount of private activity bonds issued by issuing authorities in such State during the first 9 months of calendar year 1983 multiplied by 4/3, over

(II) the State ceiling determined under subparagraph (A) for calendar year 1984.

(C) ADJUSTMENT OF CEILING TO REFLECT PARTIAL TERMINATION OF SMALL ISSUE EXEMPTION.—In the case of calendar years after 1986, subparagraph (A) shall be applied by substituting "$100" for "$150."

(5) SPECIAL RULE FOR STATES WITH CONSTITUTIONAL HOME RULE CITIES.—In the case of any State with 1 or more constitutional home rule cities (as defined in section 103A(g)(5)(C)), the rules of paragraph (5) of section 103A(g) shall apply for purposes of this subsection.

(6) STATE MAY PROVIDE FOR DIFFERENT ALLOCATION.—

(A) IN GENERAL.—A State may, by law provide a different formula for allocating the State ceiling among the governmental units or other authorities in such State having authority to issue private activity bonds.

(B) INTERIM AUTHORITY FOR GOVERNOR.—

(i) IN GENERAL.—The Governor of any State may proclaim a different formula for allocating the State ceiling among the governmental units or other authorities in such State having authority to issue private activity bonds.

(ii) TERMINATION OF AUTHORITY.—The authority provided in clause (i) shall not apply after the earlier of—

(I) the first day of the first calendar year beginning after the legislature has met in regular session for more than 60 days after the date of the enactment of this paragraph, or

(II) the effective date of any State legislation with respect to the allocation of the State ceiling.

(C) STATE MAY NOT ALTER ALLOCATION TO CONSTITUTIONAL HOME RULE CITIES.—The rules of paragraph (6)(C) of section 103A(g) shall apply for purposes of this paragraph.

(7) PRIVATE ACTIVITY BOND.—For purposes of this subsection—

(A) IN GENERAL.—Except as otherwise provided in the paragraph, the term "private activity bond" means any obligation the interest on which is exempt from tax under subsection (a) and which is—

(i) an industrial development bond, or

(ii) a student loan bond.

(B) EXCEPTION FOR MULTIFAMILY HOUSING.—The term "private activity bond" shall not include any obligation described in subsection (b)(4)(A) nor any housing program obligation under section 11(b) of the United States Housing Act of 1937.

(C) EXCEPTION FOR CERTAIN FACILITIES DESCRIBED IN SECTION 103(b)(4)(C) OR (D).—

(i) IN GENERAL.—The term "private activity bond" shall not include any obligation described in subparagraph (C) or (D) of subsection (b)(4), but only if all of the property to be financed by the obligation is owned by or on behalf of a governmental unit.

(ii) EXCEPTION NOT TO APPLY TO CERTAIN PARKING FACILITIES.—For purposes of clause (i), subparagraph (D) of subsection (b)(4) shall be applied as if it did not contain the phrase "parking facilities".

(iii) DETERMINATION OF WHETHER PROPERTY OWNED BY GOVERNMENTAL UNIT.—For purposes of clause (i), property shall not be treated as not owned by a governmental unit solely by reason of the length of the lease to which it is subject if the lessee makes an irrevocable election (binding on the lessee and all successors in interest under the lease) not to claim depreciation or an investment credit with respect to such property.

(iv) RESTRICTION WHERE SIGNIFICANT FRONT END LOADING.—Under regulations prescribed by the Secretary, clause (i) shall not apply in any case where the property is leased under a lease which has significant front end loading of rental accruals or payments.

(D) REFUNDING ISSUES.—The term "private activity bond" shall not include any obligation which is issued to refund another obligation to the extent that the amount of such obligation does not exceed the amount of the refunded obligation. In the case of any student loan bond, the preceding sentence shall apply only if the maturity date of the refunding obligation is not later than the later of—

(i) the maturity of the obligation to be refunded, or

(ii) the date 17 years after the date on which the refunded obligation was issued (or in the case of a series of refundings, the date on which the original obligation was issued).

(8) STUDENT LOAN BONDS.—For purposes of this subsection, the term "student loan bond" means an obligation which is issued as part of an issue all or a major portion of the proceeds of which are to be used, directly or indirectly to finance loans to individuals for educational expenses.

(9) POPULATION.—For purposes of this subsection, determinations of the population of any State (or issuing authority) shall be made with respect to any calendar year on the basis of the most recent census estimate of the resident population of such State (or issuing authority) published by the Bureau of the Census before the beginning of such calendar year.

(10) ELECTIVE CARRYFORWARD OF UNUSED LIMITATION FOR SPECIFIED PROJECT.—

(A) IN GENERAL.—If—

(i) an issuing authority's private activity bond limit for any calendar year after 1983, exceeds

(ii) the aggregate amount of private activity bonds issued during such calendar year by such authority,

such authority may elect to treat all (or any portion) of such excess as a carryforward for 1 or more carryforward projects.

(B) ELECTION MUST IDENTIFY PROJECT.—In any election under subparagraph (A), the issuing authority shall—

(i) identify (with reasonable specificity) the project (or projects) for which the carryforward is elected, and

(ii) specify the portion of the excess described in subparagraph (A) which is to be a carryforward for each such project.

(C) USE OF CARRYFORWARD.—

(i) IN GENERAL.—If any issuing authority elects a carryforward under subparagraph (A) with respect to any carryforward project, any private activity bonds issued by such authority with respect to such project during the 3 calendar years (or, in the case of a project described in subsection (b)(4)(F), 6 calendar years) following the calendar year in which the carryforward arose shall not be taken into account under paragraph (1) to the extent the amount of such bonds do not exceed the amount of the carryforward elected for such project.

(ii) ORDER IN WHICH CARRYFORWARD USED.—Carryforwards elected with respect to any project shall be used in the order of the calendar years in which they arose.

(D) ELECTION.—Any election made under this paragraph shall be made at such time and in such manner as the Secretary shall by regulations prescribe. Any such election (and any identification or specification contained therein), once made, shall be irrevocable.

(E) CARRYFORWARD PROJECT.—For purposes of this paragraph, the term "carryforward project" means—

(i) any project described in paragraph (4) or (5) of subsection (b), and

(ii) the purpose of issuing student loan bonds.

(11) TREATMENT OF QUALIFIED SCHOLARSHIP FUNDING BONDS.—In the case of a qualified scholarship funding bond (as defined in subsection (e)), such bond shall be treated for purposes of this subsection as issued by a State or local issuing authority (whichever is appropriate).

(12) CERTIFICATION OF NO CONSIDERATION FOR ALLOCATION.—

(A) IN GENERAL.—Any private activity bond allocated any portion of the State limit shall not be exempt from tax under subsection (a) unless the public official if any responsible for such allocation certifies under penalty of perjury that the allocation was not made in consideration of any bribe, gift, gratuity, or direct or indirect contribution to any political campaign.

(B) ANY CRIMINAL PENALTY MADE APPLICABLE.—Any person willfully making an allocation described in subparagraph (A) in consideration of any bribe, gift, gratuity, or direct or indirect contribution to any political campaign shall be subject to criminal penalty to the same extent as if such allocation were a willful attempt to evade tax imposed by this title.

(13) FACILITY MUST BE LOCATED WITHIN STATE.—

(A) IN GENERAL.—Except as provided in subparagraph (B), no portion of the State ceiling applicable to any State for any calendar year may be used with respect to financing for a facility located outside such State.

(B) EXCEPTION FOR CERTAIN FACILITIES WHERE STATE WILL GET PROPORTIONATE SHARE OF BENEFITS.—Subparagraph (A) shall not apply to any issue described in subparagraph (E), (G), or (H) of subsection (b)(4) if the issuer establishes that the State's share of the use of the facility (or its output) will equal or exceed the State's share of the private activity bonds issued to finance the facility.

Amendments

• 1984, Deficit Reduction Act of 1984 (P.L. 98-369)

P.L. 98-369, §621:

Redesignated Code Sec. 103(n) as Code Sec. 103(o) and added new Code Sec. 103(n). **Effective** for obligations issued after 12-31-83. For exceptions, however, see Act Sec. 631(a)(2)-(3), below.

P.L. 98-369, §631(a)(2)-(3)[(4)], provides:

(a) Private Activity Bond Cap.—

* * *

(2) Inducement Resolution Before June 19, 1984.—The amendment made by section 621 shall not apply to any issue of obligations if—

(A) there was an inducement resolution (or other comparable preliminary approval) for the issue before June 19, 1984, and

(B) the issue is issued before January 1, 1985.

(3) Certain Projects Preliminarily Approved Before October 19, 1983, Given Approval.—If—

(A) there was an inducement resolution (or other comparable preliminary approval) for a project before October 19, 1983, by any issuing authority,

(B) a substantial user of such project notifies the issuing authority within 30 days after the date of the enactment of this Act that it intends to claim its rights under this paragraph, and

(C) construction of such project began before October 19, 1983, or the substantial user was under a binding contract on such date to incur significant expenditures with respect to such project,

such issuing authority shall allocate its share of the limitation under section 103(n) of such Code for the calendar year during which the obligations were to be issued pursuant to such resolution (or other approval) first to such project. If the amount of obligations required by all projects which meet the requirements of the preceding sentence exceeds the issuing authority's share of the limitation under section 103(n) of such Code, priority under the preceding sentence shall be provided first to those projects for which substantial expenditures were incurred before October 19, 1983. If any issuing authority fails to meet the requirements of this paragraph, the limitation under section 103(n) of such Code for the issuing authority for the calendar year following such failure shall be reduced by the amount of obligations with respect to which such failure occurred.

(3) [(4)] Exception for Certain Bonds for a Convention Center and Resource Recovery Project.—In the case of any city, if—

(A) the city council of such city authorized a feasibility study for a convention center on June 10, 1982, and

(B) on November 4, 1983, a municipal authority acting for such city accepted a proposal for the construction of a facility that is capable of generating steam and electricity through the combustion of municipal waste,

the amendment made by section 621 shall not apply to any issue, issued during 1984, 1985, 1986, or 1987 and substantially all of the proceeds of which are to be used to finance the convention center (or access ramps and parking facilities therefor) described in subparagraph (A) or the facility described in subparagraph (B).

[Sec. 103(o)]

(o) PRIVATE LOAN BONDS.—

(1) DENIAL OF TAX EXEMPTION.—For purposes of this title, any private loan bond shall be treated as an obligation which is not described in subsection (a).

(2) PRIVATE LOAN BONDS.—For purposes of this subsection—

(A) IN GENERAL.—The term "private loan bond" means any obligation which is issued as part of an issue all or a significant portion of the proceeds of which are reasonably expected to be used directly or indirectly to make or finance loans (other than loans described in subparagraph (C)) to persons who are not exempt persons (within the meaning of subsection (b)(3)).

(B) EXCLUDED OBLIGATIONS.—The term "private loan bond" shall not include any—

(i) qualified student loan bond,

(ii) industrial development bond, or

(iii) qualified mortgage bond or qualified veterans' mortgage bond.

(C) EXCLUDED LOANS.—A loan is described in this subparagraph if the loan—

(i) enables the borrower to finance any governmental tax or assessment of general application for an essential governmental function, or

(ii) is used to acquire or carry nonpurpose obligations (within the meaning of subsection (c)(6)(H)(i)).

(3) QUALIFIED STUDENT LOAN BONDS.—For purposes of this subsection, the term "qualified student loan bond" means any obligation which is issued as part of an issue all or a major portion of the proceeds of which are reasonably expected to be used directly or indirectly to make or finance student loans under a program of general application to which the Higher Education Act of 1965 applies if—

(A) limitations are imposed under the program on—

(i) the maximum amount of loans outstanding to any student, and

(ii) the maximum rate of interest payable on any loan,

(B) the loans are directly or indirectly guaranteed by the Federal Government,

(C) the financing of loans under the program is not limited by Federal law to the proceeds of obligations the interest on which is exempt from taxation under this title, and

(D) special allowance payments under section 438 of the Higher Education Act of 1965—

(i) are authorized to be paid with respect to loans made under the program, or

(ii) would be authorized to be made with respect to loans under the program if such loans were not financed with the proceeds of obligations the interest on which is exempt from taxation under this title.

Such term shall not include any obligation issued under a State program which discriminates on the basis of the location (in the United States) at which the educational institution is located.

Amendments

• 1986, Tax Reform Act of 1986 (P.L. 99-514)

P.L. 99-514, §1896(c), as amended by P.L. 100-647 §1018(n), provides:

(c) TRANSITIONAL RULES.—

(1) TREATMENT OF CERTAIN OBLIGATIONS ISSUED BY THE CITY OF BALTIMORE.—Obligations issued by the city of Baltimore, Maryland, after June 30, 1985, shall not be treated as private loan bonds for purposes of section 103(o) of the Internal Revenue Code of 1954 (or as private activity bonds for purposes of section 103 and part IV of subchapter A of chapter 1 of the Internal Revenue Code of 1986, as amended by title XIII of this Act) by reason of the use of a portion of the proceeds of such obligations to finance or refinance temporary advances made by the city of Baltimore in connection with loans to persons who are not exempt persons (within the meaning of section 103(b)(3) of such Code) if—

(A) such obligations are not industrial development bonds (within the meaning of section 103(b)(2) of the Internal Revenue Code of 1954),

(B) the portion of the proceeds of such obligations so used is attributable to debt approved by voter referendum on or before November 2, 1982,

(C) the loans to such nonexempt persons were approved by the Board of Estimates of the city of Baltimore on or before October 19, 1983, and

(D) the aggregate amount of such temporary advances financed or refinanced by such obligations does not exceed $27,000,000.

(2) WHITE PINE POWER PROJECT.—The amendment made by section 626(a) of the Tax Reform Act of 1984 shall not apply to any obligation issued during 1984 to provide financing for the White Pine Power Project in Nevada.

(3) TAX INCREMENT BONDS.—The amendment made by section 626(a) of the Tax Reform Act of 1984 shall not apply to any tax increment financing obligation issued before August 16, 1986, if—

(A) substantially all of the proceeds of the issue are to be used to finance—

(i) sewer, street, lighting, or other governmental improvements to real property,

(ii) the acquisition of any interest in real property (by a governmental unit having the power to exercise eminent domain), the preparation of such property for new use, or the transfer of such interest to a private developer, or

(iii) payments of reasonable relocation costs of prior users of such real property,

(B) all of the activities described in subparagraph (A) are pursuant to a redevelopment plan adopted by the issuing authority before the issuance of such issue,

(C) repayment of such issue is secured exclusively by pledges of that portion of any increase in real property tax revenues (or their equivalent) attributable to the redevelopment resulting from the issue (or similar issues), and

(D) none of the property described in subparagraph (A) is subject to a real property or other tax based on a rate or valuation method which differs from the rate and valuation method applicable to any other similar property located within the jurisdiction of the issuing authority.

(4) EASTERN MAINE ELECTRIC COOPERATIVE.—The amendment made by section 626(a) of the Tax Reform Act of 1984 shall not apply to obligations issued by Massachusetts Municipal Wholesale Electric Company Project No. 6 if—

(A) such obligation is issued before January 1, 1986,

(B) such obligation is issued after such date to refund a prior obligation for such project, except that the aggregate amount of obligations to which this subparagraph applies shall not exceed $100,000,000, or

(C) such obligation is issued after such date to provide additional financing for such project except that the aggregate amount of obligations to which this subparagraph applies shall not exceed $45,000,000.

Subparagraph (B) shall not apply to any obligation issued for the advance refunding of any obligation.

(5) CLARIFICATION OF TRANSITIONAL RULE FOR CERTAIN STUDENT LOAN PROGRAMS.—Subparagraph (A) of section 626(b)(2) of the Tax Reform Act of 1984 is amended by striking out "$11 million" in the table contained in such subparagraph and inserting in lieu thereof "$70 million".

(6) TREATMENT OF OBLIGATIONS TO FINANCE ST. JOHNS RIVER POWER PARK.—

(A) IN GENERAL.—The amendment made by section 626(a) of the Tax Reform Act of 1984 shall not apply to any obligation issued to finance the project described in subparagraph (B) if—

(i) such obligation is issued before September 27, 1985,

(ii) such obligation is issued after such date to refund a prior tax exemption obligation for such project, the amount of such obligation does not exceed the outstanding amount of the refunded obligation, and such prior tax exempt obligation is retired not later than the date 30 days after the issuance of the refunding obligation, or

(iii) such obligation is issued after such date to provide additional financing for such project except that the aggregate amount of obligations to which this clause applies shall not exceed $150,000,000.

Clause (ii) shall not apply to any obligation issued for the advance refunding of any obligation.

(B) DESCRIPTION OF PROJECT.—The project described in this subparagraph in the St. Johns River Power Park system in Florida which was authorized by legislation enacted by the Florida Legislature in February of 1982.

• 1984, Deficit Reduction Act of 1984 (P.L. 98-369)

P.L. 98-369, §626(a):

Amended Code Sec. 103 by adding at the end thereof new subsection (o). **Effective** for obligations issued after the date of enactment. See, however the exceptions provided in Act Sec. 626(b)(2), below.

P.L. 98-369, §626(b)(2)-(6), provides:

(b) Effective Dates.—

* * *

(2) Exceptions for Certain Student Loan Programs.—

(A) In General.—The amendments made by this section shall not apply to obligations issued by a program described in the following table to the extent the aggregate face amount of such obligations does not exceed the amount of allowable obligations specified in the following table with respect to such program:

Program	Amount of Allowable Obligations
Colorado Student Obligation Bond Authority	$60 million
Connecticut Higher Education Supplementary Loan Authority	$15.5 million
District of Columbia	$50 million
Illinois Higher Education Authority	$11 million
State of Iowa	$16 million
Louisiana Public Facilities Authority	$75 million
Maine Health and Higher Education Facilities Authority	$5 million
Maryland Higher Education Supplemental Loan Program	$24 million
Massachusetts College Student Loan Authority	$90 million
Minnesota Higher Education Coordinating Board	$60 million
New Hampshire Higher Education and Health Facilities Authority	$39 million
New York Dormitory Authority	$120 million
Pennsylvania Higher Education Assistance Agency	$300 million
Georgia Private Colleges and University Authority	$31 million
Wisconsin State Building Commission	$60 million
South Dakota Health and Educational Facilities Authority	$6 million

(B) Pennsylvania Higher Education Assistance Agency.—Subparagraph (A) shall apply to obligations issued by the Pennsylvania Higher Education Assistance Agency only if such obligations are issued solely for the purpose of refunding student loan bonds outstanding on March 15, 1984.

(3) Certain Tax-Exempt Mortgage Subsidy Bonds.—For purposes of applying section 103(o) of the Internal Revenue Code of 1954, the term "consumer loan bond" shall not include any mortgage subsidy bond (within the meaning of section 103A(b) of such Code) to which the amendments made by section 1102 of the Mortgage Subsidy Bond Tax Act of 1980 do not apply.

(4) Refunding Exception.—The amendments made by this section shall not apply to any obligation or series of obligations the proceeds of which are used exclusively to refund obligations issued before March 15, 1984, except that—

(A) the amount of the refunding obligations may not exceed 101 percent of the aggregate face amount of the refunded obligations, and

(B) the maturity date of any refunding obligation may not be later than the date which is 17 years after the date on which the refunded obligation was issued (or, in the case of a series of refundings, the date on which the original obligation was issued).

(5) Exception for Certain Established Programs—The amendments made by this section shall not apply to any obligation substantially all of the proceeds of which are used to carry out a program established under State law which has been in effect in substantially the same form during the 30-year period ending on the date of enactment of this Act, but only if such proceeds are used to make loans or to fund similar obligations—

(A) in the same manner in which

(B) in the same (or lesser) amount per participant, and

(C) for the same purposes for which,

such program was operated on March 15, 1984. This subparagraph shall not apply to obligations issued on or after March 15, 1987.

(6) Certain Bonds for Renewable Energy Property.—The amendments made by this section shall not apply to any obligations described in section 243 of the Crude Oil Windfall Profit Tax Act of 1980.

[Sec. 103(p)]

(p) CROSS REFERENCES.—

For provisions relating to the taxable status of—

(1) Certain obligations issued by Indian tribal governments (or their subdivisions), see section 7871.

(2) Exempt interest dividends of regulated investment companies, see section 852(b)(5)(B).

(3) Puerto Rican bonds, see section 3 of the Act of March 2, 1917, as amended (48 U.S.C. 745).

(4) Virgin Islands insular and municipal bonds, see section 1 of the Act of October 27, 1949 (48 U.S.C. 1403).

(5) Certain obligations issued under title I of the Housing Act of 1949, see section 102(g) of title I of such Act (42 U.S.C. 1452(g)).

Amendments

• 1984, Deficit Reduction Act of 1984 (P.L. 98-369)

P.L. 98-369, §621:

Redesignated Code Sec. 103(n) as Code Sec. 103(o)[p]. **Effective**, generally, for obligations issued after 12-31-83.

• 1983 (P.L. 97-473)

P.L. 97-473, §202(b)(2):

Amended Code Sec. 103(m). For the **effective** date of the amendment, see the amendment note for P.L. 97-473, Act Sec. 204 following Code Sec. 7871. Prior to amendment, Code Sec. 103(m) read as follows:

(m) CROSS REFERENCES.—

For provisions relating to the taxable status of—

(1) Puerto Rican bonds, see section 3 of the Act of March 2, 1917, as amended (48 U.S.C. 745).

(2) Virgin Islands insular and municipal bonds, see section 1 of the Act of October 27, 1919 (48 U.S.C. 1403).

(3) Certain obligations issued under title I of the Housing Act of 1949, see section 102(g) of title I of such Act (42 U.S.C. 1452(g)).

• 1983, Surface Transportation Act of 1982 (P.L. 97-424)

P.L. 97-424, §547(a):

Redesignated subsection (m) as subsection (n) and added a new subsection (m). **Effective** 1-6-83.

• 1982, Tax Equity and Fiscal Responsibility Act of 1982 (P.L. 97-248)

P.L. 97-248, §215(a):

Redesignated Code Sec. 103(k) as (l). **Effective** for obligations issued after 12-31-82.

P.L. 97-248, §215(b)(1):

Redesignated Code Sec. 103(l) as (m). **Effective** for obligations issued after 12-31-82.

P.L. 97-248, §310(b)(1):

Redesignated Code Sec. 103(j) as (k). **Effective** for obligations issued after 12-31-82.

• 1981, Economic Recovery Tax Act of 1981 (P.L. 97-34)

P.L. 97-34, §812(a):

Amended Code Sec. 103 by redesignating subsection (i) as subsection (j) and by inserting after subsection (h) new subsection (i). **Effective** for obligations issued after 12-31-80.

• 1980, Crude Oil Windfall Profit Tax Act of 1980 (P.L. 96-223)

P.L. 96-223, §241(a):

Redesignated subsection (g) as Code Sec. 103(h). **Effective** 4-3-80.

P.L. 96-223, §244(a):

Redesignated Code Sec. 103(h), as redesignated by §241(a), as Code Sec. 103(i). **Effective** 4-3-80.

• 1978, New York City Loan Guarantee Act of 1978 (P.L. 95-339)

P.L. 95-339, §201(a):

Redesignated former subsection (f) as subsection (g). **Effective** for tax years ending after 8-8-78.

• 1976, Tax Reform Act of 1976 (P.L. 94-455)

P.L. 94-455, §1901(a)(17):

Redesignated former Code Sec. 103(g) as Code Sec. 103(f) and amended redesignated Code Sec. 103(f). **Effective** for tax years beginning after 12-31-76. Prior to amendment, redesignated Code Sec. 103(f) read as follows:

(f) CROSS REFERENCES.

For provisions relating to the taxable status of—

(1) Bonds and certificates of indebtedness authorized by the First Liberty Bond Act, see sections 1 and 6 of that Act (40 Stat. 35, 36; 31 U.S.C. 746, 755);

(2) Bonds issued to restore or maintain the gold reserve, see section 2 of the Act of March 14, 1900 (31 Stat. 46; 31 U.S.C. 408);

(3) Bonds, notes, certificates of indebtedness, and Treasury bills authorized by the Second Liberty Bond Act, see sections 4, 5(b) and (d), 7, 18(b), and 22(d) of that Act, as amended (40 Stat. 290; 46 Stat. 20,775; 40 Stat. 291, 1310; 55 Stat. 8; 31 U.S.C. 752a, 754, 747, 753, 757c);

(4) Bonds, notes, and certificates of indebtedness of the United States and bonds of the War Finance Corporation owned by certain nonresidents, see section 3 of the Fourth Liberty Bond Act, as amended (40 Stat. 1311, §4; 31 U.S.C. 750);

(5) Certificates of indebtedness issued after February 4, 1910, see section 2 of the Act of that date (36 Stat. 192; 31 U.S.C. 769);

(6) Consols of 1930, see section 11 of the Act of March 14, 1900 (31 Stat. 48; 31 U.S.C. 751);

(7) Obligations and evidences of ownership issued by the United States or any of its agencies or instrumentalities on or after March 28, 1942, see section 4 of the Public Debt Act of 1941, as amended (c. 147, 61 Stat. 180; 31 U.S.C. 742a);

(8) Commodity Credit Corporation obligations, see section 5 of the Act of March 8, 1938 (52 Stat. 108; 15 U.S.C. 713a-5);

(9) Debentures issued by Federal Housing Administrator, see sections 204(d) and 207(i) of the National Housing Act, as amended (52 Stat. 14, 20; 12 U.S.C. 1710, 1713);

(10) Debentures issued to mortgagees by United States Maritime Commission, see section 1105(c) of the Merchant Marine Act, 1936, as amended (52 Stat. 972; 46 U.S.C. 1275);

(11) Federal Deposit Insurance Corporation obligations, see section 15 of the Federal Deposit Insurance Act (64 Stat. 890; 12 U.S.C. 1825);

(12) Federal Home Loan Bank obligations, see section 13 of the Federal Home Loan Bank Act, as amended (49 Stat. 295, §8; 12 U.S.C. 1433);

(13) Federal savings and loan association loans, see section 5(h) of the Home Owners' Loan Act of 1933, as amended (48 Stat. 133; 12 U.S.C. 1464);

(14) Federal Savings and Loan Insurance Corporation obligations, see section 402(e) of the National Housing Act (48 Stat. 1257; 12 U.S.C. 1725);

(15) Home Owners' Loan Corporation bonds, see section 4(c) of the Home Owners' Loan Act of 1933, as amended (48 Stat. 644, c. 168; 12 U.S.C. 1463);

(16) Obligations of Central Bank for Cooperatives, production credit corporations, production credit associations, and banks for cooperatives, see section 63 of the Farm Credit Act of 1933 (48 Stat. 267; 12 U.S.C. 1138c);

(17) Panama Canal bonds, see section 1 of the Act of December 21, 1904 (34 Stat. 5; 31 U.S.C. 743), section 8 of the Act of June 28, 1902 (32 Stat. 484; 31 U.S.C. 744), and section 39 of the Tariff Act of 1909 (36 Stat. 117; 31 U.S.C. 745);

(18) Philippine bonds, etc., issued before the independence of the Philippines, see section 9 of the Philippine Independence Act (48 Stat. 463; 48 U.S.C. 1239);

(19) Postal savings bonds, see section 10 of the Act of June 25, 1910 (36 Stat. 817; 39 U.S.C. 760);

(20) Puerto Rican bonds, see section 3 of the Act of March 2, 1917, as amended (50 Stat. 844; 48 U.S.C. 745);

(21) Treasury notes issued to retire national bank notes, see section 18 of the Federal Reserve Act (38 Stat. 268; 12 U.S.C. 447);

(22) United States Housing Authority obligations, see sections 5(e) and 20(b) of the United States Housing Act of 1937 (50 Stat. 890, 898; 42 U.S.C. 1405, 1420);

(23) Virgin Islands insular and municipal bonds, see section 1 of the Act of October 27, 1949 (63 Stat. 940; 48 U.S.C. 1403);

(24) Exempt-interest dividends.—For treatment of exempt-interest dividends, see section 852(b)(5)(B).

P.L. 94-455, §2105(b):

Redesignated former Code Sec. 103(f) as Code Sec. 103(g). **Effective** with respect to obligations issued on or after 10-4-76.

P.L. 94-455, §2137(d):

Added paragraph (24). **Effective** for tax years beginning after 12-31-75.

• 1975, Revenue Adjustment Act of 1975 (P.L. 94-164)

P.L. 94-164, §7(a):

Amended Code Sec. 103 by redesignating subsection (e) as subsection (f) and by inserting new subsection (e). **Effective** with respect to obligations issued after 12-23-75.

• 1969, Tax Reform Act of 1969 (P.L. 91-172)

P.L. 91-172, §601(a):

Redesignated Code Sec. 103(d) as Code Sec. 103(e). **Effective** with respect to obligations issued after 10-9-69.

• 1968, Revenue and Expenditure Control Act of 1968 (P.L. 90-364)

P.L. 90-364, §107(a):

Redesignated Code Sec. 103(c) as Code Sec. 103(d). **Effective** 5-1-68.

• 1986, Tax Reform Act of 1986 (P.L. 99-514)

P.L. 99-514, §§1312-1317, amended by P.L. 100-647, §1013, provide:

SEC. 1312. TRANSITIONAL RULES FOR CONSTRUCTION OR BINDING AGREEMENTS AND CERTAIN GOVERNMENT BONDS ISSUED AFTER AUGUST 15, 1986.

(a) EXCEPTION FOR CONSTRUCTION OR BINDING AGREEMENTS.—

(1) IN GENERAL.—The amendments made by section 1301 shall not apply to bonds (other than a refunding bond) with respect to a facility—

(A)(i) the original use of which commences with the taxpayer, and the construction, reconstruction, or rehabilitation of which began before September 26, 1985, and was completed on or after such date,

(ii) the original use of which begins with the taxpayer and with respect to which a binding contract to incur significant expenditures for construction, reconstruction or rehabilitation was entered into before September 26, 1985, and some of such expenditures are incurred on or after such date, or

(iii) acquired on or after September 26, 1985, pursuant to a binding contract entered into before such date, and

(B) described in an inducement resolution or other comparable preliminary approval adopted by an issuing authority (or by a voter referendum) before September 26, 1985.

(2) SIGNIFICANT EXPENDITURES.—For purposes of paragraph (1)(A), the term "significant expenditures" means expenditures greater than 10 percent of the reasonably anticipated cost of the construction, reconstruction, or rehabilitation of the facility involved.

(b) CERTAIN AMENDMENTS TO APPLY TO BONDS UNDER SUBSECTION (a) TRANSITIONAL RULE.—

(1) IN GENERAL.—In the case of a bond issued after August 15, 1986, and to which subsection (a) of this section applies, the requirements of the following provisions shall be treated as included in section 103 and section 103A (as appropriate) of the 1954 Code:

(A) The requirement that 95 percent or more of the net proceeds of an issue are to be used for a purpose described in section 103(b)(4) or (5) of such Code in order for section 103(b)(4) or (5) of such Code to apply, including the application of section 142(b)(2) of the 1986 Code (relating to limitation on office space).

(B) The requirement that 95 percent or more of the net proceeds of an issue are to be used for a purpose described in section 103(b)(6)(A) of the 1954 Code in order for section 103(b)(6)(A) of such Code to apply.

(C) The requirements of section 143 of the 1986 Code (relating to qualified mortgage bonds and qualified veterans' mortgage bonds) in order for section 103A(b)(2) of the 1954 Code to apply.

(D) The requirements of section 144(a)(11) of the 1986 Code (relating to limitation on acquisition of depreciable farm property) in order for section 103(b)(6)(A) of the 1954 Code to apply.

(E) The requirements of section 147(b) of the 1986 Code (relating to maturity may not exceed 120 percent of economic life).

(F) The requirements of section 147(f) of the 1986 Code (relating to public approval required for private activity bonds).

(G) The requirements of section 147(g) of the 1986 Code (relating to restriction on issuance costs financed by issue).

(H) The requirements of section 148 of the 1986 Code (relating to arbitrage).

(I) The requirements of section 149(e) of the 1986 Code (relating to information reporting).

(J) The provisions of section 150(b) of the 1986 Code (relating to changes in use).

(2) CERTAIN REQUIREMENTS APPLY ONLY TO BONDS ISSUED AFTER DECEMBER 31, 1986.—In the case of subparagraphs (F) and (I) of paragraphs (1), paragraph (1) shall be applied by substituting "December 31, 1986" for "August 15, 1986".

(3) APPLICATION OF VOLUME CAP.—Except as provided in section 1315, any bond to which this subsection applies shall be treated as a private activity bond for purposes of section

146 of the 1986 Code if such bond would have been taken into account under section 103(n) or 103A(g) of the 1954 Code (determined without regard to any carryforward election) were such bond issued before August 16, 1986.

(4) APPLICATION OF PROVISIONS.—For purposes of applying the requirements referred to in any subparagraph of paragraph (1) or of subsection (a)(3) or (b)(3) of section 1313 to any bond, such bond shall be treated as described in the subparagraph of section 141(d)(1) of the 1986 Code to which the use of the proceeds of such bond most closely relates.

(c) SPECIAL RULES FOR CERTAIN GOVERNMENT BONDS ISSUED AFTER AUGUST 15, 1986.—

(1) IN GENERAL.—IN THE CASE OF ANY BOND DESCRIBED IN PARAGRAPH (2)—

(A) section 1311(a) and (c) and subsection (b) of this section shall be applied by substituting "August 31, 1986" for "August 15, 1986" each place it appears,

(B) subsection (b)(1) shall be applied without regard to subparagraphs (F), (G), and (J), and

(C) such bond shall not be treated as a private activity bond for purposes of applying the requirements referred to in subparagraphs (H) and (I) of subsection (b)(1).

(2) BOND DESCRIBED.—A bond is described in this paragraph if such bond is not—

(A) an industrial development bond, as defined in section 103(b)(2) of the 1954 Code but determined—

(i) by inserting "directly or indirectly" after "is" in the material preceding clause (i) of subparagraph (B) thereof, and

(ii) without regard to subparagraph (B) of section 103(b)(3) of such Code,

(B) a mortgage subsidy bond (as defined in section 103A(b)(1) of such Code, without regard to any exception from such definition), or

(C) a private loan bond (as defined in section 103(o)(2)(A) of such Code, without regard to any exception from such definition other than section 103(o)(2)(C) of such Code).

(d) ELECTION OUT.—This section shall not apply to any issue with respect to which the issuer elects not to have this section apply.

SEC. 1313. TRANSITIONAL RULES RELATING TO REFUNDINGS.

(a) CERTAIN CURRENT REFUNDINGS.—

(1) IN GENERAL.—Except as provided in paragraph (3), the amendments made by section 1301 shall not apply to any bond the proceeds of which are used exclusively to refund (other than to advance refund) a qualified bond (or a bond which is part of a series of refundings of a qualified bond) if—

(A) the amount of the refunding bond does not exceed the outstanding amount of the refunded bond, and

(B)(i) the average maturity of the issue of which the refunding bond is a part does not exceed 120 percent of the average reasonably expected economic life of the facilities being financed with the net proceeds of such issue (determined under section 147(b) of the 1986 Code), or

(ii) the refunding bond has a maturity date not later than the date which is 17 years after the date on which the qualified bond was issued.

In the case of a qualified bond which was (when issued) a qualified mortgage bond or a qualified veterans' mortgage bond, subparagraph (B)(i) shall not apply and subparagraph (B)(ii) shall be applied by substituting "32 years" for "17 years".

(2) QUALIFIED BOND.—For purposes of paragraph (1), the term "qualified bond" means any bond (other than a refunding bond)—

(A) issued before August 16, 1986, or

(B) issued after August 15, 1986, if section 1312(a) applies to such bond.

(3) CERTAIN AMENDMENTS TO APPLY.—The following provisions of the 1986 Code shall be treated as included in section 103 and section 103A (as appropriate) of the 1954 Code and shall apply to refunding bonds described in paragraph (1):

(A) The requirements of section 147(f) (relating to public approval required for private activity bonds) but only if the maturity date of the refunding bond is later than the maturity date of the refunded bond.

(B) The requirements of section 147(g) (relating to restriction on issuance costs financed by issue).

(C) The requirements of sections 143(g) and 148 (relating to arbitrage).

(D) The requirements of section 149(e) (relating to information reporting).

(E) The provisions of section 150(b) (relating to changes in use).

Subparagraphs (A) and (D) shall apply only if the refunding bond is issued after December 31, 1986. In the case of a refunding bond described in paragraph (1) with respect to a qualified bond described in paragraph (2)(B), the requirements of section 1312(b)(1) which applied to such qualified bond shall be treated as specified in this paragraph with respect to such refunding bond.

(4) SPECIAL RULES FOR CERTAIN GOVERNMENT BONDS ISSUED AFTER AUGUST 15, 1986.—In the case of any bond described in section 1312(c)(2)—

(A) paragraph (2) of this subsection shall be applied by substituting "August 31, 1986" for "August 15, 1986" and by substituting "September 1, 1986" for "August 16, 1986",

(B) paragraph (3) shall be applied without regard to subparagraphs (A), (B), and (E), and

(C) such bond shall not be treated as a private activity bond for purposes of applying the requirements referred to in subparagraphs (C) and (D) of paragraph (3).

(b) CERTAIN ADVANCE REFUNDINGS.—

(1) IN GENERAL.—Except as provided in paragraph (3), the amendments made by section 1301 shall not apply to any bond the proceeds of which are used exclusively to advance refund a bond if—

(A) the refunded bond is described in paragraph (2), and

(B) the requirements of subsection (a)(1)(B) are met.

(2) NON-IDB'S, ETC.—A bond is described in this paragraph if such bond is not described in subsection (b)(2) or (o)(2)(A) of section 103 of the 1954 Code and was issued (or was issued to refund a bond issued) before August 16, 1986. For purposes of the preceding sentence, the determination of whether a bond is described in such subsection (o)(2)(A) shall be made without regard to any exception other than section 103(o)(2)(C) of such Code.

(3) CERTAIN AMENDMENTS TO APPLY.—The following provisions of the 1986 Code shall be treated as included in section 103 and section 103A (as appropriate) of the 1954 Code and shall apply to refunding bonds described in paragraph (1):

(A) The requirements of section 147(f) (relating to public approval required for private activity bonds).

(B) The requirements of section 147(g) (relating to restrictions on issuance costs financed by issue).

(C) The requirements of section 148 (relating to arbitrage), except that section 148(d)(3) shall not apply to proceeds of such bonds to be used to discharge the refunded bonds.

(D) The requirements of paragraphs (3) and (4) of section 149(d) (relating to advanced refundings).

(E) The requirements of section 149(e) (relating to information reporting).

(F) The provisions of section 150(b) (relating to changes in use).

(G) Except as provided in the last sentence of subsection (c)(2) of this section, the requirements of section 145(b) (relating to $150,000,000 limitation on bonds other than hospital bonds)."

Subparagraphs (A) and (E) shall apply only if the refunding bond is issued after December 31, 1986.

(4) SPECIAL RULE FOR CERTAIN GOVERNMENT BONDS ISSUED AFTER AUGUST 15, 1986.—In the case of any bond described in section 1312(c)(2)—

(A) paragraph (2) of this subsection shall be applied by substituting "September 1, 1986" for "August 16, 1986",

(B) paragraph (3) shall be applied without regard to subparagraphs (A), (B), and (F), and

(C) such bond shall not be treated as a private activity bond for purposes of applying the requirements referred to in subparagraphs (C) and (E).

(5) CERTAIN REFUNDING BONDS SUBJECT TO VOLUME CAP.—Any refunding bond described in paragraph (1) the proceeds of which are used to refund a bond issued as part of an issue 5

percent or more of the net proceeds of which are or will be used to provide an output facility (within the meaning of section 141(b)(4) of the 1986 Code) shall be treated as a private activity bond for purposes of section 146 of the 1986 Code (to the extent of the nongovernmental use of such issue, under rules similar to the rules of section 146(m)(2) of such Code). For purposes of the preceding sentence, use by a 501(c)(3) organization with respect to its activities which do not constitute unrelated trades or businesses (determined by applying section 513(a) of the 1986 Code) shall not be taken into account.

(c) TREATMENT OF CERTAIN REFUNDINGS OF CERTAIN IDB'S AND 501(c)(3) BONDS.—

(1) $40,000,000 LIMIT FOR CERTAIN SMALL ISSUE BONDS.—Paragraph (10) of section 144(a) of the 1986 Code shall not apply to any bond (or series of bonds) the proceeds of which are used exclusively to refund a tax-exempt bond to which such paragraph and the corresponding provision of prior law did not apply if—

(A) the average maturity date of the issue of which the refunding bond is a part is not later than the average maturity date of the bonds to be refunded by such issue,

(B) the amount of the refunding bond does not exceed the outstanding amount of the refunded bond, and

(C) the net proceeds of the refunding bond are used to redeem the refunded bond not later than 90 days after the date of the issuance of the refunding bond.

For purposes of subparagraph (A), average maturity shall be determined in accordance with section 147(b)(2)(A) of the 1986 Code.

(2) $150,000,000 LIMITATION FOR CERTAIN 501(c)(3) BONDS.—Subsection (b) of section 145 of the 1986 Code (relating to $150,000,000 limitation for nonhospital bonds) shall not apply to any bond (or series of bonds) the proceeds of which are used exclusively to refund a tax-exempt bond to which such subsection did not apply if—

(A)(i) the average maturity of the issue of which the refunding bond is a part does not exceed 120 percent of the average reasonably expected economic life of the facilities being financed with the net proceeds of such issue (determined under section 147(b) of the 1986 Code), or

(ii) the refunding bond has a maturity date not later than the later of the date which is 17 years after the date on which the qualified bond (as defined in subsection (a)(2)) was issued, and

(B) the requirements of subparagraphs (B) and (C) of paragraph (1) are met with respect to the refunding bond.

Subsection (b) of section 145 of the 1986 Code shall not apply to the 1st advance refunding after March 14, 1986, of a bond issued before January 1, 1986.

(3) APPLICATION TO LATER ISSUES.—Any bond to which section 144(a)(10) or 145(b) of the 1986 Code does not apply by reason of this section shall be taken into account in determining whether such section applies to any later issue.

(d) MORTGAGE AND STUDENT LOAN TARGETING RULES TO APPLY TO LOANS MADE MORE THAN 3 YEARS AFTER THE DATE OF THE ORIGINAL ISSUE.—Subsections (a)(3) and (b)(3) shall be treated as including the requirements of subsections (e) and (f) of section 143 and paragraphs (3) and (4) of section 144(b) of the 1986 Code with respect to bonds the proceeds of which are used to finance loans made more than 3 years after the date of the issuance of the original bond.

SEC. 1314. SPECIAL RULES WHICH OVERRIDE OTHER RULES IN THIS SUBTITLE.

(a) ARBITRAGE RESTRICTION ON INVESTMENTS IN ANNUITIES.—In the case of a bond issued after September 25, 1985, section 103(c) of the 1954 Code shall be applied by treating the reference to securities in paragraph (2) thereof as including a reference to an annuity contract. The preceding sentence shall also apply to the first advance refunding after September 25, 1985, if a bond issued before September 26, 1985.

(b) TEMPORARY PERIOD FOR ADVANCE REFUNDINGS.—In the case of a bond issued after December 31, 1985, to advance refund a bond, the initial temporary period under section 103(c) of the 1954 Code with respect to the proceeds of the refunding bond shall end not later than 30 days after the date of issue of the refunding bond.

(c) DETERMINATION OF YIELD.—In the case of a bond issued after December 31, 1985, for purposes of section 103(c) of the 1954 Code, the yield on an issue shall be determined on the basis of the issue price (within the meaning of sections 1273 and 1274 of the 1986 Code).

(d) ARBITRAGE REBATE REQUIREMENT.—

(1) IN GENERAL.—Except as otherwise provided in this subsection, in the case of a bond issued after December 31, 1985, section 103 of the 1954 Code shall be treated as including the requirements of section 148(f) of the 1986 Code in order for section 103(a) of the 1954 Code to apply.

(2) GOVERNMENT BONDS.—In the case of a bond described in section 1312(c)(2) (and not described in paragraph (3) of this subsection), paragraph (1) shall be applied by substituting "August 31, 1986" for "December 31, 1985".

(3) CERTAIN POOLS.—

(A) IN GENERAL.—In the case of a bond described in section 1312(c)(2) and issued as part of an issue described in subparagraph (B), (C), (D), or (E), pargraph (1) shall be applied by substituting "3 p.m. E.D.T., July 17, 1986" for "December 31, 1985". Such a bond shall not be treated as a private activity bond for purposes of applying section 148(f) of the 1986 Code.

(B) LOANS TO UNRELATED GOVERNMENTAL UNITS.—An issue is described in this subparagraph if any portion of the proceeds of the issue is to be used to make or finance loans to any governmental unit other than any governmental unit which is subordinate to the issuer and the jurisdiction of which is within—

(i) the jurisdiction of the issuer, or

(ii) the jurisdiction of the governmental unit on behalf of which such issuer issued the issue.

(C) LESS THAN 75 PERCENT OF PROJECTS IDENTIFIED.—An issue is described in this subparagraph if less than 75 percent of the proceeds of the issue is to be used to make or finance loans to initial borrowers to finance projects identified (with specificity) by the issuer, on or before the date of issuance of the issue, as projects to be financed with the proceeds of the issue.

(D) LESS THAN 25 PERCENT OF FUNDS COMMITTED TO BE BORROWED.—An issue is described in this subparagraph if, on or before the date of issuance of the issue, the commitments have not have been entered into by initial borrowers to borrow at least 25 percent of the proceeds of the issue.

(E) CERTAIN LONG MATURITY ISSUES.—An issue is described in this subparagraph if—

(i) the maturity date of any bond issued as part of such issue exceeds 30 years, and

(ii) any prinicipal payment on any loan made or financed by the proceeds of the issue to be used to make or finance additional loans.

(F) SPECIAL RULES.—

(i) EXCEPTION FROM SUBPARAGRAPHS(c) AND(d) WHERE SIMILAR POOLS ISSUED BY ISSUER.—An issue shall not be treated as described in subparagraph (C) or (D) with respect to any issue to make or finance loans to governmental units if—

(I) the issuer, before 1986, issued 1 or more similar issues to make or finance loans to governmental units, and

(II) the aggregate face amount of such issues issued during 1986, does not exceed 250 percent of the average of the annual aggregate face amounts of such similar issues during 1983, 1984, or 1985.

(ii) DETERMINATION OF ISSUANCE.—For purposes of subparagraph (A), an issue shall not be treated as issued until—

(I) the bonds issued as a part of such issue are offered to the public (pursuant to final offering materials), and

(II) at least 25 percent of such bonds is sold to the public.

For purposes of the preceding sentence, the sale of a bond to a securities firm, broker, or other person acting in the capacity of an underwriter or wholesaler shall not be treated as a sale to the public.

(e) INFORMATION REPORTING.—In the case of a bond issued after December 31, 1986, nothing in section 103(a) of the 1986 Code or any other provision of law shall be construed to provide an exemption from Federal income tax for interest on any bond unless such bond satisfies the requirements of section 149(e) of the 1986 Code. A bond described in section 1312(c)(2) shall not be treated as a private activity bond for purposes of applying such requirements.

(f) ABUSIVE TRANSACTION LIMITATION ON ADVANCE REFUNDING TO APPLY.—In the case of a bond issued after August 31, 1986, nothing in section 103(a) of the 1986 Code or any other provision of law shall be construed to provide an exemption from Federal income tax for interest on any bond if the issue of which such bond is a part is described in paragraph (4) of section 149(d) of the 1986 Code (relating to abusive transactions).

(g) TERMINATION OF MORTGAGE BOND POLICY STATEMENT REQUIREMENT.—Paragraph (5) of section 103A(j) of the 1954 Code (relating to policy statement) shall not apply to any bond issued after August 15, 1986, and shall not apply to nonissued bond amounts elected under section 25 of the 1986 Code after such date.

(h) ARBITRAGE RESTRICTION ON INVESTMENTS IN INVESTMENT-TYPE PROPERTY.—In the case of a bond issued before August 16, 1986 (September 1, 1986 in the case of a bond described in section 1312(c)(2)), section 103(c) of the 1954 Code shall be applied by treating the reference to securities in paragraph (2) thereof as including a reference to investment-type property but only for purposes of determining whether any bond issued after October 16, 1987, to advance refund such bond (or a bond which is part of a series of refundings of such bond) is an arbitrage bond (within the meaning of section 148(a) of the 1986 Code).

(i) SECTION TO OVERRIDE OTHER RULES.—Except as otherwise expressly provided by reference to a provision to which a subsection of this section applies, nothing in any other section of this subtitle shall be construed as exempting any bond from the application of such provision.

SEC. 1315. TRANSITIONAL RULES RELATING TO VOLUME CAP.

(a) IN GENERAL.—Except as otherwise provided in this section, section 146(f) of the 1986 Code shall not apply with respect to an issuing authority's volume cap under section 103(n) of the 1954 Code, and no carryforward under such section 103(n) shall be recognized for bonds issued after August 15, 1986.

(b) CERTAIN BONDS FOR CARRYFORWARD PROJECTS OUTSIDE OF VOLUME CAP.—Bonds issued pursuant to an election under section 103(n)(10) of the 1954 Code (relating to elective carryforward of unused limitation for specified project) made before November 1, 1985, shall not be taken into account under section 146 of the 1986 Code if the carryforward project is a facility to which the amendments made by section 1301 do not apply by reason of section 1312(a) of this Act.

(c) VOLUME CAP NOT TO APPLY WITH RESPECT TO CERTAIN FACILITIES AND PURPOSES.—Section 146 of the 1986 Code shall not apply to any bond issued with respect to any facility or purpose described in a paragraph of subsection (d) if—

(1) such bond would not have been taken into account under section 103(n) of the 1954 Code for calendar year 1986 (determined without regard to any carryforward election) were such bond issued on August 15, 1986, or

(2) such bond would not have been taken into account under section 103(n) of the 1954 Code for calendar year 1986 (determined with regard to any carryforward election made before January 1, 1986) were such bond issued before August 16, 1986.

The preceding sentence shall not apply to the extent section 1313(b)(5) treats any bond as a private activity bond for purposes of section 146 of the 1986 Code.

(d) FACILITIES AND PURPOSES DESCRIBED.—

(1) A facility is described in this paragraph if the amendment made by section 201 of this Act (relating to depreciation) do not apply to such facility by reason of section 204(a)(8) of this Act (or, in the case of a facility which is governmentally owned, would not apply to such facility were it owned by a nongovernmental person).

(2) A facility or purpose is described in this paragraph if the facility or purpose is described in a paragraph of section 1317.

(3) A facility is described in this paragraph if the facility—

(A) serves Los Osos, California, and

(B) would be described in paragraph (1) were it a solid waste disposal facility.

The aggregate face amount of bonds to which this paragraph applies shall not exceed $35,000,000.

(4) A facility is described in this paragraph if it is a sewage disposal facility with respect to which—

(A) on September 13, 1985, the State public facilities authority took official action authorizing the issuance of bonds for such facility, and

(B) on December 30, 1985, there was an executive order of the State Governor granting allocation of the State ceiling under section 103(n) of the 1954 Code in the amount of $250,000,000 to the Industrial Development Board of the Parish of East Baton Rouge, Louisiana.

The aggregate face amount of bonds to which this paragraph applies shall not exceed $98,500,000.

(5) A facility is described in this paragraph if—

(A) such facility is a solid waste disposal facility in Charleston, South Carolina, and

(B) a State political subdivision took formal action on April 1, 1980, to commit development funds for such facility.

For purposes of determining whether a bond issued as part of an issue for a facility described in the preceding sentence is an exempt facility bond for purposess of part IV of subchapter B of chapter 1 of the 1986 Code, "90 percent" shall be substituted for "95 percent" in section 142(a) of the 1986 Code.

The aggregate face amount of bonds to which this paragraph applies shall not exceed $75,000,000.

(6) A facility is described in this paragraph if—

(A) such facility is a wastewater treatment facility for which site preparation commenced before September 1985, and

(B) a parish council approved a service agreement with respect to such facility on December 4, 1985.

The aggregate face amount of bonds to which this paragraph applies shall not exceed $120,000,000.

(e) TREATMENT OF REDEVELOPMENT BONDS.—Any bond to which section 1317(6) of this Act applies shall be treated for purposes of this section as described in subsection (c)(1). The preceding sentence shall not apply to any bond which (if issued on August 15, 1986) would have been an industrial development bond (as defined in section 103(b)(2) of the 1954 Code).

SEC. 1316. PROVISIONS RELATING TO CERTAIN ESTABLISHED STATE PROGRAMS.

(a) CERTAIN LOANS TO VETERANS FOR THE PURCHASE OF LAND.—

(1) IN GENERAL.—A bond described in paragraph (2) shall be treated as described in section 141(d)(1) of the 1986 Code and as having a carryforward purpose described in section 146(f)(5) of such Code, but subsections (a), (b), (c), and (d) of section 147 of such Code shall not apply to such bond.

(2) BOND DESCRIBED.—A bond is described in this paragraph if—

(A) such bond is a private activity bond solely by reason of section 141(c) of such Code, and

(B) such bond is issued as part of an issue 95 percent or more of the net proceeds of which are to be used to carry out a program established under State law to provide loans to veterans for the purchase of land and which has been in effect in substantially the same form during the 30-year period ending on July 18, 1984, but only if such proceeds are used to make loans or to fund similar obligations—

(i) in the same manner in which,

(ii) in the same (or lesser) amount or multiple of acres per participant, and

(iii) for the same purposes for which,

such program was operated on March 15, 1984.

(b) RENEWABLE ENERGY PROPERTY.—

(1) IN GENERAL.—A bond described in paragraph (2) shall be treated as described in section 141(d)(1) of the 1986 Code and as having a carryforward purpose described in section 146(f)(5) of such Code.

(2) BOND DESCRIBED.—A bond is described in this paragraph if paragraph (1) of section 103(b) of the 1954 Code would not (without regard to the amendments made by this title) have applied to such bond by reason of section 243 of the Crude Oil Windfall Profit Tax Act of 1980 if—

(A) such section 243 were applied by substituting "95 percent or more of the net proceeds" for "substantially all of the proceeds" in subsection (a)(1) thereof, and

(B) subparagraph (E) of subsection (a)(1) thereof referred to section 149(b) of the 1986 Code.

(c) CERTAIN STATE PROGRAMS.—

(1) IN GENERAL.—A bond described in paragraph (2) shall be treated as described in section 141(d)(1) of the 1986 Code and as having a carryforward purpose described in section 146(f)(5) of such Code.

(2) BOND DESCRIBED.—A bond is described in this paragraph if such bond is issued as part of an issue 95 percent or more of the net proceeds of which are to be used to carry out a program established under sections 280A, 280B, and 280C of the Iowa Code, but only if—

(A) such program has been in effect in substantially the same form since July 1, 1983, and

(B) such proceeds are to be used to make loans or fund similar obligations for the same purposes as permitted under such program on July 1, 1986.

(3) $100,000,000 LIMITATION.—The aggregate face amount of outstanding bonds to which this subsection applies shall not exceed $100,000,000.

(4) APPLICATION OF SECTION 147(b).—A bond to which this subsection applies (other than a refunding bond) shall be treated as meeting the requirements of section 147(b) of the 1986 Code if the average maturity (determined in accordance with section 147(b)(2)(A) of such Code) of the issue of which such bond is a part does not exceed 20 years. A bond issued to refund (or which is part of a series of bonds issued to refund) a bond described in the preceding sentence shall be treated as meeting the requirements of such section if the refunding bond has a maturity date not later than the date which is 20 years after the date on which the original bond was issued.

(d) USE BY CERTAIN FEDERAL INSTRUMENTALITIES TREATED AS USE BY GOVERNMENTAL UNITS.—Use by an instrumentality of the United States shall be treated as use by a State or local governmental unit for purposes of section 103, and part IV of subchapter B of chapter 1, of the 1986 Code with respect to a program approved by Congress before August 3, 1972, but only if—

(1) a portion of such program has been financed by bonds issued before such date, to which section 103(a) of the 1954 Code applied pursuant to a ruling issued by the Commissioner of the Internal Revenue Service, and

(2) construction of 1 or more facilities comprising a part of such program commenced before such date.

(e) REFUNDING PERMITTED OF CERTAIN BONDS INVESTED IN FEDERALLY INSURED DEPOSITS.—

(1) IN GENERAL.—Section 149(b)(2)(B)(ii) of the 1986 Code (and section 103(h)(2)(B)(ii) of the 1954 Code) shall not apply to any bond issued to refund a bond—

(A) which, when issued, would have been treated as federally guaranteed by reason of being described in clause (ii) of section 103(h)(2)(B) of the 1954 Code if such section had applied to such bond, and

(B)(i) which was issued before April 15, 1983, or

(ii) to which such clause did not apply by reason of the except clause in section 631(c)(2) of the Tax Reform Act of 1984.

Section 147(c) of the 1986 Code (and section 103(b)(16) of the 1954 Code) shall not apply to any refunding bond permitted under the preceding sentence if section 103(b)(16) of the 1954 code did not apply to the refunded bond when issued.

(2) REQUIREMENTS.—A refunding bond meets the requirements of this paragraph if—

(A) the refunding bond has a maturity date not later than the maturity date of the refunded bond,

(B) the amount of the refunding bond does not exceed the outstanding amount of the refunded bond,

(C) the weighted average interest rate on the refunding bond is lower than the weighted average interest rate on the refunded bond, and

(D) the net proceeds of the refunding bond are used to redeem the refunded bond not later than 90 days after the date of the issuance of the refunding bond.

(f) CERTAIN HYDROELECTRIC GENERATING PROPERTY.—

(1) IN GENERAL.—A bond described in paragraph (2) shall be treated as described in section 141(d)(1) of the 1986 Code and as having a carryforward purpose described in section 146(f)(5) of such Code.

(2) DESCRIPTION.—A bond described in this paragraph if such bond is issued as part of an issue 95 percent or more of the net proceeds of which are to be used to provide a facility described in section 103(b)(4)(H) of the 1954 Code determined—

(A) by substituting "an application for a license" for "an application" in section 103(b)(8)(E)(ii) of the 1954 Code, and

(B) by applying the requirements of section 142(b)(2) of the 1986 Code.

(g) TREATMENT OF BONDS SUBJECT TO TRANSITIONAL RULES UNDER TAX REFORM ACT OF 1984.—

(1) Subsections (d)(3) and (f) of section 148 of the 1986 Code shall not apply to any bond described in section 624(c)(2) of the Tax Reform Act of 1984.

(2)(A) There shall not be taken into account under section 146 of the 1986 Code any bond issued to provide a facility described in paragraph (3) of section 631(a) of the Tax Reform Act of 1984 relating to exception for certain bonds for a convention center and resource recovery project.

(B) If a bond issued as part of an issue substantially all of the proceeds of which are used to provide the convention center to which such paragraph (3) applies, such bond shall be treated as an exempt facility bond as defined in section 142(a) of the 1986 Code.

(C) If a bond which is issued as part of an issue substantially all of the proceeds of which are used to provide the resource recovery project to which such paragraph (3) applies, such bond shall be treated as an exempt facility bond as defined in section 142(a) of the 1986 Code and section 149(b) of such Code shall not apply.

(3) The amendments made by section 1301 shall not apply to bonds issued to finance any property described in section 631(d)(4) of the Tax Reform Act of 1984.

(4) The amendments made by section 1301 shall not apply to—

(A) any bond issued to finance property described in section 631(d)(5) of the Tax Reform Act of 1984,

(B) any bond described in paragraph (2), (3), (4), (5), (6), or (7) of section 632(a), or section 632(b), of such Act, and

(C) any bond to which section 632(g)(2) of such Act applies.

In the case of bonds to which this paragraph applies, the requirements of sections 148 and 149(d) shall be treated as included in section 103 of the 1954 Code and shall apply to such bonds.

(5) The preceding provisions of this subsection shall not apply to any bond issued after December 31, 1988.

(6) The amendments made by section 1301 (and the provisions of section 1314) shall not apply to any bond issued to finance property described in section 216(b)(3) of the Tax Equity and Fiscal Responsibility Act of 1982.

(7) In the case of a bond described in section 632(d) of the Tax Reform Act of 1984—

(A) section 141 of the 1986 Code shall be applied without regard to subsection (a)(2) and paragraphs (4) and (5) of subsection (b).

(B) paragraphs (1) and (2) of section 141(b) of the 1986 Code shall be applied by substituting "25 percent" for "10 percent" each place it appears, and

(C) section 149(b) of the 1986 Code shall not apply.

This paragraph shall not apply to any bond issued after December 31, 1990.

(8)(A) The amendments made by section 1301 shall not apply to any bond to which section 629(a)(1) of the Tax Reform Act of 1984 applies, but such bond shall be treated as a private activity bond for purposes of section 146 of the 1986 Code and as having a carryforward purpose described in section 146(f)(5) of such Code.

(B) Section 629 of the Tax Reform Act of 1984 is amended—

(i) in subsection (c)(2), by striking out "$625,000,000" and inserting in lieu thereof "$911,000,000",

(ii) in subsection (c)(3), by adding at the end thereof the following new subparagraphs:

"(D) Improvements to existing generating facilities.

"(E) Transmission lines.

"(F) Electric generating facilities.", and

(iii) in subsection (a), by adding at the end thereof the following new sentence: "The preceding sentence shall be applied by inserting 'and a rural electric cooperative utility' after 'regulated public utility' but only if not more than 1 percent of the load of the public power authority is sold to such rural electric cooperative utility."

(h) CERTAIN POLLUTION BONDS.—Any bond which is treated as described in section 103(b)(4)(F) of the 1954 Code by reason of section 13209 of the Consolidated Omnibus Budget Reconciliation Act of 1985 shall be treated as an exempt facility bond for purposes of part IV of subchapter B of chapter 1 of the 1986 Code, and section 147(d) of the 1986 Code shall not apply to such bond.

(i) TRANSITION RULE FOR AGGREGATE LIMIT PER TAXPAYER.—For purposes of section 144(a)(10) of the 1986 Code, tax increment bonds described in section 1869(c)(3) of this Act which are issued before August 16, 1986, shall not be taken into account under subparagraph (B)(ii) thereof.

(j) EXTENSION OF ADVANCE REFUNDING EXCEPTION FOR QUALIFIED PUBLIC FACILITY.—Paragraph (4) of section 631(c) of the Tax Reform Act of 1984 is amended—

(1) by striking out "or the Dade County, Florida, airport" in the last sentence, and

(2) by adding at the end thereof the following new sentence: "In the case of refunding obligations not to exceed $100,000,000 issued after October 21, 1986, by Dade County, Florida, for the purpose of advance refunding its Aviation Revenue Bonds (Series J), the first sentence of this paragraph shall be applied by substituting 'the date which is 1 year after the date of the enactment of the Technical and Miscellaneous Revenue Act of 1988' for 'December 31, 1984' and the amendments made by section 1301 of the Tax Reform Act of 1986 shall not apply."

(k) EXPANSION OF EXCEPTION FOR RIVER PLACE PROJECT.—Section 1104 of the Mortgage Subsidy Bond Tax Act of 1980, as added by the Tax Reform Act of 1984, is amended—

(1) by striking out "December 31, 1984," in subsection (p) and inserting in lieu thereof "December 31, 1984 (other than obligations described in subsection (r)(1)),", and

(2) by striking out "$55,000,000," in subsection (r)(1)(B) and inserting in lieu thereof "$110,000,000 of which no more than $55,000,000 shall be outstanding later than November 1, 1987."

(l) [Repealed.]

SEC. 1317. TRANSITIONAL RULES FOR SPECIFIC FACILITIES.

(1) DOCKS AND WHARVES.—A bond issued as part of an issue 95 percent or more of the net proceeds of which are to be used to provide any dock or wharf (within the meaning of section 103(b)(4)(D) of the 1954 Code) shall be treated as an exempt facility bond (for a facility described in section 142(a)(2) of the 1986 Code) for purposes of part IV of subchapter B of chapter 1 of the 1986 Code if such dock or wharf is described in any of the following subparagraphs:

(A) A dock or wharf is described in this subparagraph if—

(i) the issue to finance such dock or wharf was approved by official city action on September 3, 1985, and by voters on November 5, 1985, and

(ii) such dock or wharf is for a slack water harbor with respect to which a Corps of Engineers grant of approximately $2,000,000 has been made under section 107 of the Rivers and Harbors Act.

The aggregate face amount of bonds to which this subparagraph applies shall not exceed $2,500,000.

(B) A dock or wharf is described in this subparagraph if—

(i) inducement resolutions were adopted on May 23, 1985, September 18, 1985, and September 24, 1985, for the issuance of the bonds to finance such dock or wharf,

(ii) a harbor dredging contract with respect thereto was entered into on August 2, 1985, and

(iii) a construction management and joint venture agreement with respect thereto was entered into on October 1, 1984.

The aggregate face amount of bonds to which this subparagraph applies shall not exceed $625,000,000.

(C) A facility is described in this subparagraph if—

(i) the legislature first authorized on June 29, 1981, the State agency issuing the bond to issue at least $30,000,000 of bonds,

(ii) the developer of the facility was selected on April 26, 1985, and

(iii) an inducement resolution for the issuance of such issue was adopted on October 9, 1985.

The aggregate face amount of bonds to which this subparagraph applies shall not exceed $200,000,000.

(D) A facility is described in this subparagraph if—

(i) an inducement resolution was adopted on October 17, 1985, for such issue, and

(ii) the city council for the city in which the facility is to be located approved on July 30, 1985, an application for an urban development action grant with respect to such facility.

The aggregate face amount of bonds to which this subparagraph applies shall not exceed $36,500,000. A facility shall be treated as described in this subparagraph if it would be so described if "90 percent" were substituted for "95 percent" in the material preceding subparagraph (A) of this paragraph.

(2) POLLUTION CONTROL FACILITIES.—A bond issued as part of an issue 95 percent or more of the net proceeds of which are to be used to provide air or water pollution control facilities (within the meaning of section 103(b)(4)(F) of the 1954 Code) shall be treated as an exempt facility bond for purposes of part IV of subchapter B of chapter 1 of the 1986 Code if such facility is described in any of the following subparagraphs:

(A) A facility is described in this subparagraph if—

(i) inducement resolutions with respect to such facility were adopted on September 23, 1974, and on April 5, 1985,

(ii) a bond resolution for such facility was adopted on September 6, 1985, and

(iii) the issuance of the bonds to finance such facility was delayed by action of the Securities and Exchange Commission (file number 70-7127).

The aggregate face amount of bonds to which this subparagraph applies shall not exceed $120,000,000.

(B) A facility is described in this subparagraph if—

(i) there was an inducement resolution for such facility on November 19, 1985, and

(ii) design and engineering studies for such facility were completed in March of 1985.

The aggregate face amount of bonds to which this subparagraph applies shall not exceed $25,000,000.

(C) A facility is described in this subparagraph if—

(i) a resolution was adopted by the county board of supervisors pertaining to an issuance of bonds with respect to such facility on April 10, 1974, and

(ii) such facility was placed in service on June 12, 1985.

The aggregate face amount of bonds to which this subparagraph applies shall not exceed $90,000,000. For purposes of this subparagraph, a pollution control facility includes a sewage or solid waste disposal facility (within the meaning of section 103(b)(4)(E) of the 1954 Code).

(D) A facility is described in this subparagraph if—

(i) the issuance of the bonds for such facility was approved by a State agency on August 22, 1979, and

(ii) the authority to issue such bonds was scheduled to expire (under terms of the State approval) on August 22, 1989.

The aggregate face amount of bonds to which this subparagraph applies shall not exceed $198,000,000.

(E) A facility is described in this subparagraph if—

(i) such facility is 1 of 4 such facilities in 4 States with respect to which the Ball Corporation transmitted a letter of intent to purchase such facilities on February 26, 1986, and

(ii) inducement resolutions were issued on December 30, 1985, January 15, 1986, January 22, 1986, and March 17, 1986 with respect to bond issuance in the 4 respective States.

The aggregate face amount of bonds to which this subparagraph applies shall not exceed $6,000,000.

(F) A facility is described in this subparagraph if—

(i) inducement resolutions for bonds with respect to such facility were adopted on September 27, 1977, May 27, 1980, and October 8, 1981, and

(ii) such facility is located at a geothermal power complex owned and operated by a single investor-owned utility.

For purposes of this subparagraph and section 103 of the 1986 Code, all hydrogen sulfide air and water pollution control equipment, together with functionally related and subordinate equipment and structures, located or to be located at such power complex shall be treated as a single pollution control facility. The aggregate face amount of bonds to which this subparagraph applies shall not exceed $600,000,000.

(G) A facility is described in this subparagraph if—

(i) such facility is an air pollution control facility approved by a State bureau of pollution control on July 10, 1986, and by a State board of economic development on July 17, 1986, and

(ii) on August 15, 1986, the State bond attorney gave notice to the clerk to initiate validation proceedings with respect to such issue and on August 28, 1986, the validation decree was entered.

The aggregate face amount of bonds to which this subparagraph applies shall not exceed $900,000.

(I) A facility is described in this subparagraph if—

(i) a private company met with a State air control board on November 14, 1985, to propose construction of a sulften unit, and

(ii) the sulften unit is being constructed under a letter of intent to construct which was signed on April 8, 1986.

The aggregate face amount of bonds to which this subparagraph applies shall not exceed $11,000,000.

(J) A facility is described in this subparagraph if it is part of a 250 megawatt coal-fire electric plant in northeastern Nevada on which the Sierra Pacific Power Company, a subsidiary of Sierra Pacific Resources, began in 1980 work to design, finance, construct, and operate. The aggregate face amount of bonds to which this subparagraph applies shall not exceed $200,000,000.

(K) A facility is described in this subparagraph if—

(i) there was an inducement resolution adopted by a State industrial development authority on January 14, 1976, and

(ii) such facility is named in a resolution of such authority relating to carryforward of the State's unused 1985 private activity bond limit passed by such industrial development authority on December 18, 1985.

This subparagraph shall apply only to obligations issued at the request of the party pursuant to whose request the January 14, 1976, inducement was given. The aggregate face amount of bonds to which this subparagraph applies shall not exceed $75,000,000.

(L) A facility is described in this subparagraph if a city council passed an ordinance (ordinance number 4626) agreeing to issue bonds for such project, December 16, 1985. The aggregate face amount of obligations to which this subparagraph applies shall not exceed $45,000,000.

(3) SPORTS FACILITIES.—A bond issued as part of an issue 95 percent or more of the net proceeds of which are to be used to provide sports facilities (within the meaning of section 103(b)(4)(B) of the 1954 Code) shall be treated as an exempt facility bond for purposes of part IV of subchapter B of chapter 1 of the 1986 Code if such facilities are described in any of the following subparagraphs:

(A) A facility is described in this subparagraph if it is a stadium—

(i) which was the subject of a city ordinance passed on September 23, 1985,

(ii) for which a loan of approximately $4,000,000 for land acquisition was approved on October 28, 1985, by the State Controlling Board, and

(iii) a stadium operating corporation with respect to which was incorporated on March 20, 1985.

The aggregate face amount of bonds to which this subparagraph applies shall not exceed $200,000,000.

(B) a facility is described in this subparagraph if—

(i) it is a stadium with respect to which a lease agreement for the ground on which the stadium is to be built was entered into between a county and the stadium corporation for such stadium on July 3, 1984,

(ii) there was a resolution approved on November 14, 1984, by an industrial development authority setting forth the terms under which the bonds to be issued to finance such stadium would be issued, and

(iii) there was an agreement for consultant and engineering services for such stadium entered into on September 28, 1984.

The aggregate face amount of bonds to which this subparagraph applies shall not exceed $90,000,000.

(C) A facility is described in this subparagraph if—

(i) it is one or more stadiums to be used either by an American League baseball team or a National Football League team currently using a stadium in a city having a population in excess of 2,500,000 and described in section 146(d)(3) of the 1986 Code,

(ii) the bonds to be used to provide financing for one or more such stadiums are issued by a political subdivision or a State agency pursuant to a resolution approving an inducement resolution adopted by a State agency on November 20, 1985, as it may be amended (whether or not the beneficiaries of such issue or issues are the beneficiaries (if any) specified in such inducement resolution and whether or not the number of such stadiums and the locations thereof are as specified in such inducement resolution) or pursuant to P.A. 84-1470 of the State in which such city is located (and by an agency created thereby), and

(iii) such stadium or stadiums are located in the city described in (i).

The aggregate face amount of bonds to which this subparagraph applies shall not exceed $250,000,000. In the case of any carryforward of volume cap for one or more stadiums described in the first sentence of this subparagraph, such carryforward shall be valid with respect to bonds issued for such stadiums notwithstanding any other provision of the 1986 Code or the 1954 Code, and whether or not (i) there is a change in the number of stadiums or the beneficiaries or sites of the stadium or stadiums and (ii) the bonds are issued by either of the state agencies described in the first sentence of this subparagraph.

(D) A facility is described in this subparagraph if—

(i) such facility is a stadium or sports arena for Memphis, Tennessee,

(ii) there was an inducement resolution adopted on November 12, 1985, for the issuance of bonds to expand or renovate an existing stadium and sports arena and/or to construct a new arena, and

(iii) the city council for such city adopted a resolution on April 19, 1983, to include funds in the capital budget of the city for such facility or facilities.

The aggregate face amount of bonds to which this subparagraph applies shall not exceed $35,000,000.

(E) A facility is described in this subparagraph if such facility is a baseball stadium located in Bergen, Essex, Union, Middlesex, or Hudson County, New Jersey with respect to which governmental action occurred on November 7, 1985. The aggregate face amount of bonds to which this subparagraph applies shall not exceed $150,000,000.

(F) A facility is described in this subparagraph if—

(i) it is a facility with respect to which—

(I) an inducement resolution dated December 24, 1985, was adopted by the county industrial development authority,

(II) a public hearing of the county industrial development authority was held on February 6, 1986, regarding such facility, and

(III) a contract was entered into by the county, dated February 19, 1986, for engineering services for a highway improvement in connection with such project, or

(ii) it is a domed football stadium adjacent to Cervantes Convention Center in St. Louis, Missouri, with respect to which a proposal to evaluate market demand, financial operations, and economic impact was dated May 9, 1986.

The aggregate face amount of bonds to which this subparagraph applies shall not exceed $175,000,000.

(G) A project to provide a roof or dome for an existing sports facility is described in this subparagraph if—

(i) in December 1984 the county sports complex authority filed a carryforward election under section 103(n) of the 1954 Code with respect to such project,

(ii) in January 1985, the State authorized issuance of $30,000,000 in bonds in the next 3 years for such project, and

(iii) an 11-member task force was appointed by the county executive in June 1985, to further study the feasibility of the project.

The aggregate face amount of bonds to which this subparagraph applies shall not exceed $30,000,000.

(H) A sports facility renovation or expansion project is described in this subparagraph if—

(i) an amendment to the sports team's lease agreement for such facility was entered into on May 23, 1985, and

(ii) the lease agreement had previously been amended in January 1976, on July 6, 1984, on April 1, 1985, and on May 7, 1985.

The aggregate face amount of bonds to which this subparagraph applies shall not exceed $20,000,000.

(I) a facility is described in this subparagraph if—

(i) an appraisal for such facility was completed on March 6, 1985,

(ii) an inducement resolution was adopted with respect to such facility on June 7, 1985, and

(iii) a State bond commission granted preliminary approval for such project on September 3, 1985.

The aggregate face amount of bonds to which this subparagraph applies shall not exceed $3,200,000.

(J) A sports facility renovation or expansion project is described in this subparagraph if—

(i) such facility is a domed stadium which commenced operations in 1965,

(ii) such facility has been the subject of an ongoing construction, expansion, or renovation program of planned improvements,

(iii) part 1 of such improvements began in 1982 with a preliminary renovation program financed by tax-exempt bonds,

(iv) part 2 of such program was previously scheduled for a bond election on February 25, 1986, pursuant to a Commissioners Court Order of November 5, 1985, and

(v) the bond election for improvements to such facility was subsequently postponed on December 10, 1985, in order to provide for more comprehensive construction planning.

The aggregate face amount of bonds to which this subparagraph applies shall not exceed $60,000,000.

(K) A facility is described in this subparagraph if—

(i) the 1985 State legislature appropriated a maximum sum of $22,500,000 to the State urban development corporation to be made available for such project, and

(ii) a development and operation agreement was entered into among such corporation, the city, the State budget director, and the county industrial development agency, as of March 1, 1986.

The aggregate face amount of bonds to which this subparagraph applies shall not exceed $28,000,000.

(L) A facility is described in this subparagraph if—

(i) it is to consist of 1 or 2 stadiums appropriate for football games and baseball games with related structures and facilities,

(ii) governmental action was taken on August 7, 1985, by the county commission, and on December 19, 1985, by the city council, concerning such facility, and

(iii) such facility is located in a city having a National League baseball team.

The aggregate face amount of bonds to which this subparagraph applies shall not exceed $200,000,000.

(M) A facility is described in this subparagraph if—

(i) such facility consists of 1 or 2 stadium projects (1 of which may be a stadium renovation or expansion project) with related structures and facilities,

(ii) a special advisory commission commissioned a study by a national accounting firm with respect to a project for such facility, which study was released in September 1985, was recommended construction of either a new multipurpose or a new baseball-only stadium,

(iii) a nationally recognized design and architectural firm released a feasibility study with respect to such project in April 1985, and

(iv) the metropolitan area in which the facility is located is presently the home of an American League baseball team.

The aggregate face amount of bonds to which this subparagraph applies shall not exceed $200,000,000.

(N) A facility is described in this subparagraph if—

(i) it is to consist of 1 or 2 stadiums appropriate for football games and baseball games with related structures and facilities,

(ii) the site for such facility was approved by the council of the city in which such facility is to be located on July 9, 1985, and

(iii) the request for proposals process was authorized by the council of the city in which such facility is to be located on November 5, 1985, and such requests were distributed to potential developers on November 15, 1985, with responses due by February 14, 1986.

The aggregate face amount of bonds to which this subparagraph applies shall not exceed $200,000,000.

(O) A facility is described in this subparagraph if—

(i) such facility is described in a feasibility study dated September 1985, and

(ii) resolutions were adopted or other actions taken on February 21, 1985, July 18, 1985, August 8, 1985, October 17, 1985, and November 7, 1985, by the Board of Supervisors of the county in which such facility will be located with respect to such feasibility study, appropriations to obtain land for such facility, and approving the location of such facility in the county.

The aggregate face amount of bonds to which this subparagraph applies shall not exceed $20,000,000.

(P) A facility is described in this subparagraph if such facility constructed on a site acquired with the sale of revenue bonds authorized by a city council on December 2, 1985 (Ordinances No. 669 and 670, series 1985). The aggregate face amount of bonds to which this subparagraph applies shall not exceed $90,000,000.

(Q) A facility is described in this subparagraph if—

(i) resolutions were adopted approving a ground lease dated June 27, 1983, by a sports authority (created by a State legislature) with respect to the land on which the facility will be erected,

(ii) such facility is described in a market study dated June 13, 1983, and

(iii) such facility was the subject of an Act of the State legislature which was signed on July 1, 1983.

The aggregate face amount of bonds to which this subparagraph applies shall not exceed $81,000,000.

(R) A facility is described in this subparagraph if such facility is a baseball stadium and adjacent parking facilities with respect to which a city made a carryforward election of $52,514,000 on February 25, 1985. The aggregate face amount of bonds to which this subparagraph applies shall not exceed $50,000,000.

(S) A facility is described in this subparagraph if—

(i) such facility is to be used by both a National Hockey League team and a National Basketball Association team,

(ii) such facility is to be constructed on a platform using air rights over land acquired by a State authority and identified as site B in a report dated May 30, 1984, prepared for a State urban development corporation, and

(iii) such facility is eligible for real property tax (and power and energy) benefits pursuant to State legislation approved and effective as of July 7, 1982.

The aggregate face amount of bonds to which this subparagraph applies shall not exceed $225,000,000.

(T) A facility is described in this subparagraph if—

(i) a resolution authorizing the financing of the facility through an issuance of revenue bonds was adopted by the City Commission on August 5, 1986, and

(ii) the metropolitan area in which the facility is to be located is currently the spring training home of an American league baseball team located during the regular season in a city described in subparagraph (C).

The aggregate face amount of bonds to which this subparagraph applies shall not exceed $10,000,000.

(U) A facility is described in this subparagraph if it is a football stadium located in Oakland, California, with respect to which a design was completed by a nationally recognized architectural firm for a stadium seating approximately 72,000, to be located on property adjacent to an existing coliseum complex, or is a renovation of an existing stadium located in Oakland, California, and used by an American League baseball team. The aggregate face amount of bonds to which this subparagraph applies shall not exceed $100,000,000.

(V) A facility is described in this subparagraph if it is a sports arena (and related parking facility) for Grand Rapids, Michigan. The aggregate face amount of bonds to which this subparagraph applies shall not exceed $80,000,000.

(W) A facility is described in this subparagraph if such facility is located adjacent to the Anacostia River in the District of Columbia. The aggregate face amount of bonds to which this subparagraph applies shall not exceed $25,000,000.

(X) A facility is described in this subparagraph if it is a spectator sports facility for the City of San Antonio, Texas.

The aggregate face amount of bonds to which this subparagraph applies shall not exceed $125,000,000.

(Y) A facility is described in this subparagraph if it will be part of, or adjacent to, an existing stadium which has been owned and operated by a State university and if—

(i) the stadium was the subject of a feasibility report by a certified public accounting firm which is dated December 28, 1984, and

(ii) a report by an independent research organization was prepared in December 1985 demonstrating support among donors and season ticket holders for the addition of a dome to the stadium.

The aggregate face amount of bonds to which this subparagraph applies shall not exceed $50,000,000.

(Z) A facility is described in this subparagraph if—

(i) such facility was a redevelopment project that was approved in concept by the city council sitting as the redevelopment agency in October 1984, and

(ii) $20,000,000 in funds for such facility was identified in a 5-year budget approved by the city redevelopment agency on October 25, 1984.

The aggregate face amount of bonds to which this subparagraph applies shall not exceed $80,000,000.

(4) Residential Rental Property.—A bond issued as part of an issue 95 percent or more of the net proceeds of which are to be used to finance a residential rental project within the meaning of section 103(b)(4) of the 1954 Code shall be treated as an exempt facility bond within the meaning of section 142(a)(7) of the 1986 Code if the facility with respect to [which] the bond is issued satisfies all low-income occupancy requirements applicable to such bonds before August 15, 1986, and the bonds are issued pursuant to—

(A) a contract to purchase such property dated August 12, 1985;

(B) the county housing authority approved the property and the financing thereof on September 24, 1985; and

(C) there was an inducement resolution adopted on October 10, 1985, by the county industrial development authority.

The aggregate face amount of bonds to which this paragraph applies shall not exceed $25,400,000.

(5) AIRPORTS.—A bond issued as part of an issue 95 percent or more of the net proceeds of which are to be used to provide an airport (within the meaning of section 103(b)(4)(D) of the 1954 Code) shall be treated as an exempt facility bond (for facilities described in section 142(a)(1) of the 1986 Code) for purposes of part IV of subchapter B of chapter 1 of the 1986 Code if the facility is described in any of the following subparagraphs:

(A) A facility is described in this subparagraph if such facility is a hotel at an airport facility serving a city described in section 631(a)(3) of the Tax Reform Act of 1984 (relating to certain bonds for a convention center and resource recovery project). The aggregate face amount of bonds to which this subparagraph applies shall not exceed $40,000,000.

(B) A facility is described in this subparagraph if such facility is the primary airport for a city described in paragraph (3)(C). The aggregate face amount of bonds to which this subparagraph applies shall not exceed $500,000,000. Section 148(d)(2) of the 1986 Code shall not apply to any issue to which this subparagraph applies. A facility shall be described in this subparagraph if it would be so described if "90 percent" were substituted for "95 percent" in the material preceding subparagraph (A).

(C) A facility is described in this subparagraph if such facility is a hotel at Logan airport and such hotel is located on land leased from a State authority under a lease contemplating development of such hotel dated May 1, 1983, or under an amendment, renewal, or extension of such a lease. The aggregate face amount of bonds to which this subparagraph applies shall not exceed $40,000,000.

(D) A facility is described in this subparagraph if such facility is the airport for the County of Sacramento, California. The aggregate face amount of bonds to which this subparagraph applies shall not exceed $150,000,000.

(6) REDEVELOPMENT PROJECTS.—A bond issued as part of an issue 95 percent or more of the net proceeds of which are to be used to finance redevelopment activities as part of a project within a specific designated area shall be treated as a qualified redevelopment bond for purposes of part IV of subchapter B of chapter 1 of the 1986 Code if such project is described in any of the following subparagraphs:

(A) A project is described in this subparagraph if it was subject of a city ordinance numbered 82-115 and adopted on December 2, 1982, or numbered 9590 and adopted on April 6, 1983. The aggregate face amount of bonds to which this subparagraph applies shall not exceed $9,000,000.

(B) A project is described in this subparagraph if it is a redevelopment project for an area in a city described in paragraph (3)(C) which was designated as commercially blighted on November 14, 1975, by the city council and the redevelopment plan for which will be approved by the city council before January 31, 1987. The aggregate face amount of bonds to which this subparagraph applies shall not exceed $20,000,000.

(C) A project is described in this subparagraph if it is a redevelopment project for an area in a city described in paragraph (3)(C) which was designated as commercially blighted on March 28, 1979, by the city council and the redevelopment plan for which was approved by the city council on June 20, 1984. The aggregate face amount of bonds to which this subparagraph applies shall not exceed $100,000,000.

(D) A project is described in this subparagraph if it is any one of three redevelopment projects in areas in a city described in paragraph (3)(C) designated as blighted by a city council before January 31, 1987 and with respect to which the redevelopment plan is approved by the city council before January 31, 1987. The aggregate face amount of bonds to which this subparagraph applies shall not exceed $20,000,000.

(E) A project is described in this subparagraph if such project is for public improvements (including street reconstruction and improvement of underground utilities) for Great Falls, Montana, with respect to which engineering estimates are due on October 1, 1986. The aggregate face amount of bonds to which this subparagraph applies shall not exceed $3,000,000.

(F) A project is described in this subparagraph if—

(i) such project is located in an area designated as blighted by the governing body of the city on February 15, 1983 (Resolution No. 4573), and

(ii) such project is developed pursuant to a redevelopment plan adopted by the governing body of the city on March 1, 1983 (Ordinance No. 15073).

The aggregate face amount of bonds to which this subparagraph applies shall not exceed $5,000,000.

(G) A project is described in this subparagraph if—

(i) such project is located in an area designated by the governing body of the city in 1983,

(ii) such project is described in a letter dated August 8, 1985, from the developer's legal counsel to the development agency of the city, and

(iii) such project consists primarily of retail facilities to be built by the developer named in a resolution of the governing body of the city on August 30, 1985.

The aggregate face amount of bonds to which this subparagraph applies shall not exceed $75,000,000.

(H) A project is described in this subparagraph if—

(i) such project is a project for research and development facilities to be used primarily to benefit a State university and related hospital, with respect to which an urban renewal district was created by the city council effective October 11, 1985, and

(ii) such project was announced by the university and the city in March 1985.

The aggregate face amount of bonds to which this subparagraph applies shall not exceed $40,000,000.

(I) A project is described in this subparagraph if such project is a downtown redevelopment project with respect to which—

(i) an urban development action grant was made, but only if such grant was preliminarily approved on November 3, 1983, and received final approval before June 1, 1984, and

(ii) the issuer of bonds with respect to such facility adopted a resolution indicating the issuer's intent to adopt such redevelopment project on October 6, 1981, and the issuer adopted an ordinance adopting such redevelopment project on December 13, 1983.

The aggregate face amount of bonds to which this subparagraph applies shall not exceed $10,000,000.

(J) A project is described in this subparagraph if—

(i) with respect to such project the city council adopted on December 16, 1985, an ordinance directing the urban renewal authority to study blight and produce an urban renewal plan,

(ii) the blight survey was accepted and approved by the urban renewal authority on March 20, 1986, and

(iii) the city planning board approved the urban renewal plan on May 7, 1986.

The aggregate face amount of bonds to which this subparagraph applies shall not exceed $60,000,000.

(K) A project is described in this subparagraph if—

(i) the city redevelopment agency approved resolutions authorizing issuance of land acquisition and public improvement bonds with respect to such project on August 8, 1978,

(ii) such resolutions were later amended in June 1979, and

(iii) the State Supreme Court upheld a lower court decree validating the bonds on December 11, 1980.

The aggregate face amount of bonds to which this subparagraph applies shall not exceed $380,000,000.

(L) A project is described in this subparagraph if it is a mixed use redevelopment project either—

(i) in an area (known as the Near South Development Area) with respect to which the planning department of a city described in paragraph 3(c) promulgated a draft development plan dated March 1986, and which was the subject of public hearings held by a subcommittee of the plan commission of such city on May 28, 1986, and June 10, 1986, or

(ii) in an area located within the boundaries of any 1 or more census tracts which are directly adjacent to a river whose course runs through such city.

The aggregate face amount of bonds to which this subparagraph applies shall not exceed $75,000,000.

(M) A project is described in this subparagraph if it is a redevelopment project for an area in a city described in paragraph 3(C) and such area—

(i) was the subject of a report released in May 1986, prepared by the National Park Service, and

(ii) was the subject of a report released January 1986, prepared by a task force appointed by the Mayor of such city.

The aggregate face amount of bonds to which this subparagraph applies shall not exceed $75,000,000.

(N) A project is described in this subparagraph if it is a city-university redevelopment project approved by a city ordinance No. 152-0-84 and the development plan for which was adopted on January 28, 1985. The aggregate face amount of bonds to which this subparagraph applies shall not exceed $23,760,000.

(O) A project is described in this subparagraph if—

(i) an inducement resolution was passed on March 9, 1984, for issuance of bonds with respect to such project,

(ii) such resolution was extended by resolutions passed on August 14, 1984, April 2, 1985, August 13, 1985, and July 8, 1986,

(iii) an urban development action grant was preliminarily approved for part or all of such project on July 3, 1986, and

(iv) the project is located in a district designated as the Peabody-Gayoso District.

The aggregate face amount of bonds to which this subparagraph applies shall not exceed $140,000,000.

(P) A project is described in this subparagraph if the project is a 1-block area of a central business district containing a YMCA building with respect to which—

(i) the city council adopted a resolution expressing an intent to issue bonds for the project on September 27, 1985,

(ii) the city council approved project guidelines for the project on December 20, 1985, and

(iii) the city council by resolution (adopted on July 30, 1986) directed completion of a development agreement.

The aggregate face amount of bonds to which this subparagraph applies shall not exceed $26,000,000.

(Q) A project is described in this subparagraph if the project is a 2-block area of a central business district designated as blocks E and F with respect to which—

(i) the city council adopted guidelines and criteria and authorized a request for development proposals on July 22, 1985,

(ii) the city council adopted a resolution expressing an intent to issue bonds for the project on September 27, 1985, and

(iii) the city issued requests for development proposals on March 28, 1986.

The aggregate face amount of bonds to which this subparagraph applies shall not exceed $47,000,000.

(R) A project is described in this subparagraph if the project is an urban renewal project covering approximately 5.9 acres of land in the Shaw area of the northwest section of the District of Columbia and the 1st portion of such project was the subject of a District of Columbia public hearing on June 2, 1986. The aggregate face amount of bonds to which this subparagraph applies shall not exceed $10,000,000.

(S) A project is described in this subparagraph if such project is a hotel, commercial, and residential project on the east bank of the Grand River in Grand Rapids, Michigan, with respect to which a developer was selected by the city in June 1985 and a planning agreement was executed in August 1985. The aggregate face amount of bonds to which this subparagraph applies shall not exceed $39,000,000.

(T) A project is described in this subparagraph if such project is the Wurzburg Block Redevelopment Project in Grand Rapids, Michigan. The aggregate face amount of bonds to which this subparagraph applies shall not exceed $60,000,000.

(U) A project is described in this subparagraph if such project is consistent with an urban renewal plan adopted or ordered prepared before August 28, 1986, by the city council of the most populous city in a state which entered the Union on February 14, 1859. The aggregate face amount of bonds to which this subparagraph applies shall not exceed $83,000,000.

(V) A project is described in this subparagraph if such project is consistent with an urban renewal plan which was adopted (or ordered prepared) before August 13, 1985, by an appropriate jurisdiction of a state which entered the Union on February 14, 1859. The aggregate face amount of bonds to which this subparagraph applies shall not exceed $135,000,000 and the limitation on the period during which bonds under this section may be issued shall not apply to such bonds.

(W) A project is described in this subparagraph if such project is—

(i) a part of the Kenosha Downtown Redevelopment project, and

(ii) located in an area bounded—

(I) on the east by the east wall of the Army Corps of Engineers Confined Disposal Facility (extended),

(II) on the north by 48th Street (extended),

(III) on the west by the present Chicago & Northwestern Railroad tracks, and

(IV) on the south by the north line of Eichelman Park (60th Street) (extended).

The aggregate face amount of bonds to which this subparagraph applies shall not exceed $105,000,000.

(X) A project is described in this subparagraph if a redevelopment plan for such project was approved by the city council of Bell Gardens, California, on June 12, 1979. The aggregate face amount of bonds to which this subparagraph applies shall not exceed $10,000,000.

(Y) Nothing in this paragraph shall be construed as having the effect of exempting from tax interest on any bond issued after June 10, 1987, if such interest would not have been exempt from tax were such bond issued on August 15, 1986.

(Z) Any designated area with respect to which a project is described in any subparagraph of this paragraph shall be taken into account in applying section 144(c)(4)(C) of the 1986 Code in determining whether other areas (not so described) may be designated.

(7) CONVENTION CENTERS.—A bond issued as part of an issue 95 percent or more of the net proceeds of which are to be used to provide any convention or trade show facility (within the meaning of section 103(b)(4)(C) of the 1954 Code) shall be treated as an exempt facility bond for purposes of part IV of subchapter B of chapter 1 of the 1986 Code if such facility is described in any of the following subparagraphs:

(A) A facility is described in this subparagraph if—

(i) a feasibility consultant and a designing consultant were hired on April 3, 1985, with respect to such facility, and

(ii) a draft feasibility report with respect to such facility was presented on November 3, 1985, to the Mayor of the city in which such facility is to be located.

The aggregate face amount of bonds to which this subparagraph applies shall not exceed $190,000,000. For purposes of this subparagraph, not more than $20,000,000 of bonds issued to advance refund existing convention facility bonds sold on May 12, 1978, shall be treated as bonds described in this subparagraph, and section 149(d)(2) of the 1986 Code shall not apply to bonds so treated.

(B) A facility is described in this subparagraph if—

(i) an application for a State loan for such facility was approved by the city council on March 4, 1985, and

(ii) the city council of the city in which such facility is to be located approved on March 25, 1985, an application for an urban development action grant.

The aggregate face amount of bonds to which this subparagraph applies shall not exceed $10,000,000.

(C) A facility is described in this subparagraph if—

(i) on November 1, 1983, a convention development tax took effect and was dedicated to financing such facility,

(ii) the State supreme court of the State in which the facility is to be located validated such tax on February 8, 1985, and

(iii) an agreement was entered into on November 14, 1985, between the city and county in which such facility is to be located on the terms of the bonds to be issued with respect to such facility.

The aggregate face amount of bonds to which this subparagraph applies shall not exceed $66,000,000.

(D) A facility is described in this subparagraph if—

(i) it is a convention, trade, or spectator facility,

(ii) a regional convention, trade, and spectator facilities study committee was created before March 19, 1985, with respect to such facility, and

(iii) feasibility and preliminary design consultants were hired on May 1, 1985, and October 31, 1985, with respect to such facility.

The aggregate face amount of bonds to which this subparagraph applies shall not exceed the excess of $175,000,000 over the amount of bonds to which paragraph (48)(B) applies.

(E) A facility is described in this subparagraph if—

(i) such facility is meeting rooms for a convention center, and

(ii) resolutions and ordinances were adopted with respect to such meeting rooms on January 17, 1983, July 11, 1983, December 17, 1984, and September 23, 1985.

The aggregate face amount of bonds to which this subparagraph applies shall not exceed $75,000,000.

(F) A facility is described in this subparagraph if it is an international trade center which is part of the 125th Street redevelopment project in New York, New York. The aggregate face amount of obligations to which this subparagraph applies shall not exceed $165,000,000.

(G) A facility is described in this subparagraph if—

(i) such facility is located in a city which was the subject of a convention center market analysis or study dated March 1983, and prepared by a nationally recognized accounting firm,

(ii) such facility's location was approved in December 1985 by a task force created jointly by the Governor of the State within which such facility will be located and the mayor of the capital city of such State, and

(iii) the size of such facility is not more than 200,000 square feet.

The aggregate face amount of bonds to which this subparagraph applies shall not exceed $70,000,000.

(H) A facility is described in this subparagraph if an analysis of operations and recommendations of utilization of such facility was prepared by a certified public accounting firm pursuant to an engagement authorized on March 6, 1984, and presented on June 11, 1984, to officials of the city in which such facility is located. The aggregate face amount of bonds to which this subparagraph applies shall not exceed $75,000,000.

(I) A facility is described in this subparagraph if—

(i) voters approved a bond issue to finance the acquisition of the site for such facility on May 4, 1985,

(ii) title of the property was transferred from the Illinois Center Gulf Railroad to the city on September 30, 1985, and

(iii) a United States judge rendered a decision regarding the fair market value of the site of such facility on December 30, 1985.

The aggregate face amount of bonds to which this subparagraph applies shall not exceed $131,000,000.

(J) A facility is described in this subparagraph if—

(i) such facility is to be used for an annual aquafestival,

(ii) a referendum was held on April 6, 1985, in which voters permitted the city council to lease 130 acres of dedicated parkland for the purpose of constructing such facility, and

(iii) the city council passed an inducement resolution on June 19, 1986.

The aggregate face amount of bonds to which this subparagraph applies shall not exceed $10,000,000.

(K) A facility is described in this subparagraph if—

(i) voters approved a bond issued to finance a portion of the cost of such facility on December 1, 1984, and

(ii) such facility was the subject of a market study and financial projections dated March 21, 1986, prepared by a nationally recognized accounting firm.

The aggregate face amount of bonds to which this subparagraph applies shall not exceed $5,000,000.

(L) A facility is described in this subparagraph if—

(i) on July 12, 1984, the city council passed a resolution increasing the local hotel and motel tax to 7 percent to assist in paying for such facility,

(ii) on October 25, 1984, the city council selected a consulting firm for such facility, and

(iii) with respect to such facility, the city council appropriated funds for additional work on February 7, 1985, October 3, 1985, and June 26, 1986.

The aggregate face amount of bonds to which this subparagraph applies shall not exceed $120,000,000.

(M) A facility is described in this subparagraph if—

(i) a board of county commissioners, in an action dated January 21, 1986, supported an application for official approval of the facility, and

(ii) the State economic development commission adopted a resolution dated February 25, 1986, determining the facility to be an eligible facility pursuant to State law and the rules adopted by the commission.

The aggregate face amount of bonds to which this subparagraph applies shall not exceed $7,500,000.

(8) SPORTS OR CONVENTION FACILITIES.—A bond issued as a part of an issue 95 percent or more of the net proceeds of which are to be used to provide either a sports facility (within the meaning of section 103(b)(4)(B) of the 1954 Code) or a convention facility (within the meaning of section 103(b)(4)(C) of the 1954 Code) shall be treated as an exempt facility bond for purposes of part IV of subchapter B of chapter 1 of the 1986 Code if such facility is described in any of the following subparagraphs:

(A) A combined convention and arena facility, or any part thereof (whether on the same or different sites), is described in this subparagraph if—

(i) bonds for the expansions, acquisition, or construction of such combined facility are payable from a tax and are issued under a plan initially approved by the voters of the taxing authority on April 25, 1978, and

(ii) such bonds were authorized for expanding a convention center, for acquiring an arena site, and for building an arena or any of the foregoing pursuant to a resolution adopted by the governing body of the bond issuer on March 17, 1986, and superseded by a resolution adopted by such governing body on May 27, 1986.

The aggregate face amount of bonds to which this subparagraph applies shall not exceed $160,000,000.

(B) A sports or convention facility is described in this subparagraph if—

(i) on March 4, 1986, county commissioners held public hearings on creation of a county convention facilities authority, and

(ii) on March 7, 1986, the county commissioners voted to create a county convention facilities authority and to submit to county voters a 1/2 cent sales and use tax to finance such facility.

The aggregate face amount of bonds to which this subparagraph applies shall not exceed $150,000,000.

(C) A sports or convention facility is described in this subparagraph if—

(i) a feasibility consultant and a design consultant were hired prior to October 1980 with respect to such facility,

(ii) a feasibility report dated October 1980 with respect to such facility was presented to a city or county in which such facility is to be located, and

(iii) on September 7, 1982, a joint city/county resolution appointed a committee which was charged with the task of independently reviewing the studies and present need for the facility.

The aggregate face amount of bonds to which this subparagraph applies shall not exceed $60,000,000.

(D) A sports or convention facility is described in this subparagraph if—

(i) such facility is a multipurpose coliseum facility for which, before January 1, 1985, a city, an auditorium district created by the State legislature within which such facility will be located, and a limited partnership executed an enforceable contract,

(ii) significant governmental action regarding such facility was taken before May 23, 1983, and

(iii) inducement resolutions were passed for issuance of bonds with respect to such facility on May 26, 1986.

The aggregate face amount of bonds to which this subparagraph applies shall not exceed $25,000,000.

(9) Parking facilities.—A bond issued as part of an issue 95 percent or more of the net proceeds of which are to be used to provide a parking facility (within the meaning of section 103(b)(4)(D) of the 1954 Code) shall be treated as an exempt facility bond for purposes of part IV of subchapter B of chapter 1 of the 1986 Code if such facility is described in any of the following subparagraphs:

(A) A facility is described in this subparagraph if—

(i) there was an inducement resolution on March 9, 1984, for the issuance of bonds with respect to such facility, and

(ii) such resolution was extended by resolutions passed on August 14, 1984, April 2, 1985, August 13, 1985, and July 8, 1986.

The aggregate face amount of bonds to which this subparagraph applies shall not exceed $30,000,000.

(B) A facility is described in this subparagraph if—

(i) such facility is for a university medical school,

(ii) the last parcel of land necessary for such facility was purchased on February 4, 1985, and

(iii) the amount of bonds to be issued with respect to such facility was increased by the State legislature of the State in which the facility is to be located as part of its 1983-1984 general appropriations act.

The aggregate face amount of bonds to which this subparagraph applies shall not exceed $9,000,000.

(C) A facility is described in this subparagraph if—

(i) the development agreement with respect to the project of which such facility is a part was entered into during May 1984, and

(ii) an inducement resolution was passed on October 9, 1985, for the issuance of bonds with respect to the facility.

The aggregate face amount of bonds to which this subparagraph applies shall not exceed $35,000,000.

(D) A facility is described in this subparagraph if the city council approved a resolution of intent to issue tax-exempt bonds (Resolution 34083) for such facility on April 30, 1986. The aggregate face amount of bonds to which this subparagraph applies shall not exceed $8,000,000. Solely for purposes of this subparagraph, a heliport constructed as part of such facility shall be deemed to be functionally related and subordinate to such facility.

(E) A facility is described in this subparagraph if—

(i) resolutions were adopted by a public joint powers authority relating to such facility on March 6, 1985, May 1, 1985, October 2, 1985, December 4, 1985, and February 5, 1986; and

(ii) such facility is to be located at an exposition park which includes a coliseum and sports arena.

The aggregate face amount of bonds to which this subparagraph applies shall not exceed $150,000,000.

(F) A facility is described in this subparagraph if—

(i) it is to be constructed as part of ana overall development that is the subject of a development agreement dated October 1, 1983, between a developer and an organization described in section 501(c)(3) of the 1986 Code, and

(ii) an environmental notification form with respect to the overall development was filed with a State environmental agency on February 28, 1985.

The aggregate face amount of bonds to which this subparagraph applies shall not exceed $60,000,000.

(G) A facility is described in this subparagraph if—

(i) an inducement resolution was passed by the city redevelopment agency on December 3, 1984, and a resolution to carryforward the private activity bond limit was passed by such agency on December 21, 1984, with respect to such facility, and

(ii) the owner participation agreement with respect to such facility was entered into on July 30, 1986.

The aggregate face amount of bonds to which this subparagraph applies shall not exceed $18,000,000.

(H) A facility is described in this subparagraph if—

(i) an application (dated August 28, 1986) for financial assistance was submitted to the county industrial development agency with respect to such facility, and

(ii) the inducement resolution for such facility was passed by the industrial development agency on September 10, 1986.

The aggregate face amount of bonds to which this subparagraph applies shall not exceed $8,000,000.

(I) A facility is described in this subparagraph if—

(i) it is located in a city the parking needs of which were comprehensively described in a "Downtown Parking Plan" dated January 1983, and approved by the city's City Plan Commission on June 1, 1983, and

(ii) obligations with respect to the construction of which are issued on behalf of a State or local governmental unit by a corporation empowered to issue the same which was created by the legislative body of a State by an Act introduced on May 21, 1985, and thereafter passed, which Act became effective without the governor's signature on June 26, 1985.

The aggregate face amount of bonds to which this subparagraph applies shall not exceed $50,000,000.

(J) A facility is described in this subparagraph if—

(i) such facility is located in a city which was the subject of a convention center market analysis or study dated March 1983 and prepared by a nationally recognized accounting firm,

(ii) such facility is intended for use by, among others, persons attending a convention center located within the same town or city, and

(iii) such facility's location was approved in December 1985 by a task force created jointly by the governor of the

State within which such facility will be located and the mayor of the capital city of such State.

The aggregate face amount of bonds to which this subparagraph applies shall not exceed $30,000,000.

(K) A facility is described in this subparagraph if—

(i) scale and components for the facility were determined by a city downtown plan adopted October 31, 1984 (resolution number 3882), and

(ii) the site area for the facility is approximately 51,200 square feet.

The aggregate face amount of bonds to which this subparagraph applies shall not exceed $5,000,000.

(L) A facility is described in this subparagraph if—

(i) the property for such facility was offered for development by a city renewal agency on March 19, 1986 (resolution number 920), and

(ii) the site area for the facility is approximately 25,600 square feet.

The aggregate face amount of bonds to which this subparagraph applies shall not exceed $5,000,000.

(M) A facility is described in this subparagraph if such facility was approved by official action of the city council on July 26, 1984 (resolution number 33718), and is for the Moyer Theatre. The aggregate face amount of bonds to which this subparagraph applies shall not exceed $8,000,000.

(N) A facility is described in this subparagraph if it is part of a renovation project involving the Outlet Company building in Providence, Rhode Island. The aggregate face amount of obligations to which this subparagraph applies shall not exceed $6,000,000.

(10) CERTAIN ADVANCE REFUNDING.—

(A) Section 149(d)(3) of the 1986 Code shall not apply to a bond issued by a State admitted to the Union on November 16, 1907, for the advance refunding of not more than $186,000,000 State turnpike obligations.

(B) A refunding of the Charleston, West Virginia Town Center Garage Bonds shall not be treated for purposes of part IV of subchapter A of chapter 1 of the 1986 Code as an advance refunding if it would not be so treated if "100" were substituted for "90" in section 149(d)(5) of such Code.

(11) PRINCIPAL USER PROVISIONS.—

(A) In the case of a bond issued as part of an issue the proceeds of which are to be used to provide a facility described in subparagraph (B) or (C), the determination of whether such bond is an exempt facility bond shall be made by substituting "90 percent" for "95 percent" in section 142(a) of the 1986 Code.

(B) A facility is described in this subparagraph if—

(i) it is a waste-to-energy project for which a contract for the sale of electricity was executed in September 1984, and

(ii) the design, construction, and operation contract for such project was signed in March 1985 and the order to begin construction was issued on March 31, 1986.

The aggregate face amount of bonds to which this subparagraph applies shall not exceed $29,100,000.

(C) A facility is described in this subparagraph if it is described in section 1865(c)(2)(C) of this Act.

(12) QUALIFIED SCHOLARSHIP FUNDING BONDS.—Subsections (d)(3) and (f) of section 148 of the 1986 Code shall not apply to any bond or series of bonds the proceeds of which are used exclusively to refund qualified scholarship funding bonds (as defined in section 150 of the 1986 Code) issued before January 1, 1986, if—

(A) the amount of the refunding bonds does not exceed the aggregate face amount of the refunded bonds,

(B) the maturity date of such refunding bond is not later than later of—

(i) the maturity date of the bond to be refunded, or

(ii) the date which is 15 years after the date on which the refunded bond was issued (or, in the case of a series of refundings, the date on which the original bond was issued),

(C) the bonds to be refunded were issued by the California Student Loan Finance Corporation, and

(D) the face amount of the refunding bonds does not exceed $175,000,000.

(13) RESIDENTIAL RENTAL PROPERTY PROJECTS.—A bond issued as part of an issue 95 percent or more of the net proceeds of which are to be used to provide a project for residential rental property which satisfies the requirements of section 103(b)(4)(A) of the 1954 Code shall be treated as an exempt facility bond (for projects described in section 142(a)(7) of the 1986 Code) for purposes of part IV of subchapter B of chapter 1 of the 1986 Code if the project is described in any of the following subparagraphs:

(A) A residential rental property project is described in this subparagraph if—

(i) a public building development corporation was formed on June 6, 1984, with respect to such project,

(ii) a partnership of which the corporation is a general partner was formed on June 8, 1984, and

(iii) the partnership entered into a preliminary agreement with the State public facilities authority effective as of May 4, 1984, with respect to the issuance of the bonds for such project.

The aggregate face amount of bonds to which this subparagraph applies shall not exceed $6,200,000.

(B) A residential rental property project is described in this subparagraph if—

(i) the Board of Commissioners of the city housing authority officially selected such project's developer on December 19, 1985,

(ii) the Board of the City Redevelopment Commission agreed on February 13, 1986, to conduct a public hearing with respect to the project on March 6, 1986,

(iii) an official action resolution for such project was adopted on March 6, 1986, and

(iv) an allocation of a portion of the State ceiling was made with respect to such project on July 29, 1986.

The aggregate face amount of bonds to which this subparagraph applies shall not exceed $10,000,000.

(C) A residential rental property project is described in this subparagraph if—

(i) the issuance of $1,289,882 of bonds for such project was approved by a State agency on September 11, 1985, and

(ii) the authority to issue such bonds was scheduled to expire (under the terms of the State approval) on September 9, 1986.

The aggregate face amount of bonds to which this subparagraph applies shall not exceed $1,300,000.

(D) A residential rental property project is described in this subparagraph if—

(i) the issuance of $7,020,000 of bonds for such project was approved by a State agency on October 10, 1985, and

(ii) the authority to issue such bonds was scheduled to expire (under the terms of the State approval) on October 9, 1986.

The aggregate face amount of bonds to which this subparagraph applies shall not exceed $7,020,000.

(E) A residential rental property project is described in this subparagraph if—

(i) it is to be located in a city urban renewal project area which was established pursuant to an urban renewal plan adopted by the city council on May 17, 1960,

(ii) the urban renewal plan was revised in 1972 to permit multifamily dwellings in areas of the urban renewal project designated as a central business district,

(iii) an inducement resolution was adopted for such project on December 14, 1984, and

(iv) the city council approved on November 6, 1985, an agreement which provides for conveyance to the city of fee title to such project site.

The aggregate face amount of bonds to which this subparagraph applies shall not exceed $60,000,000.

(F) A residential rental property project is described in this subparagraph if—

(i) such project is to be located in a city urban renewal project area which was established pursuant to an urban renewal plan adopted by the city council on May 17, 1960,

(ii) the urban renewal plan was revised in 1972 to permit multifamily dwellings in areas of the urban renewal project designated as a central business district,

(iii) the amended urban renewal plan adopted by the city council on May 19, 1972, also provides for the conversion of any public area site in Block J of the urban renewal project area for the development of residential facilities, and

(iv) acquisition of all of the parcels comprising the Block J project site was completed by the city on December 28, 1984.

The aggregate face amount of bonds to which this subparagraph applies shall not exceed $60,000,000.

(G) A residential rental property project is described in this subparagraph if—

(i) such project is to be located on a city-owned site which is to become available for residential development upon the relocation of a bus maintenance facility,

(ii) preliminary design studies for such project site were complete in December 1985, and

(iii) such project is located in the same State as the projects described in subparagraphs (E) and (F).

The aggregate face amount of bonds to which this subparagraph applies shall not exceed $100,000,000.

(H) A residential rental property project is described in this subparagraph if—

(i) at least 20 percent of the residential units in such project are to be utilized to fulfill the requirements of a unilateral agreement date[d] July 21, 1983, relating to the provision of low- and moderate-income housing,

(ii) the unilateral agreement was incorporated into ordinance numbers 83-49 and 83-50, adopted by the city council and approved by the mayor on August 24, 1983, and

(iii) an inducement resolution was adopted for such project on September 25, 1985.

The aggregate face amount of bonds to which this subparagraph applies shall not exceed $8,000,000.

(I) A residential rental property project is described in this subparagraph if—

(i) a letter of understanding was entered into on December 11, 1985, between the city and county housing and community development office and the project developer regarding the conveyance of land for such project, and

(ii) such project is located in the same State as the projects described in subparagraphs (E), (F), (G), and (H).

The aggregate face amount of bonds to which this subparagraph applies shall not exceed an amount which, together with the amounts allowed under subparagraphs (E), (F), (G), and (H), does not exceed $250,000,000.

(J) A residential rental property project is described in this subparagraph if it is a multifamily residential development located in Arrowhead Springs, within the county of San Bernardino, California, and a portion of the site of which currently is owned by the Campus Crusade for Christ. The aggregate face amount of bonds to which this subparagraph applies shall not exceed $350,000,000.

(K) A residential rental property project is described in this subparagraph if—

(i) it is a new residential development with approximately 309 dwelling units located in census tract No. 3202, and

(ii) there was an inducement ordinance for such project adopted by a city council on November 20, 1985.

The aggregate face amount of bonds to which this subparagraph applies shall not exceed $32,000,000.

(L) A residential rental property project is described in this subparagraph if—

(i) it is a new residential development with approximately 70 dwelling units located in census tract No. 3901, and

(ii) there was an inducement ordinance for such project adopted by a city council on August 14, 1984.

The aggregate face amount of bonds to which this subparagraph applies shall not exceed $4,000,000.

(M) A residential rental property project is described in this subparagraph if—

(i) it is a new residential development with approximately 98 dwelling units located in census tract No. 4701, and

(ii) there was an inducement ordinance for such project adopted by a city council on August 14, 1984.

The aggregate face amount of bonds to which this subparagraph applies shall not exceed $7,000,000.

(N) A project or projects are described in this subparagraph if they are part of the Willow Road residential improvement plan in Menlo Park, California. The aggregate face amount of obligations to which this subparagraph applies shall not exceed $9,000,000.

(O) A residential rental property project is described in this subparagraph if—

(i) an inducement resolution for such project was approved on July 18, 1985, by the city council,

(ii) such project was approved by such council on August 11, 1986, and

(iii) such project consists of approximately 22 duplexes to be used for housing qualified low and moderate income tenants.

The aggregate face amount of bonds to which this subparagraph applies shall not exceed $1,500,000.

(P) A residential rental property project is described in this subparagraph if—

(i) an inducement resolution for such project was approved on April 22, 1986, by the city council,

(ii) such project was approved by such council on August 11, 1986, and

(iii) such project consists of a unit apartment complex (having approximately 60 units) to be used for housing qualified low and moderate income tenants.

The aggregate face amount of bonds to which this subparagraph applies shall not exceed $1,625,000.

(Q) A residential rental property project is described in this subparagraph if—

(i) a State housing authority granted a notice of official action for the project on May 24, 1985, and

(ii) a binding agreement was executed for such project with the State housing finance authority on May 14, 1986, and such agreement was accepted by the State housing authority on June 5, 1986.

The aggregate face amount of bonds to which this subparagraph applies shall not exceed $7,800,000.

(R) A residential rental property project is described in this subparagraph if such project is either of 2 projects (located in St. Louis, Missouri) which received commitments to provide construction and permanent financing through the issuance of bonds in principal amounts of up to $242,130 and $654,045, on July 16, 1986. The aggregate face amount of bonds to which this subparagraph applies shall not exceed $1,000,000.

(S) A residential rental property project is described in this subparagraph if—

(i) a local housing authority approved an inducement resolution for such project on January 28, 1985, and

(ii) a suit relating to such project was dismissed without right of further appeal on April 4, 1986.

The aggregate face amount of bonds to which this subparagraph applies shall not exceed $13,200,000.

(T) A residential rental property project is described in this subparagraph if—

(i) such project is the renovation of a hotel for residents for senior citizens,

(ii) an inducement resolution for such project was adopted on November 20, 1985, by the State Development Finance Authority, and

(iii) such project is to be located in the metropolitan area of the city described in paragraph (3)(C).

The aggregate face amount of bonds to which this subparagraph applies shall not exceed $9,500,000.

(U) A residential rental property project is described in this subparagraph if—

(i) such project is the renovation of apartment housing,

(ii) an inducement resolution for such project was adopted on December 20, 1985, by the State Housing Development Authority, and

(iii) such project is to be located in the metropolitan area of the city described in paragraph (3)(C).

The aggregate face amount of bonds to which this subparagraph applies shall not exceed $12,000,000.

(V) A residential rental project is described in this subparagraph if it is a renovation and construction project for low-income housing in central Louisville, Kentucky, and local board approval for such project was granted April 22, 1986.

The aggregate face amount of bonds to which this subparagraph applies shall not exceed $500,000.

(W) A residential rental project is described in this subparagraph if—

(i) such project is 1 of 6 residential rental projects having in the aggregate approximately 1,010 units,

(ii) inducement resolutions for such projects were adopted by the county residential finance authority on November 21, 1985, and

(iii) a public hearing of the county residential finance authority was held by such authority on December 19, 1985, regarding such projects to be constructed by an in-commonwealth developer.

The aggregate face amount of bonds to which this subparagraph applies shall not exceed $62,000,000.

(X) A residential rental project is described in this subparagraph if—

(i) an inducement resolution with respect to such project was adopted by the State housing development authority on January 25, 1985, and

(ii) the issuance of bonds for such project was the subject of a law suit filed on October 25, 1985.

(Y) A project or projects are described in this subparagraph if they are financed with bonds issued by the Tulare, California, County Housing Authority. The aggregate face amount of obligations to which this subparagraph applies shall not exceed $8,000,000.

(Z) A residential rental project is described in this subparagraph if such project is a multifamily mixed-use housing project located in a city described in paragraph (3)(C), the zoning for which was changed to residential-business planned development on November 26, 1985, and with respect to which both the city on December 4, 1985, and the state housing finance agency on December 20, 1985, adopted inducement resolutions. The aggregate face amount of obligations to which this subparagraph applies shall not exceed $90,000,000.

(AA) A residential rental property project is described in this subparagraph if it is the Carriage Trace residential rental project in Clinton, Tennessee. The aggregate face amount of bonds to which this subparagraph applies shall not exceed $10,000,000.

(BB) A residential rental property project is described in this subparagraph if—

(i) a contract to purchase such property was dated as of August 9, 1985,

(ii) there was an inducement resolution adopted on September 27, 1985, for the issuance of obligations to finance such property,

(iii) there was a State court final validation of such financing on November 15, 1985, and

(iv) the certificate of nonappeal from such validation was available on December 15, 1985.

The aggregate face amount of bonds to which this subparagraph applies shall not exceed $27,750,000.

(14) QUALIFIED STUDENT LOANS.—The amendments made by section 1301 shall not apply to any qualified student loan bonds (as defined in section 144 of the 1986 Code) issued by the Volunteer State Student Assistance Corporation incorporated on February 20, 1985. The aggregate face amount of bonds to which this paragraph applies shall not exceed $130,000,000. In the case of bonds to which this paragraph applies, the requirements of sections 148 and 149(d) of the 1986 Code shall be treated as included in section 103 of the 1954 Code and shall apply to such bonds.

(15) ANNUITY CONTRACTS.—The treatment of annuity contracts as investments property under section 148(b)(2) of the 1986 Code shall not apply to any bond described in any of the following subparagraphs:

(A) A bond is described in this subparagraph if such bond is issued by a city located in a noncontiguous State if—

(i) the authority to acquire such a contract was approved on September 24, 1985, by city ordinance A085-176, and

(ii) formal bid requests for such contracts were mailed to insurance companies on September 6, 1985.

The aggregate face amount of bonds to which this subparagraph applies shall not exceed $57,000,000.

(B) A bond is described in this subparagraph if—

(i) on or before May 12, 1985, the governing board of the city pension fund authorized an agreement with an underwriter to provide planning and financial guidance for a possible bond issue, and

(ii) the proceeds of the sale of such bond issue are to be used to purchase an annuity to fund the unfunded liability of the City of Berkeley, California's Safety Members Pension Fund.

The aggregate face amount of bonds to which this subparagraph applies shall not exceed $40,000,000.

(C) A bond is described in this subparagraph if such bond is issued by the South Dakota Building Authority if on September 18, 1985, representatives of such authority and its underwriters met with bond counsel and approved financing the purchase of an annuity contract through the sale and leaseback of State properties. The aggregate face amount of bonds to which this subparagraph applies shall not exceed $175,000,000.

(D) A bond is described in this subparagraph if—

(i) such bond is issued by Los Angeles County, and

(ii) such county, before September 25, 1985, paid or incurred at least $50,000 of costs related to the issuance of such bonds.

The aggregate face amount of bonds to which this subparagraph applies shall not exceed $50,000,000.

(16) SOLID WASTE DISPOSAL FACILITY.—The amendments made by section 1301 shall not apply to any solid waste disposal facility if—

(A) construction of such facility was approved by State law I.C. 36-9-31,

(B) there was an inducement resolution on November 19, 1984, for the bonds with respect to such facility, and

(C) a carryforward election of unused 1984 volume cap was made for such project on February 25, 1985.

(17) REFUNDING OF BOND ANTICIPATION NOTES.—There shall not be taken into account under section 146 of the 1986 Code any refunding of bond anticipation notes—

(A) issued in December of 1984 by the Rhode Island Housing and Mortgage Finance Corporation,

(B) which mature in December of 1986,

(C) which is not an advance refunding within the meaning of section 149(d)(5) of the 1986 Code (determined by substituting "180 days" for "90 days" therein), and

(D) the aggregate face amount of the refunding bonds does not exceed $25,500,000.

(18) CERTAIN AIRPORTS.—The amendments made by section 1301 shall not apply to a bond issued as part of an issue 95 percent or more of the net proceeds of which are to be used to provide any airport (within the meaning of section 103(b)(4)(D) of the 1954 Code) if such airport is a mid-field airport terminal and accompanying facilities at a major air carrier airport which during April 1980 opened a new precision instrument approach runway 10R28L. The aggregate face amount of bonds to which this subparagraph applies shall not exceed $425,000,000.

(19) MASS COMMUTING FACILITIES.—A bond issued as a part of an issue 95 percent or more of the net proceeds of which are to be used to provide a mass commuting facility (within the meaning of section 103(b)(4)(D) of the 1954 Code) shall be treated as an exempt facility bond (for facilities described in section 142(a)(3) of the 1986 Code) for purposes of part IV of subchapter B of chapter 1 of the 1986 Code if such facility is described in 1 of the following subparagraphs:

(A) A facility is described in this subparagraph if—

(i) such facility provides access to an international airport,

(ii) a corporation was formed in connection with such project in September 1984,

(iii) the Board of Directors of such corporation authorized the hiring of various firms to conduct a feasibility study with respect to such project in April 1985, and

(iv) such feasibility study was completed in November 1985.

The aggregate face amount of bonds to which this subparagraph applies shall not exceed $150,000,000.

(B) A facility is described in this subparagraph if—

(i) enabling legislation with respect to such project was approved by the State legislature in 1979,

(ii) a 1-percent local sales tax assessment to be dedicated to the financing of such project was approved by the voters on August 13, 1983, and

(iii) a capital fund with respect to such project was established upon the issuance of $90,000,000 of notes on October 22, 1985.

The aggregate face amount of bonds to which this subparagraph applies shall not exceed $200,000,000 and such bonds must be issued before January 1, 1996.

(C) A facility is described in this subparagraph if—

(i) bonds issued therefor are issued by or on behalf of an authority organized in 1979 pursuant to enabling legislation originally enacted by the State legislature in 1973, and

(ii) such facility is part of a system connector described in a resolution adopted by the board of directors of the authority on March 27, 1986.

The aggregate face amount of bonds to which this subparagraph applies shall not exceed $400,000,000. Notwithstanding the last paragraph of this subsection, this subparagraph shall apply to bonds issued before January 1, 1996.

(D) A facility is described in this subparagraph if—

(i) the facility is a fixed guideway project,

(ii) enabling legislation with respect to the issuing authority was approved by the State legislature in May 1973,

(iii) on October 28, 1985, a board issued a request for consultants to conduct a feasibility study on mass transit corridor analysis in connection with the facility, and

(iv) on May 12, 1986, a board approved a further binding contract for expenditures of approximately $1,494,963, to be expended on a facility study.

The aggregate face amount of bonds to which this subparagraph applies shall not exceed $250,000,000. Notwithstanding the last paragraph of this subsection, this subparagraph shall apply to bonds issued before January 1, 1996.

(20) PRIVATE COLLEGES.—Subsections (c)(2) and (f) of section 148 of the 1986 Code shall not apply to any bond which is issued as part of an issue if such bond—

(A) is issued by a political subdivision pursuant to home rule and interlocal cooperation powers conferred by the constitution and laws of a State to provide funds to finance the costs of the purchase and construction of educational facilities for private colleges and universities, and

(B) was the subject of a resolution of official action by such political subdivision (Resolution No. 86-1039) adopted by the governing body of such political subdivision on March 18, 1986.

The aggregate face amount of bonds to which this paragraph applies shall not exceed $100,000,000.

(21) POOLED FINANCING PROGRAMS.—

(A) Section 147(b) of the 1986 Code shall not apply to any hospital pooled financing program with respect to which—

(i) a formal presentation was made to a city hospital facilities authority on January 14, 1986, and

(ii) such authority passed a resolution approving the bond issue in principle on February 5, 1986.

The aggregate face amount of bonds to which this subparagraph applies shall not exceed $950,000,000.

(B) Subsections (c)(2) and (f) of section 148 of the 1986 Code shall not apply to bonds for which closing occurred on July 16, 1986, and for which a State municipal league served as administrator for use in a State described in section 103A(g)(5)(C) of the Internal Revenue Code of 1954. The aggregate face amount of obligations to which this subparagraph applies shall not exceed $585,000,000.

(22) DOWNTOWN REDEVELOPMENT PROJECT.—Subsection (b) of section 626 of the Tax Reform Act of 1984 is amended by adding at the end thereof the following new paragraph:

"(7) EXCEPTION FOR CERTAIN DOWNTOWN REDEVELOPMENT PROJECT.—The amendments made by this section shall not apply to any obligation which is issued as part of an issue 95 percent or more of the proceeds of which are to be used to provide a project to acquire and redevelop a downtown area if—

"(A) on August 15, 1985, a downtown redevelopment authority adopted a resolution to issue obligations for such project,

"(B) before September 26, 1985, the city expended, or entered into binding contracts to expend, more than $10,000,000 in connection with such project, and

"(C) the State supreme court issued a ruling regarding the proposed financing structure for such project on December 11, 1985.

The aggregate face amount of obligations to which this paragraph applies shall not exceed $85,000,000 and such obligations must be issued before January 1, 1992."

(23) MASS COMMUTING AND PARKING FACILITIES.—A bond issued as part of an issue 95 percent or more of the net proceeds of which are to be used to provide any mass commuting facility or parking facility (within the meaning of section 103(b)(4)(D) of the 1954 Code) shall be treated as an exempt facility bond for purposes of part IV of subchapter B of chapter 1 of the 1986 Code if such facility is provided in connection with the rehabilitation, renovation, or other improvement to an existing railroad station owned on the date of the enactment of this Act by the National Railroad Passenger Corporation in the Northeast Corridor and which was placed in partial service in 1934 and was placed in the National Register of Historic Places in 1978. The aggregate face amount of bonds to which this paragraph applies shall not exceed $30,000,000.

(24) TAX-EXEMPT STATUS OF BONDS OF CERTAIN EDUCATIONAL ORGANIZATIONS.—

(A) In General.—For purposes of section 103 and part IV of subchapter B of chapter 1 of the 1986 Code, a qualified educational organization shall be treated as a governmental unit, but only with respect to a trade or business carried on by such organization which is not an unrelated trade or business (determined by applying section 513(a) of such Code to such organization). The last paragraph of this section shall not apply to the treatment under the preceding sentence.

(B) Qualified Educational Organization.—For purposes of subparagraph (A), the term "qualified educational organization" means a college or university—

(i) which was reincorporated and renewed with perpetual existence as a corporation by specific act of the legislature of the State within which such college or university is located on March 19, 1913, or

(ii) which—

(I) was initially incorporated or created on February 28, 1787, on April 29, 1854, or on May 14, 1888, and

(II) as an instrumentality of the State, serves as a "State-related" university by a specific act of the legislature of the State within which such college or university is located.

(25) TAX-EXEMPT STATUS OF BONDS OF CERTAIN PUBLIC UTILITIES.—

(A) In General.—Except as provided in subparagraph (B), a bond shall be treated as a qualified bond for purposes of section 103 of the 1986 Code if such bond is issued after the date of the enactment of this Act with respect to a public utility facility if such facility is—

(i) located at any non-federally owned dam (or on project waters or adjacent lands) located wholly or partially in 1 or more of 3 counties, 2 of which are contiguous to the third, where the rated capacity of the hydroelectric generating facilities at 5 of such dams on October 18, 1979, was more than 650 megawatts each,

(ii) located at a dam (or on the project waters or adjacent lands) at which hydroelectric generating facilities were financed with the proceeds of tax-exempt obligations before December 31, 1968,

(iii) owned and operated by a State, political subdivision of a State, or any agency or instrumentality of any of the foregoing, and

(iv) located at a dam (or on project waters or adjacent lands) where the general public has access for recreational purposes to such dam or to such project waters or adjacent lands.

(B) Special Rules for Subparagraph(A).—

(i) Bonds Subject to Cap.—Section 146 of the 1986 Code shall apply to any bond described in subparagraph (A) which (without regard to subparagraph (A)) is a private activity bond. For purposes of applying section 146(k) of the 1986 Code, the public utility facility described in subparagraph (A) shall be treated as described in paragraph (2) of such section and such paragraph shall be applied without regard to the requirement that the issuer establish that a State's share of the use of a facility (or its output) will equal or exceed the State's share of the private activity bonds issued to finance the facility.

(ii) Limitation on Amount of Bonds to Which Subparagraph (A) Applies.—The aggregate face amount of bonds to which subparagraph (A) applies shall not exceed $750,000,000, not more than $350,000,000 of which may be issued before January 1, 1992.

(iii) Limitation on Purposes.—Subparagraph (A) shall only apply to bonds issued as part of an issue 95 percent or more of the net proceeds of which are used to provide 1 or more of the following:

(I) A fish by-pass facility or fisheries enchancement facility.

(II) A recreational facility or other improvement which is required by Federal licensing terms and conditions or other Federal, State, or local law requirements.

(III) A project of repair, maintenance, renewal, or replacement, and safety improvement.

(IV) Any reconstruction, replacement, or improvement, including any safety improvement, which increases, or allows an increase in, the capacity, efficiency, or productivity of the existing generating equipment.

(26) CONVENTION AND PARKING FACILITIES.—A bond shall not be treated as a private activity bond for purposes of section 103 and part IV of subchapter B of chapter 1 of the 1986 Code if—

(A) such bond is issued to provide a sports or convention facility described in section 103(b)(4)(B) or (C) of the 1954 Code,

(B) such bond is not described in section 103(b)(2) or (o)(2)(A) of such Code,

(C) legislation by a State legislature in connection with such facility was enacted on July 19, 1985, and was designated Chapter 375 of the Laws of 1985, and

(D) legislation by a State legislature in connection with the appropriation of funds to a State public benefit corporation for loans in connection with the construction of such facility was enacted on April 17, 1985, and was designated Chapter 41 of the Laws of 1985.

The aggregate face amount of bonds to which this subparagraph applies shall not exceed $35,000,000.

(27) SMALL ISSUE TERMINATION.—Section 144(a)(12) of the 1986 Code shall not apply to any bond issued as part of an issue 95 percent or more of the net proceeds of which are to be used to provide a facility described in any of the following subparagraphs:

(A) A facility is described in this subparagraph if—

(i) the facility is a hotel and office facility located in a State capital,

(ii) the economic development corporation of the city in which the facility is located adopted an initial inducement resolution on October 30, 1985, and

(iii) a feasibility consultant was retained on February 21, 1986, with respect to such facility.

The aggregate face amount of bonds to which this subparagraph applies shall not exceed $10,000,000.

(B) A facility is described in this subparagraph if such facility is financed by bonds issued by a State finance authority which was created in April 1985 by Act 1062 of the State General Assembly, and the Bond Guarantee Act (Act 505 of 1985) allowed such authority to pledge the interest from investment of the State's general fund as a guarantee for bonds issued by such authority. The aggregate face amount of bonds to which this subparagraph applies shall not exceed $75,000,000.

(C) A facility is described in this subparagraph if such facility is a downtown mall and parking project for Holland, Michigan, with respect to which an initial agreement was formulated with the city in May 1985 and a formal memorandum of understanding was executed on July 2, 1986. The aggregate face amount of bonds to which this subparagraph applies shall not exceed $18,200,000.

(D) A facility is described in this subparagraph if such facility is a downtown mall and parking ramp project for Traverse City, Michigan, with respect to which a final development agreement was signed in June 1986. The aggregate face amount of bonds to which this subparagraph applies shall not exceed $21,500,000.

(E) A facility is described in this subparagraph if such facility is the rehabilitation of the Heritage Hotel in Marquette, Michigan. The aggregate face amount of bonds to which this subparagraph applies shall not exceed $5,000,000.

(F) A facility is described in this subparagraph if it is the Lakeland Center Hotel in Lakeland, Florida. The aggregate face amount of obligations to which this subparagraph applies shall not exceed $10,000,000.

(G) A facility is described in this suparagraph if it is the Marble Arcade office building renovation project in Lakeland, Florida. The aggregate face amount of obligations to which this subparagraph applies shall not exceed $5,900,000.

(H) A facility is described in this subparagraph if it is a medical office building in Bradenton, Florida, with respect to which—

(i) a memorandum of agreement was entered into on October 17, 1985, and

(ii) the city council held a public hearing and approved issuance of the bonds on November 13, 1985.

The aggregate face amount of obligations to which this subparagraph applies shall not exceed $8,500,000.

(I) A facility is described in this subparagraph if it consists of the rehabilitation of the Andover Town Hall in Andover, Massachusetts. The provisions of section 149(b) of the 1986 Code (relating to federally guaranteed obligations) shall not apply to obligations to finance such project solely as a result of the occupation of a portion of such building by a United States Post Office. For purposes of determining whether any bond to which this subparagraph applies is a qualified small issue bond, there shall not be taken into account under section 144(a) of the 1986 Code capital expenditures with respect to any facility of the United States Government and there shall not be taken into account any bond allocable to the United States Government.

(J) A facility is described in this subparagraph if it is the Central Bank Building renovation project in Grand Rapids, Michigan. The aggregate face amount of obligations to which this subparagraph applies shall not exceed $1,000,000.

(28) CERTAIN PRIVATE LOANS NOT TAKEN INTO ACCOUNT.—For purposes of determining whether any bond is a private activity bond, an amount of loans (but not in excess of $75,000,000) provided from the proceeds of 1 or more issues shall not be taken into account if such loans are provided in furtherance of—

(A) a city Emergency Conservation Plan as set forth in an ordinance adopted by the city council of such city on February 17, 1983, or

(B) a resolution adopted by the city council of such city on March 10, 1983, committing such city to a goal of reducing the peak load of such city's electric generation and distribution system by 553 megawatts in 15 years.

(29) CERTAIN PRIVATE BUSINESS USE NOT TAKEN INTO ACCOUNT.—

(A) The nonqualified amount of the proceeds of an issue shall not be taken into account under section 141(b)(5) of the 1986 Code or in determining whether a bond described in subparagraph (B) (which is part of such issue) is a private activity bond for purposes of section 103 and part IV of subchapter B of chapter 1 of the 1986 Code.

(B) A bond is described in this subparagraph if—

(i) such bond is issued before January 1, 1993, by the State of Connecticut, and

(ii) such bond is issued pursuant to a resolution of the State Bond Commission adopted before September 26, 1985.

(C) The nonqualified amount to which this paragraph applies shall not exceed $150,000,000.

(D) For purposes of this paragraph, the term "nonqualified amount" has the meaning given such term by section 141(b)(8) of the 1986 Code, except that such term shall include the amount of the proceeds of an issue which is to be used (directly or indirectly) to make or finance loans (other than loans described in section 141(c)(2) of the 1986 Code) to persons other than governmental units.

(30) VOLUME CAP NOT TO APPLY TO CERTAIN FACILITIES.—For purposes of section 146 of the 1986 Code, any exempt facility bond for the following facility shall not be taken into account: The facility is a facility for the furnishing of water which was authorized under Public Law 90-537 of the United States if—

(A) construction of such facility began on May 6, 1973, and

(B) forward funding will be provided for the remainder of the project pursuant to a negotiated agreement between State and local water users and the Secretary of the Interior signed April 15, 1986.

The aggregate face amount of bonds to which this subparagraph applies shall not exceed $391,000,000.

(31) CERTAIN HYDROELECTRIC GENERATING PROPERTY.—A bond shall be treated as described in paragraph (2) of section 1316(f) of this Act if—

(A) such bond would be so described but for the substitution specified in such paragraph,

(B) on January 7, 1983, an application for a preliminary permit was filed for the project for which such bond is issued and received [as per] docket no. 6986, and

(C) on September 20, 1983, the Federal Energy Regulatory Commission issued an order granting the preliminary permit for the project.

The aggregate face amount of bonds to which this paragraph applies shall not exceed $12,000,000.

(32) VOLUME CAP.—The State ceiling applicable under section 146 of the 1986 Code for calendar year 1987 for the State which ratified the United States Constitution on May 29, 1790, shall be $150,000,000 higher than the State ceiling otherwise applicable under such section for such year.

(33) APPLICATION OF $150,000,000 LIMITATION FOR CERTAIN QUALIFIED 501(c)(3) BONDS.—Proceeds of an issue described in any of the following subparagraphs shall not be taken into account under section 145(b) of the 1986 Code.

(A) Proceeds of an issue are described in this subparagraph if—

(i) such proceeds are used to provide medical school facilities or medical research and clinical facilities for a university medical center,

(ii) such proceeds are of—

(I) a $21,550,000 issue dated August 1, 1980,

(II) a $84,400,000 issue dated September 1, 1984, and

(III) a $48,500,000 issue (Series 1985 A and 1985 B) dated on December 1, 1985, and

(iii) the issuer of all such issues is the same.

(B) Proceeds of an issue are described in this subparagraph if such proceeds are for use by Yale University and—

(i) the bonds are issued after August 8, 1986, by the State of Connecticut Health and Educational Facilities Authority, or

(ii) the bonds are the 1st or 2nd refundings (including advance refundings) of the bonds described in clause (i) or of original bonds issued before August 7, 1986, by such Authority.

The aggregate face amount of bonds to which this subparagraph applies shall not exceed $90,000,000.

(C) Proceeds of an issue are described in this subparagraph if—

(i) such issue is issued on behalf of a university established by Charter granted by King George II of England on October 31, 1754, to accomplish a refunding (including an advance refunding) of bonds issued to finance 1 or more projects, and

(ii) the application or other request for the issuance of the issue to the appropriate State issuer was made by or on behalf of such university before February 26, 1986.

The aggregate face amount of bonds to which this subparagraph applies shall not exceed $250,000,000.

(D) Proceeds of an issue are described in this subparagraph if—

(i) such proceeds are to be used for finance construction of a new student recreation center,

(ii) a contract for the development phase of the project was signed by the university on May 21, 1986, with a private company for 5 percent of the costs of the project, and

(iii) a committee of the university board of administrators approved the major program elements for the center on August 11, 1986.

The aggregate face amount of bonds to which this subparagraph applies shall not exceed $25,000,000.

(E) Proceeds of an issue are described in this subparagraph if—

(i) such proceeds are to be used in the construction of new life sciences facilities for a university for medical research and education,

(ii) the president of the university authorized a faculty/administration planning committee for such facilities on September 17, 1982,

(iii) the trustees of such university authorized site and architect selection on October 30, 1984, and

(iv) the university negotiated a $2,600,000 contract with the architect on August 9, 1985.

The aggregate face amount of bonds to which this subparagraph applies shall not exceed $47,500,000.

(F) Proceeds of an issue are described in this subparagraph if such proceeds are to be used to renovate undergraduate chemistry and engineering laboratories, and to rehabilitate other basic science facilities, for an institution of higher education in Philadelphia, Pennsylvania, chartered by legislative Acts of the Commonwealth of Pennsylvania, including an Act dated September 30, 1791. The aggregate face amount of bonds to which this subparagraph applies shall not exceed $6,500,000.

(G) Proceeds of an issue are described in this subparagraph if such proceeds are of bonds which are the first advance refunding of bonds issued during 1985 for the development of a computer network, and construction and renovation or rehabilitation of other facilities, for an institution of higher education described in subparagraph (H). The aggregate face amount of bonds to which this subparagraph applies shall not exceed $80,000,000.

(H) Proceeds of an issue are described in this subparagraph if—

(i) the issue is issued on behalf of a university founded in 1789, and

(ii) the proceeds of the issue are to be used to finance projects (to be determined by such university and the issuer) which are similar to those projects intended to be financed by bonds that were the subject of a request transmitted to Congress on November 7, 1985.

Bonds to which this subparagraph applies shall be treated as qualified 501(c)(3) bonds if such bonds would not (if issued on August 15, 1986) be industrial development bonds (as defined in section 103(b)(2) of the 1954 Code), and section 147(f) of the 1986 Code shall not apply to the issue of which such bonds are a part. Bonds issued to finance facilities described in this subparagraph shall be treated as issued to finance such facilities notwithstanding the fact that a period in excess of 1 year has expired since the facilities were placed in service.

The aggregate face amount of bonds to which this subparagraph applies shall not exceed $200,000,000.

(I) Proceeds of an issue are described in this subparagraph if the issue is issued on behalf of a university established on August 6, 1872, for a project approved by the trustees thereof on November 1, 1985. The aggregate face amount of bonds to which this subparagraph applies shall not exceed $100,000,000.

(J) Proceeds of an issue are described in this subparagraph if—

(i) the issue is issued on behalf of a university for which the founding grant was signed on November 11, 1885, and

(ii) such bond is issued for the purpose of providing a Near West Campus Redevelopment Project and a Student Housing Project.

The aggregate face amount of bonds to which this subparagraph applies shall not exceed $105,000,000.

(J)[(K)] Proceeds of an issue are described in this subparagraph if—

(i) they are the proceeds of advance refunding obligations issued on behalf of a university established on April 21, 1831, and

(ii) the application or other request for the issuance of such obligations was made to the appropriate State issuer before July 12, 1986.

The aggregate face amount of obligations to which this subparagraph applies shall not exceed $175,000,000.

(K)[(L)] Proceeds of an issue are described in this subparagraph if—

(i) the issue or issues are for the purpose of financing or refinancing costs associated with university facilities including at least 900 units of housing for students, faculty, and staff in up to two buildings and an office building containing up to 245,000 square feet of space, and

(ii) a bond act authorizing the issuance of such bonds for such project was adopted on July 8, 1986, and such act under Federal law was required to be transmitted to Congress.

The aggregate face amount of obligations to which this subparagraph applies shall not exceed $112,000,000.

(L)[(M)] Proceeds of an issue are described in this subparagraph if such issue is for Cornell University in an aggregate face amount of not more than $150,000,000.

(M)[(N)] Proceeds of an issue are described in this subparagraph if such issue is issued on behalf of the Society of the New York Hospital to finance completion of a project commenced by such hospital in 1981 for construction of a diagnostic and treatment center or to refund bonds issued on behalf of such hospital in connection with the construction of such diagnostic and treatment center or to finance construction and renovation projects associated with an inpatient psychiatric care facility. The aggregate face amount of bonds to which this subparagraph applies shall not exceed $150,000,000.

(N)[(O)] Any bond to which section 145(b) of the 1986 Code does not apply by reason of this paragraph (other than subparagraph (A) thereof) shall be taken into account in determining whether such section applies to any later issue.

(O)[(P)] In the case of any refunding bond—

(i) to which any subparagraph of this paragraph applies, and

(ii) to which the last sentence of section 1313(c)(2) applies,

such bond shall be treated as having such subparagraph apply (and the refunding bond shall be treated for purposes of such section as issued before January 1, 1986, and as not being an advance refunding) unless the issuer elects the opposite result.

(41) CERTAIN REFUNDING OBLIGATIONS FOR CERTAIN POWER FACILITIES.—With respect to 2 net billed nuclear power facilities located in the State of Washington on which construction has been suspended, the requirements of section 147(b) of the 1986 Code shall be treated as satisfied with respect to refunding bonds issued before 1992 if—

(A) each refunding bond has a maturity date not later than the maturity date of the refunded bond, and

(B) the facilities have not been placed in service as of the date of issuance of the refunding bond.

The aggregate face amount of bonds to which this paragraph applies shall not exceed $2,000,000,000. Section 146 of the 1986 Code and the last paragraph of this section shall not apply to bonds to which this paragraph applies.

(34) ARBITRAGE REBATE.—Section 148(f) of the 1986 Code shall not apply to any period before October 1, 1990, with respect to any bond the proceeds of which are to be used to provide a high-speed rail system for the State of Ohio. The aggregate face amount of bonds to which this paragraph applies shall not exceed $2,000,000,000.

(35) EXTENSION OF CARRYFORWARD PERIOD.—

(A) In the case of a carryforward under section 103(n)(10) of the 1954 Code of $170,000,000 of bond limit for calendar year 1984 for a project described in subparagraph (B), clause (i) of section 103(n)(10)(C) of the 1954 Code shall be applied by substituting "6 calendar years" for "3 calendar years", and such carryforward may be used by any authority designated by the State in which the facility is located.

(B) A project is described in this subparagraph if—

(i) such project is a facility for local furnishing of electricity described in section 645 of the Tax Reform Act of 1984, and

(ii) construction of such facility commenced within the 3-year period following the calendar year in which the carryforward arose.

(36) POWER PURCHASE BONDS.—A bond issued to finance purchase of power from a power facility at a dam being renovated pursuant to P.L. 98-381 shall not be treated as a private activity bond if it would not be such under section 141(b)(1) and (2) of the 1986 Code if 25 percent were substituted for 10 percent and the provisions of section 141(b)(3), (4), and (5) of the 1986 Code did not apply. The aggregate face amount of bonds to which this paragraph applies shall not exceed $400,000,000.

(37) QUALIFIED MORTGAGE BONDS.—A bond issued as part of either of 2 issues no later than September 8, 1986, shall be treated as a qualified mortgage bond within the meaning of section 141(d)(1)(B) of the 1986 Code if it satisfies the requirements of section 103A of the 1954 Code and if the issues are issued by the two most populous cities in the Tar Heel State. The aggregate face amount of bonds to which this paragraph applies shall not exceed $4,000,000.

(38) EXEMPT FACILITY BONDS.—A bond shall be treated as an exempt facility bond within the meaning of section 142(a) of the 1986 Code if it is issued to fund residential, office, retail, light industrial, recreational and parking development known as Tobacco Row. Such bond shall be subject to section 146 of the 1986 Code. The aggregate face amount of bonds to which this paragraph applies shall not exceed $100,000,000.

(39) CERTAIN BONDS TREATED AS QUALIFIED 501(c)(3) BONDS.—A bond issued as part of an issue shall be treated for purposes of part IV of subchapter B of chapter 1 of the 1986 Code as a qualified 501(c)(3) bond if—

(A) such bond would not (if issued on August 15, 1986) be an industrial development bond (as defined in section 103(b)(2) of the 1954 Code), and

(B) such issue was approved by city voters on January 19, 1985, for construction or renovation of facilities for the cultural and performing arts.

The aggregate face amount of bonds to which this paragraph applies shall not exceed $5,000,000.

(40) CERTAIN LIBRARY BONDS.—In the case of a bond issued before January 1, 1986, by the City of Los Angeles Community Redevelopment Agency to provide the library and related structures associated with the City of Los Angeles Central Library Project, the ownership and use of the land and facilities associated with such project by persons which are not governmental units (or payments from such persons) shall not adversely affect the exclusion from gross income under section 103 of the 1954 Code of interest on such bonds.

(42) RESIDENTIAL RENTAL PROPERTY.—A bond issued to finance a residential rental project within the meaning of 103(b)(4) of the 1954 Code shall be treated as an exempt facility bond within the meaning of section 142(a)(7) of the 1986 Code if the county housing finance authority adopted an inducement resolution with respect to the project on May 8, 1985, and the project is located in Polk County, Florida. The aggregate face amount of bonds to which this paragraph applies shall not exceed $4,100,000.

(43) EXTENSION OF ADVANCE REFUNDING FOR CERTAIN FACILITIES.—Paragraph (4) of section 631(c) of the Tax Reform Act of 1984 is amended—

(A) by striking out the second sentence thereof,

(B) by adding at the end thereof the following new sentence: "In the case of refunding obligations not exceeding $100,000,000 issued by the Alabama State Docks Department, the first sentence of this paragraph shall be applied by substituting "December 31, 1987" for "December 31, 1984" and the Internal Revenue Code of 1986 shall be applied without regard to section 149(d)(2).

(44) POOL BONDS.—The following amounts of pool bonds are exempt from the arbitrage rebate requirement of section 148(f) of the 1986 Code and the temporary period limitation of section 148(c)(2) of the 1986 Code:

Pool	Maximum Bond Amount
Tennessee Utility Districts Pool	$80,000,000
New Mexico Hospital Equipment Loan Council	$35,000,000
Pennsylvania Local Government Investment Trust Pool	$375,000,000
Indiana Bond Bank Pool	$240,000,000
Hernando County, Florida Bond Pool	$300,000,000
Utah Municipal Finance Cooperative Pool	$262,000,000
North Carolina League of Municipalities Pool	$200,000,000
Kentucky Municipal League Bond Pool	$170,000,000
Kentucky Association of Counties Bond Pool	$200,000,000
Homewood Municipal Bond Pool	$50,000,000
Colorado Association of School Boards Pool	$300,000,000
Tennessee Municipal League Pooled Bonds	$75,000,000
Georgia Municipal Association Pool	$130,000,000

(45) CERTAIN CARRYFORWARD ELECTIONS.—Notwithstanding any other provision of this title—

(A) In the case of a metropolitan service district created pursuant to State revised statutes, chapter 268, up to $100,000,000 unused 1985 bond authority may be carried forward to any year until 1989 (regardless of the date on which such carryforward election is made).

(B) If—

(i) official action was taken by an industrial development board on September 16, 1985, with respect to the issuance of not more than $98,500,000, of waste water treatment revenue bonds, and

(ii) an executive order of the governor granted a carryforward of State bond authority for such project on December 30, 1985,

such carryforward election shall be valid for any year through 1988. The aggregate face amount of obligations to which this subparagraph applies shall not exceed $98,500,000.

(46) TREATMENT OF CERTAIN OBLIGATIONS TO FINANCE HYDROELECTRIC GENERATING FACILITY.—If

(A) obligations are issued in an amount not exceeding $5,000,000 to finance the construction of a hydroelectric generating facility located on the North Fork of Cache Creek in Lake County, California, which was the subject of a preliminary resolution of the issuer of the obligations on June 29, 1982, or are issued to refund any of such obligations,

(B) substantially all of the electrical power generated by such facility is to be sold to a nongovernmental person pursuant to a long-term power sales agreement in accordance with the Public Utility Regulatory Policies Act of 1978, and

(C) the initially issued obligations are issued on or before December 31, 1986, and any of such refunding obligations are issued on or before December 31, 1996,

then the person referred to in subparagraph (B) shall not be treated as a principal user of such facilities by reason of such sales for purposes of subparagraphs (D) and (E) of section 103(b)(6) of the 1954 Code.

(47) TREATMENT OF CERTAIN OBLIGATIONS TO FINANCE STEAM AND ELECTRIC COGENERATION FACILITY.—If—

(A) obligations are issued on or before December 31, 1986, in an amount not exceeding $4,400,000 to finance a facility for the generation and transmission of steam and electricity having a maximum electrical capacity of approximately 5.3 megawatts and located within the City of San Jose, California, or are issued to refund any of such obligations,

(B) substantially all of the electrical power generated by such facility that is not sold to an institution of higher education created by statute of the State of California is to be sold to a nongovernmental person pursuant to a long-term power sales agreement in accordance with the Public Utility Regulatory Policies Act of 1978, and

(C) the initially issued obligations are issued on or before December 31, 1986, and any of such refunding obligations are issued on or before December 31, 1996,

then the nongovernmental person referred to in subparagraph (B) shall not be treated as a principal user of such facilities by reason of such sales for purposes of subparagraphs (D) and (E) of Section 103(b)(6) of the Internal Revenue Code of 1954.

(48) TREATMENT OF CERTAIN OBLIGATIONS.—A bond which is not an industrial development bond under section 103(b)(2) of the Internal Revenue Code of 1954 shall not be treated as a private activity bond for purposes of part IV of subchapter B of chapter 1 of the 1986 Code if 95 percent or more of the net proceeds of the issue of which such bond is a part are used to provide facilities described in any of the following subparagraphs:

(A) A facility is described in this subparagraph if it is a governmentally-owned and operated State fair and exposition center with respect to which—

(i) the 1985 session of the State legislature authorized revenue bonds to be issued in a maximum amount of $10,000,000, and

(ii) a market feasibility study dated June 30, 1986, relating to a major capital improvemental program at the facility was prepared for the advisory board of the State fair and exposition center by a certified public accounting firm.

The aggregate face amount of obligations to which this subparagraph applies shall not exceed $10,000,000.

(B) A facility is described in this subparagraph if it is a convention, trade, or spectator facility which is to be located in the State with respect to which paragraph (U)(6) applies and with respect to which feasibility and preliminary design consultants were hired on May 1, 1985 and October 31, 1985. The aggregate face amount of obligations to which this subparagraph applies shall not exceed $175,000,000.

(C) A facility which is part of a project described in paragraph (6)(O). The aggregate face amount of bonds to which this subparagraph applies shall not exceed $20,000,000.

(49) TRANSITION RULE FOR REFUNDING CERTAIN HOUSING BONDS.—Sections 146 and 149(d)(2) of the 1986 Code shall not apply to the refunding of any bond issued under section 11(b) of the United States Housing Act of 1937 before December 31, 1983, if—

(A) the bond has an original term to maturity of at least 40 years,

(B) the maturity date of the refunding bonds does not exceed the maturity date of the refunded bonds,

(C) the amount of the refunding bonds does not exceed the outstanding amount of the refunded bonds,

(D) the interest rate on the refunding bonds is lower than the interest rate of the refunded bonds, and

(E) the refunded bond is required to be redeemed not later than the earliest date on which such bond could be redeemed at par.

(50) TRANSITIONED BONDS SUBJECT TO CERTAIN RULES.—In the case of any bond to which any provision of this section applies, except as otherwise expressly provided, sections 103 and 103A of the 1954 Code shall be applied as if the requirements of sections 147(g), 148, and 149(d) of the 1986 Code were included in each such section.

(51) CERTAIN ADDITIONAL PROJECTS.—Section 141(b) of the 1986 Code shall be applied by substituting "25" for "10" each place it appears and by not applying sections 141(b)(3) and 141(c)(1)(B) to bonds substantially all of the proceeds [of which] are used for—

(A) A project [that] is described in this subparagraph if it consists of a capital improvements program for a metropolitan sewer district, with respect to which a proposition was submitted to voters on August 7, 1984. The aggregate face amount of obligations to which this subparagraph applies shall not exceed $60,000,000.

(B) Facilities[y] [that is] described in this subparagraph if it consists of additions, extensions, and improvements to the wastewater system for Lakeland, Florida. The aggregate face amount of obligations to which this subparagraph applies shall not exceed $20,000,000.

(C) A project [that] is described in this subparagraph if it is the Central Valley Water Reclamation Project in Utah. The aggregate face amount of obligations to which this subparagraph applies shall not exceed $100,000,000.

(D) A project [that] is described in this subparagraph if it is a project to construct approximately 26 miles of toll expressways, with respect to which any appeal to validation was filed July 11, 1986. The aggregate face amount of obligations to which this subparagraph applies shall not exceed $450,000,000.

(52) Termination.—Except as otherwise provided in this section, this section shall not apply to any bond issued after December 31, 1990.

P.L. 99-514, §1318, as amended by P.L. 101-239, §7831(e), provides:

SEC. 1318. DEFINITIONS, ETC., RELATING TO EFFECTIVE DATES AND TRANSITIONAL RULES.

(a) DEFINITIONS.—For purposes of this subtitle—

(1) 1954 CODE.—The term "1954 Code" means the Internal Revenue Code of 1954 as in effect on the day before the date of the enactment of this Act.

(2) 1986 CODE.—The term "1986 Code" means the Internal Revenue Code of 1986 as amended by this Act.

(3) BOND.—The term "bond" includes any obligation.

(4) ADVANCE REFUND.—A bond shall be treated as issued to advance refund another bond if it is issued more than 90 days before the redemption of the refunded bond.

(5) NET PROCEEDS.—The term "net proceeds" has the meaning given such term by section 150(a) of the 1986 Code.

(6) CONTINUED APPLICATON OF THE 1954 CODE.—Nothing in this subtitle shall be construed to exempt any bond from any provision of the 1954 Code by reason of a delay in (or

exemption from) the application of any amendment made by subtitle A.

(7) TREATMENT AS EXEMPT FACILITY.—Any bond which is treated as an exempt facility bond by section 1316 or 1317 shall not fail to be so treated by reason of subsection (b) of section 142 of the 1986 Code.

(8) APPLICATION OF FUTURE LEGISLATION TO TRANSITIONED BONDS.—In the case of any bond to which the amendments made by section 1301 do not apply by reason of a provision of this Act, any amendment of the 1986 Code (and any other provision applicable to such Code) included in any law enacted after October 22, 1986, shall be treated as included in section 103 and section 103A (as appropriate) of the 1954 Code with respect to such bond unless—

(A) such law expressly provides that such amendment (or other provision) shall not apply to such bond, or

(B) such amendment (or other provision) applies to a provision of the 1986 Code—

(i) for which there is no corresponding provision in section 103 and section 103A (as appropriate) of the 1954 Code, and

(ii) which is not otherwise treated as included in such sections 103 and 103A with respect to such bond.

(b) MINIMUM TAX TREATMENT.—

(1) IN GENERAL.—Any bond described in paragraph (2) shall not be treated as a private activity bond for purposes of section 57 of the 1986 Code unless such bond would (if issued on August 7, 1986) be—

(A) an industrial development bond (as defined in section 103(b)(2) of the 1954 Code), or

(B) a private loan bond (as defined in section 103(o)(2)(A) of the 1954 Code, without regard to any exception from such definition other than section 103(o)(2)(C) of such Code).

(2) BONDS DESCRIBED.—For purposes of paragraph (1), a bond is described in this paragraph if—

(A) the amendments made by section 1301 do not apply to such bond by reason of section 1312 or 1316(g),

(B) any provision of section 1317 applies to such bond, or

(C) the proceeds of such bond are used to refund any bond referred to in subparagraph (A) or (B) (or any bond which is part of a series of refundings of such a bond) if the requirements of paragraphs (1), (2), and (3) of subsection (c) are met with respect to the refunding bond.

(c) CURRENT REFUNDINGS NOT TAKEN INTO ACCOUNT IN APPLYING AGGREGATE LIMIT ON BONDS TO WHICH TRANSITIONAL RULES APPLY.—The limitation on the aggregate face amount of bonds to which any provision of section 1316(g) or 1317 applies shall not be reduced by the face amount of any bond the proceeds of which are to be used exclusively to refund any bond to which such provision applies (or any bond which is part of a series of refundings of such bond) if—

(1) the average maturity date of the issue of which the refunding bond is a part is not later than the average maturity date of the bonds to be refunded by such issue,

(2) the amount of the refunding bond does not exceed the outstanding amount of the refunded bond, and

(3) the net proceeds of the refunding bond are used to redeem the refunded bond not later than 90 days after the date of the issuance of the refunding bond.

For purposes of paragraph (1), average maturity shall be determined in accordance with section 147(b)(2)(A) of the 1986 Code. No limitation in section 1316(g) or 1317 on the period during which bonds may be issued under such section shall apply to any refunding bond which meets the requirements of this subsection.

(d) SPECIAL RULE PERMITTING CARRYFORWARD OF VOLUME CAP FOR CERTAIN TRANSITIONED PROJECTS.—A bond to which section 1312 or 1317 applies shall be treated as having a carryforward purpose described in section 146(f)(5) of the 1986 Code, and the requirement of section 146(f)(2)(A) of the 1986 Code shall be treated as met if such project is identified with reasonable specificity. The preceding sentence shall not apply so as to permit a carryforward with respect to any qualified small issue bond.

P.L. 99-514, §1864(a)(1):

Amended Code Sec. 103(n) by adding at the end thereof new paragraph (13). For the **effective** date, see Act Sec. 1864(a)(2), below.

P.L. 99-514, §1864(a)(2), provides:

(2) EFFECTIVE DATE.—

(A) Except as provided in subparagraph (B), the amendment made by paragraph (1) shall apply to obligations issued after the date of the enactment of this Act in taxable years ending after such date.

(B) At the election of the issuer (made at such time and in such manner as the Secretary of the Treasury or his delegate shall prescribe), the amendment made by paragraph (1) shall apply to any obligation issued on or before the date of the enactment of this Act.

P.L. 99-514, §1864(b):

Amended Code Sec. 103(n)(6)(A) and (B)(i) by striking out "governmental units" and inserting in lieu thereof "governmental units or other authorities". **Effective** as if included in the provision of P.L. 98-369 to which it relates.

P.L. 99-514, §1864(c):

Amended Code Sec. 103(n)(7)(C)(i) by striking out "the property described in such subparagraph" and inserting in lieu thereof "all of the property to be financed by the obligation". **Effective** as if included in the provision of P.L. 98-369 to which it relates.

P.L. 99-514, §1864(d):

Amended Code Sec. 103(l)(2) by striking out "and" at the end of subpargraph (D), by striking out the period at the end of subparagraph (E) and inserting in lieu thereof ", and", and by adding at the end thereof new subparagraph (F). **Effective** as if included in the provision of P.L. 98-369 to which it relates.

P.L. 99-514, §1864(e)(1)(A)-(B):

Amended Code Sec. 103(n)(10)(B) by striking out "specify the project" in clause (i) and inserting in lieu thereof "identify (with reasonable specificity) the project", and by striking out "SPECIFY PROJECT" in the subparagraph heading and inserting in lieu thereof "IDENTIFY PROJECT". **Effective** as if included in the provision of P.L. 98-369 to which it relates.

P.L. 99-514, §1864(e)(2):

Amended Code Sec. 103(n)(10)(D) by striking out "any specification" and inserting in lieu thereof "any identification or specification". **Effective** as if included in the provision of P.L. 98-369 to which it relates.

P.L. 99-514, §1865(a):

Amended Code Sec. 103(h)(5)(A) by striking out "the United States," after "a program of". **Effective** as if included in the provision of P.L. 98-369 to which it relates.

P.L. 99-514, §1865(b)-(c), provides:

(b) TREATMENT OF CERTAIN GUARANTEES BY FARMERS HOME ADMINISTRATION.—An obligation shall not be treated as federally guaranteed for purposes of section 103(h) of the Internal Revenue Code of 1954 by reason of a guarantee by the Farmers Home Administration if—

(1) such guarantee is pursuant to a commitment made by the Farmers Home Administration before July 1, 1984, and

(2) such obligation is issued to finance a convention center project in Carbondale, Illinois.

(c) TREATMENT OF CERTAIN OBLIGATIONS USED TO FINANCE SOLID WASTE DISPOSAL FACILITY.—

(1) IN GENERAL.—Any obligation which is part of an issue a substantial portion of the proceeds of which is to be used to finance a solid waste disposal facility described in paragraph (2) shall not, for purposes of section 103(h) of the Internal Revenue Code of 1954, be treated as an obligation which is federally guaranteed by reason of the sale of fuel, steam, electricity, or other forms of usable energy to the Federal Government or any agency or instrumentality thereof.

(2) SOLID WASTE DISPOSAL FACILITY.—A solid waste disposal facility is described in this paragraph if such facility is described in section 103(b)(4)(E) of such Code and—

(A) if—

(i) a public State authority created pursuant to State legislation which took effect on July 1, 1980, took formal action before October 19, 1983, to commit development funds for such facility,

(ii) such authority issues obligations for such facility before January 1, 1988, and

(iii) expenditures have been made for the development of such facility before October 19, 1983,

(B) if—

(i) such facility is operated by the South Eastern Public Service Authority of Virginia, and

(ii) on December 20, 1984, the Internal Revenue Service issued a ruling concluding that a portion of the obligations with respect to such facility would not be treated as federally guaranteed under section 103(h) of such Code by reason of the transitional rule contained in section 631(c)(3)(A)(i) of the Tax Reform Act of 1984,

(C) if—

(i) a political subdivision of a State took formal action on April 1, 1980, to commit development funds for such facility,

(ii) such facility has a contract to sell steam to a naval base,

(iii) such political subdivision issues obligations for such facility before January 1, 1988, and

(iv) expenditures have been made for the development of such facility before October 19, 1983, or

(D) if—

(i) such facility is a thermal transfer facility,

(ii) is to be built and operated by the Elk Regional Resource Authority, and

(iii) is to be on land leased from the United States Air Force at Arnold Engineering Development Center near Tullahoma, Tennessee.

(3) LIMITATIONS.—

(A) In the case of a solid waste disposal facility described in paragraph (2)(A), the aggregate face amount of obligations to which paragraph (1) applies shall not exceed $65,000,000.

(B) In the case of a solid waste disposal facility described in paragraph (2)(B), the aggregate face amount of obligations to which paragraph (1) applies shall not exceed $20,000,000. Such amount shall be in addition to the amount permitted under the Internal Revenue Service ruling referred to in paragraph (2)(B)(ii).

(C) In the case of a solid waste disposal facility described in paragraph (2)(C), the aggregate face amount of obligations to which paragraph (1) applies shall not exceed $75,000,000.

(D) In the case of a solid waste disposal facility described in paragraph (2)(D), the aggregate face amount of obligations to which paragraph (1) applies shall not exceed $25,000,000.

P.L. 99-514, §1869(a)(1)-(3):

Amended Code Sec. 103(o) by striking out "consumer loan bond" each place it appears and inserting in lieu thereof "private loan bond", by striking out "Consumer Loan Bonds" in the subsection heading and inserting in lieu thereof "Private Loan Bonds", and by striking out "Consumer Loan Bonds" in the heading for paragraph (2) and inserting in lieu thereof "Private Loan Bonds". **Effective** as if included in the provision of P.L. 98-369 to which it relates.

P.L. 99-514, §1869(b)(1):

Amended Code Sec. 103(o)(2)(C)(ii) by striking out "subsection (c)(6)(G)(i)" and inserting in lieu thereof "subsection (c)(6)(H)(i)". **Effective** as if included in the provision of P.L. 98-369 to which it relates.

P.L. 99-514, §1869(b)(2):

Amended Code Sec. 103 by redesignating subsection (o)[p] as subsection (p). **Effective** as if included in the provision of P.L. 98-369 to which it relates.

P.L. 99-514, §1869(c), provides:

(c) TRANSITIONAL RULES.—

(1) TREATMENT OF CERTAIN OBLIGATIONS ISSUED BY THE CITY OF BALTIMORE.—Obligations issued by the city of Baltimore, Maryland, after June 30, 1985, shall not be treated as private loan bonds for purposes of section 103(o) of the Internal Revenue Code of 1954 (or as private activity bonds for purposes of section 103 and part IV of subchapter A of chapter 1 of the Internal Revenue Code of 1986, as amended by title XIII of this Act) by reason of the use of a portion of the proceeds of such obligations to finance or refinance temporary advances made by the city of Baltimore in connection with loans to persons who are not exempt persons (within the meaning of section 103(b)(3) of such Code) if—

(A) such obligations are not industrial development bonds (within the meaning of section 103(b)(2) of the Internal Revenue Code of 1954).

(B) the portion of the proceeds of such obligations so used is attributable to debt approved by voter referendum on or before November 2, 1982,

(C) the loans to such nonexempt persons were approved by the Board of Estimates of the city of Baltimore on or before October 19, 1983, and

(D) the aggregate amount of such temporary advances financed or refinanced by such obligations does not exceed $27,000,000.

(2) WHITE PINE POWER PROJECT.—The amendment made by section 626(a) of the Tax Reform Act of 1984 shall not apply to any obligation issued during 1984 to provide financing for the White Pine Power Project in Nevada.

(3) TAX INCREMENT BONDS.—The amendment made by section 626(a) of the Tax Reform Act of 1984 shall not apply to any tax increment financing obligation issued before August 16, 1986, if—

(A) substantially all of the proceeds of the issue are to be used to finance—

(i) sewer, street, lighting, or other governmental improvements to real property,

(ii) the acquisition of any interest in real property pursuant to the exercise of eminent domain, the preparation of such property for new use, or the transfer of such interest to a private developer, or

(iii) payments of reasonable relocation costs of prior users of such real property,

(B) all of the activities described in subparagraph (A) are pursuant to a redevelopment plan adopted by the issuing authority before the issuance of such issue,

(C) repayment of such issue is secured exclusively by pledges of that portion of any increase in real property tax revenues (or their equivalent) attributable to the redevelopment resulting from the issue, and

(D) none of the property described in subparagraph (A) is subject to a real property or other tax based on a rate or valuation method which differs from the rate and valuation method applicable to any other similar property located within the jurisdiction of the issuing authority.

(4) EASTERN MAINE ELECTRIC COOPERATIVE.—The amendment made by section 626(a) of the Tax Reform Act of 1984 shall not apply to obligations issued by Massachusetts Municipal Wholesale Electric Company Project No. 6 if—

(A) such obligation is issued before January 1, 1986,

(B) such obligation is issued after such date to refund a prior obligation for such project, except that the aggregate amount of obligations to which this subparagraph applies shall not exceed $100,000,000, or

(C) such obligation is issued after such date to provide additional financing for such project except that the aggregate amount of obligations to which this subparagraph applies shall not exceed $45,000,000.

Subparagraph (B) shall not apply to any obligation issued for the advance refunding of any obligation.

(5) CLARIFICATION OF TRANSITIONAL RULE FOR CERTAIN STUDENT LOAN PROGRAMS.—Subparagraph (A) of section 626(b)(2) of the Tax Reform Act of 1984 is amended by striking out "$11 million" in the table contained in such subparagraph and inserting in lieu thereof "$70 million".

(6) TREATMENT OF OBLIGATIONS TO FINANCE ST. JOHNS RIVER POWER PARK.—

(A) IN GENERAL.—The amendment made by section 626(a) of the Tax Reform Act of 1984 shall not apply to any obligation issued to finance the project described in subparagraph (B) if—

(i) such obligation is issued before September 27, 1985,

(ii) such obligation is issued after such date to refund a prior tax exemption obligation for such project, the amount of such obligation does not exceed the outstanding amount of the refunded obligation, and such prior tax exempt obligation is retired not later than the date 30 days after the issuance of the refunding obligation, or

(iii) such obligation is issued after such date to provide additional financing for such project except that the aggregate amount of obligations to which this clause applies shall not exceed $150,000,000.

Clause (ii) shall not apply to any obligation issued for the advance refunding of any obligation.

(B) DESCRIPTION OF PROJECT.—The project described in this subparagraph in the St. Johns River Power Park system in Florida which was authorized by legislation enacted by the Florida Legislature in February of 1982.

P.L. 99-514, §1870:

Amended Code Sec. 103(b)(16)(A) by striking out "clause (i)" in the last sentence and inserting in lieu thereof "clause (ii)". **Effective** as if included in the provision of P.L. 98-369 to which it relates.

P.L. 99-514, §1871(a)(1):

Amended Code Sec. 103(m)(1) by striking out "(k), (l), and (n)" and inserting in lieu thereof "(j), (k), (l), (n), and (o)". **Effective** for obligations issued after 3-28-85, in tax years ending after such date.

P.L. 99-514, §1871(b):

Amended Code Sec. 103(b)(13), (14)(A), and (17)(A) by striking out "(6), and (7)" and inserting in lieu thereof "and (6)". **Effective** as if included in the provision of P.L. 98-369 to which it relates.

P.L. 99-514, §1873(c)-(g), provides:

(c) TREATMENT OF CERTAIN OBLIGATIONS TO FINANCE HYDROELECTRIC GENERATING FACILITY.—If—

(1) obligations are to be issued in an amount not to exceed $9,500,000 to finance the construction of an approximately 4 megawatt hydroelectric generating facility owned and operated by the city of Hastings, Minnesota, and located on United States Army Corps of Engineers lock and dam No. 2 or are issued to refund any of such obligations,

(2) substantially all of the electrical power generated by such facility is to be sold to a nongovernmental person pursuant to a long-term power sales agreement in accordance with the Public Utilities Regulatory Policies Act of 1978, and

(3) the initially issued obligations are issued on or before December 31, 1986, and any of such refunding obligations are issued on or before December 31, 1996,

then the person referred to in paragraph (2) shall not be treated as the principal user of such facilities by reason of such sales for purposes of subparagraphs (D) and (E) of section 103(b)(6) of the Internal Revenue Code of 1954.

(d) TREATMENT OF CERTAIN OBLIGATIONS TO FINANCE HYDROELECTRIC GENERATING FACILITY.—If—

(1) obligations are to be issued in an amount not to exceed $6,500,000 to finance the construction of an approximately 2.6 megawatt hydroelectric generating facility located on the Schroon River in Warren County, New York, near Warrensburg, New York,

(2) such facility has a Federal Energy Regulatory Commission project number 8719-0000 under a preliminary permit issued in November 8, 1985, and

(3) substantially all of the electrical power generated by such facility is to be sold to a nongovernmental person pursuant to a long-term power sales agreement in accordance with the Public Utilities Regulatory Policies Act of 1978,

then the person referred to in paragraph (3) shall not be treated as the principal user of such facilities by reason of such sales for purposes of subparagraphs (D) and (E) of section 103(b)(6) of the Internal Revenue Code of 1954.

(e) TREATMENT OF CERTAIN OBLIGATIONS TO FINANCE HYDROELECTRIC GENERATING FACILITIES.—If—

(1) obligations in the amount of $6,000,000 issued on November 30, 1984, to finance the construction of an approximately 1.0 megawatt hydroelectric generating facility and an approximately .6 megawatt hydroelectric generating facility, both of which are located near Los Banos, California,

(2) such facilities have Federal Energy Regulatory Commission project numbers 5129-001 and 5128-001, respectively, under license exemptions issued on December 6, 1983, and

(3) substantially all of the electrical power generated by such facility is to be sold to a nongovernmental person pursuant to a long-term power sales agreement in accordance with the Public Utilities Regulatory Policies Act of 1978,

then the person referred to in paragraph (3) shall not be treated as the principal user of such facilities by reason of such sales for purposes of subparagraphs (D) and (E) of section 103(b)(6) of the Internal Revenue Code of 1954.

(f) TREATMENT OF CERTAIN OBLIGATIONS TO FINANCE METHANE RECOVERY ELECTRIC GENERATING FACILITIES.—If—

(1) obligations are to be issued in an amount not to exceed $3,000,000 to finance the construction of a methane recovery electric generating facility located on a sanitary landfill near Richmond, California, and

(2) substantially all of the electrical power generated by such facility is to be sold to a nongovernmental person pursuant to a long-term power sales agreement entered into on April 16, 1985, in accordance with the Public Utilities Regulatory Policies Act of 1978,

then the person referred to in paragraph (2) shall not be treated as the principal user of such facilities by reason of such sales for purposes of subparagraphs (D) and (E) of section 103(b)(6) of the Internal Revenue Code of 1954.

(g) TREATMENT OF CERTAIN OBLIGATIONS TO FINANCE HYDROELECTRIC GENERATING FACILITIES.—If—

(1) obligations are to be issued in an amount not to exceed $6,000,000 to finance the construction of a hydroelectric generating facility having a Federal Energy Regulatory Commission license number 3189, and located near Placerville, California,

(2) an inducement resolution for such project was adopted in March 1985, and

(3) substantially all of the electrical power generated by such facility is to be sold to a nongovernmental person pursuant to a long-term power sales agreement in accordance with the Public Utilities Regulatory Policies Act of 1978,

then the person referred to in paragraph (3) shall not be treated as the principal user of such facilities by reason of such sales for purposes of subparagraphs (D) and (E) of section 103(b)(6) of the Internal Revenue Code of 1954.

P.L. 99-514, §1899A(2):

Amended Code Sec. 103(h)(2)(A) by striking out "guaranted" and inserting in lieu thereof "guaranteed". **Effective** 10-22-86.

P.L. 99-514, §1899A(3):

Amended Code Sec. 103(m)(3)(B) by striking out "section 608(6)(A)" and inserting in lieu thereof "section 608(a)(6)(A)". **Effective** 10-22-86.

P.L. 99-514, §1899A(4):

Amended Code Sec. 103(p)(4) by striking out "October" and all that follows and inserting in lieu thereof "October 27, 1949 (48 U.S.C. 1403)". **Effective** 10-22-86. Prior to amendment, Code Sec. 103(p)(4) read as follows:

(4) Virgin Islands insular and municipal bonds, see section 1 of the Act of October 27, 1919 (48 U.S.C. 1402).

[Sec. 103A—Repealed]

Amendments

• 1986, Tax Reform Act of 1986 (P.L. 99-514)

P.L. 99-514, §1301(j)(1):

Repealed Code Sec. 103A. **Effective** for bonds issued after 8-15-86. For special and transitional rules, see amendment notes for Code Sec. 103. Prior to repeal, Code Sec. 103A read as follows:

SEC. 103A. MORTGAGE SUBSIDY BONDS.

[Sec. 103A(a)]

(a) GENERAL RULE.—Except as otherwise provided in this section, any mortgage subsidy bond shall be treated as an obligation not described in subsection (a)(1) or (2) of section 103.

[Sec. 103A(b)]

(b) MORTGAGE SUBSIDY BOND DEFINED.—

(1) IN GENERAL.—For purposes of this title, the term "mortgage subsidy bond" means any obligation which is issued as part of an issue a significant portion of the proceeds of which are to be used directly or indirectly for mortgages on owner-occupied residences.

(2) EXCEPTIONS.—The following shall not be treated as mortgage subsidy bonds:

(A) any qualified mortgage bond; and

(B) any qualified veterans' mortgage bond.

[Sec. 103A(c)]

(c) QUALIFIED MORTGAGE BOND; QUALIFIED MORTGAGE ISSUE; QUALIFIED VETERANS' MORTGAGE BOND.—

(1) QUALIFIED MORTGAGE BOND DEFINED.—

(A) IN GENERAL.—For purposes of this title, the term "qualified mortgage bond" means an obligation which is issued as part of a qualified mortgage issue.

(B) TERMINATION DECEMBER 31, 1989.—No obligation issued after December 31, 1989, may be treated as a qualified mortgage bond.

(2) QUALIFIED MORTGAGE ISSUE DEFINED.—

(A) DEFINITION.—For purposes of this title, the term "qualified mortgage issue" means an issue by a State or political subdivision thereof of 1 or more obligations, but only if—

(i) all proceeds of such issue (exclusive of issuance costs and a reasonably required reserve) are to be used to finance owner-occupied residences, and

(ii) such issue meets the requirements of subsections (d), (e), (f), (g), (h), (i), and (j).

(B) GOOD FAITH EFFORT TO COMPLY WITH MORTGAGE ELIGIBILITY REQUIREMENTS.—An issue which fails to meet 1 or more of the requirements of subsections (d), (e), (f), and (j)(1) and (2) shall be treated as meeting such requirements if—

(i) the issuer in good faith attempted to meet all such requirements before the mortgages were executed,

(ii) 95 percent or more of the proceeds devoted to owner-financing was devoted to residences with respect to which (at the time the mortgages were executed) all such requirements were met, and

(iii) any failure to meet the requirements of such subsections and paragraphs is corrected within a reasonable period after such failure is first discovered.

(C) GOOD FAITH EFFORT TO COMPLY WITH OTHER REQUIREMENTS.—An issue which fails to meet 1 or more of the requirements of subsections (g), (h), (i), and (j)(3), (4), and (5) shall be treated as meeting such requirements if—

(i) the issuer in good faith attempted to meet all such requirements, and

(ii) any failure to meet such requirements is due to inadvertent error after taking reasonable steps to comply with such requirements.

(3) QUALIFIED VETERANS' MORTGAGE BOND DEFINED.—For purposes of this section, the term "qualified veterans' mortgage bond" means any obligation—

(A) which is issued as part of an issue substantially all of the proceeds of which are to be used to provide residences for veterans,

(B) the payment of the principal and interest on which is secured by the general obligation of a State, and

(C) which is part of an issue which meets the requirements of subsection (d), paragraphs (1) and (3) of subsection (j), and subsection (o).

Amendments

• 1988, Technical and Miscellaneous Revenue Act of 1988 (P.L. 100-647)

P.L. 100-647, §1013(a)(27), provides:

(27) The date contained in section 143(a)(1)(B) of the 1986 Code shall be treated as contained in section 103A(c)(1)(B) of the Internal Revenue Code of 1954, as in effect on the day before the date of the enactment of the Reform Act, for purposes of any bond issued to refund a bond to which such 103(c)(1) applies.

• 1986, Tax Reform Act of 1986 (P.L. 99-514)

P.L. 99-514, §1861(c)(1):

Amended Code Sec. 103A(c)(2)(B) by striking out "and (j)" and inserting in lieu thereof "and (j)(1) and (2)". Effective as if included in the provision of P.L. 98-369 to which it relates.

P.L. 99-514, §1861(c)(2):

Amended Code Sec. 103A(c)(2)(C) by striking out "and (i)" and inserting in lieu thereof "(i), and (j)(3), (4), and (5)". **Effective** as if included in the provision of P.L. 98-369 to which it relates.

• 1984, Deficit Reduction Act of 1984 (P.L. 98-369)

P.L. 98-369, §611(a):

Amended Code Sec. 103A(c)(1)(B) by striking out "December 31, 1983" each place it appeared and inserting in lieu thereof "December 31, 1987". **Effective** with respect to obligations issued after 12-31-83.

P.L. 98-369, §611(c)(1):

Amended Code Sec. 103(A)(c)(3)(C) by striking out "subsection (j)(1)" and inserting in lieu thereof "subsection (d), paragraphs (1) and (3) of subsection (j), and subsection (o)". **Effective** for obligations issued after 7-18-84.

• 1982, Tax Equity and Fiscal Responsibility Act of 1982 (P.L. 97-248)

P.L. 97-248, §310(c)(3)(B):

Amended Code Sec. 103A(c)(2)(B) by striking out "and (f) and paragraphs (2) and (3) of subsection (j)" and inserting "(f), and (j)". **Effective** for obligations issued after 12-31-82.

P.L. 97-248, §310(c)(3)(C):

Amended Code Sec. 103A(c)(2)(C) by striking out ", and paragraph (1) of subsection (j)". **Effective** for obligations issued after 12-31-82. Prior to amendment, Code Sec. 103A(c)(2)(C) read as follows:

"(C) Good faith effort to comply with other requirements.—An issue which fails to meet 1 or more of the requirements of subsections (g), (h), and (i), and paragraph (1) of subsection (j) shall be treated as meeting such requirements if—

* * *

P.L. 97-248, §310(c)(3)(D):

Amended Code Sec. 103A(c)(3)(C) by striking out "subsection (j)(2)" and inserting "subsection (j)(1)". **Effective** for obligations issued after 12-31-82.

P.L. 97-248, §310(c)(4):

Amended Code Sec. 103A(c)(3)(A) by striking out "in registered form". **Effective** for obligations issued after 12-31-82. Prior to amendment, Code Sec. 103A(c)(3)(A) read as follows:

"(A) which is issued in registered form as part of an issue substantially all of the proceeds of which are to be used to provide residences for veterans,"

[Sec. 103A(d)]

(d) RESIDENCE REQUIREMENTS.—

(1) FOR A RESIDENCE.—A residence meets the requirements of this subsection only if—

(A) it is a single-family residence which can reasonably be expected to become the principal residence of the mortgagor within a reasonable time after the financing is provided, and

(B) it is located within the jurisdiction of the authority issuing the obligation.

(2) FOR AN ISSUE.—An issue meets the requirements of this subsection only if all of the residences for which owner-financing is provided under the issue meet the requirements of paragraph (1).

[Sec. 103A(e)]

(e) 3-YEAR REQUIREMENT.—

(1) IN GENERAL.—An issue meets the requirements of this subsection only if 90 percent or more of the lendable proceeds of such issue are used to finance the residences of mortgagors who had no present ownership interest in their principal residences at any time during the 3-year period ending on the date their mortgage is executed.

(2) EXCEPTIONS.—For purposes of paragraph (1), the proceeds of an issue which are used—

(A) to provide financing with respect to targeted area residences,

(B) to provide qualified home improvement loans, and

(C) to provide qualified rehabilitation loans,

shall not be taken into account.

(3) MORTGAGOR'S INTEREST IN RESIDENCE BEING FINANCED.—For purposes of paragraph (1), a mortgagor's interest in the residence with respect to which the financing is being provided shall not be taken into account.

Amendments

• 1982, Tax Equity and Fiscal Responsibility Act of 1982 (P.L. 97-248)

P.L. 97-248, §220(c):

Amended Code Sec. 103A(e). Prior to amendment, Code Sec. 103A(e) read as follows:

"(e) 3-YEAR REQUIREMENT.—

(1) In general.—An issue meets the requirements of this subsection only if each mortgagor to whom financing is provided under the issue had a present ownership interest in a principal residence of such mortgagor at no time during the 3-year period ending on the date the mortgage is executed. For purposes of the preceding sentence, the mortgagor's interest in the residence with respect to which the financing is being provided shall not be taken into account.

(2) Exceptions.—Paragraph (1) shall not apply with respect to—

(A) any financing provided with respect to a targeted area residence,

(B) any qualified home improvement loan, and

(C) any qualified rehabilitation loan."

The above amendment applies to obligations issued after September 3, 1982. However, Act Sec. 220(f)(2) provides:

(2) First time homebuyer requirement.—The amendments made by subsection (c) shall also apply to obligations issued after April 24, 1979, and before the date of the enactment of this Act but only to the extent that the proceeds of such obligations are not committed as of the date of the enactment of this Act.

[Sec. 103A(f)]

(f) PURCHASE PRICE REQUIREMENT.—

(1) IN GENERAL.—An issue meets the requirements of this subsection only if the acquisition cost of each residence the owner-financing of which is to be provided under the issue does not exceed 110 percent of the average area purchase price applicable to such residence.

(2) AVERAGE AREA PURCHASE PRICE.—For purposes of paragraph (1), the term "average area purchase price" means, with respect to any residence, the average purchase price of single family residences (in the statistical area in which the residence is located) which were purchased during the most recent 12-month period for which sufficient statistical information is available. The determination under the preceding sentence shall be made as of the date on which the commitment to provide the financing is made (or, if earlier, the date of the purchase of the residence).

(3) SEPARATE APPLICATION TO NEW RESIDENCES AND OLD RESIDENCES.—For purposes of this subsection, the determination of average area purchase price shall be made separately with respect to—

(A) residences which have not been previously occupied, and

(B) residences which have been previously occupied.

(4) SPECIAL RULE FOR 2 TO 4 FAMILY RESIDENCES.—For purposes of this subsection, to the extent provided in regulations, the average area purchase price shall be made separately with respect to 1 family, 2 family, 3 family, and 4 family residences.

(5) SPECIAL RULE FOR TARGETED AREA RESIDENCES.—In the case of a targeted area residence, paragraph (1) shall be applied by substituting "120 percent" for "110 percent".

(6) EXCEPTION FOR QUALIFIED HOME IMPROVEMENT LOANS.—Paragraph (1) shall not apply with respect to any qualified home improvement loan.

Amendments

• 1982, Tax Equity and Fiscal Responsibility Act of 1982 (P.L. 97-248)

P.L. 97-248, §220(d):

Amended Code Sec. 103A(f) by striking out "90 percent" each place it appeared and inserting in lieu thereof "110 percent" and by striking out "110 percent" in paragraph (5) and inserting in lieu thereof "120 percent". **Effective** for obligations issued after 9-3-82.

[Sec. 103A(g)]

(g) LIMITATION ON AGGREGATE AMOUNT OF QUALIFIED MORTGAGE BONDS ISSUED DURING ANY CALENDAR YEAR.—

(1) IN GENERAL.—An issue meets the requirements of this subsection only if the aggregate amount of bonds issued pursuant thereto, when added to the aggregate amount of qualified mortgage bonds previously issued by the issuing authority during the calendar year, does not exceed the applicable limit for such authority for such calendar year.

(2) APPLICABLE LIMIT FOR STATE HOUSING AGENCY.—For purposes of this subsection—

(A) IN GENERAL.—The applicable limit for any State housing finance agency for any calendar year shall be 50 percent of the State ceiling for such year.

(B) SPECIAL RULE WHERE MORE THAN 1 AGENCY.—If any State has more than 1 State housing finance agency, all such agencies shall be treated as a single agency.

(3) APPLICABLE LIMIT FOR OTHER ISSUERS.—For purposes of this subsection—

(A) IN GENERAL.—The applicable limit for any issuing authority (other than a State housing finance agency) for any calendar year is an amount which bears the same ratio to 50 percent of the State ceiling for such year as—

(i) the average annual aggregate principal amount of mortgages executed during the immediately preceding 3 calendar years for single-family, owner-occupied residences located within the jurisdiction of such issuing authority, bears to

(ii) an average determined in the same way for the entire State.

(B) OVERLAPPING JURISDICTIONS.—For purposes of subparagraph (A)(i), if an area is within the jurisdiction of 2 or more governmental units, such area shall be treated as only within the jurisdiction of the unit having jurisdiction over the smallest geographical area unless such unit agrees to surrender all or part of such jurisdiction for such calendar year to the unit with overlapping jurisdiction which has the next smallest geographical area.

(4) STATE CEILING.—For purposes of this subsection, the State ceiling applicable to any State for any calendar year shall be the greater of—

(A) 9 percent of the average annual aggregate principal amount of mortgages executed during the immediately preceding 3 calendar years for single-family, owner-occupied residences located within the jurisdiction of such State, or

(B) $200,000,000.

(5) SPECIAL RULE FOR STATES WITH CONSTITUTIONAL HOME RULE CITIES.—For purposes of this subsection—

(A) IN GENERAL.—The applicable limit for any constitutional home rule city for any calendar year shall be determined under subparagraph (A) of paragraph (3) by substituting "100 percent" for "50 percent".

(B) COORDINATION WITH PARAGRAPHS (2) AND (3).—In the case of any State which contains 1 or more constitutional home rule cities, for purposes of applying paragraphs (2) and (3) with respect to issuing authorities in such State other than constitutional home rule cities, the State ceiling for any calendar year shall be reduced by the aggregate applicable limits determined for such year for all constitutional home rule cities in such State.

(C) CONSTITUTIONAL HOME RULE CITY.—For purposes of this subsection, the term "constitutional home rule city" means, with respect to any calendar year, any political subdivision of a State which, under a State constitution which was adopted in 1970 and effective on July 1, 1971, had home rule powers on the first day of the calendar year.

(6) STATE MAY PROVIDE FOR DIFFERENT ALLOCATION.—

(A) IN GENERAL.—Except as provided in subparagraph (C), a State may, by law enacted after the date of the enactment of this section, provide a different formula for allocating the State ceiling among the governmental units in such State having authority to issue qualified mortgage bonds.

(B) INTERIM AUTHORITY FOR GOVERNOR.—

(i) IN GENERAL.—Except as otherwise provided in subparagraph (C), the Governor of any State may proclaim a different formula for allocating the State ceiling among the governmental units in such State having authority to issue qualified mortgage bonds.

(ii) TERMINATION OF AUTHORITY.—The authority provided in clause (i) shall not apply after the earlier of—

(I) the first day of the first calendar year beginning after the first calendar year after 1980 during which the legislature of the State met in regular session, or

(II) the effective date of any State legislation with respect to the allocation of the State ceiling enacted after the date of the enactment of this section.

(C) STATE MAY NOT ALTER ALLOCATION TO CONSTITUTIONAL HOME RULE CITIES.—Except as otherwise provided in a State constitutional amendment (or law changing the home rule provision adopted in the manner provided by the State constitution), the authority provided in this paragraph shall not apply to that portion of the State ceiling which is allocated to any constitutional home rule city in the State unless such city agrees to such different allocation.

(7) TRANSITIONAL RULES.—In applying this subsection to any calendar year, there shall not be taken into account any bond which, by reason of section 1104 of the Mortgage Subsidy Bond Tax Act of 1980, receives the same tax treatment as bonds issued on or before April 24, 1979.

(8) REDUCTION FOR MORTGAGE CREDIT CERTIFICATES.—The applicable limit of any issuing authority for any calendar year shall be reduced by the sum of—

(A) the amount of qualified mortgage bonds which such authority elects not to issue under section 25(c)(2)(A)(ii) during such year, plus

(B) the amount of any reduction in such ceiling under section 25(f) applicable to such authority for such year.

Amendments

• 1984, Deficit Reduction Act of 1984 (P.L. 98-369)

P.L. 98-369, §612(b):

Amended Code Sec. 103A(g) by adding at the end thereof new paragraph (8). **Effective** for interest paid or accrued after 12-31-83, on indebtedness incurred after 12-31-83. It also applies to elections under Code Sec. 25(c)(2)(A)(ii) (as added by this Act section) for calendar years after 1983.

[Sec. 103A(h)]

(h) PORTION OF LOANS REQUIRED TO BE PLACED IN TARGETED AREAS.—

(1) IN GENERAL.—An issue meets the requirements of this subsection only if at least 20 percent of the proceeds of the issue which are devoted to providing owner-financing is made available (with reasonable diligence) for owner-financing of targeted area residences for at least 1 year after the date on which owner-financing is first made available with respect to targeted area residences.

(2) LIMITATION.—Nothing in paragraph (1) shall be treated as requiring the making available of an amount which exceeds 40 percent of the average annual aggregate principle amount of mortgages executed during the immediately preceding 3 calendar years for single-family, owner-occupied residences located in targeted areas within the jurisdiction of the issuing authority.

[Sec. 103A(i)]

(i) REQUIREMENTS RELATED TO ARBITRAGE.—

(1) IN GENERAL.—An issue meets the requirements of this subsection only if such issue meets the requirements of paragraphs (2), (3), and (4) of this subsection. Such requirements shall be in addition to the requirements of section 103(c) (other than section 103(c)(6)).

(2) EFFECTIVE RATE OF MORTGAGE INTEREST CANNOT EXCEED BOND YIELD BY MORE THAN 1.125 PERCENTAGE POINTS.—

(A) IN GENERAL.—An issue shall be treated as meeting the requirements of this paragraph only if the excess of—

(i) the effective rate of interest on the mortgages provided under the issue, over

(ii) the yield on the issue,

is not greater than 1.125 percentage points.

(B) EFFECTIVE RATE OF MORTGAGE INTEREST.—

(i) IN GENERAL.—In determining the effective rate of interest on any mortgage for purposes of this paragraph, there shall be taken into account all fees, charges, and other amounts borne by the mortgagor which are attributable to the mortgage or to the bond issue.

(ii) SPECIFICATION OF SOME OF THE AMOUNTS TO BE TREATED AS BORNE BY THE MORTGAGOR.—For purposes of clause (i), the following items (among others) shall be treated as borne by the mortgagor:

(I) all points or similar charges paid by the seller of the property, and

(II) the excess of the amounts received from any person other than the mortgagor by any person in connection with the acquisition of the mortgagor's interest in the property over the usual and reasonable acquisition costs of a person acquiring like property where owner-financing is not provided through the use of qualified mortgage bonds.

(iii) SPECIFICATION OF SOME OF THE AMOUNTS TO BE TREATED AS NOT BORNE BY THE MORTGAGOR.—For purposes of clause (i), the following items shall not be taken into account:

(I) any expected rebate of arbitrage profits, and

(II) any application fee, survey fee, credit report fee, insurance charge, or similar amount to the extent such amount does not exceed amounts charged in such area in cases where owner-financing is not provided through the use of qualified mortgage bonds.

Subclause (II) shall not apply to origination fees, points, or similar amounts.

(iv) PREPAYMENT ASSUMPTIONS.—In determining the effective rate of interest—

(I) it shall be assumed that the mortgage prepayment rate will be the rate set forth in the most recent mortgage maturity experience table published by the Federal Housing Administration for the State (or, if available, the area within the State) in which the residences are located, and

(II) prepayments of principal shall be treated as received on the last day of the month in which the issuer reasonably expects to receive such prepayments.

(C) YIELD ON THE ISSUE.—For purposes of this subsection, the yield on the issue shall be determined on the basis of—

(i) the issue price (within the meaning of section 1273(b) and 1274), and

(ii) an expected maturity for the bonds which is consistent with the assumption required under subparagraph (B)(iv).

(3) NON-MORTGAGE INVESTMENT REQUIREMENTS.—

(A) IN GENERAL.—An issue meets the requirements of this paragraph only if—

(i) at no time during any bond year may the amount invested in non-mortgage investments with a yield higher than the yield on the issue exceed 150 percent of the debt service on the issue for the bond year, and

(ii) the aggregate amount invested as provided in clause (i) is promptly and appropriately reduced as mortgages are repaid.

(B) EXCEPTION FOR TEMPORARY PERIODS.—Subparagraph (A) shall not apply to—

(i) proceeds of the issue invested for an initial temporary period until such proceeds are needed for mortgages, and

(ii) temporary investment periods related to debt service.

(C) DEBT SERVICE DEFINED.—For purposes of subparagraph (A), the debt service on the issue for any bond year is the scheduled amount of interest and amortization of principal payable for such year with respect to such issue. For purposes of the preceding sentence, there shall not be taken into account amounts scheduled with respect to any bond which has been retired before the beginning of the bond year.

(D) NO DISPOSITION IN CASE OF LOSS.—This paragraph shall not require the sale or disposition of any investment if such sale or disposition would result in a loss which exceeds the amount which would be paid or credited to the mortgagors under paragraph (4)(A) (but for such sale or disposition) at the time of such sale or disposition.

(4) ARBITRAGE AND INVESTMENT GAINS TO BE USED TO REDUCE COSTS OF OWNER-FINANCING.—

(A) IN GENERAL.—An issue shall be treated as meeting the requirements of this paragraph only if an amount equal to the sum of—

(i) the excess of—

(I) the amount earned on all non-mortgage investments (other than investments attributable to an excess described in this clause), over

(II) the amount which would have been earned if the investments were invested at a rate equal to the yield on the issue, plus

(ii) any income attributable to the excess described in clause (i),

shall be paid or credited to the mortgagors as rapidly as may be practicable.

(B) INVESTMENT GAINS AND LOSSES.—For purposes of subparagraph (A), in determining the amount earned on all nonmortgage investments, any gain or loss on the disposition of such investments shall be taken into account.

(C) REDUCTION WHERE ISSUER DOES NOT USE FULL 1.125 PERCENTAGE POINTS UNDER PARAGRAPH (2).—

(i) IN GENERAL.—The amount required to be paid or credited to mortgagors under subparagraph (A) (determined under this paragraph without regard to this subparagraph) shall be reduced by the unused paragraph (2) amount.

(ii) UNUSED PARAGRAPH (2) AMOUNT.—For purposes of clause (i), the unused paragraph (2) amount is the amount which (if it were treated as an interest payment made by mortgagors) would result in the excess referred to in paragraph (2)(A) being equal to 1.125 percentage points. Such amount shall be fixed and determined as of the yield determination date.

(D) ELECTION TO PAY UNITED STATES.—Subparagraph (A) shall be satisfied with respect to any issue if the issuer elects before issuing the obligations to pay over to the United States—

(i) not less frequently than once each 5 years after the date of issue, an amount equal to 90 percent of the aggregate amount which would be required to be paid or credited to mortgagors under subparagraph (A) (and not theretofore paid to the United States), and

(ii) not later than 30 days after the redemption of the last obligation, 100 percent of such aggregate amount not theretofore paid to the United States.

(E) SIMPLIFIED ACCOUNTING.—The Secretary shall permit any simplified system of accounting for purposes of this paragraph which the issuer establishes to the satisfaction of the Secretary will assure that the purposes of this paragraph are carried out.

Amendments

• 1984, Deficit Reduction Act of 1984 (P.L. 98-369)

P.L. 98-369, §42(a)(2):

Amended Code Sec. 103A(i)(2)(C)(i) by striking out "section 1232(b)(2)" and inserting in lieu thereof "sections 1273(b) and 1274". **Effective** for tax years ending after 7-18-84.

P.L. 98-369, §624(b)(1):

Amended Code Sec. 103A(i)(1) by striking out "section 103(c)" and inserting in lieu thereof "section 103(c) (other than section 103(c)(6))". **Effective** with respect to bonds issued after 12-31-84.

• 1982, Tax Equity and Fiscal Responsibility Act of 1982 (P.L. 97-248)

P.L. 97-248, §220(a)(1):

Amended Code Sec. 103A(i)(2)(A) by striking out "1 percentage point" and inserting in lieu thereof "1.125 percentage points". **Effective** for obligations issued after 9-3-82.

P.L. 97-248, §220(a)(2):

Amended Code Sec. 103A(i)(2)(B)(iv). **Effective** for obligations issued after 9-3-82. Prior to amendment, Code Sec. 103A(i)(2)(B)(iv) read as follows:

"(iv) Prepayment assumption.—In determining the effective rate of interest, it shall be assumed that the mortgage prepayment rate will be the rate set forth in the most recent mortgage maturity experience table published by the Federal Housing Administration for the State (or, if available, the area within the State) in which the residences are located."

P.L. 97-248, §220(a)(3)(A):

Amended Code Sec. 103A(i)(2) by striking out in the caption "1 PERCENTAGE POINT" and inserting in lieu thereof "1.125 PERCENTAGE POINTS". **Effective** for obligations issued after 9-3-82.

P.L. 97-248, §220(a)(3)(B):

Amended Code Sec. 103A(i)(4)(C) by striking out "1 percentage point" in clause (ii) and inserting in lieu thereof "1.125 percentage points"; and by striking out "1 PERCENTAGE POINT" in the caption and inserting in lieu thereof "1.125 PERCENTAGE POINTS". **Effective** for obligations issued after 9-3-82.

P.L. 97-248, §220(b):

Amended Code Sec. 103A(i)(3) by adding at the end thereof new subparagraph (D). **Effective** for obligations issued after 9-3-82.

• 1980 (P.L. 96-595)

P.L. 96-595, §5(a):

Amended Code Sec. 103A(i)(4) by adding new subparagraphs (C), (D), and (E). For the **effective** date, see the historical comment for P.L. 96-499 under Code Sec. 103A(n).

[Sec. 103A(j)]

(j) OTHER REQUIREMENTS.—

(1) MORTGAGES MUST BE NEW MORTGAGES.—

(A) IN GENERAL.—An issue meets the requirements of this subsection only if no part of the proceeds of such issue is to be used to acquire or replace existing mortgages.

(B) EXCEPTIONS.—Under regulations prescribed by the Secretary, the replacement of—

(i) construction period loans,

(ii) bridge loans or similar temporary initial financing, and

(iii) in the case of a qualified rehabilitation, an existing mortgage,

shall not be treated as the acquisition or replacement of an existing mortgage for purposes of subparagraph (A).

(2) CERTAIN REQUIREMENTS MUST BE MET WHERE MORTGAGE IS ASSUMED.—An issue meets the requirements of this subsection only if a mortgage with respect to which owner-financing has been provided under such issue may be assumed only if the requirements of subsections (d), (e), and (f), are met with respect to such assumption.

(3) INFORMATION REPORTING REQUIREMENT.—

(A) IN GENERAL.—An issue meets the requirements of this subsection only if the issuer submits to the Secretary, not later than the 15th day of the 2nd calendar month after the close of the calendar quarter in which the issue is issued (or such later time as the Secretary may prescribe with respect to any portion of the statement) a statement concerning the issue which contains—

(i) the name and address of the issuer,

(ii) the date of the issue, the amount of the lendable proceeds of the issue, and the stated interest rate, term, and face amount of each obligation which is part of the issue,

(iii) such information as the Secretary may require in order to determine whether such issue meets the requirements of this section and the extent to which proceeds of such issue have been made available to low-income individuals, and

(iv) such other information as the Secretary may require.

(B) EXTENSION OF TIME.—The Secretary may grant an extension of time for the filing of any statement under subparagraph (A) if there is reasonable cause for the failure to file such statement in a timely fashion.

(4) STATE CERTIFICATION REQUIREMENTS.—

(A) IN GENERAL.—An issue meets the requirements of this subsection only if, before the issue, a State official designated by State law (or, where there is no such State official, the Governor) certifies in the manner prescribed by regulations that the issue meets the requirements of subsection (g).

(B) CERTIFICATION FURNISHED TO SECRETARY.—Any certification under subparagraph (A) shall be submitted to the Secretary at the same time as the statement with respect to such issue is submitted under paragraph (3) or such other time as the Secretary may prescribe.

(C) SPECIAL RULE FOR CONSTITUTIONAL HOME RULE CITIES.—In the case of any constitutional home rule city (as defined in subsection (g)(5)(C)), the certification under subparagraph (A) shall be made by the chief executive officer of such city.

(5) POLICY STATEMENT.—

(A) IN GENERAL.—An issue meets the requirements of this subsection only if the applicable elected representative of the governmental unit—

(i) which is the issuer, or

(ii) on whose behalf such issue was issued,

has published (after a public hearing following reasonable public notice) a report described in subparagraph (B) by the last day of the year preceding the year in which such issue is issued and a copy of such report has been submitted to the Secretary on or before such last day.

(B) REPORT.—The report referred to in subparagraph (A) which is published by the applicable elected representative of the governmental unit shall include—

(i) a statement of the policies with respect to housing, development, and low-income housing assistance which such governmental unit is to follow in issuing qualified mortgage bonds and mortgage credit certificates, and

(ii) an assessment of the compliance of such governmental unit during the preceding 1-year period preceding the date of the report with—

(I) the statement of policy on qualified mortgage bonds and mortgage credit certificates that was set forth in the previous report, if any, of an applicable elected representative of such governmental unit, and

(II) the intent of Congress that State and local governments are expected to use their authority to issue qualified mortgage bonds and mortgage credit certificates to the greatest extent feasible (taking into account prevailing interest rates and conditions in the housing market) to assist lower income families to afford home ownership before assisting higher income families.

(C) EXTENSION OF TIME.—The Secretary may grant an extension of time for the publishing of a report described in subparagraph (B) or the submittal of such report to the Secretary if there is reasonable cause for the failure to publish or submit such report in a timely fashion.

Amendments

• 1986, Tax Reform Act of 1986 (P.L. 99-514)

P.L. 99-514, §1861(a):

Amended Code Sec. 103A(j)(5) by adding at the end thereof new subparagraph (C). **Effective** as if included in the provision of P.L. 98-369 to which it relates.

• 1984, Deficit Reduction Act of 1984 (P.L. 98-369)

P.L. 98-369, §611(b)(1):

Amended Code Sec. 103A(j) by adding at the end thereof new paragraphs (3)-(5). **Effective** for obligations issued after 12-31-84.

• 1982, Tax Equity and Fiscal Responsibility Act of 1982 (P.L. 97-248)

P.L. 97-248, §310(c)(3)(A):

Amended Code Sec. 103A(j) by striking out paragraph (1) and by redesignating paragraphs (2) and (3) as paragraphs (1) and (2), respectively. **Effective** for obligations issued after 12-31-82. Prior to amendment, Code Sec. 103A(j)(1) read as follows:

"(1) Obligations must be registered.—An issue meets the requirements of this subsection only if each obligation issued pursuant to such issue is in registered form."

[Sec. 103A(k)]

(k) TARGETED AREA RESIDENCES.—

(1) IN GENERAL.—For purposes of this section, the term "targeted area residence" means a residence in an area which is either—

(A) a qualified census tract, or

(B) an area of chronic economic distress.

(2) QUALIFIED CENSUS TRACT.—

(A) IN GENERAL.—For purposes of paragraph (1), the term "qualified census tract" means a census tract in which 70 percent or more of the families have income which is 80 percent or less of the statewide median family income.

(B) DATA USED.—The determination under subparagraph (A) shall be made on the basis of the most recent decennial census for which data are available.

(3) AREA OF CHRONIC ECONOMIC DISTRESS.—

(A) IN GENERAL.—For purposes of paragraph (1), the term "area of chronic economic distress" means an area of chronic economic distress—

(i) designated by the State as meeting the standards established by the State for purposes of this subsection, and

(ii) the designation of which has been approved by the Secretary and the Secretary of Housing and Urban Development.

(B) CRITERIA TO BE USED IN APPROVING STATE DESIGNATIONS.—The criteria used by the Secretary and the Secretary of Housing and Urban Development in evaluating any proposed designation of an area for purposes of this subsection shall be—

(i) the condition of the housing stock, including the age of the housing and the number of abandoned and substandard residential units,

(ii) the need of area residents for owner-financing under this section, as indicated by low per capita income, a high percentage of families in poverty, a high number of welfare recipients, and high unemployment rates,

(iii) the potential for use of owner-financing under this section to improve housing conditions in the area, and

(iv) the existence of a housing assistance plan which provides a displacement program and a public improvements and services program.

[Sec. 103A(l)]

(l) OTHER DEFINITIONS AND SPECIAL RULES.—For purposes of this section—

(1) MORTGAGE.—The term "mortgage" includes any other owner-financing.

(2) BOND.—The term "bond" includes any obligation.

(3) STATE.—The term "State" includes a possession of the United States and the District of Columbia.

(4) STATISTICAL AREA.—

(A) IN GENERAL.—The term "statistical area" means—

(i) a standard metropolitan statistical area, and

(ii) any county (or the portion thereof) which is not within a standard metropolitan statistical area.

(B) STANDARD METROPOLITAN STATISTICAL AREA.—The term "standard metropolitan statistical area" means the area in and around a city of 50,000 inhabitants or more (or equivalent area) as defined by the Secretary of Commerce.

(C) DESIGNATION WHERE ADEQUATE STATISTICAL INFORMATION NOT AVAILABLE.—For purposes of this paragraph, if there is insufficient recent statistical information with respect to a county (or portion thereof) described in subparagraph (A)(ii), the Secretary may substitute for such county (or portion thereof) another area for which there is sufficient recent statistical information.

(D) DESIGNATION WHERE NO COUNTY.—In the case of any portion of a State which is not within a county, subparagraphs (A)(ii) and (C) shall be applied by substituting for "county" an area designated by the Secretary which is the equivalent of a county.

(5) ACQUISITION COST.—

(A) IN GENERAL.—The term "acquisition cost" means the cost of acquiring the residence as a completed residential unit.

(B) EXCEPTIONS.—The term "acquisition cost" does not include—

(i) usual and reasonable settlement or financing costs,

(ii) the value of services performed by the mortgagor or members of his family in completing the residence, and

(iii) the cost of land which has been owned by the mortgagor for at least 2 years before the date on which construction of the residence begins.

(C) SPECIAL RULE FOR QUALIFIED REHABILITATION LOANS.—In the case of a qualified rehabilitation loan, for purposes of subsection (f), the term "acquisition cost" includes the cost of the rehabilitation.

(6) QUALIFIED HOME IMPROVEMENT LOAN.—The term "qualified home improvement loan" means the financing (in an amount which does not exceed $15,000)—

(A) of alterations, repairs, and improvements on or in connection with an existing residence by the owner thereof, but

(B) only of such items as substantially protect or improve the basic livability or energy efficiency of the property.

(7) QUALIFIED REHABILITATION LOAN.—

(A) IN GENERAL.—The term "qualified rehabilitation loan" means any owner-financing provided in connection with—

(i) a qualified rehabilitation, or

(ii) the acquisition of a residence with respect to which there has been a qualified rehabilitation,

but only if the mortgagor to whom such financing is provided is the first resident of the residence after the completion of the rehabilitation.

(B) QUALIFIED REHABILITATION.—For purposes of subparagraph (A), the term "qualified rehabilitation" means any rehabilitation of a building if—

(i) there is a period of at least 20 years between the date on which the building was first used and the date on which the physical work on such rehabilitation begins,

(ii) 75 percent or more of the existing external walls of such building are retained in place as external walls in the rehabilitation process, and

(iii) the expenditures for such rehabilitation are 25 percent or more of the mortgagor's adjusted basis in the residence.

For purposes of clause (iii), the mortgagor's adjusted basis shall be determined as of the completion of the rehabilitation or, if later, the date on which the mortgagor acquires the residence.

(8) DETERMINATIONS ON ACTUARIAL BASIS.—All determinations of yield, effective interest rates, and amounts required to be paid or credited to mortgagors or paid to the United States under subsection (i)(4)(A) shall be made on an actuarial basis taking into account the present value of money.

(9) SINGLE-FAMILY AND OWNER-OCCUPIED RESIDENCES INCLUDE CERTAIN RESIDENCES WITH 2 TO 4 UNITS.—Except for purposes of subsections (g) and (h)(2), the terms "single-family" and "owner-occupied", when used with respect to residences, include 2, 3, or 4 family residences—

(A) one unit of which is occupied by the owner of the units, and

(B) which were first occupied at least 5 years before the mortgage is executed.

(10) COOPERATIVE HOUSING CORPORATIONS.—

(A) IN GENERAL.—In the case of any cooperative housing corporation—

(i) each dwelling unit shall be treated as if it were actually owned by the person entitled to occupy such dwelling unit by reason of his ownership of stock in the corporation, and

(ii) any indebtedness of the corporation allocable to the dwelling unit shall be treated as if it were indebtedness of the shareholder entitled to occupy the dwelling unit.

(B) ADJUSTMENT TO TARGETED AREA REQUIREMENT.—In the case of any issue to provide financing to a cooperative housing corporation with respect to cooperative housing not located in a targeted area, to the extent provided in regulations, such issue may be combined with 1 or more other issues for purposes of determining whether the requirements of subsection (h) are met.

(C) COOPERATIVE HOUSING CORPORATION.—The term "cooperative housing corporation" has the meaning given to such term by section 216(b)(1).

Amendments

• 1982, Tax Equity and Fiscal Responsibility Act of 1982 (P.L. 97-248)

P.L. 97-248, §220(e):

Amended Code Sec. 103A(l) by adding a new paragraph (10). **Effective** for obligations issued after 9-3-82.

• 1980 (P.L. 96-595)

P.L. 96-595, §5(b):

Amended Code Sec. 103A(l)(8) by inserting "or paid to the United States" after "credited to mortgagors". For the **effective** date of this amendment, see the historical comment for P.L. 96-499 under Code Sec. 103A(n).

[Sec. 103A(m)]

(m) SPECIAL RULE FOR ISSUE USED FOR OWNER-OCCUPIED HOUSING AND RENTAL HOUSING.—In the case of an issue—

(1) part of the proceeds of which are to be used for mortgages on owner-occupied residences in a manner which meets the requirements of this section, and

(2) part of the proceeds of which are to be used for rental housing which meets the requirements of section 103(b)(4)(A),

under regulations prescribed by the Secretary, each such part shall be treated as a separate issue.

[Sec. 103A(n)]

(n) ADVANCE REFUNDING OF MORTGAGE SUBSIDY BONDS NOT PERMITTED.—On and after the date of the enactment of this section, no obligation may be issued for the advance refunding of a mortgage subsidy bond (determined without regard to subsection (b)(2)).

Amendments

• 1982, Tax Equity and Fiscal Responsibility Act of 1982 (P.L. 97-248)

P.L. 97-248, §221(c)(2), provides:

(2) Subsection (k) of section 1104 of the Mortgage Subsidy Bond Tax Act of 1980 is hereby repealed.

• 1980, Omnibus Reconciliation Act of 1980 (P.L. 96-499)

P.L. 96-499, §1102(a):

Added Code Sec. 103A. Section 1104 of P.L. 96-499, as amended by P.L. 98-369, §614, provides the **effective** dates for the amendments made by §§1102 and 1103 of that bill.

P.L. 96-499, §1104, as amended by P.L. 98-369, §614, provides:

SEC. 1104. EFFECTIVE DATES FOR BOND PROVISIONS.

(a) GENERAL RULE.—

(1) IN GENERAL.—Except as otherwise provided in this section, the amendments made by sections 1102 and 1103 shall apply to obligations issued after April 24, 1979.

(2) EXCEPTIONS FOR CERTAIN OBLIGATIONS ISSUED BEFORE JANUARY 1, 1981.—The amendments made by sections 1102 and 1103 shall not apply to obligations issued before January 1, 1981, if such obligations are part of an issue substantially all the proceeds of which (exclusive of issuance costs and a reasonably required reserve) are, before the date which is 1 year after the date of issue of the obligations, committed—

(A) except as provided in subparagraph (B), by firm commitment letters (similar to those used in financing not provided with tax-exempt bonds), and

(B) in the case of rental housing, by the commencement of construction of the project or by the acquisition of the project.

(b) EXCEPTION FOR OFFICIAL ACTION TAKEN BEFORE APRIL 25, 1979.—

(1) IN GENERAL.—The amendments made by sections 1102 and 1103 shall not apply to obligations if official action before April 25, 1979, of the governing body of the unit having authority to issue such obligations indicated an intent to issue such obligations.

(2) ACTION BY STAFF OF HOUSING AUTHORITY TREATED AS ACTION OF AUTHORITY IN CERTAIN CASES.—For purposes of paragraph (1), if, before April 25, 1979—

(A) the permanent professional staff of a State or local housing authority performed substantial work on a bond issue, and

(B) it was reasonable to expect that the bond issue, as developed by the staff, would be promptly approved by the governing body of the housing authority,

then such action by such staff shall be treated as the official action of such governing body.

(3) SPECIAL RULES RELATING TO SIZE OF ISSUE.—

(A) IN GENERAL.—Except as provided in subparagraph (B), an issue does not qualify for the exception provided by paragraph (1) if the issue size exceeds the intended issue size.

(B) EXCEPTION.—In the case of an issue to provide owner-financing for residences for which as of April 24, 1979, there was no documentation relating to intended issue size, paragraph (1) shall not apply unless—

(i) substantially all of the proceeds of the issue (exclusive of issuance costs and a reasonably required reserve) are to be used to provide owner-financing for 1 to 4 family residences (one unit of which is owner occupied) and not to acquire or replace existing mortgages (within the meaning of section 103A(j)(2) of the Internal Revenue Code of 1954), and

(ii) substantially all of the proceeds referred to in clause (i) are committed by firm commitment letters (similar to those used in owner-financing not provided with tax-exempt bonds) to such owner-financing before the day which is 9 months after the date of issue of the obligations.

(C) ISSUE SIZE DEFINED.—For purposes of this paragraph, the term "issue size" means the aggregate face amount of obligations issued pursuant to the issue.

(D) INTENDED ISSUE SIZE.—For purposes of this paragraph, the term "intended issue size" means the aggregate face amount of obligations which a reasonable individual would reasonably conclude from the documentation before April 25, 1979, was the issue size which the governing body of the issuing authority intended to issue.

(4) LOCAL REFERENDUM HELD BEFORE JUNE 13, 1979.—

(A) IN GENERAL.—For purposes of paragraph (1), if—

(i) on April 25, 1979, legislation was pending in a State legislature,

(ii) on April 27, 1979, such legislation was amended to authorize local governmental units to issue tax-exempt obligations,

(iii) before June 13, 1979, such legislation was enacted and a local governmental unit in such State held a referendum with respect to the issuance of obligations to finance owner-occupied residences, and

(iv) any action with respect to the issuance of such obligations by the governing body of such local governmental unit would have met the requirements of paragraph (1) if such legislation had been in effect, and such referendum had been held, when that action was taken,

then such legislation shall be treated as in effect, and such referendum shall be treated as having been held, at the time when such action was taken.

(B) DOLLAR LIMIT FOR LOCAL GOVERNMENTAL UNITS.—The aggregate amount of obligations which may be issued by local governmental units with respect to the area comprising any local governmental area by reason of subparagraph (A) may not exceed—

(i) $35,000,000, reduced by

(ii) the aggregate amount of obligations which are issued (before, on, or after the issue under this paragraph) by local governmental units with respect to such area after April 24, 1979, and to which the amendments made by this subtitle do not apply solely by reason of this subsection (determined without regard to the application of subparagraph (A) of this paragraph).

(C) MORTGAGE REQUIREMENTS.—Subparagraph (A) shall not apply with respect to any issue unless such issue meets the requirements of paragraph (3)(A) of subsection (c).

(5) CERTAIN LOCAL ACTION PURSUANT TO LEGISLATION ENACTED BEFORE SEPTEMBER 29, 1979.—

(A) IN GENERAL.—For purposes of paragraph (1), if—

(i) on April 24, 1979, legislation was pending in a State legislature authorizing a local governmental unit to issue tax-exempt obligations for owner-occupied residences.

(ii) before September 29, 1979, such legislation was enacted, and

(iii) any action with respect to the issuance of such obligations by the local governing body would have met the requirements of paragraph (1) if such legislation had been in effect when that action was taken,

then such legislation shall be treated as in effect at the time when such action was taken.

(B) DOLLAR LIMIT FOR LOCAL GOVERNMENTAL UNITS.—The aggregate amount of obligations which may be issued by local governmental units with respect to the area comprising any local governmental area by reason of subparagraph (A) may not exceed the lesser of—

(i) the aggregate amount authorized by the legislation referred to in subparagraph (A), or

(ii) $150,000,000.

(C) MORTGAGE REQUIREMENTS.—Subparagraph (A) shall not apply with respect to any issue unless such issue meets the requirements of paragraph (3)(A) of subsection (c).

(c) $150,000,000 EXCEPTION FOR STATE HOUSING FINANCE AGENCIES.—

(1) IN GENERAL.—To the extent of the limit set forth in paragraph (2), the amendments made by this subtitle shall not apply to obligations issued by a State housing finance agency.

(2) DOLLAR LIMIT FOR STATE HOUSING FINANCE AGENCIES.—The aggregate amount of obligations which may be issued by State housing finance agencies with respect to any State by reason of paragraph (1) may not exceed—

(A) $150,000,000, reduced by

(B) the aggregate amount of obligations which are issued (before, on, or after the issue under this subsection) by the housing finance agencies of such State after April 24, 1979, to finance owner-occupied residences and to which the amendments made by this subtitle do not apply solely by reason of subsection (b).

(3) COMMITMENTS.—Paragraph (1) shall not apply with respect to any issue unless substantially all of the proceeds of such issue (exclusive of issuance costs and a reasonably required reserve)—

(A) are to be used to provide owner-financing for 1 to 4 family residences (1 unit of which is owner-occupied) and not to acquire or replace existing mortgages (within the meaning of section 103A(j)(2) of the Internal Revenue Code of 1954), and

(B) are committed by firm commitment letters (similar to those used in owner-financing not provided by tax-exempt bonds) to owner-financing before January 1, 1981.

(4) SPECIAL RULE FOR ACTION IN 1978 PURSUANT TO MORTGAGE PROGRAM ESTABLISHED IN 1970.—

(A) IN GENERAL.—If—

(i) in 1970 State legislation established a program to issue tax-exempt obligations to finance the purchase of existing mortgages from financial institutions,

(ii) in August 1978, as a step toward issuing obligations under such program, the governing body of the housing agency administering the program made a finding that there was a shortage of mortgage funds within the State,

(iii) moneys received by any financial institution on the purchase of mortgages will be reinvested within 90 days in new mortgages, and

(iv) the issue meets the requirements of subparagraphs (B) and (C),

then paragraph (3) shall not apply with respect to an issue of obligations pursuant to the program referred to in clause (i) and the finding referred to in clause (ii).

(B) DOWNPAYMENT REQUIREMENT.—An issue meets the requirements of this subparagraph only if 75 percent or more of the financing provided under the issue is financing for residences where such financing constitutes 95 percent or more of the acquisition cost of the residences.

(C) TARGETED AREA REQUIREMENT.—An issue meets the requirements of this subparagraph only if at least 20 percent of the financing provided under the issue is ownerfinancing of targeted area residences. For purposes of the preceding sentence, the term "targeted area residence" means a residence in an area which is a census tract in which 70 percent or more of the families have income which is 80 percent or less of the statewide median family income (determined on the basis of the most recent decennial census for which data are available).

(D) DOLLAR LIMIT.—The aggregate amount of obligations which may be issued by a State housing authority by reason of subparagraph (A) may not exceed $125,000,000.

(d) SPECIAL RULES.—

(1) COURT ACTION WAS PENDING TO DETERMINE SCOPE OF AUTHORIZING LEGISLATION.—

(A) IN GENERAL.—If—

(i) before April 25, 1979, a State had enacted a law under which counties were authorized to establish public trusts to issue tax-exempt obligations for public purposes,

(ii) on such date the question of whether or not that law authorized the issuance of obligations to finance certain owner-occupied residences was being litigated in a court of competent jurisdiction,

(iii) before July 31, 1979, the Supreme Court of such State held that the counties were so authorized, and

(iv) there is written evidence (which was in existence before April 25, 1979) that before April 25, 1979, the governing body of a county in such State had taken action indicating an intent to issue (or to establish a program for issuing) tax-exempt obligations to finance owner-occupied residences,

then the amendments made by section 1102 shall not apply to obligations issued by the public trust for such county.

(B) DOLLAR LIMIT.—The aggregate amount of obligations which may be issued with respect to any county by reason of subparagraph (A) may not exceed $50,000,000.

(2) STATE LEGISLATION ENACTED BEFORE JUNE 8, 1979, WHERE LOCALITY HAD ESTABLISHED INCOME LIMITATIONS BEFORE APRIL 25, 1979.—

(A) IN GENERAL.—If—

(i) on April 25, 1979, legislation was pending in a State legislature authorizing a local governmental unit to issue tax-exempt obligations for owner-occupied residences,

(ii) there is written evidence (which was in existence before April 25, 1979) that before April 25, 1979, the governing body of the local governmental unit had taken action indicating to its delegation to the State legislature what the income limitation would be for individuals who would be eligible for mortgages under the program, and

(iii) before June 8, 1979, the legislation referred to in clause (i) was enacted,

then the amendments made by section 1102 shall not apply to obligations issued by the local governmental unit.

(B) DOLLAR LIMIT.—The aggregate amount of obligations which may be issued with respect to any local governmental area by reason of subparagraph (A) may not exceed $150,000,000.

(3) RESOLUTIONS BEFORE CITY COUNCIL BEFORE ENACTMENT OF STATE AUTHORIZING LEGISLATION.—

(A) IN GENERAL.—If—

(i) before April 25, 1979, 2 resolutions were submitted to a city council the first of which would create an urban residential finance authority and the second of which would authorize the appointment of the members of such authority,

(ii) at the time such resolutions were submitted, State authorizing legislation had not been enacted,

(iii) before April 25, 1979, the State authorizing legislation was enacted, and

(iv) after April 24, 1979, and before May 17, 1979, a resolution was adopted by the city council which created an urban residential finance authority and which authorized the appointment of members of the authority,

then the amendments made by section 1102 shall not apply with respect to obligations issued on behalf of such city.

(B) DOLLAR LIMIT.—The aggregate amount of obligations which may be issued with respect to any city by reason of subparagraph (A) may not exceed $50,000,000.

(4) SPECIAL RULE WHERE CITY POSTPONED SECOND HALF OF AUTHORIZED ISSUE TO SAVE INTEREST.—If—

(A) on March 28, 1979, the council of a city adopted a resolution authorizing the issuance of not to exceed $30,000,000 of mortgage revenue bonds,

(B) on or about August 1, 1979, approximately one-half of the obligations authorized by such resolution were issued, and

(C) the reason why the remaining obligations were not issued at that time was to save interest payments until the money was actually needed,

then the amendments made by section 1102 shall not apply with respect to the issuance of the remaining obligations which were authorized by such March 28, 1979, resolution.

(5) STATE WAS IN PROCESS OF PERMITTING LOCALITIES TO ESTABLISH NONPROFIT CORPORATIONS.—

(A) IN GENERAL.—If—

(i) a State law enacted after April 24, 1979, and before June 16, 1979, provides that local governments may establish nonprofit corporations to issue tax-exempt obligations to finance owner-occupied residences,

(ii) pursuant to such State law, a local government establishes such a nonprofit corporation and designates it for purposes of this subsection, and

(iii) on November 7 or 14, 1979, an amount was specified by or for the local government as the maximum amount of obligations which the local government expected the nonprofit corporation to issue with respect to the area under any transitional authority provided by this subtitle,

then the amendments made by section 1102 shall not apply to obligations issued by the nonprofit corporation with respect to the area for which such local government has jurisdiction.

(B) DOLLAR LIMITS.—The aggregate amount of obligations which may be issued with respect to any area by reason of subparagraph (A) may not exceed the amount referred to in subparagraph (A)(iii) which was specified on November 7 or 14, 1979, by or for the local government.

(C) SUBSTITUTION OF HOUSING AUTHORITIES, ETC.—For purposes of applying so much of paragraph (7) as relates to subparagraph (A)—

(i) if the local housing authority had the intent referred to in paragraph (7), such local housing authority shall be substituted for the local government, and

(ii) if the governing body of the local government is a commissioners court, the county judge who was on April 24, 1979, the presiding officer of such court shall be treated as the governing body of such government.

(6) OBLIGATIONS ISSUED UNDER THIS SUBSECTION MUST MEET THE REQUIREMENTS OF SUBSECTION (c)(3).—No obligation may be issued under this subsection unless the issue meets the requirements of subsection (c)(3).

(7) GOVERNING BODY MUST FILE AFFIDAVITS SHOWING INTENT ON APRIL 24, 1979.—No obligation may be issued under this subsection with respect to any area unless a majority of the members of the governing body of the local governmental unit having jurisdiction over that area file affidavits with the Secretary of the Treasury (or his delegate) indicating that it was their intent on April 24, 1979, either that tax-exempt obligations be issued to provide financing for owner-occupied residences or that a program be established to issue such obligations.

(8) LIMITATIONS REDUCED BY CERTAIN OTHER ISSUES.—Any limitation on the amount of obligations which may be issued by any issuer by reason of any paragraph of this subsection shall be reduced by the aggregate amount of obligations which are issued (before, on, or after the issue under this subsection) by local governmental units with respect to the area within the jurisdiction of such issuer after April 24, 1979, and to which the amendments made by this subtitle do not apply solely by reason of subsection (b).

(e) ONGOING LOCAL PROGRAMS FOR REHABILITATION LOANS.—

(1) IN GENERAL.—If before April 25, 1979, a local governmental unit had a qualified rehabilitation loan program, then the amendments made by this subtitle shall not apply to obligations issued by such governmental unit for qualified loans if substantially all of the proceeds of such issue (exclusive of issuance costs and a reasonably required reserve) are committed by firm commitment letters (similar to those used in owner financing not provided by tax-exempt bonds) to qualified loans before January 1, 1981.

(2) LIMITATION.—The aggregate amount of obligations which may be issued by reason of paragraph (1) by local governmental units with respect to the area comprising any local governmental area may not exceed the lesser of—

(A) $10,000,000, or

(B) the aggregate amount of loans made with respect to that area under the qualified rehabilitation loan program during the period beginning on January 1, 1977, and ending on April 24, 1979.

The limitation established by the preceding sentence shall be reduced by the aggregate amount of obligations (if any) which are issued (before, on, or after the issue under this subsection) under the qualified rehabilitation loan program after April 24, 1979, with respect to the same local governmental area and to which the amendments made by this subtitle do not apply solely by reason of subsection (b).

(3) QUALIFIED REHABILITATION LOAN PROGRAM.—For purposes of this subsection, the term "qualified rehabilitation loan program" means a program for the financing—

(A) of alterations, repairs, and improvements on or in connection with an existing residence by the owner thereof, but

(B) only of such items as substantially protect or improve the basic livability of the property.

(4) QUALIFIED LOAN.—For purposes of this subsection, the term "qualified loan" means the financing—

(A) of alterations, repairs, and improvements on or in connection with an existing 1 to 4 family residence (1 unit of which is owner-occupied) by the owner thereof, but

(B) only of such items as substantially protect or improve the basic livability of the property.

(5) DOLLAR LIMIT ON QUALIFIED LOANS.—For purposes of this subsection, a loan shall not be treated as a qualified loan if the financing is in an amount which exceeds $20,000 plus $2,500 for each unit in excess of 1.

(f) $50 PER CAPITA EXCEPTION FOR LOCAL GOVERNMENTS.—

(1) IN GENERAL.—To the extent of the limit set forth in paragraph (2), the amendments made by section 1102 shall

not apply to mortgage subsidy bonds issued by local governmental units after April 24, 1979.

(2) LIMIT.—

(A) IN GENERAL.—The aggregate amount of obligations issued with respect to any area by reason of paragraph (1) shall not exceed—

(i) the amount equal to the product of $50 and the population of that area, reduced by

(ii) the aggregate amount of obligations which are issued (before, on, or after the issue under this subsection) by local governmental units after April 24, 1979, with respect to that area and to which the amendments made by this subtitle do not apply solely by reason of subsections (b), (d), and (e).

(B) DETERMINATION OF POPULATION.—For purposes of subparagraph (A), the population of any area shall be the population as of July 1, 1976, as determined for purposes of the State and Local Fiscal Assistance Act of 1972.

(3) UNIT MUST ESTABLISH THAT ACTION WAS TAKEN BEFORE APRIL 25, 1979.—Paragraph (1) shall not apply with respect to any obligation issued by any local governmental unit unless—

(A) there is written evidence (which was in existence before April 25, 1979) that before April 25, 1979, the governing body of such local governmental unit had taken action indicating an intent to issue (or to establish a program for issuing) tax-exempt obligations to finance owner-occupied residences,

(B) on October 30, 1979, such local governmental unit had authority to issue obligations to finance owner-occupied residences, and

(C) a majority of the members of the governing body of the local governmental unit file with the Secretary of the Treasury (or his delegate) affidavits that the requirement of such subparagraph (A) is met.

For purposes of subparagraph (A), action of the governing body of a second local governmental unit with respect to the same area shall be treated as action of the issuing governmental unit.

(4) COMMITMENTS.—Paragraph (1) shall not apply with respect to any issue unless such issue meets the requirements of paragraph (3) of subsection (c).

(5) OVERLAPPING JURISDICTIONS.—For purposes of this subsection, if 2 or more local governmental units meet the requirements of paragraph (3) and have authority to issue mortgage subsidy bonds with respect to residences in the same area, only the unit having jurisdiction over the smallest geographical area shall be treated as having issuing authority with respect to such area unless such unit agrees to surrender part or all of the amount permitted under this subsection to the local governmental unit with overlapping jurisdiction which has the next smallest geographical area.

(g) ROLLOVER OF EXISTING TAX-EXEMPT OBLIGATIONS.—

(1) IN GENERAL.—The amendments made by sections 1102 and 1103 shall not apply to the issuance of obligations to refinance for the same purpose tax-exempt indebtedness which was outstanding on April 24, 1979 (or indebtedness which had previously been refinanced pursuant to this subsection), but only if—

(A) on April 24, 1979, there was an agreed on period for the maturity of the mortgages or other financing, and

(B) the new obligations have a maturity date which does not exceed by more than 2 years the agreed on period referred to in subparagraph (A).

(2) AMOUNTS FOR RESERVES, ISSUE COSTS, ETC.—An issue which otherwise meets the requirements of paragraph (1) shall not be treated as failing to meet such requirements solely because the amount of the new indebtedness exceeds the amount of the old indebtedness by such amount as is reasonably necessary to cover construction period interest, reserves, and the costs of issuing the new indebtedness.

(h) SPECIAL RULES FOR PROJECTS UNDER DEVELOPMENT.—

(1) RENTAL HOUSING.—The amendment made by section 1103 shall not apply to a project which was in the development stage on April 24, 1979, if—

(A) a plan specifying the number and location of rental units was approved on or before such date by a governing body of a State or local government or by a State or local housing agency or similar agency, and

(B) substantial expenditures for site improvement for the project had been incurred on or before such date.

(2) RENTAL HOUSING PROJECTS APPROVED BY SECRETARY OF HUD.—The amendment made by section 1103 shall not apply to a project which was in the development stage on April 24, 1979, if—

(A) a plan specifying the number and location of rental units was preliminarily approved by the Secretary of Housing and Urban Development pursuant to section 221(d)(4) or section 232 of the National Housing Act on or before such date, and

(B) fees for processing the project with the Department of Housing and Urban Development and other expenditures for the project had been incurred on or before such date.

(3) OWNER-OCCUPIED HOUSING.—The amendments made by section 1102 shall not apply to a project which was in the development stage on April 24, 1979, if on or before such date—

(A) substantial expenditures had been made for detailed plans and specifications, and

(B) either tax-exempt construction financing had been issued with respect to the project or there is written evidence that a governmental unit intended to issue tax-exempt obligations to finance the acquisition of the units by home buyers.

The amendment made by section 1103 shall not apply to construction or other initial temporary financing issued with respect to a project which meets the requirements of the preceding sentence if substantially all of the dwelling units in such project are to be owner-occupied residences.

(4) CERTAIN REDEVELOPMENT MORTGAGE BOND FINANCING PROJECTS.—Subparagraph (B) of paragraph (3) shall be treated as satisfied if, before April 25, 1979—

(A) the developer of a project acquired the land for such project,

(B) there was approval by the mayor's advisory committee of a city of a comprehensive proposal (under a State law authorizing tax-exempt obligations for use only in redevelopment areas) for such project, subject to revisions to be made, and

(C) a revised proposal was submitted to the redevelopment agency and city council containing the revisions.

The aggregate amount of obligations which may be issued by local governmental units with respect to the area comprising any local governmental area by reason of this paragraph may not exceed $20,000,000.

(i) REGISTRATION REQUIREMENTS.—

(1) IN GENERAL.—Notwithstanding any other provision of this section, the amendments made by sections 1102 and 1103, insofar as they require obligations to be in registered form, shall apply to obligations issued after December 31, 1981.

(2) BONDS UNDER TRANSITIONAL RULES.—Any obligation issued after December 31, 1981, by reason of this section shall be in registered form.

(j) ADVANCE REFUNDING.—Notwithstanding any other provision of this section—

(1) subsection (n) of section 103A of the Internal Revenue Code of 1954 (as added by section 1102) shall apply to obligations issued after the date of the enactment of this Act to refund obligations issued before, on, or after such date of enactment, and

(2) this section shall not apply to obligations issued after such date of enactment for the advance refunding of obligations issued before, on, or after such date of enactment.

(k) TRANSITIONAL RULE FOR LOW- AND MODERATE-INCOME REQUIREMENT.—In the case of obligations issued after April 24, 1979, and before January 1, 1984, the period for which the low- and moderate-income requirements of section 103(b)(4)(A) of the Internal Revenue Code of 1954 (as amended by section 1103 of this subtitle) is required to be met shall be 20 years.

(l) SUBSTITUTION OF GOVERNMENTAL INSTRUMENTALITY FOR CITY.—

(1) IN GENERAL.—If—

(A) a corporation was created on June 17, 1971, pursuant to State law to provide financing for the construction and rehabilitation of low-income housing.

(B) pursuant to a State law enacted in 1955 a city has made loans to housing developers from the proceeds of short-term bonds and notes issued by the city, and has secured 50-year mortgages from the developers, and

(C) the corporation agrees to acquire from the city certain of the loans referred to in subparagraph (B) by issuing obligations which will be secured by mortgages referred to in subparagraph (B) on 12 projects (11 of which projects are subsidized with interest-reduction subsidies under section 236 of the National Housing Act),

then the amendments made by this subtitle shall not apply to obligations issued by the corporation to acquire the loans (and mortgages) referred to in subparagraph (C).

(2) DOLLAR LIMIT.—The aggregate amount of obligations to which paragraph (1) applies shall not exceed $135,000,000.

(3) TIME LIMIT.—Paragraph (1) shall not apply to any obligation issued after December 31, 1980.

(m) STATE LEGISLATION WAS PENDING ON APRIL 1, 1979, AND ENACTED ON APRIL 26, 1979, WHERE LOCALITY HAD TAKEN ACTION TO UNDERTAKE A STUDY OF LOCAL MORTGAGE MARKET.—

(1) IN GENERAL.—If—

(A) on April 1, 1979, legislation was pending in a State legislature limiting the authority of local governments within such State to issue tax-exempt obligations for owner-occupied residence under existing home rule authority, and such legislation was enacted on April 26, 1979,

(B) there is written evidence (which was in existence before April 25, 1979) that not earlier than June 1, 1978, but before April 25, 1979, the governing body of a local government in such State had taken action authorizing the undertaking of a demographic or related study of the local mortgage market, which study was intended to serve as a basis for issuance of tax-exempt obligations for owner-occupied residences.

(C) on December 20, 1979, an amount was specified by or for the local government as the range of obligations which it expected to issue with respect to the area under any transitional authority provided by the Act, and

(D) a majority of the members of the governing body of the local government certify that the city or county was waiting enactment of the legislation described in subparagraph (A) prior to determining to proceed towards the issuance of tax-exempt obligations for owner-occupied residences.

then the amendments made by section 1102 shall not apply to obligations issued by such city or county.

(2) DOLLAR LIMITS.—The aggregate amount of obligations which may be issued with respect to any area by reason of subparagraph may not exceed the maximum amount referred to in paragraph (1)(C) which was specified on December 20, 1979, by or for such local government.

(3) TIME LIMITS.—Paragraph (1) shall not apply with respect to any issue unless substantially all of the proceeds of such issue (exclusive of issuance costs and a reasonably required reserve) are committed by firm commitment letters (similar to those used in owner-financing not provided by tax-exempt bonds) to owner-financing before January 1, 1982.

(n) CERTAIN ADDITIONAL TRANSITIONAL AUTHORITY.—

(1) IN GENERAL.—The amendments made by sections 1102 and 1103 shall not apply to issues described in the following table:

City or county	*Ceiling amount*	*Purpose of issue*
Baltimore, Maryland	$100,000,000	Financing owner-occupied residences.
Port Arthur, Texas .	175,000,000	For financing on New Town In Town project.
Minneapolis, Minnesota	25,000,000	Financing owner-occupied residences.
Minneapolis-St. Paul, Minnesota	235,000,000	Joint program for financing owner-occupied residences involving some UDAG grants and private financing.
Detroit, Michigan . .	50,000,000	To issue obligations maturing before 1986 for construction on the Riverfront West project.
Brevard County, Florida	150,000,000	Financing owner-occupied residences.
Chicago, Illinois . . .	235,000,000	For financing on the Presidential Towers project.

(2) ISSUING AUTHORITY.—The authority granted by this subsection with respect to any city or county may be used only by the appropriate issuing authority for that city or county.

(3) CEILING AMOUNT.—The ceiling amount specified in paragraph (1) with respect to any item shall be the maximum aggregate amount of obligations which may be issued by the appropriate issuing authority under the authority granted by such item.

(4) PURPOSE.—The authority under any item may be used to issue obligations only for the purpose set forth in paragraph (1) for such item.

(o) SPECIAL RULE FOR LOANS TO LENDERS PROGRAM.—

(1) IN GENERAL.—In the case of any obligations issued during 1981 or 1982 pursuant to a qualified loans to lender program—

(A) the amendments made by section 1103 shall not apply,

(B) subsection (i) of section 103A of the Internal Revenue Code of 1954 (other than the last sentence of paragraph (1) of such subsection) shall not apply, and

(C) the determination of whether the requirements of subsections (d), (e), (f), (h), (j)(2), and (j)(3) of such section 103A are met with respect to such issue shall be made by taking into account the loans made by the financial institutions with the funds provided by the issue (in lieu of the mortgages acquired from the financial institutions with the proceeds of the issue).

(2) QUALIFIED LOANS TO LENDER PROGRAM.—For purposes of paragraph (1), the term "qualified loans to lender program" means any program established pursuant to legislation enacted by New York State in 1970 which finances the purchase of existing mortgages from financial institutions and requires any money received by a financial institution on the purchase of a mortgage to be reinvested within 90 days in new mortgages.

(p) MOST EXCEPTIONS NOT TO APPLY TO BONDS ISSUED AFTER DECEMBER 31, 1984.—In addition to any obligations to which the amendments made by section 1102 apply by reason of the provisions of this section, the amendments made by section 1102 shall apply, notwithstanding any other provision of this section (other than subsection (n)), to obligations issued after December 31, 1984, all or a major portion of the proceeds of which are used to finance new mortgages on single-family residences that are owner occupied.

(q) REDUCTION OF STATE CEILING BY AMOUNT OF SPECIAL MORTGAGE BONDS ISSUED BEFORE 1985.—

(1) In General.—Notwithstanding any other provision of this section (other than subsections (n) and (r)), any obligation—

(A) which is part of an issue all or a major portion of the proceeds of which are used to finance new mortgages in single-family residences that are owner occupied,

(B) which were issued by issuing authorities in such State after June 15, 1984, and before January 1, 1985, and

(C) to which the amendments made by section 1102 do not apply by reason of any provision of this section other than subsection (n),

shall, for purposes of applying the Internal Revenue Code of 1954, be treated as an obligation which is not described in section 103(a) of such Code if the aggregate face amount of such issue exceeds the portion of the State ceiling that is allocated by the State to such issue prior to the date of issuance of such issue.

(2) Application of Section 103A(g).—For purposes of applying section 103A(g) of such Code, the State ceiling for calendar year 1984 shall be reduced by the aggregate

amount allocated by the State to any issues described in paragraph (1).

(3) State Ceiling.—For purposes of this subsection, the term "State ceiling" has the meaning given to such term by section 103A(g)(4) of the Internal Revenue Code of 1954.

(r) EXCEPTIONS TO SUBSECTION (q).—Subsection (q) shall not apply with respect to—

(1) obligations—

(A) the proceeds of which are used to finance the River Place Project located in Minneapolis, Minnesota, and

(B) the aggregate face amount of which does not exceed $55,000,000, or

(2) obligations—

(A) the proceeds of which are used to finance the Waseca, Minnesota project, and

(B) the aggregate face amount of which does not exceed $7,800,000.

[Sec. 103A(o)]

(o) ADDITIONAL REQUIREMENTS FOR QUALIFIED VETERANS' MORTGAGE BONDS.—

(1) VETERANS TO WHOM FINANCING MAY BE PROVIDED.—An obligation meets the requirements of this subsection only if each mortgagor to whom financing is provided under the issue is a qualified veteran.

(2) REQUIREMENT THAT STATE PROGRAM BE IN EFFECT BEFORE JUNE 22, 1984.—An issue meets the requirements of this subsection only if it is a general obligation of a State which issued qualified veterans' mortgage bonds before June 22, 1984.

(3) VOLUME LIMITATION.—

(A) IN GENERAL.—An issue meets the requirements of this subsection only if the aggregate amount of bonds issued pursuant thereto (when added to the aggregate amount of qualified verterans' mortgage bonds previously issued by the State during the calendar year) does not exceed the State veterans limit for such calendar year.

(B) STATE VETERANS LIMIT.—A State veterans limit for any calendar year is the amount equal to—

(i) the aggregate amount of qualified veterans bonds issued by such State during the period beginning on January 1, 1979, and ending on June 22, 1984 (not including the amount of any qualified veterans bond issued by such State during the calendar year (or portion thereof) in such period for which the amount of such bonds so issued was the lowest), divided by

(ii) the number (not to exceed 5) of calendar years after 1979 and before 1985 during which the State issued qualified veterans bonds (determined by only taking into account bonds issued on or before June 22, 1984).

(4) QUALIFIED VETERAN.—For purposes of this subsection, the term "qualified veteran" means any veteran—

(A) who served on active duty at some time before January 1, 1977, and

(B) who applied for the financing before the later of—

(i) the date 30 years after the last date on which such veteran left active service, or

(ii) January 31, 1985.

(5) GOOD FAITH EFFORT RULES MADE APPLICABLE.—Rules similar to the rules of subparagraphs (B) and (C) of subsection (c)(2) shall apply to the requirements of this subsection.

(6) SPECIAL RULE FOR CERTAIN SHORT-TERM OBLIGATIONS.—In the case of any obligation which has a term of 1 year or less and which was issued to provide financing for property taxes, the amount taken into account under this subsection with respect to such obligation shall be 1/15 of its principal amount.

Amendments

• 1986, Tax Reform Act of 1986 (P.L. 99-514)

P.L. 99-514, §1861(b):

Amended Code Sec. 103A(o)(4)(B) by striking out "January 1, 1985" and inserting in lieu thereof "January 31, 1985". **Effective** as if included in the provision of P.L. 98-369 to which it relates.

• 1984, Deficit Reduction Act of 1984 (P.L. 98-369)

P.L. 98-369, §611(c)(2):

Added Code Sec. 103A(o). **Effective** for obligations issued after 7-18-84. Special rules appear below.

P.L. 98-369, §611(d)(3)-(7), provides:

(3) Subsection (c).—

* * *

(B) Volume Limitation.—The requirements of paragraph (3) of section 103A(o) of the Internal Revenue Code of 1954 (as added by this section) shall apply to obligations issued after June 22, 1984. In applying such requirements to obligations issued after such date, obligations issued on or before such date shall not be taken into account under such paragraph (3).

(C) Qualified Veterans' Mortgage Bonds Authorized Before October 18, 1983, Not Taken Into Account.—The requirements of section 103A(o)(3) of the Internal Revenue Code of 1954 shall not apply to any qualified veterans' mortgage bond if—

(i) the issuance of such bond was authorized by a State referendum before October 18, 1983, or

(ii) the issuance of such bond was authorized pursuant to a State referendum before December 1, 1983, where such referendum was authorized by action of the State legislature before October 18, 1983.

(4) Transitional Rule Where State Formula for Allocating State Ceiling Expires.—

(A) In General.—If a State law which provided a formula for allocating the State ceiling under section 103A(g) of the Internal Revenue Code of 1954 for calendar year 1983 expires as of the close of calendar year 1983, for purposes of section 103A(g) of such Code, such State law shall be treated as remaining in effect after 1983. In any case to which the preceding sentence applies, where the State's expiring allocation formula requires action by a State official to allocate the State ceiling among issuers, actions of such State official in allocating such ceiling shall be effective.

(B) Termination.—Subparagraph (A) shall not apply on or after the effective date of any State legislation enacted after the date of the enactment of this Act with respect to the allocation of the State ceiling.

(C) Special Rule for Texas.—In the case of Texas, the Governor of such State may take the action described in subparagraph (A) pursuant to procedures established by the Governor consistent with the State laws of Texas.

(5) Special Rule for Determinations of Statistical Area.—For purposes of applying section 103A of the Internal Revenue Code of 1954 and any other provision of Federal law—

(A) Rescission.—The Director of the Office of Management and Budget shall rescind the designation of the Kansas City, Missouri primary metropolitan statistical area (KCMO PMSA) and the designation of the Kansas City, Kansas primary metropolitan statistical area (Kansas City, KS PMSA), and shall not take any action to designate such two primary metropolitan statistical areas as a consolidated metropolitan statistical area.

(B) Designation.—The Director of the Office of Management and Budget shall designate a single metropolitan statistical area which includes the following:

(i) Kansas City, Kansas.

(ii) Kansas City, Missouri.

(iii) The counties of Johnson, Wyandotte, Leavenworth, and Miami in Kansas.

(iv) The counties of Cass, Clay, Jackson, Platte, Ray, and Lafayette in Missouri.

The metropolitan statistical area designation pursuant to this subsection shall be known as the "Kansas City Missouri-Kansas Metropolitan Statistical Area".

(6) Transitional Rule for Kentucky and Nevada.—For purposes of section 103A(g) of the Internal Revenue Code of 1954, in the case of Kentucky and Nevada, subclause (I) of section 103A(g)(6)(B)(ii) of such Code shall be applied as if the first day referred to in such subclause were January 1, 1987.

(7) Report to Congress.—The Secretary of the Treasury, in consultation with the Secretary of Housing and Urban Development, shall, not later than January 1, 1987, submit a report to the Committee on Finance of the Senate and the Committee on Ways and Means of the House of Representatives regarding the performance of issuers of qualified mortgage bonds and mortgage credit certificates relative to the intent of Congress described in section 103A(j) of the Internal Revenue Code of 1954.

[Sec. 104]

SEC. 104. COMPENSATION FOR INJURIES OR SICKNESS.

[Sec. 104(a)]

(a) IN GENERAL.—Except in the case of amounts attributable to (and not in excess of) deductions allowed under section 213 (relating to medical, etc., expenses) for any prior taxable year, gross income does not include—

(1) amounts received under workmen's compensation acts as compensation for personal injuries or sickness;

(2) the amount of any damages (other than punitive damages) received (whether by suit or agreement and whether as lump sums or as periodic payments) on account of personal physical injuries or physical sickness;

(3) amounts received through accident or health insurance (or through an arrangement having the effect of accident or health insurance) for personal injuries or sickness (other than amounts received by an employee, to the extent such amounts (A) are attributable to contributions by the employer which were not includible in the gross income of the employee, or (B) are paid by the employer);

(4) amounts received as a pension, annuity, or similar allowance for personal injuries or sickness resulting from active service in the armed forces of any country or in the Coast and Geodetic Survey or the Public Health Service, or as a disability annuity payable under the provisions of section 808 of the Foreign Service Act of 1980; and

(5) amounts received by an individual as disability income attributable to injuries incurred as a direct result of a terroristic or military action (as defined in section 692(c)(2)).

For purposes of paragraph (3), in the case of an individual who is, or has been, an employee within the meaning of section 401(c)(1) (relating to self-employed individuals), contributions made on behalf of such individual while he was such an employee to a trust described in section 401(a) which is exempt from tax under section 501(a), or under a plan described in section 403(a), shall, to the extent allowed as deductions under section 404, be treated as contributions by the employer which were not includible in the gross income of the employee. For purposes of paragraph (2), emotional distress shall not be treated as a physical injury or physical sickness. The preceding sentence shall not apply to an amount of damages not in excess of the amount paid for medical care (described in subparagraph (A) or (B) of section 213(d)(1)) attributable to emotional distress.

Amendments

• 2002, Victims of Terrorism Tax Relief Act of 2001 (P.L. 107-134)

P.L. 107-134, §113(a):

Amended Code Sec. 104(a)(5) by striking "a violent attack" and all that follows through the period and inserting "a terroristic or military action (as defined in section 692(c)(2)).". **Effective** for tax years ending on or after 9-11-2001. Prior to amendment, Code Sec. 104(a)(5) read as follows:

(5) amounts received by an individual as disability income attributable to injuries incurred as a direct result of a violent attack which the Secretary of State determines to be a terrorist attack and which occurred while such individual was an employee of the United States engaged in the performance of his official duties outside the United States.

• 1997, Taxpayer Relief Act of 1997 (P.L. 105-34)

P.L. 105-34, §1529 (as amended by P.L. 105-206, §6015(c)(1)-(2)), provides:

SEC. 1529. TREATMENT OF CERTAIN DISABILITY BENEFITS RECEIVED BY FORMER POLICE OFFICERS OR FIREFIGHTERS.

(a) GENERAL RULE.—Amounts to which this section applies which are received by an individual (or the survivors of the individual) as a result of hypertension or heart disease of the individual shall be excludable from gross income under section 104(a)(1) of the Internal Revenue Code of 1986.

(b) AMOUNTS TO WHICH SECTION APPLIES.—This section shall apply to any amount—

(1) which is payable—

(A) to an individual (or to the survivors of an individual) who was a full-time employee of any police department or fire department which is organized and operated by a State, by any political subdivision thereof, or by any agency or instrumentality of a State or political subdivision thereof, and

(B) under—

(i) a State law (as amended on May 19, 1992) which irrebuttably presumed that heart disease and hypertension are work-related illnesses but only for employees hired before July 1, 1992, or

(ii) any other statute, ordinance, labor agreement, or similar provision as a disability pension payment or in the nature of a disability pension payment attributable to employment as a police officer or fireman, but only if the individual is referred to in the State law described in clause (i); and

(2) which was received in calendar year 1989, 1990, or 1991.

(c) WAIVER OF STATUTE OF LIMITATIONS.—If, on the date of the enactment of this Act (or at any time within the 1-year period beginning on such date of enactment), credit or refund of any overpayment of tax resulting from the provisions of this section is barred by any law or rule of law (including res judicata), then credit or refund of such overpayment shall, nevertheless, be allowed or made if claim therefore is filed before the date 1 year after such date of enactment.

• 1996, Health Insurance Portability and Accountability Act of 1996 (P.L. 104-191)

P.L. 104-191, §311(b):

Amended Code Sec. 104(a)(3) by inserting "(or through an arrangement having the effect of accident or health insurance)" after "health insurance". **Effective** for tax years beginning after 12-31-96.

• 1996, Small Business Job Protection Act of 1996 (P.L. 104-188)

P.L. 104-188, §1605(a):

Amended Code Sec. 104(a)(2). **Effective**, generally, for amounts received after 8-20-96, in tax years ending after such date. For an exception, see Act Sec. 1605(d)(2), below. Prior to amendment, Code Sec. 104(a)(2) read as follows:

(2) the amount of any damages received (whether by suit or agreement and whether as lump sums or as periodic payments) on account of personal injuries or sickness;

P.L. 104-188, §1605(b):

Amended Code Sec. 104(a) by striking the last sentence and inserting new sentence[s]. **Effective**, generally, for amounts received after 8-20-96, in tax years ending after such date. For an exception, see Act Sec. 1605(d)(2), below. Prior to amendment, the last sentence of Code Sec. 104(a) read as follows:

Paragraph (2) shall not apply to any punitive damages in connection with a case not involving physical injury or physical sickness.

P.L. 104-188, §1605(d)(2), provides:

(2) EXCEPTION.—The amendments made by this section shall not apply to any amount received under a written binding agreement, court decree, or mediation award in effect on (or issued on or before) September 13, 1995.

• 1989, Omnibus Budget Reconciliation Act of 1989 (P.L. 101-239)

P.L. 101-239, §7641(a):

Amended Code Sec. 104(a) by adding at the end thereof a new sentence. **Effective** for amounts received after 7-10-89, in tax years ending after such date. For an exception, see Act Sec. 7641(b)(2) below.

P.L. 101-239, §7641(b)(2), provides:

(2) EXCEPTION.—The amendment made by subsection (a) shall not apply to any amount received—

(A) under any written binding agreement, court decree, or mediation award in effect on (or issued on or before) July 10, 1989, or

(B) pursuant to any suit filed on or before July 10, 1989.

• 1983 (P.L. 97-473)

P.L. 97-473, §101(a):

Amended Code Sec. 104(a)(2) by striking out "whether by suit or agreement" and inserting "whether by suit or agreement and whether as lump sums or as periodic payments". **Effective** for tax years beginning after 12-31-82.

• 1980, Foreign Service Act of 1980 (P.L. 96-465)

P.L. 96-465, §2206(e)(1):

Amended Code Sec. 104(a)(4) by striking out "section 831 of the Foreign Service Act of 1946, as amended (22 U.S.C. 1081)" and inserting in lieu thereof "section 808 of the Foreign Service Act of 1980". **Effective** 2-15-81.

• 1976, Tax Reform Act of 1976 (P.L. 94-455)

P.L. 94-455, §505(e):

Amended Code Sec. 104(a) by striking out "and" at the end of paragraph (3), by substituting "; and" for the period at the end of paragraph (4), and by adding paragraph (5). **Effective** for tax years beginning after 12-31-76.

P.L. 94-455, §1901(a)(17):

Deleted "; 60 Stat. 1021" after "(22 U.S.C. 1081" in paragraph (4). **Effective** for tax years beginning after 12-31-76.

• 1962, Self-Employed Individuals Tax Retirement Act of 1962 (P.L. 87-792)

P.L. 87-792, §7(d):

Amended Code Sec. 104(a) by inserting the last sentence therein. **Effective** 1-1-63.

• 1960, Foreign Service Act Amendments of 1960 (P.L. 86-723)

P.L. 86-723, §51:

Amended paragraph (4) of Code Sec. 104(a) by inserting before the period at the end thereof the material beginning with the words ", or as a disability annuity". **Effective** 9-9-60.

[Sec. 104(b)]

(b) TERMINATION OF APPLICATION OF SUBSECTION (a)(4) IN CERTAIN CASES.—

(1) IN GENERAL.—Subsection (a)(4) shall not apply in the case of any individual who is not described in paragraph (2).

(2) INDIVIDUALS TO WHOM SUBSECTION (a)(4) CONTINUES TO APPLY.—An individual is described in this paragraph if—

(A) on or before September 24, 1975, he was entitled to receive any amount described in subsection (a)(4),

(B) on September 24, 1975, he was a member of any organization (or reserve component thereof) referred to in subsection (a)(4) or under a binding written commitment to become such a member,

(C) he receives an amount described in subsection (a)(4) by reason of a combat-related injury, or

(D) on application therefor, he would be entitled to receive disability compensation from the Veterans' Administration.

(3) SPECIAL RULES FOR COMBAT-RELATED INJURIES.—For purposes of this subsection, the term "combat-related injury" means personal injury or sickness—

(A) which is incurred—

(i) as a direct result of armed conflict,

(ii) while engaged in extrahazardous service, or

(iii) under conditions simulating war; or

(B) which is caused by an instrumentality of war.

In the case of an individual who is not described in subparagraph (A) or (B) of paragraph (2), except as provided in paragraph (4), the only amounts taken into account under subsection (a)(4) shall be the amounts which he receives by reason of a combat-related injury.

(4) AMOUNT EXCLUDED TO BE NOT LESS THAN VETERANS' DISABILITY COMPENSATION.—In the case of any individual described in paragraph (2), the amounts excludable under subsection (a)(4) for any period with respect to any individual shall not be less than the maximum amount which such individual, on application therefor, would be entitled to receive as disability compensation from the Veterans' Administration.

Amendments

• 1976, Tax Reform Act of 1976 (P.L. 94-455)

P.L. 94-455, §505(b):

Redesignated Code Sec. 104(b) as Code Sec. 104(c) and added a new Code Sec. 104(b). **Effective** for tax years beginning after 12-31-75.

[Sec. 104(c)]

(c) APPLICATION OF PRIOR LAW IN CERTAIN CASES.—The phrase "(other than punitive damages)" shall not apply to punitive damages awarded in a civil action—

(1) which is a wrongful death action, and

(2) with respect to which applicable State law (as in effect on September 13, 1995 and without regard to any modification after such date) provides, or has been construed to provide by a court of competent jurisdiction pursuant to a decision issued on or before September 13, 1995, that only punitive damages may be awarded in such an action.

This subsection shall cease to apply to any civil action filed on or after the first date on which the applicable State law ceases to provide (or is no longer construed to provide) the treatment described in paragraph (2).

Amendments

• 1996, Small Business Job Protection Act of 1996 (P.L. 104-188)

P.L. 104-188, §1605(c):

Amended Code Sec. 104 by redesignating subsection (c) as subsection (d) and inserting after subsection (b) a new subsection (c). **Effective**, generally, for amounts received after 8-20-96, in tax years ending after such date. For an exception, see Act Sec. 1605(d)(2), below.

P.L. 104-188, §1605(d)(2), provides:

(2) EXCEPTION.—The amendments made by this section shall not apply to any amount received under a written binding agreement, court decree, or mediation award in effect on (or issued on or before) September 13, 1995.

[Sec. 104(d)]

(d) CROSS REFERENCES.—

(1) For exclusion from employee's gross income of employer contributions to accident and health plans, see section 106.

(2) For exclusion of part of disability retirement pay from the application of subsection (a)(4) of this section, see section 1403 of title 10, United States Code (relating to career compensation laws).

Amendments

• 1996, Small Business Job Protection Act of 1996 (P.L. 104-188)

P.L. 104-188, §1605(c):

Amended Code Sec. 104 by redesignating subsection (c) as subsection (d). **Effective**, generally, for amounts received after 8-20-96, in tax years ending after such date. For an exception, see Act Sec. 1605(d)(2), below.

P.L. 104-188, §1605(d)(2), provides:

(2) EXCEPTION.—The amendments made by this section shall not apply to any amount received under a written binding agreement, court decree, or mediation award in effect on (or issued on or before) September 13, 1995.

• 1976, Tax Reform Act of 1976 (P.L. 94-455)

P.L. 94-455, §505(b):

Amended Code Sec. 104(b) to redesignate it as Code Sec. 104(c). **Effective** for tax years beginning after 12-31-75.

P.L. 94-455, §1901(a)(17):

Amended paragraph (2) to substitute "see section 1403 of title 10, United States Code (relating to career compensation laws)." for "see section 402(h) of the Career Compensation Act of 1949 (37 U.S.C. 272(h))." **Effective** for tax years beginning after 12-31-76.

[Sec. 105]

SEC. 105. AMOUNTS RECEIVED UNDER ACCIDENT AND HEALTH PLANS.

[Sec. 105(a)]

(a) AMOUNTS ATTRIBUTABLE TO EMPLOYER CONTRIBUTIONS.—Except as otherwise provided in this section, amounts received by an employee through accident or health insurance for personal injuries or sickness shall be included in gross income to the extent such amounts (1) are attributable to contributions by the employer which were not includible in the gross income of the employee, or (2) are paid by the employer.

[Sec. 105(b)]

(b) AMOUNTS EXPENDED FOR MEDICAL CARE.—Except in the case of amounts attributable to (and not in excess of) deductions allowed under section 213 (relating to medical, etc., expenses) for any prior taxable year, gross income does not include amounts referred to in subsection (a) if such amounts are paid, directly or indirectly, to the taxpayer to reimburse the taxpayer for expenses incurred by him for the medical care (as defined in section 213(d)) of the taxpayer, his spouse, his dependents (as defined in section 152, determined without regard to subsections (b)(1), (b)(2), and (d)(1)(B) thereof), and any child (as defined in section 152(f)(1)) of the taxpayer who as of the end of the taxable year has not attained age 27. Any child to whom section 152(e) applies shall be treated as a dependent of both parents for purposes of this subsection.

Amendments

• 2010, Health Care and Education Reconciliation Act of 2010 (P.L. 111-152)

P.L. 111-152, §1004(d)(1)(A)-(B):

Amended the first sentence of Code Sec. 105(b) by striking "and his dependents" and inserting "his dependents"; and by inserting before the period ", and any child (as defined in section 152(f)(1)) of the taxpayer who as of the end of the taxable year has not attained age 27". **Effective** 3-30-2010.

2004, Working Families Tax Relief Act of 2004 (P.L. 108-311)

P.L. 108-311, §207(9):

Amended Code Sec. 105(b) by inserting ", determined without regard to subsections (b)(1), (b)(2), and (d)(1)(B) thereof" after "section 152". **Effective** for tax years beginning after 12-31-2004.

• 1984, Deficit Reduction Act of 1984 (P.L. 98-369)

P.L. 98-369, §423(b)(2):

Amended Code Sec. 105(b) by adding a new sentence at the end thereof. **Effective** for tax years beginning after 12-31-84.

• 1982, Tax Equity and Fiscal Responsibility Act of 1982 (P.L. 97-248)

P.L. 97-248, §202(b)(3)(C):

Amended Code Sec. 105(b) by striking out "section 213(e)" and inserting in lieu thereof "section 213(d)". **Effective** for tax years beginning after 12-31-83.

[Sec. 105(c)]

(c) PAYMENTS UNRELATED TO ABSENCE FROM WORK.—Gross income does not include amounts referred to in subsection (a) to the extent such amounts—

(1) constitute payment for the permanent loss or loss of use of a member or function of the body, or the permanent disfigurement, of the taxpayer, his spouse, or a dependent (as defined in section 152, determined without regard to subsections (b)(1), (b)(2), and (d)(1)(B) thereof), and

(2) are computed with reference to the nature of the injury without regard to the period the employee is absent from work.

Amendments

• 2004, Working Families Tax Relief Act of 2004 (P.L. 108-311)

P.L. 108-311, §207(9):

Amended Code Sec. 105(c)(1) by inserting ", determined without regard to subsections (b)(1), (b)(2), and (d)(1)(B) thereof" after "section 152". **Effective** for tax years beginning after 12-31-2004.

[Sec. 105(d)—Repealed]

Amendments

• 1986, Tax Reform Act of 1986 (P.L. 99-514)

P.L. 99-514, §1301(j)(9):

Amended Code Sec. 105(d)(5)(C) by striking out "section 143(a)" and inserting in lieu thereof "section 7703(a)". **Effective** for bonds issued after 8-15-86.

• 1983, Social Security Amendments of 1983 (P.L. 98-21)

P.L. 98-21, §122(b):

Repealed Code Sec. 105(d). **Effective** for tax years beginning after 1983 as provided in Act Sec. 122(d). Prior to repeal, Code Sec. 105(d) read as follows:

(d) CERTAIN DISABILITY PAYMENTS.—

(1) IN GENERAL.—In the case of a taxpayer who—

(A) has not attained age 65 before the close of the taxable year, and

(B) retired on disability and, when he retired, was permanently and totally disabled,

gross income does not include amounts referred to in subsection (a) if such amounts constitute wages or payments in lieu of wages for a period during which the employee is absent from work on account of permanent and total disability.

(2) LIMITATION.—This subsection shall not apply to the extent that the amounts referred to in paragraph (1) exceed a weekly rate of $100.

(3) PHASEOUT OVER $15,000.—If the adjusted gross income of the taxpayer for the taxable year (determined without regard to this subsection and section 221) exceeds $15,000, the amount which but for this paragraph would be excluded under this subsection for the taxable year shall be reduced by an amount equal to the excess of the adjusted gross income (as so determined) over $15,000.

(4) PERMANENT AND TOTAL DISABILITY DEFINED.—For purposes of this subsection, an individual is permanently and totally disabled if he is unable to engage in any substantial gainful activity by reason of any medically determinable physical or mental impairment which can be expected to result in death or which has lasted or can be expected to last for a continuous period of not less than 12 months. An individual shall not be considered to be permanently and totally disabled unless he furnishes proof of the existence thereof in such form and manner, and at such times, as the Secretary may require.

(5) SPECIAL RULES FOR MARRIED COUPLES.—

(A) MARRIED COUPLE MUST FILE JOINT RETURN.—Except in the case of a husband and wife who live apart at all times during the taxable year, if the taxpayer is married at the close of the taxable year, the exclusion provided by this subsection shall be allowed only if the taxpayer and his spouse file a joint return for the taxable year.

(B) APPLICATION OF PARAGRAPHS (2) AND (3).—In the case of a joint return—

(i) paragraph (2) shall be applied separately with respect to each spouse, but

(ii) paragraph (3) shall be applied with respect to their combined adjusted gross income.

(C) DETERMINATION OF MARITAL STATUS.—For purposes of this subsection, marital status shall be determined under section 7703(a).

(D) JOINT RETURN DEFINED.—For purposes of this subsection, the term "joint return" means the joint return of a husband and wife made under section 6013.

(6) COORDINATION WITH SECTION 72.—In the case of an individual described in subparagraphs (A) and (B) of paragraph (1), for purposes of section 72 the annuity starting date shall not be deemed to occur before the beginning of the taxable year in which the taxpayer attains age 65, or before the beginning of an earlier taxable year for which the taxpayer makes an irrevocable election not to seek the benefits of this subsection for such year and all subsequent years.

P.L. 98-21, §122(d), provides:

(d) EFFECTIVE DATE.—

(1) IN GENERAL.—The amendments made by this section shall apply to taxable years beginning after December 31, 1983.

(2) TRANSITIONAL RULE.—If an individual's annuity starting date was deferred under section 105(d)(6) of the Internal Revenue Code of 1954 (as in effect on the day before the date of the enactment of this section), such deferral shall end on the first day of such individual's first taxable year beginning after December 31, 1983.

• 1981, Economic Recovery Tax Act of 1981 (P.L. 97-34)

P.L. 97-34, §103(c)(2):

Amended Code Sec. 105(d)(3) by inserting "and section 221" after "subsection" the first place it appeared. **Effective** for tax years beginning after 12-31-81.

• 1978, Revenue Act of 1978 (P.L. 95-600)

P.L. 95-600, §701(c)(1):

Amended Code Sec. 105(d) by striking out paragraphs (4) and (6), by redesignating paragraph (5) as paragraph (4) and paragraph (7) as paragraph (6), and by inserting after paragraph (4) a new paragraph (5) to read as above. **Effective** as if it were included in Code Sec. 105(d) as such section was amended by P.L. 94-455, §505(a), below. Prior to amendment, Code Sec. 105(d)(4)—(7) read as follows:

"(4) MARRIED COUPLE MUST FILE JOINT RETURN.—Except in the case of a husband and wife who live apart at all times during the taxable year, if the taxpayer is married at the close of the taxable year, the exclusion provided by this subsection shall be allowed only if the taxpayer and his spouse file a joint return for the taxable year. For purposes of this subsection, marital status shall be determined under section 143.

(5) PERMANENT AND TOTAL DISABILITY DEFINED.—For purposes of this subsection, an individual is permanently and totally disabled if he is unable to engage in any substantial gainful activity by reason of any medically determinable physical or mental impairment which can be expected to result in death or which has lasted or can be expected to last for a continuous period of not less than 12 months. An individual shall not be considered to be permanently and totally disabled unless he furnishes proof of the existence thereof in such form and manner, and at such times, as the Secretary may require.

(6) JOINT RETURN.—For purposes of this subsection, the term "joint return" means the joint return of a husband and wife made under section 6013.

(7) COORDINATION WITH SECTION 72.—In the case of an individual described in subparagraphs (A) and (B) of paragraph (1), for purposes of section 72 the annuity starting date shall not be deemed to occur before the beginning of the taxable year in which the taxpayer attains age 65, or before the beginning of an earlier taxable year for which the taxpayer makes an irrevocable election not to seek the benefits of this subsection for such year and all subsequent years."

• 1977, Tax Reduction and Simplification Act of 1977 (P.L. 95-30)

P.L. 95-30, §301(c)-(e), as amended by P.L. 95-600, §701(c)(2)(B), provides:

(c) REVOCATION OF ELECTION.—Any election made under section 105(d)(6) of the Internal Revenue Code of 1954 or under section 505(d) of the Tax Reform Act of 1976 for a taxable year beginning in 1976 may be revoked (in such manner as may be prescribed by regulations) at any time before the expiration of the period for assessing a deficiency with respect to such taxable year (determined without regard to subsection (d) of this section).

(d) PERIOD FOR ASSESSING DEFICIENCY.—In the case of any revocation made under subsection (c), the period for assessing a deficiency with respect to any taxable year affected by the revocation shall not expire before the date which is 1 year after the date of the making of the revocation, and, notwithstanding any law or rule of law, such deficiency, to the extent attributable to such revocation, may be assessed at any time during such 1-year period.

(e) EFFECTIVE DATE.—The amendments made by this section shall take effect on October 4, 1976, but shall not apply—

(1) with respect to any taxpayer who makes or has made an election under section 105(d)(6) of the Internal Revenue Code of 1954 or under section 505(d) of the Tax Reform Act of 1976 (as such sections were in effect before the enactment of this Act) for a taxable year beginning in 1976, if such election is not revoked under subsection (c) of this section, and

(2) with respect to any taxpayer (other than a taxpayer described in paragraph (1)) who has an annuity starting date at the beginning of a taxable year beginning in 1976 by reason of the amendments made by section 505 of the Tax Reform Act of 1976 (as in effect before the enactment of this Act), unless such person elects (in such manner as the Secretary of the Treasury or his delegate may by regulations prescribe) to have such amendments apply.

• 1976, Tax Reform Act of 1976 (P.L. 94-455)

P.L. 94-455, §505(a) (as amended by P.L. 95-30, §301 and P.L. 95-600, §701(c)(2)(A), (B)):

Amended Code Sec. 105(d). **Effective** for tax years beginning after 12-31-75, but P.L. 95-30, §301(a) [see below]delayed this effective date until tax years beginning after 12-31-76. Prior to amendment, Code Sec. 105(d) read as follows:

(d) WAGE CONTINUATION PLANS.—Gross income does not include amounts referred to in subsection (a) if such amounts constitute wages or payments in lieu of wages for a period during which the employee is absent from work on account of personal injuries or sickness; but this subsection shall not apply to the extent that such amounts exceed a weekly rate of $100. The preceding sentence shall not apply to amounts attributable to the first 30 calendar days in such period, if such amounts are at a rate which exceeds 75 percent of the regular weekly rate of wages of the employee (as determined under regulations prescribed by the Secretary or his delegate). If amounts attributable to the first 30 calendar days in such period are at a rate which does not exceed 75 percent of the regular weekly rate of wages of the employee, the first sentence of this subsection (1) shall not apply to the extent that such amounts exceed a weekly rate of $75, and (2) shall not apply to amounts attributable to the first 7 calendar days in such period unless the employee is hospitalized on account of personal injuries or sickness for at least one day during such period. If such amounts are not paid on the basis of a weekly pay period, the Secretary or his delegate shall by regulations prescribe the method of determining the weekly rate at which such amounts are paid.

P.L. 94-455, §505(c), as amended by P.L. 95-30, §301(b), provides as follows:

(c) SPECIAL RULE FOR EXISTING PERMANENT AND TOTAL DISABILITY CASES.—In the case of any individual who—

(1) retired before January 1, 1977,

(2) either retired on disability or was entitled to retire on disability, and

(3) on January 1, 1976, was permanently and totally disabled (within the meaning of Code Sec. 105(d)(4), as amended by P.L. 95-600, §701(c)(2)(A)).

such individual shall be deemed to have met the requirements of section 105(d)(1)(B) of such Code (as amended by subsection (a) of this section).

P.L. 94-455, §505(d), provides as follows:

(d) SPECIAL RULE FOR COORDINATION WITH SECTION 72.—In the case of an individual who—

(1) retired on disability before January 1, 1977, and

(2) on December 31, 1975, or December 31, 1976, was entitled to exclude any amount with respect to such retirement disability from gross income under section 105(d) of the Internal Revenue Code of 1954,

for purposes of section 72 the annuity starting date shall not be deemed to occur before the beginning of the taxable year in which the taxpayer attains age 65, or before the beginning of an earlier taxable year for which the taxpayer makes an irrevocable election not to seek the benefits of such section 105(d) for such year and all subsequent years.

P.L. 94-455, §505(f), as added by P.L. 95-30, §301(a), provides:

(f) EFFECTIVE DATE FOR SUBSECTION (a).—The amendment made by subsection (a) shall apply to taxable years beginning after December 31, 1976.

• 1964, Revenue Act of 1964 (P.L. 88-272)

P.L. 88-272, §205(a):

Substituted the second and third sentences for the former second sentence of subsection (d). **Effective** for amounts attributable to periods of absence commencing after 12-31-63. Prior to amendment, the second sentence read as follows:

"In the case of a period during which the employee is absent from work on account of sickness, the preceding sentence shall not apply to amounts attributable to the first 7 calendar days in such period unless the employee is hospitalized on account of sickness for at least one day during such period."

[Sec. 105(e)]

(e) ACCIDENT AND HEALTH PLANS.—For purposes of this section and section 104—

(1) amounts received under an accident or health plan for employees, and

(2) amounts received from a sickness and disability fund for employees maintained under the law of a State, or the District of Columbia,

shall be treated as amounts received through accident or health insurance.

Amendments

• 1976, Tax Reform Act of 1976 (P.L. 94-455)

P.L. 94-455, §1901(c)(2):

Amended Code Sec. 105(e)(2) by striking out "a Territory," following "a State,". **Effective** for tax years beginning after 12-31-76.

[Sec. 105(f)]

(f) RULES FOR APPLICATION OF SECTION 213.— For purposes of section 213(a) (relating to medical, dental, etc., expenses) amounts excluded from gross income under subsection (c) or (d) shall not be considered as compensation (by insurance or otherwise) for expenses paid for medical care.

[Sec. 105(g)]

(g) SELF-EMPLOYED INDIVIDUAL NOT CONSIDERED AN EMPLOYEE.—For purposes of this section, the term "employee" does not include an individual who is an employee within the meaning of section 401(c)(1) (relating to self-employed individuals).

[Sec. 105(h)]

(h) AMOUNT PAID TO HIGHLY COMPENSATED INDIVIDUALS UNDER A DISCRIMINATORY SELF-INSURED MEDICAL EXPENSE REIMBURSEMENT PLAN.—

(1) IN GENERAL.—In the case of amounts paid to a highly compensated individual under a self-insured medical reimbursement plan which does not satisfy the requirements of paragraph (2) for a plan year, subsection (b) shall not apply to such amounts to the extent they constitute an excess reimbursement of such highly compensated individual.

(2) PROHIBITION OF DISCRIMINATION.—A self-insured medical reimbursement plan satisfies the requirements of this paragraph only if—

(A) the plan does not discriminate in favor of highly compensated individuals as to eligibility to participate; and

(B) the benefits provided under the plan do not discriminate in favor of participants who are highly compensated individuals.

(3) NONDISCRIMINATORY ELIGIBILITY CLASSIFICATIONS.—

(A) IN GENERAL.—A self-insured medical reimbursement plan does not satisfy the requirements of subparagraph (A) of paragraph (2) unless such plan benefits—

(i) 70 percent or more of all employees, or 80 percent or more of all the employees who are eligible to benefit under the plan if 70 percent or more of all employees are eligible to benefit under the plan; or

(ii) such employees as qualify under a classification set up by the employer and found by the Secretary not to be discriminatory in favor of highly compensated individuals.

(B) EXCLUSION OF CERTAIN EMPLOYEES.—For purposes of subparagraph (A), there may be excluded from consideration—

(i) employees who have not completed 3 years of service;

(ii) employees who have not attained age 25;

(iii) part-time or seasonal employees;

(iv) employees not included in the plan who are included in a unit of employees covered by an agreement between employee representatives and one or more employers which the Secretary finds to be a collective bargaining agreement, if accident and health benefits were the subject of good faith bargaining between such employee representatives and such employer or employers; and

(v) employees who are nonresident aliens and who receive no earned income (within the meaning of section 911(d)(2)) from the employer which constitutes income from sources within the United States (within the meaning of section 861(a)(3)).

(4) NONDISCRIMINATORY BENEFITS.— A self-insured medical reimbursement plan does not meet the requirements of subparagraph (B) of paragraph (2) unless all benefits provided for participants who are highly compensated individuals are provided for all other participants.

(5) HIGHLY COMPENSATED INDIVIDUAL DEFINED.—For purposes of this subsection, the term "highly compensated individual" means an individual who is—

(A) one of the 5 highest paid officers,

(B) a shareholder who owns (with the application of section 318) more than 10 percent in value of the stock of the employer, or

(C) among the highest paid 25 percent of all employees (other than employees described in paragraph (3)(B) who are not participants).

(6) SELF-INSURED MEDICAL REIMBURSEMENT PLAN.— The term "self-insured medical reimbursement plan" means a plan of an employer to reimburse employees for expenses referred to in subsection (b) for which reimbursement is not provided under a policy of accident and health insurance.

(7) EXCESS REIMBURSEMENT OF HIGHLY COMPENSATED INDIVIDUAL.— For purposes of this section, the excess reimbursement of a highly compensated individual which is attributable to a self-insured medical reimbursement plan is—

(A) in the case of a benefit available to highly compensated individuals but not to all other participants (or which otherwise fails to satisfy the requirements of paragraph (2)(B)), the amount reimbursed under the plan to the employee with respect to such benefit, and

(B) in the case of benefits (other than benefits described in subparagraph (A) paid to a highly compensated individual by a plan which fails to satisfy the requirements of paragraph (2), the total amount reimbursed to the highly compensated individual for the plan year multiplied by a fraction—

(i) the numerator of which is the total amount reimbursed to all participants who are highly compensated individuals under the plan for the plan year, and

(ii) the denominator of which is the total amount reimbursed to all employees under the plan for such plan year.

In determining the fraction under subparagraph (B), there shall not be taken into account any reimbursement which is attributable to a benefit described in subparagraph (A).

(8) CERTAIN CONTROLLED GROUPS, ETC.—All employees who are treated as employed by a single employer under subsection (b), (c), or (m) of section 414 shall be treated as employed by a single employer for purposes of this section.

(9) REGULATIONS.—The Secretary shall prescribe such regulations as may be necessary to carry out the provisions of this section.

(10) TIME OF INCLUSION.— Any amount paid for a plan year that is included in income by reason of this subsection shall be treated as received or accrued in the taxable year of the participant in which the plan year ends.

Amendments

• 1989 (P.L. 101-140)

P.L. 101-140, §203(a)(1), provides:

Code Sec. 105(h)-(i), as amended by section 1151(c)(2) of the Tax Reform Act of 1986 (P.L. 99-514), shall be applied as if the amendment made by such section had not been enacted. **Effective** as if included in section 1151 of P.L. 99-514.

• 1989 (P.L. 101-136)

P.L. 101-136, §528, provides:

SEC. 528. No monies appropriated by this Act may be used to implement or enforce section 1151 of the Tax Reform Act of 1986 or the amendments made by such section.

• 1986, Tax Reform Act of 1986 (P.L. 99-514)

P.L. 99-514, §1151(c)(2):

Amended Code Sec. 105 by striking out subsection (h) and by redesignating subsection (i) as subsection (h). For the **effective** date, see Act Sec. 1151(k), below.

P.L. 99-514, §1151(k), provides:

(k) EFFECTIVE DATES.—

(1) IN GENERAL.—The amendments made by this section shall apply to years beginning after the later of—

(A) December 31, 1987, or

(B) the earlier of—

(i) the date which is 3 months after the date on which the Secretary of the Treasury or his delegate issues such regulations as are necessary to carry out the provisions of section 89 of the Internal Revenue Code of 1986 (as added by this section), or

(ii) December 31, 1988.

(2) SPECIAL RULE FOR COLLECTIVE BARGAINING PLAN.—In the case of a plan maintained pursuant to 1 or more collective bargaining agreements between employee representatives and 1 or more employers ratified before March 1, 1986, the amendments made by this section shall apply to employees covered by such an agreement in years beginning before the earlier of—

(A) the date on which the last of such collective bargaining agreements terminates (determined without regard to any extension thereof after February 28, 1986), or

(B) January 1, 1991.

A plan shall not be required to take into account employees to which the preceding sentence applies for purposes of applying section 89 of the Internal Revenue Code of 1986 (as added by this section) to employees to which the preceding sentence does not apply for any year preceding the year described in the preceding sentence.

(3) EXCEPTION FOR CERTAIN GROUP-TERM INSURANCE PLANS.—In the case of a plan described in section 223(d)(2) of the Tax Reform Act of 1984, such plan shall be treated as meeting the requirements of section 89 of the Internal Revenue Code of 1986 (as added by this section) with respect to individuals described in section 233(d)(2) of such Act. An employer may elect to disregard such individuals in applying section 89 of such Code (as so added) to other employees of the employer.

(4) SPECIAL RULE FOR CHURCH PLANS.—In the case of a church plan (within the meaning of section 414(e)(3) of the Internal Revenue Code of 1986) maintaining an insured accident and health plan, the amendments made by this section shall apply to years beginning after December 31, 1988.

(5) CAFETERIA PLANS.—The amendments made by subsection (d)(2) shall apply to taxable years beginning after December 31, 1983.

• 1981, Economic Recovery Tax Act of 1981 (P.L. 97-34)

P.L. 97-34, §111(b)(4):

Amended Code Sec. 105(h)(3)(B)(v) by striking out "section 911(b)" and inserting in lieu thereof "section 911(d)(2)". **Effective** with respect to tax years beginning after 12-31-81.

• **1980, Miscellaneous Revenue Act of 1980 (P.L. 96-605)**

P.L. 96-605, §201(b)(1):

Amended Code Sec. 105(h)(8) by striking out "subsection (b) or (c) of section 414" and inserting in lieu thereof "subsection (b), (c), or (m) of section 414", and by inserting " CONTROLLED GROUPS, ETC." for " CONTROLLED GROUPS" in the paragraph heading. **Effective** for plan years ending after 11-30-80. However, in the case of a plan in existence on 11-30-80, the amendments are applicable to plan years beginning after 11-30-80. P.L. 96-613, §5(b)(1), also signed 12-28-80, made the identical amendments.

• **1980, Technical Corrections Act of 1979 (P.L. 96-222)**

P.L. 96-222, §103(a)(13)(B):

Amended Code Sec. 105(h)(3)(A)(ii) by striking out "highly compensated participants" and inserting "highly compensated individuals". **Effective** for tax years beginning after 12-31-79.

P.L. 96-222, §103(a)(13)(C):

Amended Code Sec. 105(h)(7)(A). **Effective** for tax years beginning after 12-31-79. Prior to amendment, Code Sec. 105(h)(7)(A) read as follows:

(A) in the case of a benefit available to a highly compensated individual but not to a broad cross-section of employees, the amount reimbursed under the plan to the employee with respect to such benefit, and

P.L. 96-222, §103(a)(13)(D):

Amended Act Sec. 366(b) of the Revenue Act of 1978 to read as follows:

(b) EFFECTIVE DATE.—The amendment made by this section shall apply to amounts reimbursed after December 31, 1979. For purposes of applying such amendment, there shall not be taken into account any amount reimbursed before January 1, 1980.

• **1978, Revenue Act of 1978 (P.L. 95-600)**

P.L. 95-600, §366:

Amended Code Sec. 105 by adding subsection (h). **Effective** for tax years beginning after 12-31-79 [but, see P.L. 96-222, §103(b)(13)(o), above.—CCH].

• **1962, Self-Employed Individuals Tax Retirement Act of 1962 (P.L. 87-792)**

P.L. 87-792, §7:

Added subsection (g) to Code Sec. 105. **Effective** 1-1-63.

[Sec. 105(i)]

(i) SICK PAY UNDER RAILROAD UNEMPLOYMENT INSURANCE ACT.—Notwithstanding any other provision of law, gross income includes benefits paid under section 2(a) of the Railroad Unemployment Insurance Act for days of sickness; except to the extent such sickness (as determined in accordance with standards prescribed by the Railroad Retirement Board) is the result of on-the-job injury.

Amendments

• **1989 (P.L. 101-140)**

P.L. 101-140, §203(a)(1), provides:

Code Sec. 105(h)-(i), as amended by section 1151(c)(2) of P.L. 99-514, shall be applied as if the amendment had not been enacted. **Effective** as if included in section 1151 of P.L. 99-514.

• **1989 (P.L. 101-136)**

P.L. 101-136, §528, provides:

SEC. 528. No monies appropriated by this Act may be used to implement or enforce section 1151 of the Tax Reform Act of 1986 or the amendments made by such section.

• **1986, Tax Reform Act of 1986 (P.L. 99-514)**

P.L. 99-514, §1151(c)(2):

Amended Code Sec. 105 by redesignating subsection (i) as subsection (h).

• **1983, Railroad Retirement Solvency Act of 1983 (P.L. 98-76)**

P.L. 98-76, §241(a):

Added Code Sec. 105(i). **Effective** for amounts received after 12-31-83, in tax years ending after such date.

[Sec. 105(j)]

(j) SPECIAL RULE FOR CERTAIN GOVERNMENTAL PLANS.—

(1) IN GENERAL.—For purposes of subsection (b), amounts paid (directly or indirectly) to the taxpayer from an accident or health plan described in paragraph (2) shall not fail to be excluded from gross income solely because such plan, on or before January 1, 2008, provides for reimbursements of health care expenses of a deceased plan participant's beneficiary.

(2) PLAN DESCRIBED.—An accident or health plan is described in this paragraph if such plan is funded by a medical trust that is established in connection with a public retirement system and that—

(A) has been authorized by a State legislature, or

(B) has received a favorable ruling from the Internal Revenue Service that the trust's income is not includible in gross income under section 115.

Amendments

• **2008, Worker, Retiree, and Employer Recovery Act of 2008 (P.L. 110-458)**

P.L. 110-458, §124(a):

Amended Code Sec. 105 by adding at the end a new subsection (j). **Effective** for payments before, on, or after 12-23-2008.

[Sec. 106]

SEC. 106. CONTRIBUTIONS BY EMPLOYER TO ACCIDENT AND HEALTH PLANS.

[Sec. 106(a)]

(a) GENERAL RULE.—Except as otherwise provided in this section, gross income of an employee does not include employer-provided coverage under an accident or health plan.

[Sec. 106(b)]

(b) CONTRIBUTIONS TO ARCHER MSAS.—

(1) IN GENERAL.—In the case of an employee who is an eligible individual, amounts contributed by such employee's employer to any Archer MSA of such employee shall be treated as employer-provided coverage for medical expenses under an accident or health plan to the extent such amounts do not exceed the limitation under section 220(b)(1) (determined without regard to this subsection) which is applicable to such employee for such taxable year.

(2) NO CONSTRUCTIVE RECEIPT.—No amount shall be included in the gross income of any employee solely because the employee may choose between the contributions referred to in paragraph (1) and employer contributions to another health plan of the employer.

(3) SPECIAL RULE FOR DEDUCTION OF EMPLOYER CONTRIBUTIONS.—Any employer contribution to an Archer MSA, if otherwise allowable as a deduction under this chapter, shall be allowed only for the taxable year in which paid.

(4) EMPLOYER MSA CONTRIBUTIONS REQUIRED TO BE SHOWN ON RETURN.—Every individual required to file a return under section 6012 for the taxable year shall include on such return the aggregate amount contributed by employers to the Archer MSAs of such individual or such individual's spouse for such taxable year.

(5) MSA CONTRIBUTIONS NOT PART OF COBRA COVERAGE.—Paragraph (1) shall not apply for purposes of section 4980B.

(6) DEFINITIONS.—For purposes of this subsection, the terms "eligible individual" and "Archer MSA" have the respective meanings given to such terms by section 220.

(7) CROSS REFERENCE.—

For penalty on failure by employer to make comparable contributions to the Archer MSAs of comparable employees, see section 4980E.

Amendments

• 2000, Community Renewal Tax Relief Act of 2000 (P.L. 106-554)

P.L. 106-554, §202(a)(2):

Amended Code Sec. 106(b) by striking "medical savings account" each place it appears in the text and inserting "Archer MSA". **Effective** 12-21-2000.

P.L. 106-554, §202(b)(2)(A):

Amended Code Sec. 106(b)(4) and (7) by striking "medical savings accounts" each place it appears in the text and inserting "Archer MSAs". **Effective** 12-21-2000.

P.L. 106-554, §202(b)(6):

Amended the heading for Code Sec. 106(b) by striking "MEDICAL SAVINGS ACCOUNTS" and inserting "ARCHER MSAS". **Effective** 12-21-2000.

P.L. 106-554, §202(b)(10):

Amended Code Sec. 106(b) by striking "a Archer" and inserting "an Archer". **Effective** 12-21-2000.

• 1996, Health Insurance Portability and Accountability Act of 1996 (P.L. 104-191)

P.L. 104-191, §301(c)(1):

Amended Code Sec. 106. **Effective** for tax years beginning after 12-31-96. Prior to amendment, Code Sec. 106 read as follows:

SEC. 106. CONTRIBUTIONS BY EMPLOYER TO ACCIDENT AND HEALTH PLANS.

Gross income of an employee does not include employer-provided coverage under an accident or health plan.

[Sec. 106(c)]

(c) INCLUSION OF LONG-TERM CARE BENEFITS PROVIDED THROUGH FLEXIBLE SPENDING ARRANGEMENTS.—

(1) IN GENERAL.—Effective on and after January 1, 1997, gross income of an employee shall include employer-provided coverage for qualified long-term care services (as defined in section 7702B(c)) to the extent that such coverage is provided through a flexible spending or similar arrangement.

(2) FLEXIBLE SPENDING ARRANGEMENT.—For purposes of this subsection, a flexible spending arrangement is a benefit program which provides employees with coverage under which—

(A) specified incurred expenses may be reimbursed (subject to reimbursement maximums and other reasonable conditions), and

(B) the maximum amount of reimbursement which is reasonably available to a participant for such coverage is less than 500 percent of the value of such coverage.

In the case of an insured plan, the maximum amount reasonably available shall be determined on the basis of the underlying coverage.

Amendments

• 1996, Health Insurance Portability and Accountability Act of 1996 (P.L. 104-191)

P.L. 104-191, §321(c)(2):

Amended Code Sec. 106, as amended by Act Sec. 301(c), by adding at the end a new subsection (c). For the **effective** date and special rules, see Act Sec. 321(f)-(g), below.

P.L. 104-191, §321(f)-(g), provides:

(f) EFFECTIVE DATES.—

(1) GENERAL EFFECTIVE DATES.—

(A) IN GENERAL.—Except as provided in subparagraph (B), the amendments made by this section shall apply to contracts issued after December 31, 1996.

(B) RESERVE METHOD.—The amendment made by subsection (b) shall apply to contracts issued after December 31, 1997.

(2) CONTINUATION OF EXISTING POLICIES.—In the case of any contract issued before January 1, 1997, which met the long-term care insurance requirements of the State in which the contract was sitused at the time the contract was issued—

(A) such contract shall be treated for purposes of the Internal Revenue Code of 1986 as a qualified long-term care insurance contract (as defined in section 7702B(b) of such Code), and

(B) services provided under, or reimbursed by, such contract shall be treated for such purposes as qualified long-term care services (as defined in section 7702B(c) of such Code).

In the case of an individual who is covered on December 31, 1996, under a State long-term care plan (as defined in section 7702B(f)(2) of such Code), the terms of such plan on such date shall be treated for purposes of the preceding sentence as a contract issued on such date which met the long-term care insurance requirements of such State.

(3) EXCHANGES OF EXISTING POLICIES.—If, after the date of enactment of this Act and before January 1, 1998, a contract providing for long-term care insurance coverage is exchanged solely for a qualified long-term care insurance contract (as defined in section 7702B(b) of such Code), no gain or loss shall be recognized on the exchange. If, in addition to a qualified long-term care insurance contract, money or other property is received in the exchange, then any gain shall be recognized to the extent of the sum of the money and the fair market value of the other property received. For purposes of this paragraph, the cancellation of a contract providing for long-term care insurance coverage and reinvestment of the cancellation proceeds in a qualified long-term care insurance contract within 60 days thereafter shall be treated as an exchange.

(4) ISSUANCE OF CERTAIN RIDERS PERMITTED.—For purposes of applying sections 101(f), 7702, and 7702A of the Internal Revenue Code of 1986 to any contract—

(A) the issuance of a rider which is treated as a qualified long-term care insurance contract under section 7702B, and

(B) the addition of any provision required to conform any other long-term care rider to be so treated,

shall not be treated as a modification or material change of such contract.

(5) APPLICATION OF PER DIEM LIMITATION TO EXISTING CONTRACTS.—The amount of per diem payments made under a contract issuedon or before July 31, 1996, with respect to an insured which are excludable from gross income by reason of section 7702B of the Internal Revenue Code of 1986 (as added by this section) shall not be reduced under subsection (d)(2)(B) thereof by reason of reimbursements received under a contract issued on or before such date. The preceding sentence shall cease to apply as of the date (after July 31, 1996) such contract is exchanged or there is any contract modification which results in an increase in the amount of such per diem payments or the amount of such reimbursements.

(g) LONG-TERM CARE STUDY REQUEST.—The Chairman of the Committee on Ways and Means of the House of Representatives and the Chairman of the Committee on Finance of the Senate shall jointly request the National Association of Insurance Commissioners, in consultation with representatives of the insurance industry and consumer organizations, to formulate, develop, and conduct a study to determine the marketing and other effects of per diem limits on certain types of long-term care policies. If the National Association of Insurance Commissioners agrees to the study request, the National Association of Insurance Commissioners shall report the results of its study to such committees not later than 2 years after accepting the request.

• 1989 (P.L. 101-136)

P.L. 101-136, §528, provides:

SEC. 528. No monies appropriated by this Act may be used to implement or enforce section 1151 of the Tax Reform Act of 1986 or the amendments made by such section.

• 1989, Omnibus Budget Reconciliation Act of 1989 (P.L. 101-239)

P.L. 101-239, §7862(c)(1)(A):

Amended Code Sec. 106(b)(2)(C) by striking the last sentence thereof. **Effective** as if included in the provision of P.L. 99-514 to which it relates. Prior to amendment, the last sentence of Code Sec. 106(b)(2)(C) read as follows:

Under regulations, rules similar to the rules of subsections (a) and (b) of section 52 (relating to employers under common control) shall apply for purposes of subparagraph (A).

• 1988, Technical and Miscellaneous Revenue Act of 1988 (P.L. 100-647)

P.L. 100-647, §1018(t)(7)(A)(i)-(ii):

Amended Code Sec. 106(b)(1) by striking out "any amount contributed by an employer" and inserting in lieu thereof "any employer-provided coverage", and by striking out "to a group" and inserting in lieu thereof "under a group". **Effective** as if included in the provision of P.L. 99-514 to which it relates.

P.L. 100-647, §3011(b)(1):

Amended Code Sec. 106. For a special **effective** date, see Act Sec. 3011(d), below. Prior to amendment, Code Sec. 106 read as follows:

SEC. 106. CONTRIBUTIONS BY EMPLOYER TO ACCIDENT AND HEALTH PLANS.

(a) IN GENERAL.—Gross income of an employee does not include employer-provided coverage under an accident or health plan.

(b) EXCEPTION FOR HIGHLY COMPENSATED INDIVIDUALS WHERE PLAN FAILS TO PROVIDE CERTAIN CONTINUATION COVERAGE.—

(1) IN GENERAL.—Subsection (a) shall not apply to any employer-provided coverage on behalf of a highly compensated employee (within the meaning of section 414(q)) under a group health plan maintained by such employer unless all such plans maintained by such employer meet the continuing coverage requirements of section 162(k).

(2) EXCEPTION FOR CERTAIN PLANS.—Paragraph (1) shall not apply to any—

(A) group health plan for any calendar year if all employers maintaining such plan normally employed fewer than 20 employees on a typical business day during the preceding calendar year,

(B) governmental plan (within the meaning of section 414(d)), or

(C) church plan (within the meaning of section 414(e)).

(3) GROUP HEALTH PLAN.—For purposes of this subsection, the term "group health plan" has the meaning given such term by section 162(i)(3).

P.L. 100-647, §3011(d), provides:

(d) EFFECTIVE DATE.—The amendments made by this section shall apply to taxable years beginning after December 31, 1988, but shall not apply to any plan for any plan year to which section 162(k) of the Internal Revenue Code of 1986 (as in effect on the day before the date of the enactment of this Act) did not apply by reason of section 10001(e)(2) of the Consolidated Omnibus Budget Reconciliation Act of 1985.

• 1986, Tax Reform Act of 1986 (P.L. 99-514)

P.L. 99-514, §1114(b)(1):

Amended Code Sec. 106(b)(1) by striking out "highly compensated individual (within the meaning of section 105(h)(5))" and inserting in lieu thereof "highly compensated employee (within the meaning of section 414(q))". **Effective** for years beginning after 12-31-86.

P.L. 99-514, §1151(j)(2):

Amended Code Sec. 106(a). For the **effective** date, see Act Sec. 1151(k) following Code Sec. 105. Prior to amendment, Code Sec. 106(a) read as follows.

(a) IN GENERAL.—Gross income does not include contributions by the employer to accident or health plans for compensation (through insurance or otherwise) to his employees for personal injuries or sickness.

• 1986, Consolidated Omnibus Budget Reconciliation Act of 1985 (P.L. 99-272)

P.L. 99-272, §10001(b):

Amended Code Sec. 106 by inserting "(a) In General.—" before "Gross" and by inserting at the end thereof new subsection (b). **Effective** for plan years beginning on or after 7-1-86. However, Act Sec. 10001(e)(2), below, provides a special rule.

P.L. 99-272, §10001(e)(2), provides:

(2) SPECIAL RULE FOR COLLECTIVE BARGAINING AGREEMENTS.—In the case of a group health plan maintained pursuant to one or more collective bargaining agreements between employee representatives and one or more employers ratified before the date of the enactment of this Act, the amendments made by this section shall not apply to plan years beginning before the later of—

(A) the date on which the last of the collective bargaining agreements relating to the plan terminates (determined without regard to any extension thereof agreed to after the date of the enactment of this Act), or

(B) January 1, 1987.
For purposes of subparagraph (A), any plan amendment made pursuant to a collective bargaining agreement relating to the plan which amends the plan solely to conform to any requirement added by this section shall not be treated as a termination of such collective bargaining agreement.

[Sec. 106(d)]

(d) CONTRIBUTIONS TO HEALTH SAVINGS ACCOUNTS.—

(1) IN GENERAL.—In the case of an employee who is an eligible individual (as defined in section 223(c)(1)), amounts contributed by such employee's employer to any health savings account (as defined in section 223(d)) of such employee shall be treated as employer-provided coverage for medical expenses under an accident or health plan to the extent such amounts do not exceed the limitation under section 223(b) (determined without regard to this subsection) which is applicable to such employee for such taxable year.

(2) SPECIAL RULES.—Rules similar to the rules of paragraphs (2), (3), (4), and (5) of subsection (b) shall apply for purposes of this subsection.

(3) CROSS REFERENCE.—

For penalty on failure by employer to make comparable contributions to the health savings accounts of comparable employees, see section 4980G.

Amendments

• 2003, Medicare Prescription Drug, Improvement, and Modernization Act of 2003 (P.L. 108-173)

P.L. 108-173, §1201(d)(1):

Amended Code Sec. 106 by adding at the end a new subsection (d). **Effective** for tax years beginning after 12-31-2003.

[Sec. 106(e)]

(e) FSA AND HRA TERMINATIONS TO FUND HSAS.—

(1) IN GENERAL.—A plan shall not fail to be treated as a health flexible spending arrangement or health reimbursement arrangement under this section or section 105 merely because such plan provides for a qualified HSA distribution.

(2) QUALIFIED HSA DISTRIBUTION.—The term "qualified HSA distribution" means a distribution from a health flexible spending arrangement or health reimbursement arrangement to the extent that such distribution—

(A) does not exceed the lesser of the balance in such arrangement on September 21, 2006, or as of the date of such distribution, and

(B) is contributed by the employer directly to the health savings account of the employee before January 1, 2012.

Such term shall not include more than 1 distribution with respect to any arrangement.

(3) ADDITIONAL TAX FOR FAILURE TO MAINTAIN HIGH DEDUCTIBLE HEALTH PLAN COVERAGE.—

(A) IN GENERAL.—If, at any time during the testing period, the employee is not an eligible individual, then the amount of the qualified HSA distribution—

(i) shall be includible in the gross income of the employee for the taxable year in which occurs the first month in the testing period for which such employee is not an eligible individual, and

(ii) the tax imposed by this chapter for such taxable year on the employee shall be increased by 10 percent of the amount which is so includible.

(B) EXCEPTION FOR DISABILITY OR DEATH.—Clauses (i) and (ii) of subparagraph (A) shall not apply if the employee ceases to be an eligible individual by reason of the death of the employee or the employee becoming disabled (within the meaning of section 72(m)(7)).

(4) DEFINITIONS AND SPECIAL RULES.—For purposes of this subsection—

(A) TESTING PERIOD.—The term "testing period" means the period beginning with the month in which the qualified HSA distribution is contributed to the health savings account and ending on the last day of the 12th month following such month.

(B) ELIGIBLE INDIVIDUAL.—The term "eligible individual" has the meaning given such term by section 223(c)(1).

(C) TREATMENT AS ROLLOVER CONTRIBUTION.—A qualified HSA distribution shall be treated as a rollover contribution described in section 223(f)(5).

(5) TAX TREATMENT RELATING TO DISTRIBUTIONS.—For purposes of this title—

(A) IN GENERAL.—A qualified HSA distribution shall be treated as a payment described in subsection (d).

(B) COMPARABILITY EXCISE TAX.—

(i) IN GENERAL.—Except as provided in clause (ii), section 4980G shall not apply to qualified HSA distributions.

(ii) FAILURE TO OFFER TO ALL EMPLOYEES.—In the case of a qualified HSA distribution to any employee, the failure to offer such distribution to any eligible individual covered under a high deductible health plan of the employer shall (notwithstanding section 4980G(d)) be treated for purposes of section 4980G as a failure to meet the requirements of section 4980G(b).

Amendments

• 2006, Tax Relief and Health Care Act of 2006 (P.L. 109-432)

P.L. 109-432, Division A, §302(a):

Amended Code Sec. 106 by adding at the end a new subsection (e). **Effective** for distributions on or after 12-20-2006.

»»→ Caution: Code Sec. 106(f), below, as added by P.L. 111-148, applies to expenses incurred with respect to tax years beginning after December 31, 2010.

[Sec. 106(f)]

(f) REIMBURSEMENTS FOR MEDICINE RESTRICTED TO PRESCRIBED DRUGS AND INSULIN.—For purposes of this section and section 105, reimbursement for expenses incurred for a medicine or a drug shall be treated as a reimbursement for medical expenses only if such medicine or drug is a prescribed drug (determined without regard to whether such drug is available without a prescription) or is insulin.

Amendments

• 2010, Patient Protection and Affordable Care Act (P.L. 111-148)

P.L. 111-148, §9003(c):

Amended Code Sec. 106 by adding at the end a new subsection (f). **Effective** for expenses incurred with respect to tax years beginning after 12-31-2010.

[Sec. 107]

SEC. 107. RENTAL VALUE OF PARSONAGES.

In the case of a minister of the gospel, gross income does not include—

(1) the rental value of a home furnished to him as part of his compensation; or

(2) the rental allowance paid to him as part of his compensation, to the extent used by him to rent or provide a home and to the extent such allowance does not exceed the fair rental value of the home, including furnishings and appurtenances such as a garage, plus the cost of utilities.

Amendments

• 2002, Clergy Housing Allowance Clarification Act of 2002 (P.L. 107-181)

P.L. 107-181, §2(a):

Amended Code Sec. 107 by inserting before the period at the end of paragraph (2) "and to the extent such allowance does not exceed the fair rental value of the home, including furnishings and appurtenances such as a garage, plus the cost of utilities". **Effective** for tax years beginning after 12-31-2001. For a special rule, see Act Sec. 2(b)(2)-(3), below.

P.L. 107-181, §2(b)(2)-(3), provides:

(2) RETURNS POSITIONS.—The amendment made by this section also shall apply to any taxable year beginning before January 1, 2002, for which the taxpayer—

(A) on a return filed before April 17, 2002, limited the exclusion under section 107 of the Internal Revenue Code of 1986 as provided in such amendment, or

(B) filed a return after April 16, 2002.

(3) OTHER YEARS BEFORE 2002.—Except as provided in paragraph (2), notwithstanding any prior regulation, revenue ruling, or other guidance issued by the Internal Revenue Service, no person shall be subject to the limitations added to section 107 of such Code by this Act for any taxable year beginning before January 1, 2002.

[Sec. 108]

SEC. 108. INCOME FROM DISCHARGE OF INDEBTEDNESS.

[Sec. 108(a)]

(a) EXCLUSION FROM GROSS INCOME.—

(1) IN GENERAL.—Gross income does not include any amount which (but for this subsection) would be includible in gross income by reason of the discharge (in whole or in part) of indebtedness of the taxpayer if—

(A) the discharge occurs in a title 11 case,

(B) the discharge occurs when the taxpayer is insolvent,

(C) the indebtedness discharged is qualified farm indebtedness,

(D) in the case of a taxpayer other than a C corporation, the indebtedness discharged is qualified real property business indebtedness, or

»»→ *Caution: Code Sec. 108(a)(1)(E), prior to amendment by P.L. 110-343, applies to discharges of indebtedness occurring before January 1, 2010.*

(E) the indebtedness discharged is qualified principal residence indebtedness which is discharged before January 1, 2010.

»»→ *Caution: Code Sec. 108(a)(1)(E), as amended by P.L. 110-343, applies to discharges of indebtedness occurring on or after January 1, 2010.*

(E) the indebtedness discharged is qualified principal residence indebtedness which is discharged before January 1, 2013.

(2) COORDINATION OF EXCLUSIONS.—

(A) TITLE 11 EXCLUSION TAKES PRECEDENCE.—Subparagraphs (B), (C), (D), and (E) of paragraph (1) shall not apply to a discharge which occurs in a title 11 case.

(B) INSOLVENCY EXCLUSION TAKES PRECEDENCE OVER QUALIFIED FARM EXCLUSION AND QUALIFIED REAL PROPERTY BUSINESS EXCLUSION.—Subparagraphs (C) and (D) of paragraph (1) shall not apply to a discharge to the extent the taxpayer is insolvent.

(C) PRINCIPAL RESIDENCE EXCLUSION TAKES PRECEDENCE OVER INSOLVENCY EXCLUSION UNLESS ELECTED OTHERWISE.—Paragraph (1)(B) shall not apply to a discharge to which paragraph (1)(E) applies unless the taxpayer elects to apply paragraph (1)(B) in lieu of paragraph (1)(E).

(3) INSOLVENCY EXCLUSION LIMITED TO AMOUNT OF INSOLVENCY.—In the case of a discharge to which paragraph (1)(B) applies, the amount excluded under paragraph (1)(B) shall not exceed the amount by which the taxpayer is insolvent.

Amendments

• 2008, Emergency Economic Stabilization Act of 2008 (P.L. 110-343)

P.L. 110-343, Division A, §303(a):

Amended Code Sec. 108(a)(1)(E) by striking "January 1, 2010" and inserting "January 1, 2013". **Effective** for discharges of indebtedness occurring on or after 1-1-2010.

• 2007, Mortgage Forgiveness Debt Relief Act of 2007 (P.L. 110-142)

P.L. 110-142, §2(a):

Amended Code Sec. 108(a)(1) by striking "or" at the end of subparagraph (C), by striking the period at the end of subparagraph (D) and inserting ", or", and by inserting after subparagraph (D) a new subparagraph (E). **Effective** for discharges of indebtedness on or after 1-1-2007.

P.L. 110-142, §2(c)(1):

Amended Code Sec. 108(a)(2)(A) by striking "and (D)" and inserting "(D), and (E)". **Effective** for discharges of indebtedness on or after 1-1-2007.

P.L. 110-142, §2(c)(2):

Amended Code Sec. 108(a)(2) by adding at the end a new subparagraph (C). **Effective** for discharges of indebtedness on or after 1-1-2007.

• 2005, Katrina Emergency Tax Relief Act of 2005 (P.L. 109-73)

P.L. 109-73, §401 [but see P.L. 110-343, Division C, §702, in the amendment notes for Code Sec. 1400N(a)], provides:

SEC. 401. EXCLUSIONS OF CERTAIN CANCELLATIONS OF INDEBTEDNESS BY REASON OF HURRICANE KATRINA.

(a) IN GENERAL.—For purposes of the Internal Revenue Code of 1986, gross income shall not include any amount which (but for this section) would be includible in gross income by reason of the discharge (in whole or in part) of indebtedness of a natural person described in subsection (b) by an applicable entity (as defined in section 6050P(c)(1) of such Code).

(b) PERSONS DESCRIBED.—A natural person is described in this subsection if the principal place of abode of such person on August 25, 2005, was located—

(1) in the core disaster area, or

(2) in the Hurricane Katrina disaster area (but outside the core disaster area) and such person suffered economic loss by reason of Hurricane Katrina.

(c) EXCEPTIONS.—

(1) BUSINESS INDEBTEDNESS.—Subsection (a) shall not apply to any indebtedness incurred in connection with a trade or business.

(2) REAL PROPERTY OUTSIDE CORE DISASTER AREA.—Subsection (a) shall not apply to any discharge of indebtedness to the extent that real property constituting security for such indebtedness is located outside of the Hurricane Katrina disaster area.

(d) DENIAL OF DOUBLE BENEFIT.—For purposes of the Internal Revenue Code of 1986, the amount excluded from gross income under subsection (a) shall be treated in the same manner as an amount excluded under section 108(a) of such Code.

(e) EFFECTIVE DATE.—This section shall apply to discharges made on or after August 25, 2005, and before January 1, 2007.

• 1993, Omnibus Budget Reconciliation Act of 1993 (P.L. 103-66)

P.L. 103-66, §13150(a):

Amended Code Sec. 108(a)(1) by striking "or" at the end of subparagraph (B), by striking the period at the end of subparagraph (C) and inserting ", or", and by adding at the end new subparagraph (D). **Effective** for discharges after 12-31-92, in tax years ending after such date.

P.L. 103-66, §13150(c)(1):

Amended Code Sec. 108(a)(2)(A) by striking "and (C)" and inserting ", (C), and (D)". **Effective** for discharges after 12-31-92, in tax years ending after such date.

P.L. 103-66, §13150(c)(2):

Amended Code Sec. 108(a)(2)(B). **Effective** for discharges after 12-31-92, in tax years ending after such date. Prior to amendment, Code Sec. 108(a)(2)(B) read as follows:

(B) INSOLVENCY EXCLUSION TAKES PRECEDENCE OVER QUALIFIED FARM EXCLUSION.—Subparagraph (C) of paragraph (1) shall not apply to a discharge to the extent the taxpayer is insolvent.

• 1988, Technical and Miscellaneous Revenue Act of 1988 (P.L. 100-647)

P.L. 100-647, §1004(a)(1):

Amended Code Sec. 108(a)(1) by striking out "or" at the end of subparagraph (A), by striking out the period at the end of subparagraph (B) and inserting in lieu thereof ", or" and by adding at the end thereof new subparagraph (C). **Effective** as if included in the provision of P.L. 99-514 to which it relates.

P.L. 100-647, §1004(a)(2):

Amended Code Sec. 108(a)(2). **Effective** as if included in the provision of P.L. 99-514 to which it relates. Prior to amendment, Code Sec. 108(a)(2) read as follows:

(2) COORDINATION OF EXCLUSIONS.—Subparagraph (B) of paragraph (1) shall not apply to a discharge which occurs in a title 11 case.

• 1986, Tax Reform Act of 1986 (P.L. 99-514)

P.L. 99-514, §822(a):

Amended Code Sec. 108(a)(1) by striking out subparagraph (C), by inserting "or" at the end of subparagraph (A), and by striking out ", or" at the end of subparagraph (B) and inserting in lieu thereof a period. **Effective** for discharges after 12-31-86. Prior to amendment, Code Sec. 108(a)(1)(C) read as follows:

(C) the indebtedness discharged is qualified business indebtedness.

P.L. 99-514, §822(b)(i):

Amended Code Sec. 108(a)(2). **Effective** for discharges after 12-31-86. Prior to amendment, Code Sec. 108(a)(2) read as follows:

(2) COORDINATION OF EXCLUSIONS.—

(A) TITLE 11 EXCLUSION TAKES PRECEDENCE.—Subparagraphs (B) and (C) of paragraph (1) shall not apply to a discharge which occurs in a title 11 case.

(B) INSOLVENCY EXCLUSION TAKES PRECEDENCE OVER QUALIFIED BUSINESS EXCLUSION.—Subparagraph (C) of paragraph (1) shall not apply to a discharge to the extent that the taxpayer is insolvent.

• 1980, Bankruptcy Tax Act of 1980 (P.L. 96-589)

P.L. 96-589, §2(a):

Divided Code Sec. 108 into five subsections, (a) through (e). For the text of Code Sec. 108 prior to amendment and the **effective** date of Code Sec. 108(a), see the historical comment for P.L. 96-589 under Code Sec. 108(e).

[Sec. 108(b)]

(b) REDUCTION OF TAX ATTRIBUTES.—

(1) IN GENERAL.—The amount excluded from gross income under subparagraph (A), (B), or (C) of subsection (a)(1) shall be applied to reduce the tax attributes of the taxpayer as provided in paragraph (2).

(2) TAX ATTRIBUTES AFFECTED; ORDER OF REDUCTION.—Except as provided in paragraph (5), the reduction referred to in paragraph (1) shall be made in the following tax attributes in the following order:

(A) NOL.—Any net operating loss for the taxable year of the discharge, and any net operating loss carryover to such taxable year.

(B) GENERAL BUSINESS CREDIT.—Any carryover to or from the taxable year of a discharge of an amount for purposes for determining the amount allowable as a credit under section 38 (relating to general business credit).

(C) MINIMUM TAX CREDIT.—The amount of the minimum tax credit available under section 53(b) as of the beginning of the taxable year immediately following the taxable year of the discharge.

(D) CAPITAL LOSS CARRYOVERS.—Any net capital loss for the taxable year of the discharge, and any capital loss carryover to such taxable year under section 1212.

(E) BASIS REDUCTION.—

(i) IN GENERAL.—The basis of the property of the taxpayer.

(ii) CROSS REFERENCE.—

For provisions for making the reduction described in clause (i), see section 1017.

(F) PASSIVE ACTIVITY LOSS AND CREDIT CARRYOVERS.—Any passive activity loss or credit carryover of the taxpayer under section 469(b) from the taxable year of the discharge.

(G) FOREIGN TAX CREDIT CARRYOVERS.—Any carryover to or from the taxable year of the discharge for purposes of determining the amount of the credit allowable under section 27.

(3) AMOUNT OF REDUCTION.—

(A) IN GENERAL.—Except as provided in subparagraph (B), the reductions described in paragraph (2) shall be one dollar for each dollar excluded by subsection (a).

(B) CREDIT CARRYOVER REDUCTION.—The reductions described in subparagraphs (B), (C), and (G) shall be 33$^{1}/_{3}$ cents for each dollar excluded by subsection (a). The reduction described in subparagraph (F) in any passive activity credit carryover shall be 33$^{1}/_{3}$ cents for each dollar excluded by subsection (a).

(4) ORDERING RULES.—

(A) REDUCTIONS MADE AFTER DETERMINATION OF TAX FOR YEAR.—The reductions described in paragraph (2) shall be made after the determination of the tax imposed by this chapter for the taxable year of the discharge.

(B) REDUCTIONS UNDER SUBPARAGRAPH (a) OR (d) OF PARAGRAPH (2).—The reductions described in subparagraph (A) or (D) of paragraph (2) (as the case may be) shall be made first in the loss for the taxable year of the discharge and then in the carryovers to such taxable year in the order of the taxable years from which each such carryover arose.

(C) REDUCTIONS UNDER SUBPARAGRAPHS (b) AND (g) OF PARAGRAPH (2).—The reductions described in subparagraphs (B) and (G) of paragraph (2) shall be made in the order in which carryovers are taken into account under this chapter for the taxable year of the discharge.

(5) ELECTION TO APPLY REDUCTION FIRST AGAINST DEPRECIABLE PROPERTY.—

(A) IN GENERAL.—The taxpayer may elect to apply any portion of the reduction referred to in paragraph (1) to the reduction under section 1017 of the basis of the depreciable property of the taxpayer.

(B) LIMITATION.—The amount to which an election under subparagraph (A) applies shall not exceed the aggregate adjusted bases of the depreciable property held by the taxpayer as of the beginning of the taxable year following the taxable year in which the discharge occurs.

(C) OTHER TAX ATTRIBUTES NOT REDUCED.—Paragraph (2) shall not apply to any amount to which an election under this paragraph applies.

Amendments

• 1993, Omnibus Budget Reconciliation Act of 1993 (P.L. 103-66)

P.L. 103-66, §13226(b)(1):

Amended Code Sec. 108(b)(2) by redesignating subparagraphs (C)-(E) as subparagraphs (D)-(F) and by adding after subparagraph (B) new subparagraph (C). **Effective** for discharges of indebtedness in tax years beginning after 12-31-93.

P.L. 103-66, §13226(b)(2):

Amended Code Sec. 108(b)(2), as amended by Act Sec. 13226(b)(1), by redesignating subparagraph (F) as subparagraph (G) and by adding after subparagraph (E) new subparagraph (F). **Effective** for discharges of indebtedness in tax years beginning after 12-31-93.

P.L. 103-66, §13226(b)(3)(A):

Amended Code Sec. 108(b)(3)(B). **Effective** for discharges of indebtedness in tax years beginning after 12-31-93. Prior to amendment, Code Sec. 108(b)(3)(B) read as follows:

(B) CREDIT CARRYOVER REDUCTION.—The reductions described in subparagraphs (B) and (E) of paragraph (2) shall be 33 1/3 cents for each dollar excluded by subsection (a).

P.L. 103-66, §13226(b)(3)(B):

Amended Code Sec. 108(b)(4)(B) by striking "(C)" in the text and heading thereof and inserting "(D)". **Effective** for discharges of indebtedness in tax years beginning after 12-31-93.

P.L. 103-66, §13226(b)(3)(C):

Amended Code Sec. 108(b)(4)(C) by striking "(E)" in the text and heading thereof and inserting "(G)". **Effective** for discharges of indebtedness in tax years beginning after 12-31-93.

• 1988, Technical and Miscellaneous Revenue Act of 1988 (P.L. 100-647)

P.L. 100-647, §1004(a)(3)(A)-(B):

Amended Code Sec. 108(b) by striking out "subparagraph (A) or (B)" in paragraph (1) and inserting in lieu thereof "subparagraph (A), (B), or (C)", and by striking out "in Title 11 Case or Insolvency" in the subsection heading after "Attributes". **Effective** as if included in the provision of P.L. 99-514 to which it relates.

• 1986, Tax Reform Act of 1986 (P.L. 99-514)

P.L. 99-514, §104(b)(2):

Amended Code Sec. 108(b)(3)(B) by striking out "50 cents" and inserting in lieu thereof "33 1/3 cents". **Effective** for tax years beginning after 12-31-86.

P.L. 99-514, §231(d)(3)(D):

Amended Code Sec. 108(b)(2)(B). **Effective** for tax years beginning after 12-31-85. Prior to amendment, Code Sec. 108(b)(2)(B) read as follows:

(B) RESEARCH CREDIT AND GENERAL BUSINESS CREDIT.—Any carryover to or from the taxable year of a discharge of an amount for purposes of determining the amount allowable as a credit under—

(i) section 30 (relating to credit for increasing research activities), or

(ii) section 38 (relating to general business credit).

P.L. 99-514, §1171(b)(4):

Amended Code Sec. 108(b)(2)(B) by striking out the last sentence. **Effective** for compensation paid or accrued after 12-31-86, in tax years ending after such date. Prior to amendment, the last sentence read as follows:

For purposes of this subparagraph, there shall not be taken into account any portion of a carryover which is attributable to the employee stock ownership credit determined under section 41.

P.L. 99-514, §1847(b)(7):

Amended Code Sec. 108(b)(2)(E) by striking out "section 33" and inserting in lieu thereof "section 27". **Effective** as if included in the provision of P.L. 98-369 to which it relates.

• 1984, Deficit Reduction Act of 1984 (P.L. 98-369)

P.L. 98-369, §474(r)(5):

Amended Code Sec. 108(b)(2)(B). **Effective** for tax years beginning after 12-31-83, and to carrybacks from such years. Prior to amendment, Code Sec. 108(b)(2)(B) read as follows:

(B) Certain Credit Carryovers.—Any carryover to or from the taxable year of the discharge of an amount for purposes of determining the amount of a credit allowable under—

(i) section 38 (relating to investment in certain depreciable property),

(ii) section 40 (relating to expenses of work incentive programs),

(iii) section 44B (relating to credit for employment of certain new employees),

(iv) section 44E (relating to alcohol used as a fuel), or

(v) section 44F (relating to credit for increasing research activities).

For purposes of clause (i), there shall not be taken into account any portion of a carryover which is attributable to the employee plan credit (within the meaning of section 48(o)(3)).

• 1983, Technical Corrections Act of 1982 (P.L. 97-448)

P.L. 97-448, §102(h)(1):

Amended Code Sec. 108(b)(2)(B) by striking out "or" at the end of clause (iii), by striking out the period at the end of clause (iv) and inserting in lieu thereof ", or", and by inserting after clause (iv) the following new clause (v). **Effective** as if it had been included in the provision of P.L. 97-34 to which it relates.

• 1980, Bankruptcy Tax Act of 1980 (P.L. 96-589)

P.L. 96-589, §2(a):

Divided Code Sec. 108 into five subsections, (a) through (e). For the text of Code Sec. 108 prior to amendment and the **effective** date of Code Sec. 108(b), see the historical comment for P.L. 96-589 under Code Sec. 108(e).

[Sec. 108(c)]

(c) TREATMENT OF DISCHARGE OF QUALIFIED REAL PROPERTY BUSINESS INDEBTEDNESS.—

(1) BASIS REDUCTION.—

(A) IN GENERAL.—The amount excluded from gross income under subparagraph (D) of subsection (a)(1) shall be applied to reduce the basis of the depreciable real property of the taxpayer.

(B) CROSS REFERENCE.—For provisions making the reduction described in subparagraph (A), see section 1017.

(2) LIMITATIONS.—

(A) INDEBTEDNESS IN EXCESS OF VALUE.—The amount excluded under subparagraph (D) of subsection (a)(1) with respect to any qualified real property business indebtedness shall not exceed the excess (if any) of—

(i) the outstanding principal amount of such indebtedness (immediately before the discharge), over

(ii) the fair market value of the real property described in paragraph (3)(A) (as of such time), reduced by the outstanding principal amount of any other qualified real property business indebtedness secured by such property (as of such time).

(B) OVERALL LIMITATION.—The amount excluded under subparagraph (D) of subsection (a)(1) shall not exceed the aggregate adjusted bases of depreciable real property (determined after any reductions under subsections (b) and (g)) held by the taxpayer immediately before the discharge (other than depreciable real property acquired in contemplation of such discharge).

(3) QUALIFIED REAL PROPERTY BUSINESS INDEBTEDNESS.—The term "qualified real property business indebtedness" means indebtedness which—

(A) was incurred or assumed by the taxpayer in connection with real property used in a trade or business and is secured by such real property,

(B) was incurred or assumed before January 1, 1993, or if incurred or assumed on or after such date, is qualified acquisition indebtedness, and

(C) with respect to which such taxpayer makes an election to have this paragraph apply.

Such term shall not include qualified farm indebtedness. Indebtedness under subparagraph (B) shall include indebtedness resulting from the refinancing of indebtedness under subparagraph (B) (or this sentence), but only to the extent it does not exceed the amount of the indebtedness being refinanced.

(4) QUALIFIED ACQUISITION INDEBTEDNESS.—For purposes of paragraph (3)(B), the term "qualified acquisition indebtedness" means, with respect to any real property described in paragraph (3)(A), indebtedness incurred or assumed to acquire, construct, reconstruct, or substantially improve such property.

(5) REGULATIONS.—The Secretary shall issue such regulations as are necessary to carry out this subsection, including regulations preventing the abuse of this subsection through cross-collateralization or other means.

Amendments

• 1993, Omnibus Budget Reconciliation Act of 1993 (P.L. 103-66)

P.L. 103-66, §13150(b):

Amended Code Sec. 108 by inserting after subsection (b) a new subsection (c). **Effective** for discharges after 12-31-92, in tax years ending after such date.

[Sec. 108(c)—Stricken]

Amendments

• 1986, Tax Reform Act of 1986 (P.L. 99-514)

P.L. 99-514, §822(b)(2):

Amended Code Sec. 108 by striking out subsection (c). **Effective** for discharges after 12-31-86. Prior to amendment, Code Sec. 108(c) read as follows:

(c) TAX TREATMENT OF DISCHARGE OF QUALIFIED BUSINESS INDEBTEDNESS.—In the case of a discharge of qualified business indebtedness—

(1) BASIS REDUCTION.—

(A) IN GENERAL.—The amount excluded from gross income under subparagraph (C) of subsection (a)(1) shall be applied to reduce the basis of the depreciable property of the taxpayer.

(B) CROSS REFERENCE.—

For provisions for making the reduction described in subparagraph (A), see section 1017.

(2) LIMITATION.—The amount excluded under subparagraph (C) of subsection (a)(1) shall not exceed the aggregate adjusted bases of the depreciable property held by the taxpayer as of the beginning of the taxable year following the taxable year in which the discharge occurs (determined after any reductions under subsection (b)).

• 1980, Bankruptcy Tax Act of 1980 (P.L. 96-589)

P.L. 96-589, §2(a):

Divided Code Sec. 108 into five subsections, (a) through (e). For the text of Code Sec. 108 prior to amendment and the **effective** date of Code Sec. 108(c), see the historical comment for P.L. 96-589 under Code Sec. 108(e).

[Sec. 108(d)]

(d) MEANING OF TERMS; SPECIAL RULES RELATING TO CERTAIN PROVISIONS.—

(1) INDEBTEDNESS OF TAXPAYER.—For purposes of this section, the term "indebtedness of the taxpayer" means any indebtedness—

(A) for which the taxpayer is liable, or

(B) subject to which the taxpayer holds property.

(2) TITLE 11 CASE.—For purposes of this section, the term "title 11 case" means a case under title 11 of the United States Code (relating to bankruptcy), but only if the taxpayer is under the jurisdiction of the court in such case and the discharge of indebtedness is granted by the court or is pursuant to a plan approved by the court.

(3) INSOLVENT.—For purposes of this section, the term "insolvent" means the excess of liabilities over the fair market value of assets. With respect to any discharge, whether or not the taxpayer is insolvent, and the amount by which the taxpayer is insolvent, shall be determined on the basis of the taxpayer's assets and liabilities immediately before the discharge.

(4) [Stricken.]

(5) DEPRECIABLE PROPERTY.—The term "depreciable property" has the same meaning as when used in section 1017.

(6) CERTAIN PROVISIONS TO BE APPLIED AT PARTNER LEVEL.—In the case of a partnership, subsections (a), (b), (c), and (g) shall be applied at the partner level.

(7) SPECIAL RULES FOR S CORPORATION.—

(A) CERTAIN PROVISIONS TO BE APPLIED AT CORPORATE LEVEL.—In the case of an S corporation, subsections (a), (b), (c), and (g) shall be applied at the corporate level, including by not taking into account under section 1366(a) any amount excluded under subsection (a) of this section.

(B) REDUCTION IN CARRYOVER OF DISALLOWED LOSSES AND DEDUCTIONS.—In the case of an S corporation, for purposes of subparagraph (A) of subsection (b)(2), any loss or deduction which is disallowed for the taxable year of the discharge under section 1366(d)(1) shall be treated as a net operating loss for such taxable year. The preceding sentence shall not apply to any discharge to the extent that subsection (a)(1)(D) applies to such discharge.

(C) COORDINATION WITH BASIS ADJUSTMENTS UNDER SECTION 1367(b)(2).—For purposes of subsection (e)(6), a shareholder's adjusted basis in indebtedness of an S corporation shall be determined without regard to any adjustments made under section 1367(b)(2).

(8) REDUCTIONS OF TAX ATTRIBUTES IN TITLE 11 CASES OF INDIVIDUALS TO BE MADE BY ESTATE.—In any case under chapter 7 or 11 of title 11 of the United States Code to which section 1398 applies, for purposes of paragraphs (1) and (5) of subsection (b) the estate (and not the individual) shall be treated as the taxpayer. The preceding sentence shall not apply for purposes of applying section 1017 to property transferred by the estate to the individual.

(9) TIME FOR MAKING ELECTION, ETC.—

(A) TIME.—An election under paragraph (5) of subsection (b) or under paragraph (3)(C) of subsection (c) shall be made on the taxpayer's return for the taxable year in which the discharge occurs or at such other time as may be permitted in regulations prescribed by the Secretary.

(B) REVOCATION ONLY WITH CONSENT.—An election referred to in subparagraph (A), once made, may be revoked only with the consent of the Secretary.

(C) MANNER.—An election referred to in subparagraph (A) shall be made in such manner as the Secretary may by regulations prescribe.

(10) CROSS REFERENCE.—

For provision that no reduction is to be made in the basis of exempt property of an individual debtor, see section 1017(c)(1).

Amendments

• 2002, Job Creation and Worker Assistance Act of 2002 (P.L. 107-147)

P.L. 107-147, §402(a):

Amended Code Sec. 108(d)(7)(A) by inserting before the period ", including by not taking into account under section 1366(a) any amount excluded under subsection (a) of this section". **Effective**, generally, for discharges of indebtedness after 10-11-2001, in tax years ending after such date. For an exception, see Act Sec. 402(b)(2), below.

P.L. 107-147, §402(b)(2), provides:

(2) EXCEPTION.—The amendment made by this section shall not apply to any discharge of indebtedness before March 1, 2002, pursuant to a plan of reorganization filed with a bankruptcy court on or before October 11, 2001.

• 1996, Small Business Job Protection Act of 1996 (P.L. 104-188)

P.L. 104-188, §1703(n)(2):

Amended Code Sec. 108(d)(9)(A) by striking "paragraph (3)(B)" and inserting "paragraph (3)(C)". **Effective** as if included in the provision of P.L. 103-66 to which it relates.

• 1993, Omnibus Budget Reconciliation Act of 1993 (P.L. 103-66)

P.L. 103-66, §13150(c)(3)(A)-(C):

Amended Code Sec. 108(d) by striking "subsections (a), (b), and (g)" in paragraphs (6) and (7)(A) and inserting "subsections (a), (b), (c), and (g)", by striking "SUBSECTIONS (a), (b), AND (g)" in the subsection heading and inserting "CERTAIN PROVISIONS", and by striking "SUBSECTIONS (a), (b), AND (g)" in the headings of paragraphs (6) and (7)(A) and inserting "CERTAIN PROVISIONS". **E ffective** for discharges after 12-31-92, in tax years ending after such date.

P.L. 103-66, §13150(c)(4):

Amended Code Sec. 108(d)(7)(B) by adding at the end thereof a new sentence. **Effective** for discharges after 12-31-92, in tax years ending after such date.

P.L. 103-66, §13150(c)(5):

Amended Code Sec. 108(d)(9)(A) by inserting "or under paragraph (3)(B) of subsection (c)" after "subsection (b)". **Effective** for discharges after 12-31-92, in tax years ending after such date.

• 1988, Technical and Miscellaneous Revenue Act of 1988 (P.L. 100-647)

P.L. 100-647, §1004(a)(6)(A):

Amended Code Sec. 108(d)(6) and (7) by striking out "subsections (a) and (b)" and inserting in lieu thereof "subsections (a), (b), and (g)". **Effective** as if included in the provision of P.L. 99-514 to which it relates.

P.L. 100-647, §1004(a)(6)(B):

Amended Code Sec. 108(d) by striking out "Subsections (a), and (b)" in the subsection heading and inserting in lieu thereof "Subsections (a), (b), and (g)". **Effective** as if included in the provision of P.L. 99-514 to which it relates.

P.L. 100-647, §1004(a)(6)(C):

Amended Code Sec. 108(d)(6) and (7)(A) by striking out "Subsections (a) and (b)" in the paragraph headings and inserting in lieu thereof "Subsections (a), (b), and (g)". **Effective** as if included in the provision of P.L. 99-514 to which it relates.

• 1986, Tax Reform Act of 1986 (P.L. 99-514)

P.L. 99-514, §822(b)(3)(A)-(D):

Amended Code Sec. 108(d) by striking out paragraph (4), by striking out "subsections (a), (b), and (c)" each place it appears in the heading thereof and in the text and heading of paragraphs (6) and (7) and inserting in lieu thereof "subsections (a) and (b)", by striking out the last sentence of paragraph (7)(B), and by striking out "under paragraph (4) of this subsection or" in paragraph (9) thereof. **Effective** for discharges after 12-31-86. Prior to amendment, Code Sec. 108(d) read as follows:

(d) MEANING OF TERMS; SPECIAL RULES RELATING TO SUBSECTIONS (a), (b), AND (c).—

(1) INDEBTEDNESS OF TAXPAYER.—For purposes of this section, the term "indebtedness of the taxpayer" means any indebtedness—

(A) for which the taxpayer is liable, or

(B) subject to which the taxpayer holds property.

(2) TITLE 11 CASE.—For purposes of this section, the term "title 11 case" means a case under title 11 of the United States Code (relating to bankruptcy), but only if the taxpayer is under the jurisdiction of the court in such case and the discharge of indebtedness is granted by the court or is pursuant to a plan approved by the court.

(3) INSOLVENT.—For purposes of this section, the term "insolvent" means the excess of liabilities over the fair market value of assets. With respect to any discharge, whether or not the taxpayer is insolvent, and the amount by which the taxpayer is insolvent, shall be determined on the basis of the taxpayer's assets and liabilities immediately before the discharge.

(4) QUALIFIED BUSINESS INDEBTEDNESS.—Indebtedness of the taxpayer shall be treated as qualified business indebtedness if (and only if)—

(A) the indebtedness was incurred or assumed—

(i) by a corporation, or

(ii) by an individual in connection with property used in his trade or business, and

(B) such taxpayer makes an election under this paragraph with respect to such indebtedness.

(5) DEPRECIABLE PROPERTY.—The term "depreciable property" has the same meaning as when used in section 1017.

(6) SUBSECTIONS (a), (b), AND (c) TO BE APPLIED AT PARTNER LEVEL.—In the case of a partnership, subsections (a), (b), and (c) shall be applied at the partner level.

(7) SPECIAL RULES FOR S CORPORATION.—

(A) SUBSECTIONS (a), (b), AND (c) TO BE APPLIED AT CORPORATE LEVEL.—In the case of an S corporation, subsections (a), (b), and (c) shall be applied at the corporate level.

(B) REDUCTION IN CARRYOVER OF DISALLOWED LOSSES AND DEDUCTIONS.—In the case of an S corporation, for purposes of subparagraph (A) of subsection (b)(2), any loss or deduction which is disallowed for the taxable year of the discharge under section 1366(d)(1) shall be treated as a net operating loss for such taxable year. The preceding sentence shall not apply to any discharge to the extent that subsection (a)(1)(C) applies to such discharge.

(C) COORDINATION WITH BASIS ADJUSTMENTS UNDER SECTION 1367(b)(2).—For purposes of subsection (e)(6), a shareholder's adjusted basis in indebtedness of an S corporation shall be determined without regard to any adjustments made under section 1367(b)(2).

(8) REDUCTIONS OF TAX ATTRIBUTES IN TITLE 11 CASES OF INDIVIDUALS TO BE MADE BY ESTATE.—In any case under chapter 7 or 11 of title 11 of the United States Code to which section 1398 applies, for purposes of paragraphs (1) and (5) of subsection (b) the estate (and not the individual) shall be treated as the taxpayer. The preceding sentence shall not apply for purposes of applying section 1017 to property transferred by the estate to the individual.

(9) TIME FOR MAKING ELECTION, ETC.—

(A) TIME.—An election under paragraph (4) of this subsection or under paragraph (5) of subsection (b) shall be made on the taxpayer's return for the taxable year in which the discharge occurs or at such other time as may be permitted in regulations prescribed by the Secretary.

(B) REVOCATION ONLY WITH CONSENT.—An election referred to in subparagraph (A), once made, may be revoked only with the consent of the Secretary.

(C) MANNER.—An election referred to in subparagraph (A) shall be made in such manner as the Secretary may by regulations prescribe.

(10) CROSS REFERENCE.—

For provision that no reduction is to be made in the basis of exempt property of an individual debtor, see section 1017(c)(1).

• 1984, Deficit Reduction Act of 1984 (P.L. 98-369)

P.L. 98-369, §721(b)(2):

Amended Code Sec. 108(d) by redesignating paragraphs (7), (8) and (9) as paragraphs (8), (9), and (10), respectively, by striking out paragraph (6), and by inserting after paragraph (5) new paragraphs (6) and (7). **Effective** as if included in P.L. 97-354, except that Code Sec. 108(d)(7)(C) applies to contributions of capital after 12-31-80, in tax years ending after such date. Prior to amendment, paragraph (6) read as follows:

(6) Subsections (a), (b), and (c) to be Applied at Partner Level or S Corporation Shareholder Level.—In the case of a partnership, subsections (a), (b), and (c) shall be applied at the partner level. In the case of an S corporation, subsection (a), (b), and (c) shall be applied at the shareholder level.

• 1982, Subchapter S Revision Act of 1982 (P.L. 97-354)

P.L. 97-354, §3(e):

Amended Code Sec. 108(d)(6). **Effective** for tax years beginning after 12-31-82. Prior to amendment, it read as follows:

"(6) SUBSECTIONS (a), (b), AND (c) TO BE APPLIED AT PARTNER LEVEL.—In the case of a partnership, subsections (a), (b), and (c) shall be applied at the partner level."

• 1980, Bankruptcy Tax Act of 1980 (P.L. 96-589)

P.L. 96-589, §2(a):

Divided Code Sec. 108 into five subsections, (a) through (e). For the text of Code Sec. 108 prior to amendment and the **effective** date of Code Sec. 108(d), see the historical comment for P.L. 96-589 under Code Sec. 108(e).

[Sec. 108(e)]

(e) GENERAL RULES FOR DISCHARGE OF INDEBTEDNESS (INCLUDING DISCHARGES NOT IN TITLE 11 CASES OR INSOLVENCY).—For purposes of this title—

(1) NO OTHER INSOLVENCY EXCEPTION.—Except as otherwise provided in this section, there shall be no insolvency exception from the general rule that gross income includes income from the discharge of indebtedness.

(2) INCOME NOT REALIZED TO EXTENT OF LOST DEDUCTIONS.—No income shall be realized from the discharge of indebtedness to the extent that payment of the liability would have given rise to a deduction.

(3) ADJUSTMENTS FOR UNAMORTIZED PREMIUM AND DISCOUNT.—The amount taken into account with respect to any discharge shall be properly adjusted for unamortized premium and unamortized discount with respect to the indebtedness discharged.

(4) ACQUISITION OF INDEBTEDNESS BY PERSON RELATED TO DEBTOR.—

(A) TREATED AS ACQUISITION BY DEBTOR.—For purposes of determining income of the debtor from discharge of indebtedness, to the extent provided in regulations prescribed by the Secretary, the acquisition of outstanding indebtedness by a person bearing a relationship to the debtor specified in section 267(b) or 707(b)(1) from a person who does not bear such a relationship to the debtor shall be treated as the acquisition of such indebtedness by the debtor. Such regulations shall provide for such adjustments in the treatment of any subsequent transactions involving the indebtedness as may be appropriate by reason of the application of the preceding sentence.

(B) MEMBERS OF FAMILY.—For purposes of this paragraph, sections 267(b) and 707(b)(1) shall be applied as if section 267(c)(4) provided that the family of an individual consists of the individual's spouse, the individual's children, grandchildren, and parents, and any spouse of the individual's children or grandchildren.

(C) ENTITIES UNDER COMMON CONTROL TREATED AS RELATED.—For purposes of this paragraph, two entities which are treated as a single employer under subsection (b) or (c) of section 414 shall be treated as bearing a relationship to each other which is described in section 267(b).

(5) PURCHASE-MONEY DEBT REDUCTION FOR SOLVENT DEBTOR TREATED AS PRICE REDUCTION.—If—

(A) the debt of a purchaser of property to the seller of such property which arose out of the purchase of such property is reduced,

(B) such reduction does not occur—

(i) in a title 11 case, or

(ii) when the purchaser is insolvent, and

(C) but for this paragraph, such reduction would be treated as income to the purchaser from the discharge of indebtedness,

then such reduction shall be treated as a purchase price adjustment.

(6) INDEBTEDNESS CONTRIBUTED TO CAPITAL.—Except as provided in regulations, for purposes of determining income of the debtor from discharge of indebtedness, if a debtor corporation acquires its indebtedness from a shareholder as a contribution to capital—

(A) section 118 shall not apply, but

(B) such corporation shall be treated as having satisfied the indebtedness with an amount of money equal to the shareholder's adjusted basis in the indebtedness.

(7) RECAPTURE OF GAIN ON SUBSEQUENT SALE OF STOCK.—

(A) IN GENERAL.—If a creditor acquires stock of a debtor corporation in satisfaction of such corporation's indebtedness, for purposes of section 1245—

(i) such stock (and any other property the basis of which is determined in whole or in part by reference to the adjusted basis of such stock) shall be treated as section 1245 property,

(ii) the aggregate amount allowed to the creditor—

(I) as deductions under subsection (a) or (b) of section 166 (by reason of the worthlessness or partial worthlessness of the indebtedness), or

(II) as an ordinary loss on the exchange,

shall be treated as an amount allowed as a deduction for depreciation, and

(iii) an exchange of such stock qualifying under section 354(a), 355(a), or 356(a) shall be treated as an exchange to which section 1245(b)(3) applies.

The amount determined under clause (ii) shall be reduced by the amount (if any) included in the creditor's gross income on the exchange.

(B) SPECIAL RULE FOR CASH BASIS TAXPAYERS.—In the case of any creditor who computes his taxable income under the cash receipts and disbursements method, proper adjustment shall be made in the amount taken into account under clause (ii) of subparagraph (A) for any amount which was not included in the creditor's gross income but which would have been included in such gross income if such indebtedness had been satisfied in full.

(C) STOCK OF PARENT CORPORATION.—For purposes of this paragraph, stock of a corporation in control (within the meaning of section 368(c)) of the debtor corporation shall be treated as stock of the debtor corporation.

(D) TREATMENT OF SUCCESSOR CORPORATION.—For purposes of this paragraph, the term "debtor corporation" includes a successor corporation.

(E) PARTNERSHIP RULE.—Under regulations prescribed by the Secretary, rules similar to the rules of the foregoing subparagraphs of this paragraph shall apply with respect to the indebtedness of a partnership.

(8) INDEBTEDNESS SATISFIED BY CORPORATE STOCK OR PARTNERSHIP INTEREST.—For purposes of determining income of a debtor from discharge of indebtedness, if—

(A) a debtor corporation transfers stock, or

(B) a debtor partnership transfers a capital or profits interest in such partnership,

to a creditor in satisfaction of its recourse or nonrecourse indebtedness, such corporation or partnership shall be treated as having satisfied the indebtedness with an amount of money equal to the fair market value of the stock or interest. In the case of any partnership, any discharge of indebtedness income recognized under this paragraph shall be included in the distributive shares of taxpayers which were the partners in the partnership immediately before such discharge.

(9) DISCHARGE OF INDEBTEDNESS INCOME NOT TAKEN INTO ACCOUNT IN DETERMINING WHETHER ENTITY MEETS REIT QUALIFICATIONS.—Any amount included in gross income by reason of the discharge of indebtedness shall not be taken into account for purposes of paragraphs (2) and (3) of section 856(c).

(10) INDEBTEDNESS SATISFIED BY ISSUANCE OF DEBT INSTRUMENT.—

(A) IN GENERAL.—For purposes of determining income of a debtor from discharge of indebtedness, if a debtor issues a debt instrument in satisfaction of indebtedness, such debtor shall be treated as having satisfied the indebtedness with an amount of money equal to the issue price of such debt instrument.

(B) ISSUE PRICE.—For purposes of subparagraph (A), the issue price of any debt instrument shall be determined under sections 1273 and 1274. For purposes of the preceding sentence, section 1273(b)(4) shall be applied by reducing the stated redemption price of any instrument by the portion of such stated redemption price which is treated as interest for purposes of this chapter.

Amendments

• 2004, American Jobs Creation Act of 2004 (P.L. 108-357)

P.L. 108-357, §896(a):

Amended Code Sec. 108(e)(8). **Effective** with respect to cancellations of indebtedness occurring on or after 10-22-2004. Prior to amendment, Code Sec. 108(e)(8) read as follows:

(8) INDEBTEDNESS SATISFIED BY CORPORATION'S STOCK.—For purposes of determining income of a debtor from discharge of indebtedness, if a debtor corporation transfers stock to a creditor in satisfaction of its indebtedness, such corporation shall be treated as having satisfied the indebtedness with an amount of money equal to the fair market value of the stock.

• 1993, Omnibus Budget Reconciliation Act of 1993 (P.L. 103-66)

P.L. 103-66, §13226(a)(1)(A)-(B):

Amended Code Sec. 108(e) by striking paragraph (10) and by redesignating paragraph (11) as paragraph (10), and by amending paragraph (8). **Effective**, generally, for stock transferred after 12-31-94, in satisfaction of any indebtedness. For an exception see Act Sec. 13226(a)(3)(B) below. Prior to amendment, Code Sec. 108(e)(8) and (10) read as follows:

(8) STOCK FOR DEBT EXCEPTION NOT TO APPLY IN DE MINIMIS CASES.—For purposes of determining income of the debtor from discharge of indebtedness, the stock for debt exception shall not apply—

(A) to the issuance of nominal or token shares, or

(B) with respect to an unsecured creditor, where the ratio of the value of the stock received by such unsecured creditor to the amount of his indebtedness cancelled or exchanged for stock in the workout is less than 50 percent of a similar ratio computed for all unsecured creditors participating in the workout.

Any stock which is disqualified stock (as defined in paragraph (10)(B)(ii)) shall not be treated as stock for purposes of this paragraph.

* * *

(10) INDEBTEDNESS SATISFIED BY CORPORATION'S STOCK.—

(A) IN GENERAL.—For purposes of determining income of a debtor from discharge of indebtedness, if a debtor corporation transfers stock to a creditor in satisfaction of its indebtedness, such corporation shall be treated as having satisfied the indebtedness with an amount of money equal to the fair market value of the stock.

(B) EXCEPTION FOR CERTAIN STOCK IN TITLE 11 CASES AND INSOLVENT DEBTORS.—

(i) IN GENERAL.—Subparagraph (A) shall not apply to any transfer of stock of the debtor (other than disqualified stock)—

(I) by a debtor in a title 11 case, or

(II) by any other debtor but only to the extent such debtor is insolvent.

(ii) DISQUALIFIED STOCK.—For purposes of clause (i), the term "disqualified stock" means any stock with a stated redemption price if—

(I) such stock has a fixed redemption date,

(II) the issuer of such stock has the right to redeem such stock at one or more times, or

(III) the holder of such stock has the right to require its redemption at one or more times.

P.L. 103-66, §13226(a)(2)(B):

Amended Code Sec. 108(e)(6) by striking "For" and inserting "Except as provided in regulations, for". **Effective**, generally, for stock transferred after 12-31-94, in satisfaction of any indebtedness. For an exception see Act Sec. 13226(a)(3)(B) below.

P.L. 103-66, §13226(a)(3)(B), provides:

(B) EXCEPTION FOR TITLE 11 CASES.—The amendments made by this subsection shall not apply to stock transferred in satisfaction of any indebtedness if such transfer is in a title 11 or similar case (as defined in section 368(a)(3)(A) of the Internal Revenue Code of 1986) which was filed on or before December 31, 1993.

• 1990, Omnibus Budget Reconciliation Act of 1990 (P.L. 101-508)

P.L. 101-508, §11325(a)(1):

Amended Code Sec. 108(e) by adding at the end thereof a new paragraph (11). **Effective** for debt instruments issued, and stock transferred, after 10-9-90, in satisfaction of any indebtedness. However, for exceptions, see Act Sec. 11325(c)(2), below.

P.L. 101-508, §11325(b)(1):

Amended Code Sec. 108(e)(10)(B). **Effective** for debt instruments issued, and stock transferred, after 10-9-90, in satisfaction of any indebtedness. However, for exceptions, see Act Sec. 11325(c)(2), below. Prior to amendment, Code Sec. 108(e)(10)(B) read as follows:

(B) EXCEPTION FOR TITLE 11 CASES AND INSOLVENT DEBTORS.—Subparagraph (A) shall not apply in the case of a debtor in a title 11 case or to the extent the debtor is insolvent.

P.L. 101-508, §11325(b)(2):

Amended Code Sec. 108(e)(8) by adding at the end thereof a new sentence. **Effective** for debt instruments issued, and stock transferred, after 10-9-90, in satisfaction of any indebtedness. However, for exceptions, see Act Sec. 11325(c)(2), below.

P.L. 101-508, §11325(c)(2), provides:

(2) EXCEPTIONS.—The amendments made by this section shall not apply to any debt instrument issued, or stock transferred, in satisfaction of any indebtedness if such issuance or transfer (as the case may be)—

(A) is in a title 11 or similar case (as defined in section 368(a)(3)(A) of the Internal Revenue Code of 1986) which was filed on or before October 9, 1990,

(B) is pursuant to a written binding contract in effect on October 9, 1990, and at all times thereafter before such issuance or transfer,

(C) is pursuant to a transaction which was described in documents filed with the Securities and Exchange Commission on or before October 9, 1990, or

(D) is pursuant to a transaction—

(i) the material terms of which were described in a written public announcement on or before October 9, 1990,

(ii) which was the subject of a prior filing with the Securities and Exchange Commission, and

(iii) which is the subject of a subsequent filing with the Securities and Exchange Commission before January 1, 1991.

• 1986, Tax Reform Act of 1986 (P.L. 99-514)

P.L. 99-514, §621(e)(1):

Repealed Code Sec. 108(e)(10)(C). For the **effective** date, see Act Sec. 621(f) following Code Sec. 380(m). Prior to repeal, Code Sec. 108(e)(10)(C) read as follows:

(C) EXCEPTION FOR TRANSFERS IN CERTAIN WORKOUTS.—

(i) IN GENERAL.—Subparagraph (A) shall not apply to any transfer of stock in a qualified workout.

(ii) QUALIFIED WORKOUT.—For purposes of clause (i), the term "qualified workout" means any plan under which stock is transferred to creditors in satisfaction of indebtedness if—

(I) because of cash flow and credit problems, the corporation making such transfer will have trouble in meeting liabilities coming due during the next 12 months to such an extent that there is a substantial threat of involuntary proceedings relating to insolvency or bankruptcy.

(II) such corporation in any report to its shareholders for the period during which such transfer occurs includes a statement that such corporation believes it meets the requirement of subclause (I) and that it is availing itself of the workout provisions of this subparagraph,

(III) the holders of more than 50 percent of the total indebtedness of the corporation approve such plan, and

(VI) at least 25 percent of the total indebtedness of the corporation is extinguished by transfers pursuant to such plan.

P.L. 99-514, §805(c)(2):

Amended Code Sec. 108(e)(7)(A)(ii) by striking out "subsection (a), (b), or (c) of section 166" and inserting in lieu thereof "subsection (a) or (b) of section 166". **Effective** for tax years beginning after 12-31-86. However, see Act Sec. 805(d)(2), below.

P.L. 99-514, §805(c)(3):

Amended Code Sec. 108(e)(7) by striking out subparagraph (B) and by redesignating subparagraphs (C), (D), (E), and (F) as subparagraphs (B), (C), (D), and (E), respectively. **Effective** for tax years beginning after 12-31-86. However, see Act Sec. 805(d)(2), below. Prior to amendment, subparagraph (B) read as follows:

(B) TAXPAYERS ON RESERVE METHOD.—In the case of a taxpayer to whom subsection (c) of section 166 (relating to reserve for bad debts) applies, the amount determined under clause (ii) of subparagraph (A) shall be the aggregate charges to the reserve resulting from the worthlessness or partial worthlessness of the indebtedness.

P.L. 99-514, §805(c)(4):

Amended Code Sec. 108(e)(7)(E) (as so redesignated) by striking out "subparagraphs (A), (B), (C), (D), (E)" and inserting in lieu thereof "the foregoing subparagraphs". **Effective** for tax years beginning after 12-31-86. However, see Act Sec. 805(d)(2), below.

P.L. 99-514, §805(d)(2), provides:

(2) CHANGE IN METHOD OF ACCOUNTING.—In the case of any taxpayer who maintained a reserve for bad debts for such taxpayer's last taxable year beginning before January 1, 1987, and who is required by the amendments made by this section to change its method of accounting for any taxable year—

(A) such change shall be treated as initiated by the taxpayer,

(B) such change shall be treated as made with the consent of the Secretary, and

(C) the net amount of adjustments required by section 481 of the Internal Revenue Code of 1986 to be taken into account by the taxpayer shall—

(i) in the case of a taxpayer maintaining a reserve under section 166(f), be reduced by the balance in the suspense account under section 166(f)(4) of such Code as of the close of such last taxable year, and

(ii) be taken into account ratably in each of the first 4 taxable years beginning after December 31, 1986.

• 1984, Deficit Reduction Act of 1984 (P.L. 98-369)

P.L. 98-369, §59(a):

Amended Code Sec. 108(e) by adding at the end thereof a new paragraph (10). **Effective** for transfers after 7-18-84, in tax years ending after such date. Special rules appear below.

P.L. 98-369, §59(b)(1):

Amended Code Sec. 108(e)(10) (as added by Act Sec. 59(a)), by adding at the end thereof subparagraph (C). **Effective** as if it had been included in the amendments made by subsections (e) and (f) of section 806 of P.L. 94-455. For special **effective** dates, see the amendment notes for P.L. 94-455, §806(e), following Code Sec. 382(a).

P.L. 98-369, §59(b)(2)-(4), provides:

(2) TRANSITIONAL RULE.—The amendment made by subsection (a) shall not apply to the transfer by a corporation of its stock in exchange for debt of the corporation after the date of the enactment of this Act if such transfer is—

(A) pursuant to a written contract requiring such transfer which was binding on the corporation at all times on June 7, 1984, and at all times after such date but only if the transfer takes place before January 1, 1985, and only if the transferee held the debt at all times on June 7, 1984, or

(B) pursuant to the exercise of an option to exchange debt for stock but only if such option was in effect at all times on June 7, 1984, and at all times after such date and only if at all times on June 7, 1984, the option and the debt were held by the same person.

(3) Certain Transfers to Controlling Shareholder.—The amendment made by subsection (a) shall not apply to any transfer before January 1, 1985, by a corporation of its stock in exchange for debt of such corporation if—

(A) such transfer is to another corporation which at all times on June 7, 1984, owned 75 percent or more of the total value of the stock of the corporation making such transfer, and

(B) immediately after such transfer, the transferee corporation owns 80 percent or more of the total value of the stock of the transferor corporation.

(4) Certain Transfers Pursuant to Debt Restructure Agreement.—The amendment made by subsection (a) shall not apply to the transfer by a corporation of its stock in exchange for debt of the corporation after the date of the enactment of this Act and before January 1, 1985, if—

(A) such transfer is covered by a debt restructure agreement entered into by the corporation during November 1983, and

(B) such agreement was specified in a registration statement filed with the Securities and Exchange Commission by the corporation on March 7, 1984.

• 1983, Technical Corrections Act of 1982 (P.L. 97-448)

P.L. 97-448, §304(d):

Amended Code Sec. 108(e)(7)(A) by striking out "and" at the end of clause (i), by striking out the period at the end of clause (ii) and inserting in lieu thereof ", and", and by inserting after clause (ii) new clause (iii). **Effective** 1-12-83.

• 1980, Bankruptcy Tax Act of 1980 (P.L. 96-589)

P.L. 96-589, §2(a):

Divided Code Sec. 108 into five subsections, (a) through (e). For **effective** dates, see Act Sec. 7, below. Prior to amendment, Code Sec. 108 provided:

"No amount shall be included in gross income by reason of the discharge, in whole or in part, within the taxable year, of any indebtedness for which the taxpayer is liable, or subject to which the taxpayer holds property, if—

(1) the indebtedness was incurred or assumed—

(A) by a corporation, or

(B) by an individual in connection with property used in his trade or business, and

(2) such taxpayer makes and files a consent to the regulations prescribed under section 1017 (relating to adjustment of basis) then in effect at such time and in such manner as the Secretary by regulations prescribes.

In such case, the amount of any income of such taxpayer atttributable to any unamortized premium (computed as of the first day of the taxable year in which such discharge occurred) with respect to such indebtedness shall not be included in gross income, and the amount of the deduction attributable to any unamortized discount (computed as of the first day of the taxable year in which such discharge occurred) with repect to such indebtedness shall not be allowed as a deduction."

P.L. 96-589, §7, provides:

"(a) For section 2 (Relating to Tax Treatment of Discharge of Indebtedness).

(1) IN GENERAL.—Except as provided in paragraph (2), the amendments made by section 2 shall apply to any transaction which occurs after December 31, 1980, other than a transaction which occurs in a proceeding in a bankruptcy case or similar judicial proceeding (or in a proceeding under the Bankruptcy Act) commencing on or before December 31, 1980.

(2) TRANSITIONAL RULE.—In the case of any discharge of indebtedness to which subparagraph (A) or (B) of section 108(a)(1) of the Internal Revenue Code of 1954 (relating to exclusion from gross income), as amended by section 2, applies and which occurs before January 1, 1982, or which occurs in a proceeding in a bankruptcy case or similar judicial proceedings commencing before January 1, 1982, then—

(A) section 108(b)(2) of the such Code (relating to reduction of tax attributes), as so amended, shall be applied without regard to subparagraphs (A), (B), (C), and (E) thereof, and

(B) the basis of any property shall not be reduced under section 1017 of such Code (relating to reduction in basis in connection with discharges of indebtedness), as so amended, below the fair market value of such property on the date the debt is discharged.

* * *

(f) ELECTION TO SUBSTITUTE SEPTEMBER 30, 1979, FOR DECEMBER 31, 1980.—

(1) IN GENERAL.—The debtor (or debtors) in a bankruptcy case or similar judicial proceeding may (with the approval of the court) elect to apply subsections (a), (c), and (d) by substituting `September 30, 1979' for `December 31, 1980' each place it appears in such subsections.

(2) EFFECT OF ELECTION.—Any election made under paragraph (1) with respect to any proceeding shall apply to all parties to the proceeding.

(3) REVOCATION ONLY WITH CONSENT.—Any election under this subsection may be revoked only with the consent of the Secretary of the Treasury or his delegate.

(4) TIME AND MANNER OF ELECTION.—Any election under this subsection shall be made at such time, and in such manner, as the Secretary of the Treasury or his delegate may by regulations prescribe.

(g) DEFINITIONS.—For purposes of this section—

(1) BANKRUPTCY CASE.—The term `bankruptcy case' means any case under title 11 of the United States Code (as recodified by Public Law 95-598).

(2) SIMILAR JUDICIAL PROCEEDING.—The term `similar judicial proceeding' means a receivership, foreclosure, or similar proceeding in a Federal or State court (as modified by section 368(a)(3)(D) of the Internal Revenue Code of 1954)."

• 1976, Tax Reform Act of 1976 (P.L. 94-455)

P.L. 94-455, §1951(b):

Amended Code Sec. 108 by deleting "(a) SPECIAL RULE OF EXCLUSION.—" from the introductory paragraph and by deleting Code Sec. 108(b). **Effective** for tax years beginning after 12-31-76. Prior to repeal, Code Sec. 108(b) read as follows:

"(b) RAILROAD CORPORATIONS.—No amount shall be included in gross income by reason of the discharge, cancellation, or modification, in whole or in part, within the taxable year, of any indebtedness of a railroad corporation, as defined in section 77(m) of the Bankruptcy Act (11 U.S.C. 205(m)), if such discharge, cancellation, or modification is effected pursuant to an order of a court—

(A) in a receivership proceeding, or

(B) in a proceeding under section 77 of the Bankruptcy Act,

commenced before January 1, 1960. In such cases, the amount of any income of the taxpayer attributable to any unamortized premium (computed as of the first day of the taxable year in which such discharge occurred) with respect to such indebtedness shall not be included in gross income, and the amount of the deduction attributable to any unamortized discount (computed as of the first day of the taxable year in which such discharge occurred) with respect to such indebtedness shall not be allowed as a deduction. Subsection (a) of this section shall not apply with respect to any discharge of indebtedness to which this subsection applies."

P.L. 94-455, §1951(b)(2)(B), provides:

"(B) SAVINGS PROVISION.—If any discharge, cancellation, or modification of indebtedness of a railroad corporation occurs in a taxable year beginning after December 31, 1976, pursuant to an order of a court in a proceeding referred to in section 108(b)(A) or (B) which commenced before January 1, 1960, then, notwithstanding the amendments made by subparagraph (A), the provisions of subsection (b) of section 108 shall be considered as not repealed with respect to such discharge, cancellation, or modification of indebtedness."

• 1960 (P.L. 86-496)

P.L. 86-496, §[1](a):

Amended the first sentence and deleted the last sentence of Code Sec. 108(b). **Effective** 1-1-60. [Section [1](b) of P.L. 86-496 provides that the amendments made by Section [1](a) shall apply to tax years ending after 12-31-59, but only for discharges occurring after such date.] Prior to amendment and deletion, these sentences read as follows:

First sentence: "No amount shall be included in gross income by reason of the discharge, cancellation, or modification, in whole or in part, within the taxable year, of any indebtedness of a railroad corporation, as defined in section 77(m) of the Bankruptcy Act (11 U. S. C. 205(m)), if such discharge, cancellation, or modification is effected pursuant to an order of a court in a receivership proceeding or in a proceeding under section 77 of the Bankruptcy Act."

Last sentence: "This subsection shall not apply to any discharge occurring in a taxable year beginning after December 31, 1957."

P.L. 628, 84th Cong., 2d Sess., §5:

Amended subsection (b) by substituting "December 31, 1957" for "December 31, 1955".

[Sec. 108(f)]

(f) STUDENT LOANS.—

(1) IN GENERAL.—In the case of an individual, gross income does not include any amount which (but for this subsection) would be includible in gross income by reason of the discharge (in whole or in part) of any student loan if such discharge was pursuant to a provision of such loan under which all or part of the indebtedness of the individual would be discharged if the individual worked for a certain period of time in certain professions for any of a broad class of employers.

(2) STUDENT LOAN.—For purposes of this subsection, the term "student loan" means any loan to an individual to assist the individual in attending an educational organization described in section 170(b)(1)(A)(ii) made by—

(A) the United States, or an instrumentality or agency thereof,

(B) a State, territory, or possession of the United States, or the District of Columbia, or any political subdivision thereof,

(C) a public benefit corporation—

(i) which is exempt from taxation under section 501(c)(3),

(ii) which has assumed control over a State, county, or municipal hospital, and

(iii) whose employees have been deemed to be public employees under State law, or

(D) any educational organization described in section 170(b)(1)(A)(ii) if such loan is made—

(i) pursuant to an agreement with any entity described in subparagraph (A), (B), or (C) under which the funds from which the loan was made were provided to such educational organization, or

(ii) pursuant to a program of such educational organization which is designed to encourage its students to serve in occupations with unmet needs or in areas with unmet needs and under which the services provided by the students (or former students) are for or under the direction of a governmental unit or an organization described in section 501(c)(3) and exempt from tax under section 501(a).

The term "student loan" includes any loan made by an educational organization described in section 170(b)(1)(A)(ii) or by an organization exempt from tax under section 501(a) to refinance a loan to an individual to assist the individual in attending any such educational organization but only if the refinancing loan is pursuant to a program of the refinancing organization which is designed as described in subparagraph (D)(ii).

(3) EXCEPTION FOR DISCHARGES ON ACCOUNT OF SERVICES PERFORMED FOR CERTAIN LENDERS.—Paragraph (1) shall not apply to the discharge of a loan made by an organization described in paragraph (2)(D) if the discharge is on account of services performed for either such organization.

(4) PAYMENTS UNDER NATIONAL HEALTH SERVICE CORPS LOAN REPAYMENT PROGRAM AND CERTAIN STATE LOAN REPAYMENT PROGRAMS.—In the case of an individual, gross income shall not include any amount received under section 338B(g) of the Public Health Service Act, under a State program described in section 338I of such Act, or under any other State loan repayment or loan forgiveness program that is intended to provide for the increased availability of health care services in underserved or health professional shortage areas (as determined by such State).

Amendments

• 2010, Patient Protection and Affordable Care Act (P.L. 111-148)

P.L. 111-148, §10908(a):

Amended Code Sec. 108(f)(4). **Effective** for amounts received by an individual in tax years beginning after 12-31-2008. Prior to amendment, Code Sec. 108(f)(4) read as follows:

(4) PAYMENTS UNDER NATIONAL HEALTH SERVICE CORPS LOAN REPAYMENT PROGRAM AND CERTAIN STATE LOAN REPAYMENT PROGRAMS.—In the case of an individual, gross income shall not include any amount received under section 338B(g) of the Public Health Service Act or under a State program described in section 338I of such Act.

• 2004, American Jobs Creation Act of 2004 (P.L. 108-357)

P.L. 108-357, §320(a):

Amended Code Sec. 108(f) by adding at the end new paragraph (4). **Effective** for amounts received by an individual in tax years beginning after 12-31-2003.

• 1998, IRS Restructuring and Reform Act of 1998 (P.L. 105-206)

P.L. 105-206, §6004(f)(1):

Amended the last sentence of Code Sec. 108(f)(2). **Effective** as if included in the provision of P.L. 105-34 to which it relates [**effective** for discharges of indebtedness after 8-5-97.—CCH]. Prior to amendment, the last sentence of Code Sec. 108(f)(2) read as follows:

The term "student loan" includes any loan made by an educational organization so described or by an organization exempt from tax under section 501(a) to refinance a loan meeting the requirements of the preceding sentence.

P.L. 105-206, §6004(f)(2):

Amended Code Sec. 108(f)(3) by striking "(or by an organization described in paragraph (2)(E) from funds provided by an organization described in paragraph (2)(D))" following "paragraph (2)(D)". **Effective** as if included in the provision of P.L. 105-34 to which it relates [**effective** for discharges of indebtedness after 8-5-97.—CCH].

• 1997, Taxpayer Relief Act of 1997 (P.L. 105-34)

P.L. 105-34, §225(a)(1):

Amended Code Sec. 108(f)(2) by striking "or" at the end of subparagraph (B) and by striking subparagraph (D) and inserting a new subparagraph (D). **Effective** for discharges of indebtedness after 8-5-97. Prior to amendment, Code Sec. 108(f)(2)(D) read as follows:

(D) any educational organization so described pursuant to an agreement with any entity described in subparagraph (A), (B), or (C) under which the funds from which the loan was made were provided to such educational organization.

P.L. 105-34, §225(a)(2):

Amended Code Sec. 108(f) by adding a new paragraph (3). **Effective** for discharges of indebtedness after 8-5-97.

• 1984, Deficit Reduction Act of 1984 (P.L. 98-369)

P.L. 98-369, §1076(a):

Added Code Sec. 108(f). **Effective** for discharges of indebtedness made on or after 1-1-83.

[Sec. 108(g)]

(g) SPECIAL RULES FOR DISCHARGE OF QUALIFIED FARM INDEBTEDNESS.—

(1) DISCHARGE MUST BE BY QUALIFIED PERSON.—

(A) IN GENERAL.—Subparagraph (C) of subsection (a)(1) shall apply only if the discharge is by a qualified person.

(B) QUALIFIED PERSON.—For purposes of subparagraph (A), the term "qualified person" has the meaning given to such term by section 49(a)(1)(D)(iv); except that such term shall include any Federal, State, or local government or agency or instrumentality thereof.

(2) QUALIFIED FARM INDEBTEDNESS.—For purposes of this section, indebtedness of a taxpayer shall be treated as qualified farm indebtedness if—

(A) such indebtedness was incurred directly in connection with the operation by the taxpayer of the trade or business of farming, and

(B) 50 percent or more of the aggregate gross receipts of the taxpayer for the 3 taxable years preceding the taxable year in which the discharge of such indebtedness occurs is attributable to the trade or business of farming.

(3) AMOUNT EXCLUDED CANNOT EXCEED SUM OF TAX ATTRIBUTES AND BUSINESS AND INVESTMENT ASSETS.—

(A) IN GENERAL.—The amount excluded under subparagraph (C) of subsection (a)(1) shall not exceed the sum of—

(i) the adjusted tax attributes of the taxpayer, and

(ii) the aggregate adjusted bases of qualified property held by the taxpayer as of the beginning of the taxable year following the taxable year in which the discharge occurs.

(B) ADJUSTED TAX ATTRIBUTES.—For purposes of subparagraph (A), the term "adjusted tax attributes" means the sum of the tax attributes described in subparagraphs (A), (B), (C), (D), (F), and (G) of subsection (b)(2) determined by taking into account $3 for each $1 of the attributes described in subparagraphs (B), (C), and (G) of subsection (b)(2) and the attribute described in subparagraph (F) of subsection (b)(2) to the extent attributable to any passive activity credit carryover.

(C) QUALIFIED PROPERTY.—For purposes of this paragraph, the term "qualified property" means any property which is used or is held for use in a trade or business or for the production of income.

(D) COORDINATION WITH INSOLVENCY EXCLUSION.—For purposes of this paragraph, the adjusted basis of any qualified property and the amount of the adjusted tax attributes shall be determined after any reduction under subsection (b) by reason of amounts excluded from gross income under subsection (a)(1)(B).

Amendments

• 1993, Omnibus Budget Reconciliation Act of 1993 (P.L. 103-66)

P.L. 103-66, §13226(b)(3)(D)(i)-(iii):

Amended Code Sec. 108(g)(3)(B) by striking "subparagraphs (A), (B), (C), and (E)" and inserting "subparagraphs (A), (B), (C), (D), (F), and (G)", by striking "subparagraphs (B) and (E)" and inserting "subparagraphs (B), (C), and (G)", and by inserting "and the attribute described in subparagraph (F) of subsection (b)(2) to the extent attributable to any passive activity credit carryover" before the period at the end thereof. **Effective** for discharges of indebtedness in tax years beginning after 12-31-93.

• 1990, Omnibus Budget Reconciliation Act of 1990 (P.L. 101-508)

P.L. 101-508, §11813(b)(6):

Amended Code Sec. 108(g)(1)(B) by striking "section 46(c)(8)(D)(iv)" and inserting "section 49(a)(1)(D)(iv)". **Effective**, generally, for property placed in service after 12-31-90. However, for exceptions, see Act Sec. 11813(c)(2), below.

P.L. 101-508, §11813(c)(2), provides:

(2) EXCEPTIONS.—The amendments made by this section shall not apply to—

(A) any transition property (as defined in section 49(e) of the Internal Revenue Code of 1986 (as in effect on the day before the date of the enactment of this Act),

(B) any property with respect to which qualified progress expenditures were previously taken into account under section 46(d) of such Code (as so in effect), and

(C) any property described in section 46(b)(2)(C) of such Code (as so in effect).

• 1988, Technical and Miscellaneous Revenue Act of 1988 (P.L. 100-647)

P.L. 100-647, §1004(a)(4):

Amended Code Sec. 108(g). **Effective** as if included in the provision of P.L. 99-514 to which it relates. Prior to amendment, Code Sec. 108(g) read as follows:

(g) SPECIAL RULES FOR DISCHARGE OF QUALIFIED FARM INDEBTEDNESS OF SOLVENT FARMERS.—

(1) IN GENERAL.—For purposes of this section and section 1017, the discharge by a qualified person of qualified farm indebtedness of a taxpayer who is not insolvent at the time of the discharge shall be treated in the same manner as if the discharge had occurred when the taxpayer was insolvent.

(2) QUALIFIED FARM INDEBTEDNESS.—For purposes of this subsection, indebtedness of a taxpayer shall be treated as qualified farm indebtedness if—

(A) such indebtedness was incurred directly in connection with the operation by the taxpayer of the trade or business of farming, and

(B) 50 percent or more of the average annual gross receipts of the taxpayer for the 3 taxable years preceding the taxable year in which the discharge of such indebtedness occurs is attributable to the trade or business of farming.

(3) QUALIFIED PERSON.—For purposes of this subsection, the term "qualified person" means a person described in section 46(c)(8)(D)(iv).

• 1986, Tax Reform Act of 1986 (P.L. 99-514)

P.L. 99-514, §405(a):

Amended Code Sec. 108 by adding at the end thereof new subsection (g). **Effective** for discharges of indebtedness occurring after 4-9-86, in tax years ending after such date.

[Sec. 108(h)]

(h) SPECIAL RULES RELATING TO QUALIFIED PRINCIPAL RESIDENCE INDEBTEDNESS.—

(1) BASIS REDUCTION.—The amount excluded from gross income by reason of subsection (a)(1)(E) shall be applied to reduce (but not below zero) the basis of the principal residence of the taxpayer.

(2) QUALIFIED PRINCIPAL RESIDENCE INDEBTEDNESS.—For purposes of this section, the term "qualified principal residence indebtedness" means acquisition indebtedness (within the meaning of section 163(h)(3)(B), applied by substituting "$2,000,000 ($1,000,000" for "$1,000,000 ($500,000" in clause (ii) thereof) with respect to the principal residence of the taxpayer.

(3) EXCEPTION FOR CERTAIN DISCHARGES NOT RELATED TO TAXPAYER'S FINANCIAL CONDITION.—Subsection (a)(1)(E) shall not apply to the discharge of a loan if the discharge is on account of services performed for the lender or any other factor not directly related to a decline in the value of the residence or to the financial condition of the taxpayer.

(4) ORDERING RULE.—If any loan is discharged, in whole or in part, and only a portion of such loan is qualified principal residence indebtedness, subsection (a)(1)(E) shall apply only to so much of the amount discharged as exceeds the amount of the loan (as determined immediately before such discharge) which is not qualified principal residence indebtedness.

(5) PRINCIPAL RESIDENCE.—For purposes of this subsection, the term "principal residence" has the same meaning as when used in section 121.

Amendments

• 2007, Mortgage Forgiveness Debt Relief Act of 2007 (P.L. 110-142)

P.L. 110-142, §2(b):

Amended Code Sec. 108 by adding at the end a new subsection (h). **Effective** for discharges of indebtedness on or after 1-1-2007.

[Sec. 108(i)]

(i) DEFERRAL AND RATABLE INCLUSION OF INCOME ARISING FROM BUSINESS INDEBTEDNESS DISCHARGED BY THE REACQUISITION OF A DEBT INSTRUMENT.—

(1) IN GENERAL .—At the election of the taxpayer, income from the discharge of indebtedness in connection with the reacquisition after December 31, 2008, and before January 1, 2011, of an applicable debt instrument shall be includible in gross income ratably over the 5-taxable-year period beginning with—

(A) in the case of a reacquisition occurring in 2009, the fifth taxable year following the taxable year in which the reacquisition occurs, and

(B) in the case of a reacquisition occurring in 2010, the fourth taxable year following the taxable year in which the reacquisition occurs.

(2) DEFERRAL OF DEDUCTION FOR ORIGINAL ISSUE DISCOUNT IN DEBT FOR DEBT EXCHANGES.—

(A) IN GENERAL .—If, as part of a reacquisition to which paragraph (1) applies, any debt instrument is issued for the applicable debt instrument being reacquired (or is treated as so issued under subsection (e)(4) and the regulations thereunder) and there is any original issue discount determined under subpart A of part V of subchapter P of this chapter with respect to the debt instrument so issued—

(i) except as provided in clause (ii), no deduction otherwise allowable under this chapter shall be allowed to the issuer of such debt instrument with respect to the portion of such original issue discount which—

(I) accrues before the 1st taxable year in the 5-taxable-year period in which income from the discharge of indebtedness attributable to the reacquisition of the debt instrument is includible under paragraph (1), and

(II) does not exceed the income from the discharge of indebtedness with respect to the debt instrument being reacquired, and

(ii) the aggregate amount of deductions disallowed under clause (i) shall be allowed as a deduction ratably over the 5-taxable-year period described in clause (i)(I).

If the amount of the original issue discount accruing before such 1st taxable year exceeds the income from the discharge of indebtedness with respect to the applicable debt instrument being reacquired, the deductions shall be disallowed in the order in which the original issue discount is accrued.

(B) DEEMED DEBT FOR DEBT EXCHANGES .—For purposes of subparagraph (A), if any debt instrument is issued by an issuer and the proceeds of such debt instrument are used directly or indirectly by the issuer to reacquire an applicable debt instrument of the issuer, the debt instrument so issued shall be treated as issued for the debt instrument being reacquired. If only a portion of the proceeds from a debt instrument are so used, the rules of subparagraph (A) shall apply to the portion of any original issue discount on the newly issued debt instrument which is equal to the portion of the proceeds from such instrument used to reacquire the outstanding instrument.

(3) APPLICABLE DEBT INSTRUMENT .—For purposes of this subsection—

(A) APPLICABLE DEBT INSTRUMENT .—The term "applicable debt instrument" means any debt instrument which was issued by—

(i) a C corporation, or

(ii) any other person in connection with the conduct of a trade or business by such person.

(B) DEBT INSTRUMENT .—The term "debt instrument" means a bond, debenture, note, certificate, or any other instrument or contractual arrangement constituting indebtedness (within the meaning of section 1275(a)(1)).

(4) REACQUISITION .—For purposes of this subsection—

(A) IN GENERAL .—The term "reacquisition" means, with respect to any applicable debt instrument, any acquisition of the debt instrument by—

(i) the debtor which issued (or is otherwise the obligor under) the debt instrument, or

(ii) a related person to such debtor.

(B) ACQUISITION .—The term "acquisition" shall, with respect to any applicable debt instrument, include an acquisition of the debt instrument for cash, the exchange of the debt instrument for another debt instrument (including an exchange resulting from a modification of the debt instrument), the exchange of the debt instrument for corporate stock or a partnership interest, and the contribution of the debt instrument to capital. Such term shall also include the complete forgiveness of the indebtedness by the holder of the debt instrument.

(5) OTHER DEFINITIONS AND RULES .—For purposes of this subsection—

(A) RELATED PERSON .—The determination of whether a person is related to another person shall be made in the same manner as under subsection (e)(4).

(B) ELECTION.—

(i) IN GENERAL .—An election under this subsection with respect to any applicable debt instrument shall be made by including with the return of tax imposed by chapter 1 for the taxable year in which the reacquisition of the debt instrument occurs a statement which—

(I) clearly identifies such instrument, and

(II) includes the amount of income to which paragraph (1) applies and such other information as the Secretary may prescribe.

(ii) ELECTION IRREVOCABLE .—Such election, once made, is irrevocable.

(iii) PASS-THRU ENTITIES .—In the case of a partnership, S corporation, or other pass-thru entity, the election under this subsection shall be made by the partnership, the S corporation, or other entity involved.

(C) COORDINATION WITH OTHER EXCLUSIONS .—If a taxpayer elects to have this subsection apply to an applicable debt instrument, subparagraphs (A), (B), (C), and (D) of subsection (a)(1) shall not apply to the income from the discharge of such indebtedness for the taxable year of the election or any subsequent taxable year.

(D) ACCELERATION OF DEFERRED ITEMS.—

(i) IN GENERAL .—In the case of the death of the taxpayer, the liquidation or sale of substantially all the assets of the taxpayer (including in a title 11 or similar case), the cessation of business by the taxpayer, or similar circumstances, any item of income or deduction which is deferred under this subsection (and has not previously been taken into account) shall be taken into account in the taxable year in which such event occurs (or in the case of a title 11 or similar case, the day before the petition is filed).

(ii) SPECIAL RULE FOR PASSTHRU ENTITIES .—The rule of clause (i) shall also apply in the case of the sale or exchange or redemption of an interest in a partnership, S corporation, or other passthru entity by a partner, shareholder, or other person holding an ownership interest in such entity.

(6) SPECIAL RULE FOR PARTNERSHIPS .—In the case of a partnership, any income deferred under this subsection shall be allocated to the partners in the partnership immediately before the discharge in the manner such amounts would have been included in the distributive shares of such partners under section 704 if such income were recognized at such time. Any decrease in a partner's share of partnership liabilities as a result of such discharge shall not be taken into account for purposes of section 752 at the time of the discharge to the extent it would cause the partner to recognize gain under section 731. Any decrease in partnership liabilities deferred under the preceding sentence shall be taken into account by such partner at the same time, and to the extent remaining in the same amount, as income deferred under this subsection is recognized.

(7) SECRETARIAL AUTHORITY .—The Secretary may prescribe such regulations, rules, or other guidance as may be necessary or appropriate for purposes of applying this subsection, including—

(A) extending the application of the rules of paragraph (5)(D) to other circumstances where appropriate,

(B) requiring reporting of the election (and such other information as the Secretary may require) on returns of tax for subsequent taxable years, and

(C) rules for the application of this subsection to partnerships, S corporations, and other pass-thru entities, including for the allocation of deferred deductions.

Amendments

• 2009, American Recovery and Reinvestment Tax Act of 2009 (P.L. 111-5)

P.L. 111-5, §1231(a):

Amended Code Sec. 108 by adding at the end a new subsection (i). **Effective** for discharges in tax years ending after 12-31-2008.

[Sec. 109]

SEC. 109. IMPROVEMENTS BY LESSEE ON LESSOR'S PROPERTY.

Gross income does not include income (other than rent) derived by a lessor of real property on the termination of a lease, representing the value of such property attributable to buildings erected or other improvements made by the lessee.

[Sec. 110]

SEC. 110. QUALIFIED LESSEE CONSTRUCTION ALLOWANCES FOR SHORT-TERM LEASES.

[Sec. 110(a)]

(a) IN GENERAL.—Gross income of a lessee does not include any amount received in cash (or treated as a rent reduction) by a lessee from a lessor—

(1) under a short-term lease of retail space, and

(2) for the purpose of such lessee's constructing or improving qualified long-term real property for use in such lessee's trade or business at such retail space,

but only to the extent that such amount does not exceed the amount expended by the lessee for such construction or improvement.

[Sec. 110(b)]

(b) CONSISTENT TREATMENT BY LESSOR.—Qualified long-term real property constructed or improved in connection with any amount excluded from a lessee's income by reason of subsection (a) shall be treated as nonresidential real property of the lessor (including for purposes of section 168(i)(8)(B)).

[Sec. 110(c)]

(c) DEFINITIONS.—For purposes of this section—

(1) QUALIFIED LONG-TERM REAL PROPERTY.—The term "qualified long-term real property" means nonresidential real property which is part of, or otherwise present at, the retail space referred to in subsection (a) and which reverts to the lessor at the termination of the lease.

(2) SHORT-TERM LEASE.—The term "short-term lease" means a lease (or other agreement for occupancy or use) of retail space for 15 years or less (as determined under the rules of section 168(i)(3)).

(3) RETAIL SPACE.—The term "retail space" means real property leased, occupied, or otherwise used by a lessee in its trade or business of selling tangible personal property or services to the general public.

[Sec. 110(d)]

(d) INFORMATION REQUIRED TO BE FURNISHED TO SECRETARY.—Under regulations, the lessee and lessor described in subsection (a) shall, at such times and in such manner as may be provided in such regulations, furnish to the Secretary—

(1) information concerning the amounts received (or treated as a rent reduction) and expended as described in subsection (a), and

(2) any other information which the Secretary deems necessary to carry out the provisions of this section.

Amendments

• 1997, Taxpayer Relief Act of 1997 (P.L. 105-34)

P.L. 105-34, §1213(a):

Amended part III of subchapter B of chapter 1 by inserting after Code Sec. 109 a new Code Sec. 110. **Effective** for leases entered into after 8-5-97.

[Sec. 110—Repealed]

Amendments

• 1990, Omnibus Budget Reconciliation Act of 1990 (P.L. 101-508)

P.L. 101-508, §11801(a)(6):

Repealed Code Sec. 110. **Effective** 11-5-90. Prior to repeal, Code Sec. 110 read as follows:

SEC. 110. INCOME TAXES PAID BY LESSEE CORPORATION.

If—

(1) a lease was entered into before January 1, 1954,

(2) both lessee and lessor are corporations, and

(3) under the lease, the lessee is obligated to pay, or to reimburse the lessor for, any part of the tax imposed by this subtitle on the lessor with respect to the rentals derived by the lessor from the lessee,

then gross income of the lessor does not include such payment or reimbursement, and no deduction for such payment or reimbursement shall be allowed to the lessee. For purposes of the preceding sentence, a lease shall be considered to have been entered into before January 1, 1954, if it is a renewal or continuance of a lease entered into before such date and if such renewal or continuance was made in accordance with an option contained in the lease on December 31, 1953.

P.L. 101-508, §11821(b)(1)-(2), provides:

(b) SAVINGS PROVISION.—If—

(1) any provision amended or repealed by this part applied to—

(A) any transaction occurring before the date of the enactment of this Act,

(B) any property acquired before such date of enactment, or

(C) any item of income, loss, deduction, or credit taken into account before such date of enactment, and

(2) the treatment of such transaction, property, or item under such provision would (without regard to the amendments made by this part) affect liability for tax for periods ending after such date of enactment,

nothing in the amendments made by this part shall be construed to affect the treatment of such transaction, property, or item for purposes of determining liability for tax for periods ending after such date of enactment.

[Sec. 111]

SEC. 111. RECOVERY OF TAX BENEFIT ITEMS.

[Sec. 111(a)]

(a) DEDUCTIONS.—Gross income does not include income attributable to the recovery during the taxable year of any amount deducted in any prior taxable year to the extent such amount did not reduce the amount of tax imposed by this chapter.

[Sec. 111(b)]

(b) CREDITS.—

(1) IN GENERAL.—If—

(A) a credit was allowable with respect to any amount for any prior taxable year, and

(B) during the taxable year there is a downward price adjustment or similar adjustment,

the tax imposed by this chapter for the taxable year shall be increased by the amount of the credit attributable to the adjustment.

(2) EXCEPTION WHERE CREDIT DID NOT REDUCE TAX.—Paragraph (1) shall not apply to the extent that the credit allowable for the recovered amount did not reduce the amount of tax imposed by this chapter.

(3) EXCEPTION FOR INVESTMENT TAX CREDIT AND FOREIGN TAX CREDIT.—This subsection shall not apply with respect to the credit determined under section 46 and the foreign tax credit.

[Sec. 111(c)]

(c) TREATMENT OF CARRYOVERS.—For purposes of this section, an increase in a carryover which has not expired before the beginning of the taxable year in which the recovery or adjustment takes place shall be treated as reducing tax imposed by this chapter.

[Sec. 111(d)]

(d) SPECIAL RULES FOR ACCUMULATED EARNINGS TAX AND FOR PERSONAL HOLDING COMPANY TAX.—In applying subsection (a) for the purpose of determining the accumulated earnings tax under section 531 or the tax under section 541 (relating to personal holding companies)—

(1) any excluded amount under subsection (a) allowed for the purposes of this subtitle (other than section 531 or section 541) shall be allowed whether or not such amount resulted in a reduction of the tax under section 531 or the tax under section 541 for the prior taxable year; and

(2) where any excluded amount under subsection (a) was not allowable as a deduction for the prior taxable year for purposes of this subtitle other than of section 531 or section 541 but was allowable for the same taxable year under section 531 or section 541, then such excluded amount shall be allowable if it did not result in a reduction of the tax under section 531 or the tax under section 541.

Amendments

• 1986, Tax Reform Act of 1986 (P.L. 99-514)

P.L. 99-514, §1812(a)(1):

Amended Code Sec. 111(a) by striking out "did not reduce income subject to tax" and inserting in lieu thereof "did not reduce the amount of tax imposed by this chapter". **Effective** as if included in the provision of P.L. 98-369 to which it relates.

P.L. 99-514, §1812(a)(2):

Amended Code Sec. 111(c) by striking out "reducing income subject to tax or reducing tax imposed by this chapter, as the case may be" and inserting in lieu thereof "reducing tax imposed by this chapter". **Effective** as if included in the provision of P.L. 98-369 to which it relates.

• 1984, Deficit Reduction Act of 1984 (P.L. 98-369)

P.L. 98-369, §171(a):

Amended Code Sec. 111. **Effective** for amounts recovered after 12-31-83, in tax years ending after such date. Prior to amendment, Code Sec. 111 read as follows:

SEC. 111. RECOVERY OF BAD DEBTS, PRIOR TAXES, AND DELINQUENCY AMOUNTS.

[Sec. 111(a)]

(a) GENERAL RULE.—Gross income does not include income attributable to the recovery during the taxable year of a bad debt, prior tax, or delinquency amount, to the extent of the amount of the recovery exclusion with respect to such debt, tax, or amount.

[Sec. 111(b)]

(b) DEFINITIONS.—For purposes of subsection (a)—

(1) BAD DEBT.—The term "bad debt" means a debt on account of the worthlessness or partial worthlessness of which a deduction was allowed for a prior taxable year.

(2) PRIOR TAX.—The term "prior tax" means a tax on account of which a deduction or credit was allowed for a prior taxable year.

(3) DELINQUENCY AMOUNT.—The term "delinquency amount" means an amount paid or accrued on account of which a deduction or credit was allowed for a prior taxable year and which is attributable to failure to file return with respect to a tax, or pay a tax, within the time required by the law under which the tax is imposed, or to failure to file return with respect to a tax or pay a tax.

(4) RECOVERY EXCLUSION.—The term "recovery exclusion", with respect to a bad debt, prior tax, or delinquency amount, means the amount, determined in accordance with regulations prescribed by the Secretary, of the deductions or credits allowed, on account of such bad debt, prior tax, or delinquency amount, which did not result in a reduction of the taxpayer's tax under this subtitle (not including the accumulated earnings tax imposed by section 531 or the tax on personal holding companies imposed by section 541) or corresponding provisions of prior income tax laws (other than subchapter E of chapter 2 of the Internal Revenue Code of 1939, relating to World War II excess profits tax), reduced by the amount excludable in previous taxable years with respect to such debt, tax, or amount under this section.

Amendments

• 1976, Tax Reform Act of 1976 (P.L. 94-455)

P.L. 94-455, §1906(b)(13)(A):

Amended 1954 Code by substituting "Secretary" for "Secretary or his delegate" each place it appeared. **Effective** 2-1-77.

[Sec. 111(c)]

(c) SPECIAL RULES FOR ACCUMULATED EARNINGS TAX AND FOR PERSONAL HOLDING COMPANY TAX.—In applying subsections (a) and (b) for the purpose of determining the accumulated earnings tax under section 531 or the tax under section 541 (relating to personal holding companies)—

(1) a recovery exclusion allowed for purposes of this subtitle (other than section 531 or section 541) shall be allowed whether or not the bad debt, prior tax, or delinquency amount resulted in a reduction of the tax under section 531 or the tax under section 541 for the prior taxable year; and

(2) where a bad debt, prior tax, or delinquency amount was not allowable as a deduction or credit for the prior taxable year for purposes of this subtitle other than of section 531 or section 541 but was allowable for the same taxable year under section 531 or section 541, then a recovery exclusion shall be allowable if such bad debt, prior tax, or delinquency amount did not result in a reduction of the tax under section 531 or the tax under section 541.

[Sec. 111(d)]

(d) INCREASE IN CARRYOVER TREATED AS YIELDING TAX BENEFIT.—For purposes of paragraph (4) of subsection (b), an increase in a carryover which has not expired shall be treated as a reduction in tax.

Amendments

• 1980, Bankruptcy Tax Act of 1980 (P.L. 94-569)

P.L. 96-589, §2(c):

Amended Code Sec. 111 by adding a new subsection (d). For the **effective** date, see the historical comment for P.L. 96-589 under Code Sec. 108(e).

[Sec. 112]

SEC. 112. CERTAIN COMBAT ZONE COMPENSATION OF MEMBERS OF THE ARMED FORCES.

[Sec. 112(a)]

(a) ENLISTED PERSONNEL.— Gross income does not include compensation received for active service as a member below the grade of commissioned officer in the Armed Forces of the United States for any month during any part of which such member—

(1) served in a combat zone, or

(2) was hospitalized as a result of wounds, disease, or injury incurred while serving in a combat zone; but this paragraph shall not apply for any month beginning more than 2 years after the date of the termination of combatant activities in such zone.

With respect to service in the combat zone designated for purposes of the Vietnam conflict, paragraph (2) shall not apply to any month after January 1978.

Amendments

• 1996, Small Business Job Protection Act of 1996 (P.L. 104-188)

P.L. 104-188, §1704(t)(4)(A):

Amended Code Sec. 112 by striking " **COMBAT PAY**" in the heading and inserting " **COMBAT ZONE COMPENSATION**". **Effective** 8-20-96.

• 1980 (P.L. 94-569)

P.L. 94-569, §3(b):

Substituted "after January 1978" for "beginning more than 2 years after the date of the enactment of this sentence" in Code Sec. 112(a). **Effective** with respect to months after the month following the month in which this Act is enacted.

• 1975 (P.L. 93-597)

P.L. 93-597, §2(a):

Amended Code Sec. 112(a). **Effective** 7-1-73. Prior to amendment, Code Sec. 112(a) read as follows:

"(a) Enlisted Personnel.—Gross income does not include compensation received for active service as a member below the grade of commissioned officer in the Armed Forces of the United States for any month during any part of which such member—

"(1) served in a combat zone during an induction period, or

"(2) was hospitalized as a result of wounds, disease, or injury incurred while serving in a combat zone during an induction period; but this paragraph shall not apply for any month during any part of which there are no combatant activities in any combat zone as determined under section (c) (3) of this section."

[Sec. 112(b)]

(b) COMMISSIONED OFFICERS.— Gross income does not include so much of the compensation as does not exceed the maximum enlisted amount received for active service as a commissioned officer in the Armed Forces of the United States for any month during any part of which such officer—

(1) served in a combat zone, or

(2) was hospitalized as a result of wounds, disease, or injury incurred while serving in a combat zone; but this paragraph shall not apply for any month beginning more than 2 years after the date of the termination of combatant activities in such zone.

With respect to service in the combat zone designated for purposes of the Vietnam conflict, paragraph (2) shall not apply to any month after January 1978.

Amendments

• 1996 (P.L. 104-117)

P.L. 104-117, §1(d)(1):

Amended Code Sec. 112(b) by striking "$500" and inserting "the maximum enlisted amount". **Effective** 11-21-95.

• 1980 (P.L. 94-569)

P.L. 94-569, §3(b):

Substituted "after January 1978" for "beginning more than 2 years after the date of the enactment of this sentence" in Code Sec. 112(b). **Effective** with respect to months after the month following the month in which this Act is enacted.

• 1975 (P.L. 93-597)

P.L. 93-597, §2(a):

Amended Code Sec. 112(b). **Effective** 7-1-73. Prior to amendment, Code Sec. 112(b) read as follows:

"(b) Commissioned Officers.—Gross income does not include so much of the compensation as does not exceed $500 received for active service as a commissioned officer in the Armed Forces of the United States for any month during any part of which such officer—

"(1) served in a combat zone during an induction period, or

"(2) was hospitalized as a result of wounds, disease, or injury incurred while serving in a combat zone during an induction period; but this paragraph shall not apply for any month during any part of which there are no combatant activities in any combat zone as determined under subsection (c)(3) of this section."

• 1966 (P.L. 89-739)

P.L. 89-739, §[1]:

Amended Code Sec. 112(b) by substituting "$500" for "$200". **Effective** with respect to compensation received in tax years ending after 12-31-65, for periods of active service after that date.

[Sec. 112(c)]

(c) DEFINITIONS.— For purposes of this section—

(1) The term "commissioned officer" does not include a commissioned warrant officer.

(2) The term "combat zone" means any area which the President of the United States by Executive Order designates, for purposes of this section or corresponding provisions of prior income tax laws, as an area in which Armed Forces of the United States are or have (after June 24, 1950) engaged in combat.

(3) Service is performed in a combat zone only if performed on or after the date designated by the President by Executive Order as the date of the commencing of combatant activities in such zone, and on or before the date designated by the President by Executive Order as the date of the termination of combatant activities in such zone; except that June 25, 1950, shall be considered the date of the commencing of combatant activities in the combat zone designated in Executive Order 10195.

(4) The term "compensation" does not include pensions and retirement pay.

(5) The term "maximum enlisted amount" means, for any month, the sum of—

(A) the highest rate of basic pay payable for such month to any enlisted member of the Armed Forces of the United States at the highest pay grade applicable to enlisted members, and

(B) in the case of an officer entitled to special pay under section 310 of title 37, United States Code, for such month, the amount of such special pay payable to such officer for such month.

Amendments

• 2000 (P.L. 106-398)

P.L. 106-398, §1089, provides:

SEC. 1089. SENSE OF CONGRESS REGARDING TAX TREATMENT OF MEMBERS RECEIVING SPECIAL PAY FOR DUTY SUBJECT TO HOSTILE FIRE OR IMMINENT DANGER.

It is the sense of Congress that members of the Armed Forces who receive special pay under section 310 of title 37, United States Code, for duty subject to hostile fire or imminent danger should receive the same treatment under Federal income tax laws as members serving in combat zones.

• 2000 (P.L. 106-65)

P.L. 106-65, §677, provides:

SEC. 677. SENSE OF CONGRESS REGARDING TREATMENT UNDER INTERNAL REVENUE CODE OF MEMBERS RECEIVING HOSTILE FIRE OR IMMINENT DANGER SPECIAL PAY DURING CONTINGENCY OPERATIONS.

It is the sense of Congress that a member of the Armed Forces who is receiving special pay under section 310 of title 37, United States Code, while assigned to duty in support of a contingency operation should be treated under the Internal Revenue Code of 1986 in the same manner as a member of the Armed Forces serving in a combat zone (as defined in section 112 of the Internal Revenue Code of 1986).

• 1999 (P.L. 106-21)

P.L. 106-21, §1(a)(2), (b) and (d)(1), provide:

SECTION 1. AVAILABILITY OF CERTAIN TAX BENEFITS FOR SERVICES AS PART OF OPERATION ALLIED FORCE.

(a) GENERAL RULE.—For purposes of the following provisions of the Internal Revenue Code of 1986, a qualified hazardous duty area shall be treated in the same manner as if it were a combat zone (as determined under section 112 of such Code):

***

(2) Section 112 (relating to the exclusion of certain combat pay of members of the Armed Forces).

***

(b) QUALIFIED HAZARDOUS DUTY AREA.—For purposes of this section, the term "qualified hazardous duty area" means any area of the Federal Republic of Yugoslavia (Serbia/Montenegro), Albania, the Adriatic Sea, and the northern Ionian Sea (above the 39th parallel) during the period (which includes the date of the enactment of this Act) that any member of the Armed Forces of the United States is entitled to special pay under section 310 of title 37, United States Code (relating to special pay: duty subject to hostile fire or imminent danger) for services performed in such area.

***

(d) EFFECTIVE DATES.—

(1) IN GENERAL.—Except as provided in paragraph (2), this section shall take effect on March 24, 1999.

• 1996 (P.L. 104-117)

P.L. 104-117, §1(a)(2), (b) and (e)(1), provide:

SECTION 1. TREATMENT OF CERTAIN INDIVIDUALS PERFORMING SERVICES IN CERTAIN HAZARDOUS DUTY AREAS.

(a) GENERAL RULE.—For purposes of the following provisions of the Internal Revenue Code of 1986, a qualified hazardous duty area shall be treated in the same manner as if it were a combat zone (as determined under section 112 of such Code):

***

(2) Section 112 (relating to the exclusion of certain combat pay of members of the Armed Forces).

***

(b) QUALIFIED HAZARDOUS DUTY AREA.—For purposes of this section, the term "qualified hazardous duty area" means Bosnia and Herzegovina, Croatia, or Macedonia, if as of the date of the enactment of this section any member of the Armed Forces of the United States is entitled to special pay under section 310 of title 37, United States Code (relating to special pay; duty subject to hostile fire or imminent danger) for services performed in such country. Such term includes any such country only during the period such entitlement is in effect. Solely for purposes of applying section 7508 of the Internal Revenue Code of 1986, in the case of an individual who is performing services as part of Operation Joint Endeavor outside the United States while deployed away from such individual's permanent duty station, the term "qualified hazardous duty area" includes, during the period for which such entitlement is in effect, any area in which such services are performed.

***

(e) EFFECTIVE DATE.—

(1) IN GENERAL.—Except as provided in paragraph (2), the provisions of and amendments made by this section shall take effect on November 21, 1995.

P.L. 104-117, §1(d)(2):

Amended Code Sec. 112(c) by adding at the end a new paragraph (5). **Effective** 11-21-95.

• 1975 (P.L. 93-597)

P.L. 93-597, §2(a):

Amended Code Sec. 112(c) by deleting former paragraph (5). **Effective** 7-1-73. Former paragraph (5) read as follows:

"(5) The term 'induction period' means any period during which, under laws heretofore or hereafter enacted relating to the induction of individuals for training and service in the Armed Forces of the United States, individuals (other than individuals liable for induction by reason of a prior deferment) are liable for induction for such training and service."

[Sec. 112(d)]

(d) PRISONERS OF WAR, ETC.—

(1) MEMBERS OF THE ARMED FORCES.— Gross income does not include compensation received for active service as a member of the Armed Forces of the United States for any month during any part of which such member is in a missing status (as defined in section 551(2) of title 37, United States Code) during the Vietnam conflict as a result of such conflict, other than a period with respect to which it is officially determined under section 552(c) of such title 37 that he is officially absent from his post of duty without authority.

(2) CIVILIAN EMPLOYEES.— Gross income does not include compensation received for active service as an employee for any month during any part of which such employee is in a missing status during the Vietnam conflict as a result of such conflict. For purposes of this paragraph, the terms "active service", "employee", and "missing status" have the respective meanings given to such terms by section 5561 of title 5 of the United States Code.

(3) PERIOD OF CONFLICT.— For purposes of this subsection, the Vietnam conflict began February 28, 1961, and ends on the date designated by the President by Executive order as the date of the termination of combatant activities in Vietnam. For purposes of this subsection, an individual is in a missing status as a result of the Vietnam conflict if immediately before such status began he was performing service in Vietnam or was performing service in Southeast Asia in direct support of military operations in Vietnam.

Amendments

• 2006, Heroes Earned Retirement Opportunities Act (P.L. 109-227)

P.L. 109-227, §2(c), provides:

(c) CONTRIBUTIONS FOR TAXABLE YEARS ENDING BEFORE ENACTMENT.—

(1) IN GENERAL.—In the case of any taxpayer with respect to whom compensation was excluded from gross income under section 112 of the Internal Revenue Code of 1986 for any taxable year beginning after December 31, 2003, and ending before the date of the enactment of this Act [5-29-2006.—CCH], any contribution to an individual retirement plan made on account of such taxable year and not later than the last day of the 3-year period beginning on the date of the enactment of this Act shall be treated, for purposes of such Code, as having been made on the last day of such taxable year.

(2) WAIVER OF LIMITATIONS.—

(A) CREDIT OR REFUND.—If the credit or refund of any overpayment of tax resulting from a contribution to which paragraph (1) applies is prevented at any time by the operation of any law or rule of law (including res judicata), such credit or refund may nevertheless be allowed or made if the claim therefor is filed before the close of the 1-year period beginning on the date that such contribution is made (determined without regard to paragraph (1)).

(B) ASSESSMENT OF DEFICIENCY.—The period for assessing a deficiency attributable to a contribution to which paragraph (1) applies shall not expire before the close of the 3-year period beginning on the date that such contribution is made. Such deficiency may be assessed before the expiration of such 3-year period notwithstanding the provisions of any other law or rule of law which would otherwise prevent such assessment.

(3) INDIVIDUAL RETIREMENT PLAN DEFINED.—For purposes of this subsection, the term "individual retirement plan" has the meaning given such term by section 7701(a)(37) of such Code.

• 1972 (P.L. 92-279)

P.L. 92-279, §1:

Added Code Sec. 112(d). **Effective** for tax years ending on or after 2-28-61.

P.L. 92-279, §3(a)(2)-(3), provide:

"(2) If refund or credit of any overpayment for any taxable year resulting from the application of the amendment made by the first section of this Act (including interest, additions to the tax, and additional amounts) is prevented at any time before the expiration of the applicable period specified in paragraph (3) by the operation of any law or rule of law, such refund or credit of such overpayment may, nevertheless, be made or allowed if claim therefor is filed before the expiration of such applicable period.

"(3) For purposes of paragraph (2), the applicable period for any individual with respect to any compensation is the period ending on whichever of the following days is the later:

"(A) the day which is one year after the date of the enactment of this Act, or

"(B) the day which is 2 years after the date on which it is determined that the individual's missing status (within the meaning of section 112(d) of the Internal Revenue Code of 1954) has terminated for purposes of such section 112."

Title 37, U.S.C., §551(2) provides:

"missing status' means the status of a member of a uniformed service who is officially carried or determined to be absent in a status of—

"(A) missing;

"(B) missing in action;

"(C) interned in a foreign country;

"(D) captured, beleaguered, or beseiged by a hostile force; or

"(E) detained in a foreign country against his will; and".]

[Sec. 113—Repealed]

Amendments

• 1990, Omnibus Budget Reconciliation Act of 1990 (P.L. 101-508)

P.L. 101-508, §11801(a)(7):

Repealed Code Sec. 113. **Effective** 11-5-90. Prior to repeal, Code Sec. 113 read as follows:

SEC. 113. MUSTERING-OUT PAYMENTS FOR MEMBERS OF THE ARMED FORCES.

Gross income does not include amounts received during the taxable year as mustering-out payments with respect to service in the Armed Forces of the United States.

P.L. 101-508, §11821(b)(1)-(2), provides:

(b) SAVINGS PROVISION.—If—

(1) any provision amended or repealed by this part applied to—

(A) any transaction occurring before the date of the enactment of this Act,

(B) any property acquired before such date of enactment, or

(C) any item of income, loss, deduction, or credit taken into account before such date of enactment, and

(2) the treatment of such transaction, property, or item under such provision would (without regard to the amendments made by this part) affect liability for tax for periods ending after such date of enactment,

nothing in the amendments made by this part shall be construed to affect the treatment of such transaction, property, or item for purposes of determining liability for tax for periods ending after such date of enactment.

[Sec. 114—Repealed]

Amendments

• 2004, American Jobs Creation Act of 2004 (P.L. 108-357)

P.L. 108-357, §101(a):

Repealed Code Sec. 114. **Effective** for transactions after 12-31-2004. For transitional and special rules, see Act Sec. 101(d)-(f), below.

P.L. 108-357, §101(d)-(f), provides:

(d) TRANSITIONAL RULE FOR 2005 AND 2006.—

(1) IN GENERAL.—In the case of transactions during 2005 or 2006, the amount includible in gross income by reason of the amendments made by this section shall not exceed the applicable percentage of the amount which would have been so included but for this subsection.

(2) APPLICABLE PERCENTAGE.—For purposes of paragraph (1), the applicable percentage shall be as follows:

(A) For 2005, the applicable percentage shall be 20 percent.

(B) For 2006, the applicable percentage shall be 40 percent.

(e) REVOCATION OF ELECTION TO BE TREATED AS DOMESTIC CORPORATION.—If, during the 1-year period beginning on the date of the enactment of this Act, a corporation for which an election is in effect under section 943(e) of the Internal Revenue Code of 1986 revokes such election, no gain or loss shall be recognized with respect to property treated as transferred under clause (ii) of section 943(e)(4)(B) of such Code to the extent such property—

(1) was treated as transferred under clause (i) thereof, or

(2) was acquired during a taxable year to which such election applies and before May 1, 2003, in the ordinary course of its trade or business.

The Secretary of the Treasury (or such Secretary's delegate) may prescribe such regulations as may be necessary to prevent the abuse of the purposes of this subsection.

[**Note:** Act Sec. 101(f) of P.L. 108-357, below, was stricken by P.L. 109-222, §513(b), applicable to tax years beginning after 5-17-2006.—CCH.]

(f) BINDING CONTRACTS.—The amendments made by this section shall not apply to any transaction in the ordinary course of a trade or business which occurs pursuant to a binding contract—

(1) which is between the taxpayer and a person who is not a related person (as defined in section 943(b)(3) of such Code, as in effect on the day before the date of the enactment of this Act), and

(2) which is in effect on September 17, 2003, and at all times thereafter.

For purposes of this subsection, a binding contract shall include a purchase option, renewal option, or replacement option which is included in such contract and which is enforceable against the seller or lessor.

Prior to repeal, Code Sec. 114 read as follows:

SEC. 114. EXTRATERRITORIAL INCOME.

[Sec. 114(a)]

(a) EXCLUSION.—Gross income does not include extraterritorial income.

[Sec. 114(b)]

(b) EXCEPTION.—Subsection (a) shall not apply to extraterritorial income which is not qualifying foreign trade income as determined under subpart E of part III of subchapter N.

[Sec. 114(c)]

(c) DISALLOWANCE OF DEDUCTIONS.—

(1) IN GENERAL.—Any deduction of a taxpayer allocated under paragraph (2) to extraterritorial income of the taxpayer excluded from gross income under subsection (a) shall not be allowed.

(2) ALLOCATION.—Any deduction of the taxpayer properly apportioned and allocated to the extraterritorial income derived by the taxpayer from any transaction shall be allocated on a proportionate basis between—

(A) the extraterritorial income derived from such transaction which is excluded from gross income under subsection (a), and

(B) the extraterritorial income derived from such transaction which is not so excluded.

[Sec. 114(d)]

(d) DENIAL OF CREDITS FOR CERTAIN FOREIGN TAXES.—Notwithstanding any other provision of this chapter, no credit shall be allowed under this chapter for any income, war profits, and excess profits taxes paid or accrued to any foreign country or possession of the United States with respect to extraterritorial income which is excluded from gross income under subsection (a).

[Sec. 114(e)]

(e) EXTRATERRITORIAL INCOME.—For purposes of this section, the term "extraterritorial income" means the gross income of the taxpayer attributable to foreign trading gross receipts (as defined in section 942) of the taxpayer.

Amendments

• 2000, FSC Repeal and Extraterritorial Income Exclusion Act of 2000 (P.L. 106-519)

P.L. 106-519, §3(a):

Amended part III of subchapter B of chapter 1 by inserting before Code Sec. 115 a new Code Sec. 114. **Effective,** generally, to transactions after 9-30-2000. For special rules, see Act Sec. 5(b)-(d) in the amendment notes following Code Sec. 921.

[Sec. 114—Repealed]

Amendments

• 1990, Omnibus Budget Reconciliation Act of 1990 (P.L. 101-508)

P.L. 101-508, §11801(a)(8):

Repealed Code Sec. 114. **Effective** 11-5-90. Prior to repeal, Code Sec. 114 read as follows:

SEC. 114. SPORTS PROGRAMS CONDUCTED FOR THE AMERICAN NATIONAL RED CROSS.

(a) GENERAL RULE.—In the case of a taxpayer which is a corporation primarily engaged in the furnishing of sports programs, gross income does not include amounts received as proceeds from a sports program conducted by the taxpayer if—

(1) the taxpayer agrees in writing with the American National Red Cross to conduct such sports program exclusively for the benefit of the American National Red Cross;

(2) the taxpayer turns over to the American National Red Cross the proceeds from such sports program, minus the expenses paid or incurred by the taxpayer—

(A) which would not have been so paid or incurred but for such sports program, and

(B) which would be allowable as a deduction under section 162 (relating to trade or business expenses) but for subsection (b) of this section; and

(3) the facilities used for such program are not regularly used during the taxable year for the conduct of sports programs to which this subsection applies.

For purposes of this subsection, the term "proceeds from such sports program" includes all amounts paid for admission to the sports program, plus all proceeds received by the taxpayer from such program or activities carried on in connection therewith.

(b) TREATMENT OF EXPENSES.—Expenses described in subsection (a)(2) shall be allowed as a deduction under section 162 only to the extent that such expenses exceed the amount excluded from gross income by subsection (a) of this section.

P.L. 101-508, §11821(b)(1)-(2), provides:

(b) SAVINGS PROVISION.—If—

(1) any provision amended or repealed by this part applied to—

(A) any transaction occurring before the date of the enactment of this Act,

(B) any property acquired before such date of enactment, or

(C) any item of income, loss, deduction, or credit taken into account before such date of enactment, and

(2) the treatment of such transaction, property, or item under such provision would (without regard to the amendments made by this part) affect liability for tax for periods ending after such date of enactment,

nothing in the amendments made by this part shall be construed to affect the treatment of such transaction, property, or item for purposes of determining liability for tax for periods ending after such date of enactment.

[Sec. 115]

SEC. 115. INCOME OF STATES, MUNICIPALITIES, ETC.

Gross income does not include—

(1) income derived from any public utility or the exercise of any essential governmental function and accruing to a State or any political subdivision thereof, or the District of Columbia; or

(2) income accruing to the government of any possession of the United States, or any political subdivision thereof.

Amendments

• 1976, Tax Reform Act of 1976 (P.L. 94-455)

P.L. 94-455, §1901(a)(19):

Amended Code Sec. 115. **Effective** for tax years beginning after 12-31-76. Prior to amendment, Code Sec. 115 read as follows:

(a) GENERAL RULE.—Gross income does not include—

(1) income derived from any public utility or the exercise of any essential governmental function and accruing to a State or Territory, or any political subdivision thereof, or the District of Columbia; or

(2) income accruing to the government of any possession of the United States, or any political subdivision thereof.

(b) CONTRACTS MADE BEFORE SEPTEMBER 8, 1916, RELATING TO PUBLIC UTILITIES.—Where a State or Territory, or any political subdivision thereof, or the District of Columbia, before September 8, 1916, entered in good faith into a contract with any person, the object and purpose of which was to acquire, construct, operate, or maintain a public utility—

(1) If—

(A) by the terms of such contract the tax imposed by this subtitle is to be paid out of the proceeds from the operation of such public utility before any division of such proceeds between the person and the State, Territory, political subdivision, or the District of Columbia, and

(B) a part of such proceeds for the taxable year would (but for the imposition of the tax imposed by this subtitle) accrue directly to or for the use of such State, Territory, political subdivision, or the District of Columbia,

then a tax on the taxable income from the operation of such public utility shall be levied, assessed, collected, and paid in the manner and at the rates prescribed in this subtitle, but there shall be refunded to such State, Territory, political subdivision, or the District of Columbia (under regulations prescribed by the Secretary or his delegate) an amount which bears the same relation to the amount of the tax as the amount which (but for the imposition of the tax imposed by this subtitle) would have accrued directly to or for the use of such State, Territory, political subdivision, or the District of Columbia, bears to the amount of the taxable income from the operation of such public utility for such taxable year.

(2) If by the terms of such contract no part of the proceeds from the operation of the public utility for the taxable year would, irrespective of the tax imposed by this subtitle, accrue directly to or for the use of such State, Territory, political subdivision, or the District of Columbia, then the tax on the taxable income of such person from the operation of such public utility shall be levied, assessed, collected, and paid in the manner and at the rates prescribed in this subtitle.

(c) CONTRACTS MADE BEFORE MAY 29, 1928, RELATING TO BRIDGE ACQUISITIONS.—Where a State or political subdivision thereof, pursuant to a contract entered into before May 29, 1928, to which it is not a party, is to acquire a bridge—

(1) If—

(A) by the terms of such contract the tax imposed by this subtitle is to be paid out of the proceeds from the operation of such bridge before any division of such proceeds, and

(B) a part of such proceeds for the taxable year would (but for the imposition of the tax imposed by this subtitle) accrue directly to or for the use of or would be applied for the benefit of such State or political subdivision, then a tax on the taxable income from the operation of such bridge shall be levied, assessed, collected, and paid in the manner and at the rates prescribed in this subtitle, but there shall be refunded to such State or political subdivision (under regulations to be prescribed by the Secretary or his delegate) an amount which bears the same relation to the amount of the tax as the amount which (but for the imposition of the tax imposed by this subtitle) would have accrued directly to or for the use of or would be applied for the benefit of such State or political subdivision bears to the amount of the taxable income from the operation of such bridge for such taxable year. No such refund shall be made unless the entire amount of the refund is to be applied in part payment for the acquisition of such bridge.

(2) If by the terms of such contract no part of the proceeds from the operation of the bridge for the taxable year would, irrespective of the tax imposed by this subtitle, accrue directly to or for the use of or be applied for the benefit of such State or political subdivision, then the tax on the taxable income from the operation of such bridge shall be levied, assessed, collected, and paid in the manner and at the rates prescribed in this subtitle.

[Sec. 116—Repealed]

Amendments

• 1986, Tax Reform Act of 1986 (P.L. 99-514)

P.L. 99-514, §612(a):

Repealed Code Sec. 116. **Effective** for tax years beginning after 12-31-86. Prior to repeal, Code Sec. 116 read as follows:

SEC. 116. PARTIAL EXCLUSION OF DIVIDENDS RECEIVED BY INDIVIDUALS.

[Sec. 116(a)]

(a) EXCLUSION FROM GROSS INCOME.—

(1) IN GENERAL.—Gross income does not include amounts received by an individual as dividends from domestic corporations.

(2) MAXIMUM DOLLAR AMOUNT.—The aggregate amount excluded under subsection (a) for any taxable year shall not exceed $100 ($200 in the case of a joint return under section 6013).

Amendments

• 1981, Economic Recovery Tax Act of 1981 (P.L. 97-34)

P.L. 97-34, §302(b)(2):

Amended Code Sec. 116(a). **Effective** for tax years beginning after 12-31-81. Prior to amendment, Code Sec. 116(a) read:

(a) EXCLUSION FROM GROSS INCOME.—Gross income does not include amounts received by an individual as dividends from domestic corporations, to the extent that the dividends do not exceed $100. If the dividends received in a taxable year exceed $100, the exclusion provided by the preceding sentence shall apply to the dividends first received in such year.

• 1976, Tax Reform Act of 1976 (P.L. 94-455)

P.L. 94-455, §1901(a)(20):

Amended Code Sec. 116(a) by substituting "Gross" for "Effective with respect to any taxable year ending after July 31, 1954, gross". **Effective** for tax years beginning after 12-31-76.

• 1964, Revenue Act of 1964 (P.L. 88-272)

P.L. 88-272, §201(c):

Amended subsection (a) by inserting "$100" in lieu of "$50" wherever it appeared. **Effective** with respect to tax years beginning after 12-31-63.

[Sec. 116(b)]

(b) CERTAIN DIVIDENDS EXCLUDED.—Subsection (a) shall not apply to any dividend from—

(1) a corporation which, for the taxable year of the corporation in which the distribution is made, or for the next preceding taxable year of the corporation, is a corporation exempt from tax under section 501 (relating to certain charitable, etc., organizations) or section 521 (relating to farmers' cooperative associations); or

(2) a real estate investment trust which, for the taxable year of the trust in which the dividend is paid, qualifies under part II of subchapter M (sec. 856 and following).

Amendments

• 1976, Tax Reform Act of 1976 (P.L. 94-455)

P.L. 94-455, §1053(d)(1):

Amended Code Sec. 116(b) by striking out paragraph (1) and redesignating paragraphs (2) and (3) as paragraphs (1) and (2), respectively. **Effective** for tax years beginning after 12-31-77. Prior to amendment, Code Sec. 116(b)(1) read as follows:

(1) a corporation organized under the China Trade Act, 1922 (see sec. 941);

P.L. 94-455, §1051(h):

Amended Code Sec. 116(b)(2). **Effective** for tax years beginning after 12-31-75. Prior to amendment, Code Sec. 116(b)(2) read as follows:

(2) a corporation which, for the taxable year of the corporation in which the distribution is made, or for the next preceding taxable year of the corporation, is—

(A) a corporation exempt from tax under section 501 (relating to certain charitable, etc., organizations) or section 521 (relating to farmers' cooperative associations); or

(B) a corporation to which section 931 (relating to income from sources within possessions of the United States) applies; or

• 1960 (P.L. 86-779)

P.L. 86-779, §10(f):

Amended Code Sec. 116(b) by striking out "or" at the end of paragraph (1), by striking out the period at the end of paragraph (2) and substituting "; or", and by adding a new paragraph (3). **Effective** 1-1-61.

• 1959, Life Insurance Company Income Tax Act of 1959 (P.L. 86-69)

P.L. 86-69, §3(a)(2):

Amended Code Sec. 116(b) by striking out paragraph (1) and renumbering paragraphs (2) and (3) as (1) and (2), respectively. **Effective** for dividends received after 12-31-58, in tax years ending after that date. Prior to its repeal, old paragraph (1) read as follows:

"(1) an insurance company subject to a tax imposed by part I or II of subchapter L (sec. 801 and following):".

[Sec. 116(c)]

(c) SPECIAL RULES FOR CERTAIN DISTRIBUTIONS.—For purposes of subsection (a)—

(1) Any amount allowed as a deduction under section 591 (relating to deduction for dividends paid by mutual savings banks, etc.) shall not be treated as a dividend.

(2) A dividend received from a regulated investment company shall be subject to the limitations prescribed in section 854.

(3) The amount of dividends properly allocable to a beneficiary under section 652 or 662 shall be deemed to have been received by the beneficiary ratably on the same date that the dividends were received by the estate or trust.

Amendments

• 1964, Revenue Act of 1964 (P.L. 88-272)

P.L. 88-272, §201(d)(6)(C):

Amended Code Sec. 116(c) by adding paragraph (3). **Effective** with respect to dividends received after 12-31-64, in tax years ending after such date.

[Sec. 116(d)]

(d) CERTAIN NONRESIDENT ALIENS INELIGIBLE FOR EXCLUSION.—In the case of a nonresident alien individual, subsection (a) shall apply only—

(1) in determining the tax imposed for the taxable year pursuant to section 871(b)(1) and only in respect of dividends which are effectively connected with the conduct of a trade or business within the United States, or

(2) in determining the tax imposed for the taxable year pursuant to section 877(b).

Amendments

• 1966, Foreign Investors Tax Act of 1966 (P.L. 89-809)

P.L. 89-809, §103(g):

Amended Code Sec. 116(d). **Effective** 1-1-67. Prior to amendment, Sec. 116(d) read as follows:

"(d) Certain Nonresident Aliens Ineligible for Exclusion.—Subsection (a) does not apply to a nonresident alien individual with respect to whom a tax is imposed for the taxable year under section 871(a)."

[Sec. 116(e)]

(e) DIVIDENDS FROM EMPLOYEE STOCK OWNERSHIP PLANS.—Subsection (a) shall not apply to any dividend described in section 404(k).

Amendments

• 1984, Deficit Reduction Act of 1984 (P.L. 98-369)

P.L. 98-369, §542(b):

Amended Code Sec. 116 by adding new subsection (e). **Effective** for tax years beginning after 7-18-84.

• 1980, Crude Oil Windfall Profit Tax Act of 1980 (P.L. 96-223)

P.L. 96-223, §404(a):

Amended Code Sec. 116. **Effective** for tax years beginning after 12-31-80 and before 1-1-83. P.L. 97-34, Act Sec. 302(b)(1), amended Act Sec. 404(c) of P.L. 96-223, by striking out "1983" and inserting "1982".) The text of Code Sec. 116, as amended by P.L. 96-223, follows:

SEC. 116. PARTIAL EXCLUSION OF DIVIDENDS AND INTEREST RECEIVED BY INDIVIDUALS.

[Sec. 116(a)]

(a) EXCLUSION FROM GROSS INCOME.—Gross income does not include the sum of the amounts received during the taxable year by an individual as—

(1) a dividend from a domestic corporation, or

(2) interest.

[Sec. 116(b)]

(b) LIMITATIONS.—

(1) MAXIMUM DOLLAR AMOUNT.—The aggregate amount excluded under subsection (a) for any taxable year shall not exceed $200 ($400 in the case of a joint return under section 6013).

(2) CERTAIN DIVIDENDS EXCLUDED.—Subsection (a)(1) shall not apply to any dividend from a corporation which, for the taxable year of the corporation in which the distribution is made, or for the next preceding taxable year of the corporation, is a corporation exempt from tax under section 501 (relating to certain charitable, etc., organizations) or section 521 (relating to farmers' cooperative associations).

[Sec. 116(c)]

(c) DEFINITIONS; SPECIAL RULES.—For purposes of this section—

(1) INTEREST DEFINED.—The term "interest" means—

(A) interest on deposits with a bank (as defined in section 581),

(B) amounts (whether or not designated as interest) paid, in respect of deposits, investment certificates, or withdrawable or repurchasable shares, by—

(i) a mutual savings bank, cooperative bank, domestic building and loan association, industrial loan association or bank, or credit union, or

(ii) any other savings or thrift institution which is chartered and supervised under Federal or State law,

the deposits or accounts in which are insured under Federal or State law or which are protected and guaranteed under State law,

(C) interest on—

(i) evidences of indebtedness (including bonds, debentures, notes, and certificates) issued by a domestic corporation in registered form, and

(ii) to the extent provided in regulations prescribed by the Secretary, other evidences of indebtedness issued by a domestic corporation of a type offered by corporations to the public,

(D) interest on obligations of the United States, a State, or a political subdivision of a State (not excluded from gross income of the taxpayer under any other provision of law), and

(E) interest attributable to participation shares in a trust established and maintained by a corporation established pursuant to Federal law.

(2) DISTRIBUTIONS FROM REGULATED INVESTMENT COMPANIES AND REAL ESTATE INVESTMENT TRUSTS.—Subsection (a) shall apply with respect to any dividend from—

(A) a regulated investment company, subject to the limitations provided in section 854(b)(2), or

(B) real estate investment trust, subject to the limitations provided in section 857(c).

(3) CERTAIN NONRESIDENT ALIENS INELIGIBLE FOR EXCLUSION.—In the case of a nonresident alien individual, subsection (a) shall apply only—

(A) in determining the tax imposed for the taxable year pursuant to section 871(b)(1) and only in respect of dividends and interest which are effectively connected with the conduct of a trade or business within the United States, or

(B) in determining the tax imposed for the taxable year pursuant to section 877(b).

[Sec. 117]

SEC. 117. QUALIFIED SCHOLARSHIPS.

[Sec. 117(a)]

(a) GENERAL RULE.—Gross income does not include any amount received as a qualified scholarship by an individual who is a candidate for a degree at an educational organization described in section 170(b)(1)(A)(ii).

[Sec. 117(b)]

(b) QUALIFIED SCHOLARSHIP.—For purposes of this section—

(1) IN GENERAL.—The term "qualified scholarship" means any amount received by an individual as a scholarship or fellowship grant to the extent the individual establishes that, in accordance with the conditions of the grant, such amount was used for qualified tuition and related expenses.

(2) QUALIFIED TUITION AND RELATED EXPENSES.—For purposes of paragraph (1), the term "qualified tuition and related expenses" means—

(A) tuition and fees required for the enrollment or attendance of a student at an educational organization described in section 170(b)(1)(A)(ii), and

(B) fees, books, supplies, and equipment required for courses of instruction at such an educational organization.

→ Caution: Code Sec. 117(c), below, is subject to the sunset provision of the Economic Growth and Tax Relief Reconciliation Act of 2001 (P.L. 107-16), §901. Absent Congressional action, the changes made to this provision by P.L. 107-16, or that take effect as if included in P.L. 107-16, do not apply after December 31, 2010. For more information about the sunset provision, see page XXI of the Preface to this publication and P.L. 107-16, §901, in the amendment notes. See the amendments notes for a history of amendments to this section and the effective date of each change.

[Sec. 117(c)]

(c) LIMITATION.—

(1) IN GENERAL.—Except as provided in paragraph (2), subsections (a) and (d) shall not apply to that portion of any amount received which represents payment for teaching, research, or other services by the student required as a condition for receiving the qualified scholarship or qualified tuition reduction.

(2) EXCEPTIONS.—Paragraph (1) shall not apply to any amount received by an individual under—

(A) the National Health Service Corps Scholarship Program under section 338A(g)(1)(A) of the Public Health Service Act, or

(B) the Armed Forces Health Professions Scholarship and Financial Assistance program under subchapter I of chapter 105 of title 10, United States Code.

Amendments

• 2001, Economic Growth and Tax Relief Reconciliation Act of 2001 (P.L. 107-16)

P.L. 107-16, §413(a)(1)-(2):

Amended Code Sec. 117(c) by striking "Subsections (a)" and inserting "(1) IN GENERAL.—Except as provided in paragraph (2), subsections (a)", and by adding at the end a new paragraph (2). **Effective** for amounts received in tax years beginning after 12-31-2001.

P.L. 107-16, §901(a)-(b), provides:

SEC. 901. SUNSET OF PROVISIONS OF ACT.

(a) IN GENERAL.—All provisions of, and amendments made by, this Act shall not apply—

(1) to taxable, plan, or limitation years beginning after December 31, 2010, or

(2) in the case of title V, to estates of decedents dying, gifts made, or generation skipping transfers, after December 31, 2010.

(b) APPLICATION OF CERTAIN LAWS.—The Internal Revenue Code of 1986 and the Employee Retirement Income Security Act of 1974 shall be applied and administered to years, estates, gifts, and transfers described in subsection (a) as if the provisions and amendments described in subsection (a) had never been enacted.

[Sec. 117(d)]

(d) QUALIFIED TUITION REDUCTION.—

(1) IN GENERAL.—Gross income shall not include any qualified tuition reduction.

(2) QUALIFIED TUITION REDUCTION.—For purposes of this subsection, the term "qualified tuition reduction" means the amount of any reduction in tuition provided to an employee of an organization described in section 170(b)(1)(A)(ii) for the education (below the graduate level) at such organization (or another organization described in section 170(b)(1)(A)(ii)) of—

(A) such employee, or

(B) any person treated as an employee (or whose use is treated as an employee use) under the rules of section 132(h).

(3) REDUCTION MUST NOT DISCRIMINATE IN FAVOR OF HIGHLY COMPENSATED, ETC.—Paragraph (1) shall apply with respect to any qualified tuition reduction provided with respect to any highly compensated employee only if such reduction is available on substantially the same terms to each member of a group of employees which is defined under a reasonable classification set up by the employer which does not discriminate in favor of highly compensated employees (within the meaning of section 414(q)). For purposes of this paragraph, the term "highly compensated employee" has the meaning given such term by section 414(q).

(5) [(4)] SPECIAL RULES FOR TEACHING AND RESEARCH ASSISTANTS.—In the case of the education of an individual who is a graduate student at an educational organization described in section 170(b)(1)(A)(ii) and who is engaged in teaching or research activities for such organization, paragraph (2) shall be applied as if it did not contain the phrase "(below the graduate level)".

Amendments

• 1996, Small Business Job Protection Act of 1996 (P.L. 104-188)

P.L. 104-188, §1703(n)(14):

Amended Code Sec. 117(d)(2)(B) by striking "section 132(f)" and inserting "section 132(h)". **Effective** as if included in the provision of P.L. 103-66 to which it relates.

• 1989 (P.L. 101-140)

P.L. 101-140, §203(a)(1):

Provides that Code Sec. 117(d)(4), as added by Section 1151(g)(2) of P.L. 99-514, shall be applied as if the amendment made by such section had not been enacted.

P.L. 101-140, §203(a)(2):

Provides that Code Sec. 117(d)(4), as amended by Section 1011B(a)(31)(B)(i)-(ii) of P.L. 100-647, shall be applied as if the amendment made by such section had not been enacted. **Effective** as if included in section 1151 of P.L. 99-514. Code Sec. 117(d)(4) as added by Act Sec. 1151(g)(2) of P.L. 99-514 and amended by Act Sec. 1011B(a)(31)(B)(i)-(ii) of P.L. 100-647 read as follows:

(4) EXCLUSION OF CERTAIN EMPLOYEES.—For purposes of this subsection, there shall be excluded from consideration employees who are excluded from consideration under section 89(h).

• 1989 (P.L. 101-136)

P.L. 101-136, §528, provides:

SEC. 528. No monies appropriated by this Act may be used to implement or enforce section 1151 of the Tax Reform Act of 1986 or the amendments made by such section.

• 1988, Technical and Miscellaneous Revenue Act of 1988 (P.L. 100-647)

P.L. 100-647, §1011B(a)(31)(B)(i)-(ii):

Amended Code Sec. 117(d)(4) by striking out "may" the first place it appears and inserting in lieu thereof "shall", and by striking out "may be" the second place it appears and inserting in lieu thereof "are". **Effective** as if included in the provision of P.L. 99-514 to which it relates.

P.L. 100-647, §4001(b)(2):

Amended Code Sec. 117(d) by adding at the end thereof new paragraph (5). **Effective** for tax years beginning after 12-31-87.

• 1986, Tax Reform Act of 1986 (P.L. 99-514)

P.L. 99-514, §123(a):

Amended Code Sec. 117. **Effective** for tax years beginning after 12-31-86, but only in the case of scholarships and fellowships after 8-16-86. Prior to amendment, Code Sec. 117 read as follows:

SEC. 117. SCHOLARSHIPS AND FELLOWSHIP GRANTS.

[Sec. 117(a)]

(a) GENERAL RULE.—In the case of an individual, gross income does not include—

(1) any amount received—

(A) as a scholarship at an educational organization described in section 170(b)(1)(A)(ii), or

(B) as a fellowship grant,

including the value of contributed services and accommodations; and

(2) any amount received to cover expenses for—

(A) travel,

(B) research,

(C) clerical help, or

(D) equipment,

which are incident to such a scholarship or to a fellowship grant, but only to the extent that the amount is so expended by the recipient.

Amendments

• 1976, Tax Reform Act of 1976 (P.L. 94-455)

P.L. 94-455, §1901(b)(8):

Amended Code Sec. 117 by substituting "educational organization described in section 170(b)(1)(A)(ii)" for "educational institution (as defined in section 151(e)(4))". **Effective** for tax years beginning after 12-31-76.

• 1974 (P.L. 93-483)

P.L. 93-483, §4, as amended by P.L. 95-171, §5, P.L. 95-600, §161, and P.L. 96-167, §9(d), provides:

(a) IN GENERAL.—Any amount received from appropriated funds as a scholarship, including the value of contributed services and accommodations, by a member of a uniformed service who is receiving training under the Armed Forces Health Professions Scholarship Program (or any other program determined by the Secretary of the Treasury or his delegate to have substantially similar objectives) from an educational institution (as defined in section 151(c)(4) of the Internal Revenue Code of 1954) shall be treated as a scholarship under section 117 of such Code, whether that member is receiving training while on active duty or in an off-duty or inactive status, and without regard to whether a period of active duty is required of the member as a condition of receiving those payments.

(b) DEFINITION OF UNIFORMED SERVICES.—For purposes of this section, the term `uniformed service' has the meaning given it by section 101(3) of title 37, United States Code.

(c) EFFECTIVE DATE.—The provisions of this section shall apply with respect to amounts received during calendar years 1973, 1974, and 1975 and in the case of a member of a uniformed service receiving training after 1975 and before 1981 in programs described in subsection (a), with respect to amounts received after 1975 and before 1985.

[Sec. 117(b)]

(b) LIMITATIONS.—

(1) INDIVIDUALS WHO ARE CANDIDATES FOR DEGREES.—In the case of an individual who is a candidate for a degree at an educational organization described in section 170(b)(1)(A)(ii), subsection (a) shall not apply to that portion of any amount received which represents payment for teaching, research, or other services in the nature of part-time employment required as a condition to receiving the scholarship or the fellowship grant. If teaching, research, or other services are required of all candidates (whether or not recipients of scholarships or fellowship grants) for a particular degree as a condition to receiving such degree, such teaching, research, or other services shall not be regarded as part-time employment within the meaning of this paragraph.

(2) INDIVIDUALS WHO ARE NOT CANDIDATES FOR DEGREES.—In the case of an individual who is not a candidate for a degree at an educational organization described in section 170(b)(1)(A)(ii), subsection (a) shall apply only if the condition in subparagraph (A) is satisfied and then only within the limitations provided in subparagraph (B).

(A) CONDITIONS FOR EXCLUSION.—The grantor of the scholarship or fellowship grant is—

(i) an organization described in section 501(c)(3) which is exempt from tax under section 501(a),

(ii) a foreign government,

(iii) an international organization, or a binational or multinational educational and cultural foundation or commission created or continued pursuant to the Mutual Educational and Cultural Exchange Act of 1961, or

(iv) the United States, or an instrumentality or agency thereof, or a State, or a possession of the United States, or any political subdivision thereof, or the District of Columbia.

(B) EXTENT OF EXCLUSION.—The amount of the scholarship or fellowship grant excluded under subsection (a)(1) in any taxable year shall be limited to an amount equal to $300 times the number of months for which the recipient received amounts under the scholarship or fellowship grant during such taxable year, except that no exclusion shall be allowed under subsection (a) after the recipient has been entitled to exclude under this section for a period of 36 months (whether or not consecutive) amounts received as a scholarship or fellowship grant while not a candidate for a degree at an educational institution described in section 170(b)(1)(A)(ii).

Amendments

• 1976, Tax Reform Act of 1976 (P.L. 94-455)

P.L. 94-455, §1901(b)(8):

Amended Code Sec. 117(b) by substituting "educational organization described in section 170(b)(1)(A)(ii)" for "educational institution (as defined in section 151(e)(4))" in paragraphs (1) and (2). **Effective** for tax years beginning after 12-31-76.

P.L. 94-455, §1901(c):

Struck out "a Territory," after "a State,". **Effective** for tax years beginning after 12-31-76.

• 1961, Peace Corps Act (P.L. 87-256)

P.L. 87-256, §110(a):

Amended Code Sec. 117(b)(2)(A). **Effective** for tax years beginning after 1961. Prior to amendment, it read as follows:

(A) Conditions for exclusion.—The grantor of the scholarship or fellowship grant is an organization described in section 501(c)(3) which is exempt from tax under section 501(a), the United States, or an instrumentality or agency thereof, or a State, a Territory, or a possession of the United States, or any political subdivision thereof, or the District of Columbia.

[Sec. 117(c)]

(c) FEDERAL GRANTS FOR TUITION AND RELATED EXPENSES NOT INCLUDABLE MERELY BECAUSE THERE IS REQUIREMENT OF FUTURE SERVICE AS FEDERAL EMPLOYEE.—

(1) IN GENERAL.—If—

(A) an amount received by an individual under a Federal program would be excludable under subsections (a) and (b) as a scholarship or fellowship grant but for the fact that the individual is required to perform future service as a Federal employee, and

(B) the individual establishes that, in accordance with the terms of the grant, such amount was used for qualified tuition and related expenses,

gross income shall not include such amount.

(2) QUALIFIED TUITION AND RELATED EXPENSES DEFINED.—For purposes of this subsection—

(A) IN GENERAL.—The term "qualified tuition and related expenses" means—

(i) tuition and fees required for the enrollment or attendance of a student at an institution of higher education, and

(ii) fees, books, supplies, and equipment required for courses of instruction at an institution of higher education.

(B) INSTITUTION OF HIGHER EDUCATION.—The term "institution of higher education" means an educational institution in any State which—

(i) admits as regular students only individuals having a certificate of graduation from a high school, or the recognized equivalent of such a certificate,

(ii) is legally authorized within such State to provide a program of education beyond high school,

(iii) provides an educational program for which it awards a bachelor's or higher degree, provides a program which is acceptable for full credit toward such a degree, or offers a program of training to prepare students for gainful employment in a recognized health profession, and

(iv) is a public or other nonprofit institution.

(3) SERVICE AS FEDERAL EMPLOYEE.—For purposes of this subsection, service in a health manpower shortage area shall be treated as service as a Federal employee.

Amendments

• 1980 (P.L. 96-541)

P.L. 96-541, §5(a)(1):

Added Code Sec. 117(c). **Effective** for tax years beginning after 12-31-80.

[Sec. 117(d)]

(d) QUALIFIED TUITION REDUCTIONS.—

(1) IN GENERAL.—Gross income shall not include any qualified tuition reduction.

(2) QUALIFIED TUITION REDUCTION.—For purposes of this subsection, the term "qualified tuition reduction" means the amount of any reduction in tuition provided to an employee of an organization described in section 170(b)(1)(A)(ii) for the education (below the graduate level) at such organization (or another organization described in section 170(b)(1)(A)(ii)) of—

(A) such employee, or

(B) any person treated as an employee (or whose use is treated as an employee use) under the rules of section 132(f).

(3) Reduction must not discriminate in favor of highly compensated, etc.—Paragraph (1) shall apply with respect to any qualified tuition reduction provided with respect to any officer, owner, or highly compensated employee only if such reduction is available on substantially the same terms to each member of a group of employees which is defined under a reasonable classification set up by the employer which does not discriminate in favor of officers, owners, or highly compensated employees.

Amendments

• 1984 (P.L. 98-611)

P.L. 98-611, §1(g)(5), provides:

(5) COORDINATION WITH SECTION 117(d).—In the case of education described in section 127(c)(8) of the Internal Revenue Code of 1954, as added by this section, section 117(d) of such Code shall be treated as in effect on and after January 1, 1984.

• 1984, Deficit Reduction Act of 1984 (P.L. 98-369)

P.L. 98-369, §532(a):

Amended Code Sec. 117 by adding at the end thereof a new subsection (d). **Effective** for qualified tuition reductions (as defined in Code Sec. 117(d)(2)) for education furnished after 6-30-85, in tax years ending after such date.

• 1986, Tax Reform Act of 1986 (P.L. 99-514)

P.L. 99-514, §1114(b)(2)(A)-(C):

Amended Code Sec. 117(d)(3), as amended by Act Sec. 123, by striking out "officer, owner, or", by striking out "officers, owners, or", and by inserting at the end thereof a new sentence. **Effective** for tax years beginning after 12-31-87. Prior to amendment, Code Sec. 117(d)(3) read as follows:

(3) REDUCTION MUST NOT DISCRIMINATE IN FAVOR OF HIGHLY COMPENSATED, ETC.—Paragraph (1) shall apply with respect to any qualified tuition reduction provided with respect to any officer, owner, or highly compensated employee only if such reduction is available on substantially the same terms to each member of a group of employees which is defined under a reasonable classification set up by the employer which does not discriminate in favor of officers, owners, or highly compensated employees (within the meaning of section 414(q)).

P.L. 99-514, §1151(g)(2):

Amended Code Sec. 117(d) by adding at the end thereof new paragraph (4). For the **effective** date, see Act Sec. 1151(k), below.

P.L. 99-514, §1151(k), provides:

(k) EFFECTIVE DATES.—

(1) IN GENERAL.—The amendments made by this section shall apply to years beginning after the later of—

(A) December 31, 1987, or

(B) the earlier of—

(i) the date which is 3 months after the date on which the Secretary of the Treasury or his delegate issues such regulations as are necessary to carry out the provisions of section 89 of the Internal Revenue Code of 1986 (as added by this section), or

(ii) December 31, 1988.

(2) SPECIAL RULE FOR COLLECTIVE BARGAINING PLAN.—In the case of a plan maintained pursuant to 1 or more collective bargaining agreements between employee representatives and 1 or more employers ratified before March 1, 1986, the amendments made by this section shall not apply to employees covered by such an agreement in years beginning before the earlier of—

(A) the date on which the last of such collective bargaining agreements terminates (determined without regard to any extension thereof after February 28, 1986), or

(B) January 1, 1981.

A plan shall not be required to take into account employees to which the preceding sentence applies for purposes of applying section 89 of the Internal Revenue Code of 1986 (as added by this section) to employees to which the preceding sentence does not apply for any year preceding the year described in the preceding sentence.

(3) EXCEPTION FOR CERTAIN GROUP-TERM INSURANCE PLANS.—In the case of a plan described in section 223(d)(2) of the Tax Reform Act of 1984, such plan shall be treated as meeting the requirements of section 89 of the Internal Revenue Code of 1986 (as added by this section) with respect to individuals described in section 223(d)(2) of such Act. An employer may elect to disregard such individuals in applying section 89 of such Code (as so added) to other employees of the employer.

(4) SPECIAL RULE FOR CHURCH PLANS.—In the case of a church plan (within the meaning of section 414(e)(3) of the Internal Revenue Code of 1986) maintaining an insured accident and health plan, the amendments made by this section shall apply to years beginning after December 31, 1988.

(5) CAFETERIA PLANS.—The amendments made by subsection (d)(2) shall apply to taxable years beginning after December 31, 1983.

P.L. 99-514, §1853(f), provides:

(f) TRANSITIONAL RULES FOR TREATMENT OF CERTAIN REDUCTIONS IN TUITION.—

(1) A tuition reduction plan shall be treated as meeting the requirements of section 117(d)(3) of the Internal Revenue Code of 1954 if—

(A) such plan would have met the requirements of such section (as amended by this section but without regard to the lack of evidence that benefits under such plan were the subject of good faith bargaining) on the day on which eligibility to participate in the plan was closed,

(B) at all times thereafter, the tuition reductions available under such plan are available on substantially the same terms to all employees eligible to participate in such plan, and

(C) the eligibility to participate in such plan closed on June 30, 1972, June 30, 1974, or December 31, 1975.

(2) For purposes of applying section 117(d)(3) of the Internal Revenue Code of 1954 to all tuition reduction plans of an employer with at least 1 such plan described in paragraph (1) of this subsection, there shall be excluded from consideration employees not included in the plan who are included in a unit of employees covered by an agreement that the Secretary of the Treasury or his delegate finds to be a collective bargaining agreement between employee representatives and 1 or more employers, if, with respect to plans other than plans described in paragraph (1), there is evidence that such benefits were the subject of good faith bargaining.

(3) Any reduction in tuition provided with respect to a full-time course of education furnished at the graduate level before July 1, 1988, shall not be included in gross income if—

(A) such reduction would not be included in gross income under the Internal Revenue Service regulations in effect on the date of the enactment of the Tax Reform Act of 1984, and

(B) such reduction is provided with respect to a student who was accepted for admission to such course of education before July 1, 1984, and began such course of education before June 30, 1985.

[Sec. 118]

SEC. 118. CONTRIBUTIONS TO THE CAPITAL OF A CORPORATION.

[Sec. 118(a)]

(a) GENERAL RULE.—In the case of a corporation, gross income does not include any contribution to the capital of the taxpayer.

[Sec. 118(b)]

(b) CONTRIBUTIONS IN AID OF CONSTRUCTION ETC.—For purposes of subsection (a), except as provided in subsection (c), the term "contribution to the capital of the taxpayer" does not include any contribution in aid of construction or any other contribution as a customer or potential customer.

Amendments

• 1996, Small Business Job Protection Act of 1996 (P.L. 104-188)

P.L. 104-188, §1613(a)(2):

Amended Code Sec. 118(b) by inserting "except as provided in subsection (c)," before "the term". **Effective** for amounts received after 6-12-96.

• 1986, Tax Reform Act of 1986 (P.L. 99-514)

P.L. 99-514, §824(a):

Amended Code Sec. 118 by striking out subsection (b) and (c), by redesignating subsection (d) as subsection (c), and by inserting after subsection (a) new subsection (b). **Effective** for amounts received after 12-31-86, in tax years ending after such date. For an exception, see Act Sec. 824(c)(2) following Code Sec. 118(e). Prior to amendment, Code Sec. 118(b) read as follows:

(b) CONTRIBUTIONS IN AID OF CONSTRUCTION.—

(1) GENERAL RULE.—For purposes of this section, the term "contribution to the capital of the taxpayer" includes any amount of money or other property received from any person (whether or not a shareholder) by a regulated public utility which provides electric energy, gas (through a local distribution system or transportation by pipeline), water, or sewerage disposal services if—

(A) such amount is a contribution in aid of construction,

(B) where the contribution is in property which is other than electric energy, gas, steam, water, or sewerage disposal facilities, such amount meets the requirements of the expenditure rule of paragraph (2), and

(C) such amounts (or any property acquired or constructed with such amounts) are not included in the taxpayer's rate base for rate-making purposes.

(2) EXPENDITURE RULE.—An amount meets the requirements of this paragraph if—

(A) an amount equal to such amount is expended for the acquisition or construction of tangible property described in section 1231(b)—

(i) which was the purpose motivating the contribution, and

(ii) which is used predominantly in the trade or business of furnishing electric energy, gas, steam, water, or sewerage disposal services,

(B) the expenditure referred to in subparagraph (A) occurs before the end of the second taxable year after the year in which such amount was received, and

(C) accurate records are kept of the amounts contributed and expenditures made on the basis of the project for which the contribution was made and on the basis of the year of contribution or expenditure.

(3) DEFINITIONS.—For purposes of this section—

(A) CONTRIBUTION IN AID OF CONSTRUCTION.—The term "contribution in aid of construction" shall be defined by regulations prescribed by the Secretary; except that such term shall not include amounts paid as customer connection fees (including amounts paid to connect the customer's line to an electric line, a gas main, a steam line, or a main water or sewer line and amounts paid as service charges for starting or stopping services).

(B) PREDOMINANTLY.—The term "predominantly" means 80 percent or more.

(C) REGULATED PUBLIC UTILITY.—The term "regulated public utility" has the meaning given such term by section 7701(a)(33); except that such term shall not include any such utility which is not required to provide electric energy, gas, water, or sewerage disposal services to members of the general public (including in the case of a gas transmission utility, the provision of gas services by sale for resale to the general public) in its service area.

(4) DISALLOWANCE OF DEDUCTIONS AND INVESTMENT CREDIT; ADJUSTED BASIS.—Notwithstanding any other provision of this subtitle, no deduction or credit shall be allowed for, or by reason of, the expenditure which constitutes a contribution in aid of construction to which this subsection applies. The adjusted basis of any property acquired with contributions in aid of construction to which this subsection applies shall be zero.

• 1978, Revenue Act of 1978 (P.L. 95-600)

P.L. 95-600, 364(a):

Amended Code Secs. 118(b)(1)-(3). **Effective** for contributions made after 1-1-76. Prior to amendment, Code Secs. 118(b)(1)-(3) read as follows:

(b) CONTRIBUTIONS IN AID OF CONSTRUCTION.—

(1) GENERAL RULE.—For purposes of this section, the term "contribution to the capital of the taxpayer" includes any amount of money or other property received from any person (whether or not a shareholder) by a regulated public utility which provides water or sewerage disposal services if—

(A) such amount is a contribution in aid of construction,

(B) where the contribution is in property which is other than water or sewerage disposal facilities, such amount meets the requirements of the expenditure rule of paragraph (2), and

(C) such amounts (or any property acquired or constructed with such amounts) are not included in the taxpayer's rate base for ratemaking purposes.

(2) EXPENDITURE RULE.—An amount meets the requirements of this paragraph if—

(A) an amount equal to such amount is expended for the acquisition or construction of tangible property described in section 1231(b)—

(i) which was the purpose motivating the contribution, and

(ii) which is used predominantly in the trade or business of furnishing water or sewerage disposal services,

(B) the expenditure referred to in subparagraph (A) occurs before the end of the second taxable year after the year in which such amount was received, and

(C) accurate records are kept of the amounts contributed and expenditures made on the basis of the project for which the contribution was made and on the basis of the year of contribution or expenditure.

(3) DEFINITIONS.—For purposes of this section—

(A) CONTRIBUTION IN AID OF CONSTRUCTION.—The term "contribution in aid of construction" shall be defined by regulations prescribed by the Secretary; except that such term shall not include amounts paid as customer connection fees (including amounts paid to connect the customer's property to a main water or sewer line and amounts paid as service charges for starting or stopping services).

(B) PREDOMINANTLY.—The term "predominantly" means 80 percent or more.

(C) REGULATED PUBLIC UTILITY.—The term "regulated public utility" has the meaning given such term by section 7701(a)(33); except that such term shall not include any such utility which is not required to provide water or sewerage disposal services to members of the general public in its service area.

(4) DISALLOWANCE OF DEDUCTIONS AND INVESTMENT CREDIT; ADJUSTED BASIS.—Notwithstanding any other provision of this subtitle, no deduction or credit shall be allowed for, or by reason of, the expenditure which constitutes a contribution in aid of construction to which this subsection applies. The adjusted basis of any property acquired with contributions in aid of construction to which this subsection applies shall be zero.

• 1976, Tax Reform Act of 1976 (P.L. 94-455)

P.L. 94-455, §2120(a):

Amended Code Sec. 118 by redesignating subsection (b) as subsection (c) and adding a new subsection (b). **Effective** for contributions made after 1-31-76.

[Sec. 118(c)]

(c) SPECIAL RULES FOR WATER AND SEWERAGE DISPOSAL UTILITIES.—

(1) GENERAL RULE.—For purposes of this section, the term "contribution to the capital of the taxpayer" includes any amount of money or other property received from any person (whether or not a shareholder) by a regulated public utility which provides water or sewerage disposal services if—

(A) such amount is a contribution in aid of construction,

(B) in the case of contribution of property other than water or sewerage disposal facilities, such amount meets the requirements of the expenditure rule of paragraph (2), and

(C) such amount (or any property acquired or constructed with such amount) is not included in the taxpayer's rate base for ratemaking purposes.

(2) EXPENDITURE RULE.—An amount meets the requirements of this paragraph if—

(A) an amount equal to such amount is expended for the acquisition or construction of tangible property described in section 1231(b)—

(i) which is the property for which the contribution was made or is of the same type as such property, and

(ii) which is used predominantly in the trade or business of furnishing water or sewerage disposal services,

(B) the expenditure referred to in subparagraph (A) occurs before the end of the second taxable year after the year in which such amount was received, and

(C) accurate records are kept of the amounts contributed and expenditures made, the expenditures to which contributions are allocated, and the year in which the contributions and expenditures are received and made.

(3) DEFINITIONS.—For purposes of this subsection—

(A) CONTRIBUTION IN AID OF CONSTRUCTION.—The term "contribution in aid of construction" shall be defined by regulations prescribed by the Secretary, except that such term shall not include amounts paid as service charges for starting or stopping services.

(B) PREDOMINANTLY.—The term "predominantly" means 80 percent or more.

(C) REGULATED PUBLIC UTILITY.—The term "regulated public utility" has the meaning given such term by section 7701(a)(33), except that such term shall not include any utility which is not required to provide water or sewerage disposal services to members of the general public in its service area.

(4) DISALLOWANCE OF DEDUCTIONS AND CREDITS; ADJUSTED BASIS.—Notwithstanding any other provision of this subtitle, no deduction or credit shall be allowed for, or by reason of, any expenditure which constitutes a contribution in aid of construction to which this subsection applies. The adjusted basis of any property acquired with contributions in aid of construction to which this subsection applies shall be zero.

Amendments

• 1996, Small Business Job Protection Act of 1996 (P.L. 104-188)

P.L. 104-188, §1613(a)(1)(A)-(B):

Amended Code Sec. 118 by redesignating subsection (c) as subsection (e), and by inserting after subsection (b) new subsections (c) and (d). **Effective** for amounts received after 6-12-96.

[Sec. 118(d)]

(d) STATUTE OF LIMITATIONS.—If the taxpayer for any taxable year treats an amount as a contribution to the capital of the taxpayer described in subsection (c), then—

(1) the statutory period for the assessment of any deficiency attributable to any part of such amount shall not expire before the expiration of 3 years from the date the Secretary is notified by the taxpayer (in such manner as the Secretary may prescribe) of—

(A) the amount of the expenditure referred to in subparagraph (A) of subsection (c)(2),

(B) the taxpayer's intention not to make the expenditures referred to in such subparagraph, or

(C) a failure to make such expenditure within the period described in subparagraph (B) of subsection (c)(2), and

(2) such deficiency may be assessed before the expiration of such 3-year period notwithstanding the provisions of any other law or rule of law which would otherwise prevent such assessment.

Amendments

• 1996, Small Business Job Protection Act of 1996 (P.L. 104-188)

P.L. 104-188, §1613(a)(1)(B):

Amended Code Sec. 118 by inserting after subsection (b) new subsections (c) and (d). **Effective** for amounts received after 6-12-96.

[Sec. 118(e)]

(e) CROSS REFERENCES.—

(1) For basis of property acquired by a corporation through a contribution to its capital, see section 362.

(2) For special rules in the case of contributions of indebtedness, see section 108(e)(6).

Amendments

• 1996, Small Business Job Protection Act of 1996 (P.L. 104-188)

P.L. 104-188, §1613(a)(1)(A):

Amended Code Sec. 118 by redesignating subsection (c) as subsection (e). **Effective** for amounts received after 6-12-96.

• 1986, Tax Reform Act of 1986 (P.L. 99-514)

P.L. 99-514, §824(a):

Amended Code Sec. 118 by striking out subsection (c) and redesignating subsection (d) as subsection (c). **Effective** for amounts received after 12-31-86, in tax years ending after such date. For an exception, see Act Sec. 824(c)(2), below. Prior to amendment, subsection (c) read as follows:

(c) STATUTE OF LIMITATIONS.—If the taxpayer for any taxable year treats an amount as a contribution to the capital of the taxpayer described in subsection (b), then—

(1) the statutory period for the assessment of any deficiency attributable to any part of such amount shall not expire before the expiration of 3 years from the date the Secretary is notified by the taxpayer (in such manner as the Secretary may prescribe) of—

(A) the amount of the expenditure referred to in subparagraph (A) of subsection (b)(2),

(B) the taxpayer's intention not to make the expenditures referred to in such subparagraph, or

(C) a failure to make such expenditure within the period described in subparagraph (B) of subsection (b)(2); and

(2) such deficiency may be assessed before the expiration of such 3-year period notwithstanding the provisions of any other law or rule of law which would otherwise prevent such assessment.

P.L. 99-514, §824(c)(2)-(4), as amended by P.L. 100-647, §1008(j)(2), provides:

(2) TREATMENT OF CERTAIN WATER SUPPLY PROJECTS.—The amendments made by this section shall not apply to amounts which are paid by the New Jersey Department of Environmental Protection for construction of alternative water supply projects in zones of drinking water contamination and which are designated by such department as being taken into account under this paragraph. Not more than $4,631,000 of such amounts may be designated under the preceding sentence.

(3) TREATMENT OF CERTAIN CONTRIBUTIONS BY TRANSPORTATION AUTHORITY.—The amendments made by this section shall not apply to contributions in aid of construction by a qualified transportation authority which were clearly identified in a master plan in existence on September 13, 1984, and which are designated by such authority as being taken into account under this paragraph. Not more than $68,000,000 of such contributions may be designated under the preceding sentence. For purposes of this paragraph, a qualified transportation authority is an entity which was created on February 20, 1967, and which was established by an interstate compact and consented to by Congress in Public Law 89-774, 80 Stat. 1324 (1966).

(4) TREATMENT OF CERTAIN PARTNERSHIPS.—In the case of a partnership with a taxable year beginning May 1, 1986, if such partnership realized net capital gain during the period beginning on the 1st day of such taxable year and ending on May 29, 1986, pursuant to an underwriting agreement dated May 6, 1986, then such partnership may elect to treat each asset to which such net capital gain relates as having been distributed to the partners of such partnership in proportion to their distributive share of the capital gain or loss realized by the partnership with respect to such asset and to treat each such asset as having been sold by each partner on the date of the sale of the asset by the partnership. If such an election is made, the consideration received by the partnership in connection with the sale of such assets shall be treated as having been received by the partners in connection with the deemed sale of such assets. In the case of a tiered partnership, for purposes of this paragraph each partnership shall be treated as having realized net capital gain equal to its proportionate share of the net capital gain of each partnership in which it is a partner, and the election provided by this paragraph shall apply to each tier.

• 1984, Deficit Reduction Act of 1984 (P.L. 98-369)

P.L. 98-369, §163(a):

Amended Code Sec. 118 by redesignating subsection (c) as subsection (d) and by adding new subsection (c). **Effective** for expenditures with respect to which the second tax year described in Code Sec. 118(b)(2)(B) ends after 12-31-84.

• 1980, Bankruptcy Tax Act of 1980 (P.L. 96-589)

P.L. 96-589, §2(e)(2):

Amended Code Sec. 118(c). For the **effective** date of this amendment, see the historical comment for P.L. 96-589 under Code Sec. 108(e). Prior to amendment, Code Sec. 118(c) provided:

"(c) CROSS REFERENCE.—

For basis of property acquired by a corporation through a contribution to its capital, see section 362."

• 1976, Tax Reform Act of 1976 (P.L. 94-455)

P.L. 94-455, §2120(a):

Amended Code Sec. 118 by redesignating subsection (b) as subsection (c). **Effective** for contributions made after 1-31-76.

[Sec. 119]

SEC. 119. MEALS OR LODGING FURNISHED FOR THE CONVENIENCE OF THE EMPLOYER.

[Sec. 119(a)]

(a) MEALS AND LODGING FURNISHED TO EMPLOYEE, HIS SPOUSE, AND HIS DEPENDENTS, PURSUANT TO EMPLOYMENT .—There shall be excluded from gross income of an employee the value of any meals or lodging furnished to him, his spouse, or any of his dependents by or on behalf of his employer for the convenience of the employer, but only if—

(1) in the case of meals, the meals are furnished on the business premises of the employer, or

(2) in the case of lodging, the employee is required to accept such lodging on the business premises of his employer as a condition of his employment.

[Sec. 119(b)]

(b) SPECIAL RULES .—For purposes of subsection (a)—

(1) PROVISIONS OF EMPLOYMENT CONTRACT OR STATE STATUTE NOT TO BE DETERMINATIVE .—In determining whether meals or lodging are furnished for the convenience of the employer, the provisions of an employment contract or of a State statute fixing terms of employment shall not be determinative of whether the meals or lodging are intended as compensation.

(2) CERTAIN FACTORS NOT TAKEN INTO ACCOUNT WITH RESPECT TO MEALS .—In determining whether meals are furnished for the convenience of the employer, the fact that a charge is made for such meals, and the fact that the employee may accept or decline such meals, shall not be taken into account.

(3) CERTAIN FIXED CHARGES FOR MEALS.—

(A) IN GENERAL .—If—

(i) an employee is required to pay on a periodic basis a fixed charge for his meals, and

(ii) such meals are furnished by the employer for the convenience of the employer,

there shall be excluded from the employee's gross income an amount equal to such fixed charge.

(B) APPLICATION OF SUBPARAGRAPH (A) .—Subparagraph (A) shall apply—

(i) whether the employee pays the fixed charge out of his stated compensation or out of his own funds, and

(ii) only if the employee is required to make the payment whether he accepts or declines the meals.

(4) MEALS FURNISHED TO EMPLOYEES ON BUSINESS PREMISES WHERE MEALS OF MOST EMPLOYEES ARE OTHERWISE EXCLUDABLE .—All meals furnished on the business premises of an employer to such employer's employees shall be treated as furnished for the convenience of the employer if, without regard to this paragraph, more than half of the employees to whom such meals are furnished on such premises are furnished such meals for the convenience of the employer.

Amendments

• 1998, IRS Restructuring and Reform Act of 1998 (P.L. 105-206)

P.L. 105-206, §5002(a):

Amended Code Sec. 119(b) by adding at the end a new paragraph (4). **Effective** for tax years beginning before, on, or after 7-22-98.

[Sec. 119(c)]

(c) EMPLOYEES LIVING IN CERTAIN CAMPS.—

(1) IN GENERAL .—In the case of an individual who is furnished lodging in a camp located in a foreign country by or on behalf of his employer, such camp shall be considered to be part of the business premises of the employer.

(2) CAMP .—For purposes of this section, a camp constitutes lodging which is—

(A) provided by or on behalf of the employer for the convenience of the employer because the place at which such individual renders services is in a remote area where satisfactory housing is not available on the open market,

(B) located, as near as practicable, in the vicinity of the place at which such individual renders services, and

(C) furnished in a common area (or enclave) which is not available to the public and which normally accommodates 10 or more employees.

Amendments

• 1981, Economic Recovery Tax Act of 1981 (P.L. 97-34)

P.L. 97-34, §113:

Added Code Sec. 119(c). **Effective** for tax years beginning after 12-31-81.

[Sec. 119(d)]

(d) LODGING FURNISHED BY CERTAIN EDUCATIONAL INSTITUTIONS TO EMPLOYEES.—

(1) IN GENERAL .—In the case of an employee of an educational institution, gross income shall not include the value of qualified campus lodging furnished to such employee during the taxable year.

(2) EXCEPTION IN CASES OF INADEQUATE RENT .—Paragraph (1) shall not apply to the extent of the excess of—

(A) the lesser of—

(i) 5 percent of the appraised value of the qualified campus lodging, or

(ii) the average of the rentals paid by individuals (other than employees or students of the educational institution) during such calendar year for lodging provided by the educational institution which is comparable to the qualified campus lodging provided to the employee, over

(B) the rent paid by the employee for the qualified campus lodging during such calendar year.

The appraised value under subparagraph (A)(i) shall be determined as of the close of the calendar year in which the taxable year begins, or, in the case of a rental period not greater than 1 year, at any time during the calendar year in which such period begins.

(3) QUALIFIED CAMPUS LODGING .—For purposes of this subsection, the term "qualified campus lodging" means lodging to which subsection (a) does not apply and which is—

(A) located on, or in the proximity of, a campus of the educational institution, and

(B) furnished to the employee, his spouse, and any of his dependents by or on behalf of such institution for use as a residence.

(4) EDUCATIONAL INSTITUTION, ETC .—For purposes of this subsection—

(A) IN GENERAL .—The term "educational institution" means—

(i) an institution described in section 170(b)(1)(A)(ii) (or an entity organized under State law and composed of public institutions so described), or

(ii) an academic health center.

(B) ACADEMIC HEALTH CENTER .—For purposes of subparagraph (A), the term "academic health center" means an entity—

(i) which is described in section 170(b)(1)(A)(iii),

(ii) which receives (during the calendar year in which the taxable year of the taxpayer begins) payments under subsection (d)(5)(B) or (h) of section 1886 of the Social Security Act (relating to graduate medical education), and

(iii) which has as one of its principal purposes or functions the providing and teaching of basic and clinical medical science and research with the entity's own faculty.

Amendments

• 1996, Small Business Job Protection Act of 1996 (P.L. 104-188)

P.L. 104-188, §1123(a):

Amended Code Sec. 119(d)(4). **Effective** for tax years beginning after 12-31-95. Prior to amendment, Code Sec. 119(d)(4) read as follows:

(4) EDUCATIONAL INSTITUTION.—For purposes of this paragraph, the term "educational institution" means an institution described in section 170(b)(1)(A)(ii).

• 1988, Technical and Miscellaneous Revenue Act of 1988 (P.L. 100-647)

P.L. 100-647, §1011B(d)(1)-(2):

Amended Code Sec. 119(d)(2) by striking out "(as of the close of the calendar year in which the taxable year begins)" after "appraised value" in subparagraph (A)(i), and by adding at the end thereof a new sentence. **Effective** as if included in the provision of P.L. 99-514 to which it relates.

• 1986, Tax Reform Act of 1986 (P.L. 99-514)

P.L. 99-514, §1164(a):

Amended Code Sec. 119 by adding at the end thereof new subsection (d). **Effective** for tax years beginning after 12-31-85.

• 1978, Tax Treatment Extension Act of 1978 (P.L. 95-615)

P.L. 95-615, §205:

Amended Code Sec. 119(a)(1). **Effective** 11-9-78. Prior to amendment, Code Sec. 119(a) read as follows:

SEC. 119. MEALS OR LODGING FURNISHED FOR THE CONVENIENCE OF EMPLOYER.

There shall be excluded from gross income of an employee the value of any meals or lodging furnished to him by his employer for the convenience of the employer, but only if—

(1) in the case of meals, the meals are furnished on the business premises of the employer, or

(2) in the case of lodging, the employee is required to accept such lodging on the business premises of his employer as a condition of his employment.

• 1978 (P.L. 95-427)

P.L. 95-427, §4:

Amended Code Sec. 119. **Effective** for tax years beginning after 12-31-53, and ending after 8-16-54. Prior to amendment, Code Sec. 119 read as follows:

SEC. 119. MEALS OR LODGING FURNISHED FOR THE CONVENIENCE OF THE EMPLOYER.

There shall be excluded from gross income of an employee the value of any meals or lodging furnished to him by his employer for the convenience of the employer, but only if—

(1) in the case of meals, the meals are furnished on the business premises of the employer, or

(2) in the case of lodging, the employee is required to accept such lodging on the business premises of his employer as a condition of his employment.

In determining whether meals or lodging are furnished for the convenience of the employer, the provisions of an employment contract or of a State statute fixing terms of employment shall not be determinative of whether the meals or lodging are intended as compensation.

P.L. 95-427, §3, provides:

SEC. 3. TREATMENT OF CERTAIN STATUTORY SUBSISTENCE ALLOWANCES OR SUBSISTENCE ALLOWANCES NEGOTIATED IN ACCORDANCE WITH STATE LAW RECEIVED BY STATE POLICE OFFICERS BEFORE JANUARY 1, 1978.

(a) GENERAL RULE.—If—

(1) an individual who was employed as a State police officer received a statutory subsistence allowance or a subsistence allowance negotiated in accordance with State law while so employed,

(2) such individual elects, on or before April 15, 1979, and in such manner and form as the Secretary of the Treasury may prescribe, to have this section apply to such allowance, and

(3) this section applies to such allowance,

then, for purposes of the Internal Revenue Code of 1954, such allowance shall not be included in such individual's gross income.

(b) ALLOWANCES TO WHICH SECTION APPLIES.—For purposes of this section, this section applies to any statutory subsistence allowance or subsistence allowance negotiated in accordance with State law which was received—

(1) after December 31, 1969, and before January 1, 1977, to the extent such individual did not include such allowance in gross income on his income tax return for the taxable year in which such allowance was received, or

(2) during the calendar year 1977.

(c) OTHER DEFINITIONS.—For purposes of this section—

(1) STATE POLICE OFFICER.—The term "State police officer" means any police officer (including a highway patrolman) employed by a State (or the District of Columbia) on a full-time basis with the power to arrest.

(2) INCOME TAX RETURN.—The term tax return" means the return of the taxes imposed by subtitle A of the Internal Revenue Code of 1954. If an individual filed before November 29, 1977, an amended return for any taxable year, such amended return shall be treated as the return for such taxable year.

(d) LIMITATION ON DEDUCTION.—If any individual receives a subsistence allowance which is excluded from gross income under subsection (a), no deduction shall be allowed under any provision of chapter 1 of the Internal Revenue Code of 1954 for expenses in respect of which he has received such allowance, except to the extent that such expenses exceed the amount excludable from gross income under subsection (a) and the excess is otherwise allowed as a deduction under such chapter 1.

(e) STATUTE OF LIMITATIONS.—If refund or credit of any overpayment of tax resulting from the application of this section is prevented at any time on or before April 15, 1979, by the operation of any law or rule of law (including res judicata), refund or credit of such overpayment (to the extent attributable to the application of this section) may, nevertheless, be made or allowed if claim therefor is filed on or before April 15, 1979.

[Sec. 120]

SEC. 120. AMOUNTS RECEIVED UNDER QUALIFIED GROUP LEGAL SERVICES PLANS.

[Sec. 120(a)]

(a) EXCLUSION BY EMPLOYEE FOR CONTRIBUTIONS AND LEGAL SERVICES PROVIDED BY EMPLOYER.—Gross income of an employee, his spouse, or his dependents, does not include—

(1) amounts contributed by an employer on behalf of an employee, his spouse, or his dependent under a qualified group legal services plan (as defined in subsection (b)); or

(2) the value of legal service provided, or amounts paid for legal services, under a qualified group legal services plan (as defined in subsection (b)) to, or with respect to, an employee, his spouse, or his dependents.

No exclusion shall be allowed under this section with respect to an individual for any taxable year to the extent that the value of insurance (whether through an insurer or self-insurance) against legal costs incurred by the individual (or his spouse or dependents) provided under a qualified group legal services plan exceeds $70.

Amendments

• 1988, Technical and Miscellaneous Revenue Act of 1988 (P.L. 100-647)

P.L. 100-647, §4002(b)(1):

Amended Code Sec. 120(a) by adding at the end thereof a new sentence. **Effective** for tax years ending after 12-31-87.

• 1976, Tax Reform Act of 1976 (P.L. 94-455)

P.L. 94-455, §2134(a):

Added Code Sec. 120(a). **Effective** as noted in Act Sec. 2134(e), below.

P.L. 94-455, §2134(e), as amended by P.L. 95-600, §703(b)(1), and P.L. 97-34, §802(b), provides:

(e) EFFECTIVE DATES.—

(1) IN GENERAL.—Except as provided in paragraph (2), the amendments made by this section shall apply to taxable years beginning after December 31, 1976.

(2) NOTICE REQUIREMENT.—For purposes of section 120(d)(7) of the Internal Revenue Code of 1954, the time prescribed by the Secretary of the Treasury by regulations for giving the notice required by section 120(c)(4) of such Code shall not expire before the 90th day after the day on which regulations prescribed under such section 120(c)(4) first become final.

(3) EXISTING PLANS.—

(A) For purposes of section 120 of the Internal Revenue Code of 1954, a written group legal services plan which was in existence on June 4, 1976, shall be considered as satisfying the requirements of subsections (b) and (c) of such section 120 for the period ending with the compliance date (determined under subparagraph (B)).

(B) COMPLIANCE DATE.—For purposes of this paragraph, the term "compliance date" means—

(i) the date occurring 180 days after the date of the enactment of this Act, or

(ii) if later, in the case of a plan which is maintained pursuant to one or more agreements which the Secretary of Labor finds to be collective bargaining agreements, the earlier of December 31, 1981, or the date on which the last of the collective bargaining agreements relating to the plan terminates (determined without regard to any extension thereof agreed to after the date of the enactment of this Act).

P.L. 94-455, §2134(d), provides:

(d) STUDY AND REPORT BY SECRETARIES OF TREASURY AND LABOR.—

(1) A complete study and investigation with respect to the desirability and feasibility of continuing the exclusion from income of certain prepaid group legal services benefits under section 120 of the Internal Revenue Code of 1954 shall be made by the Secretary of Labor and by the Secretary of the Treasury.

(2) The Secretary of Labor and the Secretary of the Treasury shall report to the President and the Congress with respect to the study and investigation conducted under paragraph (1) not later than December 31, 1980.

[Sec. 120(b)]

(b) QUALIFIED GROUP LEGAL SERVICES PLAN.—For purposes of this section, a qualified group legal services plan is a separate written plan of an employer for the exclusive benefit of his employees or their spouses or dependents to provide such employees, spouse, or dependents with specified benefits consisting of personal legal services through prepayment of, or provision in advance for, legal fees in whole or in part by the employer, if the plan meets the requirements of subsection (c).

Amendments

• 1989 (P.L. 101-140)

P.L. 101-140, §203(a)(1):

Provides that Code Sec. 120(b), as amended by Section 1151(c)(3) of P.L. 99-514, shall be applied as if the amendment made by such section had not been enacted. **Effective** as if included in section 1151 of P.L. 99-514. Code Sec. 120(b) as amended by Act Sec. 1151(c) of P.L. 99-514 read as follows:

(b) QUALIFIED GROUP LEGAL SERVICES PLAN.—For purposes of this section, a qualified group legal services plan is a separate plan of an employer—

(1) under which the employer provides specified personal legal service to employees (or their spouses or dependents) through the prepayment of, or the provision in advance for, any portion of the legal fees for such services, and

(2) which meets the requirements of subsection (c) and section 89(k).

• 1989 (P.L. 101-136)

P.L. 101-136, §528, provides:

SEC. 528. No monies appropriated by this Act may be used to implement or enforce section 1151 of the Tax Reform Act of 1986 or the amendments made by such section.

• 1986, Tax Reform Act of 1986 (P.L. 99-514)

P.L. 99-514, §1151(c)(3):

Amended Code Sec. 120(b). For the **effective** date, see Act Sec. 1151(k) following Code Sec. 120(c).

• 1976, Tax Reform Act of 1976 (P.L. 94-455)

P.L. 94-455, §2134(a):

Added Code Sec. 120(b). For the **effective** date, see amendment note under Code Sec. 120(a).

[Sec. 120(c)]

(c) REQUIREMENTS.—

(1) DISCRIMINATION.—The contributions or benefits provided under the plan shall not discriminate in favor of employees who are highly compensated employees (within the meaning of section 414(q)).

(2) ELIGIBILITY.—The plan shall benefit employees who qualify under a classification set up by the employer and found by the Secretary not to be discriminatory in favor of employees who are described in paragraph (1). For purposes of this paragraph, there shall be excluded from consideration employees not included in the plan who are included in a unit of employees covered by an agreement which the Secretary of Labor finds to be a collective bargaining agreement between employee representatives and one or more employers, if there is evidence that group legal services plan benefits were the subject of good faith bargaining between such employee representatives and such employer or employers.

(3) CONTRIBUTION LIMITATION.—Not more than 25 percent of the amounts contributed under the plan during the year may be provided for the class of individuals who are shareholders or owners (or their spouses or dependents), each of whom (on any day of the year) owns more than 5 percent of the stock or of the capital or profits interest in the employer.

(4) NOTIFICATION.—The plan shall give notice to the Secretary, in such manner as the Secretary may by regulations prescribe, that it is applying for recognition of the status of a qualified group legal services plan.

(5) CONTRIBUTIONS.—Amounts contributed under the plan shall be paid only (A) to insurance companies, or to organizations or persons that provide personal legal services, or indemnification against the cost of personal legal services, in exchange for a prepayment or payment of a premium, (B) to organizations or trusts described in section 501(c)(20), (C) to organizations described in section 501(c) which are permitted by that section to receive payments from an employer for support of one or more qualified group legal services plan or plans, except that such organizations shall pay or credit the contribution to an organization or trust described in section 501(c)(20), (D) as prepayments to providers of legal services under the plan, or (E) a combination of the above.

Amendments

• 1989 (P.L. 101-140)

P.L. 101-140, §203(a)(1):

Provides that Code Sec. 120(c)(2) as amended by Section 1151(g)(1) of P.L. 99-514 shall be applied as if the amendment made by such section had not been enacted. **Effective** as if included in Section 1151 of P.L. 99-514.

P.L. 101-140, §203(a)(2):

Provides that Code Sec. 120(c)(2) as amended by Section 1011B(a)(31)(B)(i)-(ii) of P.L. 100-647 shall be applied as if the amendment made by such section has not been enacted. **Effective** as if included in Section 1151 of P.L. 99-514. Code Sec. 120(c)(2) as amended by Act Sec. 1151(g)(1) of P.L.

99-514 and Act Sec. 1011B(a)(31)(B)(i)-(ii) of P.L. 100-647 read as follows:

(2) ELIGIBILITY.—The plan shall benefit employees who qualify under a classification set up by the employer and found by the Secretary not to be discriminatory in favor of employees who are described in paragraph (1). For purposes of this paragraph, there shall be excluded from consideration employees who are excluded from consideration under section 89(h).

• 1989 (P.L. 101-136)

P.L. 101-136, §528, provides:

SEC. 528. No monies appropriated by this Act may be used to implement or enforce section 1151 of the Tax Reform Act of 1986 or the amendments made by such section.

• 1988, Technical and Miscellaneous Revenue Act of 1988 (P.L. 100-647)

P.L. 100-647, §1011B(a)(31)(B)(i)-(ii):

Amended Code Sec. 120(c)(2) by striking out "may" the first place it appears and inserting in lieu thereof "shall", and by striking out "may be" the second place it appears and inserting in lieu thereof "are". **Effective** as if included in the provision of P.L. 99-514 to which it relates.

• 1986, Tax Reform Act of 1986 (P.L. 99-514)

P.L. 99-514, §1114(b)(3)(A):

Amended Code Sec. 120(c)(1) by striking out "officers, shareholders, self-employed individuals, or highly compensated" and inserting in lieu thereof "highly compensated employees (within the meaning of section 414(q))". **Effective** for years beginning after 12-31-87.

P.L. 99-514, §1151(g)(1):

Amended Code Sec. 120(c)(2) by striking out the last sentence and inserting in lieu thereof "For purposes of this paragraph, there may be excluded from consideration employees who may be excluded from consideration under section 89(h)." For the **effective** date, see Act Sec. 1151(k), below. Prior to amendment, the last sentence read as follows:

For purposes of this paragraph, there shall be excluded from consideration employees not included in the plan who are included in a unit of employees covered by an agreement which the Secretary of Labor finds to be a collective bargaining agreement between employee representatives and one or more employers, if there is evidence that group legal services plan benefits were the subject of good faith bargaining between such employee representatives and such employer or employers.

P.L. 99-514, §1151(k), provides:

(k) EFFECTIVE DATES.—

(1) IN GENERAL.—The amendments made by this section shall apply to years beginning after the later of—

(A) December 31, 1987, or

(B) the earlier of—

(i) the date which is 3 months after the date on which the Secretary of the Treasury or his delegate issues such regulations as are necessary to carry out the provisions of section 89 of the Internal Revenue Code of 1986 (as added by this section), or

(ii) December 31, 1988.

(2) SPECIAL RULE FOR COLLECTIVE BARGAINING PLAN.—In the case of a plan maintained pursuant to 1 or more collective bargaining agreements between employee representatives and 1 or more employers ratified before March 1, 1986, the amendments made by this section shall not apply to employees covered by such an agreement in years beginning before the earlier of—

(A) the date on which the last of such collective bargaining agreements terminates (determined without regard to any extension thereof after February 28, 1986), or

(B) January 1, 1991.

A plan shall not be required to take into account employees to which the preceding sentence applies for purposes of applying section 89 of the Internal Revenue Code of 1986 (as added by this section) to employees to which the preceding the year described in the preceding sentence.

(3) EXCEPTION FOR CERTAIN GROUP-TERM INSURANCE PLANS.—In the case of a plan described in section 223(d)(2) of the Tax Reform Act of 1984, such plan shall be treated as meeting the requirements of section 89 of the Internal Revenue Code of 1986 (as added by this section) with respect to individuals described in section 223(d)(2) of such Act. An employer may elect to disregard such individuals in applying section 89 of such Code (as so added) to other employees of the employer.

(4) SPECIAL RULE FOR CHURCH PLANS.—In the case of a church plan (within the meaning of section 414(e)(3) of the Internal Revenue Code of 1986) maintaining an insured accident and health plan, the amendments made by this section shall apply to years beginning after December 31, 1988.

(5) CAFETERIA PLANS.—The amendments made by subsection (d)(2) shall apply to taxable years beginning after December 31, 1983.

• 1976, Tax Reform Act of 1976 (P.L. 94-455)

P.L. 94-455, §2134(a):

Added Code Sec. 120(c). For the **effective** date, see amendment note under Code Sec. 120(a).

[Sec. 120(d)]

(d) OTHER DEFINITIONS AND SPECIAL RULES.—For purposes of this section—

(1) EMPLOYEE.—The term "employee" includes, for any year, an individual who is an employee within the meaning of section 401(c)(1) (relating to self-employed individuals).

(2) EMPLOYER.—An individual who owns the entire interest in an unincorporated trade or business shall be treated as his own employer. A partnership shall be treated as the employer of each partner who is an employee within the meaning of paragraph (1).

(3) ALLOCATIONS.—Allocations of amounts contributed under the plan shall be made in accordance with regulations prescribed by the Secretary and shall take into account the expected relative utilization of benefits to be provided from such contributions or plan assets and the manner in which any premium or other charge was developed.

(4) DEPENDENT.—The term "dependent" has the meaning given to it by section 152 (determined without regard to subsections (b)(1), (b)(2), and (d)(1)(B) thereof).

(5) EXCLUSIVE BENEFIT.—In the case of a plan to which contributions are made by more than one employer, in determining whether the plan is for the exclusive benefit of an employer's employees or their spouses or dependents, the employees of any employer who maintains the plan shall be considered to be the employees of each employer who maintains the plan.

(6) ATTRIBUTION RULES.—For purposes of this section—

(A) ownership of stock in a corporation shall be determined in accordance with the rules provided under subsections (d) and (e) of section 1563 (without regard to section 1563(e)(3)(C)), and

(B) the interest of an employee in a trade or business which is not incorporated shall be determined in accordance with regulations prescribed by the Secretary, which shall be based on principles similar to the principles which apply in the case of subparagraph (A).

(7) TIME OF NOTICE TO SECRETARY.—A plan shall not be a qualified group legal services plan for any period prior to the time notification was provided to the Secretary in accordance with subsection (c)(4), if such notice is given after the time prescribed by the Secretary by regulations for giving such notice.

Amendments

• 2004, Working Families Tax Relief Act of 2004 (P.L. 108-311)

P.L. 108-311, §207(10):

Amended Code Sec. 120(d)(4) by inserting "(determined without regard to subsections (b)(1), (b)(2), and (d)(1)(B) thereof)" after "section 152". **Effective** for tax years beginning after 12-31-2004.

• 1986, Tax Reform Act of 1986 (P.L. 99-514)

P.L. 99-514, §1114(b)(3)(B)(i)-(ii):

Amended Code Sec. 120(d)(1) by striking out "The term `self-employed individual' means, and the" and inserting in lieu thereof "The", and by striking out "Self-employed individual;" in the heading thereof. **Effective** for years beginning after 12-31-87. Prior to amendment, Code Sec. 120(d)(1) read as follows:

(1) SELF-EMPLOYED INDIVIDUAL; EMPLOYEE.—The term "self-employed individual" means, and the term "employee" includes, for any year, an individual who is an employee within the meaning of section 401(c)(1) (relating to self-employed individuals).

• 1976, Tax Reform Act of 1976 (P.L. 94-455)

P.L. 94-455, §2134(a):

Added Code Sec. 120(d). For the **effective** date, see amendment note under Code Sec. 120(a).

[Sec. 120(e)]

(e) TERMINATION.—This section and section 501(c)(20) shall not apply to taxable years beginning after June 30, 1992.

Amendments

• 1991, Tax Extension Act of 1992 (P.L. 102-227)

P.L. 102-227, §104(a)(1):

Amended Code Sec. 120(e) by striking "December 31, 1991" and inserting "June 30, 1992". **Effective** for tax years beginning after 12-31-91. For a special rule, see §104(a)(2), below.

P.L. 102-227, §104(a)(2), provides:

(2) SPECIAL RULE.—In the case of any taxable year beginning in 1992, only amounts paid before July 1, 1992, by the employer for coverage for the employee, his spouse, or his dependents, under a qualified group legal services plan for periods before July 1, 1992, shall be taken into account in determining the amount excluded under section 120 of the Internal Revenue Code of 1986 with respect to such employee for such taxable year.

• 1990, Omnibus Budget Reconciliation Act of 1990 (P.L. 101-508)

P.L. 101-508, §11404(a):

Amended Code Sec. 120(e) by striking "September 30, 1990" and inserting "December 31, 1991". **Effective** for tax years beginning after 12-31-89.

• 1989, Omnibus Budget Reconciliation Act of 1989 (P.L. 101-239)

P.L. 101-239, §7102(a)(1):

Amended Code Sec. 120(e) by striking "ending after December 31, 1988" and inserting "beginning after September 30, 1990". **Effective** for tax years ending after 12-31-88.

• 1988, Technical and Miscellaneous Revenue Act of 1988 (P.L. 100-647)

P.L. 100-647, §4002(a):

Amended Code Sec. 120(e) by striking out "1987" and inserting in lieu thereof "1988". **Effective** for tax years ending after 12-31-87.

• 1986, Tax Reform Act of 1986 (P.L. 99-514)

P.L. 99-514, §1162(b):

Amended Code Sec. 120(e) by striking out "1985" and inserting in lieu thereof "1987". **Effective** for years ending after 12-31-85.

• 1984 (P.L. 98-612)

P.L. 98-612, §1(a):

Amended Code Sec. 120(e) by striking out "December 31, 1984" and inserting in lieu thereof "December 31, 1985". **Effective** for tax years ending after 12-31-84.

• 1983, Technical Corrections Act of 1982 (P.L. 97-448)

P.L. 97-448, §108(a):

Amended Code Sec. 120(e) by striking out "This section" and inserting in lieu thereof "This section and section 501(c)(20)". **Effective** as if included in the provision of P.L. 97-34 to which it relates.

• 1981, Economic Recovery Tax Act of 1981 (P.L. 97-34)

P.L. 97-34, §802(a):

Added Code Sec. 120(e). **Effective** 8-13-81.

[Sec. 120(f)]

(f) CROSS REFERENCE.—

For reporting and recordkeeping requirements, see section 6039D.

Amendments

• 1984 (P.L. 98-612)

P.L. 98-612, §1(b)(3)(A):

Amended Code Sec. 120 by adding at the end thereof new subsection (f). **Effective** 1-1-85.

[Sec. 121]

SEC. 121. EXCLUSION OF GAIN FROM SALE OF PRINCIPAL RESIDENCE.

[Sec. 121(a)]

(a) EXCLUSION.—Gross income shall not include gain from the sale or exchange of property if, during the 5-year period ending on the date of the sale or exchange, such property has been owned and used by the taxpayer as the taxpayer's principal residence for periods aggregating 2 years or more.

[Sec. 121(b)]

(b) LIMITATIONS.—

(1) IN GENERAL.—The amount of gain excluded from gross income under subsection (a) with respect to any sale or exchange shall not exceed $250,000.

(2) SPECIAL RULES FOR JOINT RETURNS.—In the case of a husband and wife who make a joint return for the taxable year of the sale or exchange of the property—

(A) $500,000 LIMITATION FOR CERTAIN JOINT RETURNS.—Paragraph (1) shall be applied by substituting "$500,000" for "$250,000" if—

(i) either spouse meets the ownership requirements of subsection (a) with respect to such property;

(ii) both spouses meet the use requirements of subsection (a) with respect to such property; and

(iii) neither spouse is ineligible for the benefits of subsection (a) with respect to such property by reason of paragraph (3).

(B) OTHER JOINT RETURNS.—If such spouses do not meet the requirements of subparagraph (A), the limitation under paragraph (1) shall be the sum of the limitations under paragraph (1) to which each spouse would be entitled if such spouses had not been married. For purposes of the preceding sentence, each spouse shall be treated as owning the property during the period that either spouse owned the property.

(3) APPLICATION TO ONLY 1 SALE OR EXCHANGE EVERY 2 YEARS.—

(A) IN GENERAL.—Subsection (a) shall not apply to any sale or exchange by the taxpayer if, during the 2-year period ending on the date of such sale or exchange, there was any other sale or exchange by the taxpayer to which subsection (a) applied.

(B) PRE-MAY 7, 1997, SALES NOT TAKEN INTO ACCOUNT.—Subparagraph (A) shall be applied without regard to any sale or exchange before May 7, 1997.

(4) SPECIAL RULE FOR CERTAIN SALES BY SURVIVING SPOUSES.—In the case of a sale or exchange of property by an unmarried individual whose spouse is deceased on the date of such sale, paragraph (1) shall be applied by substituting "$500,000" for "$250,000" if such sale occurs not later than 2 years after the date of death of such spouse and the requirements of paragraph (2)(A) were met immediately before such date of death.

(4)[(5)] EXCLUSION OF GAIN ALLOCATED TO NONQUALIFIED USE.—

(A) IN GENERAL.—Subsection (a) shall not apply to so much of the gain from the sale or exchange of property as is allocated to periods of nonqualified use.

(B) GAIN ALLOCATED TO PERIODS OF NONQUALIFIED USE.—For purposes of subparagraph (A), gain shall be allocated to periods of nonqualified use based on the ratio which—

(i) the aggregate periods of nonqualified use during the period such property was owned by the taxpayer, bears to

(ii) the period such property was owned by the taxpayer.

(C) PERIOD OF NONQUALIFIED USE.—For purposes of this paragraph—

(i) IN GENERAL.—The term "period of nonqualified use" means any period (other than the portion of any period preceding January 1, 2009) during which the property is not used as the principal residence of the taxpayer or the taxpayer's spouse or former spouse.

(ii) EXCEPTIONS.—The term "period of nonqualified use" does not include—

(I) any portion of the 5-year period described in subsection (a) which is after the last date that such property is used as the principal residence of the taxpayer or the taxpayer's spouse,

(II) any period (not to exceed an aggregate period of 10 years) during which the taxpayer or the taxpayer's spouse is serving on qualified official extended duty (as defined in subsection (d)(9)(C)) described in clause (i), (ii), or (iii) of subsection (d)(9)(A), and

(III) any other period of temporary absence (not to exceed an aggregate period of 2 years) due to change of employment, health conditions, or such other unforeseen circumstances as may be specified by the Secretary.

(D) COORDINATION WITH RECOGNITION OF GAIN ATTRIBUTABLE TO DEPRECIATION.—For purposes of this paragraph—

(i) subparagraph (A) shall be applied after the application of subsection (d)(6), and

(ii) subparagraph (B) shall be applied without regard to any gain to which subsection (d)(6) applies.

Amendments

• 2008, Housing Assistance Tax Act of 2008 (P.L. 110-289)

P.L. 110-289, §3092(a):

Amended Code Sec. 121(b) by adding at the end a new paragraph (4)[(5)]. **Effective** for sales and exchanges after 12-31-2008.

• 2007, Mortgage Forgiveness Debt Relief Act of 2007 (P.L. 110-142)

P.L. 110-142, §7(a):

Amended Code Sec. 121(b) by adding at the end a new paragraph (4). **Effective** for sales or exchanges after 12-31-2007.

• 1998, IRS Restructuring and Reform Act of 1998 (P.L. 105-206)

P.L. 105-206, §6005(e)(1):

Amended Code Sec. 121(b)(2). **Effective** as if included in the provision of P.L. 105-34 to which it relates [generally **effective** for sales and exchanges after 5-6-97.—CCH]. Prior to amendment, Code Sec. 121(b)(2) read as follows:

(2) $500,000 LIMITATION FOR CERTAIN JOINT RETURNS.—Paragraph (1) shall be applied by substituting "$500,000" for "$250,000" if—

(A) a husband and wife make a joint return for the taxable year of the sale or exchange of the property,

(B) either spouse meets the ownership requirements of subsection (a) with respect to such property,

(C) both spouses meet the use requirements of subsection (a) with respect to such property, and

(D) neither spouse is ineligible for the benefits of subsection (a) with respect to such property by reason of paragraph (3).

[Sec. 121(c)]

(c) EXCLUSION FOR TAXPAYERS FAILING TO MEET CERTAIN REQUIREMENTS.—

(1) IN GENERAL.—In the case of a sale or exchange to which this subsection applies, the ownership and use requirements of subsection (a), and subsection (b)(3), shall not apply; but the dollar limitation under paragraph (1) or (2) of subsection (b), whichever is applicable, shall be equal to—

(A) the amount which bears the same ratio to such limitation (determined without regard to this paragraph) as

(B)(i) the shorter of—

(I) the aggregate periods, during the 5-year period ending on the date of such sale or exchange, such property has been owned and used by the taxpayer as the taxpayer's principal residence; or

(II) the period after the date of the most recent prior sale or exchange by the taxpayer to which subsection (a) applied and before the date of such sale or exchange, bears to

(ii) 2 years.

(2) SALES AND EXCHANGES TO WHICH SUBSECTION APPLIES.—This subsection shall apply to any sale or exchange if—

(A) subsection (a) would not (but for this subsection) apply to such sale or exchange by reason of—

(i) a failure to meet the ownership and use requirements of subsection (a), or

(ii) subsection (b)(3), and

(B) such sale or exchange is by reason of a change in place of employment, health, or, to the extent provided in regulations, unforeseen circumstances.

Amendments

• 1998, IRS Restructuring and Reform Act of 1998 (P.L. 105-206)

P.L. 105-206, §6005(e)(2):

Amended Code Sec. 121(c)(1). **Effective** as if included in the provision of P.L. 105-34 to which it relates [generally **effective** for sales and exchanges after 5-6-97.—CCH]. Prior to amendment, Code Sec. 121(c)(1) read as follows:

(1) IN GENERAL.—In the case of a sale or exchange to which this subsection applies, the ownership and use requirements of subsection (a) shall not apply and subsection (b)(3) shall not apply; but the amount of gain excluded from gross income under subsection (a) with respect to such sale or exchange shall not exceed—

(A) the amount which bears the same ratio to the amount which would be so excluded under this section if such requirements had been met, as

(B) the shorter of—

(i) the aggregate periods, during the 5-year period ending on the date of such sale or exchange, such property has been owned and used by the taxpayer as the taxpayer's principal residence, or

(ii) the period after the date of the most recent prior sale or exchange by the taxpayer to which subsection (a) applied and before the date of such sale or exchange, bears to 2 years.

[Sec. 121(d)]

(d) SPECIAL RULES.—

(1) JOINT RETURNS.—If a husband and wife make a joint return for the taxable year of the sale or exchange of the property, subsections (a) and (c) shall apply if either spouse meets the ownership and use requirements of subsection (a) with respect to such property.

(2) PROPERTY OF DECEASED SPOUSE.—For purposes of this section, in the case of an unmarried individual whose spouse is deceased on the date of the sale or exchange of property, the period

such unmarried individual owned and used such property shall include the period such deceased spouse owned and used such property before death.

(3) PROPERTY OWNED BY SPOUSE OR FORMER SPOUSE.—For purposes of this section—

(A) PROPERTY TRANSFERRED TO INDIVIDUAL FROM SPOUSE OR FORMER SPOUSE.—In the case of an individual holding property transferred to such individual in a transaction described in section 1041(a), the period such individual owns such property shall include the period the transferor owned the property.

(B) PROPERTY USED BY FORMER SPOUSE PURSUANT TO DIVORCE DECREE, ETC.—Solely for purposes of this section, an individual shall be treated as using property as such individual's principal residence during any period of ownership while such individual's spouse or former spouse is granted use of the property under a divorce or separation instrument (as defined in section 71(b)(2)).

(4) TENANT-STOCKHOLDER IN COOPERATIVE HOUSING CORPORATION.—For purposes of this section, if the taxpayer holds stock as a tenant-stockholder (as defined in section 216) in a cooperative housing corporation (as defined in such section), then—

(A) the holding requirements of subsection (a) shall be applied to the holding of such stock, and

(B) the use requirements of subsection (a) shall be applied to the house or apartment which the taxpayer was entitled to occupy as such stockholder.

(5) INVOLUNTARY CONVERSIONS.—

(A) IN GENERAL.—For purposes of this section, the destruction, theft, seizure, requisition, or condemnation of property shall be treated as the sale of such property.

(B) APPLICATION OF SECTION 1033.—In applying section 1033 (relating to involuntary conversions), the amount realized from the sale or exchange of property shall be treated as being the amount determined without regard to this section, reduced by the amount of gain not included in gross income pursuant to this section.

(C) PROPERTY ACQUIRED AFTER INVOLUNTARY CONVERSION.—If the basis of the property sold or exchanged is determined (in whole or in part) under section 1033(b) (relating to basis of property acquired through involuntary conversion), then the holding and use by the taxpayer of the converted property shall be treated as holding and use by the taxpayer of the property sold or exchanged.

(6) RECOGNITION OF GAIN ATTRIBUTABLE TO DEPRECIATION.—Subsection (a) shall not apply to so much of the gain from the sale of any property as does not exceed the portion of the depreciation adjustments (as defined in section 1250(b)(3)) attributable to periods after May 6, 1997, in respect of such property.

(7) DETERMINATION OF USE DURING PERIODS OF OUT-OF-RESIDENCE CARE.—In the case of a taxpayer who—

(A) becomes physically or mentally incapable of self-care, and

(B) owns property and uses such property as the taxpayer's principal residence during the 5-year period described in subsection (a) for periods aggregating at least 1 year, then the taxpayer shall be treated as using such property as the taxpayer's principal residence during any time during such 5-year period in which the taxpayer owns the property and resides in any facility (including a nursing home) licensed by a State or political subdivision to care for an individual in the taxpayer's condition.

(8) SALES OF REMAINDER INTERESTS.—For purposes of this section—

(A) IN GENERAL.—At the election of the taxpayer, this section shall not fail to apply to the sale or exchange of an interest in a principal residence by reason of such interest being a remainder interest in such residence, but this section shall not apply to any other interest in such residence which is sold or exchanged separately.

(B) EXCEPTION FOR SALES TO RELATED PARTIES.—Subparagraph (A) shall not apply to any sale to, or exchange with, any person who bears a relationship to the taxpayer which is described in section 267(b) or 707(b).

(9) UNIFORMED SERVICES, FOREIGN SERVICE, AND INTELLIGENCE COMMUNITY.—

(A) IN GENERAL.—At the election of an individual with respect to a property, the running of the 5-year period described in subsections (a) and (c)(1)(B) and paragraph (7) of this subsection with respect to such property shall be suspended during any period that such individual or such individual's spouse is serving on qualified official extended duty—

(i) as a member of the uniformed services,

(ii) as a member of the Foreign Service of the United States, or

(iii) as an employee of the intelligence community.

(B) MAXIMUM PERIOD OF SUSPENSION.—The 5-year period described in subsection (a) shall not be extended more than 10 years by reason of subparagraph (A).

(C) QUALIFIED OFFICIAL EXTENDED DUTY.—For purposes of this paragraph—

(i) IN GENERAL.—The term "qualified official extended duty" means any extended duty while serving at a duty station which is at least 50 miles from such property or while residing under Government orders in Government quarters.

(ii) UNIFORMED SERVICES.—The term "uniformed services" has the meaning given such term by section 101(a)(5) of title 10, United States Code, as in effect on the date of the enactment of this paragraph.

(iii) FOREIGN SERVICE OF THE UNITED STATES.—The term "member of the Foreign Service of the United States" has the meaning given the term "member of the Service" by paragraph (1), (2), (3), (4), or (5) of section 103 of the Foreign Service Act of 1980, as in effect on the date of the enactment of this paragraph.

(iv) EMPLOYEE OF INTELLIGENCE COMMUNITY.—The term "employee of the intelligence community" means an employee (as defined by section 2105 of title 5, United States Code) of—

(I) the Office of the Director of National Intelligence,

(II) the Central Intelligence Agency,

(III) the National Security Agency,

(IV) the Defense Intelligence Agency,

(V) the National Geospatial-Intelligence Agency,

(VI) the National Reconnaissance Office,

(VII) any other office within the Department of Defense for the collection of specialized national intelligence through reconnaissance programs,

(VIII) any of the intelligence elements of the Army, the Navy, the Air Force, the Marine Corps, the Federal Bureau of Investigation, the Department of Treasury, the Department of Energy, and the Coast Guard,

(IX) the Bureau of Intelligence and Research of the Department of State, or

(X) any of the elements of the Department of Homeland Security concerned with the analyses of foreign intelligence information.

(v) EXTENDED DUTY.—The term "extended duty" means any period of active duty pursuant to a call or order to such duty for a period in excess of 90 days or for an indefinite period.

(D) SPECIAL RULES RELATING TO ELECTION.—

(i) ELECTION LIMITED TO 1 PROPERTY AT A TIME.—An election under subparagraph (A) with respect to any property may not be made if such an election is in effect with respect to any other property.

(ii) REVOCATION OF ELECTION.—An election under subparagraph (A) may be revoked at any time.

(10) PROPERTY ACQUIRED IN LIKE-KIND EXCHANGE.—If a taxpayer acquires property in an exchange with respect to which gain is not recognized (in whole or in part) to the taxpayer under subsection (a) or (b) of section 1031, subsection (a) shall not apply to the sale or exchange of such property by such taxpayer (or by any person whose basis in such property is determined, in whole or in part, by reference to the basis in the hands of such taxpayer) during the 5-year period beginning with the date of such acquisition.

»»→ Caution: Code Sec. 121(d)(11), below, was added by P.L. 107-16 and redesignated by P.L. 108-121 and P.L. 109-135, and is subject to the sunset provision of the Economic Growth and Tax Relief Reconciliation Act of 2001 (P.L. 107-16), §901. Absent Congressional action, the changes made to this provision by P.L. 107-16, or that take effect as if included in P.L. 107-16, do not apply after December 31, 2010. For more information about the sunset provision, see page XXI of the Preface to this publication and P.L. 107-16, §901, in the amendment notes. See the amendments notes for a history of amendments to this section and the effective date of each change.

(11) PROPERTY ACQUIRED FROM A DECEDENT.—The exclusion under this section shall apply to property sold by—

(A) the estate of a decedent,

(B) any individual who acquired such property from the decedent (within the meaning of section 1022), and

(C) a trust which, immediately before the death of the decedent, was a qualified revocable trust (as defined in section 645(b)(1)) established by the decedent,

determined by taking into account the ownership and use by the decedent.

(12) PEACE CORPS.—

(A) IN GENERAL.—At the election of an individual with respect to a property, the running of the 5-year period described in subsections (a) and (c)(1)(B) and paragraph (7) of this subsection with respect to such property shall be suspended during any period that such individual or such individual's spouse is serving outside the United States—

(i) on qualified official extended duty (as defined in paragraph (9)(C)) as an employee of the Peace Corps, or

(ii) as an enrolled volunteer or volunteer leader under section 5 or 6 (as the case may be) of the Peace Corps Act (22 U.S.C. 2504, 2505).

(B) APPLICABLE RULES.—For purposes of subparagraph (A), rules similar to the rules of subparagraphs (B) and (D) shall apply.

Amendments

• 2008, Heroes Earnings Assistance and Relief Tax Act of 2008 (P.L. 110-245)

P.L. 110-245, §110(a):

Amended Code Sec. 121(d) by adding at the end a new paragraph (12). **Effective** for tax years beginning after 12-31-2007.

P.L. 110-245, §113(a):

Amended Code Sec. 121(d)(9) by striking paragraph (E). **Effective** for sales or exchanges after 6-17-2008. Prior to being stricken, Code Sec. 121(d)(9)(E) read as follows:

(E) TERMINATION WITH RESPECT TO EMPLOYEES OF INTELLIGENCE COMMUNITY.—Clause (iii) of subparagraph (A) shall not apply with respect to any sale or exchange after December 31, 2010.

P.L. 110-245, §113(b):

Amended Code Sec. 121(d)(9)(C) by striking clause (vi). **Effective** for sales or exchanges after 6-17-2008. Prior to being stricken, Code Sec. 121(d)(9)(C)(vi) read as follows:

(vi) SPECIAL RULE RELATING TO INTELLIGENCE COMMUNITY.—An employee of the intelligence community shall not be treated as serving on qualified extended duty unless such duty is at a duty station located outside the United States.

• 2007, Tax Technical Corrections Act of 2007 (P.L. 110-172)

P.L. 110-172, §11(a)(11)(A):

Amended Code Sec. 121(d)(9) by adding at the end a new subparagraph (E). **Effective** 12-29-2007.

• 2006, Tax Relief and Health Care Act of 2006 (P.L. 109-432)

P.L. 109-432, Division A, §417(a):

Amended Code Sec. 121(d)(9)(A) by striking "duty" and all that follows and inserting "duty—" and new clauses (i)-(iii). **Effective** for sales or exchanges after 12-20-2006 [**effective** date amended by P.L. 110-172, §11(a)(11)(B).—CCH]. Prior to amendment, Code Sec. 121(d)(9)(A) read as follows:

(A) IN GENERAL.—At the election of an individual with respect to a property, the running of the 5-year period described in subsections (a) and (c)(1)(B) and paragraph (7) of this subsection with respect to such property shall be suspended during any period that such individual or such individual's spouse is serving on qualified official extended duty as a member of the uniformed services or of the Foreign Service of the United States.

P.L. 109-432, Division A, §417(b):

Amended Code Sec. 121(d)(9)(C) by redesignating clause (iv) as clause (v) and by inserting after clause (iii) a new clause (iv). **Effective** for sales or exchanges after 12-20-2006 [**effective** date amended by P.L. 110-172, §11(a)(11)(B).—CCH].

P.L. 109-432, Division A, §417(c):

Amended Code Sec. 121(d)(9)(C), as amended by Act Sec. 417(b), by adding at the end a new clause (vi). **Effective** for sales or exchanges after 12-20-2006 [**effective** date amended by P.L. 110-172, §11(a)(11)(B).—CCH].

P.L. 109-432, Division A, §417(d):

Amended the heading for Code Sec. 121(d)(9). **Effective** for sales or exchanges after 12-20-2006 [**effective** date amended by P.L. 110-172, §11(a)(11)(B).—CCH]. Prior to amendment, the heading for Code Sec. 121(d)(9) read as follows:

MEMBERS OF UNIFORMED SERVICES AND FOREIGN SERVICE

• 2005, Gulf Opportunity Zone Act of 2005 (P.L. 109-135)

P.L. 109-135, §403(ee)(1)-(2):

Amended Code Sec. 121(d) by redesignating paragraph (10) (relating to property acquired from a decedent) as paragraph (11) and by moving such paragraph to the end of such subsection, and by amending paragraph (10). **Effective** as if included in the provision of the American Jobs Creation Act of 2004 (P.L. 108-357) to which it relates [**effective** for sales or exchanges after 10-22-2004.—CCH]. Prior to amendment, Code Sec. 121(d)(10) read as follows:

(10) PROPERTY ACQUIRED IN LIKE-KIND EXCHANGE.—If a taxpayer acquired property in an exchange to which section 1031 applied, subsection (a) shall not apply to the sale or exchange of such property if it occurs during the 5-year period beginning with the date of the acquisition of such property.

• 2004, American Jobs Creation Act of 2004 (P.L. 108-357)

P.L. 108-357, §840(a):

Amended Code Sec. 121(d) by adding at the end a new paragraph (10)[(11)]. **Effective** for sales or exchanges after 10-22-2004.

• 2003, Military Family Tax Relief Act of 2003 (P.L. 108-121)

P.L. 108-121, §101(a):

Amended Code Sec. 121(d) by redesignating paragraph (9) as paragraph (10) and by inserting after paragaph (8) a new paragraph (9). **Effective** as if included in the amendments made by section 312 of P.L. 105-34. For a waiver of limitations, see Act Sec. 101(b)(2), below.

P.L. 108-121, §101(b)(2), provides:

(2) WAIVER OF LIMITATIONS.—If refund or credit of any overpayment of tax resulting from the amendments made by this section is prevented at any time before the close of the 1-year period beginning on the date of the enactment of this Act by the operation of any law or rule of law (including res judicata), such refund or credit may nevertheless be made or allowed if claim therefor is filed before the close of such period.

• 2001, Economic Growth and Tax Relief Reconciliation Act of 2001 (P.L. 107-16)

P.L. 107-16, §542(c):

Amended Code Sec. 121(d) by adding at the end a new paragraph (9). **Effective** for estates of decedents dying after 12-31-2009.

P.L. 107-16, §901(a)-(b), provides:

SEC. 901. SUNSET OF PROVISIONS OF ACT.

(a) IN GENERAL.—All provisions of, and amendments made by, this Act shall not apply—

(1) to taxable, plan, or limitation years beginning after December 31, 2010, or

(2) in the case of title V, to estates of decedents dying, gifts made, or generation skipping transfers, after December 31, 2010.

(b) APPLICATION OF CERTAIN LAWS.—The Internal Revenue Code of 1986 and the Employee Retirement Income Security Act of 1974 shall be applied and administered to years, estates, gifts, and transfers described in subsection (a) as if the provisions and amendments described in subsection (a) had never been enacted.

[Sec. 121(e)]

(e) DENIAL OF EXCLUSION FOR EXPATRIATES.—This section shall not apply to any sale or exchange by an individual if the treatment provided by section 877(a)(1) applies to such individual.

[Sec. 121(f)]

(f) ELECTION TO HAVE SECTION NOT APPLY.—This section shall not apply to any sale or exchange with respect to which the taxpayer elects not to have this section apply.

[Sec. 121(g)]

(g) RESIDENCES ACQUIRED IN ROLLOVERS UNDER SECTION 1034.—For purposes of this section, in the case of property the acquisition of which by the taxpayer resulted under section 1034 (as in effect on the day before the date of the enactment of this section) in the nonrecognition of any part of the gain realized on the sale or exchange of another residence, in determining the period for which the taxpayer has owned and used such property as the taxpayer's principal residence, there shall be included the aggregate periods for which such other residence (and each prior residence taken into account under section 1223(6) in determining the holding period of such property) had been so owned and used.

Amendments

• 2005, Gulf Opportunity Zone Act of 2005 (P.L. 109-135)

P.L. 109-135, §402(a)(3):

Amended Code Sec. 121(g) by striking "1223(7)" and inserting "1223(6)". **Effective** as if included in the provision of the Energy Policy Act of 2005 (P.L. 109-58) to which it relates [**effective** 2-8-2006.—CCH]. For a special rule, see Act Sec. 402(m)(2), below.

P.L. 109-135, §402(m)(2), provides:

(2) REPEAL OF PUBLIC UTILITY HOLDING COMPANY ACT OF 1935.—The amendments made by subsection (a) shall not apply with respect to any transaction ordered in compliance with the Public Utility Holding Company Act of 1935 before its repeal.

• 1998 (P.L. 105-261)

P.L. 105-261, §1074, provides:

SEC. 1074. SENSE OF CONGRESS CONCERNING TAX TREATMENT OF PRINCIPAL RESIDENCE OF MEMBERS OF ARMED FORCES WHILE AWAY FROM HOME ON ACTIVE DUTY.

It is the sense of Congress that a member of the Armed Forces should be treated for purposes of section 121 of the Internal Revenue Code of 1986 as using property as a principal residence during any continuous period that the member is serving on active duty for 180 days or more with the Armed Forces, but only if the member used the property as a principal residence for any period during or immediately before that period of active duty.

• 1997, Taxpayer Relief Act of 1997 (P.L. 105-34)

P.L. 105-34, §312(a):

Amended Code Sec. 121. **Effective**, generally, to sales and exchanges after 5-6-97. For special rules, see Act Sec. 312(d)[(e)](2)-(4), below.

P.L. 105-34, §312(d)[(e)](2)-(4) (as amended by P.L. 105-206, §6005(e)(3)), provides:

(2) SALES ON OR BEFORE DATE OF ENACTMENT.—At the election of the taxpayer, the amendments made by this section shall not apply to any sale or exchange on or before the date of the enactment of this Act.

(3) CERTAIN SALES WITHIN 2 YEARS AFTER DATE OF ENACTMENT.—Section 121 of the Internal Revenue Code of 1986 (as amended by this section) shall be applied without regard to subsection (c)(2)(B) thereof in the case of any sale or exchange of property during the 2-year period beginning on the date of the enactment of this Act if the taxpayer held such property on the date of the enactment of this Act and fails to meet the ownership and use requirements of subsection (a) thereof with respect to such property.

(4) BINDING CONTRACTS.—At the election of the taxpayer, the amendments made by this section shall not apply to a sale or exchange after the date of the enactment of this Act, if—

(A) such sale or exchange is pursuant to a contract which was binding on such date, or

(B) without regard to such amendments, gain would not be recognized under section 1034 of the Internal Revenue Code of 1986 (as in effect on the day before the date of the enactment of this Act) on such sale or exchange by reason of a new residence acquired on or before such date or with respect to the acquisition of which by the taxpayer a binding contract was in effect on such date.

This paragraph shall not apply to any sale or exchange by an individual if the treatment provided by section 877(a)(1) of the Internal Revenue Code of 1986 applies to such individual.

Prior to amendment, Code Sec. 121 read as follows:

SEC. 121. ONE-TIME EXCLUSION OF GAIN FROM SALE OF PRINCIPAL RESIDENCE BY INDIVIDUAL WHO HAS ATTAINED AGE 55.

[Sec. 121(a)]

(a) GENERAL RULE.—At the election of the taxpayer, gross income does not include gain from the sale or exchange of property if—

(1) the taxpayer has attained the age of 55 before the date of such sale or exchange, and

(2) during the 5-year period ending on the date of the sale or exchange, such property has been owned and used by the taxpayer as his principal residence for periods aggregating 3 years or more.

Amendments

• 1978, Revenue Act of 1978 (P.L. 95-600)

P.L. 95-600, §404(a):

Amended Code Sec. 121(a) and Code Sec. 121 heading. **Effective** as set forth in P.L. 95-600, §404(d), below. Prior to amendment, Code Sec. 121(a) read as follows:

SEC. 121. GAIN FROM SALE OR EXCHANGE OF RESIDENCE OF INDIVIDUAL WHO HAS ATTAINED AGE 65.

(a) GENERAL RULE.—At the election of the taxpayer, gross income does not include gain from the sale or exchange of property if—

(1) the taxpayer has attained the age of 65 before the date of such sale or exchange, and

(2) during the 8-year period ending on the date of the sale or exchange, such property has been owned and used by the taxpayer as his principal residence for periods aggregating 5 years or more.

P.L. 95-600, §404(d), provides:

(d) EFFECTIVE DATE.—

(1) IN GENERAL.—The amendments made by this section shall apply to sales or exchanges after July 26, 1978, in taxable years ending after such date.

(2) TRANSITIONAL RULE.—In the case of a sale or exchange of a residence before July 26, 1981, a taxpayer who has attained age 65 on the date of such sale or exchange may elect to have section 121 of the Internal Revenue Code of 1954 applied by substituting "8-year period" for "5-year period" and "5 years" for "3 years" in subsections (a), (d)(2), and (d)(5) of such section.

[Sec. 121(b)]

(b) LIMITATIONS.—

(1) DOLLAR LIMITATION.—The amount of the gain excluded from gross income under subsection (a) shall not exceed $125,000 ($62,500 in the case of a separate return by a married individual).

(2) APPLICATION TO ONLY ONE SALE OR EXCHANGE.—Subsection (a) shall not apply to any sale or exchange by the taxpayer if an election by the taxpayer or his spouse under subsection (a) with respect to any other sale or exchange is in effect.

(3) ADDITIONAL ELECTION IF PRIOR SALE WAS MADE ON OR BEFORE JULY 26, 1978.—In the case of any sale or exchange after July 26, 1978, this section shall be applied by not taking into account any election made with respect to a sale or exchange on or before such date.

Amendments

• 1981, Economic Recovery Tax Act of 1981 (P.L. 97-34)

P.L. 97-34, §123(a):

Amended Code Sec. 121(b)(1) by striking out "$100,000 ($50,000" and inserting in lieu thereof "$125,000 ($62,500". **Effective** with respect to residences sold or exchanged after 7-20-81.

• 1978, Revenue Act of 1978 (P.L. 95-600)

P.L. 95-600, §404(a):

Amended Code Sec. 121(b). **Effective** as set forth in P.L. 95-600, §404(d). See historical comment on P.L. 95-600, §404(d) under former Code Sec. 121(a). Prior to amendment, Code Sec. 121(b) read as follows:

(b) LIMITATIONS.—

(1) WHERE ADJUSTED SALES PRICE EXCEEDS $35,000.—If the adjusted sales price of the property sold or exchanged exceeds $35,000, subsection (a) shall apply to that portion of the gain which bears the same ratio to the total amount of such gain as $35,000 bears to such adjusted sales price. For purposes of the preceding sentence, the term "adjusted sales price" has the meaning assigned to such term by section 1034(b)(1) (determined without regard to subsection (d)(7) of this section).

(2) APPLICATION TO ONLY ONE SALE OR EXCHANGE.—Subsection (a) shall not apply to any sale or exchange by the taxpayer if an election by the taxpayer or his spouse under subsection (a) with respect to any other sale or exchange is in effect.

• 1976, Tax Reform Act of 1976 (P.L. 94-455)

P.L. 94-455, §1404:

Amended Code Sec. 121(b) by substituting "$35,000" for "$20,000" wherever it appears in paragraph (1). **Effective** for tax years beginning after 12-31-76.

[Sec. 121(c)]

(c) ELECTION.—An election under subsection (a) may be made or revoked at any time before the expiration of the period for making a claim for credit or refund of the tax imposed by this chapter for the taxable year in which the sale or exchange occurred, and shall be made or revoked in such manner as the Secretary shall by regulations prescribe. In the case of a taxpayer who is married, an election under subsection (a) or a revocation thereof may be made only if his spouse joins in such election or revocation.

Amendments

• 1976, Tax Reform Act of 1976 (P.L. 94-455)

P.L. 94-455, §1906(b)(13)(A):

Amended 1954 Code by substituting "Secretary" for "Secretary or his delegate" each place it appeared. **Effective** 2-1-77.

[Sec. 121(d)]

(d) SPECIAL RULES.—

(1) PROPERTY HELD JOINTLY BY HUSBAND AND WIFE.—For purposes of this section, if—

(A) property is held by a husband and wife as joint tenants, tenants by the entirety, or community property,

(B) such husband and wife make a joint return under section 6013 for the taxable year of the sale or exchange, and

(C) one spouse satisfies the age, holding, and use requirements of subsection (a) with respect to such property,

then both husband and wife shall be treated as satisfying the age, holding, and use requirements of subsection (a) with respect to such property.

(2) PROPERTY OF DECEASED SPOUSE.—For purposes of this section, in the case of an unmarried individual whose spouse is deceased on the date of the sale or exchange of property, if—

(A) the deceased spouse (during the 5-year period ending on the date of the sale or exchange) satisfied the holding and use requirements of subsection (a)(2) with respect to such property, and

(B) no election by the deceased spouse under subsection (a) is in effect with respect to a prior sale or exchange,

then such individual shall be treated as satisfying the holding and use requirements of subsection (a)(2) with respect to such property.

(3) TENANT-STOCKHOLDER IN COOPERATIVE HOUSING CORPORATION.—For purposes of this section, if the taxpayer holds stock as a tenant-stockholder (as defined in section 216) in a cooperative housing corporation (as defined in such section), then—

(A) the holding requirements of subsection (a)(2) shall be applied to the holding of such stock, and

(B) the use requirements of subsection (a)(2) shall be applied to the house or apartment which the taxpayer was entitled to occupy as such stockholder.

(4) INVOLUNTARY CONVERSIONS.—For purposes of this section, the destruction, theft, seizure, requisition, or condemnation of property shall be treated as the sale of such property.

(5) PROPERTY USED IN PART AS PRINCIPAL RESIDENCE.—In the case of property only a portion of which, during the 5-year period ending on the date of the sale or exchange, has been owned and used by the taxpayer as his principal residence for periods aggregating 3 years or more, this section shall apply with respect to so much of the gain from the sale or exchange of such property as is determined, under regulations prescribed by the Secretary, to be attributable to the portion of the property so owned and used by the taxpayer.

(6) DETERMINATION OF MARITAL STATUS.—In the case of any sale or exchange, for purposes of this section—

(A) the determination of whether an individual is married shall be made as of the date of the sale or exchange; and

(B) an individual legally separated from his spouse under a decree of divorce or of separate maintenance shall not be considered as married.

(7) APPLICATION OF SECTIONS 1033 AND 1034.—In applying sections 1033 (relating to involuntary conversions) and 1034 (relating to sale or exchange of residence), the amount realized from the sale or exchange of property shall be treated as being the amount determined without regard to this section, reduced by the amount of gain not included in gross income pursuant to an election under this section.

(8) PROPERTY ACQUIRED AFTER INVOLUNTARY CONVERSION.—If the basis of the property sold or exchanged is determined (in whole or in part) under subsection (b) of section 1033 (relating to basis of property acquired through involuntary conversion), then the holding and use by the taxpayer of the converted property shall be treated as holding and use by the taxpayer of the property sold or exchanged.

(9) DETERMINATION OF USE DURING PERIODS OF OUT-OF-RESIDENCE CARE.—In the case of a taxpayer who—

(A) becomes physically or mentally incapable of self-care, and

(B) owns property and uses such property as the taxpayer's principal residence during the 5-year period described in subsection (a)(2) for periods aggregating at least 1 year, then the taxpayer shall be treated as using such property as the taxpayer's principal residence during any time during such 5-year period in which the taxpayer owns the property and resides in any facility (including a nursing home) licensed by a State or political subdivision to care for an individual in the taxpayer's condition.

Amendments

• 1988, Technical and Miscellaneous Revenue Act of 1988 (P.L. 100-647)

P.L. 100-647, §6011(a):

Amended Code Sec. 121(d) by adding at the end thereof paragraph (9). **Effective** with respect to any sale or exchange after 9-30-88, in tax years ending after such date.

• 1978, Revenue Act of 1978 (P.L. 95-600)

P.L. 95-600, §404(b):

Amended Code Sec. 121(d) by adding subparagraph (8). **Effective** as set forth in P.L. 95-600, §404(d). See historical comment on P.L. 95-600, §404(d) under former Code Sec. 121(a).

P.L. 95-600, §404(c)(1), (2):

Amended Code Sec. 121(d)(2) and Code Sec. 121(d)(5) by striking out "8-year period" and inserting in lieu thereof "5-year period", and amended Code Sec. 121(d)(5) by striking out "5 years" and inserting in lieu thereof "3 years". For **effective** date, see historical comment on P.L. 95-600, § 404(d) under former Code Sec. 121(a).

• 1976, Tax Reform Act of 1976 (P.L. 94-455)

P.L. 94-455, § 1906(b)(13)(A):

Amended 1954 Code by substituting "Secretary" for "Secretary or his delegate" each place it appeared. **Effective** 2-1-77.

• 1964, Revenue Act of 1964 (P.L. 88-272)

P. L. 88-272, § 206(a):

Amended Part III of subchapter B of chapter 1 by adding subsection 121. **Effective** for dispositions after 12-31-63 in tax years ending after such date.

[Sec. 122]

SEC. 122. CERTAIN REDUCED UNIFORMED SERVICES RETIREMENT PAY.

[Sec. 122(a)]

(a) GENERAL RULE.—In the case of a member or former member of the uniformed services of the United States, gross income does not include the amount of any reduction in his retired or retainer pay pursuant to the provisions of chapter 73 of title 10, United States Code.

[Sec. 122(b)]

(b) SPECIAL RULE.—

(1) AMOUNT EXCLUDED FROM GROSS INCOME.—In the case of any individual referred to in subsection (a), all amounts received after December 31, 1965, as retired or retainer pay shall be excluded from gross income until there has been so excluded an amount equal to the consideration for the contract. The preceding sentence shall apply only to the extent that the amounts received would, but for such sentence, be includible in gross income.

(2) CONSIDERATION FOR THE CONTRACT.—For purposes of paragraph (1) and section 72(n), the term "consideration for the contract" means, in respect of any individual, the sum of—

(A) the total amount of the reductions before January 1, 1966, in his retired or retainer pay by reason of an election under chapter 73 of title 10 of the United States Code, and

(B) any amounts deposited at any time by him pursuant to section 1438 or 1452(d) of such title 10.

Amendments

• 1974, Employee Retirement Income Secuirty Act of 1974 (P.L. 93-406)

P. L. 93-406, § 2005(c)(10):

Amended Code Sec. 122(b)(2) by substituting "section 72(n)" for "section 72(o)".

P. L. 93-406, § 2008(a):

Amended Code Sec. 122(a). **Effective** for tax years ending on or after 9-21-72. Prior to amendment, Code Sec. 122(a) read as follows:

"(a) General Rule.—In the case of a member or former member of the uniformed services of the United States who has made an election under chapter 73 of title 10 of the United States Code to receive a reduced amount of retired or retainer pay, gross income does not include the amount of any reduction after December 31, 1965, in his retired or retainer pay by reason of such election."

P. L. 93-406, § 2008(b)(1):

Amended Code Sec. 122(b)(2)(B) by adding "or 1452(d)" after "section 1438". **Effective** with respect to individuals dying on or after 9-21-72.

• 1966 (P.L. 89-365)

P. L. 89-365, § [1]:

Added Code Sec. 122. **Effective** for tax years ending after 12-31-65.

[Sec. 123]

SEC. 123. AMOUNTS RECEIVED UNDER INSURANCE CONTRACTS FOR CERTAIN LIVING EXPENSES.

[Sec. 123(a)]

(a) GENERAL RULE.—In the case of an individual whose principal residence is damaged or destroyed by fire, storm, or other casualty, or who is denied access to his principal residence by governmental authorities because of the occurrence or threat of occurrence of such a casualty, gross income does not include amounts received by such individual under an insurance contract which are paid to compensate or reimburse such individual for living expenses incurred for himself and members of his household resulting from the loss of use or occupancy of such residence.

[Sec. 123(b)]

(b) LIMITATION.— Subsection (a) shall apply to amounts received by the taxpayer for living expenses incurred during any period only to the extent the amounts received do not exceed the amount by which—

(1) the actual living expenses incurred during such period for himself and members of his household resulting from the loss of use or occupancy of their residence, exceed

(2) the normal living expenses which would have been incurred for himself and members of his household during such period.

Amendments

• 1969, Tax Reform Act of 1969 (P.L. 91-172)

P. L. 91-172, §901(a):

Added Code Sec. 123. **Effective** for amounts received on or after 1-1-69.

[Sec. 124—Repealed]

Amendments

• 1990, Omnibus Budget Reconciliation Act of 1990 (P.L. 101-508)

P.L. 101-508, §11801(a)(9):

Repealed Code Sec. 124. **Effective** 11-5-90. Prior to repeal, Code Sec. 124 read as follows:

SEC. 124. QUALIFIED TRANSPORTATION PROVIDED BY EMPLOYER.

(a) GENERAL RULE.—Gross income of an employee does not include the value of qualified transportation provided by the employer between the employee's residence and place of employment.

(b) QUALIFIED TRANSPORTATION.—For purposes of this section, the term "qualified transportation" means transportation in a commuter highway vehicle (as defined in section 46(c)(6)(B) but without regard to clause (iii) or (iv) thereof).

(c) ADDITIONAL REQUIREMENTS.—Subsection (a) does not apply to the value of transportation provided by an employer unless—

(1) such transportation is provided under a separate written plan of the employer which does not discriminate in favor of employees who are officers, shareholders, or highly compensated employees, and

(2) the plan provides that the value of such transportation is provided in addition to (and not in lieu of) any compensation otherwise payable to the employee.

(d) DEFINITIONS.—For purposes of this section—

(1) PROVIDED BY THE EMPLOYER.—Transportation shall be considered to be provided by an employer if the transportation is furnished in a commuter highway vehicle (described in subsection (b)) operated by or for the employer.

(2) EMPLOYEE.—The term "employee" does not include an individual who is an employee (within the meaning of section 401(c)(1)).

(e) EFFECTIVE DATE.—Subsection (a) applies with respect to qualified transportation provided in taxable years beginning after December 31, 1978, and before January 1, 1986.

P.L. 101-508, §11821(b)(1)-(2), provides:

(b) SAVINGS PROVISION.—If—

(1) any provision amended or repealed by this part applied to—

(A) any transaction occurring before the date of the enactment of this Act,

(B) any property acquired before such date of enactment, or

(C) any item of income, loss, deduction, or credit taken into account before such date of enactment, and

(2) the treatment of such transaction, property, or item under such provision would (without regard to the amendments made by this part) affect liability for tax for periods ending after such date of enactment,

nothing in the amendments made by this part shall be construed to affect the treatment of such transaction, property, or item for purposes of determining liability for tax for periods ending after such date of enactment.

• 1978, Energy Tax Act of 1978 (P.L. 95-618)

P.L. 95-618, §242:

Added Code Sec. 124, and redesignated the former Code Sec. 124 as Code Sec. 125. **Effective** 11-10-78.

P.L. 95-618, §242(c), provides:

(c) TRANSITION RULE.—The plan requirements of section 124(c) of the Internal Revenue Code of 1954 shall be considered to be met with respect to transportation provided before July 1, 1979, if there is a plan meeting such requirements of the employer in effect on that date.

[Sec. 125]

SEC. 125. CAFETERIA PLANS.

[Sec. 125(a)]

(a) IN GENERAL.—Except as provided in subsection (b), no amount shall be included in the gross income of a participant in a cafeteria plan solely because, under the plan, the participant may choose among the benefits of the plan.

[Sec. 125(b)]

(b) EXCEPTION FOR HIGHLY COMPENSATED PARTICIPANTS AND KEY EMPLOYEES.—

(1) HIGHLY COMPENSATED PARTICIPANTS.—In the case of a highly compensated participant, subsection (a) shall not apply to any benefit attributable to a plan year for which the plan discriminates in favor of—

(A) highly compensated individuals as to eligibility to participate, or

(B) highly compensated participants as to contributions and benefits.

(2) KEY EMPLOYEES.—In the case of a key employee (within the meaning of section 416(i)(1)), subsection (a) shall not apply to any benefit attributable to a plan [year] for which the statutory nontaxable benefits provided to key employees exceed 25 percent of the aggregate of such benefits provided for all employees under the plan. For purposes of the preceding sentence, statutory nontaxable benefits shall be determined without regard to the second sentence of subsection (f).

(3) YEAR OF INCLUSION.—For purposes of determining the taxable year of inclusion, any benefit described in paragraph (1) or (2) shall be treated as received or accrued in the taxable year of the participant or key employee in which the plan year ends.

Amendments

• 2007, Tax Technical Corrections Act of 2007 (P.L. 110-172)

P.L. 110-172, §11(a)(12):

Amended the last sentence of Code Sec. 125(b)(2) by striking "last sentence" and inserting "second sentence". **Effective** 12-29-2007.

• 1984, Deficit Reduction Act of 1984 (P.L. 98-369)

P.L. 98-369, §531(b)(3):

Amended Code Sec. 125(b). **Effective** 1-1-85. Prior to amendment, subsection (b) read as follows:

(b) EXCEPTION FOR HIGHLY COMPENSATED PARTICIPANTS WHERE PLAN IS DISCRIMINATORY. —

(1) IN GENERAL. —In the case of a highly compensated participant, subsection (a) shall not apply to any benefit attributable to a plan year for which the plan discriminates in favor of—

(A) highly compensated individuals as to eligibility to participate, or

(B) highly compensated participants as to contributions and benefits.

(2) YEAR OF INCLUSION. —For purposes of determining the taxable year of inclusion, any benefit described in paragraph (1) shall be treated as received or accrued in the participant's taxable year in which the plan year ends.

[Sec. 125(c)]

(c) DISCRIMINATION AS TO BENEFITS OR CONTRIBUTIONS.—For purposes of subparagraph (B) of subsection (b)(1), a cafeteria plan does not discriminate where qualified benefits and total benefits (or employer contributions allocable to statutory nontaxable benefits and employer contributions for total benefits) do not discriminate in favor of highly compensated participants.

Amendments

• 1984, Deficit Reduction Act of 1984 (P.L. 98-369)

P.L. 98-369, §531(b)(2)(B):

Amended Code Sec. 125(c) by striking our "nontaxable benefits" each place it appeared and inserting in lieu thereof "statutory nontaxable benefits". **Effective** 1-1-85.

[Sec. 125(d)]

(d) CAFETERIA PLAN DEFINED.—For purposes of this section—

(1) IN GENERAL.—The term "cafeteria plan" means a written plan under which—

(A) all participants are employees, and

(B) the participants may choose among 2 or more benefits consisting of cash and qualified benefits.

(2) DEFERRED COMPENSATION PLANS EXCLUDED.—

(A) IN GENERAL.—The term "cafeteria plan" does not include any plan which provides for deferred compensation.

(B) EXCEPTION FOR CASH AND DEFERRED ARRANGEMENTS.—Subparagraph (A) shall not apply to a profit-sharing or stock bonus plan or rural cooperative plan (within the meaning of section 401(k)(7)) which includes a qualified cash or deferred arrangement (as defined in section 401(k)(2)) to the extent of amounts which a covered employee may elect to have the employer pay as contributions to a trust under such plan on behalf of the employee.

(C) EXCEPTION FOR CERTAIN PLANS MAINTAINED BY EDUCATIONAL INSTITUTIONS.—Subparagraph (A) shall not apply to a plan maintained by an educational organization described in section 170(b)(1)(A)(ii) to the extent of amounts which a covered employee may elect to have the employer pay as contributions for post-retirement group life insurance if—

(i) all contributions for such insurance must be made before retirement, and

(ii) such life insurance does not have a cash surrender value at any time.

For purposes of section 79, any life insurance described in the preceding sentence shall be treated as group-term life insurance.

(D) EXCEPTION FOR HEALTH SAVINGS ACCOUNTS.—Subparagraph (A) shall not apply to a plan to the extent of amounts which a covered employee may elect to have the employer pay as contributions to a health savings account established on behalf of the employee.

Amendments

• 2003, Medicare Prescription Drug, Improvement, and Modernization Act of 2003 (P.L. 108-173)

P.L. 108-173, §1201(i):

Amended Code Sec. 125(d)(2) by adding at the end a new subparagraph (D). **Effective** for tax years beginning after 12-31-2003.

• 1989 (P.L. 101-140)

P.L. 101-140, §203(b)(2):

Amended Code Sec. 125(d)(2), as in effect on the day before the date of the enactment of P.L. 99-514. **Effective** as if included in Act Sec. 1151 of P.L. 99-514. Prior to amendment, Code Sec. 125(d)(2) read as follows:

(2) DEFERRED COMPENSATION PLANS EXCLUDED. —The term "cafeteria plan" does not include any plan which provides for deferred compensation. The preceding sentence shall not apply in the case of a profit-sharing or stock bonus plan which includes a qualified cash or deferred arrangement (as defined in section 401(k)(2)) to the extent of amounts which a covered employee may elect to have the employer pay as contributions to a trust under such plan on behalf of the employee.

• 1984, Deficit Reduction Act of 1984 (P.L. 98-369)

P.L. 98-369, §531(b)(1):

Amended Code Sec. 125(d)(1). Prior to amendment, Code Sec. 125(d)(1) read as follows:

(1) IN GENERAL. —The term "cafeteria plan" means a written plan under which—

(A) all participants are employees, and

(B) the participants may choose among two or more benefits.

The benefits which may be chosen may be nontaxable benefits, or cash, property, or other taxable benefits.

• 1980, Miscellaneous Revenue Act of 1980 (P.L. 96-605)

P.L. 96-605, §226(a):

Amended Code Sec. 125(d)(2) by adding the last sentence. **Effective** for tax years beginning after 12-31-80.

[Sec. 125(e)]

(e) HIGHLY COMPENSATED PARTICIPANT AND INDIVIDUAL DEFINED.—For purposes of this section—

(1) HIGHLY COMPENSATED PARTICIPANT.—The term "highly compensated participant" means a participant who is—

(A) an officer,

(B) a shareholder owning more than 5 percent of the voting power or value of all classes of stock of the employer,

(C) highly compensated, or

(D) a spouse or dependent (within the meaning of section 152, determined without regard to subsections (b)(1), (b)(2), and (d)(1)(B) thereof) of an individual described in subparagraph (A), (B), or (C).

(2) HIGHLY COMPENSATED INDIVIDUAL.—The term "highly compensated individual" means an individual who is described in subparagraph (A), (B), (C), or (D) of paragraph (1).

Amendments

• 2004, Working Families Tax Relief Act of 2004 (P.L. 108-311)

P.L. 108-311, §207(11):

Amended Code Sec. 125(e)(1)(D) by inserting ", determined without regard to subsections (b)(1), (b)(2), and (d)(1)(B) thereof" after "section 152". **Effective** for tax years beginning after 12-31-2004.

»»→ Caution: Code Sec. 125(f), below, prior to amendment by P.L. 111-148, applies to tax years beginning on or before December 31, 2013.

[Sec. 125(f)]

(f) QUALIFIED BENEFITS DEFINED.—For purposes of this section, the term "qualified benefit" means any benefit which, with the application of subsection (a), is not includible in the gross income of the employee by reason of an express provision of this chapter (other than section 106(b), 117, 127, or 132). Such term includes any group term life insurance which is includible in gross income only because it exceeds the dollar limitation of section 79 and such term includes any other benefit permitted under regulations. Such term shall not include any product which is advertised, marketed, or offered as long-term care insurance.

»»→ Caution: Code Sec. 125(f), below, as amended by P.L. 111-148, applies to tax years beginning after December 31, 2013.

[Sec. 125(f)]

(f) QUALIFIED BENEFITS DEFINED.—For purposes of this section—

(1) IN GENERAL.—The term "qualified benefit"means any benefit which, with the application of subsection (a), is not includible in the gross income of the employee by reason of an express provision of this chapter (other than section 106(b), 117, 127, or 132). Such term includes any group term life insurance which is includible in gross income only because it exceeds the dollar limitation of section 79 and such term includes any other benefit permitted under regulations.

(2) LONG-TERM CARE INSURANCE NOT QUALIFIED.—The term "qualified benefit" shall not include any product which is advertised, marketed, or offered as long-term care insurance.

(3) CERTAIN EXCHANGE-PARTICIPATING QUALIFIED HEALTH PLANS NOT QUALIFIED.—

(A) IN GENERAL.—The term "qualified benefit" shall not include any qualified health plan (as defined in section 1301(a) of the Patient Protection and Affordable Care Act) offered through an Exchange established under section 1311 of such Act.

(B) EXCEPTION FOR EXCHANGE-ELIGIBLE EMPLOYERS.—Subparagraph (A) shall not apply with respect to any employee if such employee's employer is a qualified employer (as defined in section 1312(f)(2) of the Patient Protection and Affordable Care Act) offering the employee the opportunity to enroll through such an Exchange in a qualified health plan in a group market.

Amendments

• 2010, Patient Protection and Affordable Care Act (P.L. 111-148)

P.L. 111-148, §1515(a):

Amended Code Sec. 125(f) by adding at the end a new paragraph (3). **Effective** for tax years beginning after 12-31-2013.

P.L. 111-148, §1515(b)(1)-(2):

Amended Code Sec. 125(f) by striking "For purposes of this section, the term" and inserting "For purposes of this section—"

"(1) IN GENERAL.—The term",

and by striking "Such term shall not include" and inserting:

"(2) LONG-TERM CARE INSURANCE NOT QUALIFIED. —The term 'qualified benefit' shall not include".

Effective for tax years beginning after 12-31-2013.

• 1996, Health Insurance Portability and Accountability Act of 1996 (P.L. 104-191)

P.L. 104-191, §301(d):

Amended Code Sec. 125(f) by inserting "106(b)," before "117". **Effective** for tax years beginning after 12-31-96.

P.L. 104-191, §321(c)(1):

Amended Code Sec. 125(f) by adding at the end a new sentence. For the **effective** date and special rules, see Act Sec. 321(f)-(g).

P.L. 104-191, §321(f)-(g), provides:

(f) EFFECTIVE DATES. —

(1) GENERAL EFFECTIVE DATES. —

(A) IN GENERAL. —Except as provided in subparagraph (B), the amendments made by this section shall apply to contracts issued after December 31, 1996.

(B) RESERVE METHOD. —The amendment made by subsection (b) shall apply to contracts issued after December 31, 1997.

(2) CONTINUATION OF EXISTING POLICIES. —In the case of any contract issued before January 1, 1997, which met the long-term care insurance requirements of the State in which the contract was sitused at the time the contract was issued—

(A) such contract shall be treated for purposes of the Internal Revenue Code of 1986 as a qualified long-term care insurance contract (as defined in section 7702B(b) of such Code), and

(B) services provided under, or reimbursed by, such contract shall be treated for such purposes as qualified long-term care services (as defined in section 7702B(c) of such Code).

In the case of an individual who is covered on December 31, 1996, under a State long-term care plan (as defined in section 7702B(f)(2) of such Code), the terms of such plan on such date shall be treated for purposes of the preceding sentence as a contract issued on such date which met the long-term care insurance requirements of such State.

(3) EXCHANGES OF EXISTING POLICIES. —If, after the date of enactment of this Act and before January 1, 1998, a contract providing for long-term care insurance coverage is exchanged solely for a qualified long-term care insurance contract (as defined in section 7702B(b) of such Code), no gain or loss shall be recognized on the exchange. If, in addition to a qualified long-term care insurance contract, money or other property is received in the exchange, then any gain shall be recognized to the extent of the sum of the money and the fair market value of the other property received. For purposes of this paragraph, the cancellation of a contract providing for long-term care insurance coverage and reinvestment of the cancellation proceeds in a qualified long-term care insurance contract within 60 days thereafter shall be treated as an exchange.

(4) ISSUANCE OF CERTAIN RIDERS PERMITTED. —For purposes of applying sections 101(f), 7702, and 7702A of the Internal Revenue Code of 1986 to any contract—

(A) the issuance of a rider which is treated as a qualified long-term care insurance contract under section 7702B, and

(B) the addition of any provision required to conform any other long-term care rider to be so treated,

shall not be treated as a modification or material change of such contract.

(5) APPLICATION OF PER DIEM LIMITATION TO EXISTING CONTRACTS. —The amount of per diem payments made under a contract issuedon or before July 31, 1996, with respect to an insured which are excludable from gross income by reason of section 7702B of the Internal Revenue Code of 1986 (as added by this section) shall not be reduced under subsection (d)(2)(B) thereof by reason of reimbursements received under a contract issued on or before such date. The preceding sentence shall cease to apply as of the date (after July 31, 1996) such contract is exchanged or there is any contract modification which results in an increase in the amount of such per diem payments or the amount of such reimbursements.

(g) LONG-TERM CARE STUDY REQUEST. —The Chairman of the Committee on Ways and Means of the House of Representatives and the Chairman of the Committee on Finance of the Senate shall jointly request the National Association of Insurance Commissioners, in consultation with representatives of the insurance industry and consumer organizations, to formulate, develop, and conduct a study to determine the marketing and other effects of per diem limits on certain types of long-term care policies. If the National Association of Insurance Commissioners agrees to the study request, the National Association of Insurance Commissioners shall report the results of its study to such committees not later than 2 years after accepting the request.

• 1990, Omnibus Budget Reconciliation Act of 1990 (P.L. 101-508)

P.L. 101-508, §11801(c)(3):

Amended Code Sec. 125(f) by striking "section 117, 124," and inserting "section 117,". **Effective** 11-5-90.

P.L. 101-508, §11821(b)(1)-(2), provides:

(b) SAVINGS PROVISION. —If—

(1) any provision amended or repealed by this part applied to—

(A) any transaction occurring before the date of the enactment of this Act,

(B) any property acquired before such date of enactment, or

(C) any item of income, loss, deduction, or credit taken into account before such date of enactment, and

(2) the treatment of such transaction, property, or item under such provision would (without regard to the amendments made by this part) affect liability for tax for periods ending after such date of enactment,

nothing in the amendments made by this part shall be construed to affect the treatment of such transaction, property, or item for purposes of determining liability for tax for periods ending after such date of enactment.

• 1984, Deficit Reduction Act of 1984 (P.L. 98-369)

P.L. 98-369, §531(b)(2)(A):

Amended Code Sec. 125(f). **Effective** 1-1-85. Prior to amendment, Code Sec. 125(f) read as follows:

(f) NONTAXABLE BENEFIT DEFINED. —For purposes of this section, the term "nontaxable benefit" means any benefit which, with the application of subsection (a), is not includible in the gross income of the employee.

[Sec. 125(g)]

(g) SPECIAL RULES.—

(1) COLLECTIVELY BARGAINED PLAN NOT CONSIDERED DISCRIMINATORY.—For purposes of this section, a plan shall not be treated as discriminatory if the plan is maintained under an agreement which the Secretary finds to be a collective bargaining agreement between employee representatives and one or more employers.

(2) HEALTH BENEFITS.—For purposes of subparagraph (B) of subsection (b)(1), a cafeteria plan which provides health benefits shall not be treated as discriminatory if—

(A) contributions under the plan on behalf of each participant include an amount which—

(i) equals 100 percent of the cost of the health benefit coverage under the plan of the majority of the highly compensated participants similarly situated, or

(ii) equals or exceeds 75 percent of the cost of the health benefit coverage of the participant (similarly situated) having the highest cost health benefit coverage under the plan, and

(B) contributions or benefits under the plan in excess of those described in subparagraph (A) bear a uniform relationship to compensation.

(3) CERTAIN PARTICIPATION ELIGIBILITY RULES NOT TREATED AS DISCRIMINATORY.—For purposes of subparagraph (A) of subsection (b)(1), a classification shall not be treated as discriminatory if the plan—

(A) benefits a group of employees described in section 410(b)(2)(A)(i), and

(B) meets the requirements of clauses (i) and (ii):

(i) No employee is required to complete more than 3 years of employment with the employer or employers maintaining the plan as a condition of participation in the plan, and the employment requirement for each employee is the same.

(ii) Any employee who has satisfied the employment requirement of clause (i) and who is otherwise entitled to participate in the plan commences participation no later than the first day of the first plan year beginning after the date the employment requirement was satisfied unless the employee was separated from service before the first day of that plan year.

(4) CERTAIN CONTROLLED GROUPS, ETC.—All employees who are treated as employed by a single employer under subsection (b), (c), or (m) of section 414 shall be treated as employed by a single employer for purposes of this section.

Amendments

• 1989 (P.L. 101-140)

P.L. 101-140, §203(a)(3):

Amended Code Sec. 125(g)(3)(A), as in effect before the date of the enactment of P.L. 99-514, by striking "subparagraph (B) of section 410(b)(1)" and inserting "section 410(b)(2)(A)(i)". **Effective** as if included in Act Sec. 1151 of P.L. 99-514.

[Sec. 125(h)]

(h) SPECIAL RULE FOR UNUSED BENEFITS IN HEALTH FLEXIBLE SPENDING ARRANGEMENTS OF INDIVIDUALS CALLED TO ACTIVE DUTY.—

(1) IN GENERAL .—For purposes of this title, a plan or other arrangement shall not fail to be treated as a cafeteria plan or health flexible spending arrangement merely because such arrangement provides for qualified reservist distributions.

(2) QUALIFIED RESERVIST DISTRIBUTION .—For purposes of this subsection, the term "qualified reservist distribution" means, [sic] any distribution to an individual of all or a portion of the balance in the employee's account under such arrangement if—

(A) such individual was (by reason of being a member of a reserve component (as defined in section 101 of title 37, United States Code)) ordered or called to active duty for a period in excess of 179 days or for an indefinite period, and

(B) such distribution is made during the period beginning on the date of such order or call and ending on the last date that reimbursements could otherwise be made under such arrangement for the plan year which includes the date of such order or call.

Amendments

• 2008, Heroes Earnings Assistance and Relief Tax Act of 2008 (P.L. 110-245)

P.L. 110-245, §114(a):

Amended Code Sec. 125 by redesignating subsections (h) and (i) as subsections (i) and (j), respectively, and by inserting after subsection (g) a new subsection (h). **Effective** for distributions made after 6-17-2008.

»»→ Caution: Code Sec. 125(i), below, as added and amended by P.L. 111-148, applies to tax years beginning after December 31, 2012.

[Sec. 125(i)]

(i) LIMITATION ON HEALTH FLEXIBLE SPENDING ARRANGEMENTS.—

(1) IN GENERAL .—For purposes of this section, if a benefit is provided under a cafeteria plan through employer contributions to a health flexible spending arrangement, such benefit shall not be treated as a qualified benefit unless the cafeteria plan provides that an employee may not elect for any taxable year to have salary reduction contributions in excess of $2,500 made to such arrangement.

(2) ADJUSTMENT FOR INFLATION .—In the case of any taxable year beginning after December 31, 2013, the dollar amount in paragraph (1) shall be increased by an amount equal to—

(A) such amount, multiplied by

(B) the cost-of-living adjustment determined under section 1(f)(3) for the calendar year in which such taxable year begins by substituting "calendar year 2012" for "calendar year 1992" in subparagraph (B) thereof.

If any increase determined under this paragraph is not a multiple of $50, such increase shall be rounded to the next lowest multiple of $50.

Amendments

• 2010, Health Care and Education Reconciliation Act of 2010 (P.L. 111-152)

P.L. 111-152, §1403(b)(1)-(2):

Amended Code Sec. 125(i)(2), as added by section 9005 of the Patient Protection and Affordable Care Act (P.L. 111-148) and amended by section 10902 of such Act, by striking "December 31, 2011" and inserting "December 31, 2013" in the matter preceding subparagraph (A); and by striking "2010" and inserting "2012" in subparagraph (B). **Effective** 3-30-2010.

• 2010, Patient Protection and Affordable Care Act (P.L. 111-148)

P.L. 111-148, §9005(a)(1)-(2):

Amended Code Sec. 125 by redesignating subsections (i) and (j) as subsections (j) and (k), respectively, and by inserting after subsection (h) a new subsection (i). **Effective** for tax years beginning after 12-31-2012 [effective date changed by P.L. 111-152, §1403(a)—CCH].

P.L. 111-148, §10902(a):

Amended Code Sec. 125(i), as added by Act Sec. 9005. **Effective** for tax years beginning after 12-31-2012 [**effective** date changed by P.L. 111-152, §1403(a).—CCH]. Prior to amendment, Code Sec. 125(i) read as follows:

(i) LIMITATION ON HEALTH FLEXIBLE SPENDING ARRANGEMENTS .—For purposes of this section, if a benefit is provided under a cafeteria plan through employer contributions to a health flexible spending arrangement, such benefit shall not be treated as a qualified benefit unless the cafeteria plan provides that an employee may not elect for any taxable year to have salary reduction contributions in excess of $2,500 made to such arrangement.

»»→ Caution: Code Sec. 125(j), below, as added by P.L. 111-148, applies to years beginning after December 31, 2010.

[Sec. 125(j)]

(j) SIMPLE CAFETERIA PLANS FOR SMALL BUSINESSES.—

(1) IN GENERAL .—An eligible employer maintaining a simple cafeteria plan with respect to which the requirements of this subsection are met for any year shall be treated as meeting any applicable nondiscrimination requirement during such year.

(2) SIMPLE CAFETERIA PLAN .—For purposes of this subsection, the term "simple cafeteria plan" means a cafeteria plan—

(A) which is established and maintained by an eligible employer, and

(B) with respect to which the contribution requirements of paragraph (3), and the eligibility and participation requirements of paragraph (4), are met.

(3) CONTRIBUTION REQUIREMENTS.—

(A) IN GENERAL .—The requirements of this paragraph are met if, under the plan the employer is required, without regard to whether a qualified employee makes any salary reduction contribution, to make a contribution to provide qualified benefits under the plan on behalf of each qualified employee in an amount equal to—

(i) a uniform percentage (not less than 2 percent) of the employee's compensation for the plan year, or

(ii) an amount which is not less than the lesser of—

(I) 6 percent of the employee's compensation for the plan year, or

(II) twice the amount of the salary reduction contributions of each qualified employee.

(B) MATCHING CONTRIBUTIONS ON BEHALF OF HIGHLY COMPENSATED AND KEY EMPLOYEES .—The requirements of subparagraph (A)(ii) shall not be treated as met if, under the plan, the rate of contributions with respect to any salary reduction contribution of a highly compensated or key employee at any rate of contribution is greater than that with respect to an employee who is not a highly compensated or key employee.

(C) ADDITIONAL CONTRIBUTIONS .—Subject to subparagraph (B), nothing in this paragraph shall be treated as prohibiting an employer from making contributions to provide qualified benefits under the plan in addition to contributions required under subparagraph (A).

(D) DEFINITIONS .—For purposes of this paragraph—

(i) SALARY REDUCTION CONTRIBUTION .—The term "salary reduction contribution" means, with respect to a cafeteria plan, any amount which is contributed to the plan at the election of the employee and which is not includible in gross income by reason of this section.

(ii) QUALIFIED EMPLOYEE .—The term "qualified employee" means, with respect to a cafeteria plan, any employee who is not a highly compensated or key employee and who is eligible to participate in the plan.

(iii) HIGHLY COMPENSATED EMPLOYEE .—The term "highly compensated employee" has the meaning given such term by section 414(q).

(iv) KEY EMPLOYEE .—The term "key employee" has the meaning given such term by section 416(i).

(4) MINIMUM ELIGIBILITY AND PARTICIPATION REQUIREMENTS.—

(A) IN GENERAL .—The requirements of this paragraph shall be treated as met with respect to any year if, under the plan—

(i) all employees who had at least 1,000 hours of service for the preceding plan year are eligible to participate, and

(ii) each employee eligible to participate in the plan may, subject to terms and conditions applicable to all participants, elect any benefit available under the plan.

(B) CERTAIN EMPLOYEES MAY BE EXCLUDED .—For purposes of subparagraph (A)(i), an employer may elect to exclude under the plan employees—

(i) who have not attained the age of 21 before the close of a plan year,

(ii) who have less than 1 year of service with the employer as of any day during the plan year,

(iii) who are covered under an agreement which the Secretary of Labor finds to be a collective bargaining agreement if there is evidence that the benefits covered under the cafeteria plan were the subject of good faith bargaining between employee representatives and the employer, or

(iv) who are described in section 410(b)(3)(C) (relating to nonresident aliens working outside the United States).

A plan may provide a shorter period of service or younger age for purposes of clause (i) or (ii).

(5) ELIGIBLE EMPLOYER .—For purposes of this subsection—

(A) IN GENERAL .—The term "eligible employer" means, with respect to any year, any employer if such employer employed an average of 100 or fewer employees on business days during either of the 2 preceding years. For purposes of this subparagraph, a year may only be taken into account if the employer was in existence throughout the year.

(B) EMPLOYERS NOT IN EXISTENCE DURING PRECEDING YEAR .—If an employer was not in existence throughout the preceding year, the determination under subparagraph (A) shall be based on the average number of employees that it is reasonably expected such employer will employ on business days in the current year.

(C) GROWING EMPLOYERS RETAIN TREATMENT AS SMALL EMPLOYER.—

(i) IN GENERAL .—If—

(I) an employer was an eligible employer for any year (a "qualified year"), and

(II) such employer establishes a simple cafeteria plan for its employees for such year,

then, notwithstanding the fact the employer fails to meet the requirements of subparagraph (A) for any subsequent year, such employer shall be treated as an eligible employer for such subsequent year with respect to employees (whether or not employees during a qualified year) of any trade or business which was covered by the plan during any qualified year.

(ii) EXCEPTION .—This subparagraph shall cease to apply if the employer employs an average of 200 or more employees on business days during any year preceding any such subsequent year.

(D) SPECIAL RULES.—

(i) PREDECESSORS .—Any reference in this paragraph to an employer shall include a reference to any predecessor of such employer.

(ii) AGGREGATION RULES .—All persons treated as a single employer under subsection (a) or (b) of section 52, or subsection (n) or (o) of section 414, shall be treated as one person.

(6) APPLICABLE NONDISCRIMINATION REQUIREMENT .—For purposes of this subsection, the term "applicable nondiscrimination requirement" means any requirement under subsection (b) of this section, section 79(d), section 105(h), or paragraph (2), (3), (4), or (8) of section 129(d).

(7) COMPENSATION .—The term "compensation" has the meaning given such term by section 414(s).

Amendments

• 2010, Patient Protection and Affordable Care Act (P.L. 111-148)

P.L. 111-148, §9022(a):

Amended Code Sec. 125, as amended by this Act, by redesignating subsections (j) and (k) as subsections (k) and (l), respectively, and by inserting after subsection (i) a new subsection (j). **Effective** for years beginning after 12-31-2010.

»»→ Caution: Former Code Sec. 125(i) was redesignated as Code Sec. 125(j) by P.L. 111-148, §9005(a)(1), applicable to tax years beginning after December 31, 2010, and further redesignated as Code Sec. 125(k), below, by P.L. 111-148, §9022(a), applicable to years beginning after December 31, 2010.

[Sec. 125(k)]

(k) CROSS REFERENCE.—

For reporting and recordkeeping requirements, see section 6039D.

Amendments

• 2010, Patient Protection and Affordable Care Act (P.L. 111-148)

P.L. 111-148, §9005(a)(1):

Amended Code Sec. 125 by redesignating subsection (i) as (j). **Effective** for tax years beginning after 12-31-2010.

P.L. 111-148, §9022(a):

Amended Code Sec. 125, as amended by this Act, by redesignating subsection (j) as subsection (k). **Effective** for years beginning after 12-31-2010.

• 2008, Heroes Earnings Assistance and Relief Tax Act of 2008 (P.L. 110-245)

P.L. 110-245, §114(a):

Amended Code Sec. 125 by redesignating subsection (h) as subsection (i). **Effective** for distributions made after 6-17-2008.

• 1984 (P.L. 98-612)

P.L. 98-612, §1(b)(3)(B):

Amended Code Sec. 125 by striking out subsection (h) and inserting in lieu thereof a new subsection (h). [Note: P.L. 98-611 also struck out subsection (h) and inserted in lieu thereof a new subsection (h), the language of which is identical to that added by P.L. 98-612]. The text of former subsection (h) appears in the note for P.L. 98-611, below. **Effective** 1-1-85.

• 1984 (P.L. 98-611)

P.L. 98-611, §1(d)(3)(A):

Amended Code Sec. 125 by striking out subsection (h) and inserting in lieu thereof new subsection (h). **Effective** 1-1-85. [See, however, the note for P.L. 98-612, above.] Prior to amendment, Code Sec. 125(h) read as follows:

(h) REPORTING REQUIREMENTS. —

(1) IN GENERAL. —Each employer maintaining a cafeteria plan during any year which begins after December 31, 1984, and to which this section applies shall file a return (at such time and in such manner as the Secretary shall by regulations prescribe) with respect to such plan showing for such year—

(A) the number of employees of the employer,

(B) the number of employees participating under the plan,

(C) the total cost of the plan during the year, and

(D) the name, address, and taxpayer identification number of the employer and the type of business in which the employer is engaged.

(2) RECORDKEEPING REQUIREMENT. —Each employer maintaining a cafeteria plan during any year shall keep such records as may be necessary for purposes of determining whether the requirements of this section are met.

(3) ADDITIONAL INFORMATION WHEN REQUIRED BY THE SECRETARY. —Any employer—

(A) who maintains a cafeteria plan during any year for which a return is required under paragraph (1), and

(B) who is required by the Secretary to file an additional return for such year,

shall file such additional return. Such additional return shall be filed at such time and in such manner as the Secretary shall prescribe and shall contain such information as the Secretary shall prescribe.

• 1984, Deficit Reduction Act of 1984 (P.L. 98-369)

P.L. 98-369, §531(b)(4)(A):

Amended Code Sec. 125 by redesignating subsection (h) as subsection (i) and by adding new subsection (h). **Effective** 1-1-85.

P.L. 98-369, Act Sec. 531(b)(5) and (6), as amended by P.L. 99-514, §1853(b)(2)-(3), provides:

(5) Exception for Certain Cafeteria Plans and Benefits.—

(A) General Transitional Rule.—Any cafeteria plan in existence on February 10, 1984, which failed as of such date and continued to fail thereafter to satisfy the rules relating to section 125 under proposed Treasury regulations, and any benefit offered under such a cafeteria plan which failed as of such date and continued to fail thereafter to satisfy the rules of section 105, 106, 120, or 129 under proposed Treasury regulations, will not fail to be a cafeteria plan under section 125 or a nontaxable benefit under section 105, 106, 120, or 129 solely because of such failures. The preceding sentence shall apply only with respect to cafeteria plans and benefits provided under cafeteria plans before the earlier of—

(i) January 1, 1985, or

(ii) the effective date of any modification to provide additional benefits after February 10, 1984.

(B) Special Transition Rule for Advance Election Benefit Banks.—Any benefit offered under a cafeteria plan in existence on February 10, 1984, which failed as of such date and continued to fail thereafter to satisfy the rules of section 105, 106, 120, or 129 under proposed Treasury regulations because an employee was assured of receiving (in cash or any other benefit) amounts available but unused for covered reimbursement during the year without regard to whether he incurred covered expenses, will not fail to be a nontaxable benefit under such applicable section solely because of such failure. The preceding sentence shall apply only with respect to benefits provided under cafeteria plans before the earlier of—

(i) July 1, 1985, or

(ii) the effective date of any modification to provide additional benefits after February 10, 1984.

Except as provided in Treasury regulations, the special transition rule is available only for benefits with respect to which, after December 31, 1984, contributions are fixed before the period of coverage and taxable cash is not available until the end of such period of coverage.

(C) Plans for Which Substantial Implementation Costs Were Incurred.—For purposes of this paragraph, any plan with respect to which substantial implementation costs had been incurred before February 10, 1984, shall be treated as in existence on February 10, 1984.

(D) Collective Bargaining Agreements.—In the case of any cafeteria plan in existence on February 10, 1984, and maintained pursuant to 1 or more collective bargaining agreements between employee representatives and 1 or more employers, the date on which the last of such collective bargaining agreements terminates (determined without regard to any extension thereof agreed to after July 18, 1984) shall be substituted for "January 1, 1985" in subparagraph (A) and for "July 1, 1985" in subparagraph (B). For purposes of the preceding sentence, any plan amendment made pursuant to a collective bargaining agreement relating to the plan which amends the plan solely to conform to any requirement added by this section (or any requirement in the regulations under section 125 of the Internal Revenue Code of 1954 proposed on May 6, 1984) shall not be treated as a termination of such collective bargaining agreement.

(E) Special Rule Where Contributions or Reimbursements Suspended.—For purposes of subparagraphs (A) and (B), a plan shall not be treated as not continuing to fail to satisfy the rules referred to in such subparagraphs with respect to any benefit provided in the form of a flexible spending arrangement merely because contributions or reimbursements (or both) with respect to such plan were suspended before January 1, 1985.

(6) Study of Effects of Cafeteria Plans on Health Care Costs.—

(A) Study.—The Secretary of Health and Human Services, in cooperation with the Secretary of the Treasury, shall conduct a study of the effects of cafeteria plans (within the meaning of section 125 of the Internal Revenue Code of 1954) on the containment of health care costs.

(B) Report.—The Secretary of Health and Human Services, in cooperation with the Secretary of the Treasury, shall submit a report on the study conducted under subparagraph (A) to the Committee on Ways and Means of the House of Representatives and the Committee on Finance of the Senate by no later than April 1, 1985.

»»→ Caution: Former Code Sec. 125(j) was redesignated as Code Sec. 125(k) by P.L. 111-148, §9005(a)(1), applicable to tax years beginning after December 31, 2010, and further redesignated as Code Sec. 125(l), below, by P.L. 111-148, §9022(a), applicable to years beginning after December 31, 2010.

[Sec. 125(l)]

(l) REGULATIONS.—The Secretary shall prescribe such regulations as may be necessary to carry out the provisions of this section.

Amendments

• 2010, Patient Protection and Affordable Care Act (P.L. 111-148)

P.L. 111-148, §9005(a)(1):

Amended Code Sec. 125 by redesignating subsection (j) as (k). **Effective** for tax years beginning after 12-31-2010.

P.L. 111-148, §9022(a):

Amended Code Sec. 125, as amended by this Act, by redesignating subsection (k) as subsection (l). **Effective** for years beginning after 12-31-2010.

• 2008, Heroes Earnings Assistance and Relief Tax Act of 2008 (P.L. 110-245)

P.L. 110-245, §114(a):

Amended Code Sec. 125 by redesignating subsection (i) as subsection (j). **Effective** for distributions made after 6-17-2008.

• 1989 (P.L. 101-140)

P.L. 101-140, §203(a)(1):

Provides that Code Sec. 125 as amended by Section 1151(d)(1) of P.L. 99-514 shall be applied as if the amendment made by such section has not been enacted. **Effective** as if included in section 1151 of P.L. 99-514. Code Sec. 125 as amended by Act Sec. 1151(d)(1) of P.L. 99-514 read as follows:

SEC. 125. CAFETERIA PLANS.

[Sec. 125(a)]

(a) GENERAL RULE. —Except as provided in subsection (b), no amount shall be included in the gross income of a participant in a cafeteria plan solely because, under the plan, the participant may choose among the benefits of the plan.

Amendments

• 1988, Technical and Miscellaneous Revenue Act of 1988 (P.L. 100-647)

P.L. 100-647, §1011B(a)(11)(A):

Amended Code Sec. 125(a). **Effective** as if included in the provision of P.L. 99-514 to which it relates. Prior to amendment, Code Sec. 125(a) read as follows:

(a) GENERAL RULE. —In the case of a cafeteria plan—

(1) amounts shall not be included in gross income of a participant in such plan solely because, under the plan, the participant may choose among the benefits of the plan, and

(2) if the plan fails to meet the requirements of subsection (b) for any plan year—

(A) paragraph (1) shall not apply, and

(B) notwithstanding any other provision of part III of this subchapter, any qualified benefits received under such cafeteria plan by a highly compensated employee for such plan year shall be included in the gross income of such employee for the taxable year with or within which such plan year ends.

[Sec. 125(b)]

(b) PROHIBITION AGAINST DISCRIMINATION AS TO ELIGIBILITY TO PARTICIPATE. —

(1) HIGHLY COMPENSATED EMPLOYEES. —In the case of a highly compensated employee, subsection (a) shall not apply to any benefit attributable to a plan year unless the plan is available to a group of employees as qualify under a classification set up by the employer and which the Secretary find not to be discriminatory in favor of highly compensated employees.

(2) KEY EMPLOYEES. —In the case of a key employee (within the meaning of section 416(i)(1)), subsection (a) shall not apply to any plan year if the qualified benefits provided to key employees under the plan exceed 25 percent of the aggregate of such benefits provided for all employees under the plan. For purposes of the preceding sentence, qualified benefits shall not include benefits which (without regard to this paragraph) are includible in gross income.

(3) EXCLUDABLE EMPLOYEES. —For purposes of this subsection, there may be excluded from consideration employees who may be excluded from consideration under section 89(h).

Amendments

• 1988, Technical and Miscellaneous Revenue Act of 1988 (P.L. 100-647)

P.L. 100-647, §1011B(a)(11)(B):

Amended Code Sec. 125(b)(1) by striking out "A plan shall be treated as failing to meet the requirements of this subsection" and inserting in lieu thereof "In the case of a highly compensated employee, subsection (a) shall not apply to any benefit attributable to a plan year". **Effective** as if included in the provision of P.L. 99-514 to which it relates.

P.L. 100-647, §1011B(a)(11)(C):

Amended Code Sec. 125(b)(2) by striking out "a plan shall be treated as failing to meet the requirements of this subsection" and inserting in lieu thereof "subsection (a) shall not apply to any plan year". **Effective** as if included in the provision of P.L. 99-514 to which it relates.

P.L. 100-647, §1011B(a)(13)(B):

Amended the last sentence of Code Sec. 125(b)(2). **Effective** as if included in the provision of P.L. 99-514 to which it relates. Prior to amendment, the last sentence of Code Sec. 125(b)(2) read as follows:

For purposes of the preceding sentence, qualified benefits shall be determined without regard to the last sentence of subsection (e).

[Sec. 125(c)]

(c) CAFETERIA PLAN DEFINED. —For purposes of this section—

(1) IN GENERAL. —The term "cafeteria plan" means a plan which meets the requirements of section 89(k) and under which—

(A) all participants are employees, and

(B) the participant may choose among 2 or more benefits consisting of cash and qualified benefits.

(2) DEFERRED COMPENSATION PLANS EXCLUDED. —

(A) IN GENERAL. —The term "cafeteria plan" does not include any plan which provides for deferred compensation.

(B) EXCEPTION FOR CASH AND DEFERRED ARRANGEMENTS. —Subparagraph (A) shall not apply to a profit-sharing or stock bonus plan or rural electric cooperative plan (within the meaning of section 401(k)(7)) which includes a qualified cash or deferred arrangement (as defined in section 401(k)(2)) to the extent of amounts which a covered employee may elect to have the employer pay as contributions to a trust under such plan on behalf of the employee.

(C) EXCEPTION FOR CERTAIN PLANS MAINTAINED BY EDUCATIONAL INSTITUTIONS. —Subparagraph (A) shall not apply to a plan maintained by an educational organization described in section 170(b)(1)(A)(ii) to the extent of amounts which a covered employee may elect to have the employer pay as contributions for post-retirement group life insurance if—

(i) all contributions for such insurance must be made before retirement, and

(ii) such life insurance does not have a cash surrender value at any time.

For purposes of section 79, any life insurance described in the preceding sentence shall be treated as group-term life insurance. In applying section 89 to a plan described in this subparagraph, contributions under the plan shall be tested as of the time the contributions were made.

Amendments

• 1988, Technical and Miscellaneous Revenue Act of 1988 (P.L. 100-647)

P.L. 100-647, §1011B(a)(12):

Amended Code Sec. 125(c)(1)(B). **Effective** as if included in the provision of P.L. 99-514 to which it relates. Prior to amendment, Code Sec. 125(c)(1)(B) read as follows:

(B) the participants may choose—

(i) among 2 or more benefits consisting of cash and qualified benefits, or

(ii) among 2 or more qualified benefits.

P.L. 100-647, §1018(t)(6):

Amended Code Sec. 125(c)(2)(B) by inserting "or rural electric cooperative plan (within the meaning of section 401(k)(7))" after "stock bonus plan". **Effective** as if included in the provision of P.L. 99-514 to which it relates.

P.L. 100-647, §6051(b):

Amended Code Sec. 125(c)(2)(C) by adding at the end thereof a new sentence. **Effective** as if included in the amendments made by section 1151 of P.L. 99-514.

[Sec. 125(d)]

(d) HIGHLY COMPENSATED EMPLOYEE. —For purposes of this section, the term "highly compensated employee" has the meaning given such term by section 414(q).

[Sec. 125(e)]

(e) QUALIFIED BENEFITS DEFINED. —For purposes of this section—

(1) IN GENERAL. —The term "qualified benefit" means any benefit which, with the application of subsection (a) and without regard to section 89(a), is not includible in the gross income of the employee by reasons of an express provision of this chapter (other than section 117, 124, 127, or 132).

(2) CERTAIN BENEFITS INCLUDED. —The term "qualified benefits" includes—

(A) any group-term life insurance which is includible in gross income only because it exceeds the dollar limitation of section 79 or any insurance under a qualified group legal services plan the value of which is so includible only because it exceeds the limitation of section 120(a), and

(B) any other benefit permitted under regulations.

Amendments

• 1989, Omnibus Budget Reconciliation Act of 1989 (P.L. 101-239)

P.L. 101-239, §7814(b):

Amended Code Sec. 125(e)(2)(A) by striking "includable" and inserting "includible". **Effective** as if included in the provision of P.L. 100-647 to which it relates.

• 1988, Technical and Miscellaneous Revenue Act of 1988 (P.L. 100-647)

P.L. 100-647, §1011B(a)(13)(A):

Amended Code Sec. 125(e)(1) by inserting "and without regard to section 89(a)" after "subsection (a)". **Effective** as if included in the provision of P.L. 99-514 to which it relates.

P.L. 100-647, §4002(b)(2):

Amended Code Sec. 125(e)(2)(A) by inserting "or any insurance under a qualified group legal services plan the value of which is so includable only because it exceeds the limitation of section 120(a)" after "section 79". **Effective** for tax years ending after 12-31-87. For a special rule, see Act Sec. 6063, below.

P.L. 100-647, §6063, provides:

SEC. 6063. TREATMENT OF PRE-1989 ELECTIONS FOR DEPENDENT CARE ASSISTANCE UNDER CAFETERIA PLANS.

For purposes of section 125 of the 1986 Code, a plan shall not be treated as failing to be a cafeteria plan solely because under the plan a participant elected before January 1, 1989, to receive reimbursement under the plan for dependent care assistance for periods after December 31, 1988, and such assistance is includible in gross income under the provisions of the Family Support Act of 1988.

[Sec. 125(f)]

(f) COLLECTIVELY BARGAINED PLAN NOT CONSIDERED DISCRIMINATORY. —For purposes of this section, a plan shall not be treated as discriminatory if the plan is maintained under an agreement which the Secretary finds to be a collective bargaining agreement between employee representatives and one or more employers.

[Sec. 125(g)]

(g) CROSS REFERENCES. —For reporting and recordkeeping requirements, see section 6039D.

Amendments

P.L. 101-136, §528, provides:

SEC. 528. No monies appropriated by this Act may be used to implement or enforce section 1151 of the Tax Reform Act of 1986 or the amendments made by such section.

• 1986, Tax Reform Act of 1986 (P.L. 99-514)

P.L. 99-514, §1151(d)(1):

Amended Code Sec. 125. For the **effective** date, see Act Sec. 1151(k), below. For the text of Code Sec. 125 prior to amendment, see the amendment note for P.L. 101-140, §203(a)(1).

P.L. 99-514, §1151(k), provides:

(k) EFFECTIVE DATES. —

(1) IN GENERAL. —The amendments made by this section shall apply to years beginning after the later of—

(A) December 31, 1987, or

(B) the earlier of—

(i) the date which is 3 months after the date on which the Secretary of the Treasury or his delegate issues such regulations as are necessary to carry out the provisions of section 89 of the Internal Revenue Code of 1986 (as added by this section), or

(ii) December 31, 1988.

(2) SPECIAL RULE FOR COLLECTIVE BARGAINING PLAN. —In the case of a plan maintained pursuant to 1 or more collective bargaining agreements between employee representatives and 1 or more employers ratified before March 1, 1986, the amendments made by this section shall not apply to em-

ployees covered by such an agreement in years beginning before the earlier of—

(A) the date on which the last of such collective bargaining agreements terminates (determined without regard to any extension thereof after February 28, 1986), or

(B) January 1, 1991.

A plan shall not be required to take into account employees to which the preceding sentence applies for purposes of applying section 89 of the Internal Revenue Code of 1986 (as added by this section) to employees to which the preceding sentence does not apply for any year preceding the year described in the preceding sentence.

(3) EXCEPTION FOR CERTAIN GROUP-TERM INSURANCE PLANS. —In the case of plan described in section 223(d)(2) of the Tax Reform Act of 1984, such plan shall be treated as meeting the requirements of section 89 of the Internal Revenue Code of 1986 (as added by this section) with respect to individuals described in section 223(d)(2) of such Act. An employer may elect to disregard such individuals in applying section 89 of such Code (as so added) to other employees of the employer.

(4) SPECIAL RULE FOR CHURCH PLANS. —In the case of a church plan (within the meaning of section 414(e)(3) of the Internal Revenue Code of 1986) maintaining an insured accident and health plan, the amandments made by this section shall apply to years beginning after December 31, 1988.

(5) CAFETERIA PLANS. —The amendments made by the subsection (d)(2) shall apply to taxable years beginning after December 31, 1983.

P.L. 99-514, §1853(b)(1)(A):

Amended Code Sec. 125(c) and (d)(1)(B) by striking out "statutory nontaxable benefits" each place it appears and inserting in lieu thereof "qualified benefits". **Effective** as if included in the provision of P.L. 98-369 to which it relates.

P.L. 99-514, §1853(b)(1)(B):

Amended Code Sec. 125(f). **Effective** as if included in the provision of P.L. 98-369 to which it relates. Prior to amendment, Code Sec. 125(f) read as follows:

(f) STATUTORY NONTAXABLE BENEFITS DEFINED. —For purposes of this section, the term "statutory nontaxable benefit" means any benefit which with the application of subsection (a) is not includible in the gross income of the employee by reason of an express provision of this chapter (other than section 117, 124, 127, or 132). Such term includes any group term life insurance which is includible in gross income only because it exceeds the dollar limitation of section 79.

• 1984, Deficit Reduction Act of 1984 (P.L. 98-369)

P.L. 98-369, §531(b)(4)(A):

Redesignated Code Sec. 125(h) as 125(i). **Effective** 1-1-85.

• 1980, Miscellaneous Revenue Act of 1980 (P.L. 96-605)

P.L. 96-605, §201(b)(2):

Amended Code Sec. 125(g)(4) by striking out "subsection (b) or (c) of section 414" and inserting in lieu thereof "subsection (b), (c), or (m) of section 414", and by inserting "CONTROLLED GROUPS, ETC." in place of "CONTROLLED GROUPS" in the paragraph heading. **Effective** for plan years ending after 11-30-80. However, in the case of a plan in existence on 11-30-80, the amendments will apply to plan years beginning after that date. P.L. 96-613, §5(b)(2), also signed 12-38-80, made the identical amendments to Code Sec. 125(g)(4).

• 1980, Technical Corrections Act of 1979 (P.L. 96-222)

P.L. 96-222, §101(a)(6)(A):

Amended Code Sec. 125(g)(3)(B) by changing "service requirement" to "employment requirement" each place it appeared. **Effective** for tax years beginning after 12-31-79.

• 1978, Revenue Act of 1978 (P.L. 95-600)

P.L. 95-600, §134(a):

Redesignated Code Sec. 125 as Code Sec. 126 and added a new Code Sec. 125. **Effective** for plan years beginning after 12-31-78 (applied to "taxable" rather than "plan" years before amendment by P.L. 96-222, §101(a)(6)(B)).

[Sec. 126]

SEC. 126. CERTAIN COST-SHARING PAYMENTS.

[Sec. 126(a)]

(a) GENERAL RULE.—Gross income does not include the excludable portion of payments received under—

(1) The rural clean water program authorized by section 208(j) of the Federal Water Pollution Control Act (33 U.S.C. 1288(j)).

(2) The rural abandoned mine program authorized by section 406 of the Surface Mining Control and Reclamation Act of 1977 (30 U.S.C. 1236).

(3) The water bank program authorized by the Water Bank Act (16 U.S.C. 1301 et seq.).

(4) The emergency conservation measures program authorized by title IV of the Agricultural Credit Act of 1978.

(5) The agricultural conservation program authorized by the Soil Conservation and Domestic Allotment Act (16 U.S.C. 590(a).

(6) The great plains conservation program authorized by section 16 of the Soil Conservation and Domestic Policy Act (16 U.S.C. 590p(b)).

(7) The resource conservation and development program authorized by the Bankhead-Jones Farm Tenant Act and by the Soil Conservation and Domestic Allotment Act (7 U.S.C. 1010; 16 U.S.C. 590a et seq.).

(8) The forestry incentives program authorized by section 4 of the Cooperative Forestry Assistance Act of 1978 (16 U.S.C. 2103).

(9) Any small watershed program administered by the Secretary of Agriculture which is determined by the Secretary of the Treasury or his delegate to be substantially similar to the type of programs described in paragraphs (1) through (8).

(10) Any program of a State, possession of the United States, a political subdivision of any of the foregoing, or the District of Columbia under which payments are made to individuals primarily for the purpose of conserving soil, protecting or restoring the environment, improving forests, or providing a habitat for wildlife.

[Sec. 126(b)]

(b) EXCLUDABLE PORTION.—For purposes of this section—

(1) IN GENERAL.—The term "excludable portion" means that portion (or all) of a payment made to any person under any program described in subsection (a) which—

(A) is determined by the Secretary of Agriculture to be made primarily for the purpose of conserving soil and water resources, protecting or restoring the environment, improving forests, or providing a habitat for wildlife, and

(B) is determined by the Secretary of the Treasury or his delegate as not increasing substantially the annual income derived from the property.

(2) PAYMENTS NOT CHARGEABLE TO CAPITAL ACCOUNT.—The term "excludable portion" does not include that portion of any payment which is properly associated with an amount which is allowable as a deduction for the taxable year in which such amount is paid or incurred.

[Sec. 126(c)]

(c) ELECTION FOR SECTION NOT TO APPLY.—

(1) IN GENERAL.—The taxpayer may elect not to have this section (and section 1255) apply to any excludable portion (or portion thereof).

(2) MANNER AND TIME FOR MAKING ELECTION.—Any election under paragraph (1) shall be made in the manner prescribed by the Secretary by regulations and shall be made not later than the due date prescribed by law (including extensions) for filing the return of tax under this chapter for the taxable year in which the payment was received or accrued.

[Sec. 126(d)]

(d) DENIAL OF DOUBLE BENEFITS.—No deduction or credit shall be allowed with respect to any expenditure which is properly associated with any amount excluded from gross income under subsection (a).

[Sec. 126(e)]

(e) BASIS OF PROPERTY NOT INCREASED BY REASON OF EXCLUDABLE PAYMENTS.—Notwithstanding any provision of section 1016 to the contrary, no adjustment to basis shall be made with respect to property acquired or improved through the use of any payment, to the extent that such adjustment would reflect any amount which is excluded from gross income under subsection (a).

Amendments

• 1980, Technical Corrections Act of 1979 (P.L. 96-222)

P.L. 96-222, §105(a)(7)(A):

Amended Code Sec. 126(b) and (c) and added paragraphs (d) and (e). **Effective** with respect to grants made under the programs after 9-30-79. Prior to amendment, paragraphs (b) and (c) read as follows:

"(b) EXCLUDABLE PORTION.—For purposes of this section, the term "excludable portion" means that portion (or all) of a payment made to any person under any program described in subsection (a) which—

(1) is determined by the Secretary of Agriculture to be made primarily for the purpose of conserving soil and water resources, protecting or restoring the environment, improving forests, or providing a habitat for wildlife, and

(2) is determined by the Secretary of the Treasury as not increasing substantially the annual income derived from the property.

(c) APPLICATION WITH OTHER SECTIONS.—No deduction or credit allowable under any other provision of this chapter shall be allowed with respect to any expenditure made with the use of payments described in subsection (a) or with respect to any property acquired with any payment described in subsection (a) (to the extent that the basis is allocable to the use of such payments). Notwithstanding any provision of section 1016 to the contrary, no adjustment to basis shall be made with respect to property acquired through the use of such payments, to the extent that such adjustment would reflect the amount of such payment."

P.L. 96-222, §105(a)(7)(C):

Amended Code Sec. 126(a)(9) by adding "or his delegate" after "Secretary of the Treasury". **Effective** with respect to grants made under the programs after 9-30-79.

P.L. 96-222, §105(a)(7)(E):

Amended Code Sec. 126(a)(10). **Effective** with respect to grants made after 9-30-79. Prior to amendment, Code Sec. 126(a)(10) read as follows:

(10) Any State program under which payments are made to individuals primarily for the purpose of conserving soil, protecting or restoring the environment, improving forests, or providing a habitat for wildlife.

• 1978, Revenue Act of 1978 (P.L. 95-600)

P.L. 95-600, §543(a):

Redesignated Code Sec. 126 as Code Sec. 127 and added a new Code Sec. 126. **Effective** with respect to grants made under the programs after 9-30-79.

[Sec. 127]

SEC. 127. EDUCATIONAL ASSISTANCE PROGRAMS.

[Sec. 127(a)]

(a) EXCLUSION FROM GROSS INCOME.—

(1) IN GENERAL.—Gross income of an employee does not include amounts paid or expenses incurred by the employer for educational assistance to the employee if the assistance is furnished pursuant to a program which is described in subsection (b).

(2) $5,250 MAXIMUM EXCLUSION.—If, but for this paragraph, this section would exclude from gross income more than $5,250 of educational assistance furnished to an individual during a calendar year, this section shall apply only to the first $5,250 of such assistance so furnished.

Amendments

• 1986, Tax Reform Act of 1986 (P.L. 99-514)

P.L. 99-514, §1162(a)(2):

Amended Code Sec. 127(a)(2) by striking out "$5,000" each place it appears in the text and heading thereof and inserting in lieu thereof "$5,250". **Effective** for tax years beginning after 12-31-85.

• 1984 (P.L. 98-611)

P.L. 98-611, §1(b):

Amended Code Sec. 127(a). **Effective** for tax years beginning after 12-31-83. Prior to amendment, Code Sec. 127(a) read as follows:

(a) GENERAL RULE.—Gross income of an employee does not include amounts paid or expenses incurred by the employer for educational assistance to the employee if the assistance is furnished pursuant to a program which is described in subsection (b).

[Sec. 127(b)]

(b) EDUCATIONAL ASSISTANCE PROGRAM.—

(1) IN GENERAL.—For purposes of this section, an educational assistance program is a separate written plan of an employer for the exclusive benefit of his employees to provide such employees with educational assistance. The program must meet the requirements of paragraphs (2) through (6) of this subsection.

(2) ELIGIBILITY.—The program shall benefit employees who qualify under a classification set up by the employer and found by the Secretary not to be discriminatory in favor of employees who are highly compensated employees (within the meaning of section 414(q)) or their dependents. For purposes of this paragraph, there shall be excluded from consideration employees not included in the program who are included in a unit of employees covered by an agreement which the Secretary of Labor finds to be a collective bargaining agreement between employee representatives and one or more employers, if there is evidence that educational assistance benefits were the subject of good faith bargaining between such employee representatives and such employer or employers.

(3) PRINCIPAL SHAREHOLDERS OR OWNERS.—Not more than 5 percent of the amounts paid or incurred by the employer for educational assistance during the year may be provided for the class of individuals who are shareholders or owners (or their spouses or dependents), each of whom (on any day of the year) owns more than 5 percent of the stock or of the capital or profits interest in the employer.

(4) OTHER BENEFITS AS AN ALTERNATIVE.—A program must not provide eligible employees with a choice between educational assistance and other remuneration includible in gross income. For purposes of this section, the business practices of the employer (as well as the written program) will be taken into account.

(5) NO FUNDING REQUIRED.—A program referred to in paragraph (1) is not required to be funded.

(6) NOTIFICATION OF EMPLOYEES.—Reasonable notification of the availability and terms of the program must be provided to eligible employees.

Amendments

• 1989 (P.L. 101-140)

P.L. 101-140, §203(a)(1):

Provides that Code Sec. 127(b)(1) and (6), as amended by Section 1151(c)(4)(A)-(B) of P.L. 99-514, shall be applied as if the amendment had not been enacted. **Effective** as if included in Section 1151 of P.L. 99-514. Prior to amendment, Code Sec. 127(b)(1) and (6) as amended by Act Sec. 1151(c)(4)(A)-(B) of P.L. 99-514 read as follows:

(1) IN GENERAL.—For purposes of this section, an educational assistance program is a plan of an employer—

(A) under which the employer provides employees with educational assistance, and

(B) which meets the requirements of paragraphs (2) through (5) and section 89(k).

* * *

(6) [Stricken.]

P.L. 101-140, §203(a)(1):

Provides that Code Sec. 127(b)(2) as amended by Section 1151(g)(3) of P.L. 99-514 shall be applied as if the amendment had not been enacted. **Effective** as if included in Section 1151 of P.L. 99-514.

P.L. 101-140, §203(a)(2):

Provides that Code Sec. 127(b)(2) as amended by Section 1011B(a)(31)(B)(i)-(ii) of P.L. 100-647 shall be applied as if the amendment had not been enacted. **Effective** as if included in Section 1151 of P.L. 99-514. Prior to amendment, Code Sec. 127(b)(2) as amended by Act Sec. 1151(g)(3) of P.L. 99-514 and Act Sec. 1011B(a)(31)(B)(i)-(ii) of P.L. 100-647 read as follows:

(2) ELIGIBILITY.—The program shall benefit employees who qualify under a classification set up by the employer and found by the Secretary not to be discriminatory in favor of employees who are highly compensated employees (within the meaning of section 414(q)) or their dependents. For purposes of this paragraph, there shall be excluded from consideration employees who are excluded from consideration under section 89(h).

• 1989 (P.L. 101-136)

P.L. 101-136, §528, provides:

SEC. 528. No monies appropriated by this Act may be used to implement or enforce section 1151 of the Tax Reform Act of 1986 or the amendments made by such section.

• 1988, Technical and Miscellaneous Revenue Act of 1988 (P.L. 100-647)

P.L. 100-647, §1011B(a)(31)(B)(i)-(ii):

Amended Code Sec. 127(b)(2) by striking out "may" the first place it appears and inserting in lieu thereof "shall", and by striking out "may be" the second place it appears and inserting in lieu thereof "are". **Effective** as if included in the provision of P.L. 99-514 to which it relates.

• 1986, Tax Reform Act of 1986 (P.L. 99-514)

P.L. 99-514, §1114(b)(4):

Amended Code Sec. 127(b)(2) by striking out "officers, owners, or highly compensated," and inserting in lieu thereof "highly compensated employees (within the meaning of section 414(q))". **Effective** for years beginning after 12-31-87.

P.L. 99-514, §1151(c)(4)(A)-(B):

Amended Code Sec. 127(b) by striking out paragraph (1) and inserting in lieu thereof new paragraph (1), and by striking out paragraph (6). For the **effective** date, see Act Sec. 1151(k), below. Prior to amendment, Code Sec. 127(b)(1) and (6) read as follows:

(1) IN GENERAL.—For purposes of this section an educational assistance program is a separate written plan of an employer for the exclusive benefit of his employees to provide such employees with educational assistance. The program must meet the requirements of paragraphs (2) through (6) of this subsection.

* * *

(6) NOTIFICATION OF EMPLOYEES.—Reasonable notification of the availability and terms of the program must be provided to eligible employees.

P.L. 99-514, §1151(g)(3):

Amended Code Sec. 127(b)(2) by striking out the last sentence thereof and inserting in lieu thereof: "For purposes of this paragraph, there may be excluded from consideration employees who may be excluded from consideration under section 89(h)." For the **effective** date, see Act Sec. 1151(k), below. Prior to amendment, the last sentence read as follows:

For purposes of this paragraph, there shall be excluded from consideration employees not included in the program who are included in a unit of employees covered by an agreement which the Secretary of Labor finds to be a collective bargaining agreement between employee representatives and one or more employers, if there is evidence that educational assistance benefits were the subject of good faith bargaining between such employee representatives and such employer or employers.

P.L. 99-514, §1151(k), provides:

(k) EFFECTIVE DATES.—

(1) IN GENERAL.—The amendments made by this section shall apply to years beginning after the later of—

(A) December 31, 1987, or

(B) the earlier of—

(i) the date which is 3 months after the date on which the Secretary of the Treasury or his delegate issues such regulations as are necessary to carry out the provisions of section 89 of the Internal Revenue Code of 1986 (as added by this section), or

(ii) December 31, 1988.

(2) SPECIAL RULE FOR COLLECTIVE BARGAINING PLAN.—In the case of a plan maintained pursuant to 1 or more collective bargaining agreements between employee representatives and 1 or more employers ratified before March 1, 1986, the amendments made by this section shall not apply to employees covered by such an agreement in years beginning before the earlier of—

(A) the date on which the last of such collective bargaining agreements terminates (determined without regard to any extension thereof after February 28, 1986), or

(B) January 1, 1991.

A plan shall not be required to take into account employees to which the preceding sentence applies for purposes of applying section 89 of the Internal Revenue Code of 1986 (as added by this section) to employees to which the preceding sentence does not apply for any year preceding the year described in the preceding sentence.

(3) EXCEPTION FOR CERTAIN GROUP-TERM INSURANCE PLANS.—In the case of a plan described in section 223(d)(2) of the Tax Reform Act of 1984, such plan shall be treated as meeting the requirements of section 89 of the Internal Revenue Code of 1986 (as added by this section) with respect to individuals described in section 223(d)(2) of such Act. An employer may elect to disregard such individuals in applying section 89 of such Code (as so added) to other employees of the employer.

(4) SPECIAL RULE FOR CHURCH PLANS.—In the case of a church plan (within the meaning of section 414(e)(3) of the Internal Revenue Code of 1986) maintaining an insured accident and health plan, the amendments made by this section shall apply to years beginning after December 31, 1988.

(5) CAFETERIA PLANS.—The amendments made by subsection (d)(2) shall apply to taxable years beginning after December 31, 1983.

[Sec. 127(c)]

(c) DEFINITIONS; SPECIAL RULES.—For purposes of this section—

»»→ Caution: Code Sec. 127(c)(1), below, is subject to the sunset provision of the Economic Growth and Tax Relief Reconciliation Act of 2001 (P.L. 107-16), §901. Absent Congressional action, the changes made to this provision by P.L. 107-16, or that take effect as if included in P.L. 107-16, do not apply after December 31, 2010. For more information about the sunset provision, see page XXI of the Preface to this publication and P.L. 107-16, §901, in the amendment notes. See the amendments notes for a history of amendments to this section and the effective date of each change.

(1) EDUCATIONAL ASSISTANCE.—The term "educational assistance" means—

(A) the payment, by an employer, of expenses incurred by or on behalf of an employee for education of the employee (including, but not limited to, tuition, fees, and similar payments, books, supplies, and equipment), and

(B) the provision, by an employer, of courses of instruction for such employee (including books, supplies, and equipment),

but does not include payment for, or the provision of, tools or supplies which may be retained by the employee after completion of a course of instruction, or meals, lodging, or transportation. The term "educational assistance" also does not include any payment for, or the provision of any benefits with respect to, any course or other education involving sports, games, or hobbies.

(2) EMPLOYEE.—The term "employee" includes, for any year, an individual who is an employee within the meaning of section 401(c)(1) (relating to self-employed individuals).

(3) EMPLOYER.—An individual who owns the entire interest in an unincorporated trade or business shall be treated as his own employer. A partnership shall be treated as the employer of each partner who is an employee within the meaning of paragraph (2).

(4) ATTRIBUTION RULES.—

(A) OWNERSHIP OF STOCK.—Ownership of stock in a corporation shall be determined in accordance with the rules provided under subsections (d) and (e) of section 1563 (without regard to section 1563(e)(3)(C)).

(B) INTEREST IN UNINCORPORATED TRADE OR BUSINESS.—The interest of an employee in a trade or business which is not incorporated shall be determined in accordance with regulations prescribed by the Secretary, which shall be based on principles similar to the principles which apply in the case of subparagraph (A).

(5) CERTAIN TESTS NOT APPLICABLE.—An educational assistance program shall not be held or considered to fail to meet any requirements of subsection (b) merely because—

(A) of utilization rates for the different types of educational assistance made available under the program; or

(B) successful completion, or attaining a particular course grade, is required for or considered in determining reimbursement under the program.

(6) RELATIONSHIP TO CURRENT LAW.—This section shall not be construed to affect the deduction or inclusion in income of amounts (not within the exclusion under this section) which are paid or incurred, or received as reimbursement, for educational expenses under section 117, 162 or 212.

(7) DISALLOWANCE OF EXCLUDED AMOUNTS AS CREDIT OR DEDUCTION.—No deduction or credit shall be allowed to the employee under any other section of this chapter for any amount excluded from income by reason of this section.

Amendments

• 2001, Economic Growth and Tax Relief Reconciliation Act of 2001 (P.L. 107-16)

P.L. 107-16, §411(b):

Amended the last sentence of Code Sec. 127(c)(1) by striking before the period ", and such term also does not include any payment for, or the provision of any benefits with respect to, any graduate level course of a kind normally taken by an individual pursuing a program leading to a law, business, medical, or other advanced academic or professional degree". **Effective** with respect to expenses relating to courses beginning after 12-31-2001.

P.L. 107-16, §901(a)-(b), provides:

SEC. 901. SUNSET OF PROVISIONS OF ACT.

(a) IN GENERAL.—All provisions of, and amendments made by, this Act shall not apply—

(1) to taxable, plan, or limitation years beginning after December 31, 2010, or

(2) in the case of title V, to estates of decedents dying, gifts made, or generation skipping transfers, after December 31, 2010.

(b) APPLICATION OF CERTAIN LAWS.—The Internal Revenue Code of 1986 and the Employee Retirement Income Security Act of 1974 shall be applied and administered to years, estates, gifts, and transfers described in subsection (a) as if the provisions and amendments described in subsection (a) had never been enacted.

• 1996, Small Business Job Protection Act of 1996 (P.L. 104-188)

P.L. 104-188, §1202(b):

Amended the last sentence of Code Sec. 127(c)(1) by inserting before the period ", and such term also does not include any payment for, or the provision of any benefits with respect to, any graduate level course of a kind normally taken by an individual pursuing a program leading to a law, business, medical, or other advanced academic or professional degree". **Effective** with respect to expenses relating to courses beginning after 6-30-96.

• 1990, Omnibus Budget Reconciliation Act of 1990 (P.L. 101-508)

P.L. 101-508, §11403(b):

Amended Code Sec. 127(c)(1) by striking the last sentence. **Effective** for tax years beginning after 12-31-90. Prior to amendment, the last sentence of Code Sec. 127(c)(1) read as follows:

The term "educational assistance" also does not include any payment for, or the provision of any benefits with respect to, any graduate level course of a kind normally taken by an individual pursuing a program leading to a law, business, medical, or other advanced academic or professional degree.

• 1989, Omnibus Budget Reconciliation Act of 1989 (P.L. 101-239)

P.L. 101-239, §7814(a):

Amended Code Sec. 127(c) by striking paragraph (8). **Effective** as if included in the provision of P.L. 100-647 to which it relates. Prior to amendment, Code Sec. 127(c)(8) read as follows:

(8) COORDINATION WITH SECTION 117(d).—In the case of the education of an individual who is a graduate student at an educational organization described in section 170(b)(1)(A)(ii) and who is engaged in teaching or research activities for such organization, section 117(d)(2) shall be applied as if it did not contain the phrase "(below the graduate level)".

• 1988, Technical and Miscellaneous Revenue Act of 1988 (P.L. 100-647)

P.L. 100-647, §4001(b)(1):

Amended Code Sec. 127(c)(1) by adding at the end thereof a new sentence. **Effective** for tax years beginning after 12-31-87.

• 1984 (P.L. 98-611)

P.L. 98-611, §1(c):

Added Code Sec. 127(c)(8). **Effective** for tax years beginning after 12-31-83.

P.L. 98-611, §1(e):

Amended Code Sec. 127(c)(7) by inserting "to the employee" after "allowed". **Effective** for tax years beginning after 12-31-83.

»»→ Caution: Code Sec. 127(d), below, was stricken by P.L. 107-16, and is subject to the sunset provision of the Economic Growth and Tax Relief Reconciliation Act of 2001 (P.L. 107-16), §901. Absent Congressional action, the changes made to this provision by P.L. 107-16, or that take effect as if included in P.L. 107-16, do not apply after December 31, 2010. For more information about the sunset provision, see page XXI of the Preface to this publication and P.L. 107-16, §901, in the amendment notes. See the amendments notes for a history of amendments to this section and the effective date of each change.

[Sec. 127(d)—Stricken]

Amendments

• 2001, Economic Growth and Tax Relief Reconciliation Act of 2001 (P.L. 107-16)

P.L. 107-16, §411(a):

Amended Code Sec. 127 by striking subsection (d) and by redesignating subsection (e) as subsection (d). **Effective** with respect to expenses relating to courses beginning after 12-31-2001. Prior to being stricken, Code Sec. 127(d) read as follows:

(d) TERMINATION.—This section shall not apply to expenses paid with respect to courses beginning after December 31, 2001.

P.L. 107-16, §901(a)-(b), provides:

SEC. 901. SUNSET OF PROVISIONS OF ACT.

(a) IN GENERAL.—All provisions of, and amendments made by, this Act shall not apply—

(1) to taxable, plan, or limitation years beginning after December 31, 2010, or

(2) in the case of title V, to estates of decedents dying, gifts made, or generation skipping transfers, after December 31, 2010.

(b) APPLICATION OF CERTAIN LAWS.—The Internal Revenue Code of 1986 and the Employee Retirement Income Security Act of 1974 shall be applied and administered to years, estates, gifts, and transfers described in subsection (a) as if the provisions and amendments described in subsection (a) had never been enacted.

• 1999, Tax Relief Extension Act of 1999

P.L. 106-170, §506(a):

Amended Code Sec. 127(d) by striking "May 31, 2000" and inserting "December 31, 2001". **Effective** for courses beginning after 5-31-2000.

• 1997, Taxpayer Relief Act of 1997 (P.L. 105-34)

P.L. 105-34, §221(a):

Amended Code Sec. 127(d). **Effective** for tax years beginning after 12-31-96. Prior to amendment, Code Sec. 127(d) read as follows:

(d) TERMINATION.—This section shall not apply to taxable years beginning after May 31, 1997. In the case of any taxable year beginning in 1997, only expenses paid with respect to courses beginning before July 1, 1997, shall be taken into account in determining the amount excluded under this section.

• 1996, Small Business Job Protection Act of 1996 (P.L. 104-188)

P.L. 104-188, §1202(a):

Amended Code Sec. 127(d) by striking "December 31, 1994." and inserting "May 31, 1997. In the case of any tax year beginning in 1997, only expenses paid with respect to courses beginning before 7-1-97, shall be taken into account in determining the amount excluded under this section.". **Effective** for tax years beginning after 12-31-94.

P.L. 104-188, §1202(c)(3), provides:

(3) EXPEDITED PROCEDURES.—The Secretary of the Treasury shall establish expedited procedures for the refund of any overpayment of taxes imposed by the Internal Revenue Code of 1986 which is attributable to amounts excluded from gross income during 1995 or 1996 under section 127 of such Code, including procedures waiving the requirement that an employer obtain an employee's signature where the employer demonstrates to the satisfaction of the Secretary that any refund collected by the employer on behalf of the employee will be paid to the employee.

• 1993, Omnibus Budget Reconciliation Act of 1993 (P.L. 103-66)

P.L. 103-66, §13101(a)(1):

Amended Code Sec. 127(d). **Effective** for tax years ending after 6-30-92. Prior to amendment, Code Sec. 127(d) read as follows:

(d) TERMINATION.—This section shall not apply to taxable years beginning after June 30, 1992.

• 1991, Tax Extension Act of 1991 (P.L. 102-227)

P.L. 102-227, §103(a)(1):

Amended Code Sec. 127(d) by striking "December 31, 1991" and inserting "June 30, 1992". **Effective** for tax years beginning after 12-31-91. For a special rule, see §103(a)(2), below.

P.L. 102-227, §103(a)(2), provides:

(2) SPECIAL RULE.—In the case of any taxable year beginning in 1992, only amounts paid before July 1, 1992, by the employer for educational assistance for the employee shall be taken into account in determining the amount excluded under section 127 of the Internal Revenue Code of 1986 with respect to such employee for such taxable year.

• 1990, Omnibus Budget Reconciliation Act of 1990 (P.L. 101-508)

P.L. 101-508, §11403(a):

Amended Code Sec. 127(d) by striking "September 30, 1990" and inserting "December 31, 1991". **Effective** for tax years beginning after 12-31-89.

• 1989, Omnibus Budget Reconciliation Act of 1989 (P.L. 101-239)

P.L. 101-239, §7101(a):

Amended Code Sec. 127(d) by striking "December 31, 1988" and inserting "September 30, 1990". **Effective** for tax years beginning after 12-31-88.

• 1988, Technical and Miscellaneous Revenue Act of 1988 (P.L. 100-647)

P.L. 100-647, §4001(a):

Amended Code Sec. 127(d) by striking out "December 31, 1987" and inserting in lieu thereof "December 31, 1988". **Effective** for tax years beginning after 12-31-87.

• 1986, Tax Reform Act of 1986 (P.L. 99-514)

P.L. 99-514, §1162(a)(1):

Amended Code Sec. 127(d) by striking out "1985" and inserting in lieu thereof "1987". **Effective** for tax years beginning after 12-31-85.

• 1984 (P.L. 98-611)

P.L. 98-611, §1(a):

Amended Code Sec. 127(d) by striking out "December 31, 1983" and inserting in lieu thereof "December 31, 1985." **Effective** for tax years beginning after 12-31-83.

• 1978, Revenue Act of 1978 (P.L. 95-600)

P.L. 95-600, §164(a):

Redesignated Code Sec. 127 as Code Sec. 128 and added a new Code Sec. 127. **Effective** for tax years beginning after 12-31-78.

»»→ Caution: Former Code Sec. 127(e), below, was redesignated as Code Sec. 127(d) by P.L. 107-16, and is subject to the sunset provision of the Economic Growth and Tax Relief Reconciliation Act of 2001 (P.L. 107-16), §901. Absent Congressional action, the changes made to this provision by P.L. 107-16, or that take effect as if included in P.L. 107-16, do not apply after December 31, 2010. For more information about the sunset provision, see page XXI of the Preface to this publication and P.L. 107-16, §901, in the amendment notes. See the amendments notes for a history of amendments to this section and the effective date of each change.

[Sec. 127(d)]

(d) CROSS REFERENCE.—

For reporting and recordkeeping requirements, see section 6039D.

Amendments

• 2001, Economic Growth and Tax Relief Reconciliation Act of 2001 (P.L. 107-16)

P.L. 107-16, §411(a):

Amended Code Sec. 127 by redesignating subsection (e) as subsection (d). **Effective** with respect to expenses relating to courses beginning after 12-31-2001.

P.L. 107-16, §901(a)-(b), provides:

SEC. 901. SUNSET OF PROVISIONS OF ACT.

(a) IN GENERAL.—All provisions of, and amendments made by, this Act shall not apply—

(1) to taxable, plan, or limitation years beginning after December 31, 2010, or

(2) in the case of title V, to estates of decedents dying, gifts made, or generation skipping transfers, after December 31, 2010.

(b) APPLICATION OF CERTAIN LAWS.—The Internal Revenue Code of 1986 and the Employee Retirement Income Security Act of 1974 shall be applied and administered to years, estates, gifts, and transfers described in subsection (a) as if the provisions and amendments described in subsection (a) had never been enacted.

• 1984 (P.L. 98-611)

P.L. 98-611, §1(d)(3)(B):

Amended Code Sec. 127 by adding at the end thereof new subsection (e). **Effective** 1-1-85.

P.L. 98-611, §1(g)(4), provides:

(4) NO PENALTIES OR INTEREST ON FAILURE TO WITHHOLD.—No penalty or interest shall be imposed on any failure to withhold under subtitle C of the Internal Revenue Code of 1954 (relating to employment taxes) with respect to amounts excluded from gross income under section 127 of such Code (as amended by this section and determined without regard to subsection (a)(2) thereof) with respect to periods during 1984.

[Sec. 128—Repealed]

Amendments

• 1990, Omnibus Budget Reconciliation Act of 1990 (P.L. 101-508)

P.L. 101-508, §11801(a)(10):

Repealed Code Sec. 128. **Effective** 11-5-90. For special rules, see Act Sec. 11821(b)(1)-(2), below.

P.L. 101-508, §11821(b)(1)-(2), provides:

(b) SAVINGS PROVISION.—If—

(1) any provision amended or repealed by this part applied to—

(A) any transaction occurring before the date of the enactment of this Act,

(B) any property acquired before such date of enactment, or

(C) any item of income, loss, deduction, or credit taken into account before such date of enactment, and

(2) the treatment of such transaction, property, or item under such provision would (without regard to the amendments made by this part) affect liability for tax for periods ending after such date of enactment,

nothing in the amendments made by this part shall be construed to affect the treatment of such transaction, property, or item for purposes of determining liability for tax for periods ending after such date of enactment.

Prior to repeal, Code Sec. 128 read as follows:

SEC. 128. INTEREST ON CERTAIN SAVINGS CERTIFICATES.

[Sec. 128(a)]

(a) IN GENERAL.—Gross income does not include any amount received by any individual during the taxable year as interest on a depository institution tax-exempt savings certificate.

Amendments

• 1981, Economic Recovery Tax Act of 1981 (P.L. 97-34)

P.L. 97-34, §301(a):

Added Code Sec. 128(a). **Effective** for tax years ending after 9-30-81.

[Sec. 128(b)]

(b) MAXIMUM DOLLAR AMOUNT.—

(1) IN GENERAL.—The aggregate amount excludable under subsection (a) for any taxable year shall not exceed the excess of—

(A) $1,000 ($2,000 in the case of a joint return under section 6013), over

(B) the aggregate amount received by the taxpayer which was excludable under subsection (a) for any prior taxable year.

(2) SPECIAL RULE.—For purposes of paragraph (1)(B), one-half of the amount excluded under subsection (a) on any joint return shall treated as received by each spouse.

Amendments

• 1981, Economic Recovery Tax Act of 1981 (P.L. 97-34)

P.L. 97-34, §301(a):

Added Code Sec. 128(b). **Effective** for tax years ending after 9-30-81.

[Sec. 128(c)]

(c) DEPOSITORY INSTITUTION TAX-EXEMPT SAVINGS CERTIFICATE.—For purposes of this section—

(1) IN GENERAL.—The term "depository institution tax-exempt savings certificate" means any certificate—

(A) which is issued by a qualified savings institution after September 30, 1981, and before January 1, 1983,

(B) which has a maturity of 1 year,

(C) which has an investment yield equal to 70 percent of the average investment yield for the most recent auction (before the week in which the certificate is issued) of United States Treasury bills with maturities of 52 weeks, and

(D) which is made available in denominations of $500.

(2) QUALIFIED INSTITUTION.—The term "qualified institution" means—

(A)(i) a bank (as defined in section 581),

(ii) a mutual savings bank, cooperative bank, domestic building and loan association, or other savings institution chartered and supervised as a savings and loan or similar institution under Federal or State law,

(iii) a credit union, the deposits or accounts of which are insured under Federal or State law or are protected or guaranteed under State law, or

(iv) a banking facility (whether or not insured under Federal or State law) which is operated under a cost plus agreement with the Department of Defense for members of the Armed Forces of the United States serving outside the United States and their dependents, or

(B) an industrial loan association or bank chartered and supervised under Federal or State law in a manner similar to a savings and loan institution.

The term "qualified institution" does not include any foreign branch or international banking facility of an institution described in the preceding sentence and such a branch or facility shall not be taken into account under subsection (d).

Amendments

• 1983, Technical Corrections Act of 1982 (P.L. 97-448)

P.L. 97-448, §103(a)(5):

Amended Code Sec. 128(c)(2)(A) by striking out "or" at the end of clause (ii), and by inserting after clause (iii) the following new clause (iv). **Effective** as if included in the provision of P.L. 97-34 to which it relates.

• 1981, Economic Recovery Tax Act of 1981 (P.L. 97-34)

P.L. 97-34, §301(a):

Added Code Sec. 128(c). **Effective** for tax years ending after 9-30-81.

[Sec. 128(d)]

(d) INSTITUTIONS REQUIRED TO PROVIDE RESIDENTIAL PROPERTY FINANCING.—

(1) IN GENERAL.—If a qualified savings institution (other than an institution described in subsection (c)(2)(A)(iii)) issues any depository institution tax-exempt savings certificate during any calendar quarter, the amount of the qualified residential financing provided by such institution

shall during the succeeding calendar quarter not be less than the lesser of—

(A) 75 percent of the face amount of depository institution tax-exempt savings certificates issued during the calendar quarter, or

(B) 75 percent of the qualified net savings for the calendar quarter.

The aggregate amount of qualified tax-exempt savings certificates issued by any institution described in subsection (c)(2)(A)(iii) which are outstanding at the close of any calendar quarter may not exceed the limitation determined under paragraph (4) with respect to such institution for such quarter.

(2) PENALTY FOR FAILURE TO MEET REQUIREMENTS.—If, as of the close of any calendar quarter, a qualified institution has not met the requirements of paragraph (1) with respect to the preceding calendar quarter, such institution may not issue any certificates until it meets such requirements.

(3) QUALIFIED RESIDENTIAL FINANCING.—The term "qualified residential financing" includes, and is limited to—

(A) any loan secured by a lien on a single-family or multifamily residence,

(B) any secured or unsecured qualified home improvement loan (within the meaning of section 103A(1)(6) without regard to the $15,000 limit),

(C) any mortgage (within the meaning of section 103A(l)(1)) on a single-family or multifamily residence which is insured or guaranteed by the Federal, State, or local government or any instrumentality thereof,

(D) any loan to acquire a mobile home,

(E) any construction loan for the construction or rehabilitation of a single-family or multifamily residence,

(F) the purchase of mortgages secured by single-family or multifamily residences on the secondary market but only to the extent the amount of such purchases exceed[s] the amount of sales of such mortgages by an institution,

(G) the purchase of securities issued or guaranteed by the Federal National Mortgage Association, the Government National Mortgage Association, or the Federal Home Loan Mortgage Corporation, or securities issued by any other person if such securities are secured by mortgages originated by a qualified institution, but only to the extent the amount of such purchases exceed the amount of sales of such securities by an institution, and

(H) any loan for agricultural purposes.

For purposes of this paragraph, the term "single-family residence" includes 2-, 3-, and 4-family residences, and the term "residence" includes stock in a cooperative housing corporation (as defined in section 216(b)).

(4) LIMITATION FOR CREDIT UNIONS.—For purposes of paragraph (1), the limitation determined under this paragraph with respect to any institution described in subsection (c)(2)(A)(iii) for any calendar quarter is the sum of—

(A) the aggregate of the amounts described in subparagraph (A) of paragraph (5) with respect to such institution as of September 30, 1981, plus

(B) 10 percent of the excess of—

(i) the aggregate of such amounts as of the close of such calendar quarter, over

(ii) the amount referred to in subparagraph (A).

For purposes of this paragraph, the amounts described in subparagraph (A) of paragraph (5) shall include amounts paid into credit union share accounts.

(5) QUALIFIED NET SAVINGS.—The term "qualified net savings" means, with respect to any qualified institution, the excess of—

(A) the amounts paid into passbook savings account, 6-month money market certificates, 30-month small-saver certificates, time deposits with a face amount of less than $100,000, and depository institution tax-exempt savings certificates issued by such institution, over

(B) the amounts withdrawn or redeemed in connection with the accounts and certificates described in subparagraph (A).

(6) CONSOLIDATED GROUPS.—For purposes of this subsection, all members of the same affiliated group (as defined in section 1504) which file a consolidated return for the taxable year shall be treated as 1 corporation.

Amendments

• 1983, Technical Corrections Act of 1982 (P.L. 97-448)

P.L. 97-448, §103(a)(1):

Amended Code Sec. 128(d)(4) by adding the sentence at the end thereof. **Effective** as if included in the provision of P.L. 97-34 to which it relates.

• 1981, Economic Recovery Tax Act of 1981 (P.L. 97-34)

P.L. 97-34, §301(a):

Added Code Sec. 128(d). **Effective** for tax years ending after 9-30-81.

[Sec. 128(e)]

(e) PENALTY FOR EARLY WITHDRAWALS.—

(1) IN GENERAL.—If any portion of a depository institution tax-exempt savings certificate is redeemed before the date on which it matures—

(A) subsection (a) shall not apply to any interest on such certificate for the taxable year of redemption and any subsequent taxable year, and

(B) there shall be included in gross income for the taxable year of redemption the amount of any interest on such certificate excluded under subsection (a) for any preceding taxable year.

(2) CERTIFICATE PLEDGED AS COLLATERAL.—For purposes of paragraph (1), if the taxpayer uses any depository institution tax-exempt savings certificate (or portion thereof) as collateral or security for a loan, the taxpayer shall be treated as having redeemed such certificate.

Amendments

• 1981, Economic Recovery Tax Act of 1981 (P.L. 97-34)

P.L. 97-34, §301(a):

Added Code Sec. 128(e). **Effective** for tax years ending after 9-30-81.

[Sec. 128(f)]

(f) OTHER SPECIAL RULES.—

(1) COORDINATION WITH SECTION 116.—Section 116 shall not apply to the interest on any depository institution tax-exempt savings certificate.

(2) ESTATES AND TRUSTS.—

(A) IN GENERAL.—Except as provided in subparagraph (B), the exclusion provided by this section shall not apply to estates and trusts.

(B) CERTIFICATES ACQUIRED BY ESTATE FROM DECEDENT.—In the case of a depository institution tax-exempt savings certificate acquired by an estate by reason of the death of the decedent—

(i) subparagraph (A) shall not apply, and

(ii) subsection (b) shall be applied as if the estate were the decedent.

Amendments

• 1981, Economic Recovery Tax Act of 1981 (P.L. 97-34)

P.L. 97-34, §301(a):

Added Code Sec. 128(f). **Effective** for tax years ending after 9-30-81.

P.L. 97-34, §301(c), provides:

(c) STUDY.—The Secretary of the Treasury or his delegate shall conduct a study of the exemption from income of interest earned on depository institution tax-exempt savings certificates established by this section to determine the exemption's effectiveness in generating additional savings. Such report shall be submitted to the Congress before June 1, 1983.

[Sec. 128—Repealed]

Amendments

• 1984, Deficit Reduction Act of 1984 (P.L. 98-369)

P.L. 98-369, §16(a):

Repealed subsection (a) of P.L. 97-34, Act Sec. 302, which added Code Sec. 128 (applicable to tax years beginning after December 31, 1984). **Effective** as if the amendment by P.L. 97-34 had not been enacted. Prior to repeal, Code Sec. 128 read as follows:

SEC. 128. PARTIAL EXCLUSION OF INTEREST.

[Sec. 128(a)]

(a) IN GENERAL.—Gross income does not include the amount received during the taxable year by an individual as interest.

Amendments

• 1981, Economic Recovery Tax Act of 1981 (P.L. 97-34)

P.L. 97-34, §302(a):

Added Code Sec. 128(a). **Effective** for tax years beginning after 12-31-84.

[Sec. 128(b)]

(b) MAXIMUM DOLLAR AMOUNT.—The aggregate amount excludable under subsection (a) for any taxable year shall not exceed 15 percent of the lesser of—

(1) $3,000 ($6,000 in the case of a joint return under section 6013), or

(2) the excess of the amount of interest received by the taxpayer during such taxable year (less the amount of any deduction under section 62(12)) over the amount of qualified interest expenses of such taxpayer for the taxable year.

Amendments

• 1981, Economic Recovery Tax Act of 1981 (P.L. 97-34)

P.L. 97-34, §302(a):

Added Code Sec. 128(b). **Effective** for tax years beginning after 12-31-84.

[Sec. 128(c)]

(c) DEFINITIONS.—For purposes of this section—

(1) INTEREST DEFINED.—The term "interest" means—

(A) interest on deposits with a bank (as defined in section 581).

(B) amounts (whether or not designated as interest) paid, in respect of deposits, investment certificates, or withdrawable or repurchasable shares, by—

(i) an institution which is—

(I) a mutual savings bank, cooperative bank, domestic building and loan association, or credit union, or

(II) any other savings or thrift institution which is chartered and supervised under Federal or State law,

the deposits or accounts in which are insured under Federal or State law, or

(ii) an industrial loan association or bank chartered and supervised under Federal or State law in a manner similar to a savings and loan institution.

(C) interest on—

(i) evidences of indebtedness (including bonds, debentures, notes, and certificates) issued by a domestic corporation in registered form, and

(ii) to the extent provided in regulations prescribed by the Secretary, other evidences of indebtedness issued by a domestic corporation of a type offered by corporations to the public,

(D) interest on obligations of the United States, a State, or a political subdivision of a State (not excluded from gross income of the taxpayer under any other provision of law),

(E) interest attributable to participation shares in a trust established and maintained by a corporation established pursuant to Federal law, and

(F) interest paid by an insurance company under an agreement to pay interest on—

(i) prepaid premiums,

(ii) life insurance policy proceeds which are left on deposit with such company by a beneficiary, and

(iii) under regulations prescribed by the Secretary, policyholder dividends left on deposit with such company.

(2) QUALIFIED INTEREST EXPENSE DEFINED.—The term "qualified interest expense" means an amount equal to the excess of—

(A) the amount of the deduction allowed the taxpayer under section 163(a) (relating to interest) for the taxable year, over

(B) the amount of such deduction allowed with respect to interest paid or accrued on indebtedness incurred in—

(i) acquiring, constructing, reconstructing, or rehabilitating property which is primarily used by the taxpayer as a dwelling unit (as defined in section 280A(f)(1)), or

(ii) the taxpayer's conduct of a trade or business.

(3) LIMITATION ON QUALIFIED INTEREST EXPENSES, ETC.—

(A) LIMITATION.—The amount of the qualified interest expense of any taxpayer for any taxable year shall not exceed such taxpayer's excess itemized deductions (as defined in section 63(c)).

(B) COORDINATION WITH OTHER PROVISIONS.—For purposes of sections 37, 43, 85, 86, 105(d), 165(c)(3), 170(b), and 213, adjusted gross income shall be determined without regard to the exclusion provided by this section.

Amendments

• 1983, Social Security Amendments of 1983 (P.L. 98-21)

P.L. 98-21, §121(f)(2):

Amended Code Sec. 128(c)(3)(B) by striking out "85," and inserting in place thereof "85, 86,". **Effective** for benefits received after 1983 in tax years ending after 1983 as provided in Act Sec. 121(g).

P.L. 98-21, 122(c)(3):

Amended Code Sec. 128(c)(3)(B) by striking out "105(d),". **Effective** for tax years beginning after 1983 as provided in Act Sec. 122(d).

• 1983, Technical Corrections Act of 1982 (P.L. 97-448)

P.L. 97-448, §103(b):

Amended Code Sec. 128(c) (as added by P.L. 97-34, §302(a)) by adding at the end thereof new paragraph (3). **Effective** as if included in the provision of P.L. 97-34 to which it relates.

• 1981, Economic Recovery Tax Act of 1981 (P.L. 97-34)

P.L. 97-34, §302(a):

Added Code Sec. 128(c). **Effective** for tax years beginning after 12-31-84.

[Sec. 129]

SEC. 129. DEPENDENT CARE ASSISTANCE PROGRAMS.

[Sec. 129(a)]

(a) EXCLUSION.—

(1) IN GENERAL.—Gross income of an employee does not include amounts paid or incurred by the employer for dependent care assistance provided to such employee if the assistance is furnished pursuant to a program which is described in subsection (d).

(2) LIMITATION OF EXCLUSION.—

(A) IN GENERAL.—The amount which may be excluded under paragraph (1) for dependent care assistance with respect to dependent care services provided during a taxable year shall not exceed $5,000 ($2,500 in the case of a separate return by a married individual).

(B) YEAR OF INCLUSION.—The amount of any excess under subparagraph (A) shall be included in gross income in the taxable year in which the dependent care services were provided (even if payment of dependent care assistance for such services occurs in a subsequent taxable year).

(C) MARITAL STATUS.—For purposes of this paragraph, marital status shall be determined under the rules of paragraphs (3) and (4) of section 21(e).

Amendments

• 1989, Omnibus Budget Reconciliation Act of 1989 (P.L. 101-239)

P.L. 101-239, §7811(h)(2):

Amended Code Sec. 129(a) (prior to amendment by P.L. 100-647, §1011B(c)(2)(A)) by striking the sentence following paragraph (2). **Effective** as if included in the provision of P.L. 100-647 to which it relates. Prior to amendment, the sentence following Code Sec. 129(a)(2) read as follows:

For purposes of the preceding sentence, marital status shall be determined under the rules of paragraphs (3) and (4) of section 21(e).

• 1988, Technical and Miscellaneous Revenue Act of 1988 (P.L. 100-647)

P.L. 100-647, §1011B(c)(2)(A):

Amended Code Sec. 129(a)(2). For the **effective** date, see Act Sec. 1011B(c)(2)(C), below. Prior to amendment, Code Sec. 129(a)(2) read as follows:

(2) LIMITATION OF EXCLUSION.—The aggregate amount excluded from the gross income of the taxpayer under this section for any taxable year shall not exceed $5,000 ($2,500 in the case of a separate return by a married individual).

P.L. 100-647, §1011B(c)(2)(C), provides:

(C)(i) Except as provided in this subparagraph, the amendments made by this paragraph shall apply to taxable years beginning after December 31, 1987.

(ii) A taxpayer may elect to have the amendment made by subparagraph (A) apply to taxable years beginning in 1987.

(iii) In the case of a taxpayer not making an election under clause (ii), any dependent care assistance provided in a taxable year beginning in 1987 with respect to which reimbursement was not received in such taxable year shall be treated as provided in the taxpayer's first taxable year beginning after December 31, 1987.

• 1986, Tax Reform Act of 1986 (P.L. 99-514)

P.L. 99-514, §1163(a):

Amended Code Sec. 129(a). **Effective** for tax years beginning after 12-31-86. Prior to amendment, Code Sec. 129(a) read as follows:

(a) IN GENERAL.—Gross income of an employee does not include amounts paid or incurred by the employer for dependent care assistance provided to such employee if the assistance is furnished pursuant to a program which is described in subsection (d).

• 1981, Economic Recovery Tax Act of 1981 (P.L. 97-34)

P.L. 97-34, §124(e)(1):

Added Code Sec. 129(a). **Effective** for tax years beginning after 12-31-81.

[Sec. 129(b)]

(b) EARNED INCOME LIMITATION.—

(1) IN GENERAL.—The amount excluded from the income of an employee under subsection (a) for any taxable year shall not exceed—

(A) in the case of an employee who is not married at the close of such taxable year, the earned income of such employee for such taxable year, or

(B) in the case of an employee who is married at the close of such taxable year, the lesser of—

(i) the earned income of such employee for such taxable year, or

(ii) the earned income of the spouse of such employee for such taxable year.

(2) SPECIAL RULE FOR CERTAIN SPOUSES.—For purposes of paragraph (1), the provisions of section 21(d)(2) shall apply in determining the earned income of a spouse who is a student or incapable of caring for himself.

Amendments

• 1984, Deficit Reduction Act of 1984 (P.L. 98-369)

P.L. 98-369, §474(r)(6)(A):

Amended Code Sec. 129(b)(2) by striking out "section 44A(e)(2)" and inserting in lieu thereof "section 21(d)(2)". **Effective** for tax years beginning after 12-31-83, and to carrybacks from such years.

• 1981, Economic Recovery Tax Act of 1981 (P.L. 97-34)

P.L. 97-34, §124(e)(1):

Added Code Sec. 129(b). **Effective** for tax years beginning after 12-31-81.

[Sec. 129(c)]

(c) PAYMENTS TO RELATED INDIVIDUALS.—No amount paid or incurred during the taxable year of an employee by an employer in providing dependent care assistance to such employee shall be excluded under subsection (a) if such amount was paid or incurred to an individual—

(1) with respect to whom, for such taxable year, a deduction is allowable under section 151(c) (relating to personal exemptions for dependents) to such employee or the spouse of such employee, or

(2) who is a child of such employee (within the meaning of section 152(f)(1)) under the age of 19 at the close of such taxable year.

Amendments

• 2004, Working Families Tax Relief Act of 2004 (P.L. 108-311)

P.L. 108-311, §207(12):

Amended Code Sec. 129(c)(2) by striking "151(c)(3)" and inserting "152(f)(1)". **Effective** for tax years beginning after 12-31-2004.

• 1986, Tax Reform Act of 1986 (P.L. 99-514)

P.L. 99-514, §104(b)(1)(A):

Amended Code Sec. 129(c)(1) by striking out "section 151(e)" and inserting in lieu thereof "section 151(c)". **Effective** for tax years beginning after 12-31-86.

P.L. 99-514, §104(b)(1)(B):

Amended Code Sec. 129(c)(2) by striking out "section 151(e)(3)" and inserting in lieu thereof "section 151(c)(3)". **Effective** for tax years beginning after 12-31-86.

• 1981, Economic Recovery Tax Act of 1981 (P.L. 97-34)

P.L. 97-34, §124(e)(1):

Added Code Sec. 129(c). **Effective** for tax years beginning after 12-31-81.

[Sec. 129(d)]

(d) DEPENDENT CARE ASSISTANCE PROGRAM.—

(1) IN GENERAL.—For purposes of this section a dependent care assistance program is a separate written plan of an employer for the exclusive benefit of his employees to provide such employees with dependent care assistance which meets the requirements of paragraphs (2) through (8) of this subsection. If any plan would qualify as a dependent care assistance program but for a failure to meet the requirements of this subsection, then, notwithstanding such failure, such plan shall be treated as a dependent care assistance program in the case of employees who are not highly compensated employees.

(2) DISCRIMINATION.—The contributions or benefits provided under the plan shall not discriminate in favor of employees who are highly compensated employees (within the meaning of section 414(q)) or their dependents.

(3) ELIGIBILITY.—The program shall benefit employees who qualify under a classification set up by the employer and found by the Secretary not to be discriminatory in favor of employees described in paragraph (2), or their dependents.

(4) PRINCIPAL SHAREHOLDERS OR OWNERS.—Not more than 25 percent of the amounts paid or incurred by the employer for dependent care assistance during the year may be provided for the class of individuals who are shareholders or owners (or their spouses or dependents), each of whom (on any day of the year) owns more than 5 percent of the stock or of the capital or profits interest in the employer.

(5) NO FUNDING REQUIRED.—A program referred to in paragraph (1) is not required to be funded.

(6) NOTIFICATION OF ELIGIBLE EMPLOYEES.—Reasonable notification of the availability and terms of the program shall be provided to eligible employees.

(7) STATEMENT OF EXPENSES.—The plan shall furnish to an employee, on or before January 31, a written statement showing the amounts paid or expenses incurred by the employer in providing dependent care assistance to such employee during the previous calendar year.

(8) BENEFITS.—

(A) IN GENERAL.—A plan meets the requirements of this paragraph if the average benefits provided to employees who are not highly compensated employees under all plans of the employer is at least 55 percent of the average benefits provided to highly compensated employees under all plans of the employer.

(B) SALARY REDUCTION AGREEMENTS.—For purposes of subparagraph (A), in the case of any benefits provided through a salary reduction agreement, a plan may disregard any employees whose compensation is less than $25,000. For purposes of this subparagraph, the term "compensation" has the meaning given such term by section 414(q)(4), except that, under rules prescribed by the Secretary, an employer may elect to determine compensation on any other basis which does not discriminate in favor of highly compensated employees.

(9) EXCLUDED EMPLOYEES.—For purposes of paragraphs (3) and (8), there shall be excluded from consideration—

(A) subject to rules similar to the rules of section 410(b)(4), employees who have not attained the age of 21 and completed 1 year of service (as defined in section 410(a)(3)), and

(B) employees not included in a dependent care assistance program who are included in a unit of employees covered by an agreement which the Secretary finds to be a collective bargaining agreement between employee representatives and 1 or more employees, if there is evidence that dependent care benefits were the subject of good faith bargaining between such employee representatives and such employer or employers.

Amendments

• 1996, Small Business Job Protection Act of 1996 (P.L. 104-188)

P.L. 104-188, §1431(c)(1)(B):

Amended Code Sec. 129(d)(8)(B) by striking "section 414(q)(7)" and inserting "section 414(q)(4)". **Effective** for years beginning after 12-31-96, except that in determining whether an employee is a highly compensated employee for years beginning in 1997, this amendment is treated as having been in effect for years beginning in 1996.

• 1989 (P.L. 101-140)

P.L. 101-140, §203(a)(1):

Provides that Code Sec. 129(d)(1) and (6)-(7) as amended by Section 1151(c)(A)-(B) of P.L. 99-514 shall be applied as if the amendment made by such section had not been enacted. **Effective** as if included in section 1151 of P.L. 99-514. Prior to amendment, Code Sec. 129(d)(1) and (6) as amended by Act Sec. 1151(c)(5)(A)-(B) of P.L. 99-514 reads as follows:

(1) IN GENERAL.—For purposes of this section, a dependent care assistance program is a plan of an employer—

(A) under which the employer provides employees with dependent care assistance, and

(B) which meets the requirements of paragraphs (2) through (7) and Section 89(k).

***

(6) STATEMENT OF EXPENSES.—The plan shall furnish to an employee, on or before January 31, a written statement showing the amounts paid or expenses incurred by the employer in providing dependent care assistance to such employee during the previous calendar year.

P.L. 101-140, §203(a)(1):

Provides that Code Sec. 129(d)(3) as amended by Section 1151(g)(4) of P.L. 99-514 shall be applied as if the amendment had not been enacted. **Effective** as if included in section 1151 of P.L. 99-514. Prior to amendment, Code Sec. 129(d)(3) as amended by Act Sec. 1151(g)(4) of P.L. 99-514 read as follows:

(3) ELIGIBILITY.—The program shall benefit employees who qualify under a classification set up by the employer and found by the Secretary not to be discriminatory in favor of employees described in paragraph (2), or their dependents. For purposes of this paragraph, there may be excluded from consideration employees who may be excluded from consideration under section 89(h).

P.L. 101-140, §203(a)(2):

Provides that Code Sec. 129(d)(3) and (8) as amended by Section 1011B(a)(31)(A)(i)-(ii) of P.L. 100-647 shall be applied as if the amendment had not been enacted. **Effective** as if included in section 1151 of P.L. 99-514. The last sentence of Code Sec. 129(d)(3) and (8) as amended by Act Sec. 1011B(a)(31)(A)(i)-(ii) of P.L. 100-647 reads as follows:

For purposes of this paragraph, there may be excluded from consideration employees who may be excluded from consideration under section 89(h).

***

(8) EXCLUDED EMPLOYEES.—For purposes of paragraphs (2), (3), and (7), there shall be excluded from consideration employees who are excluded from consideration under section 89(h).

P.L. 101-140, §204(a)(1):

Amended Code Sec. 129(d)(1) (as in effect on the day before the date of the enactment of the P.L. 99-514) by adding at the end thereof a new sentence. **Effective** for years beginning after 12-31-88.

P.L. 101-140, §204(a)(2)(A):

Amended Code Sec. 129(d) by adding at the end thereof a new paragraph (9). **Effective** for years beginning after 12-31-88.

P.L. 101-140, §204(a)(2)(B):

Amended Code Sec. 129(d)(3) (as in effect on the day before the date of the enactment of P.L. 99-514) by striking the last sentence. **Effective** for years beginning after 12-31-88. Prior to amendment, the last sentence of Code Sec. 129(d)(3) (as in effect on the day before the date of enactment of the Tax Reform Act of 1986) read as follows:

For purposes of this paragraph, there shall be excluded from consideration employees not included in the program who are included in a unit of employees covered by an agreement which the Secretary of Labor finds to be a collective bargaining agreement between employee representatives and one or more employers, if there is evidence that dependent care benefits were the subject of good faith bargaining between such employee representatives and such employer or employers.

P.L. 101-140, §204(a)(3)(A):

Amended Code Sec. 129(d) (as in effect after the amendment made by paragraph (14) of section 1011B(a) of P.L. 100-647) by redesignating paragraph (7) as paragraph (8). **Effective** for plan years beginning after 12-31-89.

P.L. 101-140, §204(a)(3)(B):

Amended Code Sec. 129(d)(1) (as in effect on the day before the date of the enactment of P.L. 99-514) by striking "paragraphs (2) through (7)" and inserting "paragraphs (2) through (8)". **Effective** for plan years beginning after 12-31-89.

• 1989 (P.L. 101-136)

P.L. 101-136, §528, provides:

SEC. 528. No monies appropriated by this Act may be used to implement or enforce section 1151 of the Tax Reform Act of 1986 or the amendments made by such section.

• 1988, Technical and Miscellaneous Revenue Act of 1988 (P.L. 100-647)

P.L. 100-647, §1011B(a)(14):

Amended Code Sec. 129(d) by redesignating paragraph (8) as paragraph (7). **Effective** as if included in the provision of P.L. 99-514 to which it relates.

P.L. 100-647, §1011B(a)(15)(A)-(C):

Amended Code Sec. 129(d)(7) (as so redesignated) by inserting "under all plans of the employer" after "employees" the 2nd and 3rd time it appears in subparagraph (A), by striking out "there shall be disregarded" in subparagraph (B) and inserting in lieu thereof "a plan may disregard", and by striking out "415(q)(7)" in subparagraph (B) and inserting in lieu thereof "414(q)(7)". **Effective** as if included in the provision of P.L. 99-514 to which it relates.

P.L. 100-647, §1011B(a)(30):

Amended Code Sec. 129(d)(1)(B) by striking out "(6)" and inserting in lieu thereof "(7)". **Effective** as if included in the provision of P.L. 99-514 to which it relates.

P.L. 100-647, §1011B(a)(31)(A)(i)-(ii):

Amended Code Sec. 129(d) by striking out the last sentence of paragraph (3), and by inserting at the end thereof a new paragraph (8). **Effective** as if included in the provision of P.L. 99-514 to which it relates. Prior to amendment, the last sentence of Code Sec. 129(d)(3) read as follows:

For purposes of this paragraph, there may be excluded from consideration employees who may be excluded from consideration under section 89(h).

P.L. 100-647, §3021(a)(14)(A)-(B):

Amended Code Sec. 129(d)(7)(B) (as so redesignated) by striking out "(within the meaning of section 414(q)(7))", and by adding at the end thereof a new sentence. **Effective** as if included in the amendments made by section 1151 of P.L. 99-514. Prior to amendment, Code Sec. 129(d)(7)(B) read as follows:

(B) SALARY REDUCTION AGREEMENTS.—For purposes of subparagraph (A), in the case of any benefits provided through a salary reduction agreement, a plan may disregard any employees whose compensation (within the meaning of section 414(q)(7)) is less than $25,000.

• 1986, Tax Reform Act of 1986 (P.L. 99-514)

P.L. 99-514, §1114(b)(4):

Amended Code Sec. 129(d)(2) by striking out "officers, owners, or highly compensated," and inserting in lieu thereof "highly compensated employees (within the meaning of section 414(q))". **Effective** for years beginning after 12-31-87.

P.L. 99-514, §1151(c)(5)(A)-(B):

Amended Code Sec. 129(d) by striking out paragraph (1) and inserting in lieu thereof new paragraph (1), and by striking out paragraph (6) thereof, and redesignating paragraph (7) as paragraph (6). For the **effective** date, as well as special rules, see Act Sec. 1151(k) following Code Sec. 89. Prior to amendment, paragraphs (1) and (6) read as follows:

(1) IN GENERAL.—For purposes of this section a dependent care assistance program is a separate written plan of an employer for the exclusive benefit of his employees to provide such employees with dependent care assistance which meets the requirements of paragraphs (2) through (7) of this subsection.

***

(6) NOTIFICATION OF ELIGIBLE EMPLOYEES.—Reasonable notification of the availability and terms of the program shall be provided to eligible employees.

P.L. 99-514, §1151(f):

Amended Code Sec. 129(d) by adding at the end a new paragraph (8)[7]. For the **effective** date, as well as special rules, see Act Sec. 1151(k) following Code Sec. 89.

P.L. 99-514, §1151(g)(4):

Amended Code Sec. 129(d)(3) by striking out the last sentence and inserting in lieu thereof "For purposes of this paragraph, there may be excluded from consideration employees who may be excluded from consideration under section 89(h)." For the **effective** date, as well as special rules, see Act Sec. 1151(k) following Code Sec. 89. Prior to amendment, Code Sec. 129(d)(3) read as follows:

(3) ELIGIBILITY.—The program shall benefit employees who qualify under a classification set up by the employer and found by the Secretary not to be discriminatory in favor of employees described in paragraph (2), or their dependents. For purposes of this paragraph, there shall be excluded from consideration employees not included in the program who are included in a unit of employees covered by an agreement which the Secretary of Labor finds to be a collective bargaining agreement between employee representatives and one or more employers, if there is evidence that dependent care benefits were the subject of good faith bargaining between such employee representatives and such employer or employers.

• 1983, Technical Corrections Act of 1982 (P.L. 97-448)

P.L. 97-448, §101(e)(1)(A):

Amended Code Sec. 129(d) by redesignating paragraphs (2) through (6) as paragraphs (3) through (7), respectively, and by inserting after paragraph (1) new paragraph (2). **Effective** as if included in the provision of P.L. 97-34 to which it relates.

P.L. 97-448, §101(e)(1)(B):

Amended Code Sec. 129(d)(3) (as redesignated by Act Sec. 101(e)(1)(A)) by striking out "employees who are officers, owners, or highly compensated, or their dependents" and inserting in lieu thereof "employees described in paragraph (2), or their dependents". **Effective** as if included in the provision of P.L. 97-34 to which it relates.

P.L. 97-448, §101(e)(1)(C):

Amended Code Sec. 129(d)(1) by striking out "paragraphs (2) through (6)" and inserting in lieu thereof "paragraphs (2) through (7)". **Effective** as if included in the provision of P.L. 97-34 to which it relates.

• 1981, Economic Recovery Tax Act of 1981 (P.L. 97-34)

P.L. 97-34, §124(e)(1):

Added Code Sec. 129(d). **Effective** for tax years beginning after 12-31-81.

[Sec. 129(e)]

(e) DEFINITIONS AND SPECIAL RULES.—For purposes of this section—

(1) DEPENDENT CARE ASSISTANCE.—The term "dependent care assistance" means the payment of, or provision of, those services which if paid for by the employee would be considered employment-related expenses under section 21(b)(2) (relating to expenses for household and dependent care services necessary for gainful employment).

(2) EARNED INCOME.—The term "earned income" shall have the meaning given such term in section 32(c)(2), but such term shall not include any amounts paid or incurred by an employer for dependent care assistance to an employee.

(3) EMPLOYEE.—The term "employee" includes, for any year, an individual who is an employee within the meaning of section 401(c)(1) (relating to self-employed individuals).

(4) EMPLOYER.—An individual who owns the entire interest in an unincorporated trade or business shall be treated as his own employer. A partnership shall be treated as the employer of each partner who is an employee within the meaning of paragraph (3).

(5) ATTRIBUTION RULES.—

(A) OWNERSHIP OF STOCK.—Ownership of stock in a corporation shall be determined in accordance with the rules provided under subsections (d) and (e) of section 1563 (without regard to section 1563(e)(3)(C)).

(B) INTEREST IN UNINCORPORATED TRADE OR BUSINESS.—The interest of an employee in a trade or business which is not incorporated shall be determined in accordance with regulations prescribed by the Secretary, which shall be based on principles similar to the principles which apply in the case of subparagraph (A).

(6) UTILIZATION TEST NOT APPLICABLE.—A dependent care assistance program shall not be held or considered to fail to meet any requirements of subsection (d) (other than paragraphs (4) and (8) thereof) merely because of utilization rates for the different types of assistance made available under the program.

(7) DISALLOWANCE OF EXCLUDED AMOUNTS AS CREDIT OR DEDUCTION.—No deduction or credit shall be allowed to the employee under any other section of this chapter for any amount excluded from the gross income of the employee by reason of this section.

(8) TREATMENT OF ONSITE FACILITIES.—In the case of an onsite facility maintained by an employer, except to the extent provided in regulations, the amount of dependent care assistance provided to an employee excluded with respect to any dependent shall be based on—

(A) utilization of the facility by a dependent of the employee, and

(B) the value of the services provided with respect to such dependent.

(9) IDENTIFYING INFORMATION REQUIRED WITH RESPECT TO SERVICE PROVIDER.—No amount paid or incurred by an employer for dependent care assistance provided to an employee shall be excluded from the gross income of such employee unless—

(A) the name, address, and taxpayer identification number of the person performing the services are included on the return to which the exclusion relates, or

(B) if such person is an organization described in section 501(c)(3) and exempt from tax under section 501(a), the name and address of such person are included on the return to which the exclusion relates.

In the case of a failure to provide the information required under the preceding sentence, the preceding sentence shall not apply if it is shown that the taxpayer exercised due diligence in attempting to provide the information so required.

Amendments

• 1989 (P.L. 101-140)

P.L. 101-140, §204(a)(3)(C):

Amended Code Sec. 129(e)(6) by striking "(7)" and inserting "(8)". **Effective** for plan years beginning after 12-31-89.

• 1988, Technical and Miscellaneous Revenue Act of 1988 (P.L. 100-647)

P.L. 100-647, §1011B(a)(18):

Amended Code Sec. 129(e)(6) by striking out "of subsection (d)" and inserting in lieu thereof "of subsection (d) (other than paragraphs (4) and (7) thereof)". **Effective** as if included in the provision of P.L. 99-514 to which it relates.

P.L. 100-647, §1011B(c)(1)(A)-(D):

Amended Code Sec. 129(e)(8) by inserting "maintained by an employer" after "onsite facility", by inserting "of dependent care assistance provided to an employee" after "the amount", by inserting "of the facility by a dependent of the employee" after "utilization" in subparagraph (A), and by inserting "with respect to such dependent" after "provided" in subparagraph (B). **Effective** as if included in the provision of P.L. 99-514 to which it relates.

• 1988, Family Support Act of 1988 (P.L. 100-485)

P.L. 100-485, §703(c)(2):

Amended Code Sec. 129(e) by adding at the end thereof new paragraph (9). **Effective** for tax years beginning after 12-31-88.

• 1986, Tax Reform Act of 1986 (P.L. 99-514)

P.L. 99-514, §1163(b):

Amended Code Sec. 129(e) by adding at the end thereof new paragraph (8). **Effective** for tax years beginning after 12-31-86.

• 1984, Deficit Reduction Act of 1984 (P.L. 98-369)

P.L. 98-369, §474(r)(6)(B):

Amended Code Sec. 129(e)(1) by striking out "section 44A(c)(2)" and inserting in lieu thereof "section 21(b)(2)". **Effective** for tax years beginning after 12-31-83, and to carrybacks from such years.

P.L. 98-369, §474(r)(6)(C):

Amended Code Sec. 129(e)(2) by striking out "section 43(c)(2)" and inserting in lieu thereof "section 32(c)(2)". **Effective** for tax years beginning after 12-31-83, and to carrybacks from such years.

• 1983, Technical Corrections Act of 1982 (P.L. 97-448)

P.L. 97-448, §101(e)(2):

Amended Code Sec. 129(e)(7) by striking out "shall be allowed" and inserting in lieu thereof "shall be allowed to the employee", and by striking out "excluded from income" and inserting in lieu thereof "excluded from the gross income of the employee". **Effective** as if included in the provision of P.L. 97-34 to which it relates.

• 1981, Economic Recovery Tax Act of 1981 (P.L. 97-34)

P.L. 97-34, §124(e)(1):

Added Code Sec. 129(e). **Effective** for tax years beginning after 12-31-81.

[Sec. 130]

SEC. 130. CERTAIN PERSONAL INJURY LIABILITY ASSIGNMENTS.

[Sec. 130(a)]

(a) IN GENERAL.—Any amount received for agreeing to a qualified assignment shall not be included in gross income to the extent that such amount does not exceed the aggregate cost of any qualified funding assets.

[Sec. 130(b)]

(b) TREATMENT OF QUALIFIED FUNDING ASSET.—In the case of any qualified funding asset—

(1) the basis of such asset shall be reduced by the amount excluded from gross income under subsection (a) by reason of the purchase of such asset, and

(2) any gain recognized on a disposition of such asset shall be treated as ordinary income.

[Sec. 130(c)]

(c) QUALIFIED ASSIGNMENT.—For purposes of this section, the term "qualified assignment" means any assignment of a liability to make periodic payments as damages (whether by suit or agreement), or as compensation under any workmen's compensation act, on account of personal injury or sickness (in a case involving physical injury or physical sickness)—

(1) if the assignee assumes such liability from a person who is a party to the suit or agreement, or the workmen's compensation claim, and

(2) if—

(A) such periodic payments are fixed and determinable as to amount and time of payment,

(B) such periodic payments cannot be accelerated, deferred, increased, or decreased by the recipient of such payments,

(C) the assignee's obligation on account of the personal injuries or sickness is no greater than the obligation of the person who assigned the liability, and

(D) such periodic payments are excludable from the gross income of the recipient under paragraph (1) or (2) of section 104(a).

The determination for purposes of this chapter of when the recipient is treated as having received any payment with respect to which there has been a qualified assignment shall be made without regard to any provision of such assignment which grants the recipient rights as a creditor greater than those of a general creditor.

Amendments

• 1997, Taxpayer Relief Act of 1997 (P.L. 105-34)

P.L. 105-34, §962(a)(1)-(3):

Amended Code Sec. 130(c) by inserting ", or as compensation under any workmen's compensation act," after "(whether by suit or agreement)" in the material preceding paragraph (1), by inserting "or the workmen's compensation claim," after "agreement," in paragraph (1), and by striking "section 104(a)(2)" in paragraph (2)(D) and inserting "paragraph (1) or (2) of section 104(a)". **Effective** for claims under workmen's compensation acts filed after 8-5-97.

• 1988, Technical and Miscellaneous Revenue Act of 1988 (P.L. 100-647)

P.L. 100-647, §6079(b)(1)(A)-(B):

Amended Code Sec. 130(c) by striking out subparagraph (C) of paragraph (2) and redesignating subparagraphs (D) and (E) of paragraph (2) as subparagraphs (C) and (D), respectively, and by adding at the end thereof a new sentence. **Effective** for assignments after 11-10-88. Prior to amendment, Code Sec. 130(c)(2)(C) read as follows:

(C) the assignee does not provide to the recipient of such payments rights against the assignee which are greater than those of a general creditor,

• 1986, Tax Reform Act of 1986 (P.L. 99-514)

P.L. 99-514, §1002(a):

Amended Code Sec. 130(c) by inserting "(in a case involving physical injury or physical sickness)" after "personal injury or sickness". **Effective** for assignments entered into after 12-31-86, in tax years ending after such date.

[Sec. 130(d)]

(d) QUALIFIED FUNDING ASSET.—For purposes of this section, the term "qualified funding asset" means any annuity contract issued by a company licensed to do business as an insurance company under the laws of any State, or any obligation of the United States, if—

(1) such annuity contract or obligation is used by the assignee to fund periodic payments under any qualified assignment,

(2) the periods of the payments under the annuity contract or obligation are reasonably related to the periodic payments under the qualified assignment, and the amount of any such payment under the contract or obligation does not exceed the periodic payment to which it relates,

(3) such annuity contract or obligation is designated by the taxpayer (in such manner as the Secretary shall by regulations prescribe) as being taken into account under this section with respect to such qualified assignment, and

(4) such annuity contract or obligation is purchased by the taxpayer not more than 60 days before the date of the qualified assignment and not later than 60 days after the date of such assignment.

Amendments

• 1983 (P.L. 97-473)

P.L. 97-473, §101(b)(1):

Added Code Sec. 130. **Effective** for tax years ending after 12-31-82.

[Sec. 131]

SEC. 131. CERTAIN FOSTER CARE PAYMENTS.

[Sec. 131(a)]

(a) GENERAL RULE.—Gross income shall not include amounts received by a foster care provider during the taxable year as qualified foster care payments.

[Sec. 131(b)]

(b) QUALIFIED FOSTER CARE PAYMENT DEFINED.—For purposes of this section—

(1) IN GENERAL.—The term "qualified foster care payment" means any payment made pursuant to a foster care program of a State or political subdivision thereof—

(A) which is paid by—

(i) a State or political subdivision thereof, or

(ii) a qualified foster care placement agency, and

(B) which is—

(i) paid to the foster care provider for caring for a qualified foster individual in the foster care provider's home, or

(ii) a difficulty of care payment.

(2) QUALIFIED FOSTER INDIVIDUAL.—The term "qualified foster individual" means any individual who is living in a foster family home in which such individual was placed by—

(A) an agency of a State or a political subdivision thereof, or

(B) a qualified foster care placement agency.

(3) QUALIFIED FOSTER CARE PLACEMENT AGENCY DEFINED.—The term "qualified foster care placement agency" means any placement agency which is licensed or certified by—

(A) a State or political subdivision thereof, or

(B) an entity designated by a State or political subdivision thereof,

for the foster care program of such State or political subdivision to make foster care payments to providers of foster care.

(4) LIMITATION BASED ON NUMBER OF INDIVIDUALS OVER THE AGE OF 18.—In the case of any foster home in which there is a qualified foster care individual who has attained age 19, foster care payments (other than difficulty of care payments) for any period to which such payments relate shall not be excludable from gross income under subsection (a) to the extent such payments are made for more than 5 such qualified foster individuals.

Amendments

• 2002, Job Creation and Worker Assistance Act of 2002 (P.L. 107-147)

P.L. 107-147, §404(a):

Amended the matter preceding Code Sec. 131(b)(1)(B). **Effective** for tax years beginning after 12-31-2001. Prior to amendment, the matter preceding Code Sec. 131(b)(1)(B) read as follows:

(1) IN GENERAL.—The term "qualified foster care payment" means any amount—

(A) which is paid by a State or political subdivision thereof or by a placement agency which is described in section 501(c)(3) and exempt from tax under section 501(a), and

P.L. 107-147, §404(b):

Amended Code Sec. 131(b)(2)(B). **Effective** for tax years beginning after 12-31-2001. Prior to amendment, Code Sec. 131(b)(2)(B) read as follows:

(B) in the case of an individual who has not attained age 19, an organization which is licensed by a State (or political subdivision thereof) as a placement agency and which is described in section 501(c)(3) and exempt from tax under section 501(a).

P.L. 107-147, §404(c):

Amended Code Sec. 131(b) by redesignating paragraph (3) as paragraph (4) and by inserting after paragraph (2) a new paragraph (3). **Effective** for tax years beginning after 12-31-2001.

[Sec. 131(c)]

(c) DIFFICULTY OF CARE PAYMENTS.—For purposes of this section—

(1) DIFFICULTY OF CARE PAYMENTS.—The term "difficulty of care payments" means payments to individuals which are not described in subsection (b)(1)(B)(i), and which—

(A) are compensation for providing the additional care of a qualified foster individual which is—

(i) required by reason of a physical, mental, or emotional handicap of such individual with respect to which the State has determined that there is a need for additional compensation, and

(ii) provided in the home of the foster care provider, and

(B) are designated by the payor as compensation described in subparagraph (A).

(2) LIMITATION BASED ON NUMBER OF INDIVIDUALS.—In the case of any foster home, difficulty of care payments for any period to which such payments relate shall not be excludable from gross income under subsection (a) to the extent such payments are made for more than—

(A) 10 qualified foster individuals who have not attained age 19, and

(B) 5 qualified foster individuals not described in subparagraph (A).

Amendments

• 1986, Tax Reform Act of 1986 (P.L. 99-514)

P.L. 99-514, §1707(a):

Amended Code Sec. 131. **Effective** for tax years beginning after 12-31-85. Prior to amendment, Code Sec. 131 read as follows:

SEC. 131. CERTAIN FOSTER CARE PAYMENTS.

(a) GENERAL RULE.—Gross income shall not include amounts received by a foster parent during the taxable year as qualified foster care payments.

(b) QUALIFIED FOSTER CARE PAYMENT DEFINED.—For purposes of this section—

(1) IN GENERAL.—The term "qualified foster care payment" means any amount—

(A) which is paid by a State or political subdivision thereof or by a child-placing agency which is described in section 501(c)(3) and exempt from tax under section 501(a), and

(B) which is—

(i) paid to reimburse the foster parent for the expenses of caring for a qualified foster child in the foster parent's home, or

(ii) a difficulty of care payment.

(2) QUALIFIED FOSTER CHILD.—The term "qualified foster child" means any individual who—

(A) has not attained age 19, and

(B) is living in a foster family home in which such individual was placed by—

(i) an agency of a State or political subdivision thereof, or

(ii) an organization which is licensed by a State (or political subdivision thereof) as a child-placing agency and which is described in section 501(c)(3) and exempt from tax under section 501(a).

(c) DIFFICULTY OF CARE PAYMENTS.—For purposes of this section—

(1) DIFFICULTY OF CARE PAYMENTS.—The term "difficulty of care payments" means payments to individuals which are not described in subsection (b)(1)(B)(i), and which—

(A) are compensation for providing the additional care of a qualified foster child which is—

(i) required by reason of a physical, mental, or emotional handicap of such child with respect to which the State has determined that there is a need for additional compensation, and

(ii) provided in the home of the foster parent, and

(B) are designated by the payor as compensation described in subparagraph (A).

(2) LIMITATION BASED ON NUMBER OF CHILDREN.—In the case of any foster home, difficulty of care payments for any period to which such payments relate shall not be excludable from gross income under subsection (a) to the extent such payments are made for more than 10 qualified foster children.

• 1983 (P.L. 97-473)

P.L. 97-473, §102(a):

Added Code Sec. 131. **Effective** for tax years beginning after 12-31-78.

[Sec. 132]

SEC. 132. CERTAIN FRINGE BENEFITS.

[Sec. 132(a)]

(a) EXCLUSION FROM GROSS INCOME.—Gross income shall not include any fringe benefit which qualifies as a—

(1) no-additional-cost service,

(2) qualified employee discount,

(3) working condition fringe,

(4) de minimis fringe[,]

(5) qualified transportation fringe,

(6) qualified moving expense reimbursement,

(7) qualified retirement planning services, or

(8) qualified military base realignment and closure fringe.

Amendments

• 2006, Pension Protection Act of 2006 (P.L. 109-280)

P.L. 109-280, §811, provides:

SEC. 811. PENSIONS AND INDIVIDUAL RETIREMENT ARRANGEMENT PROVISIONS OF ECONOMIC GROWTH AND TAX RELIEF RECONCILIATION ACT OF 2001 MADE PERMANENT.

Title IX of the Economic Growth and Tax Relief Reconciliation Act of 2001 [P.L. 107-16] shall not apply to the provisions of, and amendments made by, subtitles A through F of title VI [§§601-666]of such Act (relating to pension and individual retirement arrangement provisions).

• 2003, Military Family Tax Relief Act of 2003 (P.L. 108-121)

P.L. 108-121, §103(a):

Amended Code Sec. 132(a) by striking "or" at the end of paragraph (6), by striking the period at the end of paragraph (7) and inserting ", or", and by adding at the end a new paragraph (8). **Effective** for payments made after 11-11-2003.

• 2001, Economic Growth and Tax Relief Reconciliation Act of 2001 (P.L. 107-16)

P.L. 107-16, §665(a):

Amended Code Sec. 132(a) by striking "or" at the end of paragraph (5), by striking the period at the end of paragraph (6) and inserting ", or", and by adding at the end a new paragraph (7). **Effective** for years beginning after 12-31-2001.

P.L. 107-16, §901(a)-(b), provides [but see P.L. 109-280, §811, above]:

SEC. 901. SUNSET OF PROVISIONS OF ACT.

(a) IN GENERAL.—All provisions of, and amendments made by, this Act shall not apply—

(1) to taxable, plan, or limitation years beginning after December 31, 2010, or

(2) in the case of title V, to estates of decedents dying, gifts made, or generation skipping transfers, after December 31, 2010.

(b) APPLICATION OF CERTAIN LAWS.—The Internal Revenue Code of 1986 and the Employee Retirement Income Security Act of 1974 shall be applied and administered to years, estates, gifts, and transfers described in subsection (a) as if the provisions and amendments described in subsection (a) had never been enacted.

• 1993, Omnibus Budget Reconciliation Act of 1993 (P.L. 103-66)

P.L. 103-66, §13213(d)(1):

Amended Code Sec. 132(a) by striking "or" at the end of paragraph (4), by striking the period at the end of paragraph (5) and inserting ", or", and by adding at the end thereof new paragraph (6). **Effective** for reimbursements or other payments in respect of expenses incurred after 12-31-93.

• 1992, Energy Policy Act of 1992 (P.L. 102-486)

P.L. 102-486, §1911(a):

Amended Code Sec. 132(a) by striking "or" at the end of paragraph (3), by striking the period at the end of paragraph (4) and inserting ", or", and by adding at the end thereof new paragraph (5). **Effective** for benefits provided after 12-31-92.

[Sec. 132(b)]

(b) NO-ADDITIONAL-COST SERVICE DEFINED.—For purposes of this section, the term "no-additional-cost service" means any service provided by an employer to an employee for use by such employee if—

(1) such service is offered for sale to customers in the ordinary course of the line of business of the employer in which the employee is performing services, and

(2) the employer incurs no substantial additional cost (including forgone revenue) in providing such service to the employee (determined without regard to any amount paid by the employee for such service).

[Sec. 132(c)]

(c) QUALIFIED EMPLOYEE DISCOUNT DEFINED.—For purposes of this section—

(1) QUALIFIED EMPLOYEE DISCOUNT.—The term "qualified employee discount" means any employee discount with respect to qualified property or services to the extent such discount does not exceed—

(A) in the case of property, the gross profit percentage of the price at which the property is being offered by the employer to customers, or

(B) in the case of services, 20 percent of the price at which the services are being offered by the employer to customers.

(2) GROSS PROFIT PERCENTAGE.—

(A) IN GENERAL.—The term "gross profit percentage" means the percent which—

(i) the excess of the aggregate sales price of property sold by the employer to customers over the aggregate cost of such property to the employer, is of

(ii) the aggregate sale price of such property.

(B) DETERMINATION OF GROSS PROFIT PERCENTAGE.—Gross profit percentage shall be determined on the basis of—

(i) all property offered to customers in the ordinary course of the line of business of the employer in which the employee is performing services (or a reasonable classification of property selected by the employer), and

(ii) the employer's experience during a representative period.

(3) EMPLOYEE DISCOUNT DEFINED.—The term "employee discount" means the amount by which—

(A) the price at which the property or services are provided by the employer to an employee for use by such employee, is less than

(B) the price at which such property or services are being offered by the employer to customers.

(4) QUALIFIED PROPERTY OR SERVICES.—The term "qualified property or services" means any property (other than real property and other than personal property of a kind held for investment) or services which are offered for sale to customers in the ordinary course of the line of business of the employer in which the employee is performing services.

Amendments

• 1986, Tax Reform Act of 1986 (P.L. 99-514)

P.L. 99-514, §1853(a)(2):

Amended Code Sec. 132(c)(3)(A) by striking out "are provided to the employee by the employer" and inserting in lieu thereof "are provided by the employer to an employee for use by such employee". **Effective** as if included in the provision of P.L. 98-369 to which it relates.

[Sec. 132(d)]

(d) WORKING CONDITION FRINGE DEFINED.—For purposes of this section, the term "working condition fringe" means any property or services provided to an employee of the employer to the extent that, if the employee paid for such property or services, such payment would be allowable as a deduction under section 162 or 167.

[Sec. 132(e)]

(e) DE MINIMIS FRINGE DEFINED.—For purposes of this section—

(1) IN GENERAL.—The term "de minimis fringe" means any property or service the value of which is (after taking into account the frequency with which similar fringes are provided by the employer to the employer's employees) so small as to make accounting for it unreasonable or administratively impracticable.

(2) TREATMENT OF CERTAIN EATING FACILITIES.—The operation by an employer of any eating facility for employees shall be treated as a de minimis fringe if—

(A) such facility is located on or near the business premises of the employer, and

(B) revenue derived from such facility normally equals or exceeds the direct operating costs of such facility.

The preceding sentence shall apply with respect to any highly compensated employee only if access to the facility is available on substantially the same terms to each member of a group of employees which is defined under a reasonable classification set up by the employer which does not discriminate in favor of highly compensated employees. For purposes of subparagraph (B), an employee entitled under section 119 to exclude the value of a meal provided at such facility shall be treated as having paid an amount for such meal equal to the direct operating costs of the facility attributable to such meal.

Amendments

• 1997, Taxpayer Relief Act of 1997 (P.L. 105-34)

P.L. 105-34, §970(a):

Amended Code Sec. 132(e)(2) by adding at the end a new sentence. **Effective** for tax years beginning after 12-31-97.

• 1986, Tax Reform Act of 1986 (P.L. 99-514)

P.L. 99-514, §1114(b)(5)(A)(i)-(ii):

Amended Code Sec. 132(e)(2) by striking out "officer, owner, or", and by striking out "officers, owners, or". **Effective** for years beginning after 12-31-87. Prior to amendment, Code Sec. 132(e)(2) read as follows:

(2) TREATMENT OF CERTAIN EATING FACILITIES.—The operation by an employer of any eating facility for employees shall be treated as a de minimis fringe if—

(A) such facility is located on or near the business premises of the employer, and

(B) revenue derived from such facility normally equals or exceeds the direct operating costs of such facility.

The preceding sentence shall apply with respect to any officer, owner, or highly compensated employee only if access to the facility is available on substantially the same terms to each member of a group of employees which is defined under a reasonable classification set up by the employer which does not discriminate in favor of officers, owners, or highly compensated employees.

[Sec. 132(f)]

(f) QUALIFIED TRANSPORTATION FRINGE.—

(1) IN GENERAL.—For purposes of this section, the term "qualified transportation fringe" means any of the following provided by an employer to an employee:

(A) Transportation in a commuter highway vehicle if such transportation is in connection with travel between the employee's residence and place of employment.

(B) Any transit pass.

(C) Qualified parking.

(D) Any qualified bicycle commuting reimbursement.

(2) LIMITATION ON EXCLUSION.—The amount of the fringe benefits which are provided by an employer to any employee and which may be excluded from gross income under subsection (a)(5) shall not exceed—

(A) $100 per month in the case of the aggregate of the benefits described in subparagraphs (A) and (B) of paragraph (1),

(B) $175 per month in the case of qualified parking, and

(C) the applicable annual limitation in the case of any qualified bicycle commuting reimbursement.

In the case of any month beginning on or after the date of the enactment of this sentence and before January 1, 2011, subparagraph (A) shall be applied as if the dollar amount therein were the same as the dollar amount in effect for such month under subparagraph (B).

(3) CASH REIMBURSEMENTS.—For purposes of this subsection, the term "qualified transportation fringe" includes a cash reimbursement by an employer to an employee for a benefit described in paragraph (1). The preceding sentence shall apply to a cash reimbursement for any transit pass only if a voucher or similar item which may be exchanged only for a transit pass is not readily available for direct distribution by the employer to the employee.

(4) NO CONSTRUCTIVE RECEIPT.—No amount shall be included in the gross income of an employee solely because the employee may choose between any qualified transportation fringe (other than a qualified bicycle commuting reimbursement) and compensation which would otherwise be includible in gross income of such employee.

(5) DEFINITIONS.—For purposes of this subsection—

(A) TRANSIT PASS.—The term "transit pass" means any pass, token, farecard, voucher, or similar item entitling a person to transportation (or transportation at a reduced price) if such transportation is—

(i) on mass transit facilities (whether or not publicly owned), or

(ii) provided by any person in the business of transporting persons for compensation or hire if such transportation is provided in a vehicle meeting the requirements of subparagraph (B)(i).

(B) COMMUTER HIGHWAY VEHICLE.—The term "commuter highway vehicle" means any highway vehicle—

(i) the seating capacity of which is at least 6 adults (not including the driver), and

(ii) at least 80 percent of the mileage use of which can reasonably be expected to be—

(I) for purposes of transporting employees in connection with travel between their residences and their place of employment, and

(II) on trips during which the number of employees transported for such purposes is at least 1/2 of the adult seating capacity of such vehicle (not including the driver).

(C) QUALIFIED PARKING.—The term "qualified parking" means parking provided to an employee on or near the business premises of the employer or on or near a location from which the employee commutes to work by transportation described in subparagraph (A), in a commuter highway vehicle, or by carpool. Such term shall not include any parking on or near property used by the employee for residential purposes.

(D) TRANSPORTATION PROVIDED BY EMPLOYER.—Transportation referred to in paragraph (1)(A) shall be considered to be provided by an employer if such transportation is furnished in a commuter highway vehicle operated by or for the employer.

(E) EMPLOYEE.—For purposes of this subsection, the term "employee" does not include an individual who is an employee within the meaning of section 401(c)(1).

(F) DEFINITIONS RELATED TO BICYCLE COMMUTING REIMBURSEMENT.—

(i) QUALIFIED BICYCLE COMMUTING REIMBURSEMENT.—The term "qualified bicycle commuting reimbursement" means, with respect to any calendar year, any employer reimbursement during the 15-month period beginning with the first day of such calendar year for reasonable expenses incurred by the employee during such calendar year for the purchase of a bicycle and bicycle improvements, repair, and storage, if such bicycle is regularly used for travel between the employee's residence and place of employment.

(ii) APPLICABLE ANNUAL LIMITATION.—The term "applicable annual limitation" means, with respect to any employee for any calendar year, the product of $20 multiplied by the number of qualified bicycle commuting months during such year.

(iii) QUALIFIED BICYCLE COMMUTING MONTH.—The term "qualified bicycle commuting month" means, with respect to any employee, any month during which such employee—

(I) regularly uses the bicycle for a substantial portion of the travel between the employee's residence and place of employment, and

(II) does not receive any benefit described in subparagraph (A), (B), or (C) of paragraph (1).

(6) INFLATION ADJUSTMENT.—

(A) IN GENERAL.—In the case of any taxable year beginning in a calendar year after 1999, the dollar amounts contained in subparagraphs (A) and (B) of paragraph (2) shall be increased by an amount equal to—

(i) such dollar amount, multiplied by

(ii) the cost-of-living adjustment determined under section 1(f)(3) for the calendar year in which the taxable year begins, by substituting "calendar year 1998" for "calendar year 1992".

In the case of any taxable year beginning in a calendar year after 2002, clause (ii) shall be applied by substituting "calendar year 2001" for "calendar year 1998" for purposes of adjusting the dollar amount contained in paragraph (2)(A).

(B) ROUNDING.—If any increase determined under subparagraph (A) is not a multiple of $5, such increase shall be rounded to the next lowest multiple of $5.

(7) COORDINATION WITH OTHER PROVISIONS.—For purposes of this section, the terms "working condition fringe" and "de minimis fringe" shall not include any qualified transportation fringe (determined without regard to paragraph (2)).

Amendments

• 2009, American Recovery and Reinvestment Tax Act of 2009 (P.L. 111-5)

P.L. 111-5, §1151(a):

Amended Code Sec. 132(f)(2) by adding at the end a new flush sentence. **Effective** for months beginning on or after 2-17-2009.

• 2008, Energy Improvement and Extension Act of 2008 (P.L. 110-343)

P.L. 110-343, Division B, §211(a):

Amended Code Sec. 132(f)(1) by adding at the end a new subparagraph (D). **Effective** for tax years beginning after 12-31-2008.

P.L. 110-343, Division B, §211(b):

Amended Code Sec. 132(f)(2) by striking "and" at the end of subparagraph (A), by striking the period at the end of subparagraph (B) and inserting ", and", and by adding at the end a new subparagraph (C). **Effective** for tax years beginning after 12-31-2008.

P.L. 110-343, Division B, §211(c):

Amended Code Sec. 132(f)(5) by adding at the end a new subparagraph (F). **Effective** for tax years beginning after 12-31-2008.

P.L. 110-343, Division B, §211(d):

Amended Code Sec. 132(f)(4) by inserting "(other than a qualified bicycle commuting reimbursement)" after "qualified transportation fringe". **Effective** for tax years beginning after 12-31-2008.

• 1998, Transportation Equity Act for the 21st Century (P.L. 105-178)

P.L. 105-178, §9010(a)(1):

Amended Code Sec. 132(f)(4). **Effective** for tax years beginning after 12-31-97. Prior to amendment, Code Sec. 132(f)(4) read as follows:

(4) BENEFIT NOT IN LIEU OF COMPENSATION.—Subsection (a)(5) shall not apply to any qualified transportation fringe unless such benefit is provided in addition to (and not in lieu of) any compensation otherwise payable to the employee. This paragraph shall not apply to any qualified parking provided in lieu of compensation which otherwise would have been includible in gross income of the employee, and no amount shall be included in the gross income of the employee solely because the employee may choose between the qualified parking and compensation.

P.L. 105-178, §9010(b)(1):

Amended Code Sec. 132(f)(6). **Effective** for tax years beginning after 12-31-98. Prior to amendment, Code Sec. 132(f)(6) read as follows:

(6) INFLATION ADJUSTMENT.—In the case of any taxable year beginning in a calendar year after 1993, the dollar amounts contained in paragraph (2)(A) and (B) shall be increased by an amount equal to—

(A) such dollar amount, multiplied by

(B) the cost-of-living adjustment determined under section 1(f)(3) for the calendar year in which the taxable year begins.

If any increase determined under the preceding sentence is not a multiple of $5, such increase shall be rounded to the next lowest multiple of $5.

P.L. 105-178, §9010(b)(2)(A)-(B):

Amended Code Sec. 132(f)(2) by striking "$60" in subparagraph (A) and inserting "$65", and by striking "$155" in subparagraph (B) and inserting "$175". **Effective** for tax years beginning after 12-31-98.

P.L. 105-178, §9010(c)(1):

Amended Code Sec. 132(f)(2)(A) by striking "$65" and inserting "$100". **Effective** for tax years beginning after 12-31-2001.

P.L. 105-178, §9010(c)(2):

Amended Code Sec. 132(f)(6)(A) by adding at the end a new flush sentence. **Effective** for tax years beginning after 12-31-2001.

• 1997, Taxpayer Relief Act of 1997 (P.L. 105-34)

P.L. 105-34, §1072(a):

Amended Code Sec. 132(f)(4) by adding at the end a new sentence. **Effective** for tax years beginning after 12-31-97.

• 1993, Omnibus Budget Reconciliation Act of 1993 (P.L. 103-66)

P.L. 103-66, §13201(b)(3)(F):

Amended Code Sec. 132(f)(6)(B) by striking ", determined by substituting" and all that follows down through the period at the end thereof and inserting a period. **Effective** for tax years beginning after 12-31-92. Prior to amendment, Code Sec. 132(f)(6)(B) read as follows:

(B) the cost-of-living adjustment determined under section 1(f)(3) for the calendar year in which the taxable year begins, determined by substituting "calendar year 1992" for "calendar year 1989" in subparagraph (B) thereof.

• 1992, Energy Policy Act of 1992 (P.L. 102-486)

P.L. 102-486, §1911(b):

Amended Code Sec. 132 by redesignating subsections (f), (g), (h), (i), (j), and (k) as subsections (g), (h), (i), (j), (k), and (l), respectively, and by inserting after subsection (e) new subsection (f). **Effective** for benefits provided after 12-31-92.

[Sec. 132(g)]

(g) QUALIFIED MOVING EXPENSE REIMBURSEMENT.—For purposes of this section, the term "qualified moving expense reimbursement" means any amount received (directly or indirectly) by an individual from an employer as a payment for (or a reimbursement of) expenses which would be deductible as moving expenses under section 217 if directly paid or incurred by the individual. Such term shall not include any payment for (or reimbursement of) an expense actually deducted by the individual in a prior taxable year.

Amendments

• 1993, Omnibus Budget Reconciliation Act of 1993 (P.L. 103-66)

P.L. 103-66, §13213(d)(2):

Amended Code Sec. 132 by redesignating subsections (g), (h), (i), (j), (k), and (l), as subsections (h), (i), (j), (k), (l), and (m), respectively, and by inserting after subsection (f) a new subsection (g). **Effective** for reimbursements or other payments for expenses incurred after 12-31-93.

[Sec. 132(h)]

(h) CERTAIN INDIVIDUALS TREATED AS EMPLOYEES FOR PURPOSES OF SUBSECTIONS (a)(1) AND (2).—For purposes of paragraphs (1) and (2) of subsection (a)—

(1) RETIRED AND DISABLED EMPLOYEES AND SURVIVING SPOUSE OF EMPLOYEE TREATED AS EMPLOYEE.—With respect to a line of business of an employer, the term "employee" includes—

(A) any individual who was formerly employed by such employer in such line of business and who separated from service with such employer in such line of business by reason of retirement or disability, and

(B) any widow or widower of any individual who died while employed by such employer in such line of business or while an employee within the meaning of subparagraph (A).

(2) SPOUSE AND DEPENDENT CHILDREN.—

(A) IN GENERAL.—Any use by the spouse or a dependent child of the employee shall be treated as use by the employee.

(B) DEPENDENT CHILD.—For purposes of subparagraph (A), the term "dependent child" means any child (as defined in section 152(f)(1)) of the employee—

(i) who is a dependent of the employee, or

(ii) both of whose parents are deceased and who has not attained age 25.

For purposes of the preceding sentence, any child to whom section 152(e) applies shall be treated as the dependent of both parents.

(3) SPECIAL RULE FOR PARENTS IN THE CASE OF AIR TRANSPORTATION.—Any use of air transportation by a parent of an employee (determined without regard to paragraph (1)(B)) shall be treated as use by the employee.

Amendments

• 2004, Working Families Tax Relief Act of 2004 (P.L. 108-311)

P.L. 108-311, §207(13):

Amended the first sentence of Code Sec. 132(h)(2)(B) by striking "151(c)(3)" and inserting "152(f)(1)". **Effective** for tax years beginning after 12-31-2004.

• 1993, Omnibus Budget Reconciliation Act of 1993 (P.L. 103-66)

P.L. 103-66, §13213(d)(2):

Amended Code Sec. 132 by redesignating subsection (g) as subsection (h). **Effective** for reimbursements or other payments for expenses incurred after 12-31-93.

• 1992, Energy Policy Act of 1992 (P.L. 102-486)

P.L. 102-486, §1911(b):

Amended Code Sec. 132 by redesignating subsection (f) as subsection (g). **Effective** for benefits provided after 12-31-92.

• 1989, Omnibus Budget Reconciliation Act of 1989 (P.L. 101-239)

P.L. 101-239, §7841(d)(19):

Amended Code Sec. 132(f)(2)(B) by striking "section 151(e)(3)" and inserting "section 151(c)(3)". **Effective** 12-19-89.

• 1986, Tax Reform Act of 1986 (P.L. 99-514)

P.L. 99-514, §1853(a)(1):

Amended Code Sec. 132(f)(2)(B)(ii) by striking out "are deceased" and inserting in lieu thereof "are deceased and who has not attained age 25". **Effective** as if included in the provision of P.L. 98-369 to which it relates.

• 1986, Consolidated Omnibus Budget Reconciliation Act of 1985 (P.L. 99-272)

P.L. 99-272, §13207(a)(1):

Amended Code Sec. 132(f) by adding at the end thereof new paragraph (3). **Effective** 1-1-85. For a transitional rule, see Act Sec. 13207(c) in the amendment notes following Code Sec. 132(j).

[Sec. 132(i)]

(i) RECIPROCAL AGREEMENTS.—For purposes of paragraph (1) of subsection (a), any service provided by an employer to an employee of another employer shall be treated as provided by the employer of such employee if—

(1) such service is provided pursuant to a written agreement between such employers, and

(2) neither of such employers incurs any substantial additional costs (including foregone revenue) in providing such service or pursuant to such agreement.

Amendments

• 1993, Omnibus Budget Reconciliation Act of 1993 (P.L. 103-66)

P.L. 103-66, §13213(d)(2):

Amended Code Sec. 132 by redesignating subsection (h) as subsection (i). **Effective** for reimbursements or other payments for expenses incurred after 12-31-93.

• 1992, Energy Policy Act of 1992 (P.L. 102-486)

P.L. 102-486, §1911(b):

Amended Code Sec. 132 by redesignating subsection (g) as subsection (h). **Effective** for benefits provided after 12-31-92.

• 1989 (P.L. 101-136)

P.L. 101-136, §528, provides:

SEC. 528. No monies appropriated by this Act may be used to implement or enforce section 1151 of the Tax Reform Act of 1986 or the amendments made by such section.

• 1986, Tax Reform Act of 1986 (P.L. 99-514)

P.L. 99-514, §1151(e)(2)(A):

Amended Code Sec. 132(g). For the **effective** date, see Act Sec. 1151(k) following Code Sec. 89. Prior to amendment, Code Sec. 132(g) read as follows:

(g) SPECIAL RULES RELATING TO EMPLOYER.—For purposes of this section—

(1) CONTROLLED GROUPS, ETC.—All employees treated as employed by a single employer under subsection (b), (c), or (m) of section 414 shall be treated as employed by a single employer for purposes of this section.

(2) RECIPROCAL AGREEMENTS.—For purposes of paragraph (1) of subsection (a), any service provided by an employer to an employee of another employer shall be treated as provided by the employer of such employee if—

(A) such service is provided pursuant to a written agreement between such employers, and

(B) neither of such employers incurs any substantial additional cost (including forgone revenue) in providing such service or pursuant to such agreement.

[Sec. 132(j)]

(j) SPECIAL RULES.—

(1) EXCLUSIONS UNDER SUBSECTION (a)(1) AND (2) APPLY TO HIGHLY COMPENSATED EMPLOYEES ONLY IF NO DISCRIMINATION.—Paragraphs (1) and (2) of subsection (a) shall apply with respect to any fringe benefit described therein provided with respect to any highly compensated employee only if such fringe benefit is available on substantially the same terms to each member of a group of employees which is defined under a reasonable classification set up by the employer which does not discriminate in favor of highly compensated employees.

(2) SPECIAL RULE FOR LEASED SECTIONS OF DEPARTMENT STORES.—

(A) IN GENERAL.—For purposes of paragraph (2) of subsection (a), in the case of a leased section of a department store—

(i) such section shall be treated as part of the line of business of the person operating the department store, and

(ii) employees in the leased section shall be treated as employees of the person operating the department store.

(B) LEASED SECTION OF DEPARTMENT STORE.—For purposes of subparagraph (A), a leased section of a department store is any part of a department store where over-the-counter sales of property are made under a lease or similar arrangement where it appears to the general public that individuals making such sales are employed by the person operating the department store.

(3) AUTO SALESMEN.—

(A) IN GENERAL.—For purposes of subsection (a)(3), qualified automobile demonstration use shall be treated as a working condition fringe.

(B) QUALIFIED AUTOMOBILE DEMONSTRATION USE.—For purposes of subparagraph (A), the term "qualified automobile demonstration use" means any use of an automobile by a full-time automobile salesman in the sales area in which the automobile dealer's sales office is located if—

(i) such use is provided primarily to facilitate the salesman's performance of services for the employer, and

(ii) there are substantial restrictions on the personal use of such automobile by such salesman.

(4) ON-PREMISES GYMS AND OTHER ATHLETIC FACILITIES.—

(A) IN GENERAL.—Gross income shall not include the value of any on-premises athletic facility provided by an employer to his employees.

(B) ON-PREMISES ATHLETIC FACILITY.—For purposes of this paragraph, the term "on-premises athletic facility" means any gym or other athletic facility—

(i) which is located on the premises of the employer,

(ii) which is operated by the employer, and

(iii) substantially all the use of which is by employees of the employer, their spouses, and their dependent children (within the meaning of subsection (h)).

(5) SPECIAL RULE FOR AFFILIATES OF AIRLINES.

(A) IN GENERAL.—If—

(i) a qualified affiliate is a member of an affiliated group another member of which operates an airline, and

(ii) employees of the qualified affiliate who are directly engaged in providing airline-related services are entitled to no-additional-cost service with respect to air transportation provided by such other member,

then, for purposes of applying paragraph (1) of subsection (a) to such no-additional-cost service provided to such employees, such qualified affiliate shall be treated as engaged in the same line of business as such other member.

(B) QUALIFIED AFFILIATE.—For purposes of this paragraph, the term "qualified affiliate" means any corporation which is predominantly engaged in airline-related services.

(C) AIRLINE-RELATED SERVICES.—For purposes of this paragraph, the term "airline-related services" means any of the following services provided in connection with air transportation:

(i) Catering.

(ii) Baggage handling.

(iii) Ticketing and reservations.

(iv) Flight planning and weather analysis.

(v) Restaurants and gift shops located at an airport.

(vi) Such other similar services provided to the airline as the Secretary may prescribe.

(D) AFFILIATED GROUP.—For purposes of this paragraph, the term "affiliated group" has the meaning given such term by section 1504(a).

(6) HIGHLY COMPENSATED EMPLOYEE.—For purposes of this section, the term "highly compensated employee" has the meaning given such term by section 414(q).

(7) AIR CARGO.—For purposes of subsection (b), the transportation of cargo by air and the transportation of passengers by air shall be treated as the same service.

(8) APPLICATION OF SECTION TO OTHERWISE TAXABLE EDUCATIONAL OR TRAINING BENEFITS.—Amounts paid or expenses incurred by the employer for education or training provided to the employee which are not excludable from gross income under section 127 shall be excluded from gross income under this section if (and only if) such amounts or expenses are a working condition fringe.

Amendments

• 1993, Omnibus Budget Reconciliation Act of 1993 (P.L. 103-66)

P.L. 103-66, §13101(b):

Amended Code Sec. 132(i)(8). **Effective** for tax years beginning after 12-31-88. Prior to amendment, Code Sec. 132(i)(8) read as follows:

(8) APPLICATION OF SECTION TO OTHERWISE TAXABLE EMPLOYER-PROVIDED EDUCATIONAL ASSISTANCE.—Amounts which would be excludible from gross income under section 127 but for subsection (a)(2) thereof or the last sentence of subsection (c)(1) thereof shall be excluded from gross income under this section if (and only if) such amounts are a working condition fringe.

P.L. 103-66, §13213(d)(2):

Amended Code Sec. 132 by redesignating subsection (i) as subsection (j). **Effective** for reimbursements or other payments in respect of expenses incurred after 12-31-93.

P.L. 103-66, §13213(d)(3)(B):

Amended Code Sec. 132(j)(4)(B)(iii) (as redesignated by Act Sec. 13213(d)(2)) by striking "subsection (f)" and inserting "subsection (h)". **Effective** for reimbursements or other payments in respect of expenses incurred after 12-31-93.

• 1992, Energy Policy Act of 1992 (P.L. 102-486)

P.L. 102-486, §1911(b):

Amended Code Sec. 132 by redesignating subsection (h) as subsection (i). **Effective** for benefits provided after 12-31-92.

P.L. 102-486, §1911(c):

Amended Code Sec. 132(i) (as redesignated) by striking paragraph (4) and redesignating paragraphs (5)-(9) as paragraphs (4)-(8). **Effective** for benefits provided after 12-31-92. Prior to amendment, Code Sec. 132(i)(4) read as follows:

(4) PARKING.—The term "working condition fringe" includes parking provided to an employee on or near the business premises of the employer.

• 1989, Omnibus Budget Reconciliation Act of 1989 (P.L. 101-239)

P.L. 101-239, §7101(b):

Amended Code Sec. 132(h) by adding at the end thereof a new paragraph (9). **Effective** for tax years beginning after 12-31-88.

P.L. 101-239, §7841(d)(7):

Amended Code Sec. 132(h)(1) by striking "OFFICERS, ETC.," in the heading and inserting "HIGHLY COMPENSATED EMPLOYEES". **Effective** 12-19-89.

• 1989 (P.L. 101-140)

P.L. 101-140, §203(a)(1):

Provides that Code Sec. 132(h)(1) as amended by Section 1151(g)(5) of P.L. 99-514 shall be applied as if the amendment had not been enacted.

P.L. 101-140, §203(a)(2):

Provides that Code Sec. 132(h)(1) as amended by Section 1011B(a)(31)(B)(i)-(ii) of P.L. 100-647 shall be applied as if the amendment had not been enacted. **Effective** as if included in section 1151 of P.L. 99-514. Code Sec. 132(h)(1) as amended by Act Sec. 1151(g)(5) of P.L. 99-514 and Act Sec. 1011B(a)(31)(B)(i)-(ii) of P.L. 100-647 read as follows:

(1) EXCLUSIONS UNDER SUBSECTION (a)(1) AND (2) APPLY TO OFFICERS, ETC., ONLY IF NO DISCRIMINATION.—Paragraphs (1) and (2) of subsection (A) shall apply with respect to any fringe benefit described therein provided with respect to any highly compensated employee only if such fringe benefit is available on substantially the same terms to each member of a group of employees which is defined under a reasonable classification set up by the employer which does not discriminate in favor of highly compensated employees. For purposes of this paragraph and subsection (e), there shall be excluded from consideration employees who are excluded from consideration under section 89(h).

• 1989 (P.L. 101-136)

P.L. 101-136, §528, provides:

SEC. 528. No monies appropriated by this Act may be used to implement or enforce section 1151 of the Tax Reform Act of 1986 or the amendments made by such section.

• 1988, Technical and Miscellaneous Revenue Act of 1988 (P.L. 100-647)

P.L. 100-647, §1011B(a)(31)(B)(i)-(ii):

Amended Code Sec. 132(h)(1) by striking out "may" the first place it appears and inserting in lieu thereof "shall", and by striking out "may be" the second place it appears and inserting in lieu thereof "are". **Effective** as if included in the provision of P.L. 99-514 to which it relates.

P.L. 100-647, §6066(a):

Amended Code Sec. 132(h) by adding at the end thereof new paragraph (8). **Effective** for transportation furnished after 12-31-87, in tax years ending after such date.

• 1986, Tax Reform Act of 1986 (P.L. 99-514)

P.L. 99-514, §1114(b)(5)(A)(i)-(ii):

Amended Code Sec. 132(h)(1) by striking out "officer, owner, or", and by striking out "officers, owners, or". **Effective** for years beginning after 12-31-87. Prior to amendment, Code Sec. 132(h)(1) read as follows:

(1) EXCLUSIONS UNDER SUBSECTION (a)(1) AND (2) APPLY TO OFFICERS, ETC., ONLY IF NO DISCRIMINATION.—Paragraphs (1) and (2) of subsection (a) shall apply with respect to any fringe benefit described therein provided with respect to any officer, owner, or highly compensated employee only if such fringe benefit is available on substantially the same terms to each member of a group of employees which is defined under a reasonable classification set up by the employer which does not discriminate in favor of officers, owners, or highly compensated employees.

P.L. 99-514, §1114(b)(5)(B):

Amended Code Sec. 132(h) by adding at the end thereof new paragraph (7). **Effective** for years beginning after 12-31-87.

P.L. 99-514, §1151(g)(5):

Amended Code Sec. 132(h)(1) by adding at the end thereof a new sentence. For the **effective** date, see Act Sec. 1151(k) following Code Sec. 89.

P.L. 99-514, §1899A(5):

Amended Code Sec. 132(h)(3)(B)(i) by striking out "such use in" and inserting in lieu thereof "such use is". **Effective** 10-22-86.

• 1986, Consolidated Omnibus Budget Reconciliation Act of 1985 (P.L. 99-272)

P.L. 99-272, §13207(b)(1):

Amended Code Sec. 132(h) by adding at the end thereof new paragraph (6). **Effective** 1-1-85. For a transitional rule see Act Sec. 13207(c), below.

P.L. 99-272, §13207(c), provides:

(c) TRANSITIONAL RULE FOR DETERMINATION OF LINE OF BUSINESS IN CASE OF AFFILIATED GROUP OPERATING AIRLINE.—If, as of September 12, 1984—

(1) an individual—

(A) was an employee (within the meaning of section 132 of the Internal Revenue Code of 1954, including subsection (f) thereof) of one member of an affiliated group (as defined in section 1504 of such Code), hereinafter referred to as the "first corporation", and

(B) was eligible for no-additional-cost service in the form of air transportation provided by another member of such affiliated group, hereinafter referred to as the "second corporation",

(2) at least 50 percent of the individuals performing service for the first corporation were or had been employees of, or had previously performed services for, the second corporation, and

(3) the primary business of the affiliated group was air transportation of passengers,

then, for purposes of applying paragraphs (1) and (2) of section 132(a) of the Internal Revenue Code of 1954, with respect to no-additional cost services and qualified employee discounts provided after December 31, 1984, for such individual by the second corporation, the first corporation shall be treated as engaged in the same air transportation line of business as the second corporation. For purposes of the preceding sentence, an employee of the second corporation who is performing services for the first corporation shall also be treated as en employee of the first corporation.

[Sec. 132(k)]

(k) CUSTOMERS NOT TO INCLUDE EMPLOYEES.—For purposes of this section (other than subsection (c)(2)), the term "customers" shall only include customers who are not employees.

Amendments

• 1993, Omnibus Budget Reconciliation Act of 1993 (P.L. 103-66)

P.L. 103-66, §13213(d)(2):

Amended Code Sec. 132 by redesignating subsection (j) as subsection (k). **Effective** for reimbursements or other payments in respect of expenses incurred after 12-31-93.

• 1992, Energy Policy Act of 1992 (P.L. 102-486)

P.L. 102-486, §1911(b):

Amended Code Sec. 132 by redesignating subsection (i) as subsection (j). **Effective** for benefits provided after 12-31-92.

• 1986, Tax Reform Act of 1986 (P.L. 99-514)

P.L. 99-514, §1567, provides:

SEC. 1567. CERTAIN RECORDKEEPING REQUIREMENTS.

(a) IN GENERAL.—For purposes of sections 132 and 274 of the Internal Revenue Code of 1954, use of an automobile by a special agent of the Internal Revenue Service shall be treated in the same manner as use of an automobile by an officer of any other law enforcement agency.

(b) EFFECTIVE DATE.—The provisions of this section shall take effect on January 1, 1985.

P.L. 99-514, §1853(a)(3):

Amended Code Sec. 132(i) by striking out "subsection (c)(2)(B)" and inserting in lieu thereof "subsection (c)(2)". **Effective** as if included in the provision of P.L. 98-369 to which it relates.

P.L. 99-514, §1853(e), provides:

(e) TREATMENT OF CERTAIN LEASED OPERATIONS OF DEPARTMENT STORES.—For purposes of section 132(h)(2)(B) of the Internal Revenue Code of 1954, a leased section of a department store which, in connection with the offering of beautician services, customarily makes sales of beauty aids in the ordinary course of business shall be treated as engaged in over-the-counter sales of property.

[Sec. 132(l)]

(l) SECTION NOT TO APPLY TO FRINGE BENEFITS EXPRESSLY PROVIDED FOR ELSEWHERE.—This section (other than subsections (e) and (g)) shall not apply to any fringe benefits of a type the tax treatment of which is expressly provided for in any other section of this chapter.

Amendments

• 1993, Omnibus Budget Reconciliation Act of 1993 (P.L. 103-66)

P.L. 103-66, §13213(d)(2):

Amended Code Sec. 132 by redesignating subsection (k) as subsection (l). **Effective** for reimbursements or other payments in respect of expenses incurred after 12-31-93.

P.L. 103-66, §13213(d)(3)(C):

Amended Code Sec. 132(l) (as redesignated by Act Sec. 13213(d)(2)) by striking "subsection (e)" and inserting "subsections (e) and (g)". **Effective** for reimbursements or other payments in respect of expenses incurred after 12-31-93.

• 1992, Energy Policy Act of 1992 (P.L. 102-486)

P.L. 102-486, §1911(b):

Amended Code Sec. 132 by redesignating subsection (j) as subsection (k). **Effective** for benefits provided after 12-31-92.

[Sec. 132(m)]

(m) QUALIFIED RETIREMENT PLANNING SERVICES.—

(1) IN GENERAL.—For purposes of this section, the term "qualified retirement planning services" means any retirement planning advice or information provided to an employee and his spouse by an employer maintaining a qualified employer plan.

(2) NONDISCRIMINATION RULE.—Subsection (a)(7) shall apply in the case of highly compensated employees only if such services are available on substantially the same terms to each member of the group of employees normally provided education and information regarding the employer's qualified employer plan.

(3) QUALIFIED EMPLOYER PLAN.—For purposes of this subsection, the term "qualified employer plan" means a plan, contract, pension, or account described in section 219(g)(5).

Amendments

• 2006, Pension Protection Act of 2006 (P.L. 109-280)

P.L. 109-280, §811, provides:

SEC. 811. PENSIONS AND INDIVIDUAL RETIREMENT ARRANGEMENT PROVISIONS OF ECONOMIC GROWTH AND TAX RELIEF RECONCILIATION ACT OF 2001 MADE PERMANENT.

Title IX of the Economic Growth and Tax Relief Reconciliation Act of 2001 [P.L. 107-16] shall not apply to the provisions of, and amendments made by, subtitles A through F of title VI [§§601-666]of such Act (relating to pension and individual retirement arrangement provisions).

• 2001, Economic Growth and Tax Relief Reconciliation Act of 2001 (P.L. 107-16)

P.L. 107-16, §665(b):

Amended Code Sec. 132 by redesignating subsection (m) as subsection (n) and by inserting after subsection (l) a new subsection (m). **Effective** for years beginning after 12-31-2001.

P.L. 107-16, §901(a)-(b), provides [but see P.L. 109-280, §811, above]:

SEC. 901. SUNSET OF PROVISIONS OF ACT.

(a) IN GENERAL.—All provisions of, and amendments made by, this Act shall not apply—

(1) to taxable, plan, or limitation years beginning after December 31, 2010, or

(2) in the case of title V, to estates of decedents dying, gifts made, or generation skipping transfers, after December 31, 2010.

(b) APPLICATION OF CERTAIN LAWS.—The Internal Revenue Code of 1986 and the Employee Retirement Income Security Act of 1974 shall be applied and administered to years, estates, gifts, and transfers described in subsection (a) as if the provisions and amendments described in subsection (a) had never been enacted.

[Sec. 132(n)]

(n) QUALIFIED MILITARY BASE REALIGNMENT AND CLOSURE FRINGE.—For purposes of this section—

(1) IN GENERAL.—The term "qualified military base realignment and closure fringe" means 1 or more payments under the authority of section 1013 of the Demonstration Cities and Metropolitan Development Act of 1966 (42 U.S.C. 3374) (as in effect on the date of the enactment of the American Recovery and Reinvestment Tax Act of 2009).

(2) LIMITATION.—With respect to any property, such term shall not include any payment referred to in paragraph (1) to the extent that the sum of all of such payments related to such property exceeds the maximum amount described in subsection (c) of such section (as in effect on such date).

Amendments

• 2009, Worker, Homeownership, and Business Assistance Act of 2009 (P.L. 111-92)

P.L. 111-92, §14(a)(1)-(2):

Amended Code Sec. 132(n) in subparagraph (1) by striking "this subsection) to offset the adverse effects on housing values as a result of a military base realignment or closure" and inserting "the American Recovery and Reinvestment Tax Act of 2009)", and in subparagraph (2) by striking "clause (1) of" before "subsection (c)". **Effective** for payments made after 2-17-2009.

• 2003, Military Family Tax Relief Act of 2003 (P.L. 108-121)

P.L. 108-121, §103(b):

Amended Code Sec. 132 by redesignating subsection (n) as subsection (o) and by inserting after subsection (m) a new subsection (n). **Effective** for payments made after 11-11-2003.

[Sec. 132(o)]

(o) REGULATIONS.—The Secretary shall prescribe such regulations as may be necessary or appropriate to carry out the purposes of this section.

Amendments

• 2006, Pension Protection Act of 2006 (P.L. 109-280)

P.L. 109-280, §811, provides:

SEC. 811. PENSIONS AND INDIVIDUAL RETIREMENT ARRANGEMENT PROVISIONS OF ECONOMIC GROWTH AND TAX RELIEF RECONCILIATION ACT OF 2001 MADE PERMANENT.

Title IX of the Economic Growth and Tax Relief Reconciliation Act of 2001 [P.L. 107-16] shall not apply to the provisions of, and amendments made by, subtitles A through F of title VI [§§601-666]of such Act (relating to pension and individual retirement arrangement provisions).

• 2003, Military Family Tax Relief Act of 2003 (P.L. 108-121)

P.L. 108-121, §103(b):

Amended Code Sec. 132 by redesignating subsection (n) as subsection (o). **Effective** for payments made after 11-11-2003.

• 2001, Economic Growth and Tax Relief Reconciliation Act of 2001 (P.L. 107-16)

P.L. 107-16, §665(b):

Amended Code Sec. 132 by redesignating subsection (m) as subsection (n). **Effective** for years beginning after 12-31-2001.

P.L. 107-16, §901(a)-(b), provides [but see P.L. 109-280, §811, above]:

SEC. 901. SUNSET OF PROVISIONS OF ACT.

(a) IN GENERAL.—All provisions of, and amendments made by, this Act shall not apply—

(1) to taxable, plan, or limitation years beginning after December 31, 2010, or

(2) in the case of title V, to estates of decedents dying, gifts made, or generation skipping transfers, after December 31, 2010.

(b) APPLICATION OF CERTAIN LAWS.—The Internal Revenue Code of 1986 and the Employee Retirement Income Security Act of 1974 shall be applied and administered to years, estates, gifts, and transfers described in subsection (a) as if the provisions and amendments described in subsection (a) had never been enacted.

• 1993, Omnibus Budget Reconciliation Act of 1993 (P.L. 103-66)

P.L. 103-66, §13213(d)(2):

Amended Code Sec. 132 by redesignating subsection (l) as subsection (m). **Effective** for reimbursements or other payments in respect of expenses incurred after 12-31-93.

• 1992, Energy Policy Act of 1992 (P.L. 102-486)

P.L. 102-486, §1911(b):

Amended Code Sec. 132 by redesignating subsection (k) as subsection (l). **Effective** for benefits provided after 12-31-92.

• 1984, Deficit Reduction Act of 1984 (P.L. 98-369)

P.L. 98-369, §531(a)(1):

Redesignated Code Sec. 132 as Code Sec. 133 and added new Code Sec. 132. **Effective** 1-1-85.

P.L. 98-369, §531(f)-(g) (as amended by P.L. 99-272, §13207(d)), provides:

(f) DETERMINATION OF LINE OF BUSINESS IN CASE OF AFFILIATED GROUP OPERATING RETAIL DEPARTMENT STORES.—If—

(1) as of October 5, 1983, the employees of one member of an affiliated group (as defined in section 1504 of the Internal Revenue Code of 1954 without regard to subsections (b)(2) and (b)(4) thereof) were entitled to employee discounts at the retail department stores operated by another member of such affiliated group, and

(2) the primary business of the affiliated group is the operation of retail department stores,

then, for purpose of applying section 132(a)(2) of the Internal Revenue Code of 1954, with respect to discounts provided for such employees at the retail department stores operated by such other member, the employer shall be treated as engaged in the same line of business as such other member.

(g) SPECIAL RULE FOR CERTAIN SERVICES RELATED TO AIR TRANSPORTATION.—

(1) IN GENERAL.—If—

(A) an individual performs services for a qualified air transportation organization, and

(B) such services are performed primarily for persons engaged in providing air transportation and are of the kind which (if performed on September 12, 1984) would qualify such individual for no-additional-cost services in the form of air transportation,

then, with respect to such individual, such qualified air transportation organization shall be treated as engaged in the line of business of providing air transportation.

(2) QUALIFIED AIR TRANSPORTATION ORGANIZATION.—For purposes of paragraph (1), the term `qualified air transportation organization' means any organization—

(A) if such organization (or a predecessor) was in existence on September 12, 1984,

(B) if—

(i) such organization is described in section 501(c)(6) of the Internal Revenue Code of 1954 and the membership of such organization is limited to entities engaged in the transportation by air of individuals or property for compensation or hire, or

(ii) such organization is a corporation all the stock of which is owned entirely by entities referred to in clause (i), and

(C) if such organization is operated in furtherance of the activities of its members or owners.

[Sec. 133—Repealed]

Amendments

• 1996, Small Business Job Protection Act of 1996 (P.L. 104-188)

P.L. 104-188, §1602(a):

Repealed Code Sec. 133. For the **effective** date, see Act Sec. 1602(c), below.

P.L. 104-188, §1602(c), provides:

(c) EFFECTIVE DATE.—

(1) IN GENERAL.—The amendments made by this section shall apply to loans made after the date of the enactment of this Act.

(2) REFINANCINGS.—The amendments made by this section shall not apply to loans made after the date of the enactment of this Act to refinance securities acquisition loans (determined without regard to section 133(b)(1)(B) of the Internal Revenue Code of 1986, as in effect on the day before the date of the enactment of this Act) made on or before such date or to refinance loans described in this paragraph if—

(A) the refinancing loans meet the requirements of section 133 of such Code (as so in effect),

(B) immediately after the refinancing the principal amount of the loan resulting from the refinancing does not exceed the principal amount of the refinanced loan (immediately before the refinancing), and

(C) the term of such refinancing loan does not extend beyond the last day of the term of the original securities acquisition loan.

For purposes of this paragraph, the term "securities acquisition loan" includes a loan from a corporation to an employee stock ownership plan described in section 133(b)(3) of such Code (as so in effect).

(3) EXCEPTION.—Any loan made pursuant to a binding written contract in effect before June 10, 1996, and at all times thereafter before such loan is made, shall be treated for purposes of paragraphs (1) and (2) as a loan made on or before the date of the enactment of this Act.

Prior to repeal, Code Sec. 133 read as follows:

SEC. 133. INTEREST ON CERTAIN LOANS USED TO ACQUIRE EMPLOYER SECURITIES.

[Sec. 133(a)]

(a) IN GENERAL.—Gross income does not include 50 percent of the interest received by—

(1) a bank (within the meaning of section 581),

(2) an insurance company to which subchapter L applies,

(3) a corporation actively engaged in the business of lending money, or

(4) a regulated investment company (as defined in section 851),

with respect to a securities acquisition loan.

Amendments

• 1986, Tax Reform Act of 1986 (P.L. 99-514)

P.L. 99-514, §1173(b)(1)(A):

Amended Code Sec. 133(a) by striking out "or" at the end of paragraph (2), by inserting "or" at the end of paragraph (3), and by adding at the end thereof new paragraph (4). For the **effective** date, see Act Sec. 1173(c)(2) following Code Sec. 133(b).

[Sec. 133(b)]

(b) SECURITIES ACQUISITION LOAN.—

(1) IN GENERAL.—For purposes of this section, the term "securities acquisition loan" means—

(A) any loan to a corporation or to an employee stock ownership plan to the extent that the proceeds are used to acquire employer securities for the plan, or

(B) any loan to a corporation to the extent that, within 30 days, employer securities are transferred to the plan in an amount equal to the proceeds of such loan and such securities are allocable to accounts of plan participants within 1 year of the date of such loan.

For purposes of this paragraph, the term "employer securities" has the meaning given such term by section 409(l). The term "securities acquisition loan" shall not include a loan with a term greater than 15 years.

(2) LOANS BETWEEN RELATED PERSONS.—The term "securities acquisition loan" shall not include—

(A) any loan made between corporations which are members of the same controlled group of corporations, or

(B) any loan made between an employee stock ownership plan and any person that is—

(i) the employer of any employees who are covered by the plan; or

(ii) a member of a controlled group of corporations which includes such employer.

For purposes of this paragraph, subparagraphs (A) and (B) shall not apply to any loan which, but for such subparagraphs, would be a securities acquisition loan if such loan was not originated by the employer of any employees who are covered by the plan or by any member of the controlled group of corporations which includes such employer, except that this section shall not apply to any interest received on such loan during such time as such loan is held by such employer (or any member of such controlled group).

(3) TERMS APPLICABLE TO CERTAIN SECURITIES ACQUISITION LOANS.—A loan to a corporation shall not fail to be treated as a securities acquisition loan merely because the proceeds of such loan are lent to any employee stock ownership plan sponsored by such corporation (or by any member of the controlled group of corporations which includes such corporation) if such loan includes—

(A) repayment terms which are substantially similar to the terms of the loan of such corporation from a lender described in subsection (a), or

(B) repayment terms providing for more rapid repayment of principal or interest on such loan, but only if allocations under the plan attributable to such repayment do not discriminate in favor of highly compensated employees (within the meaning of section 414(q)).

(4) CONTROLLED GROUP OF CORPORATIONS.—For purposes of this paragraph, the term "controlled group of corporations" has the meaning given such term by section 409(l)(4).

(5) TREATMENT OF REFINANCINGS.—The term "securities acquisition loan" shall include any loan which—

(A) is (or is part of a series of loans) used to refinance a loan described in subparagraph (A) or (B) of paragraph (1), and

(B) meets the requirements of paragraphs (2) and (3).

(6) PLAN MUST HOLD MORE THAN 50 PERCENT OF STOCK AFTER ACQUISITION OR TRANSFER.—

(A) IN GENERAL.—A loan shall not be treated as a securities acquisition loan for purposes of this section unless, immediately after the acquisition or transfer referred to in subparagraph (A) or (B) of paragraph (1), respectively, the employee stock ownership plan owns more than 50 percent of—

(i) each class of outstanding stock of the corporation issuing the employer securities, or

(ii) the total value of all outstanding stock of the corporation.

(B) FAILURE TO RETAIN MINIMUM STOCK INTEREST.—

(i) IN GENERAL.—Subsection (a) shall not apply to any interest received with respect to a securities acquisition loan which is allocable to any period during which the employee stock ownership plan does not own stock meeting the requirements of subparagraph (A).

(ii) EXCEPTION.—To the extent provided by the Secretary, clause (i) shall not apply to any period if, within 90 days of the first date on which the failure occurred (or such longer period not in excess of 180 days as the Secretary may prescribe), the plan acquires stock which results in its meeting the requirements of subparagraph (A).

(C) STOCK.—For purposes of subparagraph (A)—

(i) IN GENERAL.—The term "stock" means stock other than stock described in section 1504(a)(4).

(ii) TREATMENT OF CERTAIN RIGHTS.—The Secretary may provide that warrants, options, contracts to acquire stock, convertible debt interests and other similar interests be treated as stock for 1 or more purposes under subparagraph (A).

(D) AGGREGATION RULE.—For purposes of determining whether the requirements of subparagraph (A) are met, an employee stock ownership plan shall be treated as owning stock in the corporation issuing the employer securities which is held by any other employee stock ownership plan which is maintained by—

(i) the employer maintaining the plan, or

(ii) any member of a controlled group of corporations (within the meaning of section 409(l)(4)) of which the employer described in clause (i) is a member.

(7) VOTING RIGHTS OF EMPLOYER SECURITIES.—A loan shall not be treated as a securities acquisition loan for purposes of this section unless—

(A) the employee stock ownership plan meets the requirements of section 409(e)(2) with respect to all employer securities acquired by, or transferred to, the plan in connection with such loan (without regard to whether or not the employer has a registration-type class of securities), and

(B) no stock described in section 409(l)(3) is acquired by, or transferred to, the plan in connection with such loan unless—

(i) such stock has voting rights equivalent to the stock to which it may be converted, and

(ii) the requirements of subparagraph (A) are met with respect to such voting rights.

Amendments

• 1989, Omnibus Budget Reconciliation Act of 1989 (P.L. 101-239)

P.L. 101-239, §7301(a):

Amended Code Sec. 133(b) by adding at the end thereof a new paragraph (6). **Effective** for loans made after 7-10-89. For special rules, see Act Sec. 7301(f)(2)-(6), below.

P.L. 101-239, §7301(b):

Amended Code Sec. 133(b)(1) by adding at the end thereof a new sentence. **Effective** for loans made after 7-10-89. For special rules, see Act Sec. 7301(f)(2)-(6), below.

P.L. 101-239, §7301(c):

Amended Code Sec. 133(b), as amended by subsection (a), by adding at the end thereof a new paragraph (7). **Effective** for loans made after 7-10-89. For special rules, see Act Sec. 7301(f)(2)-(6), below.

P.L. 101-239, §7301(f)(2)-(6), provides:

(2) BINDING COMMITMENT EXCEPTIONS.—

(A) The amendments made by this section shall not apply to any loan—

(i) which is made pursuant to a binding written commitment in effect on June 6, 1989, and at all times thereafter before such loan is made, or

(ii) to the extent that the proceeds of such loan are used to acquire employer securities pursuant to a written binding contract (or tender offer registered with the Securities and Exchange Commission) in effect on June 6, 1989, and at all times thereafter before such securities are acquired.

(B) The amendments made by this section shall not apply to any loan to which subparagraph (A) does not apply which is made pursuant to a binding written commitment in effect on July 10, 1989, and at all times thereafter before such loan is made. The preceding sentence shall only apply to the extent that the proceeds of such loan are used to acquire employer securities pursuant to a written binding contract (or tender offer registered with the Securities and Exchange Commission) in effect on July 10, 1989, and at all times thereafter before such securities are acquired.

(C) The amendments made by this section shall not apply to any loan made on or before July 10, 1992, pursuant to a written agreement entered into on or before July 10, 1989, if such agreement evidences the intent of the borrower on a periodic basis to enter into securities acquisition loans described in section 133(b)(1)(B) of the Internal Revenue Code of 1986 (as in effect on the day before the date of the enactment of this Act). The preceding sentence shall apply only if one or more securities acquisition loans were made to the borrower on or before July 10, 1989.

(3) REFINANCINGS.—The amendments made by this section shall not apply to loans made after July 10, 1989, to refinance securities acquisition loans (determined without regard to section 133(b)(2) of the Internal Revenue Code of 1986) made on or before such date or to refinance loans described in this paragraph or paragraph (2), (4), or (5) if—

(A) such refinancing loans meet the requirements of such section 133 of such Code (as in effect before such amendments) applicable to such loans,

(B) immediately after the refinancing the principal amount of the loan resulting from the refinancing does not exceed the principal amount of the refinanced loan (immediately before the refinancing), and

(C) the term of such refinancing loan does not extend beyond the later of—

(i) the last day of the term of the original securities acquisition loan, or

(ii) the last day of the 7-year period beginning on the date the original securities acquisition loan was made.

For purposes of this paragraph, the term "securities acquisition loan" shall include a loan from a corporation to an employee stock ownership plan described in section 133(b)(3) of such Code.

(4) COLLECTIVE BARGAINING AGREEMENTS.—The amendments made by this section shall not apply to any loan to the extent such loan is used to acquire employer securities for an employee stock ownership plan pursuant to a collective bargaining agreement which sets forth the material terms of such employee stock ownership plan and which was agreed to on or before June 6, 1989, by one or more employers and employee representatives (and ratified on or before such date or within a reasonable period thereafter).

(5) FILINGS WITH UNITED STATES.—The amendments made by this section shall not apply to any loan the aggregate principal amount of which was specified in a filing with an agency of the United States on or before June 6, 1989, if—

(A) such filing specifies such loan is to be a securities acquisition loan for purposes of section 133 of the Internal Revenue Code of 1986 and such filing is for the registration required to permit the offering of such loan, or

(B) such filing is for the approval required in order for the employee stock ownership plan to acquire more than a certain percentage of the stock of the employer.

(6) 30-PERCENT TEST SUBSTITUTED FOR 50-PERCENT TEST IN CASE OF CERTAIN LOANS.—In the case of a loan to which the amendments made by this section apply—

(A) which is made before November 18, 1989, or

(B) with respect to which such amendments would not apply if paragraph (2)(A) were applied by substituting "November 17, 1989" for "June 6, 1989" each place it appears,

section 133(b)(6)(A) of the Internal Revenue Code of 1986 (as added by subsection (a)) shall be applied by substituting "at least 30 percent" for "more than 50 percent" and section 4978B(c)(1)(B) of such Code (as added by subsection (d)) shall be applied by substituting "less than 30 percent" for "50 percent or less". The preceding sentence shall apply to any loan which is used to refinance a loan described in such sentence if the requirements of subparagraphs (A), (B), and (C) of paragraph (3) are met with respect to the refinancing loan.

• 1988, Technical and Miscellaneous Revenue Act of 1988 (P.L. 100-647)

P.L. 100-647, §1011B(h)(2)(A)(i)-(iii):

Amended Code Sec. 133(b) by striking out "or are used to refinance such a loan," after "the plan," in paragraph (1)(A), by striking out ", except that this subparagraph shall not apply to any loan the commitment period of which exceeds 7 years" after "such loan," in paragraph (1)(B), and by adding at the end thereof new paragraph (5). **Effective** as if included in the provision of P.L. 99-514 to which it relates. For a special rule, see Act Sec. 6061, below.

P.L. 100-647, §1011B(h)(2)(B):

Amended Code Sec. 133(b)(3)(B). **Effective** as if included in the provision of P.L. 99-514 to which it relates. For a special rule, see Act Sec. 6061, below. Prior to amendment, Code Sec. 133(b)(3)(B) read as follows:

(B) repayment terms providing for more rapid repayment of principal or interest on such loan but only if—

(i) allocations under the plan attributable to such repayment do not discriminate in favor of highly compensated employees (within the meaning of section 414(q)), and

(ii) the total commitment period of such loan to the corporation does not exceed 7 years.

P.L. 100-647, §6061, as amended by P.L. 101-239, §7816(i), provides:

SEC. 6061. LOANS TO ACQUIRE EMPLOYER SECURITIES.

Notwithstanding the last sentence of section 1011B(h)(5)(A) of this Act, the amendments made by paragraphs (1) and (2) of section 1011B(h) of this Act shall not apply to any loan used to refinance a loan described in section 133(b)(1)(A) of the 1986 Code which is made before October 22, 1986, if the terms of the refinanced loan do not extend the total commitment period beyond the later of—

(1) the term of the original securities acquisition loan, or

(2) the amortization period used to determine the regular payments (prior to any final or balloon payment) applicable to the original securities acquisition loan.

• 1986, Tax Reform Act of 1986 (P.L. 99-514)

P.L. 99-514, §1173(b)(2):

Amended Code Sec. 133(b)(1). For the **effective** date, see Act Sec. 1173(c)(2), below. Prior to amendment, Code Sec. 133(b)(1) read as follows:

(1) IN GENERAL.—For purposes of this section, the term "securities acquisition loan" means any loan to a corporation, or to an employee stock ownership plan, to the extent that the proceeds are used to acquire employer securities (within the meaning of section 409(l)) for the plan.

P.L. 99-514, §1173(c)(2), as amended by P.L. 100-647, §1011B(h)(5)(B), provides:

(2) SUBSECTION (b).—

(A) The amendments made by subsection (b)(1) shall apply to loans used to acquire employer securities after the date of the enactment of this Act, including loans used to refinance loans used to acquire employer securities before such date if such loans were used to acquire employer securities after May 23, 1984.

(B) Section 133(b)(1)(A) of the Internal Revenue Code of 1986, as amended by subsection (b)(2), shall apply to any loan used (or part of a series of loans used) to refinance a loan which—

(i) was used to acquire employer securities after May 23, 1984, and

(ii) met the requirements of section 133 of the Internal Revenue Code of 1986 as in effect as of the later of—

(I) the date on which the loan was made, or

(II) July 19, 1984.

(C) Section 133(b)(1)(B) of the Internal Revenue Code of 1986, as added by subsection (b)(2), shall apply to loans incurred after the date of enactment of this Act.

P.L. 99-514, §1854(c)(2)(C):

Amended Code Sec. 133(b)(2) by adding at the end thereof a new flush sentence. **Effective** as if included in the provision of P.L. 98-369 to which it relates.

P.L. 99-514, §1854(c)(2)(D):

Amended Code Sec. 133(b) by redesignating paragraph (3) as paragraph (4) and by adding after paragraph (2) new paragraph (3). **Effective** as if included in the provision of P.L. 98-369 to which it relates.

[Sec. 133(c)]

(c) EMPLOYEE STOCK OWNERSHIP PLAN.—For purposes of this section, the term "employee stock ownership plan" has the meaning given to such term by section 4975(e)(7).

Amendments

• 1984, Deficit Reduction Act of 1984 (P.L. 98-369)

P.L. 98-369, §543(a):

Redesignated Code Sec. 133, as redesignated by Act Sec. 531(a)(1), as Code Sec. 134 and added new Code Sec. 133. **Effective** for loans used to acquire employer securities after 7-18-84.

[Sec. 133(d)]

(d) APPLICATION WITH SECTION 483 AND ORIGINAL ISSUE DISCOUNT RULES.—In applying section 483 and subpart A of part V of subchapter P to any obligation to which this section applies, appropriate adjustments shall be made to the applicable Federal rate to take into account the exclusion under subsection (a).

Amendments

• 1986, Tax Reform Act of 1986 (P.L. 99-514)

P.L. 99-514, §1854(c)(2)(A):

Amended Code Sec. 133 by adding at the end thereof new subsection (d). **Effective** as if included in the provision of P.L. 98-369 to which it relates.

[Sec. 133(e)]

(e) PERIOD TO WHICH INTEREST EXCLUSION APPLIES.—

(1) IN GENERAL.—In the case of—

(A) an original securities acquisition loan, and

(B) any securities acquisition loan (or series of such loans) used to refinance the original securities acquisition loan,

subsection (a) shall apply only to interest accruing during the excludable period with respect to the original securities acquisition loan.

(2) EXCLUDABLE PERIOD.—For purposes of this subsection, the term "excludable period" means, with respect to any original securities acquisition loan—

(A) IN GENERAL.—The 7-year period beginning on the date of such loan.

(B) LOANS DESCRIBED IN SUBSECTION (b)(1)(A).—If the term of an original securities acquisition loan described in subsection (b)(1)(A) is greater than 7 years, the term of such loan. This subparagraph shall not apply to a loan described in subsection (b)(3)(B).

(3) ORIGINAL SECURITIES ACQUISITION LOAN.—For the purposes of this subsection, the term "original securities acquisition loan" means a securities acquisition loan described in subparagraph (A) or (B) of subsection (b)(1).

Amendments

• 1988, Technical and Miscellaneous Revenue Act of 1988 (P.L. 100-647)

P.L. 100-647, §1011B(h)(1):

Amended Code Sec. 133 by adding at the end thereof new subsection (e). **Effective** as if included in the provision of P.L. 99-514 to which it relates.

[Sec. 134]

SEC. 134. CERTAIN MILITARY BENEFITS.

[Sec. 134(a)]

(a) GENERAL RULE.—Gross income shall not include any qualified military benefit.

[Sec. 134(b)]

(b) QUALIFIED MILITARY BENEFIT.—For purposes of this section—

(1) IN GENERAL.—The term "qualified military benefit" means any allowance or in-kind benefit (other than personal use of a vehicle) which—

(A) is received by any member or former member of the uniformed services of the United States or any dependent of such member by reason of such member's status or service as a member of such uniformed services, and

(B) was excludable from gross income on September 9, 1986, under any provision of law, regulation, or administrative practice which was in effect on such date (other than a provision of this title).

(2) NO OTHER BENEFIT TO BE EXCLUDABLE EXCEPT AS PROVIDED BY THIS TITLE.—Notwithstanding any other provision of law, no benefit shall be treated as a qualified military benefit unless such benefit—

(A) is a benefit described in paragraph (1), or

(B) is excludable from gross income under this title without regard to any provision of law which is not contained in this title and which is not contained in a revenue Act.

(3) LIMITATIONS ON MODIFICATIONS.—

(A) IN GENERAL.—Except as provided in subparagraphs (B) and (C) and paragraphs (4) and (5), no modification or adjustment of any qualified military benefit after September 9, 1986, shall be taken into account.

(B) EXCEPTION FOR CERTAIN ADJUSTMENTS TO CASH BENEFITS.—Subparagraph (A) shall not apply to any adjustment to any qualified military benefit payable in cash which—

(i) is pursuant to a provision of law or regulation (as in effect on September 9, 1986), and

(ii) is determined by reference to any fluctuation in cost, price, currency, or other similar index.

(C) EXCEPTION FOR DEATH GRATUITY ADJUSTMENTS MADE BY LAW.—Subparagraph (A) shall not apply to any adjustment to the amount of death gratuity payable under chapter 75 of title 10, United States Code, which is pursuant to a provision of law enacted after September 9, 1986.

(4) CLARIFICATION OF CERTAIN BENEFITS.—For purposes of paragraph (1), such term includes any dependent care assistance program (as in effect on the date of the enactment of this paragraph) for any individual described in paragraph (1)(A).

(5) TRAVEL BENEFITS UNDER OPERATION HERO MILES.—The term "qualified military benefit" includes a travel benefit provided under section 2613 of title 10, United States Code (as in effect on the date of the enactment of this paragraph).

(6) CERTAIN STATE PAYMENTS.—The term "qualified military benefit" includes any bonus payment by a State or political subdivision thereof to any member or former member of the uniformed services of the United States or any dependent of such member only by reason of such member's service in an [sic] combat zone (as defined in section 112(c)(2), determined without regard to the parenthetical).

Amendments

• 2008, Heroes Earnings Assistance and Relief Tax Act of 2008 (P.L. 110-245)

P.L. 110-245, §112(a):

Amended Code Sec. 134(b) by adding at the end a new paragraph (6). **Effective** for payments made before, on, or after 6-17-2008.

• 2004, Ronald W. Reagan National Defense Authorization Act for Fiscal Year 2005 (P.L. 108-375)

P.L. 108-375, §585(b)(1):

Amended Code Sec. 134(b) by adding at the end a new paragraph (5). **Effective** for travel benefits provided after 10-28-2004.

P.L. 108-375, §585(b)(2)(A):

Amended Code Sec. 134(b)(3)(A) by striking "paragraph (4)" and inserting "paragraphs (4) and (5)". **Effective** for travel benefits provided after 10-28-2004.

• 2003, Military Family Tax Relief Act of 2003 (P.L. 108-121)

P.L. 108-121, §102(b)(1):

Amended Code Sec. 134(b)(3) by adding at the end a new subparagraph (C). **Effective** with respect to deaths occurring after 9-10-2001.

P.L. 108-121, §102(b)(2):

Amended Code Sec. 134(b)(3)(A) by striking "subparagraph (B)" and inserting "subparagraphs (B) and (C)". **Effective** with respect to deaths occurring after 9-10-2001.

P.L. 108-121, §106(a):

Amended Code Sec. 134(b) by adding at the end a new paragraph (4). **Effective** for tax years beginning after 12-31-2002. For a special rule, see Act Sec. 106(d), below.

P.L. 108-121, §106(b)(1):

Amended Code Sec. 134(b)(3)(A), as amended by Act Sec. 102, by inserting "and paragraph (4)" after "subparagraphs (B) and (C)". **Effective** for tax years beginning after 12-31-2002. For a special rule, see Act Sec. 106(d), below.

P.L. 108-121, §106(d), provides:

(d) NO INFERENCE.—No inference may be drawn from the amendments made by this section with respect to the tax treatment of any amounts under the program described in section 134(b)(4) of the Internal Revenue Code of 1986 (as added by this section) for any taxable year beginning before January 1, 2003.

• 1988, Technical and Miscellaneous Revenue Act of 1988 (P.L. 100-647)

P.L. 100-647, §1011B(f)(1):

Amended Code Sec. 134(b)(1) by striking out "or regulation thereunder" and inserting in lieu thereof ", regulation, or administrative practice". **Effective** as if included in the provision of P.L. 99-514 to which it relates.

P.L. 100-647, §1011B(f)(2)(A):

Amended Code Sec. 134(b)(1) by inserting "(other than personal use of a vehicle)" after "in-kind benefit". **Effective** for tax years beginning after 12-31-86.

P.L. 100-647, §1011B(f)(3):

Amended Code Sec. 134(b)(3)(A) by striking out "under any provision of law or regulation described in paragraph (1)" after "September 9, 1986,". **Effective** as if included in the provision of P.L. 99-514 to which it relates.

• 1986, Tax Reform Act of 1986 (P.L. 99-514)

P.L. 99-514, §1168(a):

Amended part III of subchapter B of chapter 1 by redesignating Code Sec. 134 as Code Sec. 135 and by inserting after Code Sec. 133 new Code Sec. 134. **Effective** for tax years beginning after 12-31-84. [**effective** date changed by P.L. 100-647, §1011B(f)(4).]

[Sec. 135]

SEC. 135. INCOME FROM UNITED STATES SAVINGS BONDS USED TO PAY HIGHER EDUCATION TUITION AND FEES.

[Sec. 135(a)]

(a) GENERAL RULE.—In the case of an individual who pays qualified higher education expenses during the taxable year, no amount shall be includible in gross income by reason of the redemption during such year of any qualified United States savings bond.

[Sec. 135(b)]

(b) LIMITATIONS.—

(1) LIMITATION WHERE REDEMPTION PROCEEDS EXCEED HIGHER EDUCATION EXPENSES.—

(A) IN GENERAL.—If—

(i) the aggregate proceeds of qualified United States savings bonds redeemed by the taxpayer during the taxable year exceed

(ii) the qualified higher education expenses paid by the taxpayer during such taxable year, the amount excludable from gross income under subsection (a) shall not exceed the applicable fraction of the amount excludable from gross income under subsection (a) without regard to this subsection.

(B) APPLICABLE FRACTION.—For purposes of subparagraph (A), the term "applicable fraction" means the fraction the numerator of which is the amount described in subparagraph (A)(ii) and the denominator of which is the amount described in subparagraph (A)(i).

(2) LIMITATION BASED ON MODIFIED ADJUSTED GROSS INCOME.—

(A) IN GENERAL.—If the modified adjusted gross income of the taxpayer for the taxable year exceeds $40,000 ($60,000 in the case of a joint return), the amount which would (but for this paragraph) be excludable from gross income under subsection (a) shall be reduced (but not below zero) by the amount which bears the same ratio to the amount which would be so excludable as such excess bears to $15,000 ($30,000 in the case of a joint return).

(B) INFLATION ADJUSTMENT.—In the case of any taxable year beginning in a calendar year after 1990, the $40,000 and $60,000 amounts contained in subparagraph (A) shall be increased by an amount equal to—

(i) such dollar amount, multiplied by

(ii) the cost-of-living adjustment under section 1(f)(3) for the calendar year in which the taxable year begins, determined by substituting "calendar year 1989" for "calendar year 1992" in subparagraph (B) thereof.

(C) ROUNDING.—If any amount as adjusted under subparagraph (B) is not a multiple of $50, such amount shall be rounded to the nearest multiple of $50 (or if such amount is a multiple of $25, such amount shall be rounded to the next highest multiple of $50).

Amendments

• 1996, Small Business Job Protection Act of 1996 (P.L. 104-188)

P.L. 104-188, §1703(d):

Amended Code Sec. 135(b)(2)(B)(ii) by inserting before the period at the end thereof ", determined by substituting `calendar year 1989' for `calendar year 1992' in subparagraph (B) thereof". **Effective** as if included in the provision of P.L. 103-66 to which it relates.

• 1990, Omnibus Budget Reconciliation Act of 1990 (P.L. 101-508)

P.L. 101-508, §11101(d)(1)(E):

Amended Code Sec. 135(b)(2)(B)(ii) by striking ", determined by substituting `calendar year 1989' for `calendar year 1987' in subparagraph (B) thereof" before the period at the end. **Effective** for tax years beginning after 12-31-90.

P.L. 101-508, §11702(h)(1):

Amended Code Sec. 135(b)(2)(B) by striking "each dollar amount" and inserting "the $40,000 and $60,000 amounts". **Effective** as if included in the provision of P.L. 100-647 to which it relates.

P.L. 101-508, §11702(h)(2):

Amended Code Sec. 135(b)(2)(C) by striking "(A) or" after "under subparagraph". **Effective** as if included in the provision of P.L. 100-647 to which it relates.

[Sec. 135(c)]

(c) DEFINITIONS.—For purposes of this section—

(1) QUALIFIED UNITED STATES SAVINGS BOND.—The term "qualified United States savings bond" means any United States savings bond issued—

(A) after December 31, 1989,

(B) to an individual who has attained age 24 before the date of issuance, and

(C) at discount under section 3105 of title 31, United States Code.

(2) QUALIFIED HIGHER EDUCATION EXPENSES.—

(A) IN GENERAL.—The term "qualified higher education expenses" means tuition and fees required for the enrollment or attendance of—

(i) the taxpayer,

(ii) the taxpayer's spouse, or

(iii) any dependent of the taxpayer with respect to whom the taxpayer is allowed a deduction under section 151,

at an eligible educational institution.

(B) EXCEPTION FOR EDUCATION INVOLVING SPORTS, ETC.—Such term shall not include expenses with respect to any course or other education involving sports, games, or hobbies other than as part of a degree program.

(C) CONTRIBUTIONS TO QUALIFIED TUITION PROGRAM AND COVERDELL EDUCATION SAVINGS ACCOUNTS.—Such term shall include any contribution to a qualified tuition program (as defined in section 529) on behalf of a designated beneficiary (as defined in such section), or to a Coverdell education savings account (as defined in section 530) on behalf of an account beneficiary, who is an individual described in subparagraph (A); but there shall be no increase in the investment in the contract for purposes of applying section 72 by reason of any portion of such contribution which is not includible in gross income by reason of this subparagraph.

(3) ELIGIBLE EDUCATIONAL INSTITUTION.—The term "eligible educational institution" has the meaning given such term by section 529(e)(5).

(4) MODIFIED ADJUSTED GROSS INCOME.—The term "modified adjusted gross income" means the adjusted gross income of the taxpayer for the taxable year determined—

Caution: Code Sec. 135(c)(4)(A), below, is subject to the sunset provision of the Economic Growth and Tax Relief Reconciliation Act of 2001 (P.L. 107-16), §901. Absent Congressional action, the changes made to this provision by P.L. 107-16, or that take effect as if included in P.L. 107-16, do not apply after December 31, 2010. For more information about the sunset provision, see page XXI of the Preface to this publication and P.L. 107-16, §901, in the amendment notes. See the amendments notes for a history of amendments to this section and the effective date of each change.

(A) without regard to this section and sections 137, 199, 221, 222, 911, 931, and 933, and

(B) after the application of sections 86, 469, and 219.

Amendments

• 2006, Pension Protection Act of 2006 (P.L. 109-280)

P.L. 109-280, §1304(a), provides:

(a) PERMANENT EXTENSION OF MODIFICATIONS.—Section 901 of the Economic Growth and Tax Relief Reconciliation Act of 2001 [P.L. 107-16] (relating to sunset provisions) shall not apply to section 402 of such Act (relating to modifications to qualified tuition programs).

• 2004, American Jobs Creation Act of 2004 (P.L. 108-357)

P.L. 108-357, §102(d)(1):

Amended Code Sec. 135(c)(4)(A) by inserting "199," before "221". **Effective** for tax years beginning after 12-31-2004.

• 2001 (P.L. 107-22)

P.L. 107-22, §1(b)(1)(B):

Amended Code Sec. 135(c)(2)(C) by striking "an education individual retirement" and inserting "a Coverdell education savings". **Effective** 7-26-2001.

P.L. 107-22, §1(b)(3)(B):

Amended the heading for Code Sec. 135(c)(2)(C) by striking "EDUCATION INDIVIDUAL RETIREMENT" and inserting "COVERDELLEDUCATION SAVINGS". **E ffective** 7-26-2001.

• 2001, Economic Growth and Tax Relief Reconciliation Act of 2001 (P.L. 107-16)

P.L. 107-16, §402(a)(4)(A):

Amended Code Sec. 135(c)(2)(C) by striking "qualified State tuition" and inserting "qualified tuition". **Effective** for tax years beginning after 12-31-2001.

P.L. 107-16, §402(a)(4)(B):

Amended the heading for Code Sec. 135(c)(2)(C) by striking "QUALIFIED STATE TUITION" and inserting "QUALIFIED TUITION". **E ffective** for tax years beginning after 12-31-2001.

P.L. 107-16, §431(c)(1):

Amended Code Sec. 135(c)(4) by inserting "222," after "221,". **Effective** for payments made in tax years beginning after 12-31-2001.

P.L. 107-16, §901(a)-(b), provides [but see P.L. 109-280, §1304(a), above]:

SEC. 901. SUNSET OF PROVISIONS OF ACT.

(a) IN GENERAL.—All provisions of, and amendments made by, this Act shall not apply—

(1) to taxable, plan, or limitation years beginning after December 31, 2010, or

(2) in the case of title V, to estates of decedents dying, gifts made, or generation skipping transfers, after December 31, 2010.

(b) APPLICATION OF CERTAIN LAWS.—The Internal Revenue Code of 1986 and the Employee Retirement Income Security Act of 1974 shall be applied and administered to years, estates, gifts, and transfers described in subsection (a) as if the provisions and amendments described in subsection (a) had never been enacted.

• 1998, Tax and Trade Relief Extension Act of 1998 (P.L. 105-277)

P.L. 105-277, §4003(a)(2)(B):

Amended Code Sec. 135(c)(4)(A) by inserting "221," after "137,". **Effective** as if included in the provision of P.L. 105-34 to which it relates [generally **effective** for interest payments due and paid after 12-31-97, on any qualified education loan.—CCH].

• 1998, IRS Restructuring and Reform Act of 1998 (P.L. 105-206)

P.L. 105-206, §6004(c)(1):

Amended Code Sec. 135(c)(3). **Effective** as if included in the provision of P.L. 105-34 to which it relates [generally **effective** for tax years beginning after 12-31-97.—CCH]. Prior to amendment, Code Sec. 135(c)(3) read as follows:

(3) ELIGIBLE EDUCATIONAL INSTITUTION.—The term "eligible educational institution" means—

(A) an institution described in section 1201(a) or subparagraph (C) or (D) of section 481(a)(1) of the Higher Education Act of 1965 (as in effect on October 21, 1988), and

(B) an area vocational education school (as defined in subparagraph (C) or (D) of section 521(3) of the Carl D. Perkins Vocational Education Act) which is in any State (as defined in section 521(27) of such Act), as such sections are in effect on October 21, 1988.

P.L. 105-206, §6004(d)(9)(A)-(B):

Amended Code Sec. 135(c)(2)(C) by inserting "AND EDUCATION INDIVIDUAL RETIREMENT ACCOUNTS" in the heading after "PROGRAM" and by striking "section 529(c)(3)(A)" and inserting "section 72". **Effective** as if included in the provision of P.L. 105-34 to which it relates [generally **effective** for tax years beginning after 12-31-97.—CCH].

• 1997, Taxpayer Relief Act of 1997 (P.L. 105-34)

P.L. 105-34, §211(c):

Amended Code Sec. 135(c)(2) by adding a new subparagraph (C). **Effective** for tax years beginning after 12-31-97.

P.L. 105-34, §213(e)(2):

Amended Code Sec. 135(c)(2)(C), as added by Act Sec. 211(c), by inserting ", or to an education individual retirement account (as defined in section 530) on behalf of an account beneficiary," after "(as defined in such section)". **Effective** for tax years beginning after 12-31-97.

• 1996, Small Business Job Protection Act of 1996 (P.L. 104-188)

P.L. 104-188, §1807(c)(2):

Amended Code Sec. 135(c)(4)(A) by inserting "137," before "911". **Effective** for tax years beginning after 12-31-96.

[Sec. 135(d)]

(d) SPECIAL RULES.—

(1) ADJUSTMENT FOR CERTAIN SCHOLARSHIPS AND VETERANS BENEFITS.—The amount of qualified higher education expenses otherwise taken into account under subsection (a) with respect to the education of an individual shall be reduced (before the application of subsection (b)) by the sum of the amounts received with respect to such individual for the taxable year as—

(A) a qualified scholarship which under section 117 is not includable in gross income,

(B) an educational assistance allowance under chapter 30, 31, 32, 34, or 35 of title 38, United States Code,

(C) a payment (other than a gift, bequest, devise, or inheritance within the meaning of section 102(a)) for educational expenses, or attributable to attendance at an eligible educational institution, which is exempt from income taxation by any law of the United States, or

(D) a payment, waiver, or reimbursement of qualified higher education expenses under a qualified tuition program (within the meaning of section 529(b)).

(2) COORDINATION WITH OTHER HIGHER EDUCATION BENEFITS.—The amount of the qualified higher education expenses otherwise taken into account under subsection (a) with respect to the education of an individual shall be reduced (before the application of subsection (b)) by—

Caution: Code Sec. 135(d)(2)(A), below, is subject to the sunset provision of the Economic Growth and Tax Relief Reconciliation Act of 2001 (P.L. 107-16), §901. Absent Congressional action, the changes made to this provision by P.L. 107-16, or that take effect as if included in P.L. 107-16, do not apply after December 31, 2010. For more information about the sunset provision, see page XXI of the Preface to this publication and P.L. 107-16, §901, in the amendment notes. See the amendments notes for a history of amendments to this section and the effective date of each change.

(A) the amount of such expenses which are taken into account in determining the credit allowed to the taxpayer or any other person under section 25A with respect to such expenses; and

(B) the amount of such expenses which are taken into account in determining the exclusions under sections 529(c)(3)(B) and 530(d)(2).

(3) NO EXCLUSION FOR MARRIED INDIVIDUALS FILING SEPARATE RETURNS.—If the taxpayer is a married individual (within the meaning of section 7703), this section shall apply only if the taxpayer and his spouse file a joint return for the taxable year.

(4) REGULATIONS.—The Secretary may prescribe such regulations as may be necessary or appropriate to carry out this section, including regulations requiring record keeping and information reporting.

Amendments

• 2006, Pension Protection Act of 2006 (P.L. 109-280)

P.L. 109-280, §1304(a), provides:

(a) PERMANENT EXTENSION OF MODIFICATIONS.—Section 901 of the Economic Growth and Tax Relief Reconciliation Act of 2001 [P.L. 107-16] (relating to sunset provisions) shall not apply to section 402 of such Act (relating to modifications to qualified tuition programs).

• 2001, Economic Growth and Tax Relief Reconciliation Act of 2001 (P.L. 107-16)

P.L. 107-16, §401(g)(2)(B):

Amended Code Sec. 135(d)(2)(A) by striking "allowable" and inserting "allowed". **Effective** for tax years beginning after 12-31-2001.

P.L. 107-16, §402(a)(4)(A):

Amended Code Sec. 135(d)(1)(D) by striking "qualified State tuition" and inserting "qualified tuition". **Effective** for tax years beginning after 12-31-2001.

P.L. 107-16, §402(b)(2)(A):

Amended Code Sec. 135(d)(2)(B) by striking "the exclusion under section 530(d)(2)" and inserting "the exclusions under sections 529(c)(3)(B) and 530(d)(2)". **Effective** for tax years beginning after 12-31-2001.

P.L. 107-16, §901(a)-(b), provides [but see P.L. 109-280, §1304(a), above]:

SEC. 901. SUNSET OF PROVISIONS OF ACT.

(a) IN GENERAL.—All provisions of, and amendments made by, this Act shall not apply—

(1) to taxable, plan, or limitation years beginning after December 31, 2010, or

(2) in the case of title V, to estates of decedents dying, gifts made, or generation skipping transfers, after December 31, 2010.

(b) APPLICATION OF CERTAIN LAWS.—The Internal Revenue Code of 1986 and the Employee Retirement Income Security Act of 1974 shall be applied and administered to years, estates, gifts, and transfers described in subsection (a) as if the provisions and amendments described in subsection (a) had never been enacted.

• 1998, IRS Restructuring and Reform Act of 1998 (P.L. 105-206)

P.L. 105-206, §6004(d)(4):

Amended Code Sec. 135(d)(2). **Effective** as if included in the provision of P.L. 105-34 to which it relates [generally **effective** for tax years beginning after 12-31-97.—CCH]. Prior to amendment, Code Sec. 135(d)(2) read as follows:

(2) COORDINATION WITH HIGHER EDUCATION CREDIT.—The amount of the qualified higher education expenses otherwise taken into account under subsection (a) with respect to the education of an individual shall be reduced (before the application of subsection (b)) by the amount of such expenses which are taken into account in determining the credit allowable to the taxpayer or any other person under section 25A with respect to such expenses.

• 1997, Taxpayer Relief Act of 1997 (P.L. 105-34)

P.L. 105-34, §201(d):

Amended Code Sec. 135(d) by redesignating paragraphs (2) and (3) as paragraphs (3) and (4), respectively, and by inserting after paragraph (1) a new paragraph (2). **Effective** for expenses paid after 12-31-97 (in tax years ending after such date), for education furnished in academic periods beginning after such date.

• 1996, Small Business Job Protection Act of 1996 (P.L. 104-188)

P.L. 104-188, §1806(b)(1):

Amended Code Sec. 135(d)(1) by striking "or" at the end of subparagraph (B), by striking the period at the end of subparagraph (C) and inserting ", or", and by adding at the end a new subparagraph (D). **Effective**, generally, for tax years ending after 8-20-96. For a transition rule, see Act Sec. 1806(c)(2), below.

P.L. 104-188, §1806(c)(2), provides:

(2) TRANSITION RULE.—If—

(A) a State or agency or instrumentality thereof maintains, on the date of the enactment of this Act, a program under which persons may purchase tuition credits or certificates on behalf of, or make contributions for education expenses of, a designated beneficiary, and

(B) such program meets the requirements of a qualified State tuition program before the later of—

(i) the date which is 1 year after such date of enactment, or

(ii) the first day of the first calendar quarter after the close of the first regular session of the State legislature that begins after such date of enactment,

the amendments made by this section shall apply to contributions (and earnings allocable thereto) made before the date such program meets the requirements of such amendments without regard to whether any requirements of such amendments are met with respect to such contributions and earnings.

For purposes of subparagraph (B)(ii), if a State has a 2-year legislative session, each year of such session shall be deemed to be a separate regular session of the State legislature.

• 1989, Omnibus Budget Reconciliation Act of 1989 (P.L. 101-239)

P.L. 101-239, §7816(c)(2):

Amended Code Sec. 135(d)(1) by striking "subsection (a) respect to" and inserting "subsection (a) with respect to". **Effective** as if included in the provision of P.L. 100-647 to which it relates.

• 1988, Technical and Miscellaneous Revenue Act of 1988 (P.L. 100-647)

P.L. 100-647, §6009(a):

Amended Part III of subchapter B of chapter 1 by redesignating Code Sec. 135 as Code Sec. 136 and by inserting after Code Sec. 134 a new Code Sec. 135. **Effective** for tax years beginning after 12-31-89.

[Sec. 136]

SEC. 136. ENERGY CONSERVATION SUBSIDIES PROVIDED BY PUBLIC UTILITIES.

[Sec. 136(a)]

(a) EXCLUSION.—Gross income shall not include the value of any subsidy provided (directly or indirectly) by a public utility to a customer for the purchase or installation of any energy conservation measure.

Amendments

• 1996, Small Business Job Protection Act of 1996 (P.L. 104-188)

P.L. 104-188, §1617(b)(1):

Amended Code Sec. 136(a). **Effective** for amounts received after 12-31-96, unless received pursuant to a written binding contract in effect on 9-13-95, and at all times thereafter. Prior to amendment, Code Sec. 136(a) read as follows:

(a) EXCLUSION.—

(1) IN GENERAL.—Gross income shall not include the value of any subsidy provided (directly or indirectly) by a public utility to a customer for the purchase or installation of any energy conservation measure.

(2) LIMITATION ON EXCLUSION FOR NONRESIDENTIAL PROPERTY.—

(A) IN GENERAL.—In the case of any subsidy provided with respect to any energy conservation measure referred to in subsection (c)(1)(B), only the applicable percentage of such subsidy shall be excluded from gross income under paragraph (1).

(B) APPLICABLE PERCENTAGE.—For purposes of subparagraph (A), the term "applicable percentage" means—

(i) 40 percent in the case of subsidies provided during 1995,

(ii) 50 percent in the case of subsidies provided during 1996, and

(iii) 65 percent in the case of subsidies provided after 1996.

[Sec. 136(b)]

(b) DENIAL OF DOUBLE BENEFIT.—Notwithstanding any other provision of this subtitle, no deduction or credit shall be allowed for, or by reason of, any expenditure to the extent of the amount excluded under subsection (a) for any subsidy which was provided with respect to such expenditure. The adjusted basis of any property shall be reduced by the amount excluded under subsection (a) which was provided with respect to such property.

[Sec. 136(c)]

(c) ENERGY CONSERVATION MEASURE.—

(1) IN GENERAL.—For purposes of this section, the term "energy conservation measure" means any installation or modification primarily designed to reduce consumption of electricity or natural gas or to improve the management of energy demand with respect to a dwelling unit.

(2) OTHER DEFINITIONS.—For purposes of this subsection—

(A) DWELLING UNIT.—The term "dwelling unit" has the meaning given such term by section 280A(f)(1).

(B) PUBLIC UTILITY.—The term "public utility" means a person engaged in the sale of electricity or natural gas to residential, commercial, or industrial customers for use by such customers. For purposes of the preceding sentence, the term "person" includes the Federal Government, a State or local government or any political subdivision thereof, or any instrumentality of any of the foregoing.

Amendments

• 1996, Small Business Job Protection Act of 1996 (P.L. 104-188)

P.L. 104-188, §1617(a):

Amended Code Sec. 136(c)(1) by striking "energy demand—" and all that follows and inserting "energy demand with respect to a dwelling unit." **Effective** for amounts received after 12-31-96, unless received pursuant to a written binding contract in effect on 9-13-95, and at all times thereafter. Prior to amendment, Code Sec. 136(c)(1) read as follows:

(1) IN GENERAL.—For purposes of this section, the term "energy conservation measure" means any installation or modification primarily designed to reduce consumption of electricity or natural gas or to improve the management of energy demand—

(A) with respect to a dwelling unit, and

(B) on or after January 1, 1995, with respect to property other than dwelling units.

The purchase and installation of specially defined energy property shall be treated as an energy conservation measure described in subparagraph (B).

P.L. 104-188, §1617(b)(2)(A)-(B):

Amended Code Sec. 136(c)(2) by striking subparagraph (A) and by redesignating subparagraphs (B) and (C) as subparagraphs (A) and (B), respectively, and striking "AND SPECIAL RULES" after "DEFINITIONS" in the paragraph heading. **Effective** for amounts received after 12-31-96, unless received pursuant to a written binding contract in effect on 9-13-95, and at all times thereafter. Prior to amendment, Code Sec. 136(c)(2)(A) read as follows:

(A) SPECIALLY DEFINED ENERGY PROPERTY.—The term "specially defined energy property" means—

(i) a recuperator,

(ii) a heat wheel,

(iii) a regenerator,

(iv) a heat exchanger,

(v) a waste heat boiler,

(vi) a heat pipe,

(vii) an automatic energy control system,

(viii) a turbulator,

(ix) a preheater,

(x) a combustible gas recovery system,

(xi) an economizer,

(xii) modifications to alumina electrolytic cells,

(xiii) modifications to chlor-alkali electrolytic cells, or

(xiv) any other property of a kind specified by the Secretary by regulations, the principal purpose of which is reducing the amount of energy consumed in any existing industrial or commercial process and which is installed in connection with an existing industrial or commercial facility.

[Sec. 136(d)]

(d) EXCEPTION.—This section shall not apply to any payment to or from a qualified cogeneration facility or qualifying small power production facility pursuant to section 210 of the Public Utility Regulatory Policy Act of 1978.

Amendments

• 1992, Energy Policy Act of 1992 (P.L. 102-486)

P.L. 102-486, §1912(a):

Amended part III of subchapter B of chapter 1 by redesignating Code Sec. 136 as Code Sec. 137 and by inserting after Code Sec. 135 new Code Sec. 136. **Effective** for amounts received after 12-31-92.

[Sec. 137]

SEC. 137. ADOPTION ASSISTANCE PROGRAMS.

→ Caution: Code Sec. 137(a), below, is subject to the sunset provision of the Economic Growth and Tax Relief Reconciliation Act of 2001 (P.L. 107-16), §901. Absent Congressional action, the changes made to this provision by P.L. 107-16, or that take effect as if included in P.L. 107-16, do not apply after December 31, 2010. For more information about the sunset provision, see page XXI of the Preface to this publication and P.L. 107-16, §901, in the amendment notes. See the amendments notes for a history of amendments to this section and the effective date of each change.

[Sec. 137(a)]

(a) EXCLUSION.—

(1) IN GENERAL.—Gross income of an employee does not include amounts paid or expenses incurred by the employer for qualified adoption expenses in connection with the adoption of a child by an employee if such amounts are furnished pursuant to an adoption assistance program.

(2) $13,170 EXCLUSION FOR ADOPTION OF CHILD WITH SPECIAL NEEDS REGARDLESS OF EXPENSES.—In the case of an adoption of a child with special needs which becomes final during a taxable year, the qualified adoption expenses with respect to such adoption for such year shall be increased by an amount equal to the excess (if any) of $13,170 over the actual aggregate qualified adoption expenses with respect to such adoption during such taxable year and all prior taxable years.

Amendments

• 2010, Patient Protection and Affordable Care Act (P.L. 111-148)

P.L. 111-148, §10909(a)(2)(B)(i)-(ii):

Amended Code Sec. 137(a)(2), in the text by striking "$10,000" and inserting "$13,170", and in the heading by striking "$10,000" and inserting "$13,170". **Effective** for tax years beginning after 12-31-2009.

P.L. 111-148, §10909(c), provides:

(c) APPLICATION AND EXTENSION OF EGTRRA SUNSET.—Notwithstanding section 901 of the Economic Growth and Tax Relief Reconciliation Act of 2001 [P.L. 107-16], such section shall apply to the amendments made by this section and the amendments made by section 202 of such Act by substituting "December 31, 2011" for "December 31, 2010" in subsection (a)(1) thereof.

• 2002, Job Creation and Worker Assistance Act of 2002 (P.L. 107-147)

P.L. 107-147, §411(c)(2)(A):

Amended Code Sec. 137(a). **Effective** for tax years beginning after 12-31-2002. Prior to amendment, Code Sec. 137(a) read as follows:

(a) IN GENERAL.—Gross income of an employee does not include amounts paid or expenses incurred by the employer for adoption expenses in connection with the adoption of a child by an employee if such amounts are furnished pursuant to an adoption assistance program. The amount of the exclusion shall be—

(1) in the case of an adoption of a child other than a child with special needs, the amount of the qualified adoption expenses paid or incurred by the taxpayer, and

(2) in the case of an adoption of a child with special needs, $10,000.

• 2001, Economic Growth and Tax Relief Reconciliation Act of 2001 (P.L. 107-16)

P.L. 107-16, §202(a)(2):

Amended Code Sec. 137(a). **Effective** for tax years beginning after 12-31-2002. Prior to amendment, Code Sec. 137(a) read as follows:

(a) IN GENERAL.—Gross income of an employee does not include amounts paid or expenses incurred by the employer for qualified adoption expenses in connection with the adoption of a child by an employee if such amounts are furnished pursuant to an adoption assistance program.

P.L. 107-16, §901(a)-(b), provides [but see P.L. 111-148, §10909(c), above]:

SEC. 901. SUNSET OF PROVISIONS OF ACT.

(a) IN GENERAL.—All provisions of, and amendments made by, this Act shall not apply—

(1) to taxable, plan, or limitation years beginning after December 31, 2010, or

(2) in the case of title V, to estates of decedents dying, gifts made, or generation skipping transfers, after December 31, 2010.

(b) APPLICATION OF CERTAIN LAWS.—The Internal Revenue Code of 1986 and the Employee Retirement Income Security Act of 1974 shall be applied and administered to years, estates, gifts, and transfers described in subsection (a) as if the provisions and amendments described in subsection (a) had never been enacted.

[Sec. 137(b)]

(b) LIMITATIONS.—

»»→ Caution: Code Sec. 137(b)(1), below, is subject to the sunset provision of the Economic Growth and Tax Relief Reconciliation Act of 2001 (P.L. 107-16), §901. Absent Congressional action, the changes made to this provision by P.L. 107-16, or that take effect as if included in P.L. 107-16, do not apply after December 31, 2010. For more information about the sunset provision, see page XXI of the Preface to this publication and P.L. 107-16, §901, in the amendment notes. See the amendments notes for a history of amendments to this section and the effective date of each change.

(1) DOLLAR LIMITATION.—The aggregate of the amounts paid or expenses incurred which may be taken into account under subsection (a) for all taxable years with respect to the adoption of a child by the taxpayer shall not exceed $13,170.

(2) INCOME LIMITATION.—The amount excludable from gross income under subsection (a) for any taxable year shall be reduced (but not below zero) by an amount which bears the same ratio to the amount so excludable (determined without regard to this paragraph but with regard to paragraph (1)) as—

»»→ Caution: Code Sec. 137(b)(2)(A), below, is subject to the sunset provision of the Economic Growth and Tax Relief Reconciliation Act of 2001 (P.L. 107-16), §901. Absent Congressional action, the changes made to this provision by P.L. 107-16, or that take effect as if included in P.L. 107-16, do not apply after December 31, 2010. For more information about the sunset provision, see page XXI of the Preface to this publication and P.L. 107-16, §901, in the amendment notes. See the amendments notes for a history of amendments to this section and the effective date of each change.

(A) the amount (if any) by which the taxpayer's adjusted gross income exceeds $150,000, bears to

(B) $40,000.

(3) DETERMINATION OF ADJUSTED GROSS INCOME.—For purposes of paragraph (2), adjusted gross income shall be determined—

»»→ Caution: Code Sec. 137(b)(3)(A), below, is subject to the sunset provision of the Economic Growth and Tax Relief Reconciliation Act of 2001 (P.L. 107-16), §901. Absent Congressional action, the changes made to this provision by P.L. 107-16, or that take effect as if included in P.L. 107-16, do not apply after December 31, 2010. For more information about the sunset provision, see page XXI of the Preface to this publication and P.L. 107-16, §901, in the amendment notes. See the amendments notes for a history of amendments to this section and the effective date of each change.

(A) without regard to this section and sections 199, 221, 222, 911, 931, and 933, and

(B) after the application of sections 86, 135, 219, and 469.

Amendments

• 2010, Patient Protection and Affordable Care Act (P.L. 111-148)

P.L. 111-148, §10909(a)(2)(A):

Amended Code Sec. 137(b)(1) by striking "$10,000" and inserting "$13,170". **Effective** for tax years beginning after 12-31-2009.

P.L. 111-148, §10909(c), provides:

(c) APPLICATION AND EXTENSION OF EGTRRA SUNSET.—Notwithstanding section 901 of the Economic Growth and Tax Relief Reconciliation Act of 2001 [P.L. 107-16], such section shall apply to the amendments made by this section and the amendments made by section 202 of such Act by substituting "December 31, 2011" for "December 31, 2010" in subsection (a)(1) thereof.

• 2004, American Jobs Creation Act of 2004 (P.L. 108-357)

P.L. 108-357, §102(d)(1):

Amended Code Sec. 137(b)(3)(A) by inserting "199," before "221". **Effective** for tax years beginning after 12-31-2004.

• 2002, Job Creation and Worker Assistance Act of 2002 (P.L. 107-147)

P.L. 107-147, §411(c)(2)(B), as amended by P.L. 108-311, §403(e):

Amended Code Sec. 137(b)(1) by striking "subsection (a)(1)" and inserting "subsection (a)". **Effective** for tax years beginning after 12-31-2001.

• 2001, Economic Growth and Tax Relief Reconciliation Act of 2001 (P.L. 107-16)

P.L. 107-16, §202(b)(1)(B)(i)-(iii):

Amended Code Sec. 137(b)(1) by striking "$5,000" and inserting "$10,000", by striking "($6,000, in the case of a child with special needs)" before the period, and by striking "subsection (a)" and inserting "subsection (a)(1)". **Effective** for tax years beginning after 12-31-2001.

P.L. 107-16, §202(b)(2)(B):

Amended Code Sec. 137(b)(2)(A) by striking "$75,000" and inserting "$150,000". **Effective** for tax years beginning after 12-31-2001.

P.L. 107-16, §431(c)(1):

Amended Code Sec. 137(b)(3) by inserting "222," after "221,". **Effective** for payments made in tax years beginning after 12-31-2001.

P.L. 107-16, §901(a)-(b), provides [but see P.L. 111-148, §10909(c), above]:

SEC. 901. SUNSET OF PROVISIONS OF ACT.

(a) IN GENERAL.—All provisions of, and amendments made by, this Act shall not apply—

(1) to taxable, plan, or limitation years beginning after December 31, 2010, or

(2) in the case of title V, to estates of decedents dying, gifts made, or generation skipping transfers, after December 31, 2010.

(b) APPLICATION OF CERTAIN LAWS.—The Internal Revenue Code of 1986 and the Employee Retirement Income Security Act of 1974 shall be applied and administered to years, estates, gifts, and transfers described in subsection (a) as if the provisions and amendments described in subsection (a) had never been enacted.

• 1998, Tax and Trade Relief Extension Act of 1998 (P.L. 105-277)

P.L. 105-277, §4003(a)(2)(C):

Amended Code Sec. 137(b)(3)(A) by inserting "221," before "911,". **Effective** as if included in the provision of P.L. 105-34 to which it relates [generally **effective** for interest payments due and paid after 12-31-97, on any qualified education loan.—CCH].

• 1997, Taxpayer Relief Act of 1997 (P.L. 105-34)

P.L. 105-34, §1601(h)(2)(C):

Amended Code Sec. 137(b)(1) by striking "amount excludable from gross income" and inserting "of the amounts paid or expenses incurred which may be taken into account". **Effective** as if included in the provision of P.L. 104-188 to which it relates [**effective** for tax years beginning after 12-31-96.—CCH.].

[Sec. 137(c)]

(c) ADOPTION ASSISTANCE PROGRAM.—For purposes of this section, an adoption assistance program is a separate written plan of an employer for the exclusive benefit of such employer's employees—

(1) under which the employer provides such employees with adoption assistance, and

(2) which meets requirements similar to the requirements of paragraphs (2), (3), (5), and (6) of section 127(b).

An adoption reimbursement program operated under section 1052 of title 10, United States Code (relating to armed forces) or section 514 of title 14, United States Code (relating to members of the Coast Guard) shall be treated as an adoption assistance program for purposes of this section.

»»→ Caution: Code Sec. 137(d), below, was amended by P.L. 111-148. For sunset provision, see P.L. 111-148, §10909(c), in the amendment notes.

[Sec. 137(d)]

(d) QUALIFIED ADOPTION EXPENSES.—For purposes of this section, the term "qualified adoption expenses" has the meaning given such term by section 36C(d) (determined without regard to reimbursements under this section).

Amendments

• 2010, Patient Protection and Affordable Care Act (P.L. 111-148)

P.L. 111-148, §10909(b)(2)(J)(i):

Amended Code Sec. 137(d) by striking "section 23(d)" and inserting "section 36C(d)". **Effective** for tax years beginning after 12-31-2009.

P.L. 111-148, §10909(c), provides:

(c) APPLICATION AND EXTENSION OF EGTRRA SUNSET.—Notwithstanding section 901 of the Economic Growth and Tax Relief Reconciliation Act of 2001 [P.L. 107-16], such section shall apply to the amendments made by this section and the amendments made by section 202 of such Act by substituting "December 31, 2011" for "December 31, 2010" in subsection (a)(1) thereof.

• 2001, Economic Growth and Tax Relief Reconciliation Act of 2001 (P.L. 107-16)

P.L. 107-16, §901(a)-(b), provides [but see P.L. 111-148, §10909(c), above]:

SEC. 901. SUNSET OF PROVISIONS OF ACT.

(a) IN GENERAL.—All provisions of, and amendments made by, this Act shall not apply—

(1) to taxable, plan, or limitation years beginning after December 31, 2010, or

(2) in the case of title V, to estates of decedents dying, gifts made, or generation skipping transfers, after December 31, 2010.

(b) APPLICATION OF CERTAIN LAWS.—The Internal Revenue Code of 1986 and the Employee Retirement Income Security Act of 1974 shall be applied and administered to years, estates, gifts, and transfers described in subsection (a) as if the provisions and amendments described in subsection (a) had never been enacted.

»»→ Caution: Code Sec. 137(e), below, was amended by P.L. 111-148. For sunset provision, see P.L. 111-148, §10909(c), in the amendment notes.

[Sec. 137(e)]

(e) CERTAIN RULES TO APPLY.—Rules similar to the rules of subsections (e), (f), and (g) of section 36C shall apply for purposes of this section.

Amendments

• 2010, Patient Protection and Affordable Care Act (P.L. 111-148)

P.L. 111-148, §10909(b)(2)(J)(ii):

Amended Code Sec. 137(e) by striking "section 23" and inserting "section 36C". **Effective** for tax years beginning after 12-31-2009.

P.L. 111-148, §10909(c), provides:

(c) APPLICATION AND EXTENSION OF EGTRRA SUNSET.—Notwithstanding section 901 of the Economic Growth and Tax Relief Reconciliation Act of 2001 [P.L. 107-16], such section shall apply to the amendments made by this section and the amendments made by section 202 of such Act by substituting "December 31, 2011" for "December 31, 2010" in subsection (a)(1) thereof.

• 2001, Economic Growth and Tax Relief Reconciliation Act of 2001 (P.L. 107-16)

P.L. 107-16, §901(a)-(b), provides [but see P.L. 111-148, §10909(c), above]:

SEC. 901. SUNSET OF PROVISIONS OF ACT.

(a) IN GENERAL.—All provisions of, and amendments made by, this Act shall not apply—

(1) to taxable, plan, or limitation years beginning after December 31, 2010, or

(2) in the case of title V, to estates of decedents dying, gifts made, or generation skipping transfers, after December 31, 2010.

(b) APPLICATION OF CERTAIN LAWS.—The Internal Revenue Code of 1986 and the Employee Retirement Income Security Act of 1974 shall be applied and administered to years, estates, gifts, and transfers described in subsection (a) as if the provisions and amendments described in subsection (a) had never been enacted.

»»→ Caution: Code Sec. 137(f), below, was amended by P.L. 111-148. For sunset provision, see P.L. 111-148, §10909(c), in the amendment notes.

[Sec. 137(f)]

(f) ADJUSTMENTS FOR INFLATION.—

(1) DOLLAR LIMITATIONS.—In the case of a taxable year beginning after December 31, 2010, each of the dollar amounts in subsections (a)(2) and (b)(1) shall be increased by an amount equal to—

(A) such dollar amount, multiplied by

(B) the cost-of-living adjustment determined under section 1(f)(3) for the calendar year in which the taxable year begins, determined by substituting "calendar year 2009" for "calendar year 1992" in subparagraph (B) thereof.

If any amount as increased under the preceding sentence is not a multiple of $10, such amount shall be rounded to the nearest multiple of $10.

(2) INCOME LIMITATION.—In the case of a taxable year beginning after December 31, 2002, the dollar amount in subsection (b)(2)(A) shall be increased by an amount equal to—

(A) such dollar amount, multiplied by

(B) the cost-of-living adjustment determined under section 1(f)(3) for the calendar year in which the taxable year begins, determined by substituting "calendar year 2001" for "calendar year 1992" in subparagraph [(B)] thereof.

If any amount as increased under the preceding sentence is not a multiple of $10, such amount shall be rounded to the nearest multiple of $10.

Amendments

• 2010, Patient Protection and Affordable Care Act (P.L. 111-148)

P.L. 111-148, §10909(a)(2)(C):

Amended Code Sec. 137(f). **Effective** for tax years beginning after 12-31-2009. Prior to amendment, Code Sec. 137(f) read as follows:

(f) ADJUSTMENTS FOR INFLATION.—In the case of a taxable year beginning after December 31, 2002, each of the dollar amounts in subsection (a)(2) and paragraphs (1) and (2)(A) of subsection (b) shall be increased by an amount equal to—

(1) such dollar amount, multiplied by

(2) the cost-of-living adjustment determined under section 1(f)(3) for the calendar year in which the taxable year begins, determined by substituting "calendar year 2001" for "calendar year 1992" in subparagraph (B) thereof.

If any amount as increased under the preceding sentence is not a multiple of $10, such amount shall be rounded to the nearest multiple of $10.

P.L. 111-148, §10909(c), provides:

(c) APPLICATION AND EXTENSION OF EGTRRA SUNSET.—Notwithstanding section 901 of the Economic Growth and Tax Relief Reconciliation Act of 2001 [P.L. 107-16], such section shall apply to the amendments made by this section and the amendments made by section 202 of such Act by substituting "December 31, 2011" for "December 31, 2010" in subsection (a)(1) thereof.

• 2002, Job Creation and Worker Assistance Act of 2002 (P.L. 107-147)

P.L. 107-147, §418(a)(2):

Amended Code Sec. 137(f) by adding at the end a new flush sentence. **Effective** as if included in the provision of P.L. 107-16 to which it relates [**effective** for tax years beginning after 12-31-2001.—CCH].

• 2001, Economic Growth and Tax Relief Reconciliation Act of 2001 (P.L. 107-16)

P.L. 107-16, §202(d)(2):

Amended Code Sec. 137 by striking subsection (f). **Effective** for tax years beginning after 12-31-2001. Prior to being stricken, Code Sec. 137(f) read as follows:

(f) TERMINATION.—This section shall not apply to amounts paid or expenses incurred after December 31, 2001.

P.L. 107-16, §202(e)(2):

Amended Code Sec. 137, as amended by Act Sec. 202(d), by adding at the end a new subsection (f). **Effective** for tax years beginning after 12-31-2001.

P.L. 107-16, §901(a)-(b), provides [but see P.L. 111-148, §10909(c), above]:

SEC. 901. SUNSET OF PROVISIONS OF ACT.

(a) IN GENERAL.—All provisions of, and amendments made by, this Act shall not apply—

(1) to taxable, plan, or limitation years beginning after December 31, 2010, or

(2) in the case of title V, to estates of decedents dying, gifts made, or generation skipping transfers, after December 31, 2010.

(b) APPLICATION OF CERTAIN LAWS.—The Internal Revenue Code of 1986 and the Employee Retirement Income Security Act of 1974 shall be applied and administered to years, estates, gifts, and transfers described in subsection (a) as if the provisions and amendments described in subsection (a) had never been enacted.

• 1996, Small Business Job Protection Act of 1996 (P.L. 104-188)

P.L. 104-188, §1807(b):

Amended part III of subchapter B of chapter 1 by redesignating Code Sec. 137 as Code Sec. 138 and by inserting after Code Sec. 136 a new Code Sec. 137. **Effective** for tax years beginning after 12-31-96.

[Sec. 138]

SEC. 138. MEDICARE ADVANTAGE MSA.

[Sec. 138(a)]

(a) EXCLUSION.—Gross income shall not include any payment to the Medicare Advantage MSA of an individual by the Secretary of Health and Human Services under part C of title XVIII of the Social Security Act.

Amendments

• 2004, Working Families Tax Relief Act of 2004 (P.L. 108-311)

P.L. 108-311, §408(a)(5)(A):

Amended Code Sec. 138 by striking "Medicare+Choice MSA" each place it appears in the text and inserting "Medicare Advantage MSA". **Effective** 10-4-2004.

P.L. 108-311, §408(a)(5)(B):

Amended the heading for Code Sec. 138. **Effective** 10-4-2004. Prior to amendment, the heading for Code Sec. 138 read as follows:

SEC. 138. MEDICARE+CHOICE MSA.

[Sec. 138(b)]

(b) MEDICARE ADVANTAGE MSA.—For purposes of this section, the term "Medicare Advantage MSA" means an Archer MSA (as defined in section 220(d))—

(1) which is designated as a Medicare Advantage MSA,

(2) with respect to which no contribution may be made other than—

(A) a contribution made by the Secretary of Health and Human Services pursuant to part C of title XVIII of the Social Security Act, or

(B) a trustee-to-trustee transfer described in subsection (c)(4),

(3) the governing instrument of which provides that trustee-to-trustee transfers described in subsection (c)(4) may be made to and from such account, and

(4) which is established in connection with an MSA plan described in section 1859(b)(3) of the Social Security Act.

Amendments

• 2004, Working Families Tax Relief Act of 2004 (P.L. 108-311)

P.L. 108-311, §408(a)(5)(A):

Amended Code Sec. 138 by striking "Medicare+Choice MSA" each place it appears in the text and inserting "Medicare Advantage MSA". **Effective** 10-4-2004.

P.L. 108-311, §408(a)(5)(C):

Amended the heading for Code Sec. 138(b) by striking "MEDICARE+CHOICE MSA" and inserting "MEDICARE ADVANTAGE MSA". **Effective** 10-4-2004.

• 2000, Community Renewal Tax Relief Act of 2000 (P.L. 106-554)

P.L. 106-554, §202(a)(3):

Amended Code Sec. 138(b) by striking "medical savings account" and inserting "Archer MSA". **Effective** 12-21-2000.

P.L. 106-554, §202(b)(10):

Amended Code Sec. 138(b) by striking "a Archer" and inserting "an Archer". **Effective** 12-21-2000.

[Sec. 138(c)]

(c) SPECIAL RULES FOR DISTRIBUTIONS.—

(1) DISTRIBUTIONS FOR QUALIFIED MEDICAL EXPENSES.—In applying section 220 to a Medicare Advantage MSA—

(A) qualified medical expenses shall not include amounts paid for medical care for any individual other than the account holder, and

(B) section 220(d)(2)(C) shall not apply.

(2) PENALTY FOR DISTRIBUTIONS FROM MEDICARE ADVANTAGE MSA NOT USED FOR QUALIFIED MEDICAL EXPENSES IF MINIMUM BALANCE NOT MAINTAINED.—

(A) IN GENERAL.—The tax imposed by this chapter for any taxable year in which there is a payment or distribution from a Medicare Advantage MSA which is not used exclusively to pay the qualified medical expenses of the account holder shall be increased by 50 percent of the excess (if any) of—

(i) the amount of such payment or distribution, over

(ii) the excess (if any) of—

(I) the fair market value of the assets in such MSA as of the close of the calendar year preceding the calendar year in which the taxable year begins, over

(II) an amount equal to 60 percent of the deductible under the Medicare Advantage MSA plan covering the account holder as of January 1 of the calendar year in which the taxable year begins.

Section 220(f)(4) shall not apply to any payment or distribution from a Medicare Advantage MSA.

(B) EXCEPTIONS.—Subparagraph (A) shall not apply if the payment or distribution is made on or after the date the account holder—

(i) becomes disabled within the meaning of section 72(m)(7), or

(ii) dies.

(C) SPECIAL RULES.—For purposes of subparagraph (A)—

(i) all Medicare Advantage MSAs of the account holder shall be treated as 1 account,

(ii) all payments and distributions not used exclusively to pay the qualified medical expenses of the account holder during any taxable year shall be treated as 1 distribution, and

(iii) any distribution of property shall be taken into account at its fair market value on the date of the distribution.

(3) WITHDRAWAL OF ERRONEOUS CONTRIBUTIONS.—Section 220(f)(2) and paragraph (2) of this subsection shall not apply to any payment or distribution from a Medicare Advantage MSA to the Secretary of Health and Human Services of an erroneous contribution to such MSA and of the net income attributable to such contribution.

(4) TRUSTEE-TO-TRUSTEE TRANSFERS.—Section 220(f)(2) and paragraph (2) of this subsection shall not apply to any trustee-to-trustee transfer from a Medicare Advantage MSA of an account holder to another Medicare Advantage MSA of such account holder.

Amendments

• 2004, Working Families Tax Relief Act of 2004 (P.L. 108-311)

P.L. 108-311, §408(a)(5)(A):

Amended Code Sec. 138 by striking "Medicare+Choice MSA" each place it appears in the text and inserting "Medicare Advantage MSA". **Effective** 10-4-2004.

P.L. 108-311, §408(a)(5)(D):

Amended the heading for Code Sec. 138(c)(2) by striking "MEDICARE+CHOICE MSA" and inserting "MEDICARE ADVANTAGE MSA". **Effective** 10-4-2004.

P.L. 108-311, §408(a)(5)(E):

Amended Code Sec. 138(c)(2)(C)(i) by striking "Medicare+Choice MSAs" and inserting "Medicare Advantage MSAs". **Effective** 10-4-2004.

[Sec. 138(d)]

(d) SPECIAL RULES FOR TREATMENT OF ACCOUNT AFTER DEATH OF ACCOUNT HOLDER.—In applying section 220(f)(8)(A) to an account which was a Medicare Advantage MSA of a decedent, the rules of section 220(f) shall apply in lieu of the rules of subsection (c) of this section with respect to the spouse as the account holder of such Medicare Advantage MSA.

Amendments

• 2004, Working Families Tax Relief Act of 2004 (P.L. 108-311)

P.L. 108-311, §408(a)(5)(A):

Amended Code Sec. 138 by striking "Medicare+Choice MSA" each place it appears in the text and inserting "Medicare Advantage MSA". **Effective** 10-4-2004.

[Sec. 138(e)]

(e) REPORTS.—In the case of a Medicare Advantage MSA, the report under section 220(h)—

(1) shall include the fair market value of the assets in such Medicare Advantage MSA as of the close of each calendar year, and

(2) shall be furnished to the account holder—

(A) not later than January 31 of the calendar year following the calendar year to which such reports relate, and

(B) in such manner as the Secretary prescribes in such regulations.

• 2004, Working Families Tax Relief Act of 2004 (P.L. 108-311)

P.L. 108-311, §408(a)(5)(A):

Amended Code Sec. 138 by striking "Medicare+Choice MSA" each place it appears in the text and inserting "Medicare Advantage MSA". **Effective** 10-4-2004.

[Sec. 138(f)]

(f) COORDINATION WITH LIMITATION ON NUMBER OF TAXPAYERS HAVING ARCHER MSAS.—Subsection (i) of section 220 shall not apply to an individual with respect to a Medicare Advantage MSA, and Medicare Advantage MSAs shall not be taken into account in determining whether the numerical limitations under section 220(j) are exceeded.

Amendments

• 2004, Working Families Tax Relief Act of 2004 (P.L. 108-311)

P.L. 108-311, §408(a)(5)(A):

Amended Code Sec. 138 by striking "Medicare+Choice MSA" each place it appears in the text and inserting "Medicare Advantage MSA". **Effective** 10-4-2004.

P.L. 108-311, §408(a)(5)(F):

Amended Code Sec. 138(f) by striking "Medicare+Choice MSA's" and inserting "Medicare Advantage MSAs". **Effective** 10-4-2004.

• **2000, Community Renewal Tax Relief Act of 2000 (P.L. 106-554)**

P.L. 106-554, §202(b)(6):

Amended the heading for Code Sec. 138(f) by striking "MEDICAL SAVINGS ACCOUNTS" and inserting "ARCHER MSAS". **E ffective** 12-21-2000.

• **1997, Balanced Budget Act of 1997 (P.L. 105-33)**

P.L. 105-33, §4006(a):

Amended part III of subchapter B of chapter 1 by redesignating Code Sec. 138 as Code Sec. 139 and by inserting after Code Sec. 137 a new Code Sec. 138. **Effective** for tax years beginning after 12-31-98.

[Sec. 139]

SEC. 139. DISASTER RELIEF PAYMENTS.

[Sec. 139(a)]

(a) GENERAL RULE.—Gross income shall not include any amount received by an individual as a qualified disaster relief payment.

[Sec. 139(b)]

(b) QUALIFIED DISASTER RELIEF PAYMENT DEFINED.—For purposes of this section, the term "qualified disaster relief payment" means any amount paid to or for the benefit of an individual—

(1) to reimburse or pay reasonable and necessary personal, family, living, or funeral expenses incurred as a result of a qualified disaster,

(2) to reimburse or pay reasonable and necessary expenses incurred for the repair or rehabilitation of a personal residence or repair or replacement of its contents to the extent that the need for such repair, rehabilitation, or replacement is attributable to a qualified disaster,

(3) by a person engaged in the furnishing or sale of transportation as a common carrier by reason of the death or personal physical injuries incurred as a result of a qualified disaster, or

(4) if such amount is paid by a Federal, State, or local government, or agency or instrumentality thereof, in connection with a qualified disaster in order to promote the general welfare,

but only to the extent any expense compensated by such payment is not otherwise compensated for by insurance or otherwise.

[Sec. 139(c)]

(c) QUALIFIED DISASTER DEFINED.—For purposes of this section, the term "qualified disaster" means—

(1) a disaster which results from a terroristic or military action (as defined in section 692(c)(2)),

(2) federally declared disaster (as defined by section 165(h)(3)(C)(i)),

(3) a disaster which results from an accident involving a common carrier, or from any other event, which is determined by the Secretary to be of a catastrophic nature, or

(4) with respect to amounts described in subsection (b)(4), a disaster which is determined by an applicable Federal, State, or local authority (as determined by the Secretary) to warrant assistance from the Federal, State, or local government or agency or instrumentality thereof.

Amendments

• **2008, Tax Extenders and Alternative Minimum Tax Relief Act of 2008 (P.L. 110-343)**

P.L. 110-343, Division C, §706(a)(2)(D)(iv):

Amended Code Sec. 139(c)(2). **Effective** for disasters declared in tax years beginning after 12-31-2007. Prior to amendment, Code Sec. 139(c)(2) read as follows:

(2) a Presidentially declared disaster (as defined in section 1033(h)(3)),

[Sec. 139(d)]

(d) COORDINATION WITH EMPLOYMENT TAXES.—For purposes of chapter 2 and subtitle C, qualified disaster relief payments and qualified disaster mitigation payments shall not be treated as net earnings from self-employment, wages, or compensation subject to tax.

Amendments

• **2005 (P.L. 109-7)**

P.L. 109-7, §1(a)(2)(A):

Amended Code Sec. 139(d) by striking "a qualified disaster relief payment" and inserting "qualified disaster relief payments and qualified disaster mitigation payments". **Effective** for amounts received before, on, or after 4-15-2005.

[Sec. 139(e)]

(e) NO RELIEF FOR CERTAIN INDIVIDUALS.—Subsections (a), (f), and (g) shall not apply with respect to any individual identified by the Attorney General to have been a participant or conspirator in a terroristic action (as so defined), or a representative of such individual.

Amendments

• **2005 (P.L. 109-7)**

P.L. 109-7, §1(a)(2)(B):

Amended Code Sec. 139(e) by striking "and (f)" and inserting ", (f), and (g)". **Effective** for amounts received before, on, or after 4-15-2005.

[Sec. 139(f)]

(f) EXCLUSION OF CERTAIN ADDITIONAL PAYMENTS.—Gross income shall not include any amount received as payment under section 406 of the Air Transportation Safety and System Stabilization Act.

Amendments

• 2002, Victims of Terrorism Tax Relief Act of 2001 (P.L. 107-134)

P.L. 107-134, §111(a):

Amended part III of subchapter B of chapter 1 by redesignating Code Sec. 139 as Code Sec. 140 and inserting after Code Sec. 138 a new Code Sec. 139. **Effective** for tax years ending on or after 9-11-2001.

[Sec. 139(g)]

(g) QUALIFIED DISASTER MITIGATION PAYMENTS.—

(1) IN GENERAL.—Gross income shall not include any amount received as a qualified disaster mitigation payment.

(2) QUALIFIED DISASTER MITIGATION PAYMENT DEFINED.—For purposes of this section, the term "qualified disaster mitigation payment" means any amount which is paid pursuant to the Robert T. Stafford Disaster Relief and Emergency Assistance Act (as in effect on the date of the enactment of this subsection) or the National Flood Insurance Act (as in effect on such date) to or for the benefit of the owner of any property for hazard mitigation with respect to such property. Such term shall not include any amount received for the sale or disposition of any property.

(3) NO INCREASE IN BASIS.—Notwithstanding any other provision of this subtitle, no increase in the basis or adjusted basis of any property shall result from any amount excluded under this subsection with respect to such property.

Amendments

• 2005 (P.L. 109-7)

P.L. 109-7, §1(a)(1):

Amended Code Sec. 139 by adding at the end a new subsection (g). **Effective** for amounts received before, on, or after 4-15-2005.

[Sec. 139(h)]

(h) DENIAL OF DOUBLE BENEFIT.—Notwithstanding any other provision of this subtitle, no deduction or credit shall be allowed (to the person for whose benefit a qualified disaster relief payment or qualified disaster mitigation payment is made) for, or by reason of, any expenditure to the extent of the amount excluded under this section with respect to such expenditure.

Amendments

• 2005 (P.L. 109-7)

P.L. 109-7, §1(a)(1):

Amended Code Sec. 139 by adding at the end a new subsection (h). **Effective** for amounts received before, on, or after 4-15-2005.

»»→ Caution: Code Sec. 139A, below, prior to amendment by P.L. 111-148, applies to tax years beginning on or before December 31, 2010.

[Sec. 139A]

SEC. 139A. FEDERAL SUBSIDIES FOR PRESCRIPTION DRUG PLANS.

Gross income shall not include any special subsidy payment received under section 1860D-22 of the Social Security Act. This section shall not be taken into account for purposes of determining whether any deduction is allowable with respect to any cost taken into account in determining such payment.

»»→ Caution: Code Sec. 139A, below, as amended by P.L. 111-148, applies to tax years beginning after December 31, 2010.

[Sec. 139A]

SEC. 139A. FEDERAL SUBSIDIES FOR PRESCRIPTION DRUG PLANS.

Gross income shall not include any special subsidy payment received under section 1860D-22 of the Social Security Act.

Amendments

• 2010, Patient Protection and Affordable Care Act (P.L. 111-148)

P.L. 111-148, §9012(a):

Amended Code Sec. 139A by striking the second sentence. **Effective** for tax years beginning after 12-31-2012 [**effective** date changed by P.L. 111-152, §1407.—CCH]. Prior to being stricken, the second sentence of Code Sec. 139A read as follows:

This section shall not be taken into account for purposes of determining whether any deduction is allowable with respect to any cost taken into account in determining such payment.

• 2003, Medicare Prescription Drug, Improvement, and Modernization Act of 2003 (P.L. 108-173)

P.L. 108-173, §1202(a):

Amended part III of subchapter B of chapter 1 by inserting after Code Sec. 139 a new Code Sec. 139A. **Effective** for tax years ending after 12-8-2003.

[Sec. 139B]

SEC. 139B. BENEFITS PROVIDED TO VOLUNTEER FIREFIGHTERS AND EMERGENCY MEDICAL RESPONDERS.

[Sec. 139B(a)]

(a) IN GENERAL.—In the case of any member of a qualified volunteer emergency response organization, gross income shall not include—

(1) any qualified State and local tax benefit, and

(2) any qualified payment.

[Sec. 139B(b)]

(b) DENIAL OF DOUBLE BENEFITS.—In the case of any member of a qualified volunteer emergency response organization—

(1) the deduction under [section] 164 shall be determined with regard to any qualified State and local tax benefit, and

(2) expenses paid or incurred by the taxpayer in connection with the performance of services as such a member shall be taken into account under section 170 only to the extent such expenses exceed the amount of any qualified payment excluded from gross income under subsection (a).

[Sec. 139B(c)]

(c) DEFINITIONS.—For purposes of this section—

(1) QUALIFIED STATE AND LOCAL TAX BENEFIT.—The term "qualified state and local tax benefit" means any reduction or rebate of a tax described in paragraph (1), (2), or (3) of section 164(a) provided by a State or political division thereof on account of services performed as a member of a qualified volunteer emergency response organization.

(2) QUALIFIED PAYMENT.—

(A) IN GENERAL.—The term "qualified payment" means any payment (whether reimbursement or otherwise) provided by a State or political division thereof on account of the performance of services as a member of a qualified volunteer emergency response organization.

(B) APPLICABLE DOLLAR LIMITATION.—The amount determined under subparagraph (A) for any taxable year shall not exceed $30 multiplied by the number of months during such year that the taxpayer performs such services.

(3) QUALIFIED VOLUNTEER EMERGENCY RESPONSE ORGANIZATION.—The term "qualified volunteer emergency response organization" means any volunteer organization—

(A) which is organized and operated to provide firefighting or emergency medical services for persons in the State or political subdivision, as the case may be, and

(B) which is required (by written agreement) by the State or political subdivision to furnish firefighting or emergency medical services in such State or political subdivision.

[Sec. 139B(d)]

(d) TERMINATION.—This section shall not apply with respect to taxable years beginning after December 31, 2010.

Amendments

• 2007, Mortgage Forgiveness Debt Relief Act of 2007 (P.L. 110-142)

P.L. 110-142, §5(a):

Amended part III of subchapter B of chapter 1 by inserting after Code Sec. 139A a new Code Sec. 139B. **Effective** for tax years beginning after 12-31-2007.

[Sec. 139C]

SEC. 139C. COBRA PREMIUM ASSISTANCE.

In the case of an assistance eligible individual (as defined in section 3001 of title III of division B of the American Recovery and Reinvestment Act of 2009), gross income does not include any premium reduction provided under subsection (a) of such section.

Amendments

• 2010, Temporary Extension Act of 2010 (P.L. 111-144)

P.L. 111-144, §3(b)(5)(B):

Amended Code Sec. 139C by striking "section 3002 of the Health Insurance Assistance for the Unemployed Act of 2009" and inserting "section 3001 of title III of division B of the American Recovery and Reinvestment Act of 2009". **Effective** as if included in the provision of section 3001 of division B of the American Recovery and Reinvestment Act of 2009 to which it relates [**effective** for tax years ending after 2-17-2009.—CCH].

• 2009, American Recovery and Reinvestment Tax Act of 2009 (P.L. 111-5)

P.L. 111-5, §3001(a)(15)(A):

Amended part III of subchapter B of chapter 1 by inserting after Code Sec. 139B a new Code Sec. 139C. **Effective** for tax years ending after 2-17-1009.

P.L. 111-5, §3001(b), provides:

(b) ELIMINATION OF PREMIUM SUBSIDY FOR HIGH-INCOME INDIVIDUALS.—

(1) RECAPTURE OF SUBSIDY FOR HIGH-INCOME INDIVIDUALS.—If—

(A) premium assistance is provided under this section with respect to any COBRA continuation coverage which covers the taxpayer, the taxpayer's spouse, or any dependent (within the meaning of section 152 of the Internal Revenue Code of 1986, determined without regard to subsections (b)(1), (b)(2), and (d)(1)(B) thereof) of the taxpayer during any portion of the taxable year, and

(B) the taxpayer's modified adjusted gross income for such taxable year exceeds $125,000 ($250,000 in the case of a joint return),

then the tax imposed by chapter 1 of such Code with respect to the taxpayer for such taxable year shall be increased by the amount of such assistance.

(2) PHASE-IN OF RECAPTURE.—

(A) IN GENERAL.—In the case of a taxpayer whose modified adjusted gross income for the taxable year does not exceed $145,000 ($290,000 in the case of a joint return), the increase in the tax imposed under paragraph (1) shall not exceed the phase-in percentage of such increase (determined without regard to this paragraph).

(B) PHASE-IN PERCENTAGE.—For purposes of this subsection, the term "phase-in percentage" means the ratio (expressed as a percentage) obtained by dividing—

(i) the excess of described in subparagraph (B) of paragraph (1), by

(ii) $20,000 ($40,000 in the case of a joint return).

(3) OPTION FOR HIGH-INCOME INDIVIDUALS TO WAIVE ASSISTANCE AND AVOID RECAPTURE.—Notwithstanding subsection (a)(3), an individual shall not be treated as an assistance eligible individual for purposes of this section and section 6432 of the Internal Revenue Code of 1986 if such individual—

(A) makes a permanent election (at such time and in such form and manner as the Secretary of the Treasury may prescribe) to waive the right to the premium assistance provided under this section, and

(B) notifies the entity to whom premiums are reimbursed under section 6432(a) of such Code of such election.

(4) MODIFIED ADJUSTED GROSS INCOME.—For purposes of this subsection, the term "modified adjusted gross income" means the adjusted gross income (as defined in section 62 of the Internal Revenue Code of 1986) of the taxpayer for the taxable year increased by any amount excluded from gross income under section 911, 931, or 933 of such Code.

(5) CREDITS NOT ALLOWED AGAINST TAX, ETC.—For purposes determining regular tax liability under section 26(b) of such Code, the increase in tax under this subsection shall not be treated as a tax imposed under chapter 1 of such Code.

(6) REGULATIONS.—The Secretary of the Treasury shall issue such regulations or other guidance as are necessary or appropriate to carry out this subsection, including requirements that the entity to whom premiums are reimbursed under section 6432(a) of the Internal Revenue Code of 1986 report to the Secretary, and to each assistance eligible individual, the amount of premium assistance provided under subsection (a) with respect to each such individual.

(7) EFFECTIVE DATE.—The provisions of this subsection shall apply to taxable years ending after the date of the enactment of this Act.

[Sec. 139D]

SEC. 139D. INDIAN HEALTH CARE BENEFITS.

[Sec. 139D(a)]

(a) GENERAL RULE.—Except as otherwise provided in this section, gross income does not include the value of any qualified Indian health care benefit.

[Sec. 139D(b)]

(b) QUALIFIED INDIAN HEALTH CARE BENEFIT.—For purposes of this section, the term "qualified Indian health care benefit" means—

(1) any health service or benefit provided or purchased, directly or indirectly, by the Indian Health Service through a grant to or a contract or compact with an Indian tribe or tribal organization, or through a third-party program funded by the Indian Health Service,

(2) medical care provided or purchased by, or amounts to reimburse for such medical care provided by, an Indian tribe or tribal organization for, or to, a member of an Indian tribe, including a spouse or dependent of such a member,

(3) coverage under accident or health insurance (or an arrangement having the effect of accident or health insurance), or an accident or health plan, provided by an Indian tribe or tribal organization for medical care to a member of an Indian tribe, include a spouse or dependent of such a member, and

(4) any other medical care provided by an Indian tribe or tribal organization that supplements, replaces, or substitutes for a program or service relating to medical care provided by the Federal government to Indian tribes or members of such a tribe.

[Sec. 139D(c)]

(c) DEFINITIONS.—For purposes of this section—

(1) INDIAN TRIBE.—The term "Indian tribe" has the meaning given such term by section 45A(c)(6).

(2) TRIBAL ORGANIZATION.—The term "tribal organization" has the meaning given such term by section 4(l) of the Indian Self-Determination and Education Assistance Act.

(3) MEDICAL CARE.—The term "medical care" has the same meaning as when used in section 213.

(4) ACCIDENT OR HEALTH INSURANCE; ACCIDENT OR HEALTH PLAN.—The terms "accident or health insurance" and "accident or health plan" have the same meaning as when used in section 105.

(5) DEPENDENT.—The term "dependent" has the meaning given such term by section 152, determined without regard to subsections (b)(1), (b)(2), and (d)(1)(B) thereof.

[Sec. 139D(d)]

(d) DENIAL OF DOUBLE BENEFIT.—Subsection (a) shall not apply to the amount of any qualified Indian health care benefit which is not includible in gross income of the beneficiary of such benefit under any other provision of this chapter, or to the amount of any such benefit for which a deduction is allowed to such beneficiary under any other provision of this chapter.

Amendments

• 2010, Patient Protection and Affordable Care Act (P.L. 111-148)

P.L. 111-148, §9021(a):

Amended part III of subchapter B of chapter 1 by inserting after Code Sec. 139C a new Code Sec. 139D. **Effective** for benefits and coverage provided after 3-23-2010. For a special rule, see Act Sec. 9021(d), below.

P.L. 111-148, §9021(d), provides:

(d) NO INFERENCE.—Nothing in the amendments made by this section shall be construed to create an inference with respect to the exclusion from gross income of—

(1) benefits provided by an Indian tribe or tribal organization that are not within the scope of this section, and

(2) benefits provided prior to the date of the enactment of this Act.

»»→ Caution: Code Sec. 139D[E], below, as added by P.L. 111-148, applies to vouchers provided after December 31, 2013.

[Sec. 139D[E]]

SEC. 139D[E]. FREE CHOICE VOUCHERS.

Gross income shall not include the amount of any free choice voucher provided by an employer under section 10108 of the Patient Protection and Affordable Care Act to the extent that the amount of such voucher does not exceed the amount paid for a qualified health plan (as defined in section 1301 of such Act) by the taxpayer.

Amendments

• 2010, Patient Protection and Affordable Care Act (P.L. 111-148)

P.L. 111-148, §10108(a)-(e), provides:

SEC. 10108. FREE CHOICE VOUCHERS.

(a) IN GENERAL.—An offering employer shall provide free choice vouchers to each qualified employee of such employer.

(b) OFFERING EMPLOYER.—For purposes of this section, the term "offering employer" means any employer who—

(1) offers minimum essential coverage to its employees consisting of coverage through an eligible employer-sponsored plan; and

(2) pays any portion of the costs of such plan.

(c) QUALIFIED EMPLOYEE.—For purposes of this section—

(1) IN GENERAL.—The term "qualified employee" means, with respect to any plan year of an offering employer, any employee—

(A) whose required contribution (as determined under section 5000A(e)(1)(B)) for minimum essential coverage through an eligible employer-sponsored plan—

(i) exceeds 8 percent of such employee's household income for the taxable year described in section 1412(b)(1)(B) which ends with or within in the plan year; and

(ii) does not exceed 9.8 percent of such employee's household income for such taxable year;

(B) whose household income for such taxable year is not greater than 400 percent of the poverty line for a family of the size involved; and

(C) who does not participate in a health plan offered by the offering employer.

(2) INDEXING.—In the case of any calendar year beginning after 2014, the Secretary shall adjust the 8 percent under paragraph (1)(A)(i) and 9.8 percent under paragraph (1)(A)(ii) for the calendar year to reflect the rate of premium growth between the preceding calendar year and 2013 over the rate of income growth for such period.

(d) FREE CHOICE VOUCHER.—

(1) AMOUNT.—

(A) IN GENERAL.—The amount of any free choice voucher provided under subsection (a) shall be equal to the monthly portion of the cost of the eligible employersponsored plan which would have been paid by the employer if the employee were covered under the plan with respect to which the employer pays the largest portion of the cost of the plan. Such amount shall be equal to the amount the employer would pay for an employee with self-only coverage unless such employee elects family coverage (in which case such amount shall be the amount the employer would pay for family coverage).

(B) DETERMINATION OF COST.—The cost of any health plan shall be determined under the rules similar to the rules of section 2204 of the Public Health Service Act, except that such amount shall be adjusted for age and category of enrollment in accordance with regulations established by the Secretary.

(2) USE OF VOUCHERS.—An Exchange shall credit the amount of any free choice voucher provided under subsection (a) to the monthly premium of any qualified health plan in the Exchange in which the qualified employee is enrolled and the offering employer shall pay any amounts so credited to the Exchange.

(3) PAYMENT OF EXCESS AMOUNTS.—If the amount of the free choice voucher exceeds the amount of the premium of the qualified health plan in which the qualified employee is enrolled for such month, such excess shall be paid to the employee.

(e) OTHER DEFINITIONS.—Any term used in this section which is also used in section 5000A of the Internal Revenue Code of 1986 shall have the meaning given such term under such section 5000A.

P.L. 111-148, §10108(f)(1):

Amended part III of subchapter B of chapter 1 by inserting after Code Sec. 139C[D] a new Code Sec. 139D[E]. **Effective** for vouchers provided after 12-31-2013.

[Sec. 140]

SEC. 140. CROSS REFERENCES TO OTHER ACTS.

[Sec. 140(a)]

(a) For exemption of—

(1) Allowances and expenditures to meet losses sustained by persons serving the United States abroad, due to appreciation of foreign currencies, see section 5943 of title 5, United States Code.

(2) Amounts credited to the Maritime Administration under section 9(b)(6) of the Merchant Ship Sales Act of 1946, see section 9(c)(1) of that Act (50 U.S.C. App. 1742).

(3) Benefits under laws administered by the Veterans' Administration, see section 5301 of title 38, United States Code.

(4) Earnings of ship contractors deposited in special reserve funds, see section 53507 of title 46, United States Code.

(5) Income derived from Federal Reserve banks, including capital stock and surplus, see section 7 of the Federal Reserve Act (12 U.S.C. 531).

(6) Special pensions of persons on Army and Navy medal of honor roll, see 38 U.S.C. 1562(a)-(c).

Amendments

•2006 (P.L. 109-304)

P.L. 109-304, §17(e)(2):

Amended Code Sec. 140(a)(4) by striking "section 607(d) of the Merchant Marine Act, 1936 (46 U.S.C. 1177)" and substituting "section 53507 of title 46, United States Code". **Effective** 10-6-2006.

• 1997, Balanced Budget Act of 1997 (P.L. 105-33)

P.L. 105-33, §4006(a):

Amended part III of subchapter B of chapter 1 by redesignating Code Sec. 138 as Code Sec. 139. **Effective** for tax years beginning after 12-31-98.

• 1996, Small Business Job Protection Act of 1996 (P.L. 104-188)

P.L. 104-188, §1807(b):

Amended part III of subchapter B of chapter 1 by redesignating Code Sec. 137 as Code Sec. 138. **Effective** for tax years beginning after 12-31-96.

• 1992, Energy Policy Act of 1992 (P.L. 102-486)

P.L. 102-486, §1912(a):

Act Sec. 1912(a) redesignated Code Sec. 136 as Code Sec. 137. **Effective** for amounts received after 12-31-92.

• 1991 (P.L. 102-83)

P.L. 102-83, §5(c)(2):

Substituted "1562(a)-(c)" for "562(a)-(c)". **Effective** 8-6-91.

• 1991 (P.L. 102-40)

P.L. 102-40, §402(d)(2):

Substituted "5301" for "3101". **Effective** 5-7-91.

• 1988, Technical and Miscellaneous Revenue Act of 1988 (P.L. 100-647)

P.L. 100-647, §6009(a):

Amended Part III of subchapter B of chapter 1 by redesignating Code Sec. 135 as Code Sec. 136. **Effective** for tax years beginning after 12-31-89.

• 1984, Deficit Reduction Act of 1984 (P.L. 98-369)

P.L. 98-369, §531(a)(1):

Redesignated Code Sec. 132 as Code Sec. 133. **Effective** 1-1-85.

P.L. 98-369, §543(a):

Redesignated Code Sec. 133 as Code Sec. 134. **Effective** with respect to loans used to acquire employer securities after 7-18-84.

P.L. 98-369, §2661(o):

Amended Code Sec. 134, as redesignated by Act Sec. 531(a)(1) and 543(a), by striking out paragraphs (6) and (7) and by redesignating paragraph (8) as (6). **Effective** as if included in the enactment of P.L. 98-21. Prior to their deletion, paragraphs (6) and (7) read as follows:

(6) Railroad retirement annuities and pensions, see section 12 of the Railroad Retirement Act of 1935 (45 U.S.C. 2281).

(7) Railroad unemployment benefits which are not includible in gross income under section 85, see section 2(e) of the Railroad Unemployment Insurance Act (45 U.S.C. 352).

• 1983 (P.L. 97-473)

P.L. 97-473, §101(b)(1):

Redesignated Code Sec. 130(a) as Code Sec. 131(a). **Effective** for tax years beginning after 12-31-82.

P.L. 97-473, §102(a):

Redesignated Code Sec. 131(a) (as previously redesignated) as Code Sec. 132(a). **Effective** for tax years beginning after 12-31-78.

• 1981, Economic Recovery Tax Act of 1981 (P.L. 97-34)

P.L. 97-34, §124(e)(1):

Redesignated Code Sec. 129(a) as Code Sec. 130(a). **Effective** for tax years beginning after 12-31-81.

P.L. 97-34, §301(a):

Redesignated Code Sec. 128(a) as Code Sec. 129(a). **Effective** for tax years ending after 9-30-81. The addition of two Code Secs. 128 by P.L. 97-34 necessitated the redesignation of former Code Sec. 128(a) by P.L. 97-34, §§124(e)(1) and 301(a).

• 1980, Bankruptcy Tax Act of 1980 (P.L. 96-589)

P.L. 96-589, §6(i)(1):

Amended Code Sec. 128(a) by striking out paragraph (1) and redesignating paragraphs (2) through (9) as (1) through (8), respectively. **Effective** 10-1-79, but inapplicable to any proceeding under the Bankruptcy Act commenced before that date. Prior to amendment, Code Sec. 128(a)(1) provided:

"(1) Adjustments of indebtedness under wage earners' plans, see section 679 of the Bankruptcy Act (11 U.S.C. 1079)."

• 1980, Technical Corrections Act of 1979 (P.L. 96-222)

P.L. 96-222, §101(a)(3):

Amended Code Sec. 128(a)(8) by adding "which are not includible in gross income under section 85". **Effective** for payments made after 1978.

• 1976, Tax Reform Act of 1976 (P.L. 94-455)

P.L. 94-455, §1901(a)(21):

Amended Code Sec. 124(a). **Effective** for tax years beginning after 12-31-76. Prior to amendment, Code Sec. 124(a) read as follows:

(a) For exemption of—

(1) Adjustments of indebtedness under wage earners' plans, see section 679 of the Bankruptcy Act (52 Stat. 938; 11 U.S.C. 1079);

(2) Allowances and expenditures to meet losses sustained by persons serving the United States abroad, due to appreciation of foreign currencies, see the Acts of March 6, 1934 (48 Stat. 466; 5 U.S.C. 118c) and April 25, 1938 (52 Stat. 221; 5 U.S.C. 118c-1);

(3) Amounts credited to the Maritime Administration under section 9(b)(6) of the Merchant Ship Sales Act of 1946, see section 9(c)(1) of that Act (60 Stat. 48; 50 U.S.C. App. 1742);

(4) Benefits under World War Adjusted Compensation Act, see section 308 of that Act, as amended (43 Stat. 125; 44 Stat. 827, §3; 38 U.S.C. 618);

(5) Benefits under World War Veterans' Act, 1924, see section 3 of the Act of August 12, 1935 (49 Stat. 609; 38 U.S.C. 454a);

(6) Dividends and interest derived from certain preferred stock by Reconstruction Finance Corporation, see section 304 of the Act of March 9, 1933, as amended (49 Stat. 1185; 12 U.S.C. 51d);

(7) Earnings of ship contractors deposited in special reserve funds, see section 607(h) of the Merchant Marine Act, 1936, as amended (52 Stat. 961, §28; 46 U.S.C. 1177);

(8) Income derived from Federal Reserve banks, including capital stock and surplus, see section 7 of the Federal Reserve Act (38 Stat. 258; 12 U.S.C. 531);

(9) Income derived from Ogdensburg bridge across Saint Lawrence River, see section 4 of the Act of June 14, 1933, as amended (54 Stat. 259, §2);

(10) Income derived from Owensboro bridge across Ohio River and nearby ferries, see section 4 of the Act of August 14, 1937 (50 Stat. 643);

(11) Income derived from Saint Clair River bridge and ferries, see section 4 of the Act of June 25, 1930, as amended (48 Stat. 140, §1);

(12) Leave compensation payments under section 6 of Armed Forces Leave Act of 1946, see section 7 of that Act (60 Stat. 967; 37 U.S.C. 36);

(13) Mustering-out payments made to or on account of veterans under the Mustering-Out Payment Act of 1944, see section (5)(a) of that Act (58 Stat. 10; 38 U.S.C. 691e);

(14) Railroad retirement annuities and pensions, see section 12 of the Railroad Retirement Act of 1935, as amended (50 Stat. 316; 45 U.S.C. 2281);

(15) Railroad unemployment benefits, see section 2(e) of the Railroad Unemployment Insurance Act, as amended (52 Stat. 1097; 53 Stat. 845, §9; 45 U.S.C. 352);

(16) Special pensions of persons on Army and Navy medal of honor roll, see section 3 of the Act of April 27, 1916 (39 Stat. 54; 38 U.S.C. 393);

(17) Gain derived from the sale or other disposition of Treasury Bills, issued after June 17, 1930, under the Second Liberty Bond Act, as amended, see Act of June 17, 1930 (C. 512, 46 Stat. 775; 31 U.S.C. 754);

(18) Benefits under laws administered by the Veterans' Administration, see section 3101 of title 38, United States Code.

[Sec. 140(b)]

(b) For extension of military income-tax-exemption benefits to commissioned officers of Public Health Service in certain circumstances, see section 212 of the Public Health Service Act (42 U.S.C. 213).

Amendments

• 2002, Victims of Terrorism Tax Relief Act of 2001 (P.L. 107-134)

P.L. 107-134, §111(a):

Amended part III of subchapter B of chapter 1 by redesignating Code Sec. 139 as Code Sec. 140. **Effective** for tax years ending on or after 9-11-2001.

• 1996, Small Business Job Protection Act of 1996 (P.L. 104-188)

P.L. 104-188, §1807(b):

Amended part III of subchapter B of chapter 1 by redesignating Code Sec. 137 as Code Sec. 138. **Effective** for tax years beginning after 12-31-96.

• 1992, Energy Policy Act of 1992 (P.L. 102-486)

P.L. 102-486, §1912(a):

Redesignated Code Sec. 136 as Code Sec. 137.

• 1988, Technical and Miscellaneous Revenue Act of 1988 (P.L. 100-647)

P.L. 100-647, §6009(a):

Amended Part III of subchapter B of chapter 1 by redesignating Code Sec. 135 as Code Sec. 136. **Effective** for tax years beginning after 12-31-89.

• 1986, Tax Reform Act of 1986 (P.L. 99-514)

P.L. 99-514, §1168(a):

Redesignated former Code Sec. 134 as Code Sec. 135. **Effective** for tax years beginning after 12-31-86.

• 1983 (P.L. 97-473)

P.L. 97-473, §101(b)(1):

Redesignated Code Sec. 130(b) as Code Sec. 131(b). **Effective** for tax years beginning after 12-31-82.

P.L. 97-473, §102(a):

Redesignated Code Sec. 131(b) (as previously redesignated) as Code Sec. 132(b). **Effective** for tax years beginning after 12-31-78.

• 1981, Economic Recovery Tax Act of 1981 (P.L. 97-34)

P.L. 97-34, §124(e)(1):

Redesignated Code Sec. 129(b) as Code Sec. 130(b) and inserted new Code Sec. 129 after Code Sec. 128. **Effective** for tax years beginning after 12-31-81.

P.L. 97-34, §301(a):

Redesignated Code Sec. 128(b) as Code Sec. 129(b). **Effective** for tax years ending after 9-30-81. The addition of two Code Secs. 128 by P.L. 97-34, necessitated the redesignation of former Code Sec. 128(b) by P.L. 97-34, §§124(e)(1) and 301(a).

• 1978, Energy Tax Act of 1978 (P.L. 95-618)

P.L. 95-618, §242(a):

Redesignated Code Sec. 124 as Code Sec. 125.

• 1978, Revenue Act of 1978 (P.L. 95-600)

P.L. 95-600, §134(a):

Redesignated Code Sec. 125 as Code Sec. 126.

P.L. 95-600, §543(a):

Redesignated Code Sec. 126 as Code Sec. 127.

P.L. 95-600, §164(a):

Redesignated Code Sec. 127 as Code Sec. 128.

• 1976, Tax Reform Act of 1976 (P.L. 94-455)

P.L. 94-455, §1901(a)(a)(21):

Amended Code Sec. 124(b) to substitute "(42 U.S.C. 213)" for "(58 Stat. 689, 42 U.S.C. 213)". **Effective** for tax years beginning after 12-31-76.

• 1969, Tax Reform Act of 1969 (P.L. 91-172)

P.L. 91-172, §901(a):

Redesignated Code Sec. 123 as Code Sec. 124.

• 1966 (P.L. 89-365)

P.L. 89-365, §[1]:

Redesignated Code Sec. 122 as Code Sec. 123. **Effective** for tax years ending after 12-31-65.

• 1964, Revenue Act of 1964 (P.L. 88-272)

P.L. 88-272, §206(a):

Redesignated Code Sec. 121 as Code Sec. 122. **Effective** 1-1-64.

• 1958 (P.L. 85-857)

P.L. 85-857, §13(t):

Amended Code Sec. 122(a)(18). **Effective** 1-1-59.

• 1957, Veterans' Benefits Act of 1957 (P.L. 85-56)

P.L. 85-56, §2201:

Amended Code Sec. 122(a)(18) to read as follows: "Benefits under laws administered by the Veterans' Administration, see section 1001 of the Veterans' Benefits Act of 1957." **Effective** 1-1-58.

• 1956, Servicemen's and Veterans' Survivor Benefits Act (P.L. 881, 84th Cong.)

P.L. 881, 84th Cong., §501(t):

Amended Code Sec. 122(a) by adding paragraph (18) to read as follows: "Dependency and indemnity compensation paid to survivors of members of a uniformed service and certain other persons, see section 210 of the Servicemen's and Veterans' Survivor Benefits Act." **Effective** 1-1-57.

PART IV—TAX EXEMPTION REQUIREMENTS FOR STATE AND LOCAL BONDS

Subpart A—Private Activity Bonds

[Sec. 141]

SEC. 141. PRIVATE ACTIVITY BOND; QUALIFIED BOND.

[Sec. 141(a)]

(a) PRIVATE ACTIVITY BOND.—For purposes of this title, the term "private activity bond" means any bond issued as part of an issue—

(1) which meets—

(A) the private business use test of paragraph (1) of subsection (b), and

(B) the private security or payment test of paragraph (2) of subsection (b), or

(2) which meets the private loan financing test of subsection (c).

[Sec. 141(b)]

(b) PRIVATE BUSINESS TESTS.—

(1) PRIVATE BUSINESS USE TEST.—Except as otherwise provided in this subsection, an issue meets the test of this paragraph if more than 10 percent of the proceeds of the issue are to be used for any private business use.

(2) PRIVATE SECURITY OR PAYMENT TEST.—Except as otherwise provided in this subsection, an issue meets the test of this paragraph if the payment of the principal of, or the interest on, more than 10 percent of the proceeds of such issue is (under the terms of such issue or any underlying arrangement) directly or indirectly—

(A) secured by any interest in—

(i) property used or to be used for a private business use, or

(ii) payments in respect of such property, or

(B) to be derived from payments (whether or not to the issuer) in respect of property, or borrowed money, used or to be used for a private business use.

(3) 5 PERCENT TEST FOR PRIVATE BUSINESS USE NOT RELATED OR DISPROPORTIONATE TO GOVERNMENT USE FINANCED BY THE ISSUE.—

(A) IN GENERAL.—An issue shall be treated as meeting the tests of paragraphs (1) and (2) if such tests would be met if such paragraphs were applied—

(i) by substituting "5 percent" for "10 percent" each place it appears, and

(ii) by taking into account only—

(I) the proceeds of the issue which are to be used for any private business use which is not related to any government use of such proceeds,

(II) the disproportionate related business use proceeds of the issue, and

(III) payments, property, and borrowed money with respect to any use of proceeds described in subclause (I) or (II).

(B) DISPROPORTIONATE RELATED BUSINESS USE PROCEEDS.—For purposes of subparagraph (A), the disproportionate related business use proceeds of an issue is an amount equal to the aggregate of the excesses (determined under the following sentence) for each private business use of the proceeds of an issue which is related to a government use of such proceeds. The excess determined under this sentence is the excess of—

(i) the proceeds of the issue which are to be used for the private business use, over

(ii) the proceeds of the issue which are to be used for the government use to which such private business use relates.

(4) LOWER LIMITATION FOR CERTAIN OUTPUT FACILITIES.—An issue 5 percent or more of the proceeds of which are to be used with respect to any output facility (other than a facility for the furnishing of water) shall be treated as meeting the tests of paragraphs (1) and (2) if the nonqualified amount with respect to such issue exceeds the excess of—

(A) $15,000,000, over

(B) the aggregate nonqualified amounts with respect to all prior tax-exempt issues 5 percent or more of the proceeds of which are or will be used with respect to such facility (or any other facility which is part of the same project).

There shall not be taken into account under subparagraph (B) any bond which is not outstanding at the time of the later issue or which is to be redeemed (other than in an advance refunding) from the net proceeds of the later issue.

(5) COORDINATION WITH VOLUME CAP WHERE NONQUALIFIED AMOUNT EXCEEDS $15,000,000.—If the nonqualified amount with respect to an issue—

(A) exceeds $15,000,000, but

(B) does not exceed the amount which would cause a bond which is part of such issue to be treated as a private activity bond without regard to this paragraph,

such bond shall nonetheless be treated as a private activity bond unless the issuer allocates a portion of its volume cap under section 146 to such issue in an amount equal to the excess of such nonqualified amount over $15,000,000.

(6) PRIVATE BUSINESS USE DEFINED.—

(A) IN GENERAL.—For purposes of this subsection, the term "private business use" means use (directly or indirectly) in a trade or business carried on by any person other than a governmental unit. For purposes of the preceding sentence, use as a member of the general public shall not be taken into account.

(B) CLARIFICATION OF TRADE OR BUSINESS.—For purposes of the 1st sentence of subparagraph (A), any activity carried on by a person other than a natural person shall be treated as a trade or business.

(7) GOVERNMENT USE.—The term "government use" means any use other than a private business use.

(8) NONQUALIFIED AMOUNT.—For purposes of this subsection, the term "nonqualified amount" means, with respect to an issue, the lesser of—

(A) the proceeds of such issue which are to be used for any private business use, or

(B) the proceeds of such issue with respect to which there are payments (or property or borrowed money) described in paragraph (2).

(9) EXCEPTION FOR QUALIFIED 501(c)(3) BONDS.—There shall not be taken into account under this subsection or subsection (c) the portion of the proceeds of an issue which (if issued as a separate issue) would be treated as a qualified 501(c)(3) bond if the issuer elects to treat such portion as a qualified 501(c)(3) bond.

Amendments

• 1988, Technical and Miscellaneous Revenue Act of 1988 (P.L. 100-647)

P.L. 100-647, §1013(a)(38):

Amended Code Sec. 141(b)(5)(B) by striking out "which would cause bond" and inserting in lieu thereof "which would cause a bond". **Effective** as if included in the provision of P.L. 99-514 to which it relates. For a special rule, see Act Sec. 6179, below.

P.L. 100-647, §6179, provides:

SEC. 6179. APPLICATION OF SECURITY INTEREST TEST TO BOND FINANCING OF HAZARDOUS WASTE CLEAN-UP ACTIVITIES.

Before January 1, 1989, the Secretary of the Treasury or his delegate shall issue guidance concerning the application of the private security or payment test under section 141(b)(2) of the Internal Revenue Code of 1986 to tax-exempt bond financing by State and local governments of hazardous waste clean-up activities conducted by such governments where some of the activities occur on privately owned land.

[Sec. 141(c)]

(c) PRIVATE LOAN FINANCING TEST.—

(1) IN GENERAL.—An issue meets the test of this subsection if the amount of the proceeds of the issue which are to be used (directly or indirectly) to make or finance loans (other than loans described in paragraph (2)) to persons other than governmental units exceeds the lesser of—

(A) 5 percent of such proceeds, or

(B) $5,000,000.

(2) EXCEPTION FOR TAX ASSESSMENT, ETC., LOANS.—For purposes of paragraph (1), a loan is described in this paragraph if such loan—

(A) enables the borrower to finance any governmental tax or assessment of general application for a specific essential governmental function,

(B) is a nonpurpose investment (within the meaning of section 148(f)(6)(A)), or

(C) is a qualified natural gas supply contract (as defined in section 148(b)(4)).

Amendments

• 2005, Energy Tax Incentives Act of 2005 (P.L. 109-58)

P.L. 109-58, §1327(b):

Amended Code Sec. 141(c)(2) by striking "or" at the end of subparagraph (A), by striking the period at the end of subparagraph (B) and inserting ", or", and by adding at the end a new subparagraph (C). **Effective** for obligations issued after 8-8-2005.

[Sec. 141(d)]

(d) CERTAIN ISSUES USED TO ACQUIRE NONGOVERNMENTAL OUTPUT PROPERTY TREATED AS PRIVATE ACTIVITY BONDS.—

(1) IN GENERAL.—For purposes of this title, the term "private activity bond" includes any bond issued as part of an issue if the amount of the proceeds of the issue which are to be used (directly or indirectly) for the acquisition by a governmental unit of nongovernmental output property exceeds the lesser of—

(A) 5 percent of such proceeds, or

(B) $5,000,000.

(2) NONGOVERNMENTAL OUTPUT PROPERTY.—Except as otherwise provided in this subsection, for purposes of paragraph (1), the term "nongovernmental output property" means any property (or interest therein) which before such acquisition was used (or held for use) by a person other than a governmental unit in connection with an output facility (within the meaning of subsection (b)(4)) (other than a facility for the furnishing of water). For purposes of the preceding sentence, use (or the holding for use) before October 14, 1987, shall not be taken into account.

(3) EXCEPTION FOR PROPERTY ACQUIRED TO PROVIDE OUTPUT TO CERTAIN AREAS.—For purposes of paragraph (1)—

(A) IN GENERAL.—The term "nongovernmental output property" shall not include any property which is to be used in connection with an output facility 95 percent or more of the output of which will be consumed in—

(i) a qualified service area of the governmental unit acquiring the property, or

(ii) a qualified annexed area of such unit.

(B) DEFINITIONS.—For purposes of subparagraph (A)—

(i) QUALIFIED SERVICE AREA.—The term "qualified service area" means, with respect to the governmental unit acquiring the property, any area throughout which such unit provided (at all times during the 10-year period ending on the date such property is acquired by such unit) output of the same type as the output to be provided by such property. For purposes of the preceding sentence, the period before October 14, 1987, shall not be taken into account.

(ii) QUALIFIED ANNEXED AREA.—The term "qualified annexed area" means, with respect to the governmental unit acquiring the property, any area if—

(I) such area is contiguous to, and annexed for general governmental purposes into, a qualified service area of such unit,

(II) output from such property is made available to all members of the general public in the annexed area, and

(III) the annexed area is not greater than 10 percent of such qualified service area.

(C) LIMITATION ON SIZE OF ANNEXED AREA NOT TO APPLY WHERE OUTPUT CAPACITY DOES NOT INCREASE BY MORE THAN 10 PERCENT.—Subclause (III) of subparagraph (B)(ii) shall not apply to an annexation of an area by a governmental unit if the output capacity of the property acquired in connection with the annexation, when added to the output capacity of all other property which is not treated as nongovernmental output property by reason of subparagraph (A)(ii) with respect to such annexed area, does not exceed 10 percent of the output capacity of the property providing output of the same type to the qualified service area into which it is annexed.

(D) RULES FOR DETERMINING RELATIVE SIZE, ETC.—For purposes of subparagraphs (B)(ii) and (C)—

(i) The size of any qualified service area and the output capacity of property serving such area shall be determined as the close of the calendar year preceding the calendar year in which the acquisition of nongovernmental output property or the annexation occurs.

(ii) A qualified annexed area shall be treated as part of the qualified service area into which it is annexed for purposes of determining whether any other area annexed in a later year is a qualified annexed area.

(4) EXCEPTION FOR PROPERTY CONVERTED TO NONOUTPUT USE.—For purposes of paragraph (1)—

(A) IN GENERAL.—The term "nongovernmental output property" shall not include any property which is to be converted to a use not in connection with an output facility.

(B) EXCEPTION.—Subparagraph (A) shall not apply to any property which is part of the output function of a nuclear power facility.

(5) SPECIAL RULES.—In the case of a bond which is a private activity bond solely by reason of this subsection—

(A) subsections (c) and (d) of section 147 (relating to limitations on acquisition of land and existing property) shall not apply, and

(B) paragraph (8) of section 142(a) shall be applied as if it did not contain "local".

(6) TREATMENT OF JOINT ACTION AGENCIES.—With respect to nongovernmental output property acquired by a joint action agency the members of which are governmental units, this subsection shall be applied at the member level by treating each member as acquiring its proportionate share of such property.

(7) EXCEPTION FOR QUALIFIED ELECTRIC AND NATURAL GAS SUPPLY CONTRACTS.—The term "nongovernmental output property" shall not include any contract for the prepayment of electricity or natural gas which is not investment property under section 148(b)(2).

Amendments

• 2005, Energy Tax Incentives Act of 2005 (P.L. 109-58)

P.L. 109-58, §1327(c):

Amended Code Sec. 141(d) by adding at the end a new paragraph (7). **Effective** for obligations issued after 8-8-2005.

• 1987, Revenue Act of 1987 (P.L. 100-203)

P.L. 100-203, §10631(a):

Amended Code Sec. 141 by redesignating subsection (d) as subsection (e) and by inserting after subsection (c) new subsection (d). For the **effective** date, see Act Sec. 10631(c), below.

P.L. 100-203, §10631(c), provides:

(c) EFFECTIVE DATE.

(1) IN GENERAL.—Except as otherwise provided in this subsecion, the amendments made by this section shall apply to bonds issued after October 13, 1987 (other than bonds issued to refund bonds issued on or before such date).

(2) BINDING AGREEMENTS.—The amendments made by this section shall not apply to bonds (other than advance refunding bonds) with respect to a facility acquired after October 13, 1987, pursuant to a binding contract entered into on or before such date.

(3) TRANSITIONAL RULE.—The amendments made by this section shall not apply to bonds issued—

(A) after October 13, 1987, by an authority created by a statute—

(i) approved by the State Governor on July 24, 1986, and

(ii) sections 1 through 10 of which became effective on January 15, 1987, and

(B) to provide facilities serving the area specified in such statute on the date of its enactment.

[Sec. 141(e)]

(e) QUALIFIED BOND.—For purposes of this part, the term "qualified bond" means any private activity bond if—

(1) IN GENERAL.—Such bond is—

(A) an exempt facility bond,

(B) a qualified mortgage bond,

(C) a qualified veterans' mortgage bond,

(D) a qualified small issue bond,

(E) a qualified student loan bond,

(F) a qualified redevelopment bond, or

(G) a qualified 501(c)(3) bond.

(2) VOLUME CAP.—Such bond is issued as part of an issue which meets the applicable requirements of section 146, and

(3) OTHER REQUIREMENTS.—Such bond meets the applicable requirements of each subsection of section 147.

Amendments

• 1987, Revenue Act of 1987 (P.L. 100-203)

P.L. 100-203, §10631(a):

Amended Code Sec. 141 by redesignating subsection (d) as subsection (e) and by inserting after subsection (c) new subsection (d). For the **effective** date, see Act Sec. 10631(c), below.

P.L. 100-203, §10631(c), provides:

(c) EFFECTIVE DATE.

(1) IN GENERAL.—Except as otherwise provided in this subsecion, the amendments made by this section shall apply to bonds issued after October 13, 1987 (other than bonds issued to refund bonds issued on or before such date).

(2) BINDING AGREEMENTS.—The amendments made by this section shall not apply to bonds (other than advance refunding bonds) with respect to a facility acquired after October 13, 1987, pursuant to a binding contract entered into on or before such date.

(3) TRANSITIONAL RULE.—The amendments made by this section shall not apply to bonds issued—

(A) after October 13, 1987, by an authority created by a statute—

(i) approved by the State Governor on July 24, 1986, and

(ii) sections 1 through 10 of which became effective on January 15, 1987, and

(B) to provide facilities serving the area specified in such statute on the date of its enactment.

• 1986, Tax Reform Act of 1986 (P.L. 99-514)

P.L. 99-514, §1301(b):

Amended Part IV of subchapter B of chapter 1 by adding Code Sec. 141. **Effective**, generally, for bonds issued after 8-15-86. However, for transitional rules, see Act Secs. 1312-1318 following Code Sec. 103.

[Sec. 141—Repealed]

Amendments

• 1977, Tax Reduction and Simplification Act of 1977 (P.L. 95-30)

P.L. 95-30, §101(d)(1):

Repealed Code Sec. 141. **Effective** for tax years beginning after 12-31-76. Prior to repeal, Code Sec. 141 read as follows:

SEC. 141. STANDARD DEDUCTION.

(a) STANDARD DEDUCTION.—Except as otherwise provided in this section, the standard deduction referred to in this title is the larger of the percentage standard deduction or the low income allowance.

(b) PERCENTAGE STANDARD DEDUCTION.—The percentage standard deduction is an amount equal to 16 percent of adjusted gross income, but not more than—

(1) $2,800 in the case of—

(A) a joint return under section 6013, or

(B) a surviving spouse (as defined in section 2(a)),

(2) $2,400 in the case of an individual who is not married and who is not a surviving spouse (as so defined), or

(3) $1,400 in the case of a married individual filing a separate return.

(c) LOW INCOME ALLOWANCE.—The low income allowance is—

(1) $2,100 in the case of—

(A) a joint return under section 6013, or

(B) a surviving spouse (as defined in section 2(a)),

(2) $1,700 in the case of an individual who is not married and who is not a surviving spouse (as so defined), or

(3) $1,050 in the case of a married individual filing a separate return.

(d) MARRIED INDIVIDUALS FILING SEPARATE RETURNS.—Notwithstanding subsection (a)—

(1) The low income allowance shall not apply in the case of a separate return by a married individual if the tax of the

other spouse is determined with regard to the percentage standard deduction.

(2) A married individual filing a separate return may, if the low income allowance is less than the percentage standard deduction, and if the low income allowance of his spouse is greater than the percentage standard deduction of such spouse, elect (under regulations prescribed by the Secretary) to have his tax determined with regard to the low income allowance in lieu of being determined with regard to the percentage standard deduction.

(e) LIMITATIONS IN CASE OF CERTAIN DEPENDENT TAXPAYERS.—In the case of a taxpayer with respect to whom a deduction under section 151(e) is allowable to another taxpayer for the taxable year—

(1) the percentage standard deduction shall be computed only with reference to so much of his adjusted gross income as is attributable to his earned income (as defined in section 911(b)), and

(2) the low income allowance shall not exceed his earned income for the taxable year.

• 1976, Tax Reform Act of 1976 (P.L. 94-455)

P.L. 94-455, §1906(b)(13)(A):

Amended paragraph (d) by substituting "Secretary" for "Secretary or his delegate" each place it appeared. **Effective** 2-1-77.

P.L. 94-455, §401(b):

Amended Code Sec. 141(b) and (c). **Effective** for tax years ending after 12-31-75. Prior to amendment, Code Sec. 141(b) and (c) read as follows:

(b) PERCENTAGE STANDARD DEDUCTION.—The percentage standard deduction is an amount equal to the applicable percentage of adjusted gross income shown in the following table, but not to exceed the maximum amount shown in such table (or one-half of such maximum amount in the case of a separate return by a married individual):

Taxable years beginning in—	*Applicable percentage*	*Maximum amount*
1970	10	$1,000
1971	13	1,500
1972 and thereafter	15	2,000

(c) LOW INCOME ALLOWANCE.—The low income allowance is $1,300 ($650 in the case of a married individual filing a separate return).

• 1975, Revenue Adjustment Act of 1975 (P.L. 94-164)

P.L. 94-164, §2(a)(1), (b)(1):

Sec. 2(a)(1) of P.L. 94-164 amended Code Sec. 141(c), and §2(b)(1) of P.L. 94-164 amended Code Sec. 141(b). The text of these subsections, as amended **effective** for tax years ending in 1976 only, is as follows:

(b) PERCENTAGE STANDARD DEDUCTION.—

(1) GENERAL RULE.—The percentage standard deduction is an amount equal to 16 percent of adjusted gross income but not to exceed—

(A) $2,800 in the case of—

(i) a joint return under section 6013, or

(ii) a surviving spouse (as defined in section 2(a)),

(B) $2,400 in the case of an individual who is not married and who is not a surviving spouse (as so defined), or

(C) $1,400 in the case of a married individual filing a separate return.

(2) APPLICATION OF 6-MONTH RULE.—Notwithstanding the provisions of paragraph (1) of this subsection, the following amounts shall be substituted for the amounts set forth in paragraph (1)—

(A) "$2,400" for "$2,800" in subparagraph (A),

(B) "$2,200" for "$2,400" in subparagraph (B), and

(C) "$1,200" for "$1,400" in subparagraph (C).

(c) LOW INCOME ALLOWANCE.—

(1) IN GENERAL.—The low income allowance is—

(A) $2,100 in the case of—

(i) a joint return under section 6013, or

(ii) a surviving spouse (as defined in section 2(a)),

(B) $1,700 in the case of an individual who is not married and who is not a surviving spouse (as so defined), or

(C) $1,050 in the case of a married individual filing a separate return.

(2) APPLICATION OF 6-MONTH RULE.—Notwithstanding the provisions of paragraph (1), the following amounts shall be substituted for the amount set forth in paragraph (1)—

(A) "$1,700" for "$2,100" in subparagraph (A),

(B) "$1,500" for "$1,700" in subparagraph (B), and

(C) "$850" for "$1,050" in subparagraph (C).

See, also, the comments under P.L. 94-12, below.

• 1975, Tax Reduction Act of 1975 (P.L. 94-12)

P.L. 94-12, §§201(a), 202(a):

Sec. 202(a) of P.L. 94-12 amended Code Sec. 141(b), and §201(a) of P.L. 94-12 amended Code Sec. 141(c). The texts of these subsections, as amended **effective** for tax years beginning after 1974 and inapplicable to tax years ending after 1975, is as follows:

(b) PERCENTAGE STANDARD DEDUCTION.—The percentage standard deduction is an amount equal to 16 percent of adjusted gross income but not to exceed—

(1) $2,600 in the case of—

(A) a joint return under section 6013, or

(B) a surviving spouse (as defined in section 2(a)),

(2) $2,300 in the case of an individual who is not married and who is not a surviving spouse (as so defined), or

(3) $1,300 in the case of a married individual filing a separate return.

(c) LOW INCOME ALLOWANCE.—The low income allowance is—

(1) $1,900 in the case of—

(A) a joint return under section 6013, or

(B) a surviving spouse (as defined in section 2(a)),

(2) $1,600 in the case of an individual who is not married and who is not a surviving spouse (as so defined), or

(3) $950 in the case of a married individual filing a separate return.

• 1971, Revenue Act of 1971 (P.L. 92-178)

P.L. 92-178, §§202, 203:

Substituted the last line in the table in Code Sec. 141(b) as follows. **Effective** for tax years beginning after 12-31-71.

"1972	14	2,000"
"1973 and thereafter	15	2,000"

Sec. 203 of P. L. 92-178 provided two versions of Code Sec. 141(c). The version shown in the law text above is effective for taxable years beginning after December 31, 1971. The following version of Code Sec. 141(c) was effective for taxable years beginning after December 31, 1970, and before January 1, 1972:

"(c) Low Income Allowance.—The low income allowance is $1,050 ($525 in the case of a married individual filing a separate return)."

Prior to these amendments, Code Sec. 141(c) (as amended by P. L. 91-172, §802(a)) read as follows:

"(c) Low Income Allowance.—

"(1) In general.—The low income allowance is an amount equal to the sum of—

"(A) the basic allowance, and

"(B) the additional allowance.

"(2) Basic allowance.—For purposes of this subsection, the basic allowance is an amount equal to the sum of—

"(A) $200, plus

"(B) $100, multiplied by the number of exemptions.

"The basic allowance shall not exceed $1,000.

"(3) Additional allowance.—

"(A) In general.—For purposes of this subsection, the additional allowance is an amount equal to the excess (if any) of $900 over the sum of—

"(i) $100, multiplied by the number of exemptions, plus

"(ii) the income phase-out.

"(B) Income phase-out.—For purposes of subparagraph (A)(ii), the income phase-out is an amount equal to one-half of the amount by which the adjusted gross income for the taxable year exceeds the sum of—

"(i) $1,100, plus

"(ii) $625, multiplied by the number of exemptions.

"(4) Married individuals filing separate returns.—In the case of a married taxpayer filing a separate return—

"(A) the low income allowance is an amount equal to the basic allowance, and

"(B) the basic allowance is an amount (not in excess of $500) equal to the sum of—

"(i) $100, plus

"(ii) $100, multiplied by the number of exemptions.

"(5) Number of exemptions.—For purposes of this subsection, the number of exemptions is the number of exemptions allowed as a deduction for the taxable year under section 151.

"(6) Special rule for 1971.—For a taxable year beginning after December 31, 1970, and before January 1, 1972,—

"(A) paragraph (3)(A) shall be applied by substituting `$850' for `$900',

"(B) paragraph (3)(B) shall be applied by substituting `one-fifteenth' for `one-half',

"(C) paragraph (3)(B)(i) shall be applied by substituting `$1050' for `$1100', and

"(D) paragraph (3)(B)(ii) shall be applied by substituting `$650' for `$625'."

P.L. 92-178, §301(a):

Added Code Sec. 141(e). **Effective** for taxable years beginning after 12-31-71.

• 1969, Tax Reform Act of 1969 (P.L. 91-172)

P.L. 91-172, §802(a):

Amended Code Sec. 141 by striking out subsections (a), (b) and (c) and substituting new subsections (a), (b) and (c). Prior to amendment, subsections (a), (b) and (c) read as follows:

(a) Standard Deduction.—Except as otherwise provided in this section, the standard deduction referred to in this title is the larger of the 10-percent standard deduction or the minimum standard deduction. The standard deduction shall not exceed $1,000, except that in the case of a separate return by a married individual the standard deduction shall not exceed $500.

(b) Ten-percent Standard Deduction.—The 10-percent standard deduction is an amount equal to 10 percent of the adjusted gross income.

(c) Minimum Standard Deduction.—The minimum standard deduction is an amount equal to the sum of—

(1) $100, multiplied by the number of exemptions allowed for the taxable year as a deduction under section 151, plus

(2)(A) $200, in the case of a joint return of a husband and wife under section 6013,

(B) $200, in the case of a return of an individual who is not married, or

(C) $100 in the case of a separate return by a married individual.

P.L. 91-172, §802(c):

Amended Code Sec. 141(d) by inserting "low income allowance" in place of "minimum standard deduction" wherever it appeared and by inserting "percentage" in place of "10-percent" wherever it appeared. **Effective** for tax years beginning after 12-31-69.

P.L. 91-172, §802(e):

Amended Code Sec. 141(c) (see text under amendment note for P.L. 92-178, §203). **Effective** for tax years beginning after 12-31-71.

• 1964, Revenue Act of 1964 (P.L. 88-272)

P.L. 88-272, §112(a):

Amended Sec. 141. **Effective** for tax years beginning after 12-31-63. Prior to amendment, Sec. 141 read as follows:

"The standard deduction referred to in section 63(b) (defining taxable income in case of individual electing standard deduction) shall be an amount equal to 10 percent of the adjusted gross income or $1,000, whichever is the lesser, except that in the case of a separate return by a married individual the standard deduction shall not exceed $500."

[Sec. 142]

SEC. 142. EXEMPT FACILITY BOND.

[Sec. 142(a)]

(a) GENERAL RULE.—For purposes of this part, the term "exempt facility bond" means any bond issued as part of an issue 95 percent or more of the net proceeds of which are to be used to provide—

(1) airports,

(2) docks and wharves,

(3) mass commuting facilities,

(4) facilities for the furnishing of water,

(5) sewage facilities,

(6) solid waste disposal facilities,

(7) qualified residential rental projects,

(8) facilities for the local furnishing of electric energy or gas,

(9) local district heating or cooling facilities,

(10) qualified hazardous waste facilities,

(11) high-speed intercity rail facilities,

(12) environmental enhancements of hydroelectric generating facilities,

»»→ Caution: Code Sec. 142(a)(13), below, is subject to the sunset provision of the Economic Growth and Tax Relief Reconciliation Act of 2001 (P.L. 107-16), §901. Absent Congressional action, the changes made to this provision by P.L. 107-16, or that take effect as if included in P.L. 107-16, do not apply after December 31, 2010. For more information about the sunset provision, see page XXI of the Preface to this publication and P.L. 107-16, §901, in the amendment notes. See the amendments notes for a history of amendments to this section and the effective date of each change.

(13) qualified public educational facilities,

(14) qualified green building and sustainable design projects, or

(15) qualified highway or surface freight transfer facilities.

Amendments

• 2005, Safe, Accountable, Flexible, Efficient Transportation Equity Act: A Legacy for Users (P.L. 109-59)

P.L. 109-59, §11143(a):

Amended Code Sec. 142(a) by striking "or" at the end of paragraph (13), by striking the period at the end of paragraph (14) and inserting ", or", and by adding at the end a new paragraph (15). **Effective** for bonds issued after 8-10-2005.

• 2004, American Jobs Creation Act of 2004 (P.L. 108-357)

P.L. 108-357, §701(a):

Amended Code Sec. 142(a) by striking "or" at the end of paragraph (12), by striking the period at the end of paragraph (13) and inserting ", or", and by inserting at the end a new paragraph (14). **Effective** for bonds issued after 12-31-2004.

• 2001, Economic Growth and Tax Relief Reconciliation Act of 2001 (P.L. 107-16)

P.L. 107-16, §422(a):

Amended Code Sec. 142(a) by striking "or" at the end of paragraph (11), by striking the period at the end of paragraph (12) and inserting ", or", and by adding at the end a new paragraph (13). **Effective** for bonds issued after 12-31-2001.

P.L. 107-16, §901(a)-(b), provides:

SEC. 901. SUNSET OF PROVISIONS OF ACT.

(a) IN GENERAL.—All provisions of, and amendments made by, this Act shall not apply—

(1) to taxable, plan, or limitation years beginning after December 31, 2010, or

(2) in the case of title V, to estates of decedents dying, gifts made, or generation skipping transfers, after December 31, 2010.

(b) APPLICATION OF CERTAIN LAWS.—The Internal Revenue Code of 1986 and the Employee Retirement Income Security Act of 1974 shall be applied and administered to years, estates, gifts, and transfers described in subsection (a) as if the provisions and amendments described in subsection (a) had never been enacted.

• 1992, Energy Policy Act of 1992 (P.L. 102-486)

P.L. 102-486, §1921(a)(1)-(3):

Amended Code Sec. 142(a) by striking "or" at the end of paragraph (10), by striking the period at the end of paragraph (11) and inserting ", or", and by adding at the end thereof new paragraph (12). **Effective** for bonds issued after 10-24-92.

• 1988, Technical and Miscellaneous Revenue Act of 1988 (P.L. 100-647)

P.L. 100-647, §6180(a)(1)-(3):

Amended Code Sec. 142(a) by striking out "or" at the end of paragraph (9); by striking out the period at the end of paragraph (10) and inserting in lieu thereof ", or", and by adding at the end thereof new paragraph (11). **Effective** for bonds issued after 11-10-88.

[Sec. 142(b)]

(b) SPECIAL EXEMPT FACILITY BOND RULES.—For purposes of subsection (a)—

(1) CERTAIN FACILITIES MUST BE GOVERNMENTALLY OWNED.—

(A) IN GENERAL.—A facility shall be treated as described in paragraph (1), (2), (3), or (12) of subsection (a) only if all of the property to be financed by the net proceeds of the issue is to be owned by a governmental unit.

(B) SAFE HARBOR FOR LEASES AND MANAGEMENT CONTRACTS.—For purposes of subparagraph (A), property leased by a governmental unit shall be treated as owned by such governmental unit if—

(i) the lessee makes an irrevocable election (binding on the lessee and all successors in interest under the lease) not to claim depreciation or an investment credit with respect to such property,

(ii) the lease term (as defined in section 168(i)(3)) is not more than 80 percent of the reasonably expected economic life of the property (as determined under section 147(b)), and

(iii) the lessee has no option to purchase the property other than at fair market value (as of the time such option is exercised).

Rules similar to the rules of the preceding sentence shall apply to management contracts and similar types of operating agreements.

(2) LIMITATION ON OFFICE SPACE.—An office shall not be treated as described in a paragraph of subsection (a) unless—

(A) the office is located on the premises of a facility described in such a paragraph, and

(B) not more than a de minimis amount of the functions to be performed at such office is not directly related to the day-to-day operations at such facility.

Amendments

• 1992, Energy Policy Act of 1992 (P.L. 102-486)

P.L. 102-486, §1921(b)(2):

Amended Code Sec. 142(b)(1)(A) by striking "(2), or (3)" and inserting "(2), (3), or (12)". **Effective** for bonds issued after 10-24-92.

• 1988, Technical and Miscellaneous Revenue Act of 1988 (P.L. 100-647)

P.L. 100-647, §1013(a)(39):

Amended Code Sec. 142(b)(1)(B)(ii) by striking out "(as defined in 168(i)(3))" and inserting in lieu thereof "(as defined in section 168(i)(3))". **Effective** as if included in the provision of P.L. 99-514 to which it relates.

[Sec. 142(c)]

(c) AIRPORTS, DOCKS AND WHARVES, MASS COMMUTING FACILITIES AND HIGH-SPEED INTERCITY RAIL FACILITIES.—For purposes of subsection (a)—

(1) STORAGE AND TRAINING FACILITIES.—Storage or training facilities directly related to a facility described in paragraph (1), (2), (3) or (11) of subsection (a) shall be treated as described in the paragraph in which such facility is described.

(2) EXCEPTION FOR CERTAIN PRIVATE FACILITIES.—Property shall not be treated as described in paragraph (1), (2), (3) or (11) of subsection (a) if such property is described in any of the following subparagraphs and is to be used for any private business use (as defined in section 141(b)(6)).

(A) Any lodging facility.

(B) Any retail facility (including food and beverage facilities) in excess of a size necessary to serve passengers and employees at the exempt facility.

(C) Any retail facility (other than parking) for passengers or the general public located outside the exempt facility terminal.

(D) Any office building for individuals who are not employees of a governmental unit or of the operating authority for the exempt facility.

(E) Any industrial park or manufacturing facility.

Amendments

• 1988, Technical and Miscellaneous Revenue Act of 1988 (P.L. 100-647)

P.L. 100-647, §6180(b)(2)(A)-(B):

Amended Code Sec. 142(c) by striking out "paragraph (1), (2), or (3) of subsection (a)" each place it appears in paragraphs (1) and (2) and inserting in lieu thereof "paragraph (1), (2), (3) or (11) of subsection (a)", and by striking out "AND MASS COMMUTING FACILITIES" in the heading thereof and inserting in lieu thereof "MASS COMMUTING FACILITIES AND HIGH-SPEED INTERCITY RAIL FACILITIES". **Effective** for bonds issued after 11-10-88. Prior to amendment, Code Sec. 142(c) read as follows:

(c) AIRPORTS, DOCKS AND WHARVES, AND MASS COMMUTING FACILITIES.—For purposes of subsection (a)—

(1) STORAGE AND TRAINING FACILITIES.—Storage or training facilities directly related to a facility described in paragraph (1), (2), or (3) of subsection (a) shall be treated as described in the paragraph in which such facility is described.

(2) EXCEPTION FOR CERTAIN PRIVATE FACILITIES.—Property shall not be treated as described in paragraph (1), (2), or (3) of subsection (a) if such property is described in any of the following subparagraphs and is to be used for any private business use (as defined in section 141(b)(6)).

(A) Any lodging facility.

(B) Any retail facility (including food and beverage facilities) in excess of a size necessary to serve passengers and employees at the exempt facility.

(C) Any retail facility (other than parking) for passengers or the general public located outside the exempt facility terminal.

(D) Any office building for individuals who are not employees of a governmental unit or of the operating authority for the exempt facility.

(E) Any industrial park or manufacturing facility.

[Sec. 142(d)]

(d) QUALIFIED RESIDENTIAL RENTAL PROJECT.—For purposes of this section—

(1) IN GENERAL.—The term "qualified residential rental project" means any project for residential rental property if, at all times during the qualified project period, such project meets the requirements of subparagraph (A) or (B), whichever is elected by the issuer at the time of the issuance of the issue with respect to such project:

(A) 20-50 TEST.—The project meets the requirements of this subparagraph if 20 percent or more of the residential units in such project are occupied by individuals whose income is 50 percent or less of area median gross income.

(B) 40-60 TEST.—The project meets the requirements of this subparagraph if 40 percent or more of the residential units in such project are occupied by individuals whose income is 60 percent or less of area median gross income.

For purposes of this paragraph, any property shall not be treated as failing to be residential rental property merely because part of the building in which such property is located is used for purposes other than residential rental purposes.

(2) DEFINITIONS AND SPECIAL RULES.—For purposes of this subsection—

(A) QUALIFIED PROJECT PERIOD.—The term "qualified project period" means the period beginning on the 1st day on which 10 percent of the residential units in the project are occupied and ending on the latest of—

(i) the date which is 15 years after the date on which 50 percent of the residential units in the project are occupied,

(ii) the 1st day on which no tax-exempt private activity bond issued with respect to the project is outstanding, or

(iii) the date on which any assistance provided with respect to the project under section 8 of the United States Housing Act of 1937 terminates.

(B) INCOME OF INDIVIDUALS; AREA MEDIAN GROSS INCOME.—

(i) IN GENERAL.—The income of individuals and area median gross income shall be determined by the Secretary in a manner consistent with determinations of lower income families and area median gross income under section 8 of the United States Housing Act of 1937 (or, if such program is terminated, under such program as in effect immediately before such termination). Determinations under the preceding sentence shall include adjustments for family size. Subsections (g) and (h) of section 7872 shall not apply in determining the income of individuals under this subparagraph.

(ii) SPECIAL RULE RELATING TO BASIC HOUSING ALLOWANCES.—For purposes of determining income under this subparagraph, payments under section 403 of title 37, United

States Code, as a basic pay allowance for housing shall be disregarded with respect to any qualified building.

(iii) QUALIFIED BUILDING.—For purposes of clause (ii), the term "qualified building" means any building located—

(I) in any county in which is located a qualified military installation to which the number of members of the Armed Forces of the United States assigned to units based out of such qualified military installation, as of June 1, 2008, has increased by not less than 20 percent, as compared to such number on December 31, 2005, or

(II) in any county adjacent to a county described in subclause (I).

(iv) QUALIFIED MILITARY INSTALLATION.—For purposes of clause (iii), the term "qualified military installation" means any military installation or facility the number of members of the Armed Forces of the United States assigned to which, as of June 1, 2008, is not less than 1,000.

(C) STUDENTS.—Rules similar to the rules of 42(i)(3)(D) shall apply for purposes of this subsection.

(D) SINGLE-ROOM OCCUPANCY UNITS.—A unit shall not fail to be treated as a residential unit merely because such unit is a single-room occupancy unit (within the meaning of section 42).

(E) HOLD HARMLESS FOR REDUCTIONS IN AREA MEDIAN GROSS INCOME.—

(i) IN GENERAL.—Any determination of area median gross income under subparagraph (B) with respect to any project for any calendar year after 2008 shall not be less than the area median gross income determined under such subparagraph with respect to such project for the calendar year preceding the calendar year for which such determination is made.

(ii) SPECIAL RULE FOR CERTAIN CENSUS CHANGES.—In the case of a HUD hold harmless impacted project, the area median gross income with respect to such project for any calendar year after 2008 (hereafter in this clause referred to as the current calendar year) shall be the greater of the amount determined without regard to this clause or the sum of—

(I) the area median gross income determined under the HUD hold harmless policy with respect to such project for calendar year 2008, plus

(II) any increase in the area median gross income determined under subparagraph (B) (determined without regard to the HUD hold harmless policy and this subparagraph) with respect to such project for the current calendar year over the area median gross income (as so determined) with respect to such project for calendar year 2008.

(iii) HUD HOLD HARMLESS POLICY.—The term "HUD hold harmless policy" means the regulations under which a policy similar to the rules of clause (i) applied to prevent a change in the method of determining area median gross income from resulting in a reduction in the area median gross income determined with respect to certain projects in calendar years 2007 and 2008.

(iv) HUD HOLD HARMLESS IMPACTED PROJECT.—The term "HUD hold harmless impacted project" means any project with respect to which area median gross income was determined under subparagraph (B) for calendar year 2007 or 2008 if such determination would have been less but for the HUD hold harmless policy.

(3) CURRENT INCOME DETERMINATIONS.—For purposes of this subsection—

(A) IN GENERAL.—The determination of whether the income of a resident of a unit in a project exceeds the applicable income limit shall be made at least annually on the basis of the current income of the resident. The preceding sentence shall not apply with respect to any project for any year if during such year no residential unit in the project is occupied by a new resident whose income exceeds the applicable income limit.

(B) CONTINUING RESIDENT'S INCOME MAY INCREASE ABOVE THE APPLICABLE LIMIT.—If the income of a resident of a unit in a project did not exceed the applicable income limit upon commencement of such resident's occupancy of such unit (or as of any prior determination under subparagraph (A)), the income of such resident shall be treated as continuing to not exceed the applicable income limit. The preceding sentence shall cease to apply to any resident whose income as of the most recent determination under subparagraph (A) exceeds 140 percent of the applicable income limit if after such determination, but before the next determination, any residential unit of comparable or smaller size in the same project is occupied by a new resident whose income exceeds the applicable income limit.

(C) EXCEPTION FOR PROJECTS WITH RESPECT TO WHICH AFFORDABLE HOUSING CREDIT IS ALLOWED.—In the case of a project with respect to which credit is allowed under section 42, the second sentence of subparagraph (B) shall be applied by substituting "building (within the meaning of section 42)" for "project".

(4) SPECIAL RULE IN CASE OF DEEP RENT SKEWING.—

(A) IN GENERAL.—In the case of any project described in subparagraph (B), the 2d sentence of subparagraph (B) of paragraph (3) shall be applied by substituting—

(i) "170 percent" for "140 percent", and

(ii) "any low-income unit in the same project is occupied by a new resident whose income exceeds 40 percent of area median gross income" for "any residential unit of comparable or smaller size in the same project is occupied by a new resident whose income exceeds the applicable income limit".

(B) DEEP RENT SKEWED PROJECT.—A project is described in this subparagraph if the owner of the project elects to have this paragraph apply and, at all times during the qualified project period, such project meets the requirements of clauses (i), (ii), and (iii):

(i) The project meets the requirements of this clause if 15 percent or more of the low-income units in the project are occupied by individuals whose income is 40 percent or less of area median gross income.

(ii) The project meets the requirements of this clause if the gross rent with respect to each low-income unit in the project does not exceed 30 percent of the applicable income limit which applies to individuals occupying the unit.

(iii) The project meets the requirements of this clause if the gross rent with respect to each low-income unit in the project does not exceed 1/2 of the average gross rent with respect to units of comparable size which are not occupied by individuals who meet the applicable income limit.

(C) DEFINITIONS APPLICABLE TO SUBPARAGRAPH (b).—For purposes of subparagraph (B)—

(i) LOW-INCOME UNIT.—The term "low-income unit" means any unit which is required to be occupied by individuals who meet the applicable income limit.

(ii) GROSS RENT.—The term "gross rent" includes—

(I) any payment under section 8 of the United States Housing Act of 1937, and

(II) any utility allowance determined by the Secretary after taking into account such determinations under such section 8.

(5) APPLICABLE INCOME LIMIT.—For purposes of paragraphs (3) and (4), the term "applicable income limit" means—

(A) the limitation under subparagraph (A) or (B) of paragraph (1) which applies to the project, or

(B) in the case of a unit to which paragraph (4)(B)(i) applies, the limitation which applies to such unit.

(6) SPECIAL RULE FOR CERTAIN HIGH COST HOUSING AREA.—In the case of a project located in a city having 5 boroughs and a population in excess of 5,000,000, subparagraph (B) of paragraph (1) shall be applied by substituting "25 percent" for "40 percent".

(7) CERTIFICATION TO SECRETARY.—The operator of any project with respect to which an election was made under this subsection shall submit to the Secretary (at such time and in such manner as the Secretary shall prescribe) an annual certification as to whether such project continues to meet the requirements of this subsection. Any failure to comply with the provisions of the preceding sentence shall not affect the tax-exempt status of any bond but shall subject the operator to penalty, as provided in section 6652(j).

Amendments

• 2008, Housing Assistance Tax Act of 2008 (P.L. 110-289)

P.L. 110-289, §3005(a)(1)-(2):

Amended Code Sec. 142(d)(2)(B) by striking "The income" and inserting

"(i) IN GENERAL.—The income",

and by adding at the end new clauses (ii)-(iv). For the **effective** date, see Act Sec. 3005(b), below.

P.L. 110-289, §3005(b), provides:

(b) EFFECTIVE DATE.—The amendments made by this section shall apply to—

(1) determinations made after the date of the enactment of this Act [7-30-2008.—CCH] and before January 1, 2012, in the case of any qualified building (as defined in section 142(d)(2)(B)(iii) of the Internal Revenue Code of 1986)—

(A) with respect to which housing credit dollar amounts have been allocated on or before the date of the enactment of this Act, or

(B) with respect to buildings placed in service before such date of enactment, to the extent paragraph (1) of section 42(h) of such Code does not apply to such building by reason of paragraph (4) thereof, but only with respect to bonds issued before such date of enactment, and

(2) determinations made after the date of enactment of this Act, in the case of qualified buildings (as so defined)—

(A) with respect to which housing credit dollar amounts are allocated after the date of the enactment of this Act and before January 1, 2012, or

(B) with respect to which buildings placed in service after the date of enactment of this Act and before January 1, 2012, to the extent paragraph (1) of section 42(h) of such Code does not apply to such building by reason of paragraph (4) thereof, but only with respect to bonds issued after such date of enactment and before January 1, 2012.

P.L. 110-289, §3008(a):

Amended Code Sec. 142(d)(3) by adding at the end a new subparagraph (C). **Effective** for determinations of the status of qualified residential rental projects for periods beginning after 7-30-2008, with respect to bonds issued before, on, or after such date.

P.L. 110-289, §3008(b):

Amended Code Sec. 142(d)(2) by adding at the end a new subparagraph (C). **Effective** for determinations of the status of qualified residential rental projects for periods beginning after 7-30-2008, with respect to bonds issued before, on, or after such date.

P.L. 110-289, §3008(c):

Amended Code Sec. 142(d)(2), as amended by Act Sec. 3008(b), by adding at the end a new subparagraph (D). **Effective** for determinations of the status of qualified residential rental projects for periods beginning after 7-30-2008, with respect to bonds issued before, on, or after such date.

P.L. 110-289, §3009(a):

Amended Code Sec. 142(d)(2), as amended by Act Sec. 3008, by adding at the end a new subparagraph (E). **Effective** for determinations of area median gross income for calendar years after 2008.

P.L. 110-289, §3010(a):

Amended Code Sec. 142(d)(3)(A) by adding at the end a new sentence. **Effective** for years ending after 7-30-2008.

• 2006, Tax Increase Prevention and Reconciliation Act of 2005 (P.L. 109-222)

P.L. 109-222, §209(b)(2):

Amended Code Sec. 142(d)(2)(B) by striking "Section 7872(g)" and inserting "Subsections (g) and (h) of section 7872". **Effective** for calendar years beginning after 12-31-2005, with respect to loans made before, on, or after such date.

• 1989, Omnibus Budget Reconciliation Act of 1989 (P.L. 101-239)

P.L. 101-239, §7108(e)(3):

Amended Code Sec. 142(d)(2)(B) by adding at the end thereof a new sentence. **Effective** for determinations under section 42 of the Internal Revenue Code of 1986 with respect to housing credit dollar amounts allocated from State housing credit ceilings for calendar years after 1989.

P.L. 101-239, §7108(n)(1):

Amended Code Sec. 142(d)(4)(B)(iii) by striking "1/3" and inserting "1/2". **Effective** for determinations under section 42 of the Internal Revenue Code of 1986 with respect to housing credit dollar amounts allocated from State housing credit ceilings for calendar years after 1989.

• 1988, Technical and Miscellaneous Revenue Act of 1988 (P.L. 100-647)

P.L. 100-647, §1013(a)(1):

Amended Code Sec. 142(d)(4)(B)(iii) by striking out "average rent" and inserting in lieu thereof "average gross rent". **Effective** as if included in the provision of P.L. 99-514 to which it relates.

[Sec. 142(e)]

(e) FACILITIES FOR THE FURNISHING OF WATER.—For purposes of subsection (a)(4), the term "facilities for the furnishing of water" means any facility for the furnishing of water if—

(1) the water is or will be made available to members of the general public (including electric utility, industrial, agricultural, or commercial users), and

(2) either the facility is operated by a governmental unit or the rates for the furnishing or sale of the water have been established or approved by a State or political subdivision thereof, by an agency or instrumentality of the United States, or by a public service or public utility commission or other similar body of any State or political subdivision thereof.

[Sec. 142(f)]

(f) LOCAL FURNISHING OF ELECTRIC ENERGY OR GAS.—For purposes of subsection (a)(8)—

(1) IN GENERAL.—The local furnishing of electric energy or gas from a facility shall only include furnishing solely within the area consisting of—

(A) a city and 1 contiguous county, or

(B) 2 contiguous counties.

(2) TREATMENT OF CERTAIN ELECTRIC ENERGY TRANSMITTED OUTSIDE LOCAL AREA.—

(A) IN GENERAL.—A facility shall not be treated as failing to meet the local furnishing requirement of subsection (a)(8) by reason of electricity transmitted pursuant to an order of the Federal Energy Regulatory Commission under section 211 or 213 of the Federal Power Act (as in effect on the date of the enactment of this paragraph) if the portion of the cost of the facility financed with tax-exempt bonds is not greater than the portion of the cost of the facility which is allocable to the local furnishing of electric energy (determined without regard to this paragraph).

(B) SPECIAL RULE FOR EXISTING FACILITIES.—In the case of a facility financed with bonds issued before the date of an order referred to in subparagraph (A) which would (but for this subparagraph) cease to be tax-exempt by reason of subparagraph (A), such bonds shall not cease to be tax-exempt bonds (and section 150(b)(4) shall not apply) if, to the extent necessary to comply with subparagraph (A)—

(i) an escrow to pay principal of, premium (if any), and interest on the bonds is established within a reasonable period after the date such order becomes final, and

(ii) bonds are redeemed not later than the earliest date on which such bonds may be redeemed.

(3) TERMINATION OF FUTURE FINANCING.—For purposes of this section, no bond may be issued as part of an issue described in subsection (a)(8) with respect to a facility for the local furnishing of electric energy or gas on or after the date of the enactment of this paragraph unless—

(A) the facility will—

(i) be used by a person who is engaged in the local furnishing of that energy source on January 1, 1997, and

(ii) be used to provide service within the area served by such person on January 1, 1997 (or within a county or city any portion of which is within such area), or

(B) the facility will be used by a successor in interest to such person for the same use and within the same service area as described in subparagraph (A).

(4) ELECTION TO TERMINATE TAX-EXEMPT BOND FINANCING BY CERTAIN FURNISHERS.—

(A) IN GENERAL.—In the case of a facility financed with bonds issued before the date of the enactment of this paragraph which would cease to be tax-exempt by reason of the failure to meet the local furnishing requirement of subsection (a)(8) as a result of a service area expansion, such bonds shall not cease to be tax-exempt bonds (and section 150(b)(4) shall not apply) if the person engaged in such local furnishing by such facility makes an election described in subparagraph (B).

(B) ELECTION.—An election is described in this subparagraph if it is an election made in such manner as the Secretary prescribes, and such person (or its predecessor in interest) agrees that—

(i) such election is made with respect to all facilities for the local furnishing of electric energy or gas, or both, by such person,

(ii) no bond exempt from tax under section 103 and described in subsection (a)(8) may be issued on or after the date of the enactment of this paragraph with respect to all such facilities of such person,

(iii) any expansion of the service area—

(I) is not financed with the proceeds of any exempt facility bond described in subsection (a)(8), and

(II) is not treated as a nonqualifying use under the rules of paragraph (2), and

(iv) all outstanding bonds used to finance the facilities for such person are redeemed not later than 6 months after the later of—

(I) the earliest date on which such bonds may be redeemed, or

(II) the date of the election.

(C) RELATED PERSONS.—For purposes of this paragraph, the term "person" includes a group of related persons (within the meaning of section 144(a)(3)) which includes such person.

Amendments

• 2006, Pension Protection Act of 2006 (P.L. 109-280)

P.L. 109-280, §1303, provides:

SEC. 1303. EXCEPTION TO THE LOCAL FURNISHING REQUIREMENT OF THE TAX-EXEMPT BOND RULES.

(a) SNETTISHAM HYDROELECTRIC FACILITY.—For purposes of determining whether any private activity bond issued before May 31, 2006, and used to finance the acquisition of the Snettisham hydroelectric facility is a qualified bond for purposes of section 142(a)(8) of the Internal Revenue Code of 1986, the electricity furnished by such facility to the City of Hoonah, Alaska, shall not be taken into account for purposes of section 142(f)(1) of such Code.

(b) LAKE DOROTHY HYDROELECTRIC FACILITY.— For purposes of determining whether any private activity bond issued before May 31, 2006, and used to finance the Lake Dorothy hydroelectric facility is a qualified bond for purposes of section 142(a)(8) of the Internal Revenue Code of 1986, the electricity furnished by such facility to the City of Hoonah, Alaska, shall not be taken into account for purposes of paragraphs (1) and (3) of section 142(f) of such Code.

(c) DEFINITIONS.—For purposes of this section—

(1) LAKE DOROTHY HYDROELECTRIC FACILITY.—The term "Lake Dorothy hydroelectric facility" means the hydroelectric facility located approximately 10 miles south of Juneau, Alaska, and commonly referred to as the "Lake Dorothy project".

(2) SNETTISHAM HYDROELECTRIC FACILITY.— The term "Snettisham hydroelectric facility" means the hydroelectric project described in section 1804 of the Small Business Job Protection Act of 1996.

• 1998, IRS Restructuring and Reform Act of 1998 (P.L. 105-206)

P.L. 105-206, §6023(5):

Amended Code Sec. 142(f)(3)(A)(ii) by striking "1997, (" and inserting "1997 (". **Effective** 7-22-98.

• 1996, Small Business Job Protection Act of 1996 (P.L. 104-188)

P.L. 104-188, §1608(a):

Amended Code Sec. 142(f) by adding at the end new paragraphs (3) and (4). **Effective** 8-20-96. For special rules, see Act Secs. 1608(b) and 1804, below.

P.L. 104-188, §1608(b), provides:

(b) NO INFERENCE WITH RESPECT TO OUTSTANDING BONDS.—The use of the term "person" in section 142(f)(3) of the Internal Revenue Code of 1986, as added by subsection (a), shall not be construed to affect the tax-exempt status of interest on any bonds issued before the date of the enactment of this Act.

P.L. 104-188, §1804, provides:

SEC. 1804. TAX-EXEMPT BONDS FOR SALE OF ALASKA POWER ADMINISTRATION FACILITY.

Sections 142(f)(3) (as added by section 1608) and 147(d) of the Internal Revenue Code of 1986 shall not apply in determining whether any private activity bond issued after the date of the enactment of this Act and used to finance the acquisition of the Snettisham hydroelectric project from the Alaska Power Administration is a qualified bond for purposes of such Code.

• 1992, Energy Policy Act of 1992 (P.L. 102-486)

P.L. 102-486, §1919(a):

Amended Code Sec. 142(f). **Effective** for obligations issued before, on, or after 10-24-92. Prior to amendment, Code Sec. 142(f) read as follows:

(f) LOCAL FURNISHING OF ELECTRIC ENERGY OR GAS.—For purposes of subsection (a)(8), the local furnishing of electric energy or gas from a facility shall only include furnishing solely within the area consisting of—

(1) a city and 1 contiguous county, or

(2) 2 contiguous counties.

[Sec. 142(g)]

(g) LOCAL DISTRICT HEATING OR COOLING FACILITY.—

(1) IN GENERAL.—For purposes of subsection (a)(9), the term "local district heating or cooling facility" means property used as an integral part of a local district heating or cooling system.

(2) LOCAL DISTRICT HEATING OR COOLING SYSTEM.—

(A) IN GENERAL.—For purposes of paragraph (1), the term "local district heating or cooling system" means any local system consisting of a pipeline or network (which may be connected to a heating or cooling source) providing hot water, chilled water, or steam to 2 or more users for—

(i) residential, commercial, or industrial heating or cooling, or

(ii) process steam.

(B) LOCAL SYSTEM.—For purposes of this paragraph, a local system includes facilities furnishing heating and cooling to an area consisting of a city and 1 contiguous county.

[Sec. 142(h)]

(h) QUALIFIED HAZARDOUS WASTE FACILITIES.—For purposes of subsection (a)(10), the term "qualified hazardous waste facility" means any facility for the disposal of hazardous waste by incineration or entombment but only if—

(1) the facility is subject to final permit requirements under subtitle C of title II of the Solid Waste Disposal Act (as in effect on the date of the enactment of the Tax Reform Act of 1986), and

(2) the portion of such facility which is to be provided by the issue does not exceed the portion of the facility which is to be used by persons other than—

(A) the owner or operator of such facility, and

(B) any related person (within the meaning of section 144(a)(3)) to such owner or operator.

Amendments

• 1986, Tax Reform Act of 1986 (P.L. 99-514)

P.L. 99-514, §1301(b):

Amended part IV of subchapter B of chapter 1 by adding Code Sec. 142. **Effective**, generally, for bonds issued after 8-15-86. However, for transitional rules, see Act Secs. 1312-1318 in the amendments for Code Sec. 103.

[Sec. 142(i)]

(i) HIGH-SPEED INTERCITY RAIL FACILITIES.—

(1) IN GENERAL.—For purposes of subsection (a)(11), the term "high-speed intercity rail facilities" means any facility (not including rolling stock) for the fixed guideway rail transportation of passengers and their baggage between metropolitan statistical areas (within the meaning of section 143(k)(2)(B)) using vehicles that are reasonably expected to be capable of attaining a maximum speed in excess of 150 miles per hour between scheduled stops, but only if such facility will be made available to members of the general public as passengers.

(2) ELECTION BY NONGOVERNMENTAL OWNERS.—A facility shall be treated as described in subsection (a)(11) only if any owner of such facility which is not a governmental unit irrevocably elects not to claim—

(A) any deduction under section 167 or 168, and

(B) any credit under this subtitle,

with respect to the property to be financed by the net proceeds of the issue.

(3) USE OF PROCEEDS.—A bond issued as part of an issue described in subsection (a)(11) shall not be considered an exempt facility bond unless any proceeds not used within a 3-year period of the date of the issuance of such bond are used (not later than 6 months after the close of such period) to redeem bonds which are part of such issue.

Amendments

• 2009, American Recovery and Reinvestment Tax Act of 2009 (P.L. 111-5)

P.L. 111-5, §1504(a):

Amended Code Sec. 142(i)(1) by striking "operate at speeds in excess of" and inserting "be capable of attaining a maximum speed in excess of". **Effective** for obligations issued after 2-17-2009.

• 1989, Omnibus Budget Reconciliation Act of 1989 (P.L. 101-239)

P.L. 101-239, §7816(s)(1):

Amended Code Sec. 142(i)(1) by inserting "In general.—" after "(1)". **Effective** as if included in the provision of P.L. 100-647 to which it relates.

• 1988, Technical and Miscellaneous Revenue Act of 1988 (P.L. 100-647)

P.L. 100-647, §6180(b)(1):

Amended Code Sec. 142 by adding at the end thereof new subsection (i). **Effective** for bonds issued after 11-10-88.

[Sec. 142(j)]

(j) ENVIRONMENTAL ENHANCEMENTS OF HYDROELECTRIC GENERATING FACILITIES.—

(1) IN GENERAL.—For purposes of subsection (a)(12), the term "environmental enhancements of hydroelectric generating facilities" means property—

(A) the use of which is related to a federally licensed hydroelectric generating facility owned and operated by a governmental unit, and

(B) which—

(i) protects or promotes fisheries or other wildlife resources, including any fish bypass facility, fish hatchery, or fisheries enhancement facility, or

(ii) is a recreational facility or other improvement required by the terms and conditions of any Federal licensing permit for the operation of such generating facility.

(2) USE OF PROCEEDS.—A bond issued as part of an issue described in subsection (a)(12) shall not be considered an exempt facility bond unless at least 80 percent of the net proceeds of the issue of which it is a part are used to finance property described in paragraph (1)(B)(i).

Amendments

• 1992, Energy Policy Act of 1992 (P.L. 102-486)

P.L. 102-486, §1921(b)(1):

Amended Code Sec. 142 by adding at the end thereof new subsection (j). **Effective** for bonds issued after 10-24-92.

→ Caution: Code Sec. 142(k), below, is subject to the sunset provision of the Economic Growth and Tax Relief Reconciliation Act of 2001 (P.L. 107-16), §901. Absent Congressional action, the changes made to this provision by P.L. 107-16, or that take effect as if included in P.L. 107-16, do not apply after December 31, 2010. For more information about the sunset provision, see page XXI of the Preface to this publication and P.L. 107-16, §901, in the amendment notes. See the amendments notes for a history of amendments to this section and the effective date of each change.

[Sec. 142(k)]

(k) QUALIFIED PUBLIC EDUCATIONAL FACILITIES.—

(1) IN GENERAL.—For purposes of subsection (a)(13), the term "qualified public educational facility" means any school facility which is—

(A) part of a public elementary school or a public secondary school, and

(B) owned by a private, for-profit corporation pursuant to a public-private partnership agreement with a State or local educational agency described in paragraph (2).

(2) PUBLIC-PRIVATE PARTNERSHIP AGREEMENT DESCRIBED.—A public-private partnership agreement is described in this paragraph if it is an agreement—

(A) under which the corporation agrees—

(i) to do 1 or more of the following: construct, rehabilitate, refurbish, or equip a school facility, and

(ii) at the end of the term of the agreement, to transfer the school facility to such agency for no additional consideration, and

(B) the term of which does not exceed the term of the issue to be used to provide the school facility.

(3) SCHOOL FACILITY.—For purposes of this subsection, the term "school facility" means—

(A) any school building,

(B) any functionally related and subordinate facility and land with respect to such building, including any stadium or other facility primarily used for school events, and

(C) any property, to which section 168 applies (or would apply but for section 179), for use in a facility described in subparagraph (A) or (B).

(4) PUBLIC SCHOOLS.—For purposes of this subsection, the terms "elementary school" and "secondary school" have the meanings given such terms by section 14101 of the Elementary and Secondary Education Act of 1965 (20 U.S.C. 8801), as in effect on the date of the enactment of this subsection.

(5) ANNUAL AGGREGATE FACE AMOUNT OF TAX-EXEMPT FINANCING.—

(A) IN GENERAL.—An issue shall not be treated as an issue described in subsection (a)(13) if the aggregate face amount of bonds issued by the State pursuant thereto (when added to the aggregate face amount of bonds previously so issued during the calendar year) exceeds an amount equal to the greater of—

(i) $10 multiplied by the State population, or

(ii) $5,000,000.

(B) ALLOCATION RULES.—

(i) IN GENERAL.—Except as otherwise provided in this subparagraph, the State may allocate the amount described in subparagraph (A) for any calendar year in such manner as the State determines appropriate.

(ii) RULES FOR CARRYFORWARD OF UNUSED LIMITATION.—A State may elect to carry forward an unused limitation for any calendar year for 3 calendar years following the calendar year in which the unused limitation arose under rules similar to the rules of section 146(f), except that the only purpose for which the carryforward may be elected is the issuance of exempt facility bonds described in subsection (a)(13).

Amendments

• 2001, Economic Growth and Tax Relief Reconciliation Act of 2001 (P.L. 107-16)

P.L. 107-16, §422(b):

Amended Code Sec. 142 by adding at the end a new subsection (k). **Effective** for bonds issued after 12-31-2001.

P.L. 107-16, §901(a)-(b), provides:

SEC. 901. SUNSET OF PROVISIONS OF ACT.

(a) IN GENERAL.—All provisions of, and amendments made by, this Act shall not apply—

(1) to taxable, plan, or limitation years beginning after December 31, 2010, or

(2) in the case of title V, to estates of decedents dying, gifts made, or generation skipping transfers, after December 31, 2010.

(b) APPLICATION OF CERTAIN LAWS.—The Internal Revenue Code of 1986 and the Employee Retirement Income Security Act of 1974 shall be applied and administered to years, estates, gifts, and transfers described in subsection (a) as if the provisions and amendments described in subsection (a) had never been enacted.

[Sec. 142(l)]

(l) QUALIFIED GREEN BUILDING AND SUSTAINABLE DESIGN PROJECTS.—

(1) IN GENERAL.—For purposes of subsection (a)(14), the term "qualified green building and sustainable design project" means any project which is designated by the Secretary, after consultation with the Administrator of the Environmental Protection Agency, as a qualified green building and sustainable design project and which meets the requirements of clauses (i), (ii), (iii), and (iv) of paragraph (4)(A).

(2) DESIGNATIONS.—

(A) IN GENERAL.—Within 60 days after the end of the application period described in paragraph (3)(A), the Secretary, after consultation with the Administrator of the Environmental Protection Agency, shall designate qualified green building and sustainable design projects. At least one of the projects designated shall be located in, or within a 10-mile radius of, an empowerment zone as designated pursuant to section 1391, and at least one of the projects designated shall be located in a rural State. No more than one project shall be designated in a State. A project shall not be designated if such project includes a stadium or arena for professional sports exhibitions or games.

(B) MINIMUM CONSERVATION AND TECHNOLOGY INNOVATION OBJECTIVES.—The Secretary, after consultation with the Administrator of the Environmental Protection Agency, shall ensure that, in the aggregate, the projects designated shall—

(i) reduce electric consumption by more than 150 megawatts annually as compared to conventional generation,

(ii) reduce daily sulfur dioxide emissions by at least 10 tons compared to coal generation power,

(iii) expand by 75 percent the domestic solar photovoltaic market in the United States (measured in megawatts) as compared to the expansion of that market from 2001 to 2002, and

(iv) use at least 25 megawatts of fuel cell energy generation.

(3) LIMITED DESIGNATIONS.—A project may not be designated under this subsection unless—

(A) the project is nominated by a State or local government within 180 days of the enactment of this subsection, and

(B) such State or local government provides written assurances that the project will satisfy the eligibility criteria described in paragraph (4).

(4) APPLICATION.—

(A) IN GENERAL.—A project may not be designated under this subsection unless the application for such designation includes a project proposal which describes the energy efficiency, renewable energy, and sustainable design features of the project and demonstrates that the project satisfies the following eligibility criteria:

(i) GREEN BUILDING AND SUSTAINABLE DESIGN.—At least 75 percent of the square footage of commercial buildings which are part of the project is registered for United States Green Building Council's LEED certification and is reasonably expected (at the time of the designation) to receive such certification. For purposes of determining LEED certification as required under this clause, points shall be credited by using the following:

(I) For wood products, certification under the Sustainable Forestry Initiative Program and the American Tree Farm System.

(II) For renewable wood products, as credited for recycled content otherwise provided under LEED certification.

(III) For composite wood products, certification under standards established by the American National Standards Institute, or such other voluntary standards as published in the Federal Register by the Administrator of the Environmental Protection Agency.

(ii) BROWNFIELD REDEVELOPMENT.—The project includes a brownfield site as defined by section 101(39) of the Comprehensive Environmental Response, Compensation, and Liability Act of 1980 (42 U.S.C. 9601), including a site described in subparagraph (D)(ii)(II)(aa) thereof.

(iii) STATE AND LOCAL SUPPORT.—The project receives specific State or local government resources which will support the project in an amount equal to at least $5,000,000. For purposes of the preceding sentence, the term "resources" includes tax abatement benefits and contributions in kind.

(iv) SIZE.—The project includes at least one of the following:

(I) At least 1,000,000 square feet of building.

(II) At least 20 acres.

(v) USE OF TAX BENEFIT.—The project proposal includes a description of the net benefit of the tax-exempt financing provided under this subsection which will be allocated for financing of one or more of the following:

(I) The purchase, construction, integration, or other use of energy efficiency, renewable energy, and sustainable design features of the project.

(II) Compliance with certification standards cited under clause (i).

(III) The purchase, remediation, and foundation construction and preparation of the brownfields site.

(vi) PROHIBITED FACILITIES.—An issue shall not be treated as an issue described in subsection (a)(14) if any proceeds of such issue are used to provide any facility the principal business of which is the sale of food or alcoholic beverages for consumption on the premises.

(vii) EMPLOYMENT.—The project is projected to provide permanent employment of at least 1,500 full time equivalents (150 full time equivalents in rural States) when completed and construction employment of at least 1,000 full time equivalents (100 full time equivalents in rural States).

The application shall include an independent analysis which describes the project's economic impact, including the amount of projected employment.

(B) PROJECT DESCRIPTION.—Each application described in subparagraph (A) shall contain for each project a description of—

(i) the amount of electric consumption reduced as compared to conventional construction,

(ii) the amount of sulfur dioxide daily emissions reduced compared to coal generation,

(iii) the amount of the gross installed capacity of the project's solar photovoltaic capacity measured in megawatts, and

(iv) the amount, in megawatts, of the project's fuel cell energy generation.

(5) CERTIFICATION OF USE OF TAX BENEFIT.—No later than 30 days after the completion of the project, each project must certify to the Secretary that the net benefit of the tax-exempt financing was used for the purposes described in paragraph (4).

(6) DEFINITIONS.—For purposes of this subsection—

(A) RURAL STATE.—The term "rural State" means any State which has—

(i) a population of less than 4,500,000 according to the 2000 census,

(ii) a population density of less than 150 people per square mile according to the 2000 census, and

(iii) increased in population by less than half the rate of the national increase between the 1990 and 2000 censuses.

(B) LOCAL GOVERNMENT.—The term "local government" has the meaning given such term by section 1393(a)(5).

(C) NET BENEFIT OF TAX-EXEMPT FINANCING.—The term "net benefit of tax-exempt financing" means the present value of the interest savings (determined by a calculation established by the Secretary) which result from the tax-exempt status of the bonds.

(7) AGGREGATE FACE AMOUNT OF TAX-EXEMPT FINANCING.—

(A) IN GENERAL.—An issue shall not be treated as an issue described in subsection (a)(14) if the aggregate face amount of bonds issued by the State or local government pursuant thereto for a project (when added to the aggregate face amount of bonds previously so issued for such project) exceeds an amount designated by the Secretary as part of the designation.

(B) LIMITATION ON AMOUNT OF BONDS.—The Secretary may not allocate authority to issue qualified green building and sustainable design project bonds in an aggregate face amount exceeding $2,000,000,000.

(8) TERMINATION.—Subsection (a)(14) shall not apply with respect to any bond issued after September 30, 2012.

(9) TREATMENT OF CURRENT REFUNDING BONDS.—Paragraphs (7)(B) and (8) shall not apply to any bond (or series of bonds) issued to refund a bond issued under subsection (a)(14) before October 1, 2012, if—

(A) the average maturity date of the issue of which the refunding bond is a part is not later than the average maturity date of the bonds to be refunded by such issue,

(B) the amount of the refunding bond does not exceed the outstanding amount of the refunded bond, and

(C) the net proceeds of the refunding bond are used to redeem the refunded bond not later than 90 days after the date of the issuance of the refunding bond.

For purposes of subparagraph (A), average maturity shall be determined in accordance with section 147(b)(2)(A).

Amendments

• 2008, Energy Improvement and Extension Act of 2008 (P.L. 110-343)

P.L. 110-343, Division B, §307(a):

Amended Code Sec. 142(l)(8) by striking "September 30, 2009" and inserting "September 30, 2012". **Effective** 10-3-2008.

P.L. 110-343, Division B, §307(b):

Amended Code Sec. 142(l)(9) by striking "October 1, 2009" and inserting "October 1, 2012". **Effective** 10-3-2008.

• 2004, American Jobs Creation Act of 2004 (P.L. 108-357)

P.L. 108-357, §701(b):

Amended Code Sec. 142 by adding at the end a new subsection (l). **Effective** for bonds issued after 12-31-2004.

P.L. 108-357, §701(d) [as amended by P.L. 110-343, Division B, §307(c)], provides:

(d) ACCOUNTABILITY.—Each issuer shall maintain, on behalf of each project, an interest bearing reserve account equal to 1 percent of the net proceeds of any bond issued under this section for such project. Not later than 5 years after the date of issuance of the last issue with respect to such project, the Secretary of the Treasury, after consultation with the Administrator of the Environmental Protection Agency, shall determine whether the project financed with such bonds has substantially complied with the terms and conditions described in section 142(l)(4) of the Internal Revenue Code of 1986 (as added by this section). If the Secretary, after such consultation, certifies that the project has substantially complied with such terms and conditions and meets the commitments set forth in the application for such project described in section 142(l)(4) of such Code, amounts in the reserve account, including all interest, shall be released to the project. If the Secretary determines that the project has not substantially complied with such terms and conditions, amounts in the reserve account, including all interest, shall be paid to the United States Treasury.

[Sec. 142(m)]

(m) QUALIFIED HIGHWAY OR SURFACE FREIGHT TRANSFER FACILITIES.—

(1) IN GENERAL.—For purposes of subsection (a)(15), the term "qualified highway or surface freight transfer facilities" means—

(A) any surface transportation project which receives Federal assistance under title 23, United States Code (as in effect on the date of the enactment of this subsection),

(B) any project for an international bridge or tunnel for which an international entity authorized under Federal or State law is responsible and which receives Federal assistance under title 23, United States Code (as so in effect), or

(C) any facility for the transfer of freight from truck to rail or rail to truck (including any temporary storage facilities directly related to such transfers) which receives Federal assistance under either title 23 or title 49, United States Code (as so in effect).

(2) NATIONAL LIMITATION ON AMOUNT OF TAX-EXEMPT FINANCING FOR FACILITIES.—

(A) NATIONAL LIMITATION.—The aggregate amount allocated by the Secretary of Transportation under subparagraph (C) shall not exceed $15,000,000,000.

(B) ENFORCEMENT OF NATIONAL LIMITATION.—An issue shall not be treated as an issue described in subsection (a)(15) if the aggregate face amount of bonds issued pursuant to such issue for any qualified highway or surface freight transfer facility (when added to the aggregate face amount of bonds previously so issued for such facility) exceeds the amount allocated to such facility under subparagraph (C).

(C) ALLOCATION BY SECRETARY OF TRANSPORTATION.—The Secretary of Transportation shall allocate the amount described in subparagraph (A) among qualified highway or surface freight transfer facilities in such manner as the Secretary determines appropriate.

(3) EXPENDITURE OF PROCEEDS.—An issue shall not be treated as an issue described in subsection (a)(15) unless at least 95 percent of the net proceeds of the issue is expended for qualified highway or surface freight transfer facilities within the 5-year period beginning on the date of issuance. If at least 95 percent of such net proceeds is not expended within such 5-year period, an issue shall be treated as continuing to meet the requirements of this paragraph if the issuer uses all unspent proceeds of the issue to redeem bonds of the issue within 90 days after the end of such 5-year period. The Secretary, at the request of the issuer, may extend such 5-year period if the issuer establishes that any failure to meet such period is due to circumstances beyond the control of the issuer.

(4) EXCEPTION FOR CURRENT REFUNDING BONDS.—Paragraph (2) shall not apply to any bond (or series of bonds) issued to refund a bond issued under subsection (a)(15) if—

(A) the average maturity date of the issue of which the refunding bond is a part is not later than the average maturity date of the bonds to be refunded by such issue,

(B) the amount of the refunding bond does not exceed the outstanding amount of the refunded bond, and

(C) the refunded bond is redeemed not later than 90 days after the date of the issuance of the refunding bond.

For purposes of subparagraph (A), average maturity shall be determined in accordance with section 147(b)(2)(A).

Amendments

• 2005, Safe, Accountable, Flexible, Efficient Transportation Equity Act: A Legacy for Users (P.L. 109-59)

P.L. 109-59, §11143(b):

Amended Code Sec. 142 by adding at the end a new subsection (m). **Effective** for bonds issued after 8-10-2005.

[Sec. 142—Repealed]

Amendments

• 1977, Tax Reduction and Simplification Act of 1977 (P.L. 95-30)

P.L. 95-30, §101(d)(1):

Repealed Code Sec. 142. **Effective** for tax years beginning after 12-31-76. Prior to repeal, Code Sec. 142 read as follows:

SEC. 142. INDIVIDUALS NOT ELIGIBLE FOR STANDARD DEDUCTION.

(a) HUSBAND AND WIFE.—The standard deduction shall not be allowed to a husband or wife if the tax of the other spouse is determined under section 1 on the basis of the taxable income computed without regard to the standard deduction.

(b) CERTAIN OTHER TAXPAYERS INELIGIBLE.—The standard deduction shall not be allowed in computing the taxable income of—

(1) a nonresident alien individual;

(2) a citizen of the United States entitled to the benefits of section 931 (relating to income from sources within possessions of the United States);

(3) an individual making a return under section 443(a)(1) for a period of less than 12 months on account of a change in his annual accounting period; or

(4) an estate or trust, common trust fund, or partnership.

[Sec. 143]

SEC. 143. MORTGAGE REVENUE BONDS: QUALIFIED MORTGAGE BOND AND QUALIFIED VETERANS' MORTGAGE BOND.

[Sec. 143(a)]

(a) QUALIFIED MORTGAGE BOND.—

(1) QUALIFIED MORTGAGE BOND DEFINED.—For purposes of this title, the term "qualified mortgage bond" means a bond which is issued as part of a qualified mortgage issue.

(2) QUALIFIED MORTGAGE ISSUE DEFINED.—

(A) DEFINITION.—For purposes of this title, the term "qualified mortgage issue" means an issue by a State or political subdivision thereof of 1 or more bonds, but only if—

(i) all proceeds of such issue (exclusive of issuance costs and a reasonably required reserve) are to be used to finance owner-occupied residences,

(ii) such issue meets the requirements of subsections (c), (d), (e), (f), (g), (h), (i), and (m)(7),

(iii) such issue does not meet the private business tests of paragraphs (1) and (2) of section 141(b), and

(iv) except as provided in subparagraph (D)(ii), repayments of principal on financing provided by the issue are used not later than the close of the 1st semiannual period beginning after the date the prepayment (or complete repayment) is received to redeem bonds which are part of such issue.

Clause (iv) shall not apply to amounts received within 10 years after the date of issuance of the issue (or, in the case of refunding bond, the date of issuance of the original bond).

(B) GOOD FAITH EFFORT TO COMPLY WITH MORTGAGE ELIGIBILITY REQUIREMENTS.—An issue which fails to meet 1 or more of the requirements of subsections (c), (d), (e), (f), and (i) shall be treated as meeting such requirements if—

(i) the issuer in good faith attempted to meet all such requirements before the mortgages were executed,

(ii) 95 percent or more of the proceeds devoted to owner-financing was devoted to residences with respect to which (at the time the mortgages were executed) all such requirements were met, and

(iii) any failure to meet the requirements of such subsections is corrected within a reasonable period after such failure is first discovered.

(C) GOOD FAITH EFFORT TO COMPLY WITH OTHER REQUIREMENTS.—An issue which fails to meet 1 or more of the requirements of subsections (g), (h), and (m)(7) shall be treated as meeting such requirements if—

(i) the issuer in good faith attempted to meet all such requirements, and

(ii) any failure to meet such requirements is due to inadvertent error after taking reasonable steps to comply with such requirements.

(D) PROCEEDS MUST BE USED WITHIN 42 MONTHS OF DATE OF ISSUANCE.—

(i) IN GENERAL.—Except as otherwise provided in this subparagraph, an issue shall not meet the requirement of subparagraph (A)(i) unless—

(I) all proceeds of the issue required to be used to finance owner-occupied residences are so used within the 42-month period beginning on the date of issuance of the issue (or, in the case of a refunding bond, within the 42-month period beginning on the date of issuance of the original bond) or, to the extent not so used within such period, are used within such period to redeem bonds which are part of such issue, and

(II) no portion of the proceeds of the issue are used to make or finance any loan (other than a loan which is a nonpurpose investment within the meaning of section 148(f)(6)(A)) after the close of such period.

(ii) EXCEPTION.—Clause (i) (and clause (iv) of subparagraph (A)) shall not be construed to require amounts of less than $250,000 to be used to redeem bonds. The Secretary may by regulation treat related issues as 1 issue for purposes of the preceding sentence.

Amendments

• 1993, Omnibus Budget Reconciliation Act of 1993 (P.L. 103-66)

P.L. 103-66, §13141(a):

Amended Code Sec. 143(a)(1). **Effective** for bonds issued after 6-30-92. Prior to amendment, Code Sec. 143(a)(1) read as follows:

(1) QUALIFIED MORTGAGE BOND DEFINED.—

(A) IN GENERAL.—For purposes of this title, the term "qualified mortgage bond" means a bond which is issued as part of a qualified mortgage issue.

(B) TERMINATION ON JUNE 30, 1992.—No bond issued after June 30, 1992, may be treated as a qualified mortgage bond.

• 1991, Tax Extension Act of 1991 (P.L. 102-227)

P.L. 102-227, §108(a):

Amended Code Sec. 143(a)(1)(B) by striking "December 31, 1991" each place it appears and inserting "June 30, 1992". **Effective** for bonds issued after 12-31-91.

• 1990, Omnibus Budget Reconciliation Act of 1990 (P.L. 101-508)

P.L. 101-508, §11408(a):

Amended Code Sec. 143(a)(1)(B) by striking "September 30, 1990" each place it appears and inserting "December 31, 1991". **Effective** for bonds issued after 9-30-90.

• 1989, Omnibus Budget Reconciliation Act of 1989 (P.L. 101-239)

P.L. 101-239, §7104(a):

Amended Code Sec. 143(a)(1)(B) by striking "December 31, 1989" and inserting "September 30, 1990" each place it appears. **Effective** 12-19-89.

• 1988, Technical and Miscellaneous Revenue Act of 1988 (P.L. 100-647)

P.L. 100-647, §1013(a)(2):

Amended Code Sec. 143(a)(2)(A)(iii) by striking out "no bond which is part of such issue meets" and inserting in lieu thereof "such issue does not meet". **Effective** as if included in the provision of P.L. 99-514 to which it relates.

P.L. 100-647, §4005(a)(1):

Amended Code Sec. 143(a)(1)(B) by striking out "December 31, 1988" each place it appears and inserting in lieu thereof "December 31, 1989". **Effective** for bonds issued, and nonissued bond amounts elected, after 12-31-88.

P.L. 100-647, §4005(e):

Amended Code Sec. 143(a)(2) by adding at the end thereof a new subparagraph (D). **Effective** for bonds issued, and nonissued bond amounts elected, after 12-31-88.

P.L. 100-647, §4005(f):

Amended Code Sec. 143(a)(2)(A) by striking out "and" at the end of clause (ii), by striking out the period at the end of clause (iii) and inserting in lieu thereof ", and", and by adding at the end thereof a new clause (iv). **Effective**, generally, for bonds issued, and nonissued bond amounts elected, after 12-31-88. For a special rule, see Act Sec. 4005(h)(2), below:

P.L. 100-647, §4005(g)(2)(A):

Amended Code Sec. 143(a)(2)(A) by striking out "and (i)" and inserting in lieu thereof "(i), and (m)(7)". **Effective**, generally, for financing provided, and mortgage credit certificates issued, after 12-31-90. For an exception, see Act Sec. 4005(h)(3)(B), below.

P.L. 100-647, §4005(g)(2)(B):

Amended Code Sec. 143(a)(2)(C) by striking out "and (h)" and inserting in lieu thereof ", (h) and (m)(7)". **Effective**, generally, for financing provided, and mortgage credit certificates issued, after 12-31-90. For an exception, see Act Sec. 4005(h)(3)(B), below.

P.L. 100-647, §4005(h)(2), provides:

(2) SPECIAL RULES RELATING TO CERTAIN REQUIREMENTS AND REFUNDING BONDS.— In the case of a bond issued to refund (or which is part of a series of bonds issued to refund) a bond issued before January 1, 1989—

(A) the amendments made by subsections (b) and (c) shall apply to financing provided after the date of issuance of the refunding issue, and

(B) the amendment made by subsection (f) shall apply to payments (including on loans made before such date of issuance) received on or after such date of issuance.

P.L. 100-647, §4005(h)(3)(B), provides:

(B) EXCEPTION.—The amendments made by subsection (g) shall not apply to financing provided pursuant to a binding contract (entered into before June 23, 1988) with a homebuilder, lender, or mortgagor if the bonds (the proceeds of which are used to provide such financing) are issued—

(i) before June 23, 1988, or

(ii) before August 1, 1988, pursuant to a written application (made before July 1, 1988) for State bond volume authority.

[Sec. 143(b)]

(b) QUALIFIED VETERANS' MORTGAGE BOND DEFINED.—For purposes of this part, the term "qualified veterans' mortgage bond" means any bond—

(1) which is issued as part of an issue 95 percent or more of the net proceeds of which are to be used to provide residences for veterans,

(2) the payment of the principal and interest on which is secured by the general obligation of a State,

(3) which is part of an issue which meets the requirements of subsections (c), (g), (i)(1), and (l), and

(4) which is part of an issue which does not meet the private business tests of paragraphs (1) and (2) of section 141(b).

Rules similar to the rules of subparagraphs (B) and (C) of subsection (a)(2) shall apply to the requirements specified in paragraph (3) of this subsection.

Amendments

• 1988, Technical and Miscellaneous Revenue Act of 1988 (P.L. 100-647)

P.L. 100-647, §1013(a)(3):

Amended Code Sec. 143(b)(4) by inserting "is part of an issue which" after "which". **Effective** as if included in the provision of P.L. 99-514 to which it relates.

[Sec. 143(c)]

(c) RESIDENCE REQUIREMENTS.—

(1) FOR A RESIDENCE.—A residence meets the requirements of this subsection only if—

(A) it is a single-family residence which can reasonably be expected to become the principal residence of the mortgagor within a reasonable time after the financing is provided, and

(B) it is located within the jurisdiction of the authority issuing the bond.

(2) FOR AN ISSUE.—An issue meets the requirements of this subsection only if all of the residences for which owner-financing is provided under the issue meet the requirements of paragraph (1).

[Sec. 143(d)]

(d) 3-YEAR REQUIREMENT.—

(1) IN GENERAL.—An issue meets the requirements of this subsection only if 95 percent or more of the net proceeds of such issue are used to finance the residences of mortgagors who had no present ownership interest in their principal residences at any time during the 3-year period ending on the date their mortgage is executed.

(2) EXCEPTIONS.—For purposes of paragraph (1), the proceeds of an issue which are used to provide—

(A) financing with respect to targeted area residences,

(B) qualified home improvement loans and qualified rehabilitation loans,

(C) financing with respect to land described in subsection (i)(1)(C) and the construction of any residence thereon, and

(D) in the case of bonds issued after the date of the enactment of this subparagraph, financing of any residence for a veteran (as defined in section 101 of title 38, United States Code), if such veteran has not previously qualified for and received such financing by reason of this subparagraph,

shall be treated as used as described in paragraph (1).

(3) MORTGAGOR'S INTEREST IN RESIDENCE BEING FINANCED.—For purposes of paragraph (1), a mortgagor's interest in the residence with respect to which the financing is being provided shall not be taken into account.

Amendments

• 2008, Heroes Earnings Assistance and Relief Tax Act of 2008 (P.L. 110-245)

P.L. 110-245, §103(a):

Amended Code Sec. 143(d)(2)(D) by striking "and before January 1, 2008" following "enactment of this subparagraph". **Effective** for bonds issued after 12-31-2007.

• 2006, Tax Relief and Health Care Act of 2006 (P.L. 109-432)

P.L. 109-432, Division A, §416(a):

Amended Code Sec. 143(d)(2) by striking "and" at the end of subparagraph (B), by adding "and" at the end of subparagraph (C), and by inserting after subparagraph (C) a new subparagraph (D). **Effective** for bonds issued after 12-20-2006.

• 2005, Katrina Emergency Tax Relief Act of 2005 (P.L. 109-73)

P.L. 109-73, §404, as amended by P.L. 109-135, §104, provides:

SEC. 404. SPECIAL RULES FOR MORTGAGE REVENUE BONDS.

(a) IN GENERAL.—In the case of financing provided with respect to a qualified Hurricane Katrina recovery residence, subsection (d) of section 143 of the Internal Revenue Code of 1986 shall be applied as if such residence were a targeted area residence.

(b) QUALIFIED HURRICANE KATRINA RECOVERY RESIDENCE.—For purposes of this section, the term "qualified Hurricane Katrina recovery residence" means—

(1) any residence in the core disaster area, and

(2) any other residence if—

(A) such other residence is located in the same State as the principal residence referred to in subparagraph (B), and

(B) the mortgagor with respect to such other residence owned a principal residence on August 28, 2005, which—

(i) was located in the Hurricane Katrina disaster area, and

(ii) was rendered uninhabitable by reason of Hurricane Katrina.

(c) SPECIAL RULE FOR HOME IMPROVEMENT LOANS.—In the case of any loan with respect to a residence in the Hurricane Katrina disaster area, section 143(k)(4) of such Code shall be applied by substituting $150,000 for the dollar amount contained therein to the extent such loan is for the repair of damage by reason of Hurricane Katrina.

(d) APPLICATION.—Subsection (a) shall not apply to financing provided after December 31, 2010.

• 1996, Small Business Job Protection Act of 1996 (P.L. 104-188)

P.L. 104-188, §1703(n)(3):

Amended Code Sec. 143(d)(2)(C) by striking the period at the end thereof and inserting a comma. **Effective** as if included in the provision of P.L. 103-66 to which it relates.

• 1993, Omnibus Budget Reconciliation Act of 1993 (P.L. 103-66)

P.L. 103-66, §13141(d)(1)(A)-(C):

Amended Code Sec. 143(d)(2)(A)-(C) by striking "and" at the end of subparagraph (A), by adding "and" at the end of subparagraph (B), and by inserting after subparagraph (B) a new subparagraph (C). **Effective** for loans originated and credit certificates provided after 8-10-93.

[Sec. 143(e)]

(e) PURCHASE PRICE REQUIREMENT.—

(1) IN GENERAL.—An issue meets the requirements of this subsection only if the acquisition cost of each residence the owner-financing of which is provided under the issue does not exceed 90 percent of the average area purchase price applicable to such residence.

(2) AVERAGE AREA PURCHASE PRICE.—For purposes of paragraph (1), the term "average area purchase price" means, with respect to any residence, the average purchase price of single family residences (in the statistical area in which the residence is located) which were purchased during the most recent 12-month period for which sufficient statistical information is available. The determination under the preceding sentence shall be made as of the date on which the commitment to provide the financing is made (or, if earlier, the date of the purchase of the residence).

(3) SEPARATE APPLICATION TO NEW RESIDENCES AND OLD RESIDENCES.—For purposes of this subsection, the determination of average area purchase price shall be made separately with respect to—

(A) residences which have not been previously occupied, and

(B) residences which have been previously occupied.

(4) SPECIAL RULE FOR 2 TO 4 FAMILY RESIDENCES.—For purposes of this subsection, to the extent provided in regulations, the determination of average area purchase price shall be made separately with respect to 1 family, 2 family, 3 family, and 4 family residences.

(5) SPECIAL RULE FOR TARGETED AREA RESIDENCES.—In the case of a targeted area residence, paragraph (1) shall be applied by substituting "110 percent" for "90 percent".

(6) EXCEPTION FOR QUALIFIED HOME IMPROVEMENT LOANS.—Paragraph (1) shall not apply with respect to any qualified home improvement loan.

[Sec. 143(f)]

(f) INCOME REQUIREMENTS.—

(1) IN GENERAL.—An issue meets the requirements of this subsection only if all owner-financing provided under the issue is provided for mortgagors whose family income is 115 percent or less of the applicable median family income.

(2) DETERMINATION OF FAMILY INCOME.—For purposes of this subsection, the family income of mortgagors, and area median gross income, shall be determined by the Secretary after taking into account the regulations prescribed under section 8 of the United States Housing Act of 1937 (or, if such program is terminated, under such program as in effect immediately before such termination).

(3) SPECIAL RULE FOR APPLYING PARAGRAPH (1) IN THE CASE OF TARGETED AREA RESIDENCES.—In the case of any financing provided under any issue for targeted area residences—

(A) ⅓ of the amount of such financing may be provided without regard to paragraph (1), and

(B) paragraph (1) shall be treated as satisfied with respect to the remainder of the owner financing if the family income of the mortgagor is 140 percent or less of the applicable median family income.

(4) APPLICABLE MEDIAN FAMILY INCOME.—For purposes of this subsection, the term "applicable median family income" means, with respect to a residence, whichever of the following is the greater:

(A) the area median gross income for the area in which such residence is located, or

(B) the statewide median gross income for the State in which such residence is located.

(5) ADJUSTMENT OF INCOME REQUIREMENT BASED ON RELATION OF HIGH HOUSING COSTS TO INCOME.—

(A) IN GENERAL.—If the residence (for which financing is provided under the issue) is located in a high housing cost area and the limitation determined under this paragraph is greater than the limitation otherwise applicable under paragraph (1), there shall be substituted for the income limitation in paragraph (1), a limitation equal to the percentage determined under subparagraph (B) of the area median gross income for such area.

(B) INCOME REQUIREMENTS FOR RESIDENCES IN HIGH HOUSING COST AREA.—The percentage determined under this subparagraph for a residence located in a high housing cost area is the percentage (not greater than 140 percent) equal to the product of—

(I) 115 percent, and

(II) the amount by which the housing cost/income ratio for such area exceeds 0.2.

(C) HIGH HOUSING COST AREAS.—For purposes of this paragraph, the term "high housing cost area" means any statistical area for which the housing cost/income ratio is greater than 1.2.

(D) HOUSING COST/INCOME RATIO.—For purposes of this paragraph—

(i) IN GENERAL.—The term "housing cost/income ratio" means, with respect to any statistical area, the number determined by dividing—

(I) the applicable housing price ratio for such area, by

(II) the ratio which the area median gross income for such area bears to the median gross income for the United States.

(ii) APPLICABLE HOUSING PRICE RATIO.—For purposes of clause (i), the applicable housing price ratio for any area is the new housing price ratio or the existing housing price ratio, whichever results in the housing cost/income ratio being closer to 1.

(iii) NEW HOUSING PRICE RATIO.—The new housing price ratio for any area is the ratio which—

(I) the average area purchase price (as defined in subsection (e)(2)) for residences described in subsection (e)(3)(A) which are located in such area bears to

(II) the average purchase price (determined in accordance with the principles of subsection (e)(2)) for residences so described which are located in the United States.

(iv) EXISTING HOUSING PRICE RATIO.—The existing housing price ratio for any area is the ratio determined in accordance with clause (iii) but with respect to residences described in subsection (e)(3)(B).

(6) ADJUSTMENT TO INCOME REQUIREMENTS BASED ON FAMILY SIZE.—In the case of a mortgagor having a family of fewer than 3 individuals, the preceding provisions of this subsection shall be applied by substituting—

(A) "100 percent" for "115 percent" each place it appears, and

(B) "120 percent" for "140 percent" each place it appears.

Amendments

• 1988, Technical and Miscellaneous Revenue Act of 1988 (P.L. 100-647)

P.L. 100-647, §4005(b):

Amended Code Sec. 143(f) by adding at the end thereof a new paragraph (5). **Effective** for bonds issued, and nonissued bond amounts elected, after 12-31-88. For a special rule, see Act Sec. 4005(h)(2), below.

P.L. 100-647, §4005(c):

Amended Code Sec. 143(f) by adding at the end thereof a new paragraph (6). **Effective** for bonds issued, and nonissued bond amounts elected, after 12-31-88. For a special rule, see Act Sec. 4005(h)(2), below.

P.L. 100-647, §4005(h)(2), provides:

(2) SPECIAL RULES RELATING TO CERTAIN REQUIREMENTS AND REFUNDING BONDS.—In the case of a bond issued to refund (or which is part of a series of bonds issued to refund) a bond issued before January 1, 1989—

(A) the amendments made by subsections (b) and (c) shall apply to financing provided after the date of issuance of the refunding issue, and

(B) the amendment made by subsection (f) shall apply to payments (including on loans made before such date of issuance) received on or after such date of issuance.

[Sec. 143(g)]

(g) REQUIREMENTS RELATED TO ARBITRAGE.—

(1) IN GENERAL.—An issue meets the requirements of this subsection only if such issue meets the requirements of paragraph (2) of this subsection and, in the case of an issue described in subsection (b)(1), such issue also meets the requirements of paragraph (3) of this subsection. Such requirements shall be in addition to the requirements of section 148.

(2) EFFECTIVE RATE OF MORTGAGE INTEREST CANNOT EXCEED BOND YIELD BY MORE THAN 1.125 PERCENTAGE POINTS.—

(A) IN GENERAL.—An issue shall be treated as meeting the requirements of this paragraph only if the excess of—

(i) the effective rate of interest on the mortgages provided under the issue, over

(ii) the yield on the issue,

is not greater than 1.125 percentage points.

(B) EFFECTIVE RATE OF MORTGAGE INTEREST.—

(i) IN GENERAL.—In determining the effective rate of interest on any mortgage for purposes of this paragraph, there shall be taken into account all fees, charges, and other amounts borne by the mortgagor which are attributable to the mortgage or to the bond issue.

(ii) SPECIFICATION OF SOME OF THE AMOUNTS TO BE TREATED AS BORNE BY THE MORTGAGOR.—For purposes of clause (i), the following items (among others) shall be treated as borne by the mortgagor:

(I) all points or similar charges paid by the seller of the property, and

(II) the excess of the amounts received from any person other than the mortgagor by any person in connection with the acquisition of the mortgagor's interest in the property over the usual and reasonable acquisition costs of a person acquiring like property where owner-financing is not provided through the use of qualified mortgage bonds or qualified veterans' mortgage bonds.

(iii) SPECIFICATION OF SOME OF THE AMOUNTS TO BE TREATED AS NOT BORNE BY THE MORTGAGOR.—For purposes of clause (i), the following items shall not be taken into account:

(I) any expected rebate of arbitrage profits, and

(II) any application fee, survey fee, credit report fee, insurance charge, or similar amount to the extent such amount does not exceed amounts charged in such area in cases where owner-financing is not provided through the use of qualified mortgage bonds or qualified veterans' mortgage bonds.

Subclause (II) shall not apply to origination fees, points or similar amounts.

(iv) PREPAYMENT ASSUMPTIONS.—In determining the effective rate of interest—

(I) it shall be assumed that the mortgage prepayment rate will be the rate set forth in the most recent applicable mortgage maturity experience table published by the Federal Housing Administration, and

(II) prepayments of principal shall be treated as received on the last day of the month in which the issuer reasonably expects to receive such prepayments.

The Secretary may by regulation adjust the mortgage prepayment rate otherwise used in determining the effective rate of interest to the extent the Secretary determines that such an adjustment is appropriate by reason of the impact of subsection (m).

(C) YIELD ON THE ISSUE.—For purposes of this subsection, the yield on an issue shall be determined on the basis of—

(i) the issue price (within the meaning of sections 1273 and 1274), and

(ii) an expected maturity for the bonds which is consistent with the assumptions required under subparagraph (B)(iv).

(3) ARBITRAGE AND INVESTMENT GAINS TO BE USED TO REDUCE COSTS OF OWNER-FINANCING.—

(A) IN GENERAL.—An issue shall be treated as meeting the requirements of this paragraph only if an amount equal to the sum of—

(i) the excess of—

(I) the amount earned on all nonpurpose investments (other than investments attributable to an excess described in this clause), over

(II) the amount which would have been earned if such investments were invested at a rate equal to the yield on the issue, plus

(ii) any income attributable to the excess described in clause (i),

is paid or credited to the mortgagors as rapidly as may be practicable.

(B) INVESTMENT GAINS AND LOSSES.—For purposes of subparagraph (A), in determining the amount earned on all nonpurpose investments, any gain or loss on the disposition of such investments shall be taken into account.

(C) REDUCTION WHERE ISSUER DOES NOT USE FULL 1.125 PERCENTAGE POINTS UNDER PARAGRAPH (2).—

(i) IN GENERAL.—The amount required to be paid or credited to mortgagors under subparagraph (A) (determined under this paragraph without regard to this subparagraph) shall be reduced by the unused paragraph (2) amount.

(ii) UNUSED PARAGRAPH (2) AMOUNT.—For purposes of clause (i), the unused paragraph (2) amount is the amount which (if it were treated as an interest payment made by mortgagors) would result in the excess referred to in paragraph (2)(A) being equal to 1.125 percentage points. Such amount shall be fixed and determined as of the yield determination date.

(D) ELECTION TO PAY UNITED STATES.—Subparagraph (A) shall be satisfied with respect to any issue if the issuer elects before issuing the bonds to pay over to the United States—

(i) not less frequently than once each 5 years after the date of issue, an amount equal to 90 percent of the aggregate amount which would be required to be paid or credited to mortgagors under subparagraph (A) (and not theretofore paid to the United States), and

(ii) not later than 60 days after the redemption of the last bond, 100 percent of such aggregate amount not theretofore paid to the United States.

(E) SIMPLIFIED ACCOUNTING.—The Secretary shall permit any simplified system of accounting for purposes of this paragraph which the issuer establishes to the satisfaction of the Secretary will assure that the purposes of this paragraph are carried out.

(F) NONPURPOSE INVESTMENT.—For purposes of this paragraph, the term "nonpurpose investment" has the meaning given such term by section 148(f)(6)(A).

Amendments

• 1988, Technical and Miscellaneous Revenue Act of 1988 (P.L. 100-647)

P.L. 100-647, §4005(d)(1)(A)-(B):

Amended Code Sec. 143(g)(1) by striking out "paragraphs (2) and (3) of this subsection" and inserting in lieu thereof "paragraph (2) of this subsection and, in the case of an issue described in subsection (b)(1), such issue also meets the requirements of paragraph (3) of this subsection", and by striking out "(other than subsection (f) thereof)" after "section 148". **Effective** for bonds issued, and nonissued bond amounts elected, after 12-31-88. Prior to amendment, Code Sec. 143(g)(1) read as follows:

(g) REQUIREMENTS RELATED TO ARBITRAGE.—

(1) IN GENERAL.—An issue meets the requirements of this subsection only if such issue meets the requirements of paragraphs (2) and (3) of this subsection. Such requirements shall be in addition to the requirements of section 148 (other than subsection (f) thereof).

P.L. 100-647, §4005(g)(6):

Amended Code Sec. 143(g)(2)(B)(iv) by adding at the end thereof a new sentence. **Effective**, generally, for financing provided, and mortgage credit certificates issued, after 12-31-90. For an exception, see Act Sec. 4005(h)(3)(B), below.

P.L. 100-647, §4005(h)(3)(B), provides:

(B) EXCEPTION.—The amendments made by subsection (g) shall not apply to financing provided pursuant to a binding contract (entered into before June 23, 1988) with a homebuilder, lender, or mortgagor if the bonds (the proceeds of which are used to provide such financing) are issued—

(i) before June 23, 1988, or

(ii) before August 1, 1988, pursuant to a written application (made before July 1, 1988) for State bond volume authority.

[Sec. 143(h)]

(h) PORTION OF LOANS REQUIRED TO BE PLACED IN TARGETED AREAS.—

(1) IN GENERAL.—An issue meets the requirements of this subsection only if at least 20 percent of the proceeds of the issue which are devoted to providing owner-financing is made available (with reasonable diligence) for owner-financing of targeted area residences for at least 1 year after the date on which owner-financing is first made available with respect to targeted area residences.

(2) LIMITATION.—Nothing in paragraph (1) shall be treated as requiring the making available of an amount which exceeds 40 percent of the average annual aggregate principal amount of mortgages executed during the immediately preceding 3 calendar years for single-family, owner-occupied residences located in targeted areas within the jurisdiction of the issuing authority.

[Sec. 143(i)]

(i) OTHER REQUIREMENTS.—

(1) MORTGAGES MUST BE NEW MORTGAGES.—

(A) IN GENERAL.—An issue meets the requirements of this subsection only if no part of the proceeds of such issue is used to acquire or replace existing mortgages.

(B) EXCEPTIONS.—Under regulations prescribed by the Secretary, the replacement of—

(i) construction period loans,

(ii) bridge loans or similar temporary initial financing, and

(iii) in the case of a qualified rehabilitation, an existing mortgage,

shall not be treated as the acquisition or replacement of an existing mortgage for purposes of subparagraph (A),

(C) EXCEPTION FOR CERTAIN CONTRACT FOR DEED AGREEMENTS.—

(i) IN GENERAL.—In the case of land possessed under a contract for deed by a mortgagor—

(I) whose principal residence (within the meaning of section 121) is located on such land, and

(II) whose family income (as defined in subsection (f)(2)) is not more than 50 percent of applicable median family income (as defined in subsection (f)(4)),

the contract for deed shall not be treated as an existing mortgage for purposes of subparagraph (A).

(ii) CONTRACT FOR DEED DEFINED.—For purposes of this subparagraph, the term "contract for deed" means a seller-financed contract for the conveyance of land under which—

(I) legal title does not pass to the purchaser until the consideration under the contract is fully paid to the seller, and

(II) the seller's remedy for nonpayment is forfeiture rather than judicial or nonjudicial foreclosure.

(2) CERTAIN REQUIREMENTS MUST BE MET WHERE MORTGAGE IS ASSUMED.—An issue meets the requirements of this subsection only if each mortgage with respect to which owner-financing has been provided under such issue may be assumed only if the requirements of subsections (c), (d),

and (e), and the requirements of paragraph (1) or (3)(B) of subsection (f) (whichever applies), are met with respect to such assumption.

Amendments

• 1997, Taxpayer Relief Act of 1997 (P.L. 105-34)

P.L. 105-34, §312(d)(1):

Amended Code Sec. 143(i)(1)(C)(i)(I) by striking "section 1034" and inserting "section 121". **Effective**, generally, for sales and exchanges after 5-6-97.

• 1993, Omnibus Budget Reconciliation Act of 1993 (P.L. 103-66)

P.L. 103-66, §13141(d)(2):

Amended Code Sec. 143(i)(1) by adding at the end thereof a new subparagraph (C). **Effective** for loans originated and credit certificates provided after 8-10-93.

[Sec. 143(j)]

(j) TARGETED AREA RESIDENCES.—

(1) IN GENERAL.—For purposes of this section, the term "targeted area residence" means a residence in an area which is either—

(A) a qualified census tract, or

(B) an area of chronic economic distress.

(2) QUALIFIED CENSUS TRACT.—

(A) IN GENERAL.—For purposes of paragraph (1), the term "qualified census tract" means a census tract in which 70 percent or more of the families have income which is 80 percent or less of the statewide median family income.

(B) DATA USED.—The determination under subparagraph (A) shall be made on the basis of the most recent decennial census for which data are available.

(3) AREA OF CHRONIC ECONOMIC DISTRESS.—

(A) IN GENERAL.—For purposes of paragraph (1), the term "area of chronic economic distress" means an area of chronic economic distress—

(i) designated by the State as meeting the standards established by the State for purposes of this subsection, and

(ii) the designation of which has been approved by the Secretary and the Secretary of Housing and Urban Development.

(B) CRITERIA TO BE USED IN APPROVING STATE DESIGNATIONS.—The criteria used by the Secretary and the Secretary of Housing and Urban Development in evaluating any proposed designation of an area for purposes of this subsection shall be—

(i) the condition of the housing stock, including the age of the housing and the number of abandoned and substandard residential units,

(ii) the need of area residents for owner-financing under this section, as indicated by low per capita income, a high percentage of families in poverty, a high number of welfare recipients, and high unemployment rates,

(iii) the potential for use of owner-financing under this section to improve housing conditions in the area, and

(iv) the existence of a housing assistance plan which provides a displacement program and a public improvements and service program.

[Sec. 143(k)]

(k) OTHER DEFINITIONS AND SPECIAL RULES.—For purposes of this section—

(1) MORTGAGE.—The term "mortgage" means any owner-financing.

(2) STATISTICAL AREA.—

(A) IN GENERAL.—The term "statistical area" means—

(i) a metropolitan statistical area, and

(ii) any county (or the portion thereof) which is not within a metropolitan statistical area.

(B) METROPOLITAN STATISTICAL AREA.—The term "metropolitan statistical area" includes the area defined as such by the Secretary of Commerce.

(C) DESIGNATION WHERE ADEQUATE STATISTICAL INFORMATION NOT AVAILABLE.—For purposes of this paragraph, if there is insufficient recent statistical information with respect to a county (or portion thereof) described in subparagraph (A)(ii), the Secretary may substitute for such county (or portion thereof) another area of which there is sufficient recent statistical information.

(D) DESIGNATION WHERE NO COUNTY.—In the case of any portion of a State which is not within a county, subparagraphs (A)(ii) and (C) shall be applied by substituting for "county" an area designated by the Secretary which is the equivalent of a county.

(3) ACQUISITION COST.—

(A) IN GENERAL.—The term "acquisition cost" means the cost of acquiring the residence as a completed residential unit.

(B) EXCEPTIONS.—The term "acquisition cost" does not include—

(i) usual and reasonable settlement or financing costs,

(ii) the value of services performed by the mortgagor or members of his family in completing the residence, and

(iii) the cost of land (other than land described in subsection (i)(1)(C)(i)) which has been owned by the mortgagor for at least 2 years before the date on which construction of the residence begins.

(C) SPECIAL RULE FOR QUALIFIED REHABILITATION LOANS.—In the case of a qualified rehabilitation loan, for purposes of subsection (e), the term "acquisition cost" includes the cost of the rehabilitation.

(4) QUALIFIED HOME IMPROVEMENT LOAN.—The term "qualified home improvement loan" means the financing (in an amount which does not exceed $15,000)—

(A) of alterations, repairs, and improvements on or in connection with an existing residence by the owner thereof, but

(B) only of such items as substantially protect or improve the basic livability or energy efficiency of the property.

(5) QUALIFIED REHABILITATION LOAN.—

(A) IN GENERAL.—The term "qualified rehabilitation loan" means any owner-financing provided in connection with—

(i) a qualified rehabilitation, or

(ii) the acquisition of a residence with respect to which there has been a qualified rehabilitation,

but only if the mortgagor to whom such financing is provided is the first resident of the residence after the completion of the rehabilitation.

(B) QUALIFIED REHABILITATION.—For purposes of subparagraph (A), the term "qualified rehabilitation" means any rehabilitation of a building if—

(i) there is a period of at least 20 years between the date on which the building was first used and the date on which the physical work on such rehabilitation begins,

(ii) in the rehabilitation process—

(I) 50 percent or more of the existing external walls of such building are retained in place as external walls,

(II) 75 percent or more of the existing external walls of such building are retained in place as internal or external walls, and

(III) 75 percent or more of the existing internal structural framework of such building is retained in place, and

(iii) the expenditures for such rehabilitation are 25 percent or more of the mortgagor's adjusted basis in the residence.

For purposes of clause (iii) the mortgagor's adjusted basis shall be determined as of the completion of the rehabilitation or, if later, the date on which the mortgagor acquires the residence.

(6) DETERMINATION ON ACTUARIAL BASIS.—All determinations of yield, effective interest rates, and amounts required to be paid or credited to mortgagors or paid to the United States under subsection (g) shall be made on an actuarial basis taking into account the present value of money.

(7) SINGLE-FAMILY AND OWNER-OCCUPIED RESIDENCES INCLUDE CERTAIN RESIDENCES WITH 2 TO 4 UNITS.—Except for purposes of subsection (h)(2), the terms "single-family" and "owner-occupied", when used with respect to residences, include 2, 3, or 4 family residences—

(A) one unit of which is occupied by the owner of the units, and

(B) which were first occupied at least 5 years before the mortgage is executed.

Subparagraph (B) shall not apply to any 2-family residence if the residence is a targeted area residence and the family income of the mortgagor meets the requirement of subsection (f)(3)(B).

(8) COOPERATIVE HOUSING CORPORATIONS.—

(A) IN GENERAL.—In the case of any cooperative housing corporation—

(i) each dwelling unit shall be treated as if it were actually owned by the person entitled to occupy such dwelling unit by reason of his ownership of stock in the corporation, and

(ii) any indebtedness of the corporation allocable to the dwelling unit shall be treated as if it were indebtedness of the shareholder entitled to occupy the dwelling unit.

(B) ADJUSTMENT TO TARGETED AREA REQUIREMENT.—In the case of any issue to provide financing to a cooperative housing corporation with respect to cooperative housing not located in a targeted area, to the extent provided in regulations, such issue may be combined with 1 or more other issues for purposes of determining whether the requirements of subsection (h) are met.

(C) COOPERATIVE HOUSING CORPORATION.—The term "cooperative housing corporation" has the meaning given to such term by section 216(b)(1).

(9) TREATMENT OF LIMITED EQUITY COOPERATIVE HOUSING.—

(A) TREATMENT AS RESIDENTIAL RENTAL PROPERTY.—Except as provided in subparagraph (B), for purposes of this part—

(i) any limited equity cooperative housing shall be treated as residential rental property and not as owner-occupied housing, and

(ii) bonds issued to provide such housing shall be subject to the same requirements and limitations as bonds the proceeds of which are to be used to provide qualified residential rental projects (as defined in section 142(d)).

(B) BONDS SUBJECT TO QUALIFIED MORTGAGE BOND TERMINATION DATE.—Subparagraph (A) shall not apply to any bond issued after the date specified in subsection (a)(1)(B).

(C) LIMITED EQUITY COOPERATIVE HOUSING.—For purposes of this paragraph, the term "limited equity cooperative housing" means any dwelling unit which a person is entitled to occupy by reason of his ownership of stock in a qualified cooperative housing corporation.

(D) QUALIFIED COOPERATIVE HOUSING CORPORATION.—For purposes of this paragraph, the term "qualified cooperative housing corporation" means any cooperative housing corporation (as defined in section 216(b)(1)) if—

(i) the consideration paid for stock held by any stockholder entitled to occupy any house or apartment in a building owned or leased by the corporation may not exceed the sum of—

(I) the consideration paid for such stock by the first such stockholder, as adjusted by a cost-of-living adjustment determined by the Secretary,

(II) payments made by such stockholder for improvements to such house or apartment, and

(III) payments (other than amounts taken into account under subclause (I) or (II)) attributable to any stockholder to amortize the principal of the corporation's indebtedness arising from the acquisition or development of real property, including improvements thereof,

(ii) the value of the corporation's assets (reduced by any corporate liabilities), to the extent such value exceeds the combined transfer values of the outstanding corporate stock, shall be used only for public benefit or charitable purposes, or directly to benefit the corporation itself, and shall not be used directly to benefit any stockholder, and

(iii) at the time of issuance of the issue, such corporation makes an election under this paragraph.

(E) EFFECT OF ELECTION.—If a cooperative housing corporation makes an election under this paragraph, section 216 shall not apply with respect to such corporation (or any successor thereof) during the qualified project period (as defined in section 142(d)(2)).

(F) CORPORATION MUST CONTINUE TO BE QUALIFIED COOPERATIVE.—Subparagraph (A)(i) shall not apply to limited equity cooperative housing unless the cooperative housing corporation continues to be a qualified cooperative housing corporation at all times during the qualified project period (as defined in section 142(d)(2)).

(G) ELECTION IRREVOCABLE.—Any election under this paragraph, once made, shall be irrevocable.

(10) TREATMENT OF RESALE PRICE CONTROL AND SUBSIDY LIEN PROGRAMS.—

(A) IN GENERAL.—In the case of a residence which is located in a high housing cost area (as defined in section 143(f)(5)), the interest of a governmental unit in such residence by reason of financing provided under any qualified program shall not be taken into account under this section (other than subsection (m)), and the acquisition cost of the residence which is taken into account under subsection (e) shall be such cost reduced by the amount of such financing.

(B) QUALIFIED PROGRAM.—For purposes of subparagraph (A), the term "qualified program" means any governmental program providing mortgage loans (other than 1st mortgage loans) or grants—

(i) which restricts (throughout the 9-year period beginning on the date the financing is provided) the resale of the residence to a purchaser qualifying under this section and to a price determined by an index that reflects less than the full amount of any appreciation in the residence's value, or

(ii) which provides for deferred or reduced interest payments on such financing and grants the governmental unit a share in the appreciation of the residence, but only if such financing is not provided directly or indirectly through the use of any tax-exempt private activity bond.

(11) SPECIAL RULES FOR RESIDENCES LOCATED IN DISASTER AREAS.—In the case of a residence located in an area determined by the President to warrant assistance from the Federal Government under the Robert T. Stafford Disaster Relief and Emergency Assistance Act (as in effect on the date of the enactment of the Taxpayer Relief Act of 1997), this section shall be applied with

the following modifications to financing provided with respect to such residence within 2 years after the date of the disaster declaration:

(A) Subsection (d) (relating to 3-year requirement) shall not apply.

(B) Subsections (e) and (f) (relating to purchase price requirement and income requirement) shall be applied as if such residence were a targeted area residence.

The preceding sentence shall apply only with respect to bonds issued after May 1, 2008, and before January 1, 2010.

(12) SPECIAL RULES FOR SUBPRIME REFINANCINGS.—

(A) IN GENERAL.—Notwithstanding the requirements of subsection (i)(1), the proceeds of a qualified mortgage issue may be used to refinance a mortgage on a residence which was originally financed by the mortgagor through a qualified subprime loan.

(B) SPECIAL RULES.—In applying subparagraph (A) to any refinancing—

(i) subsection (a)(2)(D)(i) shall be applied by substituting "12-month period" for "42-month period" each place it appears,

(ii) subsection (d) (relating to 3-year requirement) shall not apply, and

(iii) subsection (e) (relating to purchase price requirement) shall be applied by using the market value of the residence at the time of refinancing in lieu of the acquisition cost.

(C) QUALIFIED SUBPRIME LOAN.—The term "qualified subprime loan" means an adjustable rate single-family residential mortgage loan made after December 31, 2001, and before January 1, 2008, that the bond issuer determines would be reasonably likely to cause financial hardship to the borrower if not refinanced.

(D) TERMINATION.—This paragraph shall not apply to any bonds issued after December 31, 2010.

(12)[13] SPECIAL RULES FOR RESIDENCES DESTROYED IN FEDERALLY DECLARED DISASTERS.—

(A) PRINCIPAL RESIDENCE DESTROYED.—At the election of the taxpayer, if the principal residence (within the meaning of section 121) of such taxpayer is—

(i) rendered unsafe for use as a residence by reason of a federally declared disaster occurring before January 1, 2010, or

(ii) demolished or relocated by reason of an order of the government of a State or political subdivision thereof on account of a federally declared disaster occurring before such date,

then, for the 2-year period beginning on the date of the disaster declaration, subsection (d)(1) shall not apply with respect to such taxpayer and subsection (e) shall be applied by substituting "110" for "90" in paragraph (1) thereof.

(B) PRINCIPAL RESIDENCE DAMAGED.—

(i) IN GENERAL.—At the election of the taxpayer, if the principal residence (within the meaning of section 121) of such taxpayer was damaged as the result of a federally declared disaster occurring before January 1, 2010, any owner-financing provided in connection with the repair or reconstruction of such residence shall be treated as a qualified rehabilitation loan.

(ii) LIMITATION.—The aggregate owner-financing to which clause (i) applies shall not exceed the lesser of—

(I) the cost of such repair or reconstruction, or

(II) $150,000.

(C) FEDERALLY DECLARED DISASTER.—For purposes of this paragraph, the term "federally declared disaster" has the meaning given such term by section 165(h)(3)(C)(i).

(D) ELECTION; DENIAL OF DOUBLE BENEFIT.—

(i) ELECTION.—An election under this paragraph may not be revoked except with the consent of the Secretary.

(ii) DENIAL OF DOUBLE BENEFIT.—If a taxpayer elects the application of this paragraph, paragraph (11) shall not apply with respect to the purchase or financing of any residence by such taxpayer.

Amendments

• 2008, Tax Extenders and Alternative Minimum Tax Relief Act of 2008 (P.L. 110-343)

P.L. 110-343, Division C, §709(a):

Amended Code Sec. 143(k) by adding at the end a new paragraph (12)[13]. **Effective** for disasters occurring after 12-31-2007.

P.L. 110-343, Division C, §712, provides:

SEC. 712. COORDINATION WITH HEARTLAND DISASTER RELIEF.

The amendments made by this subtitle, other than the amendments made by sections 706(a)(2), 710, and 711, shall not apply to any disaster described in section 702(c)[b](1)(A), or to any expenditure or loss resulting from such disaster.

• 2008, Housing Assistance Tax Act of 2008 (P.L. 110-289)

P.L. 110-289, §3021(b)(1):

Amended Code Sec. 143(k) by adding at the end a new paragraph (12). **Effective** for bonds issued after 7-30-2008.

P.L. 110-289, §3026(a)(1)-(2):

Amended Code Sec. 143(k)(11) by striking "December 31, 1996" and inserting "May 1, 2008", and by striking "January

1, 1999" and inserting "January 1, 2010". **Effective** for bonds issued after 5-1-2008.

• 1997, Taxpayer Relief Act of 1997 (P.L. 105-34)

P.L. 105-34, §914:

Amended Code Sec. 143(k) by adding at the end a new paragraph (11). **Effective** 8-5-97.

• 1993, Omnibus Budget Reconciliation Act of 1993 (P.L. 103-66)

P.L. 103-66, §13141(c):

Amended Code Sec. 143(k) by adding at the end thereof a new subparagraph (10). **Effective** for qualified mortgage bonds issued and mortgage credit certificates provided on or after 8-10-93.

P.L. 103-66, §13141(d)(3):

Amended Code Sec. 143(k)(3)(B)(iii) by inserting "(other than land described in subsection (i)(1)(C)(i))" after "cost of land". **Effective** for loans originated and credit certificates provided after 8-10-93.

P.L. 103-66, §13141(e):

Amended Code Sec. 143(k)(7) by adding at the end thereof a new flush sentence. **Effective** for qualified mortgage bonds issued and mortgage credit certificates provided on or after 8-10-93.

[Sec. 143(l)]

(l) ADDITIONAL REQUIREMENTS FOR QUALIFIED VETERANS' MORTGAGE BONDS.—An issue meets the requirements of this subsection only if it meets the requirements of paragraphs (1), (2), and (3).

(1) VETERANS TO WHOM FINANCING MAY BE PROVIDED.—An issue meets the requirements of this paragraph only if each mortgagor to whom financing is provided under the issue is a qualified veteran.

(2) REQUIREMENT THAT STATE PROGRAM BE IN EFFECT BEFORE JUNE 22, 1984.—An issue meets the requirements of this paragraph only if it is a general obligation of a State which issued qualified veterans' mortgage bonds before June 22, 1984.

(3) VOLUME LIMITATION.—

(A) IN GENERAL.—An issue meets the requirements of this paragraph only if the aggregate amount of bonds issued pursuant thereto (when added to the aggregate amount of qualified veterans' mortgage bonds previously issued by the State during the calendar year) does not exceed the State veterans limit for such calendar year.

(B) STATE VETERANS LIMIT.—

(i) IN GENERAL.—In the case of any State to which clause (ii) does not apply, the State veterans limit for any calendar year is the amount equal to—

(I) the aggregate amount of qualified veterans bonds issued by such State during the period beginning on January 1, 1979, and ending on June 22, 1984 (not including the amount of any qualified veterans bond issued by such State during the calendar year (or portion thereof) in such period for which the amount of such bonds so issued was the lowest), divided by

(II) the number (not to exceed 5) of calendar years after 1979 and before 1985 during which the State issued qualified veterans bonds (determined by only taking into account bonds issued on or before June 22, 1984).

(ii) ALASKA, OREGON, AND WISCONSIN.—In the case of the following States, the State veterans limit for any calendar year is the amount equal to—

(I) $100,000,000 for the State of Alaska,

(II) $100,000,000 for the State of Oregon, and

(III) $100,000,000 for the State of Wisconsin.

(iii) PHASEIN.—In the case of calendar years beginning before 2010, clause (ii) shall be applied by substituting for each of the dollar amounts therein an amount equal to the applicable percentage of such dollar amount. For purposes of the preceding sentence, the applicable percentage shall be determined in accordance with the following table:

For Calendar Year:	Applicable percentage is:
2006	20 percent
2007	40 percent
2008	60 percent
2009	80 percent.

(C) TREATMENT OF REFUNDING ISSUES.—

(i) IN GENERAL.—For purposes of subparagraph (A), the term "qualified veterans' mortgage bond" shall not include any bond issued to refund another bond but only if the maturity date of the refunding bond is not later than the later of—

(I) the maturity date of the bond to be refunded, or

(II) the date 32 years after the date on which the refunded bond was issued (or in the case of a series of refundings, the date on which the original bond was issued).

The preceding sentence shall apply only to the extent that the amount of the refunding bond does not exceed the outstanding amount of the refunded bond.

(ii) EXCEPTION FOR ADVANCE REFUNDING.—Clause (i) shall not apply to any bond issued to advance refund another bond.

(4) QUALIFIED VETERAN.—For purposes of this subsection, the term "qualified veteran" means any veteran who—

(A) served on active duty, and

(B) applied for the financing before the date 25 years after the last date on which such veteran left active service.

(5) SPECIAL RULE FOR CERTAIN SHORT-TERM BONDS.—In the case of any bond—

(A) which has a term of 1 year or less,

(B) which is authorized to be issued under O.R.S. 407.435 (as in effect on the date of the enactment of this subsection), to provide financing for property taxes, and

(C) which is redeemed at the end of such term,

the amount taken into account under this subsection with respect to such bond shall be 1/15 of its principal amount.

Amendments

• 2008, Heroes Earnings Assistance and Relief Tax Act of 2008 (P.L. 110-245)

P.L. 110-245, §103(b):

Amended Code Sec. 143(l)(3)(B)(ii) by striking "$25,000,000" each place it appears and inserting "$100,000,000". **Effective** for bonds issued after 12-31-2007.

P.L. 110-245, §103(c):

Amended Code Sec. 143(l)(4). **Effective** for bonds issued after 12-31-2007. For a transitional rule, see Act Sec. 103(e), below. Prior to amendment, Code Sec. 143(l)(4) read as follows:

(4) QUALIFIED VETERAN.—For purposes of this subsection, the term "qualified veteran" means—

(A) in the case of the States of Alaska, Oregon, and Wisconsin, any veteran—

(i) who served on active duty, and

(ii) who applied for the financing before the date 25 years after the last date on which such veteran left active service, and

(B) in the case of any other State, any veteran—

(i) who served on active duty at some time before January 1, 1977, and

(ii) who applied for the financing before the later of—

(I) the date 30 years after the last date on which such veteran left active service, or

(II) January 31, 1985.

P.L. 110-245, §103(e), provides:

(e) TRANSITION RULE.—In the case of any bond issued after December 31, 2007, and before the date of the enactment of this Act [6-17-2008.—CCH], subparagraph (B) of section 143(l)(4) of the Internal Revenue Code of 1986, as amended by this section, shall be applied by substituting "30 years" for "25 years".

• 2006, Tax Relief and Health Care Act of 2006 (P.L. 109-432)

P.L. 109-432, Division A, §411(a):

Amended Code Sec. 143(l)(3)(B) by striking clause (iv). **Effective** as if included in section 203 of the Tax Increase Prevention and Reconciliation Act of 2005 (P.L. 109-222) [**effective** for allocations of State volume limit after 4-5-2006.—CCH]. Prior to being stricken, Code Sec. 143(l)(3)(B)(iv) read as follows:

(iv) TERMINATION.—The State veterans limit for the States specified in clause (ii) for any calendar year after 2010 is zero.

• 2006, Tax Increase Prevention and Reconciliation Act of 2005 (P.L. 109-222)

P.L. 109-222, §203(a)(1):

Amended Code Sec. 143(l)(4). **Effective** for bonds issued on or after 5-17-2006. Prior to amendment, Code Sec. 143(l)(4) read as follows:

(4) QUALIFIED VETERAN.—For purposes of this subsection, the term "qualified veteran" means any veteran—

(A) who served on active duty at some time before January 1, 1977, and

(B) who applied for the financing before the later of—

(i) the date 30 years after the last date on which such veteran left active service, or

(ii) January 31, 1985.

P.L. 109-222, §203(b)(1)(A)-(C):

Amended Code Sec. 143(l)(3)(B) by redesignating clauses (i) and (ii) as subclauses (I) and (II), respectively, and moving such clauses 2 ems to the right, by amending the matter preceding subclause (I), as [re]designated by Act Sec. 203(b)(1)(A), and by adding at the end new clauses (ii)-(iv). **Effective** for allocations of State volume limit after 4-5-2006. Prior to amendment, the matter preceding subclause (I) of Code Sec. 143(l)(3)(B) read as follows:

(B) STATE VETERANS LIMIT.—A State veterans limit for any calendar year is the amount equal to—

• 1986, Tax Reform Act of 1986 (P.L. 99-514)

P.L. 99-514, §1301(b):

Amended part IV of subchapter B of chapter 1 by adding Code Sec. 143. **Effective**, generally, for bonds issued after 8-15-86. However, for transitional rules, see Act Secs. 1312-1318 in the amendments for Code Sec. 103.

[Sec. 143(m)]

(m) RECAPTURE OF PORTION OF FEDERAL SUBSIDY FROM USE OF QUALIFIED MORTGAGE BONDS AND MORTGAGE CREDIT CERTIFICATES.—

(1) IN GENERAL.—If, during the taxable year, any taxpayer disposes of an interest in a residence with respect to which there is or was any federally-subsidized indebtedness for the payment of which the taxpayer was liable in whole or part, then the taxpayer's tax imposed by this chapter for such taxable year shall be increased by the lesser of—

(A) the recapture amount with respect to such indebtedness, or

(B) 50 percent of the gain (if any) on the disposition of such interest.

(2) EXCEPTIONS.—Paragraph (1) shall not apply to—

(A) any disposition by reason of death, and

(B) any disposition which is more than 9 years after the testing date.

(3) FEDERALLY-SUBSIDIZED INDEBTEDNESS.—For purposes of this subsection—

(A) IN GENERAL.—The term "federally-subsidized indebtedness" means any indebtedness if—

(i) financing for the indebtedness was provided in whole or part from the proceeds of any tax-exempt qualified mortgage bond, or

(ii) any credit was allowed under section 25 (relating to interest on certain home mortgages) to the taxpayer for interest paid or incurred on such indebtedness.

(B) EXCEPTION FOR HOME IMPROVEMENT LOANS.—Such term shall not include any indebtedness to the extent such indebtedness is federally-subsidized indebtedness solely by reason of being a qualified home improvement loan (as defined in subsection (k)(4)).

(4) RECAPTURE AMOUNT.—For purposes of this subsection—

(A) IN GENERAL.—The recapture amount with respect to any indebtedness is the amount equal to the product of—

(i) the federally-subsidized amount with respect to the indebtedness,

(ii) the holding period percentage, and

(iii) the income percentage.

(B) FEDERALLY-SUBSIDIZED AMOUNT.—The federally-subsidized amount with respect to any indebtedness is the amount equal to 6.25 percent of the highest principal amount of the indebtedness for which the taxpayer was liable.

(C) HOLDING PERIOD PERCENTAGE.—

(i) IN GENERAL.—The term "holding period percentage" means the percentage determined in accordance with the following table:

If the disposition occurs during a year after the testing date which is:	*The holding period percentage is:*
The 1st such year	20
The 2d such year	40
The 3d such year	60
The 4th such year	80
The 5th such year	100
The 6th such year	80
The 7th such year	60
The 8th such year	40
The 9th such year	20.

(ii) RETIREMENTS OF INDEBTEDNESS.—If the federally-subsidized indebtedness is completely repaid during any year of the 4-year period beginning on the testing date, the holding period percentage for succeeding years shall be determined by reducing ratably to zero over the succeeding 5 years the holding period percentage which would have been determined under this subparagraph had the taxpayer disposed of his interest in the residence on the date of the repayment.

(D) TESTING DATE.—The term "testing date" means the earliest date on which all of the following requirements are met:

(i) The indebtedness is federally-subsidized indebtedness.

(ii) The taxpayer is liable in whole or part for payment of the indebtedness.

(E) INCOME PERCENTAGE.—The term "income percentage" means the percentage (but not greater than 100 percent) which—

(i) the excess of—

(I) the modified adjusted gross income of the taxpayer for the taxable year in which the disposition occurs, over

(II) the adjusted qualifying income for such taxable year, bears to

(ii) $5,000.

The percentage determined under the preceding sentence shall be rounded to the nearest whole percentage point (or, if it includes a half of a percentage point, shall be increased to the nearest whole percentage point).

(5) ADJUSTED QUALIFYING INCOME; MODIFIED ADJUSTED GROSS INCOME.—

(A) ADJUSTED QUALIFYING INCOME.—For purposes of paragraph (4), the term "adjusted qualifying income" means the product of—

(i) the highest family income which (as of the date the financing was provided) would have met the requirements of subsection (f) with respect to the residents, and

(ii) 1.05 to the nth power where "n" equals the number of full years during the period beginning on the date the financing was provided and ending on the date of the disposition.

For purposes of clause (i), highest family income shall be determined without regard to subsection (f)(3)(A) and on the basis of the number of members of the taxpayer's family as of the date of the disposition.

(B) MODIFIED ADJUSTED GROSS INCOME.—For purposes of paragraph 4, the term "modified adjusted gross income" means adjusted gross income—

(i) increased by the amount of interest received or accrued by the taxpayer during the taxable year which is excluded from gross income under section 103, and

(ii) decreased by the amount of gain (if any) included in gross income of the taxpayer by reason of the disposition to which this subsection applies.

(6) SPECIAL RULES RELATING TO LIMITATION ON RECAPTURE AMOUNT BASED ON GAIN REALIZED.—

(A) IN GENERAL.—For purposes of paragraph (1), gain shall be taken into account whether or not recognized, and the adjusted basis of the taxpayer's interest in the residence shall be determined without regard to sections 1033(b) and 1034(e) (as in effect on the day before the date of the enactment of the Taxpayer Relief Act of 1997) for purposes of determining gain.

(B) DISPOSITIONS OTHER THAN SALES, EXCHANGES, AND INVOLUNTARY CONVERSIONS.—In the case of a disposition other than a sale, exchange, or involuntary conversion, gain shall be determined as if the interest had been sold for its fair market value.

(C) INVOLUNTARY CONVERSIONS RESULTING FROM CASUALTIES.—In the case of property which (as a result of its destruction in whole or in part by fire, storm, or other casualty) is compulsorily or involuntarily converted, paragraph (1) shall not apply to such conversion if the taxpayer purchases (during the period specified in section 1033(a)(2)(B)) property for use as his principal residence on the site of the converted property. For purposes of subparagraph (A), the adjusted basis of the taxpayer in the residence shall not be adjusted for any gain or loss on a conversion to which this subparagraph applies.

(7) ISSUER TO INFORM MORTGAGOR OF FEDERALLY-SUBSIDIZED AMOUNT AND FAMILY INCOME LIMITS.—The issuer of the issue which provided the federally-subsidized indebtedness to the mortgagor shall—

(A) at the time of settlement, provide a written statement informing the mortgagor of the potential recapture under this subsection, and

(B) not later than 90 days after the date such indebtedness is provided, provide a written statement to the mortgagor specifying—

(i) the federally-subsidized amount with respect to such indebtedness, and

(ii) the adjusted qualifying income (as defined in paragraph (5)) for each category of family size for each year of the 9-year period beginning on the date the financing was provided.

(8) SPECIAL RULES.—

(A) NO BASIS ADJUSTMENT.—No adjustment shall be made to the basis of any property for the increase in tax under this subsection.

(B) SPECIAL RULE WHERE 2 OR MORE PERSONS HOLD INTERESTS IN RESIDENCE.—Except as provided in subparagraph (C) and in regulations prescribed by the Secretary, if 2 or more persons hold interests in any residence and are jointly liable for the federally-subsidized indebtedness, the recapture amount shall be determined separately with respect to their respective interests in the residence.

(C) TRANSFERS TO SPOUSES AND FORMER SPOUSES.—Paragraph (1) shall not apply to any transfer on which no gain or loss is recognized under section 1041. In any such case, the transferee shall be treated under this subsection in the same manner as the transferor would have been treated had such transfer not occurred.

(D) REGULATIONS.—The Secretary shall prescribe such regulations as may be necessary or appropriate to carry out this subsection, including regulations dealing with dispositions of partial interests in a residence.

Amendments

• 1997, Taxpayer Relief Act of 1997 (P.L. 105-34)

P.L. 105-34, §312(d)(3):

Amended Code Sec. 143(m)(6)(A) by inserting "(as in effect on the day before the date of the enactment of the Taxpayer Relief Act of 1997)" after "1034(e)". **Effective,** generally, for sales and exchanges after 5-6-97.

• 1996, Small Business Job Protection Act of 1996 (P.L. 104-188)

P.L. 104-188, §1702(d)(2)(A)-(C):

Amended Code Sec. 143(m)(4)(C)(ii) by striking "any month of the 10-year period" and inserting "any year of the 4-year period", by striking "succeeding months" and inserting "succeeding years", and by striking "over the remainder of such period (or, if lesser, 5 years)" and inserting "to zero over the succeeding 5 years". **Effective** as if included in the provision of P.L. 101-508 to which it relates.

• 1990, Omnibus Budget Reconciliation Act of 1990 (P.L. 101-508)

P.L. 101-508, §11408(c)(1)(A):

Amended Code Sec. 143(m)(4)(C)(i). **Effective** as if included in the amendments made by section 4005 of P.L. 100-647. Prior to amendment, Code Sec. 143(m)(4)(C)(i) read as follows:

(i) DISPOSITIONS DURING 1ST 5 YEARS.—If the disposition of the taxpayer's interest in the residence occurs during the 5-year period beginning on the testing date, the holding period percentage is the percentage determined by dividing the number of full months during which the requirements of subparagraph (D) were met by 60.

P.L. 101-508, §11408(c)(1)(B):

Amended Code Sec. 143(m)(4)(C) by striking clause (ii) and by redesignating clause (iii) as clause (ii). **Effective** as if included in the amendments made by section 4005 of P.L.

100-647. Prior to amendment, Code Sec. 143(m)(4)(C)(ii) read as follows:

(ii) DISPOSITIONS DURING 2D 5 YEARS.—If the disposition of the taxpayer's interest in the residence occurs during the 5-year period following the 5-year period described in clause (i), the holding period percentage is the percentage determined by dividing—

(I) the excess of 120 over the number of full months during which such requirements were met by

(II) 60.

P.L. 101-508, §11408(c)(1)(C):

Amended Code Sec. 143(m)(2)(B) by striking "10 years" and inserting "9 years". **Effective** as if included in the amendments made by section 4005 of P.L. 100-647.

P.L. 101-508, §11408(c)(2)(A):

Amended Code Sec. 143(m)(4)(A) by striking "and" at the end of clause (i), by striking the period at the end of clause (ii) and inserting ", and", and by adding at the end thereof new clause (iii). **Effective** as if included in the amendments made by section 4005 of P.L. 100-647.

P.L. 101-508, §11408(c)(2)(B):

Amended Code Sec. 143(m)(4) by adding new subparagraph (E). **Effective** as if included in the amendments made by section 4005 of P.L. 100-647.

P.L. 101-508, §11408(c)(2)(C)(i):

Amended Code Sec. 143(m)(5) by striking all that precedes subparagraph (C) and inserting new paragraph (5)(A). **Effective** as if included in the amendments made by section 4005 of P.L. 100-647. Prior to amendment, Code Sec. 143(m)(5)(A)-(B) read as follows:

(5) REDUCTION OF RECAPTURE AMOUNT IF TAXPAYER MEETS CERTAIN INCOME LIMITATIONS.—

(A) IN GENERAL.—The recapture amount which would (but for this paragraph) apply with respect to any disposition during a taxable year shall be reduced (but not below zero) by 2 percent of such amount for each $100 by which adjusted qualifying income exceeds the modified adjusted gross income of the taxpayer for such year.

(B) ADJUSTED QUALIFYING INCOME.—For purposes of this paragraph, the term "adjusted qualifying income" means the amount equal to the sum of—

(i) $5,000, plus

(ii) the product of—

(I) the highest family income which (as of the date the financing was provided) would have met the requirement of subsection (f) with respect to the residence, and

(II) the percentage equal to the sum of 100 percent plus 5 percent for each full year during the period beginning on such date and ending on the date of the disposition.

For purposes of clause (ii)(I), highest family income shall be determined without regard to subsection (f)(3)(A) and on the basis of the number of members of the taxpayer's family as of the date of the disposition.

P.L. 101-508, §11408(c)(2)(C)(ii):

Amended Code Sec. 143(m)(5)(C) by redesignating subparagraph (C) as subparagraph (B) and by striking "this paragraph" and inserting "paragraph (4)". **Effective** as if included in the amendments made by section 4005 of P.L. 100-647.

P.L. 101-508, §11408(c)(3)(A):

Amended Code Sec. 143(m)(1) by striking "increased by" and all that follows and inserting "increased by the lesser of—

"(A) the recapture amount with respect to such indebtedness, or

"(B) 50 percent of the gain (if any) on the disposition of such interest." **Effective** as if included in the amendments made by section 4005 of P.L. 100-647. Prior to amendment, Code Sec. 143(m)(1) read as follows:

(1) IN GENERAL.—If, during the taxable year, any taxpayer disposes of an interest in a residence with respect to which there is or was any federally-subsidized indebtedness for the payment of which the taxpayer was liable in whole or in part, then the taxpayer's tax imposed by this chapter for such taxable year shall be increased by the recapture amount with respect to such indebtedness.

P.L. 101-508, §11408(c)(3)(B)(i)-(iii):

Amended Code Sec. 143(m)(6) by striking "LIMITATION" in the heading and inserting "SPECIAL RULES RELATING TO LIMITATION", by striking the first sentence of subparagraph (A), and by striking "the preceding sentence" in subparagraph (A) and inserting "paragraph (1)". **Effective** as if included in the amendments made by section 4005 of P.L. 100-647. Prior to amendment, the first sentence of Code Sec. 143(m)(6)(A) read as follows:

In no event shall the recapture amount of the taxpayer with respect to any indebtedness exceed 50 percent of the gain (if any) on the disposition of the taxpayer's interest in the residence.

P.L. 101-508, §11408(c)(3)(C):

Amended Code Sec. 143(m)(7)(B)(ii). **Effective** as if included in the amendments made by section 4005 of P.L. 100-647. Prior to amendment, Code Sec. 143(m)(7)(B)(ii) read as follows:

(ii) the amounts described in paragraph (5)(B)(ii) for each category of family size for each year of the 10-year period beginning on the date the financing was provided.

• 1988, Technical and Miscellaneous Revenue Act of 1988 (P.L. 100-647)

P.L. 100-647, §4005(g)(1):

Amended Code Sec. 143 by adding at the end thereof a new subsection (m). **Effective**, generally, for financing provided, and mortgage credit certificates issued, after 12-31-90. For an exception, see Act Sec. 4005(h)(3)(B), below.

P.L. 100-647, §4005(h)(3)(B), provides:

(B) EXCEPTION.—The amendments made by subsection (g) shall not apply to financing provided pursuant to a binding contract (entered into before June 23, 1988) with a homebuilder, lender, or mortgagor if the bonds (the proceeds of which are used to provide such financing) are issued—

(i) before June 23, 1988, or

(ii) before August 1, 1988, pursuant to a written application (made before July 1, 1988) for State bond volume authority.

[Sec. 143—Repealed]

Amendments

• 1986, Tax Reform Act of 1986 (P.L. 99-514)

P.L. 99-514, §1301(j)(2):

Redesignated Code Sec. 143 as Code Sec. 7703. **Effective** for bonds issued after 8-15-86. For more information see Code Sec. 7703. Prior to redesignation, Code Sec. 143 read as follows:

SEC. 143. DETERMINATION OF MARITAL STATUS.

[Sec. 143(a)]

(a) GENERAL RULE.—For purposes of part V—

(1) The determination of whether an individual is married shall be made as of the close of his taxable year; except that if his spouse dies during his taxable year such determination shall be made as of the time of such death; and

(2) An individual legally separated from his spouse under a decree of divorce or of separate maintenance shall not be considered as married.

Amendments

• 1977, Tax Reduction and Simplification Act of 1977 (P.L. 95-30)

P.L. 95-30, §101(d)(4):

Amended Code Sec. 143(a) by deleting "this part and" which formerly appeared in front of "part V". **Effective** for tax years beginning after 12-31-76.

• 1976, Tax Reform Act of 1976 (P.L. 94-455)

P.L. 94-455, §1901(a)(22):

Amended Code Sec. 143(a) substituted "this part and part V" for "this part". **Effective** for tax years beginning after 12-31-76.

[Sec. 143(b)]

(b) CERTAIN MARRIED INDIVIDUALS LIVING APART.—For purposes of those provisions of this title which refer to this subsection, if—

(1) an individual who is married (within the meaning of subsection (a)) and who files a separate return maintains as his home a household which constitutes for more than one-half of the taxable year the principal place of abode of a child (within the meaning of section 151(e)(3)) with respect to whom such individual is entitled to a deduction for the taxable year under section 151 (or would be so entitled but for paragraph (2) or (4) of section 152(e)),

(2) such individual furnishes over one-half of the cost of maintaining such household during the taxable year, and

(3) during the last 6 months of the taxable year, such individual's spouse is not a member of such household, such individual shall not be considered as married.

Amendments

• 1984, Deficit Reduction Act of 1984 (P.L. 98-369)

P.L. 98-369, §423(c)(1):

Amended Code Sec. 143(b). **Effective** for tax years beginning after 12-31-84. Prior to amendment, Code Sec. 143(b) read as follows:

(b) Certain Married Individuals Living Apart.—For purposes of part V, if—

(1) an individual who is married (within the meaning of subsection (a)) and who files a separate return maintains as his home a household which constitutes for more than one-half of the taxable year the principal place of abode of a dependent (A) who (within the meaning of section 152) is a son, stepson, daughter, or step-daughter of the individual, and (B) with respect to whom such individual is entitled to a deduction for the taxable year under section 151,

(2) such individual furnishes over half of the cost of maintaining such household during the taxable year, and

(3) during the entire taxable year such individual's spouse is not a member of such household, such individual shall not be considered as married.

• 1977, Tax Reduction and Simplification Act of 1977 (P.L. 95-30)

P.L. 95-30, §101(d)(4):

Amended Code Sec. 143(b) by deleting "this part and" which formerly appeared in front of "part V". **Effective** for tax years beginning after 12-31-76.

• 1976, Tax Reform Act of 1976 (P.L. 94-455)

P.L. 94-455, §1901(a)(22):

Amended Code Sec. 143(b) by substituting "this part and part V" for "this part". **Effective** for tax years beginning after 12-31-76.

• 1976, Tax Reform Act of 1969 (P.L. 91-172)

P.L. 91-172, §802(b):

Amended Code Sec. 143 by substituting "(a) General Rule—For purposes of this part—" in place of "For purposes of this part—" and by adding Code Sec. 143(b). **Effective** for tax years beginning after 12-31-69.

[Sec. 144]

SEC. 144. QUALIFIED SMALL ISSUE BOND; QUALIFIED STUDENT LOAN BOND; QUALIFIED REDEVELOPMENT BOND.

[Sec. 144(a)]

(a) QUALIFIED SMALL ISSUE BOND.—

(1) IN GENERAL.—For purposes of this part, the term "qualified small issue bond" means any bond issued as part of an issue the aggregate authorized face amount of which is $1,000,000 or less and 95 percent or more of the net proceeds of which are to be used—

(A) for the acquisition, construction, reconstruction, or improvement of land or property of a character subject to the allowance for depreciation, or

(B) to redeem part or all of a prior issue which was issued for purposes described in subparagraph (A) or this subparagraph.

(2) CERTAIN PRIOR ISSUES TAKEN INTO ACCOUNT.—If—

(A) the proceeds of 2 or more issues of bonds (whether or not the issuer of each such issue is the same) are or will be used primarily with respect to facilities located in the same incorporated municipality or located in the same county (but not in any incorporated municipality),

(B) the principal user of such facilities is or will be the same person or 2 or more related persons, and

(C) but for this paragraph, paragraph (1) (or the corresponding provision of prior law) would apply to each such issue,

then, for purposes of paragraph (1), in determining the aggregate face amount of any later issue there shall be taken into account the aggregate face amount of tax-exempt bonds issued under all prior such issues and outstanding at the time of such later issue (not including as outstanding any bond which is to be redeemed (other than in an advance refunding) from the net proceeds of the later issue).

(3) RELATED PERSONS.—For purposes of this subsection, a person is a related person to another person if—

(A) the relationship between such persons would result in a disallowance of losses under section 267 or 707(b), or

(B) such persons are members of the same controlled group of corporations (as defined in section 1563(a), except that "more than 50 percent" shall be substituted for "at least 80 percent" each place it appears therein).

(4) $10,000,000 LIMIT IN CERTAIN CASES.—

(A) IN GENERAL.—At the election of the issuer with respect to any issue, this subsection shall be applied—

(i) by substituting "$10,000,000" for "$1,000,000" in paragraph (1), and

(ii) in determining the aggregate face amount of such issue, by taking into account not only the amount described in paragraph (2), but also the aggregate amount of capital expenditures with respect to facilities described in subparagraph (B) paid or incurred during the 6-year period beginning 3 years before the date of such issue and ending 3 years after such date (and financed otherwise than out of the proceeds of outstanding tax-exempt issues to which paragraph (1) (or the corresponding provision of prior law) applied), as if the aggregate amount of such capital expenditures constituted the face amount of a prior outstanding issue described in paragraph (2).

(B) FACILITIES TAKEN INTO ACCOUNT.—For purposes of subparagraph (A)(ii), the facilities described in this subparagraph are facilities—

(i) located in the same incorporated municipality or located in the same county (but not in any incorporated municipality), and

(ii) the principal user of which is or will be the same person or 2 or more related persons.

For purposes of clause (i), the determination of whether or not facilities are located in the same governmental unit shall be made as of the date of issue of the issue in question.

(C) CERTAIN CAPITAL EXPENDITURES NOT TAKEN INTO ACCOUNT.—For purposes of subparagraph (A)(ii), any capital expenditure—

(i) to replace property destroyed or damaged by fire, storm, or other casualty, to the extent of the fair market value of the property replaced,

(ii) required by a change made after the date of issue of the issue in question in a Federal or State law or local ordinance of general application or required by a change made after such date in rules and regulations of general application issued under such a law or ordinance,

(iii) required by circumstances which could not be reasonably foreseen on such date of issue or arising out of a mistake of law or fact (but the aggregate amount of expenditures not taken into account under this clause with respect to any issue shall not exceed $1,000,000), or

(iv) described in clause (i) or (ii) of section 41(b)(2)(A) for which a deduction was allowed under section 174(a),

shall not be taken into account.

(D) LIMITATION ON LOSS OF TAX EXEMPTION.—In applying subparagraph (A)(ii) with respect to capital expenditures made after the date of any issue, no bond issued as a part of such issue shall cease to be treated as a qualified small issue bond by reason of any such expenditure for any period before the date on which such expenditure is paid or incurred.

(E) CERTAIN REFINANCING ISSUES.—In the case of any issue described in paragraph (1)(B), an election may be made under subparagraph (A) of this paragraph only if all of the prior issues being redeemed are issues to which paragraph (1) (or the corresponding provision of prior law) applied. In applying subparagraph (A)(ii) with respect to such a refinancing issue, capital expenditures shall be taken into account only for purposes of determining whether the prior issues being redeemed qualified (and would have continued to qualify) under paragraph (1) (or the corresponding provision of prior law).

(F) AGGREGATE AMOUNT OF CAPITAL EXPENDITURES WHERE THERE IS URBAN DEVELOPMENT ACTION GRANT.—In the case of any issue 95 percent or more of the net proceeds of which are to be used to provide facilities with respect to which an urban development action grant has been made under section 119 of the Housing and Community Development Act of 1974, capital expenditures of not to exceed $10,000,000 shall not be taken into account for purposes of applying subparagraph (A)(ii). This subparagraph shall not apply to bonds issued after December 31, 2006.

(G) ADDITIONAL CAPITAL EXPENDITURES NOT TAKEN INTO ACCOUNT.—With respect to bonds issued after December 31, 2006, in addition to any capital expenditure described in subparagraph (C), capital expenditures of not to exceed $10,000,000 shall not be taken into account for purposes of applying subparagraph (A)(ii).

(5) ISSUES FOR RESIDENTIAL PURPOSES.—This subsection shall not apply to any bond issued as part of an issue 5 percent or more of the net proceeds of which are to be used directly or indirectly to provide residential real property for family units.

(6) LIMITATIONS ON TREATMENT OF BONDS AS PART OF THE SAME ISSUE.—

(A) IN GENERAL.—For purposes of this subsection, separate lots of bonds which (but for this subparagraph) would be treated as part of the same issue shall be treated as separate issues unless the proceeds of such lots are to be used with respect to 2 or more facilities—

(i) which are located in more than 1 State, or

(ii) which have, or will have, as the same principal user the same person or related persons.

(B) FRANCHISES.—For purposes of subparagraph (A), a person (other than a governmental unit) shall be considered a principal user of a facility if such person (or a group of related persons which includes such person)—

(i) guarantees, arranges, participates in, or assists with the issuance (or pays any portion of the cost of issuance) of any bond the proceeds of which are to be used to finance or refinance such facility, and

(ii) provides any property, or any franchise, trademark, or trade name (within the meaning of section 1253), which is to be used in connection with such facility.

(7) SUBSECTION NOT TO APPLY IF BONDS ISSUED WITH CERTAIN OTHER TAX-EXEMPT BONDS.—This subsection shall not apply to any bond issued as part of an issue (other than an issue to which paragraph (4) applies) if the interest on any other bond which is part of such issue is excluded from gross income under any provision of law other than this subsection.

(8) RESTRICTIONS ON FINANCING CERTAIN FACILITIES.—This subsection shall not apply to an issue if—

(A) more than 25 percent of the net proceeds of the issue are to be used to provide a facility the primary purpose of which is one of the following: retail food and beverage services, automobile sales or service, or the provision of recreation or entertainment; or

(B) any portion of the proceeds of the issue is to be used to provide the following: any private or commercial golf course, country club, massage parlor, tennis club, skating facility (including roller skating, skateboard, and ice skating), racquet sports facility (including any handball or racquetball court), hot tub facility, suntan facility, or racetrack.

(9) AGGREGATION OF ISSUES WITH RESPECT TO SINGLE PROJECT.—For purposes of this subsection, 2 or more issues part or all of the net proceeds of which are to be used with respect to a single building, an enclosed shopping mall, or a strip of offices, stores, or warehouses using substantial common facilities shall be treated as 1 issue (and any person who is a principal user with respect to any of such issues shall be treated as a principal user with respect to the aggregated issue).

(10) AGGREGATE LIMIT PER TAXPAYER.—

(A) IN GENERAL.—This subsection shall not apply to any issue if the aggregate authorized face amount of such issue allocated to any test-period beneficiary (when increased by the outstanding tax-exempt facility-related bonds of such beneficiary) exceeds $40,000,000.

(B) OUTSTANDING TAX-EXEMPT FACILITY-RELATED BONDS.—

(i) IN GENERAL.—For purposes of applying subparagraph (A) with respect to any issue, the outstanding tax-exempt facility-related bonds of any person who is a test-period beneficiary with respect to such issue is the aggregate amount of tax-exempt bonds referred to in clause (ii)—

(I) which are allocated to such beneficiary, and

(II) which are outstanding at the time of such later issue (not including as outstanding any bond which is to be redeemed (other than in an advance refunding) from the net proceeds of the later issue).

(ii) BONDS TAKEN INTO ACCOUNT.—For purposes of clause (i), the bonds referred to in this clause are—

(I) exempt facility bonds, qualified small issue bonds, and qualified redevelopment bonds, and

(II) industrial development bonds (as defined in section 103(b)(2), as in effect on the day before the date of the enactment of the Tax Reform Act of 1986) to which section 141(a) does not apply.

(C) ALLOCATION OF FACE AMOUNT OF ISSUE.—

(i) IN GENERAL.—Except as otherwise provided in regulations, the portion of the face amount of an issue allocated to any test-period beneficiary of a facility financed by the proceeds of such issue (other than an owner of such facility) is an amount which bears the same relationship to the entire face amount of such issue as the portion of such facility used by such beneficiary bears to the entire facility.

(ii) OWNERS.—Except as otherwise provided in regulations, the portion of the face amount of an issue allocated to any test-period beneficiary who is an owner of a facility financed by the proceeds of such issue is an amount which bears the same relationship to the entire face amount of such issue as the portion of such facility owned by such beneficiary bears to the entire facility.

(D) TEST-PERIOD BENEFICIARY.—For purposes of this paragraph, except as provided in regulations, the term "test-period beneficiary" means any person who is an owner or a principal user of facilities being financed by the issue at any time during the 3-year period beginning on the later of—

(i) the date such facilities were placed in service, or

(ii) the date of issue.

(E) TREATMENT OF RELATED PERSONS.—For purposes of this paragraph, all persons who are related (within the meaning of paragraph (3)) to each other shall be treated as 1 person.

(11) LIMITATION ON ACQUISITION OF DEPRECIABLE FARM PROPERTY.—

(A) IN GENERAL.—This subsection shall not apply to any issue if more than $250,000 of the net proceeds of such issue are to be used to provide depreciable farm property with respect to which the principal user is or will be the same person or 2 or more related persons.

(B) DEPRECIABLE FARM PROPERTY.—For purposes of this paragraph, the term "depreciable farm property" means property of a character subject to the allowance for depreciation which is to be used in a trade or business of farming.

(C) PRIOR ISSUES TAKEN INTO ACCOUNT.—In determining the amount of proceeds of an issue to be used as described in subparagraph (A), there shall be taken into account the aggregate amount of each prior issue to which paragraph (1) (or the corresponding provisions of prior law) applied which were or will be so used.

(12) TERMINATION DATES.—

(A) IN GENERAL.—This subsection shall not apply to—

(i) any bond (other than a bond described in clause (ii)) issued after December 31, 1986, or

(ii) any bond (or series of bonds) issued to refund a bond issued on or before such date unless—

(I) the average maturity date of the issue of which the refunding bond is a part is not later than the average maturity date of the bonds to be refunded by such issue,

(II) the amount of the refunding bond does not exceed the outstanding amount of the refunded bond, and

(III) the net proceeds of the refunding bond are used to redeem the refunded bond not later than 90 days after the date of the issuance of the refunding bond.

For purposes of clause (ii)(I), average maturity shall be determined in accordance with section 147(b)(2)(A).

(B) BONDS ISSUED TO FINANCE MANUFACTURING FACILITIES AND FARM PROPERTY.—Subparagraph (A) shall not apply to any bond issued as part of an issue 95 percent or more of the net proceeds of which are to be used to provide—

(i) any manufacturing facility, or

(ii) any land or property in accordance with section 147(c)(2).

(C) MANUFACTURING FACILITY.—For purposes of this paragraph—

(i) IN GENERAL.—The term "manufacturing facility" means any facility which is used in the manufacturing or production of tangible personal property (including the processing resulting in a change in the condition of such property). A rule similar to the rule of section 142(b)(2) shall apply for purposes of the preceding sentence.

(ii) CERTAIN FACILITIES INCLUDED.—Such term includes facilities which are directly related and ancillary to a manufacturing facility (determined without regard to this clause) if—

(I) such facilities are located on the same site as the manufacturing facility, and

(II) not more than 25 percent of the net proceeds of the issue are used to provide such facilities.

(iii) SPECIAL RULES FOR BONDS ISSUED IN 2009 AND 2010.—In the case of any issue made after the date of enactment of this clause and before January 1, 2011, clause (ii) shall not apply and the net proceeds from a bond shall be considered to be used to provide a manufacturing facility if such proceeds are used to provide—

(I) a facility which is used in the creation or production of intangible property which is described in section 197(d)(1)(C)(iii), or

(II) a facility which is functionally related and subordinate to a manufacturing facility (determined without regard to this subclause) if such facility is located on the same site as the manufacturing facility.

Amendments

• 2009, American Recovery and Reinvestment Tax Act of 2009 (P.L. 111-5)

P.L. 111-5, §1301(a)(1)-(2):

Amended Code Sec. 144(a)(12)(C) by striking "For purposes of this paragraph, the term" and inserting "For purposes of this paragraph—

(i) IN GENERAL.——The term", and

by striking the last sentence and inserting new clauses (ii)-(iii). **Effective** for obligations issued after 2-17-2009. Prior to being stricken, the last sentence of Code Sec. 144(a)(12)(C) read as follows:

For purposes of the 1st sentence of this subparagraph, the term "manufacturing facility" includes facilities which are directly related and ancillary to a manufacturing facility (determined without regard to this sentence) if—

(i) such facilities are located on the same site as the manufacturing facility, and

(ii) not more than 25 percent of the net proceeds of the issue are used to provide such facilities.

• 2006, Tax Increase Prevention and Reconciliation Act of 2005 (P.L. 109-222)

P.L. 109-222, §208(a):

Amended Code Sec. 144(a)(4)(G) by striking "September 30, 2009" and inserting "December 31, 2006". **Effective** 5-17-2006.

P.L. 109-222, §208(b):

Amended Code Sec. 144(a)(4)(F) by striking "September 30, 2009" and inserting "December 31, 2006". **Effective** 5-17-2006.

• 2004, American Jobs Creation Act of 2004 (P.L. 108-357)

P.L. 108-357, §340(a):

Amended Code Sec. 144(a)(4) by adding at the end a new subparagraph (G). **Effective** 10-22-2004.

P.L. 108-357, §340(b):

Amended Code Sec. 144(a)(4)(F) by adding at the end a new sentence. **Effective** 10-22-2004.

• 1993, Omnibus Budget Reconciliation Act of 1993 (P.L. 103-66)

P.L. 103-66, §13122(a):

Amended Code Sec. 144(a)(12)(B). **Effective** for bonds issued after 6-30-92. Prior to amendment, Code Sec. 144(a)(12)(B) read as follows:

(B) BONDS ISSUED TO FINANCE MANUFACTURING FACILITIES AND FARM PROPERTY.—In the case of any bond issued as part of an issue 95 percent or more of the net proceeds of which are to be used to provide—

(i) any manufacturing facility, or

(ii) any land or property in accordance with section 147(c)(2),

subparagraph (A) shall be applied by substituting "June 30, 1992" for "December 31, 1986".

• 1991, Tax Extension Act of 1991 (P.L. 102-227)

P.L. 102-227, §109(a):

Amended Code Sec. 144(a)(12)(B) by striking "December 31, 1991" and inserting "June 30, 1992". **Effective** for bonds issued after 12-31-91.

• 1990, Omnibus Budget Reconciliation Act of 1990 (P.L. 101-508)

P.L. 101-508, §11409(a):

Amended Code Sec. 144(a)(12)(B) by striking "September 30, 1990" and inserting "December 31, 1991". **Effective** for bonds issued after 9-30-90.

• 1989, Omnibus Budget Reconciliation Act of 1989 (P.L. 101-239)

P.L. 101-239, §7105:

Amended Code Sec. 144(a)(12)(B) by striking "substituting '1989' for '1986'" and inserting "substituting 'September 30, 1990' for 'December 31, 1986'". **Effective** 12-19-89.

• 1988, Technical and Miscellaneous Revenue Act of 1988 (P.L. 100-647)

P.L. 100-647, §1013(a)(4)(A):

Amended Code Sec. 144(a)(12)(A)(ii) by inserting "(or series of bonds)" before "issued to refund". **Effective** as if included in the provision of P.L. 99-514 to which it relates.

P.L. 100-647, §1013(a)(4)(B)(i):

Amended Code Sec. 144(a)(12)(A)(ii)(I). **Effective** as if included in the provision of P.L. 99-514 to which it relates. Prior to amendment, Code Sec. 144(a)(12)(A)(ii)(I) read as follows:

(I) the refunding bond has a maturity date not later than the maturity date of the refunded bond,

P.L. 100-647, §1013(a)(4)(B)(ii):

Amended Code Sec. 144(a)(12)(A) by adding at the end thereof a new sentence. **Effective** as if included in the provision of P.L. 99-514 to which it relates.

P.L. 100-647, §1013(a)(4)(C):

Amended Code Sec. 144(a)(12)(A)(ii) by adding "and" at the end of subclause (II), by striking out subclause (III) and by redesignating subclause (IV) as subclause (III). **Effective** as if included in the provision of P.L. 99-514 to which it relates. Prior to amendment, subclause (III) read as follows:

(III) the interest rate on the refunding bond is lower than the interest rate on the refunded bond, and

P.L. 100-647, §6176(a):

Amended Code Sec. 144(a)(12)(C) by adding at the end thereof a new sentence. For the **effective** date, see Act Sec. 6176(b), below.

P.L. 100-647, §6176(b), provides:

(b) EFFECTIVE DATE.—

(1) IN GENERAL.—The amendment made by subsection (a) shall apply to bonds issued after the date of the enactment of this Act.

(2) REFUNDINGS.—The amendment made by subsection (a) shall not apply to any bond issued to refund (or which is part of a series of bonds issued to refund) a bond issued on or before the date of the enactment of this Act if—

(A) the average maturity date of the issue of which the refunding bond is a part is not later than the average maturity date of the bonds to be refunded by such issue, and

(B) the amount of the refunding bond does not exceed the outstanding amount of the refunded bond.

For purposes of subparagraph (A), average maturity shall be determined in accordance with section 147(b) of the 1986 Code.

[Sec. 144(b)]

(b) QUALIFIED STUDENT LOAN BOND.—For purposes of this part—

(1) IN GENERAL.—The term "qualified student loan bond" means any bond issued as part of an issue the applicable percentage or more of the net proceeds of which are to be used directly or indirectly to make or finance student loans under—

(A) a program of general application to which the Higher Education Act of 1965 applies if—

(i) limitations are imposed under the program on—

(I) the maximum amount of loans outstanding to any student, and

(II) the maximum rate of interest payable on any loan,

(ii) the loans are directly or indirectly guaranteed by the Federal Government,

(iii) the financing of loans under the program is not limited by Federal law to the proceeds of tax-exempt bonds, and

(iv) special allowance payments under section 438 of the Higher Education Act of 1965—

(I) are authorized to be paid with respect to loans made under the program, or

(II) would be authorized to be made with respect to loans under the program if such loans were not financed with the proceeds of tax-exempt bonds, or

(B) a program of general application approved by the State if no loan under such program exceeds the difference between the total cost of attendance and other forms of student assistance (not including loans pursuant to section 428B(a)(1) of the Higher Education Act of 1965 (relating to parent loans) or subpart I or part C of title VII of the Public Health Service Act (relating to student assistance)) for which the student borrower may be eligible. A program shall not be treated as described in this subparagraph if such program is described in subparagraph (A).

A bond shall not be treated as a qualified student loan bond if the issue of which such bond is a part meets the private business tests of paragraphs (1) and (2) of section 141(b) (determined by treating 501(c)(3) organizations as governmental units with respect to their activities which do not constitute unrelated trades or businesses, determined by applying section 513(a)).

(2) APPLICABLE PERCENTAGE.—For purposes of paragraph (1), the term "applicable percentage" means—

(A) 90 percent in the case of the program described in paragraph (1)(A), and

(B) 95 percent in the case of the program described in paragraph (1)(B).

(3) STUDENT BORROWERS MUST BE RESIDENTS OF ISSUING STATE, ETC.—A student loan shall be treated as being made or financed under a program described in paragraph (1) with respect to an issue only if the student is—

(A) a resident of the State from which the volume cap under section 146 for such loan was derived, or

(B) enrolled at an educational institution located in such State.

(4) DISCRIMINATION ON BASIS OF SCHOOL LOCATION NOT PERMITTED.—A program shall not be treated as described in paragraph (1)(A) if such program discriminates on the basis of the location (in the United States) of the educational institution in which the student is enrolled.

Amendments

• 1988, Technical and Miscellaneous Revenue Act of 1988 (P.L. 100-647)

P.L. 100-647, §1013(a)(5)(A)-(C):

Amended Code Sec. 144(b)(1)(B) by striking out "to which part B of title IV of the Higher Education Act of 1965 (relating to guaranteed student loans) does not apply", by striking out "of such Act" and inserting in lieu thereof "of the Higher Education Act of 1965", and by striking out "eligible" and all that follows in such subparagraph and inserting in lieu thereof "eligible" and all that follows. **Effective** as if included in the provision of P.L. 99-514 to which it relates. Prior to amendment, Code Sec. 144(b)(1)(B) read as follows:

(B) a program of general application approved by the State to which part B of title IV of the Higher Education Act of 1965 (relating to guaranteed student loans) does not apply if no loan under such program exceeds the difference between the total cost of attendance and other forms of student assistance (not including loans pursuant to section 428B(a)(1) of such Act (relating to parent loans) or subpart I or part C of title VII of the Public Health Service Act (relating to student assistance)) for which the student borrower may be eligible. A bond issued as part of an issue shall be treated as a qualified student loan bond only if no bond which is part of such issue meets the private business tests of paragraphs (1) and (2) of section 141(b).

[Sec. 144(c)]

(c) QUALIFIED REDEVELOPMENT BOND.—For purposes of this part—

(1) IN GENERAL.—The term "qualified redevelopment bond" means any bond issued as part of an issue 95 percent or more of the net proceeds of which are to be used for 1 or more redevelopment purposes in any designated blighted area.

(2) ADDITIONAL REQUIREMENTS.—A bond shall not be treated as a qualified redevelopment bond unless—

(A) the issue described in paragraph (1) is issued pursuant to—

(i) a State law which authorizes the issuance of such bonds for redevelopment purposes in blighted areas, and

(ii) a redevelopment plan which is adopted before such issuance by the governing body described in paragraph (4)(A) with respect to the designated blighted area,

(B)(i) the payment of the principal and interest on such issue is primarily secured by taxes of general applicability imposed by a general purpose governmental unit, or

(ii) any increase in real property tax revenues (attributable to increases in assessed value) by reason of the carrying out of such purposes in such area is reserved exclusively for debt service on such issue (and similar issues) to the extent such increase does not exceed such debt service,

(C) each interest in real property located in such area—

(i) which is acquired by a governmental unit with the proceeds of the issue, and

(ii) which is transferred to a person other than a governmental unit,

is transferred for fair market value,

(D) the financed area with respect to such issue meets the no additional charge requirements of paragraph (5), and

(E) the use of the proceeds of the issue meets the requirements of paragraph (6).

(3) REDEVELOPMENT PURPOSES.—For purposes of paragraph (1)—

(A) IN GENERAL.—The term "redevelopment purposes" means, with respect to any designated blighted area—

(i) the acquisition (by a governmental unit having the power to exercise eminent domain) of real property located in such area,

(ii) the clearing and preparation for redevelopment of land in such area which was acquired by such governmental unit,

(iii) the rehabilitation of real property located in such area which was acquired by such governmental unit, and

(iv) the relocation of occupants of such real property.

(B) NEW CONSTRUCTION NOT PERMITTED.—The term "redevelopment purposes" does not include the construction (other than the rehabilitation) of any property or the enlargement of an existing building.

(4) DESIGNATED BLIGHTED AREA.—For purposes of this subsection—

(A) IN GENERAL.—The term "designated blighted area" means any blighted area designated by the governing body of a local general purpose governmental unit in the jurisdiction of which such area is located.

(B) BLIGHTED AREA.—The term "blighted area" means any area which the governing body described in subparagraph (A) determines to be a blighted area on the basis of the substantial presence of factors such as excessive vacant land on which structures were previously located, abandoned or vacant buildings, substandard structures, vacancies, and delinquencies in payment of real property taxes.

(C) DESIGNATED AREAS MAY NOT EXCEED 20 PERCENT OF TOTAL ASSESSED VALUE OF REAL PROPERTY IN GOVERNMENT'S JURISDICTION.—

(i) IN GENERAL.—An area may be designated by a governmental unit as a blighted area only if the designation percentage with respect to such area, when added to the designation percentages of all other designated blighted areas within the jurisdiction of such governmental unit, does not exceed 20 percent.

(ii) DESIGNATION PERCENTAGE.—For purposes of this subparagraph, the term "designation percentage" means, with respect to any area, the percentage (determined at the time such area is designated) which the assessed value of real property located in such area is of the total assessed value of all real property located within the jurisdiction of the governmental unit which designated such area.

(iii) EXCEPTION WHERE BONDS NOT OUTSTANDING.—The designation percentage of a previously designated blighted area shall not be taken into account under clause (i) if no qualified redevelopment bond (or similar bond) is or will be outstanding with respect to such area.

(D) MINIMUM DESIGNATED AREA.—

(i) IN GENERAL.—Except as provided in clause (ii), an area shall not be treated as a designated blighted area for purposes of this subsection unless such area is contiguous and compact and its area equals or exceeds 100 acres.

(ii) 10-ACRE MINIMUM IN CERTAIN CASES.—Clause (i) shall be applied by substituting "10 acres" for "100 acres" if not more than 25 percent of the financed area is to be provided (pursuant to the issue and all other such issues) to 1 person. For purposes of the preceding sentence, all related persons (as defined in subsection (a)(3)) shall be treated as 1 person. For purposes of this clause, an area provided to a developer on a short-term interim basis shall not be treated as provided to such developer.

(5) NO ADDITIONAL CHARGE REQUIREMENTS.—The financed area with respect to any issue meets the requirements of this paragraph if, while any bond which is part of such issue is outstanding—

(A) no owner or user of property located in the financed area is subject to a charge or fee which similarly situated owners or users of comparable property located outside such area are not subject, and

(B) the assessment method or rate of real property taxes with respect to property located in the financed area does not differ from the assessment method or rate of real property taxes with respect to comparable property located outside such area.

For purposes of the preceding sentence, the term "comparable property" means property which is of the same type as the property to which it is being compared and which is located within the jurisdiction of the designating governmental unit.

(6) USE OF PROCEEDS REQUIREMENTS.—The use of the proceeds of an issue meets the requirements of this paragraph if—

(A) not more than 25 percent of the net proceeds of such issue are to be used to provide (including the provision of land for) facilities described in subsection (a)(8) or section 147(e), and

(B) no portion of the proceeds of such issue is to be used to provide (including the provision of land for) any private or commercial golf course, country club, massage parlor, hot tub facility, suntan facility, racetrack or other facility used for gambling, or any store the principal business of which is the sale of alcoholic beverages for consumption off premises.

(7) FINANCED AREA.—For purposes of this subsection, the term "financed area" means, with respect to any issue, the portion of the designated blighted area with respect to which the proceeds of such issue are to be used.

(8) RESTRICTION ON ACQUISITION OF LAND NOT TO APPLY.—Section 147(c) (other than paragraphs (1)(B) and (2) thereof) shall not apply to any qualified redevelopment bond.

Amendments

• 1986, Tax Reform Act of 1986 (P.L. 99-514)

P.L. 99-514, §1301(b):

Amended Part IV of subchapter B of chapter 1 by adding Code Sec. 144. **Effective**, generally, for bonds issued after 8-15-86. However, for transitional rules, see Act Secs. 1312-1318 in the amendments for Code Sec. 103.

[Sec. 144—Repealed]

Amendments

• 1977, Tax Reduction and Simplification Act of 1977 (P.L. 95-30)

P.L. 95-30, §101(d)(1):

Repealed Code Sec. 144. **Effective** for tax years beginning after 12-31-76. Prior to repeal, Code Sec. 144 read as follows:

SEC. 144. ELECTION OF STANDARD DEDUCTION.

(a) METHOD OF ELECTION.—The standard deduction shall be allowed if the taxpayer so elects in his return, and the Secretary shall prescribe the manner of signifying such election in the return.

(b) CHANGE OF ELECTION.—Under regulations prescribed by the Secretary, a change of election with respect to the standard deduction for any taxable year may be made after the filing of the return for such year. If the spouse of the taxpayer filed a separate return for any taxable year corresponding, for purposes of section 142(a), to the taxable year of the taxpayer, the change shall not be allowed unless, in accordance with such regulations—

(1) the spouse makes a change of election with respect to the standard deduction for the taxable year covered in such separate return, consistent with the change of election sought by the taxpayer, and

(2) the taxpayer and his spouse consent in writing to the assessment, within such period as may be agreed on with the Secretary, of any deficiency, to the extent attributable to such change of election, even though at the time of the filing of such consent the assessment of such deficiency would otherwise be prevented by the operation of any law or rule of law.

This subsection shall not apply if the tax liability of the taxpayer's spouse, for the taxable year corresponding (for purposes of section 142(a)) to the taxable year of the taxpayer, has been compromised under section 7122.

(c) CHANGE OF ELECTION DEFINED.—For purposes of this title, the term "change of election with respect to the standard deduction" means—

(1) a change of an election to take (or not to take) the standard deduction; or

(2) a change of an election under section 141(d)(2).

Amendments

• 1976, Tax Reform Act of 1976 (P.L. 94-455)

P.L. 94-455, §501(b)(3):

Amended Code Sec. 144(a). **Effective** for tax years beginning after 12-31-75. Prior to amendment, Code Sec. 144(a) read as follows:

(a) METHOD AND EFFECT OF ELECTION.

(1) If the adjusted gross income shown on the return is $10,000 or more, the standard deduction shall be allowed if the taxpayer so elects in his return, and the Secretary or his delegate shall by regulations prescribe the manner of signifying such election in the return. If the adjusted gross income shown on the return is $10,000 or more, but the correct adjusted gross income is less than $10,000, then an election by the taxpayer under the preceding sentence to take the standard deduction shall be considered as his election to pay the tax imposed by section 3 (relating to tax based on tax table); and his failure to make under the preceding sentence an election to take the standard deduction shall be considered his election not to pay the tax imposed by section 3.

(2) If the adjusted gross income shown on the return is less than $10,000, the standard deduction shall be allowed only if the taxpayer elects, in the manner provided in section 4, to pay the tax imposed by section 3. If the adjusted gross income shown on the return is less than $10,000, but the correct adjusted gross income is $10,000 or more, then an election by the taxpayer to pay the tax imposed by section 3 shall be considered as his election to take the standard deduction; and his failure to elect to pay the tax imposed by section 3 shall be considered his election not to take the standard deduction.

(3) If the taxpayer on making his return fails to signify, in the manner provided by paragraph (1) or (2), his election to take the standard deduction or to pay the tax imposed by section 3, as the case may be, such failure shall be considered his election not to take the standard deduction.

(4) If the adjusted gross income shown on the return is less than $10,000, and if the taxpayer cannot elect to pay the tax imposed by section 3 by reason of section 4(d)(5), the standard deduction (after the application of section 141(e)) shall be allowed, notwithstanding paragraph (2), if the taxpayer so elects in his return.

P.L. 94-455, §501(b)(4):

Amended Code Sec. 144(c) by adding "or" after paragraph (1), striking out paragraph (2), and redesignating paragraph (3) as paragraph (2). **Effective** for tax years beginning after 12-31-75. Prior to repeal, paragraph (2) read as follows:

(2) a change of an election to pay (or not to pay) the tax under section 3; or.

P.L. 94-455, §501(b)(5):

Repealed Code Sec. 144(d). **Effective** tax years beginning after 12-31-75. Prior to repeal, Code Sec. 144(d) read as follows:

(d) INDIVIDUALS ELECTING INCOME AVERAGING.—In the case of a taxpayer who chooses to have the benefits of part I of subchapter Q (relating to income averaging) for the taxable year—

(1) subsection (a) shall not apply for such taxable year, and

(2) the standard deduction shall be allowed if the taxpayer so elects in his return for such taxable year.

The Secretary or his delegate shall by regulations prescribe the manner of signifying such election in the return. If the taxpayer on making his return fails to signify, in the manner so prescribed, his election to take the standard deduction, such failure shall be considered his election not to take the standard deduction.

P.L. 94-455, §1906(b)(13)(A):

Amended 1954 Code by substituting "Secretary" for "Secretary or his delegate" each place it appeared. **Effective** 2-1-77.

• 1971, Revenue Act of 1971 (P.L. 92-178)

P.L. 92-178, §206:

Amended Code Sec. 144(a) by substituting "$10,000" for "$5,000" in paragraphs (1) and (2). **Effective** for tax years beginning after 12-31-70.

P.L. 92-178, §301(c):

Added paragraph (4). **Effective** for tax years beginning after 12-31-71.

• 1964, Revenue Act of 1964 (P.L. 88-272)

P.L. 88-272, §112(c)(1):

Amended the first sentence of Sec. 144(b). **Effective** for tax years beginning after 12-31-63. Prior to amendment, the first sentence of Sec. 144(b) read as follows:

Under regulations prescribed by the Secretary or his delegate, a change of an election for any taxable year to take, or not to take, the standard deduction, or to pay, or not to pay, the tax under section 3, may be made after the filing of the return for such year.

P.L. 88-272, §112(c)(2):

Added Code Sec. 144(c). **Effective** for tax years beginning after 12-31-63.

P.L. 88-272, §232(c):

Added Code Sec. 144(d). **Effective** for tax years beginning after 12-31-63, except as provided in §234(g)(2), reproduced in comment following Code Sec. 1301.

[Sec. 145]

SEC. 145. QUALIFIED 501(c)(3) BOND.

[Sec. 145(a)]

(a) IN GENERAL.—For purposes of this part, except as otherwise provided in this section, the term "qualified 501(c)(3) bond" means any private activity bond issued as part of an issue if—

(1) all property which is to be provided by the net proceeds of the issue is to be owned by a 501(c)(3) organization or a governmental unit, and

(2) such bond would not be a private activity bond if—

(A) 501(c)(3) organizations were treated as governmental units with respect to their activities which do not constitute unrelated trades or businesses, determined by applying section 513(a), and

(B) paragraphs (1) and (2) of section 141(b) were applied by substituting "5 percent" for "10 percent" each place it appears and by substituting "net proceeds" for "proceeds" each place it appears.

[Sec. 145(b)]

(b) $150,000,000 LIMITATION ON BONDS OTHER THAN HOSPITAL BONDS.—

(1) IN GENERAL.—A bond (other than a qualified hospital bond) shall not be treated as a qualified 501(c)(3) bond if the aggregate authorized face amount of the issue (of which such bond is a part) allocated to any 501(c)(3) organization which is a test-period beneficiary (when increased by the outstanding tax-exempt nonhospital bonds of such organization) exceeds $150,000,000.

(2) OUTSTANDING TAX-EXEMPT NONHOSPITAL BONDS.—

(A) IN GENERAL.—For purposes of applying paragraph (1) with respect to any issue, the outstanding tax-exempt nonhospital bonds of any organization which is a test-period beneficiary with respect to such issue is the aggregate amount of tax-exempt bonds referred to in subparagraph (B)—

(i) which are allocated to such organization, and

(ii) which are outstanding at the time of such later issue (not including as outstanding any bond which is to be redeemed (other than in an advance refunding) from the net proceeds of the later issue).

(B) BONDS TAKEN INTO ACCOUNT.—For purposes of subparagraph (A), the bonds referred to in this subparagraph are—

(i) any qualified 501(c)(3) bond other than a qualified hospital bond, and

(ii) any bond to which section 141(a) does not apply if—

(I) such bond would have been an industrial development bond (as defined in section 103(b)(2), as in effect on the day before the date of the enactment of the Tax Reform Act of 1986) if 501(c)(3) organizations were not exempt persons, and

(II) such bond was not described in paragraph (4), (5), or (6) of such section 103(b) (as in effect on the date such bond was issued).

(C) ONLY NONHOSPITAL PORTION OF BONDS TAKEN INTO ACCOUNT.—

(i) IN GENERAL.—A bond shall be taken in account under subparagraph (B) only to the extent that the proceeds of the issue of which such bond is a part are not used with respect to a hospital.

(ii) SPECIAL RULE.—If 90 percent or more of the net proceeds of an issue are used with respect to a hospital, no bond which is part of such issue shall be taken into account under subparagraph (B)(ii).

(3) AGGREGATION RULE.—For purposes of this subsection, 2 or more organizations under common management or control shall be treated as 1 organization.

(4) ALLOCATION OF FACE AMOUNT OF ISSUE; TEST-PERIOD BENEFICIARY.—Rules similar to the rules of subparagraphs (C), (D) and (E) of section 144(a)(10) shall apply for purposes of this subsection.

(5) TERMINATION OF LIMITATION.—This subsection shall not apply with respect to bonds issued after the date of the enactment of this paragraph as part of an issue 95 percent or more of the net proceeds of which are to be used to finance capital expenditures incurred after such date.

Amendments

• 1997, Taxpayer Relief Act of 1997 (P.L. 105-34)

P.L. 105-34, §222:

Amended Code Sec. 145(b) by adding at the end a new paragraph (5). **Effective** 8-5-97.

• 1988, Technical and Miscellaneous Revenue Act of 1988 (P.L. 100-647)

P.L. 100-647, §1013(a)(6):

Amended Code Sec. 145(b)(2)(B)(ii)(I) by striking out "103(b)" and inserting in lieu thereof "103(b)(2)". **Effective** as if included in the provision of P.L. 99-514 to which it relates.

P.L. 100-647, §1013(a)(7):

Amended Code Sec. 145(b)(2)(C)(i) by striking out "subparagraph (B)(ii)" and inserting in lieu thereof "subparagraph (B)". **Effective** as if included in the provision of P.L. 99-514 to which it relates.

P.L. 100-647, §1013(a)(8):

Amended Code Sec. 145(b)(4) by striking out "subparagraphs (C) and (D)" and inserting in lieu thereof "subparagraphs (C), (D), and (E)". **Effective** as if included in the provision of P.L. 99-514 to which it relates.

[Sec. 145(c)]

(c) QUALIFIED HOSPITAL BOND.—For purposes of this section, the term "qualified hospital bond" means any bond issued as part of an issue 95 percent or more of the net proceeds of which are to be used with respect to a hospital.

[Sec. 145(d)]

(d) RESTRICTIONS ON BONDS USED TO PROVIDE RESIDENTIAL RENTAL HOUSING FOR FAMILY UNITS.—

(1) IN GENERAL.—Except as otherwise provided in this subsection, a bond which is part of an issue shall not be a qualified 501(c)(3) bond if any portion of the net proceeds of the issue are to be used directly or indirectly to provide residential rental property for family units.

(2) EXCEPTION FOR BONDS USED TO PROVIDE QUALIFIED RESIDENTIAL RENTAL PROJECTS.—Paragraph (1) shall not apply to any bond issued as part of an issue if the portion of such issue which is to be used as described in paragraph (1) is to be used to provide—

(A) a residential rental property for family units if the first use of such property is pursuant to such issue,

(B) qualified residential rental projects (as defined in section 142(d)), or

(C) property which is to be substantially rehabilitated in a rehabilitation beginning within the 2-year period ending 1 year after the date of the acquisition of such property.

(3) CERTAIN PROPERTY TREATED AS NEW PROPERTY.—Solely for purposes of determining under paragraph (2)(A) whether the 1st use of property is pursuant to tax-exempt financing—

(A) IN GENERAL.—If—

(i) the 1st use of property is pursuant to taxable financing,

(ii) there was a reasonable expectation (at the time such taxable financing was provided) that such financing would be replaced by tax-exempt financing, and

(iii) the taxable financing is in fact so replaced within a reasonable period after the taxable financing was provided,

then the 1st use of such property shall be treated as being pursuant to the tax-exempt financing.

(B) SPECIAL RULE WHERE NO OPERATING STATE OR LOCAL PROGRAM FOR TAX-EXEMPT FINANCING.—If, at the time of the 1st use of property, there was no operating State or local program for tax-exempt financing of the property, the 1st use of the property shall be treated as pursuant to the 1st tax-exempt financing of the property,

(C) DEFINITIONS.—For purposes of this paragraph—

(i) TAX-EXEMPT FINANCING.—The term "tax-exempt financing" means financing provided by tax-exempt bonds.

(ii) TAXABLE FINANCING.—The term "taxable financing" means financing which is not tax-exempt financing.

(4) SUBSTANTIAL REHABILITATION.—

(A) IN GENERAL.—Except as provided in subparagraph (B), rules similar to the rules of section 47(c)(1)(C) shall apply in determining for purposes of paragraph (2)(C) whether property is substantially rehabilitated.

(B) EXCEPTION.—For purposes of subparagraph (A), clause (ii) of section 47(c)(1)(C) shall not apply, but the Secretary may extend the 24-month period in section 47(c)(1)(C)(i) where appropriate due to circumstances not within the control of the owner.

Amendments

• 1990, Omnibus Budget Reconciliation Act of 1990 (P.L. 101-508)

P.L. 101-508, §11813(b)(7)(A)-(B):

Amended Code Sec. 145(d)(4) by striking "section 48(g)(1)(C)" each place it appears and inserting "section 47(c)(1)(C)", and by striking "section 48(g)(1)(C)(i)" and inserting "section 47(c)(1)(C)(i)". **Effective**, generally, for property placed in service after 12-31-90. For exceptions, see Act Sec. 11813(c)(2), below.

P.L. 101-508, §11813(c)(2), provides:

(2) EXCEPTIONS.—The amendments made by this section shall not apply to—

(A) any transition property (as defined in section 49(e) of the Internal Revenue Code of 1986 (as in effect on the day before the date of the enactment of this Act),

(B) any property with respect to which qualified progress expenditures were previously taken into account under section 46(d) of such Code (as so in effect), and

(C) any property described in section 46(b)(2)(C) of such Code (as so in effect).

• 1989, Omnibus Budget Reconciliation Act of 1989 (P.L. 101-239)

P.L. 101-239, §7815(f):

Amended Code Sec. 145(d) by redesignating paragraph (3) as paragraph (4) and by inserting after paragraph (2) a new paragraph (3). **Effective** as if included in the provision of P.L. 100-647 to which it relates.

• 1988, Technical and Miscellaneous Revenue Act of 1988 (P.L. 100-647)

P.L. 100-647, §5053(a):

Amended Code Sec. 145 by redesignating subsection (d) as subsection (e) and by inserting after subsection (c) a new subsection (d). For the **effective** date, see Act Sec. 5053(c), below.

P.L. 100-647, §5053(c), provides:

(c) EFFECTIVE DATE.—

(1) IN GENERAL.—The amendments made by this section shall apply to obligations issued after October 21, 1988.

(2) EXCEPTION FOR CONSTRUCTION OR BINDING AGREEMENT.—

(A) The amendments made by this section shall not apply to bonds (other than refunding bonds) with respect to a facility—

(i)(I) the original use of which begins with the taxpayer, and the construction, reconstruction, or rehabilitation of which began before July 14, 1988, and was completed on or after such date, or

(II) the original use of which begins with the taxpayer and with respect to which a binding contract to incur significant expenditures for construction, reconstruction, or rehabilitation was entered into before July 14, 1988, and some of such expenditures are incurred on or after such date, and

(ii) described in an inducement resolution or other comparable preliminary approval adopted by an issuing authority (or by a voter referendum) before July 14, 1988.

For purposes of the preceding sentence, the term "significant expenditures" means expenditures greater than 10 percent of the reasonably anticipated cost of the construction, reconstruction, or rehabilitation of the facility involved.

(B) Subparagraph (A) shall not apply to any bond issued after December 31, 1989, and shall not apply unless it is reasonably expected (at the time of issuance of the bond) that the facility will be placed in service before January 1, 1990.

(3) REFUNDINGS.—The amendments made by this section shall not apply to any bond issued to refund (or which is part of a series of bonds issued to refund) a bond issued before July 15, 1988, if—

(A) the average maturity date of the issue of which the refunding bond is a part is not later than the average maturity date of the bonds to be refunded by such issue,

(B) the amount of the refunding bond does not exceed the outstanding amount of the refunded bond, and

(C) the proceeds of the refunding bond are used to redeem the refunded bond not later than 90 days after the date of the issuance of the refunding bond.

For purposes of subparagraph (A), average maturity shall be determined in accordance with section 147(b) of the 1986 Code.

[Sec. 145(e)]

(e) ELECTION OUT.—This section shall not apply to an issue if—

(1) the issuer elects not to have this section apply to such issue, and

(2) such issue is an issue of exempt facility bonds, or qualified redevelopment bonds, to which section 146 applies.

Amendments

• 1988, Technical and Miscellaneous Revenue Act of 1988 (P.L. 100-647)

P.L. 100-647, §5053(a):

Amended Code Sec. 145 by redesignating subsection (d) as subsection (e). For the **effective** date, see Act Sec. 5053(c), below.

P.L. 100-647, §5053(c), provides:

(c) EFFECTIVE DATE.—

(1) IN GENERAL.—The amendments made by this section shall apply to obligations issued after October 21, 1988.

(2) EXCEPTION FOR CONSTRUCTION OR BINDING AGREEMENT.—

(A) The amendments made by this section shall not apply to bonds (other than refunding bonds) with respect to a facility—

(i)(I) the original use of which begins with the taxpayer, and the construction, reconstruction, or rehabilitation of which began before July 14, 1988, and was completed on or after such date, or

(II) the original use of which begins with the taxpayer and with respect to which a binding contract to incur significant expenditures for construction, reconstruction, or rehabilitation was entered into before July 14, 1988, and some of such expenditures are incurred on or after such date, and

(ii) described in an inducement resolution or other comparable preliminary approval adopted by an issuing authority (or by a voter referendum) before July 14, 1988.

For purposes of the preceding sentence, the term "significant expenditures" means expenditures greater than 10 percent of the reasonably anticipated cost of the construction, reconstruction, or rehabilitation of the facility involved.

(B) Subparagraph (A) shall not apply to any bond issued after December 31, 1989, and shall not apply unless it is reasonably expected (at the time of issuance of the bond) that the facility will be placed in service before January 1, 1990.

(3) REFUNDINGS.—The amendments made by this section shall not apply to any bond issued to refund (or which is part of a series of bonds issued to refund) a bond issued before July 15, 1988, if—

(A) the average maturity date of the issue of which the refunding bond is a part is not later than the average maturity date of the bonds to be refunded by such issue,

(B) the amount of the refunding bond does not exceed the outstanding amount of the refunded bond, and

(C) the proceeds of the refunding bond are used to redeem the refunded bond not later than 90 days after the date of the issuance of the refunding bond.

For purposes of subparagraph (A), average maturity shall be determined in accordance with section 147(b) of the 1986 Code.

• 1986, Tax Reform Act of 1986 (P.L. 99-514)

P.L. 99-514, §1301(b):

Amended Part IV of subchapter B of chapter 1 by adding Code Sec. 145. **Effective**, generally, for bonds issued after 8-15-86. However, for transitional rules, see Act Secs. 1312-1318 in the amendments for Code Sec. 103.

[Sec. 145—Repealed]

Amendments

• 1977, Tax Reduction and Simplification Act of 1977 (P.L. 95-30)

P.L. 95-30, §101(d)(1):

Repealed Code Sec. 145. **Effective** for tax years beginning after 12-31-76. Prior to repeal, Code Sec. 145 read as follows:

SEC. 145. CROSS REFERENCE.

For disallowance of certain credits against the tax in the case of individuals electing the standard deduction, see section 36.

[Sec. 146]

SEC. 146. VOLUME CAP.

[Sec. 146(a)]

(a) GENERAL RULE.—A private activity bond issued as part of an issue meets the requirements of this section if the aggregate face amount of the private activity bonds issued pursuant to such issue, when added to the aggregate face amount of tax-exempt private activity bonds previously issued by the issuing authority during the calendar year, does not exceed such authority's volume cap for such calendar year.

[Sec. 146(b)]

(b) VOLUME CAP FOR STATE AGENCIES.—For purposes of this section—

(1) IN GENERAL.—The volume cap for any agency of the State authorized to issue tax-exempt private activity bonds for any calendar year shall be 50 percent of the State ceiling for such calendar year.

(2) SPECIAL RULE WHERE STATE HAS MORE THAN 1 AGENCY.—If more than 1 agency of the State is authorized to issue tax-exempt private activity bonds, all such agencies shall be treated as a single agency.

[Sec. 146(c)]

(c) VOLUME CAP FOR OTHER ISSUERS.—For purposes of this section—

(1) IN GENERAL.—The volume cap for any issuing authority (other than a State agency) for any calendar year shall be an amount which bears the same ratio to 50 percent of the State ceiling for such calendar year as—

(A) the population of the jurisdiction of such issuing authority, bears to

(B) the population of the entire State.

(2) OVERLAPPING JURISDICTIONS.—For purposes of paragraph (1)(A), if an area is within the jurisdiction of 2 or more governmental units, such area shall be treated as only within the jurisdiction of the unit having jurisdiction over the smallest geographical area unless such unit agrees to surrender all or part of such jurisdiction for such calendar year to the unit with overlapping jurisdiction which has the next smallest geographical area.

[Sec. 146(d)]

(d) STATE CEILING.—For purposes of this section.—

(1) IN GENERAL.—The State ceiling applicable to any State for any calendar year shall be the greater of—

(A) an amount equal to $75 ($62.50 in the case of calendar year 2001) multiplied by the State population, or

(B) $225,000,000 ($187,500,000 in the case of calendar year 2001).

(2) COST-OF-LIVING ADJUSTMENT.—In the case of a calendar year after 2002, each of the dollar amounts contained in paragraph (1) shall be increased by an amount equal to—

(A) such dollar amount, multiplied by

(B) the cost-of-living adjustment determined under section 1(f)(3) for such calendar year by substituting "calendar year 2001" for "calendar year 1992" in subparagraph (B) thereof.

If any increase determined under the preceding sentence is not a multiple of $5 ($5,000 in the case of the dollar amount in paragraph (1)(B)), such increase shall be rounded to the nearest multiple thereof.

(3) SPECIAL RULE FOR STATES WITH CONSTITUTIONAL HOME RULE CITIES.—For purposes of this section—

(A) IN GENERAL.—The volume cap for any constitutional home rule city for any calendar year shall be determined under paragraph (1) of subsection (c) by substituting "100 percent" for "50 percent".

(B) COORDINATION WITH OTHER ALLOCATIONS.—In the case of any State which contains 1 or more constitutional home rule cities, for purposes of applying subsections (b) and (c) with respect to issuing authorities in such State other than constitutional home rule cities, the State ceiling for any calendar year shall be reduced by the aggregate volume caps determined for such year for all constitutional home rule cities in such State.

(C) CONSTITUTIONAL HOME RULE CITY.—For purposes of this section, the term "constitutional home rule city" means, with respect to any calendar year, any political subdivision of a State which, under a State constitution which was adopted in 1970 and effective on July 1, 1971, had home rule powers on the 1st day of the calendar year.

(4) SPECIAL RULE FOR POSSESSIONS WITH POPULATIONS OF LESS THAN THE POPULATION OF THE LEAST POPULOUS STATE.—

(A) IN GENERAL.—If the population of any possession of the United States for any calendar year is less than the population of the least populous State (other than a possession) for such calendar year, the limitation under paragraph (1)(A) shall not be less than the amount determined under subparagraph (B) for such calendar year.

(B) LIMITATION.—The limitation determined under this subparagraph, with respect to a possession, for any calendar year is an amount equal to the product of—

(i) the fraction—

(I) the numerator of which is the amount applicable under paragraph (1)(B) for such calendar year, and

(II) the denominator of which is the State population of the least populous State (other than a possession) for such calendar year, and

(ii) the population of such possession for such calendar year.

(5) INCREASE AND SET ASIDE FOR HOUSING BONDS FOR 2008.—

(A) INCREASE FOR 2008.—In the case of calendar year 2008, the State ceiling for each State shall be increased by an amount equal to $11,000,000,000 multiplied by a fraction—

(i) the numerator of which is the State ceiling applicable to the State for calendar year 2008, determined without regard to this paragraph, and

(ii) the denominator of which is the sum of the State ceilings determined under clause (i) for all States.

(B) SET ASIDE.—

(i) IN GENERAL.—Any amount of the State ceiling for any State which is attributable to an increase under this paragraph shall be allocated solely for one or more qualified housing issues.

(ii) QUALIFIED HOUSING ISSUE.—For purposes of this paragraph, the term "qualified housing issue" means—

(I) an issue described in section 142(a)(7) (relating to qualified residential rental projects), or

(II) a qualified mortgage issue (determined by substituting "12-month period" for "42-month period" each place it appears in section 143(a)(2)(D)(i)).

Amendments

• 2008, Housing Assistance Tax Act of 2008 (P.L. 110-289)

P.L. 110-289, §3021(a)(1):

Amended Code Sec. 146(d) by adding at the end a new paragraph (5). **Effective** for bonds issued after 7-30-2008.

• 2000, Community Renewal Tax Relief Act of 2000 (P.L. 106-554)

P.L. 106-554, §161(a):

Amended Code Sec. 146(d)(1) and (2). **Effective** for calendar years after 2000. Prior to amendment, Code Sec. 146(d)(1) and (2) read as follows:

(1) IN GENERAL.—The State ceiling applicable to any State for any calendar year shall be the greater of—

(A) an amount equal to the per capita limit for such year multiplied by the State population, or

(B) the aggregate limit for such year.

Subparagraph (B) shall not apply to any possession of the United States.

(2) PER CAPITA LIMIT; AGGREGATE LIMIT.—For purposes of paragraph (1), the per capita limit, and the aggregate limit, for any calendar year shall be determined in accordance with the following table:

Calendar Year	*Per Capita Limit*	*Aggregate Limit*
1999 through 2002 .	$50	$150,000,000
2003	55	165,000,000
2004	60	180,000,000
2005	65	195,000,000
2006	70	210,000,000
2007 and thereafter .	75	225,000,000

• 1998, Tax and Trade Relief Extension Act of 1998 (P.L. 105-277)

P.L. 105-277, §2021(a):

Amended Code Sec. 146(d) by striking paragraphs (1) and (2) and inserting new paragraphs (1) and (2). **Effective** for calendar years after 1998. Prior to being stricken, Code Sec. 146(d)(1) and (2) read as follows:

(1) IN GENERAL.—The State ceiling applicable to any State for any calendar year shall be the greater of—

(A) an amount equal to $75 multiplied by the State population, or

(B) $250,000,000.

Subparagraph (B) shall not apply to any possession of the United States.

(2) ADJUSTMENT AFTER 1987.—In the case of calendar years after 1987, paragraph (1) shall be applied by substituting—

(A) "$50" for "$75", and

(B) "$150,000,000" for "$250,000,000".

• 1988, Technical and Miscellaneous Revenue Act of 1988 (P.L. 100-647)

P.L. 100-647, §1013(a)(40):

Amended Code Sec. 146(d)(4)(B) by striking out "with respect a possession" and inserting in lieu thereof "with respect to a possession". **Effective** as if included in the provision of P.L. 99-514 to which it relates.

[Sec. 146(e)]

(e) STATE MAY PROVIDE FOR DIFFERENT ALLOCATION.—For purposes of this section—

(1) IN GENERAL.—Except as provided in paragraph (3), a State may, by law provide a different formula for allocating the State ceiling among the governmental units (or other authorities) in such State having authority to issue tax-exempt private activity bonds.

(2) INTERIM AUTHORITY FOR GOVERNOR.—

(A) IN GENERAL.—Except as otherwise provided in paragraph (3), the Governor of any State may proclaim a different formula for allocating the State ceiling among the governmental units (or other authorities) in such State having authority to issue private activity bonds.

(B) TERMINATION OF AUTHORITY.—The authority provided in subparagraph (A) shall not apply to bonds issued after the earlier of—

(i) the last day of the 1st calendar year after 1986 during which the legislature of the State met in regular session, or

(ii) the effective date of any State legislation with respect to the allocation of the State ceiling.

(3) STATE MAY NOT ALTER ALLOCATION TO CONSTITUTIONAL HOME RULE CITIES.—Except as otherwise provided in a State constitutional amendment (or law changing the home rule provision adopted in the manner provided by the State constitution), the authority provided in this subsection shall not apply to that portion of the State ceiling which is allocated to any constitutional home rule city in the State unless such city agrees to such different allocation.

[Sec. 146(f)]

(f) ELECTIVE CARRYFORWARD OF UNUSED LIMITATION FOR SPECIFIED PURPOSE.—

(1) IN GENERAL.—If—

(A) an issuing authority's volume cap for any calendar year after 1985, exceeds

(B) the aggregate amount of tax-exempt private activity bonds issued during such calendar year by such authority,

such authority may elect to treat all (or any portion) of such excess as a carryforward for 1 or more carryforward purposes.

(2) ELECTION MUST IDENTIFY PURPOSE.—In any election under paragraph (1), the issuing authority shall—

(A) identify the purpose for which the carryforward is elected, and

(B) specify the portion of the excess described in paragraph (1) which is to be a carryforward for each such purpose.

(3) USE OF CARRYFORWARD.—

(A) IN GENERAL.—If any issuing authority elects a carryforward under paragraph (1) with respect to any carryforward purpose, any private activity bonds issued by such authority with respect to such purpose during the 3 calendar years following the calendar year in which the carryforward arose shall not be taken into account under subsection (a) to the extent the amount of such bonds does not exceed the amount of the carryforward elected for such purpose.

(B) ORDER IN WHICH CARRYFORWARD USED.—Carryforwards elected with respect to any purpose shall be used in the order of the calendar years in which they arose.

(4) ELECTION.—Any election under this paragraph (and any identification or specification contained therein), once made, shall be irrevocable.

(5) CARRYFORWARD PURPOSE.—The term "carryforward purpose" means—

(A) the purpose of issuing exempt facility bonds described in 1 of the paragraphs of section 142(a).

(B) the purpose of issuing qualified mortgage bonds or mortgage credit certificates,

(C) the purpose of issuing qualified student loan bonds, and

(D) the purpose of issuing qualified redevelopment bonds.

(6) SPECIAL RULES FOR INCREASED VOLUME CAP UNDER SUBSECTION (d)(5).—No amount which is attributable to the increase under subsection (d)(5) may be used—

(A) for any issue other than a qualified housing issue (as defined in subsection (d)(5)), or

(B) to issue any bond after calendar year 2010.

Amendments

• 2008, Housing Assistance Tax Act of 2008 (P.L. 110-289)

P.L. 110-289, §3021(a)(2):

Amended Code Sec. 146(f) by adding at the end a new paragraph (6). **Effective** for bonds issued after 7-30-2008.

• 1988, Technical and Miscellaneous Revenue Act of 1988 (P.L. 100-647)

P.L. 100-647, §1013(a)(9):

Amended Code Sec. 146(f)(5)(A). **Effective** as if included in the provision of P.L. 99-514 to which it relates. Prior to amendment, Code Sec. 146(f)(5)(A) read as follows:

(A) the purpose of the issuing exempt facility bonds described in 1 of the paragraphs of section 142(a),

• 1987, Revenue Act of 1987 (P.L. 100-203)

P.L. 100-203, §10631(b):

Amended Code Sec. 146(f)(5)(A). For the **effective** date, see Act Sec. 10631(c), below. Prior to amendment, Code Sec. 146(f)(5)(A) read as follows:

(A) the purpose of issuing bonds referred to in one of the clauses of section 141(d)(1)(A),

P.L. 100-203, §10631(c), provides:

(c) EFFECTIVE DATE.—

(1) IN GENERAL.—Except as otherwise provided in this subsection, the amendments made by this section shall apply to bonds issued after October 13, 1987 (other than bonds issued to refund bonds issued on or before such date).

(2) BINDING AGREEMENTS.—The amendments made by this section shall not apply to bonds (other than advance refunding bonds) with respect to a facility acquired after October 13, 1987, pursuant to a binding contract entered into on or before such date.

(3) TRANSITIONAL RULE.—The amendments made by this section shall not apply to bonds issued—

(A) after October 13, 1987, by an authority created by a statute—

(i) approved by the State Governor on July 24, 1986, and

(ii) sections 1 through 10 of which became effective on January 15, 1987, and

(B) to provide facilities serving the area specified in such statute on the date of its enactment.

[Sec. 146(g)]

(g) EXCEPTION FOR CERTAIN BONDS.—Only for purposes of this section, the term "private activity bond" shall not include—

(1) any qualified veterans' mortgage bond,

(2) any qualified 501(c)(3) bond,

→ Caution: Code Sec. 146(g)(3), below, is subject to the sunset provision of the Economic Growth and Tax Relief Reconciliation Act of 2001 (P.L. 107-16), §901. Absent Congressional action, the changes made to this provision by P.L. 107-16, or that take effect as if included in P.L. 107-16, do not apply after December 31, 2010. For more information about the sunset provision, see page XXI of the Preface to this publication and P.L. 107-16, §901, in the amendment notes. See the amendments notes for a history of amendments to this section and the effective date of each change.

(3) any exempt facility bond issued as part of an issue described in paragraph (1), (2), (12), (13), (14), or (15) of section 142(a), and

(4) 75 percent of any exempt facility bond issued as part of an issue described in paragraph (11) of section 142(a) (relating to high-speed intercity rail facilities).

Paragraph (4) shall be applied without regard to "75 percent of" if all of the property to be financed by the net proceeds of the issue is to be owned by a governmental unit (within the meaning of section 142(b)(1)).

Amendments

• 2005, Safe, Accountable, Flexible, Efficient Transportation Equity Act: A Legacy for Users (P.L. 109-59)

P.L. 109-59, §11143(c):

Amended Code Sec. 146(g)(3) by striking "or 14" and all that follows through the end of the paragraph and inserting "(14), or (15) or section 142(a), and". **Effective** for bonds issued after 8-10-2005. Prior to amendment, Code Sec. 146(g)(3) read as follows:

(3) any exempt facility bond issued as part of an issue described in paragraph (1), (2), (12), (13), or (14) of section 142(a) (relating to airports, docks and wharves, environmental enhancements of hydroelectric generating facilities, qualified public educational facilities, and qualified green building and sustainable design projects), and

• 2004, American Jobs Creation Act of 2004 (P.L. 108-357)

P.L. 108-357, §701(c)(1)-(2):

Amended Code Sec. 146(g)(3) by striking "or (13)" and inserting "(13), or (14)", and by striking "and qualified public educational facilities" and inserting "qualified public educational facilities, and qualified green building and sustainable design projects". **Effective** for bonds issued after 12-31-2004.

• 2001, Economic Growth and Tax Relief Reconciliation Act of 2001 (P.L. 107-16)

P.L. 107-16, §422(c)(1)-(2):

Amended Code Sec. 146(g)(3) by striking "or (12)" and inserting "(12), or (13)", and by striking "and environmental enhancements of hydroelectric generating facilities" and inserting "environmental enhancements of hydroelectric generating facilities, and qualified public educational facilities". **Effective** for bonds issued after 12-31-2001.

P.L. 107-16, §901(a)-(b), provides:

SEC. 901. SUNSET OF PROVISIONS OF ACT.

(a) IN GENERAL.—All provisions of, and amendments made by, this Act shall not apply—

(1) to taxable, plan, or limitation years beginning after December 31, 2010, or

(2) in the case of title V, to estates of decedents dying, gifts made, or generation skipping transfers, after December 31, 2010.

(b) APPLICATION OF CERTAIN LAWS.—The Internal Revenue Code of 1986 and the Employee Retirement Income Security Act of 1974 shall be applied and administered to years, estates, gifts, and transfers described in subsection (a) as if the provisions and amendments described in subsection (a) had never been enacted.

• 1993, Omnibus Budget Reconciliation Act of 1993 (P.L. 103-66)

P.L. 103-66, §13121(a):

Amended Code Sec. 146(g)(4) by adding at the end thereof a new flush sentence. **Effective** for bonds issued after 12-31-93.

• 1992, Energy Policy Act of 1992 (P.L. 102-486)

P.L. 102-486, §1921(b)(3)(A)-(B):

Amended Code Sec. 146(g)(3) by striking "or (2)" and inserting ", (2), or (12)", and by striking "and docks and wharves" and inserting ", docks and wharves, and environmental enhancements of hydroelectric generating facilities". **Effective** for bonds issued after 10-24-92.

• 1989, Omnibus Budget Reconciliation Act of 1989 (P.L. 101-239)

P.L. 101-239, §7816(s)(2):

Amended Code Sec. 146(g) by redesignating paragraph (3), as added by P.L. 100-647, §6180, as paragraph (4). **Effective** as if included in the provision of P.L. 100-647 to which it relates.

• 1988, Technical and Miscellaneous Revenue Act of 1988 (P.L. 100-647)

P.L. 100-647, §6180(b)(3)(A)-(C):

Amended Code Sec. 146(g) by striking out "and" at the end of paragraph (2); by striking out the period at the end of paragraph (3) and inserting in lieu thereof ", and" and by adding at the end thereof new paragraph (3)[(4)]. **Effective** for bonds issued after 11-10-88.

[Sec. 146(h)]

(h) EXCEPTION FOR GOVERNMENT-OWNED SOLID WASTE DISPOSAL FACILITIES.—

(1) IN GENERAL.—Only for purposes of this section, the term "private activity bond" shall not include any exempt facility bond described in section 142(a)(6) which is issued as part of an issue if all of the property to be financed by the net proceeds of such issue is to be owned by a governmental unit.

(2) SAFE HARBOR FOR DETERMINATION OF GOVERNMENT OWNERSHIP.—In determining ownership for purposes of paragraph (1), section 142(b)(1)(B) shall apply, except that a lease term shall be treated as satisfying clause (ii) thereof if it is not more than 20 years.

[Sec. 146(i)]

(i) TREATMENT OF REFUNDING ISSUES.—For purposes of the volume cap imposed by this section—

(1) IN GENERAL.—The term "private activity bond" shall not include any bond which is issued to refund another bond to the extent that the amount of such bond does not exceed the outstanding amount of the refunded bond.

(2) SPECIAL RULES FOR STUDENT LOAN BONDS.—In the case of any qualified student loan bond, paragraph (1) shall apply only if the maturity date of the refunding bond is not later than the later of—

(A) the average maturity date of the qualified student loan bonds to be refunded by the issue of which the refunding bond is a part, or

(B) the date 17 years after the date on which the refunded bond was issued (or in the case of a series of refundings, the date on which the original bond was issued).

(3) SPECIAL RULES FOR QUALIFIED MORTGAGE BONDS.—In the case of any qualified mortgage bond, paragraph (1) shall apply only if the maturity date of the refunding bond is not later than the later of—

(A) the average maturity date of the qualified mortgage bonds to be refunded by the issue of which the refunding bond is a part, or

(B) the date 32 years after the date on which the refunded bond was issued (or in the case of a series of refundings, the date on which the original bond was issued).

(4) AVERAGE MATURITY.—For purposes of paragraphs (2) and (3), average maturity shall be determined in accordance with section 147(b)(2)(A).

(5) EXCEPTION FOR ADVANCE REFUNDING.—This subsection shall not apply to any bond issued to advance refund another bond.

(6) TREATMENT OF CERTAIN RESIDENTIAL RENTAL PROJECT BONDS AS REFUNDING BONDS IRRESPECTIVE OF OBLIGOR.—

(A) IN GENERAL.—If, during the 6-month period beginning on the date of a repayment of a loan financed by an issue 95 percent or more of the net proceeds of which are used to provide projects described in section 142(d), such repayment is used to provide a new loan for any project so described, any bond which is issued to refinance such issue shall be treated as a refunding issue to the extent the principal amount of such refunding issue does not exceed the principal amount of the bonds refunded.

(B) LIMITATIONS.—Subparagraph (A) shall apply to only one refunding of the original issue and only if—

(i) the refunding issue is issued not later than 4 years after the date on which the original issue was issued,

(ii) the latest maturity date of any bond of the refunding issue is not later than 34 years after the date on which the refunded bond was issued, and

(iii) the refunding issue is approved in accordance with section 147(f) before the issuance of the refunding issue.

Amendments

• 2008, Housing Assistance Tax Act of 2008 (P.L. 110-289)

P.L. 110-289, §3007(a):

Amended Code Sec. 146(i) by adding at the end a new paragraph (6). **Effective** for repayments of loans received after 7-30-2008.

• 1988, Technical and Miscellaneous Revenue Act of 1988 (P.L. 100-647)

P.L. 100-647, §1013(a)(28)(A):

Amended Code Sec. 146(i)(2)(A). **Effective** as if included in the provision of P.L. 99-514 to which it relates. Prior to amendment, Code Sec. 146(i)(2)(A) read as follows:

(A) the maturity date of the bond to be refunded, or

P.L. 100-647, §1013(a)(28)(B):

Amended Code Sec. 146(i)(3)(A). **Effective** as if included in the provision of P.L. 99-514 to which it relates. Prior to amendment, Code Sec. 146(i)(3)(A) read as follows:

(A) the maturity date of the bond to be refunded, or

P.L. 100-647, §1013(a)(28)(C):

Amended Code Sec. 146(i) by redesignating paragraph (4) as paragraph (5) and by inserting after paragraph (3) a new paragraph (4). **Effective** as if included in the provision of P.L. 99-514 to which it relates.

[Sec. 146(j)]

(j) POPULATION.—For purposes of this section, determinations of the population of any State (or issuing authority) shall be made with respect to any calendar year on the basis of the most recent census estimate of the resident population of such State (or issuing authority) released by the Bureau of Census before the beginning of such calendar year.

[Sec. 146(k)]

(k) FACILITY MUST BE LOCATED WITHIN STATE.—

(1) IN GENERAL.—Except as provided in paragraphs (2) and (3), no portion of the State ceiling applicable to any State for any calendar year may be used with respect to financing for a facility located outside such State.

(2) EXCEPTION FOR CERTAIN FACILITIES WHERE STATE WILL GET PROPORTIONATE SHARE OF BENEFITS.—Paragraph (1) shall not apply to any exempt facility bond described in paragraph (4), (5), (6), or (10) of section 142(a) if the issuer establishes that the State's share of the use of the facility (or its output) will equal or exceed the State's share of the private activity bonds issued to finance the facility.

(3) TREATMENT OF GOVERNMENTAL BONDS TO WHICH VOLUME CAP ALLOCATED.—Paragraph (1) shall not apply to any bond to which volume cap is allocated under section 141(b)(5)—

(A) for an output facility, or

(B) for a facility of a type described in paragraph (4), (5), (6), or (10) of section 142(a),

if the issuer establishes that the State's share of the private business use (as defined by section 141(b)(6)) of the facility will equal or exceed the State's share of the volume cap allocated with respect to bonds issued to finance the facility.

Amendments

• 1988, Technical and Miscellaneous Revenue Act of 1988 (P.L. 100-647)

P.L. 100-647, §1013(a)(10)(A):

Amended Code Sec. 146(k)(1) by striking out "paragraph (2)" and inserting in lieu thereof "paragraphs (2) and (3)". **Effective** as if included in the provision of P.L. 99-514 to which it relates.

P.L. 100-647, §1013(a)(10)(B):

Amended Code Sec. 146(k) by adding at the end thereof new paragraph (3). **Effective** as if included in the provision of P.L. 99-514 to which it relates.

[Sec. 146(l)]

(l) ISSUER OF QUALIFIED SCHOLARSHIP FUNDING BONDS.—In the case of a qualified scholarship funding bond, such bond shall be treated for purposes of this section as issued by a State or local issuing authority (whichever is appropriate).

[Sec. 146(m)]

(m) TREATMENT OF AMOUNTS ALLOCATED TO PRIVATE ACTIVITY PORTION OF GOVERNMENT USE BONDS.—

(1) IN GENERAL.—The volume cap of an issuer shall be reduced by the amount allocated by the issuer to an issue under section 141(b)(5).

(2) ADVANCE REFUNDINGS.—Except as otherwise provided by the Secretary, any advance refunding of any part of an issue to which an amount was allocated under section 141(b)(5) (or would have been allocated if such section applied to such issue) shall be taken into account under this section to the extent of the amount of the volume cap which was (or would have been) so allocated.

[Sec. 146(n)]

(n) REDUCTION FOR MORTGAGE CREDIT CERTIFICATES, ETC.—The volume cap of any issuing authority for any calendar year shall be reduced by the sum of—

(1) the amounts of qualified mortgage bonds which such authority elects not to issue under section 25(c)(2)(A)(ii) during such year, plus

(2) the amount of any reduction in such ceiling under section 25(f) applicable to such authority for such year.

Amendments

• 1986, Tax Reform Act of 1986 (P.L. 99-514)

P.L. 99-514, §1301(b):

Amended Part IV of subchapter B of chapter 1 by adding Code Sec. 146. **Effective**, generally, for bonds issued after 8-15-86. For transitional rules, see Act Sec. 1312-1318 in the amendments for Code Sec. 103.

[Sec. 147]

SEC. 147. OTHER REQUIREMENTS APPLICABLE TO CERTAIN PRIVATE ACTIVITY BONDS.

[Sec. 147(a)]

(a) SUBSTANTIAL USER REQUIREMENT.—

(1) IN GENERAL.—Except as provided in subsection (h), a private activity bond shall not be a qualified bond for any period during which it is held by a person who is a substantial user of the facilities or by a related person of such a substantial user.

(2) RELATED PERSON.—For purposes of paragraph (1), the following shall be treated as related persons—

(A) 2 or more persons if the relationship between such persons would result in a disallowance of losses under section 267 or 707(b),

(B) 2 or more persons which are members of the same controlled group of corporations (as defined in section 1563(a), except that "more than 50 percent" shall be substituted for "at least 80 percent" each place it appears therein),

(C) a partnership and each of its partners (and their spouses and minor children), and

(D) an S corporation and each of its shareholders (and their spouses and minor children).

[Sec. 147(b)]

(b) MATURITY MAY NOT EXCEED 120 PERCENT OF ECONOMIC LIFE.—

(1) GENERAL RULE.—Except as provided in subsection (h), a private activity bond shall not be a qualified bond if it is issued as part of an issue and—

(A) the average maturity of the bonds issued as part of such issue, exceeds

(B) 120 percent of the average reasonably expected economic life of the facilities being financed with the net proceeds of such issue.

(2) DETERMINATION OF AVERAGES.—For purposes of paragraph (1)—

(A) the average maturity of any issue shall be determined by taking into account the respective issue prices of the bonds issued as part of such issue, and

(B) the average reasonably expected economic life of the facilities being financed with any issue shall be determined by taking into account the respective cost of such facilities.

(3) SPECIAL RULES.—

(A) DETERMINATION OF ECONOMIC LIFE.—For purposes of this subsection, the reasonably expected economic life of any facility shall be determined as of the later of—

(i) the date on which the bonds are issued, or

(ii) the date on which the facility is placed in service (or expected to be placed in service).

(B) TREATMENT OF LAND.—

(i) LAND NOT TAKEN INTO ACCOUNT.—Except as provided in clause (ii), land shall not be taken into account under paragraph (1)(B).

(ii) ISSUES WHERE 25 PERCENT OR MORE OF PROCEEDS USED TO FINANCE LAND.—If 25 percent or more of the net proceeds of any issue is to be used to finance land, such land shall be taken into account under paragraph (1)(B) and shall be treated as having an economic life of 30 years.

(4) SPECIAL RULE FOR POOLED FINANCING OF 501(c)(3) ORGANIZATION.—

(A) IN GENERAL.—At the election of the issuer, a qualified 501(c)(3) bond shall be treated as meeting the requirements of paragraph (1) if such bond meets the requirements of subparagraph (B).

(B) REQUIREMENTS.—A qualified 501(c)(3) bond meets the requirements of this subparagraph if—

(i) 95 percent or more of the net proceeds of the issue of which such bond is a part are to be used to make or finance loans to 2 or more 501(c)(3) organizations or governmental units for acquisition of property to be used by such organizations,

(ii) each loan described in clause (i) satisfies the requirements of paragraph (1) (determined by treating each loan as a separate issue),

(iii) before such bond is issued, a demand survey was conducted which shows a demand for financing greater than an amount equal to 120 percent of the lendable proceeds of such issue, and

(iv) 95 percent or more of the net proceeds of such issue are to be loaned to 501(c)(3) organizations or governmental units within 1 year of issuance and, to the extent there are any unspent proceeds after such 1-year period, bonds issued as part of such issue are to be redeemed as soon as possible thereafter (and in no event later than 18 months after issuance).

A bond shall not meet the requirements of this subparagraph if the maturity date of any bond issued as part of such issue is more than 30 years after the date on which the bond was issued (or, in the case of a refunding or series of refundings, the date on which the original bond was issued).

(5) SPECIAL RULE FOR CERTAIN FHA INSURED LOANS.—Paragraph (1) shall not apply to any bond issued as part of an issue 95 percent or more of the net proceeds of which are to be used to finance mortgage loans insured under FHA 242 or under a similar Federal Housing Administration program (as in effect on the date of the enactment of the Tax Reform Act of 1986) where the loan term approved by such Administration plus the maximum maturity of debentures which could be issued by such Administration in satisfaction of its obligations exceeds the term permitted under paragraph (1).

[Sec. 147(c)]

(c) LIMITATION ON USE FOR LAND ACQUISITION.—

(1) IN GENERAL.—Except as provided in subsection (h), a private activity bond shall not be a qualified bond if—

(A) it is issued as part of an issue and 25 percent or more of the net proceeds of such issue are to be used (directly or indirectly) for the acquisition of land (or an interest therein), or

(B) any portion of the proceeds of such issue is to used (directly or indirectly) for the acquisition of land (or an interest therein) to be used for farming purposes.

(2) EXCEPTION FOR FIRST-TIME FARMERS.—

(A) IN GENERAL.—If the requirements of subparagraph (B) are met with respect to any land, paragraph (1) shall not apply to such land, and subsection (d) shall not apply to property to be used thereon for farming purposes, but only to the extent of expenditures (financed with the proceeds of the issue) not in excess of $450,000.

(B) ACQUISITION BY FIRST-TIME FARMERS.—The requirements of this subparagraph are met with respect to any land if—

(i) such land is to be used for farming purposes, and

(ii) such land is to be acquired by an individual who is a first-time farmer, who will be the principal user of such land, and who will materially and substantially participate on the farm of which such land is a part in the operation of such farm.

(C) FIRST-TIME FARMER.—For purposes of this paragraph—

(i) IN GENERAL.—The term "first-time farmer" means any individual if such individual—

(I) has not at any time had any direct or indirect ownership interest in substantial farmland in the operation of which such individual materially participated, and

(II) has not received financing under this paragraph in an amount which, when added to the financing to be provided under this paragraph, exceeds the amount in effect under subparagraph (A).

(ii) AGGREGATION RULES.—Any ownership or material participation, or financing received, by an individual's spouse or minor child shall be treated as ownership and material participation, or financing received, by the individual.

(iii) INSOLVENT FARMER.—For purposes of clause (i), farmland which was previously owned by the individual and was disposed of while such individual was insolvent shall be disregarded if section 108 applied to indebtedness with respect to such farmland.

(D) FARM.—For purposes of this paragraph, the term "farm" has the meaning given such term by section 6420(c)(2).

(E) SUBSTANTIAL FARMLAND.—For purposes of this paragraph, the term "substantial farmland" means any parcel of land unless such parcel is smaller than 30 percent of the median size of a farm in the county in which such parcel is located.

(F) USED EQUIPMENT LIMITATION.—For purposes of this paragraph, in no event may the amount of financing provided by reason of this paragraph to a first-time farmer for personal property—

(i) of a character subject to the allowance for depreciation,

(ii) the original use of which does not begin with such farmer, and

(iii) which is to be used for farming purposes,

exceed $62,500. A rule similar to the rule of subparagraph (C)(ii) shall apply for purposes of the preceding sentence.

(G) ACQUISITION FROM RELATED PERSON.—For purposes of this paragraph and section 144(a), the acquisition by a first-time farmer of land or personal property from a related person (within the meaning of section 144(a)(3)) shall not be treated as an acquisition from a related person, if—

(i) the acquisition price is for the fair market value of such land or property, and

(ii) subsequent to such acquisition, the related person does not have a financial interest in the farming operation with respect to which the bond proceeds are to be used.

(H) ADJUSTMENTS FOR INFLATION.—In the case of any calendar year after 2008, the dollar amount in subparagraph (A) shall be increased by an amount equal to—

(i) such dollar amount, multiplied by

(ii) the cost-of-living adjustment determined under section 1(f)(3) for the calendar year, determined by substituting "calendar year 2007" for "calendar year 1992" in subparagraph (B) thereof.

If any amount as increased under the preceding sentence is not a multiple of $100, such amount shall be rounded to the nearest multiple of $100.

(3) EXCEPTION FOR CERTAIN LAND ACQUIRED FOR ENVIRONMENTAL PURPOSES, ETC.—Any land acquired by a governmental unit (or issuing authority) in connection with an airport, mass commuting facility, high-speed intercity rail facility, dock, or wharf shall not be taken into account under paragraph (1) if—

(A) such land is acquired for noise abatement or wetland preservation, or for future use as an airport, mass commuting facility, high-speed intercity rail facility, dock, or wharf, and

(B) there is not other significant use of such land.

Amendments

• 2008, Heartland, Habitat, Harvest, and Horticulture Act of 2008 (P.L. 110-246)

P.L. 110-246, §15341(a):

Amended Code Sec. 147(c)(2)(A) by striking "$250,000" and inserting "$450,000". **Effective** for bonds issued after 5-22-2008.

P.L. 110-246, §15341(b):

Amended Code Sec. 147(c)(2) by adding at the end a new subparagraph (H). **Effective** for bonds issued after 5-22-2008.

P.L. 110-246, §15341(c):

Amended Code Sec. 147(c)(2)(E) by striking "unless" and all that follows through the period and inserting "unless such parcel is smaller than 30 percent of the median size of a farm in the county in which such parcel is located". **Effective** for bonds issued after 5-22-2008. Prior to amendment, Code Sec. 147(c)(2)(E) read as follows:

(E) SUBSTANTIAL FARMLAND.—For purposes of this paragraph, the term "substantial farmland" means any parcel of land unless—

(i) such parcel is smaller than 30 percent of the median size of a farm in the county in which such parcel is located, and

(ii) the fair market value of the land does not at any time while held by the individual exceed $125,000.

P.L. 110-246, §15341(d):

Amended Code Sec. 147(c)(2)(C)(i)(II) by striking "$250,000" and inserting "the amount in effect under subparagraph (A)". **Effective** for bonds issued after 5-22-2008.

• 1996, Small Business Job Protection Act of 1996 (P.L. 104-188)

P.L. 104-188, §1117(a):

Amended Code Sec. 147(c)(2) by adding at the end a new subparagraph (G). **Effective** for bonds issued after 8-20-96. For a special rule, see Act Sec. 1804, below.

P.L. 104-188, §1117(b):

Amended Code Sec. 147(c)(2)(E)(i) by striking "15 percent" and inserting "30 percent". **Effective** for bonds issued after 8-20-96. For a special rule, see Act Sec. 1804, below.

P.L. 104-188, §1804, provides:

SEC. 1804. TAX-EXEMPT BONDS FOR SALE OF ALASKA POWER ADMINISTRATION FACILITY.

Sections 142(f)(3) (as added by section 1608) and 147(d) of the Internal Revenue Code of 1986 shall not apply in determining whether any private activity bond issued after the date of the enactment of this Act and used to finance the acquisition of the Snettisham hydroelectric project from the Alaska Power Administration is a qualified bond for purposes of such Code.

• 1989, Omnibus Budget Reconciliation Act of 1989 (P.L. 101-239)

P.L. 101-239, §7816(s)(3):

Amended Code Sec. 147(c)(3) by inserting a comma after "mass commuting facility" each place it appears. **Effective** as if included in the provision of P.L. 100-647 to which it relates.

• 1988, Technical and Miscellaneous Revenue Act of 1988 (P.L. 100-647)

P.L. 100-647, §6180(b)(4):

Amended Code Sec. 147(c)(3) by inserting "high-speed intercity rail facility" after "mass commuting facility" each place it appears. **Effective** for bonds issued after 11-10-88.

[Sec. 147(d)]

(d) ACQUISITION OF EXISTING PROPERTY NOT PERMITTED.—

(1) IN GENERAL.—Except as provided in subsection (h), a private activity bond shall not be a qualified bond if issued as part of an issue and any portion of the net proceeds of such issue is to be used for the acquisition of any property (or an interest therein) unless the 1st use of such property is pursuant to such acquisition.

(2) EXCEPTION FOR CERTAIN REHABILITATIONS.—Paragraph (1) shall not apply with respect to any building (and the equipment therefor) if—

(A) the rehabilitation expenditures with respect to such building, equal or exceed

(B) 15 percent of the portion of the cost of acquiring such building (and equipment) financed with the net proceeds of the issue.

A rule similar to the rule of the preceding sentence shall apply in the case of structures other than a building except that subparagraph (B) shall be applied by substituting "100 percent" for "15 percent".

(3) REHABILITATION EXPENDITURES.—For purposes of this subsection—

(A) IN GENERAL.—Except as provided in this paragraph, the term "rehabilitation expenditures" means any amount properly chargeable to capital account which is incurred by the person acquiring the building for property (or additions or improvements to property) in connection with the rehabilitation of a building. In the case of an integrated operation contained in a building before its acquisition, such term includes rehabilitating existing equipment in such building or replacing it with equipment having substantially the same function. For purposes of this subparagraph, any amount incurred by a successor to the person acquiring the building or by the seller under a sales contract with such person shall be treated as incurred by such person.

(B) CERTAIN EXPENDITURES NOT INCLUDED.—The term "rehabilitation expenditures" does not include any expenditure described in section 47(c)(2)(B).

(C) PERIOD DURING WHICH EXPENDITURES MUST BE INCURRED.—The term "rehabilitation expenditures" shall not include any amount which is incurred after the date 2 years after the later of—

(i) the date on which the building was acquired, or

(ii) the date on which the bond was issued.

(4) SPECIAL RULE FOR CERTAIN PROJECTS.—In the case of a project involving 2 or more buildings, this subsection shall be applied on a project basis.

Amendments

• 1990, Omnibus Budget Reconciliation Act of 1990 (P.L. 101-508)

P.L. 101-508, §11813(b)(8):

Amended Code Sec. 147(d)(3)(B) by striking "section 48(g)(2)(B)" and inserting "section 47(c)(2)(B)". **Effective**, generally, for property placed in service after 12-31-90. However, for exceptions, see Act Sec. 11813(c)(2), below.

P.L. 101-508, §11813(c)(2), provides:

(2) EXCEPTIONS.—The amendments made by this section shall not apply to—

(A) any transition property (as defined in section 49(e) of the Internal Revenue Code of 1986 (as in effect on the day before the date of the enactment of this Act),

(B) any property with respect to which qualified progress expenditures were previously taken into account under section 46(d) of such Code (as so in effect), and

(C) any property described in section 46(b)(2)(C) of such Code (as so in effect).

[Sec. 147(e)]

(e) NO PORTION OF BONDS MAY BE ISSUED FOR SKYBOXES, AIRPLANES, GAMBLING ESTABLISHMENTS, ETC.—A private activity bond shall not be a qualified bond if issued as part of an issue and any portion of the proceeds of such issue is to be used to provide any airplane, skybox or other private luxury box, health club facility, facility primarily used for gambling, or store the principal business of which is the sale of alcoholic beverages for consumption off premises.

Amendments

• 1988, Technical and Miscellaneous Revenue Act of 1988 (P.L. 100-647)

P.L. 100-647, §1013(a)(11):

Amended Code Sec. 147(e) by striking out "treated as" before the words "a qualified bond". **Effective** as if included in the provision of P.L. 99-514 to which it relates.

[Sec. 147(f)]

(f) PUBLIC APPROVAL REQUIRED FOR PRIVATE ACTIVITY BONDS.—

(1) IN GENERAL.—A private activity bond shall not be a qualified bond unless such bond satisfies the requirements of paragraph (2).

(2) PUBLIC APPROVAL REQUIREMENT.—

(A) IN GENERAL.—A bond shall satisfy the requirements of this paragraph if such bond is issued as a part of an issue which has been approved by—

(i) the governmental unit—

(I) which issued such bond, or

(II) on behalf of which such bond was issued, and

(ii) each governmental unit having jurisdiction over the area in which any facility, with respect to which financing is to be provided from the net proceeds of such issue, is located (except that if more than 1 governmental unit within a State has jurisdiction over the entire area within such State in which such facility is located, only 1 such unit need approve such issue).

(B) APPROVAL BY A GOVERNMENTAL UNIT.—For purposes of subparagraph (A), an issue shall be treated as having been approved by any governmental unit if such issue is approved—

(i) by the applicable elected representative of such governmental unit after a public hearing following reasonable public notice, or

(ii) by voter referendum of such governmental unit.

(C) SPECIAL RULES FOR APPROVAL OF FACILITY.—If there has been public approval under subparagraph (A) of the plan for financing a facility, such approval shall constitute approval under subparagraph (A) for any issue—

(i) which is issued pursuant to such plan within 3 years after the date of the 1st issue pursuant to the approval, and

(ii) all or substantially all of the proceeds of which are to be used to finance such facility or to refund previous financing under such plan.

(D) REFUNDING BONDS.—No approval under subparagraph (A) shall be necessary with respect to any bond which is issued to refund (other than to advance refund) a bond approved under subparagraph (A) (or treated as approved under subparagraph (C)) unless the average maturity date of the issue of which the refunding bond is a part is later than the average maturity date of the bonds to be refunded by such issue. For purposes of the preceding sentence, average maturity shall be determined in accordance with subsection (b)(2)(A).

(E) APPLICABLE ELECTED REPRESENTATIVE.—For purposes of this paragraph—

(i) IN GENERAL.—The term "applicable elected representative" means with respect to any governmental unit—

(I) an elected legislative body of such unit, or

(II) the chief elected executive officer, the chief elected State legal officer of the executive branch, or any other elected official of such unit designated for purposes of this paragraph by such chief elected executive officer or by State law.

If the office of any elected official described in subclause (II) is vacated and an individual is appointed by the chief elected executive officer of the governmental unit and confirmed by the elected legislative body of such unit (if any) to serve the remaining term of the elected official, the individual so appointed shall be treated as the elected official for such remaining term.

(ii) NO APPLICABLE ELECTED REPRESENTATIVE.—If (but for this clause) a governmental unit has no applicable elected representative, the applicable elected representative for purposes of clause (i) shall be the applicable elected representative of the governmental unit—

(I) which is the next higher governmental unit with such a representative, and

(II) from which the authority of the governmental unit with no such representative is derived.

(3) SPECIAL RULE FOR APPROVAL OF AIRPORTS OR HIGH-SPEED INTERCITY RAIL FACILITIES.—If—

(A) the proceeds of an issue are to be used to finance a facility or facilities located at an airport or high-speed intercity rail facilities, and

(B) the governmental unit issuing such bonds is the owner or operator of such airport or high-speed intercity rail facilities,

such governmental unit shall be deemed to be the only governmental unit having jurisdiction over such airport or high-speed intercity rail facilities for purposes of this subsection.

(4) SPECIAL RULES FOR SCHOLARSHIP FUNDING BOND ISSUES AND VOLUNTEER FIRE DEPARTMENT BOND ISSUES.—

(A) SCHOLARSHIP FUNDING BONDS.—In the case of a qualified scholarship funding bond, any governmental unit which made a request described in section 150(d)(2)(B) with respect to the issuer of such bond shall be treated for purposes of paragraph (2) of this subsection as the governmental unit on behalf of which such bond was issued. Where more than one governmental unit within a State has made a request described in section 150(d)(2)(B), the State may also be treated for purposes of paragraph (2) of this subsection as the governmental unit on behalf of which such bond was issued.

(B) VOLUNTEER FIRE DEPARTMENT BONDS.—In the case of a bond of a volunteer fire department which meets the requirements of section 150(e), the political subdivision described in section 150(e)(2)(B) with respect to such department shall be treated for purposes of paragraph (2) of this subsection as the governmental unit on behalf of which such bond was issued.

Amendments

• 1988, Technical and Miscellaneous Revenue Act of 1988 (P.L. 100-647)

P.L. 100-647, §1013(a)(12):

Amended Code Sec. 147(f) by adding at the end thereof new paragraph (4). **Effective** as if included in the provision of P.L. 99-514 to which it relates.

P.L. 100-647, §1013(a)(29):

Amended Code Sec. 147(f)(2)(D) by striking out "the maturity date" and all that follows and inserting in lieu thereof "the average maturity date of the issue of which the refunded bond is a part is later than the average maturity date of the bonds to be refunded by such issue. For purposes of the preceding sentence, average maturity shall be determined in accordance with subsection (b)(2)(A)". **Effective** as if included in the provision of P.L. 99-514 to which it relates. Prior to amendment, Code Sec. 147(f)(2)(D) read as follows:

(D) REFUNDING BONDS.—No approval under subparagraph (A) shall be necessary with respect to any bond which is issued to refund (other than to advance refund) a bond approved under subparagraph (A) (or treated as approved under subparagraph (C)) unless the maturity date of such bond is later than the maturity date of the bond to be refunded.

P.L. 100-647, §1013(a)(36):

Amended Code Sec. 147(f)(2)(E)(i) by adding at the end thereof a new sentence. **Effective** as if included in the provision of P.L. 99-514 to which it relates.

P.L. 100-647, §1013(b)(1), provides:

Sections 147(f) and 149(e) of the 1986 Code applies to bonds issued after December 31, 1986.

P.L. 100-647, §6180(b)(5)(A)-(B):

Amended Code Sec. 147(f)(3) by inserting "or high-speed intercity rail facilities" after "airport" each place it appears and by inserting "OR HIGH-SPEED INTERCITY RAIL FACILITIES" after "AIRPORTS" in the heading. **Effective** for bonds issued after the date of enactment of this Act.

[Sec. 147(g)]

(g) RESTRICTION ON ISSUANCE COSTS FINANCED BY ISSUE.—

(1) IN GENERAL.—A private activity bond shall not be a qualified bond if the issuance costs financed by the issue (of which such bond is a part) exceed 2 percent of the proceeds of the issue.

(2) SPECIAL RULE FOR SMALL MORTGAGE REVENUE BOND ISSUES.—In the case of an issue of qualified mortgage bonds or qualified veterans' mortgage bonds, paragraph (1) shall be applied

by substituting "3.5 percent" for "2 percent" if the proceeds of the issue do not exceed $20,000,000.

Amendments

• 1988, Technical and Miscellaneous Revenue Act of 1988 (P.L. 100-647)

P.L. 100-647, §1013(a)(13)(A):

Amended Code Sec. 147(g)(1) by striking out "aggregate face amount of the issue" and inserting in lieu thereof "proceeds of the issue". **Effective** for bonds issued after 6-30-87.

P.L. 100-647, §1013(a)(13)(B):

Amended Code Sec. 147(g)(2) by striking out "aggregate authorized face amount of the issue does not" and inserting in lieu thereof "proceeds of the issue do not". **Effective** for bonds issued after 6-30-87.

»»→ Caution: The heading for Code Sec. 147(h), below, is subject to the sunset provision of the Economic Growth and Tax Relief Reconciliation Act of 2001 (P.L. 107-16), §901. Absent Congressional action, the changes made to this provision by P.L. 107-16, or that take effect as if included in P.L. 107-16, do not apply after December 31, 2010. For more information about the sunset provision, see page XXI of the Preface to this publication and P.L. 107-16, §901, in the amendment notes. See the amendments notes for a history of amendments to this section and the effective date of each change.

[Sec. 147(h)]

(h) CERTAIN RULES NOT TO APPLY TO CERTAIN BONDS.—

(1) MORTGAGE REVENUE BONDS AND QUALIFIED STUDENT LOAN BONDS.—Subsections (a), (b), (c), and (d) shall not apply to any qualified mortgage bond, qualified veterans' mortgage bond, or qualified student loan bond.

(2) QUALIFIED 501(c)(3) BONDS.—Subsections (a), (c), and (d) shall not apply to any qualified 501(c)(3) bond and subsection (e) shall be applied as if it did not contain "health club facility" with respect to such a bond.

»»→ Caution: Code Sec. 147(h)(3), below, is subject to the sunset provision of the Economic Growth and Tax Relief Reconciliation Act of 2001 (P.L. 107-16), §901. Absent Congressional action, the changes made to this provision by P.L. 107-16, or that take effect as if included in P.L. 107-16, do not apply after December 31, 2010. For more information about the sunset provision, see page XXI of the Preface to this publication and P.L. 107-16, §901, in the amendment notes. See the amendments notes for a history of amendments to this section and the effective date of each change.

(3) EXEMPT FACILITY BONDS FOR QUALIFIED PUBLIC-PRIVATE SCHOOLS.—Subsection (c) shall not apply to any exempt facility bond issued as part of an issue described in section 142(a)(13) (relating to qualified public educational facilities).

Amendments

• 2001, Economic Growth and Tax Relief Reconciliation Act of 2001 (P.L. 107-16)

P.L. 107-16, §422(d):

Amended Code Sec. 147(h) by adding at the end a new paragraph (3). **Effective** for bonds issued after 12-31-2001.

P.L. 107-16, §422(e):

Amended the heading for Code Sec. 147(h) by striking "MORTGAGE REVENUE BONDS, QUALIFIED STUDENT LOAN BONDS, AND QUALIFIED 501(c)(3) BONDS" and inserting "CERTAIN BONDS". **Effective** for bonds issued after 12-31-2001.

P.L. 107-16, §901(a)-(b), provides:

SEC. 901. SUNSET OF PROVISIONS OF ACT.

(a) IN GENERAL.—All provisions of, and amendments made by, this Act shall not apply—

(1) to taxable, plan, or limitation years beginning after December 31, 2010, or

(2) in the case of title V, to estates of decedents dying, gifts made, or generation skipping transfers, after December 31, 2010.

(b) APPLICATION OF CERTAIN LAWS.—The Internal Revenue Code of 1986 and the Employee Retirement Income Security Act of 1974 shall be applied and administered to years, estates, gifts, and transfers described in subsection (a) as if the provisions and amendments described in subsection (a) had never been enacted.

• 1986, Tax Reform Act of 1986 (P.L. 99-514)

P.L. 99-514, §1301(b):

Amended part IV of subchapter B of chapter 1 by adding Code Sec. 147. **Effective**, generally, for bonds issued after 8-15-86. However, for transitional rules, see Act Secs. 1312-1318 in the amendments for Code Sec. 103.

Subpart B—Requirements Applicable to All State and Local Bonds

[Sec. 148]

SEC. 148. ARBITRAGE.

[Sec. 148(a)]

(a) ARBITRAGE BOND DEFINED.—For purposes of section 103, the term "arbitrage bond" means any bond issued as part of an issue any portion of the proceeds of which are reasonably expected (at the time of issuance of the bond) to be used directly or indirectly—

(1) to acquire higher yielding investments, or

(2) to replace funds which were used directly or indirectly to acquire higher yielding investments.

For purposes of this subsection, a bond shall be treated as an arbitrage bond if the issuer intentionally uses any portion of the proceeds of the issue of which such bond is a part in a manner described in paragraph (1) or (2).

[Sec. 148(b)]

(b) HIGHER YIELDING INVESTMENTS.—For purposes of this section—

(1) IN GENERAL.—The term "higher yielding investments" means any investment property which produces a yield over the term of the issue which is materially higher than the yield on the issue.

(2) INVESTMENT PROPERTY.—The term "investment property" means—

(A) any security (within the meaning of section 165(g)(2)(A) or (B)),

(B) any obligation,

(C) any annuity contract,

(D) any investment-type property, or

(E) in the case of a bond other than a private activity bond, any residential rental property for family units which is not located within the jurisdiction of the issuer and which is not acquired to implement a court ordered or approved housing desegregation plan.

(3) ALTERNATIVE MINIMUM TAX BONDS TREATED AS INVESTMENT PROPERTY IN CERTAIN CASES.—

(A) IN GENERAL.—Except as provided in subparagraph (B), the term "investment property" does not include any tax-exempt bond.

(B) EXCEPTION.—With respect to an issue other than an issue a part of which is a specified private activity bond (as defined in section 57(a)(5)(C)), the term "investment property" includes a specified private activity bond (as so defined).

(4) SAFE HARBOR FOR PREPAID NATURAL GAS.—

(A) IN GENERAL.—The term "investment-type property" does not include a prepayment under a qualified natural gas supply contract.

(B) QUALIFIED NATURAL GAS SUPPLY CONTRACT.—For purposes of this paragraph, the term "qualified natural gas supply contract" means any contract to acquire natural gas for resale by a utility owned by a governmental unit if the amount of gas permitted to be acquired under the contract by the utility during any year does not exceed the sum of—

(i) the annual average amount during the testing period of natural gas purchased (other than for resale) by customers of such utility who are located within the service area of such utility, and

(ii) the amount of natural gas to be used to transport the prepaid natural gas to the utility during such year.

(C) NATURAL GAS USED TO GENERATE ELECTRICITY.—Natural gas used to generate electricity shall be taken into account in determining the average under subparagraph (B)(i)—

(i) only if the electricity is generated by a utility owned by a governmental unit, and

(ii) only to the extent that the electricity is sold (other than for resale) to customers of such utility who are located within the service area of such utility.

(D) ADJUSTMENTS FOR CHANGES IN CUSTOMER BASE.—

(i) NEW BUSINESS CUSTOMERS.—If—

(I) after the close of the testing period and before the date of issuance of the issue, the utility owned by a governmental unit enters into a contract to supply natural gas (other than for resale) for a business use at a property within the service area of such utility, and

(II) the utility did not supply natural gas to such property during the testing period or the ratable amount of natural gas to be supplied under the contract is significantly greater than the ratable amount of gas supplied to such property during the testing period,

then a contract shall not fail to be treated as a qualified natural gas supply contract by reason of supplying the additional natural gas under the contract referred to in subclause (I).

(ii) LOST CUSTOMERS.—The average under subparagraph (B)(i) shall not exceed the annual amount of natural gas reasonably expected to be purchased (other than for resale) by persons who are located within the service area of such utility and who, as of the date of issuance of the issue, are customers of such utility.

(E) RULING REQUESTS.—The Secretary may increase the average under subparagraph (B)(i) for any period if the utility owned by the governmental unit establishes to the satisfaction of the Secretary that, based on objective evidence of growth in natural gas consumption or population, such average would otherwise be insufficient for such period.

(F) ADJUSTMENT FOR NATURAL GAS OTHERWISE ON HAND.—

(i) IN GENERAL.—The amount otherwise permitted to be acquired under the contract for any period shall be reduced by—

(I) the applicable share of natural gas held by the utility on the date of issuance of the issue, and

(II) the natural gas (not taken into account under subclause (I)) which the utility has a right to acquire during such period (determined as of the date of issuance of the issue).

(ii) APPLICABLE SHARE.—For purposes of the clause (i), the term "applicable share" means, with respect to any period, the natural gas allocable to such period if the gas were allocated ratably over the period to which the prepayment relates.

(G) INTENTIONAL ACTS.—Subparagraph (A) shall cease to apply to any issue if the utility owned by the governmental unit engages in any intentional act to render the volume of natural gas acquired by such prepayment to be in excess of the sum of—

(i) the amount of natural gas needed (other than for resale) by customers of such utility who are located within the service area of such utility, and

(ii) the amount of natural gas used to transport such natural gas to the utility.

(H) TESTING PERIOD.—For purposes of this paragraph, the term "testing period" means, with respect to an issue, the most recent 5 calendar years ending before the date of issuance of the issue.

(I) SERVICE AREA.—For purposes of this paragraph, the service area of a utility owned by a governmental unit shall be comprised of—

(i) any area throughout which such utility provided at all times during the testing period—

(I) in the case of a natural gas utility, natural gas transmission or distribution services, and

(II) in the case of an electric utility, electricity distribution services,

(ii) any area within a county contiguous to the area described in clause (i) in which retail customers of such utility are located if such area is not also served by another utility providing natural gas or electricity services, as the case may be, and

(iii) any area recognized as the service area of such utility under State or Federal law.

Amendments

• 2005, Energy Tax Incentives Act of 2005 (P.L. 109-58)

P.L. 109-58, §1327(a):

Amended Code Sec. 148(b) by adding at the end a new paragraph (4). **Effective** for obligations issued after 8-8-2005.

• 1988, Technical and Miscellaneous Revenue Act of 1988 (P.L. 100-647)

P.L. 100-647, §1013(a)(43)(A):

Amended Code Sec. 148(b) by adding at the end thereof a new paragraph (3). **Effective** for obligations issued after 3-31-88.

P.L. 100-647, §1013(a)(43)(B):

Amended Code Sec. 148(b)(2) by striking out the last sentence. **Effective** for obligations issued after 3-31-88. Prior to amendment, the last sentence of Code Sec. 148(b)(2) read as follows:

Such term shall not include any tax-exempt bond.

P.L. 100-647, §5053(b):

Amended Code Sec. 148(b)(2) by striking out "or" at the end of subparagraph (C), by striking out the period at the end of subparagraph (D) and inserting in lieu thereof ", or" and by adding at the end thereof a new subparagraph (E). **Effective**, generally, for obligations issued after 10-21-88. However, for an exception, see Act Sec. 5053(c)(2)-(3), below.

P.L. 100-647, §5053(c)(2)-(3), provides:

(c)(2) EXCEPTION FOR CONSTRUCTION OR BINDING AGREEMENT.—

(A) The amendments made by this section shall not apply to bonds (other than refunding bonds) with respect to a facility—

(i)(I) the original use of which begins with the taxpayer, and the construction, reconstruction, or rehabilitation of which began before July 14, 1988, and was completed on or after such date, or

(II) the original use of which begins with the taxpayer and with respect to which a binding contract to incur significant expenditures for construction, reconstruction, or rehabilitation was entered into before July 14, 1988, and some of such expenditures are incurred on or after such date, and

(ii) described in an inducement resolution or other comparable preliminary approval adopted by an issuing authority (or by a voter referendum) before July 14, 1988. For purposes of the preceding sentence, the term "significant expenditures" means expenditures greater than 10 percent of the reasonably anticipated cost of the construction, reconstruction, or rehabilitation of the facility involved.

(B) Subparagraph (A) shall not apply to any bond issued after December 31, 1989, and shall not apply unless it is reasonably expected (at the time of issuance of the bond) that the facility will be placed in service before January 1, 1990.

(3) REFUNDING.—The amendments made by this section shall not apply to any bond issued to refund (or which is part of a series of bonds issued to refund) a bond issued before July 15, 1988, if—

(A) the average maturity date of the issue of which the refunding bond is a part is not later than the average maturity date of the bonds to be refunded by such issue,

(B) the amount of the refunding bond does not exceed the outstanding amount of the refunded bond, and

(C) the proceeds of the refunding bond are used to redeem the refunded bond not later than 90 days after the date of the issuance of the refunding bond. For purposes of subparagraph (A), average maturity shall be determined in accordance with section 147(b) of the 1986 Code.

[Sec. 148(c)]

(c) TEMPORARY PERIOD EXCEPTION.—

(1) IN GENERAL.—For purposes of subsection (a), a bond shall not be treated as an arbitrage bond solely by reason of the fact that the proceeds of the issue of which such bond is a part may be invested in higher yielding investments for a reasonable temporary period until such proceeds are needed for the purpose for which such issue was issued.

(2) LIMITATION ON TEMPORARY PERIOD FOR POOLED FINANCINGS.—

(A) IN GENERAL.—The temporary period referred to in paragraph (1) shall not exceed 6 months with respect to the proceeds of an issue which are to be used to make or finance loans (other than nonpurpose investments) to 2 or more persons.

(B) SHORTER TEMPORARY PERIOD FOR LOAN REPAYMENTS, ETC.—Subparagraph (A) shall be applied by substituting "3 months" for "6 months" with respect to the proceeds from the sale or repayment of any loan which are to be used to make or finance any loan. For purposes of the preceding sentence, a nonpurpose investment shall not be treated as a loan.

(C) BONDS USED TO PROVIDE CONSTRUCTION FINANCING.—In the case of an issue described in subparagraph (A) any portion of which is used to make or finance loans for construction expenditures (within the meaning of subsection (f)(4)(C)(iv)—

(i) rules similar to the rules of subsection (f)(4)(C)(v) shall apply, and

(ii) subparagraph (A) shall be applied with respect to such portion by substituting "2 years" for "6 months".

(D) EXCEPTION FOR MORTGAGE REVENUE BONDS.—This paragraph shall not apply to any qualified mortgage bond or qualified veterans' mortgage bond.

Amendments

• 1997, Taxpayer Relief Act of 1997 (P.L. 105-34)

P.L. 105-34, §1444(a):

Amended Code Sec. 148(c)(2) by striking subparagraph (B) and by redesignating subparagraphs (C), (D), and (E) as subparagraphs (B), (C), and (D), respectively. **Effective** for bonds issued after 8-5-97. Prior to being stricken, Code Sec. 148(c)(2)(B) read as follows:

(B) SPECIAL RULE FOR CERTAIN STUDENT LOAN POOLS.—In the case of the proceeds of an issue to be used to make or finance loans under a program described in section 144(b)(1)(A), subparagraph (A) shall be applied by substituting "18 months" for "6 months". The preceding sentence shall not apply to any bond issued after December 31, 1988.

• 1990, Omnibus Budget Reconciliation Act of 1990 (P.L. 101-508)

P.L. 101-508, §11701(j)(5)(A)-(B):

Amended Code Sec. 148(c)(2)(D) by striking "subsection (f)(4)(B)(iv)(IV)" and inserting "subsection (f)(4)(C)(iv)", and by striking "subsection (f)(4)(B)(iv)(VIII)" and inserting "subsection (f)(4)(C)(v)". **Effective** as if included in the provision of P.L. 101-239 to which it relates.

• 1989, Omnibus Budget Reconciliation Act of 1989 (P.L. 101-239)

P.L. 101-239, §7652(c):

Amended Code Sec. 148(c)(2) by redesignating subparagraph (D) as subparagraph (E) and by inserting after subparagraph (C) a new subparagraph (D). **Effective** for bonds issued after 12-19-89.

[Sec. 148(d)]

(d) SPECIAL RULES FOR REASONABLY REQUIRED RESERVE OR REPLACEMENT FUND.—

(1) IN GENERAL.—For purposes of subsection (a), a bond shall not be treated as an arbitrage bond solely by reason of the fact that an amount of the proceeds of the issue of which such bond is a part may be invested in higher yielding investments which are part of a reasonably required reserve or replacement fund. The amount referred to in the preceding sentence shall not exceed 10 percent of the proceeds of such issue unless the issuer establishes to the satisfaction of the Secretary that a higher amount is necessary.

(2) LIMITATION ON AMOUNT IN RESERVE OR REPLACEMENT FUND WHICH MAY BE FINANCED BY ISSUE.—A bond issued as part of an issue shall be treated as an arbitrage bond if the amount of the proceeds from the sale of such issue which is part of any reserve or replacement fund exceeds 10 percent of the proceeds of the issue (or such higher amount which the issuer establishes is necessary to the satisfaction of the Secretary).

Amendments

• 1997, Taxpayer Relief Act of 1997 (P.L. 105-34)

P.L. 105-34, §1443:

Amended Code Sec. 148(d) by striking paragraph (3). **Effective** for bonds issued after 8-5-97. Prior to being stricken, Code Sec. 148(d)(3) read as follows:

(3) LIMITATION ON INVESTMENT IN NONPURPOSE INVESTMENTS.—

(A) IN GENERAL.—A bond which is part of an issue which does not meet the requirements of subparagraph (B) shall be treated as an arbitrage bond.

(B) REQUIREMENTS.—An issue meets the requirements of this subparagraph only if—

(i) at no time during any bond year may the amount invested in nonpurpose investments with a yield materially higher than the yield on the issue exceed 150 percent of the debt service on the issue for the bond year, and

(ii) the aggregate amount invested as provided in clause (i) is promptly and appropriately reduced as the amount of outstanding bonds of the issue is reduced (or, in the case of a qualified mortgage bond or a qualified veterans' mortgage bond, as the mortgages are repaid).

(C) EXCEPTIONS FOR TEMPORARY PERIOD.—Subparagraph (B) shall not apply to—

(i) proceeds of the issue invested for an initial temporary period until such proceeds are needed for the governmental purpose of the issue, and

(ii) temporary investment periods related to debt service.

(D) DEBT SERVICE DEFINED.—For purposes of this paragraph, the debt service on the issue for any bond year is the scheduled amount of interest and amortization of principal payable for such year with respect to such issue. For purposes of the preceding sentence, there shall not be taken into account amounts scheduled with respect to any bond which has been redeemed before the beginning of the bond year.

(E) NO DISPOSITION IN CASE OF LOSS.—This paragraph shall not require the sale or disposition of any investment if such sale or disposition would result in a loss which exceeds the amount which, but for such sale or disposition, would at the time of such sale or disposition—

(i) be paid to the United States, or,

(ii) in the case of a qualified veterans' mortgage bond, be paid or credited mortgagors under section 143(g)(3)(A).

(F) EXCEPTION FOR GOVERNMENTAL USE BONDS AND QUALIFIED 501(c)(3) BONDS.—This paragraph shall not apply to any bond which is not a private activity bond or which is a qualified 501(c)(3) bond.

P.L. 105-34, §967, provides:

ACT SEC. 967. ADDITIONAL ADVANCE REFUNDING OF CERTAIN VIRGIN ISLAND BONDS.

Subclause (I) of section 149(d)(3)(A)(i) of the Internal Revenue Code of 1986 shall not apply to the second advance refunding of any issue of the Virgin Islands which was first advance refunded before June 9, 1997, if the debt provisions of the refunding bonds are changed to repeal the priority first lien requirement of the refunded bonds.

• 1989, Omnibus Budget Reconciliation Act of 1989 (P.L. 101-239)

P.L. 101-239, §7814(c)(2):

Amended Code Sec. 148(d)(3)(E)(ii) by striking "a qualified mortgage bond or" after "in the case of". **Effective** as if included in the provision of P.L. 100-647 to which it relates.

• 1988, Technical and Miscellaneous Revenue Act of 1988 (P.L. 100-647)

P.L. 100-647, §1013(a)(14):

Amended Code Sec. 148(d)(2) by striking out "any fund described in paragraph (1)" and inserting in lieu thereof "any reserve or replacement fund". **Effective** as if included in the provision of P.L. 99-514 to which it relates.

[Sec. 148(e)]

(e) MINOR PORTION MAY BE INVESTED IN HIGHER YIELDING INVESTMENTS.—Notwithstanding subsections (a), (c), and (d), a bond issued as part of an issue shall not be treated as an arbitrage bond solely by reason of the fact that an amount of the proceeds of such issue (in addition to the amounts under subsections (c) and (d)) is invested in higher yielding investments if such amount does not exceed the lesser of—

(1) 5 percent of the proceeds of the issue, or

(2) $100,000.

[Sec. 148(f)]

(f) REQUIRED REBATE TO THE UNITED STATES.—

(1) IN GENERAL.—A bond which is part of an issue shall be treated as an arbitrage bond if the requirements of paragraphs (2) and (3) are not met with respect to such issue. The preceding sentence shall not apply to any qualified veterans' mortgage bond.

(2) REBATE TO UNITED STATES.—An issue shall be treated as meeting the requirements of this paragraph only if an amount equal to the sum of—

(A) the excess of—

(i) the amount earned on all nonpurpose investments (other than investments attributable to an excess described in this subparagraph), over

(ii) the amount which would have been earned if such nonpurpose investments were invested at a rate equal to the yield on the issue, plus

(B) any income attributable to the excess described in subparagraph (A),

is paid to the United States by the issuer in accordance with the requirements of paragraph (3).

(3) DUE DATE OF PAYMENTS UNDER PARAGRAPH (2).—Except to the extent provided by the Secretary, the amount which is required to be paid to the United States by the issuer shall be paid in installments which are made at least once every 5 years. Each installment shall be in an amount which ensures that 90 percent of the amount described in paragraph (2) with respect to the issue at the time payment of such installment is required will have been paid to the United States. The last installment shall be made no later than 60 days after the day on which the last bond of the issue is redeemed and shall be in an amount sufficient to pay the remaining balance of the amount described in paragraph (2) with respect to such issue. A series of issues which are redeemed during a 6-month period (or such longer period as the Secretary may prescribe) shall be treated (at the election of the issuer) as 1 issue for purposes of the preceding sentence if no bond which is part of any issue in such series has a maturity of more than 270 days or is a private activity bond. In the case of a tax and revenue anticipation bond, the last installment shall not be required to be made before the date 8 months after the date of issuance of the issue of which the bond is a part.

(4) SPECIAL RULES FOR APPLYING PARAGRAPH (2).—

(A) IN GENERAL.—In determining the aggregate amount earned on nonpurpose investments for purposes of paragraph (2)—

(i) any gain or loss on the disposition of a nonpurpose investment shall be taken into account, and

(ii) any amount earned on a bona fide debt service fund shall not be taken into account if the gross earnings on such fund for the bond year is less than $100,000.

In the case of an issue no bond of which is a private activity bond, clause (ii) shall be applied without regard to the dollar limitation therein if the average maturity of the issue (determined in accordance with section 147(b)(2)(A)) is at least 5 years and the rates of interest on bonds which are part of the issue do not vary during the term of the issue.

(B) TEMPORARY INVESTMENTS.—Under regulations prescribed by the Secretary—

(i) IN GENERAL.—An issue shall, for purposes of this subsection, be treated as meeting the requirements of paragraph (2) if—

(I) the gross proceeds of such issue are expended for the governmental purposes for which the issue was issued no later than the day which is 6 months after the date of issuance of the issue, and

(II) the requirements of paragraph (2) are met with respect to amounts not required to be spent as provided in subclause (I) (other than earnings on amounts in any bona fide debt service fund).

Gross proceeds which are held in a bona fide debt service fund or a reasonably required reserve or replacement fund, and gross proceeds which arise after such 6 months and which are not reasonably anticipated as of the date of issuance, shall not be considered gross proceeds for purposes of subclause (I) only.

(ii) ADDITIONAL PERIOD FOR CERTAIN BONDS.—

(I) IN GENERAL.—In the case of an issue described in subclause (II), clause (i) shall be applied by substituting "1 year" for "6 months" each place it appears with respect to the portion of the proceeds of the issue which are not expended in accordance with clause (i) if such portion does not exceed 5 percent of the proceeds of the issue.

(II) ISSUES TO WHICH SUBCLAUSE (I) APPLIES.—An issue is described in this subclause if no bond which is part of such issue is a private activity bond (other than a qualified 501(c)(3) bond) or a tax or revenue anticipation bond.

(iii) SAFE HARBOR FOR DETERMINING WHEN PROCEEDS OF TAX AND REVENUE ANTICIPATION BONDS ARE EXPENDED.—

(I) IN GENERAL.—For purposes of clause (i), in the case of an issue of tax or revenue anticipation bonds, the net proceeds of such issue (including earnings thereon) shall be treated as expended for the governmental purpose of the issue on the 1st day after the date of issuance that the cumulative cash flow deficit to be financed by such issue exceeds 90 percent of the proceeds of such issue.

(II) CUMULATIVE CASH FLOW DEFICIT.—For purposes of subclause (I), the term "cumulative cash flow deficit" means, as of the date of computation, the excess of the expenses paid during the period described in subclause (III) which would ordinarily be paid out of or financed by anticipated tax or other revenues over the aggregate amount available (other than from the proceeds of the issue) during such period for the payment of such expenses.

(III) PERIOD INVOLVED.—For purposes of subclause (II), the period described in this subclause is the period beginning on the date of issuance of the issue and ending on the earlier of the date 6 months after such date of issuance or the date of the computation of cumulative cash flow deficit.

(iv) PAYMENTS OF PRINCIPAL NOT TO AFFECT REQUIREMENTS.—For purposes of this subparagraph, payments of principal on the bonds which are part of an issue shall not be treated as expended for the governmental purposes of the issue.

(C) EXCEPTION FROM REBATE FOR CERTAIN PROCEEDS TO BE USED TO FINANCE CONSTRUCTION EXPENDITURES.—

(i) IN GENERAL.—In the case of a construction issue, paragraph (2) shall not apply to the available construction proceeds of such issue if the spending requirements of clause (ii) are met.

(ii) SPENDING REQUIREMENTS.—The spending requirements of this clause are met if at least—

(I) 10 percent of the available construction proceeds of the construction issue are spent for the governmental purposes of the issue within the 6-month period beginning on the date of the bonds are issued,

(II) 45 percent of such proceeds are spent for such purposes within the 1-year period beginning on such date,

(III) 75 percent of such proceeds are spent for such purposes within the 18-month period beginning on such date, and

(IV) 100 percent of such proceeds are spent for such purposes within the 2-year period beginning on such date.

(iii) EXCEPTION FOR REASONABLE RETAINAGE.—The spending requirement of clause (ii)(IV) shall be treated as met if—

(I) such requirement would be met at the close of such 2-year period but for a reasonable retainage (not exceeding 5 percent of the available construction proceeds of the construction issue), and

(II) 100 percent of the available construction proceeds of the construction issue are spent for the governmental purposes of the issue within the 3-year period beginning on the date the bonds are issued.

(iv) CONSTRUCTION ISSUE.—For purposes of this subparagraph, the term "construction issue" means any issue if—

(I) at least 75 percent of the available construction proceeds of such issue are to be used for construction expenditures with respect to property which is to be owned by a governmental unit or a 501(c)(3) organization, and

(II) all of the bonds which are part of such issue are qualified 501(c)(3) bonds, bonds which are not private activity bonds, or private activity bonds issued to finance property to be owned by a governmental unit or a 501(c)(3) organization.

For purposes of this subparagraph, the term "construction" includes reconstruction and rehabilitation, and rules similar to the rules of section 142(b)(1)(B) shall apply.

(v) PORTIONS OF ISSUES USED FOR CONSTRUCTION.—If—

(I) all of the construction expenditures to be financed by an issue are to be financed from a portion thereof, and

(II) the issuer elects to treat such portion as a construction issue for purposes of this subparagraph,

then, for purposes of this subparagraph and subparagraph (B), such portion shall be treated as a separate issue.

(vi) AVAILABLE CONSTRUCTION PROCEEDS.—For purposes of this subparagraph—

(I) IN GENERAL.—The term "available construction proceeds" means the amount equal to the issue price (within the meaning of sections 1273 and 1274) of the construction issue, increased by earnings on the issue price, earnings on amounts in any reasonably required reserve or replacement fund not funded from the issue, and earnings on all of the foregoing earnings, and reduced by the amount of the issue price in any reasonably required reserve or replacement fund and the issuance costs financed by the issue.

(II) EARNINGS ON RESERVE INCLUDED ONLY FOR CERTAIN PERIODS.—The term "available construction proceeds" shall not include amounts earned on any reasonably required reserve or replacement fund after the earlier of the close of the 2-year period described in clause (ii) or the date the construction is substantially completed.

(III) PAYMENTS ON ACQUIRED PURPOSE OBLIGATIONS EXCLUDED.—The term "available construction proceeds" shall not include payments on any obligation acquired to carry out the governmental purposes of the issue and shall not include earnings on such payments.

(IV) ELECTION TO REBATE ON EARNINGS ON RESERVE.—At the election of the issuer, the term "available construction proceeds" shall not include earnings on any reasonably required reserve or replacement fund.

(vii) ELECTION TO PAY PENALTY IN LIEU OF REBATE.—

(I) IN GENERAL.—At the election of the issuer, paragraph (2) shall not apply to available construction proceeds which do not meet the spending requirements of clause (ii) if the issuer pays a penalty, with respect to each 6-month period after the date the bonds were issued, equal to 1½ percent of the amount of the available construction proceeds of the issue which, as of the close of such 6-month period, is not spent as required by clause (ii).

(II) TERMINATION.—The penalty imposed by this clause shall cease to apply only as provided in clause (viii) or after the latest maturity date of any bond in the issue (including any refunding bond with respect thereto).

(viii) ELECTION TO TERMINATE 1½ PERCENT PENALTY.—At the election of the issuer (made not later than 90 days after the earlier of the end of the initial temporary period or the date the construction is substantially completed), the penalty under clause (vii) shall not apply to any 6-month period after the initial temporary period under subsection (c) if the requirements of subclauses (I), (II), and (III) are met.

(I) 3 PERCENT PENALTY.—The requirement of this subclause is met if the issuer pays a penalty equal to 3 percent of the amount of available construction proceeds of the issue which is not spent for the governmental purposes of the issue as of the close of such initial temporary period multiplied by the number of years (including fractions thereof) in the initial temporary period.

(II) YIELD RESTRICTION AT CLOSE OF TEMPORARY PERIOD.—The requirement of this subclause is met if the amount of the available construction proceeds of the issue which is not spent for the governmental purposes of the issue as of the close of such initial temporary period is invested at a yield not exceeding the yield on the issue or which is invested in any tax exempt bond which is not investment property.

(III) REDEMPTION OF BONDS AT EARLIEST CALL DATE.—The requirement of this subclause is met if the amount of the available construction proceeds of the issue which is not spent for the governmental purposes of the issue as of the earliest date on which bonds may be redeemed is used to redeem bonds on such date.

(ix) ELECTION TO TERMINATE $1\frac{1}{2}$ PERCENT PENALTY BEFORE END OF TEMPORARY PERIOD.—If—

(I) the construction to be financed by a construction issue is substantially completed before the end of the initial temporary period,

(II) the issuer identifies an amount of available construction proceeds which will not be spent for the governmental purposes of the issue,

(III) the issuer has made the election under clause (viii), and

(IV) the issuer makes an election under this clause before the close of the initial temporary period and not later than 90 days after the date the construction is substantially completed,

then clauses (vii) and (viii) shall be applied to the available construction proceeds so identified as if the initial temporary period ended as of the date the election is made.

(x) FAILURE TO PAY PENALTIES.—In the case of a failure (which is not due to willful neglect) to pay any penalty required to be paid under clause (vii) or (viii) in the amount or at the time prescribed therefor, the Secretary may treat such failure as not occurring if, in addition to paying such penalty, the issuer pays a penalty equal to the sum of—

(I) 50 percent of the amount which was not paid in accordance with clauses (vii) and (viii), plus

(II) interest (at the underpayment rate established under section 6621) on the portion of the amount which was not paid on the date required for the period beginning on such date.

The Secretary may waive all or any portion of the penalty under this clause. Bonds which are part of an issue with respect to which there is a failure to pay the amount required under this clause (and any refunding bond with respect thereto) shall be treated as not being, and as never having been, tax-exempt bonds.

(xi) ELECTION FOR POOLED FINANCING BONDS.—At the election of the issuer of an issue the proceeds of which are to be used to make or finance loans (other than nonpurpose investments) to 2 or more persons, the periods described in clauses (ii) and (iii) shall begin on—

(I) the date the loan is made, in the case of loans made within the 1-year period after the date the bonds are issued, and

(II) the date following such 1-year period, in the case of loans made after such 1-year period.

If such an election applies to an issue, the requirements of paragraph (2) shall apply to amounts earned before the beginning of the periods determined under the preceding sentence.

(xii) PAYMENTS OF PRINCIPAL NOT TO AFFECT REQUIREMENTS.—For purposes of this subparagraph, payments of principal on the bonds which are part of the construction issue shall not be treated as an expenditure of the available construction proceeds of the issue.

(xiii) REFUNDING BONDS.—

(I) IN GENERAL.—Except as provided in this clause, clause (vii)(II), and the last sentence of clause (x), this subparagraph shall not apply to any refunding bond and no proceeds of a refunded bond shall be treated for purposes of this subparagraph as proceeds of a refunding bond.

(II) DETERMINATION OF CONSTRUCTION PORTION OF ISSUE.—For purposes of clause (v), any portion of an issue which is used to refund any issue (or portion thereof) shall be treated as a separate issue.

(III) COORDINATION WITH REBATE REQUIREMENT ON REFUNDING BONDS.—The requirements of paragraph (2) shall be treated as met with respect to earnings for any period if a penalty is paid under clause (vii) or (viii) with respect to such earnings for such period.

(xiv) DETERMINATION OF INITIAL TEMPORARY PERIOD.—For purposes of this subparagraph, the end of the initial temporary period shall be determined without regard to section 149(d)(3)(A)(iv).

(xv) ELECTIONS.—Any election under this subparagraph (other than clauses (viii) and (ix)) shall be made on or before the date the bonds are issued; and, once made, shall be irrevocable.

(xvi) TIME FOR PAYMENT OF PENALTIES.—Any penalty under this subparagraph shall be paid to the United States not later than 90 days after the period to which the penalty relates.

(xvii) TREATMENT OF BONA FIDE DEBT SERVICE FUNDS.—If the spending requirements of clause (ii) are met with respect to the available construction proceeds of a construction issue, then paragraph (2) shall not apply to earnings on a bona fide debt service fund for such issue.

(D) EXCEPTION FOR GOVERNMENTAL UNITS ISSUING $5,000,000 OR LESS OF BONDS.—

(i) IN GENERAL.—An issue shall, for purposes of this subsection, be treated as meeting the requirements of paragraphs (2) and (3) if—

(I) the issue is issued by a governmental unit with general taxing powers,

(II) no bond which is part of such issue is a private activity bond,

(III) 95 percent or more of the net proceeds of such issue are to be used for local governmental activities of the issuer (or of a governmental unit the jurisdiction of which is entirely within the jurisdiction of the issuer), and

(IV) the aggregate face amount of all tax-exempt bonds (other than private activity bonds) issued by such unit during the calendar year in which such issue is issued is not reasonably expected to exceed $5,000,000.

(ii) AGGREGATION OF ISSUERS.—For purposes of subclause (IV) of clause (i)—

(I) an issuer and all entities which issue bonds on behalf of such issuer shall be treated as 1 issuer,

(II) all bonds issued by a subordinate entity shall, for purposes of applying such subclause to each other entity to which such entity is subordinate, be treated as issued by such other entity, and

(III) an entity formed (or, to the extent provided by the Secretary, availed of) to avoid the purposes of such subclause (IV) and all other entities benefiting thereby shall be treated as 1 issuer.

(iii) CERTAIN REFUNDING BONDS NOT TAKEN INTO ACCOUNT IN DETERMINING SMALL ISSUER STATUS.—There shall not be taken into account under subclause (IV) of clause (i) any bond issued to refund (other than to advance refund) any bond to the extent the amount of the refunding bond does not exceed the outstanding amount of the refunded bond.

(iv) CERTAIN ISSUES ISSUED BY SUBORDINATE GOVERNMENTAL UNITS, ETC., EXEMPT FROM REBATE REQUIREMENT.—An issue issued by a subordinate entity of a governmental unit with general taxing powers shall be treated as described in clause (i)(I) if the aggregate face amount of such issue does not exceed the lesser of—

(I) $5,000,000, or

(II) the amount which, when added to the aggregate face amount of other issues issued by such entity, does not exceed the portion of the $5,000,000 limitation under clause (i)(IV) which such governmental unit allocates to such entity.

For purposes of the preceding sentence, an entity which issues bonds on behalf of a governmental unit with general taxing powers shall be treated as a subordinate entity of such unit. An allocation shall be taken into account under subclause (II) only if it is irrevocable and made before the issuance date of such issue and only to the extent that the limitation so allocated bears a reasonable relationship to the benefits received by such governmental unit from issues issued by such entity.

(v) DETERMINATION OF WHETHER REFUNDING BONDS ELIGIBLE FOR EXCEPTION FROM REBATE REQUIREMENT.—If any portion of an issue is issued to refund other bonds, such portion shall be treated as a separate issue which does not meet the requirements of paragraphs (2) and (3) by reason of this subparagraph unless—

(I) the aggregate face amount of such issue does not exceed $5,000,000,

(II) each refunded bond was issued as part of an issue which was treated as meeting the requirements of paragraphs (2) and (3) by reason of this subparagraph,

(III) the average maturity date of the refunding bonds issued as part of such issue is not later than the average maturity date of the bonds to be refunded by such issue, and

(IV) no refunding bond has a maturity date which is later than the date which is 30 years after the date the original bond was issued.

Subclause (III) shall not apply if the average maturity of the issue of which the original bond was a part (and of the issue of which the bonds to be refunded are a part) is 3 years or less. For purposes of this clause, average maturity shall be determined in accordance with section 147(b)(2)(A).

(vi) REFUNDINGS OF BONDS ISSUED UNDER LAW PRIOR TO TAX REFORM ACT OF 1986.—If section 141(a) did not apply to any refunded bond, the issue of which such refunded bond was a part shall be treated as meeting the requirements of subclause (II) of clause (v) if—

(I) such issue was issued by a governmental unit with general taxing powers,

(II) no bond issued as part of such issue was an industrial development bond (as defined in section 103(b)(2), but without regard to subparagraph (B) of section 103(b)(3)) or a private loan bond (as defined in section 103(o)(2)(A), but without regard to any exception from such definition other than section 103(o)(2)(C)), and

(III) the aggregate face amount of all tax-exempt bonds (other than bonds described in subclause (II)) issued by such unit during the calendar year in which such issue was issued did not exceed $5,000,000.

References in subclause (II) to section 103 shall be to such section as in effect on the day before the date of the enactment of the Tax Reform Act of 1986. Rules similar to the rules of clauses (ii) and (iii) shall apply for purposes of subclause (III). For purposes of subclause (II) of clause (i), bonds described in subclause (II) of this clause to which section 141(a) does not apply shall not be treated as private activity bonds.

Caution: Code Sec. 148(f)(4)(D)(vii), below, is subject to the sunset provision of the Economic Growth and Tax Relief Reconciliation Act of 2001 (P.L. 107-16), §901. Absent Congressional action, the changes made to this provision by P.L. 107-16, or that take effect as if included in P.L. 107-16, do not apply after December 31, 2010. For more information about the sunset provision, see page XXI of the Preface to this publication and P.L. 107-16, §901, in the amendment notes. See the amendments notes for a history of amendments to this section and the effective date of each change.

(vii) INCREASE IN EXCEPTION FOR BONDS FINANCING PUBLIC SCHOOL CAPITAL EXPENDITURES.—Each of the $5,000,000 amounts in the preceding provisions of this subparagraph shall be increased by the lesser of $10,000,000 or so much of the aggregate face amount of the bonds as are attributable to financing the construction (within the meaning of subparagraph (C)(iv)) of public school facilities.

(5) EXEMPTION FROM GROSS INCOME OF SUM REBATED.—Gross income shall not include the sum described in paragraph (2). Notwithstanding any other provision of this title, no deduction shall be allowed for any amount paid to the United States under paragraph (2).

(6) DEFINITIONS.—For purposes of this subsection and subsections (c) and (d)—

(A) NONPURPOSE INVESTMENT.—The term "nonpurpose investment" means any investment property which—

(i) is acquired with the gross proceeds of an issue, and

(ii) is not acquired in order to carry out the governmental purpose of the issue.

(B) GROSS PROCEEDS.—Except as otherwise provided by the Secretary, the gross proceeds of an issue include—

(i) amounts received (including repayments of principal) as a result of investing the original proceeds of the issue, and

(ii) amounts to be used to pay debt service on the issue.

(7) PENALTY IN LIEU OF LOSS OF TAX EXEMPTION.—In the case of an issue which would (but for this paragraph) fail to meet the requirements of paragraph (2) or (3), the Secretary may treat such issue as not failing to meet such requirements if—

(A) no bond which is part of such issue is a private activity bond (other than a qualified 501(c)(3) bond),

(B) the failure to meet such requirements is not due to willful neglect, and

(C) the issuer pays to the United States a penalty in an amount equal to the sum of—

(i) 50 percent of the amount which was not paid in accordance with paragraphs (2) and (3), plus

(ii) interest (at the underpayment rate established under section 6621) on the portion of the amount which was not paid on the date required under paragraph (3) for the period beginning on such date.

The Secretary may waive all or any portion of the penalty under this paragraph.

Amendments

• 2006, Tax Increase Prevention and Reconciliation Act of 2005 (P.L. 109-222)

P.L. 109-222, §508(c):

Amended Code Sec. 148(f)(4)(D)(ii) by striking subclause (II) and by redesignating subclauses (III) and (IV) as subclauses (II) and (III), respectively. **Effective** for bonds issued after 5-17-2006. Prior to being stricken, Code Sec. 148(f)(4)(D)(ii)(II) read as follows:

(II) all bonds issued by a governmental unit to make loans to other governmental units with general taxing powers not subordinate to such unit shall, for purposes of applying such subclause to such unit, be treated as not issued by such unit.

• 2001, Economic Growth and Tax Relief Reconciliation Act of 2001 (P.L. 107-16)

P.L. 107-16, §421(a):

Amended Code Sec. 148(f)(4)(D)(vii) by striking "$5,000,000" the second place it appears and inserting "$10,000,000". **Effective** for obligations issued in calendar years beginning after 12-31-2001.

P.L. 107-16, §901(a)-(b), provides:

SEC. 901. SUNSET OF PROVISIONS OF ACT.

(a) IN GENERAL.—All provisions of, and amendments made by, this Act shall not apply—

(1) to taxable, plan, or limitation years beginning after December 31, 2010, or

(2) in the case of title V, to estates of decedents dying, gifts made, or generation skipping transfers, after December 31, 2010.

(b) APPLICATION OF CERTAIN LAWS.—The Internal Revenue Code of 1986 and the Employee Retirement Income Security Act of 1974 shall be applied and administered to years, estates, gifts, and transfers described in subsection (a) as if the provisions and amendments described in subsection (a) had never been enacted.

• 1997, Taxpayer Relief Act of 1997 (P.L. 105-34)

P.L. 105-34, §223(a):

Amended Code Sec. 148(f)(4)(D) by adding at the end a new clause (vii). **Effective** for bonds issued after 12-31-97.

P.L. 105-34, §1441:

Amended Code Sec. 148(f)(4)(B)(ii)(I) by striking "the lesser of 5 percent of the proceeds of the issue or $100,000" and inserting "5 percent of the proceeds of the issue". **Effective** for bonds issued after 8-5-97.

P.L. 105-34, §1442:

Amended Code Sec. 148(f)(4)(C) by adding at the end a new clause (xvii). **Effective** for bonds issued after 8-5-97.

P.L. 105-34, §1444(b):

Amended Code Sec. 148(f)(4) by striking subparagraph (E). **Effective** for bonds issued after 8-5-97. Prior to being stricken, Code Sec. 148(f)(4)(E) read as follows:

(E) EXCEPTION FOR CERTAIN QUALIFIED STUDENT LOAN BONDS.

(i) IN GENERAL.—In determining the aggregate amount earned on nonpurpose investments acquired with gross proceeds of an issue of bonds for a program described in section 144(b)(1)(A), the amount earned from investment of net proceeds of such issue during the initial temporary period under subsection (c) shall not be taken into account to the extent that the amount so earned is used to pay the reasonable—

(I) administrative costs of such program attributable to such issue and the costs of carrying such issue, and

(II) costs of issuing such issue,

but only to the extent such costs were financed with proceeds of such issue and for which the issuer was not reimbursed. Amounts designated as interest on student loans shall not be taken into account in determining whether the issuer is reimbursed for such costs. Except as otherwise hereafter provided in regulations prescribed by the Secretary, costs described in subclause (I) paid from amounts earned as described in the first sentence of this clause may also be taken into account in determining the yield on the student loans under a program described in section 144(b)(1)(A).

(ii) ONLY ARBITRAGE ON AMOUNTS LOANED DURING TEMPORARY PERIOD TAKEN INTO ACCOUNT FOR ADMINISTRATIVE COSTS, ETC.—The amount earned from investment of net proceeds of an issue during the initial temporary period under subsection (c) shall be taken into account under clause (i)(I) only to the extent attributable to proceeds which were used to make or finance (not later than the close of such period) student loans under a program described in section 144(b)(1)(A).

(iii) ELECTION.—This subparagraph shall not apply to any issue if the issuer elects not to have this subparagraph apply to such issue.

(iv) TERMINATION.—This subparagraph shall not apply to any bond issued after December 31, 1988.

• 1990, Omnibus Budget Reconciliation Act of 1990 (P.L. 101-508)

P.L. 101-508, §11701(j)(1):

Amended Code Sec. 148(f)(4)(B)(i)(II). **Effective** as if included in the provision of P.L. 101-239 to which it relates. Prior to amendment, subclause (II) read as follows:

(II) The requirements of paragraph (2) are met after such 6 months with respect to earnings on amounts in any reasonably required reserve or replacement fund.

P.L. 101-508, §11701(j)(2):

Amended Code Sec. 148(f)(4)(B)(i) by striking "replacement fund" and all that follows in the last sentence and inserting "replacement fund, and gross proceeds which arise after such 6 months and which were not reasonably anticipated as of the date of issuance, shall not be considered gross proceeds for purposes of subclause (I) only." **Effective** as if included in the provision of P.L. 101-239 to which it relates.

P.L. 101-508, §11701(j)(3)(A)-(B):

Amended Code Sec. 148(f)(4) by redesignating subparagraphs (C) and (D) as subparagraphs (D) and (E), respectively and by inserting a new subparagraph (C). **Effective** as if included in the provision of P.L. 101-239 to which it relates.

P.L. 101-508, §11701(j)(4):

Amended Code Sec. 148(f)(B)(iv). **Effective** as if included in the provision of P.L. 101-239 to which it relates. Prior to amendment, clause (iv) read as follows:

(iv) 2-YEAR PERIOD FOR CERTAIN CONSTRUCTION BONDS.—

(I) IN GENERAL.—In the case of an issue described in subclause (IV), clause (i) shall be applied by substituting "2 years" for "6 months" each place it appears.

(II) PROCEEDS MUST BE SPENT WITHIN CERTAIN PERIODS.—Subclause (I) shall not apply to any issue if less than 10 percent of the net proceeds of the issue are spent for the governmental purposes of the issue within the 6-month period beginning on the date the bonds are issued, less than 45 percent of such proceeds are spent for such purposes within the 1-year period beginning on such date, less than 75 percent of such proceeds are spent for such purposes within the 18-month period beginning on such date, or less than 100 percent of such proceeds are spent for such purposes within the 2-year period beginning on such date. For purposes of the preceding sentence, the term "net proceeds" includes investment proceeds earned before the close of the period involved on the investment of the sale proceeds of the issue.

(III) EXCEPTION FOR REASONABLE RETAINAGE.—For purposes of subclause (II), 100 percent of the net proceeds of an issue shall be treated as spent for the governmental purposes of the issue within the 2-year period beginning on the date the bonds are issued if such requirement is met within the 3-year period beginning on such date and such requirement would have been met within such 2-year period but for a reasonable retainage (not exceeding 5 percent of the net proceeds of the issue).

(IV) ISSUES TO WHICH SUBCLAUSE (I) APPLIES.—An issue is described in this subclause if at least 75 percent of the net proceeds of the issue are to be used for construction expenditures with respect to property which is owned by a governmental unit or a 501(c)(3) organization. For purposes of the preceding sentence, the term "construction" includes reconstruction and rehabilitation, and section 142(b)(1) shall apply. An issue is not described in this subclause if any bond which is part of such issue is a bond other than a qualified 501(c)(3) bond, a bond which is not a private activity bond, or a private activity bond to finance property to be owned by a governmental unit or a 501(c)(3) organization.

(V) ELECTION TO PAY PENALTY IN LIEU OF REBATE.—In the case of an issue described in subclause (IV) which fails to meet the requirements of subclause (II), if the issuer elected the application of this subclause, the requirements of paragraph (2) shall be treated as met if the issuer pays the penalty under paragraph (7) or pays a penalty with respect to the close of each 6 month period after the date the bonds are issued equal to $1\frac{1}{2}$ percent of the amount of the net proceeds of the issue which, as of the close of such period, are not spent as required by subclause (II). The penalty under this subclause shall cease to apply only after the bonds (including any refunding bonds with respect thereto) are no longer outstanding.

(VI) ELECTION TO REBATE ON EARNINGS ON RESERVE.—If the issuer so elects, the term "net proceeds" for purposes of subclause (II) shall not include earnings on any reasonably required reserve or replacement fund and the requirements of paragraph (2) shall apply to such earnings.

(VII) POOLED FINANCING BONDS.—At the election of the issuer of an issue the proceeds of which are to be used to make or finance loans (other than nonpurpose investments) to 2 or more persons, the periods described in clause (i) and this clause shall begin on the date the loan is made in the case of loans made within the 1-year period after the date the bonds were issued. In the case of loans made after such 1-year period, the periods described in clause (i) and this clause shall begin at the close of such 1-year period.

(VIII) PORTIONS OF ISSUE MAY BE TREATED SEPARATELY.—If only a portion of an issue is to be used for construction expenditures referred to in subclause (IV), such portion and the other portion of such issue may, at the election of the issuer, be treated as separate issues for purposes of this clause and clause (i).

(IX) ELECTIONS.—Any election under this clause shall be made on or before the date the bonds are issued; and, once made, shall be irrevocable.

P.L. 101-508, §11701(j)(7)-(8), provides:

(7) In the case of a bond issued before the date of the enactment of this Act, the period for making the election under section 148(f)(4)(C)(viii) of the Internal Revenue Code of 1986 (as added by this subsection) shall not expire before the date which is 180 days after such date of enactment.

(8) Section 148(f)(4)(C)(xiii)(II) of such Code (as added by this subsection) shall apply only to refunding bonds issued after August 3, 1990.

• 1989, Omnibus Budget Reconciliation Act of 1989 (P.L. 101-239)

P.L. 101-239, §7652(a):

Amended Code Sec. 148(f)(4)(B)(i). **Effective** for bonds issued after 12-19-89. Prior to amendment, Code Sec. 148(f)(4)(B)(i) read as follows:

(i) IN GENERAL.—An issue shall, for purposes of this subsection, be treated as meeting the requirements of paragraph (2) if the gross proceeds of such issue are expended for the governmental purpose for which the issue was issued by no later than the day which is 6 months after the date of issuance of such issue. Gross proceeds which are held in a bona fide debt service fund shall not be considered gross proceeds for purposes of this subparagraph only.

P.L. 101-239, §7652(b):

Amended Code Sec. 148(f)(4)(B) by adding at the end thereof a new clause (iv). **Effective** for bonds issued after 12-19-89.

P.L. 101-239, §7652(d):

Amended Code Sec. 148(f)(4)(B)(ii)(I) by inserting "each place it appears" after "6 months". **Effective** for bonds issued after 12-19-89.

P.L. 101-239, §7816(r):

Amended Code Sec. 148(f)(4)(B)(iii)(III) by striking "such date of issuance, or the date" and inserting "such date of issuance or the date". **Effective** as if included in the provision of P.L. 100-647 to which it relates.

P.L. 101-239, §7816(t):

Amended Code Sec. 148(f)(4)(C)(ii)(II) by striking "on behalf of" and inserting "to make loans to". **Effective** as if included in the provision of P.L. 100-647 to which it relates.

• 1988, Technical and Miscellaneous Revenue Act of 1988 (P.L. 100-647)

P.L. 100-647, §1013(a)(15):

Amended Code Sec. 148(f)(3) by adding at the end thereof a new sentence. **Effective** as if included in the provision of P.L. 99-514 to which it relates.

P.L. 100-647, §1013(a)(16)(A):

Amended Code Sec. 148(f)(4)(B)(iii)(I) by striking out "aggregate face amount of such issue" and inserting in lieu thereof "proceeds of such issue". **Effective** for bonds issued after 6-30-87.

P.L. 100-647, §1013(a)(17)(A)(i)-(iii):

Amended Code Sec. 148(f)(4)(C) by striking out the heading and inserting in lieu thereof

"(C) Exception for governmental units issuing $5,000,000 or less of bonds.—

"(i) IN GENERAL.—",

by redesignating clauses (i)-(iv) as subclauses (I)-(IV), respectively, and by moving the margins of such subclauses 2 ems to the right, and by striking out the last sentence and inserting in lieu thereof new clauses (ii)-(vi). **Effective** for bonds issued after 6-30-87. However, at the election of an issuer (made at such time and in such manner as the Secretary of the Treasury or his delegate may prescribe), the amendments made by this paragraph shall apply to such issuer as if included in the amendments made by section 1301(a) of P.L. 99-514. Prior to amendment, the heading and last sentence read as follows:

Exception for small governmental units.—* * *

Clause (iv) shall not take into account any bond which is not outstanding at the time of a later issue or which is redeemed (other than in an advance refunding) from the net proceeds of the later issue.

P.L. 100-647, §1013(a)(17)(B):

Amended Code Sec. 148(f)(4)(C)(i)(IV) (as redesignated by subparagraph (A)) by striking out "(and all subordinate entities thereof)" after "Unit". **Effective** for bonds issued after 6-30-87. However, at the election of an issuer (made at such time and in such manner as the Secretary of the Treasury or his delegate may prescribe), the amendments made by this paragraph shall apply to such issuer as if included in the amendments made by section 1301(a) of P.L. 99-514.

P.L. 100-647, §1013(a)(18)(A)-(C):

Amended Code Sec. 148(f)(4)(D)(i) by inserting "for a program" before "described in section 144(b)(1)(A)", by striking out "such a program" and inserting in lieu thereof "such program", and by adding at the end thereof two sentences. **Effective** as if included in the provision of P.L. 99-514 to which it relates.

P.L. 100-647, §1013(a)(19):

Amended Code Sec. 148(f)(7)(B) by striking out "due to reasonable cause and not" and inserting in lieu thereof "not due". **Effective** as if included in the provision of P.L. 99-514 to which it relates.

P.L. 100-647, §4005(d)(2):

Amended Code Sec. 148(f)(1) by striking out "qualified mortgage bond or" before "qualified veterans'". **Effective** for bonds issued, and nonissued bond amounts elected, after 12-31-88.

P.L. 100-647, §6177(a):

Amended Code Sec. 148(f)(4)(B)(iii)(III) by striking out "the earliest of the maturity date of the issue, the date 6 months after such date of issuance," and inserting in lieu thereof "the earlier of the date 6 months after such date of issuance." **Effective** for bonds issued after the date of the enactment of this Act.

P.L. 100-647, §6177(b):

Amended Code Sec. 148(f)(3) by adding at the end thereof a new sentence. **Effective** for bonds issued after the date of the enactment of this Act.

P.L. 100-647, §6181(a):

Amended Code Sec. 148(f)(4)(A)(ii) by striking "unless the issuer otherwise elects," before "any amount". **Effective** for bonds issued after the date of enactment of this Act. For special rules see Act Sec. 6181(c)(2)-(3) below.

P.L. 100-647, §6181(b):

Amended Code Sec. 148(f)(4)(A) by adding at the end thereof a new sentence. **Effective** for bonds issued after the date of enactment of this Act. For special rules see Act Sec. 6181(c)(2)-(3) below.

P.L. 100-647, §6181(c)(2)-(3), provides:

(2) ELECTION FOR OUTSTANDING BONDS.—Any issue of bonds other than private activity bonds outstanding as of the date of the enactment of this Act shall be allowed a 1-time election to apply the amendments made by subsection (b) to amounts deposited after such date in bona fide debt service funds of such bonds.

(3) DEFINITION OF PRIVATE ACTIVITY BOND.—For purposes of this section and the last sentence of section 148(f)(4)(A) of the 1986 Code (as added by subsection (b)), the term "private activity bond" shall include any qualified 501(c)(3) bond (as defined under section 145 of the 1986 Code).

P.L. 100-647, §6183(a):

Amended Code Sec. 148(f)(4)(C)(ii), as amended by title I of this Act, by redesignating subclauses (II) and (III) as subclauses (III) and (IV), respectively, and by inserting after subclause (I) new subclause (II). **Effective** for bonds issued after 12-31-88.

[Sec. 148(g)]

(g) STUDENT LOAN INCENTIVE PAYMENTS.—Except to the extent otherwise provided in regulations, payments made by the Secretary of Education pursuant to section 438 of the Higher Education Act of 1965 are not to be taken into account, for purposes of subsection (a)(1), in determining yields on student loan notes.

[Sec. 148(h)]

(h) DETERMINATIONS OF YIELD.—For purposes of this section, the yield on an issue shall be determined on the basis of the issue price (within the meaning of sections 1273 and 1274).

[Sec. 148(i)]

(i) REGULATIONS.—The Secretary shall prescribe such regulations as may be necessary or appropriate to carry out the purposes of this section.

Amendments

• 1986, Tax Reform Act of 1986 (P.L. 99-514)

P.L. 99-514, §1301(b):

Amended Part IV of subchapter B of chapter 1 by adding Code Sec. 148. **Effective**, generally, for bonds issued after 8-15-86. However, for transitional rules, see Act Sec. 1312-1318 in the amendments for Code Sec. 103.

[Sec. 149]

SEC. 149. BONDS MUST BE REGISTERED TO BE TAX EXEMPT; OTHER REQUIREMENTS.

[Sec. 149(a)]

(a) BONDS MUST BE REGISTERED TO BE TAX EXEMPT.—

(1) GENERAL RULE.—Nothing in section 103(a) or in any other provision of law shall be construed to provide an exemption from Federal income tax for interest on any registration-required bond unless such bond is in registered form.

Caution: Code Sec. 149(a)(2), below, prior to amendment by P.L. 111-147, applies to obligations issued on or before the date which is 2 years after March 18, 2010.

(2) REGISTRATION-REQUIRED BOND.—For purposes of paragraph (1), the term "registration-required bond" means any bond other than a bond which—

(A) is not of a type offered to the public,

(B) has a maturity (at issue) of not more than 1 year, or

(C) is described in section 163(f)(2)(B).

Caution: Code Sec. 149(a)(2), below, as amended by P.L. 111-147, applies to obligations issued after the date which is 2 years after March 18, 2010.

(2) REGISTRATION-REQUIRED BOND.—For purposes of paragraph (1), the term "registration-required bond" means any bond other than a bond which—

(A) is not of a type offered to the public, or

(B) has a maturity (at issue) of not more than 1 year.

Caution: Code Sec. 149(a)(2)(C), below, was stricken by P.L. 111-147, applicable to obligations issued after the date which is 2 years after March 18, 2010.

(C) is described in section 163(f)(2)(B).

(3) SPECIAL RULES.—

(A) BOOK ENTRIES PERMITTED.—For purposes of paragraph (1), a book entry bond shall be treated as in registered form if the right to the principal of, and stated interest on, such bond may be transferred only through a book entry consistent with regulations prescribed by the Secretary.

(B) NOMINEES.—The Secretary shall prescribe such regulations as may be necessary to carry out the purpose of paragraph (1) where there is a nominee or chain of nominees.

Amendments

• 2010, Hiring Incentives to Restore Employment Act (P.L. 111-147)

P.L. 111-147, §502(a)(2)(A):

Amended Code Sec. 149(a)(2) by inserting "or" at the end of subparagraph (A), by striking ", or" at the end of subparagraph (B) and inserting a period, and by striking subparagraph (C). **Effective** for obligations issued after the date which is 2 years after 3-18-2010. Prior to being stricken, Code Sec. 149(a)(2)(C) read as follows:

(C) is described in section 163(f)(2)(B).

[Sec. 149(b)]

(b) FEDERALLY GUARANTEED BOND IS NOT TAX EXEMPT.—

(1) IN GENERAL.—Section 103(a) shall not apply to any State or local bond if such bond is federally guaranteed.

(2) FEDERALLY GUARANTEED DEFINED.—For purposes of paragraph (1), a bond is federally guaranteed if—

(A) the payment of principal or interest with respect to such bond is guaranteed (in whole or in part) by the United States (or any agency or instrumentality thereof),

(B) such bond is issued as part of an issue and 5 percent or more of the proceeds of such issue is to be—

(i) used in making loans the payment of principal or interest with respect to which are to be guaranteed (in whole or in part) by the United States (or any agency or instrumentality thereof), or

(ii) invested (directly or indirectly) in federally insured deposits or accounts, or

(C) the payment of principal or interest on such bond is otherwise indirectly guaranteed (in whole or in part) by the United States (or an agency or instrumentality thereof).

(3) EXCEPTIONS.—

(A) CERTAIN INSURANCE PROGRAMS.—A bond shall not be treated as federally guaranteed by reason of—

(i) any guarantee by the Federal Housing Administration, the Veterans' Administration, the Federal National Mortgage Association, the Federal Home Loan Mortgage Corporation, or the Government National Mortgage Association,

(ii) any guarantee of student loans and any guarantee by the Student Loan Marketing Association to finance student loans,

(iii) any guarantee by the Bonneville Power Authority pursuant to the Northwest Power Act (16 U.S.C. 839(d) as in effect on the date of the enactment of the Tax Reform Act of 1984, or

(iv) subject to subparagraph (E), any guarantee by a Federal home loan bank made in connection with the original issuance of a bond during the period beginning on the date of the enactment of this clause and ending on December 31, 2010 (or a renewal or extension of a guarantee so made).

(B) DEBT SERVICE, ETC.—Paragraph (1) shall not apply to—

(i) proceeds of the issue invested for an initial temporary period until such proceeds are needed for the purpose for which such issue was issued,

(ii) investments of a bona fide debt service fund,

(iii) investments of a reserve which meet the requirements of section 148(d),

(iv) investments in bonds issued by the United States Treasury, or

(v) other investments permitted under regulations.

(C) EXCEPTION FOR HOUSING PROGRAMS.—

(i) IN GENERAL.—Except as provided in clause (ii), paragraph (1) shall not apply to—

(I) a private activity bond for a qualified residential rental project or a housing program obligation under section 11(b) of the United States Housing Act of 1937,

(II) a qualified mortgage bond, or

(III) a qualified veterans' mortgage bond.

(ii) EXCEPTION NOT TO APPLY WHERE BOND INVESTED IN FEDERALLY INSURED DEPOSITS OR ACCOUNTS.—Clause (i) shall not apply to any bond which is federally guaranteed within the meaning of paragraph (2)(B)(ii).

(D) LOANS TO, OR GUARANTEES BY, FINANCIAL INSTITUTIONS.—Except as provided in paragraph (2)(B)(ii), a bond which is issued as part of an issue shall not be treated as federally guaranteed merely by reason of the fact that the proceeds of such issue are used in making loans to a financial institution or there is a guarantee by a financial institution unless such guarantee constitutes a federally insured deposit or account.

(E) SAFETY AND SOUNDNESS REQUIREMENTS FOR FEDERAL HOME LOAN BANKS.—Clause (iv) of subparagraph (A) shall not apply to any guarantee by a Federal home loan bank unless such bank meets safety and soundness collateral requirements for such guarantees which are at least as stringent as such requirements which apply under regulations applicable to such guarantees by Federal home loan banks as in effect on April 9, 2008.

(4) DEFINITIONS.—For purposes of this subsection—

(A) TREATMENT OF CERTAIN ENTITIES WITH AUTHORITY TO BORROW FROM UNITED STATES.—To the extent provided in regulations prescribed by the Secretary, any entity with statutory authority to borrow from the United States shall be treated as an instrumentality of the United States. Except in the case of an exempt facility bond, a qualified small issue bond, and a qualified student loan bond, nothing in the preceding sentence shall be construed as treating the District of Columbia or any possession of the United States as an instrumentality of the United States.

(B) FEDERALLY INSURED DEPOSIT OR ACCOUNT.—The term "federally insured deposit or account" means any deposit or account in a financial institution to the extent such deposit or account is insured under Federal law by the Federal Deposit Insurance Corporation, the Federal Savings and Loan Insurance Corporation, the National Credit Union Administration, or any similar federally chartered corporation.

Amendments

• **2008, Housing Assistance Tax Act of 2008 (P.L. 110-289)**

P.L. 110-289, §3023(a):

Amended Code Sec. 149(b)(3)(A) by striking "or" at the end of clause (ii), by striking the period at the end of clause (iii) and inserting ", or" and by adding at the end a new clause (iv). **Effective** for guarantees made after 7-30-2008.

P.L. 110-289, §3023(b):

Amended Code Sec. 149(b)(3) by adding at the end a new subparagraph (E). **Effective** for guarantees made after 7-30-2008.

• **1988, Technical and Miscellaneous Revenue Act of 1988 (P.L. 100-647)**

P.L. 100-647, §1013(a)(20):

Amended Code Sec. 149(b)(3)(A)(iii) by striking out "with respect to any bond issued before July 1, 1989" after "1984". **Effective** as if included in the provision of P.L. 99-514 to which it relates.

P.L. 100-647, §1013(a)(21):

Amended Code Sec. 149(b)(4)(A) by striking out "a qualified student loan bond, and a qualified redevelopment bond" and inserting in lieu thereof "and a qualified student loan bond". **Effective** as if included in the provision of P.L. 99-514 to which it relates.

[Sec. 149(c)]

(c) TAX EXEMPTION MUST BE DERIVED FROM THIS TITLE.—

(1) GENERAL RULE.—Except as provided in paragraph (2), no interest on any bond shall be exempt from taxation under this title unless such interest is exempt from tax under this title without regard to any provision of law which is not contained in this title and which is not contained in a revenue Act.

(2) CERTAIN PRIOR EXEMPTIONS.—

(A) PRIOR EXEMPTIONS CONTINUED.—For purposes of this title, notwithstanding any provision of this part, any bond the interest on which is exempt from taxation under this title by reason of any provision of law (other than a provision of this title) which is in effect on January 6, 1983 shall be treated as a bond described in section 103(a).

(B) ADDITIONAL REQUIREMENTS FOR BONDS ISSUED AFTER 1983.—Subparagraph (A) shall not apply to a bond (not described in subparagraph (C)) issued after 1983 if the appropriate requirements of this part (or the corresponding provisions of prior law) are not met with respect to such bond.

(C) DESCRIPTION OF BOND.—A bond is described in this subparagraph (and treated as described in subparagraph (A)) if—

(i) such bond is issued pursuant to the Northwest Power Act (16 U.S.C. 839(d), as in effect on July 18, 1984;

(ii) such bond is issued pursuant to section 608(a)(6)(A) of Public Law 97-468, as in effect on the date of the enactment of the Tax Reform Act of 1986; or

(iii) such bond is issued before June 19, 1984 under section 11(b) of the United States Housing Act of 1937.

[Sec. 149(d)]

(d) ADVANCE REFUNDINGS.—

(1) IN GENERAL.—Nothing in section 103(a) or in any other provision of law shall be construed to provide an exemption from Federal income tax for interest on any bond issued as part of an issue described in paragraph (2), (3), or (4).

(2) CERTAIN PRIVATE ACTIVITY BONDS.—An issue is described in this paragraph if any bond (issued as part of such issue) is issued to advance refund a private activity bond (other than a qualified 501(c)(3) bond).

(3) OTHER BONDS.—

(A) IN GENERAL.—An issue is described in this paragraph if any bond (issued as part of such issue), hereinafter in this paragraph referred to as the "refunding bond," is issued to advance refund a bond unless—

(i) the refunding bond is only—

(I) the 1st advance refunding of the original bond if the original bond is issued after 1985, or

(II) the 1st or 2nd advance refunding of the original bond if the original bond was issued before 1986,

(ii) in the case of refunded bonds issued before 1986, the refunded bond is redeemed not later than the earliest date on which such bond may be redeemed at par or at a premium of 3 percent or less,

(iii) in the case of refunded bonds issued after 1985, the refunded bond is redeemed not later than the earliest date on which such bond may be redeemed,

(iv) the initial temporary period under section 148(c) ends—

(I) with respect to the proceeds of the refunding bond not later than 30 days after the date of issue of such bond, and

(II) with respect to the proceeds of the refunded bond on the date of issue of the refunding bond, and

(v) in the case of refunded bonds to which section 148(e) did not apply, on and after the date of issue of the refunding bond, the amount of proceeds of the refunded bond invested in higher yielding investments (as defined in section 148(b)) which are nonpurpose investments (as defined in section 148(f)(6)(A)) does not exceed—

(I) the amount so invested as part of a reasonably required reserve or replacement fund or during an allowable temporary period, and

(II) the amount which is equal to the lesser of 5 percent of the proceeds of the issue of which the refunded bond is a part or $100,000 (to the extent such amount is allocable to the refunded bond).

(B) SPECIAL RULES FOR REDEMPTIONS.—

(i) ISSUER MUST REDEEM ONLY IF DEBT SERVICE SAVINGS.—Clause (ii) and (iii) of subparagraph (A) shall apply only if the issuer may realize present value debt service savings (determined without regard to administrative expenses) in connection with the issue of which the refunding bond is a part.

(ii) REDEMPTIONS NOT REQUIRED BEFORE 90TH DAY.—For purposes of clauses (ii) and (iii) of subparagraph (A), the earliest date referred to in such clauses shall not be earlier than the 90th day after the date of issuance of the refunding bond.

(4) ABUSIVE TRANSACTIONS PROHIBITED.—An issue is described in this paragraph if any bond (issued as part of such issue) is issued to advance refund another bond and a device is employed in connection with the issuance of such issue to obtain a material financial advantage (based on arbitrage) apart from savings attributable to lower interest rates.

(5) ADVANCE REFUNDING.—For purposes of this part, a bond shall be treated as issued to advance refund another bond if it is issued more than 90 days before the redemption of the refunded bond.

(6) SPECIAL RULES FOR PURPOSES OF PARAGRAPH (3).—For purposes of paragraph (3), bonds issued before the date of the enactment of this subsection shall be taken into account under subparagraph (A)(i) thereof except—

(A) a refunding which occurred before 1986 shall be treated as an advance refunding only if the refunding bond was issued more than 180 days before the redemption of the refunded bond, and

(B) a bond issued before 1986, shall be treated as advance refunded no more than once before March 15, 1986.

(7) REGULATIONS.—The Secretary shall prescribe such regulations as may be necessary or appropriate to carry out the purposes of this subsection.

[Sec. 149(e)]

(e) INFORMATION REPORTING.—

(1) IN GENERAL.—Nothing in section 103(a) or any other provision of law shall be construed to provide an exemption from Federal income tax for interest on any bond unless such bond satisfies the requirements of paragraph (2).

(2) INFORMATION REPORTING REQUIREMENTS.—A bond satisfies the requirements of this paragraph if the issuer submits to the Secretary, not later than the 15th day of the 2d calendar month after the close of the calendar quarter in which the bond is issued (or such later time as the Secretary may prescribe with respect to any portion of the statement), a statement concerning the issue of which the bond is a part which contains—

(A) the name and address of the issuer,

(B) the date of issue, the amount of net proceeds of the issue, the stated interest rate, term, and face amount of each bond which is part of the issue, the amount of issuance costs of the issue, and the amount of reserves of the issue,

(C) where required, the name of the applicable elected representative who approved the issue, or a description of the voter referendum by which the issue was approved,

(D) the name, address, and employer identification number of—

(i) each initial principal user of any facility provided with the proceeds of the issue,

(ii) the common parent of any affiliated group of corporations (within the meaning of section 1504(a)) of which such initial principal user is a member, and

(iii) if the issue is treated as a separate issue under section 144(a)(6)(A), any person treated as a principal user under section 144(a)(6)(B),

(E) a description of any property to be financed from the proceeds of the issue,

(F) a certification by a State official designated by State law (or, where there is no such official, the Governor) that the bond meets the requirements of section 146 (relating to cap on private activity bonds), if applicable, and

(G) such other information as the Secretary may require.

Subparagraphs (C) and (D) shall not apply to any bond which is not a private activity bond. The Secretary may provide that certain information specified in the 1st sentence need not be included in the statement with respect to an issue where the inclusion of such information is not necessary to carry out the purposes of this subsection.

(3) EXTENSION OF TIME.—The Secretary may grant an extension of time for the filing of any statement required under paragraph (2) if the failure to file in a timely fashion is not due to willful neglect.

Amendments

• 1988, Technical and Miscellaneous Revenue Act of 1988 (P.L. 100-647)

P.L. 100-647, §1013(a)(22):

Amended Code Sec. 149(e)(3) by striking out "there is reasonable cause for the failure to file such statement in a timely fashion" and inserting in lieu thereof "the failure to file in a timely fashion is not due to willful neglect". **Effective** as if included in the provision of P.L. 99-514 to which it relates.

P.L. 100-647, §1013(b)(1), provides:

Section 149(c) of the 1986 Code applies to bonds issued after December 31, 1986.

• 1986, Tax Reform Act of 1986 (P.L. 99-514)

P.L. 99-514, §1301(b):

Amended part IV of subchapter B of chapter 1 by adding Code Sec. 149. **Effective**, generally, for bonds issued after 8-15-86. However, for transitional rules, see Act Secs. 1312-1318 in the amendments for Code Sec. 103.

[Sec. 149(f)]

(f) TREATMENT OF CERTAIN POOLED FINANCING BONDS.—

(1) IN GENERAL.—Section 103(a) shall not apply to any pooled financing bond unless, with respect to the issue of which such bond is a part, the requirements of paragraphs (2), (3), (4), and (5) are met.

(2) REASONABLE EXPECTATION REQUIREMENT.—

(A) IN GENERAL.—The requirements of this paragraph are met with respect to an issue if the issuer reasonably expects that—

(i) as of the close of the 1-year period beginning on the date of issuance of the issue, at least 30 percent of the net proceeds of the issue (as of the close of such period) will have been used directly or indirectly to make or finance loans to ultimate borrowers, and

(ii) as of the close of the 3-year period beginning on such date of issuance, at least 95 percent of the net proceeds of the issue (as of the close of such period) will have been so used.

(B) CERTAIN FACTORS MAY NOT BE TAKEN INTO ACCOUNT IN DETERMINING EXPECTATIONS.—Expectations as to changes in interest rates or in the provisions of this title (or in the regulations or rulings thereunder) may not be taken into account in determining whether expectations are reasonable for purposes of this paragraph.

(C) NET PROCEEDS.—For purposes of subparagraph (A), the term "net proceeds" has the meaning given such term by section 150 but shall not include proceeds used to finance issuance costs and shall not include proceeds necessary to pay interest (during such period) on the bonds which are part of the issue.

(D) REFUNDING BONDS.—For purposes of subparagraph (A), in the case of a refunding bond, the date of issuance taken into account is the date of issuance of the original bond.

(3) COST OF ISSUANCE PAYMENT REQUIREMENTS.—The requirements of this paragraph are met with respect to an issue if—

(A) the payment of legal and underwriting costs associated with the issuance of the issue is not contingent, and

(B) at least 95 percent of the reasonably expected legal and underwriting costs associated with the issuance of the issue are paid not later than the 180th day after the date of the issuance of the issue.

(4) WRITTEN LOAN COMMITMENT REQUIREMENT.—

(A) IN GENERAL.—The requirement of this paragraph is met with respect to an issue if the issuer receives prior to issuance written loan commitments identifying the ultimate potential borrowers of at least 30 percent of the net proceeds of such issue.

(B) EXCEPTION.—Subparagraph (A) shall not apply with respect to any issuer which—

(i) is a State (or an integral part of a State) issuing pooled financing bonds to make or finance loans to subordinate governmental units of such State, or

(ii) is a State-created entity providing financing for water-infrastructure projects through the federally-sponsored State revolving fund program.

(5) REDEMPTION REQUIREMENT.—The requirement of this paragraph is met if to the extent that less than the percentage of the proceeds of an issue required to be used under clause (i) or (ii) of paragraph (2)(A) is used by the close of the period identified in such clause, the issuer uses an amount of proceeds equal to the excess of—

(A) the amount required to be used under such clause, over

(B) the amount actually used by the close of such period,

to redeem outstanding bonds within 90 days after the end of such period.

(6) POOLED FINANCING BOND.—For purposes of this subsection—

(A) IN GENERAL.—The term "pooled financing bond" means any bond issued as part of an issue more than $5,000,000 of the proceeds of which are reasonably expected (at the time of the issuance of the bonds) to be used (or are intentionally used) directly or indirectly to make or finance loans to 2 or more ultimate borrowers.

(B) EXCEPTIONS.—Such term shall not include any bond if—

(i) section 146 applies to the issue of which such bond is a part (other than by reason of section 141(b)(5)) or would apply but for section 146(i), or

(ii) section 143(l)(3) applies to such issue.

(7) DEFINITION OF LOAN; TREATMENT OF MIXED USE ISSUES.—

(A) LOAN.—For purposes of this subsection, the term "loan" does not include—

(i) any loan which is a nonpurpose investment (within the meaning of section 148(f)(6)(A), determined without regard to section 148(b)(3)), and

(ii) any use of proceeds by an agency of the issuer unless such agency is a political subdivision or instrumentality of the issuer.

(B) PORTION OF ISSUE TO BE USED FOR LOANS TREATED AS SEPARATE ISSUE.—If only a portion of the proceeds of an issue is reasonably expected (at the time of issuance of the bond) to be used (or is intentionally used) as described in paragraph (6)(A), such portion and the other portion of such issue shall be treated as separate issues for purposes of determining whether such portion meets the requirements of this subsection.

Amendments

• 2006, Tax Increase Prevention and Reconciliation Act of 2005 (P.L. 109-222)

P.L. 109-222, §508(a):

Amended Code Sec. 149(f)(2)(A). **Effective** for bonds issued after 5-17-2006. Prior to amendment, Code Sec. 149(f)(2)(A) read as follows:

(A) IN GENERAL.—The requirements of this paragraph are met with respect to an issue if the issuer reasonably expects that as of the close of the 3-year period beginning on the date of issuance of the issue, at least 95 percent of the net proceeds of the issue (as of the close of such period) will have been used directly or indirectly to make or finance loans to ultimate borrowers.

P.L. 109-222, §508(b):

Amended Code Sec. 149(f) by redesignating paragraphs (4) and (5) as paragraphs (6) and (7), respectively, and by inserting after paragraph (3) new paragraphs (4) and (5). **Effective** for bonds issued after 5-17-2006.

P.L. 109-222, §508(d)(1):

Amended Code Sec. 149(f)(1) by striking "paragraphs (2) and (3)" and inserting "paragraphs (2), (3), (4), and (5)". **Effective** for bonds issued after 5-17-2006.

P.L. 109-222, §508(d)(2):

Amended Code Sec. 149(f)(7)(B), as redesignated by Act Sec. 508(b), by striking "paragraph (4)(A)" and inserting "paragraph (6)(A)". **Effective** for bonds issued after 5-17-2006.

• 1988, Technical and Miscellaneous Revenue Act of 1988 (P.L. 100-647)

P.L. 100-647, §5051(a):

Amended Code Sec. 149 by adding at the end thereof a new subsection (f). **Effective**, generally, for bonds issued after 10-21-88. However see the special rule provided in Act Sec. 5051(b)(2), below.

P.L. 100-647, §5051(b)(2), provides:

(b)(2) SPECIAL RULE FOR REFUNDING BONDS.—In the case of a bond issued to refund a bond issued before October 22, 1988—

(A) if the 3-year period described in section 149(f)(2)(A) of the 1986 Code would (but for this paragraph) expire on or before October 22, 1989, such period shall expire on October 21, 1990, and

(B) if such period expires after October 22, 1989, the portion of the proceeds of the issue of which the refunded bond is a part which is available (on the date of issuance of the refunding issue) to provide loans shall be treated as proceeds of a separate issue (issued after October 21, 1988) for purposes of applying section 149(f) of the 1986 Code.

[Sec. 149(g)]

(g) TREATMENT OF HEDGE BONDS.—

(1) IN GENERAL.—Section 103(a) shall not apply to any hedge bond unless, with respect to the issue of which such bond is a part—

(A) the requirement of paragraph (2) is met, and

(B) the requirement of subsection (f)(3) is met.

(2) REASONABLE EXPECTATIONS AS TO WHEN PROCEEDS WILL BE SPENT.—An issue meets the requirement of this paragraph if the issuer reasonably expects that—

(A) 10 percent of the spendable proceeds of the issue will be spent for the governmental purposes of the issue within the 1-year period beginning on the date the bonds are issued,

(B) 30 percent of the spendable proceeds of the issue will be spent for such purposes within the 2-year period beginning on such date,

(C) 60 percent of the spendable proceeds of the issue will be spent for such purposes within the 3-year period beginning on such date, and

(D) 85 percent of the spendable proceeds of the issue will be spent for such purposes within the 5-year period beginning on such date.

(3) HEDGE BOND.—

(A) IN GENERAL.—For purposes of this subsection, the term "hedge bond" means any bond issued as part of an issue unless—

(i) the issuer reasonably expects that 85 percent of the spendable proceeds of the issue will be used to carry out the governmental purposes of the issue within the 3-year period beginning on the date the bonds are issued, and

(ii) not more than 50 percent of the proceeds of the issue are invested in nonpurpose investments (as defined in section 148(f)(6)(A)) having a substantially guaranteed yield for 4 years or more.

(B) EXCEPTION FOR INVESTMENT IN TAX-EXEMPT BONDS NOT SUBJECT TO MINIMUM TAX.—

(i) IN GENERAL.—Such term shall not include any bond issued as part of an issue 95 percent of the net proceeds of which are invested in bonds—

(I) the interest on which is not includible in gross income under section 103, and

(II) which are not specified private activity bonds (as defined in section 57(a)(5)(C)).

(ii) AMOUNTS IN BONA FIDE DEBT SERVICE FUND.—Amounts in a bona fide debt service fund shall be treated as invested in bonds described in clause (i).

(iii) AMOUNTS HELD PENDING REINVESTMENT OR REDEMPTION.—Amounts held for not more than 30 days pending reinvestment or bond redemption shall be treated as invested in bonds described in clause (i).

(C) EXCEPTION FOR REFUNDING BONDS.—

(i) IN GENERAL.—A refunding bond shall be treated as meeting the requirements of this subsection only if the original bond met such requirements.

(ii) GENERAL RULE FOR REFUNDING OF PRE-EFFECTIVE DATE BONDS.—A refunding bond shall be treated as meeting the requirements of this subsection if—

(I) this subsection does not apply to the original bond,

(II) the average maturity date of the issue of which the refunding bond is a part is not later than the average maturity date of the bonds to be refunded by such issue, and

(III) the amount of the refunding bond does not exceed the outstanding amount of the refunded bond.

(iii) REFUNDING OF PRE-EFFECTIVE DATE BONDS ENTITLED TO 5-YEAR TEMPORARY PERIOD.—A refunding bond shall be treated as meeting the requirements of this subsection if—

(I) this subsection does not apply to the original bond,

(II) the issuer reasonably expected that 85 percent of the spendable proceeds of the issue of which the original bond is a part would be used to carry out the governmental purposes of the issue within the 5-year period beginning on the date the original bonds were issued but did not reasonably expect that 85 percent of such proceeds would be so spent within the 3-year period beginning on such date, and

(III) at least 85 percent of the spendable proceeds of the original issue (and all other prior original issues issued to finance the governmental purposes of such issue) were spent before the date the refunding bonds are issued.

(4) SPECIAL RULES.—For purposes of this subsection—

(A) CONSTRUCTION PERIOD IN EXCESS OF 5 YEARS.—The Secretary may, at the request of any issuer, provide that the requirement of paragraph (2) shall be treated as met with respect to the portion of the spendable proceeds of an issue which is to be used for any construction project having a construction period in excess of 5 years if it is reasonably expected that such proceeds will be spent over a reasonable construction schedule specified in such request.

(B) RULES FOR DETERMINING EXPECTATIONS.—The rules of subsection (f)(2)(B) shall apply.

(5) REGULATIONS.—The Secretary may prescribe regulations to prevent the avoidance of the rules of this subsection, including through the aggregation of projects within a single issue.

Amendments

• 1996, Small Business Job Protection Act of 1996 (P.L. 104-188)

P.L. 104-188, §1704(b)(1):

Amended Code Sec. 149(g)(3)(B)(iii). **Effective** as if included in the amendments made by section 7651 of P.L. 101-239. Prior to amendment, Code Sec. 149(g)(3)(B)(iii) read as follows:

(iii) INVESTMENT EARNINGS HELD PENDING REINVESTMENT.—Investment earnings held for not more than 30 days pending reinvestment shall be treated as invested in bonds described in clause (i).

• 1989, Omnibus Budget Reconciliation Act of 1989 (P.L. 101-239)

P.L. 101-239, §7651(a):

Amended Code Sec. 149 by adding at the end thereof a new subsection (g). For the **effective** date, see Act Sec. 7651(b), below.

P.L. 101-239, §7651(b), provides:

(b) EFFECTIVE DATE.—

(1) IN GENERAL.—Except as otherwise provided in this subsection, the amendment made by subsection (a) shall apply to bonds issued after September 14, 1989.

(2) BONDS SOLD BEFORE SEPTEMBER 15, 1989.—The amendment made by subsection (a) shall not apply to any bond sold before September 15, 1989, and issued before October 15, 1989.

(3) BONDS WITH RESPECT TO WHICH PRELIMINARY OFFERING MATERIALS MAILED.—The amendment made by subsection (a) shall not apply to any issue issued after the date of the enactment of this Act if the preliminary offering materials with respect to such issue were mailed (or otherwise delivered) to members of the underwriting syndicate before September 15, 1989.

(4) CERTAIN OTHER BONDS.—In the case of a bond issued before January 1, 1991, with respect to which official action was taken (or a series of official actions were taken), or other

comparable preliminary approval was given, before November 18, 1989, demonstrating an intent to issue such bonds in a maximum specified amount for such issue or with a maximum specified amount of net proceeds of such issue, the issuer may elect to apply section 149(g)(2) of the Internal Revenue Code of 1986 (as added by this section) by substituting "15 percent" for "10 percent" in subparagraph (A) and "50 percent" for "60 percent" in subparagraph (C).

(5) BONDS ISSUED TO FINANCE SELF-INSURANCE FUNDS.—The amendment made by subsection (a) shall not apply to any bonds issued before July 1, 1990, to finance a self-insurance fund if official action was taken (or a series of official actions were taken), or other comparable preliminary approval was given, before September 15, 1989, demonstrating an intent to issue such bonds in a maximum specified amount for such issue or with a maximum specified amount of net proceeds of such issue.

Subpart C—Definitions and Special Rules

[Sec. 150]

SEC. 150. DEFINITIONS AND SPECIAL RULES.

[Sec. 150(a)]

(a) GENERAL RULE.—For purposes of this part—

(1) BOND.—The term "bond" includes any obligation.

(2) GOVERNMENTAL UNIT NOT TO INCLUDE FEDERAL GOVERNMENT.—The term "governmental unit" does not include the United States or any agency or instrumentality thereof.

(3) NET PROCEEDS.—The term "net proceeds" means, with respect to any issue, the proceeds of such issue reduced by amounts in a reasonably required reserve or replacement fund.

(4) 501(c)(3) ORGANIZATION.—The term "501(c)(3) organization" means any organization described in section 501(c)(3) and exempt from tax under section 501(a).

(5) OWNERSHIP OF PROPERTY.—Property shall be treated as owned by a governmental unit if it is owned on behalf of such unit.

(6) TAX-EXEMPT BOND.—The term "tax-exempt" means, with respect to any bond (or issue), that the interest on such bond (or on the bonds issued as part of such issue) is excluded from gross income.

[Sec. 150(b)]

(b) CHANGE IN USE OF FACILITIES FINANCED WITH TAX-EXEMPT PRIVATE ACTIVITY BONDS.—

(1) MORTGAGE REVENUE BONDS.—

(A) IN GENERAL.—In the case of any residence with respect to which financing is provided from the proceeds of a tax-exempt qualified mortgage bond or qualified veterans' mortgage bond, if there is a continuous period of at least 1 year during which such residence is not the principal residence of at least 1 of the mortgagors who received such financing, then no deduction shall be allowed under this chapter for interest on such financing which accrues on or after the date such period began and before the date such residence is again the principal residence of at least 1 of the mortgagors who received such financing.

(B) EXCEPTION.—Subparagraph (A) shall not apply to the extent the Secretary determines that its application would result in undue hardship and that the failure to meet the requirements of subparagraph (A) resulted from circumstances beyond the mortgagor's control.

(2) QUALIFIED RESIDENTIAL RENTAL PROJECTS.—In the case of any project for residential rental property—

(A) with respect to which financing is provided from the proceeds of any private activity bond which, when issued, purported to be a tax-exempt bond described in paragraph (7) of section 142(a), and

(B) which does not meet the requirements of section 142(d),

no deduction shall be allowed under this chapter for interest on such financing which accrues during the period beginning on the 1st day of the taxable year in which such project fails to meet such requirements and ending on the date such project meets such requirements. If the provisions of prior law corresponding to section 142(d) apply to a refunded bond, such provisions shall apply (in lieu of section 142(d)) to the refunding bond.

(3) QUALIFIED 501(c)(3) BONDS.—

(A) IN GENERAL.—In the case of any facility with respect to which financing is provided from the proceeds of any private activity bond which, when issued, purported to be a tax-exempt qualified 501(c)(3) bond, if any portion of such facility—

(i) is used in a trade or business of any person other than a 501(c)(3) organization or a governmental unit, but

(ii) continues to be owned by a 501(c)(3) organization,

then the owner of such portion shall be treated for purposes of this title as engaged in an unrelated trade or business (as defined in section 513) with respect to such portion. The amount of gross income attributable to such portion for any period shall not be less than the fair rental value of such portion for such period.

(B) DENIAL OF DEDUCTION FOR INTEREST.—No deduction shall be allowed under this chapter for interest on financing described in subparagraph (A) which accrues during the period beginning on the date such facility is used as described in subparagraph (A)(i) and ending on the date such facility is not so used.

(4) CERTAIN EXEMPT FACILITY BONDS AND SMALL ISSUE BONDS.—

(A) IN GENERAL.—In the case of any facility with respect to which financing is provided from the proceeds of any private activity bond to which this paragraph applies, if such facility is not used for a purpose for which a tax-exempt bond could be issued on the date of such issue, no deduction shall be allowed under this chapter for interest on such financing which accrues during the period beginning on the date such facility is not so used and ending on the date such facility is so used.

(B) BONDS TO WHICH PARAGRAPH APPLIES.—This paragraph applies to any private activity bond which, when issued, purported to be a tax-exempt exempt facility bond described in a paragraph (other than paragraph (7)) of section 142(a) or a qualified small issue bond.

(5) FACILITIES REQUIRED TO BE OWNED BY GOVERNMENTAL UNITS OR 501(c)(3) ORGANIZATIONS.—If—

(A) financing is provided with respect to any facility from the proceeds of any private activity bond which, when issued, purported to be a tax-exempt bond,

(B) such facility is required to be owned by a governmental unit or a 501(c)(3) organization as a condition of such tax exemption, and

(C) such facility is not so owned,

then no deduction shall be allowed under this chapter for interest on such financing which accrues during the period beginning on the date such facility is not so owned and ending on the date such facility is so owned.

(6) SMALL ISSUE BONDS WHICH EXCEED CAPITAL EXPENDITURE LIMITATION.—In the case of any financing provided from the proceeds of any bond which, when issued, purported to be a qualified small issue bond, no deduction shall be allowed under this chapter for interest on such financing which accrues during the period such bond is not a qualified small issue bond.

Amendments

• 1988, Technical and Miscellaneous Revenue Act of 1988 (P.L. 100-647)

P.L. 100-647, §1013(a)(23)(A):

Amended Code Sec. 150(b)(4)(B) by inserting before the period "or a qualified small issue bond". **Effective** as if included in the provision of P.L. 99-514 to which it relates.

P.L. 100-647, §1013(a)(23)(B):

Amended Code Sec. 150(b)(4) by inserting "AND SMALL ISSUE BONDS" after "EXEMPT FACILITY BONDS" in the heading. **Effective** as if included in the provision of P.L. 99-514 to which it relates.

P.L. 100-647, §1013(a)(23)(C):

Amended Code Sec. 150(b)(1)(A) by inserting "tax-exempt" before "qualified mortgage bond". **Effective** as if included in the provision of P.L. 99-514 to which it relates.

P.L. 100-647, §1013(a)(30):

Amended Code Sec. 150(b)(1)(A) by inserting before the period "and before the date such residence is again the principal residence of at least 1 of the mortgagors who received such financing". **Effective** as if included in the provision of P.L. 99-514 to which it relates.

P.L. 100-647, §1013(a)(31):

Amended Code Sec. 150(b)(2)(A) by striking out "described paragraph" and inserting in lieu thereof "described in paragraph". **Effective** as if included in the provision of P.L. 99-514 to which it relates.

P.L. 100-647, §1013(a)(32):

Amended Code Sec. 150(b)(2) by adding at the end thereof a new sentence. **Effective** as if included in the provision of P.L. 99-514 to which it relates.

P.L. 100-647, §1013(a)(33):

Amended Code Sec. 150(b) by adding at the end thereof a new paragraph (6). **Effective** as if included in the provision of P.L. 99-514 to which it relates.

[Sec. 150(c)]

(c) EXCEPTION AND SPECIAL RULES FOR PURPOSES OF SUBSECTION (b).—For purposes of subsection (b)—

(1) EXCEPTION.—Any use with respect to facilities financed with proceeds of an issue which are not required to be used for the exempt purpose of such issue shall not be taken into account.

(2) TREATMENT OF AMOUNTS OTHER THAN INTEREST.—If the amounts payable for the use of a facility are not interest, subsection (b) shall apply to such amounts as if they were interest but only to the extent such amounts for any period do not exceed the amount of interest accrued on the bond financing for such period.

(3) USE OF PORTION OF FACILITY.—In the case of any person which uses only a portion of the facility, only the interest accruing on the financing allocable to such portion shall be taken into account by such person.

(4) CESSATION WITH RESPECT TO PORTION OF FACILITY.—In the case of any facility where part but not all of the facility is not used for an exempt purpose, only the interest accruing on the financing allocable to such part shall be taken into account.

(5) REGULATIONS.—The Secretary shall prescribe such regulations as may be necessary or appropriate to carry out the purposes of this subsection and subsection (b).

[Sec. 150(d)]

(d) QUALIFIED SCHOLARSHIP FUNDING BOND.—For purposes of this part and section 103—

(1) TREATMENT AS STATE OR LOCAL BOND.—A qualified scholarship funding bond shall be treated as a State or local bond.

(2) QUALIFIED SCHOLARSHIP FUNDING BOND DEFINED.—The term "qualified scholarship funding bond" means a bond issued by a corporation which—

(A) is a corporation not for profit established and operated exclusively for the purpose of acquiring student loan notes incurred under the Higher Education Act of 1965, and

(B) is organized at the request of the State or 1 or more political subdivisions thereof or is requested to exercise such power by 1 or more political subdivisions and required by its corporate charter and bylaws, or required by State law, to devote any income (after payment of expenses, debt service, and the creation of reserves for the same) to the purchase of additional student loan notes or to pay over any income to the United States.

(3) ELECTION TO CEASE STATUS AS QUALIFIED SCHOLARSHIP FUNDING CORPORATION.—

(A) IN GENERAL.—Any qualified scholarship funding bond, and qualified student loan bond, outstanding on the date of the issuer's election under this paragraph (and any bond (or series of bonds) issued to refund such a bond) shall not fail to be a tax-exempt bond solely because the issuer ceases to be described in subparagraphs (A) and (B) of paragraph (2) if the issuer meets the requirements of subparagraphs (B) and (C) of this paragraph.

(B) ASSETS AND LIABILITIES OF ISSUER TRANSFERRED TO TAXABLE SUBSIDIARY.—The requirements of this subparagraph are met by an issuer if—

(i) all of the student loan notes of the issuer and other assets pledged to secure the repayment of qualified scholarship funding bond indebtedness of the issuer are transferred to another corporation within a reasonable period after the election is made under this paragraph;

(ii) such transferee corporation assumes or otherwise provides for the payment of all of the qualified scholarship funding bond indebtedness of the issuer within a reasonable period after the election is made under this paragraph;

(iii) to the extent permitted by law, such transferee corporation assumes all of the responsibilities, and succeeds to all of the rights, of the issuer under the issuer's agreements with the Secretary of Education in respect of student loans;

(iv) immediately after such transfer, the issuer, together with any other issuer which has made an election under this paragraph in respect of such transferee, hold all of the senior stock in such transferee corporation; and

(v) such transferee corporation is not exempt from tax under this chapter.

(C) ISSUER TO OPERATE AS INDEPENDENT ORGANIZATION DESCRIBED IN SECTION 501(c)(3).—The requirements of this subparagraph are met by an issuer if, within a reasonable period after the transfer referred to in subparagraph (B)—

(i) the issuer is described in section 501(c)(3) and exempt from tax under section 501(a);

(ii) the issuer no longer is described in subparagraphs (A) and (B) of paragraph (2); and

(iii) at least 80 percent of the members of the board of directors of the issuer are independent members.

(D) SENIOR STOCK.—For purposes of this paragraph, the term "senior stock" means stock—

(i) which participates pro rata and fully in the equity value of the corporation with all other common stock of the corporation but which has the right to payment of liquidation proceeds prior to payment of liquidation proceeds in respect of other common stock of the corporation;

(ii) which has a fixed right upon liquidation and upon redemption to an amount equal to the greater of—

(I) the fair market value of such stock on the date of liquidation or redemption (whichever is applicable); or

(II) the fair market value of all assets transferred in exchange for such stock and reduced by the amount of all liabilities of the corporation which has made an election under this paragraph assumed by the transferee corporation in such transfer;

(iii) the holder of which has the right to require the transferee corporation to redeem on a date that is not later than 10 years after the date on which an election under this paragraph was made and pursuant to such election such stock was issued; and

(iv) in respect of which, during the time such stock is outstanding, there is not outstanding any equity interest in the corporation having any liquidation, redemption or dividend rights in the corporation which are superior to those of such stock.

(E) INDEPENDENT MEMBER.—The term "independent member" means a member of the board of directors of the issuer who (except for services as a member of such board) receives no compensation directly or indirectly—

(i) for services performed in connection with such transferee corporation, or

(ii) for services as a member of the board of directors or as an officer of such transferee corporation.

For purposes of clause (ii), the term "officer" includes any individual having powers or responsibilities similar to those of officers.

(F) COORDINATION WITH CERTAIN PRIVATE FOUNDATION TAXES.—For purposes of sections 4942 (relating to the excise tax on a failure to distribute income) and 4943 (relating to the excise tax on excess business holdings), the transferee corporation referred to in subparagraph (B) shall be treated as a functionally related business (within the meaning of section 4942(j)(4)) with respect to the issuer during the period commencing with the date on which an election is made under this paragraph and ending on the date that is the earlier of—

(i) the last day of the last taxable year for which more than 50 percent of the gross income of such transferee corporation is derived from, or more than 50 percent of the assets (by value) of such transferee corporation consists of, student loan notes incurred under the Higher Education Act of 1965; or

(ii) the last day of the taxable year of the issuer during which occurs the date which is 10 years after the date on which the election under this paragraph is made.

(G) ELECTION.—An election under this paragraph may be revoked only with the consent of the Secretary.

Amendments

• 1996, Small Business Job Protection Act of 1996 (P.L. 104-188)

P.L. 104-188, §1614(a):

Amended Code Sec. 150(d) by adding at the end a new paragraph (3). **Effective** 8-20-96.

• 1988, Technical and Miscellaneous Revenue Act of 1988 (P.L. 100-647)

P.L. 100-647, §1013(b)(1), provides:

Section 150(d) of the 1986 Code applies to payments made after August 15, 1986.

[Sec. 150(e)]

(e) BONDS OF CERTAIN VOLUNTEER FIRE DEPARTMENTS.—For purposes of this part and section 103—

(1) IN GENERAL.—A bond of a volunteer fire department shall be treated as a bond of a political subdivision of a State if—

(A) such department is a qualified volunteer fire department with respect to an area within the jurisdiction of such political subdivision, and

(B) such bond is issued as part of an issue 95 percent or more of the net proceeds of which are to be used for the acquisition, construction, reconstruction, or improvement of a firehouse (including land which is functionally related and subordinate thereto) or firetruck used or to be used by such department.

(2) QUALIFIED VOLUNTEER FIRE DEPARTMENT.—For purposes of this subsection, the term "qualified volunteer fire department" means, with respect to a political subdivision of a State, any organization—

(A) which is organized and operated to provide firefighting or emergency medical services for persons in an area (within the jurisdiction of such political subdivision) which is not provided with any other firefighting services, and

(B) which is required (by written agreement) by the political subdivision to furnish firefighting services in such area.

For purposes of subparagraph (A), other firefighting services provided in an area shall be disregarded in determining whether an organization is a qualified volunteer fire department if such other firefighting services are provided by a qualified volunteer fire department (determined with the application of this sentence) and such organization and the provider of such other services have been continuously providing firefighting services to such area since January 1, 1981.

(3) TREATMENT AS PRIVATE ACTIVITY BONDS ONLY FOR CERTAIN PURPOSES.—Bonds which are part of an issue which meets the requirements of paragraph (1) shall not be treated as private activity bonds except for purposes of sections 147(f) and 149(d).

Amendments

• 1988, Technical and Miscellaneous Revenue Act of 1988 (P.L. 100-647)

P.L. 100-647, §1013(a)(24)(A):

Amended Code Sec. 150(e) by adding new paragraph (3) **Effective** for bonds issued after 10-21-88.

P.L. 100-647, §6182(a):

Amended Code Sec. 150(e)(2) by adding at the end thereof a new sentence. **Effective** for bonds issued after 11-10-88.

P.L. 100-647, §6182(b):

Amended Code Sec. 150(e)(1)(B) by inserting "(including land which is functionally related and subordinate thereto)" after "a firehouse". **Effective** for bonds issued after 11-10-88.

• 1986, Tax Reform Act of 1986 (P.L. 99-514)

P.L. 99-514, §1301(b):

Amended Part IV of subchapter B of chapter 1 by adding Code Sec. 150. **Effective**, generally, for bonds issued after 8-15-86. However, for an exception, see Act Sec. 1311(c), below.

P.L. 99-514, §1311(c), provides:

(c) Changes in Use, Etc., for Facilities Financed with Private Activity Bonds.—Subsection (b) of section 150 of the 1986 Code shall apply to changes in use (and ownership) after August 15, 1986, but only with respect to financing (including refinancings) provided after such date.

For transitional rules, see Act Secs. 1312-1318 in the amendments for Code Sec. 103.

PART V—DEDUCTIONS FOR PERSONAL EXEMPTIONS

[Sec. 151]

SEC. 151. ALLOWANCE OF DEDUCTIONS FOR PERSONAL EXEMPTIONS.

[Sec. 151(a)]

(a) ALLOWANCE OF DEDUCTIONS.—In the case of an individual, the exemptions provided by this section shall be allowed as deductions in computing taxable income.

[Sec. 151(b)]

(b) TAXPAYER AND SPOUSE.—An exemption of the exemption amount for the taxpayer; and an additional exemption of the exemption amount for the spouse of the taxpayer if a joint return is not made by the taxpayer and his spouse, and if the spouse, for the calendar year in which the taxable year of the taxpayer begins, has no gross income and is not the dependent of another taxpayer.

[Sec. 151(c)]

(c) ADDITIONAL EXEMPTION FOR DEPENDENTS.—An exemption of the exemption amount for each individual who is a dependent (as defined in section 152) of the taxpayer for the taxable year.

Amendments

• 2004, Working Families Tax Relief Act of 2004 (P.L. 108-311)

P.L. 108-311, §206:

Amended Code Sec.151(c). **Effective** for tax years beginning after 12-31-2004. Prior to amendment, Code Sec. 151(c) read as follows:

(c) ADDITIONAL EXEMPTION FOR DEPENDENTS.—

(1) IN GENERAL.—An exemption of the exemption amount for each dependent (as defined in section 152)—

(A) whose gross income for the calendar year in which the taxable year of the taxpayer begins is less than the exemption amount, or

(B) who is a child of the taxpayer and who (i) has not attained the age of 19 at the close of the calendar year in which the taxable year of the taxpayer begins, or (ii) is a student who has not attained the age of 24 at the close of such calendar year.

(2) EXEMPTION DENIED IN CASE OF CERTAIN MARRIED DEPENDENTS.—No exemption shall be allowed under this subsection for any dependent who has made a joint return with his spouse under section 6013 for the taxable year beginning in the calendar year in which the taxable year of the taxpayer begins.

(3) CHILD DEFINED.—For purposes of paragraph (1) (B), the term "child" means an individual who (within the meaning of section 152) is a son, stepson, daughter, or stepdaughter of the taxpayer.

(4) STUDENT DEFINED.—For purposes of paragraph (1) (B) (ii), the term "student" means an individual who during each of 5 calendar months during the calendar year in which the taxable year of the taxpayer begins—

(A) is a full-time student at an educational organization described in section 170(b)(1)(A)(ii); or

(B) is pursuing a full-time course of institutional on-farm training under the supervision of an accredited agent of an educational organization described in section 170(b)(1)(A)(ii) or of a State or political subdivision of a State.

(5) CERTAIN INCOME OF HANDICAPPED DEPENDENTS NOT TAKEN INTO ACCOUNT.—

(A) IN GENERAL.—For purposes of paragraph (1)(A), the gross income of an individual who is permanently and totally disabled shall not include income attributable to services performed by the individual at a sheltered workshop if—

(i) the availability of medical care at such workshop is the principal reason for his presence there, and

(ii) the income arises solely from activities at such workshop which are incident to such medical care.

(B) SHELTERED WORKSHOP DEFINED.—For purposes of subparagraph (A), the term "sheltered workshop" means a school—

(i) which provides special instruction or training designed to alleviate the disability of the individual, and

(ii) which is operated by—

(I) an organization described in section 501(c)(3) and exempt from tax under section 501(a), or

(II) a State, a possession of the United States, any political subdivision of any of the foregoing, the United States, or the District of Columbia.

(C) PERMANENT AND TOTAL DISABILITY DEFINED.—An individual shall be treated as permanently and totally disabled for purposes of this paragraph if such individual would be so treated under paragraph (3) of section 22(e).

(6) TREATMENT OF MISSING CHILDREN.—

(A) IN GENERAL.—Solely for the purposes referred to in subparagraph (B), a child of the taxpayer—

(i) who is presumed by law enforcement authorities to have been kidnapped by someone who is not a member of the family of such child or the taxpayer, and

(ii) who was (without regard to this paragraph) the dependent of the taxpayer for the portion of the taxable year before the date of the kidnapping,

shall be treated as a dependent of the taxpayer for all taxable years ending during the period that the child is kidnapped.

(B) PURPOSES.—Subparagraph (A) shall apply solely for purposes of determining—

(i) the deduction under this section,

(ii) the credit under section 24 (relating to child tax credit), and

(iii) whether an individual is a surviving spouse or a head of a household (as such terms are defined in section 2).

(C) COMPARABLE TREATMENT FOR PRINCIPAL PLACE OF ABODE REQUIREMENTS.—An individual—

(i) who is presumed by law enforcement authorities to have been kidnapped by someone who is not a member of the family of such individual or the taxpayer, and

(ii) who had, for the taxable year in which the kidnapping occurred, the same principal place of abode as the taxpayer for more than one-half of the portion of such year before the date of the kidnapping,

shall be treated as meeting the principal place of abode requirements of section 2(a)(1)(B), section 2(b)(1)(A), and section 32(c)(3)(A)(ii) with respect to a taxpayer for all taxable years ending during the period that the individual is kidnapped.

(D) TERMINATION OF TREATMENT.—Subparagraphs (A) and (C) shall cease to apply as of the first taxable year of the taxpayer beginning after the calendar year in which there is a determination that the child is dead (or, if earlier, in which the child would have attained age 18).

• 2002, Job Creation and Worker Assistance Act of 2002 (P.L. 107-147)

P.L. 107-147, §412(b)(1)-(2):

Amended Code Sec. 151(c)(6)(C) by striking "FOR EARNED INCOME CREDIT.—For purposes of section 32, an" and inserting "FOR PRINCIPAL PLACE OF ABODE REQUIREMENTS.—An", and by striking "requirement of section 32(c)(3)(A)(ii)" and inserting "principal place of abode requirements of section 2(a)(1)(B), section 2(b)(1)(A), and section 32(c)(3)(A)(ii)". **Effective** as if included in the provision of P.L. 106-554 to which it relates [**effective** for tax years ending after 12-31-2000.—CCH].

P.L. 107-147, §417(6):

Amended Code Sec. 151(c)(6)(B)(iii) by inserting "as" before "such terms". **Effective** 3-9-2002.

• 2000, Community Renewal Tax Relief Act of 2000 (P.L. 106-554)

P.L. 106-554, §306(a):

Amended Code Sec. 151(c) by adding at the end a new paragraph (6). **Effective** for tax years ending after 12-21-2000.

• 1988, Technical and Miscellaneous Revenue Act of 1988 (P.L. 100-647)

P.L. 100-647, §6010(a):

Amended Code Sec. 151(c)(1)(B)(ii) by inserting "who has not attained the age of 24 at the close of such calendar year" before the period. **Effective** for tax years beginning after 12-31-88.

[Sec. 151(d)]

(d) EXEMPTION AMOUNT.—For purposes of this section—

(1) IN GENERAL.—Except as otherwise provided in this subsection, the term "exemption amount" means $2,000.

(2) EXEMPTION AMOUNT DISALLOWED IN CASE OF CERTAIN DEPENDENTS.—In the case of an individual with respect to whom a deduction under this section is allowable to another taxpayer for a taxable year beginning in the calendar year in which the individual's taxable year begins, the exemption amount applicable to such individual for such individual's taxable year shall be zero.

(3) PHASEOUT.—

(A) IN GENERAL.—In the case of any taxpayer whose adjusted gross income for the taxable year exceeds the threshold amount, the exemption amount shall be reduced by the applicable percentage.

(B) APPLICABLE PERCENTAGE.—For purposes of subparagraph (A), the term "applicable percentage" means 2 percentage points for each $2,500 (or fraction thereof) by which the taxpayer's adjusted gross income for the taxable year exceeds the threshold amount. In the case of a married individual filing a separate return, the preceding sentence shall be applied by substituting "$1,250" for "$2,500". In no event shall the applicable percentage exceed 100 percent.

(C) THRESHOLD AMOUNT.—For purposes of this paragraph, the term "threshold amount" means—

(i) $150,000 in the case of a joint return or a surviving spouse (as defined in section 2(a)),

(ii) $125,000 in the case of a head of a household (as defined in section 2(b),

(iii) $100,000 in the case of an individual who is not married and who is not a surviving spouse or head of a household, and

(iv) $75,000 in the case of a married individual filing a separate return.

For purposes of this paragraph, marital status shall be determined under section 7703.

(D) COORDINATION WITH OTHER PROVISIONS.—The provisions of this paragraph shall not apply for purposes of determining whether a deduction under this section with respect to any individual is allowable to another taxpayer for any taxable year.

Caution: Code Sec. 151(d)(3)(E)-(F), below, is subject to the sunset provision of the Economic Growth and Tax Relief Reconciliation Act of 2001 (P.L. 107-16), §901. Absent Congressional action, the changes made to this provision by P.L. 107-16, or that take effect as if included in P.L. 107-16, do not apply after December 31, 2010. For more information about the sunset provision, see page XXI of the Preface to this publication and P.L. 107-16, §901, in the amendment notes. See the amendments notes for a history of amendments to this section and the effective date of each change.

(E) REDUCTION OF PHASEOUT.—

(i) IN GENERAL.—In the case of taxable years beginning after December 31, 2005, and before January 1, 2010, the reduction under subparagraph (A) shall be equal to the applicable fraction of the amount which would (but for this subparagraph) be the amount of such reduction.

(ii) APPLICABLE FRACTION.—For purposes of clause (i), the applicable fraction shall be determined in accordance with the following table:

For taxable years beginning in calendar year—	*The applicable fraction is—*
2006 and 2007	2/3
2008 and 2009	1/3.

(F) TERMINATION.—This paragraph shall not apply to any taxable year beginning after December 31, 2009.

(4) INFLATION ADJUSTMENTS.—

(A) ADJUSTMENT TO BASIC AMOUNT OF EXEMPTION.—In the case of any taxable year beginning in a calendar year after 1989, the dollar amount contained in paragraph (1) shall be increased by an amount equal to—

(i) such dollar amount, multiplied by

(ii) the cost-of-living adjustment determined under section 1(f)(3) for the calendar year in which the taxable year begins, by substituting "calendar year 1988" for "calendar year 1992" in subparagraph (B) thereof.

(B) ADJUSTMENT TO THRESHOLD AMOUNTS FOR YEARS AFTER 1991.—In the case of any taxable year beginning in a calendar year after 1991, each dollar amount contained in paragraph (3)(C) shall be increased by an amount equal to—

(i) such dollar amount, multiplied by

(ii) the cost-of-living adjustment determined under section 1(f)(3) for the calendar year in which the taxable year begins, by substituting "calendar year 1990" for "calendar year 1992" in subparagraph (B) thereof.

Amendments

• 2005, Katrina Emergency Tax Relief Act of 2005 (P.L. 109-73)

P.L. 109-73, §302 [but see P.L. 110-343, Division C, §702, in the amendment notes for Code Sec. 1400N(a)], provides:

SEC. 302. ADDITIONAL EXEMPTION FOR HOUSING HURRICANE KATRINA DISPLACED INDIVIDUALS.

(a) IN GENERAL.—In the case of taxable years of a natural person beginning in 2005 or 2006, for purposes of the Internal Revenue Code of 1986, taxable income shall be reduced by $500 for each Hurricane Katrina displaced individual of the taxpayer for the taxable year.

(b) LIMITATIONS.—

(1) DOLLAR LIMITATION.—The reduction under subsection (a) shall not exceed $2,000, reduced by the amount of the reduction under this section for all prior taxable years.

(2) INDIVIDUALS TAKEN INTO ACCOUNT ONLY ONCE.—An individual shall not be taken into account under subsection (a) if such individual was taken into account under such subsection by the taxpayer for any prior taxable year.

(3) IDENTIFYING INFORMATION REQUIRED.— An individual shall not be taken into account under subsection (a) for a taxable year unless the taxpayer identification number of such individual is included on the return of the taxpayer for such taxable year.

(c) HURRICANE KATRINA DISPLACED INDIVIDUAL.— For purposes of this section, the term "Hurricane Katrina displaced individual" means, with respect to any taxpayer for any taxable year, any natural person if—

(1) such person's principal place of abode on August 28, 2005, was in the Hurricane Katrina disaster area,

(2)(A) in the case of such an abode located in the core disaster area, such person is displaced from such abode, or

(B) in the case of such an abode located outside of the core disaster area, such person is displaced from such abode, and

(i) such abode was damaged by Hurricane Katrina, or

(ii) such person was evacuated from such abode by reason of Hurricane Katrina, and

(3) such person is provided housing free of charge by the taxpayer in the principal residence of the taxpayer for a period of 60 consecutive days which ends in such taxable year.

Such term shall not include the spouse or any dependent of the taxpayer.

(d) COMPENSATION FOR HOUSING.—No deduction shall be allowed under this section if the taxpayer receives any rent or other amount (from any source) in connection with the providing of such housing.

• 2001, Economic Growth and Tax Relief Reconciliation Act of 2001 (P.L. 107-16)

P.L. 107-16, §102(a):

Amended Code Sec. 151(d)(3) by adding at the end new subparagraphs (E) and (F). **Effective** for tax years beginning after 12-31-2005.

P.L. 107-16, §901(a)-(b), provides:

SEC. 901. SUNSET OF PROVISIONS OF ACT.

(a) IN GENERAL.—All provisions of, and amendments made by, this Act shall not apply—

(1) to taxable, plan, or limitation years beginning after December 31, 2010, or

(2) in the case of title V, to estates of decedents dying, gifts made, or generation skipping transfers, after December 31, 2010.

(b) APPLICATION OF CERTAIN LAWS.—The Internal Revenue Code of 1986 and the Employee Retirement Income Security Act of 1974 shall be applied and administered to years, estates, gifts, and transfers described in subsection (a) as if the provisions and amendments described in subsection (a) had never been enacted.

• 1996, Small Business Job Protection Act of 1996 (P.L. 104-188)

P.L. 104-188, §1702(a)(2):

Amended Code Sec. 151(d)(3)(C)(i) by striking "joint of a return" and inserting "joint return". **Effective** as if included in the provision of P.L. 101-508 to which it relates.

• 1993, Omnibus Budget Reconciliation Act of 1993 (P.L. 103-66)

P.L. 103-66, §13201(b)(3)(G):

Amended Code Sec. 151(d)(4)(A)(ii) and (B)(ii) by striking "1989" and inserting "1992". **Effective** for tax years beginning after 12-31-92.

P.L. 103-66, §13205:

Amended Code Sec. 151(d)(3) by striking subparagraph (E). **Effective** 8-10-93. Prior to being stricken, Code Sec. 151(d)(3)(E) read as follows:

(E) TERMINATION.—This paragraph shall not apply to any taxable year beginning after December 31, 1996.

• 1992, Unemployment Compensation Amendments of 1992 (P.L. 102-318)

P.L. 102-318, §511:

Amended Code Sec. 151(d)(3)(E) by striking "December 31, 1995" and inserting "December 31, 1996". **Effective** 7-3-92.

• 1990, Omnibus Budget Reconciliation Act of 1990 (P.L. 101-508)

P.L. 101-508, §11101(d)(1)(F):

Amended Code Sec. 151(d)(3)(B) by striking "1987" and inserting "1989". **Effective** for tax years beginning 12-31-90.

P.L. 101-508, §11104(a):

Amended Code Sec. 151(d). **Effective** for tax years beginning 12-31-90. Prior to amendment, Code Sec. 151(d) (as amended by Act Sec. 11101(d)(1)(F)) read as follows:

(d) EXEMPTION AMOUNT.—For purposes of this section—

(1) IN GENERAL.—Except as provided in paragraph (2), the term "exemption amount" means—

(A) $1,900 for taxable years beginning during 1987,

(B) $1,950 for taxable years beginning during 1988, and

(C) $2,000 for taxable years beginning after December 31, 1988.

(2) EXEMPTION AMOUNT DISALLOWED IN THE CASE OF CERTAIN DEPENDENTS.—In the case of an individual with respect to whom a deduction under this section is allowable to another taxpayer for a taxable year beginning in the calendar year in which the individual's taxable year begins, the exemption amount applicable to such individual for such individual's taxable year shall be zero.

(3) INFLATION ADJUSTMENT FOR YEARS AFTER 1989.—In the case of any taxable year beginning in a calendar year after 1989, the dollar amount contained in paragraph (1)(C) shall be increased by an amount equal to—

(A) such dollar amount, multiplied by

(B) the cost-of-living adjustment determined under section 1(f)(3), for the calendar year in which the taxable year begins, by substituting "calendar year 1988" for "calendar year 1989" in subparagraph (B) thereof.

• 1986, Tax Reform Act of 1986 (P.L. 99-514)

P.L. 99-514, §103(a):

Amended Code Sec. 151(f). **Effective** for tax years beginning after 12-31-86. Prior to amendment, Code Sec. 151(f) read as follows:

(f) Exemption Amount.—For purposes of this section, the term "exemption amount" means, with respect to any taxable year, $1,000 increased by an amount equal to $1,000 multiplied by the cost-of-living adjustment (as defined in section 1(f)(3)) for the calendar year in which the taxable year begins. If the amount determined under the preceding sentence is not a multiple of $10, such amount shall be rounded to the nearest multiple of $10 (or if such amount is a multiple of $5, such amount shall be increased to the next highest multiple of $10).

P.L. 99-514, §103(b):

Amended Code Sec. 151 by striking out subsections (c) and (d) and redesignating subsections (e) and (f) as subsections (c) and (d), respectively. **Effective** for tax years beginning after 12-31-86. Prior to amendment, Code Sec. 151(c) and (d) read as follows:

(c) Additional Exemption for Taxpayer or Spouse Aged 65 or More—

(1) For Taxpayer.—An additional exemption of the exemption amount for the taxpayer if he has attained the age of 65 before the close of his taxable year.

(2) For Spouse.—An additional exemption of the exemption amount for the spouse of the taxpayer if a joint return is not made by the taxpayer and his spouse, and if the spouse has attained the age of 65 before the close of such taxable year, and, for the calendar year in which the taxable year of the taxpayer begins, has no gross income and is not the dependent of another taxpayer.

(d) Additional Exemption for Blindness of Taxpayer or Spouse.—

(1) For Taxpayer.—An additional exemption of the exemption amount for the taxpayer if he is blind at the close of his taxable year.

(2) For Spouse.—An additional exemption of the exemption amount for the spouse of the taxpayer if a separate return is made by the taxpayer, and if the spouse is blind and, for the calendar year in which the taxable year of the taxpayer begins, has no gross income and is not the dependent of another taxpayer. For purposes of this paragraph, the determination of whether the spouse is blind shall be made as of the close of the taxable year of the taxpayer; except that if the spouse dies during such taxable year such determination shall be made as of the time of such death.

(3) Blindness Defined.—For purposes of this subsection, an individual is blind only if his central visual acuity does not exceed 20/200 in the better eye with correcting lenses, or if his visual acuity is greater than 20/200 but is accompanied by a limitation in the fields of vision such that the widest diameter of the visual field subtends an angle no greater than 20 degrees.

P.L. 99-514, §1847(b)(3):

Amended Code Sec. 151(e)(5)(C) by striking out "section 37(e)" and inserting in lieu thereof "section 22(e)". **Effective** as if included in the provision of P.L. 98-369 to which it relates.

• 1984, Deficit Reduction Act of 1984 (P.L. 98-369)

P.L. 98-369, §426(a):

Amended Sec. 151(e) by adding at the end thereof a new paragraph (5). **Effective** for tax years beginning after 12-31-84.

• 1981, Economic Recovery Tax Act of 1981 (P.L. 97-34)

P.L. 97-34, §104(c)(1), (2):

Amended Code Sec. 151 by striking out "$1,000" each place it appeared and inserting in lieu thereof "the exemption amount" and by adding at the end thereof new subsection (f). **Effective** for tax years beginning after 12-31-84.

• 1978, Revenue Act of 1978 (P.L. 95-600)

P.L. 95-600, §102(a):

Amended Code Sec. 151 by striking out "$750" each place it appeared and inserting in lieu thereof "$1000". **Effective** for tax years beginning after 12-31-78.

• 1976, Tax Reform Act of 1976 (P.L. 94-455)

P.L. 94-455, §1901(a)(23):

Amended Code Sec. 151(e)(4). **Effective** for tax years beginning after 12-31-76. Prior to amendment, Code Sec. 151(e)(4) read as follows:

(4) STUDENT AND EDUCATIONAL INSTITUTION DEFINED.—For purposes of paragraph (1)(B)(ii), the term "student" means an individual who during each of 5 calendar months during the calendar year in which the taxable year of the taxpayer begins—

(A) is a full-time student at an educational institution; or

(B) is pursuing a full-time course of institutional on-farm training under the supervision of an accredited agent of an educational institution or of a State or political subdivision of a State.

For purposes of this paragraph, the term "educational institution" means only an educational institution which normally maintains a regular faculty and curriculum and normally has a regularly organized body of students in attendance at the place where its educational activities are carried on.

• 1971, Revenue Act of 1971 (P.L. 92-178)

P.L. 92-178, §201(a)(1):

Substituted "$675" for "$650" throughout Code Sec. 151. **Effective** only for tax years beginning after 12-31-70, and before 1-1-72. [Note: This amendment superseded a $650 exemption figure that was scheduled for 1971 under P.L. 91-172.—CCH].

P.L. 92-178, §201(b)(1):

Substituted "$750" for "$675" throughout Code Sec. 151. **Effective** for tax years beginning after 12-31-71.

• 1969, Tax Reform Act of 1969 (P.L. 91-172)

P.L. 91-172, §801:

Amended Code Sec. 151 by substituting "$625" for "$600" wherever it appeared. **Effective** for tax years beginning after 12-31-69 and before 1-1-71.

P.L. 91-172 also scheduled increases in the personal exemption to $650 for 1971, to $700 for 1972, and to $750 after 1972, but these increases were repealed and were replaced by P.L. 92-178, which made the changes noted in the amendatory note under P.L. 92-178, above.

P.L. 91-172, §941(b):

Amended subsection (b) by inserting "if a joint return is not made by the taxpayer and his spouse" in lieu of "if a separate return is made by the taxpayer". **Effective** for tax years beginning after 12-31-69.

P.L. 91-172, §914(b):

Amended paragraph (c)(2) by inserting "if a joint return is not made by the taxpayer and his spouse" in lieu of "if a separate return is made by the taxpayer". **Effective** for tax years beginning after 12-31-69.

[Sec. 151(e)]

(e) IDENTIFYING INFORMATION REQUIRED.—No exemption shall be allowed under this section with respect to any individual unless the TIN of such individual is included on the return claiming the exemption.

Amendments

• 1996, Small Business Job Protection Act of 1996 (P.L. 104-188)

P.L. 104-188, §1615(a)(1):

Amended Code Sec. 151 by adding at the end a new subsection (e). **Effective**, generally, with respect to returns the due date for which (without regard to extensions) is on or after the 30th day after 8-20-96. For a special rule, see Act Sec. 1615(d)(2), below.

P.L. 104-188, §1615(d)(2), provides:

(2) SPECIAL RULE FOR 1995 AND 1996.—In the case of returns for taxable years beginning in 1995 or 1996, a taxpayer shall not be required by the amendments made by this section to provide a taxpayer identification number for a child who is born after October 31, 1995, in the case of a taxable year beginning in 1995 or November 30, 1996, in the case of a taxable year beginning in 1996.

[Sec. 152]

SEC. 152. DEPENDENT DEFINED.

[Sec. 152(a)]

(a) IN GENERAL.—For purposes of this subtitle, the term "dependent" means—

(1) a qualifying child, or

(2) a qualifying relative.

[Sec. 152(b)]

(b) EXCEPTIONS.—For purposes of this section—

(1) DEPENDENTS INELIGIBLE.—If an individual is a dependent of a taxpayer for any taxable year of such taxpayer beginning in a calendar year, such individual shall be treated as having no dependents for any taxable year of such individual beginning in such calendar year.

(2) MARRIED DEPENDENTS.—An individual shall not be treated as a dependent of a taxpayer under subsection (a) if such individual has made a joint return with the individual's spouse under section 6013 for the taxable year beginning in the calendar year in which the taxable year of the taxpayer begins.

(3) CITIZENS OR NATIONALS OF OTHER COUNTRIES.—

(A) IN GENERAL.—The term "dependent" does not include an individual who is not a citizen or national of the United States unless such individual is a resident of the United States or a country contiguous to the United States.

(B) EXCEPTION FOR ADOPTED CHILD.—Subparagraph (A) shall not exclude any child of a taxpayer (within the meaning of subsection (f)(1)(B)) from the definition of "dependent" if—

(i) for the taxable year of the taxpayer, the child has the same principal place of abode as the taxpayer and is a member of the taxpayer's household, and

(ii) the taxpayer is a citizen or national of the United States.

[Sec. 152(c)]

(c) QUALIFYING CHILD.—For purposes of this section—

(1) IN GENERAL.—The term "qualifying child" means, with respect to any taxpayer for any taxable year, an individual—

(A) who bears a relationship to the taxpayer described in paragraph (2),

(B) who has the same principal place of abode as the taxpayer for more than one-half of such taxable year,

(C) who meets the age requirements of paragraph (3),

(D) who has not provided over one-half of such individual's own support for the calendar year in which the taxable year of the taxpayer begins, and

(E) who has not filed a joint return (other than only for a claim of refund) with the individual's spouse under section 6013 for the taxable year beginning in the calendar year in which the taxable year of the taxpayer begins.

(2) RELATIONSHIP.—For purposes of paragraph (1)(A), an individual bears a relationship to the taxpayer described in this paragraph if such individual is—

(A) a child of the taxpayer or a descendant of such a child, or

(B) a brother, sister, stepbrother, or stepsister of the taxpayer or a descendant of any such relative.

(3) AGE REQUIREMENTS.—

(A) IN GENERAL.—For purposes of paragraph (1)(C), an individual meets the requirements of this paragraph if such individual is younger than the taxpayer claiming such individual as a qualifying child and—

(i) has not attained the age of 19 as of the close of the calendar year in which the taxable year of the taxpayer begins, or

(ii) is a student who has not attained the age of 24 as of the close of such calendar year.

(B) SPECIAL RULE FOR DISABLED.—In the case of an individual who is permanently and totally disabled (as defined in section 22(e)(3)) at any time during such calendar year, the requirements of subparagraph (A) shall be treated as met with respect to such individual.

(4) SPECIAL RULE RELATING TO 2 OR MORE WHO CAN CLAIM THE SAME QUALIFYING CHILD.—

(A) IN GENERAL.—Except as provided in subparagraphs (B) and (C), if (but for this paragraph) an individual may be claimed as a qualifying child by 2 or more taxpayers for a taxable year beginning in the same calendar year, such individual shall be treated as the qualifying child of the taxpayer who is—

(i) a parent of the individual, or

(ii) if clause (i) does not apply, the taxpayer with the highest adjusted gross income for such taxable year.

(B) MORE THAN 1 PARENT CLAIMING QUALIFYING CHILD.—If the parents claiming any qualifying child do not file a joint return together, such child shall be treated as the qualifying child of—

(i) the parent with whom the child resided for the longest period of time during the taxable year, or

(ii) if the child resides with both parents for the same amount of time during such taxable year, the parent with the highest adjusted gross income.

(C) NO PARENT CLAIMING QUALIFYING CHILD.—If the parents of an individual may claim such individual as a qualifying child but no parent so claims the individual, such individual may be claimed as the qualifying child of another taxpayer but only if the adjusted gross income of such taxpayer is higher than the highest adjusted gross income of any parent of the individual.

Amendments

• 2008, Fostering Connections to Success and Increasing Adoptions Act of 2008 (P.L. 110-351)

P.L. 110-351, §501(a):

Amended Code Sec. 152(c)(3)(A) by inserting "is younger than the taxpayer claiming such individual as a qualifying child and" after "such individual". **Effective** for tax years beginning after 12-31-2008.

P.L. 110-351, §501(b):

Amended Code Sec. 152(c)(1) by striking "and" at the end of subparagraph (C), by striking the period at the end of subparagraph (D) and inserting ", and", and by adding at the end a new subparagraph (E). **Effective** for tax years beginning after 12-31-2008.

P.L. 110-351, §501(c)(2)(A):

Amended Code Sec. 152(c)(4) by adding at the end a new subparagraph (C). **Effective** for tax years beginning after 12-31-2008.

P.L. 110-351, §501(c)(2)(B)(i):

Amended Code Sec. 152(c)(4)(A) by striking "Except" through "2 or more taxpayers" and inserting "Except as provided in subparagraphs (B) and (C), if (but for this paragraph) an individual may be claimed as a qualifying child by 2 or more taxpayers". **Effective** for tax years beginning after 12-31-2008. Prior to being stricken, the text "Except" through "2 or more taxpayers" read as follows:

Except as provided in subparagraph (B), if (but for this paragraph) an individual may be and is claimed as a qualifying child by 2 or more taxpayers

P.L. 110-351, §501(c)(2)(B)(ii):

Amended the heading for Code Sec. 152(c)(4) by striking "CLAIMING" and inserting "WHO CAN CLAIM THE SAME". **Effective** for tax years beginning after 12-31-2008.

[Sec. 152(d)]

(d) QUALIFYING RELATIVE.—For purposes of this section—

(1) IN GENERAL.—The term "qualifying relative" means, with respect to any taxpayer for any taxable year, an individual—

(A) who bears a relationship to the taxpayer described in paragraph (2),

(B) whose gross income for the calendar year in which such taxable year begins is less than the exemption amount (as defined in section 151(d)),

(C) with respect to whom the taxpayer provides over one-half of the individual's support for the calendar year in which such taxable year begins, and

(D) who is not a qualifying child of such taxpayer or of any other taxpayer for any taxable year beginning in the calendar year in which such taxable year begins.

(2) RELATIONSHIP.—For purposes of paragraph (1)(A), an individual bears a relationship to the taxpayer described in this paragraph if the individual is any of the following with respect to the taxpayer:

(A) A child or a descendant of a child.

(B) A brother, sister, stepbrother, or stepsister.

(C) The father or mother, or an ancestor of either.

(D) A stepfather or stepmother.

(E) A son or daughter of a brother or sister of the taxpayer.

(F) A brother or sister of the father or mother of the taxpayer.

(G) A son-in-law, daughter-in-law, father-in-law, mother-in-law, brother-in-law, or sister-in-law.

(H) An individual (other than an individual who at any time during the taxable year was the spouse, determined without regard to section 7703, of the taxpayer) who, for the taxable year of the taxpayer, has the same principal place of abode as the taxpayer and is a member of the taxpayer's household.

(3) SPECIAL RULE RELATING TO MULTIPLE SUPPORT AGREEMENTS.—For purposes of paragraph (1)(C), over one-half of the support of an individual for a calendar year shall be treated as received from the taxpayer if—

(A) no one person contributed over one-half of such support,

(B) over one-half of such support was received from 2 or more persons each of whom, but for the fact that any such person alone did not contribute over one-half of such support, would have been entitled to claim such individual as a dependent for a taxable year beginning in such calendar year,

(C) the taxpayer contributed over 10 percent of such support, and

(D) each person described in subparagraph (B) (other than the taxpayer) who contributed over 10 percent of such support files a written declaration (in such manner and form as the Secretary may by regulations prescribe) that such person will not claim such individual as a dependent for any taxable year beginning in such calendar year.

(4) SPECIAL RULE RELATING TO INCOME OF HANDICAPPED DEPENDENTS.—

(A) IN GENERAL.—For purposes of paragraph (1)(B), the gross income of an individual who is permanently and totally disabled (as defined in section 22(e)(3)) at any time during the taxable year shall not include income attributable to services performed by the individual at a sheltered workshop if—

(i) the availability of medical care at such workshop is the principal reason for the individual's presence there, and

(ii) the income arises solely from activities at such workshop which are incident to such medical care.

(B) SHELTERED WORKSHOP DEFINED.—For purposes of subparagraph (A), the term "sheltered workshop" means a school—

(i) which provides special instruction or training designed to alleviate the disability of the individual, and

(ii) which is operated by an organization described in section 501(c)(3) and exempt from tax under section 501(a), or by a State, a possession of the United States, any political subdivision of any of the foregoing, the United States, or the District of Columbia.

(5) SPECIAL RULES FOR SUPPORT.—For purposes of this subsection—

(A) payments to a spouse which are includible in the gross income of such spouse under section 71 or 682 shall not be treated as a payment by the payor spouse for the support of any dependent, and

(B) in the case of the remarriage of a parent, support of a child received from the parent's spouse shall be treated as received from the parent.

[Sec. 152(e)]

(e) SPECIAL RULE FOR DIVORCED PARENTS, ETC.—

(1) IN GENERAL.—Notwithstanding subsection (c)(1)(B), (c)(4), or (d)(1)(C), if—

(A) a child receives over one-half of the child's support during the calendar year from the child's parents—

(i) who are divorced or legally separated under a decree of divorce or separate maintenance,

(ii) who are separated under a written separation agreement, or

(iii) who live apart at all times during the last 6 months of the calendar year, and—

(B) such child is in the custody of 1 or both of the child's parents for more than one-half of the calendar year, such child shall be treated as being the qualifying child or qualifying relative of the noncustodial parent for a calendar year if the requirements described in paragraph (2) or (3) are met.

(2) EXCEPTION WHERE CUSTODIAL PARENT RELEASES CLAIM TO EXEMPTION FOR THE YEAR.—For purposes of paragraph (1), the requirements described in this paragraph are met with respect to any calendar year if—

(A) the custodial parent signs a written declaration (in such manner and form as the Secretary may by regulations prescribe) that such custodial parent will not claim such child as a dependent for any taxable year beginning in such calendar year, and

(B) the noncustodial parent attaches such written declaration to the noncustodial parent's return for the taxable year beginning during such calendar year.

(3) EXCEPTION FOR CERTAIN PRE-1985 INSTRUMENTS.—

(A) IN GENERAL.—For purposes of paragraph (1), the requirements described in this paragraph are met with respect to any calendar year if—

(i) a qualified pre-1985 instrument between the parents applicable to the taxable year beginning in such calendar year provides that the noncustodial parent shall be entitled to any deduction allowable under section 151 for such child, and

(ii) the noncustodial parent provides at least $600 for the support of such child during such calendar year.

For purposes of this subparagraph, amounts expended for the support of a child or children shall be treated as received from the noncustodial parent to the extent that such parent provided amounts for such support.

(B) QUALIFIED PRE-1985 INSTRUMENT.—For purposes of this paragraph, the term "qualified pre-1985 instrument" means any decree of divorce or separate maintenance or written agreement—

(i) which is executed before January 1, 1985,

(ii) which on such date contains the provision described in subparagraph (A)(i), and

(iii) which is not modified on or after such date in a modification which expressly provides that this paragraph shall not apply to such decree or agreement.

(4) CUSTODIAL PARENT AND NONCUSTODIAL PARENT.—For purposes of this subsection—

(A) CUSTODIAL PARENT.—The term "custodial parent" means the parent having custody for the greater portion of the calendar year.

(B) NONCUSTODIAL PARENT.—The term "noncustodial parent" means the parent who is not the custodial parent.

(5) EXCEPTION FOR MULTIPLE-SUPPORT AGREEMENT.—This subsection shall not apply in any case where over one-half of the support of the child is treated as having been received from a taxpayer under the provision of subsection (d)(3).

(6) SPECIAL RULE FOR SUPPORT RECEIVED FROM NEW SPOUSE OF PARENT.—For purposes of this subsection, in the case of the remarriage of a parent, support of a child received from the parent's spouse shall be treated as received from the parent.

Amendments

• 2005, Gulf Opportunity Zone Act of 2005 (P.L. 109-135)

P.L. 109-135, §404(a):

Amended Code Sec. 152(e). **Effective** as if included in the provision of the Working Families Tax Relief Act of 2004 (P.L. 108-311) to which it relates [**effective** for tax years beginning after 12-31-2004.—CCH]. Prior to amendment, Code Sec. 152(e) read as follows:

(e) SPECIAL RULE FOR DIVORCED PARENTS.—

(1) IN GENERAL.—Notwithstanding subsection (c)(1)(B), (c)(4), or (d)(1)(C), if—

(A) a child receives over one-half of the child's support during the calendar year from the child's parents—

(i) who are divorced or legally separated under a decree of divorce or separate maintenance,

(ii) who are separated under a written separation agreement, or

(iii) who live apart at all times during the last 6 months of the calendar year, and

(B) such child is in the custody of 1 or both of the child's parents for more than one-half of the calendar year,

such child shall be treated as being the qualifying child or qualifying relative of the noncustodial parent for a calendar year if the requirements described in paragraph (2) are met.

(2) REQUIREMENTS.—For purposes of paragraph (1), the requirements described in this paragraph are met if—

(A) a decree of divorce or separate maintenance or written separation agreement between the parents applicable to the taxable year beginning in such calendar year provides that—

(i) the noncustodial parent shall be entitled to any deduction allowable under section 151 for such child, or

(ii) the custodial parent will sign a written declaration (in such manner and form as the Secretary may prescribe) that such parent will not claim such child as a dependent for such taxable year, or

(B) in the case of such an agreement executed before January 1, 1985, the noncustodial parent provides at least $600 for the support of such child during such calendar year.

For purposes of subparagraph (B), amounts expended for the support of a child or children shall be treated as received from the noncustodial parent to the extent that such parent provided amounts for such support.

(3) CUSTODIAL PARENT AND NONCUSTODIAL PARENT.—For purposes of this subsection—

(A) CUSTODIAL PARENT.—The term "custodial parent" means the parent with whom a child shared the same principal place of abode for the greater portion of the calendar year.

(B) NONCUSTODIAL PARENT.—The term "noncustodial parent" means the parent who is not the custodial parent.

(4) EXCEPTION FOR MULTIPLE-SUPPORT AGREEMENTS.—This subsection shall not apply in any case where over one-half of the support of the child is treated as having been received from a taxpayer under the provision of subsection (d)(3).

[Sec. 152(f)]

(f) OTHER DEFINITIONS AND RULES.—For purposes of this section—

(1) CHILD DEFINED.—

(A) IN GENERAL.—The term "child" means an individual who is—

(i) a son, daughter, stepson, or stepdaughter of the taxpayer, or

(ii) an eligible foster child of the taxpayer.

(B) ADOPTED CHILD.—In determining whether any of the relationships specified in subparagraph (A)(i) or paragraph (4) exists, a legally adopted individual of the taxpayer, or an individual who is lawfully placed with the taxpayer for legal adoption by the taxpayer, shall be treated as a child of such individual by blood.

(C) ELIGIBLE FOSTER CHILD.—For purposes of subparagraph (A)(ii), the term "eligible foster child" means an individual who is placed with the taxpayer by an authorized placement agency or by judgment, decree, or other order of any court of competent jurisdiction.

(2) STUDENT DEFINED.—The term "student" means an individual who during each of 5 calendar months during the calendar year in which the taxable year of the taxpayer begins—

(A) is a full-time student at an educational organization described in section 170(b)(1)(A)(ii), or

(B) is pursuing a full-time course of institutional on-farm training under the supervision of an accredited agent of an educational organization described in section 170(b)(1)(A)(ii) or of a State or political subdivision of a State.

(3) DETERMINATION OF HOUSEHOLD STATUS.—An individual shall not be treated as a member of the taxpayer's household if at any time during the taxable year of the taxpayer the relationship between such individual and the taxpayer is in violation of local law.

(4) BROTHER AND SISTER.—The terms "brother" and "sister" include a brother or sister by the half blood.

(5) SPECIAL SUPPORT TEST IN CASE OF STUDENTS.—For purposes of subsections (c)(1)(D) and (d)(1)(C), in the case of an individual who is—

(A) a child of the taxpayer, and

(B) a student,

amounts received as scholarships for study at an educational organization described in section 170(b)(1)(A)(ii) shall not be taken into account.

(6) TREATMENT OF MISSING CHILDREN.—

(A) IN GENERAL.—Solely for the purposes referred to in subparagraph (B), a child of the taxpayer—

(i) who is presumed by law enforcement authorities to have been kidnapped by someone who is not a member of the family of such child or the taxpayer, and

(ii) who had, for the taxable year in which the kidnapping occurred, the same principal place of abode as the taxpayer for more than one-half of the portion of such year before the date of the kidnapping,

shall be treated as meeting the requirement of subsection (c)(1)(B) with respect to a taxpayer for all taxable years ending during the period that the child is kidnapped.

(B) PURPOSES.—Subparagraph (A) shall apply solely for purposes of determining—

(i) the deduction under section 151(c),

(ii) the credit under section 24 (relating to child tax credit),

(iii) whether an individual is a surviving spouse or a head of a household (as such terms are defined in section 2), and

(iv) the earned income credit under section 32.

(C) COMPARABLE TREATMENT OF CERTAIN QUALIFYING RELATIVES.—For purposes of this section, a child of the taxpayer—

(i) who is presumed by law enforcement authorities to have been kidnapped by someone who is not a member of the family of such child or the taxpayer, and

(ii) who was (without regard to this paragraph) a qualifying relative of the taxpayer for the portion of the taxable year before the date of the kidnapping,

shall be treated as a qualifying relative of the taxpayer for all taxable years ending during the period that the child is kidnapped.

(D) TERMINATION OF TREATMENT.—Subparagraphs (A) and (C) shall cease to apply as of the first taxable year of the taxpayer beginning after the calendar year in which there is a determination that the child is dead (or, if earlier, in which the child would have attained age 18).

(7) CROSS REFERENCES.—

For provision treating child as dependent of both parents for purposes of certain provisions, see sections 105(b), 132(h)(2)(B), and 213(d)(5).

Amendments

• 2004, Working Families Tax Relief Act of 2004 (P.L. 108-311)

P.L. 108-311, §201:

Amended Code Sec. 152. **Effective** for tax years beginning after 12-31-2004. Prior to amendment, Code Sec. 152 read as follows:

SEC. 152. DEPENDENT DEFINED.

[Sec. 152(a)]

(a) GENERAL DEFINITION.—For purposes of this subtitle, the term "dependent" means any of the following individuals over half of whose support, for the calendar year in which the taxable year of the taxpayer begins, was received from the taxpayer (or is treated under subsection (c) or (e) as received from the taxpayer):

(1) A son or daughter of the taxpayer, or a descendant of either,

(2) A stepson or stepdaughter of the taxpayer,

(3) A brother, sister, stepbrother, or stepsister of the taxpayer,

(4) The father or mother of the taxpayer, or an ancester of either,

(5) A stepfather or stepmother of the taxpayer,

(6) A son or daughter of a brother or sister of the taxpayer,

(7) A brother or sister of the father or mother of the taxpayer,

(8) A son-in-law, daughter-in-law, father-in-law, mother-in-law, brother-in-law, or sister-in-law of the taxpayer, or

(9) An individual (other than an individual who at any time during the taxable year was the spouse, determined without regard to section 7703, of the taxpayer) who, for the taxable year of the taxpayer, has as his principal place of abode the home of the taxpayer and is a member of the taxpayer's household.

Amendments

• 1986, Tax Reform Act of 1986 (P.L. 99-514)

P.L. 99-514, §1301(j)(8):

Amended Code Sec. 152(a)(9) by striking out "section 143" each place it appears and inserting in lieu thereof "section 7703". **Effective** for bonds issued after 8-15-86.

• 1976, Tax Reform Act of 1976 (P.L. 94-455)

P.L. 94-455, §1901(a)(24):

Amended Code Sec. 152(a) by inserting "or" at the end of paragraph (8), by striking out ", or" and inserting a period at the end of paragraph (9), and by striking out paragraph (10). **Effective** for tax years beginning after 12-31-76. Prior to repeal, paragraph (10) read as follows:

(10) An individual who—

(A) is a descendant of a brother or sister of the father or mother of the taxpayer,

(B) for the taxable year of the taxpayer receives institutional care required by reason of a physical or mental disability, and

(C) before receiving such institutional care, was a member of the same household as the taxpayer.

P.L. 94-455, §1901(b)(7):

Amended Code Sec. 152(a)(9) by substituting "section 143" for "section 153". **Effective** for tax years beginning after 12-31-76.

• 1967 (P.L. 90-78)

P.L. 90-78, §1(b):

Amended Code Sec. 152(a) by substituting "subsection (c) or (e)" for "subsection (c)" therein. **Effective** for tax years beginning after 12-31-66.

• 1958, Technical Amendments Act of 1958 (P.L. 85-866)

P.L. 85-866, §4(a):

Amended Code Sec. 152(a)(9) by adding the phrase "(other than an individual who at any time during the taxable year was the spouse, determined without regard to section 153, of the taxpayer)" immediately following the word "individual".**Effective** for tax years beginning after 12-31-53, and ending after 8-16-54.

[Sec. 152(b)]

(b) RULES RELATING TO GENERAL DEFINITION.—For purposes of this section—

(1) The terms "brother" and "sister" include a brother or sister by the halfblood.

(2) In determining whether any of the relationships specified in subsection (a) or paragraph (1) of this subsection exists, a legally adopted child of an individual (and a child who is a member of an individual's household, if placed with such individual by an authorized placement agency for legal adoption by such individual), or a foster child of an individual (if such child satisfies the requirements of subsection (a)(9) with respect to such individual), shall be treated as a child of such individual by blood.

(3) The term "dependent" does not include any individual who is not a citizen or national of the United States unless such individual is a resident of the United States or of a country contiguous to the United States. The preceding sentence shall not exclude from the definition of "dependent" any child of the taxpayer legally adopted by him, if, for the taxable year of the taxpayer, the child has as his principal place of abode the home of the taxpayer and is a member of the taxpayer's household, and if the taxpayer is a citizen or national of the United States.

(4) A payment to a wife which is includible in the gross income of the wife under section 71 or 682 shall not be treated as a payment by her husband for the support of any dependent.

(5) An individual is not a member of the taxpayer's household if at any time during the taxable year of the taxpayer the relationship between such individual and the taxpayer is in violation of local law.

Amendments

• 1976, Tax Reform Act of 1976 (P.L. 94-455)

P.L. 94-455, §1901(a)(24):

Amended Code Sec. 152(b)(3). **Effective** for tax years beginning after 12-31-76. Prior to amendment, Code Sec. 152(b)(3) read as follows:

(3) The term "dependent" does not include any individual who is not a citizen or national of the United States unless such individual is a resident of the United States, of a country contiguous to the United States, of the Canal Zone, or of the Republic of Panama. The preceding sentence shall not exclude from the definition of "dependent" any child of the taxpayer—

(A) born to him, or legally adopted by him, in the Philippine Islands before January 1, 1956, if the child is a resident of the Republic of the Philippines, and if the taxpayer was a member of the Armed Forces of the United States at the time the child was born to him or legally adopted by him, or

(B) legally adopted by him, if, for the taxable year of the taxpayer, the child has as his principal place of abode the home of the taxpayer and is a member of the taxpayer's household, and if the taxpayer is a citizen or national of the United States.

• 1972 (P.L. 92-580)

P.L. 92-580, §1(b):

Substituted "citizen or national of the United States" for "citizen of the United States" in the first sentence of Code Sec. 152(b)(3) and in subparagraph (B) thereof. **Effective** for tax years beginning after 12-31-71.

• 1969, Tax Reform Act of 1969 (P.L. 91-172)

P.L. 91-172, §912(a):

Amended paragraph (b)(2) by inserting ", or a foster child of an individual (if such child satisfies the requirements of subsection (a)(9) with respect to such individual),". **Effective** for tax years beginning after 12-31-69.

• 1959 (P.L. 86-376)

P.L. 86-376, §1(a):

Amended Code Sec. 152(b)(2) by striking out "a legally adopted child of an individual" and by substituting "a legally adopted child of an individual (and a child who is a member of an individual's household, if placed with such individual by an authorized placement agency for legal adoption by such individual)". **Effective** for tax years beginning after 12-31-58.

• 1958, Technical Amendments Act of 1958 (P.L. 85-866)

P.L. 85-866, §4(b):

Amended Code Sec. 152(b)(3). **Effective** for tax years beginning after 12-31-57. Prior to amendment, Sec. 152(b)(3) read as follows:

The preceding sentence shall not exclude from the definition of 'dependent' any child of the taxpayer born to him, or legally adopted by him, in the Philippine Islands before January 1, 1956, if the child is a resident of the Republic of the Philippines, and if the taxpayer was a member of the Armed Forces of the United States at the time the child was born to him or legally adopted by him.

P.L. 85-866, §4(c):

Added paragraph (5) to Code Sec. 152(b). **Effective** for tax years beginning after 12-31-53, and ending after 8-16-54.

• 1955 (P.L. 333, 84th Cong.)

P.L. 333, 84th Cong., §§2, 3(b):

Amended Code Sec. 152(b)(3) by deleting "July 5, 1946" and inserting in lieu thereof "January 1, 1956". **Effective** for tax years beginning after 12-31-53, and ending after 8-16-54.

[Sec. 152(c)]

(c) MULTIPLE SUPPORT AGREEMENTS.—For purposes of subsection (a), over half of the support of an individual for a calendar year shall be treated as received from the taxpayer if—

(1) no one person contributed over half of such support;

(2) over half of such support was received from persons each of whom, but for the fact that he did not contribute over half of such support, would have been entitled to claim such individual as a dependent for a taxable year beginning in such calendar year;

(3) the taxpayer contributed over 10 percent of such support; and

(4) each person described in paragraph (2) (other than the taxpayer) who contributed over 10 percent of such support files a written declaration (in such manner and form as the Secretary may by regulations prescribe) that he will not claim such individual as a dependent for any taxable year beginning in such calendar year.

Amendments

• 1976, Tax Reform Act of 1976 (P.L. 94-455)

P.L. 94-455, §1906(b)(13)(A):

Amended 1954 Code by substituting "Secretary" for "Secretary or his delegate" each place it appeared. **Effective** 2-1-77.

[Sec. 152(d)]

(d) SPECIAL SUPPORT TEST IN CASE OF STUDENTS.—For purposes of subsection (a), in the case of any individual who is—

(1) a son, stepson, daughter, or stepdaughter of the taxpayer (within the meaning of this section), and

(2) a student (within the meaning of section 151(c)(4)),

amounts received as scholarships for study at an educational organization described in section 170(b)(1)(A)(ii) shall not be taken into account in determining whether such individual received more than half of his support from the taxpayer.

Amendments

• 1986, Tax Reform Act of 1986 (P.L. 99-514)

P.L. 99-514, §104(b)(3):

Amended Code Sec. 152(d)(2) by striking out "section 151(e)(4)" and inserting in lieu thereof "section 151(c)(4)". **Effective** for tax years beginning after 12-31-86.

• 1976, Tax Reform Act of 1976 (P.L. 94-455)

P.L. 94-455, §1901(b)(8):

Amended Code Sec. 152(d) to substitute "educational organization described in section 170(b)(1)(A)(ii)" for "educational institution (as defined in section 151(e)(4))". **Effective** for tax years beginning after 12-31-76.

[Sec. 152(e)]

(e) SUPPORT TEST IN CASE OF CHILD OF DIVORCED PARENTS, ETC.—

(1) CUSTODIAL PARENT GETS EXEMPTION.—Except as otherwise provided in this subsection, if—

(A) a child (as defined in section 151(c)(3)) receives over half of his support during the calendar year from his parents—

(i) who are divorced or legally separated under a decree of divorce or separate maintenance,

(ii) who are separated under a written separation agreement, or

(iii) who live apart at all times during the last 6 months of the calendar year, and

(B) such child is in the custody of one or both of his parents for more than one-half of the calendar year,

such child shall be treated, for purposes of subsection (a), as receiving over half of his support during the calendar year from the parent having custody for a greater portion of the calendar year (hereinafter in this subsection referred to as the "custodial parent").

(2) EXCEPTION WHERE CUSTODIAL PARENT RELEASES CLAIM TO EXEMPTION FOR THE YEAR.—A child of parents described in paragraph (1) shall be treated as having received over half of his support during a calendar year from the noncustodial parent if—

(A) the custodial parent signs a written declaration (in such manner and form as the Secretary may by regulations prescribe) that such custodial parent will not claim such child as a dependent for any taxable year beginning in such calendar year, and

(B) the noncustodial parent attaches such written declaration to the noncustodial parent's return for the taxable year beginning during such calendar year.

For purposes of this subsection, the term "noncustodial parent" means the parent who is not the custodial parent.

(3) EXCEPTION FOR MULTIPLE-SUPPORT AGREEMENT.—This subsection shall not apply in any case where over half of the support of the child is treated as having been received from a taxpayer under the provisions of subsection (c).

(4) EXCEPTION FOR CERTAIN PRE-1985 INSTRUMENTS.—

(A) IN GENERAL.—A child of parents described in paragraph (1) shall be treated as having received over half his support during a calendar year from the noncustodial parent if—

(i) a qualified pre-1985 instrument between the parents applicable to the taxable year beginning in such calendar year provides that the noncustodial parent shall be entitled to any deduction allowable under section 151 for such child, and

(ii) the noncustodial parent provides at least $600 for the support of such child during such calendar year.

For purposes of this subparagraph, amounts expended for the support of a child or children shall be treated as received from the noncustodial parent to the extent that such parent provided amounts for such support.

(B) QUALIFIED PRE-1985 INSTRUMENT.—For purposes of this paragraph, the term "qualified pre-1985 instrument" means any decree of divorce or separate maintenance or written agreement—

(i) which is executed before January 1, 1985,

(ii) which on such date contains the provision described in subparagraph (A)(i), and

(iii) which is not modified on or after such date in a modification which expressly provides that this paragraph shall not apply to such decree or agreement.

(5) SPECIAL RULE FOR SUPPORT RECEIVED FROM NEW SPOUSE OF PARENT.—For purposes of this subsection, in the case of the remarriage of a parent, support of a child received from the parent's spouse shall be treated as received from the parent.

(6) CROSS REFERENCE.—

For provision treating child as dependent of both parents for purposes of medical expense deduction, see section 213(d)(5).

Amendments

• 1986, Tax Reform Act of 1986 (P.L. 99-514)

P.L. 99-514, §104(b)(1)(B):

Amended Code Sec. 152(e)(1)(A) by striking out "section 151(e)(3)" and inserting in lieu thereof "section 151(c)(3)". **Effective** for tax years beginning after 12-31-86.

• 1984, Deficit Reduction Act of 1984 (P.L. 98-369)

P.L. 98-369, §423(a):

Amended Code Sec. 152(e). **Effective** for tax years beginning after 12-31-84. Prior to amendment, Code Sec. 152(e) read as follows:

(e) SUPPORT TEST IN CASE OF CHILD OF DIVORCED PARENTS, ET CETERA.—

(1) GENERAL RULE.—If—

(A) a child (as defined in section 151(e)(3)) receives over half of his support during the calendar year from his parents who are divorced or legally separated under a decree of divorce or separate maintenance, or who are separated under a written separation agreement, and

(B) such child is in the custody of one or both of his parents for more than one-half of the calendar year,

such child shall be treated, for purposes of subsection (a), as receiving over half of his support during the calendar year from the parent having custody for a greater portion of the calendar year unless he is treated, under the provisions of paragraph (2), as having received over half of his support for such year from the other parent (referred to in this subsection as the parent not having custody).

(2) SPECIAL RULE.—The child of parents described in paragraph (1) shall be treated as having received over half of his support during the calendar year from the parent not having custody if—

(A)(i) the decree of divorce or of separate maintenance, or a written agreement between the parents applicable to the taxable year beginning in such calendar year, provides that the parent not having custody shall be entitled to any deduction allowable under section 151 for such child, and

(ii) such parent not having custody provides at least $600 for the support of such child during the calendar year, or

(B)(i) the parent not having custody provides $1,200 or more for the support of such child (or if there is more than one such child, $1,200 or more for each of such children) for the calendar year, and

(ii) the parent having custody of such child does not clearly establish that he provided more for the support of such child during the calendar year than the parent not having custody.

For the purposes of this paragraph, amounts expended for the support of a child or children shall be treated as received from the parent not having custody to the extent that such parent provided amounts for such support.

(3) ITEMIZED STATEMENT REQUIRED.—If a taxpayer claims that paragraph (2)(B) applies with respect to a child for a calendar year and the other parent claims that paragraph (2)(B)(i) is not satisfied or claims to have provided more for the support of such child during such calendar year than the taxpayer, each parent shall be entitled to receive, under regulations to be prescribed by the Secretary, an itemized statement of the expenditures upon which the other parent's claim of support is based.

(4) EXCEPTION FOR MULTIPLE-SUPPORT AGREEMENT.—The provisions of this subsection shall not apply in any case where over half of the support of the child is treated as having been received from a taxpayer under the provisions of subsection (c).

(5) REGULATIONS.—The Secretary shall prescribe such regulations as may be necessary to carry out the purposes of this subsection.

• 1984, Deficit Reduction Act of 1984 (P.L. 98-369)

P.L. 98-369, §482(b)(2):

Amended Code Sec. 152(e)(6), after amendment by Act Sec. 423(a), by striking out "section 213(d)(4)" and inserting in lieu thereof "section 213(d)(5)". **Effective** for tax years beginning after 12-31-83.

• 1976, Tax Reform Act of 1976 (P.L. 94-455)

P.L. 94-455, §1906(b)(13)(A):

Amended 1954 Code by substituting "Secretary" for "Secretary or his delegate" each place it appeared. **Effective** 2-1-77.

P.L. 94-455, §2139(a):

Substituted "each" for "all" in clause (2)(B)(i). **Effective** for tax years beginning after 10-4-76.

• 1967 (P.L. 90-78)

P.L. 90-78, §1(a):

Added Sec. 152(e). **Effective** for tax years beginning after 12-31-66.

[Sec. 153]

SEC. 153. CROSS REFERENCES.

(1) For deductions of estates and trusts, in lieu of the exemptions under section 151, see section 642(b).

(2) For exemptions of nonresident aliens, see section 873(b)(3).

(3) For determination of marital status, see section 7703.

Amendments

• 2004, Working Families Tax Relief Act of 2004 (P.L. 108-311)

P.L. 108-311, §207(14):

Amended Code Sec. 153 by striking paragraph (1) and by redesignating paragraphs (2), (3), and (4) as paragraphs (1), (2), and (3), respectively. **Effective** for tax years beginning after 12-31-2004. Prior to being stricken, Code Sec. 153(1), read as follows:

(1) For definitions of "husband" and "wife", as used in section 152(b)(4), see section 7701(a)(17).

• 1986, Tax Reform Act of 1986 (P.L. 99-514)

P.L. 99-514, §1272(d)(7):

Amended Code Sec. 153 by striking out paragraph (4) and by redesignating paragraph (5) as paragraph (4). **Effective** for tax years beginning after 12-31-86. Prior to amendment, paragraph (4) read as follows:

(4) For exemptions of citizens deriving income mainly from sources within possessions of the United States, see section 931(e).

P.L. 99-514, §1301(j)(8):

Amended Code Sec. 153(5), now redesignated as 153(4), by striking out "section 143" each place it appears and inserting in lieu thereof "section 7703". **Effective** for bonds issued after 8-15-86.

• 1976, Tax Reform Act of 1976 (P.L. 94-455)

P.L. 94-455, §1901(b)(7):

Repealed Code Sec. 153, redesignated Code Sec. 154 as Code Sec. 153, and added a new paragraph (5). **Effective** for tax years beginning after 12-31-76. Prior to repeal, former Code Sec. 153 read as follows:

For purposes of this part—

(1) The determination of whether an individual is married shall be made as of the close of his taxable year; except that if his spouse dies during his taxable year such determination shall be made as of the time of such death; and

(2) An individual legally separated from his spouse under a decree of divorce or of separate maintenance shall not be considered as married.

• 1966, Foreign Investors Tax Act of 1966 (P.L. 89-809)

P.L. 89-809, §103(c)(2):

Amended Code Sec. 154(3) by substituting "section 873(b)(3)" for "section 873(d)". **Effective** 1-1-67.

PART VI—ITEMIZED DEDUCTIONS FOR INDIVIDUALS AND CORPORATIONS

[Sec. 161]

SEC. 161. ALLOWANCE OF DEDUCTIONS.

In computing taxable income under section 63, there shall be allowed as deductions the items specified in this part, subject to the exceptions provided in part IX (sec. 261 and following, relating to items not deductible).

Amendments

• **1977, Tax Reduction and Simplification Act of 1977 (P.L. 95-30)**

P.L. 95-30, §102(b)(1):

Amended Code Sec. 161 by striking out "section 63(a)" and inserting in lieu thereof "section 63". **Effective** for tax years beginning after 12-31-76.

[Sec. 162]

SEC. 162. TRADE OR BUSINESS EXPENSES.

[Sec. 162(a)]

(a) IN GENERAL.—There shall be allowed as a deduction all the ordinary and necessary expenses paid or incurred during the taxable year in carrying on any trade or business, including—

(1) a reasonable allowance for salaries or other compensation for personal services actually rendered;

(2) traveling expenses (including amounts expended for meals and lodging other than amounts which are lavish or extravagant under the circumstances) while away from home in the pursuit of a trade or business; and

(3) rentals or other payments required to be made as a condition to the continued use or possession, for purposes of the trade or business, of property to which the taxpayer has not taken or is not taking title or in which he has no equity.

⋙→ Caution: The last sentence of Code Sec. 162(a), below, as added by P.L. 111-148, applies to vouchers provided after December 31, 2013.

For purposes of the preceding sentence, the place of residence of a Member of Congress (including any Delegate and Resident Commissioner) within the State, congressional district, or possession which he represents in Congress shall be considered his home, but amounts expended by such

Members within each taxable year for living expenses shall not be deductible for income tax purposes in excess of $3,000. For purposes of paragraph (2), the taxpayer shall not be treated as being temporarily away from home during any period of employment if such period exceeds 1 year. The preceding sentence shall not apply to any Federal employee during any period for which such employee is certified by the Attorney General (or the designee thereof) as traveling on behalf of the United States in temporary duty status to investigate or prosecute, or provide support services for the investigation or prosecution of, a Federal crime. For purposes of paragraph (1), the amount of a free choice voucher provided under section 10108 of the Patient Protection and Affordable Care Act shall be treated as an amount for compensation for personal services actually rendered.

Amendments

• 2010, Patient Protection and Affordable Care Act (P.L. 111-148)

P.L. 111-148, §10108(g)(1):

Amended Code Sec. 162(a) by adding at the end a new sentence. **Effective** for vouchers provided after 12-31-2013.

• 1998, IRS Restructuring and Reform Act of 1998 (P.L. 105-206)

P.L. 105-206, §6012(a):

Amended Code Sec. 162(a) by striking "investigate" and all that follows and inserting "investigate or prosecute, or provide support services for the investigation or prosecution of, a Federal crime." in the last sentence. **Effective** as if included in the provision of P.L. 105-34 to which it relates [**effective** for amounts paid or incurred with respect to tax years ending after 8-5-97.—CCH]. Prior to amendment, the last sentence of Code Sec. 162(a) read as follows:

The preceding sentence shall not apply to any Federal employee during any period for which such employee is certified by the Attorney General (or the designee thereof) as traveling on behalf of the United States in temporary duty status to investigate, or provide support services for the investigation of, a Federal crime.

• 1997, Taxpayer Relief Act of 1997 (P.L. 105-34)

P.L. 105-34, §1204(a):

Amended Code Sec. 162(a) by adding at the end a new sentence. **Effective** for amounts paid or incurred with respect to tax years ending after 8-5-97.

• 1996, Deposit Insurance Funds Act of 1996 (P.L. 104-208)

P.L. 104-208, §2711, provides (with regard to special assessments on SAIF-assessable deposits):

SEC. 2711. DEDUCTION FOR SPECIAL ASSESSMENTS.

For purposes of subtitle A of the Internal Revenue Code of 1986—

(1) the amount allowed as a deduction under section 162 of such Code for a taxable year shall include any amount under section 2702 of this subtitle, and

(2) section 172(f) of such Code shall not apply to any deduction described in paragraph (1).

Effective 9-30-96.

• 1992, Energy Policy Act of 1992 (P.L. 102-486)

P.L. 102-486, §1938(a):

Amended Code Sec. 162(a) by adding at the end thereof a new sentence. **Effective** for costs paid or incurred after 12-31-92.

• 1982 (P.L. 97-216)

P.L. 97-216, §215(a):

Amended Code Sec. 162(a) by inserting after "home" in the last sentence thereof ", but amounts expended by such Members within each taxable year for living expenses shall not be deductible for income tax purposes in excess of $3,000". **Effective** for tax years beginning after 12-31-81.

P.L. 97-216, §215(c):

Repealed P.L. 97-51, §139(a), which expressed the sense of the Congress that the dollar limits on tax deductions for Members of Congress while away from home should be the same as the limits for businessmen and other private citizens. **Effective** for tax years beginning after 12-31-81.

• 1981 (P.L. 97-51)

P.L. 97-51, §139:

Amended Code Sec. 162(a) by striking out ", but amounts expended by such Members within each taxable year for living expenses shall not be deductible for income tax purposes in excess of $3,000" in the last sentence thereof and inserting in lieu thereof a period. Originally **effective**, as provided by §139(b)(3) of P.L. 97-51, for tax years beginning after 12-31-81. However, Section 133(a) of P.L. 97-92, signed 12-15-81, amended §139(b)(3) of P.L. 97-51 by striking out "1981" and inserting in lieu thereof "1980".

• 1978 (P.L. 95-427)

P.L. 95-427, §2, as amended by P.L. 95-258, §2, and P.L. 96-167, §2, provides:

SEC. 2. COMMUTING EXPENSES.

With respect to transportation costs paid or incurred after December 31, 1976, and on or before May 31, 1981, the application of sections 62, 162, and 262 and of chapters 21, 23, and 24 of the Internal Revenue Code of 1954 to transportation expenses in traveling between a taxpayer's residence and place of work shall be determined—

(1) without regard to Revenue Ruling 76-453 (and without regard to any other regulation, ruling, or decision reaching the same result as, or a result similar to, the result set forth in such Revenue Ruling); and

(2) with full regard to the rules in effect before Revenue Ruling 76-453.

Effective 10-7-78.

• 1976, Tax Reform Act of 1976 (P.L. 94-455)

P.L. 94-455, §1901(c)(4):

Amended Code Sec. 162(a) by striking out "territory" after "district." **Effective** for tax years beginning after 12-31-76.

• 1962, Revenue Act of 1962 (P.L. 87-834)

P.L. 87-834, §4:

Amended Code Sec. 162(a)(2) by striking out "(including the entire amount expended for meals and lodging)" and inserting in lieu thereof "(including amounts expended for meals and lodging other than amounts which are lavish or extravagant under the circumstances)". **Effective** for tax years ending after 12-31-62, but only in respect of periods after such date.

[Sec. 162(b)]

(b) CHARITABLE CONTRIBUTIONS AND GIFTS EXCEPTED.—No deduction shall be allowed under subsection (a) for any contribution or gift which would be allowable as a deduction under section 170 were it not for the percentage limitations, the dollar limitations, or the requirements as to the time of payment, set forth in such section.

Amendments

• 1960 (P.L. 86-779)

P.L. 86-779, §7(b):

Amended Code Sec. 162(b) by inserting "the dollar limitations" following "the percentage limitations,". **Effective** 1-1-61.

[Sec. 162(c)]

(c) ILLEGAL BRIBES, KICKBACKS, AND OTHER PAYMENTS.—

(1) ILLEGAL PAYMENTS TO GOVERNMENT OFFICIALS OR EMPLOYEES.—No deduction shall be allowed under subsection (a) for any payment made, directly or indirectly, to an official or employee of any government, or of any agency or instrumentality of any government, if the payment constitutes an illegal bribe or kickback or, if the payment is to an official or employee of a foreign government, the payment is unlawful under the Foreign Corrupt Practices Act of 1977. The burden of proof in respect of the issue, for the purposes of this paragraph, as to whether a payment constitutes an illegal bribe or kickback (or is unlawful under the Foreign Corrupt Practices Act of 1977) shall be upon the Secretary to the same extent as he bears the burden of proof under section 7454 (concerning the burden of proof when the issue relates to fraud).

(2) OTHER ILLEGAL PAYMENTS.—No deduction shall be allowed under subsection (a) for any payment (other than a payment described in paragraph (1)) made, directly or indirectly, to any person, if the payment constitutes an illegal bribe, illegal kickback, or other illegal payment under any law of the United States, or under any law of a State (but only if such State law is generally enforced), which subjects the payor to a criminal penalty or the loss of license or privilege to engage in a trade or business. For purposes of this paragraph, a kickback includes a payment in consideration of the referral of a client, patient, or customer. The burden of proof in respect of the issue, for purposes of this paragraph, as to whether a payment constitutes an illegal bribe, illegal kickback, or other illegal payment shall be upon the Secretary to the same extent as he bears the burden of proof under section 7454 (concerning the burden of proof when the issue relates to fraud).

(3) KICKBACKS, REBATES, AND BRIBES UNDER MEDICARE AND MEDICAID.—No deduction shall be allowed under subsection (a) for any kickback, rebate, or bribe made by any provider of services, supplier, physician, or other person who furnishes items or services for which payment is or may be made under the Social Security Act, or in whole or in part out of Federal funds under a State plan approved under such Act, if such kickback, rebate, or bribe is made in connection with the furnishing of such items or services or the making or receipt of such payments. For purposes of this paragraph, a kickback includes a payment in consideration of the referral of a client, patient, or customer.

Amendments

• 1982, Tax Equity and Fiscal Responsibility Act of 1982 (P.L. 97-248)

P.L. 97-248, §288(a)(1):

Amended Code Sec. 162(c)(1) by striking out "would be unlawful under the laws of the United States if such laws were applicable to such payment and to such official or employee" and inserting "is unlawful under the Foreign Corrupt Practices Act of 1977". **Effective** for payments made after 9-3-82.

P.L. 97-248, §288(a)(2):

Amended Code Sec. 162(c)(1) by striking out "(or would be unlawful under the laws of the United States)" and inserting in lieu thereof "(or is unlawful under the Foreign Corrupt Practices Act of 1977)". **Effective** for payments made after 9-3-82.

• 1976, Tax Reform Act of 1976 (P.L. 94-455)

P.L. 94-455, §1906(b)(13)(A):

Amended 1954 Code by substituting "Secretary" for "Secretary or his delegate" each place it appeared. **Effective** 2-1-77.

• 1971, Revenue Act of 1971 (P.L. 92-178)

P.L. 92-178, §310(a):

Amended paragraphs (2) and (3) of Code Sec. 162(c). **Effective** for payments made after 12-30-69, except for new Code Sec. 162(c)(3), which is applicable only to kickbacks, rebates, and bribes paid on or after 12-10-71. Prior to amendment, paragraphs (2) and (3) of Code Sec. 162(c) read as follows:

(2) Other bribes or kickbacks.—If in a criminal proceeding a taxpayer is convicted of making a payment (other than a payment described in paragraph (1)) which is an illegal bribe or kickback, or his plea of guilty or nolo contendere to an indictment or information charging the making of such a payment is entered or accepted in such a proceeding, no deduction shall be allowed under subsection (a) on account of such payment or any related payment made prior to the date of final judgment in such proceeding.

(3) Statute of limitations.—If a taxpayer claimed a deduction for a payment described in paragraph (2) which is disallowed because of a final judgment entered after the close of the taxable year for which the deduction was claimed, and if the proceeding was based on an indictment returned or an information filed prior to the expiration of the period for the assessment of any deficiency for such taxable year, the period for the assessment of any deficiency attributable to the deduction of such payment shall not expire prior to the expiration of one year from the date of such final judgment, and such deficiency may be assessed prior to the expiration of such one-year period notwithstanding the provision of any other law or rule of law which would otherwise prevent such assessment.

Also substituted the heading in Code Sec. 162(c) for the following: "Bribes and Illegal Kickbacks.—"

• 1969, Tax Reform Act of 1969 (P.L. 91-172)

P.L. 91-172, §902(b):

Amended Code Sec. 162(c). Section 162(c)(1) is **effective** for all tax years to which the 1954 Code applies. Sections 162(c)(2) and (3) are **effective** for payments made after 12-30-69. Prior to amendment Code Sec. 162(c) read as follows:

(c) Improper Payments to Officials or Employees of Foreign Countries.—No deduction shall be allowed under subsection (a) for any expenses paid or incurred if the payment thereof is made, directly or indirectly, to an official of a foreign country, and if the making of the payment would be unlawful under the laws of the United States if such laws were applicable to such payment and to such official or employee.

• 1958, Technical Amendments Act of 1958 (P.L. 85-866)

P.L. 85-866, §5(a):

Redesignated subsection (c) as subsection (d) (now (f)) and added new subsection (c). **Effective** 9-3-58.

[Sec. 162(d)]

(d) CAPITAL CONTRIBUTIONS TO FEDERAL NATIONAL MORTGAGE ASSOCIATION.—For purposes of this subtitle, whenever the amount of capital contributions evidenced by a share of stock issued pursuant to section 303(c) of the Federal National Mortgage Association Charter Act (12 U.S.C., sec. 1718) exceeds the fair market value of the stock as of the issue date of such stock, the initial holder of the stock shall treat the excess as ordinary and necessary expenses paid or incurred during the taxable year in carrying on a trade or business.

Amendments

• 1960 (P.L. 86-779)

P.L. 86-779, §8(a):

Redesignated subsection (d) of Code Sec. 162 as subsection (e), and added a new subsection (d). **Effective** for tax years beginning after 1959.

[Sec. 162(e)]

(e) DENIAL OF DEDUCTION FOR CERTAIN LOBBYING AND POLITICAL EXPENDITURES.—

(1) IN GENERAL.—No deduction shall be allowed under subsection (a) for any amount paid or incurred in connection with—

(A) influencing legislation,

(B) participation in, or intervention in, any political campaign on behalf of (or in opposition to) any candidate for public office,

(C) any attempt to influence the general public, or segments thereof, with respect to elections, legislative matters, or referendums, or

(D) any direct communication with a covered executive branch official in an attempt to influence the official actions or positions of such official.

(2) EXCEPTION FOR LOCAL LEGISLATION.—In the case of any legislation of any local council or similar governing body—

(A) paragraph (1)(A) shall not apply, and

(B) the deduction allowed by subsection (a) shall include all ordinary and necessary expenses (including, but not limited to, traveling expenses described in subsection (a)(2) and the cost of preparing testimony) paid or incurred during the taxable year in carrying on any trade or business—

(i) in direct connection with appearances before, submission of statements to, or sending communications to the committees, or individual members, of such council or body with respect to legislation or proposed legislation of direct interest to the taxpayer, or

(ii) in direct connection with communication of information between the taxpayer and an organization of which the taxpayer is a member with respect to any such legislation or proposed legislation which is of direct interest to the taxpayer and to such organization,

and that portion of the dues so paid or incurred with respect to any organization of which the taxpayer is a member which is attributable to the expenses of the activities described in clauses (i) and (ii) carried on by such organization.

(3) APPLICATION TO DUES OF TAX-EXEMPT ORGANIZATIONS.—No deduction shall be allowed under subsection (a) for the portion of dues or other similar amounts paid by the taxpayer to an organization which is exempt from tax under this subtitle which the organization notifies the taxpayer under section 6033(e)(1)(A)(ii) is allocable to expenditures to which paragraph (1) applies.

(4) INFLUENCING LEGISLATION.—For purposes of this subsection—

(A) IN GENERAL.—The term "influencing legislation" means any attempt to influence any legislation through communication with any member or employee of a legislative body, or with any government official or employee who may participate in the formulation of legislation.

(B) LEGISLATION.—The term "legislation" has the meaning given such term by section 4911(e)(2).

(5) OTHER SPECIAL RULES.—

(A) EXCEPTION FOR CERTAIN TAXPAYERS.—In the case of any taxpayer engaged in the trade or business of conducting activities described in paragraph (1), paragraph (1) shall not apply to expenditures of the taxpayer in conducting such activities directly on behalf of another person (but shall apply to payments by such other person to the taxpayer for conducting such activities).

(B) DE MINIMIS EXCEPTION.—

(i) IN GENERAL.—Paragraph (1) shall not apply to any in-house expenditures for any taxable year if such expenditures do not exceed $2,000. In determining whether a taxpayer exceeds the $2,000 limit under this clause, there shall not be taken into account overhead costs otherwise allocable to activities described in paragraphs (1)(A) and (D).

(ii) IN-HOUSE EXPENDITURES.—For purposes of clause (i), the term "in-house expenditures" means expenditures described in paragraphs (1)(A) and (D) other than—

(I) payments by the taxpayer to a person engaged in the trade or business of conducting activities described in paragraph (1) for the conduct of such activities on behalf of the taxpayer, or

(II) dues or other similar amounts paid or incurred by the taxpayer which are allocable to activities described in paragraph (1).

(C) EXPENSES INCURRED IN CONNECTION WITH LOBBYING AND POLITICAL ACTIVITIES.—Any amount paid or incurred for research for, or preparation, planning, or coordination of, any activity described in paragraph (1) shall be treated as paid or incurred in connection with such activity.

(6) COVERED EXECUTIVE BRANCH OFFICIAL.—For purposes of this subsection, the term "covered executive branch official" means—

(A) the President,

(B) the Vice President,

(C) any officer or employee of the White House Office of the Executive Office of the President, and the 2 most senior level officers of each of the other agencies in such Executive Office, and

(D)(i) any individual serving in a position in level I of the Executive Schedule under section 5312 of title 5, United States Code, (ii) any other individual designated by the President as having Cabinet level status, and (iii) any immediate deputy of an individual described in clause (i) or (ii).

(7) SPECIAL RULE FOR INDIAN TRIBAL GOVERNMENTS.—For purposes of this subsection, an Indian tribal government shall be treated in the same manner as a local council or similar governing body.

(8) CROSS REFERENCE.—

For reporting requirements and alternative taxes related to this subsection, see section 6033(e).

Amendments

• 1993, Omnibus Budget Reconciliation Act of 1993 (P.L. 103-66)

P.L. 103-66, §13222(a):

Amended Code Sec. 162(e). **Effective** for amounts paid or incurred after 12-31-93. Prior to amendment, Code Sec. 162(e) read as follows:

(e) APPEARANCES, ETC., WITH RESPECT TO LEGISLATION.—

(1) IN GENERAL.—The deduction allowed by subsection (a) shall include all the ordinary and necessary expenses (including, but not limited to, traveling expenses described in subsection (a)(2) and the cost of preparing testimony) paid or incurred during the taxable year in carrying on any trade or business—

(A) in direct connection with appearances before, submission of statements to, or sending communications to, the committees, or individual members, of Congress or of any legislative body of a State, a possession of the United States, or a political subdivision of any of the foregoing with respect to legislation or proposed legislation of direct interest to the taxpayer, or

(B) in direct connection with communication of information between the taxpayer and an organization of which he is a member with respect to legislation or proposed legislation of direct interest to the taxpayer and to such organization,

and that portion of the dues so paid or incurred with respect to any organization of which the taxpayer is a member which is attributable to the expenses of the activities described in subparagraphs (A) and (B) carried on by such organization.

(2) LIMITATION.—The provisions of paragraph (1) shall not be construed as allowing the deduction of any amount paid or incurred (whether by way of contribution, gift, or otherwise)—

(A) for participation in, or intervention in, any political campaign on behalf of any candidate for public office, or

(B) in connection with any attempt to influence the general public, or segments thereof, with respect to legislative matters, elections, or referendums.

• 1962, Revenue Act of 1962 (P.L. 87-834)

P.L. 87-834, §3(a):

Redesignated subsection (e) as subsection (f) and added new subsection (e). **Effective** for tax years beginning after 12-31-62.

[Sec. 162(f)]

(f) FINES AND PENALTIES.—No deduction shall be allowed under subsection (a) for any fine or similar penalty paid to a government for the violation of any law.

Amendments

• 1969, Tax Reform Act of 1969 (P.L. 91-172)

P.L. 91-172, §902(a):

Added subsection (f) to Code Sec. 162. **Effective** for all tax years to which the 1954 Code applies.

[Sec. 162(g)]

(g) TREBLE DAMAGE PAYMENTS UNDER THE ANTITRUST LAWS.—If in a criminal proceeding a taxpayer is convicted of a violation of the antitrust laws, or his plea of guilty or nolo contendere to an indictment or information charging such a violation is entered or accepted in such a proceeding, no deduction shall be allowed under subsection (a) for two-thirds of any amount paid or incurred—

(1) on any judgment for damages entered against the taxpayer under section 4 of the Act entitled "An Act to supplement existing laws against unlawful restraints and monopolies, and for other purposes", approved October 15, 1914 (commonly known as the Clayton Act), on account of such violation or any related violation of the antitrust laws which occurred prior to the date of the final judgment of such conviction, or

(2) in settlement of any action brought under such section 4 on account of such violation or related violation.

The preceding sentence shall not apply with respect to any conviction or plea before January 1, 1970, or to any conviction or plea on or after such date in a new trial following an appeal of a conviction before such date.

Amendments

• 1969, Tax Reform Act of 1969 (P.L. 91-172)

P.L. 91-172, §902(a):

Added subsection (g) to Code Sec. 162. **Effective** for amounts paid or incurred after 12-31-69.

• 1962, Revenue Act of 1962 (P.L. 87-834)

P.L. 87-834, §3:

Redesignated Code Sec. 162(e) as Sec. 162(f) and added a new Sec. 162(e). **Effective** 1-1-63.

[Sec. 162(h)]

(h) STATE LEGISLATORS' TRAVEL EXPENSES AWAY FROM HOME.—

(1) IN GENERAL.—For purposes of subsection (a), in the case of any individual who is a State legislator at any time during the taxable year and who makes an election under this subsection for the taxable year—

(A) the place of residence of such individual within the legislative district which he represented shall be considered his home,

(B) he shall be deemed to have expended for living expenses (in connection with his trade or business as a legislator) an amount equal to the sum of the amounts determined by multiplying each legislative day of such individual during the taxable year by the greater of—

(i) the amount generally allowable with respect to such day to employees of the State of which he is a legislator for per diem while away from home, to the extent such amount does not exceed 110 percent of the amount described in clause (ii) with respect to such day, or

(ii) the amount generally allowable with respect to such day to employees of the executive branch of the Federal Government for per diem while away from home but serving in the United States, and

(C) he shall be deemed to be away from home in the pursuit of a trade or business on each legislative day.

(2) LEGISLATIVE DAYS.—For purposes of paragraph (1), a legislative day during any taxable year for any individual shall be any day during such year on which—

(A) the legislature was in session (including any day in which the legislature was not in session for a period of 4 consecutive days or less), or

(B) the legislature was not in session but the physical presence of the individual was formally recorded at a meeting of a committee of such legislature.

(3) ELECTION.—An election under this subsection for any taxable year shall be made at such time and in such manner as the Secretary shall by regulations prescribe.

(4) SECTION NOT TO APPLY TO LEGISLATORS WHO RESIDE NEAR CAPITOL.—For taxable years beginning after December 31, 1980, this subsection shall not apply to any legislator whose place of residence within the legislative district which he represents is 50 or fewer miles from the capitol building of the State.

Amendments

• 1981, Economic Recovery Tax Act of 1981 (P.L. 97-34)

P.L. 97-34, §127(a):

Added Code Sec. 162(h). **Effective** for tax years beginning on or after 1-1-76.

[Sec. 162(i)—Repealed]

Amendments

• 1989, Omnibus Budget Reconciliation Act of 1989 (P.L. 101-239)

P.L. 101-239, §6202(b)(3)(A):

Repealed Code Sec. 162(i). **Effective** for items and services furnished after 12-19-89. Prior to repeal, Code Sec. 162(i) read as follows:

(i) GROUP HEALTH PLANS.—

(1) COVERAGE RELATING TO THE END STAGE RENAL DISEASE.—The expenses paid or incurred by an employer for a group health plan shall not be allowed as a deduction under this section if the plan differentiates in the benefits it provides between individuals having end stage renal disease and other individuals covered by such plan on the basis of the existence of end stage renal disease, the need for renal dialysis, or in any other manner.

(2) GROUP HEALTH PLAN.—For purposes of this subsection the term "group health plan" means any plan of, or contributed to by, an employer to provide medical care (as defined in section 213(d)) to his employees, former employees, or the families of such employees or former employees, directly or through insurance, reimbursement, or otherwise.

• 1988, Technical and Miscellaneous Revenue Act of 1988 (P.L. 100-647)

P.L. 100-647, §3011(b)(2):

Amended Code Sec. 162(i) by striking out paragraph (2) and redesignating paragraph (3) as paragraph (2). **Effective** for tax years beginning after 12-31-88, but shall not apply to any plan for any plan year to which section 162(k) of the Internal Revenue Code of 1986 (as in effect on the day before the enactment of this Act) did not apply by reason of section 10001(e)(2) of P.L. 99-272. Prior to amendment, Code Sec. 162(i)(2) read as follows:

(2) PLANS MUST PROVIDE CONTINUATION COVERAGE TO CERTAIN INDIVIDUALS.—

(A) IN GENERAL.—No deduction shall be allowed under this section for expenses paid or incurred by an employer for any group health plan maintained by such employer unless all such plans maintained by such employer meet the continuing coverage requirements of subsection (k).

(B) EXCEPTION FOR CERTAIN SMALL EMPLOYERS, ETC.—Subparagraph (A) shall not apply to any plan described in section 106(b)(2).

• 1986, Consolidated Omnibus Budget Reconciliation Act of 1985 (P.L. 99-272)

P.L. 99-272, §10001(a)

Amended Code Sec. 162(i) by redesignating paragraph (2) as paragraph (3) and by inserting after paragraph (1) new paragraph (2). **Effective** for plan years beginning on or after 7-1-86. For a special rule see Act Sec. 10001(e)(2), below.

P.L. 99-272, §10001(d):

Amended Code Sec. 162(i)(1) by striking out "General rule" in the heading thereof and inserting in lieu thereof "COVERAGE RELATING TO THE END STAGE RENAL DISEASE". **Effective** for plan years beginning on or after 7-1-86. For a special rule see Act Sec. 10001(e)(2), below.

P.L. 99-272, §10001(e)(2), provides:

(2) SPECIAL RULE FOR COLLECTIVE BARGAINING AGREEMENTS.—In the case of a group health plan maintained pursuant to one or more collective bargaining agreements between employee representatives and one or more employers ratified before the date of the enactment of this Act, the amendments made by this section shall not apply to plan years beginning before the later of—

(A) the date on which the last of the collective bargaining agreements relating to the plan terminates (determined without regard to any extension thereof agreed to after the date of the enactment of this Act), or

(B) January 1, 1987.

For purposes of subparagraph (A), any plan amendment made pursuant to a collective bargaining agreement relating to the plan which amends the plan solely to conform to any requirement added by this section shall not be treated as a termination of such collective bargaining agreement.

• 1984, Deficit Reduction Act of 1984 (P.L. 98-369)

P.L. 98-369, §2354(d):

Amended Code Sec. 162(i)(2) by striking out "213(e)" and inserting in lieu thereof "213(d)". **Effective** 7-18-84.

• 1982, Tax Equity and Fiscal Responsibility Act of 1982 (P.L. 97-248)

P.L. 97-248, §128(b)(2):

Amended Code Sec. 162 by redesignating subsection (h), as added by P.L. 97-35, as subsection (i). **Effective** as if it had been originally included as a part of that provision of the Internal Revenue Code of 1954 to which it relates, as amended by P.L. 97-35.

• 1981, Omnibus Budget Reconciliation Act of 1981 (P.L. 97-35)

P.L. 97-35, §2146(b):

Added Code Sec. 162(h). **Effective** for tax years beginning on or after 1-1-82. Note: P.L. 97-34, §127(a), added an earlier Code Sec. 162(h).

[Sec. 162(j)]

(j) CERTAIN FOREIGN ADVERTISING EXPENSES.—

(1) IN GENERAL.—No deduction shall be allowed under subsection (a) for any expenses of an advertisement carried by a foreign broadcast undertaking and directed primarily to a market in the United States. This paragraph shall apply only to foreign broadcast undertakings located in a country which denies a similar deduction for the cost of advertising directed primarily to a market in the foreign country when placed with a United States broadcast undertaking.

(2) BROADCAST UNDERTAKING.—For purposes of paragraph (1), the term "broadcast undertaking" includes (but is not limited to) radio and television stations.

Amendments

• 1984 (P.L. 98-573)

P.L. 98-573, §232(a):

Amended Code Sec. 162 by adding new subsection (j). **Effective** for tax years beginning after 10-30-84.

[Sec. 162(k)]

(k) STOCK REACQUISITION EXPENSES.—

(1) IN GENERAL.—Except as provided in paragraph (2), no deduction otherwise allowable shall be allowed under this chapter for any amount paid or incurred by a corporation in connection with the reacquisition of its stock or of the stock of any related person (as defined in section 465(b)(3)(C)).

(2) EXCEPTIONS.—Paragraph (1) shall not apply to—

(A) CERTAIN SPECIFIC DEDUCTIONS.—Any—

(i) deduction allowable under section 163 (relating to interest),

(ii) deduction for amounts which are properly allocable to indebtedness and amortized over the term of such indebtedness, or

(iii) deduction for dividends paid (within the meaning of section 561).

(B) STOCK OF CERTAIN REGULATED INVESTMENT COMPANIES.—Any amount paid or incurred in connection with the redemption of any stock in a regulated investment company which issues only stock which is redeemable upon the demand of the shareholder.

Amendments

• 1996, Small Business Job Protection Act of 1996 (P.L. 104-188)

P.L. 104-188, §1704(p)(1):

Amended Code Sec. 162(k)(1) by striking "the redemption of its stock" and inserting "the reacquisition of its stock or of the stock of any related person (as defined in section 465(b)(3)(C))". **Effective** for amounts paid or incurred after 9-13-95, in tax years ending after such date.

P.L. 104-188, §1704(p)(2):

Amended Code Sec. 162(k)(2)(A) by striking "or" at the end of clause (i), by redesignating clause (ii) as clause (iii), and by inserting after clause (i) a new clause (ii). **Effective** as if included in the amendment made by section 613 of P.L. 99-514.

P.L. 104-188, §1704(p)(3):

Amended Code Sec. 162(k) by striking "REDEMPTION" in the heading and inserting "REACQUISITION". **Effective** for amounts paid or incurred after 9-13-95, in tax years ending after such date.

• 1988, Technical and Miscellaneous Revenue Act of 1988 (P.L. 100-647)

P.L. 100-647, §3011(b)(3)(A)-(C):

Amended Code Sec. 162 by striking out subsection (k) and by redesignating the subsection relating to stock redemption expenses as subsection (k), the subsection relating to special rules for health insurance costs of self-employed individuals as subsection (l), and the subsection relating to cross references as subsection (m). **Effective** for tax years beginning after 12-31-88, but shall not apply to any plan for any plan year to which section 162(k) of the Internal Revenue Code of 1986 (as in effect on the date before the date of enactment of this Act) did not apply by reason of section 10001(e)(2) of P.L. 99-272. Prior to amendment, Code Sec. 162(k) read as follows:

(k) CONTINUATION COVERAGE REQUIREMENTS OF GROUP HEALTH PLANS.—

(1) IN GENERAL.—For purposes of subsection (i)(2) and section 106(b)(1), a group health plan meets the requirements of this subsection only if each qualified beneficiary who would lose coverage under the plan as a result of a qualifying event is entitled to elect, within the election period, continuation coverage under the plan.

(2) CONTINUATION COVERAGE.—For purposes of paragraph (1), the term "continuation coverage" means coverage under the plan which meets the following requirements:

(A) TYPE OF BENEFIT COVERAGE.—The coverage must consist of coverage which, as of the time the coverage is being provided, is identical to the coverage provided under the plan to similarly situated beneficiaries under the plan with respect to whom a qualifying event has not occurred. If coverage under the plan is modified for any group of similarly situated beneficiaries, the coverage shall also be modified in the same manner for all individuals who are qualified beneficiaries under the plan pursuant to this subsection in connection with such group.

(B) PERIOD OF COVERAGE.—The coverage must extend for at least the period beginning on the date of the qualifying event and ending not earlier than the earliest of the following:

(i) MAXIMUM REQUIRED PERIOD.—

(I) GENERAL RULE FOR TERMINATIONS AND REDUCED HOURS.—In the case of a qualifying event described in paragraph (3)(B), except as provided in subclause (II), the date which is 18 months after the date of the qualifying event.

(II) SPECIAL RULE FOR MULTIPLE QUALIFYING EVENTS.—If a qualifying event (other than a qualifying event described in paragraph (3)(F)) occurs during the 18 months after the date of a qualifying event described in paragraph (3)(B), the date which is 36 months after the date of the qualifying event described in paragraph (3)(B).

(III) SPECIAL RULE FOR CERTAIN BANKRUPTCY PROCEEDINGS.—In the case of a qualifying event described in paragraph (3)(F) (relating to bankruptcy proceedings), the date of the death of the covered employee or qualified beneficiary (described in paragraph (7)(B)(iv)(III)), or in the case of the surviving spouse or dependent children of the covered employee, 36 months after the date of the death of the covered employee.

(IV) GENERAL RULE FOR OTHER QUALIFYING EVENTS.—In the case of a qualifying event not described in paragraph (3)(B) or (3)(F), the date which is 36 months after the date of the qualifying event.

(ii) END OF PLAN.—The date on which the employer ceases to provide any group health plan to any employee.

(iii) FAILURE TO PAY PREMIUM.—The date on which coverage ceases under the plan by reason of a failure to make timely payment of any premium required under the plan with respect to the qualified beneficiary. The payment of any premium (other than any payment referred to in the last sentence of subparagraph (C)) shall be considered to be timely if made within 30 days after the date due or within such longer period as applies to or under the plan.

(iv) GROUP HEALTH PLAN COVERAGE OR MEDICARE ENTITLEMENT.—The date on which the qualified beneficiary first becomes, after the date of the election—

(I) covered under any other group health plan (as an employee or otherwise) which does not contain any exclusion or limitation with respect to any preexisting condition of such beneficiary, or

(II) in the case of a qualified beneficiary other than a qualified beneficiary described in paragraph (7)(B)(iv) entitled to benefits under title XVIII of the Social Security Act.

(C) PREMIUM REQUIREMENTS.—The plan may require payment of a premium for any period of continuation coverage, except that such premium—

(i) shall not exceed 102 percent of the applicable premium for such period, and

(ii) may, at the election of the payor, be made in monthly installments.

If an election is made after the qualifying event, the plan shall permit payment for continuation coverage during the period preceding the election to be made within 45 days of the date of the election.

(D) NO REQUIREMENT OF INSURABILITY.—The coverage may not be conditioned upon, or discriminate on the basis of lack of, evidence of insurability.

(E) CONVERSION OPTION.—In the case of a qualified beneficiary whose period of continuation coverage expires under subparagraph (B)(i), the plan must, during the 180-day period ending on such expiration date, provide to the qualified beneficiary the option of enrollment under a conversion health plan otherwise generally available under the plan.

(3) QUALIFYING EVENT.—For purposes of this subsection, the term "qualifying event" means, with respect to any covered employee, any of the following events which, but for the continuation coverage required under this subsection, would result in the loss of coverage of a qualified beneficiary:

(A) The death of the covered employee.

(B) The termination (other than by reason of such employee's gross misconduct), or reduction of hours, of the covered employee's employment.

(C) The divorce or legal separation of the covered employee from the employee's spouse.

(D) The covered employee becoming entitled to benefits under title XVIII of the Social Security Act.

(E) A dependent child ceasing to be a dependent child under the generally applicable requirements of the plan.

(F) A proceeding in a case under title 11, United States Code, commencing on or after July 1, 1986, with respect to the employer from whose employment the covered employee retired at any time.

In the case of an event described in subparagraph (F), a loss of coverage includes a substantial elimination of coverage with respect to a qualified beneficiary described in paragraph (7)(B)(iv) within one year before or after the date of commencement of the proceeding.

(4) APPLICABLE PREMIUM.—For purposes of this subsection—

(A) IN GENERAL.—The term "applicable premium" means, with respect to any period of continuation coverage of qualified beneficiaries, the cost to the plan for such period of the coverage for similarly situated beneficiaries with respect to whom a qualifying event has not occurred (without regard to whether such cost is paid by the employer or employee).

(B) SPECIAL RULE FOR SELF-INSURED PLANS.—To the extent that a plan is a self-insured plan—

(i) IN GENERAL.—Except as provided in clause (ii), the applicable premium for any period of continuation coverage of qualified beneficiaries shall be equal to a reasonable estimate of the cost of providing coverage for such period for similarly situated beneficiaries which—

(I) is determined on an actuarial basis, and

(II) takes into account such factors as the Secretary may prescribe in regulations.

(ii) DETERMINATION ON BASIS OF PAST COST.—If a plan administrator elects to have this clause apply, the applicable premium for any period of continuation coverage of qualified beneficiaries shall be equal to—

(I) the cost to the plan for similarly situated beneficiaries for the same period occurring during the preceding determination period under subparagraph (C), adjusted by

(II) the percentage increase or decrease in the implicit price deflator of the gross national product (calculated by the Department of Commerce and published in the Survey of Current Business) for the 12-month period ending on the last day of the sixth month of such preceding determination period.

(iii) CLAUSE (ii) NOT TO APPLY WHERE SIGNIFICANT CHANGE.—A plan administrator may not elect to have clause (ii) apply in any case in which there is any significant difference between the determination period and the preceding determination period, in coverage under, or in employees covered by, the plan. The determination under the preceding sentence for any determination period shall be made at the same time as the determination under subparagraph (C).

(C) DETERMINATION PERIOD.—The determination of any applicable premium shall be made for a period of 12 months and shall be made before the beginning of such period.

(5) ELECTION.—For purposes of this subsection—

(A) ELECTION PERIOD.—The term "election period" means the period which—

(i) begins not later than the date on which coverage terminates under the plan by reason of a qualifying event,

(ii) is of at least 60 days' duration, and

(iii) ends not earlier than 60 days after the later of—

(I) the date described in clause (i), or

(II) in the case of any qualified beneficiary who receives notice under paragraph (6)(D), the date of such notice.

(B) EFFECT OF ELECTION ON OTHER BENEFICIARIES.—Except as otherwise specified in an election, any election of continuation coverage by a qualified beneficiary described in clause (i)(I) or (ii) of paragraph (7)(B) shall be deemed to include an election of continuation coverage on behalf of any other qualified beneficiary who would lose coverage under the plan by reason of the qualifying event. If there is a choice among types of coverage under the plan, each qualified beneficiary is entitled to make a separate selection among such types of coverage.

(6) NOTICE REQUIREMENTS.—In accordance with regulations prescribed by the Secretary—

(A) the group health plan shall provide, at the time of commencement of coverage under the plan, written notice to each covered employee and spouse of the employee (if any) of the rights provided under this subsection,

(B) the employer of an employee under a plan must notify the plan administrator of a qualifying event described in subparagraph (A), (B), (D), or (F) of paragraph (3) with respect to such employee within 30 days of the date of the qualifying event,

(C) each covered employee or qualified beneficiary is responsible for notifying the plan administrator of the occurrence of any qualifying event described in subparagraph (C) or (E) of paragraph (3) within 60 days after the date of the qualifying event, and

(D) the plan administrator shall notify—

(i) in the case of a qualifying event described in subparagraph (A), (B), (D), or (F) of paragraph (3), any qualified beneficiary with respect to such event, and

(ii) in the case of a qualifying event described in subparagraph (C) or (E) of paragraph (3) where the covered employee notifies the plan administrator under subparagraph (C), any qualified beneficiary with respect to such event,

of such beneficiary's rights under this subsection.

For purposes of subparagraph (D), any notification shall be made within 14 days of the date on which the plan administrator is notified under subparagraph (B) or (C), whichever is applicable, and any such notification to an individual who is a qualified beneficiary as the spouse of the covered employee shall be treated as notification to all other qualified beneficiaries residing with such spouse at the time such notification is made.

(7) DEFINITIONS.—For purposes of this subsection—

(A) COVERED EMPLOYEE.—The term "covered employee" means an individual who is (or was) provided coverage under a group health plan by virtue of the individual's employment or previous employment with an employer.

(B) QUALIFIED BENEFICIARY.—

(i) IN GENERAL.—The term "qualified beneficiary" means, with respect to a covered employee under a group health plan, any other individual who, on the day before the qualifying event for that employee, is a beneficiary under the plan—

(I) as the spouse of the covered employee, or

(II) as the dependent child of the employee.

(ii) SPECIAL RULE FOR TERMINATIONS AND REDUCED EMPLOYMENT.—In the case of a qualifying event described in paragraph (3)(B), the term "qualified beneficiary" includes the covered employee.

(iii) EXCEPTION FOR NONRESIDENT ALIENS.—Notwithstanding clauses (i) and (ii), the term "qualified beneficiary" does not include an individual whose status as a covered employee is attributable to a period in which such individual was a nonresident alien who received no earned income (within the meaning of section 911(d)(2)) from the employer which constituted income from sources within the United States (within the meaning of section 861(a)(3)). If an individual is not a qualified beneficiary pursuant to the previous sentence, a spouse or dependent child of such individual shall not be considered a qualified beneficiary by virtue of the relationship of the individual.

(iv) SPECIAL RULE FOR RETIREES AND WIDOWS.—In the case of a qualifying event described in paragraph (3)(F), the term "qualified beneficiary" includes a covered employee who had retired on or before the date of substantial elimination of coverage and any other individual who, on the day before such qualifying event, is a beneficiary under the plan—

(I) as the spouse of the covered employee,

(II) as the dependent child of the employee, or

(III) as the surviving spouse of the covered employee.

(C) PLAN ADMINISTRATOR.—The term "plan administrator" has the meaning given the term "administrator" by section 3(16)(A) of the Employee Retirement Income Security Act of 1974.

• 1989, Omnibus Budget Reconciliation Act of 1989 (P.L. 101-239)

P.L. 101-239, §7862(c)(3)(A)(i)-(ii):

Amended Code Sec. 162(k)(2)(B)(iv) by striking "ELIGIBILITY" in the heading and inserting "ENTITLEMENT", and by inserting "which does not contain any exclusion or limitation with respect to any preexisting condition of such beneficiary" after "or otherwise)" in subclause (I). **Effective** for qualifying events occurring after 12-31-89, and in the case of qualified beneficiaries who elected continuation coverage after 12-31-88, the period for which the required premium was paid (or was attempted to be paid but was rejected as such).

• 1986, Tax Reform Act of 1986 (P.L. 99-514)

P.L. 99-514, §1895(d)(1)(A):

Amended Code Sec. 162(k)(2)(A) by adding the sentence at the end thereof. **Effective** as if included in the enactment of P.L. 99-272.

P.L. 99-514, §1895(d)(2)(A):

Amended Code Sec. 162(k)(2)(B)(i). **Effective** as if included in the enactment of P.L. 99-272. Prior to amendment, it read as follows:

(i) MAXIMUM PERIOD.—In the case of—

(I) a qualifying event described in paragraph (3)(B) (relating to terminations and reduced hours), the date which is 18 months after the date of the qualifying event, and

(II) any qualifying event not described in subclause (I), the date which is 36 months after the date of the qualifying event.

P.L. 99-514, §1895(d)(3)(A):

Amended Code Sec. 162(k)(2)(B)(iii) by adding the sentence at the end thereof. **Effective** as if included in the enactment of P.L. 99-272.

P.L. 99-514, §1895(d)(4)(A)(i):

Amended Code Sec. 162(k)(2)(B) by striking out clause (v). **Effective** as if included in the enactment of P.L. 99-272. Prior to amendment, clause (v) read as follows:

(v) REMARRIAGE OF SPOUSE.—In the case of an individual who is a qualified beneficiary by reason of being the spouse of a covered employee, the date on which the beneficiary remarries and becomes covered under a group health plan.

P.L. 99-514, §1895(d)(4)(A)(ii):

Amended Code Sec. 162(k)(2)(B) by striking out subclause (I) of clause (iv) and inserting new subclause (I). **Effective** as if included in the enactment of P.L. 99-272. Prior to amendment, it read as follows:

(I) a covered employee under any other group health plan, or

P.L. 99-514, §1895(d)(4)(A)(iii):

Amended Code Sec. 162(k)(2)(B) by striking out the heading for clause (iv) and inserting the heading. **Effective** as if included in the enactment of P.L. 99-272. Prior to amendment, the heading read as follows:

Reemployment or Medicare Eligibility.

P.L. 99-514, §1895(d)(5)(A), as amended by P.L. 100-647, §1018(t)(7)(B):

Amended Code Sec. 162(k)(5)(B) by inserting "of continuation coverage" after "any election"; and by adding the sentence at the end thereof. **Effective** as if included in the enactment of P.L. 99-272.

P.L. 99-514, §1895(d)(6)(A):

Amended Code Sec. 162(k)(6)(C) by inserting "within 60 days after the date of the qualifying event" after "paragraph (3)". **Effective** with respect to qualifying events occurring after 10-22-86.

P.L. 99-514, §1895(d)(7):

Amended Code Sec. 162(k)(7)(B) by adding clause (iii) at the end thereof. **Effective** as if included in the enactment of P.L. 99-272.

• 1986, Omnibus Budget Reconciliation Act of 1986 (P.L. 99-509)

P.L. 99-509, §9501(a)(1):

Amended Code Sec. 162(k)(3) by adding at the end new subparagraph (f). **Effective** as if included in title X of P.L. 99-272. However, see Act Sec. 9501(e)(2)-(4), below.

P.L. 99-509, §9501(b)(1)(A)(i)-(iv):

Amended Code Sec. 162(k)(2)(B)(i) by inserting "(other than a qualifying event described in paragraph (3)(F))" after "qualifying event" the first place it appears in subclause (II), by inserting "or (3)(F)" after "(3)(B)" in subclause (III), by redesignating subclause (III) as subclause (IV), and by inserting after subclause (II) new subclause (III). **Effective** as if included in title X of P.L. 99-272. However, see Act Sec. 9501(e)(2)-(4), below.

P.L. 99-509, §9501(b)(2)(A):

Amended Code Sec. 162(k)(2)(B)(iv) by inserting "in the case of a qualified beneficiary other than a qualified beneficiary described in paragraph (7)(B)(iv)," before "entitled". **Effective** as if included in title X of P.L. 99-272. However, see Act Sec. 9501(e)(2)-(4), below.

P.L. 99-509, §9501(c)(1):

Amended Code Sec. 162(k)(7)(B) by adding at the end new clause (iv). **Effective** as if included in title X of P.L. 99-272. However, see Act Sec. 9501(e)(2)-(4), below.

P.L. 99-509, §9501(d)(1):

Amended Code Sec. 162(k)(6)(B) and (D)(i) by striking "or (D)" each place it appears and inserting in lieu thereof "(D), or (F)". **Effective** as if included in title X of P.L. 99-272. However, see Act Sec. 9501(e)(2)-(4), below.

P.L. 99-509, §9501(e)(2)-(4), provides:

(2) TREATMENT OF CERTAIN BANKRUPTCY PROCEEDINGS.—Notwithstanding paragraph (1), section 10001(e) of the Consolidated Omnibus Budget Reconciliation Act of 1985, and section 10002(d) of such Act, the amendments made by this section and by sections 10001 and 10002 of such Act shall apply in the case of plan years ending during the 12-month period beginning July 1, 1986, but only with respect to—

(A) a qualifying event described in section 162(k)(3)(F) of the Internal Revenue Code of 1986 or section 603(6) of the Employee Retirement Income Security Act of 1974, and

(B) a qualifying event described in section 162(k)(3)(A) of the Internal Revenue Code of 1986 or section 603(1) of the Employee Retirement Income Security Act of 1974 relating to the death of a retired employee occurring after the date of the qualifying event described in subparagraph (A).

(3) TREATMENT OF CURRENT RETIREES.—Section 162(k)(3)(F) of the Internal Revenue Code of 1986 and section 603(6) of the Employee Retirement Income Security Act of 1974 apply to covered employees who retired before, on, or after the date of the enactment of this Act.

(4) NOTICE.—In the case of a qualifying event described in section 603(6) of the Employee Retirement Income Security Act of 1974 that occurred before the date of the enactment of this Act, the notice required under section 606(2) of such Act (and under section 162(k)(6)(B) of the Internal Revenue Code of 1986) with respect to such event shall be provided no later than 30 days after the date of the enactment of this Act.

• 1986, Consolidated Omnibus Budget Reconciliation Act of 1985 (P.L. 99-272)

P.L. 99-272, §10001(c):

Amended Code Sec. 162 by redesignating subsection (k) as subsection (l) and by inserting after subsection (j) new subsection (k). **Effective** for plan years beginning on or after 7-1-86. For a special rule see Act Sec. 10001(e)(2), below.

P.L. 99-272, §10001(e)(2), provides:

(2) SPECIAL RULE FOR COLLECTIVE BARGAINING AGREEMENTS.—In the case of a group health plan maintained pursuant to one or more collective bargaining agreements between employee representatives and one or more employers ratified before the date of the enactment of this Act, the amendments made by this section shall not apply to plan years beginning before the later of—

(A) the date on which the last of the collective bargaining agreements relating to the plan terminates (determined without regard to any extension thereof agreed to after the date of the enactment of this Act), or

(B) January 1, 1987.

For purposes of subparagraph (A), any plan amendment made pursuant to a collective bargaining agreement relating to the plan which amends the plan solely to conform to any requirement added by this section shall not be treated as a termination of such collective bargaining agreement.

[Sec. 162(l)]

(l) SPECIAL RULES FOR HEALTH INSURANCE COSTS OF SELF-EMPLOYED INDIVIDUALS.—

(1) ALLOWANCE OF DEDUCTION.—In the case of a taxpayer who is an employee within the meaning of section 401(c)(1), there shall be allowed as a deduction under this section an amount equal to the amount paid during the taxable year for insurance which constitutes medical care for—

(A) the taxpayer,

(B) the taxpayer's spouse,

(C) the taxpayer's dependents, and

(D) any child (as defined in section 152(f)(1)) of the taxpayer who as of the end of the taxable year has not attained age 27.

(2) LIMITATIONS.—

(A) DOLLAR AMOUNT.—No deduction shall be allowed under paragraph (1) to the extent that the amount of such deduction exceeds the taxpayer's earned income (within the meaning of section 401(c)) derived by the taxpayer from the trade or business with respect to which the plan providing the medical care coverage is established.

(B) OTHER COVERAGE.—Paragraph (1) shall not apply to any taxpayer for any calendar month for which the taxpayer is eligible to participate in any subsidized health plan maintained by any employer of the taxpayer or of the spouse of, or any dependent, or individual described in subparagraph (D) of paragraph (1) with respect to, the taxpayer. The preceding sentence shall be applied separately with respect to—

(i) plans which include coverage for qualified long-term care services (as defined in section 7702B(c)) or are qualified long-term care insurance contracts (as defined in section 7702B(b)), and

(ii) plans which do not include such coverage and are not such contracts.

(C) LONG-TERM CARE PREMIUMS.—In the case of a qualified long-term care insurance contract (as defined in section 7702B(b)), only eligible long-term care premiums (as defined in section 213(d)(10)) shall be taken into account under paragraph (1).

(3) COORDINATION WITH MEDICAL DEDUCTION.—Any amount paid by a taxpayer for insurance to which paragraph (1) applies shall not be taken into account in computing the amount allowable to the taxpayer as a deduction under section 213(a).

(4) DEDUCTION NOT ALLOWED FOR SELF-EMPLOYMENT TAX PURPOSES.—The deduction allowable by reason of this subsection shall not be taken into account in determining an individual's net earnings from self-employment (within the meaning of section 1402(a)) for purposes of chapter 2 for taxable years beginning before January 1, 2010, or after December 31, 2010.

(5) TREATMENT OF CERTAIN S CORPORATION SHAREHOLDERS.—This subsection shall apply in the case of any individual treated as a partner under section 1372(a), except that—

(A) for purposes of this subsection, such individual's wages (as defined in section 3121) from the S corporation shall be treated as such individual's earned income (within the meaning of section 401(c)(1)), and

(B) there shall be such adjustments in the application of this subsection as the Secretary may by regulations prescribe.

Amendments

• 2010, Creating Small Business Jobs Act of 2010 (P.L. 111-240)

P.L. 111-240, §2042(a):

Amended Code Sec. 162(l)(4) by inserting "for taxable years beginning before January 1, 2010, or after December 31, 2010" before the period. **Effective** for tax years beginning after 12-31-2009.

• 2010, Health Care and Education Reconciliation Act of 2010 (P.L. 111-152)

P.L. 111-152, §1004(d)(2):

Amended Code Sec. 162(l)(1). **Effective** 3-30-2010. Prior to amendment, Code Sec. 162(l)(1) read as follows:

(1) ALLOWANCE OF DEDUCTION.—

(A) IN GENERAL.—In the case of an individual who is an employee within the meaning of section 401(c)(1), there shall be allowed as a deduction under this section an amount equal to the applicable percentage of the amount paid during the taxable year for insurance which constitutes medical care for the taxpayer, his spouse, and dependents.

(B) APPLICABLE PERCENTAGE.—For purposes of subparagraph (A), the applicable percentage shall be determined under the following table:

For taxable years beginning in calendar year—	*The applicable percentage is—*
1999 through 2001	60
2002	70
2003 and thereafter	100

P.L. 111-152, §1004(d)(3):

Amended Code Sec. 162(l)(2)(B) by inserting ", or any dependent, or individual described in subparagraph (D) of paragraph (1) with respect to," after "spouse of". **Effective** 3-30-2010.

• 1998, Tax and Trade Relief Extension Act of 1998 (P.L. 105-277)

P.L. 105-277, §2002(a):

Amended the table contained in Code Sec. 162(l)(1)(B). **Effective** for tax years beginning after 12-31-98. Prior to amendment, the table contained in Code Sec. 162(l)(1)(B) read as follows:

For taxable years beginning in calendar year—	*The applicable percentage is—*
1997	40
1998 and 1999	45
2000 and 2001	50
2002	60
2003 through 2005	80
2006	90
2007 and thereafter	100

• 1997, Taxpayer Relief Act of 1997 (P.L. 105-34)

P.L. 105-34, §934(a):

Amended the table contained in Code Sec. 162(l)(1)(B). **Effective** for tax years beginning after 12-31-96. Prior to amendment, Code Sec. 162(l)(1)(B) read as follows:

(B) APPLICABLE PERCENTAGE.—For purposes of subparagraph (A), the applicable percentage shall be determined under the following table:

For taxable years beginning in calendar year—	*The applicable percentage is—*
1997	40 percent
1998 through 2002	45 percent
2003	50 percent
2004	60 percent
2005	70 percent
2006 or thereafter	80 percent

P.L. 105-34, §1602(c):

Amended Code Sec. 162(l)(2)(B) by adding at the end a new sentence. **Effective** as if included in the provision of P.L. 104-191 to which it relates.

• 1996, Health Insurance Portability and Accountability Act of 1996 (P.L. 104-191)

P.L. 104-191, §311(a):

Amended Code Sec. 162(l)(1). **Effective** for tax years beginning after 12-31-96. Prior to amendment, Code Sec. 162(l)(1) read as follows:

(1) IN GENERAL.—In the case of an individual who is an employee within the meaning of section 401(c)(1), there shall be allowed as a deduction under this section an amount equal to 30 percent of the amount paid during the taxable year for insurance which constitutes medical care for the taxpayer, his spouse, and dependents.

P.L. 104-191, §322(b)(2)(B):

Amended Code Sec. 162(l)(2) by adding at the end a new subparagraph (C). **Effective** for tax years beginning after 12-31-96.

• 1995, Self-Employed Health Insurance Act (P.L. 104-7)

P.L. 104-7, §1(a):

Amended Code Sec. 162(l) by striking paragraph (6). **Effective** for tax years beginning after 12-31-93. Prior to amendment, Code Sec. 162(l)(6) read as follows:

(6) TERMINATION.—This subsection shall not apply to any taxable year beginning after December 31, 1993.

P.L. 104-7, §1(b):

Amended Code Sec. 162(l)(1) by striking "25 percent" and inserting "30 percent". **Effective** for tax years beginning after 12-31-94.

• 1993, Omnibus Budget Reconciliation Act of 1993 (P.L. 103-66)

P.L. 103-66, §13131(d)(2):

Amended Code Sec. 162(l)(3). **Effective** for tax years beginning after 12-31-93. Prior to amendment, Code Sec. 162(l)(3) read as follows:

(3) COORDINATION WITH MEDICAL DEDUCTION, ETC.—

(A) MEDICAL DEDUCTION.—Any amount paid by a taxpayer for insurance to which paragraph (1) applies shall not be taken into account in computing the amount allowable to the taxpayer as a deduction under section 213(a).

(B) HEALTH INSURANCE CREDIT.—The amount otherwise taken into account under paragraph (1) as paid for insurance which constitutes medical care shall be reduced by the amount (if any) of the health insurance credit allowable to the taxpayer for the taxable year under section 32.

P.L. 103-66, §13174(a)(1):

Amended Code Sec. 162(l)(6) by striking "June 30, 1992" and inserting "December 31, 1993". **Effective** for tax years ending after 6-30-92.

P.L. 103-66, §13174(b)(1):

Amended Code Sec. 162(l)(2)(B). **Effective** for tax years beginning after 12-31-92. Prior to amendment, Code Sec. 162(l)(2)(B) read as follows:

(B) OTHER COVERAGE.—Paragraph (1) shall not apply to any taxpayer who is eligible to participate in any subsidized health plan maintained by any employer of the taxpayer or of the spouse of the taxpayer.

• 1991, Tax Extension Act of 1991 (P.L. 102-227)

P.L. 102-227, §110(a)(1):

Amended Code Sec. 162(l)(6) by striking "December 31, 1991" and inserting "June 30, 1992". **Effective** for tax years beginning after 12-31-91. For a special rule, see P.L. 102-227, §110(a)(2), below.

P.L. 102-227, §110(a)(2), provides:

(2) SPECIAL RULE.—In the case of any taxable year beginning in 1992—

(A) only amounts paid before July 1, 1992, by the individual for insurance coverage for periods before July 1, 1992, shall be taken into account in determining the amount deductible under section 162(l) of the Internal Revenue Code of 1986 with respect to such individual for such taxable year, and

(B) for purposes of subparagraph (A) of section 162(l)(2) of such Code, the amount of the earned income described in such subparagraph taken into account for such taxable year shall be the amount which bears the same ratio to the total amount of such earned income as the number of months in such taxable year ending before July 1, 1992, bears to the number of months in such taxable year.

• 1990, Omnibus Budget Reconciliation Act of 1990 (P.L. 101-508)

P.L. 101-508, §11111(d)(2):

Amended Code Sec. 162(l)(3). **Effective** for tax years beginning after 12-31-90. Prior to amendment, Code Sec. 162(l)(3) read as follows:

(3) COORDINATION WITH MEDICAL DEDUCTION.—Any amount paid by a taxpayer for insurance to which paragraph (1) applies shall not be taken into account in computing the amount allowable to the taxpayer as a deduction under section 213(a).

P.L. 101-508, §11410(a):

Amended Code Sec. 162(l)(6)(B) by striking "September 30, 1990" and inserting "December 31, 1991". **Effective** for tax years beginning after 12-31-89.

• 1989, Omnibus Budget Reconciliation Act of 1989 (P.L. 101-239)

P.L. 101-239, §7107(b):

Amended Code Sec. 162(l) by redesignating paragraph (5) as paragraph (6) and by inserting after paragraph (4) a new paragraph (5). **Effective** for tax years beginning after 12-31-89.

P.L. 101-239, §7107(a)(1):

Amended Code Sec. 162(l)(5) by striking "December 31, 1989" and inserting "September 30, 1990". **Effective** for tax years beginning after 12-31-89.

• 1989 (P.L. 101-140)

P.L. 101-140, §203(a)(4):

Amended Code Sec. 162(l)(2) by striking subparagraph (B) and redesignating subparagraph (C) as subparagraph (B). **Effective** as if included in section 1151 of P.L. 99-514. Prior to amendment, Code Sec. 162(l)(2)(B) read as follows:

(B) REQUIRED COVERAGE.—Paragraph (1) shall not apply to any taxpayer for any taxable year unless coverage is provided under 1 or more plans meeting the requirements of section 89, treating such coverage as an employer-provided benefit.

• 1988, Technical and Miscellaneous Revenue Act of 1988 (P.L. 100-647)

P.L. 100-647, §1011B(b)(1):

Amended Code Sec. 162(m) by redesignating paragraph (4) as paragraph (5) and by inserting after paragraph (3) new paragraph (4). **Effective** as if included in the provision of P.L. 99-514 to which it relates.

P.L. 100-647, §1011B(b)(3):

Amended Code Sec. 162(m)(2)(A) by inserting "derived by the taxpayer from the trade or business with respect to which the plan providing the medical care coverage is established" after "401(c))". **Effective** as if included in the provision of P.L. 99-514 to which it relates.

P.L. 100-647, §3011(b)(3)(A)-(C):

Amended Code Sec. 162 by striking out subsection (k) and by redesignating the subsection relating to stock redemption expenses as subsection (k), the subsection relating to special rules for health insurance costs of self-employed individuals as subsection (l), and the subsection relating to cross references as subsection (m). **Effective** for tax years beginning after 12-31-88, but does not apply to any plan for any plan year to which section 162(k) of the Internal Revenue Code of 1986 (as in effect on the date before 11-10-88) does not apply by reason of section 10001(e)(2) of P.L. 99-272.

[Sec. 162(m)]

(m) CERTAIN EXCESSIVE EMPLOYEE REMUNERATION.—

(1) IN GENERAL.—In the case of any publicly held corporation, no deduction shall be allowed under this chapter for applicable employee remuneration with respect to any covered employee to the extent that the amount of such remuneration for the taxable year with respect to such employee exceeds $1,000,000.

(2) PUBLICLY HELD CORPORATION.—For purposes of this subsection, the term "publicly held corporation" means any corporation issuing any class of common equity securities required to be registered under section 12 of the Securities Exchange Act of 1934.

(3) COVERED EMPLOYEE.—For purposes of this subsection, the term "covered employee" means any employee of the taxpayer if—

(A) as of the close of the taxable year, such employee is the chief executive officer of the taxpayer or is an individual acting in such a capacity, or

(B) the total compensation of such employee for the taxable year is required to be reported to shareholders under the Securities Exchange Act of 1934 by reason of such employee being among the 4 highest compensated officers for the taxable year (other than the chief executive officer).

(4) APPLICABLE EMPLOYEE REMUNERATION.—For purposes of this subsection—

(A) IN GENERAL.—Except as otherwise provided in this paragraph, the term "applicable employee remuneration" means, with respect to any covered employee for any taxable year, the aggregate amount allowable as a deduction under this chapter for such taxable year (determined without regard to this subsection) for remuneration for services performed by such employee (whether or not during the taxable year).

(B) EXCEPTION FOR REMUNERATION PAYABLE ON COMMISSION BASIS.—The term "applicable employee remuneration" shall not include any remuneration payable on a commission basis solely on account of income generated directly by the individual performance of the individual to whom such remuneration is payable.

(C) OTHER PERFORMANCE-BASED COMPENSATION.—The term "applicable employee remuneration" shall not include any remuneration payable solely on account of the attainment of one or more performance goals, but only if—

(i) the performance goals are determined by a compensation committee of the board of directors of the taxpayer which is comprised solely of 2 or more outside directors,

(ii) the material terms under which the remuneration is to be paid, including the performance goals, are disclosed to shareholders and approved by a majority of the vote in a separate shareholder vote before the payment of such remuneration, and

(iii) before any payment of such remuneration, the compensation committee referred to in clause (i) certifies that the performance goals and any other material terms were in fact satisfied.

(D) EXCEPTION FOR EXISTING BINDING CONTRACTS.—The term "applicable employee remuneration" shall not include any remuneration payable under a written binding contract which was in effect on February 17, 1993, and which was not modified thereafter in any material respect before such remuneration is paid.

(E) REMUNERATION.—For purposes of this paragraph, the term "remuneration" includes any remuneration (including benefits) in any medium other than cash, but shall not include—

(i) any payment referred to in so much of section 3121(a)(5) as precedes subparagraph (E) thereof, and

(ii) any benefit provided to or on behalf of an employee if at the time such benefit is provided it is reasonable to believe that the employee will be able to exclude such benefit from gross income under this chapter.

For purposes of clause (i), section 3121(a)(5) shall be applied without regard to section 3121(v)(1).

(F) COORDINATION WITH DISALLOWED GOLDEN PARACHUTE PAYMENTS.—The dollar limitation contained in paragraph (1) shall be reduced (but not below zero) by the amount (if any) which would have been included in the applicable employee remuneration of the covered employee for the taxable year but for being disallowed under section 280G.

(G) COORDINATION WITH EXCISE TAX ON SPECIFIED STOCK COMPENSATION.—The dollar limitation contained in paragraph (1) with respect to any covered employee shall be reduced (but not below zero) by the amount of any payment (with respect to such employee) of the tax imposed by section 4985 directly or indirectly by the expatriated corporation (as defined in such section) or by any member of the expanded affiliated group (as defined in such section) which includes such corporation.

(5) SPECIAL RULE FOR APPLICATION TO EMPLOYERS PARTICIPATING IN THE TROUBLED ASSETS RELIEF PROGRAM.—

(A) IN GENERAL.—In the case of an applicable employer, no deduction shall be allowed under this chapter—

(i) in the case of executive remuneration for any applicable taxable year which is attributable to services performed by a covered executive during such applicable taxable year, to the extent that the amount of such remuneration exceeds $500,000, or

(ii) in the case of deferred deduction executive remuneration for any taxable year for services performed during any applicable taxable year by a covered executive, to the extent that the amount of such remuneration exceeds $500,000 reduced (but not below zero) by the sum of—

(I) the executive remuneration for such applicable taxable year, plus

(II) the portion of the deferred deduction executive remuneration for such services which was taken into account under this clause in a preceding taxable year.

(B) APPLICABLE EMPLOYER.—For purposes of this paragraph—

(i) IN GENERAL.—Except as provided in clause (ii), the term "applicable employer" means any employer from whom 1 or more troubled assets are acquired under a program established by the Secretary under section 101(a) of the Emergency Economic Stabilization Act of 2008 if the aggregate amount of the assets so acquired for all taxable years exceeds $300,000,000.

(ii) DISREGARD OF CERTAIN ASSETS SOLD THROUGH DIRECT PURCHASE.—If the only sales of troubled assets by an employer under the program described in clause (i) are through 1 or more direct purchases (within the meaning of section 113(c) of the Emergency Economic Stabilization Act of 2008), such assets shall not be taken into account under clause (i) in determining whether the employer is an applicable employer for purposes of this paragraph.

(iii) AGGREGATION RULES.—Two or more persons who are treated as a single employer under subsection (b) or (c) of section 414 shall be treated as a single employer, except that in applying section 1563(a) for purposes of either such subsection, paragraphs (2) and (3) thereof shall be disregarded.

(C) APPLICABLE TAXABLE YEAR.—For purposes of this paragraph, the term "applicable taxable year" means, with respect to any employer—

(i) the first taxable year of the employer—

(I) which includes any portion of the period during which the authorities under section 101(a) of the Emergency Economic Stabilization Act of 2008 are in effect (determined under section 120 thereof), and

(II) in which the aggregate amount of troubled assets acquired from the employer during the taxable year pursuant to such authorities (other than assets to which subparagraph (B)(ii) applies), when added to the aggregate amount so acquired for all preceding taxable years, exceeds $300,000,000, and

(ii) any subsequent taxable year which includes any portion of such period.

(D) COVERED EXECUTIVE.—For purposes of this paragraph—

(i) IN GENERAL.—The term "covered executive" means, with respect to any applicable taxable year, any employee—

(I) who, at any time during the portion of the taxable year during which the authorities under section 101(a) of the Emergency Economic Stabilization Act of 2008 are in effect (determined under section 120 thereof), is the chief executive officer of the applicable employer or the chief financial officer of the applicable employer, or an individual acting in either such capacity, or

(II) who is described in clause (ii).

(ii) HIGHEST COMPENSATED EMPLOYEES.—An employee is described in this clause if the employee is 1 of the 3 highest compensated officers of the applicable employer for the taxable year (other than an individual described in clause (i)(I)), determined—

(I) on the basis of the shareholder disclosure rules for compensation under the Securities Exchange Act of 1934 (without regard to whether those rules apply to the employer), and

(II) by only taking into account employees employed during the portion of the taxable year described in clause (i)(I).

(iii) EMPLOYEE REMAINS COVERED EXECUTIVE.—If an employee is a covered executive with respect to an applicable employer for any applicable taxable year, such employee shall be treated as a covered executive with respect to such employer for all subsequent applicable taxable years and for all subsequent taxable years in which deferred deduction executive remuneration with respect to services performed in all such applicable taxable years would (but for this paragraph) be deductible.

(E) EXECUTIVE REMUNERATION.—For purposes of this paragraph, the term "executive remuneration" means the applicable employee remuneration of the covered executive, as determined under paragraph (4) without regard to subparagraphs (B), (C), and (D) thereof. Such term shall not include any deferred deduction executive remuneration with respect to services performed in a prior applicable taxable year.

(F) DEFERRED DEDUCTION EXECUTIVE REMUNERATION.—For purposes of this paragraph, the term "deferred deduction executive remuneration" means remuneration which would be executive remuneration for services performed in an applicable taxable year but for the fact that the deduction under this chapter (determined without regard to this paragraph) for such remuneration is allowable in a subsequent taxable year.

(G) COORDINATION.—Rules similar to the rules of subparagraphs (F) and (G) of paragraph (4) shall apply for purposes of this paragraph.

(H) REGULATORY AUTHORITY.—The Secretary may prescribe such guidance, rules, or regulations as are necessary to carry out the purposes of this paragraph and the Emergency Economic Stabilization Act of 2008, including the extent to which this paragraph applies in the case of any acquisition, merger, or reorganization of an applicable employer.

(6) SPECIAL RULE FOR APPLICATION TO CERTAIN HEALTH INSURANCE PROVIDERS.—

(A) IN GENERAL.—No deduction shall be allowed under this chapter—

(i) in the case of applicable individual remuneration which is for any disqualified taxable year beginning after December 31, 2012, and which is attributable to services performed by an applicable individual during such taxable year, to the extent that the amount of such remuneration exceeds $500,000, or

(ii) in the case of deferred deduction remuneration for any taxable year beginning after December 31, 2012, which is attributable to services performed by an applicable individual during any disqualified taxable year beginning after December 31, 2009, to the extent that the amount of such remuneration exceeds $500,000 reduced (but not below zero) by the sum of—

(I) the applicable individual remuneration for such disqualified taxable year, plus

(II) the portion of the deferred deduction remuneration for such services which was taken into account under this clause in a preceding taxable year (or which would have been taken into account under this clause in a preceding taxable year if this clause were applied by substituting "December 31, 2009" for "December 31, 2012" in the matter preceding subclause (I)).

(B) DISQUALIFIED TAXABLE YEAR.—For purposes of this paragraph, the term "disqualified taxable year" means, with respect to any employer, any taxable year for which such employer is a covered health insurance provider.

(C) COVERED HEALTH INSURANCE PROVIDER.—For purposes of this paragraph—

(i) IN GENERAL.—The term "covered health insurance provider" means—

(I) with respect to taxable years beginning after December 31, 2009, and before January 1, 2013, any employer which is a health insurance issuer (as defined in section 9832(b)(2)) and which receives premiums from providing health insurance coverage (as defined in section 9832(b)(1)), and

(II) with respect to taxable years beginning after December 31, 2012, any employer which is a health insurance issuer (as defined in section 9832(b)(2)) and with respect to which not less than 25 percent of the gross premiums received from providing health insurance coverage (as defined in section 9832(b)(1)) is from minimum essential coverage (as defined in section 5000A(f)).

(ii) AGGREGATION RULES.—Two or more persons who are treated as a single employer under subsection (b), (c), (m), or (o) of section 414 shall be treated as a single employer, except that in applying section 1563(a) for purposes of any such subsection, paragraphs (2) and (3) thereof shall be disregarded.

(D) APPLICABLE INDIVIDUAL REMUNERATION.—For purposes of this paragraph, the term "applicable individual remuneration" means, with respect to any applicable individual for any disqualified taxable year, the aggregate amount allowable as a deduction under this chapter for such taxable year (determined without regard to this subsection) for remuneration (as defined in paragraph (4) without regard to subparagraphs (B), (C), and (D) thereof) for services performed by such individual (whether or not during the taxable year). Such term shall not include any deferred deduction remuneration with respect to services performed during the disqualified taxable year.

(E) DEFERRED DEDUCTION REMUNERATION.—For purposes of this paragraph, the term "deferred deduction remuneration" means remuneration which would be applicable individual remuneration for services performed in a disqualified taxable year but for the fact that the deduction under this chapter (determined without regard to this paragraph) for such remuneration is allowable in a subsequent taxable year.

(F) APPLICABLE INDIVIDUAL.—For purposes of this paragraph, the term "applicable individual" means, with respect to any covered health insurance provider for any disqualified taxable year, any individual—

(i) who is an officer, director, or employee in such taxable year, or

(ii) who provides services for or on behalf of such covered health insurance provider during such taxable year.

(G) COORDINATION.—Rules similar to the rules of subparagraphs (F) and (G) of paragraph (4) shall apply for purposes of this paragraph.

(H) REGULATORY AUTHORITY.—The Secretary may prescribe such guidance, rules, or regulations as are necessary to carry out the purposes of this paragraph.

Amendments

• 2010, Patient Protection and Affordable Care Act (P.L. 111-148)

P.L. 111-148, §9014(a):

Amended Code Sec. 162(m) by adding at the end a new subparagraph (6). **Effective** for tax years beginning after 12-31-2009, with respect to services performed after such date.

• 2008, Emergency Economic Stabilization Act of 2008 (P.L. 110-343)

P.L. 110-343, §111, Division A (as amended by P.L. 111-5, §7001), provides:

SEC. 111. EXECUTIVE COMPENSATION AND CORPORATE GOVERNANCE.

(a) DEFINITIONS.—For purposes of this section, the following definitions shall apply:

(1) SENIOR EXECUTIVE OFFICER.—The term "senior executive officer" means an individual who is 1 of the top 5 most highly paid executives of a public company, whose compensation is required to be disclosed pursuant to the Securities Exchange Act of 1934, and any regulations issued thereunder, and non-public company counterparts.

(2) GOLDEN PARACHUTE PAYMENT.—The term "golden parachute payment" means any payment to a senior executive officer for departure from a company for any reason, except for payments for services performed or benefits accrued.

(3) TARP RECIPIENT.—The term "TARP recipient" means any entity that has received or will receive financial assistance under the financial assistance provided under the TARP.

(4) COMMISSION.—The term "Commission" means the Securities and Exchange Commission.

(5) PERIOD IN WHICH OBLIGATION IS OUTSTANDING; RULE OF CONSTRUCTION.—For purposes of this section, the period in which any obligation arising from financial assistance provided under the TARP remains outstanding does not include any period during which the Federal Government only holds warrants to purchase common stock of the TARP recipient.

(b) EXECUTIVE COMPENSATION AND CORPORATE GOVERNANCE.—(1) ESTABLISHMENT OF STANDARDS.—During the period in which any obligation arising from financial assistance provided under the TARP remains outstanding, each TARP recipient shall be subject to—

(A) the standards established by the Secretary under this section; and

(B) the provisions of section 162(m)(5) of the Internal Revenue Code of 1986, as applicable.

(2) STANDARDS REQUIRED.—The Secretary shall require each TARP recipient to meet appropriate standards for executive compensation and corporate governance.

(3) SPECIFIC REQUIREMENTS.—The standards established under paragraph (2) shall include the following:

(A) Limits on compensation that exclude incentives for senior executive officers of the TARP recipient to take unnecessary and excessive risks that threaten the value of such recipient during the period in which any obligation arising from financial assistance provided under the TARP remains outstanding.

(B) A provision for the recovery by such TARP recipient of any bonus, retention award, or incentive compensation paid to a senior executive officer and any of the next 20 most highly-compensated employees of the TARP recipient based on statements of earnings, revenues, gains, or other criteria that are later found to be materially inaccurate.

(C) A prohibition on such TARP recipient making any golden parachute payment to a senior executive officer or any of the next 5 most highly-compensated employees of the TARP recipient during the period in which any obligation arising from financial assistance provided under the TARP remains outstanding.

(D)(i) A prohibition on such TARP recipient paying or accruing any bonus, retention award, or incentive compensation during the period in which any obligation arising from financial assistance provided under the TARP remains outstanding, except that any prohibition developed under this paragraph shall not apply to the payment of long-term restricted stock by such TARP recipient, provided that such longterm restricted stock—

(I) does not fully vest during the period in which any obligation arising from financial assistance provided to that TARP recipient remains outstanding;

(II) has a value in an amount that is not greater than 1/3 of the total amount of annual compensation of the employee receiving the stock; and

(III) is subject to such other terms and conditions as the Secretary may determine is in the public interest.

(ii) The prohibition required under clause (i) shall apply as follows:

(I) For any financial institution that received financial assistance provided under the TARP equal to less than $25,000,000, the prohibition shall apply only to the most highly compensated employee of the financial institution.

(II) For any financial institution that received financial assistance provided under the TARP equal to at least $25,000,000, but less than $250,000,000, the prohibition shall apply to at least the 5 most highly-compensated employees of the financial institution, or such higher number as the Secretary may determine is in the public interest with respect to any TARP recipient.

(III) For any financial institution that received financial assistance provided under the TARP equal to at least$250,000,000, but less than $500,000,000, the prohibition shall apply to the senior executive officers and at least the 10 next most highly-compensated employees, or such higher number as the Secretary may determine is in the public interest with respect to any TARP recipient.

(IV) For any financial institution that received financial assistance provided under the TARP equal to $500,000,000 or more, the prohibition shall apply to the senior executive officers and at least the 20 next most highly-compensated employees, or such higher number as the Secretary may determine is in the public interest with respect to any TARP recipient.

(iii) The prohibition required under clause (i) shall not be construed to prohibit any bonus payment required to be paid pursuant to a written employment contract executed on or before February 11, 2009, as such valid employment contracts are determined by the Secretary or the designee of the Secretary.

(E) A prohibition on any compensation plan that would encourage manipulation of the reported earnings of such TARP recipient to enhance the compensation of any of its employees.

(F) A requirement for the establishment of a Board Compensation Committee that meets the requirements of subsection (c).

(4) CERTIFICATION OF COMPLIANCE.—The chief executive officer and chief financial officer (or the equivalents thereof) of each TARP recipient shall provide a written certification of compliance by the TARP recipient with the requirements of this section—

(A) in the case of a TARP recipient, the securities of which are publicly traded, to the Securities and Exchange Commission, together with annual filings required under the securities laws; and

(B) in the case of a TARP recipient that is not a publicly traded company, to the Secretary.

(c) BOARD COMPENSATION COMMITTEE.—

(1) ESTABLISHMENT OF BOARD REQUIRED.—Each TARP recipient shall establish a Board Compensation Committee, comprised entirely of independent directors, for the purpose of reviewing employee compensation plans.

(2) MEETINGS.—The Board Compensation Committee of each TARP recipient shall meet at least semiannually to discuss and evaluate employee compensation plans in light of an assessment of any risk posed to the TARP recipient from such plans.

(3) COMPLIANCE BY NON-SEC REGISTRANTS.—In the case of any TARP recipient, the common or preferred stock of which is not registered pursuant to the Securities Exchange Act of 1934, and that has received $25,000,000 or less of TARP assistance, the duties of the Board Compensation Committee under this subsection shall be carried out by the board of directors of such TARP recipient.

(d) LIMITATION ON LUXURY EXPENDITURES.—The board of directors of any TARP recipient shall have in place a company-wide policy regarding excessive or luxury expenditures, as identified by the Secretary, which may include excessive expenditures on—

(1) entertainment or events;

(2) office and facility renovations;

(3) aviation or other transportation services; or

(4) other activities or events that are not reasonable expenditures for staff development, reasonable performance incentives, or other similar measures conducted in the normal course of the business operations of the TARP recipient.

(e) SHAREHOLDER APPROVAL OF EXECUTIVE COMPENSATION.—

(1) ANNUAL SHAREHOLDER APPROVAL OF EXECUTIVE COMPENSATION.—Any proxy or consent or authorization for an annual or other meeting of the shareholders of any TARP recipient during the period in which any obligation arising from financial assistance provided under the TARP remains outstanding shall permit a separate shareholder vote to approve the compensation of executives, as disclosed pursuant to the compensation disclosure rules of the Commission (which disclosure shall include the compensation discussion and analysis, the compensation tables, and any related material).

(2) NONBINDING VOTE.—A shareholder vote described in paragraph (1) shall not be binding on the board of directors of a TARP recipient, and may not be construed as overruling a decision by such board, nor to create or imply any additional fiduciary duty by such board, nor shall such vote be construed to restrict or limit the ability of shareholders to make proposals for inclusion in proxy materials related to executive compensation.

(3) DEADLINE FOR RULEMAKING.—Not later than 1 year after the date of enactment of the American Recovery and Reinvestment Act of 2009, the Commission shall issue any final rules and regulations required by this subsection.

(f) REVIEW OF PRIOR PAYMENTS TO EXECUTIVES.—

(1) IN GENERAL.—The Secretary shall review bonuses, retention awards, and other compensation paid to the senior executive officers and the next 20 most highly-compensated employees of each entity receiving TARP assistance before the date of enactment of the American Recovery and Reinvestment Act of 2009, to determine whether any such payments were inconsistent with the purposes of this section or the TARP or were otherwise contrary to the public interest.

(2) NEGOTIATIONS FOR REIMBURSEMENT.—If the Secretary makes a determination described in paragraph (1), the Secretary shall seek to negotiate with the TARP recipient and the subject employee for appropriate reimbursements to the Federal Government with respect to compensation or bonuses.

(g) NO IMPEDIMENT TO WITHDRAWAL BY TARP RECIPIENTS.—Subject to consultation with the appropriate Federal banking agency (as that term is defined in section 3 of the Federal Deposit Insurance Act), if any, the Secretary shall permit a TARP recipient to repay any assistance previously provided under the TARP to such financial institution, without regard to whether the financial institution has replaced such funds from any other source or to any waiting period, and when such assistance is repaid, the Secretary shall liquidate warrants associated with such assistance at the current market price.

(h) REGULATIONS.—The Secretary shall promulgate regulations to implement this section.

P.L. 110-343, Division A, §302(a):

Amended Code Sec. 162(m) by adding at the end a new paragraph (5). **Effective** for tax years ending on or after 10-3-2008.

• 2004, American Jobs Creation Act of 2004 (P.L. 108-357)

P.L. 108-357, §802(b)(2):

Amended Code Sec. 162(m)(4) by adding at the end a new subparagraph (G). **Effective** on 3-4-2003; except that periods before such date shall not be taken into account in applying the periods in Code Sec. 4985(a) and (e)(1), as added by Act Sec. 802(a).

• 1993, Omnibus Budget Reconciliation Act of 1993 (P.L. 103-66)

P.L. 103-66, §3211(a):

Amended Code Sec. 162 by redesignating subsection (m) as subsection (n) and by inserting after subsection (l) new subsection (m). **Effective** for amounts which would otherwise be deductible for tax years beginning on or after 1-1-94.

[Sec. 162(n)]

(n) SPECIAL RULE FOR CERTAIN GROUP HEALTH PLANS.—

(1) IN GENERAL.—No deduction shall be allowed under this chapter to an employer for any amount paid or incurred in connection with a group health plan if the plan does not reimburse for inpatient hospital care services provided in the State of New York—

(A) except as provided in subparagraphs (B) and (C), at the same rate as licensed commercial insurers are required to reimburse hospitals for such services when such reimbursement is not through such a plan,

(B) in the case of any reimbursement through a health maintenance organization, at the same rate as health maintenance organizations are required to reimburse hospitals for such services for individuals not covered by such a plan (determined without regard to any government-supported individuals exempt from such rate), or

(C) in the case of any reimbursement through any corporation organized under Article 43 of the New York State Insurance Law, at the same rate as any such corporation is required to reimburse hospitals for such services for individuals not covered by such a plan.

(2) STATE LAW EXCEPTION.—Paragraph (1) shall not apply to any group health plan which is not required under the laws of the State of New York (determined without regard to this subsection or other provisions of Federal law) to reimburse at the rates provided in paragraph (1).

(3) GROUP HEALTH PLAN.—For purposes of this subsection, the term "group health plan" means a plan of, or contributed to by, an employer or employee organization (including a self-insured plan) to provide health care (directly or otherwise) to any employee, any former employee, the employer, or any other individual associated or formerly associated with the employer in a business relationship, or any member of their family.

Amendments

• 1993, Omnibus Budget Reconciliation Act of 1993 (P.L. 103-66)

P.L. 103-66, §13442(a):

Amended Code Sec. 162, as amended by Act Sec. 13211, by redesignating subsection (n) as subsection (o) and by inserting after subsection (m) a new subsection (n). **Effective** for services provided after 2-2-93, and on or before 12-31-95 (as amended by P.L. 104-7, §5).

[Sec. 162(o)]

(o) TREATMENT OF CERTAIN EXPENSES OF RURAL MAIL CARRIERS.—

(1) GENERAL RULE.—In the case of any employee of the United States Postal Service who performs services involving the collection and delivery of mail on a rural route and who receives qualified reimbursements for the expenses incurred by such employee for the use of a vehicle in performing such services—

(A) the amount allowable as a deduction under this chapter for the use of a vehicle in performing such services shall be equal to the amount of such qualified reimbursements; and

(B) such qualified reimbursements shall be treated as paid under a reimbursement or other expense allowance arrangement for purposes of section 62(a)(2)(A) (and section 62(c) shall not apply to such qualified reimbursements).

(2) SPECIAL RULE WHERE EXPENSES EXCEED REIMBURSEMENTS.—Notwithstanding paragraph (1)(A), if the expenses incurred by an employee for the use of a vehicle in performing services described in paragraph (1) exceed the qualified reimbursements for such expenses, such excess shall be taken into account in computing the miscellaneous itemized deductions of the employee under section 67.

(3) DEFINITION OF QUALIFIED REIMBURSEMENTS.—For purposes of this subsection, the term "qualified reimbursements" means the amounts paid by the United States Postal Service to employees as an equipment maintenance allowance under the 1991 collective bargaining agreement between the United States Postal Service and the National Rural Letter Carriers' Association. Amounts paid as an equipment maintenance allowance by such Postal Service under later collective bargaining agreements that supersede the 1991 agreement shall be considered qualified reimbursements if such amounts do not exceed the amounts that would have been paid under the 1991 agreement, adjusted for changes in the Consumer Price Index (as defined in section 1(f)(5)) since 1991.

Amendments

• 2004, American Jobs Creation Act of 2004 (P.L. 108-357)

P.L. 108-357, §318(a):

Amended Code Sec. 162(o) by redesignating paragraph (2) as paragraph (3) and by inserting after paragraph (1) new paragraph (2). **Effective** for tax years beginning after 12-31-2003.

P.L. 108-357, §318(b):

Amended Code Sec. 162(o) by striking "REIMBURSED" in the heading before "EXPENSES". **Effective** for tax years beginning after 12-31-2003.

• 1997, Taxpayer Relief Act of 1997 (P.L. 105-34)

P.L. 105-34, §1203(a):

Amended Code Sec. 162 by redesignating subsection (o) as subsection (p) and by inserting after subsection (n) a new subsection (o). **Effective** for tax years beginning after 12-31-97.

[Sec. 162(p)]

(p) TREATMENT OF EXPENSES OF MEMBERS OF RESERVE COMPONENT OF ARMED FORCES OF THE UNITED STATES.—For purposes of subsection (a)(2), in the case of an individual who performs services as a member of a reserve component of the Armed Forces of the United States at any time during the taxable year, such individual shall be deemed to be away from home in the pursuit of a trade or business for any period during which such individual is away from home in connection with such service.

Amendments

• 2003, Military Family Tax Relief Act of 2003 (P.L. 108-121)

P.L. 108-121, §109(a):

Amended Code Sec. 162 by redesignating subsection (p) as subsection (q) and inserting after subsection (o) a new subsection (p). **Effective** for amounts paid or incurred in tax years beginning after 12-31-2002.

[Sec. 162(q)]

(q) CROSS REFERENCES.—

(1) For special rule relating to expenses in connection with subdividing real property for sale, see section 1237.

(2) For special rule relating to the treatment of payments by a transferee of a franchise, trademark, or trade name, see section 1253.

(3) For special rules relating to—

(A) funded welfare benefit plans, see section 419, and

(B) deferred compensation and other deferred benefits, see section 404.

Amendments

• 2003, Military Family Tax Relief Act of 2003 (P.L. 108-121)

P.L. 108-121, §109(a):

Amended Code Sec. 162 by redesignating subsection (p) as subsection (q). **Effective** for amounts paid or incurred in tax years beginning after 12-31-2002.

• 1997, Taxpayer Relief Act of 1997 (P.L. 105-34)

P.L. 105-34, §1203(a):

Amended Code Sec. 162 by redesignating subsection (o) as subsection (p). **Effective** for tax years beginning after 12-31-97.

• 1993, Omnibus Budget Reconciliation Act of 1993 (P.L. 103-66)

P.L. 103-66, §13442(a):

Amended Code Sec. 162 by redesignating subsection (n) as subsection (o). **Effective** for services provided after 2-2-93, and on or before 12-31-95 (as amended by P.L. 104-7, §5).

• 1988, Technical and Miscellaneous Revenue Act of 1988 (P.L. 100-647)

P.L. 100-647, §3011(b)(3)(A)-(C):

Amended Code Sec. 162 by striking out subsection (k), and by redesignating the subsection relating to stock redemption expenses as subsection (k), the subsection relating to special rules for health insurance costs of self-employed individuals as subsection (l), and the subsection relating to cross references as subsection (m). **Effective** for tax years beginning after 12-31-88, but shall not apply to any plan for any plan year to which section 162(k) of the Internal Revenue Code of 1986 (as in effect on the date before the date of enactment of this Act) did not apply by reason of section 10001(e)(2) of P.L. 99-272.

• 1986, Tax Reform Act of 1986 (P.L. 99-514)

P.L. 99-514, §613(a):

Amended Code Sec. 162 by redesignating subsection (l) as subsection (m) and inserting after subsection (k) the following new subsection (l). **Effective** for any amount paid or incurred after 2-28-86, in tax years ending after such date.

P.L. 99-514, §1161(a):

Amended Code Sec. 162 by redesignating subsection (n) [m] as subsection (m) [n] and by inserting after subsection (l) new subsection (m). **Effective** for tax years beginning after 12-31-86.

P.L. 99-514, §1161(a)(2)-(3), provides:

(2) TRANSITIONAL RULE.—In the case of any year to which section 89 of the Internal Revenue Code of 1986 does not apply, section 162(m)(2)(B) of such Code shall be applied by substituting any nondiscrimination requirements otherwise applicable for the requirements of section 89 of such Code.

(3) ASSISTANCE.—The Secretary of the Treasury or his delegate shall provide guidance to self-employed individuals to assist them in meeting the requirements of section 89 of the Internal Revenue Code of 1986 with respect to coverage required by the amendments made by this section.

• 1986, Consolidated Omnibus Budget Reconciliation Act of 1986 (P.L. 99-272)

P.L. 99-272, §10001(c):

Redesignated Code Sec. 162(k) as 162(l). **Effective** for plan years beginning on or after 7-1-86. For a special rule see Act Sec. 10001(e)(2) in the amendment notes following Code Sec. 162(k).

• 1984 (P.L. 98-573)

P.L. 98-573, §232(a):

Amended Code Sec. 162 by redesignating subsection (j) as subsection (k). **Effective** for tax years beginning after 10-30-84.

• 1984, Deficit Reduction Act of 1984 (P.L. 98-369)

P.L. 98-369, §512(b):

Amended Code Sec. 162(j) by adding a new paragraph (3). **Effective** for amounts paid or incurred after 7-18-84, in tax years ending after such date.

• 1982, Tax Equity and Fiscal Responsibility Act of 1982 (P.L. 97-248)

P.L. 97-248, §128(b)(1):

Amended Code Sec. 162 by redesignating subsection (i), as redesignated by P.L. 97-34, as subsection (j). **Effective** as if it had been originally included as a part of the Internal Revenue Code of 1954 to which it relates.

• 1981, Omnibus Budget Reconciliation Act of 1981 (P.L. 97-35)

P.L. 97-35, §2146(b):

Redesignated Code Sec. 162(h) as Code Sec. 162(i). **Effective** for tax years beginning on or after 1-1-82. Note: P.L. 97-34 made the same redesignation earlier.

• 1981, Economic Recovery Tax Act of 1981 (P.L. 97-34)

P.L. 97-34, §127(a):

Redesignated Code Sec. 162(h) as Code Sec. 162(i). **Effective** for tax years beginning on or after 1-1-76. P.L. 97-35 made the same redesignation later.

• 1969, Tax Reform Act of 1969 (P.L. 91-172)

P.L. 91-172, §516(c)(2)(A):

Amended Code Sec. 162(h) by adding "(1)" before "For" and by adding paragraph (2) at the end. **Effective** for transfers after 12-31-69, except that section 1253(d)(1) of the Internal Revenue Code of 1954 (as added by subsection (c)) shall, at the election of the taxpayer (made at such time and in such manner as the Secretary or his delegate may by regulations prescribe), apply to transfers before 1-1-70, but only with respect to payments made in tax years ending after 12-31-69, and beginning before 1-1-80.

P.L. 91-172, §902(a):

Redesignated Code Sec. 162(f) as Code Sec. 162(h).

• 1962, Revenue Act of 1962 (P.L. 87-834)

P.L. 87-834, §3:

Redesignated Code Sec. 162(e) as Code Sec. 162(f). **Effective** 1-1-63.

• 1960 (P.L. 86-779)

P.L. 86-779, §8(a):

Redesignated Code Sec. 162(d) as Code Sec. 162(e). **Effective** 1-1-60.

• 1958, Technical Amendments Act of 1958 (P.L. 85-866)

P.L. 85-866, §5(a):

Redesignated Code Sec. 162(c) as Code Sec. 162(d). **Effective** 9-3-58.

[Sec. 163]

SEC. 163. INTEREST.

[Sec. 163(a)]

(a) GENERAL RULE.—There shall be allowed as a deduction all interest paid or accrued within the taxable year on indebtedness.

[Sec. 163(b)]

(b) INSTALLMENT PURCHASES WHERE INTEREST CHARGE IS NOT SEPARATELY STATED.—

(1) General rule.—If personal property or educational services are purchased under a contract—

(A) which provides that payment of part or all of the purchase price is to be made in installments, and

(B) in which carrying charges are separately stated but the interest charge cannot be ascertained,

then the payments made during the taxable year under the contract shall be treated for purposes of this section as if they included interest equal to 6 percent of the average unpaid balance under the contract during the taxable year. For purposes of the preceding sentence, the average unpaid balance is the sum of the unpaid balance outstanding on the first day of each month beginning during the taxable year, divided by 12. For purposes of this paragraph, the term "educational services" means any service (including lodging) which is purchased from an educational organization described in section 170(b)(1)(A)(ii) and which is provided for a student of such organization.

(2) LIMITATION.—In the case of any contract to which paragraph (1) applies, the amount treated as interest for any taxable year shall not exceed the aggregate carrying charges which are properly attributable to such taxable year.

Amendments

• 1976, Tax Reform Act of 1976 (P.L. 94-455)

P.L. 94-455, §1901(b)(8):

Amended Code Sec. 163(b) by substituting "educational organization described in section 170(b)(1)(A)(ii) and which is provided for a student of such organization" for "educational institution (as defined in section 151(e)(4))". **Effective** for tax years beginning after 12-31-76.

• 1963 (P.L. 88-9)

P.L. 88-9, §1(a):

Redesignated Code Sec. 163(c) as Code Sec. 163(d) and added new Sec. 163(c). **Effective** for tax years ending on or after 1-1-62.

[Sec. 163(c)]

(c) REDEEMABLE GROUND RENTS.—For purposes of this subtitle, any annual or periodic rental under a redeemable ground rent (excluding amounts in redemption thereof) shall be treated as interest on an indebtedness secured by a mortgage.

Amendments

• 1964, Revenue Act of 1964 (P.L. 88-272)

P.L. 88-272, §224(c):

Amended subsection (b)(1) by inserting "personal property or educational services are purchased" in lieu of "personal property is purchased", and added the last sentence to subsection (b)(1). **Effective** for payments made during taxable years beginning after 12-31-63.

[Sec. 163(d)]

(d) LIMITATION ON INVESTMENT INTEREST.—

(1) IN GENERAL.—In the case of a taxpayer other than a corporation, the amount allowed as a deduction under this chapter for investment interest for any taxable year shall not exceed the net investment income of the taxpayer for the taxable year.

(2) CARRYFORWARD OF DISALLOWED INTEREST.—The amount not allowed as a deduction for any taxable year by reason of paragraph (1) shall be treated as investment interest paid or accrued by the taxpayer in the succeeding taxable year.

(3) INVESTMENT INTEREST.—For purposes of this subsection—

(A) IN GENERAL.—The term "investment interest" means any interest allowable as a deduction under this chapter (determined without regard to paragraph (1)) which is paid or accrued on indebtedness properly allocable to property held for investment.

(B) EXCEPTIONS.—The term "investment interest" shall not include—

(i) any qualified residence interest (as defined in subsection (h)(3)), or

(ii) any interest which is taken into account under section 469 in computing income or loss from a passive activity of the taxpayer.

(C) PERSONAL PROPERTY USED IN SHORT SALE.—For purposes of this paragraph, the term "interest" includes any amount allowable as a deduction in connection with personal property used in a short sale.

(4) NET INVESTMENT INCOME.—For purposes of this subsection—

(A) IN GENERAL.—The term "net investment income" means the excess of—

(i) investment income, over

(ii) investment expenses.

»»→ Caution: The flush sentence in Code Sec. 163(d)(4)(B), below, is subject to the sunset provision of the Jobs and Growth Tax Relief Reconciliation Act of 2003 (P.L. 108-27), §303. Absent Congressional action, the changes made to this provision by P.L. 108-27, or that take effect as if included in P.L. 108-27, do not apply after December 31, 2010. For more information about the sunset provision, see page XXI of the Preface to this publication and P.L. 108-27, §303, in the amendment notes. See the amendments notes for a history of amendments to this section and the effective date of each change.

(B) INVESTMENT INCOME.—The term "investment income" means the sum of—

(i) gross income from property held for investment (other than any gain taken into account under clause (ii)(I)),

(ii) the excess (if any) of—

(I) the net gain attributable to the disposition of property held for investment, over

(II) the net capital gain determined by only taking into account gains and losses from dispositions of property held for investment, plus

(iii) so much of the net capital gain referred to in clause (ii)(II) (or, if lesser, the net gain referred to in clause (ii)(I)) as the taxpayer elects to take into account under this clause.

Such term shall include qualified dividend income (as defined in section 1(h)(11)(B)) only to the extent the taxpayer elects to treat such income as investment income for purposes of this subsection.

(C) INVESTMENT EXPENSES.—The term "investment expenses" means the deductions allowed under this chapter (other than for interest) which are directly connected with the production of investment income.

(D) INCOME AND EXPENSES FROM PASSIVE ACTIVITIES.—Investment income and investment expenses shall not include any income or expenses taken into account under section 469 in computing income or loss from a passive activity.

(E) REDUCTION IN INVESTMENT INCOME DURING PHASE-IN OF PASSIVE LOSS RULES.—Investment income of the taxpayer for any taxable year shall be reduced by the amount of the passive activity loss to which section 469(a) does not apply for such taxable year by reason of section 469(m). The preceding sentence shall not apply to any portion of such passive activity loss which is attributable to a rental real estate activity with respect to which the taxpayer actively participates (within the meaning of section 469(i)(6)) during such taxable year.

(5) PROPERTY HELD FOR INVESTMENT.—For purposes of this subsection—

(A) IN GENERAL.—The term "property held for investment" shall include—

(i) any property which produces income of a type described in section 469(e)(1), and

(ii) any interest held by a taxpayer in an activity involving the conduct of a trade or business—

(I) which is not a passive activity, and

(II) with respect to which the taxpayer does not materially participate.

(B) INVESTMENT EXPENSES.—In the case of property described in subparagraph (A)(i), expenses shall be allocated to such property in the same manner as under section 469.

(C) TERMS.—For purposes of this paragraph, the terms "activity", "passive activity", and "materially participate" have the meanings given such terms by section 469.

(6) PHASE-IN OF DISALLOWANCE.—In the case of any taxable year beginning in calendar years 1987 through 1990—

(A) IN GENERAL.—The amount of interest paid or accrued during any such taxable year which is disallowed under this subsection shall not exceed the sum of—

(i) the amount which would be disallowed under this subsection if—

(I) paragraph (1) were applied by substituting "the sum of the ceiling amount and the net investment income" for "the net investment income", and

(II) paragraphs (4)(E) and (5)(A)(ii) did not apply, and

(ii) the applicable percentage of the excess of—

(I) the amount which (without regard to this paragraph) is not allowable as a deduction under this subsection for the taxable year, over

(II) the amount described in clause (i).

The preceding sentence shall not apply to any interest treated as paid or accrued during the taxable year under paragraph (2).

(B) APPLICABLE PERCENTAGE.—For purposes of this paragraph, the applicable percentage shall be determined in accordance with the following table:

In the case of taxable years beginning in:	*The applicable percentage is:*
1987	35
1988	60
1989	80
1990	90

(C) CEILING AMOUNT.—For purposes of this paragraph, the term "ceiling amount" means—

(i) $10,000 in the case of a taxpayer not described in clause (ii) or (iii),

(ii) $5,000 in the case of a married individual filing a separate return, and

(iii) zero in the case of a trust.

Amendments

• 2003, Jobs and Growth Tax Relief Reconciliation Act of 2003 (P.L. 108-27)

P.L. 108-27, §302(b):

Amended Code Sec. 163(d)(4)(B) by adding at the end a new flush sentence. For the **effective** date, see Act Sec. 302(f), as amended by P.L. 108-311, §402(a)(6), below.

P.L. 108-27, §302(f), as amended by P.L. 108-311, §402(a)(6), provides:

(f) EFFECTIVE DATE.—

(1) IN GENERAL.—Except as provided in paragraph (2), the amendments made by this section shall apply to taxable years beginning after December 31, 2002.

(2) PASS-THRU ENTITIES.—In the case of a pass-thru entity described in subparagraph (A), (B), (C), (D), (E), or (F) of section 1(h)(10) of the Internal Revenue Code of 1986, as amended by this Act, the amendments made by this section shall apply to taxable years ending after December 31, 2002; except that dividends received by such an entity on or before such date shall not be treated as qualified dividend income (as defined in section 1(h)(11)(B) of such Code, as added by this Act).

P.L. 108-27, §303, as amended by P.L. 109-222, §102, provides:

SEC. 303. SUNSET OF TITLE.

All provisions of, and amendments made by, this title shall not apply to taxable years beginning after December 31, 2010, and the Internal Revenue Code of 1986 shall be applied and administered to such years as if such provisions and amendments had never been enacted.

• 1993, Omnibus Budget Reconciliation Act of 1993 (P.L. 103-66)

P.L. 103-66, §13206(d)(1):

Amended Code Sec. 163(d)(4)(B). **Effective** for tax years beginning after 12-31-92. Prior to amendment, Code Sec. 163(d)(4)(B) read as follows:

(B) INVESTMENT INCOME.—The term "investment income" means the sum of—

(i) gross income (other than gain taken into account under clause (ii)) from property held for investment, and

(ii) any net gain attributable to the disposition of property held for investment.

• 1988, Technical and Miscellaneous Revenue Act of 1988 (P.L. 100-647)

P.L. 100-647, §1005(c)(1):

Amended Code Sec. 163(d)(3)(A) by striking out "incurred or continued to purchase or carry" and inserting in lieu thereof "properly allocable to". **Effective** as if enacted immediately before the enactment of P.L. 100-203. However, for a special rule, see Act Sec. 1005(c)(14), below.

P.L. 100-647, §1005(c)(2):

Amended Code Sec. 163(d)(4)(B). **Effective** as if enacted immediately before the enactment of P.L. 100-203. However, for a special rule, see Act Sec. 1005(c)(14), below. Prior to amendment, Code Sec. 163(d)(4)(B) read as follows:

(B) INVESTMENT INCOME.—The term "investment income" means the sum of—

(i) gross income (other than gain described in clause (ii)) from property held for investment, and

(ii) any net gain attributable to the disposition of property held for investment,

but only to the extent such amounts are not derived from the conduct of a trade or business.

P.L. 100-647, §1005(c)(3):

Amended Code Sec. 163(d)(6)(A). **Effective** as if enacted immediately before the enactment of P.L. 100-203. However, for a special rule, see Act Sec. 1005(c)(14), below. Prior to amendment, Code Sec. 163(d)(6)(A) read as follows:

(A) IN GENERAL.—The amount of interest disallowed under this subsection for any such taxable year shall be equal to the sum of—

(i) the applicable percentage of the amount which (without regard to this paragraph) is not allowed as a deduction under this subsection for the taxable year to the extent such amount does not exceed the ceiling amount,

(ii) the amount which (without regard to this paragraph) is not allowed as a deduction under this subsection in excess of the ceiling amount, plus

(iii) the amount of any carryforward to such taxable year under paragraph (2) with respect to which a deduction was disallowed under this subsection for a preceding taxable year.

For purposes of this subparagraph, the amount under clause (i) or (ii) shall be computed without regard to the amount described in clause (iii).

P.L. 100-647, §1005(c)(14), provides:

(14)(A) For purposes of applying section 163(h) of the 1986 Code to any taxable year beginning during 1987, if, incident to a divorce or legal separation—

(i) an individual acquires the interest of a spouse or former spouse in a qualified residence in a transfer to which section 1041 of the 1986 Code applies, and

(ii) such individual incurs indebtedness which is secured by such qualified residence,

the amount determined under paragraph (3)(B)(ii)(I) of section 163(h) of the 1986 Code (as in effect before the amendments made by the Revenue Act of 1987) with respect to such qualified residence shall be increased by the amount determined under subparagraph (B).

(B) The amount determined under this subparagraph shall be equal to the excess (if any) of—

(i) the lesser of the amount of the indebtedness described in subparagraph (A)(ii), or the fair market value of the spouse's or former spouse's interest in the qualified residence as of the time of the transfer, over

(ii) the basis of the spouse or former spouse in such interest in such residence (adjusted only by the cost of any improvements to such residence).

• 1987, Revenue Act of 1987 (P.L. 100-203)

P.L. 100-203, §10212(b):

Amended Code Sec. 163(d)(4)(E) by striking out "469(l)" and inserting in lieu thereof "469(m)". **Effective** as if included in the amendments made by P.L. 99-514, §501.

• **1986, Tax Reform Act of 1986 (P.L. 99-514)**

P.L. 99-514, §511(a):

Amended Code Sec. 163(d). **Effective** for tax years beginning after 12-31-86. Prior to amendment, Code Sec. 163(d) read as follows:

(d) LIMITATION ON INTEREST ON INVESTMENT INDEBTEDNESS.—

(1) IN GENERAL.—In the case of a taxpayer other than a corporation, the amount of investment interest (as defined in paragraph (3)(D)) otherwise allowable as a deduction under this chapter shall be limited, in the following order, to—

(A) $10,000 ($5,000, in the case of a separate return by a married individual), plus

(B) the amount of the net investment income (as defined in paragraph (3)(A)), plus the amount (if any) by which the deductions allowable under this section (determined without regard to this subsection) and sections 162, 164(a)(1) or (2), or 212 attributable to property of the taxpayer subject to a net lease exceeds the rental income produced by such property for the taxable year.

In the case of a trust, the $10,000 amount specified in subparagraph (A) shall be zero.

(2) CARRYOVER OF DISALLOWED INVESTMENT INTEREST.—The amount of disallowed investment interest for any taxable year shall be treated as investment interest paid or accrued in the succeeding taxable year.

(3) DEFINITIONS.—For purposes of this subsection—

(A) NET INVESTMENT INCOME.—The term "net investment income" means the excess of investment income over investment expenses. If the taxpayer has investment interest for the taxable year to which this subsection (as in effect before the Tax Reform Act of 1976) applies, the amount of the net investment income taken into account under this subsection shall be the amount of such income (determined without regard to this sentence) multiplied by a fraction the numerator of which is the excess of the investment interest for the taxable year over the investment interest to which such prior provision applies, and the denominator of which is the investment interest for the taxable year.

(B) INVESTMENT INCOME.—The term "investment income" means—

(i) the gross income from interest, dividends, rents, and royalties,

(ii) the net short-term capital gain attributable to the disposition of property held for investment, and

(iii) any amount treated under sections 1245, 1250, and 1254 as ordinary income,

but only to the extent such income, gain, and amounts are not derived from the conduct of a trade or business.

(C) INVESTMENT EXPENSES.—The term "investment expenses" means the deductions allowable under sections 162, 164(a)(1) or (2), 166, 167, 171, 212, or 611 directly connected with the production of investment income. For purposes of this subparagraph, the deduction allowable under section 167 with respect to any property may be treated as the amount which would have been allowable had the taxpayer depreciated the property under the straight line method for each taxable year of its useful life for which the taxpayer has held the property, and the deduction allowable under section 611 with respect to any property may be treated as the amount which would have been allowable had the taxpayer determined the deduction under section 611 without regard to section 613 for each taxable year for which the taxpayer has held the property.

(D) INVESTMENT INTEREST.—

(i) IN GENERAL.—The term "investment interest" means interest paid or accrued on indebtedness incurred or continued to purchase or carry property held for investment.

(ii) CERTAIN EXPENSES INCURRED IN CONNECTION WITH SHORT SALES.—For purposes of clause (i), the term "interest" includes any amount allowable as a deduction in connection with personal property used in a short sale.

(E) DISALLOWED INVESTMENT INTEREST.—The term "disallowed investment interest" means with respect to any taxable year, the amount not allowable as a deduction, solely by reason of the limitation in paragraph (1).

(4) SPECIAL RULES.—

(A) PROPERTY SUBJECT TO NET LEASE.—For purposes of this subsection, property subject to a lease shall be treated as property held for investment, and not as property used in a trade or business, for a taxable year, if—

(i) for such taxable year the sum of the deductions of the lessor with respect to such property which are allowable solely by reason of section 162 (other than rents and reimbursed amounts with respect to such property) is less than 15 percent of the rental income produced by such property, or

(ii) the lessor is either guaranteed a specified return or is guaranteed in whole or in part against loss of income.

(B) CONSTRUCTION INTEREST.—For purposes of this subsection, interest paid or accrued on indebtedness incurred or continued in the construction of property to be used in a trade or business shall not be treated as investment interest.

(5) EXCEPTIONS.—This subsection shall not apply with respect to investment interest, investment income, and investment expenses attributable to a specific item of property, if the indebtedness with respect to such property—

(A) is for a specified term, and

(B) was incurred before December 17, 1969, or is incurred after December 16, 1969, pursuant to a written contract or commitment which, on such date and at all times thereafter prior to the incurring of such indebtedness, is binding on the taxpayer.

For taxable years beginning after December 31, 1975, this paragraph shall be applied on an allocation basis rather than a specific item basis.

(6) REAL PROPERTY LEASES.—For purposes of paragraph (4)(A)—

(A) if a parcel of real property of the taxpayer is leased under two or more leases, paragraph (4)(A)(i) shall, at the election of the taxpayer, be applied by treating all leased portions of such property as subject to a single lease; and

(B) at the election of the taxpayer, paragraph (4)(A)(i), shall not apply with respect to real property of the taxpayer which has been in use for more than 5 years.

An election under subparagraph (A) or (B) shall be made at such time and in such manner as the Secretary prescribes by regulations.

(7) SPECIAL RULE WHERE TAXPAYER OWNS 50 PERCENT OR MORE OF ENTERPRISE.—

(A) GENERAL RULE.—In the case of any 50 percent owned corporations or partnership, the $10,000 figure specified in paragraph (1) shall be increased by the lesser of—

(i) $15,000, or

(ii) the interest paid or accrued during the taxable year on investment indebtedness incurred or continued in connection with the acquisition of the interest in such corporation or partnership.

In the case of a separate return by a married individual, $7,500 shall be substituted for the $15,000 figure in clause (1).

(B) OWNERSHIP REQUIREMENTS.—This paragraph shall apply with respect to indebtedness only if the taxpayer, his spouse, and his children own 50 percent or more of the total value of all classes of stock of the corporation or 50 percent or more of all capital interests in the partnership, as the case may be.

• **1984, Deficit Reduction Act of 1984 (P.L. 98-369)**

P.L. 98-369, §56(b):

Amended Code Sec. 163(d)(3)(D). **Effective** for short sales after 7-18-84, in tax years ending after such date. A transitional rule appears in Act Sec. 1066, below. Prior to amendment, it read as follows:

(D) Investment Interest.—The term "investment interest" means interest paid or accrued on indebtedness incurred or continued to purchase or carry property held for investment.

P.L. 98-369, §1066, provides:

SEC. 1066. TRANSITIONAL RULE FOR TREATMENT OF CERTAIN INCOME FROM S CORPORATIONS.

(a) IN GENERAL.—If—

(1) a corporation had an election in effect under subchapter S of the Internal Revenue Code of 1954 for the taxable years of such corporation beginning in 1982, 1983, and 1984, and

(2) a shareholder of such corporation makes an election to have this section apply,

then any qualified income which such shareholder takes into account by reason of holding stock in such corporation for any taxable year of such corporation beginning in 1983 or 1984 shall be treated for purposes of section 163(d) of the Internal Revenue Code of 1954 as such income would have been treated but for the enactment of the Subchapter S Revision Act of 1982.

(b) QUALIFIED INCOME.—For purposes of subsection (a), the term "qualified income" means any income other than income which is attributable to personal services performed by the shareholder for the corporation.

(c) ELECTION.—The election under subsection (a)(2) shall be made at such time and in such manner as the Secretary of the Treasury or his delegate may by regulations prescribe.

• 1982, Subchapter S Revision Act of 1982 (P.L. 97-354)

P.L. 97-354, § 5(a)(18):

Amended Code Sec. 163(d)(4) by striking out subparagraphs (B) and (C) and redesignating subparagraph (D) as subparagraph (B). **Effective** for tax years beginning after 12-31-82. Prior to being stricken, subparagraphs (B) and (C) read as follows:

"(B) PARTNERSHIPS.—In the case of a partnership, each partner shall, under regulations prescribed by the Secretary, take into account separately his distributive share of the partnership's investment interest and the other items of income and expense taken into account under this subsection.

(C) SHAREHOLDERS OF ELECTING SMALL BUSINESS CORPORATIONS.—In the case of an electing small business corporation (as defined in section 1371(b)), the investment interest paid or accrued by such corporation and the other items of income and expense which would be taken into account if this subsection applied to such corporation shall, under regulations prescribed by the Secretary, be treated as investment interest paid or accrued by the shareholders of such corporation and as items of such shareholders, and shall be apportioned pro rata among such shareholders in a manner consistent with section 1374(c)(1)."

• 1976, Tax Reform Act of 1976 (P.L. 94-455)

P.L. 94-455, § 205(c):

Amended Code Sec. 163(d)(3)(A)(iii) [probably (B)(iii)] by substituting "1250, and 1254" for "and 1250". **Effective** for tax years ending after 12-31-75.

P.L. 94-455, § 209(a)(1):

Amended Code Sec. 163(d)(1) and (2). **Effective** as provided in § 209(b), below. Prior to amendment, Code Sec. 163(d)(1) and (2) read as follows:

(d) LIMITATION ON INTEREST ON INVESTMENT INDEBTEDNESS.—

(1) IN GENERAL.—In the case of a taxpayer other than a corporation, the amount of investment interest (as defined in paragraph (3)(D)) otherwise allowable as a deduction under this chapter shall be limited, in the following order, to—

(A) $25,000 ($12,500, in the case of a separate return by a married individual), plus

(B) the amount of the net investment income (as defined in paragraph (3)(A)), plus the amount (if any) by which the deductions allowable under this section (determined without regard to this subsection) and sections 162, 164(a)(1) or (2), or 212 attributable to property of the taxpayer subject to a net lease exceeds the rental income produced by such property for the taxable year, plus

(C) an amount equal to the amount by which the net long-term capital gain exceeds the net short-term capital loss for the taxable year, plus

(D) one-half of the amount by which investment interest exceeds the sum of the amounts described in subparagraphs (A), (B), and (C).

In the case of a trust, the $25,000 amount specified in subparagraph (A) and in paragraph (2)(A) shall be zero. In determining the amount described in subparagraph (C), only gains and losses attributable to the disposition of property held for investment shall be taken into account.

(2) CARRYOVER OF DISALLOWED INVESTMENT INTEREST.—

(A) IN GENERAL.—The amount of disallowed investment interest for any taxable year shall be treated as investment interest paid or accrued in the succeeding taxable year. The amount of the interest so treated which is allowable as a deduction by reason of the first sentence of this paragraph for any taxable year shall not exceed one-half of the amount by which—

(i) the net investment income for such taxable year plus $25,000, exceeds

(ii) the investment interest paid or accrued during such taxable year (determined without regard to this paragraph) or $25,000, whichever is greater.

(B) REDUCTION FOR CAPITAL GAIN DEDUCTION.—If—

(i) an amount of disallowed investment interest treated under subparagraph (A) as investment interest paid or accrued in the taxable year is not allowable as a deduction for such taxable year by reason of the second sentence of subparagraph (A), and

(ii) the taxpayer is entitled to a deduction under section 1202 for such taxable year (whether or not the taxpayer claims such deduction), the amount of such disallowed investment interest shall be reduced by an amount equal to the amount of the deduction allowable under section 1202.

P.L. 94-455, § 209(a)(2):

Amended Code Sec. 163(d) by adding the last sentence to paragraph (3)(A). For **effective** date, see § 209(b), below.

P.L. 94-455, § 209(a)(3):

Amended Code Sec. 163(d) by substituting "limitation in paragraph (1)" for "limitations in paragraphs (1) and (2)(A)" in paragraph (3)(E). For **effective** date, see § 209(b), below.

P.L. 94-455, § 209(a)(5):

Amended Code Sec. 163(d) by adding the last paragraph to paragraph (6). For **effective** date, see § 209(b), below.

P.L. 94-455, § 209(a)(7):

Amended Code Sec. 163(d) by adding paragraph (7). For **effective** date, see § 209(b), below.

P.L. 94-455, § 209(a)(4):

Amended Code Sec. 163(d) by striking out paragraph (5) and redesignating paragraphs (6) and (7) as paragraphs (5) and (6), respectively. For **effective** date, see § 209(b), below. Prior to repeal, paragraph (5) read as follows:

(5) CAPITAL GAINS.—For purposes of sections 1201(b) (relating to alternative capital gains tax), 1202 (relating to deduction for capital gains), and 57(a)(9) (relating to treatment of capital gains as a tax preference), an amount equal to the amount of investment interest which is allowable as a deduction under this chapter by reason of subparagraph (C) of paragraph (1) shall be treated as gain from the sale or other disposition of property which is neither a capital asset nor property described in section 1231.

P.L. 94-455, § 209(b), provides:

(b) EFFECTIVE DATE.—

(1) IN GENERAL.—Except as provided in paragraph (2), the amendments made by subsection (a) shall apply to taxable years beginning after December 31, 1975.

(2) INDEBTEDNESS INCURRED BEFORE SEPTEMBER 11, 1975.—In the case of indebtedness attributable to a specific item of property which—

(A) is for a specified term, and

(B) was incurred before September 11, 1975, or is incurred after September 10, 1975, pursuant to a written contract or commitment which on September 11, 1975, and at all times thereafter before the incurring of such indebtedness, is binding on the taxpayer,

the amendments made by this section shall not apply, but section 163(d) of the Internal Revenue Code of 1954 (as in effect before the enactment of this Act) shall apply. For purposes of the preceding sentence, so much of the net investment income (as defined in section 163(d)(3)(A) of such Code) for any taxable year as is not taken into account under section 163(d) of such Code, as amended by this Act, by reason of the last sentence of section 163(d)(3)(A) of such Code, shall be taken into account for purposes of applying such section as in effect before the date of enactment of this Act with respect to interest on indebtedness referred to in the preceding sentence.

P.L. 94-455, §1901(b)(3)(K):

Amended Code Sec. 163(d)(3) by substituting "ordinary income" for "gain from the sale or exchange of property which is neither a capital asset nor property described in section 1231" in paragraph (B)(iii). **Effective** for tax years beginning after 12-31-76.

P.L. 94-455, §1906(b)(13)(A):

Amended 1954 Code by substituting "Secretary" for "Secretary or his delegate" each place it appeared. **Effective** 2-1-77.

• 1971, Revenue Act of 1971 (P.L. 92-178)

P.L. 92-178, §304(a)(2)(A):

Amended clause (i) of Code Sec. 163(d)(4)(A). **Effective** for tax years beginning after 12-31-71. Prior to amendment, clause (i) of such section read as follows:

"(i) for such taxable year the sum of the deductions with respect to such property which are allowable solely by reason of section 162 is less than 15 percent of the rental income produced by such property, or".

P.L. 92-178, §304(a)(2)(B):

Amended Code Sec. 163(d) by adding at the end thereof paragraph (7).

P.L. 92-178, §304(b)(2):

Amended Code Sec. 163(d)(1)(B). **Effective** for tax years beginning after 12-31-71. Prior to amendment, such section read as follows:

"(B) the amount of the net investment income (as defined in paragraph (3)(A)), plus".

P.L. 92-178, §304(d):

Added "162," in the first sentence of Code Sec. 163(d)(3)(C). **Effective** for tax years beginning after 12-31-71.

• 1969, Tax Reform Act of 1969 (P.L. 91-172)

P.L. 91-172, §221(a):

Amended Code Sec. 163 by adding new subsection (d). **Effective** for tax years beginning after 12-31-71.

[Sec. 163(e)]

(e) ORIGINAL ISSUE DISCOUNT.—

(1) IN GENERAL.—In the case of any debt instrument issued after July 1, 1982, the portion of the original issue discount with respect to such debt instrument which is allowable as a deduction to the issuer for any taxable year shall be equal to the aggregate daily portions of the original issue discount for days during such taxable year.

(2) DEFINITIONS AND SPECIAL RULES.—For purposes of this subsection—

(A) DEBT INSTRUMENT.—The term "debt instrument" has the meaning given such term by section 1275(a)(1).

(B) DAILY PORTIONS.—The daily portion of the original issue discount for any day shall be determined under section 1272(a) (without regard to paragraph (7) thereof and without regard to section 1273(a)(3)).

(C) SHORT-TERM OBLIGATIONS.—In the case of an obligor of a short-term obligation (as defined in section 1283(a)(1)(A)) who uses the cash receipts and disbursements method of accounting, the original issue discount (and any other interest payable) on such obligation shall be deductible only when paid.

(3) SPECIAL RULE FOR ORIGINAL ISSUE DISCOUNT ON OBLIGATION HELD BY RELATED FOREIGN PERSON.—

(A) IN GENERAL.—If any debt instrument having original issue discount is held by a related foreign person, any portion of such original issue discount shall not be allowable as a deduction to the issuer until paid. The preceding sentence shall not apply to the extent that the original issue discount is effectively connected with the conduct by such foreign related person of a trade or business within the United States unless such original issue discount is exempt from taxation (or is subject to a reduced rate of tax) pursuant to a treaty obligation of the United States.

(B) SPECIAL RULE FOR CERTAIN FOREIGN ENTITIES.—

(i) IN GENERAL.—In the case of any debt instrument having original issue discount which is held by a related foreign person which is a controlled foreign corporation (as defined in section 957) or a passive foreign investment company (as defined in section 1297), a deduction shall be allowable to the issuer with respect to such original issue discount for any taxable year before the taxable year in which paid only to the extent such original issue discount is includible (determined without regard to properly allocable deductions and qualified deficits under section 952(c)(1)(B)) during such prior taxable year in the gross income of a United States person who owns (within the meaning of section 958(a)) stock in such corporation.

(ii) SECRETARIAL AUTHORITY.—The Secretary may by regulation exempt transactions from the application of clause (i), including any transaction which is entered into by a payor in the ordinary course of a trade or business in which the payor is predominantly engaged.

(C) RELATED FOREIGN PERSON.—For purposes of subparagraph (A), the term "related foreign person" means any person—

(i) who is not a United States person, and

(ii) who is related (within the meaning of section 267(b)) to the issuer.

(4) EXCEPTIONS.—This subsection shall not apply to any debt instrument described in—

(A) subparagraph (D) of section 1272(a)(2) (relating to obligations issued by natural persons before March 2, 1984), and

(B) subparagraph (E) of section 1272(a)(2) (relating to loans between natural persons).

(5) SPECIAL RULES FOR ORIGINAL ISSUE DISCOUNT ON CERTAIN HIGH YIELD OBLIGATIONS.—

(A) IN GENERAL.—In the case of an applicable high yield discount obligation issued by a corporation—

(i) no deduction shall be allowed under this chapter for the disqualified portion of the original issue discount on such obligation, and

(ii) the remainder of such original issue discount shall not be allowable as a deduction until paid.

For purposes of this paragraph, rules similar to the rules of subsection (i)(3)(B) shall apply in determining the amount of the original issue discount and when the original issue discount is paid.

(B) DISQUALIFIED PORTION TREATED AS STOCK DISTRIBUTION FOR PURPOSES OF DIVIDEND RECEIVED DEDUCTION.—

(i) IN GENERAL.—Solely for purposes of sections 243, 245, 246, and 246A, the dividend equivalent portion of any amount includible in gross income of a corporation under section 1272(a) in respect of an applicable high yield discount obligation shall be treated as a dividend received by such corporation from the corporation issuing such obligation.

(ii) DIVIDEND EQUIVALENT PORTION.—For purposes of clause (i), the dividend equivalent portion of any amount includible in gross income under section 1272(a) in respect of an applicable high yield discount obligation is the portion of the amount so includible—

(I) which is attributable to the disqualified portion of the original issue discount on such obligation, and

(II) which would have been treated as a dividend if it had been a distribution made by the issuing corporation with respect to stock in such corporation.

(C) DISQUALIFIED PORTION.—

(i) IN GENERAL.—For purposes of this paragraph, the disqualified portion of the original issue discount on any applicable high yield discount obligation is the lesser of—

(I) the amount of such original issue discount, or

(II) the portion of the total return on such obligation which bears the same ratio to such total return as the disqualified yield on such obligation bears to the yield to maturity on such obligation.

(ii) DEFINITIONS.—For purposes of clause (i), the term "disqualified yield" means the excess of the yield to maturity on the obligation over the sum referred to subsection (i)(1)(B) plus 1 percentage point, and the term "total return" is the amount which would have been the original issue discount on the obligation if interest described in the parenthetical in section 1273(a)(2) were included in the stated redemption price at maturity.

(D) EXCEPTION FOR S CORPORATIONS.—This paragraph shall not apply to any obligation issued by any corporation for any period for which such corporation is an S corporation.

(E) EFFECT ON EARNINGS AND PROFITS.—This paragraph shall not apply for purposes of determining earnings and profits; except that, for purposes of determining the dividend equivalent portion of any amount includible in gross income under section 1272(a) in respect of an applicable high yield discount obligation, no reduction shall be made for any amount attributable to the disqualified portion of any original issue discount on such obligation.

(F) SUSPENSION OF APPLICATION OF PARAGRAPH.—

(i) TEMPORARY SUSPENSION.—This paragraph shall not apply to any applicable high yield discount obligation issued during the period beginning on September 1, 2008, and ending on December 31, 2009, in exchange (including an exchange resulting from a modification of the debt instrument) for an obligation which is not an applicable high yield discount obligation and the issuer (or obligor) of which is the same as the issuer (or obligor) of such applicable high yield discount obligation. The preceding sentence shall not apply to any obligation the interest on which is interest described in section 871(h)(4) (without regard to subparagraph (D) thereof) or to any obligation issued to a related person (within the meaning of section 108(e)(4)).

(ii) SUCCESSIVE APPLICATION.—Any obligation to which clause (i) applies shall not be treated as an applicable high yield discount obligation for purposes of applying this subparagraph to any other obligation issued in exchange for such obligation.

(iii) SECRETARIAL AUTHORITY TO SUSPEND APPLICATION.—The Secretary may apply this paragraph with respect to debt instruments issued in periods following the period described in clause (i) if the Secretary determines that such application is appropriate in light of distressed conditions in the debt capital markets.

(G) CROSS REFERENCE.—

For definition of applicable high yield discount obligation, see subsection (i).

(6) CROSS REFERENCES.—

For provision relating to deduction of original issue discount on tax-exempt obligation, see section 1288.

For special rules in the case of the borrower under certain loans for personal use, see section 1275(b).

Amendments

• 2009, American Recovery and Reinvestment Tax Act of 2009 (P.L. 111-5)

P.L. 111-5, §1232(a):

Amended Code Sec. 163(e)(5) by redesignating subparagraph (F) as subparagraph (G) and by inserting after subparagraph (E) a new subparagraph (F). **Effective** for obligations issued after 8-31-2008, in tax years ending after such date.

• 2004, American Jobs Creation Act of 2004 (P.L. 108-357)

P.L. 108-357, §841(a):

Amended Code Sec. 163(e)(3) by redesignating subparagraph (B) as subparagraph (C) and by inserting after subparagraph (A) a new subparagraph (B). **Effective** for payments accrued on or after 10-22-2004.

• 1990, Omnibus Budget Reconciliation Act of 1990 (P.L. 101-508)

P.L. 101-508, §11701(b)(1):

Amended Code Sec. 163(e)(5)(A) by striking the last sentence and inserting a new sentence. **Effective** as if included in the provision of P.L. 101-239 to which it relates. Prior to amendment, the last sentence of subparagraph (A) read as follows:

For purposes of clause (ii), rules similar to the rules of subsection (i)(3)(B) shall apply in determining the time when the original issue discount is paid.

• 1989, Omnibus Budget Reconciliation Act of 1989 (P.L. 101-239)

P.L. 101-239, §7202(a):

Amended Code Sec. 163(e) by redesignating paragraph (5) as paragraph (6) and inserting after paragraph (4) a new paragraph (5). **Effective**, generally, for instruments issued after 7-10-89. For exceptions, see Act Sec. 7202(c)(2), below.

P.L. 101-239, §7202(c)(2), provides:

(2) EXCEPTIONS.—

(A) The amendments made by this section shall not apply to any instrument if—

(i) such instrument is issued in connection with an acquisition—

(I) which is made on or before July 10, 1989,

(II) for which there was a written binding contract in effect on July 10, 1989, and at all times thereafter before such acquisition, or

(III) for which a tender offer was filed with the Securities and Exchange Commission on or before July 10, 1989,

(ii) the term of such instrument is not greater than—

(I) the term specified in the written documents described in clause (iii), or

(II) if no term is determined under subclause (I), 10 years, and

(iii) the use of such instrument in connection with such acquisition (and the maximum amount of proceeds from such instrument) was determined on or before July 10, 1989, and such determination is evidenced by written documents—

(I) which were transmitted on or before July 10, 1989, between the issuer and any governmental regulatory bodies or prospective parties to the issuance or acquisition, and

(II) which are customarily used for the type of acquisition or financing involved.

(B) The amendments made by this section shall not apply to any instrument issued pursuant to the terms of a debt instrument issued on or before July 10, 1989, or described in subparagraph (A) or (D).

(C) The amendments made by this section shall not apply to any instrument issued to refinance an original issue discount debt instrument to which the amendments made by this section do not apply if—

(i) the maturity date of the refinancing instrument is not later than the maturity date of the refinanced instrument,

(ii) the issue price of the refinancing instrument does not exceed the adjusted issue price of the refinanced instrument,

(iii) the stated redemption price at maturity of the refinancing instrument is not greater than the stated redemption price at maturity of the refinanced instrument, and

(iv) the interest payments required under the refinancing instrument before maturity are not less than (and are paid not later than) the interest payments required under the refinanced instrument.

(D) The amendments made by this section shall not apply to instruments issued after July 10, 1989, pursuant to a reorganization plan in a title 11 or similar case (as defined in section 368(a)(3) of the Internal Revenue Code of 1986) if the amount of proceeds of such instruments, and the maturities of such instruments, do not exceed the amount or maturities specified in the last reorganization plan filed in such case on or before July 10, 1989.

• 1988, Technical and Miscellaneous Revenue Act of 1988 (P.L. 100-647)

P.L. 100-647, §1006(u)(1):

Amended Code Sec. 163(e)(2)(B) by striking out "paragraph (6)" and inserting in lieu thereof "paragraph (7)". **Effective** as if included in the provision of P.L. 99-514 to which it relates.

• 1986, Tax Reform Act of 1986 (P.L. 99-514)

P.L. 99-514, §1803(a)(4):

Amended Code Sec. 163(e)(2) by adding at the end thereof new subparagraph (C). **Effective** as if included in the provision of P.L. 98-369 to which it relates.

P.L. 99-514, §1810(e)(1)(A):

Amended Code Sec. 163(e)(3)(A) by adding at the end thereof a new sentence. **Effective** as if included in the provision of P.L. 98-369 to which it relates.

P.L. 99-514, §1810(e)(1)(B):

Amended Code Sec. 163(e) by redesignating the paragraph relating to cross references as paragraph (5). **Effective** as if included in the provision of P.L. 98-369 to which it relates.

• 1984, Deficit Reduction Act of 1984 (P.L. 98-369)

P.L. 98-369, §42(a)(3):

Amended Code Sec. 163(e). **Effective** for tax years ending after 7-18-84. Prior to amendment, Code Sec. 163(e) read as follows:

(e) Original Issue Discount.—

(1) In General.—In the case of any bond issued after July 1, 1982, by an issuer (other than a natural person), the portion of the original issue discount with respect to such bond which is allowable as a deduction to the issuer for any taxable year shall be equal to the aggregate daily portions of the original issue discount for days during such taxable year.

(2) Definitions and Special Rules.—For purposes of this section—

(A) Bond.—The term "bond" has the meaning given to such term by section 1232A(c)(1).

(B) Daily Portions.—The daily portion of the original issue discount for any day shall be determined under section 1232A(a) (without regard to paragraphs (2)(B) and (6) thereof and without regard to the second sentence of section 1232(b)(1)).

P.L. 98-369, §128(c):

Amended Code Sec. 163(e) as amended by Act Sec. 42(a)(3) by redesignating subsection (3) as subsection (4) [and subsection (4) as subsection (5)] and by inserting after subsection (2) a new subsection (3). **Effective** for obligations issued after 6-9-84.

• 1982, Tax Equity and Fiscal Responsibility Act of 1982 (P.L. 97-248)

P.L. 97-248, §231(b):

Amended Code Sec. 163 by redesignating subsection (e) as subsection (f) (which was further redesignated by Act Sec. 310(b)(2)) and by inserting after subsection (d) new subsection (e). **Effective** for obligations issued after 7-1-82, unless issued pursuant to a written commitment binding on 7-1-82, and at all times thereafter. For a transitional rule, see Act Sec. 231(e), which appears in the amendment notes for P.L. 97-248 following Code Sec. 1232A.

[Sec. 163(f)]

(f) DENIAL OF DEDUCTION FOR INTEREST ON CERTAIN OBLIGATIONS NOT IN REGISTERED FORM.—

(1) IN GENERAL.—Nothing in subsection (a) or in any other provision of law shall be construed to provide a deduction for interest on any registration-required obligation unless such obligation is in registered form.

(2) REGISTRATION-REQUIRED OBLIGATION.—For purposes of this section—

(A) IN GENERAL.—The term "registration-required obligation" means any obligation (including any obligation issued by a governmental entity) other than an obligation which—

(i) is issued by a natural person,

(ii) is not of a type offered to the public, or

(iii) has a maturity (at issue) of not more than 1 year.

➡ Caution: Code Sec. 163(f)(2)(A)(iv), below, was stricken by P.L. 111-147, applicable to obligations issued after the date which is 2 years after March 18, 2010.

(iv) is described in subparagraph (B).

➡ Caution: Code Sec. 163(f)(2)(B), below, was stricken by P.L. 111-147, applicable to obligations issued after the date which is 2 years after March 18, 2010.

(B) CERTAIN OBLIGATIONS NOT INCLUDED.—An obligation is described in this subparagraph if—

(i) there are arrangements reasonably designed to ensure that such obligation will be sold (or resold in connection with the original issue) only to a person who is not a United States person, and

(ii) in the case of an obligation not in registered form—

(I) interest on such obligation is payable only outside the United States and its possessions, and

(II) on the face of such obligation there is a statement that any United States person who holds such obligation will be subject to limitations under the United States income tax laws.

➡ Caution: Code Sec. 163(f)(2)(C), below, prior to redesignation as Code Sec. 163(f)(2)(B) and amendment by P.L. 111-147, applies to obligations issued on or before the date which is 2 years after March 18, 2010.

(C) AUTHORITY TO INCLUDE OTHER OBLIGATIONS.—Clauses (ii) and (iii) of subparagraph (A), and subparagraph (B), shall not apply to any obligation if—

(i) in the case of—

(I) subparagraph (A), such obligation is of a type which the Secretary has determined by regulations to be used frequently in avoiding Federal taxes, or

(II) subparagraph (B), such obligation is of a type specified by the Secretary in regulations, and

(ii) such obligation is issued after the date on which the regulations referred to in clause (i) take effect.

➡ Caution: Former Code Sec. 163(f)(2)(C) was redesignated as Code Sec. 163(f)(2)(B), below, and amended by P.L. 111-147, applicable to obligations issued after the date which is 2 years after March 18, 2010.

(B) AUTHORITY TO INCLUDE OTHER OBLIGATIONS.—Clauses (ii) and (iii) of subparagraph (A) shall not apply to any obligation if—

(i) such obligation is of a type which the Secretary has determined by regulations to be used frequently in avoiding Federal taxes, and

(ii) such obligation is issued after the date on which the regulations referred to in clause (i) take effect.

➾➝ *Caution: Code Sec. 163(f)(3), below, prior to amendment by P.L. 111-147, applies to obligations issued on or before the date which is 2 years after March 18 , 2010.*

(3) BOOK ENTRIES PERMITTED, ETC.—For purposes of this subsection, rules similar to the rules of section 149(a)(3) shall apply.

➾➝ *Caution: Code Sec. 163(f)(3), below, as amended by P.L. 111-147, applies to obligations issued after the date which is 2 years after March 18, 2010.*

(3) BOOK ENTRIES PERMITTED, ETC.—For purposes of this subsection, rules similar to the rules of section 149(a)(3) shall apply, except that a dematerialized book entry system or other book entry system specified by the Secretary shall be treated as a book entry system described in such section.

Amendments

• 2010, Hiring Incentives to Restore Employment Act (P.L. 111-147)

P.L. 111-147, §502(a)(1):

Amended Code Sec. 163(f)(2) by striking subparagraph (B) and by redesignating subparagraph (C) as subparagraph (B). **Effective** for obligations issued after the date which is 2 years after 3-18-2010. Prior to being stricken, Code Sec. 163(f)(2)(B) read as follows:

(B) CERTAIN OBLIGATIONS NOT INCLUDED.—An obligation is described in this subparagraph if—

(i) there are arrangements reasonably designed to ensure that such obligation will be sold (or resold in connection with the original issue) only to a person who is not a United States person, and

(ii) in the case of an obligation not in registered form—

(I) interest on such obligation is payable only outside the United States and its possessions, and

(II) on the face of such obligation there is a statement that any United States person who holds such obligation will be subject to limitations under the United States income tax laws.

P.L. 111-147, §502(a)(2)(B):

Amended Code Sec. 163(f)(2)(A) by inserting "or" at the end of clause (ii), by striking ", or" at the end of clause (iii) and inserting a period, and by striking clause (iv). **Effective** for obligations issued after the date which is 2 years after 3-18-2010. Prior to being stricken, Code Sec. 163(f)(2)(A)(iv) read as follows:

(iv) is described in subparagraph (B).

P.L. 111-147, §502(a)(2)(C)(i)-(ii):

Amended Code Sec. 163(f)(2)(B), as redesignated by Act Sec. 502(a)(1), by striking ", and subparagraph (B)," following "of subparagraph (A)" in the matter preceding clause (i), and by amending clause (i). **Effective** for obligations issued after the date which is 2 years after 3-18-2010. Prior to amendment, Code Sec. 163(f)(2)(B)(i) read as follows:

(i) in the case of—

(I) subparagraph (A), such obligation is of a type which the Secretary has determined by regulations to be used frequently in avoiding Federal taxes, or

(II) subparagraph (B), such obligation is of a type specified by the Secretary in regulations, and

P.L. 111-147, §502(c):

Amended Code Sec. 163(f)(3) by inserting ", except that a dematerialized book entry system or other book entry system specified by the Secretary shall be treated as a book entry system described in such section" before the period at the end. **Effective** for obligations issued after the date which is 2 years after 3-18-2010.

• 1986, Tax Reform Act of 1986 (P.L. 99-514)

P.L. 99-514, §1301(j)(3):

Amended Code Sec. 163(f)(3) by striking out "section 103(j)(3)" and inserting in lieu thereof "section 149(a)(3)". **Effective** for bonds issued after 8-15-86.

• 1984, Deficit Reduction Act of 1984 (P.L. 98-369)

P.L. 98-369, §127(f):

Amended Code Sec. 163(f)(2)(C)(i). **Effective** for interest received after 7-1-84, with respect to obligations issued after such date, in tax years ending after such date. Prior to amendment, Code Sec. 163(f)(2)(C)(i) read as follows:

(i) such obligation is of a type which the Secretary has determined by regulations to be used frequently in avoiding Federal taxes, and

• 1982, Tax Equity and Fiscal Responsibility Act of 1982 (P.L. 97-248)

P.L. 97-248, §310(b)(2):

Amended Code Sec. 163 by redesignating subsection (f), as redesignated by Act Sec. 231(b), as subsection (g) and by inserting after subsection (e) a new subsection (f). **Effective** for obligations issued after 12-31-82. See also the amendment note for P.L. 97-248 following Code Sec. 103(j) for a special rule.

[Sec. 163(g)]

(g) REDUCTION OF DEDUCTION WHERE SECTION 25 CREDIT TAKEN.—The amount of the deduction under this section for interest paid or accrued during any taxable year on indebtedness with respect to which a mortgage credit certificate has been issued under section 25 shall be reduced by the amount of the credit allowable with respect to such interest under section 25 (determined without regard to section 26).

Amendments

• 1984, Deficit Reduction Act of 1984 (P.L. 98-369)

P.L. 98-369, §612(c):

Amended Code Sec. 163 by redesignating subsection (g) as subsection (h) and by inserting after subsection (f) a new subsection (g). **Effective** for interest paid or accrued after 12-31-84, on indebtedness incurred after 12-31-84.

[Sec. 163(h)]

(h) DISALLOWANCE OF DEDUCTION FOR PERSONAL INTEREST.—

(1) IN GENERAL.—In the case of a taxpayer other than a corporation, no deduction shall be allowed under this chapter for personal interest paid or accrued during the taxable year.

(2) PERSONAL INTEREST.—For purposes of this subsection, the term "personal interest" means any interest allowable as a deduction under this chapter other than—

(A) interest paid or accrued on indebtedness properly allocable to a trade or business (other than the trade or business of performing services as an employee),

(B) any investment interest (within the meaning of subsection (d)),

(C) any interest which is taken into account under section 469 in computing income or loss from a passive activity of the taxpayer,

(D) any qualified residence interest (within the meaning of paragraph (3)),

(E) any interest payable under section 6601 on any unpaid portion of the tax imposed by section 2001 for the period during which an extension of time for payment of such tax is in effect under section 6163, and

(F) any interest allowable as a deduction under section 221 (relating to interest on educational loans).

(3) QUALIFIED RESIDENCE INTEREST.—For purposes of this subsection—

(A) IN GENERAL.—The term "qualified residence interest" means any interest which is paid or accrued during the taxable year on—

(i) acquisition indebtedness with respect to any qualified residence of the taxpayer, or

(ii) home equity indebtedness with respect to any qualified residence of the taxpayer.

For purposes of the preceding sentence, the determination of whether any property is a qualified residence of the taxpayer shall be made as of the time the interest is accrued.

(B) ACQUISITION INDEBTEDNESS.—

(i) IN GENERAL.—The term "acquisition indebtedness" means any indebtedness which—

(I) is incurred in acquiring, constructing, or substantially improving any qualified residence of the taxpayer, and

(II) is secured by such residence.

Such term also includes any indebtedness secured by such residence resulting from the refinancing of indebtedness meeting the requirements of the preceding sentence (or this sentence); but only to the extent the amount of the indebtedness resulting from such refinancing does not exceed the amount of the refinanced indebtedness.

(ii) $1,000,000 LIMITATION.—The aggregate amount treated as acquisition indebtedness for any period shall not exceed $1,000,000 ($500,000 in the case of a married individual filing a separate return).

(C) HOME EQUITY INDEBTEDNESS.—

(i) IN GENERAL.—The term "home equity indebtedness" means any indebtedness (other than acquisition indebtedness) secured by a qualified residence to the extent the aggregate amount of such indebtedness does not exceed—

(I) the fair market value of such qualified residence, reduced by

(II) the amount of acquisition indebtedness with respect to such residence.

(ii) LIMITATION—The aggregate amount treated as home equity indebtedness for any period shall not exceed $100,000 ($50,000 in the case of a separate return by a married individual).

(D) TREATMENT OF INDEBTEDNESS INCURRED ON OR BEFORE OCTOBER 13, 1987.—

(i) IN GENERAL.—In the case of any pre-October 13, 1987, indebtedness—

(I) such indebtedness shall be treated as acquisition indebtedness, and

(II) the limitation of subparagraph (B)(ii) shall not apply.

(ii) REDUCTION IN $1,000,000 LIMITATION.—The limitation of subparagraph (B)(ii) shall be reduced (but not below zero) by the aggregate amount of outstanding pre-October 13, 1987, indebtedness.

(iii) PRE-OCTOBER 13, 1987, INDEBTEDNESS.—The term "pre-October 13, 1987, indebtedness" means—

(I) any indebtedness which was incurred on or before October 13, 1987, and which was secured by a qualified residence on October 13, 1987, and at all times thereafter before the interest is paid or accrued, or

(II) any indebtedness which is secured by the qualified residence and was incurred after October 13, 1987, to refinance indebtedness described in subclause (I) (or refinanced indebtedness meeting the requirements of this subclause) to the extent (immediately after the refinancing) the principal amount of the indebtedness resulting from the refinancing does not exceed the principal amount of the refinanced indebtedness (immediately before the refinancing).

(iv) LIMITATION ON PERIOD OF REFINANCING.—Subclause (II) of clause (iii) shall not apply to any indebtedness after—

(I) the expiration of the term of the indebtedness described in clause (iii)(I), or

(II) if the principal of the indebtedness described in clause (iii)(I) is not amortized over its term, the expiration of the term of the 1st refinancing of such indebtedness (or if earlier, the date which is 30 years after the date of such 1st refinancing).

(E) MORTGAGE INSURANCE PREMIUMS TREATED AS INTEREST.—

(i) IN GENERAL.—Premiums paid or accrued for qualified mortgage insurance by a taxpayer during the taxable year in connection with acquisition indebtedness with respect to a qualified residence of the taxpayer shall be treated for purposes of this section as interest which is qualified residence interest.

(ii) PHASEOUT.—The amount otherwise treated as interest under clause (i) shall be reduced (but not below zero) by 10 percent of such amount for each $1,000 ($500 in the case of a married individual filing a separate return) (or fraction thereof) that the taxpayer's adjusted gross income for the taxable year exceeds $100,000 ($50,000 in the case of a married individual filing a separate return).

(iii) LIMITATION.—Clause (i) shall not apply with respect to any mortgage insurance contracts issued before January 1, 2007.

(iv) TERMINATION.—Clause (i) shall not apply to amounts—

(I) paid or accrued after December 31, 2010, or

(II) properly allocable to any period after such date.

(4) OTHER DEFINITIONS AND SPECIAL RULES.—For purposes of this subsection—

(A) QUALIFIED RESIDENCE.—

(i) IN GENERAL.—The term "qualified residence" means—

(I) the principal residence (within the meaning of section 121) of the taxpayer, and

(II) 1 other residence of the taxpayer which is selected by the taxpayer for purposes of this subsection for the taxable year and which is used by the taxpayer as a residence (within the meaning of section 280A(d)(1)).

(ii) MARRIED INDIVIDUALS FILING SEPARATE RETURNS.—If a married couple does not file a joint return for the taxable year—

(I) such couple shall be treated as 1 taxpayer for purposes of clause (i), and

(II) each individual shall be entitled to take into account 1 residence unless both individuals consent in writing to 1 individual taking into account the principal residence and 1 other residence.

(iii) RESIDENCE NOT RENTED.—For purposes of clause (i)(II), notwithstanding section 280A(d)(1), if the taxpayer does not rent a dwelling unit at any time during a taxable year, such unit may be treated as a residence for such taxable year.

(B) SPECIAL RULE FOR COOPERATIVE HOUSING CORPORATIONS.—Any indebtedness secured by stock held by the taxpayer as a tenant-stockholder (as defined in section 216) in a cooperative housing corporation (as so defined) shall be treated as secured by the house or apartment which the taxpayer is entitled to occupy as such a tenant-stockholder. If stock described in the preceding sentence may not be used to secure indebtedness, indebtedness shall be treated as so secured if the taxpayer establishes to the satisfaction of the Secretary that such indebtedness was incurred to acquire such stock.

(C) UNENFORCEABLE SECURITY INTERESTS.—Indebtedness shall not fail to be treated as secured by any property solely because, under any applicable State or local homestead or other debtor protection law in effect on August 16, 1986, the security interest is ineffective or the enforceability of the security interest is restricted.

(D) SPECIAL RULES FOR ESTATES AND TRUSTS.—For purposes of determining whether any interest paid or accrued by an estate or trust is qualified residence interest, any residence held by such estate or trust shall be treated as a qualified residence of such estate or trust if such estate or trust establishes that such residence is a qualified residence of a beneficiary who has a present interest in such estate or trust or an interest in the residuary of such estate or trust.

(E) QUALIFIED MORTGAGE INSURANCE.—The term "qualified mortgage insurance" means—

(i) mortgage insurance provided by the Veterans Administration, the Federal Housing Administration, or the Rural Housing Administration, and

(ii) private mortgage insurance (as defined by section 2 of the Homeowners Protection Act of 1998 (12 U.S.C. 4901), as in effect on the date of the enactment of this subparagraph).

(F) SPECIAL RULES FOR PREPAID QUALIFIED MORTGAGE INSURANCE.—Any amount paid by the taxpayer for qualified mortgage insurance that is properly allocable to any mortgage the payment of which extends to periods that are after the close of the taxable year in which such amount is paid shall be chargeable to capital account and shall be treated as paid in such periods to which so allocated. No deduction shall be allowed for the unamortized balance of such account if such mortgage is satisfied before the end of its term. The preceding sentences shall not apply to amounts paid for qualified mortgage insurance provided by the Veterans Administration or the Rural Housing Administration.

(5) PHASE-IN OF LIMITATION.—In the case of any taxable year beginning in calendar years 1987 through 1990, the amount of interest with respect to which a deduction is disallowed under this subsection shall be equal to the applicable percentage (within the meaning of subsection (d)(6)(B)) of the amount which (but for this paragraph) would have been so disallowed.

Amendments

• 2007, Mortgage Forgiveness Debt Relief Act of 2007 (P.L. 110-142)

P.L. 110-142, §3(a):

Amended Code Sec. 163(h)(3)(E)(iv)(I) by striking "December 31, 2007" and inserting "December 31, 2010". **Effective** for amounts paid or accrued after 12-31-2007.

• 2006, Tax Relief and Health Care Act of 2006 (P.L. 109-432)

P.L. 109-432, Division A, §419(a):

Amended Code Sec. 163(h)(3) by adding at the end a new subparagraph (E). **Effective** for amounts paid or accrued after 12-31-2006.

P.L. 109-432, Division A, §419(b):

Amended Code Sec. 163(h)(4) by adding at the end new subparagraphs (E) and (F). **Effective** for amounts paid or accrued after 12-31-2006.

• 1998, Tax Trade and Relief Extension Act of 1998 (P.L. 105-277)

P.L. 105-277, §4003(a)(1):

Amended Code Sec. 163(h)(2) by striking "and" at the end of subparagraph (D), by striking the period at the end of subparagraph (E) and inserting ", and", and by adding at the end a new subparagraph (F). **Effective** as if included in the provision of P.L. 105-34 to which it relates [generally **effective** for interest payments due and paid after 12-31-97, on any qualified education loan.—CCH].

• 1997, Taxpayer Relief Act of 1997 (P.L. 105-34)

P.L. 105-34, §312(d)(1):

Amended Code Sec. 163(h)(4)(A)(i)(I) [sic] by striking "section 1034" and inserting "section 121". **Effective** for sales and exchanges after 5-6-97.

P.L. 105-34, §503(b)(2)(B):

Amended Code Sec. 163(h)(2)(E) by striking "or 6166" and all that follows and inserting a period. **Effective**, generally, for estates of decedents dying after 12-31-97. For a special rule, see Act Sec. 503(d)(2), below. Prior to amendment, Code Sec. 163(h)(2)(E) read as follows:

(E) any interest payable under section 6601 on any unpaid portion of the tax imposed by section 2001 for the period during which an extension of time for payment of such tax is in effect under section 6163 or 6166 or under section 6166A (as in effect before its repeal by the Economic Recovery Tax Act of 1981).

P.L. 105-34, §503(d)(2), provides:

(2) ELECTION.—In the case of the estate of any decedent dying before January 1, 1998, with respect to which there is an election under section 6166 of the Internal Revenue Code of 1986, the executor of the estate may elect to have the amendments made by this section apply with respect to installments due after the effective date of the election; except that the 2-percent portion of such installments shall be equal to the amount which would be the 4-percent portion of such installments without regard to such election. Such an election shall be made before January 1, 1999 in the manner prescribed by the Secretary of the Treasury and, once made, is irrevocable.

• 1988, Technical and Miscellaneous Revenue Act of 1988 (P.L. 100-647)

P.L. 100-647, §1005(c)(4):

Amended Code Sec. 163(h)(2)(A) by striking out "incurred or continued in connection with the conduct of" and inserting in lieu thereof "properly allocable to". **Effective** as if enacted immediately before the enactment of P.L. 100-203. However, for a special rule, see Act Sec. 1005(c)(14) in the amendment notes following Code Sec. 163(d).

P.L. 100-647, §1005(c)(5):

Amended Code Sec. 163(h)(3)(C) (as in effect immediately before the enactment of the P.L. 100-203, the Revenue Act of 1987) to read as below. For the text of Code Sec. 163(h)(3)(C) prior to amendment, see the amendment note for P.L. 100-203, §10102(a), below.

(C) COST NOT LESS THAN BALANCE OF INDEBTEDNESS INCURRED ON OR BEFORE AUGUST 16, 1986.—

(i) IN GENERAL.—The amount under subparagraph (B)(ii)(I) at any time after August 16, 1986, shall not be less than the outstanding principal amount (as of such time) of indebtedness—

(I) which was incurred on or before August 16, 1986, and which was secured by the qualified residence on August 16, 1986, or

(II) which is secured by the qualified residence and was incurred after August 16, 1986, to refinance indebtedness described in subclause (I) (or refinanced indebtedness meeting the requirements of this subclause) to the extent (immediately after the refinancing) the principal amount of the indebtedness resulting from the refinancing does not exceed the principal amount of the refinanced indebtedness (immediately before the refinancing).

(ii) LIMITATION ON PERIOD OF REFINANCING.—Subclause (II) of clause (i) shall not apply to any indebtedness after—

(I) the expiration of the term of the indebtedness described in clause (i)(I), or

(II) if the principal of the indebtedness described in clause (i)(I) is not amortized over its term, the expiration of the term of the 1st refinancing of such indebtedness (or if earlier, the date which is 30 years after the date of such refinancing).

P.L. 100-647, §1005(c)(6)(A):

Amended the heading for Code Sec. 163(h)(5)[(4)]. **Effective** as if enacted immediately before the enactment of P.L. 100-203. However, for a special rule, see Act Sec. 1005(c)(14) in the amendment notes following Code Sec. 163(d). Prior to amendment, the heading for Code Sec. 163(h)(5)[(4)] read as follows: OTHER DEFINITIONS AND SPECIAL RULES.—

P.L. 100-647, §1005(c)(6)(B)(i)-(ii):

Amended Code Sec. 163(h)(5)[(4)] by striking out "For purposes of this subsection—" in subparagraph (A), and by striking out "For purposes of this paragraph, any" in subparagraph (B) and inserting in lieu thereof "Any". **Effective** as if enacted immediately before the enactment of P.L. 100-203. However, for a special rule, see Act Sec. 1005(c)(14) in the amendment notes following Code Sec. 163(d).

P.L. 100-647, §1005(c)(7):

Amended Code Sec. 163(h)(5)[(4)](A)(iii) by striking out "USED OR" after "NOT" in the heading thereof and by striking out "or use"after "rent". **Effective** as if enacted immediately before the enactment of P.L. 100-203. However, for a special rule, see Act Sec. 1005(c)(14) in the amendment notes following Code Sec. 163(d). Prior to amendment, Code Sec. 163(h)(5)[(4)](A)(iii) read as follows:

(iii) RESIDENCE NOT USED OR RENTED.—For purposes of clause (i)(II), notwithstanding section 280A(d)(1), if the taxpayer does not rent or use a dwelling unit at any time during a taxable year, such unit may be treated as a residence for such taxable year.

P.L. 100-647, §1005(c)(8):

Amended Code Sec. 163(h)(5)[(4)] by adding at the end thereof new subparagraphs (C) and (D). **Effective** as if enacted immediately before the enactment of P.L. 100-203. However, for a special rule, see Act Sec. 1005(c)(14) in the amendment notes following Code Sec. 163(d).

P.L. 100-647, §1005(c)(9):

Amended Code Sec. 163(h)(6) by striking out "subsection" the 3rd place it appears and inserting in lieu thereof "paragraph". **Effective** as if enacted immediately before the enactment of P.L. 100-203. However, for a special rule, see Act Sec. 1005(c)(14) in the amendment notes following Code Sec. 163(d).

P.L. 100-647, §1005(c)(12):

Amended Code Sec. 163(h)(2)(E) by inserting before the period "or under section 6166A (as in effect before its repeal by the Economic Recovery Tax Act of 1981)". **Effective** as if enacted immediately before the enactment of P.L. 100-203. However, for a special rule, see Act Sec. 1005(c)(14) in the amendment notes following Code Sec. 163(d).

P.L. 100-647, §2004(b)(1):

Amended Code Sec. 163(h) by redesignating paragraph (6) as paragraph (5). **Effective** as if included in the provision of P.L. 100-203 to which it relates.

• 1987, Revenue Act of 1987 (P.L. 100-203)

P.L. 100-203, §10102(a):

Amended Code Sec. 163(h)(3). **Effective** for tax years beginning after 12-31-87. Prior to amendment, Code Sec. 163(h)(3) read as follows:

(3) QUALIFIED RESIDENCE INTEREST.—For purposes of this subsection—

(A) IN GENERAL.—The term "qualified residence interest" means interest which is paid or accrued during the taxable year on indebtedness which is secured by any property which (at the time such interest is paid or accrued) is a qualified residence of the taxpayer.

(B) LIMITATION ON AMOUNT OF INTEREST.—The term "qualified residence interest" shall not include any interest paid or accrued on indebtedness secured by any qualified residence which is allocable to that portion of the principal amount of such indebtedness which, when added to the outstanding aggregate principal amount of all other indebtedness previously incurred and secured by such qualified residence, exceeds the lesser of—

(i) the fair market value of such qualified residence, or

(ii) the sum of—

(I) the taxpayer's basis in such qualified residence (adjusted only by the cost of any improvements to such residence), plus

(II) the aggregate amount of qualified indebtedness of the taxpayer with respect to such qualified residence.

(C) COST NOT LESS THAN BALANCE OF INDEBTEDNESS INCURRED ON OR BEFORE AUGUST 16, 1986.—The amount under subparagraph (B)(ii)(I) at any time after August 16, 1986, shall not be less than the outstanding aggregate principal amount (as of such time) of indebtedness which was incurred on or before August 16, 1986, and which was secured by the qualified residence on August 16, 1986.

(D) TIME FOR DETERMINATION.—Except as provided in regulations, any determination under subparagraph (B) shall be made as of the time the indebtedness is incurred.

P.L. 100-203, §10102(b):

Amended Code Sec. 163(h) by striking out paragraph (4) and by redesignating paragraph (5) as paragraph (4). **Effective** for tax years beginning after 12-31-87. Prior to amendment, paragraph (4) read as follows:

(4) QUALIFIED INDEBTEDNESS.—For purposes of this subsection—

(A) IN GENERAL.—The term "qualified indebtedness" means indebtedness secured by a qualified residence of the taxpayer which is incurred after August 16, 1986, to pay for—

(i) qualified medical expenses, or

(ii) qualified educational expenses,

which are paid or incurred within a reasonable period of time before or after such indebtedness is incurred.

(B) QUALIFIED MEDICAL EXPENSES.—For purposes of this paragraph, the term "qualified medical expenses" means amounts, not compensated for by insurance or otherwise, incurred for medical care (within the meaning of subparagraphs (A) and (B) of section 213(d)(1)) for the taxpayer, his spouse, or a dependent.

(C) QUALIFIED EDUCATIONAL EXPENSES.—For purposes of this paragraph—

(i) IN GENERAL.—The term "qualified educational expenses" means qualified tuition and related expenses of the taxpayer, his spouse, or a dependent for attendance at an educational institution described in section 170(b)(1)(A)(ii).

(ii) QUALIFIED TUITION AND RELATED EXPENSES.—The term "qualified tuition and related expenses" has the meaning given such term by section 117(b), except that such term shall include any reasonable living expenses while away from home.

(D) DEPENDENT.—For purposes of this paragraph, the term "dependent" has the meaning given such term by section 152.

• 1986, Tax Reform Act of 1986 (P.L. 99-514)

P.L. 99-514, §511(b):

Amended Code Sec. 163 by redesignating subsection (h) as subsection (i) and by inserting after subsection (g) new subsection (h). **Effective** for tax years beginning after 12-31-86.

[Sec. 163(i)]

(i) APPLICABLE HIGH YIELD DISCOUNT OBLIGATION.—

(1) IN GENERAL.—For purposes of this section, the term "applicable high yield discount obligation" means any debt instrument if—

(A) the maturity date of such instrument is more than 5 years from the date of issue,

(B) the yield to maturity on such instrument equals or exceeds the sum of—

(i) the applicable Federal rate in effect under section 1274(d) for the calendar month in which the obligation is issued, plus

(ii) 5 percentage points, and

(C) such instrument has significant original issue discount.

For purposes of subparagraph (B)(i), the Secretary may by regulation (i) permit a rate to be used with respect to any debt instrument which is higher than the applicable Federal rate if the taxpayer establishes to the satisfaction of the Secretary that such higher rate is based on the same principles as the applicable Federal rate and is appropriate for the term of the instrument, or (ii) permit, on a temporary basis, a rate to be used with respect to any debt instrument which is higher than the applicable Federal rate if the Secretary determines that such rate is appropriate in light of distressed conditions in the debt capital markets.

(2) SIGNIFICANT ORIGINAL ISSUE DISCOUNT.—For purposes of paragraph (1)(C), a debt instrument shall be treated as having significant original issue discount if—

(A) the aggregate amount which would be includible in gross income with respect to such instrument for periods before the close of any accrual period (as defined in section 1272(a)(5)) ending after the date 5 years after the date of issue, exceeds—

(B) the sum of—

(i) the aggregate amount of interest to be paid under the instrument before the close of such accrual period, and

(ii) the product of the issue price of such instrument (as defined in sections 1273(b) and 1274(a)) and its yield to maturity.

(3) SPECIAL RULES.—For purposes of determining whether a debt instrument is an applicable high yield discount obligation—

(A) any payment under the instrument shall be assumed to be made on the last day permitted under the instrument, and

(B) any payment to be made in the form of another obligation of the issuer (or a related person within the meaning of section 453(f)(1)) shall be assumed to be made when such obligation is required to be paid in cash or in property other than such obligation.

Except for purposes of paragraph (1)(B), any reference to an obligation in subparagraph (B) of this paragraph shall be treated as including a reference to stock.

(4) DEBT INSTRUMENT.—For purposes of this subsection, the term "debt instrument" means any instrument which is a debt instrument as defined in section 1275(a).

(5) REGULATIONS.—The Secretary shall prescribe such regulations as may be appropriate to carry out the purposes of this subsection and subsection (e)(5), including—

(A) regulations providing for modifications to the provisions of this subsection and subsection (e)(5) in the case of varying rates of interest, put or call options, indefinite maturities, contingent payments, assumptions of debt instruments, conversion rights, or other circumstances where such modifications are appropriate to carry out the purposes of this subsection and subsection (e)(5), and

(B) regulations to prevent avoidance of the purposes of this subsection and subsection (e)(5) through the use of issuers other than C corporations, agreements to borrow amounts due under the debt instrument, or other arrangements.

Amendments

• 2009, American Recovery and Reinvestment Tax Act of 2009 (P.L. 111-5)

P.L. 111-5, §1232(b)(1)-(2):

Amended the last sentence of Code Sec. 163(i)(1) by inserting "(i)" after "regulation", and by inserting ", or (ii) permit, on a temporary basis, a rate to be used with respect to any debt instrument which is higher than the applicable Federal rate if the Secretary determines that such rate is appropriate in light of distressed conditions in the debt capital markets" before the period at the end. **Effective** for obligations issued after 12-31-2009, in tax years ending after such date.

• 1990, Omnibus Budget Reconciliation Act of 1990 (P.L. 101-508)

P.L. 101-508, §11701(b)(2):

Amended Code Sec. 163(i)(3) by striking "(or stock)" after "obligation" each place it appears in subparagraph (B), and by adding at the end thereof a new sentence. **Effective** as if included in the provision of P.L. 101-239 to which it relates.

• 1989, Omnibus Budget Reconciliation Act of 1989 (P.L. 101-239)

P.L. 101-239, §7202(b):

Amended Code Sec. 163 by redesignating subsection (i) as subsection (j) and by inserting after subsection (h) a new subsection (i). **Effective**, generally, for instruments issued after 7-10-89. For exceptions, see Act Sec. 7202 (c)(2) following Code Sec. 163(e).

[Sec. 163(j)]

(j) LIMITATION ON DEDUCTION FOR INTEREST ON CERTAIN INDEBTEDNESS.—

(1) LIMITATION.—

(A) IN GENERAL.—If this subsection applies to any corporation for any taxable year, no deduction shall be allowed under this chapter for disqualified interest paid or accrued by such corporation during such taxable year. The amount disallowed under the preceding sentence shall not exceed the corporation's excess interest expense for the taxable year.

(B) DISALLOWED AMOUNT CARRIED TO SUCCEEDING TAXABLE YEAR.—Any amount disallowed under subparagraph (A) for any taxable year shall be treated as disqualified interest paid or accrued in the succeeding taxable year (and clause (ii) of paragraph (2)(A) shall not apply for purposes of applying this subsection to the amount so treated).

(2) CORPORATIONS TO WHICH SUBSECTION APPLIES.—

(A) IN GENERAL.—This subsection shall apply to any corporation for any taxable year if—

(i) such corporation has excess interest expense for such taxable year, and

(ii) the ratio of debt to equity of such corporation as of the close of such taxable year (or on any other day during the taxable year as the Secretary may by regulations prescribe) exceeds 1.5 to 1.

(B) EXCESS INTEREST EXPENSE.—

(i) IN GENERAL.—For purposes of this subsection, the term "excess interest expense" means the excess (if any) of—

(I) the corporation's net interest expense, over

(II) the sum of 50 percent of the adjusted taxable income of the corporation plus any excess limitation carryforward under clause (ii).

(ii) EXCESS LIMITATION CARRYFORWARD.—If a corporation has an excess limitation for any taxable year, the amount of such excess limitation shall be an excess limitation carryforward to the 1st succeeding taxable year and to the 2nd and 3rd succeeding taxable years to the extent not previously taken into account under this clause. The amount of such a carryforward taken into account for any such succeeding taxable year shall not exceed the excess interest expense for such succeeding taxable year (determined without regard to the carryforward from the taxable year of such excess limitation).

(iii) EXCESS LIMITATION.—For purposes of clause (ii), the term "excess limitation" means the excess (if any) of—

(I) 50 percent of the adjusted taxable income of the corporation, over

(II) the corporation's net interest expense.

(C) RATIO OF DEBT TO EQUITY.—For purposes of this paragraph, the term "ratio of debt to equity" means the ratio which the total indebtedness of the corporation bears to the sum of its money and all other assets reduced (but not below zero) by such total indebtedness. For purposes of the preceding sentence—

(i) the amount taken into account with respect to any asset shall be the adjusted basis thereof for purposes of determining gain,

(ii) the amount taken into account with respect to any indebtedness with original issue discount shall be its issue price plus the portion of the original issue discount previously accrued as determined under the rules of section 1272 (determined without regard to subsection (a)(7) or (b)(4) thereof), and

(iii) there shall be such other adjustments as the Secretary may by regulations prescribe.

(3) DISQUALIFIED INTEREST.—For purposes of this subsection, the term "disqualified interest" means—

(A) any interest paid or accrued by the taxpayer (directly or indirectly) to a related person if no tax is imposed by this subtitle with respect to such interest,

(B) any interest paid or accrued by the taxpayer with respect to any indebtedness to a person who is not a related person if—

(i) there is a disqualified guarantee of such indebtedness, and

(ii) no gross basis tax is imposed by this subtitle with respect to such interest, and

(C) any interest paid or accrued (directly or indirectly) by a taxable REIT subsidiary (as defined in section 856(l)) of a real estate investment trust to such trust.

(4) RELATED PERSON.—For purposes of this subsection—

(A) IN GENERAL.—Except as provided in subparagraph (B), the term "related person" means any person who is related (within the meaning of section 267(b) or 707(b)(1)) to the taxpayer.

(B) SPECIAL RULE FOR CERTAIN PARTNERSHIPS.—

(i) IN GENERAL.—Any interest paid or accrued to a partnership which (without regard to this subparagraph) is a related person shall not be treated as paid or accrued to a related person if less than 10 percent of the profits and capital interests in such partnership are held by persons with respect to whom no tax is imposed by this subtitle on such interest. The preceding sentence shall not apply to any interest allocable to any partner in such partnership who is a related person to the taxpayer.

(ii) SPECIAL RULE WHERE TREATY REDUCTION.—If any treaty between the United States and any foreign country reduces the rate of tax imposed by this subtitle on a partner's share of any interest paid or accrued to a partnership, such partner's interests in such partnership shall, for purposes of clause (i), be treated as held in part by a tax-exempt person and in part by a taxable person under rules similar to the rules of paragraph (5)(B).

(5) SPECIAL RULES FOR DETERMINING WHETHER INTEREST IS SUBJECT TO TAX.—

(A) TREATMENT OF PASS-THRU ENTITIES.—In the case of any interest paid or accrued to a partnership, the determination of whether any tax is imposed by this subtitle on such interest shall be made at the partner level. Rules similar to the rules of the preceding sentence shall apply in the case of any pass-thru entity other than a partnership and in the case of tiered partnerships and other entities.

(B) INTEREST TREATED AS TAX-EXEMPT TO EXTENT OF TREATY REDUCTION.—If any treaty between the United States and any foreign country reduces the rate of tax imposed by this subtitle on any interest paid or accrued by the taxpayer, such interest shall be treated as interest on which no tax is imposed by this subtitle to the extent of the same proportion of such interest as—

(i) the rate of tax imposed without regard to such treaty, reduced by the rate of tax imposed under the treaty, bears to

(ii) the rate of tax imposed without regard to the treaty.

(6) OTHER DEFINITIONS AND SPECIAL RULES.—For purposes of this subsection—

(A) ADJUSTED TAXABLE INCOME.—The term "adjusted taxable income" means the taxable income of the taxpayer—

(i) computed without regard to—

(I) any deduction allowable under this chapter for the net interest expense,

(II) the amount of any net operating loss deduction under section 172,

(III) any deduction allowable under section 199, and

(IV) any deduction allowable for depreciation, amortization, or depletion, and

(ii) computed with such other adjustments as the Secretary may by regulations prescribe.

(B) NET INTEREST EXPENSE.—The term "net interest expense" means the excess (if any) of—

(i) the interest paid or accrued by the taxpayer during the taxable year, over

(ii) the amount of interest includible in the gross income of such taxpayer for such taxable year.

The Secretary may by regulations provide for adjustments in determining the amount of net interest expense.

(C) TREATMENT OF AFFILIATED GROUP.—All members of the same affiliated group (within the meaning of section 1504(a)) shall be treated as 1 taxpayer.

(D) DISQUALIFIED GUARANTEE.—

(i) IN GENERAL.—Except as provided in clause (ii), the term "disqualified guarantee" means any guarantee by a related person which is—

(I) an organization exempt from taxation under this subtitle, or

(II) a foreign person.

(ii) EXCEPTIONS.—The term "disqualified guarantee" shall not include a guarantee—

(I) in any circumstances identified by the Secretary by regulation, where the interest on the indebtedness would have been subject to a net basis tax if the interest had been paid to the guarantor, or

(II) if the taxpayer owns a controlling interest in the guarantor.

For purposes of subclause (II), except as provided in regulations, the term "a controlling interest" means direct or indirect ownership of at least 80 percent of the total voting power and value of all classes of stock of a corporation, or 80 percent of the profit and capital interests in any other entity. For purposes of the preceding sentence, the rules of paragraphs (1) and (5) of section 267(c) shall apply; except that such rules shall also apply to interest in entities other than corporations.

(iii) GUARANTEE.—Except as provided in regulations, the term "guarantee" includes any arrangement under which a person (directly or indirectly through an entity or otherwise) assures, on a conditional or unconditional basis, the payment of another person's obligation under any indebtedness.

(E) GROSS BASIS AND NET BASIS TAXATION.—

(i) GROSS BASIS TAX.—The term "gross basis tax" means any tax imposed by this subtitle which is determined by reference to the gross amount of any item of income without any reduction for any deduction allowed by this subtitle.

(ii) NET BASIS TAX.—The term "net basis tax" means any tax imposed by this subtitle which is not a gross basis tax.

(7) COORDINATION WITH PASSIVE LOSS RULES, ETC.—This subsection shall be applied before sections 465 and 469.

(8) TREATMENT OF CORPORATE PARTNERS.—Except to the extent provided by regulations, in applying this subsection to a corporation which owns (directly or indirectly) an interest in a partnership—

(A) such corporation's distributive share of interest income paid or accrued to such partnership shall be treated as interest income paid or accrued to such corporation,

(B) such corporation's distributive share of interest paid or accrued by such partnership shall be treated as interest paid or accrued by such corporation, and

(C) such corporation's share of the liabilities of such partnership shall be treated as liabilities of such corporation.

(9) REGULATIONS.—The Secretary shall prescribe such regulations as may be appropriate to carry out the purposes of this subsection, including—

(A) such regulations as may be appropriate to prevent the avoidance of the purposes of this subsection,

(B) regulations providing such adjustments in the case of corporations which are members of an affiliated group as may be appropriate to carry out the purposes of this subsection,

(C) regulations for the coordination of this subsection with section 884, and

(D) regulations providing for the reallocation of shares of partnership indebtedness, or distributive shares of the partnership's interest income or interest expense.

Amendments

• 2006, Tax Increase Prevention and Reconciliation Act of 2005 (P.L. 109-222)

P.L. 109-222, §501(a):

Amended Code Sec. 163(j) by redesignating paragraph (8) as paragraph (9) and by inserting after paragraph (7) a new paragraph (8). **Effective** for tax years beginning on or after 5-17-2006.

P.L. 109-222, §501(b):

Amended Code Sec. 163(j)(9), as redesignated by Act Sec. 501(a), by striking "and" at the end of subparagraph (B), by striking the period at the end of subparagraph (C) and inserting ", and", and by adding at the end a new subparagraph (D). **Effective** for tax years beginning on or after 5-17-2006.

• 2005, Gulf Opportunity Zone Act of 2005 (P.L. 109-135)

P.L. 109-135, §403(a)(15):

Amended Code Sec. 163(j)(6)(A)(i) by striking "and" at the end of subclause (II), by redesignating subclause (III) as subclause (IV), and by inserting after subclause (II) a new subclause (III). **Effective** as if included in the provision of the American Jobs Creation Act of 2004 (P.L. 108-357) to which it relates [**effective** for tax years beginning after 12-31-2004.—CCH].

• 1999, Tax Relief Extension Act of 1999 (P.L. 106-170)

P.L. 106-170, §544:

Amended Code Sec. 163(j)(3) by striking "and" at the end of subparagraph (A), by striking the period at the end of subparagraph (B) and inserting ", and", and by adding at the end a new subparagraph (C). **Effective** for tax years beginning after 12-31-2000.

• 1997, Taxpayer Relief Act of 1997 (P.L. 105-34)

P.L. 105-34, §1604(g)(1):

Amended Code Sec. 163(j)(2)(B)(iii) by striking "clause (i)" and inserting "clause (ii)". **Effective** 8-5-97.

• 1996, Small Business Job Protection Act of 1996 (P.L. 104-188)

P.L. 104-188, §1703(n)(4):

Amended Code Sec. 163(j)(6)(E)(ii) by striking "which is a" and inserting "which is". **Effective** as if included in the provision of P.L. 103-66 to which it relates.

P.L. 104-188, §1704(f)(2)(A):

Amended Code Sec. 163(j)(1)(B) by inserting before the period at the end thereof "(and clause (ii) of paragraph (2)(A) shall not apply for purposes of applying this subsection to the amount so treated)". **Effective** as if included in the amendments made by section 7210(a) of P.L. 101-239.

P.L. 104-188, §1704(f)(2)(B):

Amended Code Sec. 163(j) by redesignating paragraph (7) as paragraph (8) and by inserting after paragraph (6) a new paragraph (7). **Effective** as if included in the amendments made by section 7210(a) of P.L. 101-239.

• 1993, Omnibus Budget Reconciliation Act of 1993 (P.L. 103-66)

P.L. 103-66, §13228(a):

Amended Code Sec. 163(j)(3). **Effective** for interest paid or accrued in tax years beginning after 12-31-93. Prior to amendment, Code Sec. 163(j)(3) read as follows:

(3) DISQUALIFIED INTEREST.—For purposes of this subsection—

(A) IN GENERAL.—Except as provided in subparagraph (B), the term "disqualified interest" means any interest paid or accrued by the taxpayer (directly or indirectly) to a related person if no tax is imposed by this subtitle with respect to such interest.

(B) EXCEPTION FOR CERTAIN EXISTING INDEBTEDNESS.—The term "disqualified interest" does not include any interest paid or accrued under indebtedness with a fixed term—

(i) which was issued on or before July 10, 1989, or

(ii) which was issued after such date pursuant to a written binding contract in effect on such date and all times thereafter before such indebtedness was issued.

P.L. 103-66, §13228(b):

Amended Code Sec. 163(j)(6) by adding at the end thereof the following new subparagraphs (D) and (E). **Effective** for interest paid or accrued in tax years beginning after 12-31-93.

P.L. 103-66, §13228(c)(1):

Amended Code Sec. 163(j)(5)(B) by striking "to a related person" after "by the taxpayer". **Effective** for interest paid or accrued in tax years beginning after 12-31-93.

P.L. 103-66, §13228(c)(2):

Amended the subsection heading for Code Sec. 163(j). **Effective** for interest paid or accrued in tax years beginning after 12-31-93. Prior to amendment, the heading for Code Sec. 163(j) read as follows:

(j) LIMITATION ON DEDUCTION FOR CERTAIN INTEREST PAID BY CORPORATION TO RELATED PERSON.—

• 1990, Omnibus Budget Reconciliation Act of 1990 (P.L. 101-508)

P.L. 101-508, §11701(c)(1):

Amended Code Sec. 163(j)(2)(C) by striking "less such" and inserting "reduced (but not below zero) by such". **Effective** as if included in the provision of P.L. 101-239 to which it relates.

P.L. 101-508, §11701(c)(2):

Amended Code Sec. 163(j)(2)(A)(ii) by striking "and on such other days" and inserting "or on any other day". **Effective** as if included in the provision of P.L. 101-239 to which it relates.

• 1989, Omnibus Budget Reconciliation Act of 1989 (P.L. 101-239)

P.L. 101-239, §7202(b):

Amended Code Sec. 163 by redesignating subsection (i) as subsection (j). **Effective**, generally, for instruments issued after 7-10-89. For exceptions, see Act Sec. 7202(c)(2) following Code Sec. 163(e).

P.L. 101-239, §7210(a):

Amended Code Sec. 163, as amended by Act Sec. 7202, by redesignating subsection (j) as subsection (k) and by inserting after subsection (i) a new subsection (j). **Effective**, generally, for interest paid or accrued in tax years beginning after 7-10-89. For a special rule, see Act Sec. 7210(b)(2), below.

P.L. 101-239, §7210(b)(2), provides:

(2) SPECIAL RULE FOR DEMAND LOANS, ETC.—In the case of any demand loan (or other loan without a fixed term) which was outstanding on July 10, 1989, interest on such loan to the extent attributable to periods before September 1, 1989, shall not be treated as disqualified interest for purposes of section 163(j) of the Internal Revenue Code of 1986 (as added by subsection (a)).

[Sec. 163(k)]

(k) SECTION 6166 INTEREST.—No deduction shall be allowed under this section for any interest payable under section 6601 on any unpaid portion of the tax imposed by section 2001 for the period during which an extension of time for payment of such tax is in effect under section 6166.

Amendments

• 1997, Taxpayer Relief Act of 1997 (P.L. 105-34)

P.L. 105-34, §503(b)(2)(A):

Amended Code Sec. 163 by redesignating subsection (k) as subsection (l) and by inserting after subsection (j) a new subsection (k). **Effective**, generally, for estates of decedents dying after 12-31-97. For a special rule, see Act Sec. 503(d)(2) in the amendment notes following Code Sec. 163(h).

[Sec. 163(l)]

(l) DISALLOWANCE OF DEDUCTION ON CERTAIN DEBT INSTRUMENTS OF CORPORATIONS.—

(1) IN GENERAL.—No deduction shall be allowed under this chapter for any interest paid or accrued on a disqualified debt instrument.

(2) DISQUALIFIED DEBT INSTRUMENT.—For purposes of this subsection, the term "disqualified debt instrument" means any indebtedness of a corporation which is payable in equity of the issuer or a related party or equity held by the issuer (or any related party) in any other person.

(3) SPECIAL RULES FOR AMOUNTS PAYABLE IN EQUITY.—For purposes of paragraph (2), indebtedness shall be treated as payable in equity of the issuer or any other person only if—

(A) a substantial amount of the principal or interest is required to be paid or converted, or at the option of the issuer or a related party is payable in, or convertible into, such equity,

(B) a substantial amount of the principal or interest is required to be determined, or at the option of the issuer or a related party is determined, by reference to the value of such equity, or

(C) the indebtedness is part of an arrangement which is reasonably expected to result in a transaction described in subparagraph (A) or (B).

For purposes of this paragraph, principal or interest shall be treated as required to be so paid, converted, or determined if it may be required at the option of the holder or a related party and there is a substantial certainty the option will be exercised.

(4) CAPITALIZATION ALLOWED WITH RESPECT TO EQUITY OF PERSONS OTHER THAN ISSUER AND RELATED PARTIES.—If the disqualified debt instrument of a corporation is payable in equity held by the issuer (or any related party) in any other person (other than a related party), the basis of such equity shall be increased by the amount not allowed as a deduction by reason of paragraph (1) with respect to the instrument.

(5) EXCEPTION FOR CERTAIN INSTRUMENTS ISSUED BY DEALERS IN SECURITIES.—For purposes of this subsection, the term "disqualified debt instrument" does not include indebtedness issued by a dealer in securities (or a related party) which is payable in, or by reference to, equity (other than equity of the issuer or a related party) held by such dealer in its capacity as a dealer in securities. For purposes of this paragraph, the term "dealer in securities" has the meaning given such term by section 475.

(6) RELATED PARTY.—For purposes of this subsection, a person is a related party with respect to another person if such person bears a relationship to such other person described in section 267(b) or 707(b).

(7) REGULATIONS.—The Secretary shall prescribe such regulations as may be necessary or appropriate to carry out the purposes of this subsection, including regulations preventing avoidance of this subsection through the use of an issuer other than a corporation.

Amendments

• 2004, American Jobs Creation Act of 2004 (P.L. 108-357)

P.L. 108-357, §845(a):

Amended Code Sec. 163(l)(2) by inserting "or equity held by the issuer (or any related party) in any other person" after "or a related party". **Effective** for debt instruments issued after 10-3-2004.

P.L. 108-357, §845(b):

Amended Code Sec. 163(l) by redesignating paragraphs (4) and (5) as paragraphs (5) and (6) and by inserting after paragraph (3) a new paragraph (4). **Effective** for debt instruments issued after 10-3-2004.

P.L. 108-357, §845(c):

Amended Code Sec. 163(l), as amended by Act Sec. 845(b), by redesignating paragraphs (5) and (6) as paragraphs (6) and (7) and by inserting after paragraph (4) a new paragraph (5). **Effective** for debt instruments issued after 10-3-2004.

P.L. 108-357, §845(d):

Amended Code Sec. 163(l)(3) by striking "or a related party" in the material preceding subparagraph (A) and inserting "or any other person". **Effective** for debt instruments issued after 10-3-2004.

• 1997, Taxpayer Relief Act of 1997 (P.L. 105-34)

P.L. 105-34, §1005(a):

Amended Code Sec. 163, as amended by Act Sec. 503(b)(2)(A), by redesignating subsection (l) as subsection (m) and by inserting after subsection (k) a new subsection (l). **Effective**, generally, for disqualified debt instruments issued after 6-8-97. For a transitional rule, see Act Sec. 1005(b)(2)(A)-(C), below.

P.L. 105-34, §1005(b)(2)(A)-(C), provides:

(2) TRANSITION RULE.—The amendment made by this section shall not apply to any instrument issued after June 8, 1997, if such instrument is—

(A) issued pursuant to a written agreement which was binding on such date and at all times thereafter,

(B) described in a ruling request submitted to the Internal Revenue Service on or before such date, or

(C) described on or before such date in a public announcement or in a filing with the Securities and Exchange Commission required solely by reason of the issuance.

[Sec. 163(m)]

(m) INTEREST ON UNPAID TAXES ATTRIBUTABLE TO NONDISCLOSED REPORTABLE TRANSACTIONS.—No deduction shall be allowed under this chapter for any interest paid or accrued under section 6601 on any underpayment of tax which is attributable to the portion of any reportable transaction understatement (as defined in section 6662A(b)) with respect to which the requirement of section 6664(d)(2)(A) is not met.

Amendments

• 2004, American Jobs Creation Act of 2004 (P.L. 108-357)

P.L. 108-357, §838(a):

Amended Code Sec. 163 by redesignating subsection (m) as subsection (n) and by inserting after subsection (l) a new subsection (m). **Effective** for transactions in tax years beginning after 10-22-2004.

[Sec. 163(n)]

(n) CROSS REFERENCES.—

(1) For disallowance of certain amounts paid in connection with insurance, endowment, or annuity contracts, see section 264.

(2) For disallowance of deduction for interest relating to tax-exempt income, see section 265(a)(2).

(3) For disallowance of deduction for carrying charges chargeable to capital account, see section 266.

(4) For disallowance of interest with respect to transactions between related taxpayers, see section 267.

(5) For treatment of redeemable ground rents and real property held subject to liabilities under redeemable ground rents, see section 1055.

Amendments

• 2004, American Jobs Creation Act of 2004 (P.L. 108-357)

P.L. 108-357, §838(a):

Amended Code Sec. 163 by redesignating subsection (m) as subsection (n). **Effective** for transactions in tax years beginning after 10-22-2004.

• 1997, Taxpayer Relief Act of 1997 (P.L. 105-34)

P.L. 105-34, §503(b)(2)(A):

Amended Code Sec. 163 by redesignating subsection (k) as subsection (l). **Effective**, generally, for estates of decedents dying after 12-31-97. For a special rule, see Act Sec. 503(d)(2) in the amendment notes following Code Sec. 163(h).

P.L. 105-34, §1005(a):

Amended Code Sec. 163, as amended by Act Sec. 503(b)(2)(A), by redesignating subsection (l) as subsection (m). **Effective**, generally, for disqualified debt instruments issued after 6-8-97. For a transitional rule, see Act Sec. 1005(b)(2)(A)-(C) in the amendment notes following Code Sec. 163(l).

• 1989, Omnibus Budget Reconciliation Act of 1989 (P.L. 101-239)

P.L. 101-239, §7210(a):

Amended Code Sec. 163 by redesignating subsection (j) as subsection (k). **Effective**, generally, for interest paid or accrued in tax years beginning after 7-10-89. For a special rule, see Act Sec. 7210(b)(2) following Code Sec. 163(j).

• 1986, Tax Reform Act of 1986 (P.L. 99-514)

P.L. 99-514, §511(b):

Redesignated subsection (h) as subsection (i). **Effective** for tax years beginning after 12-31-86.

P.L. 99-514, §902(e)(1), as amended by P.L. 100-647, §1009(b)(6):

Amended Code Sec. 163(i)(2), as redesignated by Act Sec. 511(b) of this Act, by striking out "section 265(2)" and inserting in lieu thereof "section 265(a)(2)". **Effective** for tax years ending after 12-31-86.

• 1984, Deficit Reduction Act of 1984 (P.L. 98-369)

P.L. 98-369, §612(c):

Redesignated former subsection (g) as (h). **Effective** for interest paid or accrued after 12-31-84, on indebtedness incurred after 12-31-84.

• 1982, Tax Equity and Fiscal Responsibility Act of 1982 (P.L. 97-248)

P.L. 97-248, §231(b):

Redesignated former subsection (e) as (f). **Effective** for obligations issued after 7-1-82.

P.L. 97-248, §310(b)(2):

Redesignated former subsection (f) as (g). **Effective** for obligations issued after 1982.

• 1969, Tax Reform Act of 1969, (P.L. 91-172)

P.L. 91-172, §221(a):

Redesignated former Sec. 163(d) as (e). **Effective** for tax years beginning after 12-31-71.

• 1963, (P.L. 88-9)

P.L. 88-9, §1(a), (c):

Redesignated former Code Sec. 163(c) as Code Sec. 163(d) and added paragraph (5). **Effective** for tax years ending on or after 1-1-62.

[Sec. 164]

SEC. 164. TAXES.

[Sec. 164(a)]

(a) GENERAL RULE.—Except as otherwise provided in this section, the following taxes shall be allowed as a deduction for the taxable year within which paid or accrued:

(1) State and local, and foreign, real property taxes.

(2) State and local personal property taxes.

(3) State and local, and foreign, income, war profits, and excess profits taxes.

(4) The GST tax imposed on income distributions.

(5) The environmental tax imposed by section 59A.

(6) Qualified motor vehicle taxes.

In addition, there shall be allowed as a deduction State and local, and foreign, taxes not described in the preceding sentence which are paid or accrued within the taxable year in carrying on a trade or business or an activity described in section 212 (relating to expenses for production of income).

Notwithstanding the preceding sentence, any tax (not described in the first sentence of this subsection) which is paid or accrued by the taxpayer in connection with an acquisition or disposition of property shall be treated as part of the cost of the acquired property or, in the case of a disposition, as a reduction in the amount realized on the disposition.

Amendments

• 2009, American Recovery and Reinvestment Tax Act of 2009 (P.L. 111-5)

P.L. 111-5, §1008(a):

Amended Code Sec. 164(a) by inserting after paragraph (5) a new paragraph (6). **Effective** for purchases on or after 2-17-2009 in tax years ending after such date.

• 1996, Small Business Job Protection Act of 1996 (P.L. 104-188)

P.L. 104-188, §1704(t)(79):

Amended Code Sec. 164(a) by striking the paragraphs relating to generation-skipping tax [paragraph (4)] and the environmental tax imposed by section 59A [paragraph (5)] and inserting after paragraph (3) new paragraphs (4) and (5). **Effective** 8-20-96. Prior to amendment, Code Sec. 164(a)(4)-(5) read as follows:

(4) The GST tax imposed on income distributions.

(5) The environmental tax imposed by section 59A.

• 1988, Technical and Miscellaneous Revenue Act of 1988 (P.L. 100-647)

P.L. 100-647, §1018(u)(11):

Amended Code Sec. 164(a) by striking out "the GST tax" and inserting in lieu thereof "The GST tax". **Effective** as if included in the provision of P.L. 99-514 to which it relates.

• 1988, Omnibus Trade and Competitiveness Act of 1988 (P.L. 100-418)

P.L. 100-418, §1941(b)(2)(A):

Amended Code Sec. 164(a) by striking paragraph (4) and redesignating paragraphs (5)-(6) as (4)-(5), respectively. **Effective** for crude oil removed from the premises on or after 8-23-88. Prior to amendment, Code Sec. 164(a)(4) read as follows:

(4) The windfall profit tax imposed by section 4986.

• 1986, Tax Reform Act of 1986 (P.L. 99-514)

P.L. 99-514, §134(a)(1):

Amended Code Sec. 164(a) by striking out paragraph (4) and by redesignating paragraph (5) as paragraph (4). **Effective** for tax years beginning after 12-31-86. Prior to amendment, paragraph (4) read as follows:

(4) State and local general sales taxes.

P.L. 99-514, §134(a)(2):

Added the sentence at the end of Code Sec. 164(a). **Effective** for tax years beginning after 12-31-86.

P.L. 99-514, §1432(a)(1):

Amended Code Sec. 164(a), as amended by Act Sec. 134, by inserting after paragraph (4), new paragraph (5). **Effective** for any generation-skipping transfer (within the meaning of Code Sec. 2611) made after 10-22-86. See also the special rules provided by Act Sec. 1433(b)-(d) following Code Sec. 2515.

• 1986, Superfund Amendments and Reauthorization Act of 1986 (P.L. 99-499)

P.L. 99-499, §516(b)(2)(A):

Amended Code Sec. 164(a) (as amended by P.L. 99-514) by inserting after paragraph (4)[5] new paragraph (5)[6]. **Effective** for tax years beginning after 12-31-86.

• 1980, Crude Oil Windfall Profit Tax Act of 1980 (P.L. 96-223)

P.L. 96-223, §101(b):

Added paragraph (5). **Effective** for periods after 2-29-80.

• 1978, Revenue Act of 1978 (P.L. 95-600)

P.L. 95-600, §111(a):

Repealed Code Sec. 164(a)(5). **Effective** for tax years beginning after 12-31-78. Prior to repeal, Code Sec. 164(a)(5) read as follows:

(5) State and local taxes on the sale of gasoline, diesel fuel, and other motor fuels.

• 1964, Revenue Act of 1964 (P.L. 88-272)

P.L. 88-272, §207(a):

Amended subsection (a). **Effective** for tax years beginning after 12-31-63. Prior to amendment, subsections (a), (b), and (c) read as indicated in note following subsection (c).

[Sec. 164(b)]

(b) DEFINITIONS AND SPECIAL RULES.—For purposes of this section—

(1) PERSONAL PROPERTY TAXES.—The term "personal property tax" means an ad valorem tax which is imposed on an annual basis in respect of personal property.

(2) STATE OR LOCAL TAXES.—A State or local tax includes only a tax imposed by a State, a possession of the United States, or a political subdivision of any of the foregoing, or by the District of Columbia.

(3) FOREIGN TAXES.—A foreign tax includes only a tax imposed by the authority of a foreign country.

(4) SPECIAL RULES FOR GST TAX.—

(A) IN GENERAL.—The GST tax imposed on income distributions is—

(i) the tax imposed by section 2601, and

(ii) any State tax described in section 2604,

but only to the extent such tax is imposed on a transfer which is included in the gross income of the distributee and to which section 666 does not apply.

(B) SPECIAL RULE FOR TAX PAID BEFORE DUE DATE.—Any tax referred to in subparagraph (A) imposed with respect to a transfer occurring during the taxable year of the distributee (or, in the case of a taxable termination, the trust) which is paid not later than the time prescribed by law (including extensions) for filing the return with respect to such transfer shall be treated as having been paid on the last day of the taxable year in which the transfer was made.

(5) GENERAL SALES TAXES.—For purposes of subsection (a)—

(A) ELECTION TO DEDUCT STATE AND LOCAL SALES TAXES IN LIEU OF STATE AND LOCAL INCOME TAXES.—At the election of the taxpayer for the taxable year, subsection (a) shall be applied—

(i) without regard to the reference to State and local income taxes, and

(ii) as if State and local general sales taxes were referred to in a paragraph thereof.

(B) DEFINITION OF GENERAL SALES TAX.—The term "general sales tax" means a tax imposed at one rate with respect to the sale at retail of a broad range of classes of items.

(C) SPECIAL RULES FOR FOOD, ETC.—In the case of items of food, clothing, medical supplies, and motor vehicles—

(i) the fact that the tax does not apply with respect to some or all of such items shall not be taken into account in determining whether the tax applies with respect to a broad range of classes of items, and

(ii) the fact that the rate of tax applicable with respect to some or all of such items is lower than the general rate of tax shall not be taken into account in determining whether the tax is imposed at one rate.

(D) ITEMS TAXED AT DIFFERENT RATES.—Except in the case of a lower rate of tax applicable with respect to an item described in subparagraph (C), no deduction shall be allowed under this paragraph for any general sales tax imposed with respect to an item at a rate other than the general rate of tax.

(E) COMPENSATING USE TAXES.—A compensating use tax with respect to an item shall be treated as a general sales tax. For purposes of the preceding sentence, the term "compensating use tax" means, with respect to any item, a tax which—

(i) is imposed on the use, storage, or consumption of such item, and

(ii) is complementary to a general sales tax, but only if a deduction is allowable under this paragraph with respect to items sold at retail in the taxing jurisdiction which are similar to such item.

(F) SPECIAL RULE FOR MOTOR VEHICLES.—In the case of motor vehicles, if the rate of tax exceeds the general rate, such excess shall be disregarded and the general rate shall be treated as the rate of tax.

(G) SEPARATELY STATED GENERAL SALES TAXES.—If the amount of any general sales tax is separately stated, then, to the extent that the amount so stated is paid by the consumer (other than in connection with the consumer's trade or business) to the seller, such amount shall be treated as a tax imposed on, and paid by, such consumer.

(H) AMOUNT OF DEDUCTION MAY BE DETERMINED UNDER TABLES.—

(i) IN GENERAL.—At the election of the taxpayer for the taxable year, the amount of the deduction allowed under this paragraph for such year shall be—

(I) the amount determined under this paragraph (without regard to this subparagraph) with respect to motor vehicles, boats, and other items specified by the Secretary, and

(II) the amount determined under tables prescribed by the Secretary with respect to items to which subclause (I) does not apply.

(ii) REQUIREMENTS FOR TABLES.—The tables prescribed under clause (i)—

(I) shall reflect the provisions of this paragraph,

(II) shall be based on the average consumption by taxpayers on a State-by-State basis (as determined by the Secretary) of items to which clause (i)(I) does not apply, taking into account filing status, number of dependents, adjusted gross income, and rates of State and local general sales taxation, and

(III) need only be determined with respect to adjusted gross incomes up to the applicable amount (as determined under section 68(b)).

(I) APPLICATION OF PARAGRAPH.—This paragraph shall apply to taxable years beginning after December 31, 2003, and before January 1, 2010.

(6) QUALIFIED MOTOR VEHICLE TAXES.—

(A) IN GENERAL.—For purposes of this section, the term "qualified motor vehicle taxes" means any State or local sales or excise tax imposed on the purchase of a qualified motor vehicle.

(B) LIMITATION BASED ON VEHICLE PRICE.—The amount of any State or local sales or excise tax imposed on the purchase of a qualified motor vehicle taken into account under subparagraph (A) shall not exceed the portion of such tax attributable to so much of the purchase price as does not exceed $49,500.

(C) INCOME LIMITATION.—The amount otherwise taken into account under subparagraph (A) (after the application of subparagraph (B)) for any taxable year shall be reduced (but not below zero) by the amount which bears the same ratio to the amount which is so treated as—

(i) the excess (if any) of—

(I) the taxpayer's modified adjusted gross income for such taxable year, over

(II) $125,000 ($250,000 in the case of a joint return), bears to

(ii) $10,000.

For purposes of the preceding sentence, the term "modified adjusted gross income" means the adjusted gross income of the taxpayer for the taxable year (determined without regard to sections 911, 931, and 933).

(D) QUALIFIED MOTOR VEHICLE.—For purposes of this paragraph—

(i) IN GENERAL.—The term "qualified motor vehicle" means—

(I) a passenger automobile or light truck which is treated as a motor vehicle for purposes of title II of the Clean Air Act, the gross vehicle weight rating of which is not more than 8,500 pounds, and the original use of which commences with the taxpayer,

(II) a motorcycle the gross vehicle weight rating of which is not more than 8,500 pounds and the original use of which commences with the taxpayer, and

(III) a motor home the original use of which commences with the taxpayer.

(ii) OTHER TERMS.—The terms "motorcycle" and "motor home" have the meanings given such terms under section 571.3 of title 49, Code of Federal Regulations (as in effect on the date of the enactment of this paragraph).

(E) QUALIFIED MOTOR VEHICLE TAXES NOT INCLUDED IN COST OF ACQUIRED PROPERTY.—The last sentence of subsection (a) shall not apply to any qualified motor vehicle taxes.

(F) COORDINATION WITH GENERAL SALES TAX.—This paragraph shall not apply in the case of a taxpayer who makes an election under paragraph (5) for the taxable year.

(G) TERMINATION.—This paragraph shall not apply to purchases after December 31, 2009.

Amendments

• 2009, American Recovery and Reinvestment Tax Act of 2009 (P.L. 111-5)

P.L. 111-5, §1008(b):

Amended Code Sec. 164(b) by adding at the end a new paragraph (6). **Effective** for purchases on or after 2-17-2009 in tax years ending after such date.

• 2008, Tax Extenders and Alternative Minimum Tax Relief Act of 2008 (P.L. 110-343)

P.L. 110-343, Division C, §201(a):

Amended Code Sec. 164(b)(5)(I) by striking "January 1, 2008" and inserting "January 1, 2010". **Effective** for tax years beginning after 12-31-2007.

• 2006, Tax Relief and Health Care Act of 2006 (P.L. 109-432)

P.L. 109-432, Division A, §103(a):

Amended Code Sec. 164(b)(5)(I) by striking "2006" and inserting "2008". **Effective** for tax years beginning after 12-31-2005.

•2005, Gulf Opportunity Zone Act of 2005 (P.L. 109-135)

P.L. 109-135, §403(r)(1):

Amended Code Sec. 164(b)(5)(A). **Effective** as if included in the provision of the American Jobs Creation Act of 2004 (P.L. 108-357) to which it relates [**effective** for tax years beginning after 12-31-2003.—CCH]. Prior to amendment, Code Sec. 164(b)(5)(A) read as follows:

(A) ELECTION TO DEDUCT STATE AND LOCAL SALES TAXES IN LIEU OF STATE AND LOCAL INCOME TAXES.—

(i) IN GENERAL.—At the election of the taxpayer for the taxable year, subsection (a) shall be applied—

(I) without regard to the reference to State and local income taxes, and

(II) as if State and local general sales taxes were referred to in a paragraph thereof.

• 2004, American Jobs Creation Act of 2004 (P.L. 108-357)

P.L. 108-357, §501(a):

Amended Code Sec. 164(b) by adding at the end a new paragraph (5). **Effective** for tax years beginning after 12-31-2003.

• 1986, Tax Reform Act of 1986 (P.L. 99-514)

P.L. 99-514, §134(b)(1):

Struck out Code Sec. 164(b)(2) and (5). **Effective** for tax years beginning after 12-31-86. Prior to being stricken, Code Sec. 164(b)(2) and (5) read as follows:

(2) GENERAL SALES TAXES.—

(A) IN GENERAL.—The term "general sales tax" means a tax imposed at one rate in respect of the sale at retail of a broad range of classes of items.

(B) SPECIAL RULES FOR FOOD, ETC.—In the case of items of food, clothing, medical supplies, and motor vehicles—

(i) the fact that the tax does not apply in respect of some or all of such items shall not be taken into account in determining whether the tax applies in respect of a broad range of classes of items, and

(ii) the fact that the rate of tax applicable in respect of some or all of such items is lower than the general rate of tax shall not be taken into account in determining whether the tax is imposed at one rate.

(C) ITEMS TAXED AT DIFFERENT RATES.—Except in the case of a lower rate of tax applicable in respect of an item described in subparagraph (B), no deduction shall be allowed under this section for any general sales tax imposed in respect of an item at a rate other than the general rate of tax.

(D) COMPENSATING USE TAXES.—A compensating use tax in respect of an item shall be treated as a general sales tax. For purposes of the preceding sentence, the term "compensating use tax" means, in respect of any item, a tax which—

(i) is imposed on the use, storage, or consumption of such item, and

(ii) is complementary to a general sales tax, but only if a deduction is allowable under subsection (a)(4) in respect of items sold at retail in the taxing jurisdiction which are similar to such item.

(E) SPECIAL RULE FOR MOTOR VEHICLES.—In the case of motor vehicles, if the rate of tax exceeds the general rate, such excess shall be disregarded and the general rate shall be treated as the rate of tax.

(5) SEPARATELY STATED GENERAL SALES TAXES.—If the amount of any general sales tax is separately stated, then, to the extent that the amount so stated is paid by the consumer (otherwise than in connection with the consumer's trade or business) to his seller, such amount shall be treated as a tax imposed on, and paid by, such consumer.

P.L. 99-514, §134(b)(2):

Amended Code Sec. 164(b) by redesignating paragraphs (3) and (4) as paragraphs (2) and (3). **Effective** for tax years beginning after 12-31-86.

P.L. 99-514, §1432(a)(2):

Amended Code Sec. 164(b), as amended by Act Sec. 134, by adding at the end thereof new paragraph (4). **Effective** for any generation-skipping transfer (within the meaning of Code Sec. 2611) made after 10-22-86. See also the special rules provided by Act Sec. 1433(b)-(d) following Code Sec. 2515.

• **1978, Revenue Act of 1978 (P.L. 95-600)**

P.L. 95-600, §111(b):

Amended Code Sec. 164(b)(5). **Effective** for tax years beginning after 12-31-78. Prior to amendment, Code Sec. 164(b)(5) read as follows:

(5) SEPARATELY STATED GENERAL SALES TAXES AND GASOLINE TAXES.—If the amount of any general sales tax or of any tax on the sale of gasoline, diesel fuel, or other motor fuel is separately stated, then, to the extent that the amount so stated is paid by the consumer (otherwise than in connection with the consumer's trade or business) to his seller, such amount shall be treated as a tax imposed on, and paid by, such consumer.

• **1972 (P.L. 92-580)**

P.L. 92-580, §4:

Amended Code Sec. 164(b)(2) by adding subparagraph (E). **Effective** for tax years ending on or after 1-1-71.

• **1964, Revenue Act of 1964 (P.L. 88-272)**

P.L. 88-272, §207(a):

Act Sec. 207(a) amended subsection (b). **Effective** with respect to tax years beginning after 12-31-63. Prior to amendment, subsections (a), (b), and (c) read as indicated in note following subsection (c).

[Sec. 164(c)]

(c) DEDUCTION DENIED IN CASE OF CERTAIN TAXES.—No deduction shall be allowed for the following taxes:

(1) Taxes assessed against local benefits of a kind tending to increase the value of the property assessed; but this paragraph shall not prevent the deduction of so much of such taxes as is properly allocable to maintenance or interest charges.

(2) Taxes on real property, to the extent that subsection (d) requires such taxes to be treated as imposed on another taxpayer.

Amendments

• **1964, Revenue Act of 1964 (P.L. 88-272)**

P.L. 88-272, §207(a):

Amended subsection (c). **Effective** with respect to tax years beginning after 12-31-63, except that section 164(c)(1) shall not prevent the deduction under section 164 of taxes levied by a special taxing district which is described in section 164(b)(5) (as in effect for a tax year ending on 12-31-63) and which was in existence on 12-31-63, for the purpose of retiring indebtedness existing on such date. Prior to amendment, subsections (a), (b), and (c) read as follows:

(a) General Rule.—Except as otherwise provided in this section, there shall be allowed as a deduction taxes paid or accrued within the taxable year.

(b) Deduction Denied in Case of Certain Taxes.—No deduction shall be allowed for the following taxes:

(1) Federal income taxes, including—

(A) the tax imposed by section 3101 (relating to the tax on employees under the Federal Insurance Contributions Act);

(B) the taxes imposed by sections 3201 and 3211 (relating to the taxes on railroad employees and railroad employee representatives); and

(C) the tax withheld at source on wages under section 3402, and corresponding provisions of prior revenue laws.

(2) Federal war profits and excess profits taxes.

(3) Federal import duties, and Federal excise and stamp taxes (not described in paragraph (1), (2), (4), or (5)); but this paragraph shall not prevent such duties and taxes from being deducted under section 162 (relating to trade or business expenses) or section 212 (relating to expenses for the production of income).

(4) Estate, inheritance, legacy, succession, and gift taxes.

(5) Taxes assessed against local benefits of a kind tending to increase the value of the property assessed; but this paragraph shall not prevent—

(A) the deduction of so much of such taxes as is properly allocable to maintenance or interest charges; or

(B) the deduction of taxes levied by a special taxing district if—

(i) the district covers the whole of at least one country;

(ii) at least 1,000 persons are subject to the taxes levied by the district; and

(iii) the district levies its assessments annually at a uniform rate on the same assessed value of real property, including improvements, as is used for purposes of the real property tax generally.

(6) Income, war profits, and excess profits taxes imposed by the authority of any foreign country or possession of the United States, if the taxpayer chooses to take to any extent the benefits of section 901 (relating to the foreign tax credit).

(7) Taxes on real property, to the extent that subsection (d) requires such taxes to be treated as imposed on another taxpayer.

(c) Certain Retail Sales Taxes and Gasoline Taxes.—

(1) General rule.—In the case of any State or local sales tax, if the amount of the tax is separately stated, then, to the extent that the amount so stated is paid by the consumer (otherwise than in connection with the consumer's trade or business) to his seller, such amount shall be allowed as a deduction to the consumer as if it constituted a tax imposed on, and paid by, such consumer.

(2) Definition.—For purposes of paragraph (1), the term "State or local sales tax" means a tax imposed by a State, a Territory, a possession of the United States, or a political subdivision of any of the foregoing, or by the District of Columbia, which tax—

(A) is imposed on persons engaged in selling tangible personal property at retail (or on persons selling gasoline or other motor vehicle fuels at wholesale or retail) and is a stated sum per unit of property sold or is measured either by the gross sales price or by the gross receipts from the sale; or

(B) is imposed on persons engaged in furnishing services at retail and is measured by the gross receipts for furnishing such services.

[Sec. 164(d)]

(d) APPORTIONMENT OF TAXES ON REAL PROPERTY BETWEEN SELLER AND PURCHASER.—

(1) GENERAL RULE.—For purposes of subsection (a), if real property is sold during any real property tax year, then—

(A) so much of the real property tax as is properly allocable to that part of such year which ends on the day before the date of the sale shall be treated as a tax imposed on the seller, and

(B) so much of such tax as is properly allocable to that part of such year which begins on the date of the sale shall be treated as a tax imposed on the purchaser.

(2) SPECIAL RULES.—

(A) In the case of any sale of real property, if—

(i) a taxpayer may not, by reason of his method of accounting, deduct any amount for taxes unless paid, and

(ii) the other party to the sale is (under the law imposing the real property tax) liable for the real property tax for the real property tax year,

then for purposes of subsection (a) the taxpayer shall be treated as having paid, on the date of the sale, so much of such tax as, under paragraph (1) of this subsection, is treated as imposed on the taxpayer. For purposes of the preceding sentence, if neither party is liable for the tax, then the party holding the property at the time the tax becomes a lien on the property shall be considered liable for the real property tax for the real property tax year.

(B) In the case of any sale of real property, if the taxpayer's taxable income for the taxable year during which the sale occurs is computed under an accrual method of accounting, and if no election under section 461(c) (relating to the accrual of real property taxes) applies, then, for purposes of subsection (a), that portion of such tax which—

(i) is treated, under paragraph (1) of this subsection, as imposed on the taxpayer, and

(ii) may not, by reason of the taxpayer's method of accounting, be deducted by the taxpayer for any taxable year,

shall be treated as having accrued on the date of the sale.

Amendments

• 1976, Tax Reform Act of 1976 (P.L. 94-455)

P.L. 94-455, §1901(a)(25):

Amended Code Sec. 164(d) by striking out subparagraphs (2)(B) and (C) and by redesignating subparagraph (D) as subparagraph (B). **Effective** for tax years beginning after 12-31-76. Prior to repeal, Code Sec. 164(d)(2)(B) and (C) read as follows:

(B) Paragraph (1) shall apply to taxable years ending after December 31, 1953, but only in the case of sales after December 31, 1953.

(C) Paragraph (1) shall not apply to any real property tax, to the extent that such tax was allowable as a deduction under the Internal Revenue Code of 1939 to the seller for a taxable year which ended before January 1, 1954.

[Sec. 164(e)]

(e) TAXES OF SHAREHOLDER PAID BY CORPORATION.—Where a corporation pays a tax imposed on a shareholder on his interest as a shareholder, and where the shareholder does not reimburse the corporation, then—

(1) the deduction allowed by subsection (a) shall be allowed to the corporation; and

(2) no deduction shall be allowed the shareholder for such tax.

[Sec. 164(f)]

(f) DEDUCTION FOR ONE-HALF OF SELF-EMPLOYMENT TAXES.—

»»→ Caution: Code Sec. 164(f)(1), below, prior to amendment by P.L. 111-148, applies with respect to remuneration received, and tax years beginning, on or before December 31, 2012.

(1) IN GENERAL.—In the case of an individual, in addition to the taxes described in subsection (a), there shall be allowed as a deduction for the taxable year an amount equal to one-half of the taxes imposed by section 1401 for such taxable year.

»»→ Caution: Code Sec. 164(f)(1), below, as amended by P.L. 111-148, applies with respect to remuneration received, and tax years beginning, after December 31, 2012.

(1) IN GENERAL.—In the case of an individual, in addition to the taxes described in subsection (a), there shall be allowed as a deduction for the taxable year an amount equal to one-half of the taxes imposed by section 1401 (other than the taxes imposed by section 1401(b)(2)) for such taxable year.

(2) DEDUCTION TREATED AS ATTRIBUTABLE TO TRADE OR BUSINESS.—For purposes of this chapter, the deduction allowed by paragraph (1) shall be treated as attributable to a trade or business carried on by the taxpayer which does not consist of the performance of services by the taxpayer as an employee.

Amendments

• 2010, Patient Protection and Affordable Care Act (P.L. 111-148)

P.L. 111-148, §9015(b)(2)(A):

Amended Code Sec. 164(f)[(1)] by inserting "(other than the taxes imposed by section 1401(b)(2))" after "section 1401) [sic]". **Effective** with respect to remuneration received, and tax years beginning, after 12-31-2012.

[Sec. 164(g)]

(g) CROSS REFERENCES.—

(1) For provisions disallowing any deduction for certain taxes, see section 275.

(2) For treatment of taxes imposed by Indian tribal governments (or their subdivisions), see section 7871.

Amendments

• 1984, Deficit Reduction Act of 1984 (P.L. 98-369)

P.L. 98-369, §474(r)(29)(F):

Amended Code Sec. 164(f) (as in effect before its redesignation by the Social Security Amendments of 1983) is amended by striking out paragraph (1) and by redesignating paragraphs (2) and (3) as paragraphs (1) and (2), respectively. **Effective** for tax years beginning after 12-31-83, and to carrybacks from such years except that it does not apply for obligations issued before 1-1-84. Prior to amendment, paragraph (1) read as follows:

(1) For provisions disallowing any deduction for the payment of the tax imposed by subchapter B of chapter 3 (relating to tax-free covenant bonds), see section 1451.

• 1983, Social Security Amendments of 1983 (P.L. 98-21)

P.L. 98-21, §124(c)(1):

Redesignated former Code Sec. 164(f) as Code Sec. 164(g) and added new Code Sec. 164(f). **Effective** for tax years beginning after 1989.

• 1983 (P.L. 97-473)

P.L. 97-473, §202(b)(3):

Added paragraph (3). For the **effective** date, see the amendment note for P.L. 97-473 under Code Sec. 7871.

• 1976, Tax Reform Act of 1976 (P.L. 94-455)

P.L. 94-455, §1951(b)(3)(A):

Repealed Code Sec. 164(f) and redesignated former Code Sec. 164(g) to be Code Sec. 164(f). **Effective** for tax years beginning after 12-31-76. Prior to repeal, Code Sec. 164(f) read as follows:

(f) PAYMENTS FOR MUNICIPAL SERVICES IN ATOMIC ENERGY COMMUNITIES.—For purposes of this section, amounts paid or accrued, to compensate the Atomic Energy Commission for municipal-type services, by any owner of real property within any community (within the meaning of section 21 b of the Atomic Energy Community Act of 1955) shall be treated as State real property taxes paid or accrued. For purposes of this subsection, the term "owner" includes a person who holds the real property under a leasehold of 40 or more years and a person who has entered into a contract to purchase under section 61 of the Atomic Energy Community Act of 1955. Subsection (d) of this section shall not apply to a sale by the United States of property with respect to which this subsection applies.

P.L. 94-455, §1951(b)(3)(B), provides:

(B) SAVINGS PROVISION.—Notwithstanding subparagraph (A), any amount paid or accrued in a taxable year beginning after December 31, 1976, to the Atomic Energy Commission or its successors for municipal-type services shall be allowed as a deduction under section 164 if such amount would have been deductible by reason of section 164(f) (as in effect for a taxable year ending on December 31, 1976) and if the amount is paid or accrued with respect to real property in a community (within the meaning of section 21 b. of the Atomic Energy Community Act of 1955 (42 U.S.C. 2304(b))) in which the Commission on December 31, 1976, was rendering municipal-type services for which it received compensation from the owners of property within such community.

• 1964, Revenue Act of 1964 (P.L. 88-272)

P.L. 88-272, §207(b)(1):

Amended subsection (f) by inserting near the end of the first sentence the word "State" before the words "real property taxes paid or accrued." **Effective** 1-1-64.

P.L. 88-272, §207(b)(2):

Amended subsection (g). **Effective** 1-1-64. Prior to amendment, subsection (g) read as follows:

For provisions disallowing any deduction for the payment of the tax imposed by subchapter B of chapter 3 (relating to tax-free covenant bonds) see section 1451(f).

• 1958, Technical Amendments Act of 1958 (P.L. 85-866)

P.L. 85-866, §6(a):

Redesignated subsection (f) as subsection (g) and added new subsection (f). **Effective** for tax years beginning after 12-31-57.

[Sec. 165]

SEC. 165. LOSSES.

[Sec. 165(a)]

(a) GENERAL RULE.—There shall be allowed as a deduction any loss sustained during the taxable year and not compensated for by insurance or otherwise.

[Sec. 165(b)]

(b) AMOUNT OF DEDUCTION.—For purposes of subsection (a), the basis for determining the amount of the deduction for any loss shall be the adjusted basis provided in section 1011 for determining the loss from the sale or other disposition of property.

[Sec. 165(c)]

(c) LIMITATION ON LOSSES OF INDIVIDUALS.—In the case of an individual, the deduction under subsection (a) shall be limited to—

(1) losses incurred in a trade or business;

(2) losses incurred in any transaction entered into for profit, though not connected with a trade or business; and

(3) except as provided in subsection (h), losses of property not connected with a trade or business or a transaction entered into for profit, if such losses arise from fire, storm, shipwreck, or other casualty, or from theft.

Amendments

• 1984, Deficit Reduction Act of 1984 (P.L. 98-369)

P.L. 98-369, §711(c)(2)(A)(i):

Amended Code Sec. 165(c)(3) by striking out "trade or business" and inserting in lieu thereof "trade or business or a transaction entered into for profit". **Effective** for tax years beginning after 12-31-83.

• 1982, Tax Equity and Fiscal Responsibility Act of 1982 (P.L. 97-248)

P.L. 97-248, §203(b):

Amended Code Sec. 165(c) by inserting "except as provided in subsection (h)," before "losses" the first place it appeared in paragraph (3) thereof. **Effective** for tax years beginning after 12-31-82. Such amendments shall also apply to the taxpayer's last tax year beginning before 1-1-83, solely for purposes of determining the amount allowable as a deduction with respect to any loss taken into account for such year by reason of an election under new Code Sec. 165(i).

P.L. 97-248, §203(b):

Amended Code Sec. 165(c) by striking out the last three sentences. **Effective** for tax years beginning after 12-31-82. Such amendments shall also apply to the taxpayer's last tax year beginning before 1-1-83, solely for purposes of determining the amount allowable as a deduction with respect to any loss taken into account for such year by reason of an election under section 165(i) of the Internal Revenue Code of 1954 (as amended by this section). Prior to amendment, the last three sentences read as follows:

A loss described in this paragraph shall be allowed only to the extent that the amount of loss to such individual arising from each casualty, or from each theft, exceeds $100. For purposes of the $100 limitation of the preceding sentence, a husband and wife making a joint return under section 6013 for the taxable year in which the loss is allowed as a deduction shall be treated as one individual. No loss described in this paragraph shall be allowed if, at the time of filing the return, such loss has been claimed for estate tax purposes in the estate tax return.

• 1964, Revenue Act of 1964 (P.L. 88-272)

P.L. 88-272, §208(a):

Amended paragraph (3) of subsection (c). **Effective** for losses after 12-31-63, in tax years ending after such date. Prior to amendment, paragraph (3) read as follows:

(3) losses of property not connected with a trade or business, if such losses arise from fire, storm, shipwreck, or other casualty, or from theft. No loss described in this paragraph shall be allowed if, at the time of the filing of the return, such loss has been claimed for estate tax purposes in the estate tax return.

[Sec. 165(d)]

(d) WAGERING LOSSES.—Losses from wagering transactions shall be allowed only to the extent of the gains from such transactions.

[Sec. 165(e)]

(e) THEFT LOSSES.—For purposes of subsection (a), any loss arising from theft shall be treated as sustained during the taxable year in which the taxpayer discovers such loss.

[Sec. 165(f)]

(f) CAPITAL LOSSES.—Losses from sales or exchanges of capital assets shall be allowed only to the extent allowed in sections 1211 and 1212.

[Sec. 165(g)]

(g) WORTHLESS SECURITIES.—

(1) GENERAL RULE.—If any security which is a capital asset becomes worthless during the taxable year, the loss resulting therefrom shall, for purposes of this subtitle, be treated as a loss from the sale or exchange, on the last day of the taxable year, of a capital asset.

(2) SECURITY DEFINED.—For purposes of this subsection, the term "security" means—

(A) a share of stock in a corporation;

(B) a right to subscribe for, or to receive, a share of stock in a corporation; or

(C) a bond, debenture, note, or certificate, or other evidence of indebtedness, issued by a corporation or by a government or political subdivision thereof, with interest coupons or in registered form.

(3) SECURITIES IN AFFILIATED CORPORATION.—For purposes of paragraph (1), any security in a corporation affiliated with a taxpayer which is a domestic corporation shall not be treated as a capital asset. For purposes of the preceding sentence, a corporation shall be treated as affiliated with the taxpayer only if—

(A) the taxpayer owns directly stock in such corporation meeting the requirements of section 1504(a)(2), and

(B) more than 90 percent of the aggregate of its gross receipts for all taxable years has been from sources other than royalties, rents (except rents derived from rental of properties to employees of the corporation in the ordinary course of its operating business), dividends, interest (except interest received on deferred purchase price of operating assets sold), annuities, and gains from sales or exchanges of stocks and securities.

In computing gross receipts for purposes of the preceding sentence, gross receipts from sales or exchanges of stocks and securities shall be taken into account only to the extent of gains therefrom.

Amendments

• 2000, Community Renewal Tax Relief Act of 2000 (P.L. 106-554)

P.L. 106-554, §318(b)(1):

Amended Code Sec. 165(g)(3)(A). **Effective** for tax years beginning after 12-31-84. Prior to amendment, Code Sec. 165(g)(3)(A) read as follows:

(A) stock possessing at least 80 percent of the voting power of all classes of its stock and at least 80 percent of each class of its nonvoting stock is owned directly by the taxpayer, and

P.L. 106-554, §318(b)(2):

Amended Code Sec. 165(g)(3) by striking the last sentence. **Effective** for tax years beginning after 12-31-84. Prior to amendment, the last sentence of Code Sec. 165(g)(3) read as follows:

As used in subparagraph (A), the term "stock" does not include nonvoting stock which is limited and preferred as to dividends.

• 1971 (P.L. 91-687)

P.L. 91-687, §1:

Added the last sentence to Code Sec. 165(g)(3) and amended Code Sec. 165(g)(3)(A). **Effective** for tax years beginning on or after 1-1-70. Prior to amendment, subparagraph (A) read as follows:

(A) at least 95 percent of each class of its stock is owned directly by the taxpayer, and

• 1958, Technical Amendments Act of 1958 (P.L. 85-866)

P.L. 85-866, §7:

Deleted the word "from" as it appeared immediately preceding the word "properties" in Sec. 165(g)(3)(B) and inserted in lieu thereof the word "of". **Effective** 1-1-54.

[Sec. 165(h)]

(h) TREATMENT OF CASUALTY GAINS AND LOSSES.—

(1) $100 LIMITATION PER CASUALTY.—Any loss of an individual described in subsection (c)(3) shall be allowed only to the extent that the amount of the loss to such individual arising from each casualty, or from each theft, exceeds $500 ($100 for taxable years beginning after December 31, 2009).

(2) NET CASUALTY LOSS ALLOWED ONLY TO THE EXTENT IT EXCEEDS 10 PERCENT OF ADJUSTED GROSS INCOME.—

(A) IN GENERAL.—If the personal casualty losses for any taxable year exceed the personal casualty gains for such taxable year, such losses shall be allowed for the taxable year only to the extent of the sum of—

(i) the amount of the personal casualty gains for the taxable year, plus

(ii) so much of such excess as exceeds 10 percent of the adjusted gross income of the individual.

(B) SPECIAL RULE WHERE PERSONAL CASUALTY GAINS EXCEED PERSONAL CASUALTY LOSSES.—If the personal casualty gains for any taxable year exceed the personal casualty losses for such taxable year—

(i) all such gains shall be treated as gains from sales or exchanges of capital assets, and

(ii) all such losses shall be treated as losses from sales or exchanges of capital assets.

(3) SPECIAL RULE FOR LOSSES IN FEDERALLY DECLARED DISASTERS.—

(A) IN GENERAL.—If an individual has a net disaster loss for any taxable year, the amount determined under paragraph (2)(A)(ii) shall be the sum of—

(i) such net disaster loss, and

(ii) so much of the excess referred to in the matter preceding clause (i) of paragraph (2)(A) (reduced by the amount in clause (i) of this subparagraph) as exceeds 10 percent of the adjusted gross income of the individual.

(B) NET DISASTER LOSS.—For purposes of subparagraph (A), the term "net disaster loss" means the excess of—

(i) the personal casualty losses—

(I) attributable to a federally declared disaster occurring before January 1, 2010, and

(II) occurring in a disaster area, over

(ii) personal casualty gains.

(C) FEDERALLY DECLARED DISASTER.—For purposes of this paragraph—

(i) FEDERALLY DECLARED DISASTER.—The term "federally declared disaster" means any disaster subsequently determined by the President of the United States to warrant assistance by the Federal Government under the Robert T. Stafford Disaster Relief and Emergency Assistance Act.

(ii) DISASTER AREA.—The term "disaster area" means the area so determined to warrant such assistance.

(4) DEFINITIONS OF PERSONAL CASUALTY GAIN AND PERSONAL CASUALTY LOSS.—For purposes of this subsection—

(A) PERSONAL CASUALTY GAIN.—The term "personal casualty gain" means the recognized gain from any involuntary conversion of property, which is described in subsection (c)(3) arising from fire, storm, shipwreck, or other casualty, or from theft.

(B) PERSONAL CASUALTY LOSS.—The term "personal casualty loss" means any loss described in subsection (c)(3). For purposes of paragraphs (2) and (3), the amount of any personal casualty loss shall be determined after the application of paragraph (1).

(5) SPECIAL RULES.—

(A) PERSONAL CASUALTY LOSSES ALLOWABLE IN COMPUTING ADJUSTED GROSS INCOME TO THE EXTENT OF PERSONAL CASUALTY GAINS.—In any case to which paragraph (2)(A) applies, the deduction for personal casualty losses for any taxable year shall be treated as a deduction allowable in computing adjusted gross income to the extent such losses do not exceed the personal casualty gains for the taxable year.

(B) JOINT RETURNS.—For purposes of this subsection, a husband and wife making a joint return for the taxable year shall be treated as 1 individual.

(C) DETERMINATION OF ADJUSTED GROSS INCOME IN CASE OF ESTATES AND TRUSTS.—For purposes of paragraph (2), the adjusted gross income of an estate or trust shall be computed in the same manner as in the case of an individual, except that the deductions for costs paid or incurred in connection with the administration of the estate or trust shall be treated as allowable in arriving at adjusted gross income.

(D) COORDINATION WITH ESTATE TAX.—No loss described in subsection (c)(3) shall be allowed if, at the time of filing the return, such loss has been claimed for estate tax purposes in the estate tax return.

(E) CLAIM REQUIRED TO BE FILED IN CERTAIN CASES.—Any loss of an individual described in subsection (c)(3) to the extent covered by insurance shall be taken into account under this section only if the individual files a timely insurance claim with respect to such loss.

Amendments

• 2008, Tax Extenders and Alternative Minimum Tax Relief Act of 2008 (P.L. 110-343)

P.L. 110-343, Division C, §706(a)(1):

Amended Code Sec. 165(h) by redesignating paragraphs (3) and (4) as paragraphs (4) and (5), respectively, and by inserting after paragraph (2) a new paragraph (3). **Effective** for disasters declared in tax years beginning after 12-31-2007.

P.L. 110-343, Division C, §706(a)(2)(A):

Amended Code Sec. 165(h)(4)(B) (as so redesignated) by striking "paragraph (2)" and inserting "paragraphs (2) and (3)". **Effective** for disasters declared in tax years beginning after 12-31-2007.

P.L. 110-343, Division C, §706(c):

Amended Code Sec. 165(h)(1) by striking "$100" and inserting "$500 ($100 for taxable years beginning after December 31, 2009)". **Effective** for tax years beginning after 12-31-2008.

P.L. 110-343, Division C, §712, provides:

SEC. 712. COORDINATION WITH HEARTLAND DISASTER RELIEF.

The amendments made by this subtitle, other than the amendments made by sections 706(a)(2), 710, and 711, shall not apply to any disaster described in section 702(c)[b](1)(A), or to any expenditure or loss resulting from such disaster.

• 2005, Katrina Emergency Tax Relief Act of 2005 (P.L. 109-73)

P.L. 109-73, §402 [repealed by P.L. 109-135, §201(b)(4)(B)], provides:

SEC. 402. SUSPENSION OF CERTAIN LIMITATIONS ON PERSONAL CASUALTY LOSSES.

Paragraphs (1) and (2)(A) of section 165(h) of the Internal Revenue Code of 1986 shall not apply to losses described in section 165(c)(3) of such Code which arise in the Hurricane Katrina disaster area on or after August 25, 2005, and which are attributable to Hurricane Katrina. In the case of any other losses, section 165(h)(2)(A) of such Code shall be applied without regard to the losses referred to in the preceding sentence.

• 1986, Tax Reform Act of 1986 (P.L. 99-514)

P.L. 99-514, §1004(a):

Amended Code Sec. 165(h)(4) by adding at the end thereof new subparagraph (E). **Effective** for losses sustained in tax years beginning after 12-31-86.

• 1984, Deficit Reduction Act of 1984 (P.L. 98-369)

P.L. 98-369, §711(c)(1):

Amended Code Sec. 165(h)(2) by redesignating subparagraph (B) as subparagraph (C) and by inserting after subparagraph (A) a new subparagraph (B) to read as follows:

(B) DETERMINATION OF ADJUSTED GROSS INCOME IN CASE OF ESTATES AND TRUSTS.—For purposes of paragraph (1), the adjusted gross income of an estate or trust shall be computed in the same manner as in the case of an individual, except that the deductions for costs paid or incurred in connection with the administration of the estate or trust shall be treated as allowable in arriving at adjusted gross income.

Effective as if included in the provision of P.L. 97-248 to which it relates.

P.L. 98-369, §711(c)(2)(A)(ii):

Amended Code Sec. 165(h). **Effective** for tax years beginning after 12-31-83. For a transitional rule, see Act Sec. 711(c)(2)(B), below.

P.L. 98-369, §711(c)(2)(B), provides:

(B) Transitional Rule.—In the case of taxable years beginning before January 1, 1984—

(i) For purposes of paragraph (1)(B) of section 165(h) of the Internal Revenue Code of 1954, adjusted gross income shall be determined without regard to the application of section 1231 of such Code to any gain or loss from an involuntary conversion of property described in subsection (c)(3) of section 165 of such Code arising from fire, storm, shipwreck, or other casualty or from theft.

• 1982, Tax Equity and Fiscal Responsibility Act of 1982 (P.L. 97-248)

P.L. 97-248, §203(a):

Amended Code Sec. 165 by striking subsection (h), redesignating subsection (i) as (j) and inserting after subsection (g) new subsection (h). **Effective** for tax years beginning after 12-31-82. It shall also apply to the taxpayer's last tax year beginning before 1-1-83, solely for purposes of determining the amount allowable as a deduction with respect to any loss taken into account for such year by reason of an election under Code Sec. 165(i). Prior to amendment, Code Sec. 165(h) read as follows:

(h) DISASTER LOSSES.—Notwithstanding the provisions of subsection (a), any loss attributable to a disaster occurring in an area subsequently determined by the President of the United States to warrant assistance by the Federal Government under the Disaster Relief Act of 1974 may, at the election of the taxpayer, be deducted for the taxable year immediately preceding the taxable year in which the disaster occurred. Such deduction shall not be in excess of so much of the loss as would have been deductible in the taxable year in which the casualty occurred, based on facts existing at the date the taxpayer claims the loss. If an election is made under this subsection, the casualty resulting in the loss will be deemed to have occurred in the taxable year for which the deduction is claimed.

• 1976, Tax Reform Act of 1976 (P.L. 94-455)

P.L. 94-455, §2103, provides:

(a) APPLICATION OF SECTION.—This section shall apply to any individual—

(1) who was allowed a deduction under section 165 of the Internal Revenue Code of 1954 (relating to losses) for a loss attributable to a disaster occurring during calendar year 1972 which was determined by the President, under section 102 of the Disaster Relief Act of 1970, to warrant disaster assistance by the Federal Government,

(2) who in connection with such disaster—

(A) received income in the form of cancellation of a disaster loan under section 7 of the Small Business Act or an emergency loan under subtitle C of the Consolidated Farm and Rural Development Act, or

(B) received income in the form of compensation (not taken into account in computing the amount of the deduction) for such loss in settlement of any claim of the taxpayer against a person for that person's liability in tort for the damage or destruction of that taxpayer's property in connection with the disaster, and

(3) who elects (at such time and in such manner as the Secretary of the Treasury or his delegate may by regulations prescribe) to take the benefits of this section.

(b) EFFECT OF ELECTION.—In the case of any individual to whom this section applies—

(1) the tax imposed by chapter 1 of the Internal Revenue Code of 1954 for the taxable year in which the income taken into account is received or accrued which is attributable to such income shall not exceed the additional tax under such chapter which would have been payable for the year in which the deduction for the loss was taken if such deduction had not been taken for such year,

(2) any amount of tax imposed by chapter 1 attributable to the income taken into account which, on October 1, 1975, was unpaid may be paid in 3 equal annual installments (with the first such installment due and payable on April 15, 1977), and

(3) no interest on any deficiency shall be payable for any period before April 16, 1977, to the extent such deficiency is attributable to the receipt of such compensation, and no interest on any installment referred to in paragraph (2) shall be payable for any period before the due date of such installment.

(c) INCOME TAKEN INTO ACCOUNT.—For purposes of this section, the income taken into account is—

(1) in the case of an individual described in subsection (a)(2)(A), the amount of income (not in excess of $5,000) attributable to the cancellation of a disaster loan under section 7 of the Small Business Act or an emergency loan under subtitle C of the Consolidated Farm and Rural Development Act received by reason of the disaster described in subsection (a)(1), or

(2) in the case of an individual described in subsection (a)(2)(B), the amount of compensation (not in excess of $5,000) for the loss in settlement of any claim of the taxpayer against a person for that person's liability in tort for the damage or destruction of that taxpayer's property in connection with the disaster described in subsection (a)(1).

(d) PHASEOUT WHERE ADJUSTED GROSS INCOME EXCEEDS $15,000.—If for the taxable year for which the deduction for the loss was taken the individual's adjusted gross income exceeded $15,000, the $5,000 limit set forth in paragraph (1) or (2) of subsection (c) (whichever applies) shall be reduced by one dollar for each full dollar that such adjusted gross income exceeds $15,000. In the case of a married individual filing a separate return, the preceding sentence shall be applied by substituting "$7,500" for "$15,000".

(e) STATUTE OF LIMITATIONS.—If refund or credit of any overpayment of income tax resulting from an election made under this section is prevented on the date of the enactment of this Act, or at any time within one year after such date, by the operation of any law, or rule of law, refund or credit of such overpayment (to the extent attributable to such election) may, nevertheless, be made or allowed if claim therefor is filed within one year after such date. If the taxpayer makes an election under this section and if assessment of any deficiency for any taxable year resulting from such election is prevented on the date of the enactment of this Act, or at any time within one year after such date, by the operation of any law or rule of law, such assessment (to the extent attributable to such election) may, nevertheless, be made if made within one year after such date.

• 1974, Disaster Relief Act of 1974 (P.L. 93-288)

P.L. 93-288, §602(h):

Amended Code Sec. 165(h) by substituting "Disaster Relief Act of 1974" for "Disaster Relief Act of 1970." **Effective** 4-1-73.

• 1972 (P.L. 92-418)

P.L. 92-418, §2(a):

Amended Code Sec. 165(h). **Effective** for disasters occurring after 12-31-71, in tax years ending after such date. Prior to amendment, Code Sec. 165(h) read as follows:

(h) DISASTER LOSSES.—Notwithstanding the provisions of subsection (a), any loss

(1) attributable to a disaster which occurs during the period after the close of the taxable year and on or before the last day of the 6th calendar month beginning after the close of the taxable year, and

(2) occurring in an area subsequently determined by the President of the United States to warrant assistance by the Federal Government under the Disaster Relief Act of 1970, at the election of the taxpayer, may be deducted for the taxable year immediately preceding the taxable year in which the disaster occurred. Such deduction shall not be in excess of so much of the loss as would have been deductible in the taxable year in which the casualty occurred. If an election is made under this subsection, the casualty resulting in the loss will be deemed to have occurred in the taxable year for which the deduction is claimed.

• 1972 (P.L. 92-336)

P.L. 92-336, §2:

Amended Code Sec. 165(h)(1). **Effective** for disasters occurring after 12-31-71, in tax years ending after such date. Prior to amendment, Code Sec. 165(h)(1) read as follows:

(1) attributable to a disaster which occurs during the period following the close of the taxable year and on or before the time prescribed by law for filing the income tax return for the taxable year (determined without regard to any extension of time), and

• 1970, Disaster Relief Act of 1970 (P.L. 91-606)

P.L. 91-606, §301(h):

Amended Code Sec. 165(h)(2) by substituting "the Disaster Relief Act of 1970" for "sections 1855-1855g of title 42". **Effective** 12-31-70.

• 1962 (P.L. 87-426)

P.L. 87-426, §2:

Added Sec. 165(h). **Effective** for disasters occurring after 12-31-61.

[Sec. 165(i)]

(i) DISASTER LOSSES.—

(1) ELECTION TO TAKE DEDUCTION FOR PRECEDING YEAR.—Notwithstanding the provisions of subsection (a), any loss occurring in a disaster area (as defined by clause (ii) of subsection (h)(3)(C)) and attributable to a federally declared disaster (as defined by clause (i) of such subsection) may, at the election of the taxpayer, be taken into account for the taxable year immediately preceding the taxable year in which the disaster occurred.

(2) YEAR OF LOSS.—If an election is made under this subsection, the casualty resulting in the loss shall be treated for purposes of this title as having occurred in the taxable year for which the deduction is claimed.

(3) AMOUNT OF LOSS.—The amount of the loss taken into account in the preceding taxable year by reason of paragraph (1) shall not exceed the uncompensated amount determined on the basis of the facts existing at the date the taxpayer claims the loss.

(4) USE OF DISASTER LOAN APPRAISALS TO ESTABLISH AMOUNT OF LOSS.—Nothing in this title shall be construed to prohibit the Secretary from prescribing regulations or other guidance under which an appraisal for the purpose of obtaining a loan of Federal funds or a loan guarantee from the Federal Government as a result of a federally declared disaster (as defined by subsection (h)(3)(C)(i)[)] may be used to establish the amount of any loss described in paragraph (1) or (2).

Amendments

• 2008, Tax Extenders and Alternative Minimum Tax Relief Act of 2008 (P.L. 110-343)

P.L. 110-343, Division C, §706(a)(2)(B):

Amended Code Sec. 165(i)(1) by striking "loss" and all that follows through "Act" and inserting "loss occurring in a disaster area (as defined by clause (ii) of subsection (h)(3)(C)) and attributable to a federally declared disaster (as defined by clause (i) of such subsection)". **Effective** for disasters declared in tax years beginning after 12-31-2007. Prior to amendment, Code Sec. 165(i)(1), read as follows:

(1) ELECTION TO TAKE DEDUCTION FOR PRECEDING YEAR.—Notwithstanding the provisions of subsection (a), any loss attributable to a disaster occurring in an area subsequently determined by the President of the United States to warrant assistance by the Federal Government under the Robert T. Stafford Disaster Relief and Emergency Assistance Act may, at the election of the taxpayer, be taken into account for the taxable year immediately preceding the taxable year in which the disaster occurred.

P.L. 110-343, Division C, §706(a)(2)(C):

Amended Code Sec. 165(i)(4) by striking "Presidentially declared disaster (as defined by section 1033(h)(3))" and inserting "federally declared disaster (as defined by subsection (h)(3)(C)(i)[)]". **Effective** for disasters declared in tax years beginning after 12-31-2007.

• 2008, Housing Assistance Tax Act of 2008 (P.L. 110-289)

P.L. 110-289, §3082(a), provides:

(a) USE OF AMENDED INCOME TAX RETURNS TO TAKE INTO ACCOUNT RECEIPT OF CERTAIN HURRICANE-RELATED CASUALTY LOSS GRANTS BY DISALLOWING PREVIOUSLY TAKEN CASUALTY LOSS DEDUCTIONS.—

(1) IN GENERAL.—Notwithstanding any other provision of the Internal Revenue Code of 1986, if a taxpayer claims a deduction for any taxable year with respect to a casualty loss to a principal residence (within the meaning of section 121 of such Code) resulting from Hurricane Katrina, Hurricane Rita, or Hurricane Wilma and in a subsequent taxable year receives a grant under Public Law 109-148, 109-234, or 110-116 as reimbursement for such loss, such taxpayer may elect to file an amended income tax return for the taxable year in which such deduction was allowed (and for any taxable year to which such deduction is carried) and reduce (but not below zero) the amount of such deduction by the amount of such reimbursement.

(2) TIME OF FILING AMENDED RETURN.—Paragraph (1) shall apply with respect to any grant only if any amended income tax returns with respect to such grant are filed not later than the later of—

(A) the dute date for filing the tax return for the taxable year in which the taxpayer receives such grant, or

(B) the date which is 1 year after the date of the enactment of this Act.

(3) WAIVER OF PENALTIES AND INTEREST.—Any underpayment of tax resulting from the reduction under paragraph (1) of the amount otherwise allowable as a deduction shall not be subject to any penalty or interest under such Code if such tax is paid not later than 1 year after the filing of the amended return to which such reduction relates.

• 2004, Working Families Tax Relief Act of 2004 (P.L. 108-311)

P.L. 108-311, §408(a)(7)(A):

Amended Code Sec. 165(i)(1) by inserting "Robert T. Stafford" before "Disaster Relief and Emergency Assistance Act". **Effective** 10-4-2004.

• 1997, Taxpayer Relief Act of 1997 (P.L. 105-34)

P.L. 105-34, §912(a):

Amended Code Sec. 165(i) by adding at the end a new paragraph (4). **Effective** 8-5-97.

• 1988, Disaster Relief and Emergency Assistance Amendments of 1988 (P.L. 100-707)

P.L. 100-707, §109(l):

Amended Code Sec. 165(i)(1) by striking out "Act of 1974" and inserting in lieu thereof "and Emergency Assistance Act". **Effective** 11-23-88.

• 1982, Tax Equity and Fiscal Responsibility Act of 1982 (P.L. 97-248)

P.L. 97-248, §203(a):

Added subsection (i). **Effective** for tax years beginning after 1982. See amendment notes following Code Sec. 165(h) for a special rule.

[Sec. 165(j)]

(j) DENIAL OF DEDUCTION FOR LOSSES ON CERTAIN OBLIGATIONS NOT IN REGISTERED FORM.—

(1) IN GENERAL.—Nothing in subsection (a) or in any other provision of law shall be construed to provide a deduction for any loss sustained on any registration-required obligation unless such obligation is in registered form (or the issuance of such obligation was subject to tax under section 4701).

(2) DEFINITIONS.—For purposes of this subsection—

»»→ Caution: Code Sec. 165(j)(2)(A), below, prior to amendment by P.L. 111-147, applies to obligations issued on or before the date which is 2 years after March 18, 2010.

(A) REGISTRATION-REQUIRED OBLIGATION.—The term "registration-required obligation" has the meaning given to such term by section 163(f)(2) except that clause (iv) of subparagraph (A), and subparagraph (B), of such section shall not apply.

»»→ Caution: Code Sec. 165(j)(2)(A), below, as amended by P.L. 111-147, applies to obligations issued after the date which is 2 years after March 18, 2010.

(A) REGISTRATION-REQUIRED OBLIGATION.—The term "registration-required obligation" has the meaning given to such term by section 163(f)(2).

(B) REGISTERED FORM.—The term "registered form" has the same meaning as when used in section 163(f).

(3) EXCEPTIONS.—The Secretary may, by regulations, provide that this subsection and section 1287 shall not apply with respect to obligations held by any person if—

(A) such person holds such obligations in connection with a trade or business outside the United States,

(B) such person holds such obligations as a broker dealer (registered under Federal or State law) for sale to customers in the ordinary course of his trade or business,

(C) such person complies with reporting requirements with respect to ownership, transfers, and payments as the Secretary may require, or

(D) such person promptly surrenders the obligation to the issuer for the issuance of a new obligation in registered form,

but only if such obligations are held under arrangements provided in regulations or otherwise which are designed to assure that such obligations are not delivered to any United States person other than a person described in subparagraph (A), (B), or (C).

Amendments

• 2010, Hiring Incentives to Restore Employment Act (P.L. 111-147)

P.L. 111-147, §502(a)(2)(D):

Amended Code Sec. 165(j)(2)(A) by striking "except that clause (iv) of subparagraph (A), and subparagraph (B), of such section shall not apply" following "section 163(f)(2)". **Effective** for obligations issued after the date which is 2 years after 3-18-2010.

• 1984, Deficit Reduction Act of 1984 (P.L. 98-369)

P.L. 98-369, §42(a)(4):

Amended Code Sec. 165(j)(3) by striking out "subsection (d) of section 1232" and inserting in lieu thereof "section 1287". **Effective** for tax years ending after 7-18-84.

• 1982, Tax Equity and Fiscal Responsibility Act of 1982 (P.L. 97-248)

P.L. 97-248, §310(b)(5):

Amended Code Sec. 165 by redesignating subsection (j), as redesignated by Act Sec. 203(a), as subsection (k) and by inserting after subsection (i) new subsection (j). **Effective** as noted in Act Sec. 310(d)(3), below.

P.L. 97-248, §310(d)(1) and (3), provides:

(1) IN GENERAL.—Except as otherwise provided in this subsection, the amendments made by this section shall apply to obligations issued after December 31, 1982.

***

(3) EXCEPTION FOR CERTAIN WARRANTS, ETC.—The amendments made by subsection (b) shall not apply to any obligations issued after December 31, 1982, on the exercise of a warrant for the conversion of a convertible obligation if such warrant or obligation was offered or sold outside the United States without registration under the Securities Act of 1933 and was issued before August 10, 1982. A rule similar to the rule of the preceding sentence shall also apply in the case of any regulations issued under section 163(f)(2)(C) of the Internal Revenue Code of 1954 (as added by this section) except that the date on which such regulations take effect shall be substituted for "August 10, 1982".

[Sec. 165(k)]

(k) TREATMENT AS DISASTER LOSS WHERE TAXPAYER ORDERED TO DEMOLISH OR RELOCATE RESIDENCE IN DISASTER AREA BECAUSE OF DISASTER.—In the case of a taxpayer whose residence is located in an area which has been determined by the President of the United States to warrant assistance by the Federal Government under the Robert T. Stafford Disaster Relief and Emergency Assistance Act, if—

(1) not later than the 120th day after the date of such determination, the taxpayer is ordered, by the government of the State or any political subdivision thereof in which such residence is located, to demolish or relocate such residence, and

(2) the residence has been rendered unsafe for use as a residence by reason of the disaster,

any loss attributable to such disaster shall be treated as a loss which arises from a casualty and which is described in subsection (i).

Amendments

• 2004, Working Families Tax Relief Act of 2004 (P.L. 108-311)

P.L. 108-311, §408(a)(7)(B):

Amended Code Sec. 165(k) by inserting "Robert T. Stafford" before "Disaster Relief and Emergency Assistance Act". **Effective** 10-4-2004.

• 1988, Disaster Relief and Emergency Assistance Amendments of 1988 (P.L. 100-707)

P.L. 100-707, §109(l):

Amended Code Sec. 165(k) by striking out "Act of 1974" and inserting in lieu thereof "and Emergency Assistance Act". **Effective** 11-23-88.

• 1984, Deficit Reduction Act of 1984 (P.L. 98-369)

P.L. 98-369, §1051(a):

Amended Code Sec. 165 by redesignating subsection (k) as subsection (l) and by inserting after subsection (j) a new subsection (k). **Effective** for tax years ending after 12-31-81, with respect to residences in areas determined by the President of the United States, after such date, to warrant assistance by the Federal Government under P.L. 93-288.

[Sec. 165(l)]

(l) TREATMENT OF CERTAIN LOSSES IN INSOLVENT FINANCIAL INSTITUTIONS.—

(1) IN GENERAL.—If—

(A) as of the close of the taxable year, it can reasonably be estimated that there is a loss on a qualified individual's deposit in a qualified financial institution, and

(B) such loss is on account of the bankruptcy or insolvency of such institution,

then the taxpayer may elect to treat the amount so estimated as a loss described in subsection (c)(3) incurred during the taxable year.

(2) QUALIFIED INDIVIDUAL DEFINED.—For purposes of this subsection, the term "qualified individual" means any individual except an individual—

(A) who owns at least 1 percent in value of the outstanding stock of the qualified financial institution,

(B) who is an officer of the qualified financial institution,

(C) who is a sibling (whether by the whole or half blood), spouse, aunt, uncle, nephew, niece, ancestor, or lineal descendant of an individual described in subparagraph (A) or (B), or

(D) who otherwise is a related person (as defined in section 267(b)) with respect to an individual described in subparagraph (A) or (B).

(3) QUALIFIED FINANCIAL INSTITUTION.—For purposes of this subsection, the term "qualified financial institution" means—

(A) any bank (as defined in section 581),

(B) any institution described in section 591,

(C) any credit union the deposits or accounts in which are insured under Federal or State law or are protected or guaranteed under State law, or

(D) any similar institution chartered and supervised under Federal or State law.

(4) DEPOSIT.—For purposes of this subsection, the term "deposit" means any deposit, withdrawable account, or withdrawable or repurchasable share.

(5) ELECTION TO TREAT AS ORDINARY LOSS.—

(A) IN GENERAL.—In lieu of any election under paragraph (1), the taxpayer may elect to treat the amount referred to in paragraph (1) for the taxable year as an ordinary loss described in subsection (c)(2) incurred during the taxable year.

(B) LIMITATIONS.—

(i) DEPOSIT MAY NOT BE FEDERALLY INSURED.—No election may be made under subparagraph (A) with respect to any loss on a deposit in a qualified financial institution if part or all of such deposit is insured under Federal law.

(ii) DOLLAR LIMITATION.—With respect to each financial institution, the aggregate amount of losses attributable to deposits in such financial institution to which an election under subparagraph (A) may be made by the taxpayer for any taxable year shall not exceed $20,000 ($10,000 in the case of a separate return by a married individual). The limitation of the preceding sentence shall be reduced by the amount of any insurance proceeds under any State law which can reasonably be expected to be received with respect to losses on deposits in such institution.

(6) ELECTION.—Any election by the taxpayer under this subsection for any taxable year—

(A) shall apply to all losses for such taxable year of the taxpayer on deposits in the institution with respect to which such election was made, and

(B) may be revoked only with the consent of the Secretary.

(7) COORDINATION WITH SECTION 166.—Section 166 shall not apply to any loss to which an election under this subsection applies.

Amendments

• 1988, Technical and Miscellaneous Revenue Act of 1988 (P.L. 100-647)

P.L. 100-647, §1009(d)(1):

Amended Code Sec. 165(l) by redesignating paragraph (6) as paragraph (7) and by striking out paragraph (5) and inserting in lieu thereof new paragraphs (5) and (6). **Effective** as if included in the provision of P.L. 99-514 to which it relates. Prior to amendment, Code Sec. 165(l)(5) read as follows:

(5) ELECTION.—Any election by the taxpayer under this subsection may be revoked only with the consent of the Secretary and shall apply to all losses of the taxpayer on deposits in the institution with respect to which such election was made.

• 1986, Tax Reform Act of 1986 (P.L. 99-514)

P.L. 99-514, §905(a):

Amended Code Sec. 165 by redesignating subsection (l) as subsection (m) and by inserting after subsection (k) new subsection (l). **Effective** for tax years beginning after 12-31-82.

[Sec. 165(m)]

(m) CROSS REFERENCES.—

(1) For special rule for banks with respect to worthless securities, see section 582.

(2) For disallowance of deduction for worthlessness of securities to which subsection (g)(2)(C) applies, if issued by a political party or similar organization, see section 271.

(3) For special rule for losses on stock in a small business investment company, see section 1242.

(4) For special rule for losses of a small business investment company, see section 1243.

(5) For special rule for losses on small business stock, see section 1244.

Amendments

• 1986, Tax Reform Act of 1986 (P.L. 99-514)

P.L. 99-514, §905(a):

Redesignated subsection (l) as subsection (m). **Effective** for tax years beginning after 12-31-81.

• 1984, Deficit Reduction Act of 1984 (P.L. 98-369)

P.L. 98-369, §1051(a):

Redesignated Code Sec. 165(k) as (l). **Effective** for tax years ending after 1981.

• 1982, Tax Equity and Fiscal Responsibility Act of 1982 (P.L. 97-248)

P.L. 97-248, §203(a):

Redesignated Code Sec. 165(i) as (j). **Effective** for tax years beginning after 1982.

P.L. 97-248, §310(b)(5):

Redesignated Code Sec. 165(j) as (k). **Effective** for obligations issued after 1982.

• 1976, Tax Reform Act of 1976 (P.L. 94-455)

P.L. 94-455, §1901(a)(26):

Repealed Code Sec. 165(i) and redesignated former Code Sec. 165(j) as Code Sec. 165(i). **Effective** for tax years beginning after 12-31-76. Prior to repeal, Code Sec. 165(i) read as follows:

(i) CERTAIN PROPERTY CONFISCATED BY THE GOVERNMENT OF CUBA.—

(1) TREATMENT AS SUBSECTION (c)(3) LOSS.—For purposes of this chapter, in the case of an individual who was a citizen of the United States, or a resident alien, on December 31, 1958, any loss of property which—

(A) was sustained by reason of the expropriation, intervention, seizure, or similar taking of the property, before January 1, 1964, by the government of Cuba, any political subdivision thereof, or any agency or instrumentality of the foregoing, and

(B) was not a loss described in paragraph (1) of subsection (c), shall be treated as a loss to which paragraph (3) of subsection (c) applies. In the case of tangible property, the preceding sentence shall not apply unless the property was held by the taxpayer, and was located in Cuba, on one or more days in the period beginning on December 31, 1958, and ending on May 16, 1959.

(2) SPECIAL RULES.—

(A) For purposes of subsection (a), any loss described in paragraph (1) shall be treated as having been sustained on October 14, 1960, unless it is established that the loss was sustained on some other day.

(B) For purposes of subsection (a), the fair market value of property held by the taxpayer on one or more days during the period beginning on December 31, 1958, and ending on May 16, 1959, to which paragraph (1) applies, on the day on which the loss of such property was sustained, shall be its fair market value on the first day in such period on which the property was held by the taxpayer.

(C) For purposes of section 172, a loss described in paragraph (1) shall not be treated as an expropriation loss within the meaning of section 172(k).

(D) For purposes of section 6601, the amount of any tax imposed by this title shall not be reduced by virtue of this subsection for any period prior to February 26, 1964.

• 1971 (P.L. 91-677)

P.L. 91-677, §1(a):

(1) Deleted "or (2)" which followed "paragraph (1)" in Code Sec. 165(i)(1)(B). For **effective** dates, see below.

(2) Struck out "December 31, 1958" at the end of Code Sec. 165(i)(1) and substituted "on one or more days in the period beginning on December 31, 1958, and ending on May 16, 1959". For **effective** dates, see below.

(3) Amended Code Sec. 165(i)(2)(B). For **effective** dates, see below. Prior to amendment, this subparagraph read as follows:

"(B) For purposes of subsection (a), the fair market value of property held by the taxpayer on December 31, 1958, to which paragraph (1) applies, on the day on which the loss of such property was sustained, shall be its fair market value on December 31, 1958."

(4) Deleted Code Sec. 165(i)(3). For **effective** dates, see below. Prior to repeal, this subparagraph read as follows:

"(3) Refunds or credits.—Notwithstanding any law or rule of law, refund or credit of any overpayment attributable to the application of paragraph (1) may be made or allowed if claim therefor is filed before January 1, 1965. No interest shall be allowed with respect to any such refund or credit for any period prior to February 26, 1964."

The above amendments are **effective** as noted below:

(1) The amendments apply in respect of losses sustained in tax years ending after 12-31-58.

(2) Notwithstanding any law or rule of law, refund or credit of any overpayment attributable to the amendments may be made or allowed if claim therefor is filed after 1-12-71, and before 7-1-71. No interest shall be allowed with respect to any such refund or credit for any period before 1-1-72.

• 1964, Excise Tax Rate Extension Act of 1964 (P.L. 88-348)

P.L. 88-348, §3(a):

Amended Code Sec. 165(i). **Effective** for losses sustained in tax years ending after 12-31-58. Prior to amendment, Sec. 165(i) read as follows:

(i) Certain Property Confiscated by Cuba.—For purposes of this chapter, any loss of tangible property, if such loss arises from expropriation, intervention, seizure, or similar taking by the government of Cuba, any political subdivision thereof, or any agency or instrumentality of the foregoing, shall be treated as a loss from a casualty within the meaning of subsection (c)(3).

• 1964, Revenue Act of 1964 (P.L. 88-272)

P.L. 88-272, §238:

Added Code Sec. 165(i) and redesignated Sec. 165(j) from former Sec. 165(i).

• 1962 (P.L. 87-426)

P.L. 87-426, §2:

Redesignated Sec. 165(h) as Sec. 165(i). **Effective** 12-31-61.

• 1958, Technical Amendments Act of 1958 (P.L. 85-866)

P.L. 85-866, §57(c)(1):

Added paragraphs (3) and (4) to Sec. 165(h). **Effective** 9-2-58.

P.L. 85-866, §202(a):

Added paragraph (5) to Sec. 165(h). **Effective** 9-2-58.

[Sec. 166]

SEC. 166. BAD DEBTS.

[Sec. 166(a)]

(a) GENERAL RULE.—

(1) WHOLLY WORTHLESS DEBTS.—There shall be allowed as a deduction any debt which becomes worthless within the taxable year.

(2) PARTIALLY WORTHLESS DEBTS.—When satisfied that a debt is recoverable only in part, the Secretary may allow such debt, in an amount not in excess of the part charged off within the taxable year, as a deduction.

Amendments

• 1976, Tax Reform Act of 1976 (P.L. 94-455)

P.L. 94-455, §1906(b)(13)(A):

Amended 1954 Code by substituting "Secretary" for "Secretary or his delegate" each place it appeared. **Effective** 2-1-77.

[Sec. 166(b)]

(b) AMOUNT OF DEDUCTION.—For purposes of subsection (a), the basis for determining the amount of the deduction for any bad debt shall be the adjusted basis provided in section 1011 for determining the loss from the sale or other disposition of property.

[Sec. 166(c)—Repealed]

Amendments

• 1986, Tax Reform Act of 1986 (P.L. 99-514)

P.L. 99-514, §805(a):

Repealed Code Sec. 166(c). **Effective** for tax years beginning after 12-31-86. Prior to repeal, Code Sec. 166(c) read as follows:

(c) RESERVE FOR BAD DEBTS.—In lieu of any deduction under subsection (a), there shall be allowed (in the discretion of the Secretary) a deduction for a reasonable addition to a reserve for bad debts.

• 1976, Tax Reform Act of 1976 (P.L. 94-455)

P.L. 94-455, §1906(b)(13)(A):

Amended 1954 Code by substituting "Secretary" for "Secretary or his delegate" each place it appeared. **Effective** 2-1-77.

[Sec. 166(d)]

(d) NONBUSINESS DEBTS.—

(1) GENERAL RULE.—In the case of a taxpayer other than a corporation—

(A) subsection (a) shall not apply to any nonbusiness debt; and

(B) where any nonbusiness debt becomes worthless within the taxable year, the loss resulting therefrom shall be considered a loss from the sale or exchange, during the taxable year, of a capital asset held for not more than 1 year.

(2) NONBUSINESS DEBT DEFINED.—For purposes of paragraph (1), the term "nonbusiness debt" means a debt other than—

(A) a debt created or acquired (as the case may be) in connection with a trade or business of the taxpayer; or

(B) a debt the loss from the worthlessness of which is incurred in the taxpayer's trade or business.

Amendments

• 1988, Technical and Miscellaneous Revenue Act of 1988 (P.L. 100-647)

P.L. 100-647, §1008:

Amended Code Sec. 166(d)(1)(A) by striking out "subsections (a) and (c)" and inserting in lieu thereof "subsection (a)". **Effective** as if included in the provision of P.L. 99-514 to which it relates.

• 1984, Deficit Reduction Act of 1984 (P.L. 98-369)

P.L. 98-369, §1001(b)(1):

Amended Code Sec. 166(d)(1)(B) by striking out "1 year" each place it appeared and inserting in lieu thereof "6 months". **Effective** for property acquired after 6-22-84, and before 1-1-88.

• 1976, Tax Reform Act of 1976 (P.L. 94-455)

P.L. 94-455, §1402(b)(1):

Substituted "9 months" for "6 months" in Code Sec. 166(d)(1)(B). **Effective** for tax years beginning in 1977. Further substituted "1 year" for "9 months" in Code Sec. 166(d)(1)(B). **Effective** for tax years beginning after 12-31-77.

• 1958, Technical Amendments Act of 1958 (P.L. 85-866)

P.L. 85-866, §8:

Substituted the phrase "a trade or business of the taxpayer" for the phrase "a taxpayer's trade or business" in Sec. 166(d)(2)(A). **Effective** 1-1-54.

[Sec. 166(e)]

(e) WORTHLESS SECURITIES.—This section shall not apply to a debt which is evidenced by a security as defined in section 165(g)(2)(C).

[Sec. 166(f)]

(f) CROSS REFERENCES.—

(1) For disallowance of deduction for worthlessness of debts owed by political parties and similar organizations, see section 271.

(2) For special rule for banks with respect to worthless securities, see section 582.

Amendments

• 1986, Tax Reform Act of 1986 (P.L. 99-514)

P.L. 99-514, §805(b):

Amended Code Sec. 166, as amended by section 901(d)(4), by striking out subsection (f) and redesignating subsection (g) as subsection (f). **Effective** for tax years beginning after 12-31-86. Prior to amendment, Code Sec. 166(f) read as follows:

(f) RESERVE FOR CERTAIN GUARANTEED DEBT OBLIGATIONS.—

(1) ALLOWANCE OF DEDUCTION.—In the case of a taxpayer who is a dealer in property, in lieu of any deduction under subsection (a), there shall be allowed (in the discretion of the Secretary) for any taxable year ending after October 21, 1965, a deduction—

(A) for a reasonable addition to a reserve for bad debts which may arise out of his liability as a guarantor, endorser, or indemnitor of debt obligations arising out of the sale by him of real property or tangible personal property (including related services) in the ordinary course of his trade or business; and

(B) for the amount of any reduction in the suspense account required by paragraph (4)(B)(i).

(2) DEDUCTION DISALLOWED IN OTHER CASES.—Except as provided in paragraph (1), no deduction shall be allowed to a taxpayer for any addition to a reserve for bad debts which may arise out of his liability as guarantor, endorser, or indemnitor of debt obligations.

(3) OPENING BALANCE.—The opening balance of a reserve described in paragraph (1)(A) for the first taxable year ending after October 21, 1965, for which a taxpayer maintains such reserve shall, under regulations prescribed by the Secretary, be determined as if the taxpayer had maintained such reserve for the preceding taxable years.

(4) SUSPENSE ACCOUNT.—

(A) REQUIREMENT.—Except as provided by subparagraph (C), each taxpayer who maintains a reserve described in paragraph (1)(A) shall, for purposes of this subsection and section 81, establish and maintain a suspense account. The initial balance of such account shall be equal to the opening balance described in paragraph (3).

(B) ADJUSTMENTS.—At the close of each taxable year the suspense account shall be—

(i) reduced by the excess of the suspense account at the beginning of the year over the reserve described in paragraph (1)(A) (after making the addition for such year provided in such paragraph), or

(ii) increased (but not to an amount greater than the initial balance of the suspense account) by the excess of the reserve described in paragraph (1)(A) (after making the addition for such year provided in such paragraph) over the suspense account at the beginning of such year.

(C) LIMITATIONS.—Subparagraphs (A) and (B) shall not apply in the case of the taxpayer who maintained for his last taxable year ending before October 22, 1965, a reserve for bad debts under subsection (c) which included debt obligations described in paragraph (1)(A).

(D) SECTION 381 ACQUISITIONS.—The application of this paragraph in any acquisition to which section 381(a) applies shall be determined under regulations prescribed by the Secretary.

P.L. 99-514, §805(d)(2), provides:

(2) CHANGE IN METHOD OF ACCOUNTING.—In the case of any taxpayer who maintained a reserve for bad debts for such taxpayer's last taxable year beginning before January 1, 1987, and who is required by the amendments made by this section to change its method of accounting for any taxable year—

(A) such change shall be treated as initiated by the taxpayer,

(B) such change shall be treated as made with the consent of the Secretary, and

(C) the net amount of adjustments required by section 481 of the Internal Revenue Code of 1986 to be taken into account by the taxpayer shall—

(i) in the case of a taxpayer maintaining a reserve under section 166(f), be reduced by the balance in the suspense account under section 166(f)(4) of such Code as of the close of such last taxable year, and

(ii) be taken into account ratably in each of the first 4 taxable years beginning after December 31, 1986.

P.L. 99-514, §901(d)(4)(A):

Amended Code Sec. 166(g) by striking out paragraphs (3) and (4). **Effective** for tax years beginning after 12-31-86. Prior to being stricken, paragraphs (3) and (4) read as follows:

(3) For special rule for bad debt reserves of certain mutual savings banks, domestic building and loan associations, and cooperative banks, see section 593.

(4) For special rule for bad debt reserves of banks, small business investment companies, etc., see sections 585 and 586.

• 1976, Tax Reform Act of 1976 (P.L. 94-455)

P.L. 94-455, §605(a):

Repealed former Code Sec. 166(f). **Effective** for guarantees made after 12-31-75, in tax years beginning after such date. Prior to repeal, Code Sec. 166(f) read as follows:

(f) GUARANTOR OF CERTAIN NONCORPORATE OBLIGATIONS.—A payment by the taxpayer (other than a corporation) in discharge of part or all of his obligation as a guarantor, endorser, or indemnitor of a noncorporate obligation the proceeds of which were used in the trade or business of the borrower shall be treated as a debt becoming worthless within such taxable year for purposes of this section (except that subsection (d) shall not apply), but only if the obligation of the borrower to the person to whom such payment was made was worthless (without regard to such guaranty, endorsement, or indemnity) at the time of such payment.

P.L. 94-455, §605(a):

Repealed Code Sec. 166(f) and redesignated former Code Sec. 166(g) as Code Sec. 166(f). **Effective** for guarantees made after 12-31-75, in tax years beginning after such date.

P.L. 94-455, §605(a):

Redesignated former Code Sec. 166(h) as Code Sec. 166(g). **Effective** for guarantees made after 12-31-75, in tax years beginning after such date.

P.L. 94-455, §1906(b)(13)(A):

Amended 1954 Code by substituting "Secretary" for "Secretary or his delegate" each place it appeared. **Effective** 2-1-77.

• 1969, Tax Reform Act of 1969 (P.L. 91-172)

P.L. 91-172, §431(c)(1):

Added Code Sec. 166(h)(4). **Effective** for tax years beginning after 7-11-69.

• 1966 (P.L. 89-722)

P.L. 89-722, §[1(a)]:

Redesignated former Code Sec. 166(g) as Code Sec. 166(h). **Effective** for tax years ending after 10-21-65.

P.L. 89-722, §[1(a)]:

Redesignated former Code Sec. 166(g) as (h) and added new Code Sec. 166(g). **Effective**, generally, for tax years ending after 10-21-65. However, if the taxpayer, before 10-22-65, claimed a deduction for a tax year ending before such date, under Code Sec. 166(c) for an addition to a bad debt reserve on account of debt obligations described in Sec. 166(g)(1)(A) and the assessment of a deficiency of the tax imposed by chapter 1 for such tax year and each subsequent tax year ending before 10-22-65, is not prevented on 12-31-66, by the operation of any law or rule of law, then such deduction on account of such debt obligations shall be allowed for each such tax year under such section 166(c) to the extent that the deduction would have been allowable under the provisions of such section 166(g)(1)(A) if such provisions applied to such tax years. Sec. 166(g)(2) applies to tax years beginning after 12-31-53, and ending after 8-16-54.

If the taxpayer establishes a reserve described in section 166(g)(1) for a tax year ending after 10-21-65, and beginning before 8-2-66, the establishment of such reserve shall not be considered as a change in method of accounting for purposes of Sec. 446(e).

[Sec. 167]

SEC. 167. DEPRECIATION.

[Sec. 167(a)]

(a) GENERAL RULE.—There shall be allowed as a depreciation deduction a reasonable allowance for the exhaustion, wear and tear (including a reasonable allowance for obsolescence)—

(1) of property used in the trade or business, or

(2) of property held for the production of income.

Amendments

• 1988, Technical and Miscellaneous Revenue Act of 1988 (P.L. 100-647)

P.L. 100-647, §1002(a)(24):

Amended Code Sec. 167(a) by striking out the last sentence. **Effective** as if included in the provision of P.L. 99-514 to which it relates. Prior to amendment, the last sentence read as follows:

In the case of recovery property (within the meaning of section 168), the deduction allowable under section 168 shall be deemed to constitute the reasonable allowance provided by this section, except with respect to that portion of the basis of such property to which subsection (k) applies.

• 1981, Economic Recovery Tax Act of 1981 (P.L. 97-34)

P.L. 97-34, §203(a):

Amended Code Sec. 167(a) by adding the last sentence at the end thereof. **Effective** for property placed in service after 12-31-80, in tax years ending after such date.

[Sec. 167(b)]

(b) CROSS REFERENCE.—

For determination of depreciation deduction in case of property to which section 168 applies, see section 168.

Amendments

• 1990, Omnibus Budget Reconciliation Act of 1990 (P.L. 101-508)

P.L. 101-508, §11812(a)(1)-(2):

Amended Code Sec. 167 by striking subsections (b), (c), (d), (e), (f), (j), (k), (l), (m) (p), and (q) and by redesignating subsections (g), (h), (r), and (s) as subsections (c), (d), (e), and (f), respectively, and by inserting after subsection (a) new subsection (b). **Effective**, generally, for property placed in service after 11-5-90. However, for exceptions see Act Sec. 11812(c)(2)-(3) below.

P.L. 101-508, §11812(c)(2)-(3), provides:

(2) EXCEPTION.—The amendments made by this section shall not apply to any property to which section 168 of the Internal Revenue Code of 1986 does not apply by reason of subsection (f)(5) thereof.

(3) EXCEPTION FOR PREVIOUSLY GRANDFATHER [sic] EXPENDITURES.—The amendments made by this section shall not apply to rehabilitation expenditures described in section 252(f)(5) of the Tax Reform Act of 1986 (as added by section 1002(l)(31) of the Technical and Miscellaneous Revenue Act of 1988).

[Sec. 167(b)—Stricken]

Amendments

• 1990, Omnibus Budget Reconciliation Act of 1990 (P.L. 101-508)

P.L. 101-508, §11812(a)(1)-(2):

Amended Code Sec. 167 by striking subsection (b). **Effective**, generally, for property placed in service after 11-5-90. However, for exceptions see Act Sec. 11812(c)(2)-(3) below. Prior to being stricken, Code Sec. 167(b) read as follows:

(b) USE OF CERTAIN METHODS AND RATES.—For taxable years ending after December 31, 1953, the term "reasonable allowance" as used in subsection (a) shall include (but shall not be limited to) an allowance computed in accordance with regulations prescribed by the Secretary, under any of the following methods:

(1) the straight line method,

(2) the declining balance method, using a rate not exceeding twice the rate which would have been used had the annual allowance been computed under the method described in paragraph (1),

(3) the sum of the years-digits method, and

(4) any other consistent method productive of an annual allowance which, when added to all allowances for the period commencing with the taxpayer's use of the property and including the taxable year, does not, during the first two-thirds of the useful life of the property, exceed the total of such allowances which would have been used had such allowances been computed under the method described in paragraph (2).

Nothing in this subsection shall be construed to limit or reduce an allowance otherwise allowable under subsection (a).

P.L. 101-508, §11812(c)(2)-(3), provides:

(2) EXCEPTION.—The amendments made by this section shall not apply to any property to which section 168 of the Internal Revenue Code of 1986 does not apply by reason of subsection (f)(5) thereof.

(3) EXCEPTION FOR PREVIOUSLY GRANDFATHER [sic] EXPENDITURES.—The amendments made by this section shall not apply to rehabilitation expenditures described in section 252(f)(5) of the Tax Reform Act of 1986 (as added by section 1002(l)(31) of the Technical and Miscellaneous Revenue Act of 1988).

• 1976, Tax Reform Act of 1976 (P.L. 94-455)

P.L. 94-455, §1906(b)(13)(A):

Amended 1954 Code by substituting "Secretary" for "Secretary or his delegate" each place it appeared. **Effective** 2-1-77.

[Sec. 167(c)]

(c) BASIS FOR DEPRECIATION.—

(1) IN GENERAL.—The basis on which exhaustion, wear and tear, and obsolescence are to be allowed in respect of any property shall be the adjusted basis provided in section 1011, for the purpose of determining the gain on the sale or other disposition of such property.

(2) SPECIAL RULE FOR PROPERTY SUBJECT TO LEASE.—If any property is acquired subject to a lease—

(A) no portion of the adjusted basis shall be allocated to the leasehold interest, and

(B) the entire adjusted basis shall be taken into account in determining the depreciation deduction (if any) with respect to the property subject to the lease.

Amendments

• 1993, Omnibus Budget Reconciliation Act of 1993 (P.L. 103-66)

P.L. 103-66, §13261(b)(2):

Amended Code Sec. 167(c). **Effective**, generally, with respect to property acquired after 10-10-93. For special rules, see Act Sec. 13261(g)(2)-(3) in the amendment notes following Code Sec. 197. Prior to amendment, Code Sec. 167(c) read as follows:

(c) BASIS FOR DEPRECIATION.—The basis on which exhaustion, wear and tear, and obsolescence are to be allowed in respect of any property shall be the adjusted basis provided in section 1011 for the purpose of determining the gain on the sale or other disposition of such property.

• 1990, Omnibus Budget Reconciliation Act of 1990 (P.L. 101-508)

P.L. 101-508, §11812(a)(1)-(2):

Redesignated Code Sec. 167(g) as Code Sec. 167(c). **Effective**, generally, for property placed in service after 11-5-90. However, for exceptions see Act Sec. 11812(c)(2)-(3) below.

P.L. 101-508, §11812(c)(2)-(3), provides:

(2) EXCEPTION.—The amendments made by this section shall not apply to any property to which section 168 of the Internal Revenue Code of 1986 does not apply by reason of subsection (f)(5) thereof.

(3) EXCEPTION FOR PREVIOUSLY GRANDFATHER [sic] EXPENDITURES.—The amendments made by this section shall not apply to rehabilitation expenditures described in section 252(f)(5) of the Tax Reform Act of 1986 (as added by section 1002(l)(31) of the Technical and Miscellaneous Revenue Act of 1988).

[Sec. 167(c)—Stricken]

Amendments

• 1990, Omnibus Budget Reconciliation Act of 1990 (P.L. 101-508)

P.L. 101-508, §11812(a)(1)-(2):

Amended Code Sec. 167 by striking subsection (c). **Effective**, generally, for property placed in service after 11-5-90. However, for exceptions see Act Sec. 11812(c)(2)-(3) below. Prior to being stricken, Code Sec. 167(c) read as follows:

(c) LIMITATIONS ON USE OF CERTAIN METHODS AND RATES.—Paragraphs (2), (3), and (4) of subsection (b) shall apply only in the case of property (other than intangible property) described in subsection (a) with a useful life of 3 years or more—

(1) the construction, reconstruction, or erection of which is completed after December 31, 1953, and then only to that portion of the basis which is properly attributable to such construction, reconstruction, or erection after December 31, 1953, or

(2) acquired after December 31, 1953, if the original use of such property commences with the taxpayer and commences after such date.

Paragraphs (2), (3), and (4) of subsection (b) shall not apply to any motion picture film, video tape, or sound recording.

P.L. 101-508, §11812(c)(2)-(3), provides:

(2) EXCEPTION.—The amendments made by this section shall not apply to any property to which section 168 of the Internal Revenue Code of 1986 does not apply by reason of subsection (f)(5) thereof.

(3) EXCEPTION FOR PREVIOUSLY GRANDFATHER [sic] EXPENDITURES.—The amendments made by this section shall not apply to rehabilitation expenditures described in section 252(f)(5) of the Tax Reform Act of 1986 (as added by section 1002(l)(31) of the Technical and Miscellaneous Revenue Act of 1988).

• 1986, Tax Reform Act of 1986 (P.L. 99-514)

P.L. 99-514, §1809(d)(1):

Amended Code Sec. 167(c) by adding at the end thereof a new sentence. **Effective** as if included in the provision of P.L. 98-369 to which it relates except that it does not apply to property placed in service by the taxpayer on or before 3-28-85.

[Sec. 167(d)]

(d) LIFE TENANTS AND BENEFICIARIES OF TRUSTS AND ESTATES.—In the case of property held by one person for life with remainder to another person, the deduction shall be computed as if the life tenant were the absolute owner of the property and shall be allowed to the life tenant. In the case of property held in trust, the allowable deduction shall be apportioned between the income beneficiaries and the trustee in accordance with the pertinent provisions of the instrument creating the trust, or, in the absence of such provisions, on the basis of the trust income allocable to each. In the case of an estate, the allowable deduction shall be apportioned between the estate and the heirs, legatees, and devisees on the basis of the income of the estate allocable to each.

Amendments

• 1990, Omnibus Budget Reconciliation Act of 1990 (P.L. 101-508)

P.L. 101-508, §11812(a)(1)-(2):

Amended Code Sec. 167 by redesignating subsection (h) as subsection (d). **Effective**, generally, for property placed in service after 11-5-90. However, for exceptions see Act Sec. 11812(c)(2)-(3) below.

P.L. 101-508, §11812(c)(2)-(3), provides:

(2) EXCEPTION.—The amendments made by this section shall not apply to any property to which section 168 of the Internal Revenue Code of 1986 does not apply by reason of subsection (f)(5) thereof.

(3) EXCEPTION FOR PREVIOUSLY GRANDFATHER [sic] EXPENDITURES.—The amendments made by this section shall not apply to rehabilitation expenditures described in section 252(f)(5) of the Tax Reform Act of 1986 (as added by section 1002(l)(31) of the Technical and Miscellaneous Revenue Act of 1988).

[Sec. 167(d)—Stricken]

Amendments

• 1990, Omnibus Budget Reconciliation Act of 1990 (P.L. 101-508)

P.L. 101-508, §11812(a)(1)-(2):

Amended Code Sec. 167 by striking out subsection (d). **Effective**, generally, for property placed in service after 11-5-90. However, for exceptions see Act Sec. 11812(c)(2)-(3) below. Prior to being stricken, Code Sec. 167(d) read as follows:

(d) AGREEMENT AS TO USEFUL LIFE ON WHICH DEPRECIATION RATE IS BASED.—Where, under regulations prescribed by the Secretary, the taxpayer and the Secretary have, after August 16, 1954, entered into an agreement in writing specifically dealing with the useful life and rate of depreciation of any property, the rate so agreed upon shall be binding on both the taxpayer and the Secretary in the absence of facts or circumstances not taken into consideration in the adoption of such agreement. The responsibility of establishing the existence of such facts and circumstances shall rest with the party initiating the modification. Any change in the agreed rate and useful life specified in the agreement shall not be effective for taxable years before the taxable year in which notice in writing by certified mail or registered mail is served by the party to the agreement initiating such change. This subsection shall not apply with respect to property to which section 168 applies.

P.L. 101-508, §11812(c)(2)-(3), provides:

(2) EXCEPTION.—The amendments made by this section shall not apply to any property to which section 168 of the Internal Revenue Code of 1986 does not apply by reason of subsection (f)(5) thereof.

(3) EXCEPTION FOR PREVIOUSLY GRANDFATHER [sic] EXPENDITURES.—The amendments made by this section shall not apply to rehabilitation expenditures described in section 252(f)(5) of the Tax Reform Act of 1986 (as added by section 1002(l)(31) of the Technical and Miscellaneous Revenue Act of 1988).

• 1988, Technical and Miscellaneous Revenue Act of 1988 (P.L. 100-647)

P.L. 100-647, §1002(a)(31):

Amended Code Sec. 167(d) by striking out "recovery property defined in section 168" and inserting in lieu thereof "property to which section 168 applies". **Effective** as if included in the provision of P.L. 99-514 to which it relates.

• 1981, Economic Recovery Tax Act of 1981 (P.L. 97-34)

P.L. 97-34, §203(d):

Amended Code Sec. 167(d) by adding the last sentence at the end thereof. **Effective** for property placed in service after 12-31-80, in tax years ending after such date.

• 1976, Tax Reform Act of 1976 (P.L. 94-455)

P.L. 94-455, §1901(a)(27):

Substituted "after August 16, 1954" for "after the date of enactment of this title" in Code Sec. 167(d). **Effective** for tax years beginning after 12-31-76.

P.L. 94-455, §1906(b)(13)(A):

Amended 1954 Code by substituting "Secretary" for "Secretary or his delegate" each place it appeared. **Effective** 2-1-77.

• 1958, Technical Amendments Act of 1958 (P.L. 85-866)

P.L. 85-866, §89(b):

Struck out "registered mail" where it appeared in the last sentence of Sec. 167(d) and substituted "certified mail or registered mail". **Effective** 9-3-58.

[Sec. 167(e)]

(e) CERTAIN TERM INTERESTS NOT DEPRECIABLE.—

(1) IN GENERAL.—No depreciation deduction shall be allowed under this section (and no depreciation or amortization deduction shall be allowed under any other provision of this subtitle) to the taxpayer for any term interest in property for any period during which the remainder interest in such property is held (directly or indirectly) by a related person.

(2) COORDINATION WITH OTHER PROVISIONS.—

(A) SECTION 273.—This subsection shall not apply to any term interest to which section 273 applies.

(B) SECTION 305(e).—This subsection shall not apply to the holder of the dividend rights which were separated from any stripped preferred stock to which section 305(e)(1) applies.

(3) BASIS ADJUSTMENTS.—If, but for this subsection, a depreciation or amortization deduction would be allowable to the taxpayer with respect to any term interest in property—

(A) the taxpayer's basis in such property shall be reduced by any depreciation or amortization deductions disallowed under this subsection, and

(B) the basis of the remainder interest in such property shall be increased by the amount of such disallowed deductions (properly adjusted for any depreciation deductions allowable under subsection (d) to the taxpayer).

(4) SPECIAL RULES.—

(A) DENIAL OF INCREASE IN BASIS OF REMAINDERMAN.—No increase in the basis of the remainder interest shall be made under paragraph (3)(B) for any disallowed deductions attributable to periods during which the term interest was held—

(i) by an organization exempt from tax under this subtitle, or

(ii) by a nonresident alien individual or foreign corporation but only if income from the term interest is not effectively connected with the conduct of a trade or business in the United States.

(B) COORDINATION WITH SUBSECTION (d).—If, but for this subsection, a depreciation or amortization deduction would be allowable to any person with respect to any term interest in property, the principles of subsection (d) shall apply to such person with respect to such term interest.

(5) DEFINITIONS.—For purposes of this subsection—

(A) TERM INTEREST IN PROPERTY.—The term "term interest in property" has the meaning given such term by section 1001(e)(2).

(B) RELATED PERSON.—The term "related person" means any person bearing a relationship to the taxpayer described in subsection (b) or (e) of section 267.

(6) REGULATIONS.—The Secretary shall prescribe such regulations as may be necessary to carry out the purposes of this subsection, including regulations preventing avoidance of this subsection through cross-ownership arrangements or otherwise.

Amendments

• 1993, Omnibus Budget Reconciliation Act of 1993 (P.L. 103-66)

P.L. 103-66, §13206(c)(2):

Amended Code Sec. 167(e)(2). **Effective** 4-30-93. Prior to amendment, Code Sec. 167(e)(2) read as follows:

(2) COORDINATION WITH SECTION 273.—This subsection shall not apply to any term interest to which section 273 applies.

• 1990, Omnibus Budget Reconciliation Act of 1990 (P.L. 101-508)

P.L. 101-508, §11812(a)(1):

Amended Code Sec. 167 by redesignating subsection (r) as subsection (e). **Effective**, generally, for property placed in service after 11-5-90. However, for exceptions see Act Sec. 11812(c)(2)-(3) in the amendment notes following Code Sec. 167(b).

P.L. 101-508, §11812(b)(1):

Amended Code Sec. 167(e), as redesignated by Act Sec. 11812(a), by striking "(h)" each place it appears in paragraphs (3)(B) and (4)(B) and inserting "(d)". **Effective**, generally, for property placed in service after 11-5-90. However, for exceptions see Act Sec. 11812(c)(2)-(3) in the amendment notes following Code Sec. 167(b).

• 1989, Omnibus Budget Reconciliation Act of 1989 (P.L. 101-239)

P.L. 101-239, §7645(a):

Amended Code Sec. 167, as amended by section 7622, by inserting after subsection (q) a new subsection (r). **Effective** for interests created or acquired after 7-27-89, in tax years ending after such date.

[Sec. 167(e)—Stricken]

Amendments

• 1990, Omnibus Budget Reconciliation Act of 1990 (P.L. 101-508)

P.L. 101-508, §11812(a)(1)-(2):

Amended Code Sec. 167 by striking subsection (e). **Effective**, generally, for property placed in service after 11-5-90. However, for exceptions see Act Sec. 11812(c)(2)-(3) below. Prior to being stricken, Code Sec. 167(e) read as follows:

(e) CHANGE IN METHOD.—

(1) CHANGE FROM DECLINING BALANCE METHOD.—In the absence of an agreement under subsection (d) containing a provision to the contrary, a taxpayer may at any time elect in accordance with regulations prescribed by the Secretary to change from the method of depreciation described in subsection (b)(2) to the method described in subsection (b)(1).

(2) CHANGE WITH RESPECT TO SECTION 1245 PROPERTY.—A taxpayer may, on or before the last day prescribed by law (including extensions thereof) for filing his return for his first taxable year beginning after December 31, 1962, and in such manner as the Secretary shall by regulations prescribe, elect to change his method of depreciation in respect of section 1245 property (as defined in section 1245(a)(3)) from

any declining balance or sum of the years-digits method to the straight line method. An election may be made under this paragraph notwithstanding any provision to the contrary in an agreement under subsection (d).

(3) CHANGE WITH RESPECT TO SECTION 1250 PROPERTY.—A taxpayer may, on or before the last day prescribed by law (including extensions thereof) for filing his return for his first taxable year beginning after December 31, 1975, and in such manner as the Secretary shall by regulation prescribe, elect to change his method of depreciation in respect of section 1250 property (as defined in section 1250(c)) from any declining balance or sum of the years-digits method to the straight line method. An election may be made under this paragraph notwithstanding any provision to the contrary in an agreement under subsection (d).

P.L. 101-508, §11812(c)(2)-(3), provides:

(2) EXCEPTION.—The amendments made by this section shall not apply to any property to which section 168 of the Internal Revenue Code of 1986 does not apply by reason of subsection (f)(5) thereof.

(3) EXCEPTION FOR PREVIOUSLY GRANDFATHER [sic] EXPENDITURES.—The amendments made by this section shall not apply to rehabilitation expenditures described in section 252(f)(5) of the Tax Reform Act of 1986 (as added by section 1002(l)(31) of the Technical and Miscellaneous Revenue Act of 1988).

• 1976, Tax Reform Act of 1976 (P.L. 94-455)

P.L. 94-455, §202(c):

Substituted "December 31, 1975" for "July 24, 1969" in Code Sec. 167(e)(3). **Effective** for tax years ending after 12-31-75.

P.L. 94-455, §1906(b)(13)(A):

Amended 1954 Code by substituting "Secretary" for "Secretary or his delegate" each place it appeared. **Effective** 2-1-77.

• 1969, Tax Reform Act of 1969 (P.L. 91-172)

P.L. 91-172, §521(d):

Added Code Sec. 167(e)(3). **Effective** for tax years ending after 7-24-69.

• 1962, Revenue Act of 1962 (P.L. 87-834)

P.L. 87-834, §13(b):

Amended Code Sec. 167(e). **Effective** for tax years beginning after 12-31-62. Prior to amendment, Sec. 167(e) read as follows:

(e) CHANGE IN METHOD.—In the absence of an agreement under subsection (d) containing a provision to the contrary, a taxpayer may at any time elect in accordance with regulations prescribed by the Secretary or his delegate to change from the method of depreciation described in section (b)(2) to the method described in subsection (b)(1).

[Sec. 167(f)]

(f) TREATMENT OF CERTAIN PROPERTY EXCLUDED FROM SECTION 197.—

(1) COMPUTER SOFTWARE.—

(A) IN GENERAL.—If a depreciation deduction is allowable under subsection (a) with respect to any computer software, such deduction shall be computed by using the straight line method and a useful life of 36 months.

(B) COMPUTER SOFTWARE.—For purposes of this section, the term "computer software" has the meaning given to such term by section 197(e)(3)(B); except that such term shall not include any such software which is an amortizable section 197 intangible.

(C) TAX-EXEMPT USE PROPERTY SUBJECT TO LEASE.—In the case of computer software which would be tax-exempt use property as defined in subsection (h) of section 168 if such section applied to computer software, the useful life under subparagraph (A) shall not be less than 125 percent of the lease term (within the meaning of section 168(i)(3)).

(2) CERTAIN INTERESTS OR RIGHTS ACQUIRED SEPARATELY.—If a depreciation deduction is allowable under subsection (a) with respect to any property described in subparagraph (B), (C), or (D) of section 197(e)(4), such deduction shall be computed in accordance with regulations prescribed by the Secretary. If such property would be tax-exempt use property as defined in subsection (h) of section 168 if such section applied to such property, the useful life under such regulations shall not be less than 125 percent of the lease term (within the meaning of section 168(i)(3)).

(3) MORTGAGE SERVICING RIGHTS.—If a depreciation deduction is allowable under subsection (a) with respect to any right described in section 197(e)(6), such deduction shall be computed by using the straight line method and a useful life of 108 months.

Amendments

• 2005, Gulf Opportunity Zone Act of 2005 (P.L. 109-135)

P.L. 109-135, §412(r):

Amended Code Sec. 167(f)(3) by striking "section 197(e)(7)" and inserting "section 197(e)(6)". **Effective** 12-21-2005.

• 2004, American Jobs Creation Act of 2004 (P.L. 108-357)

P.L. 108-357, §847(b)(1):

Amended Code Sec. 167(f)(1) by adding at the end a new subparagraph (C). **Effective** generally for leases entered into after 3-12-2004, and in the case of property treated as tax-exempt use property other than by reason of a lease, to property acquired after 3-12-2004 [effective date amended by P.L. 109-135, §403(ff)]. For an exception, see Act Sec. 849(b)(1)-(2), below.

P.L. 108-357, §847(b)(2):

Amended Code Sec. 167(f)(2) by adding at the end a new sentence. **Effective** for leases entered into after 10-3-2004. For an exception, see Act Sec. 849(b)(1)-(2), below.

P.L. 108-357, §849(b)(1)-(2), provides:

(b) EXCEPTION.—

(1) IN GENERAL.—The amendments made by this part shall not apply to qualified transportation property.

(2) QUALIFIED TRANSPORTATION PROPERTY.—For purposes of paragraph (1), the term "qualified transportation property" means domestic property subject to a lease with respect to which a formal application—

(A) was submitted for approval to the Federal Transit Administration (an agency of the Department of Transportation) after June 30, 2003, and before March 13, 2004,

(B) is approved by the Federal Transit Administration before January 1, 2006, and

(C) includes a description of such property and the value of such property.

• 1993, Omnibus Budget Reconciliation Act of 1993 (P.L. 103-66)

P.L. 103-66, §13261(b)(1):

Amended Code Sec. 167 by redesignating subsection (f) as subsection (g) and by inserting after subsection (e) new subsection (f). **Effective**, generally, with respect to property acquired after the date of the enactment of this Act. For special rules, see Act Sec. 13261(g)(2)-(3) in the amendment notes following Code Sec. 197.

[Sec. 167(f)—Stricken]

Amendments

• 1990, Omnibus Budget Reconciliation Act of 1990 (P.L. 101-508)

P.L. 101-508, §11812(a)(1)-(2):

Amended Code Sec. 167 by striking out subsection (f). **Effective**, generally, for property placed in service after 11-5-90. However, for exceptions see Act Sec. 11812(c)(2)-(3) below. Prior to being stricken, Code Sec. 167(f) read as follows:

(f) SALVAGE VALUE.—

(1) GENERAL RULE.—Under regulations prescribed by the Secretary, a taxpayer may, for purposes of computing the allowance under subsection (a) with respect to personal property, reduce the amount taken into account as salvage value by an amount which does not exceed 10 percent of the basis of such property (as determined under subsection (g) as of the time as of which such salvage value is required to be determined).

(2) PERSONAL PROPERTY DEFINED.—For purposes of this subsection, the term "personal property" means depreciable personal property (other than livestock) with a useful life of 3 years or more acquired after October 16, 1962.

P.L. 101-508, §11812(c)(2)-(3), provides:

(2) EXCEPTION.—The amendments made by this section shall not apply to any property to which section 168 of the Internal Revenue Code of 1986 does not apply by reason of subsection (f)(5) thereof.

(3) EXCEPTION FOR PREVIOUSLY GRANDFATHER [sic] EXPENDITURES.—The amendments made by this section shall not apply to rehabilitation expenditures described in section 252(f)(5) of the Tax Reform Act of 1986 (as added by section 1002(l)(31) of the Technical and Miscellaneous Revenue Act of 1988).

• 1976, Tax Reform Act of 1976 (P.L. 94-455)

P.L. 94-455, §1901(a)(27):

Substituted "October 16, 1962" for "the date of the enactment of the Revenue Act of 1962" in Code Sec. 167(f)(2). **Effective** for tax years beginning after 12-31-76.

P.L. 94-455, §1906(b)(13)(A):

Amended 1954 Code by substituting "Secretary" for "Secretary or his delegate" each place it appeared. **Effective** 2-1-77.

• 1962, Revenue Act of 1962 (P.L. 87-834)

P.L. 87-834, §13(c)(1):

Redesignated Code Sec. 167(f), (g), and (h) as Code Sec. 167(g), (h), and (i), and added a new Code Sec. 167(f). **Effective** for tax years beginning after 12-31-61 and ending after 10-16-62.

[Sec. 167(g)]

(g) DEPRECIATION UNDER INCOME FORECAST METHOD.—

(1) IN GENERAL.—If the depreciation deduction allowable under this section to any taxpayer with respect to any property is determined under the income forecast method or any similar method—

(A) the income from the property to be taken into account in determining the depreciation deduction under such method shall be equal to the amount of income earned in connection with the property before the close of the 10th taxable year following the taxable year in which the property was placed in service,

(B) the adjusted basis of the property shall only include amounts with respect to which the requirements of section 461(h) are satisfied,

(C) the depreciation deduction under such method for the 10th taxable year beginning after the taxable year in which the property was placed in service shall be equal to the adjusted basis of such property as of the beginning of such 10th taxable year, and

(D) such taxpayer shall pay (or be entitled to receive) interest computed under the look-back method of paragraph (2) for any recomputation year.

(2) LOOK-BACK METHOD.—The interest computed under the look-back method of this paragraph for any recomputation year shall be determined by—

(A) first determining the depreciation deductions under this section with respect to such property which would have been allowable for prior taxable years if the determination of the amounts so allowable had been made on the basis of the sum of the following (instead of the estimated income from such property)—

(i) the actual income earned in connection with such property for periods before the close of the recomputation year, and

(ii) an estimate of the future income to be earned in connection with such property for periods after the recomputation year and before the close of the 10th taxable year following the taxable year in which the property was placed in service,

(B) second, determining (solely for purposes of computing such interest) the overpayment or underpayment of tax for each such prior taxable year which would result solely from the application of subparagraph (A), and

(C) then using the adjusted overpayment rate (as defined in section 460(b)(7)), compounded daily, on the overpayment or underpayment determined under subparagraph (B).

For purposes of the preceding sentence, any cost incurred after the property is placed in service (which is not treated as a separate property under paragraph (5)) shall be taken into account by discounting (using the Federal mid-term rate determined under section 1274(d) as of the time such cost is incurred) such cost to its value as of the date the property is placed in service. The taxpayer may elect with respect to any property to have the preceding sentence not apply to such property.

(3) EXCEPTION FROM LOOK-BACK METHOD.—Paragraph (1)(D) shall not apply with respect to any property which had a cost basis of $100,000 or less.

(4) RECOMPUTATION YEAR.—For purposes of this subsection, except as provided in regulations, the term "recomputation year" means, with respect to any property, the 3d and the 10th taxable years beginning after the taxable year in which the property was placed in service, unless the actual income earned in connection with the property for the period before the close of such 3d or 10th taxable year is within 10 percent of the income earned in connection with the property for such period which was taken into account under paragraph (1)(A).

(5) SPECIAL RULES.—

(A) CERTAIN COSTS TREATED AS SEPARATE PROPERTY.—For purposes of this subsection, the following costs shall be treated as separate properties:

(i) Any costs incurred with respect to any property after the 10th taxable year beginning after the taxable year in which the property was placed in service.

(ii) Any costs incurred after the property is placed in service and before the close of such 10th taxable year if such costs are significant and give rise to a significant increase in the income from the property which was not included in the estimated income from the property.

(B) SYNDICATION INCOME FROM TELEVISION SERIES.—In the case of property which is 1 or more episodes in a television series, income from syndicating such series shall not be required to be taken into account under this subsection before the earlier of—

(i) the 4th taxable year beginning after the date the first episode in such series is placed in service, or

(ii) the earliest taxable year in which the taxpayer has an arrangement relating to the future syndication of such series.

(C) SPECIAL RULES FOR FINANCIAL EXPLOITATION OF CHARACTERS, ETC.—For purposes of this subsection, in the case of television and motion picture films, the income from the property shall include income from the exploitation of characters, designs, scripts, scores, and other incidental income associated with such films, but only to the extent that such income is earned in connection with the ultimate use of such items by, or the ultimate sale of merchandise to, persons who are not related persons (within the meaning of section 267(b)) to the taxpayer.

(D) COLLECTION OF INTEREST.—For purposes of subtitle F (other than sections 6654 and 6655), any interest required to be paid by the taxpayer under paragraph (1) for any recomputation year shall be treated as an increase in the tax imposed by this chapter for such year.

(E) TREATMENT OF DISTRIBUTION COSTS.—For purposes of this subsection, the income with respect to any property shall be the taxpayer's gross income from such property.

(F) DETERMINATIONS.—For purposes of paragraph (2), determinations of the amount of income earned in connection with any property shall be made in the same manner as for purposes of applying the income forecast method; except that any income from the disposition of such property shall be taken into account.

(G) TREATMENT OF PASS-THRU ENTITIES.—Rules similar to the rules of section 460(b)(4) shall apply for purposes of this subsection.

(6) LIMITATION ON PROPERTY FOR WHICH INCOME FORECAST METHOD MAY BE USED.—The depreciation deduction allowable under this section may be determined under the income forecast method or any similar method only with respect to—

(A) property described in paragraph (3) or (4) of section 168(f),

(B) copyrights,

(C) books,

(D) patents, and

(E) other property specified in regulations.

Such methods may not be used with respect to any amortizable section 197 intangible (as defined in section 197(c)).

(7) TREATMENT OF PARTICIPATIONS AND RESIDUALS.—

(A) IN GENERAL.—For purposes of determining the depreciation deduction allowable with respect to a property under this subsection, the taxpayer may include participations and residuals with respect to such property in the adjusted basis of such property for the taxable year in which the property is placed in service, but only to the extent that such participations and residuals relate to income estimated (for purposes of this subsection) to be earned in connection with the property before the close of the 10th taxable year referred to in paragraph (1)(A).

(B) PARTICIPATIONS AND RESIDUALS.—For purposes of this paragraph, the term "participations and residuals" means, with respect to any property, costs the amount of which by contract varies with the amount of income earned in connection with such property.

(C) SPECIAL RULES RELATING TO RECOMPUTATION YEARS.—If the adjusted basis of any property is determined under this paragraph, paragraph (4) shall be applied by substituting "for each taxable year in such period" for "for such period".

(D) OTHER SPECIAL RULES.—

(i) PARTICIPATIONS AND RESIDUALS.—Notwithstanding subparagraph (A), the taxpayer may exclude participations and residuals from the adjusted basis of such property and deduct such participations and residuals in the taxable year that such participations and residuals are paid.

(ii) COORDINATION WITH OTHER RULES.—Deductions computed in accordance with this paragraph shall be allowable notwithstanding paragraph (1)(B), section 263, 263A, 404, 419, or 461(h).

(E) AUTHORITY TO MAKE ADJUSTMENTS.—The Secretary shall prescribe appropriate adjustments to the basis of property and to the look-back method for the additional amounts allowable as a deduction solely by reason of this paragraph.

(8) SPECIAL RULES FOR CERTAIN MUSICAL WORKS AND COPYRIGHTS.—

(A) IN GENERAL.—If an election is in effect under this paragraph for any taxable year, then, notwithstanding paragraph (1), any expense which—

(i) is paid or incurred by the taxpayer in creating or acquiring any applicable musical property placed in service during the taxable year, and

(ii) is otherwise properly chargeable to capital account,

shall be amortized ratably over the 5-year period beginning with the month in which the property was placed in service. The preceding sentence shall not apply to any expense which, without regard to this paragraph, would not be allowable as a deduction.

(B) EXCLUSIVE METHOD.—Except as provided in this paragraph, no depreciation or amortization deduction shall be allowed with respect to any expense to which subparagraph (A) applies.

(C) APPLICABLE MUSICAL PROPERTY.—For purposes of this paragraph—

(i) IN GENERAL.—The term "applicable musical property" means any musical composition (including any accompanying words), or any copyright with respect to a musical composition, which is property to which this subsection applies without regard to this paragraph.

(ii) EXCEPTIONS.—Such term shall not include any property—

(I) with respect to which expenses are treated as qualified creative expenses to which section 263A(h) applies,

(II) to which a simplified procedure established under section 263A(i)(2) applies, or

(III) which is an amortizable section 197 intangible (as defined in section 197(c)).

(D) ELECTION.—An election under this paragraph shall be made at such time and in such form as the Secretary may prescribe and shall apply to all applicable musical property placed in service during the taxable year for which the election applies.

(E) TERMINATION.—An election may not be made under this paragraph for any taxable year beginning after December 31, 2010.

Amendments

• 2007, Tax Technical Corrections Act of 2007 (P.L. 110-172)

P.L. 110-172, §11(a)(13):

Amended Code Sec. 167(g)(8)(C)(ii)(II) by striking "section 263A(j)(2)" and inserting "section 263A(i)(2)". **Effective** 12-29-2007.

• 2006, Tax Increase Prevention and Reconciliation Act of 2005 (P.L. 109-222)

P.L. 109-222, §207(a):

Amended Code Sec. 167(g) by adding at the end a new paragraph (8). **Effective** for expenses paid or incurred with respect to property placed in service in tax years beginning after 12-31-2005.

• 2004, American Jobs Creation Act of 2004 (P.L. 108-357)

P.L. 108-357, §242(a):

Amended Code Sec. 167(g) by adding at the end a new paragraph (7). **Effective** for property placed in service after 10-22-2004.

P.L. 108-357, §242(b):

Amended Code Sec. 167(g)(5) by redesignating subparagraphs (E) and (F) as subparagraphs (F) and (G), respectively, and inserting after subparagraph (D) a new subparagraph (E). **Effective** for property placed in service after 10-22-2004.

• 1997, Taxpayer Relief Act of 1997 (P.L. 105-34)

P.L. 105-34, §1086(a):

Amended Code Sec. 167(g) by adding at the end a new paragraph (6). **Effective** for property placed in service after 8-5-97.

• 1996, Small Business Job Protection Act of 1996 (P.L. 104-188)

P.L. 104-188, §1604(a):

Amended Code Sec. 167 by redesignating subsection (g) as subsection (h) and by inserting after subsection (f) a new subsection (g). For the **effective** date, see Act Sec. 1604(b)(1)-(3), below.

P.L. 104-188, §1604(b)(1)-(3) (as amended by P.L. 105-206, §6018(d)(1)-(2)), provides:

(b) EFFECTIVE DATE.—

(1) IN GENERAL.—The amendment made by subsection (a) shall apply to property placed in service after September 13, 1995.

(2) BINDING CONTRACTS.—The amendment made by subsection (a) shall not apply to any property produced or acquired by the taxpayer pursuant to a written contract which was binding on September 13, 1995, and at all times thereafter before such production or acquisition.

(3) UNDERPAYMENTS OF INCOME TAX.—No addition to tax shall be made under section 6662 of the Internal Revenue Code of 1986 as a result of the application of subsection (d) of that section (relating to substantial understatements of income tax) with respect to any underpayment of income tax for any taxable year ending before the date of the enactment of this Act, to the extent such underpayment was created or increased by the amendments made by subsection (a).

[Sec. 167(h)]

(h) AMORTIZATION OF GEOLOGICAL AND GEOPHYSICAL EXPENDITURES.—

(1) IN GENERAL.—Any geological and geophysical expenses paid or incurred in connection with the exploration for, or development of, oil or gas within the United States (as defined in section 638) shall be allowed as a deduction ratably over the 24-month period beginning on the date that such expense was paid or incurred.

(2) HALF-YEAR CONVENTION.—For purposes of paragraph (1), any payment paid or incurred during the taxable year shall be treated as paid or incurred on the mid-point of such taxable year.

(3) EXCLUSIVE METHOD.—Except as provided in this subsection, no depreciation or amortization deduction shall be allowed with respect to such payments.

(4) TREATMENT UPON ABANDONMENT.—If any property with respect to which geological and geophysical expenses are paid or incurred is retired or abandoned during the 24-month period described in paragraph (1), no deduction shall be allowed on account of such retirement or abandonment and the amortization deduction under this subsection shall continue with respect to such payment.

(5) SPECIAL RULE FOR MAJOR INTEGRATED OIL COMPANIES.—

(A) IN GENERAL.—In the case of a major integrated oil company, paragraphs (1) and (4) shall be applied by substituting "7-year" for "24 month".

(B) MAJOR INTEGRATED OIL COMPANY.—For purposes of this paragraph, the term "major integrated oil company" means, with respect to any taxable year, a producer of crude oil—

(i) which has an average daily worldwide production of crude oil of at least 500,000 barrels for the taxable year,

(ii) which had gross receipts in excess of $1,000,000,000 for its last taxable year ending during calendar year 2005, and

(iii) to which subsection (c) of section 613A does not apply by reason of paragraph (4) of section 613A(d), determined—

(I) by substituting "15 percent" for "5 percent" each place it occurs in paragraph (3) of section 613A(d), and

(II) without regard to whether subsection (c) of section 613A does not apply by reason of paragraph (2) of section 613A(d).

For purposes of clauses (i) and (ii), all persons treated as a single employer under subsections (a) and (b) of section 52 shall be treated as 1 person and, in case of a short taxable year, the rule under section 448(c)(3)(B) shall apply.

Amendments

• 2007, Energy Independence and Security Act of 2007 (P.L. 110-140)

P.L. 110-140, §1502(a):

Amended Code Sec. 167(h)(5)(A) by striking "5-year" and inserting "7-year". **Effective** for amounts paid or incurred after 12-19-2007.

• 2006, Tax Increase Prevention and Reconciliation Act of 2005 (P.L. 109-222)

P.L. 109-222, §503(a):

Amended Code Sec. 167(h) by adding at the end a new paragraph (5). **Effective** for amounts paid or incurred after 5-17-2006.

• 2005, Energy Tax Incentives Act of 2005 (P.L. 109-58)

P.L. 109-58, §1329(a):

Amended Code Sec. 167 by redesignating subsection (h) as subsection (i) and by inserting after subsection (g) a new subsection (h). **Effective** for amounts paid or incurred in tax years beginning after 8-8-2005.

[Sec. 167(i)]

(i) CROSS REFERENCES.—

(1) For additional rule applicable to depreciation of improvements in the case of mines, oil and gas wells, other natural deposits, and timber, see section 611.

(2) For amortization of goodwill and certain other intangibles, see section 197.

Amendments

• 2005, Energy Tax Incentives Act of 2005 (P.L. 109-58)

P.L. 109-58, §1329(a):

Amended Code Sec. 167 by redesignating subsection (h) as subsection (i). **Effective** for amounts paid or incurred in tax years beginning after 8-8-2005.

• 1996, Small Business Job Protection Act of 1996 (P.L. 104-188)

P.L. 104-188, §1604(a):

Amended Code Sec. 167 by redesignating subsection (g) as subsection (h). **Effective**, generally, for property placed in service after 9-13-95. For special rules, see Act Sec. 1604(b)(2)-(3) in the amendment notes following Code Sec. 167(g).

• 1993, Omnibus Budget Reconciliation Act of 1993 (P.L. 103-66)

P.L. 103-66, §13261(b)(1):

Amended Code Sec. 167 by redesignating subsection (f) as subsection (g). **Effective**, generally, for property acquired after 8-10-93. For special rules, see Act Sec. 13261(g)(2)-(3) in the amendment notes following Code Sec. 197.

P.L. 103-66, §13261(f)(1):

Amended Code Sec. 167(g) (as redesignated by Act Sec. 13261(b)(1)). **Effective**, generally, for property acquired after 8-10-93. For special rules, see Act Sec. 13261(g)(2)-(3) in the amendment notes following Code Sec. 197. Prior to amendment, Code Sec. 167(g) read as follows:

(g) DEPRECIATION OF IMPROVEMENTS IN THE CASE OF MINES, ETC.—

For additional rule applicable to depreciation of improvements in the case of mines, oil and gas wells, other natural deposits, and timber, see section 611.

• 1990, Omnibus Budget Reconciliation Act of 1990 (P.L. 101-508)

P.L. 101-508, §11812(a)(1):

Amended Code Sec. 167 by redesignating subsection (s) as subsection (f). **Effective**, generally, for property placed in service after 11-5-90. However, for exceptions see Act Sec. 11812(c)(2)-(3) in the amendment notes following Code Sec. 167(b).

• 1988, Technical and Miscellaneous Revenue Act of 1988 (P.L. 100-647)

P.L. 100-647, §1002(i):

Amended Code Sec. 167 by redesignating subsection (r) as subsection (s) and by inserting after subsection (q) new subsection (r). **Effective** as if included in the provision of P.L. 99-514 to which it relates.

• 1981, Economic Recovery Tax Act of 1981 (P.L. 97-34)

P.L. 97-34, §203(c)(1):

Amended Code Sec. 167 by striking out subsection (r) and redesignating subsection (s) as subsection (r). **Effective** 1-1-81 for tax years ending after such date. Prior to repeal, former Code Sec. 167(r) read as follows:

(r) RETIREMENT-REPLACEMENT-BETTERMENT METHOD.—In the case of railroad track used by a common carrier by railroad (including a railroad switching company or a terminal company), the term "reasonable allowance" as used in subsection (a) includes an allowance for such track computed under the retirement-replacement-betterment method.

P.L. 97-34, §203(c)(2)-(3), provides:

(2) CHANGE IN METHOD OF ACCOUNTING.—Sections 446 and 481 of the Internal Revenue Code of 1954 shall not apply to the change in the method of depreciation to comply with the provisions of this subsection.

(3) TRANSITIONAL RULE.—The adjusted basis of RRB property (as defined in section 168(g)(6) of such Code) as of December 31, 1980, shall be depreciated using a useful life of no less than 5 years and no more than 50 years and a method described in section 167(b) of such Code, including the method described in section 167(b)(2) of such Code, switching to the method described in section 167(b)(3) of such Code at a time to maximize the deduction.

• 1980 (P.L. 96-613)

P.L. 96-613, §2(a):

Redesignated former Code Sec. 167(r) as Code Sec. 167(s) and inserted a new Code Sec. 167(r). **Effective** 12-28-80, for tax years ending after 1953.

• 1978, Energy Tax Act of 1978 (P.L. 95-618)

P.L. 95-618, §301(d)(3):

Redesignated Code Sec. 167(p) as Code Sec. 167(r). **Effective** for property which is placed in service after 9-30-78.

• 1976, Tax Reform Act of 1976 (P.L. 94-455)

P.L. 94-455, §2124(c):

Redesignated former Code Sec. 167(n) as Code Sec. 167(p). **Effective** for that portion of the basis which is attributable to construction, reconstruction, or erection after 12-31-75, and before 1-1-81.

• 1971, Revenue Act of 1971 (P.L. 92-178)

P.L. 92-178, §109(a):

Redesignated Code Sec. 167(m) as Code Sec. 167(n).

• 1969, Tax Reform Act of 1969 (P.L. 91-172)

P.L. 91-172, §441(a):

Redesignated subsection (j) as (m). **Effective** for tax years ending after 7-24-69.

• 1966 (P.L. 89-800)

P.L. 89-800, §2:

Redesignated subsection (i) as (j). **Effective** for tax years ending after 10-9-66.

[Sec. 167(i)—Repealed]

Amendments

• 1978, Revenue Act of 1978 (P.L. 95-600)

P.L. 95-600, §312(c)(4):

Repealed Code Sec. 167(i). **Effective** for tax years ending after 12-31-78. Prior to repeal, Code Sec. 167(i) read as follows:

"(i) LIMITATION IN CASE OF PROPERTY CONSTRUCTED OR ACQUIRED DURING THE SUSPENSION PERIOD.—

"(1) IN GENERAL.—Under regulations prescribed by the Secretary, paragraphs (2), (3), and (4) of subsection (b) shall not apply in the case of real property which is not section 38 property (as defined in section 48(a)) if the physical construction, reconstruction, or erection of such property by any person begins during the suspension period, or begins, pursuant to an order placed during such period, before May 24, 1967.

Under regulations prescribed by the Secretary, rules similar to the rules provided by paragraphs (3), (4), (7), (8), (9), and (10) of section 48(h) shall be applied for purposes of the preceding sentence. In applying this paragraph to any property, there shall be taken into account only that portion of the basis which is properly attributable to construction, reconstruction, or erection before May 24, 1967.

"(2) EXCEPTION.—Paragraph (1) shall not apply to any item of real property selected by the taxpayer if the cost of such property (when added to the cost of all other items of real property selected by the taxpayer under this paragraph) does not exceed $50,000. Under regulations prescribed by the Secretary, rules similar to the rules provided by paragraph (2) of section 48(c) shall be applied for purposes of this paragraph.

"(3) SUSPENSION PERIOD.—For purposes of this subsection, the term `suspension period' means the period beginning on October 10, 1966, and ending on March 9, 1967."

• 1976, Tax Reform Act of 1976 (P.L. 94-455)

P.L. 94-455, §1906(b)(13)(A):

Amended 1954 Code by substituting "Secretary" for "Secretary or his delegate" each place it appeared. **Effective** 2-1-77.

• 1967 (P.L. 90-26)

P.L. 90-26, §1:

Amended Code Sec. 167(i)(3) by substituting "March 9, 1967" for "December 31, 1967". **Effective** for tax years ending after 3-9-67.

P.L. 90-26, §2(b):

Amended Code Sec. 167(i)(1). **Effective** for tax years ending after 3-9-67. Prior to amendment, Code Sec. 167(i)(1) read as follows:

"(1) In General.—Under regulations prescribed by the Secretary or his delegate, paragraphs (2), (3), and (4) of subsection (b) shall not apply in the case of real property which is not section 38 property (as defined in section 48(a)) if—

"(A) the physical construction, reconstruction, or erection of such property by any person begins during the suspension period, or

"(B) an order for such construction, reconstruction, or erection is placed by any person during the suspension period."

• 1966 (P.L. 89-800)

P.L. 89-800, §2:

Redesignated Code Sec. 167(i) as Sec. 167(j) and added new Code Sec. 167(i). **Effective** for tax years ending after 10-9-66.

[Sec. 167(j)—Stricken]

Amendments

• 1990, Omnibus Budget Reconciliation Act of 1990 (P.L. 101-508)

P.L. 101-508, §11812(a)(1)-(2):

Amended Code Sec. 167 by striking out subsection (j). **Effective**, generally, for property placed in service after 11-5-90. However, for exceptions see Act Sec. 11812(c)(2)-(3) below. Prior to being stricken, Code Sec. 167(j) read as follows:

(j) SPECIAL RULES FOR SECTION 1250 PROPERTY.—

(1) GENERAL RULE.—Except as provided in paragraphs (2) and (3), in the case of section 1250 property, subsection (b) shall not apply and the term "reasonable allowance" as used in subsection (a) shall include an allowance computed in accordance with regulations prescribed by the Secretary, under any of the following methods:

(A) the straight line method,

(B) the declining balance method, using a rate not exceeding 150 percent of the rate which would have been used had the annual allowance been computed under the method described in subparagraph (A), or

(C) any other consistent method productive of an annual allowance which, when added to all allowances for the period commencing with the taxpayer's use of the property and including the taxable year, does not, during the first two-thirds of the useful life of the property, exceed the total of such allowances which would have been used had such allowances been computed under the method described in subparagraph (B).

Nothing in this paragraph shall be construed to limit or reduce an allowance otherwise allowable under subsection (a) except where allowable solely by reason of paragraph (2), (3), or (4) of subsection (b).

(2) RESIDENTIAL RENTAL PROPERTY.—

(A) IN GENERAL.—Paragraph (1) of this subsection shall not apply, and subsection (b) shall apply in any taxable year, to a building or structure—

(i) which is residential rental property located within the United States or any of its possessions, or located within a foreign country if a method of depreciation for such property comparable to the method provided in subsection (b)(2) or (3) is provided by the laws of such country, and

(ii) the original use of which commences with the taxpayer.

In the case of residential rental property located within a foreign country, the original use of which commences with the taxpayer, if the allowance for depreciation provided under the laws of such country for such property is greater than that provided under paragraph (1) of this subsection, but less than that provided under subsection (b), the allowance for depreciation under subsection (b) shall be limited to the amount provided under the laws of such country.

(B) DEFINITION.—For purposes of subparagraph (A), a building or structure shall be considered to be residential rental property for any taxable year only if 80 percent or more of the gross rental income from such building or structure for such year is rental income from dwelling units (within the meaning of subsection (k)(3)(C)). For purposes of the preceding sentence, if any portion of such building or structure is occupied by the taxpayer, the gross rental income from such building or structure shall include the rental value of the portion so occupied.

(C) CHANGE IN METHOD OF DEPRECIATION.—Any change in the computation of the allowance for depreciation for any taxable year, permitted or required by reason of the application of subparagraph (A), shall not be considered a change in a method of accounting.

(3) PROPERTY CONSTRUCTED, ETC., BEFORE JULY 25, 1969.—Paragraph (1) of this subsection shall not apply, and subsection (b) shall apply, in the case of property—

(A) the construction, reconstruction, or erection of which was begun before July 25, 1969, or

(B) for which a written contract entered into before July 25, 1969, with respect to any part of the construction, reconstruction, or erection or for the permanent financing thereof, was on July 25, 1969, and at all times thereafter, binding on the taxpayer.

(4) USED SECTION 1250 PROPERTY.—Except as provided in paragraph (5), in the case of section 1250 property acquired after July 24, 1969, the original use of which does not commence with the taxpayer, the allowance for depreciation under this section shall be limited to an amount computed under—

(A) the straight line method, or

(B) any other method determined by the Secretary to result in a reasonable allowance under subsection (a), not including—

(i) any declining balance method,

(ii) the sum of the years-digits method, or

(iii) any other method allowable solely by reason of the application of subsection (b)(4) or paragraph (1)(C) of this subsection.

(5) USED RESIDENTIAL RENTAL PROPERTY.—In the case of section 1250 property which is residential rental property (as defined in paragraph (2)(B)) acquired after July 24, 1969, having a useful life of 20 years or more, the original use of which does not commence with the taxpayer, the allowance for depreciation under this section shall be limited to an amount computed under—

(A) the straight line method,

(B) the declining balance method, using a rate not exceeding 125 percent of the rate which would have been used had the annual allowance been computed under the method described in subparagraph (A), or

(C) any other method determined by the Secretary to result in a reasonable allowance under subsection (a), not including—

(i) the sum of the years-digits method,

(ii) any declining balance method using a rate in excess of the rate permitted under subparagraph (B), or

(iii) any other method allowable solely by reason of the application of subsection (b)(4) or paragraph (1)(C) of this subsection.

(6) SPECIAL RULES.—

(A) Under regulations prescribed by the Secretary, rules similar to the rules provided in paragraphs (5), (9), (10), and (13) of section 48(h) shall be applied for purposes of paragraphs (3), (4), and (5) of this subsection.

(B) For purposes of paragraphs (2), (4), and (5), if section 1250 property which is not property described in subsection (a) when its original use commences, becomes property described in subsection (a) after July 24, 1969, such property shall not be treated as property the original use of which commences with the taxpayer.

(C) Paragraphs (4) and (5) shall not apply in the case of section 1250 property acquired after July 24, 1969, pursuant to a written contract for the acquisition of such property or for the permanent financing thereof, which was, on July 24, 1969, and at all times thereafter, binding on the taxpayer.

P.L. 101-508, §11812(c)(2)-(3), provides:

(2) EXCEPTION.—The amendments made by this section shall not apply to any property to which section 168 of the Internal Revenue Code of 1986 does not apply by reason of subsection (f)(5) thereof.

(3) EXCEPTION FOR PREVIOUSLY GRANDFATHER [sic] EXPENDITURES.—The amendments made by this section shall not apply to rehabilitation expenditures described in section 252(f)(5) of the Tax Reform Act of 1986 (as added by section 1002(l)(31) of the Technical and Miscellaneous Revenue Act of 1988).

• 1976, Tax Reform Act of 1976 (P.L. 94-455)

P.L. 94-455, §1906(b)(13)(A):

Amended 1954 Code by substituting "Secretary" for "Secretary or his delegate" each place it appeared. **Effective** 2-1-77.

• 1969, Tax Reform Act of 1969 (P.L. 91-172)

P.L. 91-172, §521(a):

Added new subsection (j). **Effective** for tax years ending after 7-24-69.

[Sec. 167(k)—Stricken]

Amendments

• 1990, Omnibus Budget Reconciliation Act of 1990 (P.L. 101-508)

P.L. 101-508, §11812(a)(1)-(2):

Amended Code Sec. 167 by striking subsection (k). **Effective**, generally, for property placed in service after 11-5-90. However, for exceptions see Act Sec. 11812(c)(2)-(3) below. Prior to being stricken, Code Sec. 167(k) read as follows:

(k) DEPRECIATION OF EXPENDITURES TO REHABILITATE LOW-INCOME RENTAL HOUSING.—

(1) 60-MONTH RULE.—The taxpayer may elect, in accordance with regulations prescribed by the Secretary, to compute the depreciation deduction provided by subsection (a) attributable to rehabilitation expenditures incurred with respect to low-income rental housing after July 24, 1969, and before January 1, 1987, under the straight line method using a useful life of 60 months and no salvage value. Such method shall be in lieu of any other method of computing the depreciation deduction under subsection (a), and in lieu of any deduction for amortization, for such expenditures.

(2) LIMITATIONS.—

(A) Except as provided in subparagraph (B), the aggregate amount of rehabilitation expenditures paid or incurred by the taxpayer with respect to any dwelling unit in any low-income rental housing which may be taken into account under paragraph (1) shall not exceed $20,000.

(B) The aggregate amount of rehabilitation expenditures paid or incurred by the taxpayer with respect to any dwelling unit in any low-income rental housing which may be taken into account under paragraph (1) may exceed $20,000, but shall not exceed $40,000, if the rehabilitation is conducted pursuant to a program certified by the Secretary of Housing and Urban Development, or his delegate, or by the government of a State or political subdivision of the United States and if:

(i) the certification of development costs is required;

(ii) the tenants occupy units in the property as their principal residence and the program provides for sale of the units to tenants demonstrating home ownership responsibility; and

(iii) the leasing and sale of such units are pursuant to a program in which the sum of the taxable income, if any, from leasing of each such unit, for the entire period of such leasing, and the amount realized from sale or other disposition of a unit, if sold, normally does not exceed the excess of the taxpayer's cost basis for such unit of property, before adjustment under section 1016 for deductions under section 167, over the net tax benefits realized by the taxpayer, consisting of the tax benefits from such deductions under section 167 minus the tax incurred on such taxable income from leasing, if any.

(C) Rehabilitation expenditures paid or incurred by the taxpayer in any taxable year with respect to any dwelling unit in any low-income rental housing shall be taken into account under paragraph (1) only if over a period of two consecutive years, including the taxable year, the aggregate amount of such expenditures exceeds $3,000.

(3) DEFINITIONS.—For purposes of this subsection—

(A) REHABILITATION EXPENDITURES.—The term "rehabilitation expenditures" means amounts chargeable to capital account and incurred for property or additions or improvements to property (or related facilities) with a useful life of 5 years or more, in connection with the rehabilitation of an existing building for low-income rental housing; but such term does not include the cost of acquisition of such building or any interest therein.

(B) LOW-INCOME RENTAL HOUSING.—The term "low-income rental housing" means any building the dwelling units in which are held for occupancy on a rental basis by families and individuals of low or moderate income, as determined by the Secretary in a manner consistent with the Leased Housing Program under section 8 of the United States Housing Act of 1937 pursuant to regulations prescribed under this subsection.

(C) DWELLING UNIT.—The term "dwelling unit" means a house or an apartment used to provide living accommodations in a building or structure, but does not include a unit in a hotel, motel, inn, or other establishment more than one-half of the units in which are used on a transient basis.

(D) REHABILITATION EXPENDITURES INCURRED.—Rehabilitation expenditures incurred pursuant to a binding contract entered into before January 1, 1987, and rehabilitation expenditures incurred with respect to low-income rental housing the rehabilitation of which has begun before January 1, 1987, shall be deemed incurred before January 1, 1987.

P.L. 101-508, §11812(c)(2)-(3), provides:

(2) EXCEPTION.—The amendments made by this section shall not apply to any property to which section 168 of the Internal Revenue Code of 1986 does not apply by reason of subsection (f)(5) thereof.

(3) EXCEPTION FOR PREVIOUSLY GRANDFATHER [sic] EXPENDITURES.—The amendments made by this section shall not apply to rehabilitation expenditures described in section 252(f)(5) of the Tax Reform Act of 1986 (as added by section 1002(l)(31) of the Technical and Miscellaneous Revenue Act of 1988).

• 1984, Deficit Reduction Act of 1984 (P.L. 98-369)

P.L. 98-369, §1064:

Amended Code Sec. 167(k) by striking out "January 1, 1984" each place it appeared and inserting in lieu thereof "January 1, 1987". **Effective** 7-18-84.

• 1981, Economic Recovery Tax Act of 1981 (P.L. 97-34)

P.L. 97-34, §264(a):

Amended Code Sec. 167(k)(2) by striking out "The" in subparagraph (A) and inserting in lieu thereof "Except as provided in subparagraph (B), the"; by redesignating subparagraph (B) as subparagraph (C); and by inserting after subparagraph (A) new subparagraph (B). **Effective** for rehabilitation expenditures incurred after 12-31-80.

• 1980 (P.L. 96-541)

P.L. 96-541, §3:

Amended Code Sec. 167(k) by striking out "January 1, 1982" each place it appears and inserting "January 1, 1984" in its place. **Effective** 12-17-80.

• 1978, Revenue Act of 1978 (P.L. 95-600)

P.L. 95-600, §367:

Amended Code Sec. 167(k) by striking out "January 1, 1979" each place it appeared and inserting in lieu thereof "January 1, 1982". **Effective** 11-7-78.

• 1977 (P.L. 95-171)

P.L. 95-171, §4(a):

Amended Code Sec. 167(k) by substituting "January 1, 1979" for "January 1, 1978" in paragraphs (1) and (3)(D).

• 1976, Tax Reform Act of 1976 (P.L. 94-455)

P.L. 94-455, §203(a):

Substituted "January 1, 1978" for "January 1, 1976" in Code Sec. 167(k)(1), struck out "the policies of the Housing and Urban Development Act of 1968" and substituted "the Leased Housing Program under section 8 of the United States Housing Act of 1937" in Code Sec. 167(k)(3)(B), and added Code Sec. 167(k)(3)(D). **Effective** for expenditures paid or incurred after 12-31-75. Substituted "$20,000" for "$15,000" in Code Sec. 167(k)(2)(A). **Effective** for expenditures incurred after 12-31-75.

P.L. 94-455, §1906(b)(13)(A):

Amended 1954 Code by substituting "Secretary" for "Secretary or his delegate" each place it appeared. **Effective** 2-1-77.

• 1975 (P.L. 93-625)

P.L. 93-625, §3(c):

Amended Code Sec. 167(k)(1) by substituting "January 1, 1976" for "January 1, 1975". **Effective** 1-3-75.

• 1969, Tax Reform Act of 1969 (P.L. 91-172)

P.L. 91-172, §521(a):

Added new subsection (k). **Effective** for tax years ending after 7-24-69.

[Sec. 167(l)—Stricken]

Amendments

• 1990, Omnibus Budget Reconciliation Act of 1990 (P.L. 101-508)

P.L. 101-508, §11812(a)(1)-(2):

Amended Code Sec. 167 by striking subsection (l). **Effective**, generally, for property placed in service after 11-5-90. However, for exceptions see Act Sec. 11812(c)(2)-(3) below. Prior to being stricken, Code Sec. 167(l) read as follows:

(l) REASONABLE ALLOWANCE IN CASE OF PROPERTY OF CERTAIN UTILITIES.—

(1) PRE-1970 PUBLIC UTILITY PROPERTY.—

(A) IN GENERAL.—In the case of any pre-1970 public utility property, the term "reasonable allowance" as used in subsection (a) means an allowance computed under—

(i) a subsection (l) method, or

(ii) the applicable 1968 method for such property.

Except as provided in subparagraph (B), clause (ii) shall apply only if the taxpayer uses a normalization method of accounting.

(B) FLOW-THROUGH METHOD OF ACCOUNTING IN CERTAIN CASES.—In the case of any pre-1970 public utility property, the taxpayer may use the applicable 1968 method for such property if—

(i) the taxpayer used a flow-through method of accounting for such property for its July 1969 accounting period, or

(ii) the first accounting period with respect to such property is after the July 1969 accounting period, and the taxpayer used a flow-through method of accounting for its July 1969 accounting period for the property on the basis of which the applicable 1968 method for the property in question is established.

(2) POST-1969 PUBLIC UTILITY PROPERTY.—In the case of any post-1969 public utility property, the term "reasonable allowance" as used in subsection (a) means an allowance computed under—

(A) a subsection (l) method,

(B) a method otherwise allowable under this section if the taxpayer uses a normalization method of accounting, or

(C) the applicable 1968 method, if, with respect to its pre-1970 public utility property of the same (or similar) kind most recently placed in service, the taxpayer used a flow-through method of accounting for its July 1969 accounting period.

(3) DEFINITIONS.—For purposes of this subsection—

(A) PUBLIC UTILITY PROPERTY.—The term "public utility property" means property used predominantly in the trade or business of the furnishing or sale of—

(i) electrical energy, water, or sewage disposal services,

(ii) gas or steam through a local distribution system,

(iii) telephone services, or other communication services if furnished or sold by the Communications Satellite Corporation for purposes authorized by the Communications Satellite Act of 1962 (47 U. S. C. 701), or

(iv) transportation of gas or steam by pipeline,

if the rates for such furnishing or sale, as the case may be, have been established or approved by a State or political subdivision thereof, by any agency or instrumentality of the United States, or by a public service or public utility commission or other similar body of any State or political subdivision thereof.

(B) PRE-1970 PUBLIC UTILITY PROPERTY.—The term "pre-1970 public utility property" means property which was public utility property in the hands of any person at any time before January 1, 1970.

(C) POST-1969 PUBLIC UTILITY PROPERTY.—The term "post-1969 public utility property" means any public utility property which is not pre-1970 public utility property and which is placed in service before January 1, 1981.

(D) APPLICABLE 1968 METHOD.—The term "applicable 1968 method" means, with respect to any public utility property—

(i) the method of depreciation used on a return with respect to such property for the latest taxable year for which a return was filed before August 1, 1969,

(ii) if clause (i) does not apply, the method used by the taxpayer on a return for the latest taxable year for which a return was filed before August 1, 1969, with respect to its public utility property of the same kind (or if there is no property of the same kind, property of the most similar kind) most recently placed in service, or

(iii) if neither clause (i) nor (ii) applies, a subsection (l) method.

In the case of any section 1250 property to which subsection (j) applies, the term "applicable 1968 method" means the method permitted under subsection (j) which is most nearly comparable to the applicable 1968 method determined under the preceding sentence.

(E) APPLICABLE 1968 METHOD IN CERTAIN CASES.—If the taxpayer evidenced the intent to use a method of depreciation (other than its applicable 1968 method or a subsection (1) method) with respect to any public utility property in a timely application for change of accounting method filed before August 1, 1969, or in the computation of its tax expense for purposes of reflecting operating results in its regulated books of account for its July 1969 accounting period, such other method shall be deemed to be its applicable 1968 method with respect to such property and public utility property of the same (or similar) kind subsequently placed in service.

(F) SUBSECTION (1) METHOD.—The term "subsection (1) method" means any method determined by the Secretary to result in a reasonable allowance under subsection (a), other than (i) a declining balance method, (ii) the sum of the years-digits method, or (iii) any other method allowable solely by reason of the application of subsection (b)(4) or (j)(1)(C).

(G) NORMALIZATION METHOD OF ACCOUNTING.—In order to use a normalization method of accounting with respect to any public utility property—

(i) the taxpayer must use the same method of depreciation to compute both its tax expense and its depreciation expense for purposes of establishing its cost of service for ratemaking purposes and for reflecting operating results in its regulated books of account, and

(ii) if, to compute its allowance for depreciation under this section, it uses a method of depreciation other than the method it used for the purposes described in clause (i), the taxpayer must make adjustments to a reserve to reflect the deferral of taxes resulting from the use of such different methods of depreciation.

For purposes of this subparagraph, rules similar to the rules of section 168(i)(9)(B) shall apply.

(H) FLOW-THROUGH METHOD OF ACCOUNTING.—The taxpayer used a "flow-through method of accounting" with respect to any public utility property if it used the same method of depreciation (other than a subsection (1) method) to compute its allowance for depreciation under this section and to compute its tax expense for purposes of reflecting operating results in its regulated books of account.

(I) JULY 1969 ACCOUNTING PERIOD.—The term "July 1969 accounting period" means the taxpayer's latest accounting period ending before August 1, 1969, for which it computed its tax expense for purposes of reflecting operating results in its regulated books of account.

For purposes of this paragraph, different declining balance rates shall be treated as different methods of depreciation.

(4) SPECIAL RULES AS TO FLOW-THROUGH METHOD.—

(A) ELECTION AS TO NEW PROPERTY REPRESENTING GROWTH IN CAPACITY.—If the taxpayer makes an election under this subparagraph before June 29, 1970 in the manner prescribed by the Secretary, in the case of taxable years beginning after December 31, 1970, paragraph (2)(C) shall not apply with respect to any post-1969 public utility property, to the extent that such property constitutes property which increases the productive or operational capacity of the taxpayer with respect to the goods or services described in paragraph (3)(A) and does not represent the replacement of existing capacity.

(B) CERTAIN PENDING APPLICATIONS FOR CHANGES IN METHOD.—In applying paragraph (1)(B), the taxpayer shall be deemed to have used a flow-through method of accounting for its July 1969 accounting period with respect to any pre-1970 public utility property for which it filed a timely application for change of accounting method before August 1, 1969, if with respect to public utility property of the same (or similar) kind most recently placed in service, it used a flow-through method of accounting for its July 1969 accounting period.

(5) REORGANIZATIONS, ASSETS ACQUISITIONS, ETC.—If by reason of a corporate reorganization, by reason of any other acquisition of the assets of one taxpayer by another taxpayer, by reason of the fact that any trade or business of the taxpayer is subject to ratemaking by more than one body, or by reason of other circumstances, the application of any provisions of this subsection to any public utility property does not carry out the purposes of this subsection, the Secretary shall provide by regulations for the application of such provisions in a manner consistent with the purposes of this subsection.

P.L. 101-508, §11812(c)(2)-(3), provides:

(2) EXCEPTION.—The amendments made by this section shall not apply to any property to which section 168 of the Internal Revenue Code of 1986 does not apply by reason of subsection (f)(5) thereof.

(3) EXCEPTION FOR PREVIOUSLY GRANDFATHER [sic] EXPENDITURES.—The amendments made by this section shall not apply to rehabilitation expenditures described in section 252(f)(5) of the Tax Reform Act of 1986 (as added by section 1002(l)(31) of the Technical and Miscellaneous Revenue Act of 1988).

• 1988, Technical and Miscellaneous Revenue Act of 1988 (P.L. 100-647)

P.L. 100-647, §1002(a)(22):

Amended Code Sec. 167(l)(3)(G) by striking out "section 168(e)(3)(C)" in the last sentence and inserting in lieu thereof "section 168(i)(9)(B)". **Effective** as if included in the provision of P.L. 99-514 to which it relates.

• 1983, Surface Transportation Act of 1982 (P.L. 97-424)

P.L. 97-424, §541(a)(2):

Amended Code Sec. 167(l)(3)(G) by adding the sentence at the end thereof. **Effective** for tax years beginning after 12-31-78. See, however, the amendment note for Act Sec. 541(c)(2)-(5) following Code Sec. 46(f) for special rules.

• 1981, Economic Recovery Tax Act of 1981 (P.L. 97-34)

P.L. 97-34, §209(d)(3):

Amended Code Sec. 167(l)(3)(C) by inserting "and which is placed in service before January 1, 1981" immediately before the period at the end thereof. **Effective** 8-13-81.

• 1976, Tax Reform Act of 1976 (P.L. 94-455)

P.L. 94-455, §1901(a)(27):

Amended Code Sec. 167(l) by substituting "before June 29, 1970," for "within 180 days after the date of the enactment of this subparagraph" in Code Sec. 167(l)(4)(A). **Effective** for tax years beginning after 12-31-76.

P.L. 94-455, §1906(b)(13)(A):

Amended 1954 Code by substituting "Secretary" for "Secretary or his delegate" each place it appeared. **Effective** 2-1-77.

• 1969, Tax Reform Act of 1969 (P.L. 91-172)

P.L. 91-172, §441(a):

Added new subsection (l). **Effective** for all tax years for which a return has not been filed before 8-1-69.

[Sec. 167(m)—Stricken]

Amendments

• 1990, Omnibus Budget Reconciliation Act of 1990 (P.L. 101-508)

P.L. 101-508, §11812(a)(1)-(2):

Amended Code Sec. 167 by striking subsection (m). **Effective**, generally, for property placed in service after the date of the enactment of this Act. However, for exceptions see Act Sec. 11812(c)(2)-(3) below. Prior to being stricken, Code Sec. 167(m) read as follows:

(m) CLASS LIVES.—

(1) IN GENERAL.—In the case of a taxpayer who has made an election under this subsection for the taxable year, the term "reasonable allowance" as used in subsection (a) means (with respect to property which is placed in service during the taxable year and which is included in any class for which a class life has been prescribed) only an allowance based on the class life prescribed by the Secretary which reasonably reflects the anticipated useful life of that class of property to the industry or other group. The allowance so prescribed may (under regulations prescribed by the Secretary) permit a variance from any class life by not more than 20 percent (rounded to the nearest half year) of such life.

(2) CERTAIN FIRST-YEAR CONVENTIONS NOT PERMITTED.—No convention with respect to the time at which assets are deemed placed in service shall be permitted under this section which generally would provide greater depreciation allowances during the taxable year in which the assets are placed in service than would be permitted if all assets were placed in service ratably throughout the year and if depreciation allowances were computed without regard to any convention.

(3) MAKING OF ELECTION.—An election under this subsection for any taxable year shall be made at such time, in such manner, and subject to such conditions as may be prescribed by the Secretary by regulations.

(4) TERMINATION.—This subsection shall not apply with respect to any property to which section 168 applies.

P.L. 101-508, §11812(c)(2)-(3), provides:

(2) EXCEPTION.—The amendments made by this section shall not apply to any property to which section 168 of the Internal Revenue Code of 1986 does not apply by reason of subsection (f)(5) thereof.

(3) EXCEPTION FOR PREVIOUSLY GRANDFATHER [sic] EXPENDITURES.—The amendments made by this section shall not apply to rehabilitation expenditures described in section 252(f)(5) of the Tax Reform Act of 1986 (as added by section 1002(l)(31) of the Technical and Miscellaneous Revenue Act of 1988).

• 1986, Tax Reform Act of 1986 (P.L. 99-514)

P.L. 99-514, §201(d)(1):

Amended Code Sec. 167(m)(4). **Effective** for property placed in service after 12-31-86, in tax years ending after such date. Prior to amendment, Code Sec. 167(m)(4) read as follows:

(4) TERMINATION.—This subsection shall not apply with respect to recovery property (within the meaning of section 168) placed in service after December 31, 1980.

P.L. 99-514, §203(a)(2), provides:

(b) ELECTION TO HAVE AMENDMENTS MADE BY SECTION 201 APPLY.—A taxpayer may elect (at such time and in such manner as the Secretary of the Treasury or his delegate may prescribe) to have the amendments made by section 201 apply to any property placed in service after July 31, 1986, and before January 1, 1987.

See also the special and transition rules provided by Act Secs. 203-204 in the amendment notes following Code Sec. 168.

• 1981, Economic Recovery Tax Act of 1981 (P.L. 97-34)

P.L. 97-34, §203(b):

Amended Code Sec. 167(m) by adding at the end thereof new paragraph (4). **Effective** for property placed in service after 12-31-80, in tax years ending after such date.

• 1976, Tax Reform Act of 1976 (P.L. 94-455)

P.L. 94-455, §1906(b)(13)(A):

Amended 1954 Code by substituting "Secretary" for "Secretary or his delegate" each place it appeared. **Effective** 2-1-77.

• 1975 (P.L. 93-625)

P.L. 93-625, §5, provides:

"SEC. 5. APPLICATION OF CLASS LIFE SYSTEM TO REAL PROPERTY.

"(a) General Rule.—In the case of buildings and other items of section 1250 property (within the meaning of section 1250(c) of the Internal Revenue Code of 1954) placed in service before the effective date of the class lives first prescribed by the Secretary of the Treasury or his delegate under section 167(m) of such Code for the class in which such property falls, if an election under such section 167(m) applies to the taxpayer for the taxable year in which such property is placed in service, the taxpayer may, in accordance with regulations prescribed by the Secretary of the Treasury or his delegate, elect to determine the useful life of such property—

"(1) under Revenue Procedure 62-21 (as amended and supplemented) as in effect on December 31, 1970, or

"(2) on the facts and circumstances.

"(b) Repeal of Prior Transitional Rule.—Paragraph (1) of section 109(e) of the Revenue Act of 1971 (Public Law 92-178) is hereby repealed."

• 1971, Revenue Act of 1971 (P.L. 92-178)

P.L. 92-178, §109(a):

Added new Code Sec. 167(m) and redesignated former Code Sec. 167(m) as new Code Sec. 167(n). **Effective** for property placed in service after 12-31-70.

P.L. 92-178, §109(e), prior to repeal by P.L. 93-625, provides:

"(e) Transitional Rules.—

"(1) Real property.—In the case of buildings and other items of section 1250 property for which a separate guideline life is prescribed in Revenue Procedure 62-21 (as amended and supplemented), the class lives first prescribed by the Secretary of the Treasury or his delegate under section 167(m) of the Internal Revenue Code of 1954 shall be the same as the guideline lives for such property in effect on December 31, 1970. Any such property which is placed in service by the taxpayer during the period beginning on January 1, 1971, and ending on December 31, 1973 (or such earlier date on which a class life subsequently prescribed by the Secretary of the Treasury or his delegate under such section becomes effective for such property) may, in accordance with regulations prescribed by the Secretary of the Treasury or his delegate, be excluded by the taxpayer from an election under such section if a life for such property shorter than the class life prescribed in accordance with the preceding sentence is justified under Revenue Procedure 62-21 (as amended and supplemented).

"(2) Subsidiary assets.—If a significant portion of a class of property first prescribed by the Secretary of the Treasury or his delegate under section 167(m) of the Internal Revenue Code of 1954 consists of subsidiary assets, all such subsidiary assets in such class placed in service by the taxpayer during the period beginning on January 1, 1971, and ending on December 31, 1973 (or such earlier date on which a class which includes such subsidiary assets subsequently prescribed by the Secretary of the Treasury or his delegate under such section becomes effective), may, in accordance with regulations prescribed by the Secretary of the Treasury or his delegate, be excluded by the taxpayer from an election under such section."

[Sec. 167(n)—Repealed]

Amendments

• 1981, Economic Recovery Tax Act of 1981 (P.L. 97-34)

P.L. 97-34, §212(d)(1):

Repealed Code Sec. 167(n). **Effective** for expenditures incurred after 12-31-81, in tax years ending after such date.

P.L. 97-34, §212(e)(2), as amended by P.L. 97-448, §102(f)(1), provides:

(2) TRANSITIONAL RULE.—The amendments made by this section shall not apply with respect to any rehabilitation of a building if—

(A) the physical work on such rehabilitation began before January 1, 1982, and

(B) such building does not meet the requirements of paragraph (1) of section 48(g) of the Internal Revenue Code of 1954 (as amended by this Act).

Prior to repeal, Code Sec. 167(n) read as follows:

(n) STRAIGHT LINE METHOD IN CERTAIN CASES.—

(1) IN GENERAL.—In the case of any property in whole or in part constructed, reconstructed, erected, or used on a site which was, on or after June 30, 1976, occupied by a certified historic structure (or by any structure in a registered historic district) which is demolished or substantially altered after such date—

(A) subsections (b), (j), (k), and (l) shall not apply, and

(B) the term "reasonable allowance" as used in subsection (a) means only an allowance computed under the straight line method.

The preceding sentence shall not apply if the last substantial alteration of the structure is a certified rehabilitation.

(2) EXCEPTIONS.—The limitations imposed by this subsection shall not apply—

(A) to personal property, and

(B) in the case of demolition or substantial alteration of a structure located in a registered historic district, if—

(i) such structure was not a certified historic structure,

(ii) the Secretary of the Interior certified to the Secretary that such structure is not of historic significance to the district, and

(iii) if the certification referred to in clause (ii) occurs after the beginning of the demolition or substantial alteration of such structure, the taxpayer certifies to the Secretary that, at the beginning of such demolition or substantial alteration, he in good faith was not aware of the requirements of clause (ii).

(3) DEFINITIONS.—For purposes of this subsection, the terms "certified historic structure", "registered historic district", and "certified rehabilitation" have the respective meanings given such terms by section 191(d).

(4) APPLICATION OF SUBSECTION.—This subsection shall apply to that portion of the basis which is attributable to construction, reconstruction, or erection after December 31, 1975, and before January 1, 1984.

• 1980 (P.L. 96-541)

P.L. 96-541, §2(c):

Amended Code Sec 167(n) by adding a new paragraph (4). **Effective** 12-17-80.

• **1978, Revenue Act of 1978 (P.L. 95-600)**

P.L. 95-600, §701(f)(4):

Amended Code Sec. 167(n). **Effective** as set forth in P.L. 95-600, §701(f)(8), below. Prior to amendment, Code Sec. 167(n), P.L. 95-600, read as follows:

"(n) STRAIGHT LINE METHOD IN CERTAIN CASES.—

(1) IN GENERAL.—In the case of any property in whole or in part constructed, reconstructed, erected, or used on a site which was, on or after June 30, 1976, occupied by a certified historic structure (as defined in section 191(d)(1)) which is demolished or substantially altered (other than by virtue of a certified rehabilitation as defined in section 191(d)(3)) after such date—

(A) subsections (b), (j), (k), and (l) shall not apply,

(B) the term "reasonable allowance" as used in subsection (a) shall mean only an allowance computed under the straight line method.

(2) EXCEPTION.—The limitations imposed by this subsection shall not apply to personal property."

P.L. 95-600, §701(f)(8), provides:

(8) EFFECTIVE DATE.—The amendments made by this subsection shall take effect as if included in the respective provisions of the Internal Revenue Code of 1954 to which such amendments relate, as such provisions were added to such Code, or amended, by section 2124 of the Tax Reform Act of 1976.

• **1976, Tax Reform Act of 1976 (P.L. 94-455)**

P.L. 94-455, §2124(c):

Redesignated former Code Sec. 167(n) to be Code Sec. 167(p) and added a new Code Sec. 167(n). **Effective** for that portion of the basis which is attributable to construction, reconstruction, or erection after 12-31-75, and before 1-1-81.

[Sec. 167(o)—Repealed]

Amendments

• **1981, Economic Recovery Tax Act of 1981 (P.L. 97-34)**

P.L. 97-34, §212(d)(1):

Repealed Code Sec. 167(o). **Effective** for expenditures incurred after 12-31-81, in tax years ending after such date.

P.L. 97-34, §212(e)(2), as amended by P.L. 97-448, §102(f)(1), provides:

(2) TRANSITIONAL RULE.—The amendments made by this section shall not apply with respect to any rehabilitation of a building if—

(A) the physical work on such rehabilitation began before January 1, 1982, and

(B) such building does not meet the requirements of paragraph (1) of section 48(g) of the Internal Revenue Code of 1954 (as amended by this Act).

Prior to repeal, Code Sec. 167(o) read as follows:

(o) SUBSTANTIALLY REHABILITATED HISTORIC PROPERTY.—

(1) GENERAL RULE.—Pursuant to regulations prescribed by the Secretary, the taxpayer may elect to compute the depreciation deduction attributable to substantially rehabilitated historic property (other than property with respect to which an amortization deduction has been allowed to the taxpayer under section 191) as though the original use of such property commenced with him. The election shall be effective with respect to the taxable year referred to in paragraph (2) and all succeeding taxable years.

(2) SUBSTANTIALLY REHABILITATED PROPERTY.—For purposes of paragraph (1), the term "substantially rehabilitated historic property" means any certified historic structure (as defined in section 191(d)(1)) with respect to which the additions to capital account for any certified rehabilitation (as defined in section 191(d)(4)) during the 24-month period ending on the last day of any taxable year, reduced by any amounts allowed or allowable as depreciation or amortization with respect thereto, exceeds the greater of—

(A) the adjusted basis of such property, or

(B) $5,000.

The adjusted basis of the property shall be determined as of the beginning of the first day of such 24-month period, or of the holding period of the property (within the meaning of section 1250(e)), whichever is later.

(3) APPLICATION OF SUBSECTION.—This subsection shall apply with respect to additions to capital account occurring after June 30, 1976, and before January 1, 1984.

• **1980 (P.L. 96-541)**

P.L. 96-541, §2(d):

Amended Code Sec. 167(o) by adding a new paragraph (3). **Effective** 12-17-80.

• **1978, Revenue Act of 1978 (P.L. 95-600)**

P.L. 95-600, §701(f)(6)(A):

Amended Code Sec. 167(o)(1) by inserting "(other than property with respect to which an amortization deduction has been allowed to the taxpayer under section 191)" after "substantially rehabilitated historic property". **Effective** as set forth in Act Sec. 701(f)(8), below.

P.L. 95-600, §701(f)(6)(B):

Amended Code Sec. 167(o)(2) by striking out "section 191(d)(3)" and inserting in lieu thereof "section 191(d)(4)". **Effective** as set forth in Act Sec. 701(f)(8), below.

P.L. 95-600, §701(f)(8), provides:

(8) EFFECTIVE DATE.—The amendments made by this subsection shall take effect as if included in the respective provisions of the Internal Revenue Code of 1954 to which such amendments relate, as such provisions were added to such Code, or amended, by section 2124 of the Tax Reform Act of 1976.

• **1976, Tax Reform Act of 1976 (P.L. 94-455)**

P.L. 94-455, §2124(d):

Added Code Sec. 167(o). **Effective** for additions to capital account occurring after 6-30-76, and before 7-1-81.

[Sec. 167(p)—Stricken]

Amendments

• **1990, Omnibus Budget Reconciliation Act of 1990 (P.L. 101-508)**

P.L. 101-508, §11812(a)(1)-(2):

Amended Code Sec. 167 by striking subsection (p). **Effective**, generally, for property placed in service after 11-5-90. However, for exceptions see Act Sec. 11812(c)(2)-(3) below. Prior to being stricken, Code Sec. 167(p) read as follows:

(p) STRAIGHT LINE METHOD FOR BOILERS FUELED BY OIL OR GAS.—In the case of any boiler which, by reason of section 48(a)(10), is not section 38 property—

(1) subsections (b), (j), and (l) shall not apply, and

(2) the term "reasonable allowance" as used in subsection (a) shall mean only an allowance computed under the straight line method using a useful life equal to the class life prescribed by the Secretary under subsection (m) which is applicable to such property (determined without regard to the last sentence of subsection (m)(1)).

P.L. 101-508, §11812(c)(2)-(3), provides:

(2) EXCEPTION.—The amendments made by this section shall not apply to any property to which section 168 of the Internal Revenue Code of 1986 does not apply by reason of subsection (f)(5) thereof.

(3) EXCEPTION FOR PREVIOUSLY GRANDFATHER [sic] EXPENDITURES.—The amendments made by this section shall not apply to rehabilitation expenditures described in section 252(f)(5) of the Tax Reform Act of 1986 (as added by section 1002(l)(31) of the Technical and Miscellaneous Revenue Act of 1988).

• **1978, Energy Tax Act of 1978 (P.L. 95-618)**

P.L. 95-618, §301(d)(3):

Redesignated Code Sec. 167(p) as Code Sec. 167(r), and inserted a new Code Sec. 167(p). **Effective** as set forth in Act Sec. 301(d)(4), below.

P.L. 95-618, §301(d)(4), provides:

(4) EFFECTIVE DATE.—

(A) IN GENERAL.—The amendments made by this subsection shall apply to property which is placed in service after September 30, 1978.

(B) BINDING CONTRACTS.—The amendments made by this subsection shall not apply to property which is constructed, reconstructed, erected, or acquired pursuant to a contract which, on October 1, 1978, and at all times thereafter, was binding on the taxpayer.

[Sec. 167(q)—Stricken]

Amendments

• 1990, Omnibus Budget Reconciliation Act of 1990 (P.L. 101-508)

P.L. 101-508, §11812(a)(1)-(2):

Amended Code Sec. 167 by striking subsection (q). **Effective**, generally, for property placed in service after 11-5-90. However, for exceptions see Act Sec. 11812(c)(2)-(3) below. Prior to being stricken, Code Sec. 167(q) read as follows:

(q) RETIREMENT OR REPLACEMENT OF CERTAIN BOILERS, ETC., FUELED BY OIL OR GAS.—

(1) IN GENERAL.—If—

(A) a boiler or other combustor was in use on October 1, 1978, and as of such date the principal fuel for such combustor was petroleum or petroleum products (including natural gas), and

(B) the taxpayer establishes to the satisfaction of the Secretary that such combustor will be retired or replaced on or before the date specified by the taxpayer,

then for the period beginning with the taxable year in which subparagraph (B) is satisfied, the term "reasonable allowance" as used in subsection (a) includes an allowance under the straight line method using a useful life equal to the period ending with the date established under subparagraph (B).

(2) INTEREST.—If the retirement or replacement of any combustor does not occur on or before the date referred to in paragraph (1)(B)—

(A) this subsection shall cease to apply with respect to such combustor as of such date, and

(B) interest at the underpayment rate established under section 6621 on the amount of the tax benefit arising from the application of this subsection with respect to such combustor shall be due and payable for the period during which such tax benefit was available to the taxpayer and ending on the date referred to in paragraph (1)(B).

P.L. 101-508, §11812(c)(2)-(3), provides:

(2) EXCEPTION.—The amendments made by this section shall not apply to any property to which section 168 of the Internal Revenue Code of 1986 does not apply by reason of subsection (f)(5) thereof.

(3) EXCEPTION FOR PREVIOUSLY GRANDFATHER [sic] EXPENDITURES.—The amendments made by this section shall not apply to rehabilitation expenditures described in section 252(f)(5) of the Tax Reform Act of 1986 (as added by section 1002(l)(31) of the Technical and Miscellaneous Revenue Act of 1988).

• 1986, Tax Reform Act of 1986 (P.L. 99-514)

P.L. 99-514, §1511(c)(4):

Amended Code Sec. 167(q)(2)(B) by striking out "at the rate determined under section 6621" and inserting in lieu thereof "at the underpayment rate established under section 6621". **Effective** for purposes of determining interest for periods after 12-31-86.

• 1978, Energy Tax Act of 1978 (P.L. 95-618)

P.L. 95-618, §301(e):

Added Code Sec. 167(q). **Effective** for tax years ending after 11-10-78.

[Sec. 167(r)—Repealed]

Amendments

• 1989, Omnibus Budget Reconciliation Act of 1989 (P.L. 101-239)

P.L. 101-239, §7622(b)[d](1):

Repealed Code Sec. 167(r). **Effective**, generally, for transfers after 10-2-89. For a special rule see Act Sec. 7622(c)[e](2), below. Prior to repeal, Code Sec. 167(r) read as follows:

(r) TRADEMARK OR TRADE NAME EXPENDITURES NOT DEPRECIABLE.—

(1) IN GENERAL.—No depreciation deduction shall be allowable under this section (and no depreciation or amortization deduction shall be allowable under any other provision of this subtitle) with respect to any trademark or trade name expenditure.

(2) TRADEMARK OR TRADE NAME EXPENDITURE.—For purposes of this subsection, the term "trademark or trade name expenditure" means any expenditure which is directly connected with the acquisition, protection, expansion, registration (Federal, State, or foreign), or defense of a trademark or trade name.

P.L. 101-239, §7622(c)[e](2), provides:

(2) BINDING CONTRACT.—The amendments made by this section shall not apply to any transfer pursuant to a written binding contract in effect on October 2, 1989, and at all times thereafter before the transfer.

• 1988, Technical and Miscellaneous Revenue Act of 1988 (P.L. 100-647)

P.L. 100-647, §1002(i):

Amended Code Sec. 167 by redesignating subsection (r) as subsection (s) and by inserting after subsection (q) a new subsection (r).

[Sec. 168]

SEC. 168. ACCELERATED COST RECOVERY SYSTEM.

[Sec. 168(a)]

(a) GENERAL RULE.—Except as otherwise provided in this section, the depreciation deduction provided by section 167(a) for any tangible property shall be determined by using—

(1) the applicable depreciation method,

(2) the applicable recovery period, and

(3) the applicable convention.

[Sec. 168(b)]

(b) APPLICABLE DEPRECIATION METHOD.—For purposes of this section—

(1) IN GENERAL.—Except as provided in paragraphs (2) and (3), the applicable depreciation method is—

(A) the 200 percent declining balance method,

(B) switching to the straight line method for the 1st taxable year for which using the straight line method with respect to the adjusted basis as of the beginning of such year will yield a larger allowance.

(2) 150 PERCENT DECLINING BALANCE METHOD IN CERTAIN CASES.—Paragraph (1) shall be applied by substituting "150 percent" for "200 percent" in the case of—

(A) any 15-year or 20-year property not referred to in paragraph (3),

(B) any property used in a farming business (within the meaning of section 263A(e)(4)),

(C) any property (other than property described in paragraph (3)) which is a qualified smart electric meter or qualified smart electric grid system, or

(D) any property (other than property described in paragraph (3)) with respect to which the taxpayer elects under paragraph (5) to have the provisions of this paragraph apply.

(3) PROPERTY TO WHICH STRAIGHT LINE METHOD APPLIES.—The applicable depreciation method shall be the straight line method in the case of the following property:

(A) Nonresidential real property.

(B) Residential rental property.

(C) Any railroad grading or tunnel bore.

(D) Property with respect to which the taxpayer elects under paragraph (5) to have the provisions of this paragraph apply.

(E) Property described in subsection (e)(3)(D)(ii).

(F) Water utility property described in subsection (e)(5).

(G) Qualified leasehold improvement property described in subsection (e)(6).

(H) Qualified restaurant property described in subsection (e)(7).

(I) Qualified retail improvement property described in subsection (e)(8).

(4) SALVAGE VALUE TREATED AS ZERO.—Salvage value shall be treated as zero.

(5) ELECTION.—An election under paragraph (2)(C) or (3)(D) may be made with respect to 1 or more classes of property for any taxable year and once made with respect to any class shall apply to all property in such class placed in service during such taxable year. Such an election, once made, shall be irrevocable.

Amendments

• 2008, Tax Extenders and Alternative Minimum Tax Relief Act of 2008 (P.L. 110-343)

P.L. 110-343, Division C, §305(c)(3):

Amended Code Sec. 168(b)(3) by adding at the end a new subparagraph (I). **Effective** for property placed in service after 12-31-2008.

P.L. 110-343, Division B, §306(c):

Amended Code Sec. 168(b)(2) by striking "or" at the end of subparagraph (B), redesignating subparagraph (C) as subparagraph (D), and by inserting after subparagraph (B) a new subparagraph (C). **Effective** for property placed in service after 10-3-2008.

• 2004, American Jobs Creation Act of 2004 (P.L. 108-357)

P.L. 108-357, §211(d)(1):

Amended Code Sec. 168(b)(3) by adding at the end new subparagraphs (G) and (H). **Effective** for property placed in service after 10-22-2004.

P.L. 108-357, §211(d)(2):

Amended Code Sec. 168(b)(2)(A) by inserting before the comma "not referred to in paragraph (3)". **Effective** for property placed in service after 10-22-2004.

• 1998, Tax and Trade Relief Extension Act of 1998 (P.L. 105-277)

P.L. 105-277, §2022, provides:

SEC. 2022. DEPRECIATION STUDY.

The Secretary of the Treasury (or the Secretary's delegate)—

(1) shall conduct a comprehensive study of the recovery periods and depreciation methods under section 168 of the Internal Revenue Code of 1986, and

(2) not later than March 31, 2000, shall submit the results of such study, together with recommendations for determining such periods and methods in a more rational manner, to the Committee on Ways and Means of the House of Representatives and the Committee on Finance of the Senate.

• 1996, Small Business Job Protection Act of 1996 (P.L. 104-188)

P.L. 104-188, §1613(b)(1):

Amended Code Sec. 168(b)(3) by adding at the end a new subparagraph (F). **Effective** for property placed in service after 6-12-96, other than property placed in service pursuant to a binding contract in effect before 6-10-96, and at all times thereafter before the property is placed in service.

• 1989, Omnibus Budget Reconciliation Act of 1989 (P.L. 101-239)

P.L. 101-239, §7816(e)(1):

Amended Code Sec. 168(b)(5) by striking "paragraph (2)(B)" and inserting "paragraph (2)(C)". **Effective** as if included in the provision of P.L. 100-647 to which it relates.

P.L. 101-239, §7816(f):

Amended Code Sec. 168(b)(3) by redesignating subparagraph (D) as subparagraph (E). **Effective** as if included in the provision of P.L. 100-647 to which it relates.

• 1988, Technical and Miscellaneous Revenue Act of 1988 (P.L. 100-647)

P.L. 100-647, §1002(a)(11)(A):

Amended Code Sec. 168(b)(2). **Effective** as if included in the provision of P.L. 99-514 to which it relates. Prior to amendment, Code Sec. 168(b)(2) read as follows:

(2) 15-YEAR AND 20-YEAR PROPERTY.—In the case of 15-year and 20-year property, paragraph (1) shall be applied by substituting "150 percent" for "200 percent".

P.L. 100-647, §1002(a)(11)(B):

Amended Code Sec. 168(b)(5) by striking out "under paragraph (3)(C)" and inserting in lieu thereof "under paragraph (2)(B) or (3)(C)". **Effective** as if included in the provision of P.L. 99-514 to which it relates.

P.L. 100-647, §1002(i)(2)(B)(i):

Amended Code Sec. 168(b)(3) by redesignating subparagraph (C) as subparagraph (D) and by inserting after subparagraph (B) a new subparagraph (C). **Effective** as if included in the provision of P.L. 99-514 to which it relates.

P.L. 100-647, §1002(i)(2)(B)(ii):

Amended Code Sec. 168(b)(5) by striking out "(3)(C)" and inserting in lieu thereof "(3)(D)". **Effective** as if included in the provision of P.L. 99-514 to which it relates.

P.L. 100-647, §6028(a):

Amended Code Sec. 168(b)(2) by striking out "or" at the end of subparagraph (A), by redesignating subparagraph (B) as subparagraph (C), and by inserting after subparagraph (A) a new subparagraph (B). **Effective**, generally, for property placed in service after 12-31-88. However, for an exception, see Act Sec. 6028(b)(2) below.

P.L. 100-647, §6028(b)(2), provides:

(b)(2) EXCEPTION.—The amendments made by this section shall not apply to any property if such property is placed in service before July 1, 1989, and if such property—

(A) is constructed, reconstructed, or acquired by the taxpayer pursuant to a written contract which was binding on July 14, 1988, or

(B) is constructed or reconstructed by the taxpayer and such construction or reconstruction began by July 14, 1988.

P.L. 100-647, §6029(b):

Amended Code Sec. 168(b)(3) by adding at the end thereof a new subparagraph (D)[(E)]. **Effective** for property placed in service after 12-31-88.

[Sec. 168(c)]

(c) APPLICABLE RECOVERY PERIOD.—For purposes of this section, the applicable recovery period shall be determined in accordance with the following table:

In the case of:	*The applicable recovery period is:*
3-year property	3 years
5-year property	5 years
7-year property	7 years
10-year property	10 years
15-year property	15 years
20-year property	20 years
Water utility property	25 years
Residential rental property	27.5 years
Nonresidential real property	39 years
Any railroad grading or tunnel bore	50 years

Amendments

• 1998, IRS Restructuring and Reform Act of 1998 (P.L. 105-206)

P.L. 105-206, §6006(b)(1):

Amended Code Sec. 168(c) by striking paragraph (2). **Effective** as if included in the provision of P.L. 105-34 to which it relates [**effective** 8-5-97.—CCH]. Prior to being stricken, Code Sec. 168(c)(2) read as follows:

(2) PROPERTY FOR WHICH 150 PERCENT METHOD ELECTED.—In the case of property to which an election under subsection (b)(2)(C) applies, the applicable recovery period shall be determined under the table contained in subsection (g)(2)(C).

P.L. 105-206, §6006(b)(2):

Amended Code Sec. 168(c) by striking the portion of such subsection preceding the table in paragraph (1) and inserting new material. **Effective** as if included in the provision of P.L. 105-34 to which it relates [**effective** 8-5-97.—CCH]. Prior to amendment, the portion of Code Sec. 168(c) preceding the table read as follows:

(c) APPLICABLE RECOVERY PERIOD.—For purposes of this section—

(1) IN GENERAL.—Except as provided in paragraph (2), the applicable recovery period shall be determined in accordance with the following table:

• 1996, Small Business Job Protection Act of 1996 (P.L. 104-188)

P.L. 104-188, §1613(b)(2):

Amended Code Sec. 168(c)(1) by inserting a new item in the table after the item relating to 20-year property. **Effective** for property placed in service after 6-12-96, other than property placed in service pursuant to a binding contract in effect before 6-10-96, and at all times thereafter before the property is placed in service.

• 1993, Omnibus Budget Reconciliation Act of 1993 (P.L. 103-66)

P.L. 103-66, §13151(a):

Amended Code Sec. 168(c)(1) by striking the item relating to nonresidential real property and inserting a new item relating to nonresidential real property. **Effective**, generally, for property placed in service by the taxpayer on or after 5-13-93. For an exception, see Act Sec. 13151(b)(2) below. Prior to amendment, the item relating to nonresidential real property read as follows:

Nonresidential real property . . . . 31.5 years

P.L. 103-66, §13151(b)(2), provides:

(2) EXCEPTION.—The amendments made by this section shall not apply to property placed in service by the taxpayer before January 1, 1994, if—

(A) the taxpayer or a qualified person entered into a binding written contract to purchase or construct such property before May 13, 1993, or

(B) the construction of such property was commenced by or for the taxpayer or a qualified person before May 13, 1993.

For purposes of this paragraph, the term "qualified person" means any person who transfers his rights in such a contract or such property to the taxpayer but only if the property is not placed in service by such person before such rights are transferred to the taxpayer.

• 1989, Omnibus Budget Reconciliation Act of 1989 (P.L. 101-239)

P.L. 101-239, §7816(e)(2):

Amended Code Sec. 168(c)(2) by striking "subsection (b)(2)(B)" and inserting "subsection (b)(2)(C)". **Effective** as if included in the provision of P.L. 100-647 to which it relates.

• 1988, Technical and Miscellaneous Revenue Act of 1988 (P.L. 100-647)

P.L. 100-647, §1002(a)(11)(C):

Amended Code Sec. 168(c). **Effective** as if included in the provision of P.L. 99-514 to which it relates. Prior to amendment, Code Sec. 168(c) read as follows:

(c) APPLICABLE RECOVERY PERIOD.—For purposes of this section, the applicable recovery period shall be determined in accordance with the following table:

In the case of:	The applicable recovery period is:
3-year property	3 years
5-year property	5 years
7-year property	7 years
10-year property	10 years
15-year property	15 years
20-year property	20 years
Residential rental property	27.5 years
Nonresidential real property	31.5 years

P.L. 100-647, §1002(i)(2)(A):

Amended Code Sec. 168(c)(1) by adding at the end thereof a new item to the table. **Effective** as if included in the provision of P.L. 99-514 to which it relates.

[Sec. 168(d)]

(d) APPLICABLE CONVENTION.—For purposes of this section—

(1) IN GENERAL.—Except as otherwise provided in this subsection, the applicable convention is the half-year convention.

(2) REAL PROPERTY.—In the case of—

(A) nonresidential real property,

(B) residential rental property, and

(C) any railroad grading or tunnel bore,

the applicable convention is the mid-month convention.

(3) SPECIAL RULE WHERE SUBSTANTIAL PROPERTY PLACED IN SERVICE DURING LAST 3 MONTHS OF TAXABLE YEAR.—

(A) IN GENERAL.—Except as provided in regulations, if during any taxable year—

(i) the aggregate bases of property to which this section applies placed in service during the last 3 months of the taxable year, exceed

(ii) 40 percent of the aggregate bases of property to which this section applies placed in service during such taxable year,

the applicable convention for all property to which this section applies placed in service during such taxable year shall be the mid-quarter convention.

(B) CERTAIN PROPERTY NOT TAKEN INTO ACCOUNT.—For purposes of subparagraph (A), there shall not be taken into account—

(i) any nonresidential real property and residential rental property and railroad grading or tunnel bore, and

(ii) any other property placed in service and disposed of during the same taxable year.

(4) DEFINITIONS.—

(A) HALF-YEAR CONVENTION.—The half-year convention is a convention which treats all property placed in service during any taxable year (or disposed of during any taxable year) as placed in service (or disposed of) on the mid-point of such taxable year.

(B) MID-MONTH CONVENTION.—The mid-month convention is a convention which treats all property placed in service during any month (or disposed of during any month) as placed in service (or disposed of) on the mid-point of such month.

(C) MID-QUARTER CONVENTION.—The mid-quarter convention is a convention which treats all property placed in service during any quarter of a taxable year (or disposed of during any quarter of a taxable year) as placed in service (or disposed of) on the mid-point of such quarter.

Amendments

• 1988, Technical and Miscellaneous Revenue Act of 1988 (P.L. 100-647)

P.L. 100-647, §1002(a)(5):

Amended Code Sec. 168(d)(3)(A)(i) by striking out "and which are" after "applies". **Effective** as if included in the provision of P.L. 99-514 to which it relates. Prior to amendment, Code Sec. 168(d)(3)(A)(i) read as follows:

(i) the aggregate bases of property to which this section applies and which are placed in service during the last 3 months of the taxable year, exceed

P.L. 100-647, §1002(a)(23)(A):

Amended Code Sec. 168(d)(3)(B). **Effective**, generally, as if included in the provision of P.L. 99-514 to which it relates. However, for a special **effective** date, see Act Sec. 1002(a)(23)(B), below. Prior to amendment, Code Sec. 168(d)(3)(B) read as follows:

(B) CERTAIN REAL PROPERTY NOT TAKEN INTO ACCOUNT.—For purposes of subparagraph (A), nonresidential real property and residential rental property shall not be taken into account.

P.L. 100-647, §1002(a)(23)(B), provides:

(B) Clause (ii) of section 168(d)(3)(B) of the 1986 Code (as added by subparagraph (A)) shall apply to taxable years beginning after March 31, 1988, unless the taxpayer elects, at such time and in such manner as the Secretary of the Treasury or his delegate may prescribe, to have such clause apply to taxable years beginning on or before such date.

P.L. 100-647, §1002(i)(2)(D):

Amended Code Sec. 168(d)(2) by striking out "and" at the end of subparagraph (A), by inserting "and" at the end of subparagraph (B), and by inserting after subparagraph (B) a new subparagraph (C). **Effective** as if included in the provision of P.L. 99-514 to which it relates.

P.L. 100-647, §1002(i)(2)(E):

Amended Code Sec. 168(d)(3)(B)(i) by striking out "residential rental property" and inserting in lieu thereof "residential rental property and railroad grading or tunnel bore". **Effective** as if included in the provision of P.L. 99-514 to which it relates.

[Sec. 168(e)]

(e) CLASSIFICATION OF PROPERTY.—For purposes of this section—

(1) IN GENERAL.—Except as otherwise provided in this subsection, property shall be classified under the following table:

Property shall be treated as:	*If such property has a class life (in years) of:*
3-year property	4 or less
5-year property	More than 4 but less than 10
7-year property	10 or more but less than 16
10-year property	16 or more but less than 20
15-year property	20 or more but less than 25
20-year property	25 or more.

(2) RESIDENTIAL RENTAL OR NONRESIDENTIAL REAL PROPERTY.—

(A) RESIDENTIAL RENTAL PROPERTY.—

(i) RESIDENTIAL RENTAL PROPERTY.—The term "residential rental property" means any building or structure if 80 percent or more of the gross rental income from such building or structure for the taxable year is rental income from dwelling units.

(ii) DEFINITIONS.—For purposes of clause (i)—

(I) the term "dwelling unit" means a house or apartment used to provide living accommodations in a building or structure, but does not include a unit in a hotel, motel, or other establishment more than one-half of the units in which are used on a transient basis, and

(II) if any portion of the building or structure is occupied by the taxpayer, the gross rental income from such building or structure shall include the rental value of the portion so occupied.

(B) NONRESIDENTIAL REAL PROPERTY.—The term "nonresidential real property" means section 1250 property which is not—

(i) residential rental property, or

(ii) property with a class life of less than 27.5 years.

(3) CLASSIFICATION OF CERTAIN PROPERTY.—

(A) 3-YEAR PROPERTY.—The term "3-year property" includes—

(i) any race horse—

(I) which is placed in service before January 1, 2014, and

(II) which is placed in service after December 31, 2013, and which is more than 2 years old at the time such horse is placed in service by such purchaser,

(ii) any horse other than a race horse which is more than 12 years old at the time it is placed in service, and

(iii) any qualified rent-to-own property.

(B) 5-YEAR PROPERTY.—The term "5-year property" includes—

(i) any automobile or light general purpose truck,

(ii) any semi-conductor manufacturing equipment,

(iii) any computer-based telephone central office switching equipment,

(iv) any qualified technological equipment,

(v) any section 1245 property used in connection with research and experimentation,

(vi) any property which—

(I) is described in subparagraph (A) of section 48(a)(3) (or would be so described if "solar or wind energy" were substituted for "solar energy" in clause (i) thereof and the last sentence of such section did not apply to such subparagraph),

(II) is described in paragraph (15) of section 48(l) (as in effect on the day before the date of the enactment of the Revenue Reconciliation Act of 1990) and is a qualifying small power production facility within the meaning of section 3(17)(C) of the Federal Power Act (16 U.S.C. 796(17)(C)), as in effect on September 1, 1986, or

(III) is described in section 48(l)(3)(A)(ix) (as in effect on the day before the date of the enactment of the Revenue Reconciliation Act of 1990), and

(vii) any machinery or equipment (other than any grain bin, cotton ginning asset, fence, or other land improvement) which is used in a farming business (as defined in section 263A(e)(4)), the original use of which commences with the taxpayer after December 31, 2008, and which is placed in service before January 1, 2010.

Nothing in any provision of law shall be construed to treat property as not being described in clause (vi)(I) (or the corresponding provisions of prior law) by reason of being public utility property (within the meaning of section 48(a)(3)).

(C) 7-YEAR PROPERTY.—The term "7-year property" includes—

(i) any railroad track,

(ii) any motorsports entertainment complex,

(iii) any Alaska natural gas pipeline,

(iv) any natural gas gathering line the original use of which commences with the taxpayer after April 11, 2005, and

(v) any property which—

(I) does not have a class life, and

(II) is not otherwise classified under paragraph (2) or this paragraph.

(D) 10-YEAR PROPERTY.—The term "10-year property" includes—

(i) any single purpose agricultural or horticultural structure (within the meaning of subsection (i)(13)),

(ii) any tree or vine bearing fruit or nuts,

(iii) any qualified smart electric meter, and

(iv) any qualified smart electric grid system.

(E) 15-YEAR PROPERTY.—The term "15-year property" includes—

(i) any municipal wastewater treatment plant,

(ii) any telephone distribution plant and comparable equipment used for 2-way exchange of voice and data communications,

(iii) any section 1250 property which is a retail motor fuels outlet (whether or not food or other convenience items are sold at the outlet),

(iv) any qualified leasehold improvement property placed in service before January 1, 2010,

(v) any qualified restaurant property placed in service before January 1, 2010,

(vi) initial clearing and grading land improvements with respect to gas utility property,

(vii) any section 1245 property (as defined in section 1245(a)(3)) used in the transmission at 69 or more kilovolts of electricity for sale and the original use of which commences with the taxpayer after April 11, 2005,

(viii) any natural gas distribution line the original use of which commences with the taxpayer after April 11, 2005, and which is placed in service before January 1, 2011, and

(ix) any qualified retail improvement property placed in service after December 31, 2008, and before January 1, 2010.

(F) 20-YEAR PROPERTY.—The term "20-year property" means initial clearing and grading land improvements with respect to any electric utility transmission and distribution plant.

(4) RAILROAD GRADING OR TUNNEL BORE.—The term "railroad grading or tunnel bore" means all improvements resulting from excavations (including tunneling), construction of embankments, clearings, diversions of roads and streams, sodding of slopes, and from similar work necessary to provide, construct, reconstruct, alter, protect, improve, replace, or restore a roadbed or right-of-way for railroad track.

(5) WATER UTILITY PROPERTY.—The term "water utility property" means property—

(A) which is an integral part of the gathering, treatment, or commercial distribution of water, and which, without regard to this paragraph, would be 20-year property, and

(B) any municipal sewer.

(6) QUALIFIED LEASEHOLD IMPROVEMENT PROPERTY.—The term "qualified leasehold improvement property" has the meaning given such term in section 168(k)(3) except that the following special rules shall apply:

(A) IMPROVEMENTS MADE BY LESSOR.—In the case of an improvement made by the person who was the lessor of such improvement when such improvement was placed in service, such improvement shall be qualified leasehold improvement property (if at all) only so long as such improvement is held by such person.

(B) EXCEPTION FOR CHANGES IN FORM OF BUSINESS.—Property shall not cease to be qualified leasehold improvement property under subparagraph (A) by reason of—

(i) death,

(ii) a transaction to which section 381(a) applies,

(iii) a mere change in the form of conducting the trade or business so long as the property is retained in such trade or business as qualified leasehold improvement property and the taxpayer retains a substantial interest in such trade or business,

(iv) the acquisition of such property in an exchange described in section 1031, 1033, or 1038 to the extent that the basis of such property includes an amount representing the adjusted basis of other property owned by the taxpayer or a related person, or

(v) the acquisition of such property by the taxpayer in a transaction described in section 332, 351, 361, 721, or 731 (or the acquisition of such property by the taxpayer from the transferee or acquiring corporation in a transaction described in such section), to the extent that the basis of the property in the hands of the taxpayer is determined by reference to its basis in the hands of the transferor or distributor.

(7) QUALIFIED RESTAURANT PROPERTY.—

(A) IN GENERAL.—The term "qualified restaurant property" means any section 1250 property which is—

(i) a building, if such building is placed in service after December 31, 2008, and before January 1, 2010, or

(ii) an improvement to a building,

if more than 50 percent of the building's square footage is devoted to preparation of, and seating for on-premises consumption of, prepared meals.

(B) EXCLUSION FROM BONUS DEPRECIATION.—Property described in this paragraph shall not be considered qualified property for purposes of subsection (k).

(8) QUALIFIED RETAIL IMPROVEMENT PROPERTY.—

(A) IN GENERAL.—The term "qualified retail improvement property" means any improvement to an interior portion of a building which is nonresidential real property if—

(i) such portion is open to the general public and is used in the retail trade or business of selling tangible personal property to the general public, and

(ii) such improvement is placed in service more than 3 years after the date the building was first placed in service.

(B) IMPROVEMENTS MADE BY OWNER.—In the case of an improvement made by the owner of such improvement, such improvement shall be qualified retail improvement property (if at all) only so long as such improvement is held by such owner. Rules similar to the rules under paragraph (6)(B) shall apply for purposes of the preceding sentence.

(C) CERTAIN IMPROVEMENTS NOT INCLUDED.—Such term shall not include any improvement for which the expenditure is attributable to—

(i) the enlargement of the building,

(ii) any elevator or escalator,

(iii) any structural component benefitting a common area, or

(iv) the internal structural framework of the building.

(D) EXCLUSION FROM BONUS DEPRECIATION.—Property described in this paragraph shall not be considered qualified property for purposes of subsection (k).

(E) TERMINATION.—Such term shall not include any improvement placed in service after December 31, 2009.

Amendments

• 2008, Energy Improvement and Extension Act of 2008 (P.L. 110-343)

P.L. 110-343, Division B, §306(a):

Amended Code Sec. 168(e)(3)(D) by striking "and" at the end of clause (i), by striking the period at the end of clause (ii) and inserting a comma, and by inserting after clause (ii) new clauses (iii)-(iv). **Effective** for property placed in service after 10-3-2008.

• 2008, Tax Extenders and Alternative Minimum Tax Relief Act of 2008 (P.L. 110-343)

P.L. 110-343, Division C, §305(a)(1):

Amended Code Sec. 168(e)(3)(E)(iv) and (v) by striking "January 1, 2008" and inserting "January 1, 2010". **Effective** for property placed in service after 12-31-2007.

P.L. 110-343, Division C, §305(b)(1):

Amended Code Sec. 168(e)(7). **Effective** for property placed in service after 12-31-2008. Prior to amendment, Code Sec. 168(e)(7) read as follows:

(7) QUALIFIED RESTAURANT PROPERTY.—The term "qualified restaurant property" means any section 1250 property which is an improvement to a building if—

(A) such improvement is placed in service more than 3 years after the date such building was first placed in service, and

(B) more than 50 percent of the building's square footage is devoted to preparation of, and seating for on-premises consumption of, prepared meals.

P.L. 110-343, Division C, §305(c)(1):

Amended Code Sec. 168(e)(3)(E) by striking "and" at the end of clause (vii), by striking the period at the end of clause (viii) and inserting ", and", and by adding at the end a new clause (ix). **Effective** for property placed in service after 12-31-2008.

P.L. 110-343, Division C, §305(c)(2):

Amended Code Sec. 168(e) by adding at the end a new paragraph (8). **Effective** for property placed in service after 12-31-2008.

P.L. 110-343, Division C, §505(a):

Amended Code Sec. 168(e)(3)(B) by striking "and" at the end of clause (v), by striking the period at the end of clause (vi)(III) and inserting ", and", and by inserting after clause (vi) a new clause (vii). **Effective** for property placed in service after 12-31-2008.

• 2008, Heartland, Habitat, Harvest, and Horticulture Act of 2008 (P.L. 110-246)

P.L. 110-246, §15344(a):

Amended Code Sec. 168(e)(3)(A)(i). **Effective** for property placed in service after 12-31-2008. Prior to amendment, Code Sec. 168(e)(3)(A)(i) read as follows:

(i) any race horse which is more than 2 years old at the time it is placed in service,

• 2006, Tax Relief and Health Care Act of 2006 (P.L. 109-432)

P.L. 109-432, Division A, §113(a):

Amended Code Sec. 168(e)(3)(E)(iv)-(v) by striking "2006" and inserting "2008". **Effective** for property placed in service after 12-31-2005.

• 2005, Gulf Opportunity Zone Act of 2005 (P.L. 109-135)

P.L. 109-135, §410(a):

Amended Code Sec. 168(e)(3)(B)(vi)(I) by striking "if 'solar and wind' were substituted for 'solar' in clause (i) thereof" and inserting "if 'solar or wind energy' were substituted for 'solar energy' in clause (i) thereof". **Effective** as if included in section 11813 of the Omnibus Budget Reconciliation Act of 1990 (P.L. 101-508) [**effective** generally for property placed in service after 12-31-1990.—CCH].

• 2005, Energy Tax Incentives Act of 2005 (P.L. 109-58)

P.L. 109-58, §1301(f)(5):

Amended Code Sec. 168(e)(3)(B)(vi)(I). **Effective** as if included in the amendments made by section 710 of P.L. 108-357 [**effective** generally for electricity produced and sold after 10-22-2004, in tax years ending after such date.—CCH]. Prior to amendment, Code Sec. 168(e)(3)(B)(vi)(I) read as follows:

(I) is described in subparagraph (A) of section 48(a)(3) (or would be so described if "solar and wind" were substituted for "solar" in clause (i) thereof,

P.L. 109-58, §1308(a):

Amended Code Sec. 168(e)(3)(E) by striking "and" at the end of clause (v), by striking the period at the end of clause (vi) and inserting ", and", and by adding at the end a new clause (vii). **Effective** generally for property placed in service after 4-11-2005. For an exception, see Act Sec. 1308(c)(2), below.

P.L. 109-58, §1308(c)(2), provides:

(2) EXCEPTION.—The amendments made by this section shall not apply to any property with respect to which the taxpayer or a related party has entered into a binding contract for the construction thereof on or before April 11, 2005, or, in the case of self-constructed property, has started construction on or before such date.

P.L. 109-58, §1325(a):

Amended Code Sec. 168(e)(3)(E), as amended by this Act, by striking "and" at the end of clause (vi), by striking the period at the end of clause (vii) and by inserting ", and", and by adding at the end a new clause (viii). **Effective** generally for property placed in service after 4-11-2005. For an exception, see Act Sec. 1325(c)(2), below.

P.L. 109-58, §1325(c)(2), provides:

(2) EXCEPTION.—The amendments made by this section shall not apply to any property with respect to which the taxpayer or a related party has entered into a binding contract for the construction thereof on or before April 11, 2005, or, in the case of self-constructed property, has started construction on or before such date.

P.L. 109-58, §1326(a):

Amended Code Sec. 168(e)(3)(C) by striking "and" at the end of clause (iii), by redesignating clause (iv) as clause (v), and by inserting after clause (iii) a new clause (iv). **Effective** generally for property placed in service after 4-11-2005. For an exception, see Act Sec. 1326(e)(2), below.

P.L. 109-58, §1326(e)(2), provides:

(2) EXCEPTION.—The amendments made by this section shall not apply to any property with respect to which the taxpayer or a related party has entered into a binding contract for the construction thereof on or before April 11, 2005, or, in the case of self-constructed property, has started construction on or before such date.

• 2004, American Jobs Creation Act of 2004 (P.L. 108-357)

P.L. 108-357, §211(a):

Amended Code Sec. 168(e)(3)(E) by striking "and" at the end of clause (ii), by striking the period at the end of clause (iii) and inserting a comma, and by adding at the end new clauses (iv) and (v). **Effective** for property placed in service after 10-22-2004.

P.L. 108-357, §211(b):

Amended Code Sec. 168(e) by adding at the end a new paragraph (6). **Effective** for property placed in service after 10-22-2004.

P.L. 108-357, §211(c):

Amended Code Sec. 168(e), as amended by Act Sec. 211(b), by adding at the end a new paragraph (7). **Effective** for property placed in service after 10-22-2004.

P.L. 108-357, §704(a):

Amended Code Sec. 168(e)(3)(C) by redesignating clause (ii) as clause (iii) and by inserting after clause (i) a new clause (ii). **Effective** generally for property placed in service after 10-22-2004. For special rules, see Act Secs. 704(c)(2)-(3), below.

P.L. 108-357, §704(c)(2)-(3), provides:

(2) SPECIAL RULE FOR ASSET CLASS 80.0.—In the case of race track facilities placed in service after the date of the enactment of this Act [10-22-2004.—CCH], such facilities shall not be treated as theme and amusement facilities classified under asset class 80.0.

(3) NO INFERENCE.—Nothing in this section or the amendments made by this section shall be construed to affect the treatment of property placed in service on or before the date of the enactment of this Act [10-22-2004.—CCH].

P.L. 108-357, §706(a):

Amended Code Sec. 168(e)(3)(C), as amended by this Act, by striking "and" at the end of clause (ii), by redesignating clause (iii) as clause (iv), and by inserting after clause (ii) a new clause (iii). **Effective** for property placed in service after 12-31-2004.

P.L. 108-357, §901(a):

Amended Code Sec. 168(e)(3)(E), as amended by this Act, by striking "and" at the end of clause (iv), by striking the period at the end of clause (v) and inserting ", and", and by adding at the end a new clause (vi). **Effective** for property placed in service after 10-22-2004.

P.L. 108-357, §901(b):

Amended Code Sec. 168(e)(3) by adding at the end a new subparagraph (F). **Effective** for property placed in service after 10-22-2004.

• 1997, Taxpayer Relief Act of 1997 (P.L. 105-34)

P.L. 105-34, §1086(b)(1):

Amended Code Sec. 168(e)(3)(A) by striking "and" at the end of clause (i), by striking the period at the end of clause (ii) and inserting ", and", and by adding at the end a new clause. **Effective** for property placed in service after 8-5-97.

• 1996, Small Business Job Protection Act of 1996 (P.L. 104-188)

P.L. 104-188, §1120(a):

Amended Code Sec. 168(e)(3)(E) by striking "and" at the end of clause (i), by striking the period at the end of clause (ii) and inserting ", and", and by adding at the end a new clause (iii). For the **effective** date, see Act Sec. 1120(c), below.

P.L. 104-188, §1120(c), provides:

(c) EFFECTIVE DATE.—The amendments made by this section shall apply to property which is placed in service on or after the date of the enactment of this Act and to which section 168 of the Internal Revenue Code of 1986 applies after the amendment made by section 201 of the Tax Reform Act of 1986. A taxpayer may elect (in such form and manner as the Secretary of the Treasury may prescribe) to have such amendments apply with respect to any property placed in service before such date and to which such section so applies.

P.L. 104-188, §1613(b)(3)(A):

Amended Code Sec. 168(e) by adding at the end a new paragraph. **Effective** for property placed in service after 6-12-96, other than property placed in service pursuant to a binding contract in effect before 6-10-96, and at all times thereafter before the property is placed in service.

P.L. 104-188, §1613(b)(3)(B)(i):

Amended Code Sec. 168(e)(3) by striking subparagraph (F). **Effective** for property placed in service after 6-12-96, other than property placed in service pursuant to a binding contract in effect before 6-10-96, and at all times thereafter before the property is placed in service. Prior to being stricken, Code Sec. 168(e)(3)(F) read as follows:

(F) 20-YEAR PROPERTY.—The term "20-year property" includes any municipal sewers.

P.L. 104-188, §1702(h)(1)(A):

Amended Code Sec. 168(e)(3)(B)(vi) by striking "or" at the end of subclause (I), by striking the period at the end of subclause (II) and inserting ", or", and by adding at the end thereof a new subclause (III). **Effective** as if included in the provision of P.L. 101-508 to which it relates.

P.L. 104-188, §1702(h)(1)(B):

Amended Code Sec. 168(e)(3)(B) by adding at the end a new flush sentence. **Effective** as if included in the provision of P.L. 101-508 to which it relates.

• 1990, Omnibus Budget Reconciliation Act of 1990 (P.L. 101-508)

P.L. 101-508, §11812(b)(2)(A):

Amended Code Sec. 168(e)(2)(A). **Effective**, generally, for property placed in service after 11-5-90. However, for exceptions see Act Sec. 11812(c)(2)-(3) below. Prior to amendment, Code Sec. 168(e)(2)(A) read as follows:

(A) RESIDENTIAL RENTAL PROPERTY.—The term "residential rental property" has the meaning given such term by section 167(j)(2)(B).

P.L. 101-508, §11812(c)(2)-(3), provides:

(2) EXCEPTION.—The amendments made by this section shall not apply to any property to which section 168 of the Internal Revenue Code of 1986 does not apply by reason of subsection (f)(5) thereof.

(3) EXCEPTION FOR PREVIOUSLY GRANDFATHER EXPENDITURES.—The amendments made by this section shall not apply to rehabilitation expenditures described in section 252(f)(5) of the Tax Reform Act of 1986 (as added by section 1002(l)(31) of the Technical and Miscellaneous Revenue Act of 1988).

P.L. 101-508, §11813(b)(9)(A)(i)-(ii) (as amended by P.L. 104-188, §1704(t)(54)):

Amended Code Sec. 168(e)(3)(B)(vi) by striking "paragraph (3)(A)(viii), (3)(A)(ix), or (4) of section 48(l)" in subclause (I) and inserting "subparagraph (A) of section 48(a)(3) (or would be so described if `solar and wind' were substituted for `solar' in clause (i) thereof)", and by inserting "(as in effect on the day before the date of the enactment of the Revenue Reconciliation Act of 1990)" after "48(l)" in subclause (II). **Effective**, generally, for property placed in service after 12-31-90. However, for exceptions see Act Sec. 11813(c)(2) below.

P.L. 101-508, §11813(b)(9)(B)(i):

Amended Code Sec. 168(e)(3)(D)(i) by striking "section 48(p)" and inserting "subsection (i)(13)". **Effective**, generally, for property placed in service after 12-31-90. However, for exceptions see Act Sec. 11813(c)(2) below.

P.L. 101-508, §11813(c)(2), provides:

(2) EXCEPTIONS.—The amendments made by this section shall not apply to—

(A) any transition property (as defined in section 49(e) of the Internal Revenue Code of 1986 (as in effect on the day before the date of the enactment of this Act),

(B) any property with respect to which qualified progress expenditures were previously taken into account under section 46(d) of such Code (as so in effect), and

(C) any property described in section 46(b)(2)(C) of such Code (as so in effect).

• 1988, Technical and Miscellaneous Revenue Act of 1988 (P.L. 100-647)

P.L. 100-647, §1002(a)(21):

Amended Code Sec. 168(e)(3)(B)(v) by striking out "any property" and inserting in lieu thereof "any section 1245 property". **Effective** as if included in the provision of P.L. 99-514 to which it relates.

P.L. 100-647, §1002(i)(2)(C):

Amended Code Sec. 168(e) by adding at the end thereof a new paragraph (4). **Effective** as if included in the provision of P.L. 99-514 to which it relates.

P.L. 100-647, §6027(a):

Amended Code Sec. 168(e)(3) by redesignating subparagraphs (D) and (E) as subparagraphs (E) and (F), respectively, and by inserting after subparagraph (C) a new subparagraph (D). **Effective**, generally, for property placed in service after 12-31-88. However, see Act Sec. 6027(c)(2), below, for an exception.

P.L. 100-647, §6027(b)(1):

Amended Code Sec. 168(e)(3)(C) by adding "and" at the end of clause (i), by striking out clause (ii) and by redesignating clause (iii) as clause (ii). **Effective**, generally, for property placed in service after 12-31-88. However, see Act Sec. 6027(c)(2), below, for an exception. Prior to amendment, Code Sec. 168(e)(3)(C)(ii) read as follows:

(ii) any single-purpose agricultural or horticultural structure (within the meaning of section 48(p)), and

P.L. 100-647, §6027(c)(2), provides:

(c)(2) EXCEPTION.—The amendments made by this section shall not apply to any property if such property is placed in service before January 1, 1990, and if such property—

(A) is constructed, reconstructed, or acquired by the taxpayer pursuant to a written contract which was binding on July 14, 1988, or

(B) is constructed or reconstructed by the taxpayer and such construction or reconstruction began by July 14, 1988.

P.L. 100-647, §6029(a):

Amended Code Sec. 168(e)(3)(D). **Effective** for property placed in service after 12-31-88. Prior to amendment, Code Sec. 168(e)(3)(D) read as follows:

(D) 10-YEAR PROPERTY.—The term "10-year property" includes any single purpose agricultural or horticultural structure (within the meaning of section 48(p)).

[Sec. 168(f)]

(f) PROPERTY TO WHICH SECTION DOES NOT APPLY.—This section shall not apply to—

(1) CERTAIN METHODS OF DEPRECIATION.—Any property if—

(A) the taxpayer elects to exclude such property from the application of this section, and

(B) for the 1st taxable year for which a depreciation deduction would be allowable with respect to such property in the hands of the taxpayer, the property is properly depreciated under the unit-of-production method or any method of depreciation not expressed in a term of years (other than the retirement-replacement-betterment method or similar method).

(2) CERTAIN PUBLIC UTILITY PROPERTY.—Any public utility property (within the meaning of subsection (i)(10)) if the taxpayer does not use a normalization method of accounting.

(3) FILMS AND VIDEO TAPE.—Any motion picture film or video tape.

(4) SOUND RECORDINGS.—Any works which result from the fixation of a series of musical, spoken, or other sounds, regardless of the nature of the material (such as discs, tapes, or other phonorecordings) in which such sounds are embodied.

(5) CERTAIN PROPERTY PLACED IN SERVICE IN CHURNING TRANSACTIONS.—

(A) IN GENERAL.—Property—

(i) described in paragraph (4) of section 168(e) (as in effect before the amendments made by the Tax Reform Act of 1986), or

(ii) which would be described in such paragraph if such paragraph were applied by substituting "1987" for "1981" and "1986" for "1980" each place such terms appear.

(B) SUBPARAGRAPH (A)(ii) NOT TO APPLY.—Clause (ii) of subparagraph (A) shall not apply to—

(i) any residential rental property or nonresidential real property,

(ii) any property if, for the 1st taxable year in which such property is placed in service—

(I) the amount allowable as a deduction under this section (as in effect before the date of the enactment of this paragraph) with respect to such property is greater than,

(II) the amount allowable as a deduction under this section (as in effect on or after such date and using the half-year convention) for such taxable year, or

(iii) any property to which this section (as amended by the Tax Reform Act of 1986) applied in the hands of the transferor.

(C) SPECIAL RULE.—In the case of any property to which this section would apply but for this paragraph, the depreciation deduction under section 167 shall be determined under the provisions of this section as in effect before the amendments made by section 201 of the Tax Reform Act of 1986.

Amendments

• 1990, Omnibus Budget Reconciliation Act of 1990 (P.L. 101-508)

P.L. 101-508, §11812(b)(2)(C):

Amended Code Sec. 168(f)(2) by striking "section 167(l)(3)(A)" and inserting "subsection (i)(10)". **Effective**, generally, for property placed in service after 11-5-90. However, for exceptions see Act Sec. 11812(c)(2)-(3) in the amendment notes following Code Sec. 168(e).

• 1988, Technical and Miscellaneous Revenue Act of 1988 (P.L. 100-647)

P.L. 100-647, §1002(a)(6)(A)(i)-(ii):

Amended Code Sec. 168(f)(5)(B) by striking out "1st full taxable year" in clause (ii) and inserting in lieu thereof "1st taxable year", and by striking out "or" at the end of clause (i), by striking out the period at the end of clause (ii) and inserting in lieu thereof ", or", and by adding at the end thereof new clause (iii). **Effective** as if included in the provision of P.L. 99-514 to which it relates.

P.L. 100-647, §1002(a)(6)(B):

Amended Code Sec. 168(f)(5) by adding at the end thereof new subparagraph (C). **Effective** as if included in the provision of P.L. 99-514 to which it relates.

P.L. 100-647, §1002(a)(16)(B):

Amended Code Sec. 168(f)(4). **Effective** as if included in the provision of P.L. 99-514 to which it relates. Prior to amendment, Code Sec. 168(f)(4) read as follows:

(4) SOUND RECORDINGS.—Any sound recording described in section 48(r)(5).

[Sec. 168(g)]

(g) ALTERNATIVE DEPRECIATION SYSTEM FOR CERTAIN PROPERTY.—

(1) IN GENERAL.—In the case of—

(A) any tangible property which during the taxable year is used predominantly outside the United States,

(B) any tax-exempt use property,

(C) any tax-exempt bond financed property,

(D) any imported property covered by an Executive order under paragraph (6), and

(E) any property to which an election under paragraph (7) applies,

the depreciation deduction provided by section 167(a) shall be determined under the alternative depreciation system.

(2) ALTERNATIVE DEPRECIATION SYSTEM.—For purposes of paragraph (1), the alternative depreciation system is depreciation determined by using—

(A) the straight line method (without regard to salvage value),

(B) the applicable convention determined under subsection (d), and

(C) a recovery period determined under the following table:

In the case of:	*The recovery period shall be:*
(i) Property not described in clause (ii) or (iii)	The class life.
(ii) Personal property with no class life	12 years.
(iii) Nonresidential real and residential rental property	40 years.
(iv) Any railroad grading or tunnel bore or water utility property	50 years.

(3) SPECIAL RULES FOR DETERMINING CLASS LIFE.—

(A) TAX-EXEMPT USE PROPERTY SUBJECT TO LEASE.—In the case of any tax-exempt use property subject to a lease, the recovery period used for purposes of paragraph (2) shall (notwithstanding any other subparagraph of this paragraph) in no event be less than 125 percent of the lease term.

(B) SPECIAL RULE FOR CERTAIN PROPERTY ASSIGNED TO CLASSES.—For purposes of paragraph (2), in the case of property described in any of the following subparagraphs of subsection (e)(3), the class life shall be determined as follows:

If property is described in subparagraph:	*The class life is:*
(A)(iii)	4
(B)(ii)	5
(B)(iii)	9.5
(B)(vii)	10
(C)(i)	10
(C)(iii)	22
(C)(iv)	14
(D)(i)	15
(D)(ii)	20
(E)(i)	24
(E)(ii)	24
(E)(iii)	20
(E)(iv)	39
(E)(v)	39
(E)(vi)	20
(E)(vii)	30
(E)(viii)	35
(E)(ix)	39
(F)	25

(C) QUALIFIED TECHNOLOGICAL EQUIPMENT.—In the case of any qualified technological equipment, the recovery period used for purposes of paragraph (2) shall be 5 years.

(D) AUTOMOBILES, ETC.—In the case of any automobile or light general purpose truck, the recovery period used for purposes of paragraph (2) shall be 5 years.

(E) CERTAIN REAL PROPERTY.—In the case of any section 1245 property which is real property with no class life, the recovery period used for purposes of paragraph (2) shall be 40 years.

(4) EXCEPTION FOR CERTAIN PROPERTY USED OUTSIDE UNITED STATES.—Subparagraph (A) of paragraph (1) shall not apply to—

(A) any aircraft which is registered by the Administrator of the Federal Aviation Agency and which is operated to and from the United States or is operated under contract with the United States;

(B) rolling stock which is used within and without the United States and which is—

(i) of a rail carrier subject to part A of subtitle IV of title 49, or

(ii) of a United States person (other than a corporation described in clause (i)) but only if the rolling stock is not leased to one or more foreign persons for periods aggregating more than 12 months in any 24-month period;

(C) any vessel documented under the laws of the United States which is operated in the foreign or domestic commerce of the United States;

(D) any motor vehicle of a United States person (as defined in section 7701(a)(30)) which is operated to and from the United States;

(E) any container of a United States person which is used in the transportation of property to and from the United States;

(F) any property (other than a vessel or an aircraft) of a United States person which is used for the purpose of exploring for, developing, removing, or transporting resources from the outer Continental Shelf (within the meaning of section 2 of the Outer Continental Shelf Lands Act, as amended and supplemented; (43 U.S.C. 1331));

(G) any property which is owned by a domestic corporation (other than a corporation which has an election in effect under section 936) or by a United States citizen (other than a citizen entitled to the benefits of section 931 or 933) and which is used predominantly in a possession of the United States by such a corporation or such a citizen, or by a corporation created or organized in, or under the law of, a possession of the United States;

(H) any communications satellite (as defined in section 103(3) of the Communications Satellite Act of 1962, 47 U.S.C. 702(3)), or any interest therein, of a United States person;

(I) any cable, or any interest therein, of a domestic corporation engaged in furnishing telephone service to which section 168(i)(10)(C) applies (or of a wholly owned domestic subsidiary of such a corporation), if such cable is part of a submarine cable system which constitutes part of a communication link exclusively between the United States and one or more foreign countries;

(J) any property (other than a vessel or an aircraft) of a United States person which is used in international or territorial waters within the northern portion of the Western

Hemisphere for the purpose of exploring for, developing, removing, or transporting resources from ocean waters or deposits under such waters;

(K) any property described in section 48(l)(3)(A)(ix) (as in effect on the day before the date of the enactment of the Revenue Reconciliation Act of 1990) which is owned by a United States person and which is used in international or territorial waters to generate energy for use in the United States; and

(L) any satellite (not described in subparagraph (H)) or other spacecraft (or any interest therein) held by a United States person if such satellite or other spacecraft was launched from within the United States.

For purposes of subparagraph (J), the term "northern portion of the Western Hemisphere" means the area lying west of the 30th meridian west of Greenwich, east of the international dateline, and north of the Equator, but not including any foreign country which is a country of South America.

(5) TAX-EXEMPT BOND FINANCED PROPERTY.—For purposes of this subsection—

(A) IN GENERAL.—Except as otherwise provided in this paragraph, the term "tax-exempt bond financed property" means any property to the extent such property is financed (directly or indirectly) by an obligation the interest on which is exempt from tax under section 103(a).

(B) ALLOCATION OF BOND PROCEEDS.—For purposes of subparagraph (A), the proceeds of any obligation shall be treated as used to finance property acquired in connection with the issuance of such obligation in the order in which such property is placed in service.

(C) QUALIFIED RESIDENTIAL RENTAL PROJECTS.—The term "tax-exempt bond financed property" shall not include any qualified residential rental project (within the meaning of section 142(a)(7)).

(6) IMPORTED PROPERTY.—

(A) COUNTRIES MAINTAINING TRADE RESTRICTIONS OR ENGAGING IN DISCRIMINATORY ACTS.—If the President determines that a foreign country—

(i) maintains nontariff trade restrictions, including variable import fees, which substantially burden United States commerce in a manner inconsistent with provisions of trade agreements, or

(ii) engages in discriminatory or other acts (including tolerance of international cartels) or policies unjustifiably restricting United States commerce,

the President may by Executive order provide for the application of paragraph (1)(D) to any article or class of articles manufactured or produced in such foreign country for such period as may be provided by such Executive order. Any period specified in the preceding sentence shall not apply to any property ordered before (or the construction, reconstruction, or erection of which began before) the date of the Executive order unless the President determines an earlier date to be in the public interest and specifies such date in the Executive order.

(B) IMPORTED PROPERTY.—For purposes of this subsection, the term "imported property" means any property if—

(i) such property was completed outside the United States, or

(ii) less than 50 percent of the basis of such property is attributable to value added within the United States.

For purposes of this subparagraph, the term "United States" includes the Commonwealth of Puerto Rico and the possessions of the United States.

(7) ELECTION TO USE ALTERNATIVE DEPRECIATION SYSTEM.—

(A) IN GENERAL.—If the taxpayer makes an election under this paragraph with respect to any class of property for any taxable year, the alternative depreciation system under this subsection shall apply to all property in such class placed in service during such taxable year. Notwithstanding the preceding sentence, in the case of nonresidential real property or residential rental property, such election may be made separately with respect to each property.

(B) ELECTION IRREVOCABLE.—An election under subparagraph (A), once made, shall be irrevocable.

Amendments

• 2008, Tax Extenders and Alternative Minimum Tax Relief Act of 2008 (P.L. 110-343)

P.L. 110-343, Division C, §305(c)(4):

Amended the table contained in Code Sec. 168(g)(3)(B) by inserting after the item relating to subparagraph (E)(viii) a new item. **Effective** for property placed in service after 12-31-2008.

P.L. 110-343, Division C, §505(b):

Amended the table contained in Code Sec. 168(g)(3)(B) by inserting after the item relating to subparagraph (B)(iii) a new item. **Effective** for property placed in service after 12-31-2008.

• 2005, Energy Tax Incentives Act of 2005 (P.L. 109-58)

P.L. 109-58, §1308(b):

Amended the table contained in Code Sec. 168(g)(3)(B) by inserting after the item relating to subparagraph (E)(vi) a new item relating to subparagraph (E)(vii). **Effective** generally for property placed in service after 4-11-2005. For an exception, see Act Sec. 1308(c)(2), below.

P.L. 109-58, §1308(c)(2), provides:

(2) EXCEPTION.—The amendments made by this section shall not apply to any property with respect to which the taxpayer or a related party has entered into a binding contract for the construction thereof on or before April 11, 2005, or, in the case of self-constructed property, has started construction on or before such date.

P.L. 109-58, §1325(b):

Amended the table contained in Code Sec. 168(g)(3)(B), as amended by this Act, by inserting after the item relating to subparagraph (E)(vii) a new item relating to subparagraph (E)(viii). **Effective** generally for property placed in service after 4-11-2005. For an exception, see Act Sec. 1325(c)(2), below.

P.L. 109-58, §1325(c)(2), provides:

(2) EXCEPTION.—The amendments made by this section shall not apply to any property with respect to which the taxpayer or a related party has entered into a binding contract for the construction thereof on or before April 11, 2005, or, in the case of self-constructed property, has started construction on or before such date.

P.L. 109-58, §1326(c):

Amended the table contained in Code Sec. 168(g)(3)(B), as amended by this Act, by inserting after the item relating to subparagraph (C)(iii) a new item relating to subparagraph (C)(iv). **Effective** generally for property placed in service after 4-11-2005. For an exception, see Act Sec. 1326(e)(2), below.

P.L. 109-58, §1326(e)(2), provides:

(2) EXCEPTION.—The amendments made by this section shall not apply to any property with respect to which the taxpayer or a related party has entered into a binding contract for the construction thereof on or before April 11, 2005, or, in the case of self-constructed property, has started construction on or before such date.

• 2004, American Jobs Creation Act of 2004 (P.L. 108-357)

P.L. 108-357, §211(e):

Amended the table contained in Code Sec. 168(g)(3)(B) by adding at the end two new items. **Effective** for property placed in service after 10-22-2004.

P.L. 108-357, §706(c):

Amended the table contained in Code Sec. 168(g)(3)(B) by inserting after the item relating to subparagraph (C)(ii)[(i)] a new item. **Effective** for property placed in service after 12-31-2004.

P.L. 108-357, §847(a):

Amended Code Sec. 168(g)(3)(A) by inserting "(notwithstanding any other subparagraph of this paragraph)" after "shall". **Effective** generally for leases entered into after 3-12-2004, and in the case of property treated as tax-exempt use property other than by reason of a lease, to property acquired after 3-12-2004 [effective date amended by P.L. 109-135, §403(ff)]. For an exception, see Act Sec. 849(b)(1)-(2), below.

P.L. 108-357, §849(b)(1)-(2), provides:

(b) EXCEPTION.—

(1) IN GENERAL.—The amendments made by this part shall not apply to qualified transportation property.

(2) QUALIFIED TRANSPORTATION PROPERTY.—For purposes of paragraph (1), the term "qualified transportation property" means domestic property subject to a lease with respect to which a formal application—

(A) was submitted for approval to the Federal Transit Administration (an agency of the Department of Transportation) after June 30, 2003, and before March 13, 2004,

(B) is approved by the Federal Transit Administration before January 1, 2006, and

(C) includes a description of such property and the value of such property.

P.L. 108-357, §901(c):

Amended the table contained in Code Sec. 168(g)(3)(B), as amended by this Act, by inserting after the item relating to subparagraph (E)(v) two new items. **Effective** for property placed in service after 10-22-2004.

• 1997, Taxpayer Relief Act of 1997 (P.L. 105-34)

P.L. 105-34, §1086(b)(2):

Amended the table contained in Code Sec. 168(g)(3)(B) by inserting before the first item a new item. **Effective** for property placed in service after 8-5-97.

• 1996, Small Business Job Protection Act of 1996 (P.L. 104-188)

P.L. 104-188, §1120(b):

Amended Code Sec. 168(g)(3)(B) by inserting after the item relating to subparagraph (E)(ii) in the table contained therein a new item relating to subparagraph (E)(iii). For the **effective** date, see Act Sec. 1120(c), below.

P.L. 104-188, §1120(c), provides:

(c) EFFECTIVE DATE.—The amendments made by this section shall apply to property which is placed in service on or after the date of the enactment of this Act and to which section 168 of the Internal Revenue Code of 1986 applies after the amendment made by section 201 of the Tax Reform Act of 1986. A taxpayer may elect (in such form and manner as the Secretary of the Treasury may prescribe) to have such amendments apply with respect to any property placed in service before such date and to which such section so applies.

P.L. 104-188, §1613(b)(3)(B)(ii):

Amended Code Sec. 168(g)(3) by striking the item relating to subparagraph (F) in the table. **Effective** for property placed in service after 6-12-96, other than property placed in service pursuant to a binding contract in effect before 6-10-96, and at all times thereafter before the property is placed in service. Prior to amendment, the item relating to subparagraph (F) in the table read as follows:

(F) 50

P.L. 104-188, §1613(b)(4):

Amended Code Sec. 168(g)(2)(C)(iv) by inserting "or water utility property" after "tunnel bore". **Effective** for property placed in service after 6-12-96, other than property placed in service pursuant to a binding contract in effect before 6-10-96, and at all times thereafter before the property is placed in service.

P.L. 104-188, §1702(h)(1)(C):

Amended Code Sec. 168(g)(4)(K) by striking "section 48(a)(3)(A)(iii)" and inserting "section 48(l)(3)(A)(ix) (as in effect on the day before the date of the enactment of the Revenue Reconciliation Act of 1990)". **Effective** as if included in the provision of P.L. 101-508 to which it relates.

P.L. 104-188, §304(a):

Amended Code Sec. 168(g)(4)(B)(i) by striking "domestic railroad corporation providing transportation subject to subchapter I of chapter 105" and inserting in lieu thereof "rail carrier subject to part A of subtitle IV". **Effective** 1-1-96.

• 1990, Omnibus Budget Reconciliation Act of 1990 (P.L. 101-508)

P.L. 101-508, §11813(b)(9)(C):

Amended Code Sec. 168(g)(4). **Effective**, generally, for property placed in service after 12-31-90. However, for exceptions see Act Sec. 11813(c)(2) in the amendment notes following Code Sec. 168(e). Prior to amendment, Code Sec. 168(g)(4) read as follows:

(4) PROPERTY USED PREDOMINANTLY OUTSIDE THE UNITED STATES.—For purposes of this subsection, rules similar to the rules under section 48(a)(2) (including the exceptions contained in subparagraph (B) thereof) shall apply in determining whether property is used predominantly outside the United States. In addition to the exceptions contained in such subparagraph (B), there shall be excepted any satellite or other spacecraft (or any interest therein) held by a United States person if such satellite or spacecraft was launched from within the United States.

• 1988, Technical and Miscellaneous Revenue Act of 1988 (P.L. 100-647)

P.L. 100-647, §1002(i)(2)(F):

Amended the Code Sec. 168(g)(2)(C) by adding at the end of the table contained therein a new item. **Effective** as if included in the provision of P.L. 99-514 to which it relates.

P.L. 100-647, §6027(b)(2):

Amended the table contained in Code Sec. 168(g)(3)(B). **Effective**, generally, for property placed in service after 12-31-88. For an exception see Act Sec. 6027(c)(2) in the amendment notes following 168(e). Prior to amendment, the table contained in Code Sec. 168(g)(3)(B) read as follows:

If property is described in subparagraph:	*The class life is:*
(B)(ii)	5
(B)(iii)	9.5
(C)(i)	10
(C)(ii)	15
(D)(i)	24
(D)(ii)	24
(E)	50

P.L. 100-647, §6029(c):

Amended the table contained in Code Sec. 168(g)(3)(B), as amended by section 6027. **Effective** for property placed in service after 12-31-88. Prior to amendment, the table contained in Code Sec. 168(g)(3)(B) read as follows:

If property is described in subparagraph:	*The class life is:*
(B)(ii)	5
(B)(iii)	9.5
(C)(i)	10
(D)	15
(E)(i)	24
(E)(ii)	24
(F)	50

[Sec. 168(h)]

(h) TAX-EXEMPT USE PROPERTY.—

(1) IN GENERAL.—For purposes of this section—

(A) PROPERTY OTHER THAN NONRESIDENTIAL REAL PROPERTY.—Except as otherwise provided in this subsection, the term "tax-exempt use property" means that portion of any tangible property (other than nonresidential real property) leased to a tax-exempt entity.

(B) NONRESIDENTIAL REAL PROPERTY.—

(i) IN GENERAL.—In the case of nonresidential real property, the term "tax-exempt use property" means that portion of the property leased to a tax-exempt entity in a disqualified lease.

(ii) DISQUALIFIED LEASE.—For purposes of this subparagraph, the term "disqualified lease" means any lease of the property to a tax-exempt entity, but only if—

(I) part or all of the property was financed (directly or indirectly) by an obligation the interest on which is exempt from tax under section 103(a) and such entity (or a related entity) participated in such financing.

(II) under such lease there is a fixed or determinable price purchase or sale option which involves such entity (or a related entity) or there is the equivalent of such an option,

(III) such lease has a lease term in excess of 20 years, or

(IV) such lease occurs after a sale (or other transfer) of the property by, or lease of the property from, such entity (or a related entity) and such property has been used by such entity (or a related entity) before such sale (or other transfer) or lease.

(iii) 35-PERCENT THRESHOLD TEST.—Clause (i) shall apply to any property only if the portion of such property leased to tax-exempt entities in disqualified leases is more than 35 percent of the property.

(iv) TREATMENT OF IMPROVEMENTS.—For purposes of this subparagraph, improvements to a property (other than land) shall not be treated as a separate property.

(v) LEASEBACKS DURING 1ST 3 MONTHS OF USE NOT TAKEN INTO ACCOUNT.—Subclause (IV) of clause (ii) shall not apply to any property which is leased within 3 months after the date such property is first used by the tax-exempt entity (or a related entity).

(C) EXCEPTION FOR SHORT-TERM LEASES.—

(i) IN GENERAL.—Property shall not be treated as tax-exempt use property merely by reason of a short-term lease.

(ii) SHORT-TERM LEASE.—For purposes of clause (i), the term "short-term lease" means any lease the term of which is—

(I) less than 3 years, and

(II) less than the greater of 1 year or 30 percent of the property's present class life.

In the case of nonresidential real property and property with no present class life, subclause (II) shall not apply.

(D) EXCEPTION WHERE PROPERTY USED IN UNRELATED TRADE OR BUSINESS.—The term "tax-exempt use property" shall not include any portion of a property if such portion is predominantly used by the tax-exempt entity (directly or through a partnership of which such entity is a partner) in an unrelated trade or business the income of which is subject to tax under section 511. For purposes of subparagraph (B)(iii), any portion of a property so used shall not be treated as leased to a tax-exempt entity in a disqualified lease.

(E) NONRESIDENTIAL REAL PROPERTY DEFINED.—For purposes of this paragraph, the term "nonresidential real property" includes residential rental property.

(2) TAX-EXEMPT ENTITY.—

(A) IN GENERAL.—For purposes of this subsection, the term "tax-exempt entity" means—

(i) the United States, any State or political subdivision thereof, any possession of the United States, or any agency or instrumentality of any of the foregoing,

(ii) an organization (other than a cooperative described in section 521) which is exempt from tax imposed by this chapter,

(iii) any foreign person or entity, and

(iv) any Indian tribal government described in section 7701(a)(40).

For purposes of applying this subsection, any Indian tribal government referred to in clause (iv) shall be treated in the same manner as a State.

(B) EXCEPTION FOR CERTAIN PROPERTY SUBJECT TO UNITED STATES TAX AND USED BY FOREIGN PERSON OR ENTITY.—Clause (iii) of subparagraph (A) shall not apply with respect to any property if more than 50 percent of the gross income for the taxable year derived by the foreign person or entity from the use of such property is—

(i) subject to tax under this chapter, or

(ii) included under section 951 in the gross income of a United States shareholder for the taxable year with or within which ends the taxable year of the controlled foreign corporation in which such income was derived.

For purposes of the preceding sentence, any exclusion or exemption shall not apply for purposes of determining the amount of the gross income so derived, but shall apply for purposes of determining the portion of such gross income subject to tax under this chapter.

(C) FOREIGN PERSON OR ENTITY.—For purposes of this paragraph, the term "foreign person or entity" means—

(i) any foreign government, any international organization, or any agency or instrumentality of any of the foregoing, and

(ii) any person who is not a United States person.

Such term does not include any foreign partnership or other foreign pass-thru entity.

(D) TREATMENT OF CERTAIN TAXABLE INSTRUMENTALITIES.—For purposes of this subsection, a corporation shall not be treated as an instrumentality of the United States or of any State or political subdivision thereof if—

(i) all of the activities of such corporation are subject to tax under this chapter, and

(ii) a majority of the board of directors of such corporation is not selected by the United States or any State or political subdivision thereof.

(E) CERTAIN PREVIOUSLY TAX-EXEMPT ORGANIZATIONS.—

(i) IN GENERAL.—For purposes of this subsection, an organization shall be treated as an organization described in subparagraph (A)(ii) with respect to any property (other than property held by such organization) if such organization was an organization (other than a cooperative described in section 521) exempt from tax imposed by this chapter at any time during the 5-year period ending on the date such property was first used by such organization. The preceding sentence and subparagraph (D)(ii) shall not apply to the Federal Home Loan Mortgage Corporation.

(ii) ELECTION NOT TO HAVE CLAUSE (I) [sic] APPLY.—

(I) IN GENERAL.—In the case of an organization formerly exempt from tax under section 501(a) as an organization described in section 501(c)(12), clause (i) shall not apply to such organization with respect to any property if such organization elects not to be exempt from tax under section 501(a) during the tax-exempt use period with respect to such property.

(II) TAX-EXEMPT USE PERIOD.—For purposes of subclause (I), the term "tax-exempt use period" means the period beginning with the taxable year in which the property described in subclause (I) is first used by the organization and ending with the close of the 15th taxable year following the last taxable year of the applicable recovery period of such property.

(III) ELECTION.—Any election under subclause (I), once made, shall be irrevocable.

(iii) TREATMENT OF SUCCESSOR ORGANIZATIONS.—Any organization which is engaged in activities substantially similar to those engaged in by a predecessor organization shall succeed to the treatment under this subparagraph of such predecessor organization.

(iv) FIRST USED.—For purposes of this subparagraph, property shall be treated as first used by the organization—

(I) when the property is first placed in service under a lease to such organization, or

(II) in the case of property leased to (or held by) a partnership (or other pass-thru entity) in which the organization is a member, the later of when such property is first used by such partnership or pass-thru entity or when such organization is first a member of such partnership or pass-thru entity.

(3) SPECIAL RULES FOR CERTAIN HIGH TECHNOLOGY EQUIPMENT.—

(A) EXEMPTION WHERE LEASE TERM IS 5 YEARS OR LESS.—For purposes of this section, the term "tax-exempt use property" shall not include any qualified technological equipment if the lease to the tax-exempt entity has a lease term of 5 years or less. Notwithstanding subsection (i)(3)(A)(i), in determining a lease term for purposes of the preceding sentence, there shall not be taken into account any option of the lessee to renew at the fair market value rent determined at the time of renewal; except that the aggregate period not taken into account by reason of this sentence shall not exceed 24 months.

(B) EXCEPTION FOR CERTAIN PROPERTY.—

(i) IN GENERAL.—For purposes of subparagraph (A), the term "qualified technological equipment" shall not include any property leased to a tax-exempt entity if—

(I) part or all of the property was financed (directly or indirectly) by an obligation the interest on which is exempt from tax under section 103(a),

(II) such lease occurs after a sale (or other transfer) of the property by, or lease of such property from, such entity (or related entity) and such property has been used by such entity (or a related entity) before such sale (or other transfer) or lease, or

(III) such tax-exempt entity is the United States or any agency or instrumentality of the United States.

(ii) LEASEBACKS DURING 1ST 3 MONTHS OF USE NOT TAKEN INTO ACCOUNT.—Subclause (II) of clause (i) shall not apply to any property which is leased within 3 months after the date such property is first used by the tax-exempt entity (or a related entity).

(4) RELATED ENTITIES.—For purposes of this subsection—

(A)(i) Each governmental unit and each agency or instrumentality of a governmental unit is related to each other such unit, agency, or instrumentality which directly or indirectly derives its powers, rights, and duties in whole or in part from the same sovereign authority.

(ii) For purposes of clause (i), the United States, each State, and each possession of the United States shall be treated as a separate sovereign authority.

(B) Any entity not described in subparagraph (A)(i) is related to any other entity if the 2 entities have—

(i) significant common purposes and substantial common membership, or

(ii) directly or indirectly substantial common direction or control.

(C)(i) An entity is related to another entity if either entity owns (directly or through 1 or more entities) a 50 percent or greater interest in the capital or profits of the other entity.

(ii) For purposes of clause (i), entities treated as related under subparagraph (A) or (B) shall be treated as 1 entity.

(D) An entity is related to another entity with respect to a transaction if such transaction is part of an attempt by such entities to avoid the application of this subsection.

(5) TAX-EXEMPT USE OF PROPERTY LEASED TO PARTNERSHIPS, ETC., DETERMINED AT PARTNER LEVEL.—For purposes of this subsection—

(A) IN GENERAL.—In the case of any property which is leased to a partnership, the determination of whether any portion of such property is tax-exempt use property shall be made by treating each tax-exempt entity partner's proportionate share (determined under paragraph (6)(C)) of such property as being leased to such partner.

(B) OTHER PASS-THRU ENTITIES; TIERED ENTITIES.—Rules similar to the rules of subparagraph (A) shall also apply in the case of any pass-thru entity other than a partnership and in the case of tiered partnerships and other entities.

(C) PRESUMPTION WITH RESPECT TO FOREIGN ENTITIES.—Unless it is otherwise established to the satisfaction of the Secretary, it shall be presumed that the partners of a foreign partnership (and the beneficiaries of any other foreign pass-thru entity) are persons who are not United States persons.

(6) TREATMENT OF PROPERTY OWNED BY PARTNERSHIPS, ETC.—

(A) IN GENERAL.—For purposes of this subsection, if—

(i) any property which (but for this subparagraph) is not tax-exempt use property is owned by a partnership which has both a tax-exempt entity and a person who is not a tax-exempt entity as partners, and

(ii) any allocation to the tax-exempt entity of partnership items is not a qualified allocation,

an amount equal to such tax-exempt entity's proportionate share of such property shall (except as provided in paragraph (1)(D)) be treated as tax-exempt use property.

(B) QUALIFIED ALLOCATION.—For purposes of subparagraph (A), the term "qualified allocation" means any allocation to a tax-exempt entity which—

(i) is consistent with such entity's being allocated the same distributive share of each item of income, gain, loss, deduction, credit, and basis and such share remains the same during the entire period the entity is a partner in the partnership, and

(ii) has substantial economic effect within the meaning of section 704(b)(2).

For purposes of this subparagraph, items allocated under section 704(c) shall not be taken into account.

(C) DETERMINATION OF PROPORTIONATE SHARE.—

(i) IN GENERAL.—For purposes of subparagraph (A), a tax-exempt entity's proportionate share of any property owned by a partnership shall be determined on the basis of such entity's share of partnership items of income or gain (excluding gain allocated under section 704(c)), whichever results in the largest proportionate share.

(ii) DETERMINATION WHERE ALLOCATIONS VARY.—For purposes of clause (i), if a tax-exempt entity's share of partnership items of income or gain (excluding gain allocated under section 704(c)) may vary during the period such entity is a partner in the partnership, such share shall be the highest share such entity may receive.

(D) DETERMINATION OF WHETHER PROPERTY USED IN UNRELATED TRADE OR BUSINESS.—For purposes of this subsection, in the case of any property which is owned by a partnership which has both a tax-exempt entity and a person who is not a tax-exempt entity as partners, the determination of whether such property is used in an unrelated trade or business of such an entity shall be made without regard to section 514.

(E) OTHER PASS-THRU ENTITIES; TIERED ENTITIES.—Rules similar to the rules of subparagraphs (A), (B), (C), and (D) shall also apply in the case of any pass-thru entity other than a partnership and in the case of tiered partnerships and other entities.

(F) TREATMENT OF CERTAIN TAXABLE ENTITIES.—

(i) IN GENERAL.—For purposes of this paragraph and paragraph (5), except as otherwise provided in this subparagraph, any tax-exempt controlled entity shall be treated as a tax-exempt entity.

(ii) ELECTION.—If a tax-exempt controlled entity makes an election under this clause—

(I) such entity shall not be treated as a tax-exempt entity for purposes of this paragraph and paragraph (5), and

(II) any gain recognized by a tax-exempt entity on any disposition of an interest in such entity (and any dividend or interest received or accrued by a tax-exempt entity from such tax-exempt controlled entity) shall be treated as unrelated business taxable income for purposes of section 511.

Any such election shall be irrevocable and shall bind all tax-exempt entities holding interests in such tax-exempt controlled entity. For purposes of subclause (II), there shall only be taken into account dividends which are properly allocable to income of the tax-exempt controlled entity which was not subject to tax under this chapter.

(iii) TAX-EXEMPT CONTROLLED ENTITY.—

(I) IN GENERAL.—The term "tax-exempt controlled entity" means any corporation (which is not a tax-exempt entity determined without regard to this subparagraph and paragraph (2)(E)) if 50 percent or more (in value) of the stock in such corporation is held by 1 or more tax-exempt entities (other than a foreign person or entity).

(II) ONLY 5-PERCENT SHAREHOLDERS TAKEN INTO ACCOUNT IN CASE OF PUBLICLY TRADED STOCK.—For purposes of subclause (I), in the case of a corporation the stock of which is publicly traded on an established securities market, stock held by a tax-exempt entity shall not be taken into account unless such entity holds at least 5 percent (in value) of the stock in such corporation. For purposes of this subclause, related entities (within the meaning of paragraph (4)) shall be treated as 1 entity.

(III) SECTION 318 TO APPLY.—For purposes of this clause, a tax-exempt entity shall be treated as holding stock which it holds through application of section 318 (determined without regard to the 50-percent limitation contained in subsection (a)(2)(C) thereof).

(G) REGULATIONS.—For purposes of determining whether there is a qualified allocation under subparagraph (B), the regulations prescribed under paragraph (8) for purposes of this paragraph—

(i) shall set forth the proper treatment for partnership guaranteed payments, and

(ii) may provide for the exclusion or segregation of items.

(7) LEASE.—For purposes of this subsection, the term "lease" includes any grant of a right to use property.

(8) REGULATIONS.—The Secretary shall prescribe such regulations as may be necessary or appropriate to carry out the purposes of this subsection.

Amendments

• 2004, American Jobs Creation Act of 2004 (P.L. 108-357)

P.L. 108-357, §847(d):

Amended Code Sec. 168(h)(3)(A) by adding at the end a new sentence. **Effective** generally for leases entered into after 3-12-2004, and in the case of property treated as tax-exempt use property other than by reason of a lease, to property acquired after 3-12-2004 [effective date amended by P.L. 109-135, §403(ff)]. For an exception, see Act Sec. 849(b)(1)-(2), below.

P.L. 108-357, §847(e):

Amended Code Sec. 168(h)(2)(A) by striking "and" at the end of clause (ii), by striking the period at the end of clause (iii) and inserting ", and" and by inserting at the end a new clause (iv) and a flush sentence that follows clause (iv). **Effective** for leases entered into after 10-3-2004. For an exception, see Act Sec. 849(b)(1)-(2), below.

P.L. 108-357, §849(b)(1)-(2), provides:

(b) EXCEPTION.—

(1) IN GENERAL.—The amendments made by this part shall not apply to qualified transportation property.

(2) QUALIFIED TRANSPORTATION PROPERTY.—For purposes of paragraph (1), the term "qualified transportation property" means domestic property subject to a lease with respect to which a formal application—

(A) was submitted for approval to the Federal Transit Administration (an agency of the Department of Transportation) after June 30, 2003, and before March 13, 2004,

(B) is approved by the Federal Transit Administration before January 1, 2006, and

(C) includes a description of such property and the value of such property.

• 1988, Technical and Miscellaneous Revenue Act of 1988 (P.L. 100-647)

P.L. 100-647, §1002(a)(8):

Amended Code Sec. 168(h)(2)(B). **Effective** as if included in the provision of P.L. 99-514 to which it relates. Prior to amendment, Code Sec. 168(h)(2)(B) read as follows:

(B) EXCEPTIONS FOR CERTAIN PROPERTY SUBJECT TO UNITED STATES TAX AND USED BY FOREIGN PERSON OR ENTITY.—

(i) INCOME FROM PROPERTY SUBJECT TO UNITED STATES TAX.—Clause (iii) of subparagraph (A) shall not apply with respect to any property if more than 50 percent of the gross income for the taxable year derived by the foreign person or entity from the use of such property is—

(I) subject to tax under this chapter, or

(II) included under section 951 in the gross income of a United States shareholder for the taxable year with or within which ends the taxable year of the controlled foreign corporation in which such income was derived.

For purposes of the preceding sentence, any exclusion or exemption shall not apply for purposes of determining the amount of the gross income so derived, but shall apply for purposes of determining the portion of such gross income subject to tax under this chapter.

(ii) MOVIES AND SOUND RECORDINGS.—Clause (iii) of subparagraph (A) shall not apply with respect to any qualified film (as defined in section 48(k)(1)(B)) or any sound recording (as defined in section 48(r)(5)).

[Sec. 168(i)]

(i) DEFINITIONS AND SPECIAL RULES.—For purposes of this section—

(1) CLASS LIFE.—Except as provided in this section, the term "class life" means the class life (if any) which would be applicable with respect to any property as of January 1, 1986, under subsection (m) of section 167 (determined without regard to paragraph (4) and as if the taxpayer had made an election under such subsection). The Secretary, through an office established in the Treasury, shall monitor and analyze actual experience with respect to all depreciable assets. The reference in this paragraph to subsection (m) of section 167 shall be treated as a reference to such subsection as in effect on the day before the date of the enactment of the Revenue Reconciliation Act of 1990.

(2) QUALIFIED TECHNOLOGICAL EQUIPMENT.—

(A) IN GENERAL.—The term "qualified technological equipment" means—

(i) any computer or peripheral equipment,

(ii) any high technology telephone station equipment installed on the customer's premises, and

(iii) any high technology medical equipment.

(B) COMPUTER OR PERIPHERAL EQUIPMENT DEFINED.—For purposes of this paragraph—

(i) IN GENERAL.—The term "computer or peripheral equipment" means—

(I) any computer, and

(II) any related peripheral equipment.

(ii) COMPUTER.—The term "computer" means a programmable electronically activated device which—

(I) is capable of accepting information, applying prescribed processes to the information, and supplying the results of these processes with or without human intervention, and

(II) consists of a central processing unit containing extensive storage, logic, arithmetic, and control capabilities.

(iii) RELATED PERIPHERAL EQUIPMENT.—The term "related peripheral equipment" means any auxiliary machine (whether on-line or off-line) which is designed to be placed under the control of the central processing unit of a computer.

(iv) EXCEPTIONS.—The term "computer or peripheral equipment" shall not include—

(I) any equipment which is an integral part of other property which is not a computer,

(II) typewriters, calculators, adding and accounting machines, copiers, duplicating equipment, and similar equipment, and

(III) equipment of a kind used primarily for amusement or entertainment of the user.

(C) HIGH TECHNOLOGY MEDICAL EQUIPMENT.—For purposes of this paragraph, the term "high technology medical equipment" means any electronic, electromechanical, or computer-based high technology equipment used in the screening, monitoring, observation, diagnosis, or treatment of patients in a laboratory, medical, or hospital environment.

(3) LEASE TERM.—

(A) IN GENERAL.—In determining a lease term—

(i) there shall be taken into account options to renew,

(ii) the term of a lease shall include the term of any service contract or similar arrangement (whether or not treated as a lease under section 7701(e))—

(I) which is part of the same transaction (or series of related transactions) which includes the lease, and

(II) which is with respect to the property subject to the lease or substantially similar property,

(iii) 2 or more successive leases which are part of the same transaction (or a series of related transactions) with respect to the same or substantially similar property shall be treated as 1 lease.

(B) SPECIAL RULE FOR FAIR RENTAL OPTIONS ON NONRESIDENTIAL REAL PROPERTY OR RESIDENTIAL RENTAL PROPERTY.—For purposes of clause (i) of subparagraph (A), in the case of nonresidential real property or residential rental property, there shall not be taken into account any option to renew at fair market value, determined at the time of renewal.

(4) GENERAL ASSET ACCOUNTS.—Under regulations, a taxpayer may maintain 1 or more general asset accounts for any property to which this section applies. Except as provided in regulations, all proceeds realized on any disposition of property in a general asset account shall be included in income as ordinary income.

(5) CHANGES IN USE.—The Secretary shall, by regulations, provide for the method of determining the deduction allowable under section 167(a) with respect to any tangible property for any taxable year (and the succeeding taxable years) during which such property changes status under this section but continues to be held by the same person.

(6) TREATMENTS OF ADDITIONS OR IMPROVEMENTS TO PROPERTY.—In the case of any addition to (or improvement of) any property—

(A) any deduction under subsection (a) for such addition or improvement shall be computed in the same manner as the deduction of such property would be computed if such property had been placed in service at the same time as such addition or improvement, and

(B) the applicable recovery period for such addition or improvement shall begin on the later of—

(i) the date on which such addition (or improvement) is placed in service, or

(ii) the date on which the property with respect to which such addition (or improvement) was made is placed in service.

(7) TREATMENT OF CERTAIN TRANSFEREES.—

(A) IN GENERAL.—In the case of any property transferred in a transaction described in subparagraph (B), the transferee shall be treated as the transferor for purposes of computing the depreciation deduction determined under this section with respect to so much of the basis in the hands of the transferee as does not exceed the adjusted basis in the hands of the transferor. In any case where this section as in effect before the amendments made by section 201 of the Tax Reform Act of 1986 applied to the property in the hands of the transferor, the reference in the preceding sentence to this section shall be treated as a reference to this section as so in effect.

(B) TRANSACTIONS COVERED.—The transactions described in this subparagraph are—

(i) any transaction described in section 332, 351, 361, 721, or 731, and

(ii) any transaction between members of the same affiliated group during any taxable year for which a consolidated return is made by such group.

Subparagraph (A) shall not apply in the case of a termination of a partnership under section 708(b)(1)(B).

(C) PROPERTY REACQUIRED BY THE TAXPAYER.—Under regulations, property which is disposed of and then reaquired by the taxpayer shall be treated for purposes of computing the deduction allowable under subsection (a) as if such property had not been disposed of.

(D) [Repealed.]

(8) TREATMENT OF LEASEHOLD IMPROVEMENTS.—

(A) IN GENERAL.—In the case of any building erected (or improvements made) on leased property, if such building or improvement is property to which this section applies, the depreciation deduction shall be determined under the provisions of this section.

(B) TREATMENT OF LESSOR IMPROVEMENTS WHICH ARE ABANDONED AT TERMINATION OF LEASE.—An improvement—

(i) which is made by the lessor of leased property for the lessee of such property, and

(ii) which is irrevocably disposed of or abandoned by the lessor at the termination of the lease by such lessee,

shall be treated for purposes of determining gain or loss under this title as disposed of by the lessor when so disposed of or abandoned.

(C) CROSS REFERENCE.—

For treatment of qualified long-term real property constructed or improved in connection with cash or rent reduction from lessor to lessee, see section 110(b).

(9) NORMALIZATION RULES.—

(A) IN GENERAL.—In order to use a normalization method of accounting with respect to any public utility property for purposes of subsection (f)(2)—

(i) the taxpayer must, in computing its tax expense for purposes of establishing its cost of service for ratemaking purposes and reflecting operating results in its regulated books of account, use a method of depreciation with respect to such property that is the same as, and a depreciation period for such property that is no shorter than, the method and period used to compute its depreciation expense for such purposes; and

(ii) if the amount allowable as a deduction under this section with respect to such property differs from the amount that would be allowable as a deduction under section 167 using the method (including the period, first and last year convention, and salvage value) used to compute regulated tax expense under clause (i), the taxpayer must make adjustments to a reserve to reflect the deferral of taxes resulting from such difference.

(B) USE OF INCONSISTENT ESTIMATES AND PROJECTIONS, ETC.—

(i) IN GENERAL.—One way in which the requirements of subparagraph (A) are not met is if the taxpayer, for ratemaking purposes, uses a procedure or adjustment which is inconsistent with the requirements of subparagraph (A).

(ii) USE OF INCONSISTENT ESTIMATES AND PROJECTIONS.—The procedures and adjustments which are to be treated as inconsistent for purposes of clause (i) shall include any procedure or adjustment for ratemaking purposes which uses an estimate or projection of the taxpayer's tax expense, depreciation expense, or reserve for deferred taxes under subparagraph (A)(ii) unless such estimate or projection is also used, for ratemaking purposes, with respect to the other 2 such items and with respect to the rate base.

(iii) REGULATORY AUTHORITY.—The Secretary may by regulations prescribe procedures and adjustments (in addition to those specified in clause (ii)) which are to be treated as inconsistent for purposes of clause (i).

(C) PUBLIC UTILITY PROPERTY WHICH DOES NOT MEET NORMALIZATION RULES.—In the case of any public utility property to which this section does not apply by reason of subsection (f)(2), the allowance for depreciation under section 167(a) shall be an amount computed using the method and period referred to in subparagraph (A)(i).

(10) PUBLIC UTILITY PROPERTY.—The term "public utility property" means property used predominantly in the trade or business of the furnishing or sale of—

(A) electrical energy, water, or sewage disposal services,

(B) gas or steam through a local distribution system,

(C) telephone services, or other communication services if furnished or sold by the Communications Satellite Corporation for purposes authorized by the Communications Satellite Act of 1962 (47 U.S.C. 701), or

(D) transportation of gas or steam by pipeline,

if the rates for such furnishing or sale, as the case may be, have been established or approved by a State or political subdivision thereof, by any agency or instrumentality of the United States, or by a public service or public utility commission or other similar body of any State or political subdivision thereof.

(11) RESEARCH AND EXPERIMENTATION.—The term "research and experimentation" has the same meaning as the term research and experimental has under section 174.

(12) SECTION 1245 AND 1250 PROPERTY.—The terms "section 1245 property" and "section 1250 property" have the meanings given such terms by sections 1245(a)(3) and 1250(c), respectively.

(13) SINGLE PURPOSE AGRICULTURAL OR HORTICULTURAL STRUCTURE.—

(A) IN GENERAL.—The term "single purpose agricultural or horticultural structure" means—

(i) a single purpose livestock structure, and

(ii) a single purpose horticultural structure.

(B) DEFINITIONS.—For purposes of this paragraph—

(i) SINGLE PURPOSE LIVESTOCK STRUCTURE.—The term "single purpose livestock structure" means any enclosure or structure specifically designed, constructed, and used—

(I) for housing, raising, and feeding a particular type of livestock and their produce, and

(II) for housing the equipment (including any replacements) necessary for the housing, raising, and feeding referred to in subclause (I).

(ii) SINGLE PURPOSE HORTICULTURAL STRUCTURE.—The term "single purpose horticultural structure" means—

(I) a greenhouse specifically designed, constructed, and used for the commercial production of plants, and

(II) a structure specifically designed, constructed, and used for the commercial production of mushrooms.

(iii) STRUCTURES WHICH INCLUDE WORK SPACE.—An enclosure or structure which provides work space shall be treated as a single purpose agricultural or horticultural structure only if such work space is solely for—

(I) the stocking, caring for, or collecting of livestock or plants (as the case may be) or their produce,

(II) the maintenance of the enclosure or structure, and

(III) the maintenance or replacement of the equipment or stock enclosed or housed therein.

(iv) LIVESTOCK.—The term "livestock" includes poultry.

(14) QUALIFIED RENT-TO-OWN PROPERTY.—

(A) IN GENERAL.—The term "qualified rent-to-own property" means property held by a rent-to-own dealer for purposes of being subject to a rent-to-own contract.

(B) RENT-TO-OWN DEALER.—The term "rent-to-own dealer" means a person that, in the ordinary course of business, regularly enters into rent-to-own contracts with customers for the use of consumer property, if a substantial portion of those contracts terminate and the property is returned to such person before the receipt of all payments required to transfer ownership of the property from such person to the customer.

(C) CONSUMER PROPERTY.—The term "consumer property" means tangible personal property of a type generally used within the home for personal use.

(D) RENT-TO-OWN CONTRACT.—The term "rent-to-own contract" means any lease for the use of consumer property between a rent-to-own dealer and a customer who is an individual which—

(i) is titled "Rent-to-Own Agreement" or "Lease Agreement with Ownership Option," or uses other similar language,

(ii) provides for level (or decreasing where no payment is less than 40 percent of the largest payment), regular periodic payments (for a payment period which is a week or month),

(iii) provides that legal title to such property remains with the rent-to-own dealer until the customer makes all the payments described in clause (ii) or early purchase payments required under the contract to acquire legal title to the item of property,

(iv) provides a beginning date and a maximum period of time for which the contract may be in effect that does not exceed 156 weeks or 36 months from such beginning date (including renewals or options to extend),

(v) provides for payments within the 156-week or 36-month period that, in the aggregate, generally exceed the normal retail price of the consumer property plus interest,

(vi) provides for payments under the contract that, in the aggregate, do not exceed $10,000 per item of consumer property,

(vii) provides that the customer does not have any legal obligation to make all the payments referred to in clause (ii) set forth under the contract, and that at the end of each payment period the customer may either continue to use the consumer property by making the payment for the next payment period or return such property to the rent-to-own dealer in good working order, in which case the customer does not incur any further obligations under the contract and is not entitled to a return of any payments previously made under the contract, and

(viii) provides that the customer has no right to sell, sublease, mortgage, pawn, pledge, encumber, or otherwise dispose of the consumer property until all the payments stated in the contract have been made.

(15) MOTORSPORTS ENTERTAINMENT COMPLEX.—

(A) IN GENERAL.—The term "motorsports entertainment complex" means a racing track facility which—

(i) is permanently situated on land, and

(ii) during the 36-month period following the first day of the month in which the asset is placed in service, hosts 1 or more racing events for automobiles (of any type), trucks, or motorcycles which are open to the public for the price of admission.

(B) ANCILLARY AND SUPPORT FACILITIES.—Such term shall include, if owned by the taxpayer who owns the complex and provided for the benefit of patrons of the complex—

(i) ancillary facilities and land improvements in support of the complex's activities (including parking lots, sidewalks, waterways, bridges, fences, and landscaping),

(ii) support facilities (including food and beverage retailing, souvenir vending, and other nonlodging accommodations), and

(iii) appurtenances associated with such facilities and related attractions and amusements (including ticket booths, race track surfaces, suites and hospitality facilities, grandstands and viewing structures, props, walls, facilities that support the delivery of entertainment services, other special purpose structures, facades, shop interiors, and buildings).

(C) EXCEPTION.—Such term shall not include any transportation equipment, administrative services assets, warehouses, administrative buildings, hotels, or motels.

(D) TERMINATION.—Such term shall not include any property placed in service after December 31, 2009.

(16) ALASKA NATURAL GAS PIPELINE.—The term "Alaska natural gas pipeline" means the natural gas pipeline system located in the State of Alaska which—

(A) has a capacity of more than 500,000,000,000 Btu of natural gas per day, and

(B) is—

(i) placed in service after December 31, 2013, or

(ii) treated as placed in service on January 1, 2014, if the taxpayer who places such system in service before January 1, 2014, elects such treatment.

Such term includes the pipe, trunk lines, related equipment, and appurtenances used to carry natural gas, but does not include any gas processing plant.

(17) NATURAL GAS GATHERING LINE.—The term "natural gas gathering line" means—

(A) the pipe, equipment, and appurtenances determined to be a gathering line by the Federal Energy Regulatory Commission, and

(B) the pipe, equipment, and appurtenances used to deliver natural gas from the wellhead or a commonpoint to the point at which such gas first reaches—

(i) a gas processing plant,

(ii) an interconnection with a transmission pipeline for which a certificate as an interstate transmission pipeline has been issued by the Federal Energy Regulatory Commission,

(iii) an interconnection with an intrastate transmission pipeline, or

(iv) a direct interconnection with a local distribution company, a gas storage facility, or an industrial consumer.

(18) QUALIFIED SMART ELECTRIC METERS.—

(A) IN GENERAL.—The term "qualified smart electric meter" means any smart electric meter which—

(i) is placed in service by a taxpayer who is a supplier of electric energy or a provider of electric energy services, and

(ii) does not have a class life (determined without regard to subsection (e)) of less than 10 years.

(B) SMART ELECTRIC METER.—For purposes of subparagraph (A), the term "smart electric meter" means any time-based meter and related communication equipment which is capable of being used by the taxpayer as part of a system that—

(i) measures and records electricity usage data on a time-differentiated basis in at least 24 separate time segments per day,

(ii) provides for the exchange of information between supplier or provider and the customer's electric meter in support of time-based rates or other forms of demand response,

(iii) provides data to such supplier or provider so that the supplier or provider can provide energy usage information to customers electronically, and

(iv) provides net metering.

(19) QUALIFIED SMART ELECTRIC GRID SYSTEMS.—

(A) IN GENERAL.—The term "qualified smart electric grid system" means any smart grid property which—

(i) is used as part of a system for electric distribution grid communications, monitoring, and management placed in service by a taxpayer who is a supplier of electric energy or a provider of electric energy services, and

(ii) does not have a class life (determined without regard to subsection (e)) of less than 10 years.

(B) SMART GRID PROPERTY.—For the purposes of subparagraph (A), the term "smart grid property" means electronics and related equipment that is capable of—

(i) sensing, collecting, and monitoring data of or from all portions of a utility's electric distribution grid,

(ii) providing real-time, two-way communications to monitor or manage such grid, and

(iii) providing real time analysis of and event prediction based upon collected data that can be used to improve electric distribution system reliability, quality, and performance.

Amendments

• 2008, Energy Improvement and Extension Act of 2008 (P.L. 110-343)

P.L. 110-343, Division B, §306(b):

Amended Code Sec. 168(i) by inserting at the end new paragraph[s] (18)-(19). **Effective** for property placed in service after 10-3-2008.

• 2008, Tax Extenders and Alternative Minimum Tax Relief Act of 2008 (P.L. 110-343)

P.L. 110-343, Division C, §317(a):

Amended Code Sec. 168(i)(15)(D) by striking "December 31, 2007" and inserting "December 31, 2009". **Effective** for property placed in service after 12-31-2007.

•2005, Gulf Opportunity Zone Act of 2005 (P.L. 109-135)

P.L. 109-135, §412(s):

Amended Code Sec. 168(i)(15)(D) by striking "This paragraph shall not apply to" and inserting "Such term shall not include". **Effective** 12-21-2005.

• 2005, Energy Tax Incentives Act of 2005 (P.L. 109-58)

P.L. 109-58, §1326(b):

Amended Code Sec. 168(i) by inserting after paragraph (16) a new paragraph (17). **Effective** generally for property placed in service after 4-11-2005. For an exception, see Act Sec. 1326(e)(2), below.

P.L. 109-58, §1326(e)(2), provides:

(2) EXCEPTION.—The amendments made by this section shall not apply to any property with respect to which the taxpayer or a related party has entered into a binding contract for the construction thereof on or before April 11, 2005, or, in the case of self-constructed property, has started construction on or before such date.

• 2004, American Jobs Creation Act of 2004 (P.L. 108-357)

P.L. 108-357, §704(b):

Amended Code Sec. 168(i) by adding at the end a new paragraph (15). **Effective** generally for any property placed in service after 10-22-2004. For special rules, see Act Secs. 704(c)(2)-(3), below.

P.L. 108-357, §704(c)(2)-(3), provides:

(2) SPECIAL RULE FOR ASSET CLASS 80.0.—In the case of race track facilities placed in service after the date of the enactment of this Act [10-22-2004.—CCH], such facilities shall not be treated as theme and amusement facilities classified under asset class 80.0.

(3) NO INFERENCE.—Nothing in this section or the amendments made by this section shall be construed to affect the treatment of property placed in service on or before the date of the enactment of this Act [10-22-2004.—CCH].

P.L. 108-357, §706(b):

Amended Code Sec. 168(i), as amended by this Act, by inserting after paragraph (15) a new paragraph (16). **Effective** for property placed in service after 12-31-2004.

P.L. 108-357, §847(c):

Amended Code Sec. 168(i)(3)(A) by striking "and" at the end of clause (i), by redesignating clause (ii) as clause (iii) and by inserting after clause (i) a new clause (ii). **Effective** generally for leases entered into after 3-12-2004, and in the case of property treated as tax-exempt use property other than by reason of a lease, to property acquired after 3-12-2004 [effective date amended by P.L. 109-135, §403(ff)]. For an exception, see Act Sec. 849(b)(1)-(2), below.

P.L. 108-357, §849(b)(1)-(2), provides:

(b) EXCEPTION.—

(1) IN GENERAL.—The amendments made by this part shall not apply to qualified transportation property.

(2) QUALIFIED TRANSPORTATION PROPERTY.—For purposes of paragraph (1), the term "qualified transportation property" means domestic property subject to a lease with respect to which a formal application—

(A) was submitted for approval to the Federal Transit Administration (an agency of the Department of Transportation) after June 30, 2003, and before March 13, 2004,

(B) is approved by the Federal Transit Administration before January 1, 2006, and

(C) includes a description of such property and the value of such property.

• 1997, Taxpayer Relief Act of 1997 (P.L. 105-34)

P.L. 105-34, §1086(b)(3):

Amended Code Sec. 168(i) by adding at the end a new paragraph (14). **Effective** for property placed in service after 8-5-97.

P.L. 105-34, §1213(c):

Amended Code Sec. 168(i)(8) by adding at the end a new subparagraph (C). **Effective** for leases entered into after 8-5-97.

• 1996, Small Business Job Protection Act of 1996 (P.L. 104-188)

P.L. 104-188, §1121(a):

Amended Code Sec. 168(i)(8). **Effective** for improvements disposed of or abandoned after 6-12-96. Prior to amendment, Code Sec. 168(i)(8) read as follows:

(8) TREATMENT OF LEASEHOLD IMPROVEMENTS.—In the case of any building erected (or improvements made) on leased property, if such building or improvement is property to which this section applies, the depreciation deduction shall be determined under the provisions of this section.

• 1990, Omnibus Budget Reconciliation Act of 1990 (P.L. 101-508)

P.L. 101-508, §11801(c)(8)(B):

Amended Code Sec. 168(i)(7)(B) by striking "371(a), 374(a)," after "361". **Effective** 11-5-90.

P.L. 101-508, §11821(b), provides:

(b) SAVINGS PROVISION.—If—

(1) any provision amended or repealed by this part applied to—

(A) any transaction occurring before the date of the enactment of this Act,

(B) any property acquired before such date of enactment, or

(C) any item of income, loss, deduction, or credit taken into account before such date of enactment, and

(2) the treatment of such transaction, property, or item under such provision would (without regard to the amendments made by this part) affect liability for tax for periods ending after such date of enactment,

nothing in the amendments made by this part shall be construed to affect the treatment of such transaction, property, or item for purposes of determining liability for tax for periods ending after such date of enactment.

P.L. 101-508, §11812(b)(2)(B):

Amended Code Sec. 168(i)(10). **Effective**, generally, for property placed in service after 11-5-90. However, for exceptions see Act Sec. 11812(c)(2)-(3) below. Prior to amendment, Code Sec. 168(i)(10) read as follows:

(10) PUBLIC UTILITY PROPERTY.—The term "public utility property" has the meaning given such term by section 167(l)(3)(A).

P.L. 101-508, §11812(b)(2)(D):

Amended Code Sec. 168(i)(1) by adding a new sentence at the end thereof. **Effective**, generally, for property placed in service after 11-5-90. However, for exceptions see Act Sec. 11812(c)(2)-(3) below.

P.L. 101-508, §11812(b)(2)(E):

Amended Code Sec. 168(i)(9)(A)(ii) by striking "(determined without regard to section 167(l))" after "section 167". **Effective**, generally, for property placed in service after 11-5-90. However, for exceptions see Act Sec. 11812(c)(2)-(3) below.

P.L. 101-508, §11812(c)(2)-(3), provides:

(2) EXCEPTION.—The amendments made by this section shall not apply to any property to which section 168 of the Internal Revenue Code of 1986 does not apply by reason of subsection (f)(5) thereof.

(3) EXCEPTION FOR PREVIOUSLY GRANDFATHER EXPENDITURES.—The amendments made by this section shall not apply to rehabilitation expenditures described in section 252(f)(5) of the Tax Reform Act of 1986 (as added by section 1002(l)(31) of the Technical and Miscellaneous Revenue Act of 1988).

P.L. 101-508, §11813(b)(9)(B)(ii):

Amended Code Sec. 168(i) by adding at the end thereof new paragraph (13). **Effective**, generally, for property placed in service after 12-31-90. However, for exceptions see Act Sec. 11813(c)(2) below.

P.L. 101-508, §11813(c)(2), provides:

(2) EXCEPTIONS.—The amendments made by this section shall not apply to—

(A) any transition property (as defined in section 49(e) of the Internal Revenue Code of 1986 (as in effect on the day before the date of the enactment of this Act),

(B) any property with respect to which qualified progress expenditures were previously taken into account under section 46(d) of such Code (as so in effect), and

(C) any property described in section 46(b)(2)(C) of such Code (as so in effect).

• 1988, Technical and Miscellaneous Revenue Act of 1988 (P.L. 100-647)

P.L. 100-647, §1002(a)(7)(A):

Amended Code Sec. 168(i)(7)(A) by adding at the end thereof a new sentence. **Effective** as if included in the provision of P.L. 99-514 to which it relates.

P.L. 100-647, §1002(a)(7)(B):

Amended Code Sec. 168(i)(7)(B). **Effective** as if included in the provision of P.L. 99-514 to which it relates. Prior to amendment, Code Sec. 168(i)(7)(B) read as follows:

(B) TRANSACTIONS COVERED.—The transactions described in this subparagraph are any transaction described in section 332, 351, 361, 371(a), 374(a), 721, or 731. Subparagraph (A) shall not apply in the case of a termination of a partnership under section 708(b)(1)(B).

P.L. 100-647, §1002(a)(7)(C):

Repealed Code Sec. 168(i)(7)(D). **Effective** as if included in the provision of P.L. 99-514 to which it relates. Prior to repeal, Code Sec. 168(i)(7)(D) read as follows:

(D) EXCEPTION.—This paragraph shall not apply to any transaction to which subsection (f)(5) applies (relating to churning transactions).

P.L. 100-647, §1002(i)(2)(G):

Amended the Code Sec. 168(i)(1)(E) by adding at the end thereof a new clause (iii). **Effective** as if included in the provision of P.L. 99-514 to which it relates.

P.L. 100-647, §6253:

Amended Code Sec. 168(i)(1). **Effective** 11-10-88. Prior to amendment, Code Sec. 168(i)(1) read as follows:

(1) CLASS LIFE.—

(A) IN GENERAL.—Except as provided in this section, the term "class life" means the class life (if any) which would be applicable with respect to any property as of January 1, 1986, under subsection (m) of section 167 (determined without regard to paragraph (4) thereof and as if the taxpayer had made an election under such subsection).

(B) SECRETARIAL AUTHORITY.—The Secretary, through an office established in the Treasury—

(i) shall monitor and analyze actual experience with respect to all depreciable assets, and

(ii) except in the case of residential rental property or nonresidential real property—

(I) may prescribe a new class life for any property,

(II) in the case of assigned property, may modify any assigned item, or

(III) may prescribe a class life for any property which does not have a class life within the meaning of subparagraph (A).

Any class life or assigned item prescribed or modified under the preceding sentence shall reasonably reflect the anticipated useful life, and the anticipated decline in value over time, of the property to the industry or other group.

(C) EFFECT OF MODIFICATION.—Any class life or assigned item with respect to any property prescribed or modified under subparagraph (B) shall be used in classifying such property under subsection (e) and in applying subsection (g).

(D) NO MODIFICATION OF ASSIGNED PROPERTY BEFORE JANUARY 1, 1992.—

(i) IN GENERAL.—Except as otherwise provided in this subparagraph, the Secretary may not modify an assigned item under subparagraph (B)(ii)(II) for any assigned property which is placed in service before January 1, 1992.

(ii) EXCEPTION FOR SHORTER CLASS LIFE.—In the case of assigned property which is placed in service before January 1, 1992, and for which the assigned item reflects a class life which is shorter than the class life under subparagraph (A), the Secretary may modify such assigned item under subparagraph (B)(ii)(II) if such modification results in an item which reflects a shorter class life than such assigned item.

(E) ASSIGNED PROPERTY AND ITEM.—For purposes of this paragraph—

(i) ASSIGNED PROPERTY.—The term "assigned property" means property for which a class life, classification, or recovery period is assigned under subsection (e)(3) or subparagraph (B), (C), or (D) of subsection (g)(3).

(ii) ASSIGNED ITEMS.—The term "assigned item" means the class life, classification, or recovery period assigned under subsection (e)(3) or subparagraph (B), (C), or (D) of subsection (g)(3).

(iii) SPECIAL RULE FOR RAILROAD GRADING OR TUNNEL BORES.—In the case of any property which is a railroad grading or tunnel bore—

(I) such property shall be treated as an assigned property,

(II) the recovery period applicable to such property shall be treated as an assigned item, and

(III) clause (ii) of subparagraph (D) shall not apply.

• 1986, Tax Reform Act of 1986 (P.L. 99-514)

P.L. 99-514, §201(a):

Amended Code Sec. 168. For **effective** dates and transitional rules, see Act Secs. 203, 204 and 251(d)(2)-7, below. Prior to amendment, Code Sec. 168 read as follows:

SEC. 168. ACCELERATED COST RECOVERY SYSTEM.

[Sec. 168(a)]

(a) ALLOWANCE OF DEDUCTION.—There shall be allowed as a deduction for any taxable year the amount determined under this section with respect to recovery property.

Amendments

• 1981, Economic Recovery Tax Act of 1981 (P.L. 97-34)

P.L. 97-34, §201(a):

Added Code Sec. 168(a). **Effective** for property placed in service after 12-31-80, in tax years ending after such date.

[Sec. 168(b)]

(b) AMOUNT OF DEDUCTION.—

(1) IN GENERAL.—Except as otherwise provided in this section, the amount of the deduction allowable by subsection (a) for any taxable year shall be the aggregate amount determined by applying to the unadjusted basis of recovery property the applicable percentage determined in accordance with the following table:

If the recovery year is:	*The applicable percentage of the class of property is:* 3-year	5-year	10-year	15-year public utility
1	25	15	8	5
2	38	22	14	10
3	37	21	12	9
4		21	10	8
5		21	10	7
6			10	7
7			9	6
8			9	6
9			9	6
10			9	6
11				6
12				6
13				6
14				6
15				6

(2) 19-YEAR REAL PROPERTY.—

(A) IN GENERAL.—In the case of 19-year real property, the applicable percentage shall be determined in accordance with a table prescribed by the Secretary. In prescribing such table, the Secretary shall—

(i) assign to the property a 19-year recovery period, and

(ii) assign percentages generally determined in accordance with use of the 175 percent declining balance method, switching to the method described in section 167(b)(1) at a time to maximize the deduction allowable under subsection (a).

(B) MID-MONTH CONVENTION FOR 19-YEAR REAL PROPERTY.—In the case of 19-year real property, the amount of the deduction determined under any provision of this section (or for purposes of section 57(a)(12)(B) or 312(k)) for any taxable year shall be determined on the basis of the number of months (using a mid-month convention) in which the property is in service.

(3) ELECTION OF DIFFERENT RECOVERY PERCENTAGE.—

(A) IN GENERAL.—Except as provided in subsection (f)(2), in lieu of any applicable percentage under paragraph (1), (2), or (4), the taxpayer may elect, with respect to one or more classes of recovery property placed in service during the taxable year, the applicable percentage determined by use of the straight line method over the recovery period elected by the taxpayer in accordance with the following table:

In the case of:	*The taxpayer may elect a recovery period of:*
3-year property	3, 5, or 12 years.
5-year property	5, 12, or 25 years.
10-year property	10, 25, or 35 years.
15-year public utility property	15, 35, or 45 years.
19-year real property	19, 35, or 45 years.
Low-income housing	15, 35, or 45 years.

(B) OPERATING RULES.—

(i) IN GENERAL.—Except as provided in clause (ii), the taxpayer may elect under subparagraph (A) only a single percentage for property in any class of recovery property placed in service during the taxable year. The percentage so elected shall apply to all property in such class placed in service during such taxable year and shall apply throughout the recovery period elected for such property.

(ii) REAL PROPERTY.—In the case of 19-year real property or low-income housing the taxpayer shall make the election under subparagraph (A) on a property-by-property basis.

(iii) CONVENTION.—Under regulations prescribed by the Secretary, the half-year convention shall apply to any election with respect to any recovery property (other than 19-year real property or low-income housing) with respect to which an election is made under this paragraph.

(4) LOW-INCOME HOUSING.—

(A) IN GENERAL.—In the case of low-income housing, the applicable percentage shall be determined in accordance with the table prescribed in paragraph (2) (without regard to the mid-month convention), except that in prescribing such table, the Secretary shall—

(i) assign to the property a 15-year recovery period, and

(ii) assign percentages generally determined in accordance with use of the 200 percent declining balance method, switching to the method described in section 167(b)(1) at a time to maximize the deduction allowable under subsection (a).

(B) MONTHLY CONVENTION.—In the case of low-income housing, the amount of the deduction determined under any provision of this section (or for purposes of section 57(a)(12)(B) or 312(k)) for any taxable year shall be determined on the basis of the number of months (treating all property placed in service or disposed of during any month as placed in service or disposed of on the first day of such month) in which the property is in service.

Amendments

• 1985 (P.L. 99-121)

P.L. 99-121, §103(a):

Amended Code Sec. 168(b)(2)(A)(i) by striking out "18-year recovery period" and inserting in lieu thereof "19-year recovery period". **Effective** with respect to property placed in service by the taxpayer after 5-8-85. However, for an exception and special rule, see Act Sec. 105(b)(2) and (3), below.

P.L. 99-121, §103(b)(2):

Amended Code Sec. 168(b)(3) by striking out "18, 35, or 45" in the table contained in subparagraph (A) and inserting in lieu thereof "19, 35, or 45 years". **Effective** with respect to property placed in service by the taxpayer after 5-8-85. However, for an exception and special rule, see Act Sec. 105(b)(2) and (3), below.

P.L. 99-121, §105(b)(2) and (3), provides:

(2) EXCEPTION.—The amendments made by section 103 shall not apply to property placed in service by the taxpayer before January 1, 1987, if—

(A) the taxpayer or a qualified person entered into a binding contract to purchase or construct such property before May 9, 1985, or

(B) construction of such property was commenced by or for the taxpayer or a qualified person before May 9, 1985.

For purposes of this paragraph, the term "qualified person" means any person whose rights in such a contract or such property are transferred to the taxpayer, but only if such property is not placed in service before such rights are transferred to the taxpayer.

(3) SPECIAL RULE FOR COMPONENTS.—For purposes of applying section 168(f)(1)(B) of the Internal Revenue Code of 1954 (as amended by section 103) to components placed in service after December 31, 1986, property to which paragraph (2) of this subsection applies shall be treated as placed in service by the taxpayer before May 9, 1985.

• 1984, Deficit Reduction Act of 1984 (P.L. 98-369)

P.L. 98-369, §111(a):

Amended Code Sec. 168(b)(2) by striking out "15-year real property" each place it appears in the text and heading thereof and inserting in lieu thereof "18-year real property", by striking out "15-year recovery period" in subparagraph (A)(i) and inserting in lieu thereof "18-year recovery period", and by striking out "(200 percent declining balance method in the case of low-income housing)". For the **effective** date as well as special rules, see Act Sec. 111(g)[f], below.

P.L. 98-369, §111(b)(1):

Amended Code Sec. 168(b) by adding at the end thereof new paragraph (4). For the **effective** date as well as special rules, see Act Sec. 111(g)[f], below.

P.L. 98-369, §111(b)(3)(A):

Amended Code Sec. 168(b)(2)(A) by striking out the last sentence thereof. For the **effective** date as well as special rules, see Act Sec. 111(g)[f], below. Prior to amendment, the last sentence read as follows:

For purposes of this subparagraph, the term "low-income housing" means property described in clause (i), (ii), (iii), or (iv) of section 1250(a)(1)(B).

P.L. 98-369, §111(d):

Amended Code Sec. 168(b)(2)(A) and (B) by inserting "(using a midmonth convention)" after "months". For the **effective** date as well as special rules, see Act Sec. 111(g)[f], below.

P.L. 98-369, §111(e)(1):

Amended Code Sec. 168(b)(3)(B)(iii) by striking out "15-year real property" each place it appears and inserting in lieu thereof "18-year real property or low-income housing". For the **effective** date as well as special rules, see Act Sec. 111(g)[f], below.

P.L. 98-369, §111(e)(2):

Amended Code Sec. 168(b)(3)(B)(ii) by striking out "15-year real property" and inserting in lieu thereof "18-year real property or low-income housing". For the **effective** date as well as special rules, see Act Sec. 111(g)[f], below.

P.L. 98-369, §111(e)(9):

Amended Code Sec. 168(b)(3)(A) by striking out "under paragraphs (1) and (2)" and inserting in lieu thereof "under paragraph (1), (2), or (4)", and by striking out the item in the table relating to 15-year real property and inserting in lieu thereof: "18-year real property and low-income housing. . . . 18, 35, or 45 [years]." For the **effective** date as well as special rules, see Act Sec. 111(g)[f], below.

P.L. 98-369, §111(g)[f] provides:

[f] Effective Date.—

(1) In General.—Except as otherwise provided in this subsection, the amendments made by this section shall apply with respect to property placed in service by the taxpayer after March 15, 1984.

(2) Exception.—The amendments made by this section shall not apply to property placed in service by the taxpayer before January 1, 1987, if—

(A) the taxpayer or a qualified person entered into a binding contract to purchase or construct such property before March 16, 1984, or

(B) construction of such property was commenced by or for the taxpayer or a qualified person before March 16, 1984.

For purposes of this paragraph the term "qualified person" means any person who transfers his rights in such a contract or such property to the taxpayer, but only if the property is not placed in service by such person before such rights are transferred to the taxpayer.

(3) Special Rules for Application of Paragraph (2).—

(A) Certain Inventory.—In the case of any property which—

(i) is held by a person as property described in section 1221(1), and

(ii) is disposed of by such person before January 1, 1985,

such person shall not, for purposes of paragraph (2), be treated as having placed such property in service before such property is disposed of merely because such person rented such property or held such property for rental. No deduction for depreciation or amortization shall be allowed to such person with respect to such property,

(B) Certain Property Financed By Bonds.—In the case of any property with respect to which—,

(i) bonds were issued to finance such property before 1984, and

(ii) an architectural contract was entered into before March 16, 1984,

paragraph (2) shall be applied by substituting "May 2" for "March 16".

(4) SPECIAL RULE FOR COMPONENTS.—For purposes of applying section 168(f)(1)(B) of the Internal Revenue Code of 1954 (as amended by this section) to components placed in service after December 31, 1986, property to which paragraph (2) applies shall be treated as placed in service by the taxpayer before March 16, 1984.

(5) SPECIAL RULE FOR MID-MONTH CONVENTION.—In the case of the amendment made by subsection (d)—

(A) paragraph (1) shall be applied by substituting "June 22, 1984" for "March 15, 1984", and

(B) paragraph (2) shall be applied by substituting "June 23, 1984" for "March 15, 1984" each place it appears.

• 1983, Technical Corrections Act of 1982 (P.L. 97-448)

P.L. 97-448, §102(a)(5):

Amended the third sentence of Code Sec. 168(b)(2)(A) by striking out "For purposes of this subparagraph" and inserting in lieu thereof "In the case of 15-year real property". **Effective** as if it had been included in the provision of P.L. 97-34 to which it relates.

• 1982, Tax Equity and Fiscal Responsibility Act of 1982 (P.L. 97-248)

P.L. 97-248, § 206(a)(1)(3):

Amended Code Sec. 168(b)(1) by striking out "tables" and inserting in lieu thereof "table", by striking out "(A) FOR PROPERTY PLACED IN SERVICE AFTER DECEMBER 31, 1980, AND BEFORE JANUARY 1, 1985.—", and by striking out subparagraphs (B) and (C). **Effective** as of 9-3-82. Prior to amendment, subparagraphs (B) and (C) read as follows:

"(B) For property placed in service in 1985.—

If the recovery year is:	The applicable percentage for the class of property is:			
	3-year	5-year	10-year	15-year public utility
1	29	18	9	6
2	47	33	19	12
3	24	25	16	12
4		16	14	11
5		8	12	10
6			10	9
7			8	8
8			6	7
9			4	6
10			2	5
11				4
12				4
13				3
14				2
15				1

(C) For property placed in service after December 31, 1985.—

If the recovery year is:	The applicable percentage for the class of property is:			
	3-year	5-year	10-year	15-year public utility
1	33	20	10	7
2	45	32	18	12
3	23	24	16	12
4		16	14	11
5		8	12	10
6			10	9
7			8	8
8			6	7
9			4	6
10			2	5
11				4
12				3
13				3
14				2
15				1."

• 1981, Economic Recovery Tax Act of 1981 (P.L. 97-34)

P.L. 97-34, §201(a):

Added Code Sec. 168(b). **Effective** for property placed in service after 12-31-80, in tax years ending after such date.

[Sec. 168(c)]

(c) RECOVERY PROPERTY.—For purposes of this title—

(1) RECOVERY PROPERTY DEFINED.—Except as provided in subsection (e), the term "recovery property" means tangible property of a character subject to the allowance for depreciation—

(A) used in a trade or business, or

(B) held for the production of income.

(2) CLASSES OF RECOVERY PROPERTY.—Each item of recovery property shall be assigned to one of the following classes of property:

(A) 3-YEAR PROPERTY.—The term "3-year property" means section 1245 class property—

(i) with a present class life of 4 years or less; or

(ii) used in connection with research and experimentation.

(B) 5-YEAR PROPERTY.—The term "5-year property" means recovery property which is section 1245 class property and which is not 3-year property, 10-year property, or 15-year public utility property.

(C) 10-YEAR PROPERTY.—The term "10-year property" means—

(i) public utility property (other than section 1250 class property or 3-year property) with a present class life of more than 18 years but not more than 25 years; and

(ii) section 1250 class property with a present class life of 12.5 years or less.

(D) 19-YEAR REAL PROPERTY.—The term "19-year real property" means section 1250 class property which—

(i) does not have a present class life of 12.5 years or less, and

(ii) is not low-income housing.

(E) 15-YEAR PUBLIC UTILITY PROPERTY.—The term "15-year public utility property" means public utility property (other than section 1250 class property or 3-year property) with a present class life of more than 25 years.

(F) LOW-INCOME HOUSING.—The term "low-income housing" means property described in clause (i), (ii), (iii), or (iv) of section 1250(a)(1)(B).

(G) SPECIAL RULE FOR THEME PARKS, ETC.—For purposes of subparagraphs (C) and (D), a building (and its structural components) shall not be treated as having a present class life of 12.5 years or less by reason of any use other than the use for which such building was originally placed in service.

Amendments

• 1984, Deficit Reduction Act of 1984 (P.L. 98-369)

P.L. 98-369, §111(b)(2):

Amended Code Sec. 168(c)(2) by redesignating subparagraph (F) as subparagraph (G) and by inserting after subparagraph (E) new subparagraph (F). **Effective** with respect to property placed in service by the taxpayer after 3-15-84. Special rules appear in Act Sec. 111(g)[f]following former Code Sec. 168(f).

P.L. 98-369, §111(b)(3)(B):

Amended Code Sec. 168(c)(2)(D). Prior to amendment, it read as follows:

(D) 15-year Real Property.—The term "15-year real property" means section 1250 class property which does not have a present class life of 12.5 years or less. **Effective** with respect to property placed in service by the taxpayer after 3-15-84. Special rules appear in Act Sec. 111(g)[f] following former Code Sec. 168(f).

• 1983, Technical Corrections Act of 1982 (P.L. 97-448)

P.L. 97-448, §102(a)(8):

Amended Code Sec. 168(c)(2) by adding at the end thereof new subparagraph (F). **Effective** as if it had been included in the provision of P.L. 97-34 to which it relates.

• 1981, Economic Recovery Tax Act of 1981 (P.L. 97-34)

P.L. 97-34, §201(a):

Added Code Sec. 168(c). **Effective** for property placed in service after 12-31-80, in tax years ending after such date.

[Sec. 168(d)]

(d) UNADJUSTED BASIS; ADJUSTMENTS.—

(1) UNADJUSTED BASIS DEFINED.—

(A) IN GENERAL.—For purposes of this section, the term "unadjusted basis" means the excess of—

(i) the basis of the property determined under part II of subchapter O of chapter 1 for purposes of determining gain (determined without regard to the adjustments described in paragraph (2) or (3) of section 1016(a)), over

(ii) the sum of—

(I) that portion of the basis for which the taxpayer properly elects amortization (including the deduction allowed under section 167(k)) in lieu of depreciation, and

(II) that portion of the basis which the taxpayer properly elects to treat as an expense under section 179.

(B) TIME FOR TAKING BASIS INTO ACCOUNT.—

(i) IN GENERAL.—The unadjusted basis of property shall be first taken into account under subsection (b) for the taxable year in which the property is placed in service.

(ii) REDETERMINATIONS.—The Secretary shall by regulation provide for the method of determining the deduction allowable under subsection (a) for any taxable year (and succeeding taxable years) in which the basis is redetermined (including any reduction under section 1017).

(2) DISPOSITIONS.—

(A) MASS ASSET ACCOUNTS.—In lieu of recognizing gain or loss under this chapter, a taxpayer who maintains one or more mass asset accounts of recovery property may, under regulations prescribed by the Secretary, elect to include in income all proceeds realized on the disposition of such property.

(B) ADJUSTMENT TO BASIS.—Except as provided under regulations prescribed by the Secretary under paragraph (7) or (10) of subsection (f), if any recovery property (other than 19-year real property or low-income housing or property with respect to which an election under subparagraph (A) is made) is disposed of, the unadjusted basis of such property shall cease to be taken into account in determining any recovery deduction allowable under subsection (a) as of the beginning of the taxable year in which such disposition occurs.

(C) DISPOSITION INCLUDES RETIREMENT.—For purposes of this subparagraph, the term "disposition" includes retirement.

Amendments

• 1984, Deficit Reduction Act of 1984 (P.L. 98-369)

P.L. 98-369, §111(e)(3):

Amended Code Sec. 168(d)(2)(B) by striking out "15-year real property" and inserting in lieu thereof "18-year real property or low-income housing". For the **effective** date, as well as special rules, see Act Sec. 111(g)[f] following former Code Sec. 168(f).

• 1983, Technical Corrections Act of 1982 (P.L. 97-448)

P.L. 97-448, §102(a)(2):

Amended Code Sec. 168(d)(2)(B) by striking out "subsection (f)(7)" and inserting in lieu thereof "paragraph (7) or (10) of subsection (f)". **Effective** as if it had been included in the provision of P.L. 97-34 to which it relates.

• 1981, Economic Recovery Tax Act of 1981 (P.L. 97-34)

P.L. 97-34, §201(a):

Added Code Sec. 168(d). **Effective** for property placed in service after 12-31-80, in tax years ending after such date.

[Sec. 168(e)]

(e) PROPERTY EXCLUDED FROM APPLICATION OF SECTION.—For purposes of this title—

(1) PROPERTY PLACED IN SERVICE BEFORE JANUARY 1, 1981.—The term "recovery property" does not include property placed in service by the taxpayer before January 1, 1981.

(2) CERTAIN METHODS OF DEPRECIATION.—The term "recovery property" does not include property if—

(A) the taxpayer elects to exclude such property from the application of this section, and

(B) for the first taxable year for which a deduction would (but for this election) be allowable under this section with respect to such property in the hands of the taxpayer, the property is properly depreciated under the unit-of-production method or any method of depreciation not expressed in a term of years (other than the retirement-replacement-betterment method).

(3) SPECIAL RULE FOR CERTAIN PUBLIC UTILITY PROPERTY.—

(A) IN GENERAL.—The term "recovery property" does not include public utility property (within the meaning of section 167(l)(3)(A)) if the taxpayer does not use a normalization method of accounting.

(B) USE OF NORMALIZATION METHOD DEFINED.—For purposes of subparagraph (A), in order to use a normalization method of accounting with respect to any public utility property—

(i) the taxpayer must, in computing its tax expense for purposes of establishing its cost of service for rate-making purposes and reflecting operating results in its regulated books of account, use a method of depreciation with respect to such property that is the same as, and a depreciation period for such property that is no shorter than, the method and period used to compute its depreciation expense for such purposes; and

(ii) if the amount allowable as a deduction under this section with respect to such property differs from the amount that would be allowable as a deduction under section 167 (determined without regard to section 167(l)) using the method (including the period, first and last year convention, and salvage value) used to compute regulated tax expense under subparagraph (B)(i), the taxpayer must make adjustments to a reserve to reflect the deferral of taxes resulting from such difference.

(C) USE OF INCONSISTENT ESTIMATES AND PROJECTIONS, ETC.—

(i) IN GENERAL.—One way in which the requirements of subparagraph (B) are not met is if the taxpayer, for ratemaking purposes, uses a procedure or adjustment which is inconsistent with the requirements of subparagraph (B).

(ii) USE OF INCONSISTENT ESTIMATES AND PROJECTIONS.—The procedures and adjustments which are to be treated as inconsistent for purposes of clause (i) shall include any procedure or adjustment for ratemaking purposes which uses an estimate or projection of the taxpayer's tax expense, depreciation expense, or reserve for deferred taxes under subparagraph (B)(ii) unless such estimate or projection is also used, for ratemaking purposes, with respect to the other 2 such items and with respect to the rate base.

(iii) REGULATORY AUTHORITY.—The Secretary may by regulations prescribe procedures and adjustments (in addition to those specified in clause (ii)) which are to be treated as inconsistent for purposes of clause (i).

(D) PUBLIC UTILITY PROPERTY WHICH IS NOT RECOVERY PROPERTY.—In the case of public utility property which, by reason of this paragraph, is not treated as recovery property, the allowance for depreciation under section 167(a) shall be an amount computed using the method and period referred to in subparagraph (B)(i).

(4) CERTAIN TRANSACTIONS IN PROPERTY PLACED IN SERVICE BEFORE 1981.—

(A) SECTION 1245 CLASS PROPERTY.—The term "recovery property" does not include section 1245 class property acquired by the taxpayer after December 31, 1980, if—

(i) the property was owned or used at any time during 1980 by the taxpayer or a related person,

(ii) the property is acquired from a person who owned such property at any time during 1980, and, as part of the transaction, the user of such property does not change,

(iii) the taxpayer leases such property to a person (or a person related to such person) who owned or used such property at any time during 1980, or

(iv) the property is acquired in a transaction as part of which the user of such property does not change and the property is not recovery property in the hands of the person from which the property is so acquired by reason of clause (ii) or (iii).

For purposes of this subparagraph and subparagraph (B), property shall not be treated as owned before it is placed in service. For purposes of this subparagraph, whether the user of property changes as part of a transaction shall be determined in accordance with regulations prescribed by the Secretary.

(B) SECTION 1250 CLASS PROPERTY.—The term "recovery property" does not include section 1250 class property acquired by the taxpayer after December 31, 1980, if—

(i) such property was owned by the taxpayer or by a related person at any time during 1980;

(ii) the taxpayer leases such property to a person (or a person related to such person) who owned such property at any time during 1980; or

(iii) such property is acquired in an exchange described in section 1031, 1033, 1038, or 1039 to the extent that the basis of such property includes an amount representing the adjusted basis of other property owned by the taxpayer or a related person during 1980.

(C) CERTAIN NONRECOGNITION TRANSACTIONS.—The term "recovery property" does not include property placed in service by the transferor or distributor before January 1, 1981, which is acquired by the taxpayer after December 31, 1980, in a transaction described in section 332, 351, 361, 371(a), 374(a), 721, or 731 (or such property acquired from the transferee or acquiring corporation in a transaction described in such section), to the extent that the basis of the property is determined by reference to the basis of the property in the hands of the transferor or distributor. In the case of property to which this subparagraph applies, rules similar to the rules described in section 381(c)(6) shall apply.

(D) RELATED PERSON DEFINED.—Except as provided in subparagraph (E), for purposes of this paragraph a person (hereinafter referred to as the related person) is related to any person if—

(i) the related person bears a relationship to such person specified in section 267(b) or section 707(b)(1), or

(ii) the related person and such person are engaged in trades or businesses under common control (within the meaning of subsections (a) and (b) of section 52).

For purposes of clause (i), in applying section 267(b) and section 707(b)(1) "10 percent" shall be substituted for "50 percent". The determination of whether a person is related to another person shall be made as of the time the taxpayer acquires the property involved. In the case of the acquisition of property by any partnership which results from the termination of another partnership under section 708(b)(1)(B), the determination of whether the acquiring partnership is related to the other partnership shall be made immediately before the event resulting in such termination occurs.

(E) LIQUIDATION OF SUBSIDIARY, ETC.—For purposes of this paragraph, a corporation is not a related person to the taxpayer—

(i) if such corporation is a distributing corporation in a transaction to which section 334(b)(2)(B) applies and the stock of such corporation referred to in such subparagraph (B) was acquired by the taxpayer by purchase after December 31, 1980, or

(ii) if such corporation is liquidated in a liquidation to which section 331(a) applies and the taxpayer (or a related person) by himself or together with 1 or more other persons acquires the stock of the liquidated corporation by purchase (meeting the requirements of section 334(b)(2)(B)) after December 31, 1980.

A similar rule shall apply in the case of a deemed liquidation under section 338.

(F) ANTIAVOIDANCE RULE.—The term "recovery property" does not include property acquired by the taxpayer after December 31, 1980, which, under regulations prescribed by the Secretary, is acquired in a transaction one of the principal purposes of which is to avoid the principles of paragraph (1) and this paragraph.

(G) REDUCTION IN UNADJUSTED BASIS.—In the case of an acquisition of property described in subparagraph (B) or (C), the unadjusted basis of the property under subsection (d) shall be reduced to the extent that such property acquired is not recovery property.

(H) ACQUISITIONS BY REASON OF DEATH.—Subparagraphs (A) and (B) shall not apply to the acquisition of any property by the taxpayer if the basis of the property in the hands of the taxpayer is determined under section 1014(a).

(I) SECTION 1245 CLASS PROPERTY ACQUIRED INCIDENTAL TO ACQUISITION OF SECTION 1250 CLASS PROPERTY.—Under regulations prescribed by the Secretary, subparagraph (B) shall apply (and subparagraph (A) shall not apply) to section 1245 class property which is acquired incidental to the acquisition of section 1250 class property.

(5) FILMS AND VIDEO TAPES NOT RECOVERY PROPERTY.—The term "recovery property" shall not include any motion picture film or video tape.

Amendments

• 1984, Deficit Reduction Act of 1984 (P.L. 98-369)

P.L. 98-369, §113(b)(1):

Amended Code Sec. 168(e) by adding at the end thereof new paragraph (5). **Effective** for any motion picture film or video tape placed in service before, on, or after 7-18-84, except that such amendment shall not apply to—

(i) any qualified film placed in service by the taxpayer before March 15, 1984, if the taxpayer treated such film as recovery property for purposes of section 168 of the Internal Revenue Code of 1954 on a return of tax under chapter 1 of such Code filed before March 16, 1984, or

(ii) any qualified film placed in service by the taxpayer before January 1, 1985, if—

(I) 20 percent or more of the production costs of such film were incurred before March 16, 1984, and

(II) the taxpayer treats such film as recovery property for purposes of section 168 of such Code.

No credit shall be allowable under section 38 of such Code with respect to any qualified film described in clause (ii), except to the extent provided in section 48(k) of such Code.

For purposes of this paragraph, the terms "qualified film" and "production costs" have the same respective meanings as when used in section 48(k) of Internal Revenue Code of 1954.

P.L. 98-369, §113(b)(2)(A):

Amended Code Sec. 168(e) by striking out "section" and inserting in lieu thereof "title" in the matter preceding paragraph (1). **Effective** as if included in the amendments made by P.L. 97-34.

• 1983, Technical Corrections Act of 1982 (P.L. 97-448)

P.L. 97-448, §102(a)(9):

Amended Code Sec. 168(e)(4) by adding the sentence at the end of subparagraph (D), and by adding at the end thereof new subparagraphs (H) and (I). **Effective** as if it had been included in the provision of P.L. 97-34 to which it relates.

• 1982, Surface Transportation Act of 1982 (P.L. 97-424)

P.L. 97-424, §541(a)(1):

Amended Code Sec. 168(e)(3) by redesignating subparagraph (C) as subparagraph (D) and by adding a new subparagraph (C). **Effective** for tax years beginning after 12-31-79. See, however, the amendment note for Act Sec. 541(c)(2)-(5) following Code Sec. 46(f), as amended by P.L. 97-448, for special rules.

• 1982, Tax Equity and Fiscal Responsibility Act of 1982 (P.L. 97-248)

P.L. 97-248, §206(b)(1)(2):

Amended Code Sec. 168(e)(4) by striking out paragraph (H) and by striking out "1986" in the heading thereof and inserting in lieu thereof "1981". **Effective** 9-3-82. Prior to amendment, paragraph (H) read as follows:

"(H) Special rules for property placed in service before certain percentages take effect.—Under regulations prescribed by the Secretary—

(i) rules similar to the rules of this paragraph shall be applied in determining whether the tables contained in subparagraph (B) or (C) of subsection (b)(1) apply with respect to recovery property, and

(ii) if the tables contained in subparagraph (B) or (C) of subsection (b)(1) do not apply to such property by reason of clause (i), the deduction allowable under subsection (a) shall be computed—

(I) in the case of a transaction described in subparagraph (C), under rules similar to the rules described in section 381(c)(6); and

(II) in the case of a transaction otherwise described in this paragraph, under the recovery period and method (including rates prescribed under subsection (b)(1)) used by the person from whom the taxpayer acquired such property (or, where such person had no recovery method and period for such property, under the recovery period and method (including rates prescribed under subsection (b)(1)) used by the person which transferred such property to such person)."

P.L. 97-248, §224(c)(1):

Amended Code Sec. 168 by amending subparagraph (E) of section 168(e)(4) by adding at the end thereof the following new sentence: "A similar rule shall apply in the case of a deemed liquidation under section 338." **Effective** for any target corporation (within the meaning of Code Sec. 338) for which the acquisition date (within the meaning of such section) occurs after 8-31-82. For a special rule, see amendment notes under Code Sec. 338, as added by P.L. 97-248 Act Sec. 224.

• 1981, Economic Recovery Tax Act of 1981 (P.L. 97-34)

P.L. 97-34, §201(a):

Added Code Sec. 168(e). **Effective** for property placed in sevice after 12-31-80, in tax years ending after such date.

P.L. 97-34, §209(d)(1) and (2), provides the following transitional rules applicable to public utilities:

(d) SPECIAL RULE FOR PUBLIC UTILITIES.–

(1) TRANSITIONAL RULE FOR NORMALIZATION REQUIREMENTS.—If, by the terms of the applicable rate order last entered before the date of the enactment of this Act by a regulatory commission having appropriate jurisdiction, a regulated public utility would (but for this provision) fail to meet the requirements of section 168(e)(3) of the Internal Revenue Code of 1954 with respect to property because, for an accounting period ending after December 31, 1980, such public utility used a method of accounting other than a normalization method of accounting, such regulated public utility shall not fail to meet such requirements if, by the terms of its first rate order determining cost of service with respect to such property which becomes effective after the date of the enactment of this Act and on or before January 1, 1983, such regulated public utility uses a normalization method of accounting. This provision shall not apply to any rate order which, under the rules in effect before the date of the enactment of this Act, required a regulated public utility to use a method of accounting with respect to the deduction allowable by section 167 which, under section 167(l), it was not permitted to use.

(2) TRANSITIONAL RULE FOR REQUIREMENTS OF SECTION 46(f).—If, by the terms of the applicable rate order last entered before the date of the enactment of this Act by a regulatory commission having appropriate jurisdiction, a regulated public utility would (but for this provision) fail to meet the requirements of paragraph (1) or (2) of section 46(f) of the Internal Revenue Code of 1954 with respect to property for an accounting period ending after December 31, 1980, such regulated public utility shall not fail to meet such requirements if, by the terms of its first rate order determining cost of service with respect to such property which becomes effective after the date of the enactment of this Act and on or before January 1, 1983, such regulated public utility meets such requirements. This provision shall not apply to any rate order which, under the rules in effect before the date of the enactment of this Act, was inconsistent with the requirements of paragraph (1) or (2) of section 46(f) of such Code (whichever would have been applicable).

P.L. 97-34, §209(d)(4), provides:

(4) AUTHORITY TO PRESCRIBE INTERIM REGULATIONS WITH RESPECT TO NORMALIZATION.—Until Congress acts further, the Secretary of the Treasury or his delegate may prescribe such interim regulations as may be necessary or appropriate to

determine whether the requirements of section 168(e)(3)(B) of the Internal Revenue Code of 1954 have been met with respect to property placed in service after December 31, 1980.

[Sec. 168(f)]

(f) SPECIAL RULES FOR APPLICATION OF THIS SECTION.—For purposes of this section—

(1) COMPONENTS OF SECTION 1250 CLASS PROPERTY.—

(A) IN GENERAL.—Except as otherwise provided in this paragraph—

(i) the deduction allowable under subsection (a) with respect to any component (which is section 1250 class property) of a building shall be computed in the same manner as the deduction allowable with respect to such building, and

(ii) the recovery period for such component shall begin on the later of—

(I) the date such component is placed in service, or

(II) the date on which the building is placed in service.

(B) TRANSITIONAL RULES.—

(i) BUILDINGS PLACED IN SERVICE BEFORE 1981.—In the case of any building placed in service by the taxpayer before January 1, 1981, for purposes of applying subparagraph (A) to components of such buildings placed in service after December 31, 1980, and before March 16, 1984, the deduction allowable under subsection (a) with respect to such components shall be computed in the same manner as the deduction allowable with respect to the first such component placed in service after December 31, 1980.

(ii) BUILDINGS PLACED IN SERVICE BEFORE MARCH 16, 1984.—In the case of any building placed in service by the taxpayer before March 16, 1984, for purposes of applying subparagraph (A) to components of such buildings placed in service after March 15, 1984, and before May 9, 1985, the deduction allowable under subsection (a) with respect to such components shall be computed in the same manner as the deduction allowable with respect to the first such component placed in service after March 15, 1984.

(iii) BUILDINGS PLACED IN SERVICE BEFORE MAY 9, 1985.—In the case of any building placed in service by the taxpayer before May 9, 1985, for purposes of applying subparagraph (A) to components of such buildings placed in service after May 8, 1985, the deduction allowable under subsection (a) with respect to such components shall be computed in the same manner as the deduction allowable with respect to the first component placed in service after May 8, 1985.

(iv) FIRST COMPONENT TREATED AS SEPARATE BUILDING.—For purposes of clause (i), (ii), or (iii), the method of computing the deduction allowable with respect to the first component described in such clause shall be determined as if it were a separate building.

(C) EXCEPTION FOR SUBSTANTIAL IMPROVEMENTS.—

(i) IN GENERAL.—For purposes of this paragraph, a substantial improvement shall be treated as a separate building.

(ii) SUBSTANTIAL IMPROVEMENT.—For purposes of clause (i), the term "substantial improvement" means the improvements added to capital account with respect to any building during any 24-month period, but only if the sum of the amounts added to such account during such period equals or exceeds 25 percent of the adjusted basis of the building (determined without regard to the adjustments provided in paragraphs (2) and (3) of section 1016(a)) as of the first day of such period.

(iii) IMPROVEMENTS MUST BE MADE AFTER BUILDING IN SERVICE FOR 3 YEARS.—For purposes of this paragraph, the term "substantial improvement" shall not include any improvement made before the date 3 years after the building was placed in service.

(2) RECOVERY PROPERTY USED PREDOMINANTLY OUTSIDE THE UNITED STATES.—

(A) IN GENERAL.—Except as provided in subparagraphs (B) and (C), in the case of recovery property which, during the taxable year, is used predominantly outside the United States, the recovery deduction for the taxable year shall be, in lieu of the amount determined under subsection (b), the amount determined by applying to the unadjusted basis of such property the applicable percentage determined under tables prescribed by the Secretary. For purposes of the preceding sentence, in prescribing such tables, the Secretary shall—

(i) assign the property described in this subparagraph to classes in accordance with the present class life (or 12 years in the case of personal property with no present class life) of such property; and

(ii) assign percentages (taking into account the half-year convention) determined in accordance with use of the method of depreciation described in section 167(b)(2), switching to the method described in section 167(b)(1) at a time to maximize the deduction allowable under subsection (a).

(B) REAL PROPERTY.—Except as provided in subparagraph (C), in the case of 19-year real property or low-income housing which, during the taxable year, is predominantly used outside the United States, the recovery deduction for the taxable year shall be, in lieu of the amount determined under subsection (b), the amount determined by applying to the unadjusted basis of such property the applicable percentage determined under tables prescribed by the Secretary. For purposes of the preceding sentence, in prescribing such tables, the Secretary shall—

(i) assign to the property described in this subparagraph a 35-year recovery period, and

(ii) assign percentages determined in accordance with the use of the method of depreciation described in section 167(j)(1)(B), switching to the method described in section 167(b)(1) at a time to maximize the deduction allowable under subsection (a).

(C) ELECTION OF DIFFERENT RECOVERY PERCENTAGE.—

(i) GENERAL RULE.—The taxpayer may elect, with respect to one or more classes of recovery property described in this paragraph, to determine the applicable percentage under this paragraph by use of the straight-line method over the recovery period determined in accordance with the following table:

In the case of:	The taxpayer may elect a recovery period of:
3-year property	The present class life, 5 or 12 years.
5-year property	The present class life, 12 or 25 years.
10-year property	The present class life, 25 or 35 years.
15-year public utility property	The present class life, 35 or 45 years.
19-year real property or low-income housing	35 or 45 years.

(ii) OPERATING RULES.—

(I) PERIOD ELECTED BY TAXPAYER.—Except as provided in subclause (II), the taxpayer may elect under clause (i) for any taxable year only a single recovery period for recovery property described in this paragraph which is placed in service during such taxable year, which has the same present class life, and which is in the same class under subsection (c)(2). The period so elected shall not be shorter than such present class life.

(II) REAL PROPERTY.—In the case of 19-year real property or low-income housing, the election under clause (i) shall be made on a property-by-property basis.

(D) DETERMINATION OF PROPERTY USED PREDOMINANTLY OUTSIDE THE UNITED STATES.—For purposes of this paragraph, under regulations prescribed by the Secretary, rules similar to the rules under section 48(a)(2) (including the exceptions under subparagraph (B)) shall be applied in determining whether property is used predominantly outside the United States.

(E) CONVENTION.—Under regulations prescribed by the Secretary, the half year convention shall apply for purposes of any determination under subparagraph (C) (other than any determination with respect to 19-year real property or low-income housing).

(3) RRB REPLACEMENT PROPERTY.—

(A) IN GENERAL.—In the case of RRB replacement property placed in service before January 1, 1985, the recovery deduction for the taxable year shall be, in lieu of the amount determined under subsection (b), the amount determined by applying to the unadjusted basis of such property the applicable percentage determined under tables prescribed by the Secretary. For purposes of the preceding sentence, in prescribing such tables, the Secretary shall—

(i) use the recovery period determined in accordance with the following table:

If the year property is placed in service is:	The recovery period is:
1981	1
1982	2
1983	3
1984	4

and

(ii) assign percentages determined in accordance with use of the method of depreciation described in section 167(b)(2), switching to the method described in section 167(b)(3) at a time to maximize the deduction allowable under subsection (a) (taking into account the half-year convention).

(B) RRB REPLACEMENT PROPERTY DEFINED.—For purposes of this section, the term "RRB replacement property" means replacement track material (including rail, ties, other track material, and ballast) installed by a railroad (including a railroad switching terminal company) if—

(i) the replacement is made pursuant to a scheduled program for replacement,

(ii) the replacement is made pursuant to observations by maintenance-of-way personnel of specific track material needing replacement,

(iii) the replacement is made pursuant to the detection by a rail-test car of specific track material needing replacement, or

(iv) the replacement is made as a result of a casualty.

Replacements made as a result of a casualty shall be RRB replacement property only to the extent that, in the case of each casualty, the replacement cost with respect to the replacement track material exceeds $50,000.

(4) MANNER AND TIME FOR MAKING ELECTIONS.—

(A) IN GENERAL.—Any election under this section shall be made for the taxable year in which the property is placed in service.

(B) ELECTION MADE ON RETURN.—

(i) IN GENERAL.—Except as provided in clause (ii), any election under this section shall be made on the taxpayer's return of the tax imposed by this chapter for the taxable year concerned.

(ii) SPECIAL RULE FOR QUALIFIED REHABILITATED BUILDINGS.—In the case of any qualified rehabilitated building (as defined in section 48(g)(1)), an election under subsection (b)(3) may be made at any time before the date 3 years after the building was placed in service.

(C) REVOCATION ONLY WITH CONSENT.—Any election under this section, once made, may be revoked only with the consent of the Secretary.

(5) SHORT TAXABLE YEARS.—In the case of a taxable year that is less than 12 months, the amount of the deduction under this section shall be an amount which bears the same relationship to the amount of the deduction, determined without regard to this paragraph, as the number of months in the short taxable year bears to 12. In such case, the amount of the deduction for subsequent taxable years shall be appropriately adjusted in accordance with regulations prescribed by the Secretary. The determination of when a taxable year begins shall be made in accordance with regulations prescribed by the Secretary. This paragraph shall not apply to any deduction with respect to any property for the first taxable year of the lessor for which an election under paragraph (8) is in effect with respect to such property. In the case of 19-year real property or low-income housing, the first sentence of this paragraph shall not apply to the taxable year in which the property is placed in service or disposed of.

(6) LEASEHOLD IMPROVEMENTS.—For purposes of determining whether a leasehold improvement which is recovery property shall be amortized over the term of the lease, the recovery period (taking into account any election under paragraph (2)(C) of this subsection or under subsection (b)(3) with respect to such property) of such property shall be taken into account in lieu of its useful life.

(7) SPECIAL RULE FOR ACQUISITIONS AND DISPOSITIONS IN NONRECOGNITION TRANSACTIONS.—Notwithstanding any other provision of this section, the deduction allowed under this section in the taxable year in which recovery property is acquired or is disposed of in a transaction in which gain or loss is not recognized in whole or in part shall be determined in accordance with regulations prescribed by the Secretary.

[*Caution: Code Sec. 168(f)(8), below, as amended by P.L. 97-248 and P.L. 98-369, is generally effective with respect to agreements entered into after July 1, 1982, or to property placed in service after July 1, 1982, and before 1984. But see amendment notes below for special rules.—CCH.*]

(8) SPECIAL RULE FOR LEASES.—

(A) IN GENERAL.—In the case of an agreement with respect to qualified leased property, if all of the parties to the agreement characterize such agreement as a lease and elect to have the provisions of this paragraph apply with respect to such agreement, and if the requirements of subparagraph (B) are met, then, except as provided in subsection (i), for purposes of this subtitle—

(i) such agreement shall be treated as a lease entered into by the parties (and any party which is a corporation described in subparagraph (B)(i)(I) shall be deemed to have entered into the lease in the course of carrying on a trade or business), and

(ii) the lessor shall be treated as the owner of the property and the lessee shall be treated as the lessee of the property.

(B) CERTAIN REQUIREMENTS MUST BE MET.—The requirements of this subparagraph are met if—

(i) the lessor is—

(I) a corporation (other than an S corporation or a personal holding company (within the meaning of section 542(a))) which is not a related person with respect to the lessee,

(II) a partnership all of the partners of which are corporations described in subclause (I), or

(III) a grantor trust with respect to which the grantor and all beneficiaries of the trust are described in subclause (I) or (II),

(ii) the minimum investment of the lessor—

(I) at the time the property is first placed in service under the lease, and

(II) at all times during the term of the lease,

is not less than 10 percent of the adjusted basis of such property, and

(iii) the term of the lease (including any extensions) does not exceed the greater of—

(I) 120 percent of the present class life of the property, or

(II) the period equal to the recovery period determined with respect to such property under subsection (i)(2).

(C) NO OTHER FACTORS TAKEN INTO ACCOUNT.—If the requirements of subparagraphs (A) and (B) are met with respect to any transaction described in subparagraph (A), no other factors shall be taken into account in making a determination as to whether subparagraph (A)(i) or (ii) applies with respect to such transaction.

(D) QUALIFIED LEASED PROPERTY DEFINED.—For purposes of this section—

(i) IN GENERAL.—The term "qualified leased property" means recovery property—

(I) which is new section 38 property of the lessor, which is leased within 3 months after such property was placed in service, and which, if acquired by the lessee, would have been new section 38 property of the lessee, or

(II) which was new section 38 property of the lessee, which is leased within 3 months after such property is placed in service by the lessee, and with respect to which the adjusted basis of the lessor does not exceed the adjusted basis of the lessee at the time of the lease.

(ii) ONLY 45 PERCENT OF THE LESSEE'S PROPERTY MAY BE TREATED AS QUALIFIED.—The cost basis of all safe harbor lease property (determined without regard to this clause)—

(I) which is placed in service during any calendar year, and

(II) with respect to which the taxpayer is a lessee,

shall not exceed an amount equal to the 45 percent of the cost basis of the taxpayer's qualified base property placed in service during such calendar year.

(iii) ALLOCATION OF DISQUALIFIED BASIS.—The cost basis not treated as qualified leased property under clause (ii) shall be allocated to safe harbor lease property for such calendar year (determined without regard to clause (ii)) in reverse order to when the agreement described in subparagraph (A) with respect to such property was entered into.

(iv) CERTAIN PROPERTY MAY NOT BE TREATED AS QUALIFIED LEASED PROPERTY.—The term "qualified leased property" shall not include recovery property—

(I) which is a qualified rehabilitated building (within the meaning of section 48(g)(1)),

(II) which is public utility property (within the meaning of section 167(l)(3)(A)),

(III) which is property with respect to which a deduction is allowable by reason of section 291(b),

(IV) with respect to which the lessee of the property (other than property described in clause (v)) under the agreement described in subparagraph (A) is a nonqualified tax-exempt organization, or

(V) property with respect to which the user of such property is a person (other than a United States person) not subject to United States tax on income derived from the use of such property.

(v) QUALIFIED MASS COMMUTING VEHICLES INCLUDED.—The term "qualified leased property" includes recovery property which is a qualified mass commuting vehicle (as defined in section 103(b)(9)) which is financed in whole or in part by obligations the interest on which is excludable under section 103(a).

(vi) QUALIFIED BASE PROPERTY.—For purposes of this subparagraph, the term "qualified base property" means property placed in service during any calendar year which—

(I) is new section 38 property of the taxpayer,

(II) is safe harbor lease property (not described in subclause (I)) with respect to which the taxpayer is the lessee, or

(III) is designated leased property (other than property described in subclause (I) or (II)) with respect [to] which the taxpayer is the lessee.

Any designated leased property taken into account by any lessee under the preceding sentence shall not be taken into account by the lessor in determining the lessor's qualified base property. The lessor shall provide the lessee with such information with respect to the cost basis of such property as is necessary to carry out the purposes of this clause.

(vii) DEFINITION OF DESIGNATED LEASED PROPERTY.—For purposes of this subparagraph, the term "designated leased property" means property—

(I) which is new section 38 property,

(II) which is subject to a lease with respect to which the lessor of the property is treated (without regard to this paragraph) as the owner of the property for Federal tax purposes,

(III) with respect to which the term of the lease to which such property is subject is more than 50 percent of the present class life (or, if no present class life, the recovery period used in subsection (i)(2)) of such property, and

(IV) which the lessee designates on his return as designated leased property.

(viii) DEFINITION; SPECIAL RULE.—For purposes of this subparagraph—

(I) NEW SECTION 38 PROPERTY.—The term "new section 38 property" has the meaning given such term by section 48(b).

(II) PROPERTY PLACED IN SERVICE.—For purposes of this title (other than clause (i)), any property described in clause (i) to which subparagraph (A) applies shall be deemed originally placed in service not earlier than the date such property is used under the lease.

(E) MINIMUM INVESTMENT.—

(i) IN GENERAL.—For purposes of subparagraph (A), the term "minimum investment" means the amount the lessor has at risk with respect to the property (other than financing from the lessee or a related party of the lessee).

(ii) SPECIAL RULE FOR PURCHASE REQUIREMENT.—For purposes of clause (i), an agreement between the lessor and lessee requiring either or both parties to purchase or sell the qualified leased property at some price (whether or not fixed in the agreement) at the end of the lease term shall not affect the amount the lessor is treated as having at risk with respect to the property.

(F) CHARACTERIZATION BY PARTIES.—For purposes of this paragraph, any determination as to whether a person is a lessor or lessee or property is leased shall be made on the basis of the characterization of such person or property under the agreement described in subparagraph (A).

(G) REGULATIONS.—The Secretary shall prescribe such regulations as may be necessary to carry out the purposes of this paragraph, including (but not limited to) regulations consistent with such purposes which limit the aggregate amount of (and timing of) deductions and credits in respect of qualified leased property to the aggregate amount (and the timing) allowable without regard to this paragraph.

(H) DEFINITIONS.—For purposes of this paragraph—

(i) RELATED PERSON.—A person is related to another person if both persons are members of the same affiliated group (within the meaning of subsection (a) of section 1504 and determined without regard to subsection (b) of section 1504).

(ii) NONQUALIFIED TAX-EXEMPT ORGANIZATION.—

(I) IN GENERAL.—The term "nonqualified tax-exempt organization" means, with respect to any agreement to which subparagraph (A) applies, any organization (or predecessor organization which was engaged in substantially similar activities) which was exempt from taxation under this title at any time during the 5-year period ending on the date such agreement was entered into.

(II) SPECIAL RULE FOR FARMERS' COOPERATIVES.—The term "nonqualified tax-exempt organization" shall not include any farmers' cooperative organization described in section 521 whether or not exempt from taxation under section 521.

(III) SPECIAL RULE FOR PROPERTY USED IN UNRELATED TRADE OR BUSINESS.—An organization shall not be treated as a nonqualified tax-exempt organization with respect to any property if such property is used in an unrelated trade or business (within the meaning of section 513) of such organization which is subject to tax under section 511.

(I) TRANSITIONAL RULES FOR CERTAIN TRANSACTIONS.—

(i) IN GENERAL.—Except as provided in clause (ii), clause (ii) of subparagraph (D) shall not apply to any transitional safe harbor lease property (within the meaning of section 208(d)(3) of the Tax Equity and Fiscal Responsibility Act of 1982).

(ii) SPECIAL RULES.—For purposes of subparagraph (D)(ii)—

(I) DETERMINATION OF QUALIFIED BASE PROPERTY.—The cost basis of property described in clause (i) (and other property placed in service during 1982 to which subparagraph (D)(ii) does not apply) shall be taken into account in determining the qualified base property of the taxpayer for the taxable year in which such property was placed in service.

(II) REDUCTION IN QUALIFIED LEASED PROPERTY.—The cost basis of property which may be treated as qualified leased property under subparagraph (D)(ii) for the taxable year in which such property was placed in service (determined without regard to this subparagraph) shall be reduced by the cost basis of the property taken into account under subclause (I).

(J) COORDINATION WITH AT RISK RULES.—

(i) IN GENERAL.—For purposes of section 465, in the case of property placed in service after the date of the enactment of this subparagraph, if—

(I) an activity involves the leasing of section 1245 property which is safe harbor lease property, and

(II) the lessee of such property (as determined under this paragraph) would, but for this paragraph, be treated as the owner of such property for purposes of this title,

then the lessor (as so determined) shall be considered to be at risk with respect to such property in an amount equal to the amount the lessee is considered at risk with respect to such property (determined under section 465 without regard to this paragraph).

(ii) SUBPARAGRAPH NOT TO APPLY TO CERTAIN SERVICE CORPORATIONS.—Clause (i) shall not apply to any lessor which is a corporation the principal function of which is the performance of services in the field of health, law, engineering, architecture, accounting, actuarial science, performing arts, athletics, or consulting.

(iii) SPECIAL RULE FOR PROPERTY PLACED IN SERVICE BEFORE DATE OF ENACTMENT OF THIS SUBPARAGRAPH.—This subparagraph shall apply to property placed in service before the date of enactment of this subparagraph if the provisions of section 465 did not apply to the lessor before such date but become applicable to such lessor after such date.

(K) CROSS REFERENCE.—

For special recapture in cases where lessee acquires qualified leased property, see section 1245.

[*Caution: Code Sec. 168(f)(8), below, as added by P.L. 97-248 and amended by P.L. 97-354 and P.L. 98-369, applies, generally, to agreements entered into after December 31, 1987. But see amendment notes below for special rules.—CCH.*]

(8) SPECIAL RULES FOR FINANCE LEASES.—

(A) IN GENERAL.—For purposes of this title, except as provided in subsection (i), in the case of any agreement with respect to any finance lease property, the fact that—

(i) a lessee has the right to purchase the property at a fixed price which is not less than 10 percent of the original cost of the property to the lessor, or

(ii) the property is of a type not readily usable by any person other than the lessee,

shall not be taken into account in determining whether such agreement is a lease.

(B) FINANCE LEASE PROPERTY DEFINED.—For purposes of this section—

(i) IN GENERAL.—The term "finance lease property" means recovery property which is subject to an agreement which meets the requirements of subparagraph (C) and—

(I) which is new section 38 property of the lessor, which is leased within 3 months after such property was placed in service, and which, if acquired by the lessee, would have been new section 38 property of the lessee, or

(II) which was new section 38 property of the lessee, which is leased within 3 months after such property is placed in service by the lessee, and with respect to which the adjusted basis of the lessor does not exceed the adjusted basis of the lessee at the time of the lease.

(ii) ONLY 40 PERCENT OF THE LESSEE'S PROPERTY MAY BE TREATED AS QUALIFIED.—The cost basis of all finance lease property (determined without regard to this clause)—

(I) which is placed in service during any calendar year beginning before January 1, 1990, and

(II) with respect to which the taxpayer is a lessee,

shall not exceed an amount equal to 40 percent of the cost basis of the taxpayer's qualified base property placed in service during such calendar year.

(iii) ALLOCATION OF DISQUALIFIED BASIS.—The cost basis not treated as finance lease property under clause (ii) shall be allocated to finance lease property for such calendar year (determined without regard to clause (ii)) in reverse order to when the agreement described in subparagraph (A) with respect to such property was entered into.

(iv) CERTAIN PROPERTY MAY NOT BE TREATED AS FINANCE LEASE PROPERTY.—The term "finance lease proeprty" shall not include recovery property—

(I) which is a qualified rehabilitated building (within the meaning of section 48(g)(1)),

(II) which is public utility property (within the meaning of section 167(l)(3)(A)),

(III) which is property with respect to which a deduction is allowable by reason of section 291(b),

(IV) with respect to which the lessee of the property under the agreement described in subparagraph (A) is a nonqualified tax-exempt organization, or

(V) property with respect to which the user of such property is a person (other than a United States person) not subject to United States tax on income derived from the use of such property.

(v) QUALIFIED BASE PROPERTY.—For purposes of this subparagraph, the term "qualified base property" means property placed in service during any calendar year which—

(I) is new section 38 property of the taxpayer,

(II) is finance lease property (not described in subclause (I)) with respect to which the taxpayer is the lessee, or

(III) is designated leased property (other than property described in subclause (I) or (II)) with respect to which the taxpayer is the lessee.

Any designated leased property taken into account by any lessee under the preceding sentence shall not be taken into account by the lessor in determining the lessor's qualified base property. The lessor shall provide the lessee with such information with respect to the cost basis of such property as is necessary to carry out the purposes of this clause.

(vi) DEFINITION OF DESIGNATED LEASED PROPERTY.—For purposes of this subparagraph, the term "designated leased property" means property—

(I) which is new section 38 property,

(II) which is subject to a lease with respect to which the lessor of the property is treated (without regard to this paragraph) as the owner of the property for Federal tax purposes,

(III) with respect to which the term of the lease to which such property is subject is more than 50 percent of the present class life (or, if no present class life, the recovery period under subsection (a)) of such property, and

(IV) which the lessee designates on his return as designated leased property.

(vii) DEFINITION; SPECIAL RULES.—For purposes of this subparagraph—

(I) NEW SECTION 38 PROPERTY DEFINED.—The term "new section 38 property" has the meaning given such term by section 48(b).

(II) LESSEE LIMITATION NOT TO APPLY TO CERTAIN FARM PROPERTY.—Clause (ii) shall not apply to any property which is used for farming purposes (within the meaning of section 2032A(e)(5)) and which is placed in service during the calendar year but only if the cost basis of such property, when added to the cost basis of other finance lease property used for such purpose does not exceed $150,000 (determined under rules similar to the rules of section 209(d)(1)(B) of the Tax Equity and Fiscal Responsibility Act of 1982).

(III) PROPERTY PLACED IN SERVICE.—For purposes of this title (other than clause (i)), any finance lease property shall be deemed originally placed in service not earlier than the date such property is used under the lease.

(C) AGREEMENTS MUST MEET CERTAIN REQUIREMENTS.—The requirements of this subparagraph are met with respect to any agreement if—

(i) LESSOR REQUIREMENT.—Any lessor under the agreement must be—

(I) a corporation (other than an S corporation or a personal holding company within the meaning of section 542(a)),

(II) a partnership all of the partners of which are corporations described in subclause (I), or

(III) a grantor trust with respect to which the grantor and all the beneficiaries of the trust are described in subclause (I) or (II).

(ii) CHARACTERIZATION OF AGREEMENT.—The parties to the agreement characterize such agreement as a lease.

(iii) AGREEMENT CONTAINS CERTAIN PROVISIONS.—The agreement contains the provision described in clause (i) or (ii) of subparagraph (A), or both.

(iv) AGREEMENT OTHERWISE LEASE, ETC.—For purposes of this title (determined without regard to the provisions described in clause (iii)), the agreement would be treated as a lease and the lessor under the agreement would be treated as the owner of the property.

(D) PARAGRAPH NOT TO APPLY TO AGREEMENTS BETWEEN RELATED PERSONS.—This paragraph shall not apply to any agreement if the lessor and lessee are both persons who are members of the same affiliated group (within the meaning of subsection (a) of section 1504 and determined without regard to subsection (b) of section 1504).

(E) NONQUALIFIED TAX-EXEMPT ORGANIZATION.—

(i) IN GENERAL.—The term "nonqualified tax-exempt organization" means, with respect to any agreement to which subparagraph (A) applies, any organization (or predecessor organization which was engaged in substantially similar activities) which was exempt from taxation under this title at any time during the 5-year period ending on the date such agreement was entered into.

(ii) SPECIAL RULE FOR FARMERS' COOPERATIVES.—The term "nonqualified tax-exempt organization" shall not include any farmers' cooperative organization which is described in section 521 whether or not exempt from taxation under section 521.

(iii) SPECIAL RULE FOR PROPERTY USED IN UNRELATED TRADE OR BUSINESS.—An organization shall not be treated as a nonqualified tax-exempt organization with respect to any property if such property is used in an unrelated trade or business (within the meaning of section 513) of such organization which is subject to taxation under section 511.

(F) CROSS REFERENCE.—

For special recapture in case where lessee acquires financed recovery property, see section 1245.

(9) SALVAGE VALUE.—No salvage value shall be taken into account in determining the deduction allowable under subsection (a).

(10) TRANSFEREE BOUND BY TRANSFEROR'S PERIOD AND METHOD IN CERTAIN CASES.—

(A) IN GENERAL.—In the case of recovery property transferred in a transaction described in subparagraph (B), for purposes of computing the deduction allowable under subsection (a) with respect to so much of the basis in the hands of the transferee as does not exceed the adjusted basis in the hands of the transferor—

(i) if the transaction is described in subparagraph (B)(i), the transferee shall be treated in the same manner as the transferor, or

(ii) if the transaction is described in clause (ii) or (iii) of subparagraph (B) and the transferor made an election with respect to such property under subsection (b)(3) or (f)(2)(C), the transferee shall be treated as having made the same election (or its equivalent).

(B) TRANSFERS COVERED.—The transactions described in this subparagraph are—

(i) a transaction described in section 332, 351, 361, 371(a), 374(a), 721, or 731;

(ii) an acquisition (other than described in clause (i)) from a related person (as defined in subparagraph (D) of subsection (e)(4)); and

(iii) an acquisition followed by a leaseback to the person from whom the property is acquired.

Clause (i) shall not apply in the case of the termination of a partnership under section 708(b)(1)(B).

(C) PROPERTY REACQUIRED BY THE TAXPAYER.—Under regulations prescribed by the Secretary, recovery property which is disposed of and then reacquired by the taxpayer shall be treated for purposes of computing the deduction allowable under subsection (a) as if such property had not been disposed of.

(D) EXCEPTION.—This paragraph shall not apply to any transaction to which subsection (e)(4) applies.

(11) SPECIAL RULES FOR COOPERATIVES.—In the case of a cooperative organization described in section 1381(a), the Secretary may by regulations provide—

(A) for allowing allocation units to make separate elections under this section with respect to recovery property, and

(B) for the allocation of the deduction allowable under subsection (a) among allocation units.

(12) LIMITATIONS ON PROPERTY FINANCED WITH TAX-EXEMPT BONDS.—

(A) IN GENERAL.—Notwithstanding any other provision of this section, to the extent that any property is financed by the proceeds of an industrial development bond (within the meaning of section 103(b)(2)) the interest of which is exempt from taxation under section 103(a), the deduction allowed under subsection (a) (and any deduction allowable in lieu of the deduction allowable under subsection (a)) for any taxable year with respect to such property shall be determined under subparagraph (B).

(B) RECOVERY METHOD.—

(i) IN GENERAL.—Except as provided in clause (ii), the amount of the deduction allowed with respect to property described in subparagraph (A) shall be determined by using the straight-line method (with a half-year convention and without regard to salvage value) and a recovery period determined in accordance with the following table:

In the case of:	The recovery period is:
3-year property	3 years.
5-year property	5 years.
10-year property	10 years.
15-year public utility property	15 years.

(ii) 19-YEAR REAL PROPERTY.—In the case of 19-year real property, the amount of the deduction allowed shall be determined by using the straight-line method (without regard to salvage value) and a recovery period of 19 years.

(C) EXCEPTION FOR LOW- AND MODERATE-INCOME HOUSING.—Subparagraph (A) shall not apply to—

(i) any low-income housing, and

(ii) any other recovery property which is placed in service in connection with projects for residential rental property financed by the proceeds of obligations described in section 103(b)(4)(A).

(D) EXCEPTION WHERE LONGER RECOVERY PERIOD APPLICABLE.—Subparagraph (A) shall not apply to any recovery property if the recovery period which would be applicable to such property by reason of an election under subsection (b)(3) exceeds the recovery period for such property determined under subparagraph (B).

(13) CHANGES IN USE.—The Secretary shall, by regulation, provide for the method of determining the deduction allowable under subsection (a) with respect to any property for any taxable year (and for succeeding taxable years) during which such property changes status under this section but continues to be held by the same person.

(14) MOTOR VEHICLE OPERATING LEASES.—

(A) IN GENERAL.—For purposes of this title, in the case of a qualified motor vehicle operating agreement which contains a terminal rental adjustment clause—

(i) such agreement shall be treated as a lease if (but for such terminal rental adjustment clause) such agreement would be treated as a lease under this title, and

(ii) the lessee shall not be treated as the owner of the property subject to an agreement during any period such agreement is in effect.

(B) QUALIFIED MOTOR VEHICLE OPERATING AGREEMENT DEFINED.—For purposes of this paragraph—

(i) IN GENERAL.—The term "qualified motor vehicle operating agreement" means any agreement with respect to a motor vehicle (including a trailer) which meets the requirements of clauses (ii), (iii), and (iv) of this subparagraph.

(ii) MINIMUM LIABILITY OF LESSOR.—An agreement meets the requirements of this clause if under such agreement the sum of—

(I) the amount the lessor is personally liable to repay, and

(II) the net fair market value of the lessor's interest in any property pledged as security for property subject to the agreement,

equals or exceeds all amounts borrowed to finance the acquisition of property subject to the agreement. There shall not be taken into account under subclause (II) any property pledged which is property subject to the agreement or property directly or indirectly financed by indebtedness secured by property subject to the agreement.

(iii) CERTIFICATION BY LESSEE; NOTICE OF TAX OWNERSHIP.—An agreement meets the requirements of this clause if such agreement contains a separate written statement separately signed by the lessee—

(I) under which the lessee certifies, under penalty of perjury, that it intends that more than 50 percent of the use of the property subject to such agreement is to be in a trade or business of the lessee, and

(II) which clearly and legibly states that the lessee has been advised that it will not be treated as the owner of the property subject to the agreement for Federal income tax purposes.

(iv) LESSOR MUST HAVE NO KNOWLEDGE THAT CERTIFICATION IS FALSE.—An agreement meets the requirements of this clause if the lessor does not know that the certification described in clause (iii)(I) is false.

(C) TERMINAL RENTAL ADJUSTMENT CLAUSE DEFINED.—

(i) IN GENERAL.—For purposes of this paragraph, the term "terminal rental adjustment clause" means a provision of an agreement which permits or requires the rental price to be adjusted upward or downward by reference to the amount realized by the lessor under the agreement upon sale or other disposition of such property.

(ii) SPECIAL RULE FOR LESSEE DEALERS.—The term "terminal rental adjustment clause" also includes a provision of an agreement which requires a lessee who is a dealer in motor vehicles to purchase the motor vehicle for a predetermined price and then resell such vehicle where such provision achieves substantially the same results as a provision described in clause (i).

(15) SPECIAL RULES FOR SOUND RECORDINGS.—In the case of a sound recording (within the meaning of section 48(r)), the unadjusted basis of such property shall be equal to the production costs (within the meaning of section 48(r)(6)).

Amendments

• 1985 (P.L. 99-121)

P.L. 99-121, §103(b)(3)(A):

Amended Code Sec. 168(f)(1)(B) by redesignating clause (iii) as clause (iv) and by inserting after clause (ii) new clause (iii). **Effective** with respect to property placed in service by the taxpayer after 5-8-85. However, for an exception and special rule, see Act Sec. 105(b)(2) and (3), below.

P.L. 99-121, §103(b)(3)(B):

Amended Code Sec. 168(f)(1)(B)(ii) by striking out "March 15, 1984, the" and inserting in lieu thereof "March 15, 1984, and before May 9, 1985, the". **Effective** with respect to property placed in service by the taxpayer after 5-8-85. However, for an exception and special rule, see Act Sec. 105(b)(2) and (3), below.

P.L. 99-121, §103(b)(3)(C):

Amended Code Sec. 168(f)(1)(B)(iv), as redesignated by Act Sec. 103(b)(3)(A), by striking out "or (ii)" and inserting in lieu thereof ", (ii), or (iii)". **Effective** with respect to property placed in service by the taxpayer after 5-8-85. However, for an exception and special rule, see Act Sec. 105(b)(2) and (3), below.

P.L. 99-121, §103(b)(4)(A) and (B):

Amended Code Sec. 168(f)(12)(B)(ii) by striking out "15-year real property" each place it appears in the heading and the text and inserting in lieu thereof "19-year real property", and by striking out "15 years" and inserting in lieu thereof "19 years." **Effective** with respect to property placed in service by the taxpayer after 5-8-85. However, for an exception and special rule, see Act Sec. 105(b)(2) and (3), below.

P.L. 99-121, §105(b)(2) and (3), provides:

(2) EXCEPTION.—The amendments made by section 103 shall not apply to property placed in service by the taxpayer before January 1, 1987, if—

(A) the taxpayer or a qualified person entered into a binding contract to purchase or construct such property before May 9, 1985, or

(B) construction of such property was commenced by or for the taxpayer or a qualified person before May 9, 1985.

For purposes of this paragraph, the term "qualified person" means any person whose rights in such a contract or such property are transferred to the taxpayer, but only if such property is not placed in service before such rights are transferred to the taxpayer.

(3) SPECIAL RULE FOR COMPONENTS.—For purposes of applying section 168(f)(1)(B) of the Internal Revenue Code of 1954 (as amended by section 103) to components placed in service after December 31, 1986, property to which paragraph (2) of this subsection applies shall be treated as placed in service by the taxpayer before May 9, 1985.

• 1984, Deficit Reduction Act of 1984 (P.L. 98-369)

P.L. 98-369, §12(a)(3):

Amended Code Sec. 168(f)(8)(B)(ii)(I) by striking out "1986" and inserting in lieu thereof "1990". **Effective**, generally, for tax years beginning after 12-31-83. See, however, Act Sec. 12(b)-(c), below.

P.L. 98-369, §12(b)-(c), as amended by P.L. 99-514, §1801(a)(1) and P.L. 100-647, §1002(d)(7)(B), provides:

(b) Termination of Safe Harbor Leasing Rules.—Paragraph (8) of section 168(f) of the Internal Revenue Code of 1954 (relating to special rules for leasing), as in effect after the amendments made by section 208 of the Tax Equity and Fiscal Responsibility Act of 1982 but before the amendments made by section 209 of such Act, shall not apply to agreements entered into after December 31, 1983. The preceding sentence shall not apply to property described in paragraph (3)(G) or (5) of section 208(d) of such Act.

(c) Transitional Rules.—

(1) In General.—The amendments made by subsection (a) shall not apply with respect to any property if—

(A) A binding contract to acquire or to construct such property was entered into by or for the lessee before March 7, 1984, or

(B) such property was acquired by the lessee, or the construction of such property was begun, by or for the lessee, before March 7, 1984.

The preceding sentence shall not apply to any property with respect to which an election is made under this sentence at such time after the date of the enactment of the Tax Reform Act of 1986 as the Secretary of the Treasury or his delegate may prescribe.

(2) Special rule for certain automotive property.—

(A) In General.—The amendments made by subsection (a) shall not apply to property—

(i) which is automotive manufacturing property, and

(ii) with respect to which the lessee is a qualified lessee (within the meaning of section 208(d)(6) of the Tax Equity and Fiscal Responsibility Act of 1982).

(B) $150,000,000 limitation.—The provisions of subparagraph (A) shall not apply to any agreement if the sum of—

(i) the cost basis of the property subject to the agreement, plus

(ii) the cost basis of any property subject to an agreement to which subparagraph (A) previously applied and with respect to which the lessee was the lessee under the agreement described in clause (i) (or any related person within the meaning of section 168(e)(4)(D) of the Internal Revenue Code of 1954),

exceeds $150,000,000.

(C) Automotive Manufacturing Property.—For purposes of this paragraph, the term "automotive manufacturing property" means—

(i) property used principally by the taxpayer directly in connection with the trade or business of the taxpayer of the manufacturing of automobiles or trucks (other than truck tractors) with a gross vehicle weight of 13,000 pounds or less,

(ii) machinery, equipment, and special tools of the type included in former depreciation range guideline classes 37.11 and 37.12, and

(iii) any special tools owned by the taxpayer which are used by a vendor solely for the production of component parts for sale to the taxpayer.

(3) Special rule for certain cogeneration facilities.—The amendments made by subsection (a) shall not apply with respect to any property which is part of a coal-fired cogeneration facility—

(A) for which an application for a certification was filed with the Federal Energy Regulatory Commission on December 30, 1983,

(B) for which an application for a construction permit was filed with a State environmental protection agency on February 20, 1984, and

(C) which is placed in service before January 1, 1988.

P.L. 98-369, §32(a):

Amended Code Sec. 168(f) by adding at the end thereof new paragraph (13)[14]. **Effective** for agreements described in Code Sec. 168(f)(14) (as added by Act Sec. 32(a)) entered into more than 90 days after 7-18-84.

P.L. 98-369, §111(c):

Amended Code Sec. 168(f)(1)(B). For the **effective** date as well as special rules, see Act Sec. 111(g)[(f)], below. Prior to amendment, it read as follows:

(B) Transitional Rule.—In the case of any building placed in service by the taxpayer before January 1, 1981, for purposes of applying subparagraph (A) to components of such buildings placed in service after December 31, 1980, the deduction allowable under subsection (a) with respect to such components shall be computed in the same manner as the deduction allowable with respect to the first such component placed in service after December 31, 1980. For purposes of the preceding sentence, the method of computing the deduction allowable with respect to such first component shall be determined as if it were a separate building.

P.L. 98-369, §111(e)(1):

Amended Code Sec. 168(b)(3)(B)(iii), (f)(2)(B), (f)(2)(C)(ii)(II), (f)(2)(E), and (f)(5) by striking out "15-year real property" each place it appears and inserting in lieu thereof "18-year real property or low-income housing". For the **effective** date as well as special rules, see Act Sec. 111(g)[(f)] below.

P.L. 98-369, §111(e)(4):

Amended Code Sec. 168(f)(2)(C)(i) by striking out the item relating to 15-year real property in the table and inserting in lieu thereof: "18-year real property or low-income housing: 35 or 45 years.". For the **effective** date as well as special rules, see Act Sec. 111(g)[(f)], below.

P.L. 98-369, §111(g)[(f)], provides:

[(f)] Effective Date.—

(1) In General.—Except as otherwise provided in this subsection, the amendments made by this section shall apply with respect to property placed in service by the taxpayer after March 15, 1984.

(2) Exception.—The amendments made by this section shall not apply to property placed in service by the taxpayer before January 1, 1987, if—

(A) the taxpayer or a qualified person entered into a binding contract to purchase or construct such property before March 16, 1984, or

(B) construction of such property was commenced by or for the taxpayer or a qualified person before March 16, 1984.

For purposes of this paragraph the term "qualified person" means any person who transfers his rights in such a contract or such property to the taxpayer, but only if the property is not placed in service by such person before such rights are transferred to the taxpayer.

(3) Special Rules for Application of Paragraph (2).—

(A) Certain Inventory.—In the case of any property which—

(i) is held by a person as property described in section 1221(1), and

(ii) is disposed of by such person before January 1, 1985,

such person shall not, for purposes of paragraph (2), be treated as having placed such property in service before such property is disposed of merely because such person rented such property or held such property for rental.

No deduction for depreciation or amortization shall be allowed to such person with respect to such property,

(B) Certain Property Financed By Bonds.—In the case of any property with respect to which—

(i) bonds were issued to finance such property before 1984, and

(ii) an architectural contract was entered into before March 16, 1984,

paragraph (2) shall be applied by substituting "May 2" for "March 16".

(4) Special Rule for Components.—For purposes of applying section 168(f)(1)(B) of the Internal Revenue Code of 1954 (as amended by this section) to components placed in service after December 31, 1986, property to which paragraph (2) applies shall be treated as placed in service by the taxpayer before March 16, 1984.

(5) Special rule for mid-month convention.—In the case of the amendment made by subsection (d)—

(A) paragraph (1) shall be applied by substituting "June 22, 1984" for "March 15, 1984", and

(B) paragraph (2) shall be applied by substituting "June 23, 1984" for "March 15, 1984" each place it appears.

P.L. 98-369, §113(a)(2):

Amended Code Sec. 168(f) (as amended by this Act) by adding at the end thereof new paragraph (14)[15]. **Effective** for property placed in service after 3-15-84, in tax years ending after such date.

P.L. 98-369, §628(b)(1):

Amended Code Sec. 168(f)(12)(C). **Effective** for property placed in service after 12-31-83, to the extent such property is financed by the proceeds of an obligation (including a refunding obligation) issued after 10-18-83. However, see the exceptions provided by Act Sec. 631(b)(2), below. Prior to amendment, it read as follows:

(C) Exceptions.—Subparagraph (A) shall not apply to any recovery property which is placed in service—

(i) in connection with projects for residential rental property financed by the proceeds of obligations described in section 103(b)(4)(A),

(ii) in connection with a sewage or solid waste disposal facility—

(I) which provides sewage of solid waste disposal services for the residents of part or all of 1 or more governmental units, and

(II) with respect to which substantially all of the sewage or solid waste processed is collected from the general public,

(iii) as an air or water pollution control facility which is—

(I) installed in connection with an existing facility, or

(II) installed in connection with the conversion of an existing facility which uses oil or natural gas (or any product of oil or natural gas) as a primary fuel to a facility which uses coal as a primary fuel, or

(iv) in connection with a facility with respect to which an urban development action grant has been made under section 119 of the Housing and Community Development Act of 1974.

P.L. 98-369, §628(b)(2):

Amended Code Sec. 168(f)(12) by striking out subparagraph (D) and by redesignating subparagraph (E) as subparagraph (D). **Effective** for property placed in service after 12-31-83, to the extent such property is financed by the proceeds of an obligation (including a refunding obligation) issued after 10-18-83. However, see the exceptions provided by Act Sec. 631(b)(2), below. Prior to amendment Code Sec. 168(f)(12)(D) read as follows:

(D) Existing Facility.—For purposes of this paragraph, the term "existing facility" means a plant or property in operation before July 1, 1982.

P.L. 98-369, §631(b)(2), provides:

(b) Property Financed With Tax-Exempt Bonds Required To Be Depreciated on Straight-Line Basis.—

* * *

(2) Exceptions.—

(A) Construction or binding agreement.—The amendments made by section 628(b) shall not apply with respect to facilities—

(i) the original use of which commences with the taxpayer and the construction, reconstruction, or rehabilitation of which began before October 19, 1983, or

(ii) with respect to which a binding contract to incur significant expenditures was entered into before October 19, 1983.

(B) Refunding.—

(i) In General.—Except as provided in clause (ii), in the case of property placed in service after December 31, 1983, which is financed by the proceeds of an obligation which is issued solely to refund another obligation which was issued before October 19, 1983, the amendments made by section 628(b) shall apply only with respect to an amount equal to the basis in such property which has not been recovered before the date such refunded obligation is issued.

(ii) Significant expenditures.—In the case of facilities the original use of which commences with the taxpayer and with respect to which significant expenditures are made before January 1, 1984, the amendments made by section 628(b) shall not apply with respect to such facilities to the extent such facilities are financed by the proceeds of an obligation issued solely to refund another obligation which was issued before October 19, 1983.

(C) Facilities.—In the case of an inducement resolution or other comparable preliminary approval adopted by an issuing authority before October 19, 1983, for purposes of applying subparagraphs (A)(i) and (B)(ii) with respect to obligations described in such resolution, the term "facilities" means the facilities described in such resolution.

• 1983, Technical Corrections Act of 1982 (P.L. 97-448)

P.L. 97-448, §102(a)(1):

Amended Code Sec. 168(f)(5) by adding the last sentence. **Effective** as if such it had been included in the provision of P.L. 97-34 to which it relates.

P.L. 97-448, §102(a)(3):

Amended Code Sec. 168(f) by adding at the end thereof new paragraph (13). **Effective** as if it had been included in the provision of P.L. 97-34 to which it relates.

P.L. 97-448, §102(a)(10)(A):

Amended Code Sec. 168(f)(8)(D), as in effect before the amendments made by P.L. 97-248, by adding the last sentence below. **Effective** with respect to property to which the provisions of Code Sec. 168(f)(8) (as in effect before the amendments made by P.L. 97-248) apply.

P.L. 97-448, §102(f)(4):

Amended Code Sec. 168(f)(4)(B). **Effective** as if it had been included in the provision of P.L. 97-34 to which it relates. Prior to amendment, Code Sec. 168(f)(4)(B) read as follows:

"(B) Made on return.—Any election under this section shall be made on the taxpayer's return of the tax imposed by this chapter for the taxable year concerned."

• 1982, Subchapter S Revision Act of 1982 (P.L. 97-354)

P.L. 97-354, §5(a)(19):

Amended Code Sec. 168(f)(8)(B)(i)(I), as in effect before the enactment of P.L. 97-248 by striking out "an electing small business corporation (within the meaning of section 1371(b))" and inserting in lieu thereof "an S corporation". **Effective** for tax years beginning after 1982.

P.L. 97-354, §5(a)(20):

Amended Code Sec. 168(f)(8)(C)(i)(I) (as added by subsection (a) of section 209 of the Tax Equity and Fiscal Responsibility Act of 1982) by striking out "an electing small business corporation within the meaning of section 1371(b)" and inserting in lieu thereof "an S corporation". **Effective** for tax years beginning after 1982 with respect to agreements entered into after 1983.

• 1982, Tax Equity and Fiscal Responsibility Act of 1982 (P.L. 97-248)

P.L. 97-248, §208(a)(2)(A):

Amended Code Sec. 168(f)(8)(A) by inserting "except as provided in subsection (i)," before "for purposes of this subtitle". **Effective** for agreements entered into after 7-1-82, or to property placed in service after 7-1-82. For transitional rules, see amendment notes for P.L. 97-248, Act Sec. 208(d)(2)-(6)[7], following former Code Sec. 168(i).

P.L. 97-248, §208(b)(1):

Amended Code Sec. 168(f)(8)(B)(i)(I) by inserting "which is not a related person with respect to the lessee" before the comma at the end thereof. **Effective** for agreements entered into after 7-1-82, or to property placed in service after 7-1-82. For transitional rules, see amendment notes for P.L. 97-248, Act Sec. 208(d)(2)-(6)[7], following former Code Sec. 168(i).

P.L. 97-248, §208(b)(2):

Amended Code Sec. 168(f)(8)(B)(iii). **Effective** for agreements entered into after 7-1-82, or to property placed in service after 7-1-82. For transitional rules, see amendment notes for P.L. 97-248, Act Sec. 208(d)(2)-(6)[7], following former Code Sec. 168(i). Prior to amendment, it read as follows:

"(iii) the term of the lease (including any extensions) does not exceed the greater of—

(I) 90 percent of the useful life of such property for purposes of section 167, or

(II) 150 percent of the present class life of such property."

P.L. 97-248, §208(b)(3), as amended by P.L. 97-448, §102(a)(10)(A):

Amended Code Sec. 168(f)(8)(D). **Effective** for property placed in service after 12-31-80, in tax years ending after such date. For transitional rules, see amendment notes for P.L. 97-248, Act Sec. 208(d)(2)-(6)[7], following former Code Sec. 168(i). Prior to amendment by P.L. 97-248, but after amendment by P.L. 97-448, it read as follows:

"(D) Qualified leased property defined.—For purposes of subparagraph (A), the term `qualified leased property' means recovery property (other than a qualified rehabilitated building within the meaning of section 48(g)(1)) which is—

(i) new section 38 property (as defined in section 48(b)) of the lessor which is leased within 3 months after such property was placed in service and which, if acquired by the lessee, would have been new section 38 property of the lessee,

(ii) property—

(I) which was new section 38 property of the lessee,

(II) which was leased within 3 months after such property was placed in service by the lessee, and

(III) with respect to which the adjusted basis of the lessor does not exceed the adjusted basis of the lessee at the time of the lease, or

(iii) property which is a qualified mass commuting vehicle (as defined in section 103(b)(9)) and which is financed in whole or in part by obligations the interest on which is excludable from income under section 103(a).

For purposes of this title (other than this subparagraph), any property described in clause (i) or (ii) to which subparagraph (A) applies shall be deemed originally placed in service not earlier than the date such property is used under the lease. In the case of property placed in service after December 31, 1980, and before the date of the enactment of this subparagraph, this subparagraph shall be applied by submitting [substituting] `the date of the enactment of this subparagraph' for `such property was placed in service'. Under regulations prescribed by the Secretary, public utility property shall not be treated as qualified leased property unless the requirements of rules similar to the rules of subsection (e)(3) of this section and section 46(f) are met with respect to such property."

P.L. 97-248, §208(b)(4):

Amended Code Sec. 168(f)(8) by redesignating subparagraph (H) as subparagraph (K) and by inserting after subparagraph (G) new subparagraphs (H), (I) and (J). **Effective** for agreements entered into after 7-1-82, or to property placed in service after 7-1-82. For transitional rules, see amendment notes for P.L. 97-248, Act Sec. 208(d)(2)-(6)[7], following Code Sec. 168(i).

P.L. 97-248, §208(c), provides:

(c) Certain Leases Before October 20, 1981, Treated as Qualified Leases.—Nothing in paragraph (8) of section 168(f) of the Internal Revenue Code of 1954, or in any regulations prescribed thereunder, shall be treated as making such paragraph inapplicable to any agreement entered into before October 20, 1981, solely because under such agreement 1 party to such agreement is entitled to the credit allowable under section 38 of such Code with respect to property and another party to such agreement is entitled to the deduction allowable under section 168 of such Code with respect to such property. Section 168(f)(8)(B)(ii) of such Code shall not apply to the party entitled to such credit.

P.L. 97-248, §209(a):

Amended Code Sec. 168(f)(8). **Effective** for agreements entered into after 12-31-87. However, see Act Sec. 209(d)(1)(B), below. Prior to amendment by P.L. 97-248 but after the amendment made by P.L. 97-354, §5(a)(19), it read as follows:

"(8) Special rule for leases.—

(A) In general.—In the case of an agreement with respect to qualified leased property, if all of the parties to the agreement characterize such agreement as a lease and elect to have the provisions of this paragraph apply with respect to such agreement, and if the requirements of subparagraph (B) are met, then, for purposes of this subtitle—

(i) such agreement shall be treated as a lease entered into by the parties (and any party which is a corporation described in subparagraph (B)(i)(I) shall be deemed to have entered into the lease in the course of carrying on a trade or business), and

(ii) the lessor shall be treated as the owner of the property and the lessee shall be treated as the lessee of the property.

(B) Certain requirements must be met.—The requirements of this subparagraph are met if—

(i) the lessor is—

(I) a corporation (other than an S corporation or a personal holding company (within the meaning of section 542(a))),

(II) a partnership all of the partners of which are corporations described in subclause (I), or

(III) a grantor trust with respect to which the grantor and all beneficiaries of the trust are described in subclause (I) or (II),

(ii) the minimum investment of the lessor—

(I) at the time the property is first placed in service under the lease, and

(II) at all times during the term of the lease, is not less than 10 percent of the adjusted basis of such property, and

(iii) the term of the lease (including any extensions) does not exceed the greater of—

(I) 90 percent of the useful life of such property for purposes of section 167, or

(II) 150 percent of the present class life of such property.

(C) No other factors taken into account.—If the requirements of subparagraphs (A) and (B) are met with respect to any transaction described in subparagraph (A), no other factors shall be taken into account in making a determination as to whether subparagraph (A)(i) or (ii) applies with respect to such transaction.

(D) Qualified leased property defined.—For purposes of subparagraph (A), the term "qualified leased property" means recovery property (other than a qualified rehabilitated building within the meaning of section 48(g)(1)) which is—

(i) new section 38 property (as defined in section 48(b)) of the lessor which is leased within 3 months after such property was placed in service and which, if acquired by the lessee, would have been new section 38 property of the lessee,

(ii) property—

(I) which was new section 38 property of the lessee,

(II) which was leased within 3 months after such property was placed in service by the lessee, and

(III) with respect to which the adjusted basis of the lessor does not exceed the adjusted basis of the lessee at the time of the lease, or

(iii) property which is a qualified mass commuting vehicle (as defined in section 103(b)(9)) and which is financed in whole or in part by obligations the interest on which is excludable from income under section 103(a).

For purposes of this title (other than this subparagraph), any property described in clause (i) or (ii) to which subparagraph (A) applies shall be deemed originally placed in service not earlier than the date such property is used under the lease. In the case of property placed in service after December 31, 1980, and before the date of the enactment of this subparagraph, this subparagraph shall be applied by submitting "the date of the enactment of this subparagraph" for "such property was placed in service".

(E) Minimum investment.—

(i) In general.—For purposes of subparagraph (A), the term "minimum investment" means the amount the lessor has at risk with respect to the property (other than financing from the lessee or a related party of the lessee).

(ii) Special rule for purchase requirement.—For purposes of clause (i), an agreement between the lessor and lessee requiring either or both parties to purchase or sell the qualified leased property at some price (whether or not fixed in the agreement) at the end of the lease term shall not affect the amount the lessor is treated as having at risk with respect to the property.

(F) Characterization by parties.—For purposes of this paragraph, any determination as to whether a person is a lessor or lessee or property is leased shall be made on the basis of the characterization of such person or property under the agreement described in subparagraph (A).

(G) Regulations.—The Secretary shall prescribe such regulations as may be necessary to carry out the purposes of this paragraph, including (but not limited to) regulations consistent with such purposes which limit the aggregate amount of (and timing of) deductions and credits in respect of qualified leased property to the aggregate amount (and the timing) allowable without regard to this paragraph.

(H) Cross reference.—"

P.L. 97-248, §209(d)(1)(B), as amended by P.L. 98-369, §12(a), provides:

(B) Special rule for farm property aggregating $150,000 or less.—

(i) In general.—The amendments made by subsection (a) shall also apply to any agreement entered into after July 1, 1982, and before January 1, 1988, if the property subject to such agreement is section 38 property which is used for farming purposes (within the meaning of section 2032A(e)(5)).

(ii) $150,000 limitation.—The provisions of clause (i) shall not apply to any agreement if the sum of—

(I) the cost basis of the property subject to the agreement, plus

(II) the cost basis of any property subject to an agreement to which this subparagraph previously applied, which was entered into during the same calendar year, and with respect to which the lessee was the lessee of the agreement described in subclause (I) (or any related person within the meaning of section 168(e)(4)(D)), exceeds $150,000. For purposes of subclause (II), in the case of an individual, there shall not be taken into account any agreement of any individual who is a related person involving property which is used in a trade or business of farming of such related person which is separate from the trade or business of farming of the lessee described in subclause (II).

P.L. 97-248, §210, as amended by P.L. 98-369, §§32(b) and 712(d)(1), (2), provides:

SEC. 210 MOTOR VEHICLE OPERATING LEASES.

(a) In General.—In the case of any qualified motor vehicle agreement entered into on or before the 90th day after the date of the enactment of the Tax Reform Act of 1984, the fact that such agreement contains a terminal rental adjustment clause shall not be taken into account in determining whether such agreement is a lease.

(b) Definitions.—For purposes of this section—

(1) Qualified motor vehicle agreement.—The term "qualified motor vehicle agreement" means any agreement with respect to a motor vehicle (including a trailer)—

(A) which was entered into before—

(i) the enactment of any law, or

(ii) the publication by the Secretary of the Treasury or his delegate of any regulation, which provides that any agreement with a terminal rental adjustment clause is not a lease,

(B) with respect to which the lessor under the agreement—

(i) is personally liable for the repayment of, or

(ii) has pledged property (but only to the extent of the net fair market value of the lessor's interest in such property), other than property subject to the agreement or property directly or indirectly financed by indebtedness secured by property subject to the agreement, as security for,

all amounts borrowed to finance the acquisition of property subject to the agreement, and

(C) with respect to which the lessee under the agreement uses the property subject to the agreement in a trade or business or for the production of income.

(2) Terminal rental adjustment clause.—The term "terminal rental adjustment clause" means a provision of an agreement which permits or requires the rental price to be adjusted upward or downward by reference to the amount realized by the lessor under the agreement upon sale or other disposition of such property. Such term also includes a provision of an agreement which requires a lessee who is a dealer in motor vehicles to purchase the motor vehicle for a predetermined price and then resell such vehicle where such provision achieves substantially the same results as a provision described in the preceding sentence.

(c) Exception Where Lessee Took Position on Return.—Subsection (a) shall not apply to deny a deduction for interest paid or accrued claimed by a lessee with respect to a qualified motor vehicle agreement on a return of tax imposed by chapter 1 of the Internal Revenue Code of 1954 which was filed before the date of the enactment of this Act or to deny a credit for investment in depreciable property claimed by the lessee on such a return pursuant to an agreement with the lessor that the lessor would not claim the credit.

P.L. 97-248, §216(a):

Amended Code Sec. 168(f) by adding new paragraph (12). **Effective** with respect to property placed in service after 12-31-82, to the extent such property is financed by the proceeds of an obligation issued after 6-30-82. However, Act Sec. 216(b)(2) provides as follows:

(2) Exceptions.—

(A) Construction or binding agreement.—The amendments made by this section shall not apply with respect to facilities the original use of which commences with the taxpayer and—

(i) the construction, reconstruction, or rehabilitation of which began before July 1, 1982, or

(ii) with respect to which a binding agreement to incur significant expenditures was entered into before July 1, 1982.

(B) Refunding.—

(i) In general.—Except as provided in clause (ii), in the case of property placed in service after December 31, 1982 which is financed by the proceeds of an obligation which is issued solely to refund another obligation which was issued before July 1, 1982, the amendments made by this section shall apply only with respect to the basis in such property which has not been recovered before the date such refunding obligation is issued.

(ii) Significant expenditures.—In the case of facilities the original use of which commences with the taxpayer and with respect to which significant expenditures are made before January 1, 1983, the amendments made by this section shall not apply with respect to such facilities to the extent such facilities are financed by the proceeds of an obligation issued solely to refund another obligation which was issued before July 1, 1982.

In the case of an inducement resolution adopted by an issuing authority before July 1, 1982, for purposes of applying subparagraphs (A)(i) and (B)(ii) with respect to obligations described in such resolution, the term "facilities" means the facilities described in such resolution.

P.L. 97-248, §216(b)(3), provides:

(3) Certain projects for residential real property.—For purposes of clause (i) of section 168(f)(12)(C) of the Internal Revenue Code of 1954 (as added by this section), any obligation issued to finance a project described in the table contained in paragraph (1) of section 1104(n) of the Mortgage Subsidy Bond Tax Act of 1980 shall be treated as an obligation described in section 103(b)(4)(A) of the Internal Revenue Code of 1954.

P.L. 97-248, §224(c)(2):

Amended Code Sec. 168(f)(10)(B)(i) by striking out "(other than a transaction with respect to which the basis is determined under section 334(b)(2))." **Effective** for any target corporation (within the meaning of Code Sec. 338) with respect to which the acquisition date (within the meaning of such section) occurs after 8-31-82. For a special rule, see amendment notes under Code Sec. 338, as added by P.L. 97-248, Act Sec. 224.

• 1981, Black Lung Benefits Revenue Act of 1981 (P.L. 97-119)

P.L. 97-119, §112, provides:

SEC. 112. INFORMATION RETURNS WITH RESPECT TO SAFE HARBOR LEASES.

(a) REQUIREMENT OF RETURN.—

(1) IN GENERAL.—Except as provided in paragraph (2), paragraph (8) of section 168(f) of the Internal Revenue Code of 1954 (relating to special rule for leases) shall not apply with respect to an agreement unless a return, signed by the lessor and lessee and containing the information required to be included in the return pursuant to subsection (b), has been filed with the Internal Revenue Service not later than the 30th day after the date on which the agreement is executed.

(2) SPECIAL RULES FOR AGREEMENTS EXECUTED BEFORE JANUARY 1, 1982.—

(A) IN GENERAL.—In the case of an agreement executed before January 1, 1982, such agreement shall cease on February 1, 1982, to be treated as a lease under section 168(f)(8) unless a return, signed by the lessor and containing the information required to be included in subsection (b), has been filed with the Internal Revenue Service not later than January 31, 1982.

(B) FILING BY LESSEE.—If the lessor does not file a return under subparagraph (A), the return requirement under subparagraph (A) shall be satisfied if such return is filed by the Lessee before January 31, 1982.

(3) CERTAIN FAILURE TO FILE.—If—

(A) a lessor or lessee fails to file any return within the time prescribed by this subsection, and

(B) such failure is shown to be due to reasonable cause and not due to willful neglect,

the lessor or lessee shall be treated as having filed a timely return if a return is filed within a reasonable time after the failure is ascertained.

(b) INFORMATION REQUIRED.—The information required to be included in the return pursuant to this subsection is as follows:

(1) The name, address, and taxpayer identifying number of the lessor and the lessee (and parent company if a consolidated return is filed);

(2) The district director's office with which the income tax returns of the lessor and lessee are filed;

(3) A description of each individual property with respect to which the election is made;

(4) The date on which the lessee places the property in service, the date on which the lease begins and the term of the lease;

(5) The recovery property class and the ADR midpoint life of the leased property;

(6) The payment terms between the parties to the lease transaction;

(7) Whether the ACRS deductions and the investment tax credit are allowable to the same taxpayer;

(8) The aggregate amount paid to outside parties to arrange or carry out the transaction;

(9) For the lessor only: the unadjusted basis of the property as defined in section 168(d)(1);

(10) For the lessor only: if the lessor is a partnership or a grantor trust, the name, address, and taxpayer identifying number of the partners or the beneficiaries, and the district director's office with which the income tax return of each partner or beneficiary is filed; and

(11) Such other information as may be required by the return or its instructions.

Paragraph (8) shall not apply with respect to any person for any calendar year if it is reasonable to estimate that the aggregate adjusted basis of the property of such person which will be subject to subsection (a) for such year is $1,000,000 or less.

(c) COORDINATION WITH OTHER INFORMATION REQUIREMENTS.—In the case of agreements executed after December 31, 1982, to the extent provided in regulations prescribed by the Secretary of the Treasury or his delegate, the provisions of this section shall be modified to coordinate such provisions with other information requirements of the Internal Revenue Code of 1954.

• 1981, Economic Recovery Tax Act of 1981 (P.L. 97-34)

P.L. 97-34, §201(a):

Added Code Sec. 168(f). **Effective** for property placed in service after 12-31-80, in tax years ending after such date.

[Sec. 168(g)]

(g) DEFINITIONS.—For purposes of this section—

(1) PUBLIC UTILITY PROPERTY.—The term "public utility property" means property described in section 167(l)(3)(A).

(2) PRESENT CLASS LIFE.—The term "present class life" means the class life (if any) which would be applicable with respect to any property as of January 1, 1981, under subsection (m) of section 167 (determined without regard to paragraph (4) thereof and as if the taxpayer had made an election under such subsection). If any property (other than section 1250 class property) does not have a present class life within the meaning of the preceding sentence, the Secretary may prescribe a present class life for such property which reasonably reflects the anticipated useful life of such property to the industry or other group.

(3) SECTION 1250 CLASS PROPERTY.—The term "section 1245 class property" means tangible property described in section 1245(a)(3) other than subparagraphs (C) and (D).

(4) SECTION 1250 CLASS PROPERTY.—The term "section 1250 class property" means property described in section 1250(c) and property described in section 1245(a)(3)(C).

(5) RESEARCH AND EXPERIMENTATION.—The term "research and experimentation" has the same meaning as the term research or experimental has under section 174.

(6) RRB PROPERTY DEFINED.—For purposes of this section, the term "RRB property" means property which under the taxpayer's method of depreciation before January 1, 1981, would have been depreciated using the retirement-replacement-betterment method.

(7) MANUFACTURED HOMES.—The term "manufactured home" has the same meaning as in section 603(6) of the Housing and Community Development Act of 1974, which is 1250 class property used as a dwelling unit.

(8) QUALIFIED COAL UTILIZATION PROPERTY.—

(A) QUALIFIED COAL UTILIZATION PROPERTY.—The term "qualified coal utilization property" means that portion of the unadjusted basis of coal utilization property which bears the same ratio (but not greater than 1) to such unadjusted basis as—

(i) the Btu's of energy produced by the powerplant or major fuel-burning installation before the conversion or replacement involving coal utilization property, bears to

(ii) the Btu's of energy produced by such powerplant or installation after such conversion or replacement.

(B) COAL UTILIZATION PROPERTY.—The term "coal utilization property" means—

(i) a boiler or burner—

(I) the primary fuel for which is coal (including lignite), and

(II) which replaces an existing boiler or burner which is part of a powerplant or major fuel-burning installation and the primary fuel for which is oil or natural gas or any product thereof, and

(ii) equipment for converting an existing boiler or burner described in clause (i)(II) to a boiler or burner the primary fuel for which will be coal.

(C) POWERPLANT AND MAJOR FUEL-BURNING INSTALLATION.—The terms "powerplant" and "major fuel-burning installation" have the meanings given such terms by paragraphs (7) and (10) of section 103(a) of the Powerplant and Industrial Fuel Use Act of 1978, respectively.

(D) EXISTING BOILER OR BURNER.—The term "existing boiler or burner" means a boiler or burner which was placed in service before January 1, 1981.

(E) REPLACEMENT OF EXISTING BOILER OR BURNER.—A boiler or burner shall be treated as replacing a boiler or burner if the taxpayer certifies that the boiler or burner which is to be replaced—

(i) was used during calendar year 1980 for more than 2,000 hours of full load peak use (or equivalent thereof), and

(ii) will not be used for more than 2,000 hours of such use during any 12-month period after the boiler or burner which is to replace such boiler or burner is placed in service.

Amendments

• 1984, Deficit Reduction Act of 1984 (P.L. 98-369)

P.L. 98-369, §31(d):

Added the sentence at the end of Code Sec. 168(g)(2). For the **effective** date as well as special rules, see Act Sec. 31(g) following former Code Sec. 168(j).

• 1983, Technical Corrections Act of 1982 (P.L. 97-448)

P.L. 97-448, §102(a)(4)(B):

Amended the heading of Code Sec. 168(g)(8)(A). **Effective** as if it had been included in the provision of P.L. 97-34 to which it relates. Prior to amendment, the heading read as follows:

"(A) In general.—"

P.L. 97-448, §102(a)(4)(C):

Amended the heading of Code Sec. 168(g)(8)(B). **Effective** as if it had been included in the provision of P.L. 97-34 to which it relates. Prior to amendment, the heading read as follows:

(B) IN GENERAL.—

P.L. 97-34, §201(a):

Added Code Sec. 168(g). **Effective** for property placed in service after 12-31-80, in tax years ending after such date.

[Sec. 168(h)]

(h) SPECIAL RULES FOR RECOVERY PROPERTY CLASSES.—For purposes of this section—

(1) CERTAIN HORSES.—The term "3-year property" includes—

(A) any race horse which is more than 2 years old at the time such horse is placed in service; or

(B) any other horse which is more than 12 years old at such time.

(2) RAILROAD TANK CARS.—The term "10-year property" includes railroad tank cars.

(3) MANUFACTURED HOMES.—The term "10-year property" includes manufactured homes.

(4) QUALIFIED COAL UTILIZATION PROPERTY.—The term "10-year property" includes qualified coal utilization property which would otherwise be 15-year public utility property.

(5) APPLICATION WITH OTHER CLASSES.—Any property which is treated as included in a class or property by reason of this subsection shall not be treated as included in any other class.

Amendments

• 1983, Technical Corrections Act of 1982 (P.L. 97-448)

P.L. 97-448, §102(a)(4)(A):

Amended Code Sec. 168(h)(4). **Effective** as if it had been included in the provision of P.L. 97-34 to which it relates. Prior to amendment, Code Sec. 168(h)(4) read as follows:

"(4) Qualified coal utilization property.—The term '10-year property' includes qualified coal utilization property which is not 3-year property, 5-year property, or 10-year property (determined without regard to this paragraph)."

• 1981, Economic Recovery Tax Act of 1981 (P.L. 97-34)

P.L. 97-34, §201(a):

Added Code Sec. 168(h). **Effective** for property placed in service after 12-31-80, in tax years ending after such date.

[Caution: Code Sec. 168(i), below, as added by P.L. 97-248 and amended by P.L. 98-369, applies, generally, to agreements entered into after July 1, 1982, or to property placed in service after July 1, 1982. But see the amendment notes below for special rules.—CCH.]

[Sec. 168(i)]

(i) LIMITATIONS RELATING TO LEASES OF QUALIFIED LEASED PROPERTY.—For purposes of this subtitle, in the case of safe harbor lease property, the following limitations shall apply:

(1) LESSOR MAY NOT REDUCE TAX LIABILITY BY MORE THAN 50 PERCENT.—

(A) IN GENERAL.—The aggregate amount allowable as deductions or credits for any taxable year which are allocable to all safe harbor lease property with respect to which the taxpayer is the lessor may not reduce the liability for tax of the taxpayer for such taxable year (determined without regard to safe harbor lease items) by more than 50 percent of such liability.

(B) CARRYOVER OF AMOUNTS NOT ALLOWABLE AS DEDUCTIONS OR CREDITS.—Any amount not allowable as a deduction or credit under subparagraph (A)—

(i) may be carried over to any subsequent taxable year, and

(ii) shall be treated as a deduction or credit allocable to safe harbor lease property in such subsequent taxable year.

(C) ALLOCATION AMONG DEDUCTIONS AND CREDITS.—The Secretary shall prescribe regulations for determining the amount—

(i) of any deduction or credit allocable to safe harbor lease property for any taxable year to which subparagraph (A) applies, and

(ii) of any carryover of any such deduction or credit under subparagraph (B) to any subsequent taxable year.

(D) LIABILITY FOR TAX AND SAFE HARBOR LEASE ITEMS DEFINED.—For purposes of this paragraph—

(i) LIABILITY FOR TAX DEFINED.—Except as provided in this subparagraph, the term "liability for tax" means the tax imposed by this chapter, reduced by the sum of the credits allowable under subparts A, B, and D of part IV of subchapter A of this chapter.

(ii) SAFE HARBOR LEASE ITEMS DEFINED.—The term "safe harbor lease items" means any of the following items which are properly allocable to safe harbor lease property with respect to which the taxpayer is the lessor:

(I) Any deduction or credit allowable under this chapter (other than any deduction for interest).

(II) Any rental income received by the taxpayer from any lessee of such property.

(III) Any interest allowable as a deduction under this chapter on indebtedness of the taxpayer (or any related person within the meaning of subsection (e)(4)(D)) which is paid or incurred to the lessee of such property (or any person so related to the lessee).

(iii) CERTAIN TAXES NOT INCLUDED.—The term "tax imposed by this chapter" shall not include any tax treated as not imposed by this chapter under section 26(b)(2) (other than the tax imposed by section 56).

(2) METHOD OF COST RECOVERY.—The deduction allowable under subsection (a) with respect to any safe harbor lease property shall be determined by using the 150 percent declining balance method, switching to the straight-line method at a time to maximize the deduction (with a half-year convention in the first recovery year and without regard to salvage value) and a recovery period determined in accordance with the following table:

In the case of:	*The recovery period is:*
3-year property	5 years.
5-year property	8 years.
10-year property	15 years.

(3) INVESTMENT CREDIT ALLOWED ONLY OVER 5-YEAR PERIOD.—In the case of any credit which would otherwise be allowable under section 38 with respect to any safe harbor lease property for any taxable year (determined without regard to this paragraph), only 20 percent of the amount of such credit shall be allowable in such taxable year and 20 percent of such amount shall be allowable in each of the succeeding 4 taxable years.

(4) NO CARRYBACKS OF CREDIT OR NET OPERATING LOSS ALLOCABLE TO ELECTED QUALIFIED LEASED PROPERTY.—

(A) CREDIT CARRYBACKS.—In determining the amount of any credit allowable under section 38 which may be carried back to any preceding taxable year—

(i) the liability for tax for the taxable year from which any such credit is to be carried shall be reduced first by any credit not properly allocable to safe harbor lease property, and

(ii) no credit which is properly allocable to safe harbor lease property shall be taken into account in determining the amount of any credit which may be carried back.

(B) NET OPERATING LOSS CARRYBACKS.—The net operating loss carryback provided in section 172(b) for any taxable year shall be reduced by that portion of the amount of such carryback which is properly allocable to the items described in paragraph (1)(D)(ii) with respect to all safe harbor lease property with respect to which the taxpayer is the lessor.

(5) LIMITATION ON DEDUCTION FOR INTEREST PAID BY THE LESSOR TO THE LESSEE.—In the case of interest described in paragraph (1)(D)(ii)(III), the amount allowable as a deduction for any taxable year with respect to such interest shall not exceed the amount which would have been computed if the rate of interest under the agreement were equal to the rate of interest in effect under section 6621 at the time the agreement was entered into.

(6) COMPUTATION OF TAXABLE INCOME OF LESSEE FOR PURPOSES OF PERCENTAGE DEPLETION.—

(A) IN GENERAL.—For purposes of section 613 or 613A, the taxable income of any taxpayer who is a lessee of any safe harbor lease property shall be computed as if the taxpayer was the owner of such property, except that the amount of the deduction under subsection (a) of this section shall be determined after application of paragraph (2) of this subsection.

(B) COORDINATION WITH CRUDE OIL WINDFALL PROFIT TAX.—Section 4988(b)(3)(A) shall be applied without regard to subparagraph (A).

(7) TRANSITIONAL RULE FOR APPLICATION OF PARAGRAPH (1) TO CERTAIN TRANSACTIONS.—In the case of any deduction or credit with respect to—

(A) any transitional safe harbor lease property (within the meaning of section 208(d)(3) of the Tax Equity and Fiscal Responsibility Act of 1982), or

(B) any other safe harbor lease property placed in service during 1982 and to which paragraph (1) does not apply,

paragraph (1) shall not operate to disallow any such deduction or credit for the taxable year for which such deduction or credit would otherwise be allowable but deductions and credits with respect to such property shall be taken into account first in determining whether any deduction or credit is allowable under paragraph (1) with respect to any other safe harbor lease property.

(8) SAFE HARBOR LEASE PROPERTY.—For purposes of this section, the term "safe harbor lease property" means qualified leased property with respect to which an election under section 168(f)(8) is in effect.

[*Caution: Code Sec. 168(i), below, as added by P.L. 97-248 and amended by P.L. 98-369, applies, generally, to agreements entered into after December 31, 1987. But see the amendment notes below for special rules.—CCH.*]

[Sec. 168(i)]

(i) LIMITATIONS RELATING TO LEASES OF FINANCE LEASE PROPERTY.—For purposes of this subtitle, in the case of finance lease property, the following limitations shall apply:

(1) LESSOR MAY NOT REDUCE TAX LIABILITY BY MORE THAN 50 PERCENT.—

(A) IN GENERAL.—The aggregate amount allowable as deductions or credits for any taxable year which are allocable to all finance lease property with respect to which the taxpayer is the lessor may not reduce the liability for tax of the taxpayer for such taxable year (determined without regard to finance lease items) by more than 50 percent of such liability.

(B) CARRYOVER OF AMOUNTS NOT ALLOWABLE AS DEDUCTIONS OR CREDITS.—Any amount not allowable as a deduction or credit under subparagraph (A)—

(i) may be carried over to any subsequent taxable year, and

(ii) shall be treated as a deduction or credit allocable to finance lease property in such subsequent taxable year.

(C) ALLOCATION AMONG DEDUCTIONS AND CREDITS.—The Secretary shall prescribe regulations for determining the amount—

(i) of any deduction or credit allocable to finance lease property for any taxable year to which subparagraph (A) applies, and

(ii) of any carryover of any such deduction or credit under subparagraph (B) to any subsequent taxable year.

(D) LIABILITY FOR TAX AND FINANCE LEASE ITEMS DEFINED.—For purposes of this paragraph—

(i) LIABILITY FOR TAX DEFINED.—Except as provided in this subparagraph, the term "liability for tax" means the tax imposed by this chapter, reduced by the sum of the credits allowable under subparts A, B, and D of part IV of subchapter A of this chapter.

(ii) FINANCE LEASE ITEMS DEFINED.—The term "finance lease items" means any of the following items which are properly allocable to finance lease property with respect to which the taxpayer is the lessor:

(I) Any deduction or credit allowable under this chapter.

(II) Any rental income received by the taxpayer from any lessee of such property.

(iii) CERTAIN TAXES NOT INCLUDED.—The term "tax imposed by this chapter" shall not include any tax treated as not imposed by this chapter under section 26(b)(2) (other than the tax imposed by section 56).

(E) CERTAIN SAFE HARBOR LEASE PROPERTY TAKEN INTO ACCOUNT.—Under regulations prescribed by the Secretary, deductions and credits and safe harbor lease items which are allocable to safe harbor lease property to which this paragraph (as in effect for taxable years beginning in 1983) applies shall be taken into account for purposes of applying this paragraph.

(2) INVESTMENT CREDIT ALLOWED ONLY OVER 5-YEAR PERIOD.—In the case of any credit which would otherwise be allowable under section 38 with respect to any finance lease property for any taxable year (determined without regard to this paragraph), only 20 percent of the amount of such credit shall be allowable in such taxable year and 20 percent of such amount shall be allowable in each of the succeeding 4 taxable years.

(3) COMPUTATION OF TAXABLE INCOME OF LESSEE FOR PURPOSES OF PERCENTAGE DEPLETION.—

(A) IN GENERAL.—For purposes of section 613 or 613A, the taxable income of any taxpayer who is a lessee of any financed recovery property shall be computed as if the taxpayer was the owner of such property, except that the amount of the deduction under subsection (a) of this section shall be determined after application of paragraph (2) of this subsection.

(B) COORDINATION WITH CRUDE OIL WINDFALL PROFIT TAX.—Section 4988(b)(3)(A) shall be applied without regard to subparagraph (A).

(4) LIMITATIONS.—

(A) TERMINATION OF CERTAIN PROVISIONS.—

(i) PARAGRAPH (1).—Paragraph (1) shall not apply to property placed in service after September 30, 1989, in taxable years beginning after such date.

(ii) PARAGRAPH (2).—Paragraph (2) shall not apply to property placed in service after September 30, 1989.

(B) CERTAIN FARM PROPERTY.—This subsection shall not apply to property which is used for farming purposes (within the meaning of section 2032A(e)(5)) and which is placed in service during the taxable year but only if the cost basis of such property, when added to the cost basis of other finance lease property used for such purpose, does not exceed $150,000 (determined under rules similar to the rules of section 209(d)(1)(B) of the Tax Equity and Fiscal Responsibility Act of 1982).

Amendments

• 1984, Deficit Reduction Act of 1984 (P.L. 98-369)

P.L. 98-369, §12(a)(3):

Amended Code Sec. 168(i)(4) by striking out "1985" each place it appeared and inserting in lieu thereof "1989". **Effective**, generally, for tax years beginning after 12-31-83. See, however, the special rules provided in Act Sec. 12(b)-(c) following former Code Sec. 168(f).

P.L. 98-369, §474(r)(7)(A):

Amended Code Sec. 168(i)(1)(D)(i) by striking out "subpart A of part IV" and inserting in lieu thereof "subparts A, B, and D of part IV". **Effective** for tax years beginning after 12-31-83, and to carrybacks from such years.

P.L. 98-369, §474(r)(7)(B):

Amended Code Sec. 168(i)(1)(D)(iii) by striking out "under the last sentence of section 53(a)" and inserting in lieu thereof "under section 25(b)(2)". **Effective** for tax years beginning after 12-31-83, and to carrybacks from such years.

P.L. 98-369, §474(r)(7)(C):

Amended Code Sec. 168(i)(4)(A) by striking out "subpart A of part IV of subchapter A of this chapter" and inserting in lieu thereof "section 38". **Effective** for tax years beginning after 12-31-83, and to carrybacks from such years.

P.L. 98-369, §474(r)(7)(D):

Amended Code Sec. 168(i)(1)(D)(i) by striking out "subpart A of part IV" and inserting in lieu thereof "subparts A, B, and D of part IV". **Effective** for tax years beginning after 12-31-83, and to carrybacks from such years.

P.L. 98-369, §474(r)(7)(E):

Amended Code Sec. 168(i)(1)(D)(iii) by striking out "under the last sentence of section 53(a)" and inserting in lieu thereof "under section 25(b)(2)". **Effective** for tax years beginning after 12-31-83, and to carrybacks from such years.

P.L. 98-369, §612(e)(4):

Amended Code Sec. 168(i)(1)(D)(iii) as amended by Act Sec. 485(r)(7)(B), by striking out "section 25(b)(2)" and inserting in lieu thereof "section 26(b)(2)". **Effective** for interest paid or accrued after 12-31-84, on indebtedness incurred after 12-31-84.

P.L. 98-369, §612(e)(5):

Amended Code Sec. 168(i)(1)(D)(iii) as amended by Act Sec. 474(r)(7)(E) by striking out "section 25(b)(2)" and inserting in lieu thereof "section 26(b)(2)". **Effective** for interest paid or accrued after 12-31-84, on indebtedness incurred after 12-31-84.

• 1982, Tax Equity and Fiscal Responsibility Act of 1982 (P.L. 97-248)

P.L. 97-248, §208(a)(1):

Amended Code Sec. 168 by redesignating subsection (i) as subsection (j) and by inserting after subsection (h) new subsection (i). **Effective** for agreements entered into after 7-1-82, or to property placed in service after 7-1-82.

P.L. 97-248, §208(d)(2)-(8), as amended by P.L. 97-448, §306(a)(4)(A)-(C) and P.L. 98-369, §1067(a), provides:

(2) Transitional rule for certain safe harbor lease property.—

(A) In general.—The amendments made by subsections (a) and (b) shall not apply to transitional safe harbor lease property.

(B) Special rule for certain provisions.—Subparagraph (A) shall not apply with respect to the provisions of paragraph (6) of section 168(i) of the Internal Revenue Code of 1954 (as added by subsection (a)(1)), to the provisions of section 168(f)(8)(J) of such Code (as added by subsection (b)(4)), or to the amendment made by subsection (b)(1).

(3) Transitional safe harbor lease property.—For purposes of this subsection, the term "transitional safe harbor lease property" means property described in any of the following subparagraphs:

(A) In general.—Property is described in this subparagraph if such property is placed in service before January 1, 1983, if—

(i) with respect to such property a binding contract to acquire or to construct such property was entered into by the lessee after December 31, 1980, and before July 2, 1982, or

(ii) such property was acquired by the lessee, or construction of such property was commenced by or for the lessee, after December 31, 1980, and before July 2, 1982.

(B) Certain qualified lessees.—Property is described in this subparagraph if such property is placed in service before July 1, 1982, and with respect to which—

(i) an agreement to which section 168(f)(8)(A) of the Internal Revenue Code of 1954 applies was entered into before August 15, 1982, and

(ii) the lessee under such agreement is a qualified lessee (within the meaning of paragraph (6)).

(C) Automotive Manufacturing Property.—

(i) In General.—Property is described in this subparagraph if—

(I) such property is used principally by the taxpayer directly in connection with the trade or business of the taxpayer of the manufacture of automobiles or light-duty trucks,

(II) such property is automotive manufacturing property, and

(III) such property would be described in subparagraph (A) if "October 1" were substituted for "January 1".

(ii) Light-Duty Truck.—For purposes of this subparagraph, the term "light-duty truck" means any truck with a gross vehicle weight of 13,000 pounds or less. Such term shall not include any truck tractor.

(iii) Automotive Manufacturing Property.—For purposes of this subparagraph, the term "automotive manufacturing property" means machinery, equipment, and special tools of the type included in the former asset depreciation range guideline classes 37.11 and 37.12.

(iv) Special Tools Used By Certain Vendors.—For purposes of this subparagraph, any special tools owned by a taxpayer described in subclause (I) of clause (i) which are used by a vendor solely for the production of component parts for sale to the taxpayer shall be treated as automotive manufacturing property used directly by such taxpayer.

(D) Certain aircraft.—Property is described in this subparagraph if such property—

(i) is a commercial passenger aircraft (other than a helicopter), and

(ii) would be described in subparagraph (A) if "January 1, 1984" were substituted for "January 1, 1983".

For purposes of determining whether property described in this subparagraph in described in subparagraph (A), subparagraph (A)(ii) shall be applied by substituting "June 25, 1981" for "December 31, 1980" and by substituting "February 20, 1982" for "July 2, 1982" and construction of the aircraft shall be treated as having been begun during the period referred to in subparagraph (A)(ii) if during such period construction or reconstruction of a subassembly was commenced, or the stub wing join occurred.

(E) Turbines and boilers.—Property is described in this subparagraph if such property—

(i) is a turbine or boiler of a cooperative organization engaged in the furnishing of electric energy to persons in rural areas, and

(ii) would be property described in subparagraph (A) if "July 1" were substituted for "January 1".

For purposes of determining whether property described in this subparagraph is described in subparagraph (A), such property shall be treated as having been acquired during the period referred to in subparagraph (A)(ii) if at least 20 percent of the cost of such property is paid during such period.

(F) Property used in the production of steel.—Property is described in this subparagraph if such property—

(i) is used by the taxpayer directly in connection with the trade or business of the taxpayer of the manufacture or production of steel, and

(ii) would be described in subparagraph (A) if "January 1, 1984" were substituted for "January 1, 1983".

(4) Special rule for antiavoidance provisions.—The provisions of paragraph (6) of section 168(i) of such Code (as added by subsection (a)(1)), and the amendment made by subsection (b)(1), shall apply to leases entered into after February 19, 1982, in taxable years ending after such date.

(5) Special rule for mass commuting vehicles.—The amendments made by this section (other than section 168(i)(1) and (7) of such Code, as added by subsection (a)(1)), or section 168(f)(8)(J) of such Code, as added by subsection (b)(4), and section 209 shall not apply to qualified leased property described in section 168(f)(8)(D)(v) of such Code (as in effect after the amendments made by this section) which—

(A) is placed in service before January 1, 1988, or

(B) is placed in service after such date—

(i) pursuant to a binding contract or commitment entered into before April 1, 1983, and

(ii) solely because of conditions which, as determined by the Secretary of the Treasury or his delegate, are not within the control of the lessor or lessee.

(6) Qualified lessee defined.—

(A) In general.—The term "qualified lessee" means a taxpayer which is a lessee of an agreement to which section 168(f)(8)(A) of such Code applies and which—

(i) had net operating losses in each of the three most recent taxable years ending before July 1, 1982, and had an aggregate net operating loss for the five most recent taxable years ending before July 1, 1982, and

(ii) which uses the property subject to the agreement to manufacture and produce within the United States a class of products in an industry with respect to which—

(I) the taxpayer produced less than 5 percent of the total number of units (or value) of such products during the period covering the three most recent taxable years of the taxpayer ending before July 1, 1982, and

(II) four or fewer United States persons (including as one person an affiliated group as defined in section 1504(a)) other than the taxpayer manufactured 85 percent or more of the total number of all units (or value) within such class of products manufactured and produced in the United States during such period.

(B) Class of products.—For purposes of subparagraph (A)—

(i) the term "class of products" means any of the categories designated and numbered as a "class of products" in the 1977 Census of Manufacturers compiled and published by the Secretary of Commerce under title 13 of the United States Code, and

(ii) information—

(I) compiled or published by the Secretary of Commerce, as part of or in connection with the Statistical Abstract of the United States or the Census of Manufacturers, regarding the number of units (or value) of a class of products manufactured and produced in the United States during any period, or

(II) if information under subclause (I) is not available, so compiled or published with respect to the number of such units shipped or sold by such manufacturers during any period,

shall constitute prima facie evidence of the total number of all units of such class of products manufactured and produced in the United States in such period.

(6)[7] Underpayments of tax for 1982.—No addition to the tax shall be made under section 6655 of the Internal Revenue Code of 1954 (relating to failure by corporation to pay estimated income tax) or any period before October 15, 1982, with respect to any underpayment of estimated tax by a taxpayer with respect to any tax imposed by chapter 1 of such Code, to the extent that such underpayment was created or increased by any provision of this section.

(7)[8]Coordination with at risk rules.—Subparagraph (J) of section 168(f)(8) of the Internal Revenue Code of 1954 (as added by subsection (b)(4)) shall take effect as provided in such subparagraph (J).

(G) COAL GASIFICATION FACILITIES.—

(i) IN GENERAL.—Property is described in this subparagraph if such property—

(I) is used directly in connection with the manufacture or production of low sulfur gaseous fuel from coal, and

(II) would be described in subparagraph (A) if "July 1, 1984" were substituted for "January 1, 1983."

(ii) SPECIAL RULE.—For purposes of determining whether property described in this subparagraph is described in subparagraph (A), such property shall be treated as having been acquired during the period referred to in subparagraph (A)(ii) if at least 20 percent of the cost of such property is paid during such period.

(iii) LIMITATION ON AMOUNT.—Clause (i) shall only apply to the lease of an undivided interest in the property in an amount which does not exceed the lesser of—

(I) 50 percent of the cost basis of such property, or

(II) $67,500,000.

(iv) PLACED IN SERVICE.—In the case of property to which this subparagraph applies—

(I) such property shall be treated as placed in service when the taxpayer receives an operating permit with respect to such property from a State environmental protection agency, and

(II) the term of the lease with respect to such property shall be treated as being 5 years.

P.L. 97-248, §209(b):

Amended Code Sec. 168(i). **Effective** for agreements entered into after 12-31-87 (P.L. 98-369, §12(a)(1) changed the effective date.). See also the amendment notes for P.L. 97-248, Act Sec. 209(c), following former Code Sec. 168(f) for special rules.

[Sec. 168(j)]

(j) PROPERTY LEASED TO GOVERNMENTS AND OTHER TAX-EXEMPT ENTITIES.—

(1) IN GENERAL.—Notwithstanding any other provision of this section, the deduction allowed under subsection (a) (and any other deduction allowable for depreciation or amortization) for any taxable year with respect to tax-exempt use property shall be determined—

(A) by using the straight-line method (without regard to salvage value), and

(B) by using a recovery period determined under the following table:

	In the case of:	The recovery period shall be:
(I)	Property not described in subclause (II) or subclause (III)	The present class life.
(II)	Personal property with no present class life	12 years.
(III)	19-year real property	40 years.

(2) OPERATING RULES.—

(A) RECOVERY PERIOD MUST AT LEAST EQUAL 125 PERCENT OF LEASE TERM.—In the case of any tax-exempt use property, the recovery period used for purposes of paragraph (1) shall not be less than 125 percent of the lease term.

(B) CONVENTIONS.—

(i) PROPERTY OTHER THAN 19-YEAR REAL PROPERTY.—In the case of property other than 19-year real property, the half-year convention shall apply for purposes of paragraph (1).

(ii) CROSS REFERENCE.—

For other applicable conventions, see paragraphs (2)(B) and (4)(B) of subsection (b).

(C) EXCEPTION WHERE LONGER RECOVERY PERIOD APPLIES.—Paragraph (1) shall not apply to any recovery property if the recovery period which applies to such property (without regard to this subsection) exceeds the recovery period for such property determined under this subsection.

(D) DETERMINATION OF CLASS FOR REAL PROPERTY WHICH IS NOT RECOVERY PROPERTY.—In the case of any real property which is not recovery property, for purposes of this subsection, the determination of whether such property is 19-year real property shall be made as if such property were recovery property.

(E) COORDINATION WITH SUBSECTION (f)(12).—Paragraph (12) of subsection (f) shall not apply to any tax-exempt use property to which this subsection applies.

(F) 19-YEAR REAL PROPERTY.—For purposes of this subsection, the term "19-year real property" includes—

(i) low-income housing, and

(ii) any property which was treated as 15-year real property under this section (as in effect before the amendments made by the Tax Reform Act of 1984).

(3) TAX-EXEMPT USE PROPERTY.—For purposes of this subsection—

(A) PROPERTY OTHER THAN 19-YEAR REAL PROPERTY.—Except as otherwise provided in this subsection, the term "tax-exempt use property" means that portion of any tangible property (other than 19-year real property) leased to a tax-exempt entity.

(B) 19-YEAR REAL PROPERTY.—

(i) IN GENERAL.—In the case of 19-year real property, the term "tax-exempt use property" means that portion of the property leased to a tax-exempt entity in a disqualified lease.

(ii) DISQUALIFIED LEASE.—For purposes of this subparagraph, the term "disqualified lease" means any lease of the property to a tax-exempt entity, but only if—

(I) part or all of the property was financed (directly or indirectly) by an obligation the interest on which is exempt from tax under section 103 and such entity (or a related entity) participated in such financing,

(II) under such lease there is a fixed or determinable price purchase or sale option which involves such entity (or a related entity) or there is the equivalent of such an option,

(III) such lease has a lease term in excess of 20 years, or

(IV) such lease occurs after a sale (or other transfer) of the property by, or lease of the property from, such entity (or a related entity) and such property has been used by such entity (or a related entity) before such sale (or other transfer) or lease.

(iii) 35-PERCENT THRESHOLD TEST.—Clause (i) shall apply to any property only if the portion of such property leased to tax-exempt entities in disqualified leases is more than 35 percent of the property.

(iv) TREATMENT OF IMPROVEMENTS.—For purposes of this subparagraph, improvements to a property (other than land) shall not be treated as a separate property.

(v) LEASBACKS DURING 1ST 3 MONTHS OF USE NOT TAKEN INTO ACCOUNT.—Subclause (IV) of clause (ii) shall not apply to any property which is leased within 3 months after the date such property is first used by the tax-exempt entity (or a related entity).

(C) EXCEPTION FOR SHORT-TERM LEASES.—

(i) IN GENERAL.—Property shall not be treated as tax-exempt use property merely by reason of a short-term lease.

(ii) SHORT-TERM LEASE.—For purposes of clause (i), the term "short-term lease" means any lease the term of which is—

(I) less than 3 years, and

(II) less than the greater of 1 year or 30 percent of the property's present class life.

In the case of 19-year real property and property with no present class life, subclause (II) shall not apply.

(D) EXCEPTION WHERE PROPERTY USED IN UNRELATED TRADE OR BUSINESS.—The term "tax-exempt use property" shall not include any portion of a property if such portion is predominantly used by the tax-exempt entity (directly or through a partnership of which such entity is a partner) in an unrelated trade or business the income of which is subject to tax under section 511. For purposes of subparagraph (B)(iii), any portion of a property so used shall not be treated as leased to a tax-exempt entity in a disqualified lease.

(4) TAX-EXEMPT ENTITY.—

(A) IN GENERAL.—For purposes of this subsection, the term "tax-exempt entity" means–

(i) the United States, any State or political subdivision thereof, any possession of the United States, or any agency or instrumentality of any of the foregoing,

(ii) an organization (other than a cooperative described in section 521) which is exempt from tax imposed by this chapter, and

(iii) any foreign person or entity.

(B) EXCEPTIONS FOR CERTAIN PROPERTY USED BY FOREIGN PERSON OR ENTITY.—

(i) INCOME FROM PROPERTY SUBJECT TO UNITED STATES TAX.—Clause (iii) of subparagraph (A) shall not apply with respect to any property if more than 50 percent of the gross income for the taxable year derived by the foreign person or entity from the use of such property is—

(I) subject to tax under this chapter,or

(II) included under section 951 in the gross income of a United States shareholder for the taxable year with or within which ends the taxable year of the controlled foreign corporation in which such income was derived.

For purposes of the preceding sentence, any exclusion or exemption shall not apply for purposes of determining the amount of the gross income so derived, but shall apply for purposes of determining the portion of such gross income subject to tax under this chapter.

(ii) MOVIES AND SOUND RECORDINGS.—Clause (iii) of subparagraph (A) shall not apply with respect to any qualified film (as defined in section 48(k)(1)(B)) or any sound recording (as defined in section 48(r)).

(C) FOREIGN PERSON OR ENTITY.—For purposes of this paragraph, the term "foreign person or entity" means—

(i) any foreign government, any international organization, or any agency or instrumentality of any of the foregoing, and

(ii) any person who is not a United States person.

Such term does not include any foreign partnership or other foreign pass-thru entity.

(D) TREATMENT OF CERTAIN TAXABLE INSTRUMENTALITIES.—For purposes of this subsection and paragraph (5) of section 48(a), a corporation shall not be treated as an instrumentality of the United States or of any State or political subdivision thereof if—

(i) all of the activities of such corporation are subject to tax under this chapter, and

(ii) a majority of the board of directors of such corporation is not selected by the United States or any State or political subdivision thereof.

(E) CERTAIN PREVIOUSLY TAX-EXEMPT ORGANIZATIONS.—

(i) IN GENERAL.—For purposes of this subsection and paragraph (4) of section 48(a), an organization shall be treated as an organization described in subparagraph (A)(ii) with respect to any property, (other than property held by such organization) if such organization was an organization (other than a cooperative described in section 521) exempt from tax imposed by this chapter at any time during the 5-year period ending on the date such property was first used by such organization. The preceding sentence and subparagraph (d)(ii) shall not apply to the Federal Home Loan Mortgage Corporation.

(ii) ELECTION NOT TO HAVE CLAUSE (i) APPLY.—

(I) IN GENERAL.—In the case of an organization formerly exempt from tax under section 501(a) as an organization described in section 501(c)(12), clause (i) shall not apply to such organization with respect to any property if such organization elects not to be exempt from tax under section 501(a) during the tax-exempt use period with respect to such property.

(II) TAX-EXEMPT USE PERIOD.—For purposes of subclause (I), the term "tax-exempt use period" means the period beginning with the taxable year in which the property described in subclause (I) is first used by the organization and ending with the close of the 15th taxable year following the last taxable year of the recovery period of such property.

(III) ELECTION.—Any election under subclause (I), once made, shall be irrevocable.

(iii) TREATMENT OF SUCCESSOR ORGANIZATIONS.—Any organization which is engaged in activities substantially similar to those engaged in by a predecessor organization shall succeed to the treatment under this subparagraph of such predecessor organization.

(iv) FIRST USED.—For purposes of this subparagraph, property shall be treated as first used by the organization—

(I) when the property is first placed in service under a lease to such organization, or

(II) in the case of property leased to (or held by) a partnership (or other pass-thru entity) in which the organization is a member, the later of when such property is first used by such partnership or pass-thru entity or when such organization is first a member of such partnership of pass-thru entity.

(5) SPECIAL RULES FOR CERTAIN HIGH TECHNOLOGY EQUIPMENT.—

(A) EXEMPTION WHERE LEASE TERM IS 5 YEARS OR LESS.—For purposes of this subsection, the term "tax-exempt use property" shall not include any qualified technological equipment if the lease to the tax-exempt entity has a lease term of 5 years or less.

(B) RECOVERY PERIOD WHERE LEASE TERM IS GREATER THAN 5 YEARS.—In the case of any qualified technological equipment not described in subparagraph (A) and which is not property to which subsection (f)(2) applies, the recovery period used for purposes of paragraph (1) shall be 5 years.

(C) QUALIFIED TECHNOLOGICAL EQUIPMENT.—For purposes of this paragraph—

(i) IN GENERAL.—Except as otherwise provided in this subparagraph, the term "qualified technological equipment"means—

(I) any computer or peripheral equipment,

(II) any high technology telephone station equipment installed on the customer's premises, and

(III) any high technology medical equipment,

(ii) EXCEPTION FOR CERTAIN PROPERTY.—The term "qualified technological equipment" shall not include any property leased to a tax-exempt entity if—

(I) part or all of the property was financed (directly or indirectly) by an obligation the interest on which is exempt from tax under section 103,

(II) such lease occurs after a sale (or other transfer) of the property by, or lease of such property from, such entity (or related entity) and such property has been used by such entity (or a related entity) before such sale (or other transfer) or lease, or

(III) such tax-exempt entity is the United States or any agency or instrumentality of the United States.

(iii) LEASEBACKS DURING 1ST 3 MONTHS OF USE NOT TAKEN INTO ACCOUNT.—Subclause (II) of clause (ii) shall not apply to any property which is leased within 3 months after the date such property is first used by the tax-exempt entity (or a related entity).

(D) COMPUTER OR PERIPHERAL EQUIPMENT DEFINED.—For purposes of this paragraph—

(i) IN GENERAL.—The term "computer or peripheral equipment" means—

(I) any computer, and

(II) any related peripheral equipment.

(ii) COMPUTER.—The term "computer" means a programmable electronically activated device which—

(I) is capable of accepting information, applying prescribed processes to the information, and supplying the results of these processes with or without human intervention, and

(II) consists of a central processing unit containing extensive storage, logic, arithmetic, and control capabilities.

(iii) RELATED PERIPHERAL EQUIPMENT.—The term "related peripheral equipment" means any auxiliary machine (whether on-line or off-line) which is designed to be placed under the control of the central processing unit of a computer.

(iv) EXCEPTIONS.—The term "computer or peripheral equipment" shall not include—

(I) any equipment which is an integral part of other property which is not a computer,

(II) typewriters, calculators, adding and accounting machines, copiers, duplicating equipment, and similar equipment, and

(III) equipment of a kind used primarily for amusement or entertainment of the user.

(E) HIGH TECHNOLOGY MEDICAL EQUIPMENT.—For purposes of this paragraph, the term "high technology medical equipment" means any electronic, eletromechanical, or computerbased high technology equipment used in the screening, monitoring, observation, diagnosis, or treatment of patients in a laboratory, medical, or hospital environment.

(6) OTHER SPECIAL RULES.—For purposes of this subsection—

(A) LEASE.—The term "lease" includes any grant of a right to use property.

(B) LEASE TERM.—In determining a lease term—

(i) there shall be taken into account options to renew, and

(ii) 2 or more successive leases which are part of the same transaction (or a series of related transactions) with respect to the same or substantially similar property shall be treated as 1 lease.

(C) SPECIAL RULE FOR FAIR RENTAL OPTIONS ON 19-YEAR REAL PROPERTY.—For purposes of clause (i) of subparagraph (B), in the case of 19-year real property, there shall not be taken into account any option to renew at fair market value, determined at the time of renewal.

(7) RELATED ENTITIES.—For purposes of this subsection—

(A)(i) Each governmental unit and each agency or instrumentality of a governmental unit is related to each other such unit, agency, or instrumentality which directly or indirectly derives its powers, rights, and duties in whole or in part from the same sovereign authority.

(ii) For purposes of clause (i), the United States, each State, and each possession of the United States shall be treated as a separate sovereign authority.

(B) Any entity not described in subparagraph (A)(i) is related to any other entity if the 2 entities have—

(i) significant common purposes and substantial common membership, or

(ii) directly or indirectly substantial common direction or control.

(C)(i) An entity is related to another entity if either entity owns (directly or through 1 or more entities) a 50 percent or greater interest in the capital or profits of the other entity.

(ii) For purposes of clause (i), entities treated as related under subparagraph (A) or (B) shall be treated as 1 entity.

(D) An entity is related to another entity with respect to a transaction if such transaction is part of an attempt by such entities to avoid the application of this subsection, section 46(e), paragraph (4) or (5) of section 48(a), or clause (vi) of section 48(g)(2)(B).

(8) TAX-EXEMPT USE OF PROPERTY LEASED TO PARTNERSHIPS, ETC., DETERMINED AT PARTNER LEVEL.—For purposes of this subsection—

(A) IN GENERAL.—In the case of any property which is leased to a partnership, the determination of whether any portion of such property is tax-exempt use property shall be made by treating each tax-exempt entity partner's proportionate share (determined under paragraph (9)(C)) of such property as being leased to such partner.

(B) OTHER PASS-THRU ENTITIES; TIERED ENTITIES.—Rules similar to the rules of subparagraph (A) shall also apply in the case of any pass-thru entity other than a partnership and in the case of tiered partnerships and other entities.

(C) PRESUMPTION WITH RESPECT TO FOREIGN ENTITIES.—Unless it is otherwise established to the satisfaction of the Secretary, it shall be presumed that the partners of a foreign partnership (and the beneficiaries of any other foreign pass-thru entity) are persons who are not United States persons.

(9) TREATMENT OF PROPERTY OWNED BY PARTNERSHIPS, ETC.—

(A) IN GENERAL.—For purposes of this subsection, if

(i) any property which (but for this subparagraph) is not tax-exempt use property is owned by a partnership which has both tax-exempt entity and a person who is not a tax-exempt entity as partners and

(ii) any allocation to the tax-exempt entity of partnership items is not a qualified allocation,

an amount equal to such tax-exempt entity's proportionate share of such property shall (except as provided in paragraph (3)(D)) be treated as tax-exempt use property.

(B) QUALIFIED ALLOCATION.—For purposes of subparagraph (A), the term "qualified allocation" means any allocation to a tax-exempt entity which—

(i) is consistent with such entity's being allocated the same distributive share item of income, gain, loss, deduction, credit, and basis and such share remains the same during the entire period the entity is a partner in the partnership, and

(ii) has substantial economic effect within the meaning of section 704(b)(2).

For purposes of this subparagraph, items allocated under section 704(c) shall not be taken into account.

(C) DETERMINATION OF PROPORTION SHARE.—

(i) IN GENERAL.—For purposes of subparagraph (A), a tax-exempt entity's proportionate share of any property owned by a partnership shall be determined on the basis of such entity's share of partnership items of income or gain (excluding gain allocated under section 704(c)), whichever results in the largest proportionate share.

(ii) DETERMINATION WHERE ALLOCATIONS VARY.—For purposes of clause (i), if a tax-exempt entity's share of partnership items of income or gain (excluding gain allocated under section 704(c)) may vary during the period such entity is a partner in the partnership, such share shall be the highest share such entity may receive.

(D) DETERMINATION OF WHETHER PROPERTY USED IN UNRELATED TRADE OR BUSINESS.—For purposes of this subsection, in the case of any property which is owned by a partnership which has both a tax-exempt entity and a person who is not a tax-exempt entity as partners, the determination of whether such property is used in an unrelated trade or business of such an entity shall be made without regard to section 514.

(E) OTHER PASS-THRU ENTITIES; TIERED ENTITIES.—Rules similar to the rules of subparagraphs (A), (B), (C), and (D) shall also apply in the case of any pass-thru entity other than a partnership and in the case of tiered partnership and other entities.

(F) TREATMENT OF CERTAIN TAXABLE ENTITIES.—

(i) IN GENERAL.—For purposes of this paragraph and paragraph (8), except as otherwise provided in this subparagraph, any tax-exempt controlled entity shall be treated as a tax-exempt entity.

(ii) ELECTION.—If a tax-exempt controlled entity makes an election under this clause—

(I) such entity shall not be treated as a tax-exempt entity for purposes of this paragraph and paragraph (8),

(II) any gain recognized by a tax-exempt entity on any disposition of an interest in such entity (and any dividend or interest received or accrued by a tax-exempt entity from such tax-exempt controlled entity) shall be treated as unrelated business taxable income for purposes of section 511.

Any such election shall be irrevocable and shall bind all tax-exempt entities holding interests in such tax-exempt controlled entity. For purposes of subclause (II), there shall only be taken into account dividends which are properly allocable to income of the tax-exempt controlled entity which was not subject to tax under this chapter.

(iii) TAX-EXEMPT CONTROLLED ENTITY.—

(I) IN GENERAL.—The term "tax-exempt controlled entity" means any corporation (which is not a tax-exempt entity determined without regard to this subparagraph and paragraph (4)(E)) if 50 percent or more (in value) of the stock in such corporation is held by 1 or more tax-exempt entities (other than a foreign person or entity).

(II) ONLY 5-PERCENT SHAREHOLDERS TAKEN INTO ACCOUNT IN CASE OF PUBLICLY TRADED STOCK.—For purposes of subclause (I), in the case of a corporation the stock of which is publicly traded on an established securities market, stock held by a tax-exempt entity shall not be taken into account unless such entity holds at least 5 percent (in value) of the stock in such corporation. For purposes of this subclause, related entities (within the meaning of paragraph (7)) shall be treated as 1 entity.

(III) SECTION 318 TO APPLY.—For purposes of this clause, a tax-exempt entity shall be treated as holding stock which it holds through application of section 318 (determined without regard to the 50-percent limitation contained in subsection (a)(2)(C) thereof).

(G) REGULATIONS.—For purposes of determining whether there is a qualified allocation under subparagraph (B), the regulations prescribed under paragraph (10) for purposes of this paragraph—

(i) shall set forth the proper treatment for partnership guaranteed payments, and

(ii) may provide for the exclusion or segregation of items.

(10) REGULATIONS.—The Secretary shall prescribe such regulations as may be necessary or appropriate to carry out the purposes of this section.

Amendments

• 1988, Technical and Miscellaneous Revenue Act of 1988 (P.L. 100-647)

P.L. 100-647, §1018(b)(2)(A)-(B):

Amended Code Sec. 168(j)(9)(E) (as amended by P.L. 99-514, §1802(a)(2) and as in effect before the amendments made by P.L. 99-514, §201) by striking out "this paragraph" in clauses (i) and (ii)(I) and inserting in lieu thereof "this paragraph and paragraph (8)", and by striking out clause (iii) and inserting in lieu thereof new clause (iii). **Effective** as if included in the provision of P.L. 99-514 to which it relates. Prior to amendment, Code Sec. 168(j)(9)(E)(iii) read as follows:

(iii) TAX-EXEMPT CONTROLLED ENTITY.—The term "tax-exempt controlled entity" means any corporation (which is not a tax-exempt entity determined without regard to this subparagraph and paragraph (4)(E)) if 50 percent or more (by value) of the stock in such corporation is held (directly or through the application of section 318 determined without regard to the 50-percent limitation contained in subsection (a)(2)(C) thereof) by 1 or more tax-exempt entities.

• 1984, Deficit Reduction Act of 1984 (P.L. 98-369)

P.L. 98-369, §31(a):

Amended Code Sec. 168 by redesignating subsection (j) as subsection (k) and by inserting after subsection (i) new subsection (j). For the **effective** date as well as special rules, see Act Sec. 31(g), below.

P.L. 98-369, §31(g), as amended by P.L. 99-514 and P.L. 100-647, §1018(b)(1), provides:

(g) Effective Dates.—

(1) In General.—Except as otherwise provided in this subsection, the amendments made by this section shall apply—

(A) to property placed in service by the taxpayer after May 23, 1983, in taxable years ending after such date, and

(B) to property placed in service by the taxpayer on or before May 23, 1983, if the lease to the tax-exempt entity is entered into after May 23, 1983.

(2) Leases Entered into on or Before May 23, 1983.—The amendments made by this section shall not apply with

respect to any property leased to a tax-exempt entity if the property is leased pursuant to—

(A) a lease entered into on or before May 23, 1983 (or a sublease under such a lease), or

(B) any renewal or extension of a lease entered into on or before May 23, 1983, if such renewal or extension is pursuant to an option exercisable by the tax-exempt entity which was held by the tax-exempt entity on May 23, 1983.

(3) Binding Contracts, Etc.—

(A) The amendments made by this section shall not apply with respect to any property leased to a tax-exempt entity if such lease is pursuant to 1 or more written binding contracts which, on May 23, 1983, and at all times thereafter, required—

(i) the taxpayer (or his predecessor in interest under the contract) to acquire, construct, reconstruct, or rehabilitate such property, and

(ii) the tax-exempt entity (or a tax-exempt predecessor thereof) to be the lessee of such property.

(B) Paragraph (9) of section 168(j) of the Internal Revenue Code of 1954 (as added by this section) shall not apply with respect to any property owned by a partnership if—

(i) such property was acquired by such partnership on or before October 21, 1983, or

(ii) such partnership entered into a written binding contract which, on October 21, 1983, and at all times thereafter, required the partnership to acquire or construct such property.

(C) The amendments made by this section shall not apply with respect to any property leased to a tax-exempt entity (other than any foreign person or entity)—

(i) if—

(I) on or before May 23, 1983, the taxpayer (or his predecessor in interest under the contract) or the tax-exempt entity entered into a written binding contract to acquire, construct, reconstruct, or rehabilitate such property and such property had not previously been used by the tax-exempt entity, or

(II) the taxpayer or the tax-exempt entity acquired the property after June 30, 1982 and on or before May 23, 1983, or completed the construction, reconstruction, or rehabilitation of the property after December 31, 1982, and on or before May 23, 1983, and

(ii) if such lease is pursuant to a written binding contract entered into before January 1, 1985, which requires the tax-exempt entity to be the lessee of such property.

(4) Official Governmental Action on or Before November 1, 1983.—

(A) In General.—The amendments made by this section shall not apply with respect to any property leased to a tax-exempt entity (other than the United States, any agency or instrumentality thereof, or any foreign person or entity) if—

(i) on or before November 1, 1983—there was significant official governmental action with respect to the project or its design, and

(ii) the lease to the tax-exempt entity is pursuant to a written binding contract entered into before January 1, 1985, which requires the tax-exempt entity to be the lessee of the property.

(B) Significant Official Governmental Action.—For purposes of subparagraph (A), the term "significant official governmental action" does not include granting of permits, zoning changes, environmental impact statements, or similar governmental actions.

(C) Special Rule for Credit Unions.—In the case of any property leased to a credit union pursuant to a written binding contract with an expiration date of December 31, 1984, which was entered into by such organization on August 23, 1984—

(i) such credit union shall not be treated as an agency or instrumentality of the United States; and

(ii) clause (ii) of subparagraph (A) shall be applied by substituting "January 1, 1987" for "January 1, 1985".

(D) Special Rule for Greenville Auditorium Board.—For purposes of this paragraph, significant official governmental action taken by the Greenville County Auditorium Board of Greenville, South Carolina, before May 23, 1983, shall be treated as significant official governmental action with respect to the coliseum facility subject to a binding contract to lease which was in effect on January 1, 1985.

(E) Treatment of Certain Historic Structures.—If—

(i) On June 16, 1982, the legislative body of the local governmental unit adopted a bond ordinance to provide funds to renovate elevators in a deteriorating building owned by the local governmental unit and listed in the National Register, and

(ii) the chief executive officer of the local governmental unit, in connection with the renovation of such building, made an application on June 1, 1983, to a State agency for a Federal historic preservation grant and made an application on June 17, 1983, to the Economic Development Administration of the United States Department of Commerce for a grant,

the requirements of clauses (i) and (ii) of subparagraph (A) shall be treated as met.

(5) Mass Commuting Vehicles.—The amendments made by this section shall not apply to any qualified mass commuting vehicle (as defined in section 103(b)(9) of the Internal Revenue Code of 1954) which is financed in whole or in part by obligations the interest on which is excludable from gross income under section 103(a) of such Code if—

(A) such vehicle is placed in service before January 1, 1988, or

(B) such vehicle is placed in service on or after such date—

(i) pursuant to a binding contract or commitment entered into before April 1, 1983, and

(ii) solely because of conditions which, as determined by the Secretary of the Treasury or his delegate, are not within the control of the lessor or lessee.

(6) Certain Turbines and Boilers.—The amendments made by this section shall not apply to any property described in section 208(d)(3)(E) of the Tax Equity and Fiscal Responsibility Act of 1982.

(7) Certain Facilities for Which Ruling Requests Filed on or Before May 23, 1983.—The amendments made by this section shall not apply with respect to any facilities described in clause (ii) of section 168(f)(12)(C) of the Internal Revenue Code of 1954 (relating to certain sewage or solid waste disposal facilities), as in effect on the day before the date of the enactment of this Act, if a ruling request with respect to the lease of such facility to the tax-exempt entity was filed with the Internal Revenue Service on or before May 23, 1983.

(8) Recovery Period for Certain Qualified Sewage Facilities.—

(A) In General.—In the case of any property (other than 15-year real property) which is part of a qualified sewage facility, the recovery period used for purposes of paragraph (1) of section 168(j) of the Internal Revenue Code of 1954 (as added by this section) shall be 12 years. For purposes of the preceding sentence, the term "15-year real property" includes 18-year real property.

(B) Qualified Sewage Facility.—For purposes of subparagraph (A), the term "qualified sewage facility" means any facility which is part of the sewer system of a city, if—

(i) on June 15, 1983, the City Council approved a resolution under which the city authorized the procurement of equity investments for such facility, and

(ii) on July 12, 1983, the Industrial Development Board of the city approved a resolution to issue a $100,000,000 industrial development bond issue to provide funds to purchase such facility.

(9) Property Used by the Postal Service.—In the case of property used by the United States Postal Service, paragraphs (1) and (2) shall be applied by substituting "October 31" for "May 23".

(10) Existing Appropriations.—The amendments made by this section shall not apply to personal property leased to or used by the United States if—

(A) an express appropriation has been made for rentals under such lease for the fiscal year 1983 before May 23, 1983, and

(B) the United States or an agency or instrumentality thereof has not provided an indemnification against the loss of all or a portion of the tax benefits claimed under the lease or service contract.

(11) Special Rule for Certain Partnerships.—

(A) Partnerships for Which Qualifying Action Existed Before October 21, 1983.—Paragraph (9) of section 168(j) of the Internal Revenue Code of 1954 (as added by this section) shall not apply to any property acquired, directly or indirectly, before January 1, 1985, by any partnership described in subparagraph (B).

(B) Application Filed Before October 21, 1983.—A partnership is described in this subparagraph if—

(i) before October 21, 1983, the partnership was organized, a request for exemption with respect to such partnership was filed with the Department of Labor, and a private placement memorandum stating the maximum number of units in the partnership that would be offered had been circulated.

(ii) the interest in the property to be acquired, directly or indirectly (including through acquiring an interest in another partnership) by such partnership was described in such private placement memorandum, and

(iii) the marketing of partnership units in such partnership is completed not later than two years after the later of the date of the enactment of this Act or the date of publication in the Federal Register of such exemption by the Department of Labor and the aggregate number of units in such partnership sold does not exceed the amount described in clause (i).

(C) Partnerships For Which Qualifying Action Existed Before March 6, 1984.—Paragraph (9) of section 168(j) of the Internal Revenue Code of 1954 (as added by this section) shall not apply to any property acquired directly or indirectly, before January 1, 1986, by any partnership described in subparagraph (D). For purposes of this subparagraph, property shall be deemed to have been acquired prior to January 1, 1986, if the partnership had entered into a written binding contract to acquire such property prior to January 1, 1986 and the closing of such contract takes place within 6 months of the date of such contract (24 months in the case of new construction).

(D) Partnership Organized Before March 6, 1984.—A partnership is described in this subparagraph if—

(i) before March 6, 1984, the partnership was organized and publicly announced the maximum amount (as shown in the registration statement, prospectus or partnership agreement, whichever is greater) of interests which would be sold in the partnership, and

(ii) the marketing or partnership interests in such partnership was [*sic*] completed not later than the 90th day after the date of the enactment of this Act and the aggregate amount of interest in such partnership sold does not exceed the maximum amount described in clause (i).

(12) Special Rule for Amendment Made by Subsection (c)(2).—The amendment made by subsection (c)(2) to the extent it relates to subsection (f)(12) of section 168 of the Internal Revenue Code of 1954 shall take effect as if it had been included in the amendments made by section 216(a) of the Tax Equity and Fiscal Responsibility Act of 1982.

(13) Special Rule for Service Contracts Not Involving Tax-Exempt Entities.—In the case of a service contract or other arrangement described in section 7701(e) of the Internal Revenue Code of 1954 (as added by this section) with respect to which no party is a tax-exempt entity, such section 7701(e) shall not apply to—

(A) such contract or other arrangement if such contract or other arrangement was entered into before November 5, 1983, or

(B) any renewal or other extension of such contract or other arrangement pursuant to an option contained in such contract or other arrangement on November 5, 1983.

(14) Property Leased to Section 593 Organizations.—For purposes of the amendment made by subsection (f), paragraphs (1), (2), and (4) shall be applied by substituting—

(A) "November 5, 1983" for "May 23, 1983" and "November 1, 1983", as the case may be, and

(B) "organization described in section 593 of the Internal Revenue Code of 1954" for "tax-exempt entity".

(15) Special Rules Relating to Foreign Persons or Entities—

(A) In General.—In the case of tax-exempt use property which is used by a foreign person or entity, the amendments made by this section shall not apply to any property which—

(i) is placed in service by the taxpayer before January 1, 1984, and

(ii) is used by such foreign person or entity pursuant to a lease entered into before January 1, 1984.

(B) Special Rule for Subleases.—If tax-exempt use property is being used by a foreign person or entity pursuant to a sublease under a lease described in subparagraph (A)(ii), subparagraph (A) shall apply to such property only if such property was used before January 1, 1984, by any foreign person or entity pursuant to such lease.

(C) Binding Contracts, etc.—The amendments made by this section shall not apply with respect to any property (other than aircraft described in subparagraph (D)) to a foreign person or entity—

(i) if—

(I) on or before May 23, 1983, the taxpayer (or a predecessor in interest under the contract) or the foreign person or entity entered into a written binding conntract to acquire, construct, or rehabilitate such property and such property had not previously been used by the foreign person or entity, or

(II) the taxpayer or the foreign person or entity acquired the property or completed the construction, reconstruction, or rehabilitation of the property after December 31, 1982 and on or before May 23, 1983, and

(ii) if such lease is pursuant to a written binding contract entered into before January 1, 1984, which requires the foreign person or entity to be the lessee of such property.

(D) Certain Aircraft.—The amendments made by this section shall not apply with respect to any wide-body, fourengine, commercial aircraft used by a foreign person or entity if—

(i) on or before November 1, 1983, the foreign person or entity entered into a written binding contract to acquire such aircraft, and

(ii) such aircraft is originally placed in service by such foreign person or entity (or its successor in interest under the contract) after May 23, 1983, and before January 1, 1986.

(E) Use After 1983.—Qualified container equipment placed in service before January 1, 1984, which is used before such date by a foreign person shall not, for purposes of section 47 of the Internal Revenue Code of 1954, be treated as ceasing to be section 38 property by reason of the use of such equipment before January 1, 1985, by a foreign person or entity. For purposes of this subparagraph, the term "qualified container equipment" means any container, container chassis, or container trailer of United States person with a present class life of not more than 6 years.

(16) Organizations Electing Exemption From Rules Relating to Previously Tax-exempt Organizations Must Elect Taxation of Exempt Arbitrage Profits.—

(A) In General.—An organization may make the election under section 168(j)(4)(E)(ii) of the Internal Revenue Code of 1954 (relating to election not to have rules relating to previously tax-exempt organizations apply) only if such organization elects the tax treatment of exempt arbitrage profits described in subparagraph (B).

(B) Taxation of Exempt Arbitrage Profits.—

(i) In General.—In the case of an organization which elects the application of this subparagraph, there is hereby imposed a tax on the exempt arbitrage profits of such organization.

(ii) Rate of Tax, Etc.—The tax imposed by clause (i)—

(I) shall be the amount of tax which would be imposed by section 11 of such Code if the exempt arbitrage profits were taxable income (and there were no oher taxable income), and

(II) shall be imposed for the first taxable year of the taxexempt use period (as defined in section 168(j)(4)(E)(ii) of such Code).

(C) Exempt Arbitrage Profits.—

(i) In General.—For purposes of this paragraph, the term exempt arbitrage profits means the aggregate amount described in clauses (i) and (ii) of subparagraph (D) of section 103(c)(6) of such Code for all taxable years for which the organization was exempt from tax under section 501(a) of such Code with respect to obligations—

(I) associated with property described in section 168(j)(4)(E)(i), and

(II) issued before January 1, 1985.

(ii) Application of Section 103(b)(6).—For purposes of this paragraph, section 103(b)(6) of such Code shall apply to obligations issued before January 1, 1985, but the amount described in clauses (i) and (ii) of subparagraph (D) thereof shall be determined without regard to clauses (i)(II) and (ii) of subparagraph (F) thereof.

(D) Other Laws Applicable.—

(i) In General.—Except as provided in clause (ii), all provisions of law, including penalties applicable with respect to the tax imposed by section 11 of such Code shall apply with respect to the tax imposed by this paragraph.

(ii) No Credits Against Tax, Etc.—The tax imposed by this paragraph shall not be treated as imposed by section 11 of such Code for purposes of—

(I) part VI of subchapter A of chapter 1 of such Code (relating to minimum tax for tax preferences), and

(II) determining the amount of any credit allowable under subpart A of part IV of such subchapter.

(E) Election.—Any election under subparagraph (A)—

(i) shall be made at such time and in such manner as the Secretary may prescribe,

(ii) shall apply to any successor organization which is engaged in substantially similar activities, and

(iii) once made, shall be irrevocable.

(17) Certain Transitional Leased Property.—The amendments made by this section shall not apply to property described in section 168(c)(2)(D) of the Internal Revenue Code of 1954, as in effect on the day before the date of the enactment of this Act, and which is described in any of the following subparagraphs:

(A) Property is described in this subparagraph if such property is leased to a university, and—

(i) on June 16, 1983, the Board of Administrators of the university adopted a resolution approving the rehabilitation of the property in connection with an overall campus development program; and

(ii) the property houses a basketball arena and university offices.

(B) Property is described in this subparagraph if such property is leased to a charitable organization, and—

(i) on August 21, 1981, the charitable organization acquired the property, with a view towards rehabilitating the property; and

(ii) on June 12, 1982, an arson fire caused substantial damage to the property, delaying the planned rehabilitation.

(C) Property is described in this subparagraph if such property is leased to a corporation that is described in section 501(c)(3) of the Internal Revenue Code of 1954 (relating to organizations exempt from tax) pursuant to a contract—

(i) which was entered into on August 3, 1983; and

(ii) under which the corporation first occupied the property on December 22, 1983.

(D) Property is described in this subparagraph if such property is leased to an educational institution for use as an Arts and Humanities Center and with respect to which—

(i) in November 1982, an architect was engaged to design a planned renovation;

(ii) in January 1983, the architectural plans were completed;

(iii) in December 1983, a demolition contract was entered into; and

(iv) in March 1984, a renovation contract was entered into.

(E) Property is described in this subparagraph if such property is used by a college as a dormitory, and—

(i) in October 1981, the college purchased the property with a view towards renovating the property;

(ii) renovation plans were delayed because of a zoning dispute; and

(iii) in May 1983, the court of highest jurisdiction in the State in which the college is located resolved the zoning dispute in favor of the college.

(F) Property is described in this subparagraph if such property is a fraternity house related to a university with respect to which—

(i) in August 1982, the university retained attorneys to advise the university regarding the rehabilitation of the property;

(ii) on January 21, 1983, the governing body of the university established a committee to develop rehabilitation plans;

(iii) on January 10, 1984, the governor of the state in which the university is located approved historic district designation for an area that includes the property; and

(iv) on February 2, 1984, historic preservation certification applications for the property were filed with a historic landmarks commission.

(G) Property is described in this subparagraph if such property is leased to a retirement community with respect to which—

(i) on January 5, 1977, a certificate of incorporation was filed with the appropriate authority of the State in which the retirement community is located; and

(ii) on November 22, 1983, the Board of Trustees adopted a resolution evidencing the intention to begin immediate construction of the property.

(H) Property is described in this subparagraph if such property is used by a university, and—

(i) in July 1982, the Board of Trustees of the university adopted a master plan for the financing of the property; and

(ii) as of August 1, 1983, at least $60,000 in private expenditures had been expended in connection with the property.

In the case of Clemson University, the preceding sentence applies only to the Continuing Education Center and the component housing project.

(I) Property is described in this subparagraph if such property is used by a university as a fine arts center and the Board of Trustees of such university authorized the sale-leaseback agreement with respect to such property on March 7, 1984.

(J) Property is described in this subparagraph if such property is used by a tax-exempt entity as an international trade center, and

(i) prior to 1982, an environmental impact study for such property was completed;

(ii) on June 24, 1981, a developer made a written commitment to provide one-third of the financing for the development of such property; and

(iii) on October 20, 1983, such developer was approved by the Board of Directors of the tax-exempt entity.

(K) Property is described in this subparagraph if such property is used by [a] university of osteopathic medicine and health sciences, and on or before December 31, 1983, the Board of Trustees of such university approved the construction of such property.

(L) Property is described in this subparagraph if such property is used by a tax-exempt entity, and—

(i) such use is pursuant to a lease with a taxpayer which placed substantial improvements in service;

(ii) on May 23, 1983, there existed architectural plans and specifications (within the meaning of sec. 48(g)(1)(C)(ii) of the Internal Revenue Code of 1954); and

(iii) prior to May 23, 1983, at least 10 percent of the total cost of such improvements was actually paid or incurred.

Property is described in this subparagraph if such property was leased to a tax-exempt entity pursuant to a lease recorded in the Register of Deeds of Essex County, New Jersey, on May 7, 1984, and a deed of such property was recorded in the Register of Deeds of Essex County, New Jersey, on May 7, 1984.

(M) Property is described in this subparagraph if such property is used as a convention center, and on June 2, 1983, the City Council of the city in which the center is located provided for over $6 million for the project.

(18) Special Rule for Amendment Made by Subsection (c)(1).—

(A) In General.—The amendment made by subsection (c)(1) shall not apply to property—

(i) leased by the taxpayer on or before November 1, 1983, or

(ii) leased by the taxpayer after November 1, 1983, if on or before such date the taxpayer entered into a written binding contract requiring the taxpayer to lease such property.

(B) Limitation.—Subparagraph (A) shall apply to the amendment made by subsection (c)(1) only to the extent such amendment relates to property described in subclause (II), (III), or (IV) of section 168(j)(3)(B)(ii) of the Internal Revenue Code of 1954 (as added by this section).

(19) Special Rule for Certain Energy Management Contracts.—

(A) In General.—The amendments made by subsection (e) shall not apply to property used pursuant to a energy management contract that was entered into prior to May 1, 1984.

(B) Definition of energy management contract.—For purposes of subparagraph (A), the term "energy management contract" means a contract for the providing of energy conservation or energy management services.

(20) Definitions.—For purposes of this subsection—

(A) Tax-Exempt Entity.—The term "tax-exempt entity" has the same meaning as when used in section 168(j) of the Internal Revenue Code of 1954 (as added by this section), except that such term shall include any related entity (within the meaning of such section).

(B) Treatment of Improvements.—

(i) In General.—For purposes of this subsection, an improvement to property shall not be treated as a separate property unless such improvement is a substantial improvement with respect to such property.

(ii) Substantial Improvement.—For purposes of clause (i), the term "substantial improvement" has the meaning given such term by section 168(f)(1)(C) of such Code determined—

(I) by substituting "property" for "building" each place it appears therein,

(II) by substituting "20 percent" for "25 percent" in clause (ii) thereof, and

(III) without regard to clause (iii) thereof.

(C) Foreign Person or Entity.—The term "foreign person or entity" has the meaning given to such term by subparagraph (C) of section 168(j)(4) of such Code (as added by this section). For purposes of this subparagraph and subparagraph (A), such subparagraph (C) shall be applied without regard to the last sentence thereof.

(D) Leases and Subleases.—The determination of whether there is a lease or sublease to a tax-exempt entity shall take into account sections 168(j)(6)(A), 168(j)(8)(A) and 7701(e) of the Internal Revenue Code of 1954 (as added by this section).

[Sec. 168(k)]

(k) CROSS REFERENCE.—

For special rules with respect to certain gain derived from disposition of recovery property, see sections 1245 and 1250.

Amendments

• 1985 (P.L. 99-121)

P.L. 99-121, §103(b)(1)(A):

Amended Code Sec. 168 by striking out "18-year real property" each place it appeared in the text and headings thereof and inserting in lieu thereof "19-year real property". **Effective** with respect to property placed in service by the taxpayer after 5-8-85. However, for an exception and special rule, see Act Sec. 105(b)(2) and (3), below.

P.L. 99-121, §105(b)(2) and (3), provides:

(2) EXCEPTION.—The amendments made by section 103 shall not apply to property placed in service by the taxpayer before January 1, 1987, if—

(A) the taxpayer or a qualified person entered into a binding contract to purchase or construct such property before May 9, 1985, or

(B) construction of such property was commenced by or for the taxpayer or a qualified person before May 9, 1985.

For purposes of this paragraph, the term "qualified person" means any person whose rights in such a contract or such property are transferred to the taxpayer, but only if such property is not placed in service before such rights are transferred to the taxpayer.

(3) SPECIAL RULE FOR COMPONENTS.—For purposes of applying section 168(f)(1)(B) of the Internal Revenue Code of 1954 (as amended by section 103) to components placed in service after December 31, 1986, property to which paragraph (2) of this subsection applies shall be treated as placed in service by the taxpayer before May 9, 1985.

• 1984, Deficit Reduction Act of 1984 (P.L. 98-369)

P.L. 98-369, §31(a):

Redesignated Code Sec. 168(j) as 168(k). **Effective** as noted in Act Sec. 31(g) following former Code Sec. 168(j).

• 1982, Tax Equity and Fiscal Responsibility Act of 1982 (P.L. 97-248)

P.L. 97-248, §208(a)(1):

Redesignated Code Sec. 168(i) as (j). **Effective** for agreements entered into after 7-1-82, or to property placed in service after 7-1-82.

• 1981, Economic Recovery Tax Act of 1981 (P.L. 97-34)

P.L. 97-34, §201(a):

Added Code Sec. 168(i). **Effective** for property placed in service after 12-31-80, in tax years ending after such date.

• 1976, Tax Reform Act of 1976 (P.L. 94-455)

P.L. 94-455, §1951(b)(4):

Repealed Code Sec. 168. **Effective** 1-1-77. Prior to repeal, Code Sec. 168 read as follows:

SEC. 168. AMORTIZATION OF EMERGENCY FACILITIES.

(a) General Rule.—Every person, at his election, shall be entitled to a deduction with respect to the amortization of the adjusted basis (for determining gain) of any emergency facility (as defined in subsection (d)), based on a period of 60 months. Such amortization deduction shall be an amount, with respect to each month of such period within the taxable year, equal to the adjusted basis of the facility at the end of such month divided by the number of months (including the month for which the deduction is computed) remaining in the period. Such adjusted basis at the end of the month shall be computed without regard to the amortization deduction for such month. The amortization deduction above provided with respect to any month shall, except to the extent provided in subsection (f), be in lieu of the depreciation deduction with respect to such facility for such month provided by section 167. The 60-month period shall begin as to any emergency facility, at the election of the taxpayer, with the month following the month in which the facility was completed or acquired, or with the succeeding taxable year.

(b) Election of Amortization.—The election of the taxpayer to take the amortization deduction and to begin the 60-month period with the month following the month in which the facility was completed or acquired, or with the taxable year succeeding the taxable year in which such facility was completed or acquired, shall be made by filing with the Secretary or his delegate, in such manner, in such form, and within such time, as the Secretary or his delegate may by regulations prescribe, a statement of such election.

(c) Termination of Amortization Deduction.—A taxpayer which has elected under subsection (b) to take the amortization deduction provided in subsection (a) may, at any time after making such election, discontinue the amortization deduction with respect to the remainder of the amortization period, such discontinuance to begin as of the beginning of any month specified by the taxpayer in a notice in writing filed with the Secretary or his delegate before the beginning of such month. The depreciation deduction provided under section 167 shall be allowed, beginning with the first month as to which the amortization deduction does not apply, and the taxpayer shall not be entitled to any further amortization deduction with respect to such emergency facility.

(d) Definitions.—

(1) Emergency facility.—For purposes of this section, the term "emergency facility" means any facility, land, building, machinery, or equipment, or any part thereof, the construction, reconstruction, erection, installation, or acquisition of which was completed after December 31, 1949, and with respect to which a certificate under subsection (e) has been made. In no event shall an amortization deduction be allowed in respect of any emergency facility for any taxable year unless a certificate in respect thereof under this paragraph shall have been made before the filing of the taxpayer's return for such taxable year.

(2) Emergency period.—For purposes of this section, the term "emergency period" means the period beginning January 1, 1950, and ending on the date on which the President proclaims that the utilization of a substantial portion of the emergency facilities with respect to which certifications under subsection (e) have been made is no longer required in the interest of national defense.

(e) Determination of Adjusted Basis of Emergency Facility.—In determining, for purposes of subsection (a) or (g), the adjusted basis of an emergency facility—

(1) Certifications on or before August 22, 1957.—In the case of a certificate made on or before August 22, 1957, there shall be included only so much of the amount of the adjusted basis of such facility (computed without regard to this section) as is properly attributable to such construction, reconstruction, erection, installation, or acquisition after December 31, 1949, as the certifying authority, designated by the President by Executive Order, has certified as necessary in the interest of national defense during the emergency period, and only such portion of such amount as such authority has certified as attributable to defense purposes. Such certification shall be under such regulations as may be prescribed from time to time by such certifying authority with the approval of the President. An application for a certificate must be filed at such time and in such manner as may be prescribed by such certifying authority under such regulations, but in no event shall such certificate have any effect unless an application therefor is filed before March 24, 1951, or before the expiration of 6 months after the beginning of such construction, reconstruction, erection, or installation or the date of such acquisition, whichever is later.

(2) Certifications after August 22, 1957.—In the case of a certificate made after August 22, 1957, there shall be included only so much of the amount of the adjusted basis of such facility (computed without regard to this section) as is properly attributable to such construction, reconstruction, erection, installation, or acquisition after December 31, 1949, as the certifying authority designated by the President by Executive Order, has certified is to be used—

(A) to produce new or specialized defense items or components of new or specialized defense items (as defined in paragraph (4)) during the emergency period,

(B) to provide research, developmental, or experimental services during the emergency period for the Department of Defense (or one of the component departments of such Department), or for the Atomic Energy Commission as a part of the national defense program, or

(C) to provide primary processing for uranium ore or uranium concentrate under a program of the Atomic Energy Commission for the development of new sources of uranium ore or uranium concentrate,

and only such portion of such amount as such authority has certified is attributable to the national defense program. Such certification shall be under such regulations as may be prescribed from time to time by such certifying authority with the approval of the President. An application for a certificate must be filed at such time and in such manner as may be prescribed by such certifying authority under such regulations but in no event shall such certificate have any effect unless an application therefor is filed before the expiration of 6 months after the beginning of such construction, reconstruction, erection, or installation or the date of such acquisition. For purposes of the preceding sentence, an application which was timely filed under this subsection on or before August 22, 1957, and which was pending on such date, shall be considered to be an application timely filed under this paragraph.

(3) Separate facilities; special rule.—After the completion or acquisition of any emergency facility with respect to which a certificate under paragraph (1) or (2) has been made, any expenditure (attributable to such facility and to the period after such completion or acquisition) which does not represent construction, reconstruction, erection, installation, or acquisition included in such certificate, but with respect to which a separate certificate is made under paragraph (1) or (2), shall not be applied in adjustment of the basis of such facility, but a separate basis shall be computed therefor pursuant to paragraph (1) or (2), as the case may be, as if it were a new and separate emergency facility.

(4) Definitions.—For purposes of paragraph (2)—

(A) New or specialized defense item.—The term "new or specialized defense item" means only an item (excluding services)—

(i) which is produced, or will be produced, for sale to the Department of Defense (or one of the component departments of such Department), or to the Atomic Energy Commission, for use in the national defense program, and

(ii) for the production of which existing productive facilities are unsuitable because of its newness or of its specialized defense features.

(B) Component of new or specialized defense item.—The term "component of a new or specialized defense item" means only an item—

(i) which is, or will become, a physical part of a new or specialized defense item, and

(ii) for the production of which existing productive facilities are unsuitable because of its newness or of its specialized defense features.

(5) Limitation with respect to uranium ore or uranium concentrate processing facilities.—No certificate shall be made under paragraph (2)(C) with respect to any facility unless existing facilities for processing the uranium ore or uranium concentrate which will be processed by such facility are unsuitable because of their location.

(f) Depreciation Deduction.—If the adjusted basis of the emergency facility (computed without regard to this section) is in excess of the adjusted basis computed under subsection (e), the depreciation deduction provided by section 167 shall, despite the provisions of subsection (a) of this section, be allowed with respect to such emergency facility as if its adjusted basis for the purpose of such deduction were an amount equal to the amount of such excess.

(g) Payment by United States of Unamortized Cost of Facility.—If an amount is properly includible in the gross income of the taxpayer on account of a payment with respect to an emergency facility and such payment is certified as provided in paragraph (1), then, at the election of the taxpayer in its return for the taxable year in which such amount is so includible—

(1) The amortization deduction for the month in which such amount is so includible shall (in lieu of the amount of the deduction for such month computed under subsection (a)) be equal to the amount so includible but not in excess of the adjusted basis of the emergency facility as of the end of such month (computed without regard to any amortization deduction for such month). Payments referred to in this subsection shall be payments the amounts of which are certified, under such regulations as the President may prescribe, by the certifying authority designated by the President as compensation to the taxpayer for the unamortized cost of the emergency facility made because—

(A) a contract with the United States involving the use of the facility has been terminated by its terms or by cancellation, or

(B) the taxpayer had reasonable ground (either from provisions of a contract with the United States involving the use of the facility, or from written or oral representations made under authority of the United States) for anticipating future contracts involving the use of the facility, which future contracts have not been made.

(2) In case the taxpayer is not entitled to any amortization deduction with respect to the emergency facility, the depreciation deduction allowable under section 167 on account of the month in which such amount is so includible shall be increased by such amount, but such deduction on account of such month shall not be in excess of the adjusted basis of the emergency facility as of the end of such month (computed without regard to any amount allowable, on account of such month, under section 167 or this paragraph).

(h) Life Tenant and Remainderman.—In the case of property held by one person for life with remainder to another person, the deduction shall be computed as if the life tenant were the absolute owner of the property and shall be allowable to the life tenant.

(i) Termination.—No certificate under subsection (e) shall be made with respect to any emergency facility after December 31, 1959.

(j) Cross Reference.—

For special rule with respect to gain derived from the sale or exchange of property the adjusted basis of which is determined with regard to this section, see section 1238.

P.L. 94-455, §1951(b)(4)(B), provides:

(B) SAVINGS PROVISION.—Notwithstanding the repeal made by subparagraph (A), if a certificate was issued before January 1, 1960, with respect to an emergency facility which is or has been placed in service before the date of the enactment of this Act, the provisions of section 168 shall not, with respect to such facility, be considered repealed. The benefit of deductions by reason of the preceding sentence shall be allowed to estates and trusts in the same manner as in the case of an individual. The allowable deduction shall be apportioned between the income beneficiaries and the fiduciary in accordance with regulations prescribed under section 642(f).

• 1986, Tax Reform Act of 1986 (P.L. 99-514)

P.L. 99-514, §§203, 204 and 251(d)(2)-(7), as amended by P.L. 99-509 and P.L. 100-647, §1002(c)-(d), provide:

SEC. 203. EFFECTIVE DATES; GENERAL TRANSITIONAL RULES.

(a) GENERAL EFFECTIVE DATES.—

(1) Section 201.—

(A) IN GENERAL.—Except as provided in this section, section 204, and section 251(d), the amendments made by section 201 shall apply to property placed in service after December 31, 1986, in taxable years ending after such date.

(B) ELECTION TO HAVE AMENDMENTS MADE BY SECTION 201 APPLY.—A taxpayer may elect (at such time and in such manner as the Secretary of the Treasury or his delegate may prescribe) to have the amendments made by section 201 apply to any property placed in service after July 31, 1986, and before January 1, 1987. No election may be made under this subparagraph with respect to property to which section 168 of the Internal Revenue Code of 1986 would not apply by reason of section 168(f)(5) of such Code if such property were placed in service after December 31, 1986.

(2) SECTION 202.—

(A) IN GENERAL.—The amendments made by section 202 shall apply to property placed in service after December 31, 1986, in taxable years ending after such date.

(B) SPECIAL RULE FOR FISCAL YEARS INCLUDING JANUARY 1, 1987.—In the case of any taxable year (other than a calendar year) which includes January 1, 1987, for purposes of applying the amendments made by section 202 to property placed in service during such taxable year and after December 31, 1986—

(i) the limitation of section 179(b)(1) of the Internal Revenue Code of 1986 (as amended by section 202) shall be reduced by the aggregate deduction under section 179 (as in effect on the day before the date of the enactment of the Tax Reform Act of 1986) for section 179 property placed in service during such taxable year and before January 1, 1987,

(ii) the limitation of section 179(b)(2) of such Code (as so amended) shall be applied by taking into account the cost of all section 179 property placed in service during such taxable year, and

(iii) the limitation of section 179(b)(3) of such Code shall be applied by taking into account the taxable income for the entire taxable year reduced by the amount of any deduction under section 179 of such Code for property placed in service during such taxable year and before January 1, 1987.

(b) GENERAL TRANSITIONAL RULE.—

(1) IN GENERAL.—The amendments made by section 201 shall not apply to—

(A) any property which is constructed, reconstructed, or acquired by the taxpayer pursuant to a written contract which was binding on March 1, 1986,

(B) property which is constructed or reconstructed by the taxpayer if—

(i) the lesser of (I) $1,000,000, or (II) 5 percent of the cost of such property has been incurred or committed by March 1, 1986, and

(ii) the construction or reconstruction of such property began by such date, or

(C) an equipped building or plant facility if construction has commenced as of March 1, 1986, pursuant to a written specific plan and more than one-half of the cost of such equipped building or facility has been incurred or committed by such date.

For purposes of this paragraph, all members of the same affiliated group of corporations (within the meaning of section 1504 of the Internal Revenue Code of 1986) filing a consolidated return shall be treated as one taxpayer.

(2) REQUIREMENT THAT CERTAIN PROPERTY BE PLACED IN SERVICE BEFORE CERTAIN DATE.—

(A) IN GENERAL.—Paragraph (1) and section 204(a) (other than paragraph (8) or (12) thereof) shall not apply to any property unless such property has a class life of at least 7 years and is placed in service before the applicable date determined under the following table:

In the case of property with a class life of:	*The applicable date is:*
At least 7 but less than 20 years	January 1, 1989
20 years or more	January 1, 1991

(B) RESIDENTIAL RENTAL AND NONRESIDENTIAL REAL PROPERTY.—In the case of residential rental property and nonresidential real property, the applicable date is January 1, 1991.

(C) CLASS LIVES.—For purposes of subparagraph (A)—

(i) the class life of property to which section 168(g)(3)(B) of the Internal Revenue Code of 1986 (as added by section 201) applies shall be the class life in effect on January 1, 1986, except that computer-based telephone central office switching equipment described in section 168(e)(3)(B)(iii) of such Code shall be treated as having a class life of 6 years,

(ii) property described in section 204(a) shall be treated as having a class life of 20 years, and

(iii) property with no class life shall be treated as having a class life of 12 years.

(D) SUBSTITUTION OF APPLICABLE DATES.—If any provision of this Act substitutes a date for an applicable date, this paragraph shall be applied by using such date.

(3) PROPERTY QUALIFIES IF SOLD AND LEASED BACK IN 3 MONTHS.—Property shall be treated as meeting the requirements of paragraphs (1) and (2) or section 204(a) with respect to any taxpayer if such property is acquired by the taxpayer from a person—

(A) in whose hands such property met the requirements of paragraphs (1) and (2) or section 204(a) (or would have met such requirements if placed in service by such person), or

(B) who placed the property in service before January 1, 1987,

and such property is leased back by the taxpayer to such person, or is leased to such person, not later than the earlier of the applicable date under paragraph (2) or the day which is 3 months after such property was placed in service.

(4) PLANT FACILITY.—For purposes of paragraph (1), the term "plant facility" means a facility which does not include any building (or with respect to which buildings constitute an insignificant portion) and which is—

(A) a self-contained single operating unit or processing operation,

(B) located on a single site, and

(C) identified as a single unitary project as of March 1, 1986.

(c) PROPERTY FINANCED WITH TAX-EXEMPT BONDS.—

(1) IN GENERAL.—Except as otherwise provided in this subsection or section 204, subparagraph (C) of section 168(g)(1) of the Internal Revenue Code of 1986 (as added by this Act) shall apply to property placed in service after December 31, 1986, in taxable years ending after such date, to the extent such property is financed by the proceeds of an obligation (including a refunding obligation) issued after March 1, 1986.

(2) EXCEPTIONS.—

(A) CONSTRUCTION OR BINDING AGREEMENTS.—Subparagraph (C) of section 168(g)(1) of such Code (as so added) shall not apply to obligations with respect to a facility—

(i)(I) the original use of which commences with the taxpayer, and the construction, reconstruction, or rehabilitation of which began before March 2, 1986, and was completed on or after such date,

(II) with respect to which a binding contract to incur significant expenditures for construction, reconstruction, or rehabilitation was entered into before March 2, 1986, and some of such expenditures are incurred on or after such date, or

(III) acquired on or after March 2, 1986, pursuant to a binding contract entered into before such date, and

(ii) described in an inducement resolution or other comparable preliminary approval adopted by the issuing authority (or by a voter referendum) before March 2, 1986.

(B) REFUNDING.—

(i) IN GENERAL.—Except as provided in clause (ii), in the case of property placed in service after December 31, 1986, which is financed by the proceeds of an obligation which is issued solely to refund another obligation which was issued before March 2, 1986, subparagraph (C) of section 168(g)(1) of such Code (as so added) shall apply only with respect to an amount equal to the basis in such property which has not been recovered before the date such refunded obligation is issued.

(ii) SIGNIFICANT EXPENDITURES.—In the case of facilities the original use of which commences with the taxpayer and with respect to which significant expenditures are made before January 1, 1987, subparagraph (C) of section 168(g)(1) of such Code (as so added) shall not apply with respect to such facilities to the extent such facilities are financed by the proceeds of an obligation issued solely to refund another obligation which was issued before March 2, 1986.

(C) FACILITIES.—In the case of an inducement resolution or other comparable preliminary approval adopted by an issuing authority before March 2, 1986, for purposes of subparagraphs (A) and (B)(ii) with respect to obligations described in such resolution, the term "facilities" means the facilities described in such resolution.

(D) SIGNIFICANT EXPENDITURES.—For purposes of this paragraph, the term "significant expenditures" means expenditures greater than 10 percent of the reasonably anticipated cost of the construction, reconstruction, or rehabilitation of the facility involved.

(d) MID-QUARTER CONVENTION.—In the case of any taxable year beginning before October 1, 1987 in which property to which the amendments made by section 201 do not apply is placed in service, such property shall be taken into account in determining whether section 168(d)(3) of the Internal Code of 1986 (as added by section 201) applies for such taxable year to property to which such amendments apply. The preceding sentence shall only apply to property which would be taken into account if such amendments did apply.

(e) NORMALIZATION REQUIREMENTS.—

(1) IN GENERAL.—A normalization method of accounting shall not be treated as being used with respect to any public utility property for purposes of section 167 or 168 of the Internal Revenue Code of 1986 if the taxpayer, in computing its cost of service for ratemaking purposes and reflecting operating results in its regulated books of account, reduces the excess tax reserve more rapidly or to a greater extent than such reserve would be reduced under the average rate assumption method.

(2) DEFINITIONS.—For purpose of this subsection—

(A) EXCESS TAX RESERVE.—The term "excess tax reserve" means the excess of—

(i) the reserve for deferred taxes (as described in section 167(l)(3)(G)(ii) or 168(e)(3)(B)(ii) of the Internal Revenue Code of 1954 as in effect on the day before the date of the enactment of this Act), over

(ii) the amount which would be the balance in such reserve if the amount of such reserve were determined by assuming that the corporate rate reductions provided in this Act were in effect for all prior periods.

(B) AVERAGE RATE ASSUMPTION METHOD.—The average rate assumption method is the method under which the excess in the reserve for deferred taxes is reduced over the remaining lives of the property as used in its regulated books of account which gave rise to the reserve for deferred taxes. Under such method, if timing differences for the property reverse, the amount of the adjustment to the reserve for the deferred taxes is calculated by multiplying—

(i) the ratio of the aggregate deferred taxes for the property to the aggregate timing differences for the property as of the beginning of the period in question, by

(ii) the amount of the timing differences which reverse during such period.

SEC. 204. ADDITIONAL TRANSITIONAL RULES.

(a) OTHER TRANSITIONAL RULES.

(1) URBAN RENOVATION PROJECTS.—

(A) IN GENERAL.—The amendments made by section 201 shall not apply to any property which is an integral part of any qualified urban renovation project.

(B) QUALIFIED URBAN RENOVATION PROJECT.—For purposes of subparagraph (A), the term "qualified urban renovation project" means any project—

(i) described in subparagraph (C), (D), (E), or (G) which before March 1, 1986, was publicly announced by a political subdivision of a State for a renovation of an urban area within its jurisdiction,

(ii) described in subparagraph (C), (D) or (G) which before March 1, 1986, was identified as a single unitary project in the internal financing plans of the primary developer of the project,

(iii) described in subparagraph (C) or (D), which is not substantially modified on or after March 1, 1986, and

(iv) described in subparagraph (F) or (H).

(C) PROJECT WHERE AGREEMENT ON DECEMBER 19, 1984.—A project is described in this subparagraph if—

(i) a political subdivision granted on July 11, 1985, development rights to the primary developer-purchaser of such project, and

(ii) such project was the subject of a development agreement between a political subdivision and a bridge authority on December 19, 1984.

For purposes of this subparagraph, section 203(b)(2) shall be applied by substituting "January 1, 1994" for "January 1, 1991" each place it appears.

(D) CERTAIN ADDITIONAL PROJECTS.—A project is described in this subparagraph if it is described in any of the following clauses of this subparagraph and the primary developer of all such projects is the same person:

(i) A project is described in this clause if the development agreement with respect thereto was entered into during April 1984 and the estimated cost of the project is approximately $194,000,000.

(ii) A project is described in this clause if the development agreement with respect thereto was entered into during May 1984 and the estimated cost of the project is approximately $190,000,000.

(iii) A project is described in this clause if the project has an estimated cost of approximately $92,000,000 and at least $7,000,000 was spent before September 26, 1985, with respect to such project.

(iv) A project is described in this clause if the estimated project cost is approximately $39,000,000 and at least $2,000,000 of construction cost for such project were incurred before September 26, 1985.

(v) A project is described in this clause if the development agreement with respect thereto was entered into before September 26, 1985, and the estimated cost of the project is approximately $150,000,000.

(vi) A project is described in this clause if the board of directors of the primary developer approved such project in December 1982, and the estimated cost of such project is approximately $107,000,000.

(vii) A project is described in this clause if the board of directors of the primary developer approved such project in December 1982, and the estimated cost of such project is approximately $59,000,000.

(viii) A project is described in this clause if the Board of Directors of the primary developer approved such project in December 1983, following selection of the developer by a city council on September 26, 1983, and the estimated cost of such project is approximately $107,000,000.

(E) PROJECT WHERE PLAN CONFIRMED ON OCTOBER 4, 1984.—A project is described in this subparagraph if—

(i) a State or an agency, instrumentality, or political subdivision thereof approved the filing of a general project plan on June 18, 1981, and on October 4, 1984, a State or an agency, instrumentality, or political subdivision thereof confirmed such plan,

(ii) the project plan as confirmed on October 4, 1984, included construction or renovation of office buildings, a hotel, a trade mart, theaters, and a subway complex, and

(iii) significant segments of such project were the subject of one or more conditional designations granted by a State or an agency, instrumentality, or political subdivision thereof to one or more developers before January 1, 1985.

The preceding sentence shall apply with respect to a property only to the extent that a building on such property site was identified as part of the project plan before September 26, 1985, and only to the extent that the size of the building on such property site was not substantially increased by reason of a modification to the project plan with respect to such property on or after such date. For purposes of this subparagraph, section 203(b)(2) shall be applied by substituting "January 1, 1988" for "January 1, 1991" each place it appears.

(F) A project is described in this subparagraph if it is a sports and entertainment facility which—

(i) is to be used by both a National Hockey League team and a National Basketball Association team;

(ii) is to be constructed on a platform utilizing air rights over land acquired by a State authority and identified as site B in a report dated May 30, 1984, prepared for a State urban development corporation; and

(iii) is eligible for real property tax, and power and energy benefits pursuant to the provisions of State legislation approved and effective July 7, 1982.

A project is also described in this subparagraph if it is a mixed-use development which is—

(I) to be constructed above a public railroad station utilized by the national railroad passenger corporation and commuter railroads serving two States; and

(II) will include the reconstruction of such station so as to make it a more efficient transportation center and to better integrate the station with the development above, such reconstruction plans to be prepared in cooperation with a State transportation authority.

For purposes of this subparagraph, section 203(b)(2) shall be applied by substituting "January 1, 1998" for the applicable date that would otherwise apply.

(G) A project is described in this subparagraph if—

(i) an inducement resolution was passed on March 9, 1984, for the issuance of obligations with respect to such project,

(ii) such resolution was extended by resolutions passed on August 14, 1984, April 2, 1985, August 13, 1985, and July 8, 1986.

(iii) an application was submitted on January 31, 1984, for an Urban Development Action Grant with respect to such project, and

(iv) an Urban Development Action Grant was preliminarily approved for all or part of such project on July 3, 1986.

(H) A project is described in this subparagraph if it is a redevelopment project, with respect to which $10,000,000 in industrial revenue bonds were approved by a State Development Finance Authority on January 15, 1986, a village transferred approximately $4,000,000 of bond volume authority to the State in June 1986, and a binding Redevelopment Agreement was executed between a city and the development team on June 30, 1986.

(2) CERTAIN PROJECTS GRANTED FERC LICENSES, ETC.—The amendments made by section 201 shall not apply to any property which is part of a project—

(A) which is certified by the Federal Energy Regulatory Commission before March 2, 1986, as a qualifying facility for purposes of the Public Utility Regulatory Policies Act of 1978,

(B) which was granted before March 2, 1986, a hydroelectric license for such project by the Federal Energy Regulatory Commission, or

(C) which is a hydroelectric project of less than 80 megawatts that filed an application for a permit, exemption, or license with the Federal Energy Regulatory Commission before March 2, 1986.

(3) SUPPLY OR SERVICE CONTRACTS.—The amendments made by section 201 shall not apply to any property which is readily identifiable with and necessary to carry out a written supply or service contract, or agreement to lease, which was binding on March 1, 1986.

(4) PROPERTY TREATED UNDER PRIOR TAX ACTS.—The amendments made by section 201 shall not apply—

(A) to property described in section 12(c)(2) (as amended by the Technical and Miscellaneous Revenue Act of 1988), 31(g)(5), or 31(g)(17)(J) of the Tax Reform Act of 1984,

(B) to property described in section 209(d)(1)(B) of the Tax Equity and Fiscal Responsibility Act of 1982, as amended by the Tax Reform Act of 1984, and

(C) to property described in section 216(b)(3) of the Tax Equity and Fiscal Responsibility Act of 1982.

(5) SPECIAL RULES FOR PROPERTY INCLUDED IN MASTER PLANS OF INTEGRATED PROJECTS.—The amendments made by section 201 shall not apply to any property placed in service pursuant to a master plan which is clearly identifiable as of March 1, 1986, for any project described in any of the following subparagraphs of this paragraph:

(A) A project is described in this subparagraph if—

(i) the project involves production platforms for off-shore drilling, oil and gas pipeline to shore, process and storage facilities, and a marine terminal, and

(ii) at least $900,000,000 of the costs of such project were incurred before September 26, 1985.

(B) A project is described in this subparagraph if—

(i) such project involves a fiber optic network of at least 20,000 miles, and

(ii) before September 26, 1985, construction commenced pursuant to the master plan and at least $85,000,000 was spent on construction.

(C) A project is described in this subparagraph if—

(i) such project passes through at least 10 States and involves intercity communication link[s] (including one or more repeater sites, terminals and junction stations for microwave transmissions, regenerators or fiber optics and other related equipment),

(ii) the lesser of $150,000,000 or 5 percent of the total project cost has been expended, incurred, or committed before March 2, 1986, by one or more taxpayers each of which is a member of the same affiliated group (as defined in section 1504(a)), and

(iii) such project consists of a comprehensive plan for meeting network capacity requirements as encompassed within either:

(I) a November 5, 1985, presentation made to and accepted by the Chairman of the Board and the president of the taxpayer, or

(II) the approvals by the Board of Directors of the parent company of the taxpayer on May 3, 1985, and September 22, 1985, and of the executive committee of said board on December 23, 1985.

(D) A project is described in this subparagraph if—

(i) such project is part of a flat rolled product modernization plan which was initially presented to the Board of Directors of the taxpayer on July 8, 1983,

(ii) such program will be carried out at 3 locations, and

(iii) such project will involve a total estimated minimum capital cost of at least $250,000,000.

(E) A project is described in this subparagraph if the project is being carried out by a corporation engaged in the production of paint, chemicals, fiberglass, and glass, and if—

(i) the project includes a production line which applied a thin coating to glass in the manufacture of energy efficient residential products, if approved by the management committee of the corporation on January 29, 1986,

(ii) the project is a turbogenerator which was approved by the president of such corporation and at least $1,000,000 of the cost of which was incurred or committed before such date,

(iii) the project is a waste-to-energy disposal system which was initially approved by the management committee of the corporation on March 29, 1982, and at least $5,000,000 of the cost of which was incurred before September 26, 1985,

(iv) the project, which involves the expansion of an existing service facility and the addition of new lab facilities needed to accommodate topcoat and undercoat production needs of a nearby automotive assembly plant, was approved by the corporation's management committee on March 5, 1986, or

(v) the project is part of a facility to consolidate and modernize the silica production of such corporation and the project was provided by the president of such corporation on August 19, 1985.

(F) A project is described in this subparagraph if—

(i) such project involves a port terminal and oil pipeline extending generally from the area of Los Angeles, California, to the area of Midland, Texas, and

(ii) before September 26, 1985, there is a binding contract for dredging and channeling with respect thereto and a management contract with a construction manager for such project.

(G) A project is described in this subparagraph if—

(i) the project is a newspaper printing and distribution plant project with respect to which a contract for the purchase of 8 printing press units and related equipment to be installed in a single press line was entered into on January 8, 1985, and

(ii) the contract price for such units and equipment represents at least 50 percent of the total cost of such project.

(H) A project is described in this subparagraph if it is the second phase of a project involving direct current transmission lines spanning approximately 190 miles from the United States-Canadian border to Ayer, Massachusetts, alternating current transmission lines in Massachusetts from Ayer to Milbury to West Medway, DC-AC converted terminals to Monroe, New Hampshire, and Ayer, Massachusetts, and other related equipment and facilities.

(I) A project is described in this subparagraph if it involves not more than two natural gas-fired combined cycle electric generating units each having a net electrical capability of approximately 233 megawatts, and a sale contract for approximately one-half of the output of the 1st unit was entered into in December 1985.

(J) A project is described in this subparagraph if—

(i) the project involves an automobile manufacturing facility (including equipment and incidental appurtenances) to be located in the United States, and

(ii) either—

(I) the project was the subject of a memorandum of understanding between 2 autombile manufacturers that was signed before September 25, 1985, the automobile manufacturing facility (including equipment and incidental appurtenances) will involve a total estimated cost of approximately $750,000,000, and will have an annual production capacity of approximately 240,000 vehicles or

(II) The Board of Directors of an automobile manufacturer approved a written plan for the conversion of existing facilities to produce new models of a vehicle not currently produced in the United States, such facilities will be placed in service by July 1, 1987, and such Board action occurred in July 1985 with respect to a $602,000,000 expenditure, a $438,000,000 expenditure, and a $321,000,000 expenditure.

(K) A project is described in this subparagraph if—

(i) the project involves a joint venture between a utility company and a paper company for a supercalendared paper mill, and at least $50,000,000 was incurred or committed with respect to such project before March 1, 1986, or

(ii) the project involves a paper mill for the manufacture of newsprint (including a cogeneration facility) is generally based on a written design and feasibility study that was completed on December 15, 1981, and will be placed in service before January 1, 1991, or

(iii) the project is undertaken by a Maine corporation and involves the modernization of pulp and paper mills in Millinocket and/or East Millinocket, Maine, or

(iv) the project involves the installation of a paper machine for production of coated publication papers, the modernization of a pulp mill, and the installation of machinery and equipment with respect to related processes, as of December 31, 1985, in excess of $50,000,000 was incurred for the project, as of July 1986, in excess of $150,000,000 was incurred for the project, and the project is located in Pine Bluff, Arkansas, or

(v) the project involves property of a type described in ADR classes 26.1, 26.2, 25, 00.3 and 00.4 included in a paper plant which will manufacture and distribute tissue, towel or napkin products; is located in Effingham County, Georgia; and is generally based upon a written General Description which was submitted to the Georgia Department of Revenue on or about June 13, 1985.

(L) A project is described in this subparagraph if—

(i) a letter of intent with respect to such project was executed on June 4, 1985, and

(ii) a 5-percent downpayment was made in connection with such project for 2 10-unit press lines and related equipment.

(M) A project is described in this subparagraph if—

(i) the project involves the retrofit of ammonia plants,

(ii) as of March 1, 1986, more than $390,000 had been expended for engineering and equipment, and

(iii) more than $170,000 was expensed in 1985 as a portion of preliminary engineering expense.

(N) A project is described in this subparagraph if the project involves bulkhead intermodal flat cars which are placed in service before January 1, 1987, and either—

(i) more than $2,290,000 of expenditures were made before March 1, 1986, with respect to a project involving up to 300 platforms, or

(ii) more than $95,000 of expenditures were made before March 1, 1986, with respect to a project involving up to 850 platforms.

(O) A project is described in this subparagraph if—

(i) the project involves the production and transportation of oil and gas from a well located north of the Arctic Circle, and

(ii) more than $200,000,000 of cost had been incurred or committed before September 26, 1985.

(P) A project is described in this subparagraph if—

(i) a commitment letter was entered into with a financial institution on January 23, 1986, for the financing of the project,

(ii) the project involves intercity communication links (including microwave and fiber optics communications systems and related property),

(iii) the project consists of communications links between—

(I) Omaha, Nebraska, and Council Bluffs, Iowa,

(II) Waterloo, Iowa and Sioux City, Iowa,

(III) Davenport, Iowa and Springfield, Illinois, and

(iv) the estimated cost of such project is approximately $13,000,000.

(Q) A project is described in this subparagraph if—

(i) such project is a mining modernization project involving mining, transport, and milling operatons,

(ii) before September 26, 1985, at least $20,000,000 was expended for engineering studies which were approved by the Board of Directors of the taxpayer on January 27, 1983, and

(iii) such project will involve a total estimated minimum cost of $350,000,000.

(R) A project is described in this subparagraph if—

(i) such project is a dragline acquired in connection with a 3-stage program which began in 1980 to increase production from a coal mine,

(ii) at least $35,000,000 was spent before September 26, 1985, on the 1st 2 stages of the program, and

(iii) at least $4,000,000 was spent to prepare the mine site for the dragline.

(S) A project is described in this subparagraph if it is a project consisting of a mineral processing facility using a heap leaching system (including waste dumps, low-grade dumps, a leaching area, and mine roads) and if—

(i) convertible subordinated debentures were issued in August 1985, to finance the project,

(ii) construction of the project was authorized by the Board of Directors of the taxpayer on or before December 31, 1985,

(iii) at least $750,000 was paid or incurred with respect to the project on or before December 31, 1985, and

(iv) the project is placed in service on or before December 31, 1986.

(T) A project is described in this subparagraph if it is a plant facility on Alaska's North Slope which is placed in service before January 1, 1988, and—

(i) the approximate cost of which is $675,000,000, of which approximately $400,000,000 was spent on off-site construction,

(ii) the approximate cost of which is $445,000,000, of which approximately $400,000,000 was spent on off-site construction and more than 50 percent of the project cost was spent prior to December 31, 1985, or

(iii) the approximate cost of which is $375,000,000, of which approximately $260,000,000 was spent on off-site construction.

(U) A project is described in this subparagraph if it involves the connecting of existing retail stores in the downtown area of a city to a new covered area, the total project will be 250,000 square feet, a formal Memorandum of Understanding relating to development of the project was executed with the city on July 2, 1986, and the estimated cost of the project is $18,186,424.

(V) A project is described in this subparagraph if it includes a 200,000 square foot office tower, a 200-room hotel, a 300,000 square foot retail center, an 800-space parking facility, the total cost is projected to be $60,000,000, and $1,250,000 was expended with respect to the site before August 25, 1986.

(W) A project is described in this subparagraph if it is a joint use and development project including an integrated hotel, convention center, office, related retail facilities and public mass transportation terminal, and vehicle parking facilities which satisfies the following conditions:

(i) is developed within certain air space rights and upon real property exchanged for such joint use and development project which is owned or acquired by a state department of transportation, a regional mass transit district in a county with a population of at least 5,000,000 and a community redevelopment agency;

(ii) such project affects an existing, approximately forty (40) acre public mass transportation bus-way terminal facility located adjacent to an interstate highway;

(iii) a memorandum of understanding with respect to such joint use and development project is executed by a state department of transportation, such a county regional mass transit district and a community redevelopment agency on or before December 31, 1986, and

(iv) a major portion of such joint use and development project is placed in service by December 31, 1990.

(X) A project is described in this subparagraph if—

(i) it is an $8,000,000 project to provide advanced control technology for adipic acid at a plant, which was authorized by the company's Board of Directors in October 1985, at December 31, 1985, $1,400,000 was committed and $400,000 expended with respect to such project, or

(ii) it is an $8,300,000 project to achieve compliance with State and Federal regulations for particulates emissions, which was authorized by the company's Board of Directors in December 1985, by March 31, 1986, $250,000 was committed and $250,000 was expended with respect to such project, or

(iii) it is a $22,000,000 project for the retrofit of a plant that makes a raw material for aspartame, which was approved in the company's December 1985 capital budget, if approximately $3,000,000 of the $22,000,000 was spent before August 1, 1986.

(Y) A project is described in this subparagraph if such project passes through at least 9 states and involves an intercity communication link (including multiple repeater sites and junction stations for microwave transmissions and amplifiers for fiber optics); the link from Buffalo to New York/Elizabeth was completed in 1984; the link from Buffalo to Chicago was completed in 1985; and the link from New York to Washington is completed in 1986.

(Z) A project is described in this subparagraph if—

(i) such project involves a fiber optic network of at least 475 miles, passing through Minnesota and Wisconsin; and

(ii) before January 1, 1986, at least $15,000,000 was expended or committed for electronic equipment or fiber optic cable to be used in constructing the network.

(6) NATURAL GAS PIPELINE.—The amendments made by section 201 shall not apply to any interstate natural gas pipeline (and related equipment) if—

(A) 3 applications for the construction of such pipeline were filed with the Federal Energy Regulatory Commission before November 22, 1985 (and 2 of which were filed before September 26, 1985), and

(B) such pipeline has 1 of its terminal points near Bakersfield, California.

(7) CERTAIN LEASEHOLD IMPROVEMENTS.—The amendments made by section 201 shall not apply to any reasonable leasehold improvements, equipment and furnishings placed in service by a lessee or its affiliates if—

(A) the lessee or an affiliate is the original lessee of each building in which such property is to be used,

(B) such lessee is obligated to lease the building under an agreement to lease entered into before September 26, 1985, and such property is provided for such building, and

(C) such buildings are to serve as world headquarters of the lessee and its affiliates.

For purposes of this paragraph, a corporation is an affiliate of another corporation if both corporations are members of a controlled group of corporations within the meaning of section 1563(a) of the Internal Revenue Code of 1954 without regard to section 1563(b)(2) of such Code. Such lessee shall include a securities firm that meets the requirements of subparagraph (A), except the lessee is obligated to lease the building under a lessee entered into on June 18, 1986.

(8) SOLID WASTE DISPOSAL FACILITIES.—The amendments made by section 201 shall not apply to the taxpayer who originally places in service any qualified solid waste disposal facility (as defined in section 7701(e)(3)(B) of the Internal Revenue Code of 1986) if before March 2, 1986—

(A) there is a binding written contract between a service recipient and a service provider with respect to the operation of such facility to pay for the services to be provided by such facility,

(B) a service recipient or governmental unit (or any entity related to such recipient or unit) made a financial commitment of at least $200,000 for the financing or construction of such facility,

(C) such facility is the Tri-Cities Solid Waste Recovery Project involving Fremont, Newark, and Union City, California, and has received an authority to construct from the Environmental Protection Agency or from a State or local agency authorized by the Environmental Protection Agency to issue air quality permits under the Clean Air Act,

(D) a bond volume carryforward election was made for the facility and the facility is for Chattanooga, Knoxville, or Kingsport, Tennessee, or

(E) such facility is to serve Haverhill, Massachusetts.

(9) CERTAIN SUBMERSIBLE DRILLING UNITS.—In the case of a binding contract entered into on October 30, 1984, for the purchase of 6 semi-submersible drilling units at a cost of $425,000,000, such units shall be treated as having an applicable date under subsection 203(b)(2) of January 1, 1991.

(10) WASTEWATER OR SEWAGE TREATMENT FACILITY.—The amendments made by section 201 shall not apply to any property which is part of a wastewater or sewage treatment facility if—

(A) site preparation for such facility commenced before September 1985, and a parish council approved a service agreement with respect to such facility on December 4, 1985;

(B) a city-parish advertised in September 1985, for bids for construction of secondary treatment improvements for such facility, in May 1985, the city-parish received statements from 16 firms interested in privatizing the wastewater treatment facilities, and metropolitan council selected a privatizer at its meeting on November 20, 1985, and adopted a resolution authorizing the Mayor to enter into contractual negotiation with the selected privatizer;

(C) the property is part of a wastewater treatment facility serving Greenville, South Carolina with respect to which a binding service agreement between a privatizer and the Western Carolina Regional Sewer Authority with respect to such facility was signed before January 1, 1986; or

(D) such property is part of a wastewater treatment facility (located in Cameron County, Texas, within one mile of the City of Harlingen), an application for a wastewater discharge permit was filed with respect to such facility on December 4, 1985, and a City Commission approved a letter of intent relating to a service agreement with respect to such facility on August 7, 1986; or a wastewater facility (located in Harlingen, Texas) which is a subject of such letter of intent and service agreement of this paragraph and the design of which was contracted for in a letter of intent dated January 23, 1986.

(11) CERTAIN AIRCRAFT.—The amendments made by section 201 shall not apply to any new aircraft with 19 or fewer passenger seats if—

(A) The aircraft is manufactured in the United States. For purposes of this subparagraph, an aircraft is "manufactured" at the point of its final assembly,

(B) The aircraft was in inventory or in the planned production schedule of final assembly manufacturer, with orders placed for the engine(s) on or before August 16, 1986, and

(C) The aircraft is purchased or subject to a binding contract on or before December 31, 1986, and is delivered and placed in service by the purchaser, before July 1, 1987.

(12) CERTAIN SATELLITES.—The amendments made by section 201 shall not apply to any satellite with respect to which—

(A) on or before January 28, 1986, there was a binding contract to construct or acquire a satellite, and

(i) an agreement to launch was in existence on that date, or

(ii) on or before August 5, 1983, the Federal Communications Commission had authorized the construction and for which the authorized party has a specific although undesignated agreement to launch in existence on January 28, 1986;

(B) by order adopted on July 25, 1985, the Federal Communications Commission granted the taxpayer an orbital slot and authorized the taxpayer to launch and operate 2 satellites with a cost of approximately $300,000,000; or

(C) the International Telecommunications Satellite Organization or the International Maritime Satellite Organization entered into written binding contracts before May 1, 1985.

(13) CERTAIN NONWIRE LINE CELLULAR TELEPHONE SYSTEMS.—The amendments made by section 201 shall not apply to property that is part of a nonwire line system in the Domestic Public Cellular Radio Telecommunications Service for which the Federal Communications Commission has issued a construction permit before September 26, 1985, but only if such property is placed in service before January 1, 1987.

(14) CERTAIN COGENERATION FACILITIES.—The amendments made by section 201 shall not apply to projects consisting of 1 or more facilities for the cogeneration and distribution of electricity and steam or other forms of thermal energy if—

(A) at least $100,000 was paid or incurred with respect to the project before March 1, 1986, a memorandum of understanding was executed on September 13, 1985, and the project is placed in service before January 1, 1989,

(B) at least $500,000 was paid or incurred with respect to the projects before May 6, 1986, the projects involve a 22-megawatt combined cycle gas turbine plant and a 45-megawatt coal waste plant, and applications for qualifying facility status were filed with the Federal Energy Regulatory Commission on March 5, 1986,

(C) the project cost approximates $125,000,000 to $140,000,000 and an application was made to the Federal Energy Regulatory Commission in July 1985,

(D) an inducement resolution for such facility was adopted on September 10, 1985, a development authority was given an inducement date of September 10, 1985, for a loan not to exceed $80,000,000 with respect to such facility, and such facility is expected to have a capacity of approximately 30 megawatts of electric power and 70,000 pounds of steam per hour,

(E) at least $1,000,000 was incurred with respect to the project before May 6, 1986, the project involves a 52-megawatt combined cycle gas turbine plant and a petition was filed with the Connecticut Department of Public Utility Control to approve a power sales agreement with respect to the project on March 27, 1986,

(F) the project has a planned scheduled capacity of approximately 38,000 kilowatts, the project property is placed in service before January 1, 1991, and the project is operated, established, or constructed pursuant to certain agreements, the negotiation of which began before 1986, with public or municipal utilities conducting business in Massachusetts, or

(G) the Board of Regents of Oklahoma State University took official action on July 25, 1986, with respect to the project.

In the case of the project described in subparagraph (F), section 203(b)(2)(A) shall be applied by substituting "January 1, 1991" for "January 1, 1989."

(15) CERTAIN ELECTRIC GENERATING STATIONS.—The amendments made by section 201 shall not apply to a project located in New Mexico consisting of a coal-fired electric generating station (including multiple generating units, coal mine equipment, and transmission facilities) if—

(A) a tax-exempt entity will own an equity interest in all property included in the project (except the coal mine equipment), and

(B) at least $72,000,000 was expended in the acquisition of coal leases, land and water rights, engineering studies, and other development costs before May 6, 1986.

For purposes of this paragraph, section 203(b)(2) shall be applied by substituting "January 1, 1996" for "January 1, 1991" each place it appears.

(16) SPORTS ARENAS.—

(A) INDOOR SPORTS FACILITY.—The amendments made by section 201 shall not apply to up to $20,000,000 of improvements made by a lessee of any indoor sports facility pursuant to a lease from a State commission granting the right to make limited and specified improvements (including planned seat explanations), if architectural renderings of the project were commissioned and received before December 22, 1985.

(B) METROPOLITAN SPORTS ARENA.—The amendments made by section 201 shall not apply to any property which is part of an arena constructed for professional sports activities in a metropolitan area, provided that such arena is capable of seating no less than 18,000 spectators and a binding contract to incur significant expenditures for its construction was entered into before June 1, 1986.

(17) CERTAIN WASTE-TO-ENERGY FACILITIES.—The amendments made by section 201 shall not apply to 2 agricultural waste-to-energy powerplants (and required transmission facilities), in connection with which a contract to sell 100 megawatts of electricity to a city was executed in October 1984.

(18) CERTAIN COAL-FIRED PLANTS.—The amendments made by section 201 shall not apply to one of three 540 megawatt coal-fired plants that are placed in service after a sale leaseback occurring after January 1, 1986, if—

(A) the Board of Directors of an electric power cooperation authorized the investigation of a sale leaseback of a nuclear generation facility by resolution dated January 22, 1985, and

(B) a loan was extended by the Rural Electrification Administration on February 20, 1986, which contained a covenant with respect to used property leasing from unit II.

(19) CERTAIN RAIL SYSTEMS.—

(A) The amendments made by section 201 shall not apply to a light rail transit system, the approximate cost of which is $235,000,000, if, with respect to which, the board of directors of a corporation (formed in September 1984 for the purpose of developing, financing, and operating the system) authorized a $300,000 expenditure for a feasibility study in April 1985.

(B) The amendments made by section 201 shall not apply to any project for rehabilitation of regional railroad rights of way and properties including grade crossings which was authorized by the Board of Directors of such company prior to October 1985; and/or was modified, altered or enlarged as a result of termination of company contracts, but approved by said Board of Directors no later than January 30, 1986, and which is in the public interest, and which is subject to binding contracts or substantive commitments by December 31, 1987.

(20) CERTAIN DETERGENT MANUFACTURING FACILITY.—The amendments made by section 201 shall not apply to a laundry detergent manufacturing facility, the approximate cost of which is $13,200,000, with respect to which a project agreement was fully executed on March 17, 1986.

(21) CERTAIN RESOURCE RECOVERY FACILITY.—The amendments made by section 201 shall not apply to any of 3 resource recovery plants, the aggregate cost of which approximates $300,000,000, if an industrial development authority adopted a bond resolution with respect to such facilities on December 17, 1984, and the projects were ap-

proved by the department of commerce of a Commonwealth on December 27, 1984.

(22) The amendments made by section 201 shall not apply to a computer and office support center building in Minneapolis, with respect to which the first contract, with an architecture firm, was signed on April 30, 1985, and a construction contract was signed on March 12, 1986.

(23) CERTAIN DISTRICT HEATING AND COOLING FACILITIES.—The amendments made by section 201 shall not apply to pipes, mains, and related equipment included in district heating and cooling facilities, with respect to which the development authority of a State approved the project through an inducement resolution adopted on October 8, 1985, and in connection with which approximately $11,000,000 of tax-exempt bonds are to be issued.

(24) CERTAIN VESSELS.—

(A) CERTAIN OFFSHORE VESSELS.—The amendments made by section 201 shall not apply to any offshore vessel the construction contract for which was signed on February 28, 1986, and the approximate cost of which is $9,000,000.

(B) CERTAIN INLAND RIVER VESSEL.—The amendments made by section 201 shall not apply to a project involving the reconstruction of an inland river vessel docked on the Mississippi River at St. Louis, Missouri, on July 14, 1986, and with respect to which:

(i) the estimated cost of reconstruction is approximately $39,000,000;

(ii) reconstruction was commenced prior to December 1, 1985;

(iii) at least $17,000,000 was expended before December 31, 1985; and

(C) SPECIAL AUTOMOBILE CARRIER VESSELS.—The amendments made by section 201 shall not apply to two new automobile carrier vessels which will cost approximately $47,000,000 and will be constructed by a United States-flag carrier to operate, under the United States-flag with an American crew, to transport foreign automobiles to the United States, in a case where negotiations for such transportation arrangements commenced in April 1985, formal contract bids were submitted prior to the end of 1985, and definitive transportation contracts were awarded in May 1986.

(D) The amendments made by section 201 shall not apply to a 562-foot passenger cruise ship, which was purchased in 1980 for the purpose of returning the vessel to United States service, the approximate cost of refurbishment of which is approximately $47,000,000.

(E) The amendments made by section 201 shall not apply to the Muskegon, Michigan, Cross-Lake Ferry project having a projected cost of approximately $7,200,000.

(F) The amendments made by section 201 shall not apply to a new automobile carrier vessel, the contract price for which is no greater than $28,000,000, and which will be constructed for and placed in service by OSG Car Carriers, Inc., to transport, under the United States flag and with an American crew, foreign automobiles to North America in a case where negotiations for such transportation arrangements commenced in 1985, and definitive transportation contracts were awarded before June 1986.

(25) CERTAIN WOOD ENERGY PROJECTS.—The amendments made by section 201 shall not apply to two wood energy projects for which applications with the Federal Energy Regulatory Commission were filed before January 1, 1986, which are described as follows:

(A) a 26.5 megawatt plant in Fresno, California, and

(B) a 26.5 megawatt plant in Rocklin, California.

(26) The amendments made by section 201 shall not apply to property which is a geothermal project of less than 20 megawatts that was certified by the Federal Energy Regulatory Commission on July 14, 1986, as a qualifying small power production facility for purposes of the Public Utility Regulatory Policies Act of 1978 pursuant to an application filed with the Federal Energy Regulatory Commission on April 17, 1986.

(27) CERTAIN ECONOMIC DEVELOPMENT PROJECTS.—The amendments made by section 201 shall not apply to any of the following projects:

(A) A mixed use development on the East River the total cost of which is approximately $400,000,000, with respect to which a letter of intent was executed on January 24, 1984, and with respect to which approximately $2.5 million had been spent by March 1, 1986.

(B) A 356-room hotel, banquet, and conference facility (including 545,000 square feet of office space) the approximate cost of which is $158,000,000, with respect to which a letter of intent was executed on June 1, 1984 and with respect to which an inducement resolution and bond resolution was adopted on August 20, 1985.

(C) Phase 1 of a 4-phase project involving the construction of laboratory space and ground-floor retail space the estimated cost of which is $22,000,000 and with respect to which a memorandum of understanding was made on August 29, 1983.

(D) A project involving the development of a 490,000 square foot mixed-use building at 152 W. 57th Street, New York, New York, the estimated cost of which is $100,000,000, and with respect to which a building permit application was filed in May 1986.

(E) A mixed-use project containing a 300 unit, 12-story hotel, garage, two multi-rise office buildings, and also included a park, renovated riverboat, and barge with festival marketplace, the capital outlays for which approximate $68,000,000.

(F) The construction of a three-story office building that will serve as the home office for an insurance group and its affiliated companies, with respect to which a city agreed to transfer its ownership of the land for the project in a Redevelopment Agreement executed on September 18, 1985, once certain conditions are met.

(G) A commercial bank formed under the laws of the State of New York which entered into an agreement on September 5, 1985, to construct its headquarters at 60 Wall Street, New York, New York, with respect to such headquarters.

(H) Any property which is part of a commercial and residential project, the first phase of which is currently under construction, to be developed on land which is the subject ot an ordinance passed on July 20, 1981, by the city council of the city in which such land is located, designating such land and the improvements to be placed thereon as a residential- business planned development, which development is being financed in part by the proceeds of industrial development bonds in the amount of $62,600,000 issued on December 4, 1985.

(I) A 600,000 square foot mixed use building known as Flushing Center with respect to which a letter of intent was executed on March 26, 1986.

In the case of the building described in subparagraph (I), section 203(b)(2)(A) shall be applied by substituting "January 1, 1993" for the applicable date which would otherwise apply.

(28) The amendments made by section 201 shall not apply to an $80 million capital project steel seamless tubular casings minimill and melting facility located in Youngstown, Ohio, which was purchased by the taxpayer in April 1985, and—

(A) the purchase and renovation of which was approved by a committee of the Board of Directors on February 22, 1985, and

(B) as of December 31, 1985, more than $20,000,000 was incurred or committed with respect to the renovation.

(29) The amendments made by section 201 shall not apply to any project for residential rental property if—

(A) an inducement resolution with respect to such project was adopted by the State housing development authority on January 25, 1985, and

(B) such project was the subject of a lawsuit filed on October 25, 1985.

(30) The amendments made by section 201 shall not apply to a 30 megawatt electric generating facility fueled by geothermal and wood waste, the approximate cost of which is $55,000,000, and with respect to which a 30-year power sales contract was executed on March 22, 1985.

(31) The amendments made by section 201 shall not apply to railroad maintenance-of-way equipment, with respect to which a Boston bank entered into a firm binding contract with a major northeastern railroad before March 2, 1986, to finance $10,500,000 of such equipment, if all of the equipment was placed in service before August 1, 1986.

(32) The amendment made by section 201 shall not apply to—

(A) a facility constructed on approximately seven acres of land located on Ogle's Poso Creek Oil field, the primary fuel of which will be bituminous coal from Utah or Wyoming, with respect to which an application for an authority to construct was filed on December 26, 1985, an authority to construct was issued on July 2, 1986, and a prevention of significant deterioration permit application was submitted in May 1985,

(B) a facility constructed on approximately seven acres of land located on Teorco's Jasmin oil field, the primary fuel of which will be bituminous coal from Utah or Wyoming, with respect to which an authority to construct was filed on December 26, 1985, an authority to construct was issued on July 2, 1986, and a prevention of significant deterioration permit application was submitted in July 1985,

(C) the Mountain View Apartments, in Hadley, Massachusetts,

(D) a facility expected to have a capacity of not less than 65 megawatts of electricity, the steam from which is to be sold to a pulp and paper mill, with respect to which application was made to the Federal Regulatory Commission for certification as a qualified facility on November 1, 1985, and received such certification on January 24, 1986,

(E) $5,000,000 of equipment ordered in 1986, in connection with a 60,000 square foot plant in Masontown, Pennsylvania, that was completed in 1983,

(F) a magnetic resonance imaging machine, with respect to which a binding contract to purchase was entered into in April 1986, in connection with the construction of a magnetic resonance imaging clinic with respect to which a Determination of Need certification was obtained from a State Department of Public Health on October 22, 1985, if such property is placed in service before December 31, 1986,

(G) a company, located in Salina, Kansas, which has been engaged in the construction of highways and city streets since 1946, but only to the extent of $1,410,000 of investment in new section 38 property,

(H) a $300,000 project undertaken by a small metal finishing company located in Minneapolis, Minnesota, the first parts of which were received and paid for in January 1986, with respect to which the company received Board approval to purchase the largest piece of machinery it has ever ordered in 1985,

(I) a $1.2 million finishing machine that was purchased on April 2, 1986 and placed into service in September 1986 by a company located in Davenport, Iowa,

(J) a 25 megawatt small power production facility, with respect to which Qualifying Facility status no. QF86-593-000 was granted on March 5, 1986,

(K) a 250 megawatt coal-fired electric plant in northeastern Nevada estimated to cost $600,000,000 and known as the Thousand Springs project, on which the Sierra Pacific Power Company, a subsidiary of Sierra Pacific Resources, began in 1980 work to design, finance, construct, and operate (and section 203(b)(2) shall be applied with respect to such plant by substituting "January 1, 1995" for "January 1, 1991"),

(L) 128 units of rental housing in connection with the Point Gloria Limited Partnership,

(M) property which is part of the Kenosha Downtown Redevelopment Project and which is financed with the proceeds of bonds issued pursuant to section 1317(6)(W),

(N) Lakeland Park Phase II, in Baton Rouge, Louisiana,

(O) the Santa Rosa Hotel, in Pensacola, Florida,

(P) the Sheraton Baton Rouge, in Baton Rouge, Louisiana,

(Q) $300,000 of equipment placed in service in 1986, in connection with the renovation of the Best Western Townhouse Convention Center in Cedar Rapids, Iowa,

(R) the segment of a nationwide fiber optics telecommunications network placed in service by SouthernNet, the total estimated cost of which is $37,000,000,

(S) two cogeneration facilities, to be placed in service by the Reading Anthracite Coal Company (or any subsidiary thereof), costing approximately $110,000,000 each, with respect to which filings were made with the Federal Energy Regulatory Commission by December 31, 1985, and which are located in Pennsylvania,

(T) a portion of a fiber optics network placed in service by LDX NET after December 31, 1988, but only to the extent the cost of such portion does not exceed $25,000,000,

(U) 3 newly constructed fishing vessels, and one vessel that is overhauled, constructed by Mid Coast Marine, but only to the extent of $6,700,000 of investment,

(V) $350,000 of equipment acquired in connection with the reopening of a plant in Bristol, Rhode Island, which plant was purchased by Buttonwoods, Ltd., Associates on February 7, 1986,

(W) $4,046,000 of equipment placed in service by Brendle's Incorporated, acquired in connection with a Distribution Center,

(X) a multi-family mixed-use housing project located in a home rule city, the zoning for which was changed to residential business planned development on November 26, 1985, and with respect to which both the home rule city on December 4, 1985, and the State housing finance agency on December 20, 1985, adopted inducement resolutions,

(Y) the Myrtle Beach Convention Center, in South Carolina, to the extent of $25,000,000 of investment, and

(Z) railroad cars placed in service by the Pullman Leasing Company, pursuant to an April 3, 1986 purchase order, costing approximately $10,000,000.

(33) The amendments made by section 201 shall not apply to—

(A) $400,000 of equipment placed in service by Super Key Market, if such equipment is placed in service before January 1, 1987,

(B) the Trolley Square project, the total project cost of which is $24,500,000, and the amount of depreciable real property of which is $14,700,000.

(C)(i) a waste-to-energy project in Derry, New Hampshire, costing approximately $60,000,000, and

(ii) a waste-to-energy project in Manchester, New Hampshire, costing approximately $60,000,000,

(D) the City of Los Angeles Co-composting project, the estimated cost of which is $62,000,000, with respect to which, on July 17, 1985, the California Pollution Control Financing Authority issued an initial resolution in the maximum amount of $75,000,000 to finance this project,

(E) the St. Charles, Missouri Mixed-Use Center,

(F) Oxford Place in Tulsa, Oklahoma,

(G) an amount of investment generating $20,000,000 of investment tax credits attributable to property used on the Illinois Diversatech Campus,

(H) $25,000,000 of equipment used in the Melrose Park Engine Plant that is sold and leased back by Navistar,

(I) 80,000 vending machines, for a cost approximating $3,400,000 placed into service by Folz Vending Co.,

(J) a 25.85 megawatt alternative energy facility located in Deblois, Maine, with respect to which certification by the Federal Energy Regulatory Commission was made on April 3, 1986,

(K) Burbank Manors, in Illinois, and

(L) a cogeneration facility to be built at a paper company in Turners Falls, Massachusetts, with respect to which a letter of intent was executed on behalf of the paper company on September 26, 1985.

(34) The amendments made by section 201 shall not apply to an approximately 240,000 square foot beverage container manufacturing plant located in Batesville, Mississippi, or plant equipment used exclusively on the plant premises if—

(A) a 2-year supply contract was signed by the taxpayer and a customer on November 1, 1985,

(B) such contract further obligated the customer to purchase beverage containers for an additional 5-year period if physical signs of construction of the plant are present before September 1986,

(C) ground clearing for such plant began before August 1986, and

(D) construction is completed, the equipment is installed, and operations are commenced before July 1, 1987.

(35) The amendments made by section 201 shall not apply to any property which is part of the multifamily housing at the Columbia Point Project in Boston, Massachusetts. A project shall be treated as not described in the preceding sentence and as not described in section 252(f)(1)(D) unless such project includes at substantially all times throughout the compliance period (within the meaning of section 42(i)(1) of the Internal Revenue Code of 1986), a facility which provides health services to the residents of such project for fees commensurate with the ability of such individuals to pay for such services.

(36) The amendments made by section 201 shall not apply to any ethanol facility located in Blair, Nebraska, if—

(A) in July of 1984 an initial binding construction contract was entered into for such facility,

(B) in June of 1986, certain Department of Energy recommended contract changes required a change of contractor, and

(C) in September of 1986, a new contract to construct such facility, consistent with such recommended changes, was entered into.

(37) The amendments made by section 201 shall not apply to any property which is part of a sewage treatment facility if, prior to January 1, 1986, the City of Conyers, Georgia, selected a privatizer to construct such facility, received a guaranteed maximum price bid for the construction of such facility, signed a letter of intent and began substantial negotiations of a service agreement with respect to such facility.

(38) The amendments made by section 201 shall not apply to—

(A) a $28,000,000 wood resource complex for which construction was authorized by the Board of Directors on August 9, 1985,

(B) an electrical cogeneration plant in Bethel, Maine which is to generate 2 megawatts of electricity from the burning of wood residues, with respect to which a contract was entered into on July 10, 1984, and with respect to which $200,000 of the expected $2,000,000 cost had been committed before June 15, 1986,

(C) a mixed income housing project in Portland, Maine which is known as the Back Bay Tower and which is expected to cost $17,300,000,

(D) the Eastman Place project and office building in Rochester, New York, which is projected to cost $20,000,000, with respect to which an inducement resolution was adopted in December 1986, and for which a binding contract of $500,000 was entered into on April 30, 1986,

(E) the Marquis Two project in Atlanta, Georgia which has a total budget of $72,000,000 and the construction phase of which began under a contract entered into on March 26, 1986,

(F) a 166-unit continuing care retirement center in New Orleans, Louisiana, the construction contract for which was signed on February 12, 1986, and is for a maximum amount not to exceed $8,500,000,

(G) the expansion of the capacity of an oil refining facility in Rosemont, Minnesota from 137,000 to 207,000 barrels per day which is expected to be completed by December 31, 1990, and

(H) a project in Ransom, Pennsylvania which will burn coal waste (known as `culm') with an approximate cost of $64,000,000 and for which a certification from the Federal Energy Regulatory Commission was received on March 11, 1986.

(39) The amendments made by section 201 shall not apply to any facility for the manufacture of an improved particle board if a binding contract to purchase such equipment was executed March 3, 1986, such equipment will be placed in service by January 1, 1988, and such facility is located in or near Moncure, North Carolina.

(40) CERTAIN TRUCKS. ETC.—The amendments made by section 201 shall not apply to trucks, tractor units, and trailers which a privately held truck leasing company headquartered in Des Moines, Iowa, contracted to purchase in September 1985 but only to the extent the aggregate reduction in Federal tax liability by reason of the application of this paragraph does not exceed $8,500,000.

(b) SPECIAL RULE FOR CERTAIN PROPERTY.—The provisions of section 168(f)(8) of the Internal Revenue Code of 1954 (as amended by section 209 of the Tax Equity and Fiscal Responsibility Act of 1982) shall continue to apply to any transaction permitted by reason of section 12(c)(2) of the Tax Reform Act of 1984 or section 209(d)(1)(B) of the Tax Equity and Fiscal Responsibility Act of 1982 (as amended by the Tax Reform Act of 1984).

(c) APPLICABLE DATE IN CERTAIN CASES.—

(1) Section 203(b)(2) shall be applied by substituting "January 1, 1992" for "January 1, 1991" in the following cases:

(A) in the case of a 2-unit nuclear powered electric generating plant (and equipment and incidental appurtenances), located in Pennsylvania and constructed pursuant to contracts entered into by the owner operator of the facility before December 31, 1975, including contracts with the engineer/constructor and the nuclear steam system supplier, such contracts shall be treated as contracts described in section (b)(1)(A),

(B) a cogeneration facility with respect to which an application with the Federal Energy Regulatory Commission was filed on August 2, 1985, and approved October 15, 1985, and

(C) in the case of a 1,300 megawatt coal-fired steam powered electric generating plant (and related equipment and incidental appurtenances), which the three owners determined in 1984 to convert from nuclear power to coal power and for which more than $600,000,000 had been incurred or committed for construction before September 25, 1985, except that no investment tax credit will be allowable under section 49(d)(3) added by section 211(a) of this Act for any qualified progress expenditures made after December 31, 1990.

(2) Section 203(b)(2) shall be applied by substituting "April 1, 1992" for the applicable date that would otherwise apply, in the case of the second unit of a twin steam electric generating facility and related equipment which was granted a certificate of public convenience and necessity by a public service commission prior to January 1, 1982, if the first unit of the facility was placed in service prior to January 1, 1985, and before September 26, 1985, more than $100,000,000 had been expended toward the construction of the second unit.

(3) Section 203(b)(2) shall be applied by substituting "January 1, 1990," (or, in the case of a project described in subparagraph (B), by substituting "April 1, 1992") for the applicable date that would otherwise apply in the case of—

(A) new commercial passenger aircraft used by a domestic airline, if a binding contract with respect to such aircraft was entered into on or before April 1, 1986, and such aircraft has a present class life of 12 years,

(B) a pumped storage hydroelectric project with respect to which an application was made to the Federal Energy Regulatory Commission for a license on February 4, 1974, and license was issued August 1, 1977, the project number of which is 2740, and

(C) a newsprint mill in Pend Oreille county, Washington, costing about $290,000,000.

In the case of an aircraft described in subparagraph (A), section 203(b)(1)(A) shall be applied by substituting "April 1, 1986" for "March 1, 1986" and section 49(e)(1)(B) of the Internal Revenue Code of 1986 shall not apply.

(4) The amendments made by section 201 shall not apply to a limited amount of the following property or a limited amount of property set forth in a submission before September 16, 1986, by the following taxpayers:

(A) Arena project, Michigan, but only with respect to $78,000,000 of investments.

(B) Campbell Soup Company, Pennsylvania, California, North Carolina, Ohio, Maryland, Florida, Nebraska, Michigan, South Carolina, Texas, New Jersey, and Delaware, but only with respect to $9,329,000 of regular investment tax credits.

(C) The Southeast Overtown/Park West development, Florida, but only with respect to $200,000,000 of investments.

(D) Equipment placed in service and operated by Leggett and Platt before July 1, 1987, but only with respect to $2,000,000 of regular investment tax credits, and subsections (c) and (d) of section 49 of the Internal Revenue Code of 1986 shall not apply to such equipment.

(E) East Bank Housing Project.

(F) $1,561,215 of investments by Standard Telephone Company.

(G) Five aircraft placed in service before January 1, 1987, by Presidential Air.

(H) A rehabilitation project by Ann Arbor Railroad, but only with respect to $2,900,000 of investments.

(I) Property that is part of a cogeneration project located in Ada, Michigan, but only with respect to $30,000,000 of investments.

(J) Anchor Store Project, Michigan, but only with respect to $21,000,000 of investments.

(K) A waste-fired electrical generating facility of Biogen Power, but only with respect to $34,000,000 of investments.

(L) $14,000,000 of television transmitting towers placed in service by Media General, Inc., which were subject to binding contracts as of January 21, 1986, and will be placed in service before January 1, 1988,

(M) Interests of Samuel A. Hardage (whether owned individually or in partnership form).

(N) Two aircraft of Mesa Airlines with an aggregate cost of $5,723,484.

(O) Yarn-spinning equipment used at Spray Cotton Mills, but only with respect to $3,000,000 of investments.

(P) 328 units of low-income housing at Angelus Plaza, but only with respect to $20,500,000 of investments.

(Q) One aircraft of Continental Aviation Services with a cost of approximately $15,000,000 that was purchased pursuant to a contract entered into during March of 1983 and that is placed in service by December 31, 1988.

(d) RAILROAD GRADING AND TUNNEL BORES.—

(1) IN GENERAL.—In the case of expenditures of railroad grading and tunnel bores which were incurred by a common carrier by railroad to replace property destroyed in a disaster occurring on or about April 17, 1983, near Thistle, Utah, such expenditures, to the extent not in excess of $15,000,000, shall be treated as recovery property which is 5-year property under section 168 of the Internal Revenue Code of 1954 (as in effect before the amendments made by this Act) and which is placed in service at the time such expenditures were incurred.

(2) BUSINESS INTERRUPTION PROCEEDS.—Business interruption proceeds received for loss of use, revenues, or profits in connection with the disaster described in paragraph (1) and devoted by the taxpayer described in paragraph (1) to the construction of replacement track and related grading and tunnel bore expenditures shall be treated as constituting an amount received from the involuntary conversion of property under section 1033(a)(2) of such Code.

(3) EFFECTIVE DATE.—This subsection shall apply to taxable years ending after April 17, 1983.

(e) TREATMENT OF CERTAIN DISASTER LOSSES.—

(1) IN GENERAL.—In a case of a disaster described in paragraph (2), at the election of the taxpayer, the amendments made by section 201 of this Act—

(A) shall not apply to any property placed in service during 1987 and 1988, or

(B) shall not apply to any property placed in service during 1985 and 1986,

which is property to replace property lost, damaged, or destroyed in such disaster.

(2) DISASTER TO WHICH SECTION APPLIES.—This section shall apply to a flood which occurred on November 3 through 7, 1985, and which was declared a natural disaster area by the President of the United States.

SEC. 251. MODIFICATION OF INVESTMENT TAX CREDIT FOR REHABILITATION EXPENDITURES.

* * *

(d) EFFECTIVE DATE.—

* * *

(2) GENERAL TRANSITIONAL RULE.—The amendments made by this section and section 201 shall not apply to any property placed in service before January 1, 1994, if such property is placed in service as part of—

(A) a rehabilitation which was completed pursuant to a written contract which was binding on March 1, 1986, or

(B) a rehabilitation incurred in connection with property (including any leasehold interest) acquired before March 2, 1986, or acquired on or after such date pursuant to a written contract that was binding on March 1, 1986, if—

(i) parts 1 and 2 of the Historic Preservation Certification Application were filed with the department of the Interior (or its designee) before March 2, 1986, or

(ii) the lesser of $1,000,000 or 5 percent of the cost of the rehabilitation is incurred before March 2, 1986, or is required to be incurred pursuant to a written contract which was binding on March 1, 1986.

(3) CERTAIN ADDITIONAL REHABILITATIONS.—The amendments made by this section and section 201 shall not apply to—

(A) the rehabilitation of 8 bathhouses within the Hot Springs National Park or of buildings in the Central Avenue Historic District at such Park,

(B) the rehabilitation of the Upper Pontalba Building in New Orleans, Louisiana,

(C) the rehabilitation of at least 60 buildings listed on the National Register at the Frankford Arsenal,

(D) the rehabilitation of De Baliveriere Arcade, St. Louis Centre, and Drake Apartments in Missouri,

(E) the rehabilitation of The Tides in Bristol, Rhode Island,

(F) the rehabilitation and renovation of the Outlet Company building and garage in Providence, Rhode Island,

(G) the rehabilitation of 10 structures in Harrisburg, Pennsylvania, with respect to which the Harristown Development Corporation was designated redeveloper and received an option to acquire title to the entire project site for $1 on June 27, 1984,

(H) the rehabilitation of a project involving the renovation of 3 historic structures on the Minneapolis riverfront, with respect to which the developer of the project entered into a redevelopment agreement with a municipality dated January 4, 1985, and industrial development bonds were sold in 3 separate issues in May, July, and October 1985,

(I) the rehabilitation of a bank's main office facilities of approximately 120,000 square feet, in connection with which the bank's board of directors authorized a $3,300,000 expenditure for the renovation and retrofit on March 20, 1984,

(J) the rehabilitation of 10 warehouse buildings built between 1906 and 1910 and purchased under a contract dated February 17, 1986,

(K) the rehabilitation of a facility which is customarily used for conventions and sporting events if an analysis of operations and recommendations of utilization of such facility was prepared by a certified public accounting firm pursuant to an engagement authorized on March 6, 1984, and presented on June 11, 1984, to officials of the city in which such facility is located,

(L) Mount Vernon Mills in Columbia, South Carolina,

(M) the Barbara Jordan II Apartments,

(N) the rehabilitation of the Federal Building and Post Office, 120 Hanover Street, Manchester, New Hampshire,

(O) the rehabilitation of the Charleston Waterfront project in South Carolina,

(P) the Hayes Mansion in San Jose, California,

(Q) the renovation of a facility owned by the National Railroad Passenger Corporation ("Amtrak") for which project Amtrak engaged a development team by letter agreement dated August 23, 1985, as modified by letter agreement dated September 9, 1985,

(R) the rehabilitation of a structure or its components which is listed in the National Register of Historic Places, is located in Allegheny County, Pennsylvania, will be substantially rehabilitated (as defined in section 48(g)(1)(C) prior to amendment by this Act), prior to December 31, 1989; and was previously utilized as a market and an auto dealership,

(S) The Bellevue Stratford Hotel in Philadelphia, Pennsylvania,

(T) the Dixon Mill Housing project in Jersey City, New Jersey,

(U) Motor Square Garden,

(V) the Blackstone Apartments, and the Shriver-Johnson building, in Sioux Falls, South Dakota,

(W) the Holy Name Academy in Spokane, Washington,

(X) the Nike/Clemson Mill in Exeter, New Hampshire,

(Y) the Central Bank Building in Grand Rapids, Michigan, and

(Z) the Heritage Hotel, in the City of Marquette, Michigan.

(4) ADDITIONAL REHABILITATIONS.—The amendments made by this section and section 201 shall not apply to—

(A) the Fort Worth Town Square Project in Texas,

(B) the American Youth Hostel in New York, New York,

(C) The Riverwest Loft Development (including all three phases, two of which do not involve rehabilitations),

(D) the Gaslamp Quarter Historic District in California,

(E) the Eberhardt & Ober Brewery, in Pennsylvania,

(F) the Captain's Walk Limited Partnership-Harris Place Development, in Connecticut,

(G) the Velvet Mills in Connecticut,

(H) the Roycroft Inn, in New York,

(I) Old Main Village, in Mankato, Minnesota,

(J) the Washburn-Crosby A Mill, in Minneapolis, Minnesota,

(K) the Marble Arcade office building in Lakeland, Florida,

(L) the Willard Hotel, in Washington, D.C.,

(M) the H.P. Lau Building in Lincoln, Nebraska,

(N) the Starks Building, in Louisville, Kentucky,

(O) the Bellevue High School, in Bellevue, Kentucky,

(P) the Major Hampden Smith House, in Owensboro, Kentucky,

(Q) the Doe Run Inn, in Brandenburg, Kentucky,

(R) the State National Bank, in Frankfort, Kentucky,

(S) the Captain Jack House, in Fleming, Kentucky,

(T) the Elizabeth Arlinghaus House, in Covington, Kentucky,

(U) Limerick Shamrock, in Louisville, Kentucky,

(V) the Robert Mills Project, in South Carolina,

(W) the 620 Project, consisting of 3 buildings, in Kentucky,

(X) the Warrior Hotel, Ltd., the first two floors of the Martin Hotel, and the 105,000 square foot warehouse constructed in 1910, all in Sioux City, Iowa,

(Y) the waterpark condominium residential project, to the extent of $2 million of expenditures,

(Z) the Bigelow-Hartford Carpet Mill in Enfield, Connecticut,

(AA) properties abutting 125th Street in New York County from 7th Avenue west to Morningside and the pier area on the Hudson River at the end of such 125th Street,

(BB) the City of Los Angeles Central Library project pursuant to an agreement dated December 28, 1983,

(CC) the Warehouse Row project in Chattanooga, Tennessee,

(DD) any project described in section 204(a)(1)(F) of this Act,

(EE) the Wood Street Commons project in Pittsburgh, Pennsylvania,

(FF) any project described in section 803(d)(6) of this Act,

(GG) Union Station, Indianapolis, Indiana,

(HH) the Mattress Factory project in Pittsburgh, Pennsylvania,

(II) Union Station in Providence, Rhode Island,

(JJ) South Pack Plaza, Asheville, North Carolina,

(KK) Old Louisville Trust Project, Louisville, Kentucky,

(LL) Stewarts Rehabilitation Project, Louisville, Kentucky,

(MM) Bernheim Officenter, Louisville, Kentucky,

(NN) Springville Mill Project, Rockville, Connecticut, and

(OO) the D.J. Stewart Company Building, State and Main Streets, Rockford, Illinois.

(5) REDUCTION IN CREDIT FOR PROPERTY UNDER TRANSITIONAL RULES.—In the case of property placed in service after December 31, 1986, and to which the amendments made by this section do not apply, subparagraph (A) of section 46(b)(4) of the Internal Revenue Code of 1954 (as in effect before the enactment of this Act) shall be applied—

(A) by substituting "10 percent" for "15 percent", and

(B) by substituting "13 percent" for "20 percent".

(6) EXPENSING OF REHABILITATION EXPENSES FOR THE FRANKFORD ARSENAL.—In the case of any expenditures paid or incurred in connection with improvements (including repairs and maintenance) of the Frankford Arsenal pursuant to a contract and partnership agreement during the 8-year period specified in the contract or agreement, all such expenditures to be made during the period 1986 through and including 1993 shall—

(A) be treated as made (and allowable as a deduction) during 1986,

(B) be treated as qualified rehabilitation expenditures made during 1986, and

(C) be allocated in accordance with the partnership agreement regardless of when the interest in the partnership was acquired, except that—

(i) if the taxpayer is not the original holder of such interest, no person (other than the taxpayer) had claimed any benefits by reason of this paragraph,

(ii) no interest under section 6611 of the 1986 Code on any refund of income taxes which is solely attributable to this paragraph shall be paid for the period—

(I) beginning on the date which is 45 days after the later of April 15, 1987, or the date on which the return for such taxes was filed, and

(II) ending on the date the taxpayer acquired the interest in the partnership, and

(iii) if the expenditures to be made under this provision are not paid or incurred before January 1, 1994, then the tax imposed by chapter 1 of such Code for the taxpayer's last taxable year beginning in 1993 shall be increased by the amount of the tax benefits by reason of this paragraph which are attributable to the expenditures not so paid or incurred.

(7) SPECIAL RULE.—In the case of the rehabilitation of the Willard Hotel in Washington, D.C., section 205(c)(1)(B)(ii) of the Tax Equity and Fiscal Responsibility Act of 1982 shall be applied by substituting "1987" for "1986".

P.L. 99-514, §1801(a)(2), as amended by P.L. 100-647 §1018(c)(1), provides:

(2) TREATMENT OF CERTAIN FARM FINANCE LEASES.—

(A) IN GENERAL.—If—

(i) any partnership or grantor trust is the lessor under a specified agreement,

(ii) such partnership or grantor trust met the requirements of section 168(f)(8)(C)(i) of the Internal Revenue Code of 1954 (relating to special rules for finance leases) when the agreement was entered into, and

(iii) a person became a partner in such partnership (or a beneficiary in such trust) after its formation but before September 26, 1985,

then, for purposes of applying the revenue laws of the United States in respect to such agreement, the portion of the property allocable to partners (or beneficiaries) not described in clause (iii) shall be treated as if it were subject to a separate agreement and the portion of such property allocable to the partner or beneficiary described in clause (iii) shall be treated as if it were subject to a separate agreement.

(B) SPECIFIED AGREEMENT.—For purposes of subparagraph (A), the term "specified agreement" means an agreement to which subparagraph (B) of section 209(d) of the Tax Equity and Fiscal Responsibility Act of 1982 applies which is—

(i) an agreement dated as of December 20, 1982, as amended and restated as of February 1, 1983, involving approximately $8,734,000 of property at December 31, 1983,

(ii) an agreement dated as of December 15, 1983, as amended and restated as of January 3, 1984, involving approximately $13,199,000 of property at December 31, 1984, or

(iii) an agreement dated as of October 25, 1984, as amended and restated as of December 1, 1984, involving approximately $966,000 of property at December 31, 1984.

P.L. 99-514, §1802(a)(1):

Amended Code Sec. 168(j)(3)(D) by adding at the end thereof a new sentence. **Effective** as if included in the provision of P.L. 98-369 to which it relates.

P.L. 99-514, §1802(a)(2)(A)(i) and (ii):

Amended Code Sec. 168(j)(4)(E)(i) by striking out "any property of which such organization is the lessee" and inserting in lieu thereof "any property (other than property held by such organization)", and by striking out "first leased to" and inserting in lieu thereof "first used by". **Effective** as if included in the provision of P.L. 98-369 to which it relates.

P.L. 99-514, §1802(a)(2)(B):

Amended Code Sec. 168(j)(4)(E)(ii)(I) by striking out "of which such organization is the lessee". **Effective** as if included in the provision of P.L. 98-369 to which it relates. Prior to amendment, Code Sec. 168(j)(4)(E)(ii)(I) read as follows:

(I) IN GENERAL.—In the case of an organization formerly exempt from tax under section 501(a) as an organization described in section 501(c)(12), clause (i) shall not apply to such organization with respect to any property of which such organization is the lessee if such organization elects not to be exempt from tax under section 501(a) during the tax-exempt use period with respect to such property.

P.L. 99-514, §1802(a)(2)(C):

Amended Code Sec. 168(j)(4)(E)(ii)(II) by striking out "is placed in service under the lease" and inserting in lieu thereof "is first used by the organization". **Effective** as if included in the provision of P.L. 98-369 to which it relates.

P.L. 99-514, §1802(a)(2)(D):

Amended Code Sec. 168(j)(4)(E) by adding at the end thereof new clause (iv). **Effective** as if included in the provision of P.L. 98-369 to which it relates.

P.L. 99-514, §1802(a)(2)(E)(i):

Amended Code Sec. 168(j)(9) by redesignating subparagraph (E) as subparagraph (F) and by inserting after subparagraph (D) new subparagraph (E). For the **effective** date, see Act Sec. 1802(a)(E)(ii), below.

P.L. 99-514, §1802(a)(2)(E)(ii), provides:

(ii)(I) Except as otherwise provided in this clause, the amendment made by clause (i) shall apply to property placed in service after September 27, 1985; except that such amendment shall not apply to any property acquired pursuant to a binding written contract in effect on such date (and at all times thereafter).

(II) If an election under this subclause is made with respect to any property, the amendment made by clause (i) shall apply to such property whether or not placed in service on or before September 27, 1985.

P.L. 99-514, §1802(a)(2)(G):

Amended Code Sec. 168(j)(4)(E)(i) by striking out "preceding sentence" and inserting in lieu therof "preceding sentence and subparagraph (d)(ii)". **Effective** as if included in the provision of P.L. 98-369 to which it relates.

P.L. 99-514, §1802(a)(3):

Repealed Code Sec. 168(j)(5)(C)(iv). **Effective** as if included in the provision of P.L. 98-369 to which it relates. Prior to repeal, Code Sec. 168(j)(5)(C)(iv) read as follows:

(iv) PROPERTY NOT SUBJECT TO RAPID OBSOLESCENCE MAY BE EXCLUDED.—The term "qualified technological equipment" shall not include any equipment described in subclause (II) or (III) or clause (i)—

(I) which the Secretary determines by regulations is not subject to rapid obsolescence, and

(II) which is placed in service after the date on which final regulations implementing such determination are published in the Federal Register.

P.L. 99-514, §1802(a)(4)(A):

Amended Code Sec. 168(j)(8) by striking out "and paragraphs (4) and (5) of section 48(a)" in the matter preceding subparagraph (A). **Effective** as if included in the provision of P.L. 98-369 to which it relates. Prior to amendment, the matter preceding subparagraph (A) read as follows:

(8) TAX-EXEMPT USE OF PROPERTY LEASED TO PARTNERSHIPS, ETC., DETERMINED AT PARTNER LEVEL.—For purposes of this subsection and paragraphs (4) and (5) of section 48(a)—

P.L. 99-514, §1802(a)(4)(B)(i) and (ii):

Amended Code Sec. 168(j)(9) by striking out "and paragraphs (4) and (5) of section 48(a)" in subparagraph (A), and by striking out "loss deduction" in subparagraph (B)(i) and inserting in lieu thereof "loss, deduction". **Effective** as if included in the provision of P.L. 98-369 to which it relates. Prior to amendment, Code Sec. 168(j)(9)(A) read as follows:

(A) IN GENERAL.—For purposes of this subsection and paragraphs (4) and (5) of section 48(a), if—

(i) any property which (but for this subparagraph) is not tax-exempt use property is owned by a partnership which has both tax-exempt entity and a person who is not a tax-exempt entity as partners and

(ii) any allocation to the tax-exempt entity of partnership items is not a qualified allocation,

an amount equal to such tax-exempt entity's proportionate share of such property shall (except as provided in paragraph (3)(D)) be treated as tax-exempt use property.

P.L. 99-514, §1802(a)(7)(A):

Amended Code Sec. 168(j)(9) by redesignating subparagraphs (D), (E), and (F) as subparagraphs (E), (F), and (G), respectively, and by inserting after subparagraph (C) new subparagraph (D). **Effective** as if included in the provision of P.L. 98-369 to which it relates.

P.L. 99-514, §1802(a)(7)(B):

Amended Code Sec. 168(j)(9)(E) (as redesignated by Act Sec. 1802(a)(7)(A)) by striking out "and (C)" and inserting in lieu thereof "(C), and (D)". **Effective** as if included in the provision of P.L. 98-369 to which it relates.

P.L. 99-514, §1802(b)(1)(A) and (B):

Amended Code Sec. 168(f) by redesignating paragraph (13) as paragraph (14), and by redesignating paragraph (14) as paragraph (15). **Effective** as if included in the provision of P.L. 98-369 to which it relates.

P.L. 99-514, §1809(a)(1)(A) and (B):

Amended Code Sec. 168(b)(3)(A) by striking out "and low-income housing" in the last item, and by adding at the end thereof a new item. **Effective** as if included in the provision of P.L. 98-369 to which it relates. Prior to amendment, Code Sec. 168(b)(3)(A) read as follows:

(A) IN GENERAL.—Except as provided in subsection (f)(2), in lieu of any applicable percentage under paragraph (1), (2), or (4), the taxpayer may elect, with respect to one or more classes of recovery property placed in service during the taxable year, the applicable percentage determined by use of the straight line method over the recovery period elected by the taxpayer in accordance with the following table:

In the case of:	*The taxpayer may elect a recovery period of:*
3-year property	3, 5, or 12 years.
5-year property	5, 12, or 25 years.
10-year property	10, 25, or 35 years.
15-year property	15, 35, or 45 years.
19-year property	19, 35, or 45 years.

P.L. 99-514, §1809(a)(2)(A)(i)(I) and (II):

Amended Code Sec. 168(b)(2) by striking out the last sentence of subparagraph (A), and by amending subparagraph (B). **Effective** as if included in the provision of P.L. 98-369 to which it relates. Prior to amendment, the last sentence of subparagraph (A) and subparagraph (B) read as follows:

In the case of 19-year real property, the applicable percentage in the taxable year in which the property is placed in service shall be determined on the basis of the number of months (using a mid-month convention) in such year during which the property was in service.

(B) SPECIAL RULE FOR YEAR OF DISPOSITION.—In the case of a disposition of 19-year real property, the deduction allowable under subsection (a) for the taxable year in which the disposition occurs shall reflect only the months (using a mid-month convention) during such year the property was in service.

P.L. 99-514, §1809(a)(2)(A)(ii):

Amended Code Sec. 168(f)(2)(B). **Effective** as if included in the provision of P.L. 98-369 to which it relates. Prior to amendment, Code Sec. 168(f)(2)(B) read as follows:

(B) REAL PROPERTY.—

(i) IN GENERAL.—Except as provided in subparagraph (C), in the case of 19-year real property or low-income housing which, during the taxable year, is predominantly used outside the United States, the recovery deduction for the taxable year shall be, in lieu of the amount determined under subsection (b), the amount determined by applying to the unadjusted basis of such property the applicable percentage determined under tables prescribed by the Secretary. For purposes of the preceding sentence in prescribing such tables, the Secretary shall—

(I) assign to the property described in this subparagraph a 35-year recovery period, and

(II) assign percentages (taking into account the next to the last sentence of subsection (b)(2)(A)) determined in accordance with use of the method of depreciation described in section 167(j)(1)(B), switching to the method described in section 167(b)(1) at a time to maximize the deduction allowable under subsection (a).

(ii) SPECIAL RULE FOR DISPOSITION.—In the case of a disposition of 19-year real property or low-income housing described in clause (i), subsection (b)(2)(B) shall apply.

P.L. 99-514, §1809(a)(2)(B):

Amended Code Sec. 168(b)(4)(B). **Effective** as if included in the provision of P.L. 98-369 to which it relates. Prior to amendment, Code Sec. 168(b)(4)(B) read as follows:

(B) SPECIAL RULE FOR YEAR OF DISPOSITION.—In the case of a disposition of low-income housing, the deduction allowable under subsection (a) for the taxable year in which the disposition occurs shall reflect only the months during such year the property was placed in service.

P.L. 99-514, §1809(a)(2)(C)(i):

Amended Code Sec. 168(j)(2)(B)(ii). **Effective** on and after 10-22-86. Prior to amendment, Code Sec. 168(j)(2)(B)(ii) read as follows:

(ii) 19-YEAR REAL PROPERTY.—In the case of 19-year real property, the amount determined under paragraph (1) shall be determined on the basis of the number of months (using a mid-month convention) in the year in which the property is in service.

P.L. 99-514, §1809(a)(4)(A):

Amended Code Sec. 168(f)(12)(B)(ii). **Effective** as if included in the provision of P.L. 98-369 to which it relates. Prior to amendment, Code Sec. 168(f)(12)(B)(ii) read as follows:

(ii) 19-YEAR REAL PROPERTY.—In the case of 19-year real property, the amount of the deduction allowed shall be determined by using the straight-line method (determined on the basis of the number of months in the year in which such property was in service and without regard to salvage value) and a recovery period of 19 years.

P.L. 99-514, §1809(a)(4)(B):

Amended Code Sec. 168(f)(12)(C). **Effective** as if included in the provision of P.L. 98-369 to which it relates. Prior to amendment, Code Sec. 168(f)(12)(C) read as follows:

(C) EXCEPTION FOR PROJECTS FOR RESIDENTIAL RENTAL PROPERTY.—Subparagraph (A) shall not apply to any recovery property which is placed in service in connection with projects for residential rental property financed by the proceeds of obligations described in section 103(b)(4)(A).

P.L. 99-514, §1809(a)(4)(C), provides:

(C) Any property described in paragraph (3) of section 631(d) of the Tax Reform Act of 1984 shall be treated as property described in clause (ii) of section 168(f)(12)(C) of the Internal Revenue Code of 1954 as amended by subparagraph (B).

P.L. 99-514, §1809(a)(5), provides:

(5) COORDINATION WITH IMPUTED INTEREST CHANGES.—In the case of any property placed in service before May 9, 1985 (or treated as placed in service before such date by section 105(b)(3) of Public Law 99-121)—

(A) any reference in any amendment made by this subsection to 19-year real property shall be treated as a reference to 18-year real property, and

(B) section 168(f)(12)(B)(ii) of the Internal Revenue Code of 1954 (as amended by paragraph (4)(A)) shall be applied by substituting "18 years" for "19 years".

P.L. 99-514, §1809(b)(1):

Amended Code Sec. 168(f)(10)(A). **Effective** for property placed in service by the transferee after 12-31-85, in tax years ending after such date. Prior to amendment, Code Sec. 168(f)(10)(A) read as follows:

(A) IN GENERAL.—In the case of recovery property transferred in a transaction described in subparagraph (B), the transferee shall be treated as the transferor for purposes of computing the deduction allowable under subsection (a) with respect to so much of the basis in the hands of the transferee as does not exceed the adjusted basis in the hands of the transferor.

P.L. 99-514, §1809(b)(2):

Amended Code Sec. 168(f)(10)(B) by adding at the end thereof a new sentence. **Effective** for property placed in service by the transferee after 12-31-85, in tax years ending after such date.

[Sec. 168(j)]

(j) PROPERTY ON INDIAN RESERVATIONS.—

(1) IN GENERAL.—For purposes of subsection (a), the applicable recovery period for qualified Indian reservation property shall be determined in accordance with the table contained in paragraph (2) in lieu of the table contained in subsection (c).

(2) APPLICABLE RECOVERY PERIOD FOR INDIAN RESERVATION PROPERTY.—For purposes of paragraph (1)—

In the case of:	*The applicable recovery period is:*
3-year property	2 years
5-year property	3 years
7-year property	4 years
10-year property	6 years
15-year property	9 years
20-year property	12 years
Nonresidential real property	22 years

(3) DEDUCTION ALLOWED IN COMPUTING MINIMUM TAX.—For purposes of determining alternative minimum taxable income under section 55, the deduction under subsection (a) for property to which paragraph (1) applies shall be determined under this section without regard to any adjustment under section 56.

(4) QUALIFIED INDIAN RESERVATION PROPERTY DEFINED.—For purposes of this subsection—

(A) IN GENERAL.—The term "qualified Indian reservation property" means property which is property described in the table in paragraph (2) and which is—

(i) used by the taxpayer predominantly in the active conduct of a trade or business within an Indian reservation,

(ii) not used or located outside the Indian reservation on a regular basis,

(iii) not acquired (directly or indirectly) by the taxpayer from a person who is related to the taxpayer (within the meaning of section 465(b)(3)(C)), and

(iv) not property (or any portion thereof) placed in service for purposes of conducting or housing class I, II, or III gaming (as defined in section 4 of the Indian Regulatory Act (25 U.S.C. 2703)).

(B) EXCEPTION FOR ALTERNATIVE DEPRECIATION PROPERTY.—The term "qualified Indian reservation property" does not include any property to which the alternative depreciation system under subsection (g) applies, determined—

(i) without regard to subsection (g)(7) (relating to election to use alternative depreciation system), and

(ii) after the application of section 280F(b) (relating to listed property with limited business use).

(C) SPECIAL RULE FOR RESERVATION INFRASTRUCTURE INVESTMENT.—

(i) IN GENERAL.—Subparagraph (A)(ii) shall not apply to qualified infrastructure property located outside of the Indian reservation if the purpose of such property is to connect with qualified infrastructure property located within the Indian reservation.

(ii) QUALIFIED INFRASTRUCTURE PROPERTY.—For purposes of this subparagraph, the term "qualified infrastructure property" means qualified Indian reservation property (determined without regard to subparagraph (A)(ii)) which—

(I) benefits the tribal infrastructure,

(II) is available to the general public, and

(III) is placed in service in connection with the taxpayer's active conduct of a trade or business within an Indian reservation.

Such term includes, but is not limited to, roads, power lines, water systems, railroad spurs, and communications facilities.

(5) REAL ESTATE RENTALS.—For purposes of this subsection, the rental to others of real property located within an Indian reservation shall be treated as the active conduct of a trade or business within an Indian reservation.

(6) INDIAN RESERVATION DEFINED.—For purposes of this subsection, the term "Indian reservation" means a reservation, as defined in—

(A) section 3(d) of the Indian Financing Act of 1974 (25 U.S.C. 1452(d)), or

(B) section 4(10) of the Indian Child Welfare Act of 1978 (25 U.S.C. 1903(10)).

For purposes of the preceding sentence, such section 3(d) shall be applied by treating the term "former Indian reservations in Oklahoma" as including only lands which are within the jurisdictional area of an Oklahoma Indian tribe (as determined by the Secretary of the Interior) and are recognized by such Secretary as eligible for trust land status under 25 CFR Part 151 (as in effect on the date of the enactment of this sentence).

(7) COORDINATION WITH NONREVENUE LAWS.—Any reference in this subsection to a provision not contained in this title shall be treated for purposes of this subsection as a reference to such provision as in effect on the date of the enactment of this paragraph.

(8) TERMINATION.—This subsection shall not apply to property placed in service after December 31, 2009.

Amendments

• 2008, Tax Extenders and Alternative Minimum Tax Relief Act of 2008 (P.L. 110-343)

P.L. 110-343, Division C, §315(a):

Amended Code Sec. 168(j)(8) by striking "December 31, 2007" and inserting "December 31, 2009". **Effective** for property placed in service after 12-31-2007.

• 2006, Tax Relief and Health Care Act of 2006 (P.L. 109-432)

P.L. 109-432, Division A, §112(a):

Amended Code Sec. 168(j)(8) by striking "2005" and inserting "2007". **Effective** for property placed in service after 12-31-2005.

• 2004, Working Families Tax Relief Act of 2004 (P.L. 108-311)

P.L. 108-311, §316:

Amended Code Sec. 168(j)(8) by striking "December 31, 2004" and inserting "December 31, 2005". **Effective** 10-4-2004.

• 2002, Job Creation and Worker Assistance Act of 2002 (P.L. 107-147)

P.L. 107-147, §613(b):

Amended Code Sec. 168(j)(8) by striking "December 31, 2003" and inserting "December 31, 2004". **Effective** on 3-9-2002.

• 1997, Taxpayer Relief Act of 1997 (P.L. 105-34)

P.L. 105-34, §1604(c)(1):

Amended Code Sec. 168(j)(6) by adding at the end a new flush sentence. For the **effective** date, see Act Sec. 1604(c)(2)(A)-(B), below.

P.L. 105-34, §1604(c)(2)(A)-(B), provides:

(2) The amendment made by paragraph (1) shall apply as if included in the amendments made by section 13321 of the Omnibus Budget Reconciliation Act of 1993, except that such amendment shall not apply—

(A) with respect to property (with an applicable recovery period under section 168(j) of the Internal Revenue Code of 1986 of 6 years or less) held by the taxpayer if the taxpayer claimed the benefits of section 168(j) of such Code with respect to such property on a return filed before March 18, 1997, but only if such return is the first return of tax filed for the taxable year in which such property was placed in service, or

(B) with respect to wages for which the taxpayer claimed the benefits of section 45A of such Code for a taxable year on a return filed before March 18, 1997, but only if such return was the first return of tax filed for such taxable year.

• 1993, Omnibus Budget Reconciliation Act of 1993 (P.L. 103-66)

P.L. 103-66, §13321(a):

Amended Code Sec. 168 by adding at the end a new subsection (j). **Effective** for property placed in service after 12-31-93.

[Sec. 168(k)]

(k) SPECIAL ALLOWANCE FOR CERTAIN PROPERTY ACQUIRED AFTER DECEMBER 31, 2007, AND BEFORE JANUARY 1, 2011.—

(1) ADDITIONAL ALLOWANCE.—In the case of any qualified property—

(A) the depreciation deduction provided by section 167(a) for the taxable year in which such property is placed in service shall include an allowance equal to 50 percent of the adjusted basis of the qualified property, and

(B) the adjusted basis of the qualified property shall be reduced by the amount of such deduction before computing the amount otherwise allowable as a depreciation deduction under this chapter for such taxable year and any subsequent taxable year.

(2) QUALIFIED PROPERTY.—For purposes of this subsection—

(A) IN GENERAL.—The term "qualified property" means property—

(i)(I) to which this section applies which has a recovery period of 20 years or less,

(II) which is computer software (as defined in section 167(f)(1)(B)) for which a deduction is allowable under section 167(a) without regard to this subsection,

(III) which is water utility property, or

(IV) which is qualified leasehold improvement property,

(ii) the original use of which commences with the taxpayer after December 31, 2007,

(iii) which is—

(I) acquired by the taxpayer after December 31, 2007, and before January 1, 2011, but only if no written binding contract for the acquisition was in effect before January 1, 2008, or

(II) acquired by the taxpayer pursuant to a written binding contract which was entered into after December 31, 2007, and before January 1, 2011, and

(iv) which is placed in service by the taxpayer before January 1, 2011, or, in the case of property described in subparagraph (B) or (C), before January 1, 2012.

(B) CERTAIN PROPERTY HAVING LONGER PRODUCTION PERIODS TREATED AS QUALIFIED PROPERTY.—

(i) IN GENERAL.—The term "qualified property" includes any property if such property—

(I) meets the requirements of clauses (i), (ii), (iii), and (iv) of subparagraph (A),

(II) has a recovery period of at least 10 years or is transportation property,

(III) is subject to section 263A, and

(IV) meets the requirements of clause (iii) of section 263A(f)(1)(B) (determined as if such clauses also apply to property which has a long useful life (within the meaning of section 263A(f))).

(ii) ONLY PRE-JANUARY 1, 2011, BASIS ELIGIBLE FOR ADDITIONAL ALLOWANCE.—In the case of property which is qualified property solely by reason of clause (i), paragraph (1) shall apply only to the extent of the adjusted basis thereof attributable to manufacture, construction, or production before January 1, 2011.

(iii) TRANSPORTATION PROPERTY.—For purposes of this subparagraph, the term "transportation property" means tangible personal property used in the trade or business of transporting persons or property.

(iv) APPLICATION OF SUBPARAGRAPH.—This subparagraph shall not apply to any property which is described in subparagraph (C).

(C) CERTAIN AIRCRAFT.—The term "qualified property" includes property—

(i) which meets the requirements of clauses (ii), (iii), and (iv) of subparagraph (A),

(ii) which is an aircraft which is not a transportation property (as defined in subparagraph (B)(iii)) other than for agricultural or firefighting purposes,

(iii) which is purchased and on which such purchaser, at the time of the contract for purchase, has made a nonrefundable deposit of the lesser of—

(I) 10 percent of the cost, or

(II) $100,000, and

(iv) which has—

(I) an estimated production period exceeding 4 months, and

(II) a cost exceeding $200,000.

(D) EXCEPTIONS.—

(i) ALTERNATIVE DEPRECIATION PROPERTY.—The term "qualified property" shall not include any property to which the alternative depreciation system under subsection (g) applies, determined—

(I) without regard to paragraph (7) of subsection (g) (relating to election to have system apply), and

(II) after application of section 280F(b) (relating to listed property with limited business use).

(ii) QUALIFIED NEW YORK LIBERTY ZONE LEASEHOLD IMPROVEMENT PROPERTY.—The term "qualified property" shall not include any qualified New York Liberty Zone leasehold improvement property (as defined in section 1400L(c)(2)).

(iii) ELECTION OUT.—If a taxpayer makes an election under this clause with respect to any class of property for any taxable year, this subsection shall not apply to all property in such class placed in service during such taxable year.

(E) SPECIAL RULES.—

(i) SELF-CONSTRUCTED PROPERTY.—In the case of a taxpayer manufacturing, constructing, or producing property for the taxpayer's own use, the requirements of clause (iii) of subparagraph (A) shall be treated as met if the taxpayer begins manufacturing, constructing, or producing the property after December 31, 2007, and before January 1, 2011.

(ii) SALE-LEASEBACKS.—For purposes of clause (iii) and subparagraph (A)(ii), if property is—

(I) originally placed in service after December 31, 2007, by a person, and

(II) sold and leased back by such person within 3 months after the date such property was originally placed in service,

such property shall be treated as originally placed in service not earlier than the date on which such property is used under the leaseback referred to in subclause (II).

(iii) SYNDICATION.—For purposes of subparagraph (A)(ii), if—

(I) property is originally placed in service after December 31, 2007, by the lessor of such property,

(II) such property is sold by such lessor or any subsequent purchaser within 3 months after the date such property was originally placed in service (or, in the case of multiple units of property subject to the same lease, within 3 months after the date the final unit is placed in service, so long as the period between the time the first unit is placed in service and the time the last unit is placed in service does not exceed 12 months), and

(III) the user of such property after the last sale during such 3-month period remains the same as when such property was originally placed in service,

such property shall be treated as originally placed in service not earlier than the date of such last sale.

(iv) LIMITATIONS RELATED TO USERS AND RELATED PARTIES.—The term "qualified property" shall not include any property if—

(I) the user of such property (as of the date on which such property is originally placed in service) or a person which is related (within the meaning of section 267(b) or 707(b)) to such user or to the taxpayer had a written binding contract in effect for the acquisition of such property at any time on or before December 31, 2007, or

(II) in the case of property manufactured, constructed, or produced for such user's or person's own use, the manufacture, construction, or production of such property began at any time on or before December 31, 2007.

(F) COORDINATION WITH SECTION 280F.—For purposes of section 280F—

(i) AUTOMOBILES.—In the case of a passenger automobile (as defined in section 280F(d)(5)) which is qualified property, the Secretary shall increase the limitation under section 280F(a)(1)(A)(i) by $8,000.

(ii) LISTED PROPERTY.—The deduction allowable under paragraph (1) shall be taken into account in computing any recapture amount under section 280F(b)(2).

(G) DEDUCTION ALLOWED IN COMPUTING MINIMUM TAX.—For purposes of determining alternative minimum taxable income under section 55, the deduction under subsection (a) for qualified property shall be determined under this section without regard to any adjustment under section 56.

(3) QUALIFIED LEASEHOLD IMPROVEMENT PROPERTY.—For purposes of this subsection—

(A) IN GENERAL.—The term "qualified leasehold improvement property" means any improvement to an interior portion of a building which is nonresidential real property if—

(i) such improvement is made under or pursuant to a lease (as defined in subsection (h)(7))—

(I) by the lessee (or any sublessee) of such portion, or

(II) by the lessor of such portion,

(ii) such portion is to be occupied exclusively by the lessee (or any sublessee) of such portion, and

(iii) such improvement is placed in service more than 3 years after the date the building was first placed in service.

(B) CERTAIN IMPROVEMENTS NOT INCLUDED.—Such term shall not include any improvement for which the expenditure is attributable to—

(i) the enlargement of the building,

(ii) any elevator or escalator,

(iii) any structural component benefiting a common area, and

(iv) the internal structural framework of the building.

(C) DEFINITIONS AND SPECIAL RULES.—For purposes of this paragraph—

(i) COMMITMENT TO LEASE TREATED AS LEASE.—A commitment to enter into a lease shall be treated as a lease, and the parties to such commitment shall be treated as lessor and lessee, respectively.

(ii) RELATED PERSONS.—A lease between related persons shall not be considered a lease. For purposes of the preceding sentence, the term "related persons" means—

(I) members of an affiliated group (as defined in section 1504), and

(II) persons having a relationship described in subsection (b) of section 267; except that, for purposes of this clause, the phrase "80 percent or more" shall be substituted for the phrase "more than 50 percent" each place it appears in such subsection.

(4) ELECTION TO ACCELERATE THE AMT AND RESEARCH CREDITS IN LIEU OF BONUS DEPRECIATION.—

(A) IN GENERAL.—If a corporation elects to have this paragraph apply for the first taxable year of the taxpayer ending after March 31, 2008, in the case of such taxable year and each subsequent taxable year—

(i) paragraph (1) shall not apply to any eligible qualified property placed in service by the taxpayer,

(ii) the applicable depreciation method used under this section with respect to such property shall be the straight line method, and

(iii) each of the limitations described in subparagraph (B) for any such taxable year shall be increased by the bonus depreciation amount which is—

(I) determined for such taxable year under subparagraph (C), and

(II) allocated to such limitation under subparagraph (E).

(B) LIMITATIONS TO BE INCREASED.—The limitations described in this subparagraph are—

(i) the limitation imposed by section 38(c), and

(ii) the limitation imposed by section 53(c).

(C) BONUS DEPRECIATION AMOUNT.—For purposes of this paragraph—

(i) IN GENERAL.—The bonus depreciation amount for any taxable year is an amount equal to 20 percent of the excess (if any) of—

(I) the aggregate amount of depreciation which would be allowed under this section for eligible qualified property placed in service by the taxpayer during such taxable year if paragraph (1) applied to all such property, over

(II) the aggregate amount of depreciation which would be allowed under this section for eligible qualified property placed in service by the taxpayer during such taxable year if paragraph (1) did not apply to any such property.

The aggregate amounts determined under subclauses (I) and (II) shall be determined without regard to any election made under subsection (b)(2)(C), (b)(3)(D), or (g)(7) and without regard to subparagraph (A)(ii).

(ii) MAXIMUM AMOUNT.—The bonus depreciation amount for any taxable year shall not exceed the maximum increase amount under clause (iii), reduced (but not below zero) by the sum of the bonus depreciation amounts for all preceding taxable years.

(iii) MAXIMUM INCREASE AMOUNT.—For purposes of clause (ii), the term "maximum increase amount" means, with respect to any corporation, the lesser of—

(I) $30,000,000, or

(II) 6 percent of the sum of the business credit increase amount, and the AMT credit increase amount, determined with respect to such corporation under subparagraph (E).

(iv) AGGREGATION RULE.—All corporations which are treated as a single employer under section 52(a) shall be treated—

(I) as 1 taxpayer for purposes of this paragraph, and

(II) as having elected the application of this paragraph if any such corporation so elects.

(D) ELIGIBLE QUALIFIED PROPERTY.—For purposes of this paragraph, the term "eligible qualified property" means qualified property under paragraph (2), except that in applying paragraph (2) for purposes of this paragraph—

(i) "March 31, 2008" shall be substituted for "December 31, 2007" each place it appears in subparagraph (A) and clauses (i) and (ii) of subparagraph (E) thereof,

(ii) "April 1, 2008" shall be substituted for "January 1, 2008" in subparagraph (A)(iii)(I) thereof,

(iii) only adjusted basis attributable to manufacture, construction, or production after March 31, 2008, and before January 1, 2010, shall be taken into account under subparagraph (B)(ii) thereof,

(iv) "January 1, 2011" shall be substituted for "January 1, 2012" in subparagraph (A)(iv) thereof, and

(v) "January 1, 2010" shall be substituted for "January 1, 2011" each place it appears in subparagraph (A) thereof.

(E) ALLOCATION OF BONUS DEPRECIATION AMOUNTS.—

(i) IN GENERAL.—Subject to clauses (ii) and (iii), the taxpayer shall, at such time and in such manner as the Secretary may prescribe, specify the portion (if any) of the bonus depreciation amount for the taxable year which is to be allocated to each of the limitations described in subparagraph (B) for such taxable year.

(ii) LIMITATION ON ALLOCATIONS.—The portion of the bonus depreciation amount which may be allocated under clause (i) to the limitations described in subparagraph (B) for any taxable year shall not exceed—

(I) in the case of the limitation described in subparagraph (B)(i), the excess of the business credit increase amount over the bonus depreciation amount allocated to such limitation for all preceding taxable years, and

(II) in the case of the limitation described in subparagraph (B)(ii), the excess of the AMT credit increase amount over the bonus depreciation amount allocated to such limitation for all preceding taxable years.

(iii) BUSINESS CREDIT INCREASE AMOUNT.—For purposes of this paragraph, the term "business credit increase amount" means the amount equal to the portion of the credit allowable under section 38 (determined without regard to subsection (c) thereof) for the first taxable year ending after March 31, 2008, which is allocable to business credit carryforwards to such taxable year which are—

(I) from taxable years beginning before January 1, 2006, and

(II) properly allocable (determined under the rules of section 38(d)) to the research credit determined under section 41(a).

(iv) AMT CREDIT INCREASE AMOUNT.—For purposes of this paragraph, the term "AMT credit increase amount" means the amount equal to the portion of the minimum tax credit under section 53(b) for the first taxable year ending after March 31, 2008, determined by taking into account only the adjusted minimum tax for taxable years beginning before January 1, 2006. For purposes of the preceding sentence, credits shall be treated as allowed on a first-in, first-out basis.

(F) CREDIT REFUNDABLE.—For purposes of section 6401(b), the aggregate increase in the credits allowable under part IV of subchapter A for any taxable year resulting from the application of this paragraph shall be treated as allowed under subpart C of such part (and not any other subpart).

(G) OTHER RULES.—

(i) ELECTION.—Any election under this paragraph (including any allocation under subparagraph (E)) may be revoked only with the consent of the Secretary.

(ii) PARTNERSHIPS WITH ELECTING PARTNERS.—In the case of a corporation making an election under subparagraph (A) and which is a partner in a partnership, for purposes of determining such corporation's distributive share of partnership items under section 702—

(I) paragraph (1) shall not apply to any eligible qualified property, and

(II) the applicable depreciation method used under this section with respect to such property shall be the straight line method.

(iii) SPECIAL RULE FOR PASSENGER AIRCRAFT.—In the case of any passenger aircraft, the written binding contract limitation under paragraph (2)(A)(iii)(I) shall not apply for purposes of subparagraphs (C)(i)(I) and (D).

(H) SPECIAL RULES FOR EXTENSION PROPERTY.—

(i) TAXPAYERS PREVIOUSLY ELECTING ACCELERATION.—In the case of a taxpayer who made the election under subparagraph (A) for its first taxable year ending after March 31, 2008—

(I) the taxpayer may elect not to have this paragraph apply to extension property, but

(II) if the taxpayer does not make the election under subclause (I), in applying this paragraph to the taxpayer a separate bonus depreciation amount, maximum amount, and maximum increase amount shall be computed and applied to eligible qualified property which is extension property and to eligible qualified property which is not extension property.

(ii) TAXPAYERS NOT PREVIOUSLY ELECTING ACCELERATION.—In the case of a taxpayer who did not make the election under subparagraph (A) for its first taxable year ending after March 31, 2008—

(I) the taxpayer may elect to have this paragraph apply to its first taxable year ending after December 31, 2008, and each subsequent taxable year, and

(II) if the taxpayer makes the election under subclause (I), this paragraph shall only apply to eligible qualified property which is extension property.

(iii) EXTENSION PROPERTY.—For purposes of this subparagraph, the term "extension property" means property which is eligible qualified property solely by reason of the extension of the application of the special allowance under paragraph (1) pursuant to the amendments made by section 1201(a) of the American Recovery and Reinvestment Tax Act of 2009 (and the application of such extension to this paragraph pursuant to the amendment made by section 1201(b)(1) of such Act).

Amendments

• 2010, Creating Small Business Jobs Act of 2010 (P.L. 111-240)

P.L. 111-240, §2022(a)(1)-(2):

Amended Code Sec. 168(k)(2) by striking "January 1, 2011" in subparagraph (A)(iv) and inserting "January 1, 2012", and by striking "January 1, 2010" each place it appears and inserting "January 1, 2011". **Effective** for property placed in service after 12-31-2009, in tax years ending after such date.

P.L. 111-240, §2022(b)(1):

Amended the heading for Code Sec. 168(k) by striking "JANUARY 1, 2010" and inserting "JANUARY 1, 2011". **Effective** for property placed in service after 12-31-2009, in tax years ending after such date.

P.L. 111-240, §2022(b)(2):

Amended the heading for Code Sec. 168(k)(2)(B)(ii) by striking "PRE-JANUARY 1, 2010" and inserting "PRE-JANUARY 1, 2011". **Effective** for property placed in service after 12-31-2009, in tax years ending after such date.

P.L. 111-240, §2022(b)(3):

Amended Code Sec. 168(k)(4)(D) by striking "and" at the end of clause (ii), by striking the period at the end of clause (iii) and inserting a comma, and by adding at the end new clauses (iv) and (v). **Effective** for property placed in service after 12-31-2009, in tax years ending after such date.

• 2009, American Recovery and Reinvestment Tax Act of 2009 (P.L. 111-5)

P.L. 111-5, §1201(a)(1)(A)-(B):

Amended Code Sec. 168(k)(2) by striking "January 1, 2010" and inserting "January 1, 2011", and by striking "January 1, 2009" each place it appears and inserting "January 1, 2010". **Effective** for property placed in service after 12-31-2008, in tax years ending after such date.

P.L. 111-5, §1201(a)(2)(A):

Amended the heading for Code Sec. 168(k) by striking "JANUARY 1, 2009" and inserting "JANUARY 1, 2010". **Effective** for property placed in service after 12-31-2008, in tax years ending after such date.

P.L. 111-5, §1201(a)(2)(B):

Amended the heading for Code Sec. 168(k)(2)(B)(ii) by striking "PRE-JANUARY 1, 2009" and inserting "PRE-JANUARY 1, 2010". **Effective** for property placed in service after 12-31-2008, in tax years ending after such date.

P.L. 111-5, §1201(a)(3)(A)(i)-(iii):

Amended Code Sec. 168(k)(4)(D) by striking "and" at the end of clause (i), by redesignating clause (ii) as clause (iii), and by inserting after clause (i) a new clause (ii). **Effective** for tax years ending after 3-31-2008.

P.L. 111-5, §1201(b)(1)(A)-(B):

Amended Code Sec. 168(k)(4) by striking "2009" and inserting "2010" in subparagraph (D)(iii) (as redesignated by Act Sec. 1201(a)(3)), and by adding at the end a new subparagraph (H). **Effective** for property placed in service after 12-31-2008, in tax years ending after such date.

• 2008, Housing Assistance Tax Act of 2008 (P.L. 110-289)

P.L. 110-289, §3081(a):

Amended Code Sec. 168(k) by adding at the end a new paragraph (4). **Effective** for tax years ending after 3-31-2008. For a special rule, see Act Sec. 3081(b), below.

P.L. 110-289, §3081(b), provides:

(b) APPLICATION TO CERTAIN AUTOMOTIVE PARTNERSHIPS.—

(1) IN GENERAL.—If an applicable partnership elects the application of this subsection—

(A) the partnership shall be treated as having made a payment against the tax imposed by chapter 1 of the Internal Revenue Code of 1986 for any applicable taxable year of the partnership in the amount determined under paragraph (3),

(B) in the case of any eligible qualified property placed in service by the partnership during any applicable taxable year—

(i) section 168(k) of such Code shall not apply in determining the amount of the deduction allowable with respect to such property under section 168 of such Code,

(ii) the applicable depreciation method used with respect to such property shall be the straight line method, and

(C) the amount of the credit determined under section 41 of such Code for any applicable taxable year with respect to the partnership shall be reduced by the amount of the deemed payment under subparagraph (A) for the taxable year.

(2) TREATMENT OF DEEMED PAYMENT.—

(A) IN GENERAL.—Notwithstanding any other provision of the Internal Revenue Code of 1986, the Secretary of the Treasury or his delegate shall not use the payment of tax described in paragraph (1) as an offset or credit against any tax liability of the applicable partnership or any partner but shall refund such payment to the applicable partnership.

(B) NO INTEREST.—The payment described in paragraph (1) shall not be taken into account in determining any amount of interest under such Code.

(3) AMOUNT OF DEEMED PAYMENT.—The amount determined under this paragraph for any applicable taxable year shall be the least of the following:

(A) The amount which would be determined for the taxable year under section 168(k)(4)(C)(i) of the Internal Revenue Code of 1986 (as added by the amendments made by this section) if an election under section 168(k)(4) of such Code were in effect with respect to the partnership.

(B) The amount of the credit determined under section 41 of such Code for the taxable year with respect to the partnership.

(C) $30,000,000, reduced by the amount of any payment under this subsection for any preceding taxable year.

(4) DEFINITIONS.—For purposes of this subsection—

(A) APPLICABLE PARTNERSHIP.—The term "applicable partnership" means a domestic partnership that—

(i) was formed effective on August 3, 2007, and

(ii) will produce in excess of 675,000 automobiles during the period beginning on January 1, 2008, and ending on June 30, 2008.

(B) APPLICABLE TAXABLE YEAR.—The term "applicable taxable year" means any taxable year during which eligible qualified property is placed in service.

(C) ELIGIBLE QUALIFIED PROPERTY.— The term "eligible qualified property" has the meaning given such term by section 168(k)(4)(D) of the Internal Revenue Code of 1986 (as added by the amendments made by this section).

• 2008, Economic Stimulus Act of 2008 (P.L. 110-185)

P.L. 110-185, §103(a)(1)-(4):

Amended Code Sec. 168(k) by striking "September 10, 2001" each place it appears and inserting "December 31, 2007", by striking "September 11, 2001" each place it appears and inserting "January 1, 2008", by striking "January 1, 2005" each place it appears and inserting "January 1, 2009", and by striking "January 1, 2006" each place it appears and inserting "January 1, 2010". **Effective** for property placed in service after 12-31-2007, in tax years ending after such date.

P.L. 110-185, §103(b):

Amended Code Sec. 168(k)(1)(A) by striking "30 percent" and inserting "50 percent". **Effective** for property placed in service after 12-31-2007, in tax years ending after such date.

P.L. 110-185, §103(c)(1):

Amended Code Sec. 168(k)(2)(B)(i)(I) by striking "and (iii)" and inserting "(iii), and (iv)". **Effective** for property placed in service after 12-31-2007, in tax years ending after such date.

P.L. 110-185, §103(c)(2):

Amended Code Sec. 168(k)(2)(B)(i)(IV) by striking "clauses (ii) and [sic] (iii)" and inserting "clause (iii)". **Effective** for property placed in service after 12-31-2007, in tax years ending after such date.

P.L. 110-185, §103(c)(3):

Amended Code Sec. 168(k)(2)(C)(i) by striking "and (iii)" and inserting ", (iii), and (iv)". **Effective** for property placed in service after 12-31-2007, in tax years ending after such date.

P.L. 110-185, §103(c)(4):

Amended Code Sec. 168(k)(2)(F)(i) by striking "$4,600" and inserting "$8,000". **Effective** for property placed in service after 12-31-2007, in tax years ending after such date.

P.L. 110-185, §103(c)(5)(A):

Amended Code Sec. 168(k) by striking paragraph (4). **Effective** for property placed in service after 12-31-2007, in tax years ending after such date. Prior to being stricken, Code Sec. 168(k)(4) read as follows:

(4) 50-PERCENT BONUS DEPRECIATION FOR CERTAIN PROPERTY.—

(A) IN GENERAL.—In the case of 50-percent bonus depreciation property—

(i) paragraph (1)(A) shall be applied by substituting "50 percent" for "30 percent", and

(ii) except as provided in paragraph (2)(D), such property shall be treated as qualified property for purposes of this subsection.

(B) 50-PERCENT BONUS DEPRECIATION PROPERTY.—For purposes of this subsection, the term "50-percent bonus depreciation property" means property described in paragraph (2)(A)(i)—

(i) the original use of which commences with the taxpayer after May 5, 2003,

(ii) which is—

(I) acquired by the taxpayer after May 5, 2003, and before January 1, 2009, but only if no written binding contract for the acquisition was in effect before May 6, 2003, or

(II) acquired by the taxpayer pursuant to a written binding contract which was entered into after May 5, 2003, and before January 1, 2009, and

(iii) which is placed in service by the taxpayer before January 1, 2009, or, in the case of property described in paragraph (2)(B) (as modified by subparagraph (C) of this paragraph) or paragraph (2)(C) (as so modified), before January 1, 2010.

(C) SPECIAL RULES.—Rules similar to the rules of subparagraphs (B), (C), and (E) of paragraph (2) shall apply for purposes of this paragraph; except that references to December 31, 2007, shall be treated as references to May 5, 2003.

(D) AUTOMOBILES.—Paragraph (2)(F) shall be applied by substituting "$7,650" for "$4,600" in the case of 50-percent bonus depreciation property.

(E) ELECTION OF 30-PERCENT BONUS.—If a taxpayer makes an election under this subparagraph with respect to any class of property for any taxable year, subparagraph (A)(i) shall not apply to all property in such class placed in service during such taxable year.

P.L. 110-185, §103(c)(5)(B):

Amended Code Sec. 168(k)(2)(D)(iii) by striking the last sentence. **Effective** for property placed in service after 12-31-2007, in tax years ending after such date. Prior to being stricken, the last sentence of Code Sec. 168(k)(2)(D)(iii) read as follows:

The preceding sentence shall be applied separately with respect to property treated as qualified property by paragraph (4) and other qualified property.

P.L. 110-185, §103(c)(11)(A)-(B):

Amended the heading for Code Sec. 168(k) by striking "SEPTEMBER 10, 2001" and inserting "DECEMBER 31, 2007", and by striking "JANUARY 1, 2005" and inserting "JANUARY 1, 2009". **Effective** for property placed in service after 12-31-2007, in tax years ending after such date.

P.L. 110-185, §103(c)(12):

Amended the heading for Code Sec. 168(k)(2)(B)(ii) by striking "PRE-JANUARY 1, 2005" and inserting "PRE-JANUARY 1, 2009". **Effective** for property placed in service after 12-31-2007, in tax years ending after such date.

• 2005, Gulf Opportunity Zone Act of 2005 (P.L. 109-135)

P.L. 109-135, §105, provides:

SEC. 105. SPECIAL EXTENSION OF BONUS DEPRECIATION PLACED IN SERVICE DATE FOR TAXPAYERS AFFECTED BY HURRICANES KATRINA, RITA, AND WILMA.

In applying the rule under section 168(k)(2)(A)(iv) of the Internal Revenue Code of 1986 to any property described in subparagraph (B) or (C) of section 168(k)(2) of such Code—

(1) the placement in service of which—

(A) is to be located in the GO Zone (as defined in section 1400M(1) of such Code), the Rita GO Zone (as defined in section 1400M(3) of such Code), or the Wilma GO Zone (as defined in section 1400M(5) of such Code), and

(B) is to be made by any taxpayer affected by Hurricane Katrina, Rita, or Wilma, or

(2) which is manufactured in such Zone by any person affected by Hurricane Katrina, Rita, or Wilma,

the Secretary of the Treasury may, on a taxpayer by taxpayer basis, extend the required date of the placement in service of such property under such section by such period of time as is determined necessary by the Secretary but not to exceed 1 year. For purposes of the preceding sentence, the determination shall be made by only taking into account the effect of one or more hurricanes on the date of such placement by the taxpayer.

P.L. 109-135, §403(j)(1):

Amended Code Sec. 168(k)(2)(A)(iv) by striking "subparagraphs (B) and (C)" and inserting "subparagraph (B) or (C)". **Effective** as if included in the provision of the American Jobs Creation Act of 2004 (P.L. 108-357) to which it relates [**effective** for property placed in service after September 10, 2001, in tax years ending after such date.—CCH].

P.L. 109-135, §403(j)(2):

Amended Code Sec. 168(k)(4)(B)(iii) by striking "and paragraph (2)(C)" and inserting "or paragraph (2)(C) (as so modified)". **Effective** as if included in the provision of the American Jobs Creation Act of 2004 (P.L. 108-357) to which it relates [**effective** for property placed in service after September 10, 2001, in tax years ending after such date.—CCH].

P.L. 109-135, §405(a)(1):

Amended Code Sec. 168(k)(4)(B)(ii). **Effective** as if included in section 201 of the Jobs and Growth Tax Relief

Reconciliation Act of 2003 (P.L. 108-27) [**effective** for tax years ending after 5-5-2003.—CCH]. Prior to amendment Code Sec. 168(k)(4)(B)(ii) read as follows:

(ii) which is acquired by the taxpayer after May 5, 2003, and before January 1, 2005, but only if no written binding contract for the acquisition was in effect before May 6, 2003, and

• 2004, American Jobs Creation Act of 2004 (P.L. 108-357)

P.L. 108-357, §336(a)(1):

Amended Code Sec. 168(k)(2) by redesignating subparagraphs (C) through (F) as subparagraphs (D) through (G), respectively, and by inserting after subparagraph (B) a new subparagraph (C). **Effective** as if included in the amendments made by section 101 of the Job Creation and Worker Assistance Act of 2002 (P.L. 107-147) [**effective** for property placed in service after 9-10-2001, in tax years ending after such date.—CCH].

P.L. 108-357, §336(a)(2):

Amended Code Sec. 168(k)(2)(A)(iv) by striking "subparagraph (B)" and inserting "subparagraphs (B) and (C)". **Effective** as if included in the amendments made by section 101 of the Job Creation and Worker Assistance Act of 2002 (P.L. 107-147) [**effective** for property placed in service after 9-10-2001, in tax years ending after such date.—CCH].

P.L. 108-357, §336(b)(1):

Amended Code Sec. 168(k)(2)(B) by adding at the end a new clause (iv). **Effective** as if included in the amendments made by section 101 of the Job Creation and Worker Assistance Act of 2002 (P.L. 107-147) [**effective** for property placed in service after 9-10-2001, in tax years ending after such date.—CCH].

P.L. 108-357, §336(b)(2):

Amended Code Sec. 168(k)(4)(A)(ii) by striking "paragraph (2)(C)" and inserting "paragraph (2)(D)". **Effective** as if included in the amendments made by section 101 of the Job Creation and Worker Assistance Act of 2002 (P.L. 107-147) [**effective** for property placed in service after 9-10-2001, in tax years ending after such date.—CCH].

P.L. 108-357, §336(b)(3):

Amended Code Sec. 168(k)(4)(B)(iii) by inserting "and paragraph (2)(C)" after "of this paragraph)". **Effective** as if included in the amendments made by section 101 of the Job Creation and Worker Assistance Act of 2002 (P.L. 107-147) [**effective** for property placed in service after 9-10-2001, in tax years ending after such date.—CCH].

P.L. 108-357, §336(b)(4):

Amended Code Sec. 168(k)(4)(C) by striking "subparagraphs (B) and (D)" and inserting "subparagraphs (B), (C), and (E)". **Effective** as if included in the amendments made by section 101 of the Job Creation and Worker Assistance Act of 2002 (P.L. 107-147) [**effective** for property placed in service after 9-10-2001, in tax years ending after such date.—CCH].

P.L. 108-357, §336(b)(5):

Amended Code Sec. 168(k)(4)(D) by striking "Paragraph (2)(E)" and inserting "Paragraph (2)(F)". **Effective** as if included in the amendments made by section 101 of the Job Creation and Worker Assistance Act of 2002 (P.L. 107-147) [**effective** for property placed in service after 9-10-2001, in tax years ending after such date.—CCH].

P.L. 108-357, §337(a):

Amended Code Sec. 168(k)(2)(E)(iii)(II), as amended by the Working Families Tax Relief Act of 2004 (P.L. 108-311) and as redesignated by this Act, by inserting before the comma at the end the following: "(or, in the case of multiple units of property subject to the same lease, within 3 months after the date the final unit is placed in service, so long as the period between the time the first unit is placed in service and the time the last unit is placed in service does not exceed 12 months)". **Effective** for property sold after 6-4-2004.

• 2004, Working Families Tax Relief Act of 2004 (P.L. 108-311)

P.L. 108-311, §403(a)(1):

Amended Code Sec. 168(k)(2)(B)(i). **Effective** as if included in the provision of the Job Creation and Worker Assistance Act of 2002 (P.L. 107-147) to which it relates [**effective** for property placed in service after 9-10-2001, in tax years ending after that date.—CCH]. Prior to amendment, Code Sec. 168(k)(2)(B)(i) read as follows:

(i) IN GENERAL.—The term "qualified property" includes property—

(I) which meets the requirements of clauses (i), (ii), and (iii) of subparagraph (A),

(II) which has a recovery period of at least 10 years or is transportation property, and

(III) which is subject to section 263A by reason of clause (ii) or (iii) of subsection (f)(1)(B) thereof.

P.L. 108-311, §403(a)(2)(A):

Amended Code Sec. 168(k)(2)(D) by adding at the end new clauses (iii) and (iv). **Effective** as if included in the provision of the Job Creation and Worker Assistance Act of 2002 (P.L. 107-147) to which it relates [**effective** for property placed in service after 9-10-2001, in tax years ending after that date.—CCH].

P.L. 108-311, §403(a)(2)(B):

Amended Code Sec. 168(k)(2)(D)(ii) by inserting "clause (iii) and" before "subparagraph (A)(ii)". **Effective** as if included in the provision of the Job Creation and Worker Assistance Act of 2002 (P.L. 107-147) to which it relates [**effective** for property placed in service after 9-10-2001, in tax years ending after that date.—CCH].

P.L. 108-311, §408(a)(6)(A)-(B):

Amended Code Sec. 168(k)(2)(D)(ii) by inserting "is" after "if property", and by striking "is" in subclause (I) before "originally placed in service". **Effective** 10-4-2004.

P.L. 108-311, §408(a)(8):

Amended the heading for Code Sec. 168(k)(2)(F) by striking "MINIUMUM" and inserting "MINIMUM". **Effective** 10-4-2004.

• 2003, Jobs and Growth Tax Relief Reconciliation Act of 2003 (P.L. 108-27)

P.L. 108-27, §201(a):

Amended Code Sec. 168(k) by adding at the end a new paragraph (4). **Effective** for tax years ending after 5-5-2003.

P.L. 108-27, §201(b)(1)(A):

Amended Code Sec. 168(k)(2)(B)(ii) and (D)(i) by striking "September 11, 2004" each place it appears in the text and inserting "January 1, 2005". **Effective** for tax years ending after 5-5-2003.

P.L. 108-27, §201(b)(1)(B):

Amended Code Sec. 168(k)(2)(B)(ii) by striking "PRE-SEPTEMBER 11, 2004" in the heading and inserting "PRE-JANUARY 1, 2005". **Effective** for tax years ending after 5-5-2003.

P.L. 108-27, §201(b)(2):

Amended Code Sec. 168(k)(2)(A)(iii) by striking "September 11, 2004" each place it appears and inserting "January 1, 2005". **Effective** for tax years ending after 5-5-2003.

P.L. 108-27, §201(b)(3):

Amended Code Sec. 168(k)(2)(C)(iii) by adding at the end a new sentence. **Effective** for tax years ending after 5-5-2003.

P.L. 108-27, §201(c)(1):

Amended the subsection heading for Code Sec. 168(k) by striking "SEPTEMBER 11, 2004" and inserting "JANUARY 1, 2005". **Effective** for tax years ending after 5-5-2003.

• 2002, Job Creation and Worker Assistance Act of 2002 (P.L. 107-147)

P.L. 107-147, §101(a):

Amended Code Sec. 168 by adding at the end a new subsection (k). **Effective** for property placed in service after 9-10-2001, in tax years ending after such date.

[Sec. 168(l)]

(l) SPECIAL ALLOWANCE FOR CELLULOSIC BIOFUEL PLANT PROPERTY.—

(1) ADDITIONAL ALLOWANCE.—In the case of any qualified cellulosic biofuel plant property—

(A) the depreciation deduction provided by section 167(a) for the taxable year in which such property is placed in service shall include an allowance equal to 50 percent of the adjusted basis of such property, and

(B) the adjusted basis of such property shall be reduced by the amount of such deduction before computing the amount otherwise allowable as a depreciation deduction under this chapter for such taxable year and any subsequent taxable year.

(2) QUALIFIED CELLULOSIC BIOFUEL PLANT PROPERTY.—The term "qualified cellulosic biofuel plant property" means property of a character subject to the allowance for depreciation—

(A) which is used in the United States solely to produce cellulosic biofuel,

(B) the original use of which commences with the taxpayer after the date of the enactment of this subsection,

(C) which is acquired by the taxpayer by purchase (as defined in section 179(d)) after the date of the enactment of this subsection, but only if no written binding contract for the acquisition was in effect on or before the date of the enactment of this subsection, and

(D) which is placed in service by the taxpayer before January 1, 2013.

(3) CELLULOSIC BIOFUEL.—The term "cellulosic biofuel" means any liquid fuel which is produced from any lignocellulosic or hemicellulosic matter that is available on a renewable or recurring basis.

(4) EXCEPTIONS.—

(A) BONUS DEPRECIATION PROPERTY UNDER SUBSECTION(k).—Such term shall not include any property to which section 168(k) applies.

(B) ALTERNATIVE DEPRECIATION PROPERTY.—Such term shall not include any property described in section 168(k)(2)(D)(i).

(C) TAX-EXEMPT BOND-FINANCED PROPERTY.—Such term shall not include any property any portion of which is financed with the proceeds of any obligation the interest on which is exempt from tax under section 103.

(D) ELECTION OUT.—If a taxpayer makes an election under this subparagraph with respect to any class of property for any taxable year, this subsection shall not apply to all property in such class placed in service during such taxable year.

(5) SPECIAL RULES.—For purposes of this subsection, rules similar to the rules of subparagraph (E) of section 168(k)(2) shall apply, except that such subparagraph shall be applied—

(A) by substituting "the date of the enactment of subsection (l)" for "December 31, 2007" each place it appears therein,

(B) by substituting "January 1, 2013" for "January 1, 2011" in clause (i) thereof, and

(C) by substituting "qualified cellulosic biofuel plant property" for "qualified property" in clause (iv) thereof.

(6) ALLOWANCE AGAINST ALTERNATIVE MINIMUM TAX.—For purposes of this subsection, rules similar to the rules of section 168(k)(2)(G) shall apply.

(7) RECAPTURE.—For purposes of this subsection, rules similar to the rules under section 179(d)(10) shall apply with respect to any qualified cellulosic biofuel plant property which ceases to be qualified cellulosic biofuel plant property.

(8) DENIAL OF DOUBLE BENEFIT.—Paragraph (1) shall not apply to any qualified cellulosic biofuel plant property with respect to which an election has been made under section 179C (relating to election to expense certain refineries).

Amendments

• 2010, Creating Small Business Jobs Act of 2010 (P.L. 111-240)

P.L. 111-240, §2022(b)(4):

Amended Code Sec. 168(l)(5)(B) by striking "January 1, 2010" and inserting "January 1, 2011". **Effective** for property placed in service after 12-31-2009, in tax years ending after such date.

• 2009, American Recovery and Reinvestment Tax Act of 2009 (P.L. 111-5)

P.L. 111-5, §1201(a)(2)(C):

Amended Code Sec. 168(l)(5)(B) by striking "January 1, 2009" and inserting "January 1, 2010". **Effective** for property placed in service after 12-31-2008, in tax years ending after such date.

• 2008, Energy Improvement and Extension Act of 2008 (P.L. 110-343)

P.L. 110-343, Division B, §201(a):

Amended Code Sec. 168(l)(3). **Effective** for property placed in service after 10-3-2008, in tax years ending after such date. Prior to amendment, Code Sec. 168(l)(3) read as follows:

(3) CELLULOSIC BIOMASS ETHANOL.—For purposes of this subsection, the term "cellulosic biomass ethanol" means ethanol produced by hydrolysis of any lignocellulosic or hemicellulosic matter that is available on a renewable or recurring basis.

P.L. 110-343, Division B, §201(b)(1)-(3):

Amended Code Sec. 168(l) by striking "cellulosic biomass ethanol" each place it appears and inserting "cellulosic biofuel", by striking "CELLULOSIC BIOMASS ETHANOL" in the heading of such subsection and inserting "CELLULOSIC BIOFUEL", and by striking "CELLULOSIC BIOMASS ETHANOL" in the heading of paragraph (2) thereof and inserting "CELLULOSIC BIOFUEL". **Effective** for property placed in service after 10-3-2008, in tax years ending after such date.

• 2008, Economic Stimulus Act of 2008 (P.L. 110-185)

P.L. 110-185, §103(c)(6):

Amended Code Sec. 168(l)(4) by redesignating subparagraphs (A), (B), and (C) as subparagraphs (B), (C), and (D) and inserting before subparagraph (B) (as so redesignated) a new subparagraph (A). **Effective** for property placed in service after 12-31-2007, in tax years ending after such date.

P.L. 110-185, §103(c)(7)(A)-(B):

Amended Code Sec. 168(l)(5) by striking "September 10, 2001" in subparagraph (A) and inserting "December 31, 2007", and by striking "January 1, 2005" in subparagraph (B) and inserting "January 1, 2009". **Effective** for property placed in service after 12-31-2007, in tax years ending after such date.

• 2007, Tax Technical Corrections Act of 2007 (P.L. 110-172)

P.L. 110-172, §11(b)(1):

Amended Code Sec. 168(l)(3) by striking "enzymatic" before "hydrolysis". **Effective** as if included in the provision of the Tax Relief and Health Care Act of 2006 (P.L. 109-432) to which it relates [**effective** for property placed in service after 12-20-2006 in tax years after such date.—CCH].

• 2006, Tax Relief and Health Care Act of 2006 (P.L. 109-432)

P.L. 109-432, Division A, §209(a):

Amended Code Sec. 168 by adding at the end a new subsection (l). **Effective** for property placed in service after 12-20-2006 in tax years ending after such date.

[Sec. 168(m)]

(m) SPECIAL ALLOWANCE FOR CERTAIN REUSE AND RECYCLING PROPERTY.—

(1) IN GENERAL.—In the case of any qualified reuse and recycling property—

(A) the depreciation deduction provided by section 167(a) for the taxable year in which such property is placed in service shall include an allowance equal to 50 percent of the adjusted basis of the qualified reuse and recycling property, and

(B) the adjusted basis of the qualified reuse and recycling property shall be reduced by the amount of such deduction before computing the amount otherwise allowable as a depreciation deduction under this chapter for such taxable year and any subsequent taxable year.

(2) QUALIFIED REUSE AND RECYCLING PROPERTY.—For purposes of this subsection—

(A) IN GENERAL.—The term "qualified reuse and recycling property" means any reuse and recycling property—

(i) to which this section applies,

(ii) which has a useful life of at least 5 years,

(iii) the original use of which commences with the taxpayer after August 31, 2008, and

(iv) which is—

(I) acquired by purchase (as defined in section 179(d)(2)) by the taxpayer after August 31, 2008, but only if no written binding contract for the acquisition was in effect before September 1, 2008, or

(II) acquired by the taxpayer pursuant to a written binding contract which was entered into after August 31, 2008.

(B) EXCEPTIONS.—

(i) BONUS DEPRECIATION PROPERTY UNDER SUBSECTION (K).—The term "qualified reuse and recycling property" shall not include any property to which section 168(k) applies.

(ii) ALTERNATIVE DEPRECIATION PROPERTY.—The term "qualified reuse and recycling property" shall not include any property to which the alternative depreciation system under subsection (g) applies, determined without regard to paragraph (7) of subsection (g) (relating to election to have system apply).

(iii) ELECTION OUT.—If a taxpayer makes an election under this clause with respect to any class of property for any taxable year, this subsection shall not apply to all property in such class placed in service during such taxable year.

(C) SPECIAL RULE FOR SELF-CONSTRUCTED PROPERTY.—In the case of a taxpayer manufacturing, constructing, or producing property for the taxpayer's own use, the requirements of clause (iv) of subparagraph (A) shall be treated as met if the taxpayer begins manufacturing, constructing, or producing the property after August 31, 2008.

(D) DEDUCTION ALLOWED IN COMPUTING MINIMUM TAX.—For purposes of determining alternative minimum taxable income under section 55, the deduction under subsection (a) for qualified reuse and recycling property shall be determined under this section without regard to any adjustment under section 56.

(3) DEFINITIONS.—For purposes of this subsection—

(A) REUSE AND RECYCLING PROPERTY.—

(i) IN GENERAL.—The term "reuse and recycling property" means any machinery and equipment (not including buildings or real estate), along with all appurtenances thereto, including software necessary to operate such equipment, which is used exclusively to collect, distribute, or recycle qualified reuse and recyclable materials.

(ii) EXCLUSION.—Such term does not include rolling stock or other equipment used to transport reuse and recyclable materials.

(B) QUALIFIED REUSE AND RECYCLABLE MATERIALS.—

(i) IN GENERAL.—The term "qualified reuse and recyclable materials" means scrap plastic, scrap glass, scrap textiles, scrap rubber, scrap packaging, recovered fiber, scrap ferrous and nonferrous metals, or electronic scrap generated by an individual or business.

(ii) ELECTRONIC SCRAP.—For purposes of clause (i), the term "electronic scrap" means—

(I) any cathode ray tube, flat panel screen, or similar video display device with a screen size greater than 4 inches measured diagonally, or

(II) any central processing unit.

(C) RECYCLING OR RECYCLE.—The term "recycling" or "recycle" means that process (including sorting) by which worn or superfluous materials are manufactured or processed into specification grade commodities that are suitable for use as a replacement or substitute for virgin materials in manufacturing tangible consumer and commercial products, including packaging.

Amendments

• 2008, Energy Improvement and Extension Act of 2008 (P.L. 110-343)

P.L. 110-343, Division B, §308(a):

Amended Code Sec. 168 by adding at the end a new subsection (m). **Effective** for property placed in service after 8-31-2008.

[Sec. 168(n)]

(n) SPECIAL ALLOWANCE FOR QUALIFIED DISASTER ASSISTANCE PROPERTY.—

(1) IN GENERAL.—In the case of any qualified disaster assistance property—

(A) the depreciation deduction provided by section 167(a) for the taxable year in which such property is placed in service shall include an allowance equal to 50 percent of the adjusted basis of the qualified disaster assistance property, and

(B) the adjusted basis of the qualified disaster assistance property shall be reduced by the amount of such deduction before computing the amount otherwise allowable as a depreciation deduction under this chapter for such taxable year and any subsequent taxable year.

(2) QUALIFIED DISASTER ASSISTANCE PROPERTY.—For purposes of this subsection—

(A) IN GENERAL.—The term "qualified disaster assistance property" means any property—

(i)(I) which is described in subsection (k)(2)(A)(i), or

(II) which is nonresidential real property or residential rental property,

(ii) substantially all of the use of which is—

(I) in a disaster area with respect to a federally declared disaster occurring before January 1, 2010, and

(II) in the active conduct of a trade or business by the taxpayer in such disaster area,

(iii) which—

(I) rehabilitates property damaged, or replaces property destroyed or condemned, as a result of such federally declared disaster, except that, for purposes of this clause, property shall be treated as replacing property destroyed or condemned if, as part of an integrated plan, such property replaces property which is included in a continuous area which includes real property destroyed or condemned, and

(II) is similar in nature to, and located in the same county as, the property being rehabilitated or replaced,

(iv) the original use of which in such disaster area commences with an eligible taxpayer on or after the applicable disaster date,

(v) which is acquired by such eligible taxpayer by purchase (as defined in section 179(d)) on or after the applicable disaster date, but only if no written binding contract for the acquisition was in effect before such date, and

(vi) which is placed in service by such eligible taxpayer on or before the date which is the last day of the third calendar year following the applicable disaster date (the fourth calendar year in the case of nonresidential real property and residential rental property).

(B) EXCEPTIONS.—

(i) OTHER BONUS DEPRECIATION PROPERTY.—The term "qualified disaster assistance property" shall not include—

(I) any property to which subsection (k) (determined without regard to paragraph (4)), (l), or (m) applies,

(II) any property to which section 1400N(d) applies, and

(III) any property described in section 1400N(p)(3).

(ii) ALTERNATIVE DEPRECIATION PROPERTY.—The term "qualified disaster assistance property" shall not include any property to which the alternative depreciation system under subsection (g) applies, determined without regard to paragraph (7) of subsection (g) (relating to election to have system apply).

(iii) TAX-EXEMPT BOND FINANCED PROPERTY.—Such term shall not include any property any portion of which is financed with the proceeds of any obligation the interest on which is exempt from tax under section 103.

(iv) QUALIFIED REVITALIZATION BUILDINGS.—Such term shall not include any qualified revitalization building with respect to which the taxpayer has elected the application of paragraph (1) or (2) of section 1400I(a).

(v) ELECTION OUT.—If a taxpayer makes an election under this clause with respect to any class of property for any taxable year, this subsection shall not apply to all property in such class placed in service during such taxable year.

(C) SPECIAL RULES.—For purposes of this subsection, rules similar to the rules of subparagraph (E) of subsection (k)(2) shall apply, except that such subparagraph shall be applied—

(i) by substituting "the applicable disaster date" for "December 31, 2007" each place it appears therein,

(ii) without regard to "and before January 1, 2011" in clause (i) thereof, and

(iii) by substituting "qualified disaster assistance property" for "qualified property" in clause (iv) thereof.

(D) ALLOWANCE AGAINST ALTERNATIVE MINIMUM TAX.—For purposes of this subsection, rules similar to the rules of subsection (k)(2)(G) shall apply.

(3) OTHER DEFINITIONS.—For purposes of this subsection—

(A) APPLICABLE DISASTER DATE .—The term "applicable disaster date" means, with respect to any federally declared disaster, the date on which such federally declared disaster occurs.

(B) FEDERALLY DECLARED DISASTER.—The term "federally declared disaster" has the meaning given such term under section 165(h)(3)(C)(i).

(C) DISASTER AREA.—The term "disaster area" has the meaning given such term under section 165(h)(3)(C)(ii).

(D) ELIGIBLE TAXPAYER.—The term "eligible taxpayer" means a taxpayer who has suffered an economic loss attributable to a federally declared disaster.

(4) RECAPTURE.—For purposes of this subsection, rules similar to the rules under section 179(d)(10) shall apply with respect to any qualified disaster assistance property which ceases to be qualified disaster assistance property.

Amendments

• 2010, Creating Small Business Jobs Act of 2010 (P.L. 111-240)

P.L. 111-240, §2022(b)(5):

Amended Code Sec. 168(n)(2)(C) by striking "January 1, 2010" and inserting "January 1, 2011". **Effective** for property placed in service after 12-31-2009, in tax years ending after such date.

• 2009, American Recovery and Reinvestment Tax Act of 2009 (P.L. 111-5)

P.L. 111-5, §1201(a)(2)(D):

Amended Code Sec. 168(n)(2)(C) by striking "January 1, 2009" and inserting "January 1, 2010". **Effective** for property placed in service after 12-31-2008, in tax years ending after such date.

• 2008, Tax Extenders and Alternative Minimum Tax Relief Act of 2008 (P.L. 110-343)

P.L. 110-343, Division C, §710(a):

Amended Code Sec. 168, as amended by this Act, by adding at the end a new subsection (n). **Effective** for property placed in service after 12-31-2007, with respect [to] disasters declared after such date.

[Sec. 169]

SEC. 169. AMORTIZATION OF POLLUTION CONTROL FACILITIES.

[Sec. 169(a)]

(a) ALLOWANCE OF DEDUCTION.—Every person, at his election, shall be entitled to a deduction with respect to the amortization of the amortizable basis of any certified pollution control facility (as defined in subsection (d)), based on a period of 60 months. Such amortization deduction shall be an amount, with respect to each month of such period within the taxable year, equal to the amortizable basis of the pollution control facility at the end of such month divided by the number of months (including the month for which the deduction is computed) remaining in the period. Such amortizable basis at the end of the month shall be computed without regard to the amortization deduction for such month. The amortization deduction provided by this section with respect to any month shall be in lieu of the depreciation deduction with respect to such pollution control facility for such month provided by section 167. The 60-month period shall begin, as to any pollution control facility, at the election of the taxpayer, with the month following the month in which such facility was completed or acquired, or with the succeeding taxable year.

[Sec. 169(b)]

(b) ELECTION OF AMORTIZATION.—The election of the taxpayer to take the amortization deduction and to begin the 60-month period with the month following the month in which the facility is completed or acquired, or with the taxable year succeeding the taxable year in which such facility is completed or acquired, shall be made by filing with the Secretary, in such manner, in such form, and within such time, as the Secretary may by regulations prescribe, a statement of such election.

Amendments

• 1976, Tax Reform Act of 1976 (P.L. 94-455)

P.L. 94-455, §1906(b)(13)(A):

Amended 1954 Code by substituting "Secretary" for "Secretary or his delegate" each place it appeared. **Effective** 2-1-77.

[Sec. 169(c)]

(c) TERMINATION OF AMORTIZATION DEDUCTION.—A taxpayer which has elected under subsection (b) to take the amortization deduction provided in subsection (a) may, at any time after making such election, discontinue the amortization deduction with respect to the remainder of the amortization period, such discontinuance to begin as of the beginning of any month specified by the taxpayer in a notice in writing filed with the Secretary before the beginning of such month. The depreciation deduction provided under section 167 shall be allowed, beginning with the first month as to which the amortization deduction does not apply, and the taxpayer shall not be entitled to any further amortization deduction under this section with respect to such pollution control facility.

Amendments

• 1976, Tax Reform Act of 1976 (P.L. 94-455)

P.L. 94-455, §1906(b)(13)(A):

Amended 1954 Code by substituting "Secretary" for "Secretary or his delegate" each place it appeared. **Effective** 2-1-77.

[Sec. 169(d)]

(d) DEFINITIONS AND SPECIAL RULES.—For purposes of this section—

(1) CERTIFIED POLLUTION CONTROL FACILITY.—The term "certified pollution control facility" means a new identifiable treatment facility which is used, in connection with a plant or other property in operation before January 1, 1976, to abate or control water or atmospheric pollution or contamination by removing, altering, disposing, storing, or preventing the creation or emission of pollutants, contaminants, wastes, or heat and which—

(A) the State certifying authority having jurisdiction with respect to such facility has certified to the Federal certifying authority as having been constructed, reconstructed, erected, or acquired in conformity with the State program or requirements for abatement or control of water or atmospheric pollution or contamination;

(B) the Federal certifying authority has certified to the Secretary (i) as being in compliance with the applicable regulations of Federal agencies and (ii) as being in furtherance of the general policy of the United States for cooperation with the States in the prevention and abatement of water pollution under the Federal Water Pollution Control Act, as amended (33 U. S. C. 466 et seq.), or in the prevention and abatement of atmospheric pollution and contamination under the Clean Air Act, as amended (42 U.S.C. 1857 et seq.); and

(C) does not significantly—

(i) increase the output or capacity, extend the useful life, or reduce the total operating costs of such plant or other property (or any unit thereof), or

(ii) alter the nature of the manufacturing or production process or facility.

(2) STATE CERTIFYING AUTHORITY.—The term "State certifying authority" means, in the case of water pollution, the State water pollution control agency as defined in section 13(a) of the Federal Water Pollution Control Act and, in the case of air pollution, the air pollution control agency as defined in section 302(b) of the Clean Air Act. The term "State certifying authority" includes any interstate agency authorized to act in place of a certifying authority of the State.

(3) FEDERAL CERTIFYING AUTHORITY.—The term "Federal certifying authority" means, in the case of water pollution, the Secretary of the Interior and, in the case of air pollution, the Secretary of Health and Human Services.

(4) NEW IDENTIFIABLE TREATMENT FACILITY.—

(A) IN GENERAL.—For purposes of paragraph (1), the term "new identifiable treatment facility" includes only tangible property (not including a building and its structural components, other than a building which is exclusively a treatment facility) which is of a character subject to the allowance for depreciation provided in section 167, which is identifiable as a treatment facility, and which is property—

(i) the construction, reconstruction, or erection of which is completed by the taxpayer after December 31, 1968, or

(ii) acquired after December 31, 1968, if the original use of the property commences with the taxpayer and commences after such date.

In applying this section in the case of property described in clause (i) there shall be taken into account only that portion of the basis which is properly attributable to construction, reconstruction, or erection after December 31, 1968.

(B) CERTAIN FACILITIES PLACED IN OPERATION AFTER APRIL 11, 2005.—In the case of any facility described in paragraph (1) solely by reason of paragraph (5), subparagraph (A) shall be applied by substituting "April 11, 2005" for "December 31, 1968" each place it appears therein.

(5) SPECIAL RULE RELATING TO CERTAIN ATMOSPHERIC POLLUTION CONTROL FACILITIES.—In the case of any atmospheric pollution control facility which is placed in service after April 11, 2005, and used in connection with an electric generation plant or other property which is primarily coal fired—

(A) paragraph (1) shall be applied without regard to the phrase "in operation before January 1, 1976", and

(B) in the case of [any] facility placed in service in connection with a plant or other property placed in operation after December 31, 1975, this section shall be applied by substituting "84" for "60" each place it appears in subsections (a) and (b).

Amendments

• 2005, Gulf Opportunity Zone Act of 2005 (P.L. 109-135)

P.L. 109-135, §402(e):

Amended Code Sec. 169(d)(5)(B) by adding at the beginning thereof "in the case of [any] facility placed in service in connection with a plant or other property placed in operation after December 31, 1975,". **Effective** as if included in the provision of the Energy Policy Act of 2005 (P.L. 109-58) to which it relates [**effective** for facilities placed in service after 4-11-2005.—CCH].

• 2005, Energy Tax Incentives Act of 2005 (P.L. 109-58)

P.L. 109-58, §1309(a):

Amended Code Sec. 169(d) by adding at the end a new paragraph (5). **Effective** for facilities placed in service after 4-11-2005.

P.L. 109-58, §1309(b):

Amended Code Sec. 169(d)(4)(B). **Effective** for facilities placed in service after 4-11-2005. Prior to amendment, Code Sec. 169(d)(4)(B) read as follows:

(B) CERTAIN PLANTS, ETC., PLACED IN OPERATION AFTER 1968.—In the case of any treatment facility used in connection with any plant or other property not in operation before January 1, 1969, the preceding sentence shall be applied by substituting December 31, 1975, for December 31, 1968.

P.L. 109-58, §1309(c):

Amended the heading for Code Sec. 169(d) by inserting "AND SPECIAL RULES" after "DEFINITIONS". **Effective** for facilities placed in service after 4-11-2005.

P.L. 109-58, §1309(d):

Amended Code Sec. 169(d)(3) by striking "Health, Education, and Welfare" and inserting "Health and Human Services". **Effective** for facilities placed in service after 4-11-2005.

• 1976, Tax Reform Act of 1976 (P.L. 94-455)

P.L. 94-455, §1906(b)(13)(A):

Amended 1954 Code by substituting "Secretary" for "Secretary or his delegate" each place it appeared. **Effective** 2-1-77.

P.L. 94-455, §2112(b):

Substituted "January 1, 1976" for "January 1, 1969" in Code Sec. 169(d)(1), struck out "or storing" and substituted "storing, or preventing the creation or emission of" in Code Sec. 169(d)(1), struck out "and" at the end of Code Sec. 169(d)(1)(A), substituted "; and" for the period at the end of Code Sec. 169(d)(1)(B), and added Code Sec. 169(d)(1)(C). **Effective** for tax years beginning after 12-31-75 but not applicable for any property with respect to which the amortization period under section 169 of the Internal Revenue Code of 1954 has begun before 1-1-76.

P.L. 94-455, §2112(c):

Amended Code Sec. 169(d)(4). **Effective** 10-4-76. Prior to amendment, Code Sec. 169(d)(4) read as follows:

(4) NEW IDENTIFIABLE TREATMENT FACILITY.—For purposes of paragraph (1), the term "new identifiable treatment facility" includes only tangible property (not including a building and its structural components, other than a building which is exclusively a treatment facility) which is of a character subject to the allowance for depreciation provided in section 167, which is identifiable as a treatment facility, and which—

(A) is property—

(i) the construction, reconstruction, or erection of which is completed by the taxpayer after December 31, 1968, or

(ii) acquired after December 31, 1968, if the original use of the property commences with the taxpayer and commences after such date, and

(B) is placed in service by the taxpayer before January 1, 1976.

In applying this section in the case of property described in clause (i) of subparagraph (A), there shall be taken into account only that portion of the basis which is properly attributable to construction, reconstruction, or erection after December 31, 1968.

• 1975 (P.L. 93-625)

P.L. 93-625, §3(a):

Amended Code Sec. 169(d)(4)(B) by substituting "January 1, 1976" for "January 1, 1975". **Effective** 1-3-75.

[Sec. 169(e)]

(e) PROFITMAKING ABATEMENT WORKS, ETC.—The Federal certifying authority shall not certify any property under subsection (d)(1)(B) to the extent it appears that by reason of profits derived through the recovery of wastes or otherwise in the operation of such property, its costs will be recovered over its actual useful life.

[Sec. 169(f)]

(f) AMORTIZABLE BASIS.—

(1) DEFINED.—For purposes of this section, the term "amortizable basis" means that portion of the adjusted basis (for determining gain) of a certified pollution control facility which may be amortized under this section.

(2) SPECIAL RULES.—

(A) If a certified pollution control facility has a useful life (determined as of the first day of the first month for which a deduction is allowable under this section) in excess of 15 years, the amortizable basis of such facility shall be equal to an amount which bears the same ratio to the portion of the adjusted basis of such facility, which would be eligible for amortization but for the application of this subparagraph, as 15 bears to the number of years of useful life of such facility.

(B) The amortizable basis of a certified pollution control facility with respect to which an election under this section is in effect shall not be increased, for purposes of this section, for additions or improvements after the amortization period has begun.

[Sec. 169(g)]

(g) DEPRECIATION DEDUCTION.—The depreciation deduction provided by section 167 shall, despite the provisions of subsection (a), be allowed with respect to the portion of the adjusted basis which is not the amortizable basis.

[Sec. 169(h)—Repealed]

Amendments

• 1971, Revenue Act of 1971 (P.L. 92-178)

P.L. 92-178, §104(f)(2):

Repealed Code Sec. 169(h). **Effective** for property described in Code Sec. 50. Prior to repeal; Code Sec. 169(h) read as follows:

(h) INVESTMENT CREDIT NOT TO BE ALLOWED.—In the case of any property with respect to which an election has been made under subsection (a), so much of the adjusted basis of the property as (after the application of subsection (f)) constitutes the amortizable basis for purposes of this section shall not be treated as section 38 property within the meaning of section 48(a).

[Sec. 169(i)]

(i) LIFE TENANT AND REMAINDERMAN.—In the case of property held by one person for life with remainder to another person, the deduction under this section shall be computed as if the life tenant were the absolute owner of the property and shall be allowable to the life tenant.

[Sec. 169(j)]

(j) CROSS REFERENCE.—

For special rule with respect to certain gain derived from the disposition of property the adjusted basis of which is determined with regard to this section, see section 1245.

Amendments

• 1981, Economic Recovery Tax Act of 1981 (P.L. 97-34)

P.L. 97-34, §266(a), provides:

(a) GENERAL RULE.—For purposes of chapter 1 of the Internal Revenue Code of 1954, in computing the taxable income of a taxpayer who, on July 1, 1980, held one or more motor carrier operating authorities, an amount equal to the aggregate adjusted basis of all motor carrier operating authorities held by the taxpayer on July 1, 1980, or acquired subsequent thereto pursuant to a binding contract in effect on July 1, 1980, shall be allowed as a deduction ratably over a period of 60 months. Such 60-month period shall begin with the month of July 1980 (or if later, the month in which acquired), or at the election of the taxpayer, the first month of the taxpayer's first taxable year beginning after July 1, 1980.

(b) DEFINITION OF MOTOR CARRIER OPERATING AUTHORITY.—For purposes of ths section, the term "motor carrier operating authority" means a certificate or permit held by a motor common or contract carrier of property and issued pursuant to subchapter II of chapter 109 of title 49 of the United States Code.

(c) SPECIAL RULES.—

(1) ADJUSTED BASIS.—For purposes of the Internal Revenue Code of 1954, proper adjustments shall be made in the adjusted basis of any motor carrier operating authority held by the taxpayer on July 1, 1980, for the amounts allowable as a deduction under this section.

(2) CERTAIN STOCK ACQUISITIONS.—

(A) IN GENERAL.—Under regulations prescribed by the Secretary of the Treasury or his delegate, and at the election of the holder of the authority, in any case in which a corporation—

(i) on or before July 1, 1980 (or after such date pursuant to a binding contract in effect on such date), acquired stock in a corporation which held, directly or indirectly, any motor carrier operating authority at the time of such acquisition, and

(ii) would have been able to allocate to the basis of such authority that portion of the acquiring corporation's cost basis in such stock attributable to such authority if the acquiring corporation had received such authority in the liquidation of the acquired corporation immediately following such acquisition and such allocation would have been proper under section 334(b)(2) of such Code,

the holder of the authority may, for purposes of this section, allocate a portion of the basis of the acquiring corporation in the stock of the acquired corporation to the basis of such authority in such manner as the Secretary may prescribe in such regulations.

(B) ADJUSTMENT TO BASIS.—Under regulations prescribed by the Secretary of the Treasury or his delegate, proper adjustment shall be made to the basis of the stock or other assets in the manner provided by such regulations to take into account any allocation under subparagraph (A).

(d) EFFECTIVE DATE.—The provisions of this section shall apply to taxable years ending after June 30, 1980.

• 1969, Tax Reform Act of 1969 (P.L. 91-172)

P.L. 91-172, §704(a):

Substituted new Code Sec. 169 (amortization of pollution control facilities) for former Code Sec. 169 (amortization of grain-storage facilities). **Effective** for tax years ending after 12-31-68. Code Sec. 169 is reproduced immediately below.

"SEC. 169. AMORTIZATION OF GRAIN-STORAGE FACILITIES.

"(a) Allowance of Deduction.—

"(1) Original owner.—Any person who constructs, reconstructs, or erects a grain-storage facility (as defined in subsection (d)) shall, at his election, be entitled to a deduction with respect to the amortization of the adjusted basis (for determining gain) of such facility based on a period of 60 months. The 60-month period shall begin as to any such facility, at the election of the taxpayer, with the month following the month in which the facility was completed, or with the succeeding taxable year.

"(2) Subsequent owners.—Any person who acquires a grain-storage facility from a taxpayer who—

"(A) elected under subsection (b) to take the amortization deduction provided by this subsection with respect to such facility, and

"(B) did not discontinue the amortization deduction pursuant to subsection (c), shall, at his election, be entitled to a deduction with respect to the adjusted basis (determined under subsection (e)(2)) of such facility based on the period, if any, remaining (at the time of acquisition) in the 60-month period elected under subsection (b) by the person who constructed, reconstructed, or erected such facility.

"(3) Amount of deduction.—The amortization deduction provided in paragraphs (1) and (2) shall be an amount, with respect to each month of the amortization period within the taxable year, equal to the adjusted basis of the facility at the end of such month, divided by the number of months (including the month for which the deduction is computed) remaining in the period. Such adjusted basis at the end of the month shall be computed without regard to the amortization deduction for such month. The amortization deduction above provided with respect to any month shall be in lieu of the depreciation deduction with respect to such facility for such month provided by section 167.

"(b) Election of Amortization.—The election of the taxpayer under subsection (a)(1) to take the amortization deduction and to begin the 60-month period with the month following the month in which the facility was completed shall be made only by a statement to that effect in the return for the taxable year in which the facility was completed. The election of the taxpayer under subsection (a)(1) to take the amortization deduction and to begin such period with the taxable year succeeding such year shall be made only by a statement to that effect in the return for such succeeding taxable year. The election of the taxpayer under subsection (a)(2) to take the amortization deduction shall be made only by a statement to that effect in the return for the taxable year in which the facility was acquired. Notwithstanding the preceding three sentences, the election of the taxpayer under subsection (a)(1) or (2) may be made, under such regulations as the Secretary or his delegate may prescribe, before the time prescribed in the applicable sentence.

"(c) Termination of Amortization Deduction.—A taxpayer which has elected under subsection (b) to take the amortization deduction provided in subsection (a) may, at any time after making such election, discontinue the amortization deduction with respect to the remainder of the amortization period, such discontinuance to begin as of the beginning of any month specified by the taxpayer in a notice in writing filed with the Secretary or his delegate before the beginning of such month. The depreciation deduction provided under section 167 shall be allowed, beginning with the first month as to which the amortization deduction does not apply, and the taxpayer shall not be entitled to any further amortization deduction with respect to such facility.

"(d) Definition of Grain-Storage Facility.—For purposes of this section, the term `grain-storage facility' means—

"(1) any corn crib, grain bin, or grain elevator, or any similar structure suitable primarily for the storage of grain, which crib, bin, elevator, or structure is intended by the taxpayer at the time of his election to be used for the storage of grain produced by him (or, if the election is made by a partnership, produced by the members thereof); and

"(2) any public grain warehouse permanently equipped for receiving, elevating, conditioning, and loading out grain,

the construction, reconstruction, or erection of which was completed after December 31, 1952, and on or before December 31, 1956. If any structure described in clause (1) or (2) of the preceding sentence is altered or remodeled so as to increase its capacity for the storage of grain, or if any structure is converted, through alteration or remodeling, into a structure so described, and if such alteration or remodeling was completed after December 31, 1952, and on or before December 31, 1956, such alteration or remodeling shall be treated as the construction of a grain-storage facility. The term `grain-storage facility' shall include only property of a character which is subject to the allowance for depreciation provided in section 167. The term `grain-storage facility' shall not include any facility any part of which is an emergency facility within the meaning of section 168 of this title.

"(e) Determination of Adjusted Basis.—

"(1) Original owners.—For purposes of subsection (a)(1)—

"(A) in determining the adjusted basis of any grain-storage facility, the construction, reconstruction, or erection of which was begun before January 1, 1953, there shall be included only so much of the amount of the adjusted basis (computed without regard to this subsection) as is properly attributable to such construction, reconstruction, or erection after December 31, 1952; and

"(B) in determining the adjusted basis of any facility which is a grain-storage facility within the meaning of the second sentence of subsection (d), there shall be included only so much of the amount otherwise included in such basis as is properly attributable to the alteration or remodeling.

If any existing grain-storage facility as defined in the first sentence of subsection (d) is altered or remodeled as provided in the second sentence of subsection (d), the expenditures for such remodeling or alteration shall not be applied in adjustment of the basis of such existing facility but a separate basis shall be computed in respect of such facility as if the part altered or remodeled were a new and separate grain-storage facility.

"(2) Subsequent owners.—For purposes of subsection (a)(2), the adjusted basis of any grain-storage facility shall be whichever of the following amounts is the smaller:

"(A) the basis (unadjusted) of such facility for purposes of this section in the hands of the transferor, donor, or grantor, adjusted as if such facility in the hands of the taxpayer had a substituted basis within the meaning of section 1016(b), or

"(B) so much of the adjusted basis (for determining gain) of the facility in the hands of the taxpayer (as computed without regard to this subsection) as is properly attributable to construction, reconstruction, or erection after December 31, 1952.

"(f) Depreciation Deduction.—If the adjusted basis of the grain-storage facility (computed without regard to subsection (e)) exceeds the adjusted basis computed under subsection (e), the depreciation deduction provided by section 167 shall, despite the provisions of subsection (a)(3) of this section, be allowed with respect to such grain-storage facility as if the adjusted basis for the purpose of such deduction were an amount equal to the amount of such excess.

"(g) Life Tenant and Remainderman.—In the case of property held by one person for life with remainder to another person, the amortization deduction provided in subsection (a) shall be computed as if the life tenant were the absolute owner of the property and shall be allowed to the life tenant."

[Sec. 170]

SEC. 170. CHARITABLE, ETC., CONTRIBUTIONS AND GIFTS.

[Sec. 170(a)]

(a) ALLOWANCE OF DEDUCTION.—

(1) GENERAL RULE.—There shall be allowed as a deduction any charitable contribution (as defined in subsection (c)) payment of which is made within the taxable year. A charitable

contribution shall be allowable as a deduction only if verified under regulations prescribed by the Secretary.

(2) CORPORATIONS ON ACCRUAL BASIS.—In the case of a corporation reporting its taxable income on the accrual basis, if—

(A) the board of directors authorizes a charitable contribution during any taxable year, and

(B) payment of such contribution is made after the close of such taxable year and on or before the 15th day of the third month following the close of such taxable year,

then the taxpayer may elect to treat such contribution as paid during such taxable year. The election may be made only at the time of the filing of the return for such taxable year, and shall be signified in such manner as the Secretary shall by regulations prescribe.

(3) FUTURE INTERESTS IN TANGIBLE PERSONAL PROPERTY.—For purposes of this section, payment of a charitable contribution which consists of a future interest in tangible personal property shall be treated as made only when all intervening interests in, and rights to the actual possession or enjoyment of, the property have expired or are held by persons other than the taxpayer or those standing in a relationship to the taxpayer described in section 267(b) or 707(b). For purposes of the preceding sentence, a fixture which is intended to be severed from the real property shall be treated as tangible personal property.

Amendments

• 1984, Deficit Reduction Act of 1984 (P.L. 98-369)

P.L. 98-369, §174(b)(5)(A):

Amended Code Sec. 170(a)(3) by striking out "section 267(b)" and inserting in lieu thereof "section 267(b) or 707(b)". **Effective** for transactions after 12-31-83, in tax years ending after such date.

P.L. 98-369, §155, provides:

SEC. 155. SUBSTANTIATION OF CHARITABLE CONTRIBUTIONS; MODIFICATIONS OF INCORRECT VALUATION PENALTY.

(a) Substantiation of Contributions of Property.—

(1) In General.—Not later than December 31, 1984, the Secretary shall prescribe regulations under section 170(a)(1) of the Internal Revenue Code of 1954, which require any individual, closely held corporation, or personal service corporation claiming a deduction under section 170 of such Code for a contribution described in paragraph (2)—

(A) to obtain a qualified appraisal for the property contributed,

(B) to attach an appraisal summary to the return on which such deduction is first claimed for such contribution, and

(C) to include on such return such additional information (including the cost basis and acquisition date of the contributed property) as the Secretary may prescribe in such regulations.

Such regulations shall require the taxpayer to retain any qualified appraisal.

(2) Contributions to Which Paragraph (1) Applies.—For purposes of paragraph (1), a contribution is described in this paragraph—

(A) if such contribution is of property (other than publicly traded securities), and

(B) if the claimed value of such property (plus the claimed value of all similar items of property donated to 1 or more donees) exceeds $5,000.

In the case of any property which is nonpublicly traded stock, subparagraph (B) shall be applied by substituting "$10,000" for "$5,000".

(3) Appraisal Summary.—For purposes of this subsection, the appraisal summary shall be in such form and include such information as the Secretary prescribes by regulations. Such summary shall be signed by the qualified appraiser preparing the qualified appraisal and shall contain the TIN of such appraiser. Such summary shall be acknowledged by the donee of the property appraised in such manner as the Secretary prescribes in such regulations.

(4) Qualified Appraisal.—The term "qualified appraisal" means an appraisal prepared by a qualified appraiser which includes—

(A) a description of the property appraised,

(B) the fair market value of such property on the date of contribution and the specific basis for the valuation,

(C) a statement that such appraisal was prepared for income tax purposes,

(D) the qualifications of the qualified appraiser,

(E) the signature and TIN of such appraiser, and

(F) such additional information as the Secretary prescribes in such regulations.

(5) Qualified Appraiser.—

(A) In General.—For purposes of this subsection, the term "qualified appraiser" means an appraiser qualified to make appraisals of the type of property donated, who is not—

(i) the taxpayer,

(ii) a party to the transaction in which the taxpayer acquired the property,

(iii) the donee,

(iv) any person employed by any of the foregoing persons or related to any of the foregoing persons under section 267(b) of the Internal Revenue Code of 1954, or

(v) to the extent provided in such regulations, any person whose relationship to the taxpayer would cause a reeasonable person to question the independence of such appraiser.

(B) Appraisal Fees.—For purposes of this subsection, an appraisal shall not be treated as a qualified appraisal if all or part of the fee paid for such appraisal is based on a percentage of the appraised value of the property. The preceding sentence shall not apply to fees based on a sliding scale that are paid to a generally recognized association regulating appraisers.

(6) Other Definitions.—For purposes of this subsection—

(A) Closely Held Corporation.—The term "closely held corporation" means any corporation (other than an S corporation) with respect to which the stock ownership requirement of paragraph (2) of section 542(a) of such Code is met.

(B) Personal Service Corporation.—The term "personal service corporation" means any corporation (other than an S corporation) which is a service organization (within the meaning of section 414(m)(3) of such Code).

(C) Publicly Traded Securities.—The term "publicly traded securities" means securities for which (as of the date of the contribution) market quotations are readily available on an established securities market.

(D) Nonpublicly Traded Stock.—The term "nonpublicly traded stock" means any stock of a corporation which is not a publicly traded security.

(E) The Secretary.—The term "Secretary" means the Secretary of the Treasury or his delegate.

• 1976, Tax Reform Act of 1976 (P.L. 94-455)

P.L. 94-455, §1906(b)(13)(A):

Amended 1954 Code by substituting "Secretary" for "Secretary or his delegate" each place it appeared. **Effective** 2-1-77.

• 1969, Tax Reform Act of 1969 (P.L. 91-172)

P.L. 91-172, §201(a)(1):

Amended Code Sec. 170(a) by adding paragraph (a)(3). Prior to amendment, said paragraph was former Code Sec. 170(f).

• **1964, Revenue Act of 1964 (P.L. 88-272)**

P.L. 88-272, §209(e):

Added Code Sec. 170(f) [now Code Sec. 170(a)(3)]. **Effective** for transfers of future interests made after 12-31-63, in tax years ending after such date, except that such section does not apply to any transfer of a future interest made before 7-1-64, where—

(A) the sole intervening interest or right is a nontransferable life interest reserved by the donor, or

(B) in the case of a joint gift by husband and wife, the sole intervening interest or right is a nontransferable life interest reserved by the donors which expires not later than the death of whichever of such donors dies later.

For purposes of the exception contained in the preceding sentence, a right to make a transfer of the reserved life interest to the donee of the future interest is not to be treated as making a life interest transferable.

[Sec. 170(b)]

(b) PERCENTAGE LIMITATIONS.—

(1) INDIVIDUALS.—In the case of an individual, the deduction provided in subsection (a) shall be limited as provided in the succeeding subparagraphs.

(A) GENERAL RULE.—Any charitable contribution to—

(i) a church or a convention or association of churches,

(ii) an educational organization which normally maintains a regular faculty and curriculum and normally has a regularly enrolled body of pupils or students in attendance at the place where its educational activities are regularly carried on,

(iii) an organization the principal purpose or functions of which are the providing of medical or hospital care or medical education or medical research, if the organization is a hospital, or if the organization is a medical research organization directly engaged in the continuous active conduct of medical research in conjunction with a hospital, and during the calendar year in which the contribution is made such organization is committed to spend such contributions for such research before January 1 of the fifth calendar year which begins after the date such contribution is made,

(iv) an organization which normally receives a substantial part of its support (exclusive of income received in the exercise or performance by such organization of its charitable, educational, or other purpose or function constituting the basis for its exemption under section 501(a)) from the United States or any State or political subdivision thereof or from direct or indirect contributions from the general public, and which is organized and operated exclusively to receive, hold, invest, and administer property and to make expenditures to or for the benefit of a college or university which is an organization referred to in clause (ii) of this subparagraph and which is an agency or instrumentality of a State or political subdivision thereof, or which is owned or operated by a State or political subdivision thereof or by an agency or instrumentality of one or more States or political subdivisions,

(v) a governmental unit referred to in subsection (c)(1),

(vi) an organization referred to in subsection (c)(2) which normally receives a substantial part of its support (exclusive of income received in the exercise or performance by such organization of its charitable, educational, or other purpose or function constituting the basis for its exemption under section 501(a)) from a governmental unit referred to in subsection (c)(1) or from direct or indirect contributions from the general public,

(vii) a private foundation described in subparagraph (F), or

(viii) an organization described in section 509(a)(2) or (3),

shall be allowed to the extent that the aggregate of such contributions does not exceed 50 percent of the taxpayer's contribution base for the taxable year.

(B) OTHER CONTRIBUTIONS.—Any charitable contribution other than a charitable contribution to which subparagraph (A) applies shall be allowed to the extent that the aggregate of such contributions does not exceed the lesser of—

(i) 30 percent of the taxpayer's contribution base for the taxable year, or

(ii) the excess of 50 percent of the taxpayer's contribution base for the taxable year over the amount of charitable contributions allowable under subparagraph (A) (determined without regard to subparagraph (C)).

If the aggregate of such contributions exceeds the limitation of the preceding sentence, such excess shall be treated (in a manner consistent with the rules of subsection (d)(1)) as a charitable contribution (to which subparagraph (A) does not apply) in each of the 5 succeeding taxable years in order of time.

(C) SPECIAL LIMITATION WITH RESPECT TO CONTRIBUTIONS DESCRIBED IN SUBPARAGRAPH(a) OF CERTAIN CAPITAL GAIN PROPERTY.—

(i) In the case of charitable contributions described in subparagraph (A) of capital gain property to which subsection (e)(1)(B) does not apply, the total amount of contributions of such property which may be taken into account under subsection (a) for any taxable year shall not exceed 30 percent of the taxpayer's contribution base for such year. For purposes of this subsection, contributions of capital gain property to which this subparagraph applies shall be taken into account after all other charitable contributions (other than charitable contributions to which subparagraph (D) applies).

(ii) If charitable contributions described in subparagraph (A) of capital gain property to which clause (i) applies exceeds 30 percent of the taxpayer's contribution base for any taxable year, such excess shall be treated, in a manner consistent with the rules of subsection (d)(1), as a charitable contribution of capital gain property to which clause (i) applies in each of the 5 succeeding taxable years in order of time.

(iii) At the election of the taxpayer (made at such time and in such manner as the Secretary prescribes by regulations), subsection (e)(1) shall apply to all contributions of capital gain property (to which subsection (e)(1)(B) does not otherwise apply) made by the taxpayer during the taxable year. If such an election is made, clauses (i) and (ii) shall not apply to contributions of capital gain property made during the taxable year, and, in applying subsection (d)(1) for such taxable year with respect to contributions of capital gain property made in any prior contribution year for which an election was not made under this clause, such contributions shall be reduced as if subsection (e)(1) had applied to such contributions in the year in which made.

(iv) For purposes of this paragraph, the term "capital gain property" means, with respect to any contribution, any capital asset the sale of which at its fair market value at the time of the contribution would have resulted in gain which would have been long-term capital gain. For purposes of the preceding sentence, any property which is property used in the trade or business (as defined in section 1231(b)) shall be treated as a capital asset.

(D) SPECIAL LIMITATION WITH RESPECT TO CONTRIBUTIONS OF CAPITAL GAIN PROPERTY TO ORGANIZATIONS NOT DESCRIBED IN SUBPARAGRAPH(a).—

(i) IN GENERAL.—In the case of charitable contributions (other than charitable contributions to which subparagraph (A) applies) of capital gain property, the total amount of such contributions of such property taken into account under subsection (a) for any taxable year shall not exceed the lesser of—

(I) 20 percent of the taxpayer's contribution base for the taxable year, or

(II) the excess of 30 percent of the taxpayer's contribution base for the taxable year over the amount of the contributions of capital gain property to which subparagraph (C) applies.

For purposes of this subsection, contributions of capital gain property to which this subparagraph applies shall be taken into account after all other charitable contributions.

(ii) CARRYOVER.—If the aggregate amount of contributions described in clause (i) exceeds the limitation of clause (i), such excess shall be treated (in a manner consistent with the rules of subsection (d)(1)) as a charitable contribution of capital gain property to which clause (i) applies in each of the 5 succeeding taxable years in order of time.

(E) CONTRIBUTIONS OF QUALIFIED CONSERVATION CONTRIBUTIONS.—

(i) IN GENERAL.—Any qualified conservation contribution (as defined in subsection (h)(1)) shall be allowed to the extent the aggregate of such contributions does not exceed the excess of 50 percent of the taxpayer's contribution base over the amount of all other charitable contributions allowable under this paragraph.

(ii) CARRYOVER.—If the aggregate amount of contributions described in clause (i) exceeds the limitation of clause (i), such excess shall be treated (in a manner consistent with the rules of subsection (d)(1)) as a charitable contribution to which clause (i) applies in each of the 15 succeeding years in order of time.

(iii) COORDINATION WITH OTHER SUBPARAGRAPHS.—For purposes of applying this subsection and subsection (d)(1), contributions described in clause (i) shall not be treated as described in subparagraph (A), (B), (C), or (D) and such subparagraphs shall apply without regard to such contributions.

(iv) SPECIAL RULE FOR CONTRIBUTION OF PROPERTY USED IN AGRICULTURE OR LIVESTOCK PRODUCTION.—

(I) IN GENERAL.—If the individual is a qualified farmer or rancher for the taxable year for which the contribution is made, clause (i) shall be applied by substituting "100 percent" for "50 percent".

(II) EXCEPTION.—Subclause (I) shall not apply to any contribution of property made after the date of the enactment of this subparagraph which is used in agriculture or livestock production (or available for such production) unless such contribution is subject to a restriction that such property remain available for such production. This subparagraph shall be applied separately with respect to property to which subclause (I) does not apply by reason of the preceding sentence prior to its application to property to which subclause (I) does apply.

(v) DEFINITION.—For purposes of clause (iv), the term "qualified farmer or rancher" means a taxpayer whose gross income from the trade or business of farming (within the meaning of section 2032A(e)(5)) is greater than 50 percent of the taxpayer's gross income for the taxable year.

(vi) TERMINATION.—This subparagraph shall not apply to any contribution made in taxable years beginning after December 31, 2009.

(F) CERTAIN PRIVATE FOUNDATIONS.—The private foundations referred to in subparagraph (A)(vii) and subsection (e)(1)(B) are—

(i) a private operating foundation (as defined in section 4942(j)(3)),

(ii) any other private foundation (as defined in section 509(a)) which, not later than the 15th day of the third month after the close of the foundation's taxable year in which contributions are received, makes qualifying distributions (as defined in section 4942(g), without regard to paragraph (3) thereof), which are treated, after the application of section 4942(g)(3), as distributions out of corpus (in accordance with section 4942(h)) in an amount equal to 100 percent of such contributions, and with respect to which the taxpayer obtains adequate records or other sufficient evidence from the foundation showing that the foundation made such qualifying distributions, and

(iii) a private foundation all of the contributions to which are pooled in a common fund and which would be described in section 509(a)(3) but for the right of any substantial contributor (hereafter in this clause called "donor") or his spouse to designate annually the recipients, from among organizations described in paragraph (1) of section 509(a), of the income attributable to the donor's contribution to the fund and to direct (by deed or by will) the payment, to an organization described in such paragraph (1), of the corpus in the common fund attributable to the donor's contribution; but this clause shall apply only if all of the income of the common fund is required to be (and is) distributed to one or more organizations described in such paragraph (1) not later than the 15th day of the third month after the close of the taxable year in which the income is realized by the fund and only if all of the corpus attributable to any donor's contribution to the fund is required to be (and is) distributed to one or more of such organizations not later than one year after his death or after the death of his surviving spouse if she has the right to designate the recipients of such corpus.

(G) CONTRIBUTION BASE DEFINED.—For purposes of this section, the term "contribution base" means adjusted gross income (computed without regard to any net operating loss carryback to the taxable year under section 172).

(2) CORPORATIONS.—In the case of a corporation—

(A) IN GENERAL.—The total deductions under subsection (a) for any taxable year (other than for contributions to which subparagraph (B) applies) shall not exceed 10 percent of the taxpayer's taxable income.

(B) QUALIFIED CONSERVATION CONTRIBUTIONS BY CERTAIN CORPORATE FARMERS AND RANCHERS.—

(i) IN GENERAL.—Any qualified conservation contribution (as defined in subsection (h)(1))—

(I) which is made by a corporation which, for the taxable year during which the contribution is made, is a qualified farmer or rancher (as defined in paragraph (1)(E)(v)) and the stock of which is not readily tradable on an established securities market at any time during such year, and

(II) which, in the case of contributions made after the date of the enactment of this subparagraph, is a contribution of property which is used in agriculture or livestock production (or available for such production) and which is subject to a restriction that such property remain available for such production,

shall be allowed to the extent the aggregate of such contributions does not exceed the excess of the taxpayer's taxable income over the amount of charitable contributions allowable under subparagraph (A).

(ii) CARRYOVER.—If the aggregate amount of contributions described in clause (i) exceeds the limitation of clause (i), such excess shall be treated (in a manner consistent with the rules of subsection (d)(2)) as a charitable contribution to which clause (i) applies in each of the 15 succeeding years in order of time.

(iii) TERMINATION.—This subparagraph shall not apply to any contribution made in taxable years beginning after December 31, 2009.

(C) TAXABLE INCOME.—For purposes of this paragraph, taxable income shall be computed without regard to—

(i) this section,

(ii) part VIII (except section 248),

(iii) any net operating loss carryback to the taxable year under section 172,

(iv) section 199, and

(v) any capital loss carryback to the taxable year under section 1212(a)(1).

(3) TEMPORARY SUSPENSION OF LIMITATIONS ON CHARITABLE CONTRIBUTIONS.—In the case of a qualified farmer or rancher (as defined in paragraph (1)(E)(v)), any charitable contribution of food—

(A) to which subsection (e)(3)(C) applies (without regard to clause (ii) thereof), and

(B) which is made during the period beginning on the date of the enactment of this paragraph and before January 1, 2009,

shall be treated for purposes of paragraph (1)(E) or (2)(B), whichever is applicable, as if it were a qualified conservation contribution which is made by a qualified farmer or rancher and which otherwise meets the requirements of such paragraph.

Amendments

• 2010, (P.L. 111-126)

P.L. 111-126, §1(a)-(c), provides:

SECTION 1. ACCELERATION OF INCOME TAX BENEFITS FOR CHARITABLE CASH CONTRIBUTIONS FOR RELIEF OF VICTIMS OF EARTHQUAKE IN HAITI.

(a) IN GENERAL.—For purposes of section 170 of the Internal Revenue Code of 1986, a taxpayer may treat any contribution described in subsection (b) made after January 11, 2010, and before March 1, 2010, as if such contribution was made on December 31, 2009, and not in 2010.

(b) CONTRIBUTION DESCRIBED.—A contribution is described in this subsection if such contribution is a cash contribution made for the relief of victims in areas affected by the earthquake in Haiti on January 12, 2010, for which a charitable contribution deduction is allowable under section 170 of the Internal Revenue Code of 1986.

(c) RECORDKEEPING.—In the case of a contribution described in subsection (b), a telephone bill showing the name of the donee organization, the date of the contribution, and the amount of the contribution shall be treated as meeting the recordkeeping requirements of section 170(f)(17) of the Internal Revenue Code of 1986.

• 2008, Tax Extenders and Alternative Minimum Tax Relief Act of 2008 (P.L. 110-343)

P.L. 110-343, Division C, §323(b)(1):

Amended Code Sec. 170(b) by adding a new paragraph (3). **Effective** for tax years ending after 10-3-2008.

• 2008, Heartland, Habitat, Harvest, and Horticulture Act of 2008 (P.L. 110-246)

P.L. 110-246, §15302(a)(1):

Amended Code Sec. 170(b)(1)(E)(vi) by striking "December 31, 2007" and inserting "December 31, 2009". **Effective** for contributions made in tax years beginning after 12-31-2007.

P.L. 110-246, §15302(a)(2):

Amended Code Sec. 170(b)(2)(B)(iii) by striking "December 31, 2007" and inserting "December 31, 2009". **Effective** for contributions made in tax years beginning after 12-31-2007.

• 2007, Tax Technical Corrections Act of 2007 (P.L. 110-172)

P.L. 110-172, §11(a)(14)(A):

Amended Code Sec. 170(b)(1)(A)(vii) by striking "subparagraph (E)" and inserting "subparagraph (F)". **Effective** 12-29-2007.

• 2006, Pension Protection Act of 2006 (P.L. 109-280)

P.L. 109-280, §1206(a)(1):

Amended Code Sec. 170(b)(1) by redesignating subparagraphs (E) and (F) as subparagraphs (F) and (G), respectively, and by inserting after subparagraph (D) a new subparagraph (E). **Effective** for contributions made in tax years beginning after 12-31-2005.

P.L. 109-280, §1206(a)(2):

Amended Code Sec. 170(b)(2). **Effective** for contributions made in tax years beginning after 12-31-2005. Prior to amendment, Code Sec. 170(b)(2) read as follows:

(2) CORPORATIONS.—In the case of a corporation, the total deductions under subsection (a) for any taxable year shall not exceed 10 percent of the taxpayer's taxable income computed without regard to—

(A) this section,

(B) part VIII (except section 248),

(C) section 199,

(D) any net operating loss carryback to the taxable year under section 172, and

(E) any capital loss carryback to the taxable year under section 1212(a)(1).

• 2005, Gulf Opportunity Zone Act of 2005 (P.L. 109-135)

P.L. 109-135, §403(a)(16):

Amended Code Sec. 170(b)(2) by redesignating subparagraphs (C) and (D) as subparagraphs (D) and (E), respectively, and by inserting after subparagraph (B) a new subparagraph (C). **Effective** as if included in the provision of the American Jobs Creation Act of 2004 (P.L. 108-357) to which it relates [**effective** for tax years beginning after 12-31-2004.—CCH].

• 2005, Katrina Emergency Tax Relief Act of 2005 (P.L. 109-73)

P.L. 109-73, §301 [repealed by P.L. 109-135, §201(b)(4)(B)], provides:

SEC. 301. TEMPORARY SUSPENSION OF LIMITATIONS ON CHARITABLE CONTRIBUTIONS.

(a) IN GENERAL.—Except as otherwise provided in subsection (b), section 170(b) of the Internal Revenue Code of 1986 shall not apply to qualified contributions and such contributions shall not be taken into account for purposes of applying subsections (b) and (d) of section 170 of such Code to other contributions.

(b) TREATMENT OF EXCESS CONTRIBUTIONS.—For purposes of section 170 of such Code—

(1) INDIVIDUALS.—In the case of an individual—

(A) LIMITATION.—Any qualified contribution shall be allowed only to the extent that the aggregate of such contributions does not exceed the excess of the taxpayer's contribution base (as defined in subparagraph (F) of section 170(b)(1) of such Code) over the amount of all other charitable contributions allowed under such section 170(b)(1).

(B) CARRYOVER.—If the aggregate amount of qualified contributions made in the contribution year (within the meaning of section 170(d)(1) of such Code) exceeds the limitation of subparagraph (A), such excess shall be added to the excess described in the portion of subparagraph (A) of such section which precedes clause (i) thereof for purposes of applying such section.

(2) CORPORATIONS.—In the case of a corporation—

(A) LIMITATION.—Any qualified contribution shall be allowed only to the extent that the aggregate of such contributions does not exceed the excess of the taxpayer's taxable income (as determined under paragraph (2) of section 170(b) of such Code) over the amount of all other charitable contributions allowed under such paragraph.

(B) CARRYOVER.—Rules similar to the rules of paragraph (1)(B) shall apply for purposes of this paragraph.

(c) EXCEPTION TO OVERALL LIMITATION ON ITEMIZED DEDUCTIONS.—So much of any deduction allowed under section 170 of such Code as does not exceed the qualified contributions paid during the taxable year shall not be treated as an itemized deduction for purposes of section 68 of such Code.

(d) QUALIFIED CONTRIBUTIONS.—

(1) IN GENERAL.—For purposes of this section, the term "qualified contribution" means any charitable contribution (as defined in section 170(c) of such Code)—

(A) paid during the period beginning on August 28, 2005, and ending on December 31, 2005, in cash to an organization described in section 170(b)(1)(A) of such Code (other than an organization described in section 509(a)(3) of such Code),

(B) in the case of a contribution paid by a corporation, such contribution is for relief efforts related to Hurricane Katrina, and

(C) with respect to which the taxpayer has elected the application of this section.

(2) EXCEPTION.—Such term shall not include a contribution if the contribution is for establishment of a new, or maintenance in an existing, segregated fund or account with respect to which the donor (or any person appointed or designated by such donor) has, or reasonably expects to have, advisory privileges with respect to distributions or investments by reason of the donor's status as a donor.

(3) APPLICATION OF ELECTION TO PARTNERSHIPS AND S CORPORATIONS.—In the case of a partnership or S corporation, the election under paragraph (1)(C) shall be made separately by each partner or shareholder.

• 2005, (P.L. 109-1)

P.L. 109-1, §1, provides:

SECTION 1. ACCELERATION OF INCOME TAX BENEFITS FOR CHARITABLE CASH CONTRIBUTIONS FOR RELIEF OF INDIAN OCEAN TSUNAMI VICTIMS.

(a) IN GENERAL.—For purposes of section 170 of the Internal Revenue Code of 1986, a taxpayer may treat any contribution described in subsection (b) made in January 2005 as if such contribution was made on December 31, 2004, and not in January 2005.

(b) CONTRIBUTION DESCRIBED.—A contribution is described in this subsection if such contribution is a cash contribution made for the relief of victims in areas affected by the December 26, 2004, Indian Ocean tsunami for which a charitable contribution deduction is allowable under section 170 of the Internal Revenue Code of 1986.

• 1986, Tax Reform Act of 1986 (P.L. 99-514)

P.L. 99-514, §1831:

Amended Code Sec. 170(b)(1)(C)(iv) by striking out "this subparagraph" and inserting in lieu thereof "this paragraph". **Effective** as if included in the provision of P.L. 98-369 to which it relates.

P.L. 98-369, §301(a)(1), (2):

Amended Code Sec. 170(b)(1)(B)(i) by striking out "20 percent" and inserting in lieu thereof "30 percent" and by adding at the end thereof a new sentence. **Effective** for contributions made in tax years ending after 7-18-84.

P.L. 98-369, §301(c)(1)

Amended Code Sec. 170(b)(1) by redesignating subparagraphs (D) and (E) as subparagraphs (E) and (F), respectively, and by inserting after subparagraph (C) new subparagraph (D). **Effective** for contributions made in tax years ending after 7-18-84.

P.L. 98-369, §301(c)(2)(A):

Amended Code Sec. 170(b)(1)(A)(vii) by striking out "subparagraph (D)" and inserting in lieu thereof "subparagraph (E)". **Effective** for contributions made in tax years ending after 7-18-84.

P.L. 98-369, §301(c)(2)(B):

Amended the heading of Code Sec. 170(b)(1)(C) and clause (i). **Effective** for contributions made in tax years ending after 7-18-84. Prior to amendment, they read as follows:

(C) Special Limitation With Respect to Contributions of Certain Capital Gain Property.—

(i) In the case of charitable contributions of capital gain property to which subsection (e)(1)(B) does not apply, the total amount of contributions of such property which may be taken into account under subsection (a) for any taxable year shall not exceed 30 percent of the taxpayer's contribution base for such year. For purposes of this subsection, contributions of capital gain property to which this paragraph applies shall be taken into account after all other charitable contributions.

• 1981, Economic Recovery Tax Act of 1981 (P.L. 97-34)

P.L. 97-34, §263(a):

Amended Code Sec. 170(b)(2) by striking out "5 percent" and inserting in lieu thereof "10 percent". **Effective** for tax years beginning after 12-31-81.

• 1976, Tax Reform Act of 1976 (P.L. 94-455)

P.L. 94-455, §1052(c):

Amended Code Sec. 170(b)(2) by adding "and" at the end of subparagraph (C), repealing subparagraph (D), and redesignating subparagraph (E) as subparagraph (D). **Effective** for tax years beginning after 12-31-79. Prior to repeal, Code Sec. 170(b)(2)(D) read as follows:

(D) section 922 (special deduction for Western Hemisphere trade corporations), and

P.L. 94-455, §1901(a)(28):

Amended Code Sec. 170(b)(1)(A)(vii) to substitute "subparagraph (D)" for "subparagraph (E)", amended Code Sec. 170(b)(1)(B)(ii) to substitute "subparagraph (C)" for "subparagraph (D)", repealed Code Sec. 170(b)(1)(C), and redesignated Code Secs. 170(b)(1)(D), (E), and (F) as Code Secs. 170(b)(1)(C), (D), and (E). **Effective** for tax years beginning after 12-31-76. Prior to repeal, Code Sec. 170(b)(1)(C) read as follows:

(C) UNLIMITED DEDUCTION FOR CERTAIN INDIVIDUALS.—Subject to the provisions of subsections (f)(6) and (g), the limitations in subparagraphs (A), (B), and (D), and the provisions of subsection (e)(1)(B), shall not apply, in the case of an individual for a taxable year beginning before January 1, 1975, if in such taxable year and in 8 of the 10 preceding taxable years, the amount of the charitable contributions, plus the amount of income tax (determined without regard to chapter 2, relating to tax on self-employment income) paid during such year in respect of such year or preceding taxable years, exceeds the transitional deduction percentage (determined under subsection (f)(6)) of the taxpayer's taxable income for such year, computed without regard to—

(i) this section,

(ii) section 151 (allowance of deductions for personal exemption), and

(iii) any net operating loss carryback to the taxable year under section 172.

In lieu of the amount of income tax paid during any such year, there may be substituted for that year the amount of income tax paid in respect of such year, provided that any amount so included in the year in respect of which payment was made shall not be included in any other year. In the case of a separate return for the taxable year by a married individual who previously filed a joint return with a former deceased spouse for any of the 10 preceding taxable years, the amount of charitable contributions and taxes paid for any such preceding taxable year, for which a joint return was filed with the former deceased spouse, shall be determined in the same manner as if the taxpayer had not remarried after the death of such former spouse.

P.L. 94-455, §1906(b)(13)(A):

Amended 1954 Code by substituting "Secretary" for "Secretary or his delegate" each place it appeared. **Effective** 2-1-77.

• 1969, Tax Reform Act of 1969 (P.L. 91-172)

P.L. 91-172, §201(a)(1):

Amended Code Sec. 170(b). **Effective** for tax years beginning after 12-31-69. Prior to amendment, Code Sec. 170(b) read as follows:

"(b) Limitations.—

"(1) Individuals.—In the case of an individual the deduction provided in subsection (a) shall be limited as provided in subparagraphs (A), (B), (C), and (D).

"(A) Special rule.—Any charitable contribution to—

"(i) a church or a convention or association of churches,

"(ii) an educational organization referred to in section 503(b)(2),

"(iii) a hospital referred to in section 503(b)(5) or to a medical research organization (referred to in section 503(b)(5)) directly engaged in the continuous active conduct of medical research in conjunction with a hospital, if during the calendar year in which the contribution is made such organization is committed to spend such contributions for such research before January 1 of the fifth calendar year which begins after the date such contribution is made,

"(iv) an organization referred to in section 503(b)(3) organized and operated exclusively to receive, hold, invest, and administer property and to make expenditures to or for the benefit of a college or university which is an organization referred to in clause (ii) of this subparagraph and which is an agency or instrumentality of a State or political subdivision thereof, or which is owned or operated by a State or political subdivision thereof or by an agency or instrumentality of one or more States or political subdivisions,

"(v) a governmental unit referred to in subsection (c)(1), or

"(vi) an organization referred to in subsection (c)(2) which normally receives a substantial part of its support (exclusive of income received in the exercise or performance by such organization of its charitable, educational, or other purpose or function constituting the basis for its exemption under section 501(a)) from a governmental unit referred to in subsection (c)(1) or from direct or indirect contributions from the general public,

shall be allowed to the extent that the aggregate of such contributions does not exceed 10 percent of the taxpayer's adjusted gross income computed without regard to any net operating loss carryback to the taxable year under section 172.

"(B) General limitation.—The total deductions under subsection (a) for any taxable year shall not exceed 20 percent of the taxpayer's adjusted gross income computed without regard to any net operating loss carryback to the taxable year under section 172. For purposes of this subparagraph, the deduction under subsection (a) shall be computed without regard to any deduction allowed under subparagraph (A) but shall take into account any charitable contributions described in subparagraph (A) which are in excess of the amount allowable as a deduction under subparagraph (A).

"(C) Unlimited deduction for certain individuals.—The limitation in subparagraph (B) shall not apply in the case of an individual if, in the taxable year and in 8 of the 10 preceding taxable years, the amount of the charitable contributions, plus the amount of income tax (determined without regard to chapter 2, relating to tax on selfemployment income) paid during such year in respect of such year or preceding taxable years, exceeds 90 percent of the taxpayer's taxable income for such year, computed without regard to—

"(i) this section,

"(ii) section 151 (allowance of deductions for personal exemptions), and

"(iii) any net operating loss carryback to the taxable year under section 172.

In lieu of the amount of income tax paid during any such year, there may be substituted for that year the amount of income tax paid in respect of such year, provided that any amount so included in the year in respect of which payment was made shall not be included in any other year.

"(D) Denial of deduction in case of certain transfers in trust.—No deduction shall be allowed under this section for the value of any interest in property transferred after March 9, 1954, to a trust if—

"(i) the grantor has a reversionary interest in the corpus or income of that portion of the trust with respect to which a deduction would (but for this subparagraph) be allowable under this section; and

"(ii) at the time of the transfer the value of such reversionary interest exceeds 5 percent of the value of the property constituting such portion of the trust.

For purposes of this subparagraph, a power exercisable by the grantor or a nonadverse party (within the meaning of section 672(b)), or both, to revest in the grantor property or income therefrom shall be treated as a reversionary interest.

"(2) Corporations.—In the case of a corporation, the total deductions under subsection (a) for any taxable year shall not exceed 5 percent of the taxpayer's taxable income computed without regard to—

"(A) this section,

"(B) part VIII (except section 248),

"(C) any net operating loss carryback to the taxable year under section 172, and

"(D) section 922 (special deduction for Western Hemisphere trade corporations).

Any contribution made by a corporation in a taxable year (hereinafter in this sentence referred to as the `contribution year') in excess of the amount deductible for such year under the preceding sentence shall be deductible for each of the 5 succeeding taxable years in order of time, but only to the extent of the lesser of the two following amounts: (i) the excess of the maximum amount deductible for such succeeding taxable year under the preceding sentence over the sum of the contributions made in such year plus the aggregate of the excess contributions which were made in taxable years before the contribution year and which are deductible under this sentence for such succeeding taxable year; or (ii) in the case of the first succeeding taxable year, the amount of such excess contribution, and in the case of the second, third, fourth, or fifth succeeding taxable year, the portion of such excess contribution not deductible under this sentence for any taxable year intervening between the contribution year and such succeeding taxable year.

"(3) Special rule for corporations having net operating loss carryovers.—In applying the second sentence of paragraph (2) of this subsection, the excess of—

"(A) the contributions made by a corporation in a taxable year to which this section applies, over

"(B) the amount deductible in such year under the limitation in the first sentence of such paragraph (2),

shall be reduced to the extent that such excess reduces taxable income (as computed for purposes of the second sentence of section 172(b)(2)) and increases a net operating loss carryover under section 172 to a succeeding taxable year.

"(4) Reduction for certain interest.—If, in connection with any charitable contribution, a liability is assumed by the recipient or by any other person, or if a charitable contribution is of property which is subject to a liability, then, to the extent necessary to avoid the duplication of amounts, the amount taken into account for purposes of this section as the amount of the charitable contribution—

"(A) shall be reduced for interest (i) which has been paid (or is to be paid) by the taxpayer, (ii) which is attributable to the liability, and (iii) which is attributable to any period after the making of the contribution, and

"(B) in the case of a bond, shall be further reduced for interest (i) which has been paid (or is to be paid) by the taxpayer on indebtedness incurred or continued to purchase or carry such bond, and (ii) which is attributable to any period before the making of the contribution.

The reduction pursuant to subparagraph (B) shall not exceed the interest (including interest equivalent) on the bond which is attributable to any period before the making of the contribution and which is not (under the taxpayer's method of accounting) includible in the gross income of the taxpayer for any taxable year. For purposes of this paragraph, the term `bond' means any bond, debenture, note, or certificate or other evidence of indebtedness.

"(5) Carryover of certain excess contributions by individuals.—

"(A) In the case of an individual, if the amount of charitable contributions described in paragraph (1)(A) payment of which is made within a taxable year (hereinafter in this paragraph referred to as the `contribution year') beginning after December 31, 1963, exceeds 30 percent of the taxpayer's adjusted gross income for such year (computed without regard to any net operating loss carryback to such year under section 172), such excess shall be treated as a charitable contribution described in paragraph (1)(A) paid in each of the 5 succeeding taxable years in order of time, but, with respect to any such succeeding taxable year, only to the extent of the lesser of the two following amounts:

"(i) the amount by which 30 percent of the taxpayer's adjusted gross income for such succeeding taxable year (computed without regard to any net operating loss carryback to such succeeding taxable year under section 172) exceeds the sum of the charitable contributions described in paragraph (1)(A) payment of which is made by the taxpayer within such succeeding taxable year (determined without regard to this subparagraph) and the charitable contributions described in paragraph (1)(A) payment of which was made in taxable years (beginning after December 31, 1963) before the contribution year which are treated under this subparagraph as having been paid in such succeeding taxable year; or

"(ii) in the case of the first succeeding taxable year, the amount of such excess, and in the case of the second, third, fourth, or fifth succeeding taxable year, the portion of such excess not treated under this subparagraph as a charitable contribution described in paragraph (1)(A) paid in any taxable year intervening between the contribution year and such succeeding taxable year.

"(B) In applying subparagraph (A), the excess determined under subparagraph (A) for the contribution year shall be reduced to the extent that such excess reduces taxable income (as computed for purposes of the second sentence of section 172(b)(2)) and increases the net operating loss deduction for a taxable year succeeding the contribution year."

P.L. 91-172, §201(h):

Amended Code Sec. 170(b) by adding the last sentence to Sec. 170(b)(1)(C). **Effective** for tax years beginning after 12-31-68.

• 1964, Revenue Act of 1964 (P.L. 88-272)

P.L. 88-272, §209(a):

Amended subparagraph (A) of subsection (b)(1) by adding clauses (v) and (vi). **Effective** with respect to contributions which are paid in tax years beginning after 12-31-63.

P.L. 88-272, §209(c)(1):

Amended subsection (b) by adding paragraph (5) thereto. **Effective** with respect to contributions which are paid in tax years beginning after 12-31-63.

P.L. 88-272, §209(d)(1):

Amended section 170(b)(2) by inserting a new sentence to follow subparagraph (D). **Effective** for tax years beginning after 12-31-63, for contributions which are paid (or treated as paid under section 170(a)(2)) in tax years beginning after 12-31-61. Prior to amendment, the sentence following subparagraph (D) read:

"Any contribution made by a corporation in a taxable year to which this section applies in excess of the amount deductible in such year under the foregoing limitation shall be deductible in each of the two succeeding taxable years in order of time, but only to the extent of the lesser of the two following amounts: (i) the excess of the maximum amount deductible for such succeeding taxable year under the foregoing limitation over the contributions made in such year; and (ii) in the case of the first succeeding taxable year the amount of such excess contribution, and in the case of the second succeeding taxable year the portion of such excess contribution not deductible in the first succeeding taxable year."

• 1962 (P.L. 87-858)

P.L. 87-858, §2(a), (b):

Amended Code Sec. 170(b)(1)(A) by deleting "or" at the end of clause (ii), by inserting "or" at the end of clause (iii), and by inserting new clause (iv). Amended Code Sec. 170(b)(1)(B) by substituting "any charitable contributions described in subparagraph (A)" for "any charitable contributions to the organizations described in clauses (i), (ii), and (iii)." **Effective** 1-1-61.

• 1958, Technical Amendments Act of 1958 (P.L. 85-866)

P.L. 85-866, §10(a):

Added the last sentence in Sec. 170(b)(1)(C). **Effective** 1-1-58.

P.L. 85-866, §11:

Added paragraph (3) to Sec. 170(b). **Effective** 1-1-54.

P.L. 85-866, §12:

Added paragraph (4) to Sec. 170(b). **Effective** for tax years ending after 12-31-57, but only with respect to charitable contributions made after that date.

• 1956 (P.L. 1022, 84th Cong.)

P.L. 1022, 84th Cong., §[1]:

Amended Code Sec. 170(b)(1)(A)(iii) by adding after the phrase "section 503(b)(5)" the words "or to medical research organization (referred to in section 503(b)(5)) directly engaged in the continuous active conduct of medical research in conjunction with a hospital, if during the calendar year in which the contribution is made such organization is committed to spend such contributions for such research before January 1 of the fifth calendar year which begins after the date such contribution is made,". **Effective** under Sec. 2 only to tax years beginning after 1955.

[Sec. 170(c)]

(c) CHARITABLE CONTRIBUTION DEFINED.—For purposes of this section, the term "charitable contribution" means a contribution or gift to or for the use of—

(1) A State, a possession of the United States, or any political subdivision of any of the foregoing, or the United States or the District of Columbia, but only if the contribution or gift is made for exclusively public purposes.

(2) A corporation, trust, or community chest, fund, or foundation—

(A) created or organized in the United States or in any possession thereof, or under the law of the United States, any State, the District of Columbia, or any possession of the United States;

(B) organized and operated exclusively for religious, charitable, scientific, literary, or educational purposes, or to foster national or international amateur sports competition (but only if no part of its activities involve the provision of athletic facilities or equipment), or for the prevention of cruelty to children or animals;

(C) no part of the net earnings of which inures to the benefit of any private shareholder or individual; and

(D) which is not disqualified for tax exemption under section 501(c)(3) by reason of attempting to influence legislation, and which does not participate in, or intervene in (including the publishing or distributing of statements), any political campaign on behalf of (or in opposition to) any candidate for public office.

A contribution or gift by a corporation to a trust, chest, fund, or foundation shall be deductible by reason of this paragraph only if it is to be used within the United States or any of its possessions exclusively for purposes specified in subparagraph (B). Rules similar to the rules of section 501(j) shall apply for purposes of this paragraph.

(3) A post or organization of war veterans, or an auxiliary unit or society of, or trust or foundation for, any such post or organization—

(A) organized in the United States or any of its possessions, and

(B) no part of the net earnings of which inures to the benefit of any private shareholder or individual.

(4) In the case of a contribution or gift by an individual, a domestic fraternal society, order, or association, operating under the lodge system, but only if such contribution or gift is to be used exclusively for religious, charitable, scientific, literary, or educational purposes, or for the prevention of cruelty to children or animals.

(5) A cemetery company owned and operated exclusively for the benefit of its members, or any corporation chartered solely for burial purposes as a cemetery corporation and not permitted by its charter to engage in any business not necessarily incident to that purpose, if such company or corporation is not operated for profit and no part of the net earnings of such company or corporation inures to the benefit of any private shareholder or individual.

For purposes of this section, the term "charitable contribution" also means an amount treated under subsection (g) as paid for the use of an organization described in paragraph (2), (3), or (4).

Amendments

• 1987, Revenue Act of 1987 (P.L. 100-203)

P.L. 100-203, §10711(a)(1):

Amended Code Sec. 170(c)(2)(D) by striking out "on behalf of any candidate" and inserting in lieu thereof "on behalf of (or in opposition to) any candidate". **Effective** with respect to activities after 12-22-87.

• 1982, Tax Equity and Fiscal Responsibility Act of 1982 (P.L. 97-248)

P.L. 97-248, §286(b):

Amended Code Sec. 170(c) by adding at the end of paragraph (2) the following sentence: "Rules similar to the rules of section 501(j) shall apply for purposes of this paragraph." **Effective** retroactively, on 10-5-76.

• 1976, Tax Reform Act of 1976 (P.L. 94-455)

P.L. 94-455, §1307(d):

Substituted "which is not disqualified for tax exemption under section 501(c)(3) by reason of attempting to influence legislation," for "no substantial part of the activities of which is carrying on propaganda, or otherwise attempting, to influence legislation" in Code Sec. 170(c)(2)(D). **Effective** for tax years beginning after 12-31-76.

P.L. 94-455, §1313(b):

Added ", or to foster national or international amateur sports competition (but only if no part of its activities involve the provision of athletic facilities or equipment)," after "or educational purposes" in Code Sec. 170(c)(2)(B). **Effective** 10-5-76.

P.L. 94-455, §1901(a)(28):

Substituted "subsection (g)" for "subsection (h)" in the last sentence of Code Sec. 170(c). **Effective** for tax years beginning after 12-31-76.

• 1969, Tax Reform Act of 1969 (P.L. 91-172)

P.L. 91-172, §201(a)(1):

Amended Code Secs. 170(c)(1), 170(c)(2)(A) and 170(c)(2)(D). **Effective** for tax years beginning after 12-31-69. Prior to amendment, these read as follows:

(c) Charitable Contribution Defined.—For purposes of this section, the term "charitable contribution" means a contribution or gift to or for the use of—

(1) A State, a Territory, a possession of the United States, or any political subdivision of any of the foregoing, or the United States or the District of Columbia, but only if the contribution or gift is made for exclusively public purposes.

(2) A corporation, trust, or community chest, fund, or foundation—

(A) created or organized in the United States or in any possession thereof, or under the law of the United States, any State or Territory, the District of Columbia, or any possession of the United States;

* * *

(D) no substantial part of the activities of which is carrying on propaganda, or otherwise attempting, to influence legislation.

• 1960 (P.L. 86-779)

P.L. 86-779, §7(a)(1):

Added the last sentence to Code Sec. 170(c). **Effective** for tax years beginning after 1959.

[Sec. 170(d)]

(d) CARRYOVERS OF EXCESS CONTRIBUTIONS.—

(1) INDIVIDUALS.—

(A) IN GENERAL.—In the case of an individual, if the amount of charitable contributions described in subsection (b)(1)(A) payment of which is made within a taxable year (hereinafter in this paragraph referred to as the "contribution year") exceeds 50 percent of the taxpayer's contribution base for such year, such excess shall be treated as a charitable contribution described in subsection (b)(1)(A) paid in each of the 5 succeeding taxable years in order of time, but, with respect to any such succeeding taxable year, only to the extent of the lesser of the two following amounts:

(i) the amount by which 50 percent of the taxpayer's contribution base for such succeeding taxable year exceeds the sum of the charitable contributions described in subsection (b)(1)(A) payment of which is made by the taxpayer within such succeeding taxable year (determined without regard to this subparagraph) and the charitable contributions described in subsection (b)(1)(A) payment of which was made in taxable years before the contribution year which are treated under this subparagraph as having been paid in such succeeding taxable year; or

(ii) in the case of the first succeeding taxable year, the amount of such excess, and in the case of the second, third, fourth, or fifth succeeding taxable year, the portion of such excess not treated under this subparagraph as a charitable contribution described in subsection (b)(1)(A) paid in any taxable year intervening between the contribution year and such succeeding taxable year.

(B) SPECIAL RULE FOR NET OPERATING LOSS CARRYOVERS.—In applying subparagraph (A), the excess determined under subparagraph (A) for the contribution year shall be reduced to the extent that such excess reduces taxable income (as computed for purposes of the second sentence of section 172(b)(2)) and increases the net operating loss deduction for a taxable year succeeding the contribution year.

(2) CORPORATIONS.—

(A) IN GENERAL.—Any contribution made by a corporation in a taxable year (hereinafter in this paragraph referred to as the "contribution year") in excess of the amount deductible for such year under subsection (b)(2)(A) shall be deductible for each of the 5 succeeding taxable years in order of time, but only to the extent of the lesser of the two following amounts: (i) the excess of the maximum amount deductible for such succeeding taxable year under subsection (b)(2)(A) over the sum of the contributions made in such year plus the aggregate of the excess contributions which were made in taxable years before the contribution year and which are deductible under this subparagraph for such succeeding taxable year; or (ii) in the case of the first succeeding taxable year, the amount of such excess contribution, and in the case of the second, third, fourth, or fifth succeeding taxable year, the portion of such excess contribution not deductible under this subparagraph for any taxable year intervening between the contribution year and such succeeding taxable year.

(B) SPECIAL RULE FOR NET OPERATING LOSS CARRYOVERS.—For purposes of subparagraph (A), the excess of—

(i) the contributions made by a corporation in a taxable year to which this section applies, over

(ii) the amount deductible in such year under the limitation in subsection (b)(2)(A),

shall be reduced to the extent that such excess reduces taxable income (as computed for purposes of the second sentence of section 172(b)(2)) and increases a net operating loss carryover under section 172 to a succeeding taxable year.

Amendments

• 2006, Pension Protection Act of 2006 (P.L. 109-280)

P.L. 109-280, §1206(b)(1):

Amended Code Sec. 170(d)(2) by striking "subsection (b)(2)" each place it appears and inserting "subsection (b)(2)(A)". **Effective** for contributions made in tax years beginning after 12-31-2005.

• 1976, Tax Reform Act of 1976 (P.L. 94-455)

P.L. 94-455, §1901(a)(28):

Amended Code Sec. 170(d)(1)(A) by striking out "(30 percent, in the case of a contribution year beginning before January 1, 1970)" after "50 percent". **Effective** for tax years beginning after 12-31-76.

• 1969, Tax Reform Act of 1969 (P.L. 91-172)

P.L. 91-172, §201(a)(1):

Redesignated old Sec. 170(d) as Sec. 170(h) and added new Sec. 170(d). For purposes of applying section 170(d) (as amended by subsection (a)) with respect to contributions paid in a taxable year beginning before 1-1-70, subsection (b)(1)(D), subsection (e), and paragraphs (1), (2), (3), and (4) of subsection (f) of section 170 of such Code shall not apply.

[Sec. 170(e)]

(e) CERTAIN CONTRIBUTIONS OF ORDINARY INCOME AND CAPITAL GAIN PROPERTY.—

(1) GENERAL RULE.—The amount of any charitable contribution of property otherwise taken into account under this section shall be reduced by the sum of—

(A) the amount of gain which would not have been long-term capital gain (determined without regard to section 1221(b)(3)) if the property contributed had been sold by the taxpayer at its fair market value (determined at the time of such contribution), and

(B) in the case of a charitable contribution—

(i) of tangible personal property—

(I) if the use by the donee is unrelated to the purpose or function constituting the basis for its exemption under section 501 (or, in the case of a governmental unit, to any purpose or function described in subsection (c)), or

(II) which is applicable property (as defined in paragraph (7)(C), but without regard to clause (ii) thereof) which is sold, exchanged, or otherwise disposed of by the donee before the last day of the taxable year in which the contribution was made and with respect to which the donee has not made a certification in accordance with paragraph (7)(D),

(ii) to or for the use of a private foundation (as defined in section 509(a)), other than a private foundation described in subsection (b)(1)(F),

(iii) of any patent, copyright (other than a copyright described in section 1221(a)(3) or 1231(b)(1)(C)), trademark, trade name, trade secret, know-how, software (other than software described in section 197(e)(3)(A)(i)), or similar property, or applications or registrations of such property, or

(iv) of any taxidermy property which is contributed by the person who prepared, stuffed, or mounted the property or by any person who paid or incurred the cost of such preparation, stuffing, or mounting,

the amount of gain which would have been long-term capital gain if the property contributed had been sold by the taxpayer at its fair market value (determined at the time of such contribution).

→→ *Caution: The flush text of Code Sec. 170(e)(1), below, is subject to the sunset provision of the Economic Growth and Tax Relief Reconciliation Act of 2001 (P.L. 107-16), §901. Absent Congressional action, the changes made to this provision by P.L. 107-16, or that take effect as if included in P.L. 107-16, do not apply after December 31, 2010. For more information about the sunset provision, see page XXI of the Preface to this publication and P.L. 107-16, §901, in the amendment notes. See the amendments notes for a history of amendments to this section and the effective date of each change.*

For purposes of applying this paragraph (other than in the case of gain to which section 617(d)(1), 1245(a), 1250(a), 1252(a), or 1254(a) applies), property which is property used in the trade or business (as defined in section 1231(b)) shall be treated as a capital asset. For purposes of applying this paragraph in the case of a charitable contribution of stock in an S corporation, rules similar to the rules of section 751 shall apply in determining whether gain on such stock would have been long-term capital gain if such stock were sold by the taxpayer. For purposes of this paragraph, the determination of whether property is a capital asset shall be made without regard to the exception contained in section 1221(a)(3)(C) for basis determined under section 1022.

(2) ALLOCATION OF BASIS.—For purposes of paragraph (1), in the case of a charitable contribution of less than the taxpayer's entire interest in the property contributed, the taxpayer's adjusted basis in such property shall be allocated between the interest contributed and any interest not contributed in accordance with regulations prescribed by the Secretary.

(3) SPECIAL RULE FOR CERTAIN CONTRIBUTIONS OF INVENTORY AND OTHER PROPERTY.—

(A) QUALIFIED CONTRIBUTIONS.—For purposes of this paragraph, a qualified contribution shall mean a charitable contribution of property described in paragraph (1) or (2) of section 1221(a), by a corporation (other than a corporation which is an S corporation) to an organization which is described in section 501(c)(3) and is exempt under section 501(a) (other than a private foundation, as defined in section 509(a), which is not an operating foundation, as defined in section 4942(j)(3)), but only if—

(i) the use of the property by the donee is related to the purpose or function constituting the basis for its exemption under section 501 and the property is to be used by the donee solely for the care of the ill, the needy, or infants;

(ii) the property is not transferred by the donee in exchange for money, other property, or services;

(iii) the taxpayer receives from the donee a written statement representing that its use and disposition of the property will be in accordance with the provisions of clauses (i) and (ii); and

(iv) in the case where the property is subject to regulation under the Federal Food, Drug, and Cosmetic Act, as amended, such property must fully satisfy the applicable requirements of such Act and regulations promulgated thereunder on the date of transfer and for one hundred and eighty days prior thereto.

(B) AMOUNT OF REDUCTION.—The reduction under paragraph (1)(A) for any qualified contribution (as defined in subparagraph (A)) shall be no greater than the sum of—

(i) one-half of the amount computed under paragraph (1)(A) (computed without regard to this paragraph), and

(ii) the amount (if any) by which the charitable contribution deduction under this section for any qualified contribution (computed by taking into account the amount determined in clause (i), but without regard to this clause) exceeds twice the basis of such property.

(C) SPECIAL RULE FOR CONTRIBUTIONS OF FOOD INVENTORY.—

(i) GENERAL RULE.—In the case of a charitable contribution of food from any trade or business of the taxpayer, this paragraph shall be applied—

(I) without regard to whether the contribution is made by a C corporation, and

(II) only to food that is apparently wholesome food.

(ii) LIMITATION.—In the case of a taxpayer other than a C corporation, the aggregate amount of such contributions for any taxable year which may be taken into account under this section shall not exceed 10 percent of the taxpayer's aggregate net income for such taxable year from all trades or businesses from which such contributions were made for such year, computed without regard to this section.

(iii) APPARENTLY WHOLESOME FOOD.—For purposes of this subparagraph, the term "apparently wholesome food" has the meaning given to such term by section 22(b)(2) of the Bill Emerson Good Samaritan Food Donation Act (42 U.S.C. 1791(b)(2)), as in effect on the date of the enactment of this subparagraph.

(iv) TERMINATION.—This subparagraph shall not apply to contributions made after December 31, 2009.

(D) SPECIAL RULE FOR CONTRIBUTIONS OF BOOK INVENTORY TO PUBLIC SCHOOLS.—

(i) CONTRIBUTIONS OF BOOK INVENTORY.—In determining whether a qualified book contribution is a qualified contribution, subparagraph (A) shall be applied without regard to whether the donee is an organization described in the matter preceding clause (i) of subparagraph (A).

(ii) QUALIFIED BOOK CONTRIBUTION.—For purposes of this paragraph, the term "qualified book contribution" means a charitable contribution of books to a public school which is an educational organization described in subsection (b)(1)(A)(ii) and which provides elementary education or secondary education (kindergarten through grade 12).

(iii) CERTIFICATION BY DONEE.—Subparagraph (A) shall not apply to any contribution of books unless (in addition to the certifications required by subparagraph (A) (as modified by this subparagraph))), the donee certifies in writing that—

(I) the books are suitable, in terms of currency, content, and quantity, for use in the donee's educational programs, and

(II) the donee will use the books in its educational programs.

(iv) TERMINATION.—This subparagraph shall not apply to contributions made after December 31, 2009.

(E) This paragraph shall not apply to so much of the amount of the gain described in paragraph (1)(A) which would be long-term capital gain but for the application of sections 617, 1245, 1250, or 1252.

(4) SPECIAL RULE FOR CONTRIBUTIONS OF SCIENTIFIC PROPERTY USED FOR RESEARCH.—

(A) LIMIT ON REDUCTION.—In the case of a qualified research contribution, the reduction under paragraph (1)(A) shall be no greater than the amount determined under paragraph (3)(B).

(B) QUALIFIED RESEARCH CONTRIBUTIONS.—For purposes of this paragraph, the term "qualified research contribution" means a charitable contribution by a corporation of tangible personal property described in paragraph (1) of section 1221(a), but only if—

(i) the contribution is to an organization described in subparagraph (A) or subparagraph (B) of section 41(e)(6),

(ii) the property is constructed or assembled by the taxpayer,

(iii) the contribution is made not later than 2 years after the date the construction or assembly of the property is substantially completed,

(iv) the original use of the property is by the donee,

(v) the property is scientific equipment or apparatus substantially all of the use of which by the donee is for research or experimentation (within the meaning of section 174), or for research training, in the United States in physical or biological sciences,

(vi) the property is not transferred by the donee in exchange for money, other property, or services, and

(vii) the taxpayer receives from the donee a written statement representing that its use and disposition of the property will be in accordance with the provisions of clauses (v) and (vi).

(C) CONSTRUCTION OF PROPERTY BY TAXPAYER.—For purposes of this paragraph, property shall be treated as constructed by the taxpayer only if the cost of the parts used in the construction of such property (other than parts manufactured by the taxpayer or a related person) do not exceed 50 percent of the taxpayer's basis in such property.

(D) CORPORATION.—For purposes of this paragraph, the term "corporation" shall not include—

(i) an S corporation,

(ii) a personal holding company (as defined in section 542), and

(iii) a service organization (as defined in section 414(m)(3)).

(5) SPECIAL RULE FOR CONTRIBUTIONS OF STOCK FOR WHICH MARKET QUOTATIONS ARE READILY AVAILABLE.—

(A) IN GENERAL.—Subparagraph (B)(ii) of paragraph (1) shall not apply to any contribution of qualified appreciated stock.

(B) QUALIFIED APPRECIATED STOCK.—Except as provided in subparagraph (C), for purposes of this paragraph, the term "qualified appreciated stock" means any stock of a corporation—

(i) for which (as of the date of the contribution) market quotations are readily available on an established securities market, and

(ii) which is capital gain property (as defined in subsection (b)(1)(C)(iv)).

(C) DONOR MAY NOT CONTRIBUTE MORE THAN 10 PERCENT OF STOCK OF CORPORATION.—

(i) IN GENERAL.—In the case of any donor, the term "qualified appreciated stock" shall not include any stock of a corporation contributed by the donor in a contribution to which paragraph (1)(B)(ii) applies (determined without regard to this paragraph) to the extent that the amount of the stock so contributed (when increased by the aggregate amount of all prior such contributions by the donor of stock in such corporation) exceeds 10 percent (in value) of all of the outstanding stock of such corporation.

(ii) SPECIAL RULE.—For purposes of clause (i), an individual shall be treated as making all contributions made by any member of his family (as defined in section 267(c)(4)).

(6) SPECIAL RULE FOR CONTRIBUTIONS OF COMPUTER TECHNOLOGY AND EQUIPMENT FOR EDUCATIONAL PURPOSES.—

(A) LIMIT ON REDUCTION.—In the case of a qualified computer contribution, the reduction under paragraph (1)(A) shall be no greater than the amount determined under paragraph (3)(B).

(B) QUALIFIED COMPUTER CONTRIBUTION.—For purposes of this paragraph, the term "qualified computer contribution" means a charitable contribution by a corporation of any computer technology or equipment, but only if—

(i) the contribution is to—

(I) an educational organization described in subsection (b)(1)(A)(ii),

(II) an entity described in section 501(c)(3) and exempt from tax under section 501(a) (other than an entity described in subclause (I)) that is organized primarily for purposes of supporting elementary and secondary education, or

(III) a public library (within the meaning of section 213(2)(A) of the Library Services and Technology Act (20 U.S.C. 9122(2)(A)), as in effect on the date of the enactment of the Community Renewal Tax Relief Act of 2000), established and maintained by an entity described in subsection (c)(1),

(ii) the contribution is made not later than 3 years after the date the taxpayer acquired the property (or in the case of property constructed or assembled by the taxpayer, the date the construction or assembling of the property is substantially completed),

(iii) the original use of the property is by the donor or the donee,

(iv) substantially all of the use of the property by the donee is for use within the United States for educational purposes that are related to the purpose or function of the donee,

(v) the property is not transferred by the donee in exchange for money, other property, or services, except for shipping, installation and transfer costs,

(vi) the property will fit productively into the donee's education plan,

(vii) the donee's use and disposition of the property will be in accordance with the provisions of clauses (iv) and (v), and

(viii) the property meets such standards, if any, as the Secretary may prescribe by regulation to assure that the property meets minimum functionality and suitability standards for educational purposes.

(C) CONTRIBUTION TO PRIVATE FOUNDATION.—A contribution by a corporation of any computer technology or equipment to a private foundation (as defined in section 509) shall be treated as a qualified computer contribution for purposes of this paragraph if—

(i) the contribution to the private foundation satisfies the requirements of clauses (ii) and (v) of subparagraph (B), and

(ii) within 30 days after such contribution, the private foundation—

(I) contributes the property to a donee described in clause (i) of subparagraph (B) that satisfies the requirements of clauses (iv) through (vii) of subparagraph (B), and

(II) notifies the donor of such contribution.

(D) DONATIONS OF PROPERTY REACQUIRED BY MANUFACTURER.—In the case of property which is reacquired by the person who constructed or assembled the property—

(i) subparagraph (B)(ii) shall be applied to a contribution of such property by such person by taking into account the date that the original construction or assembly of the property was substantially completed, and

(ii) subparagraph (B)(iii) shall not apply to such contribution.

(E) SPECIAL RULE RELATING TO CONSTRUCTION OF PROPERTY.—For the purposes of this paragraph, the rules of paragraph (4)(C) shall apply.

(F) DEFINITIONS.—For the purposes of this paragraph—

(i) COMPUTER TECHNOLOGY OR EQUIPMENT.—The term "computer technology or equipment" means computer software (as defined by section 197(e)(3)(B)), computer or peripheral equipment (as defined by section 168(i)(2)(B)), and fiber optic cable related to computer use.

(ii) CORPORATION.—The term "corporation" has the meaning given to such term by paragraph (4)(D).

(G) TERMINATION.—This paragraph shall not apply to any contribution made during any taxable year beginning after December 31, 2009.

(7) RECAPTURE OF DEDUCTION ON CERTAIN DISPOSITIONS OF EXEMPT USE PROPERTY.—

(A) IN GENERAL.—In the case of an applicable disposition of applicable property, there shall be included in the income of the donor of such property for the taxable year of such donor in which the applicable disposition occurs an amount equal to the excess (if any) of—

(i) the amount of the deduction allowed to the donor under this section with respect to such property, over

(ii) the donor's basis in such property at the time such property was contributed.

(B) APPLICABLE DISPOSITION.—For purposes of this paragraph, the term "applicable disposition" means any sale, exchange, or other disposition by the donee of applicable property—

(i) after the last day of the taxable year of the donor in which such property was contributed, and

(ii) before the last day of the 3-year period beginning on the date of the contribution of such property,

unless the donee makes a certification in accordance with subparagraph (D).

(C) APPLICABLE PROPERTY.—For purposes of this paragraph, the term "applicable property" means charitable deduction property (as defined in section 6050L(a)(2)(A))—

(i) which is tangible personal property the use of which is identified by the donee as related to the purpose or function constituting the basis of the donee's exemption under section 501, and

(ii) for which a deduction in excess of the donor's basis is allowed.

(D) CERTIFICATION.—A certification meets the requirements of this subparagraph if it is a written statement which is signed under penalty of perjury by an officer of the donee organization and—

(i) which—

(I) certifies that the use of the property by the donee was substantial and related to the purpose or function constituting the basis for the donee's exemption under section 501, and

(II) describes how the property was used and how such use furthered such purpose or function, or

(ii) which—

(I) states the intended use of the property by the donee at the time of the contribution, and

(II) certifies that such intended use has become impossible or infeasible to implement.

Amendments

• 2008, Tax Extenders and Alternative Minimum Tax Relief Act of 2008 (P.L. 110-343)

P.L. 110-343, Division C, §321(a):

Amended Code Sec. 170(e)(6)(G) by striking "December 31, 2007" and inserting "December 31, 2009". **Effective** for contributions made during tax years beginning after 12-31-2007.

P.L. 110-343, Division C, §323(a)(1):

Amended Code Sec. 170(e)(3)(C)(iv) by striking "December 31, 2007" and inserting "December 31, 2009". **Effective** for contributions made after 12-31-2007.

P.L. 110-343, Division C, §324(a):

Amended Code Sec. 170(e)(3)(D)(iv) by striking "December 31, 2007" and inserting "December 31, 2009". **Effective** for contributions made after 12-31-2007.

P.L. 110-343, Division C, §324(b):

Amended Code Sec. 170(e)(3)(D)(iii) by inserting "of books" after "to any contribution". **Effective** for contributions made after 12-31-2007.

• 2007, Tax Technical Corrections Act of 2007 (P.L. 110-172)

P.L. 110-172, §3(c):

Amended Code Sec. 170(e)(7)(D)(i)(I) by striking "related" and inserting "substantial and related". **Effective** as if included in the provision of the Pension Protection Act of 2006 (P.L. 109-280) to which it relates [**effective** for contributions after 9-1-2006.—CCH].

P.L. 110-172, §11(a)(14)(B):

Amended Code Sec. 170(e)(1)(B)(ii) by striking "subsection (b)(1)(E)" and inserting "subsection (b)(1)(F)". **Effective** 12-29-2007.

P.L. 110-172, §11(a)(15):

Amended Code Sec. 170(e)(1)(B)(i)(II) by inserting ", but without regard to clause (ii) thereof" after "paragraph (7)(C)". **Effective** 12-29-2007.

• 2006, Tax Relief and Health Care Act of 2006 (P.L. 109-432)

P.L. 109-432, Division A, §116(a)(1):

Amended Code Sec. 170(e)(6)(G) by striking "2005" and inserting "2007". **Effective** for contributions made in tax years beginning after 12-31-2005.

P.L. 109-432, Division A, §116(b)(1)(A):

Amended Code Sec. 170(e)(4)(B)(ii) by inserting "or assembled" after "constructed". **Effective** for tax years beginning after 12-31-2005.

P.L. 109-432, Division A, §116(b)(1)(B):

Amended Code Sec. 170(e)(4)(B)(iii) by inserting "or assembly" after "construction". **Effective** for tax years beginning after 12-31-2005.

P.L. 109-432, Division A, §116(b)(2)(A):

Amended Code Sec. 170(e)(6)(B)(ii) by inserting "or assembled" after "constructed" and "or assembling" after "construction". **Effective** for tax years beginning after 12-31-2005.

P.L. 109-432, Division A, §116(b)(2)(B):

Amended Code Sec. 170(e)(6)(D) by inserting "or assembled" after "constructed" and "or assembly" after "construction". **Effective** for tax years beginning after 12-31-2005.

• 2006, Pension Protection Act of 2006 (P.L. 109-280)

P.L. 109-280, §1202(a):

Amended Code Sec. 170(e)(3)(C)(iv) by striking "2005" and inserting "2007". **Effective** for contributions made after 12-31-2005.

P.L. 109-280, §1204(a):

Amended Code Sec. 170(e)(3)(D)(iv) by striking "2005" and inserting "2007". **Effective** for contributions made after 12-31-2005.

P.L. 109-280, §1214(a):

Amended Code Sec. 170(e)(1)(B) by striking "or" at the end of clause (ii), by inserting "or" at the end of clause (iii), and by inserting after clause (iii) a new clause (iv). **Effective** for contributions made after 7-25-2006.

P.L. 109-280, §1215(a)(1):

Amended Code Sec. 170(e)(1)(B)(i). **Effective** for contributions after 9-1-2006. Prior to amendment, Code Sec. 170(e)(1)(B)(i) read as follows:

(i) of tangible personal property, if the use by the donee is unrelated to the purpose or function constituting the basis for its exemption under section 501 (or, in the case of a governmental unit, to any purpose or function described in subsection (c)),

P.L. 109-280, §1215(a)(2):

Amended Code Sec. 170(e) by adding at the end a new paragraph (7). **Effective** for contributions after 9-1-2006.

• 2006, Tax Increase Prevention and Reconciliation Act of 2005 (P.L. 109-222)

P.L. 109-222, §204(b):

Amended Code Sec. 170(e)(1)(A) by inserting "(determined without regard to section 1221(b)(3))" after "long-term capital gain". **Effective** for sales and exchanges in tax years beginning after 5-17-2006.

• 2005, Katrina Emergency Tax Relief Act of 2005 (P.L. 109-73)

P.L. 109-73, §305(a):

Amended Code Sec. 170(e)(3) by redesignating subparagraph (C) as subparagraph (D) and by inserting after subparagraph (B) a new subparagraph (C). **Effective** for contributions made on or after 8-28-2005, in tax years ending after such date.

P.L. 109-73, §306(a):

Amended Code Sec. 170(e)(3), as amended by Act Sec. 305, by redesignating subparagraph (D) as subparagraph (E) and by inserting after subparagraph (C) a new subparagraph (D). **Effective** for contributions made on or after 8-28-2005, in tax years ending after such date.

• 2004, American Jobs Creation Act of 2004 (P.L. 108-357)

P.L. 108-357, §882(a):

Amended Code Sec. 170(e)(1)(B) by striking "or" at the end of clause (i), by adding "or" at the end of clause (ii), and by inserting after clause (ii) a new clause (iii). **Effective** for contributions made after 6-3-2004.

• 2004, Working Families Tax Relief Act of 2004 (P.L. 108-311)

P.L. 108-311, §306(a):

Amended Code Sec. 170(e)(6)(G) by striking "2003" and inserting "2005". **Effective** for contributions made in tax years beginning after 12-31-2003.

• 2002, Job Creation and Worker Assistance Act of 2002 (P.L. 107-147)

P.L. 107-147, §417(7):

Amended Code Sec. 170(e)(6)(B)(i)(III) by striking "2000," and inserting"2000),". **Effective** 3-9-2002.

P.L. 107-147, §417(22), provides:

(22) The amendment to section 170(e)(6)(B)(iv) made by section 165(b)(1) of the Community Renewal Tax Relief Act of 2000 (114 Stat. 2763A-626) shall be applied as if it struck "in any of the grades K-12".

• 2001, Economic Growth and Tax Relief Reconciliation Act of 2001 (P.L. 107-16)

P.L. 107-16, §542(e)(2)(B):

Amended Code Sec. 170(e)(1) by adding at the end a new sentence. **Effective** for estates of decedents dying after 12-31-2009.

P.L. 107-16, §901(a)-(b), provides:

SEC. 901. SUNSET OF PROVISIONS OF ACT.

(a) IN GENERAL.—All provisions of, and amendments made by, this Act shall not apply—

(1) to taxable, plan, or limitation years beginning after December 31, 2010, or

(2) in the case of title V, to estates of decedents dying, gifts made, or generation skipping transfers, after December 31, 2010.

(b) APPLICATION OF CERTAIN LAWS.—The Internal Revenue Code of 1986 and the Employee Retirement Income Security Act of 1974 shall be applied and administered to years, estates, gifts, and transfers described in subsection (a) as if the provisions and amendments described in subsection (a) had never been enacted.

• 2000, Community Renewal Tax Relief Act of 2000 (P.L. 106-554)

P.L. 106-554, §165(a)(1):

Amended Code Sec. 170(e)(6) by striking "qualified elementary or secondary educational contribution" each place it occurs in the headings and text and inserting "qualified computer contribution". **Effective** for contributions made after 12-31-2000.

P.L. 106-554, §165(a)(2):

Amended Code Sec. 170(e)(6)(B)(i) by striking "or" at the end of subclause (I), by adding "or" at the end of subclause (II), and by inserting after subclause (II) a new subclause (III). **Effective** for contributions made after 12-31-2000.

P.L. 106-554, §165(a)(3):

Amended Code Sec. 170(e)(6)(B)(ii) by striking "2 years" and inserting "3 years". **Effective** for contributions made after 12-31-2000.

P.L. 106-554, §165(b)(1):

Amended Code Sec. 170(e)(6)(B)(iv) by striking "in any grades of the K-12" following "educational purposes". **Effective** for contributions made after 12-31-2000. [But see P.L. 107-147, §417(22).—CCH.]

P.L. 106-554, §165(b)(2):

Amended the heading of Code Sec. 170(e)(6) by striking "ELEMENTARY OR SECONDARY SCHOOL PURPOSES" and inserting

"EDUCATIONAL PURPOSES". E ffective for contributions made after 12-31-2000.

P.L. 106-554, §165(c):

Amended Code Sec. 170(e)(6)(F) by striking "December 31, 2000" and inserting "December 31, 2003". **Effective** for contributions made after 12-31-2000.

P.L. 106-554, §165(d):

Amended Code Sec. 170(e)(6)(B) by striking "and" at the end of clause (vi), by striking the period at the end of clause (vii) and inserting ", and", and by adding at the end a new clause (viii). **Effective** for contributions made after 12-31-2000.

P.L. 106-554, §165(e):

Amended Code Sec. 170(e)(6) by redesignating subparagraphs (D), (E), and (F) as subparagraphs (E), (F), and (G), respectively, and by inserting after subparagraph (C) a new subparagraph (D). **Effective** for contributions made after 12-31-2000.

• 1999, Tax Relief Extension Act of 1999 (P.L. 106-170)

P.L. 106-170, §532(c)(1)(A):

Amended Code Sec. 170(e)(3)(A) by striking "section 1221" and inserting "section 1221(a)". **Effective** for any instrument held, acquired, or entered into, any transaction entered into, and supplies held or acquired on or after 12-17-99.

P.L. 106-170, §532(c)(1)(B):

Amended Code Sec. 170(e)(4)(B) by striking "section 1221" and inserting "section 1221(a)". **Effective** for any instrument held, acquired, or entered into, any transaction entered into, and supplies held or acquired on or after 12-17-99.

• 1998, Tax and Trade Relief Extension Act of 1998 (P.L. 105-277)

P.L. 105-277, §1004(a)(1):

Amended Code Sec. 170(e)(5) by striking subparagraph (D). **Effective** for contributions made after 6-30-98. Prior to amendment, Code Sec. 170(e)(5)(D) read as follows:

(D) TERMINATION.—This paragraph shall not apply to contributions made—

(i) after December 31, 1994, and before July 1, 1996, or

(ii) after June 30, 1998.

• 1998, IRS Restructuring and Reform Act of 1998 (P.L. 105-206)

P.L. 105-206, §6004(e)(1):

Amended Code Sec. 170(e)(6)(B)(vi) and (vii) by striking "entity's" and inserting "donee's". **Effective** as if included in the provision of P.L. 105-34 to which it relates [**effective** for tax years beginning after 12-31-97.—CCH].

P.L. 105-206, §6004(e)(2):

Amended Code Sec. 170(e)(6)(B)(iv) by striking "organization or entity" and inserting "donee". **Effective** as if included in the provision of P.L. 105-34 to which it relates [**effective** for tax years beginning after 12-31-97.—CCH].

P.L. 105-206, §6004(e)(3):

Amended Code Sec. 170(e)(6)(C)(ii)(I) by striking "an entity" and inserting "a donee". **Effective** as if included in the provision of P.L. 105-34 to which it relates [**effective** for tax years beginning after 12-31-97.—CCH].

P.L. 105-206, §6004(e)(4):

Amended Code Sec. 170(e)(6)(F) by striking "1999" and inserting "2000". **Effective** as if included in the provision of P.L. 105-34 to which it relates [**effective** for tax years beginning after 12-31-97.—CCH].

• 1997, Taxpayer Relief Act of 1997 (P.L. 105-34)

P.L. 105-34, §224(a):

Amended Code Sec. 170(e) by adding a new paragraph (6). **Effective** for tax years beginning after 12-31-97.

P.L. 105-34, §602(a):

Amended Code Sec. 170(e)(5)(D)(ii) by striking "May 31, 1997" and inserting "June 30, 1998". **Effective** for contributions made after 5-31-97.

• 1996, Small Business Job Protection Act of 1996 (P.L. 104-188)

P.L. 104-188, §1206(a):

Amended Code Sec. 170(e)(5)(D). **Effective** for contributions made after 6-30-96. Prior to amendment, Code Sec. 170(e)(5)(D) read as follows:

(D) TERMINATION.—This paragraph shall not apply to contributions made after December 31, 1994.

P.L. 104-188, §1316(b):

Amended Code Sec. 170(e)(1) by adding at the end a new sentence. **Effective** for tax years beginning after 12-31-97.

• 1986, Tax Reform Act of 1986 (P.L. 99-514)

P.L. 99-514, §231(f):

Amended Code Sec. 170(e)(4)(B)(i). **Effective** for tax years beginning after 12-31-85. Prior to amendment, Code Sec. 170(e)(4)(B)(i) read as follows:

(i) the contribution is to an educational organization which is described in subsection (b)(1)(A)(ii) of this section and which is an institution of higher education (as defined in section 3304(f)),

P.L. 99-514, §301(b)(2):

Amended Code Sec. 170(e)(1) by striking out "40 percent ($^{28}/_{46}$ in the case of a corporation) of". **Effective** for tax years beginning after 12-31-86. Prior to amendment, Code Sec. 170(e)(1) read as follows:

(1) GENERAL RULE.—The amount of any charitable contribution of property otherwise taken into account under this section shall be reduced by the sum of—

(A) the amount of gain which would not have been long-term capital gain if the property contributed had been sold by the taxpayer at its fair market value (determined at the time of such contribution), and

(B) in the case of a charitable contribution—

(i) of tangible personal property, if the use by the donee is unrelated to the purpose or function constituting the basis for its exemption under section 501 (or, in the case of a governmental unit, to any purpose or function described in subsection (c)), or

(ii) to or for the use of a private foundation (as defined in section 509(a)), other than a private foundation described in subsection (b)(1)(E),

40 percent ($^{28}/_{46}$ in the case of a corporation) of the amount of gain which would have been long-term capital gain if the property contributed had been sold by the taxpayer at its fair market value (determined at the time of such contribution).

For purposes of applying this paragraph (other than in the case of gain to which section 617(d)(1), 1245(a), 1250(a), 1252(a), or 1254(a) applies), property which is property used in the trade or business (as defined in section 1231(b)) shall be treated as a capital asset.

• 1984, Deficit Reduction Act of 1984 (P.L. 98-369)

P.L. 98-369, §301(b):

Amended Code Sec. 170(e) by adding new paragraph (5). **Effective** for contributions made after 7-18-84, in tax years ending after such date.

P.L. 98-369, §301(c)(2)(C):

Amended Code Sec. 170(e)(1)(B)(ii) by striking out "subsection (b)(1)(D)" and inserting in lieu thereof "subsection (b)(1)(E)". **Effective** for contributions made in tax years ending after 7-18-84.

P.L. 98-369, §492(b)(1)(A):

Amended the second sentence of Code Sec. 170(e)(1) by striking out "1251(c),". **Effective** for tax years beginning after 12-31-83.

P.L. 98-369, §492(b)(1)(B):

Amended Code Sec. 170(e)(3)(C) by striking out "1251,". **Effective** for tax years beginning after 12-31-83.

• 1982, Subchapter S Revision Act of 1982 (P.L. 97-354)

P.L. 97-354, §5(a)(21)(A):

Amended Code Sec. 170(e)(3)(A) by striking out "an electing small business corporation within the meaning of section 1371(b))" and inserting in lieu thereof "an S corporation)". **Effective** for tax years beginning after 12-31-82.

P.L. 97-354, §5(a)(21)(B):

Amended Code Sec. 170(e)(4)(D)(i). **Effective** for tax years beginning after 12-31-82. Prior to amendment, it read as follows:

"(i) an electing small business corporation (as defined in section 1371(b)),"

• 1981, Economic Recovery Tax Act of 1981 (P.L. 97-34)

P.L. 97-34, §222(a):

Added Code Sec. 170(e)(4). **Effective** for charitable contributions made after 8-13-81, in tax years ending after such date.

• 1978, Revenue Act of 1978 (P.L. 95-600)

P.L. 95-600, §402(b)(2):

Amended Code Sec. 170(e)(1)(B) by striking out "50 percent" and inserting in lieu thereof "40 percent". **Effective** for contributions made after 10-31-78.

P.L. 95-600, §403(c)(1):

Amended Code Sec. 170(e)(1)(B) by striking out "62½ percent" and inserting in lieu thereof "28/46". **Effective** for gifts made after 12-31-78.

• 1976, Tax Reform Act of 1976 (P.L. 94-455)

P.L. 94-455, §205(c):

Substituted "1252(a), or 1254(a)" for "or 1252(a)" in Code Sec. 170(e)(1). **Effective** for tax years ending after 12-31-75.

P.L. 94-455, §1901(a)(28):

Substituted "subsection (b)(1)(D)" for "subsection (b)(1)(E)" in Code Sec. 170(e)(1)(B)(ii). **Effective** for tax years ending after 12-31-76.

P.L. 94-455, §1906(b)(13)(A):

Amended 1954 Code by substituting "Secretary" for "Secretary or his delegate" each place it appeared. **Effective** 2-1-77.

P.L. 94-455, §2135(a):

Added Code Sec. 170(e)(3). **Effective** for charitable contributions made after 10-4-76, in tax years ending after 10-4-76.

• 1969, Tax Reform Act of 1969 (P.L. 91-172)

P.L. 91-172, §201(a)(1):

Amended Code Sec. 170(e). **Effective** for contributions paid after 12-31-69, except that, with respect to a letter or memorandum or similar property described in section 1221(3) of such Code (as amended by section 514 of P.L. 91-172), subsection (e) shall apply to contributions paid after 7-25-69. Prior to amendment, Code Sec. 170(e) read as follows:

"(e) Special Rule for Charitable Contributions of Certain Property.—The amount of any charitable contribution taken into account under this section shall be reduced by the amount which would have been treated as gain to which section 617(d)(1), 1245(a), or 1250(a) applies if the property contributed had been sold at its fair market value (determined at the time of such contribution)."

• 1966 (P.L. 89-570)

P.L. 89-570, §[1(b)]:

Amended Code Sec. 170(e) by substituting "section 617(d)(1), 1245(a)," for "section 1245(a)", **Effective** for tax years ending after 9-12-66, but only for expenditures paid or incurred after that date.

• 1964, Revenue Act of 1964 (P.L. 88-272)

P.L. 88-272, §231(b)(1):

Amended Code Sec. 170(e) to substitute the heading "Certain Property" for "Section 1245 Property", and substituted "section 1245(a) or 1250(a)" for "section 1245(a)". **Effective** for dispositions after 12-31-63, in tax years ending after such date.

• 1962, Revenue Act of 1962 (P.L. 87-834)

P.L. 87-834, §13(d):

Redesignated Code Sec. 170(e) and (f) as Code Sec. 170(f) and (g) and added new Code Sec. 170(e). **Effective** for tax years beginning after 12-31-62.

[Sec. 170(f)]

(f) DISALLOWANCE OF DEDUCTION IN CERTAIN CASES AND SPECIAL RULES.—

(1) IN GENERAL.—No deduction shall be allowed under this section for a contribution to or for the use of an organization or trust described in section 508(d) or 4948(c)(4) subject to the conditions specified in such sections.

(2) CONTRIBUTIONS OF PROPERTY PLACED IN TRUST.—

(A) REMAINDER INTEREST.—In the case of property transferred in trust, no deduction shall be allowed under this section for the value of a contribution of a remainder interest unless the trust is a charitable remainder annuity trust or a charitable remainder unitrust (described in section 664), or a pooled income fund (described in section 642(c)(5)).

(B) INCOME INTERESTS, ETC.—No deduction shall be allowed under this section for the value of any interest in property (other than a remainder interest) transferred in trust unless the interest is in the form of a guaranteed annuity or the trust instrument specifies that the interest is a fixed percentage distributed yearly of the fair market value of the trust property (to be determined yearly) and the grantor is treated as the owner of such interest for purposes of applying section 671. If the donor ceases to be treated as the owner of such an interest for purposes of applying section 671, at the time the donor ceases to be so treated, the donor shall for purposes of this chapter be considered as having received an amount of income equal to the amount of any deduction he received under this section for the contribution reduced by the discounted value of all amounts of income earned by the trust and taxable to him before the time at which he ceases to be treated as the owner of the interest. Such amounts of income shall be discounted to the date of the contribution. The Secretary shall prescribe such regulations as may be necessary to carry out the purposes of this subparagraph.

(C) DENIAL OF DEDUCTION IN CASE OF PAYMENTS BY CERTAIN TRUSTS.—In any case in which a deduction is allowed under this section for the value of an interest in property described in subparagraph (B), transferred in trust, no deduction shall be allowed under this section to the grantor or any other person for the amount of any contribution made by the trust with respect to such interest.

(D) EXCEPTION.—This paragraph shall not apply in a case in which the value of all interests in property transferred in trust are deductible under subsection (a).

(3) DENIAL OF DEDUCTION IN CASE OF CERTAIN CONTRIBUTIONS OF PARTIAL INTERESTS IN PROPERTY.—

(A) IN GENERAL.—In the case of a contribution (not made by a transfer in trust) of an interest in property which consists of less than the taxpayer's entire interest in such property, a deduction shall be allowed under this section only to the extent that the value of the interest contributed would be allowable as a deduction under this section if such interest had been transferred in trust. For purposes of this subparagraph, a contribution by a taxpayer of the right to use property shall be treated as a contribution of less than the taxpayer's entire interest in such property.

(B) EXCEPTIONS.—Subparagraph (A) shall not apply to—

(i) a contribution of a remainder interest in a personal residence or farm,

(ii) a contribution of an undivided portion of the taxpayer's entire interest in property, and

(iii) a qualified conservation contribution.

(4) VALUATION OF REMAINDER INTEREST IN REAL PROPERTY.—For purposes of this section, in determining the value of a remainder interest in real property, depreciation (computed on the straight line method) and depletion of such property shall be taken into account, and such value shall be discounted at a rate of 6 percent per annum, except that the Secretary may prescribe a different rate.

(5) REDUCTION FOR CERTAIN INTEREST.—If, in connection with any charitable contribution, a liability is assumed by the recipient or by any other person, or if a charitable contribution is of property which is subject to a liability, then, to the extent necessary to avoid the duplication of amounts, the amount taken into account for purposes of this section as the amount of the charitable contribution—

(A) shall be reduced for interest (i) which has been paid (or is to be paid) by the taxpayer, (ii) which is attributable to the liability, and (iii) which is attributable to any period after the making of the contribution, and

(B) in the case of a bond, shall be further reduced for interest (i) which has been paid (or is to be paid) by the taxpayer on indebtedness incurred or continued to purchase or carry such bond, and (ii) which is attributable to any period before the making of the contribution.

The reduction pursuant to subparagraph (B) shall not exceed the interest (including interest equivalent) on the bond which is attributable to any period before the making of the contribution and which is not (under the taxpayer's method of accounting) includible in the gross income of the taxpayer for any taxable year. For purposes of this paragraph, the term "bond" means any bond, debenture, note, or certificate or other evidence of indebtedness.

(6) DEDUCTIONS FOR OUT-OF-POCKET EXPENDITURES.—No deduction shall be allowed under this section for an out-of-pocket expenditure made by any person on behalf of an organization described in subsection (c) (other than an organization described in section 501(h)(5) (relating to churches, etc.)) if the expenditure is made for the purpose of influencing legislation (within the meaning of section 501(c)(3)).

(7) REFORMATIONS TO COMPLY WITH PARAGRAPH (2).—

(A) IN GENERAL.—A deduction shall be allowed under subsection (a) in respect of any qualified reformation (within the meaning of section 2055(e)(3)(B)).

(B) RULES SIMILAR TO SECTION 2055(e)(3) TO APPLY.—For purposes of this paragraph, rules similar to the rules of section 2055(e)(3) shall apply.

(8) SUBSTANTIATION REQUIREMENT FOR CERTAIN CONTRIBUTIONS.—

(A) GENERAL RULE.—No deduction shall be allowed under subsection (a) for any contribution of $250 or more unless the taxpayer substantiates the contribution by a contemporaneous written acknowledgment of the contribution by the donee organization that meets the requirements of subparagraph (B).

(B) CONTENT OF ACKNOWLEDGEMENT.—An acknowledgement meets the requirements of this subparagraph if it includes the following information:

(i) The amount of cash and a description (but not value) of any property other than cash contributed.

(ii) Whether the donee organization provided any goods or services in consideration, in whole or in part, for any property described in clause (i).

(iii) A description and good faith estimate of the value of any goods or services referred to in clause (ii) or, if such goods or services consist solely of intangible religious benefits, a statement to that effect.

For purposes of this subparagraph, the term "intangible religious benefit" means any intangible religious benefit which is provided by an organization organized exclusively for religious purposes and which generally is not sold in a commercial transaction outside the donative context.

(C) CONTEMPORANEOUS.—For purposes of subparagraph (A), an acknowledgment shall be considered to be contemporaneous if the taxpayer obtains the acknowledgment on or before the earlier of—

(i) the date on which the taxpayer files a return for the taxable year in which the contribution was made, or

(ii) the due date (including extensions) for filing such return.

(D) SUBSTANTIATION NOT REQUIRED FOR CONTRIBUTIONS REPORTED BY THE DONEE ORGANIZATION.—Subparagraph (A) shall not apply to a contribution if the donee organization files a return, on such form and in accordance with such regulations as the Secretary may prescribe, which includes the information described in subparagraph (B) with respect to the contribution.

(E) REGULATIONS.—The Secretary shall prescribe such regulations as may be necessary or appropriate to carry out the purposes of this paragraph, including regulations that may provide that some or all of the requirements of this paragraph do not apply in appropriate cases.

(9) DENIAL OF DEDUCTION WHERE CONTRIBUTION FOR LOBBYING ACTIVITIES.—No deduction shall be allowed under this section for a contribution to an organization which conducts activities to which section 162(e)(1) applies on matters of direct financial interest to the donor's trade or business, if a principal purpose of the contribution was to avoid Federal income tax by securing a deduction for such activities under this section which would be disallowed by reason of section 162(e) if the donor had conducted such activities directly. No deduction shall be allowed under section 162(a) for any amount for which a deduction is disallowed under the preceding sentence.

(10) SPLIT-DOLLAR LIFE INSURANCE, ANNUITY, AND ENDOWMENT CONTRACTS.—

(A) IN GENERAL.—Nothing in this section or in section 545(b)(2), 642(c), 2055, 2106(a)(2), or 2522 shall be construed to allow a deduction, and no deduction shall be allowed, for any transfer to or for the use of an organization described in subsection (c) if in connection with such transfer—

(i) the organization directly or indirectly pays, or has previously paid, any premium on any personal benefit contract with respect to the transferor, or

(ii) there is an understanding or expectation that any person will directly or indirectly pay any premium on any personal benefit contract with respect to the transferor.

(B) PERSONAL BENEFIT CONTRACT.—For purposes of subparagraph (A), the term "personal benefit contract" means, with respect to the transferor, any life insurance, annuity, or endowment contract if any direct or indirect beneficiary under such contract is the transferor, any member of the transferor's family, or any other person (other than an organization described in subsection (c)) designated by the transferor.

(C) APPLICATION TO CHARITABLE REMAINDER TRUSTS.—In the case of a transfer to a trust referred to in subparagraph (E), references in subparagraphs (A) and (F) to an organization described in subsection (c) shall be treated as a reference to such trust.

(D) EXCEPTION FOR CERTAIN ANNUITY CONTRACTS.—If, in connection with a transfer to or for the use of an organization described in subsection (c), such organization incurs an obligation to pay a charitable gift annuity (as defined in section 501(m)) and such organization purchases any annuity contract to fund such obligation, persons receiving payments under the charitable gift annuity shall not be treated for purposes of subparagraph (B) as indirect beneficiaries under such contract if—

(i) such organization possesses all of the incidents of ownership under such contract,

(ii) such organization is entitled to all the payments under such contract, and

(iii) the timing and amount of payments under such contract are substantially the same as the timing and amount of payments to each such person under such obligation (as such obligation is in effect at the time of such transfer).

(E) EXCEPTION FOR CERTAIN CONTRACTS HELD BY CHARITABLE REMAINDER TRUSTS.—A person shall not be treated for purposes of subparagraph (B) as an indirect beneficiary under any life insurance, annuity, or endowment contract held by a charitable remainder annuity trust or a charitable remainder unitrust (as defined in section 664(d)) solely by reason of being entitled to any payment referred to in paragraph (1)(A) or (2)(A) of section 664(d) if—

(i) such trust possesses all of the incidents of ownership under such contract, and

(ii) such trust is entitled to all the payments under such contract.

(F) EXCISE TAX ON PREMIUMS PAID.—

(i) IN GENERAL.—There is hereby imposed on any organization described in subsection (c) an excise tax equal to the premiums paid by such organization on any life insurance, annuity, or endowment contract if the payment of premiums on such contract is in connection with a transfer for which a deduction is not allowable under subparagraph (A), determined without regard to when such transfer is made.

(ii) PAYMENTS BY OTHER PERSONS.—For purposes of clause (i), payments made by any other person pursuant to an understanding or expectation referred to in subparagraph (A) shall be treated as made by the organization.

(iii) REPORTING.—Any organization on which tax is imposed by clause (i) with respect to any premium shall file an annual return which includes —

(I) the amount of such premiums paid during the year and the name and TIN of each beneficiary under the contract to which the premium relates, and

(II) such other information as the Secretary may require.

The penalties applicable to returns required under section 6033 shall apply to returns required under this clause. Returns required under this clause shall be furnished at such time and in such manner as the Secretary shall by forms or regulations require.

(iv) CERTAIN RULES TO APPLY.—The tax imposed by this subparagraph shall be treated as imposed by chapter 42 for purposes of this title other than subchapter B of chapter 42.

(G) SPECIAL RULE WHERE STATE REQUIRES SPECIFICATION OF CHARITABLE GIFT ANNUITANT IN CONTRACT.—In the case of an obligation to pay a charitable gift annuity referred to in subparagraph (D) which is entered into under the laws of a State which requires, in order for the charitable gift annuity to be exempt from insurance regulation by such State, that each beneficiary under the charitable gift annuity be named as a beneficiary under an annuity contract issued by an insurance company authorized to transact business in such State, the requirements of clauses (i) and (ii) of subparagraph (D) shall be treated as met if—

(i) such State law requirement was in effect on February 8, 1999,

(ii) each such beneficiary under the charitable gift annuity is a bona fide resident of such State at the time the obligation to pay a charitable gift annuity is entered into, and

(iii) the only persons entitled to payments under such contract are persons entitled to payments as beneficiaries under such obligation on the date such obligation is entered into.

(H) MEMEBER OF FAMILY.—For purposes of this paragraph, an individual's family consists of the individual's grandparents, the grandparents of such individual's spouse, the lineal descendants of such grandparents, and any spouse of such a lineal descendant.

(I) REGULATIONS.—The Secretary shall prescribe such regulations as may be necessary or appropriate to carry out the purposes of this paragraph, including regulations to prevent the avoidance of such purposes.

(11) QUALIFIED APPRAISAL AND OTHER DOCUMENTATION FOR CERTAIN CONTRIBUTIONS.—

(A) IN GENERAL.—

(i) DENIAL OF DEDUCTION.—In the case of an individual, partnership, or corporation, no deduction shall be allowed under subsection (a) for any contribution of property for which a deduction of more than $500 is claimed unless such person meets the requirements of subparagraphs (B), (C), and (D), as the case may be, with respect to such contribution.

(ii) EXCEPTIONS.—

(I) READILY VALUED PROPERTY.—Subparagraphs (C) and (D) shall not apply to cash, property described in subsection (e)(1)(B)(iii) or section 1221(a)(1), publicly traded securities (as defined in section 6050L(a)(2)(B)), and any qualified vehicle described in paragraph (12)(A)(ii) for which an acknowledgement under paragraph (12)(B)(iii) is provided.

(II) REASONABLE CAUSE.—Clause (i) shall not apply if it is shown that the failure to meet such requirements is due to reasonable cause and not to willful neglect.

(B) PROPERTY DESCRIPTION FOR CONTRIBUTIONS OF MORE THAN $500.—In the case of contributions of property for which a deduction of more than $500 is claimed, the requirements of this subparagraph are met if the individual, partnership or corporation includes with the return for the taxable year in which the contribution is made a description of such property and such other information as the Secretary may require. The requirements of this subparagraph shall not apply to a C corporation which is not a personal service corporation or a closely held C corporation.

(C) QUALIFIED APPRAISAL FOR CONTRIBUTIONS OF MORE THAN $5,000.—In the case of contributions of property for which a deduction of more than $5,000 is claimed, the requirements of this subparagraph are met if the individual, partnership, or corporation obtains a qualified appraisal of such property and attaches to the return for the taxable year in which such contribution is made such information regarding such property and such appraisal as the Secretary may require.

(D) SUBSTANTIATION FOR CONTRIBUTIONS OF MORE THAN $500,000.—In the case of contributions of property for which a deduction of more than $500,000 is claimed, the requirements of this subparagraph are met if the individual, partnership, or corporation attaches to the return for the taxable year a qualified appraisal of such property.

(E) QUALIFIED APPRAISAL AND APPRAISER.—For purposes of this paragraph—

(i) QUALIFIED APPRAISAL.—The term "qualified appraisal" means, with respect to any property, an appraisal of such property which—

(I) is treated for purposes of this paragraph as a qualified appraisal under regulations or other guidance prescribed by the Secretary, and

(II) is conducted by a qualified appraiser in accordance with generally accepted appraisal standards and any regulations or other guidance prescribed under subclause (I).

(ii) QUALIFIED APPRAISER.—Except as provided in clause (iii), the term 'qualified appraiser' means an individual who—

(I) has earned an appraisal designation from a recognized professional appraiser organization or has otherwise met minimum education and experience requirements set forth in regulations prescribed by the Secretary,

(II) regularly performs appraisals for which the individual receives compensation, and

(III) meets such other requirements as may be prescribed by the Secretary in regulations or other guidance.

(iii) SPECIFIC APPRAISALS.—An individual shall not be treated as a qualified appraiser with respect to any specific appraisal unless—

(I) the individual demonstrates verifiable education and experience in valuing the type of property subject to the appraisal, and

(II) the individual has not been prohibited from practicing before the Internal Revenue Service by the Secretary under section 330(c) of title 31, United States Code, at any time during the 3-year period ending on the date of the appraisal.

(F) AGGREGATION OF SIMILAR ITEMS OF PROPERTY.—For purposes of determining thresholds under this paragraph, property and all similar items of property donated to 1 or more donees shall be treated as 1 property.

(G) SPECIAL RULE FOR PASS-THRU ENTITIES.—In the case of a partnership or S corporation, this paragraph shall be applied at the entity level, except that the deduction shall be denied at the partner or shareholder level.

(H) REGULATIONS.—The Secretary may prescribe such regulations as may be necessary or appropriate to carry out the purposes of this paragraph, including regulations that may provide that some or all of the requirements of this paragraph do not apply in appropriate cases.

(12) CONTRIBUTIONS OF USED MOTOR VEHICLES, BOATS, AND AIRPLANES.—

(A) IN GENERAL.—In the case of a contribution of a qualified vehicle the claimed value of which exceeds $500—

(i) paragraph (8) shall not apply and no deduction shall be allowed under subsection (a) for such contribution unless the taxpayer substantiates the contribution by a contemporaneous written acknowledgement of the contribution by the donee organization that meets the requirements of subparagraph (B) and includes the acknowledgement with the taxpayer's return of tax which includes the deduction, and

(ii) if the organization sells the vehicle without any significant intervening use or material improvement of such vehicle by the organization, the amount of the deduction allowed under subsection (a) shall not exceed the gross proceeds received from such sale.

(B) CONTENT OF ACKNOWLEDGEMENT.—An acknowledgement meets the requirements of this subparagraph if it includes the following information:

(i) The name and taxpayer identification number of the donor.

(ii) The vehicle identification number or similar number.

(iii) In the case of a qualified vehicle to which subparagraph (A)(ii) applies—

(I) a certification that the vehicle was sold in an arm's length transaction between unrelated parties,

(II) the gross proceeds from the sale, and

(III) a statement that the deductible amount may not exceed the amount of such gross proceeds.

(iv) In the case of a qualified vehicle to which subparagraph (A)(ii) does not apply—

(I) a certification of the intended use or material improvement of the vehicle and the intended duration of such use, and

(II) a certification that the vehicle would not be transferred in exchange for money, other property, or services before completion of such use or improvement.

(v) Whether the donee organization provided any goods or services in consideration, in whole or in part, for the qualified vehicle.

(vi) A description and good faith estimate of the value of any goods or services referred to in clause (v) or, if such goods or services consist solely of intangible religious benefits (as defined in paragraph (8)(B)), a statement to that effect.

(C) CONTEMPORANEOUS.—For purposes of subparagraph (A), an acknowledgement shall be considered to be contemporaneous if the donee organization provides it within 30 days of—

(i) the sale of the qualified vehicle, or

(ii) in the case of an acknowledgement including a certification described in subparagraph (B)(iv), the contribution of the qualified vehicle.

(D) INFORMATION TO SECRETARY.—A donee organization required to provide an acknowledgement under this paragraph shall provide to the Secretary the information contained in the acknowledgement. Such information shall be provided at such time and in such manner as the Secretary may prescribe.

(E) QUALIFIED VEHICLE.—For purposes of this paragraph, the term "qualified vehicle" means any—

(i) motor vehicle manufactured primarily for use on public streets, roads, and highways,

(ii) boat, or

(iii) airplane.

Such term shall not include any property which is described in section 1221(a)(1).

(F) REGULATIONS OR OTHER GUIDANCE.—The Secretary shall prescribe such regulations or other guidance as may be necessary to carry out the purposes of this paragraph. The Secretary may prescribe regulations or other guidance which exempts sales by the donee organization which are in direct furtherance of such organization's charitable purpose from the requirements of subparagraphs (A)(ii) and (B)(iv)(II).

(13) CONTRIBUTIONS OF CERTAIN INTERESTS IN BUILDINGS LOCATED IN REGISTERED HISTORIC DISTRICTS.—

(A) IN GENERAL.—No deduction shall be allowed with respect to any contribution described in subparagraph (B) unless the taxpayer includes with the return for the taxable year of the contribution a $500 filing fee.

(B) CONTRIBUTION DESCRIBED.—A contribution is described in this subparagraph if such contribution is a qualified conservation contribution (as defined in subsection (h)) which is a restriction with respect to the exterior of a building described in subsection (h)(4)(C)(ii) and for which a deduction is claimed in excess of $10,000.

(C) DEDICATION OF FEE.—Any fee collected under this paragraph shall be used for the enforcement of the provisions of subsection (h).

(14) REDUCTION FOR AMOUNTS ATTRIBUTABLE TO REHABILITATION CREDIT.—In the case of any qualified conservation contribution (as defined in subsection (h)), the amount of the deduction allowed under this section shall be reduced by an amount which bears the same ratio to the fair market value of the contribution as—

(A) the sum of the credits allowed to the taxpayer under section 47 for the 5 preceding taxable years with respect to any building which is a part of such contribution, bears to

(B) the fair market value of the building on the date of the contribution.

(15) SPECIAL RULE FOR TAXIDERMY PROPERTY.—

(A) BASIS.—For purposes of this section and notwithstanding section 1012, in the case of a charitable contribution of taxidermy property which is made by the person who prepared, stuffed, or mounted the property or by any person who paid or incurred the cost of such preparation, stuffing, or mounting, only the cost of the preparing, stuffing, or mounting shall be included in the basis of such property.

(B) TAXIDERMY PROPERTY.—For purposes of this section, the term "taxidermy property" means any work of art which—

(i) is the reproduction or preservation of an animal, in whole or in part,

(ii) is prepared, stuffed, or mounted for purposes of recreating one or more characteristics of such animal, and

(iii) contains a part of the body of the dead animal.

(16) CONTRIBUTIONS OF CLOTHING AND HOUSEHOLD ITEMS.—

(A) IN GENERAL.—In the case of an individual, partnership, or corporation, no deduction shall be allowed under subsection (a) for any contribution of clothing or a household item unless such clothing or household item is in good used condition or better.

(B) ITEMS OF MINIMAL VALUE.—Notwithstanding subparagraph (A), the Secretary may by regulation deny a deduction under subsection (a) for any contribution of clothing or a household item which has minimal monetary value.

(C) EXCEPTION FOR CERTAIN PROPERTY.—Subparagraphs (A) and (B) shall not apply to any contribution of a single item of clothing or a household item for which a deduction of more than $500 is claimed if the taxpayer includes with the taxpayer's return a qualified appraisal with respect to the property.

(D) HOUSEHOLD ITEMS.—For purposes of this paragraph—

(i) IN GENERAL.—The term "household items" includes furniture, furnishings, electronics, appliances, linens, and other similar items.

(ii) EXCLUDED ITEMS.—Such term does not include—

(I) food,

(II) paintings, antiques, and other objects of art,

(III) jewelry and gems, and

(IV) collections.

(E) SPECIAL RULE FOR PASS-THRU ENTITIES.—In the case of a partnership or S corporation, this paragraph shall be applied at the entity level, except that the deduction shall be denied at the partner or shareholder level.

(17) RECORDKEEPING.—No deduction shall be allowed under subsection (a) for any contribution of a cash, check, or other monetary gift unless the donor maintains as a record of such contribution a bank record or a written communication from the donee showing the name of the donee organization, the date of the contribution, and the amount of the contribution.

(18) CONTRIBUTIONS TO DONOR ADVISED FUNDS.—A deduction otherwise allowed under subsection (a) for any contribution to a donor advised fund (as defined in section 4966(d)(2)) shall only be allowed if—

(A) the sponsoring organization (as defined in section 4966(d)(1)) with respect to such donor advised fund is not—

(i) described in paragraph (3), (4), or (5) of subsection (c), or

(ii) a type III supporting organization (as defined in section 4943(f)(5)(A)) which is not a functionally integrated type III supporting organization (as defined in section 4943(f)(5)(B)), and

(B) the taxpayer obtains a contemporaneous written acknowledgment (determined under rules similar to the rules of paragraph (8)(C)) from the sponsoring organization (as so defined) of such donor advised fund that such organization has exclusive legal control over the assets contributed.

Amendments

• 2006, Pension Protection Act of 2006 (P.L. 109-280)

P.L. 109-280, §1213(c):

Amended Code Sec. 170(f) by adding at the end a new paragraph (13). **Effective** for contributions made 180 days after 8-17-2006.

P.L. 109-280, §1213(d):

Amended Code Sec. 170(f), as amended by Act Sec. 1213(c), by adding at the end a new paragraph (14). **Effective** for contributions made after 8-17-2006.

P.L. 109-280, §1214(b):

Amended Code Sec. 170(f), as amended by this Act, by adding at the end a new paragraph (15). **Effective** for contributions made after 7-25-2006.

P.L. 109-280, §1216(a):

Amended Code Sec. 170(f), as amended by this Act, by adding at the end a new paragraph (16). **Effective** for contributions made after 8-17-2006.

P.L. 109-280, §1217(a):

Amended Code Sec. 170(f), as amended by this Act, by adding at the end a new paragraph (17). **Effective** for contributions made in tax years beginning after 8-17-2006.

P.L. 109-280, §1219(c)(1):

Amended Code Sec. 170(f)(11)(E). **Effective** generally for appraisals prepared with respect to returns or submissions filed after 8-17-2006. Prior to amendment, Code Sec. 170(f)(11)(E) read as follows:

(E) QUALIFIED APPRAISAL.—For purposes of this paragraph, the term "qualified appraisal" means, with respect to any property, an appraisal of such property which is treated for purposes of this paragraph as a qualified appraisal under regulations or other guidance prescribed by the Secretary.

P.L. 109-280, §1234(a):

Amended Code Sec. 170(f), as amended by this Act, by adding at the end a new paragraph (18). **Effective** for contributions made after the date which is 180 days after 8-17-2006.

• 2005, Gulf Opportunity Zone Act of 2005 (P.L. 109-135)

P.L. 109-135, §403(gg):

Amended Code Sec. 170(f)(12)(B) by adding at the end new clauses (v) and (vi). **Effective** as if included in the provision of the American Jobs Creation Act of 2004 (P.L. 108-357) to which it relates [**effective** for contributions made after 12-31-2004.—CCH].

• 2005, Katrina Emergency Tax Relief Act of 2005 (P.L. 109-73)

P.L. 109-73, §303 [but see P.L. 110-343, Division C, §702, in the amendment notes for Code Sec. 1400N(a)], provides:

SEC. 303. INCREASE IN STANDARD MILEAGE RATE FOR CHARITABLE USE OF VEHICLES.

Notwithstanding section 170(i) of the Internal Revenue Code of 1986, for purposes of computing the deduction under section 170 of such Code for use of a vehicle described in subsection (f)(12)(E)(i) of such section for provision of relief related to Hurricane Katrina during the period beginning on August 25, 2005, and ending on December 31, 2006, the standard mileage rate shall be 70 percent of the standard mileage rate in effect under section 162(a) of such Code at the time of such use. Any increase under this section shall be rounded to the next highest cent.

• 2004, American Jobs Creation Act of 2004 (P.L. 108-357)

P.L. 108-357, §413(c)(30):

Amended Code Sec. 170(f)(10)(A) by striking "556(b)(2)," immediately preceding "642(c)". **Effective** for tax years of foreign corporations beginning after 12-31-2004, and for tax years of United States shareholders with or within which such tax years of foreign corporations end.

P.L. 108-357, §882(d):

Amended Code Sec. 170(f)(11)(A)(ii)(I), as added by this Act, by inserting "subsection (e)(1)(B)(iii) or" before "section 1221(a)(1)". **Effective** for contributions made after 6-3-2004.

P.L. 108-357, §883(a):

Amended Code Sec. 170(f) by adding after paragraph (10) a new paragraph (11). **Effective** for contributions made after 6-3-2004.

P.L. 108-357, §884(a):

Amended Code Sec. 170(f), as amended by this Act, by inserting after paragraph (11) a new paragraph (12). **Effective** for contributions made after 12-31-2004.

• 1999, Tax Relief Extension Act of 1999 (P.L. 106-170)

P.L. 106-170, §537(a):

Amended Code Sec. 170(f) by adding at the end a new paragraph (10). **Effective** for transfers made after 2-8-99. For exceptions, see Act Sec. 537(b)(2)-(3), below.

P.L. 106-170, §537(b)(2)-(3), provides:

(2) EXCISE TAX.—Except as provided in paragraph (3) of this subsection, section 170(f)(10)(F) of the Internal Revenue Code of 1986 (as added by this section) shall apply to premiums paid after the date of the enactment of this Act.

(3) REPORTING.—Clause (iii) of such section 170(f)(10)(F) shall apply to premiums paid after February 8, 1999 (determined as if the tax imposed by such section applies to premiums paid after such date).

• 1993, Omnibus Budget Reconciliation Act of 1993 (P.L. 103-66)

P.L. 103-66, §13172(a):

Amended Code Sec. 170(f) by adding at the end thereof new paragraph (8). **Effective** for contributions made on or after 1-1-94.

P.L. 103-66, §13222(b):

Amended Code Sec. 170(f), as amended by Act Sec. 13172, by adding at the end thereof a new paragraph (9). **Effective** for amounts paid or incurred after 12-31-93.

• 1984, Deficit Reduction Act of 1984 (P.L. 98-369)

P.L. 98-369, §1022(b):

Amended Code Sec. 170(f) by adding at the end thereof new paragraph (7). **Effective** for reformations after 12-31-78; except that it shall not apply to any reformation to which Code Sec. 2055(e)(3) (as in effect on 7-17-84) applies. For purposes of applying Code Sec. 2055(e)(C)(iii) (as amended), the 90th day described therein shall be treated as the 90th day after 7-18-84.

• 1980, Miscellaneous Revenue Act of 1980 (P.L. 96-605)

P.L. 96-605, §301(b)(2):

Amended Act Sec. 514 of P.L. 95-600 as follows:

(b) EFFECTIVE DATE.—

(2) CHARITABLE LEAD TRUSTS AND CHARITABLE REMAINDER TRUSTS IN THE CASE OF INCOME AND GIFT TAXES.—Section 514(b) (and section 514(c) insofar as it relates to section 514(b)) of the Revenue Act of 1978 shall be applied as if the amendment made by subsection (a) had been included in the amendment made by section 514(a) of such Act. [This provision extends until December 31, 1981, the time to amend, or commence judicial proceedings to amend, instruments of both charitable lead trusts or charitable remainder trusts that were executed before December 31, 1978, in order to conform such instruments to the requirements of P.L. 91-172 for income and gift tax purposes. See amendment note under Code Sec. 2055(e).]

• 1980, Technical Corrections Act of 1979 (P.L. 96-222)

P.L. 96-222, §105(a)(4)(B):

Amended Act Sec. 514 of P.L. 95-600 by adding paragraph (c) to read as below:

(c) EFFECTIVE DATES.—

* * *

(2) FOR SUBSECTION (b).—Subsection (b)—

(A) insofar as it relates to section 170 of the Internal Revenue Code of 1954 shall apply to transfers in trust and contributions made after July 31, 1969, and

(B) insofar as it relates to section 2522 of the Internal Revenue Code of 1954 shall apply to transfers made after December 31, 1969.

• 1978, Revenue Act of 1978 (P.L. 95-600)

P.L. 95-600, §514(b), provides as follows:

"(b) CHARITABLE LEAD TRUSTS AND CHARITABLE REMAINDER TRUSTS IN THE CASE OF INCOME AND GIFT TAXES.—Under regulations prescribed by the Secretary of the Treasury or his delegate, in the case of trusts created before December 31, 1977, provisions comparable to section 2055(c)(3) of the Internal Revenue Code of 1954 (as amended by subsection (a) [P.L. 95-600, §514(a) shall be deemed to be included in sections 170 and 2522 of the Internal Revenue Code of 1954."

• 1980 (P.L. 96-541)

P.L. 96-541, §6(a):

Amended Code Sec. 170(f)(3) by striking out subparagraphs (B) and (C) and inserting in lieu thereof a new subparagraph (B). **Effective** for transfers made after 12-31-80, in tax years ending after that date. Prior to amendment, subparagraphs (B) and (C) provided:

"(B) EXCEPTIONS.—Subparagraph (A) shall not apply to a contribution of—

(i) a remainder interest in a personal residence or farm,

(ii) an undivided portion of the taxpayer's entire interest in property,

(iii) a lease on, option to purchase, or easement with respect to real property granted in perpetuity to an organization described in subsection (b)(1)(A) exclusively for conservation purposes, or

(iv) a remainder interest in real property which is granted to an organization described in subsection (b)(1)(A) exclusively for conservation purposes.

(C) CONSERVATION PURPOSES DEFINED.—For purposes of subparagraph (B), the term "conservation purposes" means—

(i) the preservation of land areas for public outdoor recreation or education, or scenic enjoyment;

(ii) the preservation of historically important land areas or structures; or

(iii) the protection of natural environmental systems."

• 1977, Tax Reduction and Simplification Act of 1977 (P.L. 95-30)

P.L. 95-30, §309(a):

Amended clause (iii) of Code Sec. 170(f)(3)(B). **Effective** for contributions or transfers made after 6-13-77, and before 6-14-81. Prior to amendment, clause (iii) read as follows:

"(iii) a lease on, option to purchase, or easement with respect to real property of not less than 30 years' duration granted to an organization described in subsection (b)(1)(A) exclusively for conservation purposes, or".

• 1976, Tax Reform Act of 1976 (P.L 94-455)

P.L. 94-455, §1307(c):

Added Code Sec. 170(f)(6). Effective for tax years beginning after 12-31-76.

P.L. 94-455, §1901(a)(28):

Repealed Code Sec. 170(f)(6). **Effective** for tax years beginning after 12-31-76. Prior to repeal, former Code Sec. 170(f)(6) read as follows:

(6) PARTIAL REDUCTION OF UNLIMITED DEDUCTION.—

(A) IN GENERAL.—If the limitations in subsections (b)(1)(A) and (B) do not apply because of the application of subsection (b)(1)(C), the amount otherwise allowable as a deduction under subsection (a) shall be reduced by the amount by which the taxpayer's taxable income computed without regard to this subparagraph is less than the transitional income percentage (determined under subparagraph (C)) of the taxpayer's adjusted gross income. However, in no case shall a taxpayer's deduction under this section be reduced below the amount allowable as a deduction under this section without the applicability of subsection (b)(1)(C).

(B) TRANSITIONAL DEDUCTION PERCENTAGE.—For purposes of applying subsection (b)(1)(C), the term "transitional deduction percentage" means—

(i) in the case of a taxable year beginning before 1970, 90 percent, and

(ii) in the case of a taxable year beginning in—

1970	80 percent
1971	74 percent
1972	68 percent
1973	62 percent
1974	56 percent.

(C) TRANSITIONAL INCOME PERCENTAGE.—For purposes of applying subparagraph (A), the term "transitional income percentage" means, in the case of a taxable year beginning in—

1970	20 percent
1971	26 percent
1972	32 percent
1973	38 percent
1974	44 percent.

P.L. 94-455, §1906(b)(13)(A):

Amended 1954 Code by substituting "Secretary" for "Secretary or his delegate" each place it appeared. **Effective** 2-1-77.

P.L. 94-455, §2124(e) (as amended by P.L. 95-30, §309(b)(2)):

Struck out "or" at the end of Code Sec. 170(f)(3)(B)(i), substituted a comma for the period at the end of clause (ii), and added clauses (iii) and (iv) and subparagraph (C). **Effective** for contributions or transfers made after 6-13-76, and before 6-14-77. However, P.L. 95-30, §309(b)(2), changed this latter date to 6-14-81.

• 1969, Tax Reform Act of 1969 (P.L. 91-172)

P.L. 91-172, §201(a)(1):

Amended Code Sec. 170(f). Code Sec. 170(f)(1) is **effective** for contributions paid after 12-31-69. Paragraphs (2), (3) and (4) of Code Sec. 170(f) apply to transfers in trust and contributions made after 7-31-69.

[Sec. 170(g)]

(g) AMOUNTS PAID TO MAINTAIN CERTAIN STUDENTS AS MEMBERS OF TAXPAYER'S HOUSEHOLD.—

(1) IN GENERAL.—Subject to the limitations provided by paragraph (2), amounts paid by the taxpayer to maintain an individual (other than a dependent, as defined in section 152 (determined without regard to subsections (b)(1), (b)(2), and (d)(1)(B) thereof), or a relative of the taxpayer) as a member of his household during the period that such individual is—

(A) a member of the taxpayer's household under a written agreement between the taxpayer and an organization described in paragraph (2), (3), or (4) of subsection (c) to implement a program of the organization to provide educational opportunities for pupils or students in private homes, and

(B) a full-time pupil or student in the twelfth or any lower grade at an educational organization described in section 170(b)(1)(A)(ii) located in the United States,

shall be treated as amounts paid for the use of the organization.

(2) LIMITATIONS.—

(A) AMOUNT.—Paragraph (1) shall apply to amounts paid within the taxable year only to the extent that such amounts do not exceed $50 multiplied by the number of full calendar months during the taxable year which fall within the period described in paragraph (1). For purposes of the preceding sentence, if 15 or more days of a calendar month fall within such period such month shall be considered as a full calendar month.

(B) COMPENSATION OR REIMBURSEMENT.—Paragraph (1) shall not apply to any amount paid by the taxpayer within the taxable year if the taxpayer receives any money or other property as compensation or reimbursement for maintaining the individual in his household during the period described in paragraph (1).

(3) RELATIVE DEFINED.—For purposes of paragraph (1), the term "relative of the taxpayer" means an individual who, with respect to the taxpayer, bears any of the relationships described in subparagraphs (A) through (G) of section 152(d)(2).

(4) NO OTHER AMOUNT ALLOWED AS DEDUCTION.—No deduction shall be allowed under subsection (a) for any amount paid by a taxpayer to maintain an individual as a member of his household under a program described in paragraph (1)(A) except as provided in this subsection.

Amendments

• 2004, Working Families Tax Relief Act of 2004 (P.L. 108-311)

P.L. 108-311, §207(15):

Amended Code Sec. 170(g)(1) by inserting "(determined without regard to subsections (b)(1), (b)(2), and (d)(1)(B) thereof)" after "section 152". **Effective** for tax years beginning after 12-31-2004.

P.L. 108-311, §207(16):

Amended Code Sec. 170(g)(3) by striking "paragraphs (1) through (8) of section 152(a)" and inserting "subparagraphs (A) through (G) of section 152(d)(2)". **Effective** for tax years beginning after 12-31-2004.

• 1976, Tax Reform Act of 1976 (P.L. 94-455)

P.L. 94-455, §1901(a)(28):

Repealed Code Sec. 170(g) and redesignated former Code Sec. 170(h) as Code Sec. 170(g). **Effective** for tax years beginning after 12-31-76. Prior to repeal, Sec. 170(g) read as follows:

(g) APPLICATION OF UNLIMITED CHARITABLE CONTRIBUTION DEDUCTION.—

(1) ALLOWANCE OF DEDUCTION FOR TAXABLE YEARS BEGINNING AFTER DECEMBER 31, 1963.—If the taxable year begins after December 31, 1963—

(A) subsection (b)(1)(C) shall apply only if the taxpayer so elects (at such time and in such manner as the Secretary or his delegate by regulations prescribes); and

(B) for purposes of subsection (b)(1)(C), the amount of the charitable contributions for the taxable year (and for all prior taxable years beginning after December 31, 1963) shall be determined without the application of subsection (d)(1) and solely by reference to charitable contributions described in paragraph (2).

If the taxpayer elects to have subsection (b)(1)(C) apply for the taxable year, then for such taxable year subsection (a) shall apply only with respect to charitable contributions described in paragraph (2), and no amount of charitable contributions made in the taxable year or any prior taxable year may be treated under subsection (d)(1) as having been made in the taxable year or in any succeeding taxable year.

(2) QUALIFIED CONTRIBUTIONS.—The charitable contributions referred to in paragraph (1) are—

(A) any charitable contribution described in subsection (b)(1)(A);

[(B) deleted.]

(C) any charitable contribution, not described in subsection (b)(1)(A), to an organization described in subsection (c)(2) which meets the requirements of paragraph (3) with respect to such charitable contributions; and

(D) any charitable contribution payment of which is made on or before the date of the enactment of the Revenue Act of 1964.

(3) ORGANIZATIONS EXPENDING AT LEAST 50 PERCENT OF DONOR'S CONTRIBUTIONS.—An organization shall be an organization referred to in paragraph (2)(C), with respect to any charitable contribution, only if—

(A) not later than the close of the third year after the organization's taxable year in which the contribution is received (or before such later time as the Secretary or his delegate may allow upon good cause shown by such organization), such organization expends an amount equal to at least 50 percent of such contribution for—

(i) the active conduct of the activities constituting the purpose or function for which it is organized and operated,

(ii) assets which are directly devoted to such active conduct,

(iii) contributions to organizations which are described in subsection (b)(1)(A) or in paragraph (2)(B) of this subsection, or

(iv) any combination of the foregoing; and

(B) for the period beginning with the taxable year in which such contribution is received and ending with the taxable year in which subparagraph (A) is satisfied with respect to such contribution, such organization expends all of its net income (determined without regard to capital gains and losses) for the purposes described in clauses (i), (ii), (iii), and (iv) of subparagraph (A).

If the taxpayer so elects (at such time and in such manner as the Secretary or his delegate by regulations prescribes) with respect to contributions made by him to any organization, then, in applying subparagraph (B) with respect to contributions made by him to such organization during his taxable year for which such election is made and during all his subsequent taxable years, amounts expended by the organization after the close of any of its taxable years and on or before the 15th day of the third month following the close of such taxable year shall be treated as expended during such taxable year.

(4) DISQUALIFYING TRANSACTIONS.—An organization shall be an organization referred to in subparagraph (b) or (c) of paragraph (2) only if at no time during the period consisting of the organization's taxable year in which the contribution is received, its 3 preceding taxable years, and its 3 succeeding taxable years, such organization—

(A) lends any part of its income or corpus to,

(B) pays compensation (other than reasonable compensation for personal services actually rendered) to,

(C) makes any of its services available on a preferential basis to,

(D) purchases more than a minimal amount of securities or other property from, or

(E) sells more than a minimal amount of securities or other property to, the donor of such contribution, any member of his family (as defined in section 267(c)(4)), any employee of the donor, any officer or employee of a corporation in which he owns (directly or indirectly) 50 percent or more in value of the outstanding stock, or any partner or employee of a partnership in which he owns (directly or indirectly) 50 percent or more of the capital interest or profits interest. This paragraph shall not apply to transactions occurring on or before the date of the enactment of the Revenue Act of 1964.

P.L. 94-455, §1901(b)(8)(A):

Amended Code Sec. 170(g)(1)(B) by substituting "educational organization described in section 170(b)(1)(A)(ii)" for "educational institution (as defined in section 151(e)(4))". **Effective** for tax years ending after 12-31-76.

• 1969, Tax Reform Act of 1969 (P.L. 91-172)

P.L. 91-172, §201(a)(1):

Redesignated former subsection (d) as (h).

P.L. 91-172, §201(a)(2)(A):

Substituted "subsection (d)(1)" for "subsection (b)(5)" wherever it appeared in Code Sec. 170(g)(1), and deleted paragraph (B) of Code Sec. 170(g)(2). **Effective** for tax years beginning after 12-31-69. Former paragraph (B) of Code Sec. 170(g)(2) read as follows:

(B) any charitable contribution, not described in subsection (b)(1)(A), to an organization described in sub?ction (c)(2) substantially more than half of the assets of which is devoted directly to, and substantially all of the income of which is expended directly for, the active conduct of the activities constituting the purpose or function for which it is organized and operated;

• 1964, Revenue Act of 1964 (P.L. 88-272)

P.L. 88-272, §209(b):

Added subsection (g). **Effective** for contributions which are paid in tax years beginning after 12-31-63.

• 1960 (P.L. 86-779)

P.L. 86-779, §7(a)(2):

Redesignated subsections (d) and (e) of Code Sec. 170 as (e) and (f), respectively; and added a new subsection (d). **Effective** for tax years beginning after 1959.

[Sec. 170(h)]

(h) QUALIFIED CONSERVATION CONTRIBUTION.—

(1) IN GENERAL.—For purposes of subsection (f)(3)(B)(iii), the term "qualified conservation contribution" means a contribution—

(A) of a qualified real property interest,

(B) to a qualified organization,

(C) exclusively for conservation purposes.

(2) QUALIFIED REAL PROPERTY INTEREST.—For purposes of this subsection, the term "qualified real property interest" means any of the following interests in real property:

(A) the entire interest of the donor other than a qualified mineral interest,

(B) a remainder interest, and

(C) a restriction (granted in perpetuity) on the use which may be made of the real property.

(3) QUALIFIED ORGANIZATION.—For purposes of paragraph (1), the term "qualified organization" means an organization which—

(A) is described in clause (v) or (vi) of subsection (b)(1)(A), or

(B) is described in section 501(c)(3) and—

(i) meets the requirements of section 509(a)(2), or

(ii) meets the requirements of section 509(a)(3) and is controlled by an organization described in subparagraph (A) or in clause (i) of this subparagraph.

(4) CONSERVATION PURPOSE DEFINED.—

(A) IN GENERAL.—For purposes of this subsection, the term "conservation purpose" means—

(i) the preservation of land areas for outdoor recreation by, or the education of, the general public,

(ii) the protection of a relatively natural habitat of fish, wildlife, or plants, or similar ecosystem,

(iii) the preservation of open space (including farmland and forest land) where such preservation is—

(I) for the scenic enjoyment of the general public, or

(II) pursuant to a clearly delineated Federal, State, or local governmental conservation policy,

and will yield a significant public benefit, or

(iv) the preservation of an historically important land area or a certified historic structure.

(B) SPECIAL RULES WITH RESPECT TO BUILDINGS IN REGISTERED HISTORIC DISTRICTS.—In the case of any contribution of a qualified real property interest which is a restriction with respect to the exterior of a building described in subparagraph (C)(ii), such contribution shall not be considered to be exclusively for conservation purposes unless—

(i) such interest—

(I) includes a restriction which preserves the entire exterior of the building (including the front, sides, rear, and height of the building), and

(II) prohibits any change in the exterior of the building which is inconsistent with the historical character of such exterior,

(ii) the donor and donee enter into a written agreement certifying, under penalty of perjury, that the donee—

(I) is a qualified organization (as defined in paragraph (3)) with a purpose of environmental protection, land conservation, open space preservation, or historic preservation, and

(II) has the resources to manage and enforce the restriction and a commitment to do so, and

(iii) in the case of any contribution made in a taxable year beginning after the date of the enactment of this subparagraph, the taxpayer includes with the taxpayer's return for the taxable year of the contribution—

(I) a qualified appraisal (within the meaning of subsection (f)(11)(E)) of the qualified property interest,

(II) photographs of the entire exterior of the building, and

(III) a description of all restrictions on the development of the building.

(C) CERTIFIED HISTORIC STRUCTURE.—For purposes of subparagraph (A)(iv), the term "certified historic structure" means—

(i) any building, structure, or land area which is listed in the National Register, or

(ii) any building which is located in a registered historic district (as defined in section 47(c)(3)(B)) and is certified by the Secretary of the Interior to the Secretary as being of historic significance to the district.

A building, structure, or land area satisfies the preceding sentence if it satisfies such sentence either at the time of the transfer or on the due date (including extensions) for filing the transferor's return under this chapter for the taxable year in which the transfer is made.

(5) EXCLUSIVELY FOR CONSERVATION PURPOSES.—For purposes of this subsection—

(A) CONSERVATION PURPOSE MUST BE PROTECTED.—A contribution shall not be treated as exclusively for conservation purposes unless the conservation purpose is protected in perpetuity.

(B) NO SURFACE MINING PERMITTED.—

(i) IN GENERAL.—Except as provided in clause (ii), in the case of a contribution of any interest where there is a retention of a qualified mineral interest, subparagraph (A) shall not be treated as met if at any time there may be extraction or removal of minerals by any surface mining method.

(ii) SPECIAL RULE.—With respect to any contribution of property in which the ownership of the surface estate and mineral interests has been and remains separated, subparagraph (A) shall be treated as met if the probability of surface mining occurring on such property is so remote as to be negligible.

(6) QUALIFIED MINERAL INTEREST.—For purposes of this subsection, the term "qualified mineral interest" means—

(A) subsurface oil, gas or other minerals, and

(B) the right to access to such minerals.

Amendments

• 2006, Pension Protection Act of 2006 (P.L. 109-280)

P.L. 109-280, §1213(a)(1):

Amended Code Sec. 170(h)(4) by redesignating subparagraph (B) as subparagraph (C) and by inserting after subparagraph (A) a new subparagraph (B). **Effective** for contributions made after 7-25-2006.

P.L. 109-280, §1213(b)(1)-(3):

Amended Code Sec. 170(h)(4)(C), as redesignated by Act Sec. 1213(a), by striking "any building, structure, or land area which", by inserting "any building, structure, or land area which" before "is listed" in clause (i), and by inserting "any building which" before "is located" in clause (ii). **Effective** for contributions made after 8-17-2006.

• 1997, Taxpayer Relief Act of 1997 (P.L. 105-34)

P.L. 105-34, §508(d):

Amended Code Sec. 170(h)(5)(B)(ii). **Effective** for easements granted after 12-31-97. Prior to amendment, Code Sec. 170(h)(5)(B)(ii) read as follows:

(ii) SPECIAL RULE.—With respect to any contribution of property in which the ownership of the surface estate and mineral interests were separated before June 13, 1976, and remain so separated, subparagraph (A) shall be treated as met if the probability of surface mining occurring on such property is so remote as to be negligible.

• 1990, Omnibus Budget Reconciliation Act of 1990 (P.L. 101-508)

P.L. 101-508, §11813(b)(10):

Amended Code Sec. 170(h)(4)(B) by striking "section 48(g)(3)(B)" and inserting "section 47(c)(3)(B)". **Effective**, generally, for property placed in service after 12-31-90. However, for exceptions see Act Sec. 11813(c)(2) below.

P.L. 101-508, §11813(c)(2), provides:

(2) EXCEPTIONS.—The amendments made by this section shall not apply to—

(A) any transition property (as defined in section 49(e) of the Internal Revenue Code of 1986 (as in effect on the day before the date of the enactment of this Act),

(B) any property with respect to which qualified progress expenditures were previously taken into account under section 46(d) of such Code (as so in effect), and

(C) any property described in section 46(b)(2)(C) of such Code (as so in effect).

• 1984, Deficit Reduction Act of 1984 (P.L. 98-369)

P.L. 98-369, §1035(a):

Amended Code Sec. 170(h)(5)(B). **Effective** for contributions made after 7-18-84. Prior to amendment, it read as follows:

(B) NO SURFACE MINING PERMITTED.—In the case of a contribution of any interest where there is a retention of a qualified mineral interest, subparagraph (A) shall not be treated as met if at any time there may be extraction or removal of minerals by any surface mining method.

• 1983, Technical Corrections Act of 1982 (P.L. 97-448)

P.L. 97-448, §102(f)(7):

Amended Code Sec. 170(h)(4)(B)(ii) by striking out "section 191(d)(2)" and inserting in lieu thereof "section 48(g)(3)(B)". **Effective** as if it had been included in the provision of P.L. 97-34 to which it relates.

• 1980 (P.L. 96-541)

P.L. 96-541, §6(b):

Amended Code Sec. 170 by redesignating Code Sec. 170(h) as 170(i) and Code Sec. 170(i) as 170(j), and added a new Code Sec. 170(h). **Effective** for transfers made after 12-17-80, in tax years ending after that date.

[Sec. 170(i)—Repealed]

Amendments

• 1990, Omnibus Budget Reconciliation Act of 1990 (P.L. 101-508)

P.L. 101-508, §11801(a)(11):

Repealed Code Sec. 170(i). **Effective** 11-5-90. Prior to repeal, Code Sec. 170(i) read as follows:

(i) RULE FOR NONITEMIZATION OF DEDUCTIONS.—

(1) IN GENERAL.—In the case of an individual who does not itemize his deductions for the taxable year, the applicable percentage of the amount allowable under subsection (a) for the taxable year shall be taken into account as a direct charitable deduction under section 63.

(2) APPLICABLE PERCENTAGE.—For purposes of paragraph (1), the applicable percentage shall be determined under the following table:

For taxable years beginning in—	The applicable percentage is—
1982, 1983 or 1984	25
1985	50
1986 or thereafter	100

(3) LIMITATION FOR TAXABLE YEARS BEGINNING BEFORE 1985.—In the case of a taxable year beginning before 1985, the portion of the amount allowable under subsection (a) to which the applicable percentage shall be applied—

(A) shall not exceed $100 for taxable years beginning in 1982 or 1983, and

(B) shall not exceed $300 for taxable years beginning in 1984.

In the case of a married individual filing a separate return, the limit under subparagraph (A) shall be $50, and the limit under subparagraph (B) shall be $150.

(4) TERMINATION.—The provisions of this subsection shall not apply to contributions made after December 31, 1986.

• 1981, Economic Recovery Tax Act of 1981 (P.L. 97-34)

P.L. 97-34, §121(a):

Added Code Sec. 170(i). **Effective** for contributions made after 12-31-81, in tax years beginning after 1981 and before 1987.

[Sec. 170(i)]

(i) STANDARD MILEAGE RATE FOR USE OF PASSENGER AUTOMOBILE.—For purposes of computing the deduction under this section for use of a passenger automobile, the standard mileage rate shall be 14 cents per mile.

Amendments

• 1997, Taxpayer Relief Act of 1997 (P.L. 105-34)

P.L. 105-34, §973(a):

Amended Code Sec. 170(i). **Effective** for tax years beginning after 12-31-97. Prior to amendment, Code Sec. 170(i) read as follows:

(i) STANDARD MILEAGE RATE FOR USE OF PASSENGER AUTOMOBILE.—For purposes of computing the deduction under this section for use of a passenger automobile the standard mileage rate shall be 12 cents per mile.

• **1990, Omnibus Budget Reconciliation Act of 1990 (P.L. 101-508)**

P.L. 101-508, §11801(c)(5):

Amended Code Sec. 170 by redesignating subsection (j) as subsection (i). **Effective** 11-5-90.

P.L. 101-508, §11821(b), provides:

(b) SAVINGS PROVISION.—If—

(1) any provision amended or repealed by this part applied to—

(A) any transaction occurring before the date of the enactment of this Act,

(B) any property acquired before such date of enactment, or

(C) any item of income, loss, deduction, or credit taken into account before such date of enactment, and

(2) the treatment of such transaction, property, or item under such provision would (without regard to the amendments made by this part) affect liability for tax for periods ending after such date of enactment,

nothing in the amendments made by this part shall be construed to affect the treatment of such transaction, property, or item for purposes of determining liability for tax for periods ending after such date of enactment.

• **1984, Deficit Reduction Act of 1984 (P.L. 98-369)**

P.L. 98-369, §1031(a):

Amended Code Sec. 170 by redesignating subsections (j) and (k) as subsections (k) and (l), respectively, and inserting after subsection (i) new subsection (j). **Effective** for tax years beginning after 12-31-84.

[Sec. 170(j)]

(j) DENIAL OF DEDUCTION FOR CERTAIN TRAVEL EXPENSES.—No deduction shall be allowed under this section for traveling expenses (including amounts expended for meals and lodging) while away from home, whether paid directly or by reimbursement, unless there is no significant element of personal pleasure, recreation, or vacation in such travel.

Amendments

• **1990, Omnibus Budget Reconciliation Act of 1990 (P.L. 101-508)**

P.L. 101-508, §11801(c)(5):

Amended Code Sec. 170 by redesignating subsection (k) as subsection (j). **Effective** 11-5-90.

P.L. 101-508, §11821(b), provides:

(b) SAVINGS PROVISION.—If—

(1) any provision amended or repealed by this part applied to—

(A) any transaction occurring before the date of the enactment of this Act,

(B) any property acquired before such date of enactment, or

(C) any item of income, loss, deduction, or credit taken into account before such date of enactment, and

(2) the treatment of such transaction, property, or item under such provision would (without regard to the amendments made by this part) affect liability for tax for periods ending after such date of enactment,

nothing in the amendments made by this part shall be construed to affect the treatment of such transaction, property, or item for purposes of determining liability for tax for periods ending after such date of enactment.

• **1986, Tax Reform Act of 1986 (P.L. 99-514)**

P.L. 99-514, §142(d):

Amended Code Sec. 170 by redesignating subsections (k) and (l) as subsections (l) and (m), respectively, and by inserting after subsection (j) new subsection (k). **Effective** for tax years beginning after 12-31-86.

[Sec. 170(k)]

(k) DISALLOWANCE OF DEDUCTIONS IN CERTAIN CASES.—

For disallowance of deductions for contributions to or for the use of communist controlled organizations, see section 11(a) of the Internal Security Act of 1950 (50 U.S.C. 790).

Amendments

• **1990, Omnibus Budget Reconciliation Act of 1990 (P.L. 101-508)**

P.L. 101-508, §11801(c)(5):

Amended Code Sec. 170 by redesignating subsection (l) as subsection (k). **Effective** 11-5-90.

P.L. 101-508, §11821(b), provides:

(b) SAVINGS PROVISION.—If—

(1) any provision amended or repealed by this part applied to—

(A) any transaction occurring before the date of the enactment of this Act,

(B) any property acquired before such date of enactment, or

(C) any item of income, loss, deduction, or credit taken into account before such date of enactment, and

(2) the treatment of such transaction, property, or item under such provision would (without regard to the amendments made by this part) affect liability for tax for periods ending after such date of enactment,

nothing in the amendments made by this part shall be construed to affect the treatment of such transaction, property, or item for purposes of determining liability for tax for periods ending after such date of enactment.

• **1986, Tax Reform Act of 1986 (P.L. 99-514)**

P.L. 99-514, §142(d):

Amended Code Sec. 170 by redesignating subsections (k) and (l) as subsections (l) and (m), respectively. **Effective** for tax years beginning after 12-31-86.

• **1984, Deficit Reduction Act of 1984 (P.L. 98-369)**

P.L. 98-369, §1031(a):

Amended Code Sec. 170 by redesignating subsection (j) as (k). **Effective** for tax years after 12-31-84.

• **1981, Economic Recovery Tax Act of 1981 (P.L. 97-34)**

P.L. 97-34, §121(a):

Redesignated Code Sec. 170(i) as 170(j). **Effective** for contributions made after 12-31-81, in tax years beginning after such date.

• **1980 (P.L. 96-541)**

P.L. 96-541, §6(b):

Redesignated Code Sec. 171(h) as 171(i). **Effective** for transfers made after 12-17-80, in tax years ending after that date.

• **1976, Tax Reform Act of 1976 (P.L. 94-455)**

P.L. 94-455, §1901(a)(28):

Redesignated former Code Sec. 170(i) as Code Sec. 170(h) and substituted "50 U.S.C. 790)" for "(64 Stat. 996; 50 U.S.C. 790)". **Effective** for tax years beginning after 12-31-76.

• **1969, Tax Reform Act of 1969 (P.L. 91-172)**

P.L. 91-172, §§101(j)(2), 201(a)(1)(A):

Redesignated and amended Code Sec. 170(i). **Effective** 1-1-70. Prior to amendment, the section read as follows:

(h) Disallowance of Deductions in Certain Cases.—

(1) For disallowance of deductions in case of contributions or gifts to charitable organizations engaging in prohibited transactions, see section 503(e).

(2) For disallowance of deductions for contributions to or for the use of communist controlled organizations, see section 11(a) of the Internal Security Act of 1950 (64 Stat. 996; 50 U.S.C. 790).

• 1964, Revenue Act of 1964 (P.L. 88-272)

P.L. 88-272, §209(e):

Redesignated Code Sec. 170(f) as Sec. 170(h).

• 1962 (P.L. 87-834)

P.L. 87-834, §13(d):

Redesignated Code Sec. 170(e) as Sec. 170(f). **Effective** for tax years beginning after 12-31-62.

• 1960 (P.L. 86-779)

P.L. 86-779, §7(a)(2):

Redesignated subsection (d) of Code Sec. 170 as subsection (e). **Effective** 1-1-60.

[Sec. 170(l)]

(l) TREATMENT OF CERTAIN AMOUNTS PAID TO OR FOR THE BENEFIT OF INSTITUTIONS OF HIGHER EDUCATION.—

(1) IN GENERAL.—For purposes of this section, 80 percent of any amount described in paragraph (2) shall be treated as a charitable contribution.

(2) AMOUNT DESCRIBED.—For purposes of paragraph (1), an amount is described in this paragraph if—

(A) the amount is paid by the taxpayer to or for the benefit of an educational organization—

(i) which is described in subsection (b)(1)(A)(ii), and

(ii) which is an institution of higher education (as defined in section 3304(f)), and

(B) such amount would be allowable as a deduction under this section but for the fact that the taxpayer receives (directly or indirectly) as a result of paying such amount the right to purchase tickets for seating at an athletic event in an athletic stadium of such institution.

If any portion of a payment is for the purchase of such tickets, such portion and the remaining portion (if any) of such payment shall be treated as separate amounts for purposes of this subsection.

Amendments

• 1990, Omnibus Budget Reconciliation Act of 1990 (P.L. 101-508)

P.L. 101-508, §11801(c)(5):

Amended Code Sec. 170 by redesignating subsection (m) as subsection (l). **Effective** 11-5-90.

P.L. 101-508, §11821, provides:

(b) SAVINGS PROVISION.—If—

(1) any provision amended or repealed by this part applied to—

(A) any transaction occurring before the date of the enactment of this Act,

(B) any property acquired before such date of enactment, or

(C) any item of income, loss, deduction, or credit taken into account before such date of enactment, and

(2) the treatment of such transaction, property, or item under such provision would (without regard to the amendments made by this part) affect liability for tax for periods ending after such date of enactment,

nothing in the amendments made by this part shall be construed to affect the treatment of such transaction, property, or item for purposes of determining liability for tax for periods ending after such date of enactment.

• 1988, Technical and Miscellaneous Revenue Act of 1988 (P.L. 100-647)

P.L. 100-647, §6001(a):

Amended Code Sec. 170 by redesignating subsection (m) as subsection (n) and adding after subsection (l) new subsection (m). **Effective**, generally, for tax years beginning after 12-31-83. See Act Sec. 6001(b)(2), below, for a special rule.

P.L. 100-647, §6001(b)(2), provides:

(2) WAIVER OF STATUTE OF LIMITATIONS.—If on the date of the enactment of this Act (or at any time within 1 year after such date of enactment) refund or credit of any overpayment of tax resulting from the application of section 170(m) of the 1986 Code (as added by subsection (a)) is barred by any law or rule of law, refund or credit of such overpayment shall, nevertheless, be made or allowed if claim therefore is filed before the date 1 year after the date of the enactment of this Act.

[Sec. 170(m)]

(m) CERTAIN DONEE INCOME FROM INTELLECTUAL PROPERTY TREATED AS AN ADDITIONAL CHARITABLE CONTRIBUTION.—

(1) TREATMENT AS ADDITIONAL CONTRIBUTION.—In the case of a taxpayer who makes a qualified intellectual property contribution, the deduction allowed under subsection (a) for each taxable year of the taxpayer ending on or after the date of such contribution shall be increased (subject to the limitations under subsection (b)) by the applicable percentage of qualified donee income with respect to such contribution which is properly allocable to such year under this subsection.

(2) REDUCTION IN ADDITIONAL DEDUCTIONS TO EXTENT OF INITIAL DEDUCTION.—With respect to any qualified intellectual property contribution, the deduction allowed under subsection (a) shall be increased under paragraph (1) only to the extent that the aggregate amount of such increases with respect to such contribution exceed the amount allowed as a deduction under subsection (a) with respect to such contribution determined without regard to this subsection.

(3) QUALIFIED DONEE INCOME.—For purposes of this subsection, the term "qualified donee income" means any net income received by or accrued to the donee which is properly allocable to the qualified intellectual property.

(4) ALLOCATION OF QUALIFIED DONEE INCOME TO TAXABLE YEARS OF DONOR.—For purposes of this subsection, qualified donee income shall be treated as properly allocable to a taxable year of the

donor if such income is received by or accrued to the donee for the taxable year of the donee which ends within or with such taxable year of the donor.

(5) 10-YEAR LIMITATION.—Income shall not be treated as properly allocable to qualified intellectual property for purposes of this subsection if such income is received by or accrued to the donee after the 10-year period beginning on the date of the contribution of such property.

(6) BENEFIT LIMITED TO LIFE OF INTELLECTUAL PROPERTY.—Income shall not be treated as properly allocable to qualified intellectual property for purposes of this subsection if such income is received by or accrued to the donee after the expiration of the legal life of such property.

(7) APPLICABLE PERCENTAGE.—For purposes of this subsection, the term "applicable percentage" means the percentage determined under the following table which corresponds to a taxable year of the donor ending on or after the date of the qualified intellectual property contribution:

Taxable Year of Donor Ending on or After Date of Contribution:	Applicable Percentage:
1st	100
2nd	100
3rd	90
4th	80
5th	70
6th	60
7th	50
8th	40
9th	30
10th	20
11th	10
12th	10.

(8) QUALIFIED INTELLECTUAL PROPERTY CONTRIBUTION.—For purposes of this subsection, the term "qualified intellectual property contribution" means any charitable contribution of qualified intellectual property—

(A) the amount of which taken into account under this section is reduced by reason of subsection (e)(1), and

(B) with respect to which the donor informs the donee at the time of such contribution that the donor intends to treat such contribution as a qualified intellectual property contribution for purposes of this subsection and section 6050L.

(9) QUALIFIED INTELLECTUAL PROPERTY.—For purposes of this subsection, the term "qualified intellectual property" means property described in subsection (e)(1)(B)(iii) (other than property contributed to or for the use of an organization described in subsection (e)(1)(B)(ii)).

(10) OTHER SPECIAL RULES.—

(A) APPLICATION OF LIMITATIONS ON CHARITABLE CONTRIBUTIONS.—Any increase under this subsection of the deduction provided under subsection (a) shall be treated for purposes of subsection (b) as a deduction which is attributable to a charitable contribution to the donee to which such increase relates.

(B) NET INCOME DETERMINED BY DONEE.—The net income taken into account under paragraph (3) shall not exceed the amount of such income reported under section 6050L(b)(1).

(C) DEDUCTION LIMITED TO 12 TAXABLE YEARS.—Except as may be provided under subparagraph (D)(i), this subsection shall not apply with respect to any qualified intellectual property contribution for any taxable year of the donor after the 12th taxable year of the donor which ends on or after the date of such contribution.

(D) REGULATIONS.—The Secretary may issue regulations or other guidance to carry out the purposes of this subsection, including regulations or guidance—

(i) modifying the application of this subsection in the case of a donor or donee with a short taxable year, and

(ii) providing for the determination of an amount to be treated as net income of the donee which is properly allocable to qualified intellectual property in the case of a donee who uses such property to further a purpose or function constituting the basis of the donee's exemption under section 501 (or, in the case of a governmental unit, any purpose described in section 170(c)) and does not possess a right to receive any payment from a third party with respect to such property.

Amendments

• 2004, American Jobs Creation Act of 2004 (P.L. 108-357)

P.L. 108-357, §882(b):

Amended Code Sec. 170 by redesignating subsection (m) as subsection (n) and by inserting after subsection (l) a new subsection (m). **Effective** for contributions made after 6-3-2004.

[Sec. 170(n)]

(n) EXPENSES PAID BY CERTAIN WHALING CAPTAINS IN SUPPORT OF NATIVE ALASKAN SUBSISTENCE WHALING.—

(1) IN GENERAL.—In the case of an individual who is recognized by the Alaska Eskimo Whaling Commission as a whaling captain charged with the responsibility of maintaining and carrying out sanctioned whaling activities and who engages in such activities during the taxable year, the amount described in paragraph (2) (to the extent such amount does not exceed $10,000 for the taxable year) shall be treated for purposes of this section as a charitable contribution.

(2) AMOUNT DESCRIBED.—

(A) IN GENERAL.—The amount described in this paragraph is the aggregate of the reasonable and necessary whaling expenses paid by the taxpayer during the taxable year in carrying out sanctioned whaling activities.

(B) WHALING EXPENSES.—For purposes of subparagraph (A), the term "whaling expenses" includes expenses for—

(i) the acquisition and maintenance of whaling boats, weapons, and gear used in sanctioned whaling activities,

(ii) the supplying of food for the crew and other provisions for carrying out such activities, and

(iii) storage and distribution of the catch from such activities.

(3) SANCTIONED WHALING ACTIVITIES.—For purposes of this subsection, the term "sanctioned whaling activities" means subsistence bowhead whale hunting activities conducted pursuant to the management plan of the Alaska Eskimo Whaling Commission.

(4) SUBSTANTIATION OF EXPENSES.—The Secretary shall issue guidance requiring that the taxpayer substantiate the whaling expenses for which a deduction is claimed under this subsection, including by maintaining appropriate written records with respect to the time, place, date, amount, and nature of the expense, as well as the taxpayer's eligibility for such deduction, and that (to the extent provided by the Secretary) such substantiation be provided as part of the taxpayer's return of tax.

Amendments

• 2004, American Jobs Creation Act of 2004 (P.L. 108-357)

P.L. 108-357, §335(a):

Amended Code Sec. 170, as amended by this Act, by redesignating subsection (n) as subsection (o) and by inserting after subsection (m) a new subsection (n). **Effective** for contributions made after 12-31-2004.

[Sec. 170(o)]

(o) SPECIAL RULES FOR FRACTIONAL GIFTS.—

(1) DENIAL OF DEDUCTION IN CERTAIN CASES.—

(A) IN GENERAL.—No deduction shall be allowed for a contribution of an undivided portion of a taxpayer's entire interest in tangible personal property unless all interests in the property are held immediately before such contribution by—

(i) the taxpayer, or

(ii) the taxpayer and the donee.

(B) EXCEPTIONS.—The Secretary may, by regulation, provide for exceptions to subparagraph (A) in cases where all persons who hold an interest in the property make proportional contributions of an undivided portion of the entire interest held by such persons.

(2) VALUATION OF SUBSEQUENT GIFTS.—In the case of any additional contribution, the fair market value of such contribution shall be determined by using the lesser of—

(A) the fair market value of the property at the time of the initial fractional contribution, or

(B) the fair market value of the property at the time of the additional contribution.

(3) RECAPTURE OF DEDUCTION IN CERTAIN CASES; ADDITION TO TAX.—

(A) RECAPTURE.—The Secretary shall provide for the recapture of the amount of any deduction allowed under this section (plus interest) with respect to any contribution of an undivided portion of a taxpayer's entire interest in tangible personal property—

(i) in any case in which the donor does not contribute all of the remaining interests in such property to the donee (or, if such donee is no longer in existence, to any person described in section 170(c)) on or before the earlier of—

(I) the date that is 10 years after the date of the initial fractional contribution, or

(II) the date of the death of the donor, and

(ii) in any case in which the donee has not, during the period beginning on the date of the initial fractional contribution and ending on the date described in clause (i)—

(I) had substantial physical possession of the property, and

(II) used the property in a use which is related to a purpose or function constituting the basis for the organizations' exemption under section 501.

(B) ADDITION TO TAX.—The tax imposed under this chapter for any taxable year for which there is a recapture under subparagraph (A) shall be increased by 10 percent of the amount so recaptured.

(4) DEFINITIONS.—For purposes of this subsection—

(A) ADDITIONAL CONTRIBUTION.—The term "additional contribution" means any charitable contribution by the taxpayer of any interest in property with respect to which the taxpayer has previously made an initial fractional contribution.

(B) INITIAL FRACTIONAL CONTRIBUTION.—The term "initial fractional contribution" means, with respect to any taxpayer, the first charitable contribution of an undivided portion of the taxpayer's entire interest in any tangible personal property.

Amendments

• 2007, Tax Technical Corrections Act of 2007 (P.L. 110-172)

P.L. 110-172, §11(a)(16)(A):

Amended Code Sec. 170(o)(1)(A) by striking "all interest in the property is" and inserting "all interests in the property are". **Effective** 12-29-2007.

P.L. 110-172, §11(a)(16)(B)(i)-(ii):

Amended Code Sec. 170(o)(3)(A)(i) by striking "interest" and inserting "interests", and by striking "before" and inserting "on or before". **Effective** 12-29-2007.

• 2006, Pension Protection Act of 2006 (P.L. 109-280)

P.L. 109-280, §1218(a):

Amended Code Sec. 170 by redesignating subsection (o) as subsection (p) and by inserting after subsection (n) a new subsection (o). **Effective** for contributions, bequests, and gifts made after 8-17-2006.

[Sec. 170(p)]

(p) OTHER CROSS REFERENCES.—

(1) For treatment of certain organizations providing child care, see section 501(k).

(2) For charitable contributions of estates and trusts, see section 642(c).

(3) For nondeductibility of contributions by common trust funds, see section 584.

(4) For charitable contributions of partners, see section 702.

(5) For charitable contributions of nonresident aliens, see section 873.

(6) For treatment of gifts for benefit of or use in connection with the Naval Academy as gifts to or for the use of the United States, see section 6973 of title 10, United States Code.

(7) For treatment of gifts accepted by the Secretary of State, the Director of the International Communication Agency, or the Director of the United States International Development Cooperation Agency, as gifts to or for the use of the United States, see section 25 of the State Department Basic Authorities Act of 1956.

(8) For treatment of gifts of money accepted by the Attorney General for credit to the "Commissary Funds, Federal Prisons" as gifts to or for the use of the United States, see section 4043 of title 18, United States Code.

(9) For charitable contributions to or for the use of Indian tribal governments (or their subdivisions), see section 7871.

Amendments

• 2006, Pension Protection Act of 2006 (P.L. 109-280)

P.L. 109-280, §1218(a):

Amended Code Sec. 170 by redesignating subsection (o) as subsection (p). **Effective** for contributions, bequests, and gifts made after 8-17-2006.

• 2004, American Jobs Creation Act of 2004 (P.L. 108-357)

P.L. 108-357, §335(a):

Amended Code Sec. 170, as amended by this Act, by redesignating subsection (n) as subsection (o). **Effective** for contributions made after 12-31-2004.

P.L. 108-357, §882(b):

Amended Code Sec. 170 by redesignating subsection (m) as subsection (n). **Effective** for contributions made after 6-3-2004.

• 1990, Omnibus Budget Reconciliation Act of 1990 (P.L. 101-508)

P.L. 101-508, §11801(c)(5):

Amended Code Sec. 170 by redesignating subsection (n) as subsection (m). **Effective** 11-5-90.

P.L. 101-508, §11821(b), provides:

(b) SAVINGS PROVISION.—If—

(1) any provision amended or repealed by this part applied to—

(A) any transaction occurring before the date of the enactment of this Act,

(B) any property acquired before such date of enactment, or

(C) any item of income, loss, deduction, or credit taken into account before such date of enactment, and

(2) the treatment of such transaction, property, or item under such provision would (without regard to the amend-

ments made by this part) affect liability for tax for periods ending after such date of enactment,

nothing in the amendments made by this part shall be construed to affect the treatment of such transaction, property, or item for purposes of determining liability for tax for periods ending after such date of enactment.

• 1988, Technical and Miscellaneous Revenue Act of 1988 (P.L. 100-647)

P.L. 100-647, §6001(a):

Amended Code Sec. 170 by redesignating subsection (m) as subsection (n) and adding after subsection (l) new subsection (m). **Effective**, generally, for tax years beginning after 12-31-83. See Act Sec. 6001(b)(2), below, for a special rule.

P.L. 100-647, §6001(b)(2), provides:

(2) WAIVER OF STATUTE OF LIMITATIONS.—If on the date of the enactment of this Act (or at any time within 1 year after such date of enactment) refund or credit of any overpayment of tax resulting from the application of section 170(m) of the 1986 Code (as added by subsection (a)) is barred by any law or rule of law, refund or credit of such overpayment shall, nevertheless, be made or allowed if claim therefore is filed before the date 1 year after the date of the enactment of this Act.

• 1986, Tax Reform Act of 1986 (P.L. 99-514)

P.L. 99-514, §142(d):

Amended Code Sec. 170 by redesignating subsections (k) and (l) as subsections (l) and (m), respectively. **Effective** for tax years beginning after 12-31-86.

• 1984, Deficit Reduction Act of 1984 (P.L. 98-369)

P.L. 98-369, §1031(a):

Redesignated Code Sec. 170(k) as 170(l). **Effective** for tax years beginning after 1984.

P.L. 98-369, §1032(b)(1):

Amended Code Sec. 170(k), redesignated as (l) by Act Sec. 1031, by redesignating paragraphs (1) through (8) as paragraphs (2) through (9), respectively, and by inserting before paragraph (2) (as so redesignated) new paragraph (1). **Effective** for tax years beginning after 7-18-84.

• 1983 (P.L. 97-473)

P.L. 97-473, §202(b)(4):

Added Code Sec. 170(k)(8). For the **effective** date, see the amendment note for P.L. 97-473, Act Sec. 204 following Code Sec. 7871.

• 1982 (P.L. 97-258)

P.L. 97-258, §3(f)(1):

Amended Code Sec. 170(k)(7) by striking out "section 2 of the Act of May 15, 1952, as amended by the Act of July 9, 1952 (31 U.S.C. 725s-4)" and substituting "section 4043 of title 18, United States Code". **Effective** 9-13-82.

• 1981, Economic Recovery Tax Act of 1981 (P.L. 97-34)

P.L. 97-34, §121(a):

Redesignated Code Sec. 170(j) as 170(k). **Effective** for contributions made after 12-31-81, in tax years beginning after such date.

P.L. 96-541, §6(b):

Redesignated Code Sec. 170(i) as 170(j). **Effective** for transfers made after 12-17-80, in tax years ending after that date.

• 1980, Foreign Service Act of 1980 (P.L. 96-465)

P.L. 96-465, §2206(e)(2):

Amended Code Sec. 170(i)(6). **Effective** 2-15-81. Prior to amendment, paragraph (6) read as follows: "(6) For treatment of gifts accepted by the Secretary of State under the Foreign Service Act of 1946 as gifts to or for the use of the United States, see section 1021(e) of that Act (22 U.S.C. 809(e))."

• 1976, Tax Reform Act of 1976 (P.L. 94-455)

P.L. 94-455, §1901(a)(28):

Amended and redesignated former Code Sec. 170(j) as Code Sec. 170(i). **Effective** for tax years beginning after 12-31-76. Prior to amendment, redesignated Code Sec. 170(i) read as follows:

(j) OTHER CROSS REFERENCES.—

(1) For charitable contributions of estates and trusts, see section 642(c).

(2) For nondeductibility of contributions by common trust funds, see section 584.

(3) For charitable contributions of partners, see section 702.

(4) For charitable contributions of nonresident aliens, see section 873.

(5) For treatment of gifts for benefit of or use in connection with the Naval Academy as gifts to or for the use of the United States, see section 3 of the Act of March 31, 1944 (58 Stat. 135; 34 U.S.C. 1115b).

(6) For treatment of gifts for benefit of the library of the Post Office Department as gifts to or for the use of the United States, see section 2 of the Act of August 8, 1946 (60 Stat. 924; 5 U.S.C. 393).

(7) For treatment of gifts accepted by the Secretary of State under the Foreign Service Act of 1946 as gifts to or for the use of the United States, see section 1021(e) of that Act (60 Stat. 1032; 22 U.S.C. 809(e)).

(8) For treatment of gifts of money accepted by the Attorney General for credit to the "Commissary Funds Federal Prisons" as gifts to or for the use of the United States, see section 2 of the Act of May 15, 1952 (66 Stat. 73, as amended by the Act of July 9, 1952, 66 Stat. 479, 31 U.S.C. 725s-4).

• 1969, Tax Reform Act of 1969 (P.L. 91-172)

P.L. 91-172, §201(a)(1)(A):

Redesignated Code Sec. 170(i) as Code Sec. 170(j). **Effective** 1-1-70.

• 1964, Revenue Act of 1964 (P.L. 88-272)

P.L. 88-272, §209(e):

Redesignated Code Sec. 170(g) as Sec. 170(i). **Effective** 1-1-64.

• 1962, Revenue Act of 1962 (P.L. 87-834)

P.L. 87-834, §13(d):

Redesignated Code Sec. 170(f) as Sec. 170(g). **Effective** for tax years beginning after 12-31-62.

• 1960 (P.L. 86-779)

P.L. 86-779, §7(a)(2):

Redesignated subsection (e) of Code Sec. 170 as subsection (f). **Effective** 1-1-60.

[Sec. 171]

SEC. 171. AMORTIZABLE BOND PREMIUM.

[Sec. 171(a)]

(a) GENERAL RULE.—In the case of any bond, as defined in subsection (d), the following rules shall apply to the amortizable bond premium (determined under subsection (b)) on the bond:

(1) TAXABLE BONDS.—In the case of a bond (other than a bond the interest on which is excludable from gross income), the amount of the amortizable bond premium for the taxable year shall be allowed as a deduction.

(2) TAX-EXEMPT BONDS.—In the case of any bond the interest on which is excludable from gross income, no deduction shall be allowed for the amortizable bond premium for the taxable year.

(3) CROSS REFERENCE.—

For adjustment to basis on account of amortizable bond premium, see section 1016(a)(2).

Amendments

• 1976, Tax Reform Act of 1976 (P.L. 94-455)

P.L. 94-455, §1901(b)(1):

Amended Code Sec. 171(a) by striking out paragraph (3) and by redesignating paragraph (4) as paragraph (3). **Effective** for tax years beginning after 12-31-76. Prior to repeal, Code Sec. 171(a)(3) read as follows:

(3) ADJUSTMENT OF CREDIT OR DEDUCTION FOR INTEREST PARTIALLY TAX-EXEMPT.—

(A) INDIVIDUALS.—In the case of any bond the interest on which is allowable as a credit under section 35, the amount which would otherwise be taken into account in computing such credit shall be reduced by the amount of the amortizable bond premium for the taxable year.

(B) CORPORATIONS.—In the case of any bond the interest on which is allowable as a deduction under section 242, such deduction shall be reduced by the amount of the amortizable bond premium for the taxable year.

Amended Code Sec. 171(a) by changing the heading of paragraph (1) to read "Taxable bonds," effective for taxable years beginning after December 31, 1976. Prior to amendment it read as follows: "(1) Interest wholly or partially taxable."

Amended Code Sec. 171(a) by changing the heading of paragraph (2) to read "(2) Tax-exempt bonds, effective for taxable years beginning after December 31, 1976." Prior to amendment it read as follows: "Interest wholly tax-exempt."

[Sec. 171(b)]

(b) AMORTIZABLE BOND PREMIUM.—

(1) AMOUNT OF BOND PREMIUM.—For purposes of paragraph (2), the amount of bond premium, in the case of the holder of any bond, shall be determined—

(A) with reference to the amount of the basis (for determining loss on sale or exchange) of such bond,

(B) (i) with reference to the amount payable on maturity or on earlier call date, in the case of any bond other than a bond to which clause (ii) applies, and [sic]

(ii) with reference to the amount payable on maturity (or if it results in a smaller amortizable bond premium attributable to the period of earlier call date, with reference to the amount payable on earlier call date), in the case of any bond described in subsection (a)(1) which is acquired after December 31, 1957, and

(C) with adjustments proper to reflect unamortized bond premium, with respect to the bond, for the period before the date as of which subsection (a) becomes applicable with respect to the taxpayer with respect to such bond.

In no case shall the amount of bond premium on a convertible bond include any amount attributable to the conversion features of the bond.

(2) AMOUNT AMORTIZABLE.—The amortizable bond premium of the taxable year shall be the amount of the bond premium attributable to such year. In the case of a bond to which paragraph (1)(B)(ii) applies and which has a call date, the amount of bond premium attributable to the taxable year in which the bond is called shall include an amount equal to the excess of the amount of the adjusted basis (for determining loss on sale or exchange) of such bond as of the beginning of the taxable year over the amount received on redemption of the bond or (if greater) the amount payable on maturity.

(3) METHOD OF DETERMINATION.—

(A) IN GENERAL.—Except as provided in regulations prescribed by the Secretary, the determinations required under paragraphs (1) and (2) shall be made on the basis of the taxpayer's yield to maturity determined by—

(i) using the taxpayer's basis (for purposes of determining loss on sale or exchange) of the obligation, and

(ii) compounding at the close of each accrual period (as defined in section 1272(a)(5)).

(B) SPECIAL RULE WHERE EARLIER CALL DATE IS USED.—For purposes of subparagraph (A), if the amount payable on an earlier call date is used under paragraph (1)(B)(ii) in determining the amortizable bond premium attributable to the period before the earlier call date, such bond shall be treated as maturing on such date for the amount so payable and then reissued on such date for the amount so payable.

(4) TREATMENT OF CERTAIN BONDS ACQUIRED IN EXCHANGE FOR OTHER PROPERTY.—

(A) IN GENERAL.—If—

(i) a bond is acquired by any person in exchange for other property, and

(ii) the basis of such bond is determined (in whole or in part) by reference to the basis of such other property,

for purposes of applying this subsection to such bond while held by such person, the basis of such bond shall not exceed its fair market value immediately after the exchange. A similar rule shall apply in the case of such bond while held by any other person whose basis is determined (in whole or in part) by reference to the basis in the hands of the person referred to in clause (i).

(B) SPECIAL RULE WHERE BOND EXCHANGED IN REORGANIZATION.—Subparagraph (A) shall not apply to an exchange by the taxpayer of a bond for another bond if such exchange is a part of a reorganization (as defined in section 368). If any portion of the basis of the taxpayer in a bond transferred in such an exchange is not taken into account in determining bond premium by reason of this paragraph, such portion shall not be taken into account in determining the amount of bond premium on any bond received in the exchange.

Amendments

• 1986, Tax Reform Act of 1986 (P.L. 99-514)

P.L. 99-514, §1803(a)(11)(A):

Amended Code Sec. 171(b)(3). **Effective** for obligations issued after 9-27-85. In the case of a taxpayer with respect to whom an election is in effect on 10-22-86 under Section 171(c) of the Internal Revenue Code of 1954, such election shall apply to obligations issued after 9-27-85, only if the taxpayer chooses (at such time and in such manner as may be prescribed by the Secretary of the Treasury or his delegate) to have such election apply with respect to such obligations. Prior to amendment, Code Sec. 171(b)(3) read as follows:

(3) METHOD OF DETERMINATION.—The determinations required under paragraphs (1) and (2) shall be made—

(A) in accordance with the method of amortizing bond premium regularly employed by the holder of the bond, if such method is reasonable;

(B) in all other cases, in accordance with regulations prescribing reasonable methods of amortizing bond premium prescribed by the Secretary.

P.L. 99-514, §1803(a)(12)(A):

Amended Code Sec. 171(b) by adding at the end thereof new paragraph (4). **Effective** for exchanges after 5-6-86.

• 1976, Tax Reform Act of 1976 (P.L. 94-455)

P.L. 94-455, §1901(b)(1):

Substituted "subsection (a)(1)" for "subsection (c)(1)(B)" in clause (1)(B)(ii). **Effective** for tax years beginning after 12-31-76.

P.L. 94-455, §1951(b):

Struck out clause (1)(B)(iii), substituted "clause (ii) applies, or" for "clause (ii) or (iii) applies," in clause (1)(B)(i), substituted "and" for "or" at the end of clause (1)(B)(ii), and struck out "or (iii)" in subparagraph (b)(2). **Effective** for tax years beginning after 12-31-76. Prior to repeal, clause (b)(1)(B)(iii) read as follows:

(iii) with reference to the amount payable on maturity, in the case of any bond described in subsection (c)(1)(B) which was acquired after January 22, 1954, and before January 1, 1958, but only if such bond was issued after January 22, 1951, and has a call date not more than 3 years after the date of such issue, and

P.L. 94-455, §1951(b)(5)(B), provides:

(B) SAVINGS PROVISION.—Notwithstanding the amendments made by subparagraph (A), in the case of a bond the interest on which is not excludable from gross income—

(i) which was issued after January 22, 1951, with a call date not more than 3 years after the date of such issue, and

(ii) which was acquired by the taxpayer after January 22, 1954, and before January 1, 1958,

the bond premium for a taxable year beginning after December 31, 1975, shall not be determined under section 171(b)(1)(B)(i) but shall be determined with reference to the amount payable on maturity, and if the bond is called before its maturity, the bond premium for the year in which the bond is called shall be determined in accordance with the provisions of section 171(b)(2).

• 1958, Technical Amendments Act of 1958 (P.L. 85-866)

P.L. 85-866, §13(a)(1):

Amended Code Sec. 171(b)(1)(B). **Effective** 1-1-58. Prior to amendment, Code Sec. 171(b)(1)(B) read as follows:

"(B) with reference to the amount payable on maturity or on earlier call date (but in the case of bonds described in subsection (c)(1)(B) issued after January 22, 1951, and acquired after January 22, 1954, only if such earlier call date is a date more than 3 years after the date of such issue), and"

P.L. 85-866, §13(a)(2):

Struck out at the beginning of the second sentence of Sec. 171(b)(2) the phrase "In the case of a bond described in subsection (c)(1)(B) issued after January 22, 1951, and acquired after January 22, 1954, which has a call date not more than 3 years after the date of such issue," and substituted the phrase "In the case of a bond to which paragraph (1)(B)(ii) or (iii) applies and which has a call date,". **Effective** 1-1-58.

[Sec. 171(c)]

(c) ELECTION AS TO TAXABLE BONDS.—

(1) ELIGIBILITY TO ELECT; BONDS WITH RESPECT TO WHICH ELECTION PERMITTED.—In the case of bonds the interest on which is not excludable from gross income, this section shall apply only if the taxpayer has so elected.

(2) MANNER AND EFFECT OF ELECTION.—The election authorized under this subsection shall be made in accordance with such regulations as the Secretary shall prescribe. If such election is made with respect to any bond (described in paragraph (1)) of the taxpayer, it shall also apply to all such bonds held by the taxpayer at the beginning of the first taxable year to which the election applies and to all such bonds thereafter acquired by him and shall be binding for all subsequent taxable years with respect to all such bonds of the taxpayer, unless, on application by the taxpayer, the Secretary permits him, subject to such conditions as the Secretary deems necessary, to revoke such election. In the case of bonds held by a common trust fund, as defined in section 584(a), the election authorized under this subsection shall be exercisable with respect to such bonds only by the common trust fund. In case of bonds held by an estate or trust, the election authorized under this subsection shall be exercisable with respect to such bonds only by the fiduciary.

Amendments

• 2004, American Jobs Creation Act of 2004 (P.L. 108-357)

P.L. 108-357, §413(c)(2)(A)-(B):

Amended Code Sec. 171(c)(2) by striking ", or by a foreign personal holding company, as defined in section 552" immediately following "as defined in section 584(a),", and by striking ", or foreign personal holding company" before the period at the end of the third sentence. **Effective** for tax years of foreign corporations beginning after 12-31-2004, and for tax years of United States shareholders with or within which such tax years of foreign corporations end.

• 1976, Tax Reform Act of 1976 (P.L. 94-455)

P.L. 94-455, §1901(b)(1):

Amended Code Sec. 171(c)(1). **Effective** for tax years beginning after 12-31-76. Prior to amendment, Code Sec. 171(c)(1) read as follows:

(c) ELECTION AS TO TAXABLE AND PARTIALLY TAXABLE BONDS.—

(1) ELIGIBILITY TO ELECT BONDS WITH RESPECT TO WHICH ELECTION PERMITTED.—This section shall apply with respect to the following classes of taxpayers with respect to the following classes of bonds only if the taxpayer has elected to have this section apply:

(A) PARTIALLY TAX-EXEMPT.—In the case of a taxpayer other than a corporation, bonds with respect to the interest on which the credit provided in section 35 is allowable; and

(B) WHOLLY TAXABLE.—In the case of any taxpayer, bonds the interest on which is not excludable from gross income but with respect to which the credit provided in section 35, or the deduction provided in section 242, is not allowable.

P.L. 94-455, §1906(b)(13)(A):

Amended 1954 Code by substituting "Secretary" for "Secretary or his delegate" each place it appeared. **Effective** 2-1-77.

[Sec. 171(d)]

(d) BOND DEFINED.—For purposes of this section, the term "bond" means any bond, debenture, note, or certificate or other evidence of indebtedness, but does not include any such obligation which constitutes stock in trade of the taxpayer or any such obligation of a kind which would properly be included in the inventory of the taxpayer if on hand at the close of the taxable year, or any such obligation held by the taxpayer primarily for sale to customers in the ordinary course of his trade or business.

Amendments

• 1986, Tax Reform Act of 1986 (P.L. 99-514)

P.L. 99-514, §1803(a)(11)(B):

Amended Code Sec. 171(d) by striking out "issued by any corporation and bearing interest (including any like obligation issued by a government or political subdivision thereof)," after "evidence of indebtedness". **Effective** for obligations issued after 9-27-85. In the case of a taxpayer with respect to whom an election is in effect on the date of the enactment of this Act under Section 171(c) of the Internal Revenue Code of 1954, such election shall apply to obligations issued after 9-27-85, only if the taxpayer chooses (at such time and in such manner as may be prescribed by the Secretary of the Treasury or his delegate) to have such election apply with respect to such obligations.

[Sec. 171(e)]

(e) TREATMENT AS OFFSET TO INTEREST PAYMENTS.—Except as provided in regulations, in the case of any taxable bond—

(1) the amount of any bond premium shall be allocated among the interest payments on the bond under rules similar to the rules of subsection (b)(3), and

(2) in lieu of any deduction under subsection (a), the amount of any premium so allocated to any interest payment shall be applied against (and operate to reduce) the amount of such interest payment.

For purposes of the preceding sentence, the term "taxable bond" means any bond the interest of which is not excludable from gross income.

Amendments

• 1988, Technical and Miscellaneous Revenue Act of 1988 (P.L. 100-647)

P.L. 100-647, §1006(j)(1)(A):

Amended Code Sec. 171(e). **Effective** in the case of obligations acquired after 12-31-87; except that the taxpayer may elect to have such amendment apply to obligations acquired after 10-22-86. Prior to amendment, Code Sec. 171(e) read as follows:

(e) TREATMENT AS INTEREST.—Except as provided in regulations, the amount of any amortizable bond premium with respect to which a deduction is allowed under subsection (a)(1) for any taxable year shall be treated as interest for purposes of this title.

• 1986, Tax Reform Act of 1986 (P.L. 99-514)

P.L. 99-514, §643(a):

Amended Code Sec. 171 by redesignating subsection (e) as (f) and inserting after subsection (d) new subsection (e). **Effective** for obligations acquired after 10-22-86, in tax years ending after such date.

P.L. 99-514, §643(b)(2), as amended by P.L. 100-647, §1006(j)(2), provides:

(2) REVOCATION OF ELECTION.—In the case of a taxpayer with respect to whom an election is in effect on the date of enactment of this Act under section 171(c) of the Internal Revenue Code of 1986, such election shall apply to obligations acquired after the date of the enactment of this Act only if the taxpayer chooses (at such time and in such manner as may be prescribed by the Secretary of the Treasury or his delegate) to have such election apply with respect to such obligations.

[Sec. 171(f)]

(f) DEALERS IN TAX-EXEMPT SECURITIES.—

For special rules applicable, in the case of dealers in securities, with respect to premium attributable to certain wholly tax-exempt securities, see section 75.

Amendments

• 1986, Tax Reform Act of 1986 (P.L. 99-514)

P.L. 99-514, §643(a):

Amended Code Sec. 171 by redesignating subsection (e) as (f). **Effective** for obligations acquired after 10-22-86, in tax years ending after such date.

[Sec. 172]

SEC. 172. NET OPERATING LOSS DEDUCTION.

[Sec. 172(a)]

(a) DEDUCTION ALLOWED.—There shall be allowed as a deduction for the taxable year an amount equal to the aggregate of (1) the net operating loss carryovers to such year, plus (2) the net operating loss carrybacks to such year. For purposes of this subtitle, the term "net operating loss deduction" means the deduction allowed by this subsection.

[Sec. 172(b)]

(b) NET OPERATING LOSS CARRYBACKS AND CARRYOVERS.—

(1) YEARS TO WHICH LOSS MAY BE CARRIED.—

(A) GENERAL RULE.—Except as otherwise provided in this paragraph, a net operating loss for any taxable year—

(i) shall be a net operating loss carryback to each of the 2 taxable years preceding the taxable year of such loss, and

(ii) shall be a net operating loss carryover to each of the 20 taxable years following the taxable year of the loss.

(B) SPECIAL RULES FOR REIT'S.—

(i) IN GENERAL.—A net operating loss for a REIT year shall not be a net operating loss carryback to any taxable year preceding the taxable year of such loss.

(ii) SPECIAL RULE.—In the case of any net operating loss for a taxable year which is not a REIT year, such loss shall not be carried back to any taxable year which is a REIT year.

(iii) REIT YEAR.—For purposes of this subparagraph, the term "REIT year" means any taxable year for which the provisions of part II of subchapter M (relating to real estate investment trusts) apply to the taxpayer.

(C) SPECIFIED LIABILITY LOSSES.—In the case of a taxpayer which has a specified liability loss (as defined in subsection (f)) for a taxable year, such specified liability loss shall be a net operating loss carryback to each of the 10 taxable years preceding the taxable year of such loss.

(D) BAD DEBT LOSSES OF COMMERCIAL BANKS.—In the case of any bank (as defined in section 585(a)(2)), the portion of the net operating loss for any taxable year beginning after December 31, 1986, and before January 1, 1994, which is attributable to the deduction allowed under section 166(a) shall be a net operating loss carryback to each of the 10 taxable years preceding the taxable year of the loss and a net operating loss carryover to each of the 5 taxable years following the taxable year of such loss.

(E) EXCESS INTEREST LOSS.—

(i) IN GENERAL.—If—

(I) there is a corporate equity reduction transaction, and

(II) an applicable corporation has a corporate equity reduction interest loss for any loss limitation year ending after August 2, 1989,

then the corporate equity reduction interest loss shall be a net operating loss carryback and carryover to the taxable years described in subparagraph (A), except that such loss shall not be carried back to a taxable year preceding the taxable year in which the corporate equity reduction transaction occurs.

(ii) LOSS LIMITATION YEAR.—For purposes of clause (i) and subsection (h), the term "loss limitation year" means, with respect to any corporate equity reduction transaction, the taxable year in which such transaction occurs and each of the 2 succeeding taxable years.

(iii) APPLICABLE CORPORATION.—For purposes of clause (i), the term "applicable corporation" means—

(I) a C corporation which acquires stock, or the stock of which is acquired in a major stock acquisition,

(II) a C corporation making distributions with respect to, or redeeming, its stock in connection with an excess distribution, or

(III) a C corporation which is a successor of a corporation described in subclause (I) or (II).

(iv) OTHER DEFINITIONS.—

For definitions of terms used in this subparagraph, see subsection (h).

(F) RETENTION OF 3-YEAR CARRYBACK IN CERTAIN CASES.—

(i) IN GENERAL.—Subparagraph (A)(i) shall be applied by substituting "3 taxable years" for "2 taxable years" with respect to the portion of the net operating loss for the taxable year which is an eligible loss with respect to the taxpayer.

(ii) ELIGIBLE LOSS.—For purposes of clause (i), the term "eligible loss" means—

(I) in the case of an individual, losses of property arising from fire, storm, shipwreck, or other casualty, or from theft,

(II) in the case of a taxpayer which is a small business, net operating losses attributable to federally declared disasters (as defined by subsection [165](h)(3)(C)(i)), and

(III) in the case of a taxpayer engaged in the trade or business of farming (as defined in section 263A(e)(4)), net operating losses attributable to such federally declared disasters.

Such term shall not include any farming loss (as defined in subsection (i)) or qualified disaster loss (as defined in subsection (j)).

(iii) SMALL BUSINESS.—For purposes of this subparagraph, the term "small business" means a corporation or partnership which meets the gross receipts test of section 448(c) for the taxable year in which the loss arose (or, in the case of a sole proprietorship, which would meet such test if such proprietorship were a corporation).

(iv) COORDINATION WITH PARAGRAPH (2).—For purposes of applying paragraph (2), an eligible loss for any taxable year shall be treated in a manner similar to the manner in which a specified liability loss is treated.

(G) FARMING LOSSES.—In the case of a taxpayer which has a farming loss (as defined in subsection (i)) for a taxable year, such farming loss shall be a net operating loss carryback to each of the 5 taxable years preceding the taxable year of such loss.

(H) CARRYBACK FOR 2008 OR 2009 NET OPERATING LOSSES.—

(i) IN GENERAL.—In the case of an applicable net operating loss with respect to which the taxpayer has elected the application of this subparagraph—

(I) subparagraph (A)(i) shall be applied by substituting any whole number elected by the taxpayer which is more than 2 and less than 6 for "2",

(II) subparagraph (E)(ii) shall be applied by substituting the whole number which is one less than the whole number substituted under subclause (I) for "2", and

(III) subparagraph (F) shall not apply.

(ii) APPLICABLE NET OPERATING LOSS.—For purposes of this subparagraph, the term "applicable net operating loss" means the taxpayer's net operating loss for a taxable year ending after December 31, 2007, and beginning before January 1, 2010.

(iii) ELECTION.—

(I) IN GENERAL.—Any election under this subparagraph may be made only with respect to 1 taxable year.

(II) PROCEDURE.—Any election under this subparagraph shall be made in such manner as may be prescribed by the Secretary, and shall be made by the due date (including extension of time) for filing the return for the taxpayer's last taxable year beginning in 2009. Any such election, once made, shall be irrevocable.

(iv) LIMITATION ON AMOUNT OF LOSS CARRYBACK TO 5TH PRECEDING TAXABLE YEAR.—

(I) IN GENERAL.—The amount of any net operating loss which may be carried back to the 5th taxable year preceding the taxable year of such loss under clause (i) shall not exceed 50 percent of the taxpayer's taxable income (computed without regard to the net operating loss for the loss year or any taxable year thereafter) for such preceding taxable year.

(II) CARRYBACKS AND CARRYOVERS TO OTHER TAXABLE YEARS.—Appropriate adjustments in the application of the second sentence of paragraph (2) shall be made to take into account the limitation of subclause (I).

(III) EXCEPTION FOR 2008 ELECTIONS BY SMALL BUSINESSES.—Subclause (I) shall not apply to any loss of an eligible small business with respect to any election made under this subparagraph as in effect on the day before the date of the enactment of the Worker, Homeownership, and Business Assistance Act of 2009.

(v) SPECIAL RULES FOR SMALL BUSINESS.—

(I) IN GENERAL.—In the case of an eligible small business which made or makes an election under this subparagraph as in effect on the day before the date of the enactment of the Worker, Homeownership, and Business Assistance Act of 2009, clause (iii)(I) shall be applied by substituting "2 taxable years" for "1 taxable year".

(II) ELIGIBLE SMALL BUSINESS.—For purposes of this subparagraph, the term "eligible small business" has the meaning given such term by subparagraph (F)(iii), except that in applying such subparagraph, section 448(c) shall be applied by substituting "$15,000,000" for "$5,000,000" each place it appears.

(I) TRANSMISSION PROPERTY AND POLLUTION CONTROL INVESTMENT.—

(i) IN GENERAL.—At the election of the taxpayer for any taxable year ending after December 31, 2005, and before January 1, 2009, in the case of a net operating loss for a taxable year ending after December 31, 2002, and before January 1, 2006, there shall be a net operating loss carryback to each of the 5 taxable years preceding the taxable year of such loss to the extent that such loss does not exceed 20 percent of the sum of the electric transmission property capital expenditures and the pollution control facility capital expenditures of the taxpayer for the taxable year preceding the taxable year for which such election is made.

(ii) LIMITATIONS.—For purposes of this subsection—

(I) not more than one election may be made under clause (i) with respect to any net operating loss for a taxable year, and

(II) an election may not be made under clause (i) for more than 1 taxable year beginning in any calendar year.

(iii) COORDINATION WITH ORDERING RULE.—For purposes of applying subsection (b)(2), the portion of any loss which is carried back 5 years by reason of clause (i) shall be treated in a manner similar to the manner in which a specified liability loss is treated.

(iv) SPECIAL RULES RELATING TO CREDIT OR REFUND.—In the case of the portion of the loss which is carried back 5 years by reason of clause (i)—

(I) an application under section 6411(a) with respect to such portion shall not fail to be treated as timely filed if filed within 24 months after the due date specified under such section, and

(II) references in sections 6501(h), 6511(d)(2)(A), and 6611(f)(1) to the taxable year in which such net operating loss arises or results in a net operating loss carryback shall be treated as references to the taxable year for which such election is made.

(v) DEFINITIONS.—For purposes of this subparagraph—

(I) ELECTRIC TRANSMISSION PROPERTY CAPITAL EXPENDITURES.—The term "electric transmission property capital expenditures" means any expenditure, chargeable to capital account, made by the taxpayer which is attributable to electric transmission property used by the taxpayer in the transmission at 69 or more kilovolts of electricity for sale. Such term shall not include any expenditure which may be refunded or the purpose of which may be modified at the option of the taxpayer so as to cease to be treated as an expenditure within the meaning of such term.

(II) POLLUTION CONTROL FACILITY CAPITAL EXPENDITURES.—The term "pollution control facility capital expenditures" means any expenditure, chargeable to capital account, made by an electric utility company (as defined in section 2(3) of the Public Utility Holding Company Act (15 U.S.C. 79b(3)), as in effect on the day before the date of the enactment of the Energy Tax Incentives Act of 2005) which is attributable to a facility which will qualify as a certified pollution control facility as determined under section 169(d)(1) by striking "before January 1, 1976," and by substituting "an identifiable" for "a new identifiable". Such term shall not include any expenditure which may be refunded or the purpose of which may be modified at the option of the taxpayer so as to cease to be treated as an expenditure within the meaning of such term.

(J) CERTAIN LOSSES ATTRIBUTABLE FEDERALLY DECLARED DISASTERS.—In the case of a taxpayer who has a qualified disaster loss (as defined in subsection (j)), such loss shall be a net operating loss carryback to each of the 5 taxable years preceding the taxable year of such loss.

(2) AMOUNT OF CARRYBACKS AND CARRYOVERS.—The entire amount of the net operating loss for any taxable year (hereinafter in this section referred to as the "loss year") shall be carried to the earliest of the taxable years to which (by reason of paragraph (1)) such loss may be carried. The portion of such loss which shall be carried to each of the other taxable years shall be the excess, if any, of the amount of such loss over the sum of the taxable income for each of the prior taxable years to which such loss may be carried. For purposes of the preceding sentence, the taxable income for any such prior taxable year shall be computed—

(A) with the modifications specified in subsection (d) other than paragraphs (1), (4), and (5) thereof, and

(B) by determining the amount of the net operating loss deduction without regard to the net operating loss for the loss year or for any taxable year thereafter,

and the taxable income so computed shall not be considered to be less than zero.

(3) ELECTION TO WAIVE CARRYBACK.—Any taxpayer entitled to a carryback period under paragraph (1) may elect to relinquish the entire carryback period with respect to a net operating loss for any taxable year. Such election shall be made in such manner as may be prescribed by the Secretary, and shall be made by the due date (including extensions of time) for filing the taxpayer's return for the taxable year of the net operating loss for which the election is to be in effect. Such election, once made for any taxable year, shall be irrevocable for such taxable year.

Amendments

• 2009, Worker, Homeownership, and Business Assistance Act of 2009 (P.L. 111-92)

P.L. 111-92, §13(a):

Amended Code Sec. 172(b)(1)(H). **Effective** generally for net operating losses arising in tax years ending after 12-31-2007. For a transitional rule, see Act Sec. 13(e)(4), below. For an exception, see Act Sec. 13(f), below. Prior to amendment, Code Sec. 172(b)(1)(H) read as follows:

(H) CARRYBACK FOR 2008 NET OPERATING LOSSES OF SMALL BUSINESSES.—

(i) IN GENERAL.—If an eligible small business elects the application of this subparagraph with respect to an applicable 2008 net operating loss—

(I) subparagraph (A)(i) shall be applied by substituting any whole number elected by the taxpayer which is more than 2 and less than 6 for "2",

(II) subparagraph (E)(ii) shall be applied by substituting the whole number which is one less than the whole number substituted under subclause (I) for "2", and

(III) subparagraph (F) shall not apply.

(ii) APPLICABLE 2008 NET OPERATING LOSS.—For purposes of this subparagraph, the term "applicable 2008 net operating loss" means—

(I) the taxpayer's net operating loss for any taxable year ending in 2008, or

(II) if the taxpayer elects to have this subclause apply in lieu of subclause (I), the taxpayer's net operating loss for any taxable year beginning in 2008.

(iii) ELECTION.—Any election under this subparagraph shall be made in such manner as may be prescribed by the Secretary, and shall be made by the due date (including extension of time) for filing the taxpayer's return for the taxable year of the net operating loss. Any such election, once made, shall be irrevocable. Any election under this subparagraph may be made only with respect to 1 taxable year.

(iv) ELIGIBLE SMALL BUSINESS.—For purposes of this subparagraph, the term "eligible small business" has the meaning given such term by subparagraph (F)(iii), except that in applying such subparagraph, section 448(c) shall be applied by substituting "$15,000,000" for "$5,000,000" each place it appears.

P.L. 111-92, §13(d), provides:

(d) ANTI-ABUSE RULES.—The Secretary of Treasury or the Secretary's designee shall prescribe such rules as are necessary to prevent the abuse of the purposes of the amendments made by this section, including anti-stuffing rules, anti-churning rules (including rules relating to saleleasebacks), and rules similar to the rules under section 1091 of the Internal Revenue Code of 1986 relating to losses from wash sales.

P.L. 111-92, §13(e)(4), provides:

(4) TRANSITIONAL RULE.—In the case of any net operating loss (or, in the case of a life insurance company, any loss from operations) for a taxable year ending before the date of the enactment of this Act—

(A) any election made under section 172(b)(3) or 810(b)(3) of the Internal Revenue Code of 1986 with respect to such loss may (notwithstanding such section) be revoked before the due date (including extension of time) for filing the return for the taxpayer's last taxable year beginning in 2009, and

(B) any application under section 6411(a) of such Code with respect to such loss shall be treated as timely filed if filed before such due date.

P.L. 111-92, §13(f), provides:

(f) EXCEPTION FOR TARP RECIPIENTS.—The amendments made by this section shall not apply to—

(1) any taxpayer if—

(A) the Federal Government acquired before the date of the enactment of this Act an equity interest in the taxpayer pursuant to the Emergency Economic Stabilization Act of 2008,

(B) the Federal Government acquired before such date of enactment any warrant (or other right) to acquire any equity interest with respect to the taxpayer pursuant to the Emergency Economic Stabilization Act of 2008, or

(C) such taxpayer receives after such date of enactment funds from the Federal Government in exchange for an interest described in subparagraph (A) or (B) pursuant to a program established under title I of division A of the Emergency Economic Stabilization Act of 2008 (unless such taxpayer is a financial institution (as defined in section 3 of such Act) and the funds are received pursuant to a program established by the Secretary of the Treasury for the stated purpose of increasing the availability of credit to small businesses using funding made available under such Act), or

(2) the Federal National Mortgage Association and the Federal Home Loan Mortgage Corporation, and

(3) any taxpayer which at any time in 2008 or 2009 was or is a member of the same affiliated group (as defined in section 1504 of the Internal Revenue Code of 1986, determined without regard to subsection (b) thereof) as a taxpayer described in paragraph (1) or (2).

• 2009, American Recovery and Reinvestment Tax Act of 2009 (P.L. 111-5)

P.L. 111-5, §1211(a):

Amended Code Sec. 172(b)(1)(H). **Effective** for net operating losses arising in tax years ending after 12-31-2007. For a transitional rule, see Act Sec. 1211(d)(2), below. Prior to amendment, Code Sec. 172(b)(1)(H) read as follows:

(H) In the case of a net operating loss for any taxable year ending during 2001 or 2002, subparagraph (A)(i) shall be applied by substituting "5" for "2" and subparagraph (F) shall not apply.

P.L. 111-5, §1211(c), provides:

(c) ANTI-ABUSE RULES.—The Secretary of Treasury or the Secretary's designee shall prescribe such rules as are necessary to prevent the abuse of the purposes of the amendments made by this section, including anti-stuffing rules, anti-churning rules (including rules relating to saleleasebacks), and rules similar to the rules under section 1091 of the Internal Revenue Code of 1986 relating to losses from wash sales.

P.L. 111-5, §1211(d)(2), provides:

(2) TRANSITIONAL RULE.—In the case of a net operating loss for a taxable year ending before the date of the enactment of this Act—

(A) any election made under section 172(b)(3) of the Internal Revenue Code of 1986 with respect to such loss may (notwithstanding such section) be revoked before the applicable date,

(B) any election made under section 172(b)(1)(H) of such Code with respect to such loss shall (notwithstanding such section) be treated as timely made if made before the applicable date, and

(C) any application under section 6411(a) of such Code with respect to such loss shall be treated as timely filed if filed before the applicable date.

For purposes of this paragraph, the term "applicable date" means the date which is 60 days after the date of the enactment of this Act.

• 2008, Tax Extenders and Alternative Minimum Tax Relief Act of 2008 (P.L. 110-343)

P.L. 110-343, Division C, §706(a)(2)(D)(v):

Amended Code Sec. 172(b)(1)(F)(ii)(II) by striking "Presidentially declared disasters (as defined in section 1033(h)(3))" and inserting "federally declared disasters (as defined by subsection [165](h)(3)(C)(i))". **Effective** for disasters declared in tax years beginning after 12-31-2007.

P.L. 110-343, Division C, §706(a)(2)(D)(vi):

Amended Code Sec. 172(b)(1)(F)(ii)(III) by striking "Presidentially declared disasters" and inserting "federally declared disasters". **Effective** for disasters declared in tax years beginning after 12-31-2007.

P.L. 110-343, Division C, §708(a):

Amended Code Sec. 172(b)(1) by adding at the end a new subparagraph (J). **Effective** for losses arising in tax years beginning after 12-31-2007, in connection with disasters declared after such date.

P.L. 110-343, Division C, §708(d)(1):

Amended Code Sec. 172(b)(1)(F)(ii) by inserting "or qualified disaster loss (as defined in subsection (j))" before the period at the end of the last sentence. **Effective** for losses arising in tax years beginning after 12-31-2007, in connection with disasters declared after such date.

P.L. 110-343, Division C, §712, provides:

SEC. 712. COORDINATION WITH HEARTLAND DISASTER RELIEF.

The amendments made by this subtitle, other than the amendments made by sections 706(a)(2), 710, and 711, shall not apply to any disaster described in section 702(c)[b](1)(A), or to any expenditure or loss resulting from such disaster.

• 2005, Gulf Opportunity Zone Act of 2005 (P.L. 109-135)

P.L. 109-135, §402(f)(1):

Amended Code Sec. 172(b)(1)(I)(i). **Effective** as if included in the provision of the Energy Policy Act of 2005

(P.L. 109-58) to which it relates [**effective** 8-8-2005.—CCH]. Prior to amendment, Code Sec. 172(b)(1)(I)(i) read as follows:

(i) IN GENERAL.—At the election of the taxpayer in any taxable year ending after December 31, 2005, and before January 1, 2009, in the case of a net operating loss in a taxable year ending after December 31, 2002, and before January 1, 2006, there shall be a net operating loss carryback to each of the 5 years preceding the taxable year of such loss to the extent that such loss does not exceed 20 percent of the sum of electric transmission property capital expenditures and pollution control facility capital expenditures of the taxpayer for the taxable year preceding the taxable year in which such election is made.

P.L. 109-135, §402(f)(2):

Amended Code Sec. 172(b)(1)(I)(ii) by striking "in a taxable year" and inserting "for a taxable year". **Effective** as if included in the provision of the Energy Policy Act of 2005 (P.L. 109-58) to which it relates [**effective** 8-8-2005.—CCH].

P.L. 109-135, §402(f)(3):

Amended Code Sec. 172(b)(1)(I) by striking clause[s] (iv) and (v), by redesignating clause (vi) as clause (v), and by inserting a new clause (iv). **Effective** as if included in the provision of the Energy Policy Act of 2005 (P.L. 109-58) to which it relates [**effective** 8-8-2005.—CCH]. Prior to amendment, Code Sec. 172(b)(1)(I)(iv) and (v) read as follows:

(iv) APPLICATION FOR ADJUSTMENT.—In the case of any portion of a net operating loss to which an election under clause (i) applies, an application under section 6411(a) with respect to such loss shall not fail to be treated as timely filed if filed within 24 months after the due date specified under such section.

(v) SPECIAL RULES RELATING TO REFUND.—For purposes of a net operating loss to which an election under clause (i) applies, references in sections 6501(h), 6511(d)(2)(A), and 6611(f)(1) to the taxable year in which such net operating loss arises or result in a net loss carryback shall be treated as references to the taxable year in which such election occurs.

• 2005, Energy Tax Incentives Act of 2005 (P.L. 109-58)

P.L. 109-58, §1311:

Amended Code Sec. 172(b)(1) by adding at the end a new subparagraph (I). **Effective** 8-8-2005.

• 2004, Working Families Tax Relief Act of 2004 (P.L. 108-311)

P.L. 108-311, §403(b)(1):

Amended Code Sec. 172(b)(1)(H) by striking "a taxpayer which has" following "In the case of". **Effective** as if included in the provision of the Job Creation and Worker Assistance Act of 2002 (P.L. 107-147) to which it relates [**effective** for net operating losses for tax years ending after 12-31-2000.—CCH].

P.L. 108-311, §403(b)(2), provides:

(2) In the case of a net operating loss for a taxable year ending during 2001 or 2002—

(A) an application under section 6411(a) of the Internal Revenue Code of 1986 with respect to such loss shall not fail to be treated as timely filed if filed before November 1, 2002,

(B) any election made under section 172(b)(3) of such Code may (notwithstanding such section) be revoked before November 1, 2002, and

(C) any election made under section 172(j) of such Code shall (notwithstanding such section) be treated as timely made if made before November 1, 2002.

• 2002, Job Creation and Worker Assistance Act of 2002 (P.L. 107-147)

P.L. 107-147, §102(a):

Amended Code Sec. 172(b)(1) by adding at the end a new subparagraph (H). **Effective** for net operating losses for tax years ending after 12-31-2000.

P.L. 107-147, §417(8)(A)-(B):

Amended Code Sec. 172(b)(1)(F)(i) by striking "3 years" and inserting "3 taxable years", and by striking "2 years" and inserting "2 taxable years". **Effective** on 3-9-2002.

• 1998, Tax and Trade Relief Act of 1998 (P.L. 105-277)

P.L. 105-277, §2013(a):

Amended Code Sec. 172(b)(1) by adding at the end a new subparagraph (G). **Effective** for net operating losses for tax years beginning after 12-31-97.

P.L. 105-277, §2013(c):

Amended Code Sec. 172(b)(1)(F)(ii) by adding at the end a flush sentence. **Effective** for net operating losses for tax years beginning after 12-31-97.

P.L. 105-277, §4003(h):

Amended Code Sec. 172(b)(1)(F) by adding at the end a new clause (iv). **Effective** as if included in the provision of P.L. 105-34 to which it relates [**effective** for net operating losses for tax years beginning after 8-5-97.—CCH].

• 1997, Taxpayer Relief Act of 1997 (P.L. 105-34)

P.L. 105-34, §1082(a)(1)-(2):

Amended Code Sec. 172(b)(1)(A) by striking "3" in clause (i) and inserting "2", and by striking "15" in clause (ii) and inserting "20". **Effective** for net operating losses for tax years beginning after 8-5-97.

P.L. 105-34, §1082(b):

Amended Code Sec. 172(b)(1) by adding at the end a new subparagraph (F). **Effective** for net operating losses for tax years beginning after 8-5-97.

• 1996, Small Business Job Protection Act of 1996 (P.L. 104-188)

P.L. 104-188, §1702(h)(2):

Amended Code Sec. 172(b)(1)(E)(ii) by striking "subsection (m)" and inserting "subsection (h)". **Effective** as if included in the provision of P.L. 101-508 to which such amendment relates.

• 1990, Omnibus Budget Reconciliation Act of 1990 (P.L. 101-508)

P.L. 101-508, §11701(d):

Amended Code Sec. 172(b)(1)(M)(iii) by striking "a C corporation" after "means" in the material preceding subclause (I), by striking "which acquires" in subclause (I) and inserting "a C corporation which acquires", by striking "a corporation" in subclause (II) and inserting "a C corporation", and by striking "any successor corporation" in subclause (III) and inserting "any C corporation which is a successor". **Effective** as if included in the provision of P.L. 101-239 to which it relates.

P.L. 101-508, §11811(a):

Amended Code Sec. 172(b) (as amended by Act Sec. 11701(d)). **Effective** for net operating losses for tax years beginning after 12-31-90. Prior to amendment, Code Sec. 172(b) read as follows:

(b) NET OPERATING LOSS CARRYBACKS AND CARRYOVERS.—

(1) YEARS TO WHICH LOSS MAY BE CARRIED.—

(A) Except as otherwise provided in this paragraph, a net operating loss for any taxable year shall be a net operating loss carryback to each of the 3 taxable years preceding the taxable year of such loss.

(B) Except as otherwise provided in this paragraph, a net operating loss for any taxable year ending after December 31, 1975, shall be a net operating loss carryover to each of the 15 taxable years following the taxable year of the loss.

(C) In the case of a taxpayer which is a regulated transportation corporation (as defined in subsection (g)(1)), a net operating loss for any taxable year ending after December 31, 1955, and before January 1, 1976, shall (except as provided in subsection (g)) be a net operating loss carryover to each of the 7 taxable years following the taxable year of such loss.

(D) In the case of a taxpayer which has a foreign expropriation loss (as defined in subsection (h)) for any taxable year ending after December 31, 1958, the portion of the net operating loss for such year attributable to such foreign expropriation loss shall not be a net operating loss carryback to any taxable year preceding the taxable year of such loss and shall be a net operating loss carryover to each of the 10 taxable years following the taxable year of such loss (or, with respect to that portion of the net operating loss for such year attributable to a Cuban expropriation loss, to each of the 20 taxable years following the taxable year of such loss).

(E)(i) A net operating loss for a REIT year—

(I) shall not be a net operating loss carryback to any taxable year preceding the taxable year of such loss, and

(II) shall be a net operating loss carryover to each of the 15 taxable years following the taxable year of such loss.

(ii) In the case of any net operating loss for a taxable year which is not a REIT year, such loss shall not be carried back to any taxable year which is a REIT year.

(iii) For purposes of this subparagraph, the term "REIT year" means any taxable year for which the provisions of part II of subchapter M (relating to real estate investment trusts) apply to the taxpayer.

(F) In the case of a financial institution referred to in section 582(c)(5), a net operating loss for any taxable year beginning after December 31, 1975, and before January 1, 1987, shall be a net operating loss carryback to each of the 10 taxable years preceding the taxable year of such loss, and shall be a net operating loss carryover to each of the 5 taxable years following the taxable year of such loss.

(G) In the case of a Bank for Cooperatives (organized and chartered pursuant to section 2 of the Farm Credit Act of 1933 (12 U.S.C. 1134)), a net operating loss for any taxable year beginning after December 31, 1969, and before January 1, 1987, shall be a net operating loss carryback to each of the 10 taxable years preceding the taxable year of such loss and shall be a net operating loss carryover to each of the 5 taxable years following the taxable year of such loss.

(H) In the case of a net operating loss of the Federal National Mortgage Association for any taxable year beginning after December 31, 1981, and before January 1, 1987, or a net operating loss of the Federal Home Loan Mortgage Corporation for any taxable year beginning after December 31, 1984, and before January 1, 1987—

(i) such loss, to the extent it exceeds the mortgage disposition loss (within the meaning of subsection (i)), shall be—

(I) a net operating loss carryback to each of the 10 taxable years preceding the taxable year of the loss, and

(II) a net operating loss carryover to each of the 5 taxable years following the taxable year of the loss, and

(ii) the mortgage disposition loss shall be—

(I) a net operating loss carryback to each of the 3 taxable years preceding the taxable year of the loss, and

(II) a net operating loss carryover to each of the 15 taxable years following the taxable year of the loss.

(I) PRODUCT LIABILITY LOSSES.—In the case of a taxpayer which has a product liability loss (as defined in subsection (j)) for a taxable year beginning after September 30, 1979 (referred to in this subparagraph as the "loss year"), the product liability loss shall be a net operating loss carryback to each of the 10 taxable years preceding the loss year.

(J) SPECIAL RULE FOR DEFERRED STATUTORY OR TORT LIABILITY LOSSES.—In the case of a taxpayer which has a deferred statutory or tort liability loss (as defined in subsection (k)) for any taxable year beginning after December 31, 1983, the deferred statutory or tort liability loss shall be a net operating loss carryback to each of the 10 taxable years preceding the taxable year of such loss.

(K) BAD DEBT LOSSES OF COMMERCIAL BANKS.—In the case of any bank (as defined in section 585(a)(2)), the portion of the net operating loss for any taxable year beginning after December 31, 1986, and before January 1, 1994, which is attributable to the deduction allowed under section 166(a) shall be a net operating loss carryback to each of the 10 taxable years preceding the taxable year of the loss and a net operating loss carryover to each of the 5 taxable years following the taxable year of such loss.

(L) LOSSES OF THRIFT INSTITUTIONS.—In the case of an organization to which section 593 applies, in lieu of applying subparagraph (F), a net operating loss for any taxable year beginning after December 31, 1981, and before January 1, 1986, shall be a net operating loss carryback to each of the 10 taxable years preceding the taxable year of such loss and shall be a net operating loss carryover to each of the 8 taxable years following the taxable year of such loss.

(M) EXCESS INTEREST LOSS.—

(i) IN GENERAL.—If—

(I) there is a corporate equity reduction transaction, and

(II) an applicable corporation has a corporate equity reduction interest loss for any loss limitation year ending after August 2, 1989,

then the corporate equity reduction interest loss shall be a net operating loss carryback and carryover to the taxable years described in subparagraphs (A) and (B), except that such loss shall not be carried back to a taxable year preceding the taxable year in which the corporate equity reduction transaction occurs.

(ii) LOSS LIMITATION YEAR.—For purposes of clause (i) and subsection (m), the term "loss limitation year" means, with respect to any corporate equity reduction transaction, the taxable year in which such transaction occurs and each of the 2 succeeding taxable years.

(iii) APPLICABLE CORPORATION.—For purposes of clause (i), the term "applicable corporation" means—

(I) a C corporation which acquires stock, or the stock of which is acquired, in a major stock acquisition,

(II) a C corporation making distributions with respect to, or redeeming, its stock in connection with an excess distribution, or

(III) any C corporation which is a successor of a corporation described in subclause (I) or (II).

(iv) OTHER DEFINITIONS.—

For definitions of terms used in this subparagraph, see subsection (m).

(2) AMOUNT OF CARRYBACKS AND CARRYOVERS.—Except as provided in subsection (g), the entire amount of the net operating loss for any taxable year (hereinafter in this section referred to as the "loss year") shall be carried to the earliest of the taxable years to which (by reason of paragraph (1)) such loss may be carried. The portion of such loss which shall be carried to each of the other taxable years shall be the excess, if any, of the amount of such loss over the sum of the taxable income for each of the prior taxable years to which such loss may be carried. For purposes of the preceding sentence, the taxable income for any such prior taxable year shall be computed—

(A) with the modifications specified in subsection (d) other than paragraphs (1), (4), and (5) thereof; and

(B) by determining the amount of the net operating loss deduction—

(i) without regard to the net operating loss for the loss year or for any taxable year thereafter, and

(ii) without regard to that portion, if any, of a net operating loss for a taxable year attributable to a foreign expropriation loss, if such portion may not, under paragraph (1)(D), be carried back to such prior taxable year,

and the taxable income so computed shall not be considered to be less than zero. For purposes of this paragraph, if a portion of the net operating loss for the loss year is attributable to a foreign expropriation loss to which paragraph (1)(D) applies, such portion shall be considered to be a separate net operating loss for such year to be applied after the other portion of such net operating loss, and, if a portion of a foreign expropriation loss for the loss year is attributable to a Cuban expropriation loss, such portion shall be considered to be a separate foreign expropriation loss for such year to be applied after the other portion of such foreign expropriation loss.

(3) SPECIAL RULES.—

(A) Paragraph (1)(D) shall apply only if—

(i) the foreign expropriation loss (as defined in subsection (h)) for the taxable year equals or exceeds 50 percent of the net operating loss for the taxable year,

(ii) in the case of a foreign expropriation loss for a taxable year ending after December 31, 1963, the taxpayer elects (at such time and in such manner as the Secretary by regulations prescribes) to have paragraph (1)(D) apply, and

(iii) in the case of a foreign expropriation loss for a taxable year ending after December 31, 1958, and before January 1, 1964, the taxpayer elects (in such manner as the Secretary by regulations prescribes) on or before December 31, 1965, to have paragraph (1)(D) apply.

(B) If a taxpayer makes an election under subparagraph (A)(iii), then (notwithstanding any law or rule of law), with respect to any taxable year ending before January 1, 1964, affected by the election—

(i) the time for making or changing any choice or election under subpart A of part III of subchapter N (relating to foreign tax credit) shall not expire before January 1, 1966,

(ii) any deficiency attributable to the election under subparagraph (A)(iii) or to the application of clause (i) of this subparagraph may be assessed at any time before January 1, 1969, and

(iii) refund or credit of any overpayment attributable to the election under subparagraph (A)(iii) or to the application of clause (i) of this subparagraph may be made or allowed if claim therefor is filed before January 1, 1969.

(C) Any taxpayer entitled to a carryback period under paragraph (1) may elect to relinquish the entire carryback period with respect to a net operating loss for any taxable year ending after December 31, 1975. Such election shall be made in such manner as may be prescribed by the Secretary, and shall be made by the due date (including extensions of time) for filing the taxpayer's return for the taxable year of the net operating loss for which the election is to be in effect. Such election, once made for any taxable year, shall be irrevocable for that taxable year.

• 1989, Omnibus Budget Reconciliation Act of 1989 (P.L. 101-239)

P.L. 101-239, §7211(a):

Amended Code Sec. 172(b)(1) by adding at the end thereof a new subparagraph (M). **Effective**, generally, for corporate equity reduction transactions occurring after 8-2-89, in tax years ending after 8-2-89. For exceptions, see Act Sec. 7211(c)(2), below.

P.L. 101-239, §7211(c)(2), provides:

(2) EXCEPTIONS.—In determining whether a corporate equity reduction transaction has occurred after August 2, 1989, there shall not be taken into account—

(A) acquisitions or redemptions of stock, or distributions with respect to stock, occurring on or before August 2, 1989,

(B) acquisitions or redemptions of stock after August 2, 1989, pursuant to a binding written contract (or tender offer filed with the Securities and Exchange Commission) in effect on August 2, 1989, and at all times thereafter before such acquisition or redemption, or

(C) any distribution with respect to stock after August 2, 1989, which was declared on or before August 2, 1989.

Any distribution to which the preceding sentence applies shall be taken into account under section 172(m)(3)(C)(ii)(I) of the Internal Revenue Code of 1986 (relating to base period for distributions).

• 1988, Technical and Miscellaneous Revenue Act of 1988 (P.L. 100-647)

P.L. 100-647, §1009(c)(1):

Amended Code Sec. 172(b)(1) by redesignating subparagraphs (L) and (M) as subparagraphs (K) and (L), respectively. **Effective** as if included in the provision of P.L. 99-514 to which it relates.

P.L. 100-647, §1009(c)(2):

Amended Code Sec. 172(b)(1)(A) by striking out "Except" and all that follows down through "a net operating loss" and inserting in lieu thereof "Except as otherwise provided in this paragraph, a net operating loss". **Effective** as if included in the provision of P.L. 99-514 to which it relates. Prior to amendment, Code Sec. 172(b)(1)(A) read as follows:

(A) Except as provided in subparagraphs (D), (E), (F), (G), (H), (I), (J), (K), (L), and (M), a net operating loss for any taxable year shall be a net operating loss carryback to each of the 3 taxable years preceding the taxable year of such loss.

P.L. 100-647, §1009(c)(3):

Amended Code Sec. 172(b)(1)(B). **Effective** as if included in the provision of P.L. 99-514 to which it relates. Prior to amendment, Code Sec. 172(b)(1)(B) read as follows:

(B) Except as provided in subparagraphs (C), (D), and (E), a net operating loss for any taxable year ending after December 31, 1955, shall be a net operating loss carryover to each of the 5 taxable years following the taxable year of such loss. Except as provided in subparagraphs (C), (D), (E), (F), (G), (H), (J), (L), and (M), a net operating loss for any taxable year ending after December 31, 1975, shall be a net operating loss carryover to each of the 15 taxable years following the taxable year of such loss.

• 1986, Tax Reform Act of 1986 (P.L. 99-514)

P.L. 99-514, §901(d)(4)(B):

Amended Code Sec. 172(b)(1)(F) by striking out "to which section 585, 586, or 593 applies" and inserting in lieu thereof "referred to in section 582(c)(5)". **Effective** for tax years beginning after 12-31-86.

P.L. 99-514, §903(a)(1):

Amended Code Sec. 172(b)(1)(F) by striking out "after December 31, 1975," and inserting in lieu thereof "after December 31, 1975, and before January 1, 1987,". **Effective** for losses incurred in tax years beginning after 12-31-86.

P.L. 99-514, §903(a)(2):

Amended Code Sec. 172(b)(1)(G) by striking out "after December 31, 1969," and inserting in lieu thereof "after December 31, 1969, and before January 1, 1987,". **Effective** for losses incurred in tax years beginning after 12-31-86.

P.L. 99-514, §903(a)(3)(A)-(B):

Amended Code Sec. 172(b)(1)(H) by striking out "after December 31, 1981," and inserting in lieu thereof "after December 31, 1981, and before January 1, 1987," and by striking out "after December 31, 1984," and inserting in lieu thereof "after December 31, 1984, and before January 1, 1987,". **Effective** for losses incurred in tax years beginning after 12-31-86.

P.L. 99-514, §903(b)(1):

Amended Code Sec. 172(b)(1) by adding at the end thereof new subparagraphs (L) and (M). **Effective** for losses incurred in tax years beginning after 12-31-86. However, for a special rule affecting the losses of thrift institutions, see Act Sec. 903(c)(2), below.

P.L. 99-514, §903(b)(2)(A):

Amended Code Sec. 172(b)(1)(A) by striking out "and (K)" and inserting in lieu thereof "(K), (L), and (M)". **Effective** for losses incurred in tax years beginning after 12-31-86.

P.L. 99-514, §903(b)(2)(B):

Amended Code Sec. 172(b)(1)(B) by striking out "and (J)" and inserting in lieu thereof "(J), (L), and (M)". **Effective** for losses incurred in tax years beginning after 12-31-86.

P.L. 99-514, §903(c)(2), provides:

(2) ADDITIONAL CARRYFORWARD PERIOD FOR LOSSES OF THRIFT INSTITUTIONS.—Subparagraph (M)[L] of section 172(b)(1) of the Internal Revenue Code of 1986 (as added by this section) shall apply to losses incurred in taxable years beginning after December 31, 1981.

P.L. 99-514, §1303(b)(1):

Amended Code Sec. 172(b)(1) by striking out subparagraph (J) and by redesignating subparagraph (K) as subparagraph (J). **Effective** on 10-22-86. Prior to amendment, Code Sec. 172(b)(1)(J) read as follows:

(J) In the case of an electing GSOC which has a net operating loss for any taxable year such loss shall not be a net operating loss carryback to any taxable year preceding the year of such loss, but shall be a net operating loss carryover to each of the 10 taxable years following the year of such loss.

• 1984, Deficit Reduction Act of 1984 (P.L. 98-369)

P.L. 98-369, §91(d)(1):

Amended Code Sec. 172(b)(1) by adding at the end thereof new subparagraph (K). **Effective** for amounts with respect to which a deduction would be allowable under chapter 1 of the Internal Revenue Code of 1954 (determined without regard to such amendments) after—

(A) in the case of amounts to which section 461(h) of such Code (as added by such amendments) applies, the date of the enactment of this act, and

(B) in the case of amounts to which section 461(i) of such Code (as so added) applies, after 3-31-84.

P.L. 98-369, §91(d)(3)(A):

Amended clause (i) [sic] of Code Sec. 172(b)(1)(A) by striking out "and (J)" and inserting in lieu thereof "(J), and (K)". **Effective** for amounts with respect to which a deduction would be allowable under chapter 1 of the Internal Revenue Code of 1954 (determined without regard to such amendments) after—

(A) in the case of amounts to which section 461(h) of such Code (as added by such amendments) applies, the date of the enactment of this act, and

(B) in the case of amounts to which section 461(i) of such Code (as so added) applies, after 3-31-84.

See, also, special rules in Act Sec. 91(g)-(i) under the amendment notes for Code Sec. 461(h).

P.L. 98-369, §177(c)(1):

Amended Code Sec. 172(b)(1)(H) by inserting ", or a net operating loss of the Federal Home Loan Mortgage Corporation for any taxable year beginning after December 31, 1984" after "1981", by striking out "the FNMA mortgage disposition loss (within the meaning of subsection (i))" in clause (i) and inserting in lieu thereof "the mortgage dispositon loss (within the meaning of subsection (i))", and by striking out "FNMA mortgage disposition loss" in clause (ii) and inserting in lieu thereof "mortgage disposition loss". **Effective** 1-1-85. See also the special rules in Act Sec. 177(d) under the amendment notes following Code Sec. 246(a).

P.L. 98-369, §722(a)(4)(A):

Amended Code Sec. 172(b)(2)(A) by striking out "and (6)" and inserting in lieu thereof "and (5)". **Effective** as if included in the provision of P.L. 97-448 to which it relates.

• 1983, Technical Corrections Act of 1982 (P.L. 97-448)

P.L. 97-448, §102(d)(1):

Amended section 209(c)(1) of P.L. 97-34 by adding subparagraph (C) to read as below under the amendment note for P.L. 97-34, §207(a)(2)(B)(ii).

P.L. 97-448, §102(d)(2):

Amended section 209(c) of P.L. 97-34 by adding paragraph (3) to read as below under the amendment note for P.L. 97-34, §207(a)(2)(B)(ii).

• 1982, Miscellaneous Revenue Act of 1982 (P.L. 97-362)

P.L. 97-362, §102(a):

Amended Code Sec. 172(b)(1) by redesignating subparagraphs (H) and (I) as (I) and (J), respectively, and by inserting after subparagraph (G) new subparagraph (H). **Effective** for net operating losses for tax years beginning after 12-31-81.

P.L. 97-362, §102(c)(1):

Amended Code Sec. 172(b)(1)(A) by striking out "(H), and (I)" and inserting in lieu thereof "(H), (I), and (J)". **Effective** for net operating losses for tax years beginning after 12-31-81.

P.L. 97-362, §102(c)(2):

Amended Code Sec. 172(b)(1)(B) by striking out "and (I)" in the second sentence and inserting in lieu thereof "(H), and (J)". **Effective** for net operating losses for tax years beginning after 12-31-81.

P.L. 97-362, §102(c)(3):

Amended Code Sec. 172(b)(1)(I), as redesignated by P.L. 97-362, §102(a), by striking out "subsection (i)" and inserting in lieu thereof "subsection (j)". **Effective** for net operating losses for tax years beginning after 12-31-81.

• 1981, Economic Recovery Tax Act of 1981 (P.L. 97-34)

P.L. 97-34, §207(a)(1), (2)(A):

Amended Code Sec. 172(b)(1)(B) by striking out "7" and inserting in lieu thereof "15" and amended Code Sec. 172(b)(1)(C) by inserting "and before January 1, 1976," after "1955," and by striking out the last sentence thereof. **Effective** for net operating losses in tax years ending after 12-31-75. See, also, Act Sec. 209(c)(3), as added by P.L. 97-448, under the amendment note for P.L. 97-34, §207(a)(2)(B)(ii). Prior to amendment, the last sentence of Code Sec. 172(b)(1)(C) read as follows: "For any taxable year ending after December 31, 1975, the preceding sentence shall be applied by substituting '9 taxable years' for '7 taxable years'".

P.L. 97-34, §207(a)(2)(B)(i):

Amended Code Sec. 172(b)(1)(E)(i)(II) by striking out "8" and inserting in lieu thereof "15". **Effective** as if included in the amendments made by P.L. 96-595, §1(a), and applicable to net operating losses in tax years ending after 12-31-72. See, also, Act Sec. 209(c)(3), as added by P.L. 97-448, under the amendment note for P.L. 97-34, §207(a)(2)(B)(ii).

P.L. 97-34, §207(a)(2)(B)(ii):

Amended Code Sec. 172(b)(1)(E)(ii). **Effective** for net operating losses in taxable years ending after 12-31-75. Prior to amendment, Code Sec. 172(b)(1)(E)(ii) read as follows:

(ii) In the case of any net operating loss for a taxable year which is not a REIT year—

(I) such loss shall not be carried back to any taxable year which is a REIT year, and

(II) the number of taxable years to which such loss may be a net operating loss carryover under subparagraph (B) shall be increased (to a number not greater than 8) by the number of taxable years to which such loss may not be a net operating loss carryback by reason of subclause (I).

P.L. 97-34, §209(c)(1)(C), as added by P.L. 97-448, provides:

(C) If any net operating loss for any taxable year ending on or before December 31, 1975, could be a net operating loss carryover to a taxable year ending in 1981 by reason of subclause (II) of section 172(b)(1)(E)(ii) of the Internal Revenue Code of 1954 (as in effect on the day before the date of the enactment of this Act and as modified by section 1(b) of Public Law 96-595), such net operating loss shall be a net operating loss carryover under section 172 of such Code to each of the 15 taxable years following the taxable year of such loss.

P.L. 97-34, §209(c)(3), as added by P.L. 97-448, provides:

(3) Carryover must have been alive in 1981.—The amendments made by subsections (a), (b), and (c) of section 207 shall not apply to any amount which, under the law in effect on the day before the date of the enactment of this Act, could not be carried to a taxable year ending in 1981.

• 1980 (P.L. 96-595)

P.L. 96-595, §1(a):

Amended Code Sec. 172(b)(1)(E). For the **effective** date of this amendment, see Act Sec. 1(b), below. Prior to amendment, Code Sec. 172(b)(1)(E) read as follows:

(E) In the case of a taxpayer which has a net operating loss for any taxable year for which the provisions of part II of subchapter M (relating to real estate investment trusts) apply to such taxpayer, such loss shall not be a net operating loss carryback to any taxable year preceding the taxable year of such loss and shall be a net operating loss carryover to each of the 8 taxable years following the taxable year of such loss, except, in the case of a net operating loss for a taxable year ending before January 1, 1976, such loss shall not be carried to the 6th, 7th, or 8th taxable year following the taxable year of such loss unless part II of subchapter M applied to the taxpayer for the taxable year to which the loss is carried and for all intervening taxable years following the year of loss. A net operating loss shall not be carried back to a taxable year for which part II of subchapter M applied to the taxpayer.

P.L. 96-595, §1(b), provides:

(b) EFFECTIVE DATE.—The amendment made by subsection (a) shall apply to the determination of the net operating loss deduction for taxable years ending after October 4, 1976. For purposes of applying the preceding sentence to any net operating loss for a taxable year which is not a REIT year and which ends on or before October 4, 1976, subclause (II) of section 172(b)(1)(E)(ii) of the Internal Revenue Code of 1954 shall be applied by substituting "the number of REIT years to which such loss was a net operating loss carryback" for "the number of taxable years to which such loss may not be a net operating loss carryback by reason of subclause (I)." In the case of a net operating loss for a taxable year described in the preceding sentence, subclause (II) of section 172(b)(1)(E)(ii) of such Code shall not apply to any taxpayer which acted so as to cause it to cease to qualify as a "real estate investment trust" within the meaning of section 856 of such Code if the principal purpose for such action was to secure the benefit of the allowance of a net operating loss carryover under section 172(b)(1)(B) of such Code.

• **1980, Technical Corrections Act of 1979 (P.L. 96-222)**

P.L. 96-222, §106(a)(1):

Redesignated Code Sec. 172(b)(1)(H), as added by P.L. 95-600, §601(b)(1), as Code Sec. 172(b)(1)(I). **Effective** with respect to corporations chartered after 12-31-78, and before 1-1-84.

P.L. 96-222, §106(a)(6):

Amended Code Sec. 172(b)(1)(A) by changing "and (H)" to ", (H), and (I)". **Effective** with respect to corporations chartered after 12-31-78, and before 1-1-84.

P.L. 96-222, §106(a)(7):

Amended Code Sec. 172(b)(1)(B) by changing "and (G)" to "(G), and (I)". **Effective** with respect to corporations chartered after 12-31-78, and before 1-1-84.

• **1978, Revenue Act of 1978 (P.L. 95-600)**

P.L. 95-600, §371(a)(1):

Added Code Sec. 172(b)(1)(H). **Effective** with respect to tax years beginning after 9-30-79.

P.L. 95-600, §371(a)(2):

Amended Code Sec. 172(b)(1)(A) by striking out "and G" and inserting in lieu thereof "(G), and (H)". **Effective** with respect to tax years beginning after 9-30-79.

P.L. 95-600, §601(b)(1):

Added Code Sec. 172(b)(1)(H). **Effective** with respect to corporations chartered after 12-31-78, and before 1-1-84.

P.L. 95-600 §701(d):

Amended the second sentence of Code Sec. 172(b)(1)(B) by striking out "and (F)" and inserting in lieu thereof "(F), and (G)". **Effective** for losses incurred in tax years ending after 12-31-75.

P.L. 95-600, §703(p)(1)(A):

Amended Code Sec. 172(b)(1)(A). **Effective** with respect to losses sustained after 11-7-78. Prior to amendment, Code Sec. 172(b)(1)(A) read as follows:

"(A)(i) Except as provided in clause (ii) and in subparagraphs (D), (E), (F), and (G), a net operating loss for any taxable year ending after December 31, 1957, shall be a net operating loss carryback to each of the 3 taxable years preceding the taxable year of such loss.

(ii) In the case of a taxpayer with respect to a taxable year ending on or after December 31, 1962, for which a certification has been issued under section 317 of the Trade Expansion Act of 1962, a net operating loss for such taxable year shall be a net operating loss carryback to each of the 5 taxable years preceding the taxable year of such loss."

P.L. 95-600, §703(p)(1)(B):

Amended Code Sec. 172(b)(3) by striking out subparagraphs (A) and (B) and by redesignating subparagraphs (C), (D), and (E) as subparagraphs (A), (B), and (C), respectively. **Effective** with respect to losses sustained after 11-7-78. Prior to amendment, Code Sec. 172(b)(3)(A) and (B) read as follows:

"(3) SPECIAL RULES.—

(A) Paragraph (1)(A)(ii) shall apply only if—

(i) there has been filed, at such time and in such manner as may be prescribed by the Secretary, a notice of filing of the application under section 317 of the Trade Expansion Act of 1962 for tax assistance, and, after its issuance, a copy of the certification under such section, and

(ii) the taxpayer consents in writing to the assessment, within such period as may be agreed upon with the Secretary of any deficiency for any year to the extent attributable to the disallowance of a deduction previously allowed with respect to such net operating loss, even though at the time of filing such consent the assessment of such deficiency would otherwise be prevented by the operation of any law or rule of law.

(B) In the case of—

(i) a partnership and its partners, or

(ii) an electing small business corporation under subchapter S and its shareholders,

paragraph (1)(A)(ii) shall apply as determined under regulations prescribed by the Secretary. Such paragraph shall apply to a net operating loss of a partner or such a shareholder only if it arose predominantly from losses in respect of which certifications under section 317 of the Trade Expansion Act of 1962 were filed under this section."

P.L. 95-600, §703(p)(1)(C):

Amended Code Sec. 172(b)(3) (as designated by P.L. 95-600, §703(p)(1)(B)) by striking out "subparagraph (C)(iii)" each place it appeared and inserting in lieu thereof "subparagraph (A)(iii)". **Effective** with respect to losses sustained after 11-7-78.

• **1976, Tax Reform Act of 1976 (P.L. 94-455)**

P.L. 94-455, §806(a):

Added the last sentence to Code Sec. 172(b)(1)(B). **Effective** for losses incurred in tax years ending after 12-31-75.

P.L. 94-455, §806(b):

Added the last sentence to Code Sec. 172(b)(1)(C). **Effective** for losses incurred in tax years ending after 12-31-75.

P.L. 94-455, §806(c):

Added a new Code Sec. 172(b)(3)(E). **Effective** for losses incurred in tax years ending after 12-31-75.

P.L. 94-455, §1606(b):

Added a new Code Sec. 172(b)(1)(E).

P.L. 94-455, §1608(c), provides:

(c) ALTERNATIVE TAX AND NET OPERATING LOSS.—The amendments made by sections 1606 and 1607 shall apply to taxable years ending after the date of the enactment of this Act, except that in the case of a taxpayer which has a net operating loss (as defined in section 172(c) of the Internal Revenue Code of 1954) for any taxable year ending after the date of enactment of this Act for which the provisions of Part II of subchapter M of chapter I of subtitle A of such Code apply to such taxpayer, such loss shall not be a net operating loss carryback under section 172 of such Code to any taxable year ending on or before the date of enactment of this Act.

P.L. 94-455, §1901(a)(29):

Repealed subparagraphs 172(b)(3)(E) and (F). **Effective** for tax years ending after 10-4-76. Prior to repeal, Code Sec. 172(b)(3)(E) and (F) read as follows:

(E) Paragraph (1)(E) shall apply only if—

(i) the amount of the taxpayer's net operating loss for the taxable year exceeds the sum of the taxable income (computed as provided in paragraph (2)) for each of the 3 preceding taxable years of the taxpayer,

(ii) the amount of the taxpayer's net operating loss for the taxable year, increased by the amount of the taxpayer's net operating loss for the preceding taxable year or decreased by the amount of the taxpayer's taxable income for such preceding year, exceeds 15 percent of the sum of the money and other property (in an amount equal to its adjusted basis for determining gain) of the taxpayer, determined as of the close of the taxable year of such loss without regard to any refund or credit of any overpayment of tax to which the taxpayer may be entitled under paragraph (1)(E),

(iii) the aggregate unadjusted basis of property described in section 1231(b)(1) (without regard to any holding period therein provided), the basis for which was determined under section 1012, which was acquired by the taxpayer during the period beginning with the first day of its fifth taxable year preceding the taxable year of such loss and ending with the last day of the taxable year of such loss, equals or exceeds the aggregate adjusted basis of property of such description of the taxpayer on, and determined as of, the first day of the fifth preceding taxable year, and

(iv) the taxpayer derived 50 percent or more of its gross receipts (other than gross receipts derived from the conduct of a lending or finance business), for the taxable year of such loss and for each of its 5 preceding taxable years, from the manufacture and production of units within the same single class of products, and 3 or fewer United States persons (including as one person an affiliated group as defined in section 1504(a)) other than the taxpayer manufactured and produced in the United States, in the calendar year ending in or with the taxable year of such loss, 85 percent or more of the total number of all units within such class of products manufactured and produced in the United States in such calendar year.

(F) For purposes of subparagraph (e)(iv)—

(i) the term "class of products" means any of the categories designated and numbered as a "class of products" in the 1963 Census of Manufacturers compiled and published by the Secretary of Commerce under title 13 of the United States Code, and

(ii) information compiled or published by the Secretary of Commerce, as part of or in connection with the Statistical Abstract of the United States or the census of manufacturers, regarding the number of units of a class of products manufactured and produced in the United States during a calendar year, or, if such information should not be available, information so compiled or published regarding the number of such units shipped or sold by such manufacturers during a calendar year, shall constitute prima facie evidence of the total number of all units of such class of products manufactured and produced in the United States in such calendar year.

P.L. 94-455, §1901(a)(29):

Struck out Code Sec. 172(b)(1)(E). **Effective** for tax years beginning after 10-4-76. Prior to repeal, Code Sec. 172(b)(1)(E) read as follows:

(E) In the case of a taxpayer which is a domestic corporation qualifying under paragraph (3)(E), a net operating loss for any taxable year ending after December 31, 1966, and prior to January 1, 1969, shall be a net operating loss carryback to each of the 5 taxable years preceding the taxable year of such loss and shall be a net operating loss carryover to each of the 3 taxable years following the taxable year of such loss.

P.L. 94-455, §1901(a)(29):

Struck out "subsection (j)(1)" and "subsection (j)" and inserted "subsection (g)(1)" and "subsection (g)" in Code Sec. 172(b)(1)(C), substituted "subsection (h)" for "subsection (k)" in paragraphs (1)(D) and (3)(C)(i) of Code Sec. 172(b), and substituted "subsection (g)" for "subsections (i) and (j)" in Code Sec. 172(b)(2). **Effective** for tax years beginning after 10-4-76.

P.L. 94-455, §1906(b)(13)(A):

Amended 1954 Code by substituting "Secretary" for "Secretary or his delegate" each place it appeared. **Effective** 2-1-77.

P.L. 94-455, §2126:

Substituted "20" for "15" in Code Sec. 172(b)(1)(D). **Effective** 10-4-76.

• 1971 (P.L. 91-677)

P.L. 91-677, §2(a), (b):

Amended Code Sec. 172(b)(1)(D) by adding the parenthetical matter at the end thereof, and amended Code Sec. 172(b)(2) by adding at the end thereof the matter beginning with ", and, if a portion . . .". **Effective** with respect to foreign expropriation losses sustained in tax years ending after 12-31-58.

• 1969, Tax Reform Act of 1969 (P.L. 91-172)

P.L. 91-172, §431(b):

Amended Code Sec. 172(b)(1)(A)(i) by striking out "and (E)" and inserting in lieu thereof "(E), (F), and (G)". Added Code Secs. 172(b)(1)(F) and (G).

• 1967 (P.L. 90-225)

P.L. 90-225, §3(a):

Amended Code Sec. 172(b): by striking out "subparagraph (D)" in paragraph (1)(A)(i) and inserting in lieu thereof "subparagraphs (D) and (E)"; by striking out "subparagraphs (C) and (D)" in paragraph (1)(B) and inserting in lieu thereof "subparagraphs (C), (D), and (E)"; and by adding new subparagraph (E) at the end of paragraph (1) and by adding new subparagraph (E) at the end of paragraph (3). **Effective** for net operating losses sustained in tax years ending after 12-31-66.

P.L. 90-225, §3(b), provides:

(b) No interest shall be paid or allowed with respect to any overpayment of tax resulting from the application of the amendments made by subsection (a) for any period prior to the date of enactment of this Act.

• 1964, Revenue Act of 1964 (P.L. 88-272)

P.L. 88-272, §210(a)(1):

Amended subsection (b)(1)(A)(i) to have its beginning read "Except as provided in clause (ii) and in subparagraph (D)" in lieu of "Except as provided in clause (ii)". **Effective** 1-1-59.

P.L. 88-272, §210(a)(2):

Amended subsection (b)(1)(B) to have its beginning read "Except as provided in subparagraphs (C) and (D)" in lieu of "Except as provided in subparagraph (C)". **Effective** 1-1-59.

P.L. 88-272, §210(a)(3):

Amended subsection (b)(1) to add subparagraph (D). **Effective** 1-1-59.

P.L. 88-272, §210(a)(4):

Amended subsection (b)(3) to add subparagraphs (C) and (D). **Effective** 1-1-59.

P.L. 88-272, §210(b):

Amended subparagraph (B) of subsection (b)(2), and added the last sentence to subsection (b)(2). **Effective** 1-1-59. Prior to amendment, subparagraph (B) of subsection (b)(2) and the latter portion of subsection (b)(2) read as follows:

"(B) by determining the amount of the net operating loss deduction without regard to the net operating loss for the loss year or for any taxable year thereafter,

and the taxable income so computed shall not be considered to be less than zero."

• 1962, Trade Expansion Act of 1962 (P.L. 87-794)

P.L. 87-794, §317(b):

Amended Code Sec. 172(b). **Effective** for net operating losses for tax years ending after 12-31-55. Prior to amendment, Code Sec. 172(b) read as follows:

(b) Net Operating Loss Carrybacks and Carryovers.—

(1) Years to which loss may be carried.—A net operating loss for any taxable year—

(A) ending after December 31, 1957, shall be a net operating loss carryback to each of the 3 taxable years preceding the taxable year of the loss, and

(B) ending after December 31, 1955, shall (except as provided in subparagraph (C)) be a net operating loss carryover to each of the 5 taxable years following the taxable year of such loss, or

(C) ending after December 31, 1955, in the case of a taxpayer which is a regulated transportation corporation (as defined in subsection (j)(1)), shall (except as provided in subsection (j)) be a net operating loss carryover to each of the 7 taxable years following the taxable year of such loss.

(2) Amount of carrybacks and carryovers.—Except as provided in subsections (i) and (j), the entire amount of the net operating loss for any taxable year (hereinafter in this section referred to as the `loss year') shall be carried to the earliest of the taxable years to which (by reason of paragraph (1)) such loss may be carried. The portion of such loss which shall be carried to each of the other taxable years shall be the excess, if any, of the amount of such loss over the sum of the taxable income for each of the prior taxable years to which such loss may be carried. For purposes of the preceding sentence, the taxable income for any such prior taxable years shall be computed—

(A) with the modifications specified in subsection (d) other than paragraphs (1), (4), and (6) thereof; and

(B) by determining the amount of the net operating loss deduction without regard to the net operating loss for the loss year or for any taxable year thereafter,

and the taxable income so computed shall not be considered to be less than zero.

• 1962 (P.L. 87-710)

P.L. 87-710, §1(a):

Amended Code Sec. 172(b). **Effective** for net operating losses for tax years ending after 12-31-55. Prior to amendment, Code Sec. 172(b) read as follows:

(b) Net Operating Loss Carrybacks and Carryovers.—

(1) Years to which loss may be carried.—A net operating loss for any taxable year ending after December 31, 1957, shall be—

(A) a net operating loss carryback to each of the 3 taxable years preceding the taxable year of such loss, and

(B) a net operating loss carryover to each of the 5 taxable years following the taxable year of such loss.

(2) Amount of carrybacks and carryovers.—Except as provided in subsection (i), the entire amount of the net operating loss for any taxable year (hereinafter in this section referred to as the "loss year") shall be carried to the earliest of the 8 taxable years to which (by reason of subparagraphs (A) and (B) of paragraph (1)) such loss may be carried. The portion of such loss which shall be carried to each of the other 7 taxable years shall be the excess, if any, of the amount of such loss over the sum of the taxable income for each of the prior taxable years to which such loss may be carried. For purposes of the preceding sentence, the taxable income for any such prior taxable year shall be computed—

(A) with the modifications specified in subsection (d) other than paragraphs (1), (4), and (6) thereof; and

(B) by determining the amount of the net operating loss deduction without regard to the net operating loss for the loss year or for any taxable year thereafter,

and the taxable income so computed shall not be considered to be less than zero.

• 1958, Technical Amendments Act of 1958 (P.L. 85-866)

P.L. 85-866, §203(a):

Amended Code Sec. 172(b). **Effective** in respect of net operating losses for tax years ending after 12-31-57. Prior to amendment, Code Sec. 172(b) read as follows:

(b) Net Operating Loss Carrybacks and Carryovers.—

(1) Years to which loss may be carried.—A net operating loss for any taxable year ending after December 31, 1953, shall be—

(A) a net operating loss carryback to each of the 2 taxable years preceding the taxable year of such loss, and

(B) a net operating loss carryover to each of the 5 taxable years following the taxable year of such loss.

(2) Amount of carrybacks and carryovers.—Except as provided in subsection (f), the entire amount of the net operating loss for any taxable year (hereinafter in this section referred to as the "loss year") shall be carried to the earliest of the 7 taxable years to which (by reason of subparagraphs (A) and (B) of paragraph (1)) such loss may be carried. The portion of such loss which shall be carried to each of the other 6 taxable years shall be the excess, if any, of the amount of such loss over the sum of the taxable income for each of the prior taxable years to which such loss may be carried. For purposes of the preceding sentence, the taxable income for any such prior taxable year shall be computed—

(A) with the modifications specified in subsection (d) other than paragraphs (1), (4), and (6) thereof; and

(B) by determining the amount of the net operating loss deduction without regard to the net operating loss for the loss year or for any taxable year thereafter,

and the taxable income so computed shall not be considered to be less than zero.

[Sec. 172(c)]

(c) NET OPERATING LOSS DEFINED.—For purposes of this section, the term "net operating loss" means the excess of the deductions allowed by this chapter over the gross income. Such excess shall be computed with the modifications specified in subsection (d).

Amendments

• 1976, Tax Reform Act of 1976 (P.L. 94-455)

P.L. 94-455, §1901(a)(29):

Struck out "(for any taxable year ending after December 31, 1953)" after the word "means" in Code Sec. 172(c). **Effective** for tax years ending after 10-4-76.

[Sec. 172(d)]

(d) MODIFICATIONS.—The modifications referred to in this section are as follows:

(1) NET OPERATING LOSS DEDUCTION.—No net operating loss deduction shall be allowed.

(2) CAPITAL GAINS AND LOSSES OF TAXPAYERS OTHER THAN CORPORATONS.—In the case of a taxpayer other than a corporation—

(A) the amount deductible on account of losses from sales or exchanges of capital assets shall not exceed the amount includable on account of gains from sales or exchanges of capital assets; and

(B) the exclusion provided by section 1202 shall not be allowed.

(3) DEDUCTION FOR PERSONAL EXEMPTIONS.—No deduction shall be allowed under section 151 (relating to personal exemptions). No deduction in lieu of any such deduction shall be allowed.

(4) NONBUSINESS DEDUCTIONS OF TAXPAYERS OTHER THAN CORPORATIONS.—In the case of a taxpayer other than a corporation, the deductions allowable by this chapter which are not attributable to a taxpayer's trade or business shall be allowed only to the extent of the amount of the gross income not derived from such trade or business. For purposes of the preceding sentence—

(A) any gain or loss from the sale or other disposition of—

(i) property, used in the trade or business, of a character which is subject to the allowance for depreciation provided in section 167, or

(ii) real property used in the trade or business,

shall be treated as attributable to the trade or business;

(B) the modifications specified in paragraphs (1), (2)(B), and (3) shall be taken into account;

(C) any deduction for casualty or theft losses allowable under paragraph (2) or (3) of section 165(c) shall be treated as attributable to the trade or business; and

(D) any deduction allowed under section 404 to the extent attributable to contributions which are made on behalf of an individual who is an employee within the meaning of section 401(c)(1) shall not be treated as attributable to the trade or business of such individual.

(5) COMPUTATION OF DEDUCTION FOR DIVIDENDS RECEIVED, ETC.—The deductions allowed by sections 243 (relating to dividends received by corporations), 244 (relating to dividends received on certain preferred stock of public utilities), and 245 (relating to dividends received from certain foreign corporations) shall be computed without regard to section 246(b) (relating to limitation on aggregate amount of deductions); and the deduction allowed by section 247 (relating to dividends paid on certain preferred stock of public utilities) shall be computed without regard to subsection (a)(1)(B) of such section.

(6) MODIFICATIONS RELATED TO REAL ESTATE INVESTMENT TRUSTS.—In the case of any taxable year for which part II of subchapter M (relating to real estate investment trusts) applies to the taxpayer—

(A) the net operating loss for such taxable year shall be computed by taking into account the adjustments described in section 857(b)(2) (other than the deduction for dividends paid described in section 857(b)(2)(B)); and

(B) where such taxable year is a "prior taxable year" referred to in paragraph (2) of subsection (b), the term "taxable income" in such paragraph shall mean "real estate investment trust taxable income" (as defined in section 857(b)(2)).

(7) MANUFACTURING DEDUCTION.—The deduction under section 199 shall not be allowed.

Amendments

• 2005, Gulf Opportunity Zone Act of 2005 (P.L. 109-135)

P.L. 109-135, §403(a)(17):

Amended Code Sec. 172(d) by adding at the end a new paragraph (7). **Effective** as if included in the provision of the American Jobs Creation Act of 2004 (P.L. 108-357) to which it relates [**effective** for tax years beginning after 12-31-2004.—CCH].

• 1998, Tax and Trade Relief Extension Act of 1998 (P.L. 105-277)

P.L. 105-277, §4004(a):

Amended Code Sec. 172(d)(4)(C). **Effective** for tax years beginning after 12-31-83. Prior to amendment, Code Sec. 172(d)(4)(C) read as follows:

(C) any deduction allowable under section 165(c)(3) (relating to casualty losses) shall not be taken into account; and

• 1993, Omnibus Budget Reconciliation Act of 1993 (P.L. 103-66)

P.L. 103-66, §13113(d)(1)(A):

Amended Code Sec. 172(d)(2). **Effective** for stock issued after 8-10-93. Prior to amendment, Code Sec. 172(d)(2) read as follows:

(2) CAPITAL GAINS AND LOSSES OF TAXPAYERS OTHER THAN CORPORATIONS.—In the case of a taxpayer other than a corporation, the amount deductible on account of losses from sales or exchanges of capital assets shall not exceed the amount includible on account of gains from sales or exchanges of capital assets.

P.L. 103-66, §13113(d)(1)(B):

Amended Code Sec. 172(d)(4)(B) by inserting ", (2)(B)," after "paragraph (1)". **Effective** for stock issued after 8-10-93.

• 1988, Technical and Miscellaneous Revenue Act of 1988 (P.L. 100-647)

P.L. 100-647, §1003(a)(1):

Amended Code Sec. 172(d)(4)(B) by striking out ", (2)(B),". **Effective** as if included in the provision of P.L. 99-514 to which it relates.

• 1986, Tax Reform Act of 1986 (P.L. 99-514)

P.L. 99-514, §104(b)(4):

Amended Code Sec. 172(d) by striking out paragraph (7). **Effective** for tax years beginning after 12-31-86. Prior to amendment, Code Sec. 172(d)(7) read as follows:

(7) ZERO BRACKET AMOUNT.—In the case of a taxpayer other than a corporation, the zero bracket amount shall be treated as a deduction allowed by this chapter. For purposes of subsection (c)—

(A) the deduction provided by the preceding sentence shall be in lieu of any itemized deductions of the taxpayer, and

(B) such sentence shall not apply to an individual who elects to itemize deductions.

P.L. 99-514, §301(b)(3):

Amended Code Sec. 172(d)(2). **Effective** for tax years beginning after 12-31-86. Prior to amendment, Code Sec. 172(d)(2) read as follows:

(2) CAPITAL GAINS AND LOSSES OF TAXPAYERS OTHER THAN CORPORATIONS.—In the case of a taxpayer other than a corporation—

(A) the amount deductible on account of losses from sales or exchanges of capital assets shall not exceed the amount includible on account of gains from sales or exchanges of capital assets; and

(B) the deduction for long-term capital gains provided by section 1202 shall not be allowed.

P.L. 99-514, §1899A(6):

Amended Code Sec. 172(d)(6) by inserting "MODIFICATIONS RELATED TO REAL ESTATE INVESTMENT TRUSTS.—" after "(6)". **Effective** 10-22-86.

• 1984, Deficit Reduction Act of 1984 (P.L. 98-369)

P.L. 98-369, §491(d)(5):

Amended Code Sec. 172(d)(4)(D) by striking out "or section 405(c)". **Effective** for obligations issued after 12-31-83.

P.L. 98-369, §722(a)(4)(B):

Amended Code Sec. 172(d) by redesignating paragraphs (7) and (8) as paragraphs (6) and (7), respectively. **Effective** as if included in the provision of P.L. 97-448 to which it relates.

• 1977, Tax Reduction and Simplification Act of 1977 (P.L. 95-30)

P.L. 95-30, §102(b)(2):

Amended Code Sec. 172(d) by adding paragraph (8). **Effective** for tax years beginning after 12-31-76.

• 1976, Tax Reform Act of 1976 (P.L. 94-455)

P.L. 94-455, §1052(c):

Struck out paragraph (5) and redesignated paragraph (6) as paragraph (5). **Effective** for tax years beginning after 12-31-79. Prior to being stricken, paragraph (5) read as follows:

(5) SPECIAL DEDUCTIONS FOR CORPORATIONS.—No deduction shall be allowed under section 242 (relating to partially tax-exempt interest) or under section 922 (relating to Western Hemisphere trade corporations).

P.L. 94-455, §1606(c):

Added a new Code Sec. 172(d)(7). For **effective** date, see Act Sec. 1608(c) under amendment notes to Code Sec. 172(b).

• 1962, Self-Employed Individuals Tax Retirement Act of 1962 (P.L. 87-792)

P.L. 87-792, §7:

Amended Code Sec. 172(d)(4) by striking out "and" at the end of subparagraph (B); by striking out the period at the end of subparagraph (C) and inserting "; and"; and by adding after subparagraph (C) a new subparagraph (D). **Effective** 1-1-63.

[Sec. 172(e)]

(e) LAW APPLICABLE TO COMPUTATIONS.—In determining the amount of any net operating loss carryback or carryover to any taxable year, the necessary computations involving any other taxable year shall be made under the law applicable to such other taxable year.

Amendments

• 1976, Tax Reform Act of 1976 (P.L. 94-455)

P.L. 94-455, §1901(a)(29):

Struck out the last sentence of Code Sec. 172(e). **Effective** for tax years ending after 10-4-76. Prior to amendment, the last sentence read as follows:

The preceding sentence shall apply with respect to all taxable years, whether they begin before, on, or after January 1, 1954.

[Sec. 172(f)]

(f) RULES RELATING TO SPECIFIED LIABILITY LOSS.—For purposes of this section—

(1) IN GENERAL.—The term "specified liability loss" means the sum of the following amounts to the extent taken into account in computing the net operating loss for the taxable year:

(A) Any amount allowable as a deduction under section 162 or 165 which is attributable to—

(i) product liability, or

(ii) expenses incurred in the investigation or settlement of, or opposition to, claims against the taxpayer on account of product liability.

(B)(i) Any amount allowable as a deduction under this chapter (other than section 468(a)(1) or 468A(a)) which is in satisfaction of a liability under a Federal or State law requiring—

(I) the reclamation of land,

(II) the decommissioning of a nuclear power plant (or any unit thereof),

(III) the dismantlement of a drilling platform,

(IV) the remediation of environmental contamination, or

(V) a payment under any workers compensation act (within the meaning of section 461(h)(2)(C)(i)).

(ii) A liability shall be taken into account under this subparagraph only if—

(I) the act (or failure to act) giving rise to such liability occurs at least 3 years before the beginning of the taxable year, and

(II) the taxpayer used an accrual method of accounting throughout the period or periods during which such act (or failure to act) occurred.

(2) LIMITATION.—The amount of the specified liability loss for any taxable year shall not exceed the amount of the net operating loss for such taxable year.

(3) SPECIAL RULE FOR NUCLEAR POWERPLANTS.—Except as provided in regulations prescribed by the Secretary, that portion of a specified liability loss which is attributable to amounts incurred in the decommissioning of a nuclear powerplant (or any unit thereof) may, for purposes of subsection (b)(1)(C), be carried back to each of the taxable years during the period—

(A) beginning with the taxable year in which such plant (or unit thereof) was placed in service, and

(B) ending with the taxable year preceding the loss year.

(4) PRODUCT LIABILITY.—The term "product liability" means—

(A) liability of the taxpayer for damages on account of physical injury or emotional harm to individuals, or damage to or loss of the use of property, on account of any defect in any product which is manufactured, leased, or sold by the taxpayer, but only if

(B) such injury, harm, or damage arises after the taxpayer has completed or terminated operations with respect to, and has relinquished possession of, such product.

(5) COORDINATION WITH SUBSECTION (b)(2).—For purposes of applying subsection (b)(2), a specified liability loss for any taxable year shall be treated as a separate net operating loss for such taxable year to be taken into account after the remaining portion of the net operating loss for such taxable year.

(6) ELECTION.—Any taxpayer entitled to a 10-year carryback under subsection (b)(1)(C) from any loss year may elect to have the carryback period with respect to such loss year determined without regard to subsection (b)(1)(C). Such election shall be made in such manner as may be prescribed by the Secretary and shall be made by the due date (including extensions of time) for filing the taxpayer's return for the taxable year of the net operating loss. Such election, once made for any taxable year, shall be irrevocable for that taxable year.

Amendments

• 1998, Tax and Trade Relief Extension Act of 1998 (P.L. 105-277)

P.L. 105-277, §3004(a):

Amended Code Sec. 172(f)(1)(B). **Effective** for net operating losses arising in tax years ending after 10-21-98. Prior to amendment, Code Sec. 172(f)(1)(B) read as follows:

(B) Any amount (not described in subparagraph (A)) allowable as a deduction under this chapter with respect to a liability which arises under a Federal or State law or out of any tort of the taxpayer if—

(i) in the case of a liability arising out of a Federal or State law, the act (or failure to act) giving rise to such liability occurs at least 3 years before the beginning of the taxable year, or

(ii) in the case of a liability arising out of a tort, such liability arises out of a series of actions (or failures to act) over an extended period of time a substantial portion of which occurs at least 3 years before the beginning of the taxable year.

A liability shall not be taken into account under subparagraph (B) unless the taxpayer used an accrual method of accounting throughout the period or periods during which the acts or failures to act giving rise to such liability occurred.

• 1996, Deposit Insurance Funds Act of 1996 (P.L. 104-208)

P.L. 104-208, §2711, provides:

SEC. 2711. DEDUCTION FOR SPECIAL ASSESSMENTS.

For purposes of subtitle A of the Internal Revenue Code of 1986—

(1) the amount allowed as a deduction under section 162 of such Code for a taxable year shall include any amount under section 2702 of this subtitle, and

(2) section 172(f) of such Code shall not apply to any deduction described in paragraph (1).

• 1990, Omnibus Budget Reconciliation Act of 1990 (P.L. 101-508)

P.L. 101-508, §11811(b)(1):

Amended Code Sec. 172 by redesignating subsection (j) as subsection (f). **Effective** for net operating losses for tax years beginning after 12-31-90.

P.L. 101-508, §11811(b)(2)(A):

Amended Code Sec. 172(f), as redesignated by Act Sec. 11811(b)(1). **Effective** for net operating losses for tax years beginning after 12-31-90. Prior to amendment, Code Sec. 172(f) read as follows:

(f) RULES RELATING TO PRODUCT LIABILITY LOSSES.—For purposes of this section—

(1) PRODUCT LIABILITY LOSS.—The term "product liability loss" means, for any taxable year, the lesser of—

(A) the net operating loss for such year reduced by any portion thereof which is attributable to a foreign expropriation loss, or

(B) the sum of the amounts allowable as deductions under sections 162 and 165 which are attributable to—

(i) product liability, or

(ii) expenses incurred in the investigation or settlement of, or opposition to, claims against the taxpayer on account of product liability.

(2) PRODUCT LIABILITY.—The term "product liability" means—

(A) liability of the taxpayer for damages on account of physical injury or emotional harm to individuals, or damage to or loss of the use of property, on account of any defect in any product which is manufactured, leased, or sold by the taxpayer, but only if

(B) such injury, harm, or damage arises after the taxpayer has completed or terminated operations with respect to, and has relinquished possession of, such product.

(3) ELECTION.—Any taxpayer entitled to a 10-year carryback under subsection (b)(1)(I) from any loss year may elect to have the carryback period with respect to such loss year determined without regard to subsection (b)(1)(I). Such election shall be made in such manner as may be prescribed by the Secretary and shall be made by the due date (including extensions of time) for filing the taxpayer's return for the taxable year of the net operating loss. Such election, once made for any taxable year, shall be irrevocable for that taxable year.

P.L. 101-508, §11811(b)(2)(B), provides:

(B) The portion of any loss which is attributable to a deferred statutory or tort liability loss (as defined in section 172(k) of the Internal Revenue Code of 1986 as in effect on the day before the date of the enactment of this Act) may not be carried back to any taxable year beginning before January 1, 1984, by reason of the amendment made by subparagraph (A).

• 1984, Deficit Reduction Act of 1984 (P.L. 98-369)

P.L. 98-369, §91(d)(3)(B):

Amended Code Sec. 172(j) by striking out "subsection (b)" in the matter preceding paragraph (1) and inserting in lieu thereof "this section". For the **effective** date, see Act Sec. 91(d)(2) in the notes following Code Sec. 172(k).

• 1982, Miscellaneous Revenue Act of 1982 (P.L. 97-362)

P.L. 97-362, §102(b):

Redesignated subsection (i) as (j). **Effective** for net operating losses for tax years beginning after 1981.

P.L. 97-362, §102(c)(4):

Amended Code Sec. 172(j)(3), as redesignated by P.L. 97-362, §102(b), by striking out "subsection (b)(1)(H)" each place it appeared and inserting in lieu thereof "subsection (b)(1)(I)". **Effective** for net operating losses for tax years beginning after 1981.

• 1978, Revenue Act of 1978 (P.L. 95-600)

P.L. 95-600, §371(b):

Amended Code Sec. 172 by redesignating Code Sec. 172(i) as Code Sec. 172(j) and by adding a new Code Sec. 172(i). **Effective** for tax years beginning after 9-30-79.

[Sec. 172(f)—Repealed]

Amendments

• 1982, Subchapter S Revision Act of 1982 (P.L. 97-354)

P.L. 97-354, §5(a)(22):

Repealed Code Sec. 172(f). **Effective** for tax years beginning after 12-31-82. Prior to its repeal, Code Sec. 172(f) read as follows:

(f) DISALLOWANCE OF NET OPERATING LOSS OF ELECTING SMALL BUSINESS CORPORATIONS.—In determining the amount of the net operating loss deduction under subsection (a) of any corporation, there shall be disregarded the net operating loss of such corporation for any taxable year for which such corporation is an electing small business corporation under subchapter S.

• 1976, Tax Reform Act of 1976 (P.L. 94-455)

P.L. 94-455, §1901(a)(29):

Repealed Code Sec. 172(f) and redesignated former Code Sec. 172(h) as Code Sec. 172(f). **Effective** for tax years ending after 10-4-76. Prior to repeal, Sec. 172(f) read as follows:

(f) TAXABLE YEARS BEGINNING IN 1953 AND ENDING IN 1954.—In the case of a taxable year beginning in 1953 and ending in 1954—

(1) In lieu of the amount specified in subsection (c), the net operating loss for such year shall be the sum of—

(A) that portion of the net operating loss for such year computed without regard to this subsection which the number of days in the loss year after December 31, 1953, bears to the total number of days in such year, and

(B) that portion of the net operating loss for such year computed under section 122 of the Internal Revenue Code of 1939 as if this section had not been enacted which the number of days in the loss year before January 1, 1954, bears to the total number of days in such year.

(2) The amount of any net operating loss for such year which shall be carried to the second preceding taxable year is the amount which bears the same ratio to such net operating loss as the number of days in the loss year after December 31, 1953, bears to the total number of days in such year. In determining the amount carried to any other taxable year, the reduction for the second taxable year preceding the loss year shall not exceed the portion of the net operating loss which is carried to the second preceding taxable year.

(3) The net operating loss deduction for such year shall be, in lieu of the amount specified in section 122(c) of the Internal Revenue Code of 1939, the sum of—

(A) that portion of the net operating loss deduction for such year, computed as if subsection (a) of this section were applicable to the taxable year, which the number of days in such year after December 31, 1953, bears to the total number of days in such year, and

(B) that portion of the net operating loss deduction for such year, computed under section 122(c) of the Internal Revenue Code of 1939 as if this paragraph had not been enacted, which the number of days in such year before January 1, 1954, bears to the total number of days in such year.

(4) For purposes of the second sentence of subsection (b)(2), the taxable income for such year shall be the sum of—

(A) that portion of the net income for such year, computed without regard to this paragraph, which the number of days in such year before January 1, 1954, bears to the total number of days in such year, and

(B) that portion of the net income for such year, computed—

(i) without regard to paragraphs (1) and (2) of section 122(d) of the Internal Revenue Code of 1939, and

(ii) by allowing as a deduction an amount equal to the sum of the credits provided in subsections (b) and (h) of section 26 of such Code,

which the number of days in such year after December 31, 1953, bears to the total number of days in such year.

• 1958, Technical Amendments Act of 1958 (P.L. 85-866)

P.L. 85-866, §14(a):

Added new paragraphs (3) and (4) to Sec. 172(f). **Effective** 1-1-58.

P.L. 85-866, §14(c), provides:

If refund or credit of any overpayment resulting from the application of the amendment made by subsection (a) or (b) is prevented on the date of the enactment of this Act, or within 6 months after such date, by the operation of any law or rule of law (other than section 3760 of the Internal Revenue Code of 1939 or section 7121 of the Internal Revenue Code of 1954, relating to closing agreements, and other than section 3761 of the Internal Revenue Code of 1939 or section 7122 of the Internal Revenue Code of 1954, relating to compromises), refund or credit of such overpayment may, nevertheless, be made or allowed if claim therefor is filed within 6 months after such date. No interest shall be paid or allowed on any overpayment resulting from the application of the amendment made by subsection (a) or (b).

P.L. 85-866, §64(b):

Added new subsec. (h) to Code Sec. 172.

[Sec. 172(g)]

(g) RULES RELATING TO BAD DEBT LOSSES OF COMMERCIAL BANKS.—For purposes of this section—

(1) PORTION ATTRIBUTABLE TO DEDUCTION FOR BAD DEBTS.—The portion of the net operating loss for any taxable year which is attributable to the deduction allowed under section 166(a) shall be the excess of—

(i) the net operating loss for such taxable year, over

(ii) the net operating loss for such taxable year determined without regard to the amount allowed as a deduction under section 166(a) for such taxable year.

(2) COORDINATION WITH SUBSECTION (b)(2).—For purposes of subsection (b)(2), the portion of a net operating loss for any taxable year which is attributable to the deduction allowed under section 166(a) shall be treated in a manner similar to the manner in which a specified liability loss is treated.

Amendments

• 1990, Omnibus Budget Reconciliation Act of 1990 (P.L. 101-508)

P.L. 101-508, §11811(b)(1):

Amended Code Sec. 172 by redesignating subsection (l) as subsection (g). **Effective** for net operating losses for tax years beginning after 12-31-90.

P.L. 101-508, §11811(b)(3):

Amended Code Sec. 172(g)(2), as redesignated by Act Sec. 11811(b)(1). **Effective** for net operating losses for tax years beginning after 12-31-90. Prior to amendment, Code Sec. 172(g)(2) read as follows:

(2) COORDINATION WITH SUBSECTION (b)(2).—In applying paragraph (2) of subsection (b), the portion of the net operating loss for any taxable year which is attributable to the deduction allowed under section 166(a) shall be treated in a manner similar to the manner in which a foreign expropriation loss is treated.

• 1986, Tax Reform Act of 1986 (P.L. 99-514)

P.L. 99-514, §903(b)(2)(C):

Amended Code Sec. 172 by redesignating subsection (l) as subsection (m) and inserting after subsection (k) new subsection (l). **Effective** for losses incurred in tax years beginning after 12-31-86.

[Sec. 172(g)—Stricken]

Amendments

• 1990, Omnibus Budget Reconciliation Act of 1990 (P.L. 101-508)

P.L. 101-508, §11811(b)(1):

Amended Code Sec. 172 by striking subsection (g). **Effective** for net operating losses for tax years beginning after 12-31-90. Prior to being stricken, Code Sec. 172(g) read as follows:

(g) CARRYOVER OF NET OPERATING LOSS FOR CERTAIN REGULATED TRANSPORTATION CORPORATIONS.—

(1) DEFINITION.—For purposes of subsection (b)(1)(C), the term "regulated transportation corporation" means a corporation—

(A) 80 percent or more of the gross income of which (computed without regard to dividends and capital gains and losses) for the taxable year is derived from the furnishing or sale of transportation described in subparagraph (A), (C)(i), (E), or (F) of section 7701(a)(33) and taken into account for purposes of the limitation contained in the last two sentences of section 7701(a)(33),

(B) which is described in subparagraph (G) or (H) of section 7701 (a)(33), or

(C) which is a member of a regulated transportation system.

(2) REGULATED TRANSPORTATION SYSTEM.—For purposes of this subsection, a corporation shall be treated as a member of a regulated transportation system for a taxable year if—

(A) it is a member of an affiliated group of corporations making a consolidated return for such taxable year, and

(B) 80 percent or more of the aggregate gross income of the members of such affiliated group (computed without regard to dividends and capital gains and losses) for such taxable year is derived from sources described in paragraph (1)(A).

For purposes of subparagraph (B), income derived by a corporation described in subparagraph (G) or (H) of section 7701(a)(33) from leases described in subparagraph (G) thereof shall be considered as derived from sources described in paragraph (1)(A).

(3) LIMITATION.—For purposes of subsection (b)(1)(C)—

(A) a net operating loss may not be a net operating loss carryover to the 6th taxable year following the loss year unless the taxpayer is a regulated transportation corporation for such 6th taxable year; and

(B) a net operating loss may not be a net operating loss carryover to the 7th taxable year following the loss year unless the taxpayer is a regulated transportation corporation for the 6th taxable year following the loss year and for such 7th taxable year.

• 1981, Economic Recovery Tax Act of 1981 (P.L. 97-34)

P.L. 97-34, §207(a)(2)(C):

Amended Code Sec. 172(g)(3) by inserting "and" at the end of subparagraph (A); by striking out "; and" at the end of subparagraph (B) and inserting in lieu thereof a period; and by striking out subparagraph (C). **Effective** for net operating losses in tax years ending after 12-31-75. See also Act Sec. 209(c)(3), as added by P.L. 97-448, under the amendment note for P.L. 97-34, §207(a)(2)(B)(ii) following Code Sec. 172(b). Prior to amendment, Code Sec. 172(g)(3)(C) read as follows:

(C) in the case of a net operating loss carryover from a loss year ending after December 31, 1975, subparagraphs (A) and (B) shall be applied by substituting 8th taxable year for 6th taxable year and 9th taxable year for 7th taxable year.

• 1976, Tax Reform Act of 1976 (P.L. 94-455)

P.L. 94-455, §806(b):

Struck out "and" at the end of subparagraph (A), substituted "; and" for the period at the end of subparagraph (B), and inserted a new subparagraph (C). **Effective** for losses incurred in tax years ending after 12-31-75.

P.L. 94-455, §1901(a)(29):

Struck out paragraph (4). **Effective** for tax years ending after 10-4-76. Prior to repeal, paragraph (4) read as follows:

(4) TAXABLE YEARS BEGINNING IN 1955 AND ENDING IN 1956.—In the case of a net operating loss for a taxable year beginning in 1955 and ending in 1956, the amount of such loss which may be carried—

(A) to the 6th taxable year following the loss year shall be the amount which bears the same ratio to the amount which (but for this paragraph) would be carried to such 6th taxable year as the number of days in the loss year after December 31, 1955, bears to the total number of days in the loss year, and

(B) to the 7th taxable year following the loss year shall be the amount (if any) by which (i) the amount carried to the 6th taxable year (determined under subparagraph (A)), exceeds (ii) the taxable income (computed as provided in subsection (b)(2)) for such 6th taxable year.

P.L. 94-455, §1901(a)(29):

Repealed former Code Sec. 172(g) and redesignated former Code Sec. 172(j) to be Code Sec. 172(g). **Effective** for tax years ending after 10-4-76. Prior to repeal, Sec. 172(g) read as follows:

(g) SPECIAL TRANSITIONAL RULES.—

(1) LOSSES FOR TAXABLE YEARS ENDING BEFORE JANUARY 1, 1954.—For purposes of this section, the determination of the taxable years ending after December 31, 1953, to which a net operating loss for any taxable year ending before January 1, 1954, may be carried shall be made under the Internal Revenue Code of 1939.

(2) LOSSES FOR TAXABLE YEARS ENDING AFTER DECEMBER 31, 1953.—For purposes of section 122 of the Internal Revenue Code of 1939—

(A) the determination of the taxable years ending before January 1, 1954, to which a net operating loss for any taxable year ending after December 31, 1953, may be carried shall be made under subsection (b)(1)(A) of this section; and

(B) in determining the amount of the carryback to the first taxable year preceding the first taxable year ending after December 31, 1953, the portion of the net operating loss carried to such year shall be such net operating loss reduced by—

(i) the net income for the second preceding taxable year computed as if the second sentence of section 122(b)(2)(B) of the Internal Revenue Code of 1939 applied, or

(ii) if smaller, the portion of the net operating loss which by reason of subsection (f) of this section is carried to the second preceding taxable year.

(3) TAXABLE YEARS BEGINNING AFTER DECEMBER 31, 1953, AND ENDING BEFORE AUGUST 17, 1954.—In the case of a taxable year which begins after December 31, 1953, and ends before August 17, 1954—

(A) the net operating loss deduction for such year shall be computed as if subsection (a) of this section applied to such taxable year, and

(B) for purposes of the second sentence of subsection (b)(2), the taxable income for such taxable year shall be the net income for such taxable year, computed—

(i) without regard to paragraphs (1) and (2) of section 122(d) of the Internal Revenue Code of 1939, and

(ii) by allowing as a deduction an amount equal to the sum of the credits provided in subsections (b) and (h) of section 26 of such Code.

(4) EXCESS PROFITS TAX NOT AFFECTED.—For purposes of subchapter D of chapter 1 of the Internal Revenue Code of 1939, excess profits net income shall be computed as if this section had not been enacted and as if section 122 of such Code continued to apply to taxable years to which this subtitle applies.

• 1964, Revenue Act of 1964 (P.L. 88-272)

P.L. 88-272, §234(b)(5):

Amended paragraphs (1) and (2) of Code Sec. 172(j) (now Code Sec. 172(g)). **Effective** with respect to tax years beginning after 12-31-63. Prior to amendment, paragraphs (j)(1) and (2) read as follows:

(1) Definition.—For purposes of subsection (b)(1)(C), the term "regulated transportation corporation" means a corporation—

(A) 80 percent or more of the gross income of which (computed without regard to dividends and capital gains and losses) for the taxable year is derived from the furnishing or sale of transportation described in subparagraph (A), (C)(i), (E), or (F) of section 1503(c)(1) and taken into account for purposes of section 1503(c)(2),

(B) which is described in section 1503(c)(3), or

(C) which is a member of a regulated transportation system.

(2) Regulated transportation system.—For purposes of this subsection, a corporation shall be treated as a member of a regulated transportation system for a taxable year if—

(A) it is a member of an affiliated group of corporations making a consolidated return for such taxable year, and

(B) 80 percent or more of the aggregate gross income of the members of such affiliated group (computed without regard to dividends and capital gains and losses) for such taxable year is derived from sources described in paragraph (1)(A).

For purposes of subparagraph (B), income derived by a corporation described in section 1503(c)(3) from leases described in subparagraph (A) thereof shall be considered as derived from sources described in paragraph (1)(A).

• 1962 (P.L. 87-710)

P.L. 87-710, §1(b):

Added Code Sec. 172(j). **Effective** 1-1-56.

• 1958, Technical Amendments Act of 1958 (P.L. 85-866)

P.L. 85-866, §14(b):

Redesignated paragraph (3) as paragraph (4) and added new paragraph (3).

P.L. 85-866, §14(c), provides:

If refund or credit of any overpayment resulting from the application of the amendment made by subsection (a) or (b) is prevented on the date of the enactment of this Act, or within 6 months after such date, by the operation of any law or rule of law (other than section 3760 of the Internal Revenue Code of 1939 or section 7121 of the Internal Revenue Code of 1954, relating to closing agreements, and other than section 3761 of the Internal Revenue Code of 1939 or section 7122 of the Internal Revenue Code of 1954, relating to compromises), refund or credit of such overpayment may, nevertheless, be made or allowed if claim therefor is filed within 6 months after such date. No interest shall be paid or allowed on any overpayment resulting from the application of the amendment made by subsection (a) or (b).

[Sec. 172(h)]

(h) CORPORATE EQUITY REDUCTION INTEREST LOSSES.—For purposes of this section—

(1) IN GENERAL.—The term "corporate equity reduction interest loss" means, with respect to any loss limitation year, the excess (if any) of—

(A) the net operating loss for such taxable year, over

(B) the net operating loss for such taxable year determined without regard to any allocable interest deductions otherwise taken into account in computing such loss.

(2) ALLOCABLE INTEREST DEDUCTIONS.—

(A) IN GENERAL.—The term "allocable interest deductions" means deductions allowed under this chapter for interest on the portion of any indebtedness allocable to a corporate equity reduction transaction.

(B) METHOD OF ALLOCATION.—Except as provided in regulations and subparagraph (E), indebtedness shall be allocated to a corporate equity reduction transaction in the manner prescribed under clause (ii) of section 263A(f)(2)(A) (without regard to clause (i) thereof).

(C) ALLOCABLE DEDUCTIONS NOT TO EXCEED INTEREST INCREASES.—Allocable interest deductions for any loss limitation year shall not exceed the excess (if any) of—

(i) the amount allowable as a deduction for interest paid or accrued by the taxpayer during the loss limitation year, over

(ii) the average of such amounts for the 3 taxable years preceding the taxable year in which the corporate equity reduction transaction occurred.

(D) DE MINIMIS RULE.—A taxpayer shall be treated as having no allocable interest deductions for any taxable year if the amount of such deductions (without regard to this subparagraph) is less than $1,000,000.

(E) SPECIAL RULE FOR CERTAIN UNFORESEEABLE EVENTS.—If an unforeseeable extraordinary adverse event occurs during a loss limitation year but after the corporate equity reduction transaction—

(i) indebtedness shall be allocated in the manner described in subparagraph (B) to unreimbursed costs paid or incurred in connection with such event before being allocated to the corporate equity reduction transaction, and

(ii) the amount determined under subparagraph (C)(i) shall be reduced by the amount of interest on indebtedness described in clause (i).

(F) TRANSITION RULE.—If any of the 3 taxable years described in subparagraph (C)(ii) end on or before August 2, 1989, the taxpayer may substitute for the amount determined under such subparagraph an amount equal to the interest paid or accrued (determined on an annualized basis) during the taxpayer's taxable year which includes August 3, 1989, on indebtedness of the taxpayer outstanding on August 2, 1989.

(3) CORPORATE EQUITY REDUCTION TRANSACTION.—

(A) IN GENERAL.—The term "corporate equity reduction transaction" means—

(i) a major stock acquisition, or

(ii) an excess distribution.

(B) MAJOR STOCK ACQUISITION.—

(i) IN GENERAL.—The term "major stock acquisition" means the acquisition by a corporation pursuant to a plan of such corporation (or any group of persons acting in concert with such corporation) of stock in another corporation representing 50 percent or more (by vote or value) of the stock in such other corporation.

(ii) EXCEPTION.—The term "major stock acquisition" does not include a qualified stock purchase (within the meaning of section 338) to which an election under section 338 applies.

(C) EXCESS DISTRIBUTION.—The term "excess distribution" means the excess (if any) of—

(i) the aggregate distributions (including redemptions) made during a taxable year by a corporation with respect to its stock, over

(ii) the greater of—

(I) 150 percent of the average of such distributions during the 3 taxable years immediately preceding such taxable year, or

(II) 10 percent of the fair market value of the stock of such corporation as of the beginning of such taxable year.

(D) RULES FOR APPLYING SUBPARAGRAPH (b).—For purposes of subparagraph (B)—

(i) PLANS TO ACQUIRE STOCK.—All plans referred to in subparagraph (B) by any corporation (or group of persons acting in concert with such corporation) with respect to another corporation shall be treated as 1 plan.

(ii) ACQUISITION DURING 24-MONTH PERIOD.—All acquisitions during any 24-month period shall be treated as pursuant to 1 plan.

(E) RULES FOR APPLYING SUBPARAGRAPH (c).—For purposes of subparagraph (C)—

(i) CERTAIN PREFERRED STOCK DISREGARDED.—Stock described in section 1504(a)(4), and distributions (including redemptions) with respect to such stock, shall be disregarded.

(ii) ISSUANCE OF STOCK.—The amounts determined under clauses (i) and (ii)(I) of subparagraph (C) shall be reduced by the aggregate amount of stock issued by the corporation during the applicable period in exchange for money or property other than stock in the corporation.

(4) OTHER RULES.—

(A) ORDERING RULE.—For purposes of paragraph (1), in determining the allocable interest deductions taken into account in computing the net operating loss for any taxable year, taxable income for such taxable year shall be treated as having been computed by taking allocable interest deductions into account after all other deductions.

(B) COORDINATION WITH SUBSECTION (b)(2).—For purposes of subsection (b)(2)—

(i) a corporate equity reduction interest loss shall be treated in a manner similar to the manner in which a specified liability loss is treated, and

(ii) in determining the net operating loss deduction for any prior taxable year referred to in the 3rd sentence of subsection (b)(2), the portion of any net operating loss which may not be carried to such taxable year under subsection (b)(1)(E) shall not be taken into account.

(C) MEMBERS OF AFFILIATED GROUPS.—Except as provided by regulations, all members of an affiliated group filing a consolidated return under section 1501 shall be treated as 1 taxpayer for purposes of this subsection and subsection (b)(1)(E).

(5) REGULATIONS.—The Secretary shall prescribe such regulations as may be necessary to carry out the purposes of this subsection, including regulations—

(A) for applying this subsection to successor corporations and in cases where a taxpayer becomes, or ceases to be, a member of an affiliated group filing a consolidated return under section 1501,

(B) to prevent the avoidance of this subsection through related parties, pass-through entities, and intermediaries, and

(C) for applying this subsection where more than 1 corporation is involved in a corporate equity reduction transaction.

Amendments

• 1996, Small Business Job Protection Act of 1996 (P.L. 104-188)

P.L. 104-188, §1702(h)(16):

Amended Code Sec. 172(h)(4)(C) by striking "subsection (b)(1)(M)" and inserting "subsection (b)(1)(E)". **Effective** as if included in the provision of P.L. 101-508 to which it relates.

P.L. 104-188, §1704(t)(5):

Amended Code Sec. 172(h)(3)(B)(i) by striking the comma at the end thereof and inserting a period. **Effective** 8-20-96.

P.L. 104-188, §1704(t)(30):

Amended Code Sec. 172(h)(4)(B) by striking the material following the heading and preceding clause (i) and inserting "For purposes of subsection (b)(2)—". **Effective** 8-20-96. Prior to amendment, the material following the heading of Code Sec. 172(h)(4)(B) and preceding clause (i) read as follows:

For purposes of subsection (b)(2)—

• 1990, Omnibus Budget Reconciliation Act of 1990 (P.L. 101-508)

P.L. 101-508, §11324(a):

Amended Code Sec. 172(m)(3)(B)(ii), prior to amendment by Act Sec. 11811(b)(1). **Effective**, generally, for acquisitions after 10-9-90. However, for an exception see Act Sec. 11324(b)(2), below. Prior to amendment, Code Sec. 172(m)(3)(B)(ii) read as follows:

(ii) EXCEPTIONS.—The term "major stock acquisition" shall not include—

(I) a qualified stock purchase (within the meaning of section 338) to which an election under section 338 applies, or

(II) except as provided in regulations, an acquisition in which a corporation acquires stock of another corporation which, immediately before the acquisition, was a member of an affiliated group (within the meaning of section 1504(a)) other than the common parent of such group.

P.L. 101-508, §11324(b)(2), provides:

(2) BINDING CONTRACT EXCEPTION.—The amendment made by subsection (a) shall not apply to any acquisition pursuant to a written binding contract in effect on October 9, 1990, and at all times thereafter before such acquisition.

P.L. 101-508, §11704(a)(2):

Amended Code Sec. 172(m)(4)(B), prior to amendment by Act Sec. 11811(b)(1), by striking "subsection (B)(2)" in the heading and inserting "subsection (b)(2)". **Effective** 11-5-90.

P.L. 101-508, §11811(b)(1):

Amended Code Sec. 172 by striking subsection (h) and redesignating subsection (m) as subsection (h). **Effective** for net operating losses for tax years beginning after 12-31-90.

P.L. 101-508, §11811(b)(4):

Amended Code Sec. 172(h)(4)(B), as redesignated by Act Sec. 11811(b)(1). **Effective** for net operating losses for tax years beginning after 12-31-90. Prior to amendment, Code Sec. 172(h)(4)(B) read as follows:

(B) COORDINATION WITH SUBSECTION (b)(2).—In applying paragraph (2) of subsection (b), the corporate equity reduction interest loss shall be treated in a manner similar to the manner in which a foreign expropriation loss is treated.

• 1989, Omnibus Budget Reconciliation Act of 1989 (P.L. 101-239)

P.L. 101-239, §7211(b):

Amended Code Sec. 172 by redesignating subsection (m) as subsection (n) and by inserting after subsection (l) a new subsection (m). **Effective**, generally, for corporate equity reduction transactions occurring after 8-2-89, in tax years ending after 8-2-89. For exceptions, see Act Sec. 7211(c)(2) following Code Sec. 172(b).

[Sec. 172(h)—Stricken]

Amendments

• 1990, Omnibus Budget Reconciliation Act of 1990 (P.L. 101-508)

P.L. 101-508, §11811(b)(1):

Amended Code Sec. 172 by striking subsection (h). **Effective** for net operating losses for tax years beginning after 12-31-90. Prior to being stricken, Code Sec. 172(h) read as follows:

(h) FOREIGN EXPROPRIATION LOSS DEFINED.—For purposes of this section—

(1) The term "foreign expropriation loss" means, for any taxable year, the sum of the losses sustained by reason of the expropriation, intervention, seizure, or similar taking of property by the government of any foreign country, any political subdivision thereof, or any agency or instrumentality of the foregoing. For purposes of the preceding sentence, a debt which becomes worthless shall, to the extent of any deduction allowed under section 166(a), be treated as a loss.

(2) The portion of the net operating loss for any taxable year attributable to a foreign expropriation loss is the amount of the foreign expropriation loss for such year (but not in excess of the net operating loss for such year).

(3) The term "Cuban expropriation loss" means, for any taxable year, a foreign expropriation loss sustained by reason of the expropriation, intervention, seizure, or similar taking of property, before January 1, 1964, by the government of Cuba, any political subdivision thereof, or any agency or instrumentality of the foregoing. The portion of a foreign expropriation loss for any taxable year attributable to a Cuban expropriation loss is the amount of the Cuban expropriation loss.

• 1984, Deficit Reduction Act of 1984 (P.L. 98-369)

P.L. 98-369, §91(d)(3)(B):

Amended Code Sec. 172(h) by striking out "subsection (b)" in the matter preceding paragraph (1) and inserting in lieu thereof "this section". For the **effective** date, see Act Sec. 91(d)(2) in the notes following Code Sec. 172(k).

• 1976, Tax Reform Act of 1976 (P.L. 94-455)

P.L. 94-455, §1901(a)(29):

Redesignated former Code Sec. 172(h) as Code Sec. 172(f) and redesignated former Code Sec. 172(k) as Code Sec. 172(h). **Effective** for tax years ending after 10-4-76.

• 1971 (P.L. 91-677)

P.L. 91-677, §2(c):

Added paragraph (3) to Code Sec. 172(k). **Effective** in respect of foreign expropriation losses sustained in tax years ending after 12-31-58.

• 1964, Revenue Act of 1964 (P.L. 88-272)

P.L. 88-272, §210(a)(5):

Amended section 172 to add subsection (k). **Effective** in respect of foreign expropriation losses sustained in tax years ending after 12-31-58.

[Sec. 172(i)]

(i) RULES RELATING TO FARMING LOSSES.—For purposes of this section—

(1) IN GENERAL.—The term "farming loss" means the lesser of—

(A) the amount which would be the net operating loss for the taxable year if only income and deductions attributable to farming businesses (as defined in section 263A(e)(4)) are taken into account, or

(B) the amount of the net operating loss for such taxable year.

Such term shall not include any qualified disaster loss (as defined in subsection (j)).

(2) COORDINATION WITH SUBSECTION (b)(2).—For purposes of applying subsection (b)(2), a farming loss for any taxable year shall be treated in a manner similar to the manner in which a specified liability loss is treated.

(3) ELECTION.—Any taxpayer entitled to a 5-year carryback under subsection (b)(1)(G) from any loss year may elect to have the carryback period with respect to such loss year determined without regard to subsection (b)(1)(G). Such election shall be made in such manner as may be prescribed by the Secretary and shall be made by the due date (including extensions of time) for filing the taxpayer's return for the taxable year of the net operating loss. Such election, once made for any taxable year, shall be irrevocable for such taxable year.

Amendments

• 2008, Tax Extenders and Alternative Minimum Tax Relief Act of 2008 (P.L. 110-343)

P.L. 110-343, Division C, §708(d)(2):

Amended Code Sec. 172(i)(1) by adding at the end a new flush sentence. **Effective** for losses arising in tax years beginning after 12-31-2007, in connection with disasters declared after such date.

P.L. 110-343, Division C, §712, provides:

SEC. 712. COORDINATION WITH HEARTLAND DISASTER RELIEF.

The amendments made by this subtitle, other than the amendments made by sections 706(a)(2), 710, and 711, shall not apply to any disaster described in section 702(c)[b](1)(A), or to any expenditure or loss resulting from such disaster.

• 1998, Tax and Trade Relief Extension Act of 1998 (P.L. 105-277)

P.L. 105-277, §2013(b):

Amended Code Sec. 172 by redesignating subsection (i) as subsection (j) and by inserting after subsection (h) a new subsection (i). **Effective** for net operating losses for tax years beginning after 12-31-97.

[Sec. 172(i)—Stricken]

Amendments

• **1990, Omnibus Budget Reconciliation Act of 1990 (P.L. 101-508)**

P.L. 101-508, §11811(b)(1):

Amended Code Sec. 172 by striking subsection (i). **Effective** for net operating losses for tax years beginning after 12-31-90. Prior to being stricken, Code Sec. 172(i) read as follows:

(i) RULES RELATING TO MORTGAGE DISPOSITION LOSS OF THE FEDERAL NATIONAL MORTGAGE ASSOCIATION OR THE FEDERAL HOME LOAN MORTGAGE CORPORATION.—

(1) MORTGAGE DISPOSITION LOSS DEFINED.—

(A) IN GENERAL.—For purposes of subsection (b)(1)(H) and this subsection, the term "mortgage disposition loss" means for any taxable year the excess (if any) of—

(i) the losses for such year from the sale or exchange of mortgages, securities, and other evidences of indebtedness, over

(ii) the gains for such year from the sale or exchange of such assets.

(B) MORTGAGE DISPOSITION LOSS CANNOT EXCEED THE NET OPERATING LOSS FOR THE YEAR.—The amount of the mortgage disposition loss for any taxable year shall not be greater than the net operating loss for such year.

(C) FORECLOSURE TRANSACTIONS NOT INCLUDED.—In applying subparagraph (A), any gain or loss which is attributable to a mortgage foreclosure shall not be taken into account.

(2) COORDINATION WITH SUBSECTION (b)(2).—In applying paragraph (2) of subsection (b), a mortgage disposition loss shall be treated in a manner similar to the manner in which a foreign expropriation loss is treated.

• **1984, Deficit Reduction Act of 1984 (P.L. 98-369)**

P.L. 98-369, §177(c)(2):

Amended subsection (i) of Code Sec. 172 by striking out "FNMA mortgage disposition loss" each place it appears in paragraphs (1) and (2) (including in headings) and inserting in lieu thereof "mortgage disposition loss", and by striking out "FNMA Mortgage Disposition Loss" in the subsection heading and inserting in lieu thereof "Mortgage Disposition Loss of the Federal National Mortgage Association or the Federal Home Loan Mortgage Corporation". **Effective** 1-1-85. See also the special rules in Act Sec. 177(d) under the amendment notes following Code Sec. 246(a).

• **1982, Miscellaneous Revenue Act of 1982 (P.L. 97-362)**

P.L. 97-362, §102(b):

Added subsection (i). **Effective** for net operating losses for tax years beginning after 12-31-81.

[Sec. 172(j)]

(j) RULES RELATING TO QUALIFIED DISASTER LOSSES .—For purposes of this section—

(1) IN GENERAL .—The term "qualified disaster loss" means the lesser of—

(A) the sum of—

(i) the losses allowable under section 165 for the taxable year—

(I) attributable to a federally declared disaster (as defined in section 165(h)(3)(C)(i)) occurring before January 1, 2010, and

(II) occurring in a disaster area (as defined in section 165(h)(3)(C)(ii)), and

(ii) the deduction for the taxable year for qualified disaster expenses which is allowable under section 198A(a) or which would be so allowable if not otherwise treated as an expense, or

(B) the net operating loss for such taxable year.

(2) COORDINATION WITH SUBSECTION (b)(2).—For purposes of applying subsection (b)(2), a qualified disaster loss for any taxable year shall be treated in a manner similar to the manner in which a specified liability loss is treated.

(3) ELECTION .—Any taxpayer entitled to a 5-year carryback under subsection (b)(1)(J) from any loss year may elect to have the carryback period with respect to such loss year determined without regard to subsection (b)(1)(J). Such election shall be made in such manner as may be prescribed by the Secretary and shall be made by the due date (including extensions of time) for filing the taxpayer's return for the taxable year of the net operating loss. Such election, once made for any taxable year, shall be irrevocable for such taxable year.

(4) EXCLUSION .—The term "qualified disaster loss" shall not include any loss with respect to any property described in section 1400N(p)(3).

Amendments

• **2008, Tax Extenders and Alternative Minimum Tax Relief Act of 2008 (P.L. 110-343)**

P.L. 110-343, Division C, §708(b):

Amended Code Sec. 172 by redesignating subsections (j) and (k) as subsections (k) and (l), respectively, and by inserting after subsection (i) a new subsection (j). **Effective** for losses arising in tax years beginning after 12-31-2007, in connection with disasters declared after such date.

P.L. 110-343, Division C, §712, provides:

SEC. 712. COORDINATION WITH HEARTLAND DISASTER RELIEF.

The amendments made by this subtitle, other than the amendments made by sections 706(a)(2), 710, and 711, shall not apply to any disaster described in section 702(c)[b](1)(A), or to any expenditure or loss resulting from such disaster.

[Sec. 172(k)—Stricken]

Amendments

• **2009, American Recovery and Reinvestment Tax Act of 2009 (P.L. 111-5)**

P.L. 111-5, §1211(b):

Amended Code Sec. 172 by striking subsection (k) and redesignating subsection (l) as subsection (k). **Effective** for net operating losses arising in tax years ending after 12-31-2007. For a transitional rule, see Act Sec. 1211(d)(2), below. Prior to being stricken, Code Sec. 172(k) read as follows:

(k) ELECTION TO DISREGARD 5-YEAR CARRYBACK FOR CERTAIN NET OPERATING LOSSES.—Any taxpayer entitled to a 5-year carryback under subsection (b)(1)(H) from any loss year may elect to have the carryback period with respect to such loss year determined without regard to subsection (b)(1)(H). Such election shall be made in such manner as may be prescribed by the Secretary and shall be made by the due date (including extensions of time) for filing the taxpayer's return for the taxable year of the net operating loss. Such election, once made for any taxable year, shall be irrevocable for such taxable year.

P.L. 111-5, §1211(d)(2), provides:

(2) TRANSITIONAL RULE.—In the case of a net operating loss for a taxable year ending before the date of the enactment of this Act—

(A) any election made under section 172(b)(3) of the Internal Revenue Code of 1986 with respect to such loss may (notwithstanding such section) be revoked before the applicable date,

(B) any election made under section 172(b)(1)(H) of such Code with respect to such loss shall (notwithstanding such section) be treated as timely made if made before the applicable date, and

(C) any application under section 6411(a) of such Code with respect to such loss shall be treated as timely filed if filed before the applicable date.

For purposes of this paragraph, the term "applicable date" means the date which is 60 days after the date of the enactment of this Act.

• 2008, Tax Extenders and Alternative Minimum Tax Relief Act of 2008 (P.L. 110-343)

P.L. 110-343, Division C, §708(b):

Amended Code Sec. 172 by redesignating subsection (j) as subsection (k). **Effective** for losses arising in tax years beginning after 12-31-2007, in connection with disasters declared after such date.

P.L. 110-343, Division C, §712, provides:

SEC. 712. COORDINATION WITH HEARTLAND DISASTER RELIEF.

The amendments made by this subtitle, other than the amendments made by sections 706(a)(2), 710, and 711, shall not apply to any disaster described in section 702(c)[b](1)(A), or to any expenditure or loss resulting from such disaster.

• 2004, Working Families Tax Relief Act of 2004 (P.L. 108-311)

P.L. 108-311, §403(b)(2), provides:

(2) In the case of a net operating loss for a taxable year ending during 2001 or 2002—

(A) an application under section 6411(a) of the Internal Revenue Code of 1986 with respect to such loss shall not fail to be treated as timely filed if filed before November 1, 2002,

(B) any election made under section 172(b)(3) of such Code may (notwithstanding such section) be revoked before November 1, 2002, and

(C) any election made under section 172(j) of such Code shall (notwithstanding such section) be treated as timely made if made before November 1, 2002.

• 2002, Job Creation and Worker Assistance Act of 2002 (P.L. 107-147)

P.L. 107-147, §102(b):

Amended Code Sec. 172 by redesignating subsection (j) as subsection (k) and by inserting after subsection (i) a new subsection (j). **Effective** for net operating losses for tax years ending after 12-31-2000.

[Sec. 172(k)]

(k) CROSS REFERENCES.—

(1) For treatment of net operating loss carryovers in certain corporate acquisitions, see section 381.

(2) For special limitation on net operating loss carryovers in case of a corporate change of ownership, see section 382.

Amendments

• 2009, American Recovery and Reinvestment Tax Act of 2009 (P.L. 111-5)

P.L. 111-5, §1211(b):

Amended Code Sec. 172 by redesignating subsection (l) as subsection (k). **Effective** for net operating losses arising in tax years ending after 12-31-2007.

• 2008, Tax Extenders and Alternative Minimum Tax Relief Act of 2008 (P.L. 110-343)

P.L. 110-343, Division C, §708(b):

Amended Code Sec. 172 by redesignating subsection (k) as subsection (l). **Effective** for losses arising in tax years beginning after 12-31-2007, in connection with disasters declared after such date.

P.L. 110-343, Division C, §712, provides:

SEC. 712. COORDINATION WITH HEARTLAND DISASTER RELIEF.

The amendments made by this subtitle, other than the amendments made by sections 706(a)(2), 710, and 711, shall not apply to any disaster described in section 702(c)[b](1)(A), or to any expenditure or loss resulting from such disaster.

• 2002, Job Creation and Worker Assistance Act of 2002 (P.L. 107-147)

P.L. 107-147, §102(b):

Amended Code Sec. 172 by redesignating subsection (j) as subsection (k). **Effective** for net operating losses for tax years ending after 12-31-2000.

• 1998, Tax and Trade Relief Extension Act of 1998 (P.L. 105-277)

P.L. 105-277, §2013(b):

Amended Code Sec. 172 by redesignating subsection (i) as subsection (j). **Effective** for net operating losses for tax years beginning after 12-31-97.

• 1990, Omnibus Budget Reconciliation Act of 1990 (P.L. 101-508)

P.L. 101-508, §11811(b)(1):

Amended Code Sec. 172 by redesignating subsection (n) as subsection (i). **Effective** for net operating losses for tax years beginning after 12-31-90.

• 1989, Omnibus Budget Reconciliation Act of 1989 (P.L. 101-239)

P.L. 101-239, §7211(b):

Amended Code Sec. 172 by redesignating subsection (m) as subsection (n). **Effective**, generally, for corporate equity reduction transactions occurring after 8-2-89, in tax years ending after 8-2-89. For exceptions, see Act Sec. 7211(c)(2) following Code Sec. 172(b).

• 1986, Tax Reform Act of 1986 (P.L. 99-514)

P.L. 99-514, §903(b)(2)(C):

Amended Code Sec. 172 by redesignating subsection (l) as subsection (m). **Effective** for losses incurred in tax years beginning after 12-31-86.

• 1984, Deficit Reduction Act of 1984 (P.L. 98-369)

P.L. 98-369, §91(d)(2):

Redesignated Code Sec. 172(k) as 172(l). For the **effective** date, See Act Sec. 91(d)(2) following Code Sec. 172(k).

• 1982, Miscellaneous Revenue Act of 1982 (P.L. 97-362)

P.L. 97-362, §102(b):

Redesignated subsection (j) as (k). **Effective** for net operating losses for tax years beginning after 1981.

• 1978, Revenue Act of 1978 (P.L. 95-600)

P.L. 95-600, §371(b):

Redesignated Code Sec. 172(i) as Code Sec. 172(j). **Effective** with respect to tax years beginning after 9-30-79.

• 1976, Tax Reform Act of 1976 (P.L. 94-455)

P.L. 94-455, §1901(a)(29):

Repealed Code Sec. 172(i) and redesignated former Code Sec. 172(l) as Code Sec. 172(i). **Effective** for tax years ending after 10-4-76.

P.L. 94-455, §1901(a)(29):

Repealed former Code Sec. 172(i). **Effective** for tax years ending after 10-4-76. Prior to repeal, Code Sec. 172(i) read as follows:

(i) CARRYBACK OF NET OPERATING LOSS FOR TAXABLE YEARS BEGINNING IN 1957 AND ENDING IN 1958.—In the case of a taxable year beginning in 1957 and ending in 1958, the amount of any net operating loss for such year which shall be carried to the third preceding taxable year is the amount which bears the same ratio to such net operating loss as the number of days in the loss year after December 31, 1957, bears to the total number of days in such year. In determining the amount carried to any other taxable year, the reduction for the third taxable year preceding the loss year shall not exceed the portion of the net operating loss which is carried to the third preceding taxable year.

• 1964, Revenue Act of 1964 (P.L. 88-272)

P.L. 88-272, §210(a)(5):

Redesignated subsec. (k) as (l). **Effective** 1-1-59.

• 1962 (P.L. 87-710)

P.L. 87-710, §1(b):

Redesignated subsec. (j) as (k). **Effective** 1-1-56.

• 1958, Technical Amendments Act of 1958 (P.L. 85-866)

P.L. 85-866, §64(b):

Redesignated subsec. (h) as subsec. (i). Sec. 203(b) further redesignated it as subsec. (j). **Effective** 1-1-58.

P.L. 85-866, §203(b):

Amended Code Sec. 172 by adding new subsec. (i). **Effective** in respect of net operating losses for tax years ending after 12-31-57.

[Sec. 172(k)—Stricken]

Amendments

• 1990, Omnibus Budget Reconciliation Act of 1990 (P.L. 101-508)

P.L. 101-508, §11811(b)(1):

Amended Code Sec. 172 by striking subsection (k). **Effective** for net operating losses for tax years beginning after 12-31-90. Prior to being stricken, Code Sec. 172(k) read as follows:

(k) DEFINITIONS AND SPECIAL RULES RELATING TO DEFERRED STATUTORY OR TORT LIABILITY LOSSES.—For purposes of this section—

(1) DEFERRED STATUTORY OR TORT LIABILITY LOSS.—The term "deferred statutory or tort liability loss" means, for any taxable year, the lesser of—

(A) the net operating loss for such taxable year, reduced by any portion thereof attributable to—

(i) a foreign expropriation loss, or

(ii) a product liability loss, or

(B) the sum of the amounts allowable as a deduction under this chapter (other than any deduction described in subsection (j)(1)(B)) which—

(i) is taken into account in computing the net operating loss for such taxable year, and

(ii) is for an amount incurred with respect to a liability which arises under a Federal or State law or out of any tort of the taxpayer and—

(I) in the case of a liability arising out of a Federal or State law, the act (or failure to act) giving rise to such liability occurs at least 3 years before the beginning of such taxable year, or

(II) in the case of a liability arising out of a tort, such liability arises out of a series of actions (or failures to act) over an extended period of time a substantial portion of which occurs at least 3 years before the beginning of such taxable year.

A liability shall not be taken into account under the preceding sentence unless the taxpayer used an accrual method of accounting throughout the period or periods during which the acts or failures to act giving rise to such liability occurred.

(2) SPECIAL RULE FOR NUCLEAR POWERPLANTS.—Except as provided in regulations prescribed by the Secretary, that portion of a deferred statutory or tort liability loss which is attributable to amounts incurred in the decommissioning of a nuclear powerplant (or any unit thereof) may, for purposes of subsection (b)(1)(J), be carried back to each of the taxable years during the period—

(A) beginning with the taxable year in which such plant (or unit thereof) was placed in service, and

(B) ending with the taxable year preceding the loss year.

(3) COORDINATION WITH SUBSECTION (b)(2).—In applying paragraph (2) of subsection (b), a deferred statutory or tort liability loss shall be treated in a manner similar to the manner in which a foreign expropriation loss is treated.

(4) NO CARRYBACK TO TAXABLE YEARS BEGINNING BEFORE JANUARY 1, 1984.—No deferred statutory or tort liability loss may be carried back to a taxable year beginning before January 1, 1984, unless such loss may be carried back to such year without regard to subsection (b)(1)(J).

• 1986, Tax Reform Act of 1986 (P.L. 99-514)

P.L. 99-514, §1303(b)(2):

Amended Code Sec. 172(k)(2) and (4) by striking out "subsection (b)(1)(K)" and inserting in lieu thereof "subsection (b)(1)(J)". **Effective** on 10-22-86.

• 1984, Deficit Reduction Act of 1984 (P.L. 98-369)

P.L. 98-369, §91(d)(2):

Amended Code Sec. 172 by redesignating subsection (k) as subsection (l) and by inserting after subsection (j) new subsection (k). **Effective** for amounts with respect to which a deduction would be allowable under chapter 1 of the Internal Revenue Code of 1954 (determined without regard to such amendments) after—

(A) in the case of amounts to which section 461(h) of such Code (as added by such amendments) applies, the date of the enactment of this Act, and

(B) in the case of amounts to which section 461(i) of such Code (as so added) applies, after 3-31-84.

See, also, special rules in Act Sec. 91(g)-(i) under the amendment notes for Code Sec. 461(h).

[Sec. 173]

SEC. 173. CIRCULATION EXPENDITURES.

[Sec. 173(a)]

(a) GENERAL RULE.—Notwithstanding section 263, all expenditures (other than expenditures for the purchase of land or depreciable property or for the acquisition of circulation through the purchase of any part of the business of another publisher of a newspaper, magazine, or other periodical) to establish, maintain, or increase the circulation of a newspaper, magazine, or other periodical shall be allowed as a deduction; except that the deduction shall not be allowed with respect to the portion of such expenditures as, under regulations prescribed by the Secretary, is chargeable to capital account if the taxpayer elects, in accordance with such regulations, to treat such portion as so chargeable. Such election, if made, must be for the total amount of such portion of the expenditures which is so chargeable to capital account, and shall be binding for all subsequent taxable years unless, upon application by the taxpayer, the Secretary permits a revocation of such election subject to such conditions as he deems necessary.

[Sec. 173(b)]

(b) CROSS REFERENCE.—

For election of 3-year amortization of expenditures allowable as a deduction under subsection (a), see section 59(e).

Amendments

• 1988, Technical and Miscellaneous Revenue Act of 1988 (P.L. 100-647)

P.L. 100-647, §1007(g)(5):

Amended Code Sec. 173(b) by striking out "section 59(d)" and inserting in lieu thereof "section 59(e)". **Effective** as if included in the provision of P.L. 99-514 to which it relates.

• 1986, Tax Reform Act of 1986 (P.L. 99-514)

P.L. 99-514, §701(e)(4)(D):

Amended Code Sec. 173(b) by striking out "section 58(i)" and inserting in lieu thereof "section 59(d)". **Effective** for tax years beginning after 12-31-86.

• 1984, Deficit Reduction Act of 1984 (P.L. 98-369)

P.L. 98-369, §711(a)(3)(C):

Amended Code Sec. 173(b) by striking out "10-year" and inserting in lieu thereof "3-year". **Effective** as if included in the provision of P.L. 97-248 to which it relates.

• 1983, Technical Corrections Act of 1982 (P.L. 97-448)

P.L. 97-448, §306(a)(1)(A):

Amended section 201 of P.L. 97-248 by redesignating the second subsection (c) as subsection (d). **Effective** for tax years beginning after 12-31-82.

• 1982, Tax Equity and Fiscal Responsibility Act of 1982 (P.L. 97-248)

P.L. 97-248, §201(d)(9)(A):

Amended Code Sec. 173 by striking out "Notwithstanding section 263" and inserting in lieu thereof "(a) General Rule.—Notwithstanding section 263", and by adding at the end thereof new subsection (b). **Effective** for tax years beginning after 12-31-82.

• 1976, Tax Reform Act of 1976 (P.L. 94-455)

P.L. 94-455, §1906(b)(13)(A):

Amended 1954 Code by substituting "Secretary" for "Secretary or his delegate" each place it appeared. **Effective** 2-1-77.

[Sec. 174]

SEC. 174. RESEARCH AND EXPERIMENTAL EXPENDITURES.

[Sec. 174(a)]

(a) TREATMENT AS EXPENSES.—

(1) IN GENERAL.—A taxpayer may treat research or experimental expenditures which are paid or incurred by him during the taxable year in connection with his trade or business as expenses which are not chargeable to capital account. The expenditures so treated shall be allowed as a deduction.

(2) WHEN METHOD MAY BE ADOPTED.—

(A) WITHOUT CONSENT.—A taxpayer may, without the consent of the Secretary, adopt the method provided in this subsection for his first taxable year—

(i) which begins after December 31, 1953, and ends after August 16, 1954, and

(ii) for which expenditures described in paragraph (1) are paid or incurred.

(B) WITH CONSENT.—A taxpayer may, with the consent of the Secretary, adopt at any time the method provided in this subsection.

(3) SCOPE.—The method adopted under this subsection shall apply to all expenditures described in paragraph (1). The method adopted shall be adhered to in computing taxable income for the taxable year and for all subsequent taxable years unless, with the approval of the Secretary, a change to a different method is authorized with respect to part or all of such expenditures.

Amendments

• 1976, Tax Reform Act of 1976 (P.L. 94-455)

P.L. 94-455, §§1901(a)(29):

Substituted "August 16, 1954" for "the date on which this title is enacted" in Code Sec. 174(a)(2)(A)(i). **Effective** for tax years beginning after 12-31-76.

P.L. 94-455, §1906(b)(13)(A):

Amended 1954 Code by substituting "Secretary" for "Secretary or his delegate" each place it appeared. **Effective** 2-1-77.

[Sec. 174(b)]

(b) AMORTIZATION OF CERTAIN RESEARCH AND EXPERIMENTAL EXPENDITURES.—

(1) IN GENERAL.—At the election of the taxpayer, made in accordance with regulations prescribed by the Secretary, research or experimental expenditures which are—

(A) paid or incurred by the taxpayer in connection with his trade or business,

(B) not treated as expenses under subsection (a), and

(C) chargeable to capital account but not chargeable to property of a character which is subject to the allowance under section 167 (relating to allowance for depreciation, etc.) or section 611 (relating to allowance for depletion), may be treated as deferred expenses. In computing taxable income, such deferred expenses shall be allowed as a deduction ratably over such period of not less than 60 months as may be selected by the taxpayer (beginning with the month in which the taxpayer first realizes benefits from such expenditures). Such deferred expenses are expenditures properly chargeable to capital account for purposes of section 1016(a)(1) (relating to adjustments to basis of property).

(2) TIME FOR AND SCOPE OF ELECTION.—The election provided by paragraph (1) may be made for any taxable year beginning after December 31, 1953, but only if made not later than the time prescribed by law for filing the return for such taxable year (including extensions thereof). The method so elected, and the period selected by the taxpayer, shall be adhered to in computing taxable income for the taxable year for which the election is made and for all subsequent taxable years unless, with the approval of the Secretary, a change to a different method (or to a different period) is authorized with respect to part or all of such expenditures. The election shall not apply to any expenditure paid or incurred during any taxable year before the taxable year for which the taxpayer makes the election.

Amendments

• 1976, Tax Reform Act of 1976 (P.L. 94-455)

P.L. 94-455, §1906(b)(13)(A):

Amended 1954 Code by substituting "Secretary" for "Secretary or his delegate" each place it appeared. **Effective** 2-1-77.

[Sec. 174(c)]

(c) LAND AND OTHER PROPERTY.—This section shall not apply to any expenditure for the acquisition or improvement of land, or for the acquisition or improvement of property to be used in connection with the research or experimentation and of a character which is subject to the allowance under section 167 (relating to allowance for depreciation, etc.) or section 611 (relating to allowance for depletion); but for purposes of this section allowances under section 167, and allowances under section 611, shall be considered as expenditures.

[Sec. 174(d)]

(d) EXPLORATION EXPENDITURES.—This section shall not apply to any expenditure paid or incurred for the purpose of ascertaining the existence, location, extent, or quality of any deposit of ore or other mineral (including oil and gas).

[Sec. 174(e)]

(e) ONLY REASONABLE RESEARCH EXPENDITURES ELIGIBLE.—This section shall apply to a research or experimental expenditure only to the extent that the amount thereof is reasonable under the circumstances.

Amendments

• 1989, Omnibus Budget Reconciliation Act of 1989 (P.L. 101-239)

P.L. 101-239, §7110(d)[(e)]:

Amended Code Sec. 174 by redesignating subsection (e) as subsection (f) and by inserting after subsection (d) a new subsection (e). **Effective** for tax years beginning after 12-31-89.

[Sec. 174(f)]

(f) CROSS REFERENCES.—

(1) For adjustments to basis of property for amounts allowed as deductions as deferred expenses under subsection (b), see section 1016(a)(14).

(2) For election of 10-year amortization of expenditures allowable as a deduction under subsection (a), see section 59(e).

Amendments

• 1989, Omnibus Budget Reconciliation Act of 1989 (P.L. 101-239)

P.L. 101-239, §7110(d)[(e)]:

Amended Code Sec. 174 by redesignating subsection (e) as subsection (f). **Effective** for tax years beginning after 12-31-89.

• 1988, Technical and Miscellaneous Revenue Act of 1988 (P.L. 100-647)

P.L. 100-647, §1007(g)(5):

Amended Code Sec. 174(e)(2) by striking out "section 59(d)" and inserting in lieu thereof "section 59(e)". **Effective** as if included in the provision of P.L. 99-514 to which it relates.

• 1986, Tax Reform Act of 1986 (P.L. 99-514)

P.L. 99-514, §701(e)(4)(D):

Amended Code Sec. 174(e)(2) by striking out "section 58(i)" and inserting in lieu thereof "section 59(d)". **Effective** for tax years beginning after 12-31-86.

• 1983, Technical Corrections Act of 1982 (P.L. 97-448)

P.L. 97-448, §306(a)(1)(A):

Amended section 201 of P.L. 97-248 by redesignating the second subsection (c) as subsection (d).

• 1982, Tax Equity and Fiscal Responsibility Act of 1982 (P.L. 97-248)

P.L. 97-248, §201(d)(9)(B):

Amended Code Sec.174(e) by striking out "For adjustments" and inserting in lieu thereof "(1) For adjustments"; by adding at the end thereof the following new paragraph (2); and by striking out "CROSS REFERENCE" and inserting in lieu thereof "CROSS REFERENCES". **Effective** for tax years beginning after 12-31-82.

[Sec. 175]

SEC. 175. SOIL AND WATER CONSERVATION EXPENDITURES; ENDANGERED SPECIES RECOVERY EXPENDITURES.

[Sec. 175(a)]

(a) IN GENERAL.—A taxpayer engaged in the business of farming may treat expenditures which are paid or incurred by him during the taxable year for the purpose of soil or water conservation in respect of land used in farming, or for the prevention of erosion of land used in farming, or for endangered species recovery, as expenses which are not chargeable to capital account. The expenditures so treated shall be allowed as a deduction.

Amendments

• 2008, Heartland, Habitat, Harvest, and Horticulture Act of 2008 (P.L. 110-246)

P.L. 110-246, §15303(a)(2)(A):

Amended Code Sec. 175(a) by inserting ", or for endangered species recovery" after "prevention of erosion of land used in farming". **Effective** for expenditures paid or incurred after 12-31-2008.

P.L. 110-246, §15303(a)(2)(B):

Amended the heading of Code Sec. 175 by inserting "; ENDANGERED SPECIES RECOVERY EXPENDITURES" before the period. **Effective** for expenditures paid or incurred after 12-31-2008.

[Sec. 175(b)]

(b) LIMITATION.—The amount deductible under subsection (a) for any taxable year shall not exceed 25 percent of the gross income derived from farming during the taxable year. If for any taxable year the total of the expenditures treated as expenses which are not chargeable to capital account exceeds 25 percent of the gross income derived from farming during the taxable year, such excess shall be deductible for succeeding taxable years in order of time; but the amount deductible under this section for any one such succeeding taxable year (including the expenditures actually paid or incurred during the taxable year) shall not exceed 25 percent of the gross income derived from farming during the taxable year.

[Sec. 175(c)]

(c) DEFINITIONS.—For purposes of subsection (a)—

(1) The term "expenditures which are paid or incurred by him during the taxable year for the purpose of soil or water conservation in respect of land used in farming, or for the prevention of erosion of land used in farming, or for endangered species recovery" means expenditures paid or incurred for the treatment or moving of earth, including (but not limited to) leveling, grading and terracing, contour furrowing, the construction, control, and protection of diversion channels, drainage ditches, earthen dams, watercourses, outlets, and ponds, the eradication of brush, and the planting of windbreaks. Such term shall include expenditures paid or incurred for the purpose of achieving site-specific management actions recommended in recovery plans approved pursuant to the Endangered Species Act of 1973. Such term does not include—

(A) the purchase, construction, installation, or improvement of structures, appliances, or facilities which are of a character which is subject to the allowance for depreciation provided in section 167, or

(B) any amount paid or incurred which is allowable as a deduction without regard to this section.

Notwithstanding the preceding sentences, such term also includes any amount, not otherwise allowable as a deduction, paid or incurred to satisfy any part of an assessment levied by a soil or water conservation or drainage district to defray expenditures made by such district (i) which, if paid or incurred by the taxpayer, would without regard to this sentence constitute expenditures deductible under this section, or (ii) for property of a character subject to the allowance for depreciation provided in section 167 and used in the soil or water conservation or drainage district's business as such (to the extent that the taxpayer's share of the assessment levied on the members of the district for such property does not exceed 10 percent of such assessment).

(2) The term "land used in farming" means land used (before or simultaneously with the expenditures described in paragraph (1)) by the taxpayer or his tenant for the production of crops, fruits, or other agricultural products or for the sustenance of livestock.

(3) ADDITIONAL LIMITATIONS.—

(A) EXPENDITURES MUST BE CONSISTENT WITH SOIL CONSERVATION PLAN, OR ENDANGERED SPECIES RECOVERY PLAN.—Nothwithstanding any other provision of this section, subsection (a) shall not apply to any expenditures unless such expenditures are consistent with—

(i) the plan (if any) approved by the Soil Conservation Service of the Department of Agriculture or the recovery plan approved pursuant to the Endangered Species Act of 1973 for the area in which the land is located, or

(ii) If there is no plan described in clause (i), any soil conservation plan of a comparable State agency.

(B) CERTAIN WETLAND, ETC., ACTIVITIES NOT QUALIFIED.—Subsection (a) shall not apply to any expenditures in connection with the draining or filling of wetlands or land preparation for center pivot irrigation systems.

Amendments

• 2008, Heartland, Habitat, Harvest, and Horticulture Act of 2008 (P.L. 110-246)

P.L. 110-246, §15303(a)(1):

Amended Code Sec. 175(c)(1) by inserting after the first sentence a new sentence. **Effective** for expenditures paid or incurred after 12-31-2008.

P.L. 110-246, §15303(a)(2)(A):

Amended Code Sec. 175(c)(1) by inserting ", or for endangered species recovery" after "prevention of erosion of land used in farming". **Effective** for expenditures paid or incurred after 12-31-2008.

P.L. 110-246, §15303(b)(1)-(2):

Amended Code Sec. 175(c)(3) by inserting ", OR ENDANGERED SPECIES RECOVERY PLAN" after "CONSERVATION PLAN" in the heading of subparagraph (A), and by inserting "or the recovery plan approved pursuant to the Endangered Species Act of 1973" after "Department of Agriculture" in subparagraph (A)(i). **Effective** for expenditures paid or incurred after 12-31-2008.

• 1986, Tax Reform Act of 1986 (P.L. 99-514)

P.L. 99-514, §401(a):

Amended Code Sec. 175(c) by adding at the end thereof new paragraph (3). **Effective** for amounts paid or incurred after 12-31-86, in tax years ending after such date.

• 1968 (P.L. 90-630)

P.L. 90-630, §5(a):

Amended the last sentence in paragraph (1) of Code Sec. 175(c). **Effective** for assessments levied after 10-22-68 in tax years ending after that date. Prior to amendment, this sentence read as follows: "Notwithstanding the preceding sentences, such term also includes any amount, not otherwise allowable as a deduction, paid or incurred to satisfy any part of an assessment levied by a soil or water conservation or drainage district to defray expenditures made by such district which, if paid or incurred by the taxpayer, would without regard to this section constitute expenditures deductible under this section."

[Sec. 175(d)]

(d) WHEN METHOD MAY BE ADOPTED.—

(1) WITHOUT CONSENT.—A taxpayer may, without the consent of the Secretary, adopt the method provided in this section for his first taxable year—

(A) which begins after December 31, 1953, and ends after August 16, 1954, and

(B) for which expenditures described in subsection (a) are paid or incurred.

(2) WITH CONSENT.—A taxpayer may, with the consent of the Secretary, adopt at any time the method provided in this section.

Amendments

• 1976, Tax Reform Act of 1976 (P.L. 94-455)

P.L. 94-455, §1901(a)(30):

Substituted "August 16, 1954" for "the date on which this title is enacted" in Code Sec. 175(d)(1)(A). **Effective** for tax years beginning after 12-31-76.

P.L. 94-455, §1906(b)(13)(A):

Amended 1954 Code by substituting "Secretary" for "Secretary or his delegate" each place it appeared. **Effective** 2-1-77.

[Sec. 175(e)]

(e) SCOPE.—The method adopted under this section shall apply to all expenditures described in subsection (a). The method adopted shall be adhered to in computing taxable income for the taxable year and for all subsequent taxable years unless, with the approval of the Secretary, a change to a different method is authorized with respect to part or all of such expenditures.

Amendments

• 1976, Tax Reform Act of 1976 (P.L. 94-455)

P.L. 94-455, §1906(b)(13)(A):

Amended 1954 Code by substituting "Secretary" for "Secretary or his delegate" each place it appeared. **Effective** 2-1-77.

[Sec. 175(f)]

(f) RULES APPLICABLE TO ASSESSMENTS FOR DEPRECIABLE PROPERTY.—

(1) AMOUNTS TREATED AS PAID OR INCURRED OVER 9-YEAR PERIOD.—In the case of an assessment levied to defray expenditures for property described in clause (ii) of the last sentence of subsection (c)(1), if the amount of such assessment paid or incurred by the taxpayer during the taxable year (determined without the application of this paragraph) is in excess of an amount equal to 10 percent of the aggregate amounts which have been and will be assessed as the taxpayer's share of the expenditures by the district for such property, and if such excess is more than $500, the entire excess shall be treated as paid or incurred ratably over each of the 9 succeeding taxable years.

(2) DISPOSITION OF LAND DURING 9-YEAR PERIOD.—If paragraph (1) applies to an assessment and the land with respect to which such assessment was made is sold or otherwise disposed of by the taxpayer (other than by the reason of his death) during the 9 succeeding taxable years, any amount of the excess described in paragraph (1) which has not been treated as paid or incurred for a taxable year ending on or before the sale or other disposition shall be added to the adjusted

basis of such land immediately prior to its sale or other disposition and shall not thereafter be treated as paid or incurred ratably under paragraph (1).

(3) DISPOSITION BY REASON OF DEATH.—If paragraph (1) applies to an assessment and the taxpayer dies during the 9 succeeding taxable years, any amount of the excess described in paragraph (1) which has not been treated as paid or incurred for a taxable year ending before his death shall be treated as paid or incurred in the taxable year in which he dies.

Amendments

• 1968 (P.L. 90-630)

P.L. 90-630, §5(b):

Added Code Sec. 175(f). **Effective** for assessments levied after 10-22-68, in tax years ending after that date.

[Sec. 176]

SEC. 176. PAYMENTS WITH RESPECT TO EMPLOYEES OF CERTAIN FOREIGN CORPORATIONS.

In the case of a domestic corporation, there shall be allowed as a deduction amounts (to the extent not compensated for) paid or incurred pursuant to an agreement entered into under section 3121(l) with respect to services performed by United States citizens employed by foreign subsidiary corporations. Any reimbursement of any amount previously allowed as a deduction under this section shall be included in gross income for the taxable year in which received.

Amendments

• 1954, Social Security Amendments of 1954 (P.L. 761, 83rd Cong.)

P.L. 761, 83rd Cong., §210(a):

Added Code Sec. 176. **Effective** 1-1-55.

[Sec. 177—Repealed]

Amendments

• 1986, Tax Reform Act of 1986 (P.L. 99-514)

P.L. 99-514, §241(a):

Repealed Code Sec. 177. **Effective**, generally, for expenditures paid or incurred after 12-31-86. For a transitional rule see Act Sec. 241(c)(2), below. Prior to repeal, Code Sec. 177 read as follows:

SEC. 177. TRADEMARK AND TRADE NAME EXPENDITURES.

[Sec. 177(a)]

(a) ELECTION TO AMORTIZE.—Any trademark or trade name expenditure paid or incurred during a taxable year beginning after December 31, 1955, may, at the election of the taxpayer (made in accordance with regulations prescribed by the Secretary), be treated as a deferred expense. In computing taxable income, all expenditures paid or incurred during the taxable year which are so treated shall be allowed as a deduction ratably over such period of not less than 60 months (beginning with the first month in such taxable year) as may be selected by the taxpayer in making such election. The expenditures so treated are expenditures properly chargeable to capital account for purposes of section 1016(a)(1) (relating to adjustments to basis of property).

Amendments

• 1976, Tax Reform Act of 1976 (P.L. 94-455)

P.L. 94-455, §1906(b)(13)(A):

Amended 1954 Code by substituting "Secretary" for "Secretary or his delegate" each place it appeared. **Effective** 2-1-77.

[Sec. 177(b)]

(b) TRADEMARK AND TRADE NAME EXPENDITURES DEFINED.—For purposes of subsection (a), the term "trademark or trade name expenditure" means any expenditure which—

(1) is directly connected with the acquisition, protection, expansion, registration (Federal, State, or foreign), or defense of a trademark or trade name;

(2) is chargeable to capital account; and

(3) is not part of the consideration paid for a trademark, trade name, or business.

[Sec. 177(c)]

(c) TIME FOR AND SCOPE OF ELECTION.—The election provided by subsection (a) shall be made within the time prescribed by law (including extensions thereof) for filing the return for the taxable year during which the expenditure is paid or incurred. The period selected by the taxpayer under subsection (a) with respect to the expenditures paid or incurred during the taxable year which are treated as deferred expenses shall be adhered to in computing his taxable income for the taxable year for which the election is made and all subsequent years.

[Sec. 177(d)]

(d) CROSS REFERENCE.—

For adjustments to basis of property for amounts allowed as deductions for expenditures treated as deferred expenses under this section, see section 1016(a)(16).

Amendments

• 1956 (P.L. 629, 84th Cong.)

P.L. 629, 84th Cong., §4(a):

Amended Part VI of subchapter B of chapter 1 of the 1954 Code by adding Code Sec. 177. **Effective** 1-1-56.

• 1986, Tax Reform Act of 1986 (P.L. 99-514)

P.L. 99-514, §241(c)(2), provides:

(2) TRANSITIONAL RULE.—The amendments made by this section shall not apply to any expenditure incurred—

(A) pursuant to a binding contract entered into before March 2, 1986, or

(B) with respect to the development, protection, expansion, registration, or defense of a trademark or trade name commenced before March 2, 1986, but only if not less than the lesser of $1,000,000 or 5 percent of the aggregate cost of such development, protection, expansion, registration, or defense has been incurred or committed before such date.

The preceding sentence shall not apply to any expenditure with respect to a trademark or trade name placed in service after December 31, 1987.

[Sec. 178]

SEC. 178. AMORTIZATION OF COST OF ACQUIRING A LEASE.

[Sec. 178(a)]

(a) GENERAL RULE.—In determining the amount of the deduction allowable to a lessee for exhaustion, wear and tear, obsolescence, or amortization in respect of any cost of acquiring the lease, the term of the lease shall be treated as including all renewal options (and any other period for which the parties reasonably expect the lease to be renewed) if less than 75 percent of such cost is attributable to the period of the term of the lease remaining on the date of its acquisition.

Amendments

• 1988, Technical and Miscellaneous Revenue Act of 1988 (P.L. 100-647)

P.L. 100-647, §1002(a)(9):

Amended Code Sec. 178(a) by striking out "the deduction allowable to a lessee of a lease for any taxable year for amortization under section 167, 169, 179, 185, 190, 193, or 194" and inserting in lieu thereof "the deduction allowable to a lessee for exhaustion, wear and tear, obsolescence, or amortization". **Effective** as if included in the provision of P.L. 99-514 to which it relates.

[Sec. 178(b)]

(b) CERTAIN PERIODS EXCLUDED.—For purposes of subsection (a), in determining the period of the term of the lease remaining on the date of acquisition, there shall not be taken into account any period for which the lease may subsequently be renewed, extended, or continued pursuant to an option exercisable by the lessee.

Amendments

• 1986, Tax Reform Act of 1986 (P.L. 99-514)

P.L. 99-514, §201(d)(2)(A):

Amended Code Sec. 178. **Effective**, generally, for property placed in service after 12-31-86, in tax years ending after such date. For transitional rules, see Act Sec. 204 following Code Sec. 168. Prior to amendment, Code Sec. 178 read as follows:

SEC. 178. DEPRECIATION OR AMORTIZATION OF IMPROVEMENTS MADE BY LESSEE ON LESSOR'S PROPERTY.

[Sec. 178(a)]

(a) GENERAL RULE.—Except as provided in subsection (b), in determining the amount allowable to a lessee as a deduction for any taxable year for exhaustion, wear and tear, obsolescence, or amortization—

(1) in respect of any building erected (or other improvement made) on the leased property, if the portion of the term of the lease (excluding any period for which the lease may subsequently be renewed, extended, or continued pursuant to an option exercisable by the lessee) remaining upon the completion of such building or other improvement is less than 60 percent of the useful life of such building or other improvement, or

(2) in respect of any cost of acquiring the lease, if less than 75 percent of such cost is attributable to the portion of the term of the lease (excluding any period for which the lease may subsequently be renewed, extended, or continued pursuant to an option exercisable by the lessee) remaining on the date of its acquisition,

the term of the lease shall be treated as including any period for which the lease may be renewed, extended, or continued pursuant to an option exercisable by the lessee, unless the lessee establishes that (as of the close of the taxable year) it is more probable that the lease will not be renewed, extended, or continued for such period than that the lease will be so renewed, extended, or continued.

[Sec. 178(b)]

(b) RELATED LESSEE AND LESSOR.—

(1) GENERAL RULE.—If a lessee and lessor are related persons (as determined under paragraph (2)) at any time during the taxable year then, in determining the amount allowable to the lessee as a deduction for such taxable year for exhaustion, wear and tear, obsolescence, or amortization in respect of any building erected (or other improvement made) on the leased property, the lease shall be treated as including a period of not less duration than the remaining useful life of such improvement.

(2) RELATED PERSONS DEFINED.—For purposes of paragraph (1), a lessor and lessee shall be considered to be related persons if—

(A) the lessor and the lessee are members of an affiliated group (as defined in section 1504), or

(B) the relationship between the lessor and lessee is one described in subsection (b) of section 267, except that, for purposes of this subparagraph, the phrase "80 percent or more" shall be substituted for the phrase "more than 50 percent" each place it appears in such subsection and subsection (b)(1)(A) of such section shall not apply.

For purposes of determining the ownership of stock in applying subparagraph (B), the rules of subsection (c) of section 267 shall apply, except that the family of an individual shall include only his spouse, ancestors, and lineal descendants.

Amendments

• 1986, Tax Reform Act of 1986 (P.L. 99-514)

P.L. 99-514, §1812(c)(4)(B):

Amended Code Sec. 178(b)(2)(B) by inserting before the period "and subsection (f)(1)(A) of such section shall not apply". **Effective** as if included in the provision of P.L. 98-369 to which it relates.

[Sec. 178(c)]

(c) REASONABLE CERTAINTY TEST.—In any case in which neither subsection (a) nor subsection (b) applies, the determination as to the amount allowable to a lessee as a deduction for any taxable year for exhaustion, wear and tear, obsolescence, or amortization—

(1) in respect of any building erected (or other improvement made) on the leased property, or

(2) in respect of any cost of acquiring the lease,

shall be made with reference to the term of the lease (excluding any period for which the lease may subsequently be renewed, extended, or continued pursuant to an option exercisable by the lessee), unless the lease has been renewed, extended, or continued or the facts show with reasonable certainty that the lease will be renewed, extended, or continued.

Amendments

• 1958, Technical Amendments Act of 1958 (P.L. 85-866)

P.L. 85-866, §15(a):

Added Code Sec. 178. **Effective** 7-29-58.

P.L. 85-866, §15(c):

Provides that Sec. 178 applies to costs of acquiring a lease incurred, and improvements begun, after 7-28-58 (other than improvements which on 7-28-58, and at all times thereafter, the lessee was under a binding legal obligation to make).

[Sec. 179]

SEC. 179. ELECTION TO EXPENSE CERTAIN DEPRECIABLE BUSINESS ASSETS.

[Sec. 179(a)]

(a) TREATMENT AS EXPENSES.—A taxpayer may elect to treat the cost of any section 179 property as an expense which is not chargeable to capital account. Any cost so treated shall be allowed as a deduction for the taxable year in which the section 179 property is placed in service.

Amendments

• 1981, Economic Recovery Tax Act of 1981 (P.L. 97-34)

P.L. 97-34, §202(a):

Amended Code Sec. 179(a). **Effective** for property placed in service after 12-31-80, in tax years ending after such date. Prior to amendment, Code Sec. 179(a) read as follows:

SEC. 179. ADDITIONAL FIRST-YEAR DEPRECIATION ALLOWANCE FOR SMALL BUSINESS.

(a) GENERAL RULE.—In the case of section 179 property, the term "reasonable allowance" as used in section 167(a) may, at the election of the taxpayer, include an allowance, for the first taxable year for which a deduction is allowable under section 167 to the taxpayer with respect to such property, of 20 percent of the cost of such property.

[Sec. 179(b)]

(b) LIMITATIONS.—

(1) DOLLAR LIMITATION.—The aggregate cost which may be taken into account under subsection (a) for any taxable year shall not exceed—

(A) $250,000 in the case of taxable years beginning after 2007 and before 2010,

(B) $500,000 in the case of taxable years beginning in 2010 or 2011, and

(C) $25,000 in the case of taxable years beginning after 2011.

(2) REDUCTION IN LIMITATION.—The limitation under paragraph (1) for any taxable year shall be reduced (but not below zero) by the amount by which the cost of section 179 property placed in service during such taxable year exceeds—

(A) $800,000 in the case of taxable years beginning after 2007 and before 2010,

(B) $2,000,000 in the case of taxable years beginning in 2010 or 2011, and

(C) $200,000 in the case of taxable years beginning after 2011.

(3) LIMITATION BASED ON INCOME FROM TRADE OR BUSINESS.—

(A) IN GENERAL.—The amount allowed as a deduction under subsection (a) for any taxable year (determined after the application of paragraphs (1) and (2)) shall not exceed the aggregate amount of taxable income of the taxpayer for such taxable year which is derived from the active conduct by the taxpayer of any trade or business during such taxable year.

(B) CARRYOVER OF DISALLOWED DEDUCTION.—The amount allowable as a deduction under subsection (a) for any taxable year shall be increased by the lesser of—

(i) the aggregate amount disallowed under subparagraph (A) for all prior taxable years (to the extent not previously allowed as a deduction by reason of this subparagraph), or

(ii) the excess (if any) of—

(I) the limitation of paragraphs (1) and (2) (or if lesser, the aggregate amount of taxable income referred to in subparagraph (A)), over

(II) the amount allowable as a deduction under subsection (a) for such taxable year without regard to this subparagraph.

(C) COMPUTATION OF TAXABLE INCOME.—For purposes of this paragraph, taxable income derived from the conduct of a trade or business shall be computed without regard to the deduction allowable under this section.

(4) MARRIED INDIVIDUALS FILING SEPARATELY.—In the case of a husband and wife filing separate returns for the taxable year—

(A) such individuals shall be treated as 1 taxpayer for purposes of paragraphs (1) and (2), and

(B) unless such individuals elect otherwise, 50 percent of the cost which may be taken into account under subsection (a) for such taxable year (before application of paragraph (3)) shall be allocated to each such individual.

(5) LIMITATION ON COST TAKEN INTO ACCOUNT FOR CERTAIN PASSENGER VEHICLES.—

(A) IN GENERAL.—The cost of any sport utility vehicle for any taxable year which may be taken into account under this section shall not exceed $25,000.

(B) SPORT UTILITY VEHICLE.—For purposes of subparagraph (A)—

(i) IN GENERAL.—The term "sport utility vehicle" means any 4-wheeled vehicle—

(I) which is primarily designed or which can be used to carry passengers over public streets, roads, or highways (except any vehicle operated exclusively on a rail or rails),

(II) which is not subject to section 280F, and

(III) which is rated at not more than 14,000 pounds gross vehicle weight.

(ii) CERTAIN VEHICLES EXCLUDED.—Such term does not include any vehicle which—

(I) is designed to have a seating capacity of more than 9 persons behind the driver's seat,

(II) is equipped with a cargo area of at least 6 feet in interior length which is an open area or is designed for use as an open area but is enclosed by a cap and is not readily accessible directly from the passenger compartment, or

(III) has an integral enclosure, fully enclosing the driver compartment and load carrying device, does not have seating rearward of the driver's seat, and has no body section protruding more than 30 inches ahead of the leading edge of the windshield.

Amendments

• 2010, Creating Small Business Jobs Act of 2010 (P.L. 111-240)

P.L. 111-240, §2021(a)(1)-(2):

Amended Code Sec. 179(b) by striking "shall not exceed" and all that follows in paragraph (1) and inserting "shall not exceed—" and new subparagraphs (A)-(C), and by striking "exceeds" and all that follows in paragraph (2) and inserting "exceeds—" and new subparagraphs (A)-(C). **Effective** for property placed in service after 12-31-2009, in tax years beginning after such date. Prior to amendment, Code Sec. 179(b)(1)-(2) read as follows:

(1) DOLLAR LIMITATION.—The aggregate cost which may be taken into account under subsection (a) for any taxable year shall not exceed $25,000 ($250,000 in the case of taxable years beginning after 2007 and before 2011).

(2) REDUCTION IN LIMITATION.—The limitation under paragraph (1) for any taxable year shall be reduced (but not below zero) by the amount by which the cost of section 179 property placed in service during such taxable year exceeds $200,000 ($800,000 in the case of taxable years beginning after 2007 and before 2011).

• 2010, Hiring Incentives to Restore Employment Act (P.L. 111-147)

P.L. 111-147, §201(a)(1)-(4):

Amended Code Sec. 179(b) by striking "($125,000 in the case of taxable years beginning after 2006 and before 2011)" in paragraph (1) and inserting "($250,000 in the case of taxable years beginning after 2007 and before 2011)", by striking "($500,000 in the case of taxable years beginning after 2006 and before 2011)" in paragraph (2) and inserting "($800,000 in the case of taxable years beginning after 2007 and before 2011)", by striking paragraphs (5) and (7), and by redesignating paragraph (6) as paragraph (5). **Effective** for tax years beginning after 12-31-2009. Prior to being stricken, Code Sec. 179(b)(5) and (7) read as follows:

(5) INFLATION ADJUSTMENTS.—

(A) IN GENERAL.—In the case of any taxable year beginning in a calendar year after 2007 and before 2011, the $125,000 and $500,000 amounts in paragraphs (1) and (2) shall each be increased by an amount equal to—

(i) such dollar amount, multiplied by

(ii) the cost-of-living adjustment determined under section 1(f)(3) for the calendar year in which the taxable year begins, by substituting "calendar year 2006" for "calendar year 1992" in subparagraph (B) thereof.

(B) ROUNDING.—

(i) DOLLAR LIMITATION.—If the amount in paragraph (1) as increased under subparagraph (A) is not a multiple of $1,000, such amount shall be rounded to the nearest multiple of $1,000.

(ii) PHASEOUT AMOUNT.—If the amount in paragraph (2) as increased under subparagraph (A) is not a multiple of $10,000, such amount shall be rounded to the nearest multiple of $10,000.

* * *

(7) INCREASE IN LIMITATIONS FOR 2008, AND [sic] 2009.—In the case of any taxable year beginning in 2008, or [sic] 2009—

(A) the dollar limitation under paragraph (1) shall be $250,000,

(B) the dollar limitation under paragraph (2) shall be $800,000, and

(C) the amounts described in subparagraphs (A) and (B) shall not be adjusted under paragraph (5).

• 2009, American Recovery and Reinvestment Tax Act of 2009 (P.L. 111-5)

P.L. 111-5, §1202(a)(1)-(2):

Amended Code Sec. 179(b)(7) by striking "2008" and inserting "2008, or [sic] 2009", and by striking "2008" in the heading thereof and inserting "2008, AND [SIC] 2009". **Effective** for tax years beginning after 12-31-2008.

• 2008, Economic Stimulus Act of 2008 (P.L. 110-185)

P.L. 110-185, §102(a):

Amended Code Sec. 179(b) by adding at the end a new paragraph (7). **Effective** for tax years beginning after 12-31-2007.

• 2007, Small Business and Work Opportunity Tax Act of 2007 (P.L. 110-28)

P.L. 110-28, §8212(a):

Amended Code Sec. 179(b)(1), (2), and (5) by striking "2010" and inserting "2011". **Effective** for tax years beginning after 12-31-2006.

P.L. 110-28, §8212(b)(1)-(2):

Amended Code Sec. 179(b) by striking "$100,000 in the case of taxable years beginning after 2002" in paragraph (1) and inserting "$125,000 in the case of taxable years beginning after 2006", and by striking "$400,000 in the case of taxable years beginning after 2002" in paragraph (2) and inserting "$500,000 in the case of taxable years beginning after 2006". **Effective** for tax years beginning after 12-31-2006.

P.L. 110-28, §8212(c)(1)-(3):

Amended Code Sec. 179(b)(5)(A) by striking "2003" and inserting "2007", by striking "$100,000 and $400,000" and inserting "$125,000 and $500,000", and by striking "2002" in clause (ii) and inserting "2006". **Effective** for tax years beginning after 12-31-2006.

• 2006, Tax Increase Prevention and Reconciliation Act of 2005 (P.L. 109-222)

P.L. 109-222, §101:

Amended Code Sec. 179(b)(1), (b)(2) and (b)(5) by striking "2008" and inserting "2010". **Effective** 5-17-2006.

• 2004, American Jobs Creation Act of 2004 (P.L. 108-357)

P.L. 108-357, §201:

Amended Code Sec. 179(b) by striking "2006" each place it appears and inserting "2008". **Effective** 10-22-2004.

P.L. 108-357, §910(a):

Amended Code Sec. 179(b) by adding at the end a new paragraph (6). **Effective** for property placed in service after 10-22-2004.

• 2003, Jobs and Growth Tax Relief Reconciliation Act of 2003 (P.L. 108-27)

P.L. 108-27, §202(a):

Amended Code Sec. 179(b)(1). **Effective** for tax years beginning after 12-31-2002. Prior to amendment, Code Sec. 179(b)(1) read as follows:

(1) DOLLAR LIMITATION.—The aggregate cost which may be taken into account under subsection (a) for any taxable year shall not exceed the following applicable amount:

If the taxable year begins in:	*The applicable amount is:*
1997	18,000
1998	18,500
1999	19,000
2000	20,000
2001 or 2002	24,000
2003 or thereafter	25,000

P.L. 108-27, §202(b):

Amended Code Sec. 179(b)(2) by inserting "($400,000 in the case of taxable years beginning after 2002 and before 2006)" after "$200,000". **Effective** for tax years beginning after 12-31-2002.

P.L. 108-27, §202(d):

Amended Code Sec. 179(b) by adding at the end a new paragraph (5). **Effective** for tax years beginning after 12-31-2002.

• 1996, Small Business Job Protection Act of 1996 (P.L. 104-188)

P.L. 104-188, §1111(a):

Amended Code Sec. 179(b)(1). **Effective** for tax years beginning after 12-31-96. Prior to amendment, Code Sec. 179(b)(1) read as follows:

(1) DOLLAR LIMITATION.—The aggregate cost which may be taken into account under subsection (a) for any taxable year shall not exceed $17,500.

• 1993, Omnibus Budget Reconciliation Act of 1993 (P.L. 103-66)

P.L. 103-66, §13116(a):

Amended Code Sec. 179(b)(1) by striking "$10,000" and inserting "$17,500". **Effective** for tax years beginning after 12-31-92.

• 1988, Technical and Miscellaneous Revenue Act of 1988 (P.L. 100-647)

P.L. 100-647, §1002(b)(1):

Amended Code Sec. 179(b)(3). **Effective** as if included in the provision of P.L. 99-514 to which it relates. Prior to amendment, Code Sec. 179(b)(3) read as follows:

(3) LIMITATION BASED ON INCOME FROM TRADE OR BUSINESS.—

(A) IN GENERAL.—The aggregate cost of section 179 property taken into account under subsection (a) for any taxable year shall not exceed the aggregate amount of taxable income of the taxpayer for such taxable year which is derived from the active conduct by the taxpayer of any trade or business during such taxable year.

(B) CARRYOVER OF UNUSED COST.—The amount of any cost which (but for subparagraph (A)) would have been allowed as a deduction under subsection (a) for any taxable year shall be carried to the succeeding taxable year and added to the amount allowable as a deduction under subsection (a) for such succeeding taxable year.

(C) COMPUTATION OF TAXABLE INCOME.—For purposes of this paragraph, taxable income derived from the conduct of a trade or business shall be computed without regard to the cost of any section 179 property.

• 1986, Tax Reform Act of 1986 (P.L. 99-514)

P.L. 99-514, §202(a):

Amended Code Sec. 179(b). **Effective** for property placed in service after 12-31-86, in tax years ending after such date. Prior to amendment, Code Sec. 179(b) read as follows:

(b) DOLLAR LIMITATION.—

(1) IN GENERAL.—The aggregate cost which may be taken into account under subsection (a) for any taxable year shall not exceed the following applicable amount:

If the taxable year begins in:	*The applicable amount is:*
1983, 1984, 1985, 1986, or 1987	$5,000
1988 or 1989	7,500
1990 or thereafter	10,000

(2) MARRIED INDIVIDUALS FILING SEPARATELY.—In the case of a husband and wife filing separate returns for a taxable year, the applicable amount under paragraph (1) shall be equal to 50 percent of the amount otherwise determined under paragraph (1).

• 1984, Deficit Reduction Act of 1984 (P.L. 98-369)

P.L. 98-369, §13:

Amended Code Sec. 179(b)(1) by striking out the table contained therein and inserting in lieu thereof the new table. **Effective** for tax years ending after 12-31-83. Prior to the amendment, the table read as follows:

If the taxable year begins in:	*The applicable amount is:*
1981	$0
1982	5,000
1983	5,000
1984	7,500
1985	7,500
1986 or thereafter	10,000

• 1981, Economic Recovery Tax Act of 1981 (P.L. 97-34)

P.L. 97-34, §202(a):

Amended Code Sec. 179(b). **Effective** for property placed in service after 12-31-80, in tax years ending after such date. Prior to amendment, Code Sec. 179(b) read as follows:

(b) DOLLAR LIMITATION.—If in any one taxable year the cost of section 179 property with respect to which the taxpayer may elect an allowance under subsection (a) for such taxable year exceeds $10,000, then subsection (a) shall apply with respect to those items selected by the taxpayer, but only to the extent of an aggregate cost of $10,000. In the case of a husband and wife who file a joint return under section 6013 for the taxable year, the limitation under the preceding sentence shall be $20,000 in lieu of $10,000.

[Sec. 179(c)]

(c) ELECTION.—

(1) IN GENERAL.—An election under this section for any taxable year shall—

(A) specify the items of section 179 property to which the election applies and the portion of the cost of each of such items which is to be taken into account under subsection (a), and

(B) be made on the taxpayer's return of the tax imposed by this chapter for the taxable year.

Such election shall be made in such manner as the Secretary may by regulations prescribe.

»»→ Caution: Code Sec. 179(c)(2), below, prior to amendment by P.L. 111-240, applies to tax years beginning on or before December 31, 2010.

(2) ELECTION IRREVOCABLE.—Any election made under this section, and any specification contained in any such election, may not be revoked except with the consent of the Secretary. Any such election or specification with respect to any taxable year beginning after 2002 and before 2011 may be revoked by the taxpayer with respect to any property, and such revocation, once made, shall be irrevocable.

»»→ Caution: Code Sec. 179(c)(2), below, as amended by P.L. 111-240, applies to tax years beginning after December 31, 2010.

(2) ELECTION IRREVOCABLE.—Any election made under this section, and any specification contained in any such election, may not be revoked except with the consent of the Secretary. Any such election or specification with respect to any taxable year beginning after 2002 and before 2012 may be revoked by the taxpayer with respect to any property, and such revocation, once made, shall be irrevocable.

Amendments

• 2010, Creating Small Business Jobs Act of 2010 (P.L. 111-240)

P.L. 111-240, §2021(c):

Amended Code Sec. 179(c)(2) by striking "2011" and inserting "2012". **Effective** for tax years beginning after 12-31-2010.

• 2007, Small Business and Work Opportunity Tax Act of 2007 (P.L. 110-28)

P.L. 110-28, §8212(a):

Amended Code Sec. 179(c)(2) by striking "2010" and inserting "2011". **Effective** for tax years beginning after 12-31-2006.

• 2006, Tax Increase Prevention and Reconciliation Act of 2005 (P.L. 109-222)

P.L. 109-222, §101:

Amended Code Sec. 179(c)(2) by striking "2008" and inserting "2010". **Effective** 5-17-2006.

• 2004, American Jobs Creation Act of 2004 (P.L. 108-357)

P.L. 108-357, §201:

Amended Code Sec. 179(c) by striking "2006" and inserting "2008". **Effective** 10-22-2004.

• 2003, Jobs and Growth Tax Relief Reconciliation Act of 2003 (P.L. 108-27)

P.L. 108-27, §202(e):

Amended Code Sec. 179(c)(2) by adding at the end a new sentence. **Effective** for tax years beginning after 12-31-2002.

• 1981, Economic Recovery Tax Act of 1981 (P.L. 97-34)

P.L. 97-34, §202(a):

Amended Code Sec. 179(c). **Effective** for property placed in service after 12-31-80, in tax years ending after such date. Prior to amendment, Code Sec. 179(c) read as follows:

(c) ELECTION.—

(1) IN GENERAL.—The election under this section for any taxable year shall be made within the time prescribed by law (including extensions thereof) for filing the return for such taxable year. The election shall be made in such manner as the Secretary may by regulations prescribe.

(2) ELECTION IRREVOCABLE.—Any election made under this section may not be revoked except with the consent of the Secretary.

• 1976, Tax Reform Act of 1976 (P.L. 94-455)

P.L. 94-455, §1906(b)(13)(A):

Amended 1954 Code by substituting "Secretary" for "Secretary or his delegate" each place it appeared. **Effective** 2-1-77.

[Sec. 179(d)]

(d) DEFINITIONS AND SPECIAL RULES.—

(1) SECTION 179 PROPERTY.—For purposes of this section, the term "section 179 property" means property—

(A) which is—

(i) tangible property (to which section 168 applies), or

➾ *Caution: Code Sec. 179(d)(1)(A)(ii), below, prior to amendment by P.L. 111-240, applies to tax years beginning on or before December 31, 2010.*

(ii) computer software (as defined in section 197(e)(3)(B)) which is described in section 197(e)(3)(A)(i), to which section 167 applies, and which is placed in service in a taxable year beginning after 2002 and before 2011,

➾ *Caution: Code Sec. 179(d)(1)(A)(ii), below, as amended by P.L. 111-240, applies to tax years beginning after December 31, 2010.*

(ii) computer software (as defined in section 197(e)(3)(B)) which is described in section 197(e)(3)(A)(i), to which section 167 applies, and which is placed in service in a taxable year beginning after 2002 and before 2012,

(B) which is section 1245 property (as defined in section 1245(a)(3)), and

(C) which is acquired by purchase for use in the active conduct of a trade or business.

Such term shall not include any property described in section 50(b) and shall not include air conditioning or heating units.

(2) PURCHASE DEFINED.—For purposes of paragraph (1), the term "purchase" means any acquisition of property, but only if—

(A) the property is not acquired from a person whose relationship to the person acquiring it would result in the disallowance of losses under section 267 or 707(b) (but, in applying section 267(b) and (c) for purposes of this section, paragraph (4) of section 267(c) shall be treated as providing that the family of an individual shall include only his spouse, ancestors, and lineal descendants),

(B) the property is not acquired by one component member of a controlled group from another component member of the same controlled group, and

(C) the basis of the property in the hands of the person acquiring it is not determined—

(i) in whole or in part by reference to the adjusted basis of such property in the hands of the person from whom acquired, or

(ii) under section 1014(a) (relating to property acquired from a decedent).

(3) COST.—For purposes of this section, the cost of property does not include so much of the basis of such property as is determined by reference to the basis of other property held at any time by the person acquiring such property.

(4) SECTION NOT TO APPLY TO ESTATES AND TRUSTS.—This section shall not apply to estates and trusts.

(5) SECTION NOT TO APPLY TO CERTAIN NONCORPORATE LESSORS.—This section shall not apply to any section 179 property which is purchased by a person who is not a corporation and with respect to which such person is the lessor unless—

(A) the property subject to the lease has been manufactured or produced by the lessor, or

(B) the term of the lease (taking into account options to renew) is less than 50 percent of the class life of the property (as defined in section 168(i)(1)), and for the period consisting of the first 12 months after the date on which the property is transferred to the lessee the sum of the deductions with respect to such property which are allowable to the lessor solely by reason of section 162 (other than rents and reimbursed amounts with respect to such property) exceeds 15 percent of the rental income produced by such property.

(6) DOLLAR LIMITATION OF CONTROLLED GROUP.—For purposes of subsection (b) of this section—

(A) all component members of a controlled group shall be treated as one taxpayer, and

(B) the Secretary shall apportion the dollar limitation contained in subsection (b)(1) among the component members of such controlled group in such manner as he shall by regulations prescribe.

(7) CONTROLLED GROUP DEFINED.—For purposes of paragraphs (2) and (6), the term "controlled group" has the meaning assigned to it by section 1563(a), except that, for such purposes, the phrase "more than 50 percent" shall be substituted for the phrase "at least 80 percent" each place it appears in section 1563(a)(1).

(8) TREATMENT OF PARTNERSHIPS AND S CORPORATIONS.—In the case of a partnership, the limitations of subsection (b) shall apply with respect to the partnership and with respect to each partner. A similar rule shall apply in the case of an S corporation and its shareholders.

(9) COORDINATION WITH SECTION 38.—No credit shall be allowed under section 38 with respect to any amount for which a deduction is allowed under subsection (a).

(10) RECAPTURE IN CERTAIN CASES.—The Secretary shall, by regulations, provide for recapturing the benefit under any deduction allowable under subsection (a) with respect to any property which is not used predominantly in a trade or business at any time.

Amendments

• 2010, Creating Small Business Jobs Act of 2010 (P.L. 111-240)

P.L. 111-240, §2021(d):

Amended Code Sec. 179(d)(1)(A)(ii) by striking "2011" and inserting "2012". **Effective** for tax years beginning after 12-31-2010.

• 2007, Small Business and Work Opportunity Tax Act of 2007 (P.L. 110-28)

P.L. 110-28, §8212(a):

Amended Code Sec. 179(d)(1)(A)(ii) by striking "2010" and inserting "2011". **Effective** for tax years beginning after 12-31-2006.

• 2006, Tax Increase Prevention and Reconciliation Act of 2005 (P.L. 109-222)

P.L. 109-222, §101:

Amended Code Sec. 179(d)(1)(A)(ii) by striking "2008" and inserting "2010". **Effective** 5-17-2006.

• 2004, American Jobs Creation Act of 2004 (P.L. 108-357)

P.L. 108-357, §201:

Amended Code Sec. 179(d) by striking "2006" and inserting "2008". **Effective** 10-22-2004.

• 2003, Jobs and Growth Tax Relief Reconciliation Act of 2003 (P.L. 108-27)

P.L. 108-27, §202(c):

Amended Code Sec. 179(d)(1). **Effective** for tax years beginning after 12-31-2002. Prior to amendment, Code Sec. 179(d)(1) read as follows:

(1) SECTION 179 PROPERTY.—For purposes of this section, the term "section 179 property" means any tangible property (to which section 168 applies) which is section 1245 property (as defined in section 1245(a)(3) and which is acquired by purchase for use in the active conduct of a trade or business. Such term shall not include any property described in section 50(b) and shall not include air conditioning or heating units.

• 1996, Small Business Job Protection Act of 1996 (P.L. 104-188)

P.L. 104-188, §1702(h)(10):

Amended Code Sec. 179(d)(1) by striking "in a trade or business" and inserting "a trade or business". **Effective** as if included in the provision of P.L. 101-508 to which it relates.

P.L. 104-188, §1702(h)(19):

Amended Code Sec. 179(d)(1) by adding at the end a new sentence. **Effective** as if included in the provision of P.L. 101-508 to which it relates.

• 1990, Omnibus Budget Reconciliation Act of 1990 (P.L. 101-508)

P.L. 101-508, §11813(b)(11)(A):

Amended Code Sec. 179(d)(1) by striking "section 38 property" and inserting "section 1245 property (as defined in section 1245(a)(3))". **Effective**, generally, for property placed in service after 12-31-90. However, for exceptions see Act Sec. 11813(c)(2) below.

P.L. 101-508, §11813(b)(11)(B):

Amended Code Sec. 179(d)(5). **Effective**, generally, for property placed in service after 12-31-90. However, for exceptions see Act Sec. 11813(c)(2) below. Prior to amendment, Code Sec. 179(d)(5) read as follows:

(5) SECTION NOT TO APPLY TO CERTAIN NONCORPORATE LESSORS.—This section shall not apply to any section 179 property purchased by any person described in section 46(e)(3) unless the credit under section 38 is allowable with respect to such person for such property (determined without regard to this section).

P.L. 101-508, §11813(c)(2), provides:

(2) EXCEPTIONS.—The amendments made by this section shall not apply to—

(A) any transition property (as defined in section 49(e) of the Internal Revenue Code of 1986 (as in effect on the day before the date of the enactment of this Act),

(B) any property with respect to which qualified progress expenditures were previously taken into account under section 46(d) of such Code (as so in effect), and

(C) any property described in section 46(b)(2)(C) of such Code (as so in effect).

• 1988, Technical and Miscellaneous Revenue Act of 1988 (P.L. 100-647)

P.L. 100-647, §1002(a)(19):

Amended Code Sec. 179(d)(1) by striking out "recovery property" and inserting in lieu thereof "tangible property (to which section 168 applies)". **Effective** as if included in the provision of P.L. 99-514 to which it relates.

• 1986, Tax Reform Act of 1986 (P.L. 99-514)

P.L. 99-514, §201(d)(3):

Amended Code Sec. 179(d)(8). **Effective**, generally, for property placed in service after 12-31-86, in tax years ending after such date. For transitional rules, see Act Sec. 204 and 251(d)(2)-(6) following Code Sec. 168. Prior to amendment, Code Sec. 179(d)(8) read as follows:

(8) DOLLAR LIMITATION IN CASE OF PARTNERSHIPS AND S CORPORATIONS.—In the case of a partnership, the dollar limitation contained in subsection (b)(1) shall apply with respect to the partnership and with respect to each partner. A similar rule shall apply in the case of an S corporation and its shareholders.

P.L. 99-514, §202(b):

Amended Code Sec. 179(d)(1) by inserting "in the active conduct of" after "purchase for use." **Effective** for property placed in service after 12-31-86, in tax years ending after such date [**effective** date amended by P.L. 100-647, §1002(c)(8)].

P.L. 99-514, §202(c):

Amended Code Sec. 179(d)(10) by striking out all that follows "at any time" and inserting in lieu thereof a period. **Effective** for property placed in service after 12-31-86, in tax years ending after such date [**effective** date amended by P.L. 100-647, §1002(c)(8)]. Prior to amendment, Code Sec. 179(d)(10) read as follows:

(10) RECAPTURE IN CERTAIN CASES.—The Secretary shall, by regulations, provide for recapturing the benefit under any deduction allowable under subsection (a) with respect to any property which is not used predominantly in a trade or business at any time before the close of the second taxable year following the taxable year in which it is placed in service by the taxpayer.

• 1983, Technical Corrections Act of 1982 (P.L. 97-448)

P.L. 97-448, §102(aa):

Added Code Sec. 179(d)(10). **Effective** as if it had been included in the provision of P.L. 97-34 to which it relates.

• 1982, Subchapter S Revision Act of 1982 (P.L. 97-354)

P.L. 97-354, §3(f):

Amended Code Sec. 179(d)(8) by adding at the end thereof "A similar rule shall apply in the case of an S corporation and its shareholders.", and by striking out "PARTNERSHIPS" in the paragraph heading and inserting in lieu thereof "PARTNERSHIPS AND S CORPORATIONS". **E ffective** for tax years beginning after 12-31-82.

• 1981, Economic Recovery Tax Act of 1981 (P.L. 97-34)

P.L. 97-34, §202(a):

Amended Code Sec. 179(d). **Effective** for property placed in service after 12-31-80, in tax years ending after such date. Prior to amendment, Code Sec. 179(d) and (e) read as follows:

(d) DEFINITIONS AND SPECIAL RULES.—

(1) SECTION 179 PROPERTY.—For purposes of this section, the term "section 179 property" means tangible personal property—

(A) of a character subject to the allowance for depreciation under section 167,

(B) acquired by purchase after December 31, 1957, for use in a trade or business or for holding for production of income, and

(C) with a useful life (determined at the time of such acquisition) of 6 years or more.

(2) PURCHASE DEFINED.—For purposes of paragraph (1), the term "purchase" means any acquisition of property, but only if—

(A) the property is not acquired from a person whose relationship to the person acquiring it would result in the disallowance of losses under section 267 or 707(b) (but, in applying section 267(b) and (c) for purposes of this section, paragraph (4) of section 267(c) shall be treated as providing that the family of an individual shall include only his spouse, ancestors, and lineal descendants),

(B) the property is not acquired by one component member of a controlled group from another component member of the same controlled group, and

(C) the basis of the property in the hands of the person acquiring it is not determined—

(i) in whole or in part by reference to the adjusted basis of such property in the hands of the person from whom acquired, or

(ii) under section 1014(a) (relating to property acquired from a decedent).

(3) COST.—For purposes of this section, the cost of property does not include so much of the basis of such property as is determined by reference to the basis of other property held at any time by the person acquiring such property.

(4) SECTION NOT TO APPLY TO TRUSTS.—This section shall not apply to trusts.

(5) ESTATES.—In the case of an estate, any amount apportioned to an heir, legatee, or devisee under section 167(h) shall not be taken into account in applying subsection (b) of this section to section 179 property of such heir, legatee, or devisee not held by such estate.

(6) DOLLAR LIMITATION OF CONTROLLED GROUP.—For purposes of subsection (b) of this section—

(A) all component members of a controlled group shall be treated as one taxpayer, and

(B) the Secretary shall apportion the dollar limitation contained in such subsection (b) among the component members of such controlled group in such manner as he shall by regulations prescribe.

(7) CONTROLLED GROUP DEFINED.—For purposes of paragraphs (2) and (6), the term "controlled group" has the meaning assigned to it by section 1563(a); except that, for such purposes, the phrase "more than 50 percent" shall be substituted for the phrase "at least 80 percent" each place it appears in section 1563(a)(1).

(8) DOLLAR LIMITATION IN CASE OF PARTNERSHIPS.—In the case of a partnership, the dollar limitation contained in the first sentence of subsection (b) shall apply with respect to the partnership and with respect to each partner.

(9) ADJUSTMENT TO BASIS; WHEN MADE.—In applying section 167(g), the adjustment under section 1016(a)(2) resulting by reason of an election made under this section with respect to any section 179 property shall be made before any other deduction allowed by section 167(a) is computed.

(e) REGULATIONS.—The Secretary shall prescribe such regulations as may be necessary to carry out the purposes of this section.

• 1976, Tax Reform Act of 1976 (P.L. 94-455)

P.L. 94-455, §213(a):

Redesignated paragraph (8) to be paragraph (9) and added a new paragraph (8). **Effective** for partnership tax years beginning after 12-31-75.

P.L. 94-455, §1906(b)(13)(A):

Amended 1954 Code by substituting "Secretary" for "Secretary or his delegate" each place it appeared. **Effective** 2-1-77.

• 1969, Tax Reform Act of 1969 (P.L. 91-172)

P.L. 91-172, §401(f):

Amended subparagraph (d)(2)(B) and paragraphs (d)(6) and (7). **Effective** for tax years ending on or after 12-31-70. Prior to amendment, Sec. 179(d)(2)(B) and (d)(6) and (7) read as follows:

(2) Purchase defined.—For purposes of paragraph (1), the term "purchase" means any acquisition of property, but only if—

* * *

(B) the property is not acquired by one member of an affiliated group from another member of the same affiliated group, and

* * *

(6) Dollar limitation of affiliated group.—For purposes of subsection (b) of this section—

(A) all members of an affiliated group shall be treated as one taxpayer, and

(B) the Secretary or his delegate shall apportion the dollar limitation contained in such subsection (b) among the members of such affiliated group in such manner as he shall by regulations prescribe.

(7) Affiliated group defined.—For purposes of paragraphs (2) and (6), the term "affiliated group" has the meaning assigned to it by section 1504, except that, for such purposes, the phrase "more than 50 percent" shall be substituted for the phrase "at least 80 percent" each place it appears in section 1504(a).

• 1962, Revenue Act of 1962 (P.L. 87-834)

P.L. 87-834, §13(c)(2):

Amended Code Sec. 179(d)(5) by substituting "section 167(h)" for "section 167(g)" in line 2, and amended Code Sec. 179(d)(8) by substituting "section 167(g)" for "section 167(f)" in line 1. **Effective** for tax years beginning after 12-31-61 and ending after 10-16-62.

• 1958, Technical Amendments Act of 1958 (P.L. 85-866)

P.L. 85-866, §204(a):

Added Sec. 179. **Effective** for tax years ending after 6-30-58.

[Sec. 179(e)]

(e) SPECIAL RULES FOR QUALIFIED DISASTER ASSISTANCE PROPERTY.—

(1) IN GENERAL .—For purposes of this section—

(A) the dollar amount in effect under subsection (b)(1) for the taxable year shall be increased by the lesser of—

(i) $100,000, or

(ii) the cost of qualified section 179 disaster assistance property placed in service during the taxable year, and

(B) the dollar amount in effect under subsection (b)(2) for the taxable year shall be increased by the lesser of—

(i) $600,000, or

(ii) the cost of qualified section 179 disaster assistance property placed in service during the taxable year.

(2) QUALIFIED SECTION 179 DISASTER ASSISTANCE PROPERTY .—For purposes of this subsection, the term "qualified section 179 disaster assistance property" means section 179 property (as defined in subsection (d)) which is qualified disaster assistance property (as defined in section 168(n)(2)).

(3) COORDINATION WITH EMPOWERMENT ZONES AND RENEWAL COMMUNITIES .—For purposes of sections 1397A and 1400J, qualified section 179 disaster assistance property shall not be treated as qualified zone property or qualified renewal property, unless the taxpayer elects not to take such qualified section 179 disaster assistance property into account for purposes of this subsection.

(4) RECAPTURE .—For purposes of this subsection, rules similar to the rules under subsection (d)(10) shall apply with respect to any qualified section 179 disaster assistance property which ceases to be qualified section 179 disaster assistance property.

Amendments

• 2008, Tax Extenders and Alternative Minimum Tax Relief Act of 2008 (P.L. 110-343)

P.L. 110-343, Division C, §711(a):

Amended Code Sec. 179 by adding at the end a new subsection (e). **Effective** for property placed in service after 12-31-2007, with respect [to] disasters declared after such date.

[Sec. 179(f)]

(f) SPECIAL RULES FOR QUALIFIED REAL PROPERTY.—

(1) IN GENERAL.—If a taxpayer elects the application of this subsection for any taxable year beginning in 2010 or 2011, the term "section 179 property" shall include any qualified real property which is—

(A) of a character subject to an allowance for depreciation,

(B) acquired by purchase for use in the active conduct of a trade or business, and

(C) not described in the last sentence of subsection (d)(1).

(2) QUALIFIED REAL PROPERTY.—For purposes of this subsection, the term "qualified real property" means—

(A) qualified leasehold improvement property described in section 168(e)(6),

(B) qualified restaurant property described in section 168(e)(7) (without regard to the dates specified in subparagraph (A)(i) thereof), and

(C) qualified retail improvement property described in section 168(e)(8) (without regard to subparagraph (E) thereof).

(3) LIMITATION.—For purposes of applying the limitation under subsection (b)(1)(B), not more than $250,000 of the aggregate cost which is taken into account under subsection (a) for any taxable year may be attributable to qualified real property.

(4) CARRYOVER LIMITATION.—

(A) IN GENERAL.—Notwithstanding subsection (b)(3)(B), no amount attributable to qualified real property may be carried over to a taxable year beginning after 2011.

(B) TREATMENT OF DISALLOWED AMOUNTS.—Except as provided in subparagraph (C), to the extent that any amount is not allowed to be carried over to a taxable year beginning after 2011 by reason of subparagraph (A), this title shall be applied as if no election under this section had been made with respect to such amount.

(C) AMOUNTS CARRIED OVER FROM 2010.—If subparagraph (B) applies to any amount (or portion of an amount) which is carried over from a taxable year other than the taxpayer's last taxable year beginning in 2011, such amount (or portion of an amount) shall be treated for purposes of this title as attributable to property placed in service on the first day of the taxpayer's last taxable year beginning in 2011.

(D) ALLOCATION OF AMOUNTS.—For purposes of applying this paragraph and subsection (b)(3)(B) to any taxable year, the amount which is disallowed under subsection (b)(3)(A) for such taxable year which is attributed to qualified real property shall be the amount which bears the same ratio to the total amount so disallowed as—

(i) the aggregate amount attributable to qualified real property placed in service during such taxable year, increased by the portion of any amount carried over to such taxable year from a prior taxable year which is attributable to such property, bears to

(ii) the total amount of section 179 property placed in service during such taxable year, increased by the aggregate amount carried over to such taxable year from any prior taxable year.

For purposes of the preceding sentence, only section 179 property with respect to which an election was made under subsection (c)(1) (determined without regard to subparagraph (B) of this paragraph) shall be taken into account.

Amendments

• 2010, Creating Small Business Jobs Act of 2010 (P.L. 111-240)

P.L. 111-240, §2021(b):

Amended Code Sec. 179 by adding at the end a new subsection (f). **Effective** for property placed in service after 12-31-2009, in tax years beginning after such date.

[Sec. 179A]

SEC. 179A. DEDUCTION FOR CLEAN-FUEL VEHICLES AND CERTAIN REFUELING PROPERTY.

[Sec. 179A(a)]

(a) ALLOWANCE OF DEDUCTION.—

(1) IN GENERAL.—There shall be allowed as a deduction an amount equal to the cost of—

(A) any qualified clean-fuel vehicle property, and

(B) any qualified clean-fuel vehicle refueling property.

The deduction under the preceding sentence with respect to any property shall be allowed for the taxable year in which such property is placed in service.

(2) INCREMENTAL COST FOR CERTAIN VEHICLES.—If a vehicle may be propelled by both a clean-burning fuel and any other fuel, only the incremental cost of permitting the use of the clean-burning fuel shall be taken into account.

[Sec. 179A(b)]

(b) LIMITATIONS.—

(1) QUALIFIED CLEAN-FUEL VEHICLE PROPERTY.—

(A) IN GENERAL.—The cost which may be taken into account under subsection (a)(1)(A) with respect to any motor vehicle shall not exceed—

(i) in the case of a motor vehicle not described in clause (ii) or (iii), $2,000,

(ii) in the case of any truck or van with a gross vehicle weight rating greater than 10,000 pounds but not greater than 26,000 pounds, $5,000, or

(iii) $50,000 in the case of—

(I) a truck or van with a gross vehicle weight rating greater than 26,000 pounds, or

(II) any bus which has a seating capacity of at least 20 adults (not including the driver).

(B) PHASEOUT.—In the case of any qualified clean-fuel vehicle property placed in service after December 31, 2005, the limit otherwise allowable under subparagraph (A) shall be reduced by 75 percent.

(2) QUALIFIED CLEAN-FUEL VEHICLE REFUELING PROPERTY.—

(A) IN GENERAL.—The aggregate cost which may be taken into account under subsection (a)(1)(B) with respect to qualified clean-fuel vehicle refueling property placed in service during the taxable year at a location shall not exceed the excess (if any) of—

(i) $100,000, over

(ii) the aggregate amount taken into account under subsection (a)(1)(B) by the taxpayer (or any related person or predecessor) with respect to property placed in service at such location for all preceding taxable years.

(B) RELATED PERSON.—For purposes of this paragraph, a person shall be treated as related to another person if such person bears a relationship to such other person described in section 267(b) or 707(b)(1).

(C) ELECTION.—If the limitation under subparagraph (A) applies for any taxable year, the taxpayer shall, on the return of tax for such taxable year, specify the items of property (and the portion of costs of such property) which are to be taken into account under subsection (a)(1)(B).

Amendments

• 2004, Working Families Tax Relief Act of 2004 (P.L. 108-311)

P.L. 108-311, §319(a):

Amended Code Sec. 179A(b)(1)(B). **Effective** for property placed in service after 12-31-2003. Prior to amendment, Code Sec. 179A(b)(1)(B) read as follows:

(B) PHASEOUT.—In the case of any qualified clean-fuel vehicle property placed in service after December 31, 2003, the limit otherwise applicable under subparagraph (A) shall be reduced by—

(i) 25 percent in the case of property placed in service in calendar year 2004,

(ii) 50 percent in the case of property placed in sevice in calendar year 2005, and

(iii) 75 percent in the case of property placed in service in calendar year 2006.

• 2002, Job Creation and Worker Assistance Act of 2002 (P.L. 107-147)

P.L. 107-147, §606(a)(1)(A)-(B):

Amended Code Sec. 179A(b)(1)(B) by striking "December 31, 2001," and inserting "December 31, 2003", and in clauses (i), (ii), and (iii), by striking "2002", "2003", and "2004", respectively, and inserting "2004", "2005", and "2006", respectively. **Effective** for property placed in service after 12-31-2001.

[Sec. 179A(c)]

(c) QUALIFIED CLEAN-FUEL VEHICLE PROPERTY DEFINED.—For purposes of this section—

(1) IN GENERAL.—The term "qualified clean-fuel vehicle property" means property which is acquired for use by the taxpayer and not for resale, the original use of which commences with the taxpayer, with respect to which the environmental standards of paragraph (2) are met, and which is described in either of the following subparagraphs:

(A) RETROFIT PARTS AND COMPONENTS.—Any property installed on a motor vehicle which is propelled by a fuel which is not a clean-burning fuel for purposes of permitting such vehicle to be propelled by a clean-burning fuel—

(i) if the property is an engine (or modification thereof) which may use a clean-burning fuel, or

(ii) to the extent the property is used in the storage or delivery to the engine of such fuel, or the exhaust of gases from combustion of such fuel.

(B) ORIGINAL EQUIPMENT MANUFACTURER'S VEHICLES.—A motor vehicle produced by an original equipment manufacturer and designed so that the vehicle may be propelled by a clean- burning fuel, but only to the extent of the portion of the basis of such vehicle which is attributable to an engine which may use such fuel, to the storage or delivery to the engine of such fuel, or to the exhaust of gases from combustion of such fuel.

(2) ENVIRONMENTAL STANDARDS.—Property shall not be treated as qualified clean-fuel vehicle property unless—

(A) the motor vehicle of which it is a part meets any applicable Federal or State emissions standards with respect to each fuel by which such vehicle is designed to be propelled, or

(B) in the case of property described in paragraph (1)(A), such property meets applicable Federal and State emissions-related certification, testing, and warranty requirements.

(3) EXCEPTION FOR QUALIFIED ELECTRIC VEHICLES.—The term "qualified clean-fuel vehicle property" does not include any qualified electric vehicle (as defined in section 30(c)).

[Sec. 179A(d)]

(d) QUALIFIED CLEAN-FUEL VEHICLE REFUELING PROPERTY DEFINED.—For purposes of this section, the term "qualified clean-fuel vehicle refueling property" means any property (not including a building and its structural components) if—

(1) such property is of a character subject to the allowance for depreciation,

(2) the original use of such property begins with the taxpayer, and

(3) such property is—

(A) for the storage or dispensing of a clean-burning fuel into the fuel tank of a motor vehicle propelled by such fuel, but only if the storage or dispensing of the fuel is at the point where such fuel is delivered into the fuel tank of the motor vehicle, or

(B) for the recharging of motor vehicles propelled by electricity, but only if the property is located at the point where the motor vehicles are recharged.

[Sec. 179A(e)]

(e) OTHER DEFINITIONS AND SPECIAL RULES.—For purposes of this section—

(1) CLEAN-BURNING FUEL.—The term "clean-burning fuel" means—

(A) natural gas,

(B) liquefied natural gas,

(C) liquefied petroleum gas,

(D) hydrogen,

(E) electricity, and

(F) any other fuel at least 85 percent of which is 1 or more of the following: methanol, ethanol, any other alcohol, or ether.

(2) MOTOR VEHICLE.—The term "motor vehicle" means any vehicle which is manufactured primarily for use on public streets, roads, and highways (not including a vehicle operated exclusively on a rail or rails) and which has at least 4 wheels.

(3) COST OF RETROFIT PARTS INCLUDES COST OF INSTALLATION.—The cost of any qualified clean-fuel vehicle property refered to in subsection (c)(1)(A) shall include the cost of the original installation of such property.

(4) RECAPTURE.—The Secretary shall, by regulations, provide for recapturing the benefit of any deduction allowable under subsection (a) with respect to any property which ceases to be property eligible for such deduction.

(5) PROPERTY USED OUTSIDE UNITED STATES, ETC., NOT QUALIFIED.—No deduction shall be allowed under subsection (a) with respect to any property referred to in section 50(b) or with respect to the portion of the cost of any property taken into account under section 179.

(6) BASIS REDUCTION.—

(A) IN GENERAL.—For purposes of this title, the basis of any property shall be reduced by the portion of the cost of such property taken into account under subsection (a).

(B) ORDINARY INCOME RECAPTURE.—For purposes of section 1245, the amount of the deduction allowable under subsection (a) with respect to any property which is of a character subject to the allowance for depreciation shall be treated as a deduction allowed for depreciation under section 167.

[Sec. 179A(f)]

(f) TERMINATION.—This section shall not apply to any property placed in service after December 31, 2005.

Amendments

• 2005, Energy Tax Incentives Act of 2005 (P.L. 109-58)

P.L. 109-58, §1348:

Amended Code Sec. 179A(f) by striking "December 31, 2006" and inserting "December 31, 2005". **Effective** 8-8-2005.

• 2002, Job Creation and Worker Assistance Act of 2002 (P.L. 107-147)

P.L. 107-147, §606(a)(2):

Amended Code Sec. 179A(f) by striking "December 31, 2004" and inserting "December 31, 2006". **Effective** for property placed in service after 12-31-2001.

• 1996, Small Business Job Protection Act of 1996 (P.L. 104-188)

P.L. 104-188, §1704(j)(2):

Amended Code Sec. 179A by redesignating subsection (g) as subsection (f). **Effective** 8-20-96.

• 1992, Energy Policy Act of 1992 (P.L. 102-486)

P.L. 102-486, §1913(a)(1):

Amended part VI of subchapter B of chapter 1 by adding after Code Sec. 179 new Code Sec. 179A. **Effective** for property placed in service after 6-30-93.

[Sec. 179B]

SEC. 179B. DEDUCTION FOR CAPITAL COSTS INCURRED IN COMPLYING WITH ENVIRONMENTAL PROTECTION AGENCY SULFUR REGULATIONS.

[Sec. 179B(a)]

(a) ALLOWANCE OF DEDUCTION.—In the case of a small business refiner (as defined in section 45H(c)(1)) which elects the application of this section, there shall be allowed as a deduction an amount equal to 75 percent of qualified costs (as defined in section 45H(c)(2)) which are paid or incurred by the taxpayer during the taxable year and which are properly chargeable to capital account.

Amendments

• 2007, Tax Technical Corrections Act of 2007 (P.L. 110-172)

P.L. 110-172, §7(a)(3)(A):

Amended Code Sec. 179B(a) by striking "qualified capital costs" and inserting "qualified costs". **Effective** as if included in the provision of the American Jobs Creation Act of 2004 (P.L. 108-357) to which it relates [**effective** for expenses paid or incurred after 12-31-2002, in tax years ending after such date.—CCH].

P.L. 110-172, §7(a)(3)(C):

Amended Code Sec. 179B(a) by inserting "and which are properly chargeable to capital account" before the period at the end. **Effective** as if included in the provision of the American Jobs Creation Act of 2004 (P.L. 108-357) to which it relates [**effective** for expenses paid or incurred after 12-31-2002, in tax years ending after such date.—CCH].

[Sec. 179B(b)]

(b) REDUCED PERCENTAGE.—In the case of a small business refiner with average daily domestic refinery runs for the 1-year period ending on December 31, 2002, in excess of 155,000 barrels, the number of percentage points described in subsection (a) shall be reduced (not below zero) by the product of such number (before the application of this subsection) and the ratio of such excess to 50,000 barrels.

[Sec. 179B(c)]

(c) BASIS REDUCTION.—

(1) IN GENERAL.—For purposes of this title, the basis of any property shall be reduced by the portion of the cost of such property taken into account under subsection (a).

(2) ORDINARY INCOME RECAPTURE.—For purposes of section 1245, the amount of the deduction allowable under subsection (a) with respect to any property which is of a character subject to the allowance for depreciation shall be treated as a deduction allowed for depreciation under section 167.

[Sec. 179B(d)]

(d) COORDINATION WITH OTHER PROVISIONS.—Section 280B shall not apply to amounts which are treated as expenses under this section.

Amendments

• 2004, American Jobs Creation Act of 2004 (P.L. 108-357)

P.L. 108-357, §338(a):

Amended part VI of subchapter B of chapter 1 by inserting after Code Sec. 179A a new Code Sec. 179B. **Effective** for expenses paid or incurred after 12-31-2002 in tax years ending after such date.

[Sec. 179B(e)]

(e) ELECTION TO ALLOCATE DEDUCTION TO COOPERATIVE OWNER.—

(1) IN GENERAL.—If—

(A) a small business refiner to which subsection (a) applies is an organization to which part I of subchapter T applies, and

(B) one or more persons directly holding an ownership interest in the refiner are organizations to which part I of subchapter T apply,

the refiner may elect to allocate all or a portion of the deduction allowable under subsection (a) to such persons. Such allocation shall be equal to the person's ratable share of the total amount allocated, determined on the basis of the person's ownership interest in the taxpayer. The taxable income of the refiner shall not be reduced under section 1382 by reason of any amount to which the preceding sentence applies.

(2) FORM AND EFFECT OF ELECTION.—An election under paragraph (1) for any taxable year shall be made on a timely filed return for such year. Such election, once made, shall be irrevocable for such taxable year.

(3) WRITTEN NOTICE TO OWNERS.—If any portion of the deduction available under subsection (a) is allocated to owners under paragraph (1), the cooperative shall provide any owner receiving an allocation written notice of the amount of the allocation. Such notice shall be provided before the date on which the return described in paragraph (2) is due.

Amendments

• 2005, Energy Tax Incentives Act of 2005 (P.L. 109-58)

P.L. 109-58, §1324:

Amended Code Sec. 179B by adding at the end a new subsection (e). **Effective** as if included in the amendment made by section 338(a) of P.L. 108-357 [**effective** for expenses paid or incurred after 12-31-2002, in tax years ending after such date.—CCH].

[Sec. 179C]

SEC. 179C. ELECTION TO EXPENSE CERTAIN REFINERIES.

[Sec. 179C(a)]

(a) TREATMENT AS EXPENSES.—A taxpayer may elect to treat 50 percent of the cost of any qualified refinery property as an expense which is not chargeable to capital account. Any cost so treated shall be allowed as a deduction for the taxable year in which the qualified refinery property is placed in service.

[Sec. 179C(b)]

(b) ELECTION.—

(1) IN GENERAL.—An election under this section for any taxable year shall be made on the taxpayer's return of the tax imposed by this chapter for the taxable year. Such election shall be made in such manner as the Secretary may by regulations prescribe.

(2) ELECTION IRREVOCABLE.—Any election made under this section may not be revoked except with the consent of the Secretary.

[Sec. 179C(c)]

(c) QUALIFIED REFINERY PROPERTY.—

(1) IN GENERAL.—The term "qualified refinery property" means any portion of a qualified refinery—

(A) the original use of which commences with the taxpayer,

(B) which is placed in service by the taxpayer after the date of the enactment of this section and before January 1, 2014,

(C) in the case any portion of a qualified refinery (other than a qualified refinery which is separate from any existing refinery), which meets the requirements of subsection (e),

(D) which meets all applicable environmental laws in effect on the date such portion was placed in service,

(E) no written binding contract for the construction of which was in effect on or before June 14, 2005, and

(F)(i) the construction of which is subject to a written binding construction contract entered into before January 1, 2010,

(ii) which is placed in service before January 1, 2010, or

(iii) in the case of self-constructed property, the construction of which began after June 14, 2005, and before January 1, 2010.

(2) SPECIAL RULE FOR SALE-LEASEBACKS.—For purposes of paragraph (1)(A), if property is—

(A) originally placed in service after the date of the enactment of this section by a person, and

(B) sold and leased back by such person within 3 months after the date such property was originally placed in service,

such property shall be treated as originally placed in service not earlier than the date on which such property is used under the leaseback referred to in subparagraph (B).

(3) EFFECT OF WAIVER UNDER CLEAN AIR ACT.—A waiver under the Clean Air Act shall not be taken into account in determining whether the requirements of paragraph (1)(D) are met.

Amendments

• 2008, Energy Improvement and Extension Act of 2008 (P.L. 110-343)

P.L. 110-343, Division B, §209(a)(1)-(2):

Amended Code Sec. 179C(c)(1) by striking "January 1, 2012" in subparagraph (B) and inserting "January 1, 2014", and by striking "January 1, 2008" each place it appears in subparagraph (F) and inserting "January 1, 2010". **Effective** for property placed in service after 10-3-2008.

[Sec. 179C(d)]

(d) QUALIFIED REFINERY.—For purposes of this section, the term "qualified refinery" means any refinery located in the United States which is designed to serve the primary purpose of processing liquid fuel from crude oil or qualified fuels (as defined in section 45K(c)), or directly from shale or tar sands.

Amendments

• 2008, Energy Improvement and Extension Act of 2008 (P.L. 110-343)

P.L. 110-343, Division B, §209(b)(1):

Amended Code Sec. 179C(d) by inserting ", or directly from shale or tar sands" after "(as defined in section 45K(c))". **Effective** for property placed in service after 10-3-2008.

[Sec. 179C(e)]

(e) PRODUCTION CAPACITY.—The requirements of this subsection are met if the portion of the qualified refinery—

(1) enables the existing qualified refinery to increase total volume output (determined without regard to asphalt or lube oil) by 5 percent or more on an average daily basis, or

(2) enables the existing qualified refinery to process shale, tar sands, or qualified fuels (as defined in section 45K(c)) at a rate which is equal to or greater than 25 percent of the total throughput of such qualified refinery on an average daily basis.

Amendments

• 2008, Energy Improvement and Extension Act of 2008 (P.L. 110-343)

P.L. 110-343, Division B, §209(b)(2):

Amended Code Sec. 179C(e)(2) by inserting "shale, tar sands, or" before "qualified fuels". **Effective** for property placed in service after 10-3-2008.

[Sec. 179C(f)]

(f) INELIGIBLE REFINERY PROPERTY.—No deduction shall be allowed under subsection (a) for any qualified refinery property—

(1) the primary purpose of which is for use as a topping plant, asphalt plant, lube oil facility, crude or product terminal, or blending facility, or

(2) which is built solely to comply with consent decrees or projects mandated by Federal, State, or local governments.

[Sec. 179C(g)]

(g) ELECTION TO ALLOCATE DEDUCTION TO COOPERATIVE OWNER.—

(1) IN GENERAL.—If—

(A) a taxpayer to which subsection (a) applies is an organization to which part I of subchapter T applies, and

(B) one or more persons directly holding an ownership interest in the taxpayer are organizations to which part I of subchapter T apply,

the taxpayer may elect to allocate all or a portion of the deduction allowable under subsection (a) to such persons. Such allocation shall be equal to the person's ratable share of the total amount allocated, determined on the basis of the person's ownership interest in the taxpayer. The taxable income of the taxpayer shall not be reduced under section 1382 by reason of any amount to which the preceding sentence applies.

(2) FORM AND EFFECT OF ELECTION.—An election under paragraph (1) for any taxable year shall be made on a timely filed return for such year. Such election, once made, shall be irrevocable for such taxable year.

(3) WRITTEN NOTICE TO OWNERS.—If any portion of the deduction available under subsection (a) is allocated to owners under paragraph (1), the cooperative shall provide any owner receiving an allocation written notice of the amount of the allocation. Such notice shall be provided before the date on which the return described in paragraph (2) is due.

[Sec. 179C(h)]

(h) REPORTING.—No deduction shall be allowed under subsection (a) to any taxpayer for any taxable year unless such taxpayer files with the Secretary a report containing such information with respect to the operation of the refineries of the taxpayer as the Secretary shall require.

Amendments

• 2005, Energy Tax Incentives Act of 2005 (P.L. 109-58)

P.L. 109-58, §1323(a):

Amended part VI of subchapter B of chapter 1 by inserting after Code Sec. 179B a new Code Sec. 179C. **Effective** for properties placed in service after 8-8-2005.

[Sec. 179D]

SEC. 179D. ENERGY EFFICIENT COMMERCIAL BUILDINGS DEDUCTION.

[Sec. 179D(a)]

(a) IN GENERAL.—There shall be allowed as a deduction an amount equal to the cost of energy efficient commercial building property placed in service during the taxable year.

[Sec. 179D(b)]

(b) MAXIMUM AMOUNT OF DEDUCTION.—The deduction under subsection (a) with respect to any building for any taxable year shall not exceed the excess (if any) of—

(1) the product of—

(A) $1.80, and

(B) the square footage of the building, over

(2) the aggregate amount of the deductions under subsection (a) with respect to the building for all prior taxable years.

[Sec. 179D(c)]

(c) DEFINITIONS.—For purposes of this section—

(1) ENERGY EFFICIENT COMMERCIAL BUILDING PROPERTY.—The term "energy efficient commercial building property" means property—

(A) with respect to which depreciation (or amortization in lieu of depreciation) is allowable,

(B) which is installed on or in any building which is—

(i) located in the United States, and

(ii) within the scope of Standard 90.1-2001,

(C) which is installed as part of—

(i) the interior lighting systems,

(ii) the heating, cooling, ventilation, and hot water systems, or

(iii) the building envelope, and

(D) which is certified in accordance with subsection (d)(6) as being installed as part of a plan designed to reduce the total annual energy and power costs with respect to the interior lighting systems, heating, cooling, ventilation, and hot water systems of the building by 50 percent or more in comparison to a reference building which meets the minimum requirements of Standard 90.1-2001 using methods of calculation under subsection (d)(2).

(2) STANDARD 90.1-2001.—The term "Standard 90.1-2001" means Standard 90.1-2001 of the American Society of Heating, Refrigerating, and Air Conditioning Engineers and the Illuminating Engineering Society of North America (as in effect on April 2, 2003).

[Sec. 179D(d)]

(d) SPECIAL RULES.—

(1) PARTIAL ALLOWANCE.—

(A) IN GENERAL.—Except as provided in subsection (f), if—

(i) the requirement of subsection (c)(1)(D) is not met, but

(ii) there is a certification in accordance with paragraph (6) that any system referred to in subsection (c)(1)(C) satisfies the energy-savings targets established by the Secretary under subparagraph (B) with respect to such system,

then the requirement of subsection (c)(1)(D) shall be treated as met with respect to such system, and the deduction under subsection (a) shall be allowed with respect to energy efficient commercial building property installed as part of such system and as part of a plan to meet such targets, except that subsection (b) shall be applied to such property by substituting "$.60" for "$1.80".

(B) REGULATIONS.—The Secretary, after consultation with the Secretary of Energy, shall establish a target for each system described in subsection (c)(1)(C) which, if such targets were met for all such systems, the building would meet the requirements of subsection (c)(1)(D).

(2) METHODS OF CALCULATION.—The Secretary, after consultation with the Secretary of Energy, shall promulgate regulations which describe in detail methods for calculating and verifying energy and power consumption and cost, based on the provisions of the 2005 California Nonresidential Alternative Calculation Method Approval Manual.

(3) COMPUTER SOFTWARE.—

(A) IN GENERAL.—Any calculation under paragraph (2) shall be prepared by qualified computer software.

(B) QUALIFIED COMPUTER SOFTWARE.—For purposes of this paragraph, the term "qualified computer software" means software—

(i) for which the software designer has certified that the software meets all procedures and detailed methods for calculating energy and power consumption and costs as required by the Secretary,

(ii) which provides such forms as required to be filed by the Secretary in connection with energy efficiency of property and the deduction allowed under this section, and

(iii) which provides a notice form which documents the energy efficiency features of the building and its projected annual energy costs.

(4) ALLOCATION OF DEDUCTION FOR PUBLIC PROPERTY.—In the case of energy efficient commercial building property installed on or in property owned by a Federal, State, or local government or a political subdivision thereof, the Secretary shall promulgate a regulation to allow the allocation of the deduction to the person primarily responsible for designing the property in lieu of the owner of such property. Such person shall be treated as the taxpayer for purposes of this section.

(5) NOTICE TO OWNER.—Each certification required under this section shall include an explanation to the building owner regarding the energy efficiency features of the building and its projected annual energy costs as provided in the notice under paragraph (3)(B)(iii).

(6) CERTIFICATION.—

(A) IN GENERAL.—The Secretary shall prescribe the manner and method for the making of certifications under this section.

(B) PROCEDURES.—The Secretary shall include as part of the certification process procedures for inspection and testing by qualified individuals described in subparagraph (C) to ensure compliance of buildings with energy-savings plans and targets. Such procedures shall be comparable, given the difference between commercial and residential buildings, to the requirements in the Mortgage Industry National Accreditation Procedures for Home Energy Rating Systems.

(C) QUALIFIED INDIVIDUALS.—Individuals qualified to determine compliance shall be only those individuals who are recognized by an organization certified by the Secretary for such purposes.

[Sec. 179D(e)]

(e) BASIS REDUCTION.—For purposes of this subtitle, if a deduction is allowed under this section with respect to any energy efficient commercial building property, the basis of such property shall be reduced by the amount of the deduction so allowed.

[Sec. 179D(f)]

(f) INTERIM RULES FOR LIGHTING SYSTEMS.—Until such time as the Secretary issues final regulations under subsection (d)(1)(B) with respect to property which is part of a lighting system—

(1) IN GENERAL.—The lighting system target under subsection (d)(1)(A)(ii) shall be a reduction in lighting power density of 25 percent (50 percent in the case of a warehouse) of the minimum requirements in Table 9.3.1.1 or Table 9.3.1.2 (not including additional interior lighting power allowances) of Standard 90.1-2001.

(2) REDUCTION IN DEDUCTION IF REDUCTION LESS THAN 40 PERCENT.—

(A) IN GENERAL.—If, with respect to the lighting system of any building other than a warehouse, the reduction in lighting power density of the lighting system is not at least 40 percent, only the applicable percentage of the amount of deduction otherwise allowable under this section with respect to such property shall be allowed.

(B) APPLICABLE PERCENTAGE.—For purposes of subparagraph (A), the applicable percentage is the number of percentage points (not greater than 100) equal to the sum of—

(i) 50, and

(ii) the amount which bears the same ratio to 50 as the excess of the reduction of lighting power density of the lighting system over 25 percentage points bears to 15.

(C) EXCEPTIONS.—This subsection shall not apply to any system—

(i) the controls and circuiting of which do not comply fully with the mandatory and prescriptive requirements of Standard 90.1-2001 and which do not include provision for bilevel switching in all occupancies except hotel and motel guest rooms, store rooms, restrooms, and public lobbies, or

(ii) which does not meet the minimum requirements for calculated lighting levels as set forth in the Illuminating Engineering Society of North America Lighting Handbook, Performance and Application, Ninth Edition, 2000.

[Sec. 179D(g)]

(g) REGULATIONS.—The Secretary shall promulgate such regulations as necessary—

(1) to take into account new technologies regarding energy efficiency and renewable energy for purposes of determining energy efficiency and savings under this section, and

(2) to provide for a recapture of the deduction allowed under this section if the plan described in subsection (c)(1)(D) or (d)(1)(A) is not fully implemented.

[Sec. 179D(h)]

(h) TERMINATION.—This section shall not apply with respect to property placed in service after December 31, 2013.

Amendments

• 2008, Energy Improvement and Extension Act of 2008 (P.L. 110-343)

P.L. 110-343, Division B, §303:

Amended Code Sec. 179D(h) by striking "December 31, 2008" and inserting "December 31, 2013". **Effective** 10-3-2008.

• 2006, Tax Relief and Health Care Act of 2006 (P.L. 109-432)

P.L. 109-432, Division A, §204:

Amended Code Sec. 179D(h) by striking "December 31, 2007" and inserting "December 31, 2008". **Effective** 12-20-2006.

• 2005, Energy Tax Incentives Act of 2005 (P.L. 109-58)

P.L. 109-58, §1331(a):

Amended part VI of subchapter B of chapter 1, as amended by this Act, by inserting after Code Sec. 179C a new Code Sec. 179D. **Effective** for property placed in service after 12-31-2005.

[Sec. 179E]

SEC. 179E. ELECTION TO EXPENSE ADVANCED MINE SAFETY EQUIPMENT.

[Sec. 179E(a)]

(a) TREATMENT AS EXPENSES.—A taxpayer may elect to treat 50 percent of the cost of any qualified advanced mine safety equipment property as an expense which is not chargeable to capital account. Any cost so treated shall be allowed as a deduction for the taxable year in which the qualified advanced mine safety equipment property is placed in service.

[Sec. 179E(b)]

(b) ELECTION.—

(1) IN GENERAL.—An election under this section for any taxable year shall be made on the taxpayer's return of the tax imposed by this chapter for the taxable year. Such election shall specify the advanced mine safety equipment property to which the election applies and shall be made in such manner as the Secretary may by regulations prescribe.

(2) ELECTION IRREVOCABLE.—Any election made under this section may not be revoked except with the consent of the Secretary.

[Sec. 179E(c)]

(c) QUALIFIED ADVANCED MINE SAFETY EQUIPMENT PROPERTY.—For purposes of this section, the term "qualified advanced mine safety equipment property" means any advanced mine safety equipment property for use in any underground mine located in the United States—

(1) the original use of which commences with the taxpayer, and

(2) which is placed in service by the taxpayer after the date of the enactment of this section.

[Sec. 179E(d)]

(d) ADVANCED MINE SAFETY EQUIPMENT PROPERTY.—For purposes of this section, the term "advanced mine safety equipment property" means any of the following:

(1) Emergency communication technology or device which is used to allow a miner to maintain constant communication with an individual who is not in the mine.

(2) Electronic identification and location device which allows an individual who is not in the mine to track at all times the movements and location of miners working in or at the mine.

(3) Emergency oxygen-generating, self-rescue device which provides oxygen for at least 90 minutes.

(4) Pre-positioned supplies of oxygen which (in combination with self-rescue devices) can be used to provide each miner on a shift, in the event of an accident or other event which traps the miner in the mine or otherwise necessitates the use of such a self-rescue device, the ability to survive for at least 48 hours.

(5) Comprehensive atmospheric monitoring system which monitors the levels of carbon monoxide, methane, and oxygen that are present in all areas of the mine and which can detect smoke in the case of a fire in a mine.

[Sec. 179E(e)]

(e) COORDINATION WITH SECTION 179 .—No expenditures shall be taken into account under subsection (a) with respect to the portion of the cost of any property specified in an election under section 179.

[Sec. 179E(f)]

(f) REPORTING.—No deduction shall be allowed under subsection (a) to any taxpayer for any taxable year unless such taxpayer files with the Secretary a report containing such information with respect to the operation of the mines of the taxpayer as the Secretary shall require.

[Sec. 179E(g)]

(g) TERMINATION.—This section shall not apply to property placed in service after December 31, 2009.

Amendments

• 2008, Tax Extenders and Alternative Minimum Tax Relief Act of 2008 (P.L. 110-343)

P.L. 110-343, Division C, §311:

Amended Code Sec. 179E(g) by striking "December 31, 2008" and inserting "December 31, 2009". **Effective** 10-3-2008.

• 2006, Tax Relief and Health Care Act of 2006 (P.L. 109-432)

P.L. 109-432, Division A, §404(a):

Amended part VI of subchapter B of chapter 1 by inserting after Code Sec. 179D a new Code Sec. 179E. **Effective** for costs paid or incurred after 12-20-2006.

[Sec. 180]

SEC. 180. EXPENDITURES BY FARMERS FOR FERTILIZER, ETC.

[Sec. 180(a)]

(a) IN GENERAL.—A taxpayer engaged in the business of farming may elect to treat as expenses which are not chargeable to capital account expenditures (otherwise chargeable to capital account) which are paid or incurred by him during the taxable year for the purchase or acquisition of fertilizer, lime, ground limestone, marl, or other materials to enrich, neutralize, or condition land used in farming, or for the application of such materials to such land. The expenditures so treated shall be allowed as a deduction.

[Sec. 180(b)]

(b) LAND USED IN FARMING.—For purposes of subsection (a), the term "land used in farming" means land used (before or simultaneously with the expenditures described in subsection (a)) by the taxpayer or his tenant for the production of crops, fruits, or other agricultural products or for the sustenance of livestock.

[Sec. 180(c)]

(c) ELECTION.—The election under subsection (a) for any taxable year shall be made within the time prescribed by law (including extensions thereof) for filing the return for such taxable year. Such election shall be made in such manner as the Secretary may by regulations prescribe. Such election may not be revoked except with the consent of the Secretary.

Amendments

• 1976, Tax Reform Act of 1976 (P.L. 94-455)

P.L. 94-455, §1906(b)(13)(A):

Amended 1954 Code by substituting "Secretary" for "Secretary or his delegate" each place it appeared. **Effective** 2-1-77.

• 1960 (P.L. 86-779)

P.L. 86-779, §6(a):

Added Code Sec. 180. **Effective** for tax years beginning after 1959.

[Sec. 181]

SEC. 181. TREATMENT OF CERTAIN QUALIFIED FILM AND TELEVISION PRODUCTIONS.

[Sec. 181(a)]

(a) ELECTION TO TREAT COSTS AS EXPENSES.—

(1) IN GENERAL.—A taxpayer may elect to treat the cost of any qualified film or television production as an expense which is not chargeable to capital account. Any cost so treated shall be allowed as a deduction.

(2) DOLLAR LIMITATION.—

(A) IN GENERAL.—Paragraph (1) shall not apply to so much of the aggregate cost of any qualified film or television production as exceeds $15,000,000.

(B) HIGHER DOLLAR LIMITATION FOR PRODUCTIONS IN CERTAIN AREAS.—In the case of any qualified film or television production the aggregate cost of which is significantly incurred in an area eligible for designation as—

(i) a low-income community under section 45D, or

(ii) a distressed county or isolated area of distress by the Delta Regional Authority established under section 2009aa-1 of title 7, United States Code,

subparagraph (A) shall be applied by substituting "$20,000,000" for "$15,000,000".

Amendments

• 2008, Tax Extenders and Alternative Minimum Tax Relief Act of 2008 (P.L. 110-343)

P.L. 110-343, Division C, §502(b):

Amended Code Sec. 181(a)(2)(A). **Effective** for qualified film and television productions commencing after 12-31-2007. Prior to amendment, Code Sec. 181(a)(2)(A) read as follows:

(A) IN GENERAL.—Paragraph (1) shall not apply to any qualified film or television production the aggregate cost of which exceeds $15,000,000.

[Sec. 181(b)]

(b) NO OTHER DEDUCTION OR AMORTIZATION DEDUCTION ALLOWABLE.—With respect to the basis of any qualified film or television production to which an election is made under subsection (a), no other depreciation or amortization deduction shall be allowable.

[Sec. 181(c)]

(c) ELECTION.—

(1) IN GENERAL.—An election under this section with respect to any qualified film or television production shall be made in such manner as prescribed by the Secretary and by the due date (including extensions) for filing the taxpayer's return of tax under this chapter for the taxable year in which costs of the production are first incurred.

(2) REVOCATION OF ELECTION.—Any election made under this section may not be revoked without the consent of the Secretary.

[Sec. 181(d)]

(d) QUALIFIED FILM OR TELEVISION PRODUCTION.—For purposes of this section—

(1) IN GENERAL.—The term "qualified film or television production" means any production described in paragraph (2) if 75 percent of the total compensation of the production is qualified compensation.

(2) PRODUCTION.—

(A) IN GENERAL.—A production is described in this paragraph if such production is property described in section 168(f)(3).

(B) SPECIAL RULES FOR TELEVISION SERIES.—In the case of a television series—

(i) each episode of such series shall be treated as a separate production, and

(ii) only the first 44 episodes of such series shall be taken into account.

(C) EXCEPTION.—A production is not described in this paragraph if records are required under section 2257 of title 18, United States Code, to be maintained with respect to any performer in such production.

(3) QUALIFIED COMPENSATION.—For purposes of paragraph (1)—

(A) IN GENERAL.—The term "qualified compensation" means compensation for services performed in the United States by actors, production personnel, directors, and producers.

(B) PARTICIPATIONS AND RESIDUALS EXCLUDED.—The term "compensation" does not include participations and residuals (as defined in section 167(g)(7)(B)).

Amendments

• 2008, Tax Extenders and Alternative Minimum Tax Relief Act of 2008 (P.L. 110-343)

P.L. 110-343, Division C, §502(d):

Amended Code Sec. 181(d)(3)(A) by striking "actors" and all that follows and inserting "actors, production personnel, directors, and producers.". **Effective** for qualified film and television productions commencing after 12-31-2007. Prior to amendment, Code Sec. 181(d)(3)(A) read as follows:

(A) IN GENERAL.—The term "qualified compensation" means compensation for services performed in the United States by actors, directors, producers, and other relevant production personnel.

• 2005, Gulf Opportunity Zone Act of 2005 (P.L. 109-135)

P.L. 109-135, §403(e)(1):

Amended Code Sec. 181(d)(2) by striking the last sentence in subparagraph (A), by redesignating subparagraph (B) as subparagraph (C), and by inserting after subparagraph (A) a new subparagraph (B). **Effective** as if included in the provision of the American Jobs Creation Act of 2004 (P.L. 108-357) to which it relates [**effective** for qualified film and television productions commencing after 10-22-2004.—CCH]. Prior to amendment, the last sentence of Code Sec. 181(d)(2)(A) read as follows:

For purposes of a television series, only the first 44 episodes of such series may be taken into account.

[Sec. 181(e)]

(e) APPLICATION OF CERTAIN OTHER RULES.—For purposes of this section, rules similar to the rules of subsections (b)(2) and (c)(4) of section 194 shall apply.

[Sec. 181(f)]

(f) TERMINATION.—This section shall not apply to qualified film and television productions commencing after December 31, 2009.

Amendments

• 2008, Tax Extenders and Alternative Minimum Tax Relief Act of 2008 (P.L. 110-343)

P.L. 110-343, Division C, §502(a):

Amended Code Sec. 181(f) by striking "December 31, 2008" and inserting "December 31, 2009". **Effective** for qualified film and television productions commencing after 12-31-2007.

• 2004, American Jobs Creation Act of 2004 (P.L. 108-357)

P.L. 108-357, §244(a):

Amended part VI of subchapter B of chapter 1 by inserting after Code Sec. 180 a new Code Sec. 181. **Effective** for qualified film and television productions commencing after 10-22-2004.

[Sec. 182—Repealed]

Amendments

• 1986, Tax Reform Act of 1986 (P.L. 99-514)

P.L. 99-514, §402(a):

Repealed Code Sec. 182. **Effective** for amounts paid or incurred after 12-31-85, in tax years ending after such date. Prior to repeal, Code Sec. 182 read as follows:

SEC. 182. EXPENDITURES BY FARMERS FOR CLEARING LAND.

(a) IN GENERAL.—A taxpayer engaged in the business of farming may elect to treat expenditures which are paid or incurred by him during the taxable year in the clearing of land for the purpose of making such land suitable for use in farming as expenses which are not chargeable to capital account. The expenditures so treated shall be allowed as a deduction.

(b) LIMITATION.—The amount deductible under subsection (a) for any taxable year shall not exceed whichever of the following amounts is the lesser:

(1) $5,000, or

(2) 25 percent of the taxable income derived from farming during the taxable year.

For purposes of paragraph (2), the term "taxable income derived from farming" means the gross income derived from farming reduced by the deductions allowed by this chapter (other than by this section) which are attributable to the business of farming.

(c) DEFINITIONS.—For purposes of subsection (a)—

(1) The term "clearing of land" includes (but is not limited to) the eradication of trees, stumps, and brush, the treatment or moving of earth, and the diversion of streams and watercourses.

(2) The term "land suitable for use in farming" means land which as a result of the activities described in paragraph (1) is suitable for use by the taxpayer or his tenant for the production of crops, fruits, or other agricultural products or for the sustenance of livestock.

(d) EXCEPTIONS, ETC.—

(1) EXCEPTIONS.—The expenditures to which subsection (a) applies shall not include—

(A) the purchase, construction, installation, or improvement of structures, appliances, or facilities which are of a character which is subject to the allowance for depreciation provided in section 167, or

(B) any amount paid or incurred which is allowable as a deduction without regard to this section.

(2) CERTAIN PROPERTY USED IN THE CLEARING OF LAND.—

(A) ALLOWANCE FOR DEPRECIATION.—The expenditures to which subsection (a) applies shall include a reasonable allowance for depreciation with respect to property of the taxpayer which is used in the clearing of land for the purpose of making such land suitable for use in farming and which, if used in a trade or business, would be property subject to the allowance for depreciation provided by section 167.

(B) TREATMENT AS DEPRECIATION DEDUCTION.—For purposes of this chapter, any expenditure described in subparagraph (A) shall, to the extent allowed as a deduction under subsection (a), be treated as an amount allowed under section 167 for exhaustion, wear and tear, or obsolescence of the property which is used in the clearing of land.

(e) ELECTION.—The election under subsection (a) for any taxable year shall be made within the time prescribed by law (including extensions thereof) for filing the return for such taxable year. Such election shall be made in such manner as the Secretary may by regulations prescribe. Such election may not be revoked except with the consent of the Secretary.

• 1976, Tax Reform Act of 1976 (P.L. 94-455)

P.L. 94-455, §1906(b)(13)(A):

Amended 1954 Code by substituting "Secretary" for "Secretary or his delegate" each place it appeared. **Effective** 2-1-77.

• 1962, Revenue Act of 1962 (P.L. 87-834)

P.L. 87-834, §21:

Amended part VI of subchapter B of chapter 1 by adding at the end thereof a new Sec. 182, and amended the table of sections for such part by inserting after Sec. 181 "Sec. 182. Expenditures by farmers for clearing land." **Effective** with respect to tax years beginning after 12-31-62.

[Sec. 183]

SEC. 183. ACTIVITIES NOT ENGAGED IN FOR PROFIT.

[Sec. 183(a)]

(a) GENERAL RULE.—In the case of an activity engaged in by an individual or an S corporation, if such activity is not engaged in for profit, no deduction attributable to such activity shall be allowed under this chapter except as provided in this section.

Amendments

• 1982, Subchapter S Revision Act of 1982 (P.L. 97-354)

P.L. 97-354, §5(a)(23):

Amended Code Sec. 183(a) by striking out "an electing small business corporation (as defined in section 1371(b))" and inserting in lieu thereof "an S corporation". **Effective** for tax years beginning after 12-31-82.

[Sec. 183(b)]

(b) DEDUCTIONS ALLOWABLE.—In the case of an activity not engaged in for profit to which subsection (a) applies, there shall be allowed—

(1) the deductions which would be allowable under this chapter for the taxable year without regard to whether or not such activity is engaged in for profit, and

(2) a deduction equal to the amount of the deductions which would be allowable under this chapter for the taxable year only if such activity were engaged in for profit, but only to the extent that the gross income derived from such activity for the taxable year exceeds the deductions allowable by reason of paragraph (1).

[Sec. 183(c)]

(c) ACTIVITY NOT ENGAGED IN FOR PROFIT DEFINED.—For purposes of this section, the term "activity not engaged in for profit" means any activity other than one with respect to which deductions are allowable for the taxable year under section 162 or under paragraph (1) or (2) of section 212.

[Sec. 183(d)]

(d) PRESUMPTION.—If the gross income derived from an activity for 3 or more of the taxable years in the period of 5 consecutive taxable years which ends with the taxable year exceeds the deductions attributable to such activity (determined without regard to whether or not such activity is engaged in for profit), then, unless the Secretary establishes to the contrary, such activity shall be presumed for purposes of this chapter for such taxable year to be an activity engaged in for profit. In the case of an activity which consists in major part of the breeding, training, showing, or racing of horses, the preceding sentence shall be applied by substituting "2" for "3" and "7" for "5".

Amendments

• 1986, Tax Reform Act of 1986 (P.L. 99-514)

P.L. 99-514, §143(a)(1) and (2):

Amended Code Sec. 183(d) by striking out "2 or more of the taxable years in the period of 5 consecutive taxable years" and inserting in lieu thereof "3 or more of the taxable years in the period of 5 consecutive taxable years", and by striking out the last sentence and inserting in lieu thereof "In the case of an activity which consists in major part of the breeding, training, showing, or racing of horses, the preceding sentence shall be applied by substituting `2' for `3' and `7' for `5'." **Effective** for tax years beginning after 12-31-86. Prior to amendment, the last sentence read as follows:

In the case of an activity which consists in major part of the breeding, training, showing, or racing of horses, the preceding sentence shall be applied by substituting the period of 7 consecutive taxable years for the period of 5 consecutive years.

• 1976, Tax Reform Act of 1976 (P.L. 94-455)

P.L. 94-455, §1906(b)(13)(A):

Amended 1954 Code by substituting "Secretary" for "Secretary or his delegate" each place it appeared. **Effective** 2-1-77.

[Sec. 183(e)]

(e) SPECIAL RULE.—

(1) IN GENERAL.—A determination as to whether the presumption provided by subsection (d) applies with respect to any activity shall, if the taxpayer so elects, not be made before the close of the fourth taxable year (sixth taxable year, in the case of an activity described in the last sentence of such subsection) following the taxable year in which the taxpayer first engages in the activity.

For purposes of the preceding sentence, a taxpayer shall be treated as not having engaged in an activity during any taxable year beginning before January 1, 1970.

(2) INITIAL PERIOD.—If the taxpayer makes an election under paragraph (1), the presumption provided by subsection (d) shall apply to each taxable year in the 5-taxable year (or 7-taxable year) period beginning with the taxable year in which the taxpayer first engages in the activity, if the gross income derived from the activity for 3 (or 2 if applicable) or more of the taxable years in such period exceeds the deductions attributable to the activity (determined without regard to whether or not the activity is engaged in for profit).

(3) ELECTION.—An election under paragraph (1) shall be made at such time and manner, and subject to such terms and conditions, as the Secretary may prescribe.

(4) TIME FOR ASSESSING DEFICIENCY ATTRIBUTABLE TO ACTIVITY.—If a taxpayer makes an election under paragraph (1) with respect to an activity, the statutory period for the assessment of any deficiency attributable to such activity shall not expire before the expiration of 2 years after the date prescribed by law (determined without extensions) for filing the return of tax under chapter 1 for the last taxable year in the period of 5 taxable years (or 7 taxable years) to which the election relates. Such deficiency may be assessed notwithstanding the provisions of any law or rule of law which would otherwise prevent such an assessment.

Amendments

• 1988, Technical and Miscellaneous Revenue Act of 1988 (P.L. 100-647)

P.L. 100-647, §1001(h)(3):

Amended Code Sec. 183(e)(2) by striking out "2" and inserting in lieu thereof "3 (or 2 if applicable)". **Effective** as if included in the provision of P.L. 99-514 to which it relates.

• 1976, Tax Reform Act of 1976 (P.L. 94-455)

P.L. 94-455, §214(a):

Added Code Sec. 183(e)(4). **Effective** for tax years beginning after 12-31-69; except that it shall not apply to any tax year ending before 10-4-76, with respect to which the period for assessing a deficiency has expired before 10-4-76.

P.L. 94-455, §1906(b)(13)(A):

Amended 1954 Code by substituting "Secretary" for "Secretary or his delegate" each place it appeared. **Effective** 2-1-77.

• 1971, Revenue Act of 1971 (P.L. 92-178)

P.L. 92-178, §311(a):

Added Code Sec. 183(e). **Effective** for tax years beginning after 12-31-69.

• 1969, Tax Reform Act of 1969 (P.L. 91-172)

P.L. 91-172, §213(a):

Amended Part VI of subchapter B of chapter 1 by adding Code Sec. 183 at the end thereof. **Effective** for tax years beginning after 12-31-69.

[Sec. 184—Repealed]

Amendments

• 1990, Omnibus Budget Reconciliation Act of 1990 (P.L. 101-508)

P.L. 101-508, §11801(a)(12):

Repealed Code Sec. 184. **Effective** on the date of enactment of this Act.

P.L. 101-508, §11821(b), provides:

(b) SAVINGS PROVISION.—If—

(1) any provision amended or repealed by this part applied to—

(A) any transaction occurring before the date of the enactment of this Act,

(B) any property acquired before such date of enactment, or

(C) any item of income, loss, deduction, or credit taken into account before such date of enactment, and

(2) the treatment of such transaction, property, or item under such provision would (without regard to the amendments made by this part) affect liability for tax for periods ending after such date of enactment,

nothing in the amendments made by this part shall be construed to affect the treatment of such transaction, property, or item for purposes of determining liability for tax for periods ending after such date of enactment.

Prior to repeal, Code Sec. 184 read as follows:

SEC. 184. AMORTIZATION OF CERTAIN RAILROAD ROLLING STOCK.

[Sec. 184(a)]

(a) ALLOWANCE OF DEDUCTION.—Every person, at his election, shall be entitled to a deduction with respect to the amortization of the adjusted basis (for determining gain) of any qualified railroad rolling stock (as defined in subsection (d)), based on a period of 60 months. Such amortization deduction shall be an amount, with respect to each month of such period within the taxable year, equal to the adjusted basis of the qualified railroad rolling stock at the end of such month divided by the number of months (including the month for which the deduction is computed) remaining in the period. Such adjusted basis at the end of the month shall be computed without regard to the amortization deduction for such month. The amortization deduction provided by this section with respect to any qualified railroad rolling stock for any month shall be in lieu of the depreciation deduction with respect to such rolling stock for such month provided by section 167. The 60-month period shall begin, as to any qualified railroad rolling stock, at the election of the taxpayer, with the month following the month in which such rolling stock was placed in service or with the succeeding taxable year.

[Sec. 184(b)]

(b) ELECTION OF AMORTIZATION.—The election of the taxpayer to take the amortization deduction and to begin the 60-month period with the month following the month in which the qualified railroad rolling stock was placed in service, or with the taxable year succeeding the taxable year in which such rolling stock is placed in service, shall be made by filing with the Secretary, in such manner, in such form, and within such time, as the Secretary may by regulations prescribe, a statement of such election.

Amendments

• 1976, Tax Reform Act of 1976 (P.L. 94-455)

P.L. 94-455, §1906(b)(13)(A):

Amended 1954 Code by substituting "Secretary" for "Secretary or his delegate" each place it appeared. **Effective** 2-1-77.

[Sec. 184(c)]

(c) TERMINATION OF AMORTIZATION DEDUCTION.—A taxpayer which has elected under subsection (b) to take the amortization deduction provided by subsection (a) may, at any time after making such election, discontinue the amortization deduction with respect to the remainder of the amortization period, such discontinuance to begin as of the beginning of any month specified by the taxpayer in a notice in writing filed with the Secretary before the beginning of such month. The depreciation deduction provided under section 167 shall be allowed, beginning with the first month as to which the amortization deduction does not apply, and the taxpayer shall not be entitled to any further amortization deduction under this section with respect to such rolling stock.

Amendments

• 1976, Tax Reform Act of 1976 (P.L. 94-455)

P.L. 94-455, §1906(b)(13)(A):

Amended 1954 Code by substituting "Secretary" for "Secretary or his delegate" each place it appeared. **Effective** 2-1-77.

[Sec. 184(d)]

(d) QUALIFIED RAILROAD ROLLING STOCK.—Except as provided in subsection (e)(4), the term "qualified railroad rolling stock" means, for purposes of this section, rolling stock of the type used by a common carrier engaged in the furnishing or sale of transportation by railroad and subject to the jurisdiction of the Interstate Commerce Commission if—

(1) such rolling stock is—

(A) used by a domestic common carrier by railroad on a full-time basis, or on a part-time basis if its only additional use is an incidental use by a Canadian or Mexican common carrier by railroad on a per diem basis, or

(B) owned and used by a switching or terminal company all of whose stock is owned by one or more domestic common carriers by railroad, and

(2) the original use of such rolling stock commences with the taxpayer after December 31, 1968.

[Sec. 184(e)]

(e) SPECIAL RULES.—

(1) IN GENERAL.—Except as otherwise provided in this subsection, this section shall apply to qualified railroad rolling stock placed in service after 1968 and before 1976.

(2) PLACED IN SERVICE IN 1969.—If any qualified railroad rolling stock is placed in service in 1969—

(A) the month as to which the amortization period shall begin with respect to such rolling stock shall be determined as if such rolling stock were placed in service on December 31, 1969, and

(B) subsections (a) and (b) shall be applied by substituting "48" for "60" each place that it appears in such subsections.

This section shall not apply to any qualified railroad rolling stock placed in service in 1969 and owned by any person who is not a domestic common carrier by railroad, or a corporation at least 95 percent of the stock of which is owned by one or more such common carriers.

(3) PLACED IN SERVICE IN 1970.—If any qualified railroad rolling stock is placed in service in 1970 by a domestic common carrier by railroad or by a corporation at least 95 percent of the stock of which is owned by one or more such common carriers, then subsection (a) shall be applied, without regard to paragraph (2), as if such rolling stock were placed in service on December 31, 1969.

(4) RAILROAD ROLLING STOCK NOT IN SHORT SUPPLY.—The Secretary shall determine (with the assistance of the Secretary of Transportation) which types of railroad rolling stock are not in short supply and shall prescribe regulations designating such types. The term "qualified railroad rolling stock" shall not include any rolling stock which—

(A) is of the type of rolling stock designated by such regulations as not in short supply, and

(B) is placed in service after (i) 1972, or (ii) 30 days after the date on which such regulations are promulgated, whichever is later.

(5) ADJUSTED BASIS.—

(A) The adjusted basis of any qualified railroad rolling stock, with respect to which an election has been made under this section, shall not be increased, for purposes of this section, for amounts chargeable to capital account for additions or improvements after the amortization period has begun.

(B) Costs incurred in connection with a used unit of railroad rolling stock which are properly chargeable to capital account shall be treated as a separate unit of railroad rolling stock for purposes of this section.

(C) The depreciation deduction provided by section 167 shall, despite the provisions of subsection (a), be allowed with respect to the portion of the adjusted basis which is not taken into account in applying this section.

(6) CONSTRUCTIVE TERMINATION.—If at any time during the amortization period any qualified railroad rolling stock ceases to meet the requirements of subsection (d)(1), the taxpayer shall be deemed to have terminated under subsection (c) his election under this section. Such termination shall be effective beginning with the month following the month in which such cessation occurs.

(7) METHOD OF ACCOUNTING FOR DATE PLACED IN SERVICE.—For purposes of subsections (a) and (b), in the case of qualified railroad rolling stock placed in service after December 31, 1969, and before January 1, 1976, the taxpayer may elect (unless paragraph (3) is applicable) to begin the 60-month period with the date when such rolling stock is treated as having been placed in service under a method of accounting for acquisitions and retirements of property which—

(A) prescribes a date when property is placed in service, and

(B) is consistently followed by the taxpayer.

Amendments

• 1976, Tax Reform Act of 1976 (P.L. 94-455)

P.L. 94-455, §1906(b)(13)(A):

Amended 1954 Code by substituting "Secretary" for "Secretary or his delegate" each place it appeared. **Effective** 2-1-77.

[Sec. 184(f)]

(f) LIFE TENANT AND REMAINDERMAN.—In the case of qualified railroad rolling stock leased to a domestic common carrier, and held by one person for life with remainder to another person, the deduction under this section shall be computed as if the life tenant were the absolute owner of the property and shall be allowable to the life tenant.

[Sec. 184(g)]

(g) CROSS REFERENCE.—For treatment of certain gain derived from the disposition of property the adjusted basis of which is determined with regard to this section, see section 1245.

Amendments

• 1975 (P.L. 93-625)

P.L. 93-625, §3(b):

Amended Code Sec. 184(e) by substituting "1976" for "1975" in paragraph (1) and by substituting "January 1, 1976" for "January 1, 1975" in paragraph (7). **Effective** 1-3-75.

• 1969, Tax Reform Act of 1969 (P.L. 91-172)

P.L. 91-172, §705(a):

Added Code Sec. 184. **Effective** for tax years beginning after 12-31-69.

[Sec. 185—Repealed]

Amendments

• 1986, Tax Reform Act of 1986 (P.L. 99-514)

P.L. 99-514, §242(a):

Repealed Code Sec. 185. **Effective**, generally, for that portion of the basis of any property which is attributable to expenditures paid or incurred after 12-31-86. However, for a transitional rule, see P.L. 99-514, §242(c)(2), following the amendment notes for former Code Sec. 185(j). Prior to repeal, Code Sec. 185 read as follows:

SEC. 185. AMORTIZATION OF RAILROAD GRADING AND TUNNEL BORES.

[Sec. 185(a)]

(a) GENERAL RULE.—In the case of a domestic common carrier by railroad, the taxpayer shall, at his election, be entitled to a deduction with respect to the amortization of the adjusted basis (for determining gain) of his qualified railroad grading and tunnel bores. The amortization deduction provided by this section with respect to such property shall be in lieu of any depreciation deduction, or other amortization deduction, with respect to such property for any taxable year to which the election applies.

[Sec. 185(b)]

(b) AMOUNT OF DEDUCTION.—

(1) IN GENERAL.—The deduction allowable under subsection (a) for any taxable year shall be an amount determined by amortizing ratably over a period of 50 years the adjusted basis (for determining gain) of the qualified railroad grading and tunnel bores of the taxpayer. Such 50-year period shall commence with the first taxable year for which an election under this section is effective.

(2) SPECIAL RULE.—In the case of qualified railroad grading and tunnel bores placed in service after the beginning of the first taxable year for which an election under this section is effective, the 50-year period with respect to such property shall begin with the year following the year the property is placed in service.

[Sec. 185(c)]

(c) ELECTION OF AMORTIZATION.—The election of the taxpayer to take the amortization deduction provided in subsection (a) may be made for any taxable year beginning after December 31, 1969. Such election shall be made by filing with the Secretary, in such manner, in such form, and within such time, as the Secretary may by regulations prescribe, a statement of such election. The election shall remain in effect for all taxable years subsequent to the first year for which it is effective and shall apply to all qualified railroad grading and tunnel bores of the taxpayer, unless, on application by the taxpayer, the Secretary permits him, subject to such conditions as the Secretary deems necessary, to revoke such election.

Amendments

• 1976, Tax Reform Act of 1976 (P.L. 94-455)

P.L. 94-455, §1906(b)(13)(A):

Amended 1954 Code by substituting "Secretary" for "Secretary or his delegate" each place it appeared. **Effective** 2-1-77.

[Sec. 185(d)]

(d) ELECTION WITH RESPECT TO PRE-1969 PROPERTY.—A taxpayer may, for any taxable year beginning after December 31, 1974, elect for purposes of this section to treat the term "qualified railroad grading and tunnel bores" as including pre-1969 railroad grading and tunnel bores. An election under this subsection shall be made by filing with the Secretary, in such manner, in such form, and within such time, as the Secretary may by regulations prescribe, a statement of such election. The election under this subsection shall remain in effect for all taxable years, after the first year for which it is effective, for which an election under subsection (c) is effective. The election under this subsection shall apply to all pre-1969 railroad grading and tunnel bores of the taxpayer, unless, on application by the taxpayer, the Secretary permits him, subject to such conditions as the Secretary deems necessary, to revoke such election.

Amendments

• 1976, Tax Reform Act of 1976 (P.L. 94-455)

P.L. 94-455, §1702(a):

Added a new Code Sec. 185(d) and redesignated former Code Sec. 185(d) as Code Sec. 185(f). **Effective** 10-4-76.

[Sec. 185(e)]

(e) ADJUSTED BASIS FOR PRE-1969 RAILROAD GRADING AND TUNNEL BORES.—

(1) IN GENERAL.—The adjusted basis of any pre-1969 railroad grading and tunnel bores shall be determined under this subsection.

(2) PROPERTY ACQUIRED OR CONSTRUCTED AFTER FEBRUARY 28, 1913.—

(A) In the case of pre-1969 railroad grading and tunnel bores—

(i) acquired by the taxpayer after February 28, 1913, or

(ii) the construction of which was completed by the taxpayer after February 28, 1913,

the adjusted basis of such property shall be equal to the adjusted basis (for determining gain) of such property in the hands of the taxpayer.

(B) In the case of property described in subparagraph (A)(i)—

(i) which was in existence on February 28, 1913,

(ii) for which the taxpayer has a substituted basis, and

(iii) such substituted basis for which would, but for the provisions of this section, be determined under section 1053,

then the adjusted basis of such property shall be determined as if such property were property described in paragraph (3)(A).

(3) PROPERTY ACQUIRED OR CONSTRUCTED BEFORE MARCH 1, 1913.—

(A) In the case of pre-1969 railroad grading and tunnel bores—

(i) acquired by the taxpayer before March 1, 1913, or

(ii) the construction of which was completed by the taxpayer before March 1, 1913,

the adjusted basis of such property shall be determined under the provisions of subparagraph (B), (C), or (D) of this paragraph.

(B) In the case of any property valued under an original valuation made by the Interstate Commerce Commission pursuant to subchapter V of chapter 107 of title 49, the adjusted basis of such property shall be equal to the amount ascertained by the Interstate Commerce Commission as of the date of such valuation to be such property's cost of reproduction new (as the term "cost of reproduction new" is used in such subchapter V).

(C) In the case of property which was not valued by the Interstate Commerce Commission in the manner described in subparagraph (B), but which was valued under an original valuation made by a comparable State regulatory body, the adjusted basis of such property shall be equal to the amount ascertained by such State regulatory body as of the date of its original valuation to be such property's value.

(D) If, in the case of any property to which this paragraph applies—

(i) neither subparagraph (B) nor (C) applies, or

(ii) notwithstanding subparagraphs (B) and (C), either the taxpayer or the Secretary can establish the adjusted basis (for purposes of determining gain) of such property in the hands of the taxpayer,

then the adjusted basis of such property shall be equal to its adjusted basis (for purposes of determining gain) in the hands of the taxpayer.

Amendments

• 1978 (P.L. 95-473)

P.L. 95-473, §2(a)(2)(B):

Amended Code Section 185(e)(3)(B) by striking out "section 19a of part I of the Interstate Commerce Act (49 U.S.C. 19a)" and "such section 19a" and substituting "subchapter V of chapter 107 of title 49" and "such subchapter V", respectively. **Effective** 10-17-78.

• 1976, Tax Reform Act of 1976 (P.L. 94-455)

P.L. 94-455, §1702(a):

Added new Code Sec. 185(e) and redesignated former Code Sec. 185(e) to be Code Sec. 185(g). **Effective** 10-4-76.

[Sec. 185(f)]

(f) DEFINITIONS.—For purposes of this section—

(1) RAILROAD GRADING AND TUNNEL BORES.—The term "railroad grading and tunnel bores" means all improvements resulting from excavations (including tunneling), construction of embankments, clearings, diversions of roads and streams, sodding of slopes, and from similar work necessary to provide, construct, reconstruct, alter, protect, improve, replace, or restore a roadbed or right-of-way for railroad track. If expenditures for improvements described in the preceding sentence are incurred with respect to an existing roadbed or right-of-way for railroad track, such expenditures shall be considered, in applying this section, as costs for railroad grading or tunnel bores placed in service in the year in which such costs are incurred.

(2) QUALIFIED RAILROAD GRADING AND TUNNEL BORES.—The term "qualified railroad grading and tunnel bores" means railroad grading and tunnel bores the original use of which commences after December 31, 1968.

(3) PRE-1969 RAILROAD GRADING AND TUNNEL BORES.—The term "pre-1969 railroad grading and tunnel bores" means railroad grading and tunnel bores the original use of which commences before January 1, 1969.

Amendments

• 1976, Tax Reform Act of 1976 (P.L. 94-455)

P.L. 94-455, §1702(a):

Redesignated former Code Sec. 185(d) as Code Sec. 185(f). **Effective** 10-4-76.

P.L. 94-455, §1702(b):

Added a new paragraph (3) to Code Sec. 185(f). **Effective** 10-4-76.

[Sec. 185(g)]

(g) TREATMENT UPON RETIREMENT.—If any qualified railroad grading or tunnel bore is retired or abandoned during a taxable year for which an election under this section is in effect, no deduction shall be allowed on account of such retirement or abandonment and the amortization deduction under this section shall continue with respect to such property. This subsection shall not apply if the retirement or abandonment is attributable primarily to fire, storm, or other casualty.

Amendments

• 1976, Tax Reform Act of 1976 (P.L. 94-455)

P.L. 94-455, §1702(a):

Redesignated former Code Sec. 185(e) as Code Sec. 185(g). **Effective** 10-4-76.

[Sec. 185(h)]

(h) INVESTMENT CREDIT NOT TO BE ALLOWED.—Property eligible to be amortized under this section shall not be treated as section 38 property within the meaning of section 48(a).

Amendments

• 1976, Tax Reform Act of 1976 (P.L. 94-455)

P.L. 94-455, §1702(a):

Redesignated former Code Sec. 185(f) as Code Sec. 185(h). **Effective** 10-4-76.

[Sec. 185(i)]

(i) REGULATIONS.—The Secretary shall prescribe such regulations as may be necessary to carry out the purposes of this section.

Amendments

• 1976, Tax Reform Act of 1976 (P.L. 94-455)

P.L. 94-455, §1702(a):

Redesignated former Code Sec. 185(g) as Code Sec. 185(i). **Effective** 10-4-76.

P.L. 94-455, §1906(b)(13)(A):

Amended 1954 Code by substituting "Secretary" for "Secretary or his delegate" each place it appeared. **Effective** 2-1-77.

[Sec. 185(j)]

(j) CROSS REFERENCE.—

For special rule with respect to certain gain derived from the disposition of property the adjusted basis of which is determined with regard to this section, see section 1245.

Amendments

• 1976, Tax Reform Act of 1976 (P.L. 94-455)

P.L. 94-455, §1702(a):

Redesignated former Code Sec. 185(h) as Code Sec. 185(j). **Effective** 10-4-76.

Added Code Sec. 185. **Effective** for tax years beginning after 12-31-69.

• 1986, Tax Reform Act of 1986 (P.L. 99-514)

P.L. 99-514, §242(c)(2), provides:

(2) TRANSITIONAL RULE.—The amendments made by this section shall not apply to any expenditure incurred—

(A) pursuant to a binding contract entered into before March 2, 1986, or

(B) with respect to any improvement commenced before March 2, 1986, but only if not less than the lesser of $1,000,000 or 5 percent of the aggregate cost of such improvement has been incurred or committed before such date.

The preceding sentence shall not apply to any expenditure with respect to any improvement placed in service after December 31, 1987.

[Sec. 186]

SEC. 186. RECOVERIES OF DAMAGES FOR ANTITRUST VIOLATIONS, ETC.

[Sec. 186(a)]

(a) ALLOWANCE OF DEDUCTION.—If a compensatory amount which is included in gross income is received or accrued during the taxable year for a compensable injury, there shall be allowed as a deduction for the taxable year an amount equal to the lesser of—

(1) the amount of such compensatory amount, or

(2) the amount of the unrecovered losses sustained as a result of such compensable injury.

[Sec. 186(b)]

(b) COMPENSABLE INJURY.—For purposes of this section, the term "compensable injury" means—

(1) injuries sustained as a result of an infringement of a patent issued by the United States,

(2) injuries sustained as a result of a breach of contract or a breach of fiduciary duty or relationship, or

(3) injuries sustained in business, or to property, by reason of any conduct forbidden in the antitrust laws for which a civil action may be brought under section 4 of the Act entitled "An Act to supplement existing laws against unlawful restraints and monopolies, and for other purposes", approved October 15, 1914 (commonly known as the Clayton Act).

[Sec. 186(c)]

(c) COMPENSATORY AMOUNT.—For purposes of this section, the term "compensatory amount" means the amount received or accrued during the taxable year as damages as a result of an award in, or in settlement of, a civil action for recovery for a compensable injury, reduced by any amounts paid or incurred in the taxable year in securing such award or settlement.

[Sec. 186(d)]

(d) UNRECOVERED LOSSES.—

(1) IN GENERAL.—For purposes of this section, the amount of any unrecovered loss sustained as a result of any compensable injury is—

(A) the sum of the amount of the net operating losses (as determined under section 172) for each taxable year in whole or in part within the injury period, to the extent that such net operating losses are attributable to such compensable injury, reduced by

(B) the sum of—

(i) the amount of the net operating losses described in subparagraph (A) which were allowed for any prior taxable year as a deduction under section 172 as a net operating loss carryback or carryover to such taxable year, and

(ii) the amounts allowed as a deduction under subsection (a) for any prior taxable year for prior recoveries of compensatory amounts for such compensable injury.

(2) INJURY PERIOD.—For purposes of paragraph (1), the injury period is—

(A) with respect to any infringement of a patent, the period in which such infringement occurred,

(B) with respect to a breach of contract or breach of fiduciary duty or relationship, the period during which amounts would have been received or accrued but for the breach of contract or breach of fiduciary duty or relationship, and

(C) with respect to injuries sustained by reason of any conduct forbidden in the antitrust laws, the period in which such injuries were sustained.

(3) NET OPERATING LOSSES ATTRIBUTABLE TO COMPENSABLE INJURIES.—For purposes of paragraph (1)—

(A) a net operating loss for any taxable year shall be treated as attributable to a compensable injury to the extent of the compensable injury sustained during such taxable year, and

(B) if only a portion of a net operating loss for any taxable year is attributable to a compensable injury, such portion shall (in applying section 172 for purposes of this section) be considered to be a separate net operating loss for such year to be applied after the other portion of such net operating loss.

[Sec. 186(e)]

(e) EFFECT ON NET OPERATING LOSS CARRYOVERS.—If for the taxable year in which a compensatory amount is received or accrued any portion of a net operating loss carryover to such year is attributable to the compensable injury for which such amount is received or accrued, such portion of such net operating loss carryover shall be reduced by an amount equal to—

(1) the deduction allowed under subsection (a) with respect to such compensatory amount, reduced by

(2) any portion of the unrecovered losses sustained as a result of the compensable injury with respect to which the period for carryover under section 172 has expired.

Amendments

• 1969, Tax Reform Act of 1969 (P.L. 91-172)

P.L. 91-172, §904(a):

Added Code Sec. 186. **Effective** for tax years beginning after 12-31-68.

[Sec. 188—Repealed]

Amendments

• 1990, Omnibus Budget Reconciliation Act of 1990 (P.L. 101-508)

P.L. 101-508, §11801(a)(13):

Repealed Code Sec. 188. **Effective** on the date of enactment of this Act.

P.L. 101-508, §11821(b), provides:

(b) SAVINGS PROVISION.—If—

(1) any provision amended or repealed by this part applied to—

(A) any transaction occurring before the date of the enactment of this Act,

(B) any property acquired before such date of enactment, or

(C) any item of income, loss, deduction, or credit taken into account before such date of enactment, and

(2) the treatment of such transaction, property, or item under such provision would (without regard to the amendments made by this part) affect liability for tax for periods ending after such date of enactment,

nothing in the amendments made by this part shall be construed to affect the treatment of such transaction, property, or item for purposes of determining liability for tax for periods ending after such date of enactment.

Prior to repeal, Code Sec. 188 read as follows:

SEC. 188. AMORTIZATION OF CERTAIN EXPENDITURES FOR CHILD CARE FACILITIES.

[Sec. 188(a)]

(a) ALLOWANCE OF DEDUCTION.—At the election of the taxpayer, made in accordance with regulations prescribed by the Secretary, any expenditure chargeable to capital account made by an employer to acquire, construct, reconstruct, or rehabilitate section 188 property (as defined in subsection (b)) shall be allowable as a deduction ratably over a period of 60 months, beginning with the month in which the property is placed in service. The deduction provided by this section with respect to such expenditure shall be in lieu of any depreciation deduction otherwise allowable on account of such expenditure.

Amendments

• 1976, Tax Reform Act of 1976 (P.L. 94-455)

P.L. 94-455, §1906(b)(13)(A):

Amended 1954 Code by substituting "Secretary" for "Secretary or his delegate" each place it appeared. **Effective** 2-1-77.

[Sec. 188(b)]

(b) SECTION 188 PROPERTY.—For purposes of this section, the term "section 188 property" means tangible property which qualifies under regulations prescribed by the Secretary as a child care center facility primarily for the children of employees of the taxpayer; except that such term shall not include—

(1) any property which is not of a character subject to depreciation; or

(2) property located outside the United States.

Amendments

• 1977, Tax Reduction and Simplification Act of 1977 (P.L. 95-30)

P.L. 95-30, §402(a)(2):

Amended Code Sec. 188(b) by deleting "as a facility for on-the-job training of employees (or prospective employees) of the taxpayer, or" which formerly preceded "as a child care center facility". **Effective** for expenditures made after 12-31-76.

• 1976, Tax Reform Act of 1976 (P.L. 94-455)

P.L. 94-455, §1906(b)(13)(A):

Amended 1954 Code by substituting "Secretary" for "Secretary or his delegate" each place it appeared. **Effective** 2-1-77.

[Sec. 188(c)]

(c) APPLICATION OF SECTION.—This section shall apply only with respect to expenditures made after December 31, 1971, and before January 1, 1982.

Amendments

• 1977, Tax Reduction and Simplification Act of 1977 (P.L. 95-30)

P.L. 95-30, §402(a)(1):

Amended Code Sec. 188(c) by substituting "1982" for "1977". **Effective** for expenditures made after 12-31-76.

• 1971, Revenue Act of 1971 (P.L. 92-178)

P.L. 92-178, §303(a):

Added Code Sec. 188. **Effective** for tax years ending after 12-31-71.

[Sec. 189—Repealed]

Amendments

• 1986, Tax Reform Act of 1986 (P.L. 99-514)

P.L. 99-514, §803(b)(1):

Repealed Code Sec. 189. **Effective**, generally, for costs incurred after 12-31-86, in tax years ending after such date. However, for special and transitional rules, see Act Sec. 803(d)(2)-(7) following former Code Sec. 189(f). Prior to repeal Code Sec. 189 read as follows:

SEC. 189. AMORTIZATION OF REAL PROPERTY CONSTRUCTION PERIOD INTEREST AND TAXES.

[Sec. 189(a)]

(a) CAPITALIZATION OF CONSTRUCTION PERIOD INTEREST AND TAXES.—Except as otherwise provided in this section or in section 266 (relating to carrying charges), no deduction shall be allowed for real property construction period interest and taxes.

Amendments

• 1982, Tax Equity and Fiscal Responsibility Act of 1982 (P.L. 97-248)

P.L. 97-248, §207(a):

Amended Code Sec. 189(a). **Effective** with respect to tax years beginning after 12-31-82, with respect to construction which commences after such date. But see amendment notes for P.L. 97-248 following Code Sec. 189(e) for special rules. Prior to amendment, it read as follows:

"(a) CAPITALIZATION OF CONSTRUCTION PERIOD INTEREST AND TAXES.—Except as otherwise provided in this section or in section 266 (relating to carrying charges), in the case of an individual, no deduction shall be allowed for real property construction period interest and taxes. For purposes of this section, an electing small business corporation (as defined in section 1371(b)), a personal holding company (as defined in section 542), and a foreign personal holding company (as defined in section 552) shall be treated as an individual."

• 1978, Revenue Act of 1978 (P.L. 95-600)

P.L. 95-600, §701(m)(1):

Amended Code Sec. 189(a). **Effective** as provided in P.L. 94-455, §201(c). See historical comment for P.L. 94-455, §201(c) under Code Sec. 189(f). Prior to amendment, Code Sec. 189(a) read as follows:

(a) CAPITALIZATION OF CONSTRUCTION PERIOD INTEREST AND TAXES.—Except as otherwise provided in this section or in section 266 (relating to carrying charges), in the case of an individual, an electing small business corporation (within the meaning of section 1371(b)), or personal holding company (within the meaning of section 542), no deduction shall be allowed for real property construction period interest and taxes.

[Sec. 189(b)]

(b) AMORTIZATION OF AMOUNTS CHARGED TO CAPITAL ACCOUNT.—Any amount paid or accrued which would (but for subsection (a)) be allowable as a deduction for the taxable year shall be allowable for such taxable year and each subsequent amortization year in accordance with the following table:

If the amount is paid or accrued in a taxable year beginning in—		
Nonresidential real property	*Residential real property (other than low-income housing)*	*The percentage of such amount allowable for each amortization year shall be the following percentage of such amount*
1976	....	see subsection (f)
....	1978	25
1977	1979	20
1978	1980	$16\frac{2}{3}$
1979	1981	$14\frac{2}{7}$
1980	1982	$12\frac{1}{2}$
1981	1983	$11\frac{1}{9}$
after 1981	after 1983	10

Amendments

• 1981, Economic Recovery Tax Act of 1981 (P.L. 97-34)

P.L. 97-34, §262(a):

Amended the table in Code Sec. 189(b) by striking out the column relating to low-income housing. Prior to repeal, this column read as follows:

Low-income housing
....
1982
1983
1984
1985
1986
1987
after 1987

[Sec. 189(c)]

(c) AMORTIZATION YEAR.—

(1) IN GENERAL.—For purposes of this section, the term "amortization year" means the taxable year in which the amount is paid or accrued, and each taxable year thereafter (beginning with the taxable year after the taxable year in which paid or accrued or, if later, the taxable year in which the real property is ready to be placed in service or is ready to be held for sale) until the full amount has been allowable as a deduction (or until the property is sold or exchanged).

(2) RULES FOR SALES AND EXCHANGES.—For purposes of paragraph (1)—

(A) PROPORTION OF PERCENTAGE ALLOWED.—For the amortization year in which the property is sold or exchanged, a proportionate part of the percentage allowable for such year (determined without regard to the sale or exchange) shall be allowable. If the real property is subject to an allowance for depreciation, the proportion shall be determined in accordance with the convention used for depreciation purposes with respect to such property. In the case of all other real property, under regulations prescribed by the Secretary, the proportion shall be based on that proportion of the amortization year which elapsed before the sale or exchange.

(B) UNAMORTIZED BALANCE.—In the case of a sale or exchange of the property, the portion of the amount not allowable shall be treated as an adjustment to basis under section 1016 for purposes of determining gain or loss.

(C) CERTAIN EXCHANGES.—An exchange or transfer after which the property received has a basis determined in whole or in part by reference to the basis of the property to which the amortizable construction period interest and taxes relate, shall not be treated as an exchange.

[Sec. 189(d)]

(d) CERTAIN PROPERTY EXCLUDED.—This section shall not apply to any—

(1) low-income housing,

(2) real property acquired, constructed, or carried if such property is not, and cannot reasonably expected to be, held in a trade or business, or in an activity conducted for profit.

Amendments

• 1984, Deficit Reduction Act of 1984 (P.L. 98-369)

P.L. 98-369, §93(a):

Amended Code Sec. 189(d) by striking out paragraph (2) and by redesignating paragraph (3) as paragraph (2). **Effective** for tax years beginning after 12-31-84, with respect to construction beginning after 3-15-84. Prior to amendment, Code Sec. 189(d)(2) read as follows:

(2) residential real property (other than low income housing) acquired, constructed, or carried by a corporation other than S corporation, a personal holding company (within the meaning of section 542), or a foreign personal holding company (within the meaning of section 552), or

• 1982, Subchapter S Revision Act of 1982 (P.L. 97-354)

P.L. 97-354, §5(a)(24):

Amended Code Sec. 189(d)(2) by striking out "an electing small business corporation (within the meaning of section 1371(b))" and inserting in lieu thereof "an S corporation". **Effective** for tax years beginning after 12-31-82.

• 1982, Tax Equity and Fiscal Responsibility Act of 1982 (P.L. 97-248)

P.L. 97-248, §207(b):

Amended Code Sec. 189(d) by striking out "or" at the end of paragraph (1), by redesignating paragraph (2) as paragraph (3), and by inserting after paragraph (1) new paragraph (2). **Effective** with respect to tax years beginning after 12-31-82, with respect to construction commencing after that date. But see amendment notes for P.L. 97-248 following Code Sec. 189(e) for special rules.

• 1981, Economic Recovery Tax Act of 1981 (P.L. 97-34)

P.L. 97-34, §262(b):

Amended Code Sec. 189(d). **Effective** for tax years beginning after 12-31-81. Prior to amendment, Code Sec. 189(d) read as follows:

(d) CERTAIN RESIDENTIAL PROPERTY EXCLUDED.—This section shall not apply to any real property acquired, constructed, or carried if such property is not, and cannot reasonably be expected to be, held in a trade or business or in an activity conducted for profit.

[Sec. 189(e)]

(e) DEFINITIONS.—For purposes of this section—

(1) REAL PROPERTY CONSTRUCTION PERIOD INTEREST AND TAXES.—The term "real property construction period interest and taxes" means all—

(A) interest paid or accrued on indebtedness incurred or continued to acquire, construct, or carry real property, and

(B) real property taxes,

to the extent such interest and taxes are attributable to the construction period for such property and would be allowable as a deduction under this chapter for the taxable year in which paid or accrued (determined without regard to this section). The Secretary shall prescribe regulations which provide for the allocation of interest to real property under construction.

(2) CONSTRUCTION PERIOD.—The term "construction period", when used with respect to any real property, means the period—

(A) beginning on the date on which construction of the building or other improvement begins, and

(B) ending on the date on which the item of property is ready to be placed in service or is ready to be held for sale.

(3) NONRESIDENTIAL REAL PROPERTY.—The term "nonresidential real property" means real property which is neither residential real property nor low-income housing.

(4) RESIDENTIAL REAL PROPERTY.—The term "residential real property" means property which is or can reasonably be expected to be—

(A) residential rental property as defined in section 167(j)(2)(B),

(B) real property described in section 1221(1) held for sale as dwelling units (within the meaning of section 167(k)(3)(C)), or

(C) real property held by a cooperative housing corporation (as defined in section 216(b)) and used for dwelling purposes.

(5) LOW-INCOME HOUSING.—The term "low-income housing" means property described in clause (i), (ii), (iii), or (iv) of section 1250(a)(1)(B).

Amendments

• 1984, Deficit Reduction Act of 1984 (P.L. 98-369)

P.L. 98-369, §712(c):

Amended Code Sec. 189(e)(4) by striking out "or" at the end of subparagraph (A), by striking out the period at the end of subparagraph (B) and inserting in lieu thereof ", or", and by adding at the end thereof new subparagraph (C). **Effective** as if included in the provision of P.L. 97-248 to which it relates.

• 1982, Tax Equity and Fiscal Responsibility Act of 1982 (P.L. 97-248)

P.L. 97-248, §207(c)-(d):

Amended paragraph (1) of Code Sec. 189(e) by adding at the end thereof the following sentence: "The Secretary shall prescribe regulations which provide for the allocation of interest to real property under construction." Paragraph (1) was also amended by striking out "construction period interest and taxes" and inserting in lieu thereof "real property construction period interest and taxes", and by striking out the caption thereof and inserting in lieu thereof: "(1) Real Property Construction Period Interest and Taxes.—" **Effective** with respect to tax years beginnning after 12-31-82, with respect to construction which commences after such date.

P.L. 97-248, §207(e)(2), provides:

(2) CERTAIN PLANNED CONSTRUCTION.—The amendments made by this section shall not apply with respect to construction of property which is used in a trade or business described in section 48(a)(3)(B) of the Internal Revenue Code of 1954 or which is a hospital or nursing home if—

(A) such construction is conducted pursuant to a written plan of the taxpayer which was in existence on July 1, 1982, and as to which approval from a governmental unit has been requested in writing, and

(B) such construction commences before January 1, 1984, and shall not apply to the Alaska Natural Gas Transportation System (15 U.S.C. 719) and its related facilities.

[Sec. 189(f)]

(f) TRANSITIONAL RULE FOR 1976.—In the case of amounts paid or accrued by the taxpayer in a taxable year beginning in 1976, the percentage of such amount allowable under this section for—

(1) the taxable year beginning in 1976 shall be 50 percent, and

(2) each amortization year thereafter shall be 16⅔ percent.

Amendments

• 1978, Revenue Act of 1978 (P.L. 95-600)

P.L. 95-600, §701(e):

Amended paragraph (1) of §201(c) of P.L. 94-455 to read as follows:

"(1) in the case of nonresidential real property, if the construction period begins on or after the first day of the first taxable year beginning after December 31, 1975,".

• 1976, Tax Reform Act of 1976 (P.L. 94-455)

P.L. 94-455, §201(a):

Added Code Sec. 189. For the **effective** date, see Act Sec. 201(c), below.

P.L. 94-455, §201(c), provides:

(c) EFFECTIVE DATE.—The amendments made by this section shall apply—

(1) in the case of nonresidential real property, if the construction period begins after December 31, 1975,

(2) in the case of residential real property (other than low-income housing), to taxable years beginning after December 31, 1977, and

(3) in the case of low-income housing, to taxable years beginning after December 31, 1981.

For purposes of this subsection, the terms "nonresidential real property", "residential real property (other than lowincome housing)", "low-income housing", and "construction period" have the same meaning as when used in section 189 of the Internal Revenue Code of 1954 (as added by subsection (a) of this section).

P.L. 99-514, §803(d)(2)-(7), as amended by P.L. 100-647, §1008(b)(7), and P.L. 101-239, §7831(d)(1), provides:

(2) SPECIAL RULE FOR INVENTORY PROPERTY.—In the case of any property which is inventory in the hands of the taxpayer—

(A) IN GENERAL.—The amendments made by this section shall apply to taxable years beginning after December 31, 1986.

(B) CHANGE IN METHOD OF ACCOUNTING.—If the taxpayer is required by the amendments made by this section to change its method of accounting with respect to such property for any taxable year—

(i) such change shall be treated as initiated by the taxpayer,

(ii) such change shall be treated as made with the consent of the Secretary, and

(iii) the period for taking into account the adjustments under section 481 by reason of such change shall not exceed 4 years.

(3) SPECIAL RULE FOR SELF-CONSTRUCTED PROPERTY.—The amendments made by this section shall not apply to any property which is produced by the taxpayer for use by the taxpayer if substantial construction had occurred before March 1, 1986.

(4) TRANSITIONAL RULE FOR CAPITALIZATION OF INTEREST AND TAXES.—

(A) TRANSITION PROPERTY EXEMPTED FROM INTEREST CAPITALIZATION.—Section 263A of the Internal Revenue Code of 1986 (as added by this section) and the amendment made by subsection (b)(1) shall not apply to interest costs which are allocable to any property—

(i) to which the amendments made by section 201 do not apply by reason of sections 204(a)(1)(D) and (E) and 204(a)(5)(A), and

(ii) to which the amendments made by section 251 do not apply by reason of section 251(d)(3)(M).

(B) INTEREST AND TAXES.—Section 263A of such Code shall not apply to property described in the matter following subparagraph (B) of section 207(e)(2) of the Tax Equity and Fiscal Responsibility Act of 1982 to the extent it would require the capitalization of interest and taxes paid or incurred in connection with such property which are not required to be capitalized under section 189 of such Code (as in effect before the amendment made by subsection (b)(1)).

(5) TRANSITION RULE CONCERNING CAPITALIZATION OF INVENTORY RULES.—In the case of a corporation which on the date of the enactment of this Act was a member of an affiliated group of corporations (within the meaning of section 1504(a) of the Internal Revenue Code of 1986), the parent of which—

(A) was incorporated in California on April 15, 1925,

(B) adopted LIFO accounting as of the close of the taxable year ended December 31, 1950, and

(C) was, on May 22, 1986, merged into a Delaware corporation incorporated on March 12, 1986,

the amendments made by this section shall apply under a cut-off method whereby the uniform capitalization rules are applied only in costing layers of inventory acquired during taxable years beginning on or after January 1, 1987.

(6) TREATMENT OF CERTAIN REHABILITATION PROJECT.—The amendments made by this section shall not apply to interest and taxes paid or incurred with respect to the rehabilitation and conversion of a certified historic building which was formerly a factory into an apartment project with 155 units, 39 units of which are for low-income families, if the project was approved for annual interest assistance on June 10, 1986, by the housing authority of the State in which the project is located.

(7) SPECIAL RULE FOR CASUALTY LOSSES.—Section 263A(d)(2) of the Internal Revenue Code of 1986 (as added by this section) shall apply to expenses incurred on or after the date of the enactment of this Act.

[Sec. 190]

SEC. 190. EXPENDITURES TO REMOVE ARCHITECTURAL AND TRANSPORTATION BARRIERS TO THE HANDICAPPED AND ELDERLY.

[Sec. 190(a)]

(a) TREATMENT AS EXPENSES.—

(1) IN GENERAL.—A taxpayer may elect to treat qualified architectural and transportation barrier removal expenses which are paid or incurred by him during the taxable year as expenses which are not chargeable to capital account. The expenditures so treated shall be allowed as a deduction.

(2) ELECTION.—An election under paragraph (1) shall be made at such time and in such manner as the Secretary prescribes by regulations.

[Sec. 190(b)]

(b) DEFINITIONS.—For purposes of this section—

(1) ARCHITECTURAL AND TRANSPORTATION BARRIER REMOVAL EXPENSES.—The term "architectural and transportation barrier removal expenses" means an expenditure for the purpose of making

any facility or public transportation vehicle owned or leased by the taxpayer for use in connection with his trade or business more accessible to, and usable by, handicapped and elderly individuals.

(2) QUALIFIED ARCHITECTURAL AND TRANSPORTATION BARRIER REMOVAL EXPENSES.—The term "qualified architectural and transportation barrier removal expense" means, with respect to any such facility or public transportation vehicle, an architectural or transportation barrier removal expense with respect to which the taxpayer establishes, to the satisfaction of the Secretary, that the resulting removal of any such barrier meets the standards promulgated by the Secretary with the concurrence of the Architectural and Transportation Barriers Compliance Board and set forth in regulations prescribed by the Secretary.

(3) HANDICAPPED INDIVIDUAL.—The term "handicapped individual" means any individual who has a physical or mental disability (including, but not limited to, blindness or deafness) which for such individual constitutes or results in a functional limitation to employment, or who has any physical or mental impairment (including, but not limited to, a sight or hearing impairment) which substantially limits one or more major life activities of such individual.

[Sec. 190(c)]

(c) LIMITATION.—The deduction allowed by subsection (a) for any taxable year shall not exceed $15,000.

Amendments

• 1990, Omnibus Budget Reconciliation Act of 1990 (P.L. 101-508)

P.L. 101-508, §11611(c):

Amended Code Sec. 190(c) by striking "$35,000" and inserting "$15,000". **Effective** for tax years beginning after 11-5-90.

• 1984, Deficit Reduction Act of 1984 (P.L. 98-369)

P.L. 98-369, §1062(b):

Amended Code Sec. 190(c) by striking out "$25,000" and inserting in lieu thereof "$35,000". **Effective** for tax years beginning after 12-31-83.

• 1976, Tax Reform Act of 1976 (P.L. 94-455)

P.L. 94-455, §2122(a), as amended by P.L. 96-167, §9(c) and P.L. 98-369, §1062(a):

Added Code Sec. 190. **Effective** for tax years beginning after 12-31-76.

[Sec. 190(d)—Repealed]

Amendments

• 1990, Omnibus Budget Reconciliation Act of 1990 (P.L. 101-508)

P.L. 101-508, §11801(a)(14):

Repealed Code Sec. 190(d). **Effective** 11-5-90. Prior to repeal, Code Sec. 190(d) read as follows:

(d) APPLICATION OF SECTION.—This section shall apply to—

(1) taxable years beginning after December 31, 1976, and before January 1, 1983, and

(2) taxable years beginning after December 31, 1983.

P.L. 101-508, §11821(b), provides:

(b) SAVINGS PROVISION.—If—

(1) any provision amended or repealed by this part applied to—

(A) any transaction occurring before the date of the enactment of this Act,

(B) any property acquired before such date of enactment, or

(C) any item of income, loss, deduction, or credit taken into account before such date of enactment, and

(2) the treatment of such transaction, property, or item under such provision would (without regard to the amendments made by this part) affect liability for tax for periods ending after such date of enactment,

nothing in the amendments made by this part shall be construed to affect the treatment of such transaction, property, or item for purposes of determining liability for tax for periods ending after such date of enactment.

• 1986, Tax Reform Act of 1986 (P.L. 99-514)

P.L. 99-514, §244:

Amended Code Sec. 190(d)(2) by striking out "1983, and before January 1, 1986" and inserting in lieu thereof "1983". **Effective** 10-22-86.

• 1984, Deficit Reduction Act of 1984 (P.L. 98-369)

P.L. 98-369, §1062(a)(1):

Amended Code Sec. 190(d). **Effective** 7-18-84. Prior to amendment, Code Sec. 190(d) read as follows:

(d) REGULATIONS.—The Secretary shall prescribe such regulations as may be necessary to carry out the provisions of this section within 180 days after the date of the enactment of the Tax Reform Act of 1976.

[Sec. 191—Repealed]

Amendments

• 1983, Technical Corrections Act of 1982 (P.L. 97-448)

P.L. 97-448, §102(f)(1):

Amended subparagraph (B) of section 212(e)(2) of P.L. 97-24 to read as under the amendment note for P.L. 97-34, §212(e)(2).

• 1981, Economic Recovery Tax Act of 1981 (P.L. 97-34)

P.L. 97-34, §212(d)(1):

Repealed Code Sec. 191. **Effective** for expenditures incurred after 12-31-81, in tax years ending after such date. But see Act Sec. 212(e)(2), below. Prior to repeal, Code Sec. 191 read as follows:

SEC. 191. AMORTIZATION OF CERTAIN REHABILITATION EXPENDITURES FOR CERTIFIED HISTORIC STRUCTURES.

(a) ALLOWANCE OF DEDUCTION.—Every person, at his election, shall be entitled to a deduction with respect to the amortization of the amortizable basis of any certified historic structure (as defined in subsection (d)) based on a period of 60 months. Such amortization deduction shall be an amount, with respect to each month of such period within the taxable year, equal to the amortizable basis at the end of such month divided by the number of months (including the month for which the deduction is computed) remaining in the period. Such amortizable basis at the end of the month shall be computed without regard to the amortization deduction for such month. The amortization deduction provided by this section with respect to any month shall be in lieu of the depreciation deduction with respect to such basis for such month provided by section 167. The 60-month period shall begin, as to any historic structure, at the election of the taxpayer, with the month following the month in which the basis is acquired, or with the succeeding taxable year.

(b) ELECTION OF AMORTIZATION.—The election of the taxpayer to take the amortization deduction and to begin the 60-month period with the month following the month in which the basis is acquired, or with the taxable year succeeding the taxable year in which such basis is acquired, shall be made by filing with the Secretary, in such manner, in such form, and within such time as the Secretary may by regulations prescribe, a statement of such election.

(c) TERMINATION OF AMORTIZATION DEDUCTION.—A taxpayer who has elected under subsection (b) to take the amortization deduction provided in subsection (a) may, at any time after making such election, discontinue the amortization deduction with respect to the remainder of the amortization period, such discontinuance to begin as of the beginning of any month specified by the taxpayer in a notice in writing filed with the Secretary before the beginning of such month. The depreciation deduction provided under section 167 shall be allowed, beginning with the first month as to which the amortization deduction does not apply, and the taxpayer shall not be entitled to any further amortization deduction under this section with respect to such certified historic structure.

(d) DEFINITIONS.—For purposes of this section—

(1) CERTIFIED HISTORIC STRUCTURE.—The term "certified historic structure" means a building or structure which is of a character subject to the allowance for depreciation provided in section 167 and which—

(A) is listed in the National Register, or

(B) is located in a registered historic district and is certified by the Secretary of the Interior to the Secretary as being of historic significance to the district.

(2) REGISTERED HISTORIC DISTRICT.—The term "registered historic district" means—

(A) any district listed in the National Register, and

(B) any district—

(i) which is designated under a statute of the appropriate State or local government, if such statute is certified by the Secretary of the Interior to the Secretary as containing criteria which will substantially achieve the purpose of preserving and rehabilitating buildings of historic significance to the district, and

(ii) which is certified by the Secretary of the Interior to the Secretary as meeting substantially all of the requirements for the listing of districts in the National Register.

(3) AMORTIZABLE BASIS.—The term "amortizable basis" means the portion of the basis attributable to amounts expended in connection with certified rehabilitation.

(4) CERTIFIED REHABILITATION.—The term "certified rehabilitation" means any rehabilitation of a certified historic structure which the Secretary of the Interior has certified to the Secretary as being consistent with the historic character of such property or the district in which such property is located.

(e) DEPRECIATION DEDUCTION.—The depreciation deduction provided by section 167 shall, despite the provisions of subsection (a), be allowed with respect to the portion of the adjusted basis which is not the amortizable basis.

(f) SPECIAL RULES FOR CERTAIN INTERESTS.—

(1) LIFE TENANT AND REMAINDERMAN.—In the case of property held by one person for life with remainder to another person, the deduction under this section shall be computed as if the life tenant were the absolute owner of the property and shall be allowable to the life tenant.

(2) CERTAIN LESSEES.—

(A) IN GENERAL.—In the case of a lessee of a certified historic structure who has expended amounts in connection with the certified rehabilitation of such structure which are properly chargeable to capital account, the deduction under this section shall be allowable to such lessee with respect to such amounts.

(B) AMORTIZABLE BASIS.—For purposes of subsection (a), the amortizable basis of such lessee shall not exceed the sum of the amounts described in subparagraph (A).

(C) LIMITATION.—Subparagraph (A) shall apply only if on the date the certified rehabilitation is completed, the remaining term of the lease (determined without regard to any renewal periods) extends—

(i) beyond the last day of the useful life (determined without regard to this section) of the improvements for which the amounts described in subparagraph (A) were expended, and

(ii) for not less than 30 years.

(g) APPLICATION OF SECTION.—This section shall apply with respect to additions to capital account made after June 14, 1976, and before January 1, 1984.

(h) CROSS REFERENCES.—

(1) For rules relating to the listing of buildings, structures, and historic districts in the National Register, see the Act entitled "An Act to establish a program for the preservation of additional historic properties throughout the Nation, and for other purposes", approved October 15, 1966 (16 U.S.C. 470 et seq.).

(2) For special rules with respect to certain gain derived from the disposition of property the adjusted basis of which is determined with regard to this section, see sections 1245 and 1250.

P.L. 97-34, §212(e)(2), provides:

(2) TRANSITIONAL RULE—The amendments made by this section shall not apply with respect to any rehabilitation of a building if—

(A) the physical work on such rehabilitation began before January 1, 1982, and

(B) such building does not meet the requirements of paragraph (1) of section 48(g) of the Internal Revenue Code of 1954 (as amended by this Act).

• 1980 (P.L. 96-541)

P.L. 96-541, §2(a):

Redesignated former Code Sec. 191(g) as 191(h) and added a new subsection (g). **Effective** 12-17-80.

• 1980, Technical Corrections Act of 1979 (P.L. 96-222)

P.L. 96-222, §107(a)(1)(E):

Amended Code Sec. 191(f)(2)(C) by changing "the data of" to "the date". **Effective** as provided in P.L. 94-455, §2124(a)(1).

• 1978, Revenue Act of 1978 (P.L. 95-600)

P.L. 95-600, §701(f)(1):

Amended Code Sec. 191(d) by striking out paragraph (1), by redesignating paragraphs (2) and (3) as paragraphs (3) and (4), respectively, and by inserting new paragraphs (1) and (2). **Effective** as provided in P.L. 94-455, §2124(a)(1). Prior to amendment, Code Sec. 191(d)(1) read as follows:

"(1) CERTIFIED HISTORIC STRUCTURE.—The term `certified historic structure' means a building or structure which is of a character subject to the allowance for depreciation provided in section 167 which—

"(A) is listed in the National Register,

"(B) is located in a Registered Historic District and is certified by the Secretary of the Interior as being of historic significance to the district, or

"(C) is located in an historic district designated under a statute of the appropriate State or local government if such statute is certified by the Secretary of the Interior to the Secretary as containing criteria which will substantially achieve the purpose of preserving and rehabilitating buildings of historic significance to the district."

P.L. 95-600, §701(f)(2):

Amended Code Sec. 191(g). **Effective** as provided in P.L. 94-455, §2124(a)(1). Prior to amendment, Code Sec. 191(g) read as follows:

"(g) CROSS REFERENCES.—

"(1) For rules relating to the listing of buildings and structures in the National Register and for definitions of `National Register' and `Registered Historic District', see section 470 et seq. of title 16 of the United States Code.

"(2) For special rule with respect to certain gain derived from the disposition of property the adjusted basis of which is determined with regard to this section, see section 1245."

P.L. 95-600, §701(f)(7):

Amended Code Sec. 191(f). **Effective** as provided in P.L. 94-455, §2124(a)(1). Prior to amendment, Code Sec. 191(f) read as follows:

"(f) LIFE TENANT AND REMAINDERMAN.—In the case of property held by one person for life with remainder to another person, the deduction under this section shall be computed as if the life tenant were the absolute owner of the property and shall be allowable to the life tenant."

• 1976, Tax Reform Act of 1976 (P.L. 94-455)

P.L. 94-455, §2124(a)(1):

Added Code Sec. 191. **Effective** for additions to capital account made after 6-14-76, and before 6-15-81.

[Sec. 192]

SEC. 192. CONTRIBUTIONS TO BLACK LUNG BENEFIT TRUST.

[Sec. 192(a)]

(a) ALLOWANCE OF DEDUCTION.—There is allowed as a deduction for the taxable year an amount equal to the sum of the amounts contributed by the taxpayer during the taxable year to or under a trust or trusts described in section 501(c)(21).

[Sec. 192(b)]

(b) LIMITATION.—The maximum amount of the deduction allowed by subsection (a) for any taxpayer for any taxable year shall not exceed the greater of—

(1) the amount necessary to fund (with level funding) the remaining unfunded liability of the taxpayer for black lung claims filed (or expected to be filed) by (or with respect to) past or present employees of the taxpayer, or

(2) the aggregate amount necessary to increase each trust described in section 501(c)(21) to the amount required to pay all amounts payable out of such trust for the taxable year.

Amendments

• 1978 (P.L. 95-488)

P.L. 95-488, §1(a), (e):

Amended Code Sec. 192(b). **Effective** for tax years beginning after 12-31-77. Prior to amendment, Code Sec. 192(b) read as follows:

(b) LIMITATION.—

(1) IN GENERAL—The amount of the deduction allowed by subsection (a) for any taxable year with respect to any such trust shall not exceed the amount determined under paragraph (2) or (3), whichever is greater.

(2) CURRENT YEAR OBLIGATIONS.—The amount determined under this paragraph for the taxable year is the amount which, when added to the fair market value of the assets of the trust as of the beginning of the taxable year, is necessary to carry out the purposes of the trust described in subparagraph (A) of section 501(c)(21) for the taxable year.

(3) CERTAIN FUTURE OBLIGATIONS.—The amount determined under this paragraph for the taxable year is the sum of—

(A) the amount which is necessary to meet the expenses of the trust described in clause (iii) of section 501(c)(21)(A) for the taxable year, and

(B) the lesser of—

(i) the amount, which, when added to the fair market value of the assets of the trust as of the beginning of the taxable year, is necessary to provide all expected future payments with respect to black lung benefit claims which are approved, including any such claims which have been filed and which have not been disapproved, as of the end of the taxable year, or

(ii) twice the amount which is necessary to provide all expected future payments with respect to the greater of—

(I) black lung benefit claims filed during the taxable year or any one of the 3 immediately preceding taxable years, or

(II) such claims approved during any one of those 4 taxable years.

[Sec. 192(c)]

(c) SPECIAL RULES.—

(1) METHOD OF DETERMINING AMOUNTS REFERRED TO IN SUBSECTION (b).—

(A) IN GENERAL.—The amounts described in subsection (b) shall be determined by using reasonable actuarial methods and assumptions which are not inconsistent with regulations prescribed by the Secretary.

(B) FUNDING PERIOD.—Except as provided in subparagraph (C), the funding period for purposes of subsection (b)(1) shall be the greater of—

(i) the average remaining working life of miners who are present employees of the taxpayer, or

(ii) 10 taxable years.

For purposes of the preceding sentence, the term "miner" has the same meaning as such term has when used in section 402(d) of the Black Lung Benefits Act (30 U.S.C. 902(d)).

(C) DIFFERENT FUNDING PERIODS.—To the extent that—

(i) regulations prescribed by the Secretary provide for a different period, or

(ii) the Secretary consents to a different period proposed by the taxpayer,

such different period shall be substituted for the funding period provided in subparagraph (B).

(2) BENEFIT PAYMENTS TAKEN INTO ACCOUNT.—In determining the amounts described in subsection (b), only those black lung benefit claims the payment of which is expected to be made from the trust shall be taken into account.

(3) TIME WHEN CONTRIBUTIONS DEEMED MADE.—For purposes of this section, a taxpayer shall be deemed to have made a payment of a contribution on the last day of a taxable year if the payment is on account of that taxable year and is made not later than the time prescribed by law for filing the return for that taxable year (including extensions thereof).

(4) CONTRIBUTIONS TO BE IN CASH OR CERTAIN OTHER ITEMS.—No deduction shall be allowed under subsection (a) with respect to any contribution to a trust described in section 501(c)(21) other than a contribution in cash or in items in which such trust may invest under subclause (II) of section 501(c)(21)(A)(ii).

(5) DENIAL OF SECTION 162 DEDUCTION WITH RESPECT TO LIABILITY.—No deduction shall be allowed under section 162(a) with respect to any liability taken into account in determining the deduction under subsection (a) of this section of the taxpayer (or a predecessor).

Amendments

• 1992, Energy Policy Act of 1992 (P.L. 102-486)

P.L. 102-486, §1940(c):

Amended Code Sec. 192(c)(4) by striking "clause (ii) of section 501(c)(21)(B)" and inserting "subclause (II) of section 501(c)(21)(A)(ii)". **Effective** for tax years beginning after 12-31-91.

• 1978 (P.L. 95-488)

P.L. 95-488, §1(b), (e):

Amended Code Sec. 192(c)(1). **Effective** for tax years beginning after 12-31-77. Before amendment, Code Sec. 192(c)(1) read:

"(1) DETERMINATION OF EXPECTED FUTURE PAYMENTS.—The amounts described in subsection (b) shall be determined by using reasonable actuarial assumptions which are not inconsistent with regulations prescribed by the Secretary."

P.L. 95-488, §1(c), (e):

Added Code Sec. 192(c)(5). **Effective** for tax years beginning after 12-31-77.

[Sec. 192(d)]

(d) CARRYOVER OF EXCESS CONTRIBUTIONS—If the amount of the deduction determined under subsection (a) for the taxable year (without regard to the limitation imposed by subsection (b)) with respect to a trust exceeds the limitation imposed by subsection (b) for the taxable year, the excess shall be carried over to the succeeding taxable year and treated as contributed to the trust during that year.

[Sec. 192(e)]

(e) DEFINITION OF BLACK LUNG BENEFIT CLAIM.—For purposes of this section, the term "black lung benefit claim" means a claim for compensation for disability or death due to pneumoconiosis under part C of title IV of the Federal Mine Safety and Health Act of 1977 or under any State law providing for such compensation.

Amendments

• 1980, Technical Corrections Act of 1979 (P.L. 96-222)

P.L. 96-222, §108(b)(2)(B):

Amended Code Sec. 192(e) by changing "Federal Coal Mine Health and Safety Act of 1969" to "Federal Mine Safety and Health Act of 1977". **Effective** for contributions, acts, and expenditures made after 1977, in and for tax years beginning after such date.

• 1978, Black Lung Benefits Revenue Act of 1977 (P.L. 95-227)

P.L. 95-227, §4(b)(1):

Added Code Sec. 192. **Effective** for contributions, acts, and expenditures made after 1977, in and for tax years beginning after such date. However, this effective date was contingent upon enactment of the Black Lung Benefits Reform Act (H.R. 4544), which was enacted as P.L. 95-239, on 3-1-78.

[Sec. 193]

SEC. 193. TERTIARY INJECTANTS.

[Sec. 193(a)]

(a) ALLOWANCE OF DEDUCTION.—There shall be allowed as a deduction for the taxable year an amount equal to the qualified tertiary injectant expenses of the taxpayer for tertiary injectants injected during such taxable year.

[Sec. 193(b)]

(b) QUALIFIED TERTIARY INJECTANT EXPENSES.—For purposes of this section—

(1) IN GENERAL.—The term "qualified tertiary injectant expenses" means any cost paid or incurred (whether or not chargeable to capital account) for any tertiary injectant (other than a hydrocarbon injectant which is recoverable) which is used as a part of a tertiary recovery method.

(2) HYDROCARBON INJECTANT.—The term "hydrocarbon injectant" includes natural gas, crude oil, and any other injectant which is comprised of more than an insignificant amount of natural gas or crude oil. The term does not include any tertiary injectant which is hydrocarbon-based, or a hydrocarbon-derivative, and which is comprised of no more than an insignificant amount of natural gas or crude oil. For purposes of this paragraph, that portion of a hydrocarbon injectant which is not a hydrocarbon shall not be treated as a hydrocarbon injectant.

(3) TERTIARY RECOVERY METHOD.—The term "tertiary recovery method" means—

(A) any method which is described in subparagraphs (1) through (9) of section 212.78(c) of the June 1979 energy regulations (as defined by section 4996(b)(8)(C) as in effect before its repeal), or

(B) any other method to provide tertiary enhanced recovery which is approved by the Secretary for purposes of this section.

Amendments

• 1988, Omnibus Trade and Competitiveness Act of 1988 (P.L. 100-418)

P.L. 100-418, §1941(b)(7):

Amended 193(b)(3)(A) by striking "section 4996(b)(8)(C)" and inserting "section 4996(b)(8)(C) as in effect before its repeal". **Effective** for crude oil removed from the premises on or after 8-23-88.

• 1983, Technical Corrections Act of 1982 (P.L. 97-448)

P.L. 97-448, §202(b):

Amended Code Sec. 193(b)(1) by striking out "during the taxable year". **Effective** as if it had been included in the provision of P.L. 96-223 to which it relates.

[Sec. 193(c)]

(c) APPLICATION WITH OTHER DEDUCTIONS.—No deduction shall be allowed under subsection (a) with respect to any expenditure—

(1) with respect to which the taxpayer has made an election under section 263(c), or

(2) with respect to which a deduction is allowed or allowable to the taxpayer under any other provision of this chapter.

Amendments

• 1980, Crude Oil Windfall Profit Tax Act of 1980 (P.L. 96-223)

P.L. 96-223, §251(a)(1):

Added Code Sec. 193. **Effective** for tax years beginning after 12-31-79.

[Sec. 194]

SEC. 194. TREATMENT OF REFORESTATION EXPENDITURES.

[Sec. 194(a)]

(a) ALLOWANCE OF DEDUCTION.—In the case of any qualified timber property with respect to which the taxpayer has made (in accordance with regulations prescribed by the Secretary) an election under this subsection, the taxpayer shall be entitled to a deduction with respect to the amortization of the amortizable basis of qualified timber property based on a period of 84 months. Such amortization deduction shall be an amount, with respect to each month of such period within the taxable year, equal to the amortizable basis at the end of such month divided by the number of months (including the month for which the deduction is computed) remaining in the period. Such amortizable basis at the end of the month shall be computed without regard to the amortization deduction for such month. The 84-month period shall begin on the first day of the first month of the second half of the taxable year in which the amortizable basis is acquired.

Amendments

• 2004, American Jobs Creation Act of 2004 (P.L. 108-357)

P.L. 108-357, §322(c)(4):

Amended the heading for Code Sec. 194 by striking "**AMORTIZATION**" and inserting "**TREATMENT**". **Effective** with respect to expenditures paid or incurred after 10-22-2004.

• 1980, Recreational Boating Safety and Facilities Improvement Act of 1980 (P.L. 96-451)

P.L. 96-451, §301(a):

Added Code Sec. 194(a). **Effective** with respect to additions to capital accounts made after 12-31-79. (Note: An earlier Code Sec. 194 was added by P.L. 96-364, enacted on 9-26-80.)

[Sec. 194(b)]

(b) TREATMENT AS EXPENSES.—

(1) ELECTION TO TREAT CERTAIN REFORESTATION EXPENDITURES AS EXPENSES.—

(A) IN GENERAL.—In the case of any qualified timber property with respect to which the taxpayer has made (in accordance with regulations prescribed by the Secretary) an election under this subsection, the taxpayer shall treat reforestation expenditures which are paid or incurred during the taxable year with respect to such property as an expense which is not chargeable to capital account. The reforestation expenditures so treated shall be allowed as a deduction.

(B) DOLLAR LIMITATION.—The aggregate amount of reforestation expenditures which may be taken into account under subparagraph (A) with respect to each qualified timber property for any taxable year shall not exceed—

(i) except as provided in clause (ii) or (iii), $10,000,

(ii) in the case of a separate return by a married individual (as defined in section 7703), $5,000, and

(iii) in the case of a trust, zero.

(2) ALLOCATION OF DOLLAR LIMIT.—

(A) CONTROLLED GROUP.—For purposes of applying the dollar limitation under paragraph (1)(B)—

(i) all component members of a controlled group shall be treated as one taxpayer, and

(ii) the Secretary shall, under regulations prescribed by him, apportion such dollar limitation among the component members of such controlled group.

For purposes of the preceding sentence, the term "controlled group" has the meaning assigned to it by section 1563(a), except that the phrase "more than 50 percent" shall be substituted for the phrase "at least 80 percent" each place it appears in section 1563(a)(1).

(B) PARTNERSHIPS AND S CORPORATIONS.—In the case of a partnership, the dollar limitation contained in paragraph (1)(B) shall apply with respect to the partnership and with respect to each partner. A similar rule shall apply in the case of an S corporation and its shareholders.

Amendments

• 2005, Gulf Opportunity Zone Act of 2005 (P.L. 109-135)

P.L. 109-135, §403(i)(1)(A):

Amended Code Sec. 194(b)(1)(B). **Effective** as if included in the provision of the American Jobs Creation Act of 2004 (P.L. 108-357) to which it relates [**effective** with respect to expenditures paid or incurred after 10-22-2004.—CCH]. Prior to amendment, Code Sec. 194(b)(1)(B) read as follows:

(B) DOLLAR LIMITATION.—The aggregate amount of reforestation expenditures which may be taken into account under subparagraph (A) with respect to each qualified timber property for any taxable year shall not exceed $10,000 ($5,000 in the case of a separate return by a married individual (as defined in section 7703)).

• 2004, American Jobs Creation Act of 2004 (P.L. 108-357)

P.L. 108-357, §322(a):

Amended so much of Code Sec. 194(b) as precedes paragraph (2). **Effective** with respect to expenditures paid or incurred after 10-22-2004. Prior to amendment, so much of Code Sec. 194(b) as precedes paragraph (2) read as follows:

(b) LIMITATIONS.—

(1) MAXIMUM DOLLAR AMOUNT.—The aggregate amount of amortizable basis acquired during the taxable year which may be taken into account under subsection (a) for such taxable year shall not exceed $10,000 ($5,000 in the case of a separate return by a married individual (as defined in section 7703)).

P.L. 108-357, §322(c)(1):

Amended Code Sec. 194(b) by striking paragraphs (3) and (4). **Effective** with respect to expenditures paid or incurred after 10-22-2004. Prior to amendment Code Sec. 194(b)(3) and (4) read as follows:

(3) SECTION NOT TO APPLY TO TRUSTS.—This section shall not apply to trusts.

(4) ESTATES.—The benefit of the deduction for amortization provided by this section shall be allowed to estates in the same manner as in the case of an individual. The allowable deduction shall be apportioned between the income beneficiary and the fiduciary under regulations prescribed by the Secretary. Any amount so apportioned to a beneficiary shall be taken into account for purposes of determining the amount allowable as a deduction under this section to such beneficiary.

P.L. 108-357, §322(c)(2):

Amended Code Sec. 194(b)(2) by striking "paragraph (1)" both places it appears and inserting "paragraph (1)(B)". **Effective** with respect to expenditures paid or incurred after 10-22-2004.

• 1986, Tax Reform Act of 1986 (P.L. 99-514)

P.L. 99-514, §1301(j)(8):

Amended Code Sec. 194(b)(1) by striking out "section 143" each place it appears and inserting in lieu thereof "section 7703". **Effective** for bonds issued after 8-15-86.

• 1982, Subchapter S Revision Act of 1982 (P.L. 97-354)

P.L. 97-354, §3(g):

Amended Code Sec. 194(b)(2)(B) by adding at the end thereof "A similar rule shall apply in the case of an S corporation and its shareholders.", and by striking out "PARTNERSHIPS" in the subparagraph heading and inserting in lieu thereof "PARTNERSHIPS AND S CORPORATIONS". **E ffective** for tax years beginning after 12-31-82.

• 1980, Recreational Boating Safety and Facilities Improvement Act of 1980 (P.L. 96-451)

P.L. 96-451, §301(a):

Added Code Sec. 194(b). **Effective** for additions to capital account made after 12-31-79. (Note: An earlier Code Section 194 was added by P.L. 96-364, enacted on 9-26-80.)

[Sec. 194(c)]

(c) DEFINITIONS AND SPECIAL RULE.—For purposes of this section—

(1) QUALIFIED TIMBER PROPERTY.—The term "qualified timber property" means a woodlot or other site located in the United States which will contain trees in significant commercial quantities and which is held by the taxpayer for the planting, cultivating, caring for, and cutting of trees for sale or use in the commercial production of timber products.

(2) AMORTIZABLE BASIS.—The term "amortizable basis" means that portion of the basis of the qualified timber property attributable to reforestation expenditures which have not been taken into account under subsection (b).

(3) REFORESTATION EXPENDITURES.—

(A) IN GENERAL.—The term "reforestation expenditures" means direct costs incurred in connection with forestation or reforestation by planting or artificial or natural seeding, including costs—

(i) for the preparation of the site;

(ii) of seeds or seedlings; and

(iii) for labor and tools, including depreciation of equipment such as tractors, trucks, tree planters, and similar machines used in planting or seeding.

(B) COST-SHARING PROGRAMS.—Reforestation expenditures shall not include any expenditures for which the taxpayer has been reimbursed under any governmental reforestation cost-sharing program unless the amounts reimbursed have been included in the gross income of the taxpayer.

(4) TREATMENT OF TRUSTS AND ESTATES.—The aggregate amount of reforestation expenditures incurred by any trust or estate shall be apportioned between the income beneficiaries and the fiduciary under regulations prescribed by the Secretary. Any amount so apportioned to a beneficiary shall be taken into account as expenditures incurred by such beneficiary in applying this section to such beneficiary.

(5) APPLICATION WITH OTHER DEDUCTIONS.—No deduction shall be allowed under any other provision of this chapter with respect to any expenditure with respect to which a deduction is allowed or allowable under this section to the taxpayer.

Amendments

• 2005, Gulf Opportunity Zone Act of 2005 (P.L. 109-135)

P.L. 109-135, §403(i)(1)(B):

Amended Code Sec. 194(c)(4). **Effective** as if included in the provision of the American Jobs Creation Act of 2004 (P.L. 108-357) to which it relates [**effective** with respect to expenditures paid or incurred after 10-22-2004.—CCH]. Prior to amendment, Code Sec. 194(c)(4) read as follows:

(4) TREATMENT OF TRUSTS AND ESTATES.—

(A) IN GENERAL.—Except as provided in subparagraph (B), this section shall not apply to trusts and estates.

(B) AMORTIZATION DEDUCTION ALLOWED TO ESTATES.—The benefit of the deduction for amortization provided by subsection (a) shall be allowed to estates in the same manner as in the case of an individual. The allowable deduction shall be apportioned between the income beneficiary and the fiduciary under regulations prescribed by the Secretary. Any amount so apportioned to a beneficiary shall be taken into account for purposes of determining the amount allowable as a deduction under subsection (a) to such beneficiary.

• 2004, American Jobs Creation Act of 2004 (P.L. 108-357)

P.L. 108-357, §322(b):

Amended Code Sec. 194(c)(2) by inserting "which have not been taken into account under subsection (b)" after "expenditures". **Effective** with respect to expenditures paid or incurred after 10-22-2004.

P.L. 108-357, §322(c)(3):

Amended Code Sec. 194(c) by striking paragraph (4) and inserting new paragraphs (4) and (5). **Effective** with respect to expenditures paid or incurred after 10-22-2004. Prior to being stricken, Code Sec. 194(c)(4) read as follows:

(4) BASIS ALLOCATION.—If the amount of the amortizable basis acquired during the taxable year of all qualified timber property with respect to which the taxpayer has made an election under subsection (a) exceeds the amount of the limitation under subsection (b)(1), the taxpayer shall allocate that portion of such amortizable basis with respect to which a deduction is allowable under subsection (a) to each such qualified timber property in such manner as the Secretary may by regulations prescribe.

• 1980, Recreational Boating Safety and Facilities Improvement Act of 1980 (P.L. 96-451)

P.L. 96-451, §301(a):

Added Code Sec. 194(c). **Effective** for additions to capital account made after 12-31-79. (Note: An earlier Code Section 194 was added by P.L. 96-364, enacted on 9-26-80.)

[Sec. 194(d)]

(d) LIFE TENANT AND REMAINDERMAN.—In the case of property held by one person for life with remainder to another person, the deduction under this section shall be computed as if the life tenant were the absolute owner of the property and shall be allowed to the life tenant.

Amendments

• 1980, Recreational Boating Safety and Facilities Improvement Act of 1980 (P.L. 96-451)

P.L. 96-451, §301(a):

Added Code Sec. 194(d). **Effective** for additions to capital account made after 12-31-79. (Note: An earlier Code Section 194 was added by P.L. 96-364, enacted on 9-26-80.)

[Sec. 194A]

SEC. 194A. CONTRIBUTIONS TO EMPLOYER LIABILITY TRUSTS.

[Sec. 194A(a)]

(a) ALLOWANCE OF DEDUCTION.—There shall be allowed as a deduction for the taxable year an amount equal to the amount—

(1) which is contributed by an employer to a trust described in section 501(c)(22) (relating to withdrawal liability payment fund) which meets the requirements of section 4223(h) of the Employee Retirement Income Security Act of 1974, and

(2) which is properly allocable to such taxable year.

Amendments

• 1980, Multiemployer Pension Plan Amendments Act of 1980 (P.L. 96-364)

P.L. 96-364, §209(c):

Added Code Sec. 194(a). **Effective** for tax years ending after 9-26-80. [Note: A subsequent Code Section 194 was added by P.L. 96-451, enacted on 10-14-80, **effective** for additions to capital account made after 12-31-79.—CCH.]

[Sec. 194A(b)]

(b) ALLOCATION TO TAXABLE YEAR.—In the case of a contribution described in subsection (a) which relates to any specified period of time which includes more than one taxable year, the amount properly allocable to any taxable year in such period shall be determined by prorating such amounts to such taxable years under regulations prescribed by the Secretary.

Amendments

• 1980, Multiemployer Pension Plan Amendments Act of 1980 (P.L. 96-364)

P.L. 96-364, §209(c):

Added Code Sec. 194(b). **Effective** for tax years ending after 9-26-80. [Note: A subsequent Code Section 194 was added by P.L. 96-451, enacted on 10-14-80, **effective** for additions to capital account made after 12-31-79.—CCH.]

[Sec. 194A(c)]

(c) DISALLOWANCE OF DEDUCTION.—No deduction shall be allowed under subsection (a) with respect to any contribution described in subsection (a) which does not relate to any specified period of time.

Amendments

• 1983, Technical Corrections Act of 1982 (P.L. 97-448)

P.L. 97-448, §305(b)(1):

Redesignated Code Sec. 194 (relating to contributions to employer liability trusts) as Code Sec. 194A. **Effective** 10-14-80.

• 1980, Multiemployer Pension Plan Amendments Act of 1980 (P.L. 96-364)

P.L. 96-364, §209(c):

Added Code Sec. 194(c). **Effective** for tax years ending after 9-26-80. [Note: A subsequent Code Section 194 was added by P.L. 96-451, enacted on 10-14-80, effective for additions to capital account made after 12-31-79.—CCH.]

[Sec. 195]

SEC. 195. START-UP EXPENDITURES.

[Sec. 195(a)]

(a) CAPITALIZATION OF EXPENDITURES.—Except as otherwise provided in this section, no deduction shall be allowed for start-up expenditures.

[Sec. 195(b)]

(b) ELECTION TO DEDUCT.—

(1) ALLOWANCE OF DEDUCTION.—If a taxpayer elects the application of this subsection with respect to any start-up expenditures—

(A) the taxpayer shall be allowed a deduction for the taxable year in which the active trade or business begins in an amount equal to the lesser of—

(i) the amount of start-up expenditures with respect to the active trade or business, or

(ii) $5,000, reduced (but not below zero) by the amount by which such start-up expenditures exceed $50,000, and

(B) the remainder of such start-up expenditures shall be allowed as a deduction ratably over the 180-month period beginning with the month in which the active trade or business begins.

(2) DISPOSITIONS BEFORE CLOSE OF AMORTIZATION PERIOD.—In any case in which a trade or business is completely disposed of by the taxpayer before the end of the period to which paragraph (1) applies, any deferred expenses attributable to such trade or business which were not allowed as a deduction by reason of this section may be deducted to the extent allowable under section 165.

(3) SPECIAL RULE FOR TAXABLE YEARS BEGINNING IN 2010.—In the case of a taxable year beginning in 2010, paragraph (1)(A)(ii) shall be applied—

(A) by substituting "$10,000" for "$5,000", and

(B) by substituting "$60,000" for "$50,000".

Amendments

• 2010, Creating Small Business Jobs Act of 2010 (P.L. 111-240)

P.L. 111-240, §2031(a):

Amended Code Sec. 195(b) by adding at the end a new paragraph (3). **Effective** for amounts paid or incurred in tax years beginning after 12-31-2009.

• 2004, American Jobs Creation Act of 2004 (P.L. 108-357)

P.L. 108-357, §902(a)(1):

Amended Code Sec. 195(b)(1). **Effective** for amounts paid or incurred after 10-22-2004. Prior to amendment, Code Sec. 195(b)(1) read as follows:

(1) IN GENERAL.—Start-up expenditures may, at the election of the taxpayer, be treated as deferred expenses. Such deferred expenses shall be allowed as a deduction prorated equally over such period of not less than 60 months as may be selected by the taxpayer (beginning with the month in which the active trade or business begins).

P.L. 108-357, §902(a)(2):

Amended Code Sec. 195(b) by striking "AMORTIZE" and inserting "DEDUCT" in the heading. **Effective** for amounts paid or incurred after 10-22-2004.

[Sec. 195(c)]

(c) DEFINITIONS.—For purposes of this section—

(1) START-UP EXPENDITURES.—The term "start-up expenditure" means any amount—

(A) paid or incurred in connection with—

(i) investigating the creation or acquisition of an active trade or business, or

(ii) creating an active trade or business, or

(iii) any activity engaged in for profit and for the production of income before the day on which the active trade or business begins, in anticipation of such activity becoming an active trade or business, and

(B) which, if paid or incurred in connection with the operation of an existing active trade or business (in the same field as the trade or business referred to in subparagraph (A)), would be allowable as a deduction for the taxable year in which paid or incurred.

The term "start-up expenditure" does not include any amount with respect to which a deduction is allowable under section 163(a), 164, or 174.

(2) BEGINNING OF TRADE OR BUSINESS.—

(A) IN GENERAL.—Except as provided in subparagraph (B), the determination of when an active trade or business begins shall be made in accordance with such regulations as the Secretary may prescribe.

(B) ACQUIRED TRADE OR BUSINESS.—An acquired active trade or business shall be treated as beginning when the taxpayer acquires it.

[Sec. 195(d)]

(d) ELECTION.—

(1) TIME FOR MAKING ELECTION.—An election under subsection (b) shall be made not later than the time prescribed by law for filing the return for the taxable year in which the trade or business begins (including extensions thereof).

(2) SCOPE OF ELECTION.—The period selected under subsection (b) shall be adhered to in computing taxable income for the taxable year for which the election is made and all subsequent taxable years.

Amendments

• 1984, Deficit Reduction Act of 1984 (P.L. 98-369)

P.L. 98-369, §94(a):

Amended Code Sec. 195. **Effective** for tax years beginning after 6-30-84. Prior to amendment, Code Sec. 195 read as follows:

SEC. 195. START-UP EXPENDITURES.

(a) ELECTION TO AMORTIZE.—Start-up expenditures may, at the election of the taxpayer, be treated as deferred expenses. Such deferred expenses shall be allowed as a deduction ratably over such period of not less than 60 months as may be selected by the taxpayer (beginning with the month in which the business begins).

(b) START-UP EXPENDITURES.—For purposes of this section, the term "start-up expenditure" means any amount—

(1) paid or incurred in connection with—

(A) investigating the creation or acquisition of an active trade or business, or

(B) creating an active trade or business, and

(2) which, if paid or incurred in connection with the expansion of an existing trade or business (in the same field as the trade or business referred to in paragraph (1)), would be allowable as a deduction for the taxable year in which paid or incurred.

(c) ELECTION.—

(1) TIME FOR MAKING ELECTION.—An election under subsection (a) shall be made not later than the time prescribed by law for filing the return for the taxable year in which the business begins (including extensions thereof).

(2) SCOPE OF ELECTION.—The period selected under subsection (a) shall be adhered to in computing taxable income for the taxable year for which the election is made and all subsequent taxable years.

(3) MANNER OF MAKING ELECTION.—An election under subsection (a) shall be made in such manner as the Secretary shall by regulations prescribe.

(d) BUSINESS BEGINNING.—For purposes of this section, an acquired trade or business shall be treated as beginning when the taxpayer acquires it.

• 1980, Miscellaneous Revenue Act of 1980 (P.L. 96-605)

P.L. 96-605, §102(a):

Added Code Sec. 195(d). **Effective** for amounts paid or incurred after 7-29-80, in tax years ending after such date.

[Sec. 196]

SEC. 196. DEDUCTION FOR CERTAIN UNUSED BUSINESS CREDITS.

[Sec. 196(a)]

(a) ALLOWANCE OF DEDUCTION.—If any portion of the qualified business credits determined for any taxable year has not, after the application of section 38(c), been allowed to the taxpayer as a credit under section 38 for any taxable year, an amount equal to the credit not so allowed shall be allowed to the taxpayer as a deduction for the first taxable year following the last taxable year for which such credit could, under section 39, have been allowed as a credit.

[Sec. 196(b)]

(b) TAXPAYER'S DYING OR CEASING TO EXIST.—If a taxpayer dies or ceases to exist before the first taxable year following the last taxable year for which the qualified business credits could, under section 39, have been allowed as a credit, the amount described in subsection (a) (or the proper portion thereof) shall, under regulations prescribed by the Secretary, be allowed to the taxpayer as a deduction for the taxable year in which such death or cessation occurs.

[Sec. 196(c)]

(c) QUALIFIED BUSINESS CREDITS.—For purposes of this section, the term "qualified business credits" means—

(1) the investment credit determined under section 46 (but only to the extent attributable to property the basis of which is reduced by section 50(c)),

(2) the work opportunity credit determined under section 51(a),

(3) the alcohol fuels credit determined under section 40(a),

(4) the research credit determined under section 41(a) (other than such credit determined under section 280C(c)(3)) for taxable years beginning after December 31, 1988,

(5) the enhanced oil recovery credit determined under section 43(a),

(6) the empowerment zone employment credit determined under section 1396(a),

(7) the Indian employment credit determined under section 45A(a),
(8) the employer Social Security credit determined under section 45B(a),
(9) the new markets tax credit determined under section 45D(a),
(10) the small employer pension plan startup cost credit determined under section 45E(a),
(11) the biodiesel fuels credit determined under section 40A(a),
(12) the low sulfur diesel fuel production credit determined under section 45H(a),
(13) the new energy efficient home credit determined under section 45L(a), and
(14) the small employer health insurance credit determined under section 45R(a).

Amendments

• 2010, Patient Protection and Affordable Care Act (P.L. 111-148)

P.L. 111-148, §1421(d)(2):

Amended Code Sec. 196(c) by striking "and" at the end of paragraph (12), by striking the period at the end of paragraph (13) and inserting ", and", and by adding at the end a new paragraph (14). **Effective** for amounts paid or incurred in tax years beginning after 12-31-2009 [**effective** date amended by Act Sec. 10105(e)(4).—CCH].

• 2006, Pension Protection Act of 2006 (P.L. 109-280)

P.L. 109-280, §811, provides:

SEC. 811. PENSIONS AND INDIVIDUAL RETIREMENT ARRANGEMENT PROVISIONS OF ECONOMIC GROWTH AND TAX RELIEF RECONCILIATION ACT OF 2001 MADE PERMANENT.

Title IX of the Economic Growth and Tax Relief Reconciliation Act of 2001 [P.L. 107-16] shall not apply to the provisions of, and amendments made by, subtitles A through F of title VI [§§601-666]of such Act (relating to pension and individual retirement arrangement provisions).

• 2005, Energy Tax Incentives Act of 2005 (P.L. 109-58)

P.L. 109-58, §1332(d):

Amended Code Sec. 196(c) by striking "and" at the end of paragraph (11), by striking the period at the end of paragraph (12) and inserting ", and", and by adding at the end a new paragraph (13). **Effective** for qualified new energy efficient homes acquired after 12-31-2005, in tax years ending after such date.

• 2004, American Jobs Creation Act of 2004 (P.L. 108-357)

P.L. 108-357, §302(c)(2):

Amended Code Sec. 196(c) by striking "and" at the end of paragraph (9), by striking the period at the end of paragraph (10) and inserting ", and", and by adding at the end a new paragraph (11). **Effective** for fuel produced, and sold or used, after 12-31-2004, in tax years ending after such date.

P.L. 108-357, §339(e):

Amended Code Sec. 196(c), as amended by Act Sec. 302(c)(2), by striking "and" at the end of paragraph (10), by striking the period at the end of paragraph (11) and inserting ", and", and by adding after paragraph (11) a new paragraph (12). **Effective** for expenses paid or incurred after 12-31-2002, in tax years ending after such date.

• 2001, Economic Growth and Tax Relief Reconciliation Act of 2001 (P.L. 107-16)

P.L. 107-16, §619(c)(2):

Amended Code Sec. 196(c) by striking "and" at the end of paragraph (8), by striking the period at the end of paragraph (9) and inserting ", and", and by adding at the end a new paragraph (10). **Effective** for costs paid or incurred in tax years beginning after 12-31-2001, with respect to qualified employer plans first effective after such date [**effective** date amended by P.L. 107-147, §411(m)(2)].

P.L. 107-16, §901(a)-(b), provides [but see P.L. 109-280, §811, above]:

SEC. 901. SUNSET OF PROVISIONS OF ACT.

(a) IN GENERAL.—All provisions of, and amendments made by, this Act shall not apply—

(1) to taxable, plan, or limitation years beginning after December 31, 2010, or

(2) in the case of title V, to estates of decedents dying, gifts made, or generation skipping transfers, after December 31, 2010.

(b) APPLICATION OF CERTAIN LAWS.—The Internal Revenue Code of 1986 and the Employee Retirement Income Security Act of 1974 shall be applied and administered to years, estates, gifts, and transfers described in subsection (a) as if the provisions and amendments described in subsection (a) had never been enacted.

• 2000, Community Renewal Tax Relief Act of 2000 (P.L. 106-554)

P.L. 106-554, §121(c):

Amended Code Sec. 196(c) by striking "and" at the end of paragraph (7), by striking the period at the end of paragraph (8) and inserting ", and", and by adding at the end a new paragraph (9). **Effective** for investments made after 12-31-2000.

• 1998, IRS Restructuring and Reform Act of 1998 (P.L. 105-206)

P.L. 105-206, §6020(a):

Amended Code Sec. 196(c) by striking "and" at the end of paragraph (6), by striking the period at the end of paragraph (7) and inserting ", and", and by adding at the end a new paragraph (8). **Effective** as if included in the amendments made by section 13443 of P.L. 103-66 [**effective** for taxes paid after 12-31-93.—CCH].

• 1996, Small Business Job Protection Act of 1996 (P.L. 104-188)

P.L. 104-188, §1201(e)(1):

Amended Code Sec. 196(c)[2] by striking "targeted jobs credit" each place it appears and inserting "work opportunity credit". **Effective** for individuals who begin work for the employer after 9-30-96.

• 1993, Omnibus Budget Reconciliation Act of 1993 (P.L. 103-66)

P.L. 103-66, §13302(b)(2):

Amended Code Sec. 196(c) by striking "and" at the end of paragraph (4), by striking the period at the end of paragraph (5) and inserting ", and", and by adding at the end a new paragraph (6). **Effective** 8-10-93.

P.L. 103-66, §13322(c)(2):

Amended Code Sec. 196(c) by striking "and" at the end of paragraph (5), by striking the period at the end of paragraph (6) and inserting ", and", and by adding at the end a new paragraph (7). **Effective** for wages paid or incurred after 12-31-93.

• 1990, Omnibus Budget Reconciliation Act of 1990 (P.L. 101-508)

P.L. 101-508, §11511(b)(3):

Amended Code Sec. 196(c) by striking "and" at the end of paragraph (3), by striking the period at the end of paragraph (4) and inserting ", and", and by adding at the end thereof new paragraph (5). **Effective**, generally, for costs paid or incurred in tax years beginning after 12-31-90. However, for a special rule see Act Sec. 11511(d)(2), below.

P.L. 101-508, §11511(d)(2), provides:

(2) SPECIAL RULE FOR SIGNIFICANT EXPANSION OF PROJECTS.—For purposes of section 43(c)(2)(A)(iii) of the Internal Revenue Code of 1986 (as added by subsection (a)), any significant expansion after December 31, 1990, of a project begun before January 1, 1991, shall be treated as a project with respect to which the first injection commences after December 31, 1990.

P.L. 101-508, §11813(b)(12)(A)(i)-(ii):

Amended Code Sec. 196(c)(1) by striking "section 46(a)" and inserting "section 46", and by striking "section 48(q)" and inserting "section 50(c)". **Effective**, generally, for property placed in service after 12-31-90. However, for exceptions see Act Sec. 11813(c)(2), below.

P.L. 101-508, §11813(c)(2), provides:

(2) EXCEPTIONS.—The amendments made by this section shall not apply to—

(A) any transition property (as defined in section 49(e) of the Internal Revenue Code of 1986 (as in effect on the day before the date of the enactment of this Act),

(B) any property with respect to which qualified progress expenditures were previously taken into account under section 46(d) of such Code (as so in effect), and

(C) any property described in section 46(b)(2)(C) of such Code (as so in effect).

• 1989, Omnibus Budget Reconciliation Act of 1989 (P.L. 101-239)

P.L. 101-239, §7814(e)(2)(D):

Amended Code Sec. 196(c)(4) by inserting "(other than such credit determined under section 280C(c)(3))" after "section 41(a)". **Effective** as if included in the provision of P.L. 100-647 to which it relates.

• 1988, Technical and Miscellaneous Revenue Act of 1988 (P.L. 100-647)

P.L. 100-647, §4008(b)(2)(A):

Amended Code Sec. 196(c) by striking out "and" at the end of paragraph (2), by striking out the period at the end of paragraph (3) and inserting in lieu thereof ", and", and by adding at the end thereof new paragraph (4). **Effective** for tax years beginning after 12-31-88.

[Sec. 196(d)]

(d) SPECIAL RULE FOR INVESTMENT TAX CREDIT AND RESEARCH CREDIT.—Subsection (a) shall be applied by substituting "an amount equal to 50 percent of" for "an amount equal to" in the case of—

(1) the investment credit determined under section 46 (other than the rehabilitation credit), and

(2) the research credit determined under section 41(a) for a taxable year beginning before January 1, 1990.

Amendments

• 1990, Omnibus Budget Reconciliation Act of 1990 (P.L. 101-508)

P.L. 101-508, §11813(b)(12)(B)(i)-(ii):

Amended Code Sec. 196(d)(1) by striking "section 46(a)" and inserting "section 46", and by striking "other than a credit to which section 48(q)(3) applies" and inserting "other than the rehabilitation credit". **Effective**, generally, for property placed in service after 12-31-90. However, for exceptions see Act Sec. 11813(c)(2) in the amendment notes following Code Sec. 196(c).

• 1989, Omnibus Budget Reconciliation Act of 1989 (P.L. 101-239)

P.L. 101-239, §7110(c)[(d)](2):

Amended Code Sec. 196(d)(2) by inserting before the period "for a taxable year beginning before January 1, 1990". **Effective** for tax years beginning after 12-31-89.

P.L. 101-239, §7814(e)(1):

Amended Code Sec. 196(d) by striking "substituting" and all that follows through "in the case of—" and inserting "substituting `an amount equal to 50 percent of' for `an amount equal to' in the case of—". **Effective** as if included in the provision of P.L. 100-647 to which it relates. Prior to amendment, Code Sec. 196(d) read as follows:

(d) SPECIAL RULE FOR INVESTMENT TAX CREDIT AND RESEARCH CREDIT.—Subsection (a) shall be applied by substituting ["]an amount equal to 50 percent of["] for ["]an amount equal to["] in the case of—

(1) the investment credit determined under section 46(a) (other than a credit to which section 48(q)(3) applies), and

(2) the research credit determined under section 41(a).

• 1988, Technical and Miscellaneous Revenue Act of 1988 (P.L. 100-647)

P.L. 100-647, §4008(b)(2)(B):

Amended Code Sec. 196(d). **Effective** for tax years beginning after 12-31-88. Prior to amendment, Code Sec. 196(d) read as follows:

(d) SPECIAL RULE FOR INVESTMENT TAX CREDIT.—In the case of the investment credit determined under section 46(a) (other than a credit to which section 48(q)(3) applies), subsection (a) shall be applied by substituting "an amount equal to 50 percent of" for "an amount equal to".

• 1984, Deficit Reduction Act of 1984 (P.L. 98-369)

P.L. 98-369, §474(r)(8)(A):

Amended Code Sec. 196. **Effective** for tax years beginning after 12-31-83, and to carrybacks from such years. Prior to amendment, Code Sec. 196 read as follows:

SEC. 196. DEDUCTION FOR CERTAIN UNUSED INVESTMENT CREDITS.

(a) ALLOWANCE OF DEDUCTIONS.—If—

(1) the amount of the credit determined under section 46(a)(2) for any taxable year exceeds the limitation provided by section 46(a)(3) for such taxable year, and

(2) the amount of such excess has not, after the application of section 46(b), been allowed to the taxpayer as a credit under section 38 for any taxable year,

then an amount equal to 50 percent of the amount of such excess (to the extent attributable to property the basis of which is reduced under section 48(q)) not so allowed as a credit shall be allowed to the taxpayer as a deduction for the first taxable year following the last taxable year in which such excess could under section 46(b) have been allowed as a credit.

(b) TAXPAYERS DYING OR CEASING TO EXIST.—If a taxpayer dies or ceases to exist prior to the first taxable year following the last taxable year in which the excess described in subsection (a) could under section 46(b) have been allowed as a credit, the amount described in subsection (a), or the proper portion thereof, shall, under regulations prescribed by the Secretary, be allowed to the taxpayer as a deduction for the taxable year in which such death or cessation occurs.

(c) SPECIAL RULE FOR QUALIFIED REHABILITATED BUILDINGS.—In the case of any credit to which section 48(q)(3) applies, subsection (a) shall be applied without regard to the phrase "50 percent of".

• 1982, Tax Equity and Fiscal Responsibility Act of 1982 (P.L. 97-248)

P.L. 97-248, §205(a)(2):

Amended Part VI of Subchapter B of chapter 1 (relating to itemized deductions for individuals and corporations) by adding at the end thereof new Code section 196. **Effective** for periods after 12-31-82, under rules similar to the rules of Code Sec. 48(m). For an exception, see the amendment note for P.L. 97-248, Act Sec. 207(d) following Code Sec. 48.

[Sec. 197]

SEC. 197. AMORTIZATION OF GOODWILL AND CERTAIN OTHER INTANGIBLES.

[Sec. 197(a)]

(a) GENERAL RULE.—A taxpayer shall be entitled to an amortization deduction with respect to any amortizable section 197 intangible. The amount of such deduction shall be determined by amortizing the adjusted basis (for purposes of determining gain) of such intangible ratably over the 15-year period beginning with the month in which such intangible was acquired.

[Sec. 197(b)]

(b) NO OTHER DEPRECIATION OR AMORTIZATION DEDUCTION ALLOWABLE.—Except as provided in subsection (a), no depreciation or amortization deduction shall be allowable with respect to any amortizable section 197 intangible.

[Sec. 197(c)]

(c) AMORTIZABLE SECTION 197 INTANGIBLE.—For purposes of this section—

(1) IN GENERAL.—Except as otherwise provided in this section, the term "amortizable section 197 intangible" means any section 197 intangible—

(A) which is acquired by the taxpayer after the date of the enactment of this section, and

(B) which is held in connection with the conduct of a trade or business or an activity described in section 212.

(2) EXCLUSION OF SELF-CREATED INTANGIBLES, ETC.—The term "amortizable section 197 intangible" shall not include any section 197 intangible—

(A) which is not described in subparagraph (D), (E), or (F) of subsection (d)(1), and

(B) which is created by the taxpayer.

This paragraph shall not apply if the intangible is created in connection with a transaction (or series of related transactions) involving the acquisition of assets constituting a trade or business or substantial portion thereof.

(3) ANTI-CHURNING RULES.—

For exclusion of intangibles acquired in certain transactions, see subsection (f)(9).

[Sec. 197(d)]

(d) SECTION 197 INTANGIBLE.—For purposes of this section—

(1) IN GENERAL.—Except as otherwise provided in this section, the term "section 197 intangible" means—

(A) goodwill,

(B) going concern value,

(C) any of the following intangible items:

(i) workforce in place including its composition and terms and conditions (contractual or otherwise) of its employment,

(ii) business books and records, operating systems, or any other information base (including lists or other information with respect to current or prospective customers),

(iii) any patent, copyright, formula, process, design, pattern, knowhow, format, or other similar item,

(iv) any customer-based intangible,

(v) any supplier-based intangible, and

(vi) any other similar item,

(D) any license, permit, or other right granted by a governmental unit or an agency or instrumentality thereof,

(E) any covenant not to compete (or other arrangement to the extent such arrangement has substantially the same effect as a covenant not to compete) entered into in connection with an acquisition (directly or indirectly) of an interest in a trade or business or substantial portion thereof, and

(F) any franchise, trademark, or trade name.

(2) CUSTOMER-BASED INTANGIBLE.—

(A) IN GENERAL.—The term "customer-based intangible" means—

(i) composition of market,

(ii) market share, and

(iii) any other value resulting from future provision of goods or services pursuant to relationships (contractual or otherwise) in the ordinary course of business with customers.

(B) SPECIAL RULE FOR FINANCIAL INSTITUTIONS.—In the case of a financial institution, the term "customer-based intangible" includes deposit base and similar items.

(3) SUPPLIER-BASED INTANGIBLE.—The term "supplier-based intangible" means any value resulting from future acquisitions of goods or services pursuant to relationships (contractual or otherwise) in the ordinary course of business with suppliers of goods or services to be used or sold by the taxpayer.

[Sec. 197(e)]

(e) EXCEPTIONS.—For purposes of this section, the term "section 197 intangible" shall not include any of the following:

(1) FINANCIAL INTERESTS.—Any interest—

(A) in a corporation, partnership, trust, or estate, or

(B) under an existing futures contract, foreign currency contract, notional principal contract, or other similar financial contract.

(2) LAND.—Any interest in land.

(3) COMPUTER SOFTWARE.—

(A) IN GENERAL.—Any—

(i) computer software which is readily available for purchase by the general public, is subject to a nonexclusive license, and has not been substantially modified, and

(ii) other computer software which is not acquired in a transaction (or series of related transactions) involving the acquisition of assets constituting a trade or business or substantial portion thereof.

(B) COMPUTER SOFTWARE DEFINED.—For purposes of subparagraph (A), the term "computer software" means any program designed to cause a computer to perform a desired function. Such term shall not include any data base or similar item unless the data base or item is in the public domain and is incidental to the operation of otherwise qualifying computer software.

(4) CERTAIN INTERESTS OR RIGHTS ACQUIRED SEPARATELY.—Any of the following not acquired in a transaction (or series of related transactions) involving the acquisition of assets constituting a trade business or substantial portion thereof:

(A) Any interest in a film, sound recording, video tape, book, or similar property.

(B) Any right to receive tangible property or services under a contract or granted by a governmental unit or agency or instrumentality thereof.

(C) Any interest in a patent or copyright.

(D) To the extent provided in regulations, any right under a contract (or granted by a governmental unit or an agency or instrumentality thereof) if such right—

(i) has a fixed duration of less than 15 years, or

(ii) is fixed as to amount and, without regard to this section, would be recoverable under a method similar to the unit-of-production method.

(5) INTERESTS UNDER LEASES AND DEBT INSTRUMENTS.—Any interest under—

(A) an existing lease of tangible property, or

(B) except as provided in subsection (d)(2)(B), any existing indebtedness.

(6) MORTGAGE SERVICING.—Any right to service indebtedness which is secured by residential real property unless such right is acquired in a transaction (or series of related transactions) involving the acquisition of assests (other than rights described in this paragraph) constituting a trade or business or substantial portion thereof.

(7) CERTAIN TRANSACTION COSTS.—Any fees for professional services, and any transaction costs, incurred by parties to a transaction with respect to which any portion of the gain or loss is not recognized under part III of subchapter C.

Amendments

• 2004, American Jobs Creation Act of 2004 (P.L. 108-357)

P.L. 108-357, §886(a):

Amended Code Sec. 197(e) by striking paragraph (6) and by redesignating paragraphs (7) and (8) as paragraphs (6) and (7), respectively. **Effective** for property acquired after 10-22-2004. Prior to being stricken, Code Sec. 197(e)(6) read as follows:

(6) TREATMENT OF SPORTS FRANCHISES.—A franchise to engage in professional football, basketball, baseball, or other professional sport, and any item acquired in connection with such a franchise.

[Sec. 197(f)]

(f) SPECIAL RULES.—

(1) TREATMENT OF CERTAIN DISPOSITIONS, ETC.—

(A) IN GENERAL.—If there is a disposition of any amortizable section 197 intangible acquired in a transaction or series of related transactions (or any such intangible becomes worthless) and one or more other amortizable section 197 intangibles acquired in such transaction or series of related transactions are retained—

(i) no loss shall be recognized by reason of such disposition (or such worthlessness), and

(ii) appropriate adjustments to the adjusted bases of such retained intangibles shall be made for any loss not recognized under clause (i).

(B) SPECIAL RULE FOR COVENANTS NOT TO COMPETE.—In the case of any section 197 intangible which is a covenant not to compete (or other arrangement) described in subsection (d)(1)(E), in no event shall such covenant or other arrangement be treated as disposed of (or becoming worthless) before the disposition of the entire interest described in such subsection in connection with which such covenant (or other arrangement) was entered into.

(C) SPECIAL RULE.—All persons treated as a single taxpayer under section 41(f)(1) shall be so treated for purposes of this paragraph.

(2) TREATMENT OF CERTAIN TRANSFERS.—

(A) IN GENERAL.—In the case of any section 197 intangible transferred in a transaction described in subparagraph (B), the transferee shall be treated as the transferor for purposes of applying this section with respect to so much of the adjusted basis in the hands of the transferee as does not exceed the adjusted basis in the hands of the transferor.

(B) TRANSACTIONS COVERED.—The transactions described in this subparagraph are—

(i) any transaction described in section 332, 351, 361, 721, 731, 1031, or 1033, and

(ii) any transaction between members of the same affiliated group during any taxable year for which a consolidated return is made by such group.

(3) TREATMENT OF AMOUNTS PAID PURSUANT TO COVENANTS NOT TO COMPETE, ETC.—Any amount paid or incurred pursuant to a covenant or arrangement referred to in subsection (d)(1)(E) shall be treated as an amount chargeable to capital account.

(4) TREATMENT OF FRANCHISES, ETC.—

(A) FRANCHISE.—The term "franchise" has the meaning given to such term by section 1253(b)(1).

(B) TREATMENT OF RENEWALS.—Any renewal of a franchise, trademark, or trade name (or of a license, a permit, or other right referred to in subsection (d)(1)(D)) shall be treated as an acquisition. The preceding sentence shall only apply with respect to costs incurred in connection with such renewal.

(C) CERTAIN AMOUNTS NOT TAKEN INTO ACCOUNT.—Any amount to which section 1253(d)(1) applies shall not be taken into account under this section.

(5) TREATMENT OF CERTAIN REINSURANCE TRANSACTIONS.—In the case of any amortizable section 197 intangible resulting from an assumption reinsurance transaction, the amount taken into account as the adjusted basis of such intangible under this section shall be the excess of—

(A) the amount paid or incurred by the acquirer under the assumption reinsurance transaction, over

(B) the amount required to be capitalized under section 848 in connection with such transaction.

Subsection (b) shall not apply to any amount required to be capitalized under section 848.

(6) TREATMENT OF CERTAIN SUBLEASES.—For purposes of this section, a sublease shall be treated in the same manner as a lease of the underlying property involved.

(7) TREATMENT AS DEPRECIABLE.—For purposes of this chapter, any amortizable section 197 intangible shall be treated as property which is of a character subject to the allowance for depreciation provided in section 167.

(8) TREATMENT OF CERTAIN INCREMENTS IN VALUE.—This section shall not apply to any increment in value if, without regard to this section, such increment is properly taken into account in determining the cost of property which is not a section 197 intangible.

(9) ANTI-CHURNING RULES.—For purposes of this section—

(A) IN GENERAL.—The term "amortizable section 197 intangible" shall not include any section 197 intangible which is described in subparagraph (A) or (B) of subsection (d)(1) (or for which depreciation or amortization would not have been allowable but for this section) and which is acquired by the taxpayer after the date of the enactment of this section, if—

(i) the intangible was held or used at any time on or after July 25, 1991, and on or before such date of enactment by the taxpayer or a related person,

(ii) the intangible was acquired from a person who held such intangible at any time on or after July 25, 1991, and on or before such date of enactment, and, as part of the transaction, the user of such intangible does not change, or

(iii) the taxpayer grants the right to use such intangible to a person (or a person related to such person) who held or used such intangible at any time on or after July 25, 1991, and on or before such date of enactment.

For purposes of this subparagraph, the determination of whether the user of property changes as part of a transaction shall be determined in accordance with regulations prescribed by the Secretary. For purposes of this subparagraph, deductions allowable under section 1253(d) shall be treated as deductions allowable for amortization.

(B) EXCEPTION WHERE GAIN RECOGNIZED.—If—

(i) subparagraph (A) would not apply to an intangible acquired by the taxpayer but for the last sentence of subparagraph (C)(i), and

(ii) the person from whom the taxpayer acquired the intangible elects, notwithstanding any other provision of this title—

(I) to recognize gain on the disposition of the intangible, and

(II) to pay a tax on such gain which, when added to any other income tax on such gain under this title, equals such gain multiplied by the highest rate of income tax applicable to such person under this title,

then subparagraph (A) shall apply to the intangible only to the extent that the taxpayer's adjusted basis in the intangible exceeds the gain recognized under clause (ii)(I).

(C) RELATED PERSON DEFINED.—For purposes of this paragraph—

(i) RELATED PERSON.—A person (hereinafter in this paragraph referred to as the "related person") is related to any person if—

(I) the related person bears a relationship to such person specified in section 267(b) or section 707(b)(1), or

(II) the related person and such person are engaged in trades or businesses under common control (within the meaning of subparagraphs (A) and (B) of section 41(f)(1)).

For purposes of subclause (I), in applying section 267(b) or 707(b)(1), "20 percent" shall be substituted for "50 percent".

(ii) TIME FOR MAKING DETERMINATION.—A person shall be treated as related to another person if such relationship exists immediately before or immediately after the acquisition of the intangible involved.

(D) ACQUISITIONS BY REASON OF DEATH.—Subparagraph (A) shall not apply to the acquisition of any property by the taxpayer if the basis of the property in the hands of the taxpayer is determined under section 1014(a).

(E) SPECIAL RULE FOR PARTNERSHIPS.—With respect to any increase in the basis of partnership property under section 732, 734, or 743, determinations under this paragraph shall be made at the partner level and each partner shall be treated as having owned and used such partner's proportionate share of the partnership assets.

(F) ANTI-ABUSE RULES.—The term "amortizable section 197 intangible" does not include any section 197 intangible acquired in a transaction, one of the principal purposes of which is to avoid the requirement of subsection (c)(1) that the intangible be acquired after the date of the enactment of this section or to avoid the provisions of subparagraph (A).

(10) TAX-EXEMPT USE PROPERTY SUBJECT TO LEASE.—In the case of any section 197 intangible which would be tax-exempt use property as defined in subsection (h) of section 168 if such section applied to such intangible, the amortization period under this section shall not be less than 125 percent of the lease term (within the meaning of section 168(i)(3)).

Amendments

• 2004, American Jobs Creation Act of 2004 (P.L. 108-357)

P.L. 108-357, §847(b)(3):

Amended Code Sec. 197(f) by adding at the end a new paragraph (10). **Effective** for leases entered into after 10-3-2004. For an exception, see Act Sec. 849(b)(1)-(2) below.

P.L. 108-357, §849(b)(1)-(2), provides:

(b) EXCEPTION.—

(1) IN GENERAL.—The amendments made by this part shall not apply to qualified transportation property.

(2) QUALIFIED TRANSPORTATION PROPERTY.—For purposes of paragraph (1), the term "qualified transportation property" means domestic property subject to a lease with respect to which a formal application—

(A) was submitted for approval to the Federal Transit Administration (an agency of the Department of Transportation) after June 30, 2003, and before March 13, 2004,

(B) is approved by the Federal Transit Administration before January 1, 2006, and

(C) includes a description of such property and the value of such property.

[Sec. 197(g)]

(g) REGULATIONS.—The Secretary shall prescribe such regulations as may be appropriate to carry out the purposes of this section, including such regulations as may be appropriate to prevent avoidance of the purposes of this section through related persons or otherwise.

Amendments

• 1993, Omnibus Budget Reconciliation Act of 1993 (P.L. 103-66)

P.L. 103-66, §13261(a):

Amended part VI of subchapter B of chapter 1 by adding at the end thereof new Code Sec. 197. **Effective**, generally, for property acquired after 8-10-93. For special rules, see Act Sec. 13261(g)(2)-(3) below.

P.L. 103-66, §13261(g)(2)-(3), as amended by P.L. 104-188, §1703(l), provides:

(2) ELECTION TO HAVE AMENDMENTS APPLY TO PROPERTY ACQUIRED AFTER JULY 25, 1991.—

(A) IN GENERAL.—If an election under this paragraph applies to the taxpayer—

(i) the amendments made by this section shall apply to property acquired by the taxpayer after July 25, 1991,

(ii) subsection (c)(1)(A) of section 197 of the Internal Revenue Code of 1986 (as added by this section) (and so much of subsection (f)(9)(A) of such section 197 as precedes clause (i) thereof) shall be applied with respect to the taxpayer by treating July 25, 1991, as the date of the enactment of such section, and

(iii) in applying subsection (f)(9) of such section, with respect to any property acquired by the taxpayer or a related person on or before the date of the enactment of this Act, only holding or use on July 25, 1991, shall be taken into account.

(B) ELECTION.—An election under this pargraph shall be made at such time and in such manner as the Secretary of the Treasury or his delegate may prescribe. Such an election by any taxpayer, once made—

(i) may be revoked only with the consent of the Secretary, and

(ii) shall apply to the taxpayer making such election and any other taxpayer under common control with the taxpayer (within the meaning of subparagraphs (A) and (B) of section 41(f)(1) of such Code) at any time after August 2, 1993, and on or before the date on which such election is made.

(3) ELECTIVE BINDING CONTRACT EXCEPTION.—

(A) IN GENERAL.—The amendments made by this section shall not apply to any acquisition of property by the taxpayer if—

(i) such acquisition is pursuant to a written binding contract in effect on the date of the enactment of this Act and at all times thereafter before such acquisition,

(ii) an election under paragraph (2) does not apply to the taxpayer, and

(iii) the taxpayer makes an election under this paragraph with respect to such contract.

(B) ELECTION.—An election under this paragraph shall be made at such time and in such manner as the Secretary of the Treasury or his delegate shall prescribe. Such an election, once made—

(i) may be revoked only with the consent of the Secretary, and

(ii) shall apply to all property acquired pursuant to the contract with respect to which such election was made.

[Sec. 198]

SEC. 198. EXPENSING OF ENVIRONMENTAL REMEDIATION COSTS.

[Sec. 198(a)]

(a) IN GENERAL.—A taxpayer may elect to treat any qualified environmental remediation expenditure which is paid or incurred by the taxpayer as an expense which is not chargeable to capital account. Any expenditure which is so treated shall be allowed as a deduction for the taxable year in which it is paid or incurred.

[Sec. 198(b)]

(b) QUALIFIED ENVIRONMENTAL REMEDIATION EXPENDITURE.—For purposes of this section—

(1) IN GENERAL.—The term "qualified environmental remediation expenditure" means any expenditure—

(A) which is otherwise chargeable to capital account, and

(B) which is paid or incurred in connection with the abatement or control of hazardous substances at a qualified contaminated site.

(2) SPECIAL RULE FOR EXPENDITURES FOR DEPRECIABLE PROPERTY.—Such term shall not include any expenditure for the acquisition of property of a character subject to the allowance for depreciation which is used in connection with the abatement or control of hazardous substances at a qualified contaminated site; except that the portion of the allowance under section 167 for such property which is otherwise allocated to such site shall be treated as a qualified environmental remediation expenditure.

[Sec. 198(c)]

(c) QUALIFIED CONTAMINATED SITE.—For purposes of this section—

(1) IN GENERAL.—The term "qualified contaminated site" means any area—

(A) which is held by the taxpayer for use in a trade or business or for the production of income, or which is property described in section 1221(a)(1) in the hands of the taxpayer, and

(B) at or on which there has been a release (or threat of release) or disposal of any hazardous substance.

(2) NATIONAL PRIORITIES LISTED SITES NOT INCLUDED.—Such term shall not include any site which is on, or proposed for, the national priorities list under section 105(a)(8)(B) of the Comprehensive Environmental Response, Compensation, and Liability Act of 1980 (as in effect on the date of the enactment of this section).

(3) TAXPAYER MUST RECEIVE STATEMENT FROM STATE ENVIRONMENTAL AGENCY.—An area shall be treated as a qualified contaminated site with respect to expenditures paid or incurred during any taxable year only if the taxpayer receives a statement from the appropriate agency of the State in which such area is located that such area meets the requirement of paragraph (1)(B).

(4) APPROPRIATE STATE AGENCY.—For purposes of paragraph (3), the chief executive officer of each State may, in consultation with the Administrator of the Environmental Protection Agency, designate the appropriate State environmental agency within 60 days of the date of the enactment of this section. If the chief executive officer of a State has not designated an appropriate environmental agency within such 60-day period, the appropriate environmental agency for such State shall be designated by the Administrator of the Environmental Protection Agency.

Amendments

• 2000, Community Renewal Tax Relief Act of 2000 (P.L. 106-554)

P.L. 106-554, §162(a):

Amended Code Sec. 198(c). **Effective** for expenditures paid or incurred after 12-21-2000. Prior to amendment, Code Sec. 198(c) read as follows:

(c) QUALIFIED CONTAMINATED SITE.—For purposes of this section—

(1) QUALIFIED CONTAMINATED SITE.—

(A) IN GENERAL.—The term "qualified contaminated site" means any area—

(i) which is held by the taxpayer for use in a trade or business or for the production of income, or which is property described in section 1221(a)(1) in the hands of the taxpayer,

(ii) which is within a targeted area, and

(iii) at or on which there has been a release (or threat of release) or disposal of any hazardous substance.

(B) TAXPAYER MUST RECEIVE STATEMENT FROM STATE ENVIRONMENTAL AGENCY.—An area shall be treated as a qualified contaminated site with respect to expenditures paid or incurred during any taxable year only if the taxpayer receives a statement from the appropriate agency of the State in which such area is located that such area meets the requirements of clauses (ii) and (iii) of subparagraph (A).

(C) APPROPRIATE STATE AGENCY.—For purposes of subparagraph (B), the chief executive officer of each State may, in consultation with the Administrator of the Environmental

Protection Agency, designate the appropriate State environmental agency within 60 days of the date of the enactment of this section. If the chief executive officer of a State has not designated an appropriate State environmental agency within such 60-day period, the appropriate environmental agency for such State shall be designated by the Administrator of the Environmental Protection Agency.

(2) TARGETED AREA.—

(A) IN GENERAL.—The term "targeted area" means—

(i) any population census tract with a poverty rate of not less than 20 percent,

(ii) a population census tract with a population of less than 2,000 if—

(I) more than 75 percent of such tract is zoned for commercial or industrial use, and

(II) such tract is contiguous to 1 or more other population census tracts which meet the requirement of clause (i) without regard to this clause,

(iii) any empowerment zone or enterprise community (and any supplemental zone designated on December 21, 1994), and

(iv) any site announced before February 1, 1997, as being included as a brownfields pilot project of the Environmental Protection Agency.

(B) NATIONAL PRIORITIES LISTED SITES NOT INCLUDED.—Such term shall not include any site which is on, or proposed for, the national priorities list under section 105(a)(8)(B) of the Comprehensive Environmental Response, Compensation, and Liability Act of 1980 (as in effect on the date of the enactment of this section).

(C) CERTAIN RULES TO APPLY.—For purposes of this paragraph the rules of sections 1392(b)(4) and 1393(a)(9) shall apply.

• 1999, Tax Relief Extension Act of 1999 (P.L. 106-170)

P.L. 106-170, §532(c)(2)(A):

Amended Code Sec. 198(c)(1)(A)(i) by striking "section 1221(1)" and inserting "section 1221(a)(1)". **Effective** for any instrument held, acquired, or entered into, any transaction entered into, and supplies held or acquired on or after 12-17-99.

[Sec. 198(d)]

(d) HAZARDOUS SUBSTANCE.—For purposes of this section—

(1) IN GENERAL.—The term "hazardous substance" means—

(A) any substance which is a hazardous substance as defined in section 101(14) of the Comprehensive Environmental Response, Compensation, and Liability Act of 1980,

(B) any substance which is designated as a hazardous substance under section 102 of such Act, and

(C) any petroleum product (as defined in section 4612(a)(3)).

(2) EXCEPTION.—Such term shall not include any substance with respect to which a removal or remedial action is not permitted under section 104 of such Act by reason of subsection (a)(3) thereof.

Amendments

• 2006, Tax Relief and Health Care Act of 2006 (P.L. 109-432)

P.L. 109-432, Division A, §109(b):

Amended Code Sec. 198(d)(1) by striking "and" at the end of subparagraph (A), by striking the period at the end of subparagraph (B) and inserting ", and", and by adding at the end a new subparagraph (C). **Effective** for expenditures paid or incurred after 12-31-2005.

[Sec. 198(e)]

(e) DEDUCTION RECAPTURED AS ORDINARY INCOME ON SALE, ETC.—Solely for purposes of section 1245, in the case of property to which a qualified environmental remediation expenditure would have been capitalized but for this section—

(1) the deduction allowed by this section for such expenditure shall be treated as a deduction for depreciation, and

(2) such property (if not otherwise section 1245 property) shall be treated as section 1245 property solely for purposes of applying section 1245 to such deduction.

[Sec. 198(f)]

(f) COORDINATION WITH OTHER PROVISIONS.—Sections 280B and 468 shall not apply to amounts which are treated as expenses under this section.

[Sec. 198(g)]

(g) REGULATIONS.—The Secretary shall prescribe such regulations as may be necessary or appropriate to carry out the purposes of this section.

[Sec. 198(h)]

(h) TERMINATION.—This section shall not apply to expenditures paid or incurred after December 31, 2009.

Amendments

• 2008, Tax Extenders and Alternative Minimum Tax Relief Act of 2008 (P.L. 110-343)

P.L. 110-343, Division C, §318(a):

Amended Code Sec. 198(h) by striking "December 31, 2007" and inserting "December 31, 2009". **Effective** for expenditures paid or incurred after 12-31-2007.

• 2006, Tax Relief and Health Care Act of 2006 (P.L. 109-432)

P.L. 109-432, Division A, §109(a):

Amended Code Sec. 198(h) by striking "2005" and inserting "2007". **Effective** for expenditures paid or incurred after 12-31-2005.

• 2004, Working Families Tax Relief Act of 2004 (P.L. 108-311)

P.L. 108-311, §308(a):

Amended Code Sec. 198(h) by striking "December 31, 2003" and inserting "December 31, 2005". **Effective** for expenditures paid or incurred after 12-31-2003.

• 2000, Community Renewal Tax Relief Act of 2000 (P.L. 106-554)

P.L. 106-554, §162(b):

Amended Code Sec. 198(h) by striking "2001" and inserting "2003". **Effective** for expenditures paid or incurred after 12-21-2000.

• 1999, Tax Relief Extension Act of 1999 (P.L. 106-170)

P.L. 106-170, §511:

Amended Code Sec. 198(h) by striking "2000" and inserting "2001". **Effective** 12-17-99.

• 1997, Taxpayer Relief Act of 1997 (P.L. 105-34)

P.L. 105-34, §941(a):

Amended part VI of subchapter B of chapter 1 by adding at the end a new Code Sec. 198. **Effective** for expenditures paid or incurred after 8-5-97, in tax years ending after such date.

[Sec. 198A]

SEC. 198A. EXPENSING OF QUALIFIED DISASTER EXPENSES.

[Sec. 198A(a)]

(a) IN GENERAL.—A taxpayer may elect to treat any qualified disaster expenses which are paid or incurred by the taxpayer as an expense which is not chargeable to capital account. Any expense which is so treated shall be allowed as a deduction for the taxable year in which it is paid or incurred.

[Sec. 198A(b)]

(b) QUALIFIED DISASTER EXPENSE.—For purposes of this section, the term "qualified disaster expense" means any expenditure—

(1) which is paid or incurred in connection with a trade or business or with business-related property,

(2) which is—

(A) for the abatement or control of hazardous substances that were released on account of a federally declared disaster occurring before January 1, 2010,

(B) for the removal of debris from, or the demolition of structures on, real property which is business-related property damaged or destroyed as a result of a federally declared disaster occurring before such date, or

(C) for the repair of business-related property damaged as a result of a federally declared disaster occurring before such date, and

(3) which is otherwise chargeable to capital account.

[Sec. 198A(c)]

(c) OTHER DEFINITIONS.—For purposes of this section—

(1) BUSINESS-RELATED PROPERTY.—The term "business-related property" means property—

(A) held by the taxpayer for use in a trade or business or for the production of income, or

(B) described in section 1221(a)(1) in the hands of the taxpayer.

(2) FEDERALLY DECLARED DISASTER.—The term "federally declared disaster" has the meaning given such term by section 165(h)(3)(C)(i).

[Sec. 198A(d)]

(d) DEDUCTION RECAPTURED AS ORDINARY INCOME ON SALE, ETC.—Solely for purposes of section 1245, in the case of property to which a qualified disaster expense would have been capitalized but for this section—

(1) the deduction allowed by this section for such expense shall be treated as a deduction for depreciation, and

(2) such property (if not otherwise section 1245 property) shall be treated as section 1245 property solely for purposes of applying section 1245 to such deduction.

[Sec. 198A(e)]

(e) COORDINATION WITH OTHER PROVISIONS.—Sections 198, 280B, and 468 shall not apply to amounts which are treated as expenses under this section.

[Sec. 198A(f)]

(f) REGULATIONS.—The Secretary shall prescribe such regulations as may be necessary or appropriate to carry out the purposes of this section.

Amendments

• 2008, Tax Extenders and Alternative Minimum Tax Relief Act of 2008 (P.L. 110-343)

P.L. 110-343, Division C, §707(a):

Amended part VI of subchapter B of chapter 1 by inserting after Code Sec. 198 a new Code Sec. 198A. **Effective** for amounts paid or incurred after 12-31-2007 in connection with disaster declared after such date.

P.L. 110-343, Division C, §712, provides:

SEC. 712. COORDINATION WITH HEARTLAND DISASTER RELIEF.

The amendments made by this subtitle, other than the amendments made by sections 706(a)(2), 710, and 711, shall not apply to any disaster described in section 702(c)[b](1)(A), or to any expenditure or loss resulting from such disaster.

[Sec. 199]

SEC. 199. INCOME ATTRIBUTABLE TO DOMESTIC PRODUCTION ACTIVITIES.

[Sec. 199(a)]

(a) ALLOWANCE OF DEDUCTION.—

(1) IN GENERAL.—There shall be allowed as a deduction an amount equal to 9 percent of the lesser of—

(A) the qualified production activities income of the taxpayer for the taxable year, or

(B) taxable income (determined without regard to this section) for the taxable year.

(2) PHASEIN.—In the case of any taxable year beginning after 2004 and before 2010, paragraph (1) shall be applied by substituting for the percentage contained therein the transition percentage determined under the following table:

For taxable years beginning in:	The transition percentage is:
2005 or 2006	3
2007, 2008, or 2009	6

Amendments

• 2006, Tax Increase Prevention and Reconciliation Act of 2005 (P.L. 109-222)

P.L. 109-222, §514(b)(2):

Amended Code Sec. 199(a)(2) by striking "and subsection (d)(1)" after "paragraph (1)". **Effective** for tax years beginning after 5-17-2006.

• 2005, Gulf Opportunity Zone Act of 2005 (P.L. 109-135)

P.L. 109-135, §403(a)(11)(B):

Amended Code Sec. 199(a)(2) by striking "subsections (d)(1) and (d)(6)" and inserting "subsection (d)(1)". **Effective** as if included in the provision of the American Jobs Creation Act of 2004 (P.L. 108-357) to which it relates [**effective** for tax years beginning after 12-31-2004—CCH].

[Sec. 199(b)]

(b) DEDUCTION LIMITED TO WAGES PAID.—

(1) IN GENERAL.—The amount of the deduction allowable under subsection (a) for any taxable year shall not exceed 50 percent of the W-2 wages of the taxpayer for the taxable year.

(2) W-2 WAGES.—For purposes of this section—

(A) IN GENERAL.—The term "W-2 wages" means, with respect to any person for any taxable year of such person, the sum of the amounts described in paragraphs (3) and (8) of section 6051(a) paid by such person with respect to employment of employees by such person during the calendar year ending during such taxable year.

(B) LIMITATION TO WAGES ATTRIBUTABLE TO DOMESTIC PRODUCTION.—Such term shall not include any amount which is not properly allocable to domestic production gross receipts for purposes of subsection (c)(1).

(C) RETURN REQUIREMENT.—Such term shall not include any amount which is not properly included in a return filed with the Social Security Administration on or before the 60th day after the due date (including extensions) for such return.

(D) SPECIAL RULE FOR QUALIFIED FILM.—In the case of a qualified film, such term shall include compensation for services performed in the United States by actors, production personnel, directors, and producers.

(3) ACQUISITIONS AND DISPOSITIONS.—The Secretary shall provide for the application of this subsection in cases where the taxpayer acquires, or disposes of, the major portion of a trade or business or the major portion of a separate unit of a trade or business during the taxable year.

Amendments

• 2008, Tax Extenders and Alternative Minimum Tax Relief Act of 2008 (P.L. 110-343)

P.L. 110-343, Division C, §502(c)(1):

Amended Code Sec. 199(b)(2) by adding at the end a new subparagraph (D). **Effective** for tax years beginning after 12-31-2007.

• 2006, Tax Increase Prevention and Reconciliation Act of 2005 (P.L. 109-222)

P.L. 109-222, §514(a):

Amended Code Sec. 199(b)(2). **Effective** for tax years beginning after 5-17-2006. Prior to amendment, Code Sec. 199(b)(2) read as follows:

(2) W-2 WAGES.—For purposes of this section, the term "W-2 wages" means, with respect to any person for any taxable year of such person, the sum of the amounts described in paragraphs (3) and (8) of section 6051(a) paid by such person with respect to employment of employees by such person during the calendar year ending during such taxable year. Such term shall not include any amount which is not properly included in a return filed with the Social Security Administration on or before the 60th day after the due date (including extensions) for such return.

• 2005, Gulf Opportunity Zone Act of 2005 (P.L. 109-135)

P.L. 109-135, §403(a)(1):

Amended Code Sec. 199(b)(1) by striking "the employer" and inserting "the taxpayer". **Effective** as if included in the provision of the American Jobs Creation Act of 2004 (P.L. 108-357) to which it relates [**effective** for tax years beginning after 12-31-2004.—CCH].

P.L. 109-135, §403(a)(2):

Amended Code Sec. 199(b)(2). **Effective** as if included in the provision of the American Jobs Creation Act of 2004 (P.L. 108-357) to which it relates [**effective** for tax years beginning after 12-31-2004.—CCH]. Prior to amendment, Code Sec. 199(b)(2) read as follows:

(2) W-2 WAGES.—For purposes of paragraph (1), the term "W-2 wages" means the sum of the aggregate amounts the taxpayer is required to include on statements under paragraphs (3) and (8) of section 6051(a) with respect to employment of employees of the taxpayer during the calendar year ending during the taxpayer's taxable year.

[Sec. 199(c)]

(c) QUALIFIED PRODUCTION ACTIVITIES INCOME.—For purposes of this section—

(1) IN GENERAL.—The term "qualified production activities income" for any taxable year means an amount equal to the excess (if any) of—

(A) the taxpayer's domestic production gross receipts for such taxable year, over

(B) the sum of—

(i) the cost of goods sold that are allocable to such receipts, and

(ii) other expenses, losses, or deductions (other than the deduction allowed under this section), which are properly allocable to such receipts.

(2) ALLOCATION METHOD.—The Secretary shall prescribe rules for the proper allocation of items described in paragraph (1) for purposes of determining qualified production activities income. Such rules shall provide for the proper allocation of items whether or not such items are directly allocable to domestic production gross receipts.

(3) SPECIAL RULES FOR DETERMINING COSTS.—

(A) IN GENERAL.—For purposes of determining costs under clause (i) of paragraph (1)(B), any item or service brought into the United States shall be treated as acquired by purchase, and its cost shall be treated as not less than its value immediately after it entered the United States. A similar rule shall apply in determining the adjusted basis of leased or rented property where the lease or rental gives rise to domestic production gross receipts.

(B) EXPORTS FOR FURTHER MANUFACTURE.—In the case of any property described in subparagraph (A) that had been exported by the taxpayer for further manufacture, the increase in cost or adjusted basis under subparagraph (A) shall not exceed the difference between the value of the property when exported and the value of the property when brought back into the United States after the further manufacture.

(4) DOMESTIC PRODUCTION GROSS RECEIPTS.—

(A) IN GENERAL.—The term "domestic production gross receipts" means the gross receipts of the taxpayer which are derived from—

(i) any lease, rental, license, sale, exchange, or other disposition of—

(I) qualifying production property which was manufactured, produced, grown, or extracted by the taxpayer in whole or in significant part within the United States,

(II) any qualified film produced by the taxpayer, or

(III) electricity, natural gas, or potable water produced by the taxpayer in the United States,

(ii) in the case of a taxpayer engaged in the active conduct of a construction trade or business, construction of real property performed in the United States by the taxpayer in the ordinary course of such trade or business, or

(iii) in the case of a taxpayer engaged in the active conduct of an engineering or architectural services trade or business, engineering or architectural services performed in the United States by the taxpayer in the ordinary course of such trade or business with respect to the construction of real property in the United States.

(B) EXCEPTIONS.—Such term shall not include gross receipts of the taxpayer which are derived from—

(i) the sale of food and beverages prepared by the taxpayer at a retail establishment,

(ii) the transmission or distribution of electricity, natural gas, or potable water, or

(iii) the lease, rental, license, sale, exchange, or other disposition of land.

(C) SPECIAL RULE FOR CERTAIN GOVERNMENT CONTRACTS.—Gross receipts derived from the manufacture or production of any property described in subparagraph (A)(i)(I) shall be treated as meeting the requirements of subparagraph (A)(i) if—

(i) such property is manufactured or produced by the taxpayer pursuant to a contract with the Federal Government, and

(ii) the Federal Acquisition Regulation requires that title or risk of loss with respect to such property be transferred to the Federal Government before the manufacture or production of such property is complete.

(D) PARTNERSHIPS OWNED BY EXPANDED AFFILIATED GROUPS.—For purposes of this paragraph, if all of the interests in the capital and profits of a partnership are owned by members of a single expanded affiliated group at all times during the taxable year of such partnership, the partnership and all members of such group shall be treated as a single taxpayer during such period.

(5) QUALIFYING PRODUCTION PROPERTY.—The term "qualifying production property" means—

(A) tangible personal property,

(B) any computer software, and

(C) any property described in section 168(f)(4).

(6) QUALIFIED FILM.—The term "qualified film" means any property described in section 168(f)(3) if not less than 50 percent of the total compensation relating to the production of such property is compensation for services performed in the United States by actors, production personnel, directors, and producers. Such term does not include property with respect to which records are required to be maintained under section 2257 of title 18, United States Code. A qualified film shall include any copyrights, trademarks, or other intangibles with respect to such film. The methods and means of distributing a qualified film shall not affect the availability of the deduction under this section.

(7) RELATED PERSONS.—

(A) IN GENERAL.—The term "domestic production gross receipts" shall not include any gross receipts of the taxpayer derived from property leased, licensed, or rented by the taxpayer for use by any related person.

(B) RELATED PERSON.—For purposes of subparagraph (A), a person shall be treated as related to another person if such persons are treated as a single employer under subsection (a) or (b) of section 52 or subsection (m) or (o) of section 414, except that determinations under subsections (a) and (b) of section 52 shall be made without regard to section 1563(b).

Amendments

• 2008, Tax Extenders and Alternative Minimum Tax Relief Act of 2008 (P.L. 110-343)

P.L. 110-343, Division C, §502(c)(2):

Amended Code Sec. 199(c)(6) by adding at the end two new sentences. **Effective** for tax years beginning after 12-31-2007.

• 2005, Gulf Opportunity Zone Act of 2005 (P.L. 109-135)

P.L. 109-135, §403(a)(3):

Amended Code Sec. 199(c)(1)(B) by inserting "and" at the end of clause (i), by striking clauses (ii) and (iii), and by inserting after clause (i) a new clause (ii). **Effective** as if included in the provision of the American Jobs Creation Act of 2004 (P.L. 108-357) to which it relates [**effective** for tax years beginning after 12-31-2004.—CCH]. Prior to amendment, Code Sec. 199(c)(1)(B)(ii) and (iii) read as follows:

(ii) other deductions, expenses, or losses directly allocable to such receipts, and

(iii) a ratable portion of other deductions, expenses, and losses that are not directly allocable to such receipts or another class of income.

P.L. 109-135, §403(a)(4):

Amended Code Sec. 199(c)(2). **Effective** as if included in the provision of the American Jobs Creation Act of 2004 (P.L. 108-357) to which it relates [**effective** for tax years beginning after 12-31-2004.—CCH]. Prior to amendment, Code Sec. 199(c)(2) read as follows:

(2) ALLOCATION METHOD.—The Secretary shall prescribe rules for the proper allocation of items of income, deduction, expense, and loss for purposes of determining income attributable to domestic production activities.

P.L. 109-135, §403(a)(5):

Amended Code Sec. 199(c)(4)(A) by striking clauses (ii) and (iii) and inserting new clauses (ii) and (iii). **Effective** as if included in the provision of the American Jobs Creation Act of 2004 (P.L. 108-357) to which it relates [**effective** for tax years beginning after 12-31-2004.—CCH]. Prior to being stricken, Code Sec. 199(c)(4)(A)(ii) and (iii) read as follows:

(ii) construction performed in the United States, or

(iii) engineering or architectural services performed in the United States for construction projects in the United States.

P.L. 109-135, §403(a)(6):

Amended Code Sec. 199(c)(4)(B) by striking "and" at the end of clause (i), by striking the period at the end of clause (ii) and inserting ", or" and by adding at the end a new clause (iii). **Effective** as if included in the provision of the American Jobs Creation Act of 2004 (P.L. 108-357) to which it relates [**effective** for tax years beginning after 12-31-2004.—CCH].

P.L. 109-135, §403(a)(7):

Amended Code Sec. 199(c)(4) by adding at the end new subparagraphs (C) and (D). **Effective** as if included in the provision of the American Jobs Creation Act of 2004 (P.L. 108-357) to which it relates [**effective** for tax years beginning after 12-31-2004.—CCH].

[Sec. 199(d)]

(d) DEFINITIONS AND SPECIAL RULES.—

(1) APPLICATION OF SECTION TO PASS-THRU ENTITIES.—

(A) PARTNERSHIPS AND S CORPORATIONS.—In the case of a partnership or S corporation—

(i) this section shall be applied at the partner or shareholder level,

(ii) each partner or shareholder shall take into account such person's allocable share of each item described in subparagraph (A) or (B) of subsection (c)(1) (determined without regard to whether the items described in such subparagraph (A) exceed the items described in such subparagraph (B)),

(iii) each partner or shareholder shall be treated for purposes of subsection (b) as having W-2 wages for the taxable year in an amount equal to such person's allocable share of the W-2 wages of the partnership or S corporation for the taxable year (as determined under regulations prescribed by the Secretary), and

(iv) in the case of each partner of a partnership, or shareholder of an S corporation, who owns (directly or indirectly) at least 20 percent of the capital interests in such partnership or of the stock of such S corporation—

(I) such partner or shareholder shall be treated as having engaged directly in any film produced by such partnership or S corporation, and

(II) such partnership or S corporation shall be treated as having engaged directly in any film produced by such partner or shareholder.

(B) TRUSTS AND ESTATES.—In the case of a trust or estate—

(i) the items referred to in subparagraph (A)(ii) (as determined therein) and the W-2 wages of the trust or estate for the taxable year, shall be apportioned between the beneficiaries and the fiduciary (and among the beneficiaries) under regulations prescribed by the Secretary, and

(ii) for purposes of paragraph (2), adjusted gross income of the trust or estate shall be determined as provided in section 67(e) with the adjustments described in such paragraph.

(C) REGULATIONS.—The Secretary may prescribe rules requiring or restricting the allocation of items and wages under this paragraph and may prescribe such reporting requirements as the Secretary determines appropriate.

(2) APPLICATION TO INDIVIDUALS.—In the case of an individual, subsections (a)(1)(B) and (d)(9)(A)(iii) shall be applied by substituting "adjusted gross income" for "taxable income". For purposes of the preceding sentence, adjusted gross income shall be determined—

(A) after application of sections 86, 135, 137, 219, 221, 222, and 469, and

(B) without regard to this section.

(3) AGRICULTURAL AND HORTICULTURAL COOPERATIVES.—

(A) DEDUCTION ALLOWED TO PATRONS.—Any person who receives a qualified payment from a specified agricultural or horticultural cooperative shall be allowed for the taxable year in which such payment is received a deduction under subsection (a) equal to the portion of the deduction allowed under subsection (a) to such cooperative which is—

(i) allowed with respect to the portion of the qualified production activities income to which such payment is attributable, and

(ii) identified by such cooperative in a written notice mailed to such person during the payment period described in section 1382(d).

(B) COOPERATIVE DENIED DEDUCTION FOR PORTION OF QUALIFIED PAYMENTS.—The taxable income of a specified agricultural or horticultural cooperative shall not be reduced under section 1382 by reason of that portion of any qualified payment as does not exceed the deduction allowable under subparagraph (A) with respect to such payment.

(C) TAXABLE INCOME OF COOPERATIVES DETERMINED WITHOUT REGARD TO CERTAIN DEDUCTIONS.—For purposes of this section, the taxable income of a specified agricultural or horticultural cooperative shall be computed without regard to any deduction allowable under subsection (b) or (c) of section 1382 (relating to patronage dividends, per-unit retain allocations, and nonpatronage distributions).

(D) SPECIAL RULE FOR MARKETING COOPERATIVES.—For purposes of this section, a specified agricultural or horticultural cooperative described in subparagraph (F)(ii) shall be treated as having manufactured, produced, grown, or extracted in whole or significant part any qualifying production property marketed by the organization which its patrons have so manufactured, produced, grown, or extracted.

(E) QUALIFIED PAYMENT.—For purposes of this paragraph, the term "qualified payment" means, with respect to any person, any amount which—

(i) is described in paragraph (1) or (3) of section 1385(a),

(ii) is received by such person from a specified agricultural or horticultural cooperative, and

(iii) is attributable to qualified production activities income with respect to which a deduction is allowed to such cooperative under subsection (a).

(F) SPECIFIED AGRICULTURAL OR HORTICULTURAL COOPERATIVE.—For purposes of this paragraph, the term "specified agricultural or horticultural cooperative" means an organization to which part I of subchapter T applies which is engaged—

(i) in the manufacturing, production, growth, or extraction in whole or significant part of any agricultural or horticultural product, or

(ii) in the marketing of agricultural or horticultural products.

(4) SPECIAL RULE FOR AFFILIATED GROUPS.—

(A) IN GENERAL.—All members of an expanded affiliated group shall be treated as a single corporation for purposes of this section.

(B) EXPANDED AFFILIATED GROUP.—For purposes of this section, the term "expanded affiliated group" means an affiliated group as defined in section 1504(a), determined—

(i) by substituting "more than 50 percent" for "at least 80 percent" each place it appears, and

(ii) without regard to paragraphs (2) and (4) of section 1504(b).

(C) ALLOCATION OF DEDUCTION.—Except as provided in regulations, the deduction under subsection (a) shall be allocated among the members of the expanded affiliated group in proportion to each member's respective amount (if any) of qualified production activities income.

(5) TRADE OR BUSINESS REQUIREMENT.—This section shall be applied by only taking into account items which are attributable to the actual conduct of a trade or business.

(6) COORDINATION WITH MINIMUM TAX.—For purposes of determining alternative minimum taxable income under section 55—

(A) qualified production activities income shall be determined without regard to any adjustments under sections 56 through 59, and

(B) in the case of a corporation, subsection (a)(1)(B) shall be applied by substituting "alternative minimum taxable income" for "taxable income".

(7) UNRELATED BUSINESS TAXABLE INCOME.—For purposes of determining the tax imposed by section 511, subsection (a)(1)(B) shall be applied by substituting "unrelated business taxable income" for "taxable income".

(8) TREATMENT OF ACTIVITIES IN PUERTO RICO.—

(A) IN GENERAL.—In the case of any taxpayer with gross receipts for any taxable year from sources within the Commonwealth of Puerto Rico, if all of such receipts are taxable under section 1 or 11 for such taxable year, then for purposes of determining the domestic production gross receipts of such taxpayer for such taxable year under subsection (c)(4), the term "United States" shall include the Commonwealth of Puerto Rico.

(B) SPECIAL RULE FOR APPLYING WAGE LIMITATION.—In the case of any taxpayer described in subparagraph (A), for purposes of applying the limitation under subsection (b) for any taxable year, the determination of W-2 wages of such taxpayer shall be made without regard to any exclusion under section 3401(a)(8) for remuneration paid for services performed in Puerto Rico.

(C) TERMINATION.—This paragraph shall apply only with respect to the first 4 taxable years of the taxpayer beginning after December 31, 2005, and before January 1, 2010.

(9) SPECIAL RULE FOR TAXPAYERS WITH OIL RELATED QUALIFIED PRODUCTION ACTIVITIES INCOME.—

(A) IN GENERAL.—If a taxpayer has oil related qualified production activities income for any taxable year beginning after 2009, the amount otherwise allowable as a deduction under subsection (a) shall be reduced by 3 percent of the least of—

(i) the oil related qualified production activities income of the taxpayer for the taxable year,

(ii) the qualified production activities income of the taxpayer for the taxable year, or

(iii) taxable income (determined without regard to this section).

(B) OIL RELATED QUALIFIED PRODUCTION ACTIVITIES INCOME.—For purposes of this paragraph, the term "oil related qualified production activities income" means for any taxable year the qualified production activities income which is attributable to the production, refining, processing, transportation, or distribution of oil, gas, or any primary product thereof during such taxable year.

(C) PRIMARY PRODUCT.—For purposes of this paragraph, the term "primary product" has the same meaning as when used in section 927(a)(2)(C), as in effect before its repeal.

(10) REGULATIONS.—The Secretary shall prescribe such regulations as are necessary to carry out the purposes of this section, including regulations which prevent more than 1 taxpayer from being allowed a deduction under this section with respect to any activity described in subsection (c)(4)(A)(i).

Amendments

• 2008, Energy Improvement and Extension Act of 2008 (P.L. 110-343)

P.L. 110-343, Division B, §401(a):

Amended Code Sec. 199(d) by redesignating paragraph (9) as paragraph (10) and by inserting after paragraph (8) a new paragraph (9). **Effective** for tax years beginning after 12-31-2008.

P.L. 110-343, Division B, §401(b):

Amended Code Sec. 199(d)(2) by striking "subsection (a)(1)(B)" and inserting "subsections (a)(1)(B) and (d)(9)(A)(iii)". **Effective** for tax years beginning after 12-31-2008.

• 2008, Tax Extenders and Alternative Minimum Tax Relief Act of 2008 (P.L. 110-343)

P.L. 110-343, Division C, §312(a)(1)-(2):

Amended Code Sec. 199(d)(8)(C) by striking "first 2 taxable years" and inserting "first 4 taxable years", and by striking "January 1, 2008" and inserting "January 1, 2010". **Effective** for tax years beginning after 12-31-2007.

P.L. 110-343, Division C, §502(c)(3):

Amended Code Sec. 199(d)(1)(A) by striking "and" at the end of clause (ii), by striking the period at the end of clause (iii) and inserting ", and", and by adding at the end a new clause (iv). **Effective** for tax years beginning after 12-31-2007.

• 2006, Tax Relief and Health Care Act of 2006 (P.L. 109-432)

P.L. 109-432, Division A, §401(a):

Amended Code Sec. 199(d) by redesignating paragraph (8) as paragraph (9) and by inserting after paragraph (7) a new paragraph (8). **Effective** for tax years beginning after 12-31-2005.

• 2006, Tax Increase Prevention and Reconciliation Act of 2005 (P.L. 109-222)

P.L. 109-222, §514(b)(1):

Amended Code Sec. 199(d)(1)(A)(iii). **Effective** for tax years beginning after 5-17-2006. Prior to amendment, Code Sec. 199(d)(1)(A)(iii) read as follows:

(iii) each partner or shareholder shall be treated for purposes of subsection (b) as having W-2 wages for the taxable year in an amount equal to the lesser of—

(I) such person's allocable share of the W-2 wages of the partnership or S corporation for the taxable year (as determined under regulations prescribed by the Secretary), or

(II) 2 times 9 percent of so much of such person's qualified production activities income as is attributable to items allocated under clause (ii) for the taxable year.

• 2005, Gulf Opportunity Zone Act of 2005 (P.L. 109-135)

P.L. 109-135, §403(a)(8):

Amended Code Sec. 199(d)(1). **Effective** as if included in the provision of the American Jobs Creation Act of 2004 (P.L. 108-357) to which it relates [**effective** for tax years beginning after 12-31-2004.—CCH]. Prior to amendment, Code Sec. 199(d)(1) read as follows:

(1) APPLICATION OF SECTION TO PASS-THRU ENTITIES.—

(A) IN GENERAL.—In the case of an S corporation, partnership, estate or trust, or other pass-thru entity—

(i) subject to the provisions of paragraphs (2) and (3), this section shall be applied at the shareholder, partner, or similar level, and

(ii) the Secretary shall prescribe rules for the application of this section, including rules relating to—

(I) restrictions on the allocation of the deduction to taxpayers at the partner or similar level, and

(II) additional reporting requirements.

(B) APPLICATION OF WAGE LIMITATION.—Notwithstanding subparagraph (A)(i), for purposes of applying subsection (b), a shareholder, partner, or similar person which is allocated qualified production activities income from an S corporation, partnership, estate, trust, or other pass-thru entity shall also be treated as having been allocated W-2 wages from such entity in an amount equal to the lesser of—

(i) such person's allocable share of such wages (without regard to this subparagraph), as determined under regulations prescribed by the Secretary, or

(ii) 2 times 9 percent of the qualified production activities income allocated to such person for the taxable year.

P.L. 109-135, §403(a)(9):

Amended Code Sec. 199(d)(3). **Effective** as if included in the provision of the American Jobs Creation Act of 2004 (P.L. 108-357) to which it relates [**effective** for tax years beginning after 12-31-2004.—CCH]. Prior to amendment, Code Sec. 199(d)(3) read as follows:

(3) PATRONS OF AGRICULTURAL AND HORTICULTURAL COOPERATIVES.—

(A) IN GENERAL.—If any amount described in paragraph (1) or (3) of section 1385(a)—

(i) is received by a person from an organization to which part I of subchapter T applies which is engaged—

(I) in the manufacturing, production, growth, or extraction in whole or significant part of any agricultural or horticultural product, or

(II) in the marketing of agricultural or horticultural products, and

(ii) is allocable to the portion of the qualified production activities income of the organization which, but for this paragraph, would be deductible under subsection (a) by the organization and is designated as such by the organization in a written notice mailed to its patrons during the payment period described in section 1382(d),

then such person shall be allowed a deduction under subsection (a) with respect to such amount. The taxable income of the organization shall not be reduced under section 1382 by reason of any amount to which the preceding sentence applies.

(B) SPECIAL RULES.—For purposes of applying subparagraph (A), in determining the qualified production activities income which would be deductible by the organization under subsection (a)—

(i) there shall not be taken into account in computing the organization's taxable income any deduction allowable under subsection (b) or (c) of section 1382 (relating to patronage dividends, per-unit retain allocations, and nonpatronage distributions), and

(ii) in the case of an organization described in subparagraph (A)(i)(II), the organization shall be treated as having manufactured, produced, grown, or extracted in whole or significant part any qualifying production property marketed by the organization which its patrons have so manufactured, produced, grown, or extracted.

P.L. 109-135, §403(a)(10)(A)-(B):

Amended Code Sec. 199(d)(4)(B)(i) by striking "50 percent" and inserting "more than 50 percent", and by striking "80 percent" and inserting "at least 80 percent". **Effective** as if included in the provision of the American Jobs Creation Act of 2004 (P.L. 108-357) to which it relates [**effective** for tax years beginning after 12-31-2004.—CCH].

P.L. 109-135, §403(a)(11)(A):

Amended Code Sec. 199(d)(6). **Effective** as if included in the provision of the American Jobs Creation Act of 2004 (P.L. 108-357) to which it relates [**effective** for tax years beginning after 12-31-2004.—CCH]. Prior to amendment, Code Sec. 199(d)(6) read as follows:

(6) COORDINATION WITH MINIMUM TAX.—The deduction under this section shall be allowed for purposes of the tax imposed by section 55; except that for purposes of section 55, the deduction under subsection (a) shall be 9 percent of the lesser of—

(A) qualified production activities income (determined without regard to part IV of subchapter A), or

(B) alternative minimum taxable income (determined without regard to this section) for the taxable year.

In the case of an individual, subparagraph (B) shall be applied by substituting "adjusted gross income" for "alternative minimum taxable income". For purposes of the preceding sentence, adjusted gross income shall be determined in the same manner as provided in paragraph (2).

P.L. 109-135, §403(a)(12):

Amended Code Sec. 199(d) by redesignating paragraph (7) as paragraph (8) and by inserting after paragraph (6) a new paragraph (7). **Effective** as if included in the provision of the American Jobs Creation Act of 2004 (P.L. 108-357) to which it relates [**effective** for tax years beginning after 12-31-2004.—CCH].

P.L. 109-135, §403(a)(13):

Amended Code Sec. 199(d)(8), as redesignated by Act Sec. 403(a)(12), by inserting ", including regulations which prevent more than 1 taxpayer from being allowed a deduction under this section with respect to any activity described in subsection (c)(4)(A)(i)" before the period at the end. **Effective** as if included in the provision of the American Jobs Creation Act of 2004 (P.L. 108-357) to which it relates [**effective** for tax years beginning after 12-31-2004.—CCH].

• 2004, American Jobs Creation Act of 2004 (P.L. 108-357)

P.L. 108-357, §102(a):

Amended part VI of subchapter B of chapter 1 by adding at the end a new Code Sec. 199. **Effective** for tax years beginning after 12-31-2004.

P.L. 108-357, §102(d)(2), as added by P.L. 109-135, §403(a)(19), provides:

(2) APPLICATION TO PASS-THRU ENTITIES, ETC.—In determining the deduction under section 199 of the Internal Revenue Code of 1986 (as added by this section), items arising from a taxable year of a partnership, S corporation, estate, or trust beginning before January 1, 2005, shall not be taken into account for purposes of subsection (d)(1) of such section.

PART VII—ADDITIONAL ITEMIZED DEDUCTIONS FOR INDIVIDUALS

[Sec. 211]

SEC. 211. ALLOWANCE OF DEDUCTIONS.

In computing taxable income under section 63, there shall be allowed as deductions the items specified in this part, subject to the exceptions provided in part IX (section 261 and following, relating to items not deductible).

Amendments

• 1977, Tax Reduction and Simplification Act of 1977 (P.L. 95-30)

P.L. 95-30, §102(b)(3):

Amended Code Sec. 211 by striking out "section 63(a)" and inserting in lieu thereof "section 63". **Effective** for tax years beginning after 12-31-76.

[Sec. 212]

SEC. 212. EXPENSES FOR PRODUCTION OF INCOME.

In the case of an individual, there shall be allowed as a deduction all the ordinary and necessary expenses paid or incurred during the taxable year—

(1) for the production or collection of income;

(2) for the management, conservation, or maintenance of property held for the production of income; or

(3) in connection with the determination, collection, or refund of any tax.

[Sec. 213]

SEC. 213. MEDICAL, DENTAL, ETC., EXPENSES.

»»→ Caution: Code Sec. 213(a), below, prior to amendment by P.L. 111-148, applies to tax years beginning on or before December 31, 2012.

[Sec. 213(a)]

(a) ALLOWANCE OF DEDUCTION.—There shall be allowed as a deduction the expenses paid during the taxable year, not compensated for by insurance or otherwise, for medical care of the taxpayer, his spouse, or a dependent (as defined in section 152, determined without regard to subsections (b)(1), (b)(2), and (d)(1)(B) thereof), to the extent that such expenses exceed 7.5 percent of adjusted gross income.

»»→ Caution: Code Sec. 213(a), below, as amended by P.L. 111-148, applies to tax years beginning after December 31, 2012.

[Sec. 213(a)]

(a) ALLOWANCE OF DEDUCTION.—There shall be allowed as a deduction the expenses paid during the taxable year, not compensated for by insurance or otherwise, for medical care of the taxpayer, his spouse, or a dependent (as defined in section 152, determined without regard to subsections (b)(1), (b)(2), and (d)(1)(B) thereof), to the extent that such expenses exceed 10 percent of adjusted gross income.

Amendments

• 2010, Patient Protection and Affordable Care Act (P.L. 111-148)

P.L. 111-148, §9013(a):

Amended Code Sec. 213(a) by striking "7.5 percent" and inserting "10 percent". **Effective** for tax years beginning after 12-31-2012.

• 2004, Working Families Tax Relief Act of 2004 (P.L. 108-311)

P.L. 108-311, §207(17):

Amended Code Sec. 213(a) by inserting ", determined without regard to subsections (b)(1), (b)(2), and (d)(1)(B) thereof" after "section 152". **Effective** for tax years beginning after 12-31-2004.

• 1986, Tax Reform Act of 1986 (P.L. 99-514)

P.L. 99-514, §133:

Amended Code Sec. 213(a) by striking out "5 percent" and inserting in lieu thereof "7.5 percent". **Effective** for tax years beginning after 12-31-86.

• 1982, Tax Equity and Fiscal Responsibility Act of 1982 (P.L. 97-248)

P.L. 97-248, §202(a):

Amended Code Sec. 213(a). **Effective** for to tax years beginning after 12-31-82. Prior to amendment, Code Sec. 213(a) read as follows:

"(a) Allowance of Deduction.—There shall be allowed as a deduction the following amounts, not compensated for by insurance or otherwise—

(1) the amount by which the amount of the expenses paid during the taxable year (reduced by any amount deductible under paragraph (2)) for medical care of the taxpayer, his spouse, and dependents (as defined in section 152) exceeds 3 percent of the adjusted gross income, and

(2) an amount (not in excess of $150) equal to one-half of the expenses paid during the taxable year for insurance which constitutes medical care for the taxpayer, his spouse, and dependents."

• 1965, Social Security Amendments of 1965 (P.L. 89-97)

P.L. 89-97, §106(a):

Amended Code Sec. 213(a). **Effective** for tax years beginning after 12-31-66. Prior to amendment, Sec. 213(a) read as follows:

"(a) Allowance of Deduction.—There shall be allowed as a deduction the following amounts of the expenses paid during the taxable year, not compensated for by insurance or otherwise, for medical care of the taxpayer, his spouse, or a dependent (as defined in section 152):

"(1) If neither the taxpayer nor his spouse has attained the age of 65 before the close of the taxable year—

"(A) the amount of such expenses for the care of any dependent who—

"(i) is the mother or father of the taxpayer or of his spouse, and

"(ii) has attained the age of 65 before the close of the taxable year, and

"(B) the amount by which such expenses for the care of the taxpayer, his spouse, and such dependents (other than any dependent described in subparagraph (A)) exceed 3 percent of the adjusted gross income.

"(2) If either the taxpayer or his spouse has attained the age of 65 before the close of the taxable year—

"(A) the amount of such expenses for the care of the taxpayer and his spouse,

"(B) the amount of such expenses for the care of any dependent described in paragraph (1)(A), and

"(C) the amount by which such expenses for the care of such dependents (other than any dependent described in paragraph (1)(A)) exceed 3 percent of the adjusted gross income."

• 1960 (P.L. 86-470)

P.L. 86-470, §3:

Amended Code Sec. 213(a). **Effective** for taxable years beginning after 12-31-59. Prior to amendment, Code Sec. 213(a) read as follows:

"(a) Allowance of Deduction.—There shall be allowed as a deduction the expenses paid during the taxable year, not compensated for by insurance or otherwise, for medical care of the taxpayer, his spouse, or a dependent (as defined in section 152)—

"(1) if neither the taxpayer nor his spouse has attained the age of 65 before the close of the taxable year, to the extent that such expenses exceed 3 percent of the adjusted gross income; or

"(2) if either the taxpayer or his spouse has attained the age of 65 before the close of the taxable year—

"(A) the amount of such expenses for the care of the taxpayer and his spouse, and

"(B) the amount by which such expenses for the care of such dependents exceed 3 percent of the adjusted gross income.".

[Sec. 213(b)]

(b) LIMITATION WITH RESPECT TO MEDICINE AND DRUGS.—An amount paid during the taxable year for medicine or a drug shall be taken into account under subsection (a) only if such medicine or drug is a prescribed drug or is insulin.

Amendments

• 1982, Tax Equity and Fiscal Responsibility Act of 1982 (P.L. 97-248)

P.L. 97-248, §202(b)(1):

Amended Code Sec. 213(b). **Effective** for tax years beginning after 12-31-83. Prior to amendment, Code Sec. 213(b) read as follows:

(b) LIMITATION WITH RESPECT TO MEDICINE AND DRUGS.—Amounts paid during the taxable year for medicine and drugs which (but for this subsection) would be taken into account in computing the deduction under subsection (a) shall be taken into account only to the extent that the aggregate of such amounts exceeds 1 percent of the adjusted gross income.

• 1965, Social Security Amendments of 1965 (P.L. 89-97)

P.L. 89-97, §106(b):

Amended Code Sec. 213(b) by repealing the second sentence thereof. **Effective** for tax years beginning after 12-31-66. Prior to repeal, the second sentence read as follows: "The preceding sentence shall not apply to amounts paid for the care of—

"(1) the taxpayer and his spouse, if either of them has attained the age of 65 before the close of the taxable year, or

"(2) any dependent described in subsection (a)(1)(A)."

• 1964, Revenue Act of 1964 (P.L. 88-272)

P.L. 88-272, §211(a):

Amended subsection (b) by adding the last sentence. **Effective** for tax years beginning after 12-31-63.

[Sec. 213(c)—Repealed]

Amendments

• 1965, Social Security Amendments of 1965 (P.L. 89-97)

P.L. 89-97, §106(d):

Repealed Sec. 213(c). Prior to repeal, it read as follows:

"(c) Maximum Limitations.—Except as provided in subsection (g), the deduction under this section shall not exceed $5,000, multiplied by the number of exemptions allowed for the taxable year as a deduction under section 151 (other than exemptions allowed by reason of subsection (c) or (d), relating to additional exemptions for age or blindness); except that the maximum deduction under this section shall be—

"(1) $10,000, if the taxpayer is single and not the head of a household (as defined in section 1(b)(2)) and not a surviving spouse (as defined in section 2(b)) or is married but files a separate return; or

"(2) $20,000, if the taxpayer files a joint return with his spouse under section 6013, or is the head of a household (as defined in section 1(b)(2)) or a surviving spouse (as defined in section 2(b))."

• 1962 (P.L. 87-863)

P.L. 87-863, §1(a):

Amended Code Sec. 213(c) by substituting "$5,000" for "$2,500," "$10,000" for "$5,000," and "$20,000" for "$10,000." **Effective** 1-1-62.

• 1958, Technical Amendments Act of 1958 (P.L. 85-866)

P.L. 85-866, §17(c):

Struck out the word "The" at the beginning of Sec. 213(c) and substituted the phrase "Except as provided in subsection (g), the". **Effective** 1-1-58.

[Sec. 213(c)]

(c) SPECIAL RULE FOR DECEDENTS.—

(1) TREATMENT OF EXPENSES PAID AFTER DEATH.—For purposes of subsection (a), expenses for the medical care of the taxpayer which are paid out of his estate during the 1-year period beginning with the day after the date of his death shall be treated as paid by the taxpayer at the time incurred.

(2) LIMITATION.—Paragraph (1) shall not apply if the amount paid is allowable under section 2053 as a deduction in computing the taxable estate of the decedent, but this paragraph shall not apply if (within the time and in the manner and form prescribed by the Secretary) there is filed—

(A) a statement that such amount has not been allowed as a deduction under section 2053, and

(B) a waiver of the right to have such amount allowed at any time as a deduction under section 2053.

Amendments

• 1982, Tax Equity and Fiscal Responsibility Act of 1982 (P.L. 97-248)

P.L. 97-248, §202(b)(3)(B):

Redesignated former Code Sec. 213(d) as Code Sec. 213(c). **Effective** for tax years beginning after 1983.

• 1958, Technical Amendments Act of 1958 (P.L. 85-866)

P.L. 85-866, §16:

Struck out the phrase "claimed or" where it preceded the word "allowed" in Sec. 213(d)(2)(A). **Effective** 1-1-54.

[Sec. 213(d)]

(d) DEFINITIONS.—For purposes of this section—

(1) The term "medical care" means amounts paid—

(A) for the diagnosis, cure, mitigation, treatment, or prevention of disease, or for the purpose of affecting any structure or function of the body,

(B) for transportation primarily for and essential to medical care referred to in subparagraph (A),

(C) for qualified long-term care services (as defined in section 7702B(c)), or

(D) for insurance (including amounts paid as premiums under part B of title XVIII of the Social Security Act, relating to supplementary medical insurance for the aged) covering medical care referred to in subparagraphs (A) and (B) or for any qualified long-term care insurance contract (as defined in section 7702B(b)).

In the case of a qualified long-term care insurance contract (as defined in section 7702B(b)), only eligible long-term care premiums (as defined in paragraph (10)) shall be taken into account under subparagraph (D).

(2) AMOUNTS PAID FOR CERTAIN LODGING AWAY FROM HOME TREATED AS PAID FOR MEDICAL CARE.—Amounts paid for lodging (not lavish or extravagant under the circumstances) while away from home primarily for and essential to medical care referred to in paragraph (1)(A) shall be treated as amounts paid for medical care if—

(A) the medical care referred to in paragraph (1)(A) is provided by a physician in a licensed hospital (or in a medical care facility which is related to, or the equivalent of, a licensed hospital), and

(B) there is no significant element of personal pleasure, recreation, or vacation in the travel away from home.

The amount taken into account under the preceding sentence shall not exceed $50 for each night for each individual.

(3) PRESCRIBED DRUG.—The term "prescribed drug" means a drug or biological which requires a prescription of a physician for its use by an individual.

(4) PHYSICIAN.—The term "physician" has the meaning given to such term by section 1861(r) of the Social Security Act (42 U.S.C. 1395x(r)).

(5) SPECIAL RULE IN THE CASE OF CHILD OF DIVORCED PARENTS, ETC.—Any child to whom section 152(e) applies shall be treated as a dependent of both parents for purposes of this section.

(6) In the case of an insurance contract under which amounts are payable for other than medical care referred to in subparagraphs (A), (B), and (C) of paragraph (1)—

(A) no amount shall be treated as paid for insurance to which paragraph (1)(D) applies unless the charge for such insurance is either separately stated in the contract, or furnished to the policyholder by the insurance company in a separate statement,

(B) the amount taken into account as the amount paid for such insurance shall not exceed such charge, and

(C) no amount shall be treated as paid for such insurance if the amount specified in the contract (or furnished to the policyholder by the insurance company in a separate statement) as the charge for such insurance is unreasonably large in relation to the total charges under the contract.

(7) Subject to the limitations of paragraph (6) [(5) after 1984], premiums paid during the taxable year by a taxpayer before he attains the age of 65 for insurance covering medical care

(within the meaning of subparagraphs (A), (B), and (C) of paragraph (1)) for the taxpayer, his spouse, or a dependent after the taxpayer attains the age of 65 shall be treated as expenses paid during the taxable year for insurance which constitutes medical care if premiums for such insurance are payable (on a level payment basis) under the contract for a period of 10 years or more or until the year in which the taxpayer attains the age of 65 (but in no case for a period of less than 5 years).

(8) The determination of whether an individual is married at any time during the taxable year shall be made in accordance with the provisions of section 6013(d) (relating to determination of status as husband and wife).

(9) COSMETIC SURGERY.—

(A) IN GENERAL.—The term "medical care" does not include cosmetic surgery or other similar procedures, unless the surgery or procedure is necessary to ameliorate a deformity arising from, or directly related to, a congenital abnormality, a personal injury resulting from an accident or trauma, or disfiguring disease.

(B) COSMETIC SURGERY DEFINED.—For purposes of this paragraph, the term "cosmetic surgery" means any procedure which is directed at improving the patient's appearance and does not meaningfully promote the proper function of the body or prevent or treat illness or disease.

(10) ELIGIBLE LONG-TERM CARE PREMIUMS.—

(A) IN GENERAL.—For purposes of this section, the term "eligible long-term care premiums" means the amount paid during a taxable year for any qualified long-term care insurance contract (as defined in section 7702B(b)) covering an individual, to the extent such amount does not exceed the limitation determined under the following table:

In the case of an individual with an attained age before the close of the taxable year of:	*The limitation is:*
40 or less	$200
More than 40 but not more than 50	375
More than 50 but not more than 60	750
More than 60 but not more than 70	2,000
More than 70	2,500

(B) INDEXING.—

(i) IN GENERAL.—In the case of any taxable year beginning in a calendar year after 1997, each dollar amount contained in subparagraph (A) shall be increased by the medical care cost adjustment of such amount for such calendar year. If any increase determined under the preceding sentence is not a multiple of $10, such increase shall be rounded to the nearest multiple of $10.

(ii) MEDICAL CARE COST ADJUSTMENT.—For purposes of clause (i), the medical care cost adjustment for any calendar year is the percentage (if any) by which—

(I) the medical care component of the Consumer Price Index (as defined in section 1(f)(5)) for August of the preceding calendar year, exceeds

(II) such component for August of 1996. The Secretary shall, in consultation with the Secretary of Health and Human Services, prescribe an adjustment which the Secretary determines is more appropriate for purposes of this paragraph than the adjustment described in the preceding sentence, and the adjustment so prescribed shall apply in lieu of the adjustment described in the preceding sentence.

(11) CERTAIN PAYMENTS TO RELATIVES TREATED AS NOT PAID FOR MEDICAL CARE.—An amount paid for a qualified long-term care service (as defined in section 7702B(c)) provided to an individual shall be treated as not paid for medical care if such service is provided—

(A) by the spouse of the individual or by a relative (directly or through a partnership, corporation, or other entity) unless the service is provided by a licensed professional with respect to such service, or

(B) by a corporation or partnership which is related (within the meaning of section 267(b) or 707(b)) to the individual.

For purposes of this paragraph, the term "relative" means an individual bearing a relationship to the individual which is described in any of subparagraphs (A) through (G) of section 152(d)(2). This paragraph shall not apply for purposes of section 105(b) with respect to reimbursements through insurance.

Amendments

• 2010, Patient Protection and Affordable Care Act (P.L. 111-148)

P.L. 111-148, §8002, provides:

SEC. 8002. ESTABLISHMENT OF NATIONAL VOLUNTARY INSURANCE PROGRAM FOR PURCHASING COMMUNITY LIVING ASSISTANCE SERVICES AND SUPPORT.

(a) ESTABLISHMENT OF CLASS PROGRAM.—

(1) IN GENERAL.—The Public Health Service Act (42 U.S.C. 201 et seq.), as amended by section 4302(a), is amended by adding at the end the following:

* * *

"SEC. 3210. TAX TREATMENT OF PROGRAM.

"The CLASS program shall be treated for purposes of the Internal Revenue Code of 1986 in the same manner as a qualified long-term care insurance contract for qualified long-term care services.".

• 2004, Working Families Tax Relief Act of 2004 (P.L. 108-311)

P.L. 108-311, §207(18):

Amended the second sentence of Code Sec. 213(d)(11) by striking "paragraphs (1) through (8) of section 152(a)" and inserting "subparagraphs (A) through (G) of section 152(d)(2)". **Effective** for tax years beginning after 12-31-2004.

• 1996, Health Insurance Portability and Accountability Act of 1996 (P.L. 104-191)

P.L. 104-191, §322(a):

Amended Code Sec. 213(d)(1) by striking "or" at the end of subparagraph (B), by redesignating subparagraph (C) as subparagraph (D), and by inserting after subparagraph (B) a new subparagraph (C). **Effective** for tax years beginning after 12-31-96.

P.L. 104-191, §322(b)(1):

Amended Code Sec. 213(d)(1)(D) (as redesignated by subsection (a)) by inserting before the period "or for any qualified long-term care insurance contract (as defined in section 7702B(b))". **Effective** for tax years beginning after 12-31-96.

P.L. 104-191, §322(b)(2)(A):

Amended Code Sec. 213(d)(1) by adding at the end a new flush sentence. **Effective** for tax years beginning after 12-31-96.

P.L. 104-191, §322(b)(2)(C):

Amended Code Sec. 213(d) by adding at the end new paragraphs (10) and (11). **Effective** for tax years beginning after 12-31-96.

P.L. 104-191, §322(b)(3)(A)-(B):

Amended Code Sec. 213(d)(6) by striking "subparagraphs (A) and (B)" and inserting "subparagraphs (A), (B), and (C)" and by striking "paragraph (1)(C)" in subparagraph (A) and inserting "paragraph (1)(D)". **Effective** for tax years beginning after 12-31-96.

P.L. 104-191, §322(b)(4):

Amended Code Sec. 213(d)(7) by striking "subparagraphs (A) and (B)" and inserting "subparagraphs (A), (B), and (C)". **Effective** for tax years beginning after 12-31-96.

• 1990, Omnibus Budget Reconciliation Act of 1990 (P.L. 101-508)

P.L. 101-508, §11342(a):

Amended Code Sec. 213(d) by adding at the end thereof a new paragraph (9). **Effective** for tax years beginning after 12-31-90.

• 1984, Deficit Reduction Act of 1984 (P.L. 98-369)

P.L. 98-369, §423(b)(1):

Amended Code Sec. 213(d) by redesignating paragraphs (4), (5), and (6) as paragraphs (5), (6), and (7), respectively, and by inserting after paragraph (3) new paragraph (4). **Effective** for tax years beginning after 12-31-84.

P.L. 98-369, §423(b)(3):

Amended Code Sec. 213(d)(6) (as redesignated by Act Sec. 423(b)(1)) by striking out "the limitations of paragraph (4)" and inserting in lieu thereof "the limitations of paragraph (5)". **Effective** for tax years beginning after 12-31-84.

P.L. 98-369, §482(a):

Amended Code Sec. 213(d) (as amended by Act Sec. 423(b)) by redesignating (2), (3), (4), (5), (6), and (7) as paragraphs (3), (4), (5), (6), (7), and (8), respectively, and by inserting after paragraph (1) new paragraph (2). **Effective** for tax years beginning after 12-31-83.

P.L. 98-369, §482(b)(1):

Amended Code Sec. 213(d)(7) (as redesignated by Act Sec. 482(a)) by striking our "paragraph (5)" and inserting in lieu thereof "paragraph (6)". **Effective** for tax years beginning after 12-31-83.

P.L. 98-369, §711(b):

Amended Code Sec. 213(d)(5), before its redesignation by Act Secs. 423(b)(1) and 482(a) and before the amendment by Act Sec. 423(b)(3), by striking out "paragraph (2)" an inserting in lieu thereof "paragraph (4)". **Effective** as if included in the provision of P.L. 97-248 to which it relates.

• 1982, Tax Equity and Fiscal Responsibility Act of 1982 (P.L. 97-248)

P.L. 97-248, §202(b)(2):

Amended Code Sec. 213(e) by adding new paragraphs (2) and (3). **Effective** for tax years beginning after 1983.

P.L. 97-248, §202(b)(3)(A):

Amended Code Sec. 213(e) as in effect before the amendment made by Act Sec. 202(b)(2) by redesignating paragraphs (2), (3), and (4) as (4), (5), and (6), respectively. **Effective** for tax years beginning after 1983.

P.L. 97-248, §202(b)(3)(B):

Redesignated Code Sec. 213(e) as Code Sec. 213(d). **Effective** for tax years beginning after 1983.

• 1965, Social Security Amendments of 1965 (P.L. 89-97)

P.L. 89-97, §106(c):

Amended Sec. 213(e). **Effective** for tax years beginning after 12-31-66. Prior to amendment, Sec. 213(e) read as follows:

"(e) Definitions.—For purposes of this section—

"(1) The term "medical care" means amounts paid—

"(A) for the diagnosis, cure, mitigation, treatment, or prevention of disease, or for the purpose of affecting any structure or function of the body (including amounts paid for accident or health insurance), or

"(B) for transportation primarily for and essential to medical care referred to in subparagraph (A).

"(2) The determination of whether an individual is married at any time during the taxable year shall be made in accordance with the provisions of section 6013(d) (relating to determination of status as husband and wife)."

[Sec. 213(e)]

(e) EXCLUSION OF AMOUNTS ALLOWED FOR CARE OF CERTAIN DEPENDENTS.—Any expense allowed as a credit under section 21 shall not be treated as an expense paid for medical care.

Amendments

• 1984, Deficit Reduction Act of 1984 (P.L. 98-369)

P.L. 98-369, §474(r)(9):

Amended Code Sec. 213(e) by striking out "section 44A" and inserting in lieu thereof "section 21". **Effective** for tax years beginning after 12-31-83, and to carrybacks from such years.

• 1982, Tax Equity and Fiscal Responsibility Act of 1982 (P.L. 97-248)

P.L. 97-248, §202(b)(3)(B):

Redesignated Code Sec. 213(f) as Code Sec. 213(e). **Effective** for tax years beginning after 1983.

• 1976, Tax Reform Act of 1976 (P.L. 94-455)

P.L. 94-455, §504(c)(1):

Substituted "a credit under section 44A" for "a deduction under section 214" in Code Sec. 213(f). **Effective** for tax years beginning after 12-31-75.

»»→ Caution: Code Sec. 213(f), below, as added by P.L. 111-148, applies to tax years beginning after December 31, 2012.

[Sec. 213(f)]

(f) SPECIAL RULE FOR 2013, 2014, 2015, AND 2016.—In the case of any taxable year beginning after December 31, 2012, and ending before January 1, 2017, subsection (a) shall be applied with respect to a taxpayer by substituting "7.5 percent" for "10 percent" if such taxpayer or such taxpayer's spouse has attained age 65 before the close of such taxable year.

Amendments

• 2010, Patient Protection and Affordable Care Act (P.L. 111-148)

P.L. 111-148, §9013(b):

Amended Code Sec. 213 by adding at the end a new subsection (f). **Effective** for tax years beginning after 12-31-2012.

[Sec. 213(f)—Stricken]

Amendments

• 1993, Omnibus Budget Reconciliation Act of 1993 (P.L. 103-66)

P.L. 103-66, §13131(d)(3):

Amended Code Sec. 213 by striking subsection (f). **Effective** for tax years beginning after 12-31-93. Prior to being stricken, Code Sec. 213(f) read as follows:

(f) COORDINATION WITH HEALTH INSURANCE CREDIT UNDER SECTION 32.—The amount otherwise taken into account under subsection (a) as expenses paid for medical care shall be reduced by the amount (if any) of the health insurance credit allowable to the taxpayer for the taxable year under section 32.

• 1990, Omnibus Budget Reconciliation Act of 1990 (P.L. 101-508)

P.L. 101-508, §11111(d)(1):

Amended Code Sec. 213 by adding at the end thereof a new subsection (f). **Effective** for tax years beginning after 12-31-90.

[Sec. 213(g)—Repealed]

Amendments

• 1965, Social Security Amendments of 1965 (P.L. 89-97)

P.L. 89-97, §106(d):

Repealed Sec. 213(g). **Effective** 1-1-67. Prior to repeal, it read as follows:

"(g) Maximum Limitation if Taxpayer or Spouse Has Attained Age 65 and Is Disabled.—

"(1) Special rule.—Subject to the provisions of paragraph (2), the deduction under this section shall not exceed—

"(A) $20,000, if the taxpayer has attained the age of 65 before the close of the taxable year and is disabled, or if his spouse has attained the age of 65 before the close of the taxable year and is disabled and if his spouse does not make a separate return for the taxable year, or

"(B) $40,000, if both the taxpayer and his spouse have attained the age of 65 before the close of the taxable year and are disabled and if the taxpayer files a joint return with his spouse under section 6013.

"(2) Amounts taken into account.—For purposes of paragraph (1)—

"(A) amounts paid by the taxpayer during the taxable year for medical care, other than amounts paid for—

"(i) his medical care, if he has attained the age of 65 before the close of the taxable year and is disabled, or

"(ii) the medical care of his spouse, if his spouse has attained the age of 65 before the close of the taxable year and is disabled,

shall be taken into account only to the extent that such amounts do not exceed the maximum limitation provided in subsection (c) which would (but for the provisions of this subsection) apply to the taxpayer for the taxable year;

"(B) if the taxpayer has attained the age of 65 before the close of the taxable year and is disabled, amounts paid by him during the taxable year for his medical care shall be taken into account only to the extent that such amounts do not exceed $20,000; and

"(C) if the spouse of the taxpayer has attained the age of 65 before the close of the taxable year and is disabled, amounts paid by the taxpayer during the taxable year for the medical care of his spouse shall be taken into account only to the extent that such amounts do not exceed $20,000.

"(3) Meaning of disabled.—For purposes of paragraph (1), an individual shall be considered to be disabled if he is unable to engage in any substantial gainful activity by reason of any medically determinable physical or mental impairment which can be expected to result in death or to be of long-continued and indefinite duration. An individual shall not be considered to be disabled unless he furnishes proof of the existence thereof in such form and manner as the Secretary or his delegate may require.

"(4) Determination of status.—For purposes of paragraph (1), the determination as to whether the taxpayer or his spouse is disabled shall be made as of the close of the taxable year of the taxpayer, except that if his spouse dies during such taxable year such determination shall be made with respect to his spouse as of the time of such death."

• 1962 (P.L. 87-863)

P.L. 87-863, §1(b):

Amended Code Sec. 213(g) by substituting "$20,000" for "$15,000" each place it appears, and by substituting "$40,000" for "$30,000." **Effective** 1-1-62.

• 1958, Technical Amendments Act of 1958 (P.L. 85-866)

P.L. 85-866, §17(a):

Added subsection (g) to Sec. 213. **Effective** 1-1-58.

[Sec. 214—Repealed]

Amendments

• 1976, Tax Reform Act of 1976 (P.L. 94-455)

P.L. 94-455, §504(b):

Repealed Code Sec. 214. **Effective** for tax years beginning after 1975. Prior to repeal, Sec. 214 read as follows:

SEC. 214. EXPENSES FOR HOUSEHOLD AND DEPENDENT CARE SERVICES NECESSARY FOR GAINFUL EMPLOYMENT.

(a) ALLOWANCE OF DEDUCTION.—In the case of an individual who maintains a household which includes as a member one or more qualifying individuals (as defined in subsection (b)(1)), there shall be allowed as a deduction the employment-related expenses (as defined in subsection (b)(2)) paid by him during the taxable year.

(b) DEFINITIONS, ETC.—For purposes of this section—

(1) QUALIFYING INDIVIDUAL.—The term "qualifying individual" means—

(A) a dependent of the taxpayer who is under the age of 15 and with respect to whom the taxpayer is entitled to a deduction under section 151(e),

(B) a dependent of the taxpayer who is physically or mentally incapable of caring for himself, or

(C) the spouse of the taxpayer, if he is physically or mentally incapable of caring for himself.

(2) EMPLOYMENT-RELATED EXPENSES.—The term "employment-related expenses" means amounts paid for the following expenses, but only if such expenses are incurred to enable the taxpayer to be gainfully employed:

(A) expenses for household services, and

(B) expenses for the care of a qualifying individual.

(3) MAINTAINING A HOUSEHOLD.—An individual shall be treated as maintaining a household for any period only if over half of the cost of maintaining the household during such period is furnished by such individual (or if such individual is married during such period, is furnished by such individual and his spouse).

(c) LIMITATIONS ON AMOUNTS DEDUCTIBLE.—

(1) IN GENERAL.—A deduction shall be allowed under subsection (a) for employment-related expenses incurred during any month only to the extent such expenses do not exceed $400.

(2) EXPENSES MUST BE FOR SERVICES IN THE HOUSEHOLD.—

(A) IN GENERAL.—Except as provided in subparagraph (B), a deduction shall be allowed under subsection (a) for employment-related expenses only if they are incurred for services in the taxpayer's household.

(B) EXCEPTION.—Employment-related expenses described in subsection (b)(2)(B) which are incurred for services outside the taxpayer's household shall be taken into account only if incurred for the care of a qualifying individual described in subsection (b)(1)(A) and only to the extent such expenses incurred during any month do not exceed—

(i) $200, in the case of one such individual,

(ii) $300, in the case of two such individuals, and

(iii) $400, in the case of three or more such individuals.

(d) INCOME LIMITATION.—If the adjusted gross income of the taxpayer exceeds $35,000 for the taxable year during which the expenses are incurred, the amount of the employment-related expenses incurred during any month of such year which may be taken into account under this section shall (after the application of subsections (e)(5) and (c)) be further reduced by that portion of one-half of the excess of the adjusted gross income over $35,000 which is properly allocable to such month. For purposes of the preceding sentence, if the taxpayer is married during any period of the taxable year, there shall be taken into account the combined adjusted gross income of the taxpayer and his spouse for such period.

(e) SPECIAL RULES.—For purposes of this section—

(1) MARRIED COUPLES MUST FILE JOINT RETURN.—If the taxpayer is married at the close of the taxable year, the deduction provided by subsection (a) shall be allowed only if the taxpayer and his spouse file a single return jointly for the taxable year.

(2) GAINFUL EMPLOYMENT REQUIREMENT.—If the taxpayer is married for any period during the taxable year, there shall be taken into account employment-related expenses incurred during any month of such period only if—

(A) both spouses are gainfully employed on a substantially full-time basis, or

(B) the spouse is a qualifying individual described in subsection (b)(1)(C).

(3) CERTAIN MARRIED INDIVIDUALS LIVING APART.—An individual who for the taxable year would be treated as not married under section 143(b) if paragraph (1) of such section referred to any dependent, shall be treated as not married for such taxable year.

(4) PAYMENTS TO RELATED INDIVIDUALS.—No deduction shall be allowed under subsection (a) for any amount paid by the taxpayer to an individual bearing a relationship to the taxpayer described in paragraphs (1) through (8) of section 152(a) (relating to definition of dependent) or to a dependent described in paragraph (9) of such section.

(5) REDUCTION FOR CERTAIN PAYMENTS.—In the case of employment-related expenses incurred during any taxable year solely with respect to a qualifying individual (other than an individual who is also described in subsection (b)(1)(A)), the amount of such expenses which may be taken into account for purposes of this section shall (before the application of subsection (c)) be reduced—

(A) if such individual is described in subsection (b)(1)(B), by the amount by which the sum of—

(i) such individual's adjusted gross income for such taxable year, and

(ii) the disability payments received by such individual during such year,

exceeds $750, or

(B) in the case of a qualifying individual described in subsection (b)(1)(C), by the amount of disability payments received by such individual during the taxable year.

For purposes of this paragraph, the term "disability payment" means a payment (other than a gift) which is made on account of the physical or mental condition of an individual and which is not included in gross income.

(f) REGULATIONS.—The Secretary or his delegate shall prescribe such regulations as may be necessary to carry out the purposes of this section.

[Sec. 215]

SEC. 215. ALIMONY, ETC., PAYMENTS.

[Sec. 215(a)]

(a) GENERAL RULE.—In the case of an individual, there shall be allowed as a deduction an amount equal to the alimony or separate maintenance payments paid during such individual's taxable year.

[Sec. 215(b)]

(b) ALIMONY OR SEPARATE MAINTENANCE PAYMENTS DEFINED.—For purposes of this section, the term "alimony or separate maintenance payment" means any alimony or separate maintenance payment (as defined in section 71(b)) which is includible in the gross income of the recipient under section 71.

[Sec. 215(c)]

(c) REQUIREMENT OF IDENTIFICATION NUMBER.—The Secretary may prescribe regulations under which—

(1) any individual receiving alimony or separate maintenance payments is required to furnish such individual's taxpayer identification number to the individual making such payments, and

(2) the individual making such payments is required to include such taxpayer identification number on such individual's return for the taxable year in which such payments are made.

[Sec. 215(d)]

(d) COORDINATION WITH SECTION 682.—No deduction shall be allowed under this section with respect to any payment if, by reason of section 682 (relating to income of alimony trusts), the amount thereof is not includible in such individual's gross income.

Amendments

• 1984, Deficit Reduction Act of 1984 (P.L. 98-369)

P.L. 98-369, §422(b):

Amended Code Sec. 215. **Effective** for divorce or separation instruments (as defined in Code Sec. 71(b)(2), as amended by this section) executed after 12-31-84. However, it also applies to any divorce or separation instrument (as so defined) executed before 1-1-85, but modified on or after such date if the modification expressly provides that the amendments made by this section apply to such modification. Code Sec. 215(c), however, applies to payments made after 12-31-84. Prior to amendment Code Sec. 215 read as follows:

SEC. 215. ALIMONY, ETC., PAYMENTS.

(a) General Rule.—In the case of a husband described in section 71, there shall be allowed as a deduction amounts includible under section 71 in the gross income of his wife, payment of which is made within the husband's taxable year. No deduction shall be allowed under the preceding sentence with respect to any payment if, by reason of section 71(d) or 682, the amount thereof is not includible in the husband's gross income.

(b) Cross Reference.—

For definitions of "husband" and "wife", see section 7701(a)(17).

[Sec. 216]

SEC. 216. DEDUCTION OF TAXES, INTEREST, AND BUSINESS DEPRECIATION BY COOPERATIVE HOUSING CORPORATION TENANT-STOCKHOLDER.

[Sec. 216(a)]

(a) ALLOWANCE OF DEDUCTION.—In the case of a tenant-stockholder (as defined in subsection (b)(2)), there shall be allowed as a deduction amounts (not otherwise deductible) paid or accrued to a cooperative housing corporation within the taxable year, but only to the extent that such amounts represent the tenant-stockholder's proportionate share of—

(1) the real estate taxes allowable as a deduction to the corporation under section 164 which are paid or incurred by the corporation on the houses or apartment building and on the land on which such houses (or building) are situated, or

(2) the interest allowable as a deduction to the corporation under section 163 which is paid or incurred by the corporation on its indebtedness contracted—

(A) in the acquisition, construction, alteration, rehabilitation, or maintenance of the houses or apartment building, or

(B) in the acquisition of the land on which the houses (or apartment building) are situated.

[Sec. 216(b)]

(b) DEFINITIONS.—For purposes of this section—

(1) COOPERATIVE HOUSING CORPORATION.—The term "cooperative housing corporation" means a corporation—

(A) having one and only one class of stock outstanding,

(B) each of the stockholders of which is entitled, solely by reason of his ownership of stock in the corporation, to occupy for dwelling purposes a house, or an apartment in a building, owned or leased by such corporation,

(C) no stockholder of which is entitled (either conditionally or unconditionally) to receive any distribution not out of earnings and profits of the corporation except on a complete or partial liquidation of the corporation, and

(D) meeting 1 or more of the following requirements for the taxable year in which the taxes and interest described in subsection (a) are paid or incurred:

(i) 80 percent or more of the corporation's gross income for such taxable year is derived from tenant-stockholders.

(ii) At all times during such taxable year, 80 percent or more of the total square footage of the corporation's property is used or available for use by the tenant-stockholders for residential purposes or purposes ancillary to such residential use.

(iii) 90 percent or more of the expenditures of the corporation paid or incurred during such taxable year are paid or incurred for the acquisition, construction, management, maintenance, or care of the corporation's property for the benefit of the tenant-stockholders.

(2) TENANT-STOCKHOLDER.—The term "tenant-stockholder" means a person who is a stockholder in a cooperative housing corporation, and whose stock is fully paid-up in an amount not less than an amount shown to the satisfaction of the Secretary as bearing a reasonable relationship to the portion of the value of the corporation's equity in the houses or apartment building and the land on which situated which is attributable to the house or apartment which such person is entitled to occupy.

(3) TENANT-STOCKHOLDER'S PROPORTIONATE SHARE.—

(A) IN GENERAL.—Except as provided in subparagraph (B), the term "tenant-stockholder's proportionate share" means that proportion which the stock of the cooperative housing corporation owned by the tenant-stockholder is of the total outstanding stock of the corporation (including any stock held by the corporation).

(B) SPECIAL RULE WHERE ALLOCATION OF TAXES OR INTEREST REFLECT COST TO CORPORATION OF STOCKHOLDER'S UNIT.—

(i) IN GENERAL.—If, for any taxable year—

(I) each dwelling unit owned or leased by a cooperative housing corporation is separately allocated a share of such corporation's real estate taxes described in subsection (a)(1) or a share of such corporation's interest described in subsection (a)(2), and

(II) such allocations reasonably reflect the cost to such corporation of such taxes, or of such interest, attributable to the tenant-stockholder's dwelling unit (and such unit's share of the common areas),

then the term "tenant-stockholder's proportionate share" means the shares determined in accordance with the allocations described in subclause (II).

(ii) ELECTION BY CORPORATION REQUIRED.—Clause (i) shall apply with respect to any cooperative housing corporation only if such corporation elects its application. Such an election, once made, may be revoked only with the consent of the Secretary.

(4) STOCK OWNED BY GOVERNMENTAL UNITS.—For purposes of this subsection, in determining whether a corporation is a cooperative housing corporation, stock owned and apartments leased by the United States or any of its possessions, a State or any political subdivision thereof, or any agency or instrumentality of the foregoing empowered to acquire shares in a cooperative housing corporation for the purpose of providing housing facilities, shall not be taken into account.

(5) PRIOR APPROVAL OF OCCUPANCY.—For purposes of this section, in the following cases there shall not be taken into account the fact that (by agreement with the cooperative housing corporation) the person or his nominee may not occupy the house or apartment without the prior approval of such corporation:

(A) In any case where a person acquires stock of a cooperative housing corporation by operation of law.

(B) In any case where a person other than an individual acquires stock of a cooperative housing corporation.

(C) In any case where the original seller acquires any stock of the cooperative housing corporation from the corporation not later than 1 year after the date on which the apartments or houses (or leaseholds therein) are transferred by the original seller to the corporation.

(6) ORIGINAL SELLER DEFINED.—For purposes of paragraph (5), the term "original seller" means the person from whom the corporation has acquired the apartments or houses (or leaseholds therein).

Amendments

• 2007, Mortgage Forgiveness Debt Relief Act of 2007 (P.L. 110-142)

P.L. 110-142, §4(a):

Amended Code Sec. 216(b)(1)(D). **Effective** for tax years ending after 12-20-2007. Prior to amendment, Code Sec. 216(b)(1)(D) read as follows:

(D) 80 percent or more of the gross income of which for the taxable year in which the taxes and interest described in subsection (a) are paid or incurred is derived from tenant-stockholders.

• 1986, Tax Reform Act of 1986 (P.L. 99-514)

P.L. 99-514, §644(a)(1)(A)-(B):

Amended Code Sec. 216(b)(2) by striking out "an individual" and inserting in lieu thereof "a person", and by striking out "such individual" and inserting in lieu thereof "such person". **Effective** for tax years beginning after 12-31-86.

P.L. 99-514, §644(a)(2):

Amended Code Sec. 216(b)(5) and (6). **Effective** for tax years beginning after 12-31-86. Prior to amendment, Code Sec. 216(b)(5) and (6) read as follows:

(5) STOCK ACQUIRED THROUGH FORECLOSURE BY LENDING INSTITUTION.—If a bank or other lending institution acquires by foreclosure (or by instrument in lieu of foreclosure) the stock of a tenant-stockholder, and a lease or the right to occupy an apartment or house to which such stock is appurtenant, such bank or other lending institution shall be treated as a tenant-stockholder for a period not to exceed three years from the date of acquisition. The preceding sentence shall apply even though, by agreement with the cooperative housing corporation, the bank (or other lending institution) or its nominee may not occupy the house or apartment without the prior approval of such corporation.

(6) STOCK OWNED BY PERSON FROM WHOM THE CORPORATION ACQUIRED ITS PROPERTY.—

(A) IN GENERAL.—If the original seller acquires any stock of the corporation from the corporation or by foreclosure, the original seller shall be treated as a tenant-stockholder for a period not to exceed 3 years from the date of the acquisition of such stock.

(B) STOCK ACQUISITION MUST TAKE PLACE NOT LATER THAN 1 YEAR AFTER TRANSFER OF DWELLING UNITS.—Except in the case of an acquisition of stock of a corporation by foreclosure, subparagraph (A) shall apply only if the acquisition of stock occurs not later than 1 year after the date on which the apartments or houses (or leaseholds therein) are transferred by the original seller to the corporation. For purposes of this subparagraph and subparagraph (A), the term "by foreclosure" means by foreclosure (or by instrument in lieu of foreclosure) of any purchase-money security interest in the stock held by the original seller.

(C) ORIGINAL SELLER MUST HAVE RIGHT TO OCCUPY APARTMENT OR HOUSE.—Subparagraph (A) shall apply with respect to any acquisition of stock only if, together with such acquisition, the original seller acquires the right to occupy an apartment or house to which such stock is appurtenant. For purposes of the preceding sentence, there shall not be taken into account the fact that, by agreement with the corporation, the original seller or its nominee may not occupy the house or apartment without the prior approval of the corporation.

(D) ORIGINAL SELLER DEFINED.—For purposes of this paragraph, the term "original seller" means the person from whom the corporation has acquired the apartments or houses (or leaseholds therein). The estate of an original seller shall succeed to, and take into account, the tax treatment of the original seller under this paragraph.

P.L. 99-514, §644(d):

Amended Code Sec. 216(b)(3). **Effective** for tax years beginning after 12-31-86. Prior to amendment, Code Sec. 216(b)(3) read as follows:

(3) The term "tenant-stockholder's proportionate share" means that proportion which the stock of the cooperative housing corporation owned by the tenant-stockholder is of the total outstanding stock of the corporation (including any stock held by the corporation).

P.L. 99-514, §644(e), provides:

(e) TREATMENT OF AMOUNTS RECEIVED IN CONNECTION WITH THE REFINANCING OF INDEBTEDNESS OF CERTAIN COOPERATIVE HOUSING CORPORATIONS; TREATMENT OF AMOUNTS PAID FROM QUALIFIED REFINANCING-RELATED RESERVE.—

(1) PAYMENT OF CLOSING COSTS AND CREATION OF RESERVE EXCLUDED FROM GROSS INCOME.—For purposes of the Internal Revenue Code of 1954, no amount shall be included in the gross income of a qualified cooperative housing corporation by reason of the payment or reimbursement by a city housing development agency or corporation of amounts for—

(A) closing costs, or

(B) the creation of reserves for the qualified cooperative housing corporation,

in connection with a qualified refinancing.

(2) INCOME FROM RESERVE FUND TREATED AS MEMBER INCOME.—

(A) IN GENERAL.—Income from a qualified refinancing-related reserve shall be treated as derived from its members for purposes of—

(i) section 216 of the Internal Revenue Code of 1954 (relating to deduction of taxes, interest, and business depreciation by cooperative housing corporation tenant-stockholder), and

(ii) section 277 of such Code (relating to deductions incurred by certain membership organizations in transactions with members).

(B) NO INFERENCE.—Nothing in the provisions of this paragraph shall be construed to infer that a change in law is intended with respect to the treatment of deductions under section 277 of the Internal Revenue Code of 1954 with respect to cooperative housing corporations, and any determination of such issue shall be made as if such provisions had not been enacted.

(3) TREATMENT OF CERTAIN INTEREST CLAIMED AS DEDUCTION.—Any amount—

(A) claimed (on a return of tax imposed by chapter 1 of the Internal Revenue Code of 1954) as a deduction by a qualified cooperative housing coporation for interest for any taxable year beginning before January 1, 1986, on a second mortgage loan made by a city housing development agency or corporation in connection with a qualified refinancing, and

(B) reported (before April 16, 1986) by the qualified cooperative housing corporation to its tenant-stockholders as interest described in section 216(a)(2) of such Code,

shall be treated for purposes of such Code as if such amount were paid by such qualified cooperative housing corporation during such taxable year.

(4) QUALIFIED COOPERATIVE HOUSING CORPORATION.—

(A) IN GENERAL.—For purposes of this subsection, the term "qualified cooperative housing corporation" means any corporation if—

(i) such corporation is, after the application of paragraphs (1) and (2), a cooperative housing corporation (as defined in section 216(b) of the Internal Revenue Code of 1954),

(ii) such corporation is subject to a qualified limited-profit housing companies law, and

(iii) such corporation either—

(I) filed for incorporation on July 22, 1965, or

(II) filed for incorporation on March 5, 1964.

(B) QUALIFIED LIMITED-PROFIT HOUSING COMPANIES LAW.—For purposes of subparagraph (A), the term "qualified limited-profit housing companies law" means any limited-profit housing companies law which limits the resale price for a tenant-stockholder's stock in a cooperative housing corporation to the sum of his basis for such stock plus his proportionate share of part or all of the amortization of any mortgage on the building owned by such corporation.

(5) QUALIFIED REFINANCING.—For purposes of this subsection, the term "qualified refinancing" means any refinancing—

(A) which occurred—

(i) with respect to a qualified cooperative housing corporation described in paragraph (4)(A)(iii)(I) on September 20, 1978, or

(ii) with respect to a qualified cooperative housing corporation described in paragraph (4)(A)(iii)(II) on November 21, 1978, and

(B) in which a qualified cooperative housing corporation refinanced a first mortgage loan made to such corporation by a city housing development agency with a first mortgage loan made by a city housing development corporation and insured by an agency of the Federal Government and a second mortgage loan made by such city housing development agency, in the process of which a reserve was created (as required by such Federal agency) and closing costs were paid or reimbursed by such city housing development agency or corporation.

(6) QUALIFIED REFINANCING-RELATED RESERVE.—For purposes of this subsection, the term "qualified refinancing-related reserve" means any reserve of a qualified cooperative housing corporation with respect to the creation of which no amount was included in the gross income of such corporation by reason of paragraph (a).

(7) TREATMENT OF AMOUNTS PAID FROM QUALIFIED REFINANCING-RELATED RESERVE.—

(A) IN GENERAL.—With respect to any payment from a qualified refinancing-related reserve out of amounts excluded from gross income by reason of paragraph (1)—

(i) no deduction shall be allowed under chapter 1 of such Code, and

(ii) the basis of any property acquired with such payment (determined without regard to this subparagraph) shall be reduced by the amount of such payment.

(B) ORDERING RULES.—For purposes of subparagraph (A), payments from a reserve shall be treated as being made—

(i) first from amounts excluded from gross income by reason of paragraph (1) to the extent thereof, and

(ii) then from other amounts in the reserve.

• 1980, Technical Corrections Act of 1979 (P.L. 96-222)

P.L. 96-222, §105(a)(6)(A):

Amended Code Sec. 216(b)(6) by redesignating subparagraphs (B) and (C) as subparagraphs (C) and (D) and by deleting subparagraph (A) and inserting new subparagraphs (A) and (B). **Effective** for stock acquired after 11-6-78. Prior to amendment, subparagraph (A) read as follows:

(A) IN GENERAL.—If the original seller acquires any stock of the corporation—

(i) from the corporation by purchase, or

(ii) by foreclosure (or by instrument in lieu of foreclosure) of any purchase-money security interest in such stock held by the original seller,

the original seller shall be treated as a tenant-stockholder for a period not to exceed 3 years from the date of acquisition.

P.L. 96-222, §105(a)(6)(B):

Amended Code Sec. 216(b)(6)(D) (as redesignated by §105(a)(6)(A), P.L. 96-222) by adding at the end the following new sentence: "The estate of an original seller shall succeed to, and take into account, the tax treatment of the original seller under this paragraph.". **Effective** for stock acquired after 11-6-78.

• 1978, Revenue Act of 1978 (P.L. 95-600)

P.L. 95-600, §531(a):

Added Code Sec. 216(b)(6). **Effective** for stock acquired after 11-6-78.

• 1976, Tax Reform Act of 1976 (P.L. 94-455)

P.L. 94-455, §2101(f):

Added Code Sec. 216(b)(5). **Effective** for stock acquired by banks or other lending institutions after 10-4-76.

• 1969, Tax Reform Act of 1969 (P.L. 91-172)

P.L. 91-172, §913(a):

Added paragraph (b)(4). **Effective** for tax years beginning after 12-31-69.

[Sec. 216(c)]

(c) TREATMENT AS PROPERTY SUBJECT TO DEPRECIATION.—

(1) IN GENERAL.—So much of the stock of a tenant-stockholder in a cooperative housing corporation as is allocable, under regulations prescribed by the Secretary, to a proprietary lease or right of tenancy in property subject to the allowance for depreciation under section 167(a) shall, to the extent such proprietary lease or right of tenancy is used by such tenant-stockholder in a trade or business or for the production of income, be treated as property subject to the allowance for depreciation under section 167(a). The preceding sentence shall not be construed to limit or deny a deduction for depreciation under section 167(a) by a cooperative housing corporation with respect to property owned by such a corporation and leased to tenant-stockholders.

(2) DEDUCTION LIMITED TO ADJUSTED BASIS IN STOCK.—

(A) IN GENERAL.—The amount of any deduction for depreciation allowable under section 167(a) to a tenant-stockholder with respect to any stock for any taxable year by reason of paragraph (1) shall not exceed the adjusted basis of such stock as of the close of the taxable year of the tenant-stockholder in which such deduction was incurred.

(B) CARRYFORWARD OF DISALLOWED AMOUNT.—The amount of any deduction which is not allowed by reason of subparagraph (A) shall, subject to the provisions of subparagraph (A), be treated as a deduction allowable under section 167(a) in the succeeding taxable year.

Amendments

• 1986, Tax Reform Act of 1986 (P.L. 99-514)

P.L. 99-514, §644(b):

Amended Code Sec. 216(c). **Effective** for tax years beginning after 12-31-86. Prior to amendment, Code Sec. 216(c) read as follows:

(c) TREATMENT AS PROPERTY SUBJECT TO DEPRECIATION.—So much of the stock of a tenant-stockholder in a cooperative housing corporation as is allocable, under regulations prescribed by the Secretary, to a proprietary lease or right of tenancy in property subject to the allowance for depreciation under section 167(a) shall, to the extent such proprietary lease or right of tenancy is used by such tenant-stockholder in a trade or business or for the production of income, be treated as property subject to the allowance for depreciation under section 167(a). The preceding sentence shall not be construed to limit or deny a deduction for depreciation under 167(a) by a cooperative housing corporation with respect to property owned by such a corporation and leased to tenant-stockholders.

• 1976, Tax Reform Act of 1976 (P.L. 94-455)

P.L. 94-455, §1906(b)(13)(A):

Amended 1954 Code by substituting "Secretary" for "Secretary or his delegate" each place it appeared. **Effective** 2-1-77.

P.L. 94-455, §2101(b):

Added the final sentence of Code Sec. 216(c). **Effective** for tax years beginning after 12-31-73.

• 1962, Revenue Act of 1962 (P.L. 87-834)

P.L. 87-834, §28:

Amended the heading of Code Sec. 216 and added a new subsection (c). **Effective** for tax years beginning after 12-31-61. Prior to the amendment the heading of Sec. 216 read as follows:

"Amounts representing taxes and interest paid to cooperative housing corporation."

[Sec. 216(d)]

(d) DISALLOWANCE OF DEDUCTION FOR CERTAIN PAYMENTS TO THE CORPORATION.—No deduction shall be allowed to a stockholder in a cooperative housing corporation for any amount paid or accrued to such corporation during any taxable year (in excess of the stockholder's proportionate share of the items described in subsections (a)(1) and (a)(2)) to the extent that, under regulations prescribed by the Secretary, such amount is properly allocable to amounts paid or incurred at any time by the corporation which are chargeable to the corporation's capital account. The stockholder's adjusted basis in the stock in the corporation shall be increased by the amount of such disallowance.

Amendments

• 1986, Tax Reform Act of 1986 (P.L. 99-514)

P.L. 99-514, §644(c):

Amended Code Sec. 216 by adding at the end thereof new subsection (d). **Effective** for tax years beginning after 12-31-86.

[Sec. 216(e)]

(e) DISTRIBUTIONS BY COOPERATIVE HOUSING CORPORATIONS.—Except as provided in regulations, no gain or loss shall be recognized on the distribution by a cooperative housing corporation of a dwelling unit to a stockholder in such cooperation if such distribution is in exchange for the stockholder's stock in such corporation and such dwelling unit is used as his principal residence (within the meaning of section 121).

Amendments

• 1997, Taxpayer Relief Act of 1997 (P.L. 105-34)

P.L. 105-34, §312(d)(4):

Amended Code Sec. 216(e) by striking "such exchange qualifies for nonrecognition of gain under section 1034(f)" and inserting "such dwelling unit is used as his principal residence (within the meaning of section 121)". **Effective** for sales and exchanges after 5-6-97.

• 1990, Omnibus Budget Reconciliation Act of 1990 (P.L. 101-508)

P.L. 101-508, §11702(i):

Amended Code Sec. 216(e) by striking "Associations" in the heading and inserting "Corporations", and by striking "association" and inserting "corporation". **Effective** as if included in the provision of P.L. 100-647 to which it relates.

• 1988, Technical and Miscellaneous Revenue Act of 1988 (P.L. 100-647)

P.L. 100-647, §6282(a):

Amended Code Sec. 216 by adding at the end thereof new subsection (e). **Effective** as if included in the amendments made by P.L. 99-514, §631.

[Sec. 217]

SEC. 217. MOVING EXPENSES.

[Sec. 217(a)]

(a) DEDUCTION ALLOWED.—There shall be allowed as a deduction moving expenses paid or incurred during the taxable year in connection with the commencement of work by the taxpayer as an employee or as a self-employed individual at a new principal place of work.

[Sec. 217(b)]

(b) DEFINITION OF MOVING EXPENSES.—

(1) IN GENERAL.—For purposes of this section, the term "moving expenses" means only the reasonable expenses—

(A) of moving household goods and personal effects from the former residence to the new residence, and

(B) of traveling (including lodging) from the former residence to the new place of residence.

Such term shall not include any expenses for meals.

(2) INDIVIDUALS OTHER THAN TAXPAYER.—In the case of any individual other than the taxpayer, expenses referred to in paragraph (1) shall be taken into account only if such individual has both the former residence and the new residence as his principal place of abode and is a member of the taxpayer's household.

Amendments

• 1993, Omnibus Budget Reconciliation Act of 1993 (P.L. 103-66)

P.L. 103-66, §13213(a)(1):

Amended Code Sec. 217(b). **Effective** for expenses incurred after 12-31-93. Prior to amendment, Code Sec. 217(b) read as follows:

(b) DEFINITION OF MOVING EXPENSES.—

(1) IN GENERAL.—For purposes of this section, the term "moving expenses" means only the reasonable expenses—

(A) of moving household goods and personal effects from the former residence to the new residence,

(B) of traveling (including meals and lodging) from the former residence to the new place of residence,

(C) of traveling (including meals and lodging), after obtaining employment, from the former residence to the general location of the new principal place of work and return, for the principal purpose of searching for a new residence,

(D) of meals and lodging while occupying temporary quarters in the general location of the new principal place of work during any period of 30 consecutive days after obtaining employment, or

(E) constituting qualified residence sale, purchase, or lease expenses.

(2) QUALIFIED RESIDENCE SALE, ETC., EXPENSES.—For purposes of paragraph (1)(E), the term "qualified residence sale, purchase, or lease expenses" means only reasonable expenses incident to—

(A) the sale or exchange by the taxpayer or his spouse of the taxpayer's former residence (not including expenses for work performed on such residence in order to assist in its sale) which (but for this subsection and subsection (e)) would be taken into account in determining the amount realized on the sale or exchange,

(B) the purchase by the taxpayer or his spouse of a new residence in the general location of the new principal place of work which (but for this subsection and subsection (e)) would be taken into account in determining—

(i) the adjusted basis of the new residence, or

(ii) the cost of a loan (but not including any amounts which represent payments or prepayments of interest),

(C) the settlement of an unexpired lease held by the taxpayer or his spouse on property used by the taxpayer as his former residence, or

(D) the acquisition of a lease by the taxpayer or his spouse on property used by the taxpayer as his new residence in the general location of the new principal place of work (not including amounts which are payments or prepayments of rent).

(3) LIMITATIONS.—

(A) DOLLAR LIMITS.—The aggregate amount allowable as a deduction under subsection (a) in connection with a commencement of work which is attributable to expenses described in subparagraph (C) or (D) of paragraph (1) shall not exceed $1,500. The aggregate amount allowable as a deduction under subsection (a) which is attributable to qualified residence sale, purchase, or lease expenses shall not exceed $3,000, reduced by the aggregate amount so allowable which is attributable to expenses described in subparagraph (C) or (D) of paragraph (1).

(B) HUSBAND AND WIFE.—If a husband and wife both commence work at a new principal place of work within the same general location, subparagraph (A) shall be applied as if there was only one commencement of work. In the case of a husband and wife filing separate returns, subparagraph (A) shall be applied by substituting "$750" for "$1,500", and by substituting "$1,500" for "$3,000".

(C) INDIVIDUALS OTHER THAN TAXPAYER.—In the case of any individual other than the taxpayer, expenses referred to in subparagraphs (A) through (D) of paragraph (1) shall be taken into account only if such individual has both the former residence and the new residence as his principal place of abode and is a member of the taxpayer's household.

• 1976, Tax Reform Act of 1976 (P.L. 94-455)

P.L. 94-455, §506(b):

Substituted "$1,500" for "$1,000" and "$3,000" for "$2,500" in Code Sec. 217(b)(3)(A) and amended the second sentence of Code Sec. 217(b)(3)(B). **Effective** for tax years beginning after 12-31-76. Prior to amendment, the last sentence of Code Sec. 217(b)(3)(B) read as follows:

In the case of a husband and wife filing separate returns, subparagraph (A) shall be applied by substituting "$500" for "$1,000", and by substituting "$1,250" for "$2,500".

[Sec. 217(c)]

(c) CONDITIONS FOR ALLOWANCE.—No deduction shall be allowed under this section unless—

(1) the taxpayer's new principal place of work—

(A) is at least 50 miles farther from his former residence than was his former principal place of work, or

(B) if he had no former principal place of work, is at least 50 miles from his former residence, and

(2) either—

(A) during the 12-month period immediately following his arrival in the general location of his new principal place of work, the taxpayer is a full-time employee, in such general location, during at least 39 weeks, or

(B) during the 24-month period immediately following his arrival in the general location of his new principal place of work, the taxpayer is a full-time employee or performs services as a self-employed individual on a full-time basis, in such general location, during at least 78 weeks, of which not less than 39 weeks are during the 12-month period referred to in subparagraph (A).

For purposes of paragraph (1), the distance between two points shall be the shortest of the more commonly traveled routes between such two points.

Amendments

• 1993, Omnibus Budget Reconciliation Act of 1993 (P.L. 103-66)

P.L. 103-66, §13213(b):

Amended Code Sec. 217(c)(1) by striking "35 miles" each place it appears and inserting "50 miles". **Effective** for expenses incurred after 12-31-93.

• 1976, Tax Reform Act of 1976 (P.L. 94-455)

P.L. 94-455, §506(a):

Substituted "35 miles" for "50 miles" wherever it appeared in Code Sec. 217(c)(1). **Effective** for tax years beginning after 12-31-76.

[Sec. 217(d)]

(d) RULES FOR APPLICATION OF SUBSECTION (c)(2).—

(1) The condition of subsection (c)(2) shall not apply if the taxpayer is unable to satisfy such condition by reason of—

(A) death or disability, or

(B) involuntary separation (other than for willful misconduct) from the service of, or transfer for the benefit of, an employer after obtaining full-time employment in which the taxpayer could reasonably have been expected to satisfy such condition.

(2) If a taxpayer has not satisfied the condition of subsection (c)(2) before the time prescribed by law (including extensions thereof) for filing the return for the taxable year during which he paid or incurred moving expenses which would otherwise be deductible under this section, but may still satisfy such condition, then such expenses may (at the election of the taxpayer) be deducted for such taxable year notwithstanding subsection (c)(2).

(3) If—

(A) for any taxable year moving expenses have been deducted in accordance with the rule provided in paragraph (2), and

(B) the condition of subsection (c)(2) cannot be satisfied at the close of a subsequent taxable year,

then an amount equal to the expenses which were so deducted shall be included in gross income for the first such subsequent taxable year.

[Sec. 217(e)—Stricken]

Amendments

• 1993, Omnibus Budget Reconciliation Act of 1993 (P.L. 103-66)

P.L. 103-66, §13213(a)(2)(A):

Amended Code Sec. 217 by striking subsection (e). **Effective** for expenses incurred after 12-31-93. Prior to being stricken, Code Sec. 217(e) read as follows:

(e) DENIAL OF DOUBLE BENEFIT.—The amount realized on the sale of the residence described in subparagraph (A) of subsection (b)(2) shall not be decreased by the amount of any expenses described in such subparagraph which are allowed as a deduction under subsection (a), and the basis of a residence described in subparagraph (B) of subsection (b)(2) shall not be increased by the amount of any expenses described in such subparagraph which are allowed as a deduction under subsection (a). This subsection shall not apply to any expenses with respect to which an amount is included in gross income under subsection (d)(3).

[Sec. 217(f)]

(f) SELF-EMPLOYED INDIVIDUAL.—For purposes of this section, the term "self-employed individual" means an individual who performs personal services—

(1) as the owner of the entire interest in an unincorporated trade or business, or

(2) as a partner in a partnership carrying on a trade or business.

Amendments

• 1993, Omnibus Budget Reconciliation Act of 1993 (P.L. 103-66)

P.L. 103-66, §13213(a)(2)(B):

Amended Code Sec. 217(f). **Effective** for expenses incurred after 12-31-93. Prior to amendment, Code Sec. 217(f) read as follows:

(f) RULES FOR SELF-EMPLOYED INDIVIDUALS.—

(1) DEFINITION.—For purposes of this section, the term "self-employed individual" means an individual who performs personal services—

(A) as the owner of the entire interest in an unincorporated trade or business, or

(B) as a partner in a partnership carrying on a trade or business.

(2) RULE FOR APPLICATION OF SUBSECTIONS (b)(1)(C) AND (D).—For purposes of subparagraphs (C) and (D) of subsection (b)(1), an individual who commences work at a new principal place of work as a self-employed individual shall be treated as having obtained employment when he has made substantial arrangements to commence such work.

[Sec. 217(g)]

(g) RULES FOR MEMBERS OF THE ARMED FORCES OF THE UNITED STATES.—In the case of a member of the Armed Forces of the United States on active duty who moves pursuant to a military order and incident to a permanent change of station—

(1) the limitations under subsection (c) shall not apply;

(2) any moving and storage expenses which are furnished in kind (or for which reimbursement or an allowance is provided, but only to the extent of the expenses paid or incurred) to such member, his spouse, or his dependents, shall not be includible in gross income, and no reporting with respect to such expenses shall be required by the Secretary of Defense or the Secretary of Transportation, as the case may be; and

(3) if moving and storage expenses are furnished in kind (or if reimbursement or an allowance for such expenses is provided) to such member's spouse and his dependents with regard to moving to a location other than the one to which such member moves (or from a location other than the one from which such member moves), this section shall apply with respect to the moving expenses of his spouse and dependents—

(A) as if his spouse commenced work as an employee at a new principal place of work at such location; and

(B) without regard to the limitations under subsection (c).

Amendments

• 1993, Omnibus Budget Reconciliation Act of 1993 (P.L. 103-66)

P.L. 103-66, §13213(a)(2)(C):

Amended Code Sec. 217(g)(3) by inserting "and" at the end of subparagraph (A), by striking subparagraph (B), and by redesignating subparagraph (C) as subparagraph (B). **Effective** for expenses incurred after 12-31-93. Prior to amendment, Code Sec. 217(g)(3)(B) read as follows:

(B) for purposes of subsection (b)(3), as if such place of work was within the same general location as the member's new principal place of work, and

• 1976, Tax Reform Act of 1976 (P.L. 94-455)

P.L. 94-455, §506(c):

Added Code Sec. 217(g). **Effective** for tax years beginning after 12-31-75.

[Sec. 217(h)]

(h) SPECIAL RULES FOR FOREIGN MOVES.—

(1) ALLOWANCE OF CERTAIN STORAGE FEES.—In the case of a foreign move, for purposes of this section, the moving expenses described in subsection (b)(1)(A) include the reasonable expenses—

(A) of moving household goods and personal effects to and from storage, and

(B) of storing such goods and effects for part or all of the period during which the new place of work continues to be the taxpayer's principal place of work.

(2) FOREIGN MOVE.—For purposes of this subsection, the term "foreign move" means the commencement of work by the taxpayer at a new principal place of work located outside the United States.

(3) UNITED STATES DEFINED.—For purposes of this subsection and subsection (i), the term "United States" includes the possessions of the United States.

Amendments

• 1993, Omnibus Budget Reconciliation Act of 1993 (P.L. 103-66)

P.L. 103-66, §13213(a)(2)(D):

Amended Code Sec. 217(h) by striking paragraph (1) and redesignating paragraph (2)-(4) as paragraph (1)-(3), respectively. **Effective** for expenses incurred after 12-31-93. Prior to amendment, Code Sec. 217(h)(1) read as follows:

(1) INCREASE IN LIMITATIONS.—In the case of a foreign move—

(A) subsection (b)(1)(D) shall be applied by substituting "90 consecutive days" for "30 consecutive days",

(B) subsection (b)(3)(A) shall be applied by substituting "$4,500" for "$1,500" and by substituting "$6,000" for $3,000", and

(C) subsection (b)(3)(B) shall be applied as if the last sentence of such subsection read as follows: "In the case of a husband and wife filing separate returns, subparagraph (A) shall be applied by substituting "$2,250" for "$4,500", and by substituting "$3,000" for "$6,000".

• 1978, Tax Treatment Extension Act of 1978 (P.L. 95-615)

P.L. 95-615, §204(a):

Redesignated Code Sec. 217(h) as Code Sec. 217(j) and inserted a new Code Sec. 217(h). **Effective** as set forth in P.L. 95-615, §209(a) and (c). See historical comment on P.L. 95-615, §209, under Code Sec. 217(j).

[Sec. 217(i)]

(i) ALLOWANCE OF DEDUCTIONS IN CASE OF RETIREES OR DECEDENTS WHO WERE WORKING ABROAD.—

(1) IN GENERAL.—In the case of any qualified retiree moving expenses or qualified survivor moving expenses—

(A) this section (other than subsection (h)) shall be applied with respect to such expenses as if they were incurred in connection with the commencement of work by the taxpayer as an employee at a new principal place of work located within the United States, and

(B) the limitations of subsection (c)(2) shall not apply.

(2) QUALIFIED RETIREE MOVING EXPENSES.—For purposes of paragraph (1), the term "qualified retiree moving expenses" means any moving expenses—

(A) which are incurred by an individual whose former principal place of work and former residence were outside the United States, and

(B) which are incurred for a move to a new residence in the United States in connection with the bona fide retirement of the individual.

(3) QUALIFIED SURVIVOR MOVING EXPENSES.—For purposes of paragraph (1), the term "qualified survivor moving expenses" means moving expenses—

(A) which are paid or incurred by the spouse or any dependent of any decedent who (as of the time of his death) had a principal place of work outside the United States, and

(B) which are incurred for a move which begins within 6 months after the death of such decedent and which is to a residence in the United States from a former residence outside the United States which (as of the time of the decedent's death) was the residence of such decedent and the individual paying or incurring the expense.

Amendments

• 1978, Tax Treatment Extension Act of 1978 (P.L. 95-615)

P.L. 95-615, §204(a):

Added Code Sec. 217(i). **Effective** as set forth in P.L. 95-615, §209(a) and (c). See historical comment on P.L. 95-615, §209, under Code Sec. 217(j).

[Sec. 217(j)]

(j) REGULATIONS.—The Secretary shall prescribe such regulations as may be necessary to carry out the purposes of this section.

Amendments

• 1978, Tax Treatment Extension Act of 1978 (P.L. 95-615)

P.L. 95-615, §204(a):

Amended Code Sec. 217 by redesignating subsection (h) as subsection (j). **Effective** as set forth in P.L. 95-615, §209(a) and (c), below.

P.L. 95-615, §209(a), (c), provides:

SEC. 209. EFFECTIVE DATES.

(a) GENERAL RULE.—Except as provided in subsections (b) and (c) the amendments made by this title shall apply to taxable years beginning after December 31, 1977.

* * *

(c) ELECTION OF PRIOR LAW.—

(1) A taxpayer may elect not to have the amendments made by this title apply with respect to any taxable year beginning after December 31, 1977, and before January 1, 1979.

(2) An election under this subsection shall be filed with a taxpayer's timely filed return for the first taxable year beginning after December 31, 1977.

• 1976, Tax Reform Act of 1976 (P.L. 94-455)

P.L. 94-455, §506(c):

Redesignated former Code Sec. 217(g) as Code Sec. 217(h). **Effective** for tax years beginning after 12-31-75.

P.L. 94-455, §1906(b)(13)(A):

Amended the 1954 Code by substituting "Secretary" for "Secretary or his delegate" each place it appears. **Effective** 2-1-77.

P.L. 91-642, §2:

Amended the Tax Reform Act to modify the transitional rule (contained in the amendment note for P.L. 91-172, below) which allows a taxpayer to elect the pre-Tax Reform Act moving expense deduction rule. Under the new transitional rule, an employee may elect the former expense deduction rule where he had been notified by his employer of a move before 12-20-69, and the amounts were paid or incurred for the moving expenses before 1-1-71 (7-1-70 under the Tax Reform Act).

• 1969, Tax Reform Act of 1969 (P.L. 91-172)

P.L. 91-172, §231(a):

Amended Code Sec. 217. **Effective** for tax years beginning after 12-31-69, except that the amendments shall not apply to any item to the extent that the taxpayer received or accrued reimbursement or other expense allowance for such item in a tax year beginning on or before 12-31-69, which was not included in his gross income, and shall not apply (at the election of the taxpayer made at such time and manner as the Secretary of the Treasury or his delegate prescribes) with respect to moving expenses paid or incurred before 7-1-70 in connection with the commencement of work by the taxpayer as an employee at a new principal place of work of which the taxpayer had been notified by his employer on or before 12-19-69. Prior to amendment, Sec. 217 read as follows:

(a) Deduction Allowed.—There shall be allowed as a deduction moving expenses paid or incurred during the taxable year in connection with the commencement of work by the taxpayer as an employee at a new principal place of work.

(b) Definition of Moving Expenses.—

(1) In general.—For purposes of this section, the term "moving expenses" means only the reasonable expenses—

(A) of moving household goods and personal effects from the former residence to the new residence, and

(B) of traveling (including meals and lodging) from the former residence to the new place of residence.

(2) Individuals other than taxpayer.—In the case of any individual other than the taxpayer, expenses referred to in paragraph (1) shall be taken into account only if such individual has both the former residence and the new residence as his principal place of abode and is a member of the taxpayer's household.

(c) Conditions for Allowance.—No deduction shall be allowed under this section unless—

(1) the taxpayer's new principal place of work—

(A) is at least 20 miles farther from his former residence than was his former principal place of work, or

(B) if he had no former principal place of work, is at least 20 miles from his former residence, and

(2) during the 12-month period immediately following his arrival in the general location of his new principal place of work, the taxpayer is a full-time employee, in such general location, during at least 39 weeks.

(d) Rules for Application of Subsection (c)(2).—

(1) Subsection (c)(2) shall not apply to any item to the extent that the taxpayer receives reimbursement or other expense allowance from his employer for such item.

(2) If a taxpayer has not satisfied the condition of subsection (c)(2) before the time prescribed by law (including extensions thereof) for filing the return for the taxable year during which he paid or incurred moving expenses which would otherwise be deductible under this section, but may still satisfy such condition, then such expenses may (at the election of the taxpayer) be deducted for such taxable year notwithstanding subsection (c)(2).

(3) If—

(A) for any taxable year moving expenses have been deducted in accordance with the rule provided in paragraph (2), and

(B) the condition of subsection (c)(2) is not satisfied by the close of the subsequent taxable year,

then an amount equal to the expenses which were so deducted shall be included in gross income for such subsequent taxable year.

(e) Disallowance of Deduction With Respect to Reimbursements Not Included in Gross Income.—No deduction shall be allowed under this section for any item to the extent that the taxpayer receives reimbursement or other expense allowance for such item which is not included in his gross income.

(f) Regulations.—The Secretary or his delegate shall prescribe such regulations as may be necessary to carry out the purposes of this section.

• 1964, Revenue Act of 1964 (P.L. 88-272)

P.L. 88-272, §213(a)(1):

Added section 217. **Effective** for expenses incurred after 12-31-63, in tax years ending after such date.

[Sec. 218—Repealed]

Amendments

• 1978, Revenue Act of 1978 (P.L. 95-600)

P.L. 95-600, §113(a)(1):

Repealed Code Sec. 218. **Effective** for contributions the payment of which is made after 12-31-78, in tax years beginning after such date. The text of Code Sec. 218 prior to repeal read as follows:

SEC. 218. CONTRIBUTIONS TO CANDIDATES FOR PUBLIC OFFICE.

(a) ALLOWANCE OF DEDUCTION.—In the case of an individual, there shall be allowed as a deduction any political contribution (as defined in section 41(c)(1)) or newsletter fund contribution (as defined in section 41(c)(5)) payment of which is made by such individual within the taxable year.

(b) LIMITATIONS.—

(1) AMOUNT.—The deduction under subsection (a) shall not exceed $100 ($200 in the case of a joint return under section 6013).

(2) VERIFICATION.—The deduction under subsection (a) shall be allowed, with respect to any political contribution or newsletter fund contribution, only if such contribution is verified in such manner as the Secretary shall prescribe by regulations.

(c) ELECTION TO TAKE CREDIT IN LIEU OF DEDUCTION.—This section shall not apply in the case of any taxpayer who, for the taxable year, elects to take the credit against tax provided by section 41 (relating to credit against tax for contributions to candidates for public office). Such election shall be made in such manner and at such time as the Secretary or his delegate shall prescribe by regulations.

(d) CROSS REFERENCE.—

For disallowance of deduction to estates and trusts, see section 642(i).

• 1976, Tax Reform Act of 1976 (P.L. 94-455)

P.L. 94-455, §1906(b)(13)(A):

Amended 1954 Code by substituting "Secretary" for "Secretary or his delegate" each place it appeared. **Effective** 2-1-77.

• 1975 (P.L. 93-625)

P.L. 93-625, §§11(d), 12(b):

Amended Code Sec. 218(a) and (b). **Effective** with respect to any contribution the payment of which is made after 12-31-74, in tax years beginning after such date. Prior to amendment, Code Sec. 218(a) and (b) read as follows:

"(a) Allowance of Deduction.—In the case of an individual, there shall be allowed as a deduction any political contribution (as defined in section 41(c)(1)) payment of which is made by such individual within the taxable year.

"(b) Limitations.—

"(1) Amount.—The deduction under subsection (a) shall not exceed $50 ($100 in the case of a joint return under section 6013).

"(2) Verification. — The deduction under subsection (a) shall be allowed, with respect to any political contribution, only if such political contribution is verified in such manner as the Secretary or his delegate shall prescribe by regulations."

• 1971, Revenue Act of 1971 (P.L. 92-178)

P.L. 92-178, §702(a):

Added Code Sec. 218. **Effective** for tax years ending after 12-31-71, but only with respect to political contributions, payment of which is made after such date.

[Sec. 219]

SEC. 219. RETIREMENT SAVINGS.

[Sec. 219(a)]

(a) ALLOWANCE OF DEDUCTION.—In the case of an individual, there shall be allowed as a deduction an amount equal to the qualified retirement contributions of the individual for the taxable year.

Amendments

• 1981, Economic Recovery Tax Act of 1981 (P.L. 97-34)

P.L. 97-34, §311(a):

Amended Code Sec. 219(a). **Effective**, generally, for tax years beginning after 12-31-81. However, for purposes of the 1954 Code, any amount allowed as a deduction under Code Sec. 220 (as in effect before its repeal by P.L. 97-34) shall be treated as if it were allowed by section 219 of such Code. Prior to amendment, Code Sec. 219(a) read as follows:

(a) DEDUCTION ALLOWED.—In the case of an individual, there is allowed as a deduction amounts paid in cash for the taxable year by or on behalf of such individual for his benefit—

(1) to an individual retirement account described in section 408(a),

(2) for an individual retirement annuity described in section 408(b), or

(3) for a retirement bond described in section 409 (but only if the bond is not redeemed within 12 months of the date of its issuance).

For purposes of this title, any amount paid by an employer to such a retirement account or for such a retirement annuity or retirement bond constitutes payment of compensation to the employee (other than a self-employed individual who is an employee within the meaning of section 401(c)(1)) includible in his gross income, whether or not a deduction for such payment is allowable under this section to the employee after the application of subsection (b).

• **1976, Tax Reform Act of 1976 (P.L. 94-455)**

P.L. 94-455, §1501(b)(4)(A):

Substituted "for" for "during" in the first sentence of Code Sec. 219(a). **Effective** for tax years beginning after 12-31-76.

[Sec. 219(b)]

(b) MAXIMUM AMOUNT OF DEDUCTION—

(1) IN GENERAL.—The amount allowable as a deduction under subsection (a) to any individual for any taxable year shall not exceed the lesser of—

(A) the deductible amount, or

(B) an amount equal to the compensation includible in the individual's gross income for such taxable year.

(2) SPECIAL RULE FOR EMPLOYER CONTRIBUTIONS UNDER SIMPLIFIED EMPLOYEE PENSIONS.—This section shall not apply with respect to an employer contribution to a simplified employee pension.

(3) PLANS UNDER SECTION 501(c)(18).—Notwithstanding paragraph (1), the amount allowable as a deduction under subsection (a) with respect to any contributions on behalf of a employee to a plan described in section 501(c)(18) shall not exceed the lesser of—

(A) $7,000 or

(B) an amount equal to 25 percent of the compensation (as defined in section 415(c)(3)) includible in the individual's gross income for such taxable year.

(4) SPECIAL RULE FOR SIMPLE RETIREMENT ACCOUNTS.—This section shall not apply with respect to any amount contributed to a simple retirement account established under section 408(p).

(5) DEDUCTIBLE AMOUNT.—For purposes of paragraph (1)(A)—

(A) IN GENERAL.—The deductible amount shall be determined in accordance with the following table:

For taxable years beginning in:	*The deductible amount is:*
2002 through 2004	$3,000
2005 through 2007	$4,000
2008 and thereafter	$5,000.

(B) CATCH-UP CONTRIBUTIONS FOR INDIVIDUALS 50 OR OLDER.—

(i) IN GENERAL.—In the case of an individual who has attained the age of 50 before the close of the taxable year, the deductible amount for such taxable year shall be increased by the applicable amount.

(ii) APPLICABLE AMOUNT.—For purposes of clause (i), the applicable amount shall be the amount determined in accordance with the following table:

For taxable years beginning in:	*The applicable amount is:*
2002 through 2005	$500
2006 and thereafter	$1,000

(C) CATCHUP CONTRIBUTIONS FOR CERTAIN INDIVIDUALS.—

(i) IN GENERAL.—In the case of an applicable individual who elects to make a qualified retirement contribution in addition to the deductible amount determined under subparagraph (A)—

(I) the deductible amount for any taxable year shall be increased by an amount equal to 3 times the applicable amount determined under subparagraph (B) for such taxable year, and

(II) subparagraph (B) shall not apply.

(ii) APPLICABLE INDIVIDUAL.—For purposes of this subparagraph, the term "applicable individual" means, with respect to any taxable year, any individual who was a qualified participant in a qualified cash or deferred arrangement (as defined in section 401(k)) of an employer described in clause (iii) under which the employer matched at least 50 percent of the employee's contributions to such arrangement with stock of such employer.

(iii) EMPLOYER DESCRIBED.—An employer is described in this clause if, in any taxable year preceding the taxable year described in clause (ii)—

(I) such employer (or any controlling corporation of such employer) was a debtor in a case under title 11 of the United States Code, or similar Federal or State law, and

(II) such employer (or any other person) was subject to an indictment or conviction resulting from business transactions related to such case.

(iv) QUALIFIED PARTICIPANT.—For purposes of clause (ii), the term "qualified participant" means any applicable individual who was a participant in the cash or deferred arrangement described in such clause on the date that is 6 months before the filing of the case described in clause (iii).

(v) TERMINATION.—This subparagraph shall not apply to taxable years beginning after December 31, 2009.

(D) COST-OF-LIVING ADJUSTMENT.—

(i) IN GENERAL.—In the case of any taxable year beginning in a calendar year after 2008, the $5,000 amount under subparagraph (A) shall be increased by an amount equal to—

(I) such dollar amount, multiplied by

(II) the cost-of-living adjustment determined under section 1(f)(3) for the calendar year in which the taxable year begins, determined by substituting "calendar year 2007" for "calendar year 1992" in subparagraph (B) thereof.

(ii) ROUNDING RULES.—If any amount after adjustment under clause (i) is not a multiple of $500, such amount shall be rounded to the next lower multiple of $500.

Amendments

• 2006, Pension Protection Act of 2006 (P.L. 109-280)

P.L. 109-280, §811, provides:

SEC. 811. PENSIONS AND INDIVIDUAL RETIREMENT ARRANGEMENT PROVISIONS OF ECONOMIC GROWTH AND TAX RELIEF RECONCILIATION ACT OF 2001 MADE PERMANENT.

Title IX of the Economic Growth and Tax Relief Reconciliation Act of 2001 [P.L. 107-16] shall not apply to the provisions of, and amendments made by, subtitles A through F of title VI [§§601-666]of such Act (relating to pension and individual retirement arrangement provisions).

P.L. 109-280, §831(a):

Amended Code Sec. 219(b)(5) by redesignating subparagraph (C) as subparagraph (D) and by inserting after subparagraph (B) a new subparagraph (C). **Effective** for tax years beginning after 12-31-2006.

• 2001, Economic Growth and Tax Relief Reconciliation Act of 2001 (P.L. 107-16)

P.L. 107-16, §601(a)(1):

Amended Code Sec. 219(b)(1)(A) by striking "$2,000" and inserting "the deductible amount". **Effective** for tax years beginning after 12-31-2001.

P.L. 107-16, §601(a)(2):

Amended Code Sec. 219(b) by adding at the end a new paragraph (5). **Effective** for tax years beginning after 12-31-2001.

P.L. 107-16, §901(a)-(b), provides [but see P.L. 109-280, §811, above]:

SEC. 901. SUNSET OF PROVISIONS OF ACT.

(a) IN GENERAL.—All provisions of, and amendments made by, this Act shall not apply—

(1) to taxable, plan, or limitation years beginning after December 31, 2010, or

(2) in the case of title V, to estates of decedents dying, gifts made, or generation skipping transfers, after December 31, 2010.

(b) APPLICATION OF CERTAIN LAWS.—The Internal Revenue Code of 1986 and the Employee Retirement Income Security Act of 1974 shall be applied and administered to years, estates, gifts, and transfers described in subsection (a) as if the provisions and amendments described in subsection (a) had never been enacted.

• 1996, Small Business Job Protection Act of 1996 (P.L. 104-188)

P.L. 104-188, §1421(b)(1)(A):

Amended Code Sec. 219(b) by adding at the end a new paragraph (4). **Effective** for tax years beginning after 12-31-96.

• 1986, Tax Reform Act of 1986 (P.L. 99-514)

P.L. 99-514, §1875(c)(6)(B):

Amended Code Sec. 219(b)(2)(C) by striking out "the $15,000 amount specified in subparagraph (A)(ii)" and inserting in lieu thereof "the dollar limitation in effect under section 415(c)(1)(A)". **Effective** as if included in the amendments made by P.L. 97-248, §238.

P.L. 99-514, §1108(g)(2):

Amended Code Sec. 219(b)(2). **Effective** for tax years beginning after 12-31-86. Prior to amendment, Code Sec. 219(b)(2) read as follows:

(2) SPECIAL RULES FOR EMPLOYER CONTRIBUTIONS UNDER SIMPLIFIED EMPLOYEE PENSIONS.—

(A) LIMITATION.—If there is an employer contribution on behalf of the employee to a simplified employee pension, an employee shall be allowed as a deduction under subsection (a) (in addition to the amount allowable under paragraph (1)) an amount equal to the lesser of—

(i) 15 percent of the compensation from such employer includible in the employee's gross income for the taxable year (determined without regard to the employer contribution to the simplified employee pension), or

(ii) the amount contributed by such employer to the simplified employee pension and included in gross income (but not in excess of the limitation in effect under section 415(c)(1)(A)).

(B) CERTAIN LIMITATIONS DO NOT APPLY TO EMPLOYER CONTRIBUTION.—Paragraph (1) of this subsection and paragraph (1) of subsection (d) shall not apply with respect to the employer contribution to a simplified employee pension.

(C) SPECIAL RULE FOR APPLYING SUBPARAGRAPH (A)(ii).—In the case of an employee who is an officer, shareholder, or owner-employee described in section 408(k)(3), the dollar limitation in effect under section 415(c)(1)(A) shall be reduced by the amount of tax taken into account with respect to such individual under subparagraph (D) of section 408(k)(3).

P.L. 99-514, §1101(b)(2)(A):

Amended Code Sec. 219(b) by striking out paragraph (3). **Effective** for contributions for tax years beginning after 12-31-86. Prior to amendment, Code Sec. 219(b)(3) read as follows:

(3) SPECIAL RULE FOR INDIVIDUAL RETIREMENT PLANS.—If the individual has paid any qualified voluntary employee contributions for the taxable year, the amount of the qualified retirement contributions (other than employer contributions to a simplified employee pension) which are paid for the taxable year to an individual retirement plan and which are allowable as a deduction under subsection (a) for such taxable year shall not exceed—

(A) the amount determined under paragraph (1) for such taxable year, reduced by

(B) the amount of the qualified voluntary employee contributions for the taxable year.

P.L. 99-514, §1109(b):

Amended Code Sec. 219(b), as amended by Sec. 1101(b) of the Act, by adding at the end thereof new paragraph (3). **Effective** for years beginning after 12-31-86.

• 1984, Deficit Reduction Act of 1984 (P.L. 98-369)

P.L. 98-369, §422(d)(1):

Amended Code Sec. 219(b)(4)(B) by striking out all that follows "gross income" and inserting in lieu thereof the language above. **Effective** with respect to divorce or separation instruments (as defined in Code Sec. 71(b)(2) as amended by this section) executed after 12-31-84. The amendments, however, also apply to any divorce or separation instrument (as so defined) executed before 1-1-85, but modified on or after such date if the modification expressly provides that the amendments made by this section shall apply to such modification. Prior to amendment, subparagraph (B) read as follows:

(B) Qualifying Alimony.—For purposes of this paragraph, the term "qualifying alimony" means amounts includible in the individual's gross income under paragraph (1) of section 71(a) (relating to decree of divorce or separate maintenance).

P.L. 98-369, §529(b):

Amended Code Sec. 219(b) by striking out paragraph (4), after its amendment by Act Sec. 422(d)(1). **Effective** for tax years beginning after 12-31-84. Prior to its deletion, Code Sec. 219(b)(4) read as follows:

(4) Certain Divorced Individuals.—

(A) In General.—In the case of an individual to whom this paragraph applies, the limitation of paragraph (1) shall not be less than the lesser of—

(i) $1,125, or

(ii) the sum of the amount referred to in paragraph (1)(B) and any qualifying alimony received by the individual during the taxable year.

(B) Qualifying Alimony.—For purposes of this paragraph the term "qualifying alimony" means amounts includible in the individual's gross income under section 71 (relating to alimony and separate maintenance payments) by reason of a payment under a decree of divorce or separate maintenance or a written instrument incident to such a decree.

(C) Individuals to Whom Paragraph Applies.—This paragraph shall apply to an individual if—

(i) an individual retirement plan was established for the benefit of the individual at least 5 years before the beginning of the calendar year in which the decree of divorce or separate maintenance was issued, and

(ii) for at least 3 of the former spouse's most recent 5 taxable years ending before the taxable year in which the decree was issued, such former spouse was allowed a deduction under subsection (c) (or the corresponding provisions of prior law) for contributions to such individual retirement plan.

P.L. 98-369, §713(d)(2):

Amended Code Sec. 219(b)(2)(A)(ii) by striking out "but not in excess of $15,000" and inserting in lieu thereof "but not in excess of the limitation in effect under section 415(c)(1)(A)." **Effective** as if included in the provision of P.L. 97-248 to which it relates.

• 1983, Technical Corrections Act of 1982 (P.L. 97-448)

P.L. 97-448, §103(c)(12)(A):

Amended Code Sec. 219(b)(2)(A) by striking out "paragraph (1)" and inserting in lieu thereof "paragraph (1))". **Effective** as if it had been included in the provision of P.L. 97-34 to which it relates.

P.L. 97-448, §103(d)(3):

Amended paragraph (1) of section 312(f) of P.L. 97-34 (relating to effective date) by striking out "plans which include employees within the meaning of section 401(c)(1) with respect to".

• 1981, Economic Recovery Tax Act of 1981 (P.L. 97-34)

P.L. 97-34, §311(a):

Amended Code Sec. 219(b). **Effective** for tax years beginning after 12-31-81. The transitional rule provides that, for purposes of the 1954 Code, any amount allowed as a deduction under Code Sec. 220 (as in effect before its repeal by P.L. 97-34) shall be treated as if it were allowed by section 219 of the Code. Prior to amendment Code Sec. 219(b) read as follows:

(b) LIMITATIONS AND RESTRICTIONS.—

(1) MAXIMUM DEDUCTION.—The amount allowable as a deduction under subsection (a) to an individual for any taxable year may not exceed an amount equal to 15 percent of the compensation includible in his gross income for such taxable year, or $1,500, whichever is less.

(2) COVERED BY CERTAIN OTHER PLANS.—No deduction is allowed under subsection (a) for an individual for the taxable year if for any part of such year—

(A) he was an active participant in—

(i) a plan described in section 401(a) which includes a trust exempt from tax under section 501(a),

(ii) an annuity plan described in section 403(a),

(iii) a qualified bond purchase plan described in section 405(a), or

(iv) a plan established for its employees by the United States, by a State or political subdivision thereof, or by an agency or instrumentality of any of the foregoing, or

(B) amounts were contributed by his employer for an annuity contract described in section 403(b) (whether or not his rights in such contract are nonforfeitable).

(3) CONTRIBUTIONS AFTER AGE 70 1/2.—No deduction is allowed under subsection (a) with respect to any payment described in subsection (a) which is made during the taxable year of an individual who has attained age 70 1/2 before the close of such taxable year.

(4) RECONTRIBUTED AMOUNTS.—No deduction is allowed under this section with respect to a rollover contribution described in section 402(a)(5), 402(a)(7), 403(a)(4), 403(b)(8), 408(d)(3), or 409(b)(3)(C).

(5) AMOUNTS CONTRIBUTED UNDER ENDOWMENT CONTRACT.—In the case of an endowment contract described in section 408(b), no deduction is allowed under subsection (a) for that portion of the amounts paid under the contract for the taxable year properly allocable, under regulations prescribed by the Secretary, to the cost of life insurance.

(6) ALTERNATIVE DEDUCTION.—No deduction is allowed under subsection (a) for the taxable year if the individual claims the deduction allowed by section 220 for the taxable year.

(7) SPECIAL RULES IN CASE OF SIMPLIFIED EMPLOYEE PENSIONS.—

(A) LIMITATION.—If there is an employer contribution on behalf of the employee to a simplified employee pension, the limitation under paragraph (1) shall be the lesser of—

(i) 15 percent of the compensation includible in the employee's gross income for the taxable year (determined without regard to the employer contribution to the simplified employee pension), or

(ii) the sum of—

(I) the amount contributed by the employer to the simplified employee pension and included in gross income (but not in excess of $7,500), and

(II) $1,500, reduced (but not below zero) by the amount described in subclause (I).

(B) CERTAIN LIMITATIONS DO NOT APPLY TO EMPLOYER CONTRIBUTION.—Paragraphs (2) and (3) shall not apply with respect to the employer contribution to a simplified employee pension.

(C) SPECIAL RULE FOR APPLYING SUBPARAGRAPH (a)(ii).—In the case of an employee who is an officer, shareholder, or owner-employee described in section 408(k)(3), the $7,500 amount specified in subparagraph (A)(ii)(I) shall be reduced by the amount of tax taken into account with respect to such individual under subparagraph (D) of section 408(k)(3).

P.L. 97-34, §312(c)(1):

Amended Code Sec. 219(b)(2)(A)(ii) and (C), as amended by Act Sec. 311(a), by striking out "$7,500" and inserting "$15,000". **Effective** for tax years beginning after 12-31-81.

• **1980, Technical Corrections Act of 1979 (P.L. 96-222)**

P.L. 96-222, §101(a)(10)(D):

Amended Code Sec. 219(b)(7). **Effective** for tax years beginning after 12-31-78. Prior to amendment, Code Sec. 219(b)(7) read as follows:

(7) SIMPLIFIED EMPLOYEE PENSIONS.—In the case of an employer contribution on behalf of the employee to a simplified employee pension, paragraph (2) shall not apply with respect to the employer contribution and the limitation under paragraph (1) shall be the lesser of—

(A) 15 percent of compensation includible in the employee's gross income for the taxable year (determined without regard to the employer contribution to the simplified employee pension), or

(B) the sum of—

(i) the amount contributed by the employer to the simplified employee pension and included in gross income (but not in excess of $7,500), and

(ii) $1,500, reduced (but not below zero) by the amount described in clause (i).

In the case of an employee who is an officer, shareholder, or owner-employee described in section 408(k)(3), the amount referred to in subparagraph (B) shall be reduced by the amount of tax taken into account with respect to such individual under subparagraph (D) of section 408(k)(3).

P.L. 96-222, §101(a)(13)(A):

Amended Act Sec. 156(d) of P.L. 95-600 to change the effective date of the amendment of Code Sec. 219(b)(4) made by Act Sec. 156(c)(3) of P.L. 95-600 from "distributions or transfers made after December 31, 1978, in taxable years beginning after that date" to "distributions or transfers made after December 31, 1977, in taxable years beginning after that date."

P.L. 96-222, §101(a)(14)(B):

Amended Code Sec. 219(b)(4) by adding "402(a)(7)," after "section 402(a)(5),". **Effective** for distributions or transfers made after 12-31-77, in taxable years beginning after such date.

• **1978, Revenue Act of 1978 (P.L. 95-600)**

P.L. 95-600, §152(c), (h):

Added Code Sec. 219(b)(7). **Effective** for tax years beginning after 12-31-78.

P.L. 95-600, §156(c)(3):

Amended Code Sec. 219(b)(4) by inserting "403(b)(8)," after "403(a)(4)". **Effective** for distributions or transfers made after 12-31-78, in tax years beginning after such date.

• **1976, Tax Reform Act of 1976 (P.L. 94-455)**

P.L. 94-455, §1501(b)(4)(B):

Added Code Sec. 219(b)(6). **Effective** for tax years beginning after 12-31-76.

P.L. 94-455, §1901(a)(32):

Substituted "subdivision" for "division" in Code Sec. 219(b)(2)(A)(iv). **Effective** for tax years beginning after 12-31-76.

P.L. 94-455, §1906(b)(13)(A):

Amended 1954 Code by substituting "Secretary" for "Secretary or his delegate" each place it appeared. **Effective** 2-1-77.

[Sec. 219(c)]

(c) SPECIAL RULES FOR CERTAIN MARRIED INDIVIDUALS.—

(1) IN GENERAL.—In the case of an individual to whom this paragraph applies for the taxable year, the limitation of paragraph (1) of subsection (b) shall be equal to the lesser of—

(A) the dollar amount in effect under subsection (b)(1)(A) for the taxable year, or

(B) the sum of—

(i) the compensation includible in such individual's gross income for the taxable year, plus

(ii) the compensation includible in the gross income of such individual's spouse for the taxable year reduced by—

(I) the amount allowed as a deduction under subsection (a) to such spouse for such taxable year,

(II) the amount of any designated nondeductible contribution (as defined in section 408(o)) on behalf of such spouse for such taxable year, and

(III) the amount of any contribution on behalf of such spouse to a Roth IRA under section 408A for such taxable year.

(2) INDIVIDUALS TO WHOM PARAGRAPH (1) APPLIES.—Paragraph (1) shall apply to any individual if—

(A) such individual files a joint return for the taxable year, and

(B) the amount of compensation (if any) includible in such individual's gross income for the taxable year is less than the compensation includible in the gross income of such individual's spouse for the taxable year.

Amendments

• **2000, Community Renewal Tax Relief Act of 2000 (P.L. 106-554)**

P.L. 106-554, §316(d):

Amended Code Sec. 219(c)(1)(B)(ii) by striking "and" at the end of subclause (I), by redesignating subclause (II) as subclause (III), and by inserting after subclause (I) a new subclause (II). **Effective** as if included in the provision of P.L. 104-188 to which it relates [**effective** for tax years beginning after 12-31-96.—CCH].

• **1997, Taxpayer Relief Act of 1997 (P.L. 105-34)**

P.L. 105-34, §302(c):

Amended Code Sec. 219(c)(1)(B)(ii). **Effective** for tax years beginning after 12-31-97. Prior to amendment, Code Sec. 219(c)(1)(B)(ii) read as follows:

(ii) the compensation includible in the gross income of such individual's spouse for the taxable year reduced by the amount allowed as a deduction under subsection (a) to such spouse for such taxable year.

• **1996, Small Business Job Protection Act of 1996 (P.L. 104-188)**

P.L. 104-188, §1427(a):

Amended Code Sec. 219(c). **Effective** for tax years beginning after 12-31-96. Prior to amendment, Code Sec. 219(c) read as follows:

(c) SPECIAL RULES FOR CERTAIN MARRIED INDIVIDUALS.—

(1) IN GENERAL.—In the case of any individual with respect to whom a deduction is otherwise allowable under subsection (a)—

(A) who files a joint return under section 6013 for a taxable year, and

(B) whose spouse—

(i) has no compensation (determined without regard to section 911) for the taxable year, or

(ii) elects to be treated for purposes of subsection (b)(1)(B) as having no compensation for the taxable year,

there shall be allowed as a deduction any amount paid in cash for the taxable year by or on behalf of the individual to an individual retirement plan established for the benefit of his spouse.

(2) LIMITATION.—The amount allowable as a deduction under paragraph (1) shall not exceed the excess of—

(A) the lesser of—

(i) $2,250, or

(ii) an amount equal to the compensation includible in the individual's gross income for the taxable year, over

(B) the amount allowable as a deduction under subsection (a) for the taxable year.

In no event shall the amount allowable as a deduction under paragraph (1) exceed $2,000.

• 1986, Tax Reform Act of 1986 (P.L. 99-514)

P.L. 99-514, §1103(a):

Amended Code Sec. 219(c)(1)(B). **Effective** for tax years beginning before, on, or after 12-31-85. Prior to amendment, Code Sec. 219(c)(1)(B) read as follows:

(B) whose spouse has no compensation (determined without regard to section 911) for such taxable year,

P.L. 99-514, §1108(g)(3):

Amended Code Sec. 219(c)(2)(B) by striking out "(determined without regard to so much of the employer contributions to a simplified employee pension as is allowable by reason of paragraph (2) of subsection (b))". **Effective** for tax years beginning after 12-31-86.

• 1983, Technical Corrections Act of 1982 (P.L. 97-448)

P.L. 97-448, §103(c)(1):

Amended Code Sec. 219(c)(2)(B). **Effective** as if it had been included in the provision of P.L. 97-34 to which it relates. Prior to amendment, Code Sec. 219(c)(2)(B) read as follows:

"(B) the amount allowed as a deduction under subsection (a) for the taxable year."

• 1981, Economic Recovery Tax Act of 1981 (P.L. 97-34)

P.L. 97-34, §311(a):

Amended Code Sec. 219(c). **Effective** for tax years beginning after 12-31-81. The transitional rule provides that, for purposes of the 1954 Code, any amount allowed as a deduction under Code Sec. 220 (as in effect before its repeal by P.L. 97-34) shall be treated as if it were allowed by section 219 of the Code. Prior to amendment, Code Sec. 219(c) read as follows:

(c) DEFINITIONS AND SPECIAL RULES.—

(1) COMPENSATION.—For purposes of this section, the term "compensation" includes earned income as defined in section 401(c)(2).

(2) MARRIED INDIVIDUALS.—The maximum deduction under subsection (b)(1) shall be computed separately for each individual, and this section shall be applied without regard to any community property laws. For purposes of this section, the determination of whether an individual is married shall be made in accordance with the provisions of section 143(a).

(3) TIME WHEN CONTRIBUTIONS DEEMED MADE.—For purposes of this section, a taxpayer shall be deemed to have made a contribution on the last day of the preceding taxable year if the contribution is made on account of such taxable year and is made not later than the time prescribed by law for filing the return for such taxable year (including extensions thereof).

(4) PARTICIPATION IN GOVERNMENTAL PLANS BY CERTAIN INDIVIDUALS.—

(A) MEMBERS OF RESERVE COMPONENTS.—A member of a reserve component of the armed forces (as defined in section 261(a) of title 10) is not considered to be an active participant in a plan described in subsection (b)(2)(A)(iv) for a taxable year solely because he is a member of a reserve component unless he has served in excess of 90 days on active duty (other than active duty for training) during the year.

(B) VOLUNTEER FIREFIGHTERS.—An individual whose participation in a plan described in subsection (b)(2)(A)(iv) is based solely upon his activity as a volunteer firefighter and whose accrued benefit as of the beginning of the taxable year is not more than an annual benefit of $1,800 (when expressed as a single life annuity commencing at age 65) is not considered to be an active participant in such a plan for the taxable year.

(5) EXCESS CONTRIBUTIONS TREATED AS CONTRIBUTION MADE DURING SUBSEQUENT YEAR FOR WHICH THERE IS AN UNUSED LIMITATION.—

(A) IN GENERAL.—If for the taxable year the maximum amount allowable as a deduction under this section exceeds the amount contributed, then the taxpayer shall be treated as having made an additional contribution for the taxable year in an amount equal to the lesser of—

(i) the amount of such excess, or

(ii) the amount of the excess contributions for such taxable year (determined under section 4973(b)(2) without regard to subparagraph (C) thereof).

(B) AMOUNT CONTRIBUTED.—For purposes of this paragraph, the amount contributed—

(i) shall be determined without regard to this paragraph, and

(ii) shall not include any rollover contribution.

(C) SPECIAL RULE WHERE EXCESS DEDUCTION WAS ALLOWED FOR CLOSED YEAR.—Proper reduction shall be made in the amount allowable as a deduction by reason of this paragraph for any amount allowed as a deduction under this section or section 220 for a prior taxable year for which the period for assessing deficiency has expired if the amount so allowed exceeds the amount which should have been allowed for such prior taxable year.

• 1978, Revenue Act of 1978 (P.L. 95-600)

P.L. 95-600, §157(a)(1):

Amended Code Sec. 219(c)(3) by striking out "not later than 45 days after the end of such taxable year" and inserting in lieu thereof "not later than the time prescribed by law for filing the return for such taxable year (including extensions thereof)". **Effective** for tax years beginning after 12-31-77.

P.L. 95-600, §157(b)(1):

Added Code Sec. 219(c)(5). **Effective** as set forth in P.L. 95-600, §157(b)(4), below.

P.L. 95-600, §157(b)(4), provides:

(4) EFFECTIVE DATE.—

(A) IN GENERAL.—The amendments made by this subsection shall apply to the determination of deductions for taxable years beginning after December 31, 1975.

(B) TRANSITIONAL RULE.—If, but for this subparagraph, an amount would be allowable as a deduction by reason of section 219(c)(5) or 220(c)(6) of the Internal Revenue Code of 1954 for a taxable year beginning before January 1, 1978, such amount shall be allowable only for the taxpayer's first taxable year beginning in 1978.

P.L. 95-600, §703(c)(1):

Amended Code Sec. 219(c)(4) by striking out "subsection (b)(3)(A)(iv)" each place it appeared and inserting in lieu thereof "subsection (b)(2)(A)(iv)". **Effective** for tax years beginning after 12-31-76.

• 1976, Tax Reform Act of 1976 (P.L. 94-455)

P.L. 94-455, §1501(b)(4)(C), (D):

Added the last sentence of Code Sec. 219(c)(2) and added Code Sec. 219(c)(3). **Effective** for tax years beginning after 12-31-76.

P.L. 94-455, §1503(a):

Added Code Sec. 219(c)(4). **Effective** for tax years beginning after 12-31-75.

• 1974, Employee Retirement Income Security Act of 1974 (P.L. 93-406)

P.L. 93-406, §2002(a):

Added new Code Sec. 219. **Effective** for tax years beginning after 1974.

[Sec. 219(d)]

(d) OTHER LIMITATIONS AND RESTRICTIONS.—

(1) BENEFICIARY MUST BE UNDER AGE 70½.—No deduction shall be allowed under this section with respect to any qualified retirement contribution for the benefit of an individual if such individual has attained age 70½ before the close of such individual's taxable year for which the contribution was made.

(2) RECONTRIBUTED AMOUNTS.—No deduction shall be allowed under this section with respect to a rollover contribution described in section 402(c), 403(a)(4), 403(b)(8), 408(d)(3), or 457(e)(16).

(3) AMOUNTS CONTRIBUTED UNDER ENDOWMENT CONTRACT.—In the case of an endowment contract described in section 408(b), no deduction shall be allowed under this section for that portion of the amounts paid under the contract for the taxable year which is properly allocable, under regulations prescribed by the Secretary, to the cost of life insurance.

(4) DENIAL OF DEDUCTION FOR AMOUNT CONTRIBUTED TO INHERITED ANNUITIES OR ACCOUNTS.—No deduction shall be allowed under this section with respect to any amount paid to an inherited individual retirement account or individual retirement annuity (within the meaning of section 408(d)(3)(C)(ii)).

Amendments

• 2006, Pension Protection Act of 2006 (P.L. 109-280)

P.L. 109-280, §811, provides:

SEC. 811. PENSIONS AND INDIVIDUAL RETIREMENT ARRANGEMENT PROVISIONS OF ECONOMIC GROWTH AND TAX RELIEF RECONCILIATION ACT OF 2001 MADE PERMANENT.

Title IX of the Economic Growth and Tax Relief Reconciliation Act of 2001 [P.L. 107-16] shall not apply to the provisions of, and amendments made by, subtitles A through F of title VI [§§601-666]of such Act (relating to pension and individual retirement arrangement provisions).

• 2001, Economic Growth and Tax Relief Reconciliation Act of 2001 (P.L. 107-16)

P.L. 107-16, §641(e)(2):

Amended Code Sec. 219(d)(2) by striking "or 408(d)(3)" and inserting "408(d)(3), or 457(e)(16)". **Effective**, generally, for distributions after 12-31-2001. For a special rule, see Act Sec. 641(f)(3), below.

P.L. 107-16, §641(f)(3), provides:

(3) SPECIAL RULE.—Notwithstanding any other provision of law, subsections (h)(3) and (h)(5) of section 1122 of the Tax Reform Act of 1986 shall not apply to any distribution from an eligible retirement plan (as defined in clause (iii) or (iv) of section 402(c)(8)(B) of the Internal Revenue Code of 1986) on behalf of an individual if there was a rollover to such plan on behalf of such individual which is permitted solely by reason of any amendment made by this section.

P.L. 107-16, §901(a)-(b), provides [but see P.L. 109-280, §811, above]:

SEC. 901. SUNSET OF PROVISIONS OF ACT.

(a) IN GENERAL.—All provisions of, and amendments made by, this Act shall not apply—

(1) to taxable, plan, or limitation years beginning after December 31, 2010, or

(2) in the case of title V, to estates of decedents dying, gifts made, or generation skipping transfers, after December 31, 2010.

(b) APPLICATION OF CERTAIN LAWS.—The Internal Revenue Code of 1986 and the Employee Retirement Income Security Act of 1974 shall be applied and administered to years, estates, gifts, and transfers described in subsection (a) as if the provisions and amendments described in subsection (a) had never been enacted.

• 1992, Unemployment Compensation Amendments of 1992 (P.L. 102-318)

P.L. 102-318, §521(b)(4):

Amended Code Sec. 219(d)(2) by striking "section 402(a)(5), 402(a)(7)" and inserting "section 402(c)". **Effective** for distributions after 12-31-92.

• 1984, Deficit Reduction Act of 1984 (P.L. 98-369)

P.L. 98-369, §491(d)(6):

Amended Code Sec. 219(d)(2) by striking out "405(d)(3), 408(d)(3), or 409(b)(3)(C)" and inserting in lieu thereof "or 408(d)(3)". **Effective** for obligations issued after 12-31-83.

• 1983, Technical Corrections Act of 1982 (P.L. 97-448)

P.L. 97-448, §103(c)(2):

Amended Code Sec. 219(d)(1). **Effective** as if it had been included in the provision of P.L. 97-34 to which it relates. Prior to amendment, Code Sec. 219(d)(1) read as follows:

(1) INDIVIDUALS WHO HAVE ATTAINED AGE 70 ½.—No deduction shall be allowed under this section with respect to any qualified retirement contribution which is made for a taxable year of an individual if such individual has attained age 70½ before the close of such taxable year.

• 1982, Tax Equity and Fiscal Responsibility Act of 1982 (P.L. 97-248)

P.L. 97-248, §243(b)(2):

Added Code Sec. 219(d)(4). **Effective** for tax years beginning after 12-31-83.

• 1981, Economic Recovery Tax Act of 1981 (P.L. 97-34)

P.L. 97-34, §311(a):

Added Code Sec. 219(d). **Effective** for tax years beginning after 12-31-81. The transitional rule provides that, for purposes of the 1954 Code, any amount allowed as a deduction under Code Sec. 220 (as in effect before its repeal by P.L. 97-34) shall be treated as if it were allowed by section 219 of the Code.

P.L. 97-34, §313(b)(2):

Amended Code Sec. 219(d), as added by Act Sec. 311(a), by inserting "405(d)(3)" after "403(b)(8)". **Effective** for redemptions after 8-13-81 in tax years ending after 8-13-81.

[Sec. 219(e)]

(e) QUALIFIED RETIREMENT CONTRIBUTION.—For purposes of this section, the term "qualified retirement contribution" means—

(1) any amount paid in cash for the taxable year by or on behalf of an individual to an individual retirement plan for such individual's benefit, and

(2) any amount contributed on behalf of any individual to a plan described in section 501(c)(18).

Amendments

• 1986, Tax Reform Act of 1986 (P.L. 99-514)

P.L. 99-514, §1101(b)(1):

Amended Code Sec. 219(e). **Effective** for contributions for tax years beginning after 12-31-86. Prior to amendment, Code Sec. 219(e) read as follows:

(e) DEFINITION OF RETIREMENT SAVINGS CONTRIBUTIONS, ETC.—For purposes of this section—

(1) QUALIFIED RETIREMENT CONTRIBUTION.—The term "qualified retirement contribution" means—

(A) any qualified voluntary employee contribution paid in cash by the individual for the taxable year, and

(B) any amount paid in cash for the taxable year by or on behalf of such individual for his benefit to an individual retirement plan.

(2) QUALIFIED VOLUNTARY EMPLOYEE CONTRIBUTION.—

(A) IN GENERAL.—The term "qualified voluntary employee contribution" means any voluntary contribution—

(i) which is made by an individual as an employee under a qualified employer plan or government plan, which plan allows an employee to make contributions which may be treated as qualified voluntary employee contributions under this section, and

(ii) with respect to which the individual has not designated such contribution as a contribution which should not be taken into account under this section.

(B) VOLUNTARY CONTRIBUTION.—For purposes of subparagraph (A), the term "voluntary contribution" means any contribution which is not a mandatory contribution (within the meaning of section 411(c)(2)(C)).

(C) DESIGNATION.—For purposes of determining whether or not an individual has made a designation described in subparagraph (A)(ii) with respect to any contribution during any calendar year under a qualified employer plan or government plan, such individual shall be treated as having made such designation if he notifies the plan administrator of such plan, not later than the earlier of—

(i) April 15 of the succeeding calendar year, or

(ii) the time prescribed by the plan administrator,

that the individual does not want such contribution taken into account under this section. Any designation or notification referred to in the preceding sentence shall be made in such manner as the Secretary shall by regulations prescribe and, after the last date on which such designation or notification may be made, shall be irrevocable for such taxable year.

(3) QUALIFIED EMPLOYER PLAN.—The term "qualified employer plan" means—

(A) a plan described in section 401(a) which includes a trust exempt from tax under section 501(a),

(B) an annuity plan described in section 403(a), and

(C) a plan under which amounts are contributed by an individual's employer for an annuity contract described in section 403(b).

(4) GOVERNMENT PLAN.—The term "government plan" means any plan, whether or not qualified, established and maintained for its employees by the United States, by a State or political subdivision thereof, or by an agency or instrumentality of any of the foregoing.

(5) PAYMENTS FOR CERTAIN PLANS.—The term "amounts paid to an individual retirement plan" includes amounts paid for an individual retirement annuity or a retirement bond.

• 1984, Deficit Reduction Act of 1984 (P.L. 98-369)

P.L. 98-369, §491(d)(7):

Amended Code Sec. 219(e)(1) by striking out the last sentence. **Effective** for obligations issued after 12-31-83. Prior to amendment the last sentence read as follows:

For purposes of the preceding sentence, the term "individual retirement plan" includes a retirement bond described in section 409 only if the bond is not redeemed within 12 months of its issuance.

P.L. 98-369, §491(d)(8):

Amended Code Sec. 219(e)(3) by striking out subparagraph (C), by adding "and" at the end of subparagraph (B) and by redesignating subparagraph (D) as subparagraph (C). **Effective** for obligations issued after 12-31-83. Prior to amendment, Code Sec. 219(e)(3)(C) read as follows:

(C) a qualified bond purchase plan described in section 405(a), and

• 1983, Technical Corrections Act of 1982 (P.L. 97-448)

P.L. 97-448, §103(c)(3)(A):

Amended Code Sec. 219(e)(3) by inserting "and" at the end of subparagraph (C), by striking out subparagraph (D), and by redesignating subparagraph (E) as subparagraph (D). **Effective** as if it had been included in the provision of P.L. 97-34 to which it relates. Prior to being stricken, Code Sec. 219(e)(3)(D) read as follows:

"(D) a simplified employee pension (within the meaning of section 408(k)), and"

• 1981, Economic Recovery Tax Act of 1981 (P.L. 97-34)

P.L. 97-34, §311(a):

Added Code Sec. 219(e). **Effective** for tax years beginning after 12-31-81. The transitional rule provides that for purposes of the 1954 Code any amount allowed as a deduction under Code Sec. 220 (as in effect before its repeal by P.L. 97-34) shall be treated as if it were allowed by section 219 of the Code.

[Sec. 219(f)]

(f) OTHER DEFINITIONS AND SPECIAL RULES.—

(1) COMPENSATION.—For purposes of this section, the term "compensation" includes earned income (as defined in section 401(c)(2)). The term "compensation" does not include any amount received as a pension or annuity and does not include any amount received as deferred compensation. The term "compensation" shall include any amount includible in the individual's gross income under section 71 with respect to a divorce or separation instrument described in subparagraph (A) of section 71(b)(2). For purposes of this paragraph, section 401(c)(2) shall be applied as if the term trade or business for purposes of section 1402 included service described in subsection (c)(6). The term compensation includes any differential wage payment (as defined in section 3401(h)(2)).

(2) MARRIED INDIVIDUALS.—The maximum deduction under subsection (b) shall be computed separately for each individual, and this section shall be applied without regard to any community property laws.

(3) TIME WHEN CONTRIBUTIONS DEEMED MADE.—For purposes of this section, a taxpayer shall be deemed to have made a contribution to an individual retirement plan on the last day of the preceding taxable year if the contribution is made on account of such taxable year and is made not later than the time prescribed by law for filing the return for such taxable year (not including extensions thereof).

(4) REPORTS.—The Secretary shall prescribe regulations which prescribe the time and the manner in which reports to the Secretary and plan participants shall be made by the plan

administrator of a qualified employer or government plan receiving qualified voluntary employee contributions.

(5) EMPLOYER PAYMENTS.—For purposes of this title, any amount paid by an employer to an individual retirement plan shall be treated as payment of compensation to the employee (other than a self-employed individual who is an employee within the meaning of section 401(c)(1)) includible in his gross income in the taxable year for which the amount was contributed, whether or not a deduction for such payment is allowable under this section to the employee.

(6) EXCESS CONTRIBUTIONS TREATED AS CONTRIBUTION MADE DURING SUBSEQUENT YEAR FOR WHICH THERE IS AN UNUSED LIMITATION.—

(A) IN GENERAL.—If for the taxable year the maximum amount allowable as a deduction under this section for contributions to an individual retirement plan exceeds the amount contributed, then the taxpayer shall be treated as having made an additional contribution for the taxable year in an amount equal to the lesser of—

(i) the amount of such excess, or

(ii) the amount of the excess contributions for such taxable year (determined under section 4973(b)(2) without regard to subparagraph (C) thereof).

(B) AMOUNT CONTRIBUTED.—For purposes of this paragraph, the amount contributed—

(i) shall be determined without regard to this paragraph, and

(ii) shall not include any rollover contribution.

(C) SPECIAL RULE WHERE EXCESS DEDUCTION WAS ALLOWED FOR CLOSED YEAR.—Proper reduction shall be made in the amount allowable as a deduction by reason of this paragraph for any amount allowed as a deduction under this section for a prior taxable year for which the period for assessing deficiency has expired if the amount so allowed exceeds the amount which should have been allowed for such prior taxable year.

(7) SPECIAL RULE FOR COMPENSATION EARNED BY MEMBERS OF THE ARMED FORCES FOR SERVICE IN A COMBAT ZONE.—For purposes of subsections (b)(1)(B) and (c), the amount of compensation includible in an individual's gross income shall be determined without regard to section 112.

(8) ELECTION NOT TO DEDUCT CONTRIBUTIONS.—

For election not to deduct contributions to individual retirement plans, see section 408(o)(2)(B)(ii).

Amendments

• 2008, Heroes Earnings Assistance and Relief Tax Act of 2008 (P.L. 110-245)

P.L. 110-245, §105(b)(2):

Amended Code Sec. 219(f)(1) by adding at the end a new sentence. **Effective** for years beginning after 12-31-2008.

• 2006, Heroes Earned Retirement Opportunities Act (P.L. 109-227)

P.L. 109-227, §2(a):

Amended Code Sec. 219(f) by redesignating paragraph (7) as paragraph (8) and by inserting after paragraph (6) a new paragraph (7). **Effective** for tax years beginning after 12-31-2003. For a special rule, see Act Sec. 2(c), in the amendment notes for Code Sec. 112(d).

• 1996, Small Business Job Protection Act of 1996 (P.L. 104-188)

P.L. 104-188, §1427(b)(1):

Amended Code Sec. 219(f)(2) by striking "subsections (b) and (c)" and inserting "subsection (b)". **Effective** for tax years beginning after 12-31-96.

• 1989, Omnibus Budget Reconciliation Act of 1989 (P.L. 101-239)

P.L. 101-239, §7841(c)(1):

Amended Code Sec. 219(f)(1) by adding at the end thereof the new sentence. **Effective** for contributions after 12-19-89 in tax years ending after such date.

• 1986, Tax Reform Act of 1986 (P.L. 99-514)

P.L. 99-514, §301(b)(4):

Amended Code Sec. 219(f)(1) by striking out "paragraph (7)" [as in effect before the amendment made by Act Sec. 1875(c)(4). See note for Act Sec. 1875(c)(4).] and inserting in lieu thereof "paragraph (6)". **Effective** for tax years beginning after 12-31-86.

P.L. 99-514, §1101(a)(2):

Amended Code Sec. 219(f)(3). **Effective** for contributions for tax years beginning after 12-31-86. Prior to amendment, Code Sec. 219(f)(3) read as follows:

(3) TIME WHEN CONTRIBUTIONS DEEMED MADE.—

(A) INDIVIDUAL RETIREMENT PLANS.—For purposes of this section, a taxpayer shall be deemed to have made a contribution to an individual retirement plan on the last day of the preceding taxable year if the contribution is made on account of such taxable year and is made not later than the time prescribed by law for filing the return for such taxable year (not including extensions thereof).

(B) QUALIFIED EMPLOYER OR GOVERNMENT PLANS.—For purposes of this section, if a qualified employer or government plan elects to have the provisions of this subparagraph apply, a taxpayer shall be deemed to have made a voluntary contribution to such plan on the last day of the preceding calendar year (if, without regard to this paragraph, such contribution may be made on such date) if the contribution is made on account of the taxable year which includes such last day and by April 15 of the calendar year or such earlier time as is provided by the plan administrator.

P.L. 99-514, §1102(f):

Amended Code Sec. 219(f) by adding at the end thereof new paragraph (7). **Effective** for contributions and distributions for tax years beginning after 12-31-86.

P.L. 99-514, §1875(c)(4):

Amended Code Sec. 219(f)(1) by striking out "reduced by any amount allowable as a deduction to the individual in computing adjusted gross income under paragraph (7) of section 62". **Effective** as if included in the amendment made by P.L. 97-248, §238. Prior to amendment, Code Sec. 219(f)(1) read as follows:

(1) COMPENSATION.—For purposes of this section, the term "compensation" includes earned income (as defined in section 401(c)(2)) reduced by any amount allowable as a deduction to the individual in computing adjusted gross income under paragraph (7) of section 62. The term "compensation" does not include any amount received as a pension or annuity and does not include any amount received as deferred compensation. The term "compensation" shall include any amount includible in the individual's gross income under section 71 with respect to a divorce or separation instrument described in subparagraph (A) of section 71(b)(2).

• 1984, Deficit Reduction Act of 1984 (P.L. 98-369)

P.L. 98-369, § 147(c):

Amended Code Sec. 219(f)(3)(A) by striking out "including" and inserting in lieu thereof "not including". **Effective** for contributions made after 12-31-84.

P.L. 98-369, § 529(a):

Amended Code Sec. 219(f)(1) by adding the last sentence. **Effective** for tax years beginning after 12-31-84.

• 1983, Technical Corrections Act of 1982 (P.L. 97-448)

P.L. 97-448, § 103(c)(4):

Amended Code Sec. 219(f)(1). **Effective** as if it had been included in the provision of P.L. 97-34 to which it relates. Prior to amendment, Code Sec. 219(f)(1) read as follows:

"(1) COMPENSATION.—For purposes of this section, the term `compensation' includes earned income as defined in section 401(c)(2)."

P.L. 97-448, § 103(c)(5):

Amended Code Sec. 219(f)(3)(B) by striking out "the contribution is made" and inserting in lieu thereof "the contribution is made on account of the taxable year which includes such last day and". **Effective** as if it had been included in the provision of P.L. 97-34 to which it relates.

• 1981, Economic Recovery Tax Act of 1981 (P.L. 97-34)

P.L. 97-34, § 311(a):

Added Code Sec. 219(f). **Effective** for tax years beginning after 12-31-81. The transitional rule provides that, for purposes of the 1954 Code, any amount allowed as a deduction under Code Sec. 220 (as in effect before its repeal by P.L. 97-34) shall be treated as if it were allowed by section 219 of the Code.

[Sec. 219(g)]

(g) LIMITATION ON DEDUCTION FOR ACTIVE PARTICIPANTS IN CERTAIN PENSION PLANS.—

(1) IN GENERAL.—If (for any part of any plan year ending with or within a taxable year) an individual or the individual's spouse is an active participant, each of the dollar limitations contained in subsections (b)(1)(A) and (c)(1)(A) for such taxable year shall be reduced (but not below zero) by the amount determined under paragraph (2).

(2) AMOUNT OF REDUCTION.—

(A) IN GENERAL.—The amount determined under this paragraph with respect to any dollar limitation shall be the amount which bears the same ratio to such limitation as—

(i) the excess of—

(I) the taxpayer's adjusted gross income for such taxable year, over

(II) the applicable dollar amount, bears to

(ii) $10,000 ($20,000 in the case of a joint return for a taxable year beginning after December 31, 2006).

(B) NO REDUCTION BELOW $200 UNTIL COMPLETE PHASE-OUT.—No dollar limitation shall be reduced below $200 under paragraph (1) unless (without regard to this subparagraph) such limitation is reduced to zero.

(C) ROUNDING.—Any amount determined under this paragraph which is not a multiple of $10 shall be rounded to the next lowest $10.

(3) ADJUSTED GROSS INCOME; APPLICABLE DOLLAR AMOUNT.—For purposes of this subsection—

(A) ADJUSTED GROSS INCOME.—Adjusted gross income of any taxpayer shall be determined—

(i) after application of sections 86 and 469, and

»»→ Caution: Code Sec. 219(g)(3)(A)(ii), below, is subject to the sunset provision of the Economic Growth and Tax Relief Reconciliation Act of 2001 (P.L. 107-16), §901. Absent Congressional action, the changes made to this provision by P.L. 107-16, or that take effect as if included in P.L. 107-16, do not apply after December 31, 2010. For more information about the sunset provision, see page XXI of the Preface to this publication and P.L. 107-16, §901, in the amendment notes. See the amendments notes for a history of amendments to this section and the effective date of each change.

(ii) without regard to sections 135, 137, 199, 221, 222, and 911 or the deduction allowable under this section.

(B) APPLICABLE DOLLAR AMOUNT.—The term "applicable dollar amount" means the following:

(i) In the case of a taxpayer filing a joint return:

For taxable years beginning in:	*The applicable dollar amount is:*
1998	$50,000
1999	$51,000
2000	$52,000
2001	$53,000
2002	$54,000
2003	$60,000
2004	$65,000
2005	$70,000
2006	$75,000
2007 and thereafter	$80,000

(ii) In the case of any other taxpayer (other than a married individual filing a separate return):

For taxable years beginning in:	*The applicable dollar amount is:*
1998	$30,000
1999	$31,000
2000	$32,000
2001	$33,000
2002	$34,000
2003	$40,000
2004	$45,000
2005 and thereafter	$50,000

(iii) In the case of a married individual filing a separate return, zero.

(4) SPECIAL RULE FOR MARRIED INDIVIDUALS FILING SEPARATELY AND LIVING APART.—A husband and wife who—

(A) file separate returns for any taxable year, and

(B) live apart at all times during such taxable year,

shall not be treated as married individuals for purposes of this subsection.

(5) ACTIVE PARTICIPANT.—For purposes of this subsection, the term "active participant" means, with respect to any plan year, an individual—

(A) who is an active participant in—

(i) a plan described in section 401(a) which includes a trust exempt from tax under section 501(a),

(ii) an annuity plan described in section 403(a),

(iii) a plan established for its employees by the United States, by a State or political subdivision thereof, or by an agency or instrumentality of any of the foregoing,

(iv) an annuity contract described in section 403(b),

(v) a simplified employee pension (within the meaning of section 408(k)), or

(vi) any simple retirement account (within the meaning of section 408(p)), or

(B) who makes deductible contributions to a trust described in section 501(c)(18).

The determination of whether an individual is an active participant shall be made without regard to whether or not such individual's rights under a plan, trust, or contract are nonforfeitable. An eligible deferred compensation plan (within the meaning of section 457(b)) shall not be treated as a plan described in subparagraph (A)(iii).

(6) CERTAIN INDIVIDUALS NOT TREATED AS ACTIVE PARTICIPANTS.—For purposes of this subsection, any individual described in any of the following subparagraphs shall not be treated as an active participant for any taxable year solely because of any participation so described:

(A) MEMBERS OF RESERVE COMPONENTS.—Participation in a plan described in subparagraph (A)(iii) of paragraph (5) by reason of service as a member of a reserve component of the Armed Forces (as defined in section 10101 of title 10), unless such individual has served in excess of 90 days on active duty (other than active duty for training) during the year.

(B) VOLUNTEER FIREFIGHTERS.—A volunteer firefighter—

(i) who is a participant in a plan described in subparagraph (A)(iii) of paragraph (5) based on his activity as a volunteer firefighter, and

(ii) whose accrued benefit as of the beginning of the taxable year is not more than an annual benefit of $1,800 (when expressed as a single life annuity commencing at age 65).

(7) SPECIAL RULE FOR SPOUSES WHO ARE NOT ACTIVE PARTICIPANTS.—If this subsection applies to an individual for any taxable year solely because their spouse is an active participant, then, in applying this subsection to the individual (but not their spouse)—

(A) the applicable dollar amount under paragraph (3)(B)(i) shall be $150,000; and

(B) the amount applicable under paragraph (2)(A)(ii) shall be $10,000.

(8) INFLATION ADJUSTMENT.—In the case of any taxable year beginning in a calendar year after 2006, the dollar amount in the last row of the table contained in paragraph (3)(B)(i), the dollar amount in the last row of the table contained in paragraph (3)(B)(ii), and the dollar amount contained in paragraph (7)(A), shall each be increased by an amount equal to—

(A) such dollar amount, multiplied by

(B) the cost-of-living adjustment determined under section 1(f)(3) for the calendar year in which the taxable year begins, determined by substituting "calendar year 2005" for "calendar year 1992" in subparagraph (B) thereof.

Any increase determined under the preceding sentence shall be rounded to the nearest multiple of $1,000.

Amendments

• 2006, Pension Protection Act of 2006 (P.L. 109-280)

P.L. 109-280, §833(b):

Amended Code Sec. 219(g) by adding at the end a new paragraph (8). **Effective** for tax years beginning after 2006.

• 2004, American Jobs Creation Act of 2004 (P.L. 108-357)

P.L. 108-357, §102(d)(1):

Amended Code Sec. 219(g)(3)(A)(ii) by inserting "199," before "221". **Effective** for tax years beginning after 12-31-2004.

• 2001, Economic Growth and Tax Relief Reconciliation Act of 2001 (P.L. 107-16)

P.L. 107-16, §431(c)(1):

Amended Code Sec. 219(g)(3) by inserting "222," after "221,". **Effective** for payments made in tax years beginning after 12-31-2001.

P.L. 107-16, §901(a)-(b), provides:

SEC. 901. SUNSET OF PROVISIONS OF ACT.

(a) IN GENERAL.—All provisions of, and amendments made by, this Act shall not apply—

(1) to taxable, plan, or limitation years beginning after December 31, 2010, or

(2) in the case of title V, to estates of decedents dying, gifts made, or generation skipping transfers, after December 31, 2010.

(b) APPLICATION OF CERTAIN LAWS.—The Internal Revenue Code of 1986 and the Employee Retirement Income Security Act of 1974 shall be applied and administered to years, estates, gifts, and transfers described in subsection (a) as if the provisions and amendments described in subsection (a) had never been enacted.

• 1998, Tax and Trade Relief Extension Act of 1998 (P.L. 105-277)

P.L. 105-277, §4003(a)(2)(B):

Amended Code Sec. 219(g)(3)(A)(ii) by inserting "221," after "137,". **Effective** as if included in the provision of P.L. 105-34 to which it relates [generally **effective** for interest payments due and paid after 12-31-97, on any qualified education loan.—CCH].

• 1998, IRS Restructuring and Reform Act of 1998 (P.L. 105-206)

P.L. 105-206, §6005(a)(1)(A)-(B):

Amended Code Sec. 219(g) by inserting "or the individual's spouse" after "individual" in paragraph (1), and by striking paragraph (7) and inserting a new paragraph (7). **Effective** as if included in the provision of P.L. 105-34 to which it relates [**effective** for tax years beginning after 12-31-97.—CCH]. Prior to being stricken, Code Sec. 219(g)(7) read as follows:

(7) SPECIAL RULE FOR CERTAIN SPOUSES.—In the case of an individual who is an active participant at no time during any plan year ending with or within the taxable year but whose spouse is an active participant for any part of any such plan year—

(A) the applicable dollar amount under paragraph (3)(B)(i) with respect to the taxpayer shall be $150,000, and

(B) the amount applicable under paragraph (2)(A)(ii) shall be $10,000.

• 1997, Taxpayer Relief Act of 1997 (P.L. 105-34)

P.L. 105-34, §301(a)(1):

Amended Code Sec. 219(g)(3)(B). **Effective** for tax years beginning after 12-31-97. Prior to amendment, Code Sec. 219(g)(3)(B) read as follows:

(B) APPLICABLE DOLLAR AMOUNT.—The term "applicable dollar amount" means—

(i) in the case of a taxpayer filing a joint return, $40,000,

(ii) in the case of any other taxpayer (other than a married individual filing a separate return), $25,000, and

(iii) in the case of a married individual filing a separate return, zero.

P.L. 105-34, §301(a)(2) (as amended by P.L. 105-206, §6005(a)(2)):

Amended Code Sec. 219(g)(2)(A)(ii) by inserting "($20,000 in the case of a joint return for a taxable year beginning after December 31, 2006)" after "$10,000". **Effective** for tax years beginning after 12-31-97.

P.L. 105-34, §301(b)(1)-(2):

Amended Code Sec. 219(g) by striking "or the individual's spouse" after "an individual" in paragraph (1), and by adding at the end a new paragraph (7). **Effective** for tax years beginning after 12-31-97.

• 1996, Small Business Job Protection Act of 1996 (P.L. 104-188)

P.L. 104-188, §1421(b)(1)(B):

Amended Code Sec. 219(g)(5)(A) by striking "or" at the end of clause (iv) and by adding at the end a new clause (vi). **Effective** for tax years beginning after 12-31-96.

P.L. 104-188, §1427(b)(2):

Amended Code Sec. 219(g)(1) by striking "(c)(2)" and inserting "(c)(1)(A)". **Effective** for tax years beginning after 12-31-96.

P.L. 104-188, §1807(c)(3) (as amended by P.L. 105-206, §6018(f)(2)):

Amended Code Sec. 219(g)(3)(A)(ii) by inserting ", 137," before "and 911". **Effective** for tax years beginning after 12-31-96.

• 1994, National Defense Authorizations Act for Fiscal Year 1995 (P.L. 103-337)

P.L. 103-337, §1677(c):

Amended Code Sec. 219(g)(6)(A) by striking out "section 261(a) of title 10" and inserting in lieu thereof "section 10101 of title 10". **Effective** 12-1-94.

• 1988, Technical and Miscellaneous Revenue Act of 1988 (P.L. 100-647)

P.L. 100-647, §1011(a)(1):

Amended Code Sec. 219(g)(4). For the **effective** date, see Act Sec. 1011(a)(2), below. Prior to amendment, Code Sec. 219(g)(4) read as follows:

(4) SPECIAL RULE FOR MARRIED INDIVIDUALS FILING SEPARATELY.—In the case of a married individual filing a separate return for any taxable year, paragraph (1) shall be applied without regard to whether such individual's spouse is an active participant for any plan year ending with or within such taxable year.

P.L. 100-647, §1011(a)(2), provides:

(2)(A) Except as provided in subparagraph (B), the amendment made by paragraph (1) shall apply to taxable years beginning after December 31, 1987.

(B) A taxpayer may elect to have the amendment made by paragraph (1) apply to any taxable year beginning in 1987.

P.L. 100-647, §6009(c)(2), amended by P.L. 101-239, §7816(c)(1):

Amended Code Sec. 219(g)(3)(A)(ii) by striking out "section 911" and inserting "sections 135 and 911". **Effective** for tax years beginning after 12-31-89.

P.L. 100-203, §10103, as amended by P.L. 100-647, §2004(c), provides:

SEC. 10103. CLARIFICATION OF TREATMENT OF FEDERAL JUDGES.

(a) GENERAL RULE.—A Federal judge—

(1) shall be treated as an active participant in a plan established for its employees by the United States for purposes of section 219(g) of the Internal Revenue Code of 1986, and

(2) shall be treated as an employee for purposes of chapter 1 of such Code.

(b) EFFECTIVE DATE.—The provisions of subsection (a) shall apply to taxable years beginning after December 31, 1987.

• 1986, Tax Reform Act of 1986 (P.L. 99-514)

P.L. 99-514, §1101(a)(1):

Amended Code Sec. 219 by redesignating subsection (g) as subsection (h) and by adding new subsection (g). **Effective** for contributions for tax years beginning after 12-31-86.

[Sec. 219(h)]

(h) CROSS REFERENCE.—

For failure to provide required reports, see section 6652(g).

Amendments

• 1986, Tax Reform Act of 1986 (P.L. 99-514)

P.L. 99-514, §1101(a)(1):

Redesignated Code Sec. 219(g) as (h). **Effective** for tax years beginning after 12-31-86.

P.L. 99-514, §1501(d)(1)(B):

Amended Code Sec. 219(g)[h] by striking out "section 6652(h)" and inserting in lieu thereof "6652(g)". **Effective** for returns the due date for which (determined without regard to extensions) is after 12-31-86.

• 1981, Economic Recovery Tax Act of 1981 (P.L. 97-34)

P.L. 97-34, §311(a):

Added Code Sec. 219(g). **Effective** for tax years beginning after 12-31-81.

[Sec. 220]

SEC. 220. ARCHER MSAs.

[Sec. 220(a)]

(a) DEDUCTION ALLOWED.—In the case of an individual who is an eligible individual for any month during the taxable year, there shall be allowed as a deduction for the taxable year an amount equal to the aggregate amount paid in cash during such taxable year by such individual to an Archer MSA of such individual.

Amendments

• 2000, Community Renewal Tax Relief Act of 2000 (P.L. 106-554)

P.L. 106-554, §202(a)(4):

Amended Code Sec. 220 by striking "medical savings account" each place it appears in the text and inserting "Archer MSA". **Effective** 12-21-2000.

P.L. 106-554, §202(b)(8):

Amended the section heading for Code Sec. 220. **Effective** 12-21-2000. Prior to amendment, the section heading for Code Sec. 220 read as follows:

SEC. 220. MEDICAL SAVINGS ACCOUNTS.

P.L. 106-554, §202(b)(10):

Amended Code Sec. 220 by striking "a Archer" each place it appears and inserting "an Archer". **Effective** 12-21-2000.

[Sec. 220(b)]

(b) LIMITATIONS.—

(1) IN GENERAL.—The amount allowable as a deduction under subsection (a) to an individual for the taxable year shall not exceed the sum of the monthly limitations for months during such taxable year that the individual is an eligible individual.

(2) MONTHLY LIMITATION.—The monthly limitation for any month is the amount equal to $1/12$ of—

(A) in the case of an individual who has self-only coverage under the high deductible health plan as of the first day of such month, 65 percent of the annual deductible under such coverage, and

(B) in the case of an individual who has family coverage under the high deductible health plan as of the first day of such month, 75 percent of the annual deductible under such coverage.

(3) SPECIAL RULE FOR MARRIED INDIVIDUALS.—In the case of individuals who are married to each other, if either spouse has family coverage—

(A) both spouses shall be treated as having only such family coverage (and if such spouses each have family coverage under different plans, as having the family coverage with the lowest annual deductible), and

(B) the limitation under paragraph (1) (after the application of subparagraph (A) of this paragraph) shall be divided equally between them unless they agree on a different division.

(4) DEDUCTION NOT TO EXCEED COMPENSATION.—

(A) EMPLOYEES.—The deduction allowed under subsection (a) for contributions as an eligible individual described in subclause (I) of subsection (c)(1)(A)(iii) shall not exceed such individual's wages, salaries, tips, and other employee compensation which are attributable to such individual's employment by the employer referred to in such subclause.

(B) SELF-EMPLOYED INDIVIDUALS.—The deduction allowed under subsection (a) for contributions as an eligible individual described in subclause (II) of subsection (c)(1)(A)(iii) shall not exceed such individual's earned income (as defined in section 401(c)(1)) derived by the taxpayer from the trade or business with respect to which the high deductible health plan is established.

(C) COMMUNITY PROPERTY LAWS NOT TO APPLY.—The limitations under this paragraph shall be determined without regard to community property laws.

(5) COORDINATION WITH EXCLUSION FOR EMPLOYER CONTRIBUTIONS.—No deduction shall be allowed under this section for any amount paid for any taxable year to an Archer MSA of an individual if—

(A) any amount is contributed to any Archer MSA of such individual for such year which is excludable from gross income under section 106(b), or

(B) if such individual's spouse is covered under the high deductible health plan covering such individual, any amount is contributed for such year to any Archer MSA of such spouse which is so excludable.

(6) DENIAL OF DEDUCTION TO DEPENDENTS.—No deduction shall be allowed under this section to any individual with respect to whom a deduction under section 151 is allowable to another taxpayer for a taxable year beginning in the calendar year in which such individual's taxable year begins.

(7) MEDICARE ELIGIBLE INDIVIDUALS.—The limitation under this subsection for any month with respect to an individual shall be zero for the first month such individual is entitled to benefits under title XVIII of the Social Security Act and for each month thereafter.

Amendments

• 2000, Community Renewal Tax Relief Act of 2000 (P.L. 106-554)

P.L. 106-554, §202(a)(4):

Amended Code Sec. 220 by striking "medical savings account" each place it appears in the text and inserting "Archer MSA". **Effective** 12-21-2000.

P.L. 106-554, §202(b)(10):

Amended Code Sec. 220 by striking "a Archer" each place it appears and inserting "an Archer". **Effective** 12-21-2000.

• 1997, Balanced Budget Act of 1997 (P.L. 105-33)

P.L. 105-33, §4006(b)(2):

Amended Code Sec. 220(b) by adding at the end a new paragraph (7). **Effective** for tax years beginning after 12-31-98.

[Sec. 220(c)]

(c) DEFINITIONS.—For purposes of this section—

(1) ELIGIBLE INDIVIDUAL.—

(A) IN GENERAL.—The term "eligible individual" means, with respect to any month, any individual if—

(i) such individual is covered under a high deductible health plan as of the 1st day of such month,

(ii) such individual is not, while covered under a high deductible health plan, covered under any health plan—

(I) which is not a high deductible health plan, and

(II) which provides coverage for any benefit which is covered under the high deductible health plan, and

(iii)(I) the high deductible health plan covering such individual is established and maintained by the employer of such individual or of the spouse of such individual and such employer is a small employer, or

(II) such individual is an employee (within the meaning of section 401(c)(1)) or the spouse of such an employee and the high deductible health plan covering such individual is not established or maintained by any employer of such individual or spouse.

(B) CERTAIN COVERAGE DISREGARDED.—Subparagraph (A)(ii) shall be applied without regard to—

(i) coverage for any benefit provided by permitted insurance, and

(ii) coverage (whether through insurance or otherwise) for accidents, disability, dental care, vision care, or long-term care.

(C) CONTINUED ELIGIBILITY OF EMPLOYEE AND SPOUSE ESTABLISHING ARCHER MSAS.—If, while an employer is a small employer—

(i) any amount is contributed to an Archer MSA of an individual who is an employee of such employer or the spouse of such an employee, and

(ii) such amount is excludable from gross income under section 106(b) or allowable as a deduction under this section,

such individual shall not cease to meet the requirement of subparagraph (A)(iii)(I) by reason of such employer ceasing to be a small employer so long as such employee continues to be an employee of such employer.

(D) LIMITATIONS ON ELIGIBILITY.—For limitations on number of taxpayers who are eligible to have Archer MSAs, see subsection (i).

(2) HIGH DEDUCTIBLE HEALTH PLAN.—

(A) IN GENERAL.—The term "high deductible health plan" means a health plan—

(i) in the case of self-only coverage, which has an annual deductible which is not less than $1,500 and not more than $2,250,

(ii) in the case of family coverage, which has an annual deductible which is not less than $3,000 and not more than $4,500, and

(iii) the annual out-of-pocket expenses required to be paid under the plan (other than for premiums) for covered benefits does not exceed—

(I) $3,000 for self-only coverage, and

(II) $5,500 for family coverage.

(B) SPECIAL RULES.—

(i) EXCLUSION OF CERTAIN PLANS.—Such term does not include a health plan if substantially all of its coverage is coverage described in paragraph (1)(B).

(ii) SAFE HARBOR FOR ABSENCE OF PREVENTIVE CARE DEDUCTIBLE.—A plan shall not fail to be treated as a high deductible health plan by reason of failing to have a deductible for preventive care if the absence of a deductible for such care is required by State law.

(3) PERMITTED INSURANCE.—The term "permitted insurance" means—

(A) insurance if substantially all of the coverage provided under such insurance relates to—

(i) liabilities incurred under workers' compensation laws,

(ii) tort liabilities,

(iii) liabilities relating to ownership or use of property, or

(iv) such other similar liabilities as the Secretary may specify by regulations,

(B) insurance for a specified disease or illness, and

(C) insurance paying a fixed amount per day (or other period) of hospitalization.

(4) SMALL EMPLOYER.—

(A) IN GENERAL.—The term "small employer" means, with respect to any calendar year, any employer if such employer employed an average of 50 or fewer employees on business days during either of the 2 preceding calendar years. For purposes of the preceding sentence, a preceding calendar year may be taken into account only if the employer was in existence throughout such year.

(B) EMPLOYERS NOT IN EXISTENCE IN PRECEDING YEAR.—In the case of an employer which was not in existence throughout the 1st preceding calendar year, the determination under subparagraph (A) shall be based on the average number of employees that it is reasonably expected such employer will employ on business days in the current calendar year.

(C) CERTAIN GROWING EMPLOYERS RETAIN TREATMENT AS SMALL EMPLOYER.—The term "small employer" includes, with respect to any calendar year, any employer if—

(i) such employer met the requirement of subparagraph (A) (determined without regard to subparagraph (B)) for any preceding calendar year after 1996,

(ii) any amount was contributed to the Archer MSA of any employee of such employer with respect to coverage of such employee under a high deductible health plan of such employer during such preceding calendar year and such amount was excludable from gross income under section 106(b) or allowable as a deduction under this section, and

(iii) such employer employed an average of 200 or fewer employees on business days during each preceding calendar year after 1996.

(D) SPECIAL RULES.—

(i) CONTROLLED GROUPS.—For purposes of this paragraph, all persons treated as a single employer under subsection (b), (c), (m), or (o) of section 414 shall be treated as 1 employer.

(ii) PREDECESSORS.—Any reference in this paragraph to an employer shall include a reference to any predecessor of such employer.

(5) FAMILY COVERAGE.—The term "family coverage" means any coverage other than self-only coverage.

Amendments

• 2000, Community Renewal Tax Relief Act of 2000 (P.L. 106-554)

P.L. 106-554, §202(a)(4):

Amended Code Sec. 220 by striking "medical savings account" each place it appears in the text and inserting "Archer MSA". **Effective** 12-21-2000.

P.L. 106-554, §202(b)(2)(B):

Amended Code Sec. 220(c)(1)(D) by striking "medical savings accounts" and inserting "Archer MSAs". **Effective** 12-21-2000.

P.L. 106-554, §202(b)(7):

Amended the heading for Code Sec. 220(c)(1)(C) by striking "MEDICAL SAVINGS ACCOUNTS" and inserting "ARCHER MSAS". **E ffective** 12-21-2000.

P.L. 106-554, §202(b)(10):

Amended Code Sec. 220 by striking "a Archer" each place it appears and inserting "an Archer". **Effective** 12-21-2000.

• 1997, Taxpayer Relief Act of 1997 (P.L. 105-34)

P.L. 105-34, §1602(a)(2):

Amended Code Sec. 220(c)(3) by striking subparagraph (A) and redesignating subparagraphs (B) through (D) as subparagraphs (A) through (C), respectively. **Effective** as if included in the provision of P.L. 104-191 to which it relates [**effective** for tax years beginning after 12-31-96.—CCH]. Prior to being stricken, Code Sec. 220(c)(3)(A) read as follows:

(A) Medicare supplemental insurance,

[Sec. 220(d)]

(d) ARCHER MSA.—For purposes of this section—

(1) ARCHER MSA.—The term "Archer MSA" means a trust created or organized in the United States as a medical savings account exclusively for the purpose of paying the qualified medical expenses of the account holder, but only if the written governing instrument creating the trust meets the following requirements:

(A) Except in the case of a rollover contribution described in subsection (f)(5), no contribution will be accepted—

(i) unless it is in cash, or

(ii) to the extent such contribution, when added to previous contributions to the trust for the calendar year, exceeds 75 percent of the highest annual limit deductible permitted under subsection (c)(2)(A)(ii) for such calendar year.

(B) The trustee is a bank (as defined in section 408(n)), an insurance company (as defined in section 816), or another person who demonstrates to the satisfaction of the Secretary that the manner in which such person will administer the trust will be consistent with the requirements of this section.

(C) No part of the trust assets will be invested in life insurance contracts.

(D) The assets of the trust will not be commingled with other property except in a common trust fund or common investment fund.

(E) The interest of an individual in the balance in his account is nonforfeitable.

(2) QUALIFIED MEDICAL EXPENSES.—

Caution: Code Sec. 220(d)(2)(A), below, prior to amendment by P.L. 111-148, applies to amounts paid with respect to tax years beginning on or before December 31, 2010.

(A) IN GENERAL.—The term "qualified medical expenses" means, with respect to an account holder, amounts paid by such holder for medical care (as defined in section 213(d)) for such individual, the spouse of such individual, and any dependent (as defined in section 152, determined without regard to subsections (b)(1), (b)(2), and (d)(1)(B) thereof) of such individual, but only to the extent such amounts are not compensated for by insurance or otherwise.

Caution: Code Sec. 220(d)(2)(A), below, as amended by P.L. 111-148, applies to amounts paid with respect to tax years beginning after December 31, 2010.

(A) IN GENERAL.—The term "qualified medical expenses" means, with respect to an account holder, amounts paid by such holder for medical care (as defined in section 213(d)) for such individual, the spouse of such individual, and any dependent (as defined in section 152, determined without regard to subsections (b)(1), (b)(2), and (d)(1)(B) thereof) of such individual, but only to the extent such amounts are not compensated for by insurance or otherwise. Such term shall include an amount paid for medicine or a drug only if such medicine or drug is a prescribed drug (determined without regard to whether such drug is available without a prescription) or is insulin.

(B) HEALTH INSURANCE MAY NOT BE PURCHASED FROM ACCOUNT.—

(i) IN GENERAL.—Subparagraph (A) shall not apply to any payment for insurance.

(ii) EXCEPTIONS.—Clause (i) shall not apply to any expense for coverage under—

(I) a health plan during any period of continuation coverage required under any Federal law,

(II) a qualified long-term care insurance contract (as defined in section 7702B(b)), or

(III) a health plan during a period in which the individual is receiving unemployment compensation under any Federal or State law.

(C) MEDICAL EXPENSES OF INDIVIDUALS WHO ARE NOT ELIGIBLE INDIVIDUALS.—Subparagraph (A) shall apply to an amount paid by an account holder for medical care of an individual who is not described in clauses (i) and (ii) of subsection (c)(1)(A) for the month in which the expense for such care is incurred only if no amount is contributed (other than a rollover contribution) to any Archer MSA of such account holder for the taxable year which includes such month. This subparagraph shall not apply to any expense for coverage described in subclause (I) or (III) of subparagraph (B)(ii).

(3) ACCOUNT HOLDER.—The term "account holder" means the individual on whose behalf the Archer MSA was established.

(4) CERTAIN RULES TO APPLY.—Rules similar to the following rules shall apply for purposes of this section:

(A) Section 219(d)(2) (relating to no deduction for rollovers).

(B) Section 219(f)(3) (relating to time when contributions deemed made).

(C) Except as provided in section 106(b), section 219(f)(5) (relating to employer payments).

(D) Section 408(g) (relating to community property laws).

(E) Section 408(h) (relating to custodial accounts).

Amendments

• 2010, Patient Protection and Affordable Care Act (P.L. 111-148)

P.L. 111-148, §9003(b):

Amended Code Sec. 220(d)(2)(A) by adding at the end a new sentence. **Effective** for amounts paid with respect to tax years beginning after 12-31-2010.

• 2004, Working Families Tax Relief Act of 2004 (P.L. 108-311)

P.L. 108-311, §207(19):

Amended Code Sec. 220(d)(2)(A) by inserting ", determined without regard to subsections (b)(1), (b)(2), and (d)(1)(B) thereof" after "section 152". **Effective** for tax years beginning after 12-31-2004.

• 2000, Community Renewal Tax Relief Act of 2000 (P.L. 106-554)

P.L. 106-554, §202(a)(4):

Amended Code Sec. 220 by striking "medical savings account" each place it appears in the text and inserting "Archer MSA". **Effective** 12-21-2000.

P.L. 106-554, §202(b)(3):

Amended Code Sec. 220(d)(1) by inserting "as a medical savings account" after "United States". **Effective** 12-21-2000.

P.L. 106-554, §202(b)(4):

Amended the heading for Code Sec. 220(d) by striking "MEDICAL SAVINGS ACCOUNT" and inserting "ARCHER MSA". **E ffective** 12-21-2000.

P.L. 106-554, §202(b)(5):

Amended the heading for Code Sec. 220(d)(1) by striking "MEDICAL SAVINGS ACCOUNT" and inserting "ARCHER MSA". **E ffective** 12-21-2000.

• 1997, Taxpayer Relief Act of 1997 (P.L. 105-34)

P.L. 105-34, §1602(a)(3):

Amended Code Sec. 220(d)(2)(C) by striking "an eligible individual" and inserting "described in clauses (i) and (ii) of subsection (c)(1)(A)". **Effective** as if included in the provision of P.L. 104-191 to which it relates [**effective** for tax years beginning after 12-31-96.—CCH].

[Sec. 220(e)]

(e) TAX TREATMENT OF ACCOUNTS.—

(1) IN GENERAL.—An Archer MSA is exempt from taxation under this subtitle unless such account has ceased to be an Archer MSA. Notwithstanding the preceding sentence, any such account is subject to the taxes imposed by section 511 (relating to imposition of tax on unrelated business income of charitable, etc. organizations).

(2) ACCOUNT TERMINATIONS.—Rules similar to the rules of paragraphs (2) and (4) of section 408(e) shall apply to Archer MSAs, and any amount treated as distributed under such rules shall be treated as not used to pay qualified medical expenses.

Amendments

• 2000, Community Renewal Tax Relief Act of 2000 (P.L. 106-554)

P.L. 106-554, §202(a)(4):

Amended Code Sec. 220 by striking "medical savings account" each place it appears in the text and inserting "Archer MSA". **Effective** 12-21-2000.

P.L. 106-554, §202(b)(2)(B):

Amended Code Sec. 220(e)(2) by striking "medical savings accounts" and inserting "Archer MSAs". **Effective** 12-21-2000.

P.L. 106-554, §202(b)(10):

Amended Code Sec. 220 by striking "a Archer" and inserting "an Archer". **Effective** 12-21-2000.

P.L. 106-554, §202(b)(11):

Amended Code Sec. 220(e)(1) by striking "A Archer" and inserting "An Archer". **Effective** 12-21-2000.

[Sec. 220(f)]

(f) TAX TREATMENT OF DISTRIBUTIONS.—

(1) AMOUNTS USED FOR QUALIFIED MEDICAL EXPENSES.—Any amount paid or distributed out of an Archer MSA which is used exclusively to pay qualified medical expenses of any account holder shall not be includible in gross income.

(2) INCLUSION OF AMOUNTS NOT USED FOR QUALIFIED MEDICAL EXPENSES.—Any amount paid or distributed out of an Archer MSA which is not used exclusively to pay the qualified medical expenses of the account holder shall be included in the gross income of such holder.

(3) EXCESS CONTRIBUTIONS RETURNED BEFORE DUE DATE OF RETURN.—

(A) IN GENERAL.—If any excess contribution is contributed for a taxable year to any Archer MSA of an individual, paragraph (2) shall not apply to distributions from the Archer MSAs of such individual (to the extent such distributions do not exceed the aggregate excess contributions to all such accounts of such individual for such year) if—

(i) such distribution is received by the individual on or before the last day prescribed by law (including extensions of time) for filing such individual's return for such taxable year, and

(ii) such distribution is accompanied by the amount of net income attributable to such excess contribution.

Any net income described in clause (ii) shall be included in the gross income of the individual for the taxable year in which it is received.

(B) EXCESS CONTRIBUTION.—For purposes of subparagraph (A), the term "excess contribution" means any contribution (other than a rollover contribution) which is neither excludable from gross income under section 106(b) nor deductible under this section.

(4) ADDITIONAL TAX ON DISTRIBUTIONS NOT USED FOR QUALIFIED MEDICAL EXPENSES.—

Caution: Code Sec. 220(f)(4)(A), below, prior to amendment by P.L. 111-148, applies to distributions made on or before December 31, 2010.

(A) IN GENERAL.—The tax imposed by this chapter on the account holder for any taxable year in which there is a payment or distribution from an Archer MSA of such holder which is includible in gross income under paragraph (2) shall be increased by 15 percent of the amount which is so includible.

Caution: Code Sec. 220(f)(4)(A), below, as amended by P.L. 111-148, applies to distributions made after December 31, 2010.

(A) IN GENERAL.—The tax imposed by this chapter on the account holder for any taxable year in which there is a payment or distribution from an Archer MSA of such holder which is includible in gross income under paragraph (2) shall be increased by 20 percent of the amount which is so includible.

(B) EXCEPTION FOR DISABILITY OR DEATH.—Subparagraph (A) shall not apply if the payment or distribution is made after the account holder becomes disabled within the meaning of section 72(m)(7) or dies.

(C) EXCEPTION FOR DISTRIBUTIONS AFTER MEDICARE ELIGIBILITY.—Subparagraph (A) shall not apply to any payment or distribution after the date on which the account holder attains the age specified in section 1811 of the Social Security Act.

(5) ROLLOVER CONTRIBUTION.—An amount is described in this paragraph as a rollover contribution if it meets the requirements of subparagraphs (A) and (B).

(A) IN GENERAL.—Paragraph (2) shall not apply to any amount paid or distributed from an Archer MSA to the account holder to the extent the amount received is paid into an Archer MSA or a health savings account (as defined in section 223(d)) for the benefit of such holder not later than the 60th day after the day on which the holder receives the payment or distribution.

(B) LIMITATION.—This paragraph shall not apply to any amount described in subparagraph (A) received by an individual from an Archer MSA if, at any time during the 1-year period ending on the day of such receipt, such individual received any other amount described in subparagraph (A) from an Archer MSA which was not includible in the individual's gross income because of the application of this paragraph.

(6) COORDINATION WITH MEDICAL EXPENSE DEDUCTION.—For purposes of determining the amount of the deduction under section 213, any payment or distribution out of an Archer MSA for qualified medical expenses shall not be treated as an expense paid for medical care.

(7) TRANSFER OF ACCOUNT INCIDENT TO DIVORCE.—The transfer of an individual's interest in an Archer MSA to an individual's spouse or former spouse under a divorce or separation instrument described in subparagraph (A) of section 71(b)(2) shall not be considered a taxable transfer made by such individual notwithstanding any other provision of this subtitle, and such interest shall, after such transfer, be treated as an Archer MSA with respect to which such spouse is the account holder.

(8) TREATMENT AFTER DEATH OF ACCOUNT HOLDER.—

(A) TREATMENT IF DESIGNATED BENEFICIARY IS SPOUSE.—If the account holder's surviving spouse acquires such holder's interest in an Archer MSA by reason of being the designated beneficiary of such account at the death of the account holder, such Archer MSA shall be treated as if the spouse were the account holder.

(B) OTHER CASES.—

(i) IN GENERAL.—If, by reason of the death of the account holder, any person acquires the account holder's interest in an Archer MSA in a case to which subparagraph (A) does not apply—

(I) such account shall cease to be an Archer MSA as of the date of death, and

(II) an amount equal to the fair market value of the assets in such account on such date shall be includible if such person is not the estate of such holder, in such person's gross income for the taxable year which includes such date, or if such person is the estate of such holder, in such holder's gross income for the last taxable year of such holder.

(ii) SPECIAL RULES.—

(I) REDUCTION OF INCLUSION FOR PRE-DEATH EXPENSES.—The amount includible in gross income under clause (i) by any person (other than the estate) shall be reduced by the amount of qualified medical expenses which were incurred by the decedent before the date of the decedent's death and paid by such person within 1 year after such date.

(II) DEDUCTION FOR ESTATE TAXES.—An appropriate deduction shall be allowed under section 691(c) to any person (other than the decedent or the decedent's spouse) with respect to amounts included in gross income under clause (i) by such person.

Amendments

• 2010, Patient Protection and Affordable Care Act (P.L. 111-148)

P.L. 111-148, §9004(b):

Amended Code Sec. 220(f)(4)(A) by striking "15 percent" and inserting "20 percent". **Effective** for distributions made after 12-31-2010.

• 2003, Medicare Prescription Drug, Improvement, and Modernization Act of 2003 (P.L. 108-173)

P.L. 108-173, §1201(c):

Amended Code Sec. 220(f)(5)(A) by inserting "or a health savings account (as defined in section 223(d))" after "paid into an Archer MSA". **Effective** for tax years beginning after 12-31-2003.

• 2000, Community Renewal Tax Relief Act of 2000 (P.L. 106-554)

P.L. 106-554, §202(a)(4):

Amended Code Sec. 220 by striking "medical savings account" each place it appears in the text and inserting "Archer MSA". **Effective** 12-21-2000.

P.L. 106-554, §202(b)(2)(B):

Amended Code Sec. 220(f)(3)(A) by striking "medical savings accounts" and inserting "Archer MSAs". **Effective** 12-21-2000.

P.L. 106-554, §202(b)(10):

Amended Code Sec. 220 by striking "a Archer" each place it appears and inserting "an Archer". **Effective** 12-21-2000.

[Sec. 220(g)]

(g) COST-OF-LIVING ADJUSTMENT.—In the case of any taxable year beginning in a calendar year after 1998, each dollar amount in subsection (c)(2) shall be increased by an amount equal to—

(1) such dollar amount, multiplied by

(2) the cost-of-living adjustment determined under section 1(f)(3) for the calendar year in which such taxable year begins by substituting "calendar year 1997" for "calendar year 1992" in subparagraph (B) thereof.

If any increase under the preceding sentence is not a multiple of $50, such increase shall be rounded to the nearest multiple of $50.

[Sec. 220(h)]

(h) REPORTS.—The Secretary may require the trustee of an Archer MSA to make such reports regarding such account to the Secretary and to the account holder with respect to contributions, distributions, and such other matters as the Secretary determines appropriate. The reports required by this subsection shall be filed at such time and in such manner and furnished to such individuals at such time and in such manner as may be required by the Secretary.

Amendments

• 2000, Community Renewal Tax Relief Act of 2000 (P.L. 106-554)

P.L. 106-554, §202(a)(4):

Amended Code Sec. 220 by striking "medical savings account" each place it appears in the text and inserting "Archer MSA". **Effective** 12-21-2000.

P.L. 106-554, §202(b)(10):

Amended Code Sec. 220 by striking "a Archer" each place it appears and inserting "an Archer". **Effective** 12-21-2000.

[Sec. 220(i)]

(i) LIMITATION ON NUMBER OF TAXPAYERS HAVING ARCHER MSAs.—

(1) IN GENERAL.—Except as provided in paragraph (5), no individual shall be treated as an eligible individual for any taxable year beginning after the cut-off year unless—

(A) such individual was an active MSA participant for any taxable year ending on or before the close of the cut-off year, or

(B) such individual first became an active MSA participant for a taxable year ending after the cut-off year by reason of coverage under a high deductible health plan of an MSA-participating employer.

(2) CUT-OFF YEAR.—For purposes of paragraph (1), the term "cut-off year" means the earlier of—

(A) calendar year 2007, or

(B) the first calendar year before 2007 for which the Secretary determines under subsection (j) that the numerical limitation for such year has been exceeded.

(3) ACTIVE MSA PARTICIPANT.—For purposes of this subsection—

(A) IN GENERAL.—The term "active MSA participant" means, with respect to any taxable year, any individual who is the account holder of any Archer MSA into which any contribution was made which was excludable from gross income under section 106(b), or allowable as a deduction under this section, for such taxable year.

(B) SPECIAL RULE FOR CUT-OFF YEARS BEFORE 2007.—In the case of a cut-off year before 2007—

(i) an individual shall not be treated as an eligible individual for any month of such year or an active MSA participant under paragraph (1)(A) unless such individual is, on or before the cut-off date, covered under a high deductible health plan, and

(ii) an employer shall not be treated as an MSA-participating employer unless the employer, on or before the cut-off date, offered coverage under a high deductible health plan to any employee.

(C) CUT-OFF DATE.—For purposes of subparagraph (B)—

(i) IN GENERAL.—Except as otherwise provided in this subparagraph, the cut-off date is October 1 of the cut-off year.

(ii) EMPLOYEES WITH ENROLLMENT PERIODS AFTER OCTOBER 1.—In the case of an individual described in subclause (I) of subsection (c)(1)(A)(iii), if the regularly scheduled enrollment period for health plans of the individual's employer occurs during the last 3 months of the cut-off year, the cut-off date is December 31 of the cut-off year.

(iii) SELF-EMPLOYED INDIVIDUALS.—In the case of an individual described in subclause (II) of subsection (c)(1)(A)(iii), the cut-off date is November 1 of the cut-off year.

(iv) SPECIAL RULES FOR 1997.—If 1997 is a cut-off year by reason of subsection (j)(1)(A)—

(I) each of the cut-off dates under clauses (i) and (iii) shall be 1 month earlier than the date determined without regard to this clause, and

(II) clause (ii) shall be applied by substituting "4 months" for "3 months".

(4) MSA-PARTICIPATING EMPLOYER.—For purposes of this subsection, the term "MSA-participating employer" means any small employer if—

(A) such employer made any contribution to the Archer MSA of any employee during the cut-off year or any preceding calendar year which was excludable from gross income under section 106(b), or

(B) at least 20 percent of the employees of such employer who are eligible individuals for any month of the cut-off year by reason of coverage under a high deductible health plan of such employer each made a contribution of at least $100 to their Archer MSAs for any taxable year ending with or within the cut-off year which was allowable as a deduction under this section.

(5) ADDITIONAL ELIGIBILITY AFTER CUT-OFF YEAR.—If the Secretary determines under subsection (j)(2)(A) that the numerical limit for the calendar year following a cut-off year described in paragraph (2)(B) has not been exceeded—

(A) this subsection shall not apply to any otherwise eligible individual who is covered under a high deductible health plan during the first 6 months of the second calendar year following the cut-off year (and such individual shall be treated as an active MSA participant for purposes of this subsection if a contribution is made to any Archer MSA with respect to such coverage), and

(B) any employer who offers coverage under a high deductible health plan to any employee during such 6-month period shall be treated as an MSA-participating employer for purposes of this subsection if the requirements of paragraph (4) are met with respect to such coverage.

For purposes of this paragraph, subsection (j)(2)(A) shall be applied for 1998 by substituting "750,000" for "600,000".

Amendments

• 2006, Tax Relief and Health Care Act of 2006 (P.L. 109-432)

P.L. 109-432, Division A, §117(a):

Amended Code Sec. 220(i)(2) and (3)(B) by striking "2005" each place it appears in the text and headings [sic] and inserting "2007". **Effective** 12-20-2006.

• 2004, Working Families Tax Relief Act of 2004 (P.L. 108-311)

P.L. 108-311, §322(a):

Amended Code Sec. 220(i)(2) and (3)(B) by striking "2003" each place it appears in the text and headings and inserting "2005". **Effective** 1-1-2004.

• 2002, Job Creation and Worker Assistance Act of 2002 (P.L. 107-147)

P.L. 107-147, §612(a):

Amended Code Sec. 220(i)(2) and (3)(B) by striking "2002" each place it appears and inserting "2003". **Effective** 1-1-2002.

• 2000, Community Renewal Tax Relief Act of 2000 (P.L. 106-554)

P.L. 106-554, §201(a):

Amended Code Sec. 220(i)(2) and (3)(B) by striking "2000" each place it appears and inserting "2002". **Effective** 12-21-2000.

P.L. 106-554, §202(a)(4):

Amended Code Sec. 220 by striking "medical savings account" each place it appears in the text and inserting "Archer MSA". **Effective** 12-21-2000.

P.L. 106-554, §202(b)(2)(B):

Amended Code Sec. 220(i)(4)(B) by striking "medical savings accounts" and inserting "Archer MSAs". **Effective** 12-21-2000.

P.L. 106-554, §202(b)(6):

Amended the heading for Code Sec. 220(i) by striking "MEDICAL SAVINGS ACCOUNTS" and inserting "ARCHER MSAS". **E ffective** 12-21-2000.

[Sec. 220(j)]

(j) DETERMINATION OF WHETHER NUMERICAL LIMITS ARE EXCEEDED.—

(1) DETERMINATION OF WHETHER LIMIT EXCEEDED FOR 1997.—The numerical limitation for 1997 is exceeded if, based on the reports required under paragraph (4), the number of Archer MSAs established as of—

(A) April 30, 1997, exceeds 375,000, or

(B) June 30, 1997, exceeds 525,000.

(2) DETERMINATION OF WHETHER LIMIT EXCEEDED FOR 1998, 1999, 2001, 2002, 2004, 2005, OR 2006.—

(A) IN GENERAL.—The numerical limitation for 1998, 1999, 2001, 2002, 2004, 2005, or 2006 is exceeded if the sum of—

(i) the number of MSA returns filed on or before April 15 of such calendar year for taxable years ending with or within the preceding calendar year, plus

(ii) the Secretary's estimate (determined on the basis of the returns described in clause (i)) of the number of MSA returns for such taxable years which will be filed after such date,

exceeds 750,000 (600,000 in the case of 1998). For purposes of the preceding sentence, the term "MSA return" means any return on which any exclusion is claimed under section 106(b) or any deduction is claimed under this section.

(B) ALTERNATIVE COMPUTATION OF LIMITATION.—The numerical limitation for 1998, 1999, 2001, 2002, 2004, 2005, or 2006 is also exceeded if the sum of—

(i) 90 percent of the sum determined under subparagraph (A) for such calendar year, plus

(ii) the product of 2.5 and the number of Archer MSAs established during the portion of such year preceding July 1 (based on the reports required under paragraph (4)) for taxable years beginning in such year,

exceeds 750,000.

(C) NO LIMITATION FOR 2000 OR 2003.—The numerical limitation shall not apply for 2000 or 2003.

(3) PREVIOUSLY UNINSURED INDIVIDUALS NOT INCLUDED IN DETERMINATION.—

(A) IN GENERAL.—The determination of whether any calendar year is a cut-off year shall be made by not counting the Archer MSA of any previously uninsured individual.

(B) PREVIOUSLY UNINSURED INDIVIDUAL.—For purposes of this subsection, the term "previously uninsured individual" means, with respect to any Archer MSA, any individual who had no health plan coverage (other than coverage referred to in subsection (c)(1)(B)) at any time during the 6-month period before the date such individual's coverage under the high deductible health plan commences.

(4) REPORTING BY MSA TRUSTEES.—

(A) IN GENERAL.—Not later than August 1 of 1997, 1998, 1999, 2001, 2002, 2004, 2005, and 2006, each person who is the trustee of an Archer MSA established before July 1 of such calendar year shall make a report to the Secretary (in such form and manner as the Secretary shall specify) which specifies—

(i) the number of Archer MSAs established before such July 1 (for taxable years beginning in such calendar year) of which such person is the trustee,

(ii) the name and TIN of the account holder of each such account, and

(iii) the number of such accounts which are accounts of previously uninsured individuals.

(B) ADDITIONAL REPORT FOR 1997.—Not later than June 1, 1997, each person who is the trustee of an Archer MSA established before May 1, 1997, shall make an additional report described in subparagraph (A) but only with respect to accounts established before May 1, 1997.

(C) PENALTY FOR FAILURE TO FILE REPORT.—The penalty provided in section 6693(a) shall apply to any report required by this paragraph, except that—

(i) such section shall be applied by substituting "$25" for "$50", and

(ii) the maximum penalty imposed on any trustee shall not exceed $5,000.

(D) AGGREGATION OF ACCOUNTS.—To the extent practical, in determining the number of Archer MSAs on the basis of the reports under this paragraph, all Archer MSAs of an individual shall be treated as 1 account and all accounts of individuals who are married to each other shall be treated as 1 account.

(5) DATE OF MAKING DETERMINATIONS.—Any determination under this subsection that a calendar year is a cut-off year shall be made by the Secretary and shall be published not later than October 1 of such year.

Amendments

• 2006, Tax Relief and Health Care Act of 2006 (P.L. 109-432)

P.L. 109-432, Division A, §117(b)(1)(A)-(B):

Amended Code Sec. 220(j)(2) by striking "or 2004" each place it appears in the text and inserting "2004, 2005, or 2006", and by striking "OR 2004" in the heading and inserting "2004, 2005, OR 2006". **Effective** 12-20-2006.

P.L. 109-432, Division A, §117(b)(2):

Amended Code Sec. 220(j)(4)(A) by striking "and 2004" and inserting "2004, 2005, and 2006". **Effective** 12-20-2006.

P.L. 109-432, Division A, §117(c), provides:

(c) TIME FOR FILING REPORTS, ETC.—

(1) The report required by section 220(j)(4) of the Internal Revenue Code of 1986 to be made on August 1, 2005, or August 1, 2006, as the case may be, shall be treated as timely

if made before the close of the 90-day period beginning on the date of the enactment of this Act.

(2) The determination and publication required by section 220(j)(5) of such Code with respect to calendar year 2005 or calendar year 2006, as the case may be, shall be treated as timely if made before the close of the 120-day period beginning on the date of the enactment of this Act. If the determination under the preceding sentence is that 2005 or 2006 is a cut-off year under section 220(i) of such Code, the cut-off date under such section 220(i) shall be the last day of such 120-day period.

• 2004, Working Families Tax Relief Act of 2004 (P.L. 108-311)

P.L. 108-311, §322(b)(1)(A)-(B):

Amended Code Sec. 220(j)(2) in the text by striking "or 2002" each place it appears and inserting "2002, or 2004", and in the heading by striking "OR 2002" and inserting "2002, OR 2004". **Effective** 1-1-2004.

P.L. 108-311, §322(b)(2):

Amended Code Sec. 220(j)(4)(A) by striking "and 2002" and inserting "2002, and 2004". **Effective** 1-1-2004. For a special rule, see Act Sec. 322(d), below.

P.L. 108-311, §322(b)(3):

Amended Code Sec. 220(j)(2)(C). **Effective** 1-1-2004. Prior to amendment, Code Sec. 220(j)(2)(C) read as follows:

(C) NO LIMITATION FOR 2000.—The numerical limitation shall not apply for 2000.

P.L. 108-311, §322(d), provides:

(d) TIME FOR FILING REPORTS, ETC.—

(1) The report required by section 220(j)(4) of the Internal Revenue Code of 1986 to be made on August 1, 2004, shall be treated as timely if made before the close of the 90-day period beginning on the date of the enactment of this Act.

(2) The determination and publication required by section 220(j)(5) of such Code with respect to calendar year 2004 shall be treated as timely if made before the close of the 120-day period beginning on the date of the enactment of this Act. If the determination under the preceding sentence is that 2004 is a cut-off year under section 220(i) of such Code, the cut-off date under such section 220(i) shall be the last day of such 120-day period.

• 2002, Job Creation and Worker Assistance Act of 2002 (P.L. 107-147)

P.L. 107-147, §612(b)(1):

Amended Code Sec. 220(j)(2) by striking "1998, 1999, or 2001" each place it appears and inserting "1998, 1999, 2001, or 2002". **Effective** 1-1-2002.

P.L. 107-147, §612(b)(2):

Amended Code Sec. 220(j)(4)(A) by striking "and 2001" and inserting "2001, and 2002". **Effective** 1-1-2002.

• 2000, Community Renewal Tax Relief Act of 2000 (P.L. 106-554)

P.L. 106-554, §201(b)(1)(A)-(C):

Amended Code Sec. 220(j)(2) by striking "1998 or 1999" each place it appears and inserting "1998, 1999, or 2001", by striking "600,000 (750,000 in the case of 1999)" and inserting "750,000 (600,000 in the case of 1998)", and by inserting after subparagraph (B) a new subparagraph (C). **Effective** 12-21-2000.

P.L. 106-554, §201(b)(2):

Amended Code Sec. 220(j)(4)(A) by striking "and 1999" and inserting "1999, and 2001". **Effective** 12-21-2000.

P.L. 106-554, §202(a)(4):

Amended Code Sec. 220 by striking "medical savings account" each place it appears in the text and inserting "Archer MSA". **Effective** 12-21-2000.

P.L. 106-554, §202(b)(2)(B):

Amended Code Sec. 220(j) by striking "medical savings accounts" each place it appears in the text and inserting "Archer MSAs". **Effective** 12-21-2000.

P.L. 106-554, §202(b)(10):

Amended Code Sec. 220 by striking "a Archer" each place it appears and inserting "an Archer". **Effective** 12-21-2000.

• 1996, Health Insurance Portability and Accountability Act of 1996 (P.L. 104-191)

P.L. 104-191, §301(a):

Amended part VII of subchapter B of chapter 1 by redesignating Code Sec. 220 as Code Sec. 221 and by inserting after Code Sec. 219 a new Code Sec. 220. **Effective** for tax years beginning after 12-31-96.

[Sec. 220—Stricken]

Amendments

• 1990, Omnibus Budget Reconciliation Act of 1990 (P.L. 101-508)

P.L. 101-508, §11802(e)(2):

Amended part VII of subchapter B of chapter 1 by striking out section 220 and redesignating section 221 as section 220. **Effective** 11-5-90. Prior to amendment, Code Sec. 220 read as follows:

SEC. 220. JURY DUTY PAY REMITTED TO EMPLOYER.

If—

(1) an individual receives payment for the discharge of jury duty, and

(2) the employer of such individual requires the individual to remit any portion of such payment to the employer in exchange for payment by the employer of compensation for the period the individual was performing jury duty,

then there shall be allowed as a deduction the amount so remitted.

P.L. 101-508, §11821(b)(1)-(2), provides:

(b) SAVINGS PROVISION.—If—

(1) any provision amended or repealed by this part applies to—

(A) any transaction occurring before the date of the enactment of this Act,

(B) any property acquired before such date of enactment, or

(C) any item of income, loss, deduction, or credit taken into account before such date of enactment, and

(2) the treatment of such transition, property, or item under such provision would (without regard to the amendments made by this part) affect liability for tax for periods ending after such date of enactment,

nothing in the amendments made by this part shall be construed to affect the treatment of such transaction, property, or item for purposes of determining liability for tax for periods ending after such date of enactment.

• 1988, Technical and Miscellaneous Revenue Act of 1988 (P.L. 100-647)

P.L. 100-647, §6007(a):

Amended Part VII of subchapter B of chapter 1 by redesignating section 220 as section 221 and inserting new section 220. **Effective** as if included in the amendments made by P.L. 99-514, §132.

[Sec. 220—Repealed]

Amendments

• 1981, Economic Recovery Tax Act of 1981 (P.L. 97-34)

P.L. 97-34, §311(e):

Repealed Code Sec. 220. **Effective** for tax years beginning after 12-31-81. However, for purposes of the 1954 Code, any amount allowed as a deduction under section 220 of such Code (as in effect before its repeal by P.L. 97-34) shall be treated as if it were allowed by section 219 of the Code. Prior to amendment, Code Sec. 220 read as follows:

SEC. 220. RETIREMENT SAVINGS FOR CERTAIN MARRIED INDIVIDUALS.

[Sec. 220(a)]

(a) DEDUCTION ALLOWED.—In the case of an individual, there is allowed as a deduction amounts paid in cash for a taxable year by or on behalf of such individual for the benefit of himself and his spouse—

(1) to an individual retirement account described in section 408(a),

(2) for an individual retirement annuity described in section 408(b), or

(3) for a retirement bond described in section 409 (but only if the bond is not redeemed within 12 months of the date of its issuance).

For purposes of this title, any amount paid by an employer to such a retirement account or for such a retirement annuity or retirement bond constitutes payment of compensation to the employee (other than a self-employed individual who is an employee within the meaning of section 401(c)(1)) includible in his gross income, whether or not a deduction for such payment is allowable under this section to the employee after the application of subsection (b).

Amendments

• 1976, Tax Reform Act of 1976 (P.L. 94-455)

P.L. 94-455, §1501(a):

Added Code Sec. 220(a). **Effective** for tax years beginning after 12-31-76.

[Sec. 220(b)]

(b) LIMITATIONS AND RESTRICTIONS.—

(1) MAXIMUM DEDUCTION.—The amount allowable as a deduction under subsection (a) to an individual for any taxable year may not exceed—

(A) twice the amount paid to the account, for the annuity, or for the bond, established for the individual or for his spouse to or for which the lesser amount was paid for the taxable year,

(B) an amount equal to 15 percent of the compensation includible in the individual's gross income for the taxable year, or

(C) $1,750,

whichever is the smallest amount.

(2) ALTERNATIVE DEDUCTION.—No deduction is allowed under subsection (a) for the taxable year if the individual claims the deduction allowed by section 219 for the taxable year.

(3) COVERAGE UNDER CERTAIN OTHER PLANS.—No deduction is allowed under subsection (a) for an individual for the taxable year if for any part of such year—

(A) he or his spouse was an active participant in—

(i) a plan described in section 401(a) which includes a trust exempt from tax under section 501(a),

(ii) an annuity plan described in section 403(a),

(iii) a qualified bond purchase plan described in section 405(a), or

(iv) a plan established for its employees by the United States, by a State or political subdivision thereof, or by an agency or instrumentality of any of the foregoing, or

(B) amounts were contributed by his employer, or his spouse's employer, for an annuity contract described in section 403(b) (whether or not his, or his spouse's, rights in such contract are nonforfeitable).

(4) CONTRIBUTIONS AFTER AGE 70 1/2.—No deduction is allowed under subsection (a) with respect to any payment described in subsection (a) which is made for a taxable year of an individual if either the individual or his spouse has attained age 70 1/2 before the close of such taxable year.

(5) RECONTRIBUTED AMOUNTS.—No deduction is allowed under this section with respect to a rollover contribution described in section 402(a)(5), 402(a)(7), 403(a)(4), 403(b)(8), 408(d)(3), or 409(b)(3)(C).

(6) AMOUNTS CONTRIBUTED UNDER ENDOWMENT CONTRACT.—In the case of an endowment contract described in section 408(b), no deduction is allowed under subsection (a) for that portion of the amounts paid under the contract for the taxable year properly allocable, under regulations prescribed by the Secretary, to the cost of life insurance.

(7) EMPLOYED SPOUSES.—No deduction is allowed under subsection (a) with respect to a payment described in subsection (a) made for any taxable year of the individual if the spouse of the individual has any compensation (determined without regard to section 911) for the taxable year of such spouse ending with or within such taxable year.

Amendments

• 1980, Technical Corrections Act of 1979 (P.L. 96-222)

P.L. 96-222, §101(a)(13)(A):

Amended Act Sec. 156(d) of P.L. 95-600 to change the effective date of the amendment of Code Sec. 220(b)(5) made by Act Sec. 156(c)(3) of P.L. 95-600 from "distributions or transfers made after December 31, 1978, in taxable years beginning after that date" to "distributions or transfers made after December 31, 1977, in taxable years beginning after that date."

P.L. 96-222, §101(a)(14)(B):

Amended Code Sec. 220(b)(5) by adding "402(a)(7)," after "section 402(a)(5),". **Effective** for distributions or transfers made after 12-31-77, in tax years beginning after such date.

• 1978, Revenue Act of 1978 (P.L. 95-600)

P.L. 95-600, §156(c)(3):

Amended Code Sec. 220(b)(5) by inserting "403(b)(8)" after "403(a)(4)". **Effective** for distributions or transfers made after 12-31-78, in tax years beginning after such date.

P.L. 95-600, §703(c)(2):

Amended Code Sec. 220(b)(1)(A) by striking out "amount paid to the account or annuity, or for the bond" and inserting in lieu thereof "amount paid to the account, for the annuity, or for the bond". **Effective** for tax years beginning after 12-31-76.

P.L. 95-600, §703(c)(3):

Amended Code Sec. 220(b)(4) by inserting "described in subsection (a)" after "any payment". **Effective** for tax years beginning after 12-31-76.

• 1976, Tax Reform Act of 1976 (P.L. 94-455)

P.L. 94-455, §1501(a):

Added Code Sec. 220(b). **Effective** for tax years beginning after 12-31-76.

[Sec. 220(c)]

(c) DEFINITIONS AND SPECIAL RULES.—

(1) COMPENSATION.—For purposes of this section, the term "compensation" includes earned income as defined in section 401(c)(2).

(2) MARRIED INDIVIDUALS.—This section shall be applied without regard to any community property laws.

(3) DETERMINATION OF MARITAL STATUS.—The determination of whether an individual is married for purposes of this section shall be made in accordance with the provisions of section 143(a).

(4) TIME WHEN CONTRIBUTIONS DEEMED MADE.—For purposes of this section, a taxpayer shall be deemed to have made a contribution on the last day of the preceding taxable year if the contribution is made on account of such taxable year and is made not later than the time prescribed by law for filing the return for such taxable year (including extensions thereof).

(5) PARTICIPATION IN GOVERNMENTAL PLANS BY CERTAIN INDIVIDUALS.—A member of a reserve component of the armed forces or a volunteer firefighter is not considered to be an active participant in a plan described in subsection (b)(3)(A)(iv) if, under section 219(c)(4), he is not considered to be an active participant in such a plan.

(6) EXCESS CONTRIBUTIONS TREATED AS CONTRIBUTION MADE DURING SUBSEQUENT YEAR FOR WHICH THERE IS AN UNUSED LIMITATION.—

(A) IN GENERAL.—If for the taxable year the maximum amount allowable as a deduction under this section exceeds the amount contributed, then the taxpayer shall be treated as having made an additional contribution for the taxable year in an amount equal to the lesser of—

(i) the amount of such excess, or

(ii) the amount of the excess contributions for such taxable year (determined under section 4973(b)(2) without regard to subparagraph (C) thereof).

(B) AMOUNT CONTRIBUTED.—For purposes of this paragraph, the amount contributed—

(i) shall be determined without regard to this paragraph, and

(ii) shall not include any rollover contribution.

(C) SPECIAL RULE WHERE EXCESS DEDUCTION WAS ALLOWED FOR CLOSED YEAR.—Proper reduction shall be made in the amount allowable as a deduction by reason of this paragraph for any amount allowed as a deduction under this section or section 219 for a prior taxable year for which the period for assessing a deficiency has expired if the amount so allowed exceeds the amount which should have been allowed for such prior taxable year.

Amendments

• 1978, Revenue Act of 1978 (P.L. 95-600)

P.L. 95-600, §157(a)(2):

Amended Code Sec. 220(c)(4) by striking out "not later than 45 days after the end of such taxable year" and inserting in lieu thereof "not later than the time prescribed by law for filing the return (including extensions thereof)". **Effective** for tax years beginning after 12-31-77.

P.L. 95-600, §157(b)(2):

Added Code Sec. 220(c)(6). **Effective** as set forth in P.L. 95-600, §157(b)(4). See historical comment on P.L. 95-600, §157(b)(4), under Code Sec. 219(c).

• 1976, Tax Reform Act of 1976 (P.L. 94-455)

P.L. 94-455, §1501(a):

Added Code Sec. 220(c). **Effective** for tax years beginning after 12-31-76.

[Sec. 221]

SEC. 221. INTEREST ON EDUCATION LOANS.

[Sec. 221(a)]

(a) ALLOWANCE OF DEDUCTION.—In the case of an individual, there shall be allowed as a deduction for the taxable year an amount equal to the interest paid by the taxpayer during the taxable year on any qualified education loan.

[Sec. 221(b)]

(b) MAXIMUM DEDUCTION.—

(1) IN GENERAL.—Except as provided in paragraph (2), the deduction allowed by subsection (a) for the taxable year shall not exceed the amount determined in accordance with the following table:

In the case of taxable years beginning in:	*The dollar amount is:*
1998	$1,000
1999	$1,500
2000	$2,000
2001 or thereafter	$2,500

(2) LIMITATION BASED ON MODIFIED ADJUSTED GROSS INCOME.—

(A) IN GENERAL.—The amount which would (but for this paragraph) be allowable as a deduction under this section shall be reduced (but not below zero) by the amount determined under subparagraph (B).

(B) AMOUNT OF REDUCTION.—The amount determined under this subparagraph is the amount which bears the same ratio to the amount which would be so taken into account as—

»»→ Caution: Code Sec. 221(b)(2)(B)(i)-(ii), below, is subject to the sunset provision of the Economic Growth and Tax Relief Reconciliation Act of 2001 (P.L. 107-16), §901. Absent Congressional action, the changes made to this provision by P.L. 107-16, or that take effect as if included in P.L. 107-16, do not apply after December 31, 2010. For more information about the sunset provision, see page XXI of the Preface to this publication and P.L. 107-16, §901, in the amendment notes. See the amendments notes for a history of amendments to this section and the effective date of each change.

(i) the excess of—

(I) the taxpayer's modified adjusted gross income for such taxable year, over

(II) $50,000 ($100,000 in the case of a joint return), bears to

(ii) $15,000 ($30,000 in the case of a joint return).

(C) MODIFIED ADJUSTED GROSS INCOME.—The term "modified adjusted gross income" means adjusted gross income determined—

»»→ Caution: Code Sec. 221(b)(2)(C)(i), below, is subject to the sunset provision of the Economic Growth and Tax Relief Reconciliation Act of 2001 (P.L. 107-16), §901. Absent Congressional action, the changes made to this provision by P.L. 107-16, or that take effect as if included in P.L. 107-16, do not apply after December 31, 2010. For more information about the sunset provision, see page XXI of the Preface to this publication and P.L. 107-16, §901, in the amendment notes. See the amendments notes for a history of amendments to this section and the effective date of each change.

(i) without regard to this section and sections 199, 222, 911, 931, and 933, and

(ii) after application of sections 86, 135, 137, 219, and 469.

Amendments

• 2004, American Jobs Creation Act of 2004 (P.L. 108-357)

P.L. 108-357, §102(d)(2):

Amended Code Sec. 221(b)(2)(C)(i) by inserting "199," before "222". **Effective** for tax years beginning after 12-31-2004.

• 2001, Economic Growth and Tax Relief Reconciliation Act of 2001 (P.L. 107-16)

P.L. 107-16, §412(b)(1):

Amended Code Sec. 221(b)(2)(B) by striking clauses (i) and (ii) and inserting new clauses (i) and (ii). **Effective** for tax years ending after 12-31-2001. Prior to being stricken, Code Sec. 221(b)(2)(B)(i)-(ii) read as follows:

(i) the excess of—

(I) the taxpayer's modified adjusted gross income for such taxable year, over

(II) $40,000 ($60,000 in the case of a joint return), bears to

(ii) $15,000.

P.L. 107-16, §431(c)(2):

Amended Code Sec. 221(b)(2)(C) by inserting "222," before "911". **Effective** for payments made in tax years beginning after 12-31-2001.

P.L. 107-16, §901(a)-(b), provides:

SEC. 901. SUNSET OF PROVISIONS OF ACT.

(a) IN GENERAL.—All provisions of, and amendments made by, this Act shall not apply—

(1) to taxable, plan, or limitation years beginning after December 31, 2010, or

(2) in the case of title V, to estates of decedents dying, gifts made, or generation skipping transfers, after December 31, 2010.

(b) APPLICATION OF CERTAIN LAWS.—The Internal Revenue Code of 1986 and the Employee Retirement Income Security Act of 1974 shall be applied and administered to years, estates, gifts, and transfers described in subsection (a) as if the provisions and amendments described in subsection (a) had never been enacted.

• 1998, Tax and Trade Relief Extension Act of 1998 (P.L. 105-277)

P.L. 105-277, §4003(a)(2)(A)(i)-(iii):

Amended Code Sec. 221(b)(2)(C) by striking "135, 137," after "sections" in clause (i), by inserting "135, 137," after "sections 86," in clause (ii), and by striking the last sentence. **Effective** as if included in the provision of P.L. 105-34 to which it relates [generally **effective** for interest payments due and paid after 12-31-97, on any qualified education loan.—CCH]. Prior to being stricken, the last sentence of Code Sec. 221(b)(2)(C) read as follows:

For purposes of sections 86, 135, 137, 219, and 469, adjusted gross income shall be determined without regard to the deduction allowed under this section.

[Sec. 221(c)]

(c) DEPENDENTS NOT ELIGIBLE FOR DEDUCTION.—No deduction shall be allowed by this section to an individual for the taxable year if a deduction under section 151 with respect to such individual is allowed to another taxpayer for the taxable year beginning in the calendar year in which such individual's taxable year begins.

»»→ Caution: Code Sec. 221(d), below, was stricken by P.L. 107-16, and is subject to the sunset provision of the Economic Growth and Tax Relief Reconciliation Act of 2001 (P.L. 107-16), §901. Absent Congressional action, the changes made to this provision by P.L. 107-16, or that take effect as if included in P.L. 107-16, do not apply after December 31, 2010. For more information about the sunset provision, see page XXI of the Preface to this publication and P.L. 107-16, §901, in the amendment notes. See the amendments notes for a history of amendments to this section and the effective date of each change.

[Sec. 221(d)—Stricken]

Amendments

• 2001, Economic Growth and Tax Relief Reconciliation Act of 2001 (P.L. 107-16)

P.L. 107-16, §412(a)(1):

Amended Code Sec. 221, as amended by Act Sec. 402(b)(2)(B), by striking subsection (d) and by redesignating subsections (e), (f), and (g) as subsections (d), (e), and (f), respectively. **Effective** with respect to any loan interest paid after 12-31-2001, in tax years ending after such date. Prior to being stricken, Code Sec. 221(d) read as follows:

(d) LIMIT ON PERIOD DEDUCTION ALLOWED.—A deduction shall be allowed under this section only with respect to interest paid on any qualified education loan during the first 60 months (whether or not consecutive) in which interest payments are required. For purposes of this paragraph, any loan and all refinancings of such loan shall be treated as 1 loan. Such 60 months shall be determined in the manner prescribed by the Secretary in the case of multiple loans which are refinanced by, or serviced as, a single loan and in]the case of loans incurred before the date of the enactment of this section.

P.L. 107-16, §901(a)-(b), provides:

SEC. 901. SUNSET OF PROVISIONS OF ACT.

(a) IN GENERAL.—All provisions of, and amendments made by, this Act shall not apply—

(1) to taxable, plan, or limitation years beginning after December 31, 2010, or

(2) in the case of title V, to estates of decedents dying, gifts made, or generation skipping transfers, after December 31, 2010.

(b) APPLICATION OF CERTAIN LAWS.—The Internal Revenue Code of 1986 and the Employee Retirement Income Security Act of 1974 shall be applied and administered to years, estates, gifts, and transfers described in subsection (a) as if the provisions and amendments described in subsection (a) had never been enacted.

• 1998, IRS Restructuring and Reform Act of 1998 (P.L. 105-206)

P.L. 105-206, §6004(b)(2):

Amended Code Sec. 221(d) by adding at the end a new sentence. **Effective** as if included in the provision of P.L. 105-34 to which it relates [**effective** for interest payments due and paid after 12-31-97, and the portion of the 60-month period referred to in Code Sec. 221(d) after 12-31-97.—CCH].

»»→ Caution: Former Code Sec. 221(e), below, was redesignated as Code Sec. 221(d) by P.L. 107-16, and is subject to the sunset provision of the Economic Growth and Tax Relief Reconciliation Act of 2001 (P.L. 107-16), §901. Absent Congressional action, the changes made to this provision by P.L. 107-16, or that take effect as if included in P.L. 107-16, do not apply after December 31, 2010. For more information about the sunset provision, see page XXI of the Preface to this publication and P.L. 107-16, §901, in the amendment notes. See the amendments notes for a history of amendments to this section and the effective date of each change.

[Sec. 221(d)]

(d) DEFINITIONS.—For purposes of this section—

(1) QUALIFIED EDUCATION LOAN.—The term "qualified education loan" means any indebtedness incurred by the taxpayer solely to pay qualified higher education expenses—

(A) which are incurred on behalf of the taxpayer, the taxpayer's spouse, or any dependent of the taxpayer as of the time the indebtedness was incurred,

(B) which are paid or incurred within a reasonable period of time before or after the indebtedness is incurred, and

(C) which are attributable to education furnished during a period during which the recipient was an eligible student.

Such term includes indebtedness used to refinance indebtedness which qualifies as a qualified education loan. The term "qualified education loan" shall not include any indebtedness owed to a person who is related (within the meaning of section 267(b) or 707(b)(1)) to the taxpayer or to any person by reason of a loan under any qualified employer plan (as defined in section 72(p)(4)) or under any contract referred to in section 72(p)(5).

(2) QUALIFIED HIGHER EDUCATION EXPENSES.—The term "qualified higher education expenses" means the cost of attendance (as defined in section 472 of the Higher Education Act of 1965, 20 U.S.C. 1087ll, as in effect on the day before the date of the enactment of the Taxpayer Relief Act of 1997) at an eligible educational institution, reduced by the sum of—

(A) the amount excluded from gross income under section 127, 135, 529, or 530 by reason of such expenses, and

(B) the amount of any scholarship, allowance, or payment described in section 25A(g)(2).

For purposes of the preceding sentence, the term "eligible educational institution" has the same meaning given such term by section 25A(f)(2), except that such term shall also include an institution conducting an internship or residency program leading to a degree or certificate awarded by an institution of higher education, a hospital, or a health care facility which offers postgraduate training.

(3) ELIGIBLE STUDENT.—The term "eligible student" has the meaning given such term by section 25A(b)(3).

(4) DEPENDENT.—The term "dependent" has the meaning given such term by section 152 (determined without regard to subsections (b)(1), (b)(2), and (d)(1)(B) thereof).

Amendments

• 2006, Pension Protection Act of 2006 (P.L. 109-280)

P.L. 109-280, §1304(a), provides:

(a) PERMANENT EXTENSION OF MODIFICATIONS.—Section 901 of the Economic Growth and Tax Relief Reconciliation Act of 2001 [P.L. 107-16] (relating to sunset provisions) shall not apply to section 402 of such Act (relating to modifications to qualified tuition programs).

• 2005, Gulf Opportunity Zone Act of 2005 (P.L. 109-135)

P.L. 109-135, §412(t):

Amended Code Sec. 221(d)(2) by striking "this Act" and inserting "the Taxpayer Relief Act of 1997". **Effective** 12-21-2005.

• 2004, Working Families Tax Relief Act of 2004 (P.L. 108-311)

P.L. 108-311, §207(20):

Amended Code Sec. 221(d)(4) by inserting "(determined without regard to subsections (b)(1), (b)(2), and (d)(1)(B) thereof)" after "section 152". **Effective** for tax years beginning after 12-31-2004.

• 2001, Economic Growth and Tax Relief Reconciliation Act of 2001 (P.L. 107-16)

P.L. 107-16, §402(b)(2)(B):

Amended Code Sec. 221(e)(2)(A) by inserting "529," after "135,". **Effective** for tax years beginning after 12-31-2001.

P.L. 107-16, §412(a)(1):

Amended Code Sec. 221, as amended by Act Sec. 402(b)(2)(B), by striking subsection (d) and by redesignating subsections (e), (f), and (g) as subsections (d), (e), and (f), respectively. **Effective** with respect to any loan interest paid after 12-31-2001, in tax years ending after such date.

P.L. 107-16, §901(a)-(b), provides [but see P.L. 109-280, §1304(a), above]:

SEC. 901. SUNSET OF PROVISIONS OF ACT.

(a) IN GENERAL.—All provisions of, and amendments made by, this Act shall not apply—

(1) to taxable, plan, or limitation years beginning after December 31, 2010, or

(2) in the case of title V, to estates of decedents dying, gifts made, or generation skipping transfers, after December 31, 2010.

(b) APPLICATION OF CERTAIN LAWS.—The Internal Revenue Code of 1986 and the Employee Retirement Income Security Act of 1974 shall be applied and administered to years, estates, gifts, and transfers described in subsection (a) as if the provisions and amendments described in subsection (a) had never been enacted.

• 1998, Tax and Trade Relief Extension Act of 1998 (P.L. 105-277)

P.L. 105-277, §4003(a)(3):

Amended the last sentence of Code Sec. 221(e)(1) by inserting before the period "or to any person by reason of a loan under any qualified employer plan (as defined in section 72(p)(4)) or under any contract referred to in section 72(p)(5)". **Effective** as if included in the provision of P.L. 105-34 to which it relates [generally **effective** for interest payments due and paid after 12-31-97, on any qualified education loan.—CCH].

• 1998, IRS Restructuring and Reform Act of 1998 (P.L. 105-206)

P.L. 105-206, §6004(b)(1):

Amended Code Sec. 221(e)(1) by inserting "by the taxpayer solely" after "incurred" the first place it appears. **Effective** as if included in the provision of P.L. 105-34 to which it relates [**effective** for interest payments due and paid after 12-31-97, and the portion of the 60-month period referred to in Code Sec. 221(d) after 12-31-97.—CCH].

→ Caution: Former Code Sec. 221(f), below, was redesignated as Code Sec. 221(e) by P.L. 107-16, and is subject to the sunset provision of the Economic Growth and Tax Relief Reconciliation Act of 2001 (P.L. 107-16), §901. Absent Congressional action, the changes made to this provision by P.L. 107-16, or that take effect as if included in P.L. 107-16, do not apply after December 31, 2010. For more information about the sunset provision, see page XXI of the Preface to this publication and P.L. 107-16, §901, in the amendment notes. See the amendments notes for a history of amendments to this section and the effective date of each change.

[Sec. 221(e)]

(e) SPECIAL RULES.—

(1) DENIAL OF DOUBLE BENEFIT.—No deduction shall be allowed under this section for any amount for which a deduction is allowable under any other provision of this chapter.

(2) MARRIED COUPLES MUST FILE JOINT RETURN.—If the taxpayer is married at the close of the taxable year, the deduction shall be allowed under subsection (a) only if the taxpayer and the taxpayer's spouse file a joint return for the taxable year.

(3) MARITAL STATUS.—Marital status shall be determined in accordance with section 7703.

Amendments

• 2001, Economic Growth and Tax Relief Reconciliation Act of 2001 (P.L. 107-16)

P.L. 107-16, §412(a)(1):

Amended Code Sec. 221 by redesignating subsection (f) as subsection (e). **Effective** with respect to any loan interest paid after 12-31-2001, in tax years ending after such date.

P.L. 107-16, §901(a)-(b), provides:

SEC. 901. SUNSET OF PROVISIONS OF ACT.

(a) IN GENERAL.—All provisions of, and amendments made by, this Act shall not apply—

(1) to taxable, plan, or limitation years beginning after December 31, 2010, or

(2) in the case of title V, to estates of decedents dying, gifts made, or generation skipping transfers, after December 31, 2010.

(b) APPLICATION OF CERTAIN LAWS.—The Internal Revenue Code of 1986 and the Employee Retirement Income Security Act of 1974 shall be applied and administered to years, estates, gifts, and transfers described in subsection (a) as if the provisions and amendments described in subsection (a) had never been enacted.

→ Caution: Former Code Sec. 221(g), below, was redesignated as Code Sec. 221(f) by P.L. 107-16, and is subject to the sunset provision of the Economic Growth and Tax Relief Reconciliation Act of 2001 (P.L. 107-16), §901. Absent Congressional action, the changes made to this provision by P.L. 107-16, or that take effect as if included in P.L. 107-16, do not apply after December 31, 2010. For more information about the sunset provision, see page XXI of the Preface to this publication and P.L. 107-16, §901, in the amendment notes. See the amendments notes for a history of amendments to this section and the effective date of each change.

[Sec. 221(f)]

(f) INFLATION ADJUSTMENTS.—

→ Caution: Code Sec. 221(f)(1), below, is subject to the sunset provision of the Economic Growth and Tax Relief Reconciliation Act of 2001 (P.L. 107-16), §901. Absent Congressional action, the changes made to this provision by P.L. 107-16, or that take effect as if included in P.L. 107-16, do not apply after December 31, 2010. For more information about the sunset provision, see page XXI of the Preface to this publication and P.L. 107-16, §901, in the amendment notes. See the amendments notes for a history of amendments to this section and the effective date of each change.

(1) IN GENERAL.—In the case of a taxable year beginning after 2002, the $50,000 and $100,000 amounts in subsection (b)(2) shall each be increased by an amount equal to—

(A) such dollar amount, multiplied by

(B) the cost-of-living adjustment determined under section 1(f)(3) for the calendar year in which the taxable year begins, determined by substituting "calendar year 2001" for "calendar year 1992" in subparagraph (B) thereof.

(2) ROUNDING.—If any amount as adjusted under paragraph (1) is not a multiple of $5,000, such amount shall be rounded to the next lowest multiple of $5,000.

Amendments

• 2001, Economic Growth and Tax Relief Reconciliation Act of 2001 (P.L. 107-16)

P.L. 107-16, §412(a)(1):

Amended Code Sec. 221 by redesignating subsection (g) as subsection (f). **Effective** with respect to any loan interest paid after 12-31-2001, in tax years ending after such date.

P.L. 107-16, §412(b)(2), as amended by P.L. 108-311, §408(b)(5):

Amended Code Sec. 221(f)(1) by striking "$40,000 and $60,000 amounts" and inserting "$50,000 and $100,000 amounts". **Effective** for tax years ending after 12-31-2001.

P.L. 107-16, §901(a)-(b), provides:

SEC. 901. SUNSET OF PROVISIONS OF ACT.

(a) IN GENERAL.—All provisions of, and amendments made by, this Act shall not apply—

(1) to taxable, plan, or limitation years beginning after December 31, 2010, or

(2) in the case of title V, to estates of decedents dying, gifts made, or generation skipping transfers, after December 31, 2010.

(b) APPLICATION OF CERTAIN LAWS.—The Internal Revenue Code of 1986 and the Employee Retirement Income Security Act of 1974 shall be applied and administered to years, estates, gifts, and transfers described in subsection (a) as if the provisions and amendments described in subsection (a) had never been enacted.

• 1997, Taxpayer Relief Act of 1997 (P.L. 105-34)

P.L. 105-34, §202(a):

Amended part VII of subchapter B of chapter 1 by redesignating Code Sec. 221 as Code Sec. 222 and by inserting after Code Sec. 220 a new Code Sec. 221. For the **effective** date, see Act Sec. 202(e), below.

P.L. 105-34, §202(e), provides:

(e) EFFECTIVE DATE.—The amendments made by this section shall apply to any qualified education loan (as defined in section 221(e)(1) of the Internal Revenue Code of 1986, as added by this section) incurred on, before, or after the date of the enactment of this Act, but only with respect to—

(1) any loan interest payment due and paid after December 31, 1997, and

(2) the portion of the 60-month period referred to in section 221(d) of the Internal Revenue Code of 1986 (as added by this section) after December 31, 1997.

[Sec. 221—Repealed]

Amendments

• 1986, Tax Reform Act of 1986 (P.L. 99-514)

P.L. 99-514, §131(a):

Repealed Code Sec. 221. **Effective** for tax years beginning after 12-31-86. Prior to repeal, Code Sec. 221 read as follows:

SEC. 221. DEDUCTION FOR TWO-EARNER MARRIED COUPLES.

[Sec. 221(a)]

(a) DEDUCTION ALLOWED.—

(1) IN GENERAL.—In the case of a joint return under section 6013 for the taxable year, there shall be allowed as a deduction an amount equal to 10 percent of the lesser of—

(A) $30,000, or

(B) the qualified earned income of the spouse with the lower qualified earned income for such taxable year.

(2) SPECIAL RULE FOR 1982.—In the case of a taxable year beginning during 1982, paragraph (1) shall be applied by substituting "5 percent" for "10 percent".

[Sec. 221(b)]

(b) QUALIFIED EARNED INCOME DEFINED.—

(1) IN GENERAL.—For purposes of this section, the term "qualified earned income" means an amount equal to the excess of—

(A) the earned income of the spouse for the taxable year, over

(B) an amount equal to the sum of the deductions described in paragraphs (1), (2), (7), (10), and (15) of section 62 to the extent such deductions are properly allocable to or chargeable against earned income described in subparagraph (A).

The amount of qualified earned income shall be determined without regard to any community property laws.

(2) EARNED INCOME.—For purposes of paragraph (1), the term "earned income" means income which is earned income within the meaning of section 911(d)(2) or 401(c)(2)(C), except that—

(A) such term shall not include any amount—

(i) not includible in gross income,

(ii) received as a pension or annuity,

(iii) paid or distributed out of an individual retirement plan (within the meaning of section 7701(a)(37)),

(iv) received as deferred compensation, or

(v) received for services performed by an individual in the employ of his spouse (within the meaning of section 3121(b)(3)(A)), and

(B) section 911(d)(2)(B) shall be applied without regard to the phrase "not in excess of 30 percent of his share of net profits of such trade or business".

Amendments

• 1983, Technical Corrections Act of 1982 (P.L. 97-448)

P.L. 97-448, §305(d)(4):

Amended Code Sec. 221(b)(1)(B) by striking out "(9),". **Effective** 10-19-82.

[Sec. 221(c)]

(c) DEDUCTION DISALLOWED FOR INDIVIDUAL CLAIMING BENEFITS OF SECTION 911 OR 931.—No deduction shall be allowed under this section for any taxable year if either spouse claims the benefits of section 911 or 931 for such taxable year.

Amendments

• 1981, Economic Recovery Tax Act of 1981 (P.L. 97-34)

P.L. 97-34, §103(a):

Added Code Sec. 221. **Effective** for tax years beginning after 12-31-81.

[Sec. 222—Repealed]

Amendments

• 1986, Tax Reform Act of 1986 (P.L. 99-514)

P.L. 99-514, §135(a):

Repealed Code Sec. 222. **Effective** for tax years beginning after 12-31-86. Prior to repeal, Code Sec. 222 read as follows:

SEC. 222. ADOPTION EXPENSES.

[Sec. 222(a)]

(a) ALLOWANCE OF DEDUCTION.—In the case of an individual, there shall be allowed as a deduction for the taxable year the amount of the qualified adoption expenses paid or incurred by the taxpayer during such taxable year.

[Sec. 222(b)]

(b) LIMITATIONS.—

(1) MAXIMUM DOLLAR AMOUNT.—The aggregate amount of adoption expenses which may be taken into account under subsection (a) with respect to the adoption of a child shall not exceed $1,500.

(2) DENIAL OF DOUBLE BENEFIT.—

(A) IN GENERAL.—No deduction shall be allowable under subsection (a) for any expense for which a deduction or credit is allowable under any other provision of this chapter.

(B) GRANTS.—No deduction shall be allowable under subsection (a) for any expenses paid from any funds received under any Federal, State, or local program.

[Sec. 222(c)]

(c) DEFINITIONS.—For purposes of this section—

(1) QUALIFIED ADOPTION EXPENSES.—The term "qualified adoption expenses" means reasonable and necessary adoption fees, court costs, attorney fees, and other expenses which are directly related to the legal adoption of a child with special needs by the taxpayer and which are not incurred in violation of State or Federal law.

(2) CHILD WITH SPECIAL NEEDS.—The term "child with special needs" means any child determined by the State to be a child described in paragraphs (1) and (2) of section 473(c) of the Social Security Act.

Amendments

• 1983, Technical Corrections Act of 1982 (P.L. 97-448)

P.L. 97-448, §101(f):

Amended Code Sec. 222(c)(2). **Effective** as if it had been included in the provision of P.L. 97-34 to which it relates. Prior to amendment, Code Sec. 222(c)(2) read as follows:

"(2) CHILD WITH SPECIAL NEEDS.—The term `child with special needs' means a child with respect to whom adoption assistance payments are made under section 473 of the Social Security Act."

• 1981, Economic Recovery Tax Act of 1981 (P.L. 97-34)

P.L. 97-34, §125(a):

Added Code Sec. 222. **Effective** for tax years beginning after 12-31-80.

➻ Caution: Code Sec. 222, below, is subject to the sunset provision of the Economic Growth and Tax Relief Reconciliation Act of 2001 (P.L. 107-16), §901. Absent Congressional action, the changes made to this provision by P.L. 107-16, or that take effect as if included in P.L. 107-16, do not apply after December 31, 2010. For more information about the sunset provision, see page XXI of the Preface to this publication and P.L. 107-16, §901, in the amendment notes. See the amendments notes for a history of amendments to this section and the effective date of each change.

[Sec. 222]

SEC. 222. QUALIFIED TUITION AND RELATED EXPENSES.

[Sec. 222(a)]

(a) ALLOWANCE OF DEDUCTION.—In the case of an individual, there shall be allowed as a deduction an amount equal to the qualified tuition and related expenses paid by the taxpayer during the taxable year.

[Sec. 222(b)]

(b) DOLLAR LIMITATIONS.—

(1) IN GENERAL.—The amount allowed as a deduction under subsection (a) with respect to the taxpayer for any taxable year shall not exceed the applicable dollar limit.

(2) APPLICABLE DOLLAR LIMIT.—

(A) 2002 AND 2003.—In the case of a taxable year beginning in 2002 or 2003, the applicable dollar limit shall be equal to—

(i) in the case of a taxpayer whose adjusted gross income for the taxable year does not exceed $65,000 ($130,000 in the case of a joint return), $3,000, and—

(ii) in the case of any other taxpayer, zero.

(B) AFTER 2003.—In the case of any taxable year beginning after 2003, the applicable dollar amount shall be equal to—

(i) in the case of a taxpayer whose adjusted gross income for the taxable year does not exceed $65,000 ($130,000 in the case of a joint return), $4,000,

(ii) in the case of a taxpayer not described in clause (i) whose adjusted gross income for the taxable year does not exceed $80,000 ($160,000 in the case of a joint return), $2,000, and

(iii) in the case of any other taxpayer, zero.

(C) ADJUSTED GROSS INCOME.—For purposes of this paragraph, adjusted gross income shall be determined—

(i) without regard to this section and sections 199, 911, 931, and 933, and

(ii) after application of sections 86, 135, 137, 219, 221, and 469.

Amendments

• 2006, Tax Relief and Health Care Act of 2006 (P.L. 109-432)

P.L. 109-432, Division A, §101(b)(1)-(2):

Amended Code Sec. 222(b)(2)(B) by striking "a taxable year beginning in 2004 or 2005" and inserting "any taxable year beginning after 2003", and by striking "2004 AND 2005" in the heading and inserting "AFTER 2003". **Effective** for tax years beginning after 12-31-2005.

• 2004, American Jobs Creation Act of 2004 (P.L. 108-357)

P.L. 108-357, §102(d)(3):

Amended Code Sec. 222(b)(2)(C)(i) by inserting "199," before "911". **Effective** for tax years beginning after 12-31-2004.

[Sec. 222(c)]

(c) NO DOUBLE BENEFIT.—

(1) IN GENERAL.—No deduction shall be allowed under subsection (a) for any expense for which a deduction is allowed to the taxpayer under any other provision of this chapter.

(2) COORDINATION WITH OTHER EDUCATION INCENTIVES.—

(A) DENIAL OF DEDUCTION IF CREDIT ELECTED.—No deduction shall be allowed under subsection (a) for a taxable year with respect to the qualified tuition and related expenses with respect to an individual if the taxpayer or any other person elects to have section 25A apply with respect to such individual for such year.

(B) COORDINATION WITH EXCLUSIONS.—The total amount of qualified tuition and related expenses shall be reduced by the amount of such expenses taken into account in determining any amount excluded under section 135, 529(c)(1), or 530(d)(2). For purposes of the preceding sentence, the amount taken into account in determining the amount excluded under section 529(c)(1) shall not include that portion of the distribution which represents a return of any contributions to the plan.

(3) DEPENDENTS.—No deduction shall be allowed under subsection (a) to any individual with respect to whom a deduction under section 151 is allowable to another taxpayer for a taxable year beginning in the calendar year in which such individual's taxable year begins.

[Sec. 222(d)]

(d) DEFINITIONS AND SPECIAL RULES.—For purposes of this section—

(1) QUALIFIED TUITION AND RELATED EXPENSES.—The term "qualified tuition and related expenses" has the meaning given such term by section 25A(f). Such expenses shall be reduced in the same manner as under section 25A(g)(2).

(2) IDENTIFICATION REQUIREMENT.—No deduction shall be allowed under subsection (a) to a taxpayer with respect to the qualified tuition and related expenses of an individual unless the taxpayer includes the name and taxpayer identification number of the individual on the return of tax for the taxable year.

(3) LIMITATION ON TAXABLE YEAR OF DEDUCTION.—

(A) IN GENERAL.—A deduction shall be allowed under subsection (a) for qualified tuition and related expenses for any taxable year only to the extent such expenses are in connection with enrollment at an institution of higher education during the taxable year.

(B) CERTAIN PREPAYMENTS ALLOWED.—Subparagraph (A) shall not apply to qualified tuition and related expenses paid during a taxable year if such expenses are in connection with an academic term beginning during such taxable year or during the first 3 months of the next taxable year.

(4) NO DEDUCTION FOR MARRIED INDIVIDUALS FILING SEPARATE RETURNS.—If the taxpayer is a married individual (within the meaning of section 7703), this section shall apply only if the taxpayer and the taxpayer's spouse file a joint return for the taxable year.

(5) NONRESIDENT ALIENS.—If the taxpayer is a nonresident alien individual for any portion of the taxable year, this section shall apply only if such individual is treated as a resident alien of the United States for purposes of this chapter by reason of an election under subsection (g) or (h) of section 6013.

(6) REGULATIONS.—The Secretary may prescribe such regulations as may be necessary or appropriate to carry out this section, including regulations requiring recordkeeping and information reporting.

[Sec. 222(e)]

(e) TERMINATION.—This section shall not apply to taxable years beginning after December 31, 2009.

Amendments

• 2008, Tax Extenders and Alternative Minimum Tax Relief Act of 2008 (P.L. 110-343)

P.L. 110-343, Division C, §202(a):

Amended Code Sec. 222(e) by striking "December 31, 2007" and inserting "December 31, 2009". **Effective** for tax years beginning after 12-31-2007.

• 2006, Tax Relief and Health Care Act of 2006 (P.L. 109-432)

P.L. 109-432, Division A, §101(a):

Amended Code Sec. 222(e) by striking "2005" and inserting "2007". **Effective** for tax years beginning after 12-31-2005.

• 2001, Economic Growth and Tax Relief Reconciliation Act of 2001 (P.L. 107-16)

P.L. 107-16, §431(a):

Amended part VII of subchapter B of chapter 1 by redesignating Code Sec. 222 as Code Sec. 223 and by inserting after Code Sec. 221 a new Code Sec. 222. **Effective** for payments made in tax years beginning after 12-31-2001.

P.L. 107-16, §901(a)-(b), provides:

SEC. 901. SUNSET OF PROVISIONS OF ACT.

(a) IN GENERAL.—All provisions of, and amendments made by, this Act shall not apply—

(1) to taxable, plan, or limitation years beginning after December 31, 2010, or

(2) in the case of title V, to estates of decedents dying, gifts made, or generation skipping transfers, after December 31, 2010.

(b) APPLICATION OF CERTAIN LAWS.—The Internal Revenue Code of 1986 and the Employee Retirement Income Security Act of 1974 shall be applied and administered to years, estates, gifts, and transfers described in subsection (a) as if the provisions and amendments described in subsection (a) had never been enacted.

[Sec. 223]

SEC. 223. HEALTH SAVINGS ACCOUNTS.

[Sec. 223(a)]

(a) DEDUCTION ALLOWED.—In the case of an individual who is an eligible individual for any month during the taxable year, there shall be allowed as a deduction for the taxable year an amount equal to the aggregate amount paid in cash during such taxable year by or on behalf of such individual to a health savings account of such individual.

[Sec. 223(b)]

(b) LIMITATIONS.—

(1) IN GENERAL.—The amount allowable as a deduction under subsection (a) to an individual for the taxable year shall not exceed the sum of the monthly limitations for months during such taxable year that the individual is an eligible individual.

(2) MONTHLY LIMITATION.—The monthly limitation for any month is 1/12 of—

(A) in the case of an eligible individual who has self-only coverage under a high deductible health plan as of the first day of such month, $2,250.

(B) in the case of an eligible individual who has family coverage under a high deductible health plan as of the first day of such month, $4,500.

(3) ADDITIONAL CONTRIBUTIONS FOR INDIVIDUALS 55 OR OLDER.—

(A) IN GENERAL.—In the case of an individual who has attained age 55 before the close of the taxable year, the applicable limitation under subparagraphs (A) and (B) of paragraph (2) shall be increased by the additional contribution amount.

(B) ADDITIONAL CONTRIBUTION AMOUNT.—For purposes of this section, the additional contribution amount is the amount determined in accordance with the following table:

For taxable years beginning in:	The additional contribution amount is:
2004	$500
2005	$600
2006	$700
2007	$800
2008	$900
2009 and thereafter	$1,000.

(4) COORDINATION WITH OTHER CONTRIBUTIONS.—The limitation which would (but for this paragraph) apply under this subsection to an individual for any taxable year shall be reduced (but not below zero) by the sum of—

(A) the aggregate amount paid for such taxable year to Archer MSAs of such individual,

(B) the aggregate amount contributed to health savings accounts of such individual which is excludable from the taxpayer's gross income for such taxable year under section 106(d) (and such amount shall not be allowed as a deduction under subsection (a)), and

(C) the aggregate amount contributed to health savings accounts of such individual for such taxable year under section 408(d)(9) (and such amount shall not be allowed as a deduction under subsection (a)).

Subparagraph (A) shall not apply with respect to any individual to whom paragraph (5) applies.

(5) SPECIAL RULE FOR MARRIED INDIVIDUALS.—In the case of individuals who are married to each other, if either spouse has family coverage—

(A) both spouses shall be treated as having only such family coverage (and if such spouses each have family coverage under different plans, as having the family coverage with the lowest annual deductible), and

(B) the limitation under paragraph (1) (after the application of subparagraph (A) and without regard to any additional contribution amount under paragraph (3))—

(i) shall be reduced by the aggregate amount paid to Archer MSAs of such spouses for the taxable year, and

(ii) after such reduction, shall be divided equally between them unless they agree on a different division.

(6) DENIAL OF DEDUCTION TO DEPENDENTS.—No deduction shall be allowed under this section to any individual with respect to whom a deduction under section 151 is allowable to another taxpayer for a taxable year beginning in the calendar year in which such individual's taxable year begins.

(7) MEDICARE ELIGIBLE INDIVIDUALS.—The limitation under this subsection for any month with respect to an individual shall be zero for the first month such individual is entitled to benefits under title XVIII of the Social Security Act and for each month thereafter.

(8) INCREASE IN LIMIT FOR INDIVIDUALS BECOMING ELIGIBLE INDIVIDUALS AFTER THE BEGINNING OF THE YEAR.—

(A) IN GENERAL.—For purposes of computing the limitation under paragraph (1) for any taxable year, an individual who is an eligible individual during the last month of such taxable year shall be treated—

(i) as having been an eligible individual during each of the months in such taxable year, and

(ii) as having been enrolled, during each of the months such individual is treated as an eligible individual solely by reason of clause (i), in the same high deductible health plan in which the individual was enrolled for the last month of such taxable year.

(B) FAILURE TO MAINTAIN HIGH DEDUCTIBLE HEALTH PLAN COVERAGE.—

(i) IN GENERAL.—If, at any time during the testing period, the individual is not an eligible individual, then—

(I) gross income of the individual for the taxable year in which occurs the first month in the testing period for which such individual is not an eligible individual is increased by the aggregate amount of all contributions to the health savings account of the individual which could not have been made but for subparagraph (A), and

(II) the tax imposed by this chapter for any taxable year on the individual shall be increased by 10 percent of the amount of such increase.

(ii) EXCEPTION FOR DISABILITY OR DEATH.—Subclauses (I) and (II) of clause (i) shall not apply if the individual ceased to be an eligible individual by reason of the death of the individual or the individual becoming disabled (within the meaning of section 72(m)(7)).

(iii) TESTING PERIOD.—The term "testing period" means the period beginning with the last month of the taxable year referred to in subparagraph (A) and ending on the last day of the 12th month following such month.

Amendments

• 2006, Tax Relief and Health Care Act of 2006 (P.L. 109-432)

P.L. 109-432, Division A, §303(a)(1)-(2):

Amended Code Sec. 223(b)(2) by striking "the lesser of—" and all that follows and inserting "$2,250." in subparagraph (A), and by striking "the lesser of—" and all that follows and inserting "$4,500." in subparagraph (B). **Effective** for tax years beginning after 12-31-2006. Prior to amendment, Code Sec. 223(b)(2) read as follows:

(2) MONTHLY LIMITATION.—The monthly limitation for any month is 1/12 of—

(A) in the case of an eligible individual who has self-only coverage under a high deductible health plan as of the first day of such month, the lesser of—

(i) the annual deductible under such coverage, or

(ii) $2,250, or

(B) in the case of an eligible individual who has family coverage under a high deductible health plan as of the first day of such month, the lesser of—

(i) the annual deductible under such coverage, or

(ii) $4,500.

P.L. 109-432, Division A, §305(a):

Amended Code Sec. 223(b) by adding at the end a new paragraph (8). **Effective** for tax years beginning after 12-31-2006.

P.L. 109-432, Division A, §307(b):

Amended Code Sec. 223(b)(4) by striking "and" at the end of subparagraph (A), by striking the period at the end of subparagraph (B) and inserting ", and", and by inserting after subparagraph (B) a new subparagraph (C). **Effective** for tax years beginning after 12-31-2006.

[Sec. 223(c)]

(c) DEFINITIONS AND SPECIAL RULES.—For purposes of this section—

(1) ELIGIBLE INDIVIDUAL.—

(A) IN GENERAL.—The term "eligible individual" means, with respect to any month, any individual if—

(i) such individual is covered under a high deductible health plan as of the 1st day of such month, and

(ii) such individual is not, while covered under a high deductible health plan, covered under any health plan—

(I) which is not a high deductible health plan, and

(II) which provides coverage for any benefit which is covered under the high deductible health plan.

(B) CERTAIN COVERAGE DISREGARDED.—Subparagraph (A)(ii) shall be applied without regard to—

(i) coverage for any benefit provided by permitted insurance,

(ii) coverage (whether through insurance or otherwise) for accidents, disability, dental care, vision care, or long-term care, and

(iii) for taxable years beginning after December 31, 2006, coverage under a health flexible spending arrangement during any period immediately following the end of a plan year of such arrangement during which unused benefits or contributions remaining at the end of such plan year may be paid or reimbursed to plan participants for qualified benefit expenses incurred during such period if—

(I) the balance in such arrangement at the end of such plan year is zero, or

(II) the individual is making a qualified HSA distribution (as defined in section 106(e)) in an amount equal to the remaining balance in such arrangement as of the end of such plan year, in accordance with rules prescribed by the Secretary.

(2) HIGH DEDUCTIBLE HEALTH PLAN.—

(A) IN GENERAL.—The term "high deductible health plan" means a health plan—

(i) which has an annual deductible which is not less than—

(I) $1,000 for self-only coverage, and

(II) twice the dollar amount in subclause (I) for family coverage, and

(ii) the sum of the annual deductible and the other annual out-of-pocket expenses required to be paid under the plan (other than for premiums) for covered benefits does not exceed—

(I) $5,000 for self-only coverage, and

(II) twice the dollar amount in subclause (I) for family coverage.

(B) EXCLUSION OF CERTAIN PLANS.—Such term does not include a health plan if substantially all of its coverage is coverage described in paragraph (1)(B).

(C) SAFE HARBOR FOR ABSENCE OF PREVENTIVE CARE DEDUCTIBLE.—A plan shall not fail to be treated as a high deductible health plan by reason of failing to have a deductible for preventive care (within the meaning of section 1871 of the Social Security Act, except as otherwise provided by the Secretary).

(D) SPECIAL RULES FOR NETWORK PLANS.—In the case of a plan using a network of providers—

(i) ANNUAL OUT-OF-POCKET LIMITATION.—Such plan shall not fail to be treated as a high deductible health plan by reason of having an out-of-pocket limitation for services provided outside of such network which exceeds the applicable limitation under subparagraph (A)(ii).

(ii) ANNUAL DEDUCTIBLE.—Such plan's annual deductible for services provided outside of such network shall not be taken into account for purposes of subsection (b)(2).

(3) PERMITTED INSURANCE.—The term "permitted insurance" means—

(A) insurance if substantially all of the coverage provided under such insurance relates to—

(i) liabilities incurred under workers' compensation laws,

(ii) tort liabilities,

(iii) liabilities relating to ownership or use of property, or

(iv) such other similar liabilities as the Secretary may specify by regulations,

(B) insurance for a specified disease or illness, and

(C) insurance paying a fixed amount per day (or other period) of hospitalization.

(4) FAMILY COVERAGE.—The term "family coverage" means any coverage other than self-only coverage.

(5) ARCHER MSA.—The term "Archer MSA" has the meaning given such term in section 220(d).

Amendments

• 2006, Tax Relief and Health Care Act of 2006 (P.L. 109-432)

P.L. 109-432, Division A, §302(b):

Amended Code Sec. 223(c)(1)(B) by striking "and" at the end of clause (i), by striking the period at the end of clause (ii) and inserting ", and", and by inserting after clause (ii) a new clause (iii). **Effective** 12-20-2006.

[Sec. 223(d)]

(d) HEALTH SAVINGS ACCOUNT.—For purposes of this section—

(1) IN GENERAL.—The term "health savings account" means a trust created or organized in the United States as a health savings account exclusively for the purpose of paying the qualified medical expenses of the account beneficiary, but only if the written governing instrument creating the trust meets the following requirements:

(A) Except in the case of a rollover contribution described in subsection (f)(5) or section 220(f)(5), no contribution will be accepted—

(i) unless it is in cash, or

(ii) to the extent such contribution, when added to previous contributions to the trust for the calendar year, exceeds the sum of—

(I) the dollar amount in effect under subsection (b)(2)(B), and

(II) the dollar amount in effect under subsection (b)(3)(B).

(B) The trustee is a bank (as defined in section 408(n)), an insurance company (as defined in section 816), or another person who demonstrates to the satisfaction of the Secretary that the manner in which such person will administer the trust will be consistent with the requirements of this section.

(C) No part of the trust assets will be invested in life insurance contracts.

(D) The assets of the trust will not be commingled with other property except in a common trust fund or common investment fund.

(E) The interest of an individual in the balance in his account is nonforfeitable.

(2) QUALIFIED MEDICAL EXPENSES.—

»»→ Caution: Code Sec. 223(d)(2)(A), below, prior to amendment by P.L. 111-148, applies to amounts paid with respect to tax years beginning on or before December 31, 2010.

(A) IN GENERAL.—The term "qualified medical expenses" means, with respect to an account beneficiary, amounts paid by such beneficiary for medical care (as defined in section 213(d)[)]for such individual, the spouse of such individual, and any dependent (as defined in section 152, determined without regard to subsections (b)(1), (b)(2), and (d)(1)(B) thereof) of such individual, but only to the extent such amounts are not compensated for by insurance or otherwise.

»»→ Caution: Code Sec. 223(d)(2)(A), below, as amended by P.L. 111-148, applies to amounts paid with respect to tax years beginning after December 31, 2010.

(A) IN GENERAL.—The term "qualified medical expenses" means, with respect to an account beneficiary, amounts paid by such beneficiary for medical care (as defined in section 213(d)[)]for such individual, the spouse of such individual, and any dependent (as defined in section 152, determined without regard to subsections (b)(1), (b)(2), and (d)(1)(B) thereof) of such individual, but only to the extent such amounts are not compensated for by insurance or otherwise. Such term shall include an amount paid for medicine or a drug only if such medicine or drug is a prescribed drug (determined without regard to whether such drug is available without a prescription) or is insulin.

(B) HEALTH INSURANCE MAY NOT BE PURCHASED FROM ACCOUNT.—Subparagraph (A) shall not apply to any payment for insurance.

(C) EXCEPTIONS.—Subparagraph (B) shall not apply to any expense for coverage under—

(i) a health plan during any period of continuation coverage required under any Federal law,

(ii) a qualified long-term care insurance contract (as defined in section 7702B(b)),

(iii) a health plan during a period in which the individual is receiving unemployment compensation under any Federal or State law, or

(iv) in the case of an account beneficiary who has attained the age specified in section 1811 of the Social Security Act, any health insurance other than a medicare supplemental policy (as defined in section 1882 of the Social Security Act).

(3) ACCOUNT BENEFICIARY.—The term "account beneficiary" means the individual on whose behalf the health savings account was established.

(4) CERTAIN RULES TO APPLY.—Rules similar to the following rules shall apply for purposes of this section:

(A) Section 219(d)(2) (relating to no deduction for rollovers).

(B) Section 219(f)(3) (relating to time when contributions deemed made).

(C) Except as provided in section 106(d), section 219(f)(5) (relating to employer payments).

(D) Section 408(g) (relating to community property laws).

(E) Section 408(h) (relating to custodial accounts).

Amendments

• 2010, Patient Protection and Affordable Care Act (P.L. 111-148)

P.L. 111-148, §9003(a):

Amended Code Sec. 223(d)(2)(A) by adding at the end a new sentence. **Effective** for amounts paid with respect to tax years beginning after 12-31-2010.

• 2006, Tax Relief and Health Care Act of 2006 (P.L. 109-432)

P.L. 109-432, Division A, §303(b):

Amended Code Sec. 223(d)(1)(A)(ii)(I) by striking "subsection (b)(2)(B)(ii)" and inserting "subsection (b)(2)(B)". **Effective** for tax years beginning after 12-31-2006.

• 2005, Gulf Opportunity Zone Act of 2005 (P.L. 109-135)

P.L. 109-135, §404(c):

Amended Code Sec. 223(d)(2)(A) by inserting ", determined without regard to subsections (b)(1), (b)(2), and (d)(1)(B) thereof" after "section 152". **Effective** as if included in the provision of the Working Families Tax Relief Act of 2004 (P.L. 108-311) to which it relates [**effective** for tax years beginning after 12-31-2004.—CCH].

[Sec. 223(e)]

(e) TAX TREATMENT OF ACCOUNTS.—

(1) IN GENERAL.—A health savings account is exempt from taxation under this subtitle unless such account has ceased to be a health savings account. Notwithstanding the preceding sentence, any such account is subject to the taxes imposed by section 511 (relating to imposition of tax on unrelated business income of charitable, etc. organizations).

(2) ACCOUNT TERMINATIONS.—Rules similar to the rules of paragraphs (2) and (4) of section 408(e) shall apply to health savings accounts, and any amount treated as distributed under such rules shall be treated as not used to pay qualified medical expenses.

[Sec. 223(f)]

(f) TAX TREATMENT OF DISTRIBUTIONS.—

(1) AMOUNTS USED FOR QUALIFIED MEDICAL EXPENSES.—Any amount paid or distributed out of a health savings account which is used exclusively to pay qualified medical expenses of any account beneficiary shall not be includible in gross income.

(2) INCLUSION OF AMOUNTS NOT USED FOR QUALIFIED MEDICAL EXPENSES.—Any amount paid or distributed out of a health savings account which is not used exclusively to pay the qualified medical expenses of the account beneficiary shall be included in the gross income of such beneficiary.

(3) EXCESS CONTRIBUTIONS RETURNED BEFORE DUE DATE OF RETURN.—

(A) IN GENERAL.—If any excess contribution is contributed for a taxable year to any health savings account of an individual, paragraph (2) shall not apply to distributions from the health savings accounts of such individual (to the extent such distributions do not exceed the aggregate excess contributions to all such accounts of such individual for such year) if—

(i) such distribution is received by the individual on or before the last day prescribed by law (including extensions of time) for filing such individual's return for such taxable year, and

(ii) such distribution is accompanied by the amount of net income attributable to such excess contribution.

Any net income described in clause (ii) shall be included in the gross income of the individual for the taxable year in which it is received.

(B) EXCESS CONTRIBUTION.—For purposes of subparagraph (A), the term "excess contribution" means any contribution (other than a rollover contribution described in paragraph (5) or section 220(f)(5))which is neither excludable from gross income under section 106(d) nor deductible under this section.

(4) ADDITIONAL TAX ON DISTRIBUTIONS NOT USED FOR QUALIFIED MEDICAL EXPENSES.—

Caution: Code Sec. 223(f)(4)(A), below, prior to amendment by P.L. 111-148, applies to distributions made on or before December 31, 2010.

(A) IN GENERAL.—The tax imposed by this chapter on the account beneficiary for any taxable year in which there is a payment or distribution from a health savings account of such beneficiary which is includible in gross income under paragraph (2) shall be increased by 10 percent of the amount which is so includible.

Caution: Code Sec. 223(f)(4)(A), below, as amended by P.L. 111-148, applies to distributions made after December 31, 2010.

(A) IN GENERAL.—The tax imposed by this chapter on the account beneficiary for any taxable year in which there is a payment or distribution from a health savings account of such beneficiary which is includible in gross income under paragraph (2) shall be increased by 20 percent of the amount which is so includible.

(B) EXCEPTION FOR DISABILITY OR DEATH.—Subparagraph (A) shall not apply if the payment or distribution is made after the account beneficiary becomes disabled within the meaning of section 72(m)(7) or dies.

(C) EXCEPTION FOR DISTRIBUTIONS AFTER MEDICARE ELIGIBILITY.—Subparagraph (A) shall not apply to any payment or distribution after the date on which the account beneficiary attains the age specified in section 1811 of the Social Security Act.

(5) ROLLOVER CONTRIBUTION.—An amount is described in this paragraph as a rollover contribution if it meets the requirements of subparagraphs (A) and (B).

(A) IN GENERAL.—Paragraph (2) shall not apply to any amount paid or distributed from a health savings account to the account beneficiary to the extent the amount received is paid into a health savings account for the benefit of such beneficiary not later than the 60th day after the day on which the beneficiary receives the payment or distribution.

(B) LIMITATION.—This paragraph shall not apply to any amount described in subparagraph (A) received by an individual from a health savings account if, at any time during the 1-year period ending on the day of such receipt, such individual received any other amount described in subparagraph (A) from a health savings account which was not includible in the individual's gross income because of the application of this paragraph.

(6) COORDINATION WITH MEDICAL EXPENSE DEDUCTION.—For purposes of determining the amount of the deduction under section 213, any payment or distribution out of a health savings account for qualified medical expenses shall not be treated as an expense paid for medical care.

(7) TRANSFER OF ACCOUNT INCIDENT TO DIVORCE.—The transfer of an individual's interest in a health savings account to an individual's spouse or former spouse under a divorce or separation instrument described in subparagraph (A) of section 71(b)(2) shall not be considered a taxable transfer made by such individual notwithstanding any other provision of this subtitle, and such interest shall, after such transfer, be treated as a health savings account with respect to which such spouse is the account beneficiary.

(8) TREATMENT AFTER DEATH OF ACCOUNT BENEFICIARY.—

(A) TREATMENT IF DESIGNATED BENEFICIARY IS SPOUSE.—If the account beneficiary's surviving spouse acquires such beneficiary's interest in a health savings account by reason of being the designated beneficiary of such account at the death of the account beneficiary, such health savings account shall be treated as if the spouse were the account beneficiary.

(B) OTHER CASES.—

(i) IN GENERAL.— If, by reason of the death of the account beneficiary, any person acquires the account beneficiary's interest in a health savings account in a case to which subparagraph (A) does not apply—

(I) such account shall cease to be a health savings account as of the date of death, and

(II) an amount equal to the fair market value of the assets in such account on such date shall be includible if such person is not the estate of such beneficiary, in such person's gross income for the taxable year which includes such date, or if such person is the estate of such beneficiary, in such beneficiary's gross income for the last taxable year of such beneficiary.

(ii) SPECIAL RULES.—

(I) REDUCTION OF INCLUSION FOR PREDEATH EXPENSES.—The amount includible in gross income under clause (i) by any person (other than the estate) shall be reduced by the amount of qualified medical expenses which were incurred by the decedent before the date of the decedent's death and paid by such person within 1 year after such date.

(II) DEDUCTION FOR ESTATE TAXES.—An appropriate deduction shall be allowed under section 691(c) to any person (other than the decedent or the decedent's spouse) with respect to amounts included in gross income under clause (i) by such person.

Amendments

• 2010, Patient Protection and Affordable Care Act (P.L. 111-148)

P.L. 111-148, §9004(a):

Amended Code Sec. 223(f)(4)(A) by striking "10 percent" and inserting "20 percent". **Effective** for distributions made after 12-31-2010.

[Sec. 223(g)]

(g) COST-OF-LIVING ADJUSTMENT.—

(1) IN GENERAL.—Each dollar amount in subsections (b)(2) and (c)(2)(A) shall be increased by an amount equal to—

(A) such dollar amount, multiplied by

(B) the cost-of-living adjustment determined under section 1(f)(3) for the calendar year in which such taxable year begins determined by substituting for "calendar year 1992" in subparagraph (B) thereof—

(i) except as provided in clause (ii), "calendar year 1997", and

(ii) in the case of each dollar amount in subsection (c)(2)(A), "calendar year 2003".

In the case of adjustments made for any taxable year beginning after 2007, section 1(f)(4) shall be applied for purposes of this paragraph by substituting "March 31" for "August 31", and the Secretary shall publish the adjusted amounts under subsections (b)(2) and (c)(2)(A) for taxable years beginning in any calendar year no later than June 1 of the preceding calendar year.

(2) ROUNDING.—If any increase under paragraph (1) is not a multiple of $50, such increase shall be rounded to the nearest multiple of $50.

Amendments

• 2006, Tax Relief and Health Care Act of 2006 (P.L. 109-432)

P.L. 109-432, Division A, §304:

Amended Code Sec. 223(g)(1) by adding at the end a new flush sentence. **Effective** 12-20-2006.

[Sec. 223(h)]

(h) REPORTS.—The Secretary may require—

(1) the trustee of a health savings account to make such reports regarding such account to the Secretary and to the account beneficiary with respect to contributions, distributions, the return of excess contributions, and such other matters as the Secretary determines appropriate, and

(2) any person who provides an individual with a high deductible health plan to make such reports to the Secretary and to the account beneficiary with respect to such plan as the Secretary determines appropriate.

The reports required by this subsection shall be filed at such time and in such manner and furnished to such individuals at such time and in such manner as may be required by the Secretary.

Amendments

• 2003, Medicare Prescription Drug, Improvement, and Modernization Act of 2003 (P.L. 108-173)

P.L. 108-173, §1201(a):

Amended part VII of subchapter B of chapter 1 by redesignating Code Sec. 223 as Code Sec. 224 and by inserting after Code Sec. 222 a new Code Sec. 223. **Effective** for tax years beginning after 12-31-2003.

Caution: Former Code Sec. 222, below, was redesignated as Code Sec. 223 by P.L. 107-16 and redesignated as Code Sec. 224 by P.L. 108-173, and is subject to the sunset provision of the Economic Growth and Tax Relief Reconciliation Act of 2001 (P.L. 107-16), §901. Absent Congressional action, the changes made to this provision by P.L. 107-16, or that take effect as if included in P.L. 107-16, do not apply after December 31, 2010. For more information about the sunset provision, see page XXI of the Preface to this publication and P.L. 107-16, §901, in the amendment notes. See the amendments notes for a history of amendments to this section and the effective date of each change.

[Sec. 224]

SEC. 224. CROSS REFERENCE.

For deductions in respect of a decedent, see section 691.

Amendments

• 2003, Medicare Prescription Drug, Improvement, and Modernization Act of 2003 (P.L. 108-173)

P.L. 108-173, §1201(a):

Amended part VII of subchapter B of chapter 1 by redesignating Code Sec. 223 as Code Sec. 224. **Effective** for tax years beginning after 12-31-2003.

• 2001, Economic Growth and Tax Relief Reconciliation Act of 2001 (P.L. 107-16)

P.L. 107-16, §431(a):

Amended part VII of subchapter B of chapter 1 by redesignating Code Sec. 222 as Code Sec. 223. **Effective** for payments made in tax years beginning after 12-31-2001.

P.L. 107-16, §901(a)-(b), provides:

SEC. 901. SUNSET OF PROVISIONS OF ACT.

(a) IN GENERAL.—All provisions of, and amendments made by, this Act shall not apply—

(1) to taxable, plan, or limitation years beginning after December 31, 2010, or

(2) in the case of title V, to estates of decedents dying, gifts made, or generation skipping transfers, after December 31, 2010.

(b) APPLICATION OF CERTAIN LAWS.—The Internal Revenue Code of 1986 and the Employee Retirement Income Security Act of 1974 shall be applied and administered to years, estates, gifts, and transfers described in subsection (a) as if the provisions and amendments described in subsection (a) had never been enacted.

• 1997, Taxpayer Relief Act of 1997 (P.L. 105-34)

P.L. 105-34, §202(a):

Amended part VII of subchapter B of chapter 1 by redesignating Code Sec. 221 as Code Sec. 222. For the **effective** date, see Act Sec. 202(e), below.

P.L. 105-34, §202(e), provides:

(e) EFFECTIVE DATE.—The amendments made by this section shall apply to any qualified education loan (as defined in section 221(e)(1) of the Internal Revenue Code of 1986, as added by this section) incurred on, before, or after the date of the enactment of this Act, but only with respect to—

(1) any loan interest payment due and paid after December 31, 1997, and

(2) the portion of the 60-month period referred to in section 221(d) of the Internal Revenue Code of 1986 (as added by this section) after December 31, 1997.

• 1996, Health Insurance Portability and Accountability Act of 1996 (P.L. 104-191)

P.L. 104-191, §301(a):

Amended part VII of subchapter B of chapter 1 by redesignating Code Sec. 220 as Code Sec. 221. **Effective** for tax years beginning after 12-31-96.

• 1990, Omnibus Budget Reconciliation Act of 1990 (P.L. 101-508)

P.L. 101-508, §11802(e)(2):

Redesignated Code Sec. 221 as Code Sec. 220. **Effective** 11-5-90.

• 1988, Technical and Miscellaneous Revenue Act of 1988 (P.L. 100-647)

P.L. 100-647, §6007(a):

Redesignated section 220 as section 221. **Effective** as if included in the amendments made by P.L. 99-514, §132.

• 1986, Tax Reform Act of 1986 (P.L. 99-514)

P.L. 99-514, §135(b)(1):

Redesignated Code Sec. 223 as Code Sec. 220. **Effective** for tax years beginning after 12-31-86.

P.L. 99-514, §301(b)(5)(A):

Amended Code Sec. 223. **Effective** for tax years beginning after 12-31-86. Prior to amendment, Code Sec. 223 read as follows:

SEC. 223. CROSS REFERENCES.

(1) For deduction for long-term capital gains in the case of a taxpayer other than a corporation, see section 1202.

(2) For deductions in respect of a decedent, see section 691.

• 1981, Economic Recovery Tax Act of 1981 (P.L. 97-34)

P.L. 97-34, §103(a):

Redesignated Code Sec. 221 as Code Sec. 222. **Effective** for tax years beginning after 12-31-81.

P.L. 97-34, §125(a):

Redesignated Code Sec. 222 as Code Sec. 223. **Effective** for tax years beginning after 12-30-80.

• 1976, Tax Reform Act of 1976 (P.L. 94-455)

P.L. 94-455, §1501(a):

Redesignated former Code Sec. 220 as Code Sec. 221. **Effective** for tax years beginning after 12-31-76.

• 1974, Employee Retirement Income Security Act of 1974 (P.L. 93-406)

P.L. 93-406, §2002(a):

Redesignated Code Sec. 219 as Code Sec. 220.

• 1964, Revenue Act of 1964 (P.L. 88-272)

P.L. 88-272, §213(a)(1):

Redesignated section 218 from former section 217.

PART VIII—SPECIAL DEDUCTIONS FOR CORPORATIONS

[Sec. 241]

SEC. 241. ALLOWANCE OF SPECIAL DEDUCTIONS.

In addition to the deductions provided in part VI (sec. 161 and following), there shall be allowed as deductions in computing taxable income the items specified in this part.

[Sec. 243]

SEC. 243. DIVIDENDS RECEIVED BY CORPORATIONS.

[Sec. 243(a)]

(a) GENERAL RULE.—In the case of a corporation, there shall be allowed as a deduction an amount equal to the following percentages of the amount received as dividends from a domestic corporation which is subject to taxation under this chapter:

(1) 70 percent, in the case of dividends other than dividends described in paragraph (2) or (3);

(2) 100 percent, in the case of dividends received by a small business investment company operating under the Small Business Investment Act of 1958 (15 U.S.C. 661 and following); and

(3) 100 percent, in the case of qualifying dividends (as defined in subsection (b)(1)).

Amendments

• 1987, Revenue Act of 1987 (P.L. 100-203)

P.L. 100-203, §10221(a)(1):

Amended Code Sec. 243(a)(1) by striking out "80 percent" and inserting in lieu thereof "70 percent". **Effective** for dividends received or accrued after 12-31-87, in tax year ending after such date.

• 1986, Tax Reform Act of 1986 (P.L. 99-514)

P.L. 99-514, §611(a)(1):

Amended Code Sec. 243(a)(1) by striking out "85 percent" and inserting in lieu thereof "80 percent". **Effective** for dividends received or accrued after 12-31-86, in tax years ending after such date.

• 1976, Tax Reform Act of 1976 (P.L. 94-455)

P.L. 94-455, §1901(a)(34)(A):

Amended Code Sec. 243(a)(2) by adding "(15 U.S.C. 661 and following)" after "Small Business Investment Act of 1958". **Effective** for tax years beginning after 12-31-76.

• 1964, Revenue Act of 1964 (P.L. 88-272)

P.L. 88-272, §214(a):

Amended subsection (a). **Effective** for dividends received in tax years ending after 12-31-63. Prior to amendment, subsection (a) read as follows:

(a) General Rule.—In the case of a corporation (other than a small business investment company operating under the Small Business Investment Act of 1958) there shall be allowed as a deduction an amount equal to 85 percent of the amount received as dividends (other than dividends described in paragraph (1) of section 244, relating to dividends on the preferred stock of a public utility) from a domestic corporation which is subject to taxation under this chapter.

• 1958, Technical Amendments Act of 1958 (P.L. 85-866)

P.L. 85-866, §57(b)(1):

Struck out the phrase in the first sentence of Code Sec. 243(a), "In the case of a corporation" and substituted the phrase "In the case of a corporation (other than a small business investment company operating under the Small Business Investment Act of 1958)". **Effective** 9-3-58.

[Sec. 243(b)]

(b) QUALIFYING DIVIDENDS.—

(1) IN GENERAL.—For purposes of this section, the term "qualifying dividend" means any dividend received by a corporation—

(A) if at the close of the day on which such dividend is received, such corporation is a member of the same affiliated group as the corporation distributing such dividend, and

(B) if—

(i) such dividend is distributed out of the earnings and profits of a taxable year of the distributing corporation which ends after December 31, 1963, for which an election under section 1562 was not in effect, and on each day of which the distributing corporation and the corporation receiving the dividend were members of such affiliated group, or

(ii) such dividend is paid by a corporation with respect to which an election under section 936 is in effect for the taxable year in which such dividend is paid.

(2) AFFILIATED GROUP.—For purposes of this subsection:

(A) IN GENERAL.—The term "affiliated group" has the meaning given such term by section 1504(a), except that for such purposes sections 1504(b)(2), 1504(b)(4), and 1504(c) shall not apply.

(B) GROUP MUST BE CONSISTENT IN FOREIGN TAX TREATMENT.—The requirements of paragraph (1)(A) shall not be treated as being met with respect to any dividend received by a corporation if, for any taxable year which includes the day on which such dividend is received—

(i) 1 or more members of the affiliated group referred to in paragraph (1)(A) choose to any extent to take the benefits of section 901, and

(ii) 1 or more other members of such group claim to any extent a deduction for taxes otherwise creditable under section 901.

(3) SPECIAL RULE FOR GROUPS WHICH INCLUDE LIFE INSURANCE COMPANIES.—

(A) IN GENERAL.—In the case of an affiliated group which includes 1 or more insurance companies under section 801, no dividend by any member of such group shall be treated as a qualifying dividend unless an election under this paragraph is in effect for the taxable year in which the dividend is received. The preceding sentence shall not apply in the case of a dividend described in paragraph (1)(B)(ii).

(B) EFFECT OF ELECTION.—If an election under this paragraph is in effect with respect to any affiliated group—

(i) part II of subchapter B of chapter 6 (relating to certain controlled corporations) shall be applied with respect to the members of such group without regard to sections 1563(a)(4) and 1563(b)(2)(D), and

(ii) for purposes of this subsection, a distribution by any member of such group which is subject to tax under section 801 shall not be treated as a qualifying dividend if such distribution is out of earnings and profits for a taxable year for which an election under this paragraph is not effective and for which such distributing corporation was not a component member of a controlled group of corporations within the meaning of section 1563 solely by reason of section 1563(b)(2)(D).

(C) ELECTION.—An election under this paragraph shall be made by the common parent of the affiliated group and at such time and in such manner as the Secretary shall by regulations prescribe. Any such election shall be binding on all members of such group and may be revoked only with the consent of the Secretary.

Amendments

• 1996, Small Business Job Protection Act of 1996 (P.L. 104-188)

P.L. 104-188, §1702(h)(4):

Amended Code Sec. 243(b)(3)(A) by inserting "of" after "In the case". **Effective** as if included in the provision of P.L. 101-508 to which it relates.

P.L. 104-188, §1702(h)(8):

Amended Code Sec. 243(b)(2). **Effective** as if included in the provision of P.L. 101-508 to which it relates. Prior to amendment, Code Sec. 243(b)(2) read as follows:

(2) AFFILIATED GROUP.—For purposes of this subsection, the term "affiliated group" has the meaning given such term by section 1504(a), except that for such purposes sections 1504(b)(2), 1504(b)(4), and 1504(c) shall not apply.

• 1990, Omnibus Budget Reconciliation Act of 1990 (P.L. 101-508)

P.L. 101-508, §11814(a):

Amended Code Sec. 243(b). **Effective** for tax years beginning after 12-31-90. For a special rule, see Act Sec. 11814(b)(2), below. Prior to amendment subsection (b) read as follows:

(b) QUALIFYING DIVIDENDS.—

(1) DEFINITION.—For purposes of subsection (a)(3), the term "qualifying dividends" means dividends received by a corporation which, at the close of the day the dividends are received, is a member of the same affiliated group of corporations (as defined in paragraph (5)) as the corporation distributing the dividends, if—

(A) such affiliated group has made an election under paragraph (2) which is effective for the taxable years of its members which include such day, and either

(B) such dividends are distributed out of earnings and profits of a taxable year of the distributing corporation ending after December 31, 1963—

(i) on each day of which the distributing corporation and the corporation receiving the dividends were members of such affiliated group, and

(ii) for which an election under section 1562 (relating to election of multiple surtax exemptions) is not effective, or

(C) such dividends are paid by a corporation with respect to which an election under section 936 is in effect for the taxable year in which such dividends are paid.

(2) ELECTION.—An election under this paragraph shall be made for an affiliated group by the common parent corporation, and shall be made for any taxable year of the common parent corporation at such time and in such manner as the Secretary by regulations prescribes. Such election may not be made for an affiliated group for any taxable year of the common parent corporation for which an election under section 1562 is effective. Each corporation which is a member of such group at any time during its taxable year which includes the last day of such taxable year of the common parent corporation must consent to such election at such time and in such manner as the Secretary by regulations prescribes. An election under this paragraph shall be effective—

(A) for the taxable year of each member of such affiliated group which includes the last day of the taxable year of the common parent corporation with respect to which the election is made, and

(B) for the taxable year of each member of such affiliated group which ends after the last day of such taxable year of the common parent corporation but which does not include such date, unless the election is terminated under paragraph (4).

(3) EFFECT OF ELECTION.—If an election by an affiliated group is effective with respect to a taxable year of the common parent corporation, then under regulations prescribed by the Secretary—

(A) no member of such affiliated group may consent to an election under section 1562 for such taxable year,

(B) the members of such affiliated group shall be treated as one taxpayer for purposes of making the election under section 901(a) (relating to allowance of foreign tax credit), and

(C) the members of such affiliated group shall be limited to one—

(i) minimum accumulated earnings credit under section 535(c)(2) or (3), and

(ii) surtax exemption, and one amount under section 6154(c)(2) and section 6655(e)(2), for purposes of estimated tax payment requirements under section 6154 and the addition to the tax under section 6655 for failure to pay estimated tax.

(4) TERMINATION.—An election by an affiliated group under paragraph (2) shall terminate with respect to the taxable year of the common parent corporation and with respect to the taxable years of the members of such affiliated group which include the last day of such taxable year of the common parent corporation if—

(A) CONSENT OF MEMBERS.—Such affiliated group files a termination of such election (at such time and in such manner as the Secretary by regulations prescribes) with respect to such taxable year of the common parent corporation, and each corporation which is a member of such affiliated group at any time during its taxable year which includes the last day of such taxable year of the common parent corporation consents to such termination, or

(B) REFUSAL BY NEW MEMBER TO CONSENT.—During such taxable year of the common parent corporation such affiliated group includes a member which—

(i) was not a member of such group during such common parent corporation's immediately preceding taxable year, and

(ii) such member files a statement that it does not consent to the election at such time and in such manner as the Secretary by regulations prescribes.

(5) DEFINITION OF AFFILIATED GROUP.—For purposes of this subsection, the term "affiliated group" has the meaning assigned to it by section 1504(a), except that for such purposes sections 1504(b)(2), 1504(b)(4), and 1504(c) shall not apply.

(6) SPECIAL RULES FOR INSURANCE COMPANIES.—If an election under this subsection is effective for the taxable year of an insurance company subject to taxation under section 801—

(A) part II of subchapter B of chapter 6 (relating to certain controlled corporations) shall be applied without regard to section 1563(a)(4) (relating to certain insurance companies) and section 1563(b)(2)(D) (relating to certain excluded members) with respect to such company and the other corporations which are members of the controlled group of corporations (as determined under section 1563 without regard to subsections (a)(4) and (b)(2)(D)) of which such company is a member, and

(B) for purposes of paragraph (1), a distribution by such company out of earnings and profits of a taxable year for which an election under this subsection was not effective, and for which such company was not a component member of a controlled group of corporations within the meaning of section 1563 solely by reason of section 1563(b)(2)(D), shall not be a qualifying dividend.

P.L. 101-508, §11814(b)(2), provides:

(2) TREATMENT OF OLD ELECTIONS.—For purposes of section 243(b)(3) of the Internal Revenue Code of 1986 (as amended by subsection (a)), any reference to an election under such section shall be treated as including a reference to an election under section 243(b) of such Code (as in effect on the day before the date of the enactment of this Act).

• 1988, Technical and Miscellaneous Revenue Act of 1988 (P.L. 100-647)

P.L. 100-647, §1010(f)(4):

Amended Code Sec. 243(b)(6) by striking out "or 821" after "section 801" in the first sentence. **Effective** as if included in the provision of P.L. 99-514 to which it relates.

• 1986, Tax Reform Act of 1986 (P.L. 99-514)

P.L. 99-514, §411(b)(2)(C)(iv)(I)-(III):

Amended Code Sec. 243(b)(3)(C) by adding "and" at the end of clause (i), by striking out clause (ii), and by redesignating clause (iii) as clause (ii). **Effective** for costs paid or incurred after 12-31-86, in tax years ending after such date. However, for a transition rule, see Act Sec. 411(c)(2), below. Prior to amendment, clause (ii) read as follows:

(ii) $400,000 limitation for certain expenditures under section 617(h)(1), and

P.L. 99-514, §411(c)(2), provides:

(2) TRANSITION RULE.—The amendments made by this section shall not apply with respect to intangible drilling and development costs incurred by United States companies pursuant to a minority interest in a license for Netherlands or United Kingdom North Sea development if such interest was acquired on or before December 31, 1985.

• 1984, Deficit Reduction Act of 1984 (P.L. 98-369)

P.L. 98-369, §211(b)(3)(A):

Amended Code Sec. 243(b)(3)(C) by striking out clause (iii), by adding "and" at the end of clause (ii), and by redesignating clause (iv) as clause (iii). **Effective** for tax years beginning after 12-31-83. Prior to amendment, clause (iii) read as follows:

(iii) $25,000 limitation on small business deduction of life insurance companies under sections 804(a)(3) and 809(d)(10), and

P.L. 98-369, §211(b)(3)(B):

Amended Code Sec. 243(b)(6) by striking out "section 802" and inserting in lieu thereof "section 801". **Effective** for tax years beginning after 12-31-83.

• 1981, Economic Recovery Tax Act of 1981 (P.L. 97-34)

P.L. 97-34, §232(b)(2):

Amended Code Sec. 243(b)(3)(C)(i) by striking out "$150,000". **Effective** for tax years beginning after 12-31-81.

• 1976, Tax Reform Act of 1976 (P.L. 94-455)

P.L. 94-455, §1031(b)(2):

Amended Code Sec. 243(b)(3)(B). **Effective** for tax years beginning after 12-31-75, except that the amendment shall apply for taxable years beginning after 12-31-78: (1) in the case of a domestic corporation or an includible corporation in an affiliated group (as defined in Code Sec. 1504) which, as of 10-1-75, has been engaged in the active conduct of a trade or business of the extraction of minerals outside the United States or its possessions for less than 5 years preceding 10-4-76, has had deductions properly apportioned or allocated to its gross income from such trade or business in excess of such gross income in at least 2 taxable years, has 80 percent of its gross receipts from the sale of such minerals, and has made commitments for substantial expansion of such minerals; and (2) in the case of gross income, and the deductions properly apportioned or allocated thereto, from sources within a possession of the United States. In the case of losses sustained in tax years beginning before 1-1-79, by any corporation to which (1) applies or by a taxpayer to whom (2) applies, the provisions of Code Sec. 904(f) shall be applied to such losses under the principles of Code Sec. 904(a)(1) as in effect before 10-4-76. In the case of a taxpayer to whom (1) or (2) applies, Code Sec. 904(e) applies, except that "January 1, 1979" shall be substituted for "January 1, 1976" each place that it appears. If such a taxpayer elects the overall limitation for a tax year beginning before 1-1-79, Code Sec. 904(e) shall be applied by substituting "the January 1, of the last year for which such taxpayer is on the per-country limitation" for "January 1, 1976" each place it appears. Prior to amendment, Code Sec. 243(b)(3)(B) read as follows:

(B) the members of such affiliated group shall be treated as one taxpayer for purposes of making the elections under section 901(a) (relating to allowance of foreign tax credit) and section 904(b)(1) (relating to election of overall limitation), and

• 1976, Tax Reform Act of 1976 (P.L. 94-455)

P.L. 94-455, §1051(f)(1):

Added "either" at the end of Code Sec. 243(b)(1)(A), substituted ", or" for the period at the end of Code Sec. 243(b)(1)(B)(ii), and added Code Sec. 243(b)(1)(C). **Effective** for tax years beginning after 12-31-75, except that "qualified possession source investment income" as defined in Code Sec. 936(d)(2) shall include income from any source outside the United States if the taxpayer establishes to the satisfaction of the Secretary of the Treasury or his delegate that the income from such sources was earned before 10-1-76.

P.L. 94-455, §1051(f)(2):

Added ", 1504(b)(4)," immediately after "1504(b)(2)" in Code Sec. 243(b)(5). **Effective** for tax years beginning after 12-31-75.

P.L. 94-455, §1901(a)(34)(B):

Amended Code Sec. 243(b)(2)(A). **Effective** for tax years beginning after 12-31-76. Prior to amendment, Code Sec. 243(b)(2)(A) read as follows:

(A) for the taxable year of each member of such affiliated group which includes the last day of the taxable year of the common parent corporation with respect to which the election is made (except that in the case of a taxable year of a member beginning in 1963 and ending in 1964, if the election is effective for the taxable year of the common parent corporation which includes the last day of such taxable year of such member, such election shall be effective for such taxable year of such member, if such member consents to such election with respect to such taxable year), and

P.L. 94-455, §1901(b)(1)(J)(ii):

Substituted "section 804(a)(3)" for "section 804(a)(4)" in Code Sec. 243(b)(3)(C)(iii) as redesignated by P.L. 94-455, §1901(b)(21)(A). **Effective** for tax years beginning after 12-31-76.

P.L. 94-455, §1901(b)(21)(A):

Substituted Code Sec. 243(b)(3)(C)(ii) for former Code Secs. 243(b)(3)(C)(ii) and (iii) and redesignated Code Secs. 243(b)(3)(C)(iv) and (v) as Code Secs. 243(b)(3)(C)(iii) and (iv), respectively. **Effective** for tax years beginning after 12-31-76. Prior to amendment, Code Secs. 243(b)(3)(C)(ii) and (iii) read as follows:

(ii) $100,000 limitation for exploration expenditures under section 615(a) and (b),

(iii) $400,000 limitation for exploration expenditures under sections 615(c)(1) and 617(h)(1),

P.L. 94-455, §1906(b)(3)(C)(ii):

Substituted "section 6154(c)(2)" for "sections 6154(c)(2) and (3)" and substituted "section 6655(e)(2)" for "sections 6655(e)(2) and (3)" in Code Sec. 243(b)(3)(C)(iv), as redesignated by P.L. 94-455, §1901(b)(21)(A). **Effective** for tax years beginning after 12-31-76.

P.L. 94-455, §1906(b)(13)(A):

Amended 1954 Code by substituting "Secretary" for "Secretary or his delegate" each place it appeared. **Effective** 2-1-77.

• 1975, Tax Reduction Act of 1975 (P.L. 94-12)

P.L. 94-12, §304(b):

Amended Sec. 243(b)(3)(C)(i) by substituting "$150,000" for "$100,000". **Effective** for tax years beginning after 12-31-74.

• 1969, Tax Reform Act of 1969 (P.L. 91-172)

P.L. 91-172, §504(c)(1):

Amended Sec. 243(b)(3)(C)(iii) by adding "and 617(h)(1)" at the end thereof. **Effective** 1-1-70.

• 1968, Revenue and Expenditure Control Act of 1968 (P.L. 90-364)

P.L. 90-364, §103(e)(2):

Amended Code Sec. 243(b)(3)(C)(v). **Effective** for tax years beginning after 12-31-67. However, such amendment is to be taken into account as of 5-31-68. For the **effective** date provisions of P.L. 90-364, see the amendment note following Code Sec. 6154. Prior to amendment, Code Sec. 243(b)(3)(C)(v) read as follows:

"(v) $100,000 exemption for purposes of estimated tax filing requirements under section 6016 and the addition to tax under section 6655 for failure to pay estimated tax."

• 1964, Revenue Act of 1964 (P.L. 88-272)

P.L. 88-272, §214(a):

Amended subsection (b). **Effective** for dividends received in tax years ending after 12-31-63. Prior to amendment, subsection (b) read as follows:

"(b) Small Business Investment Companies.—In the case of a small business investment company operating under the Small Business Investment Act of 1958, there shall be allowed as a deduction an amount equal to 100 percent of the amount received as dividends (other than dividends described in paragraph (1) of section 244, relating to dividends on preferred stock of a public utility) from a domestic corporation which is subject to taxation under this chapter."

• 1958, Technical Amendments Act of 1958 (P.L. 85-866)

P.L. 85-866, §57(b)(2):

Redesignated subsection (b) of Sec. 243 as subsection (c) and added new subsection (b). **Effective** 9-3-58.

[Sec. 243(c)]

(c) RETENTION OF 80-PERCENT DIVIDENDS RECEIVED DEDUCTION FOR DIVIDENDS FROM 20-PERCENT OWNED CORPORATIONS.—

(1) IN GENERAL.—In the case of any dividend received from a 20-percent owned corporation—

(A) subsection (a)(1) of this section, and

(B) subsections (a)(3) and (b)(2) of section 244,

shall be applied by substituting "80 percent" for "70 percent".

(2) 20-PERCENT OWNED CORPORATION.—For purposes of this section, the term "20-percent owned corporation" means any corporation if 20 percent or more of the stock of such corporation (by vote and value) is owned by the taxpayer. For purposes of the preceding sentence, stock described in section 1504(a)(4) shall not be taken into account.

Amendments

• 1987, Revenue Act of 1987 (P.L. 100-203)

P.L. 100-203, §10221(b):

Amended Code Sec. 243 by redesignating subsections (c) and (d) as subsections (d) and (e), respectively, and by inserting after subsection (b) new subsection (c). **Effective** for tax years beginning after 12-31-87.

[Sec. 243(d)]

(d) SPECIAL RULES FOR CERTAIN DISTRIBUTIONS.—For purposes of subsection (a)—

(1) Any amount allowed as a deduction under section 591 (relating to deduction for dividends paid by mutual savings banks, etc.) shall not be treated as a dividend.

(2) A dividend received from a regulated investment company shall be subject to the limitations prescribed in section 854.

(3) Any dividend received from a real estate investment trust which, for the taxable year of the trust in which the dividend is paid, qualifies under part II of subchapter M (section 856 and following) shall not be treated as a dividend.

(4) Any dividend received which is described in section 244 (relating to dividends received on preferred stock of a public utility) shall not be treated as a dividend.

Amendments

• 1987, Revenue Act of 1987 (P.L. 100-203)

P.L. 100-203, §10221(b):

Amended Code Sec. 243 by redesignating subsection (c) as (d). **Effective** for dividends received or accrued after 12-31-87, in tax years ending after such date.

• 1964, Revenue Act of 1964 (P.L. 88-272)

P.L. 88-272, §214(a):

Amended subsection (c). **Effective** for dividends received in tax years ending after 12-31-63. Prior to amendment, subsection (c) read as follows:

"(c) Special Rules for Certain Distributions.—For purposes of subsections (a) and (b)—

"(1) Any amount allowed as a deduction under section 591 (relating to deduction for dividends paid by mutual savings banks, etc.) shall not be treated as a dividend.

"(2) A dividend received from a regulated investment company shall be subject to the limitations prescribed in section 854.

"(3) Any dividend received from a real estate investment trust which, for the taxable year of the trust in which the dividend is paid, qualifies under part II of subchapter M (sec. 856 and following) shall not be treated as a dividend."

• 1960 (P.L. 86-779)

P.L. 86-779, §10(g):

Added a new paragraph (3) to Code Sec. 243(c). **Effective** 1-1-61.

• 1958, Technical Amendments Act of 1958 (P.L. 85-866)

P.L. 85-866, §57(b)(3):

Struck out, in Sec. 243(c) (as redesignated by §57(b)(2)), the phrase "subsection (a)" and substituted the phrase "subsections (a) and (b)". **Effective** 9-3-58.

[Sec. 243(e)]

(e) CERTAIN DIVIDENDS FROM FOREIGN CORPORATIONS.—For purposes of subsection (a) and for purposes of section 245, any dividend from a foreign corporation from earnings and profits accumulated by a domestic corporation during a period with respect to which such domestic corporation was subject to taxation under this chapter (or corresponding provisions of prior law) shall be treated as a dividend from a domestic corporation which is subject to taxation under this chapter.

Amendments

• 1987, Revenue Act of 1987 (P.L. 100-203)

P.L. 100-203, §10221(b):

Amended Code Sec. 243 by redesignating subsection (d) as subsection (e). **Effective** for dividends received or accrued after 12-31-87, in tax years ending after such date [**effective** date changed by P.L. 100-647, §2004(i)(1)].

• 1964, Revenue Act of 1964 (P.L. 88-272)

P.L. 88-272, §214(a):

Amended subsection (d). **Effective** for dividends received in tax years ending after 12-31-63. Prior to amendment, subsection (d) read as follows:

"(d) Certain Dividends From Foreign Corporations.—For purposes of subsections (a) and (b) of this section and for purposes of section 245, any dividend from a foreign corporation from earnings and profits accumulated by a domestic corporation during a period with respect to which such domestic corporation was subject to taxation under this chapter (or corresponding provisions of prior law) shall be treated as a dividend from a domestic corporation which is subject to taxation under this chapter."

• 1960 (P.L. 86-779)

P.L. 86-779, §3(a):

Added subsection (d). **Effective** for dividends received after 1959 in tax years ending after 1959.

[Sec. 244]

SEC. 244. DIVIDENDS RECEIVED ON CERTAIN PREFERRED STOCK.

[Sec. 244(a)]

(a) GENERAL RULE.—In the case of a corporation, there shall be allowed as a deduction an amount computed as follows:

(1) First determine the amount received as dividends on the preferred stock of a public utility which is subject to taxation under this chapter and with respect to which the deduction provided in section 247 for dividends paid is allowable.

(2) Then multiply the amount determined under paragraph (1) by the fraction—

(A) the numerator of which is 14 percent, and

(B) the denominator of which is that percentage which equals the highest rate of tax specified in section 11(b).

(3) Finally ascertain the amount which is 70 percent of the excess of—

(A) the amount determined under paragraph (1), over

(B) the amount determined under paragraph (2).

Amendments

• 1987, Revenue Act of 1987 (P.L. 100-203)

P.L. 100-203, §10221(a)(2):

Amended Code Sec. 244(a)(3) by striking out "80 percent" and inserting in lieu thereof "70 percent". **Effective** for dividends received or accrued after 12-31-87, in tax years ending after such date.

• 1986, Tax Reform Act of 1986 (P.L. 99-514)

P.L. 99-514, §611(a)(2):

Amended Code Sec. 244(a)(3) by striking out "85 percent" and inserting in lieu thereof "80 percent". **Effective** for dividends received or accrued after 12-31-86, in tax years ending after such date.

• 1978, Revenue Act of 1978 (P.L. 95-600)

P.L. 95-600, §301(b)(3):

Amended Code Sec. 244(a)(2)(B) by striking out "the sum of the normal tax rate and the surtax rate for the taxable year prescribed by section 11" and inserting in lieu thereof "the highest rate of tax specified in section 11(b)". **Effective** for tax years beginning after 12-31-78.

• 1964, Revenue Act of 1964 (P.L. 88-272)

P.L. 88-272, §214(b)(1):

Amended subsection (a) by inserting the heading "(a) General Rule.—" at the beginning. **Effective** 1-1-64.

[Sec. 244(b)]

(b) EXCEPTION.—If the dividends described in subsection (a)(1) are qualifying dividends (as defined in section 243(b)(1), but determined without regard to section 243(d)(4))—

(1) subsection (a) shall be applied separately to such qualifying dividends, and

(2) for purposes of subsection (a)(3), the percentage applicable to such qualifying dividends shall be 100 percent in lieu of 70 percent.

Amendments

• 1988, Technical and Miscellaneous Revenue Act of 1988 (P.L. 100-647)

P.L. 100-647, §2004(i)(2):

Amended Code Sec. 244(b) by striking out "section 243(c)(4)" and inserting in lieu thereof "section 243(d)(4)". **Effective** as if included in the provision of P.L. 100-203 to which it relates.

• 1987, Revenue Act of 1987 (P.L. 100-203)

P.L. 100-203, §10221(a)(2):

Amended Code Sec. 244(b)(2) by striking out "80 percent" and inserting in lieu thereof "70 percent". **Effective** for dividends received or accrued after 12-31-87, in tax years ending after such date.

• 1986, Tax Reform Act of 1986 (P.L. 99-514)

P.L. 99-514, §611(a)(2):

Amended Code Sec. 244(b)(2) by striking out "85 percent" and inserting in lieu thereof "80 percent."

• 1964, Revenue Act of 1964 (P.L. 88-272)

P.L. 88-272, §214(b):

Amended section 244 by adding subsection (b) thereto. **Effective** for dividends received in tax years ending after 12-31-63.

[Sec. 245]

SEC. 245. DIVIDENDS RECEIVED FROM CERTAIN FOREIGN CORPORATIONS.

[Sec. 245(a)]

(a) DIVIDENDS FROM 10-PERCENT OWNED FOREIGN CORPORATIONS.—

(1) IN GENERAL.—In the case of dividends received by a corporation from a qualified 10-percent owned foreign corporation, there shall be allowed as a deduction an amount equal to the percent (specified in section 243 for the taxable year) of the U.S.-source portion of such dividends.

(2) QUALIFIED 10-PERCENT OWNED FOREIGN CORPORATION.—For purposes of this subsection, the term "qualified 10-percent owned foreign corporation" means any foreign corporation (other than a passive foreign investment company) if at least 10 percent of the stock of such corporation (by vote and value) is owned by the taxpayer.

(3) U.S.-SOURCE PORTION.—For purposes of this subsection, the U.S.-source portion of any dividend is an amount which bears the same ratio to such dividends as—

(A) the post-1986 undistributed U.S. earnings, bears to

(B) the total post-1986 undistributed earnings.

(4) POST-1986 UNDISTRIBUTED EARNINGS.—For purposes of this subsection, the term "post-1986 undistributed earnings" has the meaning given to such term by section 902(c)(1).

(5) POST-1986 UNDISTRIBUTED U.S. EARNINGS.—For purposes of this subsection, the term "post-1986 undistributed U.S. earnings" means the portion of the post-1986 undistributed earnings which is attributable to—

(A) income of the qualified 10-percent owned foreign corporation which is effectively connected with the conduct of a trade or business within the United States and subject to tax under this chapter, or

(B) any dividend received (directly or through a wholly owned foreign corporation) from a domestic corporation at least 80 percent of the stock of which (by vote and value) is owned (directly or through such wholly owned foreign corporation) by the qualified 10-percent owned foreign corporation.

(6) SPECIAL RULE.—If the 1st day on which the requirements of paragraph (2) are met with respect to any foreign corporation is in a taxable year of such corporation beginning after December 31, 1986, the post-1986 undistributed earnings and the post-1986 undistributed U.S. earnings of such corporation shall be determined by only taking into account periods beginning on and after the 1st day of the 1st taxable year in which such requirements are met.

(7) COORDINATION WITH SUBSECTION (b).—Earnings and profits of any qualified 10-percent owned foreign corporation for any taxable year shall not be taken into account under this subsection if the deduction provided by subsection (b) would be allowable with respect to dividends paid out of such earnings and profits.

(8) DISALLOWANCE OF FOREIGN TAX CREDIT.—No credit shall be allowed under section 901 for any taxes paid or accrued (or treated as paid or accrued) with respect to the United States-source portion of any dividend received by a corporation from a qualified 10-percent-owned foreign corporation.

(9) COORDINATION WITH SECTION 904.—For purposes of section 904, the U.S.-source portion of any dividend received by a corporation from a qualified 10-percent owned foreign corporation shall be treated as from sources in the United States.

(10) COORDINATION WITH TREATIES.—If—

(A) any portion of a dividend received by a corporation from a qualified 10-percent-owned foreign corporation would be treated as from sources in the United States under paragraph (9),

(B) under a treaty obligation of the United States (applied without regard to this subsection), such portion would be treated as arising from sources outside the United States, and

(C) the taxpayer chooses the benefits of this paragraph,

this subsection shall not apply to such dividend (but subsections (a), (b), and (c) of section 904 and sections 902, 907, and 960 shall be applied separately with respect to such portion of such dividend).

(11) COORDINATION WITH SECTION 1248.—For purposes of this subsection, the term "dividend" does not include any amount treated as a dividend under section 1248.

Amendments

• 2004, American Jobs Creation Act of 2004 (P.L. 108-357)

P.L. 108-357, §413(c)(3):

Amended Code Sec. 245(a)(2) by striking "foreign personal holding company or" immediately preceding "passive foreign investment company". **Effective** for tax years of foreign corporations beginning after 12-31-2004, and for tax years of United States shareholders with or within which such tax years of foreign corporations end.

• 1988, Technical and Miscellaneous Revenue Act of 1988 (P.L. 100-647)

P.L. 100-647, §1012(l)(2)(A), amended by P.L. 101-239, §7811(i)(14):

Amended Code Sec. 245(a)(8). **Effective** as if included in the provision of P.L. 99-514 to which it relates. Prior to amendment, Code Sec. 245(a)(8) read as follows:

(8) COORDINATION WITH SECTION 902.—In the case of a dividend received by a corporation from a qualified 10-percent owned foreign corporation, no credit shall be allowed under section 901 for any taxes treated as paid under section 902 with respect to the U.S.-source portion of such dividend.

P.L. 100-647, §1012(l)(2)(B):

Amended Code Sec. 245(a) by adding at the end thereof new paragraph (10). **Effective** as if included in the provision of P.L. 99-514 to which it relates.

P.L. 100-647, §1012(l)(3):

Amended Code Sec. 245(a) by adding at the end thereof a new paragraph (11). **Effective** as if included in the provision of P.L. 99-514 to which it relates.

• 1986, Tax Reform Act of 1986 (P.L. 99-514)

P.L. 99-514, §1226(a):

Amended Code Sec. 245(a). **Effective** for distributions out of earnings and profits for tax years beginning after 12-31-86. Prior to amendment, Code Sec. 245(a) read as follows:

(a) GENERAL RULE.—In the case of dividends received from a foreign corporation (other than a foreign personal holding company) which is subject to taxation under this chapter, if, for an uninterrupted period of not less than 36 months ending with the close of such foreign corporation's taxable year in which such dividends are paid (or, if the corporation has not been in existence for 36 months at the close of such taxable year, for the period the foreign corporation has been in existence as of the close of such taxable year) such foreign corporation has been engaged in trade or business within the United States and if 50 percent or more of the gross income of such corporation from all sources for such period is effectively connected with the conduct of a trade or business within the United States, there shall be allowed as a deduction in the case of a corporation—

(1) An amount equal to the percent (specified in section 243 for the taxable year) of the dividends received out of its earnings and profits specified in paragraph (2) of the first sentence of section 316(a), but such amount shall not exceed an amount which bears the same ratio to such percent of such dividends received out of such earnings and profits as the gross income of such foreign corporation for the taxable year which is effectively connected with the conduct of a trade or business within the United States bears to its gross income from all sources for such taxable year, and

(2) An amount equal to the percent (specified in section 243 for the taxable year) of the dividends received out of that part of its earnings and profits specified in paragraph (1) of the first sentence of section 316(a) accumulated after the beginning of such uninterrupted period, but such amount shall not exceed an amount which bears the same ratio to such percent of such dividends received out of such accumulated earnings and profits as the gross income of such foreign corporation, which is effectively connected with the conduct of a trade or business within the United States, for the portion of such uninterrupted period ending at the beginning of such taxable year bears to its gross income from all sources for such portion of such uninterrupted period.

For purposes of this subsection, the gross income of the foreign corporation for any period before the first taxable year beginning after December 31, 1966, which is effectively connected with the conduct of a trade or business within the United States is an amount equal to the gross income for such period from sources within the United States. For purposes of paragraph (2), there shall not be taken into account any taxable year within such uninterrupted period if, with respect to dividends paid out of the earnings and profits of such year, the deduction provided by subsection (b) would be allowable.

• 1966, Foreign Investors Tax Act of 1966 (P.L. 89-809)

P.L. 89-809, §104(d):

Amended Code Sec. 245(a) by substituting "and if 50 percent or more of the gross income of such corporation from all sources for such period is effectively connected with the conduct of a trade or business within the United States," for "and has derived 50 percent or more of its gross income from sources within the United States,", by substituting "which is effectively connected with the conduct of a trade or business within the United States" for "from sources within the United States", by substituting ", which is effectively connected with the conduct of a trade or business within the United States," for "from sources within the United States", and by adding after paragraph (2) the last sentence. **Effective** 1-1-67.

P.L. 89-809, §104(e)(2):

Added the last sentence (after the sentence added by §104(d) above) to Sec. 245(a). **Effective** 1-1-67.

• 1962, Revenue Act of 1962 (P.L. 87-834)

P.L. 87-834, §5:

Amended Code Sec. 245 by inserting "(a) General Rule.—" at the beginning of first paragraph. **Effective** for distributions made after 12-31-62.

[Sec. 245(b)]

(b) CERTAIN DIVIDENDS RECEIVED FROM WHOLLY OWNED FOREIGN SUBSIDIARIES.—

(1) IN GENERAL.—In the case of dividends described in paragraph (2) received from a foreign corporation by a domestic corporation which, for its taxable year in which such dividends are received, owns (directly or indirectly) all of the outstanding stock of such foreign corporation, there shall be allowed as a deduction (in lieu of the deduction provided by subsection (a)) an amount equal to 100 percent of such dividends.

(2) ELIGIBLE DIVIDENDS.—Paragraph (1) shall apply only to dividends which are paid out of the earnings and profits of a foreign corporation for a taxable year during which—

(A) all of its outstanding stock is owned (directly or indirectly) by the domestic corporation to which such dividends are paid; and

(B) all of its gross income from all sources is effectively connected with the conduct of a trade or business within the United States.

(3) EXCEPTION.—Paragraph (1) shall not apply to any dividends if an election under section 1562 is effective for either—

(A) the taxable year of the domestic corporation in which such dividends are received, or

(B) the taxable year of the foreign corporation out of the earnings and profits of which such dividends are paid.

Amendments

• **1966, Foreign Investors Tax Act of 1966 (P.L. 89-809)**

P.L. 89-809, §104(e)(1):

Redesignated former Code Sec. 245(b) as Sec. 245(c) and added new Code Sec. 245(b). **Effective** 1-1-67.

[Sec. 245(c)]

(c) CERTAIN DIVIDENDS RECEIVED FROM FSC.—

(1) IN GENERAL.—In the case of a domestic corporation, there shall be allowed as a deduction an amount equal to—

(A) 100 percent of any dividend received from another corporation which is distributed out of earnings and profits attributable to foreign trade income for a period during which such other corporation was a FSC, and

(B) 70 percent (80 percent in the case of dividends from a 20-percent owned corporation as defined in section 243(c)(2)) of any dividend received from another corporation which is distributed out of earnings and profits attributable to effectively connected income received or accrued by such other corporation while such other corporation was a FSC.

(2) EXCEPTION FOR CERTAIN DIVIDENDS.—Paragraph (1) shall not apply to any dividend which is distributed out of earnings and profits attributable to foreign trade income which—

(A) is section 923(a)(2) nonexempt income (within the meaning of section 927(d)(6)), or

(B) would not, but for section 923(a)(4), be treated as exempt foreign trade income.

(3) NO DEDUCTION UNDER SUBSECTION (a) OR (b).—No deduction shall be allowable under subsection (a) or (b) with respect to any dividend which is distributed out of earnings and profits of a corporation accumulated while such corporation was a FSC.

(4) DEFINITIONS.—For purposes of this subsection—

(A) FOREIGN TRADE INCOME; EXEMPT FOREIGN TRADE INCOME.—The terms "foreign trade income" and "exempt foreign trade income" have the respective meanings given such terms by section 923.

(B) EFFECTIVELY CONNECTED INCOME.—The term "effectively connected income" means any income which is effectively connected (or treated as effectively connected) with the conduct of a trade or business in the United States and is subject to tax under this chapter. Such term shall not include any foreign trade income.

(C) FSC.—The term "FSC" has the meaning given such term by section 922.

(5) REFERENCES TO PRIOR LAW.—Any reference in this subsection to section 922, 923, or 927 shall be treated as a reference to such section as in effect before its repeal by the FSC Repeal and Extraterritorial Income Exclusion Act of 2000.

Amendments

• **2007, Tax Technical Corrections Act of 2007 (P.L. 110-172)**

P.L. 110-172, §11(g)(3):

Amended Code Sec. 245(c)(4) by adding at the end a new subparagraph (C). **Effective** 12-29-2007.

P.L. 110-172, §11(g)(4):

Amended Code Sec. 245(c) by adding at the end a new paragraph (5). **Effective** 12-29-2007.

• **1988, Technical and Miscellaneous Revenue Act of 1988 (P.L. 100-647)**

P.L. 100-647, §1012(bb)(9)(A):

Amended Code Sec. 245(c). **Effective** as if included in the provision of P.L. 98-369 to which it relates. For a special rule, see Act Sec. 1006(b)(1)(A), below. Prior to amendment, Code Sec. 245(c) read as follows:

(c) CERTAIN DIVIDENDS RECEIVED FROM FSC.—

(1) IN GENERAL.—In the case of a domestic corporation, there shall be allowed as a deduction an amount equal to—

(A) 100 percent of any dividend received by such corporation from another corporation which is distributed out of earnings and profits attributable to foreign trade income for a period during which such other corporation was a FSC, and

(B) 70 percent (80 percent in the case of dividends from a 20-percent owned corporation as defined in section 243(c)(2)) of any dividend received by such corporation from another corporation which is distributed out of earnings and profits attributable to qualified interest and carrying charges received or accrued by such other corporation while such other corporation was a FSC.

The deduction allowable under the preceding sentence with respect to any dividend shall be in lieu of any deduction allowable under subsection (a) or (b) with respect to such dividend.

(2) EXCEPTION FOR CERTAIN DIVIDENDS.—Paragraph (1) shall not apply to any dividend which is distributed out of earnings and profits attributable to foreign trade income which—

(A) is section 923(a)(2) non-exempt income (within the meaning of section 927(d)(6)), or

(B) would not, but for section 923(a)(4), be treated as exempt foreign trade income.

(3) COORDINATION WITH SUBSECTIONS (a) AND (b).—The gross income giving rise to the earnings and profits described in subparagraph (A) or (B) of paragraph (1) (and not described in paragraph (2)) shall not be taken into account under subsections (a) and (b).

(4) DEFINITIONS.—For purposes of this subsection, the term "foreign trade income" and "exempt foreign trade income" have the meaning given such terms by section 923. For purposes of this subsection, the term "qualified interest and carrying charges" means any interest or carrying charges (as defined in section 927(d)(1)) derived from a transaction which results in foreign trade income.

P.L. 100-647, §1006(b)(1)(A), provides:

(1) In the case of dividends received or accrued during 1987—

(A) subparagraph (B) of section 245(c)(1) of the 1986 Code shall be applied by substituting "80 percent" for the percentage specified therein, . . .

• 1987, Revenue Act of 1987 (P.L. 100-203)

P.L. 100-203, §10221(d)(1):

Amended Code Sec. 245(c)(1)(B) by striking out "85 percent" and inserting in lieu thereof "70 percent (80 percent in the case of dividends from a 20-percent owned corporation as defined in section 243(c)(2))". **Effective** for dividends received or accrued after 12-31-87, in tax years ending after such date.

• 1986, Tax Reform Act of 1986 (P.L. 99-514)

P.L. 99-514, §1876(d)(1)(A):

Amended Code Sec. 245(c)(1). **Effective** as if included in the provision of P.L. 98-369 to which it relates. Prior to amendment, Code Sec. 245(c)(1) read as follows:

(1) IN GENERAL.—In the case of a domestic corporation, there shall be allowed as a deduction an amount equal to 100 percent of any dividend received by such corporation from another corporation which is distributed out of earnings and profits attributable to foreign trade income for a period during which such other corporation was a FSC. The deduction allowable under the preceding sentence with respect to any dividend shall be in lieu of any deduction allowable under subsection (a) or (b) with respect to such dividend.

P.L. 99-514, §1876(d)(1)(B):

Amended Code Sec. 245(c)(3) by adding at the end thereof a new sentence. **Effective** as if included in the provision of P.L. 98-369 to which it relates.

P.L. 99-514, §1876(j):

Amended Code Sec. 245(c) by redesignating paragraph (3) as paragraph (4) and by inserting after paragraph (2) new paragraph (3). **Effective** as if included in the provision of P.L. 98-369 to which it relates.

• 1984, Deficit Reduction Act of 1984 (P.L. 98-369)

P.L. 98-369, §801(b)(1):

Amended Code Sec. 245 by redesignating subsection (c) as subsection (d) and inserting new subsection (c). **Effective** for transactions after 12-31-84, in tax years ending after such date.

[Sec. 245(d)—Repealed]

Amendments

• 1988, Technical and Miscellaneous Revenue Act of 1988 (P.L. 100-647)

P.L. 100-647, §1006(e)(16):

Repealed Code Sec. 245(d). **Effective** as if included in the provision of P.L. 99-514 to which it relates. Prior to repeal, Code Sec. 245(d) read as follows:

(d) PROPERTY DISTRIBUTIONS.—For purposes of this section, the amount of any distribution of property other than money shall be the amount determined by applying section 301(b)(1)(B).

• 1984, Deficit Reduction Act of 1984 (P.L. 98-369)

P.L. 98-369, §801(b)(1):

Amended Code Sec. 245 by redesignating subsection (c) as subsection (d). **Effective** for transactions after 12-31-84, in tax years ending after such date.

P.L. 98-369, §801(b)(2)(B):

Amended Code Sec. 245(d), as redesignated by Act Sec. 801(b)(1), by striking out "subsections (a) and (b)" and inserting in lieu thereof "this section". **Effective** for transactions after 12-31-84, in tax years ending after such date.

• 1966, Foreign Investors Tax Act of 1966 (P.L. 89-809)

P.L. 89-809, §104(e)(1):

Redesignated former Code Sec. 245(b) as Sec. 245(c). **Effective** 1-1-67.

P.L. 89-809, §104(e)(3):

Amended Code Sec. 245(c) by substituting "subsections (a) and (b)" for "subsection (a)". **Effective** 1-1-67.

• 1962, Revenue Act of 1962 (P.L. 87-834)

P.L. 87-834, §5:

Added to Code Sec. 245 a new subsection (b). **Effective** for distributions made after 12-31-62.

[Sec. 246]

SEC. 246. RULES APPLYING TO DEDUCTIONS FOR DIVIDENDS RECEIVED.

[Sec. 246(a)]

(a) DEDUCTION NOT ALLOWED FOR DIVIDENDS FROM CERTAIN CORPORATIONS.—

(1) IN GENERAL.—The deductions allowed by sections 243, 244, and 245 shall not apply to any dividend from a corporation which, for the taxable year of the corporation in which the distribution is made, or for the next preceding taxable year of the corporation, is a corporation exempt from tax under section 501 (relating to certain charitable, etc., organizations) or section 521 (relating to farmers' cooperative associations).

(2) SUBSECTION NOT TO APPLY TO CERTAIN DIVIDENDS OF FEDERAL HOME LOAN BANKS.—

(A) DIVIDENDS OUT OF CURRENT EARNINGS AND PROFITS.—In the case of any dividend paid by any FHLB out of earnings and profits of the FHLB for the taxable year in which such dividend was paid, paragraph (1) shall not apply to that portion of such dividend which bears the same ratio to the total dividend as—

(i) the dividends received by the FHLB from the FHLMC during such taxable year, bears to

(ii) the total earnings and profits of the FHLB for such taxable year.

(B) DIVIDENDS OUT OF ACCUMULATED EARNINGS AND PROFITS.—In the case of any dividend which is paid out of any accumulated earnings and profits of any FHLB, paragraph (1) shall not apply to that portion of the dividend which bears the same ratio to the total dividend as—

(i) the amount of dividends received by such FHLB from the FHLMC which are out of earnings and profits of the FHLMC—

(I) for taxable years ending after December 31, 1984, and

(II) which were not previously treated as distributed under subparagraph (A) or this subparagraph, bears to

(ii) the total accumulated earnings and profits of the FHLB as of the time such dividend is paid.

For purposes of clause (ii), the accumulated earnings and profits of the FHLB as of Janaury 1, 1985, shall be treated as equal to its retained earnings as of such date.

(C) COORDINATION WITH SECTION 243.—To the extent that paragraph (1) does not apply to any dividend by reason of subparagraph (A) or (B) of this paragraph, the requirement contained in section 243(a) that the corporation paying the dividend be subject to taxation under this chapter shall not apply.

(D) DEFINITIONS.—For purposes of this paragraph—

(i) FHLB.—The term "FHLB" means any Federal Home Loan Bank.

(ii) FHLMC.—The term "FHLMC" means the Federal Home Loan Mortgage Corporation.

(iii) TAXABLE YEAR OF FHLB.—The taxable year of an FHLB shall, except as provided in regulations prescribed by the Secretary, be treated as the calendar year.

(iv) EARNINGS AND PROFITS.—The earnings and profits of any FHLB for any taxable year shall be treated as equal to the sum of—

(I) any dividends received by the FHLB from the FHLMC during such taxable year, and

(II) the total earnings and profits (determined without regard to dividends described in subclause (I)) of the FHLB as reported in its annual financial statement prepared in accordance with section 20 of the Federal Home Loan Bank Act (12 U.S.C. 1440).

Amendments

• 1986, Tax Reform Act of 1986 (P.L. 99-514)

P.L. 99-514, §1812(d)(1)(A)(i) and (ii):

Amended Code Sec. 246(a)(2)(B) by striking out "For purposes of subparagraph (A), in" and inserting in lieu thereof "In", and by striking out subclause (II) of clause (i) and inserting in lieu thereof new subclause (II). **Effective** as if included in the provision of P.L. 98-369 to which it relates. Prior to amendment, Code Sec. 246(a)(2)(B)(i)(II) read as follows:

(II) which were not taken into account under subparagraph (A), bears to

P.L. 99-514, §1812(d)(1)(B):

Amended Code Sec. 246(a)(2) by redesignating subparagraph (C) as subparagraph (D) and by inserting after subparagraph (B) new subparagraph (C). **Effective** as if included in the provision of P.L. 98-369 to which it relates.

P.L. 99-514, §1812(d)(1)(C):

Amended Code Sec. 246(a)(2)(D), as redesignated by Sec. 1812(d)(1)(B) of the Act, by adding at the end thereof new clause (iv). **Effective** as if included in the provision of P.L. 98-369 to which it relates.

• 1984, Deficit Reduction Act of 1984 (P.L. 98-369)

P.L. 98-369, §177(b):

Amended Code Sec. 246(a). **Effective** 1-1-85. Special rules appear in Act Sec. 177(d)(2)-(7), as amended by P.L. 99-514, §1812(d)(2), below. Prior to amendment, Code Sec. 246(a) read as follows:

(a) Deduction Not Allowed for Dividends from Certain Corporations.—The deductions allowed by sections 243, 244, and 245 shall not apply to any dividend from a corporation which, for the taxable year of the corporation in which the distribution is made, or for the next preceding taxable year of the corporation, is a corporation exempt from tax under section 501 (relating to certain charitable, etc., organizations) or section 521 (relating to farmers' cooperative associations).

P.L. 98-369, §177(d)(2)-(7), provides:

(d) Effective Dates.—

***

(2) Adjusted Basis of Assets.—

(A) In General.—Except as otherwise provided in subparagraph (B), the adjusted basis of any asset of the Federal Home Loan Mortgage Corporation held on January 1, 1985, shall—

(i) for purposes of determining any loss, be equal to the lesser of the adjusted basis of such asset or the fair market value of such asset as of such date, and

(ii) for purposes of determining any gain, be equal to the higher of the adjusted basis of such asset or the fair market value of such asset as of such date.

(B) Special Rule for Tangible Depreciable Property.—In the case of any tangible property which—

(i) is of a character subject to the allowance for depreciation provided by section 167 of the Internal Revenue Code of 1954, and

(ii) is held by the Federal Home Loan Mortgage Corporation on January 1, 1985,

the adjusted basis of such property shall be equal to the lesser of the basis of such property or the fair market value of such property as of such date.

(3) Treatment of Participation Certificates.—

(A) In General.—Paragraph (2) shall not apply to any right to receive income with respect to any mortgage pool participation certificate or other similar interest in any mortgage (not including any mortgage).

(B) Treatment of Certain Sales After March 15, 1984, and Before January 1, 1985.—If any gain is realized on the sale or exchange of any right described in subparagraph (A) after March 15, 1984, and before January 1, 1985, the gain shall not be recognized when realized but shall be recognized on January 1, 1985.

(4) Clarification of Earnings and Profits of Federal Home Loan Mortgage Corporation.—

(A) Treatment of Distribution of Preferred Stock, Etc.—For purposes of the Internal Revenue Code of 1954, the distribution of preferred stock by the Federal Home Loan Mortgage Corporation during December of 1984, and the other distributions of such stock by Federal Home Loan Banks during January of 1985, shall be treated as if they were distributions of money equal to the fair market value of the stock on the date of the distribution by the Federal Home Loan Banks (and such stock shall be treated as if it were purchased with the money treated as so distributed). No deduction shall be allowed under section 243 of the Internal Revenue Code of 1954 with respect to any dividend paid by the Federal Home Loan Mortgage Corporation out of earnings and profits accumulated before January 1, 1985.

(B) Section 246(a) Not to Apply to Distributions Out of Earnings and Profits Accumulated During 1985.—Subsection (a) of section 246 of the Internal Revenue Code of 1954 shall not apply to any dividend paid by the Federal Home Loan Mortgage Corporation during 1985 out of earnings and profits accumulated after December 31, 1984.

(5) Adjusted Basis.—For purposes of this subsection, the adjusted basis of any asset shall be determined under part II of subchapter O of the Internal Revenue Code of 1954.

(6) No Carrybacks for Years Before 1985.—No net operating loss, capital loss, or excess credit of the Federal Home Loan Mortgage Corporation for any taxable year beginning after December 31, 1984, shall be allowed as a carryback to any taxable year beginning before January 1, 1985.

(7) No Deduction Allowed for Interest on Replacement Obligations.—

(A) In General.—The Federal Home Loan Mortgage Corporation shall not be allowed any deduction for interest accruing after December 31, 1984, on any replacement obligation.

(B) Replacement Obligation Defined.—For purposes of subparagraph (A), the term "replacement obligation" means any obligation to any person created after March 15, 1984, which the Secretary of the Treasury or his delegate determines replaces any equity or debt interest of a Federal Home Loan Bank or any other person in the Federal Home Loan Mortgage Corporation existing on such date. The preceding sentence shall not apply to any obligation with respect to which the Federal Home Loan Mortgage Corporation establishes that there is no tax avoidance effect.

• 1976, Tax Reform Act of 1976 (P.L. 94-455)

P.L. 94-455, §1051(f)(3):

Amended Code Sec. 246(a). **Effective** for tax years beginning after 12-31-75. Prior to amendment, Code Sec. 246(a) read as follows:

(a) DEDUCTION NOT ALLOWED FOR DIVIDENDS FROM CERTAIN CORPORATIONS.—The deductions allowed by sections 243, 244, and 245 shall not apply to any dividend from—

(1) a corporation organized under the China Trade Act, 1922 (see sec. 941); or

(2) a corporation which, for the taxable year of the corporation in which the distribution is made, or the next preceding taxable year of the corporation, is—

(A) a corporation exempt from tax under section 501 (relating to certain charitable, etc., organizations) or section 521 (relating to farmers' cooperative associations); or

(B) a corporation to which section 931 (relating to income from sources within possessions of the United States) applies.

[Sec. 246(b)]

(b) LIMITATION ON AGGREGATE AMOUNT OF DEDUCTIONS.—

(1) GENERAL RULE.—Except as provided in paragraph (2), the aggregate amount of the deductions allowed by sections 243(a)(1), 244(a), and subsection (a) or (b) of section 245 shall not exceed the percentage determined under paragraph (3) of the taxable income computed without regard to the deductions allowed by sections 172, 199, 243(a)(1), 244(a), subsection (a) or (b) of section 245, and 247, without regard to any adjustment under section 1059, and without regard to any capital loss carryback to the taxable year under section 1212(a)(1).

(2) EFFECT OF NET OPERATING LOSS.—Paragraph (1) shall not apply for any taxable year for which there is a net operating loss (as determined under section 172).

(3) SPECIAL RULES.—The provisions of paragraph (1) shall be applied—

(A) first separately with respect to dividends from 20-percent owned corporations (as defined in section 243(c)(2)) and the percentage determined under this paragraph shall be 80 percent, and

(B) then separately with respect to dividends not from 20-percent owned corporations and the percentage determined under this paragraph shall be 70 percent and the taxable income shall be reduced by the aggregate amount of dividends from 20-percent owned corporations (as so defined).

Amendments

• 2004, American Jobs Creation Act of 2004 (P.L. 108-357)

P.L. 108-357, §102(d)(4):

Amended Code Sec. 246(b)(1) by inserting "199," after "172,". **Effective** for tax years beginning after 12-31-2004.

• 1987, Revenue Act of 1987 (P.L. 100-203)

P.L. 100-203, §10221(c)(1)(A)-(B):

Amended Code Sec. 246(b) by striking out "80 percent" in paragraph (1) and inserting in lieu thereof "the percentage determined under paragraph (3)", and by adding at the end thereof new paragraph (3). **Effective** for tax years beginning after 12-31-87 [**effective** date changed by P.L. 100-647, §2004(i)(1)].

• 1986, Tax Reform Act of 1986 (P.L. 99-514)

P.L. 99-514, §611(a)(3):

Amended Code Sec. 246(b)(1) by striking out "85 percent" and inserting in lieu thereof "80 percent". **Effective** for tax years beginning after 12-31-86.

• 1984, Deficit Reduction Act of 1984 (P.L. 98-369)

P.L. 98-369, §53(d)(2):

Amended Code Sec. 246(b)(1) by striking out "and without regard" and inserting in lieu thereof "without regard to any adjustment under section 1059, and without regard". **Effective** for distributions after 3-1-84, in tax years ending after such date.

P.L. 98-369, §801(b)(2)(A):

Amended Code Sec. 246(b)(1) by striking out "245" each place it appeared and inserting in lieu thereof "subsection (a) or (b) of section 245". **Effective** for transactions after 12-31-84, in tax years ending after such date.

• 1969, Tax Reform Act of 1969 (P.L. 91-172)

P.L. 91-172, §512(f):

Amended Code Sec. 246(b)(1) by adding ", and without regard to any capital loss carryback to the taxable year under section 1212(a)(1)" after "and 247". **Effective** with regard to net capital losses sustained in tax years beginning after 12-31-69.

• 1964, Revenue Act of 1964 (P.L. 88-272)

P.L. 88-272, §214(b)(2):

Amended subsection (b) by substituting "243(a)(1), 244(a)" in lieu of "243(a), 244". **Effective** 1-1-64.

• 1958, Technical Amendments Act of 1958 (P.L. 85-866)

P.L. 85-866, §57(c)(2):

Struck out "243" each place where it appeared in Sec. 246(b)(1) and substituted "243(a)". **Effective** 9-3-58.

[Sec. 246(c)]

(c) EXCLUSION OF CERTAIN DIVIDENDS.—

(1) IN GENERAL.—No deduction shall be allowed under section 243, 244, or 245, in respect of any dividend on any share of stock—

(A) which is held by the taxpayer for 45 days or less during the 91-day period beginning on the date which is 45 days before the date on which such share becomes ex-dividend with respect to such dividend, or

(B) to the extent that the taxpayer is under an obligation (whether pursuant to a short sale or otherwise) to make related payments with respect to positions in substantially similar or related property.

(2) 90-DAY RULE IN THE CASE OF CERTAIN PREFERENCE DIVIDENDS.—In the case of stock having preference in dividends, if the taxpayer receives dividends with respect to such stock which are attributable to a period or periods aggregating in excess of 366 days, paragraph (1)(A) shall be applied—

(A) by substituting "90 days" for "45 days" each place it appears, and

(B) by substituting "181-day period" for "91-day period".

(3) DETERMINATION OF HOLDING PERIODS.—For purposes of this subsection, in determining the period for which the taxpayer has held any share of stock—

(A) the day of disposition, but not the day of acquisition, shall be taken into account, and

(B) paragraph (3) of section 1223 shall not apply.

(4) HOLDING PERIOD REDUCED FOR PERIODS WHERE RISK OF LOSS DIMINISHED.—The holding periods determined for purposes of this subsection shall be appropriately reduced (in the manner provided in regulations prescribed by the Secretary) for any period (during such periods) in which—

(A) the taxpayer has an option to sell, is under a contractual obligation to sell, or has made (and not closed) a short sale of, substantially identical stock or securities,

(B) the taxpayer is the grantor of an option to buy substantially identical stock or securities, or

(C) under regulations prescribed by the Secretary, a taxpayer has diminished his risk of loss by holding 1 or more other positions with respect to substantially similar or related property.

The preceding sentence shall not apply in the case of any qualified covered call (as defined in section 1092(c)(4) but without regard to the requirement that gain or loss with respect to the option not be ordinary income or loss), other than a qualified covered call option to which section 1092(f) applies.

Amendments

• 2005, Gulf Opportunity Zone Act of 2005 (P.L. 109-135)

P.L. 109-135, §402(a)(4):

Amended Code Sec. 246(c)(3)(B) by striking "paragraph (4) of section 1223" and inserting "paragraph (3) of section 1223". **Effective** as if included in the provision of the Energy Policy Act of 2005 (P.L. 109-58) to which it relates [**effective** 2-8-2006.—CCH]. For a special rule, see Act Sec. 402(m)(2), below.

P.L. 109-135, §402(m)(2), provides:

(2) REPEAL OF PUBLIC UTILITY HOLDING COMPANY ACT OF 1935.—The amendments made by subsection (a) shall not apply with respect to any transaction ordered in compliance with the Public Utility Holding Company Act of 1935 before its repeal.

• 2004, American Jobs Creation Act of 2004 (P.L. 108-357)

P.L. 108-357, §888(d):

Amended Code Sec. 246(c) by inserting ", other than a qualified covered call option to which section 1092(f) applies" in the last sentence before the period at the end. **Effective** for positions established on or after 10-22-2004.

• 2004, Working Families Tax Relief Act of 2004 (P.L. 108-311)

P.L. 108-311, §406(f)(1):

Amended Code Sec. 246(c)(1)(A) by striking "90-day period", and inserting "91-day period". **Effective** as if included in the provision of the Taxpayer Relief Act of 1997 (P.L. 105-34) to which it relates [**effective** for dividends received or accrued after 9-4-97.—CCH].

P.L. 108-311, §406(f)(2)(A)-(B):

Amended Code Sec. 246(c)(2)(B) by striking "180-day period" and inserting "181-day period", and by striking "90-day period" and inserting "91-day period". **Effective** as if included in the provision of the Taxpayer Relief Act of 1997 (P.L. 105-34) to which it relates [**effective** for dividends received or accrued after 9-4-97.—CCH].

• 1997, Taxpayer Relief Act of 1997 (P.L. 105-34)

P.L. 105-34, §1015(a):

Amended Code Sec. 246(c)(1)(A). **Effective**, generally, for dividends received or accrued after the 30th day after 8-5-97. For a transitional rule, see Act Sec. 1015(c)(2), below. Prior to amendment, Code Sec. 246(c)(1)(A) read as follows:

(A) which is held by the taxpayer for 45 days or less, or

P.L. 105-34, §1015(b)(1):

Amended Code Sec. 246(c)(2). **Effective**, generally, for dividends received or accrued after the 30th day after 8-5-97. For a transitional rule, see Act Sec. 1015(c)(2), below. Prior to amendment, Code Sec. 246(c)(2) read as follows:

(2) 90-DAY RULE IN THE CASE OF CERTAIN PREFERENCE DIVIDENDS.—In the case of any stock having preference in dividends, the holding period specified in paragraph (1)(A) shall be 90 days in lieu of 45 days if the taxpayer receives dividends with respect to such stock which are attributable to a period or periods aggregating in excess of 366 days.

P.L. 105-34, §1015(b)(2):

Amended Code Sec. 246(c)(3) by adding "and" at the end of subparagraph (A), by striking subparagraph (B), and by redesignating subparagraph (C) as subparagraph (B). **Effective**, generally, for dividends received or accrued after the 30th day after 8-5-97. For a transitional rule, see Act Sec. 1015(c)(2), below. Prior to being stricken, Code Sec. 246(c)(3)(B) read as follows:

(B) there shall not be taken into account any day which is more than 45 days (or 90 days in the case of stock to which paragraph (2) applies) after the date on which such share becomes ex-dividend, and

P.L. 105-34, §1015(c)(2), provides:

(2) TRANSITIONAL RULE.—The amendments made by this section shall not apply to dividends received or accrued during the 2-year period beginning on the date of the enactment of this Act if—

(A) the dividend is paid with respect to stock held by the taxpayer on June 8, 1997, and all times thereafter until the dividend is received,

(B) such stock is continuously subject to a position described in section 246(c)(4) of the Internal Revenue Code of 1986 on June 8, 1997, and all times thereafter until the dividend is received, and

(C) such stock and position are clearly identified in the taxpayer's records within 30 days after the date of the enactment of this Act.

Stock shall not be treated as meeting the requirement of subparagraph (B) if the position is sold, closed, or otherwise terminated and reestablished.

• 1988, Technical and Miscellaneous Revenue Act of 1988 (P.L. 100-647)

P.L. 100-647, §1018(u)(10):

Amended Code Sec. 246(c)(1)(A) by striking out "Which" and inserting in lieu thereof "which". **Effective** as if included in the provision of P.L. 99-514 to which it relates.

• 1986, Tax Reform Act of 1986 (P.L. 99-514)

P.L. 99-514, §1804(b)(1)(A):

Amended Code Sec. 246(c)(1)(A). **Effective** for stock acquired after 3-1-86. Prior to amendment, Code Sec. 246(c)(1)(A) read as follows:

(A) which is sold or otherwise disposed of in any case in which the taxpayer has held such share for 45 days or less, or

P.L. 99-514, §1804(b)(1)(B):

Amended Code Sec. 246(c)(4) by striking out "determined under paragraph (3)" and inserting in lieu thereof "determined for purposes of this subsection". **Effective** for stock acquired after 3-1-86.

• 1984, Deficit Reduction Act of 1984 (P.L. 98-369)

P.L. 98-369, §53(b)(1):

Amended Code Sec. 246(c) by striking out "15" each place it appeared and inserting in lieu thereof "45". **Effective** for stock acquired after 7-18-84, in tax years ending after such date.

P.L. 98-369, §53(b)(2):

Added Code Sec. 246(c)(4). **Effective** for stock acquired after 7-18-84, in tax years ending after such date.

P.L. 98-369, §53(b)(3):

Amended Code Sec. 246(c)(1)(B). **Effective** for stock acquired after 7-18-84, in tax years ending after such date. Prior to amendment, it read as follows:

(B) to the extent that the taxpayer is under an obligation (whether pursuant to a short sale or otherwise) to make corresponding payments with respect to substantially identical stock or securities.

P.L. 98-369, §53(b)(4):

Struck out the last sentence of Code Sec. 246(c)(3). **Effective** for stock acquired after 7-18-84, in tax years ending after such date. Prior to being stricken, the last sentence read as follows:

The holding periods determined under the preceding provisions of this paragraph shall be appropriately reduced (in the manner provided in regulations prescribed by the Secretary) for any period (during such holding periods) in which the taxpayer has an option to sell, is under a contractual obligation to sell, or has made (and not closed) a short sale of, substantially identical stock or securities.

• 1976, Tax Reform Act of 1976 (P.L. 94-455)

P.L. 94-455, §1906(b)(13)(A):

Amended 1954 Code by substituting "Secretary" for "Secretary or his delegate" each place it appeared. **Effective** 2-1-77.

• 1958, Technical Amendments Act of 1958 (P.L. 85-866)

P.L. 85-866, §18(a):

Added subsection (c) to Sec. 246. **Effective** for tax years ending after 12-31-57, but only for shares of stock acquired or short sales made after that date.

[Sec. 246(d)]

(d) DIVIDENDS FROM A DISC OR FORMER DISC.—No deduction shall be allowed under section 243 in respect of a dividend from a corporation which is a DISC or former DISC (as defined in section 992(a)) to the extent such dividend is paid out of the corporation's accumulated DISC income or previously taxed income, or is a deemed distribution pursuant to section 995(b)(1).

Amendments

• 1971, Revenue Act of 1971 (P.L. 92-178)

P.L. 92-178, §502(a):

Added Code Sec. 246(d) and renumbered former Code Sec. 246(d) to be Code Sec. 246(e). **Effective** date is governed by the effective date for Code Sec. 992.

[Sec. 246(e)]

(e) CERTAIN DISTRIBUTIONS TO SATISFY REQUIREMENTS.—No deduction shall be allowed under section 243(a) with respect to a dividend received pursuant to a distribution described in section 936(h)(4).

Amendments

• 1986, Tax Reform Act of 1986 (P.L. 99-514)

P.L. 99-514, §1275(a)(2)(B):

Amended Code Sec. 246(e) by striking out "or 934(e)(3)". For the **effective** date as well as special rules, see Act Sec. 1277, as amended by P.L. 100-647, §1012(z)(1)-(2), below.

P.L. 99-514, §1277, as amended by P.L. 100-647, §1012(z)(1)-(2), provides:

(a) IN GENERAL.—Except as otherwise provided in this section, the amendments made by this subtitle shall apply to taxable years beginning after December 31, 1986.

(b) SPECIAL RULE FOR GUAM, AMERICAN SAMOA, AND THE NORTHERN MARIANA ISLANDS.—The amendments made by this subtitle shall apply with respect to Guam, American Samoa, or the Northern Mariana Islands (and to residents thereof and corporations created or organized therein) only if (and so long as) an implementing agreement under section 1271 is in effect between the United States and such possession.

(c) SPECIAL RULES FOR THE VIRGIN ISLANDS.—

(1) IN GENERAL.—The amendments made by section 1275(c) shall apply with respect to the Virgin Islands (and residents thereof and corporations created or organized therein) only if (and so long as) an implementing agreement is in effect between the United States and the Virgin Islands with respect to the establishment of rules under which the evasion or avoidance of United States income tax shall not be permitted or facilitated by such possession. Any such implementing agreement shall be executed on behalf of the United States by the Secretary of the Treasury, after consultation with the Secretary of the Interior.

(2) SECTION 1275(b).—

(A) IN GENERAL.—The amendment made by section 1275(b) shall apply with respect to—

(i) any taxable year beginning after December 31, 1986, and

(ii) any pre-1987 open year.

(B) SPECIAL RULES.—In the case of any pre-1987 open year—

(i) the amendment made by section 1275(b) shall not apply to income from sources in the Virgin Islands or income effectively connected with the conduct of a trade or business in the Virgin Islands, and

(ii) the taxpayer shall be allowed a credit—

(I) against any additional tax imposed by subtitle A of the Internal Revenue Code of 1954 (by reason of the amendment made by section 1275(b)) on income not described in clause (i) and from sources in the United States,

(II) for any tax paid to the Virgin Islands before the date of the enactment of this Act and attributable to such income.

For purposes of clause (ii)(II), any tax paid before January 1, 1987, pursuant to a process in effect before August 16, 1986, shall be treated as paid before the date of the enactment of this Act.

(C) PRE-1987 OPEN YEAR.—For purposes of this paragraph, the term "pre-1987 open year" means any taxable year beginning before January 1, 1987, if on the date of the enactment of this Act the assessment of a deficiency of income tax for such taxable year is not barred by any law or rule of law.

(D) EXCEPTION.—In the case of any pre-1987 open year, the amendment made by section 1275(b) shall not apply to any domestic corporation if—

(i) during the fiscal year which ended May 31, 1986, such corporation was actively engaged directly or through a subsidiary in the conduct of a trade or business in the Virgin Islands and such trade or business consists of business related to marine activities, and

(ii) such corporation was incorporated on March 31, 1983, in Delaware.

(E) EXCEPTION FOR CERTAIN TRANSACTIONS.—

(i) IN GENERAL.—In the case of any pre-1987 open year, the amendment made by section 1275(b) shall not apply to any income derived from transactions described in clause (ii) by 1 or more corporations which were formed in Delaware on or about March 6, 1981, and which have owned 1 or more office buildings in St. Thomas, United States Virgin Islands, for at least 5 years before the date of the enactment of this Act.

(ii) DESCRIPTION OF TRANSACTIONS.—The transactions described in this clause are—

(I) the redemptions of limited partnership interest for cash and property described in an agreement (as amended) dated March 12, 1981,

(II) the subsequent disposition of the properties distributed in such redemptions, and

(III) interest earned before January 1, 1987, on bank deposits of proceeds received from such redemptions to the extent such deposits are located in the United States Virgin Islands.

(iii) LIMITATION.—The aggregate reduction in tax by reason of this subparagraph shall not exceed $8,312,000. If the taxes which would be payable as the result of the application of the amendment made by section 1275(b) to pre-1987 open years exceeds the limitation of the preceding sentence, such excess shall be treated as attributable to income received in taxable years in reverse chronological order.

(d) REPORT ON IMPLEMENTING AGREEMENTS.—If, during the 1-year period beginning on the date of the enactment of this Act, any implementing agreement described in subsection (b) or (c) is not executed, the Secretary of the Treasury or his delegate shall report to the Committee on Finance of the United States Senate, the Committee on Ways and Means, and the Committee on Interior and Insular Affairs of the House of Representatives with respect to—

(1) the status of such negotiations, and

(2) the reason why such agreement has not been executed.

(e) TREATMENT OF CERTAIN UNITED STATES PERSONS.—Except as otherwise provided in regulations prescribed by the Secretary of the Treasury or his delegate, if a United States person becomes a resident of Guam, American Samoa, or the Northern Mariana Islands, the rules of section 877(c) of the Internal Revenue Code of 1954 shall apply to such person during the 10-year period beginning when such person became such a resident. Notwithstanding subsection (b), the preceding sentence shall apply to dispositions after December 31, 1985, in taxable years ending after such date.

(f) EXEMPTION FROM WITHHOLDING.—Notwithstanding subsection (b), the modification of section 884 of the Internal Revenue Code of 1986 by reason of the amendment to section 881 of such Code by section 1273(b)(1) of this Act shall apply to taxable years beginning after December 31, 1986.

• 1982, Tax Equity and Fiscal Responsibility Act of 1982 (P.L. 97-248)

P.L. 97-248, §213(c):

Added subsection (e). **Effective** for tax years beginning after 12-31-82.

[Sec. 246(f)—Stricken]

Amendments

• 1996, Small Business Job Protection Act of 1996 (P.L. 104-188)

P.L. 104-188, §1616(b)(4):

Amended Code Sec. 246 by striking subsection (f). **Effective** for tax years beginning after 12-31-95. Prior to amendment, Code Sec. 246(f) read as follows:

(f) CROSS REFERENCE.—For special rule relating to mutual savings banks, etc., to which section 593 applies, see section 596.

• 1982, Tax Equity and Fiscal Responsibility Act of 1982 (P.L. 97-248)

P.L. 97-248, §213(c):

Redesignated subsection (e) as (f). **Effective** for tax years beginning after 12-31-82.

• 1971, Revenue Act of 1971 (P.L. 92-178)

P.L. 92-178, §502(a):

Added new Code Sec. 246(d) and renumbered former Code Sec. 246(d) as Code Sec. 246(e).

• 1969, Tax Reform Act of 1969 (P.L. 91-172)

P.L. 91-172, §434(b)(1):

Added Code Sec. 246(d). **Effective** for tax years beginning after 7-11-69.

[Sec. 246A]

SEC. 246A. DIVIDENDS RECEIVED DEDUCTION REDUCED WHERE PORTFOLIO STOCK IS DEBT FINANCED.

[Sec. 246A(a)]

(a) GENERAL RULE.—In the case of any dividend on debt-financed portfolio stock, there shall be substituted for the percentage which (but for this subsection) would be used in determining the amount of the deduction allowable under section 243, 244, or 245(a) a percentage equal to the product of—

(1) 70 percent (80 percent in the case of any dividend from a 20-percent owned corporation as defined in section 243(c)(2)), and

(2) 100 percent minus the average indebtedness percentage.

Amendments

• 1988, Technical and Miscellaneous Revenue Act of 1988 (P.L. 100-647)

P.L. 100-647, §1012(l)(1):

Amended Code Sec. 246A(a) by striking out the last sentence. **Effective** as if included in the provision of P.L. 99-514 to which it relates. Prior to amendment, the last sentence of Code Sec. 246A(a) read as follows:

The preceding sentence shall be applied before any determination of a ratio under paragraph (1) or (2) of section 245(a).

• 1987, Revenue Act of 1987 (P.L. 100-203)

P.L. 100-203, §10221(d)(2):

Amended Code Sec. 246A(a)(1) by striking out "80 percent" and inserting in lieu thereof "70 percent (80 percent in the case of any dividend from a 20-percent owned corporation as defined in section 243(c)(2))". **Effective** for dividends received or accrued after 12-31-87, in tax years ending after such date.

• 1986, Tax Reform Act of 1986 (P.L. 99-514)

P.L. 99-514, §611(a)(4):

Amended Code Sec. 246A(a)(1) by striking out "85 percent" and inserting in lieu thereof "80 percent". **Effective** for dividends received or accrued after 12-31-86, in tax years ending after such date.

P.L. 99-514, §1804(a)(1) and (2):

Amended Code Sec. 246A(a) by striking out "or 245" and inserting in lieu thereof "or 245(a)", and by adding at the end thereof a new sentence. **Effective** as if included in the provision of P.L. 98-369 to which it relates.

[Sec. 246A(b)]

(b) SECTION NOT TO APPLY TO DIVIDENDS FOR WHICH 100 PERCENT DIVIDENDS RECEIVED DEDUCTION ALLOWABLE.—Subsection (a) shall not apply to—

(1) qualifying dividends (as defined in section 243(b) without regard to section 243(d)(4)), and

(2) dividends received by a small business investment company operating under the Small Business Investment Act of 1958.

Amendments

• 2004, Working Families Tax Relief Act of 2004 (P.L. 108-311)

P.L. 108-311, §408(a)(9):

Amended Code Sec. 246A(b)(1) by striking "section 243(c)(4)" and inserting "section 243(d)(4)". **Effective** 10-4-2004.

[Sec. 246A(c)]

(c) DEBT FINANCED PORTFOLIO STOCK.—For purposes of this section—

(1) IN GENERAL.—The term "debt financed portfolio stock" means any portfolio stock if at some time during the base period there is portfolio indebtedness with respect to such stock.

(2) PORTFOLIO STOCK.—The term "portfolio stock" means any stock of a corporation unless—

(A) as of the beginning of the ex-dividend date, the taxpayer owns stock of such corporation—

(i) possessing at least 50 percent of the total voting power of the stock of such corporation, and

(ii) having a value equal to at least 50 percent of the total value of the stock of such corporation, or

(B) as of the beginning of the ex-dividend date—

(i) the taxpayer owns stock of such corporation which would meet the requirements of subparagraph (A) if "20 percent" were substituted for "50 percent" each place it appears in such subparagraph, and

(ii) stock meeting the requirements of subparagraph (A) is owned by 5 or fewer corporate shareholders.

(3) SPECIAL RULE FOR STOCK IN A BANK OR BANK HOLDING COMPANY.—

(A) IN GENERAL.—If, as of the beginning of the ex-dividend date, the taxpayer owns stock of any bank or bank holding company having a value equal to at least 80 percent of the total value of the stock of such bank or bank holding company, for purposes of paragraph (2)(A)(i), the taxpayer shall be treated as owning any stock of such bank or bank holding company which the taxpayer has an option to acquire.

(B) DEFINITIONS.—For purposes of subparagraph (A)—

(i) BANK.—The term "bank" has the meaning given such term by section 581.

(ii) BANK HOLDING COMPANY.—The term "bank holding company" means a bank holding company (within the meaning of section 2(a) of the Bank Holding Company Act of 1956).

(4) TREATMENT OF CERTAIN PREFERRED STOCK.—For purposes of determining whether the requirements of subparagraph (A) or (B) of paragraph (2) or of subparagraph (A) of paragraph (3) are met, stock described in section 1504(a)(4) shall not be taken into account.

[Sec. 246A(d)]

(d) AVERAGE INDEBTEDNESS PERCENTAGE.—For purposes of this section—

(1) IN GENERAL.—Except as provided in paragraph (2), the term "average indebtedness percentage" means the percentage obtained by dividing—

(A) the average amount (determined under regulations prescribed by the Secretary) of the portfolio indebtedness with respect to the stock during the base period, by

(B) the average amount (determined under regulations prescribed by the Secretary) of the adjusted basis of the stock during the base period.

(2) SPECIAL RULE WHERE STOCK NOT HELD THROUGHOUT BASE PERIOD.—In the case of any stock which was not held by the taxpayer throughout the base period, paragraph (1) shall be applied as if the base period consisted only of that portion of the base period during which the stock was held by the taxpayer.

(3) PORTFOLIO INDEBTEDNESS.—

(A) IN GENERAL.—The term "portfolio indebtedness" means any indebtedness directly attributable to investment in the portfolio stock.

(B) CERTAIN AMOUNTS RECEIVED FROM SHORT SALE TREATED AS INDEBTEDNESS.—For purposes of subparagraph (A), any amount received from a short sale shall be treated as indebtedness for the period beginning on the day on which such amount is received and ending on the day the short sale is closed.

(4) BASE PERIOD.—The term "base period" means, with respect to any dividend, the shorter of—

(A) the period beginning on the ex-dividend date for the most recent previous dividend on the stock and ending on the day before the ex-dividend date for the dividend involved, or

(B) the 1-year period ending on the day before the ex-dividend date for the dividend involved.

[Sec. 246A(e)]

(e) REDUCTION IN DIVIDENDS RECEIVED DEDUCTION NOT TO EXCEED ALLOCABLE INTEREST.—Under regulations prescribed by the Secretary, any reduction under this section in the amount allowable as a deduction under section 243, 244, or 245 with respect to any dividend shall not exceed the amount of any interest deduction (including any deductible short sale expense) allocable to such dividend.

[Sec. 246A(f)]

(f) REGULATIONS.—The regulations prescribed for purposes of this section under section 7701(f) shall include regulations providing for the disallowance of interest deductions or other appropriate treatment (in lieu of reducing the dividend received deduction) where the obligor of the indebtedness is a person other than the person receiving the dividend.

Amendments

• 1984, Deficit Reduction Act of 1984 (P.L. 98-369)

P.L. 98-369, §51(a):

Amended Part VIII of subchapter B of chapter 1 by inserting after Code Sec. 246 new Code Sec. 246A. **Effective** for stock the holding period for which begins after 7-18-84 in tax years ending after such date.

[Sec. 247]

SEC. 247. DIVIDENDS PAID ON CERTAIN PREFERRED STOCK OF PUBLIC UTILITIES.

[Sec. 247(a)]

(a) AMOUNT OF DEDUCTION.—In the case of a public utility, there shall be allowed as a deduction an amount computed as follows:

(1) First determine the amount which is the lesser of—

(A) the amount of dividends paid during the taxable year on its preferred stock, or

(B) the taxable income for the taxable year (computed without the deduction allowed by this section).

(2) Then multiply the amount determined under paragraph (1) by the fraction—

(A) the numerator of which is 14 percent, and

(B) the denominator of which is that percentage which equals the highest rate of tax specified in section 11(b).

For purposes of the deduction provided in this section, the amount of dividends paid shall not include any amount distributed in the current taxable year with respect to dividends unpaid and accumulated in any taxable year ending before October 1, 1942. Amounts distributed in the current taxable year with respect to dividends unpaid and accumulated for a prior taxable year shall for purposes of this subsection be deemed to be distributed with respect to the earliest year or years for which there are dividends unpaid and accumulated.

Amendments

• 1978, Revenue Act of 1978 (P.L. 95-600)

P.L. 95-600, §301(b)(4):

Amended Code Sec. 247(a)(2)(B) by striking out "the sum of the normal tax rate and the surtax rate for the taxable year specified in section 11" and inserting in lieu thereof "the highest rate of tax specified in section 11(b)". **Effective** for tax years beginning after 12-31-78.

[Sec. 247(b)]

(b) DEFINITIONS.—For purposes of this section and section 244—

(1) PUBLIC UTILITY.—The term "public utility" means a corporation engaged in the furnishing of telephone service or in the sale of electrical energy, gas, or water, if the rates for such furnishing or sale, as the case may be, have been established or approved by a State or political subdivision thereof or by an agency or instrumentality of the United States or by a public utility or public service commission or other similar body of the District of Columbia or of any State or political subdivision thereof.

(2) PREFERRED STOCK.—

(A) IN GENERAL.—The term "preferred stock" means stock issued before October 1, 1942, which during the whole of the taxable year (or the part of the taxable year after its issue) was stock the dividends in respect of which were cumulative, limited to the same amount, and payable in preference to the payment of dividends on other stock.

(B) CERTAIN STOCK ISSUED ON OR AFTER OCTOBER 1, 1942.—Stock issued on or after October 1, 1942, shall be deemed for purposes of this paragraph to have been issued before October 1, 1942, if it was issued to refund or replace bonds or debentures issued before October 1, 1942, or to refund or replace other preferred stock (including stock which is preferred stock by reason of this subparagraph or subparagraph (D)), but only to the extent that the par or stated value of the new stock does not exceed the par, stated, or face value of the bonds or debentures issued before October 1, 1942, or the other preferred stock, which such new stock is issued to refund or replace.

(C) DETERMINATION UNDER REGULATIONS.—The determination of whether stock was issued to refund or replace bonds or debentures issued before October 1, 1942, or to refund or replace other preferred stock, shall be made under regulations prescribed by the Secretary.

(D) ISSUANCE OF STOCK.—For purposes of subparagraph (B), issuance of stock includes issuance either by the same or another corporation in a transaction which is a reorganization (as defined in section 368(a)) or a transaction subject to part VI of subchapter O as in effect before its repeal (relating to exchanges in SEC obedience orders), or the respectively corresponding provisions of the Internal Revenue Code of 1939.

Amendments

• 2005, Gulf Opportunity Zone Act of 2005 (P.L. 109-135)

P.L. 109-135, §402(a)(5):

Amended Code Sec. 247(b)(2)(D) by inserting "as in effect before its repeal" after "part VI of subchapter O". **Effective** as if included in the provision of the Energy Policy Act of 2005 (P.L. 109-58) to which it relates [**effective** 2-8-2006.—CCH]. For a special rule, see Act Sec. 402(m)(2), below.

P.L. 109-135, §402(m)(2), provides:

(2) REPEAL OF PUBLIC UTILITY HOLDING COMPANY ACT OF 1935.—The amendments made by subsection (a) shall not apply with respect to any transaction ordered in compliance with the Public Utility Holding Company Act of 1935 before its repeal.

• 1990, Omnibus Budget Reconciliation Act of 1990 (P.L. 101-508)

P.L. 101-508, §11801(c)(8)(C) (as amended by P.L. 104-188, §1704(t)(49)):

Amended Code Sec. 247(b)(2)(D) by striking ", a transaction to which section 371 (relating to insolvency reorganizations) applies," after "(as defined in section 368(a))". **Effective** 11-5-90.

P.L. 101-508, §11821(b), provides:

(b) SAVINGS PROVISION.—If—

(1) any provision amended or repealed by this part applied to—

(A) any transaction occurring before the date of the enactment of this Act,

(B) any property acquired before such date of enactment, or

(C) any item of income, loss, deduction, or credit taken into account before such date of enactment, and

(2) the treatment of such transaction, property, or item under such provision would (without regard to the amendments made by this part) affect liability for tax for periods ending after such date of enactment,

nothing in the amendments made by this part shall be construed to affect the treatment of such transaction, property, or item for purposes of determining liability for tax for periods ending after such date of enactment.

• **1976, Tax Reform Act of 1976 (P.L. 94-455)**

P.L. 94-455, §1901(a)(35):

Amended Code Sec. 247(b)(2). **Effective** for tax years beginning after 12-31-76. Prior to amendment, Code Sec. 247(b)(2) read as follows:

(2) PREFERRED STOCK.—The term "preferred stock" means stock issued before October 1, 1942, which during the whole of the taxable year (or the part of the taxable year after its issue) was stock the dividends in respect of which were cumulative, limited to the same amount, and payable in preference to the payment of dividends on other stock. Stock issued on or after October 1, 1942, shall be deemed for purposes of this paragraph to have been issued before October 1, 1942, if it was issued (including issuance either by the same or another corporation in a transaction which is a reorganization (as defined in section 368(a)), a transaction to which section 371 (relating to insolvency reorganizations) applies, or a transaction subject to part VI of subchapter O (relating to exchanges in SEC obedience orders), or the respectively corresponding provisions of the Internal Revenue Code of 1939) to refund or replace bonds or debentures issued before October 1, 1942, or to refund or replace other preferred stock (including stock which is preferred stock by reason of this sentence), but only to the extent that the par or stated value of the new stock does not exceed the par, stated, or face value of the bonds or debentures issued before October 1, 1942, or the other preferred stock, which such new stock is issued to refund or replace. The determination of whether stock was issued to refund or replace bonds or debentures issued before October 1, 1942, or to refund or replace other preferred stock, shall be made under regulations prescribed by the Secretary or his delegate.

[Sec. 248]

SEC. 248. ORGANIZATIONAL EXPENDITURES.

[Sec. 248(a)]

(a) ELECTION TO DEDUCT.—If a corporation elects the application of this subsection (in accordance with regulations prescribed by the Secretary) with respect to any organizational expenditures—

(1) the corporation shall be allowed a deduction for the taxable year in which the corporation begins business in an amount equal to the lesser of—

(A) the amount of organizational expenditures with respect to the taxpayer, or

(B) $5,000, reduced (but not below zero) by the amount by which such organizational expenditures exceed $50,000, and

(2) the remainder of such organizational expenditures shall be allowed as a deduction ratably over the 180-month period beginning with the month in which the corporation begins business.

Amendments

• **2004, American Jobs Creation Act of 2004 (P.L. 108-357)**

P.L. 108-357, §902(b):

Amended Code Sec. 248(a). **Effective** for amounts paid or incurred after 10-22-2004. Prior to amendment, Code Sec. 248(a) read as follows:

(a) ELECTION TO AMORTIZE.—The organizational expenditures of a corporation may, at the election of the corporation (made in accordance with regulations prescribed by the Secretary), be treated as deferred expenses. In computing taxable income, such deferred expenses shall be allowed as a deduction ratably over such period of not less than 60 months as may be selected by the corporation (beginning with the month in which the corporation begins business).

• **1976, Tax Reform Act of 1976 (P.L. 94-455)**

P.L. 94-455, §1906(b)(13)(A):

Amended 1954 Code by substituting "Secretary" for "Secretary or his delegate" each place it appeared. **Effective** 2-1-77.

[Sec. 248(b)]

(b) ORGANIZATIONAL EXPENDITURES DEFINED.—The term "organizational expenditures" means any expenditure which—

(1) is incident to the creation of the corporation;

(2) is chargeable to capital account; and

(3) is of a character which, if expended incident to the creation of a corporation having a limited life, would be amortizable over such life.

[Sec. 248(c)]

(c) TIME FOR AND SCOPE OF ELECTION.—The election provided by subsection (a) may be made for any taxable year beginning after December 31, 1953, but only if made not later than the time prescribed by law for filing the return for such taxable year (including extensions thereof). The period so elected shall be adhered to in computing the taxable income of the corporation for the taxable year for which the election is made and all subsequent taxable years. The election shall apply only with respect to expenditures paid or incurred on or after August 16, 1954.

Amendments

• **1976, Tax Reform Act of 1976 (P.L. 94-455)**

P.L. 94-455, §1901(a)(36):

Substituted "August 16, 1954" for "the date of enactment of this title" in Code Sec. 248(c). **Effective** for tax years beginning after 12-31-76.

[Sec. 249]

SEC. 249. LIMITATION ON DEDUCTION OF BOND PREMIUM ON REPURCHASE.

[Sec. 249(a)]

(a) GENERAL RULE.—No deduction shall be allowed to the issuing corporation for any premium paid or incurred upon the repurchase of a bond, debenture, note, or certificate or other evidence of indebtedness which is convertible into the stock of the issuing corporation, or a corporation in control of, or controlled by, the issuing corporation, to the extent the repurchase price exceeds an amount equal to the adjusted issue price plus a normal call premium on bonds or other evidences of indebtedness which are not convertible. The preceding sentence shall not apply to the extent that the corporation can demonstrate to the satisfaction of the Secretary that such excess is attributable to the cost of borrowing and is not attributable to the conversion feature.

Amendments

• 1976, Tax Reform Act of 1976 (P.L. 94-455)

P.L. 94-455, §1906(b)(13)(A):

Amended 1954 Code by substituting "Secretary" for "Secretary or his delegate" each place it appeared. **Effective** 2-1-77.

[Sec. 249(b)]

(b) SPECIAL RULES.—For purposes of subsection (a)—

(1) ADJUSTED ISSUE PRICE.—The adjusted issue price is the issue price (as defined in sections 1273(b) and 1274) increased by any amount of discount deducted before repurchase, or, in the case of bonds or other evidences of indebtedness issued after February 28, 1913, decreased by any amount of premium included in gross income before repurchase by the issuing corporation.

(2) CONTROL.—The term "control" has the meaning assigned to such term by section 368(c).

Amendments

• 1984, Deficit Reduction Act of 1984 (P.L. 98-369)

P.L. 98-369, §42(a)(5):

Amended Code Sec. 249(b)(1) by striking out "section 1232(b)" and inserting in lieu thereof "sections 1273(b) and 1274". **Effective** for tax years ending after 7-18-84.

• 1969, Tax Reform Act of 1969 (P.L. 91-172)

P.L. 91-172, §414(a):

Added Sec. 249. **Effective** for a convertible bond or other convertible evidence of indebtedness repurchased after 4-22-69, other than such a bond or other evidence of indebtedness repurchased pursuant to a binding obligation incurred on or before 4-22-69, to repurchase such bond or other evidence of indebtedness at a specified call premium, but no inference shall be drawn from the fact that section 249 of the Internal Revenue Code of 1954 (as added by subsection (a) of this section) does not apply to the repurchase of such convertible bond or other convertible evidence of indebtedness.

[Sec. 250—Repealed]

Amendments

• 1990, Omnibus Budget Reconciliation Act of 1990 (P.L. 101-508)

P.L. 101-508, §11801(a)(15):

Repealed Code Sec. 250. **Effective** 11-5-90.

P.L. 101-508, §11821(b), provides:

(b) SAVINGS PROVISION.—If—

(1) any provision amended or repealed by this part applied to—

(A) any transaction occurring before the date of the enactment of this Act,

(B) any property acquired before such date of enactment, or

(C) any item of income, loss, deduction, or credit taken into account before such date of enactment, and

(2) the treatment of such transaction, property, or item under such provision would (without regard to the amendments made by this part) affect liability for tax for periods ending after such date of enactment,

nothing in the amendments made by this part shall be construed to affect the treatment of such transaction, property, or item for purposes of determining liability for tax for periods ending after such date of enactment.

Prior to repeal, Code Sec. 250 read as follows:

SEC. 250. CERTAIN PAYMENTS TO THE NATIONAL RAILROAD PASSENGER CORPORATION.

[Sec. 250(a)]

(a) GENERAL RULE.—If—

(1) any corporation which is a rail carrier (as defined in Section 10102 (19) of title 49) makes a payment in cash, rail passenger equipment, or services to the National Railroad Passenger Corporation (hereinafter in this section referred to as the "Passenger Corporation") pursuant to a contract entered into under section 401(a) of the Rail Passenger Service Act of 1970, and

(2) no stock in the Passenger Corporation is issued at any time to such corporation in connection with any contract entered into under such section 401(a),

then the amount of such payment shall (subject to subsection (c)) be allowed as a deduction for the taxable year in which it is made.

Amendments

• 1982, Bus Regulatory Reform Act of 1982 (P.L. 97-261)

P.L. 97-261, §6(d)(3):

Amended Code Sec. 250(a)(1) by striking out "10102 (18)" and inserting in lieu thereof "10102 (19)". **Effective** 11-19-82.

• 1980, Household Goods Transportation Act of 1980 (P.L. 96-454)

P.L. 96-454, §3(b)(1):

Amended Code Sec. 250(a)(1) by striking out "10102(17)" and inserting "10102(18)" in lieu thereof. **Effective** 10-15-80.

• 1978 (P.L. 95-473)

P.L. 95-473, §(2)(a)(2)(C):

Amended Code Section 250(a)(1) by striking out "common carrier by railroad (as defined in section 1(3) of the Interstate Commerce Act (49 U.S.C. 1(3)))" and substituting "rail carrier (as defined in section 10102(17) of title 49)". **Effective** 10-17-78.

[Sec. 250(b)]

(b) WHEN PAYMENT IS MADE.—Under regulations prescribed by the Secretary, a payment in rail passenger equipment shall be treated as made when title to the equipment is transferred, and a payment in services shall be treated as made when the services are rendered.

Amendments

• 1976, Tax Reform Act of 1976 (P.L. 94-455)

P.L. 94-455, §1906(b)(13)(A):

Amended 1954 Code by substituting "Secretary" for "Secretary or his delegate" each place it appeared. **Effective** 2-1-77.

[Sec. 250(c)]

(c) EFFECT OF CERTAIN SUBSEQUENT ACQUISITIONS OF STOCK.—

(1) DISALLOWANCE OF DEDUCTIONS.—If any deduction has been allowed under subsection (a) to a corporation and such corporation (or a successor corporation) acquires any stock in the Passenger Corporation (other than in a transaction described in section 374 or 381) before the close of the 36-month period which begins with the day on which the last payment is made to the Passenger Corporation pursuant to the contract entered into under such section 401(a), then such deduction shall be disallowed (as of the close of the taxable year for which it was allowed under subsection (a)).

(2) COLLECTION OF DEFICIENCY.—If any deduction is disallowed by reason of paragraph (1), then the periods of limitation provided in sections 6501 and 6502 on the making of an assessment and the collection by levy or a proceeding in court shall, with respect to any deficiency (including interest and additions to the tax) resulting from such a disallowance, include one year following the date on which the person acquiring the stock which results in the disallowance (in accordance with regulations prescribed by the Secretary) notifies the Secretary of such acquisition; and such assessment and collection may be made notwithstanding any provision of law or rule of law which otherwise would prevent such assessment and collection.

Amendments

• 1976, Tax Reform Act of 1976 (P.L. 94-455)

P.L. 94-455, §1906(b)(13)(A):

Amended 1954 Code by substituting "Secretary" for "Secretary or his delegate" each place it appeared. **Effective** 2-1-77.

[Sec. 250(d)]

(d) MEMBERS OF CONTROLLED GROUP.—Under regulations prescribed by the Secretary, if a corporation is a member of a controlled group of corporations (within the meaning of section 1563), subsections (a)(2) and (c) shall be applied by treating all members of such controlled group as one corporation.

Amendments

• 1976, Tax Reform Act of 1976 (P.L. 94-455)

P.L. 94-455, §1906(b)(13)(A):

Amended 1954 Code by substituting "Secretary" for "Secretary or his delegate" each place it appeared. **Effective** 2-1-77.

• 1970, Rail Passenger Service Act of 1970 (P.L. 91-518)

P.L. 91-518, §901(a):

Added Code Sec. 250. **Effective** for tax years ending after 10-30-70.

PART IX—ITEMS NOT DEDUCTIBLE

[Sec. 261]

SEC. 261. GENERAL RULE FOR DISALLOWANCE OF DEDUCTIONS.

In computing taxable income no deduction shall in any case be allowed in respect of the items specified in this part.

[Sec. 262]

SEC. 262. PERSONAL, LIVING, AND FAMILY EXPENSES.

[Sec. 262(a)]

(a) GENERAL RULE.—Except as otherwise expressly provided in this chapter, no deduction shall be allowed for personal, living, or family expenses.

[Sec. 262(b)]

(b) TREATMENT OF CERTAIN PHONE EXPENSES.—For purposes of subsection (a), in the case of an individual, any charge (including taxes thereon) for basic local telephone service with respect to the 1st telephone line provided to any residence of the taxpayer shall be treated as a personal expense.

Amendments

• 1988, Technical and Miscellaneous Revenue Act of 1988 (P.L. 100-647)

P.L. 100-647, §5073:

Amended Code Sec. 262. **Effective** for tax years beginning after 12-31-88. Prior to amendment, Code Sec. 262 read as follows:

SEC. 262. PERSONAL, LIVING, AND FAMILY EXPENSES.

Except as otherwise expressly provided in this chapter, no deduction shall be allowed for personal, living, or family expenses.

[Sec. 263]

SEC. 263. CAPITAL EXPENDITURES.

[Sec. 263(a)]

(a) GENERAL RULE.—No deduction shall be allowed for—

(1) Any amount paid out for new buildings or for permanent improvements or betterments made to increase the value of any property or estate. This paragraph shall not apply to—

(A) expenditures for the development of mines or deposits deductible under section 616,

(B) research and experimental expenditures deductible under section 174,

(C) soil and water conservation expenditures deductible under section 175,

(D) expenditures by farmers for fertilizer, etc., deductible under section 180,

(E) expenditures for removal of architectural and transportation barriers to the handicapped and elderly which the taxpayer elects to deduct under section 190,

(F) expenditures for tertiary injectants with respect to which a deduction is allowed under section 193;

(G) expenditures for which a deduction is allowed under section 179;

(H) expenditures for which a deduction is allowed under section 179A,

(I) expenditures for which a deduction is allowed under section 179B,

(J) expenditures for which a deduction is allowed under section 179C,

(K) expenditures for which a deduction is allowed under section 179D, or

(L) expenditures for which a deduction is allowed under section 179E.

(2) Any amount expended in restoring property or in making good the exhaustion thereof for which an allowance is or has been made.

Amendments

• 2006, Tax Relief and Health Care Act of 2006 (P.L. 109-432)

P.L. 109-432, Division A, §404(b)(1):

Amended Code Sec. 263(a)(1) by striking "or" at the end of subparagraph (J), by striking the period at the end of subparagraph (K) and inserting ", or", and by inserting after subparagraph (K) a new subparagraph (L). **Effective** for costs paid or incurred after 12-20-2006.

• 2005, Energy Tax Incentives Act of 2005 (P.L. 109-58)

P.L. 109-58, §1323(b)(2):

Amended Code Sec. 263(a)(1) by striking "or" at the end of subparagraph (H), by striking the period at the end of subparagraph (I) and inserting ", or", and by inserting after subparagraph (I) a new subparagraph (J). **Effective** for properties placed in service after 8-8-2005.

P.L. 109-58, §1331(b)(4):

Amended Code Sec. 263(a)(1), as amended by this Act, by striking "or" at the end of subparagraph (I), by striking the period at the end of subparagraph (J) and inserting ", or", and by inserting after subparagraph (J) a new subparagraph (K). **Effective** for property placed in service after 12-31-2005.

• 2004, American Jobs Creation Act of 2004 (P.L. 108-357)

P.L. 108-357, §338(b)(1):

Amended Code Sec. 263(a)(1), as amended by this Act [sic], by striking "or" at the end of subparagraph (G), by striking the period at the end of subparagraph (H) and inserting ", or", and by adding at the end a new subparagraph (I). **Effective** for expenses paid or incurred after 12-31-2002, in tax years ending after such date.

• 1997, Taxpayer Relief Act of 1997 (P.L. 105-34)

P.L. 105-34, §1604(a)(1):

Amended Code Sec. 263(a)(1) by striking "or" at the end of subparagraph (F), by striking the period at the end of subparagraph (G) and inserting "; or", and by adding at the end a new subparagraph (H). **Effective** as if included in the amendments made by Act Sec. 1913 of P.L. 102-486 [**effective** for property placed in service after 6-30-93.—CCH].

• 1986, Tax Reform Act of 1986 (P.L. 99-514)

P.L. 99-514, §402(b)(1):

Amended Code Sec. 263(a)(1) by striking out subparagraph (E) and by redesignating subparagraphs (F), (G), and (H) as subparagraphs (E), (F), and (G), respectively. **Effective** for amounts paid or incurred after 12-31-85, in tax years ending after such date. Prior to amendment, Code Sec. 263(a)(1)(E) read as follows:

(E) Expenditures by farmers for clearing land deductible under section 182,

• 1981, Economic Recovery Tax Act of 1981 (P.L. 97-34)

P.L. 97-34, §202(d)(1):

Amended Code Sec. 263(a)(1) by striking out "or" at the end of subparagraph (F); by striking out the period at the end of subparagraph (G) and inserting in lieu thereof a semicolon and "or", and by adding at the end thereof new subparagraph (H). **Effective** for property placed in service after 12-31-80, in tax years ending after such date.

• 1980, Crude Oil Windfall Profit Tax of 1980 (P.L. 96-223)

P.L. 96-223, §251(a)(2)(B):

Amended Code Sec. 263(a)(1) by striking out "or" at the end of subparagraph (E), by striking out the period at the end of subparagraph (F) and inserting ", or", and by adding subparagraph (G). **Effective** for tax years beginning after 12-31-79.

• 1976, Tax Reform Act of 1976 (P.L. 94-455)

P.L. 94-455, §1904(b)(10)(A)(i):

Struck Code Sec. 263(a)(3). **Effective** 2-1-77. Prior to striking, Code Sec. 263(a)(3) read as follows:

(3) Except as provided in subsection (d), any amount paid as tax under section 4911 (relating to imposition of interest equalization tax).

P.L. 94-455, §2122(b)(2):

Struck "or" at the end of Code Sec. 263(a)(1)(D), substituted ", or" for the period at the end of Code Sec. 263(a)(1)(E) and added Code Sec. 263(a)(1)(F). **Effective** for tax years beginning after 12-31-76, and before 1-1-80.

• 1965, Interest Equalization Tax Extension Act of 1965 (P.L. 89-243)

P.L. 89-243, §4(p)(1):

Amended Code Sec. 263(a)(3). **Effective** for tax years ending after 9-2-64. Prior to amendment, Sec. 263(a)(3) read as follows:

"(3) Any amount paid as tax under section 4911 (relating to imposition of interest equalization tax) except to the extent that any amount attributable to the amount paid as tax is included in gross income for the taxable year."

• 1964, Interest Equalization Tax Act (P.L. 88-563)

P.L. 88-563, §4:

Amended Code Sec. 263(a) by adding paragraph (3).

• 1962, Revenue Act of 1962 (P.L. 87-834)

P.L. 87-834, §21:

Amended Code Sec. 263(a)(1) by striking out "or" at the end of subparagraph (C), by substituting ", or" for the period at the end of subparagraph (D), and by adding at the end thereof a new subparagraph (E). **Effective** for tax years beginning after 12-31-62.

• 1960 (P.L. 86-779)

P.L. 86-779, §6(c):

Amended Code Sec. 263(a)(1) by striking out "or" at the end of subparagraph (B), by striking out the period at the end of subparagraph (c) and inserting ", or", and by adding a new subparagraph (D). **Effective** for tax years beginning after 1959.

[Sec. 263(b)—Repealed]

Amendments

• 1990, Omnibus Budget Reconciliation Act of 1990 (P.L. 101-508)

P.L. 101-508, §11801(a)(16):

Repealed Code Sec. 263(b). **Effective** 11-5-90. Prior to repeal, Code Sec. 263(b) read as follows:

(b) EXPENDITURES FOR ADVERTISING AND GOOD WILL.—If a corporation has, for the purpose of computing its excess profits tax credit under chapter 2E or subchapter D of chapter 1 of the Internal Revenue Code of 1939 claimed the benefits of the election provided in section 733 or section 451 of such code, as the case may be, no deduction shall be allowable under section 162 to such corporation for expenditures for advertising or the promotion of good will which, under the rules and regulations prescribed under section 733 or section 451 of such code, as the case may be, may be regarded as capital investments.

P.L. 101-508, §11821(b)(1)-(2), provides:

(b) SAVINGS PROVISION.—If—

(1) any provision amended or repealed by this part applied to—

(A) any transaction occurring before the date of the enactment of this Act,

(B) any property acquired before such date of enactment, or

(C) any item of income, loss, deduction, or credit taken into account before such date of enactment, and

(2) the treatment of such transaction, property, or item under such provision would (without regard to the amendments made by this part) affect liability for tax periods ending after such date of enactment,

nothing in the amendments made by this part shall be construed to affect the treatment of such transaction, property, or item for purposes of determining liability for tax for periods ending after such date of enactment.

[Sec. 263(c)]

(c) INTANGIBLE DRILLING AND DEVELOPMENT COSTS IN THE CASE OF OIL AND GAS WELLS AND GEOTHERMAL WELLS.—Notwithstanding subsection (a), and except as provided in subsection (i), regulations shall be prescribed by the Secretary under this subtitle corresponding to the regulations which granted the option to deduct as expenses intangible drilling and development costs in the case of oil and gas wells and which were recognized and approved by the Congress in House Concurrent Resolution 50, Seventy-ninth Congress. Such regulations shall also grant the option to deduct as expenses intangible drilling and development costs in the case of wells drilled for any geothermal deposit (as defined in section 613(e)(2)) to the same extent and in the same manner as such expenses are deductible in the case of oil and gas wells. This subsection shall not apply with respect to any costs to which any deduction is allowed under section 59(e) or 291.

Amendments

• 1990, Omnibus Budget Reconciliation Act of 1990 (P.L. 101-508)

P.L. 101-508, §11815(b)(3):

Amended Code Sec. 263(c) by striking "section 613(e)(3)" and inserting "section 613(e)(2)". **Effective** 11-5-90.

P.L. 101-508, §11821(b), provides:

(b) SAVINGS PROVISION.—If—

(1) any provision amended or repealed by this part applied to—

(A) any transaction occurring before the date of the enactment of this Act,

(B) any property acquired before such date of enactment, or

(C) any item of income, loss, deduction, or credit taken into account before such date of enactment, and

(2) the treatment of such transaction, property, or item under such provision would (without regard to the amendments made by this part) affect liability for tax for periods ending after such date of enactment,

nothing in the amendments made by this part shall be construed to affect the treatment of such transaction, property, or item for purposes of determining liability for tax for periods ending after such date of enactment.

• 1988, Technical and Miscellaneous Revenue Act of 1988 (P.L. 100-647)

P.L. 100-647, §1007(g)(5):

Amended Code Sec. 263(c) by striking out "section 59(d)" and inserting in lieu thereof "section 59(e)". **Effective** as if included in the provision of P.L. 99-514 to which it relates.

• 1986, Tax Reform Act of 1986 (P.L. 99-514)

P.L. 99-514, §411(b)(1)(B):

Amended Code Sec. 263(c) by inserting "and except as provided in subsection (i)," after "subsection (a),". **Effective**, generally, for costs paid or incurred after 12-31-86, in tax years ending after such date. For a transitional rule see Act Sec. 411(c)(2), below.

P.L. 99-514, §411(c)(2), provides:

(2) TRANSITION RULE.—The amendments made by this section shall not apply with respect to intangible drilling and development costs incurred by United States companies pursuant to a minority interest in a license for Netherlands or United Kingdom North Sea development if such interest was acquired on or before December 31, 1985.

P.L. 99-514, §701(e)(4)(D):

Amended Code Sec. 263(c) by striking out "section 58(i)" and inserting in lieu thereof "section 59(d)". **Effective**, generally, for tax years beginning after 12-31-86. For exceptions, see Act Sec. 711(f)(2)-(7) following Code Sec. 56.

• 1982, Tax Equity and Fiscal Responsibility Act of 1982 (P.L. 97-248)

P.L. 97-248, §204(c)(1):

Amended Code Sec. 263(c) by adding the sentence at the end thereof. **Effective** for tax years beginning after 12-31-82.

• 1978, Energy Tax Act of 1978 (P.L. 95-618)

P.L. 95-618, §402(a):

Added "AND GEOTHERMAL WELLS" to the subsection heading for Code Sec. 263(c), and added the last sentence of Code Sec. 263(c). **Effective** as set forth in P.L. 95-618, §402(e), below.

P.L. 95-618, §402(e):

(e) EFFECTIVE DATE.—

(1) IN GENERAL.—The amendments made by this section shall apply with respect to wells commenced on or after October 1, 1978, in taxable years ending on or after such date.

(2) ELECTION.—The taxpayer may elect to capitalize or deduct any costs to which section 263(c) of the Internal Revenue Code of 1954 applies by reason of the amendments made by this section. Any such election shall be made before the expiration of the time for filing claim for credit or refund of any overpayment of tax imposed by chapter 1 of such Code with respect to the taxpayer's first taxable year to which the amendments made by this section apply and for which he pays or incurs costs to which such section 263(c) applies by reason of the amendments made by this section. Any election under this paragraph may be changed or revoked at any time before the expiration of the time referred to in the preceding sentence, but after the expiration of such time such election may not be changed or revoked.

• 1976, Tax Reform Act of 1976 (P.L. 94-455)

P.L. 94-455, §1906(b)(13)(A):

Amended 1954 Code by substituting "Secretary" for "Secretary or his delegate" each place it appeared. **Effective** 2-1-77.

[Sec. 263(d)]

(d) EXPENDITURES IN CONNECTION WITH CERTAIN RAILROAD ROLLING STOCK.—In the case of expenditures in connection with the rehabilitation of a unit of railroad rolling stock (except a locomotive) used by a domestic common carrier by railroad which would, but for this subsection, be properly chargeable to capital account, such expenditures, if during any 12-month period they do not exceed an amount equal to 20 percent of the basis of such unit in the hands of the taxpayer, shall, at the election of the taxpayer, be treated (notwithstanding subsection (a)) as deductible repairs under section 162 or 212. An election under this subsection shall be made for any taxable year at such time and in such manner as the Secretary prescribes by regulations. An election may not be made under this subsection for any taxable year to which an election under subsection (e) applies to railroad rolling stock (other than locomotives).

Amendments

• 1976, Tax Reform Act of 1976 (P.L. 94-455)

P.L. 94-455, §1904(b)(10)(A)(i):

Repealed Code Sec. 263(d) (see below), redesignated former Code Sec. 263(e) to be Code Sec. 263(d), and substituted "subsection (e)" for "subsection (f)" in the redesignated Code Sec. 263(d). **Effective** 2-1-77.

P.L. 94-455, §1904(b)(10)(A)(i):

Repealed former Code Sec. 263(d). **Effective** 2-1-77. Prior to repeal, Code Sec. 263(d) read as follows:

(d) REIMBURSEMENT OF INTEREST EQUALIZATION TAX.—The deduction allowed by section 162(a) or 212 (whichever is appropriate) shall include any amount paid or accrued in the taxable year or a preceding taxable year as tax under section 4911 (relating to imposition of interest equalization tax) to the extent that any amount attributable to the amount paid or accrued as tax is included in gross income for the taxable year. Under regulations prescribed by the Secretary or his delegate, the preceding sentence shall not apply with respect to any amount attributable to that part of the tax so paid or accrued which is attributable to an amount for which a deduction has been claimed for the taxable year or a preceding taxable year under section 171 (relating to amortization of bond premium).

P.L. 94-455, §1906(b)(13)(A):

Amended 1954 Code by substituting "Secretary" for "Secretary or his delegate" each place it appeared. **Effective** 2-1-77.

• 1971, Revenue Act of 1971 (P.L. 92-178)

P.L. 92-178, §109(c):

Added ", at the election of the taxpayer," in the first sentence of Code Sec. 263(e) (redesignated as Code Sec. 263(d)) and the last two sentences therein. **Effective** for tax years beginning after 12-31-69.

• 1969, Tax Reform Act of 1969 (P.L. 91-172)

P.L. 91-172, §706(a):

Added Code Sec. 263(e). **Effective** for tax years beginning after 12-31-69.

• 1965, Interest Equalization Tax Extension Act of 1965 (P.L. 89-243)

P.L. 89-243, §4(p)(2):

Added former Code Sec. 263(d). **Effective** for tax years ending after 9-2-64.

[Sec. 263(e)—Repealed]

Amendments

• 1981, Economic Recovery Tax Act of 1981 (P.L. 97-34)

P.L. 97-34, §201(c):

Repealed Code Sec. 263(e). **Effective** for property placed in service after 12-31-80, in tax years ending after such date. Prior to repeal, Code Sec. 263(e) read as follows:

(e) REASONABLE REPAIR ALLOWANCE.—The Secretary may by regulations provide that the taxpayer may make an election under which amounts representing either repair expenses or specified repair, rehabilitation, or improvement expenditures for any class of depreciable property—

(1) are allowable as a deduction under section 162(a) or 212 (whichever is appropriate) to the extent of the repair allowance for that class, and

(2) to the extent such amounts exceed for the taxable year such repair allowance, are chargeable to capital account.

Any allowance prescribed under this subsection shall reasonably reflect the anticipated repair experience of the class of property in the industry or other group.

• 1976, Tax Reform Act of 1976 (P.L. 94-455)

P.L. 94-455, §1904(b)(10)(A)(i):

Redesignated former Code Sec. 263(f) as Code Sec. 263(e). **Effective** 2-1-77.

P.L. 94-455, §1906(b)(13)(A):

Amended 1954 Code by substituting "Secretary" for "Secretary or his delegate" each place it appeared. **Effective** 2-1-77.

• 1971, Revenue Act of 1971 (P.L. 92-178)

P.L. 92-178, §109(b):

Added Code Sec. 263(f). **Effective** for tax years ending after 12-31-70.

[Sec. 263(f)]

(f) RAILROAD TIES.—In the case of a domestic common carrier by rail (including a railroad switching or terminal company) which uses the retirement-replacement method of accounting for depreciation of its railroad track, expenditures for acquiring and installing replacement ties of any material (and fastenings related to such ties) shall be accorded the same tax accounting treatment as expenditures for replacement ties of wood (and fastenings related to such ties).

Amendments

• 1976, Tax Reform Act of 1976 (P.L. 94-455)

P.L. 94-455, §1701)(a):

Added Code Sec. 263(g). **Effective** 10-4-76.

P.L. 94-455, §1904(b)(10)(A)(i):

Redesignated Code Sec. 263(g) as 263(f). **Effective** 2-1-77.

[Sec. 263(g)]

(g) CERTAIN INTEREST AND CARRYING COSTS IN THE CASE OF STRADDLES.—

(1) GENERAL RULE.—No deduction shall be allowed for interest and carrying charges properly allocable to personal property which is part of a straddle (as defined in section 1092(c)). Any amount not allowed as a deduction by reason of the preceding sentence shall be chargeable to the capital account with respect to the personal property to which such amount relates.

(2) INTEREST AND CARRYING CHARGES DEFINED.—For purposes of paragraph (1), the term "interest and carrying charges" means the excess of—

(A) the sum of—

(i) interest on indebtedness incurred or continued to purchase or carry the personal property, and

(ii) all other amounts (including charges to insure, store, or transport the personal property) paid or incurred to carry the personal property, over

(B) the sum of—

(i) the amount of interest (including original issue discount) includible in gross income for the taxable year with respect to the property described in subparagraph (A),

(ii) any amount treated as ordinary income under section 1271(a)(3)(A), 1276, or 1281(a) with respect to such property for the taxable year,

(iii) the excess of any dividends includible in gross income with respect to such property for the taxable year over the amount of any deduction allowable with respect to such dividends under section 243, 244, or 245, and

(iv) any amount which is a payment with respect to a security loan (within the meaning of section 512(a)(5)) includible in gross income with respect to such property for the taxable year.

For purposes of subparagraph (A), the term "interest" includes any amount paid or incurred in connection with personal property used in a short sale.

(3) EXCEPTION FOR HEDGING TRANSACTIONS.—This subsection shall not apply in the case of any hedging transaction (as defined in section 1256(e)).

(4) APPLICATION WITH OTHER PROVISIONS.—

(A) SUBSECTION (c).—In the case of any short sale, this subsection shall be applied after subsection (h).

(B) SECTION 1277 OR 1282 .—In the case of any obligation to which section 1277 or 1282 applies, this subsection shall be applied after section 1277 or 1282.

Amendments

• 2004, Working Families Tax Relief Act of 2004 (P.L. 108-311)

P.L. 108-311, §408(a)(10):

Amended Code Sec. 263(g)(2)(B)(ii) by striking "1278" and inserting "1276". **Effective** 10-4-2004.

• 1986, Tax Reform Act of 1986 (P.L. 99-514)

P.L. 99-514, §1808(b):

Amended Code Sec. 263(g)(2)(B) by striking out "and" at the end of clause (ii), by striking out the period at the end of clause (iii) and inserting in lieu thereof ", and", and by inserting after clause (iii) new clause (iv). **Effective** as if included in the provision of P.L. 98-369 to which it relates.

• 1984, Deficit Reduction Act of 1984 (P.L. 98-369)

P.L. 98-369, §102(e)(7):

Amended Code Sec. 263(g)(2). **Effective** for positions established after 7-18-84 in tax years ending after such date. Special rules appear in Act Sec. 102(g) following Code Sec. 1256(b). Prior to amendment, it read as follows:

(2) Interest and Carrying Charges Defined.—For purposes of paragraph (1), the term "interest and carrying charges" means the excess of—

(A) the sum of—

(i) interest on indebtedness incurred or continued to purchase or carry the personal property, and

(ii) all other amounts (including charges for temporary use of the personal property in a short sale, or to insure, store, or transport the personal property) paid or incurred to carry the personal property, over

(B) the sum of—

(i) the amount of interest (including original issue discount) includible in gross income for the taxable year with respect to the property described in subparagraph (A), and

(ii) any amount treated as ordinary income under section 1232(a)(3)(A) with respect to such property for the taxable year.

P.L. 98-369, §102(e)(8):

Added Code Sec. 263(g)(4). **Effective** for positions established after 7-18-84 in tax years ending after such date. Special rules appear in Act Sec. 102(g) following Code Sec. 1256(b).

• 1983, Technical Corrections Act of 1982 (P.L. 97-448)

P.L. 97-448, §105(b)(1):

Amended Code Sec. 263(g)(2)(A)(ii). **Effective** for property acquired, and positions established, by the taxpayer after 9-22-82, in tax years ending after such date. Prior to amendment, Code Sec. 263(g)(2)(A)(ii) read as follows:

"(ii) amounts paid or incurred to insure, store, or transport the personal property, over"

P.L. 97-448, §306(a)(9)(A):

Amended Code Sec. 263(g)(2)(B)(ii) by striking out "section 1232(a)(4)(A)" and inserting in lieu thereof "section 1232(a)(3)(A)". **Effective** as if it had been included in the provision of P.L. 97-248 to which it relates.

• 1981, Economic Recovery Tax Act of 1981 (P.L. 97-34)

P.L. 97-34, §502:

Added Code Sec. 263(g). **Effective** for property acquired or positions established after 6-23-81 in tax years ending after that date.

[Sec. 263(h)]

(h) PAYMENTS IN LIEU OF DIVIDENDS IN CONNECTION WITH SHORT SALES.—

(1) IN GENERAL.—If—

(A) a taxpayer makes any payment with respect to any stock used by such taxpayer in a short sale and such payment is in lieu of a dividend payment on such stock, and

(B) the closing of such short sale occurs on or before the 45th day after the date of such short sale,

then no deduction shall be allowed for such payment. The basis of the stock used to close the short sale shall be increased by the amount not allowed as a deduction by reason of the preceding sentence.

(2) LONGER PERIOD IN CASE OF EXTRAORDINARY DIVIDENDS.—If the payment described in paragraph (1)(A) is in respect of an extraordinary dividend, paragraph (1)(B) shall be applied by substituting "the day 1 year after the date of such short sale" for "the 45th day after the date of such short sale".

(3) EXTRAORDINARY DIVIDEND.—For purposes of this subsection, the term "extraordinary dividend" has the meaning given to such term by section 1059(c); except that such section shall be applied by treating the amount realized by the taxpayer in the short sale as his adjusted basis in the stock.

(4) SPECIAL RULE WHERE RISK OF LOSS DIMINISHED.—The running of any period of time applicable under paragraph (1)(B) (as modified by paragraph (2)) shall be suspended during any period in which—

(A) the taxpayer holds, has an option to buy, or is under a contractual obligation to buy, substantially identical stock or securities, or

(B) under regulations prescribed by the Secretary, a taxpayer has diminished his risk of loss by holding 1 or more other positions with respect to substantially similar or related property.

(5) DEDUCTION ALLOWABLE TO EXTENT OF ORDINARY INCOME FROM AMOUNTS PAID BY LENDING BROKER FOR USE OF COLLATERAL.—

(A) IN GENERAL.—Paragraph (1) shall apply only to the extent that the payments or distributions with respect to any short sale exceed the amount which—

(i) is treated as ordinary income by the taxpayer, and

(ii) is received by the taxpayer as compensation for the use of any collateral with respect to any stock used in such short sale.

(B) EXCEPTION NOT TO APPLY TO EXTRAORDINARY DIVIDENDS.—Subparagraph (A) shall not apply if one or more payments or distributions is in respect of an extraordinary dividend.

(6) APPLICATION OF THIS SUBSECTION WITH SUBSECTION (g).—In the case of any short sale, this subsection shall be applied before subsection (g).

Amendments

• 1984, Deficit Reduction Act of 1984 (P.L. 98-369)

P.L. 98-369, §56(a):

Amended Code Sec. 263 by adding subsection (h) at the end thereof. **Effective** for short sales after 7-18-84, in tax years ending after such date.

[Sec. 263(i)]

(i) SPECIAL RULES FOR INTANGIBLE DRILLING AND DEVELOPMENT COSTS INCURRED OUTSIDE THE UNITED STATES.—In the case of intangible drilling and development costs paid or incurred with respect to an oil, gas, or geothermal well located outside the United States—

(1) subsection (c) shall not apply, and

(2) such costs shall—

(A) at the election of the taxpayer, be included in adjusted basis for purposes of computing the amount of any deduction allowable under section 611 (determined without regard to section 613), or

(B) if subparagraph (A) does not apply, be allowed as a deduction ratably over the 10-taxable year period beginning with the taxable year in which such costs were paid or incurred.

This subsection shall not apply to costs paid or incurred with respect to a nonproductive well.

Amendments

• 1986, Tax Reform Act of 1986 (P.L. 99-514)

P.L. 99-514, §411(b)(1)(A):

Amended Code Sec. 263 by adding at the end thereof new subsection (i). **Effective**, generally, for costs paid or incurred after 12-31-86, in tax years ending after such date. For a transitional rule see Act Sec. 411(c)(2), after Code Sec. 263(c), above.

[Sec. 263A]

SEC. 263A. CAPITALIZATION AND INCLUSION IN INVENTORY COSTS OF CERTAIN EXPENSES.

[Sec. 263A(a)]

(a) NONDEDUCTIBILITY OF CERTAIN DIRECT AND INDIRECT COSTS.—

(1) IN GENERAL.—In the case of any property to which this section applies, any costs described in paragraph (2)—

(A) in the case of property which is inventory in the hands of the taxpayer, shall be included in inventory costs, and

(B) in the case of any other property, shall be capitalized.

(2) ALLOCABLE COSTS.—The costs described in this paragraph with respect to any property are—

(A) the direct costs of such property, and

(B) such property's proper share of those indirect costs (including taxes) part or all of which are allocable to such property.

Any cost which (but for this subsection) could not be taken into account in computing taxable income for any taxable year shall not be treated as a cost described in this paragraph.

Amendments

• 1988, Technical and Miscellaneous Revenue Act of 1988 (P.L. 100-647)

P.L. 100-647, §1008(b)(1):

Amended Code Sec. 263A(a)(2) by adding at the end thereof a new sentence. **Effective** as if included in the provision of P.L. 99-514 to which it relates.

[Sec. 263A(b)]

(b) PROPERTY TO WHICH SECTION APPLIES.—Except as otherwise provided in this section, this section shall apply to—

(1) PROPERTY PRODUCED BY TAXPAYER.—Real or tangible personal property produced by the taxpayer.

(2) PROPERTY ACQUIRED FOR RESALE.—

(A) IN GENERAL.—Real or personal property described in section 1221(a)(1) which is acquired by the taxpayer for resale.

(B) EXCEPTION FOR TAXPAYER WITH GROSS RECEIPTS OF $10,000,000 OR LESS.—Subparagraph (A) shall not apply to any personal property acquired during any taxable year by the taxpayer for resale if the average annual gross receipts of the taxpayer (or any predecessor) for the 3-taxable year period ending with the taxable year preceding such taxable year do not exceed $10,000,000.

(C) AGGREGATION RULES, ETC.—For purposes of subparagraph (B), rules similar to the rules of paragraphs (2) and (3) of section 448(c) shall apply.

For purposes of paragraph (1), the term "tangible personal property" shall include a film, sound recording, video tape, book, or similar property.

Amendments

• 1999, Tax Relief Extension Act of 1999 (P.L. 106-170)

P.L. 106-170, § 532(c)(2)(B):

Amended Code Sec. 263A(b)(2)(A) by striking "section 1221(1)" and inserting "section 1221(a)(1)". **Effective** for any instrument held, acquired, or entered into, any transaction entered into, and supplies held or acquired on or after 12-17-99.

[Sec. 263A(c)]

(c) GENERAL EXCEPTIONS.—

(1) PERSONAL USE PROPERTY.—This section shall not apply to any property produced by the taxpayer for use by the taxpayer other than in a trade or business or an activity conducted for profit.

(2) RESEARCH AND EXPERIMENTAL EXPENDITURES.—This section shall not apply to any amount allowable as a deduction under section 174.

(3) CERTAIN DEVELOPMENT AND OTHER COSTS OF OIL AND GAS WELLS OR OTHER MINERAL PROPERTY.—This section shall not apply to any cost allowable as a deduction under section 167(h), 179B, 263(c), 263(i), 291(b)(2), 616, or 617.

(4) COORDINATION WITH LONG-TERM CONTRACT RULES.—This section shall not apply to any property produced by the taxpayer pursuant to a long-term contract.

(5) TIMBER AND CERTAIN ORNAMENTAL TREES.—This section shall not apply to—

(A) trees raised, harvested, or grown by the taxpayer other than trees described in clause (ii) of subsection (e)(4)(B) (after application of the last sentence thereof), and

(B) any real property underlying such trees.

(6) COORDINATION WITH SECTION 59(e).—Paragraphs (2) and (3) shall apply to any amount allowable as a deduction under section 59(e) for qualified expenditures described in subparagraphs (B), (C), (D), and (E) of paragraph (2) thereof.

Amendments

• 2005, Energy Tax Incentives Act of 2005 (P.L. 109-58)

P.L. 109-58, § 1329(b):

Amended Code Sec. 263A(c)(3) by inserting "167(h)," after "under section". **Effective** for amounts paid or incurred in tax years beginning after 8-8-2005.

• 2004, American Jobs Creation Act of 2004 (P.L. 108-357)

P.L. 108-357, § 338(b)(2):

Amended Code Sec. 263A(c)(3) by inserting "179B," after "section". **Effective** for expenses paid or incurred after 12-31-2002, in tax years ending after such date.

• 1988, Technical and Miscellaneous Revenue Act of 1988 (P.L. 100-647)

P.L. 100-647, § 1008(b)(2)(A)-(B):

Amended Code Sec. 263A(c) by striking out "263(c), 616(a), or 617(a)" and inserting in lieu thereof "263(c), 263(i), 291(b)(2), 616, or 617", and by adding at the end thereof new paragraph (6). **Effective** as if included in the provision of P.L. 99-514 to which it relates.

[Sec. 263A(d)]

(d) EXCEPTION FOR FARMING BUSINESSES.—

(1) SECTION NOT TO APPLY TO CERTAIN PROPERTY.—

(A) IN GENERAL.—This section shall not apply to any of the following which is produced by the taxpayer in a farming business:

(i) Any animal.

(ii) Any plant which has a preproductive period of 2 years or less.

(B) EXCEPTION FOR TAXPAYERS REQUIRED TO USE ACCRUAL METHOD.—Subparagraph (A) shall not apply to any corporation, partnership, or tax shelter required to use an accrual method of accounting under section 447 or 448(a)(3).

(2) TREATMENT OF CERTAIN PLANTS LOST BY REASON OF CASUALTY.—

(A) IN GENERAL.—If plants bearing an edible crop for human consumption were lost or damaged (while in the hands of the taxpayer) by reason of freezing temperatures, disease, drought, pests, or casualty, this section shall not apply to any costs of the taxpayer of replanting plants bearing the same type of crop (whether on the same parcel of land on which such lost or damaged plants were located or any other parcel of land of the same acreage in the United States).

(B) SPECIAL RULE FOR PERSON WITH MINORITY INTEREST WHO MATERIALLY PARTICIPATES.—Subparagraph (A) shall apply to amounts paid or incurred by a person (other than the taxpayer described in subparagraph (A)) if—

(i) the taxpayer described in subparagraph (A) has an equity interest of more than 50 percent in the plants described in subparagraph (A) at all times during the taxable year in which such amounts were paid or incurred, and

(ii) such other person holds any part of the remaining equity interest and materially participates in the planting, maintenance, cultivation, or development of the plants described in subparagraph (A) during the taxable year in which such amounts were paid or incurred.

The determination of whether an individual materially participates in any activity shall be made in a manner similar to the manner in which such determination is made under section 2032A(e)(6).

(3) ELECTION TO HAVE THIS SECTION NOT APPLY.—

(A) IN GENERAL.—If a taxpayer makes an election under this paragraph, this section shall not apply to any plant produced in any farming business carried on by such taxpayer.

(B) CERTAIN PERSONS NOT ELIGIBLE.—No election may be made under this paragraph by a corporation, partnership, or tax shelter, if such corporation, partnership, or tax shelter is required to use an accrual method of accounting under section 447 or 448(a)(3).

(C) SPECIAL RULE FOR CITRUS AND ALMOND GROWERS.—An election under this paragraph shall not apply with respect to any item which is attributable to the planting, cultivation, maintenance, or development of any citrus or almond grove (or part thereof) and which is incurred before the close of the 4th taxable year beginning with the taxable year in which the trees were planted. For purposes of the preceding sentence, the portion of a citrus or almond grove planted in 1 taxable year shall be treated separately from the portion of such grove planted in another taxable year.

(D) ELECTION.—Unless the Secretary otherwise consents, an election under this paragraph may be made only for the taxpayer's 1st taxable year which begins after December 31, 1986, and during which the taxpayer engages in a farming business. Any such election, once made, may be revoked only with the consent of the Secretary.

Amendments

• 1988, Technical and Miscellaneous Revenue Act of 1988 (P.L. 100-647)

P.L. 100-647, §1008(b)(3)(A)-(B):

Amended Code Sec. 263A(d)(2)(B) by striking out "such grove, orchard, or vineyard" in clause (i) and inserting in lieu thereof "the plants described in subparagraph (A) at all times during the taxable year in which such amounts were paid or incurred", and by striking out "such grove, orchard, or vineyard during the 4-taxable year period beginning with the taxable year in which the grove, orchard, or vineyard was lost or damaged" and inserting in lieu thereof "the plants described in subparagraph (A) during the taxable year in which such amounts were paid or incurred". **Effective** as if included in the provision of P.L. 99-514 to which it relates.

P.L. 100-647, §6026(b)(1):

Amended Code Sec. 263A(d)(1)(A). **Effective**, generally, for costs incurred after 12-31-88, in tax years ending after such date. See also Act Sec. 6026(d)(2)(B), below. Prior to amendment, Code Sec. 263A(d)(1)(A) read as follows:

(A) IN GENERAL.—This section shall not apply to any plant or animal which is produced by the taxpayer in a farming business and which has a preproductive period of 2 years or less.

P.L. 100-647, §6026(b)(2)(A):

Amended the heading of Code Sec. 263A(d)(1). **Effective**, generally, for costs incurred after 12-31-88, in tax years ending after such date. See also Act Sec. 6026(d)(2)(B), below. Prior to amendment, the heading for Code Sec. 263(d)(1) read as follows:

(1) SECTION TO APPLY ONLY IF PREPRODUCTIVE PERIOD IS MORE THAN 2 YEARS.—

P.L. 100-647, §6026(b)(2)(B):

Amended Code Sec. 263A(d)(3) by striking out "or animal" after "any plant" in subparagraph (A). **Effective**, generally, for costs incurred after 12-31-88, in tax years ending after such date. See also Act Sec. 6026(d)(2)(B), below.

P.L. 100-647, §6026(d)(2)(B), as amended by P.L. 101-239, §7816(d)(2), provides:

(B) REVOCATION OF ELECTION.—If a taxpayer engaged in a farming business involving the production of animals having a preproductive period of more than 2 years made an election under section 263A(d)(3) of the 1986 Code for a taxable year beginning before January 1, 1989, such taxpayer may, without the consent of the Secretary of the Treasury or his delegate, revoke such election effective for the taxpayer's 1st taxable year beginning after December 31, 1988.

P.L. 100-647, §6026(c):

Amended Code Sec. 263A(d)(3)(B). **Effective** as if included in the amendments made by P.L. 99-514, §803. Prior to amendment, Code Sec. 263A(d)(3)(B) read as follows:

(B) CERTAIN PERSONS NOT ELIGIBLE.—No election may be made under this paragraph—

(i) by a corporation, partnership, or tax shelter, if such corporation, partnership, or tax shelter is required to use an accrual method of accounting under section 447 or 448(a)(3), or

(ii) with respect to the planting, cultivation, maintenance, or development of pistachio trees.

[Sec. 263A(e)]

(e) DEFINITIONS AND SPECIAL RULES FOR PURPOSES OF SUBSECTION (d).—

(1) RECAPTURE OF EXPENSED AMOUNTS ON DISPOSITION.—

(A) IN GENERAL.—In the case of any plant with respect to which amounts would have been capitalized under subsection (a) but for an election under subsection (d)(3)—

(i) such plant (if not otherwise section 1245 property) shall be treated as section 1245 property, and

(ii) for purposes of section 1245, the recapture amount shall be treated as a deduction allowed for depreciation with respect to such property.

(B) RECAPTURE AMOUNT.—For purposes of subparagraph (A), the term "recapture amount" means any amount allowable as a deduction to the taxpayer which, but for an election under subsection (d)(3), would have been capitalized with respect to the plant.

(2) EFFECTS OF ELECTION ON DEPRECIATION.—

(A) IN GENERAL.—If the taxpayer (or any related person) makes an election under subsection (d)(3), the provisions of section 168(g)(2) (relating to alternative depreciation) shall apply to all property of the taxpayer used predominantly in the farming business and placed in service in any taxable year during which any such election is in effect.

(B) RELATED PERSON.—For purposes of subparagraph (A), the term "related person" means—

(i) the taxpayer and members of the taxpayer's family,

(ii) any corporation (including an S corporation) if 50 percent or more (in value) of the stock of such corporation is owned (directly or through the application of section 318) by the taxpayer or members of the taxpayer's family,

(iii) a corporation and any other corporation which is a member of the same controlled group described in section 1563(a)(1), and

(iv) any partnership if 50 percent or more (in value) of the interests in such partnership is owned directly or indirectly by the taxpayer or members of the taxpayer's family.

(C) MEMBERS OF FAMILY.—For purposes of this paragraph, the term "family" means the taxpayer, the spouse of the taxpayer, and any of their children who have not attained age 18 before the close of the taxable year.

(3) PREPRODUCTIVE PERIOD.—

(A) IN GENERAL.—For purposes of this section, the term "preproductive period" means—

(i) in the case of a plant which will have more than 1 crop or yield, the period before the 1st marketable crop or yield from such plant, or

(ii) in the case of any other plant, the period before such plant is reasonably expected to be disposed of.

For purposes of this subparagraph, use by the taxpayer in a farming business of any supply produced in such business shall be treated as a disposition.

(B) RULE FOR DETERMINING PERIOD.—In the case of a plant grown in commercial quantities in the United States, the preproductive period for such plant if grown in the United States shall be based on the nationwide weighted average preproductive period for such plant.

(4) FARMING BUSINESS.—For purposes of this section—

(A) IN GENERAL.—The term "farming business" means the trade or business of farming.

(B) CERTAIN TRADES AND BUSINESSES INCLUDED.—The term "farming business" shall include the trade or business of—

(i) operating a nursery or sod farm, or

(ii) the raising or harvesting of trees bearing fruit, nuts, or other crops, or ornamental trees.

For purposes of clause (ii), an evergreen tree which is more than 6 years old at the time severed from the roots shall not be treated as an ornamental tree.

(5) CERTAIN INVENTORY VALUATION METHODS PERMITTED.—The Secretary shall by regulations permit the taxpayer to use reasonable inventory valuation methods to compute the amount required to be capitalized under subsection (a) in the case of any plant.

Amendments

• **1988, Technical and Miscellaneous Revenue Act of 1988 (P.L. 100-647)**

P.L. 100-647, §6026(b)(2)(B):

Amended Code Sec. 263A(e) by striking out "or animal" after "any plant" in paragraph (1)(A), after "such plant" in paragraph (1)(A)(i), after "the plant" in paragraph (1)(B), after "a plant" in paragraph (3)(A)(i), after "such plant" in paragraph (3)(A)(i), after "other plant" in paragraph (3)(A)(ii), after "such plant" in paragraph (3)(A)(ii), and after "any plant" in paragraph (5). **Effective**, generally, for costs incurred after 12-31-88, in tax years ending after such date.

[Sec. 263A(f)]

(f) SPECIAL RULES FOR ALLOCATION OF INTEREST TO PROPERTY PRODUCED BY THE TAXPAYER.—

(1) INTEREST CAPITALIZED ONLY IN CERTAIN CASES.—Subsection (a) shall only apply to interest costs which are—

(A) paid or incurred during the production period, and

(B) allocable to property which is described in subsection (b)(1) and which has—

(i) a long useful life,

(ii) an estimated production period exceeding 2 years, or

(iii) an estimated production period exceeding 1 year and a cost exceeding $1,000,000.

(2) ALLOCATION RULES.—

(A) IN GENERAL.—In determining the amount of interest required to be capitalized under subsection (a) with respect to any property—

(i) interest on any indebtedness directly attributable to production expenditures with respect to such property shall be assigned to such property, and

(ii) interest on any other indebtedness shall be assigned to such property to the extent that the taxpayer's interest costs could have been reduced if production expenditures (not attributable to indebtedness described in clause (i)) had not been incurred.

(B) EXCEPTION FOR QUALIFIED RESIDENCE INTEREST.—Subparagraph (A) shall not apply to any qualified residence interest (within the meaning of section 163(h)).

(C) SPECIAL RULE FOR FLOW-THROUGH ENTITIES.—Except as provided in regulations, in the case of any flow-through entity, this paragraph shall be applied first at the entity level and then at the beneficiary level.

(3) INTEREST RELATING TO PROPERTY USED TO PRODUCE PROPERTY.—This subsection shall apply to any interest on indebtedness allocable (as determined under paragraph (2)) to property used to produce property to which this subsection applies to the extent such interest is allocable (as so determined) to the produced property.

(4) DEFINITIONS.—For purposes of this subsection—

(A) LONG USEFUL LIFE.—Property has a long useful life if such property is—

(i) real property, or

(ii) property with a class life of 20 years or more (as determined under section 168).

(B) PRODUCTION PERIOD.—The term "production period" means, when used with respect to any property, the period—

(i) beginning on the date on which production of the property begins, and

(ii) ending on the date on which the property is ready to be placed in service or is ready to be held for sale.

(C) PRODUCTION EXPENDITURES.—The term "production expenditures" means the costs (whether or not incurred during the production period) required to be capitalized under subsection (a) with respect to the property.

Amendments

• 1988, Technical and Miscellaneous Revenue Act of 1988 (P.L. 100-647)

P.L. 100-647, §1008(b)(4)(A)-(B):

Amended Code Sec. 263A(f)(3) by striking out "incurred or continued in connection with" and inserting in lieu thereof "allocable (as determined under paragraph (2)) to", and by inserting "(as so determined)" after "allocable". **Effective** as if included in the provision of P.L. 99-514 to which it relates.

P.L. 100-647, §1008(b)(8), provides:

(8) The allocation used in the regulations prescribed under section 263A(h)(2) of the Internal Revenue Code of 1986 for apportioning storage costs and related handling costs shall be determined by dividing the amount of such costs by the beginning inventory balances and the purchases during the year and by multiplying the resulting allocation ratio by inventory amounts determined in accordance with the provisions of the joint explanatory statement of the committee of conference of the conference report accompanying H.R. 3838 (H.R. Rept. No. 99-841, Vol. II, 99th Cong., 2d Sess. II-306-307 (1986)).

[Sec. 263A(g)]

(g) PRODUCTION.—For purposes of this section—

(1) IN GENERAL.—The term "produce" includes construct, build, install, manufacture, develop, or improve.

(2) TREATMENT OF PROPERTY PRODUCED UNDER CONTRACT FOR THE TAXPAYER.—The taxpayer shall be treated as producing any property produced for the taxpayer under a contract with the taxpayer; except that only costs paid or incurred by the taxpayer (whether under such contract or otherwise) shall be taken into account in applying subsection (a) to the taxpayer.

[Sec. 263A(h)]

(h) EXEMPTION FOR FREE LANCE AUTHORS, PHOTOGRAPHERS, AND ARTISTS.—

(1) IN GENERAL.—Nothing in this section shall require the capitalization of any qualified creative expense.

(2) QUALIFIED CREATIVE EXPENSE.—For purposes of this subsection, the term "qualified creative expense" means any expense—

(A) which is paid or incurred by an individual in the trade or business of such individual (other than as an employee) of being a writer, photographer, or artist, and

(B) which, without regard to this section, would be allowable as a deduction for the taxable year.

Such term does not include any expense related to printing, photographic plates, motion picture films, video tapes, or similar items.

(3) DEFINITIONS.—For purposes of this subsection—

(A) WRITER.—The term "writer" means any individual if the personal efforts of such individual create (or may reasonably be expected to create) a literary manuscript, musical composition (including any accompanying words), or dance score.

(B) PHOTOGRAPHER.—The term "photographer" means any individual if the personal efforts of such individual create (or may reasonably be expected to create) a photograph or photographic negative or transparency.

(C) ARTIST.—

(i) IN GENERAL.—The term "artist" means any individual if the personal efforts of such individual create (or may reasonably be expected to create) a picture, painting, sculpture, statue, etching, drawing, cartoon, graphic design, or original print edition.

(ii) CRITERIA.—In determining whether any expense is paid or incurred in the trade or business of being an artist, the following criteria shall be taken into account:

(I) The originality and uniqueness of the item created (or to be created).

(II) The predominance of aesthetic value over utilitarian value of the item created (or to be created).

(D) TREATMENT OF CERTAIN CORPORATIONS.—

(i) IN GENERAL.—If—

(I) substantially all of the stock of a corporation is owned by a qualified employee-owner and members of his family (as defined in section 267(c)(4)), and

(II) the principal activity of such corporation is performance of personal services directly related to the activities of the qualified employee-owner and such services are substantially performed by the qualified employee-owner,

this subsection shall apply to any expense of such corporation which directly relates to the activities of such employee-owner in the same manner as if such expense were incurred by such employee-owner.

(ii) QUALIFIED EMPLOYEE-OWNER.—For purposes of this subparagraph, the term "qualified employee-owner" means any individual who is an employee-owner of the corporation (as defined in section 269A(b)(2)) and who is a writer, photographer, or artist.

Amendments

• 1989, Omnibus Budget Reconciliation Act of 1989 (P.L. 101-239)

P.L. 101-239, §7816(d)(1):

Amended Code Sec. 263A(h)(3)(D). **Effective** as if included in the provision of P.L. 100-647 to which it relates. Prior to amendment, Code Sec. 263A(h)(3)(D) read as follows:

(D) TREATMENT OF CERTAIN PERSONAL SERVICE CORPORATIONS.—

(i) IN GENERAL.—In the case of a personal service corporation, this subsection shall apply to any expense of such corporation which directly relates to the activities of the qualified employee-owner in the same manner as if such expense were incurred by such employee-owner.

(ii) QUALIFIED EMPLOYEE-OWNER.—The term "qualified employee-owner" means any individual who is an employee-owner of the personal service corporation and who is a writer, photographer, or artist, but only if substantially all of the stock of such corporation is owned by such individual and members of his family (as defined in section 267(c)(4)).

(iii) PERSONAL SERVICE CORPORATION.—For purposes of this subparagraph, the term "personal service corporation" means any personal service corporation (as defined in section 269A(b)).

• 1988, Technical and Miscellaneous Revenue Act of 1988 (P.L. 100-647)

P.L. 100-647, §6026(a):

Amended Code Sec. 263A by redesignating subsection (h) as subsection (i) and by inserting after subsection (g) new subsection (h). **Effective** as if included in the amendments made by P.L. 99-514, §803.

[Sec. 263A(i)]

(i) REGULATIONS.—The Secretary shall prescribe such regulations as may be necessary or appropriate to carry out the purposes of this section, including—

(1) regulations to prevent the use of related parties, pass-thru entities, or intermediaries to avoid the application of this section, and

(2) regulations providing for simplified procedures for the application of this section in the case of property described in subsection (b)(2).

Amendments

• 1989, Omnibus Budget Reconciliation Act of 1989 (P.L. 101-239)

P.L. 101-239, §7831(d)(2), provides:

(2) If any interest costs incurred after December 31, 1986, are attributable to costs incurred before January 1, 1987, the amendments made by section 803 of the Tax Reform Act of 1986 shall apply to such interest costs only to the extent such interest costs are attributable to costs which were required to be capitalized under section 263 of the Internal Revenue Code of 1954 and which would have been taken into account in applying section 189 of the Internal Revenue Code of 1954 (as in effect before its repeal by section 803 of the Tax Reform Act of 1986) or, if applicable, section 266 of such Code.

• 1988, Technical and Miscellaneous Revenue Act of 1988 (P.L. 100-647)

P.L. 100-647, §6026(a):

Redesignated Code Sec. 263A(h) as Code Sec. 263A(i). **Effective** as if included in the amendments made by P.L. 99-514, §803.

• 1987, Revenue Act of 1987 (P.L. 100-203)

P.L. 100-203, §10204, provides:

SEC. 10204. AMORTIZATION OF PAST SERVICE PENSION COSTS.

(a) IN GENERAL.—For purposes of sections 263A and 460 of the Internal Revenue Code of 1986, the allocable costs (within the meaning of section 263A(a)(2) or section 460(c) of such Code, whichever is applicable) with respect to any property shall include contributions paid to or under a pension or annuity plan whether or not such contributions represent past service costs.

(b) EFFECTIVE DATE.—

(1) IN GENERAL.—Except as provided in paragraph (2), subsection (a) shall apply to costs incurred after December 31, 1987, in taxable years ending after such date.

(2) SPECIAL RULE FOR INVENTORY PROPERTY.—In the case of any property which is inventory in the hands of the taxpayer—

(A) IN GENERAL.—Subsection (a) shall apply to taxable years beginning after December 31, 1987.

(B) CHANGE IN METHOD OF ACCOUNTING.—If the taxpayer is required by this section to change its method of accounting for any taxable year—

(i) such change shall be treated as initiated by the taxpayer,

(ii) such change shall be treated as made with the consent of the Secretary of the Treasury or his delegate, and

(iii) the net amount of adjustments required by section 481 of the Internal Revenue Code of 1986 shall be taken into account over a period not longer than 4 taxable years.

• 1986, Tax Reform Act of 1986 (P.L. 99-514)

P.L. 99-514, §803(a):

Amended part IX of subchapter B of chapter 1 by inserting after section 263 new section 263A. For the **effective** dates as well as special rules, see Act Sec. 803(d), below.

P.L. 99-514, §803(d), as amended by P.L. 100-647, §1008(b)(7) and P.L. 101-239, §7831(d)(1), provides:

(d) EFFECTIVE DATE.—

(1) IN GENERAL.—Except as provided in this subsection, the amendments made by this section shall apply to costs incurred after December 31, 1986, in taxable years ending after such date.

(2) SPECIAL RULE FOR INVENTORY PROPERTY.—In the case of any property which is inventory in the hands of the taxpayer—

(A) IN GENERAL.—The amendments made by this section shall apply to taxable years beginning after December 31, 1986.

(B) CHANGE IN METHOD OF ACCOUNTING.—If the taxpayer is required by the amendments made by this section to change its method of accounting with respect to such property for any taxable year—

(i) such change shall be treated as initiated by the taxpayer,

(ii) such change shall be treated as made with the consent of the Secretary, and

(iii) the period for taking into account the adjustments under section 481 by reason of such change shall not exceed 4 years.

(3) SPECIAL RULE FOR SELF-CONSTRUCTED PROPERTY.—The amendments made by this section shall not apply to any property which is produced by the taxpayer for use by the taxpayer if substantial construction had occurred before March 1, 1986.

(4) TRANSITIONAL RULE FOR CAPITALIZATION OF INTEREST AND TAXES.—

(A) TRANSITION PROPERTY EXEMPTED FROM INTEREST CAPITALIZATION.—Section 263A of the Internal Revenue Code of 1986 (as added by this section) and the amendment made by subsection (b)(1) shall not apply to interest costs which are allocable to any property—.

(i) to which the amendments made by section 201 do not apply by reason of sections 204(a)(1)(D) and (E) and 204(a)(5)(A), and

(ii) to which the amendments made by section 251 do not apply by reason of section 251(d)(3)(M).

(B) INTEREST AND TAXES.—Section 263A of such Code shall not apply to property described in the matter following subparagraph (B) of section 207(e)(2) of the Tax Equity and Fiscal Responsibility Act of 1982 to the extent it would require the capitalization of interest and taxes paid or incurred in connection with such property which are not required to be capitalized under section 189 of such Code (as in effect before the amendment made by subsection (b)(1)).

(5) TRANSITION RULE CONCERNING CAPITALIZATION OF INVENTORY RULES.—In the case of a corporation which on the date of the enactment of this Act was a member of an affiliated group of corporations (within the meaning of section 1504(a) of the Internal Revenue Code of 1986), the parent of which—

(A) was incorporated in California on April 15, 1925,

(B) adopted LIFO accounting as of the close of the taxable year ended December 31, 1950, and

(C) was, on May 22, 1986, merged into a Delaware corporation incorporated on March 12, 1986,

the amendments made by this section shall apply under a cut-off method whereby the uniform capitalization rules are applied only in costing layers of inventory acquired during taxable years beginning on or after January 1, 1987.

(6) TREATMENT OF CERTAIN REHABILITATION PROJECT.—The amendments made by this section shall not apply to interest and taxes paid or incurred with respect to the rehabilitation and conversion of a certified historic building which was formerly a factory into an apartment project with 155 units, 39 units of which are for low-income families, if the project was approved for annual interest assistance on June 10, 1986, by the housing authority of the State in which the project is located.

(7) SPECIAL RULE FOR CASUALTY LOSSES.—Section 263A(d)(2) of the Internal Revenue Code of 1986 (as added by this section) shall apply to expenses incurred on or after the date of the enactment of this Act.

[Sec. 264]

SEC. 264. CERTAIN AMOUNTS PAID IN CONNECTION WITH INSURANCE CONTRACTS.

[Sec. 264(a)]

(a) GENERAL RULE.—No deduction shall be allowed for—

(1) Premiums on any life insurance policy, or endowment or annuity contract, if the taxpayer is directly or indirectly a beneficiary under the policy or contract.

(2) Any amount paid or accrued on indebtedness incurred or continued to purchase or carry a single premium life insurance, endowment, or annuity contract.

(3) Except as provided in subsection (d), any amount paid or accrued on indebtedness incurred or continued to purchase or carry a life insurance, endowment, or annuity contract (other than a single premium contract or a contract treated as a single premium contract) pursuant to a plan of purchase which contemplates the systematic direct or indirect borrowing of part or all of the increases in the cash value of such contract (either from the insurer or otherwise).

(4) Except as provided in subsection (e), any interest paid or accrued on any indebtedness with respect to 1 or more life insurance policies owned by the taxpayer covering the life of any individual, or any endowment or annuity contracts owned by the taxpayer covering any individual.

Paragraph (2) shall apply in respect of annuity contracts only as to contracts purchased after March 1, 1954. Paragraph (3) shall apply only in respect of contracts purchased after August 6, 1963. Paragraph (4) shall apply with respect to contracts purchased after June 20, 1986.

Amendments

• 1998, IRS Restructuring and Reform Act of 1998 (P.L. 105-206)

P.L. 105-206, §6010(o)(1):

Amended Code Sec. 264(a)(3) by striking "subsection (c)" and inserting "subsection (d)". **Effective** as if included in the provision of P.L. 105-34 to which it relates [**effective** for contracts issued after 6-8-97, in tax years ending after such date.—CCH].

P.L. 105-206, §6010(o)(2):

Amended Code Sec. 264(a)(4) by striking "subsection (d)" and inserting "subsection (e)". **Effective** as if included in the provision of P.L. 105-34 to which it relates [**effective** for contracts issued after 6-8-97, in tax years ending after such date.—CCH].

• 1997, Taxpayer Relief Act of 1997 (P.L. 105-34)

P.L. 105-34, §1084(a)(1):

Amended Code Sec. 264(a)(1). For the **effective** date, see Act Sec. 1084(d)[(f)], below. Prior to amendment, Code Sec. 264(a)(1) read as follows:

(1) Premiums paid on any life insurance policy covering the life of any officer or employee, or of any person financially interested in any trade or business carried on by the taxpayer, when the taxpayer is directly or indirectly a beneficiary under such policy.

P.L. 105-34, §1084(b)(1):

Amended Code Sec. 264(a)(4) by striking "individual, who" and all that follows and inserting "individual.". For the **effective** date, see Act Sec. 1084(d)[(f)], below. Prior to amendment, Code Sec. 264(a)(4) read as follows:

(4) Except as provided in subsection (d), any interest paid or accrued on any indebtedness with respect to 1 or more life insurance policies owned by the taxpayer covering the life of any individual, or any endowment or annuity contracts owned by the taxpayer covering any individual, who—

(A) is or was an officer or employee, or

(B) is or was financially interested in,

any trade or business carried on (currently or formerly) by the taxpayer.

P.L. 105-34, §1084(d)[(f)], as amended by P.L. 105-206, §6010(o)(3)(B), provides:

(d)[(f)] EFFECTIVE DATE.—The amendments made by this section shall apply to contracts issued after June 8, 1997, in taxable years ending after such date. For purposes of the preceding sentence, any material increase in the death benefit or other material change in the contract shall be treated as a new contract except that, in the case of a master contract (within the meaning of section 264(f)(4)(E) of the Internal Revenue Code of 1986), the addition of covered lives shall be treated as a new contract only with respect to such additional covered lives. For purposes of this subsection, an increase in the death benefit under a policy or contract issued in connection with a lapse described in section 501(d)(2) of the Health Insurance Portability and Accountability Act of 1996 shall not be treated as a new contract.

P.L. 105-34, §1602(f)(1):

Amended Code Sec. 264(a)(4) by striking subparagraph (A) and all that follows through "by the taxpayer." and inserting new subparagraphs (A) and (B). **Effective** as if included in the provision of P.L. 104-191 to which it relates [generally **effective** for interest paid or accrued after 10-13-95.—CCH]. Prior to amendment, Code Sec. 264(a)(4)(A) and the material that followed it read as follows:

(4) Except as provided in subsection (d), any interest paid or accrued on any indebtedness with respect to 1 or more life insurance policies owned by the taxpayer covering the life of any individual, or any endowment or annuity contracts owned by the taxpayer covering any individual, who—

(A) is an officer or employee of, or

(B) is financially interested in,

any trade or business carried on by the taxpayer.

• 1996, Health Insurance Portability and Accountability Act of 1996 (P.L. 104-191)

P.L. 104-191, §501(a)(1)-(2):

Amended Code Sec. 264(a)(4) by inserting "or any endowment or annuity contracts owned by the taxpayer covering any individual", and by striking all that follows "carried on by the taxpayer" and inserting a period. **Effective** for interest paid or accrued after 10-13-95. For transitional and special rules, see Act Sec. 501(c)(2)-(3), below. Prior to amendment, Code Sec. 264(a)(4) read as follows:

(4) Any interest paid or accrued on any indebtedness with respect to 1 or more life insurance policies owned by the taxpayer covering the life of any individual who—

(A) is an officer or employee of, or

(B) is financially interested in,

any trade or business carried on by the taxpayer to the extent that the aggregate amount of such indebtedness with respect to policies covering such individual exceeds $50,000.

P.L. 104-191, §501(b)(1):

Amended Code Sec. 264(a)(4) by striking "Any" and inserting "Except as provided in subsection (d), any". **Effective** for interest paid or accrued after 10-13-95. For transitional and special rules, see Act Sec. 501(c)(2)-(3), below.

P.L. 104-191, §501(c)(2)-(3), as amended by P.L. 105-34, §1602(f)(4), provides:

(2) TRANSITION RULE FOR EXISTING INDEBTEDNESS.—

(A) IN GENERAL.—In the case of—

(i) indebtedness incurred before January 1, 1996, or

(ii) indebtedness incurred before January 1, 1997 with respect to any contract or policy entered into in 1994 or 1995,

the amendments made by this section shall not apply to qualified interest paid or accrued on such indebtedness after October 13, 1995, and before January 1, 1999.

(B) QUALIFIED INTEREST.—For purposes of subparagraph (A), the qualified interest with respect to any indebtedness for any month is the amount of interest (otherwise deductible) which would be paid or accrued for such month on such indebtedness if—

(i) in the case of any interest paid or accrued after December 31, 1995, indebtedness with respect to no more than 20,000 insured individuals were taken into account, and

(ii) the lesser of the following rates of interest were used for such month:

(I) The rate of interest specified under the terms of the indebtedness as in effect on October 13, 1995 (and without regard to modification of such terms after such date).

(II) The applicable percentage of the rate of interest described as Moody's Corporate Bond Yield Average-Monthly Average Corporates as published by Moody's Investors Service, Inc., or any successor thereto, for such month.

For purposes of clause (i), all persons treated as a single employer under subsection (a) or (b) of section 52 of the Internal Revenue Code of 1986 or subsection (m) or (o) of section 414 of such Code shall be treated as 1 person. Subclause (II) of clause (ii) shall not apply to any month before January 1, 1996.

(C) APPLICABLE PERCENTAGE.—For purposes of subparagraph (B), the applicable percentage is as follows:

For calendar year:	*The percentage is:*
1996	100 percent
1997	90 percent
1998	80 percent

(3) [Stricken.]

P.L. 104-191, §501(d), as amended by P.L. 105-34, §1602(f)(5), provides:

(d) SPREAD OF INCOME INCLUSION ON SURRENDER, ETC. OF CONTRACTS.—

(1) IN GENERAL.—If any amount is received under any life insurance policy or endowment or annuity contract described in paragraph (4) of section 264(a) of the Internal Revenue Code of 1986—

(A) on the complete surrender, redemption, or maturity of such policy or contract during calendar year 1996, 1997, or 1998, or

(B) in full discharge during any such calendar year of the obligation under the policy or contract which is in the nature of a refund of the consideration paid for the policy or contract,

then (in lieu of any other inclusion in gross income) such amount shall be includible in gross income ratably over the 4-taxable year period beginning with the taxable year such amount would (but for this paragraph) be includible. The preceding sentence shall only apply to the extent the amount is includible in gross income for the taxable year in which the event described in subparagraph (A) or (B) occurs.

(2) SPECIAL RULES FOR APPLYING SECTION 264.—A contract shall not be treated as—

(A) failing to meet the requirement of section 264(c)(1) of the Internal Revenue Code of 1986, or

(B) a single premium contract under section 264(b)(1) of such Code,

solely by reason of an occurrence described in subparagraph (A) or (B) of paragraph (1) of this subsection or solely by reason of a lapse occurring after October 13, 1995, by reason of no additional premiums being received under the contract.

(3) SPECIAL RULE FOR DEFERRED ACQUISITION COSTS.—In the case of the occurrence of any event described in subparagraph (A) or (B) of paragraph (1) of this subsection with respect to any policy or contract—

(A) section 848 of the Internal Revenue Code of 1986 shall not apply to the unamortized balance (if any) of the specified policy acquisition expenses attributable to such policy or contract immediately before the insurance company's taxable year in which such event occurs, and

(B) there shall be allowed as a deduction to such company for such taxable year under chapter 1 of such Code an amount equal to such unamortized balance.

• 1986, Tax Reform Act of 1986 (P.L. 99-514)

P.L. 99-514, §1003(a):

Amended Code Sec. 264(a) by adding after paragraph (3) new paragraph (4). **Effective** for contracts purchased after 6-20-86, in tax years ending after such date.

P.L. 99-514, §1003(b):

Amended Code Sec. 264(a) by adding a new sentence at the end thereof. **Effective** for contracts purchased after 6-20-86, in tax years ending after such date.

• 1964, Revenue Act of 1964 (P.L. 88-272)

P.L. 88-272, §215(a):

Amended subsection (a) to add paragraph (3) and to add at the end of subsection (a) the last sentence. **Effective** for contracts purchased after 8-6-63.

[Sec. 264(b)]

(b) EXCEPTIONS TO SUBSECTION (a)(1).—Subsection (a)(1) shall not apply to—

(1) any annuity contract described in section 72(s)(5), and

(2) any annuity contract to which section 72(u) applies.

Amendments

• 1997, Taxpayer Relief Act of 1997 (P.L. 105-34)

P.L. 105-34, §1084(a)(2):

Amended Code Sec. 264 by redesignating subsections (b), (c), and (d) as subsections (c), (d), and (e), respectively, and by inserting after subsection (a) a new subsection (b). For the **effective** date, see Act Sec. 1084(d)[(f)], in the amendment notes following Code Sec. 264(a).

[Sec. 264(c)]

(c) CONTRACTS TREATED AS SINGLE PREMIUM CONTRACTS.—For purposes of subsection (a) (2), a contract shall be treated as a single premium contract—

(1) if substantially all the premiums on the contract are paid within a period of 4 years from the date on which the contract is purchased, or

(2) if an amount is deposited after March 1, 1954, with the insurer for payment of a substantial number of future premiums on the contract.

Amendments

• 1997, Taxpayer Relief Act of 1997 (P.L. 105-34)

P.L. 105-34, §1084(a)(2):

Amended Code Sec. 264 by redesignating subsection (b) as subsection (c). For the **effective** date, see Act Sec. 1084(d)[(f)], in the amendment notes following Code Sec. 264(a).

[Sec. 264(d)]

(d) EXCEPTIONS.—Subsection (a)(3) shall not apply to any amount paid or accrued by a person during a taxable year on indebtedness incurred or continued as part of a plan referred to in subsection (a)(3)—

(1) if no part of 4 of the annual premiums due during the 7-year period (beginning with the date the first premium on the contract to which such plan relates was paid) is paid under such plan by means of indebtedness,

(2) if the total of the amounts paid or accrued by such person during such taxable year for which (without regard to this paragraph) no deduction would be allowable by reason of subsection (a)(3) does not exceed $100,

(3) if such amount was paid or accrued on indebtedness incurred because of an unforeseen substantial loss of income or unforeseen substantial increase in his financial obligations, or

(4) if such indebtedness was incurred in connection with his trade or business.

For purposes of applying paragraph (1), if there is a substantial increase in the premiums on a contract, a new 7-year period described in such paragraph with respect to such contract shall commence on the date the first such increased premium is paid.

Amendments

• 1997, Taxpayer Relief Act of 1997 (P.L. 105-34)

P.L. 105-34, §1084(a)(2):

Amended Code Sec. 264 by redesignating subsection (c) as subsection (d). For the **effective** date, see Act Sec. 1084(d)[(f)], in the amendment notes following Code Sec. 264(a).

• 1964, Revenue Act of 1964 (P.L. 88-272)

P.L. 88-272, §215(b):

Added 264(c). **Effective** for amounts paid or accrued in tax years beginning after 12-31-63.

[Sec. 264(e)]

(e) SPECIAL RULES FOR APPLICATION OF SUBSECTION (a)(4).—

(1) EXCEPTION FOR KEY PERSONS.—Subsection (a)(4) shall not apply to any interest paid or accrued on any indebtedness with respect to policies or contracts covering an individual who is a key person to the extent that the aggregate amount of such indebtedness with respect to policies and contracts covering such individual does not exceed $50,000.

(2) INTEREST RATE CAP ON KEY PERSONS AND PRE-1986 CONTRACTS.—

(A) IN GENERAL.—No deduction shall be allowed by reason of paragraph (1) or the last sentence of subsection (a) with respect to interest paid or accrued for any month beginning after December 31, 1995, to the extent the amount of such interest exceeds the amount which would have been determined if the applicable rate of interest were used for such month.

(B) APPLICABLE RATE OF INTEREST.—For purposes of subparagraph (A)—

(i) IN GENERAL.—The applicable rate of interest for any month is the rate of interest described as Moody's Corporate Bond Yield Average-Monthly Average Corporates as published by Moody's Investors Service, Inc., or any successor thereto, for such month.

(ii) PRE-1986 CONTRACTS.—In the case of indebtedness on a contract purchased on or before June 20, 1986—

(I) which is a contract providing a fixed rate of interest, the applicable rate of interest for any month shall be the Moody's rate described in clause (i) for the month in which the contract was purchased, or

(II) which is a contract providing a variable rate of interest, the applicable rate of interest for any month in an applicable period shall be such Moody's rate for the third month preceding the first month in such period.

For purposes of subclause (II), the term "applicable period" means the 12-month period beginning on the date the policy is issued (and each successive 12-month period thereafter) unless the taxpayer elects a number of months (not greater than 12) other than such 12-month period to be its applicable period. Such an election shall be made not later than the 90th day after the date of the enactment of this sentence and, if made, shall apply to the taxpayer's first taxable year ending on or after October 13, 1995, and all subsequent taxable years unless revoked with the consent of the Secretary.

(3) KEY PERSON.—For purposes of paragraph (1), the term "key person" means an officer or 20-percent owner, except that the number of individuals who may be treated as key persons with respect to any taxpayer shall not exceed the greater of—

(A) 5 individuals, or

(B) the lesser of 5 percent of the total officers and employees of the taxpayer or 20 individuals.

(4) 20- PERCENT OWNER.—For purposes of this subsection, the term "20-percent owner" means—

(A) if the taxpayer is a corporation, any person who owns directly 20 percent or more of the outstanding stock of the corporation or stock possessing 20 percent or more of the total combined voting power of all stock of the corporation, or

(B) if the taxpayer is not a corporation, any person who owns 20 percent or more of the capital or profits interest in the taxpayer.

(5) AGGREGATION RULES.—

(A) IN GENERAL.—For purposes of paragraph (4)(A) and applying the $50,000 limitation in paragraph (1)—

(i) all members of a controlled group shall be treated as 1 taxpayer, and

(ii) such limitation shall be allocated among the members of such group in such manner as the Secretary may prescribe.

(B) CONTROLLED GROUP.—For purposes of this paragraph, all persons treated as a single employer under subsection (a) or (b) of section 52 or subsection (m) or (o) of section 414 shall be treated as members of a controlled group.

Amendments

• 1997, Taxpayer Relief Act of 1997 (P.L. 105-34)

P.L. 105-34, §1084(a)(2):

Amended Code Sec. 264 by redesignating subsection (d) as subsection (e). For the **effective** date, see Act Sec. 1084(d)[(f)], in the amendment notes following Code Sec. 264(a).

P.L. 105-34, §1602(f)(2):

Amended the last two sentences of Code Sec. 264(d)(2)(B)(ii). **Effective** as if included in the provision of

P.L. 104-191 to which it relates [generally **effective** for interest paid or accrued after 10-13-95.—CCH]. Prior to amendment, the last two sentences of Code Sec. 264(d)(2)(B)(ii) read as follows:

For purposes of subclause (II), the taxpayer shall elect an applicable period for such contract on its return of tax imposed by this chapter for its first taxable year ending on or after October 13, 1995. Such applicable period shall be for any number of months (not greater than 12) specified in the election and may not be changed by the taxpayer without the consent of the Secretary.

P.L. 105-34, §1602(f)(3):

Amended Code Sec. 264(d)(4)(B) by striking "the employer" and inserting "the taxpayer". **Effective** as if included in the provision of P.L. 104-191 to which it relates [generally **effective** for interest paid or accrued after 10-13-95.—CCH].

• 1996, Health Insurance Portability and Accountability Act of 1996 (P.L. 104-191)

P.L. 104-191, §501(b)(2):

Amended Code Sec. 264 by adding at the end a new subsection (d). **Effective** for interest paid or accrued after 10-15-95. For transitional and special rules, see Act Sec. 501(c)(2)-(3), in the amendment notes following Code Sec. 264(a).

[Sec. 264(f)]

(f) PRO RATA ALLOCATION OF INTEREST EXPENSE TO POLICY CASH VALUES.—

(1) IN GENERAL.—No deduction shall be allowed for that portion of the taxpayer's interest expense which is allocable to unborrowed policy cash values.

(2) ALLOCATION.—For purposes of paragraph (1), the portion of the taxpayer's interest expense which is allocable to unborrowed policy cash values is an amount which bears the same ratio to such interest expense as—

(A) the taxpayer's average unborrowed policy cash values of life insurance policies, and annuity and endowment contracts, issued after June 8, 1997, bears to

(B) the sum of—

(i) in the case of assets of the taxpayer which are life insurance policies or annuity or endowment contracts, the average unborrowed policy cash values of such policies and contracts, and

(ii) in the case of assets of the taxpayer not described in clause (i), the average adjusted bases (within the meaning of section 1016) of such assets.

(3) UNBORROWED POLICY CASH VALUE.—For purposes of this subsection, the term "unborrowed policy cash value" means, with respect to any life insurance policy or annuity or endowment contract, the excess of—

(A) the cash surrender value of such policy or contract determined without regard to any surrender charge, over

(B) the amount of any loan with respect to such policy or contract.

If the amount described in subparagraph (A) with respect to any policy or contract does not reasonably approximate its actual value, the amount taken into account under subparagraph (A) shall be the greater of the amount of the insurance company liability or the insurance company reserve with respect to such policy or contract (as determined for purposes of the annual statement approved by the National Association of Insurance Commissioners) or shall be such other amount as is determined by the Secretary.

(4) EXCEPTION FOR CERTAIN POLICIES AND CONTRACTS.—

(A) POLICIES AND CONTRACTS COVERING 20-PERCENT OWNERS, OFFICERS, DIRECTORS, AND EMPLOYEES.—Paragraph (1) shall not apply to any policy or contract owned by an entity engaged in a trade or business if such policy or contract covers only 1 individual and if such individual is (at the time first covered by the policy or contract)—

(i) a 20-percent owner of such entity, or

(ii) an individual (not described in clause (i)) who is an officer, director, or employee of such trade or business.

A policy or contract covering a 20-percent owner of such entity shall not be treated as failing to meet the requirements of the preceding sentence by reason of covering the joint lives of such owner and such owner's spouse.

(B) CONTRACTS SUBJECT TO CURRENT INCOME INCLUSION.—Paragraph (1) shall not apply to any annuity contract to which section 72(u) applies.

(C) COORDINATION WITH PARAGRAPH (2).—Any policy or contract to which paragraph (1) does not apply by reason of this paragraph shall not be taken into account under paragraph (2).

(D) 20- PERCENT OWNER.—For purposes of subparagraph (A), the term "20-percent owner" has the meaning given such term by subsection (e)(4).

(E) MASTER CONTRACTS.—If coverage for each insured under a master contract is treated as a separate contract for purposes of sections 817(h), 7702, and 7702A, coverage for each such insured shall be treated as a separate contract for purposes of subparagraph (A). For purposes of the preceding sentence, the term "master contract" shall not include any group life insurance contract (as defined in section 848(e)(2)).

(5) EXCEPTION FOR POLICIES AND CONTRACTS HELD BY NATURAL PERSONS; TREATMENT OF PARTNERSHIPS AND S CORPORATIONS.—

(A) POLICIES AND CONTRACTS HELD BY NATURAL PERSONS.—

(i) IN GENERAL.—This subsection shall not apply to any policy or contract held by a natural person.

(ii) EXCEPTION WHERE BUSINESS IS BENEFICIARY.—If a trade or business is directly or indirectly the beneficiary under any policy or contract, such policy or contract shall be treated as held by such trade or business and not by a natural person.

(iii) SPECIAL RULES.—

(I) CERTAIN TRADES OR BUSINESSES NOT TAKEN INTO ACCOUNT.—Clause (ii) shall not apply to any trade or business carried on as a sole proprietorship and to any trade or business performing services as an employee.

(II) LIMITATION OF UNBORROWED CASH VALUE.—The amount of the unborrowed cash value of any policy or contract which is taken into account by reason of clause (ii) shall not exceed the benefit to which the trade or business is directly or indirectly entitled under the policy or contract.

(iv) REPORTING.—The Secretary shall require such reporting from policyholders and issuers as is necessary to carry out clause (ii).

(B) TREATMENT OF PARTNERSHIPS AND S CORPORATIONS.—In the case of a partnership or S corporation, this subsection shall be applied at the partnership and corporate levels.

(6) SPECIAL RULES.—

(A) COORDINATION WITH SUBSECTION (a) AND SECTION 265.—If interest on any indebtedness is disallowed under subsection (a) or section 265—

(i) such disallowed interest shall not be taken into account for purposes of applying this subsection, and

(ii) the amount otherwise taken into account under paragraph (2)(B) shall be reduced (but not below zero) by the amount of such indebtedness.

(B) COORDINATION WITH SECTION 263A.—This subsection shall be applied before the application of section 263A (relating to capitalization of certain expenses where taxpayer produces property).

(7) INTEREST EXPENSE.—The term "interest expense" means the aggregate amount allowable to the taxpayer as a deduction for interest (within the meaning of section 265(b)(4)) for the taxable year (determined without regard to this subsection, section 265(b), and section 291).

(8) AGGREGATION RULES.—

(A) IN GENERAL .—All members of a controlled group (within the meaning of subsection (e)(5)(B)) shall be treated as 1 taxpayer for purposes of this subsection.

(B) TREATMENT OF INSURANCE COMPANIES.—This subsection shall not apply to an insurance company subject to tax under subchapter L, and subparagraph (A) shall be applied without regard to any member of an affiliated group which is an insurance company.

Amendments

• 1998, Tax and Trade Relief Extension Act of 1998 (P.L. 105-277)

P.L. 105-277, §4003(i):

Amended Code Sec. 264(f)(3) by adding at the end a flush sentence. **Effective** as if included in the provision of P.L. 105-34 to which it relates [**effective** for contracts issued after 6-8-97, in tax years ending after such date.—CCH].

• 1998, IRS Restructuring and Reform Act of 1998 (P.L. 105-206)

P.L. 105-206, §6010(o)(3)(A):

Amended Code Sec. 264(f)(4) by adding at the end a new subparagraph (E). **Effective** as if included in the provision of P.L. 105-34 to which it relates [**effective** for contracts issued after 6-8-97, in tax years ending after such date.—CCH].

P.L. 105-206, §6010(o)(4)(A):

Amended Code Sec. 264(f)(5)(A)(iv) by striking the second sentence. **Effective** as if included in the provision of P.L. 105-34 to which it relates [**effective** for contracts issued after 6-8-97, in tax years ending after such date.—CCH]. Prior to being stricken, the second sentence of Code Sec. 264(f)(5)(A)(iv) read as follows:

Any report required under the preceding sentence shall be treated as a statement referred to in section 6724(d)(1).

P.L. 105-206, §6010(o)(5):

Amended Code Sec. 264(f)(8)(A) by striking "subsection (d)(5)(B)" and inserting "subsection (e)(5)(B)" **Effective** as if included in the provision of P.L. 105-34 to which it relates [**effective** for contracts issued after 6-8-97, in tax years ending after such date.—CCH].

• 1997, Taxpayer Relief Act of 1997 (P.L. 105-34)

P.L. 105-34, §1084(c):

Amended Code Sec. 264 by adding at the end a new subsection (f). For the **effective** date, see Act Sec. 1084(d)[(f)]in the amendment notes following Code Sec. 264(a).

[Sec. 265]

SEC. 265. EXPENSES AND INTEREST RELATING TO TAX-EXEMPT INCOME.

[Sec. 265(a)]

(a) GENERAL RULE.—No deduction shall be allowed for—

(1) EXPENSES.—Any amount otherwise allowable as a deduction which is allocable to one or more classes of income other than interest (whether or not any amount of income of that class or classes is received or accrued) wholly exempt from the taxes imposed by this subtitle, or any

amount otherwise allowable under section 212 (relating to expenses for production of income) which is allocable to interest (whether or not any amount of such interest is received or accrued) wholly exempt from the taxes imposed by this subtitle.

(2) INTEREST.—Interest on indebtedness incurred or continued to purchase or carry obligations the interest on which is wholly exempt from the taxes imposed by this subtitle.

(3) CERTAIN REGULATED INVESTMENT COMPANIES.—In the case of a regulated investment company which distributes during the taxable year an exempt-interest dividend (including exempt-interest dividends paid after the close of the taxable year as described in section 855), that portion of any amount otherwise allowable as a deduction which the amount of the income of such company wholly exempt from taxes under this subtitle bears to the total of such exempt income and its gross income (excluding from gross income, for this purpose, capital gain net income, as defined in section 1222(9)).

(4) INTEREST RELATED TO EXEMPT-INTEREST DIVIDENDS.—Interest on indebtedness incurred or continued to purchase or carry shares of stock of a regulated investment company which during the taxable year of the holder thereof distributes exempt-interest dividends.

(5) SPECIAL RULES FOR APPLICATION OF PARAGRAPH (2) IN THE CASE OF SHORT SALES.—For purposes of paragraph (2)—

(A) IN GENERAL.—The term "interest" includes any amount paid or incurred—

(i) by any person making a short sale in connection with personal property used in such short sale, or

(ii) by any other person for the use of any collateral with respect to such short sale.

(B) EXCEPTION WHERE NO RETURN ON CASH COLLATERAL.—If—

(i) the taxpayer provides cash as collateral for any short sale, and

(ii) the taxpayer receives no material earnings on such cash during the period of the sale,

subparagraph (A)(i) shall not apply to such short sale.

(6) SECTION NOT TO APPLY WITH RESPECT TO PARSONAGE AND MILITARY HOUSING ALLOWANCES.—No deduction shall be denied under this section for interest on a mortgage on, or real property taxes on, the home of the taxpayer by reason of the receipt of an amount as—

(A) a military housing allowance, or

(B) a parsonage allowance excludable from gross income under section 107.

Amendments

• 1990, Omnibus Budget Reconciliation Act of 1990 (P.L. 101-508)

P.L. 101-508, §11801(c)(4):

Amended Code Sec. 265(a)(2) by striking "subtitle" and all that follows down through the period at the end thereof and inserting "subtitle.". **Effective** 11-5-90. Prior to amendment, Code Sec. 265(a)(2) read as follows:

(2) INTEREST.—Interest on indebtedness incurred or continued to purchase or carry obligations the interest on which is wholly exempt from the taxes imposed by this subtitle, or to purchase or carry any certificate to the extent the interest on such certificate is excludable under section 128.

P.L. 101-508, §11821(b), provides:

(b) SAVINGS PROVISION.—If—

(1) any provision amended or repealed by this part applied to—

(A) any transaction occurring before the date of the enactment of this Act,

(B) any property acquired before such date of enactment, or

(C) any item of income, loss, deduction, or credit taken into account before such date of enactment, and

(2) the treatment of such transaction, property, or item under such provision would (without regard to the amendments made by this part) affect liability for tax for periods ending after such date of enactment,

nothing in the amendments made by this part shall be construed to affect the treatment of such transaction, property, or item for purposes of determining liability for tax for periods ending after such date of enactment.

• 1986, Tax Reform Act of 1986 (P.L. 99-514)

P.L. 99-514, §144:

Amended Code Sec. 265 by adding new paragraph (6). **Effective** for tax years beginning before, on, or after, 12-31-86.

P.L. 99-514, §902(b):

Amended Code Sec. 265 paragraph (2) by striking out the second sentence. **Effective** as indicated in Act Sec. 902(f) below. Prior to amendment, Code Sec. 265 paragraph (2) read as follows:

(2) INTEREST.—Interest on indebtness incurred or continued to purchase or carry obligations the interest on which is wholly exempt from the taxes imposed by this subtitle, or to purchase or carry any certificate to the extent the interest on such certificate is excludable under section 128. In applying the preceding sentence to a financial institution (other than a bank) which is a face-amount certificate company registered under the Investment Company Act of 1940 (15 U.S.C. 80a-1 and following) and which is subject to the banking laws of the State in which such institution is incorporated, interest on face-amount certificates (as defined in section 2(a)(15) of such Act) issued by such institution, and interest on amounts received for the purchase of such certificates to be issued by such institution, shall not be considered as interest on indebtedness incurred or continued to purchase or carry obligations the interest on which is wholly exempt from the taxes imposed by this subtitle, to the extent that the average amount of such obligations held by such institution during the taxable year (as determined under regulations prescribed by the Secretary) does not exceed 15 percent of the average of the total assets held by such institution during the taxable year (as so determined).

P.L. 99-514, §902(d):

Amended Code Sec. 265 by striking out "No deduction shall be allowed for—" and inserting in lieu thereof "(a) General Rule.—No deduction shall be allowed for—". For the **effective** date, see Act Sec. 902(f), as amended by P.L. 100-647, §1009(b)(1)-(2), below.

P.L. 99-514, §902(f), as amended by P.L. 100-647, §1009(b)(1)-(2), provides:

(f) EFFECTIVE DATE.—

(1) IN GENERAL.—Except as provided in this subsection, the amendments made by this section shall apply to taxable years ending after December 31, 1986.

(2) OBLIGATIONS ACQUIRED PURSUANT TO CERTAIN COMMITMENTS.—For purposes of sections 265(b) and 291(e)(1)(B) of the Internal Revenue Code of 1986, any tax-exempt obligation which is acquired after August 7, 1986, pursuant to a direct or indirect written committment—

(A) to purchase or repurchase such obligation, and

(B) entered into on or before September 25, 1985,

shall be treated as an obligation acquired before August 8, 1986.

(3) TRANSITIONAL RULES.—For purposes of sections 265(b) and 291(e)(1)(B) of the Internal Revenue Code of 1986, obligations with respect to any of the following projects shall be treated as obligations acquired before August 8, 1986, in the hands of the first and any subsequent financial institution acquiring such obligations:

(A) Park Forest, Illinois, redevelopment project.

(B) Clinton, Tennesee, Carriage Trace project.

(C) Savannah, Georgia, Mall Terrace Warehouse project.

(D) Chattanooga, Tennessee, Warehouse Row project.

(E) Dalton, Georgia, Towne Square project.

(F) Milwaukee, Wisconsin, Standard Electric Supply Company—distribution facility.

(G) Wausau, Wisconsin, urban renewal project.

(H) Cassville, Missouri, UDAG project.

(I) Outlook Envelope Company—plant expansion.

(J) Woodstock, Connecticut, Crabtree Warehouse partnership.

(K) Louisville, Kentucky, Speed Mansion renovation project.

(L) Charleston, South Carolina, 2 Festival Market Place projects at Union Pier Terminal and 1 project at the Remount Road Container Yard, State Pier No. 15 at North Charleston Terminal.

(M) New Orleans, Louisiana, Upper Pontalba Building renovation.

(N) Woodward Wight Building.

(O) Minneapolis, Minnesota, Miller Milling Company—flour mill project

(P) Homewood, Alabama, The Club Apartments.

(Q) Charlotte, North Carolina—qualified mortgage bonds acquired by NCNB bank ($5,250,000).

(R) Grand Rapids, Michigan, Central Bank project.

(S) Ruppman Marketing Services, Inc.—building project.

(T) Bellow Falls, Vermont—building project.

(U) East Broadway Project, Louisville, Kentucky.

(V) O.K. Industries, Oklahoma.

(4) ADDITIONAL TRANSITIONAL RULE.—Obligations issued pursuant to an allocation of a State's volume limitation for private activity bonds, which allocation was made by Executive Order 25 signed by the Governor of the State on May 22, 1986 (as such order may be amended before January 1, 1987), shall be treated as acquired on or before August 7, 1986, in the hands of the first and any subsequent financial institution acquiring such obligation. The aggregate face amount of obligations to which this paragraph applies shall not exceed $200,000,000.

• 1984, Deficit Reduction Act of 1984 (P.L. 98-369)

P.L. 98-369, §16(a):

Amended Code Sec. 265(2) by repealing Act Sec. 302(c)(2) of P.L. 97-34 (as in effect for tax years beginning after 12-31-81) which amended Code Sec. 265(2) by striking out in the first sentence "or to purchase or carry any certificate to the extent the interest on such certificate is excludable under section 128" and inserting in lieu thereof "or to purchase or carry obligations or shares, or to make other deposits or investments, the interest on which is described in section 128(c)(1) to the extent such interest is excludable from gross income under section 128". **Effective** as if the provision of P.L. 97-34 had not been enacted.

P.L. 98-369, §56(c):

Amended Code Sec. 265 by adding at the end thereof new paragraph (5). **Effective** for short sales after 7-18-84 in tax years ending after such date.

P.L. 98-369, §1052, provides:

Sec. 1052. Allocation of Expenses to Parsonage Allowances.

With respect to any mortgage interest or real property tax costs paid or incurred before January 1, 1986, by any minister of the gospel who owned and occupied a home before January 3, 1983 (or had a contract to purchase a home before such date and subsequently owned and occupied such home), the application of section 265(1) of the Internal Revenue Code of 1954 to such costs shall be determined without regard to Revenue Ruling 83-3 (and without regard to any other regulation, ruling, or decision reaching the same result, or a result similar to the result, set forth in such Revenue Ruling).

• 1981, Economic Recovery Tax Act of 1981 (P.L. 97-34)

P.L. 97-34, §301(b)(2):

Amended Code Sec. 265(2), as in effect for tax years beginning in 1981, by inserting after "under section 116" ", or to purchase or carry any certificate to the extent the interest on such certificate is excludable under section 128". **Effective** for tax years ending after 9-30-81.

P.L. 97-34, §302(c)(2) [repealed by P.L. 98-369, §16(a)]:

Amended Code Sec. 265(2), as in effect for tax years beginning after December 31, 1981, by striking out in the first sentence "or to purchase or carry any certificate to the extent the interest on such certificate is excludable under section 128" and inserting "or to purchase or carry obligations or shares, or to make other deposits or investments, the interest on which is described in section 128(c)(1) to the extent such interest is excludable from gross income under section 128". This amendment was originally **effective** for tax years beginning after 12-31-84 but it was subsequently repealed by P.L. 98-369, §16(a).

• 1980, Crude Oil Windfall Profit Tax Act of 1980 (P.L. 96-223)

P.L. 96-223, §404(b)(2):

Amended the first sentence of Code Sec. 265(2) by inserting after "subtitle" the following: ", or to purchase or carry obligations or shares, or to make deposits or other investments, the interest on which is described in section 116(c) to the extent such interest is excludable from gross income under section 116." **Effective** for tax years beginning after 12-31-80 and before 1-1-83. (P.L. 97-34, §302(b)(1), amended P.L. 96-223, §404(c), by striking out "1983" and inserting "1982".)

• 1976, Tax Reform Act of 1976 (P.L. 94-455)

P.L. 94-455, §1901(a)(37):

Amended Code Sec. 265(2) by striking "(other than obligations of the United States issued after September 24, 1917, and originally subscribed for by the taxpayer)" after "purchase or carry obligations" in the first sentence of Code Sec. 265(2). **Effective** for tax years beginning after 12-31-76.

P.L. 94-455, §1906(b)(13)(A):

Amended 1954 Code by substituting "Secretary" for "Secretary or his delegate" each place it appeared. **Effective** 2-1-77.

P.L. 94-455, §2137(e):

Added Code Secs. 265(3) and (4). **Effective** for tax years beginning after 12-31-75.

• 1964, Revenue Act of 1964 (P.L. 88-272)

P.L. 88-272, §216(a):

Amended paragraph (2) by adding the last sentence. **Effective** for tax years ending after the date of the enactment of the Act.

[Sec. 265(b)]

(b) PRO RATA ALLOCATION OF INTEREST EXPENSE OF FINANCIAL INSTITUTIONS TO TAX-EXEMPT INTEREST.—

(1) IN GENERAL.—In the case of a financial institution, no deduction shall be allowed for that portion of the taxpayer's interest expense which is allocable to tax-exempt interest.

(2) ALLOCATION.—For purposes of paragraph (1), the portion of the taxpayer's interest expense which is allocable to tax-exempt interest is an amount which bears the same ratio to such interest expense as—

(A) the taxpayer's average adjusted bases (within the meaning of section 1016) of tax-exempt obligations acquired after August 7, 1986, bears to

(B) such average adjusted bases for all assets of the taxpayer.

(3) EXCEPTION FOR CERTAIN TAX-EXEMPT OBLIGATIONS.—

(A) IN GENERAL.—Any qualified tax-exempt obligation acquired after August 7, 1986, shall be treated for purposes of paragraph (2) and section 291(e)(1)(B) as if it were acquired on August 7, 1986.

(B) QUALIFIED TAX-EXEMPT OBLIGATION.—

(i) IN GENERAL.—For purposes of subparagraph (A), the term "qualified tax-exempt obligation" means a tax-exempt obligation—

(I) which is issued after August 7, 1986, by a qualified small issuer,

(II) which is not a private activity bond (as defined in section 141), and

(III) which is designated by the issuer for purposes of this paragraph.

(ii) CERTAIN BONDS NOT TREATED AS PRIVATE ACTIVITY BONDS.—For purposes of clause (i)(II), there shall not be treated as a private activity bond—

(I) any qualified 501(c)(3) bond (as defined in section 145), or

(II) any obligation issued to refund (or which is part of a series of obligations issued to refund) an obligation issued before August 8, 1986, which was not an industrial development bond (as defined in section 103(b)(2) as in effect on the day before the date of the enactment of the Tax Reform Act of 1986) or a private loan bond (as defined in section 103(o)(2)(A), as so in effect, but without regard to any exemption from such definition other than section 103(o)(2)(A)).

(C) QUALIFIED SMALL ISSUER.—

(i) IN GENERAL.—For purposes of subparagraph (B), the term "qualified small issuer" means, with respect to obligations issued during any calendar year, any issuer if the reasonably anticipated amount of tax-exempt obligations (other than obligations described in clause (ii)) which will be issued by such issuer during such calendar year does not exceed $10,000,000.

(ii) OBLIGATIONS NOT TAKEN INTO ACCOUNT IN DETERMINING STATUS AS QUALIFIED SMALL ISSUER.—For purposes of clause (i), an obligation is described in this clause if such obligation is—

(I) a private activity bond (other than a qualified 501(c)(3) bond, as defined in section 145),

(II) an obligation to which section 141(a) does not apply by reason of section 1312, 1313, 1316(g), or 1317 of the Tax Reform Act of 1986 and which would (if issued on August 15, 1986) have been an industrial development bond (as defined in section 103(b)(2) as in effect on the day before the date of the enactment of such Act) or a private loan bond (as defined in section 103(o)(2)(A), as so in effect, but without regard to any exception from such definition other than section 103(o)(2)(A)), or

(III) an obligation issued to refund (other than to advance refund within the meaning of section 149(d)(5)) any obligation to the extent the amount of the refunding obligation does not exceed the outstanding amount of the refunded obligation.

(iii) ALLOCATION OF AMOUNT OF ISSUE IN CERTAIN CASES.—In the case of an issue under which more than 1 governmental entity receives benefits, if—

(I) all governmental entities receiving benefits from such issue irrevocably agree (before the date of issuance of the issue) on an allocation of the amount of such issue for purposes of this subparagraph, and

(II) such allocation bears a reasonable relationship to the respective benefits received by such entities,

then the amount of such issue so allocated to an entity (and only such amount with respect to such issue) shall be taken into account under clause (i) with respect to such entity.

(D) LIMITATION ON AMOUNT OF OBLIGATIONS WHICH MAY BE DESIGNATED.—

(i) IN GENERAL.—Not more than $10,000,000 of obligations issued by an issuer during any calendar year may be designated by such issuer for purposes of this paragraph.

(ii) CERTAIN REFUNDINGS OF DESIGNATED OBLIGATIONS DEEMED DESIGNATED.—Except as provided in clause (iii), in the case of a refunding (or series of refundings) of a qualified tax- exempt obligation, the refunding obligation shall be treated as a qualified tax-exempt obligation (and shall not be taken into account under clause (i)) if—

(I) the refunding obligation was not taken into account under subparagraph (C) by reason of clause (ii)(III) thereof,

(II) the average maturity date of the refunding obligations issued as part of the issue of which such refunding obligation is a part is not later than the average maturity date of the obligations to be refunded by such issue, and

(III) the refunding obligation has a maturity date which is not later than the date which is 30 years after the date the original qualified tax-exempt obligation was issued.

Subclause (II) shall not apply if the average maturity of the issue of which the original qualified tax-exempt obligation was a part (and of the issue of which the obligations to be refunded are a part) is 3 years or less. For purposes of this clause, average maturity shall be determined in accordance with section 147(b)(2)(A).

(iii) CERTAIN OBLIGATIONS MAY NOT BE DESIGNATED OR DEEMED DESIGNATED.—No obligation issued as part of an issue may be designated under this paragraph (or may be treated as designated under clause (ii)) if—

(I) any obligation issued as part of such issue is issued to refund another obligation, and

(II) the aggregate face amount of such issue exceeds $10,000,000.

(E) AGGREGATION OF ISSUERS.—For purposes of subparagraphs (C) and (D)—

(i) an issuer and all entities which issue obligations on behalf of such issuer shall be treated as 1 issuer,

(ii) all obligations issued by a subordinate entity shall, for purposes of applying subparagraphs (C) and (D) to each other entity to which such entity is subordinate, be treated as issued by such other entity, and

(iii) an entity formed (or, to the extent provided by the Secretary, availed of) to avoid the purposes of subparagraph (C) or (D) and all entities benefiting thereby shall be treated as 1 issuer.

(F) TREATMENT OF COMPOSITE ISSUES.—In the case of an obligation which is issued as part of a direct or indirect composite issue, such obligation shall not be treated as a qualified tax-exempt obligation unless—

(i) the requirements of this paragraph are met with respect to such composite issue (determined by treating such composite issue as a single issue), and

(ii) the requirements of this paragraph are met with respect to each separate lot of obligations which are part of the issue (determined by treating each such separate lot as a separate issue).

(G) SPECIAL RULES FOR OBLIGATIONS ISSUED DURING 2009 AND 2010.—

(i) INCREASE IN LIMITATION.—In the case of obligations issued during 2009 or 2010, subparagraphs (C)(i), (D)(i), and (D)(iii)(II) shall each be applied by substituting "$30,000,000" for "$10,000,000".

(ii) QUALIFIED 501(c)(3) BONDS TREATED AS ISSUED BY EXEMPT ORGANIZATION.—In the case of a qualified 501(c)(3) bond (as defined in section 145) issued during 2009 or 2010, this paragraph shall be applied by treating the 501(c)(3) organization for whose benefit such bond was issued as the issuer.

(iii) SPECIAL RULE FOR QUALIFIED FINANCINGS.—In the case of a qualified financing issue issued during 2009 or 2010—

(I) subparagraph (F) shall not apply, and

(II) any obligation issued as a part of such issue shall be treated as a qualified tax-exempt obligation if the requirements of this paragraph are met with respect to each qualified portion of the issue (determined by treating each qualified portion as a separate issue which is issued by the qualified borrower with respect to which such portion relates).

(iv) QUALIFIED FINANCING ISSUE.—For purposes of this subparagraph, the term "qualified financing issue" means any composite, pooled, or other conduit financing issue the proceeds of which are used directly or indirectly to make or finance loans to 1 or more ultimate borrowers each of whom is a qualified borrower.

(v) QUALIFIED PORTION.—For purposes of this subparagraph, the term "qualified portion" means that portion of the proceeds which are used with respect to each qualified borrower under the issue.

(vi) QUALIFIED BORROWER.—For purposes of this subparagraph, the term "qualified borrower" means a borrower which is a State or political subdivision thereof or an organization described in section 501(c)(3) and exempt from taxation under section 501(a).

(4) DEFINITIONS.—For purposes of this subsection—

(A) INTEREST EXPENSE.—The term "interest expense" means the aggregate amount allowable to the taxpayer as a deduction for interest for the taxable year (determined without regard to this subsection, section 264, and section 291). For purposes of the preceding sentence, the term "interest" includes amounts (whether or not designated as interest) paid in respect of deposits, investment certificates, or withdrawable or repurchasable shares.

(B) TAX-EXEMPT OBLIGATION.—The term "tax-exempt obligation" means any obligation the interest on which is wholly exempt from taxes imposed by this subtitle. Such term includes shares of stock of a regulated investment company which during the taxable year of the holder thereof distributes exempt-interest dividends.

(5) FINANCIAL INSTITUTION.—For purposes of this subsection, the term "financial institution" means any person who—

(A) accepts deposits from the public in the ordinary course of such person's trade or business, and is subject to Federal or State supervision as a financial institution, or

(B) is a corporation described in section 585(a)(2).

(6) SPECIAL RULES.—

(A) COORDINATION WITH SUBSECTION (a).—If interest on any indebtness is disallowed under subsection (a) with respect to any tax-exempt obligation—

(i) such disallowed interest shall not be taken into account for purposes of applying this subsection, and

(ii) for purposes of applying paragraph (2), the adjusted basis of such tax-exempt obligation shall be reduced (but not below zero) by the amount of such indebtedness.

(B) COORDINATION WITH SECTION 263A.—This section shall be applied before the application of section 263A (relating to capitalization of certain expenses where taxpayer produces property).

(7) DE MINIMIS EXCEPTION FOR BONDS ISSUED DURING 2009 OR 2010.—

(A) IN GENERAL.—In applying paragraph (2)(A), there shall not be taken into account tax-exempt obligations issued during 2009 or 2010.

(B) LIMITATION.—The amount of tax-exempt obligations not taken into account by reason of subparagraph (A) shall not exceed 2 percent of the amount determined under paragraph (2)(B).

(C) REFUNDINGS.—For purposes of this paragraph, a refunding bond (whether a current or advance refunding) shall be treated as issued on the date of the issuance of the refunded bond (or in the case of a series of refundings, the original bond).

Amendments

• 2009, American Recovery and Reinvestment Tax Act of 2009 (P.L. 111-5)

P.L. 111-5, §1501(a):

Amended Code Sec. 265(b) by adding at the end a new paragraph (7). **Effective** for obligations issued after 12-31-2008.

P.L. 111-5, §1502(a):

Amended Code Sec. 265(b)(3) by adding at the end a new subparagraph (G). **Effective** for obligations issued after 12-31-2008.

• 1997, Taxpayer Relief Act of 1997 (P.L. 105-34)

P.L. 105-34, §1084(c)[e]:

Amended Code Sec. 265(b)(4)(A) by inserting ", section 264," before "and section 291". For the **effective** date, see Act Sec. 1084(d)[(f)], below.

P.L. 105-34, §1084(d)[(f)], as amended by P.L. 105-206, §6010(o)(3)(B)), provides:

(d)[(f)] EFFECTIVE DATE.—The amendments made by this section shall apply to contracts issued after June 8, 1997, in taxable years ending after such date. For purposes of the preceding sentence, any material increase in the death benefit or other material change in the contract shall be treated as a new contract except that, in the case of a master contract (within the meaning of section 264(f)(4)(E) of the Internal Revenue Code of 1986), the addition of covered lives shall be treated as a new contract only with respect to such additional covered lives. For purposes of this subsection, an increase in the death benefit under a policy or contract issued in connection with a lapse described in section 501(d)(2) of the Health Insurance Portability and Accountability Act of 1996 shall not be treated as a new contract.

• 1988, Technical and Miscellaneous Revenue Act of 1988 (P.L. 100-647)

P.L. 100-647, §1009(b)(3)(A):

Amended Code Sec. 265(b)(3). For **effective** date, see Act Sec. 1009(b)(3)(B)-(D), below. Prior to amendment, Code Sec. 265(b)(3) read as follows:

(3) EXCEPTION FOR CERTAIN TAX-EXEMPT OBLIGATIONS.—

(A) IN GENERAL.—Any qualified tax-exempt obligation acquired after August 7, 1986, shall be treated for purposes of paragraph (2) and section 291(e)(1)(B) as if it were acquired on August 7, 1986.

(B) QUALIFIED TAX-EXEMPT OBLIGATIONS.—For purposes of subparagraph (A), the term "qualified tax-exempt obligation" means a tax-exempt obligation which—

(i) is not a private activity bond (as defined in section 141), and

(ii) is designated by the issuer for purposes of this paragraph.

For purposes of the preceding sentence and subparagraph (C), a qualified 501(c)(3) bond (as defined in section 145) shall not be treated as a private activity bond.

(C) LIMITATION ON ISSUER.—An obligation issued by an issuer during any calendar year shall not be treated as a qualified tax-exempt obligation unless the reasonably anticipated amount of qualified tax-exempt obligations (other than private activity bonds) which will be issued by such issuer during such calendar year does not exceed $10,000,000.

(D) OVERALL $10,000,000 LIMITATION.—Not more than $10,000,000 of obligations issued by an issuer during any calendar year may be designated by such issuer for purposes of this paragraph.

(E) AGGREGATION OF ISSUERS.—For purposes of subparagraphs (C) and (D), an issuer and all subordinate entities thereof shall be treated as 1 issuer.

P.L. 100-647, §1009(b)(3)(B)-(D), as amended by P.L. 101-239, §7811(f)(2), provides:

(B) In the case of any obligation issued after August 7, 1986, and before January 1, 1987, the time for making a designation with respect to such obligation under section 265(b)(3)(B)(i)(III) of the 1986 Code shall not expire before January 1, 1989.

(C) If—

(i) an obligation is issued on or after January 1, 1986, and on or before August 7, 1986,

(ii) when such obligation was issued, the issuer made a designation that it intended to qualify under section 802(e)(3) of H.R. 3838 of the 99th Congress as passed by the House of Representatives, and

(iii) the issuer makes an election under this subparagraph with respect to such obligation,

for purposes of section 265(b)(3) of the 1986 Code, such obligation shall be treated as issued on August 8, 1986.

(D)(i) Except as provided in clause (ii), the following provisions of section 265(b)(3) of the 1986 Code (as amended by this subparagraph (A)) shall apply to obligations issued after June 30, 1987:

(I) subparagraph (C)(ii)(III),

(II) clauses (ii) and (iii) of subparagraph (D), and

(III) subparagraphs (E) and (F).

(ii) At the election of an issuer (made at such time and in such manner as the Secretary of the Treasury or his delegate may prescribe), the provisions referred to in clause (i) shall apply to such issuer as if included in the amendments made by section 902(a) of the Tax Reform Act of 1986.

• 1986, Tax Reform Act of 1986 (P.L. 99-514)

P.L. 99-514, §902(a):

Amended Code Sec. 265 by adding at the end thereof new subsection (b). For the **effective** date, see Act Sec. 902(f) after Code Sec. 265(a).

[Sec. 266]

SEC. 266. CARRYING CHARGES.

No deduction shall be allowed for amounts paid or accrued for such taxes and carrying charges as, under regulations prescribed by the Secretary, are chargeable to capital account with respect to property, if the taxpayer elects, in accordance with such regulations, to treat such taxes or charges as so chargeable.

Amendments

• 1976, Tax Reform Act of 1976 (P.L. 94-455)

P.L. 94-455, §1906(b)(13)(A):

Amended 1954 Code by substituting "Secretary" for "Secretary or his delegate" each place it appeared. **Effective** 2-1-77.

[Sec. 267]

SEC. 267. LOSSES, EXPENSES, AND INTEREST WITH RESPECT TO TRANSACTIONS BETWEEN RELATED TAXPAYERS.

[Sec. 267(a)]

(a) IN GENERAL.—

(1) DEDUCTION FOR LOSSES DISALLOWED.—No deduction shall be allowed in respect of any loss from the sale or exchange of property, directly or indirectly, between persons specified in any of the paragraphs of subsection (b). The preceding sentence shall not apply to any loss of the distributing corporation (or the distributee) in the case of a distribution in complete liquidation.

(2) MATCHING OF DEDUCTION AND PAYEE INCOME ITEM IN THE CASE OF EXPENSES AND INTEREST.—If—

(A) by reason of the method of accounting of the person to whom the payment is to be made, the amount thereof is not (unless paid) includible in the gross income of such person, and

(B) at the close of the taxable year of the taxpayer for which (but for this paragraph) the amount would be deductible under this chapter, both the taxpayer and the person to whom the payment is to be made are persons specified in any of the paragraphs of subsection (b),

then any deduction allowable under this chapter in respect of such amount shall be allowable as of the day as of which such amount is includible in the gross income of the person to whom the payment is made (or, if later, as of the day on which it would be so allowable but for this paragraph). For purposes of this paragraph, in the case of a personal service corporation (within the meaning of section 441(i)(2)), such corporation and any employee-owner (within the meaning of section 269A(b)(2), as modified by section 441(i)(2)) shall be treated as persons specified in subsection (b).

(3) PAYMENTS TO FOREIGN PERSONS

(A) IN GENERAL.—The Secretary shall by regulations apply the matching principle of paragraph (2) in cases in which the person to whom the payment is to be made is not a United States person.

(B) SPECIAL RULE FOR CERTAIN FOREIGN ENTITIES.—

(i) IN GENERAL.—Notwithstanding subparagraph (A), in the case of any item payable to a controlled foreign corporation (as defined in section 957) or a passive foreign investment company (as defined in section 1297), a deduction shall be allowable to the payor with respect to such amount for any taxable year before the taxable year in which paid only to the extent that an amount attributable to such item is includible (determined without regard to properly allocable deductions and qualified deficits under section 952(c)(1)(B)) during such prior taxable year in the gross income of a United States person who owns (within the meaning of section 958(a)) stock in such corporation.

(ii) SECRETARIAL AUTHORITY.—The Secretary may by regulation exempt transactions from the application of clause (i), including any transaction which is entered into by a payor in the ordinary course of a trade or business in which the payor is predominantly engaged and in which the payment of the accrued amounts occurs within 8½ months after accrual or within such other period as the Secretary may prescribe.

Amendments

• 2004, American Jobs Creation Act of 2004 (P.L. 108-357)

P.L. 108-357, §841(b)(1)-(2):

Amended Code Sec. 267(a)(3) by striking "The Secretary" and inserting "(A) IN GENERAL.—The Secretary", and by adding at the end a new subparagraph (B). **Effective** for payments accrued on or after 10-22-2004.

• 1988, Technical and Miscellaneous Revenue Act of 1988 (P.L. 100-647)

P.L. 100-647, §1006(e)(9)(A)-(B):

Amended Code Sec. 267(a)(1) by striking out "(other than a loss in case of a distribution in corporate liquidation)" after "property", and by adding at the end thereof a new sentence. **Effective** as if included in the provision of P.L. 99-514 to which it relates. Prior to amendment, Code Sec. 267(a)(1) read as follows:

(a) IN GENERAL.—

(1) DEDUCTION FOR LOSSES DISALLOWED.—No deduction shall be allowed in respect of any loss from the sale or exchange of property (other than a loss in case of a distribution in corporate liquidation), directly or indirectly, between persons specified in any of the paragraphs of subsection (b).

P.L. 100-647, §1008(e)(9), provides:

(9) Nothing in section 806 of the Reform Act or in any legislative history relating thereto shall be construed as requiring the Secretary of the Treasury or his delegate to permit an automatic change of a taxable year.

• 1986, Tax Reform Act of 1986 (P.L. 99-514)

P.L. 99-514, §806(c)(2):

Amended Code Sec. 267(a) by adding at the end thereof the following new sentence: "For purposes of this paragraph, in the case of a personal service corporation (within the meaning of section 441(i)(2)), such corporation and any employee-owner (within the meaning of section 269A(b)(2), as modified by section 441(i)(2)) shall be treated as persons specified in subsection (b)." For the **effective** dates, see Act Sec. 806(e), as amended by P.L. 100-647, §1008(e)(7)-(8), and (10), below.

P.L. 99-514, §806(e), as amended by P.L. 100-647, §1008(e)(7)-(8) and (10), provides:

(e) EFFECTIVE DATE.—

(1) IN GENERAL.—The amendments made by this section shall apply to taxable years beginning after December 31, 1986.

(2) CHANGE IN ACCOUNTING PERIOD.—In the case of any partnership, S corporation, or personal service corporation required by the amendments made by this section to change its accounting period for the taxpayer's first taxable year beginning after December 31, 1986—

(A) such change shall be treated as initiated by the partnership, S corporation, or personal service corporation,

(B) such change shall be treated as having been made with the consent of the Secretary, and

(C) with respect to any partner or shareholder of an S corporation which is required to include the items from more than 1 taxable year of the partnership or S corporation in any 1 taxable year, income in excess of expenses of such partnership or corporation for the short taxable year required by such amendments shall be taken into account ratably in each of the first 4 taxable years beginning after December 31, 1986, unless such partner or shareholder elects to include all such income in the the partner's or shareholder's taxable year with or within which the partnership's or S corporation short taxable year ends.

Subparagraph (C) shall apply to a shareholder of an S corporation only if such corporation was an S corporation for a taxable year beginning in 1986.

(3) BASIS, ETC. RULES.—

(A) BASIS RULE.—The adjusted basis of any partner's interest in a partnership or shareholder's stock in an S corporation shall be determined as if all of the income to be taken into account ratably in the 4 taxable years referred to in paragraph (2)(C) were included in gross income for the 1st of such taxable years.

(B) TREATMENT OF DISPOSITIONS.—If any interest in a partnership or stock in an S corporation is disposed of before the last taxable year in the spread period, all amounts which would be included in the gross income of the partner or shareholder for subsequent taxable years in the spread period under paragraph (2)(C) and attributable to the interest of stock disposed of shall be included in gross income for the taxable year in which the disposition occurs. For purposes of the preceding sentence, the term "spread period" means the period consisting of the 4 taxable years referred to in paragraph (2)(C).

P.L. 99-514, §1812(c)(1):

Amended Code Sec. 267(a) by adding at the end of thereof new paragraph (3). **Effective** as if included in the provision of P.L. 98-369 to which it relates.

• 1984, Deficit Reduction Act of 1984 (P.L. 98-369)

P.L. 98-369, §174(a)(1):

Amended Code Sec. 267(a). **Effective** for amounts allowable as deductions under chapter 1 of the Internal Revenue Code of 1954 for tax years beginning after 12-31-83. For purposes of the preceding sentence, the allowability of a deduction shall be determined without regard to any disallowance or postponement of deductions under section 267 of such Code. An exception appears in Act Sec. 174(c)(3) following Code Sec. 267(f). Prior to amendment, Code Sec. 267(a) read as follows:

(a) Deductions Disallowed.—No deduction shall be allowed—

(1) Losses.—In respect of losses from sales or exchanges of property (other than losses in cases of distributions in corporate liquidations), directly or indirectly, between persons specified within any one of the paragraphs of subsection (b).

(2) Unpaid Expenses and Interest.—In respect of expenses, otherwise deductible under section 162 or 212, or of interest, otherwise deductible under section 163,—

(A) If within the period consisting of the taxable year of the taxpayer and 2½ months after the close thereof (i) such expenses or interest are not paid, and (ii) the amount thereof is not includible in the gross income of the person to whom the payment is to be made; and

(B) If, by reason of the method of accounting of the person to whom the payment is to be made, the amount thereof is not, unless paid, includible in the gross income of such person for the taxable year in which or with which the taxable year of the taxpayer ends; and

(C) If, at the close of the taxable year of the taxpayer or at any time within 2½ months thereafter, both the taxpayer and the person to whom the payment is to be made are persons specified within any one of the paragraphs of subsection (b).

[Sec. 267(b)]

(b) RELATIONSHIPS.—The persons referred to in subsection (a) are:

(1) Members of a family, as defined in subsection (c) (4);

(2) An individual and a corporation more than 50 percent in value of the outstanding stock of which is owned, directly or indirectly, by or for such individual;

(3) Two corporations which are members of the same controlled group (as defined in subsection (f));

(4) A grantor and a fiduciary of any trust;

(5) A fiduciary of a trust and a fiduciary of another trust, if the same person is a grantor of both trusts;

(6) A fiduciary of a trust and a beneficiary of such trust;

(7) A fiduciary of a trust and a beneficiary of another trust, if the same person is a grantor of both trusts;

(8) A fiduciary of a trust and a corporation more than 50 percent in value of the outstanding stock of which is owned, directly or indirectly, by or for the trust or by or for a person who is a grantor of the trust;

(9) A person and an organization to which section 501 (relating to certain educational and charitable organizations which are exempt from tax) applies and which is controlled directly or indirectly by such person or (if such person is an individual) by members of the family of such individual;

(10) A corporation and a partnership if the same persons own—

(A) more than 50 percent in value of the outstanding stock of the corporation, and

(B) more than 50 percent of the capital interest, or the profits interest, in the partnership;

(11) An S corporation and another S corporation if the same persons own more than 50 percent in value of the outstanding stock of each corporation;

(12) An S corporation and a C corporation, if the same persons own more than 50 percent in value of the outstanding stock of each corporation; or

(13) Except in the case of a sale or exchange in satisfaction of a pecuniary bequest, an executor of an estate and a beneficiary of such estate.

Amendments

• 1997, Taxpayer Relief Act of 1997 (P.L. 105-34)

P.L. 105-34, §1308(a):

Amended Code Sec. 267(b) by striking "or" at the end of paragraph (11), by striking the period at the end of paragraph (12) and inserting "; or", and by adding at the end a new paragraph (13). **Effective** for tax years beginning after 8-5-97.

• 1986, Tax Reform Act of 1986 (P.L. 99-514)

P.L. 99-514, §1812(c)(4)(A):

Amended Code Sec. 267(b)(12) by striking out "same persons owns" and inserting in lieu thereof "same persons own". **Effective** as if included in the provision of P.L. 98-369 to which it relates.

• 1984, Deficit Reduction Act of 1984 (P.L. 98-369)

P.L. 98-369, §174(b)(2)(A):

Amended Code Sec. 267(b)(3). **Effective** for transactions after 12-31-83, in tax years ending after such date. The amendment made by Act Sec. 174(b)(2) does not apply to property transferred to a foreign corporation on or before 3-1-84. For an exception, see Act Sec. 174(c)(3) following Code Sec. 267(f). Prior to amendment, Code Sec. 267(b)(3) reads as follows:

(3) Two corporations more than 50 percent in value of the outstanding stock of each of which is owned, directly or indirectly, by or for the same individual, if either one of such corporations, with respect to the taxable year of the corporation preceding the date of the sale or exchange was, under the law applicable to such taxable year, a personal holding company or a foreign personal holding company;

P.L. 98-369, §174(b)(3)(A)-(B):

Amended Code Sec. 267(b)(10) by striking out "An S corporation: and inserting in lieu thereof "A corporation", and by striking out "the S corporation" and inserting in lieu thereof "the corporation". **Effective** for transactions after 12-31-83, in tax years ending after such date.

P.L. 98-369, §174(b)(4):

Amended Code Sec. 267(b)(12) by striking out "the same individual" and inserting in lieu thereof "the same persons". **Effective** for transactions after 12-31-83, in tax years ending after such date.

• 1982, Subchapter S Revision Act of 1982 (P.L. 97-354)

P.L. 97-354, §3(h)(1):

Amended Code Sec. 267(b) by adding new paragraphs (10)-(12). **Effective** for tax years beginning after 12-31-82.

P.L. 97-354, §3(h)(3):

Amended Code Sec. 267(b) by striking out "or" at the end of paragraph (8), and by striking out the period at the end of paragraph (9) and inserting in lieu thereof a semicolon. **Effective** for tax years beginning after 12-31-82.

[Sec. 267(c)]

(c) CONSTRUCTIVE OWNERSHIP OF STOCK.—For purposes of determining, in applying subsection (b), the ownership of stock—

(1) Stock owned, directly or indirectly, by or for a corporation, partnership, estate, or trust shall be considered as being owned proportionately by or for its shareholders, partners, or beneficiaries;

(2) An individual shall be considered as owning the stock owned, directly or indirectly, by or for his family;

(3) An individual owning (otherwise than by the application of paragraph (2)) any stock in a corporation shall be considered as owning the stock owned, directly or indirectly, by or for his partner;

(4) The family of an individual shall include only his brothers and sisters (whether by the whole or half blood), spouse, ancestors, and lineal descendants; and

(5) Stock constructively owned by a person by reason of the application of paragraph (1) shall, for the purpose of applying paragraph (1), (2), or (3), be treated as actually owned by such person, but stock constructively owned by an individual by reason of the application of paragraph (2) or (3) shall not be treated as owned by him for the purpose of again applying either of such paragraphs in order to make another the constructive owner of such stock.

[Sec. 267(d)]

(d) AMOUNT OF GAIN WHERE LOSS PREVIOUSLY DISALLOWED.—If—

(1) in the case of a sale or exchange of property to the taxpayer a loss sustained by the transferor is not allowable to the transferor as a deduction by reason of subsection (a)(1) (or by reason of section 24(b) of the Internal Revenue Code of 1939); and

(2) after December 31, 1953, the taxpayer sells or otherwise disposes of such property (or of other property the basis of which in his hands is determined directly or indirectly by reference to such property) at a gain,

then such gain shall be recognized only to the extent that it exceeds so much of such loss as is properly allocable to the property sold or otherwise disposed of by the taxpayer. This subsection applies with respect to taxable years ending after December 31, 1953. This subsection shall not apply if the loss sustained by the transferor is not allowable to the transferor as a deduction by reason of section 1091 (relating to wash sales) or by reason of section 118 of the Internal Revenue Code of 1939.

[Sec. 267(e)]

(e) SPECIAL RULES FOR PASS-THRU ENTITIES.—

(1) IN GENERAL.—In the case of any amount paid or incurred by, to, or on behalf of, a pass-thru entity, for purposes of applying subsection (a)(2)—

(A) such entity,

(B) in the case of—

(i) a partnership, any person who owns (directly or indirectly) any capital interest or profits interest of such partnership, or

(ii) an S corporation, any person who owns (directly or indirectly) any of the stock of such corporation,

(C) any person who owns (directly or indirectly) any capital interest or profits interest of a partnership in which such entity owns (directly or indirectly) any capital interest or profits interest, and

(D) any person related (within the meaning of subsection (b) of this section or section 707(b)(1)) to a person described in subparagraph (B) or (C),

shall be treated as persons specified in a paragraph of subsection (b). Subparagraph (C) shall apply to a transaction only if such transaction is related either to the operations of the partnership described in such subparagraph or to an interest in such partnership.

(2) PASS-THRU ENTITY.—For purposes of this section, the term "pass-thru entity" means—

(A) a partnership, and

(B) an S corporation.

(3) CONSTRUCTIVE OWNERSHIP IN THE CASE OF PARTNERSHIPS.—For purposes of determining ownership of a capital interest or profits interest of a partnership, the principles of subsection (c) shall apply, except that—

(A) paragraph (3) of subsection (c) shall not apply, and

(B) interests owned (directly or indirectly) by or for a C corporation shall be considered as owned by or for any shareholder only if such shareholder owns (directly or indirectly) 5 percent or more in value of the stock of such corporation.

(4) SUBSECTION (a)(2) NOT TO APPLY TO CERTAIN GUARANTEED PAYMENTS OF PARTNERSHIPS.—In the case of any amount paid or incurred by a partnership, subsection (a)(2) shall not apply to the extent that section 707(c) applies to such amount.

(5) EXCEPTION FOR CERTAIN EXPENSES AND INTEREST OF PARTNERSHIPS OWNING LOW-INCOME HOUSING.—

(A) IN GENERAL.—This subsection shall not apply with respect to qualified expenses and interest paid or incurred by a partnership owning low-income housing to—

(i) any qualified 5-percent or less partner of such partnership, or

(ii) any person related (within the meaning of subsection (b) of this section or section 707(b)(1)) to any qualified 5-percent or less partner of such partnership.

(B) QUALIFIED 5-PERCENT OR LESS PARTNER.—For purposes of this paragraph, the term "qualified 5-percent or less partner" means any partner who has (directly or indirectly) an interest of 5 percent or less in the aggregate capital and profits interests of the partnership but only if—

(i) such partner owned the low-income housing at all times during the 2-year period ending on the date such housing was transferred to the partnership, or

(ii) such partnership acquired the low-income housing pursuant to a purchase, assignment, or other transfer from the Department of Housing and Urban Development or any State or local housing authority.

For purposes of the preceding sentence, a partner shall be treated as holding any interest in the partnership which is held (directly or indirectly) by any person related (within the meaning of subsection (b) of this section or section 707(b)(1)) to such partner.

(C) QUALIFIED EXPENSES AND INTEREST.—For purpose of this paragraph, the term "qualified expenses and interest" means any expense or interest incurred by the partnership with respect to low-income housing held by the partnership but—

(i) only if the amount of such expense or interest (as the case may be) is unconditionally required to be paid by the partnership not later than 10 years after the date such amount was incurred, and

(ii) in the case of such interest, only if such interest is incurred at an annual rate not in excess of 12 percent.

(D) LOW-INCOME HOUSING.—For purposes of this paragraph, the term "low-income housing" means—

(i) any interest in property described in clause (i), (ii), (iii), or (iv) of section 1250(a)(1)(B), and

(ii) any interest in a partnership owning such property.

(6) CROSS REFERENCE.—

For additional rules relating to partnerships, see section 707(b).

Amendments

• 1986, Tax Reform Act of 1986 (P.L. 99-514)

P.L. 99-514, §803(b)(5)(A)-(B):

Amended Code Sec. 267(e)(5)(D) by striking out "low-income housing (as defined in paragraph (5) of section 189 [179](e))" and inserting "property described in clause (i), (ii), (iii), or (iv) of section 1250(a)(1)(B)", and by striking out "low-income housing (as so defined)" and inserting "such property". **Effective**, generally, for costs incurred after 12-31-86, in tax years ending after such date. See, however, the special rules provided in Act Sec. 803(d)(2)-(7) following Code Sec. 263A.

P.L. 99-514, §1812(c)(3)(C):

Amended Code Sec. 267(e) by adding at the end thereof new paragraph (6). **Effective** as if included in the provision of P.L. 98-369 to which it relates.

• 1984, Deficit Reduction Act of 1984 (P.L. 98-369)

P.L. 98-369, §174(a)(2):

Repealed Code Sec. 267(e). **Effective** for amounts allowable as deductions under chapter 1 of the Internal Revenue Code of 1954 for tax years beginning after 12-31-83. For purposes of the preceding sentence, the allowability of a deduction shall be determined without regard to any disallowance or postponement of deductions under section 267 of such Code. An exception appears in Act Sec. 174(c)(3) following Code Sec. 267(f). Prior to repeal, Code Sec. 267(e) read as follows:

(e) Rule Where last Day of 2½ Month Period Falls on Sunday, Etc.—For purposes of subsection (a)(2)—

(1) where the last day of the 2½ month period falls on Saturday, Sunday, or a legal holiday, such last day shall be treated as falling on the next succeeding day which is not a Saturday, Sunday, or a legal holiday, and

(2) the determination of what constitutes a legal holiday shall be made under section 7503 with respect to the payor's return of tax under this chapter for the preceding taxable year.

P.L. 98-369, §174(b)(1):

Amended Code Sec. 267 by striking out Code Sec. 267(f) and inserting in lieu thereof subsection (e). **Effective** for amounts allowable as deductions under chapter 1 of the Internal Revenue Code of 1954 for tax years beginning after 12-31-83. For purposes of the preceding sentence, the allowability of a deduction shall be determined without regard to any disallowance or postponement of deductions under section 267 of such Code. An exception appears in Act Sec. 174(c)(3) following Code Sec. 267(f).

• 1978 (P.L. 95-628)

P.L. 95-628, §2(a), (b):

Added Code Sec. 267(e). **Effective** for payments made after 11-10-78.

[Sec. 267(f)]

(f) CONTROLLED GROUP DEFINED; SPECIAL RULES APPLICABLE TO CONTROLLED GROUPS.—

(1) CONTROLLED GROUP DEFINED.—For purposes of this section, the term "controlled group" has the meaning given to such term by section 1563(a), except that—

(A) "more than 50 percent" shall be substituted for "at least 80 percent" each place it appears in section 1563(a), and

(B) the determination shall be made without regard to subsections (a)(4) and (e)(3)(C) of section 1563.

(2) DEFERRAL (RATHER THAN DENIAL) OF LOSS FROM SALE OR EXCHANGE BETWEEN MEMBERS.—In the case of any loss from the sale or exchange of property which is between members of the same controlled group and to which subsection (a)(1) applies (determined without regard to this paragraph but with regard to paragraph (3))—

(A) subsections (a)(1) and (d) shall not apply to such loss, but

(B) such loss shall be deferred until the property is transferred outside such controlled group and there would be recognition of loss under consolidated return principles or until such other time as may be prescribed in regulations.

(3) LOSS DEFERRAL RULES NOT TO APPLY IN CERTAIN CASES.—

(A) TRANSFER TO DISC.—For purposes of applying subsection (a)(1), the term "controlled group" shall not include a DISC.

(B) CERTAIN SALES OF INVENTORY.—Except to the extent provided in regulations prescribed by the Secretary, subsection (a)(1) shall not apply to the sale or exchange of property between members of the same controlled group (or persons described in subsection (b)(10)) if—

(i) such property in the hands of the transferor is property described in section 1221(a)(1),

(ii) such sale or exchange is in the ordinary course of the transferor's trade or business,

(iii) such property in the hands of the transferee is property described in section 1221(a)(1), and

(iv) the transferee or the transferor is a foreign corporation.

(C) CERTAIN FOREIGN CURRENCY LOSSES.—To the extent povided in regulations, subsection (a)(1) shall not apply to any loss sustained by a member of a controlled group on the repayment of a loan made to another member of such group if such loan is payable in a foreign currency or is denominated in such a currency and such loss is attributable to a reduction in value of such foreign currency.

(4) DETERMINATION OF RELATIONSHIP RESULTING IN DISALLOWANCE OF LOSS, FOR PURPOSES OF OTHER PROVISIONS.—For purposes of any other section of this title which refers to a relationship which would result in a disallowance of losses under this section, deferral under paragraph (2) shall be treated as disallowance.

Amendments

• 1999, Tax Relief Extension Act of 1999 (P.L. 106-170)

P.L. 106-170, §532(c)(2)(C):

Amended Code Sec. 267(f)(3)(B)(i) and (iii) by striking "section 1221(1)" and inserting "section 1221(a)(1)". **Effective** for any instrument held, acquired, or entered into, any transaction entered into, and supplies held or acquired on or after 12-17-99.

• 1997, Taxpayer Relief Act of 1997 (P.L. 105-34)

P.L. 105-34, §1604(e)(1):

Amended Code Sec. 267(f) by adding at the end a new paragraph (4). **Effective** as if included in the provision of P.L. 98-369 to which it relates [generally **effective** for transactions after 12-31-83, in tax years ending after such date.—CCH].

• 1986, Tax Reform Act of 1986 (P.L. 99-514)

P.L. 99-514, §1812(c)(2):

Amended Code Sec. 267(f)(3)(B) by inserting "(or persons described in subsection (b)(10))" after "same controlled group". **Effective** as if included in the provision of P.L. 98-369 to which it relates.

P.L. 99-514, §1812(c)(5), provides:

(5) Exception for Certain Indebtedness.—Clause (i) of section 174(c)(3)(A) of the Tax Reform Act of 1984 shall be applied by substituting "December 31, 1983" for "September 29, 1983" in the case of indebtedness which matures on January 1, 1999, the payments on which from January 1989 through November 1993 equal U/L plus $77,600, the payments on which from December 1993 to maturity equal U/L plus $50,100, and which accrued interest at 13.75 percent through December 31, 1989.

• 1984, Deficit Reduction Act of 1984 (P.L. 98-369)

P.L. 98-369, §174(b)(1):

Amended Code Sec. 267 by striking out Code Sec. 267(f) and inserting in lieu thereof subsection (e). **Effective** for amounts allowable as deductions under chapter 1 of the Internal Revenue Code of 1954 for tax years beginning after 12-31-83. For purposes of the preceding sentence, the allowability of a deduction shall be determined without regard to any disallowance or postponement of deductions under section 267 of such Code. An exception appears in Act Sec. 174(c)(3), below. Prior to amendment, Code Sec. 267(f) read as follows:

(f) SPECIAL RULES FOR UNPAID EXPENSES AND INTEREST OF S CORPORATIONS.—

(1) IN GENERAL.—In the case of any amount paid or incurred by an S corporation, if—

(A) by reason of the method of accounting of the person to whom the payment is to be made, the amount thereof is not (unless paid) includible in the gross income of such person, and

(B) at the close of the taxable year of the S corporation for which (but for this paragraph) the amount would be deductible under section 162, 212, or 163, both the S corporation and the person to whom the payment is to be paid are persons specified in one of the paragraphs of subsection (b),

then no deduction shall be allowed in respect of expenses otherwise deductible under section 162 or 212, or of interest otherwise deductible under section 163, before the day as of which the amount thereof is includible in the gross income of the person to whom the payment is made.

(2) CERTAIN SHAREHOLDERS, ETC., TREATED AS RELATED PERSONS.—For purposes of applying paragraph (1)—

(A) an S corporation,

(B) any person who owns, directly or indirectly, 2 percent or more in value of the outstanding stock of such corporation, and

(C) any person related (within the meaning of subsection (b) of this section or section 707(b)(1)(A)) to a person described in subparagraph (B),

shall be treated as persons specified in a paragraph of subsection (b).

(3) SUBSECTION (a)(2) NOT TO APPLY.—Subsection (a)(2) shall not apply to any amount paid or incurred by an S corporation.

P.L. 98-369, §174(b)(2)(B):

Amended Code Sec. 267 by adding new subsection (f). **Effective** for transactions after 12-31-83, in tax years ending after such date, but it does not apply to property transferred to a foreign corporation on or before 3-1-84. For an exception, see Act Sec. 174(c)(3).

P.L. 98-369, §174(c)(3), provides:

(3) Exception for Existing Indebtedness, Etc.—

(A) In General.—The amendments made by this section shall not apply to any amount paid or incurred—

(i) on indebtedness incurred on or before September 29, 1983, or

(ii) pursuant to a contract which was binding on September 29, 1983, and at all times thereafter before the amount is paid or incurred.

(B) Treatment of Renegotiations Extensions, Etc.—If any indebtedness (or contract described in subparagraph (A)) is renegotiated, extended, renewed, or revised after September 29, 1983, subparagraph (A) shall not apply to any amount paid or incurred on such indebtedness (or pursuant to such contract) after the date of such renegotiaton, extension, renewal, or revision.

For an exception, see the amendment note for P.L. 99-514, §1812(c)(5), above.

P.L. 98-369, §721(s):

Amended Code Sec. 267(f)(1) (as in effect on the day before the date of enactment of this Act) by striking out all that followed subparagraph (B) and inserting in lieu thereof "then any deduction allowable under such sections in respect of such amount shall be allowable as of the day as of which such amount is includible in the gross income of the person to whom the payment is made (or, if later, as of the day on which it would be so allowable but for this paragraph)." **Effective** as if included in P.L. 97-354. Prior to amendment, the language of Code Sec. 267(f)(1) following (B) read as follows:

then no deduction shall be allowed in respect of expenses otherwise deductible under section 162 or 212, or of interest otherwise deductible under section 163, before the day as of which the amount thereof is includible in the gross income of the person to whom the payment is made.

• 1982, Subchapter S Revision Act of 1982 (P.L. 97-354)

P.L. 97-354, §3(h)(2):

Amended Code Sec. 267 by adding new subsection (f). **Effective** for tax years beginning after 12-31-82.

[Sec. 267(g)]

(g) COORDINATION WITH SECTION 1041.—Subsection (a)(1) shall not apply to any transfer described in section 1041(a) (relating to transfers of property between spouses or incident to divorce).

Amendments

• 1986, Tax Reform Act of 1986 (P.L. 99-514)

P.L. 99-514, §1842(a):

Amended Code Sec. 267 by adding at the end thereof new subsection (g). **Effective** as if included in the provision of P.L. 98-369 to which it relates.

[Sec. 268]

SEC. 268. SALE OF LAND WITH UNHARVESTED CROP.

Where an unharvested crop sold by the taxpayer is considered under the provisions of section 1231 as "property used in the trade or business", in computing taxable income no deduction (whether or not for the taxable year of the sale and whether for expenses, depreciation, or otherwise) attributable to the production of such crop shall be allowed.

[Sec. 269]

SEC. 269. ACQUISITIONS MADE TO EVADE OR AVOID INCOME TAX.

[Sec. 269(a)]

(a) IN GENERAL.—If—

(1) any person or persons acquire, or acquired on or after October 8, 1940, directly or indirectly, control of a corporation, or

(2) any corporation acquires, or acquired on or after October 8, 1940, directly or indirectly, property of another corporation, not controlled, directly or indirectly, immediately before such acquisition, by such acquiring corporation or its stockholders, the basis of which property, in the hands of the acquiring corporation, is determined by reference to the basis in the hands of the transferor corporation,

and the principal purpose for which such acquisition was made is evasion or avoidance of Federal income tax by securing the benefit of a deduction, credit, or other allowance which such person or corporation would not otherwise enjoy, then the Secretary may disallow such deduction, credit, or other allowance. For purposes of paragraphs (1) and (2), control means the ownership of stock possessing at least 50 percent of the total combined voting power of all classes of stock entitled to vote or at least 50 percent of the total value of shares of all classes of stock of the corporation.

Amendments

• 1976, Tax Reform Act of 1976 (P.L. 94-455)

P.L. 94-455, §1906(b)(13)(A):

Amended 1954 Code by substituting "Secretary" for "Secretary or his delegate" each place it appeared. **Effective** 2-1-77.

• 1964, Revenue Act of 1964 (P.L. 88-272)

P.L. 88-272, §235(c)(2):

Amended Sec. 269(a) by inserting "then the Secretary or his delegate may disallow such deduction, credit, or other allowance." at the end of the first sentence in lieu of "such deduction, credit or other allowance shall not be allowed." **Effective** with respect to tax years ending after 12-31-63.

[Sec. 269(b)]

(b) CERTAIN LIQUIDATIONS AFTER QUALIFIED STOCK PURCHASES.—

(1) IN GENERAL.—If—

(A) there is a qualified stock purchase by a corporation of another corporation,

(B) an election is not made under section 338 with respect to such purchase,

(C) the acquired corporation is liquidated pursuant to a plan of liquidation adopted not more than 2 years after the acquisition date, and

(D) the principal purpose for such liquidation is the evasion or avoidance of Federal income tax by securing the benefit of a deduction, credit, or other allowance which the acquiring corporation would not otherwise enjoy,

then the Secretary may disallow such deduction, credit, or other allowance.

(2) MEANING OF TERMS.—For purposes of paragraph (1), the terms "qualified stock purchase" and "acquisition date" have the same respective meanings as when used in section 338.

Amendments

• 1984, Deficit Reduction Act of 1984 (P.L. 98-369)

P.L. 98-369, §712(k)(8)(A):

Amended Code Sec. 269 by redesignating subsection (b) as subsection (c) and inserting new subsection (b). **Effective** for liquidations after 10-20-83, in tax years ending after such date.

[Sec. 269(c)]

(c) POWER OF SECRETARY TO ALLOW DEDUCTION, ETC., IN PART.—In any case to which subsection (a) or (b) applies the Secretary is authorized—

(1) to allow as a deduction, credit, or allowance any part of any amount disallowed by such subsection, if he determines that such allowance will not result in the evasion or avoidance of Federal income tax for which the acquisition was made; or

(2) to distribute, apportion, or allocate gross income, and distribute, apportion, or allocate the deductions, credits, or allowances the benefit of which was sought to be secured, between or among the corporations, or properties, or parts thereof, involved, and to allow such deductions, credits, or allowances so distributed, apportioned, or allocated, but to give effect to such allowance only to such extent as he determines will not result in the evasion or avoidance of Federal income tax for which the acquisition was made; or

(3) to exercise his powers in part under paragraph (1) and in part under paragraph (2).

Amendments

• 1984, Deficit Reduction Act of 1984 (P.L. 98-369)

P.L. 98-369, §712(k)(8)(A):

Amended Code Sec. 269 by redesignating subsection (b) as subsection (c) and inserting new subsection (b). **Effective** for liquidations after 10-20-83, in tax years ending after such date.

P.L. 98-369, §712(k)(8)(B):

Amended Code Sec. 269(c) (as redesignated) by striking out "subsection (a)" and inserting in lieu thereof "subsection (a) or (b)". **Effective** for liquidations after 10-20-83, in tax years ending after such date.

• 1976, Tax Reform Act of 1976 (P.L. 94-455)

P.L. 94-455, §1906(b)(13)(A):

Amended 1954 Code by substituting "Secretary" for "Secretary or his delegate" each place it appeared. **Effective** 2-1-77.

[Sec. 269(c)—Repealed]

Amendments

• 1976, Tax Reform Act of 1976 (P.L. 94-455)

P.L. 94-455, §1901(a)(38):

Repealed Code Sec. 269(c). **Effective** for tax years beginning after 12-31-76. Prior to repeal, Code Sec. 269(c) read as follows:

(c) PRESUMPTION IN CASE OF DISPROPORTIONATE PURCHASE PRICE.—The fact that the consideration paid upon an acquisition by any person or corporation described in subsection (a) is substantially disproportionate to the aggregate—

(1) of the adjusted basis of the property of the corporation (to the extent attributable to the interest acquired specified in paragraph (1) of subsection (a)), or of the property acquired specified in paragraph (2) of subsection (a); and

(2) of the tax benefits (to the extent not reflected in the adjusted basis of the property) not available to such person or corporation otherwise than as a result of such acquisition, shall be prima facie evidence of the principal purpose of evasion or avoidance of Federal income tax. This subsection shall apply only with respect to acquisitions after March 1, 1954.

[Sec. 269A]

SEC. 269A. PERSONAL SERVICE CORPORATIONS FORMED OR AVAILED OF TO AVOID OR EVADE INCOME TAX.

[Sec. 269A(a)]

(a) GENERAL RULE.—If—

(1) substantially all of the services of a personal service corporation are performed for (or on behalf of) 1 other corporation, partnership, or other entity, and

(2) the principal purpose for forming, or availing of, such personal service corporation is the avoidance or evasion of Federal income tax by reducing the income of, or securing the benefit of any expense, deduction, credit, exclusion, or other allowance for, any employee-owner which would not otherwise be available,

then the Secretary may allocate all income, deductions, credits, exclusions, and other allowances between such personal service corporation and its employee-owners, if such allocation is necessary to prevent avoidance or evasion of Federal income tax or clearly to reflect the income of the personal service corporation or any of its employee-owners.

[Sec. 269A(b)]

(b) DEFINITIONS.—For purposes of this section—

(1) PERSONAL SERVICE CORPORATION.—The term "personal service corporation" means a corporation the principal activity of which is the performance of personal services and such services are substantially performed by employee-owners.

(2) EMPLOYEE-OWNER.—The term "employee-owner" means any employee who owns, on any day during the taxable year, more than 10 percent of the outstanding stock of the personal service corporation. For purposes of the preceding sentence, section 318 shall apply, except that "5 percent" shall be substituted for "50 percent" in section 318(a)(2)(C).

(3) RELATED PERSONS.—All related persons (within the meaning of section 144(a)(3)) shall be treated as 1 entity.

Amendments

• 1986, Tax Reform Act of 1986 (P.L. 99-514)

P.L. 99-514, §1301(j)(4):

Amended Code Sec. 269A(b)(3) by striking out "section 103(b)(6)(C)" and inserting in lieu thereof "section 144(a)(3)". **Effective** for bonds issued after 8-15-86.

• 1982, Tax Equity and Fiscal Responsibility Act of 1982 (P.L. 97-248)

P.L. 97-248, §250(a):

Added Code Sec. 269A. **Effective** for tax years beginning after 12-31-82.

[Sec. 269B]

SEC. 269B. STAPLED ENTITIES.

[Sec. 269B(a)]

(a) GENERAL RULE.—Except as otherwise provided by regulations, for purposes of this title—

(1) if a domestic corporation and a foreign corporation are stapled entities, the foreign corporation shall be treated as a domestic corporation,

(2) in applying section 1563, stock in a second corporation which constitutes a stapled interest with respect to stock of a first corporation shall be treated as owned by such first corporation, and

(3) in applying subchapter M for purposes of determining whether any stapled entity is a regulated investment company or a real estate investment trust, all entities which are stapled entities with respect to each other shall be treated as 1 entity.

[Sec. 269B(b)]

(b) SECRETARY TO PRESCRIBE REGULATIONS.—The Secretary shall prescribe such regulations as may be necessary to prevent avoidance or evasion of Federal income tax through the use of stapled entities. Such regulations may include (but shall not be limited to) regulations providing the extent to which 1 of such entities shall be treated as owning the other entity (to the extent of the stapled interest) and regulations providing that any tax imposed on the foreign corporation referred to in subsection (a)(1) may, if not paid by such corporation, be collected from the domestic corporation referred to in such subsection or the shareholders of such foreign corporation.

Amendments

• 1986, Tax Reform Act of 1986 (P.L. 99-514)

P.L. 99-514, §1810(j)(1):

Amended Code Sec. 269B(b) by inserting "and regulations providing that any tax imposed on the foreign corporation referred to in subsection (a)(1) may, if not paid by such corporation, be collected from the domestic corporation referred to in such subsection or the shareholders of such foreign corporation" before the period at the end thereof. **Effective** as if included in the provision of P.L. 98-369 to which it relates.

[Sec. 269B(c)]

(c) DEFINITIONS.—For purposes of this section—

(1) ENTITY.—The term "entity" means any corporation, partnership, trust, association, estate, or other form of carrying on a business or activity.

(2) STAPLED ENTITIES.—The term "stapled entities" means any group of 2 or more entities if more than 50 percent in value of the beneficial ownership in each of such entities consists of stapled interests.

(3) STAPLED INTERESTS.—Two or more interests are stapled interests if, by reason of form of ownership, restrictions on transfer, or other terms or conditions, in connection with the transfer of 1 of such interests the other such interests are also transferred or required to be transferred.

[Sec. 269B(d)]

(d) SPECIAL RULE FOR TREATIES.—Nothing in section 894 or 7852(d) or in any other provision of law shall be construed as permitting an exemption, by reason of any treaty obligation of the United States heretofore or hereafter entered into, from the provisions of this section.

Amendments

• 1984, Deficit Reduction Act of 1984 (P.L. 98-369)

P.L. 98-369, §136(a):

Added Code Sec. 269B. **Effective** 7-18-84. However, see Act Sec. 136(c)(2)-(7), below, for exceptions.

P.L. 98-369, §136(c)(2)-(7), provides:

(2) Interests Stapled as of June 30, 1983.—Except as otherwise provided in this subsection, in the case of any interests which on June 30, 1983, were stapled interests (as defined in section 269B(c)(3) of the Internal Revenue Code of 1954 (as added by this section)), the amendments made by this section shall take effect on January 1, 1985 (January 1, 1987, in the case of stapled interests in a foreign corporation).

(3) Certain Stapled Entities Which Include Real Estate Investment Trust.—Paragraph (3) of section 269B(a) of such Code shall not apply in determining the application of the provisions of part II of subchapter M of chapter 1 of such Code to any real estate investment trust which is part of a group of stapled entities if—

(A) all members of such group were stapled entities as of June 30, 1983, and

(B) as of June 30, 1983, such group included one or more real estate investment trusts.

(4) Certain Stapled Entities Which Include Puerto Rican Corporations.—

(A) Paragraph (1) of section 269B(a) of such Code shall not apply to a domestic corporation and a qualified Puerto Rican corporation which on June 30, 1983, were stapled entities.

(B) For purposes of subparagraph (A), the term "qualified Puerto Rican corporation" means any corporation organized in Puerto Rico—

(i) which is described in section 957(c) of such Code or would be so described if any dividends it received from any other corporation described in such section 957(c) were treated as gross income of the type described in such section 957(c), and

(ii) does not, at any time during the taxable year, own (within the meaning of section 958 of such Code but before applying paragraph (2) of section 269B(a) of such Code) any stock of any corporation which is not described in such section 957(c).

(5) Treaty Rule Not to Apply to Stapled Entities Entitled to Treaty Benefits as of June 30, 1983.—In the case of any entity which was a stapled entity as of June 30, 1983, subsection (d) of section 269B of such Code shall not apply to any treaty benefit to which such entity was entitled as of June 30, 1983.

(6) Elections to Treat Stapled Foreign Entities as Subsidiaries.—

(A) In General.—In the case of any foreign corporation and domestic corporation which as of June 30, 1983, were stapled entities, such domestic corporation may elect (in lieu of applying paragraph (1) of section 269B(a) of such Code) to be treated as owning all interests in the foreign corporation which constitute stapled interests with respect to stock of the domestic corporation.

(B) Election.—Any election under subparagraph (A) shall be made not later than 180 days after the date of the enactment of this Act and shall be made in such manner as the Secretary of the Treasury or his delegate shall prescribe.

(C) Election Irrevocable.—Any election under subparagraph (A), once made, may be revoked only with the consent of the Secretary of the Treasury or his delegate.

(7) Other Stapled Entities Which Include Real Estate Investment Trust.—

(A) In General.—Paragraph (3) of section 269B(a) of such Code shall not apply in determining the application of the provisions of part II of subchapter M of chapter 1 of such Code to any qualified real estate investment trust which is a part of a group of stapled entities—

(i) which was created pursuant to a written board of directors resolution adopted on April 5, 1984, and

(ii) all members of such group were stapled entities as of June 16, 1985.

(B) Qualified Real Estate Investment Trust.—The term "qualified real estate investment trust" means any real estate trust—

(i) at least 75 percent of the gross income of which is derived from interest on obligations secured by mortgages on real property (as defined in section 856 of such Code),

(ii) with respect to which the interest on the obligations described in clause (i) made or acquired by such trust (other than to persons who are independent contractors, as defined in section 856(d)(3) of such Code) is at arm's length rate or a rate not more than 1 percentage point greater than the associated borrowing cost of the trust, and

(iii) with respect to which any real property held by the trust is not used in the trade or business of any other member of the group of stapled entities.

[Sec. 269B(e)]

(e) SUBSECTION (a)(1) NOT TO APPLY IN CERTAIN CASES.—

(1) IN GENERAL.—Subsection (a)(1) shall not apply if it is established to the satisfaction of the Secretary that the domestic corporation and the foreign corporation referred to in such subsection are foreign owned.

(2) FOREIGN OWNED.—For purposes of paragraph (1), a corporation is foreign owned if less than 50 percent of—

(A) the total combined voting power of all classes of stock of such corporation entitled to vote, and

(B) the total value of the stock of the corporation,

is held directly (or indirectly through applying paragraphs (2) and (3) of section 958(a) and paragraph (4) of section 318(a)) by United States persons (as defined in section 7701(a)(30)).

Amendments

• **1986, Tax Reform Act of 1986 (P.L. 99-514)**

P.L. 99-514, §1810(j)(2):

Amended Code Sec. 269B by adding at the end thereof new subsection (e). **Effective** as if included in the provision of P.L. 98-369 to which it relates.

[Sec. 271]

SEC. 271. DEBTS OWED BY POLITICAL PARTIES, ETC.

[Sec. 271(a)]

(a) GENERAL RULE.—In the case of a taxpayer (other than a bank as defined in section 581) no deduction shall be allowed under section 166 (relating to bad debts) or under section 165(g) (relating to worthlessness of securities) by reason of the worthlessness of any debt owed by a political party.

[Sec. 271(b)]

(b) DEFINITIONS.—

(1) POLITICAL PARTY.—For purposes of subsection (a), the term "political party" means—

(A) a political party;

(B) a national, State, or local committee of a political party; or

(C) a committee, association, or organization which accepts contributions or makes expenditures for the purpose of influencing or attempting to influence the election of presidential or vice-presidential electors or of any individual whose name is presented for election to any Federal, State, or local elective public office, whether or not such individual is elected.

(2) CONTRIBUTIONS.—For purposes of paragraph (1) (C), the term "contributions" includes a gift, subscription, loan, advance, or deposit, of money, or anything of value, and includes a contract, promise, or agreement to make a contribution, whether or not legally enforceable.

(3) EXPENDITURES.—For purposes of paragraph (1) (C), the term "expenditures" includes a payment, distribution, loan, advance, deposit, or gift, of money, or anything of value, and includes a contract, promise, or agreement to make an expenditure, whether or not legally enforceable.

[Sec. 271(c)]

(c) EXCEPTION.—In the case of a taxpayer who uses an accrual method of accounting, subsection (a) shall not apply to a debt which accrued as a receivable on a bona fide sale of goods or services in the ordinary course of a taxpayer's trade or business if—

(1) for the taxable year in which such receivable accrued, more than 30 percent of all receivables which accrued in the ordinary course of the trades and businesses of the taxpayer were due from political parties, and

(2) the taxpayer made substantial continuing efforts to collect on the debt.

Amendments

• 1976, Tax Reform Act of 1976 (P.L. 94-455)

P.L. 94-455, §2104(a):

Added Code Sec. 271(c). **Effective** for tax years beginning after 12-31-75.

[Sec. 272]

SEC. 272. DISPOSAL OF COAL OR DOMESTIC IRON ORE.

Where the disposal of coal or iron ore is covered by section 631, no deduction shall be allowed for expenditures attributable to the making and administering of the contract under which such disposition occurs and to the preservation of the economic interest retained under such contract, except that if in any taxable year such expenditures plus the adjusted depletion basis of the coal or iron ore disposed of in such taxable year exceed the amount realized under such contract, such excess, to the extent not availed of as a reduction of gain under section 1231, shall be a loss deductible under section 165(a). This section shall not apply to any taxable year during which there is no income under the contract.

Amendments

• 1964, Revenue Act of 1964 (P.L. 88-272)

P.L. 88-272, §227(a)(3):

Amended Code Sec. 272 by inserting the words "or iron ore" after the word "coal" wherever it appears. **Effective** with respect to amounts received or accrued in tax years beginning after 12-31-63, attributable to iron ore mined in such tax years.

P.L. 88-272, §227(b)(3):

Amended the heading of Code Sec. 272 by adding "OR DOMESTIC IRON ORE" in the heading of Code Sec. 272.

[Sec. 273]

SEC. 273. HOLDERS OF LIFE OR TERMINABLE INTEREST.

Amounts paid under the laws of a State, the District of Columbia, a possession of the United States, or a foreign country as income to the holder of a life or terminable interest acquired by gift, bequest, or inheritance shall not be reduced or diminished by any deduction for shrinkage (by whatever name called) in the value of such interest due to the lapse of time.

Amendments

• 1976, Tax Reform Act of 1976 (P.L. 94-455)

P.L. 94-455, §1901(c)(2):

Amended Code Sec. 273 by striking "a Territory," following "a State,". **Effective** for tax years beginning after 12-31-76.

[Sec. 274]

SEC. 274. DISALLOWANCE OF CERTAIN ENTERTAINMENT, ETC., EXPENSES.

[Sec. 274(a)]

(a) ENTERTAINMENT, AMUSEMENT, OR RECREATION.—

(1) IN GENERAL.—No deduction otherwise allowable under this chapter shall be allowed for any item—

(A) ACTIVITY.—With respect to an activity which is of a type generally considered to constitute entertainment, amusement, or recreation, unless the taxpayer establishes that the item was directly related to, or, in the case of an item directly preceding or following a substantial and bona fide business discussion (including business meetings at a convention or otherwise), that such item was associated with, the active conduct of the taxpayer's trade or business, or

(B) FACILITY.—With respect to a facility used in connection with an activity referred to in subparagraph (A).

In the case of an item described in subparagraph (A), the deduction shall in no event exceed the portion of such item which meets the requirements of subparagraph (A).

(2) SPECIAL RULES.—For purposes of applying paragraph (1)—

(A) Dues or fees to any social, athletic, or sporting club or organization shall be treated as items with respect to facilities.

(B) An activity described in section 212 shall be treated as a trade or business.

(C) In the case of a club, paragraph (1)(B) shall apply unless the taxpayer establishes that the facility was used primarily for the furtherance of the taxpayer's trade or business and that the item was directly related to the active conduct of such trade or business.

(3) DENIAL OF DEDUCTION FOR CLUB DUES.—Notwithstanding the preceding provisions of this subsection, no deduction shall be allowed under this chapter for amounts paid or incurred for membership in any club organized for business, pleasure, recreation, or other social purpose.

Amendments

• 1993, Omnibus Budget Reconciliation Act of 1993 (P.L. 103-66)

P.L. 103-66, §13210(a):

Amended Code Sec. 274(a) by adding at the end thereof new paragraph (3). **Effective** for amounts paid or incurred after 12-31-93.

• 1980, Technical Corrections Act of 1979 (P.L. 96-222)

P.L. 96-222, §103(a)(10)(A):

Amended Code Sec. 274(a)(2)(C) by striking out "country" before "club". **Effective** for items paid or incurred after 12-31-78, in tax years ending after such date. For a special rule, see P.L. 96-222, §103(a)(10)(C), below.

P.L. 96-222, §103(a)(10)(C), provides:

(C) USE OF FACILITIES IN CASE OF INDEPENDENT CONTRACTORS, ETC.—

(i) IN GENERAL.—Subsection (a) of section 274 of the Internal Revenue Code of 1954 (relating to disallowance of certain entertainment, etc., expenses) shall not apply to expenses paid or incurred by the taxpayer for goods, services, and facilities to the extent that the expenses are includible in the gross income of a recipient of the entertainment, amusement, or recreation who is not an employee of the taxpayer as compensation for services rendered or as a prize or award under section 74 of such Code.

(ii) INFORMATION RETURN REQUIREMENT.—Clause (i) shall not apply to any amount paid or incurred by the taxpayer if such amount is required to be included in any information return filed by such taxpayer under part III of subchapter A of chapter 61 of such Code and is not so included.

(iii) APPLICATION OF SUBPARAGRAPH.—This subparagraph shall only apply with respect to expenses paid or incurred during 1979 or 1980.

• 1978, Revenue Act of 1978 (P.L. 95-600)

P.L. 95-600, §361(a), (c):

Amended Code Sec. 274(a)(1). **Effective** for items paid or incurred after 12-31-78, in tax years ending after such date. Prior to amendment, Code Sec. 274(a)(1) read as follows:

(1) IN GENERAL.—No deduction otherwise allowable under this chapter shall be allowed for any item—

(A) ACTIVITY.—With respect to an activity which is of a type generally considered to constitute entertainment, amusement, or recreation, unless the taxpayer establishes that the item was directly related to, or, in the case of an item directly preceding or following a substantial and bona fide business discussion (including business meetings at a convention or otherwise), that such item was associated with, the active conduct of the taxpayer's trade or business, or

(B) FACILITY.—With respect to a facility used in connection with an activity referred to in subparagraph (A), unless the taxpayer establishes that the facility was used primarily for the furtherance of the taxpayer's trade or business and that the item was directly related to the active conduct of such trade or business,

and such deduction shall in no event exceed the portion of such item directly related to, or, in the case of an item described in subparagraph (A) directly preceding or following a substantial and bona fide business discussion (including business meetings at a convention or otherwise), the portion of such item associated with, the active conduct of the taxpayer's trade or business.

P.L. 95-600, §361(b), (c):

Added Code Sec. 274(a)(2)(C). **Effective** for items paid or incurred after 12-31-78, in tax years ending after such date.

[Sec. 274(b)]

(b) GIFTS.—

(1) LIMITATION.—No deduction shall be allowed under section 162 or section 212 for any expense for gifts made directly or indirectly to any individual to the extent that such expense, when added to prior expenses of the taxpayer for gifts made to such individual during the same taxable year, exceeds $25. For purposes of this section, the term "gift" means any item excludable from gross income of the recipient under section 102 which is not excludable from his gross income under any other provision of this chapter, but such term does not include—

(A) an item having a cost to the taxpayer not in excess of $4.00 on which the name of the taxpayer is clearly and permanently imprinted and which is one of a number of identical items distributed generally by the taxpayer, or

(B) a sign, display rack, or other promotional material to be used on the business premises of the recipient.

(2) SPECIAL RULES.—

(A) In the case of a gift by a partnership, the limitation contained in paragraph (1) shall apply to the partnership as well as to each member thereof.

(B) For purposes of paragraph (1), a husband and wife shall be treated as one taxpayer.

Amendments

• 1986, Tax Reform Act of 1986 (P.L. 99-514)

P.L. 99-514, §122(c)(1)-(4):

Amended Code Sec. 274(b) by adding "or" at the end of subparagraph (A) of paragraph (1); by striking out "or" at the end of subparagraph (B) of paragraph (1), and inserting in lieu thereof a period; by striking out subparagraph (C) of paragraph (1) and by striking out paragraph (3). **Effective** for prizes and awards granted after 12-31-86. Prior to amendment, Code Sec. 274(b)(1)(C) and Code Sec. 274(b)(3) read as follows:

(C) an item of tangible personal property which is awarded to an employee by reason of length of service, productivity, or safety achievement, but only to the extent that—

(i) the cost of such item to the taxpayer does not exceed $400, or

(ii) such item is a qualified plan award.

* * *

(3) QUALIFIED PLAN AWARD.—For purposes of this subsection—

(A) IN GENERAL.—The term "qualified plan award" means an item which is awarded as part of a permanent, written plan or program of the taxpayer which does not discriminate in favor of officers, shareholders, or highly compensated employees as to eligibility or benefits.

(B) AVERAGE AMOUNT OF AWARDS.—An item shall not be treated as a qualified plan award for any taxable year if the average cost of all items awarded under all plans described in subparagraph (A) of the taxpayer during the taxable year exceeds $400.

(C) MAXIMUM AMOUNT PER ITEM.—An item shall not be treated as a qualified plan award under this paragraph to the extent that the cost of such item exceeds $1,600.

• 1981, Economic Recovery Tax Act of 1981 (P.L. 97-34)

P.L. 97-34, §265(a):

Amended Code Sec. 274(b)(1)(C). **Effective** for tax years ending on or after 8-13-81. Prior to amendment, Code Sec. 274(b)(1)(C) read as follows:

(C) an item of tangible personal property having a cost to the taxpayer not in excess of $100 which is awarded to an employee by reason of length of service or for safety achievement.

P.L. 97-34, §265(b):

Amended Code Sec. 274(b) by adding at the end thereof new paragraph (3). **Effective** for tax years ending on or after 8-13-81.

[Sec. 274(c)]

(c) CERTAIN FOREIGN TRAVEL.—

(1) IN GENERAL.—In the case of any individual who travels outside the United States away from home in pursuit of a trade or business or in pursuit of an activity described in section 212, no deduction shall be allowed under section 162 or section 212 for that portion of the expenses of such travel otherwise allowable under such section which, under regulations prescribed by the Secretary, is not allocable to such trade or business or to such activity.

(2) EXCEPTION.—Paragraph (1) shall not apply to the expenses of any travel outside the United States away from home if—

(A) such travel does not exceed one week, or

(B) the portion of the time of travel outside the United States away from home which is not attributable to the pursuit of the taxpayer's trade or business or an activity described in section 212 is less than 25 percent of the total time on such travel.

(3) DOMESTIC TRAVEL EXCLUDED.—For purposes of this subsection, travel outside the United States does not include any travel from one point in the United States to another point in the United States.

Amendments

• 1976, Tax Reform Act of 1976 (P.L. 94-455)

P.L. 94-455, §1906(b)(13)(A):

Amended 1954 Code by substituting "Secretary" for "Secretary or his delegate" each place it appeared. **Effective** 2-1-77.

• 1964, Revenue Act of 1964 (P.L. 88-272)

P.L. 88-272, §217(a):

Amended subsection (c). **Effective** with respect to tax years ending after 12-31-62, but only in respect of periods after such date. Prior to amendment, subsection (c) read as follows:

"(c) Traveling.—In the case of any individual who is traveling away from home in pursuit of a trade or business or in pursuit of an activity described in section 212, no deduction shall be allowed under section 162 or section 212 for that portion of the expenses of such travel otherwise allowable under such section which, under regulations prescribed by the Secretary or his delegate, is not allocable to such trade or business or to such activity. This subsection shall not apply to the expenses of any travel away from home which does not exceed one week or where the portion of the time away from home which is not attributable to the pursuit of the taxpayer's trade or business or an activity described in section 212 is less than 25 percent of the total time away from home on such travel."

[Sec. 274(d)]

(d) SUBSTANTIATION REQUIRED.—No deduction or credit shall be allowed—

(1) under section 162 or 212 for any traveling expense (including meals and lodging while away from home),

(2) for any item with respect to an activity which is of a type generally considered to constitute entertainment, amusement, or recreation, or with respect to a facility used in connection with such an activity,

(3) for any expense for gifts, or

(4) with respect to any listed property (as defined in section 280F(d)(4)),

unless the taxpayer substantiates by adequate records or by sufficient evidence corroborating the taxpayer's own statement (A) the amount of such expense or other item, (B) the time and place of the travel, entertainment, amusement, recreation, or use of the facility or property, or the date and description of the gift, (C) the business purpose of the expense or other item, and (D) the business relationship to the taxpayer of persons entertained, using the facility or property, or receiving the gift. The Secretary may by regulations provide that some or all of the requirements of the preceding sentence shall not apply in the case of an expense which does not exceed an amount prescribed pursuant to such regulations. This subsection shall not apply to any qualified nonpersonal use vehicle (as defined in subsection (i)).

Amendments

• 1985 (P.L. 99-44)

P.L. 99-44, §1(a):

Amended Code Sec. 274(d) (as in effect for years beginning after 1985) by striking out "adequate contemporaneous records" and inserting in lieu thereof "adequate records or by sufficient evidence corroborating the taxpayer's own statement". **Effective** as if included in the amendments made by P.L. 98-369, §179(b), and the Internal Revenue Code of 1954 shall be applied and administered as if the word "contemporaneous" had not been added to such subsection (d).

P.L. 99-44, §2(a):

Amended Code Sec. 274(d) by adding at the end thereof a new sentence. **Effective** for tax years beginning after 12-31-85.

P.L. 99-44, §1(c), provides:

(c) REPEAL OF REGULATIONS.—Regulations issued before the date of the enactment of this Act to carry out the amendments made by paragraphs (1)(C), (2), and (3) of section 179(b) of the Tax Reform Act of 1984 shall have no force and effect.

P.L. 99-44, §5, provides:

Not later than October 1, 1985, the Secretary of the Treasury or his delegate shall prescribe regulations to carry out the provisions of this Act which shall fully reflect such provisions.

P.L. 99-44, §6(b), provides:

(b) RESTORATION OF PRIOR LAW FOR 1985.—For taxable years beginning in 1985, section 274(d) of the Internal Revenue Code of 1954 shall apply as it read before the amendments made by section 179(b)(1) of the Tax Reform Act of 1984.

• 1984, Deficit Reduction Act of 1984 (P.L. 98-369)

P.L. 98-369, §179(b)(1):

Amended Code Sec. 274(d) by striking out "No deduction" and inserting in lieu thereof "No deduction or credit"; by striking out "or" at the end of paragraph (2), by inserting "or" at the end of paragraph (3) and by adding paragraph (4), by strking out "adequate records or by sufficient evidence corroborating his own statement" and inserting in lieu thereof "adequate contemporaneous records"; and by striking out "the facility" each place it appeared following paragraph (4) (as added) and inserting in lieu thereof "the facility or property". **Effective** for tax years beginning after 12-31-84.

• 1976, Tax Reform Act of 1976 (P.L. 94-455)

P.L. 94-455, §1906(b)(13)(A):

Amended 1954 Code by substituting "Secretary" for "Secretary or his delegate" each place it appeared. **Effective** 2-1-77.

[Sec. 274(e)]

(e) SPECIFIC EXCEPTIONS TO APPLICATION OF SUBSECTION (a).—Subsection (a) shall not apply to—

(1) FOOD AND BEVERAGES FOR EMPLOYEES.—Expenses for food and beverages (and facilities used in connection therewith) furnished on the business premises of the taxpayer primarily for his employees.

(2) EXPENSES TREATED AS COMPENSATION.—

(A) IN GENERAL.—Except as provided in subparagraph (B), expenses for goods, services, and facilities, to the extent that the expenses are treated by the taxpayer, with respect to the recipient of the entertainment, amusement, or recreation, as compensation to an employee on the taxpayer's return of tax under this chapter and as wages to such employee for purposes of chapter 24 (relating to withholding of income tax at source on wages).

(B) SPECIFIED INDIVIDUALS.—

(i) IN GENERAL.—In the case of a recipient who is a specified individual, subparagraph (A) and paragraph (9) shall each be applied by substituting "to the extent that the expenses do not exceed the amount of the expenses which" for "to the extent that the expenses".

(ii) SPECIFIED INDIVIDUAL.—For purposes of clause (i), the term "specified individual" means any individual who—

(I) is subject to the requirements of section 16(a) of the Securities Exchange Act of 1934 with respect to the taxpayer or a related party to the taxpayer, or

(II) would be subject to such requirements if the taxpayer (or such related party) were an issuer of equity securities referred to in such section.

For purposes of this clause, a person is a related party with respect to another person if such person bears a relationship to such other person described in section 267(b) or 707(b).

(3) REIMBURSED EXPENSES.—Expenses paid or incurred by the taxpayer, in connection with the performance by him of services for another person (whether or not such other person is his employer), under a reimbursement or other expense allowance arrangement with such other person, but this paragraph shall apply—

(A) where the services are performed for an employer, only if the employer has not treated such expenses in the manner provided in paragraph (2), or

(B) where the services are performed for a person other than an employer, only if the taxpayer accounts (to the extent provided by subsection (d)) to such person.

(4) RECREATIONAL, ETC., EXPENSES FOR EMPLOYEES.—Expenses for recreational, social, or similar activities (including facilities therefor) primarily for the benefit of employees (other than employees who are highly compensated employees (within the meaning of section 414(q))). For pur-

poses of this paragraph, an individual owning less than a 10-percent interest in the taxpayer's trade or business shall not be considered a shareholder or other owner, and for such purposes an individual shall be treated as owning any interest owned by a member of his family (within the meaning of section 267(c)(4)). This paragraph shall not apply for purposes of subsection (a)(3).

(5) EMPLOYEE, STOCKHOLDER, ETC., BUSINESS MEETINGS.—Expenses incurred by a taxpayer which are directly related to business meetings of his employees, stockholders, agents, or directors.

(6) MEETINGS OF BUSINESS LEAGUES, ETC.—Expenses directly related and necessary to attendance at a business meeting or convention of any organization described in section 501(c)(6) (relating to business leagues, chambers of commerce, real estate boards, and boards of trade) and exempt from taxation under section 501(a).

(7) ITEMS AVAILABLE TO PUBLIC.—Expenses for goods, services, and facilities made available by the taxpayer to the general public.

(8) ENTERTAINMENT SOLD TO CUSTOMERS.—Expenses for goods or services (including the use of facilities) which are sold by the taxpayer in a bona fide transaction for an adequate and full consideration in money or money's worth.

(9) EXPENSES INCLUDIBLE IN INCOME OF PERSONS WHO ARE NOT EMPLOYEES.—Expenses paid or incurred by the taxpayer for goods, services, and facilities to the extent that the expenses are includible in the gross income of a recipient of the entertainment, amusement, or recreation who is not an employee of the taxpayer as compensation for services rendered or as a prize or award under section 74. The preceding sentence shall not apply to any amount paid or incurred by the taxpayer if such amount is required to be included (or would be so required except that the amount is less than $600) in any information return filed by such taxpayer under part III of subchapter A of chapter 61 and is not so included.

For purposes of this subsection, any item referred to in subsection (a) shall be treated as an expense.

Amendments

• 2005, Gulf Opportunity Zone Act of 2005 (P.L. 109-135)

P.L. 109-135, §403(mm)(1)-(3):

Amended Code Sec. 274(e)(2)(B)(ii) by inserting "or a related party to the taxpayer" after "the taxpayer" in subclause (I), by inserting "(or such related party)" after "the taxpayer" in subclause (II), and by adding at the end a new flush sentence. **Effective** as if included in the provision of the American Jobs Creation Act of 2004 (P.L. 108-357) to which it relates [**effective** for expenses incurred after 10-22-2004.—CCH].

• 2004, American Jobs Creation Act of 2004 (P.L. 108-357)

P.L. 108-357, §907(a):

Amended Code Sec. 274(e)(2). **Effective** for expenses incurred after 10-22-2004. Prior to amendment, Code Sec. 274(e)(2) read as follows:

(2) EXPENSES TREATED AS COMPENSATION.—Expenses for goods, services, and facilities, to the extent that the expenses are treated by the taxpayer, with respect to the recipient of the entertainment, amusement, or recreation, as compensation to an employee on the taxpayer's return of tax under this chapter and as wages to such employee for purposes of chapter 24 (relating to withholding of income tax at source on wages).

• 1993, Omnibus Budget Reconciliation Act of 1993 (P.L. 103-66)

P.L. 103-66, §13210(b):

Amended Code Sec. 274(e)(4) by adding at the end thereof a new sentence. **Effective** for amounts paid or incurred after 12-31-93.

• 1986, Tax Reform Act of 1986 (P.L. 99-514)

P.L. 99-514, §142(a)(2)(A):

Amended Code Sec. 274(e) by striking out paragraph (1) and by redesignating paragraphs (2) through (10) as paragraphs (1) through (9), respectively. **Effective** for tax years beginning after 12-31-86. Prior to amendment, Code Sec. 274(e)(1) read as follows:

(1) BUSINESS MEALS.—Expenses for food and beverages furnished to any individual under circumstances which (taking into account the surroundings in which furnished, the taxpayer's trade, business, or income-producing activity and the relationship to such trade, business, or activity of the persons to whom the food and beverages are furnished) are of a type generally considered to be conducive to a business discussion.

P.L. 99-514, §142(a)(2)(B):

Amended Code Sec. 274(e)(3), as redesignated by Act Sec. 142(a)(2)(A), by striking out "paragraph (3)" and inserting in lieu thereof "paragraph (2)". **Effective** for tax years beginning after 12-31-86.

P.L. 99-514, §1114(b)(6):

Amended Code Sec. 274(e)(5), now redesignated as Code Sec. 274(e)(4), by striking out "officers, shareholders or other owners, or highly compensated employees" and inserting in lieu thereof "highly compensated employees (within the meaning of section 414(q))". **Effective** for years beginning after 12-31-86.

P.L. 99-514, §1567, provides:

SEC. 1567. CERTAIN RECORDKEEPING REQUIREMENTS.

(a) IN GENERAL.—For purposes of sections 132 and 274 of the Internal Revenue Code of 1954, use of an automobile by a special agent of the Internal Revenue Service shall be treated in the same manner as use of an automobile by an officer of any other law enforcement agency.

(b) EFFECTIVE DATE.—The provision of this section shall take effect on January 1, 1985.

• 1983, Interest and Dividend Tax Compliance Act of 1983 (P.L. 98-67)

P.L. 98-67, §102(a):

Repealed the amendment made to Code Sec. 274(e)(3) by P.L. 97-248 (see below) as of the close of 6-30-83, as though it had not been enacted.

• 1982, Tax Equity and Fiscal Responsibility Act of 1982 (P.L. 97-248)

P.L. 97-248, §307(a)(1) [repealed by P.L. 98-67, §102(a)]:

Amended Code Sec. 274(e)(3) by inserting "subchapter A of" before "chapter 24". **Effective** for interest, dividends, and patronage dividends paid or credited after 6-30-83.

• 1980 (P.L. 96-598)

P.L. 96-598, §5(a):

Amended Code Sec. 274(e) by inserting after paragraph (9) paragraph (10). **Effective** with respect to expenses paid or incurred after 12-31-80, in tax years ending after such date. P.L. 96-605, §108(a), signed 12-28-80, made the identical change.

[Sec. 274(f)]

(f) INTEREST, TAXES, CASUALTY LOSSES, ETC.—This section shall not apply to any deduction allowable to the taxpayer without regard to its connection with his trade or business (or with his income-producing activity). In the case of a taxpayer which is not an individual, the preceding sentence shall be applied as if it were an individual.

[Sec. 274(g)]

(g) TREATMENT OF ENTERTAINMENT, ETC., TYPE FACILITY.—For purposes of this chapter, if deductions are disallowed under subsection (a) with respect to any portion of a facility, such portion shall be treated as an asset which is used for personal, living, and family purposes (and not as an asset used in the trade or business).

[Sec. 274(h)]

(h) ATTENDANCE AT CONVENTIONS, ETC.—

(1) IN GENERAL.—In the case of any individual who attends a convention, seminar, or similar meeting which is held outside the North American area, no deduction shall be allowed under section 162 for expenses allocable to such meeting unless the taxpayer establishes that the meeting is directly related to the active conduct of his trade or business and that, after taking into account in the manner provided by regulations prescribed by the Secretary—

(A) the purpose of such meeting and the activities taking place at such meeting,

(B) the purposes and activities of the sponsoring organizations or groups,

(C) the residences of the active members of the sponsoring organization and the places at which other meetings of the sponsoring organization or groups have been held or will be held, and

(D) such other relevant factors as the taxpayer may present,

it is as reasonable for the meeting to be held outside the North American area as within the North American area.

(2) CONVENTIONS ON CRUISE SHIPS.—In the case of any individual who attends a convention, seminar, or other meeting which is held on any cruise ship, no deduction shall be allowed under section 162 for expenses allocable to such meeting, unless the taxpayer meets the requirements of paragraph (5) and establishes that the meeting is directly related to the active conduct of his trade or business and that—

(A) the cruise ship is a vessel registered in the United States; and

(B) all ports of call of such cruise ship are located in the United States or in possessions of the United States.

With respect to cruises beginning in any calendar year, not more than $2,000 of the expenses attributable to an individual attending one or more meetings may be taken into account under section 162 by reason of the preceding sentence.

(3) DEFINITIONS.—For purposes of this subsection—

(A) NORTH AMERICAN AREA.—The term "North American area" means the United States, its possessions, and the Trust Territory of the Pacific Islands, and Canada and Mexico.

(B) CRUISE SHIP.—The term "cruise ship" means any vessel sailing within or without the territorial waters of the United States.

(4) SUBSECTION TO APPLY TO EMPLOYER AS WELL AS TO TRAVELER.—

(A) Except as provided in subparagraph (B), this subsection shall apply to deductions otherwise allowable under section 162 to any person, whether or not such person is the individual attending the convention, seminar, or similar meeting.

(B) This subsection shall not deny a deduction to any person other than the individual attending the convention, seminar, or similar meeting with respect to any amount paid by such person to or on behalf of such individual if includible in the gross income of such individual. The preceding sentence shall not apply if the amount is required to be included in any information return filed by such person under part III of subchapter A of chapter 61 and is not so included.

(5) REPORTING REQUIREMENTS.—No deduction shall be allowed under section 162 for expenses allocable to attendance at a convention, seminar, or similar meeting on any cruise ship unless the taxpayer claiming the deduction attaches to the return of tax on which the deduction is claimed—

(A) a written statement signed by the individual attending the meeting which includes—

(i) information with respect to the total days of the trip, excluding the days of transportation to and from the cruise ship port, and the number of hours of each day of the trip which such individual devoted to scheduled business activities,

(ii) a program of the scheduled business activities of the meeting, and

(iii) such other information as may be required in regulations prescribed by the Secretary; and

(B) a written statement signed by an officer of the organization or group sponsoring the meeting which includes—

(i) a schedule of business activities of each day of the meeting,

(ii) the number of hours which the individual attending the meeting attended such scheduled business activities, and

(iii) such other information as may be required in regulations prescribed by the Secretary.

(6) TREATMENT OF CONVENTIONS IN CERTAIN CARIBBEAN COUNTRIES.—

(A) IN GENERAL.—For purposes of this subsection, the term "North American area" includes, with respect to any convention, seminar, or similar meeting, any beneficiary country if (as of the time such meeting begins)—

(i) there is in effect a bilateral or multilateral agreement described in subparagraph (C) between such country and the United States providing for the exchange of information between the United States and such country, and

(ii) there is not in effect a finding by the Secretary that the tax laws of such country discriminate against conventions held in the United States.

(B) BENEFICIARY COUNTRY.—For purposes of this paragraph, the term "beneficiary country" has the meaning given to such term by section 212(a)(1)(A) of the Caribbean Basin Economic Recovery Act; except that such term shall include Bermuda.

(C) AUTHORITY TO CONCLUDE EXCHANGE OF INFORMATION AGREEMENTS.—

(i) IN GENERAL.—The Secretary is authorized to negotiate and conclude an agreement for the exchange of information with any beneficiary country. Except as provided in clause (ii), an exchange of information agreement shall provide for the exchange of such information (not limited to information concerning nationals or residents of the United States or the beneficiary country) as may be necessary or appropriate to carry out and enforce the tax laws of the United States and the beneficiary country (whether criminal or civil proceedings), including information which may otherwise be subject to nondisclosure provisions of the local law of the beneficiary country such as provisions respecting bank secrecy and bearer shares. The exchange of information agreement shall be terminable by either country on reasonable notice and shall provide that information received by either country will be disclosed only to persons or authorities (including courts and administrative bodies) involved in the administration or oversight of, or in the determination of appeals in respect of, taxes of the United States or the beneficiary country and will be used by such persons or authorities only for such purposes.

(ii) NONDISCLOSURE OF QUALIFIED CONFIDENTIAL INFORMATION SOUGHT FOR CIVIL TAX PURPOSES.—An exchange of information agreement need not provide for the exchange of qualified confidential information which is sought only for civil tax purposes if—

(I) the Secretary of the Treasury, after making all reasonable efforts to negotiate an agreement which includes the exchange of such information, determines that such an agreement cannot be negotiated but that the agreement which was negotiated will significantly assist in the administration and enforcement of the tax laws of the United States, and

(II) the President determines that the agreement as negotiated is in the national security interest of the United States.

(iii) QUALIFIED CONFIDENTIAL INFORMATION DEFINED.—For purposes of this subparagraph, the term "qualified confidential information" means information which is subject to the nondisclosure provisions of any local law of the beneficiary country regarding bank secrecy or ownership of bearer shares.

(iv) CIVIL TAX PURPOSES.—For purposes of this subparagraph, the determination of whether information is sought only for civil tax purposes shall be made by the requesting party.

(D) COORDINATION WITH OTHER PROVISIONS.—Any exchange of information agreement negotiated under subparagraph (C) shall be treated as an income tax convention for purposes of section 6103(k)(4). The Secretary may exercise his authority under subchapter A of chapter 78 to carry out any obligation of the United States under an agreement referred to in subparagraph (C).

(E) DETERMINATIONS PUBLISHED IN THE FEDERAL REGISTER.—The following shall be published in the Federal Register—

(i) any determination by the President under subparagraph (C)(ii) (including the reasons for such determination),

(ii) any determination by the Secretary under subparagraph (C)(ii) (including the reasons for such determination), and

(iii) any finding by the Secretary under subparagraph (A)(ii) (and any termination thereof).

(7) SEMINARS, ETC. FOR SECTION 212 PURPOSES.—No deduction shall be allowed under section 212 for expenses allocable to a convention, seminar, or similar meeting.

Amendments

• 1988, Technical and Miscellaneous Revenue Act of 1988 (P.L. 100-647)

P.L. 100-647, §1001(g)(5):

Amended Code Sec. 274(h)(1)-(2) by striking out "trade or business that" and inserting in lieu thereof "trade or business and that". **Effective** as if included in the provision of P.L. 99-514 to which it relates.

• 1986, Tax Reform Act of 1986 (P.L. 99-514)

P.L. 99-514, §142(c)(1):

Amended Code Sec. 274(h) by adding at the end thereof a paragraph (7). **Effective** for tax years beginning after 12-31-86.

P.L. 99-514, §142(c)(2)(A)-(B):

Amended Code Sec. 274(h)(1)-(2) and (4)-(5) by striking out "or 212" each place it appears, and by striking out "or to an activity described in section 212 and" each place it appears. **Effective** for tax years beginning after 12-31-86. Prior to amendment, Code Sec. 274(h)(1)-(2) and (4)-(5) read as follows:

(1) IN GENERAL.—In the case of any individual who attends a convention, seminar, or similar meeting which is held outside the North American area, no deduction shall be allowed under section 162 or 212 for expenses allocable to such meeting unless the taxpayer establishes that the meeting is directly related to the active conduct of his trade or business or to an activity described in section 212 and that, after taking into account in the manner provided by regulations prescribed by the Secretary—

(A) the purpose of such meeting and the activities taking place at such meeting,

(B) the purposes and activities of the sponsoring organizations or groups,

(C) the residences of the active members of the sponsoring organization and the places at which other meetings of the sponsoring organization or groups have been held or will be held, and

(D) such other relevant factors as the taxpayer may present,

it is as reasonable for the meeting to be held outside the North American area as within the North American area.

(2) CONVENTIONS ON CRUISE SHIPS.—In the case of any individual who attends a convention, seminar, or other meeting which is held on any cruise ship, no deduction shall be allowed under section 162 or 212 for expenses allocable to such meeting, unless the taxpayer meets the requirements of paragraph (5) and establishes that the meeting is directly related to the active conduct of his trade or business or to an activity described in section 212 and that—

(A) the cruise ship is a vessel registered in the United States; and

(B) all ports of call of such cruise ship are located in the United States or in possessions of the United States.

With respect to cruises beginning in any calendar year, not more than $2,000 of the expenses attributable to an individual attending one or more meetings may be taken into account under section 162 or 212 by reason of the preceding sentence.

* * *

(4) SUBSECTION TO APPLY TO EMPLOYER AS WELL AS TO TRAVELER.—

(A) Except as provided in subparagraph (B), this subsection shall apply to deductions otherwise allowable under section 162 or 212 to any person, whether or not such person is the individual attending the convention, seminar, or similar meeting.

(B) This subsection shall not deny a deduction to any person other than the individual attending the convention, seminar, or similar meeting with respect to any amount paid by such individual. The preceding sentence shall not apply if the amount is required to be included in any information return filed by such person under part III of subchapter A of chapter 61 and is not so included.

(5) REPORTING REQUIREMENTS.—No deduction shall be allowed under section 162 or 212 for expenses allocable to attendance at a convention, seminar, or similar meeting on any cruise ship unless the taxpayer claiming the deduction attaches to the return of tax on which the deduction is claimed—

(A) a written statement signed by the individual attending the meeting which includes—

(i) information with respect to the total days of the trip, excluding the days of transportation to and from the cruise ship port, and the number of hours of each day of the trip which such individual devoted to scheduled business activities,

(ii) a program of the scheduled business activities of the meeting, and

(iii) such other information as may be required in regulations prescribed by the Secretary; and

(B) a written statement signed by an officer of the organization or group sponsoring the meeting which includes—

(i) a schedule of business activities of each day of the meeting,

(ii) the number of hours which the individual attending the meeting attended such scheduled business activities, and

(iii) such other information as may be required in regulations prescribed by the Secretary.

• 1984, Deficit Reduction Act of 1984 (P.L. 98-369)

P.L. 98-369, §801(c):

Amended Code Sec. 274(h)(6)(D) by adding the sentence at the end thereof, and by changing the heading thereof. **Effective** for transactions after 12-31-84, in tax years ending after such date. Prior to amendment, the heading of Code Sec. 179(h)(6)(D) read as follows:

Coordination with section 6103.

• 1983, Interest and Dividend Tax Compliance Act of 1983 (P.L. 98-67)

P.L. 98-67, §222(a):

Added paragraph (6) to Code Sec. 274(h). **Effective** for conventions, seminars, or other meetings which begin after 6-30-83.

P.L. 98-67, §223, provides:

SEC. 223. REPORT WITH RESPECT TO USE OF CARIBBEAN BASIN TAX HAVENS.

The Secretary of the Treasury shall, not later than ninety days after the date of the enactment of this Act, report to the Committee on Ways and Means of the House of Representatives and the Committee on Finance of the Senate on—

(1) the level at which Caribbean Basin tax havens are being used to evade or avoid Federal taxes, and the effect on Federal revenues of such use,

(2) any information he may have on the relationship of such use to drug trafficking and other criminal activities, and

(3) current antitax haven enforcement activities of the Department of the Treasury.

• 1983, Surface Transportation Act of 1982 (P.L. 97-424)

P.L. 97-424, §543(a)(1):

Amended Code Sec. 274(h) by striking out the period at the end of paragraph (2) and inserting a comma and all the material that follows "allocable to such meeting,". **Effective** for tax years beginning after 12-31-82.

P.L. 97-424, §543(a)(2):

Amended Code Sec. 274(h) by adding a new paragraph (5). **Effective** for tax years beginning after 12-31-82.

• 1980 (P.L. 96-608)

P.L. 96-608, §4(a):

Amended Code Sec. 274(h). **Effective** with respect to conventions, seminars, and meetings beginning after 12-31-80, except that in the case of any convention, seminar, or meeting beginning after such date which was scheduled on or before such date, a person, in such manner as the Secretary of the Treasury or his delegate may prescribe, may elect to have the provisions of Code Sec. 274(h) applied to such convention, seminar or meeting without regard to such amendment. Prior to amendment, Code Sec. 274(h) read:

"(h) FOREIGN CONVENTIONS.—

"(1) DEDUCTIONS WITH RESPECT TO NOT MORE THAN 2 FOREIGN CONVENTIONS PER YEAR ALLOWED.—If any individual attends more than 2 foreign conventions during his taxable year—

"(A) he shall select not more than 2 of such conventions to be taken into account for purposes of this subsection, and

"(B) no deduction allocable to his attendance at any foreign convention during such taxable year (other than a foreign convention selected under subparagraph (A)) shall be allowed under section 162 or 212.

"(2) DEDUCTIBLE TRANSPORTATION COST CANNOT EXCEED COST OF COACH OR ECONOMY AIR FARE.—In the case of any foreign convention, no deduction for the expenses of transportation outside the United States to and from the site of such convention shall be allowed under section 162 or 212 in an amount which exceeds the lowest coach or economy rate at the time of travel charged by a commercial airline for transportation to and from such site during the calendar month in which such convention begins. If there is no such coach or economy rate, the preceding sentence shall be applied by substituting `first class' for `coach or economy'.

"(3) TRANSPORTATION COSTS DEDUCTIBLE IN FULL ONLY IF AT LEAST ONE-HALF OF THE DAYS ARE DEVOTED TO BUSINESS RELATED ACTIVITIES.—In the case of any foreign convention, a deduction for the full expenses of transportation (determined after the application of paragraph (2)) to and from the site of such convention shall be allowed only if at least one-half of the total days of the trip, excluding the days of transportation to and from the site of such convention, are devoted to business related activities. If less than one-half of the total days of the trip, excluding the days of transportation to and from the site of the convention, are devoted to business related activities, no deduction for the expenses of transportation shall be allowed which exceeds the percentage of the days of the trip devoted to business related activities.

"(4) DEDUCTIONS FOR SUBSISTENCE EXPENSES NOT ALLOWED UNLESS THE INDIVIDUAL ATTENDS TWO-THIRDS OF BUSINESS ACTIVITIES.—In the case of any foreign convention, no deduction for subsistence expenses shall be allowed except as follows:

"(A) a deduction for a full day of subsistence expenses while at the convention shall be allowed if there are at least 6 hours of scheduled business activities during such day and the individual attending the convention has attended at least two-thirds of these activities, and

"(B) a deduction for one-half day of subsistence expenses while at the convention shall be allowed if there are at least 3 hours of scheduled business activities during such day and the individual attending the convention has attended at least two-thirds of these activities.

Notwithstanding subparagraphs (A) and (B), a deduction for subsistence expenses for all of the days or half days, as the case may be, if [of] the convention shall be allowed if the individual attending the convention has attended at least two-thirds of the scheduled business activities, and each such full day consists of at least 6 hours of scheduled business activities and each such half day consists of at least 3 hours of scheduled business activities.

"(5) DEDUCTIBLE SUBSISTENCE COSTS CANNOT EXCEED PER DIEM RATE FOR UNITED STATES CIVIL SERVANTS.—In the case of any foreign convention, no deduction for subsistence expenses while at the convention or traveling to or from such convention shall be allowed at a rate in excess of the dollar per diem rate for the site of the convention which has been established under section 5702(a) of title 5 of the United States Code and which is in effect for the calendar month in which the convention begins.

"(6) DEFINITIONS AND SPECIAL RULES.—For purposes of this subsection—

"(A) FOREIGN CONVENTION DEFINED.—The term `foreign convention' means any convention, seminar, or similar meeting held outside the United States, its possessions, and the Trust Territory of the Pacific.

"(B) SUBSISTENCE EXPENSES DEFINED.—The term `subsistence expenses' means lodging, meals, and other necessary expenses for the personal sustenance and comfort of the traveler. Such term includes tips and taxi and other local transportation expenses.

"(C) ALLOCATION OF EXPENSES IN CERTAIN CASES.—In any case where the transportation expenses or the subsistence expenses are not separately stated, or where there is reason to believe that the stated charge for transportation expenses or subsistence expenses or both does not properly reflect the amounts properly allocable to such purposes, all amounts paid for transportation expenses and subsistence expenses shall be treated as having been paid solely for subsistence expenses.

"(D) SUBSECTION TO APPLY TO EMPLOYER AS WELL AS TO TRAVELER.—

"(i) Except as provided in clause (ii), this subsection shall apply to deductions otherwise allowable under section 162 or 212 to any person, whether or not such person is the individual attending the foreign convention. For the purposes of the preceding sentence such person shall be treated, with respect to each individual, as having selected the same 2 foreign conventions as were selected by such individual.

"(ii) This subsection shall not deny a deduction to any person other than the individual attending the foreign convention with respect to any amount paid by such person to or on behalf of another person if includible in the gross income of such other person. The preceding sentence shall not apply if such amount is required to be included in any information return filed by such person under part III of subchapter A of chapter 61 and is not so included.

"(E) INDIVIDUALS RESIDING IN FOREIGN COUNTRIES.—For purposes of this subsection, in the case of an individual citizen of the United States who establishes to the satisfaction of the Secretary that he was a bona fide resident of a foreign country at the time that he attended a convention in such foreign country, such individual's attendance at such convention shall not be considered as attendance at a foreign convention.

"(7) REPORTING REQUIREMENTS.—No deduction shall be allowed under section 162 or 212 for transportation or subsistence expenses allocable to attendance at a foreign convention unless the taxpayer claiming the deduction attaches to the return of tax on which the deduction is claimed—

"(A) a written statement signed by the individual attending the convention which includes—

"(i) information with respect to the total days of the trip, excluding the days of transportation to and from the site of such convention, and the number of hours of each day of the trip which such individual devoted to scheduled business activities,

"(ii) a program of the scheduled business activities of the convention, and

"(iii) such other information as may be required in regulations prescribed by the Secretary; and

"(B) a written statement signed by an officer of the organization or group sponsoring the convention which includes—

"(i) a schedule of the business activities of each day of the convention,

"(ii) the number of hours which the individual attending the convention attended such scheduled business activities, and

"(iii) such other information as may be required in regulations prescribed by the Secretary."

• 1978, Revenue Act of 1978 (P.L. 95-600)

P.L. 95-600, §701(g)(3), (4):

Amended the first sentence of Code Sec. 274(h)(3) by striking out "more than onehalf" and inserting in place thereof "at least onehalf". **Effective** for conventions beginning after 12-31-76.

P.L. 95-600, §701(g)(1), (4):

Amended Code Sec. 274(h)(6)(D). **Effective** for conventions beginning after 12-31-76. Before amendment, Code Sec. 274(h)(6)(D) read:

"(D) SUBSECTION TO APPLY TO EMPLOYER AS WELL AS TO TRAVELER.—This subsection shall apply to deductions otherwise allowable under section 162 or 212 to any person, whether or not such person is the individual attending the foreign convention. For the purposes of the preceding sentence such person shall be treated, with respect to each individual, as having selected the same 2 foreign conventions as were selected by such individual."

P.L. 95-600, §701(g)(2), (4):

Added Code Sec. 274(h)(6)(E). **Effective** for conventions beginning after 12-31-76.

• 1976, Tax Reform Act of 1976 (P.L. 94-455)

P.L. 94-455, §602(a):

Added Code Sec. 274(h). **Effective** for conventions beginning after 12-31-76.

[Sec. 274(i)]

(i) QUALIFIED NONPERSONAL USE VEHICLE.—For purposes of subsection (d), the term "qualified nonpersonal use vehicle" means any vehicle which, by reason of its nature, is not likely to be used more than a de minimis amount for personal purposes.

Amendments

• 1985 (P.L. 99-44)

P.L. 99-44, §2(b):

Amended Code Sec. 274 (as in effect for tax years beginning after 1985) by adding new subsection (i). **Effective** for tax years beginning after 12-31-85.

P.L. 99-44, §5, provides:

Not later than October 1, 1985, the Secretary of the Treasury or his delegate shall prescribe regulations to carry out the provisions of this Act which shall fully reflect such provisions.

[Sec. 274(j)]

(j) EMPLOYEE ACHIEVEMENT AWARDS.—

(1) GENERAL RULE.—No deduction shall be allowed under section 162 or section 212 for the cost of an employee achievement award except to the extent that such cost does not exceed the deduction limitations of paragraph (2).

(2) DEDUCTION LIMITATIONS.—The deduction for the cost of an employee achievement award made by an employer to an employee—

(A) which is not a qualified plan award, when added to the cost to the employer for all other employee achievement awards made to such employee during the taxable year which are not qualified plan awards, shall not exceed $400, and

(B) which is a qualified plan award, when added to the cost to the employer for all other employee achievement awards made to such employee during the taxable year (including employee achievement awards which are not qualified plan awards), shall not exceed $1,600.

(3) DEFINITIONS.—For purposes of this subsection—

(A) EMPLOYEE ACHIEVEMENT AWARD.—The term "employee achievement award" means an item of tangible personal property which is—

(i) transferred by an employer to an employee for length of service achievement or safety achievement,

(ii) awarded as part of a meaningful presentation, and

(iii) awarded under conditions and circumstances that do not create a significant likelihood of the payment of disguised compensation.

(B) QUALIFIED PLAN AWARD.—

(i) IN GENERAL.—The term "qualified plan award" means an employee achievement award awarded as part of an established written plan or program of the taxpayer which does not discriminate in favor of highly compensated employees (within the meaning of section 414(q)) as to eligibility or benefits.

(ii) LIMITATION.—An employee achievement award shall not be treated as a qualified plan award for any taxable year if the average cost of all employee achievement awards which are provided by the employer during the year, and which would be qualified plan awards but for this subparagraph, exceeds $400. For purposes of the preceding sentence, average cost shall be determined by including the entire cost of qualified plan awards, without taking into account employee achievement awards of nominal value.

(4) SPECIAL RULES.—For purposes of this subsection—

(A) PARTNERSHIPS.—In the case of an employee achievement award made by a partnership, the deduction limitations contained in paragraph (2) shall apply to the partnership as well as to each member thereof.

(B) LENGTH OF SERVICE AWARDS.—An item shall not be treated as having been provided for length of service achievement if the item is received during the recipient's 1st 5 years of employment or if the recipient received a length of service achievement award (other than an award excludable under section 132(e)(1)) during that year or any of the prior 4 years.

(C) SAFETY ACHIEVEMENT AWARDS.—An item provided by an employer to an employee shall not be treated as having been provided for safety achievement if—

(i) during the taxable year, employee achievement awards (other than awards excludable under section 132(e)(1)) for safety achievement have previously been awarded by the employer to more than 10 percent of the employees of the employer (excluding employees described in clause (ii)), or

(ii) such item is awarded to a manager, administrator, clerical employee, or other professional employee.

Amendments

• 1986, Tax Reform Act of 1986 (P.L. 99-514)

P.L. 99-514, §122(d):

Amended Code Sec. 274 by redesignating subsection (j) as subsection (k) and by inserting after subsection (i) a new subsection (j). **Effective** for prizes and awards granted after 12-31-86.

[Sec. 274(k)]

(k) BUSINESS MEALS.—

(1) IN GENERAL.—No deduction shall be allowed under this chapter for the expense of any food or beverages unless—

(A) such expense is not lavish or extravagant under the circumstances, and

(B) the taxpayer (or an employee of the taxpayer) is present at the furnishing of such food or beverages.

(2) EXCEPTIONS.—Paragraph (1) shall not apply to—

(A) any expense described in paragraph (2), (3), (4), (7), (8), or (9) of subsection (e), and

(B) any other expense to the extent provided in regulations.

Amendments

• 1988, Technical and Miscellaneous Revenue Act of 1988 (P.L. 100-647)

P.L. 100-647, §1001(g)(2):

Amended Code Sec. 274(k)(2). **Effective** as if included in the provision of P.L. 99-514 to which it relates. Prior to amendment, Code Sec. 274(k)(2) read as follows:

(2) EXCEPTIONS.—Paragraph (1) shall not apply to any expense if subsection (a) does not apply to such expense by reason of paragraph (2), (3), (4), (7), (8), or (9) of subsection (e).

• 1986, Tax Reform Act of 1986 (P.L. 99-514)

P.L. 99-514, §142(a)(1):

Amended Code Sec. 274, as amended by Act Sec. 122(d), by redesignating subsection (k) as subsection (o) and by inserting after subsection (j) new subsection (k). **Effective** for tax years beginning after 12-31-86.

[Sec. 274(l)]

(l) ADDITIONAL LIMITATIONS ON ENTERTAINMENT TICKETS.—

(1) ENTERTAINMENT TICKETS.—

(A) IN GENERAL.—In determining the amount allowable as a deduction under this chapter for any ticket for any activity or facility described in subsection (d)(2), the amount taken into account shall not exceed the face value of such ticket.

(B) EXCEPTION FOR CERTAIN CHARITABLE SPORTS EVENTS.—Subparagraph (A) shall not apply to any ticket for any sports event—

(i) which is organized for the primary purpose of benefiting an organization which is described in section 501(c)(3) and exempt from tax under section 501(a),

(ii) all of the net proceeds of which are contributed to such organization, and

(iii) which utilizes volunteers for substantially all of the work performed in carrying out such event.

(2) SKYBOXES, ETC.—In the case of a skybox or other private luxury box leased for more than 1 event, the amount allowable as a deduction under this chapter with respect to such events shall not exceed the sum of the face value of non-luxury box seat tickets for the seats in such box covered by the lease. For purposes of the preceding sentence, 2 or more related leases shall be treated as 1 lease.

Amendments

• 1990, Omnibus Budget Reconciliation Act of 1990 (P.L. 101-508)

P.L. 101-508, §11802(b)(1):

Amended Code Sec. 274(l)(2). **Effective** 11-5-90. Prior to amendment, Code Sec. 274(l)(2) read as follows:

(2) SKYBOXES, ETC.—

(A) IN GENERAL.—In the case of a skybox or other private luxury box leased for more than 1 event, the amount allowable as a deduction under this chapter with respect to such events shall not exceed the sum of the face value of non-luxury box seat tickets for the seats in such box covered by the lease. For purposes of the preceding sentence, 2 or more related leases shall be treated as 1 lease.

(B) PHASEIN.—In the case of—

(i) a taxable year beginning in 1987, the amount disallowed under subparagraph (A) shall be 1/3 of the amount which would be disallowed without regard to this subparagraph, and

(ii) in the case of a taxable year beginning in 1988, the amount disallowed under subparagraph (A) shall be 2/3 of the amount which would have been disallowed without regard to this subparagraph.

P.L. 101-508, §11821(b), provides:

(b) SAVINGS PROVISION.—If—

(1) any provision amended or repealed by this part applied to—

(A) any transaction occurring before the date of the enactment of this Act,

(B) any property acquired before such date of enactment, or

(C) any item of income, loss, deduction, or credit taken into account before such date of enactment, and

(2) the treatment of such transaction, property, or item under such provision would (without regard to the amendments made by this part affect liability for tax for periods ending after such date of enactment,

nothing in the amendments made by this part shall be construed to affect the treatment of such transaction, property, or item for purposes of determining liability for tax for periods ending after such date of enactment.

• 1986, Tax Reform Act of 1986 (P.L. 99-514)

P.L. 99-514, §142(b):

Amended Code Sec. 274 by inserting after the subsection added by Act Sec. 142(a) new subsections (l), (m), and (n). **Effective** for tax years beginning after 12-31-86.

[Sec. 274(m)]

(m) ADDITIONAL LIMITATIONS ON TRAVEL EXPENSES.—

(1) LUXURY WATER TRANSPORTATION.—

(A) IN GENERAL.—No deduction shall be allowed under this chapter for expenses incurred for transportation by water to the extent such expenses exceed twice the aggregate per diem amounts for days of such transportation. For purposes of the preceding sentence, the term "per diem amounts" means the highest amount generally allowable with respect to a day to employees of the executive branch of the Federal Government for per diem while away from home but serving in the United States.

(B) EXCEPTIONS.—Subparagraph (A) shall not apply to—

(i) any expense allocable to a convention, seminar, or other meeting which is held on any cruise ship, and

(ii) any expense described in paragraph (2), (3), (4), (7), (8), or (9) of subsection (e).

(2) TRAVEL AS FORM OF EDUCATION.—No deduction shall be allowed under this chapter for expenses for travel as a form of education.

(3) TRAVEL EXPENSES OF SPOUSE, DEPENDENT, OR OTHERS.—No deduction shall be allowed under this chapter (other than section 217) for travel expenses paid or incurred with respect to a spouse, dependent, or other individual accompanying the taxpayer (or an officer or employee of the taxpayer) on business travel, unless—

(A) the spouse, dependent, or other individual is an employee of the taxpayer,

(B) the travel of the spouse, dependent, or other individual is for a bona fide business purpose, and

(C) such expenses would otherwise be deductible by the spouse, dependent, or other individual.

Amendments

• 1993, Omnibus Budget Reconciliation Act of 1993 (P.L. 103-66)

P.L. 103-66, §13272(a):

Amended Code Sec. 274(m) by adding at the end thereof new paragraph (3). **Effective** for amounts paid or incurred after 12-31-93.

• 1988, Technical and Miscellaneous Revenue Act of 1988 (P.L. 100-647)

P.L. 100-647, §1001(g)(3):

Amended Code Sec. 274(m)(1)(B)(ii). **Effective** as if included in the provision of P.L. 99-514 to which it relates.

Prior to amendment, Code Sec. 274(m)(1)(B)(ii) read as follows:

(ii) any expense to which subsection (a) does not apply by reason of paragraph (2), (3), (4), (7), (8), or (9) of subsection (e).

• 1986, Tax Reform Act of 1986 (P.L. 99-514)

P.L. 99-514, §142(b):

Amended Code Sec. 274 by inserting after the subsection added by Act Sec. 142(a) new subsections (l), (m), and (n). **Effective** for tax years beginning after 12-31-86.

[Sec. 274(n)]

(n) ONLY 50 PERCENT OF MEAL AND ENTERTAINMENT EXPENSES ALLOWED AS DEDUCTION.—

(1) IN GENERAL.—The amount allowable as a deduction under this chapter for—

(A) any expense for food or beverages, and

(B) any item with respect to an activity which is of a type generally considered to constitute entertainment, amusement, or recreation, or with respect to a facility used in connection with such activity,

shall not exceed 50 percent of the amount of such expense or item which would (but for this paragraph) be allowable as a deduction under this chapter.

(2) EXCEPTIONS.—Paragraph (1) shall not apply to any expense if—

(A) such expense is described in paragraph (2), (3), (4), (7), (8), or (9) of subsection (e).

(B) in the case of an expense for food or beverages, such expense is excludable from the gross income of the recipient under section 132 by reason of subsection (e) thereof (relating to de minimis fringes),

(C) such expense is covered by a package involving a ticket described in subsection (l)(1)(B),

(D) in the case of an employer who pays or reimburses moving expenses of an employee, such expenses are includible in the income of the employee under section 82, or

(E) such expense is for food or beverages—

(i) required by any Federal law to be provided to crew members of a commercial vessel,

(ii) provided to crew members of a commercial vessel—

(I) which is operating on the Great Lakes, the Saint Lawrence Seaway, or any inland waterway of the United States, and

(II) which is of a kind which would be required by Federal law to provide food and beverages to crew members if it were operated at sea,

(iii) provided on an oil or gas platform or drilling rig if the platform or rig is located offshore, or

(iv) provided on an oil or gas platform or drilling rig, or at a support camp which is in proximity and integral to such platform or rig, if the platform or rig is located in the United States north of 54 degrees north latitude.

Clauses (i) and (ii) of subparagraph (E) shall not apply to vessels primarily engaged in providing luxury water transportation (determined under the principles of subsection (m)). In the case of the employee, the exception of subparagraph (A) shall not apply to expenses described in subparagraph (D).

(3) SPECIAL RULE FOR INDIVIDUALS SUBJECT TO FEDERAL HOURS OF SERVICE.—

(A) IN GENERAL.—In the case of any expenses for food or beverages consumed while away from home (within the meaning of section 162(a)(2)) by an individual during, or incident to, the period of duty subject to the hours of service limitations of the Department of Transportation, paragraph (1) shall be applied by substituting "the applicable percentage" for "50 percent".

(B) APPLICABLE PERCENTAGE.—For purposes of this paragraph, the term "applicable percentage" means the percentage determined under the following table:

For taxable years beginning in calendar year—	*The applicable percentage is—*
1998 or 1999	55
2000 or 2001	60
2002 or 2003	65
2004 or 2005	70
2006 or 2007	75
2008 or thereafter	80

Amendments

• 1997, Taxpayer Relief Act of 1997 (P.L. 105-34)

P.L. 105-34, §969(a):

Amended Code Sec. 274(n) by adding at the end a new paragraph (3). **Effective** for tax years beginning after 12-31-97.

• 1993, Omnibus Budget Reconciliation Act of 1993 (P.L. 103-66)

P.L. 103-66, §13209(a):

Amended Code Sec. 274(n)(1) by striking "80 percent" and inserting "50 percent". **Effective** for tax years beginning after 12-31-93.

P.L. 103-66, §13209(b):

Amended Code Sec. 274(n) by striking "80" in the subsection heading and inserting "50". **Effective** for tax years beginning after 12-31-93.

• 1990, Omnibus Budget Reconciliation Act of 1990 (P.L. 101-508)

P.L. 101-508, §11802(b)(2)(A)-(B):

Amended Code Sec. 274(n) in paragraph (2) by striking subparagraph (D) and redesignating subparagraphs (E) and (F) as subparagraphs (D) and (E), respectively, by striking "described in subparagraph (E)" and inserting "described in subparagraph (D)", by striking "of subparagraph (F)" and inserting "of subparagraph (E)"; and by striking paragraph (3). **Effective** 11-5-90. Prior to repeal, Code Sec. 274(n)(2)(D) and (3) read as follows:

(D) in the case of an expense for food or beverages before January 1, 1989, such expense is an integral part of a qualified meeting,

***

(3) QUALIFIED MEETING.—For purposes of paragraph (2)(D), the term "qualified meeting" means any convention, seminar, annual meeting, or similar business program with respect to which—

(A) an expense for food or beverages is not separately stated,

(B) more than 50 percent of the participants are away from home,

(C) at least 40 individuals attend, and

(D) such food and beverages are part of a program which includes a speaker.

P.L. 101-508, §11821(b), provides:

(b) SAVINGS PROVISION.—If—

(1) any provision amended or repealed by this part applied to—

(A) any transaction occurring before the date of the enactment of this Act,

(B) any property acquired before such date of enactment, or

(C) any item of income, loss, deduction, or credit taken into account before such date of enactment, and

(2) the treatment of such transaction, property, or item under such provision would (without regard to the amendments made by this part) affect liability for tax for periods ending after such date of enactment,

nothing in the amendments made by this part shall be construed to affect the treatment of such transaction, property, or item for purposes of determining liability for tax for periods ending after such date of enactment.

• 1989, Omnibus Budget Reconciliation Act of 1989 (P.L. 101-239)

P.L. 101-239, §7816(a)(1)-(2):

Amended Code Sec. 274(n)(2) by striking so much of such paragraph as follows subparagraph (D) and precedes subparagraph (F) and inserting a new subparagraph (E) and sentence. **Effective** as if included in the provision of P.L. 100-647 to which it relates. Prior to amendment, so much of Code Sec. 274(n)(2) as preceded subparagraph (F) and followed subparagraph (D) read as follows:

(E) in the case of an employer who pays or reimburses moving expenses of an employee, such expenses are includible in the income of the employee under section 82.

In the case of the employee, the exception of subparagraph (A) shall not apply to expenses described in subparagraph (E), or

P.L. 101-239, §7841(d)(18):

Amended Code Sec. 274(n)(2)(F)(i) by inserting "any" before "Federal". **Effective** 12-19-89.

• 1988, Technical and Miscellaneous Revenue Act of 1988 (P.L. 100-647)

P.L. 100-647, §1001(g)(1):

Amended Code Sec. 274(n)(2)(A). **Effective** as if included in the provision of P.L. 99-514 to which it relates. Prior to amendment, Code Sec. 274(n)(2)(A) read as follows:

(A) subsection (a) does not apply to such expense by reason of paragraph (2), (3), (4), (7), (8), or (9) of subsection (e).

P.L. 100-647, §1001(g)(4)(A)(i)-(iii):

Amended Code Sec. 274(n)(2) by striking "or" at the end of subparagraph (C), by striking the period at the end of subparagraph (D) and inserting ", or", and by adding at the end thereof new subparagraph (E). **Effective** as if included in the provision of P.L. 99-514 to which it relates.

P.L. 100-647, §6003(a):

Amended Code Sec. 274(n)(2) by striking out "or" at the end of subparagraph (D), by striking out the period at the end of subparagraph (E) and inserting in lieu thereof ", or", and by adding at the end thereof a new subparagraph (F). For the **effective** date, see Act Sec. 6003(b), below.

P.L. 100-647, §6003(b), provides:

(b) EFFECTIVE DATES.—

(1) Clauses (i) and (ii) of section 274(n)(2)(F) of the 1986 Code, as added by subsection (a), shall apply to taxable years beginning after December 31, 1988.

(2) Clauses (iii) and (iv) of section 274(n)(2)(F) of the 1986 Code, as added by subsection (a), shall apply to taxable years beginning after December 31, 1987.

• 1986, Tax Reform Act of 1986 (P.L. 99-514)

P.L. 99-514, §142(b):

Amended Code Sec. 274 by inserting after the subsection added by Act Sec. 142(a) new subsections (l), (m), and (n). **Effective** for tax years beginning after 12-31-86.

[Sec. 274(o)]

(o) REGULATORY AUTHORITY.—The Secretary shall prescribe such regulations as he may deem necessary to carry out the purposes of this section, including regulations prescribing whether subsection (a) or subsection (b) applies in cases where both such subsections would otherwise apply.

Amendments

• 1986, Tax Reform Act of 1986 (P.L. 99-514)

P.L. 99-514, §122(d):

Amended Code Sec. 274 by redesignating subsection (j) as subsection (k). **Effective** for prizes and awards granted after 12-31-86.

P.L. 99-514, §142(a)(1):

Amended Code Sec. 274, as amended by Act Sec. 122(d), by redesignating subsection (k) as subsection (o). **Effective** for tax years beginning after 12-31-86.

• 1985 (P.L. 99-44)

P.L. 99-44, §2(b):

Amended Code Sec. 274 (as in effect for tax years beginning after 1985) by redesignating subsection (i) as subsection (j). **Effective** for tax years beginning after 12-31-85.

P.L. 99-44, §5, provides:

Not later than October 1, 1985, the Secretary of the Treasury or his delegate shall prescribe regulations to carry out the provisions of this Act which shall fully reflect such provisions.

• 1976, Tax Reform Act of 1976 (P.L. 94-455)

P.L. 94-455, §602(a):

Redesignated former Code Sec. 274(h) as Code Sec. 274(i). **Effective** for conventions beginning after 12-31-76.

P.L. 94-455, §1906(b)(13)(A):

Amended 1954 Code by substituting "Secretary" for "Secretary or his delegate" each place it appeared. **Effective** 2-1-77.

• 1962, Revenue Act of 1962 (P.L. 87-834)

P.L. 87-834, §4:

Amended part IX of subchapter B of chapter 1 by adding at the end thereof a new Sec. 274. Also amended the table of sections for such part by inserting after Sec. 273 "Sec. 274. Disallowance of certain entertainment, etc., expenses." **Effective** for tax years ending after 12-31-62, but only in respect of periods after such date.

[Sec. 275]

SEC. 275. CERTAIN TAXES.

[Sec. 275(a)]

(a) GENERAL RULE.—No deduction shall be allowed for the following taxes:

(1) Federal income taxes, including—

(A) the tax imposed by section 3101 (relating to the tax on employees under the Federal Insurance Contributions Act);

(B) the taxes imposed by sections 3201 and 3211 (relating to the taxes on railroad employees and railroad employee representatives); and

(C) the tax withheld at source on wages under section 3402.

(2) Federal war profits and excess profits taxes.

(3) Estate, inheritance, legacy, succession, and gift taxes.

(4) Income, war profits, and excess profits taxes imposed by the authority of any foreign country or possession of the United States if the taxpayer chooses to take to any extent the benefits of section 901.

(5) Taxes on real property, to the extent that section 164(d) requires such taxes to be treated as imposed on another taxpayer.

(6) Taxes imposed by chapters 41, 42, 43, 44, 45, 46, and 54.

Paragraph (1) shall not apply to any taxes to the extent such taxes are allowable as a deduction under section 164(f). Paragraph (1) shall not apply to the tax imposed by section 59A.

Amendments

• 2007, Tax Technical Corrections Act of 2007 (P.L. 110-172)

P.L. 110-172, §11(g)(5):

Amended Code Sec. 275(a)(4) by striking "if" and all that follows and inserting "if the taxpayer chooses to take to any extent the benefits of section 901.". **Effective** 12-29-2007. Prior to amendment, Code Sec. 275(a)(4) read as follows:

(4) Income, war profits, and excess profits taxes imposed by the authority of any foreign country or possession of the United States if—

(A) the taxpayer chooses to take to any extent the benefits of section 901, or

(B) such taxes are paid or accrued with respect to foreign trade income (within the meaning of section 923(b)) of a FSC.

• 2004, American Jobs Creation Act of 2004 (P.L. 108-357)

P.L. 108-357, §101(b)(5)(A):

Amended Code Sec. 275(a) by inserting "or" at the end of paragraph (4)(A), by striking "or" at the end of paragraph (4)(B) and inserting a period, and by striking subparagraph (C). **Effective** for transactions after 12-31-2004. For transitional and special rules, see Act Sec. 101(d)-(f), below. Prior to being stricken, Code Sec. 275(a)(4)(C) read as follows:

(C) such taxes are paid or accrued with respect to qualifying foreign trade income (as defined in section 941).

P.L. 108-357, §101(b)(5)(B):

Amended Code Sec. 275(a) by striking the last sentence. **Effective** for transactions after 12-31-2004. For transitional and special rules, see Act Sec. 101(d)-(f), below. Prior to being stricken, the last sentence of Code Sec. 275(a) read as follows:

A rule similar to the rule of section 943(d) shall apply for purposes of paragraph (4)(C).

P.L. 108-357, §101(d)-(f), provides:

(d) TRANSITIONAL RULE FOR 2005 AND 2006.—

(1) IN GENERAL.—In the case of transactions during 2005 or 2006, the amount includible in gross income by reason of the amendments made by this section shall not exceed the applicable percentage of the amount which would have been so included but for this subsection.

(2) APPLICABLE PERCENTAGE.—For purposes of paragraph (1), the applicable percentage shall be as follows:

(A) For 2005, the applicable percentage shall be 20 percent.

(B) For 2006, the applicable percentage shall be 40 percent.

(e) REVOCATION OF ELECTION TO BE TREATED AS DOMESTIC CORPORATION.—If, during the 1-year period beginning on the date of the enactment of this Act, a corporation for which an election is in effect under section 943(e) of the Internal Revenue Code of 1986 revokes such election, no gain or loss shall be recognized with respect to property treated as transferred under clause (ii) of section 943(e)(4)(B) of such Code to the extent such property—

(1) was treated as transferred under clause (i) thereof, or

(2) was acquired during a taxable year to which such election applies and before May 1, 2003, in the ordinary course of its trade or business.

The Secretary of the Treasury (or such Secretary's delegate) may prescribe such regulations as may be necessary to prevent the abuse of the purposes of this subsection.

[**Note:** Act Sec. 101(f) of P.L. 108-357, below, was stricken by P.L. 109-222, §513(b), applicable to tax years beginning after 5-17-2006.—CCH.]

(f) BINDING CONTRACTS.—The amendments made by this section shall not apply to any transaction in the ordinary course of a trade or business which occurs pursuant to a binding contract—

(1) which is between the taxpayer and a person who is not a related person (as defined in section 943(b)(3) of such Code, as in effect on the day before the date of the enactment of this Act), and

(2) which is in effect on September 17, 2003, and at all times thereafter.

For purposes of this subsection, a binding contract shall include a purchase option, renewal option, or replacement option which is included in such contract and which is enforceable against the seller or lessor.

P.L. 108-357, §802(b)(1):

Amended Code Sec. 275(a)(6) by inserting "45," before "46,". **Effective** on 3-4-2003; except that periods before such date shall not be taken into account in applying the periods in Code Sec. 4985(a) and (e)(1), as added by Act Sec. 802(a).

• 2000, FSC Repeal and Extraterritorial Income Exclusion Act of 2000 (P.L. 106-519)

P.L. 106-519, §4(2)(A)-(B):

Amended Code Sec. 275(a) by striking "or" at the end of paragraph (4)(A), by striking the period at the end of paragraph (4)(B) and inserting ", or", and by adding at the end of paragraph (4) a new subparagraph (C); and by adding at the end a new sentence. **Effective**, generally, for transactions after 9-30-2000. For special rules, see Act Sec. 5(b)-(d) in the amendment notes following Code Sec. 921.

• 1987, Revenue Act of 1987 (P.L. 100-203)

P.L. 100-203, §10228(b):

Amended Code Sec. 275(a)(6) by striking out "and 46" and inserting in lieu thereof "46, and 54". **Effective** for consideration received after 12-22-87; except that such amendments shall not apply in the case of any acquisition pursuant to a written binding contract in effect on 12-15-87, and at all times thereafter before the acquisition.

• 1986, Superfund Amendments and Reauthorization Act of 1986 (P.L. 99-499)

P.L. 99-499, §516(b)(2)(B):

Amended Code Sec. 275(a) by adding at the end thereof a new sentence. **Effective** for tax years beginning after 12-31-86.

• 1984, Deficit Reduction Act of 1984 (P.L. 98-369)

P.L. 98-369, §67(b)(2):

Amended Code Sec. 275(a)(6) by striking out "and 44" and inserting in lieu thereof "44, and 46". **Effective** for payments under agreements entered into or renewed after 6-14-84, in tax years ending after such date. However, see Act Sec. 67(e)(2), below, for special rules.

P.L. 98-369, §67(e)(2), provides:

(2) SPECIAL RULE FOR CONTRACT AMENDMENTS.—In the case of any contract entered into before June 15, 1984, any amendment to such contract after June 14, 1984, which amends such contract in any significant relevant aspect shall be treated as a new contract.

P.L. 98-369, §801(d)(5):

Amended Code Sec. 275(a)(4). **Effective** for transactions after 12-31-84, in tax years ending after such date. Prior to amendment, Code Sec. 275(a)(4) read as follows:

(4) Income, war profits, and excess profits taxes imposed by the authority of any foreign country or possession of the United States, if the taxpayer chooses to take to any extent the benefits of section 901 (relating to the foreign tax credit).

• 1983, Interest and Dividend Tax Compliance Act of 1983 (P.L. 98-67)

P.L. 98-67, §102(a):

Repealed the amendments made to Code Sec. 275(a)(1) by P.L. 97-248 (see below) as of the close of 6-30-83, as though they had not been enacted.

• 1983, Social Security Amendments of 1983 (P.L. 98-21)

P.L. 98-21, §124(c)(5):

Amended Code Sec. 275(a) by adding the last sentence. **Effective** for tax years beginning after 1989.

• 1982, Tax Equity and Fiscal Responsibility Act of 1982 (P.L. 97-248)

P.L. 97-248, §305(a) [repealed by P.L. 98-67, §102(a)]:

Amended Code Sec. 275(a)(1) by striking out "and" at the end of subparagraph (B), by substituting ", and" for the period at the end of subparagraph (C), and by adding subparagraph (D) to read: "(D) the tax withheld at source on interest, dividends, and patronage dividends under section 3451." **Effective** for interest, dividends, and patronage dividends paid or credited after 6-30-83.

• 1978, Revenue Act of 1978 (P.L. 95-600)

P.L. 95-600, §701(t)(3)(B):

Amended P.L. 94-455 by deleting §1605(b)(1). **Effective** 10-4-76.

• 1976, Tax Reform Act of 1976 (P.L. 94-455)

P.L. 94-455, §1307(d)(2)(A):

Amended Code Sec. 275(a)(6). **Effective** for tax years beginning after 12-31-76. Prior to amendment, Code Sec. 275(a)(6) read as follows:

"(6) taxes imposed by chapter 42 and chapter 43."

P.L. 94-455, §1605(b)(1):

Substituted ", chapter 43, and chapter 44." for "and chapter 43." in Code Sec. 275(a)(6). **Effective** for tax years of real estate investment trusts beginning after 10-4-76.

P.L. 94-455, §1901(a)(39):

Amended Code Sec. 275(a)(1)(C) by striking out ", and corresponding provisions of prior revenue laws" after "section 3402". **Effective** for tax years beginning after 12-31-76.

• 1974, Employee Retirement Income Security Act of 1974 (P.L. 93-406)

P.L. 93-406, §1016(a)(1):

Added Code Sec. 275(a)(6).

• 1964, Revenue Act of 1964 (P.L. 88-272)

P.L. 88-272, §207(b)(3):

Added Code Sec. 275. **Effective** for tax years beginning after 12-31-63.

[Sec. 275(b)]

(b) CROSS REFERENCE.—

For disallowance of certain other taxes, see section 164(c).

Amendments

• 1964, Revenue Act of 1964 (P.L. 88-272)

P.L. 88-272, §207(b)(3):

Amended part IX of subchapter B of chapter 1 by adding section 275 thereto. **Effective** with respect to tax years beginning after 12-31-63.

[Sec. 276]

SEC. 276. CERTAIN INDIRECT CONTRIBUTIONS TO POLITICAL PARTIES.

[Sec. 276(a)]

(a) DISALLOWANCE OF DEDUCTION.—No deduction otherwise allowable under this chapter shall be allowed for any amount paid or incurred for—

(1) advertising in a convention program of a political party, or in any other publication if any part of the proceeds of such publication directly or indirectly inures (or is intended to inure) to or for the use of a political party or a political candidate,

(2) admission to any dinner or program, if any part of the proceeds of such dinner or program directly or indirectly inures (or is intended to inure) to or for the use of a political party or a political candidate, or

(3) admission to an inaugural ball, inaugural gala, inaugural parade, or inaugural concert, or to any similar event which is identified with a political party or a political candidate.

Amendments

• 1975 (P.L. 93-625)

P.L. 93-625, §10(g):

Repealed P.L. 90-346. This latter Public Law, which was **effective** with respect to amounts paid or incurred on or after 1-1-68, provided as follows:

"Sec. 1. Subsection (a) of section 276 of the Internal Revenue Code of 1954 (relating to certain indirect contributions to political parties) shall not apply to any amount paid or incurred for advertising in a convention program of a political party distributed in connection with a convention held for the purpose of nominating candidates for the offices of President and Vice President of the United States, if the proceeds from such program are used solely to defray the costs of conducting such convention (or a subsequent convention of such party held for such purpose) and the amount paid or incurred for such advertising is reasonable in light of the business the taxpayer may expect to receive—

"(1) directly as a result of such advertising, or

"(2) as a result of the convention being held in an area in which the taxpayer has a principal place of business.

"Sec. 2. The first section of this Act shall apply with respect to amounts paid or incurred on or after January 1, 1968."

[Sec. 276(b)]

(b) DEFINITIONS.—For purposes of this section—

(1) POLITICAL PARTY.—The term "political party" means—

(A) a political party;

(B) a National, State, or local committee of a political party; or

(C) a committee, association, or organization, whether incorporated or not, which directly or indirectly accepts contributions (as defined in section 271(b)(2)) or make[s] expenditures (as defined in section 271(b)(3)) for the purpose of influencing or attempting to influence the selection, nomination, or election of any individual to any Federal, State, or local elective public office, or the election of presidential and vice-presidential electors, whether or not such individual or electors are selected, nominated, or elected.

(2) PROCEEDS INURING TO OR FOR THE USE OF POLITICAL CANDIDATES.—Proceeds shall be treated as inuring to or for the use of a political candidate only if—

(A) such proceeds may be used directly or indirectly for the purpose of furthering his candidacy for selection, nomination, or election to any elective public office, and

(B) such proceeds are not received by such candidate in the ordinary course of a trade or business (other than the trade or business of holding elective public office).

[Sec. 276(c)]

(c) CROSS REFERENCE.—

For disallowance of certain entertainment, etc., expenses, see section 274.

Amendments

• 1974, Federal Election Campaign Act Amendments of 1974 (P.L. 93-443)

P.L. 93-443, §406(d):

Amended Code Sec. 276 by deleting subsection (c) and relettering subsection (d) as subsection (c). **Effective** for tax years beginning after 12-31-74. Prior to repeal, former subsection (c) read as follows:

(c) Advertising in a Convention Program of a National Political Convention.—Subsection (a) shall not apply to any amount paid or incurred for advertising in a convention program of a political party distributed in connection with a convention held for the purpose of nominating candidates for the offices of President and Vice President of the United States, if the proceeds from such program are used solely to defray the costs of conducting such convention (or a subsequent convention of such party held for such purpose) and the amount paid or incurred for such advertising is reasonable in light of the business the taxpayer may expect to receive—

(1) directly as a result of such advertising, or

(2) as a result of the convention being held in an area in which the taxpayer has a principal place of business.

• 1968, Revenue and Expenditure Control Act of 1968 (P.L. 90-364)

P.L. 90-364, §108(a):

Added Code Sec. 276(c) and redesignated former Sec. Code 276(c) to be Code Sec. 276(d). **Effective** with respect to amounts paid or incurred on or after 1-1-68.

• 1966, Tax Adjustment Act of 1966 (P.L. 89-368)

P.L. 89-368, §301(a):

Added Code Sec. 276. **Effective** for tax years beginning after 12-31-65, but only with respect to amounts paid or incurred after 3-15-66.

[Sec. 277]

SEC. 277. DEDUCTIONS INCURRED BY CERTAIN MEMBERSHIP ORGANIZATIONS IN TRANSACTIONS WITH MEMBERS.

[Sec. 277(a)]

(a) GENERAL RULE.—In the case of a social club or other membership organization which is operated primarily to furnish services or goods to members and which is not exempt from taxation, deductions for the taxable year attributable to furnishing services, insurance, goods, or other items of value to members shall be allowed only to the extent of income derived during such year from members or transactions with members (including income derived during such year from institutes and trade shows which are primarily for the education of members). If for any taxable year such deductions exceed such income, the excess shall be treated as a deduction attributable to furnishing services, insurance, goods, or other items of value to members paid or incurred in the succeeding taxable year. The deductions provided by sections 243, 244, and 245 (relating to dividends received by corporations) shall not be allowed to any organization to which this section applies for the taxable year.

[Sec. 277(b)]

(b) EXCEPTIONS.—Subsection (a) shall not apply to any organization—

(1) which for the taxable year is subject to taxation under subchapter H or L,

(2) which has made an election before October 9, 1969, under section 456(c) or which is affiliated with such an organization,

(3) which for each day of any taxable year is a national securities exchange subject to regulation under the Securities Exchange Act of 1934 or a contract market subject to regulation under the Commodity Exchange Act, or

(4) which is engaged primarily in the gathering and distribution of news to its members for publication.

Amendments

• 1986, Tax Reform Act of 1986 (P.L. 99-514)

P.L. 99-514, §1604(a)(1)-(3):

Amended Code Sec. 277(b) by striking out "or" at the end of paragraph (2); by striking out the period at the end of paragraph (3) and inserting in lieu thereof ", or" and by adding at the end thereof a new paragraph (4). **Effective** for tax years beginning after 10-22-86.

• 1976 (P.L. 94-568)

P.L. 94-568, §1(c):

Added the last sentence of Code Sec. 277(a). **Effective** for tax years beginning after 10-21-76.

• 1969, Tax Reform Act of 1969 (P.L. 91-172)

P.L. 91-172, §121(b)(3):

Added Code Sec. 277. **Effective** for tax years beginning after 12-31-70.

[Sec. 278—Repealed]

Amendments

• 1986, Tax Reform Act of 1986 (P.L. 99-514)

P.L. 99-514, §803(b)(6):

Repealed Code Sec. 278. **Effective**, generally, for costs incurred after 12-31-86, in tax years ending after such date. However, for special rules, see Act Sec. 803(d)(2)-(7) following Code Sec. 263A. Prior to repeal, Code Sec. 278 read as follows:

SEC. 278. CAPITAL EXPENDITURES INCURRED IN PLANTING AND DEVELOPING CITRUS AND ALMOND GROVES; CERTAIN CAPITAL EXPENDITURES OF FARMING SYNDICATES.

[Sec. 278(a)]

(a) GENERAL RULE.—Except as provided in subsection (c), any amount (allowable as a deduction without regard to this section), which is attributable to the planting, cultivation, maintenance, or development of any citrus or almond grove (or part thereof), and which is incurred before the close of the fourth taxable year beginning with the taxable year in which the trees were planted, shall be charged to capital account. For purposes of the preceding sentence, the portion of a citrus or almond grove planted in one taxable year shall be treated separately from the portion of such grove planted in another taxable year.

Amendments

• 1976, Tax Reform Act of 1976 (P.L. 94-455)

P.L. 94-455, §207(b)(2):

Amended the heading of Code Sec. 278 and substituted "subsection (c)" for "subsection (b)" in Code Sec. 278(a). **Effective** for tax years beginning after 12-31-75. The amendments shall not apply in the case of a grove, orchard or vineyard referred to in subsection (b) or (c) which was planted or replanted on or before 12-31-75. (A tree or vine which, on or before 12-31-75, was planted at a place other than the grove, orchard or vineyard of the taxpayer but which, on such date, was owned by the taxpayer, or with respect to which the taxpayer had a binding contract to purchase, shall be treated as planted on 12-31-75, in the grove, orchard or vineyard of the taxpayer.) Prior to amendment, the heading of Code Sec. 278 read as follows:

SEC. 278. CAPITAL EXPENDITURES INCURRED IN PLANTING AND DEVELOPING CITRUS AND ALMOND GROVES.

• 1971 (P.L. 91-680)

P.L. 91-680, §1:

Amended the heading of Code Sec. 278 by adding "AND ALMOND" and amended the text of Code Sec. 278 by adding "or almond" after "citrus" wherever such word appears. **Effective** for tax years beginning after 1-12-71.

[Sec. 278(b)]

(b) FARMING SYNDICATES.—Except as provided in subsection (c), in the case of any farming syndicate (as defined in section 464(c)) engaged in planting, cultivating, maintaining, or developing a grove, orchard, or vineyard in which fruit or nuts are grown, any amount—

(1) which would be allowable as a deduction but for the provisions of this subsection,

(2) which is attributable to the planting, cultivation, maintenance, or development of such grove, orchard, or vineyard, and

(3) which is incurred in a taxable year before the first taxable year in which such grove, orchard, or vineyard bears a crop or yield in commercial quantities, shall be charged to capital account.

Amendments

• 1976, Tax Reform Act of 1976 (P.L. 94-455)

P.L. 94-455, §207(b)(1):

Amended Code Sec. 278(b). **Effective** for tax years beginning after 12-31-75. The amendment shall not apply in the case of a grove, orchard or vineyard which was planted or replanted on or before 12-31-75 (see amendment note following Code Sec. 278(a)). Prior to amendment, Code Sec. 278(b) read as follows:

(b) EXCEPTIONS.—Subsection (a) shall not apply to amounts allowable as deductions (without regard to this section), and attributable to a citrus or almond grove (or part thereof) which was:

(1) replanted after having been lost or damaged (while in the hands of the taxpayer), by reason of freeze, disease, drought, pests or casualty, or

(2) planted or replanted before—

(A) December 30, 1969, in the case of a citrus grove, or

(B) December 30, 1970, in the case of an almond grove.

• 1971 (P.L. 91-680)

P.L. 91-680, §1:

Amended the text of Code Sec. 278 by adding "or almond" after "citrus" wherever such word appears and amended Code Sec. 278(b)(2). **Effective** for tax years beginning after 1-12-71. Prior to amendment, Code Sec. 278(b)(2) read as follows:

(2) planted or replanted prior to the enactment of this section.

[Sec. 278(c)]

(c) EXCEPTIONS.—Subsections (a) and (b) shall not apply to amounts allowable as deductions (without regard to this section) attributable to a grove, orchard, or vineyard which was replanted after having been lost or damaged (while in the hands of the taxpayer) by reason of freezing temperatures, disease, drought, pests, or casualty.

Amendments

• 1976, Tax Reform Act of 1976 (P.L. 94-455)

P.L. 94-455, §207(b)(1):

Added Code Sec. 278(c). **Effective** for tax years beginning after 12-31-75.

• 1969, Tax Reform Act of 1969 (P.L. 91-172)

P.L. 91-172, §216(a):

Added Code Sec. 278. **Effective** for tax years beginning after 12-31-69.

[Sec. 279]

SEC. 279. INTEREST ON INDEBTEDNESS INCURRED BY CORPORATION TO ACQUIRE STOCK OR ASSETS OF ANOTHER CORPORATION.

[Sec. 279(a)]

(a) GENERAL RULE.—No deduction shall be allowed for any interest paid or incurred by a corporation during the taxable year with respect to its corporate acquisition indebtedness to the extent that such interest exceeds—

(1) $5,000,000, reduced by

(2) the amount of interest paid or incurred by such corporation during such year on obligations (A) issued after December 31, 1967, to provide consideration for an acquisition described in paragraph (1) of subsection (b), but (B) which are not corporate acquisition indebtedness.

[Sec. 279(b)]

(b) CORPORATE ACQUISITION INDEBTEDNESS.—For purposes of this section, the term "corporate acquisition indebtedness" means any obligation evidenced by a bond, debenture, note, or certificate or other evidence of indebtedness issued after October 9, 1969, by a corporation (hereinafter in this section referred to as "issuing corporation") if—

(1) such obligation is issued to provide consideration for the acquisition of—

(A) stock in another corporation (hereinafter in this section referred to as "acquired corporation"), or

(B) assets of another corporation (hereinafter in this section referred to as "acquired corporation") pursuant to a plan under which at least two-thirds (in value) of all the assets (excluding money) used in trades and businesses carried on by such corporation are acquired,

(2) such obligation is either—

(A) subordinated to the claims of trade creditors of the issuing corporation generally, or

(B) expressly subordinated in right of payment to the payment of any substantial amount of unsecured indebtedness, whether outstanding or subsequently issued, of the issuing corporation,

(3) the bond or other evidence of indebtedness is either—

(A) convertible directly or indirectly into stock of the issuing corporation, or

(B) part of an investment unit or other arrangement which includes, in addition to such bond or other evidence of indebtedness, an option to acquire, directly or indirectly, stock in the issuing corporation, and

(4) as of a day determined under subsection (c)(1), either—

(A) the ratio of debt to equity (as defined in subsection (c)(2)) of the issuing corporation exceeds 2 to 1, or

(B) the projected earnings (as defined in subsection (c)(3)) do not exceed 3 times the annual interest to be paid or incurred (determined under subsection (c)(4)).

[Sec. 279(c)]

(c) RULES FOR APPLICATION OF SUBSECTION (b)(4).—For purposes of subsection (b)(4)—

(1) TIME OF DETERMINATION.—Determinations are to be made as of the last day of any taxable year of the issuing corporation in which it issues any obligation to provide consideration for an acquisition described in subsection (b)(1) of stock in, or assets of, the acquired corporation.

(2) RATIO OF DEBT TO EQUITY.—The term "ratio of debt to equity" means the ratio which the total indebtedness of the issuing corporation bears to the sum of its money and all its other assets (in an amount equal to their adjusted basis for determining gain) less such total indebtedness.

(3) PROJECTED EARNINGS.—

(A) The term "projected earnings" means the "average annual earnings" (as defined in subparagraph (B)) of—

(i) the issuing corporation only, if clause (ii) does not apply, or

(ii) both the issuing corporation and the acquired corporation, in any case where the issuing corporation has acquired control (as defined in section 368(c)), or has acquired substantially all of the properties, of the acquired corporation.

(B) The average annual earnings referred to in subparagraph (A) is, for any corporation, the amount of its earnings and profits for any 3-year period ending with the last day of a taxable year of the issuing corporation described in paragraph (1), computed without reduction for—

(i) interest paid or incurred,

(ii) depreciation or amortization allowed under this chapter,

(iii) liability for tax under this chapter, and

(iv) distributions to which section 301(c)(1) applies (other than such distributions from the acquired to the issuing corporation),

and reduced to an annual average for such 3-year period pursuant to regulations prescribed by the Secretary. Such regulations shall include rules for cases where any corporation was not in existence for all of such 3-year period or such period includes only a portion of a taxable year of any corporation.

(4) ANNUAL INTEREST TO BE PAID OR INCURRED.—The term "annual interest to be paid or incurred" means—

(A) if subparagraph (B) does not apply, the annual interest to be paid or incurred by the issuing corporation only, determined by reference to its total indebtedness outstanding, or

(B) if projected earnings are determined under clause (ii) of paragraph (3)(A), the annual interest to be paid or incurred by both the issuing corporation and the acquired corporation, determined by reference to their combined total indebtedness outstanding.

(5) SPECIAL RULES FOR BANKS AND LENDING OR FINANCE COMPANIES.—With respect to any corporation which is a bank (as defined in section 581) or is primarily engaged in a lending or finance business—

(A) in determining under paragraph (2) the ratio of debt to equity of such corporation (or of the affiliated group of which such corporation is a member), the total indebtedness of such corporation (and the assets of such corporation) shall be reduced by an amount equal to the total indebtedness owed to such corporation which arises out of the banking business of such corporation, or out of the lending or finance business of such corporation, as the case may be;

(B) in determining under paragraph (4) the annual interest to be paid or incurred by such corporation (or by the issuing and acquired corporations referred to in paragraph (4)(B) or by the affiliated group of which such corporation is a member) the amount of such interest (determined without regard to this paragraph) shall be reduced by an amount which bears the same ratio to the amount of such interest as the amount of the reduction for the taxable year under subparagraph (A) bears to the total indebtedness of such corporation; and

(C) in determining under paragraph (3)(B) the average annual earnings, the amount of the earnings and profits for the 3-year period shall be reduced by the sum of the reductions under subparagraph (B) for such period.

For purposes of this paragraph, the term "lending or finance business" means a business of making loans or purchasing or discounting accounts receivable, notes, or installment obligations.

Amendments

• **1976, Tax Reform Act of 1976 (P.L. 94-455)**

P.L. 94-455, §1906(b)(13)(A):

Amended 1954 Code by substituting "Secretary" for "Secretary or his delegate" each place it appeared. **Effective** 2-1-77.

[Sec. 279(d)]

(d) TAXABLE YEARS TO WHICH APPLICABLE.—In applying this section—

(1) FIRST YEAR OF DISALLOWANCE.—The deduction of interest on any obligation shall not be disallowed under subsection (a) before the first taxable year of the issuing corporation as of the last day of which the application of either subparagraph (A) or subparagraph (B) of subsection (b)(4) results in such obligation being corporate acquisition indebtedness.

(2) GENERAL RULE FOR SUCCEEDING YEARS.—Except as provided in paragraphs (3), (4), and (5), if an obligation is determined to be corporate acquisition indebtedness as of the last day of any taxable year of the issuing corporation, it shall be corporate acquisition indebtedness for such taxable year and all subsequent taxable years.

(3) REDETERMINATION WHERE CONTROL, ETC., IS ACQUIRED.—If an obligation is determined to be corporate acquisition indebtedness as of the close of a taxable year of the issuing corporation in which clause (i) of subsection (c)(3)(A) applied, but would not be corporate acquisition indebtedness if the determination were made as of the close of the first taxable year of such corporation thereafter in which clause (ii) of subsection (c)(3)(A) could apply, such obligation shall be considered not to be corporate acquisition indebtedness for such later taxable year and all taxable years thereafter.

(4) SPECIAL 3-YEAR RULE.—If an obligation which has been determined to be corporate acquisition indebtedness for any taxable year would not be such indebtedness for each of any 3 consecutive taxable years thereafter if subsection (b)(4) were applied as of the close of each of such 3 years, then such obligation shall not be corporate acquisition indebtedness for all taxable years after such 3 consecutive taxable years.

(5) 5 PERCENT STOCK RULE.—In the case of obligations issued to provide consideration for the acquisition of stock in another corporation, such obligations shall be corporate acquisition indebtedness for a taxable year only if at some time after October 9, 1969, and before the close of such year the issuing corporation owns 5 percent or more of the total combined voting power of all classes of stock entitled to vote of such other corporation.

[Sec. 279(e)]

(e) CERTAIN NONTAXABLE TRANSACTIONS.—An acquisition of stock of a corporation of which the issuing corporation is in control (as defined in section 368(c)) in a transaction in which gain or loss is not recognized shall be deemed an acquisition described in paragraph (1) of subsection (b) only if immediately before such transaction (1) the acquired corporation was in existence, and (2) the issuing corporation was not in control (as defined in section 368(c)) of such corporation.

[Sec. 279(f)]

(f) EXEMPTION FOR CERTAIN ACQUISITIONS OF FOREIGN CORPORATIONS.—For purposes of this section, the term "corporate acquisition indebtedness" does not include any indebtedness issued to any person to provide consideration for the acquisition of stock in, or assets of, any foreign corporation substantially all of the income of which, for the 3-year period ending with the date of such acquisition or for such part of such period as the foreign corporation was in existence, is from sources without the United States.

[Sec. 279(g)]

(g) AFFILIATED GROUPS.—In any case in which the issuing corporation is a member of an affiliated group, the application of this section shall be determined, pursuant to regulations prescribed by the Secretary, by treating all of the members of the affiliated group in the aggregate as the issuing corporation, except that the ratio of debt to equity of, projected earnings of, and annual interest to be paid or incurred by any corporation (other than the issuing corporation determined without regard to this subsection) shall be included in the determinations required under subparagraphs (A) and (B) of subsection (b)(4) as of any day only if such corporation is a member of the affiliated group on such day, and, in determining projected earnings of such corporation under subsection (c)(3), there shall be taken into account only the earnings and profits of such corporation for the period during which it was a member of the affiliated group. For purposes of the preceding sentence, the term "affiliated group" has the meaning assigned to such term by section 1504(a), except that all corporations other than the acquired corporation shall be treated as includible corporations (without any exclusion under section 1504(b)) and the acquired corporation shall not be treated as an includible corporation.

[Sec. 279(h)]

(h) CHANGES IN OBLIGATION.—For purposes of this section—

(1) Any extension, renewal, or refinancing of an obligation evidencing a preexisting indebtedness shall not be deemed to be the issuance of a new obligation.

(2) Any obligation which is corporate acquisition indebtedness of the issuing corporation is also corporate acquisition indebtedness of any corporation which becomes liable for such obligation as guarantor, endorser, or indemnitor or which assumes liability for such obligation in any transaction.

[Sec. 279(i)]

(i) CERTAIN OBLIGATIONS ISSUED AFTER OCTOBER 9, 1969.—For purposes of this section, an obligation shall not be corporate acquisition indebtedness if issued after October 9, 1969, to provide consideration for the acquisition of—

(1) stock or assets pursuant to a binding written contract which was in effect on October 9, 1969, and at all times thereafter before such acquisition, or

(2) stock in any corporation where the issuing corporation, on October 9, 1969, and at all times thereafter before such acquisition, owned at least 50 percent of the total combined voting power of all classes of stock entitled to vote of the acquired corporation.

Amendments

• 1976 (P.L. 94-514)

P.L. 94-514, §[1](a):

Struck out the last sentence of Code Sec. 279(i). **Effective** for tax years ending after 10-9-69. If refund or credit of any overpayment of income tax resulting from the amendment of Code Sec. 279(i) is prevented at any time within one year after 10-15-76, by the operation of any law or rule of law, refund or credit of such overpayment may, nevertheless be made or allowed if a claim is filed within one year from such date. Prior to striking, the last sentence of Code Sec. 279(i) read as follows:

Paragraph (2) shall cease to apply when (at any time on or after October 9, 1969) the issuing corporation has acquired control (as defined in section 368(c)) of the acquired corporation.

[Sec. 279(j)]

(j) EFFECT ON OTHER PROVISIONS.—No inference shall be drawn from any provision in this section that any instrument designated as a bond, debenture, note, or certificate or other evidence of indebtedness by its issuer represents an obligation or indebtedness of such issuer in applying any other provision of this title.

Amendments

• 1969, Tax Reform Act of 1969 (P.L. 91-172)

P.L. 91-172, §411(a):

Added Code Sec. 279. **Effective** for determination of the allowability of the deduction of interest paid or incurred for indebtedness incurred after 10-9-69.

[Sec. 280—Repealed]

Amendments

• 1986, Tax Reform Act of 1986 (P.L. 99-514)

P.L. 99-514, §803(b)(2)(A):

Repealed Code Sec. 280. **Effective**, generally, for costs incurred after 12-31-86, in tax years ending after such date. However, for special rules, see Act Sec. 803(d)(2)-(7) following Code Sec. 263A. Prior to repeal, Code Sec. 280 read as follows.

SEC. 280. CERTAIN EXPENDITURES INCURRED IN PRODUCTION OF FILMS, BOOKS, RECORDS, OR SIMILAR PROPERTY.

[Sec. 280(a)]

(a) GENERAL RULE.—In the case of an individual, except in the case of production costs which are charged to capital account, amounts attributable to the production of a film, sound recording, book, or similar property which are otherwise deductible under this chapter shall be allowed as deductions only in accordance with the provisions of subsection (b). For purposes of this section, an S corporation, a personal holding company (as defined in section 542), and a foreign personal holding company (as defined in section 552) shall be treated as an individual.

Amendments

• 1982, Subchapter S Revision Act of 1982 (P.L. 97-354)

P.L. 97-354, §5(a)(25):

Amended the second sentence of Code Sec. 280(a) by striking out "an electing small business corporation (as defined in section 1371(b))," and inserting in lieu thereof "an S corporation,". **Effective** for tax years beginning after 12-31-82.

• 1978, Revenue Act of 1978 (P.L. 95-600)

P.L. 95-600, §701(m)(2)(A), (B), (3)(B):

Amended Code Sec. 280(a). **Effective** as if included in amendments made by P.L. 94-455, §210(a). Prior to amendment, it read:

(a) GENERAL RULE.—Except in the case of a corporation (other than an electing small business corporation (as defined in section 1371(b)) or a personal holding company (as defined in section 542)) and except in the case of production costs which are charged to capital account, amounts attributable to the production of a film, sound recording, book, or similar property which are otherwise deductible under this chapter shall be allowed as deductions only in accordance with the provisions of subsection (b).

[Sec. 280(b)]

(b) PRORATION OF PRODUCTION COST OVER INCOME PERIOD.—Amounts referred to in subsection (a) are deductible only for those taxable years ending during the period during which the taxpayer reasonably may be expected to receive substantially all of the income he will receive from any such film, sound recording, book, or similar property. The amount deductible for any such taxable year is an amount which bears the same ratio to the sum of all such amounts (attributable to such film, sound recording, book, or similar property) as the income received from the property for that taxable year bears to the sum of the income the taxpayer may reasonably be expected to receive during such period.

[Sec. 280(c)]

(c) DEFINITIONS.—For purposes of this section—

(1) FILM.—The term "film" means any motion picture film or video tape.

(2) SOUND RECORDING.—The term "sound recording" means works that result from the fixation of a series of musical, spoken, or other sounds, regardless of the nature of the material objects, such as discs, tapes, or other phonorecordings, in which such sounds are embodied.

Amendments

• 1976, Tax Reform Act of 1976 (P.L. 94-455)

P.L. 94-455, §210(a):

Added Code Sec. 280. **Effective** with respect to amounts paid or incurred after 12-31-75, for property the principal production of which begins after 12-31-75.

[Sec. 280A]

SEC. 280A. DISALLOWANCE OF CERTAIN EXPENSES IN CONNECTION WITH BUSINESS USE OF HOME, RENTAL OF VACATION HOMES, ETC.

[Sec. 280A(a)]

(a) GENERAL RULE.—Except as otherwise provided in this section, in the case of a taxpayer who is an individual or an S corporation, no deduction otherwise allowable under this chapter shall be allowed with respect to the use of a dwelling unit which is used by the taxpayer during the taxable year as a residence.

Amendments

• 1982, Subchapter S Revision Act of 1982 (P.L. 97-354)

P.L. 97-354, §5(a)(26)(A):

Amended Code Sec. 280A(a) by striking out "an electing small business corporation," and inserting in lieu thereof "an S corporation,". **Effective** for tax years beginning after 12-31-82.

[Sec. 280A(b)]

(b) EXCEPTION FOR INTEREST, TAXES, CASUALTY LOSSES, ETC.—Subsection (a) shall not apply to any deduction allowable to the taxpayer without regard to its connection with his trade or business (or with his income-producing activity).

[Sec. 280A(c)]

(c) EXCEPTIONS FOR CERTAIN BUSINESS OR RENTAL USE; LIMITATION ON DEDUCTIONS FOR SUCH USE.—

(1) CERTAIN BUSINESS USE.—Subsection (a) shall not apply to any item to the extent such item is allocable to a portion of the dwelling unit which is exclusively used on a regular basis—

(A) as the principal place of business for any trade or business of the taxpayer,

(B) as a place of business which is used by patients, clients, or customers in meeting or dealing with the taxpayer in the normal course of his trade or business, or

(C) in the case of a separate structure which is not attached to the dwelling unit, in connection with the taxpayer's trade or business.

In the case of an employee, the preceding sentence shall apply only if the exclusive use referred to in the preceding sentence is for the convenience of his employer. For purposes of subparagraph (A), the term "principal place of business" includes a place of business which is used by the taxpayer for the administrative or management activities of any trade or business of the taxpayer if there is no other fixed location of such trade or business where the taxpayer conducts substantial administrative or management activities of such trade or business.

(2) CERTAIN STORAGE USE.—Subsection (a) shall not apply to any item to the extent such item is allocable to space within the dwelling unit which is used on a regular basis as a storage unit for the inventory or product samples of the taxpayer held for use in the taxpayer's trade or business of selling products at retail or wholesale, but only if the dwelling unit is the sole fixed location of such trade or business.

(3) RENTAL USE.—Subsection (a) shall not apply to any item which is attributable to the rental of the dwelling unit or portion thereof (determined after the application of subsection (e)).

(4) USE IN PROVIDING DAY CARE SERVICES.—

(A) IN GENERAL.—Subsection (a) shall not apply to any item to the extent that such item is allocable to the use of any portion of the dwelling unit on a regular basis in the taxpayer's trade or business of providing day care for children, for individuals who have attained age 65, or for individuals who are physically or mentally incapable of caring for themselves.

(B) LICENSING, ETC., REQUIREMENT.—Subparagraph (A) shall apply to items accruing for a period only if the owner or operator of the trade or business referred to in subparagraph (A)—

(i) has applied for (and such application has not been rejected),

(ii) has been granted (and such granting has not been revoked), or

(iii) is exempt from having,

a license, certification, registration, or approval as a day care center or as a family or group day care home under the provisions of any applicable State law. This subparagraph shall apply only to items accruing in periods beginning on or after the first day of the first month which begins more than 90 days after the date of the enactment of the Tax Reduction and Simplification Act of 1977.

(C) ALLOCATION FORMULA.—If a portion of the taxpayer's dwelling unit used for the purposes described in subparagraph (A) is not used exclusively for those purposes, the amount of the expenses attributable to that portion shall not exceed an amount which bears the same ratio to the total amount of the items allocable to such portion as the number of hours the portion is used for such purposes bears to the number of hours the portion is available for use.

(5) LIMITATION ON DEDUCTIONS.—In the case of a use described in paragraph (1), (2), or (4), and in the case of a use described in paragraph (3) where the dwelling unit is used by the taxpayer during the taxable year as a residence, the deductions allowed under this chapter for the taxable year by reason of being attributed to such use shall not exceed the excess of—

(A) the gross income derived from such use for the taxable year, over

(B) the sum of—

(i) the deductions allocable to such use which are allowable under this chapter for the taxable year whether or not such unit (or portion thereof) was so used, and

(ii) the deductions allocable to the trade or business (or rental activity) in which such use occurs (but which are not allocable to such use) for such taxable year.

Any amount not allowable as a deduction under this chapter by reason of the preceding sentence shall be taken into account as a deduction (allocable to such use) under this chapter for the succeeding taxable year. Any amount taken into account for any taxable year under the preceding sentence shall be subject to the limitation of the 1st sentence of this paragraph whether or not the dwelling unit is used as a residence during such taxable year.

(6) TREATMENT OF RENTAL TO EMPLOYER.—Paragraphs (1) and (3) shall not apply to any item which is attributable to the rental of the dwelling unit (or any portion thereof) by the taxpayer to his employer during any period in which the taxpayer uses the dwelling unit (or portion) in performing services as an employee of the employer.

Amendments

• 1997, Taxpayer Relief Act of 1997 (P.L. 105-34)

P.L. 105-34, §932(a):

Amended Code Sec. 280A(c)(1) by adding at the end a new sentence. **Effective** for tax years beginning after 12-31-98.

• 1996, Small Business Job Protection Act of 1996 (P.L. 104-188)

P.L. 104-188, §1113(a):

Amended Code Sec. 280A(c)(2) by striking "inventory" and inserting "inventory or product samples". **Effective** for tax years beginning after 12-31-95.

P.L. 104-188, §1704(t)(39):

Amended Code Sec. 280A(c)(1)(A). **Effective** 8-20-96. Prior to amendment, Code Sec. 280A(c)(1)(A) read as follows:

(A) the principal place of business for any trade or business of the taxpayer,

• 1988, Technical and Miscellaneous Revenue Act of 1988 (P.L. 100-647)

P.L. 100-647, §1001(h)(1):

Amended Code Sec. 280A(c)(5) by adding at the end thereof a new sentence. **Effective** as if included in the provision of P.L. 99-514 to which it relates.

P.L. 100-647, §1001(h)(2):

Amended Code Sec. 280A(c)(5)(B)(ii) by striking out "trade or business" and inserting in lieu thereof "trade or business (or rental activity)". **Effective** as if included in the provision of P.L. 99-514 to which it relates.

• 1986, Tax Reform Act of 1986 (P.L. 99-514)

P.L. 99-514, §143(b):

Amended Code Sec. 280A(c) by adding at the end thereof new paragraph (6). **Effective** for tax years beginning after 12-31-86.

P.L. 99-514, §143(c):

Amended Code Sec. 280A(c)(5) by striking out subparagraph (B) and inserting in lieu thereof a new subparagraph (B). **Effective** for tax years beginning after 12-31-86. Prior to amendment, Code Sec. 280A(c)(5)(B) read as follows:

(B) the deductions allocable to such use which are allowable under this chapter for the taxable year whether or not such unit (or portion thereof) was so used.

• 1981, Black Lung Benefits Revenue Act of 1981 (P.L. 97-119)

P.L. 97-119, §113(c):

Amended Code Sec. 280A(c)(1)(A). **Effective** for tax years beginning after 12-31-75, except that in the case of taxable years beginning after 12-31-75 and before 1-1-80, the amendment made by this section shall apply only to taxable years for which, on the date of the enactment of this Act, the making of a refund, or the assessment of a deficiency, was not barred by law or any rule of law. Prior to amendment, Code Sec. 280A(c)(1)(A) read as follows:

(A) as the taxpayer's principal place of business,

• 1977, Tax Reduction and Simplification Act of 1977 (P.L. 95-30)

P.L. 95-30, §306(a):

Amended Code Sec. 280A(c) by redesignating former paragraph (4) as paragraph (5), adding new paragraph (4), and amending renumbered paragraph (5) by substituting "paragraph (1), (2), or (4)" for "paragraph (1) or (2)". **Effective** for tax years beginning after 12-31-75.

[Sec. 280A(d)]

(d) USE AS RESIDENCE.—

(1) IN GENERAL.—For purposes of this section, a taxpayer uses a dwelling unit during the taxable year as a residence if he uses such unit (or portion thereof) for personal purposes for a number of days which exceeds the greater of—

(A) 14 days, or

(B) 10 percent of the number of days during such year for which such unit is rented at a fair rental.

For purposes of subparagraph (B), a unit shall not be treated as rented at a fair rental for any day for which it is used for personal purposes.

(2) PERSONAL USE OF UNIT.—For purposes of this section, the taxpayer shall be deemed to have used a dwelling unit for personal purposes for a day if, for any part of such day, the unit is used—

(A) for personal purposes by the taxpayer or any other person who has an interest in such unit, or by any member of the family (as defined in section 267(c)(4)) of the taxpayer or such other person;

(B) by any individual who uses the unit under an arrangement which enables the taxpayer to use some other dwelling unit (whether or not a rental is charged for the use of such other unit); or

(C) by any individual (other than an employee with respect to whose use section 119 applies), unless for such day the dwelling unit is rented for a rental which, under the facts and circumstances, is fair rental.

The Secretary shall prescribe regulations with respect to the circumstances under which use of the unit for repairs and annual maintenance will not constitute personal use under this paragraph, except that if the taxpayer is engaged in repair and maintenance on a substantially full time basis for any day, such authority shall not allow the Secretary to treat a dwelling unit as being used for personal use by the taxpayer on such day merely because other individuals who are on the premises on such day are not so engaged.

(3) RENTAL TO FAMILY MEMBER, ETC., FOR USE AS PRINCIPAL RESIDENCE.—

(A) IN GENERAL.—A taxpayer shall not be treated as using a dwelling unit for personal purposes by reason of a rental arrangement for any period if for such period such dwelling unit is rented, at a fair rental, to any person for use as such person's principal residence.

(B) SPECIAL RULES FOR RENTAL TO PERSON HAVING INTEREST IN UNIT.—

(i) RENTAL MUST BE PURSUANT TO SHARED EQUITY FINANCING AGREEMENT.—Subparagraph (A) shall apply to a rental to a person who has an interest in the dwelling unit only if such rental is pursuant to a shared equity financing agreement.

(ii) DETERMINATION OF FAIR RENTAL.—In the case of a rental pursuant to a shared equity financing agreement, fair rental shall be determined as of the time the agreement is entered into and by taking into account the occupant's qualified ownership interest.

(C) SHARED EQUITY FINANCING AGREEMENT.—For purposes of this paragraph, the term "shared equity financing agreement" means an agreement under which—

(i) 2 or more persons acquire qualified ownership interests in a dwelling unit, and

(ii) the person (or persons) holding 1 or more of such interests—

(I) is entitled to occupy the dwelling unit for use as a principal residence, and

(II) is required to pay rent to 1 or more other persons holding qualified ownership interests in the dwelling unit.

(D) QUALIFIED OWNERSHIP INTEREST.—For purposes of this paragraph, the term "qualified ownership interest" means an undivided interest for more than 50 years in the entire dwelling unit and appurtenant land being acquired in the transaction to which the shared equity financing agreement relates.

(4) RENTAL OF PRINCIPAL RESIDENCE.—

(A) IN GENERAL.—For purposes of applying subsection (c)(5) to deductions allocable to a qualified rental period, a taxpayer shall not be considered to have used a dwelling unit for personal purposes for any day during the taxable year which occurs before or after a qualified rental period described in subparagraph (B)(i), or before a qualified rental period described in subparagraph (B)(ii), if with respect to such day such unit constitutes the principal residence (within the meaning of section 121) of the taxpayer.

(B) QUALIFIED RENTAL PERIOD.—For purposes of subparagraph (A), the term "qualified rental period" means a consecutive period of—

(i) 12 or more months which begins or ends in such taxable year, or

(ii) less than 12 months which begins in such taxable year and at the end of which such dwelling unit is sold or exchanged, and

for which such unit is rented, or is held for rental, at a fair rental.

Amendments

• 1997, Taxpayer Relief Act of 1997 (P.L. 105-34)

P.L. 105-34, §312(d)(1):

Amended Code Sec. 280A(d)(4)(A) by striking "section 1034" and inserting "section 121". For the **effective** date, see Act Sec. 312(d)[(e)], below.

P.L. 105-34, §312(d)[(e)], provides:

(d) EFFECTIVE DATE.—

(1) IN GENERAL.—The amendments made by this section shall apply to sales and exchanges after May 6, 1997.

(2) SALES BEFORE DATE OF ENACTMENT.—At the election of the taxpayer, the amendments made by this section shall not apply to any sale or exchange before the date of the enactment of this Act.

(3) CERTAIN SALES WITHIN 2 YEARS AFTER DATE OF ENACTMENT.—Section 121 of the Internal Revenue Code of 1986 (as amended by this section) shall be applied without regard to

subsection (c)(2)(B) thereof in the case of any sale or exchange of property during the 2-year period beginning on the date of the enactment of this Act if the taxpayer held such property on the date of the enactment of this Act and fails to meet the ownership and use requirements of subsection (a) thereof with respect to such property.

(4) BINDING CONTRACTS.—At the election of the taxpayer, the amendments made by this section shall not apply to a sale or exchange after the date of the enactment of this Act, if—

(A) such sale or exchange is pursuant to a contract which was binding on such date, or

(B) without regard to such amendments, gain would not be recognized under section 1034 of the Internal Revenue Code of 1986 (as in effect on the day before the date of the enactment of this Act) on such sale or exchange by reason of a new residence acquired on or before such date or with respect to the acquisition of which by the taxpayer a binding contract was in effect on such date.

This paragraph shall not apply to any sale or exchange by an individual if the treatment provided by section 877(a)(1) of the Internal Revenue Code of 1986 applies to such individual.

• 1981, Black Lung Benefits Revenue Act of 1981 (P.L. 97-119)

P.L. 97-119, §113(a)(1):

Amended Code Sec. 280A(d) by redesignating paragraph (3) as paragraph (4) and by inserting new paragraph (3) after paragraph (2). **Effective** as noted in P.L. 97-119, §113(e), below.

P.L. 97-119, §113(a)(2):

Amended Code Sec. 280A(d)(4)(B) by striking out "to a person other than a member of the family (as defined in section 267(c)(4)) of the taxpayer." **Effective** as noted in P.L. 97-119, §113(e), below.

P.L. 97-119, §113(d):

Amended the last sentence of Code Sec. 280A(d)(2) by inserting the language after "paragraph". **Effective** as noted in P.L. 97-119, §113(e), below.

P.L. 97-119, §113(e), provides:

(e) EFFECTIVE DATE.—The amendments made by this section shall apply to taxable years beginning after December 31, 1975, except that in the case of taxable years beginning after December 31, 1975 and before January 1, 1980, the amendment made by this section shall apply only to taxable years for which, on the date of the enactment of this Act, the making of a refund, or the assessment of a deficiency, was not barred by law or any rule of law.

• 1978, Revenue Act of 1978 (P.L. 95-600)

P.L. 95-600, §701(h)(1), (2):

Added Code Sec. 280A(d)(3). **Effective** as if included in Code Sec. 280A as such provision was added by P.L. 94-455, §601(a).

[Sec. 280A(e)]

(e) EXPENSES ATTRIBUTABLE TO RENTAL.—

(1) IN GENERAL.—In any case where a taxpayer who is an individual or an S corporation uses a dwelling unit for personal purposes on any day during the taxable year (whether or not he is treated under this section as using such unit as a residence), the amount deductible under this chapter with respect to expenses attributable to the rental of the unit (or portion thereof) for the taxable year shall not exceed an amount which bears the same relationship to such expenses as the number of days during each year that the unit (or portion thereof) is rented at a fair rental bears to the total number of days during such year that the unit (or portion thereof) is used.

(2) EXCEPTION FOR DEDUCTIONS OTHERWISE ALLOWABLE.—This subsection shall not apply with respect to deductions which would be allowable under this chapter for the taxable year whether or not such unit (or portion thereof) was rented.

Amendments

• 1982, Subchapter S Revision Act of 1982 (P.L. 97-354)

P.L. 97-354, §5(a)(26)(B):

Amended Code Sec. 280A(e)(1) by striking out "an electing small business corporation" and inserting in lieu thereof "an S corporation". **Effective** for tax years beginning after 12-31-82.

[Sec. 280A(f)]

(f) DEFINITIONS AND SPECIAL RULES.—

(1) DWELLING UNIT DEFINED.—For purposes of this section—

(A) IN GENERAL.—The term "dwelling unit" includes a house, apartment, condominium, mobile home, boat, or similar property, and all structures or other property appurtenant to such dwelling unit.

(B) EXCEPTION.—The term "dwelling unit" does not include that portion of a unit which is used exclusively as a hotel, motel, inn, or similar establishment.

(2) PERSONAL USE BY SHAREHOLDERS OF S CORPORATION.—In the case of an S corporation, subparagraphs (A) and (B) of subsection (d)(2) shall be applied by substituting "any shareholder of the S corporation" for "the taxpayer" each place it appears.

(3) COORDINATION WITH SECTION 183.—If subsection (a) applies with respect to any dwelling unit (or portion thereof) for the taxable year—

(A) section 183 (relating to activities not engaged in for profit) shall not apply to such unit (or portion thereof) for such year, but

(B) such year shall be taken into account as a taxable year for purposes of applying subsection (d) of section 183 (relating to 5-year presumption).

(4) COORDINATION WITH SECTION 162(a)(2).—Nothing in this section shall be construed to disallow any deduction allowable under section 162(a)(2) (or any deduction which meets the tests of section 162(a)(2) but is allowable under another provision of this title) by reason of the taxpayer's being away from home in the pursuit of a trade or business (other than the trade or business of renting dwelling units).

Amendments

• 1982, Subchapter S Revision Act of 1982 (P.L. 97-354)

P.L. 97-354, §5(a)(26)(C):

Amended Code Sec. 280A(f)(2). **Effective** for tax years beginning after 12-31-82. Prior to amendment, it read as follows:

"(2) PERSONAL USE BY ELECTING SMALL BUSINESS CORPORATION.—In the case of an electing small business corporation, subparagraphs (A) and (B) of subsection (d)(2) shall be applied by substituting `any shareholder of the electing small business corporation' for `the taxpayer' each place it appears."

• 1982 (P.L. 97-216)

P.L. 97-216, §215(b):

Amended Code Sec. 280A(f)(4). **Effective** for tax years beginning after 12-31-81. Prior to amendment, Code Sec. 280A(f)(4) read:

(4) COORDINATION WITH SECTION 162(a)(2), ETC.—

(A) IN GENERAL.—Nothing in this section shall be construed to disallow any deduction allowable under section 162(a)(2) (or any deduction which meets the tests of section 162(a)(2) but is allowable under another provision of this title) by reason of the taxpayer's being away from home in the pursuit of a trade or business (other than the trade or business of renting dwelling units).

(B) LIMITATION.—The Secretary shall prescribe amounts deductible (without substantiation) pursuant to the last sentence of section 162(a), but nothing in subparagraph (A) or any other provision of this title shall permit such a deduction for any taxable year of amounts in excess of the amounts determined to be appropriate under the circumstances.

• 1981, Black Lung Benefits Revenue Act of 1981 (P.L. 97-119)

P.L. 97-119, §113(b):

Amended Code Sec. 280A(f) by adding new paragraph (4) at the end thereof. **Effective** for tax years beginning after 12-31-75, except that in the case of taxable years beginning after 12-31-75 and before 1-1-80, the amendment made by this section shall apply only to taxable years for which, on the date of the enactment of this Act, the making of a refund, or the assessment of a deficiency, was not barred by law or any rule of law.

[Sec. 280A(g)]

(g) SPECIAL RULE FOR CERTAIN RENTAL USE.—Notwithstanding any other provision of this section or section 183, if a dwelling unit is used during the taxable year by the taxpayer as a residence and such dwelling unit is actually rented for less than 15 days during the taxable year, then—

(1) no deduction otherwise allowable under this chapter because of the rental use of such dwelling unit shall be allowed, and

(2) the income derived from such use for the taxable year shall not be included in the gross income of such taxpayer under section 61.

Amendments

• 1976, Tax Reform Act of 1976 (P.L. 94-455)

P.L. 94-455, §601(a):

Added Code Sec. 280A. **Effective** for tax years beginning after 12-31-75.

[Sec. 280B]

SEC. 280B. DEMOLITION OF STRUCTURES.

[Sec. 280B(a)]

(a) In the case of the demolition of any structure—

(1) no deduction otherwise allowable under this chapter shall be allowed to the owner or lessee of such structure for—

(A) any amount expended for such demolition, or

(B) any loss sustained on account of such demolition; and

(2) amounts described in paragraph (1) shall be treated as properly chargeable to capital account with respect to the land on which the demolished structure was located.

Amendments

• 1984, Deficit Reduction Act of 1984 (P.L. 98-369)

P.L. 98-369, §1063(a):

Amended Code Sec. 280B by striking out all of subsection (a) which precedes paragraph (1) thereof and inserting in lieu thereof the following: "In the case of the demolition of any structure—". For the **effective** date, see Act Sec. 1063(c), below. Prior to amendment, the stricken language read as follows:

(a) General Rule.—In the case of the demolition of a certified historic structure (as defined in [section] 48(g)(3)(A))—

P.L. 98-369, §1063(b)(1):

Amended Code Sec. 280B by striking out "CERTAIN HISTORIC" from the heading thereof. For the **effective** date, see Act Sec. 1063(c), below. Prior to amendment, the heading of Code Sec. 280B read as follows:

Sec. 280B. Demolition of Certain Historic Structures.

P.L. 98-369, §1063(c), as amended by P.L. 99-514, §1878(h), provides:

(c) EFFECTIVE DATES.—

(1) The amendments made by this section shall apply to taxable years ending after December 31, 1983, but shall not apply to any demolition (other than of a certified historic structure) commencing before July 19, 1984.

(2) For purposes of paragraph (1), if a demolition is delayed until the completion of the replacement structure on the same site, the demolition shall be treated as commencing when construction of the replacement structure commences.

(3) The amendments made by this section shall not apply to any demolition commencing before September 1, 1984, pursuant to a bank headquarters building project if—

(A) on April 1, 1984, a corporation was retained to advise the bank on the final completion of the project, and

(B) on June 12, 1984, the Comptroller of the Currency approved the project.

(4) The amendments made by this section shall not apply to the remaining adjusted basis at the time of demolition of any structure if—

(A) such structure was used in the manufacture, storage, or distribution of lead alkyl anti-knock products and intermediate and related products at facilities located in or near Baton Rouge, Louisiana, and Houston, Texas, owned by the same corporation, and

(B) demolition of at least one such structure at the Baton Rouge facility commenced before January 1, 1984.

• 1983, Technical Corrections Act of 1982 (P.L. 97-448)

P.L. 97-448, §102(f)(1):

Amended subparagraph (B) of section 212(e)(2) of P.L. 97-34 to read as below.

• 1983, Orphan Drug Act of 1982 (P.L. 97-414)

P.L. 97-414, §4(b)(2)(A):

Amended the heading of Code Sec. 280C. **Effective** for amounts paid or incurred after 12-31-82, in tax years ending after such date. Prior to amendment, the section heading read as follows:

PORTION OF WAGES FOR WHICH CREDIT IS CLAIMED UNDER SECTION 40 OR 44B.

• 1981, Economic Recovery Tax Act of 1981 (P.L. 97-34)

P.L. 97-34, §212(d)(2)(C)(i):

Amended Code Sec. 280B(a) by striking out "section 191(d)(1)" and inserting in lieu thereof "48(g)(3)(A)". **Effective** for expenditures incurred after 12-31-81, in tax years ending after such date.

P.L. 97-34, §212(e)(2), provides:

(2) TRANSITIONAL RULE.—The amendments made by this section shall not apply with respect to any rehabilitation of a building if—

(A) the physical work on such rehabilitation began before January 1, 1982, and

(B) such building does not meet the requirements of paragraph (1) of section 48(g) of the Internal Revenue Code of 1954 (as amended by this Act).

• 1976, Tax Reform Act of 1976 (P.L. 94-455)

P.L. 94-455, §2124(b)(1):

Added Code Sec. 280B(a). **Effective** for demolitions commencing after 6-30-76, and before 1-1-81.

[Sec. 280B(b)—Repealed]

Amendments

• 1984, Deficit Reduction Act of 1984 (P.L. 98-369)

P.L. 98-369, §1063(a):

Repealed Code Sec. 280B(b). For the **effective** date, see Act Sec. 1063(c) following Code Sec. 280B(a). Prior to repeal, Code Sec. 280B(b) read as follows:

(b) Special Rule for Registered Historic Districts.—For purposes of this section, any building or other structure located in a registered historic district (as defined in section 48(g)(3)(B)) shall be treated as a certified historic structure unless the Secretary of the Interior has certified that such structure is not a certified historic structure, and that such structure is not of historic significance to the district, and if such certification occurs after the beginning of the demolition of such structure, the taxpayer has certified to the Secretary that, at the time of such demolition, he in good faith was not aware of the certification requirement by the Secretary of the Interior.

• 1981, Economic Recovery Tax Act of 1981 (P.L. 97-34)

P.L. 97-34, §212(d)(2)(C)(ii):

Amended Code Sec. 280B(b) by striking out "section 191(d)(2)" and inserting in lieu thereof "section 48(g)(3)(B)." **Effective** for expenditures incurred after 12-31-81, in tax years ending after such date. But, see comment for P.L. 97-34, §212(d)(2)(C)(i) following Code Sec. 280B(a) for applicability of a transitional rule.

• 1978, Revenue Act of 1978 (P.L. 95-600)

P.L. 95-600, §701(f)(5), (8):

Amended Code Sec. 280B(b). **Effective** as if included in Code Sec. 280B(b) as added by P.L. 94-455, §2124(b)(1). Prior to amendment, Code Sec. 280B(b) read:

"(b) SPECIAL RULE FOR REGISTERED HISTORIC DISTRICTS.—For purposes of this section, any building or other structure located in a registered historic district shall be treated as a certified historic structure unless the Secretary of the Interior has certified, prior to the demolition of such structure, that such structure is not of historic significance to the district."

• 1976, Tax Reform Act of 1976 (P.L. 94-455)

P.L. 94-455, §2124(b)(1):

Added Code Sec. 280B(b). **Effective** for demolitions commencing after 6-30-76, and before 1-1-81.

[Sec. 280B(c)—Repealed]

Amendments

• 1984, Deficit Reduction Act of 1984 (P.L. 98-369)

P.L. 98-369, §1063(a):

Repealed Code Sec. 280B(c). For the **effective** date, see Act Sec. 1063(c) following Code Sec. 280B(a). Prior to repeal, Code Sec. 280B(c) read as follows:

(c) Application of Section.—This section shall apply with respect to demolitions commencing after June 30, 1976, and before January 1, 1984.

• 1980 (P.L. 96-541)

P.L. 96-541, §2(b):

Added Code Sec. 280B(c). **Effective** 12-17-80.

[Sec. 280C]

SEC. 280C. CERTAIN EXPENSES FOR WHICH CREDITS ARE ALLOWABLE.

[Sec. 280C(a)]

(a) RULE FOR EMPLOYMENT CREDITS.—No deduction shall be allowed for that portion of the wages or salaries paid or incurred for the taxable year which is equal to the sum of the credits determined for the taxable year under sections 45A(a), 45P(a), 51(a), 1396(a), 1400P(b), and 1400R. In the case of a corporation which is a member of a controlled group of corporations (within the meaning of section 52(a)) or a trade or business which is treated as being under common control with other trades or businesses (within the meaning of section 52(b)), this subsection shall be applied under rules prescribed by the Secretary similar to the rules applicable under subsections (a) and (b) of section 52.

Amendments

• 2008, Heroes Earnings Assistance and Relief Tax Act of 2008 (P.L. 110-245)

P.L. 110-245, §111(c):

Amended Code Sec. 280C(a) by inserting "45P(a)," after "45A(a),". **Effective** for amounts paid after 6-17-2008.

• 2005, Gulf Opportunity Zone Act of 2005 (P.L. 109-135)

P.L. 109-135, §103(b)(2):

Amended Code Sec. 280C(a) by striking "and 1396(a)" and inserting "1396(a), and 1400P(b)". **Effective** 12-21-2005.

P.L. 109-135, §201(b)(2):

Amended Code Sec. 280C(a) by striking "and 1400P(b)" and inserting "1400P(b), and 1400R". **Effective** 12-21-2005.

• 1993, Omnibus Budget Reconciliation Act of 1993 (P.L. 103-66)

P.L. 103-66, §13302(b)(1)(A)-(B):

Amended Code Sec. 280C(a) by striking "the amount of the credit determined for the taxable year under section 51(a)" and inserting "the sum of the credits determined for the taxable year under sections 51(a) and 1396(a)", and by striking "Targeted Jobs Credit" in the subsection heading and inserting "Employment Credits." **Effective** 8-10-93.

P.L. 103-66, §13322(c)(1):

Amended Code Sec. 280C(a) by striking "51(a)" and inserting "45A(a), 51(a), and". **Effective** for wages paid or incurred after 12-31-93.

[Sec. 280C(b)]

(b) CREDIT FOR QUALIFIED CLINICAL TESTING EXPENSES FOR CERTAIN DRUGS.—

(1) IN GENERAL.—No deduction shall be allowed for that portion of the qualified clinical testing expenses (as defined in section 45C(b)) otherwise allowable as a deduction for the taxable year which is equal to the amount of the credit allowable for the taxable year under section 45C (determined without regard to section 38(c)).

(2) SIMILAR RULE WHERE TAXPAYER CAPITALIZES RATHER THAN DEDUCTS EXPENSES.—If—

(A) the amount of the credit allowable for the taxable year under section 45C (determined without regard to section 38(c)), exceeds

(B) the amount allowable as a deduction for the taxable year for qualified clinical testing expenses (determined without regard to paragraph (1)),

the amount chargeable to capital account for the taxable year for such expenses shall be reduced by the amount of such excess.

(3) CONTROLLED GROUPS.—In the case of a corporation which is a member of a controlled group of corporations (within the meaning of section 41(f)(5)) or a trade or business which is treated as being under common control with other trades or business (within the meaning of section 41(f)(1)(B)), this subsection shall be applied under rules prescribed by the Secretary similar to the rules applicable under subparagraphs (A) and (B) of section 41(f)(1).

Amendments

• 1996, Small Business Job Protection Act of 1996 (P.L. 104-188)

P.L. 104-188, §1205(d)(7)(A)-(C):

Amended Code Sec. 280C(b) by striking "section 28(b)" in paragraph (1) and inserting "section 45C(b)", by striking "section 28" in paragraphs (1) and (2)(A) and inserting "section 45C", and by striking "subsection (d)(2) thereof" in paragraphs (1) and (2)(A) and inserting "section 38(c)". **Effective** for amounts paid or incurred in tax years ending after 6-30-96.

• 1986, Tax Reform Act of 1986 (P.L. 99-514)

P.L. 99-514, §231(d)(3)(E)(i)-(iii):

Amended Code Sec. 280C(b)(3) by striking out "section 30(f)(5)" and inserting in lieu thereof "section 41(f)(5)", by striking out "section 30(f)(1)(B)" and inserting in lieu thereof "section 41(f)(1)(B)", and by striking out "section 30(f)(1)" and inserting in lieu thereof "section 41(f)(1)". **Effective** for tax years beginning after 12-31-85.

P.L. 99-514, §1847(b)(8)(A) and (B):

Amended Code Sec. 280C(b) by striking out "section 29" each place it appears and inserting in lieu thereof "section 28", and by striking out "section 29(b)" and inserting in lieu thereof "section 28(b)". **Effective** as if included in the provision of P.L. 98-369 to which it relates.

• 1984, Deficit Reduction Act of 1984 (P.L. 98-369)

P.L. 98-369, §474(r)(10)(A):

Amended Code Sec. 280C by striking out subsection (a) and redesignating subsections (b) and (c) as subsections (a) and (b), respectively. **Effective** for tax years beginning after 12-31-83, and to carrybacks from such years. Prior to amendment, Code Sec. 280C(a) read as follows:

(a) Rule for Section 40 Credit.—No deduction shall be allowed for that portion of the work incentive program expenses paid or incurred for the taxable year which is equal to the amount of the credit allowable for the taxable year under section 40 (relating to credit for expenses of work incentive programs) determined without regard to the provisions of section 50A(a)(2) (relating to limitation based on amount of tax). In the case of a corporation which is a member of a controlled group of corporations (within the meaning of section 50B(g)(1)) or a trade or business which is treated as being under common control with other trades or businesses (within the meaning of section 50B(g)(2), this subsection shall be applied under rules prescribed by the Secretary similar to the rules applicable under paragraphs (1) and (2) of section 50B(g).

P.L. 98-369, §474(r)(10)(B)(i):

Amended Code Sec. 280C(a) (as redesignated) by striking out the first sentence and inserting a new first sentence. **Effective** for tax years beginning after 12-31-83, and to carrybacks from such years. Prior to amendment, the first sentence of Code Sec. 280C(a) (redesignated) read as follows:

No deduction shall be allowed for that portion of the wages or salaries paid or incurred for the taxable year which is equal to the amount of the credit allowable for the taxable year under section 44B (relating to credit for employment of certain new employees) determined without regard to the provisions of section 53 (relating to limitation based on amount of tax).

P.L. 98-369, §474(r)(10)(B)(ii):

Amended Code Sec. 280C(a) (redesignated) by striking out "Section 44B Credit" in the subsection heading and inserting in lieu thereof "Targeted Jobs Credit". **Effective** for tax years beginning after 12-31-83, and to carrybacks from such years.

P.L. 98-369, §474(r)(10)(C):

Amended Code Sec. 280C(b) as redesignated by striking out "44H" each place it appeared and inserting in lieu thereof "29". **Effective** for tax years beginning after 12-31-83, and to carrybacks from such years.

P.L. 98-369, §474(r)(10)(D):

Amended Code Sec. 280C(b)(3) as redesignated by striking out "section 44F(f)(5)" and inserting in lieu thereof "section 30(f)(5)", by striking out "section 44F(f)(1)(B)" and inserting in lieu thereof "section 30(f)(1)(B)", and by striking out "section 44F(f)(1)" and inserting in lieu thereof "section 30(f)(1)". **Effective** for tax years beginning after 12-31-83, and to carrybacks from such years.

• 1983, Orphan Drug Act of 1982 (P.L. 97-414)

P.L. 97-414, §4(b)(1):

Added Code Sec. 280C(c). **Effective** for amounts paid or incurred after 12-31-82, in tax years ending after such date.

• 1978, Revenue Act of 1978 (P.L. 95-600)

P.L. 95-600, §322(e)(1)(A), (B), (C), (D), (f)(1):

Amended Code Sec. 280C. **Effective** for work incentive program expenses paid or incurred after 12-31-78, in tax years ending after such date. Prior to amendment, Code Sec. 280C provided:

SEC. 280C. PORTION OF WAGES FOR WHICH CREDIT IS CLAIMED UNDER SECTION 44B.

No deduction shall be allowed for that portion of the wages or salaries paid or incurred for the taxable year which is equal to the amount of the credit allowable for the taxable year under section 44B (relating to credit for employment of certain new employees) determined without regard to the provisions of section 53 (relating to limitation based on amount of tax). In the case of a corporation which is a member of a controlled group of corporations (within the meaning of section 52(a)) or a trade or business which is treated as being under common control with other trades or businesses (within the meaning of section 52(b)), this section shall be applied under rules prescribed by the Secretary similar to the rules applicable under subsections (a) and (b) of section 52.

• 1977, Tax Reduction and Simplification Act of 1977 (P.L. 95-30)

P.L. 95-30, §202(c):

Added Code Sec. 280C. **Effective** for tax years beginning after 12-31-76.

[Sec. 280C(c)]

(c) CREDIT FOR INCREASING RESEARCH ACTIVITIES.—

(1) IN GENERAL.—No deduction shall be allowed for that portion of the qualified research expenses (as defined in section 41(b)) or basic research expenses (as defined in section 41(e)(2)) otherwise allowable as a deduction for the taxable year which is equal to the amount of the credit determined for such taxable year under section 41(a).

(2) SIMILAR RULE WHERE TAXPAYER CAPITALIZES RATHER THAN DEDUCTS EXPENSES.—If—

(A) the amount of the credit determined for the taxable year under section 41(a)(1), exceeds

(B) the amount allowable as a deduction for such taxable year for qualified research expenses or basic research expenses (determined without regard to paragraph (1)),

the amount chargeable to capital account for the taxable year for such expenses shall be reduced by the amount of such excess.

(3) ELECTION OF REDUCED CREDIT.—

(A) IN GENERAL.—In the case of any taxable year for which an election is made under this paragraph—

(i) paragraphs (1) and (2) shall not apply, and

(ii) the amount of the credit under section 41(a) shall be the amount determined under subparagraph (B).

(B) AMOUNT OF REDUCED CREDIT.—The amount of credit determined under this subparagraph for any taxable year shall be the amount equal to the excess of—

(i) the amount of credit determined under section 41(a) without regard to this paragraph, over

(ii) the product of—

(I) the amount described in clause (i), and

(II) the maximum rate of tax under section 11(b)(1).

(C) ELECTION.—An election under this paragraph for any taxable year shall be made not later than the time for filing the return of tax for such year (including extensions), shall be made on such return, and shall be made in such manner as the Secretary may prescribe. Such an election, once made, shall be irrevocable.

(4) CONTROLLED GROUPS.—Paragraph (3) of subsection (b) shall apply for purposes of this subsection.

Amendments

• 2006, Tax Relief and Health Care of Act of 2006 (P.L. 109-432)

P.L. 109-432, Division A, §123(a), provides:

(a) RESEARCH CREDIT ELECTIONS.—In the case of any taxable year ending after December 31, 2005, and before the date of the enactment of this Act, any election under section 41(c)(4) or section 280C(c)(3)(C) of the Internal Revenue Code of 1986 shall be treated as having been timely made for such taxable year if such election is made not later than the later of April 15, 2007, or such time as the Secretary of the Treasury, or his designee, may specify. Such election shall be made in the manner prescribed by such Secretary or designee.

• 2000, Community Renewal Tax Relief Act of 2000 (P.L. 106-554)

P.L. 106-554, §311(a)(1):

Amended Code Sec. 280C(c)(1) by striking "or credit" after "deduction" each place it appears. **Effective** as if included in the provision of P.L. 106-170 to which it relates [**effective** for amounts paid or incurred after 6-30-99.—CCH].

• 1999, Tax Relief Extension Act of 1999 (P.L. 106-170)

P.L. 106-170, §502(c)(2):

Amended Code Sec. 280C(c)(1) by inserting "or credit" after "deduction" each place it appeared. **Effective** for amounts paid or incurred after 6-30-99.

• 1989, Omnibus Budget Reconciliation Act of 1989 (P.L. 101-239)

P.L. 101-239, §7110(c)[(d)](1):

Amended Code Sec. 280C(c) by striking "50 percent of" preceding "the amount of the credit" in paragraphs (1) and (2)(A), and by striking "50 percent of" before "the amount" in paragraph (3)(B)(ii)(I). **Effective** for tax years beginning after 12-31-89.

P.L. 101-239, §7814(e)(2)(A):

Amended Code Sec. 280C(c) by redesignating paragraph (3) as paragraph (4) and by inserting after paragraph (2) a new paragraph (3). **Effective** as if included in the provision of P.L. 100-647 to which it relates.

P.L. 101-239, §7814(e)(2)(B), provides:

(B) In the case of a taxable year for which the last date for making the election under section 280C(c)(3) of the Internal Revenue Code of 1986 (as added by subparagraph (A)) is on or before the date which is 75 days after the date of the enactment of this Act, such an election for such year may be made—

(i) at any time before the date which is 75 days after such date of enactment, and

(ii) in such form and manner as the Secretary of the Treasury or his delegate may prescribe.

• 1988, Technical and Miscellaneous Revenue Act of 1988 (P.L. 100-647)

P.L. 100-647, §4008(a):

Amended Code Sec. 280C by adding at the end thereof a new subsection (c). **Effective** for tax years beginning after 12-31-88.

[Sec. 280C(d)]

(d) CREDIT FOR LOW SULFUR DIESEL FUEL PRODUCTION.—The deductions otherwise allowed under this chapter for the taxable year shall be reduced by the amount of the credit determined for the taxable year under section 45H(a).

Amendments

• 2007, Tax Technical Corrections Act of 2007 (P.L. 110-172)

P.L. 110-172, §7(a)(1)(B):

Amended Code Sec. 280C(d). **Effective** as if included in the provision of the American Jobs Creation Act of 2004 (P.L. 108-357) to which it relates [**effective** for expenses paid or incurred after 12-31-2002, in tax years ending after such date.—CCH]. Prior to amendment, Code Sec. 280C(d) read as follows:

(d) LOW SULFUR DIESEL FUEL PRODUCTION CREDIT.—No deduction shall be allowed for that portion of the expenses otherwise allowable as a deduction for the taxable year which is equal to the amount of the credit determined for the taxable year under section 45H(a).

• 2004, American Jobs Creation Act of 2004 (P.L. 108-357)

P.L. 108-357, §339(c):

Amended Code Sec. 280C by adding at the end a new subsection (d). **Effective** for expenses paid or incurred after 12-31-2002, in tax years ending after such date.

[Sec. 280C(e)]

(e) MINE RESCUE TEAM TRAINING CREDIT.—No deduction shall be allowed for that portion of the expenses otherwise allowable as a deduction for the taxable year which is equal to the amount of the credit determined for the taxable year under section 45N(a).

Amendments

• 2006, Tax Relief and Health Care Act of 2006 (P.L. 109-432)

P.L. 109-432, Division A, §405(c):

Amended Code Sec. 280C by adding at the end a new subsection (e). **Effective** for tax years beginning after 12-31-2005.

[Sec. 280C(f)]

(f) CREDIT FOR SECURITY OF AGRICULTURAL CHEMICALS.—No deduction shall be allowed for that portion of the expenses otherwise allowable as a deduction taken into account in determining the credit under section 45O for the taxable year which is equal to the amount of the credit determined for such taxable year under section 45O(a).

Amendments

• 2008, Heartland, Habitat, Harvest, and Horticulture Act of 2008 (P.L. 110-246)

P.L. 110-246, §15343(c):

Amended Code Sec. 280C by adding at the end a new subsection (f). **Effective** for amounts paid or incurred after 5-22-2008.

»»→ Caution: Code Sec. 280C(g), below, as added by P.L. 111-148, applies to tax years ending after December 31, 2013.

[Sec. 280C(g)]

(g) CREDIT FOR HEALTH INSURANCE PREMIUMS.—No deduction shall be allowed for the portion of the premiums paid by the taxpayer for coverage of 1 or more individuals under a qualified health plan which is equal to the amount of the credit determined for the taxable year under section 36B(a) with respect to such premiums.

Amendments

• 2010, Patient Protection and Affordable Care Act (P.L. 111-148)

P.L. 111-148, §1401(b):

Amended Code Sec. 280C by adding at the end a new subsection (g). **Effective** for tax years ending after 12-31-2013.

[Sec. 280C(h)]

(h) CREDIT FOR EMPLOYEE HEALTH INSURANCE EXPENSES OF SMALL EMPLOYERS.—No deduction shall be allowed for that portion of the premiums for qualified health plans (as defined in section 1301(a) of the Patient Protection and Affordable Care Act), or for health insurance coverage in the case of taxable years beginning in 2010, 2011, 2012, or 2013, paid by an employer which is equal to the amount of the credit determined under section 45R(a) with respect to the premiums.

Amendments

• 2010, Patient Protection and Affordable Care Act (P.L. 111-148)

P.L. 111-148, §1421(d)(1):

Amended Code Sec. 280C, as amended by Act Sec. 1401(b), by adding at the end a new subsection (h). **Effective** for amounts paid or incurred in tax years beginning after 12-31-2009 [**effective** date amended by Act Sec. 10105(e)(4).—CCH].

P.L. 111-148, §10105(e)(3):

Amended Code Sec. 280C(h), as added by Act Sec. 1421(d)(1), by striking "2011" and inserting "2010, 2011". **Effective** as if included in the enactment of Act Sec. 1421 [**effective** for amounts paid or incurred in tax years beginning after 12-31-2009 [**effective** date amended by Act Sec. 10105(e)(4).—CCH]].

[Sec. 280C(g)[(i)]]

(g)[(i)] QUALIFYING THERAPEUTIC DISCOVERY PROJECT CREDIT.—

(1) IN GENERAL.—No deduction shall be allowed for that portion of the qualified investment (as defined in section 48D(b)) otherwise allowable as a deduction for the taxable year which—

(A) would be qualified research expenses (as defined in section 41(b)), basic research expenses (as defined in section 41(e)(2)), or qualified clinical testing expenses (as defined in section 45C(b)) if the credit under section 41 or section 45C were allowed with respect to such expenses for such taxable year, and

(B) is equal to the amount of the credit determined for such taxable year under section 48D(a), reduced by—

(i) the amount disallowed as a deduction by reason of section 48D(e)(2)(B), and

(ii) the amount of any basis reduction under section 48D(e)(1).

(2) SIMILAR RULE WHERE TAXPAYER CAPITALIZES RATHER THAN DEDUCTS EXPENSES.—In the case of expenses described in paragraph (1)(A) taken into account in determining the credit under section 48D for the taxable year, if—

(A) the amount of the portion of the credit determined under such section with respect to such expenses, exceeds

(B) the amount allowable as a deduction for such taxable year for such expenses (determined without regard to paragraph (1)),

the amount chargeable to capital account for the taxable year for such expenses shall be reduced by the amount of such excess.

(3) CONTROLLED GROUPS.—Paragraph (3) of subsection (b) shall apply for purposes of this subsection.

Amendments

• 2010, Patient Protection and Affordable Care Act (P.L. 111-148)

P.L. 111-148, §9023(c)(2):

Amended Code Sec. 280C by adding at the end a new subsection (g)[(i)]. **Effective** for amounts paid or incurred after 12-31-2008, in tax years beginning after such date.

[Sec. 280D—Repealed]

Amendments

• 1988, Omnibus Trade and Competitiveness Act of 1988 (P.L. 100-418)

P.L. 100-418, §1941(b)(4)(A):

Repealed Code Sec. 280D. **Effective** for crude oil removed from the premises on or after 8-23-88. Prior to repeal, Code Sec. 280D read as follows:

SEC. 280D. PORTION OF CHAPTER 45 TAXES FOR WHICH CREDIT OR REFUND IS ALLOWABLE UNDER SECTION 6429.

No deduction shall be allowed for that portion of the tax imposed by section 4986 for which a credit or refund is allowable under section 6429.

• 1980, Omnibus Reconciliation Act of 1980 (P.L. 96-499)

P.L. 96-499, §1131(b)(1):

Added Code Sec. 280D. **Effective** for tax years beginning after 2-29-80.

[Sec. 280E]

SEC. 280E. EXPENDITURES IN CONNECTION WITH THE ILLEGAL SALE OF DRUGS.

No deduction or credit shall be allowed for any amount paid or incurred during the taxable year in carrying on any trade or business if such trade or business (or the activities which comprise such trade or business) consists of trafficking in controlled substances (within the meaning of schedule I and II of the Controlled Substances Act) which is prohibited by Federal law or the law of any State in which such trade or business is conducted.

Amendments

• 1982, Tax Equity and Fiscal Responsibility Act of 1982 (P.L. 97-248)

P.L. 97-248, §351(a):

Added Code Sec. 280E. **Effective** for amounts paid or incurred after 9-3-82, in tax years ending after such date.

[Sec. 280F]

SEC. 280F. LIMITATION ON DEPRECIATION FOR LUXURY AUTOMOBILES; LIMITATION WHERE CERTAIN PROPERTY USED FOR PERSONAL PURPOSES.

[Sec. 280F(a)]

(a) LIMITATION ON AMOUNT OF DEPRECIATION FOR LUXURY AUTOMOBILES.—

(1) DEPRECIATION.—

(A) LIMITATION.—The amount of the depreciation deduction for any taxable year for any passenger automobile shall not exceed—

(i) $2,560 for the 1st taxable year in the recovery period,

(ii) $4,100 for the 2nd taxable year in the recovery period,

(iii) $2,450 for the 3rd taxable year in the recovery period, and

(iv) $1,475 for each succeeding taxable year in the recovery period.

(B) DISALLOWED DEDUCTIONS ALLOWED FOR YEARS AFTER RECOVERY PERIOD.—

(i) IN GENERAL.—Except as provided in clause (ii), the unrecovered basis of any passenger automobile shall be treated as an expense for the 1st taxable year after the recovery period. Any excess of the unrecovered basis over the limitation of clause (ii) shall be treated as an expense in the succeeding taxable year.

(ii) $1,475 LIMITATION.—The amount treated as an expense under clause (i) for any taxable year shall not exceed $1,475.

(iii) PROPERTY MUST BE DEPRECIABLE.—No amount shall be allowable as a deduction by reason of this subparagraph with respect to any property for any taxable year unless a depreciation deduction would be allowable with respect to such property for such taxable year.

(iv) AMOUNT TREATED AS DEPRECIATION DEDUCTION.—For purposes of this subtitle, any amount allowable as a deduction by reason of this subparagraph shall be treated as a depreciation deduction allowable under section 168.

(C) SPECIAL RULE FOR CERTAIN CLEAN-FUEL PASSENGER AUTOMOBILES.—

(i) MODIFIED AUTOMOBILES.—In the case of a passenger automobile which is propelled by a fuel which is not a clean-burning fuel and to which is installed qualified clean-fuel vehicle property (as defined in section 179A(c)(1)(A)) for purposes of permitting such vehicle to be propelled by a clean burning fuel (as defined in section 179A(e)(1)), subparagraph (A) shall not apply to the cost of the installed qualified clean burning vehicle property.

(ii) PURPOSE BUILT PASSENGER VEHICLES.—In the case of a purpose built passenger vehicle (as defined in section 4001(a)(2)(C)(ii)), each of the annual limitations specified in subparagraphs (A) and (B) shall be tripled.

(iii) APPLICATION OF SUBPARAGRAPH.—This subparagraph shall apply to property placed in service after August 5, 1997, and before January 1, 2007.

(2) COORDINATION WITH REDUCTIONS IN AMOUNT ALLOWABLE BY REASON OF PERSONAL USE, ETC.—This subsection shall be applied before—

(A) the application of subsection (b), and

(B) the application of any other reduction in the amount of any depreciation deduction allowable under section 168 by reason of any use not qualifying the property for such credit or depreciation deduction.

Amendments

• 2002, Job Creation and Worker Assistance Act of 2002 (P.L. 107-147)

P.L. 107-147, §602(b)(1):

Amended Code Sec. 280F(a)(1)(C) by adding at the end a new clause (iii). **Effective** for property placed in service after 12-31-2001.

• 1998, IRS Restructuring and Reform Act of 1998 (P.L. 105-206)

P.L. 105-206, §6009(c):

Amended Code Sec. 280F(a)(1)(C)(ii) by striking "subparagraph (A)" and inserting "subparagraphs (A) and (B)". **Effective** as if included in the provision of P.L. 105-34 to which it relates [**effective** for property placed in service after 8-5-97.—CCH].

• 1997, Taxpayer Relief Act of 1997 (P.L. 105-34)

P.L. 105-34, §971(a):

Amended Code Sec. 280F(a)(1) by adding at the end a new subparagraph (C). **Effective** for property placed in service after 8-5-97 [**effective** date amended by P.L. 107-47, §602(b)(2).—CCH].

• 1996, Small Business Job Protection Act of 1996 (P.L. 104-188)

P.L. 104-188, §1702(h)(5):

Amended Code Sec. 280F(a) by striking "INVESTMENT TAX CREDIT AND" before "DEPRECIATION" in the heading. **Effective** as if included in the provision of P.L. 101-508 to which it relates.

• **1990, Omnibus Budget Reconciliation Act of 1990 (P.L. 101-508)**

P.L. 101-508, §11813(b)(13)(A)(i)-(ii):

Amended Code Sec. 280F(a) by striking paragraphs (1) and (4) and redesignating paragraphs (2) and (3) as paragraphs (1) and (2), respectively, and by striking "the credit determined under section 46(a) or" after "amount" in paragraph (2)(B), as redesignated. **Effective** for property placed in service after 12-31-90. For exceptions, see Act Sec. 11813(c)(2), below. Prior to amendment, Code Sec. 280F(a)(1) and (4) read as follows:

(a) LIMITATION ON AMOUNT OF INVESTMENT TAX CREDIT AND DEPRECIATION FOR LUXURY AUTOMOBILES.—

(1) INVESTMENT TAX CREDIT.—The amount of the credit determined under section 46(a) for any passenger automobile shall not exceed $675.

* * *

(4) SPECIAL RULE WHERE ELECTION OF REDUCED CREDIT IN LIEU OF THE BASIS ADJUSTMENT.—In the case of any election under section 48(q)(4) with respect to any passenger automobile, the limitation of paragraph (1) applicable to such passenger automobile shall be ⅔ of the amount which would be so applicable but for this paragraph.

P.L. 101-508, §11813(b)(13)(E):

Amended Code Sec. 280F by striking "INVESTMENT TAX CREDIT AND" after "LIMITATION" in the section heading. **Effective** for property placed in service after 12-31-90. For exceptions, see Act Sec. 11813(c)(2), below.

P.L. 101-508, §11813(c)(2), provides:

(2) EXCEPTIONS.—The amendments made by this section shall not apply to—

(A) any transition property (as defined in section 49(e) of the Internal Revenue Code of 1986 (as in effect on the day before the date of the enactment of this Act),

(B) any property with respect to which qualified progress expenditures were previously taken into account under section 46(d) of such Code (as so in effect), and

(C) any property described in section 46(b)(2)(C) of such Code (as so in effect).

• **1986, Tax Reform Act of 1986 (P.L. 99-514)**

P.L. 99-514, §201(d)(4)(A)(i)-(ii):

Amended Code Sec. 280F(a)(2)(A) by striking out clauses (i) and (ii) and inserting in lieu thereof new clauses (i) through (iv), and by striking out"$4,800" each place it appears in Code Sec. 280F(a)(2)(B) and inserting in lieu thereof "$1,475". **Effective**, generally, for property placed in service after 12-31-86, in tax years ending after such date. See, however, the special rules provided in Act Secs. 203(a)(1)(B)-(e), 204 and 251(d) following Code Sec. 168. Prior to amendment, Code Sec. 280F(a)(2)(A)(i) and (ii) read as follows:

(i) $3,200 for the first taxable year in the recovery period, and

(ii) $4,800 for each succeeding taxable year in the recovery period.

P.L. 99-514, §201(d)(4)(K):

Amended Code Sec. 280F(a) by striking out "recovery deduction" each place it appears and inserting in lieu thereof "depreciation deduction". **Effective**, generally, for property placed in service after 12-31-86, in tax years ending after such date. See, however, the special rules provided in Act Secs. 203(a)(1)(B)-(e), 204 and 251(d) following Code Sec. 168.

• **1985 (P.L. 99-44)**

P.L. 99-44, §4(a)(1):

Amended Code Sec. 280F(a)(1) by striking out "$1,000" and inserting in lieu thereof "$675". **Effective** for property placed in service after 4-2-85, in tax years ending after such date, and property leased after 4-2-85, in tax years ending after such date. However, see P.L. 99-44, §6(e)(2), below, for exceptions.

P.L. 99-44, §4(a)(2)(A), (B):

Amended Code Sec. 280F(a)(2) by striking out "$4,000" in subparagraph (A)(i) and inserting in lieu thereof "$3,200", and by striking out "$6,000" each place it appeared in subparagraphs (A)(ii) and (B)(ii) and inserting in lieu thereof "$4,800". **Effective** for property placed in service after 4-2-85, in tax years ending after such date, and property leased after 4-2-85, in tax years ending after such date. However, see P.L. 99-44, §6(e)(2), below, for exceptions.

P.L. 99-44, §6(e)(2), provides:

(2) The amendments made by section 4 shall not apply to any property—

(A) acquired by the taxpayer pursuant to a binding contract in effect on April 1, 1985, and at all times thereafter, but only if the property is placed in service before August 1, 1985, or

(B) of which the taxpayer is the lessee, but only if the lease is pursuant to a binding contract in effect on April 1, 1985, and at all times thereafter, and only if the taxpayer first uses such property under the lease before August 1, 1985.

P.L. 99-44, §5, provides:

Not later than October 1, 1985, the Secretary of the Treasury or his delegate shall prescribe regulations to carry out the provisions of this Act which shall fully reflect such provisions.

[Sec. 280F(b)]

(b) LIMITATION WHERE BUSINESS USE OF LISTED PROPERTY NOT GREATER THAN 50 PERCENT.—

(1) DEPRECIATION.—If any listed property is not predominantly used in a qualified business use for any taxable year, the deduction allowed under section 168 with respect to such property for such taxable year and any subsequent taxable year shall be determined under section 168(g) (relating to alternative depreciation system).

(2) RECAPTURE.—

(A) WHERE BUSINESS USE PERCENTAGE DOES NOT EXCEED 50 PERCENT.—If—

(i) property is predominantly used in a qualified business use in a taxable year in which it is placed in service, and

(ii) such property is not predominantly used in a qualified business use for any subsequent taxable year,

then any excess depreciation shall be included in gross income for the taxable year referred to in clause (ii), and the depreciation deduction for the taxable year referred to in clause (ii) and any subsequent taxable years shall be determined under section 168(g) (relating to alternative depreciation system).

(B) EXCESS DEPRECIATION.—For purposes of subparagraph (A), the term "excess depreciation" means the excess (if any) of—

(i) the amount of the depreciation deductions allowable with respect to the property for taxable years before the 1st taxable year in which the property was not predominantly used in a qualified business use, over

(ii) the amount which would have been so allowable if the property had not been predominantly used in a qualified business use for the taxable year in which it was placed in service.

(3) PROPERTY PREDOMINANTLY USED IN QUALIFIED BUSINESS USE.—For purposes of this subsection, property shall be treated as predominantly used in a qualified business use for any taxable year if the business use percentage for such taxable year exceeds 50 percent.

Amendments

• 1990, Omnibus Budget Reconciliation Act of 1990 (P.L. 101-508)

P.L. 101-508, §11813(b)(13)(B):

Amended Code Sec. 280F(b) by striking paragraph (1) and redesignating the following paragraphs accordingly. **Effective** for property placed in service after 12-31-90. For exceptions, see P.L. 101-508, §11813(c)(2) in the Amendment Notes following Code Sec. 280F(a). Prior to amendment, Code Sec. 280F(b)(1) read as follows:

(1) INVESTMENT TAX CREDIT.—For purposes of this subtitle, any listed property shall not be treated as section 38 property for any taxable year unless such property is predominantly used in a qualified business use for such taxable year.

• 1988, Technical and Miscellaneous Revenue Act of 1988 (P.L. 100-647)

P.L. 100-647, §1018(u)(3):

Amended Code Sec. 280F(b)(3)(B)(i) by striking out "recovery deductions" and inserting in lieu thereof "depreciation deductions". [Caution: Before amendment, the language of Code Sec. 280F(b)(3)(B)(i) read "depreciation deductions".] **Effective** as if included in the provision of P.L. 99-514 to which it relates.

• 1986, Tax Reform Act of 1986 (P.L. 99-514)

P.L. 99-514, §201(d)(4)(B):

Amended Code Sec. 280F(b)(3)(A) by striking out "the straight line method over the earnings and profits life" and inserting in lieu thereof "section 168(g) (relating to alternative depreciation system)". **Effective**, generally, for property placed in service after 12-31-86, in tax years ending after such date. See, however, the special rules provided in Act Secs. 203(a)(1)(B)-(e), 204 and 251(d) following Code Sec. 168.

P.L. 99-514, §201(d)(4)(C):

Amended Code Sec. 280F(b)(4). **Effective**, generally, for property placed in service after 12-31-86, in tax years ending after such date. See, however, the special rules provided in Act Secs. 203(a)(1)(B)-(e), 204 and 251(d) following Code Sec. 168. Prior to amendment, Code Sec. 280F(b)(4) read as follows:

(4) DEFINITIONS.—For purposes of this subsection—

(A) PROPERTY PREDOMINANTLY USED IN QUALIFIED BUSINESS USE.—Property shall be treated as predominantly used in a qualified business use for any taxable year if the business use percentage for such taxable year exceeds 50 percent.

(B) STRAIGHT LINE METHOD OVER EARNINGS AND PROFITS LIFE.—The amount determined under the straight line method over the earnings and profits life with respect to any property shall be the amount which would be determined with respect to such property under the principles of section 312(k)(3). If the recovery period applicable to any property under section 168 is longer than the recovery period applicable to such property under section 312(k)(3), such longer recovery period shall be used for purposes of the preceding sentence.

P.L. 99-514, §201(d)(4)(J):

Amended Code Sec. 280F(b)(2) by striking out "the straight line method over the earnings and profits life for such property" and inserting in lieu thereof "section 168(g) (relating to alternative depreciation system)". **Effective**, generally, for property placed in service after 12-31-86, in tax years ending after such date. See, however, the special rules provided in Act Secs. 203(a)(1)(B)-(e), 204 and 251(d) following Code Sec. 168.

P.L. 99-514, §201(d)(4)(K):

Amended Code Sec. 280F(b) by striking out "recovery deduction" each place it appears and inserting in lieu thereof "depreciation deduction". **Effective**, generally, for property placed in service after 12-31-86, in tax years ending after such date. See, however, the special rules provided in Act Secs. 203(a)(1)(B)-(e), 204 and 251(d) following Code Sec. 168.

[Sec. 280F(c)]

(c) TREATMENT OF LEASES.—

(1) LESSOR'S DEDUCTIONS NOT AFFECTED.—This section shall not apply to any listed property leased or held for leasing by any person regularly engaged in the business of leasing such property.

(2) LESSEE'S DEDUCTIONS REDUCED.—For purposes of determining the amount allowable as a deduction under this chapter for rentals or other payments under a lease for a period of 30 days or more of listed property, only the allowable percentage of such payments shall be taken into account.

(3) ALLOWABLE PERCENTAGE.—For purposes of paragraph (2), the allowable percentage shall be determined under tables prescribed by the Secretary. Such tables shall be prescribed so that the reduction in the deduction under paragraph (2) is substantially equivalent to the applicable restrictions contained in subsections (a) and (b).

(4) LEASE TERM.—In determining the term of any lease for purposes of paragraph (2), the rules of section 168(i)(3)(A) shall apply.

(5) LESSEE RECAPTURE.—Under regulations prescribed by the Secretary, rules similar to the rules of subsection (b)(3) shall apply to any lessee to which paragraph (2) applies.

Amendments

• 1990, Omnibus Budget Reconciliation Act of 1990 (P.L. 101-508)

P.L. 101-508, §11813(b)(13)(C):

Amended Code Sec. 280F(c)(1) by striking "credits and" before "Deductions" in the paragraph heading. **Effective** for property placed in service after 12-31-90. For exceptions, see P.L. 105-108, §11813(c)(2) in the Amendment Notes following Code Sec. 280F(a).

• 1986, Tax Reform Act of 1986 (P.L. 99-514)

P.L. 99-514, §201(d)(4)(D):

Amended Code Sec. 280F(c)(4) by striking out "section 168(j)(6)(B)" and inserting in lieu thereof "section 168(i)(3)(A)". **Effective**, generally, for property placed in service after 12-31-86, in tax years ending after such date. See, however, the special rules provided in P.L. 105-108, §§203(a)(1)(B)-(e), 204 and 251(d) following Code Sec. 168.

[Sec. 280F(d)]

(d) DEFINITIONS AND SPECIAL RULES.—For purposes of this section—

(1) COORDINATION WITH SECTION 179.—Any deduction allowable under section 179 with respect to any listed property shall be subject to the limitations of subsections (a) and (b), and the limitation of paragraph (3) of this subsection, in the same manner as if it were a depreciation deduction allowable under section 168.

(2) SUBSEQUENT DEPRECIATION DEDUCTIONS REDUCED FOR DEDUCTIONS ALLOCABLE TO PERSONAL USE.—Solely for purposes of determining the amount of the depreciation deduction for subsequent taxable years, if less than 100 percent of the use of any listed property during any taxable year is used in a trade or business (including the holding for the production of income), all of the use of such property during such taxable year shall be treated as use so described.

(3) DEDUCTIONS OF EMPLOYEE.—

(A) IN GENERAL.—Any employee use of listed property shall not be treated as use in a trade or business for purposes of determining the amount of any depreciation deduction allowable to the employee (or the amount of any deduction allowable to the employee for rentals or other payments under a lease of listed property) unless such use is for the convenience of the employer and required as a condition of employment.

(B) EMPLOYEE USE.—For purposes of subparagraph (A), the term "employee use" means any use in connection with the performance of services as an employee.

(4) LISTED PROPERTY.—

(A) IN GENERAL.—Except as provided in subparagraph (B), the term "listed property" means—

(i) any passenger automobile,

(ii) any other property used as a means of transportation,

(iii) any property of a type generally used for purposes of entertainment, recreation, or amusement,

(iv) any computer or peripheral equipment (as defined in section 168(i)(2)(B)), and

(v) any other property of a type specified by the Secretary by regulations.

(B) EXCEPTION FOR CERTAIN COMPUTERS.—The term "listed property" shall not include any computer or peripheral equipment (as so defined) used exclusively at a regular business establishment and owned or leased by the person operating such establishment. For purposes of the preceding sentence, any portion of a dwelling unit shall be treated as a regular business establishment if (and only if) the requirements of section 280A(c)(1) are met with respect to such portion.

(C) EXCEPTION FOR PROPERTY USED IN BUSINESS OF TRANSPORTING PERSONS OR PROPERTY.—Except to the extent provided in regulations, clause (ii) of subparagraph (A) shall not apply to any property substantially all of the use of which is in a trade or business of providing to unrelated persons services consisting of the transportation of persons or property for compensation or hire.

(5) PASSENGER AUTOMOBILE.—

(A) IN GENERAL.—Except as provided in subparagraph (B), the term "passenger automobile" means any 4-wheeled vehicle—

(i) which is manufactured primarily for use on public streets, roads, and highways, and

(ii) which is rated at 6,000 pounds unloaded gross vehicle weight or less.

In the case of a truck or van, clause (ii) shall be applied by substituting "gross vehicle weight" for "unloaded gross vehicle weight."

(B) EXCEPTION FOR CERTAIN VEHICLES.—The term "passenger automobile" shall not include—

(i) any ambulance, hearse, or combination ambulance-hearse used by the taxpayer directly in a trade or business,

(ii) any vehicle used by the taxpayer directly in the trade or business of transporting persons or property for compensation or hire, and

(iii) under regulations, any truck or van.

(6) BUSINESS USE PERCENTAGE.—

(A) IN GENERAL.—The term "business use percentage" means the percentage of the use of any listed property during any taxable year which is a qualified business use.

(B) QUALIFIED BUSINESS USE.—Except as provided in subparagraph (C), the term "qualified business use" means any use in a trade or business of the taxpayer.

(C) EXCEPTION FOR CERTAIN USE BY 5-PERCENT OWNERS AND RELATED PERSONS.—

(i) IN GENERAL.—The term "qualified business use" shall not include—

(I) leasing property to any 5-percent owner or related person,

(II) use of property provided as compensation for the performance of services by a 5-percent owner or related person, or

(III) use of property provided as compensation for the performance of services by any person not described in subclause (II) unless an amount is included in the gross income of such person with respect to such use, and, where required, there was withholding under chapter 24.

(ii) SPECIAL RULE FOR AIRCRAFT.—Clause (i) shall not apply with respect to any aircraft if at least 25 percent of the total use of the aircraft during the taxable year consists of qualified business use not described in clause (i).

(D) DEFINITIONS.—For purposes of this paragraph—

(i) 5-PERCENT OWNER.—The term "5-percent owner" means any person who is a 5-percent owner with respect to the taxpayer (as defined in section 416(i)(1)(B)(i)).

(ii) RELATED PERSON.—The term "related person" means any person related to the taxpayer (within the meaning of section 267(b)).

(7) AUTOMOBILE PRICE INFLATION ADJUSTMENT.—

(A) IN GENERAL.—In the case of any passenger automobile placed in service after 1988, subsection (a) shall be applied by increasing each dollar amount contained in such subsection by the automobile price inflation adjustment for the calendar year in which such automobile is placed in service. Any increase under the preceding sentence shall be rounded to the nearest multiple of $100 (or if the increase is a multiple of $50, such increase shall be increased to the next higher multiple of $100).

(B) AUTOMOBILE PRICE INFLATION ADJUSTMENT.—For purposes of this paragraph—

(i) IN GENERAL.—The automobile price inflation adjustment for any calendar year is the percentage (if any) by which—

(I) the CPI automobile component for October of the preceding calendar year, exceeds

(II) the CPI automobile component for October of 1987.

(ii) CPI AUTOMOBILE COMPONENT.—The term "CPI automobile component" means the automobile component of the Consumer Price Index for All Urban Consumers published by the Department of Labor.

(8) UNRECOVERED BASIS.—For purposes of subsection (a)(2), the term "unrecovered basis" means the adjusted basis of the passenger automobile determined after the application of subsection (a) and as if all use during the recovery period were use in a trade or business (including the holding of property for the production of income).

(9) ALL TAXPAYERS HOLDING INTERESTS IN PASSENGER AUTOMOBILE TREATED AS 1 TAXPAYER.—All taxpayers holding interests in any passenger automobile shall be treated as 1 taxpayer for purposes of applying subsection (a) to such automobile, and the limitations of subsection (a) shall be allocated among such taxpayers in proportion to their interests in such automobile.

(10) SPECIAL RULE FOR PROPERTY ACQUIRED IN NONRECOGNITION TRANSACTIONS.—For purposes of subsection (a)(2) any property acquired in a nonrecognition transaction shall be treated as a single property originally placed in service in the taxable year in which it was placed in service after being so acquired.

Amendments

• 2010, Creating Small Business Jobs Act of 2010 (P.L. 111-240)

P.L. 111-240, §2043(a):

Amended Code Sec. 280F(d)(4)(A) by adding "and" at the end of clause (iv), by striking clause (v), and by redesignating clause (vi) as clause (v). **Effective** for tax years beginning after 12-31-2009. Prior to being stricken, Code Sec. 280F(d)(4)(A)(v) read as follows:

(v) any cellular telephone (or other similar telecommunications equipment), and

• 1990, Omnibus Budget Reconciliation Act of 1990 (P.L. 101-508)

P.L. 101-508, §11813(b)(13)(D):

Amended Code Sec. 280F(d)(3)(A) by striking "the amount of any credit allowable under section 38 to the employee or" after "determining". **Effective** for property placed in service after 12-31-90. For exceptions, see Act Sec. 11813(c)(2) in the Amendment Notes following Code Sec. 280F(a)

• 1989, Omnibus Budget Reconciliation Act of 1989 (P.L. 101-239)

P.L. 101-239, §7643(a):

Amended Code Sec. 280F(d)(4)(A) by striking "and" at the end of clause (iv), by redesignating clause (v) as clause (vi), and by inserting after clause (iv) a new clause (v). **Effective** for property placed in service or leased in tax years beginning after 12-31-89.

• 1988, Technical and Miscellaneous Revenue Act of 1988 (P.L. 100-647)

P.L. 100-647, §1002(a)(10):

Amended Code Sec. 280F(d)(3)(A) by striking out "any recovery deduction" and inserting in lieu thereof "any depreciation deduction". **Effective** as if included in the provision of P.L. 99-514 to which it relates.

P.L. 100-647, §1002(b)(2):

Amended Code Sec. 280F(d)(1) by striking out "subsections (a) and (b)" and inserting in lieu thereof "subsections (a) and (b), and the limitation of paragraph (3) of this subsection,". **Effective** as if included in the provision of P.L. 99-514 to which it relates.

• 1986, Tax Reform Act of 1986 (P.L. 99-514)

P.L. 99-514, §201(d)(4)(E):

Amended Code Sec. 280F(d)(1) by striking out "recovery deduction" and inserting in lieu thereof "depreciation deduction". **Effective**, generally, for property placed in service after 12-31-86, in tax years ending after such date. See, however, the special rules provided in Act Secs. 203(a)(1)(B)-(e), 204 and 251(d) following Code Sec. 168.

P.L. 99-514, §201(d)(4)(F)(i) and (ii):

Amended Code Sec. 280F(d)(2) by striking out "recovery deduction" and inserting in lieu thereof "depreciation deduction", and by striking out "use described in section 168(c)(1) (defining recovery property)" and inserting in lieu thereof "use in a trade or business (including the holding for the production of income)". **Effective**, generally, for property placed in service after 12-31-86, in tax years ending after such date. See, however, the special rules provided in Act Secs. 203(a)(1)(B)-(e), 204 and 251(d) following Code Sec. 168.

P.L. 99-514, §201(d)(4)(G):

Amended Code Sec. 280F(d)(4)(A)(iv) by striking out "section 168(j)(5)(D)" and inserting in lieu thereof "section 168(i)(2)(B)". **Effective**, generally, for property placed in service after 12-31-86, in tax years ending after such date. See, however, the special rules provided in Act Secs. 203(a)(1)(B)-(e), 204 and 251(d) following Code Sec. 168.

P.L. 99-514, §201(d)(4)(H):

Amended Code Sec. 280F(d)(8). **Effective**, generally, for property placed in service after 12-31-86, in tax years ending after such date. See, however, the special rules provided in Act Secs. 203(a)(1)(B)-(e), 204 and 251(d) following Code Sec. 168. Prior to amendment, Code Sec. 280F(d)(8) read as follows:

(8) UNRECOVERED BASIS.—For purposes of subsection (a)(2), the term "unrecovered basis" means the excess (if any) of—

(A) the unadjusted basis (as defined in section 168(d)(1)(A)) of the passenger automobile, over

(B) the amount of the recovery deductions which would have been allowable for taxable years in recovery period determined after the application of subsection (a) and as if all use during the recovery period were use described in section 168(c)(1).

P.L. 99-514, §201(d)(4)(I):

Amended Code Sec. 280F(d)(10) by striking out ", notwithstanding any regulations prescribed under section 168(f)(7),". **Effective**, generally, for property placed in service after 12-31-86, in tax years ending after such date. See, however, the special rules provided in Act Secs. 203(a)(1)(B)-(e), 204 and 251(d) following Code Sec. 168. Prior to amendment Code Sec. 280F(d)(10) read as follows:

(10) SPECIAL RULE FOR PROPERTY ACQUIRED IN NONRECOGNITION TRANSACTIONS.—For purposes of subsection (a)(2), notwithstanding any regulations prescribed under section 168(f)(7), any property acquired in a nonrecognition transaction shall be treated as a single property originally placed in service in the taxable year in which it was placed in service after being so acquired.

P.L. 99-514, §1812(e)(1)(A):

Amended Code Sec. 280F(d)(5)(A)(ii) by striking out "gross vehicle weight" and inserting in lieu thereof "unloaded gross vehicle weight". **Effective** as if included in the provision of P.L. 98-369 to which it relates.

P.L. 99-514, §1812(e)(1)(C):

Amended Code Sec. 280F(d)(5)(A) by adding "In the case of a truck or van, clause (ii) shall be applied by substituting 'gross vehicle weight' for 'unloaded gross vehicle weight'." at the end thereof. **Effective** as if included in the provision of P.L. 98-369 to which it relates.

P.L. 99-514, §1812(e)(2):

Amended Code Sec. 280F(d)(3)(A) by striking out "recovery deduction allowable to the employee" and inserting in lieu thereof "recovery deduction allowable to the employee (or the amount of any deduction allowable to the employee for rentals or other payments under a lease of listed property)". **Effective** as if included in the provision of P.L. 98-369 to which it relates.

P.L. 99-514, §1812(e)(3):

Amended Code Sec. 280F(d)(4)(B) by striking out "at a regular business establishment" and inserting in lieu thereof "at a regular business establishment and owned or leased by the person operating such establishment". **Effective** as if included in the provision of P.L. 98-369 to which it relates.

P.L. 99-514, §1812(e)(4):

Amended Code Sec. 280F(d)(4) by adding at the end thereof new subparagraph (C). **Effective** as if included in the provision of P.L. 98-369 to which it relates.

P.L. 99-514, §1812(e)(5):

Amended Code Sec. 280F(d)(2) by striking out "is not use described in" and inserting in lieu thereof "is use described in". **Effective** as if included in the provision of P.L. 98-369 to which it relates.

• 1985 (P.L. 99-44)

P.L. 99-44, §4(b)(1):

Amended Code Sec. 280F(d)(7)(A) by striking out "passenger automobile" and inserting in lieu thereof "passenger automobile placed in service after 1988". **Effective** for property placed in service after 4-2-85, in tax years ending after such date, and property leased after 4-2-85, in tax years ending after such date. However, see P.L. 99-44, §6(e)(2), below, for exceptions.

P.L. 99-44, §4(b)(2):

Amended Code Sec. 280F(d)(7)(B)(i)(II) by striking out "1983" and inserting in lieu thereof "1987". **Effective** for property placed in service after 4-2-85, in tax years ending after such date, and property leased after 4-2-85, in tax years ending after such date. However, see P.L. 99-44, §6(e)(2), below, for exceptions.

P.L. 99-44, §4(b)(3):

Amended Code Sec. 280F(d)(7)(B)(i) by striking out the last sentence. **Effective** for property placed in service after 4-2-85, in tax years ending after such date, and property leased after 4-2-85, in tax years ending after such date. However, see P.L. 99-44, §6(e)(2), below, for exceptions. Prior to amendment, the last sentence of Code Sec. 280F(d)(7)(B)(i) read as follows:

In the case of calendar year 1984, the automobile price inflation adjustment shall be zero.

P.L. 99-44, §6(e)(2), provides:

(2) The amendments made by section 4 shall not apply to any property—

(A) acquired by the taxpayer pursuant to a binding contract in effect on April 1, 1985, and at all times thereafter, but only if the property is placed in service before August 1, 1985, or

(B) of which the taxpayer is the lessee, but only if the lease is pursuant to a binding contract in effect on April 1, 1985, and at all times thereafter, and only if the taxpayer first uses such property under the lease before August 1, 1985.

P.L. 99-44, §5, provides:

Not later than October 1, 1985, the Secretary of the Treasury or his delegate shall prescribe regulations to carry out the provisions of this Act which shall fully reflect such provisions.

[Sec. 280F(e)]

(e) REGULATIONS.—The Secretary shall prescribe such regulations as may be necessary or appropriate to carry out the purposes of this section, including regulations with respect to items properly included in, or excluded from, the adjusted basis of any listed property.

Amendments

• 1984, Deficit Reduction Act of 1984 (P.L. 98-369)

P.L. 98-369, §179(a):

Added Code Sec. 280F. **Effective** for property placed in service after 6-18-84, in tax years ending after such date, and property leased after 6-18-84, in tax years ending after such date. However, see P.L. 98-369, §179(d)(1)(B), below, for exceptions.

P.L. 98-369, §179(d)(1)(B), provides:

The above amendment does not apply to any property acquired by the taxpayer pursuant to a binding contract in effect on June 18, 1984, and at all times thereafter (or under construction on such date) but only if the property is placed in service before January 1, 1985 (January 1, 1987, in the case of 15-year real property), or of which the taxpayer is the lessee but only if the lease is pursuant to a binding contract in effect on June 18, 1984, and at all times thereafter and only if the taxpayer first uses such property under the lease before January 1, 1985 (January 1, 1987, in the case of 15-year real property). For purposes of the preceding sentence, "15-year real property" includes 18-year real property.

[Sec. 280G]

SEC. 280G. GOLDEN PARACHUTE PAYMENTS.

[Sec. 280G(a)]

(a) GENERAL RULE.—No deduction shall be allowed under this chapter for any excess parachute payment.

[Sec. 280G(b)]

(b) EXCESS PARACHUTE PAYMENT.—For purposes of this section—

(1) IN GENERAL.—The term "excess parachute payment" means an amount equal to the excess of any parachute payment over the portion of the base amount allocated to such payment.

(2) PARACHUTE PAYMENT DEFINED.—

(A) IN GENERAL.—The term "parachute payment" means any payment in the nature of compensation to (or for the benefit of) a disqualified individual if—

(i) such payment is contingent on a change—

(I) in the ownership or effective control of the corporation, or

(II) in the ownership of a substantial portion of the assets of the corporation, and

(ii) the aggregate present value of the payments in the nature of compensation to (or for the benefit of) such individual which are contingent on such change equals or exceeds an amount equal to 3 times the base amount.

For purposes of clause (ii), payments not treated as parachute payments under paragraph (4)(A), (5), or (6) shall not be taken into account.

(B) AGREEMENTS.—The term "parachute payment" shall also include any payment in the nature of compensation to (or for the benefit of) a disqualified individual if such payment is made pursuant to an agreement which violates any generally enforced securities laws or regulations. In any proceeding involving the issue of whether any payment made to a disqualified individual is a parachute payment on account of a violation of any generally enforced securities laws or regulations, the burden of proof with respect to establishing the occurrence of a violation of such a law or regulation shall be upon the Secretary.

(C) TREATMENT OF CERTAIN AGREEMENTS ENTERED INTO WITHIN 1 YEAR BEFORE CHANGE OF OWNERSHIP.—For purposes of subparagraph (A)(i), any payment pursuant to—

(i) an agreement entered into within 1 year before the change described in subparagraph (A)(i), or

(ii) an amendment made within such 1-year period of a previous agreement,

shall be presumed to be contingent on such change unless the contrary is established by clear and convincing evidence.

(3) BASE AMOUNT.—

(A) IN GENERAL.—The term "base amount" means the individual's annualized includible compensation for the base period.

(B) ALLOCATION.—The portion of the base amount allocated to any parachute payment shall be an amount which bears the same ratio to the base amount as—

(i) the present value of such payment, bears to

(ii) the aggregate present value of all such payments.

(4) TREATMENT OF AMOUNTS WHICH TAXPAYER ESTABLISHES AS REASONABLE COMPENSATION.—In the case of any payment described in paragraph (2)(A)—

(A) the amount treated as a parachute payment shall not include the portion of such payment which the taxpayer establishes by clear and convincing evidence is reasonable compensation for personal services to be rendered on or after the date of the change described in paragraph (2)(A)(i), and

(B) the amount treated as an excess parachute payment shall be reduced by the portion of such payment which the taxpayer establishes by clear and convincing evidence is reasonable compensation for personal services actually rendered before the date of the change described in paragraph (2)(A)(i).

For purposes of subparagraph (B), reasonable compensation for services actually rendered before the date of the change described in paragraph (2)(A)(i) shall be first offset against the base amount.

(5) EXEMPTION FOR SMALL BUSINESS CORPORATIONS, ETC.—

(A) IN GENERAL.—Notwithstanding paragraph (2), the term "parachute payment" does not include—

(i) any payment to a disqualified individual with respect to a corporation which (immediately before the change described in paragraph (2)(A)(i)) was a small business corporation (as defined in section 1361(b) but without regard to paragraph (1)(C) thereof), and

(ii) any payment to a disqualified individual with respect to a corporation (other than a corporation described in clause (i)) if—

(I) immediately before the change described in paragraph (2)(A)(i), no stock in such corporation was readily tradeable on an established securities market or otherwise, and

(II) the shareholder approval requirements of subparagraph (B) are met with respect to such payment.

The Secretary may, by regulations, prescribe that the requirements of subclause (I) of clause (ii) are not met where a substantial portion of the assets of any entity consists (directly or indirectly) of stock in such corporation and interests in such other entity are readily tradeable on an established securities market, or otherwise. Stock described in section 1504(a)(4) shall not be taken into account under clause (ii)(I) if the payment does not adversely affect the shareholder's redemption and liquidation rights.

(B) SHAREHOLDER APPROVAL REQUIREMENTS.—The shareholder approval requirements of this subparagraph are met with respect to any payment if—

(i) such payment was approved by a vote of the persons who owned, immediately before the change described in paragraph (2)(A)(i), more than 75 percent of the voting power of all outstanding stock of the corporation, and

(ii) there was adequate disclosure to shareholders of all material facts concerning all payments which (but for this paragraph) would be parachute payments with respect to a disqualified individual.

The regulations prescribed under subsection (e) shall include regulations providing for the application of this subparagraph in the case of shareholders which are not individuals (including the treatment of nonvoting interests in an entity which is a shareholder) and where an entity holds a de minimis amount of stock in the corporation.

(6) EXEMPTION FOR PAYMENTS UNDER QUALIFIED PLANS.—Notwithstanding paragraph (2), the term "parachute payment" shall not include any payment to or from—

(A) a plan described in section 401(a) which includes a trust exempt from tax under section 501(a),

(B) an annuity plan described in section 403(a),

(C) a simplified employee pension (as defined in section 408(k)), or

(D) a simple retirement account described in section 408(p).

Amendments

• 1996, Small Business Job Protection Act of 1996 (P.L. 104-188)

P.L. 104-188, §1421(b)(9)(A):

Amended Code Sec. 280G(b)(6) by striking "or" at the end of subparagraph (B), by striking the period at the end of subparagraph (C) and inserting ", or" and by adding after subparagraph (C) a new subparagraph (D). **Effective** for tax years beginning after 12-31-96.

• 1988, Technical and Miscellaneous Revenue Act of 1988 (P.L. 100-647)

P.L. 100-647, §1018(d)(6)(A)-(B):

Amended Code Sec. 280G(b)(5)(A) by striking out "section 1361(b))" in clause (i) and inserting in lieu thereof "section 1361(b) but without regard to paragraph (1)(C) thereof)", and by adding at the end thereof a new sentence. **Effective** as if included in the provision of P.L. 99-514 to which it relates.

P.L. 100-647, §1018(d)(7):

Amended Code Sec. 280G(b)(5)(B) by adding at the end thereof a new sentence. **Effective** as if included in the provision of P.L. 99-514 to which it relates.

• 1986, Tax Reform Act of 1986 (P.L. 99-514)

P.L. 99-514, §1804(j)(1):

Amended Code Sec. 280G(b) by adding at the end thereof new paragraph (5). **Effective** as if included in the provision of P.L. 98-369 to which it relates.

P.L. 99-514, §1804(j)(2):

Amended Code Sec. 280G(b)(4). **Effective** as if included in the provision of P.L. 98-369 to which it relates. Prior to amendment, Code Sec. 280G(b)(4) read as follows:

(4) EXCESS PARACHUTE PAYMENTS REDUCED TO EXTENT TAXPAYER ESTABLISHES REASONABLE COMPENSATION.—In the case of any parachute payment described in paragraph (2)(A), the amount of any excess parachute payment shall be reduced by the portion of such payment which the taxpayer establishes by clear and convincing evidence is reasonable compensation for personal services actually rendered. For purposes of the preceding sentence, reasonable compensation shall be first offset against the base amount.

P.L. 99-514, §1804(j)(3):

Amended Code Sec. 280G(b) by adding at the end thereof new paragraph (6). **Effective** as if included in the provision of P.L. 98-369 to which it relates.

P.L. 99-514, §1804(j)(6):

Amended Code Sec. 280G(b)(2)(A) by adding at the end thereof a new sentence. **Effective** as if included in the provision of P.L. 98-369 to which it relates.

P.L. 99-514, §1804(j)(7):

Amended Code Sec. 280G(b)(2)(B). **Effective** as if included in the provision of P.L. 98-369 to which it relates. Prior to amendment, Code Sec. 280G(b)(2)(B) read as follows:

(B) AGREEMENTS.—The term "parachute payment" shall also include any payment in the nature of compensation to (or for the benefit of) a disqualified individual if such payment is pursuant to an agreement which violates any securities laws or regulations.

[Sec. 280G(c)]

(c) DISQUALIFIED INDIVIDUALS.—For purposes of this section, the term "disqualified individual" means any individual who is—

(1) an employee, independent contractor, or other person specified in regulations by the Secretary who performs personal services for any corporation, and

(2) is an officer, shareholder, or highly-compensated individual.

For purposes of this section, a personal service corporation (or similar entity) shall be treated as an individual. For purposes of paragraph (2), the term "highly-compensated individual" only includes an individual who is (or would be if the individual were an employee) a member of the group consisting of the highest paid 1 percent of the employees of the corporation or, if less, the highest paid 250 employees of the corporation.

Amendments

• 1986, Tax Reform Act of 1986 (P.L. 99-514)

P.L. 99-514, §1804(j)(5):

Amended Code Sec. 280G(c) by adding at the end thereof a new sentence. **Effective** as if included in the provision of P.L. 98-369 to which it relates.

[Sec. 280G(d)]

(d) OTHER DEFINITIONS AND SPECIAL RULES.—For purposes of this section—

(1) ANNUALIZED INCLUDIBLE COMPENSATION FOR BASE PERIOD.—The term "annualized includible compensation for the base period" means the average annual compensation which—

(A) was payable by the corporation with respect to which the change in ownership or control described in paragraph (2)(A) of subsection (b) occurs, and

(B) was includible in the gross income of the disqualified individual for taxable years in the base period.

(2) BASE PERIOD.—The term "base period" means the period consisting of the most recent 5 taxable years ending before the date on which the change in ownership or control described in paragraph (2)(A) of subsection (b) occurs (or such portion of such period during which the disqualified individual performed personal services for the corporation).

(3) PROPERTY TRANSFERS.—Any transfer of property—

(A) shall be treated as a payment, and

(B) shall be taken into account as its fair market value.

(4) PRESENT VALUE.—Present value shall be determined by using a discount rate equal to 120 percent of the applicable Federal rate (determined under section 1274(d)), compounded semiannually.

(5) TREATMENT OF AFFILIATED GROUPS.—Except as otherwise provided in regulations, all members of the same affiliated group (as defined in section 1504, determined without regard to section 1504(b)) shall be treated as 1 corporation for purposes of this section. Any person who is an officer of any member of such group shall be treated as an officer of such 1 corporation.

Amendments

• 1988, Technical and Miscellaneous Revenue Act of 1988 (P.L. 100-647)

P.L. 100-647, §1018(d)(8):

Amended Code Sec. 280G(d)(5) by striking out "officer or any member" and inserting in lieu thereof "officer of any member". **Effective** as if included in the provision of P.L. 99-514 to which it relates.

• 1986, Tax Reform Act of 1986 (P.L. 99-514)

P.L. 99-514, §1804(j)(4):

Amended Code Sec. 280G(d) by adding at the end thereof new paragraph (5). **Effective** as if included in the provision of P.L. 98-369 to which it relates.

P.L. 99-514, §1804(j)(8):

Amended Code Sec. 280G(d)(2) by striking out "was an employee of the corporation" and inserting in lieu thereof "performed personal services for the corporation". **Effective** as if included in the provision of P.L. 98-369 to which it relates.

• 1985 (P.L. 99-121)

P.L. 99-121, §102(c)(4):

Amended Code Sec. 280G(d)(4) by striking out "in accordance with section 1274(b)(2)" and inserting in lieu thereof "by using a discount rate equal to 120 percent of the applicable Federal rate (determined under section 1274(d)), compounded semiannually". **Effective** for sales and exchanges after 6-30-85, in tax years ending after such date. The amendment made by P.L. 98-612, §2, shall not apply to sales and exchanges after 6-30-85, in tax years ending after such date.

[Sec. 280G(e)]

(e) SPECIAL RULE FOR APPLICATION TO EMPLOYERS PARTICIPATING IN THE TROUBLED ASSETS RELIEF PROGRAM.—

(1) IN GENERAL.—In the case of the severance from employment of a covered executive of an applicable employer during the period during which the authorities under section 101(a) of the Emergency Economic Stabilization Act of 2008 are in effect (determined under section 120 of such Act), this section shall be applied to payments to such executive with the following modifications:

(A) Any reference to a disqualified individual (other than in subsection (c)) shall be treated as a reference to a covered executive.

(B) Any reference to a change described in subsection (b)(2)(A)(i) shall be treated as a reference to an applicable severance from employment of a covered executive, and any reference to a payment contingent on such a change shall be treated as a reference to any payment made during an applicable taxable year of the employer on account of such applicable severance from employment.

(C) Any reference to a corporation shall be treated as a reference to an applicable employer.

(D) The provisions of subsections (b)(2)(C), (b)(4), (b)(5), and (d)(5) shall not apply.

(2) DEFINITIONS AND SPECIAL RULES.—For purposes of this subsection:

(A) DEFINITIONS.—Any term used in this subsection which is also used in section 162(m)(5) shall have the meaning given such term by such section.

(B) APPLICABLE SEVERANCE FROM EMPLOYMENT.—The term "applicable severance from employment" means any severance from employment of a covered executive—

(i) by reason of an involuntary termination of the executive by the employer, or

(ii) in connection with any bankruptcy, liquidation, or receivership of the employer.

(C) COORDINATION AND OTHER RULES.—

(i) IN GENERAL.—If a payment which is treated as a parachute payment by reason of this subsection is also a parachute payment determined without regard to this subsection, this subsection shall not apply to such payment.

(ii) REGULATORY AUTHORITY.—The Secretary may prescribe such guidance, rules, or regulations as are necessary—

(I) to carry out the purposes of this subsection and the Emergency Economic Stabilization Act of 2008, including the extent to which this subsection applies in the case of any acquisition, merger, or reorganization of an applicable employer,

(II) to apply this section and section 4999 in cases where one or more payments with respect to any individual are treated as parachute payments by reason of this subsection, and other payments with respect to such individual are treated as parachute payments under this section without regard to this subsection, and

(III) to prevent the avoidance of the application of this section through the mischaracterization of a severance from employment as other than an applicable severance from employment.

Amendments

• 2008, Emergency Economic Stabilization Act of 2008 (P.L. 110-343)

P.L. 110-343, Division A, §302(b)(1)-(2):

Amended Code Sec. 280G by redesignating subsection (e) as subsection (f), and by inserting after subsection (d) a new subsection (e). **Effective** for payments with respect to severances occurring during the period during which the authorities under section 101(a) of this Act are in effect (determined under section 120 of this Act).

[Sec. 280G(f)]

(f) REGULATIONS.—The Secretary shall prescribe such regulations as may be necessary or appropriate to carry out the purposes of this section (including regulations for the application of this section in the case of related corporations and in the case of personal service corporations).

Amendments

• 2008, Emergency Economic Stabilization Act of 2008 (P.L. 110-343)

P.L. 110-343, Division A, §302(b)(1)-(2):

Amended Code Sec. 280G by redesignating subsection (e) as subsection (f). **Effective** for payments with respect to severances occurring during the period during which the authorities under section 101(a) of this Act are in effect (determined under section 120 of this Act).

• 1984, Deficit Reduction Act of 1984 (P.L. 98-369)

P.L. 98-369, §67(a):

Added Code Sec. 280G. **Effective** for payments under agreements entered into or renewed after 6-14-84, in tax years ending after such date. However, see P.L. 98-369, §67(e)(2), below for special rules.

P.L. 98-369, §67(e)(2), provides:

(2) Special rule for contract amendments.—Any contract entered into before June 15, 1984, which is amended after June 14, 1984, in any significant aspect shall be treated as a contract entered into after June 14, 1984.

[Sec. 280H]

SEC. 280H. LIMITATION ON CERTAIN AMOUNTS PAID TO EMPLOYEE-OWNERS BY PERSONAL SERVICE CORPORATIONS ELECTING ALTERNATIVE TAXABLE YEARS.

[Sec. 280H(a)]

(a) GENERAL RULE.—If—

(1) an election by a personal service corporation under section 444 is in effect for a taxable year, and

(2) such corporation does not meet the minimum distribution requirements of subsection (c) for such taxable year,

then the deduction otherwise allowed under this chapter for applicable amounts paid or incurred by such corporation to employee-owners shall not exceed the maximum deductible amount. The preceding sentence shall not apply for purposes of subchapter G (relating to personal holding companies).

[Sec. 280H(b)]

(b) CARRYOVER OF NONDEDUCTIBLE AMOUNTS.—If any amount is not allowed as a deduction for a taxable year under subsection (a), such amount shall be treated as paid or incurred in the succeeding taxable year.

[Sec. 280H(c)]

(c) MINIMUM DISTRIBUTION REQUIREMENT.—For purposes of this section—

(1) IN GENERAL.—A personal service corporation meets the minimum distribution requirements of this subsection if the applicable amounts paid or incurred during the deferral period of the taxable year (determined without regard to subsection (b)) equal or exceed the lesser of—

(A) the product of—

(i) the applicable amounts paid during the preceding taxable year, divided by the number of months in such taxable year, multiplied by

(ii) the number of months in the deferral period of the preceding taxable year, or

(B) the applicable percentage of the adjusted taxable income for the deferral period of the taxable year.

(2) APPLICABLE PERCENTAGE.—The term "applicable percentage" means the percentage (not in excess of 95 percent) determined by dividing—

(A) the applicable amounts paid or incurred during the 3 taxable years immediately preceding the taxable year, by

(B) the adjusted taxable income of such corporation for such 3 taxable years.

Amendments

• 1988, Technical and Miscellaneous Revenue Act of 1988 (P.L. 100-647)

P.L. 100-647, §2004(e)(14)(C):

Amended Code Sec. 280H(c)(1)(A)(i) by striking out "or incurred" after "amounts paid". **Effective** as if included in the provision of P.L. 100-203 to which it relates.

[Sec. 280H(d)]

(d) MAXIMUM DEDUCTIBLE AMOUNT.—For purposes of this section, the term maximum deductible amount means the sum of—

(1) the applicable amounts paid during the deferral period, plus

(2) an amount equal to the product of—

(A) the amount determined under paragraph (1), divided by the number of months in the deferral period, multiplied by

(B) the number of months in the nondeferral period.

Amendments

• 1988, Technical and Miscellaneous Revenue Act of 1988 (P.L. 100-647)

P.L. 100-647, §2004(e)(14)(C):

Amended Code Sec. 280H(d)(1) by striking out "or incurred" after "amounts paid". **Effective** as if included in the provision of P.L. 100-203 to which it relates.

[Sec. 280H(e)]

(e) DISALLOWANCE OF NET OPERATING LOSS CARRYBACKS.—No net operating loss carryback shall be allowed to (or from) any taxable year of a personal service corporation to which an election under section 444 applies.

[Sec. 280H(f)]

(f) OTHER DEFINITIONS AND SPECIAL RULES.—For purposes of this section—

(1) APPLICABLE AMOUNT.—The term "applicable amount" means any amount paid to an employee-owner which is includible in the gross income of such employee, other than—

(A) any gain from the sale or exchange of property between the owner-employee and the corporation, or

(B) any dividend paid by the corporation.

(2) EMPLOYEE-OWNER.—The term "employee-owner" has the meaning given such term by section 269A(b)(2) (as modified by section 441(i)(2)).

(3) NONDEFERRAL AND DEFERRAL PERIODS.—

(A) DEFERRAL PERIOD.—The term "deferral period" has the meaning given to such term by section 444(b)(4).

(B) NONDEFERRAL PERIOD.—The term "nondeferral period" means the portion of the taxable year of the personal service corporation which occurs after the portion of such year constituting the deferral period.

(4) ADJUSTED TAXABLE INCOME.—The term "adjusted taxable income" means taxable income determined without regard to—

(A) any amount paid to an employee-owner which is includible in the gross income of such employee-owner, and

(B) any net operating loss carryover to the extent such carryover is attributable to amounts described in subparagraph (A).

(5) PERSONAL SERVICE CORPORATION.—The term "personal service corporation" has the meaning given to such term by section 441(i)(2).

Amendments

• 1988, Technical and Miscellaneous Revenue Act of 1988 (P.L. 100-647)

P.L. 100-647, § 2004(e)(2)(B):

Amended Code Sec. 280H(f) by adding at the end thereof a new paragraph (5). **Effective** as if included in the provision of P.L. 100-203 to which it relates.

P.L. 100-647, § 2004(e)(3):

Amended Code Sec. 280H(f)(2) by striking out "section 296A(b)(2)" and inserting in lieu thereof "section 269A(b)(2) (as modified by section 441(i)(2))". **Effective** as if included in the provision of P.L. 100-203 to which it relates.

P.L. 100-647, § 2004(e)(14)(A):

Amended Code Sec. 280H(f)(4). **Effective** as if included in the provision of P.L. 100-203 to which it relates. Prior to amendment, Code Sec. 280H(f)(4) read as follows:

(4) ADJUSTED TAXABLE INCOME.—The term "adjusted taxable income" means taxable income increased by any amount paid or incurred to an employee-owner which was includible in the gross income of such employee-owner.

• 1987, Revenue Act of 1987 (P.L. 100-203)

P.L. 100-203, § 10206(c)(1):

Amended part IX of subchapter B of chapter 1 by adding at the end thereof new section 280H. For the **effective** date, see P.L. 100-203, § 10206(d), below.

P.L. 100-203, § 10206(d), provides:

(d) EFFECTIVE DATES.—

(1) IN GENERAL.—Except as provided in this subsection, the amendments made by this section shall apply to taxable years beginning after December 31, 1986.

(2) REQUIRED PAYMENTS.—The amendments made by subsection (b) shall apply to applicable election years beginning after December 31, 1986.

(3) ELECTIONS.—Any election under section 444 of the Internal Revenue Code of 1986 (as added by subsection (a)) for an entity's 1st taxable year beginning after December 31, 1986, shall not be required to be made before the 90th day after the date of the enactment of this Act.

(4) SPECIAL RULE FOR EXISTING ENTITIES ELECTING S CORPORATION STATUS.—If a C corporation (within the meaning of section 1361(a)(2)) of the Internal Revenue Code of 1986) with a taxable year other than the calendar year—

(A) made an election after September 18, 1986, and before January 1, 1988, under section 1362 of such Code to be treated as an S corporation, and

(B) elected to have the calendar year as the taxable year of the S corporation,

then section 444(b)(2)(B) of such Code shall be applied by taking into account the deferral period of the last taxable year of the C corporation rather than the deferral period of the taxable year being changed.

PART X—TERMINAL RAILROAD CORPORATIONS AND THEIR SHAREHOLDERS

[Sec. 281]

SEC. 281. TERMINAL RAILROAD CORPORATIONS AND THEIR SHAREHOLDERS.

[Sec. 281(a)]

(a) COMPUTATION OF TAXABLE INCOME OF TERMINAL RAILROAD CORPORATIONS.—

(1) IN GENERAL.—In computing the taxable income of a terminal railroad corporation—

(A) such corporation shall not be considered to have received or accrued—

(i) the portion of any liability of any railroad corporation, with respect to related terminal services provided by such corporation, which is discharged by crediting such liability with an amount of related terminal income, or

(ii) the portion of any charge which would be made by such corporation for related terminal services provided by it, but which is not made as a result of taking related terminal income into account in computing such charge; and

(B) no deduction otherwise allowable under this chapter shall be disallowed as a result of any discharge of liability described in subparagraph (A)(i) or as a result of any computation of charges in the manner described in subparagraph (A)(ii).

(2) LIMITATION.—In the case of any taxable year ending after the date of the enactment of this section, paragraph (1) shall not apply to the extent that it would (but for this paragraph) operate to create (or increase) a net operating loss for the terminal railroad corporation for the taxable year.

[Sec. 281(b)]

(b) COMPUTATION OF TAXABLE INCOME OF SHAREHOLDERS.—Subject to the limitation in subsection (a)(2), in computing the taxable income of any shareholder of a terminal railroad corporation, no amount shall be considered to have been received or accrued or paid or incurred by such shareholder as a result of any discharge of liability described in subsection (a)(1)(A)(i) or as a result of any computation of charges in the manner described in subsection (a)(1)(A)(ii).

[Sec. 281(c)]

(c) AGREEMENT REQUIRED.—In the case of any taxable year, subsections (a) and (b) shall apply with respect to any discharge of liability described in subsection (a)(1)(A)(i), and to any computation of charges in the manner described in subsection (a)(1)(A)(ii), only if such discharge or computation (as the case may be) was provided for in a written agreement, to which all of the shareholders of the terminal railroad corporation were parties, entered into before the beginning of such taxable year.

[Sec. 281(d)]

(d) DEFINITIONS.—For purposes of this section—

(1) TERMINAL RAILROAD CORPORATION.—The term "terminal railroad corporation" means a domestic railroad corporation which is not a member, other than as a common parent corporation, of an affiliated group (as defined in section 1504) and—

(A) all of the shareholders of which are rail carriers subject to part A of subtitle IV of title 49;

(B) the primary business of which is the providing of railroad terminal and switching facilities and services to rail carriers subject to part A of subtitle IV of title 49 and to the shippers and passengers of such railroad corporations;

(C) a substantial part of the services of which for the taxable year is rendered to one or more of its shareholders; and

(D) each shareholder of which computes its taxable income on the basis of a taxable year beginning or ending on the same day that the taxable year of the terminal railroad corporation begins or ends.

(2) RELATED TERMINAL INCOME.—The term "related terminal income" means the income (determined in accordance with regulations prescribed by the Secretary) of a terminal railroad corporation derived—

(A) from services or facilities of a character ordinarily and regularly provided by terminal railroad corporations for railroad corporations or for the employees, passengers, or shippers of railroad corporations;

(B) from the use by persons other than railroad corporations of portions of a facility, or a service, which is used primarily for railroad purposes;

(C) from any railroad corporation for services or facilities provided by such terminal railroad corporation in connection with railroad operations; and

(D) from the United States in payment for facilities or services in connection with mail handling.

For purposes of subparagraph (B), a substantial addition, constructed after the date of the enactment of this section, to a facility shall be treated as a separate facility.

(3) RELATED TERMINAL SERVICES.—The term "related terminal services" includes only services, and the use of facilities, taken into account in computing related terminal income.

Amendments

• 1996, Small Business Job Protection Act of 1996 (P.L. 104-188)

P.L. 104-88, §304(b):

Amended Code Sec. 281(d)(1)(A) and (B) by striking "domestic railroad corporations providing transportation subject to subchapter I of chapter 105" and inserting in lieu thereof "rail carriers subject to part A of subtitle IV". **Effective** 1-1-96.

• 1978 (P.L. 95-473)

P.L. 95-473, §2(a)(2)(D):

Amended Code Section 281(d)(1)(A) by striking out "subject to part I of the Interstate Commerce Act (49 U.S.C. 1 and following)" and substituting "providing transportation subject to subchapter I of chapter 105 of title 49". **Effective** 10-17-78.

P.L. 95-473, §2(a)(2)(E):

Amended Code Section 281(d)(1)(B) by striking out "subject to part I of the Interstate Commerce Act" and substituting "providing transportation subject to subchapter I of chapter 105 of title 49". **Effective** 10-17-78.

• 1976, Tax Reform Act of 1976 (P.L. 94-455)

P.L. 94-455, §1901(a)(40)(A):

Inserted "(49 U.S.C. 1 and following)" after "Interstate Commerce Act" in Code Sec. 281(d)(1)(A). **Effective** for tax years beginning after 12-31-76.

P.L. 94-455, §1906(b)(13)(A):

Amended 1954 Code by substituting "Secretary" for "Secretary or his delegate" each place it appeared. **Effective** 2-1-77.

[Sec. 281(e)]

(e) REGULATIONS.—The Secretary shall prescribe such regulations as may be necessary to carry out the purposes of this section.

Amendments

• 1976, Tax Reform Act of 1976 (P.L. 94-455)

P.L. 94-455, §1901(a)(40)(B):

Repealed Code Sec. 281(e) and redesignated former Code Sec. 282(f) to be Code Sec. 281(e). **Effective** for tax years beginning after 12-31-76. Prior to repeal, Code Sec. 281(e) read as follows:

(e) APPLICATION TO TAXABLE YEARS ENDING BEFORE THE DATE OF ENACTMENT.—In the case of any taxable year ending before the date of the enactment of this section—

(1) this section shall apply only to the extent that the taxpayer computed on its return, filed at or prior to the time (including extensions thereof) that the return for such taxable year was required to be filed, its taxable income in the manner described in subsection (a) in the case of a terminal railroad corporation, or in the manner described in subsection (b) in the case of a shareholder of a terminal railroad corporation; and

(2) this section shall apply to a taxable year for which the assessment of any deficiency, or for which refund or credit of any overpayment, whichever is applicable, was prevented, on the date of the enactment of this section, by the operation of any law or rule of law (other than section 3760 of the Internal Revenue Code of 1939 or section 7121 of this title, relating to closing agreements, and section 3761 of the Internal Revenue Code of 1939 or section 7122 of this title, relating to compromises), only—

(A) to the extent any overpayment of income tax would result from the recomputation of the taxable income of a terminal railroad corporation in the manner described in subsection (a),

(B) if claim for credit or refund of such overpayment, based upon such recomputation, is filed prior to one year after the date of the enactment of this section,

(C) to the extent that paragraph (1) applies, and

(D) if each shareholder of such terminal railroad corporation consents in writing to the assessment, within such period as may be agreed upon with the Secretary or his delegate, of any deficiency for any year to the extent attributable to the recomputation of its taxable income in the manner described in subsection (b) correlative to its allocable share of the adjustment of taxable income made by the terminal railroad corporation in the recomputation under subparagraph (A).

P.L. 94-455, §1906(b)(13)(A):

Amended 1954 Code by substituting "Secretary" for "Secretary or his delegate" each place it appeared. **Effective** 2-1-77.

• 1962 (P.L. 87-870)

P.L. 87-870, §1(a):

Added Part X to subchapter B of chapter 1 of the 1954 Code, including new Code Sec. 281. **Effective** with respect to tax years beginning after 12-31-53, and ending after 8-16-54. Provisions having the same effect as new Code Sec. 281 are deemed to be included in the 1939 Code, effective for all tax years to which the 1939 Code applies.

PART XI—SPECIAL RULES RELATING TO CORPORATE PREFERENCE ITEMS

[Sec. 291]

SEC. 291. SPECIAL RULES RELATING TO CORPORATE PREFERENCE ITEMS.

[Sec. 291(a)]

(a) REDUCTION IN CERTAIN PREFERENCE ITEMS, ETC.—For purposes of this subtitle, in the case of a corporation—

(1) SECTION 1250 CAPITAL GAIN TREATMENT.—In the case of section 1250 property which is disposed of during the taxable year, 20 percent of the excess (if any) of—

(A) the amount which would be treated as ordinary income if such property was section 1245 property, over

(B) the amount treated as ordinary income under section 1250 (determined without regard to this paragraph),

shall be treated as gain which is ordinary income under section 1250 and shall be recognized notwithstanding any other provision of this title. Under regulations prescribed by the Secretary, the provisions of this paragraph shall not apply to the disposition of any property to the extent section 1250(a) does not apply to such disposition by reason of section 1250(d).

(2) REDUCTION IN PERCENTAGE DEPLETION.—In the case of iron ore and coal (including lignite), the amount allowable as a deduction under section 613 with respect to any property (as defined in section 614) shall be reduced by 20 percent of the amount of the excess (if any) of—

(A) the amount of the deduction allowable under section 613 for the taxable year (determined without regard to this paragraph), over

(B) the adjusted basis of the property at the close of the taxable year (determined without regard to the depletion deduction for the taxable year).

(3) CERTAIN FINANCIAL INSTITUTION PREFERENCE ITEMS.—The amount allowable as a deduction under this chapter (determined without regard to this section) with respect to any financial institution preference item shall be reduced by 20 percent.

(4) AMORTIZATION OF POLLUTION CONTROL FACILITIES.—If an election is made under section 169 with respect to any certified pollution control facility, the amortizable basis of such facility for purposes of such section shall be reduced by 20 percent.

Amendments

• 2007, Tax Technical Corrections Act of 2007 (P.L. 110-172)

P.L. 110-172, §11(g)(6)(A):

Amended Code Sec. 291(a) by striking paragraph (4) and by redesignating paragraph (5) as paragraph (4). **Effective** 12-29-2007. Prior to being stricken, Code Sec. 291(a)(4) read as follows:

(4) CERTAIN FSC INCOME.—In the case of taxable years beginning after December 31, 1984, section 923(a) shall be applied with respect to any FSC by substituting—

(A) "30 percent" for "32 percent" in paragraph (2), and

(B) "15/23" for "16/23" in paragraph (3).

If all of the stock in the FSC is not held by 1 or more C corporations throughout the taxable year, under regulations, proper adjustments shall be made in the application of the preceding sentence to take into account stock held by persons other than C corporations.

• 1986, Tax Reform Act of 1986 (P.L. 99-514)

P.L. 99-514, §201(d)(5)(A):

Amended Code Sec. 291(a)(1)(A) by striking out "or section 1245 recovery property". **Effective**, generally, for property placed in service after 12-31-86, in tax years ending after such date. See however, the special rules provided in Act Secs. 203-204 and 251(d) following Code Sec. 168. Prior to amendment, Code Sec. 291(a)(1)(A) read as follows:

(A) the amount which would be treated as ordinary income if such property was section 1245 property or section 1245 recovery property, over

P.L. 99-514, §412(b)(1):

Amended Code Sec. 291(a)(2) by striking out "15 percent" and inserting in lieu thereof "20 percent". **Effective** for tax years beginning after 12-31-86.

P.L. 99-514, §1804(k)(1):

Amended Code Sec. 291(a)(4) by striking out "a corporation" and inserting in lieu thereof "a C corporation". **Effective** as if included in the provision of P.L. 98-369 to which it relates.

P.L. 99-514, §1804(k)(3)(A):

Amended Code Sec. 291(a) by striking out "20-PERCENT" in the subsection heading. **Effective** as if included in the provision of P.L. 98-369 to which it relates. Prior to amendment, the subsection heading for Code Sec. 291(a) read as follows:

(a) 20-PERCENT REDUCTION IN CERTAIN PREFERENCE ITEMS, ETC.—* * *

P.L. 99-514, §1876(b)(1):

Amended Code Sec. 291(a)(4). **Effective** as if included in the provision of P.L. 98-369 to which it relates. Prior to amendment, Code Sec. 291(a)(4) read as follows:

(4) CERTAIN DEFERRED FSC INCOME.—If a C Corporation is a shareholder of the FSC, in the case of taxable years beginning after December 31, 1984, section 923(a) shall be applied with respect to such corporation by substituting—

(A) "30 percent" for "32 percent" in paragraph (2), and

(B) "15/23" for "16/23" in paragraph (3).

[Sec. 291(b)]

(b) SPECIAL RULES FOR TREATMENT OF INTANGIBLE DRILLING COSTS AND MINERAL EXPLORATION AND DEVELOPMENT COSTS.—For purposes of this subtitle, in the case of a corporation—

(1) IN GENERAL.—The amount allowable as a deduction for any taxable year (determined without regard to this section)—

(A) under section 263(c) in the case of an integrated oil company, or

(B) under section 616(a) or 617(a),

shall be reduced by 30 percent.

(2) AMORTIZATION OF AMOUNTS NOT ALLOWABLE AS DEDUCTIONS UNDER PARAGRAPH (1).—The amount not allowable as a deduction under section 263(c), 616(a), or 617(a) (as the case may be) for any taxable year by reason of paragraph (1) shall be allowable as a deduction ratably over the 60-month period beginning with the month in which the costs are paid or incurred.

(3) DISPOSITIONS.—For purposes of section 1254, any deduction under paragraph (2) shall be treated as a deduction allowable under section 263(c), 616(a), or 617(a) (whichever is appropriate).

(4) INTEGRATED OIL COMPANY DEFINED.—For purposes of this subsection, the term "integrated oil company" means, with respect to any taxable year, any producer of crude oil to whom subsection (c) of section 613A does not apply by reason of paragraph (2) or (4) of section 613A(d).

(5) COORDINATION WITH COST DEPLETION.—The portion of the adjusted basis of any property which is attributable to amounts to which paragraph (1) applied shall not be taken into account for purposes of determining depletion under section 611.

Amendments

• 1988, Omnibus Trade and Competitiveness Act of 1988 (P.L. 100-418)

P.L. 100-418, §1941(b)(5):

Amended Code Sec. 291(b)(4). **Effective** for crude oil removed from the premises on or after 8-23-88. Prior to amendment, Code Sec. 291(b)(4) read as follows:

(4) INTEGRATED OIL COMPANY DEFINED.—For purposes of this subsection, the term "integrated oil company" means, with respect to any taxable year, any producer (within the meaning of section 4996(a)(1)) of crude oil other than an independent producer (within the meaning of section 4992(b)).

• 1986, Tax Reform Act of 1986 (P.L. 99-514)

P.L. 99-514, §411(a)(1):

Amended Code Sec. 291(b)(1) by striking out "20 percent" and inserting in lieu thereof "30 percent". For the **effective** date, see P.L. 99-514, §411(c), below.

P.L. 99-514, §411(a)(2):

Amended Code Sec. 291(b) by striking out paragraphs (2), (3), (4), (5), and (6) and inserting in lieu thereof new paragraphs (2), (3), (4), and (5). For the **effective** date, see P.L. 99-514, §411(c), below. Prior to amendment, Code Sec. 291(b)(2)-(6) read as follows:

(2) SPECIAL RULE FOR AMOUNTS NOT ALLOWABLE AS DEDUCTIONS UNDER PARAGRAPH (1).—

(A) INTANGIBLE DRILLING COSTS.—The amount not allowable as a deduction under section 263(c) for any taxable year by reason of paragraph (1) shall be allowable as a deduction ratably over the 36-month period beginning with the month in which the costs are paid or incurred.

(B) MINERAL EXPLORATION AND DEVELOPMENT COSTS.—In the case of any amount not allowable as a deduction under section 616(a) or 617 for any taxable year by reason of paragraph (1)—

(i) the applicable percentage of the amount not so allowable as a deduction shall be allowable as a deduction for the taxable year in which the costs are paid or incurred and in each of the 4 succeeding taxable years, and

(ii) in the case of a deposit located in the United States, such costs shall be treated, for purposes of determining the amount of the credit allowable under section 38 for the taxable year in which paid or incurred, as qualified investment (within the meaning of subsections (c) and (d) of section 46) with respect to property placed in service during such year.

(3) APPLICABLE PERCENTAGE.—For purposes of paragraph (2)(B), the term "applicable percentage" means the percentage determined in accordance with the following table:

Taxable Year:	*Applicable Percentage:*
1	15
2	22
3	21
4	21
5	21

(4) DISPOSITIONS.—

(A) OIL, GAS, AND GEOTHERMAL PROPERTY.—In the case of any disposition of any oil, gas, or geothermal property to which section 1254 applies (determined without regard to this section) any deduction under paragraph (2)(A) with respect to intangible drilling and development costs under section 263(c) which are allocable to such property shall, for purposes of section 1254, be treated as a deduction allowable under section 263(c).

(B) APPLICATION OF SECTION 617(d).—In the case of any disposition of mining property to which section 617(d) applies (determined without regard to this section), any amount allowable as a deduction under paragraph (2)(B) which is allocable to such property shall, for purposes of section 617(d), be treated as a deduction allowable under section 617(a).

(C) RECAPTURE OF INVESTMENT CREDIT.—In the case of any disposition of any property to which the credit allowable under section 38 by reason of paragraph (2)(B) is allocable, such disposition shall, for purposes of section 47, be treated as a disposition of section 38 recovery property which is not 3-year property.

(5) INTEGRATED OIL COMPANY DEFINED.—For purposes of this subsection, the term "integrated oil company" means, with respect to any taxable year, any producer (within the meaning of section 4996(a)(1)) of crude oil other than an independent producer (within the meaning of section 4992(b)).

(6) COORDINATION WITH COST DEPLETION.—The portion of the adjusted basis of any property which is attributable to amounts to which paragraph (1) applied shall not be taken into account for purposes of determining depletion under section 611.

P.L. 99-514, §411(b)(2)(C)(ii):

Amended Code Sec. 291(b)(1)(B) by striking out "617" and inserting in lieu thereof "617(a)". For the **effective** date, see P.L. 99-514, §411(c), below.

P.L. 99-514, §411(c), provides:

(c) EFFECTIVE DATE.—

(1) IN GENERAL.—The amendments made by this section shall apply to costs paid or incurred after December 31, 1986, in taxable years ending after such date.

(2) TRANSITION RULE.—The amendments made by this section shall not apply with respect to intangible drilling and development costs incurred by United States companies pursuant to a minority interest in a license for Netherlands or United Kingdom North Sea development if such interest was acquired on or before December 31, 1985.

[Sec. 291(c)]

(c) SPECIAL RULES RELATING TO POLLUTION CONTROL FACILITIES.—For purposes of this subtitle—

(1) ACCELERATED COST RECOVERY DEDUCTION.—Section 168 shall apply with respect to that portion of the basis of any property not taken into account under section 169 by reason of subsection (a)(4).

(2) 1250 RECAPTURE.—Subsection (a)(1) shall not apply to any section 1250 property which is part of a certified pollution control facility (within the meaning of section 169(d)(1)) with respect to which an election under section 169 was made.

Amendments

• 2007, Tax Technical Corrections Act of 2007 (P.L. 110-172)

P.L. 110-172, §11(g)(6)(B):

Amended Code Sec. 291(c)(1) by striking "subsection (a)(5)" and inserting "subsection (a)(4)". **Effective** 12-29-2007.

• 1986, Tax Reform Act of 1986 (P.L. 99-514)

P.L. 99-514, §201(d)(5)(B):

Amended Code Sec. 291(c)(1). **Effective**, generally, for property placed in service after 12-31-86, in tax years ending after such date. See, however, the special rules provided in Act Secs. 203-204 and 251(d) following Code Sec. 168. Prior to amendment, Code Sec. 291(c)(1) read as follows:

(1) ACCELERATED COST RECOVERY DEDUCTION.—For purposes of subclause (I) of section 168(d)(1)(A)(ii), a taxpayer shall not be treated as electing the amortization deduction under section 169 with respect to that portion of the basis not taken into account under section 169 by reason of subsection (a)(5).

[Sec. 291(d)]

(d) SPECIAL RULE FOR REAL ESTATE INVESTMENT TRUSTS.—In the case of a real estate investment trust (as defined in section 856), the difference between the amounts described in subparagraphs (A) and (B) of subsection (a)(1) shall be reduced to the extent that a capital gain dividend (as defined in section 857(b)(3)(C), applied without regard to this section) is treated as paid out of such difference. Any capital gain dividend treated as having been paid out of such difference to a shareholder which is an applicable corporation retains its character in the hands of the shareholder as gain from the disposition of section 1250 property for purposes of applying subsection (a)(1) to such shareholder.

[Sec. 291(e)]

(e) DEFINITIONS.—For purposes of this section—

(1) FINANCIAL INSTITUTION PREFERENCE ITEM.—The term "financial institution preference item" includes the following:

(A) [Repealed.]

(B) INTEREST ON DEBT TO CARRY TAX-EXEMPT OBLIGATIONS ACQUIRED AFTER DECEMBER 31, 1982, AND BEFORE AUGUST 8, 1986.—

(i) IN GENERAL.—In the case of a financial institution which is a bank (as defined in section 585(a)(2)), the amount of interest on indebtedness incurred or continued to purchase or carry obligations acquired after December 31, 1982, and before August 8, 1986 the interest on which is exempt from taxes for the taxable year, to the extent that a deduction would (but for this paragraph or section 265(b)) be allowable with respect to such interest for such taxable year.

(ii) DETERMINATION OF INTEREST ALLOCABLE TO INDEBTEDNESS ON TAX-EXEMPT OBLIGATIONS.—Unless the taxpayer (under regulations prescribed by the Secretary) establishes otherwise, the amount determined under clause (i) shall be an amount which bears the same ratio to the aggregate amount allowable (determined without regard to this section and section 265(b)) to the taxpayer as a deduction for interest for the taxable year as—

(I) the taxpayer's average adjusted basis (within the meaning of section 1016) of obligations described in clause (i), bears to

(II) such average adjusted basis for all assets of the taxpayer.

(iii) INTEREST.—For purposes of this subparagraph, the term "interest" includes amounts (whether or not designated as interest) paid in respect of deposits, investment certificates, or withdrawable or repurchasable shares.

(iv) APPLICATION OF SUBPARAGRAPH TO CERTAIN OBLIGATIONS ISSUED AFTER AUGUST 7, 1986.—For application of this subparagraph to certain obligations issued after August 7, 1986, see section 265(b)(3). That portion of any obligation not taken into account under paragraph (2)(A) of section 265(b) by reason of paragraph (7) of such section shall be treated for purposes of this section as having been acquired on August 7, 1986.

(2) SECTION 1245 AND 1250 PROPERTY.—The terms "section 1245 property" and "section 1250 property" have the meanings given such terms by sections 1245(a)(3) and 1250(c), respectively.

Amendments

• 2009, American Recovery and Reinvestment Tax Act of 2009 (P.L. 111-5)

P.L. 111-5, §1501(b):

Amended Code Sec. 291(e)(1)(B)(iv) by adding at the end a new sentence. **Effective** for obligations issued after 12-31-2008.

• 1996, Small Business Job Protection Act of 1996 (P.L. 104-188)

P.L. 104-188, §1602(b)(1):

Amended Code Sec. 291(e)(1)(B) by striking clause (iv) and redesignating clause (v) as clause (iv). For the **effective** date, see P.L. 104-188, §1602(c)(1)-(3), below. Prior to amendment, Code Sec. 291(e)(1)(B)(iv) read as follows:

(iv) SPECIAL RULES FOR OBLIGATIONS TO WHICH SECTION 133 APPLIES.—In the case of an obligation to which section 133 applies, interest on such obligation shall not be treated as exempt from taxes for purposes of this subparagraph.

P.L. 104-188, §1602(c)(1)-(3), provides:

(c) EFFECTIVE DATE.—

(1) IN GENERAL.—The amendments made by this section shall apply to loans made after the date of the enactment of this Act.

(2) REFINANCINGS.—The amendments made by this section shall not apply to loans made after the date of the enactment of this Act to refinance securities acquisition loans (determined without regard to section 133(b)(1)(B) of the Internal Revenue Code of 1986, as in effect on the day before the date of the enactment of this Act) made on or before such date or to refinance loans described in this paragraph if—

(A) the refinancing loans meet the requirements of section 133 of such Code (as so in effect),

(B) immediately after the refinancing the principal amount of the loan resulting from the refinancing does not exceed the principal amount of the refinanced loan (immediately before the refinancing), and

(C) the term of such refinancing loan does not extend beyond the last day of the term of the original securities acquisition loan.

For purposes of this paragraph, the term "securities acquisition loan" includes a loan from a corporation to an employee stock ownership plan described in section 133(b)(3) of such Code (as so in effect).

(3) EXCEPTION.—Any loan made pursuant to a binding written contract in effect before June 10, 1996, and at all times thereafter before such loan is made, shall be treated for purposes of paragraphs (1) and (2) as a loan made on or before the date of the enactment of this Act.

P.L. 104-188, §1616(b)(5):

Amended Code Sec. 291(e)(1)(B)(i) by striking "or to which section 593 applies" after "585(a)(2))". **Effective** for tax years beginning after 12-31-95.

• 1990, Omnibus Budget Reconciliation Act of 1990 (P.L. 101-508)

P.L. 101-508, §11801(c)(12)(B):

Repealed Code Sec. 291(e)(1)(A). **Effective** 11-5-90. Prior to repeal, Code Sec. 291(e)(1)(A) read as follows:

(A) EXCESS RESERVES FOR LOSSES ON BAD DEBTS OF FINANCIAL INSTITUTIONS.—In the case of a financial institution to which section 585 applies, the excess of—

(i) the amount which would, but for this section, be allowable as a deduction for the taxable year for a reasonable addition to a reserve for bad debts, over

(ii) the amount which would have been allowable had such institution maintained its bad debt reserve for all taxable years on the basis of actual experience.

P.L. 101-508, §11821(b), provides:

(b) SAVINGS PROVISION.—If—

(1) any provision amended or repealed by this part applied to—

(A) any transaction occurring before the date of the enactment of this Act,

(B) any property acquired before such date of enactment, or

(C) any item of income, loss, deduction, or credit taken into account before such date of enactment, and

(2) the treatment of such transaction, property, or item under such provision would (without regard to the amendments made by this part) affect liability for tax for periods ending after such date of enactment,

nothing in the amendments made by this part shall be construed to affect the treatment of such transaction, property, or item for purposes of determining liability for tax for periods ending after such date of enactment.

• 1988, Technical and Miscellaneous Revenue Act of 1988 (P.L. 100-647)

P.L. 100-647, §1009(b)(4):

Amended Code Sec. 291(e)(1)(B) by redesignating the clause (iv) added by P.L. 99-514 as clause (v). **Effective** as if included in the provision of P.L. 99-514 to which it relates.

P.L. 100-647, §1009(b)(5):

Amended Code Sec. 291(e)(1)(B)(i) by striking out "section 582(a)(2)" and inserting in lieu thereof "section 585(a)(2)". **Effective** as if included in the provision of P.L. 99-514 to which it relates.

• 1986, Tax Reform Act of 1986 (P.L. 99-514)

P.L. 99-514, §201(d)(5)(C):

Amended Code Sec. 291(e)(2) by striking out ", `section 1245 recovery property'," and ", section 1245(a)(5),". **Effective**, generally, for property placed in service after 12-31-86, in tax years ending after such date. See, however, the special rules provided in Act Secs. 203-204 and 251(d) following Code Sec. 168.

P.L. 99-514, §901(b)(4):

Amended Code Sec. 291(e)(1)(A) by striking out "or 593". **Effective** for tax years beginning after 12-31-86. Prior to amendment Code Sec. 291(e)(1)(A) read as follows:

(A) EXCESS RESERVES FOR LOSSES ON BAD DEBTS OF FINANCIAL INSTITUTIONS.—In the case of a financial institution to which section 585 or 593 applies, the excess of—

(i) the amount which would, but for this section, be allowable as a deduction for the taxable year for a reasonable addition to a reserve for bad debts, over

(ii) the amount which would have been allowable had such institution maintained its bad debt reserve for all taxable years on the basis of actual experience.

P.L. 99-514, §901(d)(4)(C):

Amended Code Sec. 291(e)(1)(B) by striking out "to which section 585 or 593 applies" and inserting in lieu thereof "which is a bank (as defined in section 582(a)(2)) or to which section 593 applies". **Effective** for tax years beginning after 12-31-86.

P.L. 99-514, §902(c)(1):

Amended Code Sec. 291(e)(1)(B)(i) by striking out "after December 31, 1982" and inserting in lieu thereof "after

December 31, 1982, and before August 8, 1986". For the **effective** date, see P.L. 99-514, §902(f), below.

P.L. 99-514, §902(c)(2)(A):

Amended Code Sec. 291(e)(1)(B)(i) by striking out "(but for this paragraph)" and inserting in lieu thereof "(but for this paragraph or section 265(b))". For the **effective** date, see P.L. 99-514, §902(f), below.

P.L. 99-514, §902(c)(2)(B):

Amended Code Sec. 291(e)(1)(B)(ii) by striking out "without regard to this section" and inserting in lieu thereof "without regard to this section and section 265(b)". For the **effective** date, see P.L. 99-514, §902(f), below.

P.L. 99-514, §902(c)(2)(C):

Amended Code Sec. 291(e)(1)(B) by striking out "AFTER DECEMBER 31, 1982" in the subparagraph heading and inserting in lieu thereof "AFTER DECEMBER 31, 1982, AND BEFORE AUGUST 8, 1986". For the **effective** date, see P.L. 99-514, §902(f), below.

P.L. 99-514, §902(c)(2)(D):

Amended Code Sec. 291(e)(1)(B) by adding new clause (iv)[v]. For the **effective** date, see P.L. 99-514, §902(f), below.

P.L. 99-514, §902(f), as amended by P.L. 100-647, §1009(b), provides:

(f) EFFECTIVE DATE.—

(1) IN GENERAL.—Except as provided in this subsection, the amendments made by this section shall apply to taxable years ending after December 31, 1986.

(2) OBLIGATIONS ACQUIRED PURSUANT TO CERTAIN COMMITMENTS.—For purposes of sections 265(b) and 291(e)(1)(B) of the Internal Revenue Code of 1986, any tax-exempt obligation which is acquired after August 7, 1986, pursuant to a direct or indirect written commitment—

(A) to purchase or repurchase such obligation, and

(B) entered into on or before September 25, 1985,

shall be treated as an obligation acquired before August 8, 1986.

(3) TRANSITIONAL RULES.—For purposes of sections 265(b) and 291(e)(1)(B) of the Internal Revenue Code of 1986, obligations with respect to any of the following projects shall be treated as obligations acquired before August 8, 1986, in the hands of the first and any subsequent financial institution acquiring such obligations:

(A) Park Forest, Illinois, redevelopment project.

(B) Clinton, Tennessee, Carriage Trace project.

(C) Savannah, Georgia, Mall Terrace Warehouse project.

(D) Chattanooga, Tennessee, Warehouse Row project.

(E) Dalton, Georgia, Towne Square project.

(F) Milwaukee, Wisconsin, Standard Electric Supply Company—distribution facility.

(G) Wausau, Wisconsin, urban renewal project.

(H) Cassville, Missouri, UDAG project.

(I) Outlook Envelope Company—plant expansion.

(J) Woodstock, Connecticut, Crabtree Warehouse partnership.

(K) Louisville, Kentucky, Speed Mansion renovation project.

(L) Charleston, South Carolina, 2 Festival Market Place projects at Union Pier Terminal and 1 project at the Lemont Road Container Yard, State Pier No. 15 at North Charleston Terminal.

(M) New Orleans, Louisiana, Upper Pontalba Building renovation.

(N) Woodward Wight Building.

(O) Minneapolis, Minnesota, Miller Milling Company—flour mill project.

(P) Homewood, Alabama, the Club Apartments.

(Q) Charlotte, North Carolina—qualified mortgage bonds acquired by NCNB bank ($5,250,000).

(R) Grand Rapids, Michigan, Central Bank project.

(S) Ruppman Marketing Services, Inc.—building project.

(T) Bellows Falls, Vermont—building project.

(U) East Broadway Project, Louisville, Kentucky.

(V) O.K. Industries, Oklahoma.

(4) ADDITIONAL TRANSITIONAL RULE.—Obligations issued pursuant to an allocation of a State's volume limitation for private activity bonds, which allocation was made by Executive Order 25 signed by the Governor of the State on May 22, 1986 (as such order may be amended before January 1, 1987), and qualified 501(c)(3) bonds designated by such Governor for purposes of this paragraph shall be treated as acquired on or before August 7, 1986, in the hands of the first and any subsequent financial institution acquiring such obligation. The aggregate face amount of obligations to which this paragraph applies shall not exceed $200,000,000.

P.L. 99-514, §1854(c)(1):

Amended Code Sec. 291(e)(1)(B) by adding at the end thereof new clause (iv). **Effective** as if included in the provision of P.L. 98-369 to which it relates.

• 1984, Deficit Reduction Act of 1984 (P.L. 98-369)

P.L. 98-369, §68(a):

Amended Code Sec. 291 by striking out "15 percent" each place it appeared other than in subsection (a)(2) and inserting in lieu thereof "20 percent". For the **effective** date, see P.L. 98-369, §68(e), below.

P.L. 98-369, §68(b):

Amended Code Sec. 291(a)(4). **Effective** for tax years beginning after 12-31-84. Prior to amendment, Code Sec. 291(a)(4) read as follows:

(4) Certain Deferred Disc Income.—If a corporation is a shareholder of a DISC, in the case of taxable years beginning after December 31, 1982, section 995(b)(1)(F)(i) shall be applied with respect to such corporation by substituting "57.5 percent" for "one-half".

P.L. 98-369, §68(e), as amended by P.L. 99-514, §1804(k)(2), provides:

(e) EFFECTIVE DATES.—

(1) IN GENERAL.—Except as provided in this subsection, the amendments made by this section shall apply to taxable years beginning after December 31, 1984.

(2) 1250 GAIN.—The amendments made by this section to section 291(a)(1) of the Internal Revenue Code of 1954, and the amendment made by subsection (c)(2) of this section,shall apply to sales or other dispositions after December 31, 1984, in taxable years ending after such date.

(3) POLLUTION CONTROL FACILITIES.—The amendments made by this section to section 291(a)(5) of such Code, and so much of the amendment made by subsection (c)(1) of this section as relates to pollution control facilities, shall apply to property placed in service after December 31, 1984, in taxable years ending after such date.

(4) DRILLING AND MINING COSTS.—The amendments made by this section to section 291(b) of such Code shall apply to expenditures after December 31, 1984, in taxable years ending after such date.

P.L. 98-369, §712(a)(1)(A):

Amended Code Sec. 291(a)(1) by striking out "under section 1250" in subparagraph (B) and inserting in lieu thereof "under section 1250 (determined without regard to this paragraph)" and by striking out "which is ordinary income" and inserting in lieu thereof "which is ordinary income under section 1250". **Effective** as if included in the provision of P.L. 97-248 to which it relates.

P.L. 98-369, §712(a)(2):

Amended Code Sec. 291(b)(2)(B)(ii) by inserting "in the case of a deposit located in the United States," after "(ii)". **Effective** as if included in the provision of P.L. 97-248 to which it relates.

P.L. 98-369, §712(a)(3):

Amended Code Sec. 291 (b)(6). **Effective** as if included in the provision of P.L. 97-248 to which it relates. Prior to amendment, Code Sec. 291(b)(6) read as follows:

(6) Coordination with Cost Depletion.—The portion of the adjusted basis of any property which is attributable to intangible drilling and development costs or mining exploration and development costs shall not be taken into account for purposes of determining depletion under section 611.

P.L. 98-369, §712(a)(4):

Amended Code Sec. 291(e)(1)(B) by adding at the end thereof a new clause (iii). **Effective** as if included in the provision of P.L. 97-248 to which it relates.

• 1983, Technical Corrections Act of 1982 (P.L. 97-448)

P.L. 97-448, §306(a)(2):

Amended Code Sec. 291(a)(1) by adding the last sentence. **Effective** as if it had been included in the provision of P.L. 97-248 to which it relates.

• 1982, Subchapter S Revision Act of 1982 (P.L. 97-354)

P.L. 97-354, §5(a)(27)(A):

Amended Code Sec. 291(a) and (b) by striking out "an applicable corporation" each place it appeared and inserting in lieu thereof "a corporation". **Effective** for tax years beginning after 12-31-82.

P.L. 97-354, §5(a)(27)(B):

Amended Code Sec. 291(e) by striking out paragraph (2) and by redesignating paragraph (3) as paragraph (2). **Effective** for tax years beginning after 12-31-82. Prior to amendment, paragraph (2) read as follows:

"(2) APPLICABLE CORPORATION.—For purposes of this section, the term `applicable corporation' means any corporation other than an electing small business corporation (as defined in section 1371(b))."

• 1982, Tax Equity and Fiscal Responsibility Act of 1982 (P.L. 97-248)

P.L. 97-248, §204(a):

Added Code Sec. 291. **Effective**, generally, for tax years beginning after 12-31-82. However, special **effective** dates are as follows: (1) Code Sec. 291(a)(1) applies to sales or other dispositions after 1982 in tax years ending after 1982; (2) Code Sec. 291(a)(2) applies to tax years beginning after 1983; (3) Code Sec. 291(a)(5) applies to property placed in service after 1982 in tax years ending after 1982; and (4) Code Sec. 291(b) applies to expenditures after 1982 in tax years ending after 1982.

Subchapter C—Corporate Distributions and Adjustments

PART I—DISTRIBUTIONS BY CORPORATIONS

Subpart A—Effects on Recipients

[Sec. 301]

SEC. 301. DISTRIBUTIONS OF PROPERTY.

[Sec. 301(a)]

(a) IN GENERAL.—Except as otherwise provided in this chapter, a distribution of property (as defined in section 317(a)) made by a corporation to a shareholder with respect to its stock shall be treated in the manner provided in subsection (c).

[Sec. 301(b)]

(b) AMOUNT DISTRIBUTED.—

(1) GENERAL RULE.—For purposes of this section, the amount of any distribution shall be the amount of money received, plus the fair market value of the other property received.

(2) REDUCTION FOR LIABILITIES.—The amount of any distribution determined under paragraph (1) shall be reduced (but not below zero) by—

(A) the amount of any liability of the corporation assumed by the shareholder in connection with the distribution, and

(B) the amount of any liability to which the property received by the shareholder is subject immediately before, and immediately after, the distribution.

(3) DETERMINATION OF FAIR MARKET VALUE.—For purposes of this section, fair market value shall be determined as of the date of the distribution.

Amendments

• 1988, Technical and Miscellaneous Revenue Act of 1988 (P.L. 100-647)

P.L. 100-647, §1006(e)(10):

Amended Code Sec. 301(b)(1). **Effective** as if included in the provision of P.L. 99-514 to which it relates. Prior to amendment, Code Sec. 301(b)(1) read as follows:

(1) GENERAL RULE.—For purposes of this section, the amount of any distribution shall be—

(A) NONCORPORATE DISTRIBUTEES.—If the shareholder is not a corporation, the amount of money received, plus the fair market value of the other property received.

(B) CORPORATE DISTRIBUTEES.—If the shareholder is a corporation, unless subparagraph (D) applies, the amount of money received, plus whichever of the following is the lesser:

(i) the fair market value of the other property received; or

(ii) the adjusted basis (in the hands of the distributing corporation immediately before the distribution) of the other property reveived, increased in the amount of gain recognized to the distributing corporation on the distribution.

(C) CERTAIN CORPORATE DISTRIBUTEES OF FOREIGN CORPORATION.—Notwithstanding subparagraph (B), if the shareholder is a corporation and the distributing corporation is a foreign corporation, the amount taken into account with respect to property (other than money) shall be the fair market value of such property; except that if any deduction is allowable under section 245 with respect to such distribution, then the amount taken into account shall be the sum (determined under regulations prescribed by the Secretary) of—

(i) the proportion of the adjusted basis of such property (or, if lower, its fair market value) properly attributable to gross income which is effectively connected with the conduct of a trade or business within the United States, and

(ii) the proportion of the fair market value of such property properly attributable to gross income which is not effectively connected with the conduct of a trade or business within the United States.

For purposes of clause (i), the gross income of a foreign corporation for any period before its first taxable year beginning after December 31, 1966, which is effectively connected with the conduct of a trade or business within the United States is an amount equal to the gross income for such period from sources within the United States. For purposes of clause (ii), the gross income of a foreign corporation for any period before its first taxable year beginning after December 31, 1966, which is not effectively connected with the conduct of a trade or business within the United States is an amount equal to the gross income for such period from sources without the United States.

(D) FOREIGN CORPORATE DISTRIBUTEES.—In the case of a distribution to a shareholder which is a foreign corporation, if the amount received by the foreign corporation is not effectively connected with the conduct by it of a trade or business within the United States, the amount of the money received, plus the fair market value of the other property received.

• 1978 (P.L. 95-628)

P.L. 95-628, §3(a), (d):

Amended Code Sec. 301(b)(1)(B)(ii). **Effective** for distributions made after 11-10-78. Before amendment, Code Sec. 301(b)(1)(B)(ii) read as follows:

"(ii) the adjusted basis (in the hands of the distributing corporation immediately before the distribution) of the other property received, increased in the amount of gain to the distributing corporation which is recognized under subsection (b), (c), or (d) of section 311, under section 341(f), or under section 617(d)(1), 1245(a), 1250(a), 1251(c), 1252(a), or 1254(a)."

• 1976, Tax Reform Act of 1976 (P.L. 94-455)

P.L. 94-455, §205(c)(1)(B):

Substituted "1252(a), or 1254(a)" for "or 1252(a)" in Code Sec. 301(b)(1)(B)(ii). **Effective** for tax years ending after 12-31-75.

P.L. 94-455, §1906(b)(13)(A):

Amended 1954 Code by substituting "Secretary" for "Secretary or his delegate" each place it appeared. **Effective** 2-1-77.

• 1971, Revenue Act of 1971 (P.L. 92-178)

P.L. 92-178, §312(a)(1), (2):

Amended Code Sec. 301(b) by adding ", unless subparagraph (D) applies," in subparagraph (1)(B) and by adding subparagraph (D) to paragraph (1). **Effective** for distributions made after 11-8-71.

• 1969, Tax Reform Act of 1969 (P.L. 91-172)

P.L. 91-172, §211(b):

Amended Code Sec. 301(b)(1)(B)(ii) by striking out "or 1250(a)" and inserting "1250(a), 1251(c), or 1252(a)". **Effective** for tax years beginning after 12-31-69.

P.L. 91-172, §905(b)(2):

Amended Code Sec. 301(b)(1)(B)(ii) by changing "subsection (b) or (c)" to "subsection (b), (c), or (d)". **Effective** 12-1-69.

• 1966, Foreign Investors Tax Act of 1966 (P.L. 89-809)

P.L. 89-809, §104(f):

Amended Code Sec. 301(b)(1)(C) by substituting "gross income which is effectively connected with the conduct of a trade or business within the United States" for "gross income from sources within the United States" in clause (i); by substituting "gross income which is not effectively connected with the conduct of a trade or business within the United States" for "gross income from sources without the United States" in clause (ii); and by adding the last two sentences. **Effective** 1-1-67.

• 1966 (P.L. 89-570)

P.L. 89-570, §[1(b)]:

Amended Code Sec. 301(b)(1)(B)(ii) by substituting "section 617(d)(1), 1245(a)," for "section 1245(a)". **Effective** for tax years ending after 9-12-66, the date of enactment, but only for expenditures paid or incurred after that date.

• 1964 (P.L. 88-484)

P.L. 88-484, §[1(b)]:

Amended Code Sec. 301(b) by inserting ", under section 341(f)," immediately after "section 311". **Effective** for transactions after 8-22-64, in tax years ending after such date.

• 1964, Revenue Act of 1964 (P.L. 88-272)

P.L. 88-272, §231(b)(2):

Amended Code Sec. 301(b) to add "or 1250(a)" at end of subparagraph (1)(B)(ii). **Effective** for dispositions after 12-31-63 in tax years ending after such date.

• 1962, Revenue Act of 1962 (P.L. 87-834)

P.L. 87-834, §5:

Added to Code Sec. 301(b)(1) a new subparagraph (C). **Effective** for distributions made after 12-31-62.

P.L. 87-834, §13(f)(2):

Amended Code Sec. 301(b)(1)(B)(ii) by inserting "or under section 1245(a)" immediately before the period. **Effective** for tax years beginning after 12-31-62.

[Sec. 301(c)]

(c) AMOUNT TAXABLE.—In the case of a distribution to which subsection (a) applies—

(1) AMOUNT CONSTITUTING DIVIDEND.—That portion of the distribution which is a dividend (as defined in section 316) shall be included in gross income.

(2) AMOUNT APPLIED AGAINST BASIS.—That portion of the distribution which is not a dividend shall be applied against and reduce the adjusted basis of the stock.

(3) AMOUNT IN EXCESS OF BASIS.—

(A) IN GENERAL.—Except as provided in subparagraph (B), that portion of the distribution which is not a dividend, to the extent that it exceeds the adjusted basis of the stock, shall be treated as gain from the sale or exchange of property.

(B) DISTRIBUTIONS OUT OF INCREASE IN VALUE ACCRUED BEFORE MARCH 1, 1913.—That portion of the distribution which is not a dividend, to the extent that it exceeds the adjusted basis of the stock and to the extent that it is out of increase in value accrued before March 1, 1913, shall be exempt from tax.

[Sec. 301(d)]

(d) BASIS.—The basis of property received in a distribution to which subsection (a) applies shall be the fair market value of such property.

Amendments

• 1988, Technical and Miscellaneous Revenue Act of 1988 (P.L. 100-647)

P.L. 100-647, §1006(e)(11):

Amended Code Sec. 301(d). **Effective** as if included in the provision of P.L. 99-514 to which it relates. Prior to amendment, Code Sec. 301(d) read as follows:

(d) BASIS.—The basis of property received in a distribution to which subsection (a) applies shall be—

(1) NONCORPORATE DISTRIBUTEES.—If the shareholder is not a corporation, the fair market value of such property.

(2) CORPORATE DISTRIBUTEES.—If the shareholder is a corporation, unless paragraph (3) applies, whichever of the following is the lesser:

(A) the fair market value of such property; or

(B) the adjusted basis (in the hands of the distributing corporation immediately before the distribution) of such property, increased in the amount of gain recognized to the distributing corporation on the distribution.

(3) FOREIGN CORPORATE DISTRIBUTEES.—In the case of a distribution of property to a shareholder which is a foreign corporation, if the amount received by the foreign corporation is not effectively connected with the conduct by it of a trade or business within the United States, the fair market value of the property received.

(4) CERTAIN CORPORATE DISTRIBUTEES OF FOREIGN CORPORATION.—In the case of property described in subparagraph (C) of subsection (b)(1), the basis shall be determined by substituting the amount determined under such subparagraph (C) for the amount described in paragraph (2) of this subsection.

• 1978 (P.L. 95-628)

P.L. 95-628, §3(b), (d):

Amended Code Sec. 301(d)(2)(B). **Effective** for distributions made after 11-10-78. Before amendment, Code Sec. 301(d)(2)(B) read:

"(B) the adjusted basis (in the hands of the distributing corporation immediately before the distribution) of such property, increased in the amount of gain to the distributing corporation which is recognized under subsection (b), (c), or (d) of section 311, under section 341(f), or under section 617(d)(1), 1245(a), 1250(a), 1251(c), 1252(a), or 1254(a)."

• 1976, Tax Reform Act of 1976 (P.L. 94-455)

P.L. 94-455, §205(c)(1)(C):

Substituted "1252(a), or 1254(a)" for "or 1252(a)" in Code Sec. 301(d)(2)(B). **Effective** for tax years ending after 12-31-75.

• 1971, Revenue Act of 1971 (P.L. 92-178)

P.L. 92-178, §312(a)(3), (4):

Amended Code Sec. 301(d) by adding ", unless paragraph (3) applies," in paragraph (2), adding new paragraph (3), and renumbering former paragraph (3) as paragraph (4). **Effective** for distributions made after 11-8-71.

• 1969, Tax Reform Act of 1969 (P.L. 91-172)

P.L. 91-172, §211(b):

Amended Code Sec. 301(d)(2)(B) by striking out "or 1250(a)" and inserting "1250(a), 1251(c), or 1252(a)". **Effective** for tax years beginning after 12-31-69.

P.L. 91-172, §905(b)(2):

Amended Code Sec. 301(d)(2)(B) by changing "subsection (b) or (c)" to "subsection (b), (c), or (d)". **Effective** 12-1-69.

• 1966 (P.L. 89-570)

P.L. 89-570, §[1(b)]:

Amended Code Sec. 301(d)(2)(B) by substituting "section 617(d)(1), 1245(a)," for "section 1245(a)". **Effective** for tax years ending after 9-12-66, the date of enactment, but only for expenditures paid or incurred after that date.

• 1964 (P.L. 88-484)

P.L. 88-484, §[1(b)]:

Amended Code Sec. 301(d) by inserting ", under section 341(f)," immediately after "section 311". **Effective** for transactions after 8-22-64, in tax years ending after such date.

• 1964, Revenue Act of 1964 (P.L. 88-272)

P.L. 88-272, §231(b)(2):

Amended Code Sec. 301(d) by adding "or 1250(a)" at end of subparagraph (2)(B). **Effective** for dispositions after 12-31-63, in tax years ending after such date.

• 1962, Revenue Act of 1962 (P.L. 87-834)

P.L. 87-834, §5:

Added to Code Sec. 301(d) a new paragraph (3). **Effective** for distributions made after 12-31-62.

P.L. 87-834, §13(f)(2):

Amended Code Sec. 301(d)(2)(B) by inserting "or under section 1245(a)" immediately before the period. **Effective** for tax years beginning after 12-31-62.

[Sec. 301(e)]

(e) SPECIAL RULE FOR CERTAIN DISTRIBUTIONS RECEIVED BY 20 PERCENT CORPORATE SHAREHOLDER.—

(1) IN GENERAL.—Except to the extent otherwise provided in regulations, solely for purposes of determining the taxable income of any 20 percent corporate shareholder (and its adjusted basis in the stock of the distributing corporation), section 312 shall be applied with respect to the distributing corporation as if it did not contain subsections (k) and (n) thereof.

(2) 20 PERCENT CORPORATE SHAREHOLDER.—For purposes of this subsection, the term "20 percent corporate shareholder" means, with respect to any distribution, any corporation which owns (directly or through the application of section 318)—

(A) stock in the corporation making the distribution possessing at least 20 percent of the total combined voting power of all classes of stock entitled to vote, or

(B) at least 20 percent of the total value of all stock of the distributing corporation (except nonvoting stock which is limited and preferred as to dividends), but only if, but for this subsection, the distributee corporation would be entitled to a deduction under section 243, 244, or 245 with respect to such distribution.

(3) APPLICATION OF SECTION 312(n)(7) NOT AFFECTED.—The reference in paragraph (1) to subsection (n) of section 312 shall be treated as not including a reference to paragraph (7) of such subsection.

(4) REGULATIONS.—The Secretary shall prescribe such regulations as may be necessary or appropriate to carry out the purposes of this subsection.

Amendments

• 1988, Technical and Miscellaneous Revenue Act of 1988 (P.L. 100-647)

P.L. 100-647, §1006(e)(12):

Amended Code Sec. 301 by striking out subsection (e) and by redesignating subsections (f) and (g) as subsections (e) and (f), respectively. **Effective** as if included in the provision of P.L. 99-514 to which it relates. Prior to amendment, Code Sec. 301(e) read as follows:

(e) SPECIAL RULE FOR HOLDING PERIOD OF APPRECIATED PROPERTY DISTRIBUTED TO CORPORATION.—For purposes of this subtitle—

(1) WHERE GAIN RECOGNIZED UNDER SECTION 311(d).—If—

(A) property is distributed to a corporation, and

(B) gain is recognized on such distribution under paragraph (1) of section 311(d),

then such corporation's holding period in the distributed property shall begin on the date of such distribution.

(2) WHERE GAIN NOT RECOGNIZED UNDER SECTION 311(d).—If—

(A) property is distributed to a corporation,

(B) gain is not recognized on such distribution under paragraph (1) of section 311(d), and

(C) the basis of such property in the hands of such corporation is determined under subsection (d)(2)(B),

then (except for purposes of section 1248) such corporation shall not be treated as holding the distributed property during any period before the date on which such corporation's holding period in the stock began.

P.L. 100-647, §2004(j)(3)(B):

Amended Code Sec. 301(e) by redesignating paragraph (3) as paragraph (4) and by inserting after paragraph (2) a new paragraph (3). **Effective** as if included in the provision of P.L. 100-203 to which it relates.

• 1987, Revenue Act of 1987 (P.L. 100-203)

P.L. 100-203, §10222(b)(1):

Amended Code Sec. 301(f)(1) by striking out "subsection (n) thereof" and inserting in lieu thereof "subsections (k) and (n) thereof". For the **effective** date, see P.L. 100-203, §10222(b)(2), below.

P.L. 100-203, §10222(b)(2), provides:

(2) EFFECTIVE DATES.—

(A) IN GENERAL.—The amendment made by paragraph (1) shall apply to distributions after December 15, 1987. For purposes of applying such amendment to any such distribution—

(i) for purposes of determining earnings and profits, such amendment shall be deemed to be in effect for all periods whether before, on, or after December 15, 1987, but

(ii) such amendment shall not affect the determination of whether any distribution on or before December 15, 1987, is a dividend and the amount of any reduction in accumulated earnings and profits on account of any such distribution.

(B) EXCEPTION.—The amendment made by paragraph (1) shall not apply for purposes of determining gain or loss on any disposition of stock after December 15, 1987, and before January 1, 1989, if such disposition is pursuant to a written binding contract, governmental order, letter of intent or preliminary agreement, or stock acquisition agreement, in effect on or before December 15, 1987.

• 1986, Tax Reform Act of 1986 (P.L. 99-514)

P.L. 99-514, §1804(f)(2)(B):

Amended Code Sec. 301(f)(3) by striking out "this section" and inserting in lieu thereof "this subsection". **Effective** as if included in the provision of P.L. 98-369 to which it relates.

• 1984, Deficit Reduction Act of 1984 (P.L. 98-369)

P.L. 98-369, §54(b):

Redesignated subsection (e) as subsection (f) and inserted new subsection (e). **Effective** for distributions after 7-18-84, in tax years ending after such date.

P.L. 98-369, §61(d):

Redesignated section (f), as redesignated by Act Sec. 54(b), as section (g) and inserted new section (f). **Effective** for distributions after 7-18-84, in tax years ending after such date.

[Sec. 301(f)]

(f) SPECIAL RULES.—

(1) For distributions in redemption of stock, see section 302.

(2) For distributions in complete liquidation, see part II (sec. 331 and following).

(3) For distributions in corporate organizations and reorganizations, see part III (sec. 351 and following).

»»→ Caution: Code Sec. 301(f)(4), below, is subject to the sunset provision of the Jobs and Growth Tax Relief Reconciliation Act of 2003 (P.L. 108-27), §303. Absent Congressional action, the changes made to this provision by P.L. 108-27, or that take effect as if included in P.L. 108-27, do not apply after December 31, 2010. For more information about the sunset provision, see page XXI of the Preface to this publication and P.L. 108-27, §303, in the amendment notes. See the amendments notes for a history of amendments to this section and the effective date of each change.

(4) For taxation of dividends received by individuals at capital gain rates, see section 1(h)(11).

Amendments

• 2003, Jobs and Growth Tax Relief Reconciliation Act of 2003 (P.L. 108-27)

P.L. 108-27, §302(e)(2):

Amended Code Sec. 301(f) by adding at the end a new paragraph (4). For the **effective** date, see Act Sec. 302(f), as amended by P.L. 108-311, §402(a)(6), below.

P.L. 108-27, §302(f), as amended by P.L. 108-311, §402(a)(6), provides:

(f) EFFECTIVE DATE.—

(1) IN GENERAL.—Except as provided in paragraph (2), the amendments made by this section shall apply to taxable years beginning after December 31, 2002.

(2) PASS-THRU ENTITIES.—In the case of a pass-thru entity described in subparagraph (A), (B), (C), (D), (E), or (F) of section 1(h)(10) of the Internal Revenue Code of 1986, as amended by this Act, the amendments made by this section shall apply to taxable years ending after December 31, 2002; except that dividends received by such an entity on or before such date shall not be treated as qualified dividend

income (as defined in section 1(h)(11)(B) of such Code, as added by this Act).

P.L. 108-27, §303, as amended by P.L. 109-222, §102, provides:

SEC. 303. SUNSET OF TITLE.

All provisions of, and amendments made by, this title shall not apply to taxable years beginning after December 31, 2010, and the Internal Revenue Code of 1986 shall be applied and administered to such years as if such provisions and amendments had never been enacted.

• 1988, Technical and Miscellaneous Revenue Act of 1988 (P.L. 100-647)

P.L. 100-647, §1006(e)(12):

Redesignated subsection (g) as subsection (f). **Effective** as if included in the provision of P.L. 99-514 to which it relates.

• 1986, Tax Reform Act of 1986 (P.L. 99-514)

P.L. 99-514, §612(b)(1):

Amended Code Sec. 301(g) by striking out paragraph (4). **Effective** for tax years beginning after 12-31-86. Prior to amendment, Code Sec. 301(g)(4) read as follows:

(4) For partial exclusion from gross income of dividends received by individuals, see section 116.

• 1984, Deficit Reduction Act of 1984 (P.L. 98-369)

P.L. 98-369, §54(b):

Redesignated subsection (e) as subsection (f). **Effective** for distributions after 7-18-84, in tax years ending after such date.

P.L. 98-369, §61(d):

Redesignated subsection (f) as subsection (g). **Effective** for distributions after 7-18-84, in tax years ending after such date.

P.L. 98-369, §712(i)(1):

Amended Code Sec. 301(e)(2), prior to its redesignations by Act Secs. 54(d) and 61(d), by striking out "partial or complete liquidation" and inserting in lieu thereof "complete liquidation." **Effective** as if included in the provision of P.L. 97-248 to which it relates.

• 1976, Tax Reform Act of 1976 (P.L. 94-455)

P.L. 94-455, §1901(a)(41):

Repealed former Code Sec. 301(e). **Effective** for tax years beginning after 12-31-76. Prior to repeal, Code Sec. 301(e) read as follows:

(e) EXCEPTION FOR CERTAIN DISTRIBUTIONS BY PERSONAL SERVICE CORPORATIONS.—Any distribution made by a corporation, which was classified as a personal service corporation under the provisions of the Revenue Act of 1918 or the Revenue Act of 1921, out of its earnings or profits which were taxable in accordance with the provisions of section 218 of the Revenue Act of 1918 (40 Stat. 1070), or section 218 of the Revenue Act of 1921 (42 Stat. 245), shall be exempt from tax to the distributees.

P.L. 94-455, §1901(b)(32)(A):

Repealed former Code Sec. 301(f). **Effective** for tax years beginning after 12-31-76. Prior to repeal, Code Sec. 301(f) read as follows:

(f) SPECIAL RULES FOR DISTRIBUTIONS OF ANTITRUST STOCK TO CORPORATIONS.

(1) DEFINITION OF ANTITRUST STOCK.—For purposes of this subsection, the term "antitrust stock" means stock received, by a corporation which is a party to a suit described in section 1111(d) (relating to definition of antitrust order), in a distribution made after September 6, 1961, either pursuant to the terms of, or in anticipation of, an antitrust order (as defined in subsection (d) of section 1111).

(2) AMOUNT DISTRIBUTED.—Notwithstanding subsection (b)(1) (but subject to subsection (b)(2)), for purposes of this section the amount of a distribution of antitrust stock received by a corporation shall be the fair market value of such stock.

(3) BASIS.—Notwithstanding subsection (d), the basis of antitrust stock received by a corporation in a distribution to which subsection (a) applies shall be the fair market value of such stock decreased by so much of the deduction for dividends received under the provisions of section 243, 244, or 245 as is, under the regulations prescribed by the Secretary or his delegate, attributable to the excess, if any, of—

(A) the fair market value of the stock, over

(B) the adjusted basis (in the hands of the distributing corporation immediately before the distribution) of the stock, increased by the amount of gain which is recognized to the distributing corporation by reason of the distribution.

• 1962 (P.L. 87-403)

P.L. 87-403, §2(a):

Redesignated former Code Sec. 301(f) (now Code Sec. 301(e)) as Code Sec. 301(g) and added a new Code Sec. 301(f). **Effective** for distributions made after 2-2-62.

[Sec. 302]

SEC. 302. DISTRIBUTIONS IN REDEMPTION OF STOCK.

[Sec. 302(a)]

(a) GENERAL RULE.—If a corporation redeems its stock (within the meaning of section 317(b)), and if paragraph (1), (2), (3), or (4) of subsection (b) applies, such redemption shall be treated as a distribution in part or full payment in exchange for the stock.

Amendments

• 1982, Tax Equity and Fiscal Responsibility Act of 1982 (P.L. 97-248)

P.L. 97-248, §222(c)(3):

Amended Code Sec. 302(a) by striking out "paragraph (1), (2), or (3)" and inserting "paragraph (1), (2), (3), or (4)". **Effective**, generally, for distributions after 8-31-82. See exceptions provided in P.L. 97-248, §222(f), in the amendment notes for Code Sec. 331(b).

• 1980, Bankruptcy Tax Act of 1980 (P.L. 96-589)

P.L. 96-589, §5(b)(2)(A):

Amended Code Sec. 302(a) by striking out "(2), (3), or (4)" and inserting in lieu thereof "(2), or (3)". **Effective** for redemption of stock issued after 12-31-80 (other than stock issued pursuant to a plan of reorganization approved on or before that date). Also, the amendment will apply to a bankruptcy or similar case commenced on or after 10-1-79 (but prior to 1-1-81) if the special effective date election is made. See the historical comment for P.L. 96-589 under Code Sec. 108(e) for the details of the election.

[Sec. 302(b)]

(b) REDEMPTIONS TREATED AS EXCHANGES.—

(1) REDEMPTIONS NOT EQUIVALENT TO DIVIDENDS.—Subsection (a) shall apply if the redemption is not essentially equivalent to a dividend.

(2) SUBSTANTIALLY DISPROPORTIONATE REDEMPTION OF STOCK.—

(A) IN GENERAL.—Subsection (a) shall apply if the distribution is substantially disproportionate with respect to the shareholder.

(B) LIMITATION.—This paragraph shall not apply unless immediately after the redemption the shareholder owns less than 50 percent of the total combined voting power of all classes of stock entitled to vote.

(C) DEFINITIONS.—For purposes of this paragraph, the distribution is substantially disproportionate if—

(i) the ratio which the voting stock of the corporation owned by the shareholder immediately after the redemption bears to all of the voting stock of the corporation at such time,

is less than 80 percent of—

(ii) the ratio which the voting stock of the corporation owned by the shareholder immediately before the redemption bears to all of the voting stock of the corporation at such time.

For purposes of this paragraph, no distribution shall be treated as substantially disproportionate unless the shareholder's ownership of the common stock of the corporation (whether voting or nonvoting) after and before redemption also meets the 80 percent requirement of the preceding sentence. For purposes of the preceding sentence, if there is more than one class of common stock, the determinations shall be made by reference to fair market value.

(D) SERIES OF REDEMPTIONS.—This paragraph shall not apply to any redemption made pursuant to a plan the purpose or effect of which is a series of redemptions resulting in a distribution which (in the aggregate) is not substantially disproportionate with respect to the shareholder.

(3) TERMINATION OF SHAREHOLDER'S INTEREST.—Subsection (a) shall apply if the redemption is in complete redemption of all of the stock of the corporation owned by the shareholder.

(4) REDEMPTION FROM NONCORPORATE SHAREHOLDER IN PARTIAL LIQUIDATION.—Subsection (a) shall apply to a distribution if such distribution is—

(A) in redemption of stock held by a shareholder who is not a corporation, and

(B) in partial liquidation of the distributing corporation.

(5) APPLICATION OF PARAGRAPHS.—In determining whether a redemption meets the requirements of paragraph (1), the fact that such redemption fails to meet the requirements of paragraph (2), (3), or (4) shall not be taken into account. If a redemption meets the requirements of paragraph (3) and also the requirements of paragraph (1), (2), or (4), then so much of subsection (c) (2) as would (but for this sentence) apply in respect of the acquisition of an interest in the corporation within the 10-year period beginning on the date of the distribution shall not apply.

Amendments

• 1982, Tax Equity and Fiscal Responsibility Act of 1982 (P.L. 97-248)

P.L. 97-248, §222(c)(1):

Amended Code Sec. 302(b) by redesignating paragraph (4) as (5) and by adding a new paragrah (4). **Effective**, generally, to distributions after 8-31-82. See exceptions provided in P.L. 97-248, §222(f), in the amendment notes for Code Sec. 331(b).

P.L. 97-248, §222(c)(4):

Amended Code Sec. 302 (b)(5) (as redesignated above) by striking out "paragraph (2) or (3)" and inserting "paragraph (2), (3), or (4)" and by striking out "paragraph (1) or (2)" and inserting "paragraph (1), (2), or (4)". **Effective**, generally, for distributions after 8-31-82. See exceptions provided in P.L. 97-248, §222(f), in the amendment notes for Code Sec. 331(b).

• 1980, Bankruptcy Tax Act of 1980 (P.L. 96-589)

P.L. 96-589, §5(b):

Amended Code Sec. 302(b) by striking out paragraph (4) and redesignating paragraph (5) as paragraph (4). Amended Code Sec. 302(b)(4), as redesignated, by striking out "(2), (3), or (4)" and inserting in lieu thereof "(2) or (3)" and by striking out "(1), (2), or (4)" and inserting in lieu thereof "(1) or (2)". **Effective** for redemption of stock issued after 12-31-80 (other than stock issued pursuant to a plan of reorganization approved on or before that date). Also, the amendment will apply to a bankruptcy or similar case commenced on or after 10-1-79 (but prior to 1-1-81) if the special effective date election is made. See the historical comment for P.L. 96-589 under Code Sec. 108(e) for the details of the election. Prior to amendment, Code Sec. 302(b)(4) read as follows:

"(4) STOCK ISSUED BY RAILROAD CORPORATIONS IN CERTAIN REORGANIZATIONS.—Subsection (a) shall apply if the redemption is of stock issued by a railroad corporation (as defined in section 77(m) of the Bankruptcy Act, as amended) pursuant to a plan of reorganization under section 77 of the Bankruptcy Act."

[Sec. 302(c)]

(c) CONSTRUCTIVE OWNERSHIP OF STOCK.—

(1) IN GENERAL.—Except as provided in paragraph (2) of this subsection, section 318(a) shall apply in determining the ownership of stock for purposes of this section.

(2) FOR DETERMINING TERMINATION OF INTEREST.—

(A) In the case of a distribution described in subsection (b) (3), section 318(a)(1) shall not apply if—

(i) immediately after the distribution the distributee has no interest in the corporation (including an interest as officer, director, or employee), other than an interest as a creditor,

(ii) the distributee does not acquire any such interest (other than stock acquired by bequest or inheritance) within 10 years from the date of such distribution, and

(iii) the distributee, at such time and in such manner as the Secretary by regulations prescribes, files an agreement to notify the Secretary of any acquisition described in clause (ii) and to retain such records as may be necessary for the application of this paragraph.

If the distributee acquires such an interest in the corporation (other than by bequest or inheritance) within 10 years from the date of the distribution, then the periods of limitation provided in sections 6501 and 6502 on the making of an assessment and the collection by levy or a proceeding in court shall, with respect to any deficiency (including interest and additions to the tax) resulting from such acquisition, include one year immediately following the date on which the distributee (in accordance with regulations prescribed by the Secretary) notifies the Secretary of such acquisition; and such assessment and collection may be made notwithstanding any provision of law or rule of law which otherwise would prevent such assessment and collection.

(B) Subparagraph (A) of this paragraph shall not apply if—

(i) any portion of the stock redeemed was acquired, directly or indirectly, within the 10-year period ending on the date of the distribution by the distributee from a person the ownership of whose stock would (at the time of distribution) be attributable to the distributee under section 318(a), or

(ii) any person owns (at the time of the distribution) stock the ownership of which is attributable to the distributee under section 318(a) and such person acquired any stock in the corporation, directly or indirectly, from the distributee within the 10-year period ending on the date of the distribution, unless such stock so acquired from the distributee is redeemed in the same transaction.

The preceding sentence shall not apply if the acquisition (or, in the case of clause (ii), the disposition) by the distributee did not have as one of its principal purposes the avoidance of Federal income tax.

(C) SPECIAL RULE FOR WAIVERS BY ENTITIES.—

(i) IN GENERAL.—Subparagraph (A) shall not apply to a distribution to any entity unless—

(I) such entity and each related person meet the requirements of clauses (i), (ii), and (iii) of subparagraph (A), and

(II) each related person agrees to be jointly and severally liable for any deficiency (including interest and additions to tax) resulting from an acquisition described in clause (ii) of subparagraph (A).

In any case to which the preceding sentence applies, the second sentence of subparagraph (A) and subparagraph (B)(ii) shall be applied by substituting "distributee or any related person" for "distributee" each place it appears.

(ii) DEFINITIONS.—For purposes of this subparagraph—

(I) the term "entity" means a partnership, estate, trust, or corporation; and

(II) the term "related person" means any person to whom ownership of stock in the corporation is (at the time of the distribution) attributable under section 318(a)(1) if such stock is further attributable to the entity under section 318(a)(3).

Amendments

• 1982, Tax Equity and Fiscal Responsibility Act of 1982 (P.L. 97-248)

P.L. 97-248, §228(a):

Added a new subparagraph (C) at the end of Code Sec. 302(c)(2). **Effective** with respect to distributions after 8-31-82, in tax years ending after such date.

• 1976, Tax Reform Act of 1976 (P.L. 94-455)

P.L. 94-455, §1906(b)(13)(A):

Amended 1954 Code by substituting "Secretary" for "Secretary or his delegate" each place it appeared. **Effective** 2-1-77.

[Sec. 302(d)]

(d) REDEMPTIONS TREATED AS DISTRIBUTIONS OF PROPERTY.—Except as otherwise provided in this subchapter, if a corporation redeems its stock (within the meaning of section 317(b)), and if subsection (a) of this section does not apply, such redemption shall be treated as a distribution of property to which section 301 applies.

[Sec. 302(e)]

(e) PARTIAL LIQUIDATION DEFINED.—

(1) IN GENERAL.—For purposes of subsection (b)(4), a distribution shall be treated as in partial liquidation of a corporation if—

(A) the distribution is not essentially equivalent to a dividend (determined at the corporate level rather than at the shareholder level), and

(B) the distribution is pursuant to a plan and occurs within the taxable year in which the plan is adopted or within the succeeding taxable year.

(2) TERMINATION OF BUSINESS.—The distributions which meet the requirements of paragraph (1)(A) shall include (but shall not be limited to) a distribution which meets the requirements of subparagraphs (A) and (B) of this paragraph:

(A) The distribution is attributable to the distributing corporation's ceasing to conduct, or consists of the assets of, a qualified trade or business.

(B) Immediately after the distribution, the distributing corporation is actively engaged in the conduct of a qualified trade or business.

(3) QUALIFIED TRADE OR BUSINESS.—For purposes of paragraph (2), the term "qualified trade or business" means any trade or business which—

(A) was actively conducted throughout the 5-year period ending on the date of the redemption, and

(B) was not acquired by the corporation within such period in a transaction in which gain or loss was recognized in whole or in part.

(4) REDEMPTION MAY BE PRO RATA.—Whether or not a redemption meets the requirements of subparagraphs (A) and (B) of paragraph (2) shall be determined without regard to whether or not the redemption is pro rata with respect to all of the shareholders of the corporation.

(5) TREATMENT OF CERTAIN PASS-THRU ENTITIES.—For purposes of determining under subsection (b)(4) whether any stock is held by a shareholder who is not a corporation, any stock held by a partnership, estate, or trust shall be treated as if it were actually held proportionately by its partners or beneficiaries.

Amendments

• 1982, Tax Equity and Fiscal Responsibility Act of 1982 (P.L. 97-248)

P.L. 97-248, §222(c)(2):

Amended Code Sec. 302 by redesignating subsection (e) as subsection (f) and inserting after subsection (d) new subsection (e). **Effective**, generally, for distributions after 8-31-82. See exceptions provided in P.L. 97-248, §222(f), in the amendment notes for Code Sec. 331(b).

[Sec. 302(f)]

(f) CROSS REFERENCES.—

For special rules relating to redemption—

(1) Death Taxes.—Of stock to pay death taxes, see section 303.

(2) Section 306 Stock.—Of section 306 stock, see section 306.

(3) Liquidations.—Of stock in complete liquidation, see section 331.

Amendments

• 1984, Deficit Reduction Act of 1984 (P.L. 98-369)

P.L. 98-369, §712(i)(1):

Amended Code Sec. 302(f)(3) by striking out "partial or complete liquidation" and inserting in lieu thereof "complete liquidation". **Effective** as if included in the provision of P.L. 97-248 to which it relates.

• 1982, Tax Equity and Fiscal Responsibility Act of 1982 (P.L. 97-248)

P.L. 97-248, §222(c)(2):

Redesignated subsection (e) as (f). **Effective**, generally, for distributions after 8-31-82.

[Sec. 303]

SEC. 303. DISTRIBUTIONS IN REDEMPTION OF STOCK TO PAY DEATH TAXES.

[Sec. 303(a)]

(a) IN GENERAL.—A distribution of property to a shareholder by a corporation in redemption of part or all of the stock of such corporation which (for Federal estate tax purposes) is included in determining the gross estate of a decedent, to the extent that the amount of such distribution does not exceed the sum of—

(1) the estate, inheritance, legacy, and succession taxes (including any interest collected as a part of such taxes) imposed because of such decedent's death, and

(2) the amount of funeral and administration expenses allowable as deductions to the estate under section 2053 (or under section 2106 in the case of the estate of a decedent nonresident, not a citizen of the United States),

shall be treated as a distribution in full payment in exchange for the stock so redeemed.

[Sec. 303(b)]

(b) LIMITATIONS ON APPLICATION OF SUBSECTION (a).—

(1) PERIOD FOR DISTRIBUTION.—Subsection (a) shall apply only to amounts distributed after the death of the decedent and—

(A) within the period of limitations provided in section 6501(a) for the assessment of the Federal estate tax (determined without the application of any provision other than section 6501(a)), or within 90 days after the expiration of such period,

(B) if a petition for redetermination of a deficiency in such estate tax has been filed with the Tax Court within the time prescribed in section 6213, at any time before the expiration of 60 days after the decision of the Tax Court becomes final, or

(C) if an election has been made under section 6166 and if the time prescribed by this subparagraph expires at a later date than the time prescribed by subparagraph (B) of this paragraph, within the time determined under section 6166 for the payment of the installments.

(2) RELATIONSHIP OF STOCK TO DECEDENT'S ESTATE.—

(A) IN GENERAL.—Subsection (a) shall apply to a distribution by a corporation only if the value (for Federal estate tax purposes) of all of the stock of such corporation which is included in determining the value of the decedent's gross estate exceeds 35 percent of the excess of—

(i) the value of the gross estate of such decedent, over

(ii) the sum of the amounts allowable as a deduction under section 2053 or 2054.

(B) SPECIAL RULE FOR STOCK IN 2 OR MORE CORPORATIONS.—For purposes of subparagraph (A), stock of 2 or more corporations, with respect to each of which there is included in determining the value of the decedent's gross estate 20 percent or more in value of the outstanding stock, shall be treated as the stock of a single corporation. For purposes of the 20-percent requirement of the preceding sentence, stock which, at the decedent's death, represents the surviving spouse's interest in property held by the decedent and the surviving spouse as community property or as joint tenants, tenants by the entirety, or tenants in common shall be treated as having been included in determining the value of the decedent's gross estate.

(3) RELATIONSHIP OF SHAREHOLDER TO ESTATE TAX.—Subsection (a) shall apply to a distribution by a corporation only to the extent that the interest of the shareholder is reduced directly (or through a binding obligation to contribute) by any payment of an amount described in paragraph (1) or (2) of subsection (a).

(4) ADDITIONAL REQUIREMENTS FOR DISTRIBUTIONS MADE MORE THAN 4 YEARS AFTER DECEDENT'S DEATH.—In the case of amounts distributed more than 4 years after the date of the decedent's death, subsection (a) shall apply to a distribution by a corporation only to the extent of the lesser of—

(A) the aggregate of the amounts referred to in paragraph (1) or (2) of subsection (a) which remained unpaid immediately before the distribution, or

(B) the aggregate of the amounts referred to in paragraph (1) or (2) of subsection (a) which are paid during the 1-year period beginning on the date of such distribution.

Amendments

• 1981, Economic Recovery Tax Act of 1981 (P.L. 97-34)

P.L. 97-34, §422(b)(1):

Amended Code Sec. 303(b)(2)(A) by striking out "50 percent" and inserting "35 percent". **Effective** for estates of decedents dying after 12-31-81.

P.L. 97-34, §422(b)(2):

Amended Code Sec. 303(b)(2)(B). **Effective** for estates of decedents dying after 12-31-81. Prior to amendment, Code Sec. 303(b)(2)(B) read as follows:

(B) SPECIAL RULE FOR STOCK OF TWO OR MORE CORPORATIONS.—For purposes of the 50 percent requirement of subparagraph (A), stock of two or more corporations, with respect to each of which there is included in determining the value of the decedent's gross estate more than 75 percent in value of the outstanding stock, shall be treated as the stock of a single corporation. For the purpose of the 75 percent requirement of the preceding sentence, stock which, at the decedent's death, represents the surviving spouse's interest in property held by the decedent and the surviving spouse as community property shall be treated as having been included in determining the value of the decedent's gross estate.

P.L. 97-34, §422(e)(1):

Amended Code Sec. 303(b)(1)(C) by striking out "or 6166A" each place it appears. **Effective** for estates of decedents dying after 12-31-81.

• 1976, Tax Reform Act of 1976 (P.L. 94-455)

P.L. 94-455, §2004(e):

Amended Code Sec. 303(b) by striking "or" at the end of paragraph (1)(A), substituting ", or" for the period at the end of paragraph (1)(B), adding paragraph (1)(C), amending paragraph (2)(A), substituting "the 50 percent requirement" for "the 35 percent and 50 percent requirements" in paragraph (2)(B), and adding paragraphs (3) and (4). **Effective** for the estates of decedents dying after 12-31-76. Prior to amendment, Code Sec. 303(b)(2)(A) read as follows:

(A) IN GENERAL.—Subsection (a) shall apply to a distribution by a corporation only if the value (for Federal estate tax purposes) of all of the stock of such corporation which is included in determining the value of the decedent's gross estate is either—

(i) more than 35 percent of the value of the gross estate of such decedent, or

(ii) more than 50 percent of the taxable estate of such decedent.

[Sec. 303(c)]

(c) STOCK WITH SUBSTITUTED BASIS.—If—

(1) a shareholder owns stock of a corporation (referred to in this subsection as "new stock") the basis of which is determined by reference to the basis of stock of a corporation (referred to in this subsection as "old stock"),

(2) the old stock was included (for Federal estate tax purposes) in determining the gross estate of a decedent, and

(3) subsection (a) would apply to a distribution of property to such shareholder in redemption of the old stock,

then, subject to the limitations specified in subsection (b), subsection (a) shall apply in respect of a distribution in redemption of the new stock.

Amendments

• 1976, Tax Reform Act of 1976 (P.L. 94-455)

P.L. 94-455, §2004(e)(4):

Substituted "limitations specified in subsection (b)" for "limitation specified in subsection (b)(1)" in Code Sec. 303(c). **Effective** for the estates of decedents dying after 12-31-76.

[Sec. 303(d)]

(d) SPECIAL RULES FOR GENERATION-SKIPPING TRANSFERS.—Where stock in a corporation is the subject of a generation-skipping transfer (within the meaning of section 2611(a)) occurring at the same time as and as a result of the death of an individual—

(1) the stock shall be deemed to be included in the gross estate of such individual;

(2) taxes of the kind referred to in subsection (a)(1) which are imposed because of the generation-skipping transfer shall be treated as imposed because of such individual's death (and for this purpose the tax imposed by section 2601 shall be treated as an estate tax);

(3) the period of distribution shall be measured from the date of the generation-skipping transfer; and

(4) the relationship of stock to the decedent's estate shall be measured with reference solely to the amount of the generation-skipping transfer.

Amendments

• 1990, Omnibus Budget Reconciliation Act of 1990 (P.L. 101-508)

P.L. 101-508, §11703(c)(3), provides:

(3) Subparagraph (C) of section 1433(b)(2) of the Tax Reform Act of 1986 shall not exempt any generation-skipping transfer from the amendments made by subtitle D of title XVI of such Act to the extent such transfer is attributable to property transferred by gift or by reason of the death of another person to the decedent (or trust) referred to in such subparagraph after August 3, 1990.

• 1988, Technical and Miscellaneous Revenue Act of 1988 (P.L. 100-647)

P.L. 100-647, §1014(h)(5), provides:

(5) Subparagraph (C) of section 1433(b)(2) of the Reform Act shall not exempt any direct skip from the amendments made by subtitle D of title XIV of the Reform Act if—

(A) such direct skip results from the application of section 2044 of the 1986 Code, and

(B) such direct skip is attributable to property transferred to the trust after October 21, 1988.

• 1986, Tax Reform Act of 1986 (P.L. 99-514)

P.L. 99-514, §1432(b):

Amended Code Sec. 303(d). For the **effective** dates, as well as special rules, see P.L. 99-514, §1433, as amended by P.L. 100-647, §1014(h)(1)-(4), below. Prior to amendment, Code Sec. 303(d) read as follows:

(d) SPECIAL RULES FOR GENERATION-SKIPPING TRANSFERS.—Under regulations prescribed by the Secretary, where stock in a corporation is subject to tax under section 2601 as a result of a generation-skipping transfer (within the meaning of section 2611(a)), which occurs at or after the death of the deemed transferor (within the meaning of section 2612)—

(1) the stock shall be deemed to be included in the gross estate of the deemed transferor;

(2) taxes of the kind referred to in subsection (a)(1) which are imposed because of the generation-skipping transfer shall be treated as imposed because of the deemed transferor's death (and for this purpose the tax imposed by section 2601 shall be treated as an estate tax);

(3) the period of distribution shall be measured from the date of the generation-skipping transfer; and

(4) the relationship of stock of the decedent's estate shall be measured with reference solely to the amount of the generation-skipping transfer.

P.L. 99-514, §1433, as amended by P.L. 100-647, §1014(h)(1)-(4), provides:

SEC. 1433. EFFECTIVE DATES.

(a) GENERAL RULE.—Except as provided in subsection (b), the amendments made by this subtitle shall apply to any generation-skipping transfer (within the meaning of section 2611 of the Internal Revenue Code of 1986) made after the date of the enactment of this Act.

(b) SPECIAL RULES.—

(1) TREATMENT OF CERTAIN INTER VIVOS TRANSFERS MADE AFTER SEPTEMBER 25, 1985.—For purposes of subsection (a) (and chapter 13 of the Internal Revenue Code of 1986 as amended by this part), any inter vivos transfer after September 25, 1985, and on or before the date of the enactment of this Act shall be treated as if it were made on the 1st day after the date of enactment of this Act.

(2) EXCEPTIONS.—The amendments made by this subtitle shall not apply to—

(A) any generation-skipping transfer under a trust which was irrevocable on September 25, 1985, but only to the extent that such transfer is not made out of corpus added to the trust after September 25, 1985 (or out of income attributable to corpus so added),

(B) any generation-skipping transfer under a will or revocable trust executed before the date of the enactment of this Act if the decedent dies before January 1, 1987, and

(C) any generation-skipping transfer—

(i) under a trust to the extent such trust consists of property included in the gross estate of a decedent (other than property transferred by the decedent during his life after the date of the enactment of this Act), or reinvestments thereof, or

(ii) which is a direct skip which occurs by reason of the death of any decedent;

but only if such decedent was, on the date of the enactment of this Act, under a mental disability to change the disposition of his property and did not regain his competence to dispose of such property before the date of his death.

(3) TREATMENT OF CERTAIN TRANSFERS TO GRANDCHILDREN.—

(A) IN GENERAL.—For purposes of chapter 13 of the Internal Revenue Code of 1986, the term "direct skip" shall not include any transfer before January 1, 1990, from a transferor to a grandchild of the transferor to the extent the aggregate transfers from such transferor to such grandchild do not exceed $2,000,000.

(B) TREATMENT OF TRANSFERS IN TRUST.—For purposes of subparagraph (A), a transfer in trust for the benefit of a grandchild shall be treated as a transfer to such grandchild if (and only if)—

(i) during the life of the grandchild, no portion of the corpus or income of the trust may be distributed to (or for the benefit of) any person other than such grandchild,

(ii) the assets of the trust will be includible in the gross estate of the grandchild if the grandchild dies before the trust is terminated, and

(iii) all of the income of the trust for periods after the grandchild has attained age 21 will be distributed to (or for the benefit of) such grandchild not less frequently than annually.

(C) COORDINATION WITH SECTION 2653(a) OF THE 1986 CODE.—In the case of any transfer which would be a generation-skipping transfer but for subparagraph (A), the rules of section 2653(a) of the Internal Revenue Code of 1986 shall apply as if such transfer were a generation-skipping transfer.

(D) COORDINATION WITH TAXABLE TERMINATIONS AND TAXABLE DISTRIBUTIONS.—For purposes of chapter 13 of the Internal Revenue Code of 1986, the terms "taxable termination" and "taxable distribution" shall not include any transfer which would be a direct skip but for subparagraph (A).

(4) DEFINITIONS.—Terms used in this section shall have the same respective meanings as when used in chapter 13 of the Internal Revenue Code of 1986; except that section 2612(c)(2) of such Code shall not apply in determining whether an individual is a grandchild of the transferor.

(c) REPEAL OF EXISTING TAX ON GENERATION-SKIPPING TRANSFERS.—

(1) IN GENERAL.—In the case of any tax imposed by chapter 13 of the Internal Revenue Code of 1954 (as in effect on the day before the date of the enactment of this Act), such tax (including interest, additions to tax, and additional amounts) shall not be assessed and if assessed, the assessment shall be abated, and if collected, shall be credited or refunded (with interest) as an overpayment.

(2) WAIVER OF STATUTE OF LIMITATIONS.—If on the date of the enactment of this Act (or at any time within 1 year after such date of enactment) refund or credit of any overpayment of tax resulting from the application of paragraph (1) is barred by any law or rule of law, refund or credit of such overpayment shall, nevertheless, be made or allowed if claim therefore is filed before the date 1 year after the date of the enactment of this Act.

(d) ELECTION FOR CERTAIN TRANSFERS BENEFITING GRANDCHILD.—

(1) IN GENERAL.—For purposes of chapter 13 of the Internal Revenue Code of 1986 (as amended by this Act) and subsection (b) of this section, any transfer in trust for the benefit of a grandchild of a transferor shall be treated as a direct skip to such grandchild if—

(A) the transfer occurs before the date of enactment of this Act,

(B) the transfer would be a direct skip to a grandchild except for the fact that the trust instrument provides that, if the grandchild dies before vesting of the interest transferred, the interest is transferred to the grandchild's heir (rather than the grandchild's estate), and

(C) an election under this subsection applies to such transfer.

(2) ELECTION.—An election under paragraph (1) shall be made at such time and in such manner as the Secretary of the Treasury or his delegate may prescribe.

Any transfer treated as a direct skip by reason of the preceding sentence shall be subject to Federal estate tax on the grandchild's death in the same manner as if the contingent gift over had been to the grandchild's estate. Unless the grandchild otherwise directs by will, the estate of such grandchild shall be entitled to recover from the person receiving the property on the death of the grandchild any increase in Federal estate tax on the estate of the grandchild by reason of the preceding sentence.

• 1978, Revenue Act of 1978 (P.L. 95-600)

P.L. 95-600, §702(n)(1), (5):

Amended P.L. 95-455, §2006(c) by striking out "April 30, 1976" each place it appears and inserting in place thereof "June 11, 1976".

• 1976, Tax Reform Act of 1976 (P.L. 94-455)

P.L. 94-455, §2006(b)(4), (c):

Added Code Sec. 303(d). **Effective** for any generation-skipping transfer (within the meaning of Code Sec. 2611(a)) made after 6-11-76. Code Sec. 303(d) shall not apply to any generation-skipping transfer: (1) under a trust that was irrevocable on 6-11-76, but only to the extent that the transfer is not made out of corpus added to the trust after 6-11-76, or (2) in the case of a decedent dying before 1-1-82, pursuant to a will (or revocable trust) which was in existence on 6-11-76, and was not amended at any time after that date in any respect that will result in the creation of, or increasing the amount of, any generation-skipping transfer. If a decedent, on 6-11-76, was under a mental disability to change the disposition of his property, the period set forth in (2) shall not expire before the date which is 2 years after the date on which he first regains his competence to dispose of such property. In the case of a trust equivalent within the meaning of Code Sec. 2611(d), the provisions of Code Sec. 2611(d) shall apply. [**Effective** date changed by P.L. 95-600, §702(n)(1), (5).—CCH].

[Sec. 304]

SEC. 304. REDEMPTION THROUGH USE OF RELATED CORPORATIONS.

[Sec. 304(a)]

(a) TREATMENT OF CERTAIN STOCK PURCHASES.—

(1) ACQUISITION BY RELATED CORPORATION (OTHER THAN SUBSIDIARY).—For purposes of sections 302 and 303, if—

(A) one or more persons are in control of each of two corporations, and

(B) in return for property, one of the corporations acquires stock in the other corporation from the person (or persons) so in control,

then (unless paragraph (2) applies) such property shall be treated as a distribution in redemption of the stock of the corporation acquiring such stock. To the extent that such distribution is treated as a distribution to which section 301 applies, the transferor and the acquiring corporation shall be treated in the same manner as if the transferor had transferred the stock so acquired to the acquiring corporation in exchange for stock of the acquiring corporation in a transaction to which section 351(a) applies, and then the acquiring corporation had redeemed the stock it was treated as issuing in such transaction.

(2) ACQUISITION BY SUBSIDIARY.—For purposes of sections 302 and 303, if—

(A) in return for property, one corporation acquires from a shareholder of another corporation stock in such other corporation, and

(B) the issuing corporation controls the acquiring corporation,

then such property shall be treated as a distribution in redemption of the stock of the issuing corporation.

Amendments

• 1997, Taxpayer Relief Act of 1997 (P.L. 105-34)

P.L. 105-34, §1013(a):

Amended the last sentence of Code Sec. 304(a)(1). **Effective**, generally, for distributions and acquisitions after 6-8-97. For a transition rule, see P.L. 105-34, §1013(d)(2), below. Prior to amendment, the last sentence of Code Sec. 304(a)(1) read as follows:

To the extent that such distribution is treated as a distribution to which section 301 applies, the stock so acquired shall be treated as having been transferred by the person from whom acquired, and as having been received by the corporation acquiring it, as a contribution to the capital of such corporation.

P.L. 105-34, §1013(d)(2), provides:

(2) TRANSITION RULE.—The amendments made by this section shall not apply to any distribution or acquisition after June 8, 1997, if such distribution or acquisition is—

(A) made pursuant to a written agreement which was binding on such date and at all times thereafter,

(B) described in a ruling request submitted to the Internal Revenue Service on or before such date, or

(C) described in a public announcement or filing with the Securities and Exchange Commission on or before such date.

• 1986, Tax Reform Act of 1986 (P.L. 99-514)

P.L. 99-514, §1875(b):

Amended Code Sec. 304(a)(1) by striking out "In any such case" and inserting in lieu thereof "To the extent that such distribution is treated as a distribution to which section 301 applies". **Effective** as if included in the provision of P.L. 98-369 to which it relates.

[Sec. 304(b)]

(b) SPECIAL RULES FOR APPLICATION OF SUBSECTION (a).—

(1) RULE FOR DETERMINATIONS UNDER SECTION 302(b).—In the case of any acquisition of stock to which subsection (a) of this section applies, determinations as to whether the acquisition is, by reason of section 302(b), to be treated as a distribution in part or full payment in exchange for the stock shall be made by reference to the stock of the issuing corporation. In applying section 318(a) (relating to constructive ownership of stock) with respect to section 302(b) for purposes of this paragraph, sections 318(a)(2)(C) and 318(a)(3)(C) shall be applied without regard to the 50 percent limitation contained therein.

(2) AMOUNT CONSTITUTING DIVIDEND.—In the case of any acquisition of stock to which subsection (a) applies, the determination of the amount which is a dividend (and the source thereof) shall be made as if the property were distributed—

(A) by the acquiring corporation to the extent of its earnings and profits, and

(B) then by the issuing corporation to the extent of its earnings and profits.

(3) COORDINATION WITH SECTION 351.—

(A) PROPERTY TREATED AS RECEIVED IN REDEMPTION.—Except as otherwise provided in this paragraph, subsection (a) (and not section 351 and not so much of sections 357 and 358 as relates to section 351) shall apply to any property received in a distribution described in subsection (a).

(B) CERTAIN ASSUMPTIONS OF LIABILITY, ETC.—

(i) IN GENERAL.—In the case of an acquisition described in section 351, subsection (a) shall not apply to any liability—

(I) assumed by the acquiring corporation, or

(II) to which the stock is subject,

if such liability was incurred by the transferor to acquire the stock. For purposes of the preceding sentence, the term "stock" means stock referred to in paragraph (1)(B) or (2)(A) of subsection (a).

(ii) EXTENSION OF OBLIGATIONS, ETC.—For purposes of clause (i), an extension, renewal, or refinancing of a libility which meets the requirements of clause (i) shall be treated as meeting such requirements.

(iii) CLAUSE (i) DOES NOT APPLY TO STOCK ACQUIRED FROM RELATED PERSON EXCEPT WHERE COMPLETE TERMINATION.—Clause (i) shall apply only to stock acquired by the transferor from a person—

(I) none of whose stock is attributable to the transferor under section 318(a) (other than paragraph (4) thereof), or

(II) who satisfies rules similar to the rules of section 302(c)(2) with respect to both the acquiring and the issuing corporations (determined as if such person were a distributee of each such corporation).

(C) DISTRIBUTIONS INCIDENT TO FORMATION OF BANK HOLDING COMPANIES.—If—

(i) pursuant to a plan, control of a bank is acquired and within 2 years after the date on which such control is acquired, stock constituting control of such bank is transferred to a BHC in connection with its formation,

(ii) incident to the formation of the BHC there is a distribution of property described in subsection (a), and

(iii) the shareholders of the BHC who receive distributions of such property do not have control of such BHC,

then, subsection (a) shall not apply to any securities received by a qualified minority shareholder incident to the formation of such BHC. For purposes of this subparagraph, any assumption of (or acquisition of stock subject to) a liability under subparagraph (B) shall not be treated as a distribution of property.

(D) DEFINITIONS AND SPECIAL RULE.—For purposes of subparagraph (C) and this subparagraph—

(i) QUALIFIED MINORITY SHAREHOLDER.—The term "qualified minority shareholder" means any shareholder who owns less than 10 percent (in value) of the stock of the

BHC. For purposes of the preceding sentence, the rules of paragraph (3) of subsection (c) shall apply.

(ii) BHC.—The term "BHC" means a bank holding company (within the meaning of section 2(a) of the Bank Holding Company Act of 1956).

(iii) SPECIAL RULE IN CASE OF BHC'S FORMED BEFORE 1985.—In the case of a BHC which is formed before 1985, clause (i) of subparagraph (C) shall not apply.

(4) TREATMENT OF CERTAIN INTRAGROUP TRANSACTIONS.—

(A) IN GENERAL.—In the case of any transfer described in subsection (a) of stock from 1 member of an affiliated group to another member of such group, proper adjustments shall be made to—

(i) the adjusted basis of any intragroup stock, and

(ii) the earnings and profits of any member of such group,

to the extent necessary to carry out the purposes of this section.

(B) DEFINITIONS.—For purposes of this paragraph—

(i) AFFILIATED GROUP.—The term "affiliated group" has the meaning given such term by section 1504(a).

(ii) INTRAGROUP STOCK.—The term "intragroup stock" means any stock which—

(I) is in a corporation which is a member of an affiliated group, and

(II) is held by another member of such group.

(5) ACQUISITIONS BY FOREIGN CORPORATIONS.—

(A) IN GENERAL.—In the case of any acquisition to which subsection (a) applies in which the acquiring corporation is a foreign corporation, the only earnings and profits taken into account under paragraph (2)(A) shall be those earnings and profits—

(i) which are attributable (under regulations prescribed by the Secretary) to stock of the acquiring corporation owned (within the meaning of section 958(a)) by a corporation or individual which is—

(I) a United States shareholder (within the meaning of section 951(b)) of the acquiring corporation, and

(II) the transferor or a person who bears a relationship to the transferor described in section 267(b) or 707(b), and

(ii) which were accumulated during the period or periods such stock was owned by such person while the acquiring corporation was a controlled foreign corporation.

(B) SPECIAL RULE IN CASE OF FOREIGN ACQUIRING CORPORATION.—In the case of any acquisition to which subsection (a) applies in which the acquiring corporation is a foreign corporation, no earnings and profits shall be taken into account under paragraph (2)(A) (and subparagraph (A) shall not apply) if more than 50 percent of the dividends arising from such acquisition (determined without regard to this subparagraph) would neither—

(i) be subject to tax under this chapter for the taxable year in which the dividends arise, nor

(ii) be includible in the earnings and profits of a controlled foreign corporation (as defined in section 957 and without regard to section 953(c)).

(C) REGULATIONS.—The Secretary shall prescribe such regulations as are appropriate to carry out the purposes of this paragraph.

(6) AVOIDANCE OF MULTIPLE INCLUSIONS, ETC.—In the case of any acquisition to which subsection (a) applies in which the acquiring corporation or the issuing corporation is a foreign corporation, the Secretary shall prescribe such regulations as are appropriate in order to eliminate a multiple inclusion of any item in income by reason of this subpart and to provide appropriate basis adjustments (including modifications to the application of sections 959 and 961).

Amendments

• 2010, (P.L. 111-226)

P.L. 111-226, §215(a):

Amended Code Sec. 304(b)(5) by redesignating subparagraph (B) as subparagraph (C) and by inserting after subparagraph (A) a new subparagraph (B). **Effective** for acquisitions after 8-10-2010.

• 1998, IRS Restructuring and Reform Act of 1998 (P.L. 105-206)

P.L. 105-206, §6010(d)(1):

Amended Code Sec. 304(b)(5) by striking subparagraph (B) and by redesignating subparagraph (C) as subparagraph (B). **Effective** as if included in the provision of P.L. 105-34 to which it relates [generally **effective** for distributions and acquisitions after 6-8-97.—CCH]. Prior to being stricken, Code Sec. 304(b)(5)(B) read as follows:

(B) APPLICATION OF SECTION 1248.—For purposes of subparagraph (A), the rules of section 1248(d) shall apply except to the extent otherwise provided by the Secretary.

P.L. 105-206, §6010(d)(2):

Amended Code Sec. 304(b) by adding at the end a new paragraph (6). **Effective** as if included in the provision of P.L. 105-34 to which it relates [generally **effective** for distributions and acquisitions after 6-8-97.—CCH].

• 1997, Taxpayer Relief Act of 1997 (P.L. 105-34)

P.L. 105-34, §1013(c):

Amended Code Sec. 304(b) by adding at the end a new paragraph (5). **Effective**, generally, for distributions and acquisitions after 6-8-97. For a transition rule, see P.L. 105-34, §1013(d)(2), below.

P.L. 105-34, §1013(d)(2), provides:

(2) TRANSITION RULE.—The amendments made by this section shall not apply to any distribution or acquisition after June 8, 1997, if such distribution or acquisition is—

(A) made pursuant to a written agreement which was binding on such date and at all times thereafter,

(B) described in a ruling request submitted to the Internal Revenue Service on or before such date, or

(C) described in a public announcement or filing with the Securities and Exchange Commission on or before such date.

• 1988, Technical and Miscellaneous Revenue Act of 1988 (P.L. 100-647)

P.L. 100-647, §2004(k)(2):

Amended Code Sec. 304(b)(4)(A) by striking out "stock of 1 member" and inserting in lieu thereof "stock from 1 member". **Effective** as if included in the provision of P.L. 100-203 to which it relates.

• 1987, Revenue Act of 1987 (P.L. 100-203)

P.L. 100-203, §10223(c):

Amended Code Sec. 304(b) by adding at the end thereof new paragraph (4). For the **effective** date, see P.L. 100-203, §10223(d), as amended by P.L. 100-647, §2004(k)(3)-(4), below.

P.L. 100-203, §10223(d), as amended by P.L. 100-647, §2004(k)(3)-(4), provides:

(d) EFFECTIVE DATES.—

(1) IN GENERAL.—The amendments made by this section shall apply to distributions or transfers after December 15, 1987.

(2) EXCEPTIONS.—

(A) DISTRIBUTIONS.—The amendments made by this section shall not apply to any distribution after December 15, 1987, and before January 1, 1993, if—

(i) 80 percent or more of the stock of the distributing corporation was acquired by the distributee before December 15, 1987, or

(ii) 80 percent or more of the stock of the distributing corporation was acquired by the distributee before January 1, 1989, pursuant to a binding written contract or tender offer in effect on December 15, 1987.

For purposes of the preceding sentence, stock described in section 1504(a)(4) of the Internal Revenue Code of 1986 shall not be taken into account.

(B) SECTION 304 TRANSFERS.—The amendment made by subsection (c) shall not apply to any transfer after December 15, 1987, and on or before March 31, 1988, if such transfer is—

(i) between corporations which are members of the same affiliated group on December 15, 1987, or

(ii) between corporations which become members of the same affiliated group, pursuant to a binding written contract or tender offer in effect on December 15, 1987.

(C) DISTRIBUTIONS COVERED BY PRIOR TRANSITION RULE.—The amendments made by this section shall not apply to any distribution to which the amendments made by subtitle D of title VI of the Tax Reform Act of 1986 do not apply.

(D) TREATMENT OF CERTAIN MEMBERS OF AFFILIATED GROUP.—

(i) IN GENERAL.—For purposes of subparagraph (A), all corporations which were in existence on the designated date and were members of the same affiliated group which included the distributees on such date shall be treated as 1 distributee.

(ii) LIMITATION TO STOCK HELD ON DESIGNATED DATE.—Clause (i) shall not exempt any distribution from the amendments made by this section if such distribution is with respect to stock not held by the distributee (determined without regard to clause (i)) on the designated date directly or indirectly through a corporation which goes out of existence in the transaction.

(iii) DESIGNATED DATE.—For purposes of this subparagraph, the term "designated date" means the later of—

(I) December 15, 1987, or

(II) the date on which the acquisition meeting the requirements of subparagraph (A) occurred.

• 1984, Deficit Reduction Act of 1984 (P.L. 98-369)

P.L. 98-369, §712(l)(1):

Amended Code Sec. 304(b)(2). **Effective** for stock acquired after 6-18-84, in tax years ending after such date. However, see P.L. 98-369, §712(l)(7)(B)-(C) below, for special rules. Prior to amendment, Code Sec. 304(b)(2) read as follows:

(2) Amount Constituting Dividend.—

(A) Where Subsection (a)(1) Applies.—In the case of any acquisition of stock to which paragraph (1) (and not paragraph (2)) of subsection (a) of this section applies, the determination of the amount which is a dividend shall be made as if the property were distributed by the issuing corporation to the acquiring corporation and immediately thereafter distributed by the acquiring corporation.

(B) Where Subsection (a)(2) Applies.—In the case of any acquisition of stock to which subsection (a)(2) of this section applies, the determination of the amount which is a dividend shall be made as if the property were distributed by the acquiring corporation to the issuing corporation and immediately thereafter distributed by the issuing corporation.

P.L. 98-369, §712(l)(7)(B)-(C), provides:

(B) ELECTION BY TAXPAYER TO HAVE AMENDMENTS APPLY EARLIER.—Any taxpayer may elect, at such time and in such manner as the Secretary of the Treasury or his delegate may prescribe, to have the amendments made by paragraphs (1) and (3) apply as if included in section 226 of the Tax Equity and Fiscal Responsibility Act of 1982.

(C) SPECIAL RULE FOR CERTAIN TRANSFERS TO FORM BANK HOLDING COMPANY.—Except as provided in subparagraph (D), the amendments made by paragraphs (1) and (3) shall not apply to transfers pursuant to an application to form a BHC (as defined in section 304(b)(3)(D)(ii) of the Internal Revenue Code of 1954) filed with the Federal Reserve Board before June 18, 1984, if—

(i) such BHC was formed not later than the 90th day after the date of the last required approval of any regulatory authority to form such BHC, and

(ii) such BHC did not elect (at such time and in such manner as the Secretary of the Treasury or his delegate shall prescribe) not to have the provisions of this subparagraph apply.

P.L. 98-369, §712(l)(2):

Amended Code Sec. 304(b)(3)(A) by striking out "(and not part III)" and inserting in lieu thereof "(and not section 351 and not so much of sections 357 and 358 as relates to section 351)". **Effective** as if included in the provision of P.L. 97-248 to which it relates.

P.L. 98-369, §712(l)(3)(A):

Amended Code Sec. 304(b)(3)(B)(i) by striking out "Subsection (a)" and inserting in lieu thereof "In the case of an acquisition described in section 351, subsection (a)". **Effective** for the acquisition of any stock to the extent the liability assumed, or to which such stock is subject, was incurred by the transferor after 10-20-83.

P.L. 98-369, §712(l)(3)(B):

Amended Code Sec. 304(b)(3)(B) by adding new clause (iii). **Effective** for stock acquisitions after 6-18-84, in tax years ending after such date. However, see P.L. 98-369, §712(l)(7)(B)-(D) following Code Sec. 304(c) for special rules.

P.L. 98-369, §712(l)(4):

Amended Code Sec. 304(b)(3)(C) by adding the sentence at the end thereof. **Effective** as if included in the provision of P.L. 97-248 to which it relates.

• 1982, Tax Equity and Fiscal Responsibility Act of 1982 (P.L. 97-248)

P.L. 97-248, §226(a)(1)(A):

Amended Code Sec. 304(b) by adding paragraph (3). **Effective**, generally, to transfers occurring after 8-31-82, in tax years ending after that date. But see exception provided in P.L. 97-248, §226(c)(2), below.

P.L. 97-248, §226(a)(3):

Amended Code Sec. 304(b)(2) by amending subparagraph (A). **Effective** for transfers occurring after 8-31-82, in tax years ending after such date. But see exception provided in P.L. 97-248, §226(c)(2), below. Prior to amendment, Code Sec. 304(b)(2)(A) read as follows:

(A) Where subsection (a)(1) applies.—In the case of any acquisition of stock to which paragraph (1) (and not paragraph (2)) of subsection (a) of this section applies, the determination of the amount which is a dividend shall be made solely by reference to the earnings and profits of the acquiring corporation.

P.L. 97-248, §226(c)(2), provides:

(2) Approval by federal reserve board.—The amendments made by this section shall not apply to transfers pursuant to an application to form a BHC filed with the Federal Reserve Board before August 16, 1982, if the BHC was formed not later than the later of—

(A) the 90th day after the date of the last required approval of any regulatory authority to form such BHC, or

(B) January 1, 1983.

For purposes of this paragraph, the term "BHC" means a bank holding company (within the meaning of section 2(a) of the Bank Holding Company Act of 1956).

• 1964 (P.L. 88-554)

P.L. 88-554, §5(b)(1):

Amended Code Sec. 304(b)(1) by substituting "sections 318(a)(2)(C) and 318(a)(3)(C)" for "section 318(a)(2)(C)". **Effective** 8-31-64.

[Sec. 304(c)]

(c) CONTROL.—

(1) IN GENERAL.—For purposes of this section, control means the ownership of stock possessing at least 50 percent of the total combined voting power of all classes of stock entitled to vote, or at least 50 percent of the total value of shares of all classes of stock. If a person (or persons) is in control (within the meaning of the preceding sentence) of a corporation which in turn owns at least 50 percent of the total combined voting power of all stock entitled to vote of another corporation, or owns at least 50 percent of the total value of the shares of all classes of stock of another corporation, then such person (or persons) shall be treated as in control of such other corporation.

(2) STOCK ACQUIRED IN THE TRANSACTION.—For purposes of subsection (a)(1)—

(A) GENERAL RULE.—Where 1 or more persons in control of the issuing corporation transfer stock of such corporation in exchange for stock of the acquiring corporation, the stock of the acquiring corporation received shall be taken into account in determining whether such person or persons are in control of the acquiring corporation.

(B) DEFINITION OF CONTROL GROUP.—Where 2 or more persons in control of the issuing corporation transfer stock of such corporation to acquiring corporation and, after the transfer, the transferors are in control of the acquiring corporation, the person or persons in control of each corporation shall include each of the persons who so transfer stock.

(3) CONSTRUCTIVE OWNERSHIP.—

(A) IN GENERAL.—Section 318(a) (relating to constructive ownership of stock) shall apply for purposes of determining control under this section.

(B) MODIFICATION OF 50-PERCENT LIMITATIONS IN SECTION 318.—For purposes of subparagraph (A)—

(i) paragraph (2)(C) of section 318(a) shall be applied by substituting "5 percent" for "50 percent", and

(ii) paragraph (3)(C) of section 318(a) shall be applied—

(I) by substituting "5 percent" for "50 percent", and

(II) in any case where such paragraph would not apply but for subclause (I), by considering a corporation as owning the stock (other than stock in such corporation) owned by or for any shareholder of such corporation in that proportion which the value of the stock which such shareholder owned in such corporation bears to the value of all stock in such corporation.

Amendments

• 1984, Deficit Reduction Act of 1984 (P.L. 98-369)

P.L. 98-369, §712(l)(5)(A):

Amended Code Sec. 304(c)(3). **Effective** as if included in the provision of P.L. 97-248 to which it relates. Prior to amendment, Code Sec. 304(c)(3) read as follows:

(3) Constructive Ownership.—Section 318(a) (relating to the constructive ownership of stock) shall apply for purposes of determining control under this section. For purposes of the preceding sentence, sections 318(a)(2)(C) and 318(a)(3)(C) shall be applied without regard to the 50 percent limitation contained therein.

• 1982, Tax Equity and Fiscal Responsibility Act of 1982 (P.L. 97-248)

P.L. 97-248, §226(a)(2):

Amended Code Sec. 304(c) by redesignating paragraph (2) as paragraph (3) and by inserting a new paragraph (2), and by striking out in (3), as redesignated, "paragraph (1)" and inserting "this section". **Effective** for transfers occurring after 8-31-82, in tax years ending after that date, except as provided in P.L. 97-248, §226(c)(2) (see amendment notes for Code Sec. 304(b)).

• 1964 (P.L. 88-554)

P.L. 88-554, §5(b)(1):

Amended Code Sec. 304(c)(2) by substituting "sections 318(a)(2)(C) and 318(a)(3)(C)" for "section 318(a)(2)(C)". **Effective** 8-31-64.

[Sec. 305]

SEC. 305. DISTRIBUTIONS OF STOCK AND STOCK RIGHTS.

[Sec. 305(a)]

(a) GENERAL RULE.—Except as otherwise provided in this section, gross income does not include the amount of any distribution of the stock of a corporation made by such corporation to its shareholders with respect to its stock.

Amendments

• 1969, Tax Reform Act of 1969 (P.L. 91-172)

P.L. 91-172, §421(a):

Amended Code Sec. 305(a). **Effective**, generally, with respect to distributions (or deemed distributions) made after 1-10-69, in tax years ending after that date. However, see P.L. 91-172, §421(b)(3) and (b)(5), below. Before amendment, Code Sec. 305(a) read as follows:

(a) General Rule.—Except as provided in subsection (b), gross income does not include the amount of any distribution made by a corporation to its shareholders, with respect to the stock of such corporation, in its stock or in rights to acquire its stock.

P.L. 91-172, §421(b)(3) and (b)(5), provide:

(3) In cases to which Treasury Decision 6990 (promulgated January 10, 1969) would not have applied, in applying paragraphs (1) [General effective date—CCH.] and (2) [See amendment note following Code Sec. 305(b)—CCH.] April 22, 1969, shall be substituted for January 10, 1969.

* * *

(5) With respect to distributions made or considered as made after January 10, 1969, in taxable years ending after such date, to the extent that the amendment made by subsection (a) does not apply by reason of paragraph (2), (3), or (4) [See amendment note following Code Sec. 305(b).—CCH] of this subsection, section 305 of the Internal Revenue Code of 1954 (as in effect before the amendment made by subsection (a)) shall continue to apply.

[Sec. 305(b)]

(b) EXCEPTIONS.—Subsection (a) shall not apply to a distribution by a corporation of its stock, and the distribution shall be treated as a distribution of property to which section 301 applies—

(1) DISTRIBUTIONS IN LIEU OF MONEY.—If the distribution is, at the election of any of the shareholders (whether exercised before or after the declaration thereof), payable either—

(A) in its stock, or

(B) in property.

(2) DISPROPORTIONATE DISTRIBUTIONS.—If the distribution (or a series of distributions of which such distribution is one) has the result of—

(A) the receipt of property by some shareholders, and

(B) an increase in the proportionate interests of other shareholders in the assets or earnings and profits of the corporation.

(3) DISTRIBUTIONS OF COMMON AND PREFERRED STOCK.—If the distribution (or a series of distributions of which such distribution is one) has the result of—

(A) the receipt of preferred stock by some common shareholders, and

(B) the receipt of common stock by other common shareholders.

(4) DISTRIBUTIONS ON PREFERRED STOCK.—If the distribution is with respect to preferred stock, other than an increase in the conversion ratio of convertible preferred stock made solely to take account of a stock dividend or stock split with respect to the stock into which such convertible stock is convertible.

(5) DISTRIBUTIONS OF CONVERTIBLE PREFERRED STOCK.—If the distribution is of convertible preferred stock, unless it is established to the satisfaction of the Secretary that such distribution will not have the result described in paragraph (2).

Amendments

• 1976, Tax Reform Act of 1976 (P.L. 94-455)

P.L. 94-455, §1906(b)(13)(A):

Amended 1954 Code by substituting "Secretary" for "Secretary or his delegate" each place it appeared. **Effective** 2-1-77.

• 1969, Tax Reform Act of 1969 (P.L. 91-172)

P.L. 91-172, §421(a):

Amended Code Sec. 305(b). **Effective**, generally, with respect to distributions (or deemed distributions) made after 1-10-69, in tax years ending after that date. However, see P.L. 91-172, §421(b)(2)-(5), below. Before amendment, Code Sec. 305(b) read as follows:

(b) Distributions in Lieu of Money.—Subsection (a) shall not apply to a distribution by a corporation of its stock (or rights to acquire its stock), and the distribution shall be treated as a distribution of property to which section 301 applies—

(1) to the extent that the distribution is made in discharge of preference dividends for the taxable year of the corporation in which the distribution is made or for the preceding taxable year; or

(2) if the distribution is, at the election of any of the shareholders (whether exercised before or after the declaration thereof), payable either—

(A) in its stock (or in rights to acquire its stock), or

(B) in property.

P.L. 91-172, §421(b)(2)-(5), provides:

(b)(2)(A) Section 305(b)(2) of the Internal Revenue Code of 1954 (as added by subsection (a)) shall not apply to a distribution (or deemed distribution) of stock made before January 1, 1991, with respect to stock (i) outstanding on January 10, 1969, (ii) issued pursuant to a contract binding on January 10, 1969, on the distributing corporation, (iii) which is additional stock of that class of stock which (as of January 10, 1969) had the largest fair market value of all classes of stock of the corporation (taking into account only stock outstanding on January 10, 1969, or issued pursuant to a contract binding on January 10, 1969), (iv) described in subparagraph (C)(iii), or (v) issued in a prior distribution described in clause (i), (ii), (iii), or (iv).

(B) Subparagraph (A) shall apply only if—

(i) the stock as to which there is a receipt of property was outstanding on January 10, 1969 (or was issued pursuant to a contract binding on January 10, 1969, on the distributing corporation), and

(ii) if such stock and any stock described in subparagraph (A)(i) were also outstanding on January 10, 1968, a distribution of property was made on or before January 10, 1969, with respect to such stock, and a distribution of stock was made on or before January 10, 1969, with respect to such stock described in subparagraph (A)(i).

(C) Subparagraph (A) shall cease to apply when at any time after October 9, 1969, the distributing corporation issues any of its stock (other than in a distribution of stock with respect to stock of the same class) which is not—

(i) nonconvertible preferred stock,

(ii) additional stock of that class of stock which meets the requirements of subparagraph (A)(iii), or

(iii) preferred stock which is convertible into stock which meets the requirements of subparagraph (A)(iii) at a fixed conversion ratio which takes account of all stock dividends and stock splits with respect to the stock into which such convertible stock is convertible.

(D) For purposes of this paragraph, the term "stock" includes rights to acquire such stock.

(b)(3) In cases to which Treasury Decision 6990 (promulgated January 10, 1969) would not have applied, in applying paragraphs (1) [General effective date.—CCH] and (2) April 22, 1969, shall be substituted for January 10, 1969.

(b)(4) Section 305(b)(4) of the Internal Revenue Code of 1954 (as added by subsection (a)) shall not apply to any distribution (or deemed distribution) with respect to preferred stock (including any increase in the conversion ratio of convertible stock) made before January 1, 1991, pursuant to the terms relating to the issuance of such stock which were in effect on January 10, 1969.

(b)(5) With respect to distributions made or considered as made after January 10, 1969, in taxable years ending after such date, to the extent that the amendment made by subsection (a) does not apply by reason of paragraph (2), (3), or (4) of this subsection, section 305 of the Internal Revenue Code of 1954 (as in effect before the amendment made by subsection (a)) shall continue to apply.

[Sec. 305(c)]

(c) CERTAIN TRANSACTIONS TREATED AS DISTRIBUTIONS.—For purposes of this section and section 301, the Secretary shall prescribe regulations under which a change in conversion ratio, a change in redemption price, a difference between redemption price and issue price, a redemption which is treated as a distribution to which section 301 applies, or any transaction (including a recapitalization) having a similar effect on the interest of any shareholder shall be treated as a distribution with respect to any shareholder whose proportionate interest in the earnings and profits or assets of the corporation is increased by such change, difference, redemption, or similar transaction. Regulations prescribed under the preceding sentence shall provide that—

(1) where the issuer of stock is required to redeem the stock at a specified time or the holder of stock has the option to require the issuer to redeem the stock, a redemption premium resulting from such requirement or option shall be treated as reasonable only if the amount of such premium does not exceed the amount determined under the principles of section 1273(a)(3),

(2) a redemption premium shall not fail to be treated as a distribution (or series of distributions) merely because the stock is callable, and

(3) in any case in which a redemption premium is treated as a distribution (or series of distributions), such premium shall be taken into account under principles similar to the principles of section 1272(a).

Amendments

• 1990, Omnibus Budget Reconciliation Act of 1990 (P.L. 101-508)

P.L. 101-508, §11322(a):

Amended Code Sec. 305(c) by adding at the end thereof a new sentence. **Effective** for stock issued after 10-9-90. For an exception, see P.L. 101-508, §11322(b)(2), below.

P.L. 101-508, §11322(b)(2), provides:

(2) EXCEPTION.—The amendment made by subsection (a) shall not apply to any stock issued after October 9, 1990, if—

(A) such stock is issued pursuant to a written binding contract in effect on October 9, 1990, and at all times thereafter before such issuance,

(B) such stock is issued pursuant to a registration or offering statement filed on or before October 9, 1990, with a Federal or State agency regulating the offering or sale of securities and such stock is issued before the date 90 days after the date of such filing, or

(C) such stock is issued pursuant to a plan filed on or before October 9, 1990, in a title 11 or similar case (as defined in section 368(a)(3)(A) of the Internal Revenue Code of 1986).

• 1976, Tax Reform Act of 1976 (P.L. 94-455)

P.L. 94-455, §1906(b)(13)(A):

Amended 1954 Code by substituting "Secretary" for "Secretary or his delegate" each place it appeared. **Effective** 2-1-77.

• 1969, Tax Reform Act of 1969 (P.L. 91-172)

P.L. 91-172, §421(a):

Redesignated Code Sec. 305(c) as Code Sec. 305(e) and added new Code Sec. 305(c). **Effective**, generally, with respect to distributions (or deemed distributions) made after 1-10-69, in tax years ending after that date. For possible exceptions, see amendment note following Code Sec. 305(a).

[Sec. 305(d)]

(d) DEFINITIONS.—

(1) RIGHTS TO ACQUIRE STOCK.—For purposes of this section, the term "stock" includes rights to acquire such stock.

(2) SHAREHOLDERS.—For purposes of subsections (b) and (c), the term "shareholder" includes a holder of rights or of convertible securities.

Amendments

• 1990, Omnibus Budget Reconciliation Act of 1990 (P.L. 101-508)

P.L. 101-508, §11801(c)(7)(A):

Amended Code Sec. 305(d)(1) by striking "(other than subsection (e))" after "this section". **Effective** 11-5-90.

P.L. 101-508, §11821(b), provides:

(b) SAVINGS PROVISION.—If—

(1) any provision amended or repealed by this part applied to—

(A) any transaction occurring before the date of the enactment of this Act,

(B) any property acquired before such date of enactment, or

(C) any item of income, loss, deduction, or credit taken into account before such date of enactment, and

(2) the treatment of such transaction, property, or item under such provision would (without regard to the amendments made by this part) affect liability for tax for periods ending after such date of enactment,

nothing in the amendments made by this part shall be construed to affect the treatment of such transaction, property, or item for purposes of determining liability for tax for periods ending after such date of enactment.

• 1981, Economic Recovery Tax Act of 1981 (P.L. 97-34)

P.L. 97-34, §321(b):

Amended Code Sec. 305(d) by striking out in paragraph (1) "this section" and inserting "this section (other than subsection (e))". **Effective** for distributions after 12-31-81, in tax years ending after such date.

• 1969, Tax Reform Act of 1969 (P.L. 91-172)

P.L. 91-172, §421(a):

Added Code Sec. 305(d). **Effective**, generally, with respect to distributions (or deemed distributions) made after 1-10-69, in tax years ending after that date. For possible exceptions, see amendment note following Code Sec. 305(a).

[Sec. 305(e)—Repealed]

Amendments

• 1990, Omnibus Budget Reconciliation Act of 1990 (P.L. 101-508)

P.L. 101-508, §11801(a)(17):

Repealed Code Sec. 305(e). **Effective** 11-5-90. Prior to repeal, Code Sec. 305(e) read as follows:

(e) DIVIDEND REINVESTMENT IN STOCK OF PUBLIC UTILITIES.—

(1) IN GENERAL.—Subsection (b) shall not apply to any qualified reinvested dividend.

(2) QUALIFIED REINVESTED DIVIDEND DEFINED.—For purposes of this subsection, the term "qualified reinvested dividend" means—

(A) a distribution by a qualified public utility of shares of its qualified common stock to an individual with respect to the common or preferred stock of such corporation pursuant to a plan under which shareholders may elect to receive dividends in the form of stock instead of property, but

(B) only if the shareholder elects to have this subsection apply to such shares.

(3) QUALIFIED PUBLIC UTILITY DEFINED.—

(A) IN GENERAL.—For purposes of this subsection, the term "qualified public utility" means, for any taxable year of the corporation, a domestic corporation which, for the 10-year period ending on the day before the beginning of the taxable year, placed in service qualified long-life public utility property having a cost equal to at least 60 percent of the aggregate cost of all tangible property described in subparagraph (A) or (B) of section 1245(a)(3) placed in service by the corporation during such period.

(B) SPECIAL RULES.—For purposes of subparagraph (A)—

(i) all members of an affiliated group shall be treated as one corporation,

(ii) a successor corporation shall take into account the acquisitions of its predecessor, and

(iii) a new corporation to which clause (ii) does not apply shall substitute its period of existence for the 10-year period set forth in subparagraph (A).

(C) DEFINITIONS.—For purposes of this paragraph—

(i) AFFILIATED GROUP.—The term "affiliated group" has the meaning given to such term by subsection (a) of section 1504 (determined without regard to subsection (b) of section 1504).

(ii) QUALIFIED LONG-LIFE PUBLIC UTILITY PROPERTY.—The term "qualified long-life public utility property" means any tangible property which—

(I) is described in subparagraph (A) or (B) of section 1245(a)(3),

(II) has a present class life (as defined in section 168(g)(2)) of more than 18 years, and

(III) is public utility property (within the meaning of section 167(l)(3)(A)).

(4) QUALIFIED COMMON STOCK DEFINED.—

(A) IN GENERAL.—For purposes of this subsection, the term "qualified common stock" means authorized but unissued common stock of the corporation—

(i) which has been designated by the board of directors of the corporation as issued for purposes of this subsection, but

(ii) only if the number of shares to be issued to a shareholder was determined by reference to a value which is not less than 95 percent and not more than 105 percent of the stock's fair market value during the period immediately before the distribution (determined under regulations prescribed by the Secretary).

(B) CERTAIN PURCHASES BY CORPORATION OF ITS OWN STOCK.—Except as provided in subparagraph (D), if a corporation has purchased or purchases its common stock within a 2-year period beginning 1 year before the date of the distribution and ending 1 year after such date, such distribution shall be treated as not being a qualified reinvested dividend.

(C) MEMBERS OF AFFILIATED GROUP.—For purposes of subparagraph (B), the purchase by any corporation which is a member of the same affiliated group (as defined in paragraph (3)(C)(i)) as the distributing corporation of common stock in any corporation which is a member of such group from any person (other than a member of such group) shall be treated as a purchase by the distributing corporation of its common stock.

(D) WAIVER OF SUBPARAGRAPH (B) WHERE THERE IS BUSINESS PURPOSE.—Under regulations prescribed by the Secretary, subparagraph (B) shall not apply where the distributing corporation establishes that there was a business purpose for the purchase of the stock and such purchase is not inconsistent with the purposes of this subsection.

(5) SHARE INCLUDES FRACTIONAL SHARE.—For purposes of this subsection, the term "share" includes a fractional share.

(6) LIMITATION.—

(A) IN GENERAL.—In the case of any individual, the aggregate amount of distributions to which this subsection applies for the taxable year shall not exceed $750 ($1,500 in the case of a joint return).

(B) APPLICATION OF CEILING.—If, but for this subparagraph, a share of stock would, by reason of subparagraph (A), be treated as partly within this subsection and partly outside this subsection, such share shall be treated as outside this subsection.

(7) BASIS AND HOLDING PERIOD.—In the case of stock received as a qualified reinvested dividend—

(A) notwithstanding section 307, the basis shall be zero, and

(B) the holding period shall begin on the date the dividend would (but for this subsection) be includible in income.

(8) ELECTION.—An election under this subsection with respect to any share shall be made on the shareholder's return for the taxable year in which the dividend would (but for this subsection) be includible in income. Any such election, once made, shall be revocable only with the consent of the Secretary.

(9) DISPOSITIONS WITHIN 1 YEAR OF DISTRIBUTION.—Under regulations prescribed by the Secretary—

(A) DISPOSITION OF OTHER COMMON STOCK.—If—

(i) a shareholder receives any qualified reinvested dividend from a corporation, and

(ii) during the period which begins on the record date for the qualified reinvested dividend and ends 1 year after the date of the distribution of such dividend, the shareholder disposes of any common stock of such corporation,

the shareholder shall be treated as having disposed of the stock received as a qualified reinvested dividend (to the extent there remains such stock to which this paragraph has not applied).

(B) ORDINARY INCOME TREATMENT.—If any stock received as a qualified reinvested dividend is disposed of within 1 year after the date such stock is distributed, such disposition shall be treated as a disposition of property which is not a capital asset.

(10) NO REDUCTION IN EARNINGS AND PROFITS FOR DISTRIBUTION OF QUALIFIED COMMON STOCK.—The earnings and profits of any corporation shall not be reduced by reason of the distribution of any qualified common stock of such corporation pursuant to a plan under which shareholders may elect to receive dividends in the form of stock instead of property.

(11) CERTAIN INDIVIDUALS INELIGIBLE.—

(A) IN GENERAL.—This subsection shall not apply to any individual who is—

(i) a trust or estate, or

(ii) a nonresident alien individual.

(B) 5 PERCENT SHAREHOLDERS INELIGIBLE.—Any distribution by a corporation to a 5 percent shareholder in such corporation shall not be treated as a qualified reinvested dividend.

(C) 5 PERCENT SHAREHOLDER DEFINED.—For purposes of subparagraph (B), the term "5 percent shareholder" means any individual who, immediately before the distribution, owns (directly or through the application of section 318)—

(i) stock possessing more than 5 percent of the total combined voting power of the distributing corporation, or

(ii) more than 5 percent of the total value of all classes of stock of the distributing corporation.

(12) TERMINATION.—This subsection shall not apply to distributions after December 31, 1985.

P.L. 101-508, §11821(b), provides:

(b) SAVINGS PROVISION.—If—

(1) any provision amended or repealed by this part applied to—

(A) any transaction occcurring before the date of the enactment of this Act,

(B) any property acquired before such date of enactment, or

(C) any item of income, loss, deduction, or credit taken into account before such date of enactment, and

(2) the treatment of such transaction, property, or item under such provision would (without regard to the amendments made by this part) affect liability for tax periods ending after such date of enactment,

nothing in the amendments made by this part shall be construed to affect the treatment of such transaction, property, or item for purposes of determining liability for tax for periods ending after such date of enactment.

• 1983, Technical Corrections Act of 1982 (P.L. 97-448)

P.L. 97-448, §103(f)(1):

Amended Code Sec. 305(e)(3)(A). **Effective** as if included in the provision of P.L. 97-34 to which it relates. Prior to amendment, Code Sec. 305(e)(3)(A) read as follows:

"(A) In general.—For purposes of this subsection, the term `qualified public utility' means for any taxable year of the corporation, a domestic corporation which, for the 10-year period ending on the day before the beginning of the taxable year, acquired public utility recovery property having a cost equal to at least 60 percent of the aggregate cost of all tangible property described in section 1245(a)(3) (other than subparagraphs (C) and (D) thereof) acquired by the corporation during such period."

P.L. 97-448, §103(f)(2):

Amended Code Sec. 305(e)(3)(C)(ii). **Effective** as if included in the provision of P.L. 97-34 to which it relates. Prior to amendment, Code Sec. 305(e)(3)(C)(ii) read as follows:

"(ii) Public utility recovery property.—The term `public utility recovery property' means public utility property (within the meaning of section 167(l)(3)(A)) which is recovery property which is 10-year property or 15-year public utility property (within the meaning of section 168), except that any requirement that the property be placed in service after December 31, 1980, shall not apply."

• 1981, Economic Recovery Tax Act of 1981 (P.L. 97-34)

P.L. 97-34, §321(a):

Added Code Sec. 305(e). **Effective** for distributions after 12-31-81, in tax years ending after such date.

[Sec. 305(e)]

(e) TREATMENT OF PURCHASER OF STRIPPED PREFERRED STOCK.—

(1) IN GENERAL.—If any person purchases after April 30, 1993, any stripped preferred stock, then such person, while holding such stock, shall include in gross income amounts equal to the amounts which would have been so includible if such stripped preferred stock were a bond issued on the purchase date and having original issue discount equal to the excess, if any, of—

(A) the redemption price for such stock, over

(B) the price at which such person purchased such stock.

The preceding sentence shall also apply in the case of any person whose basis in such stock is determined by reference to the basis in the hands of such purchaser.

(2) BASIS ADJUSTMENTS.—Appropriate adjustments to basis shall be made for amounts includible in gross income under paragraph (1).

(3) TAX TREATMENT OF PERSON STRIPPING STOCK.—If any person strips the rights to 1 or more dividends from any stock described in paragraph (5)(B) and after April 30, 1993, disposes of such dividend rights, for purposes of paragraph (1), such person shall be treated as having purchased the stripped preferred stock on the date of such disposition for a purchase price equal to such person's adjusted basis in such stripped preferred stock.

(4) AMOUNTS TREATED AS ORDINARY INCOME.—Any amount included in gross income under paragraph (1) shall be treated as ordinary income.

(5) STRIPPED PREFERRED STOCK.—For purposes of this subsection—

(A) IN GENERAL.—The term "stripped preferred stock" means any stock described in subparagraph (B) if there has been a separation in ownership between such stock and any dividend on such stock which has not become payable.

(B) DESCRIPTION OF STOCK.—Stock is described in this subsection if such stock—

(i) is limited and preferred as to dividends and does not participate in corporate growth to any significant extent, and

(ii) has a fixed redemption price.

(6) PURCHASE.—For purposes of this subsection, the term "purchase" means—

(A) any acquisition of stock, where

(B) the basis of such stock is not determined in whole or in part by the reference to the adjusted basis of such stock in the hands of the person from whom acquired.

(7) CROSS REFERENCE.—

For treatment of stripped interests in certain accounts or entities holding preferred stock, see section 1286(f).

Amendments

• 2004, American Jobs Creation Act of 2004 (P.L. 108-357)

P.L. 108-357, §831(b):

Amended Code Sec. 305(e) by adding at the end a new paragraph (7). **Effective** for purchases and dispositions after 10-22-2004.

• 1993, Omnibus Budget Reconciliation Act of 1993 (P.L. 103-66)

P.L. 103-66, §13206(c)(1):

Amended Code Sec. 305 by redesignating subsection (e) as subsection (f) and by inserting after subsection (d) new subsection (e). **Effective** 4-30-93.

[Sec. 305(f)]

(f) CROSS REFERENCES.—

For special rules—

(1) Relating to the receipt of stock rights in corporate organizations and reorganizations, see part III (sec. 351 and following).

(2) In the case of a distribution which results in a gift, see section 2501 and following.

(3) In the case of a distribution which has the effect of the payment of compensation, see section 61(a)(1).

Amendments

• 1993, Omnibus Budget Reconciliation Act of 1993 (P.L. 103-66)

P.L. 103-66, §13206(c)(1):

Amended Code Sec. 305 by redesignating subsection (e) as subsection (f). **Effective** 4-30-93.

• 1990, Omnibus Budget Reconciliation Act of 1990 (P.L. 101-508)

P.L. 101-508, §11801(c)(7)(B):

Amended Code Sec. 305 by redesignating subsection (f) as subsection (e). **Effective** 11-5-90.

P.L. 101-508, §11821(b), provides:

(b) SAVINGS PROVISION.—If—

(1) any provision amended or repealed by this part applied to—

(A) any transaction occcurring before the date of the enactment of this Act,

(B) any property acquired before such date of enactment, or

(C) any item of income, loss, deduction, or credit taken into account before such date of enactment, and

(2) the treatment of such transaction, property, or item under such provision would (without regard to the amendments made by this part) affect liability for tax periods ending after such date of enactment,

nothing in the amendments made by this part shall be construed to affect the treatment of such transaction, property, or item for purposes of determining liability for tax for periods ending after such date of enactment.

• 1981, Economic Recovery Tax Act of 1981 (P.L. 97-34)

P.L. 97-34, §321(a):

Redesignated Code Sec. 305(e) as Code Sec. 305(f). **Effective** for distributions after 12-31-81, in tax years ending after such date.

• 1969, Tax Reform Act of 1969 (P.L. 91-172)

P.L. 91-172, §421(a):

Redesignated Code Sec. 305(c) as Code Sec. 305(e).

[Sec. 306]

SEC. 306. DISPOSITIONS OF CERTAIN STOCK.

[Sec. 306(a)]

(a) GENERAL RULE.—If a shareholder sells or otherwise disposes of section 306 stock (as defined in subsection (c))—

(1) DISPOSITIONS OTHER THAN REDEMPTIONS.—If such disposition is not a redemption (within the meaning of section 317(b))—

(A) The amount realized shall be treated as ordinary income. This subparagraph shall not apply to the extent that—

(i) the amount realized, exceeds

(ii) such stock's ratable share of the amount which would have been a dividend at the time of distribution if (in lieu of section 306 stock) the corporation had distributed money in an amount equal to the fair market value of the stock at the time of distribution.

(B) Any excess of the amount realized over the sum of—

(i) the amount treated under subparagraph (A) as ordinary income, plus

(ii) the adjusted basis of the stock,

shall be treated as gain from the sale of such stock.

(C) No loss shall be recognized.

→ Caution: Code Sec. 306(a)(1)(D), below, is subject to the sunset provision of the Jobs and Growth Tax Relief Reconciliation Act of 2003 (P.L. 108-27), §303. Absent Congressional action, the changes made to this provision by, or that take effect as if included in P.L. 108-27, do not apply after December 31, 2010. For more information about the sunset provision, see page XXI of the Preface to this publication and P.L. 108-27, §303, in the amendment notes. See the amendments notes for a history of amendments to this section and the effective date of each change.

(D) TREATMENT AS DIVIDEND.—For purposes of section 1(h)(11) and such other provisions as the Secretary may specify, any amount treated as ordinary income under this paragraph shall be treated as a dividend received from the corporation.

(2) REDEMPTION.—If the disposition is a redemption, the amount realized shall be treated as a distribution of property to which section 301 applies.

Amendments

• 2003, Jobs and Growth Tax Relief Reconciliation Act of 2003 (P.L. 108-27)

P.L. 108-27, §302(e)(3):

Amended Code Sec. 306(a)(1) by adding at the end a new subparagraph (D). For the **effective** date, see Act Sec. 302(f), as amended by P.L. 108-311, §402(a)(6), below.

P.L. 108-27, §302(f), as amended by P.L. 108-311, §402(a)(6), provides:

(f) EFFECTIVE DATE.—

(1) IN GENERAL.—Except as provided in paragraph (2), the amendments made by this section shall apply to taxable years beginning after December 31, 2002.

(2) PASS-THRU ENTITIES.—In the case of a pass-thru entity described in subparagraph (A), (B), (C), (D), (E), or (F) of section 1(h)(10) of the Internal Revenue Code of 1986, as amended by this Act, the amendments made by this section shall apply to taxable years ending after December 31, 2002; except that dividends received by such an entity on or before such date shall not be treated as qualified dividend income (as defined in section 1(h)(11)(B) of such Code, as added by this Act).

P.L. 108-27, §303, as amended by P.L. 109-222, §102, provides:

SEC. 303. SUNSET OF TITLE.

All provisions of, and amendments made by, this title shall not apply to taxable years beginning after December 31, 2010, and the Internal Revenue Code of 1986 shall be applied and administered to such years as if such provisions and amendments had never been enacted.

• 1980, Crude Oil Windfall Profit Tax Act of 1980 (P.L. 96-223)

P.L. 96-223, §401(a):

Repealed Code Sec. 306(a)(3). **Effective** with respect to decedents dying after 12-31-76. However, see the amendment note for P.L. 96-223, §401(a), that follows Code Sec. 1014(d) for the text of Act Sec. 401(d) that authorizes the election of the carryover basis rules in the case of a decedent dying after 12-31-76 and before 11-7-78. Prior to repeal, Code Sec. 306(a)(3) read as follows:

(3) ORDINARY INCOME FROM SALE OR REDEMPTION OF SECTION 306 STOCK WHICH IS CARRYOVER BASIS PROPERTY ADJUSTED FOR 1976 VALUE.—

(A) IN GENERAL.—If any section 306 stock was distributed before January 1, 1977, and if the adjusted basis of such stock in the hands of the person disposing of it is determined under section 1023 (relating to carryover basis), then the amount treated as ordinary income under paragraph (1)(A) of this subsection (or the amount treated as a dividend under section 301 (c)(1)) shall not exceed the excess of the amount realized over the sum of—

(i) the adjusted basis of such stock on December 31, 1976, and

(ii) any increase in basis under section 1023(h).

(B) REDEMPTION MUST BE DESCRIBED IN SECTION 302(b).—Subparagraph (A) shall apply to a redemption only if such redemption is described in paragraph (1), (2), or (4) of section 302(b).

• 1978, Revenue Act of 1978 (P.L. 95-600)

P.L. 95-600, §702(a)(1), (3):

Added Code Sec. 306(a)(3). **Effective** for estates of decedents dying after 12-31-79.

• 1976, Tax Reform Act of 1976 (P.L. 94-455)

P.L. 94-455, §1901(b)(3)(J):

Substituted "ordinary income" for "gain from the sale of property which is not a capital asset" in Code Sec. 306(a)(1)(A) and in Code Sec. 306(a)(1)(B). **Effective** for tax years beginning after 12-31-76.

[Sec. 306(b)]

(b) EXCEPTIONS.—Subsection (a) shall not apply—

(1) TERMINATION OF SHAREHOLDER'S INTEREST, ETC.—

(A) NOT IN REDEMPTION.—If the disposition—

(i) is not a redemption;

(ii) is not, directly or indirectly, to a person the ownership of whose stock would (under section 318(a)) be attributable to the shareholder; and

(iii) terminates the entire stock interest of the shareholder in the corporation (and for purposes of this clause, section 318(a) shall apply).

(B) IN REDEMPTION.—If the disposition is a redemption and paragraph (3) or (4) of section 302(b) applies.

(2) LIQUIDATIONS.—If the section 306 stock is redeemed in a distribution in complete liquidation to which part II (sec. 331 and following) applies.

(3) WHERE GAIN OR LOSS IS NOT RECOGNIZED.—To the extent that, under any provision of this subtitle, gain or loss to the shareholder is not recognized with respect to the disposition of the section 306 stock.

(4) TRANSACTIONS NOT IN AVOIDANCE.—If it is established to the satisfaction of the Secretary—

(A) that the distribution, and the disposition or redemption, or

(B) in the case of a prior or simultaneous disposition (or redemption) of the stock with respect to which the section 306 stock disposed of (or redeemed) was issued, that the disposition (or redemption) of the section 306 stock,

was not in pursuance of a plan having as one of its principal purposes the avoidance of Federal income tax.

Amendments

• 1984, Deficit Reduction Act of 1984 (P.L. 98-369)

P.L. 98-369, §712(i)(2):

Amended the paragraph heading of Code Sec. 306(b)(1) by striking out "INTEREST" and inserting in lieu thereof "INTEREST, ETC." **E ffective** as if included in the provision of P.L. 97-248 to which it relates.

• 1982, Tax Equity and Fiscal Responsibility Act of 1982 (P.L. 97-248)

P.L. 97-248, §222(e)(1)(A):

Amended Code Sec. 306(b)(2) by striking out "partial or complete liquidation" and inserting in lieu thereof "complete liquidation". **Effective**, generally, for distributions after 8-31-82. However, see the exceptions in P.L. 97-248, §222(f)(2), which appears in the amendment notes for Code Sec. 331(b).

P.L. 97-248, §222(e)(2):

Amended Code Sec. 306(b)(1)(B) by striking out "section 302(b)(3)" and inserting in lieu thereof "paragraph (3) or (4) of section 302(b)". **Effective**, generally, for distributions after 8-31-82. However, see the exceptions in P.L. 97-248, §222(f)(2), which appears in the amendment notes for Code Sec. 331(b).

• 1980, Crude Oil Windfall Profit Tax Act of 1980 (P.L. 96-223)

P.L. 96-223, §401(a):

Repealed Code Sec. 306(b)(5), as added by P.L. 95-600, §702(a)(2). **Effective** with respect to decedents dying after

12-31-76. However, see the amendment note for P.L. 96-223, §401(a), that follows Code Sec. 1014(d) for the text of Act Sec. 401(d) that authorizes the election of the carryover basis rules in the case of a decedent dying after 12-31-76 and before 11-7-78. Prior to repeal, Code Sec. 306(b)(5) read as follows:

(5) SECTION 303 REDEMPTIONS.—To the extent that section 303 applies to a distribution in redemption of section 306 stock.

• 1978, Revenue Act of 1978 (P.L. 95-600)

P.L. 95-600, §702(a)(2), (3):

Added Code Sec. 306(b)(5). **Effective** for estates of decedents dying after 12-31-79.

• 1976, Tax Reform Act of 1976 (P.L. 94-455)

P.L. 94-455, §1906(b)(13)(A):

Amended 1954 Code by substituting "Secretary" for "Secretary or his delegate" each place it appeared. **Effective** 2-1-77.

[Sec. 306(c)]

(c) SECTION 306 STOCK DEFINED.—

(1) IN GENERAL.—For purposes of this subchapter, the term "section 306 stock" means stock which meets the requirements of subparagraph (A), (B), or (C) of this paragraph.

(A) DISTRIBUTED TO SELLER.—Stock (other than common stock issued with respect to common stock) which was distributed to the shareholder selling or otherwise disposing of such stock if, by reason of section 305(a), any part of such distribution was not includible in the gross income of the shareholder.

(B) RECEIVED IN A CORPORATE REORGANIZATION OR SEPARATION.—Stock which is not common stock and—

(i) which was received, by the shareholder selling or otherwise disposing of such stock, in pursuance of a plan of reorganization (within the meaning of section 368(a)), or in a distribution or exchange to which section 355 (or so much of section 356 as relates to section 355) applied, and

(ii) with respect to the receipt of which gain or loss to the shareholder was to any extent not recognized by reason of part III, but only to the extent that either the effect of the transaction was substantially the same as the receipt of a stock dividend, or the stock was received in exchange for section 306 stock.

For purposes of this section, a receipt of stock to which the foregoing provisions of this subparagraph apply shall be treated as a distribution of stock.

(C) STOCK HAVING TRANSFERRED OR SUBSTITUTED BASIS.—Except as otherwise provided in subparagraph (B), stock the basis of which (in the hands of the shareholder selling or otherwise disposing of such stock) is determined by reference to the basis (in the hands of such shareholder or any other person) of section 306 stock.

(2) EXCEPTION WHERE NO EARNINGS AND PROFITS.—For purposes of this section, the term "section 306 stock" does not include any stock no part of the distribution of which would have been a dividend at the time of the distribution if money had been distributed in lieu of the stock.

(3) CERTAIN STOCK ACQUIRED IN SECTION 351 EXCHANGE.—The term "section 306 stock" also includes any stock which is not common stock acquired in an exchange to which section 351 applied if receipt of money (in lieu of the stock) would have been treated as a dividend to any extent. Rules similar to the rules of section 304(b)(2) shall apply—

(A) for purposes of the preceding sentence, and

(B) for purposes of determining the application of this section to any subsequent disposition of stock which is section 306 stock by reason of an exchange described in the preceding sentence.

(4) APPLICATION OF ATTRIBUTION RULES FOR CERTAIN PURPOSES.—For purposes of paragraphs (1)(B)(ii) and (3), section 318(a) shall apply. For purposes of applying the preceding sentence to paragraph (3), the rules of section 304(c)(3)(B) shall apply.

Amendments

• 1984, Deficit Reduction Act of 1984 (P.L. 98-369)

P.L. 98-369, §712(l)(5)(B):

Amended Code Sec. 306(c)(4) by striking the last sentence thereof and inserting a new sentence. **Effective** as if included in the provision of P.L. 97-248 to which it relates. Prior to amendment, the last sentence of Code Sec. 306(c)(4) read as follows:

For purposes of applying the preceding sentence to paragraph (3), sections 318(a)(2)(C) and 318(a)(3)(C) shall be applied without regard to the 50 percent limitation contained therein.

P.L. 98-369, §712(l)(6):

Amended Code Sec. 306(c)(3) by striking the last sentence thereof and inserting a new sentence. **Effective** as if included in the provision of P.L. 97-248 to which it relates. Prior to amendment, the last sentence of Code Sec. 306(c)(3) read as follows:

In the case of such stock, rules similar to the rules of section 304(b)(2) shall apply for purposes of this section.

• 1982, Tax Equity and Fiscal Responsibility Act of 1982 (P.L. 97-248)

P.L. 97-248, §226(b):

Amended Code Sec. 306(c) by adding at the end thereof new paragraph (3). **Effective** for transfers occurring after 8-31-82, in tax years ending after such date. For a special rule, see P.L. 97-248, §226(c)(2), below.

P.L. 97-248, §226(c)(2), provides:

(2) APPROVAL BY FEDERAL RESERVE BOARD.—The amendments made by this section shall not apply to transfers pursuant to an application to form a BHC filed with the Federal Reserve Board before August 16, 1982, if the BHC was formed not later than the later of—

(A) the 90th day after the date of the last required approval of any regulatory authority to form such BHC, or

(B) January 1, 1983.

For purposes of this paragraph, the term "BHC" means a bank holding company (within the meaning of section 2(a) of the Bank Holding Company Act of 1956).

P.L. 97-248, §227(a):

Amended Code Sec. 306(c) by adding at the end thereof new paragraph (4). **Effective** for stock received after 8-31-82, in tax years ending after such date.

[Sec. 306(d)]

(d) STOCK RIGHTS.—For purposes of this section—

(1) stock rights shall be treated as stock, and

(2) stock acquired through the exercise of stock rights shall be treated as stock distributed at the time of the distribution of the stock rights, to the extent of the fair market value of such rights at the time of the distribution.

[Sec. 306(e)]

(e) CONVERTIBLE STOCK.—For purposes of subsection (c)—

(1) if section 306 stock was issued with respect to common stock and later such section 306 stock is exchanged for common stock in the same corporation (whether or not such exchange is pursuant to a conversion privilege contained in the section 306 stock), then (except as provided in paragraph (2)) the common stock so received shall not be treated as section 306 stock; and

(2) common stock with respect to which there is a privilege of converting into stock other than common stock (or into property), whether or not the conversion privilege is contained in such stock, shall not be treated as common stock.

[Sec. 306(f)]

(f) SOURCE OF GAIN.—The amount treated under subsection (a)(1)(A) as ordinary income shall, for purposes of part I of subchapter N (sec. 861 and following, relating to determination of sources of income), be treated as derived from the same source as would have been the source if money had been received from the corporation as a dividend at the time of the distribution of such stock. If under the preceding sentence such amount is determined to be derived from sources within the United States, such amount shall be considered to be fixed or determinable annual or periodical gains, profits, and income within the meaning of section 871(a) or section 881(a), as the case may be.

Amendments

• 1976, Tax Reform Act of 1976 (P.L. 94-455)

P.L. 94-455, §1901(b)(3)(J):

Amended Code Sec. 306(f) by substiting "ordinary income" for "gain from the sale of property which is not a capital asset". **Effective** for tax years beginning after 12-31-76.

[Sec. 306(g)]

(g) CHANGE IN TERMS AND CONDITIONS OF STOCK.—If a substantial change is made in the terms and conditions of any stock, then, for purposes of this section—

(1) the fair market value of such stock shall be the fair market value at the time of the distribution or at the time of such change, whichever such value is higher;

(2) such stock's ratable share of the amount which would have been a dividend if money had been distributed in lieu of stock shall be determined as of the time of distribution or as of the time of such change, whichever such ratable share is higher; and

(3) subsection (c) (2) shall not apply unless the stock meets the requirements of such subsection both at the time of such distribution and at the time of such change.

[Sec. 306(h)—Repealed]

Amendments

• 1990, Omnibus Budget Reconciliation Act of 1990 (P.L. 101-508)

P.L. 101-508, §11801(a)(18):

Repealed Code Sec. 306(h). **Effective** 11-5-90. Prior to repeal, Code Sec. 306(h) read as follows:

(h) STOCK RECEIVED IN DISTRIBUTIONS AND REORGANIZATIONS TO WHICH 1939 CODE APPLIED.—If stock—

(1) was received in a distribution or reorganization to which the Internal Revenue Code of 1939 (or the corresponding provisions of prior law) applied,

(2) such stock would have been section 306 stock if this Code applied to such distribution or reorganization, and

(3) such stock is disposed of or redeemed on or after June 22, 1954,

then the foregoing subsections of this section shall not apply in respect of such disposition or redemption. The extent to which such disposition or redemption shall be treated as a dividend shall be determined as if the Internal Revenue Code of 1939 (as modified by the provisions of this Code other than the foregoing subsections of this section) continued to apply in respect of such disposition or redemption.

P.L. 101-508, §11821(b), provides:

(b) SAVINGS PROVISION.—If—

(1) any provision amended or repealed by this part applied to—

(A) any transaction occurring before the date of the enactment of this Act,

(B) any property acquired before such date of enactment, or

(C) any item of income, loss, deduction, or credit taken into account before such date of enactment, and

(2) the treatment of such transaction, property, or item under such provision would (without regard to the amendments made by this part) affect liability for tax for periods ending after such date of enactment,

nothing in the amendments made by this part shall be construed to affect the treatment of such transaction, property, or item for purposes of determining liability for tax for periods ending after such date of enactment.

[Sec. 307]

SEC. 307. BASIS OF STOCK AND STOCK RIGHTS ACQUIRED IN DISTRIBUTIONS.

[Sec. 307(a)]

(a) GENERAL RULE.—If a shareholder in a corporation receives its stock or rights to acquire its stock (referred to in this subsection as "new stock") in a distribution to which section 305(a) applies, then the basis of such new stock and of the stock with respect to which it is distributed (referred to in this section as "old stock"), respectively, shall, in the shareholder's hands, be determined by allocating between the old stock and the new stock the adjusted basis of the old stock. Such allocation shall be made under regulations prescribed by the Secretary.

Amendments

• 1976, Tax Reform Act of 1976 (P.L. 94-455)

P.L. 94-455, §1906(b)(13)(A):

Amended 1954 Code by substituting "Secretary" for "Secretary or his delegate" each place it appeared. **Effective** 2-1-77.

[Sec. 307(b)]

(b) EXCEPTION FOR CERTAIN STOCK RIGHTS.—

(1) IN GENERAL.—If—

(A) a corporation distributes rights to acquire its stock to a shareholder in a distribution to which section 305(a) applies, and

(B) the fair market value of such rights at the time of the distribution is less than 15 percent of the fair market value of the old stock at such time,

then subsection (a) shall not apply and the basis of such rights shall be zero, unless the taxpayer elects under paragraph (2) of this subsection to determine the basis of the old stock and of the stock rights under the method of allocation provided in subsection (a).

(2) ELECTION.—The election referred to in paragraph (1) shall be made in the return filed within the time prescribed by law (including extensions thereof) for the taxable year in which such rights were received. Such election shall be made in such manner as the Secretary may by regulations prescribe, and shall be irrevocable when made.

Amendments

• 1976, Tax Reform Act of 1976 (P.L. 94-455)

P.L. 94-455, §1906(b)(13)(A):

Amended 1954 Code by substituting "Secretary" for "Secretary or his delegate" each place it appeared. **Effective** 2-1-77.

[Sec. 307(c)]

(c) CROSS REFERENCE.—

For basis of stock and stock rights distributed before June 22, 1954, see section 1052.

Subpart B—Effects on Corporation

[Sec. 311]

SEC. 311. TAXABILITY OF CORPORATION ON DISTRIBUTION.

[Sec. 311(a)]

(a) GENERAL RULE.—Except as provided in subsection (b), no gain or loss shall be recognized to a corporation on the distribution (not in complete liquidation) with respect to its stock of—

(1) its stock (or rights to acquire its stock), or

(2) property.

Amendments

• 1988, Technical and Miscellaneous Revenue Act of 1988 (P.L. 100-647)

P.L. 100-647, §1018(d)(5)(E):

Amended Code Sec. 311(a) by striking out "distribution, with respect to its stock," and inserting in lieu thereof "distribution (not in complete liquidation) with respect to its stock". **Effective** as if included in the provision of P.L. 99-514 to which it relates.

[Sec. 311(b)]

(b) DISTRIBUTIONS OF APPRECIATED PROPERTY.—

(1) IN GENERAL.—If—

(A) a corporation distributes property (other than an obligation of such corporation) to a shareholder in a distribution to which subpart A applies, and

(B) the fair market value of such property exceeds its adjusted basis (in the hands of the distributing corporation),

then gain shall be recognized to the distributing corporation as if such property were sold to the distributee at its fair market value.

(2) TREATMENT OF LIABILITIES.—Rules similar to the rules of section 336(b) shall apply for purposes of this subsection.

(3) SPECIAL RULE FOR CERTAIN DISTRIBUTIONS OF PARTNERSHIP OR TRUST INTERESTS.—If the property distributed consists of an interest in a partnership or trust, the Secretary may by regulations provide that the amount of the gain recognized under paragraph (1) shall be computed without regard to any loss attributable to property contributed to the partnership or trust for the principal purpose of recognizing such loss on the distribution.

Amendments

• 1988, Technical and Miscellaneous Revenue Act of 1988 (P.L. 100-647)

P.L. 100-647, §1006(e)(21)(B):

Amended Code Sec. 311(b)(2) by striking out "in Excess of Basis" after "Liabilities" in the heading. **Effective** as if included in the provision of P.L. 99-514 to which it relates.

P.L. 100-647, §1006(e)(8)(B):

Amended Code Sec. 311(b) by adding at the end thereof new paragraph (3). **Effective** as if included in the provision of P.L. 99-514 to which it relates.

• 1986, Tax Reform Act of 1986 (P.L. 99-514)

P.L. 99-514, §631(c):

Amended Code Sec. 311. For the **effective** date, as well as special rules, see Act Sec. 633, below. Text of Code Sec. 311 before amendment is reproduced below.

P.L. 99-514, §633, as amended by P.L. 100-647, §1006(g), provides:

SEC. 633. EFFECTIVE DATES.

(a) GENERAL RULE.—Except as otherwise provided in this section, the amendments made by this subtitle shall apply to—

(1) any distribution in complete liquidation, and any sale or exchange, made by a corporation after July 31, 1986, unless such corporation is completely liquidated before January 1, 1987,

(2) any transaction described in section 338 of the Internal Revenue Code of 1986 for which the acquisition date occurs after December 31, 1986, and

(3) any distribution (not in complete liquidation) made after December 31, 1986.

(b) BUILT-IN GAINS OF S CORPORATIONS.—

(1) IN GENERAL.—The amendments made by section 632 (other than subsection (b) thereof) shall apply to taxable years beginning after December 31, 1986, but only in cases where the return for the taxable year is filed pursuant to an S election made after December 31, 1986.

(2) APPLICATION OF PRIOR LAW.—In the case of any taxable year of an S corporation which begins after December 31, 1986, and to which the amendments made by section 632 (other than subsection (b) thereof) do not apply, paragraph (1) of section 1374(b) of the Internal Revenue Code of 1954 (as in effect on the date before the date of the enactment of this Act) shall be applied as if it read as follows:

"(1) an amount equal to 34 percent of the amount by which the net capital gain of the corporation for the taxable year exceeds $25,000, or".

(c) EXCEPTION FOR CERTAIN PLANS OF LIQUIDATION AND BINDING CONTRACTS.—

(1) IN GENERAL.—The amendments made by this subtitle shall not apply to—

(A) any distribution or sale or exchange made pursuant to a plan of liquidation adopted before August 1, 1986, if the liquidating corporation is completely liquidated before January 1, 1988,

(B) any distribution or sale or exchange made by any corporation if more than 50 percent of the voting stock by value of such corporation is acquired on or after August 1, 1986, pursuant to a written binding contract in effect before such date and if such corporation is completely liquidated before January 1, 1988,

(C) any distribution or sale or exchange made by any corporation if substantially all of the assets of such corporation are sold on or after August 1, 1986, pursuant to 1 or more written binding contracts in effect before such date and if such corporation is completely liquidated before January 1, 1988, or

(D) any transaction described in section 338 of the Internal Revenue Code of 1986 with respect to any target corporation if a qualified stock purchase of such target corporation is made on or after August 1, 1986, pursuant to a written binding contract in effect before such date and the acquisition date (within the meaning of such section 338) is before January 1, 1988.

(2) SPECIAL RULE FOR CERTAIN ACTIONS TAKEN BEFORE NOVEMBER 20, 1985.—For purposes of paragraph (1), transactions shall be treated as pursuant to a plan of liquidation adopted before August 1, 1986, if—

(A) before November 20, 1985—

(i) the board of directors of the liquidating corporation adopted a resolution to solicit shareholder approval for a transaction of a kind described in section 336 or 337, or

(ii) the shareholders or board of directors have approved such a transaction,

(B) before November 20, 1985—

(i) there has been an offer to purchase a majority of the voting stock of the liquidating corporation, or

(ii) the board of directors of the liquidating corporation has adopted a resolution approving an acquisition or recommending the approval of an acquisition to the shareholders, or

(C) before November 20, 1985, a ruling request was submitted to the Secretary of the Treasury or his delegate with respect to a transaction of a kind described in section 336 or 337 of the Internal Revenue Code of 1954 (as in effect before the amendments made by this subtitle).

For purposes of the preceding sentence, any action taken by the board of directors or shareholders of a corporation with respect to any subsidiary of such corporation shall be treated as taken by the board of directors or shareholders of such subsidiary.

(d) TRANSITIONAL RULE FOR CERTAIN SMALL CORPORATIONS.—

(1) IN GENERAL.—In the case of the complete liquidation before January 1, 1989, of a qualified corporation, the amendments made by this subtitle shall not apply to the applicable percentage of each gain or loss which (but for this paragraph) would be recognized by the liquidating corporation by reason of the amendments made by this subtitle. Section 333 of the Internal Revenue Code of 1954 (as in effect on the day before the date of the enactment of this Act) shall continue to apply to any complete liquidation described in the preceding sentence.

(2) PARAGRAPH (1) NOT TO APPLY TO CERTAIN ITEMS.—Paragraph (1) shall not apply to—

(A) any gain or loss which is an ordinary gain or loss (determined without regard to section 1239 of the Internal Revenue Code of 1986),

(B) any gain or loss on a capital asset held for not more than 6 months, and

(C) any gain on an asset acquired by the qualified corporation if—

(i) the basis of such asset in the hands of the qualified corporation is determined (in whole or in part) by reference to the basis of such asset in the hands of the person from whom acquired, and

(ii) a principal purpose for the transfer of such asset to the qualified corporation was to secure the benefits of this subsection.

(3) APPLICABLE PERCENTAGE.—For purposes of this subsection, the term "applicable percentage" means—

(A) 100 percent if the applicable value of the qualified corporation is less than $5,000,000, or

(B) 100 percent reduced by an amount which bears the same ratio to 100 percent as—

(i) the excess of the applicable value of the corporation over $5,000,000, bears to

(ii) $5,000,000.

(4) APPLICABLE VALUE.—For purposes of this subsection, the applicable value is the fair market value of all of the stock of the corporation on the date of the adoption of the plan of complete liquidation (or if greater, on August 1, 1986).

(5) QUALIFIED CORPORATION.—For purposes of this subsection, the term "qualified corporation" means any corporation if—

(A) on August 1, 1986, and at all times thereafter before the corporation is completely liquidated, more than 50 percent (by value) of the stock in such corporation is held by a qualified group, and

(B) the applicable value of such corporation does not exceed $10,000,000.

(6) DEFINITIONS AND SPECIAL RULES.—For purposes of this subsection—

(A) QUALIFIED GROUP.—

(i) IN GENERAL.—Except as provided in clause (ii), the term "qualified group" means any group of 10 or fewer qualified persons who at all times during the 5-year period ending on the date of the adoption of the plan of complete liquidation (or, if shorter, the period during which the corporation or any predecessor was in existence) owned (or was treated as owning under the rules of subparagraph (C)) more than 50 percent (by value) of the stock in such corporation.

(ii) 5-YEAR OWNERSHIP REQUIREMENT NOT TO APPLY IN CERTAIN CASES.—In the case of—

(I) any complete liquidation pursuant to a plan of liquidation adopted before March 31, 1988,

(II) any distribution not in liquidation made before March 31, 1988,

(III) an election to be an S corporation filed before March 31, 1988, or

(IV) a transaction described in section 338 of the Internal Revenue Code of 1986 where the acquisition date (within the meaning of such section 338) is before March 31, 1988,

the term "qualified group" means any group of 10 or fewer qualified persons.

(B) QUALIFIED PERSON.—The term "qualified person" means—

(i) an individual,

(ii) an estate, or

(iii) any trust described in clause (ii) or clause (iii) of section 1361(c)(2)(A) of the Internal Revenue Code of 1986.

(C) ATTRIBUTION RULES.—

(i) IN GENERAL.—Any stock owned by a corporation, trust (other than a trust referred to in subparagraph (B)(iii), or partnership shall be treated as owned proportionately by its shareholders, beneficiaries, or partners, and shall not be treated as owned by such corporation, trust, or partnership. Stock considered to be owned by a person by reason of the application of the preceding sentence shall, for purposes of applying such sentence, be treated as actually owned by such person.

(ii) FAMILY MEMBERS.—Stock owned (or treated as owned) by members of the same family (within the meaning of section 318(a)(1) of the Internal Revenue Code of 1986) shall be treated as owned by 1 person, and shall be treated as owned by such 1 person for any period during which it was owned (or treated as owned) by any such member.

(iii) TREATMENT OF CERTAIN TRUSTS.—Stock owned (or treated as owned) by the estate of any decedent or by any trust referred to in subparagraph (B)(iii) with respect to such decedent shall be treated as owned by 1 person and shall be treated as owned by such 1 person for the period during which it was owned (or treated as owned) by such estate or any such trust or by the decedent.

(D) SPECIAL HOLDING PERIOD RULES.—Any property acquired by reason of the death of an individual shall be treated as owned at all times during which such property was owned (or treated as owned) by the decedent.

(E) CONTROLLED GROUP OF CORPORATIONS.—All members of the same controlled group (as defined in section 267(f)(1) of such Code) shall be treated as 1 corporation for purposes of determining whether any of such corporations met the requirement of paragraph (5)(B) and for purposes of determining the applicable percentage with respect to any of such corporations. For purposes of the preceding sentence, an S corporation shall not be treated as a member of a controlled group unless such corporation was a C corporation for its taxable year which includes August 1, 1988, or it was not described for such taxable year in paragraph (1) or (2) of section 1374(c) of such Code (as in effect on the day before the date of the enactment of this Act).

(7) SECTION 338 TRANSACTIONS.—The provisions of this subsection shall also apply in the case of a transaction described in section 338 of the Internal Revenue Code of 1986 where the acquisition date (within the meaning of such section 338) is before January 1, 1989.

(8) APPLICATION OF SECTION 1374.—Rules similar to the rules of this subsection shall apply for purposes of applying section 1374 of the Internal Revenue Code of 1986 (as amended by section 632) in the case of a qualified corporation which makes an election to be an S corporation under section 1362 of such Code before January 1, 1989, without regard to whether such corporation is completely liquidated.

(9) APPLICATION TO NONLIQUIDATING DISTRIBUTIONS.—The provisions of this subsection shall also apply in the case of any distribution (not in complete liquidation) made by a qualified corporation before January 1, 1989, without regard to whether such corporation is completely liquidated.

(e) COMPLETE LIQUIDATION DEFINED.—For purposes of this section, a corporation shall be treated as completely liquidated if all of the assets of such corporation are distributed in complete liquidation, less assets retained to meet claims.

(f) OTHER TRANSITIONAL RULES.—

(1) The amendments made by this subtitle shall not apply to any liquidation of a corporation incorporated under the laws of Pennsylvania on August 3, 1970, if—

(A) the board of directors of such corporation approved a plan of liquidation before January 1, 1986,

(B) an agreement for the sale of a material portion of the assets of such corporation was signed on May 9, 1986 (whether or not the assets are sold in accordance with such agreement), and

(C) the corporation is completely liquidated on or before December 31, 1988.

(2) The amendments made by this subtitle shall not apply to any liquidation (or deemed liquidation under section 338 of the Internal Revenue Code of 1986) of a diversified financial services corporation incorporated under the laws of Delaware on May 9, 1929 (or any direct or indirect subsidiary of such corporation), pursuant to a binding written contract entered into on or before December 31, 1986; but only if the liquidation is completed (or in the case of a section 338 election, the acquisition date occurs) before January 1, 1988.

(3) The amendments made by this subtitle shall not apply to any distribution, or sale, or exchange—

(A) of the assets owned (directly or indirectly) by a testamentary trust established under the will of a decedent dying on June 15, 1956, to its beneficiaries,

(B) made pursuant to a court order in an action filed on January 18, 1984, if such order—

(i) is issued after July 31, 1986, and

(ii) directs the disposition of the assets of such trust and the division of the trust corpus into 3 separate subtrusts.

For purposes of the preceding sentence, an election under section 338(g) of the Internal Revenue Code of 1986 (or an election under section 338(h)(10) of such Code, qualifying as a section 337 liquidation pursuant to regulations prescribed by the Secretary under section 1.338(h)(10)-1T(j)) made in connection with a sale or exchange pursuant to a court order described in subparagraph (B) shall be treated as a sale of [or] exchange.

(4)(A) The amendments made by this subtitle shall not apply to any distribution, or sale, or exchange—

(i) if—

(I) an option agreement to sell substantially all of the assets of a selling corporation organized under the laws of Massachusetts on October 20, 1976, is executed before August 1, 1986, the corporation adopts (by approval of its shareholders) a conditional plan of liquidation before August 1, 1986 to become effective upon the exercise of such option agreement (or modification thereto), and the assets are sold pursuant to the exercise of the option (as originally executed or subsequently modified provided that the purchase price is not thereby increased), or

(II) in the event that the optionee does not acquire substantially all the assets of the coporation, the optionor corporation sells substantially all its assets to another purchaser at a purchase price not greater than that contemplated by such option agreement pursuant to an effective plan of liquidation, and

(ii) the complete liquidation of the corporation occurs within 12 months of the time the plan of liquidation becomes effective, but in no event later than December 31, 1989.

(B) For purposes of subparagraph (A), a distribution, or sale, or exchange, of a distributee corporation (within the meaning of section 337(c)(3) of the Internal Revenue Code of 1986) shall be treated as satisfying the requirements of subparagraph (A) if its subsidiary satisfies the requirements of subparagraph (A).

(C) For purposes of section 56 of the Internal Revenue Code of 1986 (as amended by this Act), any gain or loss not recognized by reason of this paragraph shall not be taken into account in determining the adjusted net book income of the corporation.

(5) In the case of a corporation incorporated under the laws of Wisconsin on April 3, 1948—

(A) a voting trust established not later than December 31, 1987, shall qualify as a trust permitted as a shareholder of an S corporation and shall be treated as only 1 shareholder if the holders of beneficial interests in such voting trust are—

(i) employees or retirees of such corporation, or

(ii) in the case of stock or voting trust certificates acquired from an employee or retiree of such corporation, the spouse, child, or estate of such employee or retiree or a

trust created by such employee or retiree which is described in section 1361(c)(2) of the Internal Revenue Code of 1986 (or treated as described in such section by reason of section 1361(d) of such Code), and

(B) the amendment made by section 632 (other than subsection (b) thereof) shall not apply to such corporation if it elects to be an S corporation before January 1, 1989.

(6) The amendments made by this subtitle shall not apply to the liquidation of a corporation incorporated on January 26, 1982, under the laws of the State of Alabama with a principal place of business in Colbert County, Alabama, but only if such corporation is completely liquidated on or before December 31, 1987.

(7) The amendments made by this subtitle shall not apply to the acquisition by a Delaware Bank holding company of all of the assets of an Iowa bank holding company pursuant to a written contract dated December 9, 1981.

(8) The amendments made by this subtitle shall not apply to the liquidation of a corporation incorporated under the laws of Delaware on January 20, 1984, if more than 40 percent of the stock of such corporation was acquired by purchase on June 11, 1986, and there was a tender offer with respect to all additional outstanding shares of such corporation on July 29, 1986, but only if the corporation is completely liquidated on or before December 31, 1987.

(g) TREATMENT OF CERTAIN DISTRIBUTIONS IN RESPONSE TO HOSTILE TENDER OFFER.—

(1) IN GENERAL.—No gain or loss shall be recognized under the Internal Revenue Code of 1986 to a corporation (hereinafter in this subsection referred to as "parent") on a qualified distribution.

(2) QUALIFIED DISTRIBUTION DEFINED.—For purposes of paragraph (1)—

(A) IN GENERAL.—The term "qualified distribution" means a distribution—

(i) by parent of all of the stock of a qualified subsidiary in exchange for stock of parent which was acquired for purposes of such exchange pursuant to a tender offer dated February 16, 1982, and

(ii) pursuant to a contract dated February 13, 1982, and

(iii) which was made not more than 60 days after the board of directors of parent recommended rejection of an unsolicited tender offer to obtain control of parent.

(B) QUALIFIED SUBSIDIARY.—The term "qualified subsidiary" means a corporation created or organized under the laws of Delaware on September 7, 1976, all of the stock of which was owned by parent immediately before the qualified distribution.

Reproduced immediately below is the text of Code Sec. 311 before the amendment made by P.L. 99-514.

SEC. 311. TAXABILITY OF CORPORATION ON DISTRIBUTION.

[Sec. 311(a)]

(a) GENERAL RULE.—Except as provided in subsections (b), (c), and (d) of this section and section 453B, no gain or loss shall be recognized to a corporation on the distribution, with respect to its stock, of—

(1) its stock (or rights to acquire its stock), or

(2) property.

Amendments

• 1980, Installment Sales Revision Act of 1980 (P.L. 96-471)

P.L. 96-471, §2(b)(1):

Amended Code Sec. 311(a) by substituting "section 453B" for "section 453(d)".

• 1969, Tax Reform Act of 1969 (P.L. 91-172)

P.L. 91-172, §905(b)(1):

Amended Code Sec. 311(a) by changing "subsections (b) and (c)" to "subsections (b), (c), and (d)". **Effective** 12-1-69.

[Sec. 311(b)]

(b) LIFO INVENTORY.—

(1) RECOGNITION OF GAIN.—If a corporation inventorying goods under the method provided in section 472 (relating to last-in, first-out inventories) distributes inventory assets (as defined in paragraph (2) (A)), then the amount (if any) by which—

(A) the inventory amount (as defined in paragraph (2) (B)) of such assets under a method authorized by section 471 (relating to general rule for inventories), exceeds

(B) the inventory amount of such assets under the method provided in section 472,

shall be treated as gain to the corporation recognized from the sale of such inventory assets.

(2) DEFINITIONS.—For purposes of paragraph (1)—

(A) INVENTORY ASSETS.—The term "inventory assets" means stock in trade of the corporation, or other property of a kind which would properly be included in the inventory of the corporation if on hand at the close of the taxable year.

(B) INVENTORY AMOUNT.—The term "inventory amount" means, in the case of inventory assets distributed during a taxable year, the amount of such inventory assets determined as if the taxable year closed at the time of such distribution.

(3) METHOD OF DETERMINING INVENTORY AMOUNT.—For purposes of this subsection, the inventory amount of assets under a method authorized by section 471 shall be determined—

(A) if the corporation uses the retail method of valuing inventories under section 472, by using such method, or

(B) if subparagraph (A) does not apply, by using cost or market, whichever is lower.

[Sec. 311(c)]

(c) LIABILITY IN EXCESS OF BASIS.—If—

(1) a corporation distributes property to a shareholder with respect to its stock,

(2) such property is subject to a liability, or the shareholder assumes a liability of the corporation in connection with the distribution, and

(3) the amount of such liability exceeds the adjusted basis (in the hands of the distributing corporation) of such property,

then gain shall be recognized to the distributing corporation in an amount equal to such excess as if the property distributed had been sold at the time of the distribution. In the case of a distribution of property subject to a liability which is not assumed by the shareholder, the amount of gain to be recognized under the preceding sentence shall not exceed the excess, if any, of the fair market value of such property over its adjusted basis.

[Sec. 311(d)]

(d) DISTRIBUTIONS OF APPRECIATED PROPERTY.—

(1) IN GENERAL.—If—

(A) a corporation distributes property (other than an obligation of such corporation) to a shareholder in a distribution to which subpart A applies, and

(B) the fair market value of such property exceeds its adjusted basis (in the hands of the distributing corporation),

then a gain shall be recognized to the distributing corporation in an amount equal to such excess as if the property distributed had been sold at the time of the distribution. This subsection shall be applied after the application of subsections (b) and (c).

(2) EXCEPTIONS AND LIMITATIONS.—Paragraph (1) shall not apply to—

(A) a distribution which is made with respect to qualified stock if—

(i) section 302(b)(4) applies to such distribution, or

(ii) such distribution is a qualified dividend;

(B) a distribution of stock or an obligation of a corporation if the requirements of paragraph (2) of subsection (e) are met with respect to the distribution;

(C) a distribution to the extent that section 303(a) (relating to distributions in redemption of stock to pay death taxes) applies to such distribution;

(D) a distribution to a private foundation in redemption of stock which is described in section 537(b)(2)(A) and (B); and

(E) a distribution by a corporation to which part I of subchapter M (relating to regulated investment companies) applies, if such distribution is in redemption of its stock upon the demand of the shareholder.

Amendments

• 1984, Deficit Reduction Act of 1984 (P.L. 98-369)

P.L. 98-369, §54(a)(1):

Amended Code Sec. 311(d)(1). **Effective** for distributions declared on or after 6-14-84, in tax years ending after such date. For special rules and exceptions, see Act Sec. 54(d)(3)-(6), below. Prior to amendment, Code Sec. 311 (d)(1) read as follows:

(1) In General.—If—

(A) a corporation distributes property (other than an obligation of such corporation) to a shareholder in a redemption (to which subpart A applies) of part or all of his stock in such corporation, and

(B) the fair market value of such property exceeds its adjusted basis (in the hands of the distributing corporation),

then a gain shall be recognized to the distributing corporation in an amount equal to such excess as if the property distributed had been sold at the time of the distribution. Subsections (b) and (c) shall not apply to any distribution to which this subsection applies.

P.L. 98-369, §54(a)(2)(A):

Amended Code Sec. 311(d)(2) by striking out subparagraphs (A) and (B) and inserting in lieu thereof new subparagraph (A). **Effective** for distributions declared on or after 6-14-84, in tax years ending after such date. For special rules and exceptions, see Act Sec. 54(d)(3)-(6), below. Prior to amendment, Code Sec. 311(d)(2)(A) and (B) read as follows:

(A) a distribution to a corporate shareholder if the basis of the property distributed is determined under section 301(d)(2);

(B) a distribution to which section 302(b)(4) applies and which is made with respect to qualified stock;

P.L. 98-369, §54(a)(2)(B):

Amended Code Sec. 311(d)(2) by redesignating subparagraphs (C), (D), (E), and (F) as (B), (C), (D), and (E), respectively. **Effective** for distributions declared on or after 6-14-84, in tax years ending after such date. For special rules and exceptions, see Act Sec. 54(d)(3)-(6), below.

P.L. 98-369, §54(a)(3):

Amended the heading of Code Sec. 311(d). **Effective** for distributions declared on or after 6-14-84, in tax years ending after such date. For special rules and exceptions, see Act Sec. 54(d)(3)-(6), below. Prior to amendment, the heading for Code Sec. 311(d) read as follows:

(d) Appreciated Property Used to Redeem Stock.—

P.L. 98-369, §54(d)(3)-(6), as amended by P.L. 99-514, §1804(b)(3) and P.L. 100-647, §1018(d)(2)-(3), provides:

(3) Exception for Distributions Before January 1, 1985, to 80-Percent Corporate Shareholders.—

(A) In General.—The amendments made by subsection (a) shall not apply to any distribution before January 1, 1985, to an 80-percent corporate shareholder if the basis of the property distributed is determined under section 301(d)(2) of the Internal Revenue Code of 1954.

(B) 80-Percent Corporate Shareholder.—The term "80-percent corporate shareholder" means, with respect to any distribution, any corporation which owns—

(i) stock in the corporation making the distribution possessing at least 80 percent of the total combined voting power of all classes of stock entitled to vote, and

(ii) at least 80 percent of the total number of shares of all other classes of stock of the distributing corporation (except nonvoting stock which is limited and preferred as to dividends).

(C) Special Rule for Affiliated Group Filing Consolidated Return.—For purposes of this paragraph and paragraph (4), all members of the same affiliated group (as defined in section 1504 of the Internal Revenue Code of 1954) which file a consolidated return for the taxable year which includes the date of the distribution shall be treated as 1 corporation.

(D) Special Rule for Certain Distributions Before January 1, 1988.—

(i) In General.—In the case of a transaction to which this subparagraph applies, subparagraph (A) shall be applied by substituting "1988" for "1985" and the amendments made by subtitle D of title VI of the Tax Reform Act of 1986 shall not apply.

(ii) Transaction to Which Subparagraph Applies.—This subparagraph applies to a transaction in which a Delaware corporation which was incorporated on May 31, 1927, and which was acquired by the transferee on December 10, 1968, transfers to the transferee stock in a corporation—

(I) with respect to which such Delaware corporation is a 100-percent corporate shareholder, and

(II) which is a Tennessee corporation which was incorporated on March 2, 1978, and which is a successor to an Indiana corporation which was incorporated on June 28, 1946, and acquired by the transferee on December 10, 1968.

(4) Exception for Certain Distributions Where Tender Offer Commenced on May 23, 1984.—

(A) In General.—The amendments made by subsection (a) shall not apply to any distribution made before September 1, 1986, if—

(i) such distribution consists of qualified stock held (directly or indirectly) on June 15, 1984, by the distributing corporation,

(ii) control of the distributing corporation (as defined in section 368(c) of the Internal Revenue Code of 1954) is acquired other than in a tax-free transaction after January 1, 1984, but before January 1, 1985,

(iii) a tender offer for the shares of the distributing corporation was commenced on May 23, 1984, and was amended on May 24, 1984, and

(iv) the distributing corporation and the distributee corporation are members of the same affiliated group (as defined in section 1504 of such Code) which filed a consolidated return for the taxable year which includes the date of the distribution.

If the common parent of any affiliated group filing a consolidated return meets the requirements of clauses (ii) and (iii), each other member of such group shall be treated as meeting such requirements.

(B) Qualified Stock.—For purposes of subparagraph (A), the term "qualified stock" means any stock in a corporation which on June 15, 1984, was a member of the same affiliated group as the distributing corporation and which filed a consolidated return with the distributing corporation for the taxable year which included June 15, 1984.

(5) Exception for Certain Distributions.—

(A) In General.—The amendments made by this section shall not apply to distributions before February 1, 1986, if—

(i) the distribution consists of property held on March 7, 1984 (or property acquired thereafter in the ordinary course of a trade or business) by—

(I) the controlled corporation, or

(II) any subsidiary controlled corporation,

(ii) a group of 1 or more shareholders (acting in concert)—

(I) acquired, during the 1-year period ending on February 1, 1984, at least 10 percent of the outstanding stock of the controlled corporation,

(II) held at least 10 percent of the outstanding stock of the common parent on February 1, 1984, and

(III) submitted a proposal for distributions of interests in a royalty trust from the common parent or the controlled corporation, and

(iii) the common parent acquired control of the controlled corporation during the 1-year period ending on February 1, 1984.

(B) Definitions.—For purposes of this paragraph—

(i) The term "common parent" has the meaning given such term by section 1504(a) of the Internal Revenue Code of 1954.

(ii) The term "controlled corporation" means a corporation with respect to which 50 percent or more of the outstanding stock of its common parent is tendered for pursuant to a tender offer outstanding on March 7, 1984.

(iii) The term "subsidiary controlled corporation" means any corporation with respect to which the controlled corporation has control (within the meaning of section 368(c) of such Code) on March 7, 1984.

(6) Exception for Certain Distribution of Partnership Interests.—The amendments made by this section shall not apply to any distribution before February 1 1986, of an interest in a partnership the interests of which were being traded on a national securities exchange on March 7, 1984, if—

(A) such interest was owned by the distributing corporation (or any member of an affiliated group within the meaning of section 1504(a) of such Code of which the distributing corporation was a member) on March 7, 1984,

(B) the distributing corporation (or any such affiliated member) owned more than 80 percent of the interests in such partnership on March 7, 1984, and

(C) more than 10 percent of the interests in such partnership was offered for sale to the public during the 1-year period ending on March 7, 1984.

• 1982, Tax Equity and Fiscal Responsibility Act of 1982 (P.L. 97-248)

P.L. 97-248, §223(a)(1):

Amended Code Sec. 311(d)(2)(A)-(C). **Effective**, generally, for distributions after 8-31-82. But see amendment notes for P.L. 97-248, §223(b)(2)-(5), below, for special rules. Prior to amendment Code Sec. 311(d)(2)(A)-(C) read as follows:

(A) a distribution in complete redemption of all of the stock of a shareholder who, at all times within the 12-month period ending on the date of such distribution, owns at least 10 percent in value of the outstanding stock of the distributing corporation, but only if the redemption qualifies under section 302(b)(3) (determined without the application of section 302(c)(2)(A)(ii));

(B) a distribution of stock or an obligation of a corporation—

(i) which is engaged in at least one trade or business,

(ii) which has not received property constituting a substantial part of its assets from the distributing corporation, in a transaction to which section 351 applied or as a contribution to capital, within the 5-year period ending on the date of the distribution, and

(iii) at least 50 percent in value of the outstanding stock of which is owned by the distributing corporation at any time within the 9-year period ending one year before the date of the distribution;

(C) a distribution of stock or securities pursuant to the terms of a final judgment rendered by a court with respect to the distributing corporation in a court proceeding under the Sherman Act (15 U.S.C. 1-7) or the Clayton Act (15 U.S.C. 12-27), or both, to which the United States is a party, but only if the distribution of such stock or securities in redemption of the distributing corporation's stock is in furtherance of the purposes of the judgment;

P.L. 97-248, §223(a)(3)(A)-(C):

Amended Code Sec. 311(d)(2) by inserting "and" at the end of subparagraph (E); by striking out the semicolon and "and" at the end of subparagraph (F) and inserting in lieu thereof a period; and by striking out paragraph (G). **Effective** for distributions after 8-31-82. Prior to amendment, paragraph (G) read as follows:

"(G) a distribution of stock to a distributee which is not an organization exempt from tax under section 501(a), if with respect to such distributee, subsection (a)(1) or (b)(1) of section 1101 (relating to distributions pursuant to Bank Holding Company Act) applies to such distribution."

P.L. 97-248, §223(b)(2)-(5), as amended by P.L. 97-448, §306(a)(7), provides:

(2) Distributions pursuant to ruling requests before July 23, 1982.—In the case of a ruling request under section 311(d)(2)(A) of the Internal Revenue Code of 1954 (as in effect before the amendments made by this section) made before July 23, 1982, the amendments made by this section shall not apply to distributions made—

(A) pursuant to a ruling granted pursuant to such request, and

(B) either before October 21, 1982, or within 90 days after the date of such ruling.

(3) Distributions pursuant to final judgments of court.—In the case of a final judgment described in section 311(d)(2)(C) of such Code (as in effect before the amendments made by this section) rendered before July 23, 1982, the amendments made by this section shall not apply to distributions made before January 1, 1986, pursuant to such judgment.

(4) Certain distributions with respect to stock acquired before May 1982.—The amendments made by this section shall not apply to distributions—

(A) which meet the requirements of section 311(d)(2)(A) of such Code (as in effect on the day before the date of the enactment of this Act),

(B) which are made on or before August 31, 1983, and

(C) which are made with respect to stock acquired after 1980 and before May 1982.

(5) Distributions of timberland with respect to stock of forest products company.—If—

(A) a forest products company distributes timberland to a shareholder in redemption of the common and preferred stock in such corporation held by such shareholder,

(B) section 311(d)(2)(A) of the Internal Revenue Code of 1954 (as in effect before the amendments made by this section) would have applied to such distributions, and

(C) such distributions are made pursuant to 1 of 2 options contained in a contract between such company and such shareholder which is binding on August 31, 1982, and at all times thereafter,

then such distributions of timberland having an aggregate fair market value on August 31, 1982, not in excess of $10,000,000 shall be treated as distributions to which section 311(d)(2)(A) of such Code (as in effect before the date of the enactment of this Act) applies.

• 1978, Revenue Act of 1978 (P.L. 95-600)

P.L. 95-600, §703(j)(2)(B), (C):

Redesignated Code Sec. 311(d)(2)(H) as subparagraph (G). **Effective** as if included in P.L. 94-452, §2(b).

• 1976, Tax Reform Act of 1976 (P.L. 94-455)

P.L. 94-455, §1901(a)(42):

Amended Code Sec. 311(d) by (1) substituting "then a gain shall be recognized" for "then again shall be recognized" in paragraph (1); (2) striking paragraph (2)(C) and redesignating paragraphs (2)(D), (2)(E), (2)(F), and (2)(G) as paragraphs (2)(C), (2)(D), (2)(E), and (2)(F), respectively; (3) striking "26 Stat. 209;" before "15 U.S.C. 1-7" in redesignated Code Sec. 311(d)(2)(C); and (4) striking "38 Stat. 730;" before "15 U.S.C. 12-27" in redesignated Code Sec. 311(d)(2)(C). **Effective** for tax years beginning after 12-31-76, except that the amendment made at (2) above apply only with respect to distributions after 11-30-74. Prior to repeal, Code Sec. 311(d)(2)(C) read as follows:

(C) a distribution before December 1, 1974, of stock of a corporation substantially all of the assets of which the distributing corporation (or a corporation which is a member of the same affiliated group (as defined in section 1504(a)) as the distributing corporation) held on November 30, 1969, if such assets constitute a trade or business which has been actively conducted throughout the one-year period ending on the date of the distribution;

• 1976, Bank Holding Company Tax Act of 1976 (P.L. 94-452)

P.L. 94-452, §2(b):

Amended Code Sec. 311(d)(2) by adding subparagraph (H) [(G)]. **Effective** 10-1-77 with respect to distributions after 12-31-75, in tax years ending after 12-31-75.

• 1969, Tax Reform Act of 1969 (P.L. 91-172)

P.L. 91-172, §905(a):

Amended Code Sec. 311 by adding subsection (d). P.L. 91-675, §1, approved 1-12-71, amended P.L. 91-172, §905(c), which governs the **effective** date of the amendments made to Code Sec. 311 by P.L. 91-172. The **effective** date provision, as amended by P.L. 91-675, read as follows:

"(c) Effective Date.—

"(1) Except as provided in paragraphs (2), (3), (4), and (5), the amendments made by subsections (a) and (b) shall apply with respect to distributions after November 30, 1969.

"(2) The amendments made by subsections (a) and (b) shall not apply to a distribution before April 1, 1970, pursuant to the terms of—

"(A) a written contract which was binding on the distributing corporation on November 30, 1969, and at all times thereafter before the distribution,

"(B) an offer made by the distributing corporation before December 1, 1969,

"(C) an offer made in accordance with a request for a ruling filed by the distributing corporation with the Internal Revenue Service before December 1, 1969, or

"(D) an offer made in accordance with a registration statement filed with the Securities and Exchange Commission before December 1, 1969.

"For purposes of subparagraphs (B), (C), and (D), an offer shall be treated as an offer only if it was in writing and not revocable by its express terms.

"(3) The amendments made by subsections (a) and (b) shall not apply to a distribution by a corporation of specific property in redemption of stock outstanding on November 30, 1969, if—

"(A) every holder of such stock on such date had the right to demand redemption of his stock in such specific property, and

"(B) the corporation had such specific property on hand on such date in a quantity sufficient to redeem all of such stock.

"For purposes of the preceding sentence, stock shall be considered to have been outstanding on November 30, 1969, if it could have been acquired on such date through the exercise of an existing right of conversion contained in other stock held on such date.

"(4) The amendments made by subsections (a) and (b) shall not apply to a distribution by a corporation of property (held on December 1, 1969, by the distributing corporation or a corporation which was a wholly owned subsidiary of the distributing corporation on such date) in redemption of stock outstanding on November 30, 1969, which is redeemed and canceled before July 31, 1971, if—

"(A) such redemption is pursuant to a resolution adopted before November 1, 1969, by the Board of Directors authorizing the redemption of a specific amount of stock constituting more than 10 percent of the outstanding stock of the corporation at the time of the adoption of such resolution; and

"(B) more than 40 percent of the stock authorized to be redeemed pursuant to such resolution was redeemed before December 30, 1969, and more than one-half of the stock so redeemed was redeemed with property other than money.

"(5) The amendments made by subsections (a) and (b) shall not apply to a distribution of stock by a corporation organized prior to December 1, 1969, for the principal purpose of providing an equity participation plan for employees of the corporation whose stock is being distributed (hereinafter referred to as the 'employer corporation') if—

"(A) the stock being distributed was owned by the distributing corporation on November 30, 1969,

"(B) the stock being redeemed was acquired before January 1, 1973, pursuant to such equity participation plan by the shareholder presenting such stock for redemption (or by a predecessor of such shareholder),

"(C) the employment of the shareholder presenting the stock for redemption (or the predecessor of such shareholder) by the employer corporation commenced before January 1, 1971,

"(D) at least 90 percent in value of the assets of the distributing corporation on November 30, 1969, consisted of common stock of the employer corporation, and

"(E) at least 50 percent of the outstanding voting stock of the employer corporation is owned by the distributing corporation at any time within the nine-year period ending one year before the date of such distribution."

[Sec. 311(e)]

(e) DEFINITIONS AND SPECIAL RULES FOR SUBSECTION (d)(2).—For purposes of subsection (d)(2) and this subsection—

(1) QUALIFIED STOCK.—

(A) IN GENERAL.—The term "qualified stock" means stock held by a person (other than a corporation) who at all times during the lesser of—

(i) the 5-year period ending on the date of distribution, or

(ii) the period during which the distributing corporation (or a predecessor corporation) was in existence,

held at least 10 percent in value of the outstanding stock of the distributing corporation (or predecessor corporation).

(B) DETERMINATION OF STOCK HELD.—Section 318 shall apply in determining ownership of stock under subparagraph (A); except that, in applying section 318(a)(1), the term "family" includes any individual described in section 267(c)(4) and any spouse of any such individual.

(C) RULES FOR PASSTHRU ENTITIES.—In the case of an S corporation, partnership, trust, or estate—

(i) the determination of whether subparagraph (A) is satisfied shall be made at the shareholder, partner, or beneficiary level (rather than at the entity level), and

(ii) the distribution shall be treated as made directly to the shareholders, partners, or beneficiaries in proportion to their respective interests in the entity.

(2) DISTRIBUTIONS OF STOCK OR OBLIGATIONS OF CONTROLLED CORPORATIONS.—

(A) REQUIREMENTS.—A distribution of stock or an obligation of a corporation (hereinafter in this paragraph referred to as the "controlled corporation") meets the requirements of this paragraph if—

(i) such distribution is made with respect to qualified stock,

(ii) substantially all of the assets of the controlled corporation consists of the assets of 1 or more qualified businesses,

(iii) no substantial part of the controlled corporation's nonbusiness assets were acquired from the distributing corporation, in a transaction to which section 351 applied or as a contribution to capital, within the 5-year period ending on the date of the distribution, and

(iv) more than 50 percent in value of the outstanding stock of the controlled corporation is distributed by the distributing corporation with respect to qualified stock.

(B) DEFINITIONS.—For purposes of subparagraph (A)—

(i) QUALIFIED BUSINESS.—The term "qualified business" means any trade or business which—

(I) was actively conducted throughout the 5-year period ending on the date of the distribution, and

(II) was not acquired by any person within such period in a transaction in which gain or loss was recognized in whole or in part.

(ii) NONBUSINESS ASSET.—The term "nonbusiness asset" means any asset not used in the active conduct of a trade or business.

(3) QUALIFIED DIVIDEND.—The term "qualified dividend" means any distribution of property to a shareholder other than a corporation if—

(A) such distribution is a dividend,

(B) such property was used by the distributing corporation in the active conduct of a qualified business (as defined in paragraph (2)), and

(C) such property is not property described in paragraph (1) or (4) of section 1221.

Amendments

• 1984, Deficit Reduction Act of 1984 (P.L. 98-369)

P.L. 98-369, §54(a)(2)(C):

Amended Code Sec. 311(e) by adding new paragraph (3). **Effective** for distributions declared on or after 6-14-84, in tax years ending after such date. Special rules and exceptions appear following former Code Sec. 311(d).

P.L. 98-369, §712(j):

Added subparagraph (C) to Code Sec. 311(e)(1). **Effective** as if included in the provision of P.L. 97-248 to which it relates.

• 1982, Tax Equity and Fiscal Responsibility Act of 1982 (P.L. 97-248)

P.L. 97-248, §223(a)(2):

Amended Code Sec. 311 by adding at the end thereof new paragraph (e). **Effective**, generally, for distributions after 8-31-82. But see amendment notes for P.L. 97-248, Act Sec. 223(b)(2)-(5) following former Code Sec. 311(d) for special rules.

[Sec. 312]

SEC. 312. EFFECT ON EARNINGS AND PROFITS.

[Sec. 312(a)]

(a) GENERAL RULE.—Except as otherwise provided in this section, on the distribution of property by a corporation with respect to its stock, the earnings and profits of the corporation (to the extent thereof) shall be decreased by the sum of—

(1) the amount of money,

(2) the principal amount of the obligations of such corporation (or, in the case of obligations having original issue discount, the aggregate issue price of such obligations), and

(3) the adjusted basis of the other property,

so distributed.

Amendments

• 1984, Deficit Reduction Act of 1984 (P.L. 98-369)

P.L. 98-369, §61(c)(1)(A):

Amended Code Sec. 312(a)(2). **Effective** with respect to distributions declared after 3-15-84 in tax years ending after such date. Prior to amendment, it read as follows:

(2) the principal amount of the obligations of such corporation, and

[Sec. 312(b)]

(b) DISTRIBUTIONS OF APPRECIATED PROPERTY.—On the distribution by a corporation, with respect to its stock, of any property (other than an obligation of such corporation) the fair market value of which exceeds the adjusted basis thereof—

(1) the earnings and profits of the corporation shall be increased by the amount of such excess, and

(2) subsection (a)(3) shall be applied by substituting "fair market value" for "adjusted basis". For purposes of this subsection and subsection (a), the adjusted basis of any property is its adjusted basis as determined for purposes of computing earnings and profits.

Amendments

• 1988, Technical and Miscellaneous Revenue Act of 1988 (P.L. 100-647)

P.L. 100-647, §1018(d)(4), amended by P.L. 101-239, §7811(m)(2):

Amended Code Sec. 312(b) by striking out "of any property" the first place it appears, and inserting in lieu thereof "of any property (other than an obligation of such corporation)". **Effective** as if included in the provision of P.L. 99-514 to which it relates.

• 1986, Tax Reform Act of 1986 (P.L. 99-514)

P.L. 99-514, §1804(f)(1)(A):

Amended Code Sec. 312(b). **Effective** as if included in the provision to which it relates. Prior to amendment, Code Sec. 312(b) read as follows:

(b) CERTAIN INVENTORY ASSETS.—

(1) IN GENERAL.—On the distribution by a corporation, with respect to its stock, of inventory assets (as defined in paragraph (2)(A)) the fair market value of which exceeds the adjusted basis thereof, the earnings and profits of the corporation—

(A) shall be increased by the amount of such excess; and

(B) shall be decreased by whichever of the following is the lesser:

(i) the fair market value of the inventory assets distributed, or

(ii) the earnings and profits (as increased under subparagraph (A)).

(2) DEFINITIONS.—

(A) INVENTORY ASSETS.—For purposes of paragraph (1), the term "inventory assets" means—

(i) stock in trade of the corporation, or other property of a kind which would properly be included in the inventory of the corporation if on hand at the close of the taxable year;

(ii) property held by the corporation primarily for sale to customers in the ordinary course of its trade or business; and

(iii) unrealized receivables or fees, except receivables from sales or exchanges of assets other than assets described in this subparagraph.

(B) UNREALIZED RECEIVABLES OR FEES.—For purposes of subparagraph (A)(iii), term "unrealized receivables or fees" means, to the extent not previously includible in income under the method of accounting used by the corporation, any rights (contractual or otherwise) to payment for—

(i) goods delivered, or to be delivered, to the extent that the proceeds therefrom would be treated as amounts received from the sale or exchange of property other than a capital asset, or

(ii) services rendered or to be rendered.

[Sec. 312(c)]

(c) ADJUSTMENTS FOR LIABILITIES.—In making the adjustments to the earnings and profits of a corporation under subsection (a) or (b), proper adjustment shall be made for—

(1) the amount of any liability to which the property distributed is subject, and

(2) the amount of any liability of the corporation assumed by a shareholder in connection with the distribution.

Amendments

• 1986, Tax Reform Act of 1986 (P.L. 99-514)

P.L. 99-514, §1804(f)(1)(B):

Amended Code Sec. 312(c) by inserting "and" at the end of paragraph (1), by striking out ",and" at the end of paragraph (2) and inserting in lieu thereof a period, and by striking out paragraph (3). **Effective** as if included in the provision of P.L. 98-369 to which it relates. Prior to amendment, Code Sec. 312(c)(3) read as follows:

(3) any gain recognized to the corporation on the distribution.

P.L. 99-514, §1804(f)(1)(C):

Amended Code Sec. 312(c) by striking out, ", Etc" in the heading for such subsection. **Effective** as if included in the provision of P.L. 98-369 to which it relates. Prior to amendment, the heading for Code Sec. 312(c) read as follows:

(c) ADJUSTMENTS FOR LIABILITIES, ETC.—

• 1978 (P.L. 95-628)

P.L. 95-628, §3(c), (d):

Amended Code Sec. 312(c)(3). **Effective** for distributions made after 11-10-78. Prior to amendment, paragraph (3) read:

"(3) any gain to the corporation recognized under subsection (b), (c), or (d) of section 311, under section 341(f), or under section 617(d)(1), 1245(a), 1250(a), 1251(c), 1252(a), or 1254(a)."

• 1976, Tax Reform Act of 1976 (P.L. 94-455)

P.L. 94-455, §205(c)(1)(D):

Substituted "1252(a), or 1254(a)" for "or 1252(a)" in Code Sec. 312(c)(3). **Effective** for tax years ending after 12-31-75.

• 1969, Tax Reform Act of 1969 (P.L. 91-172)

P.L. 91-172, §211(b):

Amended Code Sec. 312(c)(3) by striking out "or 1250(a)" and inserting "1250(a), 1251(c), or 1252(a)". **Effective** for tax years beginning after 12-31-69.

P.L. 91-172, §905(b)(2):

Amended Code Sec. 312(c)(3) by changing "subsection (b) or (c)" to "subsection (b), (c), or (d)". **Effective** 12-1-69.

• 1966 (P.L. 89-570)

P.L. 89-570, §[1(b)]:

Amended Code Sec. 312(c)(3) by substituting "section 617(d)(1), 1245(a)," for "section 1245(a)". **Effective** for tax years ending after 9-12-66, the date of enactment, but only for expenditures paid or incurred after that date.

• 1964 (P.L. 88-484)

P.L. 88-484, §[1(b)]:

Amended Code Sec. 312(c)(3) by inserting ", under section 341(f)" immediately after "section 311". **Effective** for transactions after 8-22-64, in tax years ending after such date.

• 1964, Revenue Act of 1964 (P.L. 88-272)

P.L. 88-272, §231(b)(3):

Amended Code Sec. 312(c) to add "or 1250(a)" at the end of paragraph (3). **Effective** for dispositions after 12-31-63, in tax years ending after such date.

• 1962, Revenue Act of 1962 (P.L. 87-834)

P.L. 87-834, §13(f)(3):

Amended Code Sec. 312(c)(3) by inserting "or under section 1245(a)" immediately before the period. **Effective** for tax years beginning after 12-31-62.

[Sec. 312(d)]

(d) CERTAIN DISTRIBUTIONS OF STOCK AND SECURITIES.—

(1) IN GENERAL.—The distribution to a distributee by or on behalf of a corporation of its stock or securities, of stock or securities in another corporation, or of property, in a distribution to which this title applies, shall not be considered a distribution of the earnings and profits of any corporation—

(A) if no gain to such distributee from the receipt of such stock or securities, or property, was recognized under this title, or

(B) if the distribution was not subject to tax in the hands of such distributee by reason of section 305(a).

(2) PRIOR DISTRIBUTIONS.—In the case of a distribution of stock or securities, or property, to which section 115(h) of the Internal Revenue Code of 1939 (or the corresponding provision of prior law) applied, the effect on earnings and profits of such distribution shall be determined under such section 115(h), or the corresponding provision of prior law, as the case may be.

(3) STOCK OR SECURITIES.—For purposes of this subsection, the term "stock or securities" includes rights to acquire stock or securities.

Amendments

• 1976, Tax Reform Act of 1976 (P.L. 94-455)

P.L. 94-455, §1901(a)(43)(A):

Substituted "this title" for "this Code" wherever it appears in Code Sec. 312(d)(1). **Effective** for tax years beginning after 12-31-76.

[Sec. 312(e)—Repealed]

Amendments

• 1984, Deficit Reduction Act of 1984 (P.L. 98-369)

P.L. 98-369, §61(a)(2)(B):

Repealed Code Sec. 312(e). Prior to repeal, Code Sec. 312(e) read as follows:

(e) Special Rule for Certain Redemptions.—In the case of amounts distributed in a redemption to which section 302(a) or 303 applies, the part of such distribution which is properly chargeable to capital account shall not be treated as a distribution of earnings and profits.

• 1982, Tax Equity and Fiscal Responsibility Act of 1982 (P.L. 97-248)

P.L. 97-248, §222(e)(3)(A)-(B):

Amended Code Sec. 312(e) by striking out "in partial liquidation (whether before, on, or after June 22, 1954) or", and by striking out "PARTIAL LIQUIDATIONS AND" in the heading thereof. **Effective**, generally, for distributions after 8-31-82. But see the exceptions noted in P.L. 97-248, Act Sec. 222(f)(2), which appears in the amendment notes for Code Sec. 331(b). Prior to amendment, Code Sec. 312(e) read as follows:

"(e) Special Rule for Partial Liquidations and Certain Redemptions.—In the case of amounts distributed in partial liquidation (whether before, on, or after June 22, 1954) or in a redemption to which section 302(a) or 303 applies, the part of such distribution which is properly chargeable to capital account shall not be treated as a distribution of earnings and profits."

[Sec. 312(f)]

(f) EFFECT ON EARNINGS AND PROFITS OF GAIN OR LOSS AND OF RECEIPT OF TAX-FREE DISTRIBUTIONS.—

(1) EFFECT ON EARNINGS AND PROFITS OF GAIN OR LOSS.—The gain or loss realized from the sale or other disposition (after February 28, 1913) of property by a corporation—

(A) for the purpose of the computation of the earnings and profits of the corporation, shall (except as provided in subparagraph (B)) be determined by using as the adjusted basis the adjusted basis (under the law applicable to the year in which the sale or other disposition was made) for determining gain, except that no regard shall be had to the value of the property as of March 1, 1913; but

(B) for purposes of the computation of the earnings and profits of the corporation for any period beginning after February 28, 1913, shall be determined by using as the adjusted basis the adjusted basis (under the law applicable to the year in which the sale or other disposition was made) for determining gain.

Gain or loss so realized shall increase or decrease the earnings and profits to, but not beyond, the extent to which such a realized gain or loss was recognized in computing taxable income under the law applicable to the year in which such sale or disposition was made. Where, in determining the adjusted basis used in computing such realized gain or loss, the adjustment to the basis differs from the adjustment proper for the purpose of determining earnings and profits, then the latter adjustment shall be used in determining the increase or decrease above provided. For purposes of this subsection, a loss with respect to which a deduction is disallowed under section 1091 (relating to wash sales of stock or securities), or the corresponding provision of prior law, shall not be deemed to be recognized.

(2) EFFECT ON EARNINGS AND PROFITS OF RECEIPT OF TAX-FREE DISTRIBUTIONS.—Where a corporation receives (after February 28, 1913) a distribution from a second corporation which (under the law applicable to the year in which the distribution was made) was not a taxable dividend to the shareholders of the second corporation, the amount of such distribution shall not increase the earnings and profits of the first corporation in the following cases:

(A) no such increase shall be made in respect of the part of such distribution which (under such law) is directly applied in reduction of the basis of the stock in respect of which the distribution was made; and

(B) no such increase shall be made if (under such law) the distribution causes the basis of the stock in respect of which the distribution was made to be allocated between such stock and the property received (or such basis would, but for section 307(b), be so allocated).

[Sec. 312(g)]

(g) EARNINGS AND PROFITS—INCREASE IN VALUE ACCRUED BEFORE MARCH 1, 1913.—

(1) If any increase or decrease in the earnings and profits for any period beginning after February 28, 1913, with respect to any matter would be different had the adjusted basis of the property involved been determined without regard to its March 1, 1913, value, then, except as provided in paragraph (2), an increase (properly reflecting such difference) shall be made in that part of the earnings and profits consisting of increase in value of property accrued before March 1, 1913.

(2) If the application of subsection (f) to a sale or other disposition after February 28, 1913, results in a loss which is to be applied in decrease of earnings and profits for any period beginning after February 28, 1913, then, notwithstanding subsection (f) and in lieu of the rule provided in paragraph (1) of this subsection, the amount of such loss so to be applied shall be reduced by the amount, if any, by which the adjusted basis of the property used in determining the loss exceeds the adjusted basis computed without regard to the value of the property on March 1, 1913, and if such amount so applied in reduction of the decrease exceeds such loss, the excess over such loss shall increase that part of the earnings and profits consisting of increase in value of property accrued before March 1, 1913.

[Sec. 312(h)]

(h) ALLOCATION IN CERTAIN CORPORATE SEPARATIONS AND REORGANIZATIONS.—

(1) SECTION 355.—In the case of a distribution or exchange to which section 355 (or so much of section 356 as relates to section 355) applies, proper allocation with respect to the earnings and profits of the distributing corporation and the controlled corporation (or corporations) shall be made under regulations prescribed by the Secretary.

(2) SECTION 368(a)(1)(C) OR (D).—In the case of a reorganization described in subparagraph (C) or (D) of section 368(a)(1), proper allocation with respect to the earnings and profits of the acquired corporation shall, under regulations prescribed by the Secretary, be made between the acquiring corporation and the acquired corporation (or any corporation which had control of the acquired corporation before the reorganization).

Amendments

• 1984, Deficit Reduction Act of 1984 (P.L. 98-369)

P.L. 98-369, §63(b):

Amended Code Sec. 312(h). **Effective** for transactions pursuant to plans adopted after 7-18-84. Prior to amendment, Code Sec. 312(h) read as follows:

(h) Allocation in Certain Corporate Separations.—In the case of a distribution or exchange to which section 355 (or so much of section 356 as relates to section 355) applies, proper allocation with respect to the earnings and profits of the distributing corporation and the controlled corporation (or corporations) shall be made under regulations prescribed by the Secretary.

• 1976, Tax Reform Act of 1976 (P.L. 94-455)

P.L. 94-455, §1901(a)(43)(B):

Repealed former Code Sec. 312(h). **Effective** for tax years beginning after 12-31-76. Prior to repeal, Code Sec. 312(h) read as follows:

(h) EARNINGS AND PROFITS OF PERSONAL SERVICE CORPORATIONS.—In the case of a personal service corporation subject for any taxable year to supplement S of the Internal Revenue Code of 1939, an amount equal to the undistributed supplement S net income of the personal service corporation for its taxable year shall be considered as paid in as of the close of such taxable year as paid-in surplus or as a contribution to capital, and the accumulated earnings and profits as of the close of such taxable year shall be correspondingly reduced, if such amount or any portion thereof is required to be included as a dividend in the gross income of the shareholders.

P.L. 94-455, §1906(b)(13)(A):

Amended 1954 Code by substituting "Secretary" for "Secretary or his delegate" each place it appeared. **Effective** 2-1-77.

[Sec. 312(i)]

(i) DISTRIBUTION OF PROCEEDS OF LOAN INSURED BY THE UNITED STATES.—If a corporation distributes property with respect to its stock and if, at the time of distribution—

(1) there is outstanding a loan to such corporation which was made, guaranteed, or insured by the United States (or by any agency or instrumentality thereof), and

(2) the amount of such loan so outstanding exceeds the adjusted basis of the property constituting security for such loan,

then the earnings and profits of the corporation shall be increased by the amount of such excess, and (immediately after the distribution) shall be decreased by the amount of such excess. For purposes of paragraph (2), the adjusted basis of the property at the time of distribution shall be determined without regard to any adjustment under section 1016(a)(2) (relating to adjustment for depreciation, etc.). For purposes of this subsection, a commitment to make, guarantee, or insure a loan shall be treated as the making, guaranteeing, or insuring of a loan.

Amendments

• 1976, Tax Reform Act of 1976 (P.L. 94-455)

P.L. 94-455, §1901(a)(43)(B):

Redesignated former Code Sec. 312(j) as Code Sec. 312(i). **Effective** for tax years beginning after 12-31-76.

P.L. 94-455, §1901(a)(43)(C):

Amended redesignated Code Sec. 312(i). **Effective** for tax years beginning after 12-31-76. Prior to amendment, redesignated Code Sec. 312(i) read as follows:

(i) DISTRIBUTION OF PROCEEDS OF LOAN INSURED BY THE UNITED STATES.—

(1) IN GENERAL.—If a corporation distributes property with respect to its stock, and if, at the time of the distribution—

(A) there is outstanding a loan to such corporation which was made, guaranteed, or insured by the United States (or by any agency or instrumentality thereof), and

(B) the amount of such loan so outstanding exceeds the adjusted basis of the property constituting security for such loan,

then the earnings and profits of the corporation shall be increased by the amount of such excess, and (immediately after the distribution) shall be decreased by the amount of such excess. For purposes of subparagraph (B) of the preceding sentence, the adjusted basis of the property at the time of distribution shall be determined without regard to any adjustment under section 1016 (a) (2) (relating to adjustment for depreciation, etc.). For purposes of this paragraph, a commitment to make, guarantee, or insure a loan shall be treated as the making, guaranteeing, or insuring of a loan.

(2) EFFECTIVE DATE.—Paragraph (1) shall apply only with respect to distributions made on or after June 22, 1954.

[Sec. 312(j)—Stricken]

Amendments

• 2004, American Jobs Creation Act of 2004 (P.L. 108-357)

P.L. 108-357, §413(c)(4):

Amended Code Sec. 312 by striking subsection (j). **Effective** for tax years of foreign corporations beginning after 12-31-2004, and for tax years of United States shareholders with or within which such tax years of foreign corporations end. Prior to being stricken, Code Sec. 312(j) read as follows:

(j) EARNINGS AND PROFITS OF FOREIGN INVESTMENT COMPANIES.—

(1) ALLOCATION WITHIN AFFILIATED GROUP.—In the case of a sale or exchange of stock in a foreign investment company (as defined in section 1246(b)) by a United States person (as defined in section 7701(a)(30)), if such company is a member of an affiliated group, then the accumulated earnings and profits of all members of such affiliated group shall be allocated, under regulations prescribed by the Secretary, in

such manner as is proper to carry out the purposes of section 1246.

(2) AFFILIATED GROUP DEFINED.—For purposes of paragraph (1) of this subsection, the term "affiliated group" has the meaning assigned to such term by section 1504(a); except that (A) "more than 50 percent" shall be substituted for "80 percent or more", and (B) all corporations shall be treated as includible corporations (without regard to the provisions of section 1504(b)).

• 1984, Deficit Reduction Act of 1984 (P.L. 98-369)

P.L. 98-369, §61(a)(2)(A):

Amended Code Sec. 312(j) by striking out paragraph (3). **Effective** 7-18-84. Prior to amendment, paragraph (3) read as follows:

(3) Redemptions.—If a foreign investment company (as defined in section 1246) distributes amounts in a redemption to which section 302(a) or 303 applies, the part of such distribution which is properly chargeable to earnings and profits shall be an amount which is not in excess of the ratable share of the earnings and profits of the company accumulated after February 28, 1913, attributable to the stock so redeemed.

• 1983, Technical Corrections Act of 1982 (P.L. 97-448)

P.L. 97-448, §306(a)(6)(B)(i):

Amended Code Sec. 312(j)(3) by striking out "in partial liquidation or". **Effective** as if included in the provision of P.L. 97-248 to which it relates.

P.L. 97-448, §306(a)(6)(B)(ii):

Amended the heading for Code Sec. 312(j)(3). **Effective** as if included in the provision of P.L. 97-248 to which it relates. Prior to amendment, the heading read as follows: "(3) Partial liquidations and redemptions.—"

• 1976, Tax Reform Act of 1976 (P.L. 94-455)

P.L. 94-455, §1901(a)(43)(D):

Amended redesignated Code Sec. 312(j)(3). **Effective** for tax years beginning after 12-31-76. Prior to amendment, redesignated Code Sec. 312(j)(3) read as follows:

(3) PARTIAL LIQUIDATIONS AND REDEMPTIONS.

(A) IN GENERAL.—If a foreign investment company (as defined in section 1246) distributes amounts in partial liquidation or in a redemption to which section 302(a) or 303 applies, the part of such distribution which is properly chargeable to earnings and profits shall be an amount which is not in excess of the ratable share of the earnings and profits of the company accumulated after February 28, 1913, attributable to the stock so redeemed.

(B) EFFECTIVE DATE.—Subparagraph (A) shall apply only with respect to distributions made after December 31, 1962.

P.L. 94-455, §1901(b)(32)(B)(i):

Repealed Code Sec. 312(k) and redesignated former Code Sec. 312(l) as Code Sec. 312(j). **Effective** for tax years beginning after 12-31-76. Prior to repeal, Code Sec. 312(k) read as follows:

(k) SPECIAL ADJUSTMENT ON DISPOSITION OF ANTITRUST STOCK RECEIVED AS A DIVIDEND.—If a corporation received antitrust stock (as defined in section 301(f)) in a distribution to which section 301 applied, and the amount of the distribution determined under section 301(f)(2) exceeded the basis of the stock determined under section 301(f)(3), then proper adjustment shall be made, under regulations prescribed by the Secretary or his delegate, to the earnings and profits of such corporation at the time such stock (or other property the basis of which is determined by reference to the basis of such stock) is disposed of by such corporation.

P.L. 94-455, §1906(b)(13)(A):

Amended 1954 Code by substituting "Secretary" for "Secretary or his delegate" each place it appeared. **Effective** 2-1-77.

• 1962, Revenue Act of 1962 (P.L. 87-834)

P.L. 87-834, §14(b)(1):

Amended Code Sec. 312 by adding subsection (l). **Effective** for tax years beginning after 12-31-62.

[Sec. 312(k)]

(k) EFFECT OF DEPRECIATION ON EARNINGS AND PROFITS.—

(1) GENERAL RULE.—For purposes of computing the earnings and profits of a corporation for any taxable year beginning after June 30, 1972, the allowance for depreciation (and amortization, if any) shall be deemed to be the amount which would be allowable for such year if the straight line method of depreciation had been used for each taxable year beginning after June 30, 1972.

(2) EXCEPTION.—If for any taxable year a method of depreciation was used by the taxpayer which the Secretary has determined results in a reasonable allowance under section 167(a) and which is the unit-of-production method or other method not expressed in a term of years, then the adjustment to earnings and profits for depreciation for such year shall be determined under the method so used (in lieu of the straight line method).

(3) EXCEPTION FOR TANGIBLE PROPERTY.—

(A) IN GENERAL.—Except as provided in subparagraph (B), in the case of tangible property to which section 168 applies, the adjustment to earnings and profits for depreciation for any taxable year shall be determined under the alternative depreciation system (within the meaning of section 168(g)(2)).

(B) TREATMENT OF AMOUNTS DEDUCTIBLE UNDER SECTION 179, 179A, 179B, 179C, 179D, OR 179E.—For purposes of computing the earnings and profits of a corporation, any amount deductible under section 179, 179A, 179B, 179C, 179D, or 179E shall be allowed as a deduction ratably over the period of 5 taxable years (beginning with the taxable year for which such amount is deductible under section 179, 179A, 179B, 179C, 179D, or 179E, as the case may be).

(4) CERTAIN FOREIGN CORPORATIONS.—The provisions of paragraph (1) shall not apply in computing the earnings and profits of a foreign corporation for any taxable year for which less than 20 percent of the gross income from all sources of such corporation is derived from sources within the United States.

(5) BASIS ADJUSTMENT NOT TAKEN INTO ACCOUNT.—In computing the earnings and profits of a corporation for any taxable year, the allowance for depreciation (and amortization, if any) shall be computed without regard to any basis adjustment under section 50(c).

Amendments

• 2006, Tax Relief and Health Care Act of 2006 (P.L. 109-432)

P.L. 109-432, Division A, §404(b)(2):

Amended Code Sec. 312(k)(3)(B) by striking "or 179D" each place it appears in the heading and text thereof and inserting "179D, or 179E". **Effective** for costs paid or incurred after 12-20-2006.

• 2005, Energy Tax Incentives Act of 2005 (P.L. 109-58)

P.L. 109-58, §1323(b)(3):

Amended Code Sec. 312(k)(3)(B) by striking "179 179A, or 179B" each place it appears in the heading and text and inserting "179, 179A, 179B, or 179C". **Effective** for properties placed in service after 8-8-2005.

P.L. 109-58, §1331(b)(5):

Amended Code Sec. 312(k)(3)(B), as amended by this Act, by striking "179, 179A, 179B, or 179C" each place it appears in the heading and text and inserting "179, 179A, 179B, 179C, or 179D". **Effective** for property placed in service after 12-31-2005.

• 2004, American Jobs Creation Act of 2004 (P.L. 108-357)

P.L. 108-357, §338(b)(3):

Amended Code Sec. 312(k)(3)(B) by striking "or 179A" each place it appears in the heading and text and inserting "[,] 179A, or 179B". **Effective** for expenses paid or incurred after 12-31-2002, in tax years ending after such date.

• 1997, Taxpayer Relief Act of 1997 (P.L. 105-34)

P.L. 105-34, §1604(a)(2)(A)-(B):

Amended Code Sec. 312(k)(3)(B) by striking "179" in the heading and the first place it appears in the text and inserting "179 or 179A", and by striking "179" the last place it appears and inserting "179 or 179A, as the case may be". **Effective** as if included in the amendments made by Act Sec. 1913 of P.L. 102-486 [**effective** for property placed in service after 6-30-93.—CCH].

• 1990, Omnibus Budget Reconciliation Act of 1990 (P.L. 101-508)

P.L. 101-508, §11812(b)(5):

Amended Code Sec. 312(k)(2). **Effective** for property placed in service after the date of enactment of this Act. For exceptions, see Act Sec. 11812(c)(2)-(3), below. Prior to amendment, Code Sec. 312(k)(2) read as follows:

(2) EXCEPTION.—If for any taxable year beginning after June 30, 1972, a method of depreciation was used by the taxpayer which the Secretary has determined results in a reasonable allowance under section 167(a), and which is not—

(A) a declining balance method,

(B) the sum of the years-digits method, or

(C) any other method allowable solely by reason of the application of subsection (b)(4) or (j)(1)(C) of section 167,

then the adjustment to earnings and profits for depreciation for such year shall be determined under the method so used (in lieu of under the straight line method).

P.L. 101-508, §11812(c)(2)-(3), provides:

(2) EXCEPTION.—The amendments made by this section shall not apply to any property to which section 168 of the Internal Revenue Code of 1986 does not apply by reason of subsection (f)(5) thereof.

(3) EXCEPTION FOR PREVIOUSLY GRANDFATHER [sic] EXPENDITURES.—The amendments made by this section shall not apply to rehabilitation expenditures described in section 252(f)(5) of the Tax Reform Act of 1986 (as added by section 1002(l)(31) of the Technical and Miscellaneous Revenue Act of 1988).

P.L. 101-508, §11813(b)(14):

Amended Code Sec. 312(k)(5) by striking "section 48(q)" and inserting "section 50(c)". **Effective**, generally, for property placed in service after 12-31-90. For exceptions, see Act Sec. 11813(c)(2), below.

P.L. 101-508, §11813(c)(2), provides:

(2) EXCEPTIONS.—The amendments made by this section shall not apply to—

(A) any transition property (as defined in section 49(e) of the Internal Revenue Code of 1986 (as in effect on the day before the date of the enactment of this Act),

(B) any property with respect to which qualified progress expenditures were previously taken into account under section 46(d) of such Code (as so in effect), and

(C) any property described in section 46(b)(2)(C) of such Code (as so in effect).

• 1988, Technical and Miscellaneous Revenue Act of 1988 (P.L. 100-647)

P.L. 100-647, §1002(a)(3):

Amended Code Sec. 312(k)(4) by striking out "paragraphs (1) and (3)" and inserting in lieu thereof "paragraph (1)". **Effective** as if included in the provision of P.L. 99-514 to which it relates.

• 1986, Tax Reform Act of 1986 (P.L. 99-514)

P.L. 99-514, §201(b):

Amended Code Sec. 312(k)(3). For the **effective** date, see Act Sec. 203-204 and 251(d) following Code Sec. 168. Prior to amendment, Code Sec. 312(k)(3) read as follows:

(3) EXCEPTION FOR RECOVERY AND SECTION 179 PROPERTY.—

(A) RECOVERY PROPERTY.—Except as provided in subparagraphs (B) and (C), in the case of recovery property (within the meaning of section 168), the adjustment to earnings and profits for depreciation for any taxable year shall be the amount determined under the straight-line method (using a half year convention in the case of property other than the 19-year real property and low-income housing and without regard to salvage value) and using a recovery period determined in accordance with the following table:

In the case of:	*The applicable recovery period is:*
3-year property	5 years
5-year property	12 years
10-year property	25 years
19-year real property and low-income housing	40 years
15-year public utility property	35 years

For purposes of this subparagraph, no adjustment shall be allowed in the year of disposition (except with respect to 19-year real property and low-income housing).

(B) TREATMENT OF AMOUNTS DEDUCTIBLE UNDER SECTION 179.—For purposes of computing the earnings and profits of a corporation, any amount deductible under section 179 shall be allowed as a deduction ratably over the period of 5 years (beginning with the year for which such amount is deductible under section 179).

(C) FLEXIBILITY.—In any case where a different recovery percentage is elected under section 168(b)(3) or (f)(2)(C) based on a recovery period longer than the recovery period provided in subparagraph (A), the adjustment to earnings and profits shall be based on such longer period under rules similar to those provided in subparagraph (A).

P.L. 99-514, §201(d)(6):

Amended Code Sec. 312(k)(4) by striking out the last sentence. For the **effective** date, see Act Sec. 203-204 and 251(d) following Code Sec. 168. Prior to amendment, it read as follows:

In determining the earnings and profits of such corporation in the case of recovery property (within the meaning of section 168), the rules of section 168(f)(2) shall apply.

P.L. 99-514, §1809(a)(2)(C)(ii):

Amended Code Sec. 312(k)(3)(A) by striking out ", and rules similar to the rules under the next to the last sentence of section 168(b)(2)(A) and section 168(b)(2)(B) shall apply". **Effective** as if included in the provision of P.L. 98-369 to which it relates.

P.L. 99-514, §1804(f)(1)(F), provides:

(F) Any reference in subsection (e) of section 61 of the Tax Reform Act of 1984 to a paragraph of section 312(n) of the Internal Revenue Code of 1954 shall be treated as a reference to such paragraph as in effect before its redesignation by subparagraph (D).

• **1985 (P.L. 99-121)**

P.L. 99-121, §103(b)(1)(C):

Amended Code Sec. 312(k)(3)(A) by striking out "18-year real property" each place it appeared in the text and headings thereof and inserting in lieu thereof "19-year real property". **Effective** with respect to property placed in service by the taxpayer after 5-8-85. However, for an exception, see Act Sec. 105(b)(2), below.

P.L. 99-121, §105(b)(2), provides:

(2) EXCEPTION.—The amendments made by section 103 shall not apply to property placed in service by the taxpayer before January 1, 1987, if—

(A) the taxpayer or a qualified person entered into a binding contract to purchase or construct such property before May 9, 1985, or

(B) construction of such property was commenced by or for the taxpayer or a qualified person before May 9, 1985.

For purposes of this paragraph, the term "qualified person" means any person whose rights in such a contract or such property are transferred to the taxpayer, but only if such property is not placed in service before such rights are transferred to the taxpayer.

• **1984, Deficit Reduction Act of 1984 (P.L. 98-369)**

P.L. 98-369, §61(b):

Amended the table contained in Code Sec. 312(k)(3)(A) (as amended by this Act) by striking out "35 years" in the item relating to 15-year real property and 20-year real property [sic] and inserting in lieu thereof "40 years". **Effective** for property placed in service in tax years beginning after 9-30-84.

P.L. 98-369, §111(e)(5):

Amended Code Sec. 312(k)(3)(A) by striking out "15-year real property" each place it appeared and inserting in lieu thereof "18-year real property and low-income housing." **Effective** with respect to property placed in service by the taxpayer after 3-15-84. For an exception, see Act Sec. 111(g)(2) in the amendment notes following Code Sec. 168(f).

• **1982, Tax Equity and Fiscal Responsibility Act of 1982 (P.L. 97-248)**

P.L. 97-248, §205(a)(3):

Amended Code Sec. 312(k) by adding at the end thereof new paragraph (5). **Effective** for periods after 12-31-82, under rules similar to the rules of Code Sec. 48(m). For an exception and special rules, see the amendment note for Act Sec. 205(c) following Code Sec. 48(d).

• **1981, Economic Recovery Tax Act of 1981 (P.L. 97-34)**

P.L. 97-34, §206(a):

Amended Code Sec. 312(k) by redesignating paragraph (3) as paragraph (4) and by inserting after paragraph (2) new paragraph (3). **Effective** for property placed in service after 12-31-80, in tax years ending after such date.

P.L. 97-34, §206(b):

Amended Code Sec. 312(k)(4) as redesignated by P.L. 97-34, §206(a), by striking out "paragraph (1)" and inserting in lieu thereof "paragraphs (1) and (3)" and by adding the last sentence at the end thereof. **Effective** for property placed in service after 12-31-80, in tax years ending after such date.

• **1976, Tax Reform Act of 1976 (P.L. 94-455)**

P.L. 94-455, §1901(b)(32)(B)(i):

Redesignated former Code Sec. 312(m) as Code Sec. 312(k). **Effective** for tax years beginning after 12-31-76.

P.L. 94-455, §1906(b)(13)(A):

Amended 1954 Code by substituting "Secretary" for "Secretary or his delegate" each place it appeared. **Effective** 2-1-77.

• **1969, Tax Reform Act of 1969 (P.L. 91-172)**

P.L. 91-172, §442(a):

Added new subsection (m). **Effective** for tax years beginning after 6-30-72.

[Sec. 312(l)]

(l) DISCHARGE OF INDEBTEDNESS INCOME.—

(1) DOES NOT INCREASE EARNINGS AND PROFITS IF APPLIED TO REDUCE BASIS.—The earnings and profits of a corporation shall not include income from the discharge of indebtedness to the extent of the amount applied to reduce basis under section 1017.

(2) REDUCTION OF DEFICIT IN EARNINGS AND PROFITS IN CERTAIN CASES.—If—

(A) the interest of any shareholder of a corporation is terminated or extinguished in a title 11 or similar case (within the meaning of section 368(a)(3)(A)), and

(B) there is a deficit in the earnings and profits of the corporation,

then such deficit shall be reduced by an amount equal to the paid-in capital which is allocable to the interest of the shareholder which is so terminated or extinguished.

Amendments

• **1980, Bankruptcy Tax Act of 1980 (P.L. 96-589)**

P.L. 96-589, §5(e)(2):

Amended Code Sec. 312 by adding a new subsection (l). For the **effective** date of this provision, see the historical comment for P.L. 96-589 under Code Sec. 370(a).

[Sec. 312(m)]

(m) NO ADJUSTMENT FOR INTEREST PAID ON CERTAIN REGISTRATION-REQUIRED OBLIGATIONS NOT IN REGISTERED FORM.—The earnings and profits of any corporation shall not be decreased by any interest with respect to which a deduction is not or would not be allowable by reason of section 163(f), unless at the time of issuance the issuer is a foreign corporation that is not a controlled foreign corporation (within the meaning of section 957), and the issuance did not have as a purpose the avoidance of section 163(f) of this subsection.

Amendments

• **2004, American Jobs Creation Act of 2004 (P.L. 108-357)**

P.L. 108-357, §413(c)(5):

Amended Code Sec. 312(m) by striking ", a foreign investment company (within the meaning of section 1246(b)), or a foreign personal holding company (within the meaning of section 552)" immediately following "(within the meaning of section 957),". **Effective** for tax years of foreign corporations beginning after 12-31-2004, and for tax years of United States shareholders with or within which such tax years of foreign corporations end.

• **1982, Tax Equity and Fiscal Responsibility Act of 1982 (P.L. 97-248)**

P.L. 97-248, §310(b)(3):

Amended Code Sec. 312 by adding subsection (m). **Effective** for obligations issued after 12-31-82. For an exception, see P.L. 97-248, Act Sec. 310(d)(3), which appears in the amendment notes for former Code Sec. 103(j).

[Sec. 312(n)]

(n) ADJUSTMENTS TO EARNINGS AND PROFITS TO MORE ACCURATELY REFLECT ECONOMIC GAIN AND LOSS.—For purposes of computing the earnings and profits of a corporation, the following adjustments shall be made:

(1) CONSTRUCTION PERIOD CARRYING CHARGES.—

(A) IN GENERAL.—In the case of any amount paid or incurred for construction period carrying charges—

(i) no deduction shall be allowed with respect to such amount, and

(ii) the basis of the property with respect to which such charges are allocable shall be increased by such amount.

(B) CONSTRUCTION PERIOD CARRYING CHARGES DEFINED.—For purposes of this paragraph, the term "construction period carrying charges" means all—

(i) interest paid or accrued on indebtedness incurred or continued to acquire, construct, or carry property,

(ii) property taxes, and

(iii) similar carrying charges,

to the extent such interest, taxes, or charges are attributable to the construction period for such property and would be allowable as a deduction in determining taxable income under this chapter for the taxable year in which paid or incurred.

(C) CONSTRUCTION PERIOD.—The term "construction period" has the meaning given the term production period under section 263A(f)(4)(B).

(2) INTANGIBLE DRILLING COSTS AND MINERAL EXPLORATION AND DEVELOPMENT COSTS.—

(A) INTANGIBLE DRILLING COSTS.—Any amount allowable as a deduction under section 263(c) in determining taxable income (other than costs incurred in connection with a nonproductive well)—

(i) shall be capitalized, and

(ii) shall be allowed as a deduction ratably over the 60-month period beginning with the month in which such amount was paid or incurred.

(B) MINERAL EXPLORATION AND DEVELOPMENT COSTS.—Any amount allowable as a deduction under section 616(a) or 617 in determining taxable income—

(i) shall be capitalized, and

(ii) shall be allowed as a deduction ratably over the 120-month period beginning with the later of—

(I) the month in which production from the deposit begins, or

(II) the month in which such amount was paid or incurred.

(3) CERTAIN AMORTIZATION PROVISIONS NOT TO APPLY.—Sections 173 and 248 shall not apply.

(4) LIFO INVENTORY ADJUSTMENTS.—

(A) IN GENERAL.—Earnings and profits shall be increased or decreased by the amount of any increase or decrease in the LIFO recapture amount as of the close of each taxable year; except that any decrease below the LIFO recapture amount as of the close of the taxable year preceding the 1st taxable year to which this paragraph applies to the taxpayer shall be taken into account only to the extent provided in regulations prescribed by the Secretary.

(B) LIFO RECAPTURE AMOUNT.—For purposes of this paragraph, the term "LIFO recapture amount" means the amount (if any) by which—

(i) the inventory amount of the inventory assets under the first-in, first-out method authorized by section 471, exceeds

(ii) the inventory amount of such assets under the LIFO method.

(C) DEFINITIONS.—For purposes of this paragraph—

(i) LIFO METHOD.—The term "LIFO method" means the method authorized by section 472 (relating to last-in, first-out inventories).

(ii) INVENTORY ASSETS.—The term "inventory assets" means stock in trade of the corporation, or other property of a kind which would properly be included in the inventory of the corporation if on hand at the close of the taxable year.

(iii) INVENTORY AMOUNT.—The inventory amount of assets under the first-in, first-out method authorized by section 471 shall be determined—

(I) if the corporation uses the retail method of valuing inventories under section 472, by using such method, or

(II) if subclause (I) does not apply, by using cost or market, whichever is lower.

(5) INSTALLMENT SALES.—In the case of any installment sale, earnings and profits shall be computed as if the corporation did not use the installment method.

(6) COMPLETED CONTRACT METHOD OF ACCOUNTING.—In the case of a taxpayer who uses the completed contract method of accounting, earnings and profits shall be computed as if such taxpayer used the percentage of completion method of accounting.

(7) REDEMPTIONS.—If a corporation distributes amounts in a redemption to which section 302(a) or 303 applies, the part of such distribution which is properly chargeable to earnings and profits shall be an amount which is not in excess of the ratable share of the earnings and profits of such corporation accumulated after February 28, 1913, attributable to the stock so redeemed.

(8) SPECIAL RULE FOR CERTAIN FOREIGN CORPORATIONS.—In the case of a foreign corporation described in subsection (k)(4)—

(A) paragraphs (4) and (6) shall apply only in the case of taxable years beginning after December 31, 1985, and

(B) paragraph (5) shall apply only in the case of taxable years beginning after December 31, 1987.

Amendments

• 1989, Omnibus Budget Reconciliation Act of 1989 (P.L. 101-239)

P.L. 101-239, §7611(f)(5)(A):

Amended Code Sec. 312(n)(2)(A)(ii) by striking "in which the production from the well begins" and inserting "in which such amount was paid or incurred". **Effective** for costs paid or incurred in tax years beginning after 12-31-89.

• 1986, Tax Reform Act of 1986 (P.L. 99-514)

P.L. 99-514, §241(b)(1):

Amended Code Sec. 312(n)(3) by striking out ", 177," after "173". **Effective** for expenditures paid or incurred after 12-31-86. For a transitional rule, see Act Sec. 241(c)(2), below.

P.L. 99-514, §241(c)(2), provides:

(2) TRANSITIONAL RULE.—The amendments made by this section shall not apply to any expenditure incurred—

(A) pursuant to a binding contract entered into before March 2, 1986, or

(B) with respect to the development, protection, expansion, registration, or defense of a trademark or trade name commenced before March 2, 1986, but only if not less than the lesser of $1,000,000 or 5 percent of the aggregate cost of such development, protection, expansion, registration, or defense has been incurred or committed before such date.

The preceding sentence shall not apply to any expenditure with respect to a trademark or trade name placed in service after December 31, 1987.

P.L. 99-514, §631(e)(1):

Amended Code Sec. 312(n)(4) (as redesignated by Act Sec. 1804(f)(1)(D)). For the **effective** date, see Act Sec. 633, which is reproduced following Code Sec. 311. Prior to amendment Code Sec. 312(n)(4) (as redesignated) read as follows:

(4) LIFO INVENTORY ADJUSTMENTS.—Earnings and profits shall be increased or decreased by the amount of any increase or decrease in the LIFO recapture amount (determined under section 336(b)(3)) as of the close of each taxable year; except that any decrease below the LIFO recapture amount as of the close of the taxable year preceding the first taxable year to which this paragraph applies to the taxpayer shall be taken into account only to the extent provided in regulations prescribed by the Secretary.

P.L. 99-514, §803(b)(3)(A)-(B):

Amended Code Sec. 312(n)(1) by striking out "(determined without regard to section 189) ["] in subparagraph (B)" [sic] after "paid or incurred", and by striking out subparagraph (C) and inserting in lieu thereof new subparagraph (C). For the **effective** date, see Act Sec. 803(d), below. Prior to amendment, Code Sec. 312(n)(1)(C) read as follows:

(C) CONSTRUCTION PERIOD.—The term "construction period" has the meaning given such term by section 189(e)(2) (determined without regard to any real property limitation).

P.L. 99-514, §803(d), as amended by P.L. 100-647, §1008(b)(7) and P.L. 101-239, §7831(d)(1), provides:

(d) EFFECTIVE DATE.—

(1) IN GENERAL.—Except as provided in this subsection, the amendments made by this section shall apply to costs incurred after December 31, 1986, in taxable years ending after such date.

(2) SPECIAL RULE FOR INVENTORY PROPERTY.—In the case of any property which is inventory in the hands of the taxpayer—

(A) IN GENERAL.—The amendments made by this section shall apply to taxable years beginning after December 31, 1986.

(B) CHANGE IN METHOD OF ACCOUNTING.—If the taxpayer is required by the amendments made by this section to change its method of accounting with respect to such property for any taxable year—

(i) such change shall be treated as initiated by the taxpayer,

(ii) such change shall be treated as made with the consent of the Secretary, and

(iii) the period for taking into account the adjustments under section 481 by reason of such change shall not exceed 4 years.

(3) SPECIAL RULE FOR SELF-CONSTRUCTED PROPERTY.—The amendments made by this section shall not apply to any property which is produced by the taxpayer for use by the taxpayer if substantial construction had occurred before March 1, 1986.

(4) TRANSITIONAL RULE FOR CAPITALIZATION OF INTEREST AND TAXES.—

(A) TRANSITION PROPERTY EXEMPTED FROM INTEREST CAPITALIZATION.—Section 263A of the Internal Revenue Code of 1986 (as added by this section) and the amendment made by subsection (b)(1) shall not apply to interest costs which are allocable to any property—

(i) to which the amendments made by section 201 do not apply by reason of sections 204(a)(1)(D) and (E) and 204(a)(5)(A), and such development, protection, expansion, registration, or defense had been incurred or committed before such date.

The preceding sentence shall not apply to any expenditure with respect to a trademark or trade name placed in service after December 31, 1987.

(ii) to which the amendments made by section 251 do not apply by reason of section 251(d)(3)(M).

(B) INTEREST AND TAXES.—Section 263A of such Code shall not apply to property described in the matter following subparagraph (B) of section 207(e)(2) of the Tax Equity and Fiscal Responsibility Act of 1982 to the extent it would require the capitalization of interest and taxes paid or incurred in connection with such property which are not required to be capitalized under section 189 of such Code (as in effect before the amendment made by subsection (b)(1)).

(5) TRANSITION RULE CONCERNING CAPITALIZATION OF INVENTORY RULES.—In the case of a corporation which on the date of the enactment of this Act was a member of an affiliated group of corporations (within the meaning of section 1504(a) of the Internal Revenue Code of 1986), the parent of which—

(A) was incorporated in California on April 15, 1925,

(B) adopted LIFO accounting as of the close of the taxable year ended December 31, 1950, and

(C) was, on May 22, 1986, merged into a Delaware corporation incorporated on March 12, 1986,

the amendments made by this section shall apply under a cut-off method whereby the uniform capitalization rules are applied only in costing layers of inventory acquired during taxable years beginning on or after January 1, 1987.

(6) TREATMENT OF CERTAIN REHABILITATION PROJECT.—The amendments made by this section shall not apply to interest and taxes paid or incurred with respect to the rehabilitation and conversion of a certified historic building which was formerly a factory into an apartment project with 155 units, 39 units of which are for low-income families, if the project was approved for annual interest assistance on June 10, 1986, by the housing authority of the State in which the project is located.

(7) SPECIAL RULE FOR CASUALTY LOSSES.—Section 263A(d)(2) of the Internal Revenue Code of 1986 (as added by this section) shall apply to expenses incurred on or after the date of the enactment of this Act.

P.L. 99-514, §1804(f)(1)(D):

Amended Code Sec. 312(n) by striking out paragraph (4) and by redesignating paragraphs (5), (6), (7), (8), and (9) as paragraphs (4), (5), (6), (7), and (8), respectively. **Effective** as if included in the provision of P.L. 98-369 to which it relates. Prior to amendment, Code Sec. 312(n)(4) read as follows:

(4) CERTAIN UNTAXED APPRECIATION OF DISTRIBUTED PROPERTY.—In the case of any distribution of property by a corporation described in section 311(d), earnings and profits shall be increased by the amount of any gain which would be includible in gross income for any taxable year if section 311(d)(2) did not apply.

P.L. 99-514, §1804(f)(1)(E):

Aended Code Sec. 312(n)(8) (as redesignated by Act Sec. 1804(f)(1)(D)) by striking out "subsection (k)(4)" and all that follows and inserting in lieu thereof text. **Effective** as if included in the provision of P.L. 98-369 to which it relates. Prior to amendment, Code Sec. 312(n)(8) (as redesignated) read as follows:

(8) SPECIAL RULE FOR CERTAIN FOREIGN CORPORATIONS.—In the case of a foreign corporation described in subsection (k)(4), paragraphs (5), (6), and (7) shall apply only in the case of taxable years beginning after December 31, 1985.

• 1984, Deficit Reduction Act of 1984 (P.L. 98-369)

P.L. 98-369, §61(a)(1):

Amended Code Sec. 312 by adding at the end thereof new subsection (n). For the **effective** date, see Act Sec. 611(e), below.

P.L. 98-369, §61(e), provides:

(e) Effective Dates.—

(1) Adjustments to Earnings and Profits.—

(A) Paragraphs (1), (2), and (3) of Section 312(n).—The provisions of paragraphs (1), (2), and (3) of section 312(n) of the Internal Revenue Code of 1954 (as added by subsection (a)) shall apply to amounts paid or incurred in taxable years beginning after September 30, 1984.

(B) Paragraph (4) of Section 312(n).—The provisions of paragraph (4) of section 312(n) of such Code (as so added) shall apply to distributions after September 30, 1984; except that such provisions shall not apply to any distribution to which the amendments made by section 54(a) of this Act do not apply.

(C) LIFO Inventory.—The provisions of paragraph (5) of section 312(n) of such Code (as so added) shall apply to taxable years beginning after September 30, 1984.

(D) Installment Sales.—The provisions of paragraph (6) of section 312(n) of such Code (as so added) shall apply to sales after September 30, 1984, in taxable years ending after such date.

(E) Completed Contract Method.—The provisions of paragraph (7) of section 312(n) of such Code (as so added) shall apply to contracts entered into after September 30, 1984, in taxable years ending after such date.

[Sec. 312(o)]

(o) DEFINITION OF ORIGINAL ISSUE DISCOUNT AND ISSUE PRICE FOR PURPOSES OF SUBSECTION (a)(2).—For purposes of subsection (a)(2), the terms "original issue discount" and "issue price" have the same respective meanings as when used in subpart A of part V of subchapter P of this chapter.

Amendments

• 1984, Deficit Reduction Act of 1984 (P.L. 98-369)

P.L. 98-369, §61(c)(1)(B):

Added Code Sec. 312(o). **Effective** with respect to distributions declared after 3-15-84 in tax years ending after such date.

Subpart C—Definitions; Constructive Ownership of Stock

Sec. 316.	Dividend defined.
Sec. 317.	Other definitions.
Sec. 318.	Constructive ownership of stock.

[Sec. 316]

SEC. 316. DIVIDEND DEFINED.

[Sec. 316(a)]

(a) GENERAL RULE.—For purposes of this subtitle, the term "dividend" means any distribution of property made by a corporation to its shareholders—

(1) out of its earnings and profits accumulated after February 28, 1913, or

(2) out of its earnings and profits of the taxable year (computed as of the close of the taxable year without diminution by reason of any distributions made during the taxable year), without regard to the amount of the earnings and profits at the time the distribution was made.

Except as otherwise provided in this subtitle, every distribution is made out of earnings and profits to the extent thereof, and from the most recently accumulated earnings and profits. To the extent that any distribution is, under any provision of this subchapter, treated as a distribution of property to which section 301 applies, such distribution shall be treated as a distribution of property for purposes of this subsection.

[Sec. 316(b)]

(b) SPECIAL RULES.—

(1) CERTAIN INSURANCE COMPANY DIVIDENDS.—The definition in subsection (a) shall not apply to the term "dividend" as used in subchapter L in any case where the reference is to dividends of insurance companies paid to policyholders as such.

(2) DISTRIBUTIONS BY PERSONAL HOLDING COMPANIES.—

(A) In the case of a corporation which—

(i) under the law applicable to the taxable year in which the distribution is made, is a personal holding company (as defined in section 542), or

(ii) for the taxable year in respect of which the distribution is made under section 563(b) (relating to dividends paid after the close of the taxable year), or section 547 (relating to deficiency dividends), or the corresponding provisions of prior law, is a personal holding company under the law applicable to such taxable year,

the term "dividend" also means any distribution of property (whether or not a dividend as defined in subsection (a)) made by the corporation to its shareholders, to the extent of its undistributed personal holding company income (determined under section 545 without regard to distributions under this paragraph) for such year.

(B) For purposes of subparagraph (A), the term "distribution of property" includes a distribution in complete liquidation occurring within 24 months after the adoption of a plan of liquidation, but—

(i) only to the extent of the amounts distributed to distributees other than corporate shareholders, and

(ii) only to the extent that the corporation designates such amounts as a dividend distribution and duly notifies such distributees of such designation, under regulations prescribed by the Secretary, but

(iii) not in excess of the sum of such distributees' allocable share of the undistributed personal holding company income for such year, computed without regard to this subparagraph or section 562(b).

(3) DEFICIENCY DIVIDEND DISTRIBUTIONS BY A REGULATED INVESTMENT COMPANY OR REAL ESTATE INVESTMENT TRUST.—The term "dividend" also means any distribution of property (whether or not a dividend as defined in subsection (a)) which constitutes a "deficiency dividend" as defined in section 860(f).

Amendments

• 1978, Revenue Act of 1978 (P.L. 95-600)

P.L. 95-600, §362(d)(1)(A), (B), (e):

Amended Code Sec. 316(b)(3). **Effective** for determinations (as defined in Code Sec. 860(d)) after 11-6-78. Prior to amendment, paragraph (3) read:

"(3) DEFICIENCY DIVIDEND DISTRIBUTIONS BY A REAL ESTATE INVESTMENT TRUST.—The term "dividend" also means any distribution of property (whether or not a dividend as defined in subsection (a)) which constitutes a "deficiency dividend" as defined in section 859(d)."

• 1976, Tax Reform Act of 1976 (P.L. 94-455)

P.L. 94-455, §1601(d):

Added Code Sec. 316(b)(3). **Effective** for determinations (as defined in Code Sec. 859(c)) occurring after 10-4-76.

P.L. 94-455, §1906(b)(13)(A):

Amended 1954 Code by substituting "Secretary" for "Secretary or his delegate" each place it appeared. **Effective** 2-1-77.

• 1964, Revenue Act of 1964 (P.L. 88-272)

P.L. 88-272, §225(f)(1):

Amended Code Sec. 316(b)(2). **Effective** for distributions made in any tax year of the distributing corporation beginning after 12-31-63. Prior to amendment, Code Sec. 316(b)(2) read as follows:

"(2) Distributions by personal holding companies.—In the case of a corporation which—

"(A) under the law applicable to the taxable year in which the distribution is made, is a personal holding company (as defined in section 542), or

"(B) for the taxable year in respect of which the distribution is made under section 563(b) (relating to dividends paid after the close of the taxable year), or section 547 (relating to deficiency dividends), or the corresponding provisions of prior law, is a personal holding company under the law applicable to such taxable year, the term `dividend' also means any distribution of property (whether or not a dividend as defined in subsection (a)) made by the corporation to its shareholders, to the extent of its undistributed personal holding company income (determined under section 545 without regard to distributions under this paragraph) for such year."

• 1956, Life Insurance Company Tax Act for 1955 (P.L. 429, 84th Cong.)

P.L. 429, 84th Cong., §5(1):

Amended Sec. 316(b)(1). **Effective** 1-1-55. Prior to amendment Sec. 316(b)(1) read as follows:

"(1) Certain insurance company dividends.—The definition in subsection (a) shall not apply to the term `dividend' as used in sections 803(e), 821(a)(2), 823(2), and 832(c)(11) (where the reference is to dividends of insurance companies paid to policyholders)."

[Sec. 317]

SEC. 317. OTHER DEFINITIONS.

[Sec. 317(a)]

(a) PROPERTY.—For purposes of this part, the term "property" means money, securities, and any other property; except that such term does not include stock in the corporation making the distribution (or rights to acquire such stock).

[Sec. 317(b)]

(b) REDEMPTION OF STOCK.—For purposes of this part, stock shall be treated as redeemed by a corporation if the corporation acquires its stock from a shareholder in exchange for property, whether or not the stock so acquired is cancelled, retired, or held as treasury stock.

[Sec. 318]

SEC. 318. CONSTRUCTIVE OWNERSHIP OF STOCK.

[Sec. 318(a)]

(a) GENERAL RULE.—For purposes of those provisions of this subchapter to which the rules contained in this section are expressly made applicable—

(1) MEMBERS OF FAMILY.—

(A) IN GENERAL.—An individual shall be considered as owning the stock owned, directly or indirectly, by or for—

(i) his spouse (other than a spouse who is legally separated from the individual under a decree of divorce or separate maintenance), and

(ii) his children, grandchildren, and parents.

(B) EFFECT OF ADOPTION.—For purposes of subparagraph (A)(ii), a legally adopted child of an individual shall be treated as a child of such individual by blood.

(2) ATTRIBUTION FROM PARTNERSHIPS, ESTATES, TRUSTS, AND CORPORATIONS.—

(A) FROM PARTNERSHIPS AND ESTATES.—Stock owned, directly or indirectly, by or for a partnership or estate shall be considered as owned proportionately by its partners or beneficiaries.

(B) FROM TRUSTS.—

(i) Stock owned, directly or indirectly, by or for a trust (other than an employees' trust described in section 401(a) which is exempt from tax under section 501(a)) shall be considered as owned by its beneficiaries in proportion to the actuarial interest of such beneficiaries in such trust.

(ii) Stock owned, directly or indirectly, by or for any portion of a trust of which a person is considered the owner under subpart E of part I of subchapter J (relating to grantors and others treated as substantial owners) shall be considered as owned by such person.

(C) FROM CORPORATIONS.—If 50 percent or more in value of the stock in a corporation is owned, directly or indirectly, by or for any person, such person shall be considered as owning the stock owned, directly or indirectly, by or for such corporation, in that proportion which the value of the stock which such person so owns bears to the value of all the stock in such corporation.

(3) ATTRIBUTION TO PARTNERSHIPS, ESTATES, TRUSTS, AND CORPORATIONS.—

(A) TO PARTNERSHIPS AND ESTATES.—Stock owned, directly or indirectly, by or for a partner or a beneficiary of an estate shall be considered as owned by the partnership or estate.

(B) TO TRUSTS.—

(i) Stock owned, directly or indirectly, by or for a beneficiary of a trust (other than an employees' trust described in section 401(a) which is exempt from tax under section 501(a)) shall be considered as owned by the trust, unless such beneficiary's interest in the trust is a remote contingent interest. For purposes of this clause, a contingent interest of a beneficiary in a trust shall be considered remote if, under the maximum exercise of discretion by the trustee in favor of such beneficiary, the value of such interest, computed actuarially, is 5 percent or less of the value of the trust property.

(ii) Stock owned, directly or indirectly, by or for a person who is considered the owner of any portion of a trust under subpart E of part I of subchapter J (relating to grantors and others treated as substantial owners) shall be considered as owned by the trust.

(C) TO CORPORATIONS.—If 50 percent or more in value of the stock in a corporation is owned, directly or indirectly, by or for any person, such corporation shall be considered as owning the stock owned, directly or indirectly, by or for such person.

(4) OPTIONS.—If any person has an option to acquire stock, such stock shall be considered as owned by such person. For purposes of this paragraph, an option to acquire such an option, and each one of a series of such options, shall be considered as an option to acquire such stock.

(5) OPERATING RULES.—

(A) IN GENERAL.—Except as provided in subparagraphs (B) and (C), stock constructively owned by a person by reason of the application of paragraph (1), (2), (3), or (4), shall, for purposes of applying paragraphs (1), (2), (3), and (4), be considered as actually owned by such person.

(B) MEMBERS OF FAMILY.—Stock constructively owned by an individual by reason of the application of paragraph (1) shall not be considered as owned by him for purposes of again applying paragraph (1) in order to make another the constructive owner of such stock.

(C) PARTNERSHIPS, ESTATES, TRUSTS, AND CORPORATIONS.—Stock constructively owned by a partnership, estate, trust, or corporation by reason of the application of paragraph (3) shall not be considered as owned by it for purposes of applying paragraph (2) in order to make another the constructive owner of such stock.

(D) OPTION RULE IN LIEU OF FAMILY RULE.—For purposes of this paragraph, if stock may be considered as owned by an individual under paragraph (1) or (4), it shall be considered as owned by him under paragraph (4).

(E) S CORPORATION TREATED AS PARTNERSHIP.—For purposes of this subsection—

(i) an S corporation shall be treated as a partnership, and

(ii) any shareholder of the S corporation shall be treated as a partner of such partnership.

The preceding sentence shall not apply for purposes of determining whether stock in the S corporation is constructively owned by any person.

Amendments

• 1984, Deficit Reduction Act of 1984 (P.L. 98-369)

P.L. 98-369, §721(j):

Added Code Sec. 318(a)(5)(E). **Effective** as if included in the provision of P.L. 97-354 to which it relates.

• 1964 (P.L. 88-554)

P.L. 88-554, §5(a):

Amended Code Sec. 318(a)(2), (3), and (4), and added Code Sec. 318(a)(5). **Effective** 8-31-64. Prior to amendment, subsections (a)(2), (3), and (4) read as follows:

(2) Partnerships, estates, trusts, and corporations.—

(A) Partnerships and estates.—Stock owned, directly or indirectly, by or for a partnership or estate shall be considered as being owned proportionately by its partners or beneficiaries. Stock owned, directly or indirectly, by or for a partner or a beneficiary of an estate shall be considered as being owned by the partnership or estate.

(B) Trusts.—Stock owned, directly or indirectly, by or for a trust shall be considered as being owned by its beneficiaries in proportion to the actuarial interest of such beneficiaries in such trust. Stock owned, directly or indirectly, by or for a beneficiary of a trust shall be considered as being owned by the trust, unless such beneficiary's interest in the trust is a remote contingent interest. For purposes of the preceding sentence, a contingent interest of a beneficiary in a trust shall be considered remote, if, under the maximum exercise of discretion by the trustee in favor of such beneficiary, the value of such interest, computed actuarially, is 5 percent or less of the value of the trust property. Stock owned, directly or indirectly, by or for any portion of a trust of which a person is considered the owner under subpart E of part I of subchapter J (relating to grantors and others treated as substantial owners) shall be considered as being owned by such person; and such trust shall be treated as owning the stock owned, directly or indirectly, by or for that person. This subparagraph shall not apply with respect to any employees' trust described in section 401(a) which is exempt from tax under section 501(a).

(C) Corporations.—If 50 percent or more in value of the stock in a corporation is owned, directly or indirectly, by or for any person, then—

(i) such person shall be considered as owning the stock owned, directly or indirectly, by or for that corporation, in that proportion which the value of the stock which such person so owns bears to the value of all the stock in such corporation; and

(ii) such corporation shall be considered as owning the stock owned, directly or indirectly, by or for that person.

(3) Options.—If any person has an option to acquire stock, such stock shall be considered as owned by such person. For purposes of this paragraph, an option to acquire such an option, and each one of a series of such options, shall be considered as an option to acquire such stock.

(4) Constructive ownership as actual ownership.—

(A) In general.—Except as provided in subparagraph (B), stock constructively owned by a person by reason of the application of paragraph (1), (2), or (3) shall, for purposes of applying paragraph (1), (2), or (3), be treated as actually owned by such person.

(B) Members of family.—Stock constructively owned by an individual by reason of the application of paragraph (1) shall not be treated as owned by him for purposes of again applying paragraph (1) in order to make another the constructive owner of such stock.

(C) Option rule in lieu of family rule.—For purposes of this paragraph, if stock may be considered as owned by an individual under paragraph (1) or (3), it shall be considered as owned by him under paragraph (3).

[Sec. 318(b)]

(b) CROSS REFERENCES.—

For provisions to which the rules contained in subsection (a) apply, see—

(1) section 302 (relating to redemption of stock);

(2) section 304 (relating to redemption by related corporations);

(3) section 306(b)(1)(A) (relating to disposition of section 306 stock);

(4) section 338(h)(3) (defining purchase);

(5) section 382(l)(3) (relating to special limitations on net operating loss carryovers);

(6) section 856(d) (relating to definition of rents from real property in the case of real estate investment trusts);

(7) section 958(b) (relating to constructive ownership rules with respect to controlled foreign corporations); and

(8) section 6038(e)(2) (relating to information with respect to certain foreign corporations).

Amendments

•2005, Gulf Opportunity Zone Act of 2005 (P.L. 109-135)

P.L. 109-135, §412(u):

Amended Code Sec. 318(b)(8) by striking "section 6038(d)(2)" and inserting "section 6038(e)(2)". **Effective** 12-21-2005.

• 1997, Taxpayer Relief Act of 1997 (P.L. 105-34)

P.L. 105-34, §1142(e)(3):

Amended Code Sec. 318(b)(8) by striking "6038(d)(1)" and inserting "6038(d)(2)". **Effective** for annual accounting periods beginning after 8-5-97.

• 1986, Tax Reform Act of 1986 (P.L. 99-514)

P.L. 99-514, §621(c)(1):

Amended Code Sec. 318(b)(5) by striking out "section 382(a)(3)" and inserting in lieu thereof "section 382(l)(3)". For the **effective** date, see Act Sec. 621(f)(1), below. For special rules, see Act Sec. 621(f)(2)-(9) following Code Sec. 368.

P.L. 99-514, §621(f)(1), provides:

(1) IN GENERAL.—The amendments made by subsections (a), (b), and (c) shall apply to any ownership change following—

(A) an owner shift involving a 5-percent shareholder occurring after December 31, 1986, or

(B) an equity structure shift occurring pursuant to a plan of reorganization adopted after December 31, 1986.

• 1984, Deficit Reduction Act of 1984 (P.L. 98-369)

P.L. 98-369, §712(k)(5)(E):

Amended Code Sec. 318(b)(4). **Effective** as if included in the provision of P.L. 97-248 to which it relates. Prior to amendment Code Sec. 318(b)(4) read as follows:

(4) section 338(h)(3)(B) (relating to purchase of stock from subsidiaries, etc.);

• 1982, Tax Equity and Fiscal Responsibility Act of 1982 (P.L. 97-248)

P.L. 97-248, §224(c)(3):

Amended Code Sec. 318(b)(4). **Effective** for any target corporation (with the meaning of Code Sec. 338) with respect to which the acquisition date (within the meaning of such section) occurs after 8-31-82. See, however, P.L. 97-248, §224(a), which appears in the amendment notes for Code Sec. 338, for special rules. Prior to amendment, it read as follows:

(4) section 334(b)(3)(C) (relating to basis of property received in certain liquidations of subsidiaries);

• 1964 (P.L. 88-554)

P.L. 88-554, §5(b)(2):

Amended Code Sec. 318(b) by striking out "and" at the end of paragraph (6), by renumbering paragraph (7) as paragraph (8), and by adding new paragraph (7). **Effective** 8-31-64.

• 1962, Revenue Act of 1962 (P.L. 87-834)

P.L. 87-834, §20:

Amended Code Sec. 318(b) by striking out "and" at the end of paragraph (5), by substituting "; and" for the period at the end of paragraph (6), and by adding at the end thereof a new paragraph (7). **Effective** 10-17-62.

• 1960 (P.L. 86-779)

P.L. 86-779, §10(h):

Amended Code Sec. 318(b) by striking out "and" at the end of paragraph (4), by striking out the period at the end of paragraph (5) and substituting "; and", and by adding a new paragraph (6). **Effective** 1-1-61.

PART II—CORPORATE LIQUIDATIONS

Subpart A—Effects on Recipients

[Sec. 331]

SEC. 331. GAIN OR LOSS TO SHAREHOLDERS IN CORPORATE LIQUIDATIONS.

[Sec. 331(a)]

(a) DISTRIBUTIONS IN COMPLETE LIQUIDATION TREATED AS EXCHANGES.—Amounts received by a shareholder in a distribution in complete liquidation of a corporation shall be treated as in full payment in exchange for the stock.

Amendments

• 1982, Tax Equity and Fiscal Responsibility Act of 1982 (P.L. 97-248)

P.L. 97-248, §222(a):

Amended Code Sec. 331(a). **Effective**, generally, for distributions after 8-31-82. But see P.L. 97-248, §222(f), in the amendment notes for Code Sec. 331(b), below, for special rules. Prior to amendment, it read as follows:

(a) General Rule.—

(1) Complete liquidations.—Amounts distributed in complete liquidation of a corporation shall be treated as in full payment in exchange for the stock.

(2) Partial liquidations.—Amounts distributed in partial liquidation of a corporation (as defined in section 346) shall be treated as in part or full payment in exchange for the stock.

[Sec. 331(b)]

(b) NONAPPLICATION OF SECTION 301.—Section 301 (relating to effects on shareholder of distributions of property) shall not apply to any distribution of property (other than a distribution referred to in paragraph (2)(B) of section 316(b)), in complete liquidation.

Amendments

• 1982, Tax Equity and Fiscal Responsibility Act of 1982 (P.L. 97-248)

P.L. 97-248, §222(e)(1)(B):

Amended Code Sec. 331(b) by striking out "partial or complete liquidation" and inserting in lieu thereof "complete liquidation". **Effective** as noted in Act Sec. 222(f), below:

P.L. 97-248, §222(f)(2), as amended by P.L. 97-448, §306(a)(6)(A), provides:

(1) In general.—The amendments made by this section shall apply to distributions after August 31, 1982.

(2) Exceptions.—

(A) Ruling requests.—The amendments made by this section shall not apply to distributions made by any corporation if—

(i)(I) on July 22, 1982, there was a ruling request by such corporation pending with the Internal Revenue Service as to whether such distributions would qualify as a partial liquidation, or

(II) within the period beginning on July 12, 1981, and ending on July 22, 1982, the Internal Revenue Service granted a ruling to such corporation that the distributions would qualify as a partial liquidation, and

(ii) such distributions are pursuant to a plan of partial liquidation adopted before October 1, 1982 (or, if later, 90 days after the date on which the Internal Revenue Service granted a ruling pursuant to the request described in clause (i)(I)).

(B) Plans adopted before July 23, 1982.—The amendments made by this section shall not apply to distributions made pursuant to a plan of partial liquidation adopted before July 23, 1982.

(C) Control acquired after 1981 and before July 23, 1982.—The amendments made by this section shall not apply to distributions made pursuant to a plan of partial liquidation adopted before October 1, 1982, where control of the corporation making the distributions was acquired after December 31, 1981, and before July 23, 1982.

(D) Tender offer of binding contract outstanding on July 22, 1982.—

(i) In general.—The amendments made by this section shall not apply to distributions made by a corporation if—

(I) such distributions are pursuant to a plan of liquidation adopted before October 1, 1982, and

(II) control of such corporation was acquired after July 22, 1982, pursuant to a tender offer of binding contract outstanding on such date.

(ii) Extension of time for adopting plan where acquisition subject to federal regulatory approval.—If the acquisition described in clause (i)(II) is subject to approval by a Federal regulatory agency, clause (i) shall be applied by substituting for "October 1, 1982" the date which is 90 days after the date on which approval by the Federal regulatory agency of such acquisition becomes final.

(iii) Special rule where offer subject to approval by foreign regulatory body.—In any case where an offer to acquire stock in a corporation was subject to intervention by a foreign regulatory body and a public announcement of such an offer resulted in the intervention by such foreign regulatory body before July 23, 1982—

(I) such public announcement shall be treated as a tender offer, and

(II) clause (i) shall be applied by substituting for "October 1, 1982" the date which is 90 days after the date on which such regulatory body approves a public offer to acquire stock in such corporation.

(iv) Special rule where one-third of shares acquired during March and April 1982.—If—

(I) one-third or more of the shares of a corporation were acquired by another corporation during March and April 1982, and

(II) during March or April 1982, the acquiring corporation filed with the Federal Trade Commission notification of its intent to acquire control of the acquired corporation,

subclause (II) of clause (i) shall not apply with respect to distributions made by the acquired corporation.

(E) Insurance companies.—The amendments made by this section shall not apply to distributions made by an insurance company pursuant to a plan of partial liquidation adopted before October 1, 1982, where control was acquired by the distributee or its parent after December 31, 1980, and before July 23, 1982, and the conduct of the insurance business by the distributee is conditioned on approval by a State regulatory authority.

For purposes of this paragraph, the term "control" has the meaning given to such term by section 368(c) of the Internal Revenue Code of 1954 except that in applying such section both direct and indirect ownership of stock shall be taken into account.

(3) Approval of plan by board of directors.—For purposes of—

(A) paragraph (2), and

(B) applying section 346(a)(2) of the Internal Revenue Code of 1954 (as in effect on the day before the date of the enactment of this Act) to distributions to which (but for paragraph (2)) the amendments made by this section would apply,

a plan of liquidation shall be treated as adopted when approved by the corporation's board of directors.

(4) Coordination with amendments made by section [224].—For purposes of section 338(e)(2)(C) of the Internal Revenue Code of 1954 (as added by section 224, any property acquired in a distribution to which the amendments made by this section do not apply by reason of paragraph (2) shall be treated as acquired before September 1, 1982.

• 1964, Revenue Act of 1964 (P.L. 88-272)

P.L. 88-272, §225(f)(2):

Amended Code Sec. 331(b) by inserting the phrase "(other than a distribution referred to in paragraph (2)(B) of section 316(b))," after "any distribution of property". **Effective** for distributions made in any tax year of the distributing corporation beginning after 12-31-63.

[Sec. 331(c)]

(c) CROSS REFERENCE.—

For general rule for determination of the amount of gain or loss recognized, see section 1001.

Amendments

• 1976, Tax Reform Act of 1976 (P.L. 94-455)

P.L. 94-455, §1901(b)(28)(A):

Amended Code Sec. 331(c). **Effective** for tax years beginning after 12-31-76. Prior to amendment, Code Sec. 331(c) read as follows:

(c) CROSS REFERENCES.—

(1) For general rule for determination of the amount of gain or loss to the distributee, see section 1001.

(2) For general rule for determination of the amount of gain or loss recognized, see section 1002.

[Sec. 332]

SEC. 332. COMPLETE LIQUIDATIONS OF SUBSIDIARIES.

[Sec. 332(a)]

(a) GENERAL RULE.—No gain or loss shall be recognized on the receipt by a corporation of property distributed in complete liquidation of another corporation.

[Sec. 332(b)]

(b) LIQUIDATIONS TO WHICH SECTION APPLIES.—For purposes of this section, a distribution shall be considered to be in complete liquidation only if—

(1) the corporation receiving such property was, on the date of the adoption of the plan of liquidation, and has continued to be at all times until the receipt of the property, the owner of stock (in such other corporation) meeting the requirements of section 1504(a)(2); and either

(2) the distribution is by such other corporation in complete cancellation or redemption of all its stock, and the transfer of all the property occurs within the taxable year; in such case the adoption by the shareholders of the resolution under which is authorized the distribution of all the assets of such corporation in complete cancellation or redemption of all its stock shall be considered an adoption of a plan of liquidation, even though no time for the completion of the transfer of the property is specified in such resolution; or

(3) such distribution is one of a series of distributions by such other corporation in complete cancellation or redemption of all its stock in accordance with a plan of liquidation under which the transfer of all the property under the liquidation is to be completed within 3 years from the close of the taxable year during which is made the first of the series of distributions under the plan, except that if such transfer is not completed within such period, or if the taxpayer does not continue qualified under paragraph (1) until the completion of such transfer, no distribution under the plan shall be considered a distribution in complete liquidation.

If such transfer of all the property does not occur within the taxable year, the Secretary may require of the taxpayer such bond, or waiver of the statute of limitations on assessment and collection, or both, as he may deem necessary to insure, if the transfer of the property is not completed within such 3-year period, or if the taxpayer does not continue qualified under paragraph (1) until the completion of such transfer, the assessment and collection of all income taxes then imposed by law for such taxable year or subsequent taxable years, to the extent attributable to property so received. A distribution otherwise constituting a distribution in complete liquidation within the meaning of this subsection shall not be considered as not constituting such a distribution merely because it does not constitute a distribution or liquidation within the meaning of the corporate law under which the distribution is made; and for purposes of this subsection a transfer of property of such other corporation to the taxpayer shall not be considered as not constituting a distribution (or one of a series of distributions) in complete cancellation or redemption of all the stock of such other corporation, merely because the carrying out of the plan involves (A) the transfer under the plan to the taxpayer by such other corporation of property, not attributable to shares owned by the taxpayer, on an exchange described in section 361, and (B) the complete cancellation or redemption under the plan, as a result of exchanges described in section 354, of the shares not owned by the taxpayer.

Amendments

• 1998, Tax and Trade Relief Extension Act of 1998 (P.L. 105-277)

P.L. 105-277, §3001(b)(1):

Amended Code Sec. 332(b) by striking "subsection (a)" and inserting "this section" in the material preceding paragraph (1). **Effective** for distributions after 5-21-98.

• 1986, Tax Reform Act of 1986 (P.L. 99-514)

P.L. 99-514, §1804(e)(6)(A):

Amended Code Sec. 332(b)(1). For the **effective** date, as well as a transitional rule, see Act Sec. 1804(e)(6)(B), below. Prior to amendment, Code Sec. 332(b)(1) read as follows:

(1) the corporation receiving such property was, on the date of the adoption of the plan of liquidation, and has continued to be at all times until the receipt of the property, the owner of stock (in such other corporation) possessing at least 80 percent of the total combined voting power of all classes of stock entitled to vote and the owner of at least 80 percent of the total number of shares of all other classes of stock (except nonvoting stock which is limited and preferred as to dividends); and either

P.L. 99-514, §1804(e)(6)(B), provides:

(B) Effective Date.—

(i) IN GENERAL.—Except as provided in clause (iii), the amendment made by subparagraph (A) shall apply with respect to plans of complete liquidation adopted after March 28, 1985.

(ii) CERTAIN DISTRIBUTIONS MADE AFTER DECEMBER 31, 1984.—Except as provided in clause (iii), the amendment made by subparagraph (A) shall also apply with respect to plans of complete liquidations adopted on or before March 28, 1985, pursuant to which any distribution is made in a taxable year beginning after December 31, 1984 (December 31, 1983, in the case of an affiliated group to which an election under section 60(b)(7) of the Tax Reform Act of 1984 applies), but only if the liquidating corporation and any corporation which receives a distribution in complete liquidation of such corporation are members of an affiliated group of corporations filing a consolidated return for the taxable year which includes the date of the distribution.

(iii) TRANSITIONAL RULE FOR AFFILIATED GROUPS.—The amendment made by subparagraph (A) shall not apply with respect to plans of complete liquidation if the liquidating corporation is a member of an affiliated group of corporations under section 60(b)(2), (5), (6), or (8) of the Tax Reform Act of 1984, for all taxable years which include the date of any distribution pursuant to such plan.

• 1976, Tax Reform Act of 1976 (P.L. 94-455)

P.L. 94-455, §1906(b)(13)(A):

Amended 1954 Code by substituting "Secretary" for "Secretary or his delegate" each place it appeared. **Effective** 2-1-77.

[Sec. 332(c)]

(c) DEDUCTIBLE LIQUIDATING DISTRIBUTIONS OF REGULATED INVESTMENT COMPANIES AND REAL ESTATE INVESTMENT TRUSTS.—If a corporation receives a distribution from a regulated investment company or a real estate investment trust which is considered under subsection (b) as being in complete liquidation of such company or trust, then, notwithstanding any other provision of this chapter, such corporation shall recognize and treat as a dividend from such company or trust an amount equal to the deduction for dividends paid allowable to such company or trust by reason of such distribution.

Amendments

• 1998, Tax and Trade Relief Extension Act of 1998 (P.L. 105-277)

P.L. 105-277, §3001(a):

Amended Code Sec. 332 by adding at the end a new subsection (c). **Effective** for distributions after 5-21-98.

[Sec. 332(c)—Repealed]

Amendments

• 1986, Tax Reform Act of 1986 (P.L. 99-514)

P.L. 99-514, §631(e)(2):

Amended Code Sec. 332 by repealing subsection (c). For the **effective** date, see Act Sec. 633 following Code Sec. 311. Prior to amendment Code Sec. 332(c) read as follows:

(c) SPECIAL RULE FOR INDEBTEDNESS OF SUBSIDIARY TO PARENT—If—

(1) a corporation is liquidated and subsection (a) applies to such liquidation, and

(2) on the date of the adoption of the plan of liquidation, such corporation was indebted to the corporation which meets the 80 percent stock ownership requirements specified in subsection (b),

then no gain or loss shall be recognized to the corporation so indebted because of the transfer of property in satisfaction of such indebtedness.

[Sec. 332(d)]

(d) RECOGNITION OF GAIN ON LIQUIDATION OF CERTAIN HOLDING COMPANIES.—

(1) IN GENERAL.—In the case of any distribution to a foreign corporation in complete liquidation of an applicable holding company—

(A) subsection (a) and section 331 shall not apply to such distribution, and

(B) such distribution shall be treated as a distribution of property to which section 301 applies.

(2) APPLICABLE HOLDING COMPANY.—For purposes of this subsection:

(A) IN GENERAL.—The term "applicable holding company" means any domestic corporation—

(i) which is a common parent of an affiliated group,

(ii) stock of which is directly owned by the distributee foreign corporation,

(iii) substantially all of the assets of which consist of stock in other members of such affiliated group, and

(iv) which has not been in existence at all times during the 5 years immediately preceding the date of the liquidation.

(B) AFFILIATED GROUP.—For purposes of this subsection, the term "affiliated group" has the meaning given such term by section 1504(a) (without regard to paragraphs (2) and (4) of section 1504(b)).

(3) COORDINATION WITH SUBPART F.—If the distributee of a distribution described in paragraph (1) is a controlled foreign corporation (as defined in section 957), then notwithstanding paragraph (1) or subsection (a), such distribution shall be treated as a distribution to which section 331 applies.

(4) REGULATIONS.—The Secretary shall provide such regulations as appropriate to prevent the abuse of this subsection, including regulations which provide, for the purposes of clause (iv) of paragraph (2)(A), that a corporation is not in existence for any period unless it is engaged in the active conduct of a trade or business or owns a significant ownership interest in another corporation so engaged.

Amendments

•2005, Gulf Opportunity Zone Act of 2005 (P.L. 109-135)

P.L. 109-135, §412(v):

Amended Code Sec. 332(d)(1)(B) by striking "distribution to which section 301 applies" and inserting "distribution of property to which section 301 applies". **Effective** 12-21-2005.

• 2004, American Jobs Creation Act of 2004 (P.L. 108-357)

P.L. 108-357, §893(a):

Amended Code Sec. 332 by adding at the end a new subsection (d). **Effective** for distributions in complete liquidation occurring on or after 10-22-2004.

[Sec. 333—Repealed]

Amendments

• 1986, Tax Reform Act of 1986 (P.L. 99-514)

P.L. 99-514, §631(e)(3):

Repealed Code Sec. 333. For the **effective** date, see Act Sec. 633 following Code Sec. 311. Prior to repeal, Code Sec. 333 read as follows:

SEC. 333. ELECTION AS TO RECOGNITION OF GAIN IN CERTAIN LIQUIDATIONS.

[Sec. 333(a)]

(a) GENERAL RULE.—In the case of property distributed in complete liquidation of a domestic corporation (other than a collapsible corporation to which section 341 (a) applies), if—

(1) the liquidation is made in pursuance of a plan of liquidation adopted, and

(2) the distribution is in complete cancellation or redemption of all the stock, and the transfer of all the property under the liquidation occurs within some one calendar month,

then in the case of each qualified electing shareholder (as defined in subsection (c)) gain on the shares owned by him at the time of the adoption of the plan of liquidation shall be recognized only to the extent provided in subsections (e) and (f).

Amendments

• 1982, Tax Equity and Fiscal Responsibility Act of 1982 (P.L. 97-248)

P.L. 97-248, §247, as amended by P.L. 98-369, §713(h), provides:

ACT SECTION 247. EXISTING PERSONAL SERVICE CORPORATIONS MAY LIQUIDATE UNDER SECTION 333 DURING 1983 OR 1984.

(a) In General.—In the case of a complete liquidation of a personal service corporation (within the meaning of section 535(c)(2)(B) of the Internal Revenue Code of 1954) which is in existence on September 3, 1982, during 1983 or 1984, the following rules shall apply with respect to any shareholder other than a corporation:

(1) The determination of whether section 333 of such Code applies shall be made without regard to whether the corporation is a collapsible corporation to which section 341(a) of such Code applies.

(2) No gain or loss shall be recognized by the liquidating corporation on the distribution of any unrealized receivable in such liquidation.

(3)(A) Except as provided in subparagraph (C), any disposition by a shareholder of any unrealized receivable received in the liquidation shall be treated as a sale at fair market value of such receivable and any gain or loss shall be treated as ordinary gain or loss.

(B) For purposes of subparagraph (A), the term "disposition" includes—

(i) failing to hold the property in the trade or business which generated the receivables, and

(ii) failing to hold a continuing interest in such trade or business.

(C) For purposes of subparagraph (A), the term "disposition" does not include transmission at death to the estate of the decedent or transfer to a person pursuant to the right of such person to receive such property by reason of the death of the decedent or by bequest, devise, or inheritance from the decedent.

(4) Unrealized receivables distributed in the liquidation shall be treated as having a zero basis.

(5) For purposes of computing earnings and profits, the liquidating corporation shall not treat unrealized receivables distributed in the liquidation as an item of income.

(b) Unrealized Receivables Defined.—For purposes of this section, the term "unrealized receivables" has the meaning given such term by the first sentence of section 751(c) of such Code.

• 1976, Tax Reform Act of 1976 (P.L. 94-455)

P.L. 94-455, §1901(a)(44):

Struck out "on or after June 22, 1954" following "plan of liquidation adopted" in Code Sec. 333(a)(1). **Effective** for tax years beginning after 12-31-76.

[Sec. 333(b)]

(b) EXCLUDED CORPORATION.—For purposes of this section, the term "excluded corporation" means a corporation which at any time between January 1, 1954, and the date of the adoption of the plan of liquidation, both dates inclusive, was the owner of stock possessing 50 percent or more of the total combined voting power of all classes of stock entitled to vote on the adoption of such plan.

[Sec. 333(c)]

(c) QUALIFIED ELECTING SHAREHOLDERS.—For purposes of this section, the term "qualified electing shareholder" means a shareholder (other than an excluded corporation) of any class of stock (whether or not entitled to vote on the adoption of the plan of liquidation) who is a shareholder at the time of the adoption of such plan, and whose written election to have the benefits of subsection (a) has been made and filed in accordance with subsection (d), but—

(1) in the case of a shareholder other than a corporation, only if written elections have been so filed by shareholders (other than corporations) who at the time of the adoption of the plan of liquidation are owners of stock possessing at least 80 percent of the total combined voting power (exclusive of voting power possessed by stock owned by corporations) of all classes of stock entitled to vote on the adoption of such plan of liquidation; or

(2) in the case of a shareholder which is a corporation, only if written elections have been so filed by corporate shareholders (other than an excluded corporation) which at the time of the adoption of such plan of liquidation are owners of stock possessing at least 80 percent of the total combined voting power (exclusive of voting power possessed by stock owned by an excluded corporation and by shareholders who are not corporations) of all classes of stock entitled to vote on the adoption of such plan of liquidation.

[Sec. 333(d)]

(d) MAKING AND FILING OF ELECTIONS.—The written elections referred to in subsection (c) must be made and filed in such manner as to be not in contravention of regulations prescribed by the Secretary. The filing must be within 30 days after the date of the adoption of the plan of liquidation.

Amendments

• 1976, Tax Reform Act of 1976 (P.L. 94-455)

P.L. 94-455, §1906(b)(13)(A):

Amended 1954 Code by substituting "Secretary" for "Secretary or his delegate" each place it appeared. **Effective** 2-1-77.

[Sec. 333(e)]

(e) NONCORPORATE SHAREHOLDERS.—In the case of a qualified electing shareholder other than a corporation—

(1) there shall be recognized, and treated as a dividend, so much of the gain as is not in excess of his ratable share of the earnings and profits of the corporation accumulated after February 28, 1913, such earnings and profits to be determined as of the close of the month in which the transfer in liquidation occurred under subsection (a)(2), but without diminution by reason of distributions made during such month; but by including in the computation thereof all amounts accrued up to the date on which the transfer of all the property under the liquidation is completed; and

(2) there shall be recognized, and treated as short-term or long-term capital gain, as the case may be, so much of the remainder of the gain as is not in excess of the amount by which the value of that portion of the assets received by him which consists of money, or of stock or securities acquired by the corporation after December 31, 1953, exceeds his ratable share of such earnings and profits.

Amendments

• 1969, Tax Reform Act of 1969 (P.L. 91-172)

P.L. 91-172, §917, provides:

SEC. 917. RECOGNITION OF GAIN IN CERTAIN LIQUIDATIONS.

For purposes of applying section 333(e) and (f) of the Internal Revenue Code of 1954 to a distribution in liquidation of a corporation during 1970, stock (including stock received in respect of such stock by reason of a stock dividend or stock split), or securities received by a qualified electing shareholder in exchange for his stock in the liquidating corporation shall be considered as having been acquired by the liquidating corporation before January 1, 1954, if—

(1) such stock or securities were acquired by the liquidating corporation after December 31, 1953, from such qualified electing shareholder (or from a person from whom such qualified electing shareholder acquired such stock in the liquidating corporation by gift, bequest, or inheritance) solely in exchange for its stock in a transaction to which section 351 of such Code (or the corresponding provisions of prior law) applied, and

(2) the holding period of such stock or securities in the hands of the liquidating corporation, determined under section 1223(2) of such Code, includes any period before January 1, 1954.

[Sec. 333(f)]

(f) CORPORATE SHAREHOLDERS.—In the case of a qualified electing shareholder which is a corporation, the gain shall be recognized only to the extent of the greater of the two following—

(1) the portion of the assets received by it which consists of money, or of stock or securities acquired by the liquidating corporation after December 31, 1953; or

(2) its ratable share of the earnings and profits of the liquidating corporation accumulated after February 28, 1913, such earnings and profits to be determined as of the close of the month in which the transfer in liquidation occurred under subsection (a)(2), but without diminution by reason of distributions made during such month; but by

including in the computation thereof all amounts accrued up to the date on which the transfer of all the property under the liquidation is completed.

[Sec. 333(g)—Repealed]

Amendments

• 1976, Tax Reform Act of 1976 (P.L. 94-455)

P.L. 94-455, §1951(b)(6)(A):

Repealed Code Sec. 333(g). **Effective** for tax years beginning after 12-31-76. Prior to repeal, Code Sec. 333(g) read as follows:

(g) SPECIAL RULE.—

(1) LIQUIDATIONS BEFORE JANUARY 1, 1967.—In the case of a liquidation occurring before January 1, 1967, of a corporation referred to in paragraph (3)—

(A) the date "December 31, 1953" referred to in subsections (e)(2) and (f)(1) shall be treated as if such date were "December 31, 1962", and

(B) in the case of stock in such corporation held for more than 6 months, the term "a dividend" as used in subsection (e)(1) shall be treated as if such term were "longterm capital gain".

Subparagraph (B) shall not apply to any earnings and profits to which the corporation succeeds after December 31, 1963, pursuant to any corporate reorganization or pursuant to any liquidation to which section 332 applies, except earnings and profits which on December 31, 1963, constituted earnings and profits of a corporation referred to in paragraph (3), and except earnings and profits which were earned after such date by a corporation referred to in paragraph (3).

(2) LIQUIDATIONS AFTER DECEMBER 31, 1966.—

(A) IN GENERAL.—In the case of a liquidation occurring after December 31, 1966, of a corporation to which this subparagraph applies—

(i) the date "December 31, 1953" referred to in subsections (e)(2) and (f)(1) shall be treated as if such date were "December 31, 1962", and

(ii) so much of the gain recognized under subsection (e)(1) as is attributable to the earnings and profits accumulated after February 28, 1913, and before January 1, 1967, shall, in the case of stock in such corporation held for more than 6 months, be treated as longterm capital gain, and only the remainder of such gain shall be treated as a dividend.

Clause (ii) shall not apply to any earnings and profits to which the corporation succeeds after December 31, 1963, pursuant to any corporate reorganization or pursuant to any liquidation to which section 332 applies, except earnings and profits which on December 31, 1963, constituted earnings and profits of a corporation referred to in paragraph (3), and except earnings and profits which were earned after such date by a corporation referred to in paragraph (3).

(B) CORPORATIONS TO WHICH APPLICABLE.—Subparagraph (A) shall apply only with respect to a corporation which is referred to in paragraph (3) and which—

(i) on January 1, 1964, owes qualified indebtedness (as defined in section 545(c)),

(ii) before January 1, 1968, notifies the Secretary or his delegate that it may wish to have subparagraph (A) apply to it and submits such information as may be required by regulations prescribed by the Secretary or his delegate, and

(iii) liquidates before the close of the taxable year in which such corporation ceases to owe such qualified indebtedness or (if earlier) the taxable year referred to in subparagraph (C).

(C) ADJUSTED POST-1963 EARNINGS AND PROFITS EXCEED QUALIFIED INDEBTEDNESS.—In the case of any corporation, the taxable year referred to in this subparagraph is the first taxable year at the close of which its adjusted post-1963 earnings and profits equal or exceed the amount of such corporation's qualified indebtedness on January 1, 1964. For purposes of the preceding sentence, the term "adjusted post-1963 earnings and profits" means the sum of—

(i) the earnings and profits of such corporation for taxable years beginning after December 31, 1963, without diminution by reason of any distributions made out of such earnings and profits, and

(ii) the deductions allowed for taxable years beginning after December 31, 1963, for exhaustion, wear and tear, obsolescence, amortization, or depletion.

(3) CORPORATIONS REFERRED TO.—For purposes of paragraphs (1) and (2), a corporation referred to in this paragraph is a corporation which for at least one of the two most recent taxable years ending before the date of the enactment of this subsection was not a personal holding company under section 542, but would have been a personal holding company under section 542 for such taxable year if the law applicable for the first taxable year beginning after December 31, 1963, had been applicable to such taxable year.

(4) MISTAKE AS TO APPLICABILITY OF SUBSECTION.—An election made under this section by a qualified electing shareholder of a corporation in which such shareholder states that such election is made on the assumption that such corporation is a corporation referred to in paragraph (3) shall have no force or effect if it is determined that the corporation is not a corporation referred to in paragraph (3).

P.L. 94-455, §1951(b)(6)(B), (C), provide as follows:

(B) SAVINGS PROVISION.—Notwithstanding subparagraph (A), if any corporation meets all the requirements of section 333(g)(2)(B), as in effect before its repeal by this Act, the liquidation of such corporation shall be treated as if paragraphs (2), (3), and (4) of section 333(g) had not been repealed.

(C) PHASE-IN OF 12-MONTH HOLDING PERIOD REQUIREMENT.—For purposes of subparagraph (B), the period for holding of stock specified in section 333(g)(2)(A)(ii), as in effect before such repeal, shall—

(i) in the case of taxable years beginning in 1977, be considered to be "9 months"; and

(ii) in the case of taxable years beginning after December 31, 1977, be considered to be "1 year".

• 1964, Revenue Act of 1964 (P.L. 88-272)

P.L. 88-272, §225(g), (h):

Added Code Sec. 333(g). **Effective** for tax years beginning after 12-31-63. Act Sec. 225(h), providing an exception for certain corporations, is reproduced below:

(h) Exception for Certain Corporations.—

(1) General rule.—Except as provided in paragraph (2) [below], in the case of a corporation referred to in section 333(g)(3) of the Internal Revenue Code of 1954 (as added by subsection (g) of this section), the amendments made by this section (other than subsections (f) and (g)) shall not apply if there is a complete liquidation of such corporation and if the distribution of all the property under such liquidation occurs before January 1, 1966.

(2) Exception.—Paragraph (1) shall not apply to any liquidation to which section 332 of the Internal Revenue Code of 1954 applies unless—

(A) the corporate distributee (referred to in subsection (b)(1) of such section 332) in such liquidation is liquidated in a complete liquidation to which such section 332 does not apply, and

(B) the distribution of all the property under such liquidation occurs before the 91st day after the last distribution referred to in paragraph (1) and before January 1, 1966.

[Sec. 334]

SEC. 334. BASIS OF PROPERTY RECEIVED IN LIQUIDATIONS.

[Sec. 334(a)]

(a) GENERAL RULE.—If property is received in a distribution in complete liquidation, and if gain or loss is recognized on receipt of such property, then the basis of the property in the hands of the distributee shall be the fair market value of such property at the time of the distribution.

Amendments

• 1986, Tax Reform Act of 1986 (P.L. 99-514)

P.L. 99-514, §631(e)(4)(A):

Amended Code Sec. 334(a) by striking out "(other than a distribution to which section 333 applies)". For the **effective** date, see Act Sec. 633 following Code Sec. 311. Prior to amendment, Code Sec. 334(a) read as follows:

(a) GENERAL RULE.—If property is received in a distribution in complete liquidation (other than a distribution to which section 333 applies), and if gain or loss is recognized on receipt of such property, then the basis of the property in the hands of the distributee shall be the fair market value of such property at the time of the distribution.

• 1982, Tax Equity and Fiscal Responsibility Act of 1982 (P.L. 97-248)

P.L. 97-248, §222(e)(1)(C):

Amended Code Sec. 334(a) by striking out "partial or complete liquidation" and inserting in lieu thereof "complete liquidation". **Effective**, generally, for distributions after 8-31-82. But see amendment notes for P.L. 97-248, Act Sec. 222(f), following Code Sec. 331(b) for exceptions.

[Sec. 334(b)]

(b) LIQUIDATION OF SUBSIDIARY.—

(1) IN GENERAL.—If property is received by a corporate distributee in a distribution in a complete liquidation to which section 332 applies (or in a transfer described in section 337(b)(1)), the basis of such property in the hands of such distributee shall be the same as it would be in the hands of the transferor; except that, in the hands of such distributee—

(A) the basis of such property shall be the fair market value of the property at the time of the distribution in any case in which gain or loss is recognized by the liquidating corporation with respect to such property, and

(B) the basis of any property described in section 362(e)(1)(B) shall be the fair market value of the property at the time of the distribution in any case in which such distributee's aggregate adjusted basis of such property would (but for this subparagraph) exceed the fair market value of such property immediately after such liquidation.

(2) CORPORATE DISTRIBUTEE.—For purposes of this subsection, the term "corporate distributee" means only the corporation which meets the stock ownership requirements specified in section 332(b).

Amendments

•2005, Gulf Opportunity Zone Act of 2005 (P.L. 109-135)

P.L. 109-135, §403(dd)(1):

Amended Code Sec. 334(b)(1) by striking "except that" and all that follows and inserting "except that, in the hands of such distributee—"and new subparagraphs (A) and (B). **Effective** as if included in the provision of the American Jobs Creation Act of 2004 (P.L. 108-357) to which it relates [**effective** for liquidations after 10-22-2004.—CCH]. Prior to amendment, Code Sec. 334(b)(1) read as follows:

(1) IN GENERAL.—If property is received by a corporate distributee in a distribution in a complete liquidation to which section 332 applies (or in a transfer described in section 337(b)(1)), the basis of such property in the hands of such distributee shall be the same as it would be in the hands of the transferor; except that the basis of such property in the hands of such distributee shall be the fair market value of the property at the time of the distribution—

(A) in any case in which gain or loss is recognized by the liquidating corporation with respect to such property, or

(B) in any case in which the liquidating corporation is a foreign corporation, the corporate distributee is a domestic corporation, and the corporate distributee's aggregate adjusted bases of property described in section 362(e)(1)(B) which is distributed in such liquidation would (but for this subparagraph) exceed the fair market value of such property immediately after such liquidation.

• 2004, American Jobs Creation Act of 2004 (P.L. 108-357)

P.L. 108-357, §836(b):

Amended Code Sec. 334(b)(1). **Effective** for liquidations after 10-22-2004. Prior to amendment, Code Sec. 334(b)(1) read as follows:

(1) IN GENERAL.—If property is received by a corporate distributee in a distribution in a complete liquidation to which section 332 applies (or in a transfer described in section 337(b)(1)), the basis of such property in the hands of such distributee shall be the same as it would be in the hands of the transferor; except that, in any case in which gain or loss is recognized by the liquidating corporation with respect to such property, the basis of such property in the hands of such distributee shall be the fair market value of the property at the time of the distribution.

• 1998, Tax and Trade Relief Extension Act of 1998 (P.L. 105-277)

P.L. 105-277, §3001(b)(2):

Amended Code Sec. 334(b)(1) by striking "section 332(a)" and inserting "section 332". **Effective** for distributions after 5-21-98.

• 1988, Technical and Miscellaneous Revenue Act of 1988 (P.L. 100-647)

P.L. 100-647, §1006(e)(6):

Amended Code Sec. 334(b). **Effective** as if included in the provision of P.L. 99-514 to which it relates. Prior to amendment, Code Sec. 334(b) read as follows:

(b) LIQUIDATION OF SUBSIDIARY.—

(1) DISTRIBUTION IN COMPLETE LIQUIDATION.—If property is received by a corporation in a distribution in a complete liquidation to which section 332(a) applies, the basis of the property in the hands of the distributee shall be the same as it would be in the hands of the transferor.

(2) TRANSFERS TO WHICH SECTION 332(c) APPLIES.—If property is received by a corporation in a transfer to which section 332(c) applies, the basis of the property in the hands of the transferee shall be the same as it would be in the hands of the transferor.

(3) DISTRIBUTEE DEFINED.—For purposes of this subsection, the term "distributee" means only the corporation which meets the 80-percent stock ownership requirements specified in section 332(b).

• 1982, Tax Equity and Fiscal Responsibility Act of 1982 (P.L. 97-248)

P.L. 97-248, §224(b):

Amended Code Sec. 334(b). **Effective** for any target corporation (within the meaning of Code Sec. 338) with respect to which the acquisition date (within the meaning of such section) occurs after 8-31-82. See P.L. 97-248, §224(a), which appears in the amendment notes for new Code Sec. 338, for special rules. Prior to amendment, it read as follows:

(b) Liquidation of Subsidiary.—

(1) In general.—If property is received by a corporation in a distribution in complete liquidation of another corporation (within the meaning of section 332(b)), then, except as provided in paragraph (2), the basis of the property in the hands of the distributee shall be the same as it would be in

the hands of the transferor. If property is received by a corporation in a transfer to which section 332(c) applies, and if paragraph (2) of this subsection does not apply, then the basis of the property in the hands of the transferee shall be the same as it would be in the hands of the transferor.

(2) Exception.—If property is received by a corporation in a distribution in complete liquidation of another corporation (within the meaning of section 332(b)), and if—

(A) the distribution is pursuant to a plan of liquidation adopted not more than 2 years after the date of the transaction described in subparagraph (B) (or, in the case of a series of transactions, the date of the last such transaction); and

(B) stock of the distributing corporation possessing at least 80 percent of the total conbined voting power of all classes of stock entitled to vote, and at least 80 percent of the total number of shares of all other classes of stock (except nonvoting stock which is limited and preferred as to dividends), was acquired by the distributee by purchase (as defined in paragraph (3)) during a 12-month period beginning with the earlier of,

(i) the date of the first acquisition by purchase of such stock, or

(ii) if any of such stock was acquired in an acquisition which is a purchase within the meaning of the second sentence of paragraph (3), the date on which the distributee is first considered under section 318(a) as owning stock owned by the corporation from which such acquisition was made,

then the basis of the property in the hands of the distributee shall be the adjusted basis of the stock with respect to which the distribution was made. For purposes of the preceding sentence, under regulations prescribed by the Secretary, proper adjustment in the adjusted basis of any stock shall be made for any distribution made to the distributee with respect to such stock before the adoption of the plan of liquidation, for any money received, for any liabilities assumed or subject to which the property was received, and for other items.

(3) Purchase defined.—For purposes of paragraph (2)(B), the term `purchase' means any acquisition of stock, but only if—

(A) the basis of the stock in the hands of the distributee is not determined (i) in whole or in part by reference to the adjusted basis of such stock in the hands of the person from whom acquired, or (ii) under section 1014(a) (relating to property acquired from a decedent),

(B) the stock is not acquired in an exchange to which section 351 applies, and

(C) the stock is not acquired from a person the ownership of whose stock would, under section 318(a), be attributed to the person acquiring such stock.

Notwithstanding subparagraph (C) of this paragraph, for purposes of paragraph (2)(B), the term `purchase' also means an acquisition of stock from a corporation when ownership of such stock would be attributed under section 318(a) to the person acquiring such stock, if the stock of such corporation by reason of which such ownership would be attributed was acquired by purchase (within the meaning of the preceding sentence).

(4) Distributee defined.—For purposes of this subsection, the term `distributee' means only the corporation which meets the 80 percent stock ownership requirements specified in section 332(b)."

• 1976, Tax Reform Act of 1976 (P.L. 94-455)

P.L. 94-455, §1901(a)(45):

Amended Code Sec. 334(b)(2)(A). **Effective** for tax years beginning after 12-31-76. Prior to amendment, Code Sec. 334(b)(2)(A) read as follows:

(A) the distribution is pursuant to a plan of liquidation adopted—

(i) on or after June 22, 1954, and

(ii) not more than 2 years after the date of the transaction described in subparagraph (B) (or, in the case of a series of transactions, the date of the last such transaction); and

P.L. 94-455, §1906(b)(13)(A):

Amended 1954 Code by substituting "Secretary" for "Secretary or his delegate" each place it appeared. **Effective** 2-1-77.

• 1966, Foreign Investors Tax Act of 1996 (P.L. 89-809)

P.L. 89-809, §202(a):

Amended Code Sec. 334(b)(3) by adding the last sentence. **Effective** for acquisitions of stock after 12-31-65.

P.L. 89-809, §202(b):

Amended Code Sec. 334(b)(2)(B) by striking out "during a period of not more than 12 months," and inserting in lieu thereof "during a 12-month period beginning with the earlier of—

"(i) the date of the first acquisition by purchase of such stock, or

"(ii) if any of such stock was acquired in an acquisition which is a purchase within the meaning of the second sentence of paragraph (3), the date on which the distributee is first considered under section 318(a) as owning stock owned by the corporation from which such acquisition was made,". **Effective** for distributions made after 11-13-66, the date of enactment.

[Sec. 334(c)—Repealed]

Amendments

• 1986, Tax Reform Act of 1986 (P.L. 99-514)

P.L. 99-514, §631 (e)(4)(B):

Repealed Code Sec. 334(c). For the **effective** date, see Act Sec. 633 following Code Sec. 311. Prior to repeal, Code Sec. 334(c) read as follows:

(c) PROPERTY RECEIVED IN LIQUIDATION UNDER SECTION 333.—If—

(1) property was acquired by a shareholder in the liquidation of a corporation in cancellation or redemption of stock, and

(2) with respect to such acquisition—

(A) gain was realized, but

(B) as the result of an election made by the shareholder under section 333, the extent to which gain was recognized was determined under section 333,

then the basis shall be the same as the basis of such stock cancelled or redeemed in the liquidation, decreased in the amount of any money received by the shareholder, and increased in the amount of gain recognized to him.

Subpart B—Effects on Corporation

[Sec. 336]

SEC. 336. GAIN OR LOSS RECOGNIZED ON PROPERTY DISTRIBUTED IN COMPLETE LIQUIDATION.

[Sec. 336(a)]

(a) GENERAL RULE.—Except as otherwise provided in this section or section 337, gain or loss shall be recognized to a liquidating corporation on the distribution of property in complete liquidation as if such property were sold to the distributee at its fair market value.

Amendments

• 2005, Safe, Accountable, Flexible, Efficient Transportation Equity Act: A Legacy for Users (P.L. 109-59)

P.L. 109-59, §11146, provides:

SEC. 11146. TAX TREATMENT OF STATE OWNERSHIP OF RAILROAD REAL ESTATE INVESTMENT TRUST.

(a) IN GENERAL.—If a State owns all of the outstanding stock of a corporation—

(1) which is a real estate investment trust on the date of the enactment of this Act,

(2) which is a non-operating class III railroad, and

(3) substantially all of the activities of which consist of the ownership, leasing, and operation by such corporation of facilities, equipment, and other property used by the corporation or other persons for railroad transportation and for economic development purposes for the benefit of the State and its citizens, then, to the extent such activities are of a type which are an essential governmental function within the meaning of section 115 of the Internal Revenue Code of 1986, income derived from such activities by the corporation shall be treated as accruing to the State for purposes of section 115 of such Code.

(b) GAIN OR LOSS NOT RECOGNIZED ON CONVERSION.—Notwithstanding section 337(d) of the Internal Revenue Code of 1986—

(1) no gain or loss shall be recognized under section 336 or 337 of such Code, and

(2) no change in basis of the property of such corporation shall occur, because of any change of status of a corporation to a tax-exempt entity by reason of the application of subsection (a).

(c) TAX-EXEMPT FINANCING.—

(1) IN GENERAL.—Any obligation issued by a corporation described in subsection (a) at least 95 percent of the net proceeds (as defined in section 150(a) of the Internal Revenue Code of 1986) of which are to be used to provide for the acquisition, construction, or improvement of railroad transportation infrastructure (including railroad terminal facilities)—

(A) shall be treated as a State or local bond (within the meaning of section 103(c) of such Code), and

(B) shall not be treated as a private activity bond (within the meaning of section 103(b)(1) of such Code) solely by reason of the ownership or use of such railroad transportation infrastructure by the corporation.

(2) NO INFERENCE.—Except as provided in paragraph (1), nothing in this subsection shall be construed to affect the treatment of the private use of proceeds or property financed with obligations issued by the corporation for purposes of section 103 of the Internal Revenue Code of 1986 and part IV of subchapter B of such Code.

(d) DEFINITIONS.—For purposes of this section:

(1) REAL ESTATE INVESTMENT TRUST.—The term "real estate investment trust" has the meaning given such term by section 856(a) of the Internal Revenue Code of 1986.

(2) NON-OPERATING CLASS III RAILROAD.—The term "non-operating class III railroad" has the meaning given such term by part A of subtitle IV of title 49, United States Code (49 U.S.C. 10101 et seq.), and the regulations thereunder.

(3) STATE.—The term "State" includes—

(A) the District of Columbia and any possession of the United States, and

(B) any authority, agency, or public corporation of a State.

(e) APPLICABILITY.—

(1) IN GENERAL.—Except as provided in paragraph (2), this section shall apply on and after the date on which a State becomes the owner of all of the outstanding stock of a corporation described in subsection (a) through action of such corporation's board of directors.

(2) EXCEPTION.—This section shall not apply to any State which—

(A) becomes the owner of all of the voting stock of a corporation described in subsection (a) after December 31, 2003, or

(B) becomes the owner of all of the outstanding stock of a corporation described in subsection (a) after December 31, 2006.

[Sec. 336(b)]

(b) TREATMENT OF LIABILITIES.—If any property distributed in the liquidation is subject to a liability or the shareholder assumes a liability of the liquidating corporation in connection with the distribution, for purposes of subsection (a) and section 337, the fair market value of such property shall be treated as not less than the amount of such liability.

Amendments

• 1988, Technical and Miscellaneous Revenue Act of 1988 (P.L. 100-647)

P.L. 100-647, §1006(e)(21)(A):

Amended Code Sec. 336(b) by striking out "in Excess of Basis" after "Liabilities" in the heading. **Effective** as if included in the provision of P.L. 99-514 to which it relates.

[Sec. 336(c)]

(c) EXCEPTION FOR LIQUIDATIONS WHICH ARE PART OF A REORGANIZATION.—For provision providing that this subpart does not apply to distributions in pursuance of a plan of reorganization, see section 361(c)(4).

Amendments

• 1988, Technical and Miscellaneous Revenue Act of 1988 (P.L. 100-647)

P.L. 100-647, §1018(d)(5)(D):

Amended Code Sec. 336(c) (as amended by P.L. 99-514, §631). **Effective** as if included in the provision of P.L. 99-514 to which it relates. Prior to amendment, Code Sec. 336(c) read as follows:

(c) EXCEPTION FOR CERTAIN LIQUIDATIONS TO WHICH PART III APPLIES.—This section shall not apply with respect to any distribution of property to the extent there is nonrecognition of gain or loss with respect to such property to the recipient under part III.

[Sec. 336(d)]

(d) LIMITATIONS ON RECOGNITION OF LOSS.—

(1) NO LOSS RECOGNIZED IN CERTAIN DISTRIBUTIONS TO RELATED PERSONS.—

(A) IN GENERAL.—No loss shall be recognized to a liquidating corporation on the distribution of any property to a related person (within the meaning of section 267) if—

(i) such distribution is not pro rata, or

(ii) such property is disqualified property.

(B) DISQUALIFIED PROPERTY.—For purposes of subparagraph (A), the term "disqualified property" means any property which is acquired by the liquidating corporation in a transaction to which section 351 applied, or as a contribution to capital, during the 5-year period ending on the date of the distribution. Such term includes any property if the adjusted basis of such property is determined (in whole or in part) by reference to the adjusted basis of property described in the preceding sentence.

(2) SPECIAL RULE FOR CERTAIN PROPERTY ACQUIRED IN CERTAIN CARRYOVER BASIS TRANSACTIONS.—

(A) IN GENERAL.—For purposes of determining the amount of loss recognized by any liquidating corporation on any sale, exchange, or distribution of property described in subparagraph (B), the adjusted basis of such property shall be reduced (but not below zero) by the excess (if any) of—

(i) the adjusted basis of such property immediately after its acquisition by such corporation, over

(ii) the fair market value of such property as of such time.

(B) DESCRIPTION OF PROPERTY.—

(i) IN GENERAL.—For purposes of subparagraph (A), property is described in this subparagraph if—

(I) such property is acquired by the liquidating corporation in a transaction to which section 351 applied or as a contribution to capital, and

(II) the acquisition of such property by the liquidating corporation was part of a plan a principal purpose of which was to recognize loss by the liquidating corporation with respect to such property in connection with the liquidation.

Other property shall be treated as so described if the adjusted basis of such other property is determined (in whole or in part) by reference to the adjusted basis of property described in the preceding sentence.

(ii) CERTAIN ACQUISITIONS TREATED AS PART OF PLAN.—For purposes of clause (i), any property described in clause (i)(I) acquired by the liquidated corporation after the date 2 years before the date of the adoption of the plan of complete liquidation shall, except as provided in regulations, be treated as acquired as part of a plan described in clause (i)(II).

(C) RECAPTURE IN LIEU OF DISALLOWANCE.—The Secretary may prescribe regulations under which, in lieu of disallowing a loss under subparagraph (A) for a prior taxable year, the gross income of the liquidating corporation for the taxable year in which the plan of complete liquidation is adopted shall be increased by the amount of the disallowed loss.

(3) SPECIAL RULE IN CASE OF LIQUIDATION TO WHICH SECTION 332 APPLIES.—In the case of any liquidation to which section 332 applies, no loss shall be recognized to the liquidating corporation on any distribution in such liquidation. The preceding sentence shall apply to any distribution to the 80-percent distributee only if subsection (a) or (b)(1) of section 337 applies to such distribution.

Amendments

• 1988, Technical and Miscellaneous Revenue Act of 1988 (P.L. 100-647)

P.L. 100-647, § 1006(e)(1):

Amended Code Sec. 336(d)(2)(B)(ii). **Effective** as if included in the provision of P.L. 99-514 to which it relates. Prior to amendment Code Sec. 336(d)(2)(B)(ii) read as follows:

(ii) CERTAIN ACQUISITIONS TREATED AS PART OF PLAN.—For purposes of clause (i), any property described in clause (i)(I) acquired by the liquidating corporation during the 2-year period ending on the date of the adoption of the plan of complete liquidation shall, except as provided in regulations, be treated as part of a plan described in clause (i)(II).

P.L. 100-647, § 1006(e)(2):

Amended Code Sec. 336(d)(3) by adding at the end thereof a new sentence. **Effective** as if included in the provision of P.L. 99-514 to which it relates.

[Sec. 336(e)]

(e) CERTAIN STOCK SALES AND DISTRIBUTIONS MAY BE TREATED AS ASSET TRANSFERS.—Under regulations prescribed by the Secretary, if—

(1) a corporation owns stock in another corporation meeting the requirements of section 1504(a)(2), and

(2) such corporation sells, exchanges, or distributes all of such stock,

an election may be made to treat such sale, exchange, or distribution as a disposition of all of the assets of such other corporation, and no gain or loss shall be recognized on the sale, exchange, or distribution of such stock.

Amendments

• 1988, Technical and Miscellaneous Revenue Act of 1988 (P.L. 100-647)

P.L. 100-647, §1006(e)(3):

Amended Code Sec. 336(e) by striking out "such corporation may elect" and inserting in lieu thereof "an election may be made". **Effective** as if included in the provision of P.L. 99-514 to which it relates.

• 1986, Tax Reform Act of 1986 (P.L. 99-514)

P.L. 99-514, §631(a):

Amended Code Sec. 336. **Effective** for (1) any distribution in complete liquidation, and any sale or exchange, made by a corporation after 7-31-86, unless such corporation is completely liquidated before 1-1-87, (2) any transaction described in section 338 of the Internal Revenue Code of 1986 for which the acquisition date occurs after 12-31-86, and (3) any distribution (not in complete liquidation) made after 12-31-86. However, for special rules and exceptions, see Act Sec. 633(b)-(f) following Code Sec. 311. Prior to amendment, Code Sec. 336 read as follows:

SEC. 336. DISTRIBUTIONS OF PROPERTY IN LIQUIDATION.

[Sec. 336(a)]

(a) GENERAL RULE.—Except as provided in subsection (b) of this section and in section 453B (relating to disposition of installment obligations), no gain or loss shall be recognized to a corporation on the distribution of property in complete liquidation.

Amendments

• 1982, Tax Equity and Fiscal Responsibility Act of 1982 (P.L. 97-248)

P.L. 97-248, §222(b):

Amended Code Sec. 336(a) by striking out "partial or complete liquidation" and inserting in lieu thereof "complete liquidation". **Effective**, generally, to distributions after 8-31-82. But see P.L. 97-248, Act Sec. 222(f), in the amendment notes under Code Sec. 331(b) for exceptions.

[Sec. 336(b)]

(b) LIFO INVENTORY.—

(1) IN GENERAL.—If a corporation inventorying goods under the LIFO method distributes inventory assets in complete liquidation, then the LIFO recapture amount with respect to such assets shall be treated as gain to the corporation recognized from the sale of such inventory assets.

(2) EXCEPTION WHERE BASIS DETERMINED UNDER SECTION 334(b).—Paragraph (1) shall not apply to any liquidation under section 332 for which the basis of property received is determined under section 334(b).

(3) LIFO RECAPTURE AMOUNT.—For purposes of this subsection, the term "LIFO recapture amount" means the amount (if any) by which—

(A) the inventory amount of the inventory assets under the first-in, first-out method authorized by section 471, exceeds

(B) the inventory amount of such assets under the LIFO method.

(4) DEFINITIONS.—For purposes of this subsection—

(A) LIFO METHOD.—The term "LIFO method" means the method authorized by section 472 (relating to last-in, first-out inventories).

(B) OTHER DEFINITIONS.—The term "inventory assets" has the meaning given to such term by subparagraph (A) of section 311(b)(2), and the term "inventory amount" has the meaning given to such term by subparagraph (B) of section 311(b)(2) (as modified by paragraph (3) of section 311(b)).

Amendments

• 1982, Tax Equity and Fiscal Responsibility Act of 1982 (P.L. 97-248)

P.L. 97-248, §222(e)(1)(D):

Amended Code Sec. 336(b)(1) by striking out "partial or complete liquidation" and inserting in lieu thereof "complete liquidation". **Effective**, generally, to distributions after 8-31-82. But see P.L. 97-248, Act Sec. 222(f), in the amendment notes under Code Sec. 331(b) for exceptions.

P.L. 97-248, §224(c)(4):

Amended Code Sec. 336(b)(2) by striking out "334(b)(1)" each place it appeared and inserting in lieu thereof "334(b)". **Effective**, generally, for any target corporation (within the meaning of Code Sec. 338) with respect to which the acquisition date (within the meaning of such section) occurs after 8-31-82. For special rules, see Act Sec. 224(a), which appears in the amendment notes for new Code Sec. 338.

• 1980, Installment Sales Revision Act of 1980 (P.L. 96-471)

P.L. 96-471, §2(b)(1):

Amended Code Sec. 336(a) by striking out "section 453(d)" and substituting "section 453B". **Effective** for dispositions made after 10-19-80.

P.L. 96-471, §2(c)(1):

Amended Code Sec. 336(a) by striking out "section 453(d)" and substituting "section 453B". **Effective** as though included as part of §403(b) of P.L. 96-223.

• 1980, Crude Oil Windfall Profit Tax Act of 1980 (P.L. 96-223)

P.L. 96-223, §403(b)(1):

Amended Code Sec. 336. **Effective** for distributions and dispositions pursuant to plans of liquidation adopted after 12-31-81. Prior to amendment, Code Sec. 336 read as follows:

SEC. 336. GENERAL RULE.

Except as provided in section 453B (relating to disposition of installment obligations), no gain or loss shall be recognized to a corporation on the distribution of property in partial or complete liquidation.

P.L. 96-223, §403(b)(4), as added by P.L. 97-362, §101, provides:

"(4) PLANS OF LIQUIDATION ADOPTED DURING 1982.—

"(A) IN GENERAL.—If—

"(i) a corporation adopts a plan of liquidation during 1982, and

"(ii) such liquidation is completed before January 1, 1984,

then the LIFO recapture amount taken into account with respect to such liquidation under the amendments made by paragraphs (1) and (2) shall be reduced (but not below zero) by $1,000,000.

"(B) MORE THAN 1 PLAN OF LIQUIDATION.—If a corporation (or group of corporations treated as 1 corporation under subparagraph (C)) has more than 1 liquidation which qualifies under subparagraph (A), the dollar amount under such subparagraph shall apply to all such liquidations in the order in which the distributions, sales, and exchanges occur until such dollar amount is used up.

"(C) APPLICATION TO MEMBERS OF CONTROLLED GROUP.—

"(i) IN GENERAL.—For purposes of this paragraph, all corporations which are competent members of the same controlled group of corporations at any time after December 31, 1981, and before January 1, 1984, shall be treated as 1 corporation.

"(ii) CORPORATIONS MEMBERS OF MORE THAN 1 GROUP.—For purposes of this subparagraph, if (but for this clause) a corporation would be a component member of more than 1 controlled group of corporations during the period described in clause (i)—

"(I) if such corporation is a component member of a controlled group on October 1, 1982, such corporation shall be treated only as a component member of such group, or

"(II) if subclause (I) does not apply, such corporation shall be treated as a component member of only the first such controlled group.

"(iii) CONTROLLED GROUP OF CORPORATIONS DEFINED.—For purposes of this subparagraph, the term `controlled group of corporations' has the meaning given such term by section 1563(a) of the Internal Revenue Code of 1954, except that—

"(I) `more than 50 percent' shall be substituted for `at least 80 percent' each place it appears in section 1563(a)(1) of such Code, and

"(II) the determination shall be made without regard to subsections (a)(4), (b), and (e)(3)(C) of section 1563 of such Code.

"(D) TREATMENT OF DEEMED LIQUIDATIONS UNDER SECTION 338.—If an election under section 338 of the Internal Revenue Code of 1954 is made during 1982 with respect to any qualified stock purchase (within the meaning of such section 338), the requirements of clauses (i) and (ii) of subparagraph (A) shall be treated as met with respect to the target corporation for purposes of applying section 338 of such Code. For purposes of this paragraph, an election to which subparagraph (A) applies by reason of this subparagraph shall be treated as a sale and a liquidation."

[Sec. 337]

SEC. 337. NONRECOGNITION FOR PROPERTY DISTRIBUTED TO PARENT IN COMPLETE LIQUIDATION OF SUBSIDIARY.

[Sec. 337(a)]

(a) IN GENERAL.—No gain or loss shall be recognized to the liquidating corporation on the distribution to the 80-percent distributee of any property in a complete liquidation to which section 332 applies.

[Sec. 337(b)]

(b) TREATMENT OF INDEBTEDNESS OF SUBSIDIARY, ETC.—

(1) INDEBTEDNESS OF SUBSIDIARY TO PARENT.—If—

(A) a corporation is liquidated in a liquidation to which section 332 applies, and

(B) on the date of the adoption of the plan of liquidation, such corporation was indebted to the 80-percent distributee.

for purposes of this section and section 336, any transfer of property to the 80-percent distributee in satisfaction of such indebtedness shall be treated as a distribution to such distributee in such liquidation.

(2) TREATMENT OF TAX-EXEMPT DISTRIBUTEE.—

(A) IN GENERAL.—Except as provided in subparagraph (B), paragraph (1) and subsection (a) shall not apply where the 80-percent distributee is an organization (other than a cooperative described in section 521) which is exempt from the tax imposed by this chapter.

(B) EXCEPTION WHERE PROPERTY WILL BE USED IN UNRELATED BUSINESS.—

(i) IN GENERAL.—Subparagraph (A) shall not apply to any distribution of property to an organization described in section 511(a)(2) if, immediately after such distribution, such organization uses such property in an activity the income from which is subject to tax under 511(a).

(ii) LATER DISPOSITION OR CHANGE IN USE.—If any property to which clause (i) applied is disposed of by the organization acquiring such property, notwithstanding any other provision of law, any gain (not in excess of the amount not recognized by reason of clause (i)) shall be included in such organization's unrelated business taxable income. For purposes of the preceding sentence, if such property ceases to be used in an activity referred to in clause (i), such organization shall be treated as having disposed of such property on the date of such cessation.

Amendments

• 1988, Technical and Miscellaneous Revenue Act of 1988 (P.L. 100-647)

P.L. 100-647, §1006(e)(4)(A)-(C):

Amended Code Sec. 337(b)(2)(B) by striking out "or 511(b)(2)" after "511(a)(2)" in clause (i), by striking out "in an unrelated trade or business (as defined in section 513)" in clause (i) and inserting in lieu thereof "in an activity the income from which is subject to tax under section 511(a)", and by striking out "an unrelated trade or business of such organization" in clause (ii) and inserting in lieu thereof "an activity referred to in clause (i)". **Effective** as if included in the provision of P.L. 99-514 to which it relates.

[Sec. 337(c)]

(c) 80-PERCENT DISTRIBUTEE.—For purposes of this section, the term "80-percent distributee" means only the corporation which meets the 80-percent stock ownership requirements specified in section 332(b). For purposes of this section, the determination of whether any corporation is an 80-percent distributee shall be made without regard to any consolidated return regulation.

Amendments

• 1987, Revenue Act of 1987 (P.L. 100-203)

P.L. 100-203, §10223(a):

Amended Code Sec. 337(c) by adding at the end thereof a new sentence. For the **effective** date, see Act Sec. 10223(d), below.

P.L. 100-203, §10223(d), as amended by P.L. 100-647, §2004(k)(3)-(4), provides:

(d) Effective Dates.—

(1) IN GENERAL.—The amendments made by this section shall apply to distributions or transfers after December 15, 1987.

(2) EXCEPTIONS.—

(A) DISTRIBUTIONS.—The amendments made by this section shall not apply to any distribution after December 15, 1987, and before January 1, 1993, if—

(i) 80 percent or more of the stock of the distributing corporation was acquired by the distributee before December 15, 1987, or

(ii) 80 percent or more of the stock of the distributing corporation was acquired by the distributee before January 1, 1989, pursuant to a binding written contract or tender offer in effect on December 15, 1987.

For purposes of the preceding sentence, stock described in section 1504(a)(4) of the Internal Revenue Code of 1986 shall not be taken into account.

(B) SECTION 304 TRANSFERS.—The amendment made by subsection (c) shall not apply to any transfer after December 15, 1987, and on or before March 31, 1988, if such transfer is—

(i) between corporations which are members of the same affiliated group on December 15, 1987, or

(ii) between corporations which become members of the same affiliated group pursuant to a binding written contract or tender offer in effect on December 15, 1987.

(C) DISTRIBUTIONS COVERED BY PRIOR TRANSITION RULE.—The amendments made by this section shall not apply to any distribution to which the amendments made by subtitle D of title VI of the Tax Reform Act of 1986 do not apply.

(D) TREATMENT OF CERTAIN MEMBERS OF AFFILIATED GROUP.—

(i) IN GENERAL.—For purposes of subparagraph (A), all corporations which were in existence on the designated date and were members of the same affiliated group which included the distributees on such date shall be treated as 1 distributee.

(ii) LIMITATION TO STOCK HELD ON DESIGNATED DATE.—Clause (i) shall not exempt any distribution from the amendments made by this section if such distribution is with respect to stock not held by the distributee (determined without regard to clause (i)) on the designated date directly or indirectly through a corporation which goes out of existence in the transaction.

(iii) DESIGNATED DATE.—For purposes of this subparagraph, the term "designated date" means the later of—

(I) December 15, 1987, or

(II) the date on which the acquisition meeting the requirements of subparagraph (A) occurred.

[Sec. 337(d)]

(d) REGULATIONS.—The Secretary shall prescribe such regulations as may be necessary or appropriate to carry out the purposes of the amendments made by subtitle D of title VI of the Tax Reform Act of 1986, including—

(1) regulations to ensure that such purposes may not be circumvented through the use of any provision of law or regulations (including the consolidated return regulations and part III of this subchapter) or through the use of a regulated investment company, real estate investment trust, or tax exempt entity, and

(2) regulations providing for appropriate coordination of the provisions of this section with the provisions of this title relating to taxation of foreign corporations and their shareholders.

Amendments

• 1988, Technical and Miscellaneous Revenue Act of 1988 (P.L. 100-647)

P.L. 100-647, §1006(e)(5)(A)(i)-(ii):

Amended Code Sec. 337(d) by striking out "made to this subpart by the Tax Reform Act of 1986" and inserting in lieu thereof "made by subtitle D of title VI of the Tax Reform Act of 1986", and by inserting "or through the use of a regulated investment company, real estate investment trust, or tax-exempt entity" after "subchapter)" in paragraph (1). For the **effective** date, see Act Sec. 1006(e)(5)(B), below.

P.L. 100-647, §1006(e)(5)(B), provides:

(B) The amendment made by subparagraph (A)(ii) shall not apply to any reorganization if before June 10, 1987—

(i) the board of directors of a party to the reorganization adopted a resolution to solicit shareholder approval for the transaction, or

(ii) the shareholders or the board of directors of a party to the reorganization approved the transaction.

• 1986, Tax Reform Act of 1986 (P.L. 99-514)

P.L. 99-514, §631(a):

Amended Code Sec. 337. **Effective**, generally, for

(1) any distribution in complete liquidation, and any sale or exchange, made by a corporation after 7-31-86, unless such corporation is completely liquidated before 1-1-87,

(2) any transaction described in section 338 of the Internal Revenue Code of 1986 for which the acquisition date occurs after 12-31-86, and

(3) any distribution (not in complete liquidation) made after 12-31-86. However, for special rules and exceptions, see Act Sec. 633(b)-(f) following Code Sec. 311. Prior to amendment, Code Sec. 337 read as follows:

SEC. 337. GAIN OR LOSS ON SALES OR EXCHANGES IN CONNECTION WITH CERTAIN LIQUIDATIONS.

[Sec. 337(a)]

(a) GENERAL RULE.—If, within the 12-month period beginning on the date on which a corporation adopts a plan of complete liquidation, all of the assets of the corporation are distributed in complete liquidation, less assets retained to meet claims, then no gain or loss shall be recognized to such corporation from the sale or exchange by it of property within such 12-month period.

Amendments

• 1976, Tax Reform Act of 1976 (P.L. 94-455)

P.L. 94-455, §1901(a)(46)(A):

Amended Code Sec. 337(a). **Effective** for tax years beginning after 12-31-76. Prior to amendment, Code Sec. 337(a) read as follows:

(a) GENERAL RULE.—If—

(1) a corporation adopts a plan of complete liquidation on or after June 22, 1954, and

(2) within the 12-month period beginning on the date of the adoption of such plan, all of the assets of the corporation are distributed in complete liquidation, less assets retained to meet claims,

then no gain or loss shall be recognized to such corporation from the sale or exchange by it of property within such 12-month period.

[Sec. 337(b)]

(b) PROPERTY DEFINED.—

(1) IN GENERAL.—For purposes of subsection (a), the term "property" does not include—

(A) stock in trade of the corporation, or other property of a kind which would properly be included in the inventory of the corporation if on hand at the close of the taxable year, and property held by the corporation primarily for sale to customers in the ordinary course of its trade or business,

(B) installment obligations acquired in respect of the sale or exchange (without regard to whether such sale or exchange occurred before, on, or after the date of the adoption of the plan referred to in subsection (a)) of stock in trade or other property described in subparagraph (A) of this paragraph, and

(C) installment obligations acquired in respect of property (other than property described in subparagraph (A)) sold or exchanged before the date of the adoption of such plan of liquidation.

(2) NONRECOGNITION WITH RESPECT TO INVENTORY IN CERTAIN CASES.—Notwithstanding paragraph (1) of this subsection, if substantially all of the property described in subparagraph (A) of such paragraph (1) which is attributable to a trade or business of the corporation is, in accordance with this section, sold or exchanged to one person in one transaction, then for purposes of subsection (a) the term "property" includes—

(A) such property so sold or exchanged, and

(B) installment obligations acquired in respect of such sale or exchange.

[Sec. 337(c)]

(c) LIMITATIONS.—

(1) COLLAPSIBLE CORPORATIONS AND LIQUIDATIONS TO WHICH SECTION 333 APPLIES.—This section shall not apply to any sale or exchange—

(A) made by a collapsible corporation (as defined in section 341 (b)), or

(B) following the adoption of a plan of complete liquidation, if section 333 applies with respect to such liquidation.

(2) LIQUIDATIONS TO WHICH SECTION 332 APPLIES.—In the case of any sale or exchange following the adoption of a plan of complete liquidation, if section 332 applies with respect to such liquidation, this section shall not apply.

(3) SPECIAL RULE FOR AFFILIATED GROUP.—

(A) IN GENERAL.—Paragraph (2) shall not apply to a sale or exchange by a corporation (hereinafter in this paragraph referred to as the "selling corporation") if—

(i) within the 12-month period beginning on the date of the adoption of a plan of complete liquidation by the selling corporation, the selling corporation and each distributee corporation is completely liquidated, and

(ii) none of the complete liquidations referred to in clause (i) is a liquidation with respect to which section 333 applies.

(B) DISTRIBUTEE CORPORATION.—For purposes of subparagraph (A), the term "distributee corporation" means any corporation which receives a distribution to which section 332 applies in a complete liquidation of the selling corporation. Such term also includes any other corporation which receives a distribution to which section 332 applies in a complete liquidation of a corporation which is a distributee corporation under the preceding sentence or prior application of this sentence.

Amendments

• 1986, Tax Reform Act of 1986 (P.L. 99-514)

P.L. 99-514, §1804(e)(7)(A):

Amended Code Sec. 337(c)(3)(B). **Effective** in the case of plans of complete liquidation pursuant to which any distribution is made in a tax year beginning after 12-31-84 (12-31-83, in the case of an affiliated group to which an election under section 60(b)(7) of P.L. 98-369 applies). Prior to amendment, Code Sec. 337(c)(3)(B) read as follows:

(B) DEFINITIONS.—For purposes of subparagraph (A)—

(i) The term "distributee corporation" means a corporation in the chain of includible corporations to which the selling corporation or a corporation above the selling corporation in such chain makes a distribution in complete liquidation within the 12-month period referred to in subparagraph (A)(i).

(ii) The term "chain of includible corporations" includes, in the case of any distribution, any corporation which (at the time of such distribution) is in a chain of includible corporations for purposes of section 1504(a) (determined without regard to the exceptions contained in section 1504(b)). Such term includes, where appropriate, the common parent corporation.

• 1982, Tax Equity and Fiscal Responsibility Act of 1982 (P.L. 97-248)

P.L. 97-248, §224(c)(5):

Amended Code Sec. 337(c)(2). **Effective** for any target corporation (within the meaning of Code Sec. 338) with respect to which the acquisition date (within the meaning of such section) occurs after 8-31-82. For special rules, see P.L. 97-248, Act Sec. 224(a) under new Code Sec. 338. Prior to amendment, it read as follows:

"(2) Liquidations to which section 332 applies.—In the case of a sale or exchange following the adoption of a plan of complete liquidation, if section 332 applies with respect to such liquidation, then—

(A) if the basis of the property of the liquidating corporation in the hands of the distributee is determined under section 334(b)(1), this section shall not apply; or

(B) if the basis of the property of the liquidating corporation in the hands of the distributee is determined under section 334(b)(2), this section shall apply only to that portion (if any) of the gain which is not greater than the excess of (i) that portion of the adjusted basis (adjusted for any adjustment required under the second sentence of section 334(b)(2) of the stock of the liquidating corporation which is allocable, under regulations prescribed by the Secretary, to the property sold or exchanged, over (ii) the adjusted basis, in the hands of the liquidating corporation, of the property sold or exchanged."

• 1978, Revenue Act of 1978 (P.L. 95-600)

P.L. 95-600, §701(i)(1), (2):

Amended Code Sec. 337(c)(2), by deleting the last sentence and added a new paragraph (3). **Effective** for sales or exchanges made pursuant to a plan of complete liquidation adopted after 12-31-75. Before deletion, the last sentence of paragraph (2) read:

"This paragraph shall not apply to a sale or exchange by a member of an affiliated group of corporations, as defined in section 1504(a) (but without regard to the exceptions contained in section 1504(b)), if each member of such group (including the common parent corporation) which receives, within the 12-month period beginning on the date of the adoption of a plan of complete liquidation by the corporation which made the sale or exchange, a distribution in complete liquidation from any other member of such group is itself completely liquidated within such 12-month period."

• 1976, Tax Reform Act of 1976 (P.L. 94-455)

P.L. 94-455, §1906(b)(13)(A):

Amended 1954 Code by substituting "Secretary" for "Secretary or his delegate" each place it appeared. **Effective** 2-1-77.

P.L. 94-455, §2118(a):

Added the final sentence of Code Sec. 337(c)(2). **Effective** for sales or exchanges made pursuant to a plan of complete liquidation adopted after 12-31-75.

[Sec. 337(d)]

(d) SPECIAL RULE FOR CERTAIN MINORITY SHAREHOLDERS.—If a corporation adopts a plan of complete liquidation, and if subsection (a) does not apply to sales or exchanges of property by such corporation, solely by reason of the application of subsection (c)(2), then for the first taxable year of any shareholder (other than a corporation which meets the 80 percent stock ownership requirement specified in section 332(b)(1)) in which he receives a distribution in complete liquidation—

(1) the amount realized by such shareholder on the distribution shall be increased by his proportionate share of the amount by which the tax imposed by this subtitle on such corporation would have been reduced if subsection (c)(2) had not been applicable, and

(2) for purposes of this title, such shareholder shall be deemed to have paid, on the last day prescribed by law for the payment of the tax imposed by this subtitle on such shareholder for such taxable year, an amount of tax equal to the amount of the increase described in paragraph (1).

Amendments

• 1982, Tax Equity and Fiscal Responsibility Act of 1982 (P.L. 97-248)

P.L. 97-248, §224(c)(6):

Amended Code Sec. 337(d) by striking out "subsection (c)(2)(A)" each place it appears and inserting in lieu thereof "subsection (c)(2)". **Effective** for any target corporation (within the meaning of Code Sec. 338) with respect to which the acquisition date (within the meaning of such section) occurs after 8-31-82. For special rules, see P.L. 97-248, Act Sec. 224(a), under new Code Sec. 338.

• 1976, Tax Reform Act of 1976 (P.L. 94-455)

P.L. 94-455, §1901(a)(46)(B):

Struck out "on or after January 1, 1958" after "a plan of complete liquidation" in the first sentence of Code Sec. 337(d). **Effective** for tax years beginning after 12-31-76.

• 1958, Technical Amendments Act of 1958 (P.L. 85-866)

P.L. 85-866, §19:

Added subsection (d) to Sec. 337. **Effective** 1-1-54.

[Sec. 337(e)]

(e) SPECIAL RULE FOR INVOLUNTARY CONVERSIONS.—If—

(1) there is an involuntary conversion (within the meaning of section 1033) of property of a distributing corporation and there is a complete liquidation of such corporation which qualifies under subsection (a),

(2) the disposition of the converted property (within the meaning of clause (ii) of section 1033(a)(2)(E)) occurs during the 60-day period which ends on the day before the first day of the 12-month period, and

(3) such corporation elects the application of this subsection at such time and in such manner as the Secretary may by regulations prescribe,

then for purposes of this section such disposition shall be treated as a sale or exchange occurring within the 12-month period.

Amendments

• 1978 (P.L. 95-628)

P.L. 95-628, §4(a), (b):

Added Code Sec. 337(e). **Effective** for dispositions of converted property (within the meaning of clause (ii) of Code Sec. 1033(a)(2)(E)) occurring after 11-10-78, in tax years ending after such date.

[Sec. 337(f)]

(f) SPECIAL RULE FOR LIFO INVENTORIES.—

(1) IN GENERAL.—In the case of a corporation inventorying goods under the LIFO method, this section shall apply to gain from the sale or exchange of inventory assets (which under subsection (b)(2) constitute property) only to the extent that such gain exceeds the LIFO recapture amount with respect to such assets.

(2) DEFINITIONS.—The terms used in this subsection shall have the same meaning as when used in section 336(b).

(3) CROSS REFERENCE.—

For treatment of gain from the sale or exchange of an installment obligation as gain resulting from the sale or exchange of the property in respect of which the obligation was received, see the last sentence of section 453B(a).

Amendments

• 1980, Installment Sales Revision Act of 1980 (P.L. 96-471)

P.L. 96-471, §2(c)(2):

Amended Code Sec. 337(f)(3) by striking out "453(d)(1)" and substituting" 453B(a)". **Effective** as though included in §403(b) of P.L. 96-223.

• 1980, Crude Oil Windfall Profit Tax Act of 1980 (P.L. 96-223)

P.L. 96-223, §403(b)(2)(A):

Added Code Sec. 337(f). **Effective** for distributions and dispositions pursuant to plans of liquidation adopted after 12-31-81.

P.L. 96-223, §403(b)(4), as added P.L. 97-362, §101, provides:

"(4) PLANS OF LIQUIDATION ADOPTED DURING 1982.—

"(A) IN GENERAL.—If—

"(i) a corporation adopts a plan of liquidation during 1982, and

"(ii) such liquidation is completed before January 1, 1984,

then the LIFO recapture amount taken into account with respect to such liquidation under the amendments made by paragraphs (1) and (2) shall be reduced (but not below zero) by $1,000,000.

"(B) MORE THAN 1 PLAN OF LIQUIDATION.—If a corporation (or group of corporations treated as 1 corporation under subparagraph (C)) has more than 1 liquidation which qualifies under subparagraph (A), the dollar amount under such subparagraph shall apply to all such liquidations in the order in which the distributions, sales, and exchanges occur until such dollar amount is used up.

"(C) APPLICATION TO MEMBERS OF CONTROLLED GROUP.—

"(i) IN GENERAL.—For purposes of this paragraph, all corporations which are competent members of the same controlled group of corporations at any time after December 31, 1981, and before January 1, 1984, shall be treated as 1 corporation.

"(ii) CORPORATIONS MEMBERS OF MORE THAN 1 GROUP.—For purposes of this subparagraph, if (but for this clause) a corporation would be a component member of more than 1 controlled group of corporations during the period described in clause (i)—

"(I) if such corporation is a component member of a controlled group on October 1, 1982, such corporation shall be treated only as a component member of such group, or

"(II) if subclause (I) does not apply, such corporation shall be treated as a component member of only the first such controlled group.

"(iii) CONTROLLED GROUP OF CORPORATIONS DEFINED.—For purposes of this subparagraph, the term `controlled group of corporations' has the meaning given such term by section 1563(a) of the Internal Revenue Code of 1954, except that—

"(I) `more than 50 percent' shall be substituted for `at least 80 percent' each place it appears in section 1563(a)(1) of such Code, and

"(II) the determination shall be made without regard to subsections (a)(4), (b), and (e)(3)(C) of section 1563 of such Code.

"(D) TREATMENT OF DEEMED LIQUIDATIONS UNDER SECTION 338.—If an election under section 338 of the Internal Revenue Code of 1954 is made during 1982 with respect to any qualified stock purchase (within the meaning of such section 338), the requirements of clauses (i) and (ii) of subparagraph (A) shall be treated as met with respect to the target corporation for purposes of applying section 338 of such Code. For purposes of this paragraph, an election to which subparagraph (A) applies by reason of this subparagraph shall be treated as a sale and a liquidation."

[Sec. 337(g)]

(g) TITLE 11 OR SIMILAR CASES.—If a corporation completely liquidates pursuant to a plan of complete liquidation adopted in a title 11 or similar case (within the meaning of section 368(a)(3)(A))—

(1) for purposes of subsection (a), the term "property" shall not include any item acquired on or after the date of the adoption of the plan of liquidation if such item is not property within the meaning of subsection (b)(2), and

(2) subsection (a) shall apply to sales and exchanges by the corporation of property within the period beginning on the date of the adoption of the plan and ending on the date of the termination of the case.

Amendments

• 1980, Bankruptcy Tax Act of 1980 (P.L. 96-589)

P.L. 96-589, §5(c):

Added Code Sec. 337(g). **Effective** for bankruptcy cases commencing after 12-31-80 and to similar cases commencing after that date. Also, the amendment will apply to a bankruptcy or similar case commenced on or after 10-1-79 (but prior to 1-1-81) if the special effective date election is made. See the historical comment for P.L. 96-589 under Code Sec. 108(e) for the details of the election.

[Sec. 338]

SEC. 338. CERTAIN STOCK PURCHASES TREATED AS ASSET ACQUISITIONS.

[Sec. 338(a)]

(a) GENERAL RULE.—For purposes of this subtitle, if a purchasing corporation makes an election under this section (or is treated under subsection (e) as having made such an election), then, in the case of any qualified stock purchase, the target corporation—

(1) shall be treated as having sold all of its assets at the close of the acquisition date at fair market value in a single transaction, and

(2) shall be treated as a new corporation which purchased all of the assets referred to in paragraph (1) as of the beginning of the day after the acquisition date.

Amendments

• 1986, Tax Reform Act of 1986 (P.L. 99-514)

P.L. 99-514, §631(b)(1):

Amended Code Sec. 338(a) by striking out "to which section 337 applies" after "single transaction". **Effective**, generally, for:

(1) any distribution in complete liquidation, and any sale or exchange, made by a corporation after 7-31-86, unless such corporation is completely liquidated before 1-1-87,

(2) any transaction described in section 338 of the Internal Revenue Code of 1986 for which the acquisition date occurs after 12-31-86, and

(3) any distribution (not in complete liquidation) made after 12-31-86. However, for special rules and exceptions, see Act Sec. 633(b)-(f) in the Amendment Notes following Code Sec. 311.

• 1984, Deficit Reduction Act of 1984 (P.L. 98-369)

P.L. 98-369, §712(k)(1)(A):

Amended Code Sec. 338(a)(1) by inserting "at fair market value" after "the acquisition date". **Effective** as if included in the provision of P.L. 97-248 to which it relates. Special rules appear in Act Sec. 712(k)(9) following Code Sec. 338(h).

[Sec. 338(b)]

(b) BASIS OF ASSETS AFTER DEEMED PURCHASE.—

(1) IN GENERAL.—For purposes of subsection (a), the assets of the target corporation shall be treated as purchased for an amount equal to the sum of—

(A) the grossed-up basis of the purchasing corporation's recently purchased stock, and

(B) the basis of the purchasing corporation's nonrecently purchased stock.

(2) ADJUSTMENT FOR LIABILITIES AND OTHER RELEVANT ITEMS.—The amount described in paragraph (1) shall be adjusted under regulations prescribed by the Secretary for liabilities of the target corporation and other relevant items.

(3) ELECTION TO STEP-UP THE BASIS OF CERTAIN TARGET STOCK.—

(A) IN GENERAL.—Under regulations prescribed by the Secretary, the basis of the purchasing corporation's nonrecently purchased stock shall be the basis amount determined under subparagraph (B) of this paragraph if the purchasing corporation makes an election to recognize gain as if such stock were sold on the acquisition date for an amount equal to the basis amount determined under subparagraph (B).

(B) DETERMINATION OF BASIS AMOUNT.—For purposes of subparagraph (A), the basis amount determined under this subparagraph shall be an amount equal to the grossed-up basis determined under subparagraph (A) of paragraph (1) multiplied by a fraction—

(i) the numerator of which is the percentage of stock (by value) in the target corporation attributable to the purchasing corporation's nonrecently purchased stock, and

(ii) the denominator of which is 100 percent minus the percentage referred to in clause (i).

(4) GROSSED-UP BASIS.—For purposes of paragraph (1), the grossed-up basis shall be an amount equal to the basis of the corporation's recently purchased stock, multiplied by a fraction—

(A) the numerator of which is 100 percent, minus the percentage of stock (by value) in the target corporation attributable to the purchasing corporation's nonrecently purchased stock, and

(B) the denominator of which is the percentage of stock (by value) in the target corporation attributable to the purchasing corporation's recently purchased stock.

(5) ALLOCATION AMONG ASSETS.—The amount determined under paragraphs (1) and (2) shall be allocated among the assets of the target corporation under regulations prescribed by the Secretary.

(6) DEFINITIONS OF RECENTLY PURCHASED STOCK AND NONRECENTLY PURCHASED STOCK.—For purposes of this subsection—

(A) RECENTLY PURCHASED STOCK.—The term "recently purchased stock" means any stock in the target corporation which is held by the purchasing corporation on the acquisition date and which was purchased by such corporation during the 12-month acquisition period.

(B) NONRECENTLY PURCHASED STOCK.—The term "nonrecently purchased stock" means any stock in the target corporation which is held by the purchasing corporation on the acquisition date and which is not recently purchased stock.

Amendments

• 1984, Deficit Reduction Act of 1984 (P.L. 98-369)

P.L. 98-369, §712(k)(1)(B):

Amended Code Sec. 338(b). **Effective** as if included in the provision of P.L. 97-248 to which it relates. Special rules appear in Act Sec. 712(k)(9) following Code Sec. 338(h). Prior to amendment, Code Sec. 338(b) read as follows:

(b) PRICE AT WHICH DEEMED SALE MADE.—

(1) IN GENERAL.—For purposes of subsection (a), the assets of the target corporation shall be treated as sold (and purchased) at an amount equal to—

(A) the grossed-up basis of the purchasing corporation's stock in the target corporation on the acquisition date,

(B) properly adjusted under regulations prescribed by the Secretary for liabilities of the target corporation and other relevant items.

(2) GROSSED-UP BASIS.—For purposes of paragraph (1), the grossed-up basis shall be an amount equal to the basis of the purchasing corporation's stock in the target corporation on the acquisition date multiplied by a fraction—

(A) the numerator of which is 100 percent, and

(B) the denominator of which is the percentage of stock (by value) of the target corporation held by the purchasing corporation on the acquisition date.

(3) ALLOCATION AMONG ASSETS.—The amount determined under paragraph (1) shall be allocated among the assets of the target corporation under regulations prescribed by the Secretary.

[Sec. 338(c)—Repealed]

Amendments

• **1986, Tax Reform Act of 1986 (P.L. 99-514)**

P.L. 99-514, §631(b)(2):

Repealed Code Sec. 338(c). **Effective**, generally, for:

(1) any distribution in complete liquidation, and any sale or exchange, made by a corporation after 7-31-86, unless such corporation is completely liquidated before 1-1-87,

(2) any transaction described in section 338 of the Internal Revenue Code of 1986 for which the acquisition date occurs after 12-31-86, and

(3) any distribution (not in complete liquidation) made after 12-31-86. However, for special rules and exceptions, see Act Sec. 633(b)-(f) in the Amendment Notes following Code Sec. 311. Prior to repeal, Code Sec. 338(c) read as follows:

(c) SPECIAL RULES.—

(1) COORDINATION WITH SECTION 337 WHERE PURCHASING CORPORATION HOLDS LESS THAN 100 PERCENT OF STOCK.—If during the 1-year period beginning on the acquisition date the maximum percentage (by value) of stock in the target corporation held by the purchasing corporation is less than 100 percent, then in applying section 337 for purposes of subsection (a)(1), the nonrecognition of gain or loss shall be limited to an amount determined by applying such maximum percentage to such gain or loss. The preceding sentence shall not apply if the target corporation is liquidated during such 1-year period and section 333 does not apply to such liquidation.

(2) CERTAIN REDEMPTIONS WHERE ELECTION MADE.—If, in connection with a qualified stock purchase with respect to which an election is made under this section, the target corporation makes a distribution in complete redemption of all of the stock of a shareholder which qualifies under section 302(b)(3) (determined without regard to the application of section 302(c)(2)(A)(ii)), section 336 shall apply to such distribution as if it were a distribution in complete liquidation.

• **1984, Deficit Reduction Act of 1984 (P.L. 98-369)**

P.L. 98-369, §712(k)(2):

Amended the last sentence of Code Sec. 338(c)(1) by striking out "such 1-year period" and inserting in lieu thereof "such 1-year period and section 333 does not apply to such liquidation". **Effective** as if included in the provision of P.L. 97-248 to which it relates. Special rules appear in Act Sec. 712(k)(9) following Code Sec. 338(h).

[Sec. 338(d)]

(d) PURCHASING CORPORATION; TARGET CORPORATION; QUALIFIED STOCK PURCHASE.—For purposes of this section—

(1) PURCHASING CORPORATION.—The term "purchasing corporation" means any corporation which makes a qualified stock purchase of stock of another corporation.

(2) TARGET CORPORATION.—The term "target corporation" means any corporation the stock of which is acquired by another corporation in a qualified stock purchase.

(3) QUALIFIED STOCK PURCHASE.—The term "qualified stock purchase" means any transaction or series of transactions in which stock (meeting the requirements of section 1504(a)(2)) of 1 corporation is acquired by another corporation by purchase during the 12-month acquisition period.

Amendments

• **1986, Tax Reform Act of 1986 (P.L. 99-514)**

P.L. 99-514, §1804(e)(8)(A):

Amended Code Sec. 338(d)(3). **Effective** in cases where the 12-month acquisition period (as defined in section 338(h)(1) of the Internal Revenue Code of 1954) begins after 12-31-85. Prior to amendment, Code Sec. 338(d)(3) read as follows:

(3) QUALIFIED STOCK PURCHASE.—The term "qualified stock purchase" means any transaction or series of transactions in which stock of 1 corporation possessing—

(A) at least 80 percent of total combined voting power of all classes of stock entitled to vote, and

(B) at least 80 percent of the total number of shares of all other classes of stock (except nonvoting stock which is limited and preferred as to dividends),

is acquired by another corporation by purchase during the 12-month acquisition period.

[Sec. 338(e)]

(e) DEEMED ELECTION WHERE PURCHASING CORPORATION ACQUIRES ASSET OF TARGET CORPORATION.—

(1) IN GENERAL.—A purchasing corporation shall be treated as having made an election under this section with respect to any target corporation if, at any time during the consistency period, it acquires any asset of the target corporation (or a target affiliate).

(2) EXCEPTIONS.—Paragraph (1) shall not apply with respect to any acquisition by the purchasing corporation if—

(A) such acquisition is pursuant to a sale by the target corporation (or the target affiliate) in the ordinary course of its trade or business,

(B) the basis of the property acquired is determined (wholly) by reference to the adjusted basis of such property in the hands of the person from whom acquired,

(C) such acquisition was before September 1, 1982, or

(D) such acquisition is described in regulations prescribed by the Secretary and meets such conditions as such regulations may provide.

(3) ANTI-AVOIDANCE RULE.—Whenever necessary to carry out the purpose of this subsection and subsection (f), the Secretary may treat stock acquisitions which are pursuant to a plan and which meet the requirements of section 1504(a)(2) as qualified stock purchases.

Amendments

• 1988, Technical and Miscellaneous Revenue Act of 1988 (P.L. 100-647)

P.L. 100-647, §1018(d)(9):

Amended Code Sec. 338(e)(3) by striking out "which meet the 80 percent requirements of subparagraphs (A) and (B) of subsection (d)(3)" and inserting in lieu thereof "which meet the requirements of section 1504(a)(2)". **Effective** as if included in the provision of P.L. 99-514 to which it relates.

• 1984, Deficit Reduction Act of 1984 (P.L. 98-369)

P.L. 98-369, §712(k)(3):

Amended Code Sec. 338(e)(2) by striking out "(in whole or in part)" in subparagraph (B) and inserting in lieu thereof "(wholly)", by inserting "or" at the end of subparagraph (C) and by striking out subparagraphs (D) and (E) and inserting in lieu thereof subparagraph (D) above. **Effective** as if included in the provision of P.L. 97-248 to which it relates. Special rules appear in Act Sec. 712(k)(9) following Code Sec. 338(h). Prior to amendment, subparagraph (D) and (E) read as follows:

(D) to the extent provided in regulations, the property acquired is located outside the United States, or

(E) such acquisition is described in regulations prescribed by the Secretary.

[Sec. 338(f)]

(f) CONSISTENCY REQUIRED FOR ALL STOCK ACQUISITIONS FROM SAME AFFILIATED GROUP.—If a purchasing corporation makes qualified stock purchases with respect to the target corporation and 1 or more target affiliates during any consistency period, then (except as otherwise provided in subsection (e))—

(1) any election under this section with respect to the first such purchase shall apply to each other such purchase, and

(2) no election may be made under this section with respect to the second or subsequent such purchase if such an election was not made with respect to the first such purchase.

[Sec. 338(g)]

(g) ELECTION.—

(1) WHEN MADE.—Except as otherwise provided in regulations, an election under this section shall be made not later than the 15th day of the 9th month, beginning after the month in which the acquisition date occurs.

(2) MANNER.—An election by the purchasing corporation under this section shall be made in such manner as the Secretary shall by regulations prescribe.

(3) ELECTION IRREVOCABLE.—An election by a purchasing corporation under this section, once made, shall be irrevocable.

Amendments

• 1984, Deficit Reduction Act of 1984 (P.L. 98-369)

P.L. 98-369, §712(k)(4):

Amended Code Sec. 338(g)(1). **Effective** as if included in the provision of P.L. 97-248 to which it relates. Special rules appear in Act Sec. 712(k)(9) following Code Sec. 338(h). Prior to amendment, Code Sec. 338(g)(1) read as follows:

(1) When Made.—Except as otherwise provided in regulations, an election under this section shall be made not later than 75 days after the acquisition date.

[Sec. 338(h)]

(h) DEFINITIONS AND SPECIAL RULES.—For purposes of this section—

(1) 12-MONTH ACQUISITION PERIOD.—The term "12-month acquisition period" means the 12-month period beginning with the date of the first acquisition by purchase of stock included in a qualified stock purchase (or, if any of such stock was acquired in an acquisition which is a purchase by reason of subparagraph (C) of paragraph (3), the date on which the acquiring corporation is first considered under section 318(a) (other than paragraph (4) thereof) as owning stock owned by the corporation from which such acquisition was made).

(2) ACQUISITION DATE.—The term "acquisition date" means, with respect to any corporation, the first day on which there is a qualified stock purchase with respect to the stock of such corporation.

(3) PURCHASE.—

(A) IN GENERAL.—The term "purchase" means any acquisition of stock, but only if—

(i) the basis of the stock in the hands of the purchasing corporation is not determined (I) in whole or in part by reference to the adjusted basis of such stock in the hands of the person from whom acquired, or (II) under section 1014(a) (relating to property acquired from a decedent),

(ii) the stock is not acquired in an exchange to which section 351, 354, 355, or 356 applies and is not acquired in any other transaction described in regulations in which the transferor does not recognize the entire amount of the gain or loss realized on the transaction, and

(iii) the stock is not acquired from a person the ownership of whose stock would, under section 318(a) (other than paragraph (4) thereof), be attributed to the person acquiring such stock.

(B) DEEMED PURCHASE UNDER SUBSECTION (a).—The term "purchase" includes any deemed purchase under subsection (a)(2). The acquisition date for a corporation which is deemed purchased under subsection (a)(2) shall be determined under regulations prescribed by the Secretary.

(C) CERTAIN STOCK ACQUISITIONS FROM RELATED CORPORATIONS.—

(i) IN GENERAL.—Clause (iii) of subparagraph (A) shall not apply to an acquisition of stock from a related corporation if at least 50 percent in value of the stock of such related corporation was acquired by purchase (within the meaning of subparagraphs (A) and (B)).

(ii) CERTAIN DISTRIBUTIONS.—Clause (i) of subparagraph (A) shall not apply to an acquisition of stock described in clause (i) of this subparagraph if the corporation acquiring such stock—

(I) made a qualified stock purchase of stock of the related corporation, and

(II) made an election under this section (or is treated under subsection (e) as having made such an election) with respect to such qualified stock purchase.

(iii) RELATED CORPORATION DEFINED.—For purposes of this subparagraph, a corporation is a related corporation if stock owned by such corporation is treated (under section 318(a) other than paragraph (4) thereof) as owned by the corporation acquiring the stock.

(4) CONSISTENCY PERIOD.—

(A) IN GENERAL.—Except as provided in subparagraph (B), the term "consistency period" means the period consisting of—

(i) the 1-year period before the beginning of the 12-month acquisition period for the target corporation,

(ii) such acquisition period (up to and including the acquisition date), and

(iii) the 1-year period beginning on the day after the acquisition date.

(B) EXTENSION WHERE THERE IS PLAN.—The period referred to in subparagraph (A) shall also include any period during which the Secretary determines that there was in effect a plan to make a qualified stock purchase plus 1 or more other qualified stock purchases (or asset acquisitions described in subsection (e)) with respect to the target corporation or any target affiliate.

(5) AFFILIATED GROUP.—The term "affiliated group" has the meaning given to such term by section 1504(a) (determined without regard to the exceptions contained in section 1504(b)).

(6) TARGET AFFILIATE.—

(A) IN GENERAL.—A corporation shall be treated as a target affiliate of the target corporation if each of such corporations was, at any time during so much of the consistency period as ends on the acquisition date of the target corporation, a member of an affiliated group which had the same common parent.

(B) CERTAIN FOREIGN CORPORATIONS, ETC.—Except as otherwise provided in regulations (and subject to such conditions as may be provided in regulations)—

(i) the term "target affiliate" does not include a foreign corporation, a DISC, or a corporation to which an election under section 936 applies, and

(ii) stock held by a target affiliate in a foreign corporation or a domestic corporation which is a DISC or described in section 1248(e) shall be excluded from the operation of this section.

(7) [Repealed.]

(8) ACQUISITIONS BY AFFILIATED GROUP TREATED AS MADE BY 1 CORPORATION.—Except as provided in regulations prescribed by the Secretary, stock and asset acquisitions made by members of the same affiliated group shall be treated as made by 1 corporation.

(9) TARGET NOT TREATED AS MEMBER OF AFFILIATED GROUP.—Except as otherwise provided in paragraph (10) or in regulations prescribed under this paragraph, the target corporation shall not be treated as a member of an affiliated group with respect to the sale described in subsection (a)(1).

(10) ELECTIVE RECOGNITION OF GAIN OR LOSS BY TARGET CORPORATION, TOGETHER WITH NONRECOGNITION OF GAIN OR LOSS ON STOCK SOLD BY SELLING CONSOLIDATED GROUP.—

(A) IN GENERAL.—Under regulations prescribed by the Secretary, an election may be made under which if—

(i) the target corporation was, before the transaction, a member of the selling consolidated group, and

(ii) the target corporation recognizes gain or loss with respect to the transaction as if it sold all of its assets in a single transaction,

then the target corporation shall be treated as a member of the selling consolidated group with respect to such sale, and (to the extent provided in regulations) no gain or loss will be recognized on stock sold or exchanged in the transaction by members of the selling consolidated group.

(B) SELLING CONSOLIDATED GROUP.—For purposes of subparagraph (A), the term "selling consolidated group" means any group of corporations which (for the taxable period which includes the transaction)—

(i) includes the target corporation, and

(ii) files a consolidated return.

To the extent provided in regulations, such term also includes any affiliated group of corporations which includes the target corporation (whether or not such group files a consolidated return).

(C) INFORMATION REQUIRED TO BE FURNISHED TO THE SECRETARY.—Under regulations, where an election is made under subparagraph (A), the purchasing corporation and the common parent of the selling consolidated group shall, at such times and in such manner as may be provided in regulations, furnish to the Secretary the following information:

(i) The amount allocated under subsection (b)(5) to goodwill or going concern value.

(ii) Any modification of the amount described in clause (i).

(iii) Any other information as the Secretary deems necessary to carry out the provisions of this paragraph.

(11) ELECTIVE FORMULA FOR DETERMINING FAIR MARKET VALUE.—For purposes of subsection (a)(1), fair market value may be determined on the basis of a formula provided in regulations prescribed by the Secretary which takes into account liabilities and other relevant items.

(12) [Repealed.]

(13) TAX ON DEEMED SALE NOT TAKEN INTO ACCOUNT FOR ESTIMATED TAX PURPOSES.—For purposes of section 6655, tax attributable to the sale described in subsection (a)(1) shall not be taken into account. The preceding sentence shall not apply with respect to a qualified stock purchase for which an election is made under paragraph (10).

»»→ Caution: Code Sec. 338(h)(14), below, was stricken by P.L. 108-27, and is subject to the sunset provision of the Jobs and Growth Tax Relief Reconciliation Act of 2003 (P.L. 108-27), §303. Absent Congressional action, the changes made to this provision by P.L. 108-27, or that take effect as if included in P.L. 108-27, do not apply after December 31, 2010. For more information about the sunset provision, see page XXI of the Preface to this publication and P.L. 108-27, §303, in the amendment notes. See the amendments notes for a history of amendments to this section and the effective date of each change.

(14) [Stricken.]

(15) COMBINED DEEMED SALE RETURN.—Under regulations prescribed by the Secretary, a combined deemed sale return may be filed by all target corporations acquired by a purchasing corporation on the same acquisition date if such target corporations were members of the same selling consolidated group (as defined in subparagraph (B) of paragraph (10)).

(16) COORDINATION WITH FOREIGN TAX CREDIT PROVISIONS.—Except as provided in regulations, this section shall not apply for purposes of determining the source or character of any item for purposes of subpart A of part III of subchapter N of this chapter (relating to foreign tax credit). The preceding sentence shall not apply to any gain to the extent such gain is includible in gross income as a dividend under section 1248 (determined without regard to any deemed sale under this section by a foreign corporation).

Amendments

• 2004, American Jobs Creation Act of 2004 (P.L. 108-357)

P.L. 108-357, §839(a):

Amended Code Sec. 338(h)(13) by adding at the end a new sentence. **Effective** for transactions occurring after 10-22-2004.

• 2003, Jobs and Growth Tax Relief Reconciliation Act of 2003 (P.L. 108-27)

P.L. 108-27, §302(e)(4)(B)(i):

Amended Code Sec. 338(h) by striking paragraph (14). For the **effective** date, see Act Sec. 302(f), as amended by P.L. 108-311, §402(a)(6), below. Prior to being stricken, Code Sec. 338(h)(14) read as follows:

(14) COORDINATION WITH SECTION 341.—For purposes of determining whether section 341 applies to a disposition within 1 year after the acquisition date of stock by a shareholder (other than the acquiring corporation) who held stock in the target corporation on the acquisition date, section 341 shall be applied without regard to this section.

P.L. 108-27, §302(f), as amended by P.L. 108-311, §402(a)(6), provides:

(f) EFFECTIVE DATE.—

(1) IN GENERAL.—Except as provided in paragraph (2), the amendments made by this section shall apply to taxable years beginning after December 31, 2002.

(2) PASS-THRU ENTITIES.—In the case of a pass-thru entity described in subparagraph (A), (B), (C), (D), (E), or (F) of section 1(h)(10) of the Internal Revenue Code of 1986, as amended by this Act, the amendments made by this section shall apply to taxable years ending after December 31, 2002; except that dividends received by such an entity on or before such date shall not be treated as qualified dividend income (as defined in section 1(h)(11)(B) of such Code, as added by this Act).

P.L. 108-27, §303, as amended by P.L. 109-222, §102, provides:

SEC. 303. SUNSET OF TITLE.

All provisions of, and amendments made by, this title shall not apply to taxable years beginning after December 31, 2010, and the Internal Revenue Code of 1986 shall be applied and administered to such years as if such provisions and amendments had never been enacted.

• 1990, Omnibus Budget Reconciliation Act of 1990 (P.L. 101-508)

P.L. 101-508, §11323(c)(1):

Amended Code Sec. 338(h)(10) by adding at the end thereof a new subparagraph (C). **Effective**, generally, for acquisitions after 10-9-90. For an exception, see Act Sec. 11323(d)(2), below.

P.L. 101-508, §11323(d)(2), provides:

(2) BINDING CONTRACT EXCEPTION.—The amendments made by this section shall not apply to any acquisition pursuant to a written binding contract in effect on October 9, 1990, and at all times thereafter before such acquisition.

• 1988, Technical and Miscellaneous Revenue Act of 1988 (P.L. 100-647)

P.L. 100-647, §1006(e)(20):

Repealed Code Sec. 338(h)(7). **Effective** as if included in the provision of P.L. 99-514 to which it relates. Prior to repeal, Code Sec. 338(h)(7) read as follows:

(7) ADDITIONAL PERCENTAGE MUST BE ATTRIBUTABLE TO PURCHASE, ETC.—For purposes of subsection (c)(1), any increase in the maximum percentage of stock taken into account over the percentage of stock (by value) of the target corporation held by the purchasing corporation on the acquisition date shall be taken into account only to the extent such increase is attributable to—

(A) purchase, or

(B) a redemption of stock of the target corporation—

(i) to which section 302(a) applies, or

(ii) in the case of a shareholder who is not a corporation, to which section 301 applies.

P.L. 100-647, §1012(bb)(5)(A):

Amended Code Sec. 338(h) by adding at the end thereof a new paragraph (16). **Effective** for qualified stock purchases (as defined in section 338(d)(3) of the 1986 Code) after 3-31-88, except that, in the case of an election under section 338(h)(10) of the 1986 Code, such amendment shall apply to qualified stock purchases (as so defined) after 6-10-87.

• 1986, Tax Reform Act of 1986 (P.L. 99-514)

P.L. 99-514, §631(b)(3):

Amended Code Sec. 338(h)(10)(B) by adding to the end thereof a new sentence. **Effective**, generally, for:

(1) any distribution in complete liquidation, and any sale or exchange, made by a corporation after 7-31-86, unless such corporation is completely liquidated before 1-1-87,

(2) any transaction described in section 338 of the Internal Revenue Code of 1986 for which the acquisition date occurs after 12-31-86, and

(3) any distribution (not in complete liquidation) made after 12-31-86. However, for special rules and exceptions, see Act Sec. 633(b)-(f) in the Amendment Notes following Code Sec. 311.

P.L. 99-514, §631(e)(5):

Repealed Code Sec. 338(h)(12). **Effective**, generally, for:

(1) any distribution in complete liquidation, and any sale or exchange, made by a corporation after 7-31-86, unless such corporation is completely liquidated before 1-1-87,

(2) any transaction described in section 338 of the Internal Revenue Code of 1986 for which the acquisition date occurs after 12-31-86, and

(3) any distribution (not in complete liquidation) made after 12-31-86. However, for special rules and exceptions, see Act Sec. 633(b)-(f) in the Amendment Notes following Code Sec. 311. Prior to repeal, Code Sec. 338(h)(12) read as follows:

(12) SECTION 337 TO APPLY WHERE TARGET HAD ADOPTED PLAN FOR COMPLETE LIQUIDATION.—If—

(A) during the 12-month period ending on the acquisition date the target corporation adopted a plan of complete liquidation,

(B) such plan was not rescinded before the close of the acquisition date, and

(C) the purchasing corporation makes an election under this section (or is treated under subsection (e) as having made such an election) with respect to the target corporation, then, subject to rules similar to the rules of subsection (c)(1), for purposes of section 337 (and other provisions which relate to section 337), the target corporation shall be treated as having distributed all of its assets as of the close of the acquisition date.

P.L. 99-514, §1275(c)(6):

Amended Code Sec. 338(h)(6)(B)(i) by striking out "a corporation described in section 934(b)," after "a DISC". **Effective**, generally, for tax years beginning after 12-31-86. For special rules and exceptions see Act Sec. 1277(b)-(c) in the Amendment Notes following Code Sec. 48.

P.L. 99-514, §1899A(7):

Amended Code Sec. 338(h)(3)(C)(i) by striking out "subparagraph (A) and (B)" and inserting in lieu thereof "subparagraphs (A) and (B)". **Effective** 10-22-86.

• 1984, Deficit Reduction Act of 1984 (P.L. 98-369)

P.L. 98-369, §712(k)(5)(A):

Amended Code Sec. 338(h)(3)(B). **Effective** as if included in the provision of P.L. 97-248 to which it relates. A special rule appears below. Prior to amendment, Code Sec. 338(h)(3)(B) read as follows:

(B) Deemed Purchase of Stock of Subsidiaries.—If stock in a corporation is acquired by purchase (within the meaning of subparagraph (A)) and, as a result of such acquisition, the corporation making such purchase is treated (by reason of section 318(a)) as owning stock in a 3rd corporation, the corporation making such purchase shall be treated as having purchased such stock in such 3rd corporation. The corporation making such purchase shall be treated as purchasing stock in the 3rd corporation by reason of the preceding sentence on the first day on which the purchasing corporation is considered under section 318(a) as owning such stock.

P.L. 98-369, §712(k)(5)(B):

Amended Code Sec. 338(h)(3)(C). **Effective** as if included in the provision of P.L. 97-248 to which it relates. A special rule appears below.

P.L. 98-369, §712(k)(5)(C):

Amended Code Sec. 338(h)(1) by inserting before the period at the end thereof the following: "(or, if any of such stock was acquired in an acquisition which is a purchase by reason of subparagraph (C) of paragraph (3), the date on which the acquiring corporation is first considered under section 318(a) (other than paragraph (4) thereof) as owning stock owned by the corporation from which such acquisition was made)". **Effective** as if included in the provision of P.L. 97-248 to which it relates. A special rule appears below.

P.L. 98-369, §712(k)(5)(D):

Amended Code Sec. 338(h)(3)(A)(ii). **Effective** as if included in the provision of P.L. 97-248 to which it relates. A special rule appears below. Prior to amendment, it read as follows:

(ii) the stock is not acquired in an exchange to which section 351 applies, and

P.L. 98-369, §712(k)(6)(A):

Amended Code Sec. 338(h) by striking out paragraph (7), by redesignating paragraphs (8) and (9) as paragraphs (9) and (10), respectively, and by inserting after paragraph (6) new paragraphs (7) and (8). **Effective** as if included in the provision of P.L. 97-248 to which it relates. A special rule appears below. Prior to its deletion, paragraph (7) read as follows:

(7) Acquisitions by Purchasing Corporation Include Acquisitions by Corporations Affiliated with Purchasing Corporation.—Except as otherwise provided in regulations, an acquisition of stock or assets by any member of an affiliated group which includes a purchasing corporation shall be treated as made by the purchasing corporation.

P.L. 98-369, §712(k)(6)(B):

Amended Code Sec. 338(h)(9), as redesignated by Act Sec. 712(k)(6)(A), by striking out "paragraph (9)" and inserting in lieu thereof "paragraph (10)". **Effective** as if included in the provision of P.L. 97-248 to which it relates. A special rule appears below.

P.L. 98-369, §712(k)(6)(C):

Added Code Secs. 338(h)(11)—(15). **Effective** as if included in the provision of P.L. 97-248 to which it relates. A special rule appears below.

P.L. 98-369, §712(k)(9)-(10), provides:

(9) Amendments Not to Apply to Acquisitions before September 1, 1982.—

(A) In General.—The amendments made by this subsection shall not apply to any qualified stock purchase (as defined in section 338(d)(3) of the Internal Revenue Code of 1954) where the acquisition date (as defined in section 338(h)(2) of such Code) is before September 1, 1982.

(B) Extension of Time for Making Election.—In the case of any qualified stock purchase described in subparagraph (A), the time for making an election under section 338 of such Code shall not expire before the close of the 60th day after the date of the enactment of this Act.

(10) Special Rules for Deemed Purchases Under Prior Law.—If, before October 20, 1983, a corporation was treated

as making a qualified stock purchase (as defined in section 338(d)(3) of the Internal Revenue Code of 1954), but would not be so treated under the amendments made by paragraphs (5) and (6) of this subsection, the amendments made by such paragraphs shall not apply to such purchase unless such corporation elects (at such time and in such manner as the Secretary of the Treasury or his delegate may by regulations prescribe) to have the amendments made by such paragraphs apply.

• **1983, Technical Corrections Act of 1982 (P.L. 97-448)**

P.L. 97-448, §306(a)(8)(B)(i):

Added Code Sec. 338(h)(8) and (9). **Effective** as if included in the provision of P.L. 97-248 to which it relates.

P.L. 97-448, §306(a)(8)(A)(ii), as amended by P.L. 98-369, §722(a)(3), provides:

(ii) If—

(I) any portion of a qualified stock purchase is pursuant to a binding contract entered into on or after September 1, 1982, and on or before the date of the enactment of this Act, and

(II) the purchasing corporation establishes by clear and convincing evidence that such contract was negotiated on the contemplation that, with respect to the deemed sale under section 338 of the Internal Revenue Code of 1954, the target corporation would be treated as a member of the affiliated group which includes the selling corporation,

then the amendment made by clause (i) shall not apply to such qualified stock purchase.

• **1982, Tax Equity and Fiscal Responsibility Act of 1982 (P.L. 97-248)**

P.L. 97-248, §222(e)(4):

Repealed Code Sec. 338 as in effect on 9-2-82. Prior to amendment, this section read as follows:

SEC. 338. EFFECT ON EARNINGS AND PROFITS.

For special rule relating to the effect on earnings and profits of certain distributions in partial liquidation, see section 312(e).

Applicable to distributions after August 31, 1982. See exceptions under P.L. 97-248, Act Sec. 222(f), following Code Sec. 331(b) for special rules.

P.L. 97-248, §224(a):

Amended Subchapter [part] B of Part II of Subchapter C of Chapter I by adding Code Sec. 338. **Effective** for any target corporation with respect to which the acquisition date occurs after 8-31-82.

P.L. 97-248, §224(d), as amended by P.L. 97-448, §306(a)(8)(B)(i) and (ii), provides:

As to certain acquisitions before September 1, 1982, if

(1) an acquisition date (within the meaning of section 338 of such Code without regard to paragraph (5) of this subsection) occurred after August 31, 1980, and before September 1, 1982,

(2) the target corporation (within the meaning of section 338 of such Code) is not liquidated before September 1, 1982, and

(3) the purchasing corporation (within the meaning of Code Sec. 338) makes, not later than November 15, 1982, an election under Code Sec. 338,

then the amendments made by this section shall apply to the acquisition of such target corporation.

In any case in which—

(1) there is, on July 22, 1982, a binding contract to acquire control (within the meaning of Code Sec. 368(c)) of any financial institution,

(2) the approval of one or more regulatory authorities is required in order to complete such acquisition, and

(3) within 90 days after the date of the final approval of the last such regulatory authority granting final approval, a plan of complete liquidation of such financial institution is adopted,

then the purchasing corporation may elect not to have the amendments made by this section apply to the acquisition pursuant to such contract.

(4) Extension of time for making elections; revocation of elections.—

(A) Extension.—The time for making an election under section 338 of such Code shall not expire before the close of February 28, 1983.

(B) Revocation.—Any election made under section 338 of such Code may be revoked by the purchasing corporation if revoked before March 1, 1983.

(5) Rules for acquisitions described in paragraph (2).—

(A) In general.—For purposes of applying section 338 of such Code with respect to any acquisition described in paragraph (2)—

(i) the date selected under subparagraph (B) of this paragraph shall be treated as the acquisition date,

(ii) a rule similar to the last sentence of section 334(b)(2) of such Code (as in effect on August 31, 1982) shall apply, and

(iii) subsections (e), (f), and (i) of such section 338, and paragraphs (4), (6), (8), and (9) of subsection (h) of such section 338, shall not apply.

(B) Selection of acquisition date by purchasing corporation.—The purchasing corporation may select any date for purposes of subparagraph (A)(i) if such date—

(i) is after the later of June 30, 1982, or the acquisition date (within the meaning of section 338 of such Code without regard to this paragraph), and

(ii) is on or before the date on which the election described in paragraph (2)(C) is made.

For additional rules, see amendment notes for P.L. 97-248, Act Sec. 222(f) under Code Sec. 331(b).

[Sec. 338(i)]

(i) REGULATIONS.—The Secretary shall prescribe such regulations as may be necessary or appropriate to carry out the purposes of this section, including—

(1) regulations to ensure that the purpose of this section to require consistency of treatment of stock and asset sales and purchases may not be circumvented through the use of any provision of law or regulations (including the consolidated return regulations) and

(2) regulations providing for the coordination of the provisions of this section with the provision of this title relating to foreign corporations and their shareholders.

Amendments

• **1984, Deficit Reduction Act of 1984 (P.L. 98-369)**

P.L. 98-369, §712(k)(7):

Amended Code Sec. 338(i). **Effective** as if included in the provision of P.L. 97-248 to which it relates. Special rules appear in Act Sec. 712(k)(9) following Code Sec. 338(h). Prior to amendment, it read as follows:

(i) Regulations.—The Secretary shall precribe such regulations as may be necessary to ensure that the purposes of this section to require consistency of treatment of stock and asset purchases with respect to a target corporation and its target affiliates (whether by treating all of them as stock purchases or as asset purchases) may not be circumvented through the use of any provision of law or regulations (including the consolidated return regulations).

Subpart C—Collapsible Corporations—[Repealed]

»»→ Caution: Code Sec. 341, below, was repealed by P.L. 108-27, and is subject to the sunset provision of the Jobs and Growth Tax Relief Reconciliation Act of 2003 (P.L. 108-27), §303. Absent Congressional action, the changes made to this provision by P.L. 108-27, or that take effect as if included in P.L. 108-27, do not apply after December 31, 2010. For more information about the sunset provision, see page XXI of the Preface to this publication and P.L. 108-27, §303, in the amendment notes. See the amendments notes for a history of amendments to this section and the effective date of each change.

[Sec. 341—Repealed]

Amendments

• 2003, Jobs and Growth Tax Relief Reconciliation Act of 2003 (P.L. 108-27)

P.L. 108-27, §302(e)(4)(A):

Repealed subpart C of part II of subchapter C of chapter 1 (Code Sec. 341). For the **effective** date, see Act Sec. 302(f), as amended by P.L. 108-311, §402(a)(6), below.

P.L. 108-27, §302(f), as amended by P.L. 108-311, §402(a)(6), provides:

(f) EFFECTIVE DATE.—

(1) IN GENERAL.—Except as provided in paragraph (2), the amendments made by this section shall apply to taxable years beginning after December 31, 2002.

(2) PASS-THRU ENTITIES.—In the case of a pass-thru entity described in subparagraph (A), (B), (C), (D), (E), or (F) of section 1(h)(10) of the Internal Revenue Code of 1986, as amended by this Act, the amendments made by this section shall apply to taxable years ending after December 31, 2002; except that dividends received by such an entity on or before such date shall not be treated as qualified dividend income (as defined in section 1(h)(11)(B) of such Code, as added by this Act).

P.L. 108-27, §303, as amended by P.L. 109-222, §102, provides:

SEC. 303. SUNSET OF TITLE.

All provisions of, and amendments made by, this title shall not apply to taxable years beginning after December 31, 2010, and the Internal Revenue Code of 1986 shall be applied and administered to such years as if such provisions and amendments had never been enacted.

Prior to repeal, Code Sec. 341 read as follows:

SEC. 341. COLLAPSIBLE CORPORATIONS.

[Sec. 341(a)]

(a) TREATMENT OF GAIN TO SHAREHOLDERS.—Gain from—

(1) the sale or exchange of stock of a collapsible corporation,

(2) a distribution—

(A) in complete liquidation of a collapsible corporation if such distribution is treated under this part as in part or full payment in exchange for stock, or

(B) in partial liquidation (within the meaning of section 302(e)) of a collapsible corporation if such distribution is treated under section 302(b)(4) as in part or full payment in exchange for the stock, and

(3) a distribution made by a collapsible corporation which, under section 301(c)(3)(A), is treated, to the extent it exceeds the basis of the stock, in the same manner as a gain from the sale or exchange of property,

to the extent that it would be considered (but for the provisions of this section) as gain from the sale or exchange of a capital asset shall, except as otherwise provided in this section, be considered as ordinary income.

Amendments

• 1986, Tax Reform Act of 1986 (P.L. 99-514)

P.L. 99-514, §1804(i)(1):

Amended Code Sec. 341(a) by striking out "held for more than 6 months". **Effective** with respect to sales, exchanges, and distributions after 9-27-85.

• 1984, Deficit Reduction Act of 1984 (P.L. 98-369)

P.L. 98-369, §1001(b)(2):

Amended Code Sec. 341(a) by striking out "1 [one] year" and inserting in lieu thereof "6 months". **Effective** for property acquired after 6-22-84, and before 1-1-88.

• 1982, Tax Equity and Fiscal Responsibility Act of 1982 (P.L. 97-248)

P.L. 97-248, §222(e)(5):

Amended paragraph (2) of Code Sec. 341(a). **Effective,** generally, for distributions after 8-31-82. Also see P.L. 97-248, Act Sec. 222(f) which appears in the amendment notes for Code Sec. 331(b). Prior to amendment, paragraph (2) read as follows:

"(2) a distribution in partial or complete liquidation of a collapsible corporation, which distribution is treated under this part as in part or full payment in exchange for stock, and".

• 1976, Tax Reform Act of 1976 (P.L. 94-455)

P.L. 94-455, §1402(b)(1)(B)

Substituted "9 months" for "6 months" in Code Sec. 341(a). **Effective** for tax years beginning in 1977.

P.L. 94-455, §1402(b)(2)

Amended Code Sec. 341(a) by substituting "1 year" for "9 months". **Effective** with respect to tax years beginning after 12-31-77.

P.L. 94-455, §1901(b)(3)(I):

Substituted "ordinary income" for "gain from the sale or exchange of property which is not a capital asset" in Code Sec. 341(a). **Effective** for tax years beginning after 12-31-76.

• 1964 (P.L. 88-484)

P.L. 88-484, §[1(a)]:

Amended Code Sec. 341(a) by substituting "except as otherwise provided in this section" for "except as provided in subsection (d)". **Effective** for transactions after 8-22-64 in tax years ending after such date.

[Sec. 341(b)]

(b) DEFINITIONS.—

(1) COLLAPSIBLE CORPORATION.—For purposes of this section, the term "collapsible corporation" means a corporation formed or availed of principally for the manufacture, construction, or production of property, for the purchase of property which (in the hands of the corporation) is property described in paragraph (3), or for the holding of stock in a corporation so formed or availed of, with a view to—

(A) the sale or exchange of stock by its shareholders (whether in liquidation or otherwise), or a distribution to its shareholders, before the realization by the corporation manufacturing, constructing, producing, or purchasing the property of 2/3 of the taxable income to be derived from such property, and

(B) the realization by such shareholders of gain attributable to such property.

(2) PRODUCTION OR PURCHASE OF PROPERTY.—For purposes of paragraph (1), a corporation shall be deemed to have manufactured, constructed, produced, or purchased property, if—

(A) it engaged in the manufacture, construction, or production of such property to any extent,

(B) it holds property having a basis determined, in whole or in part, by reference to the cost of such property in the hands of a person who manufactured, constructed, produced, or purchased the property, or

(C) it holds property having a basis determined, in whole or in part, by reference to the cost of property manufactured, constructed, produced, or purchased by the corporation.

(3) SECTION 341 ASSETS.—For purposes of this section, the term "section 341 assets" means property held for a period of less than 3 years which is—

(A) stock in trade of the corporation, or other property of a kind which would properly be included in the inventory of the corporation if on hand at the close of the taxable year;

(B) property held by the corporation primarily for sale to customers in the ordinary course of its trade or business;

(C) unrealized receivables or fees, except receivables from sales of property other than property described in this paragraph; or

(D) property described in section 1231(b) (without regard to any holding period therein provided), except such property which is or has been used in connection with the manufacture, construction, production, or sale of property described in subparagraph (A) or (B).

In determining whether the 3-year holding period specified in this paragraph has been satisfied, section 1223 shall apply, but no such period shall be deemed to begin before the completion of the manufacture, construction, production, or purchase.

(4) UNREALIZED RECEIVABLES.—For purposes of paragraph (3)(C), the term "unrealized receivables or fees" means, to the extent not previously includible in income under the method of accounting used by the corporation, any rights (contractual or otherwise) to payment for—

(A) goods delivered, or to be delivered, to the extent the proceeds therefrom would be treated as amounts received from the sale or exchange of property other than a capital asset, or

(B) services rendered or to be rendered.

Amendments

• 1984, Deficit Reduction Act of 1984 (P.L. 98-369)

P.L. 98-369, §65(a):

Amended Code Sec. 341(b)(1)(A) by striking out "a substantial part" and inserting in lieu thereof "⅔". **Effective** with respect to sales, exchanges, and distributions made after 7-18-84.

[Sec. 341(c)]

(c) PRESUMPTION IN CERTAIN CASES.—

(1) IN GENERAL.—For purposes of this section, a corporation shall, unless shown to the contrary, be deemed to be a collapsible corporation if (at the time of the sale or exchange, or the distribution, described in subsection (a)) the fair market value of its section 341 assets (as defined in subsection (b)(3)) is—

(A) 50 percent or more of the fair market value of its total assets, and

(B) 120 percent or more of the adjusted basis of such section 341 assets.

Absence of the conditions described in subparagraphs (A) and (B) shall not give rise to a presumption that the corporation was not a collapsible corporation.

(2) DETERMINATION OF TOTAL ASSETS.—In determining the fair market value of the total assets of a corporation for purposes of paragraph (1)(A), there shall not be taken into account—

(A) cash,

(B) obligations which are capital assets in the hands of the corporation, and

(C) stock in any other corporation.

Amendments

• 1981, Economic Recovery Tax Act of 1981 (P.L. 97-34)

P.L. 97-34, §505(c)(2):

Amended Code Sec. 341(c)(2)(B) by striking out "(and governmental obligations described in section 1221(5))". **Effective** for property acquired and positions established by the taxpayer after 6-23-81, in tax years ending after such date.

[Sec. 341(d)]

(d) LIMITATIONS ON APPLICATION OF SECTION.—In the case of gain realized by a shareholder with respect to his stock in a collapsible corporation, this section shall not apply—

(1) unless, at any time after the commencement of the manufacture, construction, or production of the property, or at the time of the purchase of the property described in subsection (b)(3) or at any time thereafter, such shareholder (A) owned (or was considered as owning) more than 5 percent in value of the outstanding stock of the corporation, or (B) owned stock which was considered as owned at such time by another shareholder who then owned (or was considered as owning) more than 5 percent in value of the outstanding stock of the corporation;

(2) to the gain recognized during a taxable year, unless more than 70 percent of such gain is attributable to the property described in subsection (b)(1); and

(3) to gain realized after the expiration of 3 years following the completion of such manufacture, construction, production, or purchase.

For purposes of paragraph (1), the ownership of stock shall be determined in accordance with the rules prescribed in paragraphs (1), (2), (3), (5), and (6) of section 544(a) (relating to personal holding companies); except that, in addition to the persons prescribed by paragraph (2) of that section, the family of an individual shall include the spouses of that individual's brothers and sisters (whether by the whole or half blood) and the spouses of that individual's lineal descendants. In determining whether property is described in subsection (b)(1) for purposes of applying paragraph (2), all property described in section 1221(a)(1) shall, to the extent provided in regulations prescribed by the Secretary, be treated as one item of property.

Amendments

• 1999, Tax Relief Extension Act of 1999 (P.L. 106-170)

P.L. 106-170, §532(c)(2)(D) (as amended by P.L. 107-147, §417(24)(B)(i)):

Amended Code Sec. 341(d) by striking "section 1221(1)" and inserting "section 1221(a)(1)". **Effective** for any instrument held, acquired, or entered into, any transaction entered into, and supplies held or acquired on or after 12-17-99.

• 1984, Deficit Reduction Act of 1984 (P.L. 98-369)

P.L. 98-369, §65(b):

Amended Code Sec. 341(d) by adding the last sentence. **Effective** with respect to sales, exchanges, and distributions made after 7-18-84.

P.L. 98-369, §65(c):

Amended Code Sec. 341(d)(2) by striking out "so manufactured, constructed, produced, or purchased" and inserting in lieu thereof "described in subsection (b)(1)". **Effective** with respect to sales, exchanges, and distributions made after 7-18-84.

[Sec. 341(e)]

(e) EXCEPTIONS TO APPLICATION OF SECTION.—

(1) SALES OR EXCHANGES OF STOCK.—For purposes of subsection (a)(1), a corporation shall not be considered to be a collapsible corporation with respect to any sale or exchange of stock of the corporation by a shareholder, if, at the time of such sale or exchange, the sum of—

(A) the net unrealized appreciation in subsection (e) assets of the corporation (as defined in paragraph (5)(A)), plus

(B) if the shareholder owns more than 5 percent in value of the outstanding stock of the corporation, the net unrealized appreciation in assets of the corporation (other than assets described in subparagraph (A)) which would be subsection (e) assets under clauses (i) and (iii) of paragraph (5)(A) if the shareholder owned more than 20 percent in value of such stock, plus

(C) if the shareholder owns more than 20 percent in value of the outstanding stock of the corporation and owns, or at any time during the preceding 3-year period owned, more than 20 percent in value of the outstanding stock of any other corporation more than 70 percent in value of the assets of which are, or were at any time during which such shareholder owned during such 3-year period more than 20 percent in value of the outstanding stock, assets similar or related in service or use to assets comprising more than 70 percent in value of the assets of the corporation, the net unrealized appreciation in assets of the corporation (other than assets described in subparagraph (A)) which would be subsection (e) assets under clauses (i) and (iii) of paragraph (5)(A) if the determination whether the property, in the hands of such shareholder, would be property gain from the sale or exchange of which would under any provision of this chapter be considered in whole or in part as ordinary income, were made—

(i) by treating any sale or exchange by such shareholder of stock in such other corporation within the preceding 3-year period (but only if at the time of such sale or exchange the shareholder owned more than 20 percent in value of the outstanding stock in such other corporation) as a sale or exchange by such shareholder of his proportionate share of the assets of such other corporation, and

(ii) by treating any liquidating sale or exchange of property by such other corporation within such 3-year period (but only if at the time of such sale or exchange the shareholder owned more than 20 percent in value of the outstanding stock in such other corporation), as a sale or exchange by such shareholder of his proportionate share of the property sold or exchanged,

does not exceed an amount equal to 15 percent of the net worth of the corporation. This paragraph shall not apply to any sale or exchange of stock to the issuing corporation or, in the case of a shareholder who owns more than 20 percent in value of the outstanding stock of the corporation, to any sale or exchange of stock by such shareholder to any person related to him (within the meaning of paragraph (8)).

(2) [Repealed.]

(3) [Repealed.]

(4) [Repealed.]

(5) SUBSECTION (e) ASSET DEFINED.—

(A) For purposes of paragraph (1), the term "subsection (e) asset" means, with respect to property held by any corporation—

(i) property (except property used in the trade or business, as defined in paragraph (9)) which in the hands of the corporation is, or, in the hands of a shareholder who owns more than 20 percent in value of the outstanding stock of the corporation, would be, property gain from the sale or exchange of which would under any provision of this chapter be considered in whole or in part as ordinary income;

(ii) property used in the trade or business (as defined in paragraph (9)), but only if the unrealized depreciation on all such property on which there is unrealized depreciation exceeds the unrealized appreciation on all such property on which there is unrealized appreciation;

(iii) if there is net unrealized appreciation on all property used in the trade or business (as defined in paragraph (9)), property used in the trade or business (as defined in paragraph (9)) which, in the hands of a shareholder who owns more than 20 percent in value of the outstanding stock of the corporation, would be property gain from the sale or exchange of which would under any provision of this chapter be considered in whole or in part as ordinary income; and

(iv) property (unless included under clause (i), (ii), or (iii)) which consists of a copyright, a literary, musical, or artistic composition, a letter or memorandum, or similar property, or any interest in any such property, if the property was created in whole or in part by the personal efforts of, or (in the case of a letter, memorandum, or similar property) was prepared, or produced in whole or in part for, any individual who owns more than 5 percent in value of the stock of the corporation.

The determination as to whether property of the corporation in the hands of the corporation is, or in the hands of a shareholder would be, property gain from the sale or exchange of which would under any provision in this chapter be considered in whole or in part as ordinary income shall be made as if all property of the corporation had been sold or exchanged to one person in one transaction.

(B) [Repealed.]

(6) NET UNREALIZED APPRECIATION DEFINED.—

(A) For purposes of this subsection, the term "net unrealized appreciation" means, with respect to the assets of a corporation, the amount by which—

(i) the unrealized appreciation in such assets on which there is unrealized appreciation, exceeds

(ii) the unrealized depreciation in such assets on which there is unrealized depreciation.

(B) For purposes of subparagraph (A) and paragraph (5)(A), the term "unrealized appreciation" means, with respect to any asset, the amount by which—

(i) the fair market value of such asset, exceeds

(ii) the adjusted basis for determining gain from the sale or other disposition of such asset.

(C) For purposes of subparagraph (A) and paragraph (5)(A), the term "unrealized depreciation" means, with respect to any asset, the amount by which—

(i) the adjusted basis for determining gain from the sale or other disposition of such asset, exceeds

(ii) the fair market value of such asset.

(D) For purposes of this paragraph (but not paragraph (5)(A)), in the case of any asset on the sale or exchange of which only a portion of the gain would under any provision of this chapter be considered as ordinary income, there shall be taken into account only an amount of the unrealized appreciation in such asset which is equal to such portion of the gain.

(7) NET WORTH DEFINED.—For purposes of this subsection, the net worth of a corporation, as of any day, is the amount by which—

(A)(i) the fair market value of all its assets at the close of such day, plus

(ii) the amount of any distribution in complete liquidation made by it on or before such day, exceeds

(B) all its liabilities at the close of such day.

For purposes of this paragraph, the net worth of a corporation as of any day shall not take into account any increase in net worth during the one-year period ending on such day to the extent attributable to any amount received by it for stock, or as a contribution to capital or as paid-in surplus, if it appears that there was not a bona fide business purpose for the transaction in respect of which such amount was received.

(8) RELATED PERSON DEFINED.—For purposes of paragraphs (1) and (4), the following persons shall be considered to be related to a shareholder:

(A) If the shareholder is an individual—

(i) his spouse, ancestors, and lineal descendants, and

(ii) a corporation which is controlled by such shareholder.

(B) If the shareholder is a corporation—

(i) a corporation which controls, or is controlled by, the shareholder, and

(ii) if more than 50 percent in value of the outstanding stock of the shareholder is owned by any person, a corporation more than 50 percent in value of the outstanding stock of which is owned by the same person.

For purposes of determining the ownership of stock in applying subparagraphs (A) and (B), the rules of section 267(c) shall apply, except that the family of an individual shall include only his spouse, ancestors, and lineal descendants. For purposes of this paragraph, control means the ownership of stock possessing at least 50 percent of the total combined voting power of all classes of stock entitled to vote or at least 50 percent of the total value of shares of all classes of stock of the corporation.

(9) PROPERTY USED IN THE TRADE OR BUSINESS.—For purposes of this subsection, the term "property used in the trade or business" means property described in section 1231(b), without regard to any holding period therein provided.

(10) OWNERSHIP OF STOCK.—For purposes of this subsection (other than paragraph (8)), the ownership of stock shall be determined in the manner prescribed in subsection (d).

(11) CORPORATIONS AND SHAREHOLDERS NOT MEETING REQUIREMENTS.—In determining whether or not any corporation is a collapsible corporation within the meaning of subsection (b), the fact that such corporation, or such corporation with respect to any of its shareholders, does not meet the requirements of paragraph (1), (2), (3), or (4) of this subsection shall not be taken into account, and such determination, in the case of a corporation which does not meet such requirements, shall be made as if this subsection had not been enacted.

(12) NONAPPLICATION OF SECTION 1245(a), ETC.—For purposes of this subsection, the determination of whether gain from the sale or exchange of property would under any provision of this chapter be considered as ordinary income shall be made without regard to the application of sections 617(d)(1), 1245(a), 1250(a),1252(a),1254(a), and 1276(a).

Amendments

• 1988, Technical and Miscellaneous Revenue Act of 1988 (P.L. 100-647)

P.L. 100-647, §1006(e)(18)(A)-(B):

Amended Code Sec. 341(e)(1)(C)(ii) by striking out "sale or exchange" the first place it appears and inserting in lieu thereof "liquidating sale or exchange", and by striking out, "gain or loss on which was not recognized to such other corporation under section 337(a)," after "corporation)". **Effective** as if included in the provision of P.L. 99-514 to which it relates.

• 1986, Tax Reform Act of 1986 (P.L. 99-514)

P.L. 99-514, §631(c)(6)(A):

Amended Code Sec. 341(e) by striking out paragraphs (2), (3), and (4). **Effective**, generally, for:

(1) any distribution in complete liquidation, and any sale or exchange, made by a corporation after 7-31-86, unless such corporation is completely liquidated before 1-1-86,

(2) any transaction described in section 338 of the Internal Revenue Code of 1986 for which the acquisition date occurs after 12-31-86, and

(3) any distribution (not in complete liquidation) made after 12-31-86. For special rules and exceptions see Act Sec. 633(b)-(f) in the Amendment Notes following Code Sec. 311. Prior to amendment, paragraphs (2), (3), and (4) read as follows:

(2) DISTRIBUTIONS IN LIQUIDATION.—For purposes of subsection (a)(2), a corporation shall not be considered to be a collapsible corporation with respect to any distribution to a shareholder pursuant to a plan of complete liquidation if, by reason of the application of paragraph (4) of this subsection, section 337(a) applies to sales or exchanges of property by the corporation within the 12-month period beginning on the date of the adoption of such plan, and if, at all times after the adoption of the plan of liquidation, the sum of—

(A) the net unrealized appreciation in subsection (e) assets of the corporation (as defined in paragraph (5)(A)), plus

(B) if the shareholder owns more than 5 percent in value of the outstanding stock of the corporation, the net unrealized appreciation in assets of the corporation described in paragraph (1)(B) (other than assets described in subparagraph (A) of this paragraph), plus

(C) if the shareholder owns more than 20 percent in value of the outstanding stock of the corporation and owns, or at any time during the preceding 3-year period owned, more than 20 percent in value of the outstanding stock of any other corporation more than 70 percent in value of the assets of which are, or were at any time during which such shareholder owned during such 3-year period more than 20 percent in value of the outstanding stock, assets similar or related in service or use to assets comprising more than 70 percent in value of the assets of the corporation, the net unrealized appreciation in assets of the corporation described in paragraph (1)(C) (other than assets described in subparagraph (A) of this paragraph),

does not exceed an amount equal to 15 percent of the net worth of the corporation.

(3) RECOGNITION OF GAIN IN CERTAIN LIQUIDATIONS.—For purposes of section 333, a corporation shall not be considered to be a collapsible corporation if at all times after the adoption of the plan of liquidation, the net unrealized appreciation in subsection (e) assets of the corporation (as defined in paragraph (5)(B)) does not exceed an amount equal to 15 percent of the net worth of the corporation.

(4) GAIN OR LOSS ON SALES OR EXCHANGES IN CONNECTION WITH CERTAIN LIQUIDATIONS.—For purposes of section 337, a corporation shall not be considered to be a collapsible corporation with respect to any sale or exchange by it of property within the 12-month period beginning on the date of the adoption of a plan of complete liquidation, if—

(A) at all times after the adoption of such plan, the net unrealized appreciation in subsection (e) assets of the corporation (as defined in paragraph (5)(A)) does not exceed an amount equal to 15 percent of the net worth of the corporation,

(B) within the 12-month period beginning on the date of the adoption of such plan, the corporation sells substantially all of the properties held by it on such date, and

(C) following the adoption of such plan, no distribution is made of any property which in the hands of the corporation or in the hands of the distributee is property in respect of which a deduction for exhaustion, wear and tear, obsolescence, amortization, or depletion is allowable.

This paragraph shall not apply with respect to any sale or exchange of property by the corporation to any shareholder who owns more than 20 percent in value of the outstanding stock of the corporation or to any person related to such shareholder (within the meaning of paragraph (8)), if such property in the hands of the corporation or in the hands of such shareholder or related person is property in respect of which a deduction for exhaustion, wear and tear, obsolescence, amortization, or depletion is allowable.

P.L. 99-514, §631(e)(6)(B)(i) and (ii):

Amended Code Sec. 341(e)(5) by striking out "paragraphs (1), (2), and (4)" and inserting in lieu thereof "paragraph (1)", and by striking out subparagraph (B). **Effective**, generally, for:

(1) any distribution in complete liquidation, and any sale or exchange, made by a corporation after 7-31-86, unless such corporation is completely liquidated before 1-1-86,

(2) any transaction described in section 338 of the Internal Revenue Code of 1986 for which the acquisition date occurs after 12-31-86, and

(3) any distribution (not in complete liquidation) made after 12-31-86. For special rules and exceptions see Act Sec. 633(b)-(f) in the Amendment Notes following Code Sec. 311. Prior to amendment, Code Sec. 341(e)(5)(B) read as follows:

(B) For purposes of paragraph (3), the term "subsection (e) asset" means, with respect to property held by any corporation, property described in clauses (i), (ii), (iii), and (iv) of subparagraph (A), except that clauses (i) and (iii) shall apply in respect of any shareholder who owns more than 5 percent in value of the outstanding stock of the corporation (in lieu of any shareholder who owns more than 20 percent in value of such stock.

P.L. 99-514, §1899A(8):

Amended Code Sec. 341(e)(12) by striking out "1245(a).—" in the heading and inserting in lieu thereof "1245(a), Etc.—". **Effective** 10-22-86.

• 1984, Deficit Reduction Act of 1984 (P.L. 98-369)

P.L. 98-369, §43(c)(1):

Amended Code Sec. 341(e)(12) by striking out "and 1254(a)" and inserting in lieu thereof "1254(a), and 1276(a)". **Effective** for tax years ending after 7-18-84.

P.L. 98-369, §492(b)(2):

Amended Code Sec. 341(e)(12) by striking out "1251(c)," after "1250(a),". **Effective** for tax years beginning after 12-31-83.

• 1976, Tax Reform Act of 1976 (P.L. 94-455)

P.L. 94-455, §205(c)(2):

Substituted "1252(a), and 1254(a)" for "and 1252(a)" in Code Sec. 341(e)(12). **Effective** for tax years ending after 12-31-75.

P.L. 94-455, §1901(b)(3)(A):

Substituted "ordinary income" for "gain from the sale or exchange of property which is neither a capital asset nor property described in section 1231(b)" wherever it appears in paragraphs (1)(C), (5)(A), (6)(D) and (12) of Code Sec. 341(e). **Effective** for tax years beginning after 12-31-76.

• 1969, Tax Reform Act of 1969 (P.L. 91-172)

P.L. 91-172, §211(b):

Amended Code Sec. 341(e)(12) by striking out "and 1250(a)" and inserting "1250(a), 1251(c), and 1252(a)". **Effective** for tax years beginning after 12-31-69.

P.L. 91-172, §514(b)(1):

Amended Code Sec. 341(e)(5)(A)(iv). **Effective** for sales and other dispositions occurring after 7-25-69. Prior to amendment, Code Sec. 341(e)(5)(A)(iv) read as follows:

"(iv) property (unless included under clause (i), (ii), or (iii)) which consists of a copyright, a literary, musical, or artistic composition, or similar property, or any interest in any such property, if the property was created in whole or in part by the personal efforts of any individual who owns more than 5 percent in value of the stock of the corporation."

• 1966 (P.L. 89-570)

P.L. 89-570, §[1(b)]:

Amended Code Sec. 341(e)(12) by substituting "section 617(d)(1), 1245(a)," for "section 1245(a)". **Effective** for tax years ending after 9-12-66, the date of enactment, but only for expenditures paid or incurred after that date.

• 1964, Revenue Act of 1964 (P.L. 88-272)

P.L. 88-272, §231(b)(4):

Amended Code Sec. 341(e) to insert "sections 1245(a) and 1250(a)" in lieu of "section 1245(a)" at end of paragraph (12). **Effective** for dispositions after 12-31-63, in tax years ending after such date.

• 1962, Revenue Act of 1962 (P.L. 87-834)

P.L. 87-834, §13(f)(4):

Amended Code Sec. 341(e) by adding a new paragraph (12). **Effective** for tax years beginning after 12-31-62.

• 1958, Technical Amendments Act of 1958 (P.L. 85-866)

P.L. 85-866, §20(a):

Added subsection (e) to Sec. 341. **Effective** for tax years beginning after 12-31-57, but only for sales, exchanges, and distributions after 9-2-58.

[Sec. 341(f)]

(f) CERTAIN SALES OF STOCK OF CONSENTING CORPORATIONS.—

(1) IN GENERAL.—Subsection (a)(1) shall not apply to a sale of stock of a corporation (other than a sale to the issuing corporation) if such corporation (hereinafter in this subsection referred to as "consenting corporation") consents (at such time and in such manner as the Secretary may by regulations prescribe) to have the provisions of paragraph (2) apply. Such consent shall apply with respect to each sale of stock of such corporation made within the 6-month period beginning with the date on which such consent is filed.

(2) RECOGNITION OF GAIN.—Except as provided in paragraph (3), if a subsection (f) asset (as defined in paragraph (4)) is disposed of at any time by a consenting corporation (or, if paragraph (3) applies, by a transferee corporation), then the amount by which—

(A) in the case of a sale, exchange, or involuntary conversion, the amount realized, or

(B) in the case of any other disposition, the fair market value of such asset,

exceeds the adjusted basis of such asset shall be treated as gain from the sale or exchange of such asset. Such gain shall be recognized notwithstanding any other provision of this subtitle, but only to the extent such gain is not recognized under any other provision of this subtitle.

(3) EXCEPTION FOR CERTAIN TAX-FREE TRANSACTIONS.—If the basis of a subsection (f) asset in the hands of a transferee is determined by reference to its basis in the hands of the transferor by reason of the application of section 332, 351, or 361, then the amount of gain taken into account by the transferor under paragraph (2) shall not exceed the amount of gain recognized to the transferor on the transfer of such asset (determined without regard to this subsection). This paragraph shall apply only if the transferee—

(A) is not an organization which is exempt from tax imposed by this chapter, and

(B) agrees (at such time and in such manner as the Secretary may by regulations prescribe) to have the provisions of paragraph (2) apply to any disposition by it of such subsection (f) asset.

(4) SUBSECTION (f) ASSET DEFINED.—For purposes of this subsection—

(A) IN GENERAL.—The term "subsection (f) asset" means any property which, as of the date of any sale of stock referred to in paragraph (1), is not a capital asset and is property owned by, or subject to an option to acquire held by, the consenting corporation. For purposes of this subparagraph, land or any interest in real property (other than a security interest), and unrealized receivables or fees (as defined in subsection (b)(4)), shall be treated as property which is not a capital asset.

(B) PROPERTY UNDER CONSTRUCTION.—If manufacture, construction, or production with respect to any property described in subparagraph (A) has commenced before any date of sale described therein, the term "subsection (f) asset" includes the property resulting from such manufacture, construction, or production.

(C) SPECIAL RULE FOR LAND.—In the case of land or any interest in real property (other than a security interest) described in subparagraph (A), the term "subsection (f) asset" includes any improvements resulting from construction with respect to such property if such construction is commenced (by the consenting corporation or by a transferee corporation which has agreed to the application of paragraph (2)) within 2 years after the date of any sale described in subparagraph (A).

(5) 5-YEAR LIMITATION AS TO SHAREHOLDER.—Paragraph (1) shall not apply to the sale of stock of a corporation by a shareholder if, during the 5-year period ending on the date of such sale, such shareholder (or any related person within the meaning of subsection (e)(8)(A)) sold any stock of another consenting corporation within any 6-month period beginning on a date on which a consent was filed under paragraph (1) by such other corporation.

(6) SPECIAL RULE FOR STOCK OWNERSHIP IN OTHER CORPORATIONS.—If a corporation (hereinafter in this paragraph referred to as "owning corporation") owns 5 percent or more in value of the outstanding stock of another corporation on the date of any sale of stock of the owning corporation during a 6-month period with respect to which a consent under paragraph (1) was filed by the owning corporation, such consent shall not be valid with respect to such sale unless such other corporation has (within the 6-month period ending on the date of such sale) filed a valid consent under paragraph (1) with respect to sales of its stock. For purposes of applying paragraph (4) to such other corporation, a sale of stock of the owning corporation to which paragraph (1) applies shall be treated as a sale of stock of such other corporation. In the case of a chain of corporations connected by the 5-percent ownership requirements of this paragraph, rules similar to the rules of the two preceding sentences shall be applied.

(7) ADJUSTMENTS TO BASIS.—The Secretary shall prescribe such regulations as he may deem necessary to provide for adjustments to the basis of property to reflect gain recognized under paragraph (2).

(8) SPECIAL RULE FOR FOREIGN CORPORATIONS.—Except to the extent provided in regulations prescribed by the Secretary—

(A) any consent given by a foreign corporation under paragraph (1) shall not be effective, and

(B) paragraph (3) shall not apply if the transferee is a foreign corporation.

Amendments

• 1996, Small Business Job Protection Act of 1996 (P.L. 104-188)

P.L. 104-188, §1702(h)(7):

Amended Code Sec. 341(f)(3) by striking "351, 361, 371(a), or 374(a)" and inserting "351, or 361". **Effective** as if included in the provision of P.L. 101-508 to which it relates.

• 1984, Deficit Reduction Act of 1984 (P.L. 98-369)

P.L. 98-369, §135(a):

Added Code Sec. 341(f)(8). **Effective** 7-18-84.

• 1976, Tax Reform Act of 1976 (P.L. 94-455)

P.L. 94-455, §1906(b)(13)(A):

Amended 1954 Code by substituting "Secretary" for "Secretary or his delegate" each place it appeared. **Effective** 2-1-77.

• 1964 (P.L. 88-484)

P.L. 88-484, §[1(a)]:

Added Code Sec. 341(f). **Effective** for transactions after 8-22-64 in tax years ending after such date.

Subpart D—Definition and Special Rule

[Sec. 346]

SEC. 346. DEFINITION AND SPECIAL RULE.

[Sec. 346(a)]

(a) COMPLETE LIQUIDATION.—For purposes of this subchapter, a distribution shall be treated as in complete liquidation of a corporation if the distribution is one of a series of distributions in redemption of all of the stock of the corporation pursuant to a plan.

[Sec. 346(b)]

(b) TRANSACTIONS WHICH MIGHT REACH SAME RESULT AS PARTIAL LIQUIDATIONS.—The Secretary shall prescribe such regulations as may be necessary to ensure that the purposes of subsections (a) and (b) of section 222 of the Tax Equity and Fiscal Responsibility Act of 1982 (which repeal the special tax treatment for partial liquidations) may not be circumvented through the use of section 355, 351, or any other provision of law or regulations (including the consolidated return regulations).

Amendments

• 1986, Tax Reform Act of 1986 (P.L. 99-514)

P.L. 99-514, §631(e)(7):

Amended Code Sec. 346(b) by striking out "337,". **Effective**, generally, for:

(1) any distribution in complete liquidation, and any sale or exchange, made by a corporation after 7-31-86, unless such corporation is completely liquidated before 1-1-87,

(2) any transaction described in section 338 of the Internal Revenue Code of 1986 for which the acquisition date occurs after 12-31-86, and

(3) any distribution (not in complete liquidation) made after 12-31-86. For special rules and exceptions see Act Sec. 633(b)-(f) in the Amendment Notes following Code Sec. 311.

• 1982, Tax Equity and Fiscal Responsibility Act of 1982 (P.L. 97-248)

P.L. 97-248, §222(d):

Amended Code Sec. 346. **Effective**, generally, for distributions after 8-31-82. But see special rules for P.L. 97-248, Act Sec. 222(f), in the amendment notes for Code Sec. 331(b). Prior to amendment, Code Sec. 346 read as follows:

SEC. 346. PARTIAL LIQUIDATION DEFINED.

(a) IN GENERAL.—For purposes of this subchapter, a distribution shall be treated as in partial liquidation of a corporation if—

(1) the distribution is one of a series of distributions in redemption of all of the stock of the corporation pursuant to a plan; or

(2) the distribution is not essentially equivalent to a dividend, is in redemption of a part of the stock of the corporation pursuant to a plan, and occurs within the taxable year in which the plan is adopted or within the succeeding taxable year, including (but not limited to) a distribution which meets the requirements of subsection (b).

For purposes of section 562(b) (relating to the dividends paid deduction) and section 6043 (relating to information returns), a partial liquidation includes a redemption of stock to which section 302 applies.

(b) TERMINATION OF A BUSINESS.—A distribution shall be treated as a distribution described in subsection (a)(2) if the requirements of paragraphs (1) and (2) of this subsection are met.

(1) The distribution is attributable to the corporation's ceasing to conduct, or consists of the assets of, a trade or business which has been actively conducted throughout the 5-year period immediately before the distribution, which trade or business was not acquired by the corporation within such period in a transaction in which gain or loss was recognized in whole or in part.

(2) Immediately after the distribution the liquidating corporation is actively engaged in the conduct of a trade or business, which trade or business was actively conducted throughout the 5-year period ending on the date of the distribution and was not acquired by the corporation within such period in a transaction in which gain or loss was recognized in whole or in part.

Whether or not a distribution meets the requirements of paragraphs (1) and (2) of this subsection shall be determined without regard to whether or not the distribution is pro rata with respect to all of the shareholders of the corporation.

(c) TREATMENT OF CERTAIN REDEMPTIONS.—The fact that, with respect to a shareholder, a distribution qualifies under section 302(a) (relating to redemptions treated as distributions in part or full payment in exchange for stock) by reason of section 302(b) shall not be taken into account in determining whether the distribution, with respect to such shareholder, is also a distribution in partial liquidation of the corporation.

P.L. 97-248, §222(e)(8)(A):

Amended the heading and table of sections for subpart D of part II of subchapter C of chapter 1. **Effective** as noted above under Act Sec. 222(d). Prior to amendment, the heading and table of sections read as follows:

Subpart D—Definition and Special Rule

Sec. 346. Definition and special rule.

PART III—CORPORATE ORGANIZATIONS AND REORGANIZATIONS

Subpart A—Corporate Organizations

[Sec. 351]

SEC. 351. TRANSFER TO CORPORATION CONTROLLED BY TRANSFEROR.

[Sec. 351(a)]

(a) GENERAL RULE.—No gain or loss shall be recognized if property is transferred to a corporation by one or more persons solely in exchange for stock in such corporation and immediately after the exchange such person or persons are in control (as defined in section 368(c)) of the corporation.

Amendments

• 1989, Omnibus Budget Reconciliation Act of 1989 (P.L. 101-239)

P.L. 101-239, §7203(a):

Amended Code Sec. 351(a) by striking "or securities" after "for stock". **Effective**, generally, for transfers after 10-2-89, in tax years ending after such date. For exceptions, see Act Sec. 7203(c)(2)-(3), below.

P.L. 101-239, §7203(c)(2)-(3), provides:

(2) BINDING CONTRACT.—The amendments made by this section shall not apply to any transfer pursuant to a written binding contract in effect on October 2, 1989, and at all times thereafter before such transfer.

(3) CORPORATE TRANSFERS.—In the case of property transferred (directly or indirectly through a partnership or otherwise) by a C corporation, paragraphs (1) and (2) shall be applied by substituting "July 11, 1989" for "October 2, 1989". The preceding sentence shall not apply where the corporation meets the requirements of section 1504(a)(2) of the Internal Revenue Code of 1986 with respect to the transferee corporation (and where the transfer is not part of a plan pursuant to which the transferor subsequently fails to meet such requirements).

• 1980, Bankruptcy Tax Act of 1980 (P.L. 96-589)

P.L. 96-589, §5(e)(2).

Amended Code Sec. 351(a) by striking out the last sentence. For the **effective** date, see the historical comment for P.L. 96-589 under Code Sec. 370(a). Prior to amendment, the last sentence of Code Sec. 351(a) provided:

"For purposes of this section, stock or securities issued for services shall not be considered as issued in return for property."

• 1976, Tax Reform Act of 1976 (P.L. 94-455)

P.L. 94-455, §1901(a)(48)(A):

Struck out "(including, in the case of transfers made on or before June 30, 1967, an investment company" after "transferred to a corporation" in Code Sec. 351(a). **Effective** for transfers of property occurring after 10-4-76.

• 1966, Foreign Investors Tax Act of 1966 (P.L. 89-809)

P.L. 89-809, §203(a):

Amended the first sentence of Code Sec. 351(a) by inserting "(including, in the case of transfers made on or before June 30, 1967, an investment company)" immediately after "to a corporation". **Effective** with respect to transfers of property to investment companies, whether made before, on, or after 11-13-66, the date of enactment.

[Sec. 351(b)]

(b) RECEIPT OF PROPERTY.—If subsection (a) would apply to an exchange but for the fact that there is received, in addition to the stock permitted to be received under subsection (a), other property or money, then—

(1) gain (if any) to such recipient shall be recognized, but not in excess of—

(A) the amount of money received, plus

(B) the fair market value of such other property received; and

(2) no loss to such recipient shall be recognized.

Amendments

• 1989, Omnibus Budget Reconciliation Act of 1989 (P.L. 101-239)

P.L. 101-239, §7203(b)(1):

Amended Code Sec. 351(b) by striking "or securities" after "stock". **Effective**, generally, for transfers after 10-2-89, in tax years ending after such date. For exceptions, see Act Sec. 7203(c)(2)-(3) in the amendment notes following Code Sec. 351(a).

[Sec. 351(c)]

(c) SPECIAL RULES WHERE DISTRIBUTION TO SHAREHOLDERS.—

(1) IN GENERAL.—In determining control for purposes of this section, the fact that any corporate transferor distributes part or all of the stock in the corporation which it receives in the exchange to its shareholders shall not be taken into account.

(2) SPECIAL RULE FOR SECTION 355.—If the requirements of section 355 (or so much of section 356 as relates to section 355) are met with respect to a distribution described in paragraph (1), then, solely for purposes of determining the tax treatment of the transfers of property to the controlled corporation by the distributing corporation, the fact that the shareholders of the distributing corporation dispose of part or all of the distributed stock, or the fact that the corporation whose stock was distributed issues additional stock, shall not be taken into account in determining control for purposes of this section.

Amendments

• 1998, Tax and Trade Relief Extension Act of 1998 (P.L. 105-277)

P.L. 105-277, §4003(f)(1):

Amended Code Sec. 351(c)(2) by inserting ", or the fact that the corporation whose stock was distributed issues additional stock," after "dispose of part or all of the distributed stock". **Effective** as if included in the provision of P.L. 105-34 to which it relates [generally **effective** for transfers after 8-5-97.—CCH].

• 1998, IRS Restructuring and Reform Act of 1998 (P.L. 105-206)

P.L. 105-206, §6010(c)(3)(A):

Amended Code Sec. 351(c). **Effective** as if included in the provision of P.L. 105-34 to which it relates [generally **effective** for transfers after 8-5-97.—CCH]. Prior to amendment, Code Sec. 351(c) read as follows:

(c) SPECIAL RULES WHERE DISTRIBUTION TO SHAREHOLDERS.—In determining control for purposes of this section—

(1) the fact that any corporate transferor distributes part or all of the stock in the corporation which it receives in the exchange to its shareholders shall not be taken into account, and

(2) if the requirements of section 355 are met with respect to such distribution, the shareholders shall be treated as in control of such corporation immediately after the exchange if the shareholders own (immediately after the distribution) stock possessing—

(A) more than 50 percent of the total combined voting power of all classes of stock of such corporation entitled to vote, and

(B) more than 50 percent of the total value of shares of all classes of stock of such corporation.

• 1997, Taxpayer Relief Act of 1997 (P.L. 105-34)

P.L. 105-34, §1012(c)(1):

Amended Code Sec. 351(c). **Effective**, generally, for transfers after 8-5-97. For a transition rule, see Act Sec.1012(d)(3), below. Prior to amendment, Code Sec. 351(c) read as follows:

(c) SPECIAL RULE.—In determining control, for purposes of this section, the fact that any corporate transferor distributes part or all of the stock which it receives in the exchange to its shareholders shall not be taken into account.

P.L. 105-34, §1012(d)(3), provides:

(3) TRANSITION RULE.—The amendments made by this section shall not apply to any distribution pursuant to a plan (or series of related transactions) which involves an acquisition described in section 355(e)(2)(A)(ii) of the Internal Revenue Code of 1986 (or, in the case of the amendments made by subsection (c), any transfer) occurring after April 16, 1997, if such acquisition or transfer is—

(A) made pursuant to an agreement which was binding on such date and at all times thereafter,

(B) described in a ruling request submitted to the Internal Revenue Service on or before such date, or

(C) described on or before such date in a public announcement or in a filing with the Securities and Exchange Commission required solely by reason of the acquisition or transfer.

This paragraph shall not apply to any agreement, ruling request, or public announcement or filing unless it identifies the acquirer of the distributing corporation or any controlled corporation, or the transferee, whichever is applicable.

[Sec. 351(d)]

(d) SERVICES, CERTAIN INDEBTEDNESS, AND ACCRUED INTEREST NOT TREATED AS PROPERTY.—For purposes of this section, stock issued for—

(1) services,

(2) indebtedness of the transferee corporation which is not evidenced by a security, or

(3) interest on indebtedness of the transferee corporation which accrued on or after the beginning of the transferor's holding period for the debt,

shall not be considered as issued in return for property.

Amendments

• 1989, Omnibus Budget Reconciliation Act of 1989 (P.L. 101-239)

P.L. 101-239, §7203(b)(1):

Amended Code Sec. 351(d) by striking "or securities" after "stock". **Effective**, generally, for transfers after 10-2-89, in tax years ending after such date. For exceptions, see Act Sec. 7203(c)(2)-(3) in the amendment notes following Code Sec. 351(a).

• 1980, Bankruptcy Tax Act of 1980 (P.L. 96-589)

P.L. 96-589, §5(e)(1):

Amended Code Sec. 351 by striking out subsection (d) and inserting in lieu thereof a new subsection (d). For the **effective** date, see the historical comment for P.L. 96-589 under Code Sec. 370(a). Prior to amendment, Code Sec. 351(d) provided:

"(d) EXCEPTION.—This section shall not apply to a transfer of property to an investment company."

• 1976, Tax Reform Act of 1976 (P.L. 94-455)

P.L. 94-455, §1901(a)(48)(B):

Amended Code Sec. 351(d). **Effective** for transfers of property occurring after 10-4-76. Prior to amendment, Code Sec. 351(d) read as follows:

(d) APPLICATION OF JUNE 30, 1967, DATE.—For purposes of this section, if, in connection with the transaction, a registration statement is required to be filed with the Securities and Exchange Commission, a transfer of property to an investment company shall be treated as made on or before June 30, 1967, only if—

(1) such transfer is made on or before such date,

(2) the registration statement was filed with the Securities and Exchange Commission before January 1, 1967, and the aggregate issue price of the stock and securities of the investment company which are issued in the transaction does not exceed the aggregate amount therefor specified in the registration statement as of the close of December 31, 1966, and

(3) the transfer of property to the investment company in the transaction includes only property deposited before May 1, 1967.

• 1966, Foreign Investors Tax Act of 1966 (P.L. 89-809)

P.L. 89-809, §203(b):

Redesignated former Code Sec. 351(d) as Sec. 351(e) and added new Code Sec. 351(d). **Effective** for transfers of property to investment companies, whether made on, before, or after 11-13-66, the date of enactment.

[Sec. 351(e)]

(e) EXCEPTIONS.—This section shall not apply to—

(1) TRANSFER OF PROPERTY TO AN INVESTMENT COMPANY.—A transfer of property to an investment company. For purposes of the preceding sentence, the determination of whether a company is an investment company shall be made—

(A) by taking into account all stock and securities held by the company, and

(B) by treating as stock and securities—

(i) money,

(ii) stocks and other equity interests in a corporation, evidences of indebtedness, options, forward or futures contracts, notional principal contracts and derivatives,

(iii) any foreign currency,

(iv) any interest in a real estate investment trust, a common trust fund, a regulated investment company, a publicly-traded partnership (as defined in section 7704(b)) or any other equity interest (other than in a corporation) which pursuant to its terms or any other arrangement is readily convertible into, or exchangeable for, any asset described in any preceding clause, this clause or clause (v) or (viii),

(v) except to the extent provided in regulations prescribed by the Secretary, any interest in a precious metal, unless such metal is used or held in the active conduct of a trade or business after the contribution,

(vi) except as otherwise provided in regulations prescribed by the Secretary, interests in any entity if substantially all of the assets of such entity consist (directly or indirectly) of any assets described in any preceding clause or clause (viii),

(vii) to the extent provided in regulations prescribed by the Secretary, any interest in any entity not described in clause (vi), but only to the extent of the value of such interest that is attributable to assets listed in clauses (i) through (v) or clause (viii), or

(viii) any other asset specified in regulations prescribed by the Secretary.

The Secretary may prescribe regulations that, under appropriate circumstances, treat any asset described in clauses (i) through (v) as not so listed.

(2) TITLE 11 OR SIMILAR CASE.—A transfer of property of a debtor pursuant to a plan while the debtor is under the jurisdiction of a court in a title 11 or similar case (within the meaning of section 368(a)(3)(A)), to the extent that the stock received in the exchange is used to satisfy the indebtedness of such debtor.

Amendments

• 1997, Taxpayer Relief Act of 1997 (P.L. 105-34)

P.L. 105-34, §1002(a):

Amended Code Sec. 351(e)(1) by adding at the end new material. **Effective**, generally, for transfers after 6-8-97, in tax years ending after such date. For a special rule, see Act Sec. 1002(b)(2), below. Prior to amendment, Code Sec. 351(e)(1) read as follows:

(1) TRANSFER OF PROPERTY TO AN INVESTMENT COMPANY.—A transfer of property to an investment company.

P.L. 105-34, §1002(b)(2), provides:

(2) BINDING CONTRACTS.—The amendment made by subsection (a) shall not apply to any transfer pursuant to a written binding contract in effect on June 8, 1997, and at all times thereafter before such transfer if such contract provides for the transfer of a fixed amount of property.

• 1990, Omnibus Budget Reconciliation Act of 1990 (P.L. 101-508)

P.L. 101-508, §11704(a)(3):

Amended Code Sec. 351(e)(2) by striking "are used" and inserting "is used". **Effective** 11-5-90.

• 1989, Omnibus Budget Reconciliation Act of 1989 (P.L. 101-239)

P.L. 101-239, §7203(b)(1):

Amended Code Sec. 351(e)(2) by striking "or securities" after "stock". **Effective**, generally, for transfers after 10-2-89, in tax years ending after such date. For exceptions, see Act Sec. 7203(c)(2)-(3) in the amendment notes following Code Sec. 351(a).

• 1980, Bankruptcy Tax Act of 1980 (P.L. 96-589)

P.L. 96-589, §5(e)(1):

Redesignated former Code Sec. 351(e) as Code Sec. 351(f) and added a new Code Sec. 351(e). For the **effective** date, see the historical comment for P.L. 96-589 under Code Sec. 370(a).

[Sec. 351(f)]

(f) TREATMENT OF CONTROLLED CORPORATION.—If—

(1) property is transferred to a corporation (hereinafter in this subsection referred to as the "controlled corporation") in an exchange with respect to which gain or loss is not recognized (in whole or in part) to the transferor under this section, and

(2) such exchange is not in pursuance of a plan of reorganization,

section 311 shall apply to any transfer in such exchange by the controlled corporation in the same manner as if such transfer were a distribution to which subpart A of part I applies.

Amendments

• 1988, Technical and Miscellaneous Revenue Act of 1988 (P.L. 100-647)

P.L. 100-647, §1018(d)(5)(G):

Amended Code Sec. 351 by redesignating subsection (f) as subsection (g) and inserting after subsection (e) new subsection (f). **Effective** with respect to transfers on or after 6-21-88.

[Sec. 351(g)]

(g) NONQUALIFIED PREFERRED STOCK NOT TREATED AS STOCK.—

(1) IN GENERAL.—In the case of a person who transfers property to a corporation and receives nonqualified preferred stock—

(A) subsection (a) shall not apply to such transferor, and

(B) if (and only if) the transferor receives stock other than nonqualified preferred stock—

(i) subsection (b) shall apply to such transferor; and

(ii) such nonqualified preferred stock shall be treated as other property for purposes of applying subsection (b).

(2) NONQUALIFIED PREFERRED STOCK.—For purposes of paragraph (1)—

(A) IN GENERAL.—The term "nonqualified preferred stock" means preferred stock if—

(i) the holder of such stock has the right to require the issuer or a related person to redeem or purchase the stock,

(ii) the issuer or a related person is required to redeem or purchase such stock,

(iii) the issuer or a related person has the right to redeem or purchase the stock and, as of the issue date, it is more likely than not that such right will be exercised, or

(iv) the dividend rate on such stock varies in whole or in part (directly or indirectly) with reference to interest rates, commodity prices, or other similar indices.

(B) LIMITATIONS.—Clauses (i), (ii), and (iii) of subparagraph (A) shall apply only if the right or obligation referred to therein may be exercised within the 20-year period beginning on the issue date of such stock and such right or obligation is not subject to a contingency which, as of the issue date, makes remote the likelihood of the redemption or purchase.

(C) EXCEPTIONS FOR CERTAIN RIGHTS OR OBLIGATIONS.—

(i) IN GENERAL.—A right or obligation shall not be treated as described in clause (i), (ii), or (iii) of subparagraph (A) if—

(I) it may be exercised only upon the death, disability, or mental incompetency of the holder, or

(II) in the case of a right or obligation to redeem or purchase stock transferred in connection with the performance of services for the issuer or a related person (and which represents reasonable compensation), it may be exercised only upon the holder's separation from service from the issuer or a related person.

(ii) EXCEPTION.—Clause (i)(I) shall not apply if the stock relinquished in the exchange, or the stock acquired in the exchange is in—

(I) a corporation if any class of stock in such corporation or a related party is readily tradable on an established securities market or otherwise, or

(II) any other corporation if such exchange is part of a transaction or series of transactions in which such corporation is to become a corporation described in subclause (I).

(3) DEFINITIONS.—For purposes of this subsection—

(A) PREFERRED STOCK.—The term "preferred stock" means stock which is limited and preferred as to dividends and does not participate in corporate growth to any significant extent. Stock shall not be treated as participating in corporate growth to any significant extent unless there is a real and meaningful likelihood of the shareholder actually participating in the earnings and growth of the corporation. If there is not a real and meaningful likelihood that dividends beyond any limitation or preference will actually be paid, the possibility of such payments will be disregarded in determining whether stock is limited and preferred as to dividends.

(B) RELATED PERSON.—A person shall be treated as related to another person if they bear a relationship to such other person described in section 267(b) or 707(b).

(4) REGULATIONS.—The Secretary may prescribe such regulations as may be necessary or appropriate to carry out the purposes of this subsection and sections 354(a)(2)(C), 355(a)(3)(D), and 356(e). The Secretary may also prescribe regulations, consistent with the treatment under this subsection and such sections, for the treatment of nonqualified preferred stock under other provisions of this title.

Amendments

•2005, Gulf Opportunity Zone Act of 2005 (P.L. 109-135)

P.L. 109-135, §403(kk):

Amended Code Sec. 351(g)(3)(A) by adding at the end a new sentence. **Effective** as if included in the provision of the American Jobs Creation Act of 2004 (P.L. 108-357) to which it relates [**effective** for transactions after 5-14-2003.—CCH].

• 2004, American Jobs Creation Act of 2004 (P.L. 108-357)

P.L. 108-357, §899(a):

Amended Code Sec. 351(g)(3)(A) by adding at the end a new sentence. **Effective** for transactions after 5-14-2003.

• 1998, IRS Restructuring and Reform Act of 1998 (P.L. 105-206)

P.L. 105-206, §6010(e)(1):

Amended Code Sec. 351(g)(1) by adding "and" at the end of subparagraph (A) and by striking subparagraphs (B) and (C) and inserting a new subparagraph (B). **Effective** as if included in the provision of P.L. 105-34 to which it relates [generally **effective** for transactions after 6-8-97.—CCH]. Prior to being stricken, Code Sec. 351(g)(1)(B)-(C) read as follows:

(B) subsection (b) shall apply to such transferor, and

(C) such nonqualified preferred stock shall be treated as other property for purposes of applying subsection (b).

• 1997, Taxpayer Relief Act of 1997 (P.L. 105-34)

P.L. 105-34, §1014(a):

Act Sec. 1014(a) amended Code Sec. 351 by redesignating subsection (g) as subsection (h), and by inserting after subsection (f) a new subsection (g). **Effective**, generally, for transactions after 6-8-97. For a transition rule, see Act Sec. 1014(f)(2), below.

P.L. 105-34, §1014(f)(2), provides:

(2) TRANSITION RULE.—The amendments made by this section shall not apply to any transaction after June 8, 1997, if such transaction is—

(A) made pursuant to a written agreement which was binding on such date and at all times thereafter,

(B) described in a ruling request submitted to the Internal Revenue Service on or before such date, or

(C) described on or before such date in a public announcement or in a filing with the Securities and Exchange Commission required solely by reason of the transaction.

[Sec. 351(h)]

(h) CROSS REFERENCES.—

(1) For special rule where another party to the exchange assumes a liability, see section 357.

(2) For the basis of stock or property received in an exchange to which this section applies, see sections 358 and 362.

(3) For special rule in the case of an exchange described in this section but which results in a gift, see section 2501 and following.

(4) For special rule in the case of an exchange described in this section but which has the effect of the payment of compensation by the corporation or by a transferor, see section 61(a)(1).

(5) For coordination of this section with section 304, see section 304(b)(3).

Amendments

• 2002, Job Creation and Worker Assistance Act of 2002 (P.L. 107-147)

P.L. 107-147, §417(9):

Amended Code Sec. 351(h)(1) by inserting a comma after "liability". **Effective** 3-9-2002.

• 1999, Miscellaneous Trade and Technical Corrections Act of 1999 (P.L. 106-36)

P.L. 106-36, §3001(d)(1):

Amended Code Sec. 351(h)(1) by striking ", or acquires property subject to a liability," following "liability". **Effective** for transfers after 10-18-98.

• 1997, Taxpayer Relief Act of 1997 (P.L. 105-34)

P.L. 105-34, §1014(a):

Amended Code Sec. 351 by redesignating subsection (g) as subsection (h). **Effective**, generally, for transactions after 6-8-97. For a transitional rule, see Act Sec. 1014(f)(2) in the amendment notes following Code Sec. 351(g).

• 1989, Omnibus Budget Reconciliation Act of 1989 (P.L. 101-239)

P.L. 101-239, §7203(b)(2):

Amended Code Sec. 351(g)(2) by striking "stock, securities, or property" and inserting "stock or property". **Effective**, generally, for transfers after 10-2-89, in tax years ending after such date. For exceptions, see Act Sec. 7203(c)(2)-(3) in the amendment notes following Code Sec. 351(a).

• 1988, Technical and Miscellaneous Revenue Act of 1988 (P.L. 100-647)

P.L. 100-647, §1018(d)(5)(G):

Amended Code Sec. 351 by redesignating subsection (f) as subsection (g). **Effective** with respect to transfers on or after 6-21-88.

• 1982, Tax Equity and Fiscal Responsibility Act of 1982 (P.L. 97-248)

P.L. 97-248, §226(a)(1)(B):

Added Code Sec. 351(f)(5). **Effective** for transfers occurring after 8-31-82, in tax years ending after such date. See P.L. 97-248, Act Sec. 226(c)(2), in the amendment notes under Code Sec. 306(c) for an exception.

• 1980, Bankruptcy Tax Act of 1980 (P.L. 96-589)

P.L. 96-589, §5(e)(1):

Redesignated former Code Sec. 351(e) as Code Sec. 351(f). For the **effective** date, see the historical comment for P.L. 96-589 under Code Sec. 370(a).

• 1966, Foreign Investors Tax Act of 1966 (P.L. 89-809)

P.L. 89-809, §203(b):

Redesignated former Code Sec. 351(d) as Sec. 351(e). **Effective** for transfers of property to investment companies, whether made before, on, or after 11-13-66, the date of enactment.

Subpart B—Effects on Shareholders and Security Holders

[Sec. 354]

SEC. 354. EXCHANGES OF STOCK AND SECURITIES IN CERTAIN REORGANIZATIONS.

[Sec. 354(a)]

(a) GENERAL RULE.—

(1) IN GENERAL.—No gain or loss shall be recognized if stock or securities in a corporation a party to a reorganization are, in pursuance of the plan of reorganization, exchanged solely for stock or securities in such corporation or in another corporation a party to the reorganization.

(2) LIMITATIONS.—

(A) EXCESS PRINCIPAL AMOUNT.—Paragraph (1) shall not apply if—

(i) the principal amount of any such securities received exceeds the principal amount of any such securities surrendered, or

(ii) any such securities are received and no such securities are surrendered.

(B) PROPERTY ATTRIBUTABLE TO ACCRUED INTEREST.—Neither paragraph (1) nor so much of section 356 as relates to paragraph (1) shall apply to the extent that any stock (including nonqualified preferred stock, as defined in section 351(g)(2)), securities, or other property received is attributable to interest which has accrued on securities on or after the beginning of the holder's holding period.

(C) NONQUALIFIED PREFERRED STOCK.—

(i) IN GENERAL.—Nonqualified preferred stock (as defined in section 351(g)(2)) received in exchange for stock other than nonqualified preferred stock (as so defined) shall not be treated as stock or securities.

(ii) RECAPITALIZATIONS OF FAMILY-OWNED CORPORATIONS.—

(I) IN GENERAL.—Clause (i) shall not apply in the case of a recapitalization under section 368(a)(1)(E) of a family-owned corporation.

(II) FAMILY-OWNED CORPORATION.—For purposes of this clause, except as provided in regulations, the term "family-owned corporation" means any corporation which is described in clause (i) of section 447(d)(2)(C) throughout the 8-year period beginning on the date which is 5 years before the date of the recapitalization. For purposes of the preceding sentence, stock shall not be treated as owned by a family member during any period described in section 355(d)(6)(B).

(III) EXTENSION OF STATUTE OF LIMITATIONS.—The statutory period for the assessment of any deficiency attributable to a corporation failing to be a family-owned corporation shall not expire before the expiration of 3 years after the date the Secretary is notified by the corporation (in such manner as the Secretary may prescribe) of such failure, and such deficiency may be assessed before the expiration of such 3-year period notwithstanding the provisions of any other law or rule of law which would otherwise prevent such assessment.

(3) CROSS REFERENCES.—

(A) For treatment of the exchange if any property is received which is not permitted to be received under this subsection (including nonqualified preferred stock and an excess principal amount of securities received over securities surrendered, but not including property to which paragraph (2)(B) applies), see section 356.

(B) For treatment of accrued interest in the case of an exchange described in paragraph (2)(B), see section 61.

Amendments

• 1998, IRS Restructuring and Reform Act of 1998 (P.L. 105-206)

P.L. 105-206, §6010(e)(2):

Amended Code Sec. 354(a)(2)(C)(ii) by adding at the end a new subclause (III). **Effective** as if included in the provision of P.L. 105-34 to which it relates [generally **effective** for transactions after 6-8-97.—CCH].

• 1997, Taxpayer Relief Act of 1997 (P.L. 105-34)

P.L. 105-34, §1014(b):

Amended Code Sec. 354(a)(2) by adding at the end a new subparagraph (C). **Effective**, generally, for transactions after 6-8-97. For a transitional rule, see Act Sec. 1014(f)(2), below.

P.L. 105-34, §1014(e)(1):

Amended Code Sec. 354(a)(2)(B) by inserting "(including nonqualified preferred stock, as defined in section 351(g)(2))" after "stock". **Effective**, generally, for transactions after 6-8-97. For a transitional rule, see Act Sec. 1014(f)(2), below.

P.L. 105-34, §1014(e)(2):

Amended Code Sec. 354(a)(3)(A) by inserting "nonqualified preferred stock and" after "including". **Effective**, generally, for transactions after 6-8-97. For a transitional rule, see Act Sec. 1014(f)(2), below.

P.L. 105-34, §1014(f)(2), provides:

(2) TRANSITION RULE.—The amendments made by this section shall not apply to any transaction after June 8, 1997, if such transaction is—

(A) made pursuant to a written agreement which was binding on such date and at all times thereafter,

(B) described in a ruling request submitted to the Internal Revenue Service on or before such date, or

(C) described on or before such date in a public announcement or in a filing with the Securities and Exchange Commission required solely by reason of the transaction.

• 1980, Bankruptcy Tax Act of 1980 (P.L. 96-589)

P.L. 96-589, §4(e)(1):

Amended Code Sec. 354(a) by striking out paragraphs (2) and (3) and inserting in lieu thereof new paragraphs (2) and (3). Prior to amendment, Code Sec. 354(a)(2) and (3) provided:

"(2) LIMITATION.—Paragraph (1) shall not apply if—

(A) the principal amount of any such securities received exceeds the principal amount of any such securities surrendered, or

(B) any such securities are received and no such securities are surrendered.

(3) CROSS REFERENCE.—

For treatment of the exchange if any property is received which is not permitted to be received under this subsection (including an excess principal amount of securities received over securities surrendered), see section 356."

P.L. 96-589, §7(c), (f)-(g), provides:

"(c) FOR SECTION 4 (RELATING TO CORPORATE REORGANIZATION PROVISIONS).—

"(1) IN GENERAL.—The amendments made by section 4 shall apply to any bankruptcy case or similar judicial proceeding commencing after December 31, 1980.

"(2) EXCHANGES OF PROPERTY FOR ACCRUED INTEREST.—The amendments made by subsection (e) of section 4 (relating to treatment of property attributable to accrued interest) shall also apply to any exchange—

"(A) which occurs after December 31, 1980, and

"(B) which does not occur in a bankruptcy case or similar judicial proceeding (or in a proceeding under the Bankruptcy Act) commenced on or before December 31, 1980.

* * *

"(f) ELECTION TO SUBSTITUTE SEPTEMBER 30, 1979, FOR DECEMBER 31, 1980.—

"(1) IN GENERAL.—The debtor (or debtors) in a bankruptcy case or similar judicial proceeding may (with the approval of the court) elect to apply subsections (a), (c), and (d) by substituting `September 30, 1979' for `December 31, 1980' each place it appears in such subsections.

"(2) EFFECT OF ELECTION.—Any election made under paragraph (1) with respect to any proceeding shall apply to all parties to the proceeding.

"(3) REVOCATION ONLY WITH CONSENT.—Any election under this subsection may be revoked only with the consent of the Secretary of the Treasury or his delegate.

"(4) TIME AND MANNER OF ELECTION.—Any election under this subsection shall be made at such time, and in such manner, as the Secretary of the Treasury or his delegate may by regulations prescribe.

"(g) DEFINITIONS.—For purposes of this section—

"(1) BANKRUPTCY CASE.—The term `bankruptcy case' means any case under title 11 of the United States Code (as recodified by Public Law 95-598).

"(2) SIMILAR JUDICIAL PROCEEDING.—The term `similar judicial proceeding' means a receivership, foreclosure, or similar proceeding in a Federal or State court (as modified by section 368(a)(3)(D) of the Internal Revenue Code of 1954)."

[Sec. 354(b)]

(b) EXCEPTION.—

(1) IN GENERAL.—Subsection (a) shall not apply to an exchange in pursuance of a plan of reorganization within the meaning of subparagraph (D) or (G) of section 368(a)(1), unless—

(A) the corporation to which the assets are transferred acquires substantially all of the assets of the transferor of such assets; and

(B) the stock, securities, and other properties received by such transferor, as well as the other properties of such transferor, are distributed in pursuance of the plan of reorganization.

(2) CROSS REFERENCE.—

For special rules for certain exchanges in pursuance of plans of reorganization within the meaning of subparagraph (D) or (G) of section 368(a)(1), see section 355.

Amendments

• 1980, Bankruptcy Tax Act of 1980 (P.L. 96-589)

P.L. 96-589, §4(h):

Amended Code Sec. 354(b), paragraphs (1) and (2), by striking out "section 368(a)(1)(D)" and inserting in lieu thereof "subparagraph (D) or (G) of section 368(a)(1)". For the **effective** date of this provision, see the historical comment for P.L. 96-589 under Code Sec. 370(a).

[Sec. 354(c)]

(c) CERTAIN RAILROAD REORGANIZATIONS.—Notwithstanding any other provision of this subchapter, subsection (a)(1) (and so much of section 356 as relates to this section) shall apply with respect to a plan of reorganization (whether or not a reorganization within the meaning of section 368(a)) for a railroad confirmed under section 1173 of title 11 of the United States Code, as being in the public interest.

Amendments

• 1995, ICC Termination Act of 1995 (P.L. 104-88)

P.L. 104-88, §304(c):

Act Sec. 304(c) amended Code Sec. 354(c) by striking "or approved by the Interstate Commerce Commission under subchapter IV of chapter 113 of title 49," after "United States Code,". **Effective** 1-1-96.

• 1980, Bankruptcy Tax Act of 1980 (P.L. 96-589)

P.L. 96-589, §6(i)(2):

Amended Code Sec. 354(c) by striking out "approved by the Interstate Commerce Commission under section 77 of the Bankruptcy Act, or" and inserting in lieu thereof "confirmed under section 1173 of title 11 of the United States Code, or approved by the Interstate Commerce Commission". **Effective** 10-1-79 but inapplicable to any proceeding under the Bankruptcy Act commenced before that date.

• 1978 (P.L. 95-473)

P.L. 95-473, §2(a)(2)(F):

Amended Code Sec. 354(c) by striking out "section 20b of the Interstate Commerce Act" and substituting "subchapter IV of chapter 113 of title 49". **Effective** 10-17-78.

[Sec. 354(d)—Repealed]

Amendments

• 1990, Omnibus Budget Reconciliation Act of 1990 (P.L. 101-508)

P.L. 101-508, §11801(c)(8)(D):

Repealed Code Sec. 354(d). **Effective** 11-5-90. Prior to repeal, Code Sec. 354(d) read as follows:

(d) EXCHANGES UNDER THE FINAL SYSTEM PLAN FOR CONRAIL.—No gain or loss shall be recognized if stock or securities in a corporation are, in pursuance of an exchange to which paragraph (1) or (2) of section 374(c) applies, exchanged solely for stock of the Consolidated Rail Corporation, securities of such Corporation, certificates of value of the United States Railway Association, or any combination thereof.

P.L. 101-508, §11821(b), provides:

(b) SAVINGS PROVISION.—If—

(1) any provision amended or repealed by this part applied to—

(A) any transaction occurring before the date of the enactment of this Act,

(B) any property acquired before such date of enactment, or

(C) any item of income, loss, deduction, or credit taken into account before such date of enactment, and

(2) the treatment of such transaction, property, or item under such provision would (without regard to the amendments made by this part) affect liability for tax for periods ending after such date of enactment,

nothing in the amendments made by this part shall be construed to affect the treatment of such transaction, property, or item for purposes of determining liability for tax for periods ending after such date of enactment.

• 1976 (P.L. 94-253)

P.L. 94-253, §1:

Added subsection (d). **Effective** for tax years ending after 3-31-76.

[Sec. 355]

SEC. 355. DISTRIBUTION OF STOCK AND SECURITIES OF A CONTROLLED CORPORATION.

[Sec. 355(a)]

(a) EFFECT ON DISTRIBUTEES.—

(1) GENERAL RULE.—If—

(A) a corporation (referred to in this section as the "distributing corporation")

(i) distributes to a shareholder, with respect to its stock, or

(ii) distributes to a security holder, in exchange for its securities,

solely stock or securities of a corporation (referred to in this section as "controlled corporation") which it controls immediately before the distribution,

(B) the transaction was not used principally as a device for the distribution of the earnings and profits of the distributing corporation or the controlled corporation or both (but the mere fact that subsequent to the distribution stock or securities in one or more of such corporations are sold or exchanged by all or some of the distributees (other than pursuant to an arrangement negotiated or agreed upon prior to such distribution) shall not be construed to mean that the transaction was used principally as such a device),

(C) the requirements of subsection (b) (relating to active businesses) are satisfied, and

(D) as part of the distribution, the distributing corporation distributes—

(i) all of the stock and securities in the controlled corporation held by it immediately before the distribution, or

(ii) an amount of stock in the controlled corporation constituting control within the meaning of section 368(c), and it is established to the satisfaction of the Secretary that the retention by the distributing corporation of stock (or stock and securities) in the controlled corporation was not in pursuance of a plan having as one of its principal purposes the avoidance of Federal income tax,

then no gain or loss shall be recognized to (and no amount shall be includible in the income of) such shareholder or security holder on the receipt of such stock or securities.

(2) NON PRO RATA DISTRIBUTIONS, ETC.—Paragraph (1) shall be applied without regard to the following:

(A) whether or not the distribution is pro rata with respect to all of the shareholders of the distributing corporation,

(B) whether or not the shareholder surrenders stock in the distributing corporation, and

(C) whether or not the distribution is in pursuance of a plan of reorganization (within the meaning of section 368(a)(1)(D)).

(3) LIMITATIONS.—

(A) EXCESS PRINCIPAL AMOUNT.—Paragraph (1) shall not apply if—

(i) the principal amount of the securities in the controlled corporation which are received exceeds the principal amount of the securities which are surrendered in connection with such distribution, or

(ii) securities in the controlled corporation are received and no securities are surrendered in connection with such distribution.

(B) STOCK ACQUIRED IN TAXABLE TRANSACTIONS WITHIN 5 YEARS TREATED AS BOOT.—For purposes of this section (other than paragraph (1)(D) of this subsection) and so much of section 356 as relates to this section, stock of a controlled corporation acquired by the distributing corporation by reason of any transaction—

(i) which occurs within 5 years of the distribution of such stock, and

(ii) in which gain or loss was recognized in whole or in part,

shall not be treated as stock of such controlled corporation, but as other property.

(C) PROPERTY ATTRIBUTABLE TO ACCRUED INTEREST.—Neither paragraph (1) nor so much of section 356 as relates to paragraph (1) shall apply to the extent that any stock (including nonqualified preferred stock, as defined in section 351(g)(2)), securities, or other property received is attributable to interest which has accrued on securities on or after the beginning of the holder's holding period.

(D) NONQUALIFIED PREFERRED STOCK.—Nonqualified preferred stock (as defined in section 351(g)(2)) received in a distribution with respect to stock other than nonqualified preferred stock (as so defined) shall not be treated as stock or securities.

(4) CROSS REFERENCES.—

(A) For treatment of the exchange if any property is received which is not permitted to be received under this subsection (including nonqualified preferred stock and an excess principal amount of securities received over securities surrendered, but not including property to which paragraph (3)(C) applies), see section 356.

(B) For treatment of accrued interest in the case of an exchange described in paragraph (3)(C), see section 61.

Amendments

• 1997, Taxpayer Relief Act of 1997 (P.L. 105-34)

P.L. 105-34, §1014(c):

Amended Code Sec. 355(a)(3) by adding at the end a new subparagraph (D). **Effective**, generally, for transactions after 6-8-97. For a transitional rule, see Act Sec. 1014(f)(2), below.

P.L. 105-34, §1014(e)(1):

Amended Code Sec. 355(a)(3)(C) by inserting "(including nonqualified preferred stock, as defined in section 351(g)(2))" after "stock". **Effective**, generally, for transactions after 6-8-97. For a transitional rule, see Act Sec. 1014(f)(2), below.

P.L. 105-34, §1014(e)(2):

Amended Code Sec. 355(a)(4)(A) by inserting "nonqualified preferred stock and" after "including". **Effective**, generally, for transactions after 6-8-97. For a transitional rule, see Act Sec. 1014(f)(2), below.

P.L. 105-34, §1014(f)(2), provides:

(2) TRANSITION RULE.—The amendments made by this section shall not apply to any transaction after June 8, 1997, if such transaction is—

(A) made pursuant to a written agreement which was binding on such date and at all times thereafter,

(B) described in a ruling request submitted to the Internal Revenue Service on or before such date, or

(C) described on or before such date in a public announcement or in a filing with the Securities and Exchange Commission required solely by reason of the transaction.

• 1980, Bankruptcy Tax Act of 1980 (P.L. 96-589)

P.L. 96-589, §4(e)(2):

Amended Code Sec. 355(a) by striking out paragraphs (3) and (4), and inserting in lieu thereof new paragraphs (3) and (4). Prior to amendment, Code Sec. 355(a)(3) and (4) provided:

"(3) LIMITATION.—Paragraph (1) shall not apply if—

"(A) the principal amount of the securities in the controlled corporation which are received exceeds the principal amount of the securities which are surrendered in connection with such distribution, or

"(B) securities in the controlled corporation are received and no securities are surrendered in connection with such distribution.

For purposes of this section (other than paragraph (1)(D) of this subsection) and so much of section 356 as relates to this section, stock of a controlled corporation acquired by the distributing corporation by reason of any transaction which occurs within 5 years of the distribution of such stock and in which gain or loss was recognized in whole or in part, shall not be treated as stock of such controlled corporation, but as other property.

"(4) CROSS REFERENCE.—

For treatment of the distribution if any property is received which is not permitted to be received under this subsection (including an excess principal amount of securities received over securities surrendered), see section 356."

P.L. 96-589, §7(c), (f)-(g), provides:

"(c) FOR SECTION 4 (RELATING TO CORPORATE REORGANIZATION PROVISIONS).—

"(1) IN GENERAL.—The amendments made by section 4 shall apply to any bankruptcy case or similar judicial proceeding commencing after December 31, 1980.

"(2) EXCHANGE OF PROPERTY FOR ACCRUED INTEREST.—The amendments made by subsection (e) of section 4 (relating to treatment of property attributable to accrued interest) shall also apply to any exchange—

"(A) which occurs after December 31, 1980, and

"(B) which does not occur in a bankruptcy case or similar judicial proceeding (or in a proceeding under the Bankruptcy Act) commenced on or before December 31, 1980.

***

"(f) ELECTION TO SUBSTITUTE SEPTEMBER 30, 1979, FOR DECEMBER 31, 1980.—

"(1) IN GENERAL.—The debtor (or debtors) in a bankruptcy case or similar judicial proceeding may (with the approval of the court) elect to apply subsections (a), (c), and (d) by substituting 'September 30, 1979' for 'December 31, 1980' each place it appears in such subsections.

"(2) EFFECT OF ELECTION.—Any election made under paragraph (1) with respect to any proceeding shall apply to all parties to the proceeding.

"(3) REVOCATION ONLY WITH CONSENT.—Any election under this subsection may be revoked only with the consent of the Secretary of the Treasury or his delegate.

"(4) TIME AND MANNER OF ELECTION.—Any election under this subsection shall be made at such time, and in such manner, as the Secretary of the Treasury or his delegate may by regulations prescribe.

"(g) DEFINITIONS.—For purposes of this section—

"(1) BANKRUPTCY CASE.—The term 'bankruptcy case' means any case under title 11 of the United States Code (as recodified by Public Law 95-598).

"(2) SIMILAR JUDICIAL PROCEEDING.—The term 'similar judicial proceeding' means a receivership, foreclosure, or similar proceeding in a Federal or State court (as modified by section 368(a)(3)(D) of the Internal Revenue Code of 1954)."

• 1976, Tax Reform Act of 1976 (P.L. 94-455)

P.L. 94-455, §1906(b)(13)(A):

Amended 1954 Code by substituting "Secretary" for "Secretary or his delegate" each place it appeared. **Effective** 2-1-77.

[Sec. 355(b)]

(b) REQUIREMENTS AS TO ACTIVE BUSINESS.—

(1) IN GENERAL.—Subsection (a) shall apply only if either—

(A) the distributing corporation, and the controlled corporation (or, if stock of more than one controlled corporation is distributed, each of such corporations), is engaged immediately after the distribution in the active conduct of a trade or business, or

(B) immediately before the distribution, the distributing corporation had no assets other than stock or securities in the controlled corporations and each of the controlled corporations is engaged immediately after the distribution in the active conduct of a trade or business.

(2) DEFINITION.—For purposes of paragraph (1), a corporation shall be treated as engaged in the active conduct of a trade or business if and only if—

(A) it is engaged in the active conduct of a trade or business,

(B) such trade or business has been actively conducted throughout the 5-year period ending on the date of the distribution,

(C) such trade or business was not acquired within the period described in subparagraph (B) in a transaction in which gain or loss was recognized in whole or in part, and

(D) control of a corporation which (at the time of acquisition of control) was conducting such trade or business—

(i) was not acquired by any distributee corporation directly (or through 1 or more corporations, whether through the distributing corporation or otherwise) within the period described in subparagraph (B) and was not acquired by the distributing corporation directly (or through 1 or more corporations) within such period, or

(ii) was so acquired by any such corporation within such period, but, in each case in which such control was so acquired, it was so acquired, only by reason of transactions in which gain or loss was not recognized in whole or in part, or only by reason of such transactions combined with acquisitions before the beginning of such period.

For purposes of subparagraph (D), all distributee corporations which are members of the same affiliated group (as defined in section 1504(a) without regard to section 1504(b)) shall be treated as 1 distributee corporation.

(3) SPECIAL RULES FOR DETERMINING ACTIVE CONDUCT IN THE CASE OF AFFILIATED GROUPS.—

(A) IN GENERAL.—For purposes of determining whether a corporation meets the requirements of paragraph (2)(A), all members of such corporation's separate affiliated group shall be treated as one corporation.

(B) SEPARATE AFFILIATED GROUP.—For purposes of this paragraph, the term "separate affiliated group" means, with respect to any corporation, the affiliated group which would be determined under section 1504(a) if such corporation were the common parent and section 1504(b) did not apply.

(C) TREATMENT OF TRADE OR BUSINESS CONDUCTED BY ACQUIRED MEMBER.—If a corporation became a member of a separate affiliated group as a result of one or more transactions in which gain or loss was recognized in whole or in part, any trade or business conducted by such corporation (at the time that such corporation became such a member) shall be treated for purposes of paragraph (2) as acquired in a transaction in which gain or loss was recognized in whole or in part.

(D) REGULATIONS.—The Secretary shall prescribe such regulations as are necessary or appropriate to carry out the purposes of this paragraph, including regulations which provide for the proper application of subparagraphs (B), (C), and (D) of paragraph (2), and modify the application of subsection (a)(3)(B), in connection with the application of this paragraph.

Amendments

• 2007, Tax Technical Corrections Act of 2007 (P.L. 110-172)

P.L. 110-172, §4(b)(1):

Amended Code Sec. 355(b)(2)(A). **Effective** generally for distributions made after 5-17-2006. For a transition rule, see Act Sec. 4(d)(2)(B)-(D), below. Prior to amendment, Code Sec. 355(b)(2)(A) read as follows:

(A) it is engaged in the active conduct of a trade or business, or substantially all of its assets consist of stock and securities of a corporation controlled by it (immediately after the distribution) which is so engaged,

P.L. 110-172, §4(b)(2):

Amended Code Sec. 355(b)(3). **Effective** generally for distributions made after 5-17-2006. For a transition rule, see Act Sec. 4(d)(2)(B)-(D), below. Prior to amendment, Code Sec. 355(b)(3) read as follows:

(3) SPECIAL RULE RELATING TO ACTIVE BUSINESS REQUIREMENT.—

(A) IN GENERAL.—In the case of any distribution made after the date of the enactment of this paragraph, a corporation shall be treated as meeting the requirement of paragraph (2)(A) if and only if such corporation is engaged in the active conduct of a trade or business.

(B) AFFILIATED GROUP RULE.—For purposes of subparagraph (A), all members of such corporation's separate affiliated group shall be treated as one corporation. For purposes of the preceding sentence, a corporation's separate affiliated group is the affiliated group which would be determined under section 1504(a) if such corporation were the common parent and section 1504(b) did not apply.

(C) TRANSITION RULE.—Subparagraph (A) shall not apply to any distribution pursuant to a transaction which is—

(i) made pursuant to an agreement which was binding on the date of the enactment of this paragraph and at all times thereafter,

(ii) described in a ruling request submitted to the Internal Revenue Service on or before such date, or

(iii) described on or before such date in a public announcement or in a filing with the Securities and Exchange Commission.

The preceding sentence shall not apply if the distributing corporation elects not to have such sentence apply to distributions of such corporation. Any such election, once made, shall be irrevocable.

(D) SPECIAL RULE FOR CERTAIN PREENACTMENT DISTRIBUTIONS.—For purposes of determining the continued qualification under paragraph (2)(A) of distributions made on or before the date of the enactment of this paragraph as a result of an acquisition, disposition, or other restructuring after such date, such distribution shall be treated as made on the date of such acquisition, disposition, or restructuring for purposes of applying subparagraphs (A) through (C) of this paragraph.

P.L. 110-172, §4(b)(3), provides:

(3) The Internal Revenue Code of 1986 shall be applied and administered as if the amendments made by section 202 of the Tax Increase Prevention and Reconciliation Act of 2005 and by section 410 of division A of the Tax Relief and Health Care Act of 2006 had never been enacted.

P.L. 110-172, §4(d)(2)(B)-(D), provides:

(B) TRANSITION RULE.—The amendments made by subsection (b) shall not apply to any distribution pursuant to a transaction which is—

(i) made pursuant to an agreement which was binding on May 17, 2006, and at all times thereafter,

(ii) described in a ruling request submitted to the Internal Revenue Service on or before such date, or

(iii) described on or before such date in a public announcement or in a filing with the Securities and Exchange Commission.

(C) ELECTION OUT OF TRANSITION RULE.—Subparagraph (B) shall not apply if the distributing corporation elects not to have such subparagraph apply to distributions of such corporation. Any such election, once made, shall be irrevocable.

(D) SPECIAL RULE FOR CERTAIN PRE-ENACTMENT DISTRIBUTIONS.—For purposes of determining the continued qualification under section 355(b)(2)(A) of the Internal Revenue Code of 1986 of distributions made on or before May 17, 2006, as a result of an acquisition, disposition, or other restructuring after such date, such distribution shall be treated as made on the date of such acquisition, disposition, or restructuring for purposes of applying subparagraphs (A) through (C) of this paragraph. The preceding sentence shall only apply with respect to the corporation that undertakes such acquisition, disposition, or other restructuring, and only if such application results in continued qualification under section 355(b)(2)(A) of such Code.

• 2006, Tax Relief and Health Care Act of 2006 (P.L. 109-432)

P.L. 109-432, Division A, §410(a) [but see P.L. 110-172, §4(b)(3), above]:

Amended Code Sec. 355(b)(3) by striking "and on or before December 31, 2010" after "this paragraph" in subparagraph (A) and after "such date" in subparagraph (D). **Effective** as if included in section 202 of the Tax Increase Prevention and Reconciliation Act of 2005 (P.L. 109-222) [**effective** 5-17-2006.—CCH].

• 2006, Tax Increase Prevention and Reconciliation Act of 2005 (P.L. 109-222)

P.L. 109-222, §202 [but see P.L. 110-172, §4(b)(3), above]:

Amended Code Sec. 355(b) by adding at the end a new paragraph (3). **Effective** 5-17-2006.

• 1988, Technical and Miscellaneous Revenue Act of 1988 (P.L. 100-647)

P.L. 100-647, §2004(k)(1):

Amended Code Sec. 355(b)(2)(D) by striking out clauses (i) and (ii) and inserting in lieu thereof new clauses (i) and (ii). **Effective** as if included in the provision of P.L. 100-203 to which it relates. Prior to amendment, Code Sec. 355(b)(2)(D)(i) and (ii) read as follows:

(i) was not acquired by any distributee corporation directly (or through 1 or more corporations, whether through the distributing corporation or otherwise) within the period described in subparagraph (B), or

(ii) was so acquired such distributee corporation within such period, but such control was so acquired only by reason of transactions in which gain or loss was not recognized in whole or in part, or only by reason of such transactions combined with acquisitions before the beginning of such period.

• 1987, Revenue Act of 1987 (P.L. 100-203)

P.L. 100-203, §10223(b)(1)-(3):

Amended Code Sec. 355(b)(2)(D) by amending clause (i) by striking out "by another corporation" in clause (ii) and inserting in lieu thereof "such distributee corporation", and by adding at the end thereof a new sentence. For the **effective** date, see Act Sec. 10223(d), as amended by P.L. 100-647, §2004(k)(3)-(4), below. Prior to amendment, Code Sec. 355(b)(2)(D)(i) read as follows:

(i) was not acquired directly (or through one or more corporations) by another corporation within the period described in subparagraph (B), or

P.L. 100-203, §10223(d), as amended by P.L. 100-647, §2004(k)(3)-(4), provides:

(d) EFFECTIVE DATES.—

(1) IN GENERAL.—The amendments made by this section shall apply to any distribution after December 15, 1987.

(2) EXCEPTIONS.—

(A) DISTRIBUTIONS.—The amendments made by this section shall not apply to any distribution after December 15, 1987, and before January 1, 1993, if—

(i) 80 percent or more of the stock of the distributing corporation was acquired by the distibutee before December 15, 1987, or

(ii) 80 percent or more of the stock of the distributing corporation was acquired by the distributee before January 1, 1989, pursuant to a binding written contract or tender offer in effect on December 15, 1987.

For purposes of the preceding sentence, stock described in section 1504(a)(4) of the Internal Revenue Code of 1986 shall not be taken into account.

(B) SECTION 304 TRANSFERS.—The amendment made by subsection (c) shall not apply to any transfer after December 15, 1987, and on or before March 31, 1988, if such transfer is—

(i) between corporations which are members of the same affiliated group on December 15, 1987, or

(ii) between corporations which become members of the same affiliated group, pursuant to a binding written contract or tender offer in effect on December 15, 1987.

(C) DISTRIBUTIONS COVERED BY PRIOR TRANSITION RULE.—The amendments made by this section shall not apply to any distribution to which the amendments made by subtitle D of title VI of the Tax Reform Act of 1986 do not apply.

(D) TREATMENT OF CERTAIN MEMBERS OF AFFILIATED GROUP.—

(i) IN GENERAL.—For purposes of subparagraph (A), all corporations which were in existence on the designated date and were members of the same affiliated group which included the distributees on such date shall be treated as 1 distributee.

(ii) LIMITATION TO STOCK HELD ON DESIGNATED DATE.—Clause (i) shall not exempt any distribution from the amendments made by this section if such distribution is with respect to stock not held by the distributee (determined without regard to clause (i)) on the designated date directly or indirectly through a corporation which goes out of existence in the transaction.

(iii) DESIGNATED DATE.—For purposes of this subparagraph, the term "designated date" means the later of—

(I) December 15, 1987, or

(II) the date on which the acquisition meeting the requirements of subparagraph (A) occurred.

[Sec. 355(c)]

(c) TAXABILITY OF CORPORATION ON DISTRIBUTION.—

(1) IN GENERAL.—Except as provided in paragraph (2), no gain or loss shall be recognized to a corporation on any distribution to which this section (or so much of section 356 as relates to this section) applies and which is not in pursuance of a plan of reorganization.

(2) DISTRIBUTION OF APPRECIATED PROPERTY.—

(A) IN GENERAL.—If—

(i) in a distribution referred to in paragraph (1), the corporation distributes property other than qualified property, and

(ii) the fair market value of such property exceeds its adjusted basis (in the hands of the distributing corporation),

then gain shall be recognized to the distributing corporation as if such property were sold to the distributee at its fair market value.

(B) QUALIFIED PROPERTY.—For purposes of subparagraph (A), the term "qualified property" means any stock or securities in the controlled corporation.

(C) TREATMENT OF LIABILITIES.—If any property distributed in the distribution referred to in paragraph (1) is subject to a liability or the shareholder assumes a liability of the distributing corporation in connection with the distribution, then, for purposes of subparagraph (A), the fair market value of such property shall be treated as not less than the amount of such liability.

(3) COORDINATION WITH SECTIONS 311 AND 336(a).—Sections 311 and 336(a) shall not apply to any distribution referred to in paragraph (1).

Amendments

• 1990, Omnibus Budget Reconciliation Act of 1990 (P.L. 101-508)

P.L. 101-508, §11321(a):

Amended Code Sec. 355 by striking subsection (c) (as amended by Act Sec. 11702(e)(2)) and inserting a new subsection (c). **Effective** for distributions after 10-9-90. For exceptions, see Act Sec. 11321(c)(2)-(3), below. Prior to amendment subsection (c) read as follows:

(c) TAXABILITY OF CORPORATION ON DISTRIBUTION.—

(1) IN GENERAL.—Except as provided in paragraph (2), no gain or loss shall be recognized to a corporation on any distribution to which this section (or so much of section 356 as relates to this section) applies and which is not in pursuance of a plan of reorganization.

(2) DISTRIBUTION OF APPRECIATED PROPERTY.—

(A) IN GENERAL.—If—

(i) in a distribution referred to in paragraph (1), the corporation distributes property other than stock or securities in the controlled corporation, and

(ii) the fair market value of such property exceeds its adjusted basis (in the hands of the distributing corporation),

then gain shall be recognized to the distributing corporation as if such property were sold to the distributee at its fair market value.

(B) TREATMENT OF LIABILITIES.—If any property distributed in the distribution referred to in paragraph (1) is subject to a liability or the shareholder assumes a liability of the distributing corporation in connection with the distribution, then, for purposes of subparagraph (A), the fair market value of such property shall be treated as not less than the amount of such liability.

(3) COORDINATION WITH SECTIONS 311 AND 336(a).—Sections 311 and 336(a) shall not apply to any distribution referred to in paragraph (1).

P.L. 101-508, §11321(c)(2)-(3), provides:

(2) BINDING CONTRACT EXCEPTION.—The amendments made by this section shall not apply to any distribution pursuant to a written binding contract in effect on October 9, 1990, and at all times thereafter before such distribution.

(3) TRANSITIONAL RULES.—For purposes of subparagraphs (A) and (B) of section 355(d)(3) of the Internal Revenue Code of 1986 (as amended by subsection (a)), an acquisition shall be treated as occurring on or before October 9, 1990, if—

(A) such acquisition is pursuant to a written binding contract in effect on October 9, 1990, and at all times thereafter before such acquisition,

(B) such acquisition is pursuant to a transaction which was described in documents filed with the Securities and Exchange Commission on or before October 9, 1990, or

(C) such acquisition is pursuant to a transaction—

(i) the material terms of which were described in a written public announcement on or before October 9, 1990,

(ii) which was the subject of a prior filing with the Securities and Exchange Commission, and

(iii) which is the subject of a subsequent filing with the Securities and Exchange Commission before January 1, 1991.

P.L. 101-508, §11702(e)(2):

Amended Code Sec. 355(c). **Effective** as if included in the provision of P.L. 100-647 to which it relates. Prior to amendment, subsection (c) read as follows:

(c) TAXABILITY OF CORPORATION ON DISTRIBUTION.—Section 311 shall apply to any distribution—

(1) to which this section (or so much of section 356 as relates to this section) applies, and

(2) which is not in pursuance of a plan of reorganization,

in the same manner as if such distribution were a distribution to which subpart A of part 1 applies; except that subsection (b) of section 311 shall not apply to any distribution of stock or securities in the controlled corporation.

• 1988, Technical and Miscellaneous Revenue Act of 1988 (P.L. 100-647)

P.L. 100-647, §1018(d)(5)(C):

Amended Code Sec. 355 by adding at the end thereof new subsection (c). **Effective** as if included in the provision of P.L. 99-514 to which it relates.

[Sec. 355(d)]

(d) RECOGNITION OF GAIN ON CERTAIN DISTRIBUTIONS OF STOCK OR SECURITIES IN CONTROLLED CORPORATION.—

(1) IN GENERAL.—In the case of a disqualified distribution, any stock or securities in the controlled corporation shall not be treated as qualified property for purposes of subsection (c)(2) of this section or section 361(c)(2).

(2) DISQUALIFIED DISTRIBUTION.—For purposes of this subsection, the term "disqualified distribution" means any distribution to which this section (or so much of section 356 as relates to this section) applies if, immediately after the distribution—

(A) any person holds disqualified stock in the distributing corporation which constitutes a 50-percent or greater interest in such corporation, or

(B) any person holds disqualified stock in the controlled corporation (or, if stock of more than 1 controlled corporation is distributed, in any controlled corporation) which constitutes a 50-percent or greater interest in such corporation.

(3) DISQUALIFIED STOCK.—For purposes of this subsection, the term "disqualified stock" means—

(A) any stock in the distributing corporation acquired by purchase after October 9, 1990, and during the 5-year period ending on the date of the distribution, and

(B) any stock in any controlled corporation—

(i) acquired by purchase after October 9, 1990, and during the 5-year period ending on the date of the distribution, or

(ii) received in the distribution to the extent attributable to distributions on—

(I) stock described in subparagraph (A), or

(II) any securities in the distributing corporation acquired by purchase after October 9, 1990, and during the 5-year period ending on the date of the distribution.

(4) 50-PERCENT OR GREATER INTEREST.—For purposes of this subsection, the term "50-percent or greater interest" means stock possessing at least 50 percent of the total combined voting power of all classes of stock entitled to vote or at least 50 percent of the total value of shares of all classes of stock.

(5) PURCHASE.—For purposes of this subsection—

(A) IN GENERAL.—Except as otherwise provided in this paragraph, the term "purchase" means any acquisition but only if—

(i) the basis of the property acquired in the hands of the acquirer is not determined (I) in whole or in part by reference to the adjusted basis of such property in the hands of the person from whom acquired, or (II) under section 1014(a), and

(ii) the property is not acquired in an exchange to which section 351, 354, 355, or 356 applies.

(B) CERTAIN SECTION 351 EXCHANGES TREATED AS PURCHASES.—The term "purchase" includes any acquisition of property in an exchange to which section 351 applies to the extent such property is acquired in exchange for—

(i) any cash or cash item,

(ii) any marketable stock or security, or

(iii) any debt of the transferor.

(C) CARRYOVER BASIS TRANSACTIONS.—If—

(i) any person acquires property from another person who acquired such property by purchase (as determined under this paragraph with regard to this subparagraph), and

(ii) the adjusted basis of such property in the hands of such acquirer is determined in whole or in part by reference to the adjusted basis of such property in the hands of such other person,

such acquirer shall be treated as having acquired such property by purchase on the date it was so acquired by such other person.

(6) SPECIAL RULE WHERE SUBSTANTIAL DIMINUTION OF RISK.—

(A) IN GENERAL.—If this paragraph applies to any stock or securities for any period, the running of any 5-year period set forth in subparagraph (A) or (B) of paragraph (3) (whichever applies) shall be suspended during such period.

(B) PROPERTY TO WHICH SUSPENSION APPLIES.—This paragraph applies to any stock or securities for any period during which the holder's risk of loss with respect to such stock or securities, or with respect to any portion of the activities of the corporation, is (directly or indirectly) substantially diminished by—

(i) an option,

(ii) a short sale,

(iii) any special class of stock, or

(iv) any other device or transaction.

(7) AGGREGATION RULES.—

(A) IN GENERAL.—For purposes of this subsection, a person and all persons related to such person (within the meaning of section 267(b) or 707(b)(1)) shall be treated as one person.

(B) PERSONS ACTING PURSUANT TO PLANS OR ARRANGEMENTS.—If two or more persons act pursuant to a plan or arrangement with respect to acquisitions of stock or securities in the distributing corporation or controlled corporation, such persons shall be treated as one person for purposes of this subsection.

(8) ATTRIBUTION FROM ENTITIES.—

(A) IN GENERAL.—Paragraph (2) of section 318(a) shall apply in determining whether a person holds stock or securities in any corporation (determined by substituting "10 percent" for "50 percent" in subparagraph (C) of such paragraph (2) and by treating any reference to stock as including a reference to securities).

(B) DEEMED PURCHASE RULE.—If—

(i) any person acquires by purchase an interest in any entity, and

(ii) such person is treated under subparagraph (A) as holding any stock or securities by reason of holding such interest,

such stock or securities shall be treated as acquired by purchase by such person on the later of the date of the purchase of the interest in such entity or the date such stock or securities are acquired by purchase by such entity.

(9) REGULATIONS.—The Secretary shall prescribe such regulations as may be necessary to carry out the purposes of this subsection, including—

(A) regulations to prevent the avoidance of the purposes of this subsection through the use of related persons, intermediaries, pass-thru entities, options, or other arrangements, and

(B) regulations modifying the definition of the term "purchase".

Amendments

• 1996, Small Business Job Protection Act of 1996 (P.L. 104-188)

P.L. 104-188, §1704(t)(31):

Amended Code Sec. 355(d)(7)(A) by inserting "section" before "267(b)". **Effective** 8-20-96.

• 1990, Omnibus Budget Reconciliation Act of 1990 (P.L. 101-508)

P.L. 101-508, §11321(a):

Amended Code Sec. 355 by inserting a new subsection (d). **Effective** for distributions after 10-9-90. For exceptions, see Act Sec. 11321(c)(2)-(3), below.

P.L. 101-508, §11321(c)(2)-(3), provides:

(2) BINDING CONTRACT EXCEPTION.—The amendments made by this section shall not apply to any distribution pursuant to a written binding contract in effect on October 9, 1990, and at all times thereafter before such distribution.

(3) TRANSITIONAL RULES.—For purposes of subparagraphs (A) and (B) of section 355(d)(3) of the Internal Revenue Code of 1986 (as amended by subsection (a)), an acquisition shall be treated as occurring on or before October 9, 1990, if—

(A) such acquisition is pursuant to a written binding contract in effect on October 9, 1990, and at all times thereafter before such acquisition,

(B) such acquisition is pursuant to a transaction which was described in documents filed with the Securities and Exchange Commission on or before October 9, 1990, or

(C) such acquisition is pursuant to a transaction—

(i) the material terms of which were described in a written public announcement on or before October 9, 1990,

(ii) which was the subject of a prior filing with the Securities and Exchange Commission, and

(iii) which is the subject of a subsequent filing with the Securities and Exchange Commission before January 1, 1991.

[Sec. 355(e)]

(e) RECOGNITION OF GAIN ON CERTAIN DISTRIBUTIONS OF STOCK OR SECURITIES IN CONNECTION WITH ACQUISITIONS.—

(1) GENERAL RULE.—If there is a distribution to which this subsection applies, any stock or securities in the controlled corporation shall not be treated as qualified property for purposes of subsection (c)(2) of this section or section 361(c)(2).

(2) DISTRIBUTIONS TO WHICH SUBSECTION APPLIES.—

(A) IN GENERAL.—This subsection shall apply to any distribution—

(i) to which this section (or so much of section 356 as relates to this section) applies, and

(ii) which is part of a plan (or series of related transactions) pursuant to which 1 or more persons acquire directly or indirectly stock representing a 50-percent or greater interest in the distributing corporation or any controlled corporation.

(B) PLAN PRESUMED TO EXIST IN CERTAIN CASES.—If 1 or more persons acquire directly or indirectly stock representing a 50-percent or greater interest in the distributing corporation or any controlled corporation during the 4-year period beginning on the date which is 2 years before the date of the distribution, such acquisition shall be treated as pursuant to a plan described in subparagraph (A)(ii) unless it is established that the distribution and the acquisition are not pursuant to a plan or series of related transactions.

(C) CERTAIN PLANS DISREGARDED.—A plan (or series of related transactions) shall not be treated as described in subparagraph (A)(ii) if, immediately after the completion of such plan or transactions, the distributing corporation and all controlled corporations are members of a single affiliated group (as defined in section 1504 without regard to subsection (b) thereof).

(D) COORDINATION WITH SUBSECTION (d).—This subsection shall not apply to any distribution to which subsection (d) applies.

(3) SPECIAL RULES RELATING TO ACQUISITIONS.—

(A) CERTAIN ACQUISITIONS NOT TAKEN INTO ACCOUNT.—Except as provided in regulations, the following acquisitions shall not be taken into account in applying paragraph (2)(A)(ii):

(i) The acquisition of stock in any controlled corporation by the distributing corporation.

(ii) The acquisition by a person of stock in any controlled corporation by reason of holding stock or securities in the distributing corporation.

(iii) The acquisition by a person of stock in any successor corporation of the distributing corporation or any controlled corporation by reason of holding stock or securities in such distributing or controlled corporation.

(iv) The acquisition of stock in the distributing corporation or any controlled corporation to the extent that the percentage of stock owned directly or indirectly in such corporation by each person owning stock in such corporation immediately before the acquisition does not decrease.

This subparagraph shall not apply to any acquisition if the stock held before the acquisition was acquired pursuant to a plan (or series of related transactions) described in paragraph (2)(A)(ii).

(B) ASSET ACQUISITIONS.—Except as provided in regulations, for purposes of this subsection, if the assets of the distributing corporation or any controlled corporation are acquired by a successor corporation in a transaction described in subparagraph (A), (C), or (D) of section 368(a)(1) or any other transaction specified in regulations by the Secretary, the shareholders (immediately before the acquisition) of the corporation acquiring such assets shall be treated as acquiring stock in the corporation from which the assets were acquired.

(4) DEFINITION AND SPECIAL RULES.—For purposes of this subsection—

(A) 50-PERCENT OR GREATER INTEREST.—The term "50-percent or greater interest" has the meaning given such term by subsection (d)(4).

(B) DISTRIBUTIONS IN TITLE 11 OR SIMILAR CASE.—Paragraph (1) shall not apply to any distribution made in a title 11 or similar case (as defined in section 368(a)(3)).

(C) AGGREGATION AND ATTRIBUTION RULES.—

(i) AGGREGATION.—The rules of paragraph (7)(A) of subsection (d) shall apply.

(ii) ATTRIBUTION.—Section 318(a)(2) shall apply in determining whether a person holds stock or securities in any corporation. Except as provided in regulations, section 318(a)(2)(C) shall be applied without regard to the phrase "50 percent or more in value" for purposes of the preceding sentence.

(D) SUCCESSORS AND PREDECESSORS.—For purposes of this subsection, any reference to a controlled corporation or a distributing corporation shall include a reference to any predecessor or successor of such corporation.

(E) STATUTE OF LIMITATIONS.—If there is a distribution to which paragraph (1) applies—

(i) the statutory period for the assessment of any deficiency attributable to any part of the gain recognized under this subsection by reason of such distribution shall not expire before the expiration of 3 years from the date the Secretary is notified by the taxpayer (in such manner as the Secretary may by regulations prescribe) that such distribution occurred, and

(ii) such deficiency may be assessed before the expiration of such 3-year period notwithstanding the provisions of any other law or rule of law which would otherwise prevent such assessment.

(5) REGULATIONS.—The Secretary shall prescribe such regulations as may be necessary to carry out the purposes of this subsection, including regulations—

(A) providing for the application of this subsection where there is more than 1 controlled corporation,

(B) treating 2 or more distributions as 1 distribution where necessary to prevent the avoidance of such purposes, and

(C) providing for the application of rules similar to the rules of subsection (d)(6) where appropriate for purposes of paragraph (2)(B).

Amendments

• 1998, IRS Restructuring and Reform Act of 1998 (P.L. 105-206)

P.L. 105-206, §6010(c)(2)(A)-(B):

Amended Code Sec. 355(e)(3)(A) by striking "shall not be treated as described in" and inserting "shall not be taken into account in applying", and by striking clause (iv) and inserting a new clause (iv). **Effective** as if included in the provision of P.L. 105-34 to which it relates [generally **effective** for distributions after 4-16-97.—CCH]. Prior to being stricken, Code Sec. 355(e)(3)(A)(iv) read as follows:

(iv) The acquisition of stock in a corporation if shareholders owning directly or indirectly stock possessing—

(I) more than 50 percent of the total combined voting power of all classes of stock entitled to vote, and

(II) more than 50 percent of the total value of shares of all classes of stock,

in the distributing corporation or any controlled corporation before such acquisition own directly or indirectly stock possessing such vote and value in such distributing or controlled corporation after such acquisition.

• 1997, Taxpayer Relief Act of 1997 (P.L. 105-34)

P.L. 105-34, §1012(a):

Amended Code Sec. 355 by adding at the end a new subsection (e). **Effective** for distributions after 4-16-97, only if pursuant to a plan (or series of related transactions) which involves an acquisition described in Code Sec. 355(e)(2)(A)(ii) occurring after such date [**effective** date changed by P.L. 105-206, §6010(c)(1)]. For a transitional rule, see Act Sec. 1012(d)(3), below.

P.L. 105-34, §1012(d)(3), provides:

(3) TRANSITION RULE.—The amendments made by this section shall not apply to any distribution pursuant to a plan (or series of related transactions) which involves an acquisition described in section 355(e)(2)(A)(ii) of the Internal Revenue Code of 1986 (or, in the case of the amendments made by subsection (c), any transfer) occurring after April 16, 1997, if such acquisition or transfer is—

(A) made pursuant to an agreement which was binding on such date and at all times thereafter,

(B) described in a ruling request submitted to the Internal Revenue Service on or before such date, or

(C) described on or before such date in a public announcement or in a filing with the Securities and Exchange Commission required solely by reason of the acquisition or transfer.

This paragraph shall not apply to any agreement, ruling request, or public announcement or filing unless it identifies the acquirer of the distributing corporation or any controlled corporation, or the transferee, whichever is applicable.

[Sec. 355(f)]

(f) SECTION NOT TO APPLY TO CERTAIN INTRAGROUP DISTRIBUTIONS.—Except as provided in regulations, this section (or so much of section 356 as relates to this section) shall not apply to the distribution of stock from 1 member of an affiliated group (as defined in section 1504(a)) to another member of such group if such distribution is part of a plan (or series of related transactions) described in subsection (e)(2)(A)(ii) (determined after the application of subsection (e)).

Amendments

• 1997, Taxpayer Relief Act of 1997 (P.L. 105-34)

P.L. 105-34, §1012(b)(1):

Amended Code Sec. 355, as amended by Act Sec. 1012(a), by adding at the end a new subsection (f). **Effective**, generally, for distributions after 4-16-97 [**effective** date changed by P.L. 105-206, §6010(c)(1)]. For a transitional rule, see Act Sec. 1012(d)(3) in the amendment notes following Code Sec. 355(e).

[Sec. 355(g)]

(g) SECTION NOT TO APPLY TO DISTRIBUTIONS INVOLVING DISQUALIFIED INVESTMENT CORPORATIONS.—

(1) IN GENERAL.—This section (and so much of section 356 as relates to this section) shall not apply to any distribution which is part of a transaction if—

(A) either the distributing corporation or controlled corporation is, immediately after the transaction, a disqualified investment corporation, and

(B) any person holds, immediately after the transaction, a 50-percent or greater interest in any disqualified investment corporation, but only if such person did not hold such an interest in such corporation immediately before the transaction.

(2) DISQUALIFIED INVESTMENT CORPORATION.—For purposes of this subsection—

(A) IN GENERAL.—The term "disqualified investment corporation" means any distributing or controlled corporation if the fair market value of the investment assets of the corporation is—

(i) in the case of distributions after the end of the 1-year period beginning on the date of the enactment of this subsection, $2/3$ or more of the fair market value of all assets of the corporation, and

(ii) in the case of distributions during such 1-year period, $3/4$ or more of the fair market value of all assets of the corporation.

(B) INVESTMENT ASSETS.—

(i) IN GENERAL.—Except as otherwise provided in this subparagraph, the term "investment assets" means—

(I) cash,

(II) any stock or securities in a corporation,

(III) any interest in a partnership,

(IV) any debt instrument or other evidence of indebtedness,

(V) any option, forward or futures contract, notional principal contract, or derivative,

(VI) foreign currency, or

(VII) any similar asset.

(ii) EXCEPTION FOR ASSETS USED IN ACTIVE CONDUCT OF CERTAIN FINANCIAL TRADES OR BUSINESSES.—Such term shall not include any asset which is held for use in the active and regular conduct of—

(I) a lending or finance business (within the meaning of section 954(h)(4)),

(II) a banking business through a bank (as defined in section 581), a domestic building and loan association (within the meaning of section 7701(a)(19)), or any similar institution specified by the Secretary, or

(III) an insurance business if the conduct of the business is licensed, authorized, or regulated by an applicable insurance regulatory body.

This clause shall only apply with respect to any business if substantially all of the income of the business is derived from persons who are not related (within the meaning of section 267(b) or 707(b)(1)) to the person conducting the business.

(iii) EXCEPTION FOR SECURITIES MARKED TO MARKET.—Such term shall not include any security (as defined in section 475(c)(2)) which is held by a dealer in securities and to which section 475(a) applies.

(iv) STOCK OR SECURITIES IN A 20-PERCENT CONTROLLED ENTITY.—

(I) IN GENERAL.—Such term shall not include any stock and securities in, or any asset described in subclause (IV) or (V) of clause (i) issued by, a corporation which is a 20-percent controlled entity with respect to the distributing or controlled corporation.

(II) LOOK-THRU RULE.—The distributing or controlled corporation shall, for purposes of applying this subsection, be treated as owning its ratable share of the assets of any 20-percent controlled entity.

(III) 20-PERCENT CONTROLLED ENTITY.—For purposes of this clause, the term "20-percent controlled entity" means, with respect to any distributing or controlled corporation, any corporation with respect to which the distributing or controlled corporation owns directly or indirectly stock meeting the requirements of section 1504(a)(2), except that such section shall be applied by substituting "20 percent" for "80 percent" and without regard to stock described in section 1504(a)(4).

(v) INTERESTS IN CERTAIN PARTNERSHIPS.—

(I) IN GENERAL.—Such term shall not include any interest in a partnership, or any debt instrument or other evidence of indebtedness, issued by the partnership, if 1 or more of the trades or businesses of the partnership are (or, without regard to the 5-year requirement under subsection (b)(2)(B), would be) taken into account by the distributing or controlled corporation, as the case may be, in determining whether the requirements of subsection (b) are met with respect to the distribution.

(II) LOOK-THRU RULE.—The distributing or controlled corporation shall, for purposes of applying this subsection, be treated as owning its ratable share of the assets of any partnership described in subclause (I).

(3) 50-PERCENT OR GREATER INTEREST.—For purposes of this subsection—

(A) IN GENERAL.—The term "50-percent or greater interest" has the meaning given such term by subsection (d)(4).

(B) ATTRIBUTION RULES.—The rules of section 318 shall apply for purposes of determining ownership of stock for purposes of this paragraph.

(4) TRANSACTION.—For purposes of this subsection, the term "transaction" includes a series of transactions.

(5) REGULATIONS.—The Secretary shall prescribe such regulations as may be necessary to carry out, or prevent the avoidance of, the purposes of this subsection, including regulations—

(A) to carry out, or prevent the avoidance of, the purposes of this subsection in cases involving—

(i) the use of related persons, intermediaries, pass-thru entities, options, or other arrangements, and

(ii) the treatment of assets unrelated to the trade or business of a corporation as investment assets if, prior to the distribution, investment assets were used to acquire such unrelated assets,

(B) which in appropriate cases exclude from the application of this subsection a distribution which does not have the character of a redemption which would be treated as a sale or exchange under section 302, and

(C) which modify the application of the attribution rules applied for purposes of this subsection.

Amendments

• 2006, Tax Increase Prevention and Reconciliation Act of 2005 (P.L. 109-222)

P.L. 109-222, §507(a):

Amended Code Sec. 355 by adding at the end a new subsection (g). **Effective**, generally, for distributions after 5-17-2006. For a transition rule, see Act Sec. 507(b)(2), below.

P.L. 109-222, §507(b)(2), provides:

(2) TRANSITION RULE.—The amendments made by this section shall not apply to any distribution pursuant to a transaction which is—

(A) made pursuant to an agreement which was binding on such date of enactment and at all times thereafter,

(B) described in a ruling request submitted to the Internal Revenue Service on or before such date, or

(C) described on or before such date in a public announcement or in a filing with the Securities and Exchange Commission.

[Sec. 356]

SEC. 356. RECEIPT OF ADDITIONAL CONSIDERATION.

[Sec. 356(a)]

(a) GAIN ON EXCHANGES.—

(1) RECOGNITION OF GAIN.—If—

(A) section 354 or 355 would apply to an exchange but for the fact that

(B) the property received in the exchange consists not only of property permitted by section 354 or 355 to be received without the recognition of gain but also of other property or money,

then the gain, if any, to the recipient shall be recognized, but in an amount not in excess of the sum of such money and the fair market value of such other property.

(2) TREATMENT AS DIVIDEND.—If an exchange is described in paragraph (1) but has the effect of the distribution of a dividend (determined with the application of section 318(a)), then there shall be treated as a dividend to each distributee such an amount of the gain recognized under paragraph (1) as is not in excess of his ratable share of the undistributed earnings and profits of the corporation accumulated after February 28, 1913. The remainder, if any, of the gain recognized under paragraph (1) shall be treated as gain from the exchange of property.

Amendments

• 1982, Tax Equity and Fiscal Responsibility Act of 1982 (P.L. 97-248)

P.L. 97-248, §227(b):

Amended paragraph (2) of Code Sec. 356(a) by inserting "(determined with the application of section 318(a))" after "distribution of a dividend". **Effective** for distributions made after 8-31-82, in tax years ending after such date.

[Sec. 356(b)]

(b) ADDITIONAL CONSIDERATION RECEIVED IN CERTAIN DISTRIBUTIONS.—If—

(1) section 355 would apply to a distribution but for the fact that

(2) the property received in the distribution consists not only of property permitted by section 355 to be received without the recognition of gain, but also of other property or money,

then an amount equal to the sum of such money and the fair market value of such other property shall be treated as a distribution of property to which section 301 applies.

[Sec. 356(c)]

(c) LOSS.—If—

(1) section 354 would apply to an exchange, or section 355 would apply to an exchange or distribution, but for the fact that

(2) the property received in the exchange or distribution consists not only of property permitted by section 354 or 355 to be received without the recognition of gain or loss, but also of other property or money,

then no loss from the exchange or distribution shall be recognized.

[Sec. 356(d)]

(d) SECURITIES AS OTHER PROPERTY.—For purposes of this section—

(1) IN GENERAL.—Except as provided in paragraph (2), the term "other property" includes securities.

(2) EXCEPTIONS.—

(A) SECURITIES WITH RESPECT TO WHICH NONRECOGNITION OF GAIN WOULD BE PERMITTED.—The term "other property" does not include securities to the extent that, under section 354 or 355, such securities would be permitted to be received without the recognition of gain.

(B) GREATER PRINCIPAL AMOUNT IN SECTION 354 EXCHANGE.—If—

(i) in an exchange described in section 354 (other than subsection (c) thereof), securities of a corporation a party to the reorganization are surrendered and securities of any corporation a party to the reorganization are received, and

(ii) the principal amount of such securities received exceeds the principal amount of such securities surrendered,

then, with respect to such securities received, the term "other property" means only the fair market value of such excess. For purposes of this subparagraph and subparagraph (C), if no securities are surrendered, the excess shall be the entire principal amount of the securities received.

(C) GREATER PRINCIPAL AMOUNT IN SECTION 355 TRANSACTION.—If, in an exchange or distribution described in section 355, the principal amount of the securities in the controlled corporation which are received exceeds the principal amount of the securities in the distributing corporation which are surrendered, then, with respect to such securities received, the term "other property" means only the fair market value of such excess.

Amendments

• 1990, Omnibus Budget Reconciliation Act of 1990 (P.L. 101-508)

P.L. 101-508, §11801(c)(8)(E):

Amended Code Sec. 356(d)(2)(B)(i) by striking "or (d)" after "subsection (c)". **Effective** on the date of enactment of this Act.

P.L. 101-508, §11821(b)(1)-(2), provides:

(b) SAVINGS PROVISION.—If—

(1) any provision amended or repealed by this part applied to—

(A) any transaction occurring before the date of the enactment of this Act,

(B) any property acquired before such date of enactment, or

(C) any item of income, loss, deduction, or credit taken into account before such date of enactment, and

(2) the treatment of such transaction, property, or item under such provision would (without regard to the amendments made by this part) affect liability for tax for periods ending after such date of enactment,

nothing in the amendments made by this part shall be construed to affect the treatment of such transaction, property, or item for purposes of determining liability for tax for periods ending after such date of enactment.

• 1976 (P.L. 94-253)

P.L. 94-253, §1:

Amended Code Sec. 356(d)(2)(B) by striking out "subsection (c) thereof" and inserting in lieu thereof "subsection (c) or (d) thereof". **Effective** for tax years ending after 3-31-76.

[Sec. 356(e)]

(e) NONQUALIFIED PREFERRED STOCK TREATED AS OTHER PROPERTY.—For purposes of this section—

(1) IN GENERAL.—Except as provided in paragraph (2), the term "other property" includes nonqualified preferred stock (as defined in section 351(g)(2)).

(2) EXCEPTION.—The term "other property" does not include nonqualified preferred stock (as so defined) to the extent that, under section 354 or 355, such preferred stock would be permitted to be received without the recognition of gain.

Amendments

• 1997, Taxpayer Relief Act of 1997 (P.L. 105-34)

P.L. 105-34, §1014(d):

Amended Code Sec. 356 by redesignating subsections (e) and (f) as subsections (f) and (g), respectively, and by inserting after subsection (d) a new subsection (e). **Effective**, generally, for transactions after 6-8-97. For a transition rule, see Act Sec. 1014(f)(2), below.

P.L. 105-34, §1014(f)(2), provides:

(2) TRANSITION RULE.—The amendments made by this section shall not apply to any transaction after June 8, 1997, if such transaction is—

(A) made pursuant to a written agreement which was binding on such date and at all times thereafter,

(B) described in a ruling request submitted to the Internal Revenue Service on or before such date, or

(C) described on or before such date in a public announcement or in a filing with the Securities and Exchange Commission required solely by reason of the transaction.

[Sec. 356(f)]

(f) EXCHANGES FOR SECTION 306 STOCK.—Notwithstanding any other provision of this section, to the extent that any of the other property (or money) is received in exchange for section 306 stock, an amount equal to the fair market value of such other property (or the amount of such money) shall be treated as a distribution of property to which section 301 applies.

Amendments

• 1997, Taxpayer Relief Act of 1997 (P.L. 105-34)

P.L. 105-34, §1014(d):

Amended Code Sec. 356 by redesignating subsection (e) as subsection (f). **Effective**, generally, for transactions after 6-8-97. For a transition rule, see Act Sec. 1014(f)(2) in the amendment notes following Code Sec. 356(e).

[Sec. 356(g)]

(g) TRANSACTIONS INVOLVING GIFT OR COMPENSATION.—For special rules for a transaction described in section 354, 355, or this section, but which—

(1) results in a gift, see section 2501 and following, or

(2) has the effect of the payment of compensation, see section 61(a)(1).

Amendments

• 1997, Taxpayer Relief Act of 1997 (P.L. 105-34)

P.L. 105-34, §1014(d):

Amended Code Sec. 356 by redesignating subsection (f) as subsection (g). **Effective**, generally, for transactions after 6-8-97. For a transition rule, see Act Sec. 1014(f)(2) in the amendment notes following Code Sec. 356(e).

[Sec. 357]

SEC. 357. ASSUMPTION OF LIABILITY.

[Sec. 357(a)]

(a) GENERAL RULE.—Except as provided in subsections (b) and (c), if—

(1) the taxpayer receives property which would be permitted to be received under section 351 or 361 without the recognition of gain if it were the sole consideration, and

(2) as part of the consideration, another party to the exchange assumes a liability of the taxpayer,

then such assumption shall not be treated as money or other property, and shall not prevent the exchange from being within the provisions of section 351 or 361, as the case may be.

Amendments

• 1999, Miscellaneous Trade and Technical Corrections Act of 1999 (P.L. 106-36)

P.L. 106-36, §3001(a)(1):

Amended Code Sec. 357(a)(2) by striking ", or acquires from the taxpayer property subject to a liability" following "taxpayer". **Effective** for transfers after 10-18-98.

P.L. 106-36, §3001(d)(2):

Amended Code Sec. 357(a) by striking " or acquisition" following "then such assumption". **Effective** for transfers after 10-18-98.

• 1990, Omnibus Budget Reconciliation Act of 1990 (P.L. 101-508)

P.L. 101-508, §11801(c)(8)(F)(i):

Amended Code Sec. 357 by striking "351, 361, 371, or 374" each place it appears and inserting "351 or 361". **Effective** 11-5-90.

P.L. 101-508, §11821(b)(1)-(2), provides:

(b) SAVINGS PROVISION.—If—

(1) any provision amended or repealed by this part applied to—

(A) any transaction occurring before the date of the enactment of this Act,

(B) any property acquired before such date of enactment, or

(C) any item of income, loss, deduction, or credit taken into account before such date of enactment, and

(2) the treatment of such transaction, property, or item under such provision would (without regard to the amendments made by this part) affect liability for tax for periods ending after such date of enactment,

nothing in the amendments made by this part shall be construed to affect the treatment of such transaction, property, or item for purposes of determining liability for tax for periods ending after such date of enactment.

• 1956 (P.L. 628, 84th Cong.)

P.L. 628, 84th Cong., §2(1):

Amended subsection (a) by substituting wherever it appears therein "371, or 374" for "or 371".

[Sec. 357(b)]

(b) TAX AVOIDANCE PURPOSE.—

(1) IN GENERAL.—If, taking into consideration the nature of the liability and the circumstances in the light of which the arrangement for the assumption was made, it appears that the principal purpose of the taxpayer with respect to the assumption described in subsection (a)—

(A) was a purpose to avoid Federal income tax on the exchange, or

(B) if not such purpose, was not a bona fide business purpose,

then such assumption (in the total amount of the liability assumed pursuant to such exchange) shall, for purposes of section 351 or 361 (as the case may be), be considered as money received by the taxpayer on the exchange.

(2) BURDEN OF PROOF.—In any suit or proceeding where the burden is on the taxpayer to prove such assumption is not to be treated as money received by the taxpayer, such burden shall

not be considered as sustained unless the taxpayer sustains such burden by the clear preponderance of the evidence.

Amendments

• 1999, Miscellaneous Trade and Technical Corrections Act of 1999 (P.L. 106-36)

P.L. 106-36, §3001(d)(2):

Act Sec. 3001(d)(2) amended Code Sec. 357(b) by striking "or acquisition" following "assumption" each place it appeared. **Effective** for transfers after 10-18-98.

P.L. 106-36, §3001(d)(3):

Act Sec. 3001(d)(3) amended Code Sec. 357(b)(1) by striking "or acquired" following "assumed". **Effective** for transfers after 10-18-98.

• 1990, Omnibus Budget Reconciliation Act of 1990 (P.L. 101-508)

P.L. 101-508, §11801(c)(8)(F)(i):

Act Sec. 11801(c)(8)(F)(i) amended Code Sec. 357 by striking "351, 361, 371, or 374" each place it appears and inserting "351 or 361". **Effective** 11-5-90.

P.L. 101-508, §11821(b)(1)-(2), provides:

(b) SAVINGS PROVISION.—If—

(1) any provision amended or repealed by this part applied to—

(A) any transaction occurring before the date of the enactment of this Act,

(B) any property acquired before such date of enactment, or

(C) any item of income, loss, deduction, or credit taken into account before such date of enactment, and

(2) the treatment of such transaction, property, or item under such provision would (without regard to the amendments made by this part) affect liability for tax for periods ending after such date of enactment,

nothing in the amendments made by this part shall be construed to affect the treatment of such transaction, property, or item for purposes of determining liability for tax for periods ending after such date of enactment.

P.L. 628, 84th Cong., 2d Sess., §2(1):

Amended subsection (b) by substituting "371, or 374" for "or 371". **Effective** 6-29-56.

[Sec. 357(c)]

(c) LIABILITIES IN EXCESS OF BASIS.—

(1) IN GENERAL.—In the case of an exchange—

(A) to which section 351 applies, or

(B) to which section 361 applies by reason of a plan of reorganization within the meaning of section 368(a)(1)(D) with respect to which stock or securities of the corporation to which the assets are transferred are distributed in a transaction which qualifies under section 355,

if the sum of the amount of the liabilities assumed exceeds the total of the adjusted basis of the property transferred pursuant to such exchange, then such excess shall be considered as a gain from the sale or exchange of a capital asset or of property which is not a capital asset, as the case may be.

(2) EXCEPTIONS.—Paragraph (1) shall not apply to any exchange—

(A) to which subsection (b)(1) of this section applies, or

(B) which is pursuant to a plan of reorganization within the meaning of section 368(a)(1)(G) where no former shareholder of the transferor corporation receives any consideration for his stock.

(3) CERTAIN LIABILITIES EXCLUDED.—

(A) IN GENERAL.—If a taxpayer transfers, in an exchange to which section 351 applies, a liability the payment of which either—

(i) would give rise to a deduction, or

(ii) would be described in section 736(a),

then, for purposes of paragraph (1), the amount of such liability shall be excluded in determining the amount of liabilities assumed.

(B) EXCEPTION.—Subparagraph (A) shall not apply to any liability to the extent that the incurrence of the liability resulted in the creation of, or an increase in, the basis of any property.

Amendments

• 2004, American Jobs Creation Act of 2004 (P.L. 108-357)

P.L. 108-357, §898(b):

Amended Code Sec. 357(c)(1)(B) by inserting "with respect to which stock or securities of the corporation to which the assets are transferred are distributed in a transaction which qualifies under section 355" after "section 368(a)(1)(D)". **Effective** for transfers of money or other property, or liabilities assumed, in connection with a reorganization occurring on or after 10-22-2004.

• 1999, Miscellaneous Trade and Technical Corrections Act of 1999 (P.L. 106-36)

P.L. 106-36, §3001(d)(4):

Amended Code Sec. 357(c)(1) by striking ", plus the amount of the liabilities to which the property is subject," following "assumed". **Effective** for transfers after 10-18-98.

P.L. 106-36, §3001(d)(5):

Amended Code Sec. 357(c)(3) by striking "or to which the property transferred is subject" following "assumed". **Effective** for transfers after 10-18-98.

• 1990, Omnibus Budget Reconciliation Act of 1990 (P.L. 101-508)

P.L. 101-508, §11801(c)(8)(F)(ii):

Amended Code Sec. 357(c)(2) by inserting "or" at the end of subparagraph (A), by striking subparagraph (B), and by redesignating subparagraph (C) as subparagraph (B). **Effective** 11-5-90. Prior to amendment, Code Sec. 357(c)(2)(B) read as follows:

(B) to which section 371 or 374 applies, or

P.L. 101-508, §11821(b)(1)-(2), provides:

(b) SAVINGS PROVISION.—If—

(1) any provision amended or repealed by this part applied to—

(A) any transaction occurring before the date of the enactment of this Act,

(B) any property acquired before such date of enactment, or

(C) any item of income, loss, deduction, or credit taken into account before such date of enactment, and

(2) the treatment of such transaction, property, or item under such provision would (without regard to the amendments made by this part) affect liability for tax for periods ending after such date of enactment,

nothing in the amendments made by this part shall be construed to affect the treatment of such transaction, property, or item for purposes of determining liability for tax for periods ending after such date of enactment.

• 1980, Bankruptcy Tax Act of 1980 (P.L. 96-589)

P.L. 96-589, §4(h)(2):

Amended Code Sec. 357(c)(2). For the **effective** date, see the historical comment for P.L. 96-589 under Code Sec. 370(a). Prior to amendment, Code Sec. 357(c)(2) provided:

(2) EXCEPTIONS.—Paragraph (1) shall not apply to any exchange to which—

(A) subsection (b)(1) of this section applies, or

(B) section 371 or 374 applies.

• 1980, Technical Corrections Act of 1979 (P.L. 96-222)

P.L. 96-222, §103(a)(12):

Amended Code Sec. 357(c)(3)(A). **Effective** for transfers made after 11-6-78. Prior to amendment, Code Sec. 357(c)(3)(A) read as follows:

(A) IN GENERAL.—If—

(i) the taxpayer's taxable income is computed under the cash receipts and disbursements method of accounting, and

(ii) such taxpayer transfers, in an exchange to which section 351 applies, a liability which is either—

(I) an account payable payment of which would give rise to a deduction, or

(II) an amount payable which is described in section 736(a),

then, for purposes of paragraph (1), the amount of such liability shall be excluded in determining the amount of liabilities assumed or to which the property transferred is subject.

• 1978, Revenue Act of 1978 (P.L. 95-600)

P.L. 95-600, §365(a), (c):

Added Code Sec. 357(c)(3). **Effective** for transfers occurring on or after 11-6-78.

• 1956 (P.L. 628, 84th Cong.)

P.L. 628, 84th Cong., §2(2):

Amended subsection (c)(2)(B) by substituting "371 or 374" for "371".

[Sec. 357(d)]

(d) DETERMINATION OF AMOUNT OF LIABILITY ASSUMED.—

(1) IN GENERAL.—For purposes of this section, section 358(d), section 358(h), section 361(b)(3), section 362(d), section 368(a)(1)(C), and section 368(a)(2)(B), except as provided in regulations—

(A) a recourse liability (or portion thereof) shall be treated as having been assumed if, as determined on the basis of all facts and circumstances, the transferee has agreed to, and is expected to, satisfy such liability (or portion), whether or not the transferor has been relieved of such liability; and

(B) except to the extent provided in paragraph (2), a nonrecourse liability shall be treated as having been assumed by the transferee of any asset subject to such liability.

(2) EXCEPTION FOR NONRECOURSE LIABILITY.—The amount of the nonrecourse liability treated as described in paragraph (1)(B) shall be reduced by the lesser of—

(A) the amount of such liability which an owner of other assets not transferred to the transferee and also subject to such liability has agreed with the transferee to, and is expected to, satisfy, or

(B) the fair market value of such other assets (determined without regard to section 7701(g)).

(3) REGULATIONS.—The Secretary shall prescribe such regulations as may be necessary to carry out the purposes of this subsection and section 362(d). The Secretary may also prescribe regulations which provide that the manner in which a liability is treated as assumed under this subsection is applied, where appropriate, elsewhere in this title.

Amendments

•2005, Gulf Opportunity Zone Act of 2005 (P.L. 109-135)

P.L. 109-135, §403(jj)(2):

Amended Code Sec. 357(d)(1) by inserting "section 361(b)(3)," after "section 358(h),". **Effective** as if included in the provision of the American Jobs Creation Act of 2004 (P.L. 108-357) to which it relates [**effective** for transfers of money or other property, or liabilities assumed, in connection with a reorganization occurring on or after 10-22-2004.—CCH].

• 2000, Community Renewal Tax Relief Act of 2000 (P.L. 106-554)

P.L. 106-554, §309(b):

Amended Code Sec. 357(d)(1) by inserting "section 358(h)," after "section 358(d),". **Effective**, generally, for assumptions of liability after 10-18-99. For special rules, see Act Sec. 309(c)(1)-(2) and (d)(2), below.

Act Sec. 309(c)(1)-(2) and (d)(2) provide:

(c) APPLICATION OF COMPARABLE RULES TO PARTNERSHIPS AND S CORPORATIONS.—The Secretary of the Treasury or his delegate—

(1) shall prescribe rules which provide appropriate adjustments under subchapter K of chapter 1 of the Internal Revenue Code of 1986 to prevent the acceleration or duplication of losses through the assumption of (or transfer of assets subject to) liabilities described in section 358(h)(3) of such Code (as added by subsection (a)) in transactions involving partnerships, and

(2) may prescribe rules which provide appropriate adjustments under subchapter S of chapter 1 of such Code in transactions described in paragraph (1) involving S corporations rather than partnerships.

(d) EFFECTIVE DATES.—

***

(2) RULES.—The rules prescribed under subsection (c) shall apply to assumptions of liability after October 18, 1999, or such later date as may be prescribed in such rules.

• 1999, Miscellaneous Trade and Technical Corrections Act of 1999 (P.L. 106-36)

P.L. 106-36, §3001(b)(1):

Amended Code Sec. 357 by adding at the end new subsection (d). **Effective** for transfers after 10-18-98.

[Sec. 358]

SEC. 358. BASIS TO DISTRIBUTEES.

[Sec. 358(a)]

(a) GENERAL RULE.—In the case of an exchange to which section 351, 354, 355, 356, or 361 applies—

(1) NONRECOGNITION PROPERTY.—The basis of the property permitted to be received under such section without the recognition of gain or loss shall be the same as that of the property exchanged—

(A) decreased by—

(i) the fair market value of any other property (except money) received by the taxpayer,

(ii) the amount of any money received by the taxpayer, and

(iii) the amount of loss to the taxpayer which was recognized on such exchange, and

(B) increased by—

(i) the amount which was treated as a dividend, and

(ii) the amount of gain to the taxpayer which was recognized on such exchange (not including any portion of such gain which was treated as a dividend).

(2) OTHER PROPERTY.—The basis of any other property (except money) received by the taxpayer shall be its fair market value.

Amendments

• 1990, Omnibus Budget Reconciliation Act of 1990 (P.L. 101-508)

P.L. 101-508, §11801(c)(8)(G)(i):

Amended Code Sec. 358(a) by striking "361, 371(b), or 374" and inserting "or 361." **Effective** 11-5-90.

P.L. 101-508, §11821(b)(1)-(2), provides:

(b) SAVINGS PROVISION.—If—

(1) any provision amended or repealed by this part applied to—

(A) any transaction occurring before the date of the enactment of this Act,

(B) any property acquired before such date of enactment, or

(C) any item of income, loss, deduction, or credit taken into account before such date of enactment, and

(2) the treatment of such transaction, property, or item under such provision would (without regard to the amendments made by this part) affect liability for tax for periods ending after such date of enactment,

nothing in the amendments made by this part shall be construed to affect the treatment of such transaction, property, or item for purposes of determining liability for tax for periods ending after such date of enactment.

• 1976 (P.L. 94-253)

P.L. 94-253, §1:

Amended Code Sec. 358(a) by striking out "or 371(b)" and inserting in lieu thereof "371(b), or 374". **Effective** for tax years ending after 3-31-76.

• 1958, Technical Amendments Act of 1958 (P.L. 85-866)

P.L. 85-866, §21(a):

Struck out the word "and" at the end of clause (i) of Sec. 358(a)(1)(A) and added clause (iii). **Effective** 6-22-54.

P.L. 85-866, §21(b):

Provides that the amendment made by §21(a) applies as provided in 1954 Code Sec. 393 as if the clause (iii) added by that amendment had been included in the 1954 Code at the time of its enactment.

[Sec. 358(b)]

(b) ALLOCATION OF BASIS.—

(1) IN GENERAL.—Under regulations prescribed by the Secretary, the basis determined under subsection (a)(1) shall be allocated among the properties permitted to be received without the recognition of gain or loss.

(2) SPECIAL RULE FOR SECTION 355.—In the case of an exchange to which section 355 (or so much of section 356 as relates to section 355) applies, then in making the allocation under paragraph (1) of this subsection, there shall be taken into account not only the property so permitted to be received without the recognition of gain or loss, but also the stock or securities (if any) of the distributing corporation which are retained, and the allocation of basis shall be made among all such properties.

Amendments

• 1990, Omnibus Budget Reconciliation Act of 1990 (P.L. 101-508)

P.L. 101-508, §11801(c)(8)(G)(ii):

Struck Code Sec. 358(b)(3). **Effective** 11-5-90. Prior to being stricken, Code Sec. 358(b)(3) read as follows:

(3) CERTAIN EXCHANGES INVOLVING CONRAIL.—To the extent provided in regulations prescribed by the Secretary, in the case of an exchange to which section 354(d) (or so much of section 356 as relates to section 354(d)) or section 374(c) applies, for purposes of allocating basis under paragraph (1), stock of the Consolidated Rail Corporation and the certificate of value of the United States Railway Association

which relates to such stock shall, so long as they are held by the same person, be treated as one property.

P.L. 101-508, §11821(b)(1)-(2), provides:

(b) SAVINGS PROVISION.—If—

(1) any provision amended or repealed by this part applied to—

(A) any transaction occurring before the date of the enactment of this Act,

(B) any property acquired before such date of enactment, or

(C) any item of income, loss, deduction, or credit taken into account before such date of enactment, and

(2) the treatment of such transaction, property, or item under such provision would (without regard to the amendments made by this part) affect liability for tax for periods ending after such date of enactment,

nothing in the amendments made by this part shall be construed to affect the treatment of such transaction, property, or item for purposes of determining liability for tax for periods ending after such date of enactment.

• 1976, Tax Reform Act of 1976 (P.L. 94-455)

P.L. 94-455, §1906(b)(13)(A):

Amended 1954 Code by substituting "Secretary" for "Secretary or his delegate" each place it appeared. **Effective** 2-1-77.

• 1976 (P.L. 94-253)

P.L. 94-253, §1:

Added paragraph (3). **Effective** for tax years ending after 3-31-76.

[Sec. 358(c)]

(c) SECTION 355 TRANSACTIONS WHICH ARE NOT EXCHANGES.—For purposes of this section, a distribution to which section 355 (or so much of section 356 as relates to section 355) applies shall be treated as an exchange, and for such purposes the stock and securities of the distributing corporation which are retained shall be treated as surrendered, and received back, in the exchange.

[Sec. 358(d)]

(d) ASSUMPTION OF LIABILITY.—

(1) IN GENERAL.—Where, as part of the consideration to the taxpayer, another party to the exchange assumed a liability of the taxpayer, such assumption shall, for purposes of this section, be treated as money received by the taxpayer on the exchange.

(2) EXCEPTION.—Paragraph (1) shall not apply to the amount of any liability excluded under section 357(c)(3).

Amendments

• 1999, Miscellaneous Trade and Technical Corrections Act of 1999 (P.L. 106-36)

P.L. 106-36, §3001(a)(2):

Amended Code Sec. 358(d)(1) by striking "or acquired from the taxpayer property subject to a liability" following "liability of the taxpayer". **Effective** for transfers after 10-18-98.

P.L. 106-36, §3001(d)(6):

Amended Code Sec. 358(d)(1) by striking "or acquisition (in the amount of the liability)" following "such assumption". **Effective** for transfers after 10-18-98.

• 1978, Revenue Act of 1978 (P.L. 95-600)

P.L. 95-600, §365(b):

Amended Code Sec. 358(d). **Effective** for transfers occurring on or after 11-6-78. Before amendment, such section read:

(d) ASSUMPTION OF LIABILITY.—Where, as part of the consideration to the taxpayer, another party to the exchange assumed a liability of the taxpayer or acquired from the taxpayer property subject to a liability, such assumption or acquisition (in the amount of the liability) shall, for purposes of this section, be treated as money received by the taxpayer on the exchange.

[Sec. 358(e)]

(e) EXCEPTION.—This section shall not apply to property acquired by a corporation by the exchange of its stock or securities (or the stock or securities of a corporation which is in control of the acquiring corporation) as consideration in whole or in part for the transfer of the property to it.

Amendments

• 1968 (P.L. 90-621)

P.L. 90-621, §2(a):

Amended subsection (e). **Effective** only to plans of reorganization adopted after 10-22-68. Prior to amendment, the subsection read as follows:

(e) EXCEPTION.—This section shall not apply to property acquired by a corporation by the issuance of its stock or securities as consideration in whole or in part for the transfer of the property to it.

[Sec. 358(f)]

(f) DEFINITION OF NONRECOGNITION PROPERTY IN CASE OF SECTION 361 EXCHANGE.—For purposes of this section, the property permitted to be received under section 361 without the recognition of gain or loss shall be treated as consisting only of stock or securities in another corporation a party to the reorganization.

Amendments

• 1988, Technical and Miscellaneous Revenue Act of 1988 (P.L. 100-647)

P.L. 100-647, §1018(d)(5)(B):

Amended Code Sec. 358 by adding at the end thereof new subsection (f). **Effective** as if included in the provision of P.L. 99-514 to which it relates.

[Sec. 358(g)]

(g) ADJUSTMENTS IN INTRAGROUP TRANSACTIONS INVOLVING SECTION 355.—In the case of a distribution to which section 355 (or so much of section 356 as relates to section 355) applies and which involves the distribution of stock from 1 member of an affiliated group (as defined in section 1504(a) without regard to subsection (b) thereof) to another member of such group, the Secretary may, notwithstanding any other provision of this section, provide adjustments to the adjusted basis of any stock which—

(1) is in a corporation which is a member of such group, and

(2) is held by another member of such group, to appropriately reflect the proper treatment of such distribution.

Amendments

• 1997, Taxpayer Relief Act of 1997 (P.L. 105-34)

P.L. 105-34, §1012(b)(2):

Amended Code Sec. 358 by adding at the end a new subsection (g). **Effective**, generally, for distributions after 4-16-97 [**effective** date changed by P.L. 105-206, §6010(c)(1)]. For a transitional rule, see Act Sec. 1012(d)(3), below.

P.L. 105-34, §1012(d)(3), provides:

(3) TRANSITION RULE.—The amendments made by this section shall not apply to any distribution pursuant to a plan (or series of related transactions) which involves an acquisition described in section 355(e)(2)(A)(ii) of the Internal Revenue Code of 1986 (or, in the case of the amendments made by subsection (c), any transfer) occurring after April 16, 1997, if such acquisition or transfer is—

(A) made pursuant to an agreement which was binding on such date and at all times thereafter,

(B) described in a ruling request submitted to the Internal Revenue Service on or before such date, or

(C) described on or before such date in a public announcement or in a filing with the Securities and Exchange Commission required solely by reason of the acquisition or transfer.

This paragraph shall not apply to any agreement, ruling request, or public announcement or filing unless it identifies the acquirer of the distributing corporation or any controlled corporation, or the transferee, whichever is applicable.

[Sec. 358(h)]

(h) SPECIAL RULES FOR ASSUMPTION OF LIABILITIES TO WHICH SUBSECTION (d) DOES NOT APPLY.—

(1) IN GENERAL.—If, after application of the other provisions of this section to an exchange or series of exchanges, the basis of property to which subsection (a)(1) applies exceeds the fair market value of such property, then such basis shall be reduced (but not below such fair market value) by the amount (determined as of the date of the exchange) of any liability—

(A) which is assumed by another person as part of the exchange, and

(B) with respect to which subsection (d)(1) does not apply to the assumption.

(2) EXCEPTIONS.—Except as provided by the Secretary, paragraph (1) shall not apply to any liability if—

(A) the trade or business with which the liability is associated is transferred to the person assuming the liability as part of the exchange, or

(B) substantially all of the assets with which the liability is associated are transferred to the person assuming the liability as part of the exchange.

(3) LIABILITY.—For purposes of this subsection, the term "liability" shall include any fixed or contingent obligation to make payment, without regard to whether the obligation is otherwise taken into account for purposes of this title.

Amendments

• 2002, Job Creation and Worker Assistance Act of 2002 (P.L. 107-147)

P.L. 107-147, §412(c):

Amended Code Sec. 358(h)(1)(A). **Effective** as if included in the provision of P.L. 106-554 to which it relates [**effective** for assumptions of liabilities after 10-18-99.—CCH]. Prior to amendment, Code Sec. 358(h)(1)(A) read as follows:

(A) which is assumed in exchange for such property, and

• 2000, Community Renewal Tax Relief Act of 2000 (P.L. 106-554)

P.L. 106-554, §309(a):

Amended Code Sec. 358 by adding at the end a new subsection (h). **Effective**, generally, for assumptions of liability after 10-18-99. For special rules, see Act Sec. 309(c)(1)-(2) and (d)(2), below.

P.L. 106-554, §309(c)(1)-(2) and (d)(2), provide:

(c) APPLICATION OF COMPARABLE RULES TO PARTNERSHIPS AND S CORPORATIONS.—The Secretary of the Treasury or his delegate—

(1) shall prescribe rules which provide appropriate adjustments under subchapter K of chapter 1 of the Internal Revenue Code of 1986 to prevent the acceleration or duplication of losses through the assumption of (or transfer of assets subject to) liabilities described in section 358(h)(3) of such Code (as added by subsection (a)) in transactions involving partnerships, and

(2) may prescribe rules which provide appropriate adjustments under subchapter S of chapter 1 of such Code in transactions described in paragraph (1) involving S corporations rather than partnerships.

(d) EFFECTIVE DATES.—

***

(2) RULES.—The rules prescribed under subsection (c) shall apply to assumptions of liability after October 18, 1999, or such later date as may be prescribed in such rules.

Subpart C—Effects on Corporations

[Sec. 361]

SEC. 361. NONRECOGNITION OF GAIN OR LOSS TO CORPORATIONS; TREATMENT OF DISTRIBUTIONS.

[Sec. 361(a)]

(a) GENERAL RULE.—No gain or loss shall be recognized to a corporation if such corporation is a party to a reorganization and exchanges property, in pursuance of the plan of reorganization, solely for stock or securities in another corporation a party to the reorganization.

[Sec. 361(b)]

(b) EXCHANGES NOT SOLELY IN KIND.—

(1) GAIN.—If subsection (a) would apply to an exchange but for the fact that the property received in exchange consists not only of stock or securities permitted by subsection (a) to be received without the recognition of gain, but also of other property or money, then—

(A) PROPERTY DISTRIBUTED.—If the corporation receiving such other property or money distributes it in pursuance of the plan of reorganization, no gain to the corporation shall be recognized from the exchange, but

(B) PROPERTY NOT DISTRIBUTED.—If the corporation receiving such other property or money does not distribute it in pursuance of the plan of reorganization, the gain, if any, to the corporation shall be recognized.

The amount of gain recognized under subparagraph (B) shall not exceed the sum of the money and the fair market value of the other property so received which is not so distributed.

(2) LOSS.—If subsection (a) would apply to an exchange but for the fact that the property received in exchange consists not only of property permitted by subsection (a) to be received without the recognition of gain or loss, but also of other property or money, then no loss from the exchange shall be recognized.

(3) TREATMENT OF TRANSFERS TO CREDITORS.—For purposes of paragraph (1), any transfer of the other property or money received in the exchange by the corporation to its creditors in connection with the reorganization shall be treated as a distribution in pursuance of the plan of reorganization. The Secretary may prescribe such regulations as may be necessary to prevent avoidance of tax through abuse of the preceding sentence or subsection (c)(3). In the case of a reorganization described in section 368(a)(1)(D) with respect to which stock or securities of the corporation to which the assets are transferred are distributed in a transaction which qualifies under section 355, this paragraph shall apply only to the extent that the sum of the money and the fair market value of other property transferred to such creditors does not exceed the adjusted bases of such assets transferred (reduced by the amount of the liabilities assumed (within the meaning of section 357(c))).

Amendments

•2005, Gulf Opportunity Zone Act of 2005 (P.L. 109-135)

P.L. 109-135, §403(jj)(1):

Amended Code Sec. 361(b)(3) by inserting "(reduced by the amount of the liabilities assumed (within the meaning of section 357(c)))" before the period at the end. **Effective** as if included in the provision of the American Jobs Creation Act of 2004 (P.L. 108-357) to which it relates [**effective** for transfers of money or other property, or liabilities assumed, in connection with a reorganization occurring on or after 10-22-2004.—CCH].

• 2004, American Jobs Creation Act of 2004 (P.L. 108-357)

P.L. 108-357, §898(a):

Amended Code Sec. 361(b)(3) by adding at the end a new sentence. **Effective** for transfers of money or other property, or liabilities assumed, in connection with a reorganization occurring on or after 10-22-2004.

[Sec. 361(c)]

(c) TREATMENT OF DISTRIBUTIONS.—

(1) IN GENERAL.—Except as provided in paragraph (2), no gain or loss shall be recognized to a corporation a party to a reorganization on the distribution to its shareholders of property in pursuance of the plan of reorganization.

(2) DISTRIBUTIONS OF APPRECIATED PROPERTY.—

(A) IN GENERAL.—If—

(i) in a distribution referred to in paragraph (1), the corporation distributes property other than qualified property, and

(ii) the fair market value of such property exceeds its adjusted basis (in the hands of the distributing corporation),

then gain shall be recognized to the distributing corporation as if such property were sold to the distributee at its fair market value.

(B) QUALIFIED PROPERTY.—For purposes of this subsection, the term "qualified property" means—

(i) any stock in (or right to acquire stock in) the distributing corporation or obligation of the distributing corporation, or

(ii) any stock in (or right to acquire stock in) another corporation which is a party to the reorganization or obligation of another corporation which is such a party if such stock (or right) or obligation is received by the distributing corporation in the exchange.

(C) TREATMENT OF LIABILITIES.—If any property distributed in the distribution referred to in paragraph (1) is subject to a liability or the shareholder assumes a liability of the distributing corporation in connection with the distribution, then, for purposes of subparagraph (A), the fair market value of such property shall be treated as not less than the amount of such liability.

(3) TREATMENT OF CERTAIN TRANSFERS TO CREDITORS.—For purposes of this subsection, any transfer of qualified property by the corporation to its creditors in connection with the reorganization shall be treated as a distribution to its shareholders pursuant to the plan of reorganization.

(4) COORDINATION WITH OTHER PROVISIONS.—Section 311 and subpart B of part II of this subchapter shall not apply to any distribution referred to in paragraph (1).

(5) CROSS REFERENCE.—

For provision providing for recognition of gain in certain distributions, see section 355(d).

Amendments

• 1990, Omnibus Budget Reconciliation Act of 1990 (P.L. 101-508)

P.L. 101-508, §11321(b):

Amended Code Sec. 361(c) by adding at the end thereof a new paragraph (5). **Effective** for distributions after 10-9-90. For exceptions, see Act Sec. 11321(c)(2)-(3), below.

P.L. 101-508, §11321(c)(2)-(3), provides:

(2) BINDING CONTRACT EXCEPTION.—The amendments made by this section shall not apply to any distribution pursuant to a written binding contract in effect on October 9, 1990, and at all times thereafter before such distribution.

(3) TRANSITIONAL RULES.—For purposes of subparagraphs (A) and (B) of section 355(d)(3) of the Internal Revenue Code of 1986 (as amended by subsection (a)), an acquisition shall be treated as occurring on or before October 9, 1990, if—

(A) such acquisition is pursuant to a written binding contract in effect on October 9, 1990, and at all times thereafter before such acquisition,

(B) such acquisition is pursuant to a transaction which was described in documents filed with the Securities and Exchange Commission on or before October 9, 1990, or

(C) such acquisition is pursuant to a transaction—

(i) the material terms of which were described in a written public announcement on or before October 9, 1990,

(ii) which was the subject of a prior filing with the Securities and Exchange Commission, and

(iii) which is the subject of a subsequent filing with the Securities and Exchange Commission before January 1, 1991.

• 1988, Technical and Miscellaneous Revenue Act of 1988 (P.L. 100-647)

P.L. 100-647, §1018(d)(5)(A):

Amended Code Sec. 361. **Effective** as if included in the provision of P.L. 99-514 to which it relates. Prior to amendment, Code Sec. 361 read as follows:

SEC. 361. NONRECOGNITION OF GAIN OR LOSS TO TRANSFEROR CORPORATION; OTHER TREATMENT OF TRANSFEROR CORPORATION; ETC.

[Sec. 361(a)]

(a) GENERAL RULE.—No gain or loss shall be recognized to a transferor corporation which is a party to a reorganization on any exchange of property pursuant to the plan of reorganization.

Amendments

• 1986, Tax Reform Act of 1986 (P.L. 99-514)

P.L. 99-514, §1804(g)(1):

Amended Code Sec. 361(a). **Effective** for plans of reorganizations adopted after 10-22-86. Prior to amendment, Code Sec. 361(a) read as follows:

SEC. 361. NONRECOGNITION OF GAIN OR LOSS TO CORPORATIONS.

(a) GENERAL RULE.—No gain or loss shall be recognized if a corporation a party to a reorganization exchanges property, in pursuance of the plan of reorganization, solely for stock or securities in another corporation a party to the reorganization.

[Sec. 361(b)]

(b) OTHER TREATMENT OF TRANSFEROR CORPORATION.—In the case of a transferor corporation which is a party to a reorganization—

(1) sections 336 and 337 shall not apply with respect to any liquidation of such corporation pursuant to the plan of reorganization,

(2) the basis of the property (other than stock and securities described in paragraph (3)) received by the corporation pursuant to such plan of reorganization shall be the same as it would be in the hands of the transferor of such property, adjusted by the amount of gain or loss recognized to such transferor on such transfer, and

(3) no gain or loss shall be recognized by such corporation on any disposition (pursuant to the plan of reorganization) of stock or securities which were received pursuant to such plan and which are in another corporation which is a party to such reorganization.

For purposes of paragraph (3), if the transferor corporation is merged, consolidated, or liquidated pursuant to the plan of reorganization, or if a transaction meets the requirements of section 368(a)(1)(C) pursuant to a waiver granted by the Secretary under section 368(a)(2)(G)(ii), any distribution of such stock or securities by the transferor corporation to its creditors in connection with such transaction shall be treated as pursuant to such plan of reorganization.

Amendments

• 1986, Tax Reform Act of 1986 (P.L. 99-514)

P.L. 99-514, §1804(g)(1):

Amended Code Sec. 361(b). **Effective** for plans of reorganizations adopted after 10-22-86. Prior to amendment, Code Sec. 361(b) read as follows:

(b) EXCHANGES NOT SOLELY IN KIND.—

(1) GAIN.—If subsection (a) would apply to an exchange but for the fact that the property received in exchange consists not only of stock or securities permitted by subsection (a) to be received without the recognition of gain, but also of other property or money, then—

(A) if the corporation receiving such other property or money distributes it in pursuance of the plan of reorganization, no gain to the corporation shall be recognized from the exchange, but

(B) if the corporation receiving such other property or money does not distribute it in pursuance of the plan of reorganization, the gain, if any, to the corporation shall be recognized, but in an amount not in excess of the sum of such money and the fair market value of such other property so received, which is not so distributed.

(2) LOSS.—If subsection (a) would apply to an exchange but for the fact that the property received in exchange consists not only of property permitted by subsection (a) to be received without the recognition of gain or loss, but also of other property or money, then no loss from the exchange shall be recognized.

[Sec. 361(c)]

(c) TREATMENT OF DISTRIBUTIONS OF APPRECIATED PROPERTY.—Notwithstanding any other provision of this subtitle, gain shall be recognized on the distribution of property (other than property permitted by section 354, 355, or 356 to be received without the recognition of gain) pursuant to a plan of reorganization in the same manner as if such property had been sold to the distributee at its fair market value.

Amendments

• 1986, Tax Reform Act of 1986 (P.L. 99-514)

P.L. 99-514, §1804(g)(1):

Added Code Sec. 361(c). **Effective** for plans of reorganizations adopted after 10-22-86.

[Sec. 362]

SEC. 362. BASIS TO CORPORATIONS.

[Sec. 362(a)]

(a) PROPERTY ACQUIRED BY ISSUANCE OF STOCK OR AS PAID-IN SURPLUS.—If property was acquired on or after June 22, 1954, by a corporation—

(1) in connection with a transaction to which section 351 (relating to transfer of property to corporation controlled by transferor) applies, or

(2) as paid-in surplus or as a contribution to capital,

then the basis shall be the same as it would be in the hands of the transferor, increased in the amount of gain recognized to the transferor on such transfer.

[Sec. 362(b)]

(b) TRANSFERS TO CORPORATIONS.—If property was acquired by a corporation in connection with a reorganization to which this part applies, then the basis shall be the same as it would be in the hands of the transferor, increased in the amount of gain recognized to the transferor on such transfer. This subsection shall not apply if the property acquired consists of stock or securities in a corporation a party to the reorganization, unless acquired by the exchange of stock or securities of the transferee (or of a corporation which is in control of the transferee) as the consideration in whole or in part for the transfer.

Amendments

• 1968 (P.L. 90-621)

P.L. 90-621, §2(b):

Amended the last sentence in subsection (b). **Effective** only for plans of reorganization adopted after 10-22-68. Prior to amendment, this sentence read as follows:

This subsection shall not apply if the property acquired consists of stock or securities in a corporation a party to the reorganization, unless acquired by the issuance of stock or securities of the transferee as the consideration in whole or in part for the transfer.

[Sec. 362(c)]

(c) SPECIAL RULE FOR CERTAIN CONTRIBUTIONS TO CAPITAL.—

(1) PROPERTY OTHER THAN MONEY.—Notwithstanding subsection (a)(2), if property other than money—

(A) is acquired by a corporation, on or after June 22, 1954, as a contribution to capital, and

(B) is not contributed by a shareholder as such,

then the basis of such property shall be zero.

(2) MONEY.—Notwithstanding subsection (a)(2), if money—

(A) is received by a corporation, on or after June 22, 1954, as a contribution to capital, and

(B) is not contributed by a shareholder as such,

then the basis of any property acquired with such money during the 12-month period beginning on the day the contribution is received shall be reduced by the amount of such contribution. The excess (if any) of the amount of such contribution over the amount of the reduction under the preceding sentence shall be applied to the reduction (as of the last day of the period specified in the preceding sentence) of the basis of any other property held by the taxpayer. The particular properties to which the reductions required by this paragraph shall be allocated shall be determined under regulations prescribed by the Secretary.

Amendments

• 1986, Tax Reform Act of 1986 (P.L. 99-514)

P.L. 99-514, §824(b)-(c)(2)-(3):

Amended Code Sec. 362(c) by striking out paragraph (3). **Effective**, generally, for amounts received after 12-31-86, in tax years ending after such date. However, for special rules, see Act Sec. 824(c)(2)-(3), below. Prior to amendment, Code Sec. 362(c)(3) read as follows:

(3) EXCEPTION FOR CONTRIBUTIONS IN AID OF CONSTRUCTION.—The provisions of this subsection shall not apply to contributions in aid of construction to which section 118(b) applies.

P.L. 99-514, §824(c)(2)-(4), as amended by P.L. 100-647, §1008(j)(2), provides:

(2) TREATMENT OF CERTAIN WATER SUPPLY PROJECTS.—The amendments made by this section shall not apply to amounts which are paid by the New Jersey Department of Environmental Protection for construction of alternative water supply projects in zones of drinking water contamination and which are designated by such department as being taken into account under this paragraph. Not more than $4,631,000 of such amounts may be designated under the preceding sentence.

(3) TREATMENT OF CERTAIN CONTRIBUTIONS BY TRANSPORTATION AUTHORITY.—The amendments made by this section shall not apply to contributions in aid of construction by a qualified transportation authority which were clearly identified in a master plan in existence on September 13, 1984, and which are designated by such authority as being taken into account under this paragraph. Not more than $68,000,000 of such contributions may be designated under the preceding sentence. For purposes of this paragraph, a qualified transportation authority is an entity which was created on February 20, 1967, and which was established by an interstate compact and consented to by Congress in Public Law 89-774, 80 Stat. 1324 (1966).

(4) TREATMENT OF CERTAIN PARTNERSHIPS.—In the case of a partnership with a taxable year beginning May 1, 1986, if such partnership realized net capital gain during the period beginning on the 1st day of such taxable year and ending on May 29, 1986, pursuant to an underwriting agreement dated May 6, 1986, then such partnership may elect to treat each asset to which such net capital gain relates as having been distributed to the partners of such partnership in proportion to their distributive share of the capital gain or loss realized by the partnership with respect to such asset and to treat each such asset as having been sold by each partner on the date of the sale of the asset by the partnership. If such an election is made, the consideration received by the partnership in connection with the sale of such assets shall be treated as having been received by the partners in connection with the deemed sale of such assets. In the case of a tiered partnership, for purposes of this paragraph each partnership shall be treated as having realized net capital gain equal to its proportionate share of the net capital gain of each partnership in which it is a partner, and the election provided by this paragraph shall apply to each tier.

• 1976, Tax Reform Act of 1976 (P.L. 94-455)

P.L. 94-455, §1906(b)(13)(A):

Amended 1954 Code by substituting "Secretary" for "Secretary or his delegate" each place it appeared. **Effective** 2-1-77.

P.L. 94-455, §2120(b):

Added Code Sec. 362(c)(3). **Effective** for contributions made after 1-31-76.

[Sec. 362(d)]

(d) LIMITATION ON BASIS INCREASE ATTRIBUTABLE TO ASSUMPTION OF LIABILITY.—

(1) IN GENERAL.—In no event shall the basis of any property be increased under subsection (a) or (b) above the fair market value of such property (determined without regard to section 7701(g)) by reason of any gain recognized to the transferor as a result of the assumption of a liability.

(2) TREATMENT OF GAIN NOT SUBJECT TO TAX.—Except as provided in regulations, if—

(A) gain is recognized to the transferor as a result of an assumption of a nonrecourse liability by a transferee which is also secured by assets not transferred to such transferee; and

(B) no person is subject to tax under this title on such gain,

then, for purposes of determining basis under subsections (a) and (b), the amount of gain recognized by the transferor as a result of the assumption of the liability shall be determined as if the liability assumed by the transferee equaled such transferee's ratable portion of such liability determined on the basis of the relative fair market values (determined without regard to section 7701(g)) of all of the assets subject to such liability.

Amendments

• 1999, Miscellaneous Trade and Technical Corrections Act of 1999 (P.L. 106-36)

P.L. 106-36, §3001(b)(2):

Amended Code Sec. 362 by adding at the end new subsection (d). **Effective** for transfers after 10-18-98.

[Sec. 362(e)]

(e) LIMITATIONS ON BUILT-IN LOSSES.—

(1) LIMITATION ON IMPORTATION OF BUILT-IN LOSSES.—

(A) IN GENERAL.—If in any transaction described in subsection (a) or (b) there would (but for this subsection) be an importation of a net built-in loss, the basis of each property described in subparagraph (B) which is acquired in such transaction shall (notwithstanding subsections (a) and (b)) be its fair market value immediately after such transaction.

(B) PROPERTY DESCRIBED.—For purposes of subparagraph (A), property is described in this subparagraph if—

(i) gain or loss with respect to such property is not subject to tax under this subtitle in the hands of the transferor immediately before the transfer, and

(ii) gain or loss with respect to such property is subject to such tax in the hands of the transferee immediately after such transfer.

In any case in which the transferor is a partnership, the preceding sentence shall be applied by treating each partner in such partnership as holding such partner's proportionate share of the property of such partnership.

(C) IMPORTATION OF NET BUILT-IN LOSS.—For purposes of subparagraph (A), there is an importation of a net built-in loss in a transaction if the transferee's aggregate adjusted bases of property described in subparagraph (B) which is transferred in such transaction would (but for this paragraph) exceed the fair market value of such property immediately after such transaction.

(2) LIMITATION ON TRANSFER OF BUILT-IN LOSSES IN SECTION 351 TRANSACTIONS.—

(A) IN GENERAL.—If—

(i) property is transferred by a transferor in any transaction which is described in subsection (a) and which is not described in paragraph (1) of this subsection, and

(ii) the transferee's aggregate adjusted bases of such property so transferred would (but for this paragraph) exceed the fair market value of such property immediately after such transaction,

then, notwithstanding subsection (a), the transferee's aggregate adjusted bases of the property so transferred shall not exceed the fair market value of such property immediately after such transaction.

(B) ALLOCATION OF BASIS REDUCTION.—The aggregate reduction in basis by reason of subparagraph (A) shall be allocated among the property so transferred in proportion to their respective built-in losses immediately before the transaction.

(C) ELECTION TO APPLY LIMITATION TO TRANSFEROR'S STOCK BASIS.—

(i) IN GENERAL.—If the transferor and transferee of a transaction described in subparagraph (A) both elect the application of this subparagraph—

(I) subparagraph (A) shall not apply, and

(II) the transferor's basis in the stock received for property to which subparagraph (A) does not apply by reason of the election shall not exceed its fair market value immediately after the transfer.

(ii) ELECTION.—Any election under clause (i) shall be made at such time and in such form and manner as the Secretary may prescribe, and, once made, shall be irrevocable.

Amendments

•2005, Gulf Opportunity Zone Act of 2005 (P.L. 109-135)

P.L. 109-135, §403(dd)(2):

Amended Code Sec. 362(e)(2)(C)(ii). **Effective** as if included in the provision of the American Jobs Creation Act of 2004 (P.L. 108-357) to which it relates [**effective** for transactions after 10-22-2004.—CCH]. Prior to amendment, Code Sec. 362(e)(2)(C)(ii) read as follows:

(ii) ELECTION.—An election under clause (i) shall be included with the return of tax for the taxable year in which the transaction occurred, shall be in such form and manner as the Secretary may prescribe, and, once made, shall be irrevocable.

• 2004, American Jobs Creation Act of 2004 (P.L. 108-357)

P.L. 108-357, §836(a):

Amended Code Sec. 362 by adding at the end a new subsection (e). **Effective** for transactions after 10-22-2004.

Subpart D—Special Rule; Definitions

[Sec. 367]

SEC. 367. FOREIGN CORPORATIONS.

[Sec. 367(a)]

(a) TRANSFERS OF PROPERTY FROM THE UNITED STATES.—

(1) GENERAL RULE.—If, in connection with any exchange described in section 332, 351, 354, 356, or 361, a United States person transfers property to a foreign corporation, such foreign corporation shall not, for purposes of determining the extent to which gain shall be recognized on such transfer, be considered to be a corporation.

(2) EXCEPTION FOR CERTAIN STOCK OR SECURITIES.—Except to the extent provided in regulations, paragraph (1) shall not apply to the transfer of stock or securities of a foreign corporation which is a party to the exchange or a party to the reorganization.

(3) EXCEPTION FOR TRANSFERS OF CERTAIN PROPERTY USED IN THE ACTIVE CONDUCT OF A TRADE OR BUSINESS.—

(A) IN GENERAL.—Except as provided in regulations prescribed by the Secretary, paragraph (1) shall not apply to any property transferred to a foreign corporation for use by such foreign corporation in the active conduct of a trade or business outside of the United States.

(B) PARAGRAPH NOT TO APPLY TO CERTAIN PROPERTY.—Except as provided in regulations prescribed by the Secretary, subparagraph (A) shall not apply to any—

(i) property described in paragraph (1) or (3) of section 1221(a) (relating to inventory and copyrights, etc.),

(ii) installment obligations, accounts receivable, or similar property,

(iii) foreign currency or other property denominated in foreign currency,

(iv) intangible property (within the meaning of section 936(h)(3)(B)), or

(v) property with respect to which the transferor is a lessor at the time of the transfer, except that this clause shall not apply if the transferee was the lessee.

(C) TRANSFER OF FOREIGN BRANCH WITH PREVIOUSLY DEDUCTED LOSSES.—Except as provided in regulations prescribed by the Secretary, subparagraph (A) shall not apply to gain realized on the transfer of the assets of a foreign branch of a United States person to a foreign corporation in an exchange described in paragraph (1) to the extent that—

(i) the sum of losses—

(I) which were incurred by the foreign branch before the transfer, and

(II) with respect to which a deduction was allowed to the taxpayer, exceeds

(ii) the sum of—

(I) any taxable income of such branch for a taxable year after the taxable year in which the loss was incurred and through the close of the taxable year of the transfer, and

(II) the amount which is recognized under section 904(f)(3) on account of the transfer.

Any gain recognized by reason of the preceding sentence shall be treated for purposes of this chapter as income from sources outside the United States having the same character as such losses had.

(4) SPECIAL RULE FOR TRANSFER OF PARTNERSHIP INTERESTS.—Except as provided in regulations prescribed by the Secretary, a transfer by a United States person of an interest in a partnership to a foreign corporation in an exchange described in paragraph (1) shall, for purposes of this subsection, be treated as a transfer to such corporation of such person's pro rata share of the assets of the partnership.

(5) PARAGRAPHS (2) AND (3) NOT TO APPLY TO CERTAIN SECTION 361 TRANSACTIONS.—Paragraphs (2) and (3) shall not apply in the case of an exchange described in subsection (a) or (b) of section 361. Subject to such basis adjustments and such other conditions as shall be provided in regulations, the preceding sentence shall not apply if the transferor corporation is controlled (within the meaning of section 368(c)) by 5 or fewer domestic corporations. For purposes of the preceding sentence, all members of the same affiliated group (within the meaning of section 1504) shall be treated as 1 corporation.

(6) SECRETARY MAY EXEMPT CERTAIN TRANSACTIONS FROM APPLICATION OF THIS SUBSECTION.—Paragraph (1) shall not apply to the transfer of any property which the Secretary, in order to carry out the purposes of this subsection, designates by regulation.

Amendments

• 1999, Tax Relief Extension Act of 1999 (P.L. 106-170)

P.L. 106-170, §532(c)(1)(C):

Amended Code Sec. 367(a)(3)(B)(i) by striking "section 1221" and inserting "section 1221(a)". **Effective** for any instrument held, acquired, or entered into, any transaction entered into, and supplies held or acquired on or after 12-17-99.

• 1990, Omnibus Budget Reconciliation Act of 1990 (P.L. 101-508)

P.L. 101-508, §11702(a)(1):

Amended Code Sec. 367(a)(5) by striking "section 361", and inserting "subsection (a) or (b) of section 361". **Effective** as if included in the provision of P.L. 101-239 to which it relates.

• 1988, Technical and Miscellaneous Revenue Act of 1988 (P.L. 100-647)

P.L. 100-647, §1006(e)(13)(A):

Amended Code Sec. 367(a) by redesignating paragraph (5) as paragraph (6) and by inserting after paragraph (4) new paragraph (5). **Effective** for exchanges on or after 6-21-88.

• 1986, Tax Reform Act of 1986 (P.L. 99-514)

P.L. 99-514, §1810(g)(4)(A):

Amended Code Sec. 367(a)(1) by striking out "355,". **Effective** as if included in the provision of P.L. 98-369 to which it relates.

• 1984, Deficit Reduction Act of 1984 (P.L. 98-369)

P.L. 98-369, §131(a):

Amended Code Sec. 367(a). **Effective** for transfers or exchanges after 12-31-84, in tax years ending after such date. However, see Act Sec. 131(g)(2)-(3) following Code Sec. 367(e) for special rules. Prior to amendment, Code Sec. 367(a) read as follows:

(a) Transfers of Property From the United States.—

(1) General Rule.—If, in connection with any exchange described in section 332, 351, 354, 355, 356, or 361, there is a transfer of property (other than stock or securities of a foreign corporation which is a party to the exchange or a party to the reorganization) by a United States person to a foreign corporation, for purposes of determining the extent to which gain shall be recognized on such transfer, a foreign corporation shall not be considered to be a corporation unless, pursuant to a request filed not later than the close of the 183d day after the beginning of such transfer (and filed in such form and manner as may be prescribed by regulations by the Secretary), it is established to the satisfaction of the Secretary that such exchange is not in pursuance of a plan having as one of its principal purposes the avoidance of Federal income taxes.

(2) Exception for Transactions Designated by the Secretary.—Paragraph (1) shall not apply to any exchange (otherwise within paragraph (1)), or to any type of property, which the Secretary by regulations designates as not requiring the filing of a request.

• 1976, Tax Reform Act of 1976 (P.L. 94-455)

P.L. 94-455, §1042(a):

Amended Code Sec. 367. **Effective** for transfers beginning after 10-9-75, and for sales, exchanges, and distributions taking place after that date. In the case of any exchange described in Code Sec. 367 (as in effect on 12-31-74) in any tax year beginning after 12-31-62, and before 10-4-76, which does not involve the transfer of property to or from a United States person, a taxpayer shall have until 183 days after 10-4-76 to file a request with the Secretary of the Treasury or his delegate seeking to establish to the satisfaction of the Secretary or his delegate that such exchange was not in pursuance of a plan having as one of its principal purposes the avoidance of federal income taxes and that for purposes of Code Sec. 367, a foreign corporation is to be treated as a foreign corporation. Prior to amendment, Code Sec. 367(a) read as follows:

SEC. 367. FOREIGN CORPORATIONS.

(a) GENERAL RULE.—In determining the extent to which gain shall be recognized in the case of any of the exchanges described in section 332, 351, 354, 355, 356, or 361, a foreign corporation shall not be considered as a corporation unless—

(1) before such exchange, or

(2) in the case of an exchange described in subsection (b), either before or after such exchange,

it has been established to the satisfaction of the Secretary or his delegate that such exchange is not in pursuance of a plan having as one of its principal purposes the avoidance of Federal income taxes.

• 1971 (P.L. 91-681)

P.L. 91-681, §1(a):

Amended Code Sec. 367. **Effective** for transfers made after 12-31-67. Prior to amendment, Code Sec. 367 read as follows:

SEC. 367. FOREIGN CORPORATIONS.—

In determining the extent to which gain shall be recognized in the case of any of the exchanges described in section 332, 351, 354, 355, 356, or 361, a foreign corporation shall not be considered as a corporation unless, before such exchange, it has been established to the satisfaction of the Secretary or his delegate that such exchange is not in pursuance of a plan having as one of its principal purposes the avoidance of Federal income taxes. For purposes of this section, any distribution described in section 355 (or so much of section 356 as relates to section 355) shall be treated as an exchange whether or not it is an exchange.

[Sec. 367(b)]

(b) OTHER TRANSFERS.—

(1) EFFECT OF SECTION TO BE DETERMINED UNDER REGULATIONS.—In the case of any exchange described in section 332, 351, 354, 355, 356, or 361 in connection with which there is no transfer of property described in subsection (a)(1), a foreign corporation shall be considered to be a corporation except to the extent provided in regulations prescribed by the Secretary which are necessary or appropriate to prevent the avoidance of Federal income taxes.

(2) REGULATIONS RELATING TO SALE OR EXCHANGE OF STOCK IN FOREIGN CORPORATIONS.—The regulations prescribed pursuant to paragraph (1) shall include (but shall not be limited to) regulations dealing with the sale or exchange of stock or securities in a foreign corporation by a United States person, including regulations providing—

(A) the circumstances under which—

(i) gain shall be recognized currently, or amounts included in gross income currently as a dividend, or both, or

(ii) gain or other amounts may be deferred for inclusion in the gross income of a shareholder (or his successor in interest) at a later date, and

(B) the extent to which adjustments shall be made to earnings and profits, basis of stock or securities, and basis of assets.

Amendments

• 1976, Tax Reform Act of 1976 (P.L. 94-455)

P.L. 94-455, §1042(a):

Amended Code Sec. 367(b). **Effective** for transfers beginning after 10-9-75, and for sales, exchanges, and distributions taking place after that date (see note for P.L. 94-455, §1042(a), following Code Sec. 367(a)). Prior to amendment, Code Sec. 367(b) read as follows:

(b) APPLICATION OF SUBSECTION (a)(2).—Subsection (a)(2) shall apply in the case of a mere change in form in which there is an exchange by a foreign corporation of—

(1) stock in one foreign corporation for,

(2) stock in another foreign corporation,

if the corporations referred to in paragraphs (1) and (2) differ only in their form of organization, and if the ownership of the corporation referred to in paragraph (1) immediately before such exchange is identical to the ownership of the corporation referred to in paragraph (2) immediately after such exchange.

• 1971 (P.L. 91-681)

P.L. 91-681, §1(a):

Amended Code Sec. 367. **Effective** for transfers made after 12-31-67 (see note for P.L. 91-681, §1(a), following Code Sec. 367(a)).

[Sec. 367(c)]

(c) TRANSACTIONS TO BE TREATED AS EXCHANGES.—

(1) SECTION 355 DISTRIBUTION.—For purposes of this section, any distribution described in section 355 (or so much of section 356 as relates to section 355) shall be treated as an exchange whether or not it is an exchange.

(2) CONTRIBUTION OF CAPITAL TO CONTROLLED CORPORATIONS.—For purposes of this chapter, any transfer of property to a foreign corporation as a contribution to the capital of such corporation by one or more persons who, immediately after the transfer, own (within the meaning of section 318) stock possessing at least 80 percent of the total combined voting power of all classes of stock of such corporation entitled to vote shall be treated as an exchange of such property for stock of the foreign corporation equal in value to the fair market value of the property transferred.

Amendments

• 1976, Tax Reform Act of 1976 (P.L. 94-455)

P.L. 94-455, §1042(a):

Amended Code Sec. 367(c). **Effective** for transfers beginning after 10-9-75, and for sales, exchanges, and distributions taking place after that date (see note for P.L. 94-455, §1042(a), following Code Sec. 367(a)). Prior to amendment, Code Sec. 367(c) read as follows:

(c) SECTION 355 DISTRIBUTIONS TREATED AS EXCHANGES.—For purposes of this section, any distribution described in section 355 (or so much of section 356 as relates to section 355) shall be treated as an exchange whether or not it is an exchange.

• 1971 (P.L. 91-681)

P.L. 91-681, §1(a):

Amended Code Sec. 367. **Effective** for transfers made after 12-31-67 (see note for P.L. 91-681, §1(a), following Code Sec. 367(a)).

[Sec. 367(d)]

(d) SPECIAL RULES RELATING TO TRANSFERS OF INTANGIBLES.—

(1) IN GENERAL.—Except as provided in regulations prescribed by the Secretary, if a United States person transfers any intangible property (within the meaning of section 936(h)(3)(B)) to a foreign corporation in an exchange described in section 351 or 361—

(A) subsection (a) shall not apply to the transfer of such property, and

(B) the provisions of this subsection shall apply to such transfer.

(2) TRANSFER OF INTANGIBLES TREATED AS TRANSFER PURSUANT TO SALE OF CONTINGENT PAYMENTS.—

(A) IN GENERAL.—If paragraph (1) applies to any transfer, the United States person transferring such property shall be treated as—

(i) having sold such property in exchange for payments which are contingent upon the productivity, use, or disposition of such property, and

(ii) receiving amounts which reasonably reflect the amounts which would have been received—

(I) annually in the form of such payments over the useful life of such property, or

(II) in the case of a disposition following such transfer (whether direct or indirect), at the time of the disposition.

The amounts taken into account under clause (ii) shall be commensurate with the income attributable to the intangible.

(B) EFFECT ON EARNINGS AND PROFITS.—For purposes of this chapter, the earnings and profits of a foreign corporation to which the intangible property was transferred shall be reduced by the amount required to be included in the income of the transferor of the intangible property under subparagraph (A)(ii).

(C) AMOUNTS RECEIVED TREATED AS ORDINARY INCOME.—For purposes of this chapter, any amount included in gross income by reason of this subsection shall be treated as ordinary income. For purposes of applying section 904(d), any such amount shall be treated in the same manner as if such amount were a royalty.

(3) REGULATIONS RELATING TO TRANSFERS OF INTANGIBLES TO PARTNERSHIPS.—The Secretary may provide by regulations that the rules of paragraph (2) also apply to the transfer of intangible property by a United States person to a partnership in circumstances consistent with the purposes of this subsection.

Amendments

• 2004, American Jobs Creation Act of 2004 (P.L. 108-357)

P.L. 108-357, §406(a):

Amended Code Sec. 367(d)(2)(C) by adding at the end a new sentence. **Effective** for amounts treated as received pursuant to Code Sec. 367(d)(2) on or after 8-5-97.

• 1997, Taxpayer Relief Act of 1997 (P.L. 105-34)

P.L. 105-34, §1131(b)[(c)](4):

Amended Code Sec. 367(d)(2)(C). **Effective** 8-5-97. Prior to amendment, Code Sec. 367(d)(2)(C) read as follows:

(C) AMOUNTS RECEIVED TREATED AS UNITED STATES SOURCE ORDINARY INCOME.—For purposes of this chapter, any amount included in gross income by reason of this subsection shall be treated as ordinary income from sources within the United States.

P.L. 105-34, §1131(b)[(c)](5)(A):

Amended Code Sec. 367(d) by adding at the end a new paragraph (3). **Effective** 8-5-97.

• 1986, Tax Reform Act of 1986 (P.L. 99-514)

P.L. 99-514, §1231(e)(2):

Amended Code Sec. 367(d)(2)(A) by adding at the end thereof a new sentence. **Effective**, generally, for tax years beginning after 12-31-86. For special and transitional rules, see Act Sec. 1231(g)(2)-(5), below.

P.L. 99-514, §1231(g)(2)-(5), as amended by P.L. 100-647 §1012(n), provides:

(2) SPECIAL RULE FOR TRANSFER OF INTANGIBLES.—

(A) IN GENERAL.—The amendments made by subsection (e) shall apply to taxable years beginning after December 31, 1986, but only with respect to transfers after November 16, 1985, or licenses granted after such date (or before such date with respect to property not in existence or owned by the taxpayer on such date).

In the case of any transfer (or license) which is not to a foreign person, the preceding sentence shall be applied by substituting "August 16, 1986" for "November 16, 1985".

(B) SPECIAL RULE FOR SECTION 936.—For purposes of section 936(h)(5)(C) of the Internal Revenue Code of 1986 the amendments made by subsection (e) shall apply to taxable years beginning after December 31, 1986, without regard to when the transfer (or license), if any, was made.

(3) SUBSECTION (f).—The amendment made by subsection (f) shall apply to taxable years beginning after December 31, 1982.

(4) TRANSITIONAL RULE.—In the case of a corporation—

(A) with respect to which an election under section 936 of the Internal Revenue Code of 1986 (relating to possessions tax credit) is in effect,

(B) which produced an end-product form in Puerto Rico on or before September 3, 1982,

(C) which began manufacturing a component of such product in Puerto Rico in its taxable year beginning in 1983, and

(D) with respect to which a Puerto Rican tax exemption was granted on June 27, 1983.

such corporation shall treat such component as a separate product for such taxable year for purposes of determining whether such corporation had a significant business presence in Puerto Rico with respect to such product and its income with respect to such product.

(5) TRANSITIONAL RULE FOR INCREASE IN GROSS INCOME TEST.—

(A) IN GENERAL.—If—

(i) a corporation fails to meet the requirements of subparagraph (B) of section 936(a)(2) of the Internal Revenue Code of 1986 (as amended by subsection (d)(1)) for any taxable year beginning in 1987 or 1988,

(ii) such corporation would have met the requirements of such subparagraph (B) if such subparagraph had been applied without regard to the amendment made by subsection (d)(1), and

(iii) 75 percent or more of the gross income of such corporation for such taxable year (or, in the case of a taxable year beginning in 1988, for the period consisting of such taxable year and the preceding taxable year) was derived from the active conduct of a trade or business within a possession of the United States, such corporation shall nevertheless be treated as meeting the requirements of such subparagraph (B) for such taxable year if it elects to reduce the amount of the qualified possession source investment income for the taxable year by the amount of the shortfall determined under subparagraph (B) of this paragraph.

(B) DETERMINATION OF SHORTFALL.—The shortfall determined under this subparagraph for any taxable year is an amount equal to the excess of—

(i) 75 percent of the gross income of the corporation for the 3-year period (or part thereof) referred to in section 936(a)(2)(A) of such Code, over

(ii) the amount of the gross income of such corporation for such period (or part therof) which was derived from the active conduct of a trade or business within a possession of the United States.

(C) SPECIAL RULE.—Any income attributable to the investment of the amount not treated as qualified possession source investment income under subparagraph (A) shall not be treated as qualified possession source investment income for any taxable year.

• 1984, Deficit Reduction Act of 1984 (P.L. 98-369)

P.L. 98-369, §131(b):

Amended Code Sec. 367(d). **Effective** for transfers or exchanges after 12-31-84, in tax years ending after such date. However, see Act Sec. 131(g)(2)-(3) following Code Sec. 367(e) for special rules. Prior to amendment, Code Sec. 367(d) read as follows:

(d) Special Rule Relating to Transfer of Intangibles by Possession Corporations.—

(1) In General.—If, after August 14, 1982, any possession corporation transfers, directly or indirectly, any intangible property (within the meaning of section 936(h)(3)(B)) to any foreign corporation, such transfer shall be treated for purposes of subsection (a) as pursuant to a plan having as one of its principal purposes the avoidance of Federal income taxes.

(2) Possession Corporation.—

(A) In General.—The term "possession corporation" means any corporation—

(i) to which an election under section 936 applies, or

(ii) which is described in subsection (b) of section 934 and which is an inhabitant of the Virgin Islands (within the meaning of section 28(a) of the Revised Organic Act of the Virgin Islands).

(B) Former Possession Corporation.—A corporation shall be treated as a possession corporation with respect to any transfer if such corporation was a possession corporation (within the meaning of subparagraph (A)) at any time during the 5-year period ending on the date of such transfer.

(3) Transfer by United States Affiliates.—A rule similar to the rule of paragraph (1) shall apply in the case of a direct or indirect transfer by a United States affiliate to a foreign person of intangible property which, after August 14, 1982, was being used (or held for use) by a possession corporation under an arrangement with a United States affiliate. For purposes of the preceding sentence, the term "United States affiliate" means any United States person who is a member of an affiliated group (within the meaning of section 936(h)(5)(C)(i)(I)(b)) which includes the possession corporation.

(4) Waiver Authority.—Subject to such terms and conditions as the Secretary may provide, paragraph (1) or (3) shall not apply to any case where the Secretary is satisfied that the transfer will not result in the reduction of current or future Federal income taxes.

• 1982, Tax Equity and Fiscal Responsibility Act of 1982 (P.L. 97-248)

P.L. 97-248, §213(d):

Added new subsection (d). **Effective** for tax years beginning after 8-14-82.

[Sec. 367(e)]

(e) TREATMENT OF DISTRIBUTIONS DESCRIBED IN SECTION 355 OR LIQUIDATIONS UNDER SECTION 332.—

(1) DISTRIBUTIONS DESCRIBED IN SECTION 355.—In the case of any distribution described in section 355 (or so much of section 356 as relates to section 355) by a domestic corporation to a person who is not a United States person, to the extent provided in regulations, gain shall be recognized under principles similar to the principles of this section.

(2) LIQUIDATIONS UNDER SECTION 332.—In the case of any liquidation to which section 332 applies, except as provided in regulations, subsections (a) and (b)(1) of section 337 shall not apply where the 80-percent distributee (as defined in section 337(c)) is a foreign corporation.

Amendments

• 1986, Tax Reform Act of 1986 (P.L. 99-514)

P.L. 99-514, §631(d)(1):

Amended Code Sec. 367(e). **Effective**, generally, for:

(1) any distribution in complete liquidation, and any sale or exchange, made by a corporation after 7-31-86, unless such corporation is completely liquidated before 1-1-87,

(2) any transaction described in section 338 of the Internal Revenue Code of 1986 for which the acquisition date occurs after 12-31-86, and

(3) any distribution (not in complete liquidation) made after 12-31-86. For special rules and exceptions, see Act Sec. 633(b)-(f) following Code Sec. 26. Prior to amendment, Code Sec. 367(e) read as follows:

(e) TREATMENT OF DISTRIBUTIONS DESCRIBED IN SECTION 336 OR 355.—In the case of any distribution described in section 336 or 355 (or so much of section 356 as relates to section 355) by a domestic corporation which is made to a person who is not a United States person, to the extent provided in regulations, gain shall be recognized under principles similar to the principles of this section.

P.L. 99-514, §1810(g)(4)(B)(i) and (ii):

Amended Code Sec. 367(e) by striking out "described in section 336" and inserting in lieu thereof "described in section 336 or 355 (or so much of section 356 as relates to section 355)", and by striking out "Liquidations Under Section 366 [336]" in the subsection heading and inserting in lieu thereof "Distributions Described in Section 336 or 355". **Effective** as if included in the provision of P.L. 98-369 to which it relates.

• 1984, Deficit Reduction Act of 1984 (P.L. 98-369)

P.L. 98-369, §131(c):

Redesignated Code Sec. 367(e) as Code Sec. 367(f) and added new subsection (e). **Effective** for transfers or exchanges after 12-31-84, in tax years ending after such date. However, see Act Sec. 131(g)(2)-(3), below, for special rules.

P.L. 98-369, §131(g)(2)-(3), provides:

(2) Special Rule for Certain Transfers of Intangibles.—

(A) In General.—If, after June 6, 1984, and before January 1, 1985, a United States person transfers any intangible property (within the meaning of section 936(h)(3)(B) of the Internal Revenue Code of 1954) to a foreign corporation or in a transfer described in section 1491, such transfer shall be treated for purposes of sections 367(a), 1492(2), and 1494(b) of such Code as pursuant to a plan having as one of its principal purposes the avoidance of Federal income tax.

(B) Waiver.—Subject to such terms and conditions as the Secretary of the Treasury or his delegate may prescribe, the Secretary may waive the application of subparagraph (A) with respect to any transfer.

(3) Ruling Request Before March 1, 1984.—The amendments made by this section (and the provisions of paragraph (2) of this subsection) shall not apply to any transfer or exchange of property described in a request filed before March 1, 1984, under section 367(a), 1492(2), or 1494(b) of the Internal Revenue Code of 1954 (as in effect before such amendments).

[Sec. 367(f)]

(f) OTHER TRANSFERS.—To the extent provided in regulations, if a United States person transfers property to a foreign corporation as paid-in surplus or as a contribution to capital (in a transaction not otherwise described in this section), such transfer shall be treated as a sale or exchange for an amount equal to the fair market value of the property transferred, and the transferor shall recognize as gain the excess of—

(1) the fair market value of the property so transferred, over

(2) the adjusted basis (for purposes of determining gain) of such property in the hands of the transferor.

Amendments

• 1997, Taxpayer Relief Act of 1997 (P.L. 105-34)

P.L. 105-34, §1131(b)[(c)](2):

Amended Code Sec. 367 by adding at the end a new subsection (f). **Effective** 8-5-97.

[Sec. 367(f)—Repealed]

Amendments

• 1986, Tax Reform Act of 1986 (P.L. 99-514)

P.L. 99-514, §1810(g)(1):

Repealed Code Sec. 367(f). **Effective** as if included in the provision of P.L. 98-369 to which it relates. Prior to repeal, Code Sec. 367(f) read as follows:

(f) TRANSITIONAL RULE.—In the case of any exchange beginning before January 1, 1978—

(1) subsection (a) shall be applied without regard to whether or not there is a transfer of property described in subsection (a)(1), and

(2) subsection (b) shall not apply.

• 1984, Deficit Reduction Act of 1984 (P.L. 98-369)

P.L. 98-369, §131(c):

Redesignated Code Sec. 367(e) as Code Sec. 367(f). **Effective** for transfers or exchanges after 12-31-84, in tax years ending after such date.

• 1982, Tax Equity and Fiscal Responsibility Act of 1982 (P.L. 97-248)

P.L. 97-248, §213(d):

Amended Code Sec. 367 by redesignating subsection (d) as subsection (e). **Effective** for tax years beginning after 8-14-82.

• 1976, Tax Reform Act of 1976 (P.L. 94-455)

P.L. 94-455, §1042(a):

Amended Code Sec. 367(d). **Effective** for pleadings filed with the Tax Court after 10-4-76, but only with respect to transfers beginning after 10-9-75 (see amendatory note for P.L. 94-455, §1042(a), following Code Sec. 367(a)). Prior to amendment, Code Sec. 367(d) read as follows:

(d) CONTRIBUTIONS OF CAPITAL TO CONTROLLED CORPORATIONS.—For purposes of this chapter, any transfer of property to a foreign corporation as a contribution to the capital of such corporation by one or more persons who, immediately after the transfer, own (within the meaning of section 318) stock possessing at least 80 percent of the total combined voting power of all classes of stock of such corporation entitled to vote shall be treated as an exchange of such property for stock of the foreign corporation equal in value to the fair market value of the property transferred unless, before such transfer, it has been established to the satisfaction of the Secretary or his delegate that such transfer is not in pursuance of a plan having as one of its principal purposes the avoidance of Federal income taxes.

• 1971 (P.L. 91-681)

P.L. 91-681, §1(a):

Amended Code Sec. 367. **Effective** for transfers made after 12-31-70 (see note for P.L. 91-681, §1(a), following Code Sec. 367(a)).

[Sec. 368]

SEC. 368. DEFINITIONS RELATING TO CORPORATE REORGANIZATIONS.

[Sec. 368(a)]

(a) REORGANIZATION.—

(1) IN GENERAL.—For purposes of parts I and II and this part, the term "reorganization" means—

(A) a statutory merger or consolidation;

(B) the acquisition by one corporation, in exchange solely for all or a part of its voting stock (or in exchange solely for all or a part of the voting stock of a corporation which is in control of the acquiring corporation), of stock of another corporation if, immediately after the acquisition, the acquiring corporation has control of such other corporation (whether or not such acquiring corporation had control immediately before the acquisition);

(C) the acquisition by one corporation, in exchange solely for all or a part of its voting stock (or in exchange solely for all or a part of the voting stock of a corporation which is in control of the acquiring corporation), of substantially all of the properties of another corporation, but in determining whether the exchange is solely for stock the assumption by the acquiring corporation of a liability of the other shall be disregarded;

(D) a transfer by a corporation of all or a part of its assets to another corporation if immediately after the transfer the transferor, or one or more of its shareholders (including persons who were shareholders immediately before the transfer), or any combination thereof, is in control of the corporation to which the assets are transferred; but only if, in pursuance of the plan, stock or securities of the corporation to which the assets are transferred are distributed in a transaction which qualifies under section 354, 355, or 356;

(E) a recapitalization;

(F) a mere change in identity, form, or place of organization of one corporation, however effected; or

(G) a transfer by a corporation of all or part of its assets to another corporation in a title 11 or similar case; but only if, in pursuance of the plan, stock or securities of the corporation to which the assets are transferred are distributed in a transaction which qualifies under section 354, 355, or 356.

(2) SPECIAL RULES RELATING TO PARAGRAPH (1).—

(A) REORGANIZATIONS DESCRIBED IN BOTH PARAGRAPH (1)(C) AND PARAGRAPH (1)(D).—If a transaction is described in both paragraph (1)(C) and paragraph (1)(D), then, for purposes of this subchapter (other than for purposes of subparagraph (C)), such transaction shall be treated as described only in paragraph (1)(D).

(B) ADDITIONAL CONSIDERATION IN CERTAIN PARAGRAPH (1)(C) CASES.—If—

(i) one corporation acquires substantially all of the properties of another corporation,

(ii) the acquisition would qualify under paragraph (1)(C) but for the fact that the acquiring corporation exchanges money or other property in addition to voting stock, and

(iii) the acquiring corporation acquires, solely for voting stock described in paragraph (1)(C), property of the other corporation having a fair market value which is at least 80 percent of the fair market value of all of the property of the other corporation,

then such acquisition shall (subject to subparagraph (A) of this paragraph) be treated as qualifying under paragraph (1)(C). Solely for the purpose of determining whether clause (iii) of the preceding sentence applies, the amount of any liability assumed by the acquiring corporation shall be treated as money paid for the property.

(C) TRANSFERS OF ASSETS OR STOCK TO SUBSIDIARIES IN CERTAIN PARAGRAPH (1)(A), (1)(B), (1)(C), AND (1)(G) CASES.—A transaction otherwise qualifying under paragraph (1)(A), (1)(B), or (1)(C) shall not be disqualified by reason of the fact that part or all of the assets or stock which were acquired in the transaction are transferred to a corporation controlled by the corporation acquiring such assets or stock. A similar rule shall apply to a transaction otherwise qualifying under paragraph (1)(G) where the requirements of subparagraphs (A) and (B) of section 354(b)(1) are met with respect to the acquisition of the assets.

(D) USE OF STOCK OF CONTROLLING CORPORATION IN PARAGRAPH (1)(A) AND (1)(G) CASES.—The acquisition by one corporation, in exchange for stock of a corporation (referred to in this subparagraph as "controlling corporation") which is in control of the acquiring corporation, of substantially all of the properties of another corporation shall not disqualify a transaction under paragraph (1)(A) or (1)(G) if—

(i) no stock of the acquiring corporation is used in the transaction, and

(ii) in the case of a transaction under paragraph (1)(A), such transaction would have qualified under paragraph (1)(A) had the merger been into the controlling corporation.

(E) STATUTORY MERGER USING VOTING STOCK OF CORPORATION CONTROLLING MERGED CORPORATION.—A transaction otherwise qualifying under paragraph (1)(A) shall not be disqualified by reason of the fact that stock of a corporation (referred to in this subparagraph as the "controlling corporation") which before the merger was in control of the merged corporation is used in the transaction, if—

(i) after the transaction, the corporation surviving the merger holds substantially all of its properties and of the properties of the merged corporation (other than stock of the controlling corporation distributed in the transaction); and

(ii) in the transaction, former shareholders of the surviving corporation exchanged, for an amount of voting stock of the controlling corporation, an amount of stock in the surviving corporation which constitutes control of such corporation.

(F) CERTAIN TRANSACTIONS INVOLVING 2 OR MORE INVESTMENT COMPANIES.—

(i) If immediately before a transaction described in paragraph (1) (other than subparagraph (E) thereof), 2 or more parties to the transaction were investment companies, then the transaction shall not be considered to be a reorganization with respect to any such investment company (and its shareholders and security holders) unless it was a regulated investment company, a real estate investment trust, or a corporation which meets the requirements of clause (ii).

(ii) A corporation meets the requirements of this clause if not more than 25 percent of the value of its total assets is invested in the stock and securities of any one issuer and not more than 50 percent of the value of its total assets is invested in the stock and securities of 5 or fewer issuers. For purposes of this clause, all members of a controlled group of corporations (within the meaning of section 1563(a)) shall be treated as one issuer. For purposes of this clause, a person holding stock in a regulated investment company, a real estate investment trust, or an investment company which meets the requirements of this clause shall, except as provided in regulations, be treated as holding its proportionate share of the assets held by such company or trust.

(iii) For purposes of this subparagraph the term "investment company" means a regulated investment company, a real estate investment trust, or a corporation 50 percent or more of the value of whose total assets are stock and securities and 80 percent or more of the value of whose total assets are assets held for investment. In making the 50-percent and 80-percent determinations under the preceding sentence, stock and securities in any subsidiary corporation shall be disregarded and the parent corporation shall be deemed to own its ratable share of the subsidiary's assets, and a corporation shall be considered a subsidiary if the parent owns 50 percent or more of the combined voting power of all classes of stock entitled to vote, or 50 percent or more of the total value of shares of all classes of stock outstanding.

(iv) For purposes of this subparagraph, in determining total assets there shall be excluded cash and cash items (including receivables), Government securities, and, under regulations prescribed by the Secretary, assets acquired (through incurring indebtedness or otherwise) for purposes of meeting the requirements of clause (ii) or ceasing to be an investment company.

(v) This subparagraph shall not apply if the stock of each investment company is owned substantially by the same persons in the same proportions.

(vi) If an investment company which does not meet the requirements of clause (ii) acquires assets of another corporation, clause (i) shall be applied to such investment company and its shareholders and security holders as though its assets had been acquired by such other corporation. If such investment company acquires stock of another corporation in a reorganization described in section 368(a)(1)(B), clause (i) shall be applied to the shareholders of such investment company as though they had exchanged with such other corporation all of their stock in such company for stock having a fair market value equal to the fair market value of their stock of such investment company immediately after the exchange. For purposes of section 1001, the deemed acquisition or exchange referred to in the two preceding sentences shall be treated as a sale or exchange of property by the corporation and by the shareholders and security holders to which clause (i) is applied.

(vii) For purposes of clauses (ii) and (iii), the term "securities" includes obligations of State and local governments, commodity futures contracts, shares of regulated investment companies and real estate investment trusts, and other investments constituting a security within the meaning of the Investment Company Act of 1940 (15 U.S.C. 80a-2(36)).

(G) DISTRIBUTION REQUIREMENT FOR PARAGRAPH (1)(C).—

(i) IN GENERAL.—A transaction shall fail to meet the requirements of paragraph (1)(C) unless the acquired corporation distributes the stock, securities, and other properties it receives, as well as its other properties, in pursuance of the plan of reorganization. For purposes of the preceding sentence, if the acquired corporation is liquidated pursuant to the plan of reorganization, any distribution to its creditors in connection with such liquidation shall be treated as pursuant to the plan of reorganization.

(ii) EXCEPTION.—The Secretary may waive the application of clause (i) to any transaction subject to any conditions the Secretary may prescribe.

(H) SPECIAL RULES FOR DETERMINING WHETHER CERTAIN TRANSACTIONS ARE QUALIFIED UNDER PARAGRAPH (1)(D).—For purposes of determining whether a transaction qualifies under paragraph (1)(D)—

(i) in the case of a transaction with respect to which the requirements of subparagraphs (A) and (B) of section 354(b)(1) are met, the term "control" has the meaning given such term by section 304(c), and

(ii) in the case of a transaction with respect to which the requirements of section 355 (or so much of section 356 as relates to section 355) are met, the fact that the shareholders of the distributing corporation dispose of part or all of the distributed stock, or the fact that the corporation whose stock was distributed issues additional stock, shall not be taken into account.

(3) ADDITIONAL RULES RELATING TO TITLE 11 AND SIMILAR CASES.—

(A) TITLE 11 OR SIMILAR CASE DEFINED.—For purposes of this part, the term "title 11 or similar case" means—

(i) a case under title 11 of the United States Code, or

(ii) a receivership, foreclosure, or similar proceeding in a Federal or State court.

(B) TRANSFER OF ASSETS IN A TITLE 11 OR SIMILAR CASE.—In applying paragraph (1)(G), a transfer of the assets of a corporation shall be treated as made in a title 11 or similar case if and only if—

(i) any party to the reorganization is under the jurisdiction of the court in such case, and

(ii) the transfer is pursuant to a plan of reorganization approved by the court.

(C) REORGANIZATIONS QUALIFYING UNDER PARAGRAPH (1)(G) AND ANOTHER PROVISION.—If a transaction would (but for this subparagraph) qualify both—

(i) under subparagraph (G) of paragraph (1), and

(ii) under any other subparagraph of paragraph (1) or under section 332 or 351,

then, for purposes of this subchapter (other than section 357(c)(1)), such transaction shall be treated as qualifying only under subparagraph (G) of paragraph (1).

(D) AGENCY RECEIVERSHIP PROCEEDINGS WHICH INVOLVE FINANCIAL INSTITUTIONS.—For purposes of subparagraphs (A) and (B), in the case of a receivership, foreclosure, or similar proceeding before a Federal or State agency involving a financial institution referred to in section 581 or 591, the agency shall be treated as a court.

(E) APPLICATION OF PARAGRAPH (2)(E)(ii).—In the case of a title 11 or similar case, the requirement of clause (ii) of paragraph (2)(E) shall be treated as met if—

(i) no former shareholder of the surviving corporation received any consideration for his stock, and

(ii) the former creditors of the surviving corporation exchanged, for an amount of voting stock of the controlling corporation, debt of the surviving corporation which had a fair market value equal to 80 percent or more of the total fair market value of the debt of the surviving corporation.

Amendments

• 1999, Miscellaneous Trade and Technical Corrections Act of 1999 (P.L. 106-36)

P.L. 106-36, §3001(a)(3)(A):

Amended Code Sec. 368(a)(1)(C) by striking ", or the fact that property acquired is subject to a liability," following "liability of the other". **Effective** for transfers after 10-18-98.

P.L. 106-36, §3001(a)(3)(B):

Amended the last sentence of Code Sec. 368(a)(2)(B) by striking ", and the amount of any liability to which any property acquired from [by] the acquiring corporation is subject," following "acquiring corporation". **Effective** for transfers after 10-18-98.

• 1998, Tax and Trade Relief Extension Act of 1998. (P.L. 105-277)

P.L. 105-277, §4003(f)(2):

Amended Code Sec. 368(a)(2)(H)(ii) by inserting ", or the fact that the corporation whose stock was distributed issues additional stock," after "dispose of part or all of the distributed stock". **Effective** as if included in the provision of P.L. 105-34 to which it relates [generally **effective** for transfers after 8-5-97.—CCH].

• 1998, IRS Restructuring and Reform Act of 1998 (P.L. 105-206)

P.L. 105-206, §6010(c)(3)(B):

Amended Code Sec. 368(a)(2)(H)(ii). **Effective** as if included in the provision of P.L. 105-34 to which it relates [generally **effective** for transfers after 8-5-97.—CCH]. Prior to amendment, Code Sec. 368(a)(2)(H)(ii) read as follows:

(ii) in the case of a transaction with respect to which the requirements of section 355 are met, the shareholders described in paragraph (1)(D) shall be treated as having control of the corporation to which the assets are transferred if such shareholders own (immediately after the distribution) stock possessing—

(I) more than 50 percent of the total combined voting power of all classes of stock of such corporation entitled to vote, and

(II) more than 50 percent of the total value of shares of all classes of stock of such corporation.

• 1997, Taxpayer Relief Act of 1997 (P.L. 105-34)

P.L. 105-34, §1012(c)(2):

Amended Code Sec. 368(a)(2)(H). **Effective**, generally, for transfers after 8-5-97. For a transitional rule, see Act Sec. 1012(d)(3), below. Prior to amendment, Code Sec. 368(a)(2)(H) read as follows:

(H) SPECIAL RULE FOR DETERMINING WHETHER CERTAIN TRANSACTIONS ARE QUALIFIED UNDER PARAGRAPH (1)(D).—In the case of any transaction with respect to which the requirements of subparagraphs (A) and (B) of section 354(b)(1) are met, for purposes of determining whether such transaction qualifies under subparagraph (D) of paragraph (1), the term "control" has the meaning given to such term by section 304(c).

P.L. 105-34, §1012(d)(3), provides:

(3) TRANSITION RULE.—The amendments made by this section shall not apply to any distribution pursuant to a plan (or series of related transactions) which involves an acquisition described in section 355(e)(2)(A)(ii) of the Internal Revenue Code of 1986 (or, in the case of the amendments made by subsection (c), any transfer) occurring after April 16, 1997, if such acquisition or transfer is—

(A) made pursuant to an agreement which was binding on such date and at all times thereafter,

(B) described in a ruling request submitted to the Internal Revenue Service on or before such date, or

(C) described on or before such date in a public announcement or in a filing with the Securities and Exchange Commission required solely by reason of the acquisition or transfer.

This paragraph shall not apply to any agreement, ruling request, or public announcement or filing unless it identifies the acquirer of the distributing corporation or any controlled corporation, or the transferee, whichever is applicable.

• 1989, Financial Institutions Reform, Recovery, and Enforcement Act of 1989 (P.L. 101-73)

P.L. 101-73, §1401(a)(1):

Amended Code Sec. 368(a)(3)(D). **Effective** for acquisitions on or after 5-10-89. Prior to amendment, Code Sec. 368(a)(3)(D) read as follows:

(D) AGENCY PROCEEDINGS WHICH INVOLVE FINANCIAL INSTITUTIONS.—

(i) For purpose[s]of subparagraphs (A) and (B)—

(I) In the case of a receivership, foreclosure, or similar proceeding before a Federal or State agency involving a financial institution to which section 585 applies, the agency shall be treated as a court, and

(II) In the case of a financial institution to which section 593 applies, the term "title 11 or similar case" means only a case in which the Board (which will be treated as the court in such case) makes the certification described in clause (ii).

(ii) A transaction otherwise meeting the requirements of subparagraph (G) of paragraph (1), in which the transferor corporation is a financial institution to which section 593 applies, will not be disqualified as a reorganization if no stock or securities of the corporation to which the assets are transferred (transferee) are received or distributed, but only if all of the following conditions are met:

(I) the requirements of subparagraphs (A) and (B) of section 354(b)(1) are met with respect to the acquisition of the assets,

(II) substantially all of the liabilities of the transferor immediately before the transfer become, as a result of the transfer, liabilities of the transferee, and

(III) the Board certifies that the grounds set forth in section 1464(d)(6)(A)(i), (ii), or (iii) of title 12, United States Code, exist with respect to the transferor or will exist in the near future in the absence of action by the Board.

(iii) For purpose[s] of this subparagraph, the "Board" means the Federal Home Loan Bank Board or the Federal Savings and Loan Insurance Corporation or, if neither has supervisory authority with respect to the transferor, the equivalent State authority.

(iv) In the case of a financial institution to which section 585 applies—

(I) the term "title 11 or similar case" means only a case in which the applicable authority (which shall be treated as the court in such case) makes the certification described in subclause (II), and

(II) clause (ii) shall apply to such institution, except that for purposes of clause (ii)(III), the applicable authority must certify that the grounds set forth in such clause (modified in such manner as the Secretary determines necessary because such institution is not an institution to which section 593 applies) exist with respect to such transferor or will exist in the near future in the absence of action by the applicable authority.

For purposes of this clause, the term "applicable authority" means the Comptroller of the Currency or the Federal Deposit Insurance Corporation, or if neither has the supervisory authority with respect to the transfer, the equivalent State authority.

(v) For purposes of this subparagraph, in applying section 593, the determination as to whether a corporation is a domestic building and loan association shall be made without regard to section 7701(a)(19)(C).

P.L. 101-73, §1401(b)(1):

Repealed Section 904 of P.L. 99-514 [see amendment note below], which amended Code Sec. 368(a)(3)(D) to read as follows:

(D) AGENCY RECEIVERSHIP PROCEEDINGS WHICH INVOLVE FINANCIAL INSTITUTIONS.—For purposes of subparagraphs (A) and (B), in the case of a receivership, foreclosure, or similar proceeding before a Federal or State agency involving a financial institution referred to in section 581 or 591, the agency shall be treated as a court. **Effective** 10-22-86, the date of enactment of P.L. 99-514.

• 1988, Technical and Miscellaneous Revenue Act of 1988 (P.L. 100-647)

P.L. 100-647, §1018(q)(5)(A)-(B):

Amended Code Sec. 368(a)(2)(F)(ii) by striking out the two parenthetical phrases in the first sentence and by adding at the end thereof a new sentence. **Effective** as if included in the provision of P.L. 99-514 to which it relates. Prior to amendment, the first sentence read as follows:

A corporation meets the requirements of this clause if not more than 25 percent of the value of its total assets is invested in the stock and securities of any one issuer (other than stock in a regulated investment company, a real estate investment trust, or an investment company which meets the requirements of this clause (ii)), and not more than 50 percent of the value of its total assets is invested in the stock and securities of 5 or fewer issuers (other than stock in a regulated investment company, a real estate investment trust, or an investment company, which meets the requirements of this clause (ii)).

P.L. 100-647, §4012(b)(1)(A):

Amended Code Sec. 368(a)(3)(D) (as in effect before the amendment made by P.L. 99-514, §904) by adding at the end thereof new clauses (iv)-(v). **Effective** for acquisitions after the date of the enactment of this Act and before 1-1-90.

P.L. 100-647, §6126, provides:

SEC. 6126. DUAL RESIDENT COMPANIES.

(a) GENERAL RULE.—In the case of a transaction which—

(1) involves the transfer after the date of the enactment of this Act by a domestic corporation, with respect to which there is a qualified excess loss account, of its assets and liabilities to a foreign corporation in exchange for all of the stock of such foreign corporation, followed by the complete liquidation of the domestic corporation into the common parent, and

(2) qualifies, pursuant to Revenue Ruling 87-27, as a reorganization which is described in section 368(a)(1)(F) of the 1986 Code,

then, solely for purposes of applying Treasury Regulation section 1.1502-19 to such qualified excess loss account, such foreign corporation shall be treated as a domestic corporation in determining whether such foreign corporation is a member of the affiliated group of the common parent.

(b) TREATMENT OF INCOME OF NEW FOREIGN CORPORATION.—

(1) IN GENERAL.—In any case to which subsection (a) applies, for purposes of the 1986 Code—

(A) the source and character of any item of income of the foreign corporation referred to in subsection (a) shall be determined as if such foreign corporation were a domestic corporation,

(B) the net amount of any such income shall be treated as subpart F income (without regard to section 952(c) of the 1986 Code), and

(C) the amount in the qualified excess loss account referred to in subsection (a) shall—

(i) be reduced by the net amount of any such income, and

(ii) be increased by the amount of any such income distributed directly or indirectly to the common parent described in subsection (a).

(2) LIMITATION.—Paragraph (1) shall apply to any item of income only to the extent that the net amount of such income does not exceed the amount in the qualified excess loss account after being reduced under paragraph (1)(C) for prior income.

(3) BASIS ADJUSTMENTS NOT APPLICABLE.—To the extent paragraph (1) applies to any item of income, there shall be no increase in basis under section 961(a) of such Code on account of such income (and there shall be no reduction in basis under section 961(b) of such Code on account of an exclusion attributable to the inclusion of such income).

(4) RECOGNITION OF GAIN.—For purposes of paragraph (1), if the foreign corporation referred to in subsection (a) transfers any property acquired by such foreign corporation in the transaction referred to in subsection (a) (or transfers any other property the basis of which is determined in whole or in part by reference to the basis of property so acquired) and (but for this paragraph) there is not full recognition of gain on such transfer, the excess (if any) of—

(A) the fair market value of the property transferred, over

(B) its adjusted basis,

shall be treated as gain from the sale or exchange of such property and shall be recognized notwithstanding any other provision of law. Proper adjustment shall be made to the basis of any such property for gain recognized under the preceding sentence.

(c) DEFINITIONS.—For purposes of this section—

(1) COMMON PARENT.—The term "common parent" means the common parent of the affiliated group which included the domestic corporation referred to in subsection (a)(1).

(2) QUALIFIED EXCESS LOSS ACCOUNT.—The term "qualified excess loss account" means any excess loss account (within the meaning of the consolidated return regulations) to the extent such account is attributable—

(A) to taxable years beginning before January 1, 1988, and

(B) to periods during which the domestic corporation was subject to an income tax of a foreign country on its income on a residence basis or without regard to whether such income is from sources in or outside of such foreign country.

The amount of such account shall be determined as of immediately after the transaction referred to in subsection (a) and without, except as provided in subsection (b), diminution for any future adjustment.

(3) NET AMOUNT.T he net amount of any item of income is the amount of such income reduced by allocable deductions as determined under the rules of section 954(b)(5) of the 1986 Code.

(4) SECOND SAME COUNTRY CORPORATION MAY BE TREATED AS DOMESTIC CORPORATION IN CERTAIN CASES.—If—

(A) another foreign corporation acquires from the common parent stock of the foreign corporation referred to in subsection (a) after the transaction referred to in subsection (a),

(B) both of such foreign corporations are subject to the income tax of the same foreign country on a residence basis, and

(C) such common parent complies with such reporting requirements as the Secretary of the Treasury or his delegate may prescribe for purposes of this paragraph,

such other foreign corporation shall be treated as a domestic corporation in determining whether the foreign corporation referred to in subsection (a) is a member of the affiliated group referred to in subsection (a) (and the rules of subsection (b) shall apply (i) to any gain of such other foreign corporation on any disposition of such stock, and (ii) to any other income of such other foreign corporation except to the extent it establishes to the satisfaction of the Secretary of the Treasury or his delegate that such income is not attributable to property acquired from the foreign corporation referred to in subsection (a)).

• 1986, Tax Reform Act of 1986 (P.L. 99-514)

P.L. 99-514, §904(a) [repealed by P.L. 101-73, §1401(b)(1)]:

Amended Code Sec. 368(a)(3)(D). **Effective** for acquisitions after 12-31-88, in tax years ending after such date. Prior to amendment, Code Sec. 368(a)(3)(D) read as follows:

(D) AGENCY PROCEEDINGS WHICH INVOLVE FINANCIAL INSTITUTIONS.—

(i) For purpose[s] of subparagraphs (A) and (B)—

(I) In the case of a receivership, foreclosure, or similar proceeding before a Federal or State agency involving a financial institution to which section 585 applies, the agency shall be treated as a court, and

(II) In the case of a financial institution to which section 593 applies, the term "title 11 or similar case" means only a case in which the Board (which will be treated as the court in such case) makes the certification described in clause (ii).

(ii) A transaction otherwise meeting the requirements of subparagraph (G) of paragraph (1), in which the transferor corporation is a financial institution to which section 593 applies, will not be disqualified as a reorganization if no stock or securities of the corporation to which the assets are transferred (transferee) are received or distributed, but only if all of the following conditions are met:

(I) the requirements of subparagraphs (A) and (B) of section 354(b)(1) are met with respect to the acquisition of the assets,

(II) substantially all of the liabilities of the transferor immediately before the transfer become, as a result of the transfer, liabilities of the transferee, and

(III) the Board certifies that the grounds set forth in section 1464(d)(6)(A)(i), (ii) or (iii) of title 12, United States Code, exist with respect to the transferor or will exist in the near future in the absence of action by the Board.

(iii) For purposes of this subparagraph, the "Board" means the Federal Home Loan Bank Board or the Federal Savings and Loan Insurance Corporation or, if neither has supervisory authority with respect to the transferor, the equivalent State authority.

(iv) In the case of a financial institution to which section 585 applies—

(I) the term "title 11 or similar case" means only a case in which the applicable authority (which shall be treated as the court in such case) makes the certification described in subclause (II), and

(II) clause (ii) shall apply to such institution, except that for purposes of clause (ii)(III), the applicable authority must certify that the grounds set forth in such clause (modified in such manner as the Secretary determines necessary because such institution is not an institution to which section 593 applies) exist with respect to such transferor or will exist in the near future in the absence of action by the applicable authority.

For purposes of this clause, the term "applicable authority" means the Comptroller of the Currency or the Federal Deposit Insurance Corporation, or if neither has the supervisory authority with respect to the transfer, the equivalent State authority.

(v) For purposes of this subparagraph, in applying section 593, the determination as to whether a corporation is a domestic building and loan association shall be made without regard to section 7701(a)(19)(C).

P.L. 99-514, §1804(g)(2):

Amended Code Sec. 368(a)(2)(G)(i) by adding at the end thereof a new sentence. **Effective** for plans of reorganizations adopted after 10-22-86.

P.L. 99-514, §1804(h)(2):

Amended Code Sec. 368(a)(2) by adding at the end thereof new subparagraph (H). **Effective** as if included in the provision of P.L. 98-369 to which it relates.

P.L. 99-514, §1804(h)(3):

Amended Code Sec. 368(a)(2) by inserting "(other than for purposes of subparagraph (C))" in subparagraph (A) after "subchapter". **Effective** as if included in the provision of P.L. 98-369 to which it relates.

P.L. 99-514, §1879(l)(1):

Amended Code Sec. 368(a)(2)(F)(ii). **Effective** as if included in P.L. 94-455, §2131. Prior to amendment, Code Sec. 368(a)(2)(F)(ii) read as follows:

(ii) A corporation meets the requirements of this clause if not more than 25 percent of the value of its total assets is invested in the stock and securities of any one issuer, and not more than 50 percent of the value of its total assets is invested in the stock and securities of 5 or fewer issuers. For purposes of this clause, all members of a controlled group of corporations (within the meaning of section 1563(a)) shall be treated as one issuer.

• 1984, Deficit Reduction Act of 1984 (P.L. 98-369)

P.L. 98-369, §63(a):

Amended Code Sec. 368(a)(2) by adding at the end thereof new subparagraph (G). **Effective** for transactions pursuant to plans adopted after 7-18-84.

P.L. 98-369, §174(b)(5)(D):

Amended Code Sec. 368(a)(2)(F) by striking out clause (viii). **Effective** for transactions after 12-31-83, in tax years ending after such date. However, see exceptions for transfers to foreign corporations on or before 3-1-84, described in Act Sec. 174(c)(2)(B) under the amendment notes for Code Sec. 267. Prior to amendment, clause (viii) read as follows:

(viii) In applying paragraph (3) of section 267(b) in respect of any transaction to which this subparagraph applies, the reference to a personal holding company in such paragraph (3) shall be treated as including a reference to an investment company and the determination of whether a corporation is an investment company shall be made as of the time immediately before the transaction instead of with respect to the taxable year referred to in such paragraph (3).

• 1983, Technical Corrections Act of 1982 (P.L. 97-448)

P.L. 97-448, §304(b):

Amended Code Sec. 368(a)(2)(C) by striking out "or stock". **Effective** as if included in the amendments made by §4 of P.L. 96-589.

P.L. 97-448, §304(c):

Amended Code Sec. 368(a)(3)(B)(i) by striking out "such corporation" and inserting in lieu thereof "any party to the reorganization". **Effective** 1-12-83.

• 1982, Tax Equity and Fiscal Responsibility Act of 1982 (P.L. 97-248)

P.L. 97-248, §225(a):

Amended subparagraph (F) of Code Sec. 368(a)(1) by inserting "of one corporation" after "place of organization". **Effective** for transactions occurring after 8-31-82, and shall not apply with respect to plans of reorganization adopted on or before 8-31-82, but only if the transaction occurs before 1-1-83.

• 1981, Economic Recovery Tax Act of 1981 (P.L. 97-34)

P.L. 97-34, §241:

Amended Code Sec. 368(a)(3)(D). **Effective** for any transfer made on or after 1-1-81. Prior to amendment, Code Sec. 368(a)(3)(D) read as follows:

(D) AGENCY RECEIVERSHIP PROCEEDINGS WHICH INVOLVE FINANCIAL INSTITUTIONS.—For purposes of subparagraphs (A) and (B), in the case of a receivership, foreclosure, or similar proceeding before a Federal or State agency involving a financial institution to which section 585 or 593 applies, the agency shall be treated as a court.

• 1980, Bankruptcy Tax Act of 1980 (P.L. 96-589)

P.L. 96-589, §4(a), (b), (c), (d):

Amended Code Sec. 368(a)(1) by adding a new subparagraph (G). Amended Code Sec. 368(a) by adding a new paragraph (3). Amended Code Sec. 368(a)(2)(C) to read as indicated. Prior to amendment, Code Sec. 368(a)(2)(C) provided:

"(C) TRANSFERS OF ASSETS OR STOCK TO SUBSIDIARIES IN CERTAIN PARAGRAPH (1)(A), (1)(B), AND (1)(C) CASES.—A transaction otherwise qualifying under paragraph (1)(A), (1)(B), or (1)(C) shall not be disqualified by reason of the fact that part or all of the assets or stock which were acquired in the transaction are transferred to a corporation controlled by the corporation acquiring such assets or stock."

Amended Code Sec. 368(a)(2)(D) to read as indicated. Prior to amendment, Code Sec. 368(a)(2)(D) provided:

"(D) STATUTORY MERGER USING STOCK OF CONTROLLING CORPORATION.—The acquisition by one corporation, in exchange for stock of a corporation (referred to in this subparagraph as `controlling corporation') which is in control of the acquiring corporation, of substantially all of the properties of another corporation which in the transaction is merged into the acquiring corporation shall not disqualify a transaction under paragraph (1)(A) if (i) such transaction would have qualified under paragraph (1)(A) if the merger had been into the controlling corporation, and (ii) no stock of the acquiring corporation is used in the transaction."

Section 7 of the Bankruptcy Tax Act of 1980, P.L. 96-589, provides for the following **effective** dates for amendments relating to corporate reorganization provisions:

"(c) FOR SECTION 4 (RELATING TO CORPORATE REORGANIZATION PROVISIONS).—

(1) IN GENERAL.—The amendments made by section 4 shall apply to any bankruptcy case or similar judicial proceeding commencing after December 31, 1980.

* * *

(f) ELECTION TO SUBSTITUTE SEPTEMBER 30, 1979, FOR DECEMBER 31, 1980.

(1) IN GENERAL.—The debtor (or debtors) in a bankruptcy case or similar judicial proceeding may (with the approval of the court) elect to apply subsections (a), (c), and (d) by substituting `September 30, 1979' for `December 31, 1980' each place it appears in such subsections.

(2) EFFECT OF ELECTION.—Any election made under paragraph (1) with respect to any proceeding shall apply to all parties to the proceeding.

(3) REVOCATION ONLY WITH CONSENT.—Any election under this subsection may be revoked only with the consent of the Secretary of the Treasury or his delegate.

(4) TIME AND MANNER OF ELECTION.—Any election under this subsection shall be made at such time, and in such manner, as the Secretary of the Treasury or his delegate may by regulations prescribe.

(g) DEFINITIONS.—For purposes of this section—

(1) BANKRUPTCY CASE.—The term `bankruptcy case' means any case under title 11 of the Unites States Code (as recodified by Public Law 95-598).

(2) SIMILAR JUDICIAL PROCEEDING.—The term `similar judicial proceeding' means a receivership, foreclosure, or similar proceeding in a Federal or State court (as modified by section 368(a)(3)(D) of the Internal Revenue Code of 1954)."

P.L. 96-589, §4(h)(3):

Amended Code Sec. 368(a)(1) by striking out "or" at the end of subparagraph (E) and by striking out the period at the end of subparagraph (F) and inserting in lieu thereof "; or". For the **effective** date of these amendments, see the historical comment for P.L. 96-589 under Code Sec. 370(a).

• 1978, Revenue Act of 1978 (P.L. 95-600)

P.L. 95-600, §701(j)(1)(A), (j)(2)(A):

Amended the first sentence of clause (iii) of Code Sec. 368(a)(2)(F) by striking out "more than 50 percent" and inserting in place thereof "50 percent or more" and by striking out "more than 80 percent" and inserting in place thereof "80 percent or more". **Effective** as if included in Code Sec. 368(a)(2)(F) as added by P.L. 94-455, Sec. 2131(a).

P.L. 95-600, §701(j)(1)(B), (C), (j)(2)(A):

Amended Code Sec. 368(a)(2)(F)(vi). **Effective** as if included in Code Sec. 368(a)(2)(F) as added by P.L. 94-455, Sec. 2131(a). Prior to amendment, clause (vi) read:

"(vi) If an investment company which is not diversified within the meaning of clause (ii) acquires assets of another corporation, clause (i) shall be applied to such investment company and its shareholders and security holders as though its assets had been acquired by such other corporation. If such investment company acquires stock of another corporation in a reorganization described in section 368(a)(1)(B) (hereafter referred to as the "actual acquisition"), clause (i) shall be applied to the shareholders and security holders of such investment company as though they had exchanged with such other corporation all of their stock in such investment company for a percentage of the value of the total outstanding stock of the other corporation equal to the percentage of the value of the total outstanding stock of such investment company which such shareholders own immediately after the actual acquisition. For purposes of section 1001, the deemed acquisition or exchange referred to in the two preceding sentences shall be treated as a sale or exchange of property by the corporation and by the shareholders and security holders to which clause (i) is applied."

P.L. 95-600, §701(j)(1)(D), (j)(2)(B), (C):

Added Code Sec. 368(a)(2)(F)(vii). **Effective** for transfers made after 9-26-77. Also added Code Sec. 368(a)(2)(F)(viii). **Effective** for losses sustained after 9-26-77.

• 1976, Tax Reform Act of 1976 (P.L. 94-455)

P.L. 94-455, §2131(a):

Added Code Sec. 368(a)(2)(F). **Effective** for transfers made after 2-17-76, in tax years ending after such date. The amendment shall not apply to transfers made in accordance with a ruling issued by the IRS before 2-18-76, holding that a proposed transaction would be a reorganization described in Code Sec. 368(a)(1).

• 1971 (P.L. 91-693)

P.L. 91-693, §1(a):

Amended Code Sec. 368(a)(2) by adding at the end thereof new subparagraph (E). **Effective** for statutory mergers occurring after 12-31-70.

• 1968 (P.L. 90-621)

P.L. 90-621, §1(a):

Amended subsection (a)(2) by adding at the end thereof new subparagraph (D). **Effective** for statutory mergers occurring after 10-22-68.

• 1964, Revenue Act of 1964 (P.L. 88-272)

P.L. 88-272, §218(a):

Amended subparagraph (B) of subsection (a)(1). **Effective** for transactions after 12-31-63, in tax years ending after such date. Prior to amendment, subparagraph (B) read as follows:

"(B) the acquisition by one corporation, in exchange solely for all or a part of its voting stock, of stock of another corporation if, immediately after the acquisition, the acquiring corporation has control of such other corporation (whether or not such acquiring corporation had control immediately before the acquisition);".

P.L. 88-272, §218(b)(1):

Amended subparagraph (C) of subsection (a)(2). **Effective** for transactions after 12-31-63, in tax years ending after such date. Prior to amendment, subparagraph (C) read as follows:

"(C) Transfers of assets to subsidiaries in certain paragraph (1)(A) and (1)(C) cases.—A transaction otherwise qualifying under paragraph (1)(A) or paragraph (1)(C) shall not be disqualified by reason of the fact that part or all of the assets which were acquired in the transaction are transferred to a corporation controlled by the corporation acquiring such assets."

[Sec. 368(b)]

(b) PARTY TO A REORGANIZATION.—For purposes of this part, the term "a party to a reorganization" includes—

(1) a corporation resulting from a reorganization, and

(2) both corporations, in the case of a reorganization resulting from the acquisition by one corporation of stock or properties of another.

In the case of a reorganization qualifying under paragraph (1)(B) or (1)(C) of subsection (a), if the stock exchanged for the stock or properties is stock of a corporation which is in control of the acquiring corporation, the term "a party to a reorganization" includes the corporation so controlling the acquiring corporation. In the case of a reorganization qualifying under paragraph (1)(A), (1)(B), (1)(C), or (1)(G) of subsection (a) by reason of paragraph (2)(C) of subsection (a), the term "a party to a reorganization" includes the corporation controlling the corporation to which the acquired assets or stock are transferred. In the case of a reorganization qualifying under paragraph (1)(A) or (1)(G) of subsection (a) by reason of paragraph (2)(D) of that subsection, the term "a party to a reorganization" includes the controlling corporation referred to in such paragraph (2)(D). In the case of a reorganization qualifying under subsection (a)(1)(A) by reason of subsection (a)(2)(E), the term "party to a reorganization" includes the controlling corporation referred to in subsection (a)(2)(E).

Amendments

• 1980, Bankruptcy Tax Act of 1980 (P.L. 96-589)

P.L. 96-589, §4(b)(3):

Amended Code Sec. 368(b) by striking out "or (1)(C)" in the third sentence and inserting in lieu thereof "(1)(C), or (1)(G)", and by striking out "paragraph (1)(A)" in the fourth sentence and inserting in lieu thereof "paragraph (1)(A) or (1)(G)". For the **effective** date, see the historical comment for P.L. 96-589 under Code Sec. 370(a).

• 1971 (P.L. 91-693)

P.L. 91-693, §1(b):

Amended Code Sec. 368(b) by adding the last sentence. **Effective** for statutory mergers occurring after 12-31-70.

• 1968 (P.L. 90-621)

P.L. 90-621, §1(b):

Amended subsection (b) by adding the next to last sentence therein. **Effective** for statutory mergers occurring after 10-22-68.

• 1964, Revenue Act of 1964 (P.L. 88-272)

P.L. 88-272, §218(b)(2):

Amended subsection (b). **Effective** for transactions after 12-31-63, in tax years ending after such date. Prior to amendment, subsection (b) read as follows:

"(b) Party to a Reorganization.—For purposes of this part, the term `a party to a reorganization' includes—

"(1) a corporation resulting from a reorganization, and

"(2) both corporations, in the case of a reorganization resulting from the acquisition by one corporation of stock or properties of another.

"In the case of a reorganization qualifying under paragraph (1)(C) of subsection (a), if the stock exchanged for the properties is stock of a corporation which is in control of the acquiring corporation, the term `a party to a reorganization' includes the corporation so controlling the acquiring corporation. In the case of a reorganization qualifying under paragraph (1)(A) or (1)(C) of subsection (a) by reason of paragraph (2)(C) of subsection (a), the term `a party to a reorganization' includes the corporation controlling the corporation to which the acquired assets are transferred."

[Sec. 368(c)]

(c) CONTROL DEFINED.—For purposes of part I (other than section 304), part II, this part, and part V, the term "control" means the ownership of stock possessing at least 80 percent of the total combined voting power of all classes of stock entitled to vote and at least 80 percent of the total number of shares of all other classes of stock of the corporation.

Amendments

• 1986, Tax Reform Act of 1986 (P.L. 99-514)

P.L. 99-514, §1804(h)(1):

Amended Code Sec. 368(c). **Effective** as if included within the provision of P.L. 98-369 to which it applies. Prior to amendment, Code Sec. 368(c) read as follows:

(c) CONTROL DEFINED.—

(1) IN GENERAL.—For purposes of part I (other than section 304), part II, this part, and part V, the term "control" means the ownership of stock possessing at least 80 percent of the total combined voting power of all classes of stock entitled to vote and at least 80 percent of the total number of shares of all other classes of stock of the corporation.

(2) SPECIAL RULE FOR DETERMINING WHETHER CERTAIN TRANSACTIONS ARE DESCRIBED IN SUBSECTION (a)(1)(D).—In the case of any transaction with respect to which the requirements of subparagraphs (A) and (B) of section 354(b)(1) are met, for purposes of determining whether such transaction is described in subparagraph (D) of subsection (a)(1), the term "control" has the meaning given to such term by section 304(c).

• 1984, Deficit Reduction Act of 1984 (P.L. 98-369)

P.L. 98-369, §64(a):

Amended Code Sec. 368(c). **Effective** for transactions pursuant to plans adopted after 7-18-84. Prior to amendment, Code Sec. 368(c) read as follows:

(c) Control.—For purposes of part I (other than section 304), part II, this part, and part V, the term "control" means the ownership of stock possessing at least 80 percent of the total combined voting power of all classes of stock entitled to vote and at least 80 percent of the total number of shares of all other classes of stock of the corporation.

• 1976, Tax Reform Act of 1976 (P.L. 94-455)

P.L. 94-455, §806(f)(1):

Substituted "this part, and part V," for "and this part" in Code Sec. 368(c). **Effective** for tax years beginning after 6-30-78.

PART IV—INSOLVENCY REORGANIZATIONS—[Repealed]

[Sec. 370—Repealed]

Amendments

• 1990, Omnibus Budget Reconciliation Act of 1990 (P.L. 101-508)

P.L. 101-508, §11801(a)(19):

Repealed Code Sec. 370. **Effective** on the date of enactment of this Act.

P.L. 101-508, §11821(b)(1)-(2), provides:

(b) SAVINGS PROVISION.—If—

(1) any provision amended or repealed by this part applied to—

(A) any transaction occurring before the date of the enactment of this Act,

(B) any property acquired before such date of enactment, or

(C) any item of income, loss, deduction, or credit taken into account before such date of enactment, and

(2) the treatment of such transaction, property, or item under such provision would (without regard to the amendments made by this part) affect liability for tax for periods ending after such date of enactment,

nothing in the amendments made by this part shall be construed to affect the treatment of such transaction, property, or item for purposes of determining liability for tax for periods ending after such date of enactment.

Prior to repeal, Code Sec. 370 read as follows:

SEC. 370. TERMINATION OF PART.

[Sec. 370(a)]

(a) GENERAL RULE.—Except as provided in subsection (b), this part shall not apply to any proceeding which is begun after September 30, 1979.

Amendments

• 1980, Bankruptcy Tax Act of 1980 (P.L. 96-589)

P.L. 96-589, §4(f):

Added Code Sec. 370(a). Section 7 of the Bankruptcy Tax Act of 1980, P.L. 96-589, provides for the following **effective** dates for provisions relating to corporate reorganizations:

"(c) FOR SECTION 4 (RELATING TO CORPORATE REORGANIZATION PROVISIONS).—

(1) IN GENERAL.—The amendments made by section 4 shall apply to any bankruptcy case or similar judicial proceeding commencing after December 31, 1980.

(2) EXCHANGES OF PROPERTY FOR ACCRUED INTEREST.—The amendments made by subsection (e) of section 4 (relating to treatment of property attributable to accrued interest) shall also apply to any exchange—

(A) which occurs after December 31, 1980, and

(B) which does not occur in a bankruptcy case or similar judicial proceeding (or in a proceeding under the Bankruptcy Act) commenced on or before December 31, 1980.

* * *

(f) ELECTION TO SUBSTITUTE SEPTEMBER 30, 1979, FOR DECEMBER 31, 1980.—

(1) IN GENERAL.—The debtor (or debtors) in a bankruptcy case or similar judicial proceeding may (with the approval of the court) elect to apply subsections (a), (c), and (d) by substituting `September 30, 1979' for `December 31, 1980' each place it appears in such subsections.

(2) EFFECT OF ELECTION.—Any election made under paragraph (1) with respect to any proceeding shall apply to all parties to the proceeding.

(3) REVOCATION ONLY WITH CONSENT.—Any election under this subsection may be revoked only with the consent of the Secretary of the Treasury or his delegate.

(4) TIME AND MANNER OF ELECTION.—Any election under this subsection shall be made at such time, and in such manner, as the Secretary of the Treasury or his delegate may by regulations prescribe.

(g) DEFINITIONS.—For purposes of this section—

(1) BANKRUPTCY CASE.—The term `bankruptcy case' means any case under title 11 of the United States Code (as recodified by Public Law 95-598).

(2) SIMILAR JUDICIAL PROCEEDING.—The term `similar judicial proceeding' means a receivership, foreclosure, or similar proceeding in a Federal or State court (as modified by section 368(a)(3)(D) of the Internal Revenue Code of 1954)."

[Sec. 370(b)]

(b) EXCEPTIONS.—Subsection (a) shall not apply to subsections (c) and (e) of section 374.

Amendments

• 1980, Bankruptcy Tax Act of 1980 (P.L. 96-589)

P.L. 96-589, §4(f):

Added Code Sec. 370(b). For the **effective** date, see the historical comment for P.L. 96-589 under Code Sec. 370(a).

[Sec. 371—Repealed]

Amendments

• 1990, Omnibus Budget Reconciliation Act of 1990 (P.L. 101-508)

P.L. 101-508, §11801(a)(19):

Repealed Code Sec. 371. **Effective** on the date of enactment of this Act.

P.L. 101-508, §11821(b)(1)-(2), provides:

(b) SAVINGS PROVISION.—If—

(1) any provision amended or repealed by this part applied to—

(A) any transaction occurring before the date of the enactment of this Act,

(B) any property acquired before such date of enactment, or

(C) any item of income, loss, deduction, or credit taken into account before such date of enactment, and

(2) the treatment of such transaction, property, or item under such provision would (without regard to the amendments made by this part) affect liability for tax for periods ending after such date of enactment,

nothing in the amendments made by this part shall be construed to affect the treatment of such transaction, property, or item for purposes of determining liability for tax for periods ending after such date of enactment.

Prior to repeal, Code Sec. 371 read as follows:

SEC. 371. REORGANIZATION IN CERTAIN RECEIVERSHIP AND BANKRUPTCY PROCEEDINGS.

[Sec. 371(a)]

(a) EXCHANGES BY CORPORATIONS.—

(1) IN GENERAL.—No gain or loss shall be recognized if property of a corporation (other than a railroad corporation, as defined in section 77(m) of the Bankruptcy Act (11 U.S.C. 205) is transferred in pursuance of an order of the court having jurisdiction of such corporation—

(A) in a receivership, foreclosure, or similar proceeding, or

(B) in a proceeding under chapter X of the Bankruptcy Act (11 U.S.C. 501 and following), to another corporation organized or made use of to effectuate a plan of reorganization approved by the court in such proceeding, in exchange solely for stock or securities in such other corporation.

(2) GAIN FROM EXCHANGES NOT SOLELY IN KIND.—If an exchange would be within the provisions of paragraph (1) if it were not for the fact that the property received in exchange consists not only of stock or securities permitted by paragraph (1) to be received without the recognition of gain, but also of other property or money, then—

(A) if the corporation receiving such other property or money distributes it in pursuance of the plan of reorganization, no gain to the corporation shall be recognized from the exchange, but

(B) if the corporation receiving such other property or money does not distribute it in pursuance of the plan of reorganization, the gain, if any, to the corporation shall be recognized, but in an amount not in excess of the sum of such money and the fair market value of such other property so received, which is not so distributed.

Amendments

• 1976, Tax Reform Act of 1976 (P.L. 94-455)

P.L. 94-455, §1901(a)(50):

Struck out "49 Stat. 922;" before "11 U.S.C. 205" and substituted "(11 U.S.C. 501 and following)" for "(52 Stat. 883-905; 11 U.S.C., chapter 10) or the corresponding provisions of prior law" in Code Sec. 371(a)(1). **Effective** for tax years beginning after 12-31-76.

[Sec. 371(b)]

(b) EXCHANGES BY SECURITY HOLDERS.—

(1) IN GENERAL.—No gain or loss shall be recognized on an exchange consisting of the relinquishment or extinguishment of stock or securities in a corporation the plan of reorganization of which is approved by the court in a proceeding described in subsection (a), in consideration of the acquisition solely of stock or securities in a corporation organized or made use of to effectuate such plan of reorganization.

(2) GAIN FROM EXCHANGES NOT SOLELY IN KIND.—If an exchange would be within the provisions of paragraph (1) if it were not for the fact that the property received in exchange consists not only of property permitted by paragraph (1) to

be received without the recognition of gain, but also of other property or money, then the gain, if any, to the recipient shall be recognized, but in an amount not in excess of the sum of such money and the fair market value of such other property.

[Sec. 371(c)]

(c) LOSS FROM EXCHANGES NOT SOLELY IN KIND.—If an exchange would be within the provisions of subsection (a)(1) or (b)(1) if it were not for the fact that the property received in exchange consists not only of property permitted by subsection (a)(1) or (b)(1) to be received without the recognition of gain or loss, but also of other property or money, then no loss from the exchange shall be recognized.

[Sec. 371(d)]

(d) ASSUMPTION OF LIABILITIES.—In the case of a transaction involving an assumption of a liability or the acquisition of property subject to a liability, the rules provided in section 357 shall apply.

[Sec. 372—Repealed]

Amendments

• 1990, Omnibus Budget Reconciliation Act of 1990 (P.L. 101-508)

P.L. 101-508, §11801(a)(19):

Repealed Code Sec. 372. **Effective** on the date of enactment of this Act.

P.L. 101-508, §11821(b)(1)-(2), provides:

(b) SAVINGS PROVISION.—If—

(1) any provision amended or repealed by this part applied to—

(A) any transaction occurring before the date of the enactment of this Act,

(B) any property acquired before such date of enactment, or

(C) any item of income, loss, deduction, or credit taken into account before such date of enactment, and

(2) the treatment of such transaction, property, or item under such provision would (without regard to the amendments made by this part) affect liability for tax for periods ending after such date of enactment,

nothing in the amendments made by this part shall be construed to affect the treatment of such transaction, property, or item for purposes of determining liability for tax for periods ending after such date of enactment.

Prior to repeal, Code Sec. 372 read as follows:

SEC. 372. BASIS IN CONNECTION WITH CERTAIN RECEIVERSHIP AND BANKRUPTCY PROCEEDINGS.

[Sec. 372(a)]

(a) CORPORATION.—If property was acquired by a corporation in a transfer to which—

(1) section 371(a) applies,

(2) so much of section 371(c) as relates to section 371(a)(1) applies, or

(3) the corresponding provisions of prior law apply,

then notwithstanding the provisions of section 270 of the Bankruptcy Act (11 U.S.C. 670), the basis in the hands of the acquiring corporation shall be the same as it would be in the hands of the corporation whose property was so acquired, increased in the amount of gain recognized to the corporation whose property was so acquired under the law applicable to the year in which the acquisition occurred, and such basis shall not be adjusted under section 1017 by reason of a discharge of indebtedness in pursuance of the plan of reorganization under which such transfer was made.

Amendments

• 1976, Tax Reform Act of 1976 (P.L. 94-455)

P.L. 94-455, §1901(a)(51):

Struck out "54 Stat. 709;" before "11 U.S.C. 670" in Code Sec. 372(a). **Effective** for tax years beginning after 12-31-76.

[Sec. 372(b)]

(b) ADJUSTMENT FOR DEPRECIATION SUSTAINED BEFORE MARCH 1, 1913, IN CERTAIN CASES OF PROPERTY ACQUIRED FROM RETIREMENT METHOD CORPORATIONS.—

(1) IN GENERAL.—If the taxpayer has acquired property in a transaction described in section 374(b), and if any such property constitutes retirement-straight line property, then, in determining the adjusted basis of all retirement-straight line property held by the taxpayer on his adjustment date, adjustment shall be made (in lieu of the adjustment provided in section 1016(a)(3)(A)) for depreciation sustained before March 1, 1913, on retirement-straight line property which was held on such date for which cost was or is claimed as basis, and which either—

(A) RETIRED BEFORE ACQUISITION BY TAXPAYER.—Was retired before the acquisition of the retirement-straight line property by the taxpayer, but only if a deduction was allowed in computing net income by reason of such retirement, and such deduction was computed on the basis of cost without adjustment for depreciation sustained before March 1, 1913. In the case of any such property retired during any taxable year beginning after December 31, 1929, the adjustment under this subparagraph shall not exceed that portion of the amount attributable to depreciation sustained before March 1, 1913, which resulted (by reason of the deduction so allowed) in a reduction in taxes under this subtitle or prior income, war-profits, or excess-profits tax laws.

(B) ACQUIRED BY TAXPAYER.—Was acquired by the taxpayer.

The adjustment determined under this paragraph shall be allocated (in the manner prescribed by the Secretary) among all retirement-straight line property held by the taxpayer on his adjustment date. Such adjustment shall apply to all periods on and after the adjustment date.

(2) RETIREMENT-STRAIGHT LINE PROPERTY DEFINED.—For purposes of this subsection, the term "retirement-straight line property" means any property of a kind or class with respect to which (A) the corporation transferring such property to the taxpayer was using (at the time of transfer) the retirement method of computing the allowance of deductions for depreciation, and (B) the acquiring corporation has adopted any other method of computing such allowance.

(3) OTHER DEFINITIONS.—For purposes of this subsection:

(A) DEPRECIATION.—The term "depreciation" means exhaustion, wear and tear, and obsolescence.

(B) ADJUSTMENT DATE.—In the case of any kind or class of property, the term "adjustment date" means whichever of the following is the later:

(i) the first day of the taxpayer's first taxable year beginning after December 31, 1955, or

(ii) the first day of the first taxable year in which the taxpayer uses a method of computing the allowance of deductions for depreciation other than the retirement method.

Amendments

• 1976, Tax Reform Act of 1976 (P.L. 94-455)

P.L. 94-455, §1901(b)(14)(A):

Struck out "373(b) or" before "374(b)" in Code Sec. 372(b)(1). **Effective** for tax years beginning after 12-31-76.

P.L. 94-455, §1906(b)(13)(A):

Amended 1954 Code by substituting "Secretary" for "Secretary or his delegate" each place it appeared. **Effective** 2-1-77.

• 1958, Technical Amendments Act of 1958 (P.L. 85-866)

P.L. 85-866, §95(a):

Added new subsection (b) to Sec. 372. **Effective**, generally, for tax years beginning after 12-31-55, but see §95(b) below.

P.L. 85-866, §95(b), provides:

"The amendments made by subsection (a) shall not apply with respect to any taxpayer if, before the date of the enactment of this Act, there has been a determination, for any taxable year, of the adjusted basis of retirement-straight line property of the taxpayer of the type described in section 372(b) of the Internal Revenue Code of 1954 (as added by subsection (a)) by the Tax Court of the United States, or by any other court of competent jurisdiction, in any proceeding in which the decision of the court became final after December 31, 1955, and which established the right of the taxpayer to use the straight line depreciation method of computing the annual depreciation allowance with respect to such property for Federal tax purposes for any year."

[Sec. 372(c)]

(c) STOCK OR SECURITY HOLDER.—

For basis of stock or securities acquired under section 371(b), see section 358.

Amendments

• 1958, Technical Amendments Act of 1958 (P.L. 85-866)

P.L. 85-866, §95(a):

Redesignated subsection (b) of Sec. 372 as subsection (c). **Effective** 1-1-56.

[Sec. 374—Repealed]

Amendments

• 1990, Omnibus Budget Reconciliation Act of 1990 (P.L. 101-508)

P.L. 101-508, §11801(a)(19):

Repealed Code Sec. 374. **Effective** on the date of enactment of this Act.

P.L. 101-508, §11821(b)(1)-(2), provides:

(b) SAVINGS PROVISION.—If—

(1) any provision amended or repealed by this part applied to—

(A) any transaction occurring before the date of the enactment of this Act,

(B) any property acquired before such date of enactment, or

(C) any item of income, loss, deduction, or credit taken into account before such date of enactment, and

(2) the treatment of such transaction, property, or item under such provision would (without regard to the amendments made by this part) affect liability for tax for periods ending after such date of enactment,

nothing in the amendments made made by this part shall be construed to affect the treatment of such transaction, property, or item for purposes of determining liability for tax for periods ending after such date of enactment.

Prior to repeal, Code Sec. 374 read as follows:

SEC. 374. GAIN OR LOSS NOT RECOGNIZED IN CERTAIN RAILROAD REORGANIZATIONS.

[Sec. 374(a)]

(a) EXCHANGES BY CORPORATIONS.—

(1) NONRECOGNITION OF GAIN OR LOSS.—No gain or loss shall be recognized if property of a railroad corporation, as defined in section 77(m) of the Bankruptcy Act (11 U.S.C. 205), is transferred after July 31, 1955, in pursuance of an order of the court having jurisdiction of such corporation—

(A) in a receivership proceeding, or

(B) in a proceeding under section 77 of the Bankruptcy Act,

to another railroad corporation (as defined in section 77(m) of the Bankruptcy Act) organized or made use of to effectuate a plan of reorganization approved by the court in such proceeding, in exchange solely for stock or securities in such other railroad corporation.

(2) GAIN FROM EXCHANGES NOT SOLELY IN KIND.—If an exchange would be within the provisions of paragraph (1) if it were not for the fact that the property received in exchange consists not only of stock or securities permitted by paragraph (1) to be received without the recognition of gain, but also of other property or money, then—

(A) if the corporation receiving such other property or money distributes it in pursuance of the plan of reorganization, no gain to the corporation shall be recognized from the exchange, but

(B) if the corporation receiving such other property or money does not distribute it in pursuance of the plan of reorganization, the gain, if any, to the corporation shall be recognized, but in an amount not in excess of the sum of such money and the fair market value of such other property so received, which is not so distributed.

(3) LOSS FROM EXCHANGES NOT SOLELY IN KIND.—If an exchange would be within the provisions of paragraph (1) if it were not for the fact that the property received in exchange consists not only of property permitted by such paragraph to be received without the recognition of gain or loss, but also of other property or money, then no loss from the exchange shall be recognized.

Amendments

• 1976, Tax Reform Act of 1976 (P.L. 94-455)

P.L. 94-455, §1901(a)(53):

Struck out "49 Stat. 922;" before "11 U.S.C. 205" in Code Sec. 374(a)(1). **Effective** for tax years beginning after 12-31-76.

• 1956 (P.L. 628, 84th Cong.)

P.L. 628, 84th Cong., §[1]:

Added Code Sec. 374(a).

[Sec. 374(b)]

(b) BASIS.—

(1) RAILROAD CORPORATIONS.—If the property of a railroad corporation, as defined in section 77(m) of the Bankruptcy Act (11 U.S.C. 205(m)), was acquired after December 31, 1938, in pursuance of an order of the court having jurisdiction of such corporation—

(A) in a receivership proceeding, or

(B) in a proceeding under section 77 of the Bankruptcy Act,

and the acquiring corporation is a railroad corporation (as defined in section 77(m) of the Bankruptcy Act) organized or made use of to effectuate a plan of reorganization approved by the court in such proceeding, the basis shall be the same as it would be in the hands of the railroad corporation whose property was so acquired, increased in the amount of gain recognized under subsection (a)(2) to the transferor on such transfer.

(2) PROPERTY ACQUIRED BY STREET, SUBURBAN, OR INTERURBAN ELECTRIC RAILWAY CORPORATION.—If the property of any street, suburban, or interurban electric railway corporation engaged as a common carrier in the transportation of persons or property in interstate commerce was acquired after December 31, 1934, in pursuance of an order of the court having jurisdiction of such corporation in a proceeding under section 77 of the Bankruptcy Act (11 U.S.C. 501 and following), and the acquiring corporation is a street, suburban, or interurban electric railway engaged as a common carrier in the transportation of persons or property in interstate commerce, organized or made use of to effectuate a plan of reorganization approved by the court in such proceeding, then, notwithstanding the provisions of section 270 of the Bankruptcy Act (11 U.S.C. 670), the basis shall be the same as it would be in the hands of the corporation whose property was so acquired.

Amendments

• 1976, Tax Reform Act of 1976 (P.L. 94-455)

P.L. 94-455, §1901(b)(14)(B):

Amended Code Sec. 374(b). **Effective** for tax years beginning after 12-31-76. Prior to amendment, Code Sec. 374(b) read as follows:

(b) BASES.—If the property of a railroad corporation (as defined in section 77(m) of the Bankruptcy Act) was acquired after July 31, 1955, in pursuance of an order of the court having jurisdiction of such corporation—

(1) in a receivership proceeding, or

(2) in a proceeding under section 77 of the Bankruptcy Act,

and the acquiring corporation is a railroad corporation (as defined in section 77(m) of the Bankruptcy Act) organized or made use of to effectuate a plan of reorganization approved by the court in such proceeding, the basis shall be the same as it would be in the hands of the railroad corporation whose property was so acquired, increased in the amount of gain recognized under subsection (a)(2) to the transferor on such transfer.

• 1956 (P.L. 628, 84th Cong.)

P.L. 628, 84th Cong., 2d Sess., §[1]:

Added Code Sec. 374(b). **Effective** 8-1-55.

[Sec. 374(c)]

(c) EXCHANGES UNDER THE FINAL SYSTEM PLAN FOR CONRAIL.—

(1) IN GENERAL.—No gain or loss shall be recognized if, in order to carry out the final system plan, rail properties of a transferor railroad corporation are transferred to the Consolidated Rail Corporation (or any subsidiary thereof) pursuant to an order of the special court under section 303 or 305(d) of the Regional Rail Reorganization Act of 1973 in exchange solely for stock of the Consolidated Rail Corporation, securities of such Corporation, certificates of value of the United States Railway Association, or any combination thereof.

(2) EXCHANGES NOT SOLELY IN KIND.—If paragraph (1) would apply to an exchange if it were not for the fact that the property received in exchange consists not only of property permitted by paragraph (1) to be received without the recognition of gain or loss, but also of other property or money, then rules similar to the rules set forth in paragraph (2) or (3) of subsection (a) (whichever is appropriate) shall be applied.

(3) BASIS.—The basis of the property transferred to the Consolidated Rail Corporation (or any subsidiary thereof) in an exchange to which paragraph (1) or (2) applies shall be determined under rules similar to the rules set forth in subsection (b)(1).

(4) DENIAL OF NET OPERATING LOSS CARRYOVERS TO CONRAIL.—Neither the Consolidated Rail Corporation nor any subsidiary thereof shall succeed to any net operating loss carryover of any transferor railroad corporation.

(5) DEFINITIONS.—For purposes of this subsection—

(A) RAIL PROPERTIES.—The term "rail properties" means rail properties within the meaning of paragraph (12) of section 102 of the Regional Rail Reorganization Act of 1973.

(B) TRANSFEROR RAILROAD CORPORATION.—The term "transferor railroad corporation" means a corporation which, on March 11, 1976, was—

(i) a railroad in reorganization (within the meaning of paragraph (14) of section 102 of the Regional Rail Reorganization Act of 1973) in the region (within the meaning of paragraph (15) of such section 102), or

(ii) a corporation leased, operated, or controlled by such a railroad in reorganization.

(C) FINAL SYSTEM PLAN.—The term "final system plan" means the final system plan (within the meaning of paragraph (6) of section 102 of such Act). Such term includes supplemental transactions under section 305 of such Act.

(D) SUBSIDIARY.—The term "subsidiary" means any corporation 100 percent of whose total combined voting shares are, directly or indirectly, owned or controlled by the Consolidated Rail Corporation.

Amendments

• 1976, Tax Reform Act of 1976 (P.L. 94-455)

P.L. 94-455, §1901(b)(14)(C):

Substituted "subsection (b)(1)" for "subsection (b)" in Code Sec. 374(c)(3). **Effective** for tax years beginning after 12-31-76.

• 1976 (P.L. 94-253)

P.L. 94-253, §1:

Amended Code Sec. 374 by redesignating subsection (c) as subsection (d) and by adding new subsection (c). **Effective** for tax years ending after 3-31-76.

[Sec. 374(d)]

(d) ASSUMPTION OF LIABILITIES.—In the case of a transaction involving an assumption of a liability or the acquisition of property subject to a liability, the rules provided in section 357 shall apply.

Amendments

• 1976 (P.L. 94-253)

P.L. 94-253, §1:

Redesignated former Code Sec. 374(c) as Code Sec. 374(d). **Effective** for tax years ending after 3-31-76.

• 1956 (P.L. 628, 84th Cong.)

P.L. 628, 84th Cong., §[1]:

Added Code Sec. 374(c). **Effective** 8-1-55.

[Sec. 374(e)]

(e) USE OF EXPIRED NET OPERATING LOSS CARRYOVERS TO OFFSET INCOME ARISING FROM CERTAIN RAILROAD REORGANIZATION PROCEEDINGS.—

(1) IN GENERAL.—If—

(A) any corporation receives or accrues any amount pursuant to—

(i) an award in (or settlement of) a proceeding under section 77 of the Bankruptcy Act.

(ii) an award in (or settlement of) a proceeding before the special court to carry out section 303(c), 305, or 306 of the Regional Rail Reorganization Act of 1973.

(iii) an award in (or settlement of) a proceeding in the United States Claims Court under section 1491 of title 28 of the United States Code, to the extent such proceeding involves a claim arising under the Regional Rail Reorganization Act of 1973, or

(iv) a redemption of a certificate of value of the United States Railway Association issued under section 306 of such Act to such corporation (or issued to another member of the same affiliated group (within the meaning of section 1504) as such corporation for their taxable years which included March 31, 1976),

(B) any portion of such amount is includible in the gross income of such corporation for the taxable year in which such portion is received or accrued, and such taxable year begins not more than 5 years after the date of such award, settlement, or redemption, and

(C) the net operating loss of such corporation for any taxable year—

(i) was a net operating loss carryover to, or arose in, the first taxable year of such corporation ending after March 31, 1976 (or, in the case of a proceeding referred to in subparagraph (A)(i) which began after March 31, 1976, ending after the beginning of such proceeding), but

(ii) solely by reason of the lapse of time, is not a net operating loss carryover to the taxable year referred to in subparagraph (B),

then such net operating loss shall be a net operating loss carryover to the taxable year described in subparagraph (B) but only for use (to the extent not theretofore used under this subsection to offset other amounts) to offset the portion referred to in subparagraph (B).

(2) SPECIAL RULE.—For purposes of paragraph (1)(C)(i), a corporation which was a regulated transportation corporation (within the meaning of section 172(g)) for its last taxable year ending on or before March 31, 1976, shall be treated as such a regulated transportation corporation for its first taxable year ending after such date.

Amendments

• 1986, Tax Reform Act of 1986 (P.L. 99-514)

P.L. 99-514, §1899A(9):

Amended Code Sec. 374(e)(1)(A)(iii) by striking out "Court of Claims" and inserting in lieu thereof "United States Claims Court". **Effective** 10-22-86.

• 1980, Technical Corrections Act of 1979 (P.L. 96-222)

P.L. 96-222, §103(a)(14):

Amended Code Sec. 374(e)(1)(A)(iv) by striking out "March 31, 1967" and inserting "March 31, 1976". **Effective** for tax years ending after 3-31-76.

• 1978, Revenue Act of 1978 (P.L. 95-600)

P.L. 95-600, §369(a), (b):

Amended Code Sec. 374(e)(1)(A)(iv). **Effective** for tax years ending after 3-31-76. Before amendment, clause (iv) read:

"(iv) a redemption of a certificate of value of the United States Railway Association issued to such corporation under section 306 of such Act,"

• 1976, Tax Reform Act of 1976 (P.L. 94-455)

P.L. 94-455, §1901(b)(10)(A):

Substituted "172(g)" for "172(j)" in Code Sec. 374(e)(2). **Effective** for tax years beginning after 12-31-76.

• 1976 (P.L. 94-253)

P.L. 94-253, §1:

Added subsection (e). **Effective** for tax years ending after 3-31-76.

PART V—CARRYOVERS

[Sec. 381]

SEC. 381. CARRYOVERS IN CERTAIN CORPORATE ACQUISITIONS.

[Sec. 381(a)]

(a) GENERAL RULE.—In the case of the acquisition of assets of a corporation by another corporation—

(1) in a distribution to such other corporation to which section 332 (relating to liquidations of subsidiaries) applies; or

(2) in a transfer to which section 361 (relating to nonrecognition of gain or loss to corporations) applies, but only if the transfer is in connection with a reorganization described in subparagraph (A), (C), (D), (F), or (G) of section 368(a)(1),

the acquiring corporation shall succeed to and take into account, as of the close of the day of distribution or transfer, the items described in subsection (c) of the distributor or transferor corporation, subject to the conditions and limitations specified in subsections (b) and (c). For purposes of the preceding sentence, a reorganization shall be treated as meeting the requirements of subparagraph (D) or (G) of section 368(a)(1) only if the requirements of subparagraphs (A) and (B) of section 354(b)(1) are met.

Amendments

• 1982, Tax Equity and Fiscal Responsibility Act of 1982 (P.L. 97-248)

P.L. 97-248, §224(c)(7):

Amended Code Sec. 381(a)(1) by striking out ", except in the case in which the basis of the assets distributed is determined under section 334(b)(2)". **Effective** for any target corporation (within the meaning of Code Sec. 338) with respect to which the acquisition date (within the meaning of such section) occurs after 8-31-82. See, also, amendment notes under Code Sec. 338 for P.L. 97-248, Act Sec. 224(a) for special rules.

• 1980, Bankruptcy Tax Act of 1980 (P.L. 96-589)

P.L. 96-589, §4(g):

Amended Code Sec. 381(a) by adding a new last sentence to Code Sec. 381(a), and by striking out "subparagraph (A), (C), (D) (but only if the requirements of subparagraphs (A) and (B) of section 354(b)(1) are met), or (F) of section 368(a)(1)," in paragraph (2), and inserting in lieu thereof: "subparagraph (A), (C), (D), (F), or (G) of section 368(a)(1).". For the **effective** date, see the historical comment for P.L. 96-589 under Code Sec. 370(a). Prior to amendment, Code Sec. 381(a)(2) provided:

"(2) in a transfer to which section 361 (relating to nonrecognition of gain or loss to corporations) applies, but only if the transfer is in connection with a reorganization described in subparagraph (A), (C), (D) (but only if the requirements of subparagraphs (A) and (B) of section 354(b)(1) are met), or (F) of section 368(a)(1),"

[Sec. 381(b)]

(b) OPERATING RULES.—Except in the case of an acquisition in connection with a reorganization described in subparagraph (F) of section 368(a)(1)—

(1) The taxable year of the distributor or transferor corporation shall end on the date of distribution or transfer.

(2) For purposes of this section, the date of distribution or transfer shall be the day on which the distribution or transfer is completed; except that, under regulations prescribed by the Secretary, the date when substantially all of the property has been distributed or transferred may be used if the distributor or transferor corporation ceases all operations, other than liquidating activities, after such date.

(3) The corporation acquiring property in a distribution or transfer described in subsection (a) shall not be entitled to carry back a net operating loss or a net capital loss for a taxable year ending after the date of distribution or transfer to a taxable year of the distributor or transferor corporation.

Amendments

• 1976, Tax Reform Act of 1976 (P.L. 94-455)

P.L. 94-455, §1906(b)(13)(A):

Amended 1954 Code by substituting "Secretary" for "Secretary or his delegate" each place it appeared. **Effective** 2-1-77.

• 1969, Tax Reform Act of 1969 (P.L. 91-172)

P.L. 91-172, §512(c):

Amended Sec. 381(b)(3) by adding the words "or a net capital loss". **Effective** for net capital losses sustained in tax years beginning after 12-31-69.

[Sec. 381(c)]

(c) ITEMS OF THE DISTRIBUTOR OR TRANSFEROR CORPORATION.—The items referred to in subsection (a) are:

(1) NET OPERATING LOSS CARRYOVERS.—The net operating loss carryovers determined under section 172, subject to the following conditions and limitations:

(A) The taxable year of the acquiring corporation to which the net operating loss carryovers of the distributor or transferor corporation are first carried shall be the first taxable year ending after the date of distribution or transfer.

(B) In determining the net operating loss deduction, the portion of such deduction attributable to the net operating loss carryovers of the distributor or transferor corporation to the first taxable year of the acquiring corporation ending after the date of distribution or transfer shall be limited to an amount which bears the same ratio to the taxable income (determined without regard to a net operating loss deduction) of the acquiring corporation in such taxable year as the number of days in the taxable year after the date of distribution or transfer bears to the total number of days in the taxable year.

(C) For the purpose of determining the amount of the net operating loss carryovers under section 172(b)(2), a net operating loss for a taxable year (hereinafter in this subparagraph referred to as the "loss year") of a distributor or transferor corporation which ends on or before the end of a loss year of the acquiring corporation shall be considered to be a net operating loss for a year prior to such loss year of the acquiring corporation. For the same purpose, the taxable income for a "prior taxable year" (as the term is used in section 172(b)(2)) shall be computed as provided in such section; except that, if the date of distribution or transfer is on a day other than the last day of a taxable year of the acquiring corporation—

(i) such taxable year shall (for the purpose of this subparagraph only) be considered to be 2 taxable years (hereinafter in this subparagraph referred to as the "pre-acquisition part year" and the "post-acquisition part year");

(ii) the pre-acquisition part year shall begin on the same day as such taxable year begins and shall end on the date of distribution or transfer;

(iii) the post-acquisition part year shall begin on the day following the date of distribution or transfer and shall end on the same day as the end of such taxable year;

(iv) the taxable income for such taxable year (computed with the modifications specified in section 172(b)(2)(A) but without a net operating loss deduction) shall be divided between the pre-acquisition part year and the post-acquisition part year in proportion to the number of days in each;

(v) the net operating loss deduction for the pre-acquisition part year shall be determined as provided in section 172(b)(2)(B), but without regard to a net operating loss year of the distributor or transferor corporation; and

(vi) the net operating loss deduction for the post-acquisition part year shall be determined as provided in section 172(b)(2)(B).

(2) EARNINGS AND PROFITS.—In the case of a distribution or transfer described in subsection (a)—

(A) the earnings and profits or deficit in earnings and profits, as the case may be, of the distributor or transferor corporation shall, subject to subparagraph (B), be deemed to have been received or incurred by the acquiring corporation as of the close of the date of the distribution or transfer; and

(B) a deficit in earnings and profits of the distributor, transferor, or acquiring corporation shall be used only to offset earnings and profits accumulated after the date of transfer. For this purpose, the earnings and profits for the taxable year of the acquiring corporation in which the distribution or transfer occurs shall be deemed to have been accumulated after such distribution or transfer in an amount which bears the same ratio to the undistributed earnings and profits of the acquiring corporation for such taxable year (computed without regard to any earnings and profits received from the distributor or transferor corporation, as described in subparagraph (A) of this paragraph) as the number of days in the taxable year after the date of distribution or transfer bears to the total number of days in the taxable year.

(3) CAPITAL LOSS CARRYOVER.—The capital loss carryover determined under section 1212, subject to the following conditions and limitations:

(A) The taxable year of the acquiring corporation to which the capital loss carryover of the distributor or transferor corporation is first carried shall be the first taxable year ending after the date of distribution or transfer.

(B) The capital loss carryover shall be a short-term capital loss in the taxable year determined under subparagraph (A) but shall be limited to an amount which bears the same ratio to the capital gain net income (determined without regard to a short-term capital loss attributable to capital loss carryover), if any, of the acquiring corporation in such taxable year as the number of days in the taxable year after the date of distribution or transfer bears to the total number of days in the taxable year.

(C) For purposes of determining the amount of such capital loss carryover to taxable years following the taxable year determined under subparagraph (A), the capital gain net income in the taxable year determined under subparagraph (A) shall be considered to be an amount equal to the amount determined under subparagraph (B).

(4) METHOD OF ACCOUNTING.—The acquiring corporation shall use the method of accounting used by the distributor or transferor corporation on the date of distribution or transfer unless different methods were used by several distributor or transferor corporations or by a distributor or transferor corporation and the acquiring corporation. If different methods were used, the acquiring corporation shall use the method or combination of methods of computing taxable income adopted pursuant to regulations prescribed by the Secretary.

(5) INVENTORIES.—In any case in which inventories are received by the acquiring corporation, such inventories shall be taken by such corporation (in determining its income) on the same basis on which such inventories were taken by the distributor or transferor corporation, unless different methods were used by several distributor or transferor corporations or by a distributor or transferor corporation and the acquiring corporation. If different methods were used, the acquiring corporation shall use the method or combination of methods of taking inventory adopted pursuant to regulations prescribed by the Secretary.

(6) METHOD OF COMPUTING DEPRECIATION ALLOWANCE.—The acquiring corporation shall be treated as the distributor or transferor corporation for purposes of computing the depreciation allowance under sections 167 and 168 on property acquired in a distribution or transfer with respect to so much of the basis in the hands of the acquiring corporation as does not exceed the adjusted basis in the hands of the distributor or transferor corporation.

(7) [Repealed.]

(8) INSTALLMENT METHOD.—If the acquiring corporation acquires installment obligations (the income from which the distributor or transferor corporation reports on the installment basis under section 453) the acquiring corporation shall, for purposes of section 453, be treated as if it were the distributor or transferor corporation.

(9) AMORTIZATION OF BOND DISCOUNT OR PREMIUM.—If the acquiring corporation assumes liability for bonds of the distributor or transferor corporation issued at a discount or premium, the acquiring corporation shall be treated as the distributor or transferor corporation after the date of distribution or transfer for purposes of determining the amount of amortization allowable or includible with respect to such discount or premium.

(10) TREATMENT OF CERTAIN MINING DEVELOPMENT AND EXPLORATION EXPENSES OF DISTRIBUTOR OR TRANSFEROR CORPORATION.—The acquiring corporation shall be entitled to deduct, as if it were the distributor or transferor corporation, expenses deferred under section 616 (relating to certain development expenditures) if the distributor or transferor corporation has so elected.

(11) CONTRIBUTIONS TO PENSION PLANS, EMPLOYEES' ANNUITY PLANS, AND STOCK BONUS AND PROFIT-SHARING PLANS.—The acquiring corporation shall be considered to be the distributor or transferor corporation after the date of distribution or transfer for the purpose of determining the amounts deductible under section 404 with respect to pension plans, employees' annuity plans, and stock bonus and profit-sharing plans.

(12) RECOVERY OF TAX BENEFIT ITEMS.—If the acquiring corporation is entitled to the recovery of any amounts previously deducted by (or allowable as credits to) the distributor or transferor corporation, the acquiring corporation shall succeed to the treatment under section 111 which would apply to such amounts in the hands of the distributor or transferor corporation.

(13) INVOLUNTARY CONVERSIONS UNDER SECTION 1033.—The acquiring corporation shall be treated as the distributor or transferor corporation after the date of distribution or transfer for purposes of applying section 1033.

(14) DIVIDEND CARRYOVER TO PERSONAL HOLDING COMPANY.—The dividend carryover (described in section 564) to taxable years ending after the date of distribution or transfer.

(15) [Repealed.]

(16) CERTAIN OBLIGATIONS OF DISTRIBUTOR OR TRANSFEROR CORPORATION.—If the acquiring corporation—

(A) assumes an obligation of the distributor or transferor corporation which, after the date of the distribution or transfer, gives rise to a liability, and

(B) such liability, if paid or accrued by the distributor or transferor corporation, would have been deductible in computing its taxable income,

the acquiring corporation shall be entitled to deduct such items when paid or accrued, as the case may be, as if such corporation were the distributor or transferor corporation. A corporation which would have been an acquiring corporation under this section if the date of distribution or transfer had occurred on or after the effective date of the provisions of this subchapter applicable to a liquidation or reorganization, as the case may be, shall be entitled, even though the date of distribution or transfer occurred before such effective date, to apply this paragraph with respect to amounts paid or accrued in taxable years beginning after December 31, 1953, on account of such obligations of the distributor or transferor corporation. This paragraph shall not apply if such obligations are reflected in the amount of stock, securities, or property transferred by the acquiring corporation to the transferor corporation for the property of the transferor corporation.

(17) DEFICIENCY DIVIDEND OF PERSONAL HOLDING COMPANY.—If the acquiring corporation pays a deficiency dividend (as defined in section 547(d)) with respect to the distributor or transferor corporation, such distributor or transferor corporation shall, with respect to such payments, be entitled to the deficiency dividend deduction provided in section 547.

(18) PERCENTAGE DEPLETION ON EXTRACTION OF ORES OR MINERALS FROM THE WASTE OR RESIDUE OF PRIOR MINING.—The acquiring corporation shall be considered to be the distributor or transferor corporation for the purpose of determining the applicability of section 613(c)(3) (relating to extraction of ores or minerals from the ground).

(19) CHARITABLE CONTRIBUTIONS IN EXCESS OF PRIOR YEARS' LIMITATION.—Contributions made in the taxable year ending on the date of distribution or transfer and the 4 prior taxable years by the distributor or transferor corporation in excess of the amount deductible under section 170(b)(2) for such taxable years shall be deductible by the acquiring corporation for its taxable years which begin after the date of distribution or transfer, subject to the limitations imposed in section 170(b)(2). In applying the preceding sentence, each taxable year of the distributor or transferor corporation beginning on or before the date of distribution or transfer shall be treated as a prior taxable year with reference to the acquiring corporation's taxable years beginning after such date.

(20) [Stricken.]

(21) [Stricken.]

(22) SUCCESSOR INSURANCE COMPANY.—If the acquiring corporation is an insurance company taxable under subchapter L, there shall be taken into account (to the extent proper to carry out the purposes of this section and of subchapter L, and under such regulations as may be prescribed by the Secretary) the items required to be taken into account for purposes of subchapter L in respect of the distributor or transferor corporation.

(23) DEFICIENCY DIVIDEND OF REGULATED INVESTMENT COMPANY OR REAL ESTATE INVESTMENT TRUST.—If the acquiring corporation pays a deficiency dividend (as defined in section 860(f)) with respect to the distributor or transferor corporation, such distributor or transferor corporation shall, with respect to such payments, be entitled to the deficiency dividend deduction provided in section 860.

(24) CREDIT UNDER SECTION 38.—The acquiring corporation shall take into account (to the extent proper to carry out the purposes of this section and section 38, and under such regulations as may be prescribed by the Secretary) the items required to be taken into account for purposes of section 38 in respect of the distributor or transferor corporation.

(25) CREDIT UNDER SECTION 53.—The acquiring corporation shall take into account (to the extent proper to carry out the purposes of this section and section 53, and under such regulations as may be prescribed by the Secretary) the items required to be taken into account for purposes of section 53 in respect of the distributor or transferor corporation.

(26) ENTERPRISE ZONE PROVISIONS.—The acquiring corporation shall take into account (to the extent proper to carry out the purposes of this section and subchapter U, and under such regulations as may be prescribed by the Secretary) the items required to be taken into account for purposes of subchapter U in respect of the distributor or transferor corporation.

Amendments

• 1993, Omnibus Budget Reconciliation Act of 1993 (P.L. 103-66)

P.L. 103-66, §13302(e):

Amended Code Sec. 381(c) by adding at the end a new paragraph (26). **Effective** 8-10-93.

• 1990, Omnibus Budget Reconciliation Act of 1990 (P.L. 101-508)

P.L. 101-508, §11801(c)(10)(A):

Repealed Code Sec. 381(c)(15). **Effective** 11-5-90. Prior to repeal, Code Sec. 381(c)(15) read as follows:

(15) INDEBTEDNESS OF CERTAIN PERSONAL HOLDING COMPANIES.—The acquiring corporation shall be considered to be the distributor or transferor corporation for the purpose of determining the applicability of subsection (c) of section 545, relating to deduction with respect to payment of certain indebtedness.

P.L. 101-508, §11821(b)(1)-(2), provides:

(b) SAVINGS PROVISION.—If—

(1) any provision amended or repealed by this part applied to—

(A) any transaction occurring before the date of the enactment of this Act,

(B) any property acquired before such date of enactment, or

(C) any item of income, loss, deduction, or credit taken into account before such date of enactment, and

(2) the treatment of such transaction, property, or item under such provision would (without regard to the amendments made by this part) affect liability for tax for periods ending after such date of enactment,

nothing in the amendments made by this part shall be construed to affect the treatment of such transaction, property, or item for purposes of determining liability for tax for periods ending after such date of enactment.

P.L. 101-508, §11812(b)(6)(A):

Amended Code Sec. 381(c)(6) by striking "subsections (b), (j), and (k) of section 167" and inserting "sections 167 and

168". **Effective** for property placed in service after 11-5-90. For exceptions, see Act Sec. 11821(c)(2)-(3), below.

P.L. 101-508, §11812(b)(6)(B):

Amended Code Sec. 381(c) by striking paragraph (24) and redesignating paragraphs (25) and (26) as paragraphs (24) and (25), respectively. **Effective** for property placed in service after 11-5-90. For exceptions, see Act Sec. 11821(c)(2)-(3), below. Prior to amendment, Code Sec. 381(c)(24) read as follows:

(24) METHOD OF COMPUTING DEPRECIATION DEDUCTION.—The acquiring corporation shall be treated as the distributor or transferor corporation for purposes of computing the deduction allowable under section 168(a) on property acquired in a distribution or transfer with respect to so much of the basis in the hands of the acquiring corporation as does not exceed the adjusted basis in the hands of the distributor or transferor corporation.

P.L. 101-508, §11812(c)(2)-(3), provides:

(2) EXCEPTION.—The amendments made by this section shall not apply to any property to which section 168 of the Internal Revenue Code of 1986 does not apply by reason of subsection (f)(5) thereof.

(3) EXCEPTION FOR PREVIOUSLY GRANDFATHER [sic] EXPENDITURES.—The amendments made by this section shall not apply to rehabilitation expenditures described in section 252(f)(5) of the Tax Reform Act of 1986 (as added by section 1002(l)(31) of the Technical and Miscellaneous Revenue Act of 1988).

• 1989, Omnibus Budget Reconciliation Act of 1989 (P.L. 101-239)

P.L. 101-239, §7841(d)(10) (as amended by P.L. 104-188, §1704(t)(26)):

Amended Code Sec. 381(c) by redesignating paragraph (27) as paragraph (26). **Effective** 12-19-89.

• 1988, Technical and Miscellaneous Revenue Act of 1988 (P.L. 100-647)

P.L. 100-647, §1002(a)(13):

Amended Code Sec. 381(c)(24) by striking out "RECOVERY ALLOWANCE FOR RECOVERY PROPERTY" in the paragraph heading and inserting in lieu thereof "DEPRECIATION DEDUCTION". E **ffective** as if included in the provision of P.L. 99-514 to which it relates.

• 1987, Revenue Act of 1987 (P.L. 100-203)

P.L. 100-203, §10202(c)(3):

Amended Code Sec. 381(c)(8) by striking out "or 453A" after "453" each place it appears. For the **effective** date, see Act Sec. 10202(e), as amended by P.L. 100-647, §2004(d)(4), below.

P.L. 100-203, §10202(e), as amended by P.L. 100-647, §2004(d)(4), provides:

(e) EFFECTIVE DATES.—

(1) IN GENERAL.—Except as provided in this subsection, the amendments made by this section shall apply to dispositions in taxable years beginning after December 31, 1987.

(2) SPECIAL RULES FOR DEALERS.—

(A) IN GENERAL.—In the case of dealer dispositions (within the meaning of section 453A of the Internal Revenue Code of 1986), the amendments made by subsections (a) and (b) shall apply to installment obligations arising from dispositions after December 31, 1987.

(B) SPECIAL RULES FOR OBLIGATIONS ARISING FROM DEALER DISPOSITIONS AFTER FEBRUARY 28, 1986, AND BEFORE JANUARY 1, 1988.—

(i) IN GENERAL.—In the case of an applicable installment obligation arising from a disposition described in subclause (I) or (II) of section 453C(e)(A)(i) of the Internal Revenue Code of 1986 (as in effect before the amendments made by this section) before January 1, 1988, the amendments made by subsections (a) and (b) shall apply to taxable years beginning after December 31, 1987.

(ii) CHANGE IN METHOD OF ACCOUNTING.—In the case of any taxpayer who is required by clause (i) to change its method of accounting for any taxable year with respect to obligations described in clause (i)—

(I) such change shall be treated as initiated by the taxpayer,

(II) such change shall be treated as made with the consent of the Secretary of the Treasury or his delegate, and

(III) the net amount of adjustments required by section 481 of the Internal Revenue Code of 1986 shall be taken into account over a period not longer than 4 taxable years

(C) CERTAIN RULES MADE APPLICABLE.—For purposes of this paragraph, rules similar to the rules of paragraphs (4) and (5) of secton 812(c) of the Tax Reform Act of 1986 (as added by the Technical and Miscellaneous Revenue Act of 1988) shall apply.

(3) SPECIAL RULE FOR NONDEALERS.—

(A) ELECTION.—A taxpayer may elect, at such time and in such manner as the Secretary of the Treasury or his delegate may prescribe, to have the amendments made by subsections (a) and (c) apply to taxable years ending after December 31, 1986, with respect to dispositions and pledges occurring after August 16, 1986.

(B) PLEDGING RULES.—Except as provided in subparagraph (A)—

(i) IN GENERAL.—Section 453A(d) of the Internal Revenue Code of 1986 shall apply to any installment obligation which is pledged to secure any secured indebtedness (within the meaning of section 453A(d)(4) of such Code) after December 17, 1987, in taxable years ending after such date.

(ii) COORDINATION WITH SECTION 453C.—For purposes of section 453C of such Code (as in effect before its repeal), the face amount of any obligation to which section 453A(d) of such Code applies shall be reduced by the amount treated as payments on such obligation under section 453A(d) of such Code and the amount of any indebtedness secured by it shall not be taken into account.

(4) MINIMUM TAX.—The amendment made by subsection (d) shall apply to dispositions in taxable years beginning after December 31, 1986.

(5) COORDINATION WITH TAX REFORM ACT OF 1986.—The amendments made by this section shall not apply to any installment obligation or to any taxpayer during any period to the extent the amendments made by section 811 of the Tax Reform Act of 1986 do not apply to such obligation or during such period.

• 1986, Tax Reform Act of 1986 (P.L. 99-514)

P.L. 99-514, §231(d)(3)(F):

Amended Code Sec. 381(c) by striking out paragraph (25) and by redesignating paragraph (26) as paragraph (25). **Effective** for tax years beginning after 12-31-85. Prior to amendment, Code Sec. 381(c)(25) read as follows:

(25) CREDIT UNDER SECTION 30.—The acquiring corporation shall take into account (to the extent proper to carry out the purposes of this section 30, and under such regulations as may be prescribed by the Secretary) the items required to be taken into account for purposes of section 30 in respect of the distributor or transferor corporation.

P.L. 99-514, §411(b)(2)(C)(iii):

Amended Code Sec. 381(c)(10) by striking out the last sentence thereof. **Effective** for costs paid or incurred after 12-31-86, in tax years ending after such date. For a transitional rule, see Act Sec. 411(c)(2), below. Prior to amendment, Code Sec. 381(c)(10) read as follows:

(10) TREATMENT OF CERTAIN MINING DEVELOPMENT AND EXPLORATION EXPENSES OF DISTRIBUTOR OR TRANSFEROR CORPORATION.—The acquiring corporation shall be entitled to deduct, as if it were the distributor or transferor corporation, expenses deferred under section 616 (relating to certain development expenditures) if the distributor or transferor corporation has so elected. For the purpose of applying the limitation provided in section 617(h), if, for any taxable year, the distributor or transferor corporation was allowed a deduction under section 617(a), the acquiring corporation shall be deemed to have been allowed such deduction.

P.L. 99-514, §411(c)(2), provides:

(2) TRANSITION RULE.—The amendments made by this section shall not apply with respect to intangible drilling and development costs incurred by United States companies pursuant to minority interest in a license for Netherlands or United Kingdom North Sea development if such interest was acquired on or before December 31, 1985.

P.L. 99-514, §701(e)(1):

Amended Code Sec. 381(c) by adding at the end thereof new paragraph (27)[26]. **Effective**, generally, for tax years beginning after 12-31-86. For exceptions, see Act Sec. 701(f)(2)(7) following Code Sec. 56.

P.L. 99-514, §1812(a)(3):

Amended Code Sec. 381(c)(12). **Effective** as if included in the provision of P.L. 98-369 to which it relates. Prior to amendment, Code Sec. 381(c)(12) read as follows:

(12) RECOVERY OF BAD DEBTS, PRIOR TAXES, OR DELINQUENCY AMOUNTS.—If the acquiring corporation is entitled to the recovery of bad debts, prior taxes, or delinquency amounts previously deducted or credited by the distributor or transferor corporation, the acquiring corporation shall include in its income such amounts as would have been includible by the distributor or transferor corporation in accordance with section 111 (relating to the recovery of bad debts, prior taxes, and delinquency amounts).

• 1984, Deficit Reduction Act of 1984 (P.L. 98-369)

P.L. 98-369, §474(r)(11)(A):

Amended Code Sec. 381(c) by striking out former paragraphs (23), (24), (26), (27) and (30). **Effective** for tax years beginning after 12-31-83, and to carrybacks from such years. Prior to their deletion, paragraphs (23), (24), (26), (27) and (30) read as follows:

(23) Credit Under Section 38 for Investment in Certain Depreciable Property.—The acquiring corporation shall take into account (to the extent proper to carry out the purposes of this section and section 38, and under such regulations as may be prescribed by the Secretary) the items required to be taken into account for purposes of section 38 in respect of the distributor or transferor corporation.

(24) Credit Under Section 40 for Work Incentive Program Expenses.—The acquiring corporation shall take into account (to the extent proper to carry out the purposes of this section and section 40, and under such regulations as may be prescribed by the Secretary) the items required to be taken into account for purposes of section 40 in respect of the distributor or transferor corporation.

(26) Credit Under Section 44B for Employment of Certain New Employees.—The acquiring corporation shall take into account (to the extent proper to carry out the purposes of this section and section 44B, and under such regulations as may be prescribed by the Secretary) the items required to be taken into account for purposes of section 44B in respect of the distributor or transferor corporation.

(27) Credit Under Section 44E for Alcohol Used as Fuel.—The acquiring corporation shall take into account (to the extent proper to carry out the purposes of this section and section 44E, and under such regulations as may be prescribed by the Secretary) the items required to be taken into account for purposes of section 44E in respect of the distributor or transferor corporation.

* * *

(30) Credit Under Section 44G.—The acquiring corporation shall take into account (to the extent proper to carry out the purposes of this section and section 44G, and under such regulations as may be prescribed by the Secretary) the items required to be taken into account for purposes of section 44G in respect of the distributor or transferor corporation.

P.L. 98-369, §474(r)(11)(B):

Amended Code Sec. 381(c) by redesignating paragraphs (25), (28), and (29) as paragraphs (23), (24), and (25), respectively. **Effective** for tax years beginning after 12-31-83, and to carrybacks from such years.

P.L. 98-369, §474(r)(11)(C):

Amended Code Sec. 381(c) by striking out "44F" each place it appears in paragraph (25) (as so redesignated) and inserting in lieu thereof "30". **Effective** for tax years beginning after 12-31-83, and to carrybacks from such years.

P.L. 98-369, §474(r)(11)(D):

Added Code Sec. 381(c)(26). **Effective** for tax years beginning after 12-31-83, and to carrybacks from such years.

• 1983, Technical Corrections Act of 1982 (P.L. 97-448)

P.L. 97-448, §102(h)(3):

Amended Code Sec. 381(c)(28) by redesignating it as paragraph (29). **Effective** as if included in the provision of P.L. 97-34 to which it relates.

P.L. 97-448, §103(g)(2)(F):

Redesignated paragraph (29) of Code Sec. 381(c) (as such paragraph was added by P.L. 97-34, §331) as paragraph (30). **Effective** as if included in the provision of P.L. 97-34 to which it relates.

• 1981, Economic Recovery Tax Act of 1981 (P.L. 97-34)

P.L. 97-34, §208:

Amended Code Sec. 381(c) by adding at the end thereof new paragraph (28). **Effective** for property placed in service after 12-31-80, in tax years ending after such date.

P.L. 97-34, §221(b)(1)(B):

Amended Code Sec. 381(c) by adding at the end thereof new paragraph (28). **Effective** for amounts paid or incurred after 6-30-81 [**effective** date changed by P.L. 99-514, §231(a)(2)]. Note: P.L. 97-34, §208 added an earlier Code Sec. 318(c)(28).

P.L. 97-34, §221(d)(2), as amended by P.L. 99-514, §231 (a)(2), provides the following transitional rule:

(2) TRANSITIONAL RULE.—

(A) IN GENERAL.—If, with respect to the first taxable year to which the amendments made by this section apply and which ends in 1981 or 1982, the taxpayer may only take into account qualified research expenses paid or incurred during a portion of such taxable year, the amount of the qualified research expenses taken into account for the base period of such taxable year shall be the amount which bears the same ratio to the total qualified research expenses for such base period as the number of months in such portion of such taxable year bears to the toal number of months in such taxable year.

(B) DEFINITIONS.—For purposes of the preceding sentence, the terms "qualified research expenses" and "base period" have the meanings given to such terms by section 44F of the Internal Revenue Code of 1954 (as added by this section).

P.L. 97-34, §331(d)(1)(B):

Added Code Sec. 381(c)(29). **Effective** for tax years ending after 12-31-82.

• 1980, Installment Sales Revision Act of 1980 (P.L. 96-471)

P.L. 96-471, §2(b)(2)(A):

Amended Code Sec. 381(c)(8) by striking out "has elected, under section 453, to report on the installment basis" and substituting "reports on the installment basis under section 453 or 453A". **Effective** for dispositions made after 10-19-80, in tax years ending after that date.

P.L. 96-471, §2(b)(2)(B):

Amended Code Sec. 381(c)(8) by striking out "for purposes of section 453" and substituting "for purposes of section 453 or 543A". **Effective** for dispositions made after 10-19-80, in tax years ending after that date.

• 1980, Crude Oil Windfall Profit Tax Act of 1980 (P.L. 96-223)

P.L. 96-223, §232(b)(2)(B):

Amended Code Sec. 381(c) by adding paragraph (27). **Effective** for sales and uses after 9-30-80, in tax years ending after such date.

• 1978, Revenue Act of 1978 (P.L. 95-600)

P.L. 95-600, §362(d)(2)(A), (B), (C), (e):

Amended Code Sec. 381(c)(25). **Effective** for determinations (as defined in Code Sec. 860(d)) after 11-6-78. Prior to amendment, paragraph (25) read:

"(25) DEFICIENCY DIVIDEND OF REAL ESTATE INVESTMENT TRUST.—If the acquiring corporation pays a deficiency dividend (as defined in section 859(d)) with respect to the distributor or transferor corporation, such distributor or transferor corporation shall, with respect to such payments, be entitled to the deficiency dividend deduction provided in section 859."

• 1977, Tax Reduction and Simplification Act of 1975 (P.L. 95-30)

P.L. 95-30, §202(d)(3)(A):

Added Code Sec. 381(c)(26). **Effective** for tax years beginning after 12-31-76, and for credit carrybacks from such years.

• 1976, Tax Reform Act of 1976 (P.L. 94-455)

P.L. 94-455, §1601(e):

Added Code Sec. 381(c)(25). **Effective** for determinations (as defined in Code Sec. 859(c)) occurring after 10-4-76.

P.L. 94-455, §1901(a)(54):

Struck out Code Sec. 381(c)(20). **Effective** for tax years beginning after 12-31-76. Prior to striking, Code Sec. 381(c)(20) read as follows:

(20) CARRY-OVER OF UNUSED PENSION TRUST DEDUCTIONS IN CERTAIN CASES.—Notwithstanding the other provisions of this section, or section 394(a), a corporation which has acquired the properties and assumed the liabilities of a wholly owned subsidiary shall be considered to have succeeded to and to be entitled to take into account contributions of the subsidiary to a pension plan, and shall be considered to be the distributor or transferor corporation after the date of distribution or transfer (but not for taxable years with respect to which this paragraph does not apply) for the purpose of determining the amounts deductible under section 404 with respect to contributions to a pension plan if—

(A) the corporate laws of the State of incorporation of the subsidiary required the surviving corporation in the case of merger to be incorporated under the laws of the State of incorporation of the subsidiary; and

(B) the properties were acquired in a liquidation of the subsidiary in a transaction subject to section 112(b)(6) of the Internal Revenue Code of 1939.

P.L. 94-455, §1901(b)(16):

Struck out Code Sec. 381(c)(21). **Effective** for tax years beginning after 12-31-76. Prior to striking, Code Sec. 381(c)(21) read as follows:

(21) PRE-1954 ADJUSTMENTS RESULTING FROM CHANGE IN METHOD OF ACCOUNTING.—The acquiring corporation shall take into account any net amount of any adjustment described in section 481(b)(4) of the distributor or transferor corporation—

(A) to the extent such net amount of such adjustment has not been taken into account by the distributor or transferor corporation, and

(B) in the same manner and at the same time as such net amount would have been taken into account by the distributor or transferor corporation.

P.L. 94-455, §1901(b)(17):

Substituted "subsection (c)" for "subsections (b)(7) and (c)" in Code Sec. 381(c)(15). **Effective** for tax years beginning after 12-31-76.

P.L. 94-455, §1901(b)(21)(B):

Amended Code Sec. 381(c)(10). **Effective** for tax years beginning after 12-31-76. Prior to amendment, Code Sec. 381(c)(10) read as follows:

(10) TREATMENT OF CERTAIN MINING EXPLORATION AND DEVELOPMENT EXPENSES OF DISTRIBUTOR OR TRANSFEROR CORPORATION.—The acquiring corporation shall be entitled to deduct, as if it were the distributor or transferor corporation, expenses deferred under sections 615 and 616 (relating to pre-1970 exploration expenditures and development expenditures, respectively) if the distributor or transferor corporation has so elected. For the purpose of applying the limitation provided in section 615, if, for any taxable year, the distributor or transferor corporation was allowed the deduction in section 615(a) or made the election in section 615(b), the acquiring corporation shall be deemed to have been allowed such deduction or to have made such election, as the case may be. For the purpose of applying the limitation provided in section 617, if, for any taxable year, the distributor or transferor corporation was allowed the deduction in section 615(a) or section 617(a) or made the election provided in section 615(b), the acquiring corporation shall be deemed to have been allowed such deduction or deductions or to have made such election, as the case may be.

P.L. 94-455, §1901(b)(33)(N):

Substituted "capital gain net income" for "net capital gain" in Code Secs. 381(c)(3)(B) and 381(c)(3)(C). **Effective** for tax years beginning after 12-31-76.

P.L. 94-455, §1906(b)(13)(A):

Amended 1954 Code by substituting "Secretary" for "Secretary or his delegate" each place it appeared. **Effective** 2-1-77.

• 1971, Revenue Act of 1971 (P.L. 92-178)

P.L. 92-178, §601(c)(3):

Amended Code Sec. 381(c) by adding paragraph (24). **Effective** for tax years beginning after 12-31-71.

• 1969, Tax Reform Act of 1969 (P.L. 91-172)

P.L. 91-172, §521(f):

Amended Code Sec. 381(c)(6). **Effective** for tax years ending after 7-24-69. Prior to amendment Code Sec. 381(c)(6) read as follows:

(c)(6) Method of computing depreciation allowance.—The acquiring corporation shall be treated as the distributor or transferor corporation for purposes of computing the depreciation allowance under paragraphs (2), (3), and (4) of section 167(b) on property acquired in a distribution or transfer with respect to that part or all of the basis in the hands of the acquiring corporation as does not exceed the basis in the hands of the distributor or transferor corporation.

P.L. 91-172, §504(c)(2):

Amended Sec. 381(c)(10) by inserting "mining exploration and development expenses" in lieu of "expenses deferred by the election" in the heading, by inserting "pre-1970" in the parenthetical language in the first sentence, and by adding the last sentence. **Effective** for exploration expenditures paid or incurred after 12-31-69.

• 1968 (P.L. 90-240)

P.L. 90-240, §5(d):

Amended paragraph (22) of section 381(c). **Effective** for tax years beginning after 12-31-66. Prior to amendment, paragraph (22) read as follows:

"(22) Successor Life Insurance Company.—If the acquiring corporation is a life insurance company (as defined in section 801(a)), there shall be taken into account (to the extent proper to carry out the purposes of this section and part I of subchapter L, and under such regulations as may be prescribed by the Secretary or his delegate) the items required to be taken into account for purposes of part I of subchapter L (relating to life insurance companies) in respect of the distributor or transferor corporation."

• 1964, Revenue Act of 1964 (P.L. 88-272)

P.L. 88-272, §209(d)(2):

Amended paragraph (19) of section 381(c). **Effective** for tax years beginning after 12-31-63, with respect to contributions which are paid (or treated as paid under section 170(a)(2)) in tax years beginning after 12-31-61. Prior to amendment, paragraph (19) of section 381(c) read as follows:

"(19) Charitable contributions in excess of prior years' limitation.—Contributions made in the taxable year ending on the date of distribution or transfer and the prior taxable year by the distributor or transferor corporation in excess of the amount deductible under section 170(b)(2) in such taxable years shall be deductible by the acquiring corporation in its first two taxable years which begin after the date of distribution or transfer, subject to the limitations imposed in section 170(b)(2)."

P.L. 88-272, §225(i)(3):

Amended Code Sec. 381(c)(15). **Effective** for tax years beginning after 12-31-63. Prior to amendment, Code Sec. 381(c)(15) read as follows:

"(15) Indebtedness of certain personal holding companies.—The acquiring corporation shall be considered to be the distributor or transferor corporation for the purpose of determining the applicability of section 545(b)(7), relating to a deduction for payment of certain indebtedness incurred before January 1, 1934."

• 1962, Revenue Act of 1962 (P.L. 87-834)

P.L. 87-834, §2:

Added to Code Sec. 381(c) a new paragraph (23). **Effective** for tax years ending after 12-31-61.

• 1959, Life Insurance Company Income Tax Act of 1959 (P.L. 86-69)

P.L. 86-69, §3(c)(1):

Added paragraph (22) to Code Sec. 381(c). **Effective** for tax years beginning after 12-31-57.

• 1958, Technical Amendments Act of 1958 (P.L. 85-866)

P.L. 85-866, §29(c):

Amended Code Sec. 381(c) by adding paragraph (21). **Effective** for any change in method of accounting where the year of the change is a tax year beginning after 12-31-54 and ending after 8-16-54. However, the amendment does not apply if before 9-2-58 the taxpayer applied for a change in method of accounting in the manner provided by regulations and the taxpayer and the Secretary or his delegate agreed to the terms and conditions for making the change.

• 1956 (P.L. 396, 84th Cong.)

P.L. 396, 84th Cong., §[1]:

Added paragraph (20). **Effective** for tax years beginning after 12-31-53, and ending after 8-16-54.

• 1955 (P.L. 74, 84th Cong.)

P.L. 74, 84th Cong., §2(1):

Amended Sec. 381(c) by deleting paragraph (7). **Effective** for tax years beginning after 12-31-53, and ending after 8-16-54. Former Code Sec. 381(c)(7) read as follows:

"(7) Prepaid income.—If the acquiring corporation assumes the liability described in section 452(e)(2) with respect to prepaid income of a distributor or transferor corporation which had elected, under section 452(d), to report such income as provided in section 452, the acquiring corporation shall be treated, for this purpose, as if it were the distributor or transferor corporation, unless the acquiring corporation, after the date of distribution or transfer, uses the cash receipts and disbursements method of accounting. In the latter case, the acquiring corporation shall include in gross income for the first taxable year ending after the date of distribution or transfer, so much of such prepaid income as was not includible in gross income of the distributor or transferor corporation under section 452 for preceding taxable years."

[Sec. 381(d)]

(d) OPERATIONS LOSS CARRYBACKS AND CARRYOVERS OF LIFE INSURANCE COMPANIES.—

For application of this part to operations loss carrybacks and carryovers of life insurance companies, see section 810.

Amendments

• 1984, Deficit Reduction Act of 1984 (P.L. 98-369)

P.L. 98-369, §211(b)(4):

Amended Code Sec. 381(d) by striking out "section 812(f)" and inserting in lieu thereof "section 810". **Effective** for tax years beginning after 12-31-83.

• 1959, Life Insurance Company Income Tax Act of 1959 (P.L. 86-69)

P.L. 86-69, §3(c)(2):

Added subsection (d) to Code Sec. 381. **Effective** for tax years beginning after 12-31-57.

[Sec. 382]

SEC. 382. LIMITATION ON NET OPERATING LOSS CARRYFORWARDS AND CERTAIN BUILT-IN LOSSES FOLLOWING OWNERSHIP CHANGE.

[Sec. 382(a)]

(a) GENERAL RULE.—The amount of the taxable income of any new loss corporation for any post-change year which may be offset by pre-change losses shall not exceed the section 382 limitation for such year.

[Sec. 382(b)]

(b) SECTION 382 LIMITATION.—For purposes of this section—

(1) IN GENERAL.—Except as otherwise provided in this section, the section 382 limitation for any post-change year is an amount equal to—

(A) the value of the old loss corporation, multiplied by

(B) the long-term tax-exempt rate.

(2) CARRYFORWARD OF UNUSED LIMITATION.—If the section 382 limitation for any post-change year exceeds the taxable income of the new loss corporation for such year which was offset by pre-change losses, the section 382 limitation for the next post-change year shall be increased by the amount of such excess.

(3) SPECIAL RULE FOR POST-CHANGE YEAR WHICH INCLUDES CHANGE DATE.—In the case of any post-change year which includes the change date—

(A) LIMITATION DOES NOT APPLY TO TAXABLE INCOME BEFORE CHANGE.—Subsection (a) shall not apply to the portion of the taxable income for such year which is allocable to the period in such year on or before the change date. Except as provided in subsection (h)(5) and in regulations, taxable income shall be allocated ratably to each day in the year.

(B) LIMITATION FOR PERIOD AFTER CHANGE.—For purposes of applying the limitation of subsection (a) to the remainder of the taxable income for such year, the section 382 limitation shall be an amount which bears the same ratio to such limitation (determined without regard to this paragraph) as—

(i) the number of days in such year after the change date, bears to

(ii) the total number of days in such year.

[Sec. 382(c)]

(c) CARRYFORWARDS DISALLOWED IF CONTINUITY OF BUSINESS REQUIREMENTS NOT MET.—

(1) IN GENERAL.—Except as provided in paragraph (2), if the new loss corporation does not continue the business enterprise of the old loss corporation at all times during the 2-year period beginning on the change date, the section 382 limitation for any post-change year shall be zero.

(2) EXCEPTION FOR CERTAIN GAINS.—The section 382 limitation for any post-change year shall not be less than the sum of—

(A) any increase in such limitation under—

(i) subsection (h)(1)(A) for recognized built-in gains for such year, and

(ii) subsection (h)(1)(C) for gain recognized by reason of an election under section 338, plus

(B) any increase in such limitation under subsection (b)(2) for amounts described in subparagraph (A) which are carried forward to such year.

[Sec. 382(d)]

(d) PRE-CHANGE LOSS AND POST-CHANGE YEAR.—For purposes of this section—

(1) PRE-CHANGE LOSS.—The term "pre-change loss" means—

(A) any net operating loss carryforward of the old loss corporation to the taxable year ending with the ownership change or in which the change date occurs, and

(B) the net operating loss of the old loss corporation for the taxable year in which the ownership change occurs to the extent such loss is allocable to the period in such year on or before the change date.

Except as provided in subsection (h)(5) and in regulations, the net operating loss shall, for purposes of subparagraph (B), be allocated ratably to each day in the year.

(2) POST-CHANGE YEAR.—The term "post-change year" means any taxable year ending after the change date.

[Sec. 382(e)]

(e) VALUE OF OLD LOSS CORPORATION.—For purposes of this section—

(1) IN GENERAL.—Except as otherwise provided in this subsection, the value of the old loss corporation is the value of the stock of such corporation (including any stock described in section 1504(a)(4)) immediately before the ownership change.

(2) SPECIAL RULE IN THE CASE OF REDEMPTION OR OTHER CORPORATE CONTRACTION.—If a redemption or other corporate contraction occurs in connection with an ownership change, the value under paragraph (1) shall be determined after taking such redemption or other corporate contraction into account.

(3) TREATMENT OF FOREIGN CORPORATIONS.—Except as otherwise provided in regulations, in determining the value of any old loss corporation which is a foreign corporation, there shall be taken into account only items treated as connected with the conduct of a trade or business in the United States.

Amendments

• 1988, Technical and Miscellaneous Revenue Act of 1988 (P.L. 100-647)

P.L. 100-647, § 1006(d)(1)(A)(i)-(ii):

Amended Code Sec. 382(e)(2) by inserting "or other corporate contraction" after "redemption" each place it appears, and by inserting "OR OTHER CORPORATE CONTRACTION" after "REDEMPTION" in the heading thereof. **Effective** with respect to ownership changes after 6-10-87.

P.L. 100-647, § 1006(d)(17)(A):

Amended Code Sec. 382(e) by adding at the end thereof new paragraph (3). **Effective** for any ownership change after 6-10-87. For purposes of the preceding sentence, any equity structure shift pursuant to a plan of reorganization adopted on or before 6-10-87, shall be treated as occurring when such plan was adopted.

[Sec. 382(f)]

(f) LONG-TERM TAX-EXEMPT RATE.—For purposes of this section—

(1) IN GENERAL.—The long-term tax-exempt rate shall be the highest of the adjusted Federal long-term rates in effect for any month in the 3-calendar-month period ending with the calendar month in which the change date occurs.

(2) ADJUSTED FEDERAL LONG-TERM RATE.—For purposes of paragraph (1), the term "adjusted Federal long-term rate" means the Federal long-term rate determined under section 1274(d), except that—

(A) paragraphs (2) and (3) thereof shall not apply, and

(B) such rate shall be properly adjusted for differences between rates on long-term taxable and tax-exempt obligations.

[Sec. 382(g)]

(g) OWNERSHIP CHANGE.—For purposes of this section—

(1) IN GENERAL.—There is an ownership change if, immediately after any owner shift involving a 5-percent shareholder or any equity structure shift—

(A) the percentage of the stock of the loss corporation owned by 1 or more 5-percent shareholders has increased by more than 50 percentage points, over

(B) the lowest percentage of stock of the loss corporation (or any predecessor corporation) owned by such shareholders at any time during the testing period.

(2) OWNER SHIFT INVOLVING 5-PERCENT SHAREHOLDER.—There is an owner shift involving a 5-percent shareholder if—

(A) there is any change in the respective ownership of stock of a corporation, and

(B) such change affects the percentage of stock of such corporation owned by any person who is a 5-percent shareholder before or after such change.

(3) EQUITY STRUCTURE SHIFT DEFINED.—

(A) IN GENERAL.—The term "equity structure shift" means any reorganization (within the meaning of section 368). Such term shall not include—

(i) any reorganization described in subparagraph (D) or (G) of section 368(a)(1) unless the requirements of section 354(b)(1) are met, and

(ii) any reorganization described in subparagraph (F) of section 368(a)(1).

(B) TAXABLE REORGANIZATION-TYPE TRANSACTIONS, ETC.—To the extent provided in regulations, the term "equity structure shift" includes taxable reorganization-type transactions, public offerings, and similar transactions.

(4) SPECIAL RULES FOR APPLICATION OF SUBSECTION.—

(A) TREATMENT OF LESS THAN 5-PERCENT SHAREHOLDERS.—Except as provided in subparagraphs (B)(i) and (C), in determining whether an ownership change has occurred, all stock owned by shareholders of a corporation who are not 5-percent shareholders of such corporation shall be treated as stock owned by 1 5-percent shareholder of such corporation.

(B) COORDINATION WITH EQUITY STRUCTURE SHIFTS.—For purposes of determining whether an equity structure shift (or subsequent transaction) is an ownership change—

(i) LESS THAN 5-PERCENT SHAREHOLDERS.—Subparagraph (A) shall be applied separately with respect to each group of shareholders (immediately before such equity structure shift) of each corporation which was a party to the reorganization involved in such equity structure shift.

(ii) ACQUISITIONS OF STOCK.—Unless a different proportion is established, acquisitions of stock after such equity structure shift shall be treated as being made proportionately from all shareholders immediately before such acquisition.

(C) COORDINATION WITH OTHER OWNER SHIFTS.—Except as provided in regulations, rules similar to the rules of subparagraph (B) shall apply in determining whether there has been an owner shift involving a 5-percent shareholder and whether such shift (or subsequent transaction) results in an ownership change.

(D) TREATMENT OF WORTHLESS STOCK.—If any stock held by a 50-percent shareholder is treated by such shareholder as becoming worthless during any taxable year of such shareholder and such stock is held by such shareholder as of the close of such taxable year, for purposes of determining whether an ownership change occurs after the close of such taxable year, such shareholder—

(i) shall be treated as having acquired such stock on the 1st day of his 1st succeeding taxable year, and

(ii) shall not be treated as having owned such stock during any prior period.

For purposes of the preceding sentence, the term "50-percent shareholder" means any person owning 50 percent or more of the stock of the corporation at any time during the 3-year period ending on the last day of the taxable year with respect to which the stock was so treated.

Amendments

• 1988, Technical and Miscellaneous Revenue Act of 1988 (P.L. 100-647)

P.L. 100-647, §1006(d)(2):

Amended Code Sec. 382(g)(4)(C) by inserting "rules similar to" before "the rules". **Effective** as if included in the provision of P.L. 99-514 to which it relates.

P.L. 100-647, §1006(d)(21)(A)-(B):

Amended Code Sec. 382(g)(1) by striking out "new loss corporation" and inserting in lieu thereof "loss corporation", and by striking out "old loss corporation" and inserting in lieu thereof "loss corporation". **Effective** as if included in the provision of P.L. 99-514 to which it relates.

• 1987, Revenue Act of 1987 (P.L. 100-203)

P.L. 100-203, §10225(a):

Amended Code Sec. 382(g)(4) by adding at the end thereof new subparagraph (D). **Effective** in the case of stock treated as becoming worthless in tax years beginning after 12-31-87.

[Sec. 382(h)]

(h) SPECIAL RULES FOR BUILT-IN GAINS AND LOSSES AND SECTION 338 GAINS.—For purposes of this section—

(1) IN GENERAL.—

(A) NET UNREALIZED BUILT-IN GAIN.—

(i) IN GENERAL.—If the old loss corporation has a net unrealized built-in gain, the section 382 limitation for any recognition period taxable year shall be increased by the recognized built-in gains for such taxable year.

(ii) LIMITATION.—The increase under clause (i) for any recognition period taxable year shall not exceed—

(I) the net unrealized built-in gain, reduced by

(II) recognized built-in gains for prior years ending in the recognition period.

(B) NET UNREALIZED BUILT-IN LOSS.—

(i) IN GENERAL.—If the old loss corporation has a net unrealized built-in loss, the recognized built-in loss for any recognition period taxable year shall be subject to limitation under this section in the same manner as if such loss were a pre-change loss.

(ii) LIMITATION.—Clause (i) shall apply to recognized built-in losses for any recognition period taxable year only to the extent such losses do not exceed—

(I) the net unrealized built-in loss, reduced by

(II) recognized built-in losses for prior taxable years ending in the recognition period.

(C) SPECIAL RULES FOR CERTAIN SECTION 338 GAINS.—If an election under section 338 is made in connection with an ownership change and the net unrealized built-in gain is zero by reason of paragraph (3)(B), then, with respect to such change, the section 382 limitation for the post-change year in which gain is recognized by reason of such election shall be increased by the lesser of—

(i) the recognized built-in gains by reason of such election, or

(ii) the net unrealized built-in gain (determined without regard to paragraph (3)(B)).

(2) RECOGNIZED BUILT-IN GAIN AND LOSS.—

(A) RECOGNIZED BUILT-IN GAIN.—The term "recognized built-in gain" means any gain recognized during the recognition period on the disposition of any asset to the extent the new loss corporation establishes that—

(i) such asset was held by the old loss corporation immediately before the change date, and

(ii) such gain does not exceed the excess of—

(I) the fair market value of such asset on the change date, over

(II) the adjusted basis of such asset on such date.

(B) RECOGNIZED BUILT-IN LOSS.—The term "recognized built-in loss" means any loss recognized during the recognition period on the disposition of any asset except to the extent the new loss corporation establishes that—

(i) such asset was not held by the old loss corporation immediately before the change date, or

(ii) such loss exceeds the excess of—

(I) the adjusted basis of such asset on the change date, over

(II) the fair market value of such asset on such date.

Such term includes any amount allowable as depreciation, amortization, or depletion for any period within the recognition period except to the extent the new loss corporation establishes that the amount so allowable is not attributable to the excess described in clause (ii).

(3) NET UNREALIZED BUILT-IN GAIN AND LOSS DEFINED.—

(A) NET UNREALIZED BUILT-IN GAIN AND LOSS.—

(i) IN GENERAL.—The terms "net unrealized built-in gain" and "net unrealized built-in loss" mean, with respect to any old loss corporation, the amount by which—

(I) the fair market value of the assets of such corporation immediately before an ownership change is more or less, respectively, than

(II) the aggregate adjusted basis of such assets at such time.

(ii) SPECIAL RULE FOR REDEMPTIONS OR OTHER CORPORATE CONTRACTIONS.—If a redemption or other corporate contraction occurs in connection with an ownership change, to the extent provided in regulations, determinations under clause (i) shall be made after taking such redemption or other corporate contraction into account.

(B) THRESHOLD REQUIREMENT.—

(i) IN GENERAL.—If the amount of the net unrealized built-in gain or net unrealized built-in loss (determined without regard to this subparagraph) of any old loss corporation is not greater than the lesser of—

(I) 15 percent of the amount determined for purposes of subparagraph (A)(i)(I), or

(II) $10,000,000,

the net unrealized built-in gain or net unrealized built-in loss shall be zero.

(ii) CASH AND CASH ITEMS NOT TAKEN INTO ACCOUNT.—In computing any net unrealized built-in gain or unrealized built-in loss under clause (i), except as provided in regulations, there shall not be taken into account—

(I) any cash or cash item, or

(II) any marketable security which has a value which does not substantially differ from adjusted basis.

(4) DISALLOWED LOSS ALLOWED AS A CARRYFORWARD.—If a deduction for any portion of a recognized built-in loss is disallowed for any post-change year, such portion—

(A) shall be carried forward to subsequent taxable years under rules similar to the rules for the carrying forward of net operating losses (or to the extent the amount so disallowed is attributable to capital losses, under rules similar to the rules for the carrying forward of net capital losses), but

(B) shall be subject to limitation under this section in the same manner as a pre-change loss.

(5) SPECIAL RULES FOR POST-CHANGE YEAR WHICH INCLUDES CHANGE DATE.—For purposes of subsection (b)(3)—

(A) in applying subparagraph (A) thereof, taxable income shall be computed without regard to recognized built-in gains to the extent such gains increased the section 382 limitation for the year (or recognized built-in losses to the extent such losses are treated as pre-change losses), and gain described in paragraph (1)(C), for the year, and

(B) in applying subparagraph (B) thereof, the section 382 limitation shall be computed without regard to recognized built-in gains, and gain described in paragraph (1)(C), for the year.

(6) TREATMENT OF CERTAIN BUILT-IN ITEMS.—

(A) INCOME ITEMS.—Any item of income which is properly taken into account during the recognition period but which is attributable to periods before the change date shall be treated as a recognized built-in gain for the taxable year in which it is properly taken into account.

(B) DEDUCTION ITEMS.—Any amount which is allowable as a deduction during the recognition period (determined without regard to any carryover) but which is attributable to periods before the change date shall be treated as a recognized built-in loss for the taxable year for which it is allowable as a deduction.

(C) ADJUSTMENTS.—The amount of the net unrealized built-in gain or loss shall be properly adjusted for amounts which would be treated as recognized built-in gains or losses under this paragraph if such amounts were properly taken into account (or allowable as a deduction) during the recognition period.

(7) RECOGNITION PERIOD, ETC.—

(A) RECOGNITION PERIOD.—The term "recognition period" means, with respect to any ownership change, the 5-year period beginning on the change date.

(B) RECOGNITION PERIOD TAXABLE YEAR.—The term "recognition period taxable year" means any taxable year any portion of which is in the recognition period.

(8) DETERMINATION OF FAIR MARKET VALUE IN CERTAIN CASES.—If 80 percent or more in value of the stock of a corporation is acquired in 1 transaction (or in a series of related transactions during any 12-month period), for purposes of determining the net unrealized built-in loss, the fair market value of the assets of such corporation shall not exceed the grossed up amount paid for such stock properly adjusted for indebtedness of the corporation and other relevent items.

(9) TAX-FREE EXCHANGES OR TRANSFERS.—The Secretary shall prescribe such regulations as may be necessary to carry out the purposes of this subsection where property held on the change date was acquired (or is subsequently transferred) in a transaction where gain or loss is not recognized (in whole or in part).

Amendments

• 2009, American Recovery and Reinvestment Tax Act of 2009 (P.L. 111-5)

P.L. 111-5, §1261, provides:

SEC. 1261. CLARIFICATION OF REGULATIONS RELATED TO LIMITATIONS ON CERTAIN BUILT-IN LOSSES FOLLOWING AN OWNERSHIP CHANGE.

(a) FINDINGS.—Congress finds as follows:

(1) The delegation of authority to the Secretary of the Treasury under section 382(m) of the Internal Revenue Code of 1986 does not authorize the Secretary to provide exemptions or special rules that are restricted to particular industries or classes of taxpayers.

(2) Internal Revenue Service Notice 2008-83 is inconsistent with the congressional intent in enacting such section 382(m).

(3) The legal authority to prescribe Internal Revenue Service Notice 2008-83 is doubtful.

(4) However, as taxpayers should generally be able to rely on guidance issued by the Secretary of the Treasury legislation is necessary to clarify the force and effect of Internal Revenue Service Notice 2008-83 and restore the proper ap-

plication under the Internal Revenue Code of 1986 of the limitation on built-in losses following an ownership change of a bank.

(b) DETERMINATION OF FORCE AND EFFECT OF INTERNAL REVENUE SERVICE NOTICE 2008–83 EXEMPTING BANKS FROM LIMITATION ON CERTAIN BUILT–IN LOSSES FOLLOWING OWNERSHIP CHANGE.—

(1) IN GENERAL.—Internal Revenue Service Notice 2008–83—

(A) shall be deemed to have the force and effect of law with respect to any ownership change (as defined in section 382(g) of the Internal Revenue Code of 1986) occurring on or before January 16, 2009, and

(B) shall have no force or effect with respect to any ownership change after such date.

(2) BINDING CONTRACTS.—Notwithstanding paragraph (1), Internal Revenue Service Notice 2008–83 shall have the force and effect of law with respect to any ownership change (as so defined) which occurs after January 16, 2009, if such change—

(A) is pursuant to a written binding contract entered into on or before such date, or

(B) is pursuant to a written agreement entered into on or before such date and such agreement was described on or before such date in a public announcement or in a filing with the Securities and Exchange Commission required by reason of such ownership change.

• 1989, Omnibus Budget Reconciliation Act of 1989 (P.L. 101-239)

P.L. 101-239, §7205(a):

Amended Code Sec. 382(h)(3)(B)(i). **Effective**, generally, for ownership changes and acquisitions after 10-2-89, in tax years ending after such date. For exceptions, see Act Sec. 7205(c)(2)-(4), below. Prior to amendment, Code Sec. 382(h)(3)(B)(i) read as follows:

(i) If the amount of the net unrealized built-in gain or net unrealized built-in loss (determined without regard to this subparagraph) of any old loss corporation is not greater than 25 percent of the amount determined for purposes of subparagraph (A)(i)(I), the net unrealized built-in gain or net unrealized built-in loss shall be zero.

P.L. 101-239, §7205(c)(2)-(4), provides:

(2) BINDING CONTRACT.—The amendments made by this section shall not apply to any ownership change or acquisition pursuant to a written binding contract in effect on October 2, 1989, and at all times thereafter before such change or acquisition.

(3) BANKRUPTCY PROCEEDINGS.—In the case of a reorganization described in section 368(a)(1)(G) of the Internal Revenue Code of 1986, or an exchange of debt for stock in a title 11 or similar case (as defined in section 368(a)(3) of such Code), the amendments made by this section shall not apply to any ownership change resulting from such a reorganization or proceeding if a petition in such case was filed with the court before October 3, 1989.

(4) SUBSIDIARIES OF BANKRUPT PARENT.—The amendments made by this section shall not apply to any built-in loss of a corporation which is a member (on October 2, 1989) of an affiliated group the common parent of which (on such date) was subject to title 11 or similar case (as defined in section 368(a)(3) of such Code). The preceding sentence shall apply only if the ownership change or acquisition is pursuant to the plan approved in such proceeding and is before the date 2 years after the date on which the petition which commenced such proceeding was filed.

P.L. 101-239, §7811(c)(5)(A)(i)-(ii):

Amended Code Sec. 382(h)(6) by striking "during the recognition period" in subparagraph (B) and inserting "during the recognition period (determined without regard to any carryover)", and by striking "treated as recognized built-in gains or losses under this paragraph" in subparagraph (C) and inserting "which would be treated as recognized built-in gains or losses under this paragraph if such amounts were properly taken into account (or allowable as a deduction) during the recognition period". **Effective** as if included in the provision of P.L. 100-647 to which it relates.

• 1988, Technical and Miscellaneous Revenue Act of 1988 (P.L. 100-647)

P.L. 100-647, §1006(d)(1)(B)(i)-(ii):

Amended Code Sec. 382(h)(3)(A)(ii) by inserting "or other corporate contraction" after "redemption" each place it appears, and by inserting "OR OTHER CORPORATE CONTRACTIONS" after "REDEMPTIONS" in the heading thereof. **Effective** with respect to ownership changes after 6-10-87.

P.L. 100-647, §1006(d)(3)(A):

Amended Code Sec. 382(h)(1)(C). **Effective** as if included in the provision of P.L. 99-514 to which it relates. Prior to amendment, Code Sec. 382(h)(1)(C) read as follows:

(C) SECTION 338 GAIN.—The section 382 limitation for any taxable year in which gain is recognized by reason of an election under section 338 shall be increased by the excess of—

(i) the amount of such gain, over

(ii) the portion of such gain taken into account in computing recognized built-in gains for such taxable year.

P.L. 100-647, §1006(d)(3)(B):

Amended Code Sec. 382(h)(5) by striking out "recognized built-in gains and losses" and inserting in lieu thereof "recognized built-in gains to the extent such gains increased the section 382 limitation for the year (or recognized built-in losses to the extent such losses are treated as pre-change losses)". **Effective** as if included in the provision of P.L. 99-514 to which it relates.

P.L. 100-647, §1006(d)(20)(A)-(B):

Amended Code Sec. 382(h)(4) by inserting before the comma at the end of subparagraph (A) "(or to the extent the amount so disallowed is attributable to capital losses, under rules similar to the rules for the carrying forward of net capital losses)", and by striking out "TREATED AS A NET OPERATING LOSS" in the paragraph heading and inserting in lieu thereof "ALLOWED AS A CARRYFORWARD". **E ffective** as if included in the provision of P.L. 99-514 to which it relates.

P.L. 100-647, §1006(d)(22):

Amended Code Sec. 382(h)(6). **Effective** as if included in the provision of P.L. 99-514 to which it relates. Prior to amendment, Code Sec. 382(h)(6) read as follows:

(6) SECRETARY MAY TREAT CERTAIN DEDUCTIONS AS BUILT-IN LOSSES.—The Secretary may by regulation treat amounts which accrue on or before the change date but which are allowable as a deduction after such date as recognized built-in losses.

P.L. 100-647, §1006(d)(23):

Amended Code Sec. 382(h)(9) by striking out "is transferred" and inserting in lieu thereof "was acquired (or is subsequently transferred)". **Effective** as if included in the provision of P.L. 99-514 to which it relates.

P.L. 100-647, §1006(d)(26):

Amended Code Sec. 382(h)(3)(B)(ii) by striking out "there shall not" and inserting in lieu thereof "except as provided in regulations, there shall not". **Effective** as if included in the provision of P.L. 99-514 to which it relates.

P.L. 100-647, §1006(d)(28)(A):

Amended Code Sec. 382(h)(3)(A)(ii) by striking out "determinations under clause (i)" and inserting in lieu thereof "to the extent provided in regulations, determinations under clause (i)". **Effective** in the case of ownership changes on or after 6-21-88.

• 1987, Revenue Act of 1987 (P.L. 100-203)

P.L. 100-203, §10225(b):

Amended Code Sec. 382(h)(2)(B) by adding at the end thereof a new sentence. **Effective** in the case of ownership changes (as defined in section 382 of the Internal Revenue Code of 1986 as amended by subsection (a)) after 12-15-87; except that such amendment shall not apply in the case of any ownership change pursuant to a binding written contract which was in effect on 12-15-87, and at all times thereafter before such ownership change.

[Sec. 382(i)]

(i) TESTING PERIOD.—For purposes of this section—

(1) 3-YEAR PERIOD.—Except as otherwise provided in this section, the testing period is the 3-year period ending on the day of any owner shift involving a 5-percent shareholder or equity structure shift.

(2) SHORTER PERIOD WHERE THERE HAS BEEN RECENT OWNERSHIP CHANGE.—If there has been an ownership change under this section, the testing period for determining whether a 2nd ownership change has occurred shall not begin before the 1st day following the change date for such earlier ownership change.

(3) SHORTER PERIOD WHERE ALL LOSSES ARISE AFTER 3-YEAR PERIOD BEGINS.—The testing period shall not begin before the earlier of the 1st day of the 1st taxable year from which there is a carryforward of a loss or of an excess credit to the 1st post-change year or the taxable year in which the transaction being tested occurs. Except as provided in regulations, this paragraph shall not apply to any loss corporation which has a net unrealized built-in loss (determined after application of subsection (h)(3)(B)).

Amendments

• **1988, Technical and Miscellaneous Revenue Act of 1988 (P.L. 100-647)**

P.L. 100-647, §1006(d)(4)(A)-(B):

Amended Code Sec. 382(i)(3) by inserting "the earlier of" before "the 1st day", and by inserting "or the taxable year in which the transaction being tested occurs" after "1st post-change year". **Effective** as if included in the provision of P.L. 99-514 to which it relates.

[Sec. 382(j)]

(j) CHANGE DATE.—For purposes of this section, the change date is—

(1) in the case where the last component of an ownership change is an owner shift involving a 5-percent shareholder, the date on which such shift occurs, and

(2) in the case where the last component of an ownership change is an equity structure shift, the date of the reorganization.

[Sec. 382(k)]

(k) DEFINITIONS AND SPECIAL RULES.—For purposes of this section—

(1) LOSS CORPORATION.—The term "loss corporation" means a corporation entitled to use a net operating loss carryover or having a net operating loss for the taxable year in which the ownership change occurs. Except to the extent provided in regulations, such term includes any corporation with a net unrealized built-in loss.

(2) OLD LOSS CORPORATION.—The term "old loss corporation" means any corporation—

(A) with respect to which there is an ownership change, and

(B) which (before the ownership change) was a loss corporation.

(3) NEW LOSS CORPORATION.—The term "new loss corporation" means a corporation which (after an ownership change) is a loss corporation. Nothing in this section shall be treated as implying that the same corporation may not be both the old loss corporation and the new loss corporation.

(4) TAXABLE INCOME.—Taxable income shall be computed with the modifications set forth in section 172(d).

(5) VALUE.—The term "value" means fair market value.

(6) RULES RELATING TO STOCK.—

(A) PREFERRED STOCK.—Except as provided in regulations and subsection (e), the term "stock" means stock other than stock described in section 1504(a)(4).

(B) TREATMENT OF CERTAIN RIGHTS, ETC.—The Secretary shall prescribe such regulations as may be necessary—

(i) to treat warrants, options, contracts to acquire stock, convertible debt interests, and other similar interests as stock, and

(ii) to treat stock as not stock.

(C) DETERMINATIONS ON BASIS OF VALUE.—Determinations of the percentage of stock of any corporation held by any person shall be made on the basis of value.

(7) 5-PERCENT SHAREHOLDER.—The term "5-percent shareholder" means any person holding 5 percent or more of the stock of the corporation at any time during the testing period.

Amendments

• **1988, Technical and Miscellaneous Revenue Act of 1988 (P.L. 100-647)**

P.L. 100-647, §1006(d)(5)(A):

Amended Code Sec. 382(k)(1) by inserting "or having a net operating loss for the taxable year in which the ownership change occurs" after "carryover". **Effective** as if included in the provision of P.L. 99-514 to which it relates.

P.L. 100-647, §1006(d)(5)(B):

Amended Code Sec. 382(k)(2). **Effective** as if included in the provision of P.L. 99-514 to which it relates. Prior to amendment, Code Sec. 382(k)(2) read as follows:

(2) OLD LOSS CORPORATION.—The term "old loss corporation" means any corporation with respect to which there is an ownership change—

(A) which (before the ownership change) was a loss corporation, or

(B) with respect to which there is a pre-change loss described in subsection (d)(1)(B).

[Sec. 382(l)]

(l) CERTAIN ADDITIONAL OPERATING RULES.—For purposes of this section—

(1) CERTAIN CAPITAL CONTRIBUTIONS NOT TAKEN INTO ACCOUNT.—

(A) IN GENERAL.—Any capital contribution received by an old loss corporation as part of a plan a principal purpose of which is to avoid or increase any limitation under this section shall not be taken into account for purposes of this section.

(B) CERTAIN CONTRIBUTIONS TREATED AS PART OF PLAN.—For purposes of subparagraph (A), any capital contribution made during the 2-year period ending on the change date shall, except as provided in regulations, be treated as part of a plan described in subparagraph (A).

(2) ORDERING RULES FOR APPLICATION OF SECTION.—

(A) COORDINATION WITH SECTION 172(b) CARRYOVER RULES.—In the case of any pre-change loss for any taxable year (hereinafter in this subparagraph referred to as the "loss year" subject to limitation under this section, for purposes of determining under the 2nd sentence of section 172(b)(2) the amount of such loss which may be carried to any taxable year, taxable income for any taxable year shall be treated as not greater than—

(i) the section 382 limitation for such taxable year, reduced by

(ii) the unused pre-change losses for taxable years preceding the loss year.

Similar rules shall apply in the case of any credit or loss subject to limitation under section 383.

(B) ORDERING RULE FOR LOSSES CARRIED FROM SAME TAXABLE YEAR.—In any case in which—

(i) a pre-change loss of a loss corporation for any taxable year is subject to a section 382 limitation, and

(ii) a net operating loss of such corporation from such taxable year is not subject to such limitation,

taxable income shall be treated as having been offset first by the loss subject to such limitation.

(3) OPERATING RULES RELATING TO OWNERSHIP OF STOCK.—

(A) CONSTRUCTIVE OWNERSHIP.—Section 318 (relating to constructive ownership of stock) shall apply in determining ownership of stock, except that—

(i) paragraphs (1) and (5)(B) of section 318(a) shall not apply and an individual and all members of his family described in paragraph (1) of section 318(a) shall be treated as 1 individual for purposes of applying this section,

(ii) paragraph (2) of section 318(a) shall be applied—

(I) without regard to the 50-percent limitation contained in subparagraph (C) thereof, and

(II) except as provided in regulations, by treating stock attributed thereunder as no longer being held by the entity from which attributed,

(iii) paragraph (3) of section 318(a) shall be applied only to the extent provided in regulations,

(iv) except to the extent provided in regulations, an option to acquire stock shall be treated as exercised if such exercise results in an ownership change, and

(v) in attributing stock from an entity under paragraph (2) of section 318(a), there shall not be taken into account—

(I) in the case of attribution from a corporation, stock which is not treated as stock for purposes of this section, or

(II) in the case of attribution from another entity, an interest in such entity similar to stock described in subclause (I).

A rule similar to the rule of clause (iv) shall apply in the case of any contingent purchase, warrant, convertible debt, put, stock subject to a risk of forfeiture, contract to acquire stock, or similar interests.

(B) STOCK ACQUIRED BY REASON OF DEATH, GIFT, DIVORCE, SEPARATION, ETC.—If—

(i) the basis of any stock in the hands of any person is determined—

(I) under section 1014 (relating to property acquired from a decedent),

(II) section 1015 (relating to property acquired by a gift or transfer in trust), or

(III) section 1041(b)(2) (relating to transfers of property between spouses or incident to divorce),

(ii) stock is received by any person in satisfaction of a right to receive a pecuniary bequest, or

(iii) stock is acquired by a person pursuant to any divorce or separation instrument (within the meaning of section 71(b)(2)),

such person shall be treated as owning such stock during the period such stock was owned by the person from whom it was acquired.

(C) CERTAIN CHANGES IN PERCENTAGE OWNERSHIP WHICH ARE ATTRIBUTABLE TO FLUCTUATIONS IN VALUE NOT TAKEN INTO ACCOUNT.—Except as provided in regulations, any change in proportionate ownership which is attributable solely to fluctuations in the relative fair market values of different classes of stock shall not be taken into account.

(4) REDUCTION IN VALUE WHERE SUBSTANTIAL NONBUSINESS ASSETS.—

(A) IN GENERAL.—If, immediately after an ownership change, the new loss corporation has substantial nonbusiness assets, the value of the old loss corporation shall be reduced by the excess (if any) of—

(i) the fair market value of the nonbusiness assets of the old loss corporation, over

(ii) the nonbusiness asset share of indebtedness for which such corporation is liable.

(B) CORPORATION HAVING SUBSTANTIAL NONBUSINESS ASSETS.—For purposes of subparagraph (A)—

(i) IN GENERAL.—The old loss corporation shall be treated as having substantial nonbusiness assets if at least 1/3 of the value of the total assets of such corporation consists of nonbusiness assets.

(ii) EXCEPTION FOR CERTAIN INVESTMENT ENTITIES.—A regulated investment company to which part I of subchapter M applies, a real estate investment trust to which part II of subchapter M applies, or a REMIC to which part IV of subchapter M applies, shall not be treated as a new loss corporation having substantial nonbusiness assets.

(C) NONBUSINESS ASSETS.—For purposes of this paragraph, the term "nonbusiness assets" means assets held for investment.

(D) NONBUSINESS ASSET SHARE.—For purposes of this paragraph, the nonbusiness asset share of the indebtedness of the corporation is an amount which bears the same ratio to such indebtedness as—

(i) the fair market value of the nonbusiness assets of the corporation, bears to

(ii) the fair market value of all assets of such corporation.

(E) TREATMENT OF SUBSIDIARIES.—For purposes of this paragraph, stock and securities in any subsidiary corporation shall be disregarded and the parent corporation shall be deemed to own its ratable share of the subsidiary's assets. For purposes of the preceding sentence, a corporation shall be treated as a subsidiary if the parent owns 50 percent or more of the combined voting power of all classes of stock entitled to vote, and 50 percent or more of the total value of shares of all classes of stock.

(5) TITLE 11 OR SIMILAR CASE.—

(A) IN GENERAL.—Subsection (a) shall not apply to any ownership change if—

(i) the old loss corporation is (immediately before such ownership change) under the jurisdiction of the court in a title 11 or similar case, and

(ii) the shareholders and creditors of the old loss corporation (determined immediately before such ownership change) own (after such ownership change and as a result of being shareholders or creditors immediately before such change) stock of the new loss corporation (or stock of a controlling corporation if also in bankruptcy) which meets the requirements of section 1504(a)(2) (determined by substituting "50 percent" for "80 percent" each place it appears).

(B) REDUCTION FOR INTEREST PAYMENTS TO CREDITORS BECOMING SHAREHOLDERS.—In any case to which subparagraph (A) applies, the pre-change losses and excess credits (within the meaning of section 383(a)(2)) which may be carried to a post-change year shall be computed as if no deduction was allowable under this chapter for the interest paid or accrued by the old loss corporation on indebtedness which was converted into stock pursuant to title 11 or similar case during—

(i) any taxable year ending during the 3-year period preceding the taxable year in which the ownership change occurs, and

(ii) the period of the taxable year in which the ownership change occurs on or before the change date.

(C) COORDINATION WITH SECTION 108.—In applying section 108(e)(8) to any case to which subparagraph (A) applies, there shall not be taken into account any indebtedness for interest described in subparagraph (B).

(D) SECTION 382 LIMITATION ZERO IF ANOTHER CHANGE WITHIN 2 YEARS.—If, during the 2-year period immediately following an ownership change to which this paragraph applies, an ownership change of the new loss corporation occurs, this paragraph shall not apply and the section 382 limitation with respect to the 2nd ownership change for any post-change year ending after the change date of the 2nd ownership change shall be zero.

(E) ONLY CERTAIN STOCK TAKEN INTO ACCOUNT.—For purposes of subparagraph (A)(ii), stock transferred to a creditor shall be taken into account only to the extent such stock is transferred in satisfaction of indebtedness and only if such indebtedness—

(i) was held by the creditor at least 18 months before the date of the filing of the title 11 or similar case, or

(ii) arose in the ordinary course of the trade or business of the old loss corporation and is held by the person who at all times held the beneficial interest in such indebtedness.

(F) SPECIAL RULE FOR CERTAIN FINANCIAL INSTITUTIONS.—

(i) IN GENERAL.—In the case of any ownership change to which this subparagraph applies, this paragraph shall be applied—

(I) by substituting "1504(a)(2)(B)" for "1504(a)(2)" and "20 percent" for "50 percent" in subparagraph (A)(ii), and

(II) without regard to subparagraphs (B) and (C).

(ii) SPECIAL RULE FOR DEPOSITORS.—For purposes of applying this paragraph to an ownership change to which this subparagraph applies—

(I) a depositor in the old loss corporation shall be treated as a stockholder in such loss corporation immediately before the change,

(II) deposits which, after the change, become deposits of the new loss corporation shall be treated as stock of the new loss corporation, and

(III) the fair market value of the outstanding stock of the new loss corporation shall include the amount of deposits in the new loss corporation immediately after the change.

(iii) CHANGES TO WHICH SUBPARAGRAPH APPLIES.—This subparagraph shall apply to—

(I) an equity structure shift which is a reorganization described in section 368(a)(3)(D)(ii) (as modified by section 368(a)(3)(D)(iv)), or

(II) any other equity structure shift (or transaction to which section 351 applies) which occurs as an integral part of a transaction involving a change to which subclause (I) applies.

This subparagraph shall not apply to any equity structure shift or transaction occurring on or after May 10, 1989.

(G) TITLE 11 OR SIMILAR CASE.—For purposes of this paragraph, the term "title 11 or similar case" has the meaning given such term by section 368(a)(3)(A).

(H) ELECTION NOT TO HAVE PARAGRAPH APPLY.—A new loss corporation may elect, subject to such terms and conditions as the Secretary may prescribe, not to have the provisions of this paragraph apply.

(6) SPECIAL RULE FOR INSOLVENCY TRANSACTIONS.—If paragraph (5) does not apply to any reorganization described in subparagraph (G) of section 368(a)(1) or any exchange of debt for stock in a title 11 or similar case (as defined in section 368(a)(3)(A)), the value under subsection (e) shall reflect the increase (if any) in value of the old loss corporation resulting from any surrender or cancellation of creditors' claims in the transaction.

(7) COORDINATION WITH ALTERNATIVE MINIMUM TAX.—The Secretary shall by regulation provide for the application of this section to the alternative tax net operating loss deduction under section 56(d).

(8) PREDECESSOR AND SUCCESSOR ENTITIES.—Except as provided in regulations, any entity and any predecessor or successor entities of such entity shall be treated as 1 entity.

Amendments

• 2004, American Jobs Creation Act of 2004 (P.L. 108-357)

P.L. 108-357, §835(b)(2):

Amended Code Sec. 382(l)(4)(B)(ii) by striking "a REMIC to which part IV of subchapter M applies, or a FASIT to which part V of subchapter M applies," and inserting "or a REMIC to which part IV of subchapter M applies,". For the **effective** date, see Act Sec. 835(c), below.

P.L. 108-357, §835(c), provides:

(c) EFFECTIVE DATE.—

(1) IN GENERAL.—Except as provided in paragraph (2), the amendments made by this section shall take effect on January 1, 2005.

(2) EXCEPTION FOR EXISTING FASITS.—Paragraph (1) shall not apply to any FASIT in existence on the date of the enactment of this Act [10-22-2004.—CCH] to the extent that regular interests issued by the FASIT before such date continue to remain outstanding in accordance with the original terms of issuance.

• 1996, Small Business Job Protection Act of 1996 (P.L. 104-188)

P.L. 104-188, §1621(b)(3):

Amended Code Sec. 382(l)(4)(B)(ii) by striking "or a REMIC to which part IV of subchapter M applies" and inserting "a REMIC to which part IV of subchapter M applies, or a FASIT to which part V of subchapter M applies". **Effective** 9-1-97.

• 1993, Omnibus Budget Reconciliation Act of 1993 (P.L. 103-66)

P.L. 103-66, §13226(a)(2)(A):

Amended Code Sec. 382(l)(5)(C). **Effective**, generally, for stock transferred after 12-31-94 in satisfaction of any indebtedness. However, for an exception see Act Sec. 13226(a)(3)(B), below. Prior to amendment, Code Sec. 382(l)(5)(C) read as follows:

(C) REDUCTION OF TAX ATTRIBUTES WHERE DISCHARGE OF INDEBTEDNESS.—

(i) IN GENERAL.—In any case to which subparagraph (A) applies, 50 percent of the amount which, but for the application of section 108(e)(10)(B), would have been applied to reduce tax attributes under section 108(b) shall be so applied.

(ii) CLARIFICATION WITH SUBPARAGRAPH (B).—In applying clause (i), there shall not be taken into account any indebtedness for interest described in subparagraph (B).

P.L. 103-66, §13226(a)(3)(B), provides:

(B) EXCEPTION FOR TITLE 11 CASES.—The amendments made by this subsection shall not apply to stock transferred in satisfaction of any indebtedness if such transfer is in a title 11 or similar case (as defined in section 368(a)(3)(A) of the Internal Revenue Code of 1986) which was filed on or before December 31, 1993.

• 1989, Omnibus Budget Reconciliation Act of 1989 (P.L. 101-239)

P.L. 101-239, §7304(d)(1):

Amended Code Sec. 382(l)(3) by striking subparagraph (C) and by redesignating subparagraph (D) as subparagraph (C). **Effective** for acquisitions of employer securities after 7-12-89, except that such amendments shall not apply to acquisitions after 7-12-89, pursuant to a written binding contract in effect on 7-12-89, and at all times thereafter before such acquisition. Prior to amendment, Code Sec. 382(l)(3)(C) read as follows:

(C) SPECIAL RULE FOR EMPLOYEE STOCK OWNERSHIP PLANS.—

(i) IN GENERAL.—Except as provided in clause (ii), the acquisition of employer securities (within the meaning of section 409(l)) by—

(I) a tax credit employee stock ownership plan or an employee stock ownership plan (within the meaning of section 4975(e)(7)), or

(II) a participant of any such plan pursuant to the requirements of section 409(h), shall not be taken into account in determining whether an ownership change has occurred.

(ii) OWNERSHIP AND ALLOCATION REQUIREMENTS.—Subclause (I) of clause (i) shall not apply to any acquisition unless—

(I) immediately after such acquisition the plan holds stock meeting the requirements of section 1042(b)(2), except that such section shall be applied by substituting "50 percent" for "30 percent",

(II) the plan meets requirements similar to the requirements of section 409(n); and

(III) immediately after the acquisition the plan has a number of participants which is not less than 50 percent of the average number of employees of the loss corporation during the 3-year period ending with such acquisition.

For purposes of subclause (III), except as provided in regulations, all members of an affiliated group which includes the loss corporation and which files a consolidated return shall be treated as 1 loss corporation.

P.L. 101-239, §7815(h):

Amended Code Sec. 382(l)(3)(C)(ii) by striking "for purposes of subclause (III)," and inserting "For purposes of subclause (III),". **Effective** as if included in the provision of P.L. 100-647 to which it relates.

P.L. 101-239, §7841(d)(11):

Amended Code Sec. 382(l)(3)(B)(i)(III) by striking "divorce," and inserting "divorce),". **Effective** 12-19-89.

• 1989, Financial Institutions Reform, Recovery, and Enforcement Act of 1989 (P.L. 101-73)

P.L. 101-73, §1401(a)(2):

Amended Code Sec. 382(l)(5)(F) by striking out "after December 31, 1989" in the last sentence and inserting "on or after May 10, 1989". **Effective** for transactions on or after 5-10-89.

• 1988, Technical and Miscellaneous Revenue Act of 1988 (P.L. 100-647)

P.L. 100-647, §1006(d)(6):

Amended Code Sec. 382(1)(3)(A) by striking out "and" at the end of clause (iii), and by striking out clause (iv) and inserting in lieu thereof new clauses (iv)-(v). **Effective** as if included in the provision of P.L. 99-514 to which it relates. Prior to amendment, Code Sec. 382(1)(3)(A)(iv) read as follows:

(iv) except to the extent provided in regulations, paragraph (4) of section 318(a) shall apply to an option if such application results in an ownership change.

P.L. 100-647, §1006(d)(7):

Amended Code Sec. 382(l)(5)(A)(ii) by striking out "immediately after such ownership change" and inserting in lieu thereof "after such ownership change and as a result of being shareholders or creditors immediately before such change". **Effective** as if included in the provision of P.L. 99-514 to which it relates.

P.L. 100-647, §1006(d)(8)(A)-(B):

Amended Code Sec. 382(l)(5)(F) by inserting "`1504(a)(2)(B)' for `1504(a)(2)' and" after "substituting" in clause (i)(I), and by striking out "deposits described in subclause (II)" in clause (ii)(III) and inserting in lieu thereof "the amount of deposits in the new loss corporation immediately after the change". **Effective** as if included in the provision of P.L. 99-514 to which it relates.

P.L. 100-647, §1006(d)(9):

Amended Code Sec. 382(l)(6) by striking out "shall be the value of the new loss corporation immediately after the ownership change" and inserting in lieu thereof "shall reflect the increase (if any) in value of the old loss corporation resulting from any surrender or cancellation of creditors' claims in the transaction". **Effective** as if included in the provision of P.L. 99-514 to which it relates.

P.L. 100-647, §1006(d)(10):

Amended Code Sec. 382(l) by adding at the end thereof new paragraph (8). **Effective** as if included in the provision of P.L. 99-514 to which it relates.

P.L. 100-647, §1006(d)(18):

Amended Code Sec. 382(l)(5)(C). **Effective** as if included in the provision of P.L. 99-514 to which it relates. Prior to amendment, Code Sec. 382(l)(5)(C) read as follows:

(C) REDUCTION OF CARRYFORWARDS WHERE DISCHARGE OF INDEBTEDNESS.—In any case to which subparagraph (A) applies, the pre-change losses and excess credits (within the meaning of section 383(a)(2)) which may be carried to a post-change year shall be computed as if 50 percent of the amount which, but for the application of section 108(e)(10)(B), would have been includible in gross income for any taxable year had been so included.

P.L. 100-647, §1006(d)(19):

Amended Code Sec. 382(l)(5)(E). **Effective** as if included in the provision of P.L. 99-514 to which it relates. Prior to amendment, Code Sec. 382(l)(5)(E) read as follows:

(E) ONLY CERTAIN STOCK OF CREDITORS TAKEN INTO ACCOUNT.—For purposes of subparagraph (A)(ii) stock transferred to a creditor in satisfaction of indebtedness shall be taken into account only if such indebtedeness—

(i) was held by the creditor at least 18 months before the date of the filing of the title 11 or similar case, or

(ii) arose in the ordinary course of the trade or business of the old loss corporation and is held by the person who at all times held the beneficial interest in such indebtedness.

P.L. 100-647, §1006(d)(25):

Amended Code Sec. 382(l)(5)(A)(ii) by striking out "stock of controlling corporation" and inserting in lieu thereof "stock of a controlling corporation". **Effective** as if included in the provision of P.L. 99-514 to which it relates.

P.L. 100-647, §1006(d)(27):

Amended Code Sec. 382(l)(5)(B) by striking out "the net operating loss deduction under section 172(a) for any post-change year shall be determined" and inserting in lieu thereof "the pre-change losses and excess credits (within the meaning of section 383(a)(2)) which may be carried to a post-change year shall be computed". **Effective** as if included in the provision of P.L. 99-514 to which it relates.

P.L. 100-647, §1006(d)(29):

Amended Code Sec. 382(l)(5)(F)(iii)(I) by striking out "section 368(a)(D)(ii)" and inserting in lieu thereof "section 368(a)(3)(D)(ii)". **Effective** as if included in the provision of P.L. 99-514 to which it relates.

P.L. 100-647, §1006(t)(22)(A):

Amended Code Sec. 382(l)(4)(B)(ii) by striking out "real estate mortgage pool" and inserting in lieu thereof

"REMIC". **Effective** as if included in the provision of P.L. 99-514 to which it relates.

P.L. 100-647, §4012(a)(3):

Amended Code Sec. 382(l)(5)(F) by striking out "December 31, 1988" and inserting in lieu thereof "December 31, 1989" in the last sentence. **Effective** on the date of enactment of this Act.

P.L. 100-647, §4012(b)(1)(B):

Amended Code Sec. 382(l)(5)(F)(iii)(I) by inserting "(as modified by section 368(a)(3)(D)(iv))" after "section 368(a)(3)(D)(ii)". **Effective** for any ownership change occurring after the date of the enactment of this Act and before 1-1-90.

P.L. 100-647, §5077(a):

Amended Code Sec. 382(l)(3)(C)(ii) by striking "and" at the end of subclause (I), by striking the period at the end of subclause (ii) and inserting in lieu thereof "; and", and by adding at the end thereof a new subclause (III) and a new flush left sentence. For the **effective** date, see Act Sec. 5077(b), below.

P.L. 100-647, §5077(b), provides:

(b) EFFECTIVE DATE.—

(1) IN GENERAL.—The amendment made by subsection (a) shall apply to acquisition after December 31, 1988.

(2) EXCEPTION.—The amendment made by subsection (a) shall not apply to acquisitions after December 31, 1988, pursuant to a binding written contract entered into on or before October 21, 1988.

[Sec. 382(m)]

(m) REGULATIONS.—The Secretary shall prescribe such regulations as may be necessary or appropriate to carry out the purposes of this section and section 383, including (but not limited to) regulations—

(1) providing for the application of this section and section 383 where an ownership change with respect to the old loss corporation is followed by an ownership change with respect to the new loss corporation, and

(2) providing for the application of this section and section 383 in the case of a short taxable year,

(3) providing for such adjustments to the application of this section and section 383 as is necessary to prevent the avoidance of the purposes of this section and section 383, including the avoidance of such purposes through the use of related persons, pass-thru entities, or other intermediaries,

(4) providing for the application of subsection (g)(4) where there is only 1 corporation involved, and

(5) providing, in the case of any group of corporations described in section 1563(a) (determined by substituting "50 percent" for "80 percent" each place it appears and determined without regard to paragraph (4) thereof), appropriate adjustments to value, built-in gain or loss, and other items so that items are not omitted or taken into account more than once.

Amendments

• 1988, Technical and Miscellaneous Revenue Act of 1988 (P.L. 100-647)

P.L. 100-647, §1006(d)(1)(C):

Amended Code Sec. 382(m) by inserting "and" at the end of paragraph (3), by striking out paragraph (4), and by redesignating paragraph (5) as paragraph (4). **Effective** with respect to ownership changes after 6-10-87. Prior to amendment, Code Sec. 382(m)(4) read as follows:

(4) providing for the treatment of corporate contractions as redemptions for purposes of subsections (e)(2) and (h)(3)(A), and

P.L. 100-647, §1006(d)(24):

Amended Code Sec. 382(m) (as amended by paragraph (1)) by striking out "and" at the end of subparagraph (3), by striking out the period at the end of paragraph (4) and inserting in lieu thereof ", and", and by adding at the end thereof new paragraph (5). **Effective** as if included in the provision of P.L. 99-514 to which it relates.

• 1986, Tax Reform Act of 1986 (P.L. 99-514)

P.L. 99-514, §621(a):

Amended Code Sec. 382 to read as above. For the **effective** date, see Act Sec. 621(f), below.

P.L. 99-514, §621(f), as amended by P.L. 100-647, §§1006(d)(11)-(16) and 6277(a)-(b), provides:

(f) EFFECTIVE DATES.—

(1) AMENDMENTS MADE BY SUBSECTIONS (a), (b), and (c).—

(A) IN GENERAL.—

(i) CHANGES AFTER 1986.—The amendments made by subsections (a), (b), and (c) shall apply to any ownership change after December 31, 1986.

(ii) PLANS OF REORGANIZATION ADOPTED BEFORE 1987.—For purposes of clause (i), any equity structure shift pursuant to a plan of reorganization adopted before January 1, 1987, shall be treated as occurring when such plan was adopted.

(B) TERMINATION OF OLD SECTION 382.—Except in a case described in any of the following paragraphs—

(i) section 382(a) of the Internal Revenue Code of 1954 (as in effect before the amendment made by subsection (a) and the amendments made by section 806 of the Tax Reform Act of 1976) shall not apply to any increase in percentage points occurring after December 1, 1988, and

(ii) section 382(b) of such Code (as so in effect) shall not apply to any reorganization occurring pursuant to a plan of reorganization adopted after December 31, 1986.

In no event shall sections 382 (a) and (b) of such Code (as so in effect) apply to any ownership change described in subparagraph (A).

(C) COORDINATION WITH SECTION 382(i).—For purposes of section 382(i) of the Internal Revenue Code of 1986 (as added by this section), any equity structure shift pursuant to a plan of reorganization adopted before January 1, 1987, shall be treated as occurring when such plan was adopted.

(2) FOR AMENDMENTS TO TAX REFORM ACT OF 1976.—

(A) IN GENERAL.—The repeals made by subsection (e)(1) and the amendment made by subsection (e)(2) shall take effect on January 1, 1986.

(B) ELECTION TO HAVE AMENDMENTS APPLY.—

(i) If a taxpayer described in clause (ii) elects to have the provisions of this subparagraph apply, the amendments made by subsections (e) and (f) of section 806 of the Tax Reform Act of 1976 shall apply to the reorganization described in clause (ii).

(ii) A taxpayer is described in this clause if the taxpayer filed a title 11 or similar case on December 8, 1981, filed a plan of reorganization on February 5, 1986, filed an amended plan on March 14, 1986, and received court approval for the amended plan and disclosure statement on April 16, 1986.

(C) APPLICATION OF OLD RULES TO CERTAIN DEBT.—In the case of debt of a corporation incorporated in Colorado on November 8, 1924, and reincorporated in Delaware in 1987, with headquarters in Denver, Colorado—

(i) the amendments made by subsections (a), (b), and (c) shall not apply to any debt restructuring of such debt which was approved by the debtor's Board of Directors and the lenders in 1986, and

(ii) the amendments made by subsections (e) and (f) of section 806 of the Tax Reform Act of 1976 shall not apply to such debt restructuring, except that the amendment treated as part of such subsections under section 59(b) of the Tax Reform Act of 1984 (relating to qualified workouts) shall apply to such debt restructuring.

(D) SPECIAL RULE FOR OIL AND GAS WELL DRILLING BUSINESS.—In the case of a Texas corporation incorporated on July 23, 1935, in applying section 382 of the Internal Revenue Code of 1986 (as in effect before and after the amendments made by subsections (a), (b), and (c)) to a loan restructuring agreement during 1985, section 382(a)(5)(C) of the Internal Revenue Code of 1954 (as added by the amendments made by subsections (e) and (f) of section 806 of the Tax Reform Act of 1976) shall be applied as if it were in effect with respect to such restructuring. For purposes of the preceding sentence, in applying section 382 (as so in effect), if a person has a warrant to acquire stock, such stock shall be considered as owned by such person.

(3) TESTING PERIOD.—For purposes of determining whether there is an ownership change, the testing period shall not begin before the later of—

(A) May 6, 1986, or

(B) in the case of an ownership change which occurs after May 5, 1986, and to which the amendments made by subsections (a), (b), and (c) do not apply, the first day following the date on which such ownership change occurs.

(4) SPECIAL TRANSITION RULES.—The amendments made by subsections (a), (b), and (c) shall not apply to any—

(A) stock-for-debt exchanges and stock sales made pursuant to a plan of reorganization with respect to a petition for reorganization filed by a corporation under chapter 11 of title 11, United States Code, on August 26, 1982, and which filed with a United States district court a first amended and related plan of reorganization before March 1, 1986, or

(B) ownership change of a Delaware corporation incorporated in August 1983, which may result from the exercise of put or call option under an agreement entered into on September 14, 1983, but only with respect to taxable years beginning after 1991 regardless of when such ownership change takes place.

Any regulations prescribed under section 382 of the Internal Revenue Code of 1986 (as added by subsection (a)) which have the effect of treating a group of shareholders as a separate 5-percent shareholder by reason of a public offering shall not apply to any public offering before January 1, 1989, for the benefit of institutions described in section 591 of such Code. Unless the corporation otherwise elects, an underwriter of any offering of stock in a corporation before September 19, 1986 (January 1, 1989, in the case of an offering for the benefit of an institution described in the preceding sentence), shall not be treated as acquiring any stock of such corporation by reason of a firm commitment underwriting to the extent the stock is disposed of pursuant to the offering (but in no event later than 60 days after the initial offering).

(5) BANKRUPTCY PROCEEDINGS.—Unless the taxpayer elects not to have the provisions of this paragraph apply, in the case of a reorganization described in subparagraph (G) of section 368(a)(1) of the Internal Revenue Code of 1986 or an exchange of debt for stock in a title 11 or similar case, as defined in section 368(a)(3) of such Code, the amendments made by subsections (a), (b), and (c) shall not apply to any ownership change resulting from such a reorganization or proceeding if a petition in such case was filed with the court before August 14, 1986. The determination as to whether an ownership change has occurred during the period beginning January 1, 1987, and ending on the final settlement of any reorganization or proceeding described in the preceding sentence shall be redetermined as of the time of such final settlement.

(6) CERTAIN PLANS.—The amendments made by subsections (a), (b), and (c) shall not apply to any ownership change with respect to—

(A) the acquisition of a corporation the stock of which is acquired pursuant to a plan of divestiture which identified such corporation and its assets, and was agreed to by the board of directors of such corporation's parent corporation on May 17, 1985,

(B) a merger which occurs pursuant to a merger agreement (entered into before September 24, 1985) and an application for approval by the Federal Home Loan Bank Board was filed on October 4, 1985,

(C) a reorganization involving a party to a reorganization of a group of corporations engaged in enhanced oil recovery operations in California, merged in furtherance of a plan of reorganization adopted by a board of directors vote on September 24, 1985, and a Delaware corporation whose principal oil and gas producing fields are located in California, or

(D) the conversion of a mutual savings and loan association holding a Federal charter dated March 22, 1985, to a stock savings and loan association pursuant to the rules and regulations of the *Federal Home Loan Bank Board*.

(7) OWNERSHIP CHANGE OF REGULATED AIR CARRIER.—The amendments made by subsections (a), (b), and (c) shall not apply to an ownership change of a regulated air carrier if—

(A) on July 16, 1986, at least 40 percent of the outstanding common stock (excluding all preferred stock, whether or not convertible) of such carrier had been acquired by a parent corporation incorporated in March 1980 under the laws of Delaware, and

(B) the acquisition (by or for such parent corporation) or retirement of the remaining common stock of such carrier is completed before the later of March 31, 1987, or 90 days after the requisite governmental approvals are finally granted,

but only if the ownership change occurs on or before the later of March 31, 1987, or such 90th day. The aggregate reduction in tax for any taxable year by reason of this paragraph shall not exceed $10,000,000. The testing period for determining whether a subsequent ownership change has occurred shall not begin before the 1st day following an ownership change to which this paragraph applies.

(8) The amendments made by subsections (a), (b), and (c) shall not apply to any ownership change resulting from the conversion of a Minnesota mutual savings bank holding a Federal charter dated December 31, 1985, to a stock savings bank pursuant to the rules and regulations of the Federal Home Loan Bank Board, and from the issuance of stock pursuant to that conversion to a holding company incorporated in Delaware on February 21, 1984. For purposes of determining whether any ownership change occurs with respect to the holding company or any subsidiary thereof (whether resulting from the transaction described in the preceding sentence or otherwise), any issuance of stock made by such holding company in connection with the transaction described in the preceding sentence shall not be taken into account.

(9) DEFINITIONS.—Except as otherwise provided, terms used in this subsection shall have the same meaning as when used in section 382 of the Internal Revenue Code of 1986 (as amended by this section).

Reproduced below is the text of Code Sec. 382 as it read before amendment by P.L. 99-514.

[Caution: Reproduced below is the text of Code Sec. 382 prior to amendment by P.L. 94-455. The text of post-1983 law as a result of amendments made by P.L. 94-455 follows.]

[Sec. 382]

SEC. 382. SPECIAL LIMITATIONS ON NET OPERATING LOSS CARRYOVER.

[Sec. 382(a)]

(a) PURCHASE OF A CORPORATION AND CHANGE IN ITS TRADE OR BUSINESS.—

(1) IN GENERAL.—If, at the end of a taxable year of a corporation—

(A) any one or more of those persons described in paragraph (2) own a percentage of the total fair market value of the outstanding stock of such corporation which is at least 50 percentage points more than such person or persons owned at—

(i) the beginning of such taxable year, or

(ii) the beginning of the prior taxable year,

(B) the increase in percentage points at the end of such taxable year is attributable to—

(i) a purchase by such person or persons of such stock, the stock of another corporation owning stock in such corporation, or an interest in a partnership or trust owning stock in such corporation, or

(ii) a decrease in the amount of such stock outstanding or the amount of stock outstanding of another corporation owning stock in such corporation, except a decrease resulting from a redemption to pay death taxes to which section 303 applies, and

(C) such corporation has not continued to carry on a trade or business substantially the same as that conducted before any change in the percentage ownership of the fair market value of such stock,

the net operating loss carryovers, if any, from prior taxable years of such corporation to such taxable year and subsequent taxable years shall not be included in the net operating loss deduction for such taxable year and subsequent taxable years.

(2) DESCRIPTION OF PERSON OR PERSONS.—The person or persons referred to in paragraph (1) shall be the 10 persons (or such lesser number as there are persons owning the outstanding stock at the end of such taxable year) who own the greatest percentage of the fair market value of such stock at the end of such taxable year; except that, if any other person owns the same percentage of such stock at such time as is owned by one of the 10 persons, such person shall also be included. If any of the persons are so related that such stock owned by one is attributed to the other under the rules specified in paragraph (3), such person shall be considered as only one person solely for the purpose of selecting the 10 persons (more or less) who own the greatest percentage of the fair market value of such outstanding stock.

(3) ATTRIBUTION OF OWNERSHIP.—Section 318 (relating to constructive ownership of stock) shall apply in determining the ownership of stock, except that section 318(a)(2)(C) and 318(a)(3)(C) shall be applied without regard to the 50 percent limitation contained therein.

(4) DEFINITION OF PURCHASE.—For purposes of this subsection, the term "purchase" means the acquisition of stock, the basis of which is determined solely by reference to its cost to the holder thereof, in a transaction from a person or persons other than the person or persons the ownership of whose stock would be attributed to the holder by application of paragraph (3).

[Sec. 382(b)]

(b) CHANGE OF OWNERSHIP AS THE RESULT OF A REORGANIZATION.—

(1) IN GENERAL.—If, in the case of a reorganization specified in paragraph (2) of section 381(a), the transferor corporation or the acquiring corporation—

(A) has a net operating loss which is a net operating loss carryover to the first taxable year of the acquiring corporation ending after the date of transfer, and

(B) the stockholders (immediately before the reorganization) of such corporation (hereinafter in this subsection referred to as the "loss corporation"), as the result of owning stock of the loss corporation, own (immediately after the reorganization) less than 20 percent of the fair market value of the outstanding stock of the acquiring corporation,

the total net operating loss carryover from prior taxable years of the loss corporation to the first taxable year of the acquiring corportion ending after the date of transfer shall be reduced by the percentage determined under paragraph (2).

(2) REDUCTION OF NET OPERATING LOSS CARRYOVER.—The reduction applicable under paragraph (1) shall be the percentage determined by subracting from 100 percent—

(A) the percent of the fair market value of the outstanding stock of the acquiring corporation owned (immediately after the reorganization) by the stockholders (immediately before the reorganization) of the loss corporation, as the result of owning stock of the loss corporation, multiplied by

(B) five.

(3) EXCEPTION TO LIMITATION IN THIS SUBSECTION.—The limitation in this subsection shall not apply if the transferor corporation and the acquiring corporation are owned substantially by the same persons in the same proportion.

(4) NET OPERATING LOSS CARRYOVERS TO SUBSEQUENT YEARS.—In computing the net operating loss carryovers to taxable years subsequent to a taxable year in which there was a limitation applicable to a net operating loss carryover by operation of this subsection, the income in such taxable year, as computed under section 172(b)(2), shall be increased by the amount of the reduction of the total net operating loss carryover determined under paragraph (2).

(5) ATTRIBUTION OF OWNERSHIP.—If the transferor corporation or the acquiring corporation owns (immediately before the reorganization) any of the outstanding stock of the loss corporation, such transferor corporation or acquiring corporation shall, for purposes of this subsection, be treated as owning (immediately after the reorganization) a percentage of the fair market value of the acquiring corporation's outstanding stock which bears the same ratio to the percentage of the fair market value of the outstanding stock of the loss corporation (immediately before the reorganization) owned by such transferor corporation or acquiring corporation as the fair market value of the total outstanding stock of the loss corporation (immediately before the reorganization) bears to the fair market value of the total outstanding stock of the acquiring corporation (immediately after the reorganization).

(6) STOCK OF CORPORATION CONTROLLING ACQUIRING CORPORATION.—If the stockholders of the loss corporation (immediately before the reorganization) own, as a result of the reorganization, stock in a corporation controlling the acquiring corporation, such stock of the controlling corporation shall, for purposes of this subsection, be treated as stock of the acquiring corporation in an amount valued at an equivalent fair market value.

(7) SPECIAL RULE FOR REORGANIZATIONS IN TITLE 11 OR SIMILAR CASES.—For purposes of this subsection—

(A) a creditor who receives stock in a reorganization in a title 11 or similar case (within the meaning of section 368(a)(3)(A)) shall be treated as a stockholder immediately before the reorganization and

(B) in a transaction qualifying under section 368(a)(3)(D)(ii)—

(i) a depositor in the transferor shall be treated as a stockholder immediately before the reorganization of the loss corporation,

(ii) deposits in the transferor which become, as a result of the transfer, deposits in the transferee shall be treated as stock of the acquiring corporation owned as a result of owning stock of the loss corporation, and

(iii) the fair market value of the outstanding stock of the acquiring corporation shall include the amount of deposits in the acquiring corporation immediately after the reorganization.

[Sec. 382(c)]

(c) DEFINITION OF STOCK.—For purposes of this section, "stock" means all shares except nonvoting stock which is limited and preferred as to dividends.

[Sec. 382]

SEC. 382. SPECIAL LIMITATIONS ON NET OPERATING LOSS CARRYOVER.

[Caution: Code Sec. 382(a), below, reads as amended by the Tax Reform Act of 1976 (P.L. 94-455) and P.L. 96-167 and is applicable to taxable years beginning after December 31, 1985.]

[Sec. 382(a)]

(a) CERTAIN ACQUISITIONS OF STOCK OF A CORPORATION.—

(1) IN GENERAL.—If—

(A) on the last day of a taxable year of a corporation,

(B) any one or more of the persons described in paragraph (4)(B) own, directly or indirectly, a percentage of the total fair market value of the participating stock or of all the stock of the corporation which exceeds by more than 60 percentage points the percentage of such stock owned by such person or persons at—

(i) the beginning of such taxable year, or

(ii) the beginning of the first or second preceding taxable year, and

(C) such increase in percentage points is attributable to—

(i) a purchase by such person or persons of such stock, or of the stock of another corporation owning stock in such corporation, or of an interest in a partnership or trust owning stock in such corporation,

(ii) an acquisition (by contribution, merger, or consolidation) of an interest in a partnership owning stock in such corporation, or an acquisition (by contribution, merger, or consolidation) by a partnership of such stock,

(iii) an exchange to which section 351 (relating to transfer to corporation controlled by transferor) applies, or an acquisition by a corporation of such stock in an exchange in which section 351 applies to the transferor,

(iv) a contribution to the capital of such corporation,

(v) a decrease in the amount of such stock outstanding or in the amount of stock outstanding of another corporation owning stock in such corporation (except a decrease resulting from a redemption to pay death taxes to which section 303 applies),

(vi) a liquidation of the interest of a partner in a partnership owning stock in such corporation, or

(vii) any combination of the transactions described in clauses (i) through (vi),

then the net operating loss carryover, if any, from such taxable year and the net operating loss carryovers, if any, from prior taxable years to such taxable year and subsequent taxable years of such corporation shall be reduced by the percentage determined under paragraph (2),

(2) REDUCTION OF NET OPERATING LOSS CARRYOVER.—The reduction applicable under paragraph (1) shall be the sum of the percentages determined by multiplying—

(A) by three and one-half the increase in percentage points (including fractions thereof) in excess of 60 and up to and including 80, and

(B) by one and one-half the increase in percentage points (including fractions thereof) in excess of 80.

The reduction under this paragraph shall be determined by reference to the increase in percentage points of the total fair market value of the participating stock or of all the stock, whichever increase is greater.

(3) MINIMUM OWNERSHIP RULE.—Notwithstanding the provisions of paragraph (1), a net operating loss carryover from a taxable year shall not be reduced under this subsection if, at all times during the last half of such taxable year, any of the persons described in paragraph (4)(B) (determined on the last day of the taxable year referred to in paragraph (1)(A)) owned at least 40 percent of the total fair market value of the participating stock and of all the stock of the corporation. For purposes of the preceding sentence, persons owning stock of a corporation on the last day of its first taxable year shall be considered to have owned such stock at all times during the last half of such first taxable year.

(4) OPERATING RULES.—For purposes of this subsection—

(A) DEFINITION OF PURCHASE.—The term "purchase" means an acquisition of stock the basis of which is determined by reference to its cost to the holder thereof.

(B) DESCRIPTION OF PERSON OR PERSONS.—The person or persons referred to in paragraph (1)(B) shall be the 15 persons (or such lesser number as there are persons owning the stock on the last day of the taxable year) who own the greatest percentage of the total fair market value of all the stock on the last day of that year, except that if any other person owns the same percentage of such stock at such time as is owned by one of the 15 persons, that other person shall also be included. If any of the persons are so related that the stock owned by one is attributed to the other under the rules specified in subparagraph (C), such persons shall be considered as only one person solely for the purpose of selecting the 15 persons (more or less) who own the greatest percentage of the total fair market value of all the stock.

(C) CONSTRUCTIVE OWNERSHIP.—Section 318 (relating to constructive ownership of stock) shall apply in determining the ownership of stock, except that section 318(a)(2)(C) and 318(a)(3)(C) shall be applied without regard to the 50 percent limitation contained therein.

(D) SHORT TAXABLE YEARS.—If one of the taxable years of the corporation referred to in paragraph (1)(B) is a short taxable year, then such paragraph and paragraph (6) shall be applied by substituting "first, second, or third" for "first or second" each time such phrase occurs.

(5) EXCEPTIONS.—This subsection shall not apply to a purchase or other acquisition of stock (or of an interest in a partnership or trust owning stock in the corporation)—

(A) from a person whose ownership of stock would be attributed to the holder by application of paragraph (4)(C) to the extent that such stock would be so attributed;

(B) if (and to the extent) the basis thereof is determined under section 1014 or 1023 (relating to property acquired from a decedent), or section 1015(a) or (b) (relating to property acquired by gift or transfers in trust);

(C) by a security holder or creditor in exchange for the relinquishment or extinguishment in whole or part of a claim against the corporation, unless the claim was acquired for the purpose of acquiring such stock;

(D) by one or more persons who were full-time employees of the corporation at all times during the period of 36 months ending on the last day of the taxable year of the corporation (or at all times during the period of the corporation's existence, if shorter);

(E) by a trust described in section 401(a) which is exempt from tax under section 501(a) and which benefits exclusively the employees (or the beneficiaries) of the corporation, including a member of a controlled group of corporations (within the meaning of section 1563(a) determined without regard to section 1563(a)(4) and (e)(3)(C)) which includes such corporation;

(F) by an employee stock ownership plan meeting the requirements of section 301(d) of the Tax Reduction Act of 1975; or

(G) in a recapitalization described in section 368(a)(1)(E).

(6) SUCCESSIVE APPLICATIONS OF SUBSECTION.—If—

(A) a net operating loss carryover is reduced under this subsection at the end of a taxable year of a corporation, and

(B) any person described in paragraph (4)(B) who owns stock of the corporation on the last day of such taxable year does not own, on the last day of the first or second succeeding taxable year of the corporation, a greater percentage of the total fair market value of the participating stock or of all the stock of the corporation than such person owned on the last day of such taxable year,

then, for purposes of applying this subsection as of the end of the first or second succeeding taxable year (as the case may be), stock owned by such person at the end of such succeeding taxable year shall be considered owned by such person at the beginning of the first or second preceding taxable year. Other rules relating to the manner and extent of successive applications of this section in the case of increases in ownership and transfers of stock by the persons described in paragraph (4)(B) shall be prescribed by regulations issued by the Secretary.

Amendments

• 1978, Revenue Act of 1978 (P.L. 95-600)

P.L. 95-600, §368, as amended by P.L. 96-167, §9(e):

(a) IN GENERAL.—Except as provided in subsection (b), paragraphs (2) and (3) of section 806(g) of the Tax Reform Act of 1976 (relating to effective dates for the amendments to sections 382 and 383 of the Code) are amended by striking out "1980" each place it appears and inserting in lieu thereof "1982".

(b) ELECTION OF PRIOR LAW.—

(1) A taxpayer may elect not to have the amendment made by subsection (a) apply with respect to any acquisition or reorganization occurring before the end of the taxpayer's first taxable year beginning after June 30, 1978, where such acquisition or reorganization occurs pursuant to a written binding contract or option to acquire stock or assets which was entered into before September 27, 1978.

(2) An election under this subsection shall be filed with a taxpayer's timely filed return for the first taxable year in which a reorganization or acquisition described in paragraph (1) occurs, or, if later, within 90 days after the date of enactment of this Act. Such election shall apply to all acquisitions and reorganizations to which, but for such election, subsection (a) would apply.

• 1976, Tax Reform Act of 1976 (P.L. 94-455)

P.L. 94-455, §806(e):

Amended Code Sec. 382(a). **Effective** as noted in P.L. 94-455, §806(g)(2)-(3), below.

P.L. 94-455, §806(g)(2)-(3), as amended by P.L. 95-600, §368(a), P.L. 96-167, §9(e), P.L. 97-119, §111, and P.L. 98-369, §62(a), provides:

(2) For purposes of applying sections 382(a) and 383 (as it relates to section 382(a)) of the Internal Revenue Code of 1954, as amended by subsections (e) and (f), the amendments made by subsections (e) and (f) shall take effect for taxable years beginning after December 31, 1985, except that the beginning of the taxable years specified in clause (ii) of

section 382(a)(1)(B) of such Code, as so amended, shall be considered to be the later of:

(A) the beginning of such taxable years, or

(B) January 1, 1986.

(3) Sections 382(b) and 383 (as it relates to section 382(b)) of the Internal Revenue Code of 1954, as amended by subsections (e) and (f), shall apply (and such sections as in effect prior to such amendment shall not apply) to reorganization pursuant to a plan of reorganization adopted by one or more of the parties thereto on or after January 1, 1986. For purposes of the preceding sentence, a corporation shall be considered to have adopted a plan of reorganization on the date on which a resolution of the board of directors is passed adopting the plan or recommending its adoption to the shareholders, or on the date on which the shareholders approve the plan of reorganization, whichever is earlier.

• 1964 (P.L. 88-554)

P.L. 88-554, §5(b)(3):

Amended Code Sec. 382(a)(3) by substituting "sections 318(a)(2)(C) and 318(a)(3)(C)" for "section 318(a)(2)(C)." **Effective** 8-31-64.

[Caution: Code Sec. 382(b), below, reads as amended by the Tax Reform Act of 1976 (P.L. 94-455), P.L. 96-167 and P.L. 98-369 and is effective for reorganizations pursuant to a plan of reorganization adopted on or after January 1, 1986.]

[Sec. 382(b)]

(b) REORGANIZATIONS.—

(1) IN GENERAL.—If one corporation acquires the stock or assets of another corporation in a reorganization described in subparagraph (A), (B), (C), or (F) of section 368(a)(1) or subparagraph (D) or (G) of section 368(a)(1) (but only if the requirements of section 354(b)(1) are met), and if—

(A) the acquiring or acquired corporation has a net operating loss for the taxable year which includes the date of the acquisition, or a net operating loss carryover from a prior taxable year to such taxable year, and

(B) the shareholders (immediately before the reorganization) of such corporation (the "loss corporation"), as the result of owning stock of the loss corporation, own (immediately after the reorganization) less than 40 percent of the total fair market value of the participating stock or of all the stock of the acquiring corporation,

then the net operating loss carryover (if any) of the loss corporation from the taxable year which includes the date of the acquisition, and the net operating loss carryovers (if any) of the loss corporation from prior taxable years to such taxable year and subsequent taxable years, shall be reduced by the percentage determined under paragraph (2).

(2) REDUCTION OF NET OPERATING LOSS CARRYOVER.—

(A) OWNERSHIP OF 20 PERCENT OR MORE.—If such shareholders own less than 40 percent, but not less than 20 percent, of the total fair market value of participating stock or of all the stock of the acquiring corporation, the reduction applicable under paragraph (1) shall be the percentage equal to the number of percentage points (including fractions thereof) less than 40 percent, multiplied by three and one-half.

(B) OWNERSHIP OF LESS THAN 20 PERCENT.—If such shareholders own less than 20 percent of the total fair market value of the participating stock or of all the stock of the acquiring corporation, the reduction applicable under paragraph (1) shall be the sum of—

(i) the percentage that would be determined under subparagraph (A) if the shareholders owned 20 percent of such stock, plus

(ii) the percentage equal to the number of percentage points (including fractions thereof) of such stock less than 20 percent, multiplied by one and one-half.

The reduction under this paragraph shall be determined by reference to the lesser of the percentage of the total fair market value of the participating stock or of all the stock of the acquiring corporation owned by such shareholders.

(3) LOSSES OF CONTROLLED CORPORATIONS.—For purposes of this subsection—

(A) HOLDING COMPANIES.—If, immediately before the reorganization, the acquiring or acquired corporation controls a corporation which has a net operating loss for the taxable year which includes the date of the acquisition, or a net operating loss carryover from a prior taxable year to such taxable year, the acquiring or acquired corporation, as the case may be, shall be treated as the loss corporation (whether or not such corporation is a loss corporation). The reduction, if any, so determined under paragraph (2) shall be applied to the losses of such controlled corporation.

(B) TRIANGULAR REORGANIZATIONS.—Except as otherwise provided in paragraph (5), if the shareholders of the loss corporation (immediately before the reorganization) own, as a result of the reorganization, stock in a corporation controlling the acquiring corporation, such shareholders shall be treated as owning (immediately after the reorganization) a percentage of the total fair market value of the participating stock and of all the stock of the acquiring corporation owned by the controlling corporation equal to the percentage of the total fair market value of the participating stock and of all the stock, respectively, of the controlling corporation owned by such shareholders.

(4) SPECIAL RULES.—For purposes of applying paragraph (1)(B)—

(A) CERTAIN RELATED TRANSACTIONS.—If, immediately before the reorganization—

(i) one or more shareholders of the loss corporation own stock of such corporation which such shareholder acquired during the 36-month period ending on the date of the acquisition in a transaction described in paragraph (1) or in subsection (a)(1)(C) (unless excepted by subsection (a)(5)), and

(ii) such shareholders own more than 50 percent of the total fair market value of the stock of another corporation a party to the reorganization, or any such shareholder is a corporation controlled by another corporation a party to the reorganization,

then such shareholders shall not be treated as shareholders of the loss corporation with respect to such stock.

(B) CERTAIN PRIOR OWNERSHIP OF LOSS CORPORATION.—If, immediately before the reorganization, the acquiring or acquired corporation owns stock of the loss corporation, then paragraph (1)(B) shall be applied by treating the shareholders of the loss corporation as owning an additional amount of the total fair market value of the participating stock and of all the stock of the acquiring corporation, as a result of owning stock in the loss corporation, equal to the total fair market value of the participating stock and of all the stock, respectively, of the loss corporation owned (immediately before the reorganization) by the acquiring or acquired corporation. This subparagraph shall not apply to stock of the loss corporation owned by the acquiring or acquired corporation if such stock was acquired by such corporation within the 36-month period ending on the date of the reorganization in a transaction described in subsection (a)(1)(C) (unless excepted by subsection (a)(5)); or to a reorganization described in section 368(a)(1)(B) or (C) to the extent the acquired corporation does not distribute the stock received by it to its own shareholders.

(C) CERTAIN ASSET ACQUISITIONS.—If a loss corporation receives stock of the acquiring corporation in a reorganization described in section 368(a)(1)(C) and does not distribute such stock to its shareholders, paragraph (1)(B) shall be applied by treating the shareholders of the loss corporation as owning (immediately after the reorganization) such undistributed stock in proportion to the fair market value of the stock which such shareholders own in the loss corporation.

(5) CERTAIN STOCK-FOR-STOCK REORGANIZATIONS.—In the case of a reorganization described in section 368(a)(1)(B) in which the acquired corporation is a loss corporation—

(A) STOCK WHICH IS EXCHANGED.—Paragraphs (1)(B) and (2) shall be applied by reference to the ownership of stock of the loss corporation (rather than the acquiring corporation) immediately after the reorganization. Shareholders of the loss corporation who exchange stock of the loss corporation shall be treated as owning (immediately after the reorganization) a percentage of the total fair market value of the participating stock and of all the stock of the loss corporation acquired in the exchange by the acquiring corporation which is equal to the percentage of the total fair market value of the participating stock and of all the stock, respectively, of the acquiring corporation owned (immediately after the reorganization) by such shareholders.

(B) STOCK WHICH IS NOT EXCHANGED.—Stock of the loss corporation owned by shareholders immediately before the reorganization which was not exchanged in the reorganization shall be taken into account in applying paragraph

(1)(B). For purposes of the preceding sentence, the acquiring corporation (or a corporation controlled by the acquiring corporation) shall not be treated as a shareholder of the loss corporation with respect to stock of the loss corporation acquired in a transaction described in paragraph (1), or in subsection (a)(1)(C) (unless excepted by subsection (a)(5)), during the 36-month period ending on the date of the exchange.

(C) TRIANGULAR EXCHANGES.—For purposes of applying the rules in this paragraph, if the shareholders of the loss corporation receive stock of a corporation controlling the acquiring corporation, such shareholders shall be treated as owning a percentage of the participating stock and of all the stock of the acquiring corporation owned by the controlling corporation equal to the percentage of the total fair market value of the participating stock and of all the stock, respectively, which such shareholders own of the controlling corporation immediately after the reorganization.

(6) EXCEPTIONS.—The limitations in this subsection shall not apply—

(A) if the same persons own substantially all the stock of the acquiring corporation and of the other corporation in substantially the same proportions: or

(B) to a net operating loss carryover from a taxable year if the acquiring or acquired corporation owned at least 40 percent of the total fair market value of the participating stock and of all the stock of the loss corporation at all times during the last half of such taxable year.

For purposes of subparagraph (A), if the acquiring or acquired corporation is controlled by another corporation, the shareholders of the controlling corporation shall be considered as also owning the stock owned by the controlling corporation in that proportion which the total fair market value of the stock which each shareholder owns in the controlling corporation bears to the total fair market value of all the stock in the controlling corporation.

Amendments

• 1984, Deficit Reduction Act of 1984 (P.L. 98-369)

P.L. 98-369, §62(b)(1):

Amended paragraph (1) of Code Sec. 382(b) (as amended by the Tax Reform Act of 1976) by striking out "section 368(a)(1)(A), (B), (C), (D) (but only if the requirements of section 354(b)(1) are met), or (F)" and inserting in lieu thereof "subparagraph (A), (B), (C), or (F) of section 368(a)(1) or subparagraph (D) or (G) of section 368(a)(1) (but only if the requirements of section 354(b)(1) are met)". **Effective** as if included in the amendments made by section 4 of the Bankruptcy Tax Act of 1980.

• 1980, Bankruptcy Tax Act of 1980 (P.L. 96-589)

P.L. 96-589, §2(d):

Amended Code Sec. 382(b), as in effect before amendment by the Tax Reform Act of 1976, P.L. 94-455, by adding a new paragraph (7). For the text of Code Sec. 382(b), as amended by P.L. 96-589 (but not by P.L. 94-455), see the historical comment for P.L. 94-455. For the **effective** date, see the historical comment for P.L. 96-589 under Code Sec. 108(e).

Code Sec. 382(b)(7), as added by P.L. 96-589, §2(d), and subsequently amended by P.L. 97-34, §242, reads as follows. **Effective** for any transfer made on or after 1-1-81.

(7) SPECIAL RULE FOR REORGANIZATIONS IN TITLE 11 OR SIMILAR CASES.—For purposes of this subsection—

(A) a creditor who receives stock in a reorganization in a title 11 or similar case (within the meaning of section 368(a)(3)(A)) shall be treated as a stockholder immediately before the reorganization, and

(B) in a transaction qualifying under section 368(a)(3)(D)(ii)—

(i) a depositor in the transferor shall be treated as a stockholder immediately before the reorganization of the loss corporation,

(ii) deposits in the transferor which become, as a result of the transfer, deposits in the transferee shall be treated as stock of the acquiring corporation owned as a result of owning stock of the loss corporation, and

(iii) the fair market value of the outstanding stock of the acquiring corporation shall include the amount of deposits in the acquiring corporation immediately after the reorganization.

Prior to amendment by P.L. 97-34, §242, Code Sec. 382(b)(7) read as follows:

(7) SPECIAL RULE FOR REORGANIZATIONS IN TITLE 11 OR SIMILAR CASES.—For purposes of this subsection, a creditor who receives stock in a reorganization in a title 11 or similar case (within the meaning of section 368(a)(3)(A)) shall be treated as a stockholder immediately before the reorganization.

P.L. 94-455, §806(e). See historical comment for P.L. 94-455, §806(g)(2)-(3) under Code Sec. 382(a):

Added Code Sec. 382(b). **Effective** for reorganization plans adopted on or after 1-1-84. In this connection, a corporation shall be considered to have adopted a plan of reorganization on the date on which a resolution of the board of directors is passed adopting the plan or recommending its adoption to the shareholders, or on the date on which the shareholders approve the plan of reorganization, whichever is earlier.

[*Caution: Code Sec. 382(c), below, reads as amended by the Tax Reform Act of 1976.—CCH.*]

[Sec. 382(c)]

(c) RULES RELATING TO STOCK.—For purposes of this section—

(1) The term "stock" means all shares of stock, except stock which—

(A) is not entitled to vote,

(B) is fixed and preferred as to dividends and does not participate in corporate growth to any significant extent,

(C) has redemption and liquidation rights which do not exceed the paid-in capital or par value represented by such stock (except for a reasonable redemption premium in excess of such paid-in capital or par value), and

(D) is not convertible into another class of stock.

(2) The term "participating stock" means stock (including common stock) which represents an interest in the earnings and assets of the issuing corporation which is not limited to a stated amount of money or property or percentage of paid-in capital or par value, or by any similar formula.

(3) The Secretary shall prescribe regulations under which—

(A) stock or convertible securities shall be treated as stock or participating stock, or

(B) stock (however denoted) shall not be treated as stock or participating stock,

by reason of conversion and call rights, rights in earnings and assets, priorities and preferences as to distributions of earnings or assets, and similar factors.

Amendments

• 1976, Tax Reform Act of 1976 (P.L. 94-455)

P.L. 94-455, §806(e):

Amended Code Sec. 382(c). **Effective** 10-4-76.

[Sec. 382(n)]

(n) SPECIAL RULE FOR CERTAIN OWNERSHIP CHANGES.—

(1) IN GENERAL .—The limitation contained in subsection (a) shall not apply in the case of an ownership change which is pursuant to a restructuring plan of a taxpayer which—

(A) is required under a loan agreement or a commitment for a line of credit entered into with the Department of the Treasury under the Emergency Economic Stabilization Act of 2008, and

(B) is intended to result in a rationalization of the costs, capitalization, and capacity with respect to the manufacturing workforce of, and suppliers to, the taxpayer and its subsidiaries.

(2) SUBSEQUENT ACQUISITIONS .—Paragraph (1) shall not apply in the case of any subsequent ownership change unless such ownership change is described in such paragraph.

(3) LIMITATION BASED ON CONTROL IN CORPORATION.—

(A) IN GENERAL .—Paragraph (1) shall not apply in the case of any ownership change if, immediately after such ownership change, any person (other than a voluntary employees' beneficiary association under section 501(c)(9)) owns stock of the new loss corporation possessing 50 percent or more of the total combined voting power of all classes of stock entitled to vote, or of the total value of the stock of such corporation.

(B) TREATMENT OF RELATED PERSONS.—

(i) IN GENERAL .—Related persons shall be treated as a single person for purposes of this paragraph.

(ii) RELATED PERSONS .—For purposes of clause (i), a person shall be treated as related to another person if—

(I) such person bears a relationship to such other person described in section 267(b) or 707(b), or

(II) such persons are members of a group of persons acting in concert.

Amendments

• 2009, American Recovery and Reinvestment Tax Act of 2009 (P.L. 111-5)

P.L. 111-5, §1262(a):

Amended Code Sec. 382 by adding at the end a new subsection (n). **Effective** for ownership changes after 2-17-2009.

[Sec. 383]

SEC. 383. SPECIAL LIMITATIONS ON CERTAIN EXCESS CREDITS, ETC.

[Sec. 383(a)]

(a) EXCESS CREDITS.—

(1) IN GENERAL.—Under regulations, if an ownership change occurs with respect to a corporation, the amount of any excess credit for any taxable year which may be used in any post-change year shall be limited to an amount determined on the basis of the tax liability which is attributable to so much of the taxable income as does not exceed the section 382 limitation for such post-change year to the extent available after the application of section 382 and subsections (b) and (c) of this section.

(2) EXCESS CREDIT.—For purposes of paragraph (1), the term "excess credit" means—

(A) any unused general business credit of the corporation under section 39, and

(B) any unused minimum tax credit of the corporation under section 53.

[Sec. 383(b)]

(b) LIMITATION ON NET CAPITAL LOSS.—If an ownership change occurs with respect to a corporation, the amount of any net capital loss under section 1212 for any taxable year before the 1st post-change year which may be used in any post-change year shall be limited under regulations which shall be based on the principles applicable under section 382. Such regulations shall provide that any such net capital loss used in a post-change year shall reduce the section 382 limitation which is applied to pre-change losses under section 382 for such year.

[Sec. 383(c)]

(c) FOREIGN TAX CREDITS.—If an ownership change occurs with respect to a corporation, the amount of any excess foreign taxes under section 904(c) for any taxable year before the 1st post-change taxable year shall be limited under regulations which shall be consistent with purposes of this section and section 382.

[Sec. 383(d)]

(d) PRO RATION RULES FOR YEAR WHICH INCLUDES CHANGE.—For purposes of this section, rules similar to the rules of subsections (b)(3) and (d)(1)(B) of section 382 shall apply.

[Sec. 383(e)]

(e) DEFINITIONS.—Terms used in this section shall have the same respective meanings as when used in section 382, except that appropriate adjustments shall be made to take into account that the limitations of this section apply to credits and net capital losses.

Amendments

• 1986, Tax Reform Act of 1986 (P.L. 99-514)

P.L. 99-514, §621(b):

Amended Code Sec. 383. For the **effective** date, see Act Sec. 621(f) following Code Sec. 382. Prior to amendment, Code Sec. 383 read as follows:

[Caution: Code Sec. 383, below, reads prior to amendment by the Tax Reform Act of 1976 (P.L. 94-455), but as amended by P.L. 97-34, P.L. 95-30, P.L. 96-222, P.L. 96-223, and P.L. 98-369, and applies, generally, to tax years beginning after 1983.]

[Sec. 383]

SEC. 383. SPECIAL LIMITATIONS ON UNUSED BUSINESS CREDITS, RESEARCH CREDITS, FOREIGN TAXES, AND CAPITAL LOSSES.

If—

(1) the ownership and business of a corporation are changed in the manner described in section 382(a)(1), or

(2) in the case of a reorganization specified in paragraph (2) of section 381(a), there is a change in ownership described in section 382(b)(1)(B),

then the limitations provided in section 382 in such cases with respect to the carryover of net operating losses shall apply in the same manner, as provided under regulations prescribed by the Secretary or his delegate, with respect to any unused business credit of the corporation which can otherwise be carried forward under section 39, to any unused credit of the corporation which could otherwise be carried forward under section 30(g)(2), to any excess foreign taxes of the corporation which could otherwise be carried forward under section 904(c), and to any net capital loss of the corporation which can otherwise be carried forward under section 1212.

Amendments

• 1984, Deficit Reduction Act of 1984 (P.L. 98-369)

P.L. 98-369, §474(r)(12)(A):

Amended Code Sec. 383 (prior to amendment by P.L. 94-455). **Effective** for tax years beginning after 12-31-83, and to carrybacks from such years. Prior to amendment, which struck out the section heading and "with respect to any unused investment credit" and all that followed, Code Sec. 383 read as follows:

Sec. 383. Special Limitations On Carryovers of Unused Investment Credits, Work Incentive Program Credits, New Employee Credits, Alcohol Fuel Credits, Research Credits, Employee Stock Ownership Credits, Foreign Taxes, and Capital Losses.

If—

(1) the ownership and business of a corporation are changed in the manner described in section 382(a)(1), or

(2) in the case of a reorganization specified in paragraph (2) of section 381(a), there is a change in ownership described in section 382(b)(1)(B),

then the limitations provided in section 382 in such cases with respect to the carryover of net operating losses shall apply in the same manner, as provided under regulations prescribed by the Secretary or his delegate, with respect to any unused investment credit of the corporation which can otherwise be carried forward under section 46(b), to any unused work incentive program credit of the corporation which can otherwise be carried forward under section 50A(b), to any unused new employee credit of the corporation which could otherwise be carried forward under section 53(b), to any unused credit of the corporation which could otherwise be carried forward under section 44E(e)(2), to any unused credit of the corporation which could otherwise be carried forward under section 44F(g)(2), to any unused credit of the corporation which could otherwise be carried forward under section 44G(b)(2), to any excess foreign taxes of the corporation which can otherwise be carried forward under section 904(d), and to any net capital loss of the corporation which can otherwise be carried forward under section 1212.

• 1981, Economic Recovery Tax Act of 1981 (P.L. 97-34)

P.L. 97-34, §221(b)(1)(D):

Amended Code Sec. 383 (as in effect on the day before the date of the enactment of P.L. 94-455) by inserting "to any unused credit of the corporation which could otherwise be carried forward under section 44F(g)(2)," after "44E(e)(2),"; and by inserting "RESEARCH CREDITS," after "ALCOHOL FUEL CREDITS," in the section heading. **Effective** for amounts paid or incurred after 6-30-81 [**effective** date changed by P.L. 99-514, §231(a)(2)].

P.L. 97-34, §221(d)(2), as amended by P.L. 99-514, §231(a)(2), provides the following transitional rule:

(2) TRANSITIONAL RULE.—

(A) IN GENERAL.—If, with respect to the first taxable year to which the amendments made by this section apply and which ends in 1981 or 1982, the taxpayer may only take into account qualified research expenses paid or incurred during a portion of such taxable year, the amount of the qualified research expenses taken into account for the base period of such taxable year shall be the amount which bears the same ratio to the total qualified research expenses for such base period as the number of months in such portion of such taxable year bears to the total number of months in such taxable year.

(B) DEFINITIONS.—For purposes of the preceding sentence, the terms "qualified research expenses" and "base period" have the meanings given to such terms by section 44F of the Internal Revenue Code of 1954 (as added by this section).

P.L. 97-34, §331(d)(1)(D):

Amended Code Sec. 383 (as in effect on the day before the date of the enactment of P.L. 94-455) by inserting "to any unused credit of the corporation which could otherwise be carried forward under section 44G(b)(2)," after "44F(g)(2)"; and by inserting "EMPLOYEE STOCK OWNERSHIP CREDITS," after "RESEARCH CREDITS," in the section heading. **Effective** for tax years beginning after 12-31-81.

• 1980, Crude Oil Windfall Profit Tax Act of 1980 (P.L. 96-223)

P.L. 96-223, §232(b)(2)(D):

Amended Code Sec. 383 by inserting "to any unused credit of the corporation which could otherwise be carried forward under section 44E(e)(2)," after "section 53(b)," and by striking out in the section heading **"NEW EMPLOYEE CREDITS"** and inserting **"NEW EMPLOYEE CREDITS, ALCOHOL FUEL CREDITS"**. **Effective** for sales and uses after 9-30-80, in tax years ending after such date.

• 1980, Technical Corrections Act of 1979 (P.L. 96-222)

P.L. 96-222, §103(a)(6)(G)(xiii):

Amended Code Sec. 383 by striking out "53(c)" and inserting "53(b)."

• 1977, Tax Reduction and Simplification Act of 1975 (P.L. 95-30)

P.L. 95-30, §202(d)(3)(B):

Amended Code Sec. 383 by adding **"NEW EMPLOYEE CREDITS,"** in the heading and by adding "to any unused new employee credit of the corporation under section 53(c)," after "section 50A(b),". **Effective** for tax years beginning after 12-31-76 and for credit carrybacks from such years.

• 1971, Revenue Act of 1971 (P.L. 92-178)

P.L. 92-178, §302(a):

Added Code Sec. 383. **Effective** only for reorganizations and other changes in ownership occurring after 12-10-71 pursuant to a plan or reorganization or contract entered into on or after 9-29-71.

[***Caution: Code Sec. 383, below, reads as amended by the Tax Reform Act of 1976 (P.L. 94-455), P.L. 97-34, P.L. 96-167, P.L. 96-223 and P.L. 98-369 and applies to tax years beginning after December 31, 1985.***]

[Sec. 383]

SEC. 383. SPECIAL LIMITATIONS ON UNUSED BUSINESS CREDITS, RESEARCH CREDITS, FOREIGN TAXES, AND CAPITAL LOSSES.

In the case of a change of ownership of a corporation in the manner described in section 382(a) or (b), the limitations provided in section 382 in such cases with respect to net operating losses shall apply in the same manner, as provided under regulations prescribed by the Secretary, with respect to any unused business credit of the corporation under section 39, to any unused credit of the corporation under section 30(g)(2), to any excess foreign taxes of the corporation under section 904(c), and to any net capital loss of the corporation under section 1212.

Amendments

• 1984, Deficit Reduction Act of 1984 (P.L. 98-369)

P.L. 98-369, §474(r)(12)(B):

Amended Code Sec. 383 (as amended by P.L. 94-455). **Effective** for tax years beginning after 12-31-83, and to carrybacks from such years. Prior to amendment, which struck out "with respect to any unused investment credit" and all that followed and the section heading, Code Sec. 383 read as follows:

Sec. 383. Special Limitations On Unused Investment Credits, Work Incentive Program Credits, New Employee Credits, Alcohol Fuel Credits, Research Credits, Employee

Stock Ownership Credits, Foreign Taxes, and Capital Losses.

In the case of a change of ownership of a corporation in the manner described in section 382(a) or (b), the limitations provided in section 382 in such cases with respect to net operating losses shall apply in the same manner, as provided under regulations prescribed by the Secretary, with respect to any unused investment credit of the corporation under section 46(b), to any unused work incentive program credit of the corporation under section 50A(b), to any unused new employee credit of the corporation under section 53(b), to any unused credit of the corporation under section 44E(e)(2), to any unused credit of the corporation under section 44F(g)(2), to any unused credit of the corporation under section 44G(b)(2), to any excess foreign taxes of the corporation under section 904(c), and to any net capital loss of the corporation under section 1212.

• 1981, Economic Recovery Tax Act of 1981 (P.L. 97-34)

P.L. 97-34, §221(b)(1)(C):

Amended Code Sec. 383, as in effect for taxable years beginning after 6-30-82, by inserting "to any unused credit of the corporation under section 44F(g)(2)," after "44E(e)(2),"; and by inserting "RESEARCH CREDITS," after "ALCOHOL FUEL CREDITS," in the section heading. **Effective** for amounts paid or incurred after 6-30-81 [**effective** date changed by P.L. 99-514, §231(a)(2)].

P.L. 97-34, §221(d)(2), as amended by P.L. 99-514, §231(a)(2), provides the following transitional rule:

(2) TRANSITIONAL RULE.—

(A) IN GENERAL.—If, with respect to the first taxable year to which the amendments made by this section apply and which ends in 1981 or 1982, the taxpayer may only take into account qualified research expenses paid or incurred during a portion of such taxable year, the amount of the qualified research expenses taken into account for the base period of such taxable year shall be the amount which bears the same ratio to the total qualified research expenses for such base period as the number of months in such portion of such taxable year bears to the total number of months in such taxable year.

(B) DEFINITIONS.—For purposes of the preceding sentence, the terms "qualified research expenses" and "base period" have the meanings given to such terms by section 44F of the Internal Revenue Code of 1954 (as added by this section).

P.L. 97-34, §331(d)(1)(C):

Amended Code Sec. 383, as in effect for taxable years to which the amendments made by P.L. 94-455 apply, by inserting "to any unused credit of the corporation under section 44G(b)(2)," after "44F(g)(2),"; and by inserting "EMPLOYEE STOCK OWNERSHIP CREDITS," after "RESEARCH CREDITS," in the section heading. **Effective** for tax years beginning after 12-31-81.

• 1980, Crude Oil Windfall Profit Tax Act of 1980 (P.L. 96-223)

P.L. 96-223, §232(b)(2)(C):

Amended Code Sec. 383 by inserting "to any unused credit of the corporation under section 44E(e)(2)," after "section 53(b)," and by striking out in the section heading **"NEW EMPLOYEE CREDITS"** and inserting **"NEW EMPLOYEE CREDITS, ALCOHOL FUEL CREDITS"**. **Effective** for sales and uses after 9-30-80, in tax years ending after such date.

• 1980, Technical Corrections Act of 1979 (P.L. 96-222)

P.L. 96-222, §103(a)(6)(G)(xiii):

Amended Code Sec. 383 by striking out "53(c)" and inserting "53(b)".

• 1977, Tax Reduction and Simplification Act of 1977 (P.L. 95-30)

P.L. 95-30, §202(d)(3)(B):

Amended Code Sec. 383 by adding **"NEW EMPLOYEE CREDITS,"** in the heading and by adding "to any unused new employee credit of the corporation under section 53(c)," after "section 50A(b),". **Effective** for tax years beginning after 12-31-76 and for credit carrybacks from such years.

• 1976, Tax Reform Act of 1976 (P.L. 94-455)

P.L. 94-455, §806(f)(2): See historical comment under Code Sec. 382(a):

Amended Code Sec. 383. P.L. 94-455, §806(g)(2), (3), amended by P.L. 95-600, §368(a), P.L. 96-167, §9(e), and P.L. 97-119, §111 provides that the amendment, as it relates to Code Sec. 382(a), is **effective** for tax years beginning after 6-30-84, except that the beginning of the tax years specified in Code Sec. 382(a)(1)(B)(ii) shall be considered to be the later of (1) the beginning of such tax years, or (2) 1-1-84. The amendment, as it relates to Code Sec. 382(b), applies to reorganizations pursuant to a plan of reorganization adopted by one or more of the parties thereto on or after 1-1-84. For this purpose, a corporation shall be considered to have adopted a plan of reorganization on the date on which a resolution of the board of directors is passed adopting the plan or recommending its adoption to the shareholders, or on the date the shareholders approve the plan of reorganization, whichever is earlier.

P.L. 94-455, §1031(b)(5):

Substituted "section 904(c)" for "section 904(d)" in Code Sec. 383.

P.L. 94-455, §1031(c), provides:

(c) EFFECTIVE DATES.—

(1) IN GENERAL.—Except as provided in paragraphs (2) and (3), the amendments made by this section shall apply to taxable years beginning after December 31, 1975.

(2) EXCEPTION FOR CERTAIN MINING OPERATIONS.—In the case of a domestic corporation or includible corporation in an affiliated group (as defined in section 1504 of the Internal Revenue Code of 1954) which has as of October 1, 1975—

(A) been engaged in the active conduct of the trade or business of the extraction of minerals (of a character with respect to which a deduction for depletion is allowable under section 613 of such Code) outside the United States or its possessions for less than 5 years preceding the date of enactment of this Act,

(B) had deductions properly apportioned or allocated to its gross income from such trade or business in excess of such gross income in at least 2 taxable years,

(C) 80 percent of its gross receipts are from the sale of such minerals, and

(D) made commitments for substantial expansion of such mineral extraction activities,

the amendments made by this section shall apply to taxable years beginning after December 31, 1978. In the case of losses sustained in taxable years beginning before January 1, 1979, by any corporation to which this paragraph applies, the provisions of section 904(f) of such Code shall be applied with respect to such losses under the principles of section 904(a)(1) of such Code as in effect before the enactment of this Act.

(3) EXCEPTION FOR INCOME FROM POSSESSIONS.—In the case of gross income from sources within a possession of the United States (and the deductions properly apportioned or allocated thereto), the amendments made by this section shall apply to taxable years beginning after December 31, 1978. In the case of losses sustained in a possession of the United States in taxable years beginning before January 1, 1979, the provisions of section 904(f) of such Code shall be applied with respect to such losses under the principles of section 904(a)(1) of such Code as in effect before the enactment of this Act.

(4) CARRYBACKS AND CARRYOVERS IN THE CASE OF MINING OPERATIONS AND INCOME FROM A POSSESSION.—In the case of a taxpayer to whom paragraph (2) or (3) of this subsection applies, section 904(e) of such Code shall apply except that "January 1, 1979" shall be substituted for "January 1, 1976" each place it appears therein. If such a taxpayer elects the overall limitation for a taxable year beginning before January 1, 1979, such section 904(e) shall be applied by substituting "the January 1, of the last year for which such taxpayer is on the per-country limitation" for "January 1, 1976" each place it appears therein.

• 1971, Revenue Act of 1971 (P.L. 92-178)

P.L. 92-178, §302(a):

Added Code Sec. 383. **Effective** only with respect to reorganizations and other changes in ownership occurring after 12-10-71 pursuant to a plan or reorganization or contract entered into on or after 9-29-71.

[Sec. 384]

SEC. 384. LIMITATION ON USE OF PREACQUISITION LOSSES TO OFFSET BUILT-IN GAINS.

[Sec. 384(a)]

(a) GENERAL RULE.—If—

(1)(A) a corporation acquires directly (or through 1 or more other corporations) control of another corporation, or

(B) the assets of a corporation are acquired by another corporation in a reorganization described in subparagraph (A), (C), or (D) of section 368(a)(1), and

(2) either of such corporations is a gain corporation,

income for any recognition period taxable year (to the extent attributable to recognized built-in gains) shall not be offset by any preacquisition loss (other than a preacquisition loss of the gain corporation).

Amendments

• 1988, Technical and Miscellaneous Revenue Act of 1988 (P.L. 100-647)

P.L. 100-647, §2004(m)(1)(A):

Amended Code Sec. 384(a). **Effective** as if included in the provision of P.L. 100-203 to which it relates. Prior to amendment, Code Sec. 384(a) read as follows:

(a) GENERAL RULE.—

(1) STOCK ACQUISITIONS, ETC.—If—

(A) a corporation (hereinafter in this section referred to as the "gain corporation") becomes a member of an affiliated group, and

(B) such corporation has a net unrealized built-in gain,

the income of such corporation for any recognition period taxable year (to the extent attributable to recognized built-in gains) shall not be offset by any preacquisition loss of any other member of such group.

(2) ASSET ACQUISITIONS.—If—

(A) the assets of a corporation (hereinafter in this section referred to as the "gain corporation") are acquired by another corporation—

(i) in a liquidation to which section 332 applies, or

(ii) in a reorganization described in subparagraph (A), (C), or (D) of section 368(a)(1), and

(B) the gain corporation has a net unrealized built-in gain,

the income of the acquiring corporation for any recognition period taxable year (to the extent attributable to recognized built-in gains of the gain corporation) shall not be offset by any preacquisition loss of any corporation (other than the gain corporation).

[Sec. 384(b)]

(b) EXCEPTION WHERE CORPORATIONS UNDER COMMON CONTROL.—

(1) IN GENERAL.—Subsection (a) shall not apply to the preacquisition loss of any corporation if such corporation and the gain corporation were members of the same controlled group at all times during the 5-year period ending on the acquisition date.

(2) CONTROLLED GROUP.—For purposes of this subsection, the term "controlled group" means a controlled group of corporations (as defined in section 1563(a)); except that—

(A) "more than 50 percent" shall be substituted for "at least 80 percent" each place it appears,

(B) the ownership requirements of section 1563(a) must be met both with respect to voting power and value, and

(C) the determination shall be made without regard to subsection (a)(4) of section 1563.

(3) SHORTER PERIOD WHERE CORPORATIONS NOT IN EXISTENCE FOR 5 YEARS.—If either of the corporations referred to in paragraph (1) was not in existence throughout the 5-year period referred to in paragraph (1), the period during which such corporation was in existence (or if both, the shorter of such periods) shall be substituted for such 5-year period.

Amendments

• 1988, Technical and Miscellaneous Revenue Act of 1988 (P.L. 100-647)

P.L. 100-647, §2004(m)(3):

Amended Code Sec. 384(b). **Effective** as if included in the provision of P.L. 100-203 to which it relates. Prior to amendment, Code Sec. 384(b) read as follows:

(b) EXCEPTION WHERE 50 PERCENT OF GAIN CORPORATION HELD.—Subsection (a) shall not apply if more than 50 percent of the stock (by vote and value) of the gain corporation was held throughout the 5-year period ending on the acquisition date—

(1) in any case described in subsection (a)(1), by members of the affiliated group referred to in subsection (a)(1), or

(2) in any case described in subsection (a)(2), by the acquiring corporation or members of such acquiring corporation's affiliated group.

For purposes of the preceding sentence, stock described in section 1504(a)(4) shall not be taken into account.

[Sec. 384(c)]

(c) DEFINITIONS.—For purposes of this section—

(1) RECOGNIZED BUILT-IN GAIN.—

(A) IN GENERAL.—The term "recognized built-in gain" means any gain recognized during the recognition period on the disposition of any asset except to the extent the gain corporation (or, in any case described in subsection (a)(1)(B), the acquiring corporation) establishes that—

(i) such asset was not held by the gain corporation on the acquisition date, or

(ii) such gain exceeds the excess (if any) of—

(I) the fair market value of such asset on the acquisition date, over

(II) the adjusted basis of such asset on such date.

(B) TREATMENT OF CERTAIN INCOME ITEMS.—Any item of income which is properly taken into account for any recognition period taxable year but which is attributable to periods before the acquisition date shall be treated as a recognized built-in gain for the taxable year in which it is properly taken into account and shall be taken into account in determining the amount of the net unrealized built-in gain.

(C) LIMITATION.—The amount of the recognized built-in gains for any recognition period taxable year shall not exceed—

(i) the net unrealized built-in gain, reduced by

(ii) the recognized built-in gains for prior years ending in the recognition period which (but for this section) would have been offset by preacquisition losses.

(2) ACQUISITION DATE.—The term "acquisition date" means—

(A) in any case described in subsection (a)(1)(A), the date on which the acquisition of control occurs, or

(B) in any case described in subsection (a)(1)(B), the date of the transfer in the reorganization.

(3) PREACQUISITION LOSS.—

(A) IN GENERAL.—The term "preacquisition loss" means—

(i) any net operating loss carryforward to the taxable year in which the acquisition date occurs, and

(ii) any net operating loss for the taxable year in which the acquisition date occurs to the extent such loss is allocable to the period in such year on or before the acquisition date.

Except as provided in regulations, the net operating loss shall, for purposes of clause (ii), be allocated ratably to each day in the year.

(B) TREATMENT OF RECOGNIZED BUILT-IN LOSS.—In the case of a corporation with a net unrealized built-in loss, the term "preacquisition loss" includes any recognized built-in loss.

(4) GAIN CORPORATION.—The term "gain corporation" means any corporation with a net unrealized built-in gain.

(5) CONTROL.—The term "control" means ownership of stock in a corporation which meets the requirements of section 1504(a)(2).

(6) TREATMENT OF MEMBERS OF SAME GROUP.—Except as provided in regulations and except for purposes of subsection (b), all corporations which are members of the same affiliated group immediately before the acquisition date shall be treated as 1 corporation. To the extent provided in regulations, section 1504 shall be applied without regard to subsection (b) thereof for purposes of the preceding sentence.

(7) TREATMENT OF PREDECESSORS AND SUCCESSORS.—Any reference in this section to a corporation shall include a reference to any predecessor or successor thereof.

(8) OTHER DEFINITIONS.—Except as provided in regulations, the terms "net unrealized built-in gain", "net unrealized built-in loss", "recognized built-in loss", "recognition period", and "recognition period taxable year", have the same respective meanings as when used in section 382(h), except that the acquisition date shall be taken into account in lieu of the change date.

Amendments

• 1988, Technical and Miscellaneous Revenue Act of 1988 (P.L. 100-647)

P.L. 100-647, §2004(m)(1)(B):

Amended Code Sec. 384(c) by redesignating paragraph (4) as paragraph (8) and inserting after paragraph (3) new paragraphs (4)-(7). **Effective** as if included in the provision of P.L. 100-203 to which it relates.

P.L. 100-647, §2004(m)(1)(C):

Amended Code Sec. 384(c)(2). **Effective** as if included in the provision of P.L. 100-203 to which it relates. Prior to amendment, Code Sec. 384(c)(2) read as follows:

(2) ACQUISITION DATE.—The term "acquisition date" means the date on which the gain corporation becomes a member of the affiliated group or, in any case described in subsection (a)(2), the date of the distribution or transfer in the liquidation or reorganization.

P.L. 100-647, §2004(m)(1)(D):

Amended Code Sec. 384(c)(1) by striking out "subsection (a)(2)" and inserting in lieu thereof "subsection (a)(1)(B)". **Effective** as if included in the provision of P.L. 100-203 to which it relates.

P.L. 100-647, §2004(m)(5), provides:

(5) In any case where the acquisition date (as defined in section 384(c)(2) of the 1986 Code as amended by this subsection) is before March 31, 1988, the acquiring corporation may elect to have the amendments made by this subsection not apply. Such an election shall be made in such manner as the Secretary of the Treasury or his delegate shall prescribe and shall be made not later than the later of the due date (including extensions) for filing the return for the taxable year of the acquiring corporation in which the acquisition date occurs, or the date 120 days after the date of the enactment of this Act. Such an election, once made, shall be irrevocable.

[Sec. 384(d)]

(d) LIMITATION ALSO TO APPLY TO EXCESS CREDITS OR NET CAPITAL LOSSES.—Rules similar to the rules of subsection (a) shall also apply in the case of any excess credit (as defined in section 383(a)(2)) or net capital loss.

[Sec. 384(e)]

(e) ORDERING RULES FOR NET OPERATING LOSSES, ETC.—

(1) CARRYOVER RULES.—If any preacquisition loss may not offset a recognized built-in gain by reason of this section, such gain shall not be taken into account in determining under section 172(b)(2) the amount of such loss which may be carried to other taxable years. A similar rule shall apply in the case of any excess credit or net capital loss limited by reason of subsection (d).

(2) ORDERING RULE FOR LOSSES CARRIED FROM SAME TAXABLE YEAR.—In any case in which—

(A) a preacquisition loss for any taxable year is subject to limitation under subsection (a), and

(B) a net operating loss from such taxable year is not subject to such limitation,

taxable income shall be treated as having been offset 1st by the loss subject to such limitation.

Amendments

• 1989, Omnibus Budget Reconciliation Act of 1989 (P.L. 101-239)

P.L. 101-239, §7812(c)(1):

Act Sec. 7812(c)(1) amended Code Sec. 384(e)(1) by striking "build-in gain" and inserting "built-in gain". **Effective** as if included in the provision of P.L. 100-647 to which it relates.

• 1988, Technical and Miscellaneous Revenue Act of 1988 (P.L. 100-647)

P.L. 100-647, §2004(m)(4):

Amended Code Sec. 384 by redesignating subsection (e) as subsection (f) and by inserting after subsection (d) a new subsection (e). **Effective** as if included in the provision of P.L. 100-203 to which it relates.

• 1987, Revenue Act of 1987 (P.L. 100-203)

P.L. 100-203, §10226(a):

Amended part V of subchapter C of chapter 1 by adding at the end thereof new Code Sec. 384. For the **effective** date, see Act Sec. 10226(c), below.

P.L. 100-203, §10226(c), provides:

(c) EFFECTIVE DATE.—The amendments made by this section shall apply in cases where the acquisition date (as defined in section 384(c)(2) of the Internal Revenue Code of 1986 as added by this section) is after December 15, 1987; except that such amendments shall not apply in the case of any transaction pursuant to—

(1) a binding written contract in effect on or before December 15, 1987, or

(2) a letter of intent or agreement of merger signed on or before December 15, 1987.

[Sec. 384(f)]

(f) REGULATIONS.—The Secretary shall prescribe such regulations as may be necessary to carry out the purposes of this section, including regulations to ensure that the purposes of this section may not be circumvented through—

(1) the use of any provision of law or regulations (including subchapter K of this chapter), or

(2) contributions of property to a corporation.

Amendments

• 1988, Technical and Miscellaneous Revenue Act of 1988 (P.L. 100-647)

P.L. 100-647, §2004(m)(2):

Amended Code Sec. 384(e)(2), prior to redesignation by striking out "the gain corporation" and inserting in lieu thereof "a corporation". **Effective** as if included in the provision of P.L. 100-203 to which it relates.

P.L. 100-647, §2004(m)(4):

Amended Code Sec. 384 by redesignating subsection (e) as subsection (f). **Effective** as if included in the provision of P.L. 100-203 to which it relates.

PART VI—TREATMENT OF CERTAIN CORPORATE INTERESTS AS STOCK OR INDEBTEDNESS

[Sec. 385]

SEC. 385. TREATMENT OF CERTAIN INTERESTS IN CORPORATIONS AS STOCK OR INDEBTEDNESS.

[Sec. 385(a)]

(a) AUTHORITY TO PRESCRIBE REGULATIONS.—The Secretary is authorized to prescribe such regulations as may be necessary or appropriate to determine whether an interest in a corporation is to be treated for purposes of this title as stock or indebtedness (or as in part stock and in part indebtedness).

Amendments

• 1989, Omnibus Budget Reconciliation Act of 1989 (P.L. 101-239)

P.L. 101-239, §7208(a)(1):

Amended Code Sec. 385(a) by inserting "(or as in part stock and in part indebtedness)" before the period at the end thereof. **Effective** 12-19-89.

P.L. 101-239, §7208(a)(2), provides:

(2) REGULATIONS NOT TO BE APPLIED RETROACTIVELY.—Any regulations issued pursuant to the authority granted by the amendment made by paragraph (1) shall only apply with respect to instruments issued after the date on which the Secretary of the Treasury or his delegate provides public guidance as to the characterization of such instruments whether by regulation, ruling, or otherwise.

[Sec. 385(b)]

(b) FACTORS.—The regulations prescribed under this section shall set forth factors which are to be taken into account in determining with respect to a particular factual situation whether a debtor-creditor relationship exists or a corporation-shareholder relationship exists. The factors so set forth in the regulations may include among other factors:

(1) whether there is a written unconditional promise to pay on demand or on a specified date a sum certain in money in return for an adequate consideration in money or money's worth, and to pay a fixed rate of interest,

(2) whether there is subordination to or preference over any indebtedness of the corporation,

(3) the ratio of debt to equity of the corporation,

(4) whether there is convertibility into the stock of the corporation, and

(5) the relationship between holdings of stock in the corporation and holdings of the interest in question.

Amendments

• 1969, Tax Reform Act of 1969 (P.L. 91-172)

P.L. 91-172, §415(a):

Added Sec. 385. **Effective** 12-31-69.

[Sec. 385(c)]

(c) EFFECT OF CLASSIFICATION BY ISSUER.—

(1) IN GENERAL.—The characterization (as of the time of issuance) by the issuer as to whether an interest in a corporation is stock or indebtedness shall be binding on such issuer and on all holders of such interest (but shall not be binding on the Secretary).

(2) NOTIFICATION OF INCONSISTENT TREATMENT.—Except as provided in regulations, paragraph (1) shall not apply to any holder of an interest if such holder on his return discloses that he is treating such interest in a manner inconsistent with the characterization referred to in paragraph (1).

(3) REGULATIONS.—The Secretary is authorized to require such information as the Secretary determines to be necessary to carry out the provisions of this subsection.

Amendments

• 1992, Energy Policy Act of 1992 (P.L. 102-486)

P.L. 102-486, §1936(a):

Amended Code Sec. 385 by adding at the end thereof new subsection (c). **Effective** for instruments issued after 10-24-92.

PART VII—MISCELLANEOUS CORPORATE PROVISIONS—[Repealed]

[Sec. 386—Repealed]

Amendments

• 1988, Technical and Miscellaneous Revenue Act of 1988 (P.L. 100-647)

P.L. 100-647, §1006(e)(8)(A):

Repealed Part VII of subchapter C of Chapter 1 (Code Sec. 386). **Effective** as if included in the provision of P.L. 99-514 to which it relates. Prior to repeal, Part VII of subchapter C of Chapter 1 read as follows:

PART VII—MISCELLANEOUS CORPORATE PROVISIONS

SEC. 386. TRANSFERS OF PARTNERSHIP AND TRUST IN INTERESTS BY CORPORATIONS.

(a) CORPORATE DISTRIBUTIONS.—For purposes of determining the amount (and character) of gain recognized by a corporation on any distribution of an interest in a partnership, the distribution shall be treated in the same manner as if it included a property distribution consisting of the corporation's proportionate share of the recognition property of such partnership.

(b) SALES OR EXCHANGE TO WHICH SECTION 337 APPLIES.—For purposes of determining the amount (and character) of gain recognized on a sale or exchange described in section 337, any sale or exchange by a corporation of an interest in a partnership shall be treated as a sale or exchange of the corporation's proportionate share of the recognition property of such partnership.

(c) RECOGNITION PROPERTY.—For purposes of this section, the term "recognition property" means any property with respect to which gain would be recognized to the corporation if such property—

(1) were distributed by the corporation in a distribution described in section 311 or 336, or

(2) were sold in a sale described in section 337,

whichever is appropriate. In determining whether property of a partnership is recognition property, such partnership shall be treated as owning its proportionate share of the property of any other partnership in which it is a partner.

(d) LIMITATIONS ON AMOUNT OF GAIN RECOGNIZED IN CASE OF NON-LIQUIDATING DISTRIBUTIONS.—In the case of any distribution by a corporation to which section 311 applies, the amount of any gain recognized by reason of subsection (a) shall not exceed the amount of the gain which would have been recognized if the partnership interest had been sold. The Secretary may by regulations provide that the amount of such gain shall be computed without regard to any loss attributable to property contributed to the partnership for the principal purpose of recognizing such loss on the distribution.

(e) EXTENSION TO TRUSTS.—Under regulations, rules similar to the rules of this section shall also apply in the case of the distribution or sale or exchange by a corporation of an interest in a trust.

Amendments

• 1986, Tax Reform Act of 1986 (P.L. 99-514)

P.L. 99-514, §1805(c)(1):

Amended Code Sec. 386 by redesignating subsection (d) as subsection (e) and by inserting after subsection (c) new subsection (d). **Effective** as if included in the provision of P.L. 98-369 to which it relates.

• 1984, Deficit Reduction Act of 1984 (P.L. 98-369)

P.L. 98-369, §75(a):

Added Code Sec. 386. **Effective** for distributions, sales and exchanges made after 3-31-84, in tax years ending after such date.

Subchapter D—Deferred Compensation, Etc.

PART I—PENSION, PROFIT-SHARING, STOCK BONUS PLANS, ETC.

Subpart A—General Rule

[Sec. 401]

SEC. 401. QUALIFIED PENSION, PROFIT-SHARING, AND STOCK BONUS PLANS.

[Sec. 401(a)]

(a) REQUIREMENTS FOR QUALIFICATION.—A trust created or organized in the United States and forming part of a stock bonus, pension, or profit-sharing plan of an employer for the exclusive benefit of his employees or their beneficiaries shall constitute a qualified trust under this section—

(1) if contributions are made to the trust by such employer, or employees, or both, or by another employer who is entitled to deduct his contributions under section 404(a)(3)(B) (relating to deduction for contributions to profit-sharing and stock bonus plans), or by a charitable remainder trust pursuant to a qualified gratuitous transfer (as defined in section 664(g)(1)), for the purpose of distributing to such employees or their beneficiaries the corpus and income of the fund accumulated by the trust in accordance with such plan;

(2) if under the trust instrument it is impossible, at any time prior to the satisfaction of all liabilities with respect to employees and their beneficiaries under the trust, for any part of the corpus or income to be (within the taxable year or thereafter) used for, or diverted to, purposes other than for the exclusive benefit of his employees or their beneficiaries (but this paragraph shall not be construed, in the case of a multiemployer plan, to prohibit the return of a contribution within 6 months after the plan administrator determines that the contribution was made by a mistake of fact or law (other than a mistake relating to whether the plan is described in section 401(a) or the trust which is part of such plan is exempt from taxation under section 501(a), or the return of any withdrawal liability payment determined to be an overpayment within 6 months of such determination));

(3) if the plan of which such trust is a part satisfies the requirements of section 410 (relating to minimum participation standards); and

(4) if the contributions or benefits provided under the plan do not discriminate in favor of highly compensated employees (within the meaning of section 414(q)). For purposes of this paragraph, there shall be excluded from consideration employees described in section 410(b)(3)(A) and (C).

(5) SPECIAL RULES RELATING TO NONDISCRIMINATION REQUIREMENTS.—

(A) SALARIED OR CLERICAL EMPLOYEES.—A classification shall not be considered discriminatory within the meaning of paragraph (4) or section 410(b)(2)(A)(i) merely because it is limited to salaried or clerical employees.

(B) CONTRIBUTIONS AND BENEFITS MAY BEAR UNIFORM RELATIONSHIP TO COMPENSATION.—A plan shall not be considered discriminatory within the meaning of paragraph (4) merely because the contributions or benefits of, or on behalf of, the employees under the plan bear a uniform relationship to the compensation (within the meaning of section 414(s)) of such employees.

(C) CERTAIN DISPARITY PERMITTED.—A plan shall not be considered discriminatory within the meaning of paragraph (4) merely because the contributions or benefits of, or on behalf of, the employees under the plan favor highly compensated employees (as defined in section 414(q)) in the manner permitted under subsection (l).

(D) INTEGRATED DEFINED BENEFIT PLAN.—

(i) IN GENERAL.—A defined benefit plan shall not be considered discriminatory within the meaning of paragraph (4) merely because the plan provides that the employer-derived accrued retirement benefit for any participant under the plan may not exceed the excess (if any) of—

(I) the participant's final pay with the employer, over

(II) the employer-derived retirement benefit created under Federal law attributable to service by the participant with the employer.

For purposes of this clause, the employer-derived retirement benefit created under Federal law shall be treated as accruing ratably over 35 years.

(ii) FINAL PAY.—For purposes of this subparagraph, the participant's final pay is the compensation (as defined in section 414(q)(4)) paid to the participant by the employer for any year—

(I) which ends during the 5-year period ending with the year in which the participant separated from service for the employer, and

(II) for which the participant's total compensation from the employer was highest.

(E) 2 OR MORE PLANS TREATED AS SINGLE PLAN.—For purposes of determining whether 2 or more plans of an employer satisfy the requirements of paragraph (4) when considered as a single plan—

(i) CONTRIBUTIONS.—If the amount of contributions on behalf of the employees allowed as a deduction under section 404 for the taxable year with respect to such plans, taken together, bears a uniform relationship to the compensation (within the meaning of section 414(s)) of such employees, the plans shall not be considered discriminatory merely because the rights of employees to, or derived from, the employer contributions under the separate plans do not become nonforfeitable at the same rate.

(ii) BENEFITS.—If the employees' rights to benefits under the separate plans do not become nonforfeitable at the same rate, but the levels of benefits provided by the separate plans satisfy the requirements of regulations prescribed by the Secretary to take account of the differences in such rates, the plans shall not be considered discriminatory merely because of the difference in such rates.

(F) SOCIAL SECURITY RETIREMENT AGE.—For purposes of testing for discrimination under paragraph (4)—

(i) the social security retirement age (as defined in section 415(b)(8)) shall be treated as a uniform retirement age, and

(ii) subsidized early retirement benefits and joint and survivor annuities shall not be treated as being unavailable to employees on the same terms merely because such benefits or annuities are based in whole or in part on an employee's social security retirement age (as so defined).

(G) GOVERNMENTAL PLANS.—Paragraphs (3) and (4) shall not apply to a governmental plan (within the meaning of section 414(d)).

(6) A plan shall be considered as meeting the requirements of paragraph (3) during the whole of any taxable year of the plan if on one day in each quarter it satisfied such requirements.

(7) A trust shall not constitute a qualified trust under this section unless the plan of which such trust is a part satisfies the requirements of section 411 (relating to minimum vesting standards).

(8) A trust forming part of a defined benefit plan shall not constitute a qualified trust under this section unless the plan provides that forfeitures must not be applied to increase the benefits any employee would otherwise receive under the plan.

(9) REQUIRED DISTRIBUTIONS.—

(A) IN GENERAL.—A trust shall not constitute a qualified trust under this subsection unless the plan provides that the entire interest of each employee—

(i) will be distributed to such employee not later than the required beginning date, or

(ii) will be distributed, beginning not later than the required beginning date, in accordance with regulations, over the life of such employee or over the lives of such employee and a designated beneficiary (or over a period not extending beyond the life expectancy of such employee or the life expectancy of such employee and a designated beneficiary).

(B) REQUIRED DISTRIBUTION WHERE EMPLOYEE DIES BEFORE ENTIRE INTEREST IS DISTRIBUTED.—

(i) WHERE DISTRIBUTIONS HAVE BEGUN UNDER SUBPARAGRAPH (A)(ii).—A trust shall not constitute a qualified trust under this section unless the plan provides that if—

(I) the distribution of the employee's interest has begun in accordance with subparagraph (A)(ii), and

(II) the employee dies before his entire interest has been distributed to him,

the remaining portion of such interest will be distributed at least as rapidly as under the method of distributions being used under subparagraph (A)(ii) as of the date of his death.

(ii) 5-YEAR RULE FOR OTHER CASES.—A trust shall not constitute a qualified trust under this section unless the plan provides that, if an employee dies before the distribution of the employee's interest has begun in accordance with subparagraph (A)(ii), the entire interest of the employee will be distributed within 5 years after the death of such employee.

(iii) EXCEPTION TO 5-YEAR RULE FOR CERTAIN AMOUNTS PAYABLE OVER LIFE OF BENEFICIARY.—If—

(I) any portion of the employee's interest is payable to (or for the benefit of) a designated beneficiary,

(II) such portion will be distributed (in accordance with regulations) over the life of such designated beneficiary (or over a period not extending beyond the life expectancy of such beneficiary), and

(III) such distributions begin not later than 1 year after the date of the employee's death or such later date as the Secretary may by regulations prescribe,

for purposes of clause (ii), the portion referred to in subclause (I) shall be treated as distributed on the date on which such distributions begin.

(iv) SPECIAL RULE FOR SURVIVING SPOUSE OF EMPLOYEE.—If the designated beneficiary referred to in clause (iii)(I) is the surviving spouse of the employee—

(I) the date on which the distributions are required to begin under clause (iii)(III) shall not be earlier than the date on which the employee would have attained age $70^1/_2$, and

(II) if the surviving spouse dies before the distributions to such spouse begin, this subparagraph shall be applied as if the surviving spouse were the employee.

(C) REQUIRED BEGINNING DATE.—For purposes of this paragraph—

(i) IN GENERAL.—The term "required beginning date" means April 1 of the calendar year following the later of—

(I) the calendar year in which the employee attains age $70^1/_2$, or

(II) the calendar year in which the employee retires.

(ii) EXCEPTION.—Subclause (II) of clause (i) shall not apply—

(I) except as provided in section 409(d), in the case of an employee who is a 5-percent owner (as defined in section 416) with respect to the plan year ending in the calendar year in which the employee attains age 70$^1/_2$, or

(II) for purposes of section 408(a)(6) or (b)(3).

(iii) ACTUARIAL ADJUSTMENT.—In the case of an employee to whom clause (i)(II) applies who retires in a calendar year after the calendar year in which the employee attains age 70$^1/_2$, the employee's accrued benefit shall be actuarially increased to take into account the period after age 70$^1/_2$ in which the employee was not receiving any benefits under the plan.

(iv) EXCEPTION FOR GOVERNMENTAL AND CHURCH PLANS.—Clauses (ii) and (iii) shall not apply in the case of a governmental plan or church plan. For purposes of this clause, the term "church plan" means a plan maintained by a church for church employees, and the term "church" means any church (as defined in section 3121(w)(3)(A)) or qualified church-controlled organization (as defined in section 3121(w)(3)(B)).

(D) LIFE EXPECTANCY.—For purposes of this paragraph, the life expectancy of an employee and the employee's spouse (other than in the case of a life annuity) may be redetermined but not more frequently than annually.

(E) DESIGNATED BENEFICIARY.—For purposes of this paragraph, the term "designated beneficiary" means any individual designated as a beneficiary by the employee.

(F) TREATMENT OF PAYMENTS TO CHILDREN.—Under regulations prescribed by the Secretary, for purposes of this paragraph, any amount paid to a child shall be treated as if it had been paid to the surviving spouse if such amount will become payable to the surviving spouse upon such child reaching majority (or other designated event permitted under regulations).

(G) TREATMENT OF INCIDENTAL DEATH BENEFIT DISTRIBUTIONS.—For purposes of this title, any distribution required under the incidental death benefit requirements of this subsection shall be treated as a distribution required under this paragraph.

(H) TEMPORARY WAIVER OF MINIMUM REQUIRED DISTRIBUTION.—

(i) IN GENERAL.—The requirements of this paragraph shall not apply for calendar year 2009 to—

(I) a defined contribution plan which is described in this subsection or in section 403(a) or 403(b),

(II) a defined contribution plan which is an eligible deferred compensation plan described in section 457(b) but only if such plan is maintained by an employer described in section 457(e)(1)(A), or

(III) an individual retirement plan.

(ii) SPECIAL RULES REGARDING WAIVER PERIOD.—For purposes of this paragraph—

(I) the required beginning date with respect to any individual shall be determined without regard to this subparagraph for purposes of applying this paragraph for calendar years after 2009, and

(II) if clause (ii) of subparagraph (B) applies, the 5-year period described in such clause shall be determined without regard to calendar year 2009.

(10) OTHER REQUIREMENTS.—

(A) PLANS BENEFITING OWNER-EMPLOYEES.—In the case of any plan which provides contributions or benefits for employees some or all of whom are owner-employees (as defined in subsection (c)(3)), a trust forming part of such plan shall constitute a qualified trust under this section only if the requirements of subsection (d) are also met.

(B) TOP-HEAVY PLANS.—

(i) IN GENERAL.—In the case of any top-heavy plan, a trust forming part of such plan shall constitute a qualified trust under this section only if the requirements of section 416 are met.

(ii) PLANS WHICH MAY BECOME TOP-HEAVY.—Except to the extent provided in regulations, a trust forming part of a plan (whether or not a top-heavy plan) shall constitute a qualified trust under this section only if such plan contains provisions—

(I) which will take effect if such plan becomes a top-heavy plan, and

(II) which meet the requirements of section 416.

(iii) EXEMPTION FOR GOVERNMENTAL PLANS.—This subparagraph shall not apply to any governmental plan.

(11) REQUIREMENT OF JOINT AND SURVIVOR ANNUITY AND PRERETIREMENT SURVIVOR ANNUITY.—

(A) IN GENERAL.—In the case of any plan to which this paragraph applies, except as provided in section 417, a trust forming part of such plan shall not constitute a qualified trust under this section unless—

(i) in the case of a vested participant who does not die before the annuity starting date, the accrued benefit payable to such participant is provided in the form of a qualified joint and survivor annuity, and

(ii) in the case of a vested participant who dies before the annuity starting date and who has a surviving spouse, a qualified preretirement survivor annuity is provided to the surviving spouse of such participant.

(B) PLANS TO WHICH PARAGRAPH APPLIES.—This paragraph shall apply to—

(i) any defined benefit plan,

(ii) any defined contribution plan which is subject to the funding standards of section 412, and

(iii) any participant under any other defined contribution plan unless—

(I) such plan provides that the participant's nonforfeitable accrued benefit (reduced by any security interest held by the plan by reason of a loan outstanding to such participant) is payable in full, on the death of the participant, to the participant's surviving spouse (or, if there is no surviving spouse or the surviving spouse consents in the manner required under section 417(a)(2), to a designated beneficiary),

(II) such participant does not elect a payment of benefits in the form of a life annuity, and

(III) with respect to such participant, such plan is not a direct or indirect transferee (in a transfer after December 31, 1984) of a plan which is described in clause (i) or (ii) or to which this clause applied with respect to the participant.

Clause (iii)(III) shall apply only with respect to the transferred assets (and income therefrom) if the plan separately accounts for such assets and any income therefrom.

(C) EXCEPTION FOR CERTAIN ESOP BENEFITS.—

(i) IN GENERAL.—In the case of—

(I) a tax credit employee stock ownership plan (as defined in section 409(a)), or

(II) an employee stock ownership plan (as defined in section 4975(e)(7)),

subparagraph (A) shall not apply to that portion of the employee's accrued benefit to which the requirements of section 409(h) apply.

(ii) NONFORFEITABLE BENEFIT MUST BE PAID IN FULL, ETC.—In the case of any participant, clause (i) shall apply only if the requirements of subclauses (I), (II), and (III) of subparagraph (B)(iii) are met with respect to such participant.

(D) SPECIAL RULE WHERE PARTICIPANT AND SPOUSE MARRIED LESS THAN 1 YEAR.—A plan shall not be treated as failing to meet the requirements of subparagraphs (B)(iii) or (C) merely because the plan provides that benefits will not be payable to the surviving spouse of the participant unless the participant and such spouse had been married throughout the 1-year period ending on the earlier of the participant's annuity starting date or the date of the participant's death.

(E) EXCEPTION FOR PLANS DESCRIBED IN SECTION 404(c).—This paragraph shall not apply to a plan which the Secretary has determined is a plan described in section 404(c) (or a continuation thereof) in which participation is substantially limited to individuals who, before January 1, 1976, ceased employment covered by the plan.

(F) CROSS REFERENCE.—For—

(i) provisions under which participants may elect to waive the requirements of this paragraph, and

(ii) other definitions and special rules for purposes of this paragraph,

see section 417.

(12) A trust shall not constitute a qualified trust under this section unless the plan of which such trust is a part provides that in the case of any merger or consolidation with, or transfer of assets or liabilities to, any other plan after September 2, 1974, each participant in the plan would (if the plan then terminated) receive a benefit immediately after the merger, consolidation, or transfer which is equal to or greater than the benefit he would have been entitled to receive immediately before the merger, consolidation, or transfer (if the plan had then terminated). The preceding sentence does not apply to any multiemployer plan with respect to any transaction to the extent that participants either before or after the transaction are covered under a multiemployer plan to which title IV of the Employee Retirement Income Security Act of 1974 applies.

(13) ASSIGNMENT AND ALIENATION.—

(A) IN GENERAL.—A trust shall not constitute a qualified trust under this section unless the plan of which such trust is a part provides that benefits provided under the plan may not be assigned or alienated. For purposes of the preceding sentence, there shall not be taken into account any voluntary and revocable assignment of not to exceed 10 percent of any benefit payment made by any participant who is receiving benefits under the plan unless the assignment or alienation is made for purposes of defraying plan administration costs. For purposes of this paragraph a loan made to a participant or beneficiary shall not be treated as an assignment or alienation if such loan is secured by the participant's accrued nonforfeitable benefit and is exempt from the tax imposed by section 4975 (relating to tax on prohibited transactions) by reason of section 4975(d)(1). This paragraph shall take effect on January 1, 1976 and shall not apply to assignments which were irrevocable on September 2, 1974.

(B) SPECIAL RULES FOR DOMESTIC RELATIONS ORDERS.—Subparagraph (A) shall apply to the creation, assignment, or recognition of a right to any benefit payable with respect to a participant pursuant to a domestic relations order, except that subparagraph (A) shall not apply if the order is determined to be a qualified domestic relations order.

(C) SPECIAL RULE FOR CERTAIN JUDGMENTS AND SETTLEMENTS.—Subparagraph (A) shall not apply to any offset of a participant's benefits provided under a plan against an amount that the participant is ordered or required to pay to the plan if—

(i) the order or requirement to pay arises—

(I) under a judgment of conviction for a crime involving such plan,

(II) under a civil judgment (including a consent order or decree) entered by a court in an action brought in connection with a violation (or alleged violation) of part 4 of subtitle B of title I of the Employee Retirement Income Security Act of 1974, or

(III) pursuant to a settlement agreement between the Secretary of Labor and the participant, or a settlement agreement between the Pension Benefit Guaranty Corporation and the participant, in connection with a violation (or alleged violation) of part 4 of such subtitle by a fiduciary or any other person,

(ii) the judgment, order, decree, or settlement agreement expressly provides for the offset of all or part of the amount ordered or required to be paid to the plan against the participant's benefits provided under the plan, and

(iii) in a case in which the survivor annuity requirements of section 401(a)(11) apply with respect to distributions from the plan to the participant, if the participant has a spouse at the time at which the offset is to be made—

(I) either such spouse has consented in writing to such offset and such consent is witnessed by a notary public or representative of the plan (or it is established to the satisfaction of a plan representative that such consent may not be obtained by reason of circumstances described in section 417(a)(2)(B)), or an election to waive the right of the spouse to either a qualified joint and survivor annuity or a qualified preretirement survivor annuity is in effect in accordance with the requirements of section 417(a),

(II) such spouse is ordered or required in such judgment, order, decree, or settlement to pay an amount to the plan in connection with a violation of part 4 of such subtitle, or

(III) in such judgment, order, decree, or settlement, such spouse retains the right to receive the survivor annuity under a qualified joint and survivor annuity provided pursuant to section 401(a)(11)(A)(i) and under a qualified preretirement survivor annuity provided pursuant to section 401(a)(11)(A)(ii), determined in accordance with subparagraph (D).

A plan shall not be treated as failing to meet the requirements of this subsection, subsection (k), section 403(b), or section 409(d) solely by reason of an offset described in this subparagraph.

(D) SURVIVOR ANNUITY.—

(i) IN GENERAL.—The survivor annuity described in subparagraph (C)(iii)(III) shall be determined as if—

(I) the participant terminated employment on the date of the offset,

(II) there was no offset,

(III) the plan permitted commencement of benefits only on or after normal retirement age,

(IV) the plan provided only the minimum-required qualified joint and survivor annuity, and

(V) the amount of the qualified preretirement survivor annuity under the plan is equal to the amount of the survivor annuity payable under the minimum-required qualified joint and survivor annuity.

(ii) DEFINITION.—For purposes of this subparagraph, the term "minimum-required qualified joint and survivor annuity" means the qualified joint and survivor annuity which is the actuarial equivalent of the participant's accrued benefit (within the meaning of section 411(a)(7)) and under which the survivor annuity is 50 percent of the amount of the annuity which is payable during the joint lives of the participant and the spouse.

(14) A trust shall not constitute a qualified trust under this section unless the plan of which such trust is a part provides that, unless the participant otherwise elects, the payment of benefits under the plan to the participant will begin not later than the 60th day after the latest of the close of the plan year in which—

(A) the date on which the participant attains the earlier of age 65 or the normal retirement age specified under the plan,

(B) occurs the 10th anniversary of the year in which the participant commenced participation in the plan, or

(C) the participant terminates his service with the employer.

In the case of a plan which provides for the payment of an early retirement benefit, a trust forming a part of such plan shall not constitute a qualified trust under this section unless a participant who satisfied the service requirements for such early retirement benefit, but separated from the service (with any nonforfeitable right to an accrued benefit) before satisfying the age requirement for such early retirement benefit, is entitled upon satisfaction of such age requirement to receive a benefit not less than the benefit to which he would be entitled at the normal retirement age, actuarially reduced under regulations prescribed by the Secretary.

(15) A trust shall not constitute a qualified trust under this section unless under the plan of which such trust is a part—

(A) in the case of a participant or beneficiary who is receiving benefits under such plan, or

(B) in the case of a participant who is separated from the service and who has nonforfeitable rights to benefits,

such benefits are not decreased by reason of any increase in the benefit levels payable under title II of the Social Security Act or any increase in the wage base under such title II, if such increase takes place after September 2, 1974, or (if later) the earlier of the date of first receipt of such benefits or the date of such separation, as the case may be.

(16) A trust shall not constitute a qualified trust under this section if the plan of which such trust is a part provides for benefits or contributions which exceed the limitations of section 415.

(17) COMPENSATION LIMIT.—

(A) IN GENERAL.—A trust shall not constitute a qualified trust under this section unless, under the plan of which such trust is a part, the annual compensation of each employee taken into account under the plan for any year does not exceed $200,000.

(B) COST-OF-LIVING ADJUSTMENT.—The Secretary shall adjust annually the $200,000 amount in subparagraph (A) for increases in the cost-of-living at the same time and in the same manner as adjustments under section 415(d); except that the base period shall be the calendar quarter beginning July 1, 2001, and any increase which is not a multiple of $5,000 shall be rounded to the next lowest multiple of $5,000.

(18) [Repealed.]

(19) A trust shall not constitute a qualified trust under this section if under the plan of which such trust is a part any part of a participant's accrued benefit derived from employer contributions (whether or not otherwise nonforfeitable), is forfeitable solely because of withdrawal by such participant of any amount attributable to the benefit derived from contributions made by such participant. The preceding sentence shall not apply to the accrued benefit of any participant unless, at the time of such withdrawal, such participant has a nonforfeitable right to at least 50 percent of such accrued benefit (as determined under section 411). The first sentence of this paragraph shall not apply to the extent that an accrued benefit is permitted to be forfeited in accordance with section 411(a)(3)(D)(iii) (relating to proportional forfeitures of benefits accrued before September 2, 1974, in the event of withdrawal of certain mandatory contributions).

(20) A trust forming part of a pension plan shall not be treated as failing to constitute a qualified trust under this section merely because the pension plan of which such trust is a part makes 1 or more distributions within 1 taxable year to a distributee on account of a termination of the plan of which the trust is a part, or in the case of a profit-sharing or stock bonus plan, a complete discontinuance of contributions under such plan. This paragraph shall not apply to a defined benefit plan unless the employer maintaining such plan files a notice with the Pension Benefit Guaranty Corporation (at the time and in the manner prescribed by the Pension Benefit Guaranty Corporation) notifying the Corporation of such payment or distribution and the Corporation has approved such payment or distribution or, within 90 days after the date on which such notice was filed, has failed to disapprove such payment or distribution. For purposes of this paragraph, rules similar to the rules of section 402(a)(6)(B) (as in effect before its repeal by section 521 of the Unemployment Compensation Amendments of 1992) shall apply.

(21) [Repealed.]

(22) If a defined contribution plan (other than a profit-sharing plan)—

(A) is established by an employer whose stock is not readily tradable on an established market, and

(B) after acquiring securities of the employer, more than 10 percent of the total assets of the plan are securities of the employer,

any trust forming part of such plan shall not constitute a qualified trust under this section unless the plan meets the requirements of subsection (e) of section 409. The requirements of subsection (e) of section 409 shall not apply to any employees of an employer who are participants in any defined contribution plan established and maintained by such employer if the stock of such employer is not readily tradable on an established market and the trade or business of such employer consists of publishing on a regular basis a newspaper for general circulation. For purposes of the preceding sentence, subsections (b), (c), (m), and (o) of section 414 shall not apply except for determining whether stock of the employer is not readily tradable on an established market.

(23) A stock bonus plan shall not be treated as meeting the requirements of this section unless such plan meets the requirements of subsections (h) and (o) of section 409, except that in applying section 409(h) for purposes of this paragraph, the term "employer securities" shall include any securities of the employer held by the plan.

(24) Any group trust which otherwise meets the requirements of this section shall not be treated as not meeting such requirements on account of the participation or inclusion in such trust of the moneys of any plan or governmental unit described in section 818(a)(6).

(25) REQUIREMENT THAT ACTUARIAL ASSUMPTIONS BE SPECIFIED.—A defined benefit plan shall not be treated as providing definitely determinable benefits unless, whenever the amount of any benefit is to be determined on the basis of actuarial assumptions, such assumptions are specified in the plan in a way which precludes employer discretion.

(26) ADDITIONAL PARTICIPATION REQUIREMENTS.—

(A) IN GENERAL.—In the case of a trust which is a part of a defined benefit plan, such trust shall not constitute a qualified trust under this subsection unless on each day of the plan year such trust benefits at least the lesser of—

(i) 50 employees of the employer, or

(ii) the greater of—

(I) 40 percent of all employees of the employer, or

(II) 2 employees (or if there is only 1 employee, such employee).

(B) TREATMENT OF EXCLUDABLE EMPLOYEES.—

(i) IN GENERAL.—A plan may exclude from consideration under this paragraph employees described in paragraphs (3) and (4)(A) of section 410(b).

(ii) SEPARATE APPLICATION FOR CERTAIN EXCLUDABLE EMPLOYEES.—If employees described in section 410(b)(4)(B) are covered under a plan which meets the requirements of subparagraph (A) separately with respect to such employees, such employees may be excluded from consideration in determining whether any plan of the employer meets such requirements if—

(I) the benefits for such employees are provided under the same plan as benefits for other employees,

(II) the benefits provided to such employees are not greater than comparable benefits provided to other employees under the plan, and

(III) no highly compensated employee (within the meaning of section 414(q)) is included in the group of such employees for more than 1 year.

(C) SPECIAL RULE FOR COLLECTIVE BARGAINING UNITS.—Except to the extent provided in regulations, a plan covering only employees described in section 410(b)(3)(A) may exclude from consideration any employees who are not included in the unit or units in which the covered employees are included.

(D) PARAGRAPH NOT TO APPLY TO MULTIEMPLOYER PLANS.—Except to the extent provided in regulations, this paragraph shall not apply to employees in a multiemployer plan (within the meaning of section 414(f)) who are covered by collective bargaining agreements.

(E) SPECIAL RULE FOR CERTAIN DISPOSITIONS OR ACQUISITIONS.—Rules similar to the rules of section 410(b)(6)(C) shall apply for purposes of this paragraph.

(F) SEPARATE LINES OF BUSINESS.—At the election of the employer and with the consent of the Secretary, this paragraph may be applied separately with respect to each separate line of business of the employer. For purposes of this paragraph, the term "separate line of business" has the meaning given such term by section 414(r) (without regard to paragraph (2)(A) or (7) thereof).

(G) EXCEPTION FOR GOVERNMENTAL PLANS.—This paragraph shall not apply to a governmental plan (within the meaning of section 414(d)).

(H) REGULATIONS.—The Secretary may by regulation provide that any separate benefit structure, any separate trust, or any other separate arrangement is to be treated as a separate plan for purposes of applying this paragraph.

(27) DETERMINATIONS AS TO PROFIT-SHARING PLANS.—

(A) CONTRIBUTIONS NEED NOT BE BASED ON PROFITS.—The determination of whether the plan under which any contributions are made is a profit-sharing plan shall be made without regard to current or accumulated profits of the employer and without regard to whether the employer is a tax-exempt organization.

(B) PLAN MUST DESIGNATE TYPE.—In the case of a plan which is intended to be a money purchase pension plan or a profit-sharing plan, a trust forming part of such plan shall not constitute a qualified trust under this subsection unless the plan designates such intent at such time and in such manner as the Secretary may prescribe.

(28) ADDITIONAL REQUIREMENTS RELATING TO EMPLOYEE STOCK OWNERSHIP PLANS.—

(A) IN GENERAL.—In the case of a trust which is part of an employee stock ownership plan (within the meaning of section 4975(e)(7)) or a plan which meets the requirements of section 409(a), such trust shall not constitute a qualified trust under this section unless such plan meets the requirements of subparagraphs (B) and (C).

(B) DIVERSIFICATION OF INVESTMENTS.—

(i) IN GENERAL.—A plan meets the requirements of this subparagraph if each qualified participant in the plan may elect within 90 days after the close of each plan year in the qualified election period to direct the plan as to the investment of at least 25 percent of the participant's account in the plan (to the extent such portion exceeds the amount to which a prior election under this subparagraph applies). In the case of the election year in which the participant can make his last election, the preceding sentence shall be applied by substituting "50 percent" for "25 percent".

(ii) METHOD OF MEETING REQUIREMENTS.—A plan shall be treated as meeting the requirements of clause (i) if—

(I) the portion of the participant's account covered by the election under clause (i) is distributed within 90 days after the period during which the election may be made, or

(II) the plan offers at least 3 investment options (not inconsistent with regulations prescribed by the Secretary) to each participant making an election under clause (i) and within 90 days after the period during which the election may be made, the plan invests the portion of the participant's account covered by the election in accordance with such election.

(iii) QUALIFIED PARTICIPANT.—For purposes of this subparagraph, the term "qualified participant" means any employee who has completed at least 10 years of participation under the plan and has attained age 55.

(iv) QUALIFIED ELECTION PERIOD.—For purposes of this subparagraph, the term "qualified election period" means the 6-plan-year period beginning with the later of—

(I) the 1st plan year in which the individual first became a qualified participant, or

(II) the 1st plan year beginning after December 31, 1986.

For purposes of the preceding sentence, an employer may elect to treat an individual first becoming a qualified participant in the 1st plan year beginning in 1987 as having become a participant in the 1st plan year beginning in 1988.

(v) EXCEPTION.—This subparagraph shall not apply to an applicable defined contribution plan (as defined in paragraph (35)(E)).

(C) USE OF INDEPENDENT APPRAISER.—A plan meets the requirements of this subparagraph if all valuations of employer securities which are not readily tradable on an established securities market with respect to activities carried on by the plan are by an independent appraiser. For purposes of the preceding sentence, the term "independent appraiser" means any appraiser meeting requirements similar to the requirements of the regulations prescribed under section 170(a)(1).

(29) BENEFIT LIMITATIONS.—In the case of a defined benefit plan (other than a multiemployer plan) to which the requirements of section 412 apply, the trust of which the plan is a part shall not constitute a qualified trust under this subsection unless the plan meets the requirements of section 436.

(30) LIMITATIONS ON ELECTIVE DEFERRALS.—In the case of a trust which is part of a plan under which elective deferrals (within the meaning of section 402(g)(3)) may be made with respect to any individual during a calendar year, such trust shall not constitute a qualified trust under this subsection unless the plan provides that the amount of such deferrals under such plan and all other plans, contracts, or arrangements of an employer maintaining such plan may not exceed the amount of the limitation in effect under section 402(g)(1)(A) for taxable years beginning in such calendar year.

(31) DIRECT TRANSFER OF ELIGIBLE ROLLOVER DISTRIBUTIONS.—

(A) IN GENERAL.—A trust shall not constitute a qualified trust under this section unless the plan of which such trust is a part provides that if the distributee of any eligible rollover distribution—

(i) elects to have such distribution paid directly to an eligible retirement plan, and

(ii) specifies the eligible retirement plan to which such distribution is to be paid (in such form and at such time as the plan administrator may prescribe),

such distribution shall be made in the form of a direct trustee-to-trustee transfer to the eligible retirement plan so specified.

(B) CERTAIN MANDATORY DISTRIBUTIONS.—

(i) IN GENERAL.—In case of a trust which is part of an eligible plan, such trust shall not constitute a qualified trust under this section unless the plan of which such trust is a part provides that if—

(I) a distribution described in clause (ii) in excess of $1,000 is made, and

(II) the distributee does not make an election under subparagraph (A) and does not elect to receive the distribution directly,

the plan administrator shall make such transfer to an individual retirement plan of a designated trustee or issuer and shall notify the distributee in writing (either separately or as part of the notice under section 402(f)) that the distribution may be transferred to another individual retirement plan.

(ii) ELIGIBLE PLAN.—For purposes of clause (i), the term "eligible plan" means a plan which provides that any nonforfeitable accrued benefit for which the present value (as determined under section 411(a)(11)) does not exceed $5,000 shall be immediately distributed to the participant.

(C) LIMITATION.—Subparagraphs (A) and (B) shall apply only to the extent that the eligible rollover distribution would be includible in gross income if not transferred as provided in subparagraph (A) (determined without regard to sections 402(c), 403(a)(4), 403(b)(8), and 457(e)(16)). The preceding sentence shall not apply to such distribution if the plan to which such distribution is transferred—

(i) is a qualified trust which is part of a plan which is a defined contribution plan and agrees to separately account for amounts so transferred, including separately accounting for the portion of such distribution which is includible in gross income and the portion of such distribution which is not so includible, or

(ii) is an eligible retirement plan described in clause (i) or (ii) of section 402(c)(8)(B).

(D) ELIGIBLE ROLLOVER DISTRIBUTION.—For purposes of this paragraph, the term "eligible rollover distribution" has the meaning given such term by section 402(f)(2)(A).

(E) ELIGIBLE RETIREMENT PLAN.—For purposes of this paragraph, the term "eligible retirement plan" has the meaning given such term by section 402(c)(8)(B), except that a qualified trust shall be considered an eligible retirement plan only if it is a defined contribution plan, the terms of which permit the acceptance of rollover distributions.

(32) TREATMENT OF FAILURE TO MAKE CERTAIN PAYMENTS IF PLAN HAS LIQUIDITY SHORTFALL.—

(A) IN GENERAL.—A trust forming part of a pension plan to which section 430(j)(4) applies shall not be treated as failing to constitute a qualified trust under this section merely because such plan ceases to make any payment described in subparagraph (B) during any period that such plan has a liquidity shortfall (as defined in section 430(j)(4)).

(B) PAYMENTS DESCRIBED.—A payment is described in this subparagraph if such payment is—

(i) any payment, in excess of the monthly amount paid under a single life annuity (plus any social security supplements described in the last sentence of section 411(a)(9)), to a participant or beneficiary whose annuity starting date (as defined in section 417(f)(2)) occurs during the period referred to in subparagraph (A),

(ii) any payment for the purchase of an irrevocable commitment from an insurer to pay benefits, and

(iii) any other payment specified by the Secretary by regulations.

(C) PERIOD OF SHORTFALL.—For purposes of this paragraph, a plan has a liquidity shortfall during the period that there is an underpayment of an installment under section 430(j)(3) by reason of section 430(j)(4)(A) thereof.

(33) PROHIBITION ON BENEFIT INCREASES WHILE SPONSOR IS IN BANKRUPTCY.—

(A) IN GENERAL.—A trust which is part of a plan to which this paragraph applies shall not constitute a qualified trust under this section if an amendment to such plan is adopted while the employer is a debtor in a case under title 11, United States Code, or similar Federal or State law, if such amendment increases liabilities of the plan by reason of—

(i) any increase in benefits,

(ii) any change in the accrual of benefits, or

(iii) any change in the rate at which benefits become nonforfeitable under the plan, with respect to employees of the debtor, and such amendment is effective prior to the effective date of such employer's plan of reorganization.

(B) EXCEPTIONS.—This paragraph shall not apply to any plan amendment if—

(i) the plan, were such amendment to take effect, would have a funding target attainment percentage (as defined in section 430(d)(2)) of 100 percent or more,

(ii) the Secretary determines that such amendment is reasonable and provides for only de minimis increases in the liabilities of the plan with respect to employees of the debtor,

(iii) such amendment only repeals an amendment described in section 412(d)(2), or

(iv) such amendment is required as a condition of qualification under this part.

(C) PLANS TO WHICH THIS PARAGRAPH APPLIES.—This paragraph shall apply only to plans (other than multiemployer plans) covered under section 4021 of the Employee Retirement Income Security Act of 1974.

(D) EMPLOYER.—For purposes of this paragraph, the term "employer" means the employer referred to in section 412(b)(1), without regard to section 412(b)(2).

(34) BENEFITS OF MISSING PARTICIPANTS ON PLAN TERMINATION.—In the case of a plan covered by title IV of the Employee Retirement Income Security Act of 1974, a trust forming part of such plan shall not be treated as failing to constitute a qualified trust under this section merely because the pension plan of which such trust is a part, upon its termination, transfers benefits of missing participants to the Pension Benefit Guaranty Corporation in accordance with section 4050 of such Act.

(35) DIVERSIFICATION REQUIREMENTS FOR CERTAIN DEFINED CONTRIBUTION PLANS.—

(A) IN GENERAL.—A trust which is part of an applicable defined contribution plan shall not be treated as a qualified trust unless the plan meets the diversification requirements of subparagraphs (B), (C), and (D).

(B) EMPLOYEE CONTRIBUTIONS AND ELECTIVE DEFERRALS INVESTED IN EMPLOYER SECURITIES.—In the case of the portion of an applicable individual's account attributable to employee contributions and elective deferrals which is invested in employer securities, a plan meets the requirements of this subparagraph if the applicable individual may elect to direct the plan to divest any such securities and to reinvest an equivalent amount in other investment options meeting the requirements of subparagraph (D).

(C) EMPLOYER CONTRIBUTIONS INVESTED IN EMPLOYER SECURITIES.—In the case of the portion of the account attributable to employer contributions other than elective deferrals which is invested in employer securities, a plan meets the requirements of this subparagraph if each applicable individual who—

(i) is a participant who has completed at least 3 years of service, or

(ii) is a beneficiary of a participant described in clause (i) or of a deceased participant,

may elect to direct the plan to divest any such securities and to reinvest an equivalent amount in other investment options meeting the requirements of subparagraph (D).

(D) INVESTMENT OPTIONS.—

(i) IN GENERAL.—The requirements of this subparagraph are met if the plan offers not less than 3 investment options, other than employer securities, to which an applicable individual may direct the proceeds from the divestment of employer securities pursuant to this paragraph, each of which is diversified and has materially different risk and return characteristics.

(ii) TREATMENT OF CERTAIN RESTRICTIONS AND CONDITIONS.—

(I) TIME FOR MAKING INVESTMENT CHOICES.—A plan shall not be treated as failing to meet the requirements of this subparagraph merely because the plan limits the time for divestment and reinvestment to periodic, reasonable opportunities occurring no less frequently than quarterly.

(II) CERTAIN RESTRICTIONS AND CONDITIONS NOT ALLOWED.—Except as provided in regulations, a plan shall not meet the requirements of this subparagraph if the plan imposes restrictions or conditions with respect to the investment of employer securities which are not imposed on the investment of other assets of the plan. This subclause shall not apply to any restrictions or conditions imposed by reason of the application of securities laws.

(E) APPLICABLE DEFINED CONTRIBUTION PLAN.—For purposes of this paragraph—

(i) IN GENERAL.—The term "applicable defined contribution plan" means any defined contribution plan which holds any publicly traded employer securities.

(ii) EXCEPTION FOR CERTAIN ESOPS.—Such term does not include an employee stock ownership plan if—

(I) there are no contributions to such plan (or earnings thereunder) which are held within such plan and are subject to subsection (k) or (m), and

(II) such plan is a separate plan for purposes of section 414(l) with respect to any other defined benefit plan or defined contribution plan maintained by the same employer or employers.

(iii) EXCEPTION FOR ONE PARTICIPANT PLANS.—Such term does not include a one-participant retirement plan.

(iv) ONE-PARTICIPANT RETIREMENT PLAN.—For purposes of clause (iii), the term "one-participant retirement plan" means a retirement plan that on the first day of the plan year—

(I) covered only one individual (or the individual and the individual's spouse) and the individual (or the individual and the individual's spouse) owned 100 percent of the plan sponsor (whether or not incorporated), or

(II) covered only one or more partners (or partners and their spouses) in the plan sponsor.

(F) CERTAIN PLANS TREATED AS HOLDING PUBLICLY TRADED EMPLOYER SECURITIES.—

(i) IN GENERAL.—Except as provided in regulations or in clause (ii), a plan holding employer securities which are not publicly traded employer securities shall be treated as holding publicly traded employer securities if any employer corporation, or any member of a controlled group of corporations which includes such employer corporation, has issued a class of stock which is a publicly traded employer security.

(ii) EXCEPTION FOR CERTAIN CONTROLLED GROUPS WITH PUBLICLY TRADED SECURITIES.—Clause (i) shall not apply to a plan if—

(I) no employer corporation, or parent corporation of an employer corporation, has issued any publicly traded employer security, and

(II) no employer corporation, or parent corporation of an employer corporation, has issued any special class of stock which grants particular rights to, or bears particular risks for, the holder or issuer with respect to any corporation described in clause (i) which has issued any publicly traded employer security.

(iii) DEFINITIONS.—For purposes of this subparagraph, the term—

(I) "controlled group of corporations" has the meaning given such term by section 1563(a), except that "50 percent" shall be substituted for "80 percent" each place it appears,

(II) "employer corporation" means a corporation which is an employer maintaining the plan, and

(III) "parent corporation" has the meaning given such term by section 424(e).

(G) OTHER DEFINITIONS.—For purposes of this paragraph—

(i) APPLICABLE INDIVIDUAL.—The term "applicable individual" means—

(I) any participant in the plan, and

(II) any beneficiary who has an account under the plan with respect to which the beneficiary is entitled to exercise the rights of a participant.

(ii) ELECTIVE DEFERRAL.—The term "elective deferral" means an employer contribution described in section 402(g)(3)(A).

(iii) EMPLOYER SECURITY.—The term "employer security" has the meaning given such term by section 407(d)(1) of the Employee Retirement Income Security Act of 1974.

(iv) EMPLOYEE STOCK OWNERSHIP PLAN.—The term "employee stock ownership plan" has the meaning given such term by section 4975(e)(7).

(v) PUBLICLY TRADED EMPLOYER SECURITIES.—The term "publicly traded employer securities" means employer securities which are readily tradable on an established securities market.

(vi) YEAR OF SERVICE.—The term "year of service" has the meaning given such term by section 411(a)(5).

(H) TRANSITION RULE FOR SECURITIES ATTRIBUTABLE TO EMPLOYER CONTRIBUTIONS.—

(i) RULES PHASED IN OVER 3 YEARS.—

(I) IN GENERAL.—In the case of the portion of an account to which subparagraph (C) applies and which consists of employer securities acquired in a plan year beginning before January 1, 2007, subparagraph (C) shall only apply to the applicable percentage of such securities. This subparagraph shall be applied separately with respect to each class of securities.

(II) EXCEPTION FOR CERTAIN PARTICIPANTS AGED 55 OR OVER.—Subclause (I) shall not apply to an applicable individual who is a participant who has attained age 55 and completed at least 3 years of service before the first plan year beginning after December 31, 2005.

(ii) APPLICABLE PERCENTAGE.—For purposes of clause (i), the applicable percentage shall be determined as follows:

Plan year to which subparagraph (C) applies:	The applicable percentage is:
1st	33
2d	66
3d and following	100.

(36) DISTRIBUTIONS DURING WORKING RETIREMENT.—A trust forming part of a pension plan shall not be treated as failing to constitute a qualified trust under this section solely because the plan provides that a distribution may be made from such trust to an employee who has attained age 62 and who is not separated from employment at the time of such distribution.

(37) DEATH BENEFITS UNDER USERRA-QUALIFIED ACTIVE MILITARY SERVICE.—A trust shall not constitute a qualified trust unless the plan provides that, in the case of a participant who dies while performing qualified military service (as defined in section 414(u)), the survivors of the participant are entitled to any additional benefits (other than benefit accruals relating to the period of qualified military service) provided under the plan had the participant resumed and then terminated employment on account of death.

Paragraphs (11), (12), (13), (14), (15), (19), and (20) shall apply only in the case of a plan to which section 411 (relating to minimum vesting standards) applies without regard to subsection (e)(2) of such section.

Amendments

• 2008, Worker, Retiree, and Employer Recovery Act of 2008 (P.L. 110-458)

P.L. 110-458, §101(d)(2)(A):

Amended the heading of Code Sec. 401(a)(29) by striking "ON PLANS IN AT-RISK STATUS" following "BENEFIT LIMITATIONS". **Effective** as if included in the provision of the 2006 Act to which the amendment relates [**effective** for plan years beginning after 2007.—CCH].

P.L. 110-458, §101(d)(2)(B)(i)-(ii):

Amended Code Sec. 401(a)(32)(C) by striking "section 430(j)" and inserting "section 430(j)(3)", and by striking "paragraph (5)(A)" and inserting "section 430(j)(4)(A)". **Effective** as if included in the provision of the 2006 Act to which the amendment relates [**effective** for plan years beginning after 2007.—CCH].

P.L. 110-458, §101(d)(2)(C)(i)-(ii):

Amended Code Sec. 401(a)(33) by striking "section 412(c)(2)" in subparagraph (B)(iii) and inserting "section 412(d)(2)", and by striking "section 412(b)(2) (without regard to subparagraph (B) thereof)" in subparagraph (D) and inserting "section 412(b)(1), without regard to section 412(b)(2)". **Effective** as if included in the provision of the 2006 Act to which the amendment relates [**effective** for plan years beginning after 2007.—CCH].

P.L. 110-458, §109(a):

Amended Code Sec. 401(a)(35)(E)(iv). **Effective** as if included in the provision of the 2006 Act to which the amendment relates For the **effective** date, see §901(c) of the Pension Protection Act of 2006 (P.L. 109-280).—CCH]. Prior to amendment, Code Sec. 401(a)(35)(E)(iv) read as follows:

(iv) ONE-PARTICIPANT RETIREMENT PLAN.—For purposes of clause (iii), the term "one-participant retirement plan" means a retirement plan that—

(I) on the first day of the plan year covered only one individual (or the individual and the individual's spouse) and the individual owned 100 percent of the plan sponsor (whether or not incorporated), or covered only one or more partners (or partners and their spouses) in the plan sponsor,

(II) meets the minimum coverage requirements of section 410(b) without being combined with any other plan of the business that covers the employees of the business,

(III) does not provide benefits to anyone except the individual (and the individual's spouse) or the partners (and their spouses),

(IV) does not cover a business that is a member of an affiliated service group, a controlled group of corporations, or a group of businesses under common control, and

(V) does not cover a business that uses the services of leased employees (within the meaning of section 414(n)).

For purposes of this clause, the term "partner" includes a 2-percent shareholder (as defined in section 1372(b)) of an S corporation.

P.L. 110-458, §201(a):

Amended Code Sec. 401(a)(9) by adding at the end a new subparagraph (H). **Effective** generally for calendar years beginning after 12-31-2008. For a special rule, see Act Sec. 201(c)(2), below.

P.L. 110-458, §201(c)(2), provides:

(2) PROVISIONS RELATING TO PLAN OR CONTRACT AMENDMENTS.—

(A) IN GENERAL.—If this paragraph applies to any pension plan or contract amendment, such pension plan or contract shall not fail to be treated as being operated in accordance with the terms of the plan during the period described in subparagraph (B)(ii) solely because the plan operates in accordance with this section.

(B) AMENDMENTS TO WHICH PARAGRAPH APPLIES.—

(i) IN GENERAL.—This paragraph shall apply to any amendment to any pension plan or annuity contract which—

(I) is made pursuant to the amendments made by this section, and

(II) is made on or before the last day of the first plan year beginning on or after January 1, 2011.

In the case of a governmental plan, subclause (II) shall be applied by substituting "2012" for "2011".

(ii) CONDITIONS.—This paragraph shall not apply to any amendment unless during the period beginning on the effective date of the amendment and ending on December 31, 2009, the plan or contract is operated as if such plan or contract amendment were in effect.

• 2008, Heroes Earnings Assistance and Relief Tax Act of 2008 (P.L. 110-245)

P.L. 110-245, §104(a):

Amended Code Sec. 401(a) by inserting after paragraph (36) a new paragraph (37). **Effective** generally with respect to deaths and disabilities occurring on or after 1-1-2007. For a special rule, see Act Sec. 104(d)(2), below.

P.L. 110-245, §104(d)(2), provides:

(2) PROVISIONS RELATING TO PLAN AMENDMENTS.—

(A) IN GENERAL.—If this subparagraph applies to any plan or contract amendment, such plan or contract shall be treated as being operated in accordance with the terms of the plan during the period described in subparagraph (B)(iii).

(B) AMENDMENTS TO WHICH SUBPARAGRAPH (A) APPLIES.—

(i) IN GENERAL.—Subparagraph (A) shall apply to any amendment to any plan or annuity contract which is made—

(I) pursuant to the amendments made by subsection (a) or pursuant to any regulation issued by the Secretary of the Treasury under subsection (a), and

(II) on or before the last day of the first plan year beginning on or after January 1, 2010.

In the case of a governmental plan (as defined in section 414(d) of the Internal Revenue Code of 1986), this clause shall be applied by substituting "2012" for "2010" in subclause (II).

(ii) CONDITIONS.—This paragraph shall not apply to any amendment unless—

(I) the plan or contract is operated as if such plan or contract amendment were in effect for the period described in clause (iii), and

(II) such plan or contract amendment applies retroactively for such period.

(iii) PERIOD DESCRIBED.—The period described in this clause is the period—

(I) beginning on the effective date specified by the plan, and

(II) ending on the date described in clause (i)(II) (or, if earlier, the date the plan or contract amendment is adopted).

• 2006, Pension Protection Act of 2006 (P.L. 109-280)

P.L. 109-280, §114(a)(1):

Amended Code Sec. 401(a)(29). **Effective** for plan years beginning after 2007 [**effective** date amended by P.L. 110-458, §101(d)(3).—CCH]. Prior to amendment, Code Sec. 401(a)(29) read as follows:

(29) SECURITY REQUIRED UPON ADOPTION OF PLAN AMENDMENT RESULTING IN SIGNIFICANT UNDERFUNDING.—

(A) IN GENERAL.—If—

(i) a defined benefit plan (other than a multiemployer plan) to which the requirements of section 412 apply adopts an amendment an effect of which is to increase current liability under the plan for a plan year, and

(ii) the funded current liability percentage of the plan for the plan year in which the amendment takes effect is less than 60 percent, including the amount of the unfunded current liability under the plan attributable to the plan amendment,

the trust of which such plan is a part shall not constitute a qualified trust under this subsection unless such amendment does not take effect until the contributing sponsor (or any member of the controlled group of the contributing sponsor) provides security to the plan.

(B) FORM OF SECURITY.—The security required under subparagraph (A) shall consist of—

(i) a bond issued by a corporate surety company that is an acceptable surety for purposes of section 412 of the Employee Retirement Income Security Act of 1974,

(ii) cash, or United States obligations which mature in 3 years or less, held in escrow by a bank or similar financial institution, or

(iii) such other form of security as is satisfactory to the Secretary and the parties involved.

(C) AMOUNT OF SECURITY.—The security shall be in an amount equal to the excess of—

(i) the lesser of—

(I) the amount of additional plan assets which would be necessary to increase the funded current liability percentage under the plan to 60 percent, including the amount of the unfunded current liability under the plan attributable to the plan amendment, or

(II) The amount of the increase in current liability under the plan attributable to the plan amendment and any other plan amendments adopted after December 22, 1987, and before such plan amendment, over

(ii) $10,000,000.

(D) RELEASE OF SECURITY.—The security shall be released (and any amounts thereunder shall be refunded together with any interest accrued thereon) at the end of the first plan year which ends after the provision of the security and for which the funded current liability percentage under the plan is not less than 60 percent. The Secretary may prescribe regulations for partial releases of the security by reason of increases in the funded current liability percentage.

(E) DEFINITIONS.—For purposes of this paragraph, the terms "current liability", "funded current liability percentage", and "unfunded current liability" shall have the meanings given such terms by section 412(l), except that in computing unfunded current liability there shall not be taken into account any unamortized portion of the unfunded old liability amount as of the close of the plan year.

P.L. 109-280, §114(a)(2)(A)-(B):

Amended Code Sec. 401(a)(32) by striking "[section]412(m)(5)" each place it appears and inserting "section 430(j)(4)" in subparagraph (A), and by striking "section 412(m)" and inserting "section 430(j)" in subparagraph (C). **Effective** for plan years beginning after 2007 [**effective** date amended by P.L. 110-458, §101(d)(3).—CCH].

P.L. 109-280, §114(a)(3)(A)-(C):

Amended Code Sec. 401(a)(33) by striking "funded current liability percentage (within the meaning of [as defined in] section 412(l)(8))" and inserting "funding target attainment percentage (as defined in section 430(d)(2))" in subparagraph (B)(i), by striking "subsection 412(c)(8)" and inserting "section 412(c)(2)" in subparagraph (B)(iii), and by striking "section 412(c)(11) (without regard to subparagraph (B) thereof)" and inserting "section 412(b)(2) (without regard to subparagraph (B) thereof)" in subparagraph (D). **Effective** for plan years beginning after 2007 [**effective** date amended by P.L. 110-458, §101(d)(3).—CCH].

P.L. 109-280, §811, provides:

SEC. 811. PENSIONS AND INDIVIDUAL RETIREMENT ARRANGEMENT PROVISIONS OF ECONOMIC GROWTH AND TAX RELIEF RECONCILIATION ACT OF 2001 MADE PERMANENT.

Title IX of the Economic Growth and Tax Relief Reconciliation Act of 2001 [P.L. 107-16] shall not apply to the provisions of, and amendments made by, subtitles A through F of title VI [§§601-666]of such Act (relating to pension and individual retirement arrangement provisions).

P.L. 109-280, §823, provides:

SEC. 823. CLARIFICATION OF MINIMUM DISTRIBUTION RULES FOR GOVERNMENTAL PLANS.

The Secretary of the Treasury shall issue regulations under which a governmental plan (as defined in section 414(d) of the Internal Revenue Code of 1986) shall, for all years to which section 401(a)(9) of such Code applies to such plan, be treated as having complied with such section 401(a)(9) if such plan complies with a reasonable good faith interpretation of such section 401(a)(9).

P.L. 109-280, §861(a)(1):

Amended Code Sec. 401(a)(5)(G) by striking "section 414(d))" and all that follows and inserting "section 414(d)).". **Effective** for any year beginning after 8-17-2006. Prior to amendment, Code Sec. 401(a)(5)(G) read as follows:

(G) STATE AND LOCAL GOVERNMENTAL PLANS.—Paragraphs (3) and (4) shall not apply to a governmental plan (within the meaning of section 414(d)) maintained by a State or local government or political subdivision thereof (or agency or instrumentality thereof).

P.L. 109-280, §861(a)(1):

Amended Code Sec. 401(a)(26)(G) by striking "section 414(d))" and all that follows and inserting "section 414(d)).". **Effective** for any year beginning after 8-17-2006. Prior to amendment, Code Sec. 401(a)(26)(G) read as follows:

(G) EXCEPTION FOR STATE AND LOCAL GOVERNMENTAL PLANS.—This paragraph shall not apply to a governmental plan (within the meaning of section 414(d)) maintained by a State or local government or political subdivision thereof (or agency or instrumentality thereof).

P.L. 109-280, §861(b)(1):

Amended the heading of Code Sec. 401(a)(5)(G) by striking "STATE AND LOCAL GOVERNMENTAL" and inserting "GOVERNMENTAL". **Effective** for any year beginning after 8-17-2006.

P.L. 109-280, §861(b)(2):

Amended the heading of Code Sec. 401(a)(26)(G) by striking "EXCEPTION FOR STATE AND LOCAL" and inserting "EXCEPTION FOR". **Effective** for any year beginning after 8-17-2006.

P.L. 109-280, §865, provides:

SEC. 865. GRANDFATHER RULE FOR CHURCH PLANS WHICH SELF-ANNUITIZE.

(a) IN GENERAL.—In the case of any plan year ending after the date of the enactment of this Act, annuity payments provided with respect to any account maintained for a participant or beneficiary under a qualified church plan shall not fail to satisfy the requirements of section 401(a)(9) of the Internal Revenue Code of 1986 merely because the payments are not made under an annuity contract purchased from an insurance company if such payments would not fail such requirements if provided with respect to a retirement income account described in section 403(b)(9) of such Code.

(b) QUALIFIED CHURCH PLAN.—For purposes of this section, the term "qualified church plan" means any money purchase pension plan described in section 401(a) of such Code which—

(1) is a church plan (as defined in section 414(e) of such Code) with respect to which the election provided by section 410(d) of such Code has not been made, and

(2) was in existence on April 17, 2002.

P.L. 109-280, §901(a)(1):

Amended Code Sec. 401(a) by inserting after paragraph (34) a new paragraph (35). For the **effective** date, see Act Sec. 901(c), below.

P.L. 109-280, §901(a)(2)(A):

Amended Code Sec. 401(a)(28)(B) by adding at the end a new clause (v). For the **effective** date, see Act Sec. 901(c), below.

P.L. 109-280, §901(c), provides:

(c) EFFECTIVE DATES.—

(1) IN GENERAL.—Except as provided in paragraphs (2) and (3), the amendments made by this section shall apply to plan years beginning after December 31, 2006.

(2) SPECIAL RULE FOR COLLECTIVELY BARGAINED AGREEMENTS.—In the case of a plan maintained pursuant to 1 or more collective bargaining agreements between employee representatives and 1 or more employers ratified on or before the date of the enactment of this Act, paragraph (1) shall be applied to benefits pursuant to, and individuals covered by, any such agreement by substituting for "December 31, 2006" the earlier of—

(A) the later of—

(i) December 31, 2007, or

(ii) the date on which the last of such collective bargaining agreements terminates (determined without regard to any extension thereof after such date of enactment), or

(B) December 31, 2008.

(3) SPECIAL RULE FOR CERTAIN EMPLOYER SECURITIES HELD IN AN ESOP.—

(A) IN GENERAL.—In the case of employer securities to which this paragraph applies, the amendments made by this section shall apply to plan years beginning after the earlier of—

(i) December 31, 2007, or

(ii) the first date on which the fair market value of such securities exceeds the guaranteed minimum value described in subparagraph (B)(ii).

(B) APPLICABLE SECURITIES.—This paragraph shall apply to employer securities which are attributable to employer contributions other than elective deferrals, and which, on September 17, 2003—

(i) consist of preferred stock, and

(ii) are within an employee stock ownership plan (as defined in section 4975(e)(7) of the Internal Revenue Code of 1986), the terms of which provide that the value of the securities cannot be less than the guaranteed minimum value specified by the plan on such date.

(C) COORDINATION WITH TRANSITION RULE.—In applying section 401(a)(35)(H) of the Internal Revenue Code of 1986 and section 204(j)(7) of the Employee Retirement Income Security Act of 1974 (as added by this section) to employer securities to which this paragraph applies, the applicable percentage shall be determined without regard to this paragraph.

P.L. 109-280, §905(b):

Amended Code Sec. 401(a), as amended by this Act, by inserting after paragraph (35) a new paragraph (36). **Effective** for distributions in plan years beginning after 12-31-2006.

• 2005, Katrina Emergency Tax Relief Act of 2005 (P.L. 109-73)

P.L. 109-73, §101(f)(1) [repealed by P.L. 109-135, §201(b)(4)(A)], provides:

(1) EXEMPTION OF DISTRIBUTIONS FROM TRUSTEE TO TRUSTEE TRANSFER AND WITHHOLDING RULES.—For purposes of sections 401(a)(31), 402(f), and 3405 of such Code, qualified Hurricane Katrina distributions shall not be treated as eligible rollover distributions.

• 2004 (P.L. 108-476)

P.L. 108-476, §1, provides:

SECTION 1. CERTAIN ARRANGEMENTS MAINTAINED BY THE YMCA RETIREMENT FUND TREATED AS CHURCH PLANS.

(a) RETIREMENT PLANS.—

(1) IN GENERAL.—For purposes of sections 401(a) and 403(b) of the Internal Revenue Code of 1986, any retirement plan maintained by the YMCA Retirement Fund as of January 1, 2003, shall be treated as a church plan (within the meaning of section 414(e) of such Code) which is maintained by an organization described in section 414(e)(3)(A) of such Code.

(2) TAX-DEFERRED RETIREMENT PLAN.—In the case of a retirement plan described in paragraph (1) which allows contributions to be made under a salary reduction agreement—

(A) such treatment shall not apply for purposes of section 415(c)(7) of such Code, and

(B) any account maintained for a participant or beneficiary of such plan shall be treated for purposes of such Code as a retirement income account described in section 403(b)(9) of such Code, except that such account shall not, for purposes of section 403(b)(12) of such Code, be treated as a contract purchased by a church for purposes of section 403(b)(1)(D) of such Code.

(3) MONEY PURCHASE PENSION PLAN.—In the case of a retirement plan described in paragraph (1) which is subject to the requirements of section 401(a) of such Code—

(A) such plan (but not any reserves held by the YMCA Retirement Fund)—

(i) shall be treated for purposes of such Code as a defined contribution plan which is a money purchase pension plan, and

(ii) shall be treated as having made an election under section 410(d) of such Code for plan years beginning after December 31, 2005, except that notwithstanding the election—

(I) nothing in the Employee Retirement Income Security Act of 1974 or such Code shall prohibit the YMCA Retirement Fund from commingling for investment purposes the assets of the electing plan with the assets of such Fund and with the assets of any employee benefit plan maintained by such Fund, and

(II) nothing in this section shall be construed as subjecting any assets described in subclause (I), other than the assets of the electing plan, to any provision of such Act,

(B) notwithstanding section 401(a)(11) or 417 of such Code or section 205 of such Act, such plan may offer a lump-sum distribution option to participants who have not attained age 55 without offering such participants an annuity option, and

(C) any account maintained for a participant or beneficiary of such plan shall, for purposes of section 401(a)(9) of such Code, be treated as a retirement income account described in section 403(b)(9) of such Code.

(4) SELF-FUNDED DEATH BENEFIT PLAN.—For purposes of section 7702(j) of such Code, a retirement plan described in paragraph (1) shall be treated as an arrangement described in section 7702(j)(2).

(b) YMCA RETIREMENT FUND.—For purposes of this section, the term "YMCA Retirement Fund" means the Young Men's Christian Association Retirement Fund, a corporation created by an Act of the State of New York which became law on April 30, 1921.

(c) EFFECTIVE DATE.—This section shall apply to plan years beginning after December 31, 2003.

• 2004, Working Families Tax Relief Act of 2004 (P.L. 108-311)

P.L. 108-311, §407(b):

Amended Code Sec. 401(a)(26) by striking subparagraph (C) and by resdesignating subparagraphs (D) through (I) as subparagraphs (C) through (H), respectively. **Effective** as if included in the provision of the Small Business Job Protection Act of 1996 (P.L. 104-188) to which it relates [**effective** for years beginning after 12-31-1996.—CCH]. Prior to being stricken, Code Sec. 401(a)(26)(C) read as follows:

(C) ELIGIBILITY TO PARTICIPATE.—In the case of contributions under section 401(k) or 401(m), employees who are eligible to contribute (or may elect to have contributions made on their behalf) shall be treated as benefiting under the plan.

• 2002, Job Creation and Worker Assistance Act of 2002 (P.L. 107-147)

P.L. 107-147, §411(o)(2):

Amended Code Sec. 401(a)(30) by striking "402(g)(1)" and inserting "402(g)(1)(A)". **Effective** as if included in the provision of P.L. 107-16 to which it relates [**effective** for contributions in tax years beginning after 12-31-2001.—CCH].

P.L. 107-147, §411(q)(1):

Amended Code Sec. 401(a)(31)(C)(i) by inserting "is a qualified trust which is part of a plan which is a defined contribution plan and" before "agrees". **Effective** as if included in the provision of P.L. 107-16 to which it relates [applicable to distributions made after 12-31-2001.—CCH].

• 2001, Economic Growth and Tax Relief Reconciliation Act of 2001 (P.L. 107-16)

P.L. 107-16, §611(c)(1):

Amended Code Sec. 401(a)(17) by striking "$150,000" each place it appears and inserting "$200,000". **Effective** for years beginning after 12-31-2001. For a special rule, see Act Sec. 611(i)(3), below.

P.L. 107-16, §611(c)(2)(A)-(B):

Amended Code Sec. 401(a)(17)(B) by striking "October 1, 1993" and inserting "July 1, 2001", and by striking "$10,000" both places it appears and inserting "$5,000". **Effective** for years beginning after 12-31-2001. For a special rule, see Act Sec. 611(i)(3), below.

P.L. 107-16, §611(i)(3), as added by P.L. 107-147, §411(j)(3), provides:

(3) SPECIAL RULE.—In the case of plan that, on June 7, 2001, incorporated by reference the limitation of section 415(b)(1)(A) of the Internal Revenue Code of 1986, section 411(d)(6) of such Code and section 204(g)(1) of the Employee Retirement Income Security Act of 1974 do not apply to a plan amendment that—

(A) is adopted on or before June 30, 2002,

(B) reduces benefits to the level that would have applied without regard to the amendments made by subsection (a) of this section, and

(C) is effective no earlier than the years described in paragraph (2).

P.L. 107-16, §641(e)(3):

Amended Code Sec. 401(a)(31)(B) by striking "and 403(a)(4)" and inserting ", 403(a)(4), 403(b)(8), and 457(e)(16)". **Effective**, generally, for distributions after 12-31-2001. For a special rule, see Act Sec. 641(f)(3), below.

P.L. 107-16, §641(f)(3), provides:

(3) SPECIAL RULE.—Notwithstanding any other provision of law, subsections (h)(3) and (h)(5) of section 1122 of the Tax Reform Act of 1986 shall not apply to any distribution from an eligible retirement plan (as defined in clause (iii) or (iv) of section 402(c)(8)(B) of the Internal Revenue Code of 1986) on behalf of an individual if there was a rollover to such plan on behalf of such individual which is permitted solely by reason of any amendment made by this section.

P.L. 107-16, §643(b):

Amended Code Sec. 401(a)(31)(B) by adding at the end a new sentence containing (i) and (ii). **Effective** for distributions made after 12-31-2001.

P.L. 107-16, §657(a)(1):

Amended Code Sec. 401(a)(31), as amended by Act Sec. 643, by redesignating subparagraphs (B), (C), and (D) as subparagraphs (C), (D), and (E), respectively, and by inserting after subparagraph (A) a new subparagraph (B). **Effective** for distributions made after final regulations implementing Act Sec. 657(c)(2)(A) are prescribed.

P.L. 107-16, §657(a)(2)(A):

Amended the heading of Code Sec. 401(a)(31) by striking "OPTIONAL DIRECT" and inserting "DIRECT". **E ffective** for distributions made after final regulations implementing Act Sec. 657(c)(2)(A) are prescribed.

P.L. 107-16, §657(a)(2)(B):

Amended Code Sec. 401(a)(31)(C), as redesignated by Act Sec. 657(a)(1), by striking "Subparagraph (A)" and inserting "Subparagraphs (A) and (B)". **Effective** for distributions made after final regulations implementing Act Sec. 657(c)(2)(A) are prescribed.

P.L. 107-16, §657(c)(2), provides:

(2) REGULATIONS.—

(A) AUTOMATIC ROLLOVER SAFE HARBOR.—Not later than 3 years after the date of enactment of this Act, the Secretary of Labor shall prescribe regulations providing for safe harbors under which the designation of an institution and investment of funds in accordance with section 401(a)(31)(B) of the Internal Revenue Code of 1986 is deemed to satisfy the fiduciary requirements of section 404(a) of the Employee Retirement Income Security Act of 1974 (29 U.S.C. 1104(a)).

(B) USE OF LOW-COST INDIVIDUAL RETIREMENT PLANS.—The Secretary of the Treasury and the Secretary of Labor may provide, and shall give consideration to providing, special relief with respect to the use of low-cost individual retirement plans for purposes of transfers under section 401(a)(31)(B) of the Internal Revenue Code of 1986 and for other uses that promote the preservation of assets for retirement income purposes.

P.L. 107-16, §901(a)-(b), provides [but see P.L. 109-280, §811, above]:

SEC. 901. SUNSET OF PROVISIONS OF ACT.

(a) IN GENERAL.—All provisions of, and amendments made by, this Act shall not apply—

(1) to taxable, plan, or limitation years beginning after December 31, 2010, or

(2) in the case of title V, to estates of decedents dying, gifts made, or generation skipping transfers, after December 31, 2010.

(b) APPLICATION OF CERTAIN LAWS.—The Internal Revenue Code of 1986 and the Employee Retirement Income Security Act of 1974 shall be applied and administered to years, estates, gifts, and transfers described in subsection (a) as if the provisions and amendments described in subsection (a) had never been enacted.

• 1997, Taxpayer Relief Act of 1997 (P.L. 105-34)

P.L. 105-34, §1502(b):

Amended Code Sec. 401(a)(13) by adding at the end new subparagraphs (C)-(D). **Effective** for judgments, orders, and decrees issued, and settlement agreements entered into, on or after 8-5-97.

P.L. 105-34, §1505(a)(1):

Amended Code Sec. 401(a)(5) by adding at the end a new subparagraph (G). **Effective** for tax years beginning on or after 8-5-97. For a special rule, see Act Sec. 1505(d)(2), below.

P.L. 105-34, §1505(a)(2):

Amended Code Sec. 401(a)(26)(H). **Effective** for tax years beginning on or after 8-5-97. For a special rule, see Act Sec. 1505(d)(2), below. Prior to amendment, Code Sec. 401(a)(26)(H) read as follows:

(H) SPECIAL RULE FOR CERTAIN POLICE OR FIREFIGHTERS.—

(i) IN GENERAL.—An employer may elect to have this paragraph applied separately with respect to any classification of qualified public safety employees for whom a separate plan is maintained.

(ii) QUALIFIED PUBLIC SAFETY EMPLOYEE.—For purposes of this subparagraph, the term "qualified public safety employee" means any employee of any police department or fire department organized and operated by a State or political subdivision if the employee provides police protection, firefighting services, or emergency medical services for any area within the jurisdiction of such State or political subdivision.

P.L. 105-34, §1505(d)(2), as amended by P.L. 105-206, §6015(b), and further amended by P.L. 109-280, §861(a)(2), provides:

(2) TREATMENT FOR YEARS BEGINNING BEFORE DATE OF ENACTMENT.—A governmental plan (within the meaning of section 414(d) of the Internal Revenue Code of 1986) shall be treated

as satisfying the requirements of sections 401(a)(3), 401(a)(4), 401(a)(26), 401(k), 401(m), 403(b)(1)(D) and (b)(12)(A)(i), and 410 of such Code for all taxable years beginning before the date of enactment of this Act.

P.L. 105-34, §1530(c)(1):

Amended Code Sec. 401(a)(1) by inserting "or by a charitable remainder trust pursuant to a qualified gratuitous transfer (as defined in section 664(g)(1)), after "stock bonus plans),". **Effective** for transfers made by trusts to, or for the use of, an employee stock ownership plan after 8-5-97.

• 1996, Small Business Job Protection Act of 1996 (P.L. 104-188)

P.L. 104-188, §1401(b)(5):

Amended Code Sec. 401(a)(28)(B) by striking clause (v). **Effective,** generally, for tax years beginning after 12-31-99. For a special transitional rule, see Act Sec. 1401(c)(2) in the amendment notes following Code Sec. 402(d). Prior to being stricken, Code Sec. 401(a)(28)(B)(v) read as follows:

(v) COORDINATION WITH DISTRIBUTION RULES.—Any distribution required by this subparagraph shall not be taken into account in determining whether a subsequent distribution is a lump sum distribution under section 402(d)(4)(A) or in determining whether section 402(c)(10) applies.

P.L. 104-188, §1404(a):

Amended Code Sec. 401(a)(9)(C). **Effective** for years beginning after 12-31-96. Prior to amendment, Code Sec. 401(a)(9)(C) read as follows:

(C) REQUIRED BEGINNING DATE.—For purposes of this paragraph, the term "required beginning date" means April 1 of the calendar year following the calendar year in which the employee attains age 70½. In the case of a governmental plan or church plan, the required beginning date shall be the later of the date determined under the preceding sentence or April 1 of the calendar year following the calendar year in which the employee retires. For purposes of this subparagraph, the term "church plan" means a plan maintained by a church for church employees, and the term "church" means any church (as defined in section 3121(w)(3)(A)) or qualified church-controlled organization (as defined in section 3121(w)(3)(B)).

P.L. 104-188, §1431(b)(2):

Amended Code Sec. 401(a)(17)(A) by striking the last sentence. **Effective** for years beginning after 12-31-96. Prior to amendment, the last sentence of Code Sec. 401(a)(17)(A) read as follows:

In determining the compensation of an employee, the rules of section 414(q)(6) shall apply, except that in applying such rules, the term "family" shall include only the spouse of the employee and any lineal descendants of the employee who have not attained age 19 before the close of the year.

P.L. 104-188, §1431(c)(1)(B):

Amended Code Sec. 401(a)(5)(D)(ii) by striking "section 414(q)(7)" and inserting "section 414(q)(4)". **Effective** for years beginning after 12-31-96, except that in determining whether an employee is a highly compensated employee for years beginning in 1997, this amendment is treated as having been in effect for years beginning in 1996.

P.L. 104-188, §1432(a):

Amended Code Sec. 401(a)(26)(A). **Effective** for years beginning after 12-31-96. Prior to amendment, Code Sec. 401(a)(26)(A) read as follows:

(A) IN GENERAL.—A trust shall not constitute a qualified trust under this subsection unless such trust is part of a plan which on each day of the plan year benefits the lesser of—

(i) 50 employees of the employer, or

(ii) 40 percent or more of all employees of the employer.

P.L. 104-188, §1432(b):

Amended Code Sec. 401(a)(26)(G) by striking "paragraph (7)" and inserting "paragraph (2)(A) or (7)". **Effective** for years beginning after 12-31-96.

P.L. 104-188, §1445(a):

Amended Code Sec. 401(a)(5) by adding at the end a new subparagraph (F). **Effective** for years beginning after 12-31-96.

P.L. 104-188, §1704(t)(67):

Amended Code Sec. 401(a)(20) by striking "section 211" in the last sentence and inserting "section 521". **Effective** 8-20-96.

• 1994, Uruguay Round Agreements Act (P.L. 103-465)

P.L. 103-465, §732(a):

Amended Code Sec. 401(a)(17)(B). **Effective** for years beginning after 12-31-94. See also, Act. Sec. 732(e)(2), below. Prior to amendment, Code Sec. 401(a)(17)(B) read as follows:

(B) COST-OF-LIVING ADJUSTMENT.—

(i) IN GENERAL.—If, for any calendar year after 1994, the excess (if any) of—

(I) $150,000, increased by the cost-of-living adjustment for the calendar year, over

(II) the dollar amount in effect under subparagraph (A) for taxable years beginning in the calendar year, is equal to or greater than $10,000, then the $150,000 amount under subparagraph (A) (as previously adjusted under this subparagraph) for any taxable year beginning in any subsequent calendar year shall be increased by the amount of such excess, rounded to the next lowest multiple of $10,000.

(ii) COST-OF-LIVING ADJUSTMENT.—The cost-of-living adjustment for any calendar year shall be the adjustment made under section 415(d) for such calendar year, except that the base period for purposes of section 415(d)(1)(A) shall be the calendar quarter beginning October 1, 1993.

P.L. 103-465, §732(e)(2), provides:

(2) ROUNDING NOT TO RESULT IN DECREASES.—The amendments made by this section providing for the rounding of indexed amounts shall not apply to any year to the extent the rounding would require the indexed amount to be reduced below the amount in effect for years beginning in 1994.

P.L. 103-465, §751(a)(9)(C):

Amended Code Sec. 401(a) by adding at the end a new paragraph (32). **Effective** for plan years beginning after 12-31-94.

P.L. 103-465, §766(b):

Amended Code Sec. 401(a), as amended by Act Sec. 751(a)(9)(C), by adding at the end a new paragraph (33). **Effective** for plan amendments adopted on or after 12-8-94.

P.L. 103-465, §776(d):

Amended Code Sec. 401(a), as amended by Act Sec. 766(b), by inserting after paragraph (33) a new paragraph (34). **Effective** with respect to distributions that occur in plan years commencing after final regulations implementing these provisions are prescribed by the Pension Benefit Guaranty Corporation.

• 1993, Omnibus Budget Reconciliation Act of 1993 (P.L. 103-66)

P.L. 103-66, §13212(a)(1)(A)-(C):

Amended Code Sec. 401(a)(17) by striking "$200,000" in the first sentence and inserting "$150,000", by striking the second sentence, and by adding at the end thereof new subparagraph (B). **Effective**, generally, for benefits accruing in plan years beginning after 12-31-93. However, for special rules see Act Sec. 13212(d)(2)-(3) below. Prior to amendment, the second sentence of Code Sec. 401(a)(17) read as follows:

The Secretary shall adjust the $200,000 amount at the same time and in the same manner as under section 415(d).

P.L. 103-66, §13212(a)(2):

Amended Code Sec. 401(a)(17) by striking "(17) A trust" and inserting:

(17) COMPENSATION LIMIT.—

(A) IN GENERAL.—A trust. **Effective**, generally, for benefits accruing in plan years beginning after 12-31-93. However, for special rules see Act Sec. 13212(d)(2)-(3), below.

P.L. 103-66, §13212(d)(2)-(3), provides:

(2) COLLECTIVELY BARGAINED PLANS.—In the case of a plan maintained pursuant to 1 or more collective bargaining agreements between employee representatives and 1 or more employers ratified before the date of the enactment of this Act, the amendments made by this section shall not apply to contributions or benefits pursuant to such agreements for plan years beginning before the earlier of—

(A) the latest of—

(i) January 1, 1994,

(ii) the date on which the last of such collective bargaining agreements terminates (without regard to any extension, amendment, or modification of such agreements on or after such date of enactment), or

(iii) in the case of a plan maintained pursuant to collective bargaining under the Railway Labor Act, the date of execution of an extension or replacement of the last of such collective bargaining agreements in effect on such date of enactment, or

(B) January 1, 1997.

(3) TRANSITION RULE FOR STATE AND LOCAL PLANS.—

(A) IN GENERAL.—In the case of an eligible participant in a governmental plan (within the meaning of section 414(d) of the Internal Revenue Code of 1986), the dollar limitation under section 401(a)(17) of such Code shall not apply to the extent the amount of compensation which is allowed to be taken into account under the plan would be reduced below the amount which was allowed to be taken into account under the plan as in effect on July 1, 1993.

(B) Eligible participant.—For purposes of subparagraph (A), an eligible participant is an individual who first became a participant in the plan during a plan year beginning before the 1st plan year begining after the earlier of—

(i) the plan year in which the plan is amended to reflect the amendments made by this section, or

(ii) December 31, 1995.

(C) PLAN MUST BE AMENDED TO INCORPORATE LIMITS.—This paragraph shall not apply to any eligible participant of a plan unless the plan is amended so that the plan incorporates by reference the dollar limitation under section 401(a)(17) of the Internal Revenue Code of 1986, effective with respect to noneligible participants for plan years beginning after December 31, 1995 (or earlier if the plan amendment so provides).

• 1992, Unemployment Compensation Amendments of 1992 (P.L. 102-318)

P.L. 102-318, §521(b)(5)(A)-(B):

Amended Code Sec. 401(a)(20) by striking "a qualified total distribution described in section 402(a)(5)(E)(i)(I)" and inserting "1 or more distributions within 1 taxable year to a distributee on account of a termination of the plan of which the trust is a part, or in the case of a profit-sharing or stock bonus plan, a complete discontinuance of contributions under such plan", and by adding at the end a new sentence. **Effective** for distributions after 12-31-92.

P.L. 102-318, §521(b)(6):

Amended Code Sec. 401(a)(28)(B)(v). **Effective** for distributions after 12-31-92. Prior to amendment, Code Sec. 401(a)(28)(B)(v) read as follows:

(v) COORDINATION WITH DISTRIBUTION RULES.—Any distribution required by this subparagraph shall not be taken into account in determining whether—

(I) a subsequent distribution is a lump-sum distribution under section 402(e)(4)(A), or

(II) section 402(a)(5)(D)(iii) applies to a subsequent distribution.

P.L. 102-318, §522(a)(1):

Amended Code Sec. 401(a) by inserting after paragraph (30) new paragraph (31). **Effective** for distributions after 12-31-92.

• 1989, Omnibus Budget Reconciliation Act of 1989 (P.L. 101-239)

P.L. 101-239, §7811(g)(1):

Amended Code Sec. 401(a) by moving paragraph (30) from the end thereof and inserting it after paragraph (29). **Effective** as if included in the provision of P.L. 100-647 to which it relates.

P.L. 101-239, §7881(i)(1)(A):

Amended Code Sec. 401(a)(29)(C)(i)(II) by inserting "and any other plan amendments adopted after December 22, 1987, and before such plan amendment" after "amendment". **Effective** as if included in the provision of P.L. 100-203 to which it relates.

P.L. 101-239, §7881(i)(4)(A):

Amended Code Sec. 401(a)(29)(A)(i) by inserting "to which the requirements of section 412 apply" after "multiemployer plan)". **Effective** as if included in the provision of P.L. 100-203 to which it relates.

• 1989 (P.L. 101-140)

P.L. 101-140, §203(a)(5)(A)-(B):

Amended Code Sec. 401(a)(9)(C) by striking "(as defined in section 89(i)(4))" after "church plan", and by adding at the end a new sentence. **Effective** as if included in section 1151 of P.L. 99-514.

• 1988, Technical and Miscellaneous Revenue Act of 1988 (P.L. 100-647)

P.L. 100-647, §1011(c)(7)(A):

Amended Code Sec. 401(a) by adding at the end thereof new paragraph (30). **Effective** as provided in Act Sec. 1011(c)(7)(E), as follows:

(E)(i) Except as provided in clause (ii), the amendments made by this paragraph shall apply to plan years beginning after December 31, 1987.

(ii) In the case of a plan described in section 1105(c)(2) of the Reform Act, the amendments made by this paragraph shall not apply to contributions made pursuant to an agreement described in such section for plan years beginning before the earlier of—

(I) the later of January 1, 1988, or the date on which the last of such agreements terminates (determined without regard to any extension thereof after February 28, 1986), or

(II) January 1, 1989.

P.L. 100-647, §1011(d)(4):

Amended Code Sec. 401(a)(17) by adding at the end thereof a new sentence. **Effective** as if included in the provision of P.L. 99-514 to which it relates.

P.L. 100-647, §1011(h)(3):

Amended Code Sec. 401(a)(26) by redesignating subparagraph (F) as subparagraph (H) and by adding after subparagraph (E) new subparagraphs (F)-(G). **Effective** as if included in the provision of P.L. 99-514 to which it relates.

P.L. 100-647, §1011A(j)(1):

Amended Code Sec. 401(a)(27) by adding at the end thereof new subparagraph (B). **Effective** as if included in the provision of P.L. 99-514 to which it relates.

P.L. 100-647, §1011A(j)(2):

Amended Code Sec. 401(a)(27) by striking out "(27)" and inserting in lieu thereof:

(27) Determination as to profit-sharing plans.—

(A) Contributions need not be based on profits.—. **Effective** as if included in the provision of P.L. 99-514 to which it relates.

P.L. 100-647, §1011A(1):

Amended Code Sec. 401(a)(11) by redesignating subparagraph (E) (relating to cross reference) as subparagraph (F). **Effective** as if included in the provision of P.L. 99-514 to which it relates.

P.L. 100-647, §1011B(j)(1):

Amended Code Sec. 401(a)(28)(B)[ii](II) by inserting "and within 90 days after the period during which the election may be made, the plan invests the portion of the participant's account covered by the election in accordance with such election" after "clause (i)". **Effective** as if included in the provision of P.L. 99-514 to which it relates.

P.L. 100-647, §1011B(j)(2):

Amended Code Sec. 401(a)(28)(B)(iv). **Effective** as if included in the provision of P.L. 99-514 to which it relates. Prior to amendment, Code Sec. 401(a)(28)(B)(iv) read as follows:

(iv) QUALIFIED ELECTION PERIOD.—For purposes of this subparagraph, the term "qualified election period" means the 5-plan-year period beginning with the plan year after the plan year in which the participant attains age 55 (or, if later, beginning with the plan year after the 1st plan year in which the individual 1st became a qualified participant).

P.L. 100-647, §1011B(j)(6):

Amended Code Sec. 401(a)(28)(B) by adding at the end thereof a new clause (v). **Effective** as if included in the provision of P.L. 99-514 to which it relates.

P.L. 100-647, §1011B(k)(1):

Amended Code Sec. 401(a)(22) by striking out "is not publicly traded" each place it appears and inserting in lieu thereof "is not readily tradable on an established market". **Effective** as if included in the provision of P.L. 99-514 to which it relates.

P.L. 100-647, §1011B(k)(2):

Amended Code Sec. 401(a)(22) by adding at the end thereof a new sentence. **Effective** as if included in the provision of P.L. 99-514 to which it relates.

P.L. 100-647, §6053(a):

Amended Code Sec. 401(a)(9)(C) by adding at the end thereof a new sentence. **Effective** as if included in the amendments made by section 1121 of P.L. 99-514.

P.L. 100-647, §6055(a):

Amended Code Sec. 401(a)(26) by redesignating subparagraph (H) as subparagraph (I) and by inserting after subparagraph (G) a new subparagraph (H). **Effective** as if included in the amendments made by section 1112(b) of P.L. 99-514.

P.L. 100-647, §6056, provides:

SEC. 6056. STUDY OF EFFECT OF MINIMUM PARTICIPATION RULE ON EMPLOYERS REQUIRED TO PROVIDE CERTAIN RETIREMENT BENEFITS.

(a) STUDY.—The Secretary of the Treasury or his delegate shall conduct a study on the application of section 401(a)(26) of the Internal Revenue Code of 1986 to Government contractors who—

(1) are required by Federal law to provide certain employees specified retirement benefits, and

(2) establish a separate plan for such employees while maintaining a separate plan for employees who are not entitled to such benefits.

Such study shall consider the Federal requirements with respect to employee benefits for employees of Government contractors, whether a special minimum participation rule should apply to such employees, and methods by which plans may be modified to satisfy minimum participation requirements.

(b) REPORT.—The Secretary of the Treasury or his delegate shall report the results of the study under subsection (a) to the Committee on Finance of the Senate and the Committee on Ways and Means of the House of Representatives not later than September 1, 1989.

P.L. 100-647, §6065, provides:

SEC. 6065. EXCEPTION FOR GOVERNMENTAL PLANS.

In the case of plan years beginning before January 1, 1993, section 401(a)(26) of the 1986 Code shall not apply to any governmental plan (within the meaning of section 414(d) of such Code) with respect to employees who were participants in such plan on July 14, 1988.

• 1987, Revenue Act of 1987 (P.L. 100-203)

P.L. 100-203, §9341(a):

Amended Code Sec. 401(a) by inserting after paragraph (28) new paragraph (29). **Effective** for plan amendments adopted after 12-22-87. For a special rule, see Act Sec. 9341(c)(2) below.

P.L. 100-203, §9341(c)(2), as amended by P.L. 101-239, §7881(i)(5), provides:

(2) COLLECTIVE BARGAINING AGREEMENTS.—In the case of a plan maintained pursuant to 1 or more collective bargaining agreements between employee representatives and 1 or more employers ratified before the date of the enactment (without regard to any extension, amendment, or modification of such agreements on or after such date of enactment) of this Act, the amendments made by this section shall not apply to plan amendments adopted pursuant to collective bargaining agreements ratified before the date of enactment.

• 1986, Tax Reform Act of 1986 (P.L. 99-514)

P.L. 99-514, §1106(d)(1):

Amended Code Sec. 401(a) by inserting after paragraph (16) new paragraph (17). For the **effective** date, see Act Sec. 1106(i), below.

P.L. 99-514, §1106(i), as amended by P.L. 100-647, §§1011(d)(5) and 6062(a), provides:

(i) EFFECTIVE DATES.—

(1) IN GENERAL.—Except as provided in this subsection, the amendments made by this section shall apply to years beginning after December 31, 1986.

(2) COLLECTIVE BARGAINING AGREEMENTS.—In the case of a plan in effect before March 1, 1986, pursuant to 1 or more collective bargaining agreements between employee repre-

sentatives and 1 or more employers, the amendments made by this section (other than subsection (d)) shall not apply to contributions or benefits pursuant to such agreement in years beginning before October 1, 1991.

(3) RIGHT TO HIGHER ACCRUED DEFINED BENEFIT PRESERVED.—

(A) IN GENERAL.—In the case of an individual who is a participant (as of the 1st day of the 1st year to which the amendments made by this section apply) in a defined benefit plan which is in existence on May 6, 1986, and with respect to which the requirements of section 415 of the Internal Revenue Code of 1986 have been met for all plan years, if such individual's current accrued benefit under the plan exceeds the limitation of subsection (b) of section 415 of such Code (as amended by this section), then (in the case of such plan), for purposes of subsections (b) and (e) if such section, the limitation of such subsection (b)(1)(A) with respect to such individual shall be equal to such current accrued benefit.

(B) CURRENT ACCRUED BENEFIT DEFINED.—

(i) IN GENERAL.—For purposes of this paragraph, the term "current accrued benefit" means the individual's accrued benefit (at the close of the last year to which the amendments made by this section do not apply) when expressed as an annual benefit (within the meaning of section 415(b)(2) of such Code).

(ii) SPECIAL RULE.—For purposes of determining the amount of any individual's current accrued benefit—

(I) no change in the terms and conditions of the plan after May 5, 1986, and

(II) no cost-of-living adjustment occurring after May 5, 1986,

shall be taken into account. For purposes of subclause (I), any change in the terms and conditions of the plan pursuant to a collective bargaining agreement ratified before May 6, 1986, shall be treated as a change made before May 6, 1986.

(4) TRANSITION RULE WHERE THE SUM OF DEFINED CONTRIBUTION AND DEFINED BENEFIT PLAN FRACTIONS EXCEEDS 1.0.—In the case of a plan which satisfied the requirements of section 415 of the Internal Revenue Code of 1986 for its last year beginning before January 1, 1987, the Secretary of the Treasury or his delegate shall prescribe regulations under which an amount is subtracted from the numerator of the defined contribution plan fraction (not exceeding such numerator) so that the sum of the defined benefit plan fraction and the defined contribution plan fraction computed under section 415(e)(1) of such Code does not exceed 1.0 for such year (determined as if the amendments made by this section were in effect for such year).

(5) EFFECTIVE DATE FOR SUBSECTION (d).—

(A) IN GENERAL.—Except as provided in subparagraph (B), the amendment made by subsection (d) shall apply to benefits accruing in years beginning after December 31, 1988.

(B) COLLECTIVE BARGAINING AGREEMENTS.—In the case of a plan described in paragraph (2), the amendments made by subsection (d) shall apply to benefits accruing in years beginning on or after the earlier of—

(i) the later of—

(I) the date determined under paragraph (2)(A), or

(II) January 1, 1989, or

(ii) January 1, 1991.

P.L. 99-514, §1111(b):

Amended Code Sec. 401(a)(5). For the **effective** date, see Act Sec. 1111(c), below. Prior to amendment, Code Sec. 401(a)(5) read as follows:

(5) A classification shall not be considered discriminatory within the meaning of paragraph (4) or section 410(b) (without regard to paragraph (1)(A) thereof) merely because it excludes employees the whole of whose remuneration constitutes "wages" under section 3121(a)(1) (relating to the Federal Insurance Contributions Act) or merely because it is limited to salaried or clerical employees. Neither shall a plan be considered discriminatory within the meaning of such provisions merely because the contributions or benefits of or on behalf of the employees under the plan bear a uniform relationship to the total compensation, or the basic or regular rate of compensation, of such employees, or merely because the contributions or benefits based on that part of an employee's remuneration which is excluded from "wages" by section 3121(a)(1) differ from the contributions or benefits based on employee's remuneration not so excluded, or differ because of any retirement benefits created under the State or Federal law. For purposes of this paragraph and paragraph (10), the total compensation of an individual who is an employee within the meaning of subsection (c)(1) means such individual's earned income (as defined in subsection (c)(2)), and the basic or regular rate of compensation of such an individual shall be determined, under regulations prescribed by the Secretary, with respect to that portion of his earned income which bears the same ratio to his earned income as the basic or regular compensation of the employees under the plan bears to the total compensation of such employees. For purposes of determining whether two or more plans of an employer satisfy the requirements of paragraph (4) when considered as a single plan, if the amount of contributions on behalf of the employees allowed as a deduction under section 404 for the taxable year with respect to such plans, taken together, bears a uniform relationship to the total compensation, or the basic or regular rate of compensation, of such employees, the plans shall not be considered discriminatory merely because the rights of employees to, or derived from, the employer contributions under the separate plans do not become nonforfeitable at the same rate. For the purposes of determining whether two or more plans of an employer satisfy the requirements of paragraph (4) when considered as a single plan, if the employees' rights to benefits under the separate plans do not become nonforfeitable at the same rate, but the levels of benefits provided by the separate plans satisfy the requirements of regulations prescribed by the Secretary to take account of the differences in such rates, the plans shall not be considered discriminatory merely because of the difference in such rates. For purposes of determining whether one or more plans of an employer satisfy the requirements of paragraph (4) and of section 410(b), an employer may take into account all simplified employee pensions to which only the employer contributes.

P.L. 99-514, §1111(c), as amended by P.L. 100-647, §1011(g)(4), provides:

(c) EFFECTIVE DATE.—

(1) SUBSECTION (a).—The amendments made by subsection (a) shall apply to benefits attributable to plan years beginning after December 31, 1988.

(2) SUBSECTION (b).—The amendments made by subsection (b) shall apply to years beginning after December 31, 1988.

(3) SPECIAL RULE COLLECTIVE BARGAINING AGREEMENTS.—In the case of a plan maintained pursuant to 1 or more collective bargaining agreements between employee representatives and 1 or more employers ratified before March 1, 1986, the amendments made by this section shall not apply to plan years beginning before the earlier of—

(A) the later of—

(i) January 1, 1989, or

(ii) the date on which the last of such collective bargaining agreements terminates (determined without regard to any extension thereof after February 28, 1986), or

(B) January 1, 1991.

P.L. 99-514, §1112(b):

Amended Code Sec. 401(a) by adding at the end thereof new paragraph (26). **Effective**, generally, for plan years beginning after 12-31-88. However, for special rules, see Act Sec. 1112(e)(2)-(4), below.

P.L. 99-514, §1112(e)(2)-(4), as amended by P.L. 100-647, §1011(h)(6)-(9), provides:

(2) SPECIAL RULE FOR COLLECTIVE BARGAINING AGREEMENTS.—In the case of a plan maintained pursuant to 1 or more collective bargaining agreements between employee representatives and 1 or more employers ratified before March 1, 1986, the amendments made by this section shall not apply to plan years beginning before the earlier of—

(A) the later of—

(i) January 1, 1989, or

(ii) the date on which the last of such collective bargaining agreement terminates (determined without regard to any extension thereof after February 28, 1986), or

(B) January 1, 1991.

(3) WAIVER OF EXCISE TAX ON REVERSIONS.—

(A) IN GENERAL.—If—

(i) a plan is in existence on August 16, 1986,

(ii) such plan would fail to meet the requirements of section 401(a)(26) of the Internal Revenue Code of 1986 (as added by subsection (b)) if such section were in effect for the plan year including August 16, 1986, and

(iii) there is no transfer of assets to or liabilities from the plan or spinoff or merger involving such plan after August 16, 1986,

then no tax shall be imposed under section 4980 of such Code on any employer reversion by reason of the termination or merger of such plan before the 1st year to which the amendment made by subsection (b) applies.

(B) INTEREST RATE FOR DETERMINING ACCRUED BENEFIT OF HIGHLY COMPENSATED EMPLOYEES FOR CERTAIN PURPOSES.—In the case of a termination, transfer, or distribution of assets of a plan described in subparagraph (A)(ii) before the 1st year to which the amendment made by subsection (b) applies—

(i) AMOUNT ELIGIBLE FOR ROLLOVER, INCOME AVERAGING, OR TAX-FREE TRANSFER.—For purposes of determining any eligible amount, the present value of the accrued benefit of any highly compensated employee shall be determined by using an interest rate not less than the highest of—

(I) the applicable rate under the plan's method in effect under the plan on August 16, 1986,

(II) the highest rate (as of the date of the termination, transfer, or distribution) determined under any of the methods applicable under the plan at any time after August 15, 1986, and before the termination, transfer, or distribution in calculating the present value of the accrued benefit of an employee who is not a highly compensated employee under the plan (or any other plan used in determining whether the plan meets the requirements of section 401 of the Internal Revenue Code of 1986), or

(III) 5 percent.

(ii) ELIGIBLE AMOUNT.—For purposes of clause (i), the term "eligible amount" means any amount with respect to a highly compensated employee which—

(I) may be rolled over under section 402(a)(5) of such Code.

(II) is eligible for income averaging under section 402(e)(1) of such Code, or capital gains treatment under section 402(a)(2) or 403(a)(2) of such Code (as in effect before this Act), or

(III) may be transferred to another plan without inclusion in gross income.

(iii) AMOUNTS SUBJECT TO EARLY WITHDRAWAL OR EXCESS DISTRIBUTION TAX.—For purposes of sections 72(t) and 4980A of such Code, there shall not be taken into account the excess (if any) of—

(I) the amount distributed to a highly compensated employee by reason of such termination or distribution, over

(II) the amount determined by using the interest rate applicable under clause (i).

(iv) DISTRIBUTIONS OF ANNUITY CONTRACTS.—If an annuity contract purchased after August 16, 1986, is distributed to a highly compensated employee in connection with such termination or distribution, there shall be included in gross income for the taxable year of such distribution an amount equal to the excess of—

(I) the purchase price of such contract, over

(II) the present value of the benefits payable under such contract determined by using the interest rate applicable under clause (i).

Such excess shall not be taken into account for purposes of sections 72(t) and 4980A of such Code.

(v) HIGHLY COMPENSATED EMPLOYEE.—For purposes of this subparagraph, the term "highly compensated employee" has the meaning given such term by section 414(q) of such Code.

(4) SPECIAL RULE FOR PLANS WHICH MAY NOT TERMINATE.—To the extent provided in regulations prescribed by the Secretary of the Treasury or his delegate, if a plan is prohibited from terminating under title IV of the Employee Retirement Income Security Act of 1974 before the 1st year to which the amendment made by subsection (b) would apply, the amendment made by subsection (b) shall only apply to years after the 1st year in which the plan is able to terminate.

P.L. 99-514, §1114(b)(7):

Amended Code Sec. 401(a)(4). **Effective** for tax years beginning after 12-31-88. However, for a special rule, see Act Sec. 1114(c)(4), below. Prior to amendment, Code Sec. 401(a)(4) read as follows:

(4) if the contributions or benefits provided under the plan do not discriminate in favor of employees who are—

(A) officers,

(B) shareholders, or

(C) highly compensated.

For purposes of this paragraph, there shall be excluded from consideration employees described in section 410(b)(3)(A) and (C).

P.L. 99-514, §1114(c)(4), repealed by P.L. 107-16, §663(a), provides:

(4) SPECIAL RULE FOR DETERMINING HIGHLY COMPENSATED EMPLOYEES.—For purposes of sections 401(k) and 401(m) of the Internal Revenue Code of 1986, in the case of an employer incorporated on December 15, 1924, if more than 50 percent of its employees in the top-paid group (within the meaning of section 414(q)(4) of such Code) earn less than $25,000 (indexed at the same time and in the same manner as under section 415(d) of such Code), then the highly compensated employees shall include employees described in section 414(q)(1)(C) of such Code determined without regard to the level of compensation of such employees.

P.L. 99-514, §1119(a):

Amended Code Sec. 401(a)(8) by striking out "pension plan" and inserting in lieu thereof "defined benefit plan". **Effective** for plan years beginning after 12-31-85.

P.L. 99-514, §1121(b):

Amended Code Sec. 401(a)(9)(C). **Effective**, generally, for tax years beginning after 12-31-88. However, for a special rule, see Act Sec. 1121(d)(3)-(5), below. Prior to amendment, Code Sec. 401(a)(9)(C) read as follows:

(C) Required Beginning Date.—For purposes of this paragraph, the term "required beginning date" means April 1 of the calendar year following the later of—

(i) the calendar year in which the employee attains age $70^{1}/_{2}$, or

(ii) the calendar year in which the employee retires.

Clause (ii) shall not apply in the case of an employee who is a 5-percent owner (as defined in section 416(i)(1)(B)) at any time during the 5-plan-year period ending in the calendar year in which the employee attains age $70^{1}/_{2}$. If the employee becomes a 5-percent owner during any subsequent plan year, the required beginning date shall be April 1 of the calendar year following the calendar year in which such subsequent plan year ends.

P.L. 99-514, §1121(d)(3)-(5), as amended by P.L. 100-647, §1011A(a)(3)-(4), provides:

(3) COLLECTIVE BARGAINING AGREEMENTS.—In the case of a plan maintained pursuant to 1 or more collective bargaining agreements between employee representatives and 1 or more employers ratified before March 1, 1986, the amendments made by this section shall not apply to distributions to individuals covered by such agreements in years beginning before the earlier of—

(A) the later of—

(i) the date on which the last of such collective bargaining agreements terminates (determined without regard to any extension thereof after February 28, 1986), or

(ii) January 1, 1989, or

(B) January 1, 1991.

(4) TRANSITION RULES.—

(A) The amendments made by subsections (a) and (b) shall not apply with respect to any benefits with respect to which a designation is in effect under section 242(b)(2) of the Tax Equity and Fiscal Responsibility Act of 1982.

(B)(i) Except as provided in clause (ii), the amendment made by subsection (b) shall not apply in the case of any individual who has attained age $70^{1}/_{2}$ before January 1, 1988.

(ii) Clause (i) shall not apply to any individual who is a 5-percent owner (as defined in section 416(i) of the Internal Revenue Code of 1986), at any time during—

(I) the plan year ending with or within the calendar year in which such owner attains age $66^{1}/_{2}$, and

(II) any subsequent plan year.

(5) PLANS MAY INCORPORATE SECTION 401(a)(9) REQUIREMENTS BY REFERENCE.—Notwithstanding any other provision of law, except as provided in regulations prescribed by the Secretary of the Treasury or his delegate, a plan may incorporate by reference the requirements of section 401(a)(9) of the Internal Revenue Code of 1986.

P.L. 99-514, §1136(a):

Amended Code Sec. 401(a) by adding at the end thereof new paragraph (27). **Effective** for tax years beginning after 12-31-85.

P.L. 99-514, §1145(a):

Amended Code Sec. 401(a)(11), as amended by Act Sec. 1898(b)(14)(A), by redesignating subparagraph (D)[E] as subparagraph (E) [F] and by inserting new subparagraph (E). **Effective** as if included in the provision of P.L. 98-397 to which it relates.

P.L. 99-514, §1171(b)(5):

Repealed Code Sec. 401(a)(21). **Effective** for compensation paid or accrued after 12-31-86, in tax years ending after such date. Prior to amendment it read as follows:

(21) A trust forming part of a tax credit employee stock ownership plan shall not fail to be considered a permanent program merely because employer contributions under the plan are determined solely by reference to the amount of credit which would be allowable under section 41 if the employer made the transfer described in section 41(c)(1)(B).

P.L. 99-514, §1174(c)(2)(A):

Amended Code Sec. 401(a)(23). **Effective** for distributions attributable to stock acquired after 12-31-86, except that a plan may elect to have such amendment apply to all distributions after 10-22-86. Prior to amendment, Code Sec. 401(a)(23) read as follows:

(23) A stock bonus plan which otherwise meets the requirements of this section shall not be considered to fail to meet the requirements of this section because it provides a cash distribution option to participants if that option meets the requirements of section 409(h), except that in applying section 409(h) for purposes of this paragraph, the term "employer securities" shall include any securities of the employer held by the plan.

P.L. 99-514, §1175(a)(1):

Amended Code Sec. 401(a) by adding at the end thereof new paragraph (28). **Effective** for stock acquired after 12-31-86.

P.L. 99-514, §1176(a):

Amended Code Sec. 401(a)(22) by inserting a new sentence at the end thereof. **Effective** 12-31-86.

P.L. 99-514, §1852(a)(4)(A):

Amended Code Sec. 401(a)(9)(C) by striking out the last sentence and inserting in lieu thereof "Clause (ii) shall not apply in the case of an employee who is a 5-percent owner (as defined in section 416(i)(1)(B)) at any time during the 5-plan-year period ending in the calendar year in which the employee attains age $70^{1}/_{2}$. If the employee becomes a 5-percent owner during any subsequent plan year, the required beginning date shall be April 1 of the calendar year following the calendar year in which such subsequent plan year ends." **Effective** as if included in the provision of P.L. 98-369 to which it relates. Prior to amendment, the last sentence read as follows:

Except as provided in section 409(d), clause (ii) shall not apply in the case of an employee who is a 5-percent owner (as defined in section 416) with respect to the plan year ending in the calendar year in which the employee attains $70^{1}/_{2}$.

P.L. 99-514, §1852(a)(4)(C), as added by P.L. 100-647, §1018(t)(3)(A), provides:

(C) An individual whose required beginning date would, but for the amendment made by subparagraph (A), occur after December 31, 1986, but whose required beginning date after such amendment occurs before January 1, 1987, shall be treated as if such individual had become a 5-percent owner during the plan year ending in 1986.

P.L. 99-514, §1852(a)(6):

Amended Code Sec. 401(a)(9) by adding at the end thereof new subparagraph (G). **Effective** as if included in the provision of P.L. 98-369 to which it relates.

P.L. 99-514, §1852(b)(8):

Amended Code Sec. 401(a)(20) by striking out "qualifying rollover distribution (determined as if section 402(a)(5)(D)(i) did not contain subclause (II) thereof) described in section 402(a)(5)(A)(i) or 403(a)(4)(A)(i)" and inserting in lieu thereof "qualified total distribution described in section 402(a)(5)(E)(i)(I)". **Effective** as if included in the provision of P.L. 98-369 to which it relates.

P.L. 99-514, §1898(b)(2)(A)(i):

Amended Code Sec. 401(a)(11)(B)(iii)(III) by striking out "indirect transferee" and inserting in lieu thereof "indirect transferee (in a transfer after December 31, 1984)". **Effective** as if included in the provision of P.L. 98-397 to which it relates.

P.L. 99-514, §1898(b)(2)(A)(ii):

Amended Code Sec. 401(a)(11)(B) by adding at the end thereof a new sentence. **Effective** as if included in the provision of P.L. 98-397 to which it relates.

P.L. 99-514, §1898(b)(3)(A):

Amended Code Sec. 401(a)(11)(A)(i) by striking out "who retires under the plan" and inserting in lieu thereof "who does not die before the annuity starting date". **Effective** as if included in the provision of P.L. 98-397 to which it relates.

P.L. 99-514, §1898(b)(7)(A):

Amended Code Sec. 401(a)(11)(B)(iii)(I) by striking out "the participant's nonforfeitable accrued benefit" and inserting in lieu thereof "the participant's nonforfeitable accrued benefit (reduced by any security interest held by the plan by reason of a loan outstanding to such participant)". **Effective** as if included in the provision of P.L. 98-397 to which it relates.

P.L. 99-514, §1898(b)(13)(A):

Amended Code Sec. 401(a)(11)(B)(iii)(I) by striking out "section 417(a)(2)(A)" and inserting in lieu thereof "section 417(a)(2)". **Effective** as if included in the provision of P.L. 98-397 to which it relates.

P.L. 99-514, §1898(b)(14)(A):

Amended Code Sec. 401(a)(11) by redesignating subparagraph (D) as subparagraph (E) and by inserting after subparagraph (C) new subparagraph (D). **Effective** as if included in the provision of P.L. 98-397 to which it relates.

P.L. 99-514, §1899A(10):

Amended Code Sec. 401(a)(22) by striking out "if" and inserting in lieu thereof "If". **Effective** 10-22-86.

• 1984, Retirement Equity Act of 1984 (P.L. 98-397)

P.L. 98-397, §203(a):

Amended Code Sec. 401(a)(11). **Effective** only in the case of participants who have at least 1 hour of service under the plan on or after the date of enactment or have at least 1 hour of paid leave on or after such date. Special rules appear in Act Sec. 302(b), below. Prior to amendment, Code Sec. 401(a)(11) read as follows:

(11)(A) A trust shall not constitute a qualified trust under this section if the plan of which such trust is a part provides for the payment of benefits in the form of an annuity unless such plan provides for the payment of annuity benefits in a form having the effect of a qualified joint and survivor annuity.

(B) Notwithstanding the provisions of subparagraph (A), in the case of a plan which provides for the payment of benefits before the normal retirement age (as defined in section 411(a)(8)), the plan is not required to provide for the payment of annuity benefits in a form having the effect of a qualified joint and survivor annuity during the period beginning on the date on which the employee enters into the plan as a participant and ending on the later of—

(i) the date the employee reaches the earliest retirement age under the plan, or

(ii) the first day of the 120th month beginning before the date on which the employee reaches normal retirement age.

(C) A plan described in subparagraph (B) does not meet the requirements of subparagraph (A) unless, under the plan, a participant has a reasonable period during which he may elect the qualified joint and survivor annuity form with respect to the period beginning on the date on which the period described in subparagraph (B) ends and ending on the date on which he reaches normal retirement age (as defined in section 411(a)(8)) if he continues his employment during that period. A plan does not meet the requirements of this subparagraph unless, in the case of such an election, the payments under the survivor annuity are not less than the payments which would have been made under the joint annuity to which the participant would have been entitled if he made an election described in this subparagraph immediately prior to his retirement and if his retirement had occurred on the day before his death and within the period within which an election can be made.

(D) A plan shall not be treated as not satisfying the requirements of this paragraph solely because the spouse of the participant is not entitled to receive a survivor annuity (whether or not an election described in subparagraph (C) has been made under subparagraph (C)) unless the participant and his spouse have been married throughout the 1-year period ending on the date of such participant's death.

(E) A plan shall not be treated as satisfying the requirements of this paragraph unless, under the plan, each participant has a reasonable period (as described by the Secretary by regulations) before the annuity starting date during which he may elect in writing (after having received a written explanation of the terms and conditions of the joint and survivor annuity and the effect of an election under this subparagraph) not to take such joint and survivor annuity.

(F) A plan shall not be treated as not satisfying the requirements of this paragraph solely because under the plan there is a provision that any election described in subparagraph (C) or (E), and any revocation of any such election, does not become effective (or ceases to be effective) if the participant dies within a period (not in excess of 2 years) beginning on the date of such election or revocation, as the case may be. The preceding sentence does not apply unless the plan provision described in the preceding sentence also provides that such an election or revocation will be given effect in any case in which—

(i) the participant dies from accidental causes,

(ii) a failure to give effect to the election or revocation would deprive the participant's survivor of a survivor annuity, and

(iii) such election or revocation is made before such accident occurred.

(G) For purposes of this paragraph—

(i) the term "annuity starting date" means the first day of the first period for which an amount is received as an annuity (whether by reason of retirement or by reason of disability),

(ii) the term "earliest retirement age" means the earliest date on which, under the plan, the participant could elect to receive retirement benefits, and

(iii) the term "qualified joint and survivor annuity" means an annuity for the life of the participant with a survivor annuity for the life of his spouse which is not less than one-half of, or greater than, the amount of the annuity payable during the joint lives of the participant and his spouse and which is the actuarial equivalent of a single life annuity for the life of the participant.

For purposes of this paragraph, a plan may take into account in any equitable manner (as determined by the Secretary) any increased costs resulting from providing joint and survivor annuity benefits.

(H) This paragraph shall apply only if—

(i) the annuity starting date did not occur before the effective date of this paragraph, and

(ii) the participant was an active participant in the plan on or after such effective date.

P.L. 98-397, §204(a):

Amended Code Sec. 401(a)(13) by striking out "(13) A trust" and inserting in lieu thereof "(13) ASSIGNMENT AND ALIENATION.—(A) IN GENERAL.—A trust"; by correcting the margin for subparagraph (A); and by adding at the end thereof new subparagraph (B). **Effective** 1-1-85, except that, in the case of a domestic relations order entered before such date the plan administrator—

(1) shall treat such order as a qualified domestic relations order if such administrator is paying benefits pursuant to such order on such date, and

(2) may treat any other such order entered before such date as a qualified domestic relations order even if such order does not meet the requirements of such amendments.

P.L. 98-397, §301(b):

Amended Code Sec. 401(a) by inserting after paragraph (24) new paragraph (25). **Effective** for plan amendments made after 7-30-84. For special rules, see Act Secs. 302(b), 302(d)(2), 303(c)(2)-(3), 303(e) and 303(f), below.

P.L. 98-397, §302(b), as amended by P.L. 99-514, §1898(g), provides:

(b) SPECIAL RULE FOR COLLECTIVE BARGAINING AGREEMENTS.—In the case of a plan maintained pursuant to 1 or more collective bargaining agreements between employee representatives and 1 or more employers ratified before the date of the enactment of this Act, except as provided in subsection (d) or section 303, the amendments made by this Act shall not apply to plan years beginning before the earlier of—

(1) the date on which the last of the collective bargaining agreements relating to the plan terminates (determined without regard to any extension thereof agreed to after the date of the enactment of this Act), or

(2) July 1, 1988.

For purposes of paragraph (1), any plan amendment made pursuant to a collective bargaining agreement relating to the plan which amends the plan solely to conform to any requirement added by title I or II shall not be treated as a termination of such collective bargaining agreement.

P.L. 98-397, §302(d)(2), provides:

(2) SPECIAL RULE FOR COLLECTIVE BARGAINING AGREEMENTS.—In the case of a plan maintained pursuant to 1 or more collective bargaining agreements entered into before January 1, 1985, which are—

(A) between employee representatives and 1 or more employers, and

(B) successor agreements to 1 or more collective bargaining agreements which terminate after July 30, 1984, and before January 1, 1985,

the amendments made by section 301 shall not apply to plan amendments adopted before April 1, 1985, pursuant to such successor agreements (without regard to any modification or reopening after December 31, 1984).

P.L. 98-397, §303(c)(2)-(3), as amended by P.L. 99-514, §1898(h), provides:

(2) REQUIREMENT THAT PRERETIREMENT SURVIVOR ANNUITY BE PROVIDED IN CASE OF CERTAIN PARTICIPANTS DYING ON OR AFTER DATE OF ENACTMENT.—In the case of any participant—

(A) who has at least 1 hour of service under the plan on or after the date of the enactment of this Act or has at least 1 hour of paid leave on or after such date of enactment,

(B) who dies before the annuity starting date, and

(C) who dies on or after the date of the enactment of this Act and before the first day of the first plan year to which the amendments made by this Act apply,

the amendments made by sections 103 and 203 shall be treated as in effect as of the time of such participant's death.

(3) SPOUSAL CONSENT REQUIRED FOR CERTAIN ELECTIONS AFTER DECEMBER 31, 1984.—Any election after December 31, 1984, and before the first day of the first plan year to which the amendments made by this Act apply not to take a joint and survivor annuity shall not be effective unless the requirements of section 205(c)(2) of the Employee Retirement Income Security Act of 1974 (as amended by section 103 of this Act) and section 417(a)(2) of the Internal Revenue Code of 1954 (as added by section 203 of this Act) are met with respect to such election.

(4) Elimination of Double Death Benefits.—

(A) In General.—In the case of a participant described in paragraph (2), death benefits (other than a qualified joint and survivor annuity or a qualified preretirement survivor annuity) payable to any beneficiary shall be reduced by the amount payable to the surviving spouse of such participant by reason of paragraph (2). The reduction under the preceding sentence shall be made on the basis of the respective present values (as of the date of the participant's death) of such death benefits and the amount so payable to the surviving spouse.

(B) Spouse May Waive Provisions of Paragraph (2).—In the case of any participant described in paragraph (2), the surviving spouse of such participant may waive the provisions of paragraph (2). Such waiver shall be made on or before the close of the second plan year to which the amendments made by section 103 of this Act apply. Such a waiver shall not be treated as a transfer of property for purposes of chapter 12 of the Internal Revenue Code of 1954 and shall not be treated as an assignment or alienation for purposes of section 401(a)(13) of the Internal Revenue Code of 1954 or section 206(d) of the Employee Retirement Income Security Act of 1974.

P.L. 98-397, §303(e), provides:

(e) TREATMENT OF CERTAIN PARTICIPANTS WHO SEPARATE FROM SERVICE BEFORE DATE OF ENACTMENT.—

(1) JOINT AND SURVIVOR ANNUITY PROVISIONS OF EMPLOYEE RETIREMENT INCOME SECURITY ACT OF 1974 APPLY TO CERTAIN PARTICIPANTS,—If—

(A) a participant had at least 1 hour of service under the plan on or after September 2, 1974,

(B) section 205 of the Employee Retirement Income Security Act of 1974 and section 401(a)(11) of the Internal Revenue Code of 1954 (as in effect on the day before the date of the enactment of this Act) would not (but for this paragraph) apply to such participant,

(C) the amendments made by sections 103 and 203 of this Act do not apply to such participant, and

(D) as of the date of the enactment of this Act, the participant's annuity starting date has not occurred and the participant is alive,

then such participant may elect to have section 205 of the Employee Retirement Income Security Act of 1974 and section 401(a)(11) of the Internal Revenue Code of 1954 (as in effect on the day before the date of the enactment of this Act) apply.

(2) TREATMENT OF CERTAIN PARTICIPANTS WHO PERFORM SERVICE ON OR AFTER JANUARY 1, 1976.—If—

(A) a participant had at least 1 hour of service in the first plan year beginning on or after January 1, 1976,

(B) the amendments made by sections 103 and 203 would not (but for this paragraph) apply to such participant,

(C) when such participant separated from service, such participant had at least 10 years of service under the plan and had a nonforfeitable right to all (or any portion) of such participant's accrued benefit derived from employer contributions, and

(D) as of the date of the enactment of this Act, such participant's annuity starting date has not occurred and such participant is alive,

then such participant may elect to have the qualified preretirement survivor annuity requirements of the amendments made by sections 103 and 203 apply.

(3) PERIOD DURING WHICH ELECTION MAY BE MADE.—An election under paragraph (1) or (2) may be made by any participant during the period—

(A) beginning on the date of the enactment of this Act, and

(B) ending on the earlier of the participant's annuity starting date or the date of the participant's death.

(4) REQUIREMENT OF NOTICE.—

(A) IN GENERAL.—

(i) TIME AND MANNER.—Every plan shall give notice of the provisions of this subsection at such time or times and in such manner or manners as the Secretary of the Treasury may prescribe.

(ii) PENALTY.—If any plan fails to meet the requirements of clause (i), such plan shall pay a civil penalty to the Secretary of the Treasury equal to $1 per participant for each day during the period beginning with the first day on which such failure occurs and ending on the day before notice is given by the plan; except that the amount of such penalty imposed on any plan shall not exceed $2,500.

(B) RESPONSIBILITIES OF SECRETARY OF LABOR.—The Secretary of Labor shall take such steps (by public announcements and otherwise) as may be necessary or appropriate to bring to public attention the provisions of this subsection.

P.L. 98-397, §303(f), as added by P.L. 99-514, §1145(c), and amended by P.L. 101-239, §7861(d)(1), provides:

(f) The amendments made by section 301 of this Act shall not apply to the termination of a defined benefit plan if such termination—

(1) is pursuant to a resolution directing the termination of such plan which was adopted by the Board of Directors of a corporation on July 17, 1984, and

(2) occurred on November 30, 1984.

• 1984, Deficit Reduction Act of 1984 (P.L. 98-369)

P.L. 98-369, §211(b)(5):

Amended Code Sec. 401(a)(24) by striking out "section 805(d)(6)" and inserting in lieu thereof "section 818(a)(6)". **Effective** for tax years beginning after 12-31-83.

P.L. 98-369, §474(4)(13):

Amended Code Sec. 401(a)(21) by striking out "allowable—" and all that followed and inserting in lieu thereof "allowable under section 41 if the employer made the transfer described in section 41(c)(1)(B)." **Effective** for tax years beginning after 12-31-83, and to carrybacks from such years. Prior to amendment, paragraph (21) read as follows:

(21) A trust forming part of a tax credit employee stock ownership plan shall not fail to be considered a permanent program merely because employer contributions under the plan are determined solely by reference to the amount of credit which would be allowable—

(A) under section 46(a) if the employer made the transfer described in section 48(n)(1), or

(B) under section 44G if the employer made the transfer described in section 44G(c)(1)(B).

P.L. 98-369, §491(e)(4):

Amended Code Sec. 401(a)(22) by striking out "section 409A" and inserting in lieu thereof "section 409". **Effective** 1-1-84.

P.L. 98-369, §491(e)(5):

Amended Code Sec. 401(a)(23) by striking out "section 409A(h)" each place it appeared and inserting in lieu thereof "section 409(h)". **Effective** 1-1-84.

P.L. 98-369, §521(a)(1):

Amended Code Sec. 401(a)(9) as in effect before the amendments made by section 242 of P.L. 97-248. **Effective** for years beginning after 12-31-84. But see the special rules provided by Act Sec. 521(d)(2)(5), below. Prior to amendment, it read as follows:

(9) In the case of a plan which provides contributions or benefits for employees some or all of whom are employees within the meaning of subsection (c)(1), a trust forming part of such plan shall not constitute a qualified trust under this section unless, under the plan, the entire interest of each employee—

(A) either will be distributed to him not later than his taxable year in which he attains the age of $70^{1}/_{2}$ years, or, in the case of an employee other than an owner-employee (as defined in subsection (c)(3)), in which he retires, whichever is the later, or

(B) will be distributed, commencing not later than such taxable year, (i) in accordance with regulations prescribed by the Secretary, over the life of such employee or over the lives of such employee and his spouse, or (ii) in accordance with such regulations, over a period not extending beyond the life expectancy of such employee or the life expectancy of such employee and his spouse.

A trust shall not be disqualified under this paragraph by reason of distributions under a designation, prior to the date of the enactment of this paragraph, by any employee under the plan of which such trust is a part, of a method of distribution which does not meet the terms of the preceding sentence.

P.L. 98-369, §521(a)(2):

Repealed Act Sec. 242 of P.L. 97-248, which added Code Sec. 401(a)(9), below. **Effective** for plan years beginning after 12-31-83. Prior to repeal, Code Sec. 401(a)(9) read as follows:

(9) Required Distributions.—

(A) Before Death.—A trust forming part of a plan shall not constitute a qualified trust under this section unless the plan provides that the entire interest of each employee—

(i) either will be distributed to him not later than his taxable year in which he attains age $70^{1}/_{2}$ or, in the case of an employee other than a key employee who is a participant in a top-heavy plan, in which he retires, whichever is the later, or

(ii) will be distributed, commencing not later than such taxable year—

(I) in accordance with regulations prescribed by the Secretary, over the life of such employee or over the lives of such employee and his spouse, or

(II) in accordance with such regulations, over a period not extending beyond the life expectancy of such employee or the life expectancy of such employee and his spouse.

(B) After Death.—A trust forming part of a plan shall not constitute a qualified trust under this section unless the plan provides that if—

(i) an employee dies before his entire interest has been distributed to him, or

(ii) distribution has been commenced in accordance with subparagraph (A)(ii) to his surviving spouse and such surviving spouse dies before his entire interest has been distributed to such surviving spouse,

his entire interest (or the remaining part of such interest if distribution thereof has commenced) will be distributed within 5 years after his death (or the death of his surviving spouse). The preceding sentence shall not apply if the distribution of the interest of the employee has commenced and such distribution is for a term certain over a period permitted under subparagraph (A)(ii)(II).

P.L. 98-369, §521(d)(2)-(5), provides:

(2) Repeal of Section 242 of TEFRA.—The amendment made by subsection (a)(2) shall take effect as if included in the Tax Equity and Fiscal Responsibility Act of 1982.

(3) Transition Rule.—A trust forming part of a plan shall not be disqualified under paragraph (9) of section 401(a) of

the Internal Revenue Code of 1954, as amended by subsection (a)(1), by reason of distributions under a designation (before January 1, 1984) by any employee in accordance with a designation described in section 242(b)(2) of the Tax Equity and Fiscal Responsibility Act of 1982 (as in effect before the amendments made by this Act).

(4) Special Rule for Governmental Plans.—In the case of a governmental plan (within the meaning of section 414(d) of the Internal Revenue Code of 1954), paragraph (1) shall be applied by substituting "1986" for "1984".

(5) Special Rule for Collective Bargaining Agreements.—In the case of a plan maintained pursuant to one or more collective bargaining agreements ratified on or before the date of the enactment of this Act between employee representatives and one or more employers, the amendments made by this section shall not apply to years beginning before the earlier of—

(A) the date on which the last of the collective bargaining agreements relating to the plan terminates (determined without regard to any extension thereof agreed to after the date of the enactment of this Act), or

(B) January 1, 1988.

For purposes of subparagraph (A), any plan amendment made pursuant to a collective bargaining agreement relating to the plan which amends the plan solely to conform to any requirement added by this section shall not be treated as a termination of such collective bargaining agreement.

Effective as if included in P.L. 97-248.

P.L. 98-369, §524(d)(1):

Amended Code Sec. 401(a)(10)(B) by adding at the end thereof new clause (iii). **Effective** for plan years beginning after 12-31-83.

P.L. 98-369, §524(e), provides:

(e) QUALIFICATION REQUIREMENTS MODIFIED IF REGULATIONS NOT ISSUED.—

(1) IN GENERAL.—If the Secretary of the Treasury or his delegate does not publish final regulations under section 416 of the Internal Revenue Code of 1954 (as in effect on the day before the date of the enactment of this Act) before January 1, 1985, the Secretary shall publish before such date plan amendment provisions which may be incorporated in a plan to meet the requirements of section 401(a)(10)(B)(ii) of such Code.

(2) EFFECT OF INCORPORATION.—If a plan is amended to incorporate the plan amendment provisions described in paragraph (1), such plan shall be treated as meeting the requirements of section 401(a)(10)(B)(ii) of the Internal Revenue Code of 1954 during the period such amendment is in effect but not later than 6 months after the final regulations described in paragraph (1) are published.

(3) FAILURE BY SECRETARY TO PUBLISH.—If the Secretary of the Treasury or his delegate does not publish plan amendment provisions described in paragraph (1), the plan shall be treated as meeting the requirements of section 401(a)(10)(B) of the Internal Revenue Code of 1954 if—

(A) such plan is amended to incorporate such requirements by reference, except that

(B) in the case of any optional requirement under section 416 of such Code, if such amendment does not specify the manner in which such requirement will be met, the employer shall be treated as having elected the requirement with respect to each employee which provides the maximum vested accrued benefit for such employee.

• 1983, Technical Corrections Act of 1982 (P.L. 97-448)

P.L. 97-448, §103(g)(2)(A):

Amended Code Sec. 401(a)(21) by striking out "which would be allowable under section 46(a) if the employer made the transfer described in section 48(n)(1)." and inserting in lieu thereof the following: "which would be allowable—

(A) under section 46(a) if the employer made the transfer described in section 48(n)(1), or

(B) under section 44G if the employer made the transfer described in section 44G(c)(1)(B)." **Effective** as if included in the provision of P.L. 97-34 to which it relates.

• 1982, Tax Equity and Fiscal Responsibility Act of 1982 (P.L. 97-248)

P.L. 97-248, §237(b):

Repealed paragraphs (17) and (18) of Code Section 401(a). **Effective** for years beginning after 12-31-83. Prior to repeal, Code Sec. 401(a)(17)-(18) read as follows:

(17) In the case of a plan which provides contributions or benefits for employees some or all of whom are employees within the meaning of subsection (c)(1), or are shareholder-employees within the meaning of section 1379(d), only if—

(A) the annual compensation of each employee taken into account under the plan does not exceed the first $200,000 of compensation, and

(B) in the case of—

(i) a defined contribution plan with respect to which compensation in excess of $100,000 is taken into account, contributions on behalf of each employee (other than an employee within the meaning of section 401(c)(1)) to the plan or plans are at a rate (expressed as a percentage of compensation) not less than 7.5 percent, or

(ii) a defined benefit plan with respect to which compensation in excess of $100,000 is taken into account, the annual benefit accrual for each employee (other than an employee within the meaning of section 401(c)(1)) is a percentage of compensation which is not less than one-half of the applicable percentage provided by subsection (j)(3).

(18) In the case of a trust which is part of a plan providing a defined benefit for employees some or all of whom are employees within the meaning of subsection (c)(1), or are shareholder-employees within the meaning of section 1379(d), only if such plan satisfies the requirements of subsection (j).

P.L. 97-248, §237(e)(1):

Amended Code Sec. 401(a)(10) to read as 401(a)(10)(A). **Effective** for years beginning after 12-31-83.

P.L. 97-248, §240(b):

Amended Code Sec. 401(a)(10) by adding at the end thereof new subparagraph (B). **Effective** for years beginning after 12-31-83.

P.L. 97-248, §242(a):

Amended Code Sec. 401(a)(9). **Effective** for plan years beginning after 12-31-83. For a transition rule, see Act Sec. 242(b)(2), below.

P.L. 97-248, §242(b)(2), provides:

(2) Transition rule.—A trust forming part of a plan shall not be disqualified under paragraph (9) of section 401(a) of the Internal Revenue Code of 1954, as amended by subsection (a), by reason of distributions under a designation (before January 1, 1984) by any employee of a method of distribution—

(A) which does not meet the requirements of such paragraph (9), but

(B) which would not have disqualified such trust under paragraph (9) of section 401(a) of such Code as in effect before the amendment made by subsection (a).

P.L. 97-248, §254(a):

Amended Code Sec. 401(a) by inserting after paragraph (23) a new paragraph (24). **Effective** for tax years beginning after 12-31-81.

• 1981, Economic Recovery Tax Act of 1981 (P.L. 97-34)

P.L. 97-34, §312(b)(1):

Amended Code Sec. 401(a)(17). **Effective** for plans which include employees within the meaning of Code Sec. 401(c)(1), with respect to tax years beginning after 12-31-81. Prior to amendment Code Sec. 401(a)(17) read as follows:

(17) In the case of a plan which provides contributions or benefits for employees some or all of whom are employees within the meaning of subsection (c)(1), or are shareholder-employees within the meaning of section 1379(d), only if the annual compensation of each employee taken into account under the plan does not exceed the first $100,000 of such compensation.

P.L. 97-34, §335:

Amended Code Sec. 401(a)(23) by striking out "409A(h)(2)" and inserting "409A(h), except that in applying section 409A(h) for purposes of this paragraph, the term 'employer securities' shall include any securities of the employer held by the plan". **Effective** for tax years beginning after 12-31-81.

P.L. 97-34, §338(a):

Amended Code Sec. 401(a)(22). **Effective** for acquisitions of securities after 12-31-79. Prior to amendment, Code Sec. 401(a)(22) read as follows:

(22) If a defined contributions plan—

(A) is established by an employer whose stock is not publicly traded, and

(B) after acquiring securities of the employer, more than 10 percent of the total assets of the plan are securities of the employer,

any trust forming part of said plan shall not constitute a qualified trust under this section unless the plan meets the requirements of subsection (e) of section 409A.

• 1980, Miscellaneous Revenue Act of 1980 (P.L. 96-605)

P.L. 96-605, §221(a):

Amended Code Sec. 401(a) by inserting immediately before the last sentence thereof paragraph (23). **Effective** with respect to plan years beginning after 12-31-80.

P.L. 96-605, §225(b)(1):

Amended Code Sec. 401(a)(4) by striking out "section 410(b)(2)(A)" and inserting in lieu thereof "section 410(b)(3)(A)". **Effective** with respect to plan years beginning after 12-31-80.

• 1980, Multiemployer Pension Plan Amendments Act of 1980 (P.L. 96-364)

P.L. 96-364, §208(a):

Amended Code Sec. 401(a)(12). **Effective** 9-26-80. Prior to amendment, the last sentence read as follows:

This paragraph shall apply in the case of a multiemployer plan only to the extent determined by the Pension Benefit Guaranty Corporation.

P.L. 96-364, §208(e):

Amended Code Sec. 401(a), as amended by Act Sec. 410(b), by adding in subparagraph (2) ", or the return of any withdrawal liability payment determined to be an overpayment within 6 months of such determination" after "501(a)". **Effective** 9-26-80.

P.L. 96-364, §410(b):

Amended Code Sec. 401(a) by inserting the language in parentheses following "employees or their beneficiaries" and preceding the semicolon in subparagraph (2). For the **effective** date, see Act Sec. 410(c), below.

P.L. 96-364, §410(c), provides:

(c) The amendment made by this section shall take effect on January 1, 1975, except that in the case of contributions received by a collectively bargained plan maintained by more than one employer before the date of enactment of this Act, any determination by the plan administrator that any such contribution was made by mistake of fact or law before such date shall be deemed to have been made on such date of enactment.

• 1980, Technical Corrections Act of 1979 (P.L. 96-222)

P.L. 96-222, §101(a)(7)(L)(i)(V):

Amended Code Sec. 401(a)(21) by striking out "an ESOP" and inserting "a tax credit employee stock ownership plan". **Effective** for tax years beginning after 12-31-78.

P.L. 96-222, §101(a)(9):

Amended Code Sec. 401(a)(22)(B) by changing "as securities" to "are securities". **Effective** for acquisitions of securities after 12-31-79.

P.L. 96-222, §101(a)(14)(E)(iii):

Amended Code Sec. 401(a)(20) by striking out "makes a payment or distribution described in section 402(a)(5)(A)(i) or 403(a)(4)(A)(i) and inserting "makes a qualifying rollover distribution (determined as if section 402(a)(5)(D)(i) did not contain subclause (II) thereof) described in section 402(a)(5)(A)(i) or 403(a)(4)(A)(i)". **Effective** for payments made in tax years beginning after 12-31-77.

• 1978, Revenue Act of 1978 (P.L. 95-600)

P.L. 95-600, §141(f)(3):

Amended Code Sec. 401(a)(21). **Effective** 11-7-78. Prior to amendment, Code Sec. 401(a)(21) read as follows:

(21) A trust forming part of an employee stock ownership plan which satisfies the requirements of section 301(d) of the Tax Reduction Act of 1975 shall not fail to be considered a permanent program merely because employer contributions under the plan are determined solely by reference to the amount of credit which would be allowable under section 46(a) if the employer made the transfer described in subsection (d)(6) or (e)(3) of section 301 of the Tax Reduction Act of 1975.

P.L. 95-600, §143(a):

Added Code Sec. 401(a)(22). **Effective** for acquisitions of securities after 12-31-79.

P.L. 95-600, §152(e):

Added a new last sentence to the end of Code Sec. 401(a)(5). **Effective** for tax years beginning after 12-31-78.

• 1976, Tax Reform Act of 1976 (P.L. 94-455)

P.L. 94-455, §803(b)(2):

Amended Code Sec. 401(a) by adding paragraph (21). **Effective** for tax years beginning after 12-31-74.

P.L. 94-455, §1901(a)(56):

Substituted "September 2, 1974" for "the date of the enactment of the Employee Retirement Income Security Act of 1974" in paragraphs (12), (13), and (15) and for "enactment . . . 1974" in (19) of Code Sec. 411(a) and amended the last sentence of Code Sec. 401(a) to have its phraseology read "(19), and (20)". **Effective** for tax years beginning after 12-31-76.

P.L. 94-455, §1906(b)(13)(A):

Amended 1954 Code by substituting "Secretary" for "Secretary or his delegate" each place it appeared. **Effective** 2-1-77.

• 1976 (P.L. 94-267)

P.L. 94-267, §1(c):

Amended Code Sec. 401(a) by adding paragraph (20), and by striking out "and (19)" and inserting in lieu thereof "(19), and (20)". **Effective** for payments made to an employee on or after 7-4-74.

• 1974, Employee Retirement Income Security Act of 1974 (P.L. 93-406)

P.L. 93-406, §§1012(b), 1016(a)(2), 1021(a)(1), 1021(a)(2), 1021(b)-1021(f), 1022(a), 1022(b)(1), 2001(c), 2001(d), 2001(e)(4):

Amended Code Sec. 401(a). **Effective** dates and transitional rules appear in the historical note relating to §1017, P.L. 93-406, following the text of Code Sec. 410. Prior to amendment, Code Sec. 401(a) read as follows:

"(a) Requirements for Qualification.—A trust created or organized in the United States and forming part of a stock bonus, pension, or profit-sharing plan of an employer for the exclusive benefit of his employees or their beneficiaries shall constitute a qualified trust under this section—

"(1) if contributions are made to the trust by such employer, or employees, or both, or by another employer who is entitled to deduct his contributions under section 404(a)(3)(B) (relating to deduction for contributions to profit-sharing and stock bonus plans), for the purpose of distributing to such employees or their beneficiaries the corpus and income of the fund accumulated by the trust in accordance with such plan;

"(2) if under the trust instrument it is impossible, at any time prior to the satisfaction of all liabilities with respect to employees and their beneficiaries under the trust, for any part of the corpus or income to be (within the taxable year or thereafter) used for, or diverted to, purposes other than for the exclusive benefit of his employees or their beneficiaries;

"(3) if the trust, or two or more trusts, or the trust or trusts and annuity plan or plans are designated by the employer as constituting parts of a plan intended to qualify under this subsection which benefits either—

"(A) 70 percent or more of all the employees, or 80 percent or more of all the employees who are eligible to benefit under the plan if 70 percent or more of all the employees are eligible to benefit under the plan, excluding in each case employees who have been employed not more than a minimum period prescribed by the plan, not exceeding 5 years, employees whose customary employment is for not more than 20 hours in any one week, and employees whose customary employment is for not more than 5 months in any calendar year, or

"(B) such employees as qualify under a classification set up by the employer and found by the Secretary or his delegate not to be discriminatory in favor of employees who are officers, shareholders, persons whose principal duties consist in supervising the work of other employees, or highly compensated employees;

and

"(4) if the contributions or benefits provided under the plan do not discriminate in favor of employees who are officers, shareholders, persons whose principal duties consist in supervising the work of other employees, or highly compensated employees.

"(5) A classification shall not be considered discriminatory within the meaning of paragraph (3)(B) or (4) merely because it excludes employees the whole of whose remuneration constitutes `wages' under section 3121(a)(1) (relating to the Federal Insurance Contributions Act) or merely because it is limited to salaried or clerical employees. Neither shall a plan be considered discriminatory within the meaning of such provisions merely because the contributions or benefits of or on behalf of the employees under the plan bear a uniform relationship to the total compensation, or the basic or regular rate of compensation, of such employees, or merely because the contributions or benefits based on that part of an employee's remuneration which is excluded from `wages' by section 3121(a)(1) differ from the contributions or benefits based on employee's remuneration not so excluded, or differ because of any retirement benefits created under State or Federal law. For purposes of this paragraph and paragraph (10), the total compensation of an individual who is an employee within the meaning of subsection (c)(1) means such individual's earned income (as defined in subsection (c)(2)), and the basic or regular rate of compensation of such an individual shall be determined, under regulations prescribed by the Secretary or his delegate, with respect to that portion of his earned income which bears the same ratio to his earned income as the basic or regular compensation of the employees under the plan bears to the total compensation of such employees.

"(6) A plan shall be considered as meeting the requirements of paragraph (3) during the whole of any taxable year of the plan if on one day in each quarter it satisfied such requirements.

"(7) A trust shall not constitute a qualified trust under this section unless the plan of which such trust is a part provides that, upon its termination or upon complete discontinuance of contributions under the plan, the rights of all employees to benefits accrued to the date of such termination or discontinuance, to the extent then funded, or the amounts credited to the employees' accounts are nonforfeitable. This paragraph shall not apply to benefits or contributions which, under provisions of the plan adopted pursuant to regulations prescribed by the Secretary or his delegate to preclude the discrimination prohibited by paragraph (4), may not be used for designated employees in the event of early termination of the plan.

"(8) A trust forming part of a pension plan shall not constitute a qualified trust under this section unless the plan provides that forfeitures must not be applied to increase the benefits any employee would otherwise receive under the plan.

"(9) In the case of a plan which provides contributions or benefits for employees some or all of whom are employees within the meaning of subsection (c)(1), a trust forming part of such plan shall not constitute a qualified trust under this section unless, under the plan, the entire interest of each employee—

"(A) either will be distributed to him not later than his taxable year in which he attains the age of 70½ years, or, in the case of an amployee other than an owner-employee (as defined in subsection (c)(3)), in which he retires, whichever is the later, or

"(B) will be distributed, commencing not later than such taxable year, (i) in accordance with regulations prescribed by the Secretary or his delegate, over the life of such employee or over the lives of such employee and his spouse, or (ii) in accordance with such regulations, over a period not extending beyond the life expectancy of such employee or the life expectancy of such employee and his spouse.

A trust shall not be disqualified under this paragraph by reason of distributions under a designation, prior to the date of the enactment of this paragraph, by any employee under the plan of which such trust is a part, of a method of distribution which does not meet the terms of the preceding sentence.

"(10) In the case of a plan which provides contributions or benefits for employees some or all of whom are owner-employees (as defined in subsection (c)(3))—

"(A) paragraph (3) and the first and second sentences of paragraph (5) shall not apply, but—

"(i) such plan shall not be considered discriminatory within the meaning of paragraph (4) merely because the contributions or benefits of or on behalf of employees under the plan bear a uniform relationship to the total compensation, or the basic or regular rate of compensation, of such employees, and

"(ii) such plan shall not be considered discriminatory within the meaning of paragraph (4) solely because under the plan contributions described in subsection (e)(3)(A) which are in excess of the amounts which may be deducted under section 404 for the taxable year may be made on behalf of any owner-employee; and

"(B) a trust forming a part of such plan shall constitute a qualified trust under this section only if the requirements in subsection (d) are also met."

• 1966, Foreign Investors Tax Act of 1966 (P.L. 89-809)

P.L. 89-809, §204(b)(1)(A):

Amended Code Sec. 401(a)(10)(A)(ii) by deleting "(determined without regard to section 404(a)(10))". **Effective** 1-1-68.

• 1962, Self-Employed Individuals Tax Retirement Act of 1962 (P.L. 87-792)

P.L. 87-792, §2:

Amended Code Sec. 401(a)(5) by inserting the following sentence: "For purposes of this paragraph and paragraph (10), the total compensation of an individual who is an employee within the meaning of subsection (c)(1) means such individual's earned income (as defined in subsection (c)(2)), and the basic or regular rate of compensation of such an individual shall be determined, under regulations prescribed by the Secretary or his delegate, with respect to that portion of his earned income which bears the same ratio to his earned income as the basic or regular compensation of the employees under the plan bears to the total compensation of such employees.", and by adding paragraphs (7), (8), (9), and (10) to Sec. 401(a). **Effective** 1-1-63.

[Sec. 401(b)]

(b) CERTAIN RETROACTIVE CHANGES IN PLAN.—A stock bonus, pension, profit-sharing, or annuity plan shall be considered as satisfying the requirements of subsection (a) for the period beginning with the date on which it was put into effect, or for the period beginning with the earlier of the date on which there was adopted or put into effect any amendment which caused the plan to fail to satisfy such requirements, and ending with the time prescribed by law for filing the return of the employer for his taxable year in which such plan or amendment was adopted (including extensions thereof) or such later time as the Secretary may designate, if all provisions of the plan which are necessary to satisfy such requirements are in effect by the end of such period and have been made effective for all purposes for the whole of such period.

Amendments

• 1976, Tax Reform Act of 1976 (P.L. 94-455)

P.L. 94-455, §1906(b)(13)(A):

Amended 1954 Code by substituting "Secretary" for "Secretary or his delegate" each place it appeared. **Effective** 2-1-77.

• 1974, Employee Retirement Income Security Act of 1974 (P.L. 93-406)

P.L. 93-406, §1023:

Amended Code Sec. 401(b). **Effective** 9-2-74. Prior to amendment, Code Sec. 401(b) read as follows:

(b) CERTAIN RETROACTIVE CHANGES IN PLAN.—A stock bonus, pension, profit-sharing, or annuity plan shall be considered as satisfying the requirements of paragraphs (3), (4), (5), and (6) of subsection (a) for the period beginning with the date on which it was put into effect and ending with the 15th day of the third month following the close of the taxable year of the employer in which the plan was put in effect, if all provisions of the plan which are necessary to satisfy such requirements are in effect by the end of such period and have been made effective for all purposes with respect to the whole of such period.

[Sec. 401(c)]

(c) DEFINITIONS AND RULES RELATING TO SELF-EMPLOYED INDIVIDUALS AND OWNER-EMPLOYEES.—For purposes of this section—

(1) SELF-EMPLOYED INDIVIDUAL TREATED AS EMPLOYEE.—

(A) IN GENERAL.—The term "employee" includes, for any taxable year, an individual who is a self-employed individual for such taxable year.

(B) SELF-EMPLOYED INDIVIDUAL.—The term "self-employed individual" means, with respect to any taxable year, an individual who has earned income (as defined in paragraph (2)) for such taxable year. To the extent provided in regulations prescribed by the Secretary, such term also includes, for any taxable year—

(i) an individual who would be a self-employed individual within the meaning of the preceding sentence but for the fact that the trade or business carried on by such individual did not have net profits for the taxable year, and

(ii) an individual who has been a self-employed individual within the meaning of the preceding sentence for any prior taxable year.

(2) EARNED INCOME.—

(A) IN GENERAL.—The term "earned income" means the net earnings from self-employment (as defined in section 1402(a)), but such net earnings shall be determined—

(i) only with respect to a trade or business in which personal services of the taxpayer are a material income-producing factor,

(ii) without regard to paragraphs (4) and (5) of section 1402(c),

(iii) in the case of any individual who is treated as an employee under sections 3121(d)(3)(A), (C), or (D), without regard to paragraph (2) of section 1402(c),

(iv) without regard to items which are not included in gross income for purposes of this chapter, and the deductions properly allocable to or chargeable against such items,

(v) with regard to the deductions allowed by section 404 to the taxpayer, and

(vi) with regard to the deduction allowed to the taxpayer by section 164(f).

For purposes of this subparagraph, section 1402, as in effect for a taxable year ending on December 31, 1962, shall be treated as having been in effect for all taxable years ending before such date. For purposes of this part only (other than sections 419 and 419A), this subparagraph shall be applied as if the term "trade or business" for purposes of section 1402 included service described in section 1402(c)(6).

(C) [B] INCOME FROM DISPOSITION OF CERTAIN PROPERTY.—For purposes of this section, the term "earned income" includes gains (other than any gain which is treated under any provision of this chapter as gain from the sale or exchange of a capital asset) and net earnings derived from the sale or other disposition of, the transfer of any interest in, or the licensing of the use of property (other than good will) by an individual whose personal efforts created such property.

(3) OWNER-EMPLOYEE.—The term "owner-employee" means an employee who—

(A) owns the entire interest in an unincorporated trade or business, or

(B) in the case of a partnership, is a partner who owns more than 10 percent of either the capital interest or the profits interest in such partnership.

To the extent provided in regulations prescribed by the Secretary, such term also means an individual who has been an owner-employee within the meaning of the preceding sentence.

(4) EMPLOYER.—An individual who owns the entire interest in an unincorporated trade or business shall be treated as his own employer. A partnership shall be treated as the employer of each partner who is an employee within the meaning of paragraph (1).

(5) CONTRIBUTIONS ON BEHALF OF OWNER-EMPLOYEES.—The term "contribution on behalf of an owner-employee" includes, except as the context otherwise requires, a contribution under a plan—

(A) by the employer for an owner-employee, and

(B) by an owner-employee as an employee.

(6) SPECIAL RULE FOR CERTAIN FISHERMEN.—For purposes of this subsection, the term "self-employed individual" includes an individual described in section 3121(b)(20) (relating to certain fishermen).

Amendments

• 2006, Pension Protection Act of 2006 (P.L. 109-280)

P.L. 109-280, §811, provides:

SEC. 811. PENSIONS AND INDIVIDUAL RETIREMENT ARRANGEMENT PROVISIONS OF ECONOMIC GROWTH AND TAX RELIEF RECONCILIATION ACT OF 2001 MADE PERMANENT.

Title IX of the Economic Growth and Tax Relief Reconciliation Act of 2001 [P.L. 107-16] shall not apply to the provisions of, and amendments made by, subtitles A through F of title VI [§§601-666]of such Act (relating to pension and individual retirement arrangement provisions).

• 2001, Economic Growth and Tax Relief Reconciliation Act of 2001 (P.L. 107-16)

P.L. 107-16, §611(g)(1):

Amended Code Sec. 401(c)(2)(A) by adding at the end a new sentence. **Effective** for years beginning after 12-31-2001. For a special rule, see Act Sec. 611(i)(3), below.

P.L. 107-16, §611(i)(3), as added by P.L. 107-147, §411(j)(3), provides:

(3) SPECIAL RULE.—In the case of plan that, on June 7, 2001, incorporated by reference the limitation of section 415(b)(1)(A) of the Internal Revenue Code of 1986, section 411(d)(6) of such Code and section 204(g)(1) of the Em-

ployee Retirement Income Security Act of 1974 do not apply to a plan amendment that—

(A) is adopted on or before June 30, 2002,

(B) reduces benefits to the level that would have applied without regard to the amendments made by subsection (a) of this section, and

(C) is effective no earlier than the years described in paragraph (2).

P.L. 107-16, §901(a)-(b), provides [but see P.L. 109-280, §811, above]:

SEC. 901. SUNSET OF PROVISIONS OF ACT.

(a) IN GENERAL.—All provisions of, and amendments made by, this Act shall not apply—

(1) to taxable, plan, or limitation years beginning after December 31, 2010, or

(2) in the case of title V, to estates of decedents dying, gifts made, or generation skipping transfers, after December 31, 2010.

(b) APPLICATION OF CERTAIN LAWS.—The Internal Revenue Code of 1986 and the Employee Retirement Income Security Act of 1974 shall be applied and administered to years, estates, gifts, and transfers described in subsection (a) as if the provisions and amendments described in subsection (a) had never been enacted.

• 1986, Tax Reform Act of 1986 (P.L. 99-514)

P.L. 99-514, §1143(a):

Amended Code Sec. 401(c) by adding at the end thereof new paragraph (6). **Effective** for tax years beginning after 12-31-86.

P.L. 99-514, §1848(b):

Amended Code Sec. 401(c)(2)(A) by striking out "sections 404 and 405(c)" and inserting in lieu thereof "section 404". **Effective** as if included in the provision of P.L. 98-369 to which it relates.

• 1983, Social Security Amendments of 1983 (P.L. 98-21)

P.L. 98-21, §124(c)(4)(A):

Amended Code Sec. 401(c)(2)(A) by striking out "and" at the end of clause (iv), by striking out the period at the end of clause (v) and inserting in place thereof ", and", and by inserting clause (vi) after clause (v). **Effective** for tax years beginning after 1989.

• 1982, Tax Equity and Fiscal Responsibility Act of 1982 (P.L. 97-248)

P.L. 97-248, §238(d)(1):

Amended Code Sec. 401(c)(1). **Effective** for years beginning after 12-31-83. Prior to amendment, Code Sec. 401(c)(1) read as follows:

(1) EMPLOYEE.—The term "employee" includes, for any taxable year, an individual who has earned income (as defined in paragraph (2)) for the taxable year. To the extent provided in regulations prescribed by the Secretary, such term also includes, for any taxable year—

(A) an individual who would be an employee within the meaning of the preceding sentence but for the fact that the trade or business carried on by such individual did not have net profits for the taxable year, and

(B) an individual who has been an employee within the meaning of the preceding sentence for any prior taxable year.

P.L. 97-248, §238(d)(2):

Amended subparagraph (A) of section 401(c)(2) by striking out "and" at the end of clause (iii), by striking out the period at the end of clause (iv) and inserting in lieu thereof ", and", and by adding at the end thereof the new clause (v). **Effective** for years beginning after 12-31-83.

• 1976, Tax Reform Act of 1976 (P.L. 94-455)

P.L. 94-455, §1906(b)(13)(A):

Amended 1954 Code by substituting "Secretary" for "Secretary or his delegate" each place it appeared. **Effective** 2-1-77.

• 1968 (P.L. 90-607)

P.L. 90-607, provides:

"The amendment made by subsection (c) [of Sec. 204, P.L. 89-809] shall apply with respect to taxable years beginning after December 31, 1967, and in the case of a taxpayer who applies the averaging provisions of section 401(e)(3) of the Internal Revenue Code of 1954 for a taxable year beginning after December 31, 1967, the computation of the amount deductible under section 404 of such Code for any prior taxable year which began before January 1, 1968, shall be made, for purposes of such averaging provisions, as if the amendment made by subsection (c) were applicable to such prior taxable year."

• 1966, Foreign Investors Tax Act of 1966 (P.L. 89-809)

P.L. 89-809, §204(c):

Amended Code Sec. 401(c)(2) by striking out subparagraphs (A) and (B) and inserting new subparagraph (A). **Effective** as provided in P.L. 90-607, above. Prior to being stricken, subparagraphs (A) and (B) read as follows:

"(A) In General.—The term `earned income' means the net earnings from self-employment (as defined in section 1402(a)) to the extent that such net earnings constitute earned income (as defined in section 911(b) but determined with the application of subparagraph (B)), but such net earnings shall be determined—

"(i) without regard to paragraphs (4) and (5) of section 1402(c),

"(ii) in the case of any individual who is treated as an employee under sections 3121(d)(3)(A), (C), or (D), without regard to paragraph (2) of section 1402(c), and

"(iii) without regard to items which are not included in gross income for purposes of this chapter, and the deductions properly allocable to or chargeable against such items.

"For purposes of this subparagraph, sections 911(b) and 1402, as in effect for a taxable year ending on December 31, 1962, and subparagraph (B), as in effect for a taxable year beginning on January 1, 1963, shall be treated as having been in effect for all taxable years ending before such date.

"(B) Earned Income When Both Personal Services and Capital Are Material Income-Producing Factors.—In applying section 911(b) for purposes of subparagraph (A), in the case of an individual who is an employee within the meaning of paragraph (1) and who is engaged in a trade or business in which both personal services and capital are material income-producing factors and with respect to which the individual actually renders personal services on a full-time, or substantially full-time, basis, so much of his share of the net profits of such trade or business as does not exceed $2,500 shall be considered as earned income. In the case of any such individual who is engaged in more than one trade or business with respect to which he actually renders substantial personal services, if with respect to all such trades or businesses he actually renders personal services on a full-time, or substantially full-time, basis, there shall be considered as earned income with respect to the trades or businesses in which both personal services and capital are material income-producing factors—

"(i) so much of his share of the net profits of such trades or businesses as does not exceed $2,500, reduced by

"(ii) his share of the net profits of any trade or business in which only personal services is [are] a material income-producing factor.

"The preceding sentences shall not be construed to reduce the share of net profits of any trade or business which under the second sentence of section 911(b) would be considered as earned income of any such individual."

P.L. 89-809, §205(a):

Amended Code Sec. 401(c)(2) by adding new subparagraph (C). **Effective** 11-13-66.

• **1962, Self-Employed Individuals Tax Retirement Act of 1962 (P.L. 87-792)**

P.L. 87-792, §2:

Added Code Sec. 401(c) and redesignated former Code Sec. 401(c) as Code Sec. 401(h). **Effective** for tax years beginning after 12-31-62.

[Sec. 401(d)]

(d) CONTRIBUTION LIMIT ON OWNER-EMPLOYEES.—A trust forming part of a pension or profit-sharing plan which provides contributions or benefits for employees some or all of whom are owner-employees shall constitute a qualified trust under this section only if, in addition to meeting the requirements of subsection (a), the plan provides that contributions on behalf of any owner-employee may be made only with respect to the earned income of such owner-employee which is derived from the trade or business with respect to which such plan is established.

Amendments

• **1996, Small Business Job Protection Act of 1996 (P.L. 104-188)**

P.L. 104-188, §1441(a):

Amended Code Sec. 401(d). **Effective** for years beginning after 12-31-96. Prior to amendment, Code Sec. 401(d) read as follows:

(d) ADDITIONAL REQUIREMENTS FOR QUALIFICATION OF TRUSTS AND PLANS BENEFITING OWNER-EMPLOYEES.—A trust forming part of a pension or profit-sharing plan which provides contributions or benefits for employees some or all of whom are owner-employees shall constitute a qualified trust under this section only if, in addition to meeting the requirements of subsection (a), the following requirements of this subsection are met by the trust and by the plan of which such trust is a part:

(1)(A) If the plan provides contributions or benefits for an owner-employee who controls, or for two or more owner-employees who together control, the trade or business with respect to which the plan is established, and who also control as an owner-employee or as owner-employees one or more other trades or businesses, such plan and the plans established with respect to such other trades or businesses, when coalesced, constitute a single plan which meets the requirements of subsection (a) (including paragraph (10) thereof) and of this subsection with respect to the employees of all such trades or businesses (including the trade or business with respect to which the plan intended to qualify under this section is established).

(B) For purposes of subparagraph (A), an owner-employee, or two or more owner-employees, shall be considered to control a trade or business if such owner-employee, or such two or more owner-employees together—

(i) own the entire interest in an unincorporated trade or business, or

(ii) in the case of a partnership, own more than 50 percent of either the capital interest or the profits interest in such partnership.

For purposes of the preceding sentence, an owner-employee, or two or more owner-employees, shall be treated as owning any interest in a partnership which is owned, directly or indirectly, by a partnership which such owner-employee, or such two or more owner-employees, are considered to control within the meaning of the preceding sentence.

(2) The plan does not provide contributions or benefits for any owner-employee who controls (within the meaning of paragraph (1)(B)), or for two or more owner-employees who together control, as an owner-employee or as owner-employees, any other trade or business, unless the employees of each trade or business which such owner-employee or such owner-employees control are included under a plan which meets the requirements of subsection (a) (including paragraph (10) thereof) and of this subsection, and provides contributions and benefits for employees which are not less favorable than contributions and benefits provided for owner-employees under the plan.

(3) Under the plan, contributions on behalf of any owner-employee may be made only with respect to the earned income of such owner-employee which is derived from the trade or business with respect to which such plan is established.

• **1983, Technical Corrections Act of 1982 (P.L. 97-448)**

P.L. 97-448, §103(c)(10)(A):

Amended the second sentence of Code Sec. 401(d)(5). **Effective** as if included in the provision of P.L. 97-34 to which it relates. Prior to amendment, the second sentence of Code Sec. 401(d)(5) read as follows:

"Subparagraphs (A) and (B) do not apply to contributions described in subsection (e)."

P.L. 97-448, §306(a)(12):

Amended Code Sec. 401(d)(2) (as redesignated by P.L. 97-248, §237) by striking out "paragraph (9)(B)" and inserting in lieu thereof "paragraph (1)(B)". **Effective** as if included in the provision of P.L. 97-248 to which it relates.

• **1982, Tax Equity and Fiscal Responsibility Act of 1982 (P.L. 97-248)**

P.L. 97-248, §237(a):

Amended Code Sec. 401(d) by striking out paragraphs (1) through (7), and by redesignating paragraphs (9), (10), and (11) as paragraphs (1), (2), and (3), respectively. **Effective** for years beginning after 12-31-83. Prior to amendment, Code Sec. 401(d)(1)-(7) read as follows:

(1) In the case of a trust which is created on or after October 10, 1962, or which was created before such date but is not exempt from tax under section 501(a) as an organization described in subsection (a) on the day before such date, the assets thereof are held by a bank or other person who demonstrates to the satisfaction of the Secretary that the manner in which he will administer the trust will be consistent with the requirements of this section. A trust shall not be disqualified under this paragraph merely because a per-

son (including the employer) other than the trustee or custodian so administering the trust may be granted, under the trust instrument, the power to control the investment of the trust funds either by directing investments (including reinvestments, disposals, and exchanges) or by disapproving proposed investments (including reinvestments, disposals, and exchanges). This paragraph shall not apply to a trust created or organized outside the United States before October 10, 1962, if, under section 402(c), it is treated as exempt from tax under section 501(a) on the day before such date; or, to the extent provided under regulations prescribed by the Secretary, to a trust which uses annuity, endowment, or life insurance contracts of a life insurance company exclusively to fund the benefits prescribed by the trust, if the life insurance company supplies annually such information about trust transactions affecting owner-employees as the Secretary shall by forms or regulations prescribe. For purposes of this paragraph, the term "bank" means a bank as defined in section 581, an insured credit union (within the meaning of section 101(6) of the Federal Credit Union Act), a corporation which under the laws of the State of its incorporation is subject to supervision and examination by the commissioner of banking or other officer of such State in charge of the administration of the banking laws of such State, and, in the case of a trust created or organized outside the United States, a bank or trust company, wherever incorporated, exercising fiduciary powers and subject to supervision and examination by governmental authority.

(2) Under the plan—

(A) the employees' rights to or derived from the contributions under the plan are nonforfeitable at the time the contributions are paid to or under the plan; and

(B) in the case of a profit-sharing plan, there is a definite formula for determining the contributions to be made by the employer on behalf of employees (other than owner-employees).

Subparagraph (A) shall not apply to contributions which, under provisions of the plan adopted pursuant to regulations prescribed by the Secretary to preclude the discrimination prohibited by subsection (a)(4), may not be used to provide benefits for designated employees in the event of early termination of the plan.

(3)(A) The plan benefits each employee having 3 or more years of service (within the meaning of section 410(a)(3)).

(B) For purposes of subparagraph (A), the term "employee" does not include—

(i) any employee included in a unit of employees covered by a collective-bargaining agreement described in section 410(b)(3)(A), and

(ii) any employee who is a nonresident alien individual described in section 410(b)(3)(C).

(4) Under the plan—

(A) contributions or benefits are not provided for any owner-employee unless such owner-employee has consented to being included under the plan; and

(B) no benefits in excess of contributions made by an owner-employee as an employee may be paid to any owner-employee, except in the case of his becoming disabled (within the meaning of section 72(m)(7)), prior to his attaining the age of 59½ years.

Subparagraph (B) shall not apply to any distribution to which section 72(m)(9) applies.

(5) The plan does not permit—

(A) contributions to be made by the employer on behalf of any owner-employee in excess of the amounts which may be deducted under section 404 for the taxable year;

(B) in the case of a plan which provides contributions or benefits only for owner-employees, contributions to be made on behalf of any owner-employee in excess of the amounts which may be deducted under section 404 for the taxable year; and

(C) if a distribution under the plan is made to any employee and if any portion of such distribution is an amount described in section 72(m)(5)(A)(i), contributions to be made on behalf of such employee for the 5 taxable years succeeding the taxable year in which such distribution is made.

Subparagraphs (A) and (B) shall not apply to contributions described in subsection (e), and shall not apply to any deductible employee contribution (as defined in section 72(o)(5)). Subparagraph (C) shall not apply to a distribution on account of the termination of the plan.

(6) Except as provided in this paragraph, the plan meets the requirements of subsection (a)(4) without taking into account for any purpose contributions or benefits under chapter 2 (relating to tax on self-employment income), chapter 21 (relating to Federal Insurance Contributions Act), title II of the Social Security Act, as amended, or any other Federal or State law. If—

(A) of the contributions deductible under section 404, not more than one-third is deductible by reason of contributions by the employer on behalf of owner-employees, and

(B) taxes paid by the owner-employees under chapter 2 (relating to tax on self-employment income), and the taxes which would be payable under such chapter 2 by the owner-employees but for paragraphs (4) and (5) of section 1402(c), are taken into account as contributions by the employer on behalf of such owner-employees,

then taxes paid under section 3111 (relating to tax on employers) with respect to an employee may, for purposes of subsection (a)(4), be taken into account as contributions by the employer for such employee under the plan.

(7) Under the plan, if an owner-employee dies before his entire interest has been distributed to him, or if distribution has been commenced in accordance with subsection (a)(9)(B) to his surviving spouse and such surviving spouse dies before his entire interest has been distributed to such surviving spouse, his entire interest (or the remaining part of such interest if distribution thereof has commenced) will, within 5 years after his death (or the death of his surviving spouse), be distributed, or applied to the purchase of an immediate annuity for his beneficiary or beneficiaries (or the beneficiary or beneficiaries of his surviving spouse) which will be payable for the life of such beneficiary or beneficiaries (or for a term certain not extending beyond the life expectancy of such beneficiary or beneficiaries) and which will be immediately distributed to such beneficiary or beneficiaries. The preceding sentence shall not apply if distribution of the interest of an owner-employee has commenced and such distribution is for a term certain over a period permitted under subsection (a)(9)(B)(ii).

• 1981, Economic Recovery Tax Act of 1981 (P.L. 97-34)

P.L. 97-34, §312(e)(2):

Amended Code Sec. 401(d)(4) by adding a new sentence at the end. **Effective** for plans which include employees within the meaning of Code Sec. 401(c)(1) with respect to tax years beginning after 12-31-81.

P.L. 97-34, §314(a)(1):

Amended Code Sec. 401(d)(5) by adding a new sentence at the end. **Effective** for distributions made after 12-31-80, in tax years beginning after that date.

• 1980, Miscellaneous Revenue Act of 1980 (P.L. 96-605)

P.L. 96-605, §225(b)(2):

Amended Code Sec. 401(d)(3)(B) by: (1) striking out "section 410(b)(2)(A)" and inserting in lieu thereof "section 410(b)(3)(A)"; and (2) striking out "section 410(b)(2)(C)" and inserting in lieu thereof "section 410(b)(3)(C)". **Effective** with respect to plan years beginning after 12-31-80.

• 1976, Tax Reform Act of 1976 (P.L. 94-455)

P.L. 94-455, §1906(b)(13)(A):

Amended 1954 Code by substituting "Secretary" for "Secretary or his delegate" each place it appeared. **Effective** 2-1-77.

• 1974, Employee Retirement Income Security Act of 1974 (P.L. 93-406)

P.L. 93-406, §§1022(b)(2), 1022(c)(1), (2), 1022(f), 2001(h)(1), 2001(e)(1), (2):

Amended paragraphs (1), (3), (4) and (5) and repealed paragraph (8) of Code Sec. 401(d). The amendments are subject to the special **effective** dates and transitional rules applicable to Code Sec. 410. For such special effective dates and transitional rules, see the historical note for §1017, P.L. 93-406, following the text of Code Sec. 410. Prior to repeal by P.L. 93-406, effective for contributions made in tax years beginning after 1975, Code Sec. 401(d)(8) read as follows:

(8) Under the plan—

(A) any contribution which is an excess contribution, together with the income attributable to such excess contribution, is (unless subsection (e)(2)(E) applies) to be repaid to the owner-employee on whose behalf such excess contribution is made;

(B) if for any taxable year the plan does not, by reason of subsection (e)(2)(A), meet (for purposes of section 404) the requirements of this subsection with respect to an owner-employee, the income for the taxable year attributable to the interest of such owner-employee under the plan is to be paid to such owner-employee; and

(C) the entire interest of an owner-employee is to be repaid to him when required by the provisions of subsection (e)(2)(E)."

P.L. 93-406, §1022(f):

Amended the last sentence of Code Sec. 401(d)(1) by adding "an insured credit union (within the meaning of section 101(6) of the Federal Credit Union Act),". **Effective** 1-1-74.

• 1966, Foreign Investors Tax Act of 1966 (P.L. 89-809)

P.L. 89-809, §204(b)(1)(B), (C):

Amended Code Sec. 401(d)(5)(A), (B) and (6)(A) by deleting "(determined without regard to section 404(a)(10))". **Effective** 1-1-68.

• 1965, Social Security Amendments of 1965 (P.L. 89-97)

P.L. 89-97, §106(d):

Amended Code Sec. 401(d)(4)(B) by substituting "section 72(m)(7)" for "section 213(g)(3)". **Effective** for tax years beginning after 12-31-66.

• 1962, Self-Employed Individuals Tax Retirement Act of 1962 (P.L. 87-792)

P.L. 87-792, §2:

Added Code Sec. 401(d). **Effective** for tax years beginning after 12-31-62.

[Sec. 401(e)—Repealed]

Amendments

• 1984, Deficit Reduction Act of 1984 (P.L. 98-369)

P.L. 98-369, §713(d)(3):

Repealed Code Sec. 401(e). **Effective** as if included in the provision of P.L. 97-248 to which it relates. Prior to repeal, it read as follows:

(e) Contributions for Premiums on Annuity, Etc., Contracts.—A contribution by the employer on behalf of an owner-employee is described in this subsection if—

(1) under the plan such contribution is required to be applied (directly or through a trustee) to pay premiums or other consideration for one or more annuity, endowment, or life insurance contracts on the life of such owner-employee issued under the plan,

(2) the amount of such contribution exceeds the amount deductible under section 404 with respect to contributions made by the employer on behalf of such owner-employee under the plan, and

(3) the amount of such contribution does not exceed the average of the amounts which were deductible under section 404 with respect to contributions made by the employer on behalf of such owner-employee under the plan (or which would have been deductible if such section had been in effect) for the first three taxable years (A) preceding the year in which the last such annuity, endowment, or life insurance contract was issued under the plan, and (B) in which such owner-employee derived earned income from the trade or business with respect to which the plan is established, or for so many of such taxable years as such owner-employee was engaged in such trade or business and derived earned income therefrom.

In the case of any individual on whose behalf contributions described in paragraph (1) are made under more than one plan as an owner-employee during any taxable year, the preceding sentence does not apply if the amount of such contributions under all such plans for all such years exceeds $15,000. Any contribution which is described in this subsection shall, for purposes of section 4972(b), be taken into account as a contribution made by such owner-employee as an employee to the extent that the amount of such contribution is not deductible under section 404 for the taxable year, but only for the purpose of applying section 4972(b) to other contributions made by such owner-employee as an employee.

• 1981, Economic Recovery Tax Act of 1981 (P.L. 97-34)

P.L. 97-34, §312(c)(2):

Amended Code Sec. 401(e) by striking out "$7,500" and inserting "$15,000". **Effective** for plans which include employees within the meaning of Code Sec. 401(c)(1) with respect to tax years beginning after 12-31-81.

• 1974, Employee Retirement Income Security Act of 1974 (P.L. 93-406)

P.L. 93-406, §2001(e)(3):

Amended Code Sec. 401(e). **Effective** for contributions made in tax years beginning after 12-31-75. Prior to amendment, Code Sec. 401(e) read as follows:

"(e) Excess Contributions on Behalf of Owner-Employees.—

"(1) Excess contribution defined.—For purposes of this section, the term `excess contribution' means, except as provided in paragraph (3)—

"(A) if, in the taxable year, contributions are made under the plan only on behalf of owner-employees, the amount of any contribution made on behalf of any owner-employee which (without regard to this subsection) is not deductible under section 404 for the taxable year; or

"(B) if, in the taxable year, contributions are made under the plan on behalf of employees other than owner-employees—

"(i) the amount of any contribution made by the employer on behalf of any owner-employee which (without regard to this subsection) is not deductible under section 404 for the taxable year;

"(ii) the amount of any contribution made by any owner-employee (as an employee) at a rate which exceeds the rate of contributions permitted to be made by employees other than owner-employees;

"(iii) the amount of any contribution made by any owner-employee (as an employee) which exceeds the lesser of $2,500 or 10 percent of the earned income for such taxable year derived by such owner-employee from the trade or business with respect to which the plan is established; and

"(iv) in the case of any individual on whose behalf contributions are made under more than one plan as an owner-employee, the amount of any contribution made by such owner-employee (as an employee) under all such plans which exceeds $2,500; and

"(C) the amount of any contribution made on behalf of an owner-employee in any taxable year for which, under paragraph (2)(A) or (E), the plan does not (for purposes of section 404) meet the requirements of subsection (d) with respect to such owner-employee.

For purposes of this subsection, the amount of any contribution which is allocable (determined in accordance with regulations prescribed by the Secretary or his delegate) to the purchase of life, accident, health, or other insurance shall not be taken into account.

"(2) Effect of excess contribution.—

"(A) In general.—If an excess contribution (other than an excess contribution to which subparagraph (E) applies) is made on behalf of an owner-employee in any taxable year, the plan with respect to which such excess contribution is made shall, except as provided in subparagraphs (C) and (D), be considered, for purposes of section 404, as not meeting the requirements of subsection (d) with respect to such owner-employee for the taxable year and for all succeeding taxable years.

"(B) Inclusion of amounts in gross income of owner-employees.—For any taxable year for which any plan does not meet the requirements of subsection (d) with respect to an owner-employee by reason of subparagraph (A), the gross income of such owner-employee shall, for purposes of this chapter, include the amount of net income for such taxable year attributable to the interest of such owner-employee under such plan.

"(C) Repayment within prescribed period.—Subparagraph (A) shall not apply to an excess contribution with respect to any taxable year, if, on or before the close of the 6-month period beginning on the day on which the Secretary or his delegate sends notice (by certified or registered mail) to the person to whom such excess contribution was paid of the amount of such excess contribution, the amount of such excess contribution, and the net income attributable thereto, is repaid to the owner-employee on whose behalf such excess contribution was made. If the excess contribution is an excess contribution as defined in paragraph (1)(A) or (B)(i), or is an excess contribution as defined in paragraph (1)(C) with respect to which a deduction has been claimed under section 404, the notice required by the preceding sentence shall not be mailed prior to the time that the amount of the tax under this chapter of such owner-employee for the taxable year in which such excess contribution was made has been finally determined.

"(D) Repayment after prescribed period.—If an excess contribution, together with the net income attributable thereto, is not repaid within the 6-month period referred to in subparagraph (C), subparagraph (A) shall not apply to an excess contribution with respect to any taxable year beginning with the taxable year in which the person to whom such excess contribution was paid repays the amount of such excess contribution to the owner-employee on whose behalf such excess contribution was made, and pays to such owner-employee the amount of net income attributable to the interest of such owner-employee which, under subparagraph (B), has been included in the gross income of such owner-employee for any prior taxable year.

"(E) Special rule if excess contribution was willfully made.—If an excess contribution made on behalf of an owner-employee is determined to have been willfully made, then—

"(i) subparagraphs (A), (B), (C), and (D) shall not apply with respect to such excess contribution;

"(ii) there shall be distributed to the owner-employee on whose behalf such excess contribution was willfully made his entire interest in all plans with respect to which he is an owner-employee; and

"(iii) no plan shall, for purposes of section 404, be considered as meeting the requirements of subsection (d) with respect to such owner-employee for the taxable year in which it is determined that such excess contribution was willfully made and for the 5 taxable years following such taxable year.

"(F) Statute of limitations.—In any case in which subparagraph (A) applies, the period of assessing any deficiency arising by reason of—

"(i) the disallowance of any deduction under section 404 on account of a plan not meeting the requirements of subsection (d) with respect to the owner-employee on whose behalf an excess contribution was made, or

"(ii) the inclusion, under subparagraph (B), in gross income of such owner-employee of income attributable to the interest of such owner-employee under a plan,

for the taxable year in which such excess contribution was made or for any succeeding taxable year shall not expire prior to one year after the close of the 6-month period referred to in subparagraph (C).

"(3) Contributions for premiums on annuity, etc., contracts.—A contribution by the employer on behalf of an owner-employee shall not be considered to be an excess contribution within the meaning of paragraph (1), if—

"(A) under the plan such contribution is required to be applied (directly or through a trustee) to pay premiums or other consideration for one or more annuity, endowment, or life insurance contracts on the life of such owner-employee issued under the plan,

"(B) the amount of such contribution exceeds the amount deductible under section 404 with respect to contributions made by the employer on behalf of such owner-employee under the plan, and

"(C) the amount of such contribution does not exceed the average of the amounts which were deductible under section 404 with respect to contributions made by the employer on behalf of such owner-employee under the plan (or which would have been deductible under such section if such section had been in effect) for the first 3 taxable years (i) preceding the year in which the last such annuity, endowment, or life insurance contract was issued under the plan and (ii) in which such owner-employee derived earned income from the trade or business with respect to which the plan is established, or for so many of such taxable years as such owner-employee was engaged in such trade or business and derived earned income therefrom.

In the case of any individual on whose behalf contributions described in subparagraph (A) are made under more than one plan as an owner-employee during any taxable year, the preceding sentence shall not apply if the amount of such contributions under all such plans for such taxable year exceeds $2,500. Any contribution which is not considered to be an excess contribution by reason of the application of this paragraph shall, for purposes of subparagraphs (B)(ii), (iii), and (iv) of paragraph (1), be taken into account as a contribution made by such owner-employee as an employee to the extent that the amount of such contribution is not deductible under section 404 for the taxable year, but only for the purpose of applying such subparagraphs to other contributions made by such owner-employee as an employee."

• 1966, Foreign Investors Tax Act of 1966 (P.L. 89-809)

P.L. 89-809, §204(b)(1)(D), (E):

Amended Code Sec. 401(e)(1)(A), (B)(i), and Code Sec. 401(e)(3)(B), (C), and the last sentence of (e)(3) by deleting "(determined without regard to section 404(a)(10))" immediately following "section 404". **Effective** 1-1-68.

• 1962, Self-Employed Individuals Tax Retirement Act of 1962 (P.L. 87-792)

P.L. 87-792, §2:

Added Code Sec. 401(e). **Effective** for tax years beginning after 12-31-62.

[Sec. 401(f)]

(f) CERTAIN CUSTODIAL ACCOUNTS AND CONTRACTS.—For purposes of this title, a custodial account, an annuity contract, or a contract (other than a life, health or accident, property, casualty, or liability insurance contract) issued by an insurance company qualified to do business in a State shall be treated as a qualified trust under this section if—

(1) the custodial account or contract would, except for the fact that it is not a trust, constitute a qualified trust under this section, and

(2) in the case of a custodial account the assets thereof are held by a bank (as defined in section 408(n)) or another person who demonstrates, to the satisfaction of the Secretary, that the manner in which he will hold the assets will be consistent with the requirements of this section.

For purposes of this title, in the case of a custodial account or contract treated as a qualified trust under this section by reason of this subsection, the person holding the assets of such account or holding such contract shall be treated as the trustee thereof.

Amendments

• 1984, Deficit Reduction Act of 1984 (P.L. 98-369)

P.L. 98-369, §713(c)(2)(A):

Amended Code Sec. 401(f)(2) by striking out "(as defined in subsection (d)(1))" and inserting in lieu thereof "(as defined in section 408(n))". **Effective** as if included in the provision of P.L. 97-248 to which it relates.

• 1976, Tax Reform Act of 1976 (P.L. 94-455)

P.L. 94-455, §1505(b):

Amended Code Sec. 401(f). **Effective** for tax years beginning after 12-31-75. Prior to amendment, Sec. 401(f) read as follows:

(f) CERTAIN CUSTODIAL ACCOUNTS AND ANNUITY CONTRACTS.—For purposes of this title, a custodial account or an annuity contract shall be treated as a qualified trust under this section if—

(1) the custodial account or annuity contract would, except for the fact that it is not a trust, constitute a qualified trust under this section, and

(2) in the case of a custodial account the assets thereof are held by a bank (as defined in subsection (d)(1)) or another person who demonstrates, to the satisfaction of the Secretary or his delegate, that the manner in which he will hold the assets will be consistent with the requirements of this section.

For purposes of this title, in the case of a custodial account or annuity contract treated as a qualified trust under this section by reason of this subsection, the person holding the assets of such account or holding such contract shall be treated as the trustee thereof.

• 1974, Employee Retirement Income Security Act of 1974 (P.L. 93-406)

P.L. 93-406, 1022(d):

Amended Code Sec. 401(f). **Effective** 1-1-74. Prior to amendment, Code Sec. 401(f) read as follows:

"(f) Certain Custodial Accounts.—

"(1) Treatment as qualified trust.—For purposes of this title, a custodial account shall be treated as a qualified trust under this section, if—

"(A) such custodial account would, except for the fact that it is not a trust, constitute a qualified trust under this section;

"(B) the custodian is a bank (as defined in subsection (d)(1));

"(C) the investment of the funds in such account (including all earnings) is to be made—

"(i) solely in regulated investment company stock with respect to which an employee is the beneficial owner, or

"(ii) solely in annuity, endowment, or life insurance contracts issued by an insurance company;

"(D) the shareholder of record of any such stock described in subparagraph (C)(i) is the custodian or its nominee; and

"(E) the contracts described in subparagraph (C)(ii) are held by the custodian until distributed under the plan.

For purposes of this title, in the case of a custodial account treated as a qualified trust under this section by reason of the preceding sentence, the custodian of such account shall be treated as the trustee thereof.

"(2) Definition.—For purposes of paragraph (1), the term `regulated investment company' means a domestic corporation which—

"(A) is a regulated investment company within the meaning of section 851(a), and

"(B) issues only redeemable stock."

• **1962, Self-Employed Individuals Tax Retirement Act of 1962 (P.L. 87-792)**

P.L. 87-792, §2:

Added Code Sec. 401(f). **Effective** for tax years beginning after 12-31-62.

[Sec. 401(g)]

(g) ANNUITY DEFINED.—For purposes of this section and sections 402, 403, and 404, the term "annuity" includes a face-amount certificate, as defined in section 2(a)(15) of the Investment Company Act of 1940 (15 U. S. C., sec. 80a-2); but does not include any contract or certificate issued after December 31, 1962, which is transferable, if any person other than the trustee of a trust described in section 401(a) which is exempt from tax under section 501(a) is the owner of such contract or certificate.

Amendments

• **1962, Self-Employed Individuals Tax Retirement Act of 1962 (P.L. 87-792)**

P.L. 87-792, §2:

Added Code Sec. 401(g). **Effective** for tax years beginning after 12-31-62.

[Sec. 401(h)]

(h) MEDICAL, ETC., BENEFITS FOR RETIRED EMPLOYEES AND THEIR SPOUSES AND DEPENDENTS.—Under regulations prescribed by the Secretary, and subject to the provisions of section 420, a pension or annuity plan may provide for the payment of benefits for sickness, accident, hospitalization, and medical expenses of retired employees, their spouses and their dependents, but only if—

(1) such benefits are subordinate to the retirement benefits provided by the plan,

(2) a separate account is established and maintained for such benefits,

(3) the employer's contributions to such separate account are reasonable and ascertainable,

(4) it is impossible, at any time prior to the satisfaction of all liabilities under the plan to provide such benefits, for any part of the corpus or income of such separate account to be (within the taxable year or thereafter) used for, or diverted to, any purpose other than the providing of such benefits,

(5) notwithstanding the provisions of subsection (a)(2), upon the satisfaction of all liabilities under the plan to provide such benefits, any amount remaining in such separate account must, under the terms of the plan, be returned to the employer, and

(6) in the case of an employee who is a key employee, a separate account is established and maintained for such benefits payable to such employee (and his spouse and dependents) and such benefits (to the extent attributable to plan years beginning after March 31, 1984, for which the employee is a key employee) are only payable to such employee (and his spouse and dependents) from such separate account.

For purposes of paragraph (6), the term "key employee" means any employee, who at any time during the plan year or any preceding plan year during which contributions were made on behalf of such employee, is or was a key employee as defined in section 416(i). In no event shall the requirements of paragraph (1) be treated as met if the aggregate actual contributions for medical benefits, when added to actual contributions for life insurance protection under the plan, exceed 25 percent of the total actual contributions to the plan (other than contributions to fund past service credits) after the date on which the account is established. For purposes of this subsection, the term "dependent" shall include any individual who is a child (as defined in section 152(f)(1)) of a retired employee who as of the end of the calendar year has not attained age 27.

Amendments

• **2010, Health Care and Education Reconciliation Act of 2010 (P.L. 111-152)**

P.L. 111-152, §1004(d)(5):

Amended Code Sec. 401(h) by adding at the end a new sentence. **Effective** 3-30-2010.

• **1990, Omnibus Budget Reconciliation Act of 1990 (P.L. 101-508)**

P.L. 101-508, §12011(b):

Amended Code Sec. 401(h) by inserting ", and subject to the provisions of section 420" after "Secretary". **Effective,** generally, for transfers in tax years beginning after 12-31-90. For a special rule, see Act Sec. 12011(c)(2), below.

P.L. 101-508, §12011(c)(2), provides:

(2) WAIVER OF ESTIMATED TAX PENALTIES.—No addition to tax shall be made under section 6654 or section 6655 of the Internal Revenue Code of 1986 for the taxable year preceding the taxpayer's 1st taxable year beginning after December 31, 1990, with respect to any underpayment to the extent such underpayment was created or increased by reason of section 420(b)(4)(B) of such Code (as added by subsection (a)).

• 1989, Omnibus Budget Reconciliation Act of 1989 (P.L. 101-239)

P.L. 101-239, §7311(a):

Amended Code Sec. 401(h) by adding at the end thereof a new sentence. **Effective**, generally, for contributions after 10-3-89. However, for a transitional rule, see Act Sec. 7311(b)(2), below.

P.L. 101-239, §7311(b)(2), provides:

(2) TRANSITION.—The amendment made by this section shall not apply to contributions made before January 1, 1990, if—

(A) the employer requested before October 3, 1989, a private letter ruling or determination letter with respect to the qualification of the plan maintaining the account under section 401(h) of the Internal Revenue Code of 1986,

(B) the request sets forth a method under which the amount of contributions to the account are to be determined on the basis of cost,

(C) such method is permissible under section 401(h) of such Code under the provisions of General Counsel Memorandum 39785, and

(D) the Internal Revenue Service issued before October 4, 1989, a private letter ruling, determination letter, or other letter providing that the specific plan involved qualifies under section 401(a) of such Code when such method is used, that contributions to the account are deductible, or acknowledging that the account would not adversely affect the qualified status of the plan (contingent on all phases of the particular plan being approved).

• 1986, Tax Reform Act of 1986 (P.L. 99-514)

P.L. 99-514, §1852(h)(1)(A) and (B):

Amended Code Sec. 401(h) by striking out "5-percent owner" each place it appears in paragraph (6) and inserting in lieu thereof "key employee", and by striking out the last sentence and inserting in lieu thereof "For purposes of paragraph (6), the term `key employee' means any employee, who at any time during the plan year or any preceding plan year during which contributions were made on behalf of such employee, is or was a key employee as defined in section 416(i)." **Effective** for years beginning after 12-31-85. Prior to amendment, the last sentence read as follows:

For purposes of paragraph (6), the term "5-percent owner" means any employee who, at any time during the plan year or any preceding plan year during which contributions were made on behalf of such employee, is or was a 5-percent owner (as defined in section 416(i)(1)(B)).

• 1984, Deficit Reduction Act of 1984 (P.L. 98-369)

P.L. 98-369, §528(b):

Amended Code Sec. 401(h) by striking out "and" at the end of paragraph (4), by striking out the period at the end of paragraph (5) and inserting in lieu thereof ", and", and by adding at the end thereof new paragraph (6). **Effective** for years beginning after 3-31-84.

• 1976, Tax Reform Act of 1976 (P.L. 94-455)

P.L. 94-455, §1906(b)(13)(A):

Amended 1954 Code by substituting "Secretary" for "Secretary or his delegate" each place it appeared. **Effective** 2-1-77.

• 1962 (P.L. 87-863)

P.L. 87-863, §2(a):

Added Code Sec. 401(h) and redesignated former Code Sec. 401(h) as Code Sec. 401(i). **Effective** for tax years beginning after 10-23-62.

[Sec. 401(i)]

(i) CERTAIN UNION-NEGOTIATED PENSION PLANS.—In the case of a trust forming part of a pension plan which has been determined by the Secretary to constitute a qualified trust under subsection (a) and to be exempt from taxation under section 501(a) for a period beginning after contributions were first made to or for such trust, if it is shown to the satisfaction of the Secretary that—

(1) such trust was created pursuant to a collective bargaining agreement between employee representatives and one or more employers,

(2) any disbursements of contributions, made to or for such trust before the time as of which the Secretary determined that the trust constituted a qualified trust, substantially complied with the terms of the trust, and the plan of which the trust is a part, as subsequently qualified, and

(3) before the time as of which the Secretary determined that the trust constitutes a qualified trust, the contributions to or for such trust were not used in a manner which would jeopardize the interests of its beneficiaries,

then such trust shall be considered as having constituted a qualified trust under subsection (a) and as having been exempt from taxation under section 501(a) for the period beginning on the date on which contributions were first made to or for such trust and ending on the date such trust first constituted (without regard to this subsection) a qualified trust under subsection (a).

Amendments

• 1976, Tax Reform Act of 1976 (P.L. 94-455)

P.L. 94-455, §1906(b)(13)(A):

Amended 1954 Code by substituting "Secretary" for "Secretary or his delegate" each place it appeared. **Effective** 2-1-77.

• 1971 (P.L. 91-691)

P.L. 91-691, §1(a):

Amended the heading of Code Sec. 401(i) by deleting "Multiemployer" which formerly appeared after "Union-Negotiated", and amended paragraph (1). **Effective** for tax years beginning after 12-31-53, and ending after 8-16-54, but only with respect to contributions made after 12-31-54. Prior to amendment, the paragraph read as follows:

(1) such trust was created pursuant to a collective bargaining agreement between employee representatives and two or more employers who are not related (determined under regulations prescribed by the Secretary or his delegate).

• 1964, Revenue Act of 1964 (P.L. 88-272)

P.L. 88-272, §219(a):

Added Code Sec. 401(i) and redesignated former Code Sec. 401(i) as Code Sec. 401(j). **Effective** with respect to tax years beginning after 12-31-53, and ending after 8-16-54, but only with respect to contributions made after 12-31-54.

[Sec. 401(j)—Repealed]

Amendments

• 1983, Technical Corrections Act of 1982 (P.L. 97-448)

P.L. 97-448, §103(d)(2):

Amended the last sentence of Code Sec. 401(j)(3) by striking out "subsection (j)(2)" and inserting in lieu thereof "paragraph (2)", and by inserting "with respect only to such change" after "participation". **Effective** as if included in the provision of P.L. 97-34 to which it relates.

• 1982, Tax Equity and Fiscal Responsibility Act of 1982 (P.L. 97-248)

P.L. 97-248, §238(b):

Repealed Code Sec. 401(j). **Effective** for years beginning after 12-31-83. Prior to repeal, Code Sec. 401(j) read as follows:

(j) DEFINED BENEFIT PLANS PROVIDING BENEFITS FOR SELF-EMPLOYED INDIVIDUALS AND SHAREHOLDER-EMPLOYEES.—

(1) IN GENERAL.—A defined benefit plan satisfies the requirements of this subsection only if the basic benefit accruing under the plan for each plan year of participation by an employee within the meaning of subsection (c)(1) (or a shareholder-employee) is permissible under regulations prescribed by the Secretary under this subsection to insure that there will be reasonable comparability (assuming level funding) between the maximum retirement benefits which may be provided with favorable tax treatment under this title for such employees under—

(A) defined contribution plans,

(B) defined benefit plans, and

(C) a combination of defined contribution plans and defined benefit plans.

(2) GUIDELINES FOR REGULATIONS.—The regulations prescribed under this subsection shall provide that a plan does not satisfy the requirements of this subsection if, under the plan, the basic benefit of any employee within the meaning of subsection (c)(1) (or a shareholder-employee) may exceed the sum of the products for each plan year of participation of—

(A) his annual compensation (not in excess of $100,000) for such year, and

(B) the applicable percentage determined under paragraph (3).

(3) APPLICABLE PERCENTAGE.—

(A) TABLE.—For purposes of paragraph (2), the applicable percentage for any individual for any plan year shall be based on the percentage shown in the following table opposite his age when his current period of participation in the plan began.

Age when participation began:	*Applicable percentage*
30 or less	6.5
35	5.4
40	4.4
45	3.6
50	3.0
55	2.5
60 or over	2.0

(B) ADDITIONAL REQUIREMENTS.—The regulations prescribed under this subsection shall include provisions—

(i) for applicable percentages for ages between any two ages shown on the table,

(ii) for adjusting the applicable percentages in the case of plans providing benefits other than a basic benefit,

(iii) that any increase in the rate of accrual, and any increase in the compensation base which may be taken into account, shall, with respect only to such increase, begin a new period of participation in the plan, and

(iv) when appropriate, in the case of periods beginning after December 31, 1977, for adjustments in the applicable percentages based on changes in prevailing interest and mortality rates occurring after 1973.

For purposes of this paragraph, a change in the annual compensation taken into account under subparagraph (A) of paragraph (2) shall be treated as beginning a new period of plan participation with respect only to such change.

(4) CERTAIN CONTRIBUTIONS AND BENEFITS MAY NOT BE TAKEN INTO ACCOUNT.—A defined benefit plan which provides contributions or benefits for owner-employees does not satisfy the requirements of this subsection unless such plan meets the requirements of subsection (a)(4) without taking into account contributions or benefits under chapter 2 (relating to tax on self-employment income), chapter 21 (relating to Federal Insurance Contributions Act), title II of the Social Security Act, or any other Federal or State law.

(5) DEFINITIONS.—For purposes of this subsection—

(A) BASIC BENEFIT.—The term "basic benefit" means a benefit in the form of a straight life annuity commencing at the later of—

(i) age 65, or

(ii) the day 5 years after the day the participant's current period of participation began under a plan which provides no ancillary benefits and to which employees do not contribute.

(B) SHAREHOLDER-EMPLOYEE.—The term "shareholder-employee" has the same meaning as when used in section 1379(d).

(C) COMPENSATION.—The term "compensation" means—

(i) in the case of an employee within the meaning of subsection (c)(1), the earned income of such individual, or

(ii) in the case of a shareholder-employee, the compensation received or accrued by the individual from the electing small business corporation.

(6) SPECIAL RULES.—Section 404(e) (relating to special limitations for self-employed individuals) and section 1379(b) (relating to taxability of shareholder-employee beneficiaries) do not apply to a trust to which this subsection applies.

• 1981, Economic Recovery Tax Act of 1981 (P.L. 97-34)

P.L. 97-34, §312(c)(3):

Amended Code Sec. 401(j)(2)(A) by striking out "$50,000" and inserting "$100,000". **Effective** with respect to plans which include employees within the meaning of Code Sec. 401(c)(1) for tax years beginning after 12-31-81.

P.L. 97-34, §312(c)(4):

Amended Code Sec. 401(j)(3) by adding the last sentence. **Effective** for plans which include employees within the meaning of Code Sec. 401(c)(1) with respect to tax years beginning after 12-31-81.

• 1976, Tax Reform Act of 1976 (P.L. 94-455)

P.L. 94-455, §1906(b)(13)(A):

Amended 1954 Code by substituting "Secretary" for "Secretary or his delegate" each place it appeared. **Effective** 2-1-77.

• 1974, Employee Retirement Income Security Act of 1974 (P.L. 93-406)

P.L. 93-406, §2001(d)(2):

Added Code Sec. 401(j) and redesignated former Code Sec. 401(j) as Code Sec. 401(k). **Effective** for tax years beginning after 12-31-75.

[Sec. 401(k)]

(k) CASH OR DEFERRED ARRANGEMENTS.—

(1) GENERAL RULE.—A profit-sharing or stock bonus plan, a pre-ERISA money purchase plan, or a rural cooperative plan shall not be considered as not satisfying the requirements of subsection (a) merely because the plan includes a qualified cash or deferred arrangement.

(2) QUALIFIED CASH OR DEFERRED ARRANGEMENT.—A qualified cash or deferred arrangement is any arrangement which is part of a profit-sharing or stock bonus plan, a pre-ERISA money purchase plan, or a rural cooperative plan which meets the requirements of subsection (a)—

(A) under which a covered employee may elect to have the employer make payments as contributions to a trust under the plan on behalf of the employee, or to the employee directly in cash;

(B) under which amounts held by the trust which are attributable to employer contributions made pursuant to the employee's election—

(i) may not be distributable to participants or other beneficiaries earlier than—

(I) severance from employment, death, or disability,

(II) an event described in paragraph (10),

(III) in the case of a profit-sharing or stock bonus plan, the attainment of age $59^1/_2$,

(IV) in the case of contributions to a profit-sharing or stock bonus plan to which section 402(e)(3) applies, upon hardship of the employee, or

(V) in the case of a qualified reservist distribution (as defined in section 72(t)(2)(G)(iii)), the date on which a period referred to in subclause (III) of such section begins, and

(ii) will not be distributable merely by reason of the completion of a stated period of participation or the lapse of a fixed number of years;

(C) which provides that an employee's right to his accrued benefit derived from employer contributions made to the trust pursuant to his election is nonforfeitable, and

(D) which does not require, as a condition of participation in the arrangement, that an employee complete a period of service with the employer (or employers) maintaining the plan extending beyond the period permitted under section 410(a)(1) (determined without regard to subparagraph (B)(i) thereof).

(3) APPLICATION OF PARTICIPATION AND DISCRIMINATION STANDARDS.—

(A) A cash or deferred arrangement shall not be treated as a qualified cash or deferred arrangement unless—

(i) those employees eligible to benefit under the arrangement satisfy the provisions of section 410(b)(1), and

(ii) the actual deferral percentage for eligible highly compensated employees (as defined in paragraph (5)) for the plan year bears a relationship to the actual deferral percentage for all other eligible employees for the preceding plan year which meets either of the following tests:

(I) The actual deferral percentage for the group of eligible highly compensated employees is not more than the actual deferral percentage of all other eligible employees multiplied by 1.25.

(II) The excess of the actual deferral percentage for the group of eligible highly compensated employees over that of all other eligible employees is not more than 2 percentage points, and the actual deferral percentage for the group of eligible highly compensated employees is not more than the actual deferral percentage of all other eligible employees multiplied by 2.

If 2 or more plans which include cash or deferred arrangements are considered as 1 plan for purposes of section 401(a)(4) or 410(b), the cash or deferred arrangements included in such plans shall be treated as 1 arrangement for purposes of this subparagraph.

If any highly compensated employee is a participant under 2 or more cash or deferred arrangements of the employer, for purposes of determining the deferral percentage with respect to such employee, all such cash or deferred arrangements shall be treated as 1 cash or deferred arrangement. An arrangement may apply clause (ii) by using the plan year rather than the preceding plan year if the employer so elects, except that if such an election is made, it may not be changed except as provided by the Secretary.

(B) For purposes of subparagraph (A), the actual deferral percentage for a specified group of employees for a plan year shall be the average of the ratios (calculated separately for each employee in such group) of—

(i) the amount of employer contributions actually paid over to the trust on behalf of each such employee for such plan year, to

(ii) the employee's compensation for such plan year.

(C) A cash or deferred arrangement shall be treated as meeting the requirements of subsection (a)(4) with respect to contributions if the requirements of subparagraph (A)(ii) are met.

(D) For purposes of subparagraph (B), the employer contributions on behalf of any employee—

(i) shall include any employer contributions made pursuant to the employee's election under paragraph (2), and

(ii) under such rules as the Secretary may prescribe, may, at the election of employer, include—

(I) matching contributions (as defined in section 401(m)(4)(A)) which meet the requirements of paragraph (2)(B) and (C), and

(II) qualified nonelective contributions (within the meaning of section 401(m)(4)(C)).

(E) For purposes of this paragraph, in the case of the first plan year of any plan (other than a successor plan), the amount taken into account as the actual deferral percentage of nonhighly compensated employees for the preceding plan year shall be—

(i) 3 percent, or

(ii) if the employer makes an election under this subclause, the actual deferral percentage of nonhighly compensated employees determined for such first plan year.

(F) SPECIAL RULE FOR EARLY PARTICIPATION.—If an employer elects to apply section 410(b)(4)(B) in determining whether a cash or deferred arrangement meets the requirements of subparagraph (A)(i), the employer may, in determining whether the arrangement meets the requirements of subparagraph (A)(ii), exclude from consideration all eligible employees (other than highly compensated employees) who have not met the minimum age and service requirements of section 410(a)(1)(A).

(G) GOVERNMENTAL PLAN.—A governmental plan (within the meaning of section 414(d)) shall be treated as meeting the requirements of this paragraph.

(4) OTHER REQUIREMENTS.—

(A) BENEFITS (OTHER THAN MATCHING CONTRIBUTIONS) MUST NOT BE CONTINGENT ON ELECTION TO DEFER.—A cash or deferred arrangement of any employer shall not be treated as a qualified cash or deferred arrangement if any other benefit is conditioned (directly or indirectly) on the employee electing to have the employer make or not make contributions under the arrangement in lieu of receiving cash. The preceding sentence shall not apply to any matching contribution (as defined in section 401(m)) made by reason of such an election.

(B) ELIGIBILITY OF STATE AND LOCAL GOVERNMENTS AND TAX-EXEMPT ORGANIZATIONS.—

(i) TAX-EXEMPTS ELIGIBLE.—Except as provided in clause (ii), any organization exempt from tax under this subtitle may include a qualified cash or deferred arrangement as part of a plan maintained by it.

(ii) GOVERNMENTS INELIGIBLE.—A cash or deferred arrangement shall not be treated as a qualified cash or deferred arrangement if it is part of a plan maintained by a State or local government or political subdivision thereof, or any agency or instrumentality thereof. This clause shall not apply to a rural cooperative plan or to a plan of an employer described in clause (iii).

(iii) TREATMENT OF INDIAN TRIBAL GOVERNMENTS.—An employer which is an Indian tribal government (as defined in section 7701(a)(40)), a subdivision of an Indian tribal government (determined in accordance with section 7871(d)), an agency or instrumentality of an Indian tribal government or subdivision thereof, or a corporation chartered under Federal, State, or tribal law which is owned in whole or in part by any of the foregoing may include a qualified cash or deferred arrangement as part of a plan maintained by the employer.

(C) COORDINATION WITH OTHER PLANS.—Except as provided in section 401(m), any employer contribution made pursuant to an employee's election under a qualified cash or deferred arrangement shall not be taken into account for purposes of determining whether any other plan meets the requirements of section 401(a) or 410(b). This subparagraph shall not apply for purposes of determining whether a plan meets the average benefit requirement of section 410(b)(2)(A)(ii).

(5) HIGHLY COMPENSATED EMPLOYEE.—For purposes of this subsection, the term "highly compensated employee" has the meaning given such term by section 414(q).

(6) PRE-ERISA MONEY PURCHASE PLAN.—For purposes of this subsection, the term "pre-ERISA money purchase plan" means a pension plan—

(A) which is a defined contribution plan (as defined in section 414(i)),

(B) which was in existence on June 27, 1974, and which, on such date, included a salary reduction arrangement, and

(C) under which neither the employee contributions nor the employer contributions may exceed the levels provided for by the contribution formula in effect under the plan on such date.

(7) RURAL COOPERATIVE PLAN.—For purposes of this subsection—

(A) IN GENERAL.—The term "rural cooperative plan" means any pension plan—

(i) which is a defined contribution plan (as defined in section 414(i)), and

(ii) which is established and maintained by a rural cooperative.

(B) RURAL COOPERATIVE DEFINED.—For purposes of subparagraph (A), the term "rural cooperative" means—

(i) any organization which—

(I) is engaged primarily in providing electric service on a mutual or cooperative basis, or

(II) is engaged primarily in providing electric service to the public in its area of service and which is exempt from tax under this subtitle or which is a State or local government (or an agency or instrumentality thereof), other than a municipality (or an agency or instrumentality thereof),

(ii) any organization described in paragraph (4) or (6) of section 501(c) and at least 80 percent of the members of which are organizations described in clause (i),

(iii) a cooperative telephone company described in section 501(c)(12),

(iv) any organization which—

(I) is a mutual irrigation or ditch company described in section 501(c)(12) (without regard to the 85 percent requirement thereof), or

(II) is a district organized under the laws of a State as a municipal corporation for the purpose of irrigation, water conservation, or drainage, and

(v) an organization which is a national association of organizations described in clause (i), (ii),, [sic] (iii), or (iv).

(C) SPECIAL RULE FOR CERTAIN DISTRIBUTIONS.—A rural cooperative plan which includes a qualified cash or deferred arrangement shall not be treated as violating the requirements of section 401(a) or of paragraph (2) merely by reason of a hardship distribution or a distribution to a participant after attainment of age 59½. For purposes of this section, the term "hardship distribution" means a distribution described in paragraph (2)(B)(i)(IV) (without regard to the limitation of its application to profit-sharing or stock bonus plans).

(8) ARRANGEMENT NOT DISQUALIFIED IF EXCESS CONTRIBUTIONS DISTRIBUTED.—

(A) IN GENERAL.—A cash or deferred arrangement shall not be treated as failing to meet the requirements of clause (ii) of paragraph (3)(A) for any plan year if, before the close of the following plan year—

(i) the amount of excess contributions for such plan year (and any income allocable to such contributions through the end of such year) is distributed, or

(ii) to the extent provided in regulations, the employee elects to treat the amount of the excess contributions as an amount distributed to the employee and then contributed by the employee to the plan.

Any distribution of excess contributions (and income) may be made without regard to any other provision of law.

(B) EXCESS CONTRIBUTIONS.—For purposes of subparagraph (A), the term "excess contributions" means, with respect to any plan year, the excess of—

(i) the aggregate amount of employer contributions actually paid over to the trust on behalf of highly compensated employees for such plan year, over

(ii) the maximum amount of such contributions permitted under the limitations of clause (ii) of paragraph (3)(A) (determined by reducing contributions made on behalf of highly compensated employees in order of the actual deferral percentages beginning with the highest of such percentages).

(C) METHOD OF DISTRIBUTING EXCESS CONTRIBUTIONS.—Any distribution of the excess contributions for any plan year shall be made to highly compensated employees on the basis of the amount of contributions by, or on behalf of, each of such employees.

(D) ADDITIONAL TAX UNDER SECTION 72(t) NOT TO APPLY.—No tax shall be imposed under section 72(t) on any amount required to be distributed under this paragraph.

(E) TREATMENT OF MATCHING CONTRIBUTIONS FORFEITED BY REASON OF EXCESS DEFERRAL OR CONTRIBUTION OR PERMISSIBLE WITHDRAWAL.—For purposes of paragraph (2)(C), a matching contribution (within the meaning of subsection (m)) shall not be treated as forfeitable merely because such contribution is forfeitable if the contribution to which the matching contribution relates is treated as an excess contribution under subparagraph (B), an excess deferral under section 402(g)(2)(A), a permissible withdrawal under section 414(w), or an excess aggregate contribution under section 401(m)(6)(B).

(F) CROSS REFERENCE.—

For excise tax on certain excess contributions, see section 4979.

(9) COMPENSATION.—For purposes of this subsection, the term "compensation" has the meaning given such term by section 414(s).

(10) DISTRIBUTIONS UPON TERMINATION OF PLAN.—

(A) IN GENERAL.—An event described in this subparagraph is the termination of the plan without establishment or maintenance of another defined contribution plan (other than an employee stock ownership plan as defined in section 4975(e)(7)).

(B) DISTRIBUTIONS MUST BE LUMP SUM DISTRIBUTIONS.—

(i) IN GENERAL.—A termination shall not be treated as described in subparagraph (A) with respect to any employee unless the employee receives a lump sum distribution by reason of the termination.

(ii) LUMP-SUM DISTRIBUTION.—For purposes of this subparagraph, the term "lump-sum distribution" has the meaning given such term by section 402(e)(4)(D) (without regard to subclauses (I), (II), (III), and (IV) of clause (i) thereof). Such term includes a distribution of an annuity contract from—

(I) a trust which forms a part of a plan described in section 401(a) and which is exempt from tax under section 501(a), or

(II) an annuity plan described in section 403(a).

(11) ADOPTION OF SIMPLE PLAN TO MEET NONDISCRIMINATION TESTS.—

(A) IN GENERAL.—A cash or deferred arrangement maintained by an eligible employer shall be treated as meeting the requirements of paragraph (3)(A)(ii) if such arrangement meets—

(i) the contribution requirements of subparagraph (B),

(ii) the exclusive plan requirements of subparagraph (C), and

(iii) the vesting requirements of section 408(p)(3).

(B) CONTRIBUTION REQUIREMENTS.—

(i) IN GENERAL.—The requirements of this subparagraph are met if, under the arrangement—

(I) an employee may elect to have the employer make elective contributions for the year on behalf of the employee to a trust under the plan in an amount which is expressed as a percentage of compensation of the employee but which in no event exceeds the amount in effect under section 408(p)(2)(A)(ii),

(II) the employer is required to make a matching contribution to the trust for the year in an amount equal to so much of the amount the employee elects under subclause (I) as does not exceed 3 percent of compensation for the year, and

(III) no other contributions may be made other than contributions described in subclause (I) or (II).

(ii) EMPLOYER MAY ELECT 2-PERCENT NONELECTIVE CONTRIBUTION.—An employer shall be treated as meeting the requirements of clause (i)(II) for any year if, in lieu of the contributions described in such clause, the employer elects (pursuant to the terms of the arrangement) to make nonelective contributions of 2 percent of compensation for each employee who is eligible to participate in the arrangement and who has at least $5,000 of compensation from the employer for the year. If an employer makes an election under this subparagraph for any year, the employer shall notify employees of such election within a reasonable period of time before the 60th day before the beginning of such year.

(iii) ADMINISTRATIVE REQUIREMENTS.—

(I) IN GENERAL.—Rules similar to the rules of subparagraphs (B) and (C) of section 408(p)(5) shall apply for purposes of this subparagraph.

(II) NOTICE OF ELECTION PERIOD.—The requirements of this subparagraph shall not be treated as met with respect to any year unless the employer notifies each employee eligible to participate, within a reasonable period of time before the 60th day before the beginning of such year (and, for the first year the employee is so eligible, the 60th day before the first day such employee is so eligible), of the rules similar to the rules of section 408(p)(5)(C) which apply by reason of subclause (I).

(C) EXCLUSIVE PLAN REQUIREMENT.—The requirements of this subparagraph are met for any year to which this paragraph applies if no contributions were made, or benefits were accrued, for services during such year under any qualified plan of the employer on behalf of any employee eligible to participate in the cash or deferred arrangement, other than contributions described in subparagraph (B).

(D) DEFINITIONS AND SPECIAL RULE.—

(i) DEFINITIONS.—For purposes of this paragraph, any term used in this paragraph which is also used in section 408(p) shall have the meaning given such term by such section.

(ii) COORDINATION WITH TOP-HEAVY RULES.—A plan meeting the requirements of this paragraph for any year shall not be treated as a top-heavy plan under section 416 for such year if such plan allows only contributions required under this paragraph.

(12) ALTERNATIVE METHODS OF MEETING NONDISCRIMINATION REQUIREMENTS.—

(A) IN GENERAL.—A cash or deferred arrangement shall be treated as meeting the requirements of paragraph (3)(A)(ii) if such arrangement—

(i) meets the contribution requirements of subparagraph (B) or (C), and

(ii) meets the notice requirements of subparagraph (D).

(B) MATCHING CONTRIBUTIONS.—

(i) IN GENERAL.—The requirements of this subparagraph are met if, under the arrangement, the employer makes matching contributions on behalf of each employee who is not a highly compensated employee in an amount equal to—

(I) 100 percent of the elective contributions of the employee to the extent such elective contributions do not exceed 3 percent of the employee's compensation, and

(II) 50 percent of the elective contributions of the employee to the extent that such elective contributions exceed 3 percent but do not exceed 5 percent of the employee's compensation.

(ii) RATE FOR HIGHLY COMPENSATED EMPLOYEES.—The requirements of this subparagraph are not met if, under the arrangement, the rate of matching contribution with respect to any elective contribution of a highly compensated employee at any rate of elective contribution is greater than that with respect to an employee who is not a highly compensated employee.

(iii) ALTERNATIVE PLAN DESIGNS.—If the rate of any matching contribution with respect to any rate of elective contribution is not equal to the percentage required under clause (i), an arrangement shall not be treated as failing to meet the requirements of clause (i) if—

(I) the rate of an employer's matching contribution does not increase as an employee's rate of elective contributions increase, and

(II) the aggregate amount of matching contributions at such rate of elective contribution is at least equal to the aggregate amount of matching contributions which would be made if matching contributions were made on the basis of the percentages described in clause (i).

(C) NONELECTIVE CONTRIBUTIONS.—The requirements of this subparagraph are met if, under the arrangement, the employer is required, without regard to whether the employee makes an elective contribution or employee contribution, to make a contribution to a defined contribution plan on behalf of each employee who is not a highly compensated employee and who is eligible to participate in the arrangement in an amount equal to at least 3 percent of the employee's compensation.

(D) NOTICE REQUIREMENT.—An arrangement meets the requirements of this paragraph if, under the arrangement, each employee eligible to participate is, within a reasonable period before any year, given written notice of the employee's rights and obligations under the arrangement which—

(i) is sufficiently accurate and comprehensive to appraise the employee of such rights and obligations, and

(ii) is written in a manner calculated to be understood by the average employee eligible to participate.

(E) OTHER REQUIREMENTS.—

(i) WITHDRAWAL AND VESTING RESTRICTIONS.—An arrangement shall not be treated as meeting the requirements of subparagraph (B) or (C) of this paragraph unless the requirements of subparagraphs (B) and (C) of paragraph (2) are met with respect to all employer contributions (including matching contributions) taken into account in determining whether the requirements of subparagraphs (B) and (C) of this paragraph are met.

(ii) SOCIAL SECURITY AND SIMILAR CONTRIBUTIONS NOT TAKEN INTO ACCOUNT.—An arrangement shall not be treated as meeting the requirements of subparagraph (B) or (C) unless such requirements are met without regard to subsection (l), and, for purposes of subsection (l), employer contributions under subparagraph (B) or (C) shall not be taken into account.

(F) OTHER PLANS.—An arrangement shall be treated as meeting the requirements under subparagraph (A)(i) if any other plan maintained by the employer meets such requirements with respect to employees eligible under the arrangement.

(13) ALTERNATIVE METHOD FOR AUTOMATIC CONTRIBUTION ARRANGEMENTS TO MEET NONDISCRIMINATION REQUIREMENTS.—

(A) IN GENERAL.—A qualified automatic contribution arrangement shall be treated as meeting the requirements of paragraph (3)(A)(ii).

(B) QUALIFIED AUTOMATIC CONTRIBUTION ARRANGEMENT.—For purposes of this paragraph, the term "qualified automatic contribution arrangement" means any cash or deferred arrangement which meets the requirements of subparagraphs (C) through (E).

(C) AUTOMATIC DEFERRAL.—

(i) IN GENERAL.—The requirements of this subparagraph are met if, under the arrangement, each employee eligible to participate in the arrangement is treated as having elected to have the employer make elective contributions in an amount equal to a qualified percentage of compensation.

(ii) ELECTION OUT.—The election treated as having been made under clause (i) shall cease to apply with respect to any employee if such employee makes an affirmative election—

(I) to not have such contributions made, or

(II) to make elective contributions at a level specified in such affirmative election.

(iii) QUALIFIED PERCENTAGE.—For purposes of this subparagraph, the term "qualified percentage" means, with respect to any employee, any percentage determined under the arrangement if such percentage is applied uniformly, does not exceed 10 percent, and is at least—

(I) 3 percent during the period ending on the last day of the first plan year which begins after the date on which the first elective contribution described in clause (i) is made with respect to such employee,

(II) 4 percent during the first plan year following the plan year described in subclause (I),

(III) 5 percent during the second plan year following the plan year described in subclause (I), and

(IV) 6 percent during any subsequent plan year.

(iv) AUTOMATIC DEFERRAL FOR CURRENT EMPLOYEES NOT REQUIRED.—Clause (i) may be applied without taking into account any employee who—

(I) was eligible to participate in the arrangement (or a predecessor arrangement) immediately before the date on which such arrangement becomes a qualified automatic contribution arrangement (determined after application of this clause), and

(II) had an election in effect on such date either to participate in the arrangement or to not participate in the arrangement.

(D) MATCHING OR NONELECTIVE CONTRIBUTIONS.—

(i) IN GENERAL.—The requirements of this subparagraph are met if, under the arrangement, the employer—

(I) makes matching contributions on behalf of each employee who is not a highly compensated employee in an amount equal to the sum of 100 percent of the elective contributions of the employee to the extent that such contributions do not exceed 1 percent of compensation plus 50 percent of so much of such contributions as exceed 1 percent but do not exceed 6 percent of compensation, or

(II) is required, without regard to whether the employee makes an elective contribution or employee contribution, to make a contribution to a defined contribution plan on behalf of each employee who is not a highly compensated employee and who is eligible to participate in the arrangement in an amount equal to at least 3 percent of the employee's compensation.

(ii) APPLICATION OF RULES FOR MATCHING CONTRIBUTIONS.—The rules of clauses (ii) and (iii) of paragraph (12)(B) shall apply for purposes of clause (i)(I).

(iii) WITHDRAWAL AND VESTING RESTRICTIONS.—An arrangement shall not be treated as meeting the requirements of clause (i) unless, with respect to employer contributions (including matching contributions) taken into account in determining whether the requirements of clause (i) are met—

(I) any employee who has completed at least 2 years of service (within the meaning of section 411(a)) has a nonforfeitable right to 100 percent of the employee's accrued benefit derived from such employer contributions, and

(II) the requirements of subparagraph (B) of paragraph (2) are met with respect to all such employer contributions.

(iv) APPLICATION OF CERTAIN OTHER RULES.—The rules of subparagraphs (E)(ii) and (F) of paragraph (12) shall apply for purposes of subclauses (I) and (II) of clause (i).

(E) NOTICE REQUIREMENTS.—

(i) IN GENERAL.—The requirements of this subparagraph are met if, within a reasonable period before each plan year, each employee eligible to participate in the arrangement for such year receives written notice of the employee's rights and obligations under the arrangement which—

(I) is sufficiently accurate and comprehensive to apprise the employee of such rights and obligations, and

(II) is written in a manner calculated to be understood by the average employee to whom the arrangement applies.

(ii) TIMING AND CONTENT REQUIREMENTS.—A notice shall not be treated as meeting the requirements of clause (i) with respect to an employee unless—

(I) the notice explains the employee's right under the arrangement to elect not to have elective contributions made on the employee's behalf (or to elect to have such contributions made at a different percentage),

(II) in the case of an arrangement under which the employee may elect among 2 or more investment options, the notice explains how contributions made under the arrangement will be invested in the absence of any investment election by the employee, and

(III) the employee has a reasonable period of time after receipt of the notice described in subclauses (I) and (II) and before the first elective contribution is made to make either such election.

Amendments

• 2008, Worker, Retiree, and Employer Recovery Act of 2008 (P.L. 110-458)

P.L. 110-458, §109(b)(1):

Amended Code Sec. 401(k)(13)(D)(i)(I) by striking "such compensation as exceeds 1 percent but does not" and inserting "such contributions as exceed 1 percent but do not". **Effective** as if included in the provision of the 2006 Act to which the amendment relates [**effective** for plan years beginning after 12-31-2007.—CCH].

P.L. 110-458, §109(b)(2)(A)-(B):

Amended Code Sec. 401(k)(8)(E) by striking "an erroneous automatic contribution" and inserting "a permissible withdrawal", and by striking "ERRONEOUS AUTOMATIC CONTRIBUTION" in the heading and inserting "PERMISSIBLE WITHDRAWAL". **Effective** as if included in the provision of the 2006 Act to which the amendment relates [**effective** for plan years beginning after 12-31-2007.—CCH].

• 2006, Pension Protection Act of 2006 (P.L. 109-280)

P.L. 109-280, §811, provides:

SEC. 811. PENSIONS AND INDIVIDUAL RETIREMENT ARRANGEMENT PROVISIONS OF ECONOMIC GROWTH AND TAX RELIEF RECONCILIATION ACT OF 2001 MADE PERMANENT.

Title IX of the Economic Growth and Tax Relief Reconciliation Act of 2001 [P.L. 107-16] shall not apply to the provisions of, and amendments made by, subtitles A through F of title VI [§§601-666]of such Act (relating to pension and individual retirement arrangement provisions).

P.L. 109-280, §827(b)(1):

Amended Code Sec. 401(k)(2)(B)(i) by striking "or" at the end of subclause (III), by striking "and" at the end of subclause (IV) and inserting "or", and by inserting after subclause (IV) a new subclause (V). **Effective** for distributions after 9-11-2001. For a waiver of limitations, see Act Sec. 827(c)(2), below.

P.L. 109-280, §827(c)(2), provides:

(2) WAIVER OF LIMITATIONS.—If refund or credit of any overpayment of tax resulting from the amendments made by this section is prevented at any time before the close of the 1-year period beginning on the date of the enactment of this Act by the operation of any law or rule of law (including res judicata), such refund or credit may nevertheless be made or allowed if claim therefor is filed before the close of such period.

P.L. 109-280, §861(a)(2):

Amended Code Sec. 401(k)(3)(G) by striking "maintained by a State or local government or political subdivision thereof (or agency or instrumentality thereof)" after "section 414(d))". **Effective** for any year beginning after 8-17-2006.

P.L. 109-280, §861(b)(3):

Amended Code Sec. 401(k)(3)(G) by inserting "GOVERNMENTAL PLAN.—"after "(G)". **Effective** for any year beginning after 8-17-2006.

P.L. 109-280, §902(a):

Amended Code Sec. 401(k) by adding at the end a new paragraph (13). **Effective** for plan years beginning after 12-31-2007.

P.L. 109-280, §902(d)(2)(C):

Amended Code Sec. 401(k)(8)(E) by inserting "an erroneous automatic contribution under section 414(w)," after "402(g)(2)(A),". **Effective** for plan years beginning after 12-31-2007.

P.L. 109-280, §902(d)(2)(D):

Amended the heading of Code Sec. 401(k)(8)(E) by inserting "OR ERRONEOUS AUTOMATIC CONTRIBUTION" before the period. **Effective** for plan years beginning after 12-31-2007.

P.L. 109-280, §902(e)(3)(B)(i):

Amended Code Sec. 401(k)(8)(A)(i) by adding "through the end of such year" after "such contributions". **Effective** for plan years beginning after 12-31-2007.

• 2005, Katrina Emergency Tax Relief Act of 2005 (P.L. 109-73)

P.L. 109-73, §101(f)(2) [repealed by P.L. 109-135, §201(b)(4)(A)], provides:

(2) QUALIFIED HURRICANE KATRINA DISTRIBUTIONS TREATED AS MEETING PLAN DISTRIBUTION REQUIREMENTS.—For purposes of such Code, a qualified Hurricane Katrina distribution shall be treated as meeting the requirements of sections 401(k)(2)(B)(i), 403(b)(7)(A)(ii), 403(b)(11), and 457(d)(1)(A) of such Code.

P.L. 109-73, §102 [repealed by P.L. 109-135, §201(b)(4)(A)], provides:

SEC. 102. RECONTRIBUTIONS OF WITHDRAWALS FOR HOME PURCHASES CANCELLED DUE TO HURRICANE KATRINA.

(a) RECONTRIBUTIONS.—

(1) IN GENERAL.—Any individual who received a qualified distribution may, during the period beginning on August 25, 2005, and ending on February 28, 2006, make one or more contributions in an aggregate amount not to exceed the amount of such qualified distribution to an eligible retirement plan (as defined in section 402(c)(8)(B) of the Internal Revenue Code of 1986) of which such individual is a beneficiary and to which a rollover contribution of such distribution could be made under section 402(c), 403(a)(4), 403(b)(8), or 408(d)(3) of such Code, as the case may be.

(2) TREATMENT OF REPAYMENTS.—Rules similar to the rules of paragraphs (2) and (3) of section 101(c) of this Act shall apply for purposes of this section.

(b) QUALIFIED DISTRIBUTION DEFINED.—For purposes of this section, the term "qualified distribution" means any distribution—

(1) described in section 401(k)(2)(B)(i)(IV), 403(b)(7)(A)(ii) (but only to the extent such distribution relates to financial hardship), 403(b)(11)(B), or 72(t)(2)(F) of such Code,

(2) received after February 28, 2005, and before August 29, 2005, and

(3) which was to be used to purchase or construct a principal residence in the Hurricane Katrina disaster area, but which was not so purchased or constructed on account of Hurricane Katrina.

• 2001, Economic Growth and Tax Relief Reconciliation Act of 2001 (P.L. 107-16)

P.L. 107-16, §611(f)(3)(A):

Amended Code Sec. 401(k)(11)(B)(i)(I) by striking "$6,000" and inserting "the amount in effect under section 408(p)(2)(A)(ii)". **Effective** for years beginning after 12-31-2001. For a special rule, see Act Sec. 611(i)(3), below.

P.L. 107-16, §611(f)(3)(B):

Amended Code Sec. 401(k)(11) by striking subparagraph (E). **Effective** for years beginning after 12-31-2001. For a special rule, see Act Sec. 611(i)(3), below. Prior to being stricken, Code Sec. 401(k)(11)(E) read as follows:

(E) COST-OF-LIVING ADJUSTMENT.—The Secretary shall adjust the $6,000 amount under subparagraph (B)(i)(I) at the same time and in the same manner as under section 408(p)(2)(E).

P.L. 107-16, §611(i)(3), as added by P.L. 107-147, §411(j)(3), provides:

(3) SPECIAL RULE.—In the case of [a]plan that, on June 7, 2001, incorporated by reference the limitation of section 415(b)(1)(A) of the Internal Revenue Code of 1986, section 411(d)(6) of such Code and section 204(g)(1) of the Employee Retirement Income Security Act of 1974 do not apply to a plan amendment that—

(A) is adopted on or before June 30, 2002,

(B) reduces benefits to the level that would have applied without regard to the amendments made by subsection (a) of this section, and

(C) is effective no earlier than the years described in paragraph (2).

P.L. 107-16, §646(a)(1)(A):

Amended Code Sec. 401(k)(2)(B)(i)(I) by striking "separation from service" and inserting "severance from employment". **Effective** for distributions after 12-31-2001.

P.L. 107-16, §646(a)(1)(B):

Amended Code Sec. 401(k)(10)(A). **Effective** for distributions after 12-31-2001. Prior to amendment, Code Sec. 401(k)(10)(A) read as follows:

(A) IN GENERAL.—The following events are described in this paragraph:

(i) TERMINATION.—The termination of the plan without establishment or maintenance of another defined contribution plan (other than an employee stock ownership plan as defined in section 4975(e)(7)).

(ii) DISPOSITION OF ASSETS.—The disposition by a corporation of substantially all of the assets (within the meaning of section 409(d)(2)) used by such corporation in a trade or business of such corporation, but only with respect to an employee who continues employment with the corporation acquiring such assets.

(iii) DISPOSITION OF SUBSIDIARY.—The disposition by a corporation of such corporation's interest in a subsidiary (within the meaning of section 409(d)(3)), but only with respect to an employee who continues employment with such subsidiary.

P.L. 107-16, §646(a)(1)(C)(i)-(iii):

Amended Code Sec. 401(k)(10) by striking "An event" and inserting "A termination", and by striking "the event" and inserting "the termination" in subparagraph (B)(i); by striking subparagraph (C); and by striking "OR DISPOSITION OF ASSETS OR SUBSIDIARY" before the period in the heading. **Effective** for distributions after 12-31-2001. Prior to being stricken, Code Sec. 401(k)(10)(C) read as follows:

(C) TRANSFEROR CORPORATION MUST MAINTAIN PLAN.—An event shall not be treated as described in clause (ii) or (iii) of subparagraph (A) unless the transferor corporation continues to maintain the plan after the disposition.

P.L. 107-16, §901(a)-(b), provides [but see P.L. 109-280, §811, above]:

SEC. 901. SUNSET OF PROVISIONS OF ACT.

(a) IN GENERAL.—All provisions of, and amendments made by, this Act shall not apply—

(1) to taxable, plan, or limitation years beginning after December 31, 2010, or

(2) in the case of title V, to estates of decedents dying, gifts made, or generation skipping transfers, after December 31, 2010.

(b) APPLICATION OF CERTAIN LAWS.—The Internal Revenue Code of 1986 and the Employee Retirement Income Security Act of 1974 shall be applied and administered to years, estates, gifts, and transfers described in subsection (a) as if the provisions and amendments described in subsection (a) had never been enacted.

• 2000, Community Renewal Tax Relief Act of 2000 (P.L. 106-554)

P.L. 106-554, §316(c):

Amended Code Sec. 401(k)(10)(B)(ii) by adding at the end a new sentence. **Effective** as if included in the provision of P.L. 104-188 to which it relates [**effective** for tax years beginning after 12-31-99.—CCH].

• 1997, Taxpayer Relief Act of 1997 (P.L. 105-34)

P.L. 105-34, §1505(b):

Amended Code Sec. 401(k)(3) by adding at the end a new subparagraph (G). **Effective** for tax years beginning on or after 8-5-97. For a special rule, see Act Sec. 1505(d)(2), below.

P.L. 105-34, §1505(d)(2), as amended by P.L. 105-206, §6015(b), and further amended by P.L. 109-280, §861(a)(2), provides:

(2) TREATMENT FOR YEARS BEGINNING BEFORE DATE OF ENACTMENT.—A governmental plan (within the meaning of section 414(d) of the Internal Revenue Code of 1986) shall be treated as satisfying the requirements of sections 401(a)(3), 401(a)(4), 401(a)(26), 401(k), 401(m), 403(b)(1)(D) and (b)(12)(A)(i), and 410 of such Code for all taxable years beginning before the date of enactment of this Act.

P.L. 105-34, §1525(a)(1)-(2):

Amended Code Sec. 401(k)(7)(B) by striking "and" at the end of clause (iii), by redesignating clause (iv) as clause (v), by inserting after clause (iii) a new clause (iv), and by striking "or (iii)" in clause (v), as so redesignated, and inserting ", (iii), or (iv)". **Effective** for years beginning after 12-31-97.

P.L. 105-34, §1601(d)(2)(A):

Amended Code Sec. 401(k)(11)(D)(ii) by striking the period and inserting "if such plan allows only contributions required under this paragraph.". **Effective** as if included in the provision of P.L. 104-188 to which it relates [**effective** for plan years beginning after 12-31-96.—CCH].

P.L. 105-34, §1601(d)(2)(B):

Amended Code Sec. 401(k)(11) by adding at the end a new subparagraph (E). **Effective** as if included in the provision of P.L. 104-188 to which it relates [**effective** for plan years beginning after 12-31-96.—CCH].

P.L. 105-34, §1601(d)(2)(D):

Amended Code Sec. 401(k)(11)(B) by adding at the end a new clause (iii). **Effective** for calendar years beginning after 8-5-97.

• 1996, Small Business Job Protection Act of 1996 (P.L. 104-188)

P.L. 104-188, §1401(b)(6):

Amended Code Sec. 401(k)(10)(B)(ii). **Effective**, generally, for tax years beginning after 12-31-99. For a special transitional rule, see Act Sec. 1401(c)(2) in the amendment notes following Code Sec. 402(d). Prior to amendment, Code Sec. 401(k)(10)(B)(ii) read as follows:

(ii) LUMP SUM DISTRIBUTION.—For purposes of this subparagraph, the term "lump sum distribution" has the meaning given such term by section 402(d)(4), without regard to clauses (i), (ii), (iii), and (iv) of subparagraph (A), subparagraph (B), or subparagraph (F) thereof.

P.L. 104-188, §1422(a):

Amended Code Sec. 401(k) by adding at the end a new paragraph (11). **Effective** for plan years beginning after 12-31-96.

P.L. 104-188, §1426(a):

Amended Code Sec. 401(k)(4)(B). **Effective** for plan years beginning after 12-31-96, but does not apply to any cash or deferred arrangement to which clause (i) of section 1116(f)(2)(B) of the Tax Reform Act of 1986 applies. Prior to amendment, Code Sec. 401(k)(4)(B) read as follows:

(B) STATE AND LOCAL GOVERNMENTS AND TAX-EXEMPT ORGANIZATIONS NOT ELIGIBLE.—A cash or deferred arrangement shall not be treated as a qualified cash or deferred arrangement if it is part of a plan maintained by—

(i) a State or local government or political subdivision thereof, or any agency or instrumentality thereof, or

(ii) any organization exempt from tax under this subtitle.

This subparagraph shall not apply to a rural cooperative plan.

P.L. 104-188, §1433(a):

Amended Code Sec. 401(k), as amended by Act Sec. 1422(a), by adding at the end a new paragraph (12). **Effective** for years beginning after 12-31-98.

P.L. 104-188, §1433(c)(1)(A)-(B):

Amended Code Sec. 401(k)(3)(A)(ii) by striking "such year" and inserting "the plan year", and striking "for such plan year" and inserting "for the preceding plan year". **Effective** for years beginning after 12-31-96.

P.L. 104-188, §1433(c)(1)(C):

Amended Code Sec. 401(k)(3)(A) by adding at the end a new sentence. **Effective** for years beginning after 12-31-96.

P.L. 104-188, §1433(d)(1):

Amended Code Sec. 401(k)(3) by adding at the end a new subparagraph (E). **Effective** for years beginning after 12-31-96.

P.L. 104-188, §1433(e)(1):

Amended Code Sec. 401(k)(8)(C) by striking "on the basis of the respective portions of the excess contributions attributable to each of such employees" and inserting "on the basis of the amount of contributions by, or on behalf of, each of such employees". **Effective** for years beginning after 12-31-96.

P.L. 104-188, §1443(a):

Amended Code Sec. 401(k)(7) by adding at the end a new subparagraph (C). **Effective** for distributions after 8-20-96.

P.L. 104-188, §1443(b):

Amended Code Sec. 401(k)(7)(B)(i). **Effective** for plan years beginning after 12-31-96. Prior to amendment, Code Sec. 401(k)(7)(B)(i) read as follows:

(i) any organization which—

(I) is exempt from tax under this subtitle or which is a State or local government or political subdivision thereof (or agency or instrumentality thereof), and

(II) is engaged primarily in providing electric service on a mutual or cooperative basis,

P.L. 104-188, §1459(a):

Amended Code Sec. 401(k)(3), as amended by Act Sec. 1433(d)(1), by adding at the end a new subparagraph (F). **Effective** for plan years beginning after 12-31-98.

• 1992, Unemployment Compensation Amendments of 1992 (P.L. 102-318)

P.L. 102-318, §521(b)(7):

Amended Code Sec. 401(k)(2)(B)(i)(IV) by striking "section 402(a)(8)" and inserting "section 402(e)(3)". **Effective** for distributions after 12-31-92.

P.L. 102-318, §521(b)(8)(A)-(B):

Amended Code Sec. 401(k)(10)(B)(ii) by striking "section 402(e)(4)" and inserting "section 402(d)(4)", and by striking "subparagraph (H)" and inserting "subparagraph (F)". **Effective** for distributions after 12-31-92.

• 1988, Technical and Miscellaneous Revenue Act of 1988 (P.L. 100-647)

P.L. 100-647, §1011(e)(3):

Amended Code Sec. 401(k)(7). **Effective** as if included in the provision of P.L. 99-514 to which it relates. Prior to amendment, Code Sec. 401(k)(7) read as follows:

(7) RURAL ELECTRIC COOPERATIVE PLAN.—For purposes of this subsection, the term "rural electric cooperative plan" means any pension plan—

(A) which is a defined contribution plan (as defined in section 414(i)), and

(B) which is established and maintained by a rural electric cooperative (as defined in section 457(d)(9)(B)) or a national association of such rural electric cooperatives.

P.L. 100-647, §1011(k)(1)(A)(i)-(ii):

Amended Code Sec. 401(k)(2)(B) by striking out subclauses (II), (III), and (IV) of clause (i) and inserting in lieu thereof new subclause (II), and by redesignating subclauses (V) and (VI) as subclauses (III) and (IV), respectively. **Effective** as if included in the provision of P.L. 99-514 to which it relates. Prior to amendment, Code Sec. 401(k)(2)(B)(i)(II)-(IV) read as follows:

(II) termination of the plan without establishment of a successor plan,

(III) the date of the sale by a corporation of substantially all of the assets (within the meaning of section 409(d)(2)) used by such corporation in a trade or business of such corporation with respect to an employee who continues employment with the corporation acquiring such assets,

(IV) the date of the sale by a corporation of such corporation's interest in a subsidiary (within the meaning of section 409(d)(3)) with respect to an employee who continues employment with such subsidiary.

P.L. 100-647, §1011(k)(1)(B):

Amended Code Sec. 401(k) by adding at the end thereof new paragraph (10). **Effective** as if included in the provision of P.L. 99-514 to which it relates. See, also, Act Sec. 1011(k)(1)(C), below.

P.L. 100-647, §1011(k)(1)(C), provides:

(C)(i) Subparagraph (A)(i) of section 401(k)(10) of the 1986 Code (as added by subparagraph (B)) shall apply to distributions after October 16, 1987.

(ii) Subparagraph (B) of section 401(k)(10) of the 1986 Code (as added by subparagraph (B)) shall apply to distributions after March 31, 1988.

P.L. 100-647, §1011(k)(2)(A)-(C):

Amended Code Sec. 401(k)(2)(B) by inserting "amounts held by the trust which are attributable to employer contributions made pursuant to the employee's election" after "under which", by striking out "amounts held by the trust which are attributable to employer contributions made pursuant to the employee's election" in clause (i) after "(i)", and by striking out "amounts" in clause (ii) after "(ii)". **Effective** as if included in the provision of P.L. 99-514 to which it relates.

P.L. 100-647, §1011(k)(3)(A):

Amended Code Sec. 401(k)(3)(A)(ii) by inserting "eligible" before "highly compensated employees" each place it appears. **Effective** as if included in the provision of P.L. 99-514 to which it relates.

P.L. 100-647, §1011(k)(4):

Redesignated Code Sec. 401(k)(3)(C) as Code Sec. 401(k)(3)(D). **Effective** as if included in the provision of P.L. 99-514 to which it relates.

P.L. 100-647, §1011(k)(5):

Amended Code Sec. 401(k)(3)(D)(ii)(I), as redesignated, by striking out "meets" and inserting in lieu thereof "meet". **Effective** as if included in the provision of P.L. 99-514 to which it relates.

P.L. 100-647, §1011(k)(6):

Amended Code Sec. 401(k)(4)(A) by striking out "provided by such employer" after "benefit". **Effective** as if included in the provision of P.L. 99-514 to which it relates.

P.L. 100-647, §1011(k)(7):

Amended Code Sec. 401(k)(8) by redesignating subparagraph (E) as subparagraph (F) and by inserting after subparagraph (D) new subparagraph (E). **Effective** as if included in the provision of P.L. 99-514 to which it relates.

P.L. 100-647, §1011(k)(9):

Amended Code Sec. 401(k)(4)(B) by adding at the end thereof a new sentence. **Effective** as if included in the provision of P.L. 99-514 to which it relates.

P.L. 100-647, §6071(a):

Amended Code Sec. 401(k)(1) and (2) by striking out "or a rural electric cooperative plan" and inserting in lieu thereof "or a rural cooperative plan". **Effective** for tax years beginning after 11-10-88.

P.L. 100-647, §6071(b)(1):

Amended Code Sec. 401(k)(7). **Effective** for tax years beginning after 11-10-88. Prior to amendment, Code Sec. 401(k)(7) read as follows:

(7) RURAL ELECTRIC COOPERATIVE PLAN.—For purposes of this subsection—

(A) IN GENERAL.—The term "rural electric cooperative plan" means any pension plan—

(i) which is a defined contribution plan (as defined in section 414(i)), and

(ii) which is established and maintained by a rural electric cooperative.

(B) RURAL ELECTRIC COOPERATIVE DEFINED.—For purposes of subparagraph (A), the term "rural electric cooperative" means—

(i) any organization which—

(I) is exempt from tax under this subtitle or which is a State or local government or political subdivision thereof (or agency or instrumentality thereof), and

(II) is engaged primarily in providing electric service on a mutual or cooperative basis,

(ii) any organization described in paragraph (4) or (6) of section 501(c) and at least 80 percent of the members of which are organizations described in clause (i), and

(iii) an organization which is a national association of organizations described in clause (i) or (ii).

P.L. 100-647, §6071(b)(2), as amended by P.L. 101-239, §7816(l):

Amended Code Sec. 401(k)(4)(B), as amended by title I, by striking out "rural electric cooperative plan" and inserting in lieu thereof "rural cooperative plan". **Effective** for tax years beginning after 11-10-88.

• 1986, Tax Reform Act of 1986 (P.L. 99-514)

P.L. 99-514, §1112(d)(1):

Amended Code Sec. 401(k)(3)(A) by striking out "subparagraph (A) or (B) of" before "section 410(b)(1)". **Effective**, generally, for plan years beginning after 12-31-88. However, for special rules, see Act Sec. 1112(e)(2)-(4), reproduced under the amendment note for Code Sec. 401(a).

P.L. 99-514, §1116(a)(1)-(3):

Amended Code Sec. 401(k)(3)(A) by striking out "1.5" in clause (ii)(I) and inserting in lieu thereof "1.25", by striking out "3 percentage points" in clause (ii)(II) and inserting in lieu thereof "2 percentage points", and by striking out "2.5" in clause (ii)(II) and inserting in lieu thereof "2". **Effective**, generally, for years beginning after 12-31-88. However, for special rules, see Act Sec. 1116(f)(2)-(7), below.

P.L. 99-514, §1116(b)(1):

Amended Code Sec. 401(k)(2)(B). **Effective**, generally, for years beginning after 12-31-88. However, for special rules, see Act Sec. 1116(f)(2)-(7), below. Prior to amendment, Code Sec. 401(k)(2)(B) read as follows:

(B) under which amounts held by the trust which are attributable to employer contributions made pursuant to the employee's election may not be distributable to participants or other beneficiaries earlier than upon retirement, death, disability, or separation from service (or in the case of a profit sharing or stock bonus plan, hardship or the attainment of age 59½) and will not be distributable merely by reason of the completion of a stated period of participation or the lapse of a fixed number of years;

P.L. 99-514, §1116(b)(2):

Amended Code Sec. 401(k)(2) by striking out "and" at the end of subparagraph (B), by striking out the period at the end of subparagraph (C) and inserting in lieu thereof ", and", and by adding at the end thereof new subparagraph (D). **Effective**, generally, for years beginning after 12-31-88. However, for special rules, see Act Sec. 1116(f)(2)-(7), below.

P.L. 99-514, §1116(b)(3):

Amended Code Sec. 401(k) by redesignating paragraphs (4), (5), and (6) as paragraphs (5), (6), and (7), respectively, and by inserting after paragraph (3) new paragraph (4). **Effective**, generally, for years beginning after 12-31-88. However, for special rules, see Act Sec. 1116(f)(2)-(7), below.

P.L. 99-514, §1116(b)(4):

Amended Code Sec. 401(k)(3)(A) by striking out "an employee" and inserting in lieu thereof "any highly compensated employee" in the last sentence. **Effective**, generally, for years beginning after 12-31-88. However, for special rules, see Act Sec. 1116(f)(2)-(7), below.

P.L. 99-514, §1116(c)(1):

Amended Code Sec. 401(k) by adding at the end thereof new paragraph (8). **Effective**, generally, for years beginning after 12-31-88. However, for special rules, see Act Sec. 1116(f)(2)-(7), below.

P.L. 99-514, §1116(c)(2):

Amended Code Sec. 401(k)(3)(A)(ii) by striking out "paragraph (4)" and inserting in lieu thereof "paragraph (5)". **Effective**, generally, for years beginning after 12-31-88. However, for special rules, see Act Sec. 1116(f)(2)-(7), below.

P.L. 99-514, §1116(d)(1):

Amended Code Sec. 401(k)(5), as redesignated by this Act. **Effective**, generally, for years beginning after 12-31-88. However, for special rules, see Act Sec. 1116(f)(2)-(7), below. Prior to amendment, Code Sec. 401(k)(5) read as follows:

(5) HIGHLY COMPENSATED EMPLOYEE.—For purposes of this subsection, the term "highly compensated employee" means any employee who is more highly compensated than two-thirds of all eligible employees, taking into account only compensation which is considered in applying paragraph (3).

P.L. 99-514, §1116(d)(2):

Amended Code Sec. 401(k) by adding at the end thereof new paragraph (9). **Effective**, generally, for years beginning after 12-31-88. However, for special rules, see Act Sec. 1116(f)(2)-(7), below.

P.L. 99-514, §1116(d)(3):

Amended Code Sec. 401(k)(3)(B) by striking out the last sentence thereof. **Effective**, generally, for years beginning after 12-31-88. However, for special rules, see Act Sec. 1116(f)(2)-(7), below. Prior to amendment, the last sentence of Code Sec. 401(k)(3)(B) read as follows:

For purposes of the preceding sentence, the compensation of any employee for a plan year shall be the amount of his compensation which is taken into account under the plan in calculating the contribution which may be made on his behalf for such plan year.

P.L. 99-514, §1116(e):

Amended Code Sec. 401(k)(3) by adding at the end thereof new subparagraph (C)[D]. **Effective**, generally, for years beginning after 12-31-88. However, for special rules, see Act Sec. 1116(f)(2)-(7), below.

P.L. 99-514, §1116(f)(2)-(7), as amended by P.L. 100-647, §1011(k)(8) and (10), provides:

(2) NONDISCRIMINATION RULES.—

(A) IN GENERAL.—Except as provided in subparagraph (B), the amendments made by subsections (a), (b)(4), and (d), and the provisions of section 401(k)(4)(B) of the Internal Revenue Code of 1986 (as added by this section), shall apply to years beginning after December 31, 1986.

(B) TRANSITION RULES FOR CERTAIN GOVERNMENTAL AND TAX-EXEMPT PLANS.—Subparagraph (B) of section 401(k)(4) of the Internal Revenue Code of 1986 (relating to governments and tax-exempt organizations not eligible for cash or deferred arrangements), as added by this section, shall not apply to any cash or deferred arrangement adopted by—

(i) a State or local government or political subdivision thereof, or any agency or instrumentality thereof, before May 6, 1986, or

(ii) a tax-exempt organization before July 2, 1986.

In the case of an arrangement described in clause (i), the amendments made by subsections (a), (b)(4), and (d) shall apply to years beginning after December 31, 1988. If clause (i) or (ii) applies to any arrangement adopted by a governmental unit, then any cash or deferred arrangement adopted by such unit on or after the date referred to in the applicable clause shall be treated as adopted before such date.

(3) AGGREGATION AND EXCESS CONTRIBUTIONS.—The amendments made by subsections (c) and (e) shall apply to years beginning after December 31, 1986.

(4) COLLECTIVE BARGAINING AGREEMENTS.—

(A) IN GENERAL.—In the case of a plan maintained pursuant to 1 or more collective bargaining agreements between employee representatives and 1 or more employers ratified before March 1, 1986, the amendments made by this section shall not apply to years beginning before the earlier of—

(i) the later of—

(I) January 1, 1989, or

(II) the date on which the last of such collective bargaining agreements terminates (determined without regard to any extension thereof after February 28, 1986), or

(ii) January 1, 1991.

(B) SPECIAL RULE FOR NONDISCRIMINATION RULES.—In the case of a plan described in subparagraph (A), the amendments and provisions described in paragraph (2) shall not apply to years beginning before the earlier of—

(i) the date determined under subparagraph (A)(i)(II), or

(ii) January 1, 1989.

(5) SPECIAL RULE FOR QUALIFIED OFFSET ARRANGEMENTS.—

(A) IN GENERAL.—A cash or deferred arrangement shall not be treated as failing to meet the requirements of section 401(k)(4) of the Internal Revenue Code of 1986 (as added by this section) to the extent such arrangement is part of a qualified offset arrangement consisting of such cash or deferred arrangement and a defined benefit plan.

(B) QUALIFIED OFFSET ARRANGEMENT.—For purposes of subparagraph (A), a cash or deferred arrangement is part of a qualified offset arrangement with a defined benefit plan to the extent such offset arrangement satisfies each of the following conditions with respect to the employer maintaining the arrangement on April 16, 1986, and at all times thereafter:

(i) The benefit under the defined benefit plan is directly and uniformly conditioned on the initial elective deferrals (up to 4 percent of compensation).

(ii) The benefit provided under the defined benefit plan (before the offset) is at least 60 percent of an employee's cumulative elective deferrals (up to 4 percent of compensation).

(iii) The benefit under the defined benefit plan is reduced by the benefit attributable to the employee's elective deferrals under the plan (up to 4-percent of compensation) and the income allocable thereto. The interest rate used to calculate the reduction shall not exceed the greater of the rate under section 411(a)(11)(B)(ii) of such Code or the interest rate applicable under section 411(c)(2)(C)(ii) of such Code, taking into account section 411(c)(2)(D) of such Code.

For purposes of applying section 401(k)(3) of such Code to the cash or deferred arrangement, the benefits under the defined benefit plan conditioned on initial elective deferrals may be treated as matching contributions under such rules as the Secretary of the Treasury or his delegate may prescribe. The Secretary shall provide rules for the application of this paragraph in the case of successor plans.

(C) DEFINITION OF EMPLOYER.—For purposes of this paragraph, the term "employer" includes any research and development center which is federally funded and engaged in cancer research, but only with respect to employees of contractor-operators whose salaries are reimbursed as direct costs against the operator's contract to perform work at such center.

(6) WITHDRAWALS ON SALE OF ASSETS.—Subclauses (II), (III), and (IV) of section 401(k)(2)(B)(i) of the Internal Revenue Code of 1986 (as added by subsection (b)(1)) shall apply to distributions after December 31, 1984.

(7) DISTRIBUTIONS BEFORE PLAN AMENDMENT.—

(A) IN GENERAL.—If a plan amendment is required to allow a plan to make any distribution described in section 401(k)(8) of the Internal Revenue Code of 1986, any such distribution which is made before the close of the 1st plan year for which such amendment is required to be in effect under section 1140, shall be treated as made in accordance with the provisions of such plan.

(B) DISTRIBUTIONS PURSUANT TO MODEL AMENDMENT.—

(i) SECRETARY TO PRESCRIBE AMENDMENT.—The Secretary of the Treasury or his delegate shall prescribe an amendment which allows a plan to make any distribution described in section 401(k)(8) of such Code.

(ii) ADOPTION BY PLAN.—If a plan adopts the amendment prescribed under clause (i) and makes a distribution in accordance with such amendment, such distribution shall be treated as made in accordance with the provisions of the plan.

P.L. 99-514, §1852(g)(i):

Amended Code Sec. 401(k)(3) by adding at the end thereof new subparagraph (C). **Effective** as if included in the provision of P.L. 98-369 to which it relates.

P.L. 99-514, §1852(g)(2):

Amended Code Sec. 401(k)(3)(A) by striking out the last sentence and inserting in lieu thereof "If an[y] employee is a participant under 2 or more cash or deferred arrangements of the employer, for purposes of determining the deferral percentage with respect to such employee, all such cash or deferred arrangements shall be treated as 1 cash or deferred arrangement." **Effective** as if included in the provision of P.L. 98-369 to which it relates. Prior to amendment, the last sentence read as follows:

The deferral percentage taken into account under this subparagraph for any employee who is a participant under 2 or more cash or deferred arrangements of the employer shall be the sum of the deferral percentages for such employee under each of such arrangements.

P.L. 99-514, §1852(g)(3):

Amended Code Sec. 401(k)(2)(C) by striking out "are nonforfeitable" and inserting in lieu thereof "is nonforfeitable". **Effective** as if included in the provision of P.L. 98-369 to which it relates.

P.L. 99-514, §1879(g)(1):

Amended Code Sec. 401(k)(1) and (2) by striking out "(or a pre-ERISA money purchase plan)" and inserting in lieu thereof ", a pre-ERISA money purchase plan, or a rural electric cooperative plan". **Effective** for plan years beginning after 12-31-84.

P.L. 99-514, §1879(g)(2):

Amended Code Sec. 401(k) by adding at the end thereof new paragraph (6). **Effective** for plan years beginning after 12-31-84.

• 1984, Deficit Reduction Act of 1984 (P.L. 98-369)

P.L. 98-369, §527(a):

Amended Code Sec. 401(k)(3)(A). **Effective** for plan years beginning after 12-31-84. However, it does not apply to any plan which was maintained by a State on 6-8-84, and with respect to which a determination letter had been issued by the Secretary on 12-6-82. Prior to amendment, it read as follows:

(3) Application of Participation and Discrimination Standards.—

(A) A qualified cash or deferred arrangement shall be considered to satisfy the requirements of subsection (a)(4), with respect to the amount of contributions, and of subparagraph (B) of section 410(b)(1) for a plan year if those employees eligible to benefit under the plan satisfy the provisions of subparagraph (A) or (B) of section 410(b)(1) and if the actual deferral percentage for highly compensated employees (as defined in paragraph (4)) for such plan year bears a relationship to the actual deferral percentage for all other eligible employees for such plan year which meets either of the following tests.

(i) The actual deferral percentage for the group of highly compensated employees is not more than the actual deferral percentage of all other eligible employees multiplied by 1.5.

(ii) The excess of the actual deferral percentage for the group of highly compensated employees over that of all other eligible employees is not more than 3 percentage points, and the actual deferral percentage for the group of highly compensated employees is not more than the actual deferral percentage of all other eligible employees multiplied by 2.5.

P.L. 98-369, §527(b)(1):

Amended Code Sec. 401(k)(1) and (2) by inserting "(or a pre-ERISA money purchase plan)" after "stock bonus plan". **Effective**, generally, for plan years beginning after 7-18-84. However, see the transitional rule in Act Sec. 527(c)(2)(B), below.

P.L. 98-369, §527(b)(2):

Amended Code Sec. 401(k) by adding new paragraph (5) at the end thereof. **Effective**, generally, for plan years beginning after 7-18-84. However, see the transitional rule in Act Sec. 527(c)(2)(B), below.

P.L. 98-369, §527(b)(3):

Amended Code Sec. 401(k)(2)(B) by striking out ", hardship or the attainment of age 59½," and inserting in lieu thereof "(or in the case of a profit sharing or stock bonus plan, hardship or the attainment of age 59½)". **Effective**, generally, for plan years beginning after 7-18-84. However, see the transitional rule in Act Sec. 527(c)(2)(B), below.

P.L. 98-369, §527(c)(2)(B), provides:

(B) Transitional Rule.—Rules similar to the rules under section 135(c)(2) of the Revenue Act of 1978 shall apply with respect to any pre-ERISA money purchase plan (as defined in section 401(k)(5) of the Internal Revenue Code of 1954) for plan years beginning after December 31, 1979, and on or before July 18, 1984.

• 1978, Revenue Act of 1978 (P.L. 95-600)

P.L. 95-600, §135(a):

Redesignated Code Sec. 401(k) as 401(l) and added a new Code Sec. 401(k). **Effective** as provided by Act Sec. 135(c), below.

P.L. 95-600, §135(c), provides:

(c) EFFECTIVE DATE.—

(1) IN GENERAL.—The amendments made by this section shall apply to plan years beginning after December 31, 1979.

(2) TRANSITIONAL RULE.—In the case of cash or deferred arrangements in existence on June 27, 1974—

(A) the qualification of the plan and the trust under section 401 of the Internal Revenue Code of 1954;

(B) the exemption of the trust under section 501(a) of such Code;

(C) the taxable year of inclusion in gross income of the employee of any amount so contributed by the employer to the trust; and

(D) the excludability of the interest of the employee in the trust under sections 2039 and 2517 of such Code,

shall be determined for plan years beginning before January 1, 1980 in a manner consistent with Revenue Ruling 56-497 (1956-2 C.B. 284), Revenue Ruling 63-180 (1963-2 C.B. 189), and Revenue Ruling 68-89 (1968-1 C.B. 402).

[Sec. 401(l)]

(l) PERMITTED DISPARITY IN PLAN CONTRIBUTIONS OR BENEFITS.—

(1) IN GENERAL.—The requirements of this subsection are met with respect to a plan if—

(A) in the case of a defined contribution plan, the requirements of paragraph (2) are met, and

(B) in the case of a defined benefit plan, the requirements of paragraph (3) are met.

(2) DEFINED CONTRIBUTION PLAN.—

(A) IN GENERAL.—A defined contribution plan meets the requirements of this paragraph if the excess contribution percentage does not exceed the base contribution percentage by more than the lesser of—

(i) the base contribution percentage, or

(ii) the greater of—

(I) 5.7 percentage points, or

(II) the percentage equal to the portion of the rate of tax under section 3111(a) (in effect as of the beginning of the year) which is attributable to old-age insurance.

(B) CONTRIBUTION PERCENTAGES.—For purposes of this paragraph—

(i) EXCESS CONTRIBUTION PERCENTAGE.—The term "excess contribution percentage" means the percentage of compensation which is contributed by the employer under the plan with respect to that portion of each participant's compensation in excess of the integration level.

(ii) BASE CONTRIBUTION PERCENTAGE.—The term "base contribution percentage" means the percentage of compensation contributed by the employer under the plan with respect to that portion of each participant's compensation not in excess of the integration level.

(3) DEFINED BENEFIT PLAN.—A defined benefit plan meets the requirements of this paragraph if—

(A) EXCESS PLANS.—

(i) IN GENERAL.—In the case of a plan other than an offset plan—

(I) the excess benefit percentage does not exceed the base benefit percentage by more than the maximum excess allowance,

(II) any optional form of benefit, preretirement benefit, actuarial factor, or other benefit or feature provided with respect to compensation in excess of the integration level is provided with respect to compensation not in excess of such level, and

(III) benefits are based on average annual compensation.

(ii) BENEFIT PERCENTAGES.—For purposes of this subparagraph, the excess and base benefit percentages shall be computed in the same manner as the excess and base contribution percentages under paragraph (2)(B), except that such determination shall be made on the basis of benefits attributable to employer contributions rather than contributions.

(B) OFFSET PLANS.—In the case of an offset plan, the plan provides that—

(i) a participant's accrued benefit attributable to employer contributions (within the meaning of section 411(c)(1)) may not be reduced (by reason of the offset) by more than the maximum offset allowance, and

(ii) benefits are based on average annual compensation.

(4) DEFINITIONS RELATING TO PARAGRAPH (3).—For purposes of paragraph (3)—

(A) MAXIMUM EXCESS ALLOWANCE.—The maximum excess allowance is equal to—

(i) in the case of benefits attributable to any year of service with the employer taken into account under the plan, 3/4 of a percentage point, and

(ii) in the case of total benefits, 3/4 of a percentage point, multiplied by the participant's years of service (not in excess of 35) with the employer taken into account under the plan.

In no event shall the maximum excess allowance exceed the base benefit percentage.

(B) MAXIMUM OFFSET ALLOWANCE.—The maximum offset allowance is equal to—

(i) in the case of benefits attributable to any year of service with the employer taken into account under the plan, 3/4 percent of the participant's final average compensation, and

(ii) in the case of total benefits, 3/4 percent of the participant's final average compensation, multiplied by the participant's years of service (not in excess of 35) with the employer taken into account under the plan.

In no event shall the maximum offset allowance exceed 50 percent of the benefit which would have accrued without regard to the offset reduction.

(C) REDUCTIONS.—

(i) IN GENERAL.—The Secretary shall prescribe regulations requiring the reduction of the 3/4 percentage factor under subparagraph (A) or (B)—

(I) in the case of a plan other than an offset plan which has an integration level in excess of covered compensation, or

(II) with respect to any participant in an offset plan who has final average compensation in excess of covered compensation.

(ii) BASIS OF REDUCTIONS.—Any reductions under clause (i) shall be based on the percentages of compensation replaced by the employer-derived portions of primary insurance amounts under the Social Security Act for participants with compensation in excess of covered compensation.

(D) OFFSET PLAN.—The term "offset plan" means any plan with respect to which the benefit attributable to employer contributions for each participant is reduced by an amount specified in the plan.

(5) OTHER DEFINITIONS AND SPECIAL RULES.—For purposes of this subsection—

(A) INTEGRATION LEVEL.—

(i) IN GENERAL.—The term "integration level" means the amount of compensation specified under the plan (by dollar amount or formula) at or below which the rate at which contributions or benefits are provided (expressed as a percentage) is less than such rate above such amount.

(ii) LIMITATION.—The integration level for any year may not exceed the contribution and benefit base in effect under section 230 of the Social Security Act for such year.

(iii) LEVEL TO APPLY TO ALL PARTICIPANTS.—A plan's integration level shall apply with respect to all participants in the plan.

(iv) MULTIPLE INTEGRATION LEVELS.—Under rules prescribed by the Secretary, a defined benefit plan may specify multiple integration levels.

(B) COMPENSATION.—The term "compensation" has the meaning given such term by section 414(s).

(C) AVERAGE ANNUAL COMPENSATION.—The term "average annual compensation" means the participant's highest average annual compensation for—

(i) any period of at least 3 consecutive years, or

(ii) if shorter, the participant's full period of service.

(D) FINAL AVERAGE COMPENSATION.—

(i) IN GENERAL.—The term "final average compensation" means the participant's average annual compensation for—

(I) the 3-consecutive year period ending with the current year, or

(II) if shorter, the participant's full period of service.

(ii) LIMITATION.—A participant's final average compensation shall be determined by not taking into account in any year compensation in excess of the contribution and benefit base in effect under section 230 of the Social Security Act for such year.

(E) COVERED COMPENSATION.—

(i) IN GENERAL.—The term "covered compensation" means, with respect to an employee, the average of the contribution and benefit bases in effect under section 230 of the Social Security Act for each year in the 35-year period ending with the year in which the employee attains the social security retirement age.

(ii) COMPUTATION FOR ANY YEAR.—For purposes of clause (i), the determination for any year preceding the year in which the employee attains the social security retirement age shall be made by assuming that there is no increase in the bases described in clause (i) after the determination year and before the employee attains the social security retirement age.

(iii) SOCIAL SECURITY RETIREMENT AGE.—For purposes of this subparagraph, the term "social security retirement age" has the meaning given such term by section 415(b)(8).

(F) REGULATIONS.—The Secretary shall prescribe such regulations as are necessary or appropriate to carry out the purposes of this subsection, including—

(i) in the case of a defined benefit plan which provides for unreduced benefits commencing before the social security retirement age (as defined in section 415(b)(8)), rules providing for the reduction of the maximum excess allowance and the maximum offset allowance, and

(ii) in the case of an employee covered by 2 or more plans of the employer which fail to meet the requirements of subsection (a)(4) (without regard to this subsection), rules preventing the multiple use of the disparity permitted under this subsection with respect to any employee.

For purposes of clause (i), unreduced benefits shall not include benefits for disability (within the meaning of section 223(d) of the Social Security Act).

(6) SPECIAL RULE FOR PLAN MAINTAINED BY RAILROADS.—In determining whether a plan which includes employees of a railroad employer who are entitled to benefits under the Railroad Retirement Act of 1974 meets the requirements of this subsection, rules similar to the rules set forth in this subsection shall apply. Such rules shall take into account the employer-derived portion of the employees' tier 2 railroad retirement benefits and any supplemental annuity under the Railroad Retirement Act of 1974.

Amendments

• 1988, Technical and Miscellaneous Revenue Act of 1988 (P.L. 100-647)

P.L. 100-647, §1011(g)(1)(A):

Amended Code Sec. 401(l)(2)(B) by inserting "by the employer" after "contributed" each place it appears. **Effective** as if included in the provision of P.L. 99-514 to which it relates.

P.L. 100-647, §1011(g)(1)(B):

Amended Code Sec. 401(l)(3)(A)(ii) by inserting "attributable to employer contributions" after "benefits". **Effective** as if included in the provision of P.L. 99-514 to which it relates.

P.L. 100-647, §1011(g)(2):

Amended Code Sec. 401(l)(5)(C). **Effective** as if included in the provision of P.L. 99-514 to which it relates. Prior to amendment, Code Sec. 401(l)(5)(C) read as follows:

(C) AVERAGE ANNUAL COMPENSATION.—The term "average annual compensation" means the greater of—

(i) the participant's final average compensation (determined without regard to subparagraph (D)(ii)), or

(ii) the participant's highest average annual compensation for any other period of at least 3 consecutive years.

P.L. 100-647, §1011(g)(3)(A)-(B):

Amended Code Sec. 401(l)(5)(E) by striking out "age 65" each place it appears and inserting in lieu thereof "the social security retirement age", and by adding at the end thereof new clause (iii). **Effective** as if included in the provision of P.L. 99-514 to which it relates.

• 1986, Tax Reform Act of 1986 (P.L. 99-514)

P.L. 99-514, §1111(a):

Amended Code Sec. 401(l). For the **effective** date, see Act Sec. 1111(c) reproduced under the amendment notes for Code Sec. 401(a). Prior to amendment, Code Sec. 401(l) read as follows:

(l) NONDISCRIMINATORY COORDINATION OF DEFINED CONTRIBUTION PLANS WITH OASDI.—

(1) IN GENERAL.—Notwithstanding subsection (a)(5), the coordination of a defined contribution plan with OASDI meets the requirements of subsection (a)(4) only if the total contributions with respect to each participant, when in-

creased by the OASDI contributions, bear a uniform relationship—

(A) to the total compensation of such employee, or

(B) to the basic or regular rate of compensation of such employee.

(2) DEFINITIONS.—For purposes of paragraph (1)—

(A) OASDI CONTRIBUTIONS.—The term "OASDI contributions" means the product of—

(i) so much of the remuneration paid by the employer to the employee during the plan year as—

(I) constitutes wages (within the meaning of section 3121(a) without regard to paragraph (1) thereof), and

(II) does not exceed the contribution and benefit base applicable under OASDI at the beginning of the plan year, multiplied by

(ii) the rate of tax applicable under section 3111(a) (relating to employer's OASDI tax) at the beginning of the plan year.

In the case of an individual who is an employee within the meaning of subsection (c)(1), the preceding sentence shall be applied by taking into account his earned income (as defined in subsection (c)(2)).

(B) OASDI.—The term "OASDI" means the system of old-age, survivors, and disability insurance established under title II of the Social Security Act and the Federal Insurance Contributions Act.

(C) REMUNERATION.—The term "remuneration" means—

(i) total compensation, or

(ii) basic or regular rate of compensation,

whichever is used in determining contributions or benefits under the plan.

(3) DETERMINATION OF COMPENSATION, ETC., OF SELF-EMPLOYED INDIVIDUALS.—For purposes of this subsection, in the case of an individual who is an employee within the meaning of subsection (c)(1)—

(A) his total compensation shall include his earned income (as defined in subsection (c)(2)), and

(B) his basic or regular rate of compensation shall be determined (under regulations prescribed by the Secretary) with respect to that portion of his earned income which bears the same ratio to his earned income as the basic or regular compensation of the employees under the plan (other than employees within the meaning of subsection (c)(1)) bears to the total compensation of such employees.

• 1982, Tax Equity and Fiscal Responsibility Act of 1982 (P.L. 97-248)

P.L. 97-248, §249(a):

Added subsection (l). **Effective** for plan years beginning after 12-31-83.

[Sec. 401(m)]

(m) NONDISCRIMINATION TEST FOR MATCHING CONTRIBUTIONS AND EMPLOYEE CONTRIBUTIONS.—

(1) IN GENERAL.—A defined contribution plan shall be treated as meeting the requirements of subsection (a)(4) with respect to the amount of any matching contribution or employee contribution for any plan year only if the contribution percentage requirement of paragraph (2) of this subsection is met for such plan year.

(2) REQUIREMENTS.—

(A) CONTRIBUTION PERCENTAGE REQUIREMENT.—A plan meets the contribution percentage requirement of this paragraph for any plan year only if the contribution percentage for eligible highly compensated employees for such plan year does not exceed the greater of—

(i) 125 percent of such percentage for all other eligible employees for the preceding plan year, or

(ii) the lesser of 200 percent of such percentage for all other eligible employees for the preceding plan year, or such percentage for all other eligible employees for the preceding plan year plus 2 percentage points.

This subparagraph may be applied by using the plan year rather than the preceding plan year if the employer so elects, except that if such an election is made, it may not be changed except as provided the Secretary.

(B) MULTIPLE PLANS TREATED AS A SINGLE PLAN.—If two or more plans of an employer to which matching contributions, employee contributions, or elective deferrals are made are treated as one plan for purposes of section 410(b), such plans shall be treated as one plan for purposes of this subsection. If a highly compensated employee participates in two or more plans of an employer to which contributions to which this subsection applies are made, all such contributions shall be aggregated for purposes of this subsection.

(3) CONTRIBUTION PERCENTAGE.—For purposes of paragraph (2), the contribution percentage for a specified group of employees for a plan year shall be the average for the ratios (calculated separately for each employee in such group) of—

(A) the sum of the matching contributions and employee contributions paid under the plan on behalf of each such employee for such plan year, to

(B) the employee's compensation (within the meaning of section 414(s)) for such plan year.

Under regulations, an employer may elect to take into account (in computing the contribution percentage) elective deferrals and qualified nonelective contributions under the plan or any other plan of the employer. If matching contributions are taken into account for purposes of subsection (k)(3)(A)(ii) for any plan year, such contributions shall not be taken into account under subparagraph (A) for such year. Rules similar to the rules of subsection (k)(3)(E) shall apply for purposes of this subsection.

(4) DEFINITIONS.—For purposes of this subsection—

(A) MATCHING CONTRIBUTION.—The term "matching contribution" means—

(i) any employer contribution made to a defined contribution plan on behalf of an employee on account of an employee contribution made by such employee, and

(ii) any employer contribution made to a defined contribution plan on behalf of an employee on account of an employee's elective deferral.

(B) ELECTIVE DEFERRAL.—The term "elective deferral" means any employer contribution described in section 402(g)(3).

(C) QUALIFIED NONELECTIVE CONTRIBUTIONS.—The term "qualified nonelective contribution" means any employer contribution (other than a matching contribution) with respect to which—

(i) the employee may not elect to have the contribution paid to the employee in cash instead of being contributed to the plan, and

(ii) the requirements of subparagraphs (B) and (C) of subsection (k)(2) are met.

(5) EMPLOYEES TAKEN INTO CONSIDERATION.—

(A) IN GENERAL.—Any employee who is eligible to make an employee contribution (or, if the employer takes elective contributions into account, elective contributions) or to receive a matching contribution under the plan being tested under paragraph (1) shall be considered an eligible employee for purposes of this subsection.

(B) CERTAIN NONPARTICIPANTS.—If an employee contribution is required as a condition of participation in the plan, any employee who would be a participant in the plan if such employee made such a contribution shall be treated as an eligible employee on behalf of whom no employer contributions are made.

(C) SPECIAL RULE FOR EARLY PARTICIPATION.—If an employer elects to apply section 410(b)(4)(B) in determining whether a plan meets the requirements of section 410(b), the employer may, in determining whether the plan meets the requirements of paragraph (2), exclude from consideration all eligible employees (other than highly compensated employees) who have not met the minimum age and service requirements of section 410(a)(1)(A).

(6) PLAN NOT DISQUALIFIED IF EXCESS AGGREGATE CONTRIBUTIONS DISTRIBUTED BEFORE END OF FOLLOWING PLAN YEAR.—

(A) IN GENERAL.—A plan shall not be treated as failing to meet the requirements of paragraph (1) for any plan year if, before the close of the following plan year, the amount of the excess aggregate contributions for such plan year (and any income allocable to such contributions through the end of such year) is distributed (or, if forfeitable, is forfeited). Such contributions (and such income) may be distributed without regard to any other provision of law.

(B) EXCESS AGGREGATE CONTRIBUTIONS.—For purposes of subparagraph (A), the term "excess aggregate contributions" means, with respect to any plan year, the excess of—

(i) the aggregate amount of the matching contributions and employee contributions (and any qualified nonelective contribution or elective contribution taken into account in computing the contribution percentage) actually made on behalf of highly compensated employees for such plan year, over

(ii) the maximum amount of such contributions permitted under the limitations of paragraph (2)(A) (determined by reducing contributions made on behalf of highly compensated employees in order of their contribution percentages beginning with the highest of such percentages).

(C) METHOD OF DISTRIBUTING EXCESS AGGREGATE CONTRIBUTIONS.—Any distribution of the excess aggregate contributions for any plan year shall be made to highly compensated employees on the basis of the amount of contributions on behalf of, or by, each such employee. Forfeitures of excess aggregate contributions may not be allocated to participants whose contributions are reduced under this paragraph.

(D) COORDINATION WITH SUBSECTION (k) AND 402(g).—The determination of the amount of excess aggregate contributions with respect to a plan shall be made after—

(i) first determining the excess deferrals (within the meaning of section 402(g)), and

(ii) then determining the excess contributions under subsection (k).

(7) TREATMENT OF DISTRIBUTIONS.—

(A) ADDITIONAL TAX OF SECTION 72(t) NOT APPLICABLE.—No tax shall be imposed under section 72(t) on any amount required to be distributed under paragraph (6).

(B) EXCLUSION OF EMPLOYEE CONTRIBUTIONS.—Any distribution attributable to employee contributions shall not be included in gross income except to the extent attributable to income on such contributions.

(8) HIGHLY COMPENSATED EMPLOYEE.—For purposes of this subsection, the term "highly compensated employee" has the meaning given to such term by section 414(q).

(9) REGULATIONS.—The Secretary shall prescribe such regulations as may be necessary to carry out the purposes of this subsection and subsection (k), including regulations permitting appropriate aggregation of plans and contributions.

(10) ALTERNATIVE METHOD OF SATISFYING TESTS.—A defined contribution plan shall be treated as meeting the requirements of paragraph (2) with respect to matching contributions if the plan—

(A) meets the contribution requirements of subparagraph (B) of subsection (k)(11),

(B) meets the exclusive plan requirements of subsection (k)(11)(C), and

(C) meets the vesting requirements of section 408(p)(3).

(11) ADDITIONAL ALTERNATIVE METHOD OF SATISFYING TESTS.—

(A) IN GENERAL.—A defined contribution plan shall be treated as meeting the requirements of paragraph (2) with respect to matching contributions if the plan—

(i) meets the contribution requirements of subparagraph (B) or (C) of subsection (k)(12),

(ii) meets the notice requirements of subsection (k)(12)(D), and

(iii) meets the requirements of subparagraph (B).

(B) LIMITATION ON MATCHING CONTRIBUTIONS.—The requirements of this subparagraph are met if—

(i) matching contributions on behalf of any employee may not be made with respect to an employee's contributions or elective deferrals in excess of 6 percent of the employee's compensation,

(ii) the rate of an employer's matching contribution does not increase as the rate of an employee's contributions or elective deferrals increase, and

(iii) the matching contribution with respect to any highly compensated employee at any rate of an employee contribution or rate of elective deferral is not greater than that with respect to an employee who is not a highly compensated employee.

(12) ALTERNATIVE METHOD FOR AUTOMATIC CONTRIBUTION ARRANGEMENTS.—A defined contribution plan shall be treated as meeting the requirements of paragraph (2) with respect to matching contributions if the plan—

(A) is a qualified automatic contribution arrangement (as defined in subsection (k)(13)), and

(B) meets the requirements of paragraph (11)(B).

(13) CROSS REFERENCE.—

For excise tax on certain excess contributions, see section 4979.

Amendments

• 2006, Pension Protection Act of 2006 (P.L. 109-280)

P.L. 109-280, §811, provides:

SEC. 811. PENSIONS AND INDIVIDUAL RETIREMENT ARRANGEMENT PROVISIONS OF ECONOMIC GROWTH AND TAX RELIEF RECONCILIATION ACT OF 2001 MADE PERMANENT.

Title IX of the Economic Growth and Tax Relief Reconciliation Act of 2001 [P.L. 107-16] shall not apply to the provisions of, and amendments made by, subtitles A through F of title VI [§§601-666]of such Act (relating to pension and individual retirement arrangement provisions).

P.L. 109-280, §902(b):

Amended Code Sec. 401(m) by redesignating paragraph (12) as paragraph (13) and by inserting after paragraph (11) a new paragraph (12). **Effective** for plan years beginning after 12-31-2007.

P.L. 109-280, §902(e)(3)(B)(ii):

Amended Code Sec. 401(m)(6)(A) by adding "through the end of such year" after "to such contributions". **Effective** for plan years beginning after 12-31-2007.

• 2001, Economic Growth and Tax Relief Reconciliation Act of 2001 (P.L. 107-16)

P.L. 107-16, §666(a):

Amended Code Sec. 401(m)(9). **Effective** for years beginning after 12-31-2001. Prior to amendment, Code Sec. 401(m)(9) read as follows:

(9) REGULATIONS.—The Secretary shall prescribe such regulations as may be necessary to carry out the purposes of this subsection and subsection (k) including—

(A) such regulations as may be necessary to prevent the multiple use of the alternative limitation with respect to any highly compensated employee, and

(B) regulations permitting appropriate aggregation of plans and contributions.

For purposes of the preceding sentence, the term "alternative limitation" means the limitation of section 401(k)(3)(A)(ii)(II) and the limitation of paragraph (2)(A)(ii) of this subsection.

P.L. 107-16, §901(a)-(b), provides [but see P.L. 109-280, §811, above]:

SEC. 901. SUNSET OF PROVISIONS OF ACT.

(a) IN GENERAL.—All provisions of, and amendments made by, this Act shall not apply—

(1) to taxable, plan, or limitation years beginning after December 31, 2010, or

(2) in the case of title V, to estates of decedents dying, gifts made, or generation skipping transfers, after December 31, 2010.

(b) APPLICATION OF CERTAIN LAWS.—The Internal Revenue Code of 1986 and the Employee Retirement Income Security Act of 1974 shall be applied and administered to years, estates, gifts, and transfers described in subsection (a) as if the provisions and amendments described in subsection (a) had never been enacted.

• 1997, Taxpayer Relief Act of 1997 (P.L. 105-34)

P.L. 105-34, §1601(d)(3):

Amended Code Sec. 401(m)(11) by striking "ALTERNATIVE" and inserting "ADDITIONAL ALTERNATIVE" in the heading. **Effective** as if included in the provision of P.L. 104-188 to which it relates [**effective** for years beginning after 12-31-98.—CCH].

• 1996, Small Business Job Protection Act of 1996 (P.L. 104-188)

P.L. 104-188, §1422(b):

Amended Code Sec. 401(m) by redesignating paragraph (10) as paragraph (11) and by adding after paragraph (9) a new paragraph (10). **Effective** for plan years beginning after 12-31-96.

P.L. 104-188, §1433(b):

Amended Code Sec. 401(m), as amended by Act Sec. 1422(b), by redesignating paragraph (11) as paragraph (12) and by adding after paragraph (10) a new paragraph (11). **Effective** for years beginning after 12-31-98.

P.L. 104-188, §1433(c)(2)(A)-(C):

Amended Code Sec. 401(m)(2)(A) by inserting "for such plan year" after "highly compensated employees", inserting "for the preceding plan year" after "eligible employees" each place it appears in clause (i) and clause (ii), and adding at the end a new flush sentence. **Effective** for years beginning after 12-31-96.

P.L. 104-188, §1433(d)(2):

Amended Code Sec. 401(m)(3) by adding at the end a new sentence. **Effective** for years beginning after 12-31-96.

P.L. 104-188, §1433(e)(2):

Amended Code Sec. 401(m)(6)(C) by striking "on the basis of the respective portions of such amounts attributable to each of such employees" and inserting "on the basis of the amount of contributions on behalf of, or by, each such employee". **Effective** for years beginning after 12-31-96.

P.L. 104-188, §1459(b):

Amended Code Sec. 401(m)(5) by adding at the end a new subparagraph (C). **Effective** for plan years beginning after 12-31-98.

• 1988, Technical and Miscellaneous Revenue Act of 1988 (P.L. 100-647)

P.L. 100-647, §1011(l)(1):

Amended Code Sec. 401(m)(1) by striking out "A plan" and inserting in lieu thereof "A defined contribution plan". **Effective** as if included in the provision of P.L. 99-514 to which it relates.

P.L. 100-647, §1011(l)(2):

Amended Code Sec. 401(m)(3) by adding at the end thereof a new sentence. **Effective** as if included in the provision of P.L. 99-514 to which it relates.

P.L. 100-647, §1011(l)(3):

Amended Code Sec. 401(m)(2)(B) by striking out "such contributions" the first place it appears in the last sentence and inserting in lieu thereof "contributions to which this subsection applies". **Effective** as if included in the provision of P.L. 99-514 to which it relates.

P.L. 100-647, §1011(l)(4):

Amended Code Sec. 401(m)(4)(A) by striking out "the plan" each place it appears and inserting in lieu thereof "a defined contribution plan". **Effective** as if included in the provision of P.L. 99-514 to which it relates.

P.L. 100-647, §1011(l)(5)(A):

Amended Code Sec. 401(m)(4)(B) by striking out "section 402(g)(3)(A)" and inserting in lieu thereof "section 402(g)(3)". **Effective** as if included in the provision of P.L. 99-514 to which it relates.

P.L. 100-647, §1011(l)(6):

Amended Code Sec. 401(m)(6)(C) by striking out "excess" in the subparagraph heading and inserting in lieu thereof "excess aggregate". **Effective** as if included in the provision of P.L. 99-514 to which it relates.

P.L. 100-647, §1011(l)(7):

Amended Code Sec. 401(m)(7)(A) by striking out "paragraph (8)" and inserting in lieu thereof "paragraph (6)". **Effective** as if included in the provision of P.L. 99-514 to which it relates.

• 1986, Tax Reform Act of 1986 (P.L. 99-514)

P.L. 99-514, §1117(a):

Amended Code Sec. 401 by redesignating subsections (m) and (n) as subsections (n) and (o), respectively, and by inserting after subsection (l) new subsection (m). **Effective,** generally, for plan years beginning 12-31-86. However, see Act Sec. 1117(d)(2)-(4), below.

P.L. 99-514, §1117(d)(2)-(4), as amended by P.L. 100-647, §1011(l)(12), provides:

(2) COLLECTIVE BARGAINING AGREEMENTS.—In the case of a plan maintained pursuant to 1 or more collective bargaining agreements between employee representatives and 1 or more employers ratified before March 1, 1986, the amendments made by this section shall not apply to plan years beginning before the earlier of—

(A) January 1, 1989, or

(B) the date on which the last of such collective bargaining agreements terminates (determined without regard to any extension thereof after February 28, 1986).

(3) ANNUITY CONTRACTS.—In the case of an annuity contract under section 403(b) of the Internal Revenue Code of 1986—

(A) the amendments made by this section shall apply to plan years beginning after December 31, 1988, and

(B) in the case of a collective bargaining agreement described in paragraph (2), the amendments made by this section shall not apply to years beginning before the earlier of—

(i) the later of—

(I) January 1, 1989, or

(II) the date determined under paragraph (2)(B), or

(ii) January 1, 1991.

(4) DISTRIBUTIONS BEFORE PLAN AMENDMENT.—

(A) IN GENERAL.—If a plan amendment is required to allow a plan to make any distribution described in section 401(m)(6) of the Internal Revenue Code of 1986, any such distribution which is made before the close of the 1st plan year for which such amendment is required to be in effect under section 1140 shall be treated as made in accordance with the provisions of the plan.

(B) DISTRIBUTIONS PURSUANT TO MODEL AMENDMENT.—

(i) SECRETARY TO PRESCRIBE AMENDMENT.—The Secretary of the Treasury or his delegate shall prescribe an amendment which allows a plan to make any distribution described in section 401(m)(6) of the Internal Revenue Code of 1986.

(ii) ADOPTION BY PLAN.—If a plan adopts the amendment prescribed under clause (i) and makes a distribution in accordance with such amendment, such distribution shall be treated as made in accordance with the provisions of the plan.

[Sec. 401(n)]

(n) COORDINATION WITH QUALIFIED DOMESTIC RELATIONS ORDERS.—The Secretary shall prescribe such rules or regulations as may be necessary to coordinate the requirements of subsection (a)(13)(B) and section 414(p) (and the regulations issued by the Secretary of Labor thereunder) with the other provisions of this chapter.

Amendments

• 1986, Tax Reform Act of 1986 (P.L. 99-514)

P.L. 99-514, §1117(a):

Amended Code Sec. 401 by redesignating subsections (m) and (n) as subsections (n) and (o), respectively. **Effective**, generally, for plan years beginning after 12-31-86. However, see Act Sec. 1117(d)(2)-(3), reproduced under the amendment notes for Code Sec. 401(m).

P.L. 99-514, §1898(c)(3):

Amended Code Sec. 401 by redesignating subsection (o)[m] (relating to cross references) as subsection (n) and by inserting after subsection (l) new subsection (m). **Effective** as if included in the provision of P.L. 98-397 to which it relates.

[Sec. 401(o)]

(o) CROSS REFERENCE.—

For exemption from tax of a trust qualified under this section, see section 501(a).

Amendments

• 1986, Tax Reform Act of 1986 (P.L. 99-514)

P.L. 99-514, §1117(a):

Amended Code Sec. 401 by redesignating subsections (m) and (n) as subsections (n) and (o), respectively. **Effective**, generally, for plan years beginning after 12-31-86. However, see Act Sec. 1117(d)(2)-(4), reproduced under the amendment note for Code Sec. 401(m).

P.L. 99-514, §1898(c)(3):

Amended Code Sec. 401 by redesignating subsection (o)[m] (relating to cross references) as subsection (n). **Effective** as if included in the provision of P.L. 98-397 to which it relates.

• 1982, Tax Equity and Fiscal Responsibility Act of 1982 (P.L. 97-248)

P.L. 97-248, §249(a):

Amended Code Sec. 401 by redesignating subsection (l) as subsection (o)[m]. **Effective** for plan years beginning after 12-31-83.

• 1978, Revenue Act of 1978 (P.L. 95-600)

P.L. 95-600, §135(a):

Redesignated Code Sec. 401(k) as Code Sec. 401(l).

• 1974, Employee Retirement Income Security Act of 1974 (P.L. 93-406)

P.L. 93-406, §2001(d)(2):

Redesignated Code Sec. 401(j) as Code Sec. 401(k).

• 1964, Revenue Act of 1964 (P.L. 88-272)

P.L. 88-272, §219(a):

Redesignated Code Sec. 401(i) as Code Sec. 401(j).

[Sec. 402]

SEC. 402. TAXABILITY OF BENEFICIARY OF EMPLOYEES' TRUST.

[Sec. 402(a)]

(a) TAXABILITY OF BENEFICIARY OF EXEMPT TRUST.—Except as otherwise provided in this section, any amount actually distributed to any distributee by any employees' trust described in section 401(a) which is exempt from tax under section 501(a) shall be taxable to the distributee, in the taxable year of the distributee in which distributed, under section 72 (relating to annuities).

Amendments

• 1992, Unemployment Compensation Amendments Act of 1992 (P.L. 102-318)

P.L. 102-318, §521(a):

Amended so much of Code Sec. 402 as precedes subsection (g). **Effective** for distributions after 12-31-92. For a special rule, see P.L. 102-318, §521(e)(2), below. Prior to amendment, the section heading and Code Sec. 402(a) read as follows:

SEC. 402. TAXABILITY OF BENEFICIARY OF EMPLOYEES' TRUST.

(a) TAXABILITY OF BENEFICIARY OF EXEMPT TRUST.—

(1) GENERAL RULE.—Except as provided in paragraph (4), the amount actually distributed to any distributee by any employees' trust described in section 401(a) which is exempt from tax under section 501(a) shall be taxable to him, in the year in which so distributed, under section 72 (relating to annuities). The amount actually distributed to any distributee shall not include net unrealized appreciation in securities of the employer corporation attributable to the amount contributed by the employee (other than deductible employee contributions within the meaning of section 72(o)(5)). Such net unrealized appreciation and the resulting adjustments to basis of such securities shall be determined in accordance with regulations prescribed by the Secretary.

(2) [Repealed.]

(3) DEFINITIONS.—For purposes of this subsection—

(A) The term "securities" means only shares of stock and bonds or debentures issued by a corporation with interest coupons or in registered form.

(B) The term "securities of the employer corporation" includes securities of a parent or subsidiary corporation (as defined in subsections (e) and (f) of section 424) of the employer corporation.

(4) DISTRIBUTIONS BY UNITED STATES TO NONRESIDENT ALIENS.—The amount includible under paragraph (1) of this

subsection in the gross income of a nonresident alien individual with respect to a distribution made by the United States in respect of services performed by an employee of the United States shall not exceed an amount which bears the same ratio to the amount includible in gross income without regard to this paragraph as—

(A) the aggregate basic pay paid by the United States to such employee for such services, reduced by the amount of such basic pay which was not includible in gross income by reason of being from sources without the United States, bears to

(B) the aggregate basic pay paid by the United States to such employee for such services.

In the case of distributions under the civil service retirement laws, the term "basic pay" shall have the meaning provided in section 8331(3) of title 5, United States Code.

(5) ROLLOVER AMOUNTS.—

(A) GENERAL RULE.—If—

(i) any portion of the balance to the credit of an employee in a qualified trust is paid to him,

(ii) the employee transfers any portion of the property he receives in such distribution to an eligible retirement plan, and

(iii) in the case of a distribution of property other than money, the amount so transferred consists of the property distributed,

then such distribution (to the extent so transferred) shall not be includible in gross income for the taxable year in which paid.

(B) MAXIMUM AMOUNT WHICH MAY BE ROLLED OVER.—In the case of any qualified total distribution, the maximum amount transferred to which subparagraph (A) applies shall not exceed the fair market value of all the property the employee receives in the distribution, reduced by the employee contributions (other than accumulated deductible employee contributions within the meaning of section 72(o)(5)). In the case of any partial distribution, the maximum amount transferred to which subparagraph (A) applies shall not exceed the portion of such distribution which is includible in gross income (determined without regard to subparagraph (A)).

(C) TRANSFER MUST BE MADE WITHIN 60 DAYS OF RECEIPT.—Subparagraph (A) shall not apply to any transfer of a distribution made after the 60th day following the day on which the employee received the property distributed.

(D) SPECIAL RULES FOR PARTIAL DISTRIBUTIONS.—

(i) REQUIREMENTS.—Subparagraph (A) shall apply to a partial distribution only if—

(I) such distribution is payable as provided in clause (i), (iii), or (iv) of subsection (e)(4)(A) (without regard to the second sentence thereof) and is of an amount equal to at least 50 percent of the balance to the credit of the employee in a qualified trust (determined immediately before such distribution and without regard to subsection (e)(4)(C)),

(II) such distribution is not one of a series of periodic payments, and

(III) the employee elects (at such time and in such manner as the Secretary shall by regulations prescribe) to have subparagraph (A) apply to such partial distribution.

For purposes of subclause (I), the balance to the credit of the employee shall not include any accumulated deductible employee contributions (within the meaning of section 72(o)(5)). Any distribution described in section 401(a)(28)(B)(ii) shall be treated as meeting the requirements of subclause (I) and (II).

(ii) PARTIAL DISTRIBUTIONS MAY BE TRANSFERRED ONLY TO INDIVIDUAL RETIREMENT PLANS.—In the case of a partial distribution, a trust or plan described in subclause (III) or (IV) of subparagraph (E)(iv) shall not be treated as an eligible retirement plan.

(iii) DENIAL OF AVERAGING FOR SUBSEQUENT DISTRIBUTIONS.—If an election under clause (i) is made with respect to any partial distribution paid to any employee, paragraph (1) and (3) of subsection (e) shall not apply to any distribution (paid after such partial distribution) of the balance to the credit of such employee under the plan under which such partial distribution was made (or under any other plan which, under subsection (e)(4)(C), would be aggregated with such plan).

(iv) SPECIAL RULE FOR UNREALIZED APPRECIATION.—If an election under clause (i) is made with respect to any partial distribution, the second and third sentences of paragraph (1) shall not apply to such distribution.

(E) DEFINITIONS.—For purposes of this paragraph—

(i) QUALIFIED TOTAL DISTRIBUTION.—The term "qualified total distribution" means 1 or more distributions—

(I) within 1 taxable year of the employee on account of a termination of the plan of which the trust is a part or, in the case of a profit-sharing or stock bonus plan, a complete discontinuance of contributions under such plan,

(II) which constitute a lump sum distribution within the meaning of subsection (e)(4)(A) (determined without reference to subparagraphs (B) and (H) of subsection (e)(4)), or

(III) which constitute a distribution of accumulated deductible employee contributions (within the meaning of section 72(o)(5)).

(ii) EMPLOYEE CONTRIBUTIONS.—The term "employee contributions" means—

(I) the excess of the amounts considered by the employee (determined by applying section 72(f)), over

(II) any amounts theretofore distributed to the employee which were not includible in gross income (determined without regard to this paragraph).

(iii) QUALIFIED TRUST.—The term "qualified trust" means an employees' trust described in section 401(a) which is exempt from tax under section 501(a).

(iv) ELIGIBLE RETIREMENT PLAN.—The term "eligible retirement plan" means—

(I) an individual retirement account described in section 408(a),

(II) an individual retirement annuity described in section 408(b) (other than an endowment contract),

(III) a qualified trust, and

(IV) an annuity plan described in section 403(a).

(v) PARTIAL DISTRIBUTION.—The term "partial distribution" means any distribution to an employee of all or any portion of the balance to the credit of such employee in a qualified trust; except that such term shall not include any distribution which is a qualified total distribution.

(F) TRANSFER TREATED AS ROLLOVER CONTRIBUTION UNDER SECTION 408.—For purposes of this title, a transfer resulting in any portion of a distribution being excluded from gross income under subparagraph (A) to an eligible retirement plan described in subclause (I) or (II) of subparagraph (E)(iv) shall be treated as a rollover contribution described in section 408(d)(3).

(G) REQUIRED DISTRIBUTIONS NOT ELIGIBLE FOR ROLLOVER TREATMENT.—Subparagraph (A) shall not apply to any distribution to the extent such distribution is required under section 401(a)(9).

(6) SPECIAL ROLLOVER RULES.—

(A) TIME OF TERMINATION.—For purposes of paragraph (5)(E)(i), a complete discontinuance of contributions under a profit-sharing or stock bonus plan shall be deemed to occur on the day the plan administrator notifies the Secretary (in accordance with regulations prescribed by the Secretary) that all contributions to the plan have been completely discontinued. For purposes of section 411(d)(3), the plan shall be considered to be terminated no later than the day such notice is filed with the Secretary.

(B) SALE OF SUBSIDIARY OR ASSETS.—For purposes of paragraph (5)(E)(i)—

(i) A payment of the balance to the credit of an employee of a corporation (hereinafter referred to as the employer corporation) which is a subsidiary corporation (within the meaning of section 424(f)) or which is a member of a controlled group of corporations (within the meaning of section 1563(a), determined by substituting "50 percent" for "80 percent" each place it appears therein) in connection with the liquidation, sale, or other means of terminating the parent-subsidiary or controlled group relationship of the employer corporation with the parent corporation or controlled group, or

(ii) a payment of the balance to the credit of an employee of a corporation (hereinafter referred to as the acquiring corporation) in connection with the sale or other transfer to the acquiring corporation of all or substantially all of the assets used by the previous employer of the employee (hereinafter referred to as the selling corporation) in a trade or business conducted by the selling corporation

shall be treated as a payment or distribution on account of the termination of the plan with respect to such employee if the employees of the employer corporation or the acquiring corporation (whichever applies) are not active participants in such plan at the time of such payment or distribution. For purposes of this subparagraph, in no event shall a payment or distribution be deemed to be in connection with a sale or other transfer of assets, or a liquidation, sale, or other means of terminating such parent-subsidiary or controlled group relationship, if such payment or distribution is made later than the end of the second calendar year after the calendar year in which occurs such sale or other transfer of assets, or such liquidation, sale, or other means of terminating such parent-subsidiary or controlled group relationship.

(C) TREATMENT OF PORTION NOT ROLLED OVER.—If any portion of a lump sum distribution is transferred in a transfer to which paragraph (5)(A) applies, paragraph (1) and (3) of subsection (e) shall not apply with respect to such lump sum distribution.

(D) SALES OF DISTRIBUTED PROPERTY.—For purposes of subparagraphs (5) and (7)—

(i) TRANSFER OF PROCEEDS FROM SALE OF DISTRIBUTED PROPERTY TREATED AS TRANSFER OF DISTRIBUTED PROPERTY.—The transfer of an amount equal to any portion of the proceeds from the sale of property received in the distribution shall be treated as the transfer of property received in the distribution.

(ii) PROCEEDS ATTRIBUTABLE TO INCREASE IN VALUE.—The excess of fair market value of property on sale over its fair market value on distribution shall be treated as property received in the distribution.

(iii) DESIGNATION WHERE AMOUNT OF DISTRIBUTION EXCEEDS ROLLOVER CONTRIBUTION.—In any case where part or all of the distribution consists of property other than money, the taxpayer may designate—

(I) the portion of the money or other property which is to be treated as attributable to employee contributions (or, in the case of a partial distribution, the amount not includible in gross income), and

(II) the portion of the money or other property which is to be treated as included in the rollover contribution.

Any designation under this clause for a taxable year shall be made not later than the time prescribed by law for filing the return for such taxable year (including extensions thereof). Any such designation, once made, shall be irrevocable.

(iv) TREATMENT WHERE NO DESIGNATION.—In any case where part or all of the distribution consists of property other than money and the taxpayer fails to make a designation under clause (iii) within the time provided therein, then—

(I) the portion of the money or other property which is to be treated as attributable to employee contributions (or, in the case of a partial distribution, the amount not includible in gross income), and

(II) the portion of the money or other property which is to be treated as included in the rollover contribution

shall be determined on a ratable basis.

(v) NONRECOGNITION OF GAIN OR LOSS.—In the case of any sale described in clause (i), to the extent that an amount equal to the proceeds is transferred pursuant to paragraph (5)(B) or (7) (as the case may be), neither gain nor loss on such sale shall be recognized.

(E) SPECIAL RULE WHERE EMPLOYER MAINTAINS MONEY PURCHASE PENSION PLAN AND OTHER PENSION PLAN.—

(i) IN GENERAL.—In the case of any distribution from a money purchase pension plan which is maintained by an employer, for purposes of paragraph (5)(D) or (5)(E)(i)(II), subsection (e)(4)(C) shall be applied by not taking into account any pension plan maintained by such employer which is not a money purchase pension plan. The preceding sentence shall not apply to any distribution which is a qualified total distribution without regard to this subparagraph.

(ii) TREATMENT OF SUBSEQUENT DISTRIBUTIONS.—If—

(I) any distribution of the balance to the credit or an employee from a money purchase pension plan maintained by an employer is treated as a qualifying rollover distribution by reason of clause (i), and

(II) any portion of such distribution is transferred in a transfer to which paragraph (5)(A) applies,

then paragraphs (1) and (3) of subsection (e) shall not apply to any distribution (after the taxable year in which the distribution described in subparagraph (A) of paragraph (5) is made) of the balance to the credit of such employee from any other pension plan maintained by such employer.

(F) QUALIFIED DOMESTIC RELATIONS ORDERS.—If—

(i) within 1 taxable year of the recipient, the balance to the credit of the recipient by reason of any qualified domestic relations order (within the meaning of section 414(p)) is distributed or paid to the recipient,

(ii) the recipient transfers any portion of the property the recipient receives in such distributions to an eligible retirement plan described in subclause (I) or (II) of paragraph (5)(E)(iv), and

(iii) in the case of a distribution of property other than money, the amount so transferred consists of the property distributed,

then the portion of the distribution so transferred shall be treated as a distribution described in paragraph (5).

(G) PAYMENTS FROM CERTAIN PENSION PLAN TERMINATION TRUSTS.—If—

(i) any amount is paid or distributed to a recipient from a trust described in section 501(c)(24),

(ii) the recipient transfers any portion of the property received in such distribution to an eligible retirement plan described in subclause (I) or (II) of paragraph (5)(E)(iv), and

(iii) in the case of a distribution of property other than money, the amount so transferred consists of the property distributed,

then the portion of the distribution so transferred shall be treated as a distribution described in paragraph (5)(A).

(H) SPECIAL RULE FOR FROZEN DEPOSITS.—

(i) IN GENERAL.—The 60-day period described in paragraph (5)(C) shall not—

(I) include any period during which the amount transferred to the employee is a frozen deposit, or

(II) end earlier than 10 days after such amount ceases to be a frozen deposit.

(ii) FROZEN DEPOSIT.—For purposes of this subparagraph, the term "frozen deposit" means any deposit which may not be withdrawn because of—

(I) the bankruptcy or insolvency of any financial institution, or

(II) any requirement imposed by the State in which such institution is located by reason of the bankruptcy or insolvency (or threat thereof) of 1 or more financial institutions in such State.

A deposit shall not be treated as a frozen deposit unless on at least 1 day during the 60-day period described in paragraph (5)(C) (without regard to this subparagraph) such deposit is described in the preceding sentence.

(I) TREATMENT OF POTENTIAL FUTURE VESTING.—

(i) IN GENERAL.—For purposes of paragraph (5), in determining whether any portion of a distribution on account of the employee's separation from service may be transferred in a transfer to which paragraph (5)(A) applies, the balance to the credit of the employee shall be determined without regard to any increase in vesting which may occur if the employee is re-employed by the employer.

(ii) TREATMENT OF SUBSEQUENT DISTRIBUTIONS.—If—

(I) any portion of a distribution is transferred in a transfer to which paragraph (5)(A) applies by reason of clause (i),

(II) the employee is subsequently re-employed by the employer, and

(III) as a result of service performed after being so re-employed, there is an increase in the employee's vesting for benefits accrued before the separation referred to in clause (i),

then the provisions of paragraph (5)(D)(iii) shall apply to any distribution from the plan after the distribution referred to in clause (i). The preceding sentence shall not apply if the distribution referred to in subclause (I) is made without the consent of the participant.

(7) ROLLOVER WHERE SPOUSE RECEIVES DISTRIBUTIONS AFTER DEATH OF EMPLOYEE.—If any distribution attributable to an employee is paid to the spouse of the employee after the employee's death, paragraph (5) shall apply to such distribution in the same manner as if the spouse were the employee; except that a trust or plan described in subclause

(III) or (IV) of paragraph (5)(E)(iv) shall not be treated as an eligible retirement plan with respect to such distribution.

(8) CASH OR DEFERRED ARRANGEMENTS.—For purposes of this title, contributions made by an employer on behalf of an employee to a trust which is a part of a qualified cash or deferred arrangement (as defined in section 401(k)(2)) shall not be treated as distributed or made available to the employee nor as contributions made to the trust by the employee merely because the arrangement includes provisions under which the employee has an election whether the contribution will be made to the trust or received by the employee in cash.

(9) ALTERNATE PAYEE UNDER QUALIFIED DOMESTIC RELATIONS ORDER TREATED AS DISTRIBUTEE.—For purposes of subsection (a)(1) and section 72, any alternate payee who is the spouse or former spouse of the participant shall be treated as the distributee of any distribution or payment made to the alternate payee under a qualified domestic relations order (as defined in section 414(p)).

P.L. 102-318, §521(e)(2), provides:

(2) SPECIAL RULE FOR PARTIAL DISTRIBUTIONS.—For purposes of section 402(a)(5)(D)(i)(II) of the Internal Revenue Code of 1986 (as in effect before the amendments made by this section), a distribution before January 1, 1993, which is made before or at the same time as a series of periodic payments shall not be treated as one of such series if it is not substantially equal in amount to other payments in such series.

• 1990, Omnibus Budget Reconciliation Act of 1990 (P.L. 101-508)

P.L. 101-508, §11801(c)(9)(I)(i)-(ii):

Amended Code Sec. 402(a) by striking in subparagraph (3)(B) "section 425" and inserting "section 424" and by striking in clause (6)(B)(i) "section 425(f)" and inserting "section 424(f)". **Effective** on 11-5-90.

P.L. 101-508, §11821(b), provides:

(b) SAVINGS PROVISION.—If—

(1) any provision amended or repealed by this part applied to—

(A) any transaction occurring before the date of the enactment of this Act,

(B) any property acquired before such date of enactment, or

(C) any item of income, loss, deduction, or credit taken into account before such date of enactment, and

(2) the treatment of such transaction, property, or item under such provision would (without regard to the amendments made by this part) affect liability for tax for periods ending after such date of enactment,

nothing in the amendments made by this part shall be construed to affect the treatment of such transaction, property, or item for purposes of determining liability for tax for periods ending after such date of enactment.

• 1988, Technical and Miscellaneous Revenue Act of 1988 (P.L. 100-647)

P.L. 100-647, §1011A(a)(1):

Amended Code Sec. 402(a)(5)(F) by striking out "described in subparagraph (A)" and inserting in lieu thereof "resulting in any portion of a distribution being excluded from gross income under subparagraph (A)". **Effective** as if included in the provision of P.L. 99-514 to which it relates.

P.L. 100-647, §1011A(b)(4)(A):

Repealed the amendment made by section 1122(e)(1) of P.L. 99-514 to Code Sec. 402(a)(5)(D)(i). **Effective** as if the amendment made by P.L. 99-514 had not been enacted. Under section 1122(e)(1) of P.L. 99-514, Code Sec. 402(a)(5)(D)(i) was amended to read as follows:

(i) REQUIREMENTS.—Subparagraph (A) shall apply to a partial distribution only if the employee elects to have subparagraph (A) apply to such distribution and such distribution would be a lump sum distribution if subsection (e)(4)(A) were applied—

(I) by substituting "50 percent of the balance to the credit of an employee" for "the balance to the credit of an employee",

(II) without regard to clause (ii) thereof, the second sentence thereof, and subparagraph (B) of subsection (e)(4).

Any distribution described in section 401(a)(28)(B)(ii) shall be treated as meeting the requirements of this clause.

P.L. 100-647, §1011A(b)(4)(B):

Amended Code Sec. 402(a)(5)(D)(i)(I) by inserting "is payable as provided in clause (i), (iii), or (iv) of subsection (e)(4)(A) (without regard to the second sentence thereof) and" after "such distribution" the first place it appears. **Effective** as if included in the provision of P.L. 99-514 to which it relates.

P.L. 100-647, §1011A(b)(4)(C):

Amended Code Sec. 402(a)(5)(D)(i) by adding at the end thereof a new sentence. **Effective** as if included in the provision of P.L. 99-514 to which it relates.

P.L. 100-647, §1011A(b)(4)(D):

Amended Code Sec. 402(a)(5)(D)(iii) by striking out "10-year" in the heading after "of". **Effective** as if included in the provision of P.L. 99-514 to which it relates.

P.L. 100-647, §1011A(b)(4)(E), provides:

(E) Section 402(a)(5)(D)(i)(II) of the 1986 Code (as in effect after the amendment made by subparagraph (A)) shall not apply to distributions after December 31, 1986, and before March 31, 1988.

P.L. 100-647, §1011A(b)(5):

Amended Code Sec. 402(a)(6)(H)(ii) by adding at the end thereof a new flush sentence. **Effective** as if included in the provision of P.L. 99-514 to which it relates.

P.L. 100-647, §1011A(b)(8)(A):

Amended Code Sec. 402(a)(1) by striking out "paragraphs (2) and (4)" and inserting in lieu thereof "paragraph (4)". **Effective** as if included in the provision of P.L. 99-514 to which it relates.

P.L. 100-647, §1011A(b)(8)(B):

Amended Code Sec. 402(a)(4) by striking out "or (2)" after "paragraph (1)". **Effective** as if included in the provision of P.L. 99-514 to which it relates.

P.L. 100-647, §1011A(b)(8)(C):

Amended Code Sec. 402(a)(6)(C) by striking out "paragraph (2) of subsection (a), and" after "applies,". **Effective** as if included in the provision of P.L. 99-514 to which it relates.

P.L. 100-647, §1011A(b)(8)(D):

Amended Code Sec. 402(a)(6)(E)(ii) by striking out "paragraph (2) of subsection (a), and" and by striking out the comma after "subsection (e)". **Effective** as if included in the provision of P.L. 99-514 to which it relates. Prior to amendment, Code Sec. 402(a)(6)(E)(ii) read as follows:

(ii) TREATMENT OF SUBSEQUENT DISTRIBUTIONS.—If—

(I) any distribution of the balance to the credit of an employee from a money purchase pension plan maintained by an employer is treated as a qualifying rollover distribution by reason of clause (i), and

(II) any portion of such distribution is transferred in a transfer to which paragraph (5)(A) applies,

then paragraph (2) of subsection (a), and paragraphs (1) and (3) of subsection (e), shall not apply to any distribution (after the taxable year in which the distribution described in subparagraph (A) of paragraph (5) is made) of the balance to the credit of such employee from any other pension plan maintained by such employer.

P.L. 100-647, §1018(t)(8)(A):

Redesignated Code Sec. 402(a)(6)(G), as Code Sec. 402(a)(6)(I). **Effective** as if included in the provision of P.L. 99-514 to which it relates.

• 1986, Tax Reform Act of 1986 (P.L. 99-514)

P.L. 99-514, §1121(c)(1):

Amended Code Sec. 402(a)(5)(F). **Effective** for years beginning after 12-31-86. For special rules, see Act Sec. 1121(d)(3)-(5), following Code Sec. 401(a). Prior to amendment, Code Sec. 402(a)(5)(F) read as follows:

(F) SPECIAL RULES.—

(i) TRANSFER TREATED AS ROLLOVER CONTRIBUTION UNDER SECTION 408.—For purposes of this title, a transfer described in subparagraph (A) to an eligible retirement plan described in subclause (I) or (II) of subparagraph (E)(iv) shall be treated as a rollover contribution described in section 408(d)(3).

(ii) KEY EMPLOYEES.—An eligible retirement plan described in subclause (III) or (IV) of subparagraph (E)(iv) shall not be treated as an eligible retirement plan for the transfer of a distribution if any part of the distribution is attributable to contributions made on behalf of the employee while he was a key employee in a top-heavy plan. For purposes of the preceding sentence, the terms "key employee" and "top-heavy plan" have the same respective meanings as when used in section 416.

P.L. 99-514, §1122(b)(1)(A):

Repealed Code Sec. 402(a)(2). For the **effective** date, see Act Sec. 1122(h), below. Prior to repeal, Code Sec. 402(a)(2) read as follows:

(2) CAPITAL GAINS TREATMENT FOR PORTION OF LUMP SUM DISTRIBUTION.—In the case of an employee trust described in section 401(a), which is exempt from tax under section 501(a), so much of the total taxable amount (as defined in subparagraph (D) of subsection (e)(4)) of a lump sum distribution as is equal to the product of such total taxable amount multiplied by a fraction—

(A) the numerator of which is the number of calendar years of active participation by the employee in such plan before January 1, 1974, and

(B) the denominator of which is the number of calendar years of active participation by the employee in such plan,

shall be treated as a gain from the sale or exchange of a capital asset held for more than 6 months. For purposes of computing the fraction described in this paragraph and the fraction under subsection (e)(4)(E), the Secretary may prescribe regulations under which plan years may be used in lieu of calendar years. For purposes of this paragraph, in the case of an individual who is an employee without regard to section 401(c)(1), determination of whether or not any distribution is a lump sum distribution shall be made without regard to the requirement that an election be made under subsection (e)(4)(B), but no distribution to any taxpayer other than an individual, estate, or trust may be treated as a lump sum distribution under this paragraph.

P.L. 99-514, §1122(b)(2)(A):

Amended Code Sec. 402(a)(5)(D)(iii). For the **effective** date, see Act Sec. 1122(h), below. Prior to amendment it read as follows:

(iii) DENIAL OF 10-YEAR AVERAGING AND CAPITAL GAINS TREATMENT FOR SUBSEQUENT DISTRIBUTIONS.—If an election under clause (i) is made with respect to any partial distribution paid to any employee—

(I) paragraphs (2) of this subsection,

(II) paragraphs (1) and (3) of subsection (e), and

(III) paragraph (2) of section 403(a),

shall not apply to any distribution (paid after such partial distribution) of the balance to the credit of such employee under the plan under which such partial distribution was made (or under any other plan which, under subsection (e)(4)(C), would be aggregated with such plan).

P.L. 99-514, §1122(e)(1):

Amended Code Sec. 402(a)(5)(D)(i). For the **effective** date, see Act Sec. 1122(h), below. Prior to amendment, Code Sec. 402(a)(5)(D)(i) read as follows:

(D) SPECIAL RULES FOR PARTIAL DISTRIBUTIONS.—

(i) REQUIREMENTS.—Subparagraph (A) shall apply to a partial distribution only if—

(I) such distribution is of an amount equal to at least 50 percent of the balance to the credit of the employee in a qualified trust (determined immediately before such distribution and without regard to subsection (e)(4)(C)),

(II) such distribution is not one of a series of periodic payments, and

(III) the employee elects (at such time and in such manner as the Secretary shall by regulations prescribe) to have subparagraph (A) apply to such partial distribution.

For purposes of subclause (I), the balance to the credit of the employee shall not include any accumulated deductible employee contributions (within the meaning of section 72(o)(5)).

P.L. 99-514, §1122(e)(2)(A):

Amended Code Sec. 402(a)(6) by adding at the end thereof new subparagraph (H)[(I)]. For the **effective** date, see Act Sec. 1122(h), below.

P.L. 99-514, §1122(h), as amended by P.L. 100-647, §1011A(b)(11), (13)-(15), provides:

(h) EFFECTIVE DATES.—

(1) IN GENERAL.—Except as otherwise provided in this subsection, the amendments made by this section shall apply to amounts distributed after December 31, 1986, in taxable years ending after such date.

(2) SUBSECTION (c).—

(A) SUBSECTION (c)(1).—The amendment made by subsection (c)(1) shall apply to individuals whose annuity starting date is after July 1, 1986.

(B) SUBSECTION (c)(2).—The amendment made by subsection (c)(2) shall apply to individuals whose annuity starting date is after December 31, 1986.

(C) SPECIAL RULE FOR AMOUNTS NOT RECEIVED AS ANNUITIES.—In the case of any plan not described in section 72(e)(8)(D) of the Internal Revenue Code of 1986 (as added by subsection (c)(3)), the amendments made by subsection (c)(3) shall apply to amounts received after July 1, 1986.

(3) SPECIAL RULE FOR INDIVIDUALS WHO ATTAINED AGE 50 BEFORE JANUARY 1, 1986.—

(A) IN GENERAL.—In the case of a lump sum distribution to which this paragraph applies—

(i) the existing capital gains provisions shall continue to apply, and

(ii) the requirement of subparagraph (B) of section 402(e)(4) of the Internal Revenue Code of 1986 (as amended by subsection (a)) that the distribution be received after attaining age 59½ shall not apply.

(B) COMPUTATION OF TAX.—If subparagraph (A) applies to any lump sum distribution of any taxpayer for any taxable year, the tax imposed by section 1 of the Internal Revenue Code of 1986 on such taxable year shall be equal to the sum of—

(i) the tax imposed by such section 1 on the taxable income of the taxpayer (reduced by the portion of such lump sum distribution to which clause (ii) applies), plus

(ii) 20 percent of the portion of such lump sum distribution to which the existing capital gains provisions continue to apply by reason of this paragraph.

(C) LUMP SUM DISTRIBUTIONS TO WHICH PARAGRAPH APPLIES.—This paragraph shall apply to any lump sum distribution if—

(i) such lump sum distribution is received by an employee who has attained age 50 before January 1, 1986 or by an individual estate, or trust with respect to such employee, and

(ii) the taxpayer makes an election under this paragraph.

Not more than 1 election may be made under this paragraph with respect to an employee. An election under this subparagraph shall be treated as an election under section 402(e)(4)(B) of such Code with for purposes of such Code.

(4) 5-YEAR PHASE-OUT OF CAPITAL GAINS TREATMENT.—

(A) Notwithstanding the amendment made by subsection (b), if the taxpayer elects the application of this paragraph with respect to any distribution after December 31, 1986, and before January 1, 1992, the phase-out percentage of the amount which would have been treated, without regard to this subparagraph, as long-term capital gain under the existing capital gains provisions shall be treated as long-term capital gain.

(B) FOR PURPOSES OF THIS PARAGRAPH—

In the case of distributions during calendar year:	*The phase-out percentage is:*
1987	100
1988	95
1989	75
1990	50
1991	25

(C) No more than 1 election may be made under this paragraph with respect to an employee. An election under this paragraph shall be treated as an election under section

402(e)(4)(B) of the Internal Revenue Code of 1986 for purposes of such Code.

(5) ELECTION OF 10-YEAR AVERAGING.—An employee who has attained age 50 before January 1, 1986, and elects the application of paragraph (3) or section 402(e)(1) of the Internal Revenue Code of 1986 (as amended by this Act) may elect to have such section applied by substituting "10 times" for "5 times" and "1/10" for "1/5" in subparagraph (B) thereof. For purposes of the preceding sentence, section 402(e)(1) of such Code shall be applied by using the rate of tax in effect under section 1 of the Internal Revenue Code of 1954 for taxable years beginning during 1986 and by including in gross income the zero bracket amount in effect under section 63(d) of such Code for such years. This paragraph shall also apply to an individual, estate, or trust which receives a distribution with respect to an employee described in this paragraph.

(6) EXISTING CAPITAL GAIN PROVISIONS.—For purposes of paragraphs (3) and (4), the term "existing capital gains provisions" means the provisions of paragraph (2) of section 402(a) of the Internal Revenue Code of 1954 (as in effect on the day before the date of the enactment of this Act) and paragraph (2) of section 403(a) of such Code (as so in effect).

(7) SUBSECTION(d).—The amendments made by subsection (d) shall apply to taxable years beginning after December 31, 1985.

(8) FROZEN DEPOSITS.—The amendments made by subsection (e)(2) shall apply to amounts transferred to an employee before, on, or after the date of the enactment of this Act, except that in the case of an amount transferred on or before such date, the 60-day period referred to in section 402(a)(5)(C) of the Internal Revenue Code of 1986 shall not expire before the 60th day after the date of the enactment of this Act.

(9) SPECIAL RULE FOR STATE PLANS.—In the case of a plan maintained by a State which on May 5, 1986, permitted withdrawal by the employee of employee contributions (other than as an annuity), section 72(e) of the Internal Revenue Code of 1986 shall be applied—

(A) without regard to the phrase "before separation from service" in paragraph (8)(D), and

(B) by treating any amount received (other than as an annuity) before or with the 1st annuity payment as having been received before the annuity starting date.

P.L. 99-514, §1124, as amended by P.L. 100-647, §1011A(d), provides:

SEC. 1124. ELECTION TO TREAT CERTAIN LUMP SUM DISTRIBUTIONS RECEIVED DURING 1987 AS RECEIVED DURING 1986.

(a) IN GENERAL.—If an employee dies, separates from service, or becomes disabled before 1987 and an individual, trust, or estate receives a lump-sum distribution with respect to such employee after December 31, 1986, and before March 16, 1987, on account of such death, separation from service, or disability, then, for purposes of the Internal Revenue Code of 1986, such individual, estate, or trust may treat such distribution as if it were received in 1986.

(b) SPECIAL RULE FOR TERMINATED PLAN.—In the case of an individual, estate, or trust who receives with respect to an employee a distribution from a terminated plan which was maintained by a corporation organized under the laws of the State of Nevada, the principal place of business of which is Denver, Colorado, and which filed for relief from creditors under the United States Bankruptcy Code on August 28, 1986, the individual, estate, or trust may treat a lump sum distribution received from such plan before June 30, 1987, as if it were received in 1986.

(c) LUMP SUM DISTRIBUTION.—For purposes of this section, the term "lump sum distribution" has the meaning given such term by section 402(e)(4)(A) of the Internal Revenue Code of 1986, without regard to subparagraph (B) or (H) of section 402(e)(4) of such Code.

P.L. 99-514, §1852(a)(5)(A):

Amended Code Sec. 402(a)(5) by adding at the end thereof new subparagraph (G). **Effective** as if included in the provision of P.L. 98-369 to which it relates.

P.L. 99-514, §1852(b)(1):

Amended Code Sec. 402(a)(5)(E)(v) by striking out "of any portion of" and inserting in lieu thereof "of all or any portion of". **Effective** as if included in the provision of P.L. 98-369 to which it relates.

P.L. 99-514, §1852(b)(2):

Amended Code Sec. 402(a)(5)(D)(i) by adding at the end thereof a new sentence. **Effective** as if included in the provision of P.L. 98-369 to which it relates.

P.L. 99-514, §1852(b)(4):

Amended Code Sec. 402(a)(7) by striking out "the spouse were the employee" and inserting in lieu thereof "the spouse were the employee; except that a trust or plan described in subclause (III) or (IV) of paragraph (5)(E)(iv) shall not be treated as an eligible retirement plan with respect to such distribution". **Effective** as if included in the provision of P.L. 98-369 to which it relates.

P.L. 99-514, §1852(b)(5):

Amended Code Sec. 402(a)(5)(D)(ii) by striking out "a plan described in subclause (IV) or (V)" and inserting in lieu thereof "a trust or plan described in subclause (III) or (IV)". **Effective** as if included in the provision of P.L. 98-369 to which it relates.

P.L. 99-514, §1852(b)(6):

Amended Code Sec. 402(a)(5)(F)(i) by striking out "a transfer described in subparagraph (A)" and inserting in lieu thereof "a transfer resulting in any portion of a distribution being excluded from gross income under subparagraph (A)". **Effective** as if included in the provision of P.L. 98-369 to which it relates.

P.L. 99-514, §1852(b)(7):

Amended Code Sec. 402(a)(6)(D)(v) by striking out "(7)(B)" and inserting in lieu thereof "(7)". **Effective** as if included in the provision of P.L. 98-369 to which it relates.

P.L. 99-514, §1875(c)(1)(A):

Amended Code Sec. 402(a)(5)(F)(ii). **Effective** for distributions after the date of the enactment of this Act. It shall also be **effective** for distributions after 1983 and on or before the date of the enactment of this Act to individuals who are not 5-percent owners (as defined in section 402(a)(5)(F)(ii) of the Internal Revenue Code of 1954). Prior to amendment, Code Sec. 402(a)(5)(F)(ii) read as follows:

(ii) KEY EMPLOYEES.—An eligible retirement plan described in subclause (III) or (IV) of subparagraph (E)(iv) shall not be treated as an eligible retirement plan for the transfer of a distribution if any part of the distribution is attributable to contributions made on behalf of the employee while he was a key employee in a top-heavy plan. For purposes of the preceding sentence, the terms "key employee" and "top-heavy plan" have the same respective meanings as when used in section 416.

P.L. 99-514, §1898(a)(3):

Amended Code Sec. 402(a)(6) by adding at the end thereof new subparagraph (G)[(H)]. **Effective** as if included in the provision of P.L. 98-397 to which it relates.

P.L. 99-514, §1898(c)(1)(A):

Amended Code Sec. 402(a)(9) by striking out "the alternate payee shall be treated" and inserting in lieu thereof "any alternate payee who is the spouse or former spouse of the participant shall be treated". **Effective** for payments made after 10-22-86.

P.L. 99-514, §1898(c)(7)(A)(i):

Amended Code Sec. 402(a)(6)(F) by striking out "paragraph (5)(A)" and inserting in lieu thereof "paragraph (5)". **Effective** as if included in the provision of P.L. 98-397 to which it relates.

• 1986, Consolidated Omnibus Budget Reconciliation Act of 1985 (P.L. 99-272)

P.L. 99-272, §11012(c):

Amended Code Sec. 402(a)(6) by adding at the end thereof new subparagraph (G). For the **effective** date, see Act Sec. 11019, below.

P.L. 99-272, §11019, provides:

SEC. 11019. EFFECTIVE DATE OF TITLE; TEMPORARY PROCEDURES.

(a) IN GENERAL.—Except as otherwise provided in this title, the amendments made by this title shall be effective as of January 1, 1986, except that such amendments shall not apply with respect to terminations for which—

(1) notices of intent to terminate were filed with the Pension Benefit Guaranty Corporation under section 4041 of the Employee Retirement Income Security Act of 1974 before such date, or

(2) proceedings were commenced under section 4042 of such Act before such date.

(b) TRANSITIONAL RULES.—

(1) IN GENERAL.—In the case of a single-employer plan termination for which a notice of intent to terminate was filed with the Pension Benefit Guaranty Corporation under section 4041 of the Employee Retirement Income Security Act of 1974 (as in effect before the amendments made by this title) on or after January 1, 1986, but before the date of the enactment of this Act, the amendments made by this title shall apply with respect to such termination, as modified by paragraphs (2) and (3).

(2) DEEMED COMPLIANCE WITH NOTICE REQUIREMENTS.—The requirements of subsections (a)(2), (b)(1)(A), and (c)(1)(A) of section 4041 of the Employee Retirement Income Security Act of 1974 (as amended by this title) shall be considered to have been met with respect to a termination described in paragraph (1) if—

(A) the plan administrator provided notice to the participants in the plan regarding the termination in compliance with applicable regulations of the Pension Benefit Guaranty Corporation as in effect on the date of the notice, and

(B) the notice of intent to terminate provided to the Pension Benefit Guaranty Corporation in connection with the termination was filed with the Corporation not less than 10 days before the proposed date of termination specified in the notice.

For purposes of section 4041 of such Act (as amended by this title), the proposed date of termination specified in the notice of intent to terminate referred to in subparagraph (B) shall be considered the proposed termination date.

(3) SPECIAL TERMINATION PROCEDURES.—

(A) IN GENERAL.—This paragraph shall apply with respect to any termination described in paragraph (1) if, within 90 days after the date of enactment of this Act, the plan administrator notifies the Corporation in writing—

(i) that the plan administrator wishes the termination to proceed as a standard termination under section 4041(b) of the Employee Retirement Income Security Act of 1974 (as amended by this title) in accordance with subparagraph (B),

(ii) that the plan administrator wishes the termination to proceed as a distress termination under section 4041(c) of such Act (as amended by this title) in accordance with subparagraph (C), or

(iii) that the plan administrator wishes to stop the termination proceedings in accordance with subparagraph (D).

(B) TERMINATIONS PROCEEDING AS STANDARD TERMINATION.—

(i) TERMINATIONS FOR WHICH SUFFICIENCY NOTICES HAVE NOT BEEN ISSUED.—

(I) IN GENERAL.—In the case of a plan termination described in paragraph (1) wiih respect to which the Corporation has been provided the notification described in subparagraph (A)(i) and with respect to which a notice of sufficiency has not been issued by the Corporation before the date of the enactment of this Act, if, during the 90-day period commencing on the date of the notice required in subclause (II), all benefit commitments under the plan have been satisfied, the termination shall be treated as a standard termination under section 4041(b) of such Act (as amended by this title).

(II) SPECIAL NOTICE REGARDING SUFFICIENCY FOR TERMINATIONS FOR WHICH NOTICES OF SUFFICIENCY HAVE NOT BEEN ISSUED AS OF DATE OF ENACTMENT.—In the case of a plan termination described in paragraph (1) with respect to which the Corporation has been provided the notification described in subparagraph (A)(i) and with respect to which a notice of sufficiency has not been issued by the Corporation before the date of the enactment of this Act, the Corporation shall make the determinations described in section 4041(c)(3)(A)(i) and (ii) (as amended by this title) and notify the plan administrator of such determinations as provided in section 4041(c)(3)(A)(iii) (as amended by this title).

(ii) TERMINATIONS FOR WHICH NOTICES OF SUFFICIENCY HAVE BEEN ISSUED.—In the case of a plan termination described in paragraph (1) with respect to which the Corporation has been provided the notification described in subparagraph (A)(i) and with respect to which a notice of sufficiency has been issued by the Corporation before the date of the enactment of this Act, clause (i)(I) shall apply, except that the 90-day period referred to in clause (i)(I) shall begin on the date of the enactment of this Act.

(C) TERMINATIONS PROCEEDING AS DISTRESS TERMINATION.—In the case of a plan termination described in paragraph (1) with respect to which the Corporation has been provided the notification described in subparagraph (A)(ii), if the requirements of section 4041(c)(2)(B) of such Act (as amended by this title) are met, the termination shall be treated as a distress termination under section 4041(c) of such Act (as amended by this title).

(D) TERMINATION OF PROCEEDINGS BY PLAN ADMINISTRATOR.—

(i) IN GENERAL.—Except as provided in clause (ii), in the case of a plan termination described in paragraph (1) with respect to which the Corporation has been provided the notification described in subparagraph (A)(iii), the termination shall not take effect.

(ii) TERMINATIONS WITH RESPECT TO WHICH FINAL DISTRIBUTION OF ASSETS HAS COMMENCED.—Clause (i) shall not apply with respect to a termination with respect to which the final distribution of assets has commenced before the date of the enactment of this Act unless, within 90 days after the date of the enactment of this Act, the plan has been restored in accordance with procedures issued by the Corporation pursuant to subsection (c).

(E) AUTHORITY OF CORPORATION TO EXTEND 90-DAY PERIODS TO PERMIT STANDARD TERMINATION.—The Corporation may, on a case-by-case basis in accordance with subsection (c), provide for extensions of the applicable 90-day period referred to in clause (i) or (ii) of subparagraph (B) if it is demonstrated to the satisfaction of the Corporation that—

(i) the plan could not otherwise, pursuant to the preceding provisions of this paragraph, terminate in a termination treated as a standard termination under section 4041(b) of the Employee Retirement Income Security Act of 1974 (as amended by this title), and

(ii) the extension would result in a greater likelihood that benefit commitments under the plan would be paid in full,

except that any such period may not be so extended beyond one year after the date of the enactment of this Act.

(c) AUTHORITY TO PRESCRIBE TEMPORARY PROCEDURES.—The Pension Benefit Guaranty Corporation may prescribe temporary procedures for purposes of carrying out the amendments made by this title during the 180-day period beginning on the date described in subsection (a).

• 1984, Retirement Equity Act of 1984 (P.L. 98-397)

P.L. 98-397, §204(c)(1):

Amended Code Sec. 402(a) by adding at the end thereof new paragraph (9). **Effective** 1-1-85, except that in the case of a domestic relations order entered before such date, the plan administrator—

(1) shall treat such order as a qualified domestic relations order if such administrator is paying benefits pursuant to such order on such date, and

(2) may treat any other such order entered before such date as a qualified domestic relations order even if such order does not meet the requirements of such amendments.

P.L. 98-397, §204(c)(3):

Amended Code Sec. 402(a)(6) by adding at the end thereof new subparagraph (F). **Effective** 1-1-85, except that in the case of a domestic relations order entered before such date, the plan administrator—

(1) shall treat such order as a qualified domestic relations order if such administrator is paying benefits pursuant to such order on such date, and

(2) may treat any other such order entered before such date as a qualified domestic relations order even if such order does not meet the requirements of such amendments.

• 1984, Deficit Reduction Act of 1984 (P.L. 98-369)

P.L. 98-369, §491(d)(9):

Amended Code Sec. 402(a)(5)(E)(iv), as redesignated by Act Sec. 522(b), by striking out subclause (III) and by redesignating subclauses (IV) and (V) as subclauses (III) and (IV). **Effective** for obligations issued after 12-31-83. Prior to repeal, subclause (III) read as follows:

(III) a retirement bond described in section 409,

P.L. 98-369, §491(d)(10):

Amended Code Sec. 402(a)(5)(F)(i), as redesignated by Act Sec. 491(b), by striking out ", (II), or (III)" and inserting in lieu thereof "or (II)". **Effective** for obligations issued after 12-31-83.

P.L. 98-369, §491(d)(11):

Amended Code Sec. 402(a)(5)(F)(ii), as redesignated by Act Sec. 522(b), by striking out "(IV) or (V)" and inserting in lieu thereof "(III) or (IV)". **Effective** for obligations issued after 12-31-83.

P.L. 98-369, §522(a)(1):

Amended Code Sec. 402(a)(5)(A)(1). **Effective** for distributions made after 7-18-84, in tax years ending after such date. Prior to amendment, it read as follows:

(i) the balance to the credit of an employee in a qualified trust is paid to him in a qualifying rollover distribution,

P.L. 98-369, §522(b):

Amended Code Sec. 402(a)(5) by redesignating subpararaphs (D) and (E) as subparagraphs (E) and (F), respectively, and by inserting new paragraph (D) after subparagraph (C). **Effective** for distributions made after 7-18-84, in tax years ending after such date.

P.L. 98-369, §522(c):

Amended Code Sec. 402(a)(7). **Effective** for distributions made after 7-18-84, in tax years ending after such date. Prior to amendment, Code Sec. 402(a)(7) read as follows:

(7) Rollover Where Spouse Receives Lump-Sum Distribution at Death of Employee.—

(A) General Rule.—If—

(i) any portion of a qualifying rollover distribution attributable to an employee is paid to the spouse of the employee after the employee's death,

(ii) the spouse transfers any portion of the property which the spouse receives in such distribution to an individual retirement plan, and

(iii) in the case of a distribution of property other than money, the amount so transferred consists of the property distributed,

then such distribution (to the extent so transferred) shall not be includible in gross income for the taxable year in which paid.

(B) Certain Rules Made Applicable.—Rules similar to the rules of subparagraphs (B) through (E) of paragraph (5) and of paragraph (6) shall apply for purposes of this paragraph.

P.L. 98-369, §522(d)(1):

Amended Code Secs. 402(a)(5)(B), 402(a)(5)(E)(i) (as redesignated by Act Sec. 522(b)), and 402(a)(6)(E)(i) by striking out "qualifying rollover distribution" each place it appeared and inserting in lieu thereof "qualified total distribution". **Effective** for distributions made after 7-18-84, in tax years ending after such date.

P.L. 98-369, §522(d)(2):

Amended Code Sec. 402(a)(5)(B) by adding the last sentence. **Effective** for distributions made after 7-18-84, in tax years ending after such date.

P.L. 98-369, §522(d)(3):

Amended Code Sec. 402(a)(5)(E)(ii) (as redesignated by Act Sec. 522(b)) by striking out "gross income" and inserting in lieu thereof "gross income (determined without regard to this paragraph)". **Effective** for distributions made after 7-18-84, in tax years ending after such date.

P.L. 98-369, §522(d)(4):

Amended Code Sec. 402(a)(5)(E)(v) (as redesignated by Act Sec. 522(b)). **Effective** for distributions made after 7-18-84, in tax years ending after such date. Prior to amendment, Code Sec. 402(a)(5)(E)(v) read as follows:

(v) Rollover of Partial Distributions of Deductible Employee Contributions Permitted.—In the case of any qualifying rollover distribution described in subclause (III) of clause (i), clause (i) of subparagraph (A) shall be applied by substituting "any portion of the balance" for "the balance".

P.L. 98-369, §522(d)(5):

Amended Code Sec. 402(a)(5)(F) (as redesignated by Act Sec. 522(b)) by striking out "subparagraph (D)(iv)" each place it appeared and inserting in lieu thereof "subparagraph (E)(iv)". **Effective** for distributions made after 7-18-84, in tax years ending after such date.

P.L. 98-369, §522(d)(6):

Amended Code Sec. 402(a)(6) by striking out "paragraph (5)(D)(i)" each place it appeared and inserting in lieu thereof "paragraph (5)(E)(i)". **Effective** for distributions made after 7-18-84, in tax years ending after such date.

P.L. 98-369, §522(d)(7):

Amended Code Sec. 402(a)(6)(D)(iii) and (iv) by striking out "employee contributions" and inserting in lieu thereof "employee contributions (or, in the case of a partial distribution, the amount not includible in gross income)". **Effective** for distributions made after 7-18-84, in tax years ending after such date.

P.L. 98-369, §522(d)(8):

Amended Code Sec. 402(a)(6)(E)(i) by striking out "paragraph (5)(D)(i)(II)" and inserting in lieu thereof "paragraph (5)(D) or (5)(E)(i)(II)". **Effective** for distributions made after 7-18-84, in tax years ending after such date.

P.L. 98-369, §713(c)(3):

Amended Code Sec. 402(a)(5)(E)(ii) (before its redesignation by Act Sec. 522(b)). **Effective** for distributions after 7-18-84 [**effective** date changed by P.L. 99-514, §1875(c)(2)]. Prior to amendment, Code Sec. 402(a)(5)(E)(ii) read as follows:

(ii) Self-Employed Individuals and Owner-Employees.—An eligible retirement plan described in subclause (IV) or (V) of subparagraph (D)(iv) shall not be treated as an eligible retirement plan for the transfer of a distribution if any part of the distribution is attributable to a trust forming part of a plan under which the employee was an employee within the meaning of section 401(c)(1) at the time contributions were made on his behalf under the plan.

P.L. 98-369, §1001(b)(3):

Amended Code Sec. 402(a)(2) and (e)(4)(L) by striking out "1 year" each place it appeared and inserting in lieu thereof "6 months". **Effective** for property acquired after 6-22-84 and before 1-1-88.

P.L. 98-369, §551, provides:

SEC. 551. TREATMENT OF CERTAIN DISTRIBUTIONS FROM A QUALIFIED TERMINATED PLAN.

(a) In General.—For purposes of the Internal Revenue Code 1954, if—

(1) a distribution was made from a qualified terminated plan to an employee on December 16, 1976, and on January 6, 1977, such employee transferred all of the property received in such distribution to an individual retirement account (within the meaning of section 408(a) of such Code) established for the benefit of such employee, and

(2) the remaining balance to the credit of such employee in such qualified terminated plan was distributed to such employee on Janaury 21, 1977, and all the property received by such employee in such distribution was transferred by such employee to such individual retirement account on January 21, 1977, then such distributions shall be treated as qualifying rollover distributions (within the meaning of section 402(a)(5) of such Code) and shall not be includible in the gross income of such employee for the taxable year in which paid.

(b) Qualified Terminated Plan.—For purposes of this section, the term "qualified terminated plan" means a pension plan—

(1) with respect to which a notice of sufficiency was issued by the Pension Benefit Guaranty Corporation on December 2, 1976, and

(2) which was terminated by corporate action on February 20, 1976.

(c) Refund or Credit of Overpayment Barred by Statute of Limitations.—Notwithstanding section 6511(a) of the Internal Revenue Code of 1954 or any other period of limitation or lapse of time, a claim for credit or refund of overpayment of the tax imposed by such Code which arises by reason of this section may be filed by any person at any time within the 1-year period beginning on the date of enactment of this Act. Sections 6511(b) and 6514 of such Code shall not apply to any claim for credit or refund filed under this subsection within such 1-year period.

• 1983, Technical Corrections Act of 1982 (P.L. 97-448)

P.L. 97-448, §103(c)(8)(A):

Amended Code Sec. 402(a)(5)(D) by adding at the end thereof new clause (v). **Effective** as if included in the provision of P.L. 97-34 to which it relates.

• 1981, Economic Recovery Tax Act of 1981 (P.L. 97-34)

P.L. 97-34, §311(b)(3)(A):

Amended Code Sec. 402(a)(5) by inserting "(other than accumulated deductible employee contributions within the meaning of section 72(o)(5))" after "contributions" in subparagraph (b), by striking out "or" at the end of subparagraph (D)(i)(I), by striking out the period at the end of subparagraph (D)(i)(II) and inserting ", or", and by inserting at the end (D)(i)(III). **Effective** for tax years beginning after 12-31-81. The transitional rule provides, that, for purposes of the 1954 Code, any amount allowed as a deduction under section 220 of the Code (as in effect before its repeal by P.L. 97-34) shall be treated as if it were allowed by section 219 of the Code.

P.L. 97-34, §311(c)(1):

Amended Code Sec. 402(a)(1) by striking out in the second sentence "by the employee" and inserting "by the employee (other than deductible employee contributions within the meaning of section 72(o)(5))". **Effective** for tax years beginning after 12-31-81. For the transitional rule, see the amendment note at P.L. 97-34, §311(b)(3)(A).

P.L. 97-34, §314(c)(1):

Amended Code Sec. 402(a)(1) by striking out each place it appears "or made available". **Effective** for tax years beginning after 12-31-81.

• 1980 (P.L. 96-608)

P.L. 96-608, §2(a):

Amended Code Sec. 402(a)(6) by adding subparagraph (E). **Effective** for payments made in tax years beginning after 12-31-78. However, a transitional rule provides that in the case of any payment made before 1-1-82, in a tax year beginning after 12-31-78, which is treated as a qualifying rollover distribution (as defined in Code Sec. 402(a)(5)(D)(i)) by reason of the amendment made by §2(a) herein, the applicable period specified in Code Sec. 402(a)(5)(C) shall not expire before the close of 12-31-81.

• 1980, Technical Corrections Act of 1979 (P.L. 96-222)

P.L. 96-222, §101(a)(14)(A) and (D):

Amended Act Sec. 157(h)(3) of P.L. 95-600 by striking out "the amendments made by this section" each place it appeared, and inserting "the amendments made by this subsection", by striking out in subparagraph (B) "any payment" and inserting "any payment made during 1978", and by striking out in subparagraph (B) "December 31, 1978" and inserting "December 31, 1980".

P.L. 96-222, §101(a)(14)(C):

Amended Code Sec. 402(a)(7)(A) by changing paragraph (i). **Effective** for lump-sum distributions completed after 12-31-78, in tax years ending after such date. Prior to amendment, paragraph (i) read as follows:

(i) any portion of a lump-sum distribution from a qualified trust is paid to the spouse of the employee on account of the employee's death,

P.L. 96-222, §101(a)(14)(E)(i):

Amended Code Sec. 402(a)(6)(D)(iii) by changing "many designate" to "may designate". **Effective** for qualifying rollover distributions completed after 12-31-78, in tax years ending after such date.

• 1978, Revenue Act of 1978 (P.L. 95-600)

P.L. 95-600, §135(b):

Added Code Sec. 402(a)(8). **Effective** as set forth in P.L. 95-600, §135(c). See historical comment on P.L. 95-600, §135(c) under Code Sec. 401(k).

P.L. 95-600, §157(f):

Added Code Sec. 402(a)(6)(D). **Effective** for qualifying rollover distributions (as defined in Code Sec. 402(a)(5)(D)(i)) completed after 12-31-78, in tax years ending after such date.

P.L. 95-600, §157(g)(1):

Added Code Sec. 402(a)(7). **Effective** for lump-sum distributions completed after 12-31-78, in tax years ending after such date.

P.L. 95-600, §157(h)(1):

Amended Code Sec. 402(a)(5)(D)(i) by striking out "subsection (e)(4)(B)" and inserting in lieu thereof "subparagraphs (B) and (H) of subsection (e)(4)". **Effective** as set forth in P.L. 95-600, §157(h)(3).

P.L. 95-600, §157(h)(3), provides:

(3) EFFECTIVE DATE.—

(A) IN GENERAL.—The amendments made by this section shall apply to payments made in taxable years beginning after December 31, 1977.

(B) TRANSITIONAL RULE.—In the case of any payment which is described in section 402(a)(5)(A) or 403(a)(4)(A) of the Internal Revenue Code of 1954 by reason of the amendments made by this section, the applicable period specified in section 402(a)(5)(C) of such Code (or in the case of an individual retirement annuity, such section as made applicable by section 403(a)(4)(B) of such Code) shall not expire before the close of December 31, 1978.

• 1978 (P.L. 95-458)

P.L. 95-458, §4(a):

Amended paragraph (a)(5). **Effective** as indicated in §4(d), below. Before amendment, paragraph (a)(5) read as follows:

"(5) ROLLOVER AMOUNTS.—In the case of an employees' trust described in section 401(a) which is exempt from tax under section 501(a), if—

(A) the balance to the credit of an employee is paid to him—

(i) within one taxable year of the employee on account of a termination of the plan of which the trust is a part or, in the case of a profit-sharing or stock bonus plan, a complete discontinuance of contributions under such plan, or

(ii) in one or more distributions which constitute a lump-sum distribution within the meaning of subsection (e)(4)(A) (determined without reference to subsection (e)(4)(B)),

(B)(i) the employee transfers all the property he receives in such distribution to an individual retirement account described in section 408(a), an individual retirement annuity described in section 408(b) (other than an endowment contract), or a retirement bond described in section 409, on or before the 60th day after the day on which he received such property, to the extent the fair market value of such property exceeds the amount referred to in subsection (e)(4)(D)(i), or

(ii) the employee transfers all the property he receives in such distribution to an employees' trust described in section 401(a) which is exempt from tax under section 501(a), or to an annuity plan described in section 403(a) on or before the 60th day after the day on which he received such property, to the extent the fair market value of such property exceeds the amount referred to in subsection (e)(4)(D)(i), and

(C) the amount so transferred consists of the property (other than money) distributed, to the extent that the fair market value of such property does not exceed the amount required to be transferred pursuant to subparagraph (B),

then such distributions are not includible in gross income for the year in which paid. For purposes of this title, a transfer described in subparagraph (B)(i) shall be treated as a rollover contribution as described in section 408(d)(3). Subparagraph (B)(ii) does not apply in the case of a transfer to an employees' trust, or annuity plan if any part of a payment described in subparagraph (A) is attributable to a trust forming part of a plan under which the employee was an employee within the meaning of section 401(c)(1) at the time contributions were made on his behalf under the plan."

P.L. 95-458, §4(c)(1):

Added subparagraph (C) at the end of paragraph (a)(6). **Effective** as indicated in §4(d), below.

P.L. 95-458, §4(c)(2)(A)-(C):

Amended paragraph (a)(6) and subparagraphs (a)(6)(A) and (B). **Effective** as indicated in §4(d), below. Prior to amendment, the aforementioned read as follows:

"(6) SPECIAL ROLLOVER RULES.—For purposes of paragraph (5)(A)(i)—

(A) TIME OF TERMINATION.—A complete discontinuance of contributions under a profit-sharing or stock bonus plan shall be deemed to occur on the day the plan administrator notifies the Secretary (in accordance with regulations prescribed by the Secretary) that all contributions to the plan have been completely discontinued. For purposes of section 411(d)(3), the plan shall be considered to be terminated no later than the day such notice is filed with the Secretary.

(B) SALE OF SUBSIDIARY OR ASSETS.—"

P.L. 95-458, §4(d), provides:

"(d) EFFECTIVE DATES.—

(1) IN GENERAL.—The amendments made by subsections (a), (b), and (c) shall apply with respect to taxable years beginning after December 31, 1974.

(2) VALIDATION OF CERTAIN ATTEMPTED ROLLOVERS.—If the taxpayer—

(A) attempted to comply with the requirements of section 402(a)(5) or 403(a)(4) of the Internal Revenue Code of 1954 for a taxable year beginning before October 14, 1978, and

(B) failed to meet the requirements of such section that all property received in the distribution be transferred,

such section (as amended by this section) shall be applied by treating any transfer of property made on or before December 31, 1978, as if it were made on or before the 60th day after the day on which the taxpayer received such property. For purposes of the preceding sentence, a transfer of money shall be treated as a transfer of property received in a distribution to the extent that the amount of the money transferred does not exceed the highest fair market value of the property distributed during the 60-day period beginning on the date on which the taxpayer received such property."

• 1976, Tax Reform Act of 1976 (P.L. 94-455)

P.L. 94-455, §1402(b)(1)(C):

Substituted "9 months" for "6 months" in Code Sec. 402(a)(2). **Effective** with respect to tax years beginning in 1977.

P.L. 94-455, §1402(b)(2):

Substituted "1 year" for "9 months" in Code Sec. 402(a)(2). **Effective** for tax years beginning after 12-31-77.

P.L. 94-455, §1901(a)(57)(A):

Substituted "basic pay" for "basic salary" wherever it appeared in Code Sec. 402(a)(4), and amended the last sentence of such paragraph. **Effective** for tax years beginning after 12-31-76. Prior to amendment the last sentence read:

In the case of distributions under the Civil Service Retirement Act (5 U.S.C. 2251), the term "basic salary" shall have the meaning provided in section 1(d) of such Act.

P.L. 94-455, §1906(b)(13)(A):

Amended the 1954 Code by substituting "Secretary" for "Secretary or his delegate" each place it appeared. **Effective** 2-1-77.

• 1976 (P.L. 94-267)

P.L. 94-267, §1(a):

Amended Code Sec. 402(a)(5)(A). **Effective** for payments made to an employee on or after 7-4-74. Prior to amendment Code Sec. 402(a)(5)(A) read as follows:

"(A) the balance of the credit of an employee is paid to him in one or more distributions which constitute a lump sum distribution within the meaning of subsection (e)(4)(A) (determined without reference to subsection (e)(4)(B)),".

Amended the last sentence of paragraph (5) by striking out "the lump-sum distribution" and inserting in lieu thereof "a payment". **Effective** for payments made to an employee on or after 7-4-74.

Added Code Sec. 402(a)(6). **Effective** for payments made to an employee on or after 7-4-74.

P.L. 94-267, §1(d), provides:

"(d) TRANSITIONAL RULES.

"(1) In general.—

"(A) Period for rollover contribution.—In the case of a payment described in section 402(a)(5)(A) (other than a payment described in section 402(a)(5)(A) as in effect on the day before the date of the enactment of this Act) or section 403(a)(4)(A) (other than a payment described in section 403(a)(4)(A) as in effect on the day before the date of the enactment of this Act) of the Internal Revenue Code of 1954 (relating to distributions of the balance to the credit of the employee) which is contributed by an employee after the date of the enactment of this Act to a trust, plan, account, annuity, or bond described in section, 402(a)(5)(B) or 403(a)(4)(B) of such Code, the applicable period specified in section 402(a)(5)(B) or 403(a)(4)(B) of such Code (relating to rollover distributions to another plan or retirement account) shall not expire before December 31, 1976.

"(B) Time of contribution.—

"(i) General rule.—If the initial portion of a payment the applicable period for which is determined under subparagraph (A) is contributed before December 31, 1976, by an individual to a trust, plan, account, annuity, or bond described in subparagraph (A) and the remaining portion of such payment is contributed by such individual to such a trust, plan, account, annuity, or bond not later than 30 days after the date a credit or refund is allowed by the Secretary of the Treasury or his delegate under section 6402 of the Internal Revenue Code of 1954 with respect to the contribution, then, for purposes of subparagraph (A) and sections 402(a)(5) and 403(a)(4) of such Code, at the election of the individual (made in accordance with regulations prescribed by the Secretary or his delegate), such remaining portion shall be considered to have been contributed on the date the initial portion of the payment was contributed. For purposes of this subparagraph, the initial portion of a payment is the amount by which such payment exceeds the amount of the tax imposed on such payment by chapter 1 of such Code (determined without regard to this subparagraph).

"(ii) Regulations.—For purposes of this subparagraph, the tax imposed on a payment by chapter 1 of the Internal Revenue Code of 1954, and the date a credit or refund is allowed by the Secretary of the Treasury or his delegate under section 6402 with respect to a contribution, shall be determined under regulations prescribed by the Secretary of the Treasury or his delegate.

"(C) Period of limitations.—If an individual has made the election provided by subparagraph (B), then—

"(i) the period provided by the Internal Revenue Code of 1954 for the assessment of any deficiency for the taxable year in which the payment described in subparagraph (A) was made and each subsequent taxable year for which tax is determined by reference to the treatment of such payment under such Code or the status under such Code of any trust, plan, account, annuity, or bond described in subparagraph (A) shall, to the extent attributable to such treatment, not expire before the expiration of 3 years from the date the Secretary of the Treasury or his delegate is notified by the individual (in such manner as the Secretary of the Treasury or his delegate may prescribe) that such individual has made (or failed to make) the contribution of the remaining portion of the payment within the period specified in subparagraph (B)(i), and

"(ii) such deficiency may be assessed before the expiration of such 3-year period notwithstanding the provisions of section 6212(c) of such Code or the provisions of any other law or rule of law which would otherwise prevent such assessment.

"(2) Rollover contribution for certain property sold.—Sections 402(a)(5)(C) and 403(a)(4)(C) of the Internal Revenue Code of 1954 (relating to the requirement that rollover amount must consist of property received in a distribution) shall not apply with respect to that portion of the property received in a payment described in section 402(a)(5)(A) (other than a payment described in section 402(a)(5)(A) as in effect on the day before the date of the enactment of this Act) or 403(a)(4)(A) (other than a payment described in section 403(a)(4)(A) as in effect on the day before the date of the enactment of this Act) of such Code which is sold or exchanged by the employee on or before the date of the enactment of this Act, if the employee transfers an amount of cash equal to the proceeds received from the sale or exchange of such property in excess of the amount considered contributed by the employee (within the meaning of section 402(a)(4)(D)(i) of such Code).

"(3) Nonrecognition of gain or loss.—For purposes of the Internal Revenue Code of 1954, no gain or loss shall be recognized with respect to the sale or exchange of property described in paragraph (2) if the proceeds of such sale or exchange are transferred by an employee in accordance with this subsection and the applicable provisions of section 402(a)(5) or 403(a)(4) of such Code."

• 1974, Employee Retirement Income Security Act of 1974 (P.L. 93-406)

P.L. 93-406, §2005(b)(1):

Amended Code Sec. 402(a)(2). **Effective** for distributions or payments made after 12-31-73, in tax years beginning after such date.

P.L. 93-406, §2005(c)(1),(2):

Repealed Code Secs. 402(a)(3)(C) and 402(a)(5). **Effective** for distributions or payments made after 12-31-73, in tax years beginning after such date.

P.L. 93-406, §2002(g)(5):

Added new Code Sec. 402(a)(5). **Effective** on and after 9-2-74, with respect to contributions to an employees' trust described in Code Sec. 401(a) which is exempt from tax under Code Sec. 501(a) or an annuity plan described in Code Sec. 403(a). Prior to amendment or repeal, Code Secs. 402(a)(2), 402(a)(3)(C) and 402(a)(5) read as follows:

"(2) Capital gains treatment for certain distributions.—In the case of an employees' trust described in section 401(a), which is exempt from tax under section 501(a), if the total distributions payable with respect to any employee are paid to the distributee within 1 taxable year of the distributee on account of the employee's death or other separation from the service, or on account of the death of the employee after his separation from the service, the amount of such distribution, to the extent exceeding the amounts contributed by the employee (determined by applying section 72(f)), which employee contributions shall be reduced by any amounts theretofore distributed to him which were not includible in gross income, shall be considered a gain from the sale or exchange of a capital asset held for more than 6 months. Where such total distributions include securities of the employer corporation, there shall be excluded from such excess the net unrealized appreciation attributable to that part of the total distributions which consists of the securities of the employer corporation so distributed. The amount of such net unrealized appreciation and the resulting adjustments to basis of the securities of the employer corporation so distributed shall be determined in accordance with regulations prescribed by the Secretary or his delegate. This paragraph shall not apply to distributions paid to any distributee to the extent such distributions are attributable to contributions made on behalf of the employee while he was an employee within the meaning of section 401(c)(1)."

"(3) Definitions.—For purposes of this subsection—

* * *

"(C) The term `total distributions payable' means the balance to the credit of an employee which becomes payable to a distributee on account of the employee's death or other separation from the service, or on account of his death after separation from the service."

"(5) Limitation on capital gains treatment.—The first sentence of paragraph (2) shall apply to a distribution paid after December 31, 1969, only to the extent that it does not exceed the sum of—

"(A) the benefits accrued by the employee on behalf of whom it is paid during plan years beginning before January 1, 1970, and

"(B) the portion of the benefits accrued by such employee during plan years beginning after December 31, 1969, which the distributee establishes does not consist of the employee's allocable share of employer contributions to the trust by which such distribution is paid.

The Secretary or his delegate shall prescribe such regulations as may be necessary to carry out the purposes of this paragraph."

• 1969, Tax Reform Act of 1969 (P.L. 91-172)

P.L. 91-172, §515(a)(1):

Amended Code Sec. 402(a) by adding paragraph (5). **Effective** for tax years ending after 12-31-69.

• 1964, Revenue Act of 1964 (P.L. 88-272)

P.L. 88-272, §221(c)(1):

Amended Code Sec. 402(a)(3)(B) by substituting "subsections (e) and (f) of section 425" for "section 421(d)(2) and (3)". **Effective** for tax years ending after 12-31-63.

P.L. 88-272, §232(e)(1):

Amended Code Sec. 402(a)(1) by deleting "except that section 72(e)(3) shall not apply" from the end of the first sentence. **Effective** with respect to tax years beginning after 12-31-63.

• 1962, Self-Employed Individuals Tax Retirement Act of 1962 (P.L. 87-792)

P.L. 87-792, §4:

Amended Code Sec. 402(a)(2) by inserting the last sentence therein. **Effective** 1-1-63.

• 1960 (P.L. 86-437)

P.L. 86-437, §§1, 2(a):

Amended Code Sec. 402(a) by adding a new paragraph (4), by striking out the phrase "paragraph 2" in Code Sec. 402(a)(1), and by substituting the phrase "paragraphs (2) and (4)". **Effective** for tax years beginning after 12-31-59.

[Sec. 402(b)]

(b) TAXABILITY OF BENEFICIARY OF NONEXEMPT TRUST.—

(1) CONTRIBUTIONS.—Contributions to an employees' trust made by an employer during a taxable year of the employer which ends with or within a taxable year of the trust for which the trust is not exempt from tax under section 501(a) shall be included in the gross income of the employee in accordance with section 83 (relating to property transferred in connection with performance of services), except that the value of the employee's interest in the trust shall be substituted for the fair market value of the property for purposes of applying such section.

(2) DISTRIBUTIONS.—The amount actually distributed or made available to any distributee by any trust described in paragraph (1) shall be taxable to the distributee, in the taxable year in which so distributed or made available, under section 72 (relating to annuities), except that distributions of income of such trust before the annuity starting date (as defined in section 72(c)(4)) shall be included in the gross income of the employee without regard to section 72(e)(5) (relating to amounts not received as annuities).

(3) GRANTOR TRUSTS.—A beneficiary of any trust described in paragraph (1) shall not be considered the owner of any portion of such trust under subpart E of part I of subchapter J (relating to grantors and others treated as substantial owners).

(4) FAILURE TO MEET REQUIREMENTS OF SECTION 410(b).—

(A) HIGHLY COMPENSATED EMPLOYEES.—If 1 of the reasons a trust is not exempt from tax under section 501(a) is the failure of the plan of which it is a part to meet the requirements of section 401(a)(26) or 410(b), then a highly compensated employee shall, in lieu of the amount determined under paragraph (1) or (2) include in gross income for the taxable year with or within which the taxable year of the trust ends an amount equal to the vested accrued benefit of such employee (other than the employee's investment in the contract) as of the close of such taxable year of the trust.

(B) FAILURE TO MEET COVERAGE TESTS.—If a trust is not exempt from tax under section 501(a) for any taxable year solely because such trust is part of a plan which fails to meet the requirements of section 401(a)(26) or 410(b), paragraphs (1) and (2) shall not apply by reason of such failure to any employee who was not a highly compensated employee during—

(i) such taxable year, or

(ii) any preceding period for which service was creditable to such employee under the plan.

(C) HIGHLY COMPENSATED EMPLOYEE.—For purposes of this paragraph, the term "highly compensated employee" has the meaning given such term by section 414(q).

Amendments

• 1992, Unemployment Compensation Amendments of 1992 (P.L. 102-318)

P.L. 102-318, §521(a):

Amended Code Sec. 402(b). **Effective** for distributions after 12-31-92. Prior to amendment, Code Sec. 402(b) read as follows:

(b) TAXABILITY OF BENEFICIARY OF NONEXEMPT TRUST.—

(1) IN GENERAL.—Contributions to an employees' trust made by an employer during a taxable year of the employer which ends within or with a taxable year of the trust for which the trust is not exempt from tax under section 501(a) shall be included in the gross income of the employee in accordance with section 83 (relating to property transferred in connection with performance of services), except that the value of the employee's interest in the trust shall be substituted for the fair market value of the property for purposes of applying such section. The amount actually distributed or made available to any distributee by any such trust shall be taxable to him in the year in which so distributed or made available, under section 72 (relating to annuities), except that distributions of income of such trust before the annuity starting date (as defined in section 72(c)(4)) shall be included in the gross income of the employee without regard to section 72(e)(5) (relating to amount not received as annuities). A beneficiary of any such trust shall not be considered the owner of any portion of such trust under subpart E of part I of subchapter J (relating to grantors and others treated as substantial owners).

(2) FAILURE TO MEET REQUIREMENTS OF SECTION 410(b).—

(A) HIGHLY COMPENSATED EMPLOYEES.—If 1 of the reasons a trust is not exempt from tax under section 501(a) is the failure of the plan of which it is a part to meet the requirements of section 401(a)(26) or 410(b), then a highly compensated employee shall, in lieu of the amount determined under paragraph (1), include in gross income for the taxable year with or within which the taxable year of the trust ends an amount equal to the vested accrued benefit of such employee (other than the employee's investment in the contract) as of the close of such taxable year of the trust.

(B) FAILURE TO MEET COVERAGE TESTS.—If a trust is not exempt from tax under section 501(a) for any taxable year solely because such trust is part of a plan which fails to meet the requirements of section 401(a)(26) or 410(b), paragraph (1) shall not apply by reason of such failure to any employee who was not a highly compensated employee during—

(i) such taxable year, or

(ii) any preceding period for which service was creditable to such employee under the plan.

(C) HIGHLY COMPENSATED EMPLOYEE.—For purposes of this paragraph, the term "highly compensated employee" has the meaning given such term by section 414(q).

• 1988, Technical and Miscellaneous Revenue Act of 1988 (P.L. 100-647)

P.L. 100-647, §1011(h)(4):

Amended Code Sec. 402(b)(2) by striking out subparagraphs (A) and (B) and inserting in lieu thereof new subparagraphs (A) and (B). **Effective** as if included in the provision of P.L. 99-514 to which it relates. Prior to amendment, Code Sec. 402(b)(2)(A) and (B) read as follows:

(A) IN GENERAL.—In the case of a trust which is not exempt from tax under section 501(a) solely because such trust is part of a plan which fails to meet the requirements of section 410(b)—

(i) such trust shall be treated as exempt from tax under section 501(a) for purposes of applying paragraph (1) to employees who are not highly compensated employees, and

(ii) paragraph (1) shall be applied to the vested accrued benefit (other than employee contributions) of any highly compensated employee as of the close of the employer's taxable year described in paragraph (1) (rather than contributions made during such year).

(B) FAILURE IN MORE THAN 1 YEAR.—If a plan fails to meet the requirements of section 410(b) for more than 1 taxable year, any portion of the vested accrued benefit to which subparagraph (A) applies shall be included in gross income only once.

• 1986, Tax Reform Act of 1986 (P.L. 99-514)

P.L. 99-514, §1112(c)(1):

Amended Code Sec. 402(b) by adding at the end thereof new subparagraph (2). **Effective,** generally, for plan years beginning after 12-31-88. However, for special rules see Act Sec. 1112(e)(2)-(3) following Code Sec. 401.

P.L. 99-514, §1112(c)(2):

Amended the heading for Code Sec. 402(b). **Effective,** generally, for plan years beginning after 12-31-88. However, for special rules see Act Sec. 1112(e)(2)-(3) following Code Sec. 401. Prior to amendment it read as follows:

(b) TAXABILITY OF BENEFICIARY OF NONEXEMPT TRUST.—

P.L. 99-514, §1852(c)(5):

Amended Code Sec. 402(b) by striking out "section 72(e)(1)" and inserting in lieu thereof "section 72(e)(5)". **Effective** as if included in the provision of P.L. 98-369 to which it relates.

• 1969, Tax Reform Act of 1969 (P.L. 91-172)

P.L. 91-172, §321(b)(1):

Amended Code Sec. 402(b). **Effective** with respect to contributions made and premiums paid after 8-1-69. Prior to amendment, Code Sec. 402(b) read as follows:

(b) Taxability of Beneficiary of Non-Exempt Trust.—Contributions to an employees' trust made by an employer during a taxable year of the employer which ends within or with a taxable year of the trust for which the trust is not exempt from tax under section 501(a) shall be included in the gross income of an employee for the taxable year in which the contribution is made to the trust in the case of an employee whose beneficial interest in such contribution is nonforfeitable at the time the contribution is made. The amount actually distributed or made available to any distributee by any such trust shall be taxable to him, in the year in which so distributed or made available, under section 72 (relating to annuities).

• 1964, Revenue Act of 1964 (P.L. 88-272)

P.L. 88-272, §232(e)(2):

Amended Code Sec. 402(b) by deleting "except that section 72(e)(3) shall not apply" from the end of the second sentence. **Effective** with respect to tax years beginning after 12-31-63.

[Sec. 402(c)]

(c) RULES APPLICABLE TO ROLLOVERS FROM EXEMPT TRUSTS.—

(1) EXCLUSION FROM INCOME.—If—

(A) any portion of the balance to the credit of an employee in a qualified trust is paid to the employee in an eligible rollover distribution,

(B) the distributee transfers any portion of the property received in such distribution to an eligible retirement plan, and

(C) in the case of a distribution of property other than money, the amount so transferred consists of the property distributed,

then such distribution (to the extent so transferred) shall not be includible in gross income for the taxable year in which paid.

(2) MAXIMUM AMOUNT WHICH MAY BE ROLLED OVER.—In the case of any eligible rollover distribution, the maximum amount transferred to which paragraph (1) applies shall not exceed the portion of such distribution which is includible in gross income (determined without regard to paragraph (1)). The preceding sentence shall not apply to such distribution to the extent—

(A) such portion is transferred in a direct trustee-to-trustee transfer to a qualified trust or to an annuity contract described in section 403(b) and such trust or contract provides for separate accounting for amounts so transferred (and earnings thereon), including separately accounting for the portion of such distribution which is includible in gross income and the portion of such distribution which is not so includible, or

(B) such portion is transferred to an eligible retirement plan described in clause (i) or (ii) of paragraph (8)(B).

In the case of a transfer described in subparagraph (A) or (B), the amount transferred shall be treated as consisting first of the portion of such distribution that is includible in gross income (determined without regard to paragraph (1)).

(3) TRANSFER MUST BE MADE WITHIN 60 DAYS OF RECEIPT.—

(A) IN GENERAL.—Except as provided in subparagraph (B), paragraph (1) shall not apply to any transfer of a distribution made after the 60th day following the day on which the distributee received the property distributed.

(B) HARDSHIP EXCEPTION.—The Secretary may waive the 60-day requirement under subparagraph (A) where the failure to waive such requirement would be against equity or good conscience, including casualty, disaster, or other events beyond the reasonable control of the individual subject to such requirement.

(4) ELIGIBLE ROLLOVER DISTRIBUTION.—For purposes of this subsection, the term "eligible rollover distribution" means any distribution to an employee of all or any portion of the balance to the credit of the employee in a qualified trust; except that such term shall not include—

(A) any distribution which is one of a series of substantially equal periodic payments (not less frequently than annually) made—

(i) for the life (or life expectancy) of the employee or the joint lives (or joint life expectancies) of the employee and the employee's designated beneficiary, or

(ii) for a specified period of 10 years or more,

(B) any distribution to the extent such distribution is required under section 401(a)(9), and

(C) any distribution which is made upon hardship of the employee.

If all or any portion of a distribution during 2009 is treated as an eligible rollover distribution but would not be so treated if the minimum distribution requirements under section 401(a)(9) had applied during 2009, such distribution shall not be treated as an eligible rollover distribution for purposes of section 401(a)(31) or 3405(c) or subsection (f) of this section.

(5) TRANSFER TREATED AS ROLLOVER CONTRIBUTION UNDER SECTION 408.—For purposes of this title, a transfer to an eligible retirement plan described in clause (i) or (ii) of paragraph (8)(B) resulting in any portion of a distribution being excluded from gross income under paragraph (1) shall be treated as a rollover contribution described in section 408(d)(3).

(6) SALES OF DISTRIBUTED PROPERTY.—For purposes of this subsection—

(A) TRANSFER OF PROCEEDS FROM SALE OF DISTRIBUTED PROPERTY TREATED AS TRANSFER OF DISTRIBUTED PROPERTY.—The transfer of an amount equal to any portion of the proceeds from the sale of property received in the distribution shall be treated as the transfer of property received in the distribution.

(B) PROCEEDS ATTRIBUTABLE TO INCREASE IN VALUE.—The excess of fair market value of property on sale over its fair market value on distribution shall be treated as property received in the distribution.

(C) DESIGNATION WHERE AMOUNT OF DISTRIBUTION EXCEEDS ROLLOVER CONTRIBUTION.—In any case where part or all of the distribution consists of property other than money—

(i) the portion of the money or other property which is to be treated as attributable to amounts not included in gross income, and

(ii) the portion of the money or other property which is to be treated as included in the rollover contribution,

shall be determined on a ratable basis unless the taxpayer designates otherwise. Any designation under this subparagraph for a taxable year shall be made not later than the time prescribed by law for filing the return for such taxable year (including extensions thereof). Any such law for designation, once made, shall be irrevocable.

(D) NONRECOGNITION OF GAIN OR LOSS.—No gain or loss shall be recognized on any sale described in subparagraph (A) to the extent that an amount equal to the proceeds is transferred pursuant to paragraph (1).

(7) SPECIAL RULE FOR FROZEN DEPOSITS.—

(A) IN GENERAL.—The 60-day period described in paragraph (3) shall not—

(i) include any period during which the amount transferred to the employee is a frozen deposit, or

(ii) end earlier than 10 days after such amount ceases to be a frozen deposit.

(B) FROZEN DEPOSITS.—For purposes of this subparagraph, the term "frozen deposit" means any deposit which may not be withdrawn because of—

(i) the bankruptcy or insolvency of any financial institution, or

(ii) any requirement imposed by the State in which such institution is located by reason of the bankruptcy or insolvency (or threat thereof) of 1 or more financial institutions in such State.

A deposit shall not be treated as a frozen deposit unless on at least 1 day during the 60-day period described in paragraph (3) (without regard to this paragraph) such deposit is described in the preceding sentence.

(8) DEFINITIONS.—For purposes of this subsection—

(A) QUALIFIED TRUST.—The term "qualified trust" means an employees' trust described in section 401(a) which is exempt from tax under section 501(a).

(B) ELIGIBLE RETIREMENT PLAN.—The term "eligible retirement plan" means—

(i) an individual retirement account described in section 408(a),

(ii) an individual retirement annuity described in section 408(b) (other than an endowment contract),

(iii) a qualified trust,

(iv) an annuity plan described in section 403(a),

(v) an eligible deferred compensation plan described in section 457(b) which is maintained by an eligible employer described in section 457(e)(1)(A), and

(vi) an annuity contract described in section 403(b).

If any portion of an eligible rollover distribution is attributable to payments or distributions from a designated Roth account (as defined in section 402A), an eligible retirement plan with respect to such portion shall include only another designated Roth account and a Roth IRA.

(9) ROLLOVER WHERE SPOUSE RECEIVES DISTRIBUTION AFTER DEATH OF EMPLOYEE.—If any distribution attributable to an employee is paid to the spouse of the employee after the employee's death, the preceding provisions of this subsection shall apply to such distribution in the same manner as if the spouse were the employee.

(10) SEPARATE ACCOUNTING.—Unless a plan described in clause (v) of paragraph (8)(B) agrees to separately account for amounts rolled into such plan from eligible retirement plans not described in such clause, the plan described in such clause may not accept transfers or rollovers from such retirement plans.

(11) DISTRIBUTIONS TO INHERITED INDIVIDUAL RETIREMENT PLAN OF NONSPOUSE BENEFICIARY.—

(A) IN GENERAL.—If, with respect to any portion of a distribution from an eligible retirement plan described in paragraph (8)(B)(iii) of a deceased employee, a direct trustee-to-trustee transfer is made to an individual retirement plan described in clause (i) or (ii) of paragraph (8)(B) established for the purposes of receiving the distribution on behalf of an individual who is a designated beneficiary (as defined by section 401(a)(9)(E)) of the employee and who is not the surviving spouse of the employee—

(i) the transfer shall be treated as an eligible rollover distribution,

(ii) the individual retirement plan shall be treated as an inherited individual retirement account or individual retirement annuity (within the meaning of section 408(d)(3)(C)) for purposes of this title, and

(iii) section 401(a)(9)(B) (other than clause (iv) thereof) shall apply to such plan.

(B) CERTAIN TRUSTS TREATED AS BENEFICIARIES.—For purposes of this paragraph, to the extent provided in rules prescribed by the Secretary, a trust maintained for the benefit of one or more designated beneficiaries shall be treated in the same manner as a designated beneficiary.

Amendments

• 2008, Worker, Retiree, and Employer Recovery Act of 2008 (P.L. 110-458)

P.L. 110-458, §108(f)(1)(A)-(B):

Amended Code Sec. 402(c)(11) by inserting "described in paragraph (8)(B)(iii)" after "eligible retirement plan" in subparagraph (A), and by striking "trust" before "designated beneficiary" in subparagraph (B). **Effective** as if included in the provision of the 2006 Act to which the amendment relates [**effective** for distributions after 12-31-2006.—CCH].

P.L. 110-458, §108(f)(2)(B):

Amended Code Sec. 402(c)(11)(A)(i) by striking "for purposes of this subsection" following "distribution". **Effective** with respect to plan years beginning after 12-31-2009.

P.L. 110-458, §201(b):

Amended Code Sec. 402(c)(4) by adding at the end a new flush sentence. **Effective** generally for calendar years beginning after 12-31-2008. For a special rule, see Act Sec. 201(c)(2), below.

P.L. 110-458, §201(c)(2), provides:

(2) PROVISIONS RELATING TO PLAN OR CONTRACT AMENDMENTS.—

(A) IN GENERAL.—If this paragraph applies to any pension plan or contract amendment, such pension plan or contract shall not fail to be treated as being operated in accordance with the terms of the plan during the period described in subparagraph (B)(ii) solely because the plan operates in accordance with this section.

(B) AMENDMENTS TO WHICH PARAGRAPH APPLIES.—

(i) IN GENERAL.—This paragraph shall apply to any amendment to any pension plan or annuity contract which—

(I) is made pursuant to the amendments made by this section, and

(II) is made on or before the last day of the first plan year beginning on or after January 1, 2011.

In the case of a governmental plan, subclause (II) shall be applied by substituting "2012" for "2011".

(ii) CONDITIONS.—This paragraph shall not apply to any amendment unless during the period beginning on the effective date of the amendment and ending on December 31, 2009, the plan or contract is operated as if such plan or contract amendment were in effect.

• 2006, Pension Protection Act of 2006 (P.L. 109-280)

P.L. 109-280, §811, provides:

SEC. 811. PENSIONS AND INDIVIDUAL RETIREMENT ARRANGEMENT PROVISIONS OF ECONOMIC GROWTH AND TAX RELIEF RECONCILIATION ACT OF 2001 MADE PERMANENT.

Title IX of the Economic Growth and Tax Relief Reconciliation Act of 2001 [P.L. 107-16] shall not apply to the provisions of, and amendments made by, subtitles A through F of title VI [§§601-666]of such Act (relating to pension and individual retirement arrangement provisions).

P.L. 109-280, §822(a)(1)-(2):

Amended Code Sec. 402(c)(2)(A) by striking "which is part of a plan which is a defined contribution plan and which agrees to separately account" and inserting "or to an annuity contract described in section 403(b) and such trust or contract provides for separate accounting"; and by inserting "(and earnings thereon)" after "so transferred". **Effective** for tax years beginning after 12-31-2006.

P.L. 109-280, §829(a)(1):

Amended Code Sec. 402(c) by adding at the end a new paragraph (11). **Effective** for distributions after 12-31-2006.

• 2005, Katrina Emergency Tax Relief Act of 2005 (P.L. 109-73)

P.L. 109-73, §102 [repealed by P.L. 109-135, §201(b)(4)(A)], provides:

SEC. 102. RECONTRIBUTIONS OF WITHDRAWALS FOR HOME PURCHASES CANCELLED DUE TO HURRICANE KATRINA.

(a) RECONTRIBUTIONS.—

(1) IN GENERAL.—Any individual who received a qualified distribution may, during the period beginning on August 25, 2005, and ending on February 28, 2006, make one or more contributions in an aggregate amount not to exceed the amount of such qualified distribution to an eligible retirement plan (as defined in section 402(c)(8)(B) of the Internal Revenue Code of 1986) of which such individual is a beneficiary and to which a rollover contribution of such distribution could be made under section 402(c), 403(a)(4), 403(b)(8), or 408(d)(3) of such Code, as the case may be.

(2) TREATMENT OF REPAYMENTS.—Rules similar to the rules of paragraphs (2) and (3) of section 101(c) of this Act shall apply for purposes of this section.

(b) QUALIFIED DISTRIBUTION DEFINED.—For purposes of this section, the term "qualified distribution" means any distribution—

(1) described in section 401(k)(2)(B)(i)(IV), 403(b)(7)(A)(ii) (but only to the extent such distribution relates to financial hardship), 403(b)(11)(B), or 72(t)(2)(F) of such Code,

(2) received after February 28, 2005, and before August 29, 2005, and

(3) which was to be used to purchase or construct a principal residence in the Hurricane Katrina disaster area, but which was not so purchased or constructed on account of Hurricane Katrina.

• 2002, Job Creation and Worker Assistance Act of 2002 (P.L. 107-147)

P.L. 107-147, §411(q)(2):

Amended Code Sec. 402(c)(2) by adding at the end a new flush sentence. **Effective** as if included in the provision of P.L. 107-16 to which it relates [**effective** for distributions made after 12-31-2001.—CCH].

• 2001, Economic Growth and Tax Relief Reconciliation Act of 2001 (P.L. 107-16)

P.L. 107-16, §617(c):

Amended Code Sec. 402(c)(8)(B) by adding at the end a new sentence. **Effective** for tax years beginning after 12-31-2005.

P.L. 107-16, §636(b)(1):

Amended Code Sec. 402(c)(4)(C). **Effective** for distributions made after 12-31-2001. Prior to amendment, Code Sec. 402(c)(4)(C) read as follows:

(C) any hardship distribution described in section 401(k)(2)(B)(i)(IV).

P.L. 107-16, §641(a)(2)(A):

Amended Code Sec. 402(c)(8)(B) by striking "and" at the end of clause (iii), by striking the period at the end of clause (iv) and inserting ", and", and by inserting after clause (iv) a new clause (v). **Effective**, generally, for distributions after 12-31-2001. For a special rule, see Act Sec. 641(f)(3), below.

P.L. 107-16, §641(a)(2)(B):

Amended Code Sec. 402(c) by adding at the end a new paragraph (10). **Effective**, generally, for distributions after 12-31-2001. For a special rule, see Act Sec. 641(f)(3), below.

P.L. 107-16, §641(b)(2):

Amended Code Sec. 402(c)(8)(B), as amended by Act Sec. 641(a), by striking "and" at the end of clause (iv), by striking the period at the end of clause (v) and inserting ", and", and by inserting after clause (v) a new clause (vi). **Effective**, generally, for distributions after 12-31-2001. For a special rule, see Act Sec. 641(f)(3), below.

P.L. 107-16, §641(d):

Amended Code Sec. 402(c)(9) by striking "; except that" and all that follows up to the end period. **Effective**, generally, for distributions after 12-31-2001. For a special rule, see Act Sec. 641(f)(3), below. Prior to amendment, Code Sec. 402(c)(9) read as follows:

(9) ROLLOVER WHERE SPOUSE RECEIVES DISTRIBUTION AFTER DEATH OF EMPLOYEE.—If any distribution attributable to an employee is paid to the spouse of the employee after the employee's death, the preceding provisions of this subsection shall apply to such distribution in the same manner as if the spouse were the employee; except that a trust or plan described in clause (iii) or (iv) of paragraph (8)(B) shall not be treated as an eligible retirement plan with respect to such distribution.

P.L. 107-16, §641(f)(3), provides:

(3) SPECIAL RULE.—Notwithstanding any other provision of law, subsections (h)(3) and (h)(5) of section 1122 of the Tax Reform Act of 1986 shall not apply to any distribution from

an eligible retirement plan (as defined in clause (iii) or (iv) of section 402(c)(8)(B) of the Internal Revenue Code of 1986) on behalf of an individual if there was a rollover to such plan on behalf of such individual which is permitted solely by reason of any amendment made by this section.

P.L. 107-16, §643(a):

Amended Code Sec. 402(c)(2) by adding at the end a new sentence containing subparagraphs (A) and (B). **Effective** for distributions after 12-31-2001.

P.L. 107-16, §644(a):

Amended Code Sec. 402(c)(3). **Effective** for distributions after 12-31-2001. Prior to amendment, Code Sec. 402(c)(3) read as follows:

(3) TRANSFER MUST BE MADE WITHIN 60 DAYS OF RECEIPT.—Paragraph (1) shall not apply to any transfer of a distribution made after the 60th day following the day on which the distributee received the property distributed.

P.L. 107-16, §901(a)-(b), provides [but see P.L. 109-280, §811, above]:

SEC. 901. SUNSET OF PROVISIONS OF ACT.

(a) IN GENERAL.—All provisions of, and amendments made by, this Act shall not apply—

(1) to taxable, plan, or limitation years beginning after December 31, 2010, or

(2) in the case of title V, to estates of decedents dying, gifts made, or generation skipping transfers, after December 31, 2010.

(b) APPLICATION OF CERTAIN LAWS.—The Internal Revenue Code of 1986 and the Employee Retirement Income Security Act of 1974 shall be applied and administered to years, estates, gifts, and transfers described in subsection (a) as if the provisions and amendments described in subsection (a) had never been enacted.

• 1998, IRS Restructuring and Reform Act of 1998 (P.L. 105-206)

P.L. 105-206, §6005(c)(2)(A):

Amended Code Sec. 402(c)(4) by striking "and" at the end of subparagraph (A), by striking the period at the end of subparagraph (B) and inserting ", and", and by inserting at the end a new subparagraph (C). **Effective** for distributions after 12-31-98.

• 1996, Small Business Job Protection Act of 1996 (P.L. 104-188)

P.L. 104-188, §1401(b)(2):

Amended Code Sec. 402(c) by striking paragraph (10). **Effective,** generally, for tax years beginning after 12-31-99. For a special transitional rule, see Act Sec. 1401(c)(2) in the amendment notes following Code Sec. 402(d). Prior to being stricken, Code Sec. 402(c)(10) read as follows:

(10) DENIAL OF AVERAGING FOR SUBSEQUENT DISTRIBUTIONS.—If paragraph (1) applies to any distribution paid to any employee, paragraphs (1) and (3) of subsection (d) shall not apply to any distribution (paid after such distribution) of the balance to the credit of the employee under the plan under which the preceding distribution was made (or under any other plan which, under subsection (d)(4)(C), would be aggregated with such plan).

• 1992, Unemployment Compensation Amendments of 1992 (P.L. 102-318)

P.L. 102-318, §521(a):

Amended Code Sec. 402(c). **Effective** for distributions after 12-31-92. Prior to amendment, Code Sec. 402(c) read as follows:

(c) TAXABILITY OF BENEFICIARY OF CERTAIN FOREIGN SITUS TRUSTS.—For purposes of subsections (a) and (b), a stock bonus, pension, or profit-sharing trust which would qualify for exemption from tax under section 501 (a) except for the fact that it is a trust created or organized outside the United States shall be treated as if it were a trust exempt from tax under section 501 (a).

[Sec. 402(d)]

(d) TAXABILITY OF BENEFICIARY OF CERTAIN FOREIGN SITUS TRUSTS.—For purposes of subsections (a), (b), and (c), a stock bonus, pension, or profit-sharing trust which would qualify for exemption from tax under section 501(a) except for the fact that it is a trust created or organized outside the United States shall be treated as if it were a trust exempt from tax under section 501(a).

Amendments

• 1996, Small Business Job Protection Act of 1996 (P.L. 104-188)

P.L. 104-188, §1401(a):

Amended Code Sec. 402(d). **Effective,** generally, for tax years beginning after 12-31-99. For a special transitional rule, see Act Sec. 1401(c)(2), below. Prior to amendment, Code Sec. 402(d) read as follows:

(d) TAX ON LUMP SUM DISTRIBUTIONS.—

(1) IMPOSITION OF SEPARATE TAX ON LUMP-SUM DISTRIBUTIONS.—

(A) SEPARATE TAX.—There is hereby imposed a tax (in the amount determined under subparagraph (B)) on a lump sum distribution.

(B) AMOUNT OF TAX.—The amount of tax imposed by subparagraph (A) for any taxable year is an amount equal to 5 times the tax which would be imposed by subsection (c) of section 1 if the recipient were an individual referred to in such subsection and the taxable income were an amount equal to 1/5 of the excess of—

(i) the total taxable amount of the lump sum distribution for the taxable year, over

(ii) the minimum distribution allowance.

(C) MINIMUM DISTRIBUTION ALLOWANCE.—For purposes of this paragraph, the minimum distribution allowance for any taxable year is an amount equal to—

(i) the lesser of $10,000 or one-half of the total taxable amount of the lump sum distribution for the taxable year, reduced (but not below zero) by

(ii) 20 percent of the amount (if any) by which such total taxable amount exceeds $20,000.

(D) LIABILITY FOR TAX.—The recipient shall be liable for the tax imposed by this paragraph.

(2) DISTRIBUTIONS OF ANNUITY CONTRACTS.—

(A) IN GENERAL.—In the case of any recipient of a lump sum distribution for any taxable year, if the distribution (or any part thereof) is an annuity contract, the total taxable amount of the distribution shall be aggregated for purposes of computing the tax imposed by paragraph (1)(A), except that the amount of tax so computed shall be reduced (but not below zero) by that portion of the tax on the aggregate total taxable amount which is attributable to annuity contracts.

(B) BENEFICIARIES.—For purposes of this paragraph, a beneficiary of a trust to which a lump sum distribution is made shall be treated as the recipient of such distribution if the beneficiary is an employee (including an employee within the meaning of section 401(c)(1)) with respect to the plan under which the distribution is made or if the beneficiary is treated as the owner of such trust for purposes of subpart E of part I of subchapter J.

(C) ANNUITY CONTRACTS.—For purposes of this paragraph, in the case of the distribution of an annuity contract, the taxable amount of such distribution shall be deemed to be the current actuarial value of the contract, determined on the date of such distribution.

(D) TRUSTS.—In the case of a lump sum distribution with respect to any individual which is made only to 2 or more trusts, the tax imposed by paragraph (1)(A) shall be computed as if such distribution was made to a single trust, but the liability for such tax shall be apportioned among such trusts according to the relative amounts received by each.

(E) REGULATIONS.—The Secretary shall prescribe such regulations as may be necessary to carry out the purposes of this paragraph.

(3) ALLOWANCE OF DEDUCTION.—The total taxable amount of a lump sum distribution for any taxable year shall be allowed as a deduction from gross income for such taxable year, but only to the extent included in the taxpayer's gross income for such taxable year.

(4) DEFINITIONS AND SPECIAL RULES.—

(A) LUMP SUM DISTRIBUTION.—For purposes of this section and section 403, the term "lump sum distribution" means the distribution or payment within 1 taxable year of the recipient of the balance to the credit of an employee which becomes payable to the recipient—

(i) on account of the employee's death,

(ii) after the employee attains age 59½,

(iii) on account of the employee's separation from the service, or

(iv) after the employee has become disabled (within the meaning of section 72(m)(7)),

from a trust which forms a part of a plan described in section 401(a) and which is exempt from tax under section 501 or from a plan described in section 403(a). Clause (iii) of this subparagraph shall be applied only with respect to an individual who is an employee without regard to section 401(c)(1), and clause (iv) shall be applied only with respect to an employee within the meaning of section 401(c)(1). A distribution of an annuity contract from a trust or annuity plan referred to in the first sentence of this subparagraph shall be treated as a lump sum distribution. For purposes of this subparagraph, a distribution to 2 or more trusts shall be treated as a distribution to 1 recipient. For purposes of this subsection, the balance to the credit of the employee does not include the accumulated deductible employee contributions under the plan (within the meaning of section 72(o)(5)).

(B) AVERAGING TO APPLY TO 1 LUMP SUM DISTRIBUTION AFTER AGE 59½.—Paragraph (1) shall apply to a lump sum distribution with respect to an employee under subparagraph (A) only if—

(i) such amount is received on or after the date on which the employee has attained age 59½, and

(ii) the taxpayer elects for the taxable year to have all such amounts received during such taxable year so treated.

Not more than 1 election may be made under this subparagraph by any taxpayer with respect to any employee. No election may be made under this subparagraph by any taxpayer other than an individual, an estate, or a trust. In the case of a lump sum distribution made with respect to an employee to 2 or more trusts, the election under this subparagraph shall be made by the personal representative of the taxpayer.

(C) AGGREGATION OF CERTAIN TRUSTS AND PLANS.—For purposes of determining the balance to the credit of an employee under subparagraph (A)—

(i) all trusts which are part of a plan shall be treated as a single trust, all pension plans maintained by the employer shall be treated as a single plan, all profit-sharing plans maintained by the employer shall be treated as a single plan, and all stock bonus plans maintained by the employer shall be treated as a single plan, and

(ii) trusts which are not qualified trusts under section 401(a) and annuity contracts which do not satisfy the requirements of section 404(a)(2) shall not be taken into account.

(D) TOTAL TAXABLE AMOUNT.—For purposes of this section and section 403, the term "total taxable amount" means, with respect to a lump sum distribution, the amount of such distribution which exceeds the sum of—

(i) the amounts considered contributed by the employee (determined by applying section 72(f)), reduced by any amounts previously distributed which were not includible in gross income, and

(ii) the net unrealized appreciation attributable to that part of the distribution which consists of the securities of the employer corporation so distributed.

(E) COMMUNITY PROPERTY LAWS.—The provisions of this subsection, other than paragraph (3), shall be applied without regard to community property laws.

(F) MINIMUM PERIOD OF SERVICE.—For purposes of this subsection, no amount distributed to an employee from or under a plan may be treated as a lump sum distribution under subparagraph (A) unless the employee has been a participant in the plan for 5 or more taxable years before the taxable year in which such amounts are distributed.

(G) AMOUNTS SUBJECT TO PENALTY.—This subsection shall not apply to amounts described in subparagraph (A) of section 72(m)(5) to the extent that section 72(m)(5) applies to such amounts.

(H) BALANCE TO CREDIT OF EMPLOYEE NOT TO INCLUDE AMOUNTS PAYABLE UNDER QUALIFIED DOMESTIC RELATIONS ORDER.—For purposes of this subsection, the balance to the credit of an employee shall not include any amount payable to an alternate payee under a qualified domestic relations order (within the meaning of section 414(p)).

(I) TRANSFERS TO COST-OF-LIVING ARRANGEMENT NOT TREATED AS DISTRIBUTION.—For purposes of this subsection, the balance to the credit of an employee under a defined contribution plan shall not include any amount transferred from such defined contribution plan to a qualified cost-of-living arrangement (within the meaning of section 415(k)(2)) under a defined benefit plan.

(J) LUMP SUM DISTRIBUTIONS OF ALTERNATE PAYEES.—If any distribution or payment of the balance to the credit of an employee would be treated as a lump sum distribution, then, for purposes of this subsection, the payment under a qualified domestic relations order (within the meaning of section 414(p)) of the balance to the credit of an alternate payee who is the spouse or former spouse of the employee shall be treated as a lump sum distribution. For purposes of this subparagraph, the balance to the credit of the alternate payee shall not include any amount payable to the employee.

(K) TREATMENT OF PORTION NOT ROLLED OVER.—If any portion of a lump sum distribution is transferred in a transfer to which subsection (c) applies, paragraphs (1) and (3) shall not apply with respect to the distribution.

(L) SECURITIES.—For purposes of this subsection, the terms "securities" and "securities of the employer corporation" have the respective meanings provided by subsection (e)(4)(E).

(5) SPECIAL RULE WHERE PORTIONS OF LUMP SUM DISTRIBUTION ATTRIBUTABLE TO ROLLOVER OF BOND PURCHASED UNDER QUALIFIED BOND PURCHASE PLAN.—If any portion of a lump sum distribution is attributable to a transfer described in section 405(d)(3)(A)(ii) (as in effect before its repeal by the Tax Reform Act of 1984), paragraphs (1) and (3) of this subsection shall not apply to such portion.

(6) TREATMENT OF POTENTIAL FUTURE VESTING.—

(A) IN GENERAL.—For purposes of determining whether any distribution which becomes payable to the recipient on account of the employee's separation from service is a lump sum distribution, the balance to the credit of the employee shall be determined without regard to any increase in vesting which may occur if the employee is reemployed by the employer.

(B) RECAPTURE IN CERTAIN CASES.—If—

(i) an amount is treated as a lump sum distribution by reason of subparagraph (A),

(ii) special lump sum treatment applies to such distribution,

(iii) the employee is subsequently reemployed by the employer, and

(iv) as a result of services performed after being so reemployed, there is an increase in the employee's vesting for benefits accrued before the separation referred to in subparagraph (A),

under regulations prescribed by the Secretary, the tax imposed by this chapter for the taxable year (in which the increase in vesting first occurs) shall be increased by the reduction in tax which resulted from the special lump sum treatment (and any election under paragraph (4)(B) shall not be taken into account for purposes of determining whether the employee may make another election under paragraph (4)(B)).

(C) SPECIAL LUMP SUM TREATMENT.—For purposes of this paragraph, special lump sum treatment applies to any distribution if any portion of such distribution is taxed under the subsection by reason of an election under paragraph (4)(B).

(D) VESTING.—For purposes of this paragraph, the term "vesting" means the portion of the accrued benefits derived from employer contributions to which the participant has a nonforfeitable right.

(7) COORDINATION WITH FOREIGN TAX CREDIT LIMITATIONS.—Subsections (a), (b), and (c) of section 904 shall be applied separately with respect to any lump sum distribution on which tax is imposed under paragraph (1), and the amount of such distribution shall be treated as the taxable income for purposes of such separate application.

P.L. 104-188, §1401(c)(2), provides:

(2) RETENTION OF CERTAIN TRANSITION RULES.—The amendments made by this section shall not apply to any distribution for which the taxpayer is eligible to elect the benefits of section 1122(h)(3) or (h)(5) of the Tax Reform Act of 1986. Notwithstanding the preceding sentence, individuals who elect such benefits after December 31, 1999, shall not be eligible for 5-year averaging under section 402(d) of the Internal Revenue Code of 1986 (as in effect immediately before such amendments).

• 1992, Unemployment Compensation Amendments of 1992 (P.L. 102-318)

P.L. 102-318, §521(a):

Added Code Sec. 402(d). **Effective** for distributions after 12-31-92.

• 1976, Tax Reform Act of 1976 (P.L. 94-455)

P.L. 94-455, §1901(a)(57)(B):

Repealed Code Sec. 402(d). **Effective** for tax years beginning after 12-31-76. Prior to repeal, Code Sec. 402(d) read as follows:

(d) CERTAIN EMPLOYEES' ANNUITIES.—Notwithstanding subsection (b) or any other provision of this subtitle, a contribution to a trust by an employer shall not be included in the gross income of the employee in the year in which the contribution is made if—

(1) such contribution is to be applied by the trustee for the purchase of annuity contracts for the benefit of such employee;

(2) such contribution is made to the trustee pursuant to a written agreement entered into prior to October 21, 1942, between the employer and the trustee, or between the employer and the employee; and

(3) under the terms of the trust agreement the employee is not entitled during his lifetime, except with the consent of the trustee, to any payments under annuity contracts purchased by the trustee other than annuity payments.

The employee shall include in his gross income the amounts received under such contracts for the year received as provided in section 72 (relating to annuities). This subsection shall have no application with respect to amounts contributed to a trust after June 1, 1949, if the trust on such date was exempt under section 165 (a) of the Internal Revenue Code of 1939. For purposes of this subsection, amounts paid by an employer for the purchase of annuity contracts which are transferred to the trustee shall be deemed to be contributions made to a trust or trustee and contributions applied by the trustee for the purchase of annuity contracts; the term "annuity contracts purchased by the trustee" shall include annuity contracts so purchased by the employer and transferred to the trustee; and the term "employee" shall include only a person who was in the employ of the employer, and was covered by the agreement referred to in paragraph (2), prior to October 21, 1942.

• 1964, Revenue Act of 1964 (P.L. 88-272)

P.L. 88-272, §232(e)(3):

Amended Code Sec. 402(d) to delete "except that section 72(e)(3) shall not apply" from the end of the second sentence. **Effective** with respect to tax years beginning after 12-31-63.

[Sec. 402(e)]

(e) OTHER RULES APPLICABLE TO EXEMPT TRUSTS.—

(1) ALTERNATE PAYEES.—

(A) ALTERNATE PAYEE TREATED AS DISTRIBUTEE.—For purposes of subsection (a) and section 72, an alternate payee who is the spouse or former spouse of the participant shall be treated as the distributee of any distribution or payment made to the alternate payee under a qualified domestic relations order (as defined in section 414(p)).

(B) ROLLOVERS.—If any amount is paid or distributed to an alternate payee who is the spouse or former spouse of the participant by reason of any qualified domestic relations order (within the meaning of section 414(p)), subsection (c) shall apply to such distribution in the same manner as if such alternate payee were the employee.

(2) DISTRIBUTIONS BY UNITED STATES TO NONRESIDENT ALIENS.—The amount includible under subsection (a) in the gross income of a nonresident alien with respect to a distribution made by the United States in respect of services performed by an employee of the United States shall not exceed an amount which bears the same ratio to the amount includible in gross income without regard to this paragraph as—

(A) the aggregate basic pay paid by the United States to such employee for such services, reduced by the amount of such basic pay which was not includible in gross income by reason of being from sources without the United States, bears to

(B) the aggregate basic pay paid by the United States to such employee for such services.

In the case of distributions under the civil service retirement laws, the term "basic pay" shall have the meaning provided in section 8331(3) of title 5, United States Code.

(3) CASH OR DEFERRED ARRANGEMENTS.—For purposes of this title, contributions made by an employer on behalf of an employee to a trust which is a part of a qualified cash or deferred arrangement (as defined in section 401(k)(2)) or which is part of a salary reduction agreement under section 403(b) shall not be treated as distributed or made available to the employee nor as contributions made to the trust by the employee merely because the arrangement includes provisions under which the employee has an election whether the contribution will be made to the trust or received by the employee in cash.

(4) NET UNREALIZED APPRECIATION.—

(A) AMOUNTS ATTRIBUTABLE TO EMPLOYEE CONTRIBUTIONS.—For purposes of subsection (a) and section 72, in the case of a distribution other than a lump sum distribution, the amount actually distributed to any distributee from a trust described in subsection (a) shall not include any net unrealized appreciation in securities of the employer corporation attributable to amounts contributed by the employee (other than deductible employee contributions within the meaning of section 72(o)(5)). This subparagraph shall not apply to a distribution to which subsection (c) applies.

(B) AMOUNTS ATTRIBUTABLE TO EMPLOYER CONTRIBUTIONS.—For purposes of subsection (a) and section 72, in the case of any lump sum distribution which includes securities of the employer corporation, there shall be excluded from gross income the net unrealized appreciation attributable to that part of the distribution which consists of securities of the employer corporation. In accordance with rules prescribed by the Secretary, a taxpayer may elect, on the return of tax on which a lump sum distribution is required to be included, not to have this subparagraph apply to such distribution.

(C) DETERMINATION OF AMOUNTS AND ADJUSTMENTS.—For purposes of subparagraphs (A) and (B), net unrealized appreciation and the resulting adjustments to basis shall be determined in accordance with regulations prescribed by the Secretary.

(D) LUMP-SUM DISTRIBUTION.—For purposes of this paragraph—

(i) IN GENERAL.—The term "lump sum distribution" means the distribution or payment within one taxable year of the recipient of the balance to the credit of an employee which becomes payable to the recipient—

(I) on account of the employee's death,

(II) after the employee attains age 59½,

(III) on account of the employee's separation from service, or

(IV) after the employee has become disabled (within the meaning of section 72(m)(7)),

from a trust which forms a part of a plan described in section 401(a) and which is exempt from tax under section 501 or from a plan described in section 403(a). Subclause (III) of this clause shall be applied only with respect to an individual who is an employee without regard to section 401(c)(1), and subclause (IV) shall be applied only with respect to an employee within the meaning of section 401(c)(1). For purposes of this clause, a distribution to two or more trusts shall be treated as a distribution to one recipient. For purposes of this paragraph, the balance to the credit of the employee does not include the accumulated deductible employee contributions under the plan (within the meaning of section 72(o)(5)).

(ii) AGGREGATION OF CERTAIN TRUSTS AND PLANS.—For purposes of determining the balance to the credit of an employee under clause (i)—

(I) all trusts which are part of a plan shall be treated as a single trust, all pension plans maintained by the employer shall be treated as a single plan, all profit-sharing plans maintained by the employer shall be treated as a single plan, and all stock bonus plans maintained by the employer shall be treated as a single plan, and

(II) trusts which are not qualified trusts under section 401(a) and annuity contracts which do not satisfy the requirements of section 404(a)(2) shall not be taken into account.

(iii) COMMUNITY PROPERTY LAWS.—The provisions of this paragraph shall be applied without regard to community property laws.

(iv) AMOUNTS SUBJECT TO PENALTY.—This paragraph shall not apply to amounts described in subparagraph (A) of section 72(m)(5) to the extent that section 72(m)(5) applies to such amounts.

(v) BALANCE TO CREDIT OF EMPLOYEE NOT TO INCLUDE AMOUNTS PAYABLE UNDER QUALIFIED DOMESTIC RELATIONS ORDER.—For purposes of this paragraph, the balance to the credit of an employee shall not include any amount payable to an alternate payee under a qualified domestic relations order (within the meaning of section 414(p)).

(vi) TRANSFERS TO COST-OF-LIVING ARRANGEMENT NOT TREATED AS DISTRIBUTION.—For purposes of this paragraph, the balance to the credit of an employee under a defined contribution plan shall not include any amount transferred from such defined contribution plan to a qualified cost-of-living arrangement (within the meaning of section 415(k)(2)) under a defined benefit plan.

(vii) LUMP-SUM DISTRIBUTIONS OF ALTERNATE PAYEES.—If any distribution or payment of the balance to the credit of an employee would be treated as a lump-sum distribution, then, for purposes of this paragraph, the payment under a qualified domestic relations order (within the meaning of section 414(p)) of the balance to the credit of an alternate payee who is the spouse or former spouse of the employee shall be treated as a lump-sum distribution. For purposes of this clause, the balance to the credit of the alternate payee shall not include any amount payable to the employee.

(E) DEFINITIONS RELATING TO SECURITIES.—For purposes of this paragraph—

(i) SECURITIES.—The term "securities" means only shares of stock and bonds or debentures issued by a corporation with interest coupons or in registered form.

(ii) SECURITIES OF THE EMPLOYER.—The term "securities of the employer corporation" includes securities of a parent or subsidiary corporation (as defined in subsections (e) and (f) of section 424) of the employer corporation.

(5) [Stricken.]

(6) DIRECT TRUSTEE-TO-TRUSTEE TRANSFERS.—Any amount transferred in a direct trustee-to-trustee transfer in accordance with section 401(a)(31) shall not be includible in gross income for the taxable year of such transfer.

Amendments

• 1996, Small Business Job Protection Act of 1996 (P.L. 104-188)

P.L. 104-188, §1401(b)(1):

Amended Code Sec. 402(e)(4)(D). **Effective,** generally, for tax years beginning after 12-31-99. For a special transitional rule, see Act Sec. 1401(c)(2) in the amendment notes following Code Sec. 402(d). Prior to amendment, Code Sec. 402(e)(4)(D) read as follows:

(D) LUMP SUM DISTRIBUTION.—For purposes of this paragraph, the term "lump sum distribution" has the meaning given such term by subsection (d)(4)(A) (without regard to subsection (d)(4)(F)).

P.L. 104-188, §1401(b)(13):

Amended Code Sec. 402(e) by striking paragraph (5). **Effective,** generally, for tax years beginning after 12-31-99. For a special transitional rule, see Act Sec. 1401(c)(2) in the amendment notes following Code Sec. 402(d). Prior to being stricken, Code Sec. 402(e)(5) read as follows:

(5) TAXABILITY OF BENEFICIARY OF CERTAIN FOREIGN SITUS TRUSTS.—For purposes of subsections (a), (b), and (c), a stock bonus, pension, or profit-sharing trust which would qualify for exemption from tax under section 501(a) except for the fact that it is a trust created or organized outside the United States shall be treated as if it were a trust exempt from tax under section 501(a).

P.L. 104-188, §1450(a)(2):

Amended Code Sec. 402(e)(3) by inserting "or which is part of a salary reduction agreement under section 403(b)" after "section 401(k)(2))". **Effective** for years beginning after 12-31-95, except a contract shall not be required to meet any change in any requirement by reason of such amendment before the 90th day after 8-20-96.

• 1992, Unemployment Compensation Amendments of 1992 (P.L. 102-318)

P.L. 102-318, §521(a):

Amended Code Sec. 402(e). **Effective** for distributions after 12-31-92. Prior to amendment Code Sec. 402(e) read as follows:

(e) TAX ON LUMP SUM DISTRIBUTIONS.—

(1) IMPOSITION OF SEPARATE TAX ON LUMP SUM DISTRIBUTIONS.—

(A) SEPARATE TAX.—There is hereby imposed a tax (in the amount determined under subparagraph (B)) on the lump sum distribution.

(B) AMOUNT OF TAX.—The amount of tax imposed by subparagraph (A) for any taxable year is an amount equal to 5 times the tax which would be imposed by subsection (c) of section 1 if the recipient were an individual referred to in such subsection and the taxable income were an amount equal to 1/5 of the excess of—

(i) the total taxable amount of the lump sum distribution for the taxable year, over

(ii) the minimum distribution allowance.

For purposes of the preceding sentence, in determining the amount of tax under section 1(c), section 1(g) shall be applied without regard to paragraph (2)(B) thereof.

(C) MINIMUM DISTRIBUTION ALLOWANCE.—For purposes of this paragraph, the minimum distribution allowance for the taxable year is an amount equal to—

(i) the lesser of $10,000 or one-half of the total taxable amount of the lump sum distribution for the taxable year, reduced (but not below zero) by

(ii) 20 percent of the amount (if any) by which such total taxable amount exceeds $20,000.

(D) LIABILITY FOR TAX.—The recipient shall be liable for the tax imposed by this paragraph.

(2) MULTIPLE DISTRIBUTIONS AND DISTRIBUTIONS OF ANNUITY CONTRACTS.—In the case of any recipient of a lump sum distribution for the taxable year with respect to whom during the 6-taxable-year period ending on the last day of the taxable year there has been one or more other lump sum distributions after December 31, 1973, or if the distribution (or any part thereof) is an annuity contract, in computing the tax imposed by paragraph (1)(A), the total taxable amounts of all such distributions during such 6-taxable-year period shall be aggregated, but the amount of tax so computed shall be reduced (but not below zero) by the sum of—

(A) the amount of the tax imposed by paragraph (1)(A) paid with respect to such other distributions, plus

(B) that portion of the tax on the aggregated total taxable amounts which is attributable to annuity contracts.

For purposes of this paragraph, a beneficiary of a trust to which a lump sum distribution is made shall be treated as the recipient of such distribution if the beneficiary is an employee (including an employee within the meaning of section 401(c)(1)) with respect to the plan under which the distribution is made or if the beneficiary is treated as the owner of such trust for purposes of subpart E of part I of subchapter J. In the case of the distribution of an annuity contract, the taxable amount of such distribution shall be deemed to be the current actuarial value of the contract, determined on the date of such distribution. In the case of a lump sum distribution with respect to any individual which is made only to two or more trusts, the tax imposed by paragraph (1)(A) shall be computed as if such distribution was made to a single trust, but the liability for such tax shall be apportioned among such trusts according to the relative amounts received by each. The Secretary shall prescribe such regulations as may be necessary to carry out the purposes of this paragraph.

(3) ALLOWANCE OF DEDUCTION.—The total taxable amount of a lump sum distribution for the taxable year shall be allowed as a deduction from gross income for such taxable year, but only to the extent included in the taxpayer's gross income for such taxable year.

(4) DEFINITIONS AND SPECIAL RULES.—

(A) LUMP SUM DISTRIBUTION.—For purposes of this section and section 403, the term "lump sum distribution" means the distribution or payment within one taxable year of the recipient of the balance to the credit of an employee which becomes payable to the recipient—

(i) on account of the employee's death,

(ii) after the employee attains age 59½,

(iii) on account of the employee's separation from the service, or

(iv) after the employee has become disabled (within the meaning of section 72(m)(7))

from a trust which forms a part of a plan described in section 401(a) and which is exempt from tax under section 501 or from a plan described in section 403(a). Clause (iii) of this subparagraph shall be applied only with respect to an individual who is an employee without regard to section 401(c)(1), and clause (iv) shall be applied only with respect to an employee within the meaning of section 401(c)(1). A distribution of an annuity contract from a trust or annuity plan referred to in the first sentence of this subparagraph shall be treated as a lump sum distribution. For purposes of this subparagraph, a distribution to two or more trusts shall be treated as a distribution to one recipient. For purposes of this subsection, the balance to the credit of the employee does not include the accumulated deductible employee contributions under the plan (within the meaning of section 72(o)(5)).

(B) AVERAGING TO APPLY TO 1 LUMP SUM DISTRIBUTION AFTER AGE 59½.—Paragraph (1) shall apply to a lump sum distribution with respect to an employee under subparagraph (A) only if—

(i) such amount is received on or after the employee has attained age 59½, and

(ii) the taxpayer elects for the taxable year to have all such amounts received during such taxable year so treated.

Not more than 1 election may be made under this subparagraph by any taxpayer with respect to any employee. No election may be made under this subparagraph by any taxpayer other than an individual, an estate, or a trust. In the case of a lump sum distribution made with respect to an employee to 2 or more trusts, the election under this subparagraph shall be made by the personal representative of the taxpayer.

(C) AGGREGATION OF CERTAIN TRUSTS AND PLANS.—For purposes of determining the balance to the credit of an employee under subparagraph (A)—

(i) all trusts which are part of a plan shall be treated as a single trust, all pension plans maintained by the employer shall be treated as a single plan, all profit-sharing plans maintained by the employer shall be treated as a single plan, and all stock bonus plans maintained by the employer shall be treated as a single plan, and

(ii) trusts which are not qualified trusts under section 401(a) and annuity contracts which do not satisfy the requirements of section 404(a)(2) shall not be taken into account.

(D) TOTAL TAXABLE AMOUNT.—For purposes of this section and section 403, the term "total taxable amount" means, with respect to a lump sum distribution, the amount of such distribution which exceeds the sum of—

(i) the amounts considered contributed by the employee (determined by applying section 72(f)), which employee contributions shall be reduced by any amounts theretofore distributed to him which were not includible in gross income, and

(ii) the net unrealized appreciation attributable to that part of the distribution which consists of the securities of the employer corporation so distributed.

(E) [Repealed.]

(F) [Repealed.]

(G) COMMUNITY PROPERTY LAWS.—The provisions of this subsection, other than paragraph (3), shall be applied without regard to community property laws.

(H) MINIMUM PERIOD OF SERVICE.—For purposes of this subsection, no amount distributed to an employee from or under a plan may be treated as a lump sum distributed under subparagraph (A) unless he has been a participant in the plan for 5 or more taxable years before the taxable year in which such amounts are distributed.

(I) AMOUNTS SUBJECT TO PENALTY.—This subsection shall not apply to amounts described in subparagraph (A) of section 72(m)(5) to the extent that section 72(m)(5) applies to such amounts.

(J) UNREALIZED APPRECIATION OF EMPLOYER SECURITIES.—In the case of any distribution including securities of the employer corporation which, without regard to the requirement of subparagraph (H), would be treated as a lump sum distribution under subparagraph (A), there shall be excluded from gross income the net unrealized appreciation attributable to that part of the distribution which consists of securities of the employer corporation so distributed. In the case of any such distribution or any lump sum distribution including securities of the employer corporation, the amount of net unrealized appreciation of such securities and the resulting adjustments to the basis of such securities shall be determined under regulations prescribed by the Secretary. This subparagraph shall not apply to distributions of accumulated deductible employee contributions (within the meaning of section 72(o)(5)). In accordance with rules prescribed by the Secretary, a taxpayer may elect, on the return of tax on which a distribution is required to be included, not to have this subparagraph apply with respect to such distribution.

(K) SECURITIES.—For purposes of this subsection, the terms "securities" and "securities of the employer corporation" have the respective meanings provided by subsection (a)(3).

(L) [Repealed.]

(M) BALANCE TO CREDIT OF EMPLOYEE NOT TO INCLUDE AMOUNTS PAYABLE UNDER QUALIFIED DOMESTIC RELATIONS ORDER—For purposes of this subsection, the balance to the credit of an employee shall not include any amount payable to an alternate payee under a qualified domestic relations order (within the meaning of section 414(p)).

(N) TRANSFERS TO COST-OF-LIVING ARRANGEMENT NOT TREATED AS DISTRIBUTION.—For purposes of this subsection, the balance to the credit of an employee under a defined contribution plan shall not include any amount transferred from such defined contribution plan to a qualified cost-of-living arrangement (within the meaning of section 415(k)(2)) under a defined benefit plan.

(O) LUMP-SUM DISTRIBUTIONS OF ALTERNATE PAYEES.—If any distribution or payment of the balance to the credit of an employee would be treated as a lump-sum distribution, then, for purposes of this subsection, the payment under a qualified domestic relations order (within the meaning of section 414(p)) of the balance to the credit of an alternate payee who is the spouse or former spouse of the employee shall be treated as a lump-sum distribution. For purposes of this subparagraph, the balance to the credit of the alternate payee shall not include any amount payable to the employee.

(5) SPECIAL RULE WHERE PORTIONS OF LUMP-SUM DISTRIBUTION ATTRIBUTABLE TO ROLLOVER OF BOND PURCHASED UNDER QUALIFIED BOND PURCHASE PLAN.—If any portion of a lump-sum distribution is attributable to a transfer described in section 405(d)(3)(A)(ii) (as in effect before its repeal by the Tax Reform Act of 1984), paragraphs (1) and (3) of this subsection shall not apply to such portion.

(6) TREATMENT OF POTENTIAL FUTURE VESTING.—

(A) IN GENERAL.—For purposes of determining whether any distribution which becomes payable to the recipient on account of the employee's separation from service is a lump sum distribution, the balance to the credit of the employee shall be determined without regard to any increase in vesting which may occur if the employee is re-employed by the employer.

(B) RECAPTURE IN CERTAIN CASES.—If—

(i) an amount is treated as a lump sum distribution by reason of subparagraph (A),

(ii) special lump sum treatment applies to such distribution,

(iii) the employee is subsequently re-employed by the employer; and

(iv) as a result of services performed after being so re-employed, there is an increase in the employee's vesting for benefits accrued before the separation referred to in subparagraph (A),

under regulations prescribed by the Secretary, the tax imposed by this chapter for the taxable year (in which the increase in vesting first occurs) shall be increased by the reduction in tax which resulted from the special lump sum treatment (and any election under paragraph (4)(B) shall not be taken into account for purposes of determining whether the employee may make another election under paragraph (4)(B)).

(C) SPECIAL LUMP-SUM TREATMENT.—For purposes of this paragraph, special lump sum treatment applies to any distribution if any portion of such distribution is taxed under the subsection by reason of an election under paragraph (4)(B).

(D) VESTING.—For purposes of this paragraph the term "vesting" means the portion of the accrued benefits derived from employer contributions to which the participant has a nonforfeitable right.

(7) COORDINATION WITH FOREIGN TAX CREDIT LIMITATIONS.—Subsections (a), (b), and (c) of section 904 shall be applied separately with respect to any lump sum distribution on which tax is imposed under paragraph (1), and the amount of such distribution shall be treated as the taxable income for purposes of such separate application.

P.L. 102-318, § 522(c)(1):

Amended Code Sec. 402(e), as amended by Act Sec. 521, by adding at the end new paragraph (6). **Effective** for distributions after 12-31-92.

• 1989, Omnibus Budget Reconciliation Act of 1989 (P.L. 101-239)

P.L. 101-239, § 7811(i)(13):

Amended Code Sec. 402(e) by adding at the end thereof a new paragraph (7). **Effective** with respect to tax years ending after 12-19-89 (or, at the election of the taxpayer, beginning after 12-31-86).

• **1988, Technical and Miscellaneous Revenue Act of 1988 (P.L. 100-647)**

P.L. 100-647, §1011A(b)(6):

Amended Code Sec. 402(e)(4)(B)(i) by striking out "taxpayer" and inserting in lieu thereof "employee". **Effective** as if included in the provision of P.L. 99-514 to which it relates.

P.L. 100-647, §1011A(b)(7):

Amended the last sentence of Code Sec. 402(e)(4)(J). **Effective** as if included in the provision of P.L. 99-514 to which it relates. Prior to amendment, the last sentence of Code Sec. 402(e)(4)(J) read as follows:

To the extent provided by the Secretary, a taxpayer may elect before any distribution not to have this paragraph apply with respect to such distribution.

P.L. 100-647, §1011A(b)(8)(E):

Amended Code Sec. 402(e)(1)(A) by striking out "ordinary income portion of a" after "on the". **Effective** as if included in the provision of P.L. 99-514 to which it relates.

P.L. 100-647, §1011A(b)(8)(F)(i)-(ii):

Amended Code Sec. 402(e)(4)(A) by striking out "Except for purposes of subsection (a)(2) and section 403(a)(2), a" and inserting in lieu thereof "A", and by striking out "subsection (a)(2) of this section, and subsection (a)(2) of section 403," after "of this subsection". **Effective** as if included in the provision of P.L. 99-514 to which it relates.

P.L. 100-647, §1011A(b)(8)(G):

Repealed Code Sec. 402(e)(4)(L). **Effective** as if included in the provision of P.L. 99-514 to which it relates. Prior to repeal, Code Sec. 402(e)(4)(L) read as follows:

(L) ELECTION TO TREAT PRE-1974 PARTICIPATION AS POST-1973 PARTICIPATION.—For purposes of subparagraph (E), subsection (a)(2), and section 403(a)(2), if a taxpayer elects (at the time and in the manner provided under regulations prescribed by the Secretary), all calendar years of an employee's active participation in all plans in which the employee has been an active participant shall be considered years of active participation by such employee after December 31, 1973. An election made under this subparagraph, once made, shall be irrevocable and shall apply to all lump-sum distributions received by the taxpayer with respect to the employee. This subparagraph shall not apply if the taxpayer received a lump-sum distribution in a previous taxable year of the employee beginning after December 31, 1975, unless no portion of such lump-sum distribution was treated under section 402(a)(2) or 403(a)(2) as gain from the sale or exchange of a capital asset held for more than 6 months.

P.L. 100-647, §1011A(b)(8)(H):

Amended Code Sec. 402(e)(4)(M) by striking out ", subsection (a)(2) of this section, and section 403(a)(2)" after "of this section". **Effective** as if included in the provision of P.L. 99-514 to which it relates.

P.L. 100-647, §1011A(b)(8)(I):

Amended Code Sec. 402(e)(5) by striking out "and paragraph (2) of subsection (a)" after "of this section". **Effective** as if included in the provision of P.L. 99-514 to which it relates.

P.L. 100-647, §1011A(b)(8)(J):

Amended Code Sec. 402(e)(6)(C). **Effective** as if included in the provision of P.L. 99-514 to which it relates. Prior to amendment, Code Sec. 402(e)(6)(C) read as follows:

(C) SPECIAL LUMP SUM TREATMENT.—For purposes of this paragraph, special lump sum treatment applies to any distribution if any portion of such distribution—

(i) is taxed under this subsection by reason of an election under paragraph (4)(b), or

(ii) is treated as long-term capital gain under subsection (a)(2) of this section or section 403(a)(2).

P.L. 100-647, §1011A(b)(10):

Amended Code Sec. 402(e)(1)(B) by adding at the end thereof a new flush sentence. **Effective** as if included in the provision of P.L. 99-514 to which it relates.

P.L. 100-647, §1011A(c)(9):

Amended Code Sec. 402(e)(4)(I) by striking out "clause (ii) of" after "amounts described in". **Effective** as if included in the provision of P.L. 99-514 to which it relates.

P.L. 100-647, §6068(a):

Amended Code Sec. 402(e)(4) by adding at the end thereof new subparagraph (O). **Effective** for tax years ending after 12-31-84.

• **1986, Tax Reform Act of 1986 (P.L. 99-514)**

P.L. 99-514, §104(b)(5):

Amended Code Sec. 402(e)(1)(B) by striking out "the zero bracket amount applicable to such individual for the taxable year plus". **Effective** for tax years beginning after 12-31-86.

P.L. 99-514, §1106(c)(2):

Amended Code Sec. 402(e)(4) by adding at the end thereof new subparagraph (N). **Effective** for years beginning after 12-31-86.

P.L. 99-514, §1122(a)(1):

Amended Code Sec. 402(e)(4)(B). For the **effective** date, see Act Sec. 1122(h), reproduced in the amendment notes for Code Sec. 402(a). Prior to amendment, Code Sec. 402(e)(4)(B) read as follows:

(B) ELECTION OF LUMP SUM TREATMENT.—For purposes of this section and section 403, no amount which is not an annuity contract may be treated as a lump sum distribution under subparagraph (A) unless the taxpayer elects for the taxable year to have all such amounts received during such year so treated at the time and in the manner provided under regulations prescribed by the Secretary. Not more than one election may be made under this subparagraph with respect to any individual after such individual has attained age $59\frac{1}{2}$. No election may be made under this subparagraph by any taxpayer other than an individual, an estate, or a trust. In the case of a lump sum distribution made with respect to an employee to two or more trusts, the election under this subparagraph shall be made by the personal representative of the employee.

P.L. 99-514, §1122(a)(2)(A)-(B):

Amended Code Sec. 402(e)(1)(C) by striking out "10 times" and inserting in lieu thereof "5 times", and by striking out "one-tenth" and inserting in lieu thereof "$\frac{1}{5}$". For the **effective** date, see Act Sec. 1122(h), reproduced in the amendment notes for Code Sec. 402(a).

P.L. 99-514, §1122(b)(2)(B)(i)-(iii):

Amended Code Sec. 402(e)(1) by striking out subparagraph (B) and by redesignating subparagraphs (C), (D), and (E) as subparagraphs (B), (C), and (D), respectively, by striking out "The initial separate tax" in subparagraph (B), as so redesignated, and inserting in lieu thereof "The amount of tax imposed by subparagraph (A)", and by striking out "Initial separate" in the heading of subparagraph (B), as so redesignated, and inserting in lieu thereof "Amount of tax". For the **effective** date, see Act Sec. 1122(h), reproduced in the amendment notes for Code Sec. 402(a). Prior to amendment, Code Sec. 402(e)(1)(B) read as follows:

(B) AMOUNT OF TAX.—The amount of tax imposed by subparagraph (A) for any taxable year shall be an amount equal to the amount of the initial separate tax for such taxable year multiplied by a fraction, the numerator of which is the ordinary income portion of the lump sum distribution for the taxable year and the denominator of which is the total taxable amount of such distribution for such year.

P.L. 99-514, §1122(b)(2)(C) (as amended by P.L. 100-647, §1018(a)(7)):

Amended Code Sec. 402(e)(3) by striking out "ordinary income portion" and inserting in lieu thereof "total taxable amount". For the **effective** date, see Act Sec. 1122(h), reproduced in the amendment notes for Code Sec. 402(a).

P.L. 99-514, §1122(b)(2)(D):

Amended Code Sec. 402(e)(4) by stiking out subparagraph (E). For the **effective** date, see Act Sec. 1122(h), reproduced in the amendment notes for Code Sec. 402(a). Prior to amendment, Code Sec. 402(e)(4)(E) read as follows:

(E) ORDINARY INCOME PORTION.—For purposes of this section, the term "ordinary income portion" means, with respect to a lump sum distribution, so much of the total taxable amount of such distribution as is equal to the product of such total taxable amount multiplied by a fraction—

(i) the numerator of which is the number of calendar years of active participation by the employee in such plan after December 31, 1973, and

(ii) the denominator of which is the number of calendar years of active participation by the employee in such plan.

P.L. 99-514, §1122(b)(2)(E):

Amended Code Sec. 402(e)(4)(H) by striking out "(but not for purposes of subsection (a)(2) or section 403(a)(2)(A))". For the **effective** date, see Act Sec. 1122(h), reproduced in the amendment notes for Code Sec. 402(a).

P.L. 99-514, §1122(g):

Amended Code Sec. 402(e)(4)(J) by adding at the end thereof the following new sentence: "To the extent provided by the Secretary, a taxpayer may elect before any distribution not to have this paragraph apply with respect to such distribution." For the **effective** date, see Act Sec. 1122(h), reproduced in the amendment notes for Code Sec. 402(a).

P.L. 99-514, §1852(b)(3)(B):

Amended Code Sec. 402(e)(4) by striking out subparagraph (F). **Effective** as if included in the provision of P.L. 98-369 to which it relates. Prior to amendment, Code Sec. 402(e)(4)(F) read as follows:

(F) EMPLOYEE.—For purposes of this subsection and subsection (a)(2), except as otherwise provided in subparagraph (A), the term "employee" includes an individual who is an employee within the meaning of section 401(c)(1) and the employer of such individual is the person treated as his employer under section 401(c)(4).

P.L. 99-514, §1898(a)(2):

Amended Code Sec. 402(e) by adding at the end thereof new paragraph (6). **Effective** as if included in the provision of P.L. 98-397 to which it relates.

• 1984, Retirement Equity Act of 1984 (P.L. 98-397)

P.L. 98-397, §204(c)(4):

Amended Code Sec. 402(e)(4) by adding at the end thereof new subparagraph (M). **Effective** 1-1-85, except that in the case of a domestic relations order entered before such date, the plan administrator—

(1) shall treat such order as a qualified domestic relations order if such administrator is paying benefits pursuant to such order on such date, and

(2) may treat any other such order entered before such date as a qualified domestic relations order even if such order does not meet the requirements of such amendments.

• 1984, Deficit Reduction Act of 1984 (P.L. 98-369)

P.L. 98-369, §491(c)(2):

Amended Code Sec. 402(e) by adding new paragraph (5). **Effective** for redemptions after 7-18-84, in tax years ending after such date.

P.L. 98-369, §1001(b)(3):

Amended Code Sec. 402(a)(2) and (e)(4)(L) by striking out "1 year" each place it appeared and inserting in lieu thereof "6 months". **Effective** for property acquired after 6-22-84 and before 1-1-88.

• 1983, Technical Corrections Act of 1982 (P.L. 97-448)

P.L. 97-448, §101(b):

Amended Code Sec. 402(e)(1)(C) by striking out "$2,300" and inserting in lieu thereof "the zero bracket amount applicable to such an individual for the taxable year". **Effective** as if included in the provision of P.L. 97-34 to which it relates.

P.L. 97-448, §103(c)(7):

Amended the last sentence of Code Sec. 402(e)(4)(A) by striking out "this section and section 403" and inserting in lieu thereof "this subsection, subsection (a)(2) of this section, and subsection (a)(2) of section 403". **Effective** as if included in the provision of P.L. 97-34 to which it relates.

P.L. 97-448, §103(c)(12)(D):

Amended Code Sec. 402(e)(4)(J) (by amending P.L. 97-34, §311(c)(2)), by adding the sentence at the end thereof. **Effective** as if included in the provision of P.L. 97-34 to which it relates.

• 1981, Economic Recovery Tax Act of 1981 (P.L. 97-34)

P.L. 97-34, §311(b)(2):

Amended Code Sec. 402(e)(4)(A) by adding at the end the following new sentence: "For purposes of this section and section 403, the balance to the credit of the employee does not include the accumulated deductible employee contributions under the plan (within the meaning of section 72(o)(5)).". **Effective** for tax years beginning after 12-31-81. The transitional rule provides that, for purposes of the 1954 Code, any amount allowed as a deduction under section 220 of the Code (as in effect before its repeal by P.L. 97-34) shall be treated as if it were allowed by section 219 of the Code.

P.L. 97-34, §311(c)(2):

Amended Code Sec. 402(e)(4)(J) by adding at the end a new sentence. **Effective** for tax years beginning after 12-31-81. For the transitional rule, see the amendment note at P.L. 97-34, §311(b)(2), above.

• 1978, Revenue Act of 1978 (P.L. 95-600)

P.L. 95-600, §101(d)(1):

Amended Code Sec. 402(e)(1) by striking out "$2,200" and inserting in lieu thereof "$2,300". **Effective** for tax years beginning after 12-31-78.

• 1977, Tax Reduction and Simplification Act of 1977 (P.L. 95-30)

P.L. 95-30, §102(b)(4):

Amended subparagraph (C) of Code Sec. 402(e)(1) by striking out "amount equal to one-tenth of the excess of" and inserting in lieu thereof "amount equal to $2,200 plus one-tenth of the excess of". **Effective** for tax years beginning after 12-31-76.

P.L. 94-455, §1402(b)(1)(C):

Substituted "9 months" for "6 months" in Code Sec. 402(e)(4)(L). **Effective** for tax years beginning in 1977.

P.L. 94-455, §1402(b)(2):

Substituted "1 year" for "9 months" in Code Sec. 402(e)(4)(L). **Effective** for tax years beginning after 12-31-77.

P.L. 94-455, §1512(a):

Added Code Sec. 402(e)(4)(L). **Effective** for distributions and payments made after 12-31-75, in tax years beginning after such date.

P.L. 94-455, §1901(a)(57)(C):

Substituted "Except for purposes of subsection (a)(2) and section 403(a)(2)," for "For purposes of this subparagraph," in the beginning of the third sentence of Code Sec. 402(e)(4)(A). **Effective** with respect to distributions or payments made after 12-31-73, in tax years beginning after such date.

P.L. 94-455, §1906(b)(13)(A):

Amended the 1954 Code by substituting "Secretary" for "Secretary or his delegate" each place it appeared. **Effective** 2-1-77.

• 1974, Employee Retirement Income Security Act of 1974 (P.L. 93-406)

P.L. 93-406, §2005(a):

Amended Code Sec. 402(e). **Effective** with respect to distributions or payments made after 12-31-73, in tax years beginning after such date. Prior to amendment, Code Sec. 402(e) read as follows:

"(e) Certain Plan Terminations.—For purposes of subsection (a)(2), distributions made after December 31, 1953, and before January 1, 1955, as a result of the complete termination of a stock bonus, pension, or profit-sharing plan of an employer which is a corporation, if the termination of the plan is incident to the complete liquidation, occurring before the date of enactment of this title, of the corporation, whether or not such liquidation is incident to a reorganization as defined in section 368(a), shall be considered to be distributions on account of separation from service."

[Sec. 402(f)]

(f) WRITTEN EXPLANATION TO RECIPIENTS OF DISTRIBUTIONS ELIGIBLE FOR ROLLOVER TREATMENT.—

(1) IN GENERAL.—The plan administrator of any plan shall, within a reasonable period of time before making an eligible rollover distribution, provide a written explanation to the recipient—

(A) of the provisions under which the recipient may have the distribution directly transferred to an eligible retirement plan and that the automatic distribution by direct transfer applies to certain distributions in accordance with section 401(a)(31)(B),

(B) of the provision which requires the withholding of tax on the distribution if it is not directly transferred to an eligible retirement plan,

(C) of the provisions under which the distribution will not be subject to tax if transferred to an eligible retirement plan within 60 days after the date on which the recipient received the distribution,

(D) if applicable, of the provisions of subsections (d) and (e) of this section, and

(E) of the provisions under which distributions from the eligible retirement plan receiving the distribution may be subject to restrictions and tax consequences which are different from those applicable to distributions from the plan making such distribution.

(2) DEFINITIONS.—For purposes of this subsection—

(A) ELIGIBLE ROLLOVER DISTRIBUTION.—The term "eligible rollover distribution" has the same meaning as when used in subsection (c) of this section, paragraph (4) of section 403(a), subparagraph (A) of section 403(b)(8), or subparagraph (A) of section 457(e)(16). Such term shall include any distribution to a designated beneficiary which would be treated as an eligible rollover distribution by reason of subsection (c)(11), or section 403(a)(4)(B), 403(b)(8)(B), or 457(e)(16)(B), if the requirements of subsection (c)(11) were satisfied.

(B) ELIGIBLE RETIREMENT PLAN.—The term "eligible retirement plan" has the meaning given such term by subsection (c)(8)(B).

Amendments

• 2008, Worker, Retiree, and Employer Recovery Act of 2008 (P.L. 110-458)

P.L. 110-458, §108(f)(2)(A):

Amended Code Sec. 402(f)(2)(A) by adding at the end a new sentence. **Effective** with respect to plan years beginning after 12-31-2009.

• 2006, Pension Protection Act of 2006 (P.L. 109-280)

P.L. 109-280, §811, provides:

SEC. 811. PENSIONS AND INDIVIDUAL RETIREMENT ARRANGEMENT PROVISIONS OF ECONOMIC GROWTH AND TAX RELIEF RECONCILIATION ACT OF 2001 MADE PERMANENT.

Title IX of the Economic Growth and Tax Relief Reconciliation Act of 2001 [P.L. 107-16] shall not apply to the provisions of, and amendments made by, subtitles A through F of title VI [§§601-666]of such Act (relating to pension and individual retirement arrangement provisions).

P.L. 109-280, §1102(a)(1)(B) and (3), provides:

(B) MODIFICATION OF REGULATIONS.—The Secretary of the Treasury shall modify the regulations under sections 402(f), 411(a)(11), and 417 of the Internal Revenue Code of 1986 by substituting "180 days" for "90 days" each place it appears in Treasury Regulations sections 1.402(f)-1, 1.411(a)-11(c), and 1.417(e)-1(b).

(3) EFFECTIVE DATE.—The amendments and modifications made or required by this subsection shall apply to years beginning after December 31, 2006.

• 2005, Katrina Emergency Tax Relief Act of 2005 (P.L. 109-73)

P.L. 109-73, §101(f)(1) [repealed by P.L. 109-135, §201(b)(4)(A)], provides:

(1) EXEMPTION OF DISTRIBUTIONS FROM TRUSTEE TO TRUSTEE TRANSFER AND WITHHOLDING RULES.—For purposes of sections 401(a)(31), 402(f), and 3405 of such Code, qualified Hurricane Katrina distributions shall not be treated as eligible rollover distributions.

• 2001, Economic Growth and Tax Relief Reconciliation Act of 2001 (P.L. 107-16)

P.L. 107-16, §641(c):

Amended Code Sec. 402(f)(1) by striking "and" at the end of subparagraph (C), by striking the period at the end of subparagraph (D) and inserting ", and", and by adding at the end a new subparagraph (E). **Effective**, generally, for distributions after 12-31-2001. For a special rule, see Act Sec. 641(f)(3), below.

P.L. 107-16, §641(e)(4):

Amended Code Sec. 402(f)(2)(A) by striking "or paragraph (4) of section 403(a)" and inserting ", paragraph (4) of section 403(a), subparagraph (A) of section 403(b)(8), or subparagraph (A) of section 457(e)(16)". **Effective**, generally, for distributions after 12-31-2001. For a special rule, see Act Sec. 641(f)(3), below.

P.L. 107-16, §641(e)(5):

Amended Code Sec. 402(f)(1) by striking "from an eligible retirement plan" after "rollover distribution". **Effective**, generally, for distributions after 12-31-2001. For a special rule, see Act Sec. 641(f)(3), below.

P.L. 107-16, §641(e)(6):

Amended Code Sec. 402(f)(1)(A) and (B) by striking "another eligible retirement plan" and inserting "an eligible retirement plan". **Effective**, generally, for distributions after 12-31-2001. For a special rule, see Act Sec. 641(f)(3), below.

P.L. 107-16, §641(f)(3), provides:

(3) SPECIAL RULE.—Notwithstanding any other provision of law, subsections (h)(3) and (h)(5) of section 1122 of the Tax Reform Act of 1986 shall not apply to any distribution from an eligible retirement plan (as defined in clause (iii) or (iv) of section 402(c)(8)(B) of the Internal Revenue Code of 1986) on behalf of an individual if there was a rollover to such plan on behalf of such individual which is permitted solely by reason of any amendment made by this section.

P.L. 107-16, §657(b):

Amended Code Sec. 402(f)(1)(A) by inserting "and that the automatic distribution by direct transfer applies to certain distributions in accordance with section 401(a)(31)(B)" before the comma at the end. **Effective** for distributions made after final regulations implementing Act Sec. 657(c)(2)(A) are prescribed.

P.L. 107-16, §657(c)(2), provides:

(2) REGULATIONS.—

(A) AUTOMATIC ROLLOVER SAFE HARBOR.—Not later than 3 years after the date of enactment of this Act, the Secretary of Labor shall prescribe regulations providing for safe harbors under which the designation of an institution and investment of funds in accordance with section 401(a)(31)(B) of the Internal Revenue Code of 1986 is deemed to satisfy the fiduciary requirements of section 404(a) of the Employee Retirement Income Security Act of 1974 (29 U.S.C. 1104(a)).

(B) USE OF LOW-COST INDIVIDUAL RETIREMENT PLANS.—The Secretary of the Treasury and the Secretary of Labor may provide, and shall give consideration to providing, special relief with respect to the use of low-cost individual retirement plans for purposes of transfers under section 401(a)(31)(B) of the Internal Revenue Code of 1986 and for other uses that promote the preservation of assets for retirement income purposes.

P.L. 107-16, §901(a)-(b), provides [but see P.L. 109-280, §811, above]:

SEC. 901. SUNSET OF PROVISIONS OF ACT.

(a) IN GENERAL.—All provisions of, and amendments made by, this Act shall not apply—

(1) to taxable, plan, or limitation years beginning after December 31, 2010, or

(2) in the case of title V, to estates of decedents dying, gifts made, or generation skipping transfers, after December 31, 2010.

(b) APPLICATION OF CERTAIN LAWS.—The Internal Revenue Code of 1986 and the Employee Retirement Income Security Act of 1974 shall be applied and administered to years, estates, gifts, and transfers described in subsection (a) as if the provisions and amendments described in subsection (a) had never been enacted.

• 1992, Unemployment Compensation Amendments of 1992 (P.L. 102-318)

P.L. 102-318, §521(a):

Amended Code Sec. 402(f). **Effective** for distributions after 12-31-92. Prior to amendment, Code Sec. 402(f) read as follows:

(f) WRITTEN EXPLANATION TO RECIPIENTS OF DISTRIBUTIONS ELIGIBLE FOR ROLLOVER TREATMENT.—

(1) IN GENERAL.—The plan administrator of any plan shall, when making an eligible rollover distribution, provide a written explanation to the recipient—

(A) of the provisions under which such distribution will not be subject to tax if transferred to an eligible retirement plan within 60 days after the date on which the recipient received the distribution, and

(B) if applicable, the provisions of subsections (a)(2) and (e) of this section.

(2) DEFINITIONS.—For purposes of this subsection—

(A) ELIGIBLE ROLLOVER DISTRIBUTION.—The term "eligible rollover distribution" means any distribution any portion of which may be excluded from gross income under subsection (a)(5) of this section or subsection (a)(4) of section 403 if transferred to an eligible retirement plan in accordance with the requirements of such subsection.

(B) ELIGIBLE RETIREMENT PLAN.—The term "eligible retirement plan" has the meaning given such term by subsection (a)(5)(E)(iv).

• 1988, Technical and Miscellaneous Revenue Act of 1988 (P.L. 100-647)

P.L. 100-647, §1018(t)(8)(C):

Amended Code Sec. 402(f)(1) by striking out "a eligible" and inserting in lieu thereof "an eligible". **Effective** as if included in the provision of P.L. 99-514 to which it relates.

• 1986, Tax Reform Act of 1986 (P.L. 99-514)

P.L. 99-514, §1898(e)(1):

Amended Code Sec. 402(f)(1) by striking out "qualifying rollover distribution" and inserting in lieu thereof "eligible rollover distribution". **Effective** as if included in the provision of P.L. 98-397 to which it relates.

P.L. 99-514, §1898(e)(2):

Amended Code Sec. 402(f)(2). **Effective** as if included in the provision of P.L. 98-397 to which it relates. Prior to amendment, Code Sec. 402(f)(2) read as follows:

(2) DEFINITIONS.—For purposes of this subsection, the terms "qualifying rollover distribution" and "eligible retirement plan" have the respective meanings given such terms by subsection (a)(5)(E).

• 1984, Retirement Equity Act of 1984 (P.L. 98-397)

P.L. 98-397, §207(a):

Amended Code Sec. 402 by adding at the end thereof new subsection (f). **Effective** for distributions after 12-31-84. Special rules appear in the notes for P.L. 98-397 following Code Sec. 401(a).

[Sec. 402(g)]

(g) LIMITATION ON EXCLUSION FOR ELECTIVE DEFERRALS.—

(1) IN GENERAL.—

(A) LIMITATION.—Notwithstanding subsections (e)(3) and (h)(1)(B), the elective deferrals of any individual for any taxable year shall be included in such individual's gross income to the extent the amount of such deferrals for the taxable year exceeds the applicable dollar amount. The preceding sentence shall not apply to the portion of such excess as does not exceed the designated Roth contributions of the individual for the taxable year.

(B) APPLICABLE DOLLAR AMOUNT.—For purposes of subparagraph (A), the applicable dollar amount shall be the amount determined in accordance with the following table:

For taxable years beginning in calendar year:	*The applicable dollar amount:*
2002	$11,000
2003	$12,000
2004	$13,000
2005	$14,000
2006 or thereafter	$15,000.

(C) CATCH-UP CONTRIBUTIONS.—In addition to subparagraph (A), in the case of an eligible participant (as defined in section 414(v)), gross income shall not include elective deferrals in excess of the applicable dollar amount under subparagraph (B) to the extent that the amount of such elective deferrals does not exceed the applicable dollar amount under section 414(v)(2)(B)(i) for the taxable year (without regard to the treatment of the elective deferrals by an applicable employer plan under section 414(v)).

(2) DISTRIBUTION OF EXCESS DEFERRALS.—

(A) IN GENERAL.—If any amount (hereinafter in this paragraph referred to as "excess deferrals") is included in the gross income of an individual under paragraph (1) (or would be included but for the last sentence thereof) for any taxable year—

(i) not later than the 1st March 1 following the close of the taxable year, the individual may allocate the amount of such excess deferrals among the plans under which the deferrals were made and may notify each such plan of the portion allocated to it, and

(ii) not later than the 1st April 15 following the close of the taxable year, each such plan may distribute to the individual the amount allocated to it under clause (i) (and any income allocable to such amount through the end of such taxable year).

The distribution described in clause (ii) may be made notwithstanding any other provision of law.

(B) TREATMENT OF DISTRIBUTION UNDER SECTION 401(k).—Except to the extent provided under rules prescribed by the Secretary, notwithstanding the distribution of any portion of an excess deferral from a plan under subparagraph (A)(ii), such portion shall, for purposes of applying section 401(k)(3)(A)(ii), be treated as an employer contribution.

(C) TAXATION OF DISTRIBUTION.—In the case of a distribution to which subparagraph (A) applies—

(i) except as provided in clause (ii), such distribution shall not be included in gross income, and

(ii) any income on the excess deferral shall, for purposes of this chapter, be treated as earned and received in the taxable year in which such income is distributed.

No tax shall be imposed under section 72(t) on any distribution described in the preceding sentence.

(D) PARTIAL DISTRIBUTIONS.—If a plan distributes only a portion of any excess deferral and income allocable thereto, such portion shall be treated as having been distributed ratably from the excess deferral and the income.

(3) ELECTIVE DEFERRALS.—For purposes of this subsection, the term "elective deferrals" means, with respect to any taxable year, the sum of—

(A) any employer contribution under a qualified cash or deferred arrangement (as defined in section 401(k)) to the extent not includible in gross income for the taxable year under subsection (e)(3) (determined without regard to this subsection),

(B) any employer contribution to the extent not includible in gross income for the taxable year under subsection (h)(1)(B) (determined without regard to this subsection),

(C) any employer contribution to purchase an annuity contract under section 403(b) under a salary reduction agreement (within the meaning of section 3121(a)(5)(D)), and

(D) any elective employer contribution under section 408(p)(2)(A)(i).

An employer contribution shall not be treated as an elective deferral described in subparagraph (C) if under the salary reduction agreement such contribution is made pursuant to a one-time irrevocable election made by the employee at the time of initial eligibility to participate in the agreement or is made pursuant to a similar arrangement involving a one-time irrevocable election specified in regulations.

(4) COST-OF-LIVING ADJUSTMENT.—In the case of taxable years beginning after December 31, 2006, the Secretary shall adjust the $15,000 amount under paragraph (1)(B) at the same time and in the same manner as under section 415(d), except that the base period shall be the calendar quarter beginning July 1, 2005, and any increase under this paragraph which is not a multiple of $500 shall be rounded to the next lowest multiple of $500.

(5) DISREGARD OF COMMUNITY PROPERTY LAWS.—This subsection shall be applied without regard to community property laws.

(6) COORDINATION WITH SECTION 72.—For purposes of applying section 72, any amount includible in gross income for any taxable year under this subsection but which is not distributed from the plan during such taxable year shall not be treated as investment in the contract.

(7) SPECIAL RULE FOR CERTAIN ORGANIZATIONS.—

(A) IN GENERAL.—In the case of a qualified employee of a qualified organization, with respect to employer contributions described in paragraph (3)(C) made by such organization, the limitation of paragraph (1) for any taxable year shall be increased by whichever of the following is the least:

(i) $3,000,

(ii) $15,000 reduced by the sum of—

(I) the amounts not included in gross income for prior taxable years by reason of this paragraph, plus

(II) the aggregate amount of designated Roth contributions (as defined in section 402A(c)) permitted for prior taxable years by reason of this paragraph, or

(iii) the excess of $5,000 multiplied by the number of years of service of the employee with the qualified organization over the employer contributions described in paragraph (3) made by the organization on behalf of such employee for prior taxable years (determined in the manner prescribed by the Secretary).

(B) QUALIFIED ORGANIZATION.—For purposes of this paragraph, the term "qualified organization" means any educational organization, hospital, home health service agency, health and welfare service agency, church, or convention or association of churches. Such term includes any organization described in section 414(e)(3)(B)(ii). Terms used in this subparagraph shall have the same meaning as when used in section 415(c)(4) (as in effect before the enactment of the Economic Growth and Tax Relief Reconciliation Act of 2001).

(C) QUALIFIED EMPLOYEE.—For purposes of this paragraph, the term "qualified employee" means any employee who has completed 15 years of service with the qualified organization.

(D) YEARS OF SERVICE.—For purposes of this paragraph, the term "years of service" has the meaning given such term by section 403(b).

(8) MATCHING CONTRIBUTIONS ON BEHALF OF SELF-EMPLOYED INDIVIDUALS NOT TREATED AS ELECTIVE EMPLOYER CONTRIBUTIONS.—Except as provided in section 401(k)(3)(D)(ii), any matching contribution described in section 401(m)(4)(A) which is made on behalf of a self-employed individual (as defined in section 401(c)) shall not be treated as an elective employer contribution under a qualified cash or deferred arrangement (as defined in section 401(k)) for purposes of this title.

Amendments

• 2008, Worker, Retiree, and Employer Recovery Act of 2008 (P.L. 110-458)

P.L. 110-458, §109(b)(3):

Amended Code Sec. 402(g)(2)(A)(ii) by inserting "through the end of such taxable year" after "such amount". **Effective** as if included in the provision of the 2006 Act to which the amendment relates [**effective** for plan years beginning after 12-31-2007.—CCH].

• 2007, Tax Technical Corrections Act of 2007 (P.L. 110-172)

P.L. 110-172, §8(a)(1):

Amended Code Sec. 402(g)(7)(A)(ii)(II) by striking "for prior taxable years" and inserting "permitted for prior taxable years by reason of this paragraph". **Effective** as if included in the provision of the Economic Growth and Tax Relief Reconciliation Act of 2001 (P.L. 107-16) to which it relates [**effective** for tax years beginning after 12-31-2005.—CCH].

• 2006, Pension Protection Act of 2006 (P.L. 109-280)

P.L. 109-280, §811, provides:

SEC. 811. PENSIONS AND INDIVIDUAL RETIREMENT ARRANGEMENT PROVISIONS OF ECONOMIC GROWTH AND TAX RELIEF RECONCILIATION ACT OF 2001 MADE PERMANENT.

Title IX of the Economic Growth and Tax Relief Reconciliation Act of 2001 [P.L. 107-16] shall not apply to the provisions of, and amendments made by, subtitles A through F of title VI [§§601-666]of such Act (relating to pension and individual retirement arrangement provisions).

• 2005, Gulf Opportunity Zone Act of 2005 (P.L. 109-135)

P.L. 109-135, §407(a)(1):

Amended Code Sec. 402(g)(7)(A)(ii). **Effective** as if included in the provision of the Economic Growth and Tax Relief Reconciliation Act of 2001 (P.L. 107-16) to which it relates [**effective** for tax years beginning after 12-31-2005.—CCH]. Prior to amendment, Code Sec. 402(g)(7)(A)(ii) read as follows:

(ii) $15,000 reduced by amounts not included in gross income for prior taxable years by reason of this paragraph, or

P.L. 109-135, §407(a)(2):

Amended Code Sec. 402(g)(1)(A) by inserting "to" after "shall not apply". **Effective** as if included in the provision of the Economic Growth and Tax Relief Reconciliation Act of 2001 (P.L. 107-16) to which it relates [**effective** for tax years beginning after 12-31-2005.—CCH].

• 2002, Job Creation and Worker Assistance Act of 2002 (P.L. 107-147)

P.L. 107-147, §411(o)(1):

Amended Code Sec. 402(g)(1) by adding at the end a new subparagraph (C). **Effective** as if included in the provision of P.L. 107-16 to which it relates [**effective** for contributions in tax years beginning after 12-31-2001.—CCH].

P.L. 107-147, §411(p)(6):

Amended Code Sec. 402(g)(7)(B) by striking "2001." and inserting "2001).". **Effective** as if included in the provision of P.L. 107-16 to which it relates [**effective** for years beginning after 12-31-2001.—CCH].

• 2001, Economic Growth and Tax Relief Reconciliation Act of 2001 (P.L. 107-16)

P.L. 107-16, §611(d)(1):

Amended Code Sec. 402(g)(1). **Effective** for years beginning after 12-31-2001. For a special rule, see Act Sec. 611(i)(3), below. Prior to amendment, Code Sec. 402(g)(1) read as follows:

(1) IN GENERAL.—Notwithstanding subsections (e)(3) and (h)(1)(B), the elective deferrals of any individual for any taxable year shall be included in such individual's gross income to the extent the amount of such deferrals for the taxable year exceeds $7,000.

P.L. 107-16, §611(d)(2):

Amended Code Sec. 402(g)(5). **Effective** for years beginning after 12-31-2001. For a special rule, see Act Sec. 611(i)(3), below. Prior to amendment, Code Sec. 402(g)(5) read as follows:

(5) COST-OF-LIVING ADJUSTMENT.—The Secretary shall adjust the $7,000 amount under paragraph (1) at the same time and in the same manner as under section 415(d); except that any increase under this paragraph which is not a multiple of $500 shall be rounded to the next lowest multiple of $500.

P.L. 107-16, §611(d)(3)(A):

Amended Code Sec. 402(g), as amended by Act Sec. 611(d)(1) and (2), by striking paragraph (4) and redesignating paragraphs (5), (6), (7), (8), and (9) as paragraphs (4), (5), (6), (7), and (8), respectively. **Effective** for years beginning after 12-31-2001. For a special rule, see Act Sec. 611(i)(3), below. Prior to being stricken, Code Sec. 402(g)(4) read as follows:

(4) INCREASE IN LIMIT FOR AMOUNTS CONTRIBUTED UNDER SECTION 403(b) CONTRACTS.—The limitation under paragraph (1) shall be increased (but not to an amount in excess of $9,500) by the amount of any employer contributions for the taxable year described in paragraph (3)(C).

P.L. 107-16, §611(i)(3) (as added by P.L. 107-147, §411(j)(3)), provides:

(3) SPECIAL RULE.—In the case of plan that, on June 7, 2001, incorporated by reference the limitation of section 415(b)(1)(A) of the Internal Revenue Code of 1986, section 411(d)(6) of such Code and section 204(g)(1) of the Employee Retirement Income Security Act of 1974 do not apply to a plan amendment that—

(A) is adopted on or before June 30, 2002,

(B) reduces benefits to the level that would have applied without regard to the amendments made by subsection (a) of this section, and

(C) is effective no earlier than the years described in paragraph (2).

P.L. 107-16, §617(b)(1)-(2):

Amended Code Sec. 402(g) by adding at the end of paragraph (1)(A), as added by Act Sec. 201(c)(1) [611(d)(1)], a new sentence; and by inserting "(or would be included but for the last sentence thereof)" after "paragraph (1)" in paragraph (2)(A). **Effective** for tax years beginning after 12-31-2005.

P.L. 107-16, §632(a)(3)(G):

Amended Code Sec. 402(g)(7)(B), as redesignated by Act Sec. 611(c)(3)[611(d)(3)(A)], by inserting "(as in effect before the enactment of the Economic Growth and Tax Relief Reconciliation Act of 2001[)]" before the period at the end. **Effective** for years beginning after 12-31-2001.

P.L. 107-16, §901(a)-(b), provides [but see P.L. 109-280, §811, above]:

SEC. 901. SUNSET OF PROVISIONS OF ACT.

(a) IN GENERAL.—All provisions of, and amendments made by, this Act shall not apply—

(1) to taxable, plan, or limitation years beginning after December 31, 2010, or

(2) in the case of title V, to estates of decedents dying, gifts made, or generation skipping transfers, after December 31, 2010.

(b) APPLICATION OF CERTAIN LAWS.—The Internal Revenue Code of 1986 and the Employee Retirement Income Security Act of 1974 shall be applied and administered to years, estates, gifts, and transfers described in subsection (a) as if the provisions and amendments described in subsection (a) had never been enacted.

• 1997, Taxpayer Relief Act of 1997 (P.L. 105-34)

P.L. 105-34, §1501(a):

Amended Code Sec. 402(g) by adding at the end a new paragraph (9). **Effective** for years beginning after 12-31-97.

• 1996, Small Business Job Protection Act of 1996 (P.L. 104-188)

P.L. 104-188, §1421(b)(9)(B):

Amended Code Sec. 402(g)(3) by striking "and" at the end of subparagraph (B), by striking the period at the end of subparagraph (C) and inserting ", and", and by adding after subparagraph (C) a new subparagraph (D). **Effective** for tax years beginning after 12-31-96.

P.L. 104-188, §1704(t)(68):

Amended Code Sec. 402(g)(3)(A) by striking "subsection (a)(8)" and inserting "subsection (e)(3)". **Effective** 8-20-96.

• 1994, Uruguay Round Agreements Act (P.L. 103-465)

P.L. 103-465, §732(c):

Amended Code Sec. 402(g)(5) by inserting before the period "; except that any increase under this paragraph which is not a multiple of $500 shall be rounded to the next lowest multiple of $500". **Effective** for years beginning after 12-31-94. For a special rule, see Act Sec. 732(e)(2), below.

P.L. 103-465, §732(e)(2), provides:

(2) ROUNDING NOT TO RESULT IN DECREASES.—The amendments made by this section providing for the rounding of indexed amounts shall not apply to any year to the extent the rounding would require the indexed amount to be reduced below the amount in effect for years beginning in 1994.

• 1992, Unemployment Compensation Amendments of 1992 (P.L. 102-318)

P.L. 102-318, §521(b)(9):

Amended Code Sec. 402(g)(1) by striking "subsections (a)(8)" and inserting "subsections (e)(3)". **Effective** for distributions after 12-31-92.

• 1989, Omnibus Budget Reconciliation Act of 1989 (P.L. 101-239)

P.L. 101-239, §7811(g)(2):

Amended Code Sec. 402(g)(3) by inserting "involving a one-time irrevocable election" after "similar arrangement" in the last sentence. **Effective** as if included in the provision of P.L. 100-647 to which it relates.

• 1988, Technical and Miscellaneous Revenue Act of 1988 (P.L. 100-647)

P.L. 100-647, §1011(c)(1)(A)-(C):

Amended Code Sec. 402(g)(2)(C) by striking out "(and no tax shall be imposed under section 72(t))" in clause (i) after "gross income", by striking out "such excess deferral is made" in clause (ii) and inserting in lieu thereof "such income is distributed", and by inserting at the end thereof a new flush sentence. **Effective** as if included in the provision of P.L. 99-514 to which it relates.

P.L. 100-647, §1011(c)(2):

Amended Code Sec. 402(g)(2) by striking out "Required distribution" in the heading thereof and inserting in lieu thereof "Distribution". **Effective** as if included in the provision of P.L. 99-514 to which it relates.

P.L. 100-647, §1011(c)(3):

Amended Code Sec. 402(g)(2) by adding at the end thereof new subparagraph (D). **Effective** as if included in the provision of P.L. 99-514 to which it relates.

P.L. 100-647, §1011(c)(4):

Amended Code Sec. 402(g)(3) by striking out "paragraph" and inserting in lieu thereof "subsection". **Effective** as if included in the provision of P.L. 99-514 to which it relates.

P.L. 100-647, §1011(c)(5)(A):

Amended Code Sec. 402(g)(8)(A)(iii) by inserting "(determined in the manner prescribed by the Secretary)" after "taxable years". **Effective** as if included in the provision of P.L. 99-514 to which it relates.

P.L. 100-647, §1011(c)(5)(B):

Amended Code Sec. 402(g)(8) by adding at the end thereof new subparagraph (D). **Effective** as if included in the provision of P.L. 99-514 to which it relates.

P.L. 100-647, §1011(c)(10), provides:

(10) Notwithstanding any other provision of law, a plan may incorporate by reference the dollar limitation under section 402(g) of the Internal Revenue Code of 1986. **Effective** as if included in the provision of P.L. 99-514 to which it relates.

P.L. 100-647, §1011(c)(11):

Amended Code Sec. 402(g)(3) by adding at the end thereof a new sentence. **Effective** as if included in the provision of P.L. 99-514 to which it relates.

• 1986, Tax Reform Act of 1986 (P.L. 99-514)

P.L. 99-514, §1105(a):

Amended Code Sec. 402 by adding at the end thereof new subsection (g). **Effective,** generally, for tax years beginning after 12-31-86. However, see Act Sec. 1105(c)(2)-(6), below.

P.L. 99-514, §1105(c)(2)-(6), as amended by P.L. 100-647, §1011(c)(8)-(9), provides:

(2) DEFERRALS UNDER COLLECTIVE BARGAINING AGREEMENTS.—In the case of a plan maintained pursuant to 1 or more collective bargaining agreements between employee representatives and 1 or more employers ratified before March 1, 1986, the amendment made by subsection (a) shall not apply to contributions made pursuant to such an agreement for taxable years beginning before the earlier of—

(A) the date on which such agreement terminates (determined without regard to any extension thereof after February 28, 1986), or

(B) January 1, 1989.

Such contributions shall be taken into account for purposes of applying the amendment made by this section to other plans.

(3) DISTRIBUTIONS MADE BEFORE PLAN AMENDMENT.—

(A) IN GENERAL.—If a plan amendment is required to allow the plan to make any distribution described in section 402(g)(2)(A)(ii) of the Internal Revenue Code of 1986, any such distribution which is made before the close of the 1st plan year for which such amendment is required to be in effect under section 1140 shall be treated as made in accordance with the provisions of such plan.

(B) DISTRIBUTIONS PURSUANT TO MODEL AMENDMENT.—

(i) SECRETARY TO PRESCRIBE AMENDMENT.—The Secretary of the Treasury or his delegate shall prescribe an amendment which allows a plan to make any distribution described in section 402(g)(2)(A)(ii) of such Code.

(ii) ADOPTION BY PLAN.—If a plan adopts the amendment prescribed under clause (i) and makes a distribution in accordance with such amendment, such distribution shall be treated as made in accordance with the provisions of the plan.

(4) SPECIAL RULE FOR TAXABLE YEARS OF PARTNERSHIPS WHICH INCLUDE JANUARY 1, 1987.—In the case of the taxable year of any partnership which begins before January 1, 1987, and ends after January 1, 1987, elective deferrals (within the meaning of section 402(g)(3) of the Internal Revenue Code of 1986) made on behalf of a partner for such taxable year shall, for purposes of section 402(g)(3) of such Code, be treated as having been made ratably during such taxable year.

(5) CASH OR DEFERRED ARRANGEMENT.—The amendments made by this section shall not apply to employer contributions made during 1987 and attributable to services performed during 1986 under a qualified cash or deferred arrangement (as defined in section 401(k) of the Internal Revenue Code of 1986) if, under the terms of such arrangement as in effect on August 16, 1986—

(A) the employee makes an election with respect to such contribution before January 1, 1987, and

(B) the employer identifies the amount of such contribution before January 1, 1987.

(6) REPORTING REQUIREMENTS.—The amendments made by subsection (b) shall apply to calendar years beginning after December 31, 1986.

[Sec. 402(h)]

(h) SPECIAL RULES FOR SIMPLIFIED EMPLOYEE PENSIONS.—For purposes of this chapter—

(1) IN GENERAL.—Except as provided in paragraph (2), contributions made by an employer on behalf of an employee to an individual retirement plan pursuant to a simplified employee pension (as defined in section 408(k))—

(A) shall not be treated as distributed or made available to the employee or as contributions made by the employee, and

(B) if such contributions are made pursuant to an arrangement under section 408(k)(6) under which an employee may elect to have the employer make contributions to the simplified employer pension on behalf of the employee, shall not be treated as distributed or made available or as contributions made by the employee merely because the simplified employee pension includes provisions for such election.

(2) LIMITATIONS ON EMPLOYER CONTRIBUTIONS.—Contributions made by an employer to a simplified employee pension with respect to an employee for any year shall be treated as distributed or made available to such employee and as contributions made by the employee to the extent such contributions exceed the lesser of—

(A) 25 percent of the compensation (within the meaning of section 414(s)) from such employer includible in the employee's gross income for the year (determined without regard to the employer contributions to the simplified employee pension), or

(B) the limitation in effect under section 415(c)(1)(A), reduced in the case of any highly compensated employee (within the meaning of section 414(q)) by the amount taken into account with respect to such employee under section 408(k)(3)(D).

(3) DISTRIBUTIONS.—Any amount paid or distributed out of an individual retirement plan pursuant to a simplified employee pension shall be included in gross income by the payee or distributee, as the case may be, in accordance with the provisions of section 408(d).

Amendments

• 2006, Pension Protection Act of 2006 (P.L. 109-280)

P.L. 109-280, §811, provides:

SEC. 811. PENSIONS AND INDIVIDUAL RETIREMENT ARRANGEMENT PROVISIONS OF ECONOMIC GROWTH AND TAX RELIEF RECONCILIATION ACT OF 2001 MADE PERMANENT.

Title IX of the Economic Growth and Tax Relief Reconciliation Act of 2001 [P.L. 107-16] shall not apply to the provisions of, and amendments made by, subtitles A through F of title VI [§§601-666]of such Act (relating to pension and individual retirement arrangement provisions).

• 2002, Job Creation and Worker Assistance Act of 2002 (P.L. 107-147)

P.L. 107-147, §411(l)(3):

Amended Code Sec. 402(h)(2)(A) by striking "15 percent" and inserting "25 percent". **Effective** as if included in the provision of P.L. 107-16 to which it relates [**effective** for years beginning after 12-31-2001.—CCH].

• 2001, Economic Growth and Tax Relief Reconciliation Act of 2001 (P.L. 107-16)

P.L. 107-16, §901(a)-(b), provides [but see P.L. 109-280, §811, above]:

SEC. 901. SUNSET OF PROVISIONS OF ACT.

(a) IN GENERAL.—All provisions of, and amendments made by, this Act shall not apply—

(1) to taxable, plan, or limitation years beginning after December 31, 2010, or

(2) in the case of title V, to estates of decedents dying, gifts made, or generation skipping transfers, after December 31, 2010.

(b) APPLICATION OF CERTAIN LAWS.—The Internal Revenue Code of 1986 and the Employee Retirement Income Security Act of 1974 shall be applied and administered to years, estates, gifts, and transfers described in subsection (a) as if the provisions and amendments described in subsection (a) had never been enacted.

• 1986, Tax Reform Act of 1986 (P.L. 99-514)

P.L. 99-514, §1108(b):

Amended Code Sec. 402 by inserting at the end thereof new subsection (h). **Effective** for years beginning after 12-31-86.

[Sec. 402(i)]

(i) TREATMENT OF SELF-EMPLOYED INDIVIDUALS.—For purposes of this section, except as otherwise provided in subparagraph (A) of subsection (d)(4), the term "employee" includes a self-employed individual (as defined in section 401(c)(1)(B)) and the employer of such individual shall be the person treated as his employer under section 401(c)(4).

Amendments

• 1992, Unemployment Compensation Amendments of 1992 (P.L. 102-318)

P.L. 102-318, §521(b)(10):

Amended Code Sec. 402(i) by striking "subsection (e)(4)" and inserting "subsection (d)(4)". **Effective** for distributions after 12-31-92.

• 1988, Technical and Miscellaneous Revenue Act of 1988 (P.L. 100-647)

P.L. 100-647, §1011(c)(6)(A):

Amended Code Sec. 402 by redesignating subsection (g), as added by P.L. 99-514, §1852(b)(3)(A), as subsection (i). **Effective** as if included in the provision of P.L. 99-514 to which it relates.

• 1986, Tax Reform Act of 1986 (P.L. 99-514)

P.L. 99-514, §1852(b)(3)(A):

Amended Code Sec. 402 by adding at the end thereof new subsection (g). **Effective** as if included in the provision of P.L. 98-369 to which it relates.

[Sec. 402(j)]

(j) EFFECT OF DISPOSITION OF STOCK BY PLAN ON NET UNREALIZED APPRECIATION.—

(1) IN GENERAL.—For purposes of subsection (e)(4), in the case of any transaction to which this subsection applies, the determination of net unrealized appreciation shall be made without regard to such transaction.

(2) TRANSACTION TO WHICH SUBSECTION APPLIES.—This subsection shall apply to any transaction in which—

(A) the plan trustee exchanges the plan's securities of the employer corporation for other such securities, or

(B) the plan trustee disposes of securities of the employer corporation and uses the proceeds of such disposition to acquire securities of the employer corporation within 90 days (or such longer period as the Secretary may prescribe), except that this subparagraph shall not apply to any employee with respect to whom a distribution of money was made during the period after such disposition and before such acquisition.

Amendments

• 1992, Unemployment Compensation Amendments of 1992 (P.L. 102-318)

P.L. 102-318, §521(b)(11):

Amended Code Sec. 402(j) by striking "(a)(1) or (e)(4)(J)" and inserting "(e)(4)". **Effective** for distributions after 12-31-92.

• 1988, Technical and Miscellaneous Revenue Act of 1988 (P.L. 100-647)

P.L. 100-647, §1011(c)(6)(B):

Amended Code Sec. 402 by redesignating subsection (g), as added by P.L. 99-514, §1854(f)(2), as subsection (j). **Effective** as if included in the provision of P.L. 99-514 to which it relates.

• 1986, Tax Reform Act of 1986 (P.L. 99-514)

P.L. 99-514, §1854(f)(2):

Amended Code Sec. 402 by adding at the end thereof new subsection (g). **Effective** for any transaction occurring after 12-31-84, except that in the case of any transaction occurring before 10-22-86, the period under which proceeds are required to be invested under section 402(j) of the Internal Revenue Code of 1954 (as added by paragraph (2)) shall not end before the earlier of 1 year after the date of such transaction or 180 days after the date of the enactment of this Act [**effective** date amended by P.L. 100-647, §1011(c)(6)(C).—CCH.].

[Sec. 402(k)]

(k) TREATMENT OF SIMPLE RETIREMENT ACCOUNTS.—Rules similar to the rules of paragraphs (1) and (3) of subsection (h) shall apply to contributions and distributions with respect to a simple retirement account under section 408(p).

Amendments

• 1996, Small Business Job Protection Act of 1996 (P.L. 104-188)

P.L. 104-188, §1421(b)(3)(A):

Amended Code Sec. 402 by adding at the end a new subsection (k). **Effective** for tax years beginning after 12-31-96.

[Sec. 402(l)]

(l) DISTRIBUTIONS FROM GOVERNMENTAL PLANS FOR HEALTH AND LONG-TERM CARE INSURANCE.—

(1) IN GENERAL.—In the case of an employee who is an eligible retired public safety officer who makes the election described in paragraph (6) with respect to any taxable year of such employee, gross income of such employee for such taxable year does not include any distribution from an eligible retirement plan maintained by the employer described in paragraph (4)(B) to the extent that the aggregate amount of such distributions does not exceed the amount paid by such employee for qualified health insurance premiums for such taxable year.

(2) LIMITATION.—The amount which may be excluded from gross income for the taxable year by reason of paragraph (1) shall not exceed $3,000.

(3) DISTRIBUTIONS MUST OTHERWISE BE INCLUDIBLE.—

(A) IN GENERAL.—An amount shall be treated as a distribution for purposes of paragraph (1) only to the extent that such amount would be includible in gross income without regard to paragraph (1).

(B) APPLICATION OF SECTION 72.—Notwithstanding section 72, in determining the extent to which an amount is treated as a distribution for purposes of subparagraph (A), the aggregate amounts distributed from an eligible retirement plan in a taxable year (up to the amount excluded under paragraph (1)) shall be treated as includible in gross income (without regard to subparagraph (A)) to the extent that such amount does not exceed the aggregate amount which would have been so includible if all amounts to the credit of the eligible public safety officer in all eligible retirement plans maintained by the employer described in paragraph (4)(B) were distributed during such taxable year and all such plans were treated as 1 contract for purposes of determining under section 72 the aggregate amount which would have been so includible. Proper adjustments shall be made in applying section 72 to other distributions in such taxable year and subsequent taxable years.

(4) DEFINITIONS.—For purposes of this subsection—

(A) ELIGIBLE RETIREMENT PLAN.—For purposes of paragraph (1), the term "eligible retirement plan" means a governmental plan (within the meaning of section 414(d)) which is described in clause (iii), (iv), (v), or (vi) of subsection (c)(8)(B).

(B) ELIGIBLE RETIRED PUBLIC SAFETY OFFICER.—The term "eligible retired public safety officer" means an individual who, by reason of disability or attainment of normal retirement age, is separated from service as a public safety officer with the employer who maintains the eligible retirement plan from which distributions subject to paragraph (1) are made.

(C) PUBLIC SAFETY OFFICER.—The term "public safety officer" shall have the same meaning given such term by section 1204(9)(A) of the Omnibus Crime Control and Safe Streets Act of 1968 (42 U.S.C. 3796b(9)(A)).

(D) QUALIFIED HEALTH INSURANCE PREMIUMS.—The term "qualified health insurance premiums" means premiums for coverage for the eligible retired public safety officer, his spouse, and dependents (as defined in section 152), by an accident or health plan or qualified long-term care insurance contract (as defined in section 7702B(b)).

(5) SPECIAL RULES.—For purposes of this subsection—

(A) DIRECT PAYMENT TO INSURER REQUIRED.—Paragraph (1) shall only apply to a distribution if payment of the premiums is made directly to the provider of the accident or health plan or qualified long-term care insurance contract by deduction from a distribution from the eligible retirement plan.

(B) RELATED PLANS TREATED AS 1.—All eligible retirement plans of an employer shall be treated as a single plan.

(6) ELECTION DESCRIBED.—

(A) IN GENERAL.—For purposes of paragraph (1), an election is described in this paragraph if the election is made by an employee after separation from service with respect to amounts not distributed from an eligible retirement plan to have amounts from such plan distributed in order to pay for qualified health insurance premiums.

(B) SPECIAL RULE.—A plan shall not be treated as violating the requirements of section 401, or as engaging in a prohibited transaction for purposes of section 503(b), merely because it provides for an election with respect to amounts that are otherwise distributable under the plan or merely because of a distribution made pursuant to an election described in subparagraph (A).

(7) COORDINATION WITH MEDICAL EXPENSE DEDUCTION.—The amounts excluded from gross income under paragraph (1) shall not be taken into account under section 213.

(8) COORDINATION WITH DEDUCTION FOR HEALTH INSURANCE COSTS OF SELF-EMPLOYED INDIVIDUALS.—The amounts excluded from gross income under paragraph (1) shall not be taken into account under section 162(l).

Amendments

• 2008, Worker, Retiree, and Employer Recovery Act of 2008 (P.L. 110-458)

P.L. 110-458, §108(j)(1)(A)-(C):

Amended Code Sec. 402(l) in paragraph (1) by inserting "maintained by the employer described in paragraph (4)(B)" after "an eligible retirement plan", and by striking "of the employee, his spouse, or dependents (as defined in section 152)" after "premiums", in paragraph (4)(D) by inserting "(as defined in section 152)" after "dependents", and by striking "health insurance plan" and inserting "health plan", and in paragraph (5)(A) by striking "health insurance plan" and inserting "health plan". **Effective** as if included in the provision of the 2006 Act to which the amendment relates [**effective** for distributions in tax years beginning after 12-31-2006.—CCH].

P.L. 110-458, §108(j)(2):

Amended Code Sec. 402(l)(3)(B) by striking "all amounts distributed from all eligible retirement plans were treated as 1 contract for purposes of determining the inclusion of such distribution under section 72" and inserting "all amounts to the credit of the eligible public safety officer in all eligible retirement plans maintained by the employer described in paragraph (4)(B) were distributed during such taxable year and all such plans were treated as 1 contract for purposes of determining under section 72 the aggregate amount which would have been so includible". **Effective** as if included in the provision of the 2006 Act to which the amendment relates [**effective** for distributions in tax years beginning after 12-31-2006.—CCH].

• 2006, Pension Protection Act of 2006 (P.L. 109-280)

P.L. 109-280, §845(a):

Amended Code Sec. 402 by adding at the end a new subsection (l). **Effective** for distributions in tax years beginning after 12-31-2006.

[Sec. 402A]

SEC. 402A. OPTIONAL TREATMENT OF ELECTIVE DEFERRALS AS ROTH CONTRIBUTIONS.

[Sec. 402A(a)]

(a) GENERAL RULE.—If an applicable retirement plan includes a qualified Roth contribution program—

(1) any designated Roth contribution made by an employee pursuant to the program shall be treated as an elective deferral for purposes of this chapter, except that such contribution shall not be excludable from gross income, and

(2) such plan (and any arrangement which is part of such plan) shall not be treated as failing to meet any requirement of this chapter solely by reason of including such program.

[Sec. 402A(b)]

(b) QUALIFIED ROTH CONTRIBUTION PROGRAM.—For purposes of this section—

(1) IN GENERAL.—The term "qualified Roth contribution program" means a program under which an employee may elect to make designated Roth contributions in lieu of all or a portion of elective deferrals the employee is otherwise eligible to make under the applicable retirement plan.

(2) SEPARATE ACCOUNTING REQUIRED.—A program shall not be treated as a qualified Roth contribution program unless the applicable retirement plan—

(A) establishes separate accounts ("designated Roth account") for the designated Roth contributions of each employee and any earnings properly allocable to the contributions, and

(B) maintains separate recordkeeping with respect to each account.

[Sec. 402A(c)]

(c) DEFINITIONS AND RULES RELATING TO DESIGNATED ROTH CONTRIBUTIONS.—For purposes of this section—

(1) DESIGNATED ROTH CONTRIBUTION.—The term "designated Roth contribution" means any elective deferral which—

(A) is excludable from gross income of an employee without regard to this section, and

(B) the employee designates (at such time and in such manner as the Secretary may prescribe) as not being so excludable.

(2) DESIGNATION LIMITS.—The amount of elective deferrals which an employee may designate under paragraph (1) shall not exceed the excess (if any) of—

(A) the maximum amount of elective deferrals excludable from gross income of the employee for the taxable year (without regard to this section), over

(B) the aggregate amount of elective deferrals of the employee for the taxable year which the employee does not designate under paragraph (1).

(3) ROLLOVER CONTRIBUTIONS.—

(A) IN GENERAL.—A rollover contribution of any payment or distribution from a designated Roth account which is otherwise allowable under this chapter may be made only if the contribution is to—

(i) another designated Roth account of the individual from whose account the payment or distribution was made, or

(ii) a Roth IRA of such individual.

(B) COORDINATION WITH LIMIT.—Any rollover contribution to a designated Roth account under subparagraph (A) shall not be taken into account for purposes of paragraph (1).

(4) TAXABLE ROLLOVERS TO DESIGNATED ROTH ACCOUNTS.—

(A) IN GENERAL.—Notwithstanding sections 402(c), 403(b)(8), and 457(e)(16), in the case of any distribution to which this paragraph applies—

(i) there shall be included in gross income any amount which would be includible were it not part of a qualified rollover contribution,

(ii) section 72(t) shall not apply, and

(iii) unless the taxpayer elects not to have this clause apply, any amount required to be included in gross income for any taxable year beginning in 2010 by reason of this paragraph shall be so included ratably over the 2-taxable-year period beginning with the first taxable year beginning in 2011.

Any election under clause (iii) for any distributions during a taxable year may not be changed after the due date for such taxable year.

(B) DISTRIBUTIONS TO WHICH PARAGRAPH APPLIES.—In the case of an applicable retirement plan which includes a qualified Roth contribution program, this paragraph shall apply to a distribution from such plan other than from a designated Roth account which is contributed in a qualified rollover contribution (within the meaning of section 408A(e)) to the designated

Roth account maintained under such plan for the benefit of the individual to whom the distribution is made.

(C) COORDINATION WITH LIMIT.—Any distribution to which this paragraph applies shall not be taken into account for purposes of paragraph (1).

(D) OTHER RULES.—The rules of subparagraphs (D), (E), and (F) of section 408A(d)(3) (as in effect for taxable years beginning after 2009) shall apply for purposes of this paragraph.

Amendments

• 2010, Creating Small Business Jobs Act of 2010 (P.L. 111-240)

P.L. 111-240, §2112(a):

Amended Code Sec. 402A(c) by adding at the end a new paragraph (4). **Effective** for distributions after 9-27-2010.

[Sec. 402A(d)]

(d) DISTRIBUTION RULES.—For purposes of this title—

(1) EXCLUSION.—Any qualified distribution from a designated Roth account shall not be includible in gross income.

(2) QUALIFIED DISTRIBUTION.—For purposes of this subsection—

(A) IN GENERAL.—The term "qualified distribution" has the meaning given such term by section 408A(d)(2)(A) (without regard to clause (iv) thereof).

(B) DISTRIBUTIONS WITHIN NONEXCLUSION PERIOD.—A payment or distribution from a designated Roth account shall not be treated as a qualified distribution if such payment or distribution is made within the 5-taxable-year period beginning with the earlier of—

(i) the first taxable year for which the individual made a designated Roth contribution to any designated Roth account established for such individual under the same applicable retirement plan, or

(ii) if a rollover contribution was made to such designated Roth account from a designated Roth account previously established for such individual under another applicable retirement plan, the first taxable year for which the individual made a designated Roth contribution to such previously established account.

(C) DISTRIBUTIONS OF EXCESS DEFERRALS AND CONTRIBUTIONS AND EARNINGS THEREON.—The term "qualified distribution" shall not include any distribution of any excess deferral under section 402(g)(2) or any excess contribution under section 401(k)(8), and any income on the excess deferral or contribution.

(3) TREATMENT OF DISTRIBUTIONS OF CERTAIN EXCESS DEFERRALS.—Notwithstanding section 72, if any excess deferral under section 402(g)(2) attributable to a designated Roth contribution is not distributed on or before the 1st April 15 following the close of the taxable year in which such excess deferral is made, the amount of such excess deferral shall—

(A) not be treated as investment in the contract, and

(B) be included in gross income for the taxable year in which such excess is distributed.

(4) AGGREGATION RULES.—Section 72 shall be applied separately with respect to distributions and payments from a designated Roth account and other distributions and payments from the plan.

[Sec. 402A(e)]

(e) OTHER DEFINITIONS.—For purposes of this section—

(1) APPLICABLE RETIREMENT PLAN.—The term "applicable retirement plan" means—

(A) an employees' trust described in section 401(a) which is exempt from tax under section 501(a),

(B) a plan under which amounts are contributed by an individual's employer for an annuity contract described in section 403(b), and

➽ *Caution: Code Sec. 402A(e)(1)(C), below, as added by P.L. 111-240, applies to tax years beginning after December 31, 2010.*

(C) an eligible deferred compensation plan (as defined in section 457(b)) of an eligible employer described in section 457(e)(1)(A).

➽ *Caution: Code Sec. 402A(e)(2), below, prior to amendment by P.L. 111-240, applies to tax years beginning on or before December 31, 2010.*

(2) ELECTIVE DEFERRAL.—The term "elective deferral" means any elective deferral described in subparagraph (A) or (C) of section 402(g)(3).

➽ *Caution: Code Sec. 402A(e)(2), below, as amended by P.L. 111-240, applies to tax years beginning after December 31, 2010.*

(2) ELECTIVE DEFERRAL.—The term "elective deferral" means—

(A) any elective deferral described in subparagraph (A) or (C) of section 402(g)(3), and

(B) any elective deferral of compensation by an individual under an eligible deferred compensation plan (as defined in section 457(b)) of an eligible employer described in section 457(e)(1)(A).

Amendments

• 2010, Creating Small Business Jobs Act of 2010 (P.L. 111-240)

P.L. 111-240, §2111(a):

Amended Code Sec. 402A(e)(1) by striking "and" at the end of subparagraph (A), by striking the period at the end of subparagraph (B) and inserting ", and", and by adding at the end a new subparagraph (C). **Effective** for tax years beginning after 12-31-2010.

P.L. 111-240, §2111(b):

Amended Code Sec. 402A(e)(2). **Effective** for tax years beginning after 12-31-2010. Prior to amendment, Code Sec. 402A(e)(2) read as follows:

(2) ELECTIVE DEFERRAL.—The term "elective deferral" means any elective deferral described in subparagraph (A) or (C) of section 402(g)(3).

• 2006, Pension Protection Act of 2006 (P.L. 109-280)

P.L. 109-280, §811, provides:

SEC. 811. PENSIONS AND INDIVIDUAL RETIREMENT ARRANGEMENT PROVISIONS OF ECONOMIC GROWTH AND TAX RELIEF RECONCILIATION ACT OF 2001 MADE PERMANENT.

Title IX of the Economic Growth and Tax Relief Reconciliation Act of 2001 [P.L. 107-16] shall not apply to the provisions of, and amendments made by, subtitles A through F of title VI [§§601-666]of such Act (relating to pension and individual retirement arrangement provisions).

• 2001, Economic Growth and Tax Relief Reconciliation Act of 2001 (P.L. 107-16)

P.L. 107-16, §617(a):

Amended subpart A of part I of subchapter D of chapter 1 by inserting after Code Sec. 402 a new Code Sec. 402A. **Effective** for tax years beginning after 12-31-2005.

P.L. 107-16, §901(a)-(b), provides [but see P.L. 109-280, §811, above]:

SEC. 901. SUNSET OF PROVISIONS OF ACT.

(a) IN GENERAL.—All provisions of, and amendments made by, this Act shall not apply—

(1) to taxable, plan, or limitation years beginning after December 31, 2010, or

(2) in the case of title V, to estates of decedents dying, gifts made, or generation skipping transfers, after December 31, 2010.

(b) APPLICATION OF CERTAIN LAWS.—The Internal Revenue Code of 1986 and the Employee Retirement Income Security Act of 1974 shall be applied and administered to years, estates, gifts, and transfers described in subsection (a) as if the provisions and amendments described in subsection (a) had never been enacted.

[Sec. 403]

SEC. 403. TAXATION OF EMPLOYEE ANNUITIES.

[Sec. 403(a)]

(a) TAXABILITY OF BENEFICIARY UNDER A QUALIFIED ANNUITY PLAN.—

(1) DISTRIBUTEE TAXABLE UNDER SECTION 72.—If an annuity contract is purchased by an employer for an employee under a plan which meets the requirements of section 404(a)(2) (whether or not the employer deducts the amounts paid for the contract under such section), the amount actually distributed to any distributee under the contract shall be taxable to the distributee (in the year in which so distributed) under section 72 (relating to annuities).

(2) SPECIAL RULE FOR HEALTH AND LONG-TERM CARE INSURANCE.—To the extent provided in section 402(l), paragraph (1) shall not apply to the amount distributed under the contract which is otherwise includible in gross income under this subsection.

(3) SELF-EMPLOYED INDIVIDUALS.—For purposes of this subsection, the term "employee" includes an individual who is an employee within the meaning of section 401(c)(1), and the employer of such individual is the person treated as his employer under section 401(c)(4).

(4) ROLLOVER AMOUNTS.—

(A) GENERAL RULE.—If—

(i) any portion of the balance to the credit of an employee in an employee annuity described in paragraph (1) is paid to him in an eligible rollover distribution (within the meaning of section 402(c)(4)),

(ii) the employee transfers any portion of the property he receives in such distribution to an eligible retirement plan, and

(iii) in the case of a distribution of property other than money, the amount so transferred consists of the property distributed,

then such distribution (to the extent so transferred) shall not be includible in gross income for the taxable year in which paid.

(B) CERTAIN RULES MADE APPLICABLE.—The rules of paragraphs (2) through (7) and (11) and (9) of section 402(c) and section 402(f) shall apply for purposes of subparagraph (A).

(5) DIRECT TRUSTEE-TO-TRUSTEE TRANSFER.—Any amount transferred in a direct trustee-to-trustee transfer in accordance with section 401(a)(31) shall not be includible in gross income for the taxable year of such transfer.

Amendments

• 2006, Pension Protection Act of 2006 (P.L. 109-280)

P.L. 109-280, §811, provides:

SEC. 811. PENSIONS AND INDIVIDUAL RETIREMENT ARRANGEMENT PROVISIONS OF ECONOMIC GROWTH AND TAX RELIEF RECONCILIATION ACT OF 2001 MADE PERMANENT.

Title IX of the Economic Growth and Tax Relief Reconciliation Act of 2001 [P.L. 107-16] shall not apply to the provisions of, and amendments made by, subtitles A through F of title VI [§§601-666]of such Act (relating to pension and individual retirement arrangement provisions).

P.L. 109-280, §829(a)(2):

Amended Code Sec. 403(a)(4)(B) by inserting "and (11)" after "(7)". **Effective** for distributions after 12-31-2006.

P.L. 109-280, §845(b)(1):

Amended Code Sec. 403(a) by inserting after paragraph (1) a new paragraph (2). **Effective** for distributions in tax years beginning after 12-31-2006.

• 2005, Katrina Emergency Tax Relief Act of 2005 (P.L. 109-73)

P.L. 109-73, §102 [repealed by P.L. 109-135, §201(b)(4)(A)], provides:

SEC. 102. RECONTRIBUTIONS OF WITHDRAWALS FOR HOME PURCHASES CANCELLED DUE TO HURRICANE KATRINA.

(a) RECONTRIBUTIONS.—

(1) IN GENERAL.—Any individual who received a qualified distribution may, during the period beginning on August 25, 2005, and ending on February 28, 2006, make one or more contributions in an aggregate amount not to exceed the amount of such qualified distribution to an eligible retirement plan (as defined in section 402(c)(8)(B) of the Internal Revenue Code of 1986) of which such individual is a beneficiary and to which a rollover contribution of such distribution could be made under section 402(c), 403(a)(4), 403(b)(8), or 408(d)(3) of such Code, as the case may be.

(2) TREATMENT OF REPAYMENTS.—Rules similar to the rules of paragraphs (2) and (3) of section 101(c) of this Act shall apply for purposes of this section.

(b) QUALIFIED DISTRIBUTION DEFINED.—For purposes of this section, the term "qualified distribution" means any distribution—

(1) described in section 401(k)(2)(B)(i)(IV), 403(b)(7)(A)(ii) (but only to the extent such distribution relates to financial hardship), 403(b)(11)(B), or 72(t)(2)(F) of such Code,

(2) received after February 28, 2005, and before August 29, 2005, and

(3) which was to be used to purchase or construct a principal residence in the Hurricane Katrina disaster area, but which was not so purchased or constructed on account of Hurricane Katrina.

• 2004, Working Families Tax Relief Act of 2004 (P.L. 108-311)

P.L. 108-311, §404(e):

Amended Code Sec. 403(a)(4)(B). **Effective** as if included in the provision of the Economic Growth and Tax Relief Reconciliation Act of 2001 (P.L. 107-16) to which it relates [**effective** for distributions after 12-31-2001.—CCH]. For sunset provision, see P.L. 107-16, §901, below. Prior to amendment, Code Sec. 403(a)(4)(B) read as follows:

(B) CERTAIN RULES MADE APPLICABLE.—Rules similar to the rules of paragraphs (2) through (7) of section 402(c) shall apply for purposes of subparagraph (A).

• 2001, Economic Growth and Tax Relief Reconciliation Act of 2001 (P.L. 107-16)

P.L. 107-16, §901(a)-(b), provides [but see P.L. 109-280, §811, above]:

SEC. 901. SUNSET OF PROVISIONS OF ACT.

(a) IN GENERAL.—All provisions of, and amendments made by, this Act shall not apply—

(1) to taxable, plan, or limitation years beginning after December 31, 2010, or

(2) in the case of title V, to estates of decedents dying, gifts made, or generation skipping transfers, after December 31, 2010.

(b) APPLICATION OF CERTAIN LAWS.—The Internal Revenue Code of 1986 and the Employee Retirement Income Security Act of 1974 shall be applied and administered to years, estates, gifts, and transfers described in subsection (a) as if the provisions and amendments described in subsection (a) had never been enacted.

• 1992, Unemployment Compensation Amendments of 1992 (P.L. 102-318)

P.L. 102-318, §521 (b)(12)(A):

Amended Code Sec. 403(a)(4)(A)(i) by inserting "in an eligible rollover distribution (within the meaning of section 402(c)(4))" before the comma at the end thereof. **Effective** for distributions after 12-31-92.

P.L. 102-318, §521(b)(12)(B):

Amended Code Sec. 403(a)(4)(B). **Effective** for distributions after 12-31-92. Prior to amendment, Code Sec. 403(a)(4)(B) read as follows:

(B) CERTAIN RULES MADE APPLICABLE.—Rules similar to the rules of subparagraphs (B) through (G) of section 402(a)(5) and of paragraphs (6) and (7) of section 402(a) shall apply for purposes of subparagraph (A).

P.L. 102-318, §522(c):

Amended Code Sec. 403(a) by adding at the end thereof new paragraph (5). **Effective** for distributions after 12-31-92.

• 1986, Tax Reform Act of 1986 (P.L. 99-514)

P.L. 99-514, §1122(b)(1)(B):

Repealed Code Sec. 403(a)(2). **Effective** generally for amounts distributed after 12-31-86, in tax years ending after such date. For special rules, see Act Sec. 1122(h)(3)-(9), below. Prior to repeal, Code Sec. 403(a)(2) read as follows:

(2) CAPITAL GAINS TREATMENT FOR CERTAIN DISTRIBUTIONS.—

(A) GENERAL RULE.—If—

(i) an annuity contract is purchased by an employer for an employee under a plan described in paragraph (1);

(ii) such plan requires that refunds of contributions with respect to annuity contracts purchased under such plan be used to reduce subsequent premiums on the contracts under the plan; and

(iii) a lump sum distribution (as defined in section 402(e)(4)(A)) is paid to the recipient,

so much of the total taxable amount (as defined in section 402(e)(4)(D)) of such distribution as is equal to the product of such total taxable amount multiplied by the fraction described in section 402(a)(2) shall be treated as a gain from the sale or exchange of a capital asset held for more than 6 months. For purposes of this paragraph, in the case of an individual who is an employee without regard to section 401(c)(1), determination of whether or not any distribution is a lump sum distribution shall be made without regard to requirement that an election be made under subsection (e)(4)(B) of section 402, but no distribution to any taxpayer other than an individual, estate, or trust may be treated as a lump sum distribution under this paragraph.

(B) CROSS REFERENCE.—

For imposition of separate tax on ordinary income portion of lump sum distribution, see section 402(e).

P.L. 99-514, §1122(d)(1):

Amended Code Sec. 403(a)(1). **Effective**, generally, for amounts distributed after 12-31-86, in tax years ending after such date. For special rules, see Act Sec. 1122(h)(3)-(9), below. Prior to amendment, Code Sec. 403(a)(1) read as follows:

(1) GENERAL RULE.—Except as provided in paragraph (2), if an annuity contract is purchased by an employer for an employee under a plan which meets the requirements of section 404(a)(2) (whether or not the employer deducts the amounts paid for the contract under such section), the employee shall include in his gross income the amounts received under such contract for the year received as provided in section 72 (relating to annuities).

P.L. 99-514, §1122(h)(3)-(9), as amended by P.L. 100-647, §1011A(b)(11), (12)-(15), provides:

(3) SPECIAL RULE FOR INDIVIDUALS WHO ATTAINED AGE 50 BEFORE JANUARY 1, 1986.—

(A) IN GENERAL.—In the case of a lump sum distribution to which this paragraph applies—

(i) the existing capital gains provisions shall continue to apply, and

(ii) the requirement of subparagraph (B) of section 402(e)(4) of the Internal Revenue Code of 1986 (as amended by subsection (a)) that the distribution be received after attaining age 59½ shall not apply.

(B) COMPUTATION OF TAX.—If subparagraph (A) applies to any lump sum distribution of any taxpayer for any taxable year, the tax imposed by section 1 of the Internal Revenue Code of 1986 on such taxpayer for such taxable year shall be equal to the sum of—

(i) the tax imposed by such section 1 on the taxable income of the taxpayer (reduced by the portion of such lump sum distribution to which clause (ii) applies), plus

(ii) 20 percent of the portion of such lump sum distribution to which the existing capital gains provisions continue to apply by reason of this paragraph.

(C) LUMP SUM DISTRIBUTIONS TO WHICH PARAGRAPH APPLIES.—This paragraph shall apply to any lump sum distribution if—

(i) such lump sum distribution is received by an employee who has attained age 50 before January 1, 1986 or by an individual estate, or trust with respect to such an employee, and

(ii) the taxpayer makes an election under this paragraph.

Not more than 1 election may be made under this paragraph with respect to an employee. An election under this subparagraph shall be treated as an election under section 402(e)(4)(B) of such Code for purposes of such Code.

(4) 5-YEAR PHASE-OUT OF CAPITAL GAINS TREATMENT.—

(A) Notwithstanding the amendment made by subsection (b), if the taxpayer elects the application of this paragraph with respect to any distribution after December 31, 1986, and before January 1, 1992, the phase-out percentage of the amount which would have been treated, without regard to this subparagraph, as long-term capital gain under the existing capital gains provisions shall be treated as long-term capital gain.

(B) FOR PURPOSES OF THIS PARAGRAPH.—

In the case of distributions during calendar year:	*The phase-out percentage is:*
1987	100
1988	95
1989	75
1990	50
1991	25

(C) No more than 1 election may be made under this paragraph with respect to an employee. An election under this paragraph shall be treated as an election under section 402(e)(4)(B) of the Internal Revenue Code of 1986 for purposes of such Code.

(5) ELECTION OF 10-YEAR AVERAGING.—An employee who has attained age 50 before January 1, 1986, and elects the application of paragraph (3) or section 402(e)(1) of the Internal Revenue Code of 1986 (as amended by this Act) may elect to have such section applied by substituting "10 times" for "5 times" and "1/10" for "1/5" in subparagraph (B) thereof. For purposes of the preceding sentence, section 402(e)(1) of such Code shall be applied by using the rate of tax in effect under section 1 of the Internal Revenue Code of 1954 for taxable years beginning during 1986 and by including in gross income the zero bracket amount in effect under section 63(d) of such Code for such years. This paragraph shall also apply to an individual, estate, or trust which receives a distribution with respect to an employee described in this paragraph.

(6) EXISTING CAPITAL GAIN PROVISIONS.—For purposes of paragraphs (3) and (4), the term "existing capital gains provisions" means the provisions of paragraph (2) of section 402(a) of the Internal Revenue Code of 1954 (as in effect on the day before the date of the enactment of this Act) and paragraph (2) of section 403(a) of such Code (as so in effect).

(7) SUBSECTION (d).—The amendments made by subsection (d) shall apply to taxable years beginning after December 31, 1985.

(8) FROZEN DEPOSITS.—The amendments made by subsection (e)(2) shall apply to amounts transferred to an employee before, on, or after the date of the enactment of this Act, except that in the case of an amount transferred on or before such date, the 60-day period referred to in section 402(a)(5)(C) of the Internal Revenue Code of 1986 shall not expire before the 60th day after the date of the enactment of this Act.

(9) SPECIAL RULE FOR STATE PLANS.—In the case of a plan maintained by a State which on May 5, 1986, permitted withdrawal by the employee of employee contributions (other than as an annuity), section 72(e) of the Internal Revenue Code of 1986 shall be applied—

(A) without regard to the phrase "before separation from service" in paragraph (8)(D), and

(B) by treating any amount received (other than as an annuity) before or with the 1st annuity payment as having been received before the annuity starting date.

P.L. 99-514, §1852(a)(5)(B)(i):

Amended Code Sec. 403(a)(4)(B) by striking out "through (F)" and inserting in lieu thereof "through (G)". **Effective** as if included in the provision of P.L. 98-369 to which it relates.

• 1984, Deficit Reduction Act of 1984 (P.L. 98-369)

P.L. 98-369, §522(a)(2):

Amended Code Sec. 403(a)(4)(A)(i). **Effective** for distributions made after 7-18-84, in tax years ending after such date. Prior to amendment, Code Sec. 403(a)(4)(A)(i) read as follows:

(i) the balance to the credit of an employee in an employee annuity described in paragraph (1) is paid to him in a qualifying rollover distribution.

P.L. 98-369, §522(d)(9):

Amended Code Sec. 403(a)(4)(B) by striking out "(B) through (E)" and inserting in lieu thereof "(B) through (F)". **Effective** for distributions made after 7-18-84, in tax years ending after such date.

P.L. 98-369, §1001(b)(4):

Amended Code Sec. 403(a)(2)(A) by striking out "1 year" and inserting in lieu thereof "6 months". **Effective** for property acquired after 6-22-84 and before 1-1-88.

• 1978, Revenue Act of 1978 (P.L. 95-600)

P.L. 95-600, §157(g)(2):

Amended Code Sec. 403(a)(4)(B) by striking out "paragraph (6)" and inserting in lieu thereof "paragraphs (6) and (7)". **Effective** for lump-sum distributions completed after 12-31-78, in tax years ending after such date.

• 1978 (P.L. 95-458)

P.L. 95-458, §4(b):

Amended subsection (a) by striking out paragraphs (4) and (5) and inserting in place thereof new paragraph (4). **Effective** as indicated in §4(d), below. Prior to amendment, paragraphs (4) and (5) read as follows:

"(4) ROLLOVER AMOUNTS.—In the case of an employee annuity described in 403(a), if—

(A) the balance to the credit of an employee is paid to him—

(i) within one taxable year of the employee on account of a termination of the plan of which such trust is a part or, in the case of a profit-sharing plan, a complete discontinuance of contributions under such plan, or

(ii) in one or more distributions which constitutes a lump-sum distribution within the meaning of section 402(e)(4)(A) (determined without reference to section 402(e)(4)(B)),

(B)(i) the employee transfers all the property he receives in such distribution to an individual account described in section 408(a), an individual retirement annuity described in section 408(b) (other than an endowment contract), or a retirement bond described in section 409, on or before the 60th day after the day on which he received such property to the extent the fair market value of such property exceeds the amount referred to in section 402(e)(4)(D)(i), or

(ii) the employee transfers all the property he receives in such distribution to an employees' trust described in section 401(a) which is exempt from tax under section 501(a), or to an annuity plan described in subsection (a) on or before the 60th day after the day on which he received such property to the extent the fair market value of such property exceeds the amount referred to in section 402(e)(4)(D)(i), and

(C) the amount so transferred consists of the property distributed to the extent that the fair market value of such property does not exceed the amount required to be transferred pursuant to subparagraph (B),

then such distribution is not includible in gross income for the year in which paid. For purposes of this title, a transfer described in subparagraph (B)(i) shall be treated as a rollover contribution described in section 408(d)(3). Subparagraph (B)(ii) does not apply in the case of a transfer to an employees' trust, or annuity plan if any part of a payment described in subparagraph (A) is attributable to an annuity plan under which the employee was an employee within the meaning of section 401(c)(1) at the time contributions were made on his behalf under the plan.

"(5) SPECIAL ROLLOVER RULES.—For purposes of paragraph (4)(A)(i)—

(A) TIME OF TERMINATION.—A complete discontinuance of contributions under a profit-sharing plan shall be deemed to occur on the day the plan administrator notifies the Secretary (in accordance with regulations prescribed by the Secretary) that all contributions to the plan have been completely discontinued. For purposes of section 411(d)(3), the plan shall be considered to be terminated no later than the day such notice is filed with the Secretary.

(B) SALE OF SUBSIDIARY OR ASSETS.—

(i) A payment of the balance to the credit of an employee of a corporation (hereinafter referred to as the employer corporation) which is a subsidiary corporation (within the meaning of section 425(f)) or which is a member of a controlled group of corporations (within the meaning of section 1563(a), determined by substituting "50 percent" for "80 percent" each place it appears therein) in connection with the liquidation, sale, or other means of terminating the parent-subsidiary or controlled group relationship of the employer corporation with the parent corporation or controlled group, or

(ii) a payment of the balance to the credit of an employee of a corporation (hereinafter referred to as the acquiring corporation) in connection with the sale or other transfer to the acquiring corporation of all or substantially all of the assets used by the previous employer of the employee (hereinafter referred to as the selling corporation) in a trade or business conducted by the selling corporation,

shall be treated as a payment or distribution on account of the termination of the plan with respect to such employee if the employees of the employer corporation or the acquiring corporation (whichever applies) are not active participants in such plan at the time of such payment or distribution. For purposes of this subparagraph, in no event shall a payment or distribution be deemed to be in accordance with a sale or other transfer of assets, or a liquidation, sale, or other means of terminating such parent-subsidiary or controlled group relationship, if such payment or distribution is made later than the end of the second calendar year after the calendar year in which occurs such sale or other transfer of assets, or such liquidation, sale, or other means of terminating such parent-subsidiary or controlled group relationship."

P.L. 95-458, §4(d), provides:

(d) EFFECTIVE DATES.—

(1) IN GENERAL.—The amendments made by subsections (a), (b), and (c) shall apply with respect to taxable years beginning after December 31, 1974.

(2) VALIDATION OF CERTAIN ATTEMPTED ROLLOVERS.—If the taxpayer—

(A) attempted to comply with the requirements of section 402(a)(5) or 403(a)(4) of the Internal Revenue Code of 1954 for a taxable year beginning before October 14, 1978, and

(B) failed to meet the requirements of such section that all property received in the distribution be transferred,

such section (as amended by this section) shall be applied by treating any transfer of property made on or before December 31, 1978, as if it were made on or before the 60th day after the day on which the taxpayer received such property. For purposes of the preceding sentence, a transfer of money shall be treated as a transfer of property received in a distribution to the extent that the amount of the money transferred does not exceed the highest fair market value of the property distributed during the 60-day period beginning on the date on which the taxpayer received such property.

• 1976, Tax Reform Act of 1976 (P.L. 94-455)

P.L. 94-455, §1402(b)(1)(D):

Substituted "9 months for taxable years beginning in 1977" for "6 months" in Code Sec. 403(a)(2)(A). **Effective** for tax years beginning after 12-31-77.

P.L. 94-455, §1402(b)(2):

Substituted "1 year" for "9 months" in Code Sec. 403(a)(2)(A). **Effective** for tax years beginning after 12-31-77.

P.L. 94-455, §1901(a)(58):

Amended the last two sentences of Code Sec. 403(a)(4). **Effective** for tax years beginning after 12-31-76. Prior to amendment, the last two sentences of Code Sec. 403(a)(4) read as follows:

For purposes of this title, a transfer described in subparagraph (B)(i) shall be treated as a rollover contribution described in section 408(d)(3). Subparagraph (B)(ii) does not apply in the case of a transfer to an employees' trust, or annuity plan if any part of a payment described in subparagraph (A) is attributable to an annuity plan under which the employee was an employee within the meaning of section 401(c)(1) at the time contributions were made on his behalf under the plan.

P.L. 94-455, §1906(b)(13)(A):

Amended the 1954 Code by substituting "Secretary" for "Secretary or his delegate" each place it appeared. **Effective** 2-1-77.

• 1976 (P.L. 94-267)

P.L. 94-267, §1(b):

Amended Code Sec. 403(a)(4)(A). **Effective** for payments made to an employee on or after 7-4-74. Prior to amendment Code Sec. 403(a)(4)(A) read as follows:

"(A) the balance to the credit of an employee is paid to him in one or more distributions which constitute a lump sum distribution within the meaning of section 402(e)(4)(A) (determined without reference to section 402(e)(4)(B)),".

P.L. 94-267, §1(b):

Amended the last sentence of paragraph (4) by striking out "the lump-sum distribution" and inserting in lieu thereof "a payment,", **Effective** for payments made to an employee on or after 7-4-74.

P.L. 94-267, §1(b):

Added Code Sec. 403(a)(5). **Effective** for payments made to an employee on or after 7-4-74.

• 1974, Employee Retirement Income Security Act of 1974 (P.L. 93-406)

P.L. 93-406, §§2002(g)(6):

Amended Code Sec. 403(a)(2). **Effective** with respect to distributions or payments made after 12-31-73, in tax years beginning after such date. Prior to amendment, Code Sec. 403(a)(2) read as follows:

"(2) Capital gains treatment for certain distributions.—

"(A) General rule.—If—

"(i) an annuity contract is purchased by an employer for an employee under a plan described in paragraph (1);

"(ii) such plan requires that refunds of contributions with respect to annuity contracts purchased under such plan be used to reduce subsequent premiums on the contracts under the plan; and

"(iii) the total amounts payable by reason of an employee's death or other separation from the service, or by reason of the death of an employee after the employee's separation from the service, are paid to the payee within one taxable year of the payee,

then the amount of such payments, to the extent exceeding the amount contributed by the employee (determined by applying section 72(f)), which employee contributions shall be reduced by any amounts theretofore paid to him which were not includible in gross income, shall be considered a gain from the sale or exchange of a capital asset held for more than 6 months. This subparagraph shall not apply to amounts paid to any payee to the extent such amounts are attributable to contributions made on behalf of the employee while he was an employee within the meaning of section 401(c)(1).

"(B) Definition.—For purposes of subparagraph (A), the term `total amounts' means the balance to the credit of an employee which becomes payable to the payee by reason of the employee's death or other separation from the service, or by reason of his death after separation from the service.

"(C) Limitation on capital gains treatment.—Subparagraph (A) shall apply to a payment paid after December 31, 1969, only to the extent it does not exceed the sum of—

"(i) the benefits accrued by the employee on behalf of whom it is paid during plan years beginning before January 1, 1970, and

"(ii) the portion of the benefits accrued by such employee during plan years beginning after December 31, 1969, which the payee establishes does not consist of the employee's allocable share of employer contributions under the plan under which the annuity contract is purchased.

The Secretary or his delegate shall prescribe such regulations as may be necessary to carry out the purposes of this subparagraph."

P.L. 93-406, §2005(b)(2):

Added Code Sec. 403(a)(4). **Effective** on and after 9-2-74, with respect to contributions to an employees' trust described in Code Sec. 401(a) which is exempt from tax under Code Sec. 401(a) or an annuity plan described in Code Sec. 403(a).

• 1969, Tax Reform Act of 1969 (P.L. 91-172)

P.L. 91-172, §515(a)(2):

Amended Code Sec. 403(a)(2) by adding subparagraph (a)(2)(C). **Effective** for tax years ending after 12-31-69.

• 1964, Revenue Act of 1964 (P.L. 88-272)

P.L. 88-272, §232(e)(4):

Amended Code Sec. 403(a)(1) to delete "except that section 72(e)(3) shall not apply" from the end of the paragraph. **Effective** for tax years beginning after 12-31-63.

• 1962, Self-Employed Individuals Tax Retirement Act of 1962 (P.L. 87-792)

P.L. 87-792, §4:

Amended Code Sec. 403(a) by striking out in paragraph (2)(A)(i) "which meets the requirements of section 401(a)(3), (4), (5), and (6)" and inserting in lieu thereof "described in paragraph (1)"; adding the last sentence at the end of paragraph (2)(A); and adding after paragraph (2) the new paragraph (3). **Effective** 1-1-63.

• 1958, Technical Amendments Act of 1958 (P.L. 85-866)

P.L. 85-866, §23(b):

Amended Sec. 403(a)(1). **Effective** 1-1-58. Prior to amendment, Sec. 403(a)(1) read as follows:

"(1) General rule.—Except as provided in paragraph (2), if an annuity contract is purchased by an employer for an employee under a plan with respect to which the employer's contribution is deductible under section 404(a)(2), or if an annuity contract is purchased for an employee by an employer described in section 501(c)(3) which is exempt from tax under section 501(a), the employee shall include in his gross income the amounts received under such contract for the year received as provided in section 72 (relating to annuities) except that section 72(e)(3) shall not apply."

[Sec. 403(b)]

(b) TAXABILITY OF BENEFICIARY UNDER ANNUITY PURCHASED BY SECTION 501(c)(3) ORGANIZATION OR PUBLIC SCHOOL.—

(1) GENERAL RULE.—If—

(A) an annuity contract is purchased—

(i) for an employee by an employer described in section 501(c)(3) which is exempt from tax under section 501(a),

(ii) for an employee (other than an employee described in clause (i)), who performs services for an educational organization described in section 170(b)(1)(A)(ii), by an employer which is a State, a political subdivision of a State, or an agency or instrumentality of any one or more of the foregoing, or

(iii) for the minister described in section 414(e)(5)(A) by the minister or by an employer,

(B) such annuity contract is not subject to subsection (a),

(C) the employee's rights under the contract are nonforfeitable, except for failure to pay future premiums,

(D) except in the case of a contract purchased by a church, such contract is purchased under a plan which meets the nondiscrimination requirements of paragraph 12, and

(E) in the case of a contract purchased under a salary reduction agreement, the contract meets the requirements of section 401(a)(30),

then contributions and other additions by such employer for such annuity contract shall be excluded from the gross income of the employee for the taxable year to the extent that the aggregate of such contributions and additions (when expressed as an annual addition (within the meaning of section 415(c)(2))) does not exceed the applicable limit under section 415. The amount actually distributed to any distributee under such contract shall be taxable to the distributee (in the year in which so distributed) under section 72 (relating to annuities). For purposes of applying the rules of this subsection to contributions and other additions by an employer for a taxable year, amounts transferred to a contract described in this paragraph by reason of a rollover contribution described in paragraph (8) of this subsection or section 408(d)(3)(A)(ii) shall not be considered contributed by such employer.

(2) SPECIAL RULE FOR HEALTH AND LONG-TERM CARE INSURANCE.—To the extent provided in section 402(l), paragraph (1) shall not apply to the amount distributed under the contract which is otherwise includible in gross income under this subsection.

(3) INCLUDIBLE COMPENSATION.—For purposes of this subsection, the term "includible compensation" means, in the case of any employee, the amount of compensation which is received from the employer described in paragraph (1)(A), and which is includible in gross income (computed without regard to section 911) for the most recent period (ending not later than the close of the taxable year) which under paragraph (4) may be counted as one year of service, and which precedes the taxable year by no more than five years. Such term does not include any amount contributed by the employer for any annuity contract to which this subsection applies. Such term includes—

(A) any elective deferral (as defined in section 402(g)(3)), and

(B) any amount which is contributed or deferred by the employer at the election of the employee and which is not includible in the gross income of the employee by reason of section 125, 132(f)(4), or 457.

(4) YEARS OF SERVICE.—In determining the number of years of service for purposes of this subsection, there shall be included—

(A) one year for each full year during which the individual was a full-time employee of the organization purchasing the annuity for him, and

(B) a fraction of a year (determined in accordance with regulations prescribed by the Secretary) for each full year during which such individual was a part-time employee of such organization and for each part of a year during which such individual was a full-time or part-time employee of such organization.

In no case shall the number of years of service be less than one.

(5) APPLICATION TO MORE THAN ONE ANNUITY CONTRACT.—If for any taxable year of the employee this subsection applies to 2 or more annuity contracts purchased by the employer, such contracts shall be treated as one contract.

(6) [Stricken.]

(7) CUSTODIAL ACCOUNTS FOR REGULATED INVESTMENT COMPANY STOCK.—

(A) AMOUNTS PAID TREATED AS CONTRIBUTIONS.—For purposes of this title, amounts paid by an employer described in paragraph (1)(A) to a custodial account which satisfies the requirements of section 401(f)(2) shall be treated as amounts contributed by him for an annuity contract for his employee if—

(i) the amounts are to be invested in regulated investment company stock to be held in that custodial account, and

(ii) under the custodial account no such amounts may be paid or made available to any distributee (unless such amount is a distribution to which section 72(t)(2)(G) applies) before the employee dies, attains age 59½, has a severance from employment, becomes disabled (within the meaning of section 72(m)(7)), or in the case of contributions made pursuant to a salary reduction agreement (within the meaning of section 3121(a)(5)(D)), encounters financial hardship.

(B) ACCOUNT TREATED AS PLAN.—For purposes of this title, a custodial account which satisfies the requirements of section 401(f)(2) shall be treated as an organization described in section 401(a) solely for purposes of subchapter F and subtitle F with respect to amounts received by it (and income from investment thereof).

(C) REGULATED INVESTMENT COMPANY.—For purposes of this paragraph, the term "regulated investment company" means a domestic corporation which is a regulated investment company within the meaning of section 851(a).

(8) ROLLOVER AMOUNTS.—

(A) GENERAL RULE.—If—

(i) any portion of the balance to the credit of an employee in an annuity contract described in paragraph (1) is paid to him in an eligible rollover distribution (within the meaning of section 402(c)(4)),

(ii) the employee transfers any portion of the property he receives in such distribution to an eligible retirement plan described in section 402(c)(8)(B), and

(iii) in the case of a distribution of property other than money, the property so transferred consists of the property distributed,

then such distribution (to the extent so transferred) shall not be includible in gross income for the taxable year in which paid.

(B) CERTAIN RULES MADE APPLICABLE.—The rules of paragraphs (2) through (7), (9), and (11) of section 402(c) and section 402(f) shall apply for purposes of subparagraph (A), except that section 402(f) shall be applied to the payor in lieu of the plan administrator.

(9) RETIREMENT INCOME ACCOUNTS PROVIDED BY CHURCHES, ETC.—

(A) AMOUNTS PAID TREATED AS CONTRIBUTIONS.—For purposes of this title—

(i) a retirement income account shall be treated as an annuity contract described in this subsection, and

(ii) amounts paid by an employer described in paragraph (1)(A) to a retirement income account shall be treated as amounts contributed by the employer for an annuity contract for the employee on whose behalf such account is maintained.

(B) RETIREMENT INCOME ACCOUNT.—For purposes of this paragraph, the term "retirement income account" means a defined contribution program established or maintained by a church, or a convention or association of churches, including an organization described in section 414(e)(3)(A), to provide benefits under section 403(b) for an employee described in paragraph (1) or his beneficiaries.

(10) DISTRIBUTION REQUIREMENTS.—Under regulations prescribed by the Secretary, this subsection shall not apply to any annuity contract (or to any custodial account described in paragraph (7) or retirement income account described in paragraph (9)) unless requirements similar to the requirements of sections 401(a)(9) and 401(a)(31) are met (and requirements similar to the incidential death benefit requirements of section 401(a) are met) with respect to such annuity contract (or custodial account or retirement income account). Any amount transferred in a direct trustee-to-trustee transfer in accordance with section 401(a)(31) shall not be includible in gross income for the taxable year of the transfer.

(11) REQUIREMENT THAT DISTRIBUTIONS NOT BEGIN BEFORE AGE 59½, SEVERANCE FROM EMPLOYMENT, DEATH, OR DISABILITY.—This subsection shall not apply to any annuity contract unless under such contract distributions attributable to contributions made pursuant to a salary reduction agreement (within the meaning of section 402(g)(3)(C)) may be paid only—

(A) when the employee attains age 59½, has a severance from employment, dies, or becomes disabled (within the meaning of section 72(m)(7)),

(B) in the case of hardship, or

(C) for distributions to which section 72(t)(2)(G) applies.

Such contract may not provide for the distribution of any income attributable to such contributions in the case of hardship.

(12) NONDISCRIMINATION REQUIREMENTS.—

(A) IN GENERAL.—For purposes of paragraph (1)(D), a plan meets the nondiscrimination requirements of this paragraph if—

(i) with respect to contributions not made pursuant to a salary reduction agreement, such plan meets the requirements of paragraphs (4), (5), (17), and (26) of section 401(a), section 401(m), and section 410(b) in the same manner as if such plan were described in section 401(a), and

(ii) all employees of the organization may elect to have the employer make contributions of more than $200 pursuant to a salary reduction agreement if any employee of the organization may elect to have the organization make contributions for such contracts pursuant to such agreement.

For purposes of clause (i), a contribution shall be treated as not made pursuant to a salary reduction agreement if under the agreement it is made pursuant to a 1-time irrevocable election made by the employee at the time of initial eligibility to participate in the agreement or is made pursuant to a similar arrangement involving a one-time irrevocable election specified in regulations. For purposes of clause (ii), there may be excluded any employee who is a participant in an eligible deferred compensation plan (within the meaning of section 457) or a qualified cash or deferred arrangement of the organization or another annuity contract described in this subsection. Any nonresident alien described in section 410(b)(3)(C) may also be excluded. Subject to the conditions applicable under section 410(b)(4), there may be excluded for purposes of this subparagraph employees who are students performing services described in section 3121(b)(10) and employees who normally work less than 20 hours per week.

(B) CHURCH.—For purposes of paragraph (1)(D), the term "church" has the meaning given to such term by section 3121(w)(3)(A). Such term shall include any qualified church-controlled organization (as defined in section 3121(w)(3)(B)).

(C) STATE AND LOCAL GOVERNMENTAL PLANS.—For purposes of paragraph (1)(D), the requirements of subparagraph (A)(i) (other than those relating to section 401(a)(17)) shall not apply to a governmental plan (within the meaning of section 414(d)) maintained by a State or local government or political subdivision thereof (or agency or instrumentality thereof).

(13) TRUSTEE-TO-TRUSTEE TRANSFERS TO PURCHASE PERMISSIVE SERVICE CREDIT.—No amount shall be includible in gross income by reason of a direct trustee-to-trustee transfer to a defined benefit governmental plan (as defined in section 414(d)) if such transfer is—

(A) for the purchase of permissive service credit (as defined in section 415(n)(3)(A)) under such plan, or

(B) a repayment to which section 415 does not apply by reason of subsection (k)(3) thereof.

(14) DEATH BENEFITS UNDER USERRA-QUALIFIED ACTIVE MILITARY SERVICE.—This subsection shall not apply to an annuity contract unless such contract meets the requirements of section 401(a)(37).

Amendments

• 2008, Heroes Earnings Assistance and Relief Tax Act of 2008 (P.L. 110-245)

P.L. 110-245, §104(c)(2):

Amended Code Sec. 403(b) by adding at the end a new paragraph (14). **Effective** generally with respect to deaths and disabilities occurring on or after 1-1-2007. For a special rule, see Act Sec. 104(d)(2), below.

P.L. 110-245, §104(d)(2), provides:

(2) PROVISIONS RELATING TO PLAN AMENDMENTS.—

(A) IN GENERAL.—If this subparagraph applies to any plan or contract amendment, such plan or contract shall be treated as being operated in accordance with the terms of the plan during the period described in subparagraph (B)(iii).

(B) AMENDMENTS TO WHICH SUBPARAGRAPH (A) APPLIES.—

(i) IN GENERAL.—Subparagraph (A) shall apply to any amendment to any plan or annuity contract which is made—

(I) pursuant to the amendments made by subsection (a) or pursuant to any regulation issued by the Secretary of the Treasury under subsection (a), and

(II) on or before the last day of the first plan year beginning on or after January 1, 2010.

In the case of a governmental plan (as defined in section 414(d) of the Internal Revenue Code of 1986), this clause shall be applied by substituting "2012" for "2010" in subclause (II).

(ii) CONDITIONS.—This paragraph shall not apply to any amendment unless—

(I) the plan or contract is operated as if such plan or contract amendment were in effect for the period described in clause (iii), and

(II) such plan or contract amendment applies retroactively for such period.

(iii) PERIOD DESCRIBED.—The period described in this clause is the period—

(I) beginning on the effective date specified by the plan, and

(II) ending on the date described in clause (i)(II) (or, if earlier, the date the plan or contract amendment is adopted).

• 2006, Pension Protection Act of 2006 (P.L. 109-280)

P.L. 109-280, §811, provides:

SEC. 811. PENSIONS AND INDIVIDUAL RETIREMENT ARRANGEMENT PROVISIONS OF ECONOMIC GROWTH AND TAX RELIEF RECONCILIATION ACT OF 2001 MADE PERMANENT.

Title IX of the Economic Growth and Tax Relief Reconciliation Act of 2001 [P.L. 107-16] shall not apply to the provisions of, and amendments made by, subtitles A through F of title VI [§§601-666]of such Act (relating to pension and individual retirement arrangement provisions).

P.L. 109-280, §827(b)(2):

Amended Code Sec. 403(b)(7)(A)(ii) by inserting "(unless such amount is a distribution to which section 72(t)(2)(G) applies)" after "distributee". **Effective** for distributions after 9-11-2001. For a waiver of limitations, see Act Sec. 827(c)(2), below.

P.L. 109-280, §827(b)(3):

Amended Code Sec. 403(b)(11) by striking "or" at the end of subparagraph (A), by striking the period at the end of subparagraph (B) and inserting ", or", and by inserting after subparagraph (B) a new subparagraph (C). **Effective** for distributions after 9-11-2001. For a waiver of limitations, see Act Sec. 827(c)(2), below.

P.L. 109-280, §827(c)(2), provides:

(2) WAIVER OF LIMITATIONS.—If refund or credit of any overpayment of tax resulting from the amendments made by this section is prevented at any time before the close of the 1-year period beginning on the date of the enactment of this Act by the operation of any law or rule of law (including res judicata), such refund or credit may nevertheless be made or allowed if claim therefor is filed before the close of such period.

P.L. 109-280, §829(a)(3):

Amended Code Sec. 403(b)(8)(B) by striking "and (9)" and inserting ", (9), and (11)". **Effective** for distributions after 12-31-2006.

P.L. 109-280, §845(b)(2):

Amended Code Sec. 403(b) by inserting after paragraph (1) a new paragraph (2). **Effective** for distributions in tax years beginning after 12-31-2006.

• 2005, Gulf Opportunity Zone Act of 2005 (P.L. 109-135)

P.L. 109-135, §412(w):

Amended Code Sec. 403(b)(9)(B) by inserting "or" before "a convention". **Effective** 12-21-2005.

• 2005, Katrina Emergency Tax Relief Act of 2005 (P.L. 109-73)

P.L. 109-73, §101(f)(2) [repealed by P.L. 109-135, §201(b)(4)(A)], provides:

(2) QUALIFIED HURRICANE KATRINA DISTRIBUTIONS TREATED AS MEETING PLAN DISTRIBUTION REQUIREMENTS.—For purposes of such Code, a qualified Hurricane Katrina distribution shall be treated as meeting the requirements of sections 401(k)(2)(B)(i), 403(b)(7)(A)(ii), 403(b)(11), and 457(d)(1)(A) of such Code.

P.L. 109-73, §102 [repealed by P.L. 109-135, §201(b)(4)(A)], provides:

SEC. 102. RECONTRIBUTIONS OF WITHDRAWALS FOR HOME PURCHASES CANCELLED DUE TO HURRICANE KATRINA.

(a) RECONTRIBUTIONS.—

(1) IN GENERAL.—Any individual who received a qualified distribution may, during the period beginning on August 25, 2005, and ending on February 28, 2006, make one or more contributions in an aggregate amount not to exceed the amount of such qualified distribution to an eligible retirement plan (as defined in section 402(c)(8)(B) of the Internal Revenue Code of 1986) of which such individual is a beneficiary and to which a rollover contribution of such distribution could be made under section 402(c), 403(a)(4), 403(b)(8), or 408(d)(3) of such Code, as the case may be.

(2) TREATMENT OF REPAYMENTS.—Rules similar to the rules of paragraphs (2) and (3) of section 101(c) of this Act shall apply for purposes of this section.

(b) QUALIFIED DISTRIBUTION DEFINED.—For purposes of this section, the term "qualified distribution" means any distribution—

(1) described in section 401(k)(2)(B)(i)(IV), 403(b)(7)(A)(ii) (but only to the extent such distribution relates to financial hardship), 403(b)(11)(B), or 72(t)(2)(F) of such Code,

(2) received after February 28, 2005, and before August 29, 2005, and

(3) which was to be used to purchase or construct a principal residence in the Hurricane Katrina disaster area, but which was not so purchased or constructed on account of Hurricane Katrina.

• 2004 (P.L. 108-476)

P.L. 108-476, §1, provides:

SECTION 1. CERTAIN ARRANGEMENTS MAINTAINED BY THE YMCA RETIREMENT FUND TREATED AS CHURCH PLANS.

(a) RETIREMENT PLANS.—

(1) IN GENERAL.—For purposes of sections 401(a) and 403(b) of the Internal Revenue Code of 1986, any retirement plan maintained by the YMCA Retirement Fund as of January 1, 2003, shall be treated as a church plan (within the meaning of section 414(e) of such Code) which is main-

tained by an organization described in section 414(e)(3)(A) of such Code.

(2) TAX-DEFERRED RETIREMENT PLAN.—In the case of a retirement plan described in paragraph (1) which allows contributions to be made under a salary reduction agreement—

(A) such treatment shall not apply for purposes of section 415(c)(7) of such Code, and

(B) any account maintained for a participant or beneficiary of such plan shall be treated for purposes of such Code as a retirement income account described in section 403(b)(9) of such Code, except that such account shall not, for purposes of section 403(b)(12) of such Code, be treated as a contract purchased by a church for purposes of section 403(b)(1)(D) of such Code.

(3) MONEY PURCHASE PENSION PLAN.—In the case of a retirement plan described in paragraph (1) which is subject to the requirements of section 401(a) of such Code—

(A) such plan (but not any reserves held by the YMCA Retirement Fund)—

(i) shall be treated for purposes of such Code as a defined contribution plan which is a money purchase pension plan, and

(ii) shall be treated as having made an election under section 410(d) of such Code for plan years beginning after December 31, 2005, except that notwithstanding the election—

(I) nothing in the Employee Retirement Income Security Act of 1974 or such Code shall prohibit the YMCA Retirement Fund from commingling for investment purposes the assets of the electing plan with the assets of such Fund and with the assets of any employee benefit plan maintained by such Fund, and

(II) nothing in this section shall be construed as subjecting any assets described in subclause (I), other than the assets of the electing plan, to any provision of such Act,

(B) notwithstanding section 401(a)(11) or 417 of such Code or section 205 of such Act, such plan may offer a lump-sum distribution option to participants who have not attained age 55 without offering such participants an annuity option, and

(C) any account maintained for a participant or beneficiary of such plan shall, for purposes of section 401(a)(9) of such Code, be treated as a retirement income account described in section 403(b)(9) of such Code.

(4) SELF-FUNDED DEATH BENEFIT PLAN.—For purposes of section 7702(j) of such Code, a retirement plan described in paragraph (1) shall be treated as an arrangement described in section 7702(j)(2).

(b) YMCA RETIREMENT FUND.—For purposes of this section, the term "YMCA Retirement Fund" means the Young Men's Christian Association Retirement Fund, a corporation created by an Act of the State of New York which became law on April 30, 1921.

(c) EFFECTIVE DATE.—This section shall apply to plan years beginning after December 31, 2003.

• 2004, Working Families Tax Relief Act of 2004 (P.L. 108-311)

P.L. 108-311, §408(a)(11):

Amended Code Sec. 403(b)(7)(A)(ii) by striking "section 3121(a)(1)(D)" and inserting "section 3121(a)(5)(D)". **Effective** 10-4-2004.

• 2002, Job Creation and Worker Assistance Act of 2002 (P.L. 107-147)

P.L. 107-147, §411(p)(1):

Amended Code Sec. 403(b)(1) by striking, in the matter that follows subparagraph (E), "then amounts contributed" and all that follows and inserting new text. **Effective** as if included in the provision of P.L. 107-16 to which it relates [generally applicable to years beginning after 12-31-2001.—CCH]. Prior to amendment, the matter that followed Code Sec. 403(b)(1)(E) read as follows:

then amounts contributed by such employer for such annuity contract on or after such rights become nonforfeitable shall be excluded from the gross income of the employee for the taxable year to the extent that the aggregate of such amounts does not exceed the applicable limit under section 415. The amount actually distributed to any distributee under such contract shall be taxable to the distributee (in the year in which so distributed) under section 72 (relating to annuities). For purposes of applying the rules of this subsection to amounts contributed by an employer for a taxable year, amounts transferred to a contract described in this paragraph by reason of a rollover contribution described in paragraph (8) of this subsection or section 408(d)(3)(A)(ii) shall not be considered contributed by such employer.

P.L. 107-147, §411(p)(2):

Amended Code Sec. 403(b) by striking paragraph (6). **Effective** as if included in the provision of P.L. 107-16 to which it relates [generally applicable to years beginning after 12-31-2001.—CCH]. Prior to amendment, Code Sec. 403(b)(6) read as follows:

(6) FORFEITABLE RIGHTS WHICH BECOME NONFORFEITABLE.—For purposes of this subsection and section 72(f) (relating to special rules for computing employees' contributions to annuity contracts), if rights of the employee under an annuity contract described in subparagraphs (A) and (B) of paragraph (1) change from forfeitable to nonforfeitable rights, then the amount (determined without regard to this subsection) includible in gross income by reason of such change shall be treated as an amount contributed by the employer for such annuity contract as of the time such rights become nonforfeitable.

P.L. 107-147, §411(p)(3)(A)-(B):

Amended Code Sec. 403(b)(3) by inserting ", and which precedes the taxable year by no more than five years" before the period at the end of the first sentence, and by striking "or any amount received by a former employee after the fifth taxable year following the taxable year in which such employee was terminated" in the second sentence following "this subsection applies". **Effective** as if included in the provision of P.L. 107-16 to which it relates [applicable to years beginning after 12-31-2001.—CCH].

• 2001, Economic Growth and Tax Relief Reconciliation Act of 2001 (P.L. 107-16)

P.L. 107-16, §632(a)(2)(A)-(C):

Amended Code Sec. 403(b) by striking "the exclusion allowance for such taxable year" in paragraph (1) and inserting "the applicable limit under section 415", by striking paragraph (2), and by inserting "or any amount received by a former employee after the fifth taxable year following the taxable year in which such employee was terminated" before the period at the end of the second sentence of paragraph (3). **Effective** for years beginning after 12-31-2001. Prior to being stricken, Code Sec. 403(b)(2) read as follows:

(2) EXCLUSION ALLOWANCE.—

(A) IN GENERAL.—For purposes of this subsection, the exclusion allowance for any employee for the taxable year is an amount equal to the excess, if any, of—

(i) the amount determined by multiplying 20 percent of his includible compensation by the number of years of service, over

(ii) the aggregate of the amount contributed by the employer for annuity contracts and excludable from the gross income of the employee for any prior taxable year.

(B) ELECTION TO HAVE ALLOWANCE DETERMINED UNDER SECTION 415 RULES.—In the case of an employee who makes an election under section 415(c)(4)(D) to have the provisions of section 415(c)(4)(C) (relating to special rule for section 403(b) contracts purchased by educational institutions, hospitals, home health service agencies, and certain churches, etc.) apply, the exclusion allowance for any such employee for the taxable year is the amount which could be contributed (under section 415 without regard to section 415(c)(8)[(7)]) by his employer under a plan described in section 403(a) if the annuity contract for the benefit of such employee were treated as a defined contribution plan maintained by the employer.

(C) NUMBER OF YEARS OF SERVICE FOR DULY ORDAINED, COMMISSIONED, OR LICENSED MINISTERS OR LAY EMPLOYEES.—For purposes of this subsection and section 415(c)(4)(A)—

(i) all years of service by—

(I) a duly ordained, commissioned, or licensed minister of a church, or

(II) a lay person,

as an employee of a church, a convention or association of churches, including an organization described in section

414(e)(3)(B)(ii), shall be considered as years of service for 1 employer, and

(ii) all amounts contributed for annuity contracts by each such church (or convention or association of churches) or such organization during such years for such minister or lay person shall be considered to have been contributed by 1 employer.

For purposes of the preceding sentence, the terms "church" and "convention or association of churches" have the same meaning as when used in section 414(e).

(D) ALTERNATIVE EXCLUSION ALLOWANCE.—

(i) IN GENERAL.—In the case of any individual described in subparagraph (C), the amount determined under subparagraph (A) shall not be less than the lesser of—

(I) $3,000, or

(II) the includible compensation of such individual.

(ii) SUBPARAGRAPH NOT TO APPLY TO INDIVIDUALS WITH ADJUSTED GROSS INCOME OVER $17,000.—This subparagraph shall not apply with respect to any taxable year to any individual whose adjusted gross income for such taxable year (determined separately and without regard to any community property laws) exceeds $17,000.

(iii) SPECIAL RULE FOR FOREIGN MISSIONARIES.—In the case of an individual described in subparagraph (C)(i) performing services outside the United States, there shall be included as includible compensation for any year under clause (i)(II) any amount contributed during such year by a church (or convention or association of churches) for an annuity contract with respect to such individual.

P.L. 107-16, §632(b)(2)(B) and (3), provides:

(B) EXCLUSION ALLOWANCE.—Effective for limitation years beginning in 2000, in the case of any annuity contract described in section 403(b) of the Internal Revenue Code of 1986, the amount of the contribution disqualified by reason of section 415(g) of such Code shall reduce the exclusion allowance as provided in section 403(b)(2) of such Code.

(3) ELECTION TO MODIFY SECTION 403(b) EXCLUSION ALLOWANCE TO CONFORM TO SECTION 415 MODIFICATION.—In the case of taxable years beginning after December 31, 1999, and before January 1, 2002, a plan may disregard the requirement in the regulations regarding the exclusion allowance under section 403(b)(2) of the Internal Revenue Code of 1986 that contributions to a defined benefit pension plan be treated as previously excluded amounts for purposes of the exclusion allowance.

P.L. 107-16, §641(b)(1):

Amended Code Sec. 403(b)(8)(A)(ii) by striking "such distribution" and all that follows and inserting "such distribution to an eligible retirement plan described in section 402(c)(8)(B), and". **Effective**, generally, for distributions after 12-31-2001. For a special rule, see Act Sec. 641(f)(3), below. Prior to amendment, Code Sec. 403(b)(8)(A)(ii) read as follows:

(ii) the employee transfers any portion of the property he receives in such distribution to an individual retirement plan or to an annuity contract described in paragraph (1), and

P.L. 107-16, §641(e)(7):

Amended Code Sec. 403(b)(8)(B). **Effective**, generally, for distributions after 12-31-2001. For a special rule, see Act Sec. 641(f)(3), below. Prior to amendment, Code Sec. 403(b)(8)(B) read as follows:

(B) CERTAIN RULES MADE APPLICABLE.—Rules similar to the rules of paragraphs (2) through (7) of section 402(c) (including paragraph (4)(C) thereof) shall apply for purposes of subparagraph (A).

P.L. 107-16, §641(f)(3), provides:

(3) SPECIAL RULE.—Notwithstanding any other provision of law, subsections (h)(3) and (h)(5) of section 1122 of the Tax Reform Act of 1986 shall not apply to any distribution from an eligible retirement plan (as defined in clause (iii) or (iv) of section 402(c)(8)(B) of the Internal Revenue Code of 1986) on behalf of an individual if there was a rollover to such plan on behalf of such individual which is permitted solely by reason of any amendment made by this section.

P.L. 107-16, §642(b)(1):

Amended Code Sec. 403(b)(1) by striking "section 408(d)(3)(A)(iii)" and inserting "section 408(d)(3)(A)(ii)". **Effective** for distributions after 12-31-2001. For a special rule, see Act Sec. 642(c)(2), below.

P.L. 107-16, §642(c)(2), provides:

(2) SPECIAL RULE.—Notwithstanding any other provision of law, subsections (h)(3) and (h)(5) of section 1122 of the Tax Reform Act of 1986 shall not apply to any distribution from an eligible retirement plan (as defined in clause (iii) or (iv) of section 402(c)(8)(B) of the Internal Revenue Code of 1986) on behalf of an individual if there was a rollover to such plan on behalf of such individual which is permitted solely by reason of the amendments made by this section.

P.L. 107-16, §646(a)(2)(A):

Amended Code Sec. 403(b) by striking "separates from service" and inserting "has a severance from employment" in paragraphs (7)(A)(ii) and (11)(A). **Effective** for distributions after 12-31-2001.

P.L. 107-16, §646(a)(2)(B):

Amended the heading for Code Sec. 403(b)(11) by striking "SEPARATION FROM SERVICE" and inserting "SEVERANCE FROM EMPLOYMENT". **E ffective** for distributions after 12-31-2001.

P.L. 107-16, §647(a):

Amended Code Sec. 403(b) by adding at the end a new paragraph (13). **Effective** for trustee-to-trustee transfers after 12-31-2001.

P.L. 107-16, §901(a)-(b), provides [but see P.L. 109-280, §811, above]:

SEC. 901. SUNSET OF PROVISIONS OF ACT.

(a) IN GENERAL.—All provisions of, and amendments made by, this Act shall not apply—

(1) to taxable, plan, or limitation years beginning after December 31, 2010, or

(2) in the case of title V, to estates of decedents dying, gifts made, or generation skipping transfers, after December 31, 2010.

(b) APPLICATION OF CERTAIN LAWS.—The Internal Revenue Code of 1986 and the Employee Retirement Income Security Act of 1974 shall be applied and administered to years, estates, gifts, and transfers described in subsection (a) as if the provisions and amendments described in subsection (a) had never been enacted.

• 2000, Community Renewal Tax Relief Act of 2000 (P.L. 106-554)

P.L. 106-554, §314(e)(1):

Amended Code Sec. 403(b)(3)(B) by striking "section 125 or" and inserting "section 125, 132(f)(4), or". **Effective** as if included in the provision of P.L. 105-34 to which it relates [**effective** for years beginning after 12-31-97.—CCH.].

• 1998, IRS Restructuring and Reform Act of 1998 (P.L. 105-206)

P.L. 105-206, §6005(c)(2)(B):

Amended Code Sec. 403(b)(8)(B) by inserting "(including paragraph (4)(C) thereof)" after "section 402(c)". **Effective** for distributions after 12-31-98.

• 1997, Taxpayer Relief Act of 1997 (P.L. 105-34)

P.L. 105-34, §1504(a)(1):

Amended Code Sec. 403(b)(3) by adding at the end "Such term includes—" and the material that follows through the period at the end of the sentence. **Effective** for years beginning after 12-31-97.

P.L. 105-34, §1504(b), provides:

(b) REPEAL OF RULES IN SECTION 415(e).—The Secretary of the Treasury shall modify the regulations regarding the exclusion allowance under section 403(b)(2) of the Internal Revenue Code of 1986 to reflect the amendment made by section 1452(a) of the Small Business Job Protection Act of 1996. Such modification shall take effect for years beginning after December 31, 1999.

P.L. 105-34, §1505(c):

Amended Code Sec. 403(b)(12) by adding at the end a new subparagraph (C). **Effective**, generally, for tax years beginning on or after 8-5-97. For a special rule, see Act Sec. 1505(d)(2), below.

P.L. 105-34, §1505(d)(2), as amended by P.L. 105-206, §6015(b), and further amended by P.L. 109-280, §861(a)(2), provides:

(2) TREATMENT FOR YEARS BEGINNING BEFORE DATE OF ENACTMENT.—A governmental plan (within the meaning of section 414(d) of the Internal Revenue Code of 1986) shall be treated as satisfying the requirements of sections 401(a)(3), 401(a)(4), 401(a)(26), 401(k), 401(m), 403(b)(1)(D) and (b)(12)(A)(i), and 410 of such Code for all taxable years beginning before the date of enactment of this Act.

P.L. 105-34, §1601(d)(4) (as amended by P.L. 105-206, §6016(a)(2)(A)-(B)), provides:

(4) CLARIFICATION OF SECTION 1450.—

(A) Paragraphs (7)(A)(ii) and (11) of section 403(b) of the Internal Revenue Code of 1986 shall not apply with respect to a distribution from a contract described in section 1450(b)(1) of such Act to the extent that such distribution is not includible in income by reason of—

(i) in the case of distributions before January 1, 1998, section 403(b)(8) or (b)(10) of such Code (determined after the application of section 1450(b)(2) of such Act), and

(ii) in the case of distributions on and after such date, such section 403(b)(10).

(B) This paragraph shall apply as if included in section 1450 of the Small Business Job Protection Act of 1996.

P.L. 105-34, §1601(d)(6)(B):

Amended Code Sec. 403(b)(1)(A) by striking "or" at the end of clause (i), by inserting "or" at the end of clause (ii), and by adding at the end a new clause (iii). **Effective** as if included in the provision of P.L. 104-188 to which it relates [**effective** for years beginning after 12-31-96.—CCH].

• 1996, Small Business Job Protection Act of 1996 (P.L. 104-188)

P.L. 104-188, §1450(a)(1) and (b)(1), provide:

(a) MULTIPLE SALARY REDUCTION AGREEMENTS PERMITTED.—

(1) GENERAL RULE.—For purposes of section 403(b) of the Internal Revenue Code of 1986, the frequency that an employee is permitted to enter into a salary reduction agreement, the salary to which such an agreement may apply, and the ability to revoke such an agreement shall be determined under the rules applicable to cash or deferred elections under section 401(k) of such Code.

* * *

(b) TREATMENT OF INDIAN TRIBAL GOVERNMENTS.—

(1) IN GENERAL.—In the case of any contract purchased in a plan year beginning before January 1, 1995, section 403(b) of the Internal Revenue Code of 1986 shall be applied as if any reference to an employer described in section 501(c)(3) of the Internal Revenue Code of 1986 which is exempt from tax under section 501 of such Code included a reference to an employer which is an Indian tribal government (as defined by section 7701(a)(40) of such Code), a subdivision of an Indian tribal government (determined in accordance with section 7871(d) of such Code), an agency or instrumentality of an Indian tribal government or subdivision thereof, or a corporation chartered under Federal, State, or tribal law which is owned in whole or in part by any of the foregoing.

P.L. 104-188, §1450(c)(1):

Amended Code Sec. 403(b)(1)(E). **Effective** for years beginning after 12-31-95, except a contract shall not be required to meet any change in any requirement by reason of this amendment before the 90th day after 8-20-96. Prior to amendment, Code Sec. 403(b)(1)(E) read as follows:

(E) in the case of a contract purchased under a plan which provides a salary reduction agreement, the plan meets the requirements of section 401(a)(30),

P.L. 104-188, §1704(t)(69):

Amended Code Sec. 403(b)(10) by striking "an direct" in the last sentence and inserting "a direct". **Effective** 8-20-96.

• 1992, Unemployment Compensation Amendments Act of 1992 (P.L. 102-318)

P.L. 102-318, §521(b)(13)(A):

Amended Code Sec. 403(b)(8)(A)(i) by inserting "in an eligible rollover distribution (within the meaning of section 402(c)(4))" before the comma at the end thereof. **Effective** for distributions after 12-31-92. For a transitional rule, see Act Sec. 522(d)(2), below.

P.L. 102-318, §521(b)(13)(B):

Amended Code Sec. 403(b)(8)(B)-(D) by striking subparagraphs (B), (C), and (D) and inserting new paragraph (B). **Effective** for distributions after 12-31-92. For a transitional rule, see Act Sec. 522(d)(2), below.

P.L. 102-318, §522(a)(3):

Amended Code Sec. 403(b)(10) by striking "section 401(a)(9)" and inserting "sections 401(a)(9) and 401(a)(31)". **Effective** for distributions after 12-31-92. For a transitional rule, see Act Sec. 522(d)(2), below.

P.L. 102-318, §522(c)(3):

Amended Code Sec. 403(b)(10) by adding at the end thereof a new sentence. **Effective** for distributions after 12-31-92. For a transitional rule, see Act Sec. 522(d)(2), below.

P.L. 102-318, §522(d)(2), provides:

(2) TRANSITION RULE FOR CERTAIN ANNUITY CONTRACTS.—If, as of July 1, 1992, a State law prohibits a direct trustee-to-trustee transfer from an annuity contract described in section 403(b) of the Internal Revenue Code of 1986 which was purchased for an employee by an employer which is a State or a political subdivision thereof (or an agency or instrumentality of any 1 or more of either), the amendments made by this section shall not apply to distributions before the earlier of—

(A) 90 days after the first day after July 1, 1992, on which such transfer is allowed under State law, or

(B) January 1, 1994.

• 1990, Omnibus Budget Reconciliation Act of 1990 (P.L. 101-508)

P.L. 101-508, §11701(k):

Amended Code Sec. 403(b)(12)(A) by inserting "involving a one-time irrevocable election" after "similar arrangement". **Effective** as if included in the provision of P.L. 101-239 to which it relates.

• 1988, Technical and Miscellaneous Revenue Act of 1988 (P.L. 100-647)

P.L. 100-647, §1011(c)(7)(B):

Amended Code Sec. 403(b)(1) by striking out "and" at the end of subparagraph (C), by inserting "and" at the end of subparagraph (D), and by inserting after subparagraph (D) new subparagraph (E). For the **effective** date, see Act Sec. 1011(c)(7)(E), below.

P.L. 100-647, §1011(c)(7)(E), provides:

(E)(i) Except as provided in clause (ii), the amendments made by this paragraph shall apply to plan years beginning after December 31, 1987.

(ii) In the case of a plan described in section 1105(c)(2) of the Reform Act, the amendments made by this paragraph shall not apply to contributions made pursuant to an agreement described in such section for plan years beginning before the earlier of—

(I) the later of January 1, 1988, or the date on which the last of such agreements terminates (determined without regard to any extension thereof after February 28, 1986), or

(II) January 1, 1989.

P.L. 100-647, §1011(c)(12):

Amended Code Sec. 403(b)(12)(A) by inserting after clause (ii) a new sentence. **Effective** as if included in the provision of P.L. 99-514 to which it relates.

P.L. 100-647, §1011(m)(1)(A):

Redesignated Code Sec. 403(b)(10) as Code Sec. 403(b)(12). **Effective** as if included in the provision of P.L. 99-514 to which it relates.

P.L. 100-647, §1011(m)(1)(B):

Amended Code Sec. 403(b)(1)(D) by striking out "paragraph (10)" and inserting in lieu thereof "paragraph (12)". **Effective** as if included in the provision of P.L. 99-514 to which it relates.

P.L. 100-647, §1011(m)(2)(A)-(B):

Amended Code Sec. 403(b)(12)(A)(i), as redesignated, by inserting "(17)," after "(5),", and by inserting ", section 401(m)," after "section 401(a)" the first place it appears. **Effective** as if included in the provision of P.L. 99-514 to which it relates.

P.L. 100-647, §6052(a)(1):

Amended the last sentence of Code Sec. 403(b)(12)(A). **Effective** as if included in the amendments made by section 1120(b) of P.L. 99-514. Prior to amendment, the last sentence of Code Sec. 403 (b)(12)(A) read as follows:

For purposes of this subparagraph, students who normally work less than 20 hours per week may (subject to the conditions applicable under section 410(b)(4)) be excluded.

P.L. 100-647, §6052(b), provides:

(b) SAMPLING.—In the case of plan years beginning in 1989, 1990, or 1991, determinations as to whether a plan meets the requirements of section 403(b)(12) of the 1986 Code may be made on the basis of a statistically valid random sample. The preceding sentence shall apply only if—

(1) the sampling is conducted by an independent person in a manner not inconsistent with regulations prescribed by the Secretary, and

(2) the statistical method and sample size result in a 95 percent probability that the results will have a margin of error not greater than 3 percent.

• 1986, Tax Reform Act of 1986 (P.L. 99-514)

P.L. 99-514, §1120(a):

Amended Code Sec. 403(b)(1) by striking out "and" at the end of subparagraph (B), by inserting "and" at the end of subparagraph (C), and by inserting after subparagraph (C) new subparagraph (D). For the **effective** date, see Act Sec. 1120(c), below.

P.L. 99-514, §1120(b):

Amended Code Sec. 403(b) by inserting at the end thereof new paragraph (10)[(11)]. For the **effective** date, see Act Sec. 1120(c), below.

P.L. 99-514, §1120(c), as amended by P.L. 100-647, §1011(m)(3), provides:

(c) EFFECTIVE DATES.—

(1) IN GENERAL.—Except as provided in paragraph (2), the amendments made by this section shall apply to years beginning after December 31, 1988.

(2) COLLECTIVE BARGAINING AGREEMENTS.—In the case of a plan maintained pursuant to 1 or more collective bargaining agreements between employee representatives and 1 or more employers ratified before March 1, 1986, the amendments made by this section shall not apply to plan years beginning before the earlier of—

(A) January 1, 1991, or

(B) the later of—

(i) January 1, 1989, or

(ii) the date on which the last of such collective bargaining agreements terminates (determined without regard to any extension thereof after February 28, 1986).

P.L. 99-514, §1122(d)(2):

Amended the second sentence of Code Sec. 403(b)(1). **Effective**, generally, for amounts distributed after 12-31-86, in tax years ending after such date. For special rules, see Act Sec. 1122(h)(3)-(9), reproduced under the amendment notes for Code Sec. 403(a). Prior to amendment, the second sentence read as follows:

The employee shall include in his gross income the amounts received under such contract for the year received as provided in section 72 (relating to annuities).

P.L. 99-514, §1123(c)(1):

Amended Code Sec. 403(b) by inserting at the end thereof new paragraph (11)[(12)]. **Effective** for years beginning after 12-31-88, but only for distributions from contracts described in section 403(b) of the Internal Revenue Code of 1986 which are attributable to assets other than assets held as of the close of the last year beginning before 1-1-89 [**effective** date changed by P.L. 100-647, §1011A(c)(11)]. However, for an exception and transitional rule, see Act Sec. 1123(e)(3)-(4), below.

P.L. 99-514, §1123(c)(2):

Amended Code Sec. 403(b)(7)[(A)](ii) by inserting "in the case of contributions made pursuant to a salary reduction agreement (within the meaning of section 3121(a)(1)(D))" before "encounters". **Effective** for years beginning after 12-31-88, but only for distributions from contracts described in section 403(b) of the Internal Revenue Code of 1986 which are attributable to assets other than assets held as of the close of the last year beginning before 1-1-89 [**effective** date changed by P.L. 100-647, §1011A(c)(11)]. However, for an exception and transitional rule, see Act Sec. 1123(e)(3)-(4), below.

P.L. 99-514, §1123(e)(3)-(4), provides:

(3) EXCEPTION WHERE DISTRIBUTION COMMENCES.—The amendments made by this section shall not apply to distributions to any employee from a plan maintained by any employer if—

(A) as of March 1, 1986, the employee separated from service with the employer,

(B) as of March 1, 1986, the accrued benefit of the employee was in pay status pursuant to a written election providing a specific schedule for the distribution of the entire accrued benefit of the employee, and

(C) such distribution is made pursuant to such written election.

(4) TRANSITION RULE.—The amendments made by this section shall not apply with respect to any benefits with respect to which a designation is in effect under section 242(b)(2) of the Tax Equity and Fiscal Responsibility Act of 1982.

P.L. 99-514, §1852(a)(3)(A):

Amended Code Sec. 403(b) by inserting at the end thereof new paragraph (10). **Effective** for benefits accruing after 12-31-86, in tax years ending after such date.

P.L. 99-514, §1852(a)(3)(B):

Amended Code Sec. 403(b)(7) by striking out subparagraph (D). **Effective** for benefits accruing after 12-31-86, in tax years ending after such date. Prior to amendment, Code Sec. 403(b)(7)(D) read as follows:

(D) DISTRIBUTION REQUIREMENTS.—For purposes of determining when the interest of an employee in a custodial account must be distributed, such account shall be treated in the same manner as an annuity contract.

P.L. 99-514, §1852(a)(5)(B)(ii):

Amended Code Sec. 403(b)(8) by adding at the end thereof new subparagraph (D). **Effective** as if included in the provision of P.L. 98-369 to which it relates.

P.L. 99-514, §1852(b)(10):

Amended Code Sec. 403(b)(8)(C) by striking out "(F)(i)" and inserting in lieu thereof "and (F)(i)". **Effective** as if included in the provision of P.L. 98-369 to which it relates.

• 1984, Deficit Reduction Act of 1984 (P.L. 98-369)

P.L. 98-369, §491(d)(12):

Amended Code Sec. 403(b)(1) by striking out "or 409(b)(3)(C)" in the last sentence. **Effective** for obligations issued after 12-31-83.

P.L. 98-369, §521(c):

Added Code Sec. 403(b)(7)(D). **Effective** for years beginning after 12-31-84.

P.L. 98-369, §522(a)(3):

Amended Code Sec. 403(b)(8)(A)(i). **Effective** for distributions made after 7-18-84, in tax years ending after such date. Prior to amendment, Code Sec. 403(b)(8)(A)(i) read as follows:

(i) the balance to the credit of an employee is paid to him in a qualifying distribution.

P.L. 98-369, §522(d)(10):

Amended Code Sec. 403(b)(8)(B). **Effective** for distributions made after 7-18-84, in tax years ending after such date. Prior to amendment, Code Sec. 403(b)(8)(B) read as follows:

(B) Qualifying Distribution Defined.—

(i) In General.—For purposes of subparagraph (A), the term "qualifying distribution" means 1 or more distributions from an annuity contract described in paragraph (1) which would constitute a lump sum distribution within the meaning of section 402(e)(4)(A) (determined without regard to subparagraphs (B) and (H) of section 402(e)(4)) if such annuity contract were described in subsection (a), or 1 or more distributions of accumulated deductible employee contributions (within the meaning of section 72(o)(5)).

(ii) Aggregation of Annuity Contracts.—For purposes of this paragraph, all annuity contracts described in paragraph (1) purchased by an employer shall be treated as a single contract, and section 402(e)(4)(C) shall not apply.

P.L. 98-369, §522(d)(11):

Amended Code Sec. 403(b)(8)(C) by striking out "(D)(v), and (E)(i)" and inserting in lieu thereof "[and](F)(i)". **Effec-**

tive for distributions made after 7-18-84, in tax years ending after such date.

• 1983, Social Security Amendments of 1983 (P.L. 98-21)

P.L. 98-21, §122(c)(4):

Amended Code Sec. 403(b)(3) by striking out "sections 105(d) and 911" and inserting in place thereof "section 911". **Effective** for tax years beginning after 1983.

• 1983, Technical Corrections Act of 1982 (P.L. 97-448)

P.L. 97-448, §103(c)(8)(B):

Amended Code Sec. 403(b)(8)(C) by striking out "subparagraphs (B), (C)," and inserting in lieu thereof "subparagraphs (B), (C), (D)(v),". **Effective** as if included in the provision of P.L. 97-34 to which it relates.

• 1982, Tax Equity and Fiscal Responsibility Act of 1982 (P.L. 97-248)

P.L. 97-248, §251(a)(1)-(2):

Amended Code Sec. 403(b)(2) by striking out in subparagraph (B) the phrase "(under section 415)" and inserting in lieu thereof "(under section 415 without regard to section 415(c)(8))" and further amended it by adding at the end thereof new subparagraphs (C) and (D). **Effective** for tax years beginning after 12-31-81.

P.L. 97-248, §251(b):

Amended Code Sec. 403(b) by adding at the end thereof new paragraph (9). **Effective** for tax years beginning after 12-31-74.

P.L. 97-248, §251(d), provides:

(d) CORRECTION PERIOD FOR CHURCHES.—A church plan (within the meaning of section 414(e) of the Internal Revenue Code of 1954) shall not be treated as not meeting the requirements of section 401 or 403 of such Code if—

(1) by reason of any change in any law, regulation, ruling, or otherwise such plan is required to be amended to meet such requirements, and

(2) such plan is so amended at the next earliest church convention or such other time as the Secretary of the Treasury or his delegate may prescribe.

This provision is **effective** July 1, 1982.

P.L. 97-248, §251(e)(5), provides:

(5) SPECIAL RULE FOR EXISTING DEFINED BENEFIT ARRANGEMENTS.—Any defined benefit arrangement which is established by a church or a convention or association of churches (including an organization described in section 414(e)(3)(B)(ii) of the Internal Revenue Code of 1954) and which is in effect on the date of the enactment of this Act shall not be treated as failing to meet the requirements of section 403(b)(2) of such Code merely because it is a defined benefit arrangement.

P.L. 97-248, §251(c)(3):

Amended Code Sec. 403(b)(2) by striking out in subparagraph (B) "and home health service agencies" and inserting in lieu thereof "home health service agencies, and certain churches, etc.". **Effective** for years beginning after 12-31-81.

• 1981, Economic Recovery Tax Act of 1981 (P.L. 97-34)

P.L. 97-34, §311(b)(3)(B):

Amended Code Sec. 403(b)(8)(B)(i) by inserting ", or 1 or more distributions of accumulated deductible employee contributions (within the meaning of section 72(o)(5))" after "subsection (a)". **Effective** for tax years beginning after 12-31-81. The transitional rule provides that, for purposes of the 1954 Code, any amount allowed as a deduction under section 220 of the Code (as in effect before its repeal by P.L. 97-34) shall be treated as if it were allowed under Code Sec. 219.

• 1980, Technical Corrections Act of 1979 (P.L. 96-222)

P.L. 96-222, §101(a)(12):

Amended Code Sec. 403(b)(7)(A) by changing "which satisfied" to "which satisfies". **Effective** for tax years beginning after 12-31-78.

P.L. 96-222, §101(a)(13)(B), provides:

(B) TRANSITIONAL RULE FOR MAKING SECTION 403(b)(8) ROLLOVER IN THE CASE OF PAYMENTS DURING 1978.—In the case of any payment made during 1978 in a qualifying distribution described in section 403(b)(8) of the Internal Revenue Code of 1954, the applicable period specified in section 402(a)(5)(C) of such Code shall not expire before the close of December 31, 1980.

P.L. 96-222, §101(a)(13)(C):

Amended Code Sec. 403(b)(1) by changing "409(d)(3)(C)" to "409(b)(3)(C)". **Effective** for distributions and transfers made after 12-31-78, in tax years beginning after such date.

• 1978, Revenue Act of 1978 (P.L. 95-600)

P.L. 95-600, §154(a):

Amended Code Sec. 403(b)(7)(A). **Effective** for tax years beginning after 12-31-78. Prior to amendment, Code Sec. 403(b)(7)(A) read:

"(A) AMOUNTS PAID TREATED AS CONTRIBUTIONS.—For purposes of this title, amounts paid by an employer described in paragraph (1)(A) to a custodial account which satisfies the requirements of section 401(f)(2) shall be treated as amounts contributed by him for an annuity contract for his employee if the amounts are paid to provide a retirement benefit for that employee and are to be invested in regulated investment company stock to be held in that custodial account."

P.L. 95-600, §156(a):

Added Code Sec. 403(b)(8). **Effective** for distributions or transfers made after 12-31-77, in tax years beginning after such date [**effective** date amended by P.L. 96-222, §101(a)(13)(A).—CCH].

P.L. 95-600, §156(b):

Added a new last sentence to Code Sec. 403(b)(1). **Effective** for distributions or transfers made after 12-31-77, in tax years beginning after such date [**effective** date amended by P.L. 96-222, §101(a)(13)(A).—CCH].

• 1976, Tax Reform Act of 1976 (P.L. 94-455)

P.L. 94-455, §1504(a):

Amended Code Sec. 403(b)(7)(C), by striking out at the end thereof, ", and which issues only redeemable stock". **Effective** for tax years beginning after 12-31-75.

P.L. 94-455, §1901(b)(8)(A):

Amended Code Sec. 403(b)(1)(A)(ii), by substituting "educational organization described in section 170(b)(1)(A)(ii)" for "educational institution (as defined in section 151(e)(4))". **Effective** for tax years beginning after 12-31-76.

P.L. 94-455, §1906(b)(13)(A):

Amended the 1954 Code by substituting "Secretary" for "Secretary or his delegate" each place it appeared. **Effective** 2-1-77.

• 1974, Employee Retirement Income Security Act of 1974 (P.L. 93-406)

P.L. 93-406, §1022(e):

Added paragraph (7). **Effective** 1-1-74.

P.L. 93-406, §2004(c)(4):

Amended Code Sec. 403(b)(2). **Effective** for years beginning after 1975. Prior to amendment, Code Sec. 403(b)(2) read as follows:

"(2) Exclusion allowance.—For purposes of this subsection, the exclusion allowance for any employee for the taxable year is an amount equal to the excess, if any, of—

"(A) the amount determined by multiplying (i) 20 percent of his includible compensation, by (ii) the number of years of service, over

"(B) the aggregate of the amounts contributed by the employer for annuity contracts and excludable from the gross income of the employee for any prior taxable year."

• 1964, Revenue Act of 1964 (P.L. 88-272)

P.L. 88-272, §232(e)(5):

Amended Code Sec. 403(b)(1) to delete "except that section 72(e)(3) shall not apply" from the end of the second sentence. **Effective** with respect to tax years beginning after 12-31-63.

• 1961 (P.L. 87-370)

P.L. 87-370, §3(a):

Amended Code Sec. 403(b) by amending subparagraph (A) of paragraph (1), striking out "the employer described in section 501(c)(3) and exempt from tax under section 501(a)" in paragraph (3) and inserting in lieu thereof the following: "the employer described in paragraph (1)(A),", and inserting before the period in the heading of Sec. 403(b) the following: "or Public School". **Effective** for tax years beginning after 1957. Prior to amendment, subparagraph (A) of paragraph (1) of Code Sec. 403(b) read as follows:

"(A) an annuity contract is purchased for an employee by an employer described in section 501(c)(3) which is exempt from tax under section 501(a),".

• 1958, Technical Amendments Act of 1958 (P.L. 85-866)

P.L. 85-866, §23(a):

Redesignated subsection (b) of Sec. 403 as subsection (c) and added new subsection (b). **Effective** 1-1-58.

[Sec. 403(c)]

(c) TAXABILITY OF BENEFICIARY UNDER NONQUALIFIED ANNUITIES OR UNDER ANNUITIES PURCHASED BY EXEMPT ORGANIZATIONS.—Premiums paid by an employer for an annuity contract which is not subject to subsection (a) shall be included in the gross income of the employee in accordance with section 83 (relating to property transferred in connection with performance of services), except that the value of such contract shall be substituted for the fair market value of the property for purposes of applying such section. The preceding sentence shall not apply to that portion of the premiums paid which is excluded from gross income under subsection (b). In the case of any portion of any contract which is attributable to premiums to which this subsection applies, the amount actually paid or made available under such contract to any beneficiary which is attributable to such premiums shall be taxable to the beneficiary (in the year in which so paid or made available) under section 72 (relating to annuities).

Amendments

• 1986, Tax Reform Act of 1986 (P.L. 99-514)

P.L. 99-514, §1122(d)(3):

Amended the last sentence of Code Sec. 403(c). **Effective**, generally, for amounts distributed after 12-31-86, in tax years ending after such date. For special rules, see Act Sec. 1122(h)(3)-(9), reproduced under the amendment notes for Code Sec. 403(a). Prior to amendment, Code Sec. 403(c) read as follows:

(c) TAXABILITY OF BENEFICIARY UNDER NONQUALIFIED ANNUITIES OR UNDER ANNUITIES PURCHASED BY EXEMPT ORGANIZATIONS.—Premiums paid by an employer for an annuity contract which is not subject to subsection (a) shall be included in the gross income of the employee in accordance with section 83 (relating to property transferred in connection with performance of services), except that the value of such contract shall be substituted for the fair market value of the property for purposes of applying such section. The preceding sentence shall not apply to that portion of the premiums paid which is excluded from gross income under subsection (b). The amount actually paid or made available to any beneficiary under such contract shall be taxable to him in the year in which so paid or made available under section 72 (relating to annuities).

• 1969, Tax Reform Act of 1969 (P.L. 91-172)

P.L. 91-172, §321(b)(2):

Amended Sec. 403(c), and deleted Sec. 403(d). **Effective** for contributions made and premiums paid after 8-1-69. Prior to amendment, Code Sec. 403(c) and (d) read as follows:

(c) Taxability of Beneficiary Under a Nonqualified Annuity.—If an annuity contract purchased by an employer for an employee is not subject to subsection (a) and the employee's rights under the contract are nonforfeitable, except for failure to pay future premiums, the amount contributed by the employer for such annuity contract on or after such rights become nonforfeitable shall be included in the gross income of the employee in the year in which the amount is contributed. The employee shall include in his gross income the amounts received under such contract for the year received as provided in section 72 (relating to annuities).

(d) Taxability of Beneficiary Under Certain Forfeitable Contracts Purchased by Exempt Organizations.—Notwithstanding the first sentence of subsection (c), if rights of an employee under an annuity contract purchased by an employer which is exempt from tax under section 501(a) or 521(a) change from forfeitable to nonforfeitable rights, the value of such contract on the date of such change (to the extent attributable to amounts contributed by the employer after December 31, 1957) shall, except as provided in subsection (b), be included in the gross income of the employee in the year of such change.

• 1964, Revenue Act of 1964 (P.L. 88-272)

P.L. 88-272, §232(e)(6):

Amended Code Sec. 403(c) to delete "except that section 72(e)(3) shall not apply" from the end of the second sentence. **Effective** for tax years beginning after 12-31-63.

• 1958, Technical Amendments Act of 1958 (P.L. 85-866)

P.L. 85-866, §23(a):

Redesignated former subsection (b) as subsection (c). **Effective** 1-1-58.

[Sec. 404]

SEC. 404. DEDUCTION FOR CONTRIBUTIONS OF AN EMPLOYER TO AN EMPLOYEES' TRUST OR ANNUITY PLAN AND COMPENSATION UNDER A DEFERRED-PAYMENT PLAN.

[Sec. 404(a)]

(a) GENERAL RULE.—If contributions are paid by an employer to or under a stock bonus, pension, profit-sharing, or annuity plan, or if compensation is paid or accrued on account of any employee under a plan deferring the receipt of such compensation, such contributions or compensation shall not be deductible under this chapter; but if they would otherwise be deductible, they shall be deductible under this section, subject, however, to the following limitations as to the amounts deductible in any year:

(1) PENSION TRUSTS.—

(A) IN GENERAL.—In the taxable year when paid, if the contributions are paid into a pension trust (other than a trust to which paragraph (3) applies), and if such taxable year ends within or with a taxable year of the trust for which the trust is exempt under section 501(a), in the case of a defined benefit plan other than a multiemployer plan, in an amount determined under subsection (o), and in the case of any other plan in an amount determined as follows:

(i) the amount necessary to satisfy the minimum funding standard provided by section 412(a) for plan years ending within or with such taxable year (or for any prior plan year), if such amount is greater than the amount determined under clause (ii) or (iii) (whichever is applicable with respect to the plan),

(ii) the amount necessary to provide with respect to all of the employees under the trust the remaining unfunded cost of their past and current service credits distributed as a level amount, or a level percentage of compensation, over the remaining future service of each such employee, as determined under regulations prescribed by the Secretary, but if such remaining unfunded cost with respect to any 3 individuals is more than 50 percent of such remaining unfunded cost, the amount of such unfunded cost attributable to such individuals shall be distributed over a period of at least 5 taxable years,

(iii) an amount equal to the normal cost of the plan, as determined under regulations prescribed by the Secretary, plus, if past service or other supplementary pension or annuity credits are provided by the plan, an amount necessary to amortize the unfunded costs attributable to such credits in equal annual payments (until fully amortized) over 10 years, as determined under regulations prescribed by the Secretary.

In determining the amount deductible in such year under the foregoing limitations the funding method and the actuarial assumptions used shall be those used for such year under section 431, and the maximum amount deductible for such year shall be an amount equal to the full funding limitation for such year determined under section 431.

(B) SPECIAL RULE IN CASE OF CERTAIN AMENDMENTS.—In the case of a multiemployer plan which the Secretary of Labor finds to be collectively bargained which makes an election under this subparagraph (in such manner and at such time as may be provided under regulations prescribed by the Secretary), if the full funding limitation determined under section 431(c)(6) for such year is zero, if as a result of any plan amendment applying to such plan year, the amount determined under section 431(c)(6)(A)(ii) exceeds the amount determined under section 431(c)(6)(A)(i), and if the funding method and the actuarial assumptions used are those used for such year under section 431, the maximum amount deductible in such year under the limitations of this paragraph shall be an amount equal to the lesser of—

(i) the full funding limitation for such year determined by applying section 431(c)(6) but increasing the amount referred to in subparagraph (A) thereof by the decrease in the present value of all unamortized liabilities resulting from such amendment, or

(ii) the normal cost under the plan reduced by the amount necessary to amortize in equal annual installments over 10 years (until fully amortized) the decrease described in clause (i).

In the case of any election under this subparagraph, the amount deductible under the limitations of this paragraph with respect to any of the plan years following the plan year for which such election was made shall be determined as provided under such regulations as may be prescribed by the Secretary to carry out the purposes of this subparagraph.

(C) CERTAIN COLLECTIVELY-BARGAINED PLANS.—In the case of a plan which the Secretary of Labor finds to be collectively bargained, established or maintained by an employer doing business in not less than 40 States and engaged in the trade or business of furnishing or selling services described in section 168(i)(10)(C), with respect to which the rates have been established or approved by a State or political subdivision thereof, by any agency or instrumentality of the United States, or by a public service or public utility commission or other similar body of any State or political subdivision thereof, and in the case of any employer which is a member of a controlled group with such employer, subparagraph (B) shall be applied by substituting for the words "plan amendment" the words "plan amendment or increase in benefits payable under title II of the Social Security Act". For purposes of this subparagraph, the term "controlled group" has the meaning provided by section 1563(a), determined without regard to section 1563(a)(4) and (e)(3)(C).

(D) AMOUNT DETERMINED ON BASIS OF UNFUNDED CURRENT LIABILITY.—In the case of a defined benefit plan which is a multiemployer plan, except as provided in regulations, the maximum amount deductible under the limitations of this paragraph shall not be less than the excess (if any) of—

(i) 140 percent of the current liability of the plan determined under section 431(c)(6)(D), over

(ii) the value of the plan's assets determined under section 431(c)(2).

(E) CARRYOVER.—Any amount paid in a taxable year in excess of the amount deductible in such year under the foregoing limitations shall be deductible in the succeeding taxable years in order of time to the extent of the difference between the amount paid and deductible in each such succeeding year and the maximum amount deductible for such year under the foregoing limitations.

(2) EMPLOYEES' ANNUITIES.—In the taxable year when paid, in an amount determined in accordance with paragraph (1), if the contributions are paid toward the purchase of retirement annuities, or retirement annuities and medical benefits as described in section 401(h), and such purchase is a part of a plan which meets the requirements of section 401(a)(3), (4), (5),(6), (7), (8), (9), (11), (12), (13), (14), (15), (16), (17), (19), (20), (22), (26), (27), (31), and (37), and, if applicable, the requirements of section 401(a)(10) and of section 401(d), and if refunds of premiums, if any, are applied within the current taxable year or next succeeding taxable year towards the purchase of such retirement annuities, or such retirement annuities and medical benefits.

(3) STOCK BONUS AND PROFIT-SHARING TRUSTS.—

(A) LIMITS ON DEDUCTIBLE CONTRIBUTIONS.—

(i) IN GENERAL.—In the taxable year when paid, if the contributions are paid into a stock bonus or profit-sharing trust, and if such taxable year ends within or with a taxable year of the trust with respect to which the trust is exempt under section 501(a), in an amount not in excess of the greater of—

(I) 25 percent of the compensation otherwise paid or accrued during the taxable year to the beneficiaries under the stock bonus or profit-sharing plan, or

(II) the amount such employer is required to contribute to such trust under section 401(k)(11) for such year.

(ii) CARRYOVER OF EXCESS CONTRIBUTIONS.—Any amount paid into the trust in any taxable year in excess of the limitation of clause (i) (or the corresponding provision of prior law) shall be deductible in the succeeding taxable years in order of time, but the amount so deductible under this clause in any 1 such succeeding taxable year together with the amount allowable under clause (i) shall not exceed the amount described in subclause (I) or (II) of clause (i), whichever is greater, with respect to such taxable year.

(iii) CERTAIN RETIREMENT PLANS EXCLUDED.—For purposes of this subparagraph, the term "stock bonus or profit-sharing trust" shall not include any trust designed to provide benefits upon retirement and covering a period of years, if under the plan the amounts to be contributed by the employer can be determined actuarially as provided in paragraph (1).

(iv) 2 OR MORE TRUSTS TREATED AS 1 TRUST.—If the contributions are made to 2 or more stock bonus or profit-sharing trusts, such trusts shall be considered a single trust for purposes of applying the limitations in this subparagraph.

(v) DEFINED CONTRIBUTION PLANS SUBJECT TO THE FUNDING STANDARDS.—Except as provided by the Secretary, a defined contribution plan which is subject to the funding standards of section 412 shall be treated in the same manner as a stock bonus or profit-sharing plan for purposes of this subparagraph.

(B) PROFIT-SHARING PLAN OF AFFILIATED GROUP.—In the case of a profit-sharing plan, or a stock bonus plan in which contributions are determined with reference to profits, of a group of corporations which is an affiliated group within the meaning of section 1504, if any member of such affiliated group is prevented from making a contribution which it would otherwise have made under the plan, by reason of having no current or accumulated earnings or profits or because such earnings or profits are less than the contributions which it would otherwise have made, then so much of the contribution which such member was so prevented from making may be made, for the benefit of the employees of such member, by the other members of the group, to the extent of current or accumulated earnings or profits, except that such contribution by each such other member shall be limited, where the group does not file a consolidated return, to that proportion of its total current and accumulated earnings or profits remaining after adjustment for its contribution deductible without regard to this subparagraph which the total prevented contribution bears to the total current and accumulated earnings or profits of all the members of the group remaining after adjustment for all contributions deductible without regard to this subparagraph. Contributions made under the preceding sentence shall be deductible under subparagraph (A) of this paragraph by the employer making such contribution, and, for the purpose of determining amounts which may be carried forward and deducted under the second sentence of subparagraph (A) of this paragraph in succeeding taxable years, shall be deemed to have been made by the employer on behalf of whose employees such contributions were made.

(4) TRUSTS CREATED OR ORGANIZED OUTSIDE THE UNITED STATES.—If a stock bonus, pension, or profit-sharing trust would qualify for exemption under section 501 (a) except for the fact that it is a trust created or organized outside the United States, contributions to such a trust by an employer which is a resident, or corporation, or other entity of the United States, shall be deductible under the preceding paragraphs.

(5) OTHER PLANS.—If the plan is not one included in paragraph (1), (2), or (3), in the taxable year in which an amount attributable to the contribution is includible in the gross income of employees participating in the plan, but, in the case of a plan in which more than one employee

participates only if separate accounts are maintained for each employee. For purposes of this section, any vacation pay which is treated as deferred compensation shall be deductible for the taxable year of the employer in which paid to the employee.

(6) TIME WHEN CONTRIBUTIONS DEEMED MADE.—For purposes of paragraphs (1), (2), and (3), a taxpayer shall be deemed to have made a payment on the last day of the preceding taxable year if the payment is on account of such taxable year and is made not later than the time prescribed by law for filing the return for such taxable year (including extensions thereof).

(7) LIMITATION ON DEDUCTIONS WHERE COMBINATION OF DEFINED CONTRIBUTION PLAN AND DEFINED BENEFIT PLAN.—

(A) IN GENERAL.—If amounts are deductible under the foregoing paragraphs of this subsection (other than paragraph (5)) in connection with 1 or more defined contribution plans and 1 or more defined benefit plans or in connection with trusts or plans described in 2 or more of such paragraphs, the total amount deductible in a taxable year under such plans shall not exceed the greater of—

(i) 25 percent of the compensation otherwise paid or accrued during the taxable year to the beneficiaries under such plans, or

(ii) the amount of contributions made to or under the defined benefit plans to the extent such contributions do not exceed the amount of employer contributions necessary to satisfy the minimum funding standard provided by section 412 with respect to any such defined benefit plans for the plan year which ends with or within such taxable year (or for any prior plan year).

A defined contribution plan which is a pension plan shall not be treated as failing to provide definitely determinable benefits merely by limited employer contributions to amounts deductible under this section. In the case of a defined benefit plan which is a single employer plan, the amount necessary to satisfy the minimum funding standard provided by section 412 shall not be less than the excess (if any) of the plan's funding target (as defined in section 430(d)(1)) over the value of the plan's assets (as determined under section 430(g)(3)).

(B) CARRYOVER OF CONTRIBUTIONS IN EXCESS OF THE DEDUCTIBLE LIMIT.—Any amount paid under the plans in any taxable year in excess of the limitation of subparagraph (A) shall be deductible in the succeeding taxable years in order of time, but the amount so deductible under this subparagraph in any 1 such succeeding taxable year together with the amount allowable under subparagraph (A) shall not exceed 25 percent of the compensation otherwise paid or accrued during such taxable year to the beneficiaries under the plans.

(C) PARAGRAPH NOT TO APPLY IN CERTAIN CASES.—

(i) BENEFICIARY TEST.—This paragraph shall not have the effect of reducing the amount otherwise deductible under paragraphs (1), (2), and (3), if no employee is a beneficiary under more than 1 trust or under a trust and an annuity plan.

(ii) ELECTIVE DEFERRALS.—If, in connection with 1 or more defined contribution plans and 1 or more defined benefit plans, no amounts (other than elective deferrals (as defined in section 402(g)(3))) are contributed to any of the defined contribution plans for the taxable year, then subparagraph (A) shall not apply with respect to any of such defined contribution plans and defined benefit plans.

(iii) LIMITATION.—In the case of employer contributions to 1 or more defined contribution plans—

(I) if such contributions do not exceed 6 percent of the compensation otherwise paid or accrued during the taxable year to the beneficiaries under such plans, this paragraph shall not apply to such contributions or to employer contributions to the defined benefit plans to which this paragraph would otherwise apply by reason of contributions to the defined contribution plans, and

(II) if such contributions exceed 6 percent of such compensation, this paragraph shall be applied by only taking into account such contributions to the extent of such excess.

For purposes of this clause, amounts carried over from preceding taxable years under subparagraph (B) shall be treated as employer contributions to 1 or more defined contributions plans to the extent attributable to employer contributions to such plans in such preceding taxable years.

(iv) GUARANTEED PLANS.—In applying this paragraph, any single-employer plan covered under section 4021 of the Employee Retirement Income Security Act of 1974 shall not be taken into account.

(v) MULTIEMPLOYER PLANS.—In applying this paragraph, any multiemployer plan shall not be taken into account.

(D) INSURANCE CONTRACT PLANS.—For purposes of this paragraph, a plan described in section 412(e)(3) shall be treated as a defined benefit plan.

(8) SELF-EMPLOYED INDIVIDUALS.—In the case of a plan included in paragraph (1), (2), or (3) which provides contributions or benefits for employees some or all of whom are employees within the meaning of section 401(c)(1), for purposes of this section—

(A) the term "employee" includes an individual who is an employee within the meaning of section 401(c)(1), and the employer of such individual is the person treated as his employer under section 401(c)(4);

(B) the term "earned income" has the meaning assigned to it by section 401(c)(2);

(C) the contributions to such plan on behalf of an individual who is an employee within the meaning of section 401(c)(1) shall be considered to satisfy the conditions of section 162 or 212 to the extent that such contributions do not exceed the earned income of such individual (determined without regard to the deductions allowed by this section) derived from the trade or business with respect to which such plan is established, and to the extent that such contributions are not allocable (determined in accordance with regulations prescribed by the Secretary) to the purchase of life, accident, health, or other insurance; and

(D) any reference to compensation shall, in the case of an individual who is an employee within the meaning of section 401(c)(1), be considered to be a reference to the earned income of such individual derived from the trade or business with respect to which the plan is established.

(9) CERTAIN CONTRIBUTIONS TO EMPLOYEE STOCK OWNERSHIP PLANS.—

(A) PRINCIPAL PAYMENTS.—Notwithstanding the provisions of paragraphs (3) and (7), if contributions are paid into a trust which forms a part of an employee stock ownership plan (as described in section 4975(e)(7)), and such contributions are, on or before the time prescribed in paragraph (6), applied by the plan to the repayment of the principal of a loan incurred for the purpose of acquiring qualifying employer securities (as described in section 4975(e)(8)), such contributions shall be deductible under this paragraph for the taxable year determined under paragraph (6). The amount deductible under this paragraph shall not, however, exceed 25 percent of the compensation otherwise paid or accrued during the taxable year to the employees under such employee stock ownership plan. Any amount paid into such trust in any taxable year in excess of the amount deductible under this paragraph shall be deductible in the succeeding taxable years in order of time to the extent of the difference between the amount paid and deductible in each such succeeding year and the maximum amount deductible for such year under the preceding sentence.

(B) INTEREST PAYMENT.—Notwithstanding the provisions of paragraphs (3) and (7), if contributions are made to an employee stock ownership plan (described in subparagraph (A)) and such contributions are applied by the plan to the repayment of interest on a loan incurred for the purpose of acquiring qualifying employer securities (as described in subparagraph (A)), such contributions shall be deductible for the taxable year with respect to which such contributions are made as determined under paragraph (6).

(C) S CORPORATIONS.—This paragraph shall not apply to an S corporation.

(D) QUALIFIED GRATUITOUS TRANSFERS.—A qualified gratuitous transfer (as defined in section 664(g)(1)) shall have no effect on the amount or amounts otherwise deductible under paragraph (3) or (7) or under this paragraph.

(10) CONTRIBUTIONS BY CERTAIN MINISTERS TO RETIREMENT INCOME ACCOUNTS.—In the case of contributions made by a minister described in section 414(e)(5) to a retirement income account described in section 403(b)(9) and not by a person other than such minister, such contributions—

(A) shall be treated as made to a trust which is exempt from tax under section 501(a) and which is part of a plan which is described in section 401(a), and

(B) shall be deductible under this subsection to the extent such contributions do not exceed the limit on elective deferrals under section 402(g) or the limit on annual additions under section 415.

For purposes of this paragraph, all plans in which the minister is a participant shall be treated as one plan.

(11) DETERMINATIONS RELATING TO DEFERRED COMPENSATION.—For purposes of determining under this section—

(A) whether compensation of an employee is deferred compensation; and

(B) when deferred compensation is paid,

no amount shall be treated as received by the employee, or paid, until it is actually received by the employee.

(12) DEFINITION OF COMPENSATION.—For purposes of paragraphs (3), (7), (8), and (9) and subsection (h)(1)(C), the term "compensation" shall include amounts treated as "participant's compensation" under subparagraph (C) or (D) of section 415(c)(3).

Amendments

• 2008, Worker, Retiree, and Employer Recovery Act of 2008 (P.L. 110-458)

P.L. 110-458, §108(a)(2)(A)-(B):

Amended Code Sec. 404(a)(7)(A) by striking the next to last sentence, and by striking "the plan's funding shortfall determined under section 430" in the last sentence and inserting "the excess (if any) of the plan's funding target (as defined in section 430(d)(1)) over the value of the plan's assets (as determined under section 430(g)(3))". **Effective** as if included in the provision of the 2006 Act to which the amendment relates [**effective** for years beginning after 12-31-2007.—CCH]. Prior to being stricken, the next to last sentence in Code Sec. 404(a)(7)(A) read as follows:

For purposes of clause (ii), if paragraph (1)(D) applies to a defined benefit plan for any plan year, the amount necessary to satisfy the minimum funding standard provided by section 412 with respect to such plan for such plan year shall not be less than the unfunded current liability of such plan under section 412(l).

P.L. 110-458, §108(b):

Amended Code Sec. 404(a)(1)(D)(i) by striking "431(c)(6)(C)" and inserting "431(c)(6)(D)". **Effective** as if included in the provision of the 2006 Act to which the amendment relates [**effective** for years beginning after 12-31-2007.—CCH].

P.L. 110-458, §108(c):

Amended Code Sec. 404(a)(7)(C)(iii). **Effective** as if included in the provision of the 2006 Act to which the amendment relates [**effective** for contributions for tax years beginning after 12-31-2005.—CCH]. Prior to amendment, Code Sec. 404(a)(7)(C)(iii) read as follows:

(iii) LIMITATION.—In the case of employer contributions to 1 or more defined contribution plans, this paragraph shall only apply to the extent that such contributions exceed 6 percent of the compensation otherwise paid or accrued during the taxable year to the beneficiaries under such plans. For purposes of this clause, amounts carried over from preceding taxable years under subparagraph (B) shall be treated as employer contributions to 1 or more defined contributions to the extent attributable to employer contributions to such plans in such preceding taxable years.

• 2008, Heroes Earnings Assistance and Relief Tax Act of 2008 (P.L. 110-245)

P.L. 110-245, §104(c)(1):

Amended Code Sec. 404(a)(2) by striking "and (31)" and inserting "(31), and (37)". **Effective** generally with respect to deaths and disabilities occurring on or after 1-1-2007. For a special rule, see Act Sec. 104(d)(2), below.

P.L. 110-245, §104(d)(2), provides:

(2) PROVISIONS RELATING TO PLAN AMENDMENTS.—

(A) IN GENERAL.—If this subparagraph applies to any plan or contract amendment, such plan or contract shall be treated as being operated in accordance with the terms of the plan during the period described in subparagraph (B)(iii).

(B) AMENDMENTS TO WHICH SUBPARAGRAPH (A) APPLIES.—

(i) IN GENERAL.—Subparagraph (A) shall apply to any amendment to any plan or annuity contract which is made—

(I) pursuant to the amendments made by subsection (a) or pursuant to any regulation issued by the Secretary of the Treasury under subsection (a), and

(II) on or before the last day of the first plan year beginning on or after January 1, 2010.

In the case of a governmental plan (as defined in section 414(d) of the Internal Revenue Code of 1986), this clause shall be applied by substituting "2012" for "2010" in subclause (II).

(ii) CONDITIONS.—This paragraph shall not apply to any amendment unless—

(I) the plan or contract is operated as if such plan or contract amendment were in effect for the period described in clause (iii), and

(II) such plan or contract amendment applies retroactively for such period.

(iii) PERIOD DESCRIBED.—The period described in this clause is the period—

(I) beginning on the effective date specified by the plan, and

(II) ending on the date described in clause (i)(II) (or, if earlier, the date the plan or contract amendment is adopted).

• 2006, Pension Protection Act of 2006 (P.L. 109-280)

P.L. 109-280, §801(a)(1):

Amended Code Sec. 404(a)(1)(A) by inserting "in the case of a defined benefit plan other than a multiemployer plan, in an amount determined under subsection (o), and in the case of any other plan" after "section 501(a),". **Effective** for years beginning after 12-31-2007.

P.L. 109-280, §801(b):

Amended Code Sec. 404(a)(7)(C), as amended by this Act, by adding at the end a new clause (iv). **Effective** for years beginning after 12-31-2007.

P.L. 109-280, §801(c)(1):

Amended the last sentence of Code Sec. 404(a)(1)(A) by striking "section 412" each place it appears and inserting "section 431". **Effective** for years beginning after 12-31-2007.

P.L. 109-280, §801(c)(2)(A)-(E):

Amended Code Sec. 404(a)(1)(B) by striking "In the case of a plan" and inserting "In the case of a multiemployer plan", by striking "section 412(c)(7)" each place it appears and inserting "section 431(c)(6)", by striking "section 412(c)(7)(B)" and inserting "section 431(c)(6)(A)(ii)", by striking "412(c)(7)(A)" and inserting "section 431(c)(6)(A)(i)", and by striking "section 412" and inserting "section 431". **Effective** for years beginning after 12-31-2007.

P.L. 109-280, §801(c)(3)(A)-(B):

Amended Code Sec. 404(a)(7), as amended by this Act, by adding at the end of subparagraph (A) a new sentence, and by striking subparagraph (D) and inserting a new subparagraph (D). **Effective** for years beginning after 12-31-2007. Prior to being stricken, Code Sec. 404(a)(7)(D) read as follows:

(D) SECTION 412(i) PLANS.—For purposes of this paragraph, any plan described in section 412(i) shall be treated as a defined benefit plan.

P.L. 109-280, §801(d)(1):

Amended Code Sec. 404(a)(1)(D)(i) by striking "section 412(l)" and inserting "section 412(l)(8)(A), except that section 412(l)(8)(A) shall be applied for purposes of this clause by substituting '150 percent (140 percent in the case of a multiemployer plan) of current liability' for 'the current liability' in clause (i)". **Effective** for years beginning after 12-31-2005.

P.L. 109-280, §801(d)(2):

Amended Code Sec. 404(a)(1) by striking subparagraph (F). **Effective** for years beginning after 12-31-2005. Prior to being stricken, Code Sec. 404(a)(1)(F) read as follows:

(F) ELECTION TO DISREGARD MODIFIED INTEREST RATE.—An employer may elect to disregard subsections (b)(5)(B)(ii)(II) and (l)(7)(C)(i)(IV) of section 412 solely for purposes of determining the interest rate used in calculating the maximum amount of the deduction allowable under this paragraph.

P.L. 109-280, §802(a):

Amended Code Sec. 404(a)(1)(D), as amended by this Act. **Effective** for years beginning after 12-31-2007. Prior to amendment, Code Sec. 404(a)(1)(D) read as follows:

(D) SPECIAL RULE IN CASE OF CERTAIN PLANS.—

(i) IN GENERAL.—In the case of any defined benefit plan, except as provided in regulations, the maximum amount deductible under the limitations of this paragraph shall not be less than the unfunded current liability determined under section 412(l)(8)(A), except that section 412(l)(8)(A) shall be applied for purposes of this clause by substituting "150 percent (140 percent in the case of a multiemployer plan) of current liability" for "the current liability" in clause (i).

(ii) PLANS WITH 100 OR LESS PARTICIPANTS.—For purposes of this subparagraph, in the case of a plan which has 100 or less participants for the plan year, unfunded current liability shall not include the liability attributable to benefit increases for highly compensated employees (as defined in section

414(q)) resulting from a plan amendment which is made or becomes effective, whichever is later, within the last 2 years.

(iii) RULE FOR DETERMINING NUMBER OF PARTICIPANTS.—For purposes of determining the number of plan participants, all defined benefit plans maintained by the same employer (or any member of such employer's controlled group (within the meaning of section 412(l)(8)(C))) shall be treated as one plan, but only employees of such member or employer shall be taken into account.

(iv) SPECIAL RULE FOR TERMINATING PLANS.—In the case of a plan which, subject to section 4041 of the Employee Retirement Income Security Act of 1974, terminates during the plan year, clause (i) shall be applied by substituting for unfunded current liability the amount required to make the plan sufficient for benefit liabilities (within the meaning of section 4041(d) of such Act).

P.L. 109-280, §803(a):

Amended Code Sec. 404(a)(7)(C) by adding after clause (ii) a new clause (iii). **Effective** for contributions for tax years beginning after 12-31-2005.

P.L. 109-280, §803(b):

Amended Code Sec. 404(a)(7)(C), as amended by this Act, by adding at the end a new clause (v). **Effective** for contributions for tax years beginning after 12-31-2005.

P.L. 109-280, §811, provides:

SEC. 811. PENSIONS AND INDIVIDUAL RETIREMENT ARRANGEMENT PROVISIONS OF ECONOMIC GROWTH AND TAX RELIEF RECONCILIATION ACT OF 2001 MADE PERMANENT.

Title IX of the Economic Growth and Tax Relief Reconciliation Act of 2001 [P.L. 107-16] shall not apply to the provisions of, and amendments made by, subtitles A through F of title VI [§§601-666]of such Act (relating to pension and individual retirement arrangement provisions).

• 2004, Pension Funding Equity Act of 2004 (P.L. 108-218)

P.L. 108-218, §101(b)(5):

Amended Code Sec. 404(a)(1) by adding at the end a new subparagraph (F). **Effective** for plan years beginning after 12-31-2003.

• 2002, Job Creation and Worker Assistance Act of 2002 (P.L. 107-147)

P.L. 107-147, §411(l)(1):

Amended Code Sec. 404(a)(12) by striking "(9)," and inserting "(9) and subsection (h)(1)(C),". **Effective** as if included in the provision of P.L. 107-16 to which it relates [**effective** for years beginning after 12-31-2001.—CCH].

P.L. 107-147, §411(l)(4):

Amended Code Sec. 404(a)(7)(C). **Effective** as if included in the provision of P.L. 107-16 to which it relates [**effective** for years beginning after 12-31-2001.—CCH]. Prior to amendment, Code Sec. 404(a)(7)(C) read as follows:

(C) PARAGRAPH NOT TO APPLY IN CERTAIN CASES.—This paragraph shall not have the effect of reducing the amount otherwise deductible under paragraphs (1), (2), and (3), if no employee is a beneficiary under more than 1 trust or under a trust and an annuity plan.

P.L. 107-147, §411(s):

Amended Code Sec. 404(a)(1)(D)(iv) by striking "PLANS MAINTAINED BY PROFESSIONAL SERVICE EMPLOYERS" and inserting "SPECIAL RULE FOR TERMINATING PLANS". **E ffective** as if included in the provision of P.L. 107-16 to which it relates [**effective** for plan years beginning after 12-31-2001.—CCH].

• 2001, Economic Growth and Tax Relief Reconciliation Act of 2001 (P.L. 107-16)

P.L. 107-16, §616(a)(1)(A):

Amended Code Sec. 404(a)(3)(A)(i)(I) by striking "15 percent" and inserting "25 percent". **Effective** for years beginning after 12-31-2001.

P.L. 107-16, §616(a)(2)(A):

Amended Code Sec. 404(a)(3)(A)(v). **Effective** for years beginning after 12-31-2001. Prior to amendment, Code Sec. 404(a)(3)(A)(v) read as follows:

(v) PRE-87 LIMITATION CARRYFORWARDS.—

(I) IN GENERAL.—The limitation of clause (i) for any taxable year shall be increased by the unused pre-87 limitation carryforwards (but not to an amount in excess of 25 percent of the compensation described in clause (i)).

(II) UNUSED PRE-87 LIMITATION CARRYFORWARDS.—For purposes of subclause (I), the term "unused pre-87 limitation carryforwards" means the amount by which the limitation of the first sentence of this subparagraph (as in effect on the day before the date of the enactment of the Tax Reform Act of 1986) for any taxable year beginning before January 1, 1987, exceeded the amount paid to the trust for such taxable year (to the extent such excess was not taken into account in prior taxable years).

P.L. 107-16, §616(a)(2)(B)(i):

Amended Code Sec. 404(a)(1)(A) by inserting "(other than a trust to which paragraph (3) applies)" after "pension trust". **Effective** for years beginning after 12-31-2001.

P.L. 107-16, §616(b)(1):

Amended Code Sec. 404(a) by adding at the end a new paragraph (12). **Effective** for years beginning after 12-31-2001.

P.L. 107-16, §616(b)(2)(A):

Amended Code Sec. 404(a)(3)(B) by striking the last sentence. **Effective** for years beginning after 12-31-2001. Prior to being stricken, the last sentence of Code Sec. 404(a)(3)(B) read as follows:

The term "compensation otherwise paid or accrued during the taxable year to all employees" shall include any amount with respect to which an election under section 415(c)(3)(C) is in effect, but only to the extent that any contribution with respect to such amount is nonforfeitable.

P.L. 107-16, §632(a)(3)(B):

Amended Code Sec. 404(a)(10)(B) by striking ", the exclusion allowance under section 403(b)(2)," after "section 402(g),". **Effective** for years beginning after 12-31-2001.

P.L. 107-16, §652(a):

Amended Code Sec. 404(a)(1)(D). **Effective** for plan years beginning after 12-31-2001. Prior to amendment, Code Sec. 404(a)(1)(D) read as follows:

(D) SPECIAL RULE IN CASE OF CERTAIN PLANS.—In the case of any defined benefit plan (other than a multiemployer plan) which has more than 100 participants for the plan year, except as provided in regulations, the maximum amount deductible under the limitations of this paragraph shall not be less than the unfunded current liability determined under section 412(l). For purposes of determining whether a plan has more than 100 participants, all defined benefit plans maintained by the same employer (or any member of such employer's controlled group (within the meaning of section 412(l)(8)(C))) shall be treated as 1 plan, but only employees of such member or employer shall be taken into account.

P.L. 107-16, §658, provides:

SEC. 658. CLARIFICATION OF TREATMENT OF CONTRIBUTIONS TO MULTIEMPLOYER PLAN.

(a) NOT CONSIDERED METHOD OF ACCOUNTING.—For purposes of section 446 of the Internal Revenue Code of 1986, a determination under section 404(a)(6) of such Code regarding the taxable year with respect to which a contribution to a multiemployer pension plan is deemed made shall not be treated as a method of accounting of the taxpayer. No deduction shall be allowed for any taxable year for any contribution to a multiemployer pension plan with respect to which a deduction was previously allowed.

(b) REGULATIONS.—The Secretary of the Treasury shall promulgate such regulations as necessary to clarify that a taxpayer shall not be allowed an aggregate amount of deductions for contributions to a multiemployer pension plan which exceeds the amount of such contributions made or deemed made under section 404(a)(6) of the Internal Revenue Code of 1986 to such plan.

(c) EFFECTIVE DATE.—Subsection (a), and any regulations promulgated under subsection (b), shall be effective for years ending after the date of the enactment of this Act.

P.L. 107-16, §901(a)-(b), provides [but see P.L. 109-280, §811, above]:

SEC. 901. SUNSET OF PROVISIONS OF ACT.

(a) IN GENERAL.—All provisions of, and amendments made by, this Act shall not apply—

(1) to taxable, plan, or limitation years beginning after December 31, 2010, or

(2) in the case of title V, to estates of decedents dying, gifts made, or generation skipping transfers, after December 31, 2010.

(b) APPLICATION OF CERTAIN LAWS.—The Internal Revenue Code of 1986 and the Employee Retirement Income Security Act of 1974 shall be applied and administered to years, estates, gifts, and transfers described in subsection (a) as if the provisions and amendments described in subsection (a) had never been enacted.

• 1998, IRS Restructuring and Reform Act of 1998 (P.L. 105-206)

P.L. 105-206, §6015(d):

Amended Code Sec. 404(a)(9) by redesignating subparagraph (C) as added by Act Sec. 1530(c)(2) of the Taxpayer Relief Act of 1997 (P.L. 105-34) as subparagraph (D) and by striking "A qualified" and inserting "QUALIFIED GRATUITOUS TRANSFERS.—A qualified". **Effective** as if included in the provision of P.L. 105-34 to which it relates [**effective** for transfers made by trusts to, or for the use of, an employee stock ownership plan after 8-5-97.—CCH].

P.L. 105-206, §7001(a):

Amended Code Sec. 404(a) by adding at the end a new paragraph (11). **Effective**, generally, for tax years ending after 7-22-98. For a special rule, see Act Sec. 7001(b)(2)(A)-(C), below.

P.L. 105-206, §7001(b)(2)(A)-(C), provides:

(2) CHANGE IN METHOD OF ACCOUNTING.—In the case of any taxpayer required by the amendment made by subsection (a) to change its method of accounting for its first taxable year ending after the date of the enactment of this Act—

(A) such change shall be treated as initiated by the taxpayer,

(B) such change shall be treated as made with the consent of the Secretary of the Treasury; and

(C) the net amount of the adjustments required to be taken into account by the taxpayer under section 481 of the Internal Revenue Code of 1986 shall be taken into account ratably over the 3-taxable year period beginning with such first taxable year.

• 1997, Taxpayer Relief Act of 1997 (P.L. 105-34)

P.L. 105-34, §1530(c)(2):

Amended Code Sec. 404(a)(9) by inserting after subparagraph (B) a new subparagraph (C) [(D)]. **Effective** for transfers made by trusts to, or for the use of, an employee stock ownership plan after 8-5-97.

P.L. 105-34, §1601(d)(2)(C)(i):

Amended Code Sec. 404(a)(3)(A)(i) by striking "not in excess of" and all that follows and inserting "not in excess of the greater of—" and new subclauses (I) and (II). **Effective** as if included in the provision of P.L. 104-188 to which it relates [**effective** for plan years beginning after 12-31-96.—CCH]. Prior to amendment, Code Sec. 404(a)(3)(A)(i) read as follows:

(i) IN GENERAL.—In the taxable year when paid, if the contributions are paid into a stock bonus or profit-sharing trust, and if such taxable year ends within or with a taxable year of the trust with respect to which the trust is exempt under section 501(a), in an amount not in excess of 15 percent of the compensation otherwise paid or accrued during the taxable year to the beneficiaries under the stock bonus or profit-sharing plan.

P.L. 105-34, §1601(d)(2)(C)(ii):

Amended Code Sec. 404(a)(3)(A)(ii) by striking "15 percent" and all that follows and inserting "the amount described in subclause (I) or (II) of clause (i), whichever is greater, with respect to such taxable year.". **Effective** as if included in the provision of P.L. 104-188 to which it relates [**effective** for plan years beginning after 12-31-96.—CCH]. Prior to amendment, Code Sec. 404(a)(3)(A)(ii) read as follows:

(ii) CARRYOVER OF EXCESS CONTRIBUTIONS.—Any amount paid into the trust in any taxable year in excess of the limitation of clause (i) (or the corresponding provision of prior law) shall be deductible in the succeeding taxable years in order of time, but the amount so deductible under this clause in any 1 such succeeding taxable year together with the amount allowable under clause (i) shall not exceed 15 percent of the compensation otherwise paid or accrued during such taxable year to the beneficiaries under the plan.

• 1996, Small Business Job Protection Act of 1996 (P.L. 104-188)

P.L. 104-188, §1316(d)(1):

Amended Code Sec. 404(a)(9) by adding at the end a new subparagraph (C). **Effective** for tax years beginning after 12-31-97.

P.L. 104-188, §1461(b):

Amended Code Sec. 404(a) by adding at the end a new paragraph (10). **Effective** for years beginning after 12-31-96.

P.L. 104-188, §1704(t)(76):

Amended Code Sec. 404(a)(2) by striking "(18)," after "(17),". **Effective** 8-20-96.

• 1992, Unemployment Compensation Amendments of 1992 (P.L. 102-318)

P.L. 102-318, §522(a)(2):

Amended Code Sec. 404(a)(2) by striking "and (27)" and inserting "(27), and (31)". **Effective** for distributions after 12-31-92.

• 1990, Omnibus Budget Reconciliation Act of 1990 (P.L. 101-508)

P.L. 101-508, §11812(b)(7):

Amended Code Sec. 404(a)(1)(C) by striking "section 167(l)(3)(A)(iii)" and inserting "section 168(i)(10)(C)". **Effective**, generally, for property placed in service after 11-5-90. For exceptions, see Act Sec. 11812(c)(2)-(3), below.

P.L. 101-508, §11812(c)(2)-(3), provides:

(2) EXCEPTION.—The amendments made by this section shall not apply to any property to which section 168 of the Internal Revenue Code of 1986 does not apply by reason of subsection (f)(5) thereof.

(3) EXCEPTION FOR PREVIOUSLY GRANDFATHER EXPENDITURES.—The amendments made by this section shall not apply to rehabilitation expenditures described in section 252(f)(5) of the Tax Reform Act of 1986 (as added by section 1002(l)(31) of the Technical and Miscellaneous Revenue Act of 1988).

• 1988, Technical and Miscellaneous Revenue Act of 1988 (P.L. 100-647)

P.L. 100-647, §1011A(e)(4)(A)(i)-(ii):

Amended Code Sec. 404(a)(7)(A) by striking out "provisions" and inserting in lieu thereof "paragraphs", and by inserting "or in connection with trusts or plans described in 2 or more of such paragraphs" after "1 or more defined benefit plans". **Effective** as if included in the provision of P.L. 99-514 to which it relates.

P.L. 100-647, §2005(b)(1):

Amended Code Sec. 404(a)(1)(D) by striking out "For purposes of this subparagraph" and inserting in lieu thereof "For purposes of determining whether a plan has more than 100 participants". **Effective** as if included in the provision of P.L. 100-203 to which it relates.

P.L. 100-647, §2005(b)(2):

Amended Code Sec. 404(a)(7)(A) by adding at the end thereof a new sentence. **Effective** as if included in the provision of P.L. 100-203 to which it relates.

P.L. 100-647, §2005(b)(3):

Amended Code Sec. 404(a)(1)(D) by striking out "(without regard to any reduction by the credit balance in the funding standard account)" after "section 412(l)". **Effective** as if included in the provision of P.L. 100-203 to which it relates.

• 1987, Revenue Act of 1987 (P.L. 100-203)

P.L. 100-203, §9307(c):

Amended Code Sec. 404(a)(1) by redesignating subparagraph (D) as subparagraph (E) and inserting after subparagraph (C) new subparagraph (D). **Effective** for years beginning after 12-31-87.

P.L. 100-203, §9307(d):

Amended Code Sec. 404(a)(1)(A)(iii) by striking out "to amortize such credits" and inserting in lieu thereof "to amortize the unfunded costs attributable to such credits". **Effective** for years beginning after 12-31-87.

P.L. 100-203, §10201(b)(3):

Amended Code Sec. 404(a)(5) by adding at the end a new sentence. **Effective**, generally, for tax years beginning after 12-31-87. However, for a special rule, see Act Sec. 10201(c)(2), below.

P.L. 100-203, §10201(c)(2), provides:

(2) CHANGE IN METHOD OF ACCOUNTING.—In the case of any taxpayer who elected to have section 463 of the Internal Revenue Code of 1986 apply for such taxpayer's last taxable year beginning before January 1, 1988, and who is required to change his method of accounting by reason of the amendments made by this section—

(A) such change shall be treated as initiated by the taxpayer,

(B) such change shall be treated as having been made with the consent of the Secretary, and

(C) the net amount of adjustments required by section 481 of such Code to be taken into account by the taxpayer—

(i) shall be reduced by the balance in the suspense account under section 463(c) of such Code as of the close of such last taxable year, and

(ii) shall be taken into account over the 4-taxable year period beginning with the taxable year following such last taxable year as follows:

In the case of the:	*The percentage taken into account is:*
1st year	25
2nd year	5
3rd year	35
4th year	35.

Notwithstanding subparagraph (C)(ii), if the period the adjustments are required to be taken into account under section 481 of such Code is less than 4 years, such adjustments shall be taken into account ratably over such shorter period.

• 1986, Tax Reform Act of 1986 (P.L. 99-514)

P.L. 99-514, §1112(d)(2):

Amended Code Sec. 404(a)(2) by striking out "and (22)" and inserting in lieu thereof "(22), and (26)". **Effective**, generally, for plan years beginning after 12-31-88. For special rules, see Act Sec. 1112(e)(2)-(3) following Code Sec. 401.

P.L. 99-514, §1131(a):

Amended Code Sec. 404(a)(3)(A). **Effective** for tax years beginning 12-31-86. For a special rule, see Act Sec. 1131(d)(2), below. Prior to amendment, Code Sec. 404(a)(3)(A) read as follows:

(A) LIMITS ON DEDUCTIBLE CONTRIBUTIONS.—In the taxable year when paid, if the contributions are paid into a stock bonus or proft-sharing trust, and if such taxable year ends within or with a taxable year of the trust with respect to which the trust is exempt under section 501(a), in an amount not in excess of 15 percent of the compensation otherwise paid or accrued during the taxable year to all employees under the stock bonus or profit-sharing plan. If in any taxable year there is paid into the trust, or a similar trust then in effect, amounts less than the amounts deductible under the preceding sentence, the excess, or if no amount is paid, the amounts deductible, shall be carried forward and be deductible when paid in the succeeding taxable years in order of time, but the amount so deductible under this sentence in any such succeeding taxable year shall not exceed 15 percent of the compensation otherwise paid or accrued during such succeeding taxable year to the beneficiaries under the plan, but the amount so deductible under this sentence in any one succeeding taxable year together with the amount so deductible under the first sentence of this subparagraph shall not exceed 25 percent of the compensation otherwise paid or accrued during such taxable year to the beneficiaries under the plan. In addition, any amount paid into the trust in any taxable year in excess of the amount allowable with respect to such year under the preceding provisions of this subparagraph shall be deductible in the succeeding taxable years in order of time, but the amount so deductible under this sentence in any one such succeeding taxable year together with the amount allowable under the first sentence of this subparagraph shall not exceed 15 percent of the compensation otherwise paid or accrued during such taxable year to the beneficiaries under the plan. The term "stock bonus or profit-sharing trust", as used in this subparagraph, shall not include any trust designed to provide benefits upon retirement and covering a period of years, if under the plan the amounts to be contributed by the employer can be determined actuarially as provided in paragraph (1). If the contributions are made to 2 or more stock bonus or profit-sharing trusts, such trusts shall be considered a single trust for purposes of applying the limitations in this subparagraph.

P.L. 99-514, §1131(b):

Amended Code Sec. 404(a)(7). **Effective** for tax years beginning 12-31-86. For a special rule, see Act Sec. 1131(d)(2), below. Prior to amendment, Code Sec. 404(a)(7) read as follows:

(7) LIMIT ON DEDUCTIONS.—If amounts are deductible under paragraphs (1) and (3), or (2) and (3), or (1), (2), and (3), in connection with two or more trusts, or one or more trusts and an annuity plan, the total amount deductible in a taxable year under such trusts and plans shall not exceed the greater of 25 percent of the compensation otherwise paid or accrued during the taxable year to the beneficiaries of the trusts or plans, or the amount of contributions made to or under the trusts or plans to the extent such contributions do not exceed the amount of employer contributions necessary to satisfy the minimum funding standard provided by section 412 for the plan year which ends with or within such taxable year (or for any prior plan year). In addition, any amount paid into such trust or under such annuity plans in any taxable year in excess of the amount allowable with respect to such year under the preceding provisions of this paragraph shall be deductible in succeeding taxable years in order of time, but the amount so deductible under this sentence in any one such succeeding taxable year together with the amount allowable under the first sentence of this paragraph shall not exceed 25 percent of the compensation otherwise paid or accrued during such taxable years to the beneficiaries under the trusts or plans. This paragraph shall not have the effect of reducing the amount otherwise deductible under paragraphs (1), (2), and (3), if no employee is a beneficiary under more than one trust or a trust and an annuity plan.

P.L. 99-514, §1131(d)(2), as added by P.L. 100-647, §1011A(e)(3), provides:

(2) SPECIAL RULES FOR COLLECTIVE BARGAINING AGREEMENTS.—In the case of a plan maintained pursuant to 1 or more collective bargaining agreements between employee representatives and 1 or more employers ratified before March 1, 1986, the amendments made by this section shall not apply to contributions pursuant to any such agreement for taxable years beginning before the earlier of—

(A) January 1, 1989, or

(B) the date on which the last of such collective bargaining agreements terminates (determined without regard to any extension thereof after February 28, 1986).

P.L. 99-514, §1136(b):

Amended Code Sec. 404(a)(2), as amended, by striking out "and (26)" and inserting in lieu thereof "(26), and (27)". **Effective** 10-22-86.

P.L. 99-514, §1848(c):

Amended Code Sec. 404(a)(8)(D) by striking out "the deductions allowed by this section and section 405(c)" and inserting in lieu thereof "the deduction allowed by this section". **Effective** as if included in the provision of P.L. 98-369 to which it relates.

P.L. 99-514, §1851(b)(2)(C)(i):

Amended Code Sec. 404(a) by striking out "section 162 (relating to trade or business expenses) or section 212 (relating to expenses for the production of income); but if they satisfy the conditions of either of such sections," and inserting in lieu thereof "this chapter; but, if they would otherwise be deductible". **Effective** as if included in the provision of P.L. 98-369 to which it relates.

P.L. 99-514, §1875(c)(7)(A):

Amended Code Sec. 404(a)(8)(C) by striking out "the earned income of such individual" and inserting in lieu thereof "the earned income of such individual (determined without regard to the deductions allowed by this section)". **Effective** as if included in the provision of P.L. 98-369 to which it relates.

P.L. 99-514, §1875(c)(7)(B):

Amended Code Sec. 404(a)(8)(D) by striking "(determined without regard to the deductions allowed by this section)" after "of such individual". **Effective** with respect to tax years beginning after 12-31-84.

• 1984, Deficit Reduction Act of 1984 (P.L. 98-369)

P.L. 98-369, §713(d)(4)(A):

Amended Code Sec. 404(a) by striking out paragraph (9) and by redesignating paragraph (10) as paragraph (9). **Effective** as if included in the provision of P.L. 97-248 to which it relates. Prior to amendment, paragraph (9) read as follows:

(9) Plans Benefiting Self-Employed Individuals.—In the case of a plan included in paragraph (1), (2), or (3) which provides contributions or benefits for employees some or all of whom are employees within the meaning of section 401(c)(1)—

(A) the limitations provided by paragraphs (1), (2), (3), and (7) on the amounts deductible for any taxable year shall be computed, with respect to contributions on behalf of employees (other than employees within the meaning of section 401(c)(1)), as if such employees were the only employees for whom contributions and benefits are provided under the plan;

(B) the limitations provided by paragraphs (1), (2), (3), and (7) on the amounts deductible for any taxable year shall be computed, with respect to contributions on behalf of employees within the meaning of section 401(c)(1)—

(i) as if such employees were the only employees for whom contributions and benefits are provided under the plan, and

(ii) without regard to the second sentence of paragraph (3); and

(C) the amounts deductible under paragraphs (1), (2), (3) and (7), with respect to contributions on behalf of any employee within the meaning of section 401(c)(1), shall not exceed the applicable limitation provided in subsection (e).

P.L. 98-369, §713(d)(6):

Amended Code Sec. 404(a)(8)(D) by striking out "the earned income of such individual" and inserting in lieu thereof "the earned income of such individual (determined without regard to the deductions allowed by this section and section 405(c))". **Effective** as if included in the provision of P.L. 97-248 to which it relates.

• 1982, Tax Equity and Fiscal Responsibility Act of 1982 (P.L. 97-248)

P.L. 97-248, §237(e)(2):

Amended Code Sec. 404(a)(2) by striking out "(8), (11)" and inserting in lieu thereof "(8), (9), (11)" and striking out "section 401(a)(9), (10), (17), and (18), and of section 401(d) (other than paragraph (1))" and inserting in lieu thereof "section 401(a)(10) and of section 401(d)". **Effective** for years beginning after 12-31-83.

P.L. 97-248, §253(b):

Amended Code Sec. 404(a)(3)(B) by adding the last sentence at the end thereof. **Effective** for tax years beginning after 12-31-81.

• 1981, Economic Recovery Tax Act of 1981 (P.L. 97-34)

P.L. 97-34, §333(a):

Added Code Sec. 404(a)(10). **Effective** for tax years beginning after 12-31-81.

• 1980, Technical Corrections Act of 1979 (P.L. 96-222)

P.L. 96-222, §101(a)(7)(B):

Amended Act Sec. 141 of P.L. 95-600 by revising paragraph (g). For the **effective** date, see the amendment note at §101(a)(7)(B), P.L. 96-222, following the text of Code Sec. 409A(n).

• 1978, Revenue Act of 1978 (P.L. 95-600)

P.L. 95-600, §141(f)(9):

Amended Code Sec. 404(a)(2) by striking out "and (20)" and inserting in lieu thereof "(20), and (22)". **Effective** for qualified investment for tax years beginning after 12-31-78.

• 1976, Tax Reform Act of 1976 (P.L. 94-455)

P.L. 94-455, §1906(b)(13)(A):

Amended 1954 Code by substituting "Secretary" for "Secretary or his delegate" each place it appeared. **Effective** 2-1-77.

• 1976 (P.L. 94-267)

P.L. 94-267, §1(c):

Amended Code Sec. 404(a)(2) by striking out "and (19)" and inserting in lieu thereof "(19), and (20)." **Effective** for payments made to an employee on or after 7-4-74.

• 1974, Employee Retirement Income Security Act of 1974 (P.L. 93-406)

P.L. 93-406, §1022(i), provides:

"(i) Certain Puerto Rican Pension, Etc., Plans To Be Exempt From Tax Under Section 501(a).—

"(1) General rule.—Effective for taxable years beginning after December 31, 1973, for purposes of section 501(a) of the Internal Revenue Code of 1954 (relating to exemption from tax), any trust forming part of a pension, profitsharing, or stock bonus plan all of the participants of which are residents of the Commonwealth of Puerto Rico shall be treated as an organization described in section 401(a) of such Code if such trust—

"(A) forms part of a pension, profitsharing, or stock bonus plan, and

"(B) is exempt from income tax under the laws of the Commonwealth of Puerto Rico.

"(2) Election to have provisions of, and amendments made by, title II of this act apply.—

"(A) If the administrator of a pension, profitsharing, or stock bonus plan which is created or organized in Puerto Rico elects, at such time and in such manner as the Secretary of the Treasury may require, to have the provisions of this paragraph apply, for plan years beginning after the date of election, any trust forming a part of such plan shall be treated as a trust created or organized in the United States for purposes of section 401(a) of the Internal Revenue Code of 1954.

"(B) An election under subparagraph (A), once made, is irrevocable.

"(C) This paragraph applies to plan years beginning after the date of enactment of this Act.

"(D) The source of any distributions made under a plan which makes an election under this paragraph to participants and beneficiaries residing outside of the United States shall be determined, for purposes of subchapter N of chapter 1 of the Internal Revenue Code of 1954, by the Secretary of the Treasury in accordance with regulations prescribed by him. For purposes of this subparagraph the United States means the United States as defined in section 7701(a)(9) of the Internal Revenue Code of 1954."

P.L. 93-406, §1013(c):

Amended paragraphs (1), (6) and (7) of Code Sec. 404(a). For **effective** dates and transitional rules, see the historical note under §1017, P.L. 93-406, following the text of Code Sec. 410. Prior to amendment, paragraphs (1), (6), and (7) of Code Sec. 404(a) read as follows:

"(1) Pension trusts.—In the taxable year when paid, if the contributions are paid into a pension trust, and if such taxable year ends within or with a taxable year of the trust for which the trust is exempt under section 501(a), in an amount determined as follows:

"(A) an amount not in excess of 5 percent of the compensation otherwise paid or accrued during the taxable year to all the employees under the trust, but such amount may be reduced for future years if found by the Secretary or his delegate upon periodical examinations at not less than 5-year intervals to be more than the amount reasonably necessary to provide the remaining unfunded cost of past and current service credits of all employees under the plan, plus

"(B) any excess over the amount allowable under subparagraph (A) necessary to provide with respect to all of the employees under the trust the remaining unfunded cost of their past and current service credits distributed as a level amount, or a level percentage of compensation, over the remaining future service of each such employee, as determined under regulations prescribed by the Secretary or his delegate, but if such remaining unfunded cost with respect to any 3 individuals is more than 50 percent of such remaining unfunded cost, the amount of such unfunded cost attributable to such individuals shall be distributed over a period of at least 5 taxable years, or

"(C) in lieu of the amounts allowable under subparagraphs (A) and (B) above, an amount equal to the normal cost of the plan, as determined under regulations prescribed by the Secretary or his delegate, plus, if past service or other supplementary pension or annuity credits are provided by the plan, an amount not in excess of 10 percent of the cost which would be required to completely fund or purchase such pension or annuity credits as of the date when they are included in the plan, as determined under regulations prescribed by the Secretary or his delegate, except that in no case shall a deduction be allowed for any amount (other than the normal cost) paid in after such pension or annuity credits are completely funded or purchased.

"(D) Any amount paid in a taxable year in excess of the amount deductible in such year under the foregoing limitations shall be deductible in the succeeding taxable years in order of time to the extent of the difference between the amount paid and deductible in each such succeeding year and the maximum amount deductible for such year in accordance with the foregoing limitations."

"(6) Taxpayers on accrual basis.—For purposes of paragraphs (1), (2), and (3), a taxpayer on the accrual basis shall be deemed to have made a payment on the last day of the year of accrual if the payment is on account of such taxable year and is made not later than the time prescribed by law for filing the return for such taxable year (including extensions thereof).

"(7) Limit of deduction.—If amounts are deductible under paragraphs (1) and (3), or (2) and (3), or (1), (2), and (3), in connection with 2 or more trusts, or one or more trusts and an annuity plan, the total amount deductible in a taxable year under such trusts and plans shall not exceed 25 percent of the compensation otherwise paid or accrued during the taxable year to the persons who are the beneficiaries of the trusts or plans. In addition, any amount paid into such trust or under such annuity plans in any taxable year in excess of the amount allowable with respect to such year under the preceding provisions of this paragraph shall be deductible in the succeeding taxable years in order of time, but the amount so deductible under this sentence in any one such succeeding taxable year together with the amount allowable under the first sentence of this paragraph shall not exceed 30 percent of the compensation otherwise paid or accrued during such taxable years to the beneficiaries under the trusts or plans. This paragraph shall not have the effect of reducing the amount otherwise deductible under paragraphs (1), (2), and (3), if no employee is a beneficiary under more than one trust, or a trust and an annuity plan."

P.L. 93-406, §1016(a)(3), 2001(g)(2), 2004(c)(1):

Amended paragraph (2). **Effective** for years beginning after 12-31-75. Prior to amendment, paragraph (2) read as follows:

"(2) Employees' annuities.—In the taxable year when paid, in an amount determined in accordance with paragraph (1), if the contributions are paid toward the purchase of retirement annuities, or retirement annuities and medical benefits as described in section 401(h), and such purchase is a part of a plan which meets the requirements of section 401(a)(3), (4), (5), (6), (7), and (8), and, if applicable, the requirements of section 401(a)(9) and (10) and of section 401(d) (other than paragraph (1)), and if refunds of premiums, if any, are applied within the current taxable year or next succeeding taxable year towards the purchase of such retirement annuities, or such retirement annuities and medical benefits."

P.L. 93-406, §2001(g)(2):

Amended Code Sec. 404(a)(9)(B)(ii). **Effective** for years beginning after 12-31-75. Prior to amendment, clause (ii) read as follows:

"(ii) without regard to paragraph (1)(D), the second and third sentences of paragraph (3), and the second sentence of paragraph (7); and".

P.L. 93-406, §2004(b):

Amended subparagraph (3)(A) by adding at the end of the second sentence the following: ", but the amount so deductible under this sentence in any one succeeding taxable year together with the amount so deductible under the first sentence of this subparagraph shall not exceed 25 percent of the compensation otherwise paid or accrued during such taxable year to the beneficiaries under the plan". **Effective** for years beginning after 12-31-75.

• 1969, Tax Reform Act of 1969 (P.L. 91-172)

P.L. 91-172, §321(b)(3):

Amended Code Sec. 404(a)(5). **Effective** for contributions made and premiums paid after 8-1-69. Prior to amendment, Code Sec. 404(a)(5) read as follows:

"(5) Other plans.—In the taxable year when paid, if the plan is not one included in paragraph (1), (2), or (3), if the employees' rights to or derived from such employer's contribution or such compensation are nonforfeitable at the time the contribution or compensation is paid."

• 1966, Foreign Investors Tax Act of 1966 (P.L. 89-809)

P.L. 89-809, §204(a):

Repealed Sec. 404(a)(10). **Effective** 1-1-68. Prior to repeal, Sec. 404(a)(10) read as follows:

"(10) Special limitation on amount allowed as deduction for self-employed individuals.—Notwithstanding any other provision of this section, the amount allowable as a deduction under paragraphs (1), (2), (3), and (7) in any taxable year with respect to contributions made on behalf of an individual who is an employee within the meaning of section 401(c)(1) shall be an amount equal to one-half of the contributions made on behalf of such individual in such taxable year which are deductible under such paragraphs (determined with the application of paragraph (9) and of subsection (e) but without regard to this paragraph). For purposes of section 401, the amount which may be deducted, or the amount deductible, under this section with respect to contributions made on behalf of such individual shall be determined without regard to the preceding sentence."

• 1962 (P.L. 87-863)

P.L. 87-863, §2(b):

Amended Code Sec. 404(a)(2) by inserting ", or retirement annuities and medical benefits as described in section 401(h)" after "purchase of retirement annuities" and by deleting the period and adding ", or such retirement annuities and medical benefits." at the end of the sentence. **Effective** for tax years beginning after 10-23-62.

• 1962, Self-Employed Individuals Tax Retirement Act of 1962 (P.L. 87-792)

P.L. 87-792, §3:

Amended Code Sec. 404(a) by striking out in paragraph (2) "and (6)," and inserting in lieu thereof "(6), (7), and (8), and, if applicable, the requirements of section 401(a)(9) and (10) and of section 401(d) (other than paragraph (1))," and by adding after paragraph (7) new paragraphs (8), (9), and (10). **Effective** 1-1-63.

• 1958, Technical Amendments Act of 1958 (P.L. 85-866)

P.L. 85-866, §24:

Struck out in the second parenthetical phrase of Sec. 404(a) the words "income) but if" and substituted the words "income); but, if". **Effective** 1-1-54.

[Sec. 404(b)]

(b) METHOD OF CONTRIBUTIONS, ETC., HAVING THE EFFECT OF A PLAN; CERTAIN DEFERRED BENEFITS.—

(1) METHOD OF CONTRIBUTIONS, ETC., HAVING THE EFFECT OF A PLAN.—If—

(A) there is no plan, but

(B) there is a method or arrangement of employer contributions or compensation which has the effect of a stock bonus, pension, profit-sharing, or annuity plan, or other plan deferring the receipt of compensation (including a plan described in paragraph (2)),

subsection (a) shall apply as if there were such a plan.

(2) PLANS PROVIDING CERTAIN DEFERRED BENEFITS.—

(A) IN GENERAL.—For purposes of this section, any plan providing for deferred benefits (other than compensation) for employees, their spouses, or their dependents shall be treated as a plan deferring the receipt of compensation. In the case of such a plan, for purposes of this section, the determination of when an amount is includible in gross income shall be made without regard to any provisions of this chapter excluding such benefits from gross income.

(B) EXCEPTION.—Subparagraph (A) shall not apply to any benefit provided through a welfare benefit fund (as defined in section 419(e)).

Amendments

• 1987, Revenue Act of 1987 (P.L. 100-203)

P.L. 100-203, §10201(b)(2):

Amended Code Sec. 404(b)(2)(B). **Effective**, generally, for tax years beginning after 12-31-87. However, for a special rule, see Act Sec. 10201(c)(2) following Code Sec. 404(a). Prior to amendment, Code Sec. 404(b)(2)(B) read as follows:

(B) Exception for Certain Benefits—Subparagraph (A) shall not apply to—

(i) any benefit provided through a welfare benefit fund (as defined in section 419(e)), or

(ii) any benefit with respect to which an election under section 463 applies.

• 1986, Tax Reform Act of 1986 (P.L. 99-514)

P.L. 99-514, §1851(b)(2)(A):

Amended Code Sec. 404(b)(2)(B)(ii) by striking out "to any benefit" and inserting in lieu thereof "any benefit". **Effective** as if included in the provision of P.L. 98-369 to which it relates.

P.L. 99-514, §1851(b)(2)(B)(i) and (ii):

Amended Code Sec. 404(b) by striking out "UNFUNDED" in the subsection heading and inserting in lieu thereof "CERTAIN", and by striking out "UNFUNDED" in the heading of paragraph (2) and inserting in lieu thereof "CERTAIN". **Effective** as if included in the provision of P.L. 98-369 to which it relates.

• 1984, Deficit Reduction Act of 1984 (P.L. 98-369)

P.L. 98-369, §512(a):

Amended Code Sec. 404(b). **Effective** for amounts paid or incurred after 7-18-84, in tax years ending after such date. However, see Act Sec. 512(c)(2), below, for exceptions. Prior to amendment, it read as follows:

(b) Method of Contributions, Etc., Having the Effect of a Plan.—If there is no plan but a method of employer contributions or compensation has the effect of a stock bonus, pension, profit-sharing, or annuity plan, or other plan deferring the receipt of compensation, subsection (a) shall apply as if there were such a plan.

P.L. 98-369, §512(c)(2), provides:

(2) Exception for Certain Extended Vacation Pay Plans.—In the case of any extended vacation pay plan maintained pursuant to a collective bargaining agreement—

(A) between employee representatives and 1 or more employers, and

(B) in effect on June 22, 1984, the amendments made by this section shall not apply before the date on which such collective bargaining agreement terminates (determined without regard to any extension thereof agreed to after June 22, 1984). For purposes of the preceding sentence, any plan amendment made pursuant to a collective bargaining agreement relating to the plan which amends the plan solely to conform to any requirement added by this section shall not be treated as a termination of such collective bargaining agreement.

• 1980, Technical Corrections Act of 1979 (P.L. 96-222)

P.L. 96-222, §101(a)(5):

Amended Act Sec. 133 of P.L. 95-600 by revising paragraph (c) which relates to the effective date for clarification of deductability of payments of deferred compensation, etc., to independent contractors. Revised paragraph (c) reads as follows:

(c) EFFECTIVE DATES.—

(1) IN GENERAL.—Except as provided in paragraph (2), the amendments made by this section shall apply to deductions for taxable years beginning after December 31, 1978.

(2) SPECIAL RULE FOR CERTAIN TITLE INSURANCE COMPANIES.—

(A) IN GENERAL.—In the case of a qualified title insurance company plan, the amendment made by subsection (a) shall apply to deductions for taxable years beginning after December 31, 1979.

(B) QUALIFIED TITLE INSURANCE COMPANY PLAN.—For purposes of subparagraph (A), the term "qualified title insurance company plan" means a plan of a qualified title insurance company—

(i) which defers the payment of amounts credited by such company to separate accounts for members of such company in consideration of their issuance of policies of title insurance, and

(ii) under which no part of such amounts is payable to or withdrawable by the members until after the period for the adverse possession of real property under applicable State law.

(C) QUALIFIED TITLE INSURANCE COMPANY.—For purposes of subparagraph (B), the term "qualified title insurance company" means an unincorporated title insurance company organized as a business trust—

(i) which is engaged in the business of providing title insurance coverage on interests in and liens upon real property obtained by clients of the members of such company, and

(ii) which is subject to tax under section 831 of the Internal Revenue Code of 1954.

• 1978, Revenue Act of 1978 (P.L. 95-600)

P.L. 95-600, §133(b):

Amended Code Sec. 404(b) by striking out "similar plan" and inserting in lieu thereof "other plan". **Effective** for deductions for tax years beginning after 12-31-78. [but see P.L. 96-222, §101(a)(15), above].

[Sec. 404(c)]

(c) CERTAIN NEGOTIATED PLANS.—If contributions are paid by an employer—

(1) under a plan under which such contributions are held in trust for the purpose of paying (either from principal or income or both) for the benefit of employees and their families and dependents at least medical or hospital care, or pensions on retirement or death of employees; and

(2) such plan was established prior to January 1, 1954, as a result of an agreement between employee representatives and the Government of the United States during a period of Government operation, under seizure powers, of a major part of the productive facilities of the industry in which such employer is engaged,

such contributions shall not be deductible under this section nor be made nondeductible by this section, but the deductibility thereof shall be governed solely by section 162 (relating to trade or business expenses). For purposes of this chapter and subtitle B, in the case of any individual who before July 1, 1974, was a participant in a plan described in the preceding sentence—

(A) such individual, if he is or was an employee within the meaning of section 401(c)(1), shall be treated (with respect to service covered by the plan) as being an employee other than an employee within the meaning of section 401(c)(1) and as being an employee of a participating employer under the plan,

(B) earnings derived from service covered by the plan shall be treated as not being earned income within the meaning of section 401(c)(2), and

(C) such individual shall be treated as an employee of a participating employer under the plan with respect to service before July 1, 1975, covered by the plan.

Section 277 (relating to deductions incurred by certain membership organizations in transactions with members) does not apply to any trust described in this subsection. The first and third sentences of this subsection shall have no application with respect to amounts contributed to a trust on or after any date on which such trust is qualified for exemption from tax under section 501(a).

Amendments

• 1974, Employee Retirement Income Security Act of 1974 (P.L. 93-406)

P.L. 93-406, §§2007(a), 2007(b):

Amended Code Sec. 404(c). **Effective** for tax years ending on or after 6-30-72. Prior to amendment, Code Sec. 404(c) read as follows:

"(c) Certain Negotiated Plans.—If contributions are paid by an employer—

"(1) under a plan under which such contributions are held in trust for the purpose of paying (either from principal or income or both) for the benefit of employees and their families and dependents at least medical or hospital care, and pensions on retirement or death of employees; and

"(2) such plan was established prior to January 1, 1954, as a result of an agreement between employee representatives and the Government of the United States during a period of Government operation, under seizure powers, of a major part of the productive facilities of the industry in which such employer is engaged,

such contributions shall not be deductible under this section nor be made nondeductible by this section, but the deductibility thereof shall be governed solely by section 162 (relating to trade or business expenses). This subsection shall have no application with respect to amounts contributed to a trust on or after any date on which such trust is qualified for exemption from tax under section 501(a)."

[Sec. 404(d)]

(d) DEDUCTIBILITY OF PAYMENTS OF DEFERRED COMPENSATION, ETC., TO INDEPENDENT CONTRACTORS.—If a plan would be described in so much of subsection (a) as precedes paragraph (1) thereof (as modified by subsection (b)) but for the fact that there is no employer-employee relationship, the contributions or compensation—

(1) shall not be deductible by the payor thereof under this chapter, but

(2) shall (if they would be deductible under this chapter but for paragraph (1)) be deductible under this subsection for the taxable year in which an amount attributable to the contribution or compensation is includible in the gross income of the persons participating in the plan.

Amendments

• 1986, Tax Reform Act of 1986 (P.L. 99-514)

P.L. 99-514, §1851(b)(2)(C)(ii):

Amended Code Sec. 404(d) by striking out "under section 162 or 212" each place it appears and inserting in lieu thereof "under this chapter". **Effective** as if included in the provision of P.L. 98-369 to which it relates.

• 1980, Technical Corrections Act of 1979 (P.L. 96-222)

P.L. 96-222, §101(a)(5):

Amended Act Sec. 133 of P.L. 95-600 by revising paragraph (c). For **effective** date, see the effective date and special rule in the historical note for §101, P.L. 96-222, following the text of Code Sec. 404(b).

• 1978, Revenue Act of 1978 (P.L. 95-600)

P.L. 95-600, §133(a):

Added a new Code Sec. 404(d). **Effective** for deductions for tax years beginning after 12-31-78. [but see P.L. 96-222, §101(a)(15), above].

• 1976, Tax Reform Act of 1976 (P.L. 94-455)

P.L. 94-455, §1901(a)(59):

Repealed Code Sec. 404(d). **Effective** with respect to tax years beginning after 12-31-76. Prior to repeal, Code Sec. 404(d) read as follows:

(d) CARRYOVER OF UNUSED DEDUCTIONS.—The amount of any unused deductions or contributions in excess of the deductible amounts for taxable years to which this part does not apply which under section 23 (p) of the Internal Revenue Code of 1939 would be allowable as deductions in later years had such section 23 (p) remained in effect, shall be allowable as deductions in taxable years to which this part applies as if such section 23 (p) were continued in effect for such years. However, the deduction under the preceding sentence shall not exceed an amount which, when added to the deduction allowable under subsection (a) for contributions made in taxable years to which this part applies, is not greater than the amount which would be deductible under subsection (a) if the contributions which give rise to the deduction under the preceding sentence were made in a taxable year to which this part applies.

[Sec. 404(e)]

(e) CONTRIBUTIONS ALLOCABLE TO LIFE INSURANCE PROTECTION FOR SELF-EMPLOYED INDIVIDUALS.—In the case of a self-employed individual described in section 401(c)(1), contributions which are allocable (determined under regulations prescribed by the Secretary) to the purchase of life, accident, health, or other insurance shall not be taken into account under paragraph (1), (2), or (3) of subsection (a).

Amendments

• 1984, Deficit Reduction Act of 1984 (P.L. 98-369)

P.L. 98-369, §713(d)(9):

Amended Code Sec. 404(e) by striking out "under this section" and inserting in lieu thereof "under paragraph (1), (2), or (3) of subsection (a)". **Effective** as if included in the provision of P.L. 97-248 to which it relates. However, Code Sec. 404(e) (as in effect on 9-2-82, does not apply to any plan to which Code Sec. 401(j) applies (or would apply but for its repeal).

• 1983, Technical Corrections Act of 1982 (P.L. 97-448)

P.L. 97-448, §103(d)(3):

Amended paragraph (1) of section 312(f) of P.L. 97-34 (relating to **effective** date) by striking out "plans which include employees within the meaning of section 401(c)(1) with respect to".

• 1982, Tax Equity and Fiscal Responsibility Act of 1982 (P.L. 97-248)

P.L. 97-248, §238(a):

Amended Code Sec. 404(e). **Effective** for years beginning after 12-31-83. Prior to amendment, Code Sec. 404(e) read as follows:

(e) SPECIAL LIMITATIONS FOR SELF-EMPLOYED INDIVIDUALS.—

(1) IN GENERAL.—In the case of a plan included in subsection (a)(1), (2), or (3), which provides contributions or benefits for employees some or all of whom are employees within the meaning of section 401(c)(1), the amounts deductible under subsection (a) in any taxable year with respect to contributions on behalf of any employee within the meaning of section 401(c)(1) shall, subject to paragraphs (2) and (4), not exceed $15,000, or 15 percent of the earned income derived by such employee from the trade or business with respect to which the plan is established, whichever is the lesser.

(2) CONTRIBUTIONS MADE UNDER MORE THAN ONE PLAN.—

(A) OVERALL LIMITATION.—In any taxable year in which amounts are deductible with respect to contributions under two or more plans on behalf of an individual who is an employee within the meaning of section 401(c)(1) with respect to such plans, the aggregate amount deductible for such taxable year under all such plans with respect to contributions on behalf of such employee shall (subject to paragraph (4)) not exceed $15,000, or 15 percent of the earned income derived by such employee from the trades or businesses with respect to which the plans are established, whichever is the lesser.

(B) ALLOCATION OF AMOUNTS DEDUCTIBLE.—In any case in which the amounts deductible under subsection (a) (with the application of the limitations of this subsection) with respect to contributions made on behalf of an employee within the meaning of section 401(c)(1) under two or more plans are, by reason of subparagraph (A), less than the amounts deductible under such subsection determined without regard to such subparagraph, the amount deductible under subsection (a) with respect to such contributions under each such plan shall be determined in accordance with regulations prescribed by the Secretary.

(3) CONTRIBUTIONS ALLOCABLE TO INSURANCE PROTECTION.—For purposes of this subsection, contributions which are allocable (determined under regulations prescribed by the Secretary) to the purchase of life, accident, health, or other insurance shall not be taken into account.

(4) LIMITATIONS CANNOT BE LOWER THAN $750 OR 100 PERCENT OF EARNED INCOME.—The limitations under paragraphs (1) and (2)(A) for any employee shall not be less than the lesser of—

(A) $750, or

(B) 100 percent of the earned income derived by such employee from the trades or businesses taken into account for purposes of paragraph (1) or (2)(A) as the case may be.

This paragraph does not apply for any taxable year to any employee whose adjusted gross income for such taxable year (determined separately for each individual, without regard to any community property laws, and without regard to the deduction allowable under subsection (a)) exceeds $15,000.

• 1981, Economic Recovery Tax Act of 1981 (P.L. 97-34)

P.L. 97-34, §312(a):

Amended Code Sec. 404(e)(1) and (2)(A) by striking out "$7,500" and inserting "$15,000". **Effective** for tax years beginning after 12-31-81.

• 1976, Tax Reform Act of 1976 (P.L. 94-455)

P.L. 94-455, §1502(a):

Amended Code Sec. 404(e)(4) by adding thereto the last sentence. **Effective** for tax years beginning after 12-31-75.

P.L. 94-455, §1906(b)(13)(A):

Amended the 1954 Code by substituting "Secretary" for "Secretary or his delegate" each place it appeared. **Effective** 2-1-77.

• 1974, Employee Retirement Income Security Act of 1974 (P.L. 93-406)

P.L. 93-406, §2001(a):

Amended Code Sec. 404(e). **Effective** for tax years beginning after 12-31-73. Prior to amendment, Code Sec. 404(e) read as follows:

"(e) Special Limitations for Self-Employed Individuals.—

"(1) In general.—In the case of a plan included in subsection (a)(1), (2), or (3), which provides contributions or benefits for employees some or all of whom are employees within the meaning of section 401(c)(1), the amounts deductible under subsection (a) in any taxable year with respect to contributions on behalf of any employee within the meaning of section 401(c)(1) shall, subject to the provisions of paragraph (2), not exceed $2,500, or 10 percent of the earned income derived by such employee from the trade or business with respect to which the plan is established, whichever is the lesser.

"(2) Contributions made under more than one plan.—

"(A) Overall limitation.—In any taxable year in which amounts are deductible with respect to contributions under two or more plans on behalf of an individual who is an employee within the meaning of section 401(c)(1) with respect to such plans, the aggregate amount deductible for such taxable year under all such plans with respect to contributions on behalf of such employee shall not exceed $2,500, or 10 percent of the earned income derived by such employee from the trades or businesses with respect to which the plans are established, whichever is the lesser.

"(B) Allocation of amounts deductible.—In any case in which the amounts deductible under subsection (a) (with the application of the limitations of this subsection) with respect to contributions made on behalf of an employee within the meaning of section 401(c)(1) under two or more plans are, by reason of subparagraph (A), less than the amounts deductible under such subsection determined without regard to such subparagraph, the amount deductible under subsection (a) with respect to such contributions under each such plan shall be determined in accordance with regulations prescribed by the Secretary or his delegate.

"(3) Contributions, allocable to insurance protection.—For purposes of this subsection, contributions which are allocable (determined under regulations prescribed by the Secretary or his delegate) to the purchase of life, accident, health, or other insurance shall not be taken into account."

• 1966, Foreign Investors Tax Act of 1966 (P.L. 89-809)

P.L. 89-809, §204(b)(2):

Amended Code Sec. 404(e)(2)(A) by deleting "determined without regard to subsection (a)(10))". **Effective** 1-1-68.

P.L. 89-809, §204(b)(3):

Amended Code Sec. 404(e)(1) and (2)(B) by deleting "(determined without regard to paragraph (10) thereof)".

• 1962, Self-Employed Individuals Tax Retirement Act of 1962 (P.L. 87-792)

P.L. 87-792, §3:

Added Code Sec. 404(e). **Effective** for tax years beginning after 12-31-62.

[Sec. 404(f)—Repealed]

Amendments

• 1984, Deficit Reduction Act of 1984 (P.L. 98-369)

P.L. 98-369, §713(b)(3):

Repealed Code Sec. 404(f). **Effective** as if included in the provision of P.L. 97-248 to which it relates. Prior to repeal, Code Sec. 404(f) read as follows:

(f) Certain Loan Repayments Considered as Contributions.—For purposes of this section, any amount paid, directly or indirectly, by an owner-employee (within the meaning of section 401(c)(3)) in repayment of any loan which under section 72(m)(4)(B) was treated as an amount received under a contract purchased by a trust described in section 401(a) which is exempt from tax under section 501(a) or purchased as a part of a plan described in section 403(a) shall be treated as a contribution to which this section applies on behalf of such owner-employee to such trust or to or under such plan.

• 1962, Self-Employed Individuals Tax Retirement Act of 1962 (P.L. 87-792)

P.L. 87-792, §3:

Added Code Sec. 404(f). **Effective** for tax years beginning after 12-31-62.

[Sec. 404(g)]

(g) CERTAIN EMPLOYER LIABILITY PAYMENTS CONSIDERED AS CONTRIBUTIONS.—

(1) IN GENERAL.—For purposes of this section, any amount paid by an employer under section 4041(b), 4062, 4063, or 4064, or part 1 of subtitle E of title IV of the Employee Retirement Income Security Act of 1974 shall be treated as a contribution to which this section applies by such employer to or under a stock bonus, pension, profit-sharing, or annuity plan.

(2) CONTROLLED GROUP DEDUCTIONS.—In the case of a payment described in paragraph (1) made by an entity which is liable because it is a member of a commonly controlled group of corporations, trades, or businesses, within the meaning of subsection (b) or (c) of section 414, the fact that the entity did not directly employ participants of the plan with respect to which the liability payment was made shall not affect the deductibility of a payment which otherwise satisfies the conditions of section 162 (relating to trade or business expenses) or section 212 (relating to expenses for the production of income).

(3) TIMING OF DEDUCTION OF CONTRIBUTIONS.—

(A) IN GENERAL.—Except as otherwise provided in this paragraph, any payment described in paragraph (1) shall (subject to the last sentence of subsection (a)(1)(A)) be deductible under this section when paid.

(B) CONTRIBUTIONS UNDER STANDARD TERMINATIONS.—Subparagraph (A) shall not apply (and subsection (a)(1)(A) shall apply) to any payments described in paragraph (1) which are paid to terminate a plan under section 4041(b) of the Employee Retirement Income Security Act of 1974 to the extent such payments result in the assets of the plan being in excess of the total amount of benefits under such plan which are guaranteed by the Pension Benefit Guaranty Corporation under section 4022 of such Act.

(C) CONTRIBUTIONS TO CERTAIN TRUSTS.—Subparagraph (A) shall not apply to any payment described in paragraph (1) which is made under section 4062(c) of such Act and such payment shall be deductible at such time as may be prescribed in regulations which are based on principles similar to the principles of subsection (a)(1)(A).

(4) REFERENCES TO EMPLOYEE RETIREMENT INCOME SECURITY ACT OF 1974.—For purposes of this subsection, any reference to a section of the Employee Retirement Income Security Act of 1974 shall be treated as a reference to such section as in effect on the date of the enactment of the Retirement Protection Act of 1994.

Amendments

• 1994, Uruguay Round Agreements Act (P.L. 103-465)

P.L. 103-465, §751(a)(11):

Amended Code Sec. 404(g)(4) by striking "the Single-Employer Pension Plan Amendments Act of 1986" and inserting "the Retirement Protection Act of 1994". **Effective** 12-8-94.

• 1989, Omnibus Budget Reconciliation Act of 1989 (P.L. 101-239)

P.L. 101-239, §7841(b)(1):

Amended Code Sec. 404(g)(1) by inserting "4041(b)," before "4062". **Effective** for payments made after 1-1-86, in tax years ending after such date.

• 1986, Consolidated Omnibus Budget Reconciliation Act of 1985 (P.L. 99-272)

P.L. 99-272, §11011(c)(1):

Amended Code Sec. 404(g)(3). **Effective** for payments made after 1-1-86, in tax years ending after such date. Prior to amendment, Code Sec. 404(g)(3) read as follows:

(3) COORDINATION WITH SUBSECTION (a).—Any payment described in paragraph (1) shall (subject to the last sentence of subsection (a)(1)(A)) be deductible under this section when paid.

P.L. 99-272, §11011(c)(2):

Amended Code Sec. 404(g) by adding at the end thereof new paragraph (4). **Effective** for payments made after 1-1-86, in tax years ending after such date.

• 1980, Multiemployer Pension Plan Amendments Act of 1980 (P.L. 96-364)

P.L. 96-364, §205:

Amended Code Sec. 404(g). Prior to amendment Code Sec. 404(g) read:

"(g) CERTAIN EMPLOYER LIABILITY PAYMENTS CONSIDERED AS CONTRIBUTIONS.—For purposes of this section any amount paid by an employer under section 4062, 4063, or 4064 of the Employee Retirement Income Security Act of 1974 shall be treated as a contribution to which this section applies by such employer to or under a stock bonus, pension, profit-sharing, or annuity plan."

P.L. 96-364, §408, provides:

"(a) For purposes of subsection (g) of section 404 of the Internal Revenue Code of 1954 (relating to certain employer liability payments considered as contributions), as amended by section 205 of this Act, any payment made to a plan covering employees of a corporation operating a public transportation system shall be treated as a payment described in paragraph (1) of such subsection if—

"(1) such payment is made to fund accrued benefits under the plan in conjunction with an acquisition by a State (or agency or instrumentality thereof) of the stock or assets of such corporation, and

"(2) such acquisition is pursuant to a State public transportation law enacted after June 30, 1979, and before January 1, 1980.

"(b) The provisions of this section shall apply to payments made after June 29, 1980."

• 1974, Employee Retirement Income Security Act of 1974 (P.L. 93-406)

P.L. 93-406, §4081(a):

Added Code Sec. 404(g). **Effective** on 9-2-74.

[Sec. 404(h)]

(h) SPECIAL RULES FOR SIMPLIFIED EMPLOYEE PENSIONS.—

(1) IN GENERAL.—Employer contributions to a simplified employee pension shall be treated as if they are made to a plan subject to the requirements of this section. Employer contributions to a simplified employee pension are subject to the following limitations:

(A) Contributions made for a year are deductible—

(i) in the case of a simplified employee pension maintained on a calendar year basis, for the taxable year with or within which the calendar year ends, or

(ii) in the case of a simplified employee pension which is maintained on the basis of the taxable year of the employer, for such taxable year.

(B) Contributions shall be treated for purposes of this subsection as if they were made for a taxable year if such contributions are made on account of such taxable year and are made not later than the time prescribed by law for filing the return for such taxable year (including extensions thereof).

(C) The amount deductible in a taxable year for a simplified employee pension shall not exceed 25 percent of the compensation paid to the employees during the calendar year ending with or within the taxable year (or during the taxable year in the case of a taxable year described in subparagraph (A)(ii)). The excess of the amount contributed over the amount deductible for a taxable year shall be deductible in the succeeding taxable years in order of time, subject to the 25 percent limit of the preceding sentence.

(2) EFFECT ON CERTAIN TRUSTS.—For any taxable year for which the employer has a deduction under paragraph (1), the otherwise applicable limitations in subsection (a)(3)(A) shall be reduced by the amount of the allowable deductions under paragraph (1) with respect to participants in the trust subject to subsection (a)(3)(A).

(3) COORDINATION WITH SUBSECTION (a)(7).—For purposes of subsection (a)(7), a simplified employee pension shall be treated as if it were a separate stock bonus or profit-sharing trust.

Amendments

• 2006, Pension Protection Act of 2006 (P.L. 109-280)

P.L. 109-280, §811, provides:

SEC. 811. PENSIONS AND INDIVIDUAL RETIREMENT ARRANGEMENT PROVISIONS OF ECONOMIC GROWTH AND TAX RELIEF RECONCILIATION ACT OF 2001 MADE PERMANENT.

Title IX of the Economic Growth and Tax Relief Reconciliation Act of 2001 [P.L. 107-16] shall not apply to the provisions of, and amendments made by, subtitles A through F of title VI [§§601-666]of such Act (relating to pension and individual retirement arrangement provisions).

• 2001, Economic Growth and Tax Relief Reconciliation Act of 2001 (P.L. 107-16)

P.L. 107-16, §616(a)(1)(B):

Amended Code Sec. 404(h)(1)(C) by striking "15 percent" each place it appears and inserting "25 percent". **Effective** for years beginning after 12-31-2001.

P.L. 107-16, §616(a)(2)(B)(ii):

Amended Code Sec. 404(h)(2) by striking "stock bonus or profit-sharing trust" and inserting "trust subject to subsection (a)(3)(A)". **Effective** for years beginning after 12-31-2001.

P.L. 107-16, §616(a)(2)(B)(iii):

Amended the heading of Code Sec. 404(h)(2) by striking "STOCK BONUS AND PROFIT-SHARING TRUST" and inserting "CERTAIN TRUSTS". **E ffective** for years beginning after 12-31-2001.

P.L. 107-16, §901(a)-(b), provides [but see P.L. 109-280, §811, above]:

SEC. 901. SUNSET OF PROVISIONS OF ACT.

(a) IN GENERAL.—All provisions of, and amendments made by, this Act shall not apply—

(1) to taxable, plan, or limitation years beginning after December 31, 2010, or

(2) in the case of title V, to estates of decedents dying, gifts made, or generation skipping transfers, after December 31, 2010.

(b) APPLICATION OF CERTAIN LAWS.—The Internal Revenue Code of 1986 and the Employee Retirement Income Security Act of 1974 shall be applied and administered to years, estates, gifts, and transfers described in subsection (a) as if the provisions and amendments described in subsection (a) had never been enacted.

• 1988, Technical and Miscellaneous Revenue Act of 1988 (P.L. 100-647)

P.L. 100-647, §1011(f)(6):

Amended Code Sec. 404(h)(1)(C) by inserting "(or during the taxable year in the case of a taxable year described in subparagraph (A)(ii))" after "taxable year" the second place it appears. **Effective** as if included in the provision of P.L. 99-514 to which it relates.

P.L. 100-647, §1011A(e)(4)(B):

Amended Code Sec. 404(h)(3). **Effective** as if included in the provision of P.L. 99-514 to which it relates. Prior to amendment, Code Sec. 404(h)(3) read as follows:

(3) EFFECT ON LIMIT ON DEDUCTIONS.—For any taxable year for which the employer has a deduction under paragraph (1), the otherwise applicable 25 percent limitations in subsection (a)(7) shall be reduced by the amount of the allowable deductions under paragraph (1) with respect to participants in the stock bonus or profit-sharing trust.

• 1986, Tax Reform Act of 1986 (P.L. 99-514)

P.L. 99-514, §1108(c):

Amended Code Sec. 404(h)(1)(A) and (B). **Effective** for tax years beginning after 12-31-86. Prior to amendment, Code Sec. 404(h)(1)(A) and (B) read as follows:

(A) Contributions made for a calendar year are deductible for the taxable year with which or within which the calendar year ends.

(B) Contributions made within 3½ months after the close of a calendar year are treated as if they were made on the last day of such calendar year if they are made on account of such calendar year.

• 1984, Deficit Reduction Act of 1984 (P.L. 98-369)

P.L. 98-369, §713(d)(5):

Repealed Code Sec. 404(h)(4). **Effective** as if included in the provision of P.L. 97-248 to which it relates. Prior to amendment, Code Sec. 404(h)(4) read as follows:

(4) Effect on Self-Employed Individuals or Shareholder-Employees.—The limitations described in paragraphs (1), (2)(A), and (4) of subsection (e) or described in section 1379(b)(1) for any taxable year shall be reduced by the amount of the allowable deductions under paragraph (1) with respect to an employee within the meaning of section 401(c)(1) or a shareholder-employee (as defined in section 1379(d)).

• 1980, Technical Corrections Act of 1979 (P.L. 96-222)

P.L. 96-222, §101(a)(10)(E):

Amended Code Sec. 404(h)(4). **Effective** for tax years beginning after 12-31-78. Prior to amendment, Code Sec. 404(h)(4) read as follows:

(4) EFFECT ON SELF-EMPLOYED INDIVIDUALS.—The limitations described in paragraphs (1), (2)(A), and (4) of subsection (e) for any taxable year shall be reduced by the amount of the allowable deductions under subparagraph (1) with respect to an employee within the meaning of section 401(c)(1).

P.L. 96-222, §101(a)(10)(J)(ii):

Amended Code Sec. 404(h) by changing "subparagraph (1)" each place it appears to "paragraph (1)" in paragraphs (2), (3), and (4). **Effective** for tax years beginning after 12-31-78.

• 1978, Revenue Act of 1978 (P.L. 95-600)

P.L. 95-600, §152(f):

Added Code Sec. 404(h). **Effective** for tax years beginning after 12-31-78.

[Sec. 404(i)—Repealed]

Amendments

• 1986, Tax Reform Act of 1986 (P.L. 99-514)

P.L. 99-514, §1171(b)(6):

Repealed Code Sec. 404(i). **Effective**, generally, for compensation paid or accrued after 12-31-86, in tax years ending after such date. For an exception, see Act Sec. 1171(c)(2), below. Prior to amendment Code Sec. 404(i) read as follows:

(i) DEDUCTIBILITY OF UNUSED PORTIONS OF EMPLOYEE STOCK OWNERSHIP CREDIT.—

(1) UNUSED CREDIT CARRYOVERS.—If any portion of the employee stock ownership credit determined under section 41 for any taxable year has not, after the application of section 38(c), been allowed under section 38 for any taxable year, such portion shall be allowed as a deduction (without regard to any limitations provided under this section) for the last taxable year to which such portion could have been allowed as a credit under section 39.

(2) REDUCTIONS IN CREDIT.—There shall be allowed as a deduction (subject to the limitations provided under this section) an amount equal to any reduction of the credit allowed under section 41 resulting from a final determination of such credit to the extent such reduction is not taken into account under section 41(c)(3).

P.L. 99-514, §1171(c)(2), provides:

(2) SECTIONS 404(i) AND 6699 TO CONTINUE TO APPLY TO PRE-1987 CREDITS.—The provisions of sections 404(i) and 6699 of the Internal Revenue Code of 1986 shall continue to apply with respect to credits under section 41 of such Code attributable to compensation paid or accrued before January 1, 1987 (or under section 38 of such Code with respect to qualified investment before January 1, 1983).

• 1984, Deficit Reduction Act of 1984 (P.L. 98-369)

P.L. 98-369, §474(r)(14):

Amended Code Sec. 404(i)[(h)]. **Effective** for tax years beginning after 12-31-83, and to carrybacks from such years. Prior to amendment, it read as follows:

(i) Deductibility of Unused Portions of Employee Stock Ownership Credit.—

(1) Unused Credit Carryovers.—There shall be allowed as a deduction (without regard to any limitations provided under this section) for the last taxable year to which an unused employee stock ownership credit carryover (within the meaning of section 44G(b)(2)(A)) may be carried, an amount equal to the portion of such unused credit carryover which expires at the close of such taxable year.

(2) Reductions in Credit.—There shall be allowed as a deduction (subject to the limitations provided under this section) an amount equal to any reduction of the credit allowed under section 44G resulting from a final determinaton of such credit to the extent such reduction is not taken into account in section 44G(c)(3).

• 1981, Economic Recovery Tax Act of 1981 (P.L. 97-34)

P.L. 97-34, §331(b):

Added Code Sec. 404(i). **Effective** for tax years ending after 12-31-82.

[Sec. 404(j)]

(j) SPECIAL RULES RELATING TO APPLICATION WITH SECTION 415.—

(1) NO DEDUCTION IN EXCESS OF SECTION 415 LIMITATION.—In computing the amount of any deduction allowable under paragraph (1), (2), (3), (4), (7), or (9) of subsection (a) for any year—

(A) in the case of a defined benefit plan, there shall not be taken into account any benefits for any year in excess of any limitation on such benefits under section 415 for such year, or

(B) in the case of a defined contribution plan, the amount of any contributions otherwise taken into account shall be reduced by any annual additions in excess of the limitation under section 415 for such year.

(2) NO ADVANCE FUNDING OF COST-OF-LIVING ADJUSTMENTS.—For purposes of clause (i), (ii) or (iii) of subsection (a)(1)(A), and in computing the full funding limitation, there shall not be taken into account any adjustments under section 415(d)(1) for any year before the year for which such adjustment first takes effect.

Amendments

• 1996, Small Business Job Protection Act of 1996 (P.L. 104-188)

P.L. 104-188, §1704(q)(1):

Amended Code Sec. 404(j)(1) by striking "(10)" and inserting "(9)". **Effective** as if included in the amendments made by section 713(d)(4)(A) of P.L. 98-369.

• 1982, Tax Equity and Fiscal Responsibility Act of 1982 (P.L. 97-248)

P.L. 97-248, §235(f):

Amended Code Sec. 404 by adding at the end thereof new subsection (j). **Effective** as noted in P.L. 97-248, Act Sec. 235(g), as follows:

(g) EFFECTIVE DATES.—

(1) IN GENERAL.—

(A) NEW PLANS.—In the case of any plan which is not in existence on July 1, 1982, the amendments made by this section shall apply to years ending after July 1, 1982.

(B) EXISTING PLANS.—

(i) In the case of any plan which is in existence on July 1, 1982, the amendments made by this section shall apply to years beginning after December 31, 1982.

(ii) PLAN REQUIREMENTS.—A plan shall not be treated as failing to meet the requirements of section 401(a)(16) of the Internal Revenue Code of 1954 for any year beginning before January 1, 1984, merely because such plan provides for benefit or contribution limits which are in excess of the limitations under section 415 of such Code, as amended by this section. The preceding sentence shall not apply to any plan which provides such limits in excess of the limitation under section 415 of such Code before such amendments.

But see amendment notes under Code Sec. 415 for P.L. 97-248, Act Sec. 235(g) for special rules.

[Sec. 404(k)]

(k) DEDUCTION FOR DIVIDENDS PAID ON CERTAIN EMPLOYER SECURITIES.—

(1) GENERAL RULE.—In the case of a C corporation, there shall be allowed as a deduction for a taxable year the amount of any applicable dividend paid in cash by such corporation with respect to applicable employer securities. Such deduction shall be in addition to the deductions allowed under subsection (a).

(2) APPLICABLE DIVIDEND.—For purposes of this subsection—

(A) IN GENERAL.—The term "applicable dividend" means any dividend which, in accordance with the plan provisions—

(i) is paid in cash to the participants in the plan or their beneficiaries,

(ii) is paid to the plan and is distributed in cash to participants in the plan or their beneficiaries not later than 90 days after the close of the plan year in which paid,

(iii) is, at the election of such participants or their beneficiaries—

(I) payable as provided in clause (i) or (ii), or

(II) paid to the plan and reinvested in qualifying employer securities, or

(iv) is used to make payments on a loan described in subsection (a)(9) the proceeds of which were used to acquire the employer securities (whether or not allocated to participants) with respect to which the dividend is paid.

(B) LIMITATION ON CERTAIN DIVIDENDS.—A dividend described in subparagraph (A)(iv) which is paid with respect to any employer security which is allocated to a participant shall not be treated as an applicable dividend unless the plan provides that employer securities with a fair market value of not less than the amount of such dividend are allocated to such participant for the year which (but for subparagraph (A)) such dividend would have been allocated to such participant.

(3) APPLICABLE EMPLOYER SECURITIES.—For purposes of this subsection, the term "applicable employer securities" means, with respect to any dividend, employer securities which are held on the record date for such dividend by an employee stock ownership plan which is maintained by—

(A) the corporation paying such dividend, or

(B) any other corporation which is a member of a controlled group of corporations (within the meaning of section 409(l)(4)) which includes such corporation.

(4) TIME FOR DEDUCTION.—

(A) IN GENERAL.—The deduction under paragraph (1) shall be allowable in the taxable year of the corporation in which the dividend is paid or distributed to a participant or his beneficiary.

(B) REINVESTMENT DIVIDENDS.—For purposes of subparagraph (A), an applicable dividend reinvested pursuant to clause (iii)(II) of paragraph (2)(A) shall be treated as paid in the taxable year of the corporation in which such dividend is reinvested in qualifying employer securities or in which the election under clause (iii) of paragraph (2)(A) is made, whichever is later.

(C) REPAYMENT OF LOANS.—In the case of an applicable dividend described in clause (iv) of paragraph (2)(A), the deduction under paragraph (1) shall be allowable in the taxable year of the corporation in which such dividend is used to repay the loan described in such clause.

(5) OTHER RULES.—For purposes of this subsection—

(A) DISALLOWANCE OF DEDUCTION.—The Secretary may disallow the deduction under paragraph (1) for any dividend if the Secretary determines that such dividend constitutes, in substance, an avoidance or evasion of taxation.

(B) PLAN QUALIFICATION.—A plan shall not be treated as violating the requirements of section 401, 409, or 4975(e)(7), or as engaging in a prohibited transaction for purposes of section 4975(d)(3), merely by reason of any payment or distribution described in paragraph (2)(A).

(6) DEFINITIONS.—For purposes of this subsection—

(A) EMPLOYER SECURITIES.—The term "employer securities" has the meaning given such term by section 409(l).

(B) EMPLOYEE STOCK OWNERSHIP PLAN.—The term "employee stock ownership plan" has the meaning given such term by section 4975(e)(7). Such term includes a tax credit employee stock ownership plan (as defined in section 409).

(7) FULL VESTING.—In accordance with section 411, an applicable dividend described in clause (iii)(II) of paragraph (2)(A) shall be subject to the requirements of section 411(a)(1).

Amendments

• 2006, Pension Protection Act of 2006 (P.L. 109-280)

P.L. 109-280, §811, provides:

SEC. 811. PENSIONS AND INDIVIDUAL RETIREMENT ARRANGEMENT PROVISIONS OF ECONOMIC GROWTH AND TAX RELIEF RECONCILIATION ACT OF 2001 MADE PERMANENT.

Title IX of the Economic Growth and Tax Relief Reconciliation Act of 2001 [P.L. 107-16] shall not apply to the provisions of, and amendments made by, subtitles A through F of title VI [§§601-666]of such Act (relating to pension and individual retirement arrangement provisions).

• 2002, Job Creation and Worker Assistance Act of 2002 (P.L. 107-147)

P.L. 107-147, §411(w)(1)(A)-(D):

Amended Code Sec. 404(k) by striking "during the taxable year" before "with respect to" in paragraph (1), by striking "(A)(iii)" and inserting "(A)(iv)" in paragraph (2)(B), by striking "(iii)" and inserting "(iv)" in paragraph (4)(B), by redesignating subparagraph (B) of paragraph (4) (as amended) as subparagraph (C) of paragraph (4), and by inserting after subparagraph (A) a new subparagraph (B). **Effective** as if included in the provision of P.L. 107-16 to which it relates [**effective** for tax years beginning after 12-31-2001.—CCH].

P.L. 107-147, §411(w)(2):

Amended Code Sec. 404(k) by adding at the end a new paragraph (7). **Effective** as if included in the provision of P.L. 107-16 to which it relates [**effective** for tax years beginning after 12-31-2001.—CCH].

• 2001, Economic Growth and Tax Relief Reconciliation Act of 2001 (P.L. 107-16)

P.L. 107-16, §662(a):

Amended Code Sec. 404(k)(2)(A) by striking "or" at the end of clause (ii), by redesignating clause (iii) as clause (iv), and by inserting after clause (ii) a new clause (iii). **Effective** for tax years beginning after 12-31-2001.

P.L. 107-16, §662(b):

Amended Code Sec. 404(k)(5)(A) by inserting "avoidance or" before "evasion". **Effective** for tax years beginning after 12-31-2001.

P.L. 107-16, §901(a)-(b), provides [but see P.L. 109-280, §811, above]:

SEC. 901. SUNSET OF PROVISIONS OF ACT.

(a) IN GENERAL.—All provisions of, and amendments made by, this Act shall not apply—

(1) to taxable, plan, or limitation years beginning after December 31, 2010, or

(2) in the case of title V, to estates of decedents dying, gifts made, or generation skipping transfers, after December 31, 2010.

(b) APPLICATION OF CERTAIN LAWS.—The Internal Revenue Code of 1986 and the Employee Retirement Income Security Act of 1974 shall be applied and administered to years, estates, gifts, and transfers described in subsection (a) as if the provisions and amendments described in subsection (a) had never been enacted.

• 1996, Small Business Job Protection Act of 1996 (P.L. 104-188)

P.L. 104-188, §1316(d)(2):

Amended Code Sec. 404(k)(1) by striking "a corporation" and inserting "a C corporation". **Effective** for tax years beginning after 12-31-97.

• 1989, Omnibus Budget Reconciliation Act of 1989 (P.L. 101-239)

P.L. 101-239, §7302(a):

Amended Code Sec. 404(k). **Effective**, generally, for employer securities acquired after 8-4-89. However, for a special rule, see Act Sec. 7302(b)(2), below. Prior to amendment, Code Sec. 404(k) read as follows:

(k) DIVIDENDS PAID DEDUCTIONS.—In addition to the deductions provided under subsection (a), there shall be allowed as a deduction to a corporation the amount of any dividend paid in cash by such corporation during the taxable year with respect to the stock of such corporation if—

(1) such stock is held on the record date for the dividend by a tax credit employee stock ownership plan (as defined in section 409) or an employee stock ownership plan (as defined in section 4975(e)(7)) which is maintained by such corporation or by any other corporation that is a member of a controlled group of corporations (within the meaning of section 409(l)(4)) that includes such corporation, and

(2) in accordance with the plan provisions—

(A) the dividend is paid in cash to the participants in the plan or their beneficiaries,

(B) the dividend is paid to the plan and is distributed in cash to participants in the plan or their beneficiaries not later than 90 days after the close of the plan year in which paid, or

(C) the dividend with respect to employer securities (whether or not allocated to participants) is used to make payments on a loan described in section 404(a)(9).

Any deduction under subparagraph (A) or (B) of paragraph (2) shall be allowed in the taxable year of the corporation in which the dividend is paid or distributed to the participant under paragraph (2). A plan to which this subsection applies shall not be treated as violating the requirements of section 401, 409, or 4975(e)(7) or as engaging in a prohibited transaction for purposes of section 4975(d)(3) merely by reason of any distribution or payment described in paragraph (2). The Secretary may disallow the deduction under this subsection for any dividend if the Secretary determines that such dividend constitutes, in substance, an evasion of taxation. Any deduction under paragraph (2)(C) shall be allowable in the taxable year of the corporation in which the dividend is used to repay the loan described in such paragraph. Paragraph (2)(C) shall not apply to dividends from employer securities which are allocated to any participant unless the plan provides that employer securities with a fair market value not less than the amount of such dividends are allocated to such participant for the year which (but for paragraph (2)(C)) such dividends would have been allocated to such participant.

P.L. 101-239, §7302(b)(2), provides:

(2) SECURITIES ACQUIRED WITH CERTAIN LOANS.—The amendment made by this section shall not apply to employer securities acquired after August 4, 1989, which are acquired—

(A) with the proceeds of any loan which was made pursuant to a binding written commitment in effect on August 4, 1989, and at all times thereafter before such loan is made, and

(B) pursuant to a written binding contract (or tender offer registered with the Securities and Exchange Commission) in effect on August 4, 1989, and at all times thereafter before such securities are acquired.

• 1988, Technical and Miscellaneous Revenue Act of 1988 (P.L. 100-647)

P.L. 100-647, §1011B(h)(3)(A)-(B):

Amended Code Sec. 404(k) by inserting "(whether or not allocated to participants)" after "employer securities" in paragraph (2)(C), and by adding at the end thereof a new sentence. **Effective** as if included in the provision of P.L. 99-514 to which it relates.

P.L. 100-647, §1011B(h)(6):

Amended Code Sec. 404(k) by striking out "merely by reason of any distribution" in the third sentence and inserting in lieu thereof "or as engaging in a prohibited transaction for purposes of section 4975(d)(3) merely by reason of any distribution or payment". **Effective** as if included in the provision of P.L. 99-514 to which it relates.

P.L. 100-647, §1018(t)(4)(A):

Amended Code Sec. 404(k) by striking out "avoidance" in the 4th sentence and inserting in lieu thereof "evasion". **Effective** as if included in the provision of P.L. 99-514 to which it relates.

• 1986, Tax Reform Act of 1986 (P.L. 99-514)

P.L. 99-514, §1173(a)(1):

Amended Code Sec. 404(k)(2) by striking out "or" at the end of subparagraph (A), by striking out the period at the end of subparagraph (B) and inserting in lieu thereof ", or", and by inserting at the end thereof new subparagraph (C). **Effective** for dividends paid in tax years beginning after 10-22-86.

P.L. 99-514, §1173(a)(2):

Amended Code Sec. 404(k) by adding at the end thereof a new sentence. **Effective** for dividends paid in tax years beginning after 10-22-86.

P.L. 99-514, §1854(b)(2)(A) and (B):

Amended Code Sec. 404(k) by adding at the end thereof a new flush sentence, and by striking out "during the taxable year" after "such corporation" in the matter preceding paragraph (1). **Effective** as if included in the provision of P.L. 98-369 to which it relates. However, the above amendment shall not apply to dividends paid before 1-1-86, if the taxpayer treated such dividends in a manner inconsistent with such amendments on a return filed with the Secretary before 10-22-86.

P.L. 99-514, §1854(b)(3):

Amended Code Sec. 404(k), as amended by Act Sec. 1854(b)(2), by adding at the end thereof a new sentence. **Effective** as if included in the provision of P.L. 98-369 to which it relates.

P.L. 99-514, §1854(b)(4):

Amended Code Sec. 404(k) by adding at the end thereof a new sentence. **Effective** as if included in the provision of P.L. 98-369 to which it relates.

P.L. 99-514, §1854(b)(5):

Amended Code Sec. 404(k)(2) by striking out "participants in the plan" each place it appears and inserting in lieu thereof "participants in the plan or their beneficiaries". **Effective** as if included in the provision of P.L. 98-369 to which it relates.

• 1984, Deficit Reduction Act of 1984 (P.L. 98-369)

P.L. 98-369, §542(a):

Amended Code Sec. 404 by adding new subsection (k)[(j)]. **Effective** for tax years beginning after 7-18-84.

[Sec. 404(l)]

(l) LIMITATION ON AMOUNT OF ANNUAL COMPENSATION TAKEN INTO ACCOUNT.—For purposes of applying the limitations of this section, the amount of annual compensation of each employee taken into account under the plan for any year shall not exceed $200,000. The Secretary shall adjust the $200,000 amount at the same time, and by the same amount, as the adjustment under section 401(a)(17)(B). For purposes of clause (i), (ii), or (iii) of subsection (a)(1)(A), and in computing the full funding limitation, any adjustment under the preceding sentence shall not be taken into account for any year before the year for which such adjustment first takes effect.

Amendments

• 2006, Pension Protection Act of 2006 (P.L. 109-280)

P.L. 109-280, §811, provides:

SEC. 811. PENSIONS AND INDIVIDUAL RETIREMENT ARRANGEMENT PROVISIONS OF ECONOMIC GROWTH AND TAX RELIEF RECONCILIATION ACT OF 2001 MADE PERMANENT.

Title IX of the Economic Growth and Tax Relief Reconciliation Act of 2001 [P.L. 107-16] shall not apply to the provisions of, and amendments made by, subtitles A through F of title VI [§§601-666]of such Act (relating to pension and individual retirement arrangement provisions).

• 2001, Economic Growth and Tax Relief Reconciliation Act of 2001 (P.L. 107-16)

P.L. 107-16, §611(c)(1):

Amended Code Sec. 404(l) by striking "$150,000" each place it appears and inserting "$200,000". **Effective** for years beginning after 12-31-2001. For a special rule, see Act. Sec. 611(i)(3), below.

P.L. 107-16, §611(i)(3) (as added by P.L. 107-147, §411(j)(3)), provides:

(3) SPECIAL RULE.—In the case of [a] plan that, on June 7, 2001, incorporated by reference the limitation of section 415(b)(1)(A) of the Internal Revenue Code of 1986, section 411(d)(6) of such Code and section 204(g)(1) of the Employee Retirement Income Security Act of 1974 do not apply to a plan amendment that—

(A) is adopted on or before June 30, 2002,

(B) reduces benefits to the level that would have applied without regard to the amendments made by subsection (a) of this section, and

(C) is effective no earlier than the years described in paragraph (2).

P.L. 107-16, §901(a)-(b), provides [but see P.L. 109-280, §811, above]:

SEC. 901. SUNSET OF PROVISIONS OF ACT.

(a) IN GENERAL.—All provisions of, and amendments made by, this Act shall not apply—

(1) to taxable, plan, or limitation years beginning after December 31, 2010, or

(2) in the case of title V, to estates of decedents dying, gifts made, or generation skipping transfers, after December 31, 2010.

(b) APPLICATION OF CERTAIN LAWS.—The Internal Revenue Code of 1986 and the Employee Retirement Income Security Act of 1974 shall be applied and administered to years, estates, gifts, and transfers described in subsection (a) as if the provisions and amendments described in subsection (a) had never been enacted.

• 1996, Small Business Job Protection Act of 1996 (P.L. 104-188)

P.L. 104-188, §1431(b)(3):

Amended Code Sec. 404(l) by striking the last sentence. **Effective** for years beginning after 12-31-96, except that in determining whether an employee is a highly compensated employee for years beginning in 1997, such amendments shall be treated as having been in effect for years beginning in 1996. Prior to amendment, the last sentence of Code Sec. 404(l) read as follows:

In determining the compensation of an employee, the rules of section 414(q)(6) shall apply, except that in applying such rules, the term "family" shall include only the spouse of the employee and any lineal descendants of the employee who have not attained age 19 before the close of the year.

• 1993, Omnibus Budget Reconciliation Act of 1993 (P.L. 103-66)

P.L. 103-66, §13212(c)(1)(A)-(B):

Amended Code Sec. 404(l) by striking "$200,000" in the first sentence and inserting "$150,000", and by striking the second sentence and inserting a new sentence. **Effective,** generally, for benefits accruing in plan years beginning after 12-31-93. However, for special rules see Act Sec. 13212(d)(2)-(3) below. Prior to amendment, the second sentence read as follows:

The Secretary shall adjust the $200,000 amount at the same time and in the same amount as under section 415(d).

P.L. 103-66, §13212(d)(2)-(3), provides:

(2) COLLECTIVELY BARGAINED PLANS.—In the case of a plan maintained pursuant to 1 or more collective bargaining agreements between employee representatives and 1 or more employers ratified before the date of the amendment of this Act, the amendments made by this section shall not apply to contributions or benefits pursuant to such agreements for plan years beginning before the earlier of—

(A) the latest of—

(i) January 1, 1994,

(ii) the date on which the last of such collective bargaining agreements terminates (without regard to any extension, amendment, or modification of such agreements on or after such date of enactment), or

(iii) in the case of a plan maintained pursuant to collective bargaining under the Railway Labor Act, the date of execution of an extension or replacement of the last of such collective bargaining agreements in effect on such date of enactment, or

(B) January 1, 1997.

(3) TRANSITION RULE FOR STATE AND LOCAL PLANS.—

(A) IN GENERAL.—In the case of an eligible participant in a governmental plan (within the meaning of section 414(d) of the Internal Revenue Code of 1986), the dollar limitation under section 401(a)(17) of such Code shall not apply to the extent the amount of compensation which is allowed to be taken into account under the plan would be reduced below the amount which was allowed to be taken into account under the plan as in effect on July 1, 1993.

(B) ELIGIBLE PARTICIPANT.—For purposes of subparagraph (A), an eligible participant is an individual who first became a participant in the plan during a plan year beginning before the 1st plan year beginning after the earlier of—

(i) the plan year in which the plan is amended to reflect the amendments made by this section, or

(ii) December 31, 1995.

(C) PLAN MUST BE AMENDED TO INCORPORATE LIMITS.—This paragraph shall not apply to any eligible participant of a plan unless the plan is amended so that the plan incorporates by reference the dollar limitation under section 401(a)(17) of the Internal Revenue Code of 1986, effective with respect to noneligible participants for plan years beginning after December 31, 1995 (or earlier if the plan amendments so provides).

• 1988, Technical and Miscellaneous Revenue Act of 1988 (P.L. 100-647)

P.L. 100-647, §1011(d)(1):

Amended Code Sec. 404(l) by adding at the end thereof a new sentence. **Effective** as if included in the provision of P.L. 99-514 to which it relates.

P.L. 100-647, §1011(d)(4):

Amended Code Sec. 404(l) by adding at the end thereof a new sentence. **Effective** as if included in the provision of P.L. 99-514 to which it relates.

• 1986, Tax Reform Act of 1986 (P.L. 99-514)

P.L. 99-514, §1106(d)(2):

Amended Code Sec. 404 by adding new subsection (l). **Effective,** generally, for benefits accruing in years beginning after 12-31-88. However, for an exception, see Act Sec. 1106(i)(5)(B), below.

P.L. 99-514, §1106(i)(5)(B), provides:

(B) COLLECTIVE BARGAINING AGREEMENTS.—In the case of a plan described in paragraph (2), the amendments made by subsection (d) shall apply to benefits accruing in years beginning on or after the earlier of—

(i) the later of—

(I) the date determined under paragraph (2)(A), or

(II) January 1, 1989, or

(ii) January 1, 1991.

[Sec. 404(m)]

(m) SPECIAL RULES FOR SIMPLE RETIREMENT ACCOUNTS.—

(1) IN GENERAL.—Employer contributions to a simple retirement account shall be treated as if they are made to a plan subject to the requirements of this section.

(2) TIMING.—

(A) DEDUCTION.—Contributions described in paragraph (1) shall be deductible in the taxable year of the employer with or within which the calendar year for which the contributions were made ends.

(B) CONTRIBUTIONS AFTER END OF YEAR.—For purposes of this subsection, contributions shall be treated as made for a taxable year if they are made on account of the taxable year and are made not later than the time prescribed by law for filing the return for the taxable year (including extensions thereof).

Amendments

• 1996, Small Business Job Protection Act of 1996 (P.L. 104-188)

P.L. 104-188, §1421(b)(2):

Amended Code Sec. 404 by adding at the end a new subsection (m). **Effective** for tax years beginning after 12-31-96.

[Sec. 404(n)]

(n) ELECTIVE DEFERRALS NOT TAKEN INTO ACCOUNT FOR PURPOSES OF DEDUCTION LIMITS.—Elective deferrals (as defined in section 402(g)(3)) shall not be subject to any limitation contained in paragraph (3), (7), or (9) of subsection (a) or paragraph (1)(C) of subsection (h), and such elective deferrals shall not be taken into account in applying any such limitation to any other contributions.

Amendments

• 2006, Pension Protection Act of 2006 (P.L. 109-280)

P.L. 109-280, §811, provides:

SEC. 811. PENSIONS AND INDIVIDUAL RETIREMENT ARRANGEMENT PROVISIONS OF ECONOMIC GROWTH AND TAX RELIEF RECONCILIATION ACT OF 2001 MADE PERMANENT.

Title IX of the Economic Growth and Tax Relief Reconciliation Act of 2001 [P.L. 107-16] shall not apply to the provisions of, and amendments made by, subtitles A through F of title VI [§§601-666]of such Act (relating to pension and individual retirement arrangement provisions).

• 2002, Job Creation and Worker Assistance Act of 2002 (P.L. 107-147)

P.L. 107-147, §411(l)(2):

Amended Code Sec. 404(n) by striking "subsection (a)," and inserting "subsection (a) or paragraph (1)(C) of subsection (h)". **Effective** as if included in the provision of P.L. 107-16 to which it relates [**effective** for years beginning after 12-31-2001.—CCH].

• 2001, Economic Growth and Tax Relief Reconciliation Act of 2001 (P.L. 107-16)

P.L. 107-16, §614(a):

Amended Code Sec. 404 by adding at the end a new subsection (n). **Effective** for years beginning after 12-31-2001.

P.L. 107-16, §901(a)-(b), provides [but see P.L. 109-280, §811, above]:

SEC. 901. SUNSET OF PROVISIONS OF ACT.

(a) IN GENERAL.—All provisions of, and amendments made by, this Act shall not apply—

(1) to taxable, plan, or limitation years beginning after December 31, 2010, or

(2) in the case of title V, to estates of decedents dying, gifts made, or generation skipping transfers, after December 31, 2010.

(b) APPLICATION OF CERTAIN LAWS.—The Internal Revenue Code of 1986 and the Employee Retirement Income Security Act of 1974 shall be applied and administered to years, estates, gifts, and transfers described in subsection (a) as if the provisions and amendments described in subsection (a) had never been enacted.

[Sec. 404(o)]

(o) DEDUCTION LIMIT FOR SINGLE-EMPLOYER PLANS.—For purposes of subsection (a)(1)(A)—

(1) IN GENERAL.—In the case of a defined benefit plan to which subsection (a)(1)(A) applies (other than a multiemployer plan), the amount determined under this subsection for any taxable year shall be equal to the greater of—

(A) the sum of the amounts determined under paragraph (2) with respect to each plan year ending with or within the taxable year, or

(B) the sum of the minimum required contributions under section 430 for such plan years.

(2) DETERMINATION OF AMOUNT.—

(A) IN GENERAL.—The amount determined under this paragraph for any plan year shall be equal to the excess (if any) of—

(i) the sum of—

(I) the funding target for the plan year,

(II) the target normal cost for the plan year, and

(III) the cushion amount for the plan year, over

(ii) the value (determined under section 430(g)(3)) of the assets of the plan which are held by the plan as of the valuation date for the plan year.

(B) SPECIAL RULE FOR CERTAIN EMPLOYERS.—If section 430(i) does not apply to a plan for a plan year, the amount determined under subparagraph (A)(i) for the plan year shall in no event be less than the sum of—

(i) the funding target for the plan year (determined as if section 430(i) applied to the plan), plus

(ii) the target normal cost for the plan year (as so determined).

(3) CUSHION AMOUNT.—For purposes of paragraph (2)(A)(i)(III)—

(A) IN GENERAL.—The cushion amount for any plan year is the sum of—

(i) 50 percent of the funding target for the plan year, and

(ii) the amount by which the funding target for the plan year would increase if the plan were to take into account—

(I) increases in compensation which are expected to occur in succeeding plan years, or

(II) if the plan does not base benefits for service to date on compensation, increases in benefits which are expected to occur in succeeding plan years (determined on the basis of the average annual increase in benefits over the 6 immediately preceding plan years).

(B) LIMITATIONS.—

(i) IN GENERAL.—In making the computation under subparagraph (A)(ii), the plan's actuary shall assume that the limitations under subsection (l) and section 415(b) shall apply.

(ii) EXPECTED INCREASES.—In the case of a plan year during which a plan is covered under section 4021 of the Employee Retirement Income Security Act of 1974, the plan's actuary may, notwithstanding subsection (l), take into account increases in the limitations which are expected to occur in succeeding plan years.

(4) SPECIAL RULES FOR PLANS WITH 100 OR FEWER PARTICIPANTS.—

(A) IN GENERAL.—For purposes of determining the amount under paragraph (3) for any plan year, in the case of a plan which has 100 or fewer participants for the plan year, the liability of the plan attributable to benefit increases for highly compensated employees (as defined in section 414(q)) resulting from a plan amendment which is made or becomes effective, whichever is later, within the last 2 years shall not be taken into account in determining the target liability.

(B) RULE FOR DETERMINING NUMBER OF PARTICIPANTS.—For purposes of determining the number of plan participants, all defined benefit plans maintained by the same employer (or any member of such employer's controlled group (within the meaning of section 412(d)(3))) shall be treated as one plan, but only participants of such member or employer shall be taken into account.

(5) SPECIAL RULE FOR TERMINATING PLANS.—In the case of a plan which, subject to section 4041 of the Employee Retirement Income Security Act of 1974, terminates during the plan year, the amount determined under paragraph (2) shall in no event be less than the amount required to make the plan sufficient for benefit liabilities (within the meaning of section 4041(d) of such Act).

(6) ACTUARIAL ASSUMPTIONS.—Any computation under this subsection for any plan year shall use the same actuarial assumptions which are used for the plan year under section 430.

(7) DEFINITIONS.—Any term used in this subsection which is also used in section 430 shall have the same meaning given such term by section 430.

Amendments

• 2008, Worker, Retiree, and Employer Recovery Act of 2008 (P.L. 110-458)

P.L. 110-458, §108(a)(1)(A)-(B):

Amended Code Sec. 404(o) by striking "430(g)(2)" in paragraph (2)(A)(ii) and inserting "430(g)(3)", and by striking "412(f)(4)" in paragraph (4)(B) and inserting "412(d)(3)". **Effective** as if included in the provision of the 2006 Act to which the amendment relates [**effective** for years beginning after 12-31-2007.—CCH].

• 2006, Pension Protection Act of 2006 (P.L. 109-280)

P.L. 109-280, §801(a)(2):

Amended Code Sec. 404 by inserting at the end a new subsection (o). **Effective** for years beginning after 12-31-2007.

[Sec. 404A]

SEC. 404A. DEDUCTION FOR CERTAIN FOREIGN DEFERRED COMPENSATION PLANS.

[Sec. 404A(a)]

(a) GENERAL RULE.—Amounts paid or accrued by an employer under a qualified foreign plan—

(1) shall not be allowable as a deduction under this chapter, but

(2) if they would otherwise be deductible, shall be allowed as a deduction under this section for the taxable year for which such amounts are properly taken into account under this section.

Amendments

• 1986, Tax Reform Act of 1986 (P.L. 99-514)

P.L. 99-514, §1851(b)(2)(C)(iii)(I)-(II):

Amended Code Sec. 404A(a) by striking out "under section 162, 212, or 404" and inserting in lieu thereof "under this chapter" and by striking out "they satisfy the conditions of section 162" and inserting in lieu thereof "they would otherwise be deductible". **Effective** as if included in the provision of P.L. 98-369 to which it relates.

• 1980 (P.L. 96-603)

P.L. 96-603, §2(a):

Added Code Sec. 404A(a). **Effective** for employer contributions or accruals for tax years beginning after 1979. However, see the historical comment for P.L. 96-603 under Code Sec. 404A(h) for details on elections permitting retroactive application of this section with respect to foreign subsidiaries and permitting allowance of prior deductions in case of certain funded branch plans.

[Sec. 404A(b)]

(b) RULES FOR QUALIFIED FUNDED PLANS.—For purposes of this section—

(1) IN GENERAL.—Except as otherwise provided in this section, in the case of a qualified funded plan contributions are properly taken into account for the taxable year in which paid.

(2) PAYMENT AFTER CLOSE OF TAXABLE YEAR.—For purposes of paragraph (1), a payment made after the close of a taxable year shall be treated as made on the last day of such year if the payment is made—

(A) on account of such year, and

(B) not later than the time prescribed by law for filing the return for such year (including extensions thereof).

(3) LIMITATIONS.—In the case of a qualified funded plan, the am ount allowable as a deduction for the taxable year shall be subject to—

(A) in the case of—

(i) a plan under which the benefits are fixed or determinable, limitations similar to those contained in clauses (ii) and (iii) of subparagraph (A) of section 404(a)(1) (determined without regard to the last sentence of such subparagraph (A)), or

(ii) any other plan, limitations similar to the limitations contained in paragraph (3) of section 404(a), and

(B) limitations similar to those contained in paragraph (7) of section 404(a).

(4) CARRYOVER.—If—

(A) the aggregate of the contributions paid during the taxable year reduced by any contributions not allowable as a deduction under paragraphs (1) and (2) of subsection (g), exceeds

(B) the amount allowable as a deduction under subsection (a) (determined without regard to subsection (d)),

such excess shall be treated as an amount paid in the succeeding taxable year.

(5) AMOUNTS MUST BE PAID TO QUALIFIED TRUST, ETC.—In the case of a qualified funded plan, a contribution shall be taken into account only if it is paid—

(A) to a trust (or the equivalent of a trust) which meets the requirements of section 401(a)(2),

(B) for a retirement annuity, or

(C) to a participant or beneficiary.

Amendments

• 1980 (P.L. 96-603)

P.L. 96-603, §2(a):

Added Code Sec. 404A(b). **Effective** for employer contributions or accruals for tax years beginning after 1979. However, see the historical comment for P.L. 96-603 under Code Sec. 404A(h) for details on elections permitting retroactive application of this section with respect to foreign subsidiaries and permitting allowance of prior deductions in case of certain funded branch plans.

[Sec. 404A(c)]

(c) RULES RELATING TO QUALIFIED RESERVE PLANS.—For purposes of this section—

(1) IN GENERAL.—In the case of a qualified reserve plan, the amount properly taken into account for the taxable year is the reasonable addition for such year to a reserve for the taxpayer's liability under the plan. Unless otherwise required or permitted in regulations prescribed by the Secretary, the reserve for the taxpayer's liability shall be determined under the unit credit method modified to reflect the requirements of paragraphs (3) and (4). All benefits paid under the plan shall be charged to the reserve.

(2) INCOME ITEM.—In the case of a plan which is or has been a qualified reserve plan, an amount equal to that portion of any decrease for the taxable year in the reserve which is not attributable to the payment of benefits shall be included in gross income.

(3) RIGHTS MUST BE NONFORFEITABLE, ETC.—In the case of a qualified reserve plan, an item shall be taken into account for a taxable year only if—

(A) there is no substantial risk that the rights of the employee will be forfeited, and

(B) such item meets such additional requirements as the Secretary may by regulations prescribe as necessary or appropriate to ensure that the liability will be satisfied.

(4) SPREADING OF CERTAIN INCREASES AND DECREASES IN RESERVES.—There shall be amortized over a 10-year period any increase or decrease to the reserve on account of—

(A) the adoption of the plan or a plan amendment,

(B) experience gains and losses, and

(C) any change in actuarial assumptions,

(D) changes in the interest rate under subsection (g)(3)(B), and

(E) such other factors as may be prescribed by regulations.

Amendments

• 1980 (P.L. 96-603)

P.L. 96-603, §2(a):

Added Code Sec. 404A(c). **Effective** for employer contributions or accruals for tax years beginning after 1979. However, see the historical comment for P.L. 96-603 for details of elections permitting retroactive allocation of this section with respect to foreign subsidiaries and permitting allowance of prior deductions in case of certain funded branch plans.

[Sec. 404A(d)]

(d) AMOUNTS TAKEN INTO ACCOUNT MUST BE CONSISTENT WITH AMOUNTS ALLOWED UNDER FOREIGN LAW.—

(1) GENERAL RULE.—In the case of any plan, the amount allowed as a deduction under subsection (a) for any taxable year shall equal—

(A) the lesser of—

(i) the cumulative United States amount, or

(ii) the cumulative foreign amount, reduced by

(B) the aggregate amount determined under this section for all prior taxable years.

(2) CUMULATIVE AMOUNTS DEFINED.—For purposes of paragraph (1)—

(A) CUMULATIVE UNITED STATES AMOUNT.—The term "cumulative United States amount" means the aggregate amount determined with respect to the plan under this section for the taxable year and for all prior taxable years to which this section applies. Such determination shall be made for each taxable year without regard to the application of paragraph (1).

(B) CUMULATIVE FOREIGN AMOUNT.—The term "cumulative foreign amount" means the aggregate amount allowed as a deduction under the appropriate foreign tax laws for the taxable year and all prior taxable years to which this section applies.

(3) EFFECT ON EARNINGS AND PROFITS, ETC.—In determining the earnings and profits and accumulated profits of any foreign corporation with respect to a qualified foreign plan, except as provided in regulations, the amount determined under paragraph (1) with respect to any plan for any taxable year shall in no event exceed the amount allowed as a deduction under the appropriate foreign tax laws for such taxable year.

Amendments

• 1988, Technical and Miscellaneous Revenue Act of 1988 (P.L. 100-647)

P.L. 100-647, §1012(b)(4):

Amended Code Sec. 404A(d)(3) by striking out "the amount determined" and inserting in lieu thereof "except as provided in regulations, the amount determined". **Effective** as if included in the provision of P.L. 99-514 to which it relates.

• 1980 (P.L. 96-603)

P.L. 96-603, §2(a):

Added Code Sec. 404A(d). **Effective** for employer contributions or accruals for tax years beginning after 1979. However, see the historical comment for P.L. 96-603 under Code Sec. 404A(h) for details of elections permitting retroactive application of this section with respect to foreign subsidiaries and permitting allowance of prior deductions in case of certain funded branch plans.

[Sec. 404A(e)]

(e) QUALIFIED FOREIGN PLAN.—For purposes of this section, the term "qualified foreign plan" means any written plan of an employer for deferring the receipt of compensation but only if—

(1) such plan is for the exclusive benefit of the employer's employees or their beneficiaries,

(2) 90 percent or more of the amounts taken into account for the taxable year under the plan are attributable to services—

(A) performed by nonresident aliens, and

(B) the compensation for which is not subject to tax under this chapter, and

(3) the employer elects (at such time and in such manner as the Secretary shall by regulations prescribe) to have this section apply to such plan.

Amendments

• 1980 (P.L. 96-603)

P.L. 96-603, §2(a):

Added Code Sec. 404A(e). **Effective** for employer contributions or accruals for tax years beginning after 1979. However, see the historical comment for P.L. 96-603 under Code Sec. 404A(h) for the details of elections permitting retroactive application of this section with respect to foreign subsidiaries and permitting allowance of prior deductions in case of certain funded branch plans.

[Sec. 404A(f)]

(f) FUNDED AND RESERVE PLANS.—For purposes of this section—

(1) QUALIFIED FUNDED PLAN.—The term "qualified funded plan" means a qualified foreign plan which is not a qualified reserve plan.

(2) QUALIFIED RESERVE PLAN.—The term "qualified reserve plan" means a qualified foreign plan with respect to which an election made by the taxpaper is in effect for the taxable year. An election under the preceding sentence shall be made in such manner and form as the Secretary may by regulations prescribe and, once made, may be revoked only with the consent of the Secretary.

Amendments

• 1980 (P.L. 96-603)

P.L. 96-603, §2(a):

Added Code Sec. 404A(f). **Effective** with respect to employer contributions or accruals for tax years beginning after 1979. However, see the historical comment for P.L. 96-603 under Code Sec. 404A(h) for the details of elections permitting retroactive application of this section with respect to foreign subsidiaries and permitting allowance of prior deductions in case of certain funded branch plans.

[Sec. 404A(g)]

(g) OTHER SPECIAL RULES.—

(1) NO DEDUCTION FOR CERTAIN AMOUNTS.—Except as provided in section 404(a)(5), no deduction shall be allowed under this section for any item to the extent such item is attributable to services—

(A) performed by a citizen or resident of the United States who is a highly compensated employee (within the meaning of section 414(q)), or

(B) performed in the United States the compensation for which is subject to tax under this chapter.

(2) TAXPAYER MUST FURNISH INFORMATION.—

(A) IN GENERAL.—No deduction shall be allowed under this section with respect to any plan for any taxable year unless the taxpayer furnishes to the Secretary with respect to such plan (at such time as the Secretary may by regulations prescribe)—

(i) a statement from the foreign tax authorities specifying the amount of the deduction allowed in computing taxable income under foreign law for such year with respect to such plan,

(ii) if the return under foreign tax law shows the deduction for plan contributions or reserves as a separate, identifiable item, a copy of the foreign tax return for the taxable year, or

(iii) such other statement, return, or other evidence as the Secretary prescribes by regulation as being sufficient to establish the amount of the deduction under foreign law.

(B) REDETERMINATION WHERE FOREIGN TAX DEDUCTION IS ADJUSTED.—If the deduction under foreign tax law is adjusted, the taxpayer shall notify the Secretary of such adjustment on or before the date prescribed by regulations, and the Secretary shall redetermine the amount of the tax year or years affected. In any case described in the preceding sentence, rules similar to the rules of subsection (c) of section 905 shall apply.

(3) ACTUARIAL ASSUMPTIONS MUST BE REASONABLE; FULL FUNDING.—

(A) IN GENERAL.—Except as provided in subparagraph (B), principles similar to those set forth in paragraphs (3) and (6) of section 431(c) shall apply for purposes of this section.

(B) INTEREST RATE FOR RESERVE PLAN.—

(i) IN GENERAL.—In the case of a qualified reserve plan, in lieu of taking rates of interest into account under subparagraph (A), the rate of interest for the plan shall be the rate selected by the taxpayer which is within the permissible range.

(ii) RATE REMAINS IN EFFECT SO LONG AS IT FALLS WITHIN PERMISSIBLE RANGE.—Any rate selected by the taxpayer for the plan under this subparagraph shall remain in effect for such plan until the first taxable year for which such rate is no longer within the permissible range. At such time, the taxpayer shall select a new rate of interest which is within the permissible range applicable at such time.

(iii) PERMISSIBLE RANGE.—For purposes of this subparagraph, the term "permissible range" means a rate of interest which is not more than 20 percent above, and not more than 20 percent below, the average rate of interest for long-term corporate bonds in the appropriate country for the 15-year period ending on the last day before the beginning of the taxable year.

(4) ACCOUNTING METHOD.—Any change in the method (but not the actuarial assumptions) used to determine the amount allowed as a deduction under subsection (a) shall be treated as a change in accounting method under section 446(e).

(5) SECTION 481 APPLIES TO ELECTION.—For purposes of section 481, any election under this section shall be treated as a change in the taxpayer's method of accounting. In applying section 481 with respect to any such election, the period for taking into account any increase or decrease in accumulated profits, earnings and profits or taxable income resulting from the application of section 481(a)(2) shall be the year for which the election is made and the fourteen succeeding years.

Amendments

• 2006, Pension Protection Act of 2006 (P.L. 109-280)

P.L. 109-280, §801(c)(4):

Amended Code Sec. 404A(g)(3)(A) by striking "paragraphs (3) and (7) of section 412(c)" and inserting "paragraphs (3) and (6) of section 431(c)". **Effective** for years beginning after 12-31-2007.

• 1986, Tax Reform Act of 1986 (P.L. 99-514)

P.L. 99-514, §1114(b)(8):

Amended Code Sec. 404A(g)(1)(A) by striking out "an officer, shareholder, or highly compensated" and inserting in lieu thereof "highly compensated employee (within the meaning of section 414(q))". **Effective** for years beginning after 12-31-88.

• 1980 (P.L. 96-603)

P.L. 96-603, §2(a):

Added Code Sec. 404A(g). **Effective** with respect to employer contributions or accruals for tax years beginning after 1979. However, see the historical comment for P.L. 96-603 under Code Sec. 404A(h) for the details of elections permitting retroactive application of this section with respect to foreign subsidiaries and permitting allowance of prior deductions in case of certain funded branch plans.

[Sec. 404A(h)]

(h) REGULATIONS.—The Secretary shall prescribe such regulations as may be necessary to carry out the purposes of this section (including regulations providing for the coordination of the provisions of this section with section 404 in the case of a plan which has been subject to both of such sections).

Amendments

• 1983, Technical Corrections Act of 1982 (P.L. 97-448)

P.L. 97-448, §305(a):

Amended subparagraph E of section 2(e)(2) of P.L. 96-603 by striking out "was barred" and inserting "was not barred". For amended section 2(e)(2)(E), see below under the amendment note for P.L. 96-603.

• 1980 (P.L. 96-603)

P.L. 96-603, §2(a):

Added Code Sec. 404A(h). **Effective** with respect to employer contributions or accruals for tax years beginning after 1979.

P.L. 96-603, §2(e)(2)-(4), provides:

(2) ELECTION TO APPLY AMENDMENTS RETROACTIVELY WITH REPESCT TO FOREIGN SUBSIDIARIES.—

(A) IN GENERAL.—The taxpayer may elect to have the amendments made by this section apply retroactively with respect to its foreign subsidiaries.

(B) SCOPE OF RETROACTIVE APPLICATION.—Any election made under this paragraph shall apply with respect to all foreign subsidiaries of the taxpayer for the taxpayer's open period.

(C) DISTRIBUTIONS BY FOREIGN SUBSIDIARY MUST BE OUT OF POST-1971 EARNINGS AND PROFITS.—The election under this paragraph shall apply to distributions made by a foreign subsidiary only if made out of accumulated profits (or earnings and profits) earned December 31, 1970.

(D) REVOCATION ONLY WITH CONSENT.—An election under this paragraph may be revoked only with the consent of the Secretary of the Treasury or his delegate.

(E) OPEN PERIOD.—For purposes of this subsection, the term "open period" means, with respect to any taxpayer, all taxable years which begin before January 1, 1980, and which begin after December 31, 1971, and for which, on December 31, 1980, the making of a refund, or the assessment of a deficiency, was not barred by any law or rule of law.

(3) ALLOWANCE OF PRIOR DEDUCTIONS IN CASE OF CERTAIN FUNDED BRANCH PLANS.—

(A) IN GENERAL.—If—

(i) the taxpayer elects to have this paragraph apply, and

(ii) the taxpayer agrees to the assessment of all deficiencies (including interest thereon) arising from all erroneous deductions,

then an amount equal to 1/15th of the aggregate of the prior deductions which would have been allowable if the amendments made by this section applied to taxable years beginning before January 1, 1980, shall be allowed as a deduction for the taxpayer's first taxable year beginning in 1980, and an equal amount shall be allowed for each of the succeeding 14 taxable years.

(B) PRIOR DEDUCTION.—For purposes of subparagraph (A), the term "prior deduction" means a deduction with respect to a qualified funded plan (within the meaning of section 404A(f)(1) of the Internal Revenue Code of 1954) of the taxpayer—

(i) which the taxpayer claimed for a taxable year (or could have claimed if the amendments made by this section applied to taxable years beginning before January 1, 1980) beginning before January 1, 1980,

(ii) which was not allowable, and

(iii) with respect to which, on December 1, 1980, the assessment of a deficiency was not barred by any law or rule or law.

(4) TIME AND MANNER FOR MAKING ELECTIONS.—

(A) TIME.—An election under paragraph (2) or (3) may be made only on or before the due date (including extensions) for filing the taxpayer's return of tax under chapter 1 of the Internal Revenue Code of 1954 for its first taxable year ending on or after December 31, 1980.

(B) MANNER.—An election under paragraph (2) may be made only by a statement attached to the taxpayer's return for its first taxable year ending on or after December 31, 1980. An election under paragraph (3) may be made only if the taxpayer, on or before the last day for making the election, files with the Secretary of the Treasury or his delegate such amended return and such other information as the Secretary of the Treasury or his delegate may require, and agrees to the assessment of a deficiency for any closed year falling within the open period, to the extent such deficiency is attributable to the operation of such election.

[Sec. 405—Repealed]

Amendments

• 1984, Deficit Reduction Act of 1984 (P.L. 98-369)

P.L. 98-369, §491(a):

Repealed Code Sec. 405. **Effective** for obligations issued after 12-31-83. Prior to repeal, Code Sec. 405 read as follows:

SEC. 405. QUALIFIED BOND PURCHASE PLANS.

[Sec. 405(a)]

(a) REQUIREMENTS FOR QUALIFICATION.—A plan of an employer for the purchase for and distribution to his employees or their beneficiaries of United States bonds described in subsection (b) shall constitute a qualified bond purchase plan under this section if—

(1) the plan meets the requirements of section 401(a) (3), (4), (5), (6), (7), (8), (16), and (19) and, if applicable, the requirements of section 401(a)(9) and (10) and of section 401(d) (other than paragraphs (1), (5)(B), and (8)); and

(2) contributions under the plan are used solely to purchase for employees or their beneficiaries United States bonds described in subsection (b).

Amendments

• 1974, Employee Retirement Income Security Act of 1974 (P.L. 93-406)

P.L. 93-406, §2004(c)(2):

Amended paragraph (1) of Code Sec. 405(a) by substituting "(8), (16), and (19)" for "and (8)". **Effective** for years beginning after 12-31-75.

• 1962, Self-Employed Individuals Tax Retirement Act of 1962 (P.L. 87-792)

P.L. 87-792, §5:

Added Sec. 405(a). **Effective** 1-1-63.

[Sec. 405(b)]

(b) BONDS TO WHICH APPLICABLE.—

(1) CHARACTERISTICS OF BONDS.—This section shall apply only to a bond issued under chapter 31 of title 31, which by its terms, or by regulations prescribed by the Secretary under such chapter—

(A) provides for payment of interest, or investment yield, only upon redemption;

(B) may be purchased only in the name of an individual;

(C) ceases to bear interest, or provide investment yield, not later than 5 years after the death of the individual in whose name it is purchased;

(D) may be redeeemed before the death of the individual in whose name it is purchased only if such individual—

(i) has attained the age of 59½ years, or

(ii) has become disabled (within the meaning of section 72(m)(7)); and

(E) is nontransferable.

(2) MUST BE PURCHASED IN NAME OF EMPLOYEE.—This section shall apply to a bond described in paragraph (1) only if it is purchased in the name of the employee.

Amendments

• 1983 (P.L. 97-452)

P.L. 97-452, §2(c)(1):

Amended Code Sec. 405(b)(1) by striking out "the Second Liberty Bond Act, as amended" and "Act" and inserting "chapter 31 of title 31" and "chapter", respectively. **Effective** 1-12-83.

• 1965, Social Security Amendments of 1965 (P.L. 89-97)

P.L. 89-97, §106(d):

Amended Sec. 405(b)(1)(D)(ii) by substituting "section 72(m)(7)" for "section 213(g)(3)". **Effective** for tax years beginning after 12-31-66.

• 1962, Self-Employed Individuals Tax Retirement Act of 1962 (P.L. 87-792)

P.L. 87-792, §5:

Added Sec. 405(b). **Effective** 1-1-63.

[Sec. 405(c)]

(c) DEDUCTION FOR CONTRIBUTIONS TO BOND PURCHASE PLANS.—Contributions paid by an employer to or under a qualified bond purchase plan shall be allowed as a deduction in an amount determined under section 404 in the same manner and to the same extent as if such contributions were made to a trust described in section 401(a) which is exempt from tax under section 501(a).

Amendments

• 1962, Self-Employed Individuals Tax Retirement Act of 1962 (P.L. 87-792)

P.L. 87-792, §5:

Added Sec. 405(c). **Effective** 1-1-63.

[Sec. 405(d)]

(d) TAXABILITY OF BENEFICIARY OF QUALIFIED BOND PURCHASE PLAN.—

(1) GROSS INCOME NOT TO INCLUDE BONDS AT TIME OF DISTRIBUTION.—For purposes of this chapter, in the case of a distributee of a bond described in subsection (b) under a qualified bond purchase plan, or from a trust described in section 401(a) which is exempt from tax under section 501(a), gross income does not include any amount attributable to the receipt of such bond. Upon redemption of such bond, except as provided in paragraph (3), the proceeds shall be subject to taxation under this chapter, but the provisions of section 72 (relating to annuities, etc.) and section 1271 (relating to treatment of amounts received on retirement or sale or exchange of debt instruments) shall not apply.

(2) BASIS.—The basis of any bond received by a distributee under a qualified bond purchase plan—

(A) if such bond is distributed to an employee, or with respect to an employee, who, at the time of purchase of the bond, was an employee other than an employee within the meaning of section 401(c)(1), shall be the amount of the contributions by the employee which were used to purchase the bond, and

(B) if such bond is distributed to an employee, or with respect to an employee, who, at the time of purchase of the bond, was an employee within the meaning of section 401(c)(1), shall be the amount of the contributions used to purchase the bond which were made on behalf of such employee and were not allowed as a deduction under subsection (c).

The basis of any bond described in subsection (b) received by a distributee from a trust described in section 401(a) which is exempt from tax under section 501(a) shall be determined under regulations prescribed by the Secretary.

(3) ROLLOVER INTO AN INDIVIDUAL RETIREMENT ACCOUNT OR ANNUITY.—

(A) IN GENERAL.—If—

(i) any qualified bond is redeemed,

(ii) any portion of the excess of the proceeds from such redemption over the basis of such bond is transferred to an individual retirement plan which is maintained for the benefit of the individual redeeming such bond, or to a qualified trust (as defined in section 402(a)(5)(D)(iii)) for the benefit of such individual, and

(iii) such transfer is made on or before the 60th day after the individual received the proceeds of such redemption,

then gross income shall not include the proceeds to the extent so transferred and the transfer shall be treated as a rollover contribution described in section 408(d)(3).

(B) QUALIFIED BOND.—For purposes of this paragraph, the term "qualified bond" means any bond described in subsection (b) which is distributed under a qualified bond purchase plan or from a trust described in section 401(a) which is exempt from tax under section 501(a).

Amendments

• 1984, Deficit Reduction Act of 1984 (P.L. 98-369)

P.L. 98-369, §42(a)(6):

Amended Code Sec. 405(d)(1), prior to repeal, by striking out "section 1232 (relating to bonds and other evidences of indebtedness)" and inserting in lieu thereof "section 1271 (relating to treatment of amounts received on retirement or sale or exchange of debt instruments)". **Effective** for tax years ending after 7-18-84.

P.L. 98-369, §491(c)(1):

Amended Code Sec. 405(d)(3)(A) (prior to repeal). **Effective** for redemptions after 7-18-84, in tax years ending after such date. However, for a special provision dealing with redemptions of bonds under qualified bond purchase plans, see Act Sec. 491(f)(4), below. Prior to amendment, Code Sec. 405(d)(3)(A) read as follows:

(A) In General.—If—

(i) any qualified bond is redeemed,

(ii) any portion of the excess of the proceeds from such redemption over the basis of such bond is transferred to an individual retirement plan which is maintained for the benefit of the individual redeeming such bond, and

(iii) such transfer is made on or before the 60th day after the day on which the individual received the proceeds of such redemption,

then, gross income shall not include the proceeds to the extent so transferred and the transfer shall be treated as a rollover contribution described in section 408(d)(3).

P.L. 98-369, §491(f)(4), provides:

(4) Bonds Under Qualified Bond Purchase Plans May Be Redeemed at Any Time.—Notwithstanding—

(A) subparagraph (D) of section 405(b)(1) of the Internal Revenue Code of 1954 (as in effect before its repeal by this section), and

(B) the terms of any bond described in subsection (b) of such section 405,

such a bond may be redeemed at any time after the date of the enactment of this Act in the same manner as if the individual redeeming the bond had attained age 59½.

• 1981, Economic Recovery Tax Act of 1981 (P.L. 97-34)

P.L. 97-34, §313(a):

Added Code Sec. 405(d)(3). **Effective** for redemptions occurring after 8-13-81 in tax years ending after 8-13-81.

P.L. 97-34, §313(b)(1):

Amended the second sentence of Code Sec. 405(d)(1) by striking out "the proceeds" and inserting "except as provided in paragraph (3), the proceeds". **Effective** for redemptions occurring after 8-13-81 in tax years ending after 8-13-81.

• 1976, Tax Reform Act of 1976 (P.L. 94-455)

P.L. 94-455, §1906(b)(13)(A):

Amended 1954 Code by substituting "Secretary" for "Secretary or his delegate" each place it appeared. **Effective** 2-1-77.

• 1962, Self-Employed Individuals Tax Retirement Act of 1962 (P.L. 87-792)

P.L. 87-792, §5:

Added Sec. 405(d). **Effective** 1-1-63.

[Sec. 405(e)]

(e) CAPITAL GAINS TREATMENT AND LIMITATION OF TAX NOT TO APPLY TO BONDS DISTRIBUTED BY TRUSTS.—Subsections (a)(2) and (e) of section 402 shall not apply to any bond described in subsection (b) distributed to any distributee and, for purposes of applying such sections, any such bond distributed to any distributee and any such bond to the credit of any employee shall not be taken into account.

Amendments

• Employee Retirement Income Security Act of 1974 (P.L. 93-406)

P.L. 93-406, §2005(c)(11):

Substituted "Subsections (a)(2) and (e) of section 402" for "Section 72(n) and section 402(a)(2)" at the beginning thereof. **Effective** for distributions or payments made after 12-31-73, in tax years beginning after such date.

• 1969, Tax Reform Act of 1969 (P.L. 91-172)

P.L. 91-172, §515(c)(1):

Amended Code Sec. 405(e). **Effective** for tax years ending after 12-31-69. Prior to amendment, Code Sec. 405(e) read as follows:

(e) Capital Gains Treatment Not to Apply to Bonds Distributed by Trusts.—Section 402(a)(2) shall not apply to any bond described in subsection (b) distributed to any distributee and, for purposes of applying such section, any such bond distributed to any distributee and any such bond to the credit of any employee shall not be taken into account.

• 1962, Self-Employed Individuals Tax Retirement Act of 1962 (P.L. 87-792)

P.L. 87-792, §5:

Added Sec. 405(e). **Effective** 1-1-63.

[Sec. 405(f)]

(f) EMPLOYEE DEFINED.—For purposes of this section, the term "employee" includes an individual who is an employee within the meaning of section 401(c)(1), and the employer of such individual shall be the person treated as his employer under section 401(c)(4).

Amendments

• 1962, Self-Employed Individuals Tax Retirement Act of 1962 (P.L. 87-792)

P.L. 87-792, §5:

Added Sec. 405(f). **Effective** 1-1-63.

[Sec. 405(g)]

(g) PROOF OF PURCHASE.—At the time of purchase of any bond to which this section applies, proof of such purchase shall be furnished in such form as will enable the purchaser, and the employee in whose name such bond is purchased, to comply with the provisions of this section.

Amendments

• 1962, Self-Employed Individuals Tax Retirement Act of 1962 (P.L. 87-792)

P.L. 87-792, §5:

Added Sec. 405(g). **Effective** 1-1-63.

[Sec. 405(h)]

(h) REGULATIONS.—The Secretary shall prescribe such regulations as may be necessary to carry out the provisions of this section.

Amendments

• 1976, Tax Reform Act of 1976 (P.L. 94-455)

P.L. 94-455, §1906(b)(13)(A):

Amended 1954 Code by substituting "Secretary" for "Secretary or his delegate" each place it appeared. **Effective** 2-1-77.

• 1962, Self-Employed Individuals Tax Retirement Act of 1962 (P.L. 87-792)

P.L. 87-792, §5:

Added Sec. 405(h). **Effective** 1-1-63.

[Sec. 406]

SEC. 406. EMPLOYEES OF FOREIGN AFFILIATES COVERED BY SECTION 3121(l) AGREEMENTS.

[Sec. 406(a)]

(a) TREATMENT AS EMPLOYEES OF AMERICAN EMPLOYER.—For purposes of applying this part with respect to a pension, profit-sharing, or stock bonus plan described in section 401(a) or an annuity plan described in section 403(a) of an American employer (as defined in section 3121(h)), an individual who is a citizen or resident of the United States and who is an employee of a foreign affiliate (as defined in section 3121(l)(6)) of such American employer shall be treated as an employee of such American employer, if—

(1) such American employer has entered into an agreement under section 3121(l) which applies to the foreign affiliate of which such individual is an employee;

(2) the plan of such American employer expressly provides for contributions or benefits for individuals who are citizens or residents of the United States and who are employees of its foreign affiliates to which an agreement entered into by such American employer under section 3121(l) applies; and

(3) contributions under a funded plan of deferred compensation (whether or not a plan described in section 401(a) or 403(a)) are not provided by any other person with respect to the remuneration paid to such individual by the foreign affiliate.

Amendments

• 1989, Omnibus Budget Reconciliation Act of 1989 (P.L. 101-239)

P.L. 101-239, §10201(b)(1):

Amended Code Sec. 406(a) by striking "section 3121(l)(8)" and inserting "section 3121(l)(6)". **Effective** with respect to any agreement in effect under section 3121(l) of the Internal Revenue Code of 1986 on or after 6-15-89, with respect to which no notice of termination is in effect on such date.

• 1984, Deficit Reduction Act of 1984 (P.L. 98-369)

P.L. 98-369, §491(d)(13):

Amended Code Sec. 406(a) by striking out ", an annuity plan described in section 403(a), or a bond purchase plan described in section 405(a)" and inserting in lieu thereof "or an annuity plan described in section 403(a)". **Effective** for obligations issued after 12-31-83.

P.L. 98-369, §491(d)(14):

Amended Code Sec. 406(a)(3) by striking out ", 403(a), or 405(a)" and inserting in lieu thereof "or 403(a)". **Effective** for obligations issued after 12-31-83.

• 1983, Social Security Amendments of 1983 (P.L. 98-21)

P.L. 98-21, §321(c):

Amended Code Sec. 406(a). **Effective** for agreements entered into after 4-20-83. Under a special election provided in Act Sec. 321(f)(1)(B), such amendments may apply to agreements executed on or before 4-20-83. Prior to amendment, Code Sec. 406(a) read as follows:

(a) TREATMENT AS EMPLOYEES OF DOMESTIC CORPORATION.—For purposes of applying this part with respect to a pension, profit-sharing, or stock bonus plan described in section 401(a), an annuity plan described in section 403(a), or a bond purchase plan described in section 405(a), of a domestic corporation, an individual who is a citizen of the United States and who is an employee of a foreign subsidiary (as defined in section 3121(l)(8)) of such domestic corporation shall be treated as an employee of such domestic corporation, if—

(1) such domestic corporation has entered into an agreement under section 3121(l) which applies to the foreign subsidiary of which such individual is an employee;

(2) the plan of such domestic corporation expressly provides for contributions or benefits for individuals who are citizens of the United States and who are employees of its foreign subsidiaries to which an agreement entered into by such domestic corporation under section 3121(l) applies; and

(3) contributions under a funded plan of deferred compensation (whether or not a plan described in section 401(a), 403(a), or 405(a)) are not provided by any other person with respect to the remuneration paid to such individual by the foreign subsidiary.

P.L. 98-21, §321(e)(2)(D)(i):

Amended the heading of Code Sec. 406. **Effective** for agreements entered into after 4-20-83. Before amendment, such heading read as follows:

SEC. 406. CERTAIN EMPLOYEES OF FOREIGN SUBSIDIARIES.

P.L. 98-21, §321(f)(1):

The effective date of changes made by Act Sec. 321(c) and (e) and a special election are provided as follows:

(f)(1)(A) The amendments made by this section (other than subsection (d)) shall apply to agreements entered into after the date of the enactment of this Act.

(B) At the election of any American employer, the amendments made by this section (other than subsection (d)) shall also apply to any agreement entered into on or before the date of the enactment of this Act. Any such election shall be made at such time and in such manner as the Secretary may by regulations prescribe.

• 1964, Revenue Act of 1964 (P.L. 88-272)

P.L. 88-272, §220(a):

Added Sec. 406(a). **Effective** for tax years ending after 12-31-63.

[Sec. 406(b)]

(b) SPECIAL RULES FOR APPLICATION OF SECTION 401(a).—

(1) NONDISCRIMINATION REQUIREMENTS.—For purposes of applying section 401(a)(4) and section 410(b) with respect to an individual who is treated as an employee of an American employer under subsection (a)—

(A) if such individual is a highly compensated employee (within the meaning of section 414(q)), he shall be treated as having such capacity with respect to such American employer; and

(B) the determination of whether such individual is a highly compensated employee (as so defined) shall be made by treating such individual's total compensation (determined with the application of paragraph (2) of this subsection) as compensation paid by such American employer and by determining such individual's status with regard to such American employer.

(2) DETERMINATION OF COMPENSATION.—For purposes of applying paragraph (5) of section 401(a) with respect to an individual who is treated as an employee of an American employer under subsection (a)—

(A) the total compensation of such individual shall be the remuneration paid to such individual by the foreign affiliate which would constitute his total compensation if his services had been performed for such American employer, and the basic or regular rate of compensation such individual shall be determined under regulations prescribed by the Secretary; and

(B) such individual shall be treated as having paid the amount paid by such American employer which is equivalent to the tax imposed by section 3101.

Amendments

• 1986, Tax Reform Act of 1986 (P.L. 99-514)

P.L. 99-514, §1112(d)(3):

Amended Code Sec. 406(b)(1) by striking out "(without regard to paragraph (1)(A) thereof)" after "section 410(b)". **Effective**, generally, for plan years beginning after 12-31-88. However, for special rules see Act Sec. 1112(e)(2)-(3) following Code Sec. 401. Prior to amendment Code Sec. 406(b)(1) read as follows:

(1) NONDISCRIMINATION REQUIREMENTS.—For purposes of applying section 401(a)(4) and section 410(b) (without regard to paragraph (1)(A) thereof) with respect to an individual who is treated as an employee of an American employer under subsection (a)—

P.L. 99-514, §1114(b)(9)(A):

Amended Code Sec. 406(b)(1)(A) by striking out "an officer, shareholder, or person whose principal duties consist of supervising the work of other employees of a foreign affiliate of such American employer" and insert in lieu thereof "a highly compensated employee (within the meaning of section 414(q))". **Effective** for years beginning after 12-31-88.

P.L. 99-514, §1114(b)(9)(C):

Amended Code Sec. 406(b)(1)(B) by inserting "(as so defined)" after "employee". **Effective** for years beginning after 12-31-88.

• 1983, Social Security Amendments of 1983 (P.L. 98-21)

P.L. 98-21, §321(e)(2)(A):

Amended Code Sec. 406(b) by striking out "domestic corporation" wherever it appears and inserting "American employer", by striking out "subsidiary" wherever it appears and inserting "affiliate", and by striking out the word "a" where it appears before "domestic" and inserting "an". **Effective** for agreements entered into after 4-20-83. See, however, the special rules provided in Act Sec. 321(f)(1) following Code Sec. 406(a).

• 1976, Tax Reform Act of 1976 (P.L. 94-455)

P.L. 94-455, §1906(b)(13)(A):

Amended 1954 Code by substituting "Secretary" for "Secretary or his delegate" each place it appeared. **Effective** 2-1-77.

• Employee Retirement Income Security Act of 1974 (P.L. 93-406)

P.L. 93-406, §1016(a)(4):

Amended paragraph (1) of Code Sec. 406(b) by substituting "section 401(a)(4) and section 410(b) (without regard to paragraph (1)(A) thereof)" for "paragraphs (3)(B) and (4) of section 401(a)". For **effective** date, see the special effective dates and transitional rules in the historical note for §1017, P.L. 93-406, in the amendments for Code Sec. 410.

• 1964, Revenue Act of 1964 (P.L. 88-272)

P.L. 88-272, §220(a):

Added Code Sec. 406(b). **Effective** for tax years ending after 12-31-63.

[Sec. 406(c)—Repealed]

Amendments

• 1996, Small Business Job Protection Act of 1996 (P.L. 104-188)

P.L. 104-188, §1401(b)(7):

Repealed Code Sec. 406(c). **Effective**, generally, for tax years beginning after 12-31-99. For a special transitional rule, see Act Sec. 1401(c)(2) in the amendment notes following Code Sec. 402(d). Prior to repeal, Code Sec. 406(c) read as follows:

(c) TERMINATION OF STATUS AS DEEMED EMPLOYEE NOT TO BE TREATED AS SEPARATION FROM SERVICE FOR PURPOSES OF LIMITATION OF TAX.—For purposes of applying section 402(d) with respect to an individual who is treated as an employee of an American employer under subsection (a), such individual shall not be considered as separated from the service of such American employer solely by reason of the fact that—

(1) the agreement entered into by such American employer under section 3121(l) which covers the employment of such individual is terminated under the provisions of such section,

(2) such individual becomes an employee of a foreign affiliate with respect to which such agreement does not apply,

(3) such individual ceases to be an employee of the foreign affiliate by reason of which he is treated as an employee of such American employer, if he becomes an employee of another entity in which such American employer has not less than a 10-percent interest (within the meaning of section 3121(l)(6)), or

(4) the provision of the plan described in subsection (a)(2) is terminated.

• 1992, Unemployment Compensation Amendments of 1992 (P.L. 102-318)

P.L. 102-318, §521(b)(14):

Amended Code Sec. 406(c) by striking "section 402(e)" and inserting "section 402(d)". **Effective** for distributions after 12-31-92.

• 1989, Omnibus Budget Reconciliation Act of 1989 (P.L. 101-239)

P.L. 101-239, §7811(g)(3):

Amended Code Sec. 406(c) by striking "PURPOSES LIMITATION" and inserting "PURPOSES OF LIMITATION" in the heading. **Effective** as if included in the provision of P.L. 100-647 to which it relates.

P.L. 101-239, §10201(b)(2):

Amended Code Sec. 406(c)(3) by striking "section 3121(l)(8)(B)" and inserting "section 3121(l)(6)". **Effective** for any agreement in effect under section 3121(l) of the Internal Revenue Code of 1986 on or after 6-15-89, with respect to which no notice of termination is in effect on such date.

• 1988, Technical and Miscellaneous Revenue Act of 1988 (P.L. 100-647)

P.L. 100-647, §1011A(b)(16)(A)-(B):

Amended Code Sec. 406(c) by striking out "subsections (a)(2) and (e) of section 402, and section 403(a)(2)" and inserting in lieu thereof "section 402(e)", and by striking out "OF CAPITAL GAIN PROVISIONS AND" in the heading thereof. **Effective** as if included in the provision of P.L. 99-514 to which it relates.

• 1983, Social Security Amendments of 1983 (P.L. 98-21)

P.L. 98-21, §321(e)(2)(A):

Amended Code Sec. 406(c) by striking out "domestic corporation" wherever it appeared and inserting "American employer", by striking out "subsidiary" wherever it appeared and inserting "affiliate", and by striking out the word "a" where it appeared before "domestic" and inserting "an". **Effective** for agreements entered into after 4-20-83. For a special rule, see Act Sec. 321(f)(1)(B), below.

[Act §321(e)(2)(B) amended Code Sec. 406(c) also. It appears that the amendment made by that Act section to Code Sec. 406(c)(3) was intended to be made prior to the amendment made by Act §321(e)(2)(A).]

P.L. 98-21, §321(e)(2)(B):

Amended Code Sec. 406(c)(3) (as in effect before the amendment made by Act Sec. 321(e)(2)(A)) by striking out "another corporation controlled by such domestic corporation" and inserting in place thereof "another entity in which such American employer has not less than a 10-percent interest (within the meaning of section 3121(l)(8)(B))". **Effective** for agreements entered into after 4-20-83. For a special rule, see Act Sec. 321(f)(1)(B), below.

P.L. 98-21, §321(f)(1)(B), provides:

(B) At the election of any American employer, the amendments made by this section (other than subsection (d)) shall also apply to any agreement entered into on or before the date of the enactment of this Act. Any such election shall be made at such time and in such manner as the Secretary may by regulations prescribe.

• Employee Retirement Income Security Act of 1974 (P.L. 93-406)

P. L. 93-406, §2005(c)(12):

Amended Code Sec. 406(c) by substituting "subsections (a)(2) and (e) of section 402" for "section 72(n), section 402(a)(2)". **Effective** for distributions or payments made after 12-31-73, in tax years beginning after such date.

• 1969, Tax Reform Act of 1969 (P.L. 91-172)

P.L. 91-172, §515(c)(2):

Amended Code Sec. 406(c). **Effective** for tax years ending after 12-31-69. Prior to amendment, that portion of Sec. 406(c) as precedes paragraph (1) read as follows:

(c) TERMINATION OF STATUS AS DEEMED EMPLOYEE NOT TO BE TREATED AS SEPARATION FROM SERVICE FOR PURPOSES OF CAPITAL GAIN PROVISIONS.—For purposes of applying section 402(a)(2) and section 403(a)(2) with respect to an individual who is treated as an employee of a domestic corporation under subsection (a), such individual shall not be considered as separated from the service of such domestic corporation solely by reason of the fact that—

• 1964, Revenue Act of 1964 (P.L. 88-272)

P.L. 88-272, §220(a):

Added Sec. 406(c). **Effective** for tax years ending after 12-31-63.

[Sec. 406(d)]

(d) DEDUCTIBILITY OF CONTRIBUTIONS.—For purposes of applying section 404 with respect to contributions made to or under a pension, profit-sharing, stock bonus, or annuity plan by an American employer, or by another taxpayer which is entitled to deduct its contributions under section 404(a)(3)(B), on behalf of an individual who is treated as an employee of such American employer under subsection (a)—

(1) except as provided in paragraph (2), no deduction shall be allowed to such American employer or to any other taxpayer which is entitled to deduct its contributions under such sections,

(2) there shall be allowed as a deduction to the foreign affiliate of which such individual is an employee an amount equal to the amount which (but for paragraph (1)) would be deductible under section 404 by the American employer if he were an employee of the American employer, and

(3) any reference to compensation shall be considered to be a reference to the total compensation of such individual (determined with the application of subsection (b)(2)).

Any amount deductible by a foreign affiliate under this subsection shall be deductible for its taxable year with or within which the taxable year of such American employer ends.

Amendments

• 1984, Deficit Reduction Act of 1984 (P.L. 98-369)

P.L. 98-369, §491(d)(15):

Amended Code Sec. 406(d) by striking out "sections 404 and 405(c)" and inserting in lieu thereof "section 404", by striking out "annuity, or bond purchase" and inserting in lieu thereof "or annuity", and by striking out "(or section 405(c))" in paragraph (2). **Effective** for obligations issued after 12-31-83.

• 1983, Social Security Amendments of 1983 (P.L. 98-21)

P.L. 98-21, §321(e)(2)(A):

Amended Code Sec. 406(d) by striking out "domestic corporation" wherever it appears and inserting "American employer", by striking out "subsidiary" wherever it appears and inserting "affiliate", and by striking out the word "a" where it appears before "domestic" and inserting "an". **Effective** for agreements entered into after 4-20-83. See, however, the special rules provided in Act Sec. 321(f)(1) following Code Sec. 406(a).

P.L. 98-21, §321(e)(2)(C):

Amended so much of Code Sec. 406(d) as preceded paragraph (1) by striking out "another corporation" and inserting in lieu thereof "another taxpayer", and amended Code Sec. 406(d)(1) by striking out "any other corporation" and inserting in lieu thereof "any other taxpayer". **Effective** for agreements entered into after 4-20-83. But see special rules provided in Act Sec. 321(f)(1)(B) following Code Sec. 406(a).

• 1964, Revenue Act of 1964 (P.L. 88-272)

P.L. 88-272, §220(a):

Added Sec. 406(d). **Effective** for tax years ending after 12-31-63.

[Sec. 406(e)]

(e) TREATMENT AS EMPLOYEE UNDER RELATED PROVISIONS.—An individual who is treated as an employee of an American employer under subsection (a) shall also be treated as an employee of such American employer, with respect to the plan described in subsection (a)(2), for purposes of applying the following provisions of this title:

(1) Section 72(f) (relating to special rules for computing employees' contributions).

(2) Section 2039 (relating to annuities).

Amendments

• 1996, Small Business Job Protection Act of 1996 (P.L. 104-188)

P.L. 104-188, §1402(b)(2):

Amended Code Sec. 406(e) by striking paragraph (2) and by redesignating paragraph (3) as paragraph (2). **Effective** with respect to decedents dying after 8-20-96. Prior to amendment, Code Sec. 406(e)(2) read as follows:

(2) Section 101(b) (relating to employees' death benefits).

• 1988, Technical and Miscellaneous Revenue Act of 1988 (P.L. 100-647)

P.L. 100-647, §1011A(b)(1)(C):

Amended Code Sec. 406(e) by striking out paragraph (1) and by redesignating paragraphs (2), (3), and (4) as paragraphs (1), (2), and (3), respectively. **Effective** as if included in the provision of P.L. 99-514 to which it relates. Prior to amendment, Code Sec. 406(e)(1) read as follows:

(1) Section 72(d) (relating to employees' annuities).

• 1986, Tax Reform Act of 1986 (P.L. 99-514)

P.L. 99-514, §1852(e)(2)(C):

Amended Code Sec. 406(e) by striking out paragraph (5). **Effective** as if included in the provision of P.L. 98-369 to which it relates. Prior to amendment, Code Sec. 406(e)(5) read as follows:

(5) Section 2517 (relating to certain annuities under qualified plans).

• 1983, Social Security Amendments of 1983 (P.L. 98-21)

P.L. 98-21, §321(e)(2)(A):

Amended Code Sec. 406(e) by striking out "domestic corporation" wherever it appears and inserting "American employer", and by striking out the word "a" before "domestic" and inserting "an". **Effective** for agreements entered into after 4-20-83. See, however, the special rules provided in Act Sec. 321(f)(1)(B) following Code Sec. 406(a).

• 1964, Revenue Act of 1964 (P.L. 88-272)

P.L. 88-272, §220(a):

Added Sec. 406(e). **Effective** for tax years ending after 12-31-63.

[Sec. 407]

SEC. 407. CERTAIN EMPLOYEES OF DOMESTIC SUBSIDIARIES ENGAGED IN BUSINESS OUTSIDE THE UNITED STATES.

[Sec. 407(a)]

(a) TREATMENT AS EMPLOYEES OF DOMESTIC PARENT CORPORATION.—

(1) IN GENERAL.—For purposes of applying this part with respect to a pension, profit-sharing, or stock bonus plan described in section 401(a) or an annuity plan described in section 403(a), of a domestic parent corporation, an individual who is a citizen or resident of the United States and who is an employee of a domestic subsidiary (within the meaning of paragraph (2)) of such domestic parent corporation shall be treated as an employee of such domestic parent corporation, if—

(A) the plan of such domestic parent corporation expressly provides for contributions or benefits for individuals who are citizens or residents of the United States and who are employees of its domestic subsidiaries; and

(B) contributions under a funded plan of deferred compensation (whether or not a plan described in section 401(a) or 403(a)) are not provided by any other person with respect to the remuneration paid to such individual by the domestic subsidiary.

(2) DEFINITIONS.—For purposes of this section—

(A) DOMESTIC SUBSIDIARY.—A corporation shall be treated as a domestic subsidiary for any taxable year only if—

(i) such corporation is a domestic corporation 80 percent or more of the outstanding voting stock of which is owned by another domestic corporation;

(ii) 95 percent or more of its gross income for the three-year period immediately preceding the close of its taxable year which ends on or before the close of the taxable year of such other domestic corporation (or for such part of such period during which the corporation was in existence) was derived from sources without the United States; and

(iii) 90 percent or more of its gross income for such period (or such part) was derived from the active conduct of a trade or business.

If for the period (or part thereof) referred to in clauses (ii) and (iii) such corporation has no gross income, the provisions of clauses (ii) and (iii) shall be treated as satisfied if it is reasonable to anticipate that, with respect to the first taxable year thereafter for which such corporation has gross income, the provisions of such clauses will be satisfied.

(B) DOMESTIC PARENT CORPORATION.—The domestic parent corporation of any domestic subsidiary is the domestic corporation which owns 80 percent or more of the outstanding voting stock of such domestic subsidiary.

Amendments

• 1984, Deficit Reduction Act of 1984 (P.L. 98-369)

P.L. 98-369, §491(d)(16):

Amended Code Sec. 407(a)(1) by striking out ", an annuity plan described in section 403(a), or a bond purchase plan described in section 405(a)" and inserting in lieu thereof "or an annuity plan described in section 403(a)". **Effective** for obligations issued after 12-31-83.

P.L. 98-369, §491(d)(17):

Amended Code Sec. 407(a)(1)(B) by striking out ", or 403(a), or 405(a)" and inserting in lieu thereof "or 403(a)". **Effective** for obligations issued after 12-31-83.

• 1983, Social Security Amendments of 1983 (P.L. 98-21)

P.L. 98-21, §321(d):

Amended Code Sec. 407(a)(1). **Effective** for plans established after 4-20-83. Under a special election provided in Act Sec. 321(f)(2)(B), such amendments may apply to agreements executed on or before 4-20-83. Prior to amendment, Code Sec. 407(a)(1) read as follows:

(a) TREATMENT AS EMPLOYEES OF DOMESTIC PARENT CORPORATION.—

(1) IN GENERAL.—For purposes of applying this part with respect to a pension, profit-sharing, or stock bonus plan described in section 401(a), an annuity plan described in section 403(a), or a bond purchase plan described in section 405(a), of a domestic parent corporation, an individual who is a citizen of the United States and who is an employee of a domestic subsidiary (within the meaning of paragraph (2)) of such domestic parent corporation shall be treated as an employee of such domestic parent corporation, if—

(A) the plan of such domestic parent corporation expressly provides for contributions or benefits for individuals who are citizens of the United States and who are employees of its domestic subsidiaries; and

(B) contributions under a funded plan of deferred compensation (whether or not a plan described in section 401(a), 403(a), or 405(a)) are not provided by any other person with respect to the remuneration paid to such individual by the domestic subsidiary.

P.L. 98-21, §321(f)(2)(B), provides:

(B) At the election of any domestic parent corporation the amendments made by subsection (d) shall also apply to any plan established on or before the date of the enactment of this Act. Any such election shall be made at such time and in such manner as the Secretary may by regulations prescribe.

• 1964, Revenue Act of 1964 (P.L. 88-272)

P.L. 88-272, §220(b):

Added Code Sec. 407(a). **Effective** for tax years ending after 12-31-63.

[Sec. 407(b)]

(b) SPECIAL RULES FOR APPLICATION OF SECTION 401(a).—

(1) NONDISCRIMINATION REQUIREMENTS.—For purposes of applying section 401(a)(4) and section 410(b)with respect to an individual who is treated as an employee of a domestic parent corporation under subsection (a)—

(A) if such individual is a highly compensated employee (within the meaning of section 414(q)), he shall be treated as having such capacity with respect to such domestic parent corporation; and

(B) the determination of whether such individual is a highly compensated employee (as so defined) shall be made by treating such individual's total compensation (determined with the application of paragraph (2) of this subsection) as compensation paid by such domestic parent corporation and by determining such individual's status with regard to such domestic parent corporation.

(2) DETERMINATION OF COMPENSATION.—For purposes of applying paragraph (5) of section 401(a) with respect to an individual who is treated as an employee of a domestic parent corporation under subsection (a), the total compensation of such individual shall be the remuneration paid to such individual by the domestic subsidiary which would constitute his total compensation if his services had been performed for such domestic parent corporation, and the basic or regular rate of compensation of such individual shall be determined under regulations prescribed by the Secretary.

Amendments

• 1986, Tax Reform Act of 1986 (P.L. 99-514)

P.L. 99-514, §1112(d)(3):

Amended Code Sec. 407(b)(1) by striking out "(without regard to paragraph (1)(A) thereof)" after "section 410(b)". **Effective**, generally, for plan years beginning after 12-31-88. However, for special rules see Act Sec. 1112(e)(2)-(3) following Code Sec. 401.

P.L. 99-514, §1114(b)(9)(B):

Amended Code Sec. 407(b)(1)(A) by striking out "an officer, shareholder, or person whose principal duties consist in supervising the work of other employees of a domestic subsidiary" and inserting in lieu thereof "a highly compensated employee (within the meaning of section 414(q))". **Effective** for years beginning after 12-31-88.

P.L. 99-514, §1114(b)(9)(C):

Amended Code Sec. 407(b)(1)(B) by inserting "(as so defined)" after "employee". **Effective** for years beginning after 12-31-88.

• 1976, Tax Reform Act of 1976 (P.L. 94-455)

P.L. 94-455, §1906(b)(13)(A):

Amended 1954 Code by substituting "Secretary" for "Secretary or his delegate" each place it appeared. **Effective** 2-1-77.

• 1974, Employee Retirement Income Security Act of 1974 (P.L. 93-406)

P.L. 93-406, §1016(a)(5):

Amended Code Sec. 407(b) by substituting "section 401(a)(4) and section 410(b) (without regard to paragraph (1)(A) thereof)" for "paragraph (3)(B) and (4) of section 401(a)". For **effective** date, see the special effective dates and transitional rules in the historical note for §1017, P.L. 93-406, following the text of Code Sec. 410.

• 1964, Revenue Act of 1964 (P.L. 88-272)

P.L. 88-272, §220(b):

Added Sec. 407(b). **Effective** for tax years ending after 12-31-63.

[Sec. 407(c)—Repealed]

Amendments

• 1996, Small Business Job Protection Act of 1996 (P.L. 104-188)

P.L. 104-188, §1401(b)(8):

Repealed Code Sec. 407(c). **Effective**, generally, for tax years beginning after 12-31-99. For a special transitional rule, see Act Sec. 1401(c)(2) in the amendment notes following Code Sec. 402(d). Prior to repeal, Code Sec. 407(c) read as follows:

(c) TERMINATION OF STATUS AS DEEMED EMPLOYEE NOT TO BE TREATED AS SEPARATION FROM SERVICE FOR PURPOSES OF LIMITATION OF TAX.—For purposes of applying section 402(d) with respect to an individual who is treated as an employee of a domestic parent corporation under subsection (a), such individual shall not be considered as separated from the service of such domestic parent corporation solely by reason of the fact that—

(1) the corporation of which such individual is an employee ceases, for any taxable year, to be a domestic subsidiary within the meaning of subsection (a)(2)(A),

(2) such individual ceases to be an employee of a domestic subsidiary of such domestic parent corporation, if he becomes an employee of another corporation controlled by such domestic parent corporation, or

(3) the provision of the plan described in subsection (a)(1)(A) is terminated.

• 1992, Unemployment Compensation Amendments of 1992 (P.L. 102-318)

P.L. 102-318, §521(b)(15):

Amended Code Sec. 407(c) by striking "section 402(e) and inserting "section 402(d)". **Effective** for distributions after 12-31-92.

• 1989, Omnibus Budget Reconciliation Act of 1989 (P.L. 101-239)

P.L. 101-239, §7811(g)(3):

Amended Code Sec. 407(c) by striking "PURPOSES LIMITATION" and inserting "PURPOSES OF LIMITATION" in the heading. **Effective** as if included in the provision of P.L. 100-647 to which it relates.

• 1988, Technical and Miscellaneous Revenue Act of 1988 (P.L. 100-647)

P.L. 100-647, §1011A(b)(16)(A)-(B):

Amended Code Sec. 407(c) by striking out "subsections (a)(2) and (e) of section 402, and section 403(a)(2)" and inserting in lieu thereof "section 402(e)", and by striking out "OF CAPITAL PROVISIONS AND" in the heading thereof. **Effective** as if included in the provision of P.L. 99-514 to which it relates.

• 1974, Employee Retirement Income Security Act of 1974 (P.L. 93-406)

P.L. 93-406, §2005(c)(13):

Amended Code Sec. 407(c) by substituting "subsections (a)(2) and (e) of section 402" for "section 72(n), section 402(a)(2)". **Effective** for distributions or payments made after 12-31-73, in tax years beginning after such date.

• 1969, Tax Reform Act of 1969 (P.L. 91-172)

P.L. 91-172, §515(c)(3):

Amended Code Sec. 407(c). **Effective** for to tax years ending after 12-31-69. Prior to amendment, that portion of Sec. 407(c) as precedes paragraph (1) read as follows:

(c) TERMINATION OF STATUS AS DEEMED EMPLOYEE NOT TO BE TREATED AS SEPARATION FROM SERVICE FOR PURPOSES OF CAPITAL GAIN PROVISIONS.—For purposes of applying section 402(a)(2) and section 403(a)(2) with respect to an individual who is treated as an employee of a domestic parent corporation under subsection (a), such individual shall not be considered as separated from the service of such domestic parent corporation solely by reason of the fact that—

• 1964, Revenue Act of 1964 (P.L. 88-272)

P.L. 88-272, §220(b):

Added Sec. 407(c). **Effective** for tax years ending after 12-31-63.

[Sec. 407(d)]

(d) DEDUCTIBILITY OF CONTRIBUTIONS.—For purposes of applying section 404 with respect to contributions made to or under a pension, profit-sharing, stock bonus or annuity plan by a domestic parent corporation, or by another corporation which is entitled to deduct its contributions under section 404(a)(3)(B), on behalf of an individual who is treated as an employee of such domestic corporation under subsection (a)—

(1) except as provided in paragraph (2), no deduction shall be allowed to such domestic parent corporation or to any other corporation which is entitled to deduct its contributions under such sections,

(2) there shall be allowed as a deduction to the domestic subsidiary of which such individual is an employee an amount equal to the amount which (but for paragraph (1)) would be deductible under section 404 by the domestic parent corporation if he were an employee of the domestic parent corporation, and

(3) any reference to compensation shall be considered to be a reference to the total compensation of such individual (determined with the application of subsection (b)(2)).

Any amount deductible by a domestic subsidiary under this subsection shall be deductible for its taxable year with or within which the taxable year of such domestic parent corporation ends.

Amendments

• **1984, Deficit Reduction Act of 1984 (P.L. 98-369)**

P.L. 98-369, §491(d)(18):

Amended Code Sec. 407(d) by striking out "sections 404 and 405(c)" and inserting in lieu thereof "section 404", by striking out ", annuity, or bond purchase" and inserting in lieu thereof "or annuity", and by striking out "(or section 405(c))" in paragraph (2). **Effective** for obligations issued after 12-31-83.

• **1964, Revenue Act of 1964 (P.L. 88-272)**

P.L. 88-272, §220(b):

Added Sec. 407(d). **Effective** for tax years ending after 12-31-63.

[Sec. 407(e)]

(e) TREATMENT AS EMPLOYEE UNDER RELATED PROVISIONS.—An individual who is treated as an employee of a domestic parent corporation under subsection (a) shall also be treated as an employee of such domestic parent corporation, with respect to the plan described in subsection (a)(1)(A), for purposes of applying the following provisions of this title:

(1) Section 72(f) (relating to special rules for computing employees' contributions).

(2) Section 2039 (relating to annuities).

Amendments

• **1996, Small Business Job Protection Act of 1996 (P.L. 104-188)**

P.L. 104-188, §1402(b)(2):

Amended Code Sec. 407(e) by striking paragraph (2) and by redesignating paragraph (3) as paragraph (2). **Effective** with respect to decedents dying after 8-20-96. Prior to amendment, Code Sec. 407(e)(2) read as follows:

(2) Section 101(b) (relating to employees' death benefits).

• **1988, Technical and Miscellaneous Revenue Act of 1988 (P.L. 100-647)**

P.L. 100-647, §1011A(b)(1)(C):

Amended Code Sec. 407(e) by striking out paragraph (1) and by redesignating paragraphs (2), (3), and (4) as paragraphs (1), (2), and (3), respectively. **Effective** as if included in the provision of P.L. 99-514 to which it relates. Prior to amendment, Code Sec. 407(e)(1) read as follows:

(1) Section 72(d) (relating to employees' annuities).

• **1986, Tax Reform Act of 1986 (P.L. 99-514)**

P.L. 99-514, §1852(e)(2)(D):

Amended Code Sec. 407(e) by striking out paragraph (5). **Effective** for transfers after 10-22-86. Prior to amendment, Code Sec. 407(e)(5) read as follows:

(5) Section 2517 (relating to certain annuities under qualified plans).

• **1964, Revenue Act of 1964 (P.L. 88-272)**

P.L. 88-272, §220(b):

Added Sec. 407(e). **Effective** for tax years ending after 12-31-63.

[Sec. 408]

SEC. 408. INDIVIDUAL RETIREMENT ACCOUNTS.

[Sec. 408(a)]

(a) INDIVIDUAL RETIREMENT ACCOUNT.—For purposes of this section, the term "individual retirement account" means a trust created or organized in the United States for the exclusive benefit of an individual or his beneficiaries, but only if the written governing instrument creating the trust meets the following requirements:

(1) Except in the case of a rollover contribution described in subsection (d)(3), in section 402(c), 403(a)(4), 403(b)(8), or 457(e)(16), no contribution will be accepted unless it is in cash, and contributions will not be accepted for the taxable year on behalf of any individual in excess of the amount in effect for such taxable year under section 219(b)(1)(A).

(2) The trustee is a bank (as defined in subsection (n)) or such other person who demonstrates to the satisfaction of the Secretary that the manner in which such other person will administer the trust will be consistent with the requirements of this section.

(3) No part of the trust funds will be invested in life insurance contracts.

(4) The interest of an individual in the balance of his account is nonforfeitable.

(5) The assets of the trust will not be commingled with other property except in a common trust fund or common investment fund.

(6) Under regulations prescribed by the Secretary, rules similar to the rules of section 401(a)(9) and the incidental death benefit requirements of section 401(a) shall apply to the distribution of the entire interest of an individual for whose benefit the trust is maintained.

Amendments

• **2006, Pension Protection Act of 2006 (P.L. 109-280)**

P.L. 109-280, §811, provides:

SEC. 811. PENSIONS AND INDIVIDUAL RETIREMENT ARRANGEMENT PROVISIONS OF ECONOMIC GROWTH AND TAX RELIEF RECONCILIATION ACT OF 2001 MADE PERMANENT.

Title IX of the Economic Growth and Tax Relief Reconciliation Act of 2001 [P.L. 107-16] shall not apply to the provisions of, and amendments made by, subtitles A through F of title VI [§§601-666]of such Act (relating to pension and individual retirement arrangement provisions).

• **2004, Working Families Tax Relief Act of 2004 (P.L. 108-311)**

P.L. 108-311, §408(a)(12):

Amended Code Sec. 408(a)(1) by striking "457(e)(16)" and inserting "457(e)(16),". **Effective** 10-4-2004.

• **2001, Economic Growth and Tax Relief Reconciliation Act of 2001 (P.L. 107-16)**

P.L. 107-16, §601(b)(1):

Amended Code Sec. 408(a)(1) by striking "in excess of $2,000 on behalf of any individual" and inserting "on behalf of any individual in excess of the amount in effect for such taxable year under section 219(b)(1)(A)". **Effective** for tax years beginning after 12-31-2001.

P.L. 107-16, §641(e)(8):

Amended Code Sec. 408(a)(1) by striking "or 403(b)(8)," and inserting "403(b)(8), or 457(e)(16)". **Effective**, generally, for distributions after 12-31-2001. For a special rule, see Act Sec. 641(f)(3) in the amendment notes following Code Sec. 457(e).

P.L. 107-16, §901(a)-(b), provides [but see P.L. 109-280, §811, above]:

SEC. 901. SUNSET OF PROVISIONS OF ACT.

(a) IN GENERAL.—All provisions of, and amendments made by, this Act shall not apply—

(1) to taxable, plan, or limitation years beginning after December 31, 2010, or

(2) in the case of title V, to estates of decedents dying, gifts made, or generation skipping transfers, after December 31, 2010.

(b) APPLICATION OF CERTAIN LAWS.—The Internal Revenue Code of 1986 and the Employee Retirement Income Security Act of 1974 shall be applied and administered to years, estates, gifts, and transfers described in subsection (a) as if the provisions and amendments described in subsection (a) had never been enacted.

• 1992, Unemployment Compensation Amendments of 1992 (P.L. 102-318)

P.L. 102-318, §521(b)(16):

Amended Code Sec. 408(a)(1) by striking "section 402(a)(5), 402(a)(7)" and inserting "section 402(c)". **Effective** for distributions after 12-31-92.

• 1989, Omnibus Budget Reconciliation Act of 1989 (P.L. 101-239)

P.L. 101-239, §7811(m)(7):

Amended Code Sec. 408(a)(6) by striking "(without regard to subparagraph (C)(ii) thereof)" after "section 401(a)(9)". **Effective** as if included in the provision of P.L. 100-647 to which it relates.

• 1986, Tax Reform Act of 1986 (P.L. 99-514)

P.L. 99-514, §1852(a)(1)(A):

Amended Code Sec. 408(a)(6) by striking out "(relating to required distributions)" and inserting in lieu thereof "(without regard to subparagraph (C)(ii) thereof) and the incidental death benefit requirements of section 401(a)". **Effective** as if included in the provision of P.L. 98-369 to which it relates.

• 1984, Deficit Reduction Act of 1984 (P.L. 98-369)

P.L. 98-369, §491(d)(19):

Amended Code Sec. 408(a)(1) by striking out "403(b)(8), 405(d)(3), or 409(b)(3)(C)" and inserting in lieu thereof "or 403(b)(8)". **Effective** for obligations issued after 12-31-83.

P.L. 98-369, §521(b)(1):

Amended Code Sec. 408(a) by striking out paragraphs (6) and (7) and inserting new paragraph (6). **Effective** for years beginning after 12-31-84. Prior to amendment, paragraphs (6) and (7) read as follows:

(6) The entire interest of an individual for whose benefit the trust is maintained will be distributed to him not later than the close of his taxable year in which he attains age 70½ or will be distributed, commencing before the close of such taxable year, in accordance with regulations prescribed by the Secretary, over—

(A) the life of such individual or the lives of such individual and his spouse, or

(B) a period not extending beyond the life expectancy of such individual or the life expectancy of such individual and his spouse.

(7) If—

(A) an individual for whose benefit the trust is maintained dies before his entire interest has been distributed to him, or

(B) distribution has been commenced as provided in paragraph (6) to his surviving spouse and such surviving spouse dies before the entire interest has been distributed to such spouse,

the entire interest (or the remaining part of such interest if distribution thereof has commenced) will be distributed within 5 years after his death (or the death of the surviving spouse). The preceding sentence shall not apply if distributions over a term certain commenced before the death of the individual for whose benefit the trust was maintained and the term certain is for a period permitted under paragraph (6).

• 1982, Tax Equity and Fiscal Responsibility Act of 1982 (P.L. 97-248)

P.L. 97-248, §237(e)(3)(A):

Amended Code Sec. 408(a)(2) by striking out "as defined in section 401(d)(1)" and inserting "as defined in subsection (n)". **Effective** for years beginning after 12-31-83.

P.L. 97-248, §243(a)(1):

Amended Code Sec. 408(a)(7). **Effective** for individuals dying after 12-31-83. Prior to amendment, Code Sec. 408(a)(7) read as follows:

(7) If an individual for whose benefit the trust is maintained dies before his entire interest has been distributed to him, or if distribution has been commenced as provided in paragraph (6) to his surviving spouse and such surviving spouse dies before the entire interest has been distributed to such spouse, the entire interest (or the remaining part of such interest if distribution thereof has commenced) will, within 5 years after his death (or the death of the surviving spouse), be distributed, or applied to the purchase of an immediate annuity for his beneficiary or beneficiaries (or the beneficiary or beneficiaries of his surviving spouse) which will be payable for the life of such beneficiary or beneficiaries (or for term certain not extending beyond the life expectancy of such beneficiary or beneficiaries) and which annuity will be immediately distributed to such beneficiary or beneficiaries. The preceding sentence does not apply if distributions over a term certain commenced before the death of the individual for whose benefit the trust was maintained and the term certain is for a period permitted under paragraph (6).

• 1981, Economic Recovery Tax Act of 1981 (P.L. 97-34)

P.L. 97-34, §311(g)(1)(A):

Amended Code Sec. 408(a)(1) by striking out "$1,500" and inserting "$2,000". **Effective** for tax years beginning after 12-31-81.

P.L. 97-34, §313(b)(2):

Amended Code Sec. 408(a)(1) by adding "405(d)(3)" after "403(b)(8),". **Effective** for redemptions after 8-13-81 in tax years ending after 8-13-81.

• 1980, Technical Corrections Act of 1979 (P.L. 96-222)

P.L. 96-222, §101(a)(14)(B):

Amended Code Sec. 408(a)(1) by adding "402(a)(7)," after "section 402(a)(5),". **Effective** for distributions or transfers made after 12-31-77, in tax years beginning after such date.

• 1978, Revenue Act of 1978 (P.L. 95-600)

P.L. 95-600, §156(c)(3):

Amended Code Sec. 408(a)(1) by inserting "403(b)(8)" after "403(a)(4)". **Effective** for distributions or transfers made after 12-31-77, in tax years beginning after such date [**effective** date changed by P.L. 96-222, §101(a)(13)(A).—CCH].

• 1976, Tax Reform Act of 1976 (P.L. 94-455)

P.L. 94-455, §1906(b)(13)(A):

Amended 1954 Code by substituting "Secretary" for "Secretary or his delegate" each place it appeared. **Effective** 2-1-77.

[Sec. 408(b)]

(b) INDIVIDUAL RETIREMENT ANNUITY.—For purposes of this section, the term "individual retirement annuity" means an annuity contract, or an endowment contract (as determined under regulations prescribed by the Secretary), issued by an insurance company which meets the following requirements:

(1) The contract is not transferable by the owner.

(2) Under the contract—

(A) the premiums are not fixed,

(B) the annual premium on behalf of any individual will not exceed the dollar amount in effect under section 219(b)(1)(A), and

(C) any refund of premiums will be applied before the close of the calendar year following the year of the refund toward the payment of future premiums or the purchase of additional benefits.

(3) Under regulations prescribed by the Secretary, rules similar to the rules of section 401(a)(9) and the incidental death benefit requirements of section 401(a) shall apply to the distribution of the entire interest of the owner.

(4) The entire interest of the owner is nonforfeitable.

Such term does not include such an annuity contract for any taxable year of the owner in which it is disqualified on the application of subsection (e) or for any subsequent taxable year. For purposes of this subsection, no contract shall be treated as an endowment contract if it matures later than the taxable year in which the individual in whose name such contract is purchased attains age 70½; if it is not for the exclusive benefit of the individual in whose name it is purchased or his beneficiaries; or if the aggregate annual premiums under all such contracts purchased in the name of such individual for any taxable year exceed the dollar amount in effect under section 219(b)(1)(A).

Amendments

• 2006, Pension Protection Act of 2006 (P.L. 109-280)

P.L. 109-280, §811, provides:

SEC. 811. PENSIONS AND INDIVIDUAL RETIREMENT ARRANGEMENT PROVISIONS OF ECONOMIC GROWTH AND TAX RELIEF RECONCILIATION ACT OF 2001 MADE PERMANENT.

Title IX of the Economic Growth and Tax Relief Reconciliation Act of 2001 [P.L. 107-16] shall not apply to the provisions of, and amendments made by, subtitles A through F of title VI [§§601-666]of such Act (relating to pension and individual retirement arrangement provisions).

• 2001, Economic Growth and Tax Relief Reconciliation Act of 2001 (P.L. 107-16)

P.L. 107-16, §601(b)(2):

Amended Code Sec. 408(b)(2)(B) by striking "$2,000" and inserting "the dollar amount in effect under section 219(b)(1)(A)". **Effective** for tax years beginning after 12-31-2001.

P.L. 107-16, §601(b)(3):

Amended Code Sec. 408(b) by striking "$2,000" in the matter following paragraph (4) and inserting "the dollar amount in effect under section 219(b)(1)(A)". **Effective** for tax years beginning after 12-31-2001.

P.L. 107-16, §901(a)-(b), provides [but see P.L. 109-280, §811, above]:

SEC. 901. SUNSET OF PROVISIONS OF ACT.

(a) IN GENERAL.—All provisions of, and amendments made by, this Act shall not apply—

(1) to taxable, plan, or limitation years beginning after December 31, 2010, or

(2) in the case of title V, to estates of decedents dying, gifts made, or generation skipping transfers, after December 31, 2010.

(b) APPLICATION OF CERTAIN LAWS.—The Internal Revenue Code of 1986 and the Employee Retirement Income Security Act of 1974 shall be applied and administered to years, estates, gifts, and transfers described in subsection (a) as if the provisions and amendments described in subsection (a) had never been enacted.

• 1989, Omnibus Budget Reconciliation Act of 1989 (P.L. 101-239)

P.L. 101-239, §7811(m)(7):

Amended Code Sec. 408(b)(3) by striking "(without regard to subparagraph (C)(ii) thereof)" after "section 401(a)(9)". **Effective** as if included in the provision of P.L. 100-647 to which it relates.

• 1986, Tax Reform Act of 1986 (P.L. 99-514)

P.L. 99-514, §1852(a)(1)(B):

Amended Code Sec. 408(b)(3) by striking out "(relating to required distributions)" and inserting in lieu thereof "(without regard to subparagraph (C)(ii) thereof) and the incidental death benefit requirements of section 401(a)". **Effective** as if included in the provision of P.L. 98-369 to which it relates.

• 1984, Deficit Reduction Act of 1984 (P.L. 98-369)

P.L. 98-369, §521(b)(2):

Amended Code Sec. 408(b) by striking out paragraphs (3) and (4), by redesignating paragraph (5) as paragraph (4), and by inserting after paragraph (2) new paragraph (3). **Effective** for years beginning after 12-31-84. Prior to amendment, paragraphs (3) and (4) read as follows:

(3) The entire interest of the owner will be distributed to him not later than the close of his taxable year in which he attains age 70½ or will be distributed, in accordance with regulations prescribed by the Secretary, over—

(A) the life of such owner or the lives of such owner and his spouse, or

(B) a period not extending beyond the life expectancy of such owner or the life expectancy of such owner and his spouse.

(4) If—

(A) the owner dies before his entire interest has been distributed to him, or

(B) distribution has been commenced as provided in paragraph (3) to his surviving spouse and such surviving spouse dies before the entire interest has been distributed to such spouse,

the entire interest (or the remaining part of such interest if distribution thereof has commenced) will be distributed within 5 years after his death (or the death of his surviving spouse). The preceding sentence shall not apply if distributions over a term certain commenced before the death of the owner and the term certain is for a period permitted under paragraph (3).

• 1982, Tax Equity and Fiscal Responsibility Act of 1982 (P.L. 97-248)

P.L. 97-248, §243(a)(2):

Amended Code Sec. 408(b)(4). **Effective** for individuals dying after 12-31-83. Prior to amendment, Code Sec. 408(b)(4) read as follows:

(4) If the owner dies before his entire interest has been distributed to him, or if distribution has been commenced as provided in paragraph (3) to his surviving spouse and such surviving spouse dies before the entire interest has been distributed to such spouse, the entire interest (or the remain-

ing part of such interest if distribution thereof has commenced) will, within 5 years after his death (or the death of the surviving spouse), be distributed, or applied to the purchase of an immediate annuity for his beneficiary or beneficiaries (or the beneficiary or beneficiaries of his surviving spouse) which will be payable for the life of such beneficiary or beneficiaries (or for a term certain not extending beyond the life expectancy of such beneficiary or beneficiaries) and which annuity will be immediately distributed to such beneficiary or beneficiaries. The preceding sentence shall have no application if distributions over a term certain commenced before the death of the owner and the term certain is for a period permitted under paragraph (3).

• 1981, Economic Recovery Tax Act of 1981 (P.L. 97-34)

P.L. 97-34, §311(g)(1)(B):

Amended Code Sec. 408(b) by striking out "$1,500" each place it appears and inserting "$2,000". **Effective** for tax years beginning after 12-31-81.

• 1978, Revenue Act of 1978 (P.L. 95-600)

P.L. 95-600, §157(d)(1), (e)(1)(A):

Amended Code Sec. 408(b)(2). **Effective** for contracts issued after 11-7-78. Prior to amendment, Code Sec. 408(b)(2) read as follows:

(2) The annual premium under the contract will not exceed $1,500 and any refund of premiums will be applied before the close of the calendar year following the year of the refund toward the payment of future premiums or the purchase of additional benefits.

P.L. 95-600, §157(d)(3), provides:

(3) TAX RELIEF FOR FIXED PREMIUM CONTRACTS HERETOFORE ISSUED.—In the case of any annuity or endowment contract issued on or before the date of the enactment of this Act which would be an individual retirement annuity within the meaning of section 408(b) of the Internal Revenue Code of 1954 (as amended by paragraph (1)) but for the fact that the premiums under the contract are fixed, at the election of the taxpayer an exchange before January 1, 1981, of that contract for an individual retirement annuity within the meaning of such section 408(b) (as amended by paragraph (1)) shall be treated as a nontaxable exchange which does not constitute a distribution.

• 1976, Tax Reform Act of 1976 (P.L. 94-455)

P.L. 94-455, §1906(b)(13)(A):

Amended 1954 Code by substituting "Secretary" for "Secretary or his delegate" each place it appeared. **Effective** 2-1-77.

[Sec. 408(c)]

(c) ACCOUNTS ESTABLISHED BY EMPLOYERS AND CERTAIN ASSOCIATIONS OF EMPLOYEES.—A trust created or organized in the United States by an employer for the exclusive benefit of his employees or their beneficiaries, or by an association of employees (which may include employees within the meaning of section 401(c)(1)) for the exclusive benefit of its members or their beneficiaries, shall be treated as an individual retirement account (described in subsection (a)), but only if the written governing instrument creating the trust meets the following requirements:

(1) The trust satisfies the requirements of paragraphs (1) through (6) of subsection (a).

(2) There is a separate accounting for the interest of each employee or member (or spouse of an employee or member).

The assets of the trust may be held in a common fund for the account of all individuals who have an interest in the trust.

Amendments

• 1986, Tax Reform Act of 1986 (P.L. 99-514)

P.L. 99-514, §1852(a)(7)(A):

Amended Code Sec. 408(c)(1) by striking out "paragraphs (1) through (7)" and inserting in lieu thereof "paragraphs (1) through (6)". **Effective** as if included in the provision of P.L. 98-369 to which it relates.

• 1976, Tax Reform Act of 1976 (P.L. 94-455)

P.L. 94-455, §1501(b)(2):

Amended Code Sec. 408(c) by inserting "(or spouse of an employee or member)" after "member". **Effective** for tax years beginning after 12-31-76.

[Sec. 408(d)]

(d) TAX TREATMENT OF DISTRIBUTIONS.—

(1) IN GENERAL.—Except as otherwise provided in this subsection, any amount paid or distributed out of an individual retirement plan shall be included in gross income by the payee or distributee, as the case may be, in the manner provided under section 72.

(2) SPECIAL RULES FOR APPLYING SECTION 72.—For purposes of applying section 72 to any amount described in paragraph (1)—

(A) all individual retirement plans shall be treated as 1 contract,

(B) all distributions during any taxable year shall be treated as 1 distribution, and

(C) the value of the contract, income on the contract, and investment in the contract shall be computed as of the close of the calendar year in which the taxable year begins.

For purposes of subparagraph (C), the value of the contract shall be increased by the amount of any distributions during the calendar year.

(3) ROLLOVER CONTRIBUTION.—An amount is described in this paragraph as a rollover contribution if it meets the requirements of subparagraphs (A) and (B).

(A) IN GENERAL.—Paragraph (1) does not apply to any amount paid or distributed out of an individual retirement account or individual retirement annuity to the individual for whose benefit the account or annuity is maintained if—

(i) the entire amount received (including money and any other property) is paid into an individual retirement account or individual retirement annuity (other than an endowment contract) for the benefit of such individual not later than the 60th day after the day on which he receives the payment or distribution; or

(ii) the entire amount received (including money and any other property) is paid into an eligible retirement plan for the benefit of such individual not later than the 60th day after the date on which the payment or distribution is received, except that the maximum amount which may be paid into such plan may not exceed the portion of the amount received which is includible in gross income (determined without regard to this paragraph).

For purposes of clause (ii), the term "eligible retirement plan" means an eligible retirement plan described in clause (iii), (iv), (v), or (vi) of section 402(c)(8)(B).

(B) LIMITATION.—This paragraph does not apply to any amount described in subparagraph (A)(i) received by an individual from an individual retirement account or individual retirement annuity if at any time during the 1-year period ending on the day of such receipt such individual received any other amount described in that subparagraph from an individual retirement account or an individual retirement annuity which was not includible in his gross income because of the application of this paragraph.

(C) DENIAL OF ROLLOVER TREATMENT FOR INHERITED ACCOUNTS, ETC.—

(i) IN GENERAL.—In the case of an inherited individual retirement account or individual retirement annuity—

(I) this paragraph shall not apply to any amount received by an individual from such an account or annuity (and no amount transferred from such account or annuity to another individual retirement account or annuity shall be excluded from gross income by reason of such transfer), and

(II) such inherited account or annuity shall not be treated as an individual retirement account or annuity for purposes of determining whether any other amount is a rollover contribution.

(ii) INHERITED INDIVIDUAL RETIREMENT ACCOUNT OR ANNUITY.—An individual retirement account or individual retirement annuity shall be treated as inherited if—

(I) the individual for whose benefit the account or annuity is maintained acquired such account by reason of the death of another individual, and

(II) such individual was not the surviving spouse of such other individual.

(D) PARTIAL ROLLOVERS PERMITTED.—

(i) IN GENERAL.—If any amount paid or distributed out of an individual retirement account or individual retirement annuity would meet the requirements of subparagraph (A) but for the fact that the entire amount was not paid into an eligible plan as required by clause (i) or (ii) of subparagraph (A), such amount shall be treated as meeting the requirements of subparagraph (A) to the extent it is paid into an eligible plan referred to in such clause not later than the 60th day referred to in such clause.

(ii) ELIGIBLE PLAN.—For purposes of clause (i), the term "eligible plan" means any account, annuity, contract, or plan referred to in subparagraph (A).

(E) DENIAL OF ROLLOVER TREATMENT FOR REQUIRED DISTRIBUTIONS.—This paragraph shall not apply to any amount to the extent such amount is required to be distributed under subsection (a)(6) or (b)(3).

(F) FROZEN DEPOSITS.—For purposes of this paragraph, rules similar to the rules of section 402(c)(7) (relating to frozen deposits) shall apply.

(G) SIMPLE RETIREMENT ACCOUNTS.—In the case of any payment or distribution out of a simple retirement account (as defined in subsection (p)) to which section 72(t)(6) applies, this paragraph shall not apply unless such payment or distribution is paid into another simple retirement account.

(H) APPLICATION OF SECTION 72.—

(i) IN GENERAL.—If—

(I) a distribution is made from an individual retirement plan, and

(II) a rollover contribution is made to an eligible retirement plan described in section 402(c)(8)(B)(iii), (iv), (v), or (vi) with respect to all or part of such distribution,

then, notwithstanding paragraph (2), the rules of clause (ii) shall apply for purposes of applying section 72.

(ii) APPLICABLE RULES.—In the case of a distribution described in clause (i)—

(I) section 72 shall be applied separately to such distribution,

(II) notwithstanding the pro rata allocation of income on, and investment in, the contract to distributions under section 72, the portion of such distribution rolled over to an eligible retirement plan described in clause (i) shall be treated as from income on the contract (to the extent of the aggregate income on the contract from all individual retirement plans of the distributee), and

(III) appropriate adjustments shall be made in applying section 72 to other distributions in such taxable year and subsequent taxable years.

(I) WAIVER OF 60-DAY REQUIREMENT.—The Secretary may waive the 60-day requirement under subparagraphs (A) and (D) where the failure to waive such requirement would be against equity or good conscience, including casualty, disaster, or other events beyond the reasonable control of the individual subject to such requirement.

(4) CONTRIBUTIONS RETURNED BEFORE DUE DATE OF RETURN.—Paragraph (1) does not apply to the distribution of any contribution paid during a taxable year to an individual retirement account or for an individual retirement annuity if—

(A) such distribution is received on or before the day prescribed by law (including extensions of time) for filing such individual's return for such taxable year,

(B) no deduction is allowed under section 219 with respect to such contribution, and

(C) such distribution is accompanied by the amount of net income attributable to such contribution.

In the case of such a distribution, for purposes of section 61, any net income described in subparagraph (C) shall be deemed to have been earned and receivable in the taxable year in which such contribution is made.

(5) DISTRIBUTIONS OF EXCESS CONTRIBUTIONS AFTER DUE DATE FOR TAXABLE YEAR AND CERTAIN EXCESS ROLLOVER CONTRIBUTIONS.—

(A) IN GENERAL.—In the case of any individual, if the aggregate contributions (other than rollover contributions) paid for any taxable year to an individual retirement account or for an individual retirement annuity do not exceed the dollar amount in effect under section 219(b)(1)(A), paragraph (1) shall not apply to the distribution of any such contribution to the extent that such contribution exceeds the amount allowable as a deduction under section 219 for the taxable year for which the contribution was paid—

(i) if such distribution is received after the date described in paragraph (4),

(ii) but only to the extent that no deduction has been allowed under section 219 with respect to such excess contribution.

If employer contributions on behalf of the individual are paid for the taxable year to a simplified employee pension, the dollar limitation of the preceding sentence shall be increased by the lesser of the amount of such contributions or the dollar limitation in effect under section 415(c)(1)(A) for such taxable year.

(B) EXCESS ROLLOVER CONTRIBUTIONS ATTRIBUTABLE TO ERRONEOUS INFORMATION.—If—

(i) the taxpayer reasonably relies on information supplied pursuant to subtitle F for determining the amount of a rollover contribution, but

(ii) the information was erroneous,

subparagraph (A) shall be applied by increasing the dollar limit set forth therein by that portion of the excess contribution which was attributable to such information.

For purposes of this paragraph, the amount allowable as a deduction under section 219 shall be computed without regard to section 219(g).

(6) TRANSFER OF ACCOUNT INCIDENT TO DIVORCE.—The transfer of an individual's interest in an individual retirement account or an individual retirement annuity to his spouse or former spouse under a divorce or separation instrument described in subparagraph (A) of section 71(b)(2) is not to be considered a taxable transfer made by such individual notwithstanding any other provision of this subtitle, and such interest at the time of the transfer is to be treated as an individual retirement account of such spouse, and not of such individual. Thereafter such account or annuity for purposes of this subtitle is to be treated as maintained for the benefit of such spouse.

(7) SPECIAL RULES FOR SIMPLIFIED EMPLOYEE PENSIONS OR SIMPLE RETIREMENT ACCOUNTS.—

(A) TRANSFER OR ROLLOVER OF CONTRIBUTIONS PROHIBITED UNTIL DEFERRAL TEST MET.—Notwithstanding any other provision of this subsection or section 72(t), paragraph (1) and section 72(t)(1) shall apply to the transfer or distribution from a simplified employee pension of any contribution under a salary reduction arrangement described in subsection (k)(6) (or any income allocable thereto) before a determination as to whether the requirements of subsection (k)(6)(A)(iii) are met with respect to such contribution.

(B) CERTAIN EXCLUSIONS TREATED AS DEDUCTIONS.—For purposes of paragraphs (4) and (5) and section 4973, any amount excludable or excluded from gross income under section 402(h) or 402(k) shall be treated as an amount allowable or allowed as a deduction under section 219.

(8) DISTRIBUTIONS FOR CHARITABLE PURPOSES.—

(A) IN GENERAL.—So much of the aggregate amount of qualified charitable distributions with respect to a taxpayer made during any taxable year which does not exceed $100,000 shall not be includible in gross income of such taxpayer for such taxable year.

(B) QUALIFIED CHARITABLE DISTRIBUTION.—For purposes of this paragraph, the term "qualified charitable distribution" means any distribution from an individual retirement plan (other than a plan described in subsection (k) or (p))—

(i) which is made directly by the trustee to an organization described in section 170(b)(1)(A) (other than any organization described in section 509(a)(3) or any fund or account described in section 4966(d)(2)), and

(ii) which is made on or after the date that the individual for whose benefit the plan is maintained has attained age 70½.

A distribution shall be treated as a qualified charitable distribution only to the extent that the distribution would be includible in gross income without regard to subparagraph (A).

(C) CONTRIBUTIONS MUST BE OTHERWISE DEDUCTIBLE.—For purposes of this paragraph, a distribution to an organization described in subparagraph (B)(i) shall be treated as a qualified charitable distribution only if a deduction for the entire distribution would be allowable under section 170 (determined without regard to subsection (b) thereof and this paragraph).

(D) APPLICATION OF SECTION 72.—Notwithstanding section 72, in determining the extent to which a distribution is a qualified charitable distribution, the entire amount of the distribution shall be treated as includible in gross income without regard to subparagraph (A) to the extent that such amount does not exceed the aggregate amount which would have been so includible if all amounts in all individual retirement plans of the individual were distributed during such taxable year and all such plans were treated as 1 contract for purposes of determining under section 72 the aggregate amount which would have been so includible. Proper adjustments shall be made in applying section 72 to other distributions in such taxable year and subsequent taxable years.

(E) DENIAL OF DEDUCTION.—Qualified charitable distributions which are not includible in gross income pursuant to subparagraph (A) shall not be taken into account in determining the deduction under section 170.

(F) TERMINATION.—This paragraph shall not apply to distributions made in taxable years beginning after December 31, 2009.

(9) DISTRIBUTION FOR HEALTH SAVINGS ACCOUNT FUNDING.—

(A) IN GENERAL.—In the case of an individual who is an eligible individual (as defined in section 223(c)) and who elects the application of this paragraph for a taxable year, gross income of the individual for the taxable year does not include a qualified HSA funding distribution to the extent such distribution is otherwise includible in gross income.

(B) QUALIFIED HSA FUNDING DISTRIBUTION.—For purposes of this paragraph, the term "qualified HSA funding distribution" means a distribution from an individual retirement plan (other than a plan described in subsection (k) or (p)) of the employee to the extent that such distribution is contributed to the health savings account of the individual in a direct trustee-to-trustee transfer.

(C) LIMITATIONS.—

(i) MAXIMUM DOLLAR LIMITATION.—The amount excluded from gross income by subparagraph (A) shall not exceed the excess of—

(I) the annual limitation under section 223(b) computed on the basis of the type of coverage under the high deductible health plan covering the individual at the time of the qualified HSA funding distribution, over

(II) in the case of a distribution described in clause (ii)(II), the amount of the earlier qualified HSA funding distribution.

(ii) ONE-TIME TRANSFER.—

(I) IN GENERAL.—Except as provided in subclause (II), an individual may make an election under subparagraph (A) only for one qualified HSA funding distribution during the lifetime of the individual. Such an election, once made, shall be irrevocable.

(II) CONVERSION FROM SELF-ONLY TO FAMILY COVERAGE.—If a qualified HSA funding distribution is made during a month in a taxable year during which an individual has self-only coverage under a high deductible health plan as of the first day of the month, the individual may elect to make an additional qualified HSA funding distribution during a subsequent month in such taxable year during which the individual has family coverage under a high deductible health plan as of the first day of the subsequent month.

(D) FAILURE TO MAINTAIN HIGH DEDUCTIBLE HEALTH PLAN COVERAGE.—

(i) IN GENERAL.—If, at any time during the testing period, the individual is not an eligible individual, then the aggregate amount of all contributions to the health savings account of the individual made under subparagraph (A)—

(I) shall be includible in the gross income of the individual for the taxable year in which occurs the first month in the testing period for which such individual is not an eligible individual, and

(II) the tax imposed by this chapter for any taxable year on the individual shall be increased by 10 percent of the amount which is so includible.

(ii) EXCEPTION FOR DISABILITY OR DEATH.—Subclauses (I) and (II) of clause (i) shall not apply if the individual ceased to be an eligible individual by reason of the death of the individual or the individual becoming disabled (within the meaning of section 72(m)(7)).

(iii) TESTING PERIOD.—The term "testing period" means the period beginning with the month in which the qualified HSA funding distribution is contributed to a health savings account and ending on the last day of the 12th month following such month.

(E) APPLICATION OF SECTION 72.—Notwithstanding section 72, in determining the extent to which an amount is treated as otherwise includible in gross income for purposes of subparagraph (A), the aggregate amount distributed from an individual retirement plan shall be treated as includible in gross income to the extent that such amount does not exceed the aggregate amount which would have been so includible if all amounts from all individual retirement plans were distributed. Proper adjustments shall be made in applying section 72 to other distributions in such taxable year and subsequent taxable years.

Amendments

• 2008, Tax Extenders and Alternative Minimum Tax Relief Act of 2008 (P.L. 110-343)

P.L. 110-343, Division C, §205(a):

Amended Code Sec. 408(d)(8)(F) by striking "December 31, 2007" and inserting "December 31, 2009". **Effective** for distributions made in tax years beginning after 12-31-2007.

• 2007, Tax Technical Corrections Act of 2007 (P.L. 110-172)

P.L. 110-172, §3(a):

Amended Code Sec. 408(d)(8)(D) by striking "all amounts distributed from all individual retirement plans were treated as 1 contract under paragraph (2)(A) for purposes of determining the inclusion of such distributions under section 72" and inserting "all amounts in all individual retirement plans of the individual were distributed during such taxable year and all such plans were treated as 1 contract for purposes of determining under section 72 the aggregate amount which would have been so includible". **Effective** as if included in the provision of the Pension Protection Act of 2006 (P.L. 109-280) to which it relates [**effective** for distributions made in tax years beginning after 12-31-2005.—CCH].

• 2006, Tax Relief and Health Care Act of 2006 (P.L. 109-432)

P.L. 109-432, Division A, §307(a):

Amended Code Sec. 408(d) by adding at the end a new paragraph (9). **Effective** for tax years beginning after 12-31-2006.

• 2006, Pension Protection Act of 2006 (P.L. 109-280)

P.L. 109-280, §811, provides:

SEC. 811. PENSIONS AND INDIVIDUAL RETIREMENT ARRANGEMENT PROVISIONS OF ECONOMIC GROWTH AND TAX RELIEF RECONCILIATION ACT OF 2001 MADE PERMANENT.

Title IX of the Economic Growth and Tax Relief Reconciliation Act of 2001 [P.L. 107-16] shall not apply to the provisions of, and amendments made by, subtitles A through F of title VI [§§601-666]of such Act (relating to pension and individual retirement arrangement provisions).

P.L. 109-280, §1201(a):

Amended Code Sec. 408(d) by adding at the end a new paragraph (8). **Effective** for distributions made in tax years beginning after 12-31-2005.

• 2005, Katrina Emergency Tax Relief Act of 2005 (P.L. 109-73)

P.L. 109-73, §102 [repealed by P.L. 109-135, §201(b)(4)(A)], provides:

SEC. 102. RECONTRIBUTIONS OF WITHDRAWALS FOR HOME PURCHASES CANCELLED DUE TO HURRICANE KATRINA.

(a) RECONTRIBUTIONS.—

(1) IN GENERAL.—Any individual who received a qualified distribution may, during the period beginning on August 25, 2005, and ending on February 28, 2006, make one or more contributions in an aggregate amount not to exceed the amount of such qualified distribution to an eligible retirement plan (as defined in section 402(c)(8)(B) of the Internal Revenue Code of 1986) of which such individual is a beneficiary and to which a rollover contribution of such distribution could be made under section 402(c), 403(a)(4), 403(b)(8), or 408(d)(3) of such Code, as the case may be.

(2) TREATMENT OF REPAYMENTS.—Rules similar to the rules of paragraphs (2) and (3) of section 101(c) of this Act shall apply for purposes of this section.

(b) QUALIFIED DISTRIBUTION DEFINED.—For purposes of this section, the term "qualified distribution" means any distribution—

(1) described in section 401(k)(2)(B)(i)(IV), 403(b)(7)(A)(ii) (but only to the extent such distribution relates to financial hardship), 403(b)(11)(B), or 72(t)(2)(F) of such Code,

(2) received after February 28, 2005, and before August 29, 2005, and

(3) which was to be used to purchase or construct a principal residence in the Hurricane Katrina disaster area, but which was not so purchased or constructed on account of Hurricane Katrina.

• 2001, Economic Growth and Tax Relief Reconciliation Act of 2001 (P.L. 107-16)

P.L. 107-16, §642(a):

Amended Code Sec. 408(d)(3)(A) by adding "or" at the end of clause (i), by striking clauses (ii) and (iii), and by adding at the end a new clause (ii) and flush sentence. **Effective** for distributions after 12-31-2001. For a special rule, see Act Sec. 642(c)(2), below. Prior to being stricken, Code Sec. 408(d)(3)(A)(ii)-(iii) read as follows:

(ii) no amount in the account and no part of the value of the annuity is attributable to any source other than a rollover contribution (as defined in section 402) from an employee's trust described in section 401(a) which is exempt from tax under section 501(a) or from an annuity plan described in section 403(a) (and any earnings on such contribution), and the entire amount received (including property and other money) is paid (for the benefit of such individual) into another such trust or annuity plan not later than the 60th day on which the individual receives the payment or the distribution; or

(iii)(I) the entire amount received (including money and other property) represents the entire interest in the account or the entire value of the annuity,

(II) no amount in the account and no part of the value of the annuity is attributable to any source other than a rollover contribution from an annuity contract described in section 403(b) and any earnings on such rollover, and

(III) the entire amount thereof is paid into another annuity contract described in section 403(b) (for the benefit of such individual) not later than the 60th day after he receives the payment or distribution.

P.L. 107-16, §642(b)(2):

Amended Code Sec. 408(d)(3)(D)(i) by striking "(i), (ii), or (iii)" and inserting "(i) or (ii)". **Effective** for distributions after 12-31-2001. For a special rule, see Act Sec. 642(c)(2), below.

P.L. 107-16, §642(b)(3):

Amended Code Sec. 408(d)(3)(G). **Effective** for distributions after 12-31-2001. For a special rule, see Act Sec. 642(c)(2), below. Prior to amendment, Code Sec. 408(d)(3)(G) read as follows:

(G) SIMPLE RETIREMENT ACCOUNTS.—This paragraph shall not apply to any amount paid or distributed out of a simple retirement account (as defined in subsection (p)) unless—

(i) it is paid into another simple retirement account, or

(ii) in the case of any payment or distribution to which section 72(t)(6) does not apply, it is paid into an individual retirement plan.

P.L. 107-16, §642(c)(2), provides:

(2) SPECIAL RULE.—Notwithstanding any other provision of law, subsections (h)(3) and (h)(5) of section 1122 of the Tax Reform Act of 1986 shall not apply to any distribution from an eligible retirement plan (as defined in clause (iii) or (iv) of section 402(c)(8)(B) of the Internal Revenue Code of 1986) on behalf of an individual if there was a rollover to such plan on behalf of such individual which is permitted solely by reason of the amendments made by this section.

P.L. 107-16, §643(c):

Amended Code Sec. 408(d)(3) by inserting at the end a new subparagraph (H). **Effective** for distributions made after 12-31-2001.

P.L. 107-16, §644(b):

Amended Code Sec. 408(d)(3), as amended by Act Sec. 643, by adding after subparagraph (H) a new subparagraph (I). **Effective** for distributions after 12-31-2001.

P.L. 107-16, §901(a)-(b), provides [but see P.L. 109-280, §811, above]:

SEC. 901. SUNSET OF PROVISIONS OF ACT.

(a) IN GENERAL.—All provisions of, and amendments made by, this Act shall not apply—

(1) to taxable, plan, or limitation years beginning after December 31, 2010, or

(2) in the case of title V, to estates of decedents dying, gifts made, or generation skipping transfers, after December 31, 2010.

(b) APPLICATION OF CERTAIN LAWS.—The Internal Revenue Code of 1986 and the Employee Retirement Income Security Act of 1974 shall be applied and administered to years, estates, gifts, and transfers described in subsection (a) as if the provisions and amendments described in subsection (a) had never been enacted.

• 2000, Community Renewal Tax Relief Act of 2000 (P.L. 106-554)

P.L. 106-554, §319(3):

Amended the heading for Code Sec. 408(d)(5). **Effective** 12-21-2000. Prior to amendment, the heading for Code Sec. 408(d)(5) read as follows:

(5) CERTAIN DISTRIBUTIONS OF EXCESS CONTRIBUTIONS AFTER DUE DATE FOR TAXABLE YEAR.

• 1998, IRS Restructuring and Reform Act of 1998 (P.L. 105-206)

P.L. 105-206, §6018(b)(1)–(2):

Amended Code Sec. 408(d)(7) by inserting "or 402(k)" after "section 402(h)" in subparagraph (B), and by inserting "OR SIMPLE RETIREMENT ACCOUNTS" after "PENSIONS" in the heading. **Effective** as if included in the provision of P.L. 104-188 to which it relates [**effective** for tax years beginning after 12-31-96.—CCH].

• 1996, Small Business Job Protection Act of 1996 (P.L. 104-188)

P.L. 104-188, §1421(b)(3)(B):

Amended Code Sec. 408(d)(3) by adding at the end a new subparagraph (G). **Effective** for tax years beginning after 12-31-96.

P.L. 104-188, §1427(b)(3):

Amended Code Sec. 408(d)(5)[(A)] by striking "$2,250" and inserting "the dollar amount in effect under section 219(b)(1)(A)". **Effective** for tax years beginning after 12-31-96.

• 1992, Unemployment Compensation Amendments of 1992 (P.L. 102-318)

P.L. 102-318, §521(b)(17):

Amended Code Sec. 408(d)(3)(A)(ii). **Effective** for distributions after 12-31-92. Prior to amendment, Code Sec. 408(d)(3)(A)(ii) read as follows:

(ii) the entire amount received (including money and any other property) represents the entire amount in the account or the entire value of the annuity and no amount in the account and no part of the value of the annuity is attributable to any source other than a rollover contribution of a qualified total distribution (as defined in section 402(a)(5)(E)(i)) from an employee's trust described in section 401(a) which is exempt from tax under section 501(a), or an annuity plan described in section 403(a) and any earnings on such sums and the entire amount thereof is paid into another such trust (for the benefit of such individual) or annuity plan not later than the 60th day on which he receives the payment or distribution; or

P.L. 102-318, §521(b)(18):

Amended Code Sec. 408(d)(3)(B) by striking the second sentence thereof. **Effective** for distributions after 12-31-92. Prior to amendment, the second sentence of Code Sec. 408(d)(3)(B) read as follows:

Clause (ii) of subparagraph (A) shall not apply to any amount paid or distributed out of an individual retirement account or an individual retirement annuity to which an amount was contributed which was treated as a rollover contribution by section 402(a)(7) (or in the case of an individual retirement annuity, such section as made applicable by section 403(a)(4)(B)).

P.L. 102-318, §521(b)(19):

Amended Code Sec. 408(d)(3)(F) by striking "section 402(a)(6)(H)" and inserting "section 402(c)(7)". **Effective** for distributions after 12-31-92.

• 1989, Omnibus Budget Reconciliation Act of 1989 (P.L. 101-239)

P.L. 101-239, §7841(a)(1):

Amended Code Sec. 408(d)(6) by striking "his former spouse under a divorce decree or under a written instrument incident to such divorce" and inserting "his spouse or former spouse under a divorce or separation instrument described in subparagraph (A) of section 71(b)(2)". **Effective** for transfers after 12-19-89, in tax years ending after such date.

• 1988, Technical and Miscellaneous Revenue Act of 1988 (P.L. 100-647)

P.L. 100-647, §1011(b)(1):

Amended Code Sec. 408(d)(2)(C) by striking out "with or within which the taxable year ends" and inserting in lieu thereof "in which the taxable year begins". **Effective** as if included in the provision of P.L. 99-514 to which it relates.

P.L. 100-647, §1011(b)(2)(A):

Amended Code Sec. 408(d)(4) by striking out "to the extent that such contribution exceeds the amount allowable as a deduction under section 219" after "retirement annuity". **Effective** as if included in the provision of P.L. 99-514 to which it relates.

P.L. 100-647, §1011(b)(2)(B)(i)-(ii):

Amended Code Sec. 408(d)(4) by striking out "excess" each place it appears, and by striking out "EXCESS CONTRIBUTIONS" in the heading and inserting in lieu thereof "CONTRIBUTIONS". **Effective** as if included in the provision of P.L. 99-514 to which it relates. Prior to amendment, Code Sec. 408(d)(4) read as follows:

(4) EXCESS CONTRIBUTIONS RETURNED BEFORE DUE DATE OF RETURN.—Paragraph (1) does not apply to the distribution of any contribution paid during a taxable year to an individual retirement account or for an individual retirement annuity to the extent that such contribution exceeds the amount allowable as a deduction under section 219 if—

(A) such distribution is received on or before the day prescribed by law (including extensions of time) for filing such individual's return for such taxable year,

(B) no deduction is allowed under section 219 with respect to such excess contribution, and

(C) such distribution is accompanied by the amount of net income attributable to such excess contribution.

In the case of such a distribution, for purposes of section 61, any net income described in subparagraph (C) shall be deemed to have been earned and receivable in the taxable year in which such excess contribution is made.

P.L. 100-647, §1011(b)(3):

Amended Code Sec. 408(d)(5) by striking out all that follows "section 219" in the last sentence thereof and inserting in lieu thereof "shall be computed without regard to section 219(g).". **Effective** as if included in the provision of

P.L. 99-514 to which it relates. Prior to amendment, the last sentence of Code Sec. 408(d)(5) read as follows:

For purposes of this paragraph, the amount allowable as a deduction under section 219 (after application of section 408(o)(2)(B)(ii)) shall be increased by the nondeductible limit under section 408(o)(2)(B).

P.L. 100-647, §1011(f)(5):

Amended Code Sec. 408(d) by adding at the end thereof new paragraph (7). **Effective** as if included in the provision of P.L. 99-514 to which it relates.

P.L. 100-647, §1011A(a)(2)(A):

Amended Code Sec. 408(d)(3)(A) by striking out the last sentence thereof. **Effective** for rollover contributions made in tax years beginning after 12-31-86. Prior to amendment, the last sentence of Code Sec. 408(d)(3)(A) read as follows:

Clause (ii) shall not apply during the 5-year period beginning on the date of the qualified total distribution referred to in such clause if the individual was treated as a 5-percent owner with respect to such distribution under section 402(a)(5)(F)(ii).

P.L. 100-647, §1018(t)(3)(D):

Amended Code Sec. 408(d)(3)(E) by striking out "subparagraph" and inserting in lieu thereof "paragraph". **Effective** as if included in the provision of P.L. 99-514 to which it relates.

• 1986, Tax Reform Act of 1986 (P.L. 99-514)

P.L. 99-514, §1102(b)(2):

Amended Code Sec. 408(d)(5) by adding at the end thereof a new sentence. **Effective** for contributions and distributions for tax years beginning after 12-31-86.

P.L. 99-514, §1102(c):

Amended Code Sec. 408(d)(1) and (2). **Effective** for contributions and distributions for tax years beginning after 12-31-86. Prior to amendment, Code Sec. 408(d)(1) and (2) read as follows:

(1) IN GENERAL.—Except as otherwise provided in this subsection, any amount paid or distributed out of an individual retirement account or under an individual retirement annuity shall be included in gross income by the payee or distributee, as the case may be, for the taxable year in which the payment of distribution is received. Notwithstanding any other provision of this title (including chapters 11 and 12), the basis of any person in such an account or annuity is zero.

(2) DISTRIBUTIONS OF ANNUITY CONTRACTS.—Paragraph (1) does not apply to any annuity contract which meets the requirements of paragraphs (1), (3), (4), and (5) of subsection (b) and which is distributed from an individual retirement account. Section 72 applies to any such annuity contract, and for purposes of section 72 the investment in such contract is zero.

P.L. 99-514, §1121(c)(2):

Amended Code Sec. 408(d)(3)(A)(ii) by striking out the third and fourth parenthetical phrases. [However, this change was already made by Act Sec. 1875(c)(8)(A)-(C).] **Effective** for years beginning after 12-31-86. Prior to amendment, Code Sec. 408(d)(3)(A)(ii) read as follows:

(ii) the entire amount received (including money and any other property) represents the entire amount in the account or the entire value of the annuity and no amount in the account and no part of the value of the annuity is attributable to any source other than a rollover contribution of a qualified total distribution (as defined in section 402(a)(5)(E)(i)) from an employee's trust described in section 401(a) which is exempt from tax under section 501(a) (other than a trust forming part of a plan under which the individual was an employee within the meaning of section 401(c)(1) at the time contributions were made on his behalf under the plan), or an annuity plan described in section 403(a) (other than a plan under which the individual was an employee within the meaning of section 401(c)(1) at the time contributions were made on his behalf under the plan) and any earnings on such sums and the entire amount thereof is paid into another such trust (for the benefit of such individual) or annuity plan not later than the 60th day on which he receives the payment or distribution; or

P.L. 99-514, §1121(d)(3) and (5), as amended by P.L. 100-647, §1011A(a)(3)-(4), provides:

(3) COLLECTIVE BARGAINING AGREEMENTS.—In the case of a plan maintained pursuant to 1 or more collective bargaining agreements between employee representatives and 1 or more employers ratified before March 1, 1986, the amendments made by this section shall not apply to distributions to individuals covered by such agreements in plan years beginning before the earlier of—

(A) the later of—

(i) the date on which the last of such collective bargaining agreements terminates (determined without regard to any extension thereof after February 28, 1986), or

(ii) January 1, 1989, or

(B) January 1, 1991.

* * *

(5) PLANS MAY INCORPORATE SECTION 401(a)(9) REQUIREMENTS BY REFERENCE.—Notwithstanding any other provision of law, except as provided in regulations prescribed by the Secretary of the Treasury or his delegate, a plan may incorporate by reference the requirements of section 401(a)(9) of the Internal Revenue Code of 1986.

P.L. 99-514, §1122(e)(2)(B):

Amended Code Sec. 408(d)(3) by adding at the end thereof the new subparagraph (F). **Effective** for amounts distributed after 12-31-86, in tax years ending after such date. For special rules, see Act Sec. 1122(h)(3)-(8) following Code Sec. 403.

P.L. 99-514, §1852(a)(5)(C):

Amended Code Sec. 408(d)(3) by adding at the end thereof new subparagraph (E). **Effective** as if included in the provision of P.L. 98-369 to which it relates.

P.L. 99-514, §1875(c)(6)(A):

Amended Code Sec. 408(d)(5) by striking out "$15,000" and inserting in lieu thereof "the dollar limitation in effect under section 415(c)(1)(A) for such taxable year". **Effective** as if included in the amendments made by P.L. 97-248, §238.

P.L. 99-514, §1875(c)(8)(A)-(C):

Amended Code Sec. 408(d)(3)(A) by striking out "(other than a trust forming part of a plan under which the individual was an employee within the meaning of section 401(c)(1) at the time contributions were made on his behalf under the plan)" after "section 501(a)" in clause (ii), by striking out "(other than a plan under which the individual was an employee within the meaning of section 401(c)(1) at the time contributions were made on his behalf under the plan)" after "section 403(a)" in clause (ii), and by adding at the end thereof a new sentence. **Effective** as if included in the provision of P.L. 98-369 to which it relates.

• 1984, Deficit Reduction Act of 1984 (P.L. 98-369)

P.L. 98-369, §491(d)(20):

Amended Code Sec. 408(d)(3)(A)(i) by striking out "or retirement bond". **Effective** for obligations issued after 12-31-83.

P.L. 98-369, §491(d)(21):

Amended Code Sec. 408(d)(3)(B) by striking out ", individual retirement annuity, or a retirement bond" and inserting in lieu thereof "or an individual retirement annuity". **Effective** for obligations issued after 12-31-83.

P.L. 98-369, §491(d)(22):

Amended Code Sec. 408(d)(3)(D)(ii), as redesignated, by striking out "bond,". **Effective** for obligations issued after 12-31-83.

P.L. 98-369, §491(d)(23):

Amended Code Sec. 408(d)(6) by striking out ", individual retirement annuity, or retirement bond" and inserting in lieu thereof "or an individual retirement annuity", and by striking out ", annuity, or bond" and inserting in lieu thereof "or annuity". **Effective** for obligations issued after 12-31-83.

P.L. 98-369, §522(d)(12):

Amended Code Sec. 408(d)(3)(A)(ii) by striking out "rollover contribution from an employee's trust" and inserting in lieu thereof "rollover contribution of a qualified total distribution (as defined in section 402(a)(5)(E)(i)) from an employee's trust". **Effective** for distributions made after 7-18-84, in tax years ending after such date.

P.L. 98-369, §713(g)(2):

Redesignated Code Sec. 408(d)(3)(C), as added by P.L. 97-248, Act Sec. 408(d)(3), as Code Sec. 408(d)(3)(D). **Effective** as if included in the provision of P.L. 97-248 to which it relates.

• 1983, Technical Corrections Act of 1982 (P.L. 97-448)

P.L. 97-448, §103(d)(3):

Amended paragraph (1) of section 312(f) of P.L. 97-34 by striking out "plans which include employees within the meaning of section 401(c)(1) with respect to".

• 1982, Tax Equity and Fiscal Responsibility Act of 1982 (P.L. 97-248)

P.L. 97-248, §243(b)(1)(A) (as amended by P.L. 98-369, §713(g)):

Amended Code Sec. 408(d)(3) by adding new subparagraph (C). **Effective** with respect to individuals dying after 12-31-83.

P.L. 97-248, §335(a)(1):

Amended Code Sec. 408(d)(3) by adding new subparagraph (C)[D]. **Effective** for distributions made after 12-31-82, in tax years ending after that date.

• 1981, Economic Recovery Tax Act of 1981 (P.L. 97-34)

P.L. 97-34, §311(g)(2):

Amended Code Sec. 408(d)(5)(A) by striking out "$1,750" and inserting "$2,250". **Effective** for tax years beginning after 12-31-81.

P.L. 97-34, §311(h)(2):

Amended Code Sec. 408(d)(4) and (5) by striking out "section 219 or 220" each place it appeared and inserting "section 219". **Effective** for tax years beginning after 12-31-81. The transitional rule provides that, for purposes of the 1954 Code, any amount allowed as a deduction under section 220 of the Code (as in effect before its repeal by P.L. 97-34) shall be treated as if it were allowed by Code Sec. 219.

P.L. 97-34, §312(c)(5):

Amended Code Sec. 408(d)(5) by striking out "$7,500" and inserting "$15,000". **Effective** for tax years beginning after 12-31-81.

• 1980, Technical Corrections Act of 1979 (P.L. 96-222)

P.L. 96-222, §101(a)(10)(C):

Amended Code Sec. 408(d)(5)(A) by adding the last sentence. **Effective** as set forth in P.L. 95-600, §157(c)(2), below.

P.L. 96-222, §101(a)(14)(E)(ii):

Amended Code Sec. 408(d)(5)(B) by deleting all that follows clause (i) and adding clause (ii) and another sentence. **Effective** as set forth in P.L. 95-600, §157(c)(2), below. Prior to amendment, all that followed clause (i) read as follows:

(ii) such information was erroneous, subparagraph (A) shall be applied by increasing the dollar limit set forth therein by that portion of the excess contribution which was attributable to such information.

• 1978, Revenue Act of 1978 (P.L. 95-600)

P.L. 95-600, §156(c)(1):

Amended Code Sec. 408(d)(3)(A) by striking out "or" at the end of clause (i), by substituting ";or" for the period at the end of clause (ii), and by adding clause (iii). **Effective** for distributions or transfers made after 12-31-77, in tax years beginning after such date [**effective** date changed by P.L. 96-222, §101(a)(13)(A).—CCH].

P.L. 95-600, §157(c)(1):

Redesignated Code Sec. 408(d)(5) as 408(d)(6) and added a new Code Sec. 408(d)(5). **Effective** as set forth in P.L. 95-600, §157(c)(2), below.

P.L. 95-600, §157(c)(2), provides:

(2) EFFECTIVE DATE.—

(A) IN GENERAL.T he amendments made by paragraph (1) shall apply to distributions in taxable years beginning after December 31, 1975.

(B) TRANSITIONAL RULE.—In the case of contributions for taxable years beginning before January 1, 1978, paragraph (5) of section 408(d) of the Internal Revenue Code of 1954 shall be applied as if such paragraph did not contain any dollar limitation.

P.L. 95-600, §157(g)(3):

Added a new last sentence to Code Sec. 408(d)(3)(B). **Effective** for lump-sum distributions completed after 12-31-78, in tax years ending after such date.

P.L. 95-600, §157(h)(2):

Amended Code Sec. 408(d)(3)(B) by striking out "3-year period" and inserting in lieu thereof "1-year period". **Effective** for payments made in tax years beginning after 12-31-77.

• 1976, Tax Reform Act of 1976 (P.L. 94-455)

P.L. 94-455, §1501(b), as amended by P.L. 95-600, §703(c)(4):

Amended Code Sec. 408(d)(4) by inserting "or 220" after "219" each place it appeared and by inserting a new last sentence. **Effective** for tax years beginning after 12-31-76. Prior to amendment, the last sentence of Code Sec. 408(d)(4) read:

Any net income described in subparagraph (C) shall be included in the gross income of the individual for the taxable year in which received.

[Sec. 408(e)]

(e) TAX TREATMENT OF ACCOUNTS AND ANNUITIES.—

(1) EXEMPTION FROM TAX.—Any individual retirement account is exempt from taxation under this subtitle unless such account has ceased to be an individual retirement account by reason of paragraph (2) or (3). Notwithstanding the preceding sentence, any such account is subject to the taxes imposed by section 511 (relating to imposition of tax on unrelated business income of charitable, etc. organizations).

(2) LOSS OF EXEMPTION OF ACCOUNT WHERE EMPLOYEE ENGAGES IN PROHIBITED TRANSACTION.—

(A) IN GENERAL.—If, during any taxable year of the individual for whose benefit any individual retirement account is established, that individual or his beneficiary engages in any transaction prohibited by section 4975 with respect to such account, such account ceases to be an individual retirement account as of the first day of such taxable year. For purposes of this paragraph—

(i) the individual for whose benefit any account was established is treated as the creator of such account, and

(ii) the separate account for any individual within an individual retirement account maintained by an employer or association of employees is treated as a separate individual retirement account.

(B) ACCOUNT TREATED AS DISTRIBUTING ALL ITS ASSETS.—In any case in which any account ceases to be an individual retirement account by reason of subparagraph (A) as of the first day of any taxable year, paragraph (1) of subsection (d) applies as if there were a distribution on such first day in an amount equal to the fair market value (on such first day) of all assets in the account (on such first day).

(3) EFFECT OF BORROWING ON ANNUITY CONTRACT.—If during any taxable year the owner of an individual retirement annuity borrows any money under or by use of such contract, the contract ceases to be an individual retirement annuity as of the first day of such taxable year. Such owner shall include in gross income for such year an amount equal to the fair market value of such contract as of such first day.

(4) EFFECT OF PLEDGING ACCOUNT AS SECURITY.—If, during any taxable year of the individual for whose benefit an individual retirement account is established, that individual uses the account or any portion thereof as security for a loan, the portion so used is treated as distributed to that individual.

(5) PURCHASE OF ENDOWMENT CONTRACT BY INDIVIDUAL RETIREMENT ACCOUNT.—If the assets of an individual retirement account or any part of such assets are used to purchase an endowment contract for the benefit of the individual for whose benefit the account is established—

(A) to the extent that the amount of the assets involved in the purchase are not attributable to the purchase of life insurance, the purchase is treated as a rollover contribution described in subsection (d)(3), and

(B) to the extent that the amount of the assets involved in the purchase are attributable to the purchase of life, health, accident, or other insurance such amounts are treated as distributed to that individual (but the provisions of subsection (f) do not apply).

(6) COMMINGLING INDIVIDUAL RETIREMENT ACCOUNT AMOUNTS IN CERTAIN COMMON TRUST FUNDS AND COMMON INVESTMENT FUNDS.—Any common trust fund or common investment fund of individual retirement account assets which is exempt from taxation under this subtitle does not cease to be exempt on account of the participation or inclusion of assets of a trust exempt from taxation under section 501(a) which is described in section 401(a).

[Sec. 408(f)—Repealed]

Amendments

• 1986, Tax Reform Act of 1986 (P.L. 99-514)

P.L. 99-514, §1123(d)(2);

Repealed Code Sec. 408(f). **Effective** for tax years beginning after 12-31-86. However, for an exception, see Act Sec. 1123(e)(3)-(4), below. Prior to repeal, Code Sec. 408(f) read follows:

(f) ADDITIONAL TAX ON CERTAIN AMOUNTS INCLUDED IN GROSS INCOME BEFORE AGE 59½.—

(1) EARLY DISTRIBUTIONS FROM AN INDIVIDUAL RETIREMENT ACCOUNT, ETC.—If a distribution from an individual retirement account or under an individual retirement annuity to the individual for whose benefit such account or annuity was established is made before such individual attains age 59½ his tax under this chapter for the taxable year in which such distribution is received shall be increased by an amount equal to 10 percent of the amount of the distribution which is includible in his gross income for such taxable year.

(2) DISQUALIFICATION CASES.—If an amount is includible in gross income for a taxable year under subsection (e) and the taxpayer has not attained age 59½ before the beginning of such taxable year, his tax under this chapter for such taxable year shall be increased by an amount equal to 10 percent of such amount so required to be included in his gross income.

(3) DISABILITY CASES.—Paragraphs (1) and (2) do not apply if the amount paid or distributed, or the disqualification of the account or annuity under subsection (e), is attributable to the taxpayer becoming disabled within the meaning of section 72(m)(7).

P.L. 99-514, §1123(e)(3)-(4), provides:

(3) EXCEPTION WHERE DISTRIBUTION COMMENCES.—The amendments made by this section shall not apply to distributions to any employee from a plan maintained by any employer if—

(A) as of March 1, 1986, the employee separated from service with the employer,

(B) as of March 1, 1986, the accrued benefit of the employee was in pay status pursuant to a written election providing a specific schedule for the distribution of the entire accrued benefit of the employee, and

(C) such distribution is made pursuant to such written election.

(4) TRANSITION RULE.—The amendments made by this section shall not apply with respect to any benefits with respect to which a designation is in effect under section 242(b)(2) of the Tax Equity and Fiscal Responsibility Act of 1982.

[Sec. 408(g)]

(g) COMMUNITY PROPERTY LAWS.—This section shall be applied without regard to any community property laws.

[Sec. 408(h)]

(h) CUSTODIAL ACCOUNTS.—For purposes of this section, a custodial account shall be treated as a trust if the assets of such account are held by a bank (as defined in subsection (n)) or another person who demonstrates, to the satisfaction of the Secretary, that the manner in which he will administer the account will be consistent with the requirements of this section, and if the custodial account would, except for the fact that it is not a trust, constitute an individual retirement account described in subsection (a). For purposes of this title, in the case of a custodial account treated as a trust by reason of the preceding sentence, the custodian of such account shall be treated as the trustee thereof.

Amendments

• 1984, Deficit Reduction Act of 1984 (P.L. 98-369)

P.L. 98-369, §713(c)(2)(B):

Amended Code Sec. 408(h) by striking out "(as defined in section 401(d)(1))" and inserting in lieu thereof "(as defined in subsection (n))". **Effective** as if included in the provision of P.L. 97-248 to which it relates.

• 1976, Tax Reform Act of 1976 (P.L. 94-455)

P.L. 94-455, §1906(b)(13)(A):

Amended 1954 Code by substituting "Secretary" for "Secretary or his delegate" each place it appeared. **Effective** 2-1-77.

[Sec. 408(i)]

(i) REPORTS.—The trustee of an individual retirement account and the issuer of an endowment contract described in subsection (b) or an individual retirement annuity shall make such reports regarding such account, contract, or annuity to the Secretary and to the individuals for whom the account, contract, or annuity is, or is to be, maintained with respect to contributions (and the years to which they relate), distributions aggregating $10 or more in any calendar year, and such other matters as the Secretary may require. The reports required by this subsection—

(1) shall be filed at such time and in such manner as the Secretary prescribes, and

(2) shall be furnished to individuals—

(A) not later than January 31 of the calendar year following the calendar year to which such reports relate, and

(B) in such manner as the Secretary prescribes.

In the case of a simple retirement account under subsection (p), only one report under this subsection shall be required to be submitted each calendar year to the Secretary (at the time provided under paragraph (2)) but, in addition to the report under this subsection, there shall be furnished, within 31 days after each calendar year, to the individual on whose behalf the account is maintained a statement with respect to the account balance as of the close of, and the account activity during, such calendar year.

Amendments

• 1997, Taxpayer Relief Act of 1997 (P.L. 105-34)

P.L. 105-34, §302(d)(1)-(2):

Amended Code Sec. 408(i)(1)-(2) by striking "under regulations" following "as the Secretary may require", and by striking "in such regulations" each place it appears. **Effective** for tax years beginning after 12-31-97. Prior to amendment, Code. Sec. 408(i)(1)-(2) read as follows

(i) REPORTS.—The trustee of an individual retirement account and the issuer of an endowment contract described in subsection (b) or an individual retirement annuity shall make such reports regarding such account, contract, or annuity to the Secretary and to the individuals for whom the account, contract, or annuity is, or is to be, maintained with respect to contributions (and the years to which they relate), distributions aggregating $10 or more in any calendar year, and such other matters as the Secretary may require under regulations. The reports required by this subsection—

(1) shall be filed at such time and in such manner as the Secretary prescribes in such regulations, and

(2) shall be furnished to individuals—

(A) not later than January 31 of the calendar year following the calendar year to which such reports relate, and

(B) in such manner as the Secretary prescribes in such regulations.

P.L. 105-34, §1601(d)(1)(A):

Amended Code Sec. 408(i) by striking "30 days" in the last sentence and inserting "31 days". **Effective** as if included in the provision of P.L. 104-188 to which it relates [**effective** for tax years beginning after 12-31-96.—CCH].

• 1996, Small Business Job Protection Act of 1996 (P.L. 104-188)

P.L. 104-188, §1421(b)(6):

Amended Code Sec. 408(i) by adding at the end a new flush sentence. **Effective** for tax years beginning after 12-31-96.

P.L. 104-188, §1455(b)(1):

Amended Code Sec. 408(i) by inserting "aggregating $10 or more in any calendar year" after "distributions". **Effective** for returns, reports, and other statements the due date for which (determined without regard to extensions) is after 12-31-96.

• 1986, Tax Reform Act of 1986 (P.L. 99-514)

P.L. 99-514, §1102(e)(2):

Amended the last sentence of Code Sec. 408(i). **Effective** for contributions and distributions for tax years beginning after 12-31-86. Prior to amendment, the last sentence of Code Sec. 408(i) read as follows:

The reports required by this subsection shall be filed at such time and in such manner and furnished to such individuals at such time and in such manner as may be required by those regulations.

• 1984, Deficit Reduction Act of 1984 (P.L. 98-369)

P.L. 98-369, §147(a):

Amended Code Sec. 408(i) by inserting "(and the years to which they relate)" after "contributions". **Effective** for contributions made after 12-31-84.

• 1976, Tax Reform Act of 1976 (P.L. 94-455)

P.L. 94-455, §1906(b)(13)(A):

Amended 1954 Code by substituting "Secretary" for "Secretary or his delegate" each place it appeared. **Effective** 2-1-77.

[Sec. 408(j)]

(j) INCREASE IN MAXIMUM LIMITATIONS FOR SIMPLIFIED EMPLOYEE PENSIONS.—In the case of any simplified employee pension, subsections (a)(1) and (b)(2) of this section shall be applied by increasing the amounts contained therein by the amount of the limitation in effect under section 415(c)(1)(A).

Amendments

• 2006, Pension Protection Act of 2006 (P.L. 109-280)

P.L. 109-280, §811, provides:

SEC. 811. PENSIONS AND INDIVIDUAL RETIREMENT ARRANGEMENT PROVISIONS OF ECONOMIC GROWTH AND TAX RELIEF RECONCILIATION ACT OF 2001 MADE PERMANENT.

Title IX of the Economic Growth and Tax Relief Reconciliation Act of 2001 [P.L. 107-16] shall not apply to the provisions of, and amendments made by, subtitles A through F of title VI [§§601-666]of such Act (relating to pension and individual retirement arrangement provisions).

• 2001, Economic Growth and Tax Relief Reconciliation Act of 2001 (P.L. 107-16)

P.L. 107-16, §601(b)(4):

Amended Code Sec. 408(j) by striking "$2,000" after "by increasing the". **Effective** for tax years beginning after 12-31-2001.

P.L. 107-16, §901(a)-(b), provides [but see P.L. 109-280, §811, above]:

SEC. 901. SUNSET OF PROVISIONS OF ACT.

(a) IN GENERAL.—All provisions of, and amendments made by, this Act shall not apply—

(1) to taxable, plan, or limitation years beginning after December 31, 2010, or

(2) in the case of title V, to estates of decedents dying, gifts made, or generation skipping transfers, after December 31, 2010.

(b) APPLICATION OF CERTAIN LAWS.—The Internal Revenue Code of 1986 and the Employee Retirement Income Security Act of 1974 shall be applied and administered to years, estates, gifts, and transfers described in subsection (a) as if the provisions and amendments described in subsection (a) had never been enacted.

• 1983, Technical Corrections Act of 1982 (P.L. 97-448)

P.L. 97-448, §103(d)(1)(B):

Amended Code Sec. 408(j) by striking out "$15,000" and inserting "$17,000". **Effective** as if included in the provision of P.L. 97-34 to which it relates.

P.L. 97-448, §103(d)(3):

Amended paragraph (1) of section 312(f) of P.L. 97-34 (relating to **effective** date) by striking out "plans which include employees within the meaning of section 401(c)(1) with respect to".

• 1982, Tax Equity and Fiscal Responsibility Act of 1982 (P.L. 97-248)

P.L. 97-248, §238(d)(3):

Amended Code Sec. 408(j). **Effective** for years beginning after 12-31-83. Prior to amendment, Code Sec. 408(j) read as follows:

(j) INCREASE IN MAXIMUM LIMITATIONS FOR SIMPLIFIED EMPLOYEE PENSIONS.—In the case of a simplified employee pension, this section shall be applied by substituting "$17,000" for "$2,000" in the following provisions:

(1) paragraph (1) of subsection (a), and

(2) paragraph (2) of subsection (b).

• 1981, Economic Recovery Tax Act of 1981 (P.L. 97-34)

P.L. 97-34, §311(g)(1)(C):

Amended Code Sec. 408(j) by striking out "$1,500" and inserting "$2,000". **Effective** for tax years beginning after 12-31-81.

P.L. 97-34, §312(c)(5):

Amended Code Sec. 408(j) by striking out "$7,500" and inserting "$15,000". **Effective** for tax years beginning after 12-31-81.

• 1980, Technical Corrections Act of 1979 (P.L. 96-222)

P.L. 96-222, §101(a)(10)(J)(i):

Amended Code Sec. 408(j) by adding "and" to paragraph (1), by deleting ", and" from paragraph (2), and by deleting paragraph (3). **Effective** for tax years beginning after 12-31-78. Prior to deletion, paragraph (3) of Code Sec. 408(j) read as follows:

(3) paragraph (5) of subsection (b).

• 1978, Revenue Act of 1978 (P.L. 95-600)

P.L. 95-600, §152(a):

Redesignated Code Sec. 408(j) as 408(m) and added a new Code Sec. 408(j). **Effective** for tax years beginning after 12-31-78.

[Sec. 408(k)]

(k) SIMPLIFIED EMPLOYEE PENSION DEFINED.—

(1) IN GENERAL.—For purposes of this title, the term "simplified employee pension" means an individual retirement account or individual retirement annuity—

(A) with respect to which the requirements of paragraphs (2), (3), (4), and (5) of this subsection are met, and

(B) if such account or annuity is part of a top-heavy plan (as defined in section 416), with respect to which the requirements of section 416(c)(2) are met.

(2) PARTICIPATION REQUIREMENTS.—This paragraph is satisfied with respect to a simplified employee pension for a year only if for such year the employer contributes to the simplified employee pension of each employee who—

(A) has attained age 21,

(B) has performed service for the employer during at least 3 of the immediately preceding 5 years, and

(C) received at least $450 in compensation (within the meaning of section 414(q)(4)) from the employer for the year.

For purposes of this paragraph, there shall be excluded from consideration employees described in subparagraph (A) or (C) of section 410(b)(3). For purposes of any arrangement described in subsection (k)(6), any employee who is eligible to have employer contributions made on the employee's behalf under such arrangement shall be treated as if such a contribution was made.

(3) CONTRIBUTIONS MAY NOT DISCRIMINATE IN FAVOR OF THE HIGHLY COMPENSATED, ETC.—

(A) IN GENERAL.—The requirements of this paragraph are met with respect to a simplified employee pension for a year if for such year the contributions made by the employer to simplified employee pensions for his employees do not discriminate in favor of any highly compensated employee (within the meaning of section 414(q)).

(B) SPECIAL RULES.—For purposes of subparagraph (A), there shall be excluded from consideration employees described in subparagraph (A) or (C) of section 410(b)(3).

(C) CONTRIBUTIONS MUST BEAR UNIFORM RELATIONSHIP TO TOTAL COMPENSATION.—For purposes of subparagraph (A), and except as provided in subparagraph (D), employer contributions, to simplified employee pensions (other than contributions under an arrangement described in paragraph (6)) shall be considered discriminatory unless contributions thereto bear a uniform relationship to the compensation (not in excess of the first $200,000) of each employee maintaining a simplified employee pension.

(D) PERMITTED DISPARITY.—For purposes of subparagraph (C), the rules of section 401(l)(2) shall apply to contributions to simplified employee pensions (other than contributions under an arrangement described in paragraph (6)).

(4) WITHDRAWALS MUST BE PERMITTED.—A simplified employee pension meets the requirements of this paragraph only if—

(A) employer contributions thereto are not conditioned on the retention in such pension of any portion of the amount contributed, and

(B) there is no prohibition imposed by the employer on withdrawals from the simplified employee pension.

(5) CONTRIBUTIONS MUST BE MADE UNDER WRITTEN ALLOCATION FORMULA.—The requirements of this paragraph are met with respect to a simplified employee pension only if employer contributions to such pension are determined under a definite written allocation formula which specifies—

(A) the requirements which an employee must satisfy to share in an allocation, and

(B) the manner in which the amount allocated is computed.

(6) EMPLOYEE MAY ELECT SALARY REDUCTION ARRANGEMENT.—

(A) ARRANGEMENTS WHICH QUALIFY.—

(i) IN GENERAL.—A simplified employee pension shall not fail to meet the requirements of this subsection for a year merely because, under the terms of the pension, an employee may elect to have the employer make payments—

(I) as elective employer contributions to the simplified employee pension on behalf of the employee, or

(II) to the employee directly in cash.

(ii) 50 PERCENT OF ELIGIBLE EMPLOYEES MUST ELECT.—Clause (i) shall not apply to a simplified employee pension unless an election described in clause (i)(I) is made or is in effect with respect to not less than 50 percent of the employees of the employer eligible to participate.

(iii) REQUIREMENTS RELATING TO DEFERRAL PERCENTAGE.—Clause (i) shall not apply to a simplified employee pension for any year unless the deferral percentage for such year of each highly compensated employee eligible to participate is not more than the product of—

(I) the average of the deferral percentages for such year of all employees (other than highly compensated employees) eligible to participate, multiplied by

(II) 1.25.

(iv) LIMITATIONS ON ELECTIVE DEFERRALS.—Clause (i) shall not apply to a simplified employee pension unless the requirements of section 401(a)(30) are met.

(B) EXCEPTION WHERE MORE THAN 25 EMPLOYEES.—This paragraph shall not apply with respect to any year in the case of a simplified employee pension maintained by an employer with more than 25 employees who were eligible to participate (or would have been required to be eligible to participate if a pension was maintained) at any time during the preceding year.

(C) DISTRIBUTIONS OF EXCESS CONTRIBUTIONS.—

(i) IN GENERAL.—Rules similar to the rules of section 401(k)(8) shall apply to any excess contribution under this paragraph. Any excess contribution under a simplified employee pension shall be treated as an excess contribution for purposes of section 4979.

(ii) EXCESS CONTRIBUTION.—For purposes of clause (i), the term "excess contributions" means, with respect to a highly compensated employee, the excess of elective employer contributions under this paragraph over the maximum amount of such contributions allowable under subparagraph (A)(iii).

(D) DEFERRAL PERCENTAGE.—For purposes of this paragraph, the deferral percentage for an employee for a year shall be the ratio of—

(i) the amount of elective employer contributions actually paid over to the simplified employee pension on behalf of the employee for the year, to

(ii) the employee's compensation (not in excess of the first $200,000) for the year.

(E) EXCEPTION FOR STATE AND LOCAL AND TAX-EXEMPT PENSIONS.—This paragraph shall not apply to a simplified employee pension maintained by—

(i) a State or local government or political subdivision thereof, or any agency or instrumentality thereof, or

(ii) an organization exempt from tax under this title.

(F) EXCEPTION WHERE PENSION DOES NOT MEET REQUIREMENTS NECESSARY TO INSURE DISTRIBUTION OF EXCESS CONTRIBUTIONS.—This paragraph shall not apply with respect to any year for which the simplified employee pension does not meet such requirements as the Secretary may prescribe as are necessary to insure that excess contributions are distributed in accordance with subparagraph (C), including—

(i) reporting requirements, and

(ii) requirements which, notwithstanding paragraph (4), provide that contributions (and any income allocable thereto) may not be withdrawn from a simplified employee pension until a determination has been made that the requirements of subparagraph (A)(iii) have been met with respect to such contributions.

(G) HIGHLY COMPENSATED EMPLOYEE.—For purposes of this paragraph, the term "highly compensated employee" has the meaning given such term by section 414(q).

(H) TERMINATION.—This paragraph shall not apply to years beginning after December 31, 1996. The preceding sentence shall not apply to a simplified employee pension of an employer if the terms of simplified employee pensions of such employer, as in effect on December 31, 1996, provide that an employee may make the election described in subparagraph (A).

(7) DEFINITIONS.—For purposes of this subsection and subsection (l)—

(A) EMPLOYEE, EMPLOYER, OR OWNER-EMPLOYEE.—The terms "employee", "employer", and "owner-employee" shall have the respective meanings given such terms by section 401(c).

(B) COMPENSATION.—Except as provided in paragraph (2)(C), the term "compensation" has the meaning given such term by section 414(s).

(C) YEAR.—The term "year" means—

(i) the calendar year, or

(ii) if the employer elects, subject to such terms and conditions as the Secretary may prescribe, to maintain the simplified employee pension on the basis of the employer's taxable year.

(8) COST-OF-LIVING ADJUSTMENT.—The Secretary shall adjust the $450 amount in paragraph (2)(C) at the same time and in the same manner as under section 415(d) and shall adjust the $200,000 amount in paragraphs (3)(C) and (6)(D)(ii) at the same time, and by the same amount, as any adjustment under section 401(a)(17)(B); except that any increase in the $450 amount which is not a multiple of $50 shall be rounded to the next lowest multiple of $50.

(9) CROSS REFERENCE.—

For excise tax on certain excess contributions, see section 4979.

Amendments

• 2006, Pension Protection Act of 2006 (P.L. 109-280)

P.L. 109-280, §811, provides:

SEC. 811. PENSIONS AND INDIVIDUAL RETIREMENT ARRANGEMENT PROVISIONS OF ECONOMIC GROWTH AND TAX RELIEF RECONCILIATION ACT OF 2001 MADE PERMANENT.

Title IX of the Economic Growth and Tax Relief Reconciliation Act of 2001 [P.L. 107-16] shall not apply to the provisions of, and amendments made by, subtitles A through F of title VI [§§601-666]of such Act (relating to pension and individual retirement arrangement provisions).

• 2002, Job Creation and Worker Assistance Act of 2002 (P.L. 107-147)

P.L. 107-147, §411(j)(1)(A)-(B):

Amended Code Sec. 408(k) by striking "$300" and inserting "$450" in paragraph (2)(C), and by striking "$300" both places it appears and inserting "$450" in paragraph (8). **Effective** as if included in the provision of P.L. 107-16 to which it relates [**effective** for years beginning after 12-31-2001.—CCH].

• 2001, Economic Growth and Tax Relief Reconciliation Act of 2001 (P.L. 107-16)

P.L. 107-16, §611(c)(1):

Amended Code Sec. 408(k) by striking "$150,000" each place it appears and inserting "$200,000". **Effective** for years beginning after 12-31-2001. For a special rule, see Act Sec. 611(i)(3), below.

P.L. 107-16, §611(i)(3) (as added by P.L. 107-147, §411(j)(3)), provides:

(3) SPECIAL RULE.—In the case of plan that, on June 7, 2001, incorporated by reference the limitation of section 415(b)(1)(A) of the Internal Revenue Code of 1986, section 411(d)(6) of such Code and section 204(g)(1) of the Employee Retirement Income Security Act of 1974 do not apply to a plan amendment that—

(A) is adopted on or before June 30, 2002,

(B) reduces benefits to the level that would have applied without regard to the amendments made by subsection (a) of this section, and

(C) is effective no earlier than the years described in paragraph (2).

P.L. 107-16, §901(a)-(b), provides [but see P.L. 109-280, §811, above]:

SEC. 901. SUNSET OF PROVISIONS OF ACT.

(a) IN GENERAL.—All provisions of, and amendments made by, this Act shall not apply—

(1) to taxable, plan, or limitation years beginning after December 31, 2010, or

(2) in the case of title V, to estates of decedents dying, gifts made, or generation skipping transfers, after December 31, 2010.

(b) APPLICATION OF CERTAIN LAWS.—The Internal Revenue Code of 1986 and the Employee Retirement Income Security Act of 1974 shall be applied and administered to years, estates, gifts, and transfers described in subsection (a) as if the provisions and amendments described in subsection (a) had never been enacted.

• 1997, Taxpayer Relief Act of 1997 (P.L. 105-34)

P.L. 105-34, §1601(d)(1)(B):

Amended Code Sec. 408(k)(6)(H) by striking "if the terms of such pension" and inserting "of an employer if the terms of simplified employee pensions of such employer". **Effective** as if included in the provision of P.L. 104-188 to which it relates [**effective** for tax years beginning after 12-31-96.—CCH].

• 1996, Small Business Job Protection Act of 1996 (P.L. 104-188)

P.L. 104-188, §1421(c):

Amended Code Sec. 408(k)(6) by adding at the end a new subparagraph (H). **Effective** for tax years beginning after 12-31-96.

P.L. 104-188, §1431(c)(1)(B):

Amended Code Sec. 408(k)(2)(C) by striking "section 414(q)(7)" and inserting "section 414(q)(4)". **Effective** for years beginning after 12-31-96, except that in determining whether an employee is a highly compensated employee for years beginning in 1997, this amendment shall be treated as having been in effect for years beginning in 1996.

• 1994, Uruguay Round Agreement Act (P.L. 103-465)

P.L. 103-465, §732(d):

Amended Code Sec. 408(k)(8) by inserting before the period "; except that any increase in the $300 amount which is not a multiple of $50 shall be rounded to the next lowest multiple of $50". **Effective** for years beginning after 12-31-94. For a special rule, see Act Sec. 732(e)(2), below.

P.L. 103-465, §732(e)(2), provides:

(2) ROUNDING NOT TO RESULT IN DECREASES.—The amendments made by this section providing for the rounding of indexed amounts shall not apply to any year to the extent the rounding would require the indexed amount to be reduced below the amount in effect for years beginning in 1994.

• 1993, Omnibus Budget Reconciliation Act of 1993 (P.L. 103-66)

P.L. 103-66, §13212(b)(1):

Amended Code Sec. 408(k)(3)(C) and (6)(D)(ii) by striking "$200,000" and inserting "$150,000". **Effective**, generally, for benefits accruing in plan years beginning after 12-31-93. However, for special rules see Act Sec. 13212(d)(2)-(3) below.

P.L. 103-66, §13212(b)(2):

Amended Code Sec. 408(k)(8). **Effective**, generally, for benefits accruing in plan years beginning after 12-31-93. However, for special rules see Act Sec. 13212(d)(2)-(3) below. Prior to amendment, Code Sec. 408(k)(8) read as follows:

(8) COST-OF-LIVING ADJUSTMENT.—The Secretary shall adjust the $300 amount in paragraph (2)(C) and the $200,000 amount in paragraphs (3)(C) and (6)(D)(ii) at the same time and in the same manner as under section 415(d), except that in the case of years beginning after 1988, the $200,000 amount (as so adjusted) shall not exceed the amount in effect under section 401(a)(17).

P.L. 103-66, §13212(d)(2)-(3), provides:

(2) COLLECTIVELY BARGAINED PLANS.—In the case of a plan maintained pursuant to 1 or more collective bargaining agreements between employee representatives and 1 or more employers ratified before the date of the enactment of this Act, the amendments made by this section shall not apply to contributions or benefits pursuant to such agreements for plan years beginning before the earlier of—

(A) the latest of—

(i) January 1, 1994,

(ii) the date on which the last of such collective bargaining agreements terminates (without regard to any extension, amendment, or modification of such agreements on or after such date of enactment), or

(iii) in the case of a plan maintained pursuant to collective bargaining under the Railway Labor Act, the date of execution of an extension or replacement of the last of such collective bargaining agreements in effect on such date of enactment, or

(B) January 1, 1997.

(3) TRANSITION RULE FOR STATE AND LOCAL PLANS.—

(A) IN GENERAL.—In the case of an eligible participant in a governmental plan (within the meaning of section 414(d) of the Internal Revenue Code of 1986), the dollar limitation under section 401(a)(17) of such Code shall not apply to the extent the amount of compensation which is allowed to be taken into account under the plan would be reduced below the amount which was allowed to be taken into account under the plan as in effect on July 1, 1993.

(B) ELIGIBLE PARTICIPANT.—For purposes of subparagraph (A), an eligible participant is an individual who first became a participant in the plan during a plan year beginning before the 1st plan year beginning after the earlier of—

(i) the plan year in which the plan is amended to reflect the amendments made by this section, or

(ii) December 31, 1995.

(C) PLAN MUST BE AMENDED TO INCORPORATE LIMITS.—This paragraph shall not apply to any eligible participant of a plan unless the plan is amended so that the plan incorporates by reference the dollar limitation under section 401(a)(17) of the Internal Revenue Code of 1986, effective with respect to noneligible participants for plan years beginning after December 31, 1995 (or earlier if the plan amendment so provides).

• 1988, Technical and Miscellaneous Revenue Act of 1988 (P.L. 100-647)

P.L. 100-647, §1011(c)(7)(C):

Amended Code Sec. 408(k)(6)(A) by adding at the end thereof new clause (iv). For the **effective** date, see Act Sec. 1011(c)(7)(E), below.

P.L. 100-647, §1011(c)(7)(E), provides:

(E)(i) Except as provided in clause (ii), the amendments made by this paragraph shall apply to plan years beginning after December 31, 1987.

(ii) In the case of a plan described in section 1105(c)(2) of the Reform Act, the amendments made by this paragraph shall not apply to contributions made pursuant to an agreement described in such section for plan years beginning before the earlier of—

(I) the later of January 1, 1988, or the date on which the last of such agreements terminates (determined without regard to any extension thereof after February 28, 1986), or

(II) January 1, 1989.

P.L. 100-647, §1011(f)(1):

Amended Code Sec. 408(k)(6)(A). **Effective** as if included in the provision of P.L. 99-514 to which it relates. Prior to amendment, Code Sec. 408(k)(6)(A) read as follows:

(A) IN GENERAL.—A simplified employee pension shall not fail to meet the requirements of this subsection for a year merely because, under the terms of the pension—

(i) an employee may elect to have the employer make payments—

(I) as elective employer contributions to the simplified employee pension on behalf of the employee, or

(II) to the employee directly in cash,

(ii) an election described in clause (i)(I) is made or is in effect with respect to not less than 50 percent of the employees of the employer, and

(iii) the deferral percentage for such year of each highly compensated employee eligible to participate is not more than the product derived by multiplying the average of the deferral percentages for such year of all employees (other than highly compensated employees) eligible to participate by 1.25.

P.L. 100-647, §1011(f)(2):

Amended Code Sec. 408(k)(6)(B) by inserting "who were eligible to participate (or would have been required to be eligible to participate if a pension was maintained)" after "25 employees". **Effective** as if included in the provision of P.L. 99-514 to which it relates.

P.L. 100-647, §1011(f)(3)(A):

Amended Code Sec. 408(k)(6)(D)(ii) by striking out "(within the meaning of section 414(s))" and inserting in lieu thereof "(not in excess of the first $200,000)". **Effective** as if included in the provision of P.L. 99-514 to which it relates.

P.L. 100-647, §1011(f)(3)(B):

Amended Code Sec. 408(k)(7)(B). **Effective** as if included in the provision of P.L. 99-514 to which it relates. Prior to amendment, Code Sec. 408(k)(7)(B) read as follows:

(B) COMPENSATION.—The term "compensation" means, in the case of an employee within the meaning of section 401(c)(1), earned income within the meaning of section 401(c)(2).

P.L. 100-647, §1011(f)(3)(C):

Amended Code Sec. 408(k)(3)(C) by striking out "total" before "compensation". **Effective** as if included in the provision of P.L. 99-514 to which it relates.

P.L. 100-647, §1011(f)(3)(D):

Amended Code Sec. 408(k)(8) by striking out "paragraph (3)(c)" and inserting in lieu thereof "paragraphs (3)(C) and (6)(D)(ii)". **Effective** as if included in the provision of P.L. 99-514 to which it relates.

P.L. 100-647, §1011(f)(4):

Amended Code Sec. 408(k)(6) by redesignating subparagraph (F) as subparagraph (G) and by inserting after subparagraph (E) new subparagraph (F). **Effective** as if included in the provision of P.L. 99-514 to which it relates.

P.L. 100-647, §1011(f)(10):

Amended Code Sec. 408(k)(8) by inserting ", except that in the case of years beginning after 1988, the $200,000 amount (as so adjusted) shall not exceed the amount in effect under section 401(a)(17)" after "section 415(d)". **Effective** as if included in the provision of P.L. 99-514 to which it relates.

P.L. 100-647, §1011(i)(5):

Amended Code Sec. 408(k)(3)(B). **Effective** as if included in the provision of P.L. 99-514 to which it relates. Prior to amendment, Code Sec. 408(k)(3)(B) read as follows:

(B) SPECIAL RULES.—For purposes of subparagraph (A)—

(i) there shall be excluded from consideration employees described in subparagraph (A) or (C) of section 410(b)(3), and

(ii) an individual shall be considered a shareholder if he owns (with the application of section 318) more than 10 percent of the value of the stock of the employer.

• 1986, Tax Reform Act of 1986 (P.L. 99-514)

P.L. 99-514, §1108(a):

Amended Code Sec. 408(k) by inserting after paragraph (5) new paragraph (6). **Effective** for years beginning after 12-31-86. For a special rule, see Act Sec. 1108(h)(2), below.

P.L. 99-514, §1108(d):

Amended Code Sec. 408(k)(2). **Effective** for years beginning after 12-31-86. For a special rule, see Act Sec. 1108(h)(2), below. Prior to amendment, Code Sec. 408(k)(2) read as follows:

(2) PARTICIPATION REQUIREMENTS.—This paragraph is satisfied with respect to a simplified employee pension for a calendar year only if for such year the employer contributes to the simplified employee pension of each employee who—

(A) has attained age 21, and

(B) has performed service for the employer during at least 3 of the immediately preceding 5 calendar years.

For purposes of this paragraph, there shall be excluded from consideration employees described in subparagraph (A) or (C) of section 410(b)(3).

P.L. 99-514, §1108(e):

Amended Code Sec. 408(k) by adding at the end thereof new paragraph (8). **Effective** for years beginning after 12-31-86. For a special rule, see Act Sec. 1108(h)(2), below.

P.L. 99-514, §1108(f):

Amended Code Sec. 408(k)(7) by adding at the end thereof new subparagraph (C). **Effective** for years beginning after 12-31-86. For a special rule, see Act Sec. 1108(h)(2), below.

P.L. 99-514, §1108(g)(1)(A)-(C):

Amended Code Sec. 408(k)(3) by striking out all that follows "in favor of" in subparagraph (A) and inserting in lieu thereof "any highly compensated employee (within the meaning of section 414(q)).", by inserting "and except as provided in subparagraph (D)," after "subparagraph (A)," in subparagraph (C), by inserting "(other than contributions under an arrangement described in paragraph (6))" after "employer contributions to simplified employee pensions" in subparagraph (C), by striking out the last sentence of subparagraph (C), and by striking out subparagraphs (D) and (E) and inserting in lieu thereof new subparagraph (D). **Effective** for years beginning after 12-31-86. For a special rule, see Act Sec. 1108(h)(2), below. Prior to amendment, Code Sec. 408(k)(3) read as follows:

(3) CONTRIBUTIONS MAY NOT DISCRIMINATE IN FAVOR OF THE HIGHLY COMPENSATED, ETC.—

(A) IN GENERAL.—The requirements of this paragraph are met with respect to a simplified employee pension for a calendar year if for such year the contributions made by the employer to simplified employee pensions for his employees do not discriminate in favor of any employee who is—

(i) an officer,

(ii) a shareholder,

(iii) a self-employed individual, or

(iv) highly compensated.

(B) SPECIAL RULES.—For purposes of subparagraph (A)—

(i) there shall be excluded from consideration employees described in subparagraph (A) or (C) of section 410(b)(3), and

(ii) an individual shall be considered a shareholder if he owns (with the application of section 318) more than 10 percent of the value of the stock of the employer.

(C) CONTRIBUTIONS MUST BEAR UNIFORM RELATIONSHIP TO TOTAL COMPENSATION.—For purposes of subparagraph (A), employer contributions to simplified employee pensions shall be considered discriminatory unless contributions thereto bear a uniform relationship to the total compensation (not in excess of the first $200,000) of each employee maintaining a simplified employee pension. The Secretary shall annually adjust the $200,000 amount contained in the preceding sentence at the same time and in the same manner as he adjusts the dollar amount contained in section 415(c)(1)(A).

(D) TREATMENT OF CERTAIN CONTRIBUTIONS AND TAXES.—Except as provided in this subparagraph, employer contributions do not meet the requirements of this paragraph unless such contributions meet the requirements of this paragraph without taking into account contributions or benefits under chapter 2 (relating to tax on self-employment income), chapter 21 (relating to Federal Insurance Contributions Act), title II of the Social Security Act, or any other Federal or State law. If the employer does not maintain an integrated plan at any time during the taxable year, OASDI contributions (as defined in section 401(1)(2)) may, for purposes of this paragraph, be taken into account as contributions by the employer to the employee's simplified employee pension, but only if such contributions are so taken into account with respect to each employee maintaining a simplified employee pension.

(E) INTEGRATED PLAN DEFINED.—For purposes of subparagraph (D), the term "integrated plan" means a plan which meets the requirements of section 401(a) or 403(a) but would not meet such requirements if contributions or benefits under chapter 2 (relating to tax on self-employment income), chapter 21 (relating to Federal Insurance Contributions Act), title II of the Social Security Act, or any other Federal or State law were not taken into account.

P.L. 99-514, §1108(g)(4):

Amended Code Sec. 408(k)(3)(A) by striking out "calendar". **Effective** for years beginning after 12-31-86. For a special rule, see Act Sec. 1108(h)(2), below.

P.L. 99-514, §1108(g)(6):

Amended Code Sec. 408(k) by adding at the end thereof new paragraph (9). **Effective** for years beginning after 12-31-86. For a special rule, see Act Sec. 1108(h)(2), below.

P.L. 99-514, §1108(h)(2), as added by P.L. 100-647, §1011(f)(7), provides:

(2) INTEGRATION RULES.—Subparagraphs (D) and (E) of section 408(k)(3) of the Internal Revenue Code of 1954 (as in effect before the amendments made by this section) shall continue to apply for years beginning after December 31, 1986, and before January 1, 1989, except that employer contributions under an arrangement under section 408(k)(6) of the Internal Revenue Code of 1986 (as added by this section) may not be integrated under such subparagraphs.

P.L. 99-514, §1898(a)(5):

Amended Code Sec. 408(k)(2)(A) by striking out "age 25" and inserting in lieu thereof "age 21". **Effective** with respect to plan years beginning after 10-22-86.

• 1984, Deficit Reduction Act of 1984 (P.L. 98-369)

P.L. 98-369, §491(d)(24):

Amended Code Sec. 408(k)(3)(E) by striking out ", 403(a), or 405(a)" and inserting in lieu thereof "or 403(a)". **Effective** for obligations issued after 12-31-83.

P.L. 98-369, §713(f)(2):

Amended Code Sec. 408(k)(1). **Effective** as if included in the provision of P.L. 97-248 to which it relates. Prior to amendment, it read as follows:

(1) IN GENERAL.—For purposes of this title, the term "simplified employee pension" means an individual retirement account or individual retirement annuity with respect to which the requirements of paragraphs (2), (3), (4), and (5) of this subsection are met.

P.L. 98-369, §713(f)(5)(B):

Amended Code Sec. 408(k)(3)(C) by adding at the end thereof a new sentence. **Effective** as if included in the provision of P.L. 97-248 to which it relates.

P.L. 98-369, §713(j):

Amended Code Sec. 408(k)(3)(D) by striking out the second and third sentences and inserting in lieu thereof a new sentence. **Effective** as if included in the provision of P.L. 97-248 to which it relates. Prior to amendment, the second and third sentences of Code Sec. 408(k)(3)(D) read as follows:

If the employer does not maintain an integrated plan at any time during the taxable year, taxes paid under section 3111 (relating to tax on employers) with respect to an employee may, for purposes of this paragraph, be taken into account as a contribution by the employer to an employee's simplified employee pension. If contributions are made to the simplified employee pension of an owner-employee, the preceding sentence shall not apply unless taxes paid by all such owner-employees under chapter 2, and the taxes which would be payable under chapter 2 by such owner-employees but for paragraphs (4) and (5) of section 1402(c), are taken into account as contributions by the employer on behalf of such owner-employees.

• 1983, Technical Corrections Act of 1982 (P.L. 97-448)

P.L. 97-448, §103(d)(1)(A):

Amended Code Sec. 408(k)(3)(C)(ii) by striking out "on behalf of each employee" and inserting in lieu thereof "on behalf of each employee (other than an employee within the meaning of section 401(c)(1))". **Effective** as if included in the provision of P.L. 97-34 to which it relates.

P.L. 97-448, §103(d)(3):

Amended paragraph (1) of section 312(f) of P.L. 97-34 (relating to **effective** date) by striking out "plans which include employees within the meaning of section 401(c)(1) with respect to".

• 1982, Tax Equity and Fiscal Responsibility Act of 1982 (P.L. 97-248)

P.L. 97-248, §238(d)(4)(A):

Repealed Code Sec. 408(k)(6). **Effective** for years beginning after 12-31-83. Prior to repeal, Code Sec. 408(k)(6) read as follows:

(6) EMPLOYER MAY NOT MAINTAIN PLAN TO WHICH SECTION 401(j) APPLIES.—The requirements of this paragraph are met with respect to a simplified employee pension for a calendar year unless the employer maintains during any part of such year a plan—

(A) some or all of the active participants in which are employees (within the meaning of section 401(c)(1)) or shareholder-employees (as defined in section 1379(d)), and

(B) to which section 401(j) applies.

P.L. 97-248, §238(d)(4)(B):

Amended Code Sec. 408(k)(1) by striking out "(5), and (6)" and inserting "and (5)". **Effective** for years beginning after 12-31-83.

P.L. 97-248, §238(d)(4)(C):

Amended Code Sec. 408(k)(3)(C). **Effective** for years beginning after 12-31-83. Prior to amendment, Code Sec. 401(k)(3)(C) read as follows:

(C) CONTRIBUTIONS MUST BEAR A UNIFORM RELATIONSHIP TO TOTAL COMPENSATION.—For purposes of subparagraph (A), employer contributions to simplified employee pensions shall be considered discriminatory unless—

(i) contributions thereto bear a uniform relationship to the total compensation (not in excess of the first $200,000) of each employee maintaining a simplified employee pension, and

(ii) if compensation in excess of $100,000 is taken into account under a simplified employee pension for an employee, contributions to a simplified employee pension on behalf of each employee (other than an employee within the meaning of section 401(c)(1)) for whom a contribution is required are at a rate (expressed as a percentage of compensation) not less than 7.5 percent.

• 1981, Economic Recovery Tax Act of 1981 (P.L. 97-34)

P.L. 97-34, §312(b)(2):

Amended Code Sec. 408(k)(3)(C). **Effective** for tax years beginning after 12-31-81. Prior to amendment, Code Sec. 408(k)(3)(C) read:

(C) CONTRIBUTIONS MUST BEAR A UNIFORM RELATIONSHIP TO TOTAL COMPENSATION.—For purposes of subparagraph (A), employer contributions to simplified employee pensions shall be considered discriminatory unless contributions thereto bear a uniform relationship to the total compensation (not in excess of the first $100,000) of each employee maintaining a simplified employee pension.

• 1980, Miscellaneous Revenue Act of 1980 (P.L. 96-605)

P.L. 96-605, §225(b)(3) and (4):

Amended the last sentence of Code Sec. 408(k)(2) by striking out "section 410(b)(2)" and inserting in lieu thereof "section 410(b)(3)", and amended Code Sec. 408(k)(3)(B)(i) by striking out "section 410(b)(2)" and inserting in lieu thereof "section 410(b)(3)". **Effective** for plan years beginning after 12-31-80.

• 1980, Technical Corrections Act of 1979 (P.L. 96-222)

P.L. 96-222, §101(a)(10)(A):

Amended Code Sec. 408(k)(2) by adding the last sentence. **Effective** for tax years beginning after 12-31-78.

P.L. 96-222, §101(a)(10)(F):

Amended Code Sec. 408(k) by changing "and (5)" in paragraph (1) to "(5) and (6)", by redesignating paragraph (6) as paragraph (7), and by adding new paragraph (6) after paragraph (5). **Effective** for tax years beginning after 12-31-78.

P.L. 96-222, §101(a)(10)(G):

Amended Code Sec. 408(k) by striking out in the second sentence of paragraph (D) "Taxes paid" and inserting "If the employer does not maintain an integrated plan at any time during the taxable year, taxes paid", and by adding a new paragraph (E). **Effective** for tax years beginning after 12-31-78.

• 1978, Revenue Act of 1978 (P.L. 95-600)

P.L. 95-600, §152(b):

Added Code Sec. 408(k). **Effective** for tax years beginning after 12-31-78.

[Sec. 408(l)]

(l) SIMPLIFIED EMPLOYER REPORTS.—

(1) IN GENERAL.—An employer who makes a contribution on behalf of an employee to a simplified employee pension shall provide such simplified reports with respect to such contributions as the Secretary may require by regulations. The reports required by this subsection shall be filed at such time and in such manner, and information with respect to such contributions shall be furnished to the employee at such time and in such manner, as may be required by regulations.

(2) SIMPLE RETIREMENT ACCOUNTS.—

(A) NO EMPLOYER REPORTS.—Except as provided in this paragraph, no report shall be required under this section by an employer maintaining a qualified salary reduction arrangement under subsection (p).

(B) SUMMARY DESCRIPTION.—The trustee of any simple retirement account established pursuant to a qualified salary reduction arrangement under subsection (p) and the issuer of an annuity established under such an arrangement shall provide to the employer maintaining the arrangement, each year a description containing the following information:

(i) The name and address of the employer and the trustee or issuer.

(ii) The requirements for eligibility for participation.

(iii) The benefits provided with respect to the arrangement.

(iv) The time and method of making elections with respect to the arrangement.

(v) The procedures for, and effects of, withdrawals (including rollovers) from the arrangement.

(C) EMPLOYEE NOTIFICATION.—The employer shall notify each employee immediately before the period for which an election described in subsection (p)(5)(C) may be made of the employee's opportunity to make such election. Such notice shall include a copy of the description described in subparagraph (B).

Amendments

• 1997, Taxpayer Relief Act of 1997 (P.L. 105-34)

P.L. 105-34, §1601(d)(1)(C)(i)(I)-(II):

Amended Code Sec. 408(l)(2)(B) by inserting "and the issuer of an annuity established under such an arrangement" after "under subsection (p)", and by inserting in clause (i) "or issuer" after "trustee". **Effective** as if included in the provision of P.L. 104-188 to which it relates [**effective** for tax years beginning after 12-31-96.—CCH].

• 1996, Small Business Job Protection Act of 1996 (P.L. 104-188)

P.L. 104-188, §1421(b)(5)(A):

Amended Code Sec. 408(l) by adding at the end a new paragraph (2). **Effective** for tax years beginning after 12-31-96.

P.L. 104-188, §1421(b)(5)(B):

Amended Code Sec. 408(l) by striking "An employer" and inserting "(1) IN GENERAL.—An employer". **Effective** for tax years beginning after 12-31-96.

• 1978, Revenue Act of 1978 (P.L. 95-600)

P.L. 95-600, §152(b):

Added a new Code Sec. 408(l). **Effective** for tax years beginning after 12-31-78.

[Sec. 408(m)]

(m) INVESTMENT IN COLLECTIBLES TREATED AS DISTRIBUTIONS.—

(1) IN GENERAL.—The acquisition by an individual retirement account or by an individually-directed account under a plan described in section 401(a) of any collectible shall be treated (for purposes of this section and section 402) as a distribution from such account in an amount equal to the cost to such account of such collectible.

(2) COLLECTIBLE DEFINED.—For purposes of this subsection, the term "collectible" means—

(A) any work of art,

(B) any rug or antique,

(C) any metal or gem,

(D) any stamp or coin,

(E) any alcoholic beverage, or

(F) any other tangible personal property specified by the Secretary for purposes of this subsection.

(3) EXCEPTION FOR CERTAIN COINS AND BULLION.—For purposes of this subsection, the term "collectible" shall not include—

(A) any coin which is—

(i) a gold coin described in paragraph (7), (8), (9), or (10) of section 5112(a) of title 31, United States Code,

(ii) a silver coin described in section 5112(e) of title 31, United States Code,

(iii) a platinum coin described in section 5112(k) of title 31, United States Code, or

(iv) a coin issued under the laws of any State, or

(B) any gold, silver, platinum, or palladium bullion of a fineness equal to or exceeding the minimum fineness that a contract market (as described in section 7 of the Commodity Exchange Act, 7 U.S.C. 7) requires for metals which may be delivered in satisfaction of a regulated futures contract,

if such bullion is in the physical possession of a trustee described under subsection (a) of this section.

Amendments

• 1997, Taxpayer Relief Act of 1997 (P.L. 105-34)

P.L. 105-34, §304(a):

Amended Code Sec. 408(m)(3). **Effective** for tax years beginning after 12-31-97. Prior to amendment, Code Sec. 408(m)(3) read as follows:

(3) EXCEPTION FOR CERTAIN COINS.—In the case of an individual retirement account, paragraph (2) shall not apply to—

(A) any gold coin described in paragraph (7), (8), (9), or (10) of section 5112(a) of title 31,

(B) any silver coin described in section 5112(e) of title 31, or

(C) any coin issued under the laws of any State.

• 1988, Technical and Miscellaneous Revenue Act of 1988 (P.L. 100-647)

P.L. 100-647, §6057(a):

Amended Code Sec. 408(m)(3). **Effective** for acquisitions after 11-10-88. Prior to amendment, Code Sec. 408(m)(3) read as follows:

(3) EXCEPTION FOR CERTAIN COINS.—In the case of an individual retirement account, paragraph (2) shall not apply to any gold coin described in paragraph (7), (8), (9), or (10) of section 5112(a) of title 31 or any silver coin described in section 5112(e) of title 31.

• 1986, Tax Reform Act of 1986 (P.L. 99-514)

P.L. 99-514, §1144(a):

Amended Code Sec. 408(m) by adding at the end thereof new paragraph (3). **Effective** for acquisitions after 12-31-86.

• 1983, Technical Corrections Act of 1982 (P.L. 97-448)

P.L. 97-448, §103(e)(2):

Amended Code Sec. 408 by redesignating subsection (n) as subsection (m). **Effective** as if included in the provision of P.L. 97-34 to which it relates.

• 1981, Economic Recovery Tax Act of 1981 (P.L. 97-34)

P.L. 97-34, §314(b)(1):

Added Code Sec. 408(n)[m]. **Effective** for property acquired after 12-31-81, in tax years ending after that date.

[Sec. 408(n)]

(n) BANK.—For purposes of subsection (a)(2), the term "bank" means—

(1) any bank (as defined in section 581),

(2) an insured credit union (within the meaning of paragraph (6) or (7) of section 101 of the Federal Credit Union Act), and

(3) a corporation which, under the laws of the State of its incorporation, is subject to supervision and examination by the Commissioner of Banking or other officer of such State in charge of the administration of the banking laws of such State.

Amendments

• 2004, Working Families Tax Relief Act of 2004 (P.L. 108-311)

P.L. 108-311, §408(a)(13):

Amended Code Sec. 408(n)(2) by striking "section 101(6)" and inserting "paragraph (6) or (7) of section 101". **Effective** 10-4-2004.

• 1982, Tax Equity and Fiscal Responsibility Act of 1982 (P.L. 97-248)

P.L. 97-248, §237(e)(3)(B):

Added subsection (n). **Effective** for years beginning after 1983.

[Sec. 408(o)]

(o) DEFINITIONS AND RULES RELATING TO NONDEDUCTIBLE CONTRIBUTIONS TO INDIVIDUAL RETIREMENT PLANS.—

(1) IN GENERAL.—Subject to the provisions of this subsection, designated nondeductible contributions may be made on behalf of an individual to an individual retirement plan.

(2) LIMITS ON AMOUNTS WHICH MAY BE CONTRIBUTED.—

(A) IN GENERAL.—The amount of the designated nondeductible contributions made on behalf of any individual for any taxable year shall not exceed the nondeductible limit for such taxable year.

(B) NONDEDUCTIBLE LIMIT.—For purposes of this paragraph—

(i) IN GENERAL.—The term "nondeductible limit" means the excess of—

(I) the amount allowable as a deduction under section 219 (determined without regard to section 219(g)), over

(II) the amount allowable as a deduction under section 219 (determined with regard to section 219(g)).

(ii) TAXPAYER MAY ELECT TO TREAT DEDUCTIBLE CONTRIBUTIONS AS NONDEDUCTIBLE.—If a taxpayer elects not to deduct an amount which (without regard to this clause) is allowable as a deduction under section 219 for any taxable year, the nondeductible limit for such taxable year shall be increased by such amount.

(C) DESIGNATED NONDEDUCTIBLE CONTRIBUTIONS.—

(i) IN GENERAL.—For purposes of this paragraph, the term "designated nondeductible contribution" means any contribution to an individual retirement plan for the taxable year which is designated (in such manner as the Secretary may prescribe) as a contribution for which a deduction is not allowable under section 219.

(ii) DESIGNATION.—Any designation under clause (i) shall be made on the return of tax imposed by chapter 1 for the taxable year.

(3) TIME WHEN CONTRIBUTIONS MADE.—In determining for which taxable year a designated nondeductible contribution is made, the rule of section 219(f)(3) shall apply.

(4) INDIVIDUAL REQUIRED TO REPORT AMOUNT OF DESIGNATED NONDEDUCTIBLE CONTRIBUTIONS.—

(A) IN GENERAL.—Any individual who—

(i) makes a designated nondeductible contribution to any individual retirement plan for any taxable year, or

(ii) receives any amount from any individual retirement plan for any taxable year, shall include on his return of the tax imposed by chapter 1 for such taxable year and any succeeding taxable year (or on such other form as the Secretary may prescribe for any such taxable year) information described in subparagraph (B).

(B) INFORMATION REQUIRED TO BE SUPPLIED.—The following information is described in this subparagraph:

(i) The amount of designated nondeductible contributions for the taxable year.

(ii) The amount of distributions from individual retirement plans for the taxable year.

(iii) The excess (if any) of—

(I) the aggregate amount of designated nondeductible contributions for all preceding taxable years, over

(II) the aggregate amount of distributions from individual retirement plans which was excludable from gross income for such taxable years.

(iv) The aggregate balance of all individual retirement plans of the individual as of the close of the calendar year in which the taxable year begins.

(v) Such other information as the Secretary may prescribe.

(C) PENALTY FOR REPORTING CONTRIBUTIONS NOT MADE.—

For penalty where individual reports designated nondeductible contributions not made, see section 6693(b).

Amendments

• 1988, Technical and Miscellaneous Revenue Act of 1988 (P.L. 100-647)

P.L. 100-647, §1011(b)(1):

Amended Code Sec. 408(o)(4)(B)(iv) by striking out "with or within which the taxable year ends" and inserting in lieu thereof "in which the taxable year begins". **Effective** as if included in the provision of P.L. 99-514 to which it relates.

• 1986, Tax Reform Act of 1986 (P.L. 99-514)

P.L. 99-514, §1102(a):

Amended Code Sec. 408 by redesignating subsection (o) as subsection (p) and by inserting after subsection (n) new subsection (o). **Effective** for contributions and distributions for tax years beginning after 12-31-86.

[Sec. 408(p)]

(p) SIMPLE RETIREMENT ACCOUNTS.—

(1) IN GENERAL.—For purposes of this title, the term "simple retirement account" means an individual retirement plan (as defined in section 7701(a)(37))—

(A) with respect to which the requirements of paragraphs (3), (4), and (5) are met; and

(B) with respect to which the only contributions allowed are contributions under a qualified salary reduction arrangement.

(2) QUALIFIED SALARY REDUCTION ARRANGEMENT.—

(A) IN GENERAL.—For purposes of this subsection, the term "qualified salary reduction arrangement" means a written arrangement of an eligible employer under which—

(i) an employee eligible to participate in the arrangement may elect to have the employer make payments—

(I) as elective employer contributions to a simple retirement account on behalf of the employee, or

(II) to the employee directly in cash,

(ii) the amount which an employee may elect under clause (i) for any year is required to be expressed as a percentage of compensation and may not exceed a total of the applicable dollar amount for any year,

(iii) the employer is required to make a matching contribution to the simple retirement account for any year in an amount equal to so much of the amount the employee elects under clause (i)(I) as does not exceed the applicable percentage of compensation for the year, and

(iv) no contributions may be made other than contributions described in clause (i) or (iii).

(B) EMPLOYER MAY ELECT 2-PERCENT NONELECTIVE CONTRIBUTION.—

(i) IN GENERAL.—An employer shall be treated as meeting the requirements of subparagraph (A)(iii) for any year if, in lieu of the contributions described in such clause, the employer elects to make nonelective contributions of 2 percent of compensation for each employee who is eligible to participate in the arrangement and who has at least $5,000 of compensation from the employer for the year. If an employer makes an election under this subparagraph for any year, the employer shall notify employees of such election within a reasonable period of time before the 60-day period for such year under paragraph (5)(C).

(ii) COMPENSATION LIMITATION.—The compensation taken into account under clause (i) for any year shall not exceed the limitation in effect for such year under section 401(a)(17).

(C) DEFINITIONS.—For purposes of this subsection—

(i) ELIGIBLE EMPLOYER.—

(I) IN GENERAL.—The term "eligible employer" means, with respect to any year, an employer which had no more than 100 employees who received at least $5,000 of compensation from the employer for the preceding year.

(II) 2-YEAR GRACE PERIOD.—An eligible employer who establishes and maintains a plan under this subsection for 1 or more years and who fails to be an eligible employer for any subsequent year shall be treated as an eligible employer for the 2 years following the last year the employer was an eligible employer. If such failure is due to any acquisition, disposition, or similar transaction involving an eligible employer, the preceding sentence shall not apply.

(ii) APPLICABLE PERCENTAGE.—

(I) IN GENERAL.—The term "applicable percentage" means 3 percent.

(II) ELECTION OF LOWER PERCENTAGE.—An employer may elect to apply a lower percentage (not less than 1 percent) for any year for all employees eligible to participate in the plan for such year if the employer notifies the employees of such lower percentage within a reasonable period of time before the 60-day election period for such year under paragraph (5)(C). An employer may not elect a lower percentage under this subclause for any year if that election would result in the applicable percentage being lower than 3 percent in more than 2 of the years in the 5-year period ending with such year.

(III) SPECIAL RULE FOR YEARS ARRANGEMENT NOT IN EFFECT.—If any year in the 5-year period described in subclause (II) is a year prior to the first year for which any qualified salary reduction arrangement is in effect with respect to the employer (or any predecessor), the employer shall be treated as if the level of the employer matching contribution was at 3 percent of compensation for such prior year.

(D) ARRANGEMENT MAY BE ONLY PLAN OF EMPLOYER.—

(i) IN GENERAL.—An arrangement shall not be treated as a qualified salary reduction arrangement for any year if the employer (or any predecessor employer) maintained a qualified plan with respect to which contributions were made, or benefits were accrued, for service in any year in the period beginning with the year such arrangement became effective and ending with the year for which the determination is being made. If only individuals other than employees described in subparagraph (A) of section 410(b)(3) are eligible to participate in such arrangement, then the preceding sentence shall be applied without regard to any qualified plan in which only employees so described are eligible to participate.

(ii) QUALIFIED PLAN.—For purposes of this subparagraph, the term "qualified plan" means a plan, contract, pension, or trust described in subparagraph (A) or (B) of section 219(g)(5).

(E) APPLICABLE DOLLAR AMOUNT; COST-OF-LIVING ADJUSTMENT.—

(i) IN GENERAL.—For purposes of subparagraph (A)(ii), the applicable dollar amount shall be the amount determined in accordance with the following table:

For years beginning in calendar year:	*The applicable dollar amount:*
2002	$7,000
2003	$8,000
2004	$9,000
2005 or thereafter	$10,000.

(ii) COST-OF-LIVING ADJUSTMENT.—In the case of a year beginning after December 31, 2005, the Secretary shall adjust the $10,000 amount under clause (i) at the same time and in the same manner as under section 415(d), except that the base period taken into account shall be the calendar quarter beginning July 1, 2004, and any increase under this subparagraph which is not a multiple of $500 shall be rounded to the next lower multiple of $500.

(3) VESTING REQUIREMENTS.—The requirements of this paragraph are met with respect to a simple retirement account if the employee's rights to any contribution to the simple retirement account are nonforfeitable. For purposes of this paragraph, rules similar to the rules of subsection (k)(4) shall apply.

(4) PARTICIPATION REQUIREMENTS.—

(A) IN GENERAL.—The requirements of this paragraph are met with respect to any simple retirement account for a year only if, under the qualified salary reduction arrangement, all employees of the employer who—

(i) received at least $5,000 in compensation from the employer during any 2 preceding years, and

(ii) are reasonably expected to receive at least $5,000 in compensation during the year,

are eligible to make the election under paragraph (2)(A)(i) or receive the nonelective contribution described in paragraph (2)(B).

(B) EXCLUDABLE EMPLOYEES.—An employer may elect to exclude from the requirement under subparagraph (A) employees described in section 410(b)(3).

(5) ADMINISTRATIVE REQUIREMENTS.—The requirements of this paragraph are met with respect to any simple retirement account if, under the qualified salary reduction arrangement—

(A) an employer must—

(i) make the elective employer contributions under paragraph (2)(A)(i) not later than the close of the 30-day period following the last day of the month with respect to which the contributions are to be made, and

(ii) make the matching contributions under paragraph (2)(A)(iii) or the nonelective contributions under paragraph (2)(B) not later than the date described in section 404(m)(2)(B),

(B) an employee may elect to terminate participation in such arrangement at any time during the year, except that if an employee so terminates, the arrangement may provide that the employee may not elect to resume participation until the beginning of the next year, and

(C) each employee eligible to participate may elect, during the 60-day period before the beginning of any year (and the 60-day period before the first day such employee is eligible to participate), to participate in the arrangement, or to modify the amounts subject to such arrangement, for such year.

(6) DEFINITIONS.—For purposes of this subsection—

(A) COMPENSATION.—

(i) IN GENERAL.—The term "compensation" means amounts described in paragraphs (3) and (8) of section 6051(a). For purposes of the preceding sentence, amounts described in section 6051(a)(3) shall be determined without regard to section 3401(a)(3).

(ii) SELF-EMPLOYED.—In the case of an employee described in subparagraph (B), the term "compensation" means net earnings from self-employment determined under section 1402(a) without regard to any contribution under this subsection. The preceding sentence shall be applied as if the term "trade or business" for purposes of section 1402 included service described in section 1402(c)(6).

(B) EMPLOYEE.—The term "employee" includes an employee as defined in section 401(c)(1).

(C) YEAR.—The term "year" means the calendar year.

(7) USE OF DESIGNATED FINANCIAL INSTITUTION.—A plan shall not be treated as failing to satisfy the requirements of this subsection or any other provision of this title merely because the employer makes all contributions to the individual retirement accounts or annuities of a designated trustee or issuer. The preceding sentence shall not apply unless each plan participant is notified in writing (either separately or as part of the notice under subsection (l)(2)(C)) that the participant's balance may be transferred without cost or penalty to another individual account or annuity in accordance with subsection (d)(3)(G).

(8) COORDINATION WITH MAXIMUM LIMITATION UNDER SUBSECTION (a).—In the case of any simple retirement account, subsections (a)(1) and (b)(2) shall be applied by substituting "the sum of the dollar amount in effect under paragraph (2)(A)(ii) of this subsection [(p)]and the employer contribution required under subparagraph (A)(iii) or (B)(i) of paragraph (2) of this subsection [(p)] , whichever is applicable" for "the dollar amount in effect under section 219(b)(1)(A)".

(9) MATCHING CONTRIBUTIONS ON BEHALF OF SELF-EMPLOYED INDIVIDUALS NOT TREATED AS ELECTIVE EMPLOYER CONTRIBUTIONS.—Any matching contribution described in paragraph (2)(A)(iii) which is made on behalf of a self-employed individual (as defined in section 401(c)) shall not be treated as an elective employer contribution to a simple retirement account for purposes of this title.

(10) SPECIAL RULES FOR ACQUISITIONS, DISPOSITIONS, AND SIMILAR TRANSACTIONS.—

(A) IN GENERAL.—An employer which fails to meet any applicable requirement by reason of an acquisition, disposition, or similar transaction shall not be treated as failing to meet such requirement during the transition period if—

(i) the employer satisfies requirements similar to the requirements of section 410(b)(6)(C)(i)(II); and

(ii) the qualified salary reduction arrangement maintained by the employer would satisfy the requirements of this subsection after the transaction if the employer which maintained the arrangement before the transaction had remained a separate employer.

(B) APPLICABLE REQUIREMENT.—For purposes of this paragraph, the term "applicable requirement" means—

(i) the requirement under paragraph (2)(A)(i) that an employer be an eligible employer;

(ii) the requirement under paragraph (2)(D) that an arrangement be the only plan of an employer; and

(iii) the participation requirements under paragraph (4).

(C) TRANSITION PERIOD.—For purposes of this paragraph, the term "transition period" means the period beginning on the date of any transaction described in subparagraph (A) and ending on the last day of the second calendar year following the calendar year in which such transaction occurs.

Amendments

• 2006, Pension Protection Act of 2006 (P.L. 109-280)

P.L. 109-280, §811, provides:

SEC. 811. PENSIONS AND INDIVIDUAL RETIREMENT ARRANGEMENT PROVISIONS OF ECONOMIC GROWTH AND TAX RELIEF RECONCILIATION ACT OF 2001 MADE PERMANENT.

Title IX of the Economic Growth and Tax Relief Reconciliation Act of 2001 [P.L. 107-16] shall not apply to the provisions of, and amendments made by, subtitles A through F of title VI [§§601-666]of such Act (relating to pension and individual retirement arrangement provisions).

• 2004, Working Families Tax Relief Act of 2004 (P.L. 108-311)

P.L. 108-311, §404(d):

Amended Code Sec. 408(p)(6)(A)(i) by adding at the end a new sentence. **Effective** as if included in the provision of the Economic Growth and Tax Relief Reconciliation Act of 2001 (P.L. 107-16) to which it relates [**effective** for tax years beginning after 12-31-2001.—CCH].

• 2001, Economic Growth and Tax Relief Reconciliation Act of 2001 (P.L. 107-16)

P.L. 107-16, §601(b)(5):

Amended Code Sec. 408(p)(8) by striking "$2,000" and inserting "the dollar amount in effect under section 219(b)(1)(A)". **Effective** for tax years beginning after 12-31-2001.

P.L. 107-16, §611(f)(1):

Amended Code Sec. 408(p)(2)(A)(ii) by striking "$6,000" and inserting "the applicable dollar amount". **Effective** for years beginning after 12-31-2001. For a special rule, see Act Sec. 611(i)(3), below.

P.L. 107-16, §611(f)(2):

Amended Code Sec. 408(p)(2)(E). **Effective** for years beginning after 12-31-2001. For a special rule, see Act Sec. 611(i)(3), below. Prior to amendment, Code Sec. 408(p)(2)(E) read as follows:

(E) COST-OF-LIVING ADJUSTMENT.—The Secretary shall adjust the $6,000 amount under subparagraph (A)(ii) at the same time and in the same manner as under section 415(d), except that the base period taken into account shall be the calendar quarter ending September 30, 1996, and any increase under this subparagraph which is not a multiple of $500 shall be rounded to the next lower multiple of $500.

P.L. 107-16, §611(g)(2):

Amended Code Sec. 408(p)(6)(A)(ii) by adding at the end a new sentence. **Effective** for years beginning after 12-31-2001. For a special rule, see Act Sec. 611(i)(3), below.

P.L. 107-16, §611(i)(3) (as added by P.L. 107-147, §411(j)(3)), provides:

(3) SPECIAL RULE.—In the case of plan that, on June 7, 2001, incorporated by reference the limitation of section 415(b)(1)(A) of the Internal Revenue Code of 1986, section 411(d)(6) of such Code and section 204(g)(1) of the Employee Retirement Income Security Act of 1974 do not apply to a plan amendment that—

(A) is adopted on or before June 30, 2002,

(B) reduces benefits to the level that would have applied without regard to the amendments made by subsection (a) of this section, and

(C) is effective no earlier than the years described in paragraph (2).

P.L. 107-16, §901(a)-(b), provides [but see P.L. 109-280, §811, above]:

SEC. 901. SUNSET OF PROVISIONS OF ACT.

(a) IN GENERAL.—All provisions of, and amendments made by, this Act shall not apply—

(1) to taxable, plan, or limitation years beginning after December 31, 2010, or

(2) in the case of title V, to estates of decedents dying, gifts made, or generation skipping transfers, after December 31, 2010.

(b) APPLICATION OF CERTAIN LAWS.—The Internal Revenue Code of 1986 and the Employee Retirement Income Security Act of 1974 shall be applied and administered to years, estates, gifts, and transfers described in subsection (a) as if the provisions and amendments described in subsection (a) had never been enacted.

• 1998, IRS Restructuring and Reform Act of 1998 (P.L. 105-206)

P.L. 105-206, §6015(a):

Amended Code Sec. 408(p) by redesignating paragraph (8), as added by Act Sec. 1501(b) of P.L. 105-34, as paragraph (9). **Effective** as if included in the provision of P.L. 105-34 to which it relates [**effective** for tax years beginning after 12-31-96.—CCH].

P.L. 105-206, §6016(a)(1)(A):

Amended Code Sec. 408(p)(2)(D)(i) by striking "or (B)" after "subparagraph (A)" in the last sentence. **Effective** as if included in the provision of P.L. 105-34 to which it relates [**effective** for tax years beginning after 12-31-96.—CCH].

P.L. 105-206, §6016(a)(1)(B):

Amended Code Sec. 408(p) by adding at the end a new paragraph (10). **Effective** as if included in the provision of P.L. 105-34 to which it relates [**effective** for tax years beginning after 12-31-96.—CCH].

P.L. 105-206, §6016(a)(1)(C)(i)-(ii):

Amended Code Sec. 408(p)(2) by striking "the preceding sentence shall apply only in accordance with rules similar to the rules of section 410(b)(6)(C)(i)" in the last sentence of subparagraph (C)(i)(II) and inserting "the preceding sentence shall not apply", and by striking clause (iii) of subparagraph (D). **Effective** as if included in the provision of P.L. 105-34 to which it relates [**effective** for tax years beginning after 12-31-96.—CCH]. Prior to being stricken, Code Sec. 408(p)(2)(D)(iii) read as follows:

(iii) GRACE PERIOD.—In the case of an employer who establishes and maintains a plan under this subsection for 1 or more years and who fails to meet any requirement of this subsection for any subsequent year due to any acquisition, disposition, or similar transaction involving another such employer, rules similar to the rules of section 410(b)(6)(C) shall apply for purposes of this subsection.

• 1997, Taxpayer Relief Act of 1997 (P.L. 105-34)

P.L. 105-34, §1501(b):

Amended Code Sec. 408(p) by adding at the end a new paragraph (8)[(9)]. **Effective** for years beginning after 12-31-96.

P.L. 105-34, §1601(d)(1)(D):

Amended Code Sec. 408(p) by adding at the end a new paragraph (8). **Effective** as if included in the provision of P.L. 104-188 to which it relates [**effective** for tax years beginning after 12-31-96.—CCH].

P.L. 105-34, §1601(d)(1)(E):

Amended Code Sec. 408(p)(2)(D)(i) by adding at the end a new sentence. **Effective** as if included in the provision of P.L. 104-188 to which it relates [**effective** for tax years beginning after 12-31-96.—CCH].

P.L. 105-34, §1601(d)(1)(F):

Amended Code Sec. 408(p)(2)(D) by adding at the end a new clause (iii). **Effective** as if included in the provision of P.L. 104-188 to which it relates [**effective** for tax years beginning after 12-31-96.—CCH].

P.L. 105-34, §1601(d)(1)(G):

Amended Code Sec. 408(p)(5) by striking "simplified" and inserting "simple" in the text preceding subparagraph (A). **Effective** as if included in the provision of P.L. 104-188 to which it relates [**effective** for tax years beginning after 12-31-96.—CCH].

• 1996, Small Business Job Protection Act of 1996 (P.L. 104-188)

P.L. 104-188, §1421(a):

Amended Code Sec. 408 by redesignating subsection (p) as subsection (q) and by inserting after subsection (o) a new subsection (p). **Effective** for tax years beginning after 12-31-96.

[Sec. 408(q)]

(q) DEEMED IRAS UNDER QUALIFIED EMPLOYER PLANS.—

(1) GENERAL RULE.—If—

(A) a qualified employer plan elects to allow employees to make voluntary employee contributions to a separate account or annuity established under the plan, and

(B) under the terms of the qualified employer plan, such account or annuity meets the applicable requirements of this section or section 408A for an individual retirement account or annuity,

then such account or annuity shall be treated for purposes of this title in the same manner as an individual retirement plan and not as a qualified employer plan (and contributions to such account or annuity as contributions to an individual retirement plan and not to the qualified employer plan). For purposes of subparagraph (B), the requirements of subsection (a)(5) shall not apply.

(2) SPECIAL RULES FOR QUALIFIED EMPLOYER PLANS.—For purposes of this title, a qualified employer plan shall not fail to meet any requirement of this title solely by reason of establishing and maintaining a program described in paragraph (1).

(3) DEFINITIONS.—For purposes of this subsection—

(A) QUALIFIED EMPLOYER PLAN.—The term "qualified employer plan" has the meaning given such term by section 72(p)(4)(A)(i); except that such term shall also include an eligible deferred compensation plan (as defined in section 457(b)) of an eligible employer described in section 457(e)(1)(A).

(B) VOLUNTARY EMPLOYEE CONTRIBUTION.—The term "voluntary employee contribution" means any contribution (other than a mandatory contribution within the meaning of section 411(c)(2)(C))—

(i) which is made by an individual as an employee under a qualified employer plan which allows employees to elect to make contributions described in paragraph (1), and

(ii) with respect to which the individual has designated the contribution as a contribution to which this subsection applies.

Amendments

• 2006, Pension Protection Act of 2006 (P.L. 109-280)

P.L. 109-280, §811, provides:

SEC. 811. PENSIONS AND INDIVIDUAL RETIREMENT ARRANGEMENT PROVISIONS OF ECONOMIC GROWTH AND TAX RELIEF RECONCILIATION ACT OF 2001 MADE PERMANENT.

Title IX of the Economic Growth and Tax Relief Reconciliation Act of 2001 [P.L. 107-16] shall not apply to the provisions of, and amendments made by, subtitles A through F of title VI [§§601-666]of such Act (relating to pension and individual retirement arrangement provisions).

• 2002, Job Creation and Worker Assistance Act of 2002 (P.L. 107-147)

P.L. 107-147, §411(i)(1):

Amended Code Sec. 408(q)(3)(A). **Effective** as if included in the provision of P.L. 107-16 to which it relates [applicable to plan years beginning after 12-31-2002.—CCH]. Prior to amendment, Code Sec. 408(q)(3)(A) read as follows:

(A) QUALIFIED EMPLOYER PLAN.—The term "qualified employer plan" has the meaning given such term by section 72(p)(4); except such term shall not include a government plan which is not a qualified plan unless the plan is an eligible deferred compensation plan (as defined in section 457(b)).

• 2001, Economic Growth and Tax Relief Reconciliation Act of 2001 (P.L. 107-16)

P.L. 107-16, §602(a):

Amended Code Sec. 408 by redesignating subsection (q) as subsection (r) and by inserting after subsection (p) a new subsection (q). **Effective** for plan years beginning after 12-31-2002.

P.L. 107-16, §901(a)-(b), provides [but see P.L. 109-280, §811, above]:

SEC. 901. SUNSET OF PROVISIONS OF ACT.

(a) IN GENERAL.—All provisions of, and amendments made by, this Act shall not apply—

(1) to taxable, plan, or limitation years beginning after December 31, 2010, or

(2) in the case of title V, to estates of decedents dying, gifts made, or generation skipping transfers, after December 31, 2010.

(b) APPLICATION OF CERTAIN LAWS.—The Internal Revenue Code of 1986 and the Employee Retirement Income Security Act of 1974 shall be applied and administered to years, estates, gifts, and transfers described in subsection (a) as if the provisions and amendments described in subsection (a) had never been enacted.

[Sec. 408(r)]

(r) CROSS REFERENCES.—

(1) For tax on excess contributions in individual retirement accounts or annuities, see section 4973.

(2) For tax on certain accumulations in individual retirement accounts or annuities, see section 4974.

Amendments

• 2006, Pension Protection Act of 2006 (P.L. 109-280)

P.L. 109-280, §811, provides:

SEC. 811. PENSIONS AND INDIVIDUAL RETIREMENT ARRANGEMENT PROVISIONS OF ECONOMIC GROWTH AND TAX RELIEF RECONCILIATION ACT OF 2001 MADE PERMANENT.

Title IX of the Economic Growth and Tax Relief Reconciliation Act of 2001 [P.L. 107-16] shall not apply to the provisions of, and amendments made by, subtitles A through F of title VI [§§601-666]of such Act (relating to pension and individual retirement arrangement provisions).

• 2001, Economic Growth and Tax Relief Reconciliation Act of 2001 (P.L. 107-16)

P.L. 107-16, §602(a):

Amended Code Sec. 408 by redesignating subsection (q) as subsection (r). **Effective** for plan years beginning after 12-31-2002.

P.L. 107-16, §901(a)-(b), provides [but see P.L. 109-280, §811, above]:

SEC. 901. SUNSET OF PROVISIONS OF ACT.

(a) IN GENERAL.—All provisions of, and amendments made by, this Act shall not apply—

(1) to taxable, plan, or limitation years beginning after December 31, 2010, or

(2) in the case of title V, to estates of decedents dying, gifts made, or generation skipping transfers, after December 31, 2010.

(b) APPLICATION OF CERTAIN LAWS.—The Internal Revenue Code of 1986 and the Employee Retirement Income Security Act of 1974 shall be applied and administered to years, estates, gifts, and transfers described in subsection (a) as if the provisions and amendments described in subsection (a) had never been enacted.

• 1996, Small Business Job Protection Act of 1996 (P.L. 104-188)

P.L. 104-188, §1421(a):

Amended Code Sec. 408 by redesignating subsection (p) as subsection (q). **Effective** for tax years beginning after 12-31-96.

• 1986, Tax Reform Act of 1986 (P.L. 99-514)

P.L. 99-514, §1102(a):

Amended Code Sec. 408 by redesignating subsection (o) as subsection (p). **Effective** for contributions and distributions for tax years beginning after 12-31-86.

• 1983, Technical Corrections Act of 1982 (P.L. 97-448)

P.L. 97-448, §103(e)(1):

Amended section 314(b)(1) of P.L. 97-34 by striking out "by redesignating subsection (n) as subsection (o) and by inserting after subsection (m)" and inserting "by redesignating subsection (m) as subsection (n) and by inserting after subsection (l)".

• 1982, Tax Equity and Fiscal Responsibility Act of 1982 (P.L. 97-248)

P.L. 97-248, §237(e)(3)(B):

Amended Code Sec. 408 by redesignating subsection (n) as (o). **Effective** for years beginning after 1983.

• 1981, Economic Recovery Tax Act of 1981 (P.L. 97-34)

P.L. 97-34, §314(b)(1):

Redesignated Code Sec. 408(m) as Code Sec. 408(n). **Effective** for property acquired after 12-31-81 in tax years ending after such date.

• 1978, Revenue Act of 1978 (P.L. 95-600)

P.L. 95-600, §152(a):

Redesignated Code Sec. 408(j) as 408(m).

• 1974, Employee Retirement Income Security Act of 1974 (P.L. 93-406)

P.L. 93-406, §2002(b):

Added Code Sec. 408. **Effective** for tax years beginning after 12-31-74.

[Sec. 408A]

SEC. 408A. ROTH IRAS.

[Sec. 408A(a)]

(a) GENERAL RULE.—Except as provided in this section, a Roth IRA shall be treated for purposes of this title in the same manner as an individual retirement plan.

[Sec. 408A(b)]

(b) ROTH IRA.—For purposes of this title, the term "Roth IRA" means an individual retirement plan (as defined in section 7701(a)(37)) which is designated (in such manner as the Secretary may prescribe) at the time of establishment of the plan as a Roth IRA. Such designation shall be made in such manner as the Secretary may prescribe.

[Sec. 408A(c)]

(c) TREATMENT OF CONTRIBUTIONS.—

(1) NO DEDUCTION ALLOWED.—No deduction shall be allowed under section 219 for a contribution to a Roth IRA.

(2) CONTRIBUTION LIMIT.—The aggregate amount of contributions for any taxable year to all Roth IRAs maintained for the benefit of an individual shall not exceed the excess (if any) of—

(A) the maximum amount allowable as a deduction under section 219 with respect to such individual for such taxable year (computed without regard to subsection (d)(1) or (g) of such section), over

(B) the aggregate amount of contributions for such taxable year to all other individual retirement plans (other than Roth IRAs) maintained for the benefit of the individual.

(3) LIMITS BASED ON MODIFIED ADJUSTED GROSS INCOME.—

(A) DOLLAR LIMIT.—The amount determined under paragraph (2) for any taxable year shall not exceed an amount equal to the amount determined under paragraph (2)(A) for such taxable year, reduced (but not below zero) by the amount which bears the same ratio to such amount as—

(i) the excess of—

(I) the taxpayer's adjusted gross income for such taxable year, over

(II) the applicable dollar amount, bears to

(ii) $15,000 ($10,000 in the case of a joint return or a married individual filing a separate return).

The rules of subparagraphs (B) and (C) of section 219(g)(2) shall apply to any reduction under this subparagraph.

(B) DEFINITIONS.—For purposes of this paragraph—

(i) adjusted gross income shall be determined in the same manner as under section 219(g)(3), except that any amount included in gross income under subsection (d)(3) shall not be taken into account, and

(ii) the applicable dollar amount is—

(I) in the case of a taxpayer filing a joint return, $150,000,

(II) in the case of any other taxpayer (other than a married individual filing a separate return), $95,000, and

(III) in the case of a married individual filing a separate return, zero.

(C) MARITAL STATUS.—Section 219(g)(4) shall apply for purposes of this paragraph.

(D) INFLATION ADJUSTMENT.—In the case of any taxable year beginning in a calendar year after 2006, the dollar amounts in subclauses (I) and (II) of subparagraph (B)(ii) shall each be increased by an amount equal to—

(i) such dollar amount, multiplied by

(ii) the cost-of-living adjustment determined under section 1(f)(3) for the calendar year in which the taxable year begins, determined by substituting "calendar year 2005" for "calendar year 1992" in subparagraph (B) thereof.

Any increase determined under the preceding sentence shall be rounded to the nearest multiple of $1,000.

(4) CONTRIBUTIONS PERMITTED AFTER AGE 70 1/2.—Contributions to a Roth IRA may be made even after the individual for whom the account is maintained has attained age 70 1/2.

(5) MANDATORY DISTRIBUTION RULES NOT TO APPLY BEFORE DEATH.—Notwithstanding subsections (a)(6) and (b)(3) of section 408 (relating to required distributions), the following provisions shall not apply to any Roth IRA:

(A) Section 401(a)(9)(A).

(B) The incidental death benefit requirements of section 401(a).

(6) ROLLOVER CONTRIBUTIONS.—

(A) IN GENERAL.—No rollover contribution may be made to a Roth IRA unless it is a qualified rollover contribution.

(B) COORDINATION WITH LIMIT.—A qualified rollover contribution shall not be taken into account for purposes of paragraph (2).

(7) TIME WHEN CONTRIBUTIONS MADE.—For purposes of this section, the rule of section 219(f)(3) shall apply.

Amendments

• 2008, Worker, Retiree, and Employer Recovery Act of 2008 (P.L. 110-458)

P.L. 110-458, §108(d)(1)(A)-(C):

Amended Code Sec. 408A(c)(3)(B), as in effect after the amendments made by Act Sec. 824(b)(1) of the 2006 Act (P.L. 109-280), by striking the second "an" before "eligible", by striking "other than a Roth IRA" before "during", and by adding at the end a new flush sentence. **Effective** as if included in the provision of the 2006 Act to which the amendment relates [**effective** for distributions after 12-31-2007.—CCH].

P.L. 110-458, §108(h)(1):

Amended Code Sec. 408A(c)(3)(C), as added by Act Sec. 833(c) of the 2006 Act (P.L. 109-280), by redesignating it as subparagraph (E). **Effective** as if included in the provision of the 2006 Act to which the amendment relates [**effective** for tax years beginning after 2006.—CCH].

P.L. 110-458, §108(h)(2)(A)-(B):

Amended Code Sec. 408A(c)(3)(E), in the case of tax years beginning after 12-31-2009, as redesignated by Act Sec. 108(h)(1), by redesignating it as subparagraph (D), and by striking "subparagraph (C)(ii)" and inserting "subparagraph (B)(ii)". **Effective** for tax years beginning after 12-31-2009.

• 2006, Pension Protection Act of 2006 (P.L. 109-280)

P.L. 109-280, §824(b)(1)(A)-(B):

Amended Code Sec. 408A(c)(3)(B), as in effect before the Tax Increase Prevention and Reconciliation Act of 2005 (P.L. 109-222), in the text by striking "individual retirement plan" and inserting "an eligible retirement plan (as defined by section 402(c)(8)(B))", and in the heading by striking "IRA" the first place it appears [sic] and inserting "ELIGIBLE RETIREMENT PLAN". **Effective** for distributions after 12-31-2007.

P.L. 109-280, §833(c):

Amended Code Sec. 408A(c)(3) by adding at the end a new subparagraph (C)[(D)]. **Effective** for tax years beginning after 2006.

• 2006, Tax Increase Prevention and Reconciliation Act of 2005 (P.L. 109-222)

P.L. 109-222, §512(a)(1):

Amended Code Sec. 408A(c)(3) by striking subparagraph (B) and redesignating subparagraphs (C) and (D) as subparagraphs (B) and (C), respectively. **Effective** for tax years beginning after 12-31-2009. Prior to being stricken, Code Sec. 408A(c)(3)(B) read as follows:

(B) ROLLOVER FROM ELIGIBLE RETIREMENT PLAN.—A taxpayer shall not be allowed to make a qualified rollover contribution to a Roth IRA from an an [sic] eligible retirement plan (as defined by section 402(c)(8)(B)) other than a Roth IRA during any taxable year if, for the taxable year of the distribution to which such contribution relates—

(i) the taxpayer's adjusted gross income exceeds $100,000, or

(ii) the taxpayer is a married individual filing a separate return.

P.L. 109-222, §512(a)(2):

Amended Code Sec. 408A(c)(3)(B)(i), as redesignated by Act Sec. 512(a)(1), by striking "except that—"and all that follows and inserting "except that any amount included in gross income under subsection (d)(3) shall not be taken into account, and". **Effective** for tax years beginning after 12-31-2009. Prior to being amended, Code Sec. 408A(c)(3)(B)(i) read as follows:

(i) adjusted gross income shall be determined in the same manner as under section 219(g)(3), except that—

(I) any amount included in gross income under subsection (d)(3) shall not be taken into account; and

(II) any amount included in gross income by reason of a required distribution under a provision described in paragraph (5) shall not be taken into account for purposes of subparagraph (B)(i), and

• 1998, Tax and Trade Relief Extension Act of 1998 (P.L. 105-277)

P.L. 105-277, §4002(j):

Amended Code Sec. 408A(c)(3)(C)(i) by striking the period at the end of subclause (II) and inserting ", and". **Effective** as if included in the provision of P.L. 105-206 to which it relates [**effective** for tax years beginning after 12-31-2004.—CCH].

• 1998, IRS Restructuring and Reform Act of 1998 (P.L. 105-206)

P.L. 105-206, §6005(b)(1):

Amended Code Sec. 408A(c)(3)(A) by striking "shall be reduced" and inserting "shall not exceed an amount equal to the amount determined under paragraph (2)(A) for such taxable year, reduced". **Effective** as if included in the provision of P.L. 105-34 to which it relates [**effective** for tax years beginning after 12-31-97.—CCH].

P.L. 105-206, §6005(b)(2)(A)-(C):

Amended Code Sec. 408A(c)(3) by inserting "or a married individual filing a separate return" after "joint return" in subparagraph (A)(ii), by inserting ", for the taxable year of the distribution to which such contribution relates" after "if" in subparagraph (B), by striking "for such taxable year" after "gross income" in clause (i) of subparagraph (B), and by striking "and the deduction under section 219 shall be taken into account" before ", and" in subparagraph (C)(i). **Effective** as if included in the provision of P.L. 105-34 to which it relates [**effective** for tax years beginning after 12-31-97.—CCH].

P.L. 105-206, §7004(a):

Amended Code Sec. 408A(c)(3)(C)(i). **Effective** for tax years beginning after 12-31-2004. Prior to amendment, Code Sec. 408A(c)(3)(C)(i) read as follows:

(i) adjusted gross income shall be determined in the same manner as under section 219(g)(3), except that any amount included in gross income under subsection (d)(3) shall not be taken into account, and

[Sec. 408A(d)]

(d) DISTRIBUTION RULES.—For purposes of this title—

(1) EXCLUSION.—Any qualified distribution from a Roth IRA shall not be includible in gross income.

(2) QUALIFIED DISTRIBUTION.—For purposes of this subsection—

(A) IN GENERAL.—The term "qualified distribution" means any payment or distribution—

(i) made on or after the date on which the individual attains age 59½,

(ii) made to a beneficiary (or to the estate of the individual) on or after the death of the individual,

(iii) attributable to the individual's being disabled (within the meaning of section 72(m)(7)), or

(iv) which is a qualified special purpose distribution.

(B) DISTRIBUTIONS WITHIN NONEXCLUSION PERIOD.—A payment or distribution from a Roth IRA shall not be treated as a qualified distribution under subparagraph (A) if such payment or distribution is made within the 5-taxable year period beginning with the 1st taxable year for which the individual made a contribution to a Roth IRA (or such individual's spouse made a contribution to a Roth IRA) established for such individual.

(C) DISTRIBUTIONS OF EXCESS CONTRIBUTIONS AND EARNINGS.—The term "qualified distribution" shall not include any distribution of any contribution described in section 408(d)(4) and any net income allocable to the contribution.

(3) ROLLOVERS FROM AN ELIGIBLE RETIREMENT PLAN OTHER THAN A ROTH IRA.—

(A) IN GENERAL.—Notwithstanding sections 402(c), 403(b)(8), 408(d)(3), and 457(e)(16), in the case of any distribution to which this paragraph applies—

(i) there shall be included in gross income any amount which would be includible were it not part of a qualified rollover contribution,

(ii) section 72(t) shall not apply, and

(iii) unless the taxpayer elects not to have this clause apply, any amount required to be included in gross income for any taxable year beginning in 2010 by reason of this paragraph shall be so included ratably over the 2-taxable-year period beginning with the first taxable year beginning in 2011.

Any election under clause (iii) for any distributions during a taxable year may not be changed after the due date for such taxable year.

(B) DISTRIBUTIONS TO WHICH PARAGRAPH APPLIES.—This paragraph shall apply to a distribution from an eligible retirement plan (as defined by section 402(c)(8)(B)) maintained for the benefit of an individual which is contributed to a Roth IRA maintained for the benefit of such individual in a qualified rollover contribution. This paragraph shall not apply to a distribution which is a qualified rollover contribution from a Roth IRA or a qualified rollover contribution from a designated Roth account which is a rollover contribution described in section 402A(c)(3)(A).

(C) CONVERSIONS.—The conversion of an individual retirement plan (other than a Roth IRA) to a Roth IRA shall be treated for purposes of this paragraph as a distribution to which this paragraph applies.

(D) ADDITIONAL REPORTING REQUIREMENTS.—Trustees of Roth IRAs, trustees of individual retirement plans, persons subject to section 6047(d)(1), or all of the foregoing persons, whichever is appropriate, shall include such additional information in reports required under section 408(i) or 6047 as the Secretary may require to ensure that amounts required to be included in gross income under subparagraph (A) are so included.

(E) SPECIAL RULES FOR CONTRIBUTIONS TO WHICH 2-YEAR AVERAGING APPLIES.—In the case of a qualified rollover contribution to a Roth IRA of a distribution to which subparagraph (A)(iii) applied, the following rules shall apply:

(i) ACCELERATION OF INCLUSION.—

(I) IN GENERAL.—The amount otherwise required to be included in gross income for any taxable year beginning in 2010 or the first taxable year in the 2-year period under subparagraph (A)(iii) shall be increased by the aggregate distributions from Roth IRAs for such taxable year which are allocable under paragraph (4) to the portion of such qualified rollover contribution required to be included in gross income under subparagraph (A)(i).

(II) LIMITATION ON AGGREGATE AMOUNT INCLUDED.—The amount required to be included in gross income for any taxable year under subparagraph (A)(iii) shall not exceed the aggregate amount required to be included in gross income under subparagraph (A)(iii) for all taxable years in the 2-year period (without regard to subclause (I)) reduced by amounts included for all preceding taxable years.

(ii) DEATH OF DISTRIBUTEE.—

(I) IN GENERAL.—If the individual required to include amounts in gross income under such subparagraph dies before all of such amounts are included, all remaining amounts shall be included in gross income for the taxable year which includes the date of death.

(II) SPECIAL RULE FOR SURVIVING SPOUSE.—If the spouse of the individual described in subclause (I) acquires the individual's entire interest in any Roth IRA to which such qualified rollover contribution is properly allocable, the spouse may elect to treat the remaining amounts described in subclause (I) as includible in the spouse's gross income in the taxable years of the spouse ending with or within the taxable years of such individual in which such amounts would otherwise have been includible. Any such election may not be made or changed after the due date for the spouse's taxable year which includes the date of death.

(F) SPECIAL RULE FOR APPLYING SECTION 72.—

(i) IN GENERAL.—If—

(I) any portion of a distribution from a Roth IRA is properly allocable to a qualified rollover contribution described in this paragraph; and

(II) such distribution is made within the 5-taxable year period beginning with the taxable year in which such contribution was made,

then section 72(t) shall be applied as if such portion were includible in gross income.

(ii) LIMITATION.—Clause (i) shall apply only to the extent of the amount of the qualified rollover contribution includible in gross income under subparagraph (A)(i).

(4) AGGREGATION AND ORDERING RULES.—

(A) AGGREGATION RULES.—Section 408(d)(2) shall be applied separately with respect to Roth IRAs and other individual retirement plans.

(B) ORDERING RULES.—For purposes of applying this section and section 72 to any distribution from a Roth IRA, such distribution shall be treated as made—

(i) from contributions to the extent that the amount of such distribution, when added to all previous distributions from the Roth IRA, does not exceed the aggregate contributions to the Roth IRA; and

(ii) from such contributions in the following order:

(I) Contributions other than qualified rollover contributions to which paragraph (3) applies.

(II) Qualified rollover contributions to which paragraph (3) applies on a first-in, first-out basis.

Any distribution allocated to a qualified rollover contribution under clause (ii)(II) shall be allocated first to the portion of such contribution required to be included in gross income.

(5) QUALIFIED SPECIAL PURPOSE DISTRIBUTION.—For purposes of this section, the term "qualified special purpose distribution" means any distribution to which subparagraph (F) of section 72(t)(2) applies.

(6) TAXPAYER MAY MAKE ADJUSTMENTS BEFORE DUE DATE.—

(A) IN GENERAL.—Except as provided by the Secretary, if, on or before the due date for any taxable year, a taxpayer transfers in a trustee-to-trustee transfer any contribution to an individual retirement plan made during such taxable year from such plan to any other individual retirement plan, then, for purposes of this chapter, such contribution shall be treated as having been made to the transferee plan (and not the transferor plan).

(B) SPECIAL RULES.—

(i) TRANSFER OF EARNINGS.—Subparagraph (A) shall not apply to the transfer of any contribution unless such transfer is accompanied by any net income allocable to such contribution.

(ii) NO DEDUCTION.—Subparagraph (A) shall apply to the transfer of any contribution only to the extent no deduction was allowed with respect to the contribution to the transferor plan.

(7) DUE DATE.—For purposes of this subsection, the due date for any taxable year is the date prescribed by law (including extensions of time) for filing the taxpayer's return for such taxable year.

Amendments

• 2008, Worker, Retiree, and Employer Recovery Act of 2008 (P.L. 110-458)

P.L. 110-458, §108(d)(2):

Amended Code Sec. 408A(d)(3)(B), as in effect after the amendments made by Act Sec. 824(b)(2)(B) of the 2006 Act (P.L. 109-280), by striking "(other than a Roth IRA)" after "section 402(c)(8)(B))", and by inserting at the end a new sentence. **Effective** as if included in the provision of the 2006 Act to which the amendment relates [**effective** for distributions after 12-31-2007.—CCH].

• 2006, Pension Protection Act of 2006 (P.L. 109-280)

P.L. 109-280, §824(b)(2)(A)-(E):

Amended Code Sec. 408A(d)(3) by striking "section 408(d)(3)" [and]inserting "sections 402(c), 403(b)(8), 408(d)(3), and 457(e)(16)" in subparagraph (A), by striking "individual retirement plan" and inserting "eligible retirement plan (as defined by section 402(c)(8)(B))" in subparagraph (B), by inserting "or 6047" after "408(i)" in subparagraph (D), by striking "or both" and inserting "persons subject to section 6047(d)(1), or all of the foregoing persons" in subparagraph (D), and by striking "IRA" the first place it appears in the heading and inserting "ELIGIBLE RETIREMENT PLAN". **Effective** for distributions after 12-31-2007.

• 2006, Tax Increase Prevention and Reconciliation Act of 2005 (P.L. 109-222)

P.L. 109-222, §512(b)(1):

Amended Code Sec. 408A(d)(3)(A)(iii). **Effective** for tax years beginning after 12-31-2009. Prior to amendment, Code Sec. 408A(d)(3)(A)(iii) read as follows:

(iii) unless the taxpayer elects not to have this clause apply for any taxable year, any amount required to be included in gross income for such taxable year by reason of this paragraph for any distribution before January 1, 1999, shall be so included ratably over the 4-taxable year period beginning with such taxable year.

P.L. 109-222, §512(b)(2)(A):

Amended Code Sec. 408A(d)(3)(E)(i). **Effective** for tax years beginning after 12-31-2009. Prior to amendment, Code Sec. 408A(d)(3)(E)(i) read as follows:

(i) ACCELERATION OF INCLUSION.—

(I) IN GENERAL.—The amount required to be included in gross income for each of the first 3 taxable years in the 4-year period under subparagraph (A)(iii) shall be increased by the aggregate distributions from Roth IRAs for such taxable year which are allocable under paragraph (4) to the portion of such qualified rollover contribution required to be included in gross income under subparagraph (A)(i).

(II) LIMITATION ON AGGREGATE AMOUNT INCLUDED.—The amount required to be included in gross income for any taxable year under subparagraph (A)(iii) shall not exceed the aggregate amount required to be included in gross income under subparagraph (A)(iii) for all taxable years in the 4-year period (without regard to subclause (I)) reduced by amounts included for all preceding taxable years.

P.L. 109-222, §512(b)(2)(B):

Amended the heading for Code Sec. 408A(d)(3)(E) by striking "4-YEAR" and inserting "2-YEAR". **Effective** for tax years beginning after 12-31-2009.

• 1998, IRS Restructuring and Reform Act of 1998 (P.L. 105-206)

P.L. 105-206, §6005(b)(3)(A):

Amended Code Sec. 408A(d)(2) by striking subparagraph (B) and inserting a new subparagraph (B). **Effective** as if included in the provision of P.L. 105-34 to which it relates [**effective** for tax years beginning after 12-31-97.—CCH]. Prior to being stricken, Code Sec. 408(d)(2)(B) read as follows:

(B) CERTAIN DISTRIBUTIONS WITHIN 5 YEARS.—A payment or distribution shall not be treated as a qualified distribution under subparagraph (A) if—

(i) it is made within the 5-taxable year period beginning with the 1st taxable year for which the individual made a contribution to a Roth IRA (or such individual's spouse made a contribution to a Roth IRA) established for such individual, or

(ii) in the case of a payment or distribution properly allocable (as determined in the manner prescribed by the Secretary) to a qualified rollover contribution from an individual retirement plan other than a Roth IRA (or income allocable thereto), it is made within the 5-taxable year period beginning with the taxable year in which the rollover contribution was made.

P.L. 105-206, §6005(b)(3)(B):

Amended Code Sec. 408A(d)(2) by adding at the end a new subparagraph (C). **Effective** as if included in the provision of P.L. 105-34 to which it relates [**effective** for tax years beginning after 12-31-97.—CCH].

P.L. 105-206, §6005(b)(4)(A)-(B):

Amended Code Sec. 408A(d)(3) by striking clause (iii) of subparagraph (A) and inserting a new clause (iii) and new material, and by adding at the end new subparagraphs (F) and (G). **Effective** as if included in the provision of P.L. 105-34 to which it relates [**effective** for tax years beginning after 12-31-97.—CCH]. Prior to being stricken, Code Sec. 408A(d)(3)(A)(iii) read as follows:

(iii) in the case of a distribution before January 1, 1999, any amount required to be included in gross income by reason of this paragraph shall be so included ratably over the 4-taxable year period beginning with the taxable year in which the payment or distribution is made.

P.L. 105-206, §6005(b)(5)(A):

Amended Code Sec. 408A(d)(4). **Effective** as if included in the provision of P.L. 105-34 to which it relates [**effective** for tax years beginning after 12-31-97.—CCH]. Prior to amendment, Code Sec. 408A(d)(4) read as follows:

(4) COORDINATION WITH INDIVIDUAL RETIREMENT ACCOUNTS.—Section 408(d)(2) shall be applied separately with respect to Roth IRAs and other individual retirement plans.

P.L. 105-206, §6005(b)(5)(B):

Amended Code Sec. 408A(d)(1). **Effective** as if included in the provision of P.L. 105-34 to which it relates [**effective** for tax years beginning after 12-31-97.—CCH]. Prior to amendment, Code Sec. 408A(d)(1) read as follows:

(1) GENERAL RULES.—

(A) EXCLUSIONS FROM GROSS INCOME.—Any qualified distribution from a Roth IRA shall not be includible in gross income.

(B) NONQUALIFIED DISTRIBUTIONS.—In applying section 72 to any distribution from a Roth IRA which is not a qualified distribution, such distribution shall be treated as made from contributions to the Roth IRA to the extent that such distribution, when added to all previous distributions from the Roth IRA, does not exceed the aggregate amount of contributions to the Roth IRA.

P.L. 105-206, §6005(b)(6)(A):

Amended Code Sec. 408A(d) by adding at the end a new paragraph (6). **Effective** as if included in the provision of P.L. 105-34 to which it relates [**effective** for tax years beginning after 12-31-97.—CCH].

P.L. 105-206, §6005(b)(6)(B):

Amended Code Sec. 408A(d)(3), as amended by Act Sec. 6005(b), by striking subparagraph (D) and by redesignating subparagraphs (E), (F), and (G) as subparagraphs (D), (E), and (F), respectively. **Effective** as if included in P.L. 105-34 to which it relates [**effective** for tax years beginning after 12-31-97.—CCH]. Prior to being stricken, Code Sec. 408A(d)(3)(D) read as follows:

(D) CONVERSION OF EXCESS CONTRIBUTIONS.—If, no later than the due date for filing the return of tax for any taxable year (without regard to extensions), an individual transfers, from an individual retirement plan (other than a Roth IRA), contributions for such taxable year (and any earnings allocable thereto) to a Roth IRA, no such amount shall be includible in gross income to the extent no deduction was allowed with respect to such amount.

P.L. 105-206, §6005(b)(7):

Amended Code Sec. 408A(d), as amended by Act Sec. 6005(b)(6), by adding at the end a new paragraph (7). **Effective** as if included in the provision of P.L. 105-34 to which it relates [**effective** for tax years beginning after 12-31-97.—CCH].

[Sec. 408A(e)]

(e) QUALIFIED ROLLOVER CONTRIBUTION.—For purposes of this section—

(1) IN GENERAL.—The term "qualified rollover contribution" means a rollover contribution—

(A) to a Roth IRA from another such account,

(B) from an eligible retirement plan, but only if—

(i) in the case of an individual retirement plan, such rollover contribution meets the requirements of section 408(d)(3), and

(ii) in the case of any eligible retirement plan (as defined in section 402(c)(8)(B) other than clauses (i) and (ii) thereof), such rollover contribution meets the requirements of section 402(c), 403(b)(8), or 457(e)(16), as applicable.

For purposes of section 408(d)(3)(B), there shall be disregarded any qualified rollover contribution from an individual retirement plan (other than a Roth IRA) to a Roth IRA.

(2) MILITARY DEATH GRATUITY.—

(A) IN GENERAL.—The term "qualified rollover contribution" includes a contribution to a Roth IRA maintained for the benefit of an individual made before the end of the 1-year period beginning on the date on which such individual receives an amount under section 1477 of title 10, United States Code, or section 1967 of title 38 of such Code, with respect to a person, to the extent that such contribution does not exceed—

(i) the sum of the amounts received during such period by such individual under such sections with respect to such person, reduced by

(ii) the amounts so received which were contributed to a Coverdell education savings account under section 530(d)(9).

(B) ANNUAL LIMIT ON NUMBER OF ROLLOVERS NOT TO APPLY.—Section 408(d)(3)(B) shall not apply with respect to amounts treated as a rollover by the [sic] subparagraph (A).

(C) APPLICATION OF SECTION 72.—For purposes of applying section 72 in the case of a distribution which is not a qualified distribution, the amount treated as a rollover by reason of subparagraph (A) shall be treated as [an] investment in the contract.

Amendments

• 2008, Worker, Retiree, and Employer Recovery Act of 2008 (P.L. 110-458)

P.L. 110-458, §125, provides:

SEC. 125. ROLLOVER OF AMOUNTS RECEIVED IN AIRLINE CARRIER BANKRUPTCY TO ROTH IRAS.

(a) GENERAL RULE.—If a qualified airline employee receives any airline payment amount and transfers any portion of such amount to a Roth IRA within 180 days of receipt of such amount (or, if later, within 180 days of the date of the enactment of this Act), then such amount (to the extent so transferred) shall be treated as a qualified rollover contribution described in section 408A(e) of the Internal Revenue Code of 1986, and the limitations described in section 408A(c)(3) of such Code shall not apply to any such transfer.

(b) DEFINITIONS AND SPECIAL RULES.—For purposes of this section—

(1) AIRLINE PAYMENT AMOUNT.—

(A) IN GENERAL.—The term "airline payment amount" means any payment of any money or other property which is payable by a commercial passenger airline carrier to a qualified airline employee—

(i) under the approval of an order of a Federal bankruptcy court in a case filed after September 11, 2001, and before January 1, 2007, and

(ii) in respect of the qualified airline employee's interest in a bankruptcy claim against the carrier, any note of the carrier (or amount paid in lieu of a note being issued), or any other fixed obligation of the carrier to pay a lump sum amount.

The amount of such payment shall be determined without regard to any requirement to deduct and withhold tax from such payment under sections 3102(a) and 3402(a).

(B) EXCEPTION.—An airline payment amount shall not include any amount payable on the basis of the carrier's future earnings or profits.

(2) QUALIFIED AIRLINE EMPLOYEE.—The term "qualified airline employee" means an employee or former employee of a commercial passenger airline carrier who was a participant in a defined benefit plan maintained by the carrier which—

(A) is a plan described in section 401(a) of the Internal Revenue Code of 1986 which includes a trust exempt from tax under section 501(a) of such Code, and

(B) was terminated or became subject to the restrictions contained in paragraphs (2) and (3) of section 402(b) of the Pension Protection Act of 2006.

(3) REPORTING REQUIREMENTS.—If a commercial passenger airline carrier pays 1 or more airline payment amounts, the carrier shall, within 90 days of such payment (or, if later, within 90 days of the date of the enactment of this Act), report—

(A) to the Secretary of the Treasury, the names of the qualified airline employees to whom such amounts were paid, and

(B) to the Secretary and to such employees, the years and the amounts of the payments.

Such reports shall be in such form, and contain such additional information, as the Secretary may prescribe.

(c) EFFECTIVE DATE.—This section shall apply to transfers made after the date of the enactment of this Act with respect to airline payment amounts paid before, on, or after such date.

• 2008, Heroes Earnings Assistance and Relief Tax Act of 2008 (P.L. 110-245)

P.L. 110-245, §109(a):

Amended Code Sec. 408A(e), as in effect before the amendments made by section 824 of the Pension Protection Act of 2006 (P.L. 109-280). **Effective** generally with respect to deaths from injuries occurring on or after 6-17-2008. For a special rule, see Act Sec. 109(d)(2), below. Prior to amendment, Code Sec. 408A(e) read as follows:

(e) QUALIFIED ROLLOVER CONTRIBUTION.—For purposes of this section, the term "qualified rollover contribution" means a rollover contribution to a Roth IRA from another such account, or from an individual retirement plan, but only if such rollover contribution meets the requirements of section 408(d)(3). Such term includes a rollover contribution described in section 402A(c)(3)(A). For purposes of section 408(d)(3)(B), there shall be disregarded any qualified rollover contribution from an individual retirement plan (other than a Roth IRA) to a Roth IRA.

P.L. 110-245, §109(b):

Amended Code Sec. 408A(e), as in effect after the amendments made by section 824 of the Pension Protection Act of 2006 (P.L 109-280). **Effective** generally with respect to deaths from injuries occurring on or after 6-17-2008. For a special rule, see Act Sec. 109(d)(3), below. Prior to amendment, Code Sec. 408A(e) read as follows:

(e) QUALIFIED ROLLOVER CONTRIBUTION.—For purposes of this section, the term "qualified rollover contribution" means a rollover contribution—

(1) to a Roth IRA from another such account,

(2) from an eligible retirement plan, but only if—

(A) in the case of an individual retirement plan, such rollover contribution meets the requirements of section 408(d)(3), and

(B) in the case of any eligible retirement plan (as defined in section 402(c)(8)(B) other than clauses (i) and (ii) thereof), such rollover contribution meets the requirements of section 402(c), 403(b)(8), or 457(e)(16), as applicable.

For purposes of section 408(d)(3)(B), there shall be disregarded any qualified rollover contribution from an individual retirement plan (other than a Roth IRA) to a Roth IRA.

P.L. 110-245, §109(d)(2)-(3), provides:

(2) APPLICATION OF AMENDMENTS TO DEATHS FROM INJURIES OCCURRING ON OR AFTER OCTOBER 7, 2001, AND BEFORE ENACTMENT.—The amendments made by this section shall apply to any contribution made pursuant to section 408A(e)(2) or 530(d)(5) [sic] of the Internal Revenue Code of 1986, as amended by this Act, with respect to amounts received under section 1477 of title 10, United States Code, or under section 1967 of title 38 of such Code, for deaths from injuries occurring on or after October 7, 2001, and before the date of the enactment of this Act [6-17-2008.—CCH] if such contribution is made not later than 1 year after the date of the enactment of this Act.

(3) PENSION PROTECTION ACT CHANGES.—Section 408A(e)(1) of the Internal Revenue Code of 1986 (as in effect after the amendments made by subsection (b)) shall apply to taxable years beginning after December 31, 2007.

• 2006, Pension Protection Act of 2006 (P.L. 109-280)

P.L. 109-280, §811, provides:

SEC. 811. PENSIONS AND INDIVIDUAL RETIREMENT ARRANGEMENT PROVISIONS OF ECONOMIC GROWTH AND TAX RELIEF RECONCILIATION ACT OF 2001 MADE PERMANENT.

Title IX of the Economic Growth and Tax Relief Reconciliation Act of 2001 [P.L. 107-16] shall not apply to the provisions of, and amendments made by, subtitles A through F of title VI [§§601-666]of such Act (relating to pension and individual retirement arrangement provisions).

P.L. 109-280, §824(a):

Amended Code Sec. 408A(e). **Effective** for distributions after 12-31-2007. Prior to amendment [but as amended by Act Sec. 109(a) of the Heroes Earnings Assistance and Relief Tax Act of 2008 (P.L. 110-245)], Code Sec. 408A(e) read as follows:

(e) QUALIFIED ROLLOVER CONTRIBUTION.—For purposes of this section—

(1) IN GENERAL.—The term "qualified rollover contribution" means a rollover contribution to a Roth IRA from another such account, or from an individual retirement plan, but only if such rollover contribution meets the requirements of section 408(d)(3). Such term includes a rollover contribution described in section 402A(c)(3)(A). For purposes of section 408(d)(3)(B), there shall be disregarded any qualified rollover contribution from an individual retirement plan (other than a Roth IRA) to a Roth IRA.

(2) MILITARY DEATH GRATUITY.—

(A) IN GENERAL.—The term "qualified rollover contribution" includes a contribution to a Roth IRA maintained for the benefit of an individual made before the end of the 1-year period beginning on the date on which such individual receives an amount under section 1477 of title 10, United States Code, or section 1967 of title 38 of such Code, with respect to a person, to the extent that such contribution does not exceed—

(i) the sum of the amounts received during such period by such individual under such sections with respect to such person, reduced by

(ii) the amounts so received which were contributed to a Coverdell education savings account under section 530(d)(9).

(B) ANNUAL LIMIT ON NUMBER OF ROLLOVERS NOT TO APPLY.—Section 408(d)(3)(B) shall not apply with respect to amounts treated as a rollover by subparagraph (A).

(C) APPLICATION OF SECTION 72.—For purposes of applying section 72 in the case of a distribution which is not a qualified distribution, the amount treated as a rollover by reason of subparagraph (A) shall be treated as investment in the contract.

• 2001, Economic Growth and Tax Relief Reconciliation Act of 2001 (P.L. 107-16)

P.L. 107-16, §617(e)(1):

Amended Code Sec. 408A(e) by adding after the first sentence a new sentence. **Effective** for tax years beginning after 12-31-2005.

P.L. 107-16, §901(a)-(b), provides [but see P.L. 109-280, §811, above]:

SEC. 901. SUNSET OF PROVISIONS OF ACT.

(a) IN GENERAL.—All provisions of, and amendments made by, this Act shall not apply—

(1) to taxable, plan, or limitation years beginning after December 31, 2010, or

(2) in the case of title V, to estates of decedents dying, gifts made, or generation skipping transfers, after December 31, 2010.

(b) APPLICATION OF CERTAIN LAWS.—The Internal Revenue Code of 1986 and the Employee Retirement Income Security Act of 1974 shall be applied and administered to years, estates, gifts, and transfers described in subsection (a) as if the provisions and amendments described in subsection (a) had never been enacted.

[Sec. 408A(f)]

(f) INDIVIDUAL RETIREMENT PLAN.—For purposes of this section—

(1) a simplified employee pension or a simple retirement account may not be designated as a Roth IRA; and

(2) contributions to any such pension or account shall not be taken into account for purposes of subsection (c)(2)(B).

Amendments

• 1998, IRS Restructuring and Reform Act of 1998 (P.L. 105-206)

P.L. 105-206, §6005(b)(9):

Amended Code Sec. 408A by adding at the end a new subsection (f). **Effective** as if included in the provision of P.L. 105-34 to which it relates [**effective** for tax years beginning after 12-31-97.—CCH].

• 1997, Taxpayer Relief Act of 1997 (P.L. 105-34)

P.L. 105-34, §302(a):

Amended subpart A of part I of subchapter D of chapter 1 by inserting after Code Sec. 408 a new Code Sec. 408A. **Effective** for tax years beginning after 12-31-97.

[Sec. 409]

SEC. 409. QUALIFICATIONS FOR TAX CREDIT EMPLOYEE STOCK OWNERSHIP PLANS.

[Sec. 409(a)]

(a) TAX CREDIT EMPLOYEE STOCK OWNERSHIP PLAN DEFINED.—Except as otherwise provided in this title, for purposes of this title, the term "tax credit employee stock ownership plan" means a defined contribution plan which—

(1) meets the requirements of section 401(a),

(2) is designed to invest primarily in employer securities, and

(3) meets the requirements of subsections (b), (c), (d), (e), (f), (g), (h), and (o) of this section.

Amendments

• 1986, Tax Reform Act of 1986 (P.L. 99-514)

P.L. 99-514, §1174(b)(2):

Amended Code Sec. 409(a)(3) by striking out "and (h)" and inserting in lieu thereof "(h), and (o)". **Effective** for distributions attributable to stock acquired after 12-31-86.

• 1984, Deficit Reduction Act of 1984 (P.L. 98-369)

P.L. 98-369, §491(e)(1):

Amended the section heading for Code Sec. 409A by striking out "Sec. 409A." and inserting in lieu thereof "Sec. 409.". **Effective** 1-1-84.

[Sec. 409(b)]

(b) REQUIRED ALLOCATION OF EMPLOYER SECURITIES.—

(1) IN GENERAL.—A plan meets the requirements of this subsection if—

(A) the plan provides for the allocation for the plan year of all employer securities transferred to it or purchased by it (because of the requirements of section 41(c)(1)(B) to the accounts of all participants who are entitled to share in such allocation, and

(B) for the plan year the allocation to each participant so entitled is an amount which bears substantially the same proportion to the amount of all such securities allocated to all such participants in the plan for that year as the amount of compensation paid to such participant during that year bears to the compensation paid to all such participants during that year.

(2) COMPENSATION IN EXCESS OF $100,000 DISREGARDED.—For purposes of paragraph (1), compensation of any participant in excess of the first $100,000 per year shall be disregarded.

(3) DETERMINATION OF COMPENSATION.—For purposes of this subsection, the amount of compensation paid to a participant for any period is the amount of such participant's compensation (within the meaning of section 415(c)(3)) for such period.

(4) SUSPENSION OF ALLOCATION IN CERTAIN CASES.—Notwithstanding paragraph (1), the allocation to the account of any participant which is attributable to the basic employee plan credit or the credit allowed under section 41 (relating to the employee stock ownership credit) may be extended over whatever period may be necessary to comply with the requirements of section 415.

Amendments

• 1984, Deficit Reduction Act of 1984 (P.L. 98-369)

P.L. 98-369, §474(r)(15)(A):

Amended Code Sec. 409 (as redesignated by Act Sec. 491) by striking out "44G" each place it appeared in subsection (b) and inserting in lieu thereof "41". **Effective** for tax years beginning after 12-31-83, and to carrybacks from such years.

P.L. 98-369, §474(r)(15)(B):

Amended Code Sec. 409(b)(1), as redesignated, by striking out "48(n)(1)(A) or". **Effective** for tax years beginning after 12-31-83, and to carrybacks from such years.

• 1981, Economic Recovery Tax Act of 1981 (P.L. 97-34)

P.L. 97-34, §331(c)(1)(A):

Amended Code Sec. 409A(b)(1)(A) by inserting "or 44G(c)(1)(B)" after "section 48(n)(1)(A)". **Effective** for tax years ending after 12-31-82.

P.L. 97-34, §331(c)(1)(B):

Amended Code Sec. 409A(b)(4) by inserting "or the credit allowed under section 44G (relating to the employee stock ownership credit" after "basic employee plan credit". **Effective** for tax years ending after 12-31-82.

[Sec. 409(c)]

(c) PARTICIPANTS MUST HAVE NONFORFEITABLE RIGHTS.—A plan meets the requirements of this subsection only if it provides that each participant has a nonforfeitable right to any employer security allocated to his account.

[Sec. 409(d)]

(d) EMPLOYER SECURITIES MUST STAY IN THE PLAN.—A plan meets the requirements of this subsection only if it provides that no employer security allocated to a participant's account under subsection (b) (or allocated to a participant's account in connection with matched employer and employee contributions) may be distributed from that account before the end of the 84th month beginning after the month in which the security is allocated to the account. To the extent provided in the plan, the preceding sentence shall not apply in the case of—

(1) death, disability, separation from service, or termination of the plan;

(2) a transfer of a participant to the employment of an acquiring employer from the employment of the selling corporation in the case of a sale to the acquiring corporation of substantially all of the assets used by the selling corporation in a trade or business conducted by the selling corporation, or

(3) with respect to the stock of a selling corporation, a disposition of such selling corporation's interest in a subsidiary when the participant continues employment with such subsidiary.

This subsection shall not apply to any distribution required under section 401(a)(9) or to any distribution or reinvestment required under section 401(a)(28).

Amendments

• 1988, Technical and Miscellaneous Revenue Act of 1988 (P.L. 100-647)

P.L. 100-647, §1011B(j)(3):

Amended Code Sec. 409(d) by inserting "or to any distribution or reinvestment required under section 401(a)(28)" after "section 401(a)(9)" in the last sentence thereof. **Effective** as if included in the provision of P.L. 99-514 to which it relates.

• 1986, Tax Reform Act of 1986 (P.L. 99-514)

P.L. 99-514, §1174(a)(1):

Amended Code Sec. 409(d)(1) by striking out "or separation from service" and inserting in lieu thereof "separation from service, or termination of the plan". **Effective** for distributions after 12-31-84 [**effective** date changed by P.L. 100-647, §1011B(i)(2)].

P.L. 99-514, §1852(a)(4)(B):

Amended Code Sec. 409(d) by adding at the end thereof a new sentence. **Effective** as if included in the provision of P.L. 98-369 to which it relates.

P.L. 99-514, §1899A(11):

Amended Code Sec. 409(d) by striking out "particicipants's" and inserting in lieu thereof "participant's". **Effective** 10-22-86.

• 1983, Technical Corrections Act of 1982 (P.L. 97-448)

P.L. 97-448, §103(i):

Amended Code Sec. 409A(d)(2). **Effective** as if included in the provision of P.L. 97-34 to which it relates. Prior to amendment, Code Sec. 409A(d)(2) read as follows:

"(2) a transfer of a participant to the employment of an acquiring employer from the employment of the selling corporation in the case of—

(A) a sale to the acquiring employer of substantially all of the assets used by the selling corporation in a trade or business conducted by the selling corporation, or

(B) the sale of substantially all of the stock of a subsidiary of the employer, or".

• 1981, Economic Recovery Tax Act of 1981 (P.L. 97-34)

P.L. 97-34, §337(a):

Amended Code Sec. 409A(d) by striking out the last sentence and by inserting a new last sentence. **Effective** for distributions described in Code Sec. 409A(d) (or any corresponding provision of prior law) made after 3-29-75. Prior to amendment, the last sentence of Code Sec. 409A(d) read: "To the extent provided in the plan, the preceding sentence shall not apply in the case of separation from service, death, or disability."

[Sec. 409(e)]

(e) VOTING RIGHTS.—

(1) IN GENERAL.—A plan meets the requirements of this subsection if it meets the requirements of paragraph (2) or (3), whichever is applicable.

(2) REQUIREMENTS WHERE EMPLOYER HAS A REGISTRATION-TYPE CLASS OF SECURITIES.—If the employer has a registration-type class of securities, the plan meets the requirements of this paragraph only if each participant or beneficiary in the plan is entitled to direct the plan as to the manner in which securities of the employer which are entitled to vote and are allocated to the account of such participant or beneficiary are to be voted.

(3) REQUIREMENT FOR OTHER EMPLOYERS.—If the employer does not have a registration-type class of securities, the plan meets the requirements of this paragraph only if each participant or beneficiary in the plan is entitled to direct the plan as to the manner in which voting rights under securities of the employer which are allocated to the account of such participant or beneficiary are to be exercised with respect to any corporate matter which involves the voting of such shares with respect to the approval or disapproval of any corporate merger or consolidation, recapitalization, reclassification, liquidation, dissolution, sale of substantially all assets of a trade or business, or such similar transaction as the Secretary may prescribe in regulations.

(4) REGISTRATION-TYPE CLASS OF SECURITIES DEFINED.—For purposes of this subsection, the term "registration-type class of securities" means—

(A) a class of securities required to be registered under section 12 of the Securities Exchange Act of 1934, and

(B) a class of securities which would be required to be so registered except for the exemption from registration provided in subsection (g)(2)(H) of such section 12.

(5) 1 VOTE PER PARTICIPANT.—A plan meets the requirements of paragraph (3) with respect to an issue if—

(A) the plan permits each participant 1 vote with respect to such issue, and

(B) the trustee votes the shares held by the plan in the proportion determined after application of subparagraph (A).

Amendments

• 1988, Technical and Miscellaneous Revenue Act of 1988 (P.L. 100-647)

P.L. 100-647, §1018(t)(4)(H):

Amended Code Sec. 409(e)(5) by striking out "(2) or" after "paragraph". **Effective** as if included in the provision of P.L. 99-514 to which it relates.

• 1986, Tax Reform Act of 1986 (P.L. 99-514)

P.L. 99-514, §1854(b)(1)(A):

Amended Code Sec. 409(e) by adding at the end thereof new paragraph (5). **Effective** on 10-22-86.

P.L. 99-514, §1854(f)(1)(B):

Amended Code Sec. 409(e)(3) by striking out all that follows "with respect to" and inserting in lieu thereof "any corporate matter which involves the voting of such shares and which relates to any corporate merger or consolidation, recapitalization, reclassification, liquidation, dissolution, sale of substantially all assets of a trade or business, or such similar transaction as the Secretary may prescribe in regulations." **Effective** after 12-31-86, to stock acquired after 12-31-79. Prior to amendment, Code Sec. 409(e)(3) read as follows:

(3) REQUIREMENT FOR OTHER EMPLOYERS.—If the employer does not have a registration-type class of securities, the plan meets the requirements of this paragraph only if each participant in the plan is entitled to direct the plan as to the manner in which voting rights under employer securities which are allocated to the account of such participant are to be exercised with respect to a corporate matter which (by law or charter) must be decided by more than a majority vote of outstanding common shares voted.

P.L. 99-514, §1854(f)(1)(C):

Amended Code Sec. 409(e)(2) and (3) by striking out "employer securities" and inserting in lieu thereof "securities of the employer". **Effective** after 12-31-86, to stock acquired after 12-31-79.

P.L. 99-514, §1854(f)(1)(D):

Amended Code Sec. 409(e)(2) and (3) by inserting "or beneficiary" after "participant" each place it appears. **Effective** after 12-31-86, to stock acquired after 12-31-79.

[Sec. 409(f)]

(f) PLAN MUST BE ESTABLISHED BEFORE EMPLOYER'S DUE DATE.—

(1) IN GENERAL.—A plan meets the requirements of this subsection only if it is established on or before the due date (including any extension of such date) for the filing of the employer's tax return for the first taxable year of the employer for which an employee plan credit is claimed by the employer with respect to the plan.

(2) SPECIAL RULE FOR FIRST YEAR.—A plan which otherwise meets the requirements of this section shall not be considered to have failed to meet the requirements of section 401(a) merely because it was not established by the close of the first taxable year of the employer for which an employee plan credit is claimed by the employer with respect to the plan.

[Sec. 409(g)]

(g) TRANSFERRED AMOUNTS MUST STAY IN PLAN EVEN THOUGH INVESTMENT CREDIT IS REDETERMINED OR RECAPTURED.—A plan meets the requirement of this subsection only if it provides that amounts which are transferred to the plan (because of the requirements of section 48(n)(1) or 41(c)(1)(B)) shall remain in the plan (and, if allocated under the plan, shall remain so allocated) even though part or all of the employee plan credit or the credit allowed under section 41 (relating to employee stock ownership credit) is recaptured or redetermined. For purposes of the preceding sentence, the references to section 48(n)(1) and the employee plan credit shall refer to such section and credit as in effect before the enactment of the Tax Reform Act of 1984.

Amendments

• 1984, Deficit Reduction Act of 1984 (P.L. 98-369)

P.L. 98-369, §474(r)(15)(A):

Amended Code Sec. 409 (as redesignated by Act Sec. 491) by striking out "44G" each place it appeared in subsection (g) and inserting in lieu thereof "41". **Effective** for tax years beginning after 12-31-83, and to carrybacks from such years.

P.L. 98-369, §474(r)(15)(C):

Amended Code Sec. 409(g), as redesignated, by adding at the end thereof a new sentence. **Effective** for tax years beginning after 12-31-83, and to carrybacks from such years.

• 1981, Economic Recovery Tax Act of 1981 (P.L. 97-34)

P.L. 97-34, §331(c)(1)(C):

Amended Code Sec. 409A(g) by inserting "or 44G(c)(1)(B)" after "section 48(n)(1)". **Effective** for tax years ending after 12-31-82.

P.L. 97-34, §331(c)(1)(D):

Amended Code Sec. 409A(g) by inserting "or the credit allowed under section 44G (relating to employee stock ownership credit)" after "employee plan credit". **Effective** for tax years ending after 12-31-82.

[Sec. 409(h)]

(h) RIGHT TO DEMAND EMPLOYER SECURITIES; PUT OPTION.—

(1) IN GENERAL.—A plan meets the requirements of this subsection if a participant who is entitled to a distribution from the plan—

(A) has a right to demand that his benefits be distributed in the form of employer securities, and

(B) if the employer securities are not readily tradable on an established market, has a right to require that the employer repurchase employer securities under a fair valuation formula.

(2) PLAN MAY DISTRIBUTE CASH IN CERTAIN CASES.—

(A) IN GENERAL.—A plan which otherwise meets the requirements of this subsection or of section 4975(e)(7) shall not be considered to have failed to meet the requirements of section 401(a) merely because under the plan the benefits may be distributed in cash or in the form of employer securities.

(B) EXCEPTION FOR CERTAIN PLANS RESTRICTED FROM DISTRIBUTING SECURITIES.—

(i) IN GENERAL.—A plan to which this subparagraph applies shall not be treated as failing to meet the requirements of this subsection or section 401(a) merely because it does not permit a participant to exercise the right described in paragraph (1)(A) if such plan provides that the participant entitled to a distribution has a right to receive the distribution in cash, except that such plan may distribute employer securities subject to a requirement that such securities may be resold to the employer under terms which meet the requirements of paragraph (1)(B).

(ii) APPLICABLE PLANS.—This subparagraph shall apply to a plan which otherwise meets the requirements of this subsection or section 4975(e)(7) and which is established and maintained by—

(I) an employer whose charter or bylaws restrict the ownership of substantially all outstanding employer securities to employees or to a trust described in section 401(a), or

(II) an S corporation.

(3) SPECIAL RULE FOR BANKS.—In the case of a plan established and maintained by a bank (as defined in section 581) which is prohibited by law from redeeming or purchasing its own securities, the requirements of paragraph (1)(B) shall not apply if the plan provides that participants entitled to a distribution from the plan shall have a right to receive a distribution in cash.

(4) PUT OPTION PERIOD.—An employer shall be deemed to satisfy the requirements of paragraph (1)(B) if it provides a put option for a period of at least 60 days following the date of distribution of stock of the employer and, if the put option is not exercised within such 60-day period, for an additional period of at least 60 days in the following plan year (as provided in regulations promulgated by the Secretary).

(5) PAYMENT REQUIREMENT FOR TOTAL DISTRIBUTION.—If an employer is required to repurchase employer securities which are distributed to the employee as part of a total distribution, the requirements of paragraph (1)(B) shall be treated as met if—

(A) the amount to be paid for the employer securities is paid in substantially equal periodic payments (not less frequently than annually) over a period beginning not later than 30 days after the exercise of the put option described in paragraph (4) and not exceeding 5 years, and

(B) there is adequate security provided and reasonable interest paid on the unpaid amounts referred to in subparagraph (A).

For purposes of this paragraph, the term "total distribution" means the distribution within 1 taxable year to the recipient of the balance to the credit of the recipient's account.

(6) PAYMENT REQUIREMENT FOR INSTALLMENT DISTRIBUTIONS.—If an employer is required to repurchase employer securities as part of an installment distribution, the requirements of paragraph (1)(B) shall be treated as met if the amount to be paid for the employer securities is paid not later than 30 days after the exercise of the put option described in paragraph (4).

(7) EXCEPTION WHERE EMPLOYEE ELECTED DIVERSIFICATION.—Paragraph (1)(A) shall not apply with respect to the portion of the participant's account which the employee elected to have reinvested under section 401(a)(28)(B) or subparagraph (B) or (C) of section 401(a)(35).

Amendments

• 2006, Pension Protection Act of 2006 (P.L. 109-280)

P.L. 109-280, §901(a)(2)(B):

Amended Code Sec. 409(h)(7) by inserting "or subparagraph (B) or (C) of section 401(a)(35)" before the period at the end. For the **effective** date, see Act Sec. 901(c), below.

P.L. 109-280, §901(c), provides:

(c) EFFECTIVE DATES.—

(1) IN GENERAL.—Except as provided in paragraphs (2) and (3), the amendments made by this section shall apply to plan years beginning after December 31, 2006.

(2) SPECIAL RULE FOR COLLECTIVELY BARGAINED AGREEMENTS.—In the case of a plan maintained pursuant to 1 or more collective bargaining agreements between employee representatives and 1 or more employers ratified on or before the date of the enactment of this Act, paragraph (1) shall be applied to benefits pursuant to, and individuals covered by, any such agreement by substituting for "December 31, 2006" the earlier of—

(A) the later of—

(i) December 31, 2007, or

(ii) the date on which the last of such collective bargaining agreements terminates (determined without regard to any extension thereof after such date of enactment), or

(B) December 31, 2008.

(3) SPECIAL RULE FOR CERTAIN EMPLOYER SECURITIES HELD IN AN ESOP.—

(A) IN GENERAL.—In the case of employer securities to which this paragraph applies, the amendments made by this section shall apply to plan years beginning after the earlier of—

(i) December 31, 2007, or

(ii) the first date on which the fair market value of such securities exceeds the guaranteed minimum value described in subparagraph (B)(ii).

(B) APPLICABLE SECURITIES.—This paragraph shall apply to employer securities which are attributable to employer contributions other than elective deferrals, and which, on September 17, 2003—

(i) consist of preferred stock, and

(ii) are within an employee stock ownership plan (as defined in section 4975(e)(7) of the Internal Revenue Code of 1986), the terms of which provide that the value of the securities cannot be less than the guaranteed minimum value specified by the plan on such date.

(C) COORDINATION WITH TRANSITION RULE.—In applying section 401(a)(35)(H) of the Internal Revenue Code of 1986 and section 204(j)(7) of the Employee Retirement Income Security Act of 1974 (as added by this section) to employer securities to which this paragraph applies, the applicable percentage shall be determined without regard to this paragraph.

• 1997, Taxpayer Relief Act of 1997 (P.L. 105-34)

P.L. 105-34, §1506(a)(1):

Amended Code Sec. 409(h)(2) by adding at the end a new subparagraph (B). **Effective** for tax years beginning after 12-31-97.

P.L. 105-34, §1506(a)(2)(A)-(B):

Amended Code Sec. 409(h)(2), as in effect before the amendment made by Act Sec. 1506(a)(1), by striking "A plan which" in the first sentence and inserting "(A) IN GENERAL.—A plan which", and by striking the last sentence. **Effective** for tax years beginning after 12-31-97. Prior to amendment, the last sentence of Code Sec. 409(h)(2) read as follows:

In the case of an employer whose charter or bylaws restrict the ownership of substantially all outstanding employer securities to employees or to a trust described in section 401(a), a plan which otherwise meets the requirements of this subsection or section 4975(e)(7) shall not be considered to have failed to meet the requirements of this subsection or of section 401(a) merely because it does not permit a participant to exercise the right described in paragraph (1)(A) if such plan provides that participants entitled to a distribution from the plan shall have a right to receive such distribution in cash except that such plan may distribute employer securities subject to a requirement that such securities may be resold to the employer under terms which meet the requirements of paragraph (1)(B).

• 1988, Technical and Miscellaneous Revenue Act of 1988 (P.L. 100-647)

P.L. 100-647, §1011B(j)(5):

Amended Code Sec. 409(h) by adding at the end thereof new paragraph (7). **Effective** as if included in the provision of P.L. 99-514 to which it relates.

P.L. 100-647, §1018(t)(4)(B):

Amended Code Sec. 409(h)(2) by striking out "section 409(o)" and inserting in lieu thereof "paragraph (1)(B)". **Effective** as if included in the provision of P.L. 99-514 to which it relates.

• 1986, Tax Reform Act of 1986 (P.L. 99-514)

P.L. 99-514, §1174(c)(1)(A):

Amended Code Sec. 409(h) by adding at the end thereof new paragraphs (5) and (6). **Effective** for distributions attributable to stock acquired after 12-31-86, except that a plan may elect to have such amendment apply to all distributions after 10-22-86.

P.L. 99-514, §1854(f)(3)(C):

Amended Code Sec. 409(h)(2) by striking out "in cash" and inserting in lieu thereof "in cash, except that such plan may distribute employer securities subject to a requirement that such securities may be resold to the employer under the terms which meet the requirements of section 409(o)". **Effective** 10-22-86.

• 1983, Technical Corrections Act of 1982 (P.L. 97-448)

P.L. 97-448, §103(h):

Amended the last sentence of Code Sec. 409A(h)(2) by striking out "the requirements of section 401(a)" and inserting in lieu thereof "the requirements of this subsection or of section 401(a)". **Effective** as if included in the provision of P.L. 97-34 to which it relates.

• 1981, Economic Recovery Tax Act of 1981 (P.L. 97-34)

P.L. 97-34, §334:

Amended Code Sec. 409A(h)(2) by striking out in the first sentence "this section" and inserting "this subsection" and by adding a new last sentence. **Effective** for tax years beginning after 12-31-81.

P.L. 97-34, §336:

Added paragraphs (3) and (4). **Effective** for tax years beginning after 12-31-81.

[Sec. 409(i)]

(i) REIMBURSEMENT FOR EXPENSES OF ESTABLISHING AND ADMINISTERING PLAN.—A plan which otherwise meets the requirements of this section shall not be treated as failing to meet such requirements merely because it provides that—

(1) EXPENSES OF ESTABLISHING PLAN.—As reimbursement for the expenses of establishing the plan, the employer may withhold from amounts due the plan for the taxable year for which the plan is established (or the plan may pay) so much of the amounts paid or incurred in connection with the establishment of the plan as does not exceed the sum of—

(A) 10 percent of the first $100,000 which the employer is required to transfer to the plan for that taxable year under section 41(c)(1)(B), and

(B) 5 percent of any amount so required to be transferred in excess of the first $100,000; and

(2) ADMINISTRATIVE EXPENSES.—As reimbursement for the expenses of administering the plan, the employer may withhold from amounts due the plan (or the plan may pay) so much of the amounts paid or incurred during the taxable year as expenses of administering the plan as does not exceed the lesser of—

(A) the sum of—

(i) 10 percent of the first $100,000 of the dividends paid to the plan with respect to stock of the employer during the plan year ending with or within the employer's taxable year, and

(ii) 5 percent of the amount of such dividends in excess of $100,000 or

(B) $100,000.

Amendments

• 1984, Deficit Reduction Act of 1984 (P.L. 98-369)

P.L. 98-369, §474(r)(15)(A):

Amended Code Sec. 409 (as redesignated by Act Sec. 491) by striking out "44G" each place it appeared in subsection (i) and inserting in lieu thereof "41". **Effective** for tax years beginning after 12-31-83, and to carrybacks from such years.

P.L. 98-369, §474(r)(15)(D):

Amended Code Sec. 409(i)(1)(A), as redesignated, by striking out "48(n)(1) or". **Effective** for tax years beginning after 12-31-83, and to carrybacks from such years.

• 1981, Economic Recovery Tax Act of 1981 (P.L. 97-34)

P.L. 97-34, §331(c)(1)(E):

Amended Code Sec. 409A(i)(1)(A) by inserting "44G(c)(1)(B)" after "section 48(n)(1)". **Effective** for tax years ending after 12-31-82.

[Sec. 409(j)]

(j) CONDITIONAL CONTRIBUTIONS TO THE PLAN.—A plan which otherwise meets the requirements of this section shall not be treated as failing to satisfy such requirements (or as failing to satisfy the requirements of section 401(a) of this title or of section 403(c)(1) of the Employee Retirement Income Security Act of 1974) merely because of the return of a contribution (or a provision permitting such a return) if—

(1) the contribution to the plan is conditioned on a determination by the Secretary that such plan meets the requirements of this section,

(2) the application for a determination described in paragraph (1) is filed with the Secretary not later than 90 days after the date on which an employee plan credit is claimed, and

(3) the contribution is returned within 1 year after the date on which the Secretary issues notice to the employer that such plan does not satisfy the requirements of this section.

[Sec. 409(k)]

(k) REQUIREMENTS RELATING TO CERTAIN WITHDRAWALS.—Notwithstanding any other law or rule of law—

(1) the withdrawal from a plan which otherwise meets the requirements of this section by the employer of an amount contributed for purposes of the matching employee plan credit shall not be considered to make the benefits forfeitable, and

(2) the plan shall not, by reason of such withdrawal, fail to be for the exclusive benefit of participants or their beneficiaries,

if the withdrawn amounts were not matched by employee contributions or were in excess of the limitations of section 415. Any withdrawal described in the preceding sentence shall not be considered to violate the provisions of section 403(c)(1) of the Employee Retirement Income Security Act of 1974. For purposes of this subsection, the reference to the matching employee plan credit shall refer to such credit as in effect before the enactment of the Tax Reform Act of 1984.

Amendments

• 1984, Deficit Reduction Act of 1984 (P.L. 98-369)

P.L. 98-369, §474(r)(15)(E):

Amended Code Sec. 409(k) by adding at the end thereof a new sentence. **Effective** for tax years beginning after 12-31-83, and to carrybacks from such years.

[Sec. 409(l)]

(l) EMPLOYER SECURITIES DEFINED.—For purposes of this section—

(1) IN GENERAL.—The term "employer securities" means common stock issued by the employer (or by a corporation which is a member of the same controlled group) which is readily tradable on an established securities market.

(2) SPECIAL RULE WHERE THERE IS NO READILY TRADABLE COMMON STOCK.—If there is no common stock which meets the requirements of paragraph (1), the term "employer securities" means common stock issued by the employer (or by a corporation which is a member of the same controlled group) having a combination of voting power and dividend rights equal to or in excess of—

(A) that class of common stock of the employer (or of any other such corporation) having the greatest voting power, and

(B) that class of common stock of the employer (or of any other such corporation) having the greatest dividend rights.

(3) PREFERRED STOCK MAY BE ISSUED IN CERTAIN CASES.—Noncallable preferred stock shall be treated as employer securities if such stock is convertible at any time into stock which meets the requirements of paragraph (1) or (2) (whichever is applicable) and if such conversion is at a conversion price which (as of the date of the acquisition by the tax credit employee stock ownership plan) is reasonable. For purposes of the preceding sentence, under regulations prescribed by the Secretary, preferred stock shall be treated as noncallable if after the call there will be a reasonable opportunity for a conversion which meets the requirements of the preceding sentence.

(4) APPLICATION TO CONTROLLED GROUP OF CORPORATIONS.—

(A) IN GENERAL.—For purposes of this subsection, the term "controlled group of corporations" has the meaning given to such term by section 1563(a) (determined without regard to subsections (a)(4) and (e)(3)(C) of section 1563).

(B) WHERE COMMON PARENT OWNS AT LEAST 50 PERCENT OF FIRST TIER SUBSIDIARY.—For purposes of subparagraph (A), if the common parent owns directly stock possessing at least 50 percent of the voting power of all classes of stock and at least 50 percent of each class of nonvoting stock in a first tier subsidiary, such subsidiary (and all other corporations below it in the chain which would meet the 80 percent test of section 1563(a) if the first tier subsidiary were the common parent) shall be treated as includible corporations.

(C) WHERE COMMON PARENT OWNS 100 PERCENT OF FIRST TIER SUBSIDIARY.—For purposes of subparagraph (A), if the common parent owns directly stock possessing all of the voting power of all classes of stock and all of the nonvoting stock, in a first tier subsidiary, and if the first tier subsidiary owns directly stock possessing at least 50 percent of the voting power of all classes of stock, and at least 50 percent of each class of nonvoting stock, in a second tier subsidiary of the common parent, such second tier subsidiary (and all other corporations below it in the chain which would meet the 80 percent test of section 1563(a) if the second tier subsidiary were the common parent) shall be treated as includible corporations.

(5) NONVOTING COMMON STOCK MAY BE ACQUIRED IN CERTAIN CASES.—Nonvoting common stock of an employer described in the second sentence of section 401(a)(22) shall be treated as employer securities if an employer has a class of nonvoting common stock outstanding and the specific shares that the plan acquires have been issued and outstanding for at least 24 months.

Amendments

• 1989, Omnibus Budget Reconciliation Act of 1989 (P.L. 101-239)

P.L. 101-239, §7811(h)(1):

Amended Code Sec. 409(l)(5) by striking "the last sentence" and inserting "the second sentence". **Effective** as if included in the provision of P.L. 100-647 to which it relates.

• 1988, Technical and Miscellaneous Revenue Act of 1988 (P.L. 100-647)

P.L. 100-647, §1011B(k)(3):

Amended Code Sec. 409(l) by redesignating paragraph (4) as paragraph (5). **Effective** as if included in the provision of P.L. 99-514 to which it relates.

• 1986, Tax Reform Act of 1986 (P.L. 99-514)

P.L. 99-514, §1176(b):

Amended Code Sec. 409(l) by adding at the end thereof the new paragraph (4). **Effective** for acquisitions of securities after 12-31-86.

• 1980, Miscellaneous Revenue Act of 1980 (P.L. 96-605)

P.L. 96-605, §224(a):

Amended Code Sec. 409A(1)(4) by striking out the caption "CONTROLLED GROUP OF CORPORATIONS DEFINED.—" and inserting in lieu thereof "APPLICATION TO CONTROLLED GROUP OF CORPORATIONS.—", by striking out "COMMON PARENT MAY OWN ONLY" in the caption of subparagraph (B) and inserting in lieu thereof "WHERE COMMON PARENT OWNS AT LEAST", and by adding at the end thereof subparagraph (C). **Effective** with respect to qualified investment for tax years beginning after 12-31-78.

[Sec. 409(m)]

(m) NONRECOGNITION OF GAIN OR LOSS ON CONTRIBUTION OF EMPLOYER SECURITIES TO TAX CREDIT EMPLOYEE STOCK OWNERSHIP PLAN.—No gain or loss shall be recognized to the taxpayer with respect to the transfer of employer securities to a tax credit employee stock ownership plan maintained by the taxpayer to the extent that such transfer is required under section 41(c)(1)(B), or subparagraph (A) or (B) of section 48(n)(1).

Amendments

• 1984, Deficit Reduction Act of 1984 (P.L. 98-369)

P.L. 98-369, §474(r)(15)(A):

Amended Code Sec. 409 (as redesignated by Act Sec. 491) by striking out "44G" each place it appeared in subsection (m) and inserting in lieu thereof "41". **Effective** for tax years beginning after 12-31-83, and to carrybacks from such years.

• 1981, Economic Recovery Tax Act of 1981 (P.L. 97-34)

P.L. 97-34, §331(c)(1)(F):

Amended Code Sec. 409A(m) by inserting "section 44G(c)(1)(B), or" after "required under". **Effective** for tax years ending after 12-31-82.

[Sec. 409(n)]

(n) SECURITIES RECEIVED IN CERTAIN TRANSACTIONS.—

(1) IN GENERAL.—A plan to which section 1042 applies and an eligible worker-owned cooperative (within the meaning of section 1042(c)) shall provide that no portion of the assets of the plan or cooperative attributable to (or allocable in lieu of) employer securities acquired by the plan or cooperative in a sale to which section 1042 applies may accrue (or be allocated directly or indirectly under any plan of the employer meeting the requirements of section 401(a))—

(A) during the nonallocation period, for the benefit of—

(i) any taxpayer who makes an election under section 1042(a) with respect to employer securities,

(ii) any individual who is related to the taxpayer (within the meaning of section 267(b)), or

(B) for the benefit of any other person who owns (after application of section 318(a)) more than 25 percent of—

(i) any class of outstanding stock of the corporation which issued such employer securities or of any corporation which is a member of the same controlled group of corporations (within the meaning of subsection (l)(4)) as such corporation, or

(ii) the total value of any class of outstanding stock of any such corporation.

For purposes of subparagraph (B), section 318(a) shall be applied without regard to the employee trust exception in paragraph (2)(B)(i).

(2) FAILURE TO MEET REQUIREMENTS.—If a plan fails to meet the requirements of paragraph (1)—

(A) the plan shall be treated as having distributed to the person described in paragraph (1) the amount allocated to the account of such person in violation of paragraph (1) at the time of such allocation,

(B) the provisions of section 4979A shall apply, and

(C) the statutory period for the assessment of any tax imposed by section 4979A shall not expire before the date which is 3 years from the later of—

(i) the 1st allocation of employer securities in connection with a sale to the plan to which section 1042 applies, or

(ii) the date on which the Secretary is notified of such failure.

(3) DEFINITIONS AND SPECIAL RULES.—For purposes of this subsection—

(A) LINEAL DESCENDANTS.—Paragraph (1)(A)(ii) shall not apply to any individual if—

(i) such individual is a lineal descendant of the taxpayer, and

(ii) the aggregate amount allocated to the benefit of all such lineal descendants during the nonallocation period does not exceed more than 5 percent of the employer securities (or amounts allocated in lieu thereof) held by the plan which are attributable to a sale to the plan by any person related to such descendants (within the meaning of section 267(c)(4) in a transaction to which section 1042 applied.

(B) 25-PERCENT SHAREHOLDERS.—A person shall be treated as failing to meet the stock ownership limitation under paragraph (1)(B) if such person fails such limitation—

(i) at any time during the 1-year period ending on the date of sale of qualified securities to the plan or cooperative, or

(ii) on the date as of which qualified securities are allocated to participants in the plan or cooperative.

(C) NONALLOCATION PERIOD.—The term "nonallocation period" means the period beginning on the date of the sale of the qualified securities and ending on the later of—

(i) the date which is 10 years after the date of sale, or

(ii) the date of the plan allocation attributable to the final payment of acquisition indebtedness incurred in connection with such sale.

Amendments

• 1989, Omnibus Budget Reconciliation Act of 1989 (P.L. 101-239)

P.L. 101-239, §7304(a)(2)(A)(i)-(iii):

Amended Code Sec. 409(n)(1) by striking "or section 2057" after "1042" each place it appears, by striking "or any decedent if the executor of the estate of such decedent makes a qualified sale to which section 2057 applies" after "securities" in subparagraph (A)(i), and by striking "or the decedent" after "taxpayer" in subparagraph (A)(ii). **Effective** for estates of decedents dying after 12-19-89.

P.L. 101-239, §7304(a)(2)(B):

Amended Code Sec. 409(n)(2)(C)(i) by striking "or section 2057" after "1042 applies", and Code Sec. 409(n)(3)(A)(ii) by striking "or section 2057" after "section 1042". **Effective** for estates of decedents dying after 12-19-89.

• 1988, Technical and Miscellaneous Revenue Act of 1988 (P.L. 100-647)

P.L. 100-647, §1011B(g)(2):

Amended Code Sec. 409(n)(2) and (3) by inserting "or section 2057" after "section 1042" each place it appears. **Effective** as if included in the provision of P.L. 99-514 to which it relates.

P.L. 100-647, §1018(t)(4)(C):

Amended Code Sec. 409(n)(3)(C). **Effective** as if included in the provision of P.L. 99-514 to which it relates. Prior to amendment, Code Sec. 409(n)(3)(C) read as follows:

(C) NONALLOCATION PERIOD.—The term "nonallocation period" means the 10-year period beginning on the later of—

(i) the date of the sale of the qualified securities, or

(ii) the date of the plan allocation attributable to the final payment of acquisition indebtedness incurred in connection with such sale.

• 1986, Tax Reform Act of 1986 (P.L. 99-514)

P.L. 99-514, §1172(b)(1)(A)-(C):

Amended Code Sec. 409(n)(1), as added by Act Sec. 1854(a)(3)(A), by inserting "or section 2057" after "section 1042", by inserting "or any decedent if the executor of the estate of such decedent makes a qualified sale to which section 2057 applies," after "securities" in subparagraph (A)(i) thereof, and by inserting "or the decedent" after "taxpayer" in subparagraph (A)(ii) thereof. **Effective** for sales after 10-22-86, with respect to which an election is made by the executor of an estate who is required to file the return of the tax imposed by the Internal Revenue Code of 1954 on a date (including extensions) after 10-22-86.

P.L. 99-514, §1854(a)(3)(A):

Amended Code Sec. 409 by redesignating subsection (n) as subsection (o) and by inserting after subsection (m) new subsection (n). **Effective**, generally, for sales of securities after 10-22-86. For a special rule, see Act Sec. 1854(a)(3)(C)(ii), below. [Amended by P.L. 100-647, §1018(t)(4)(G).]

P.L. 99-514, §1854(a)(3)(C)(ii), provides:

(ii) A taxpayer or executor may elect to have section 1042(b)(3) of the Internal Revenue Code of 1954 (as in effect before the amendment made by subparagraph (B)) apply to sales before the date of the enactment of this Act as if such section included the last sentence of section 409(n)(1) of the Internal Revenue Code of 1986 (as added by subparagraph (A)).

[Sec. 409(o)]

(o) DISTRIBUTION AND PAYMENT REQUIREMENTS.—A plan meets the requirements of this subsection if—

(1) DISTRIBUTION REQUIREMENT.—

(A) IN GENERAL.—The plan provides that, if the participant and, if applicable pursuant to section 401(a)(11) and 417, with the consent of the participant's spouse elects the distribution of the participant's account balance in the plan will commence not later than 1 year after the close of the plan year—

(i) in which the participant separates from service by reason of the attainment of normal retirement age under the plan, disability, or death, or

(ii) which is the 5th plan year following the plan year in which the participant otherwise separates from service, except that this clause shall not apply if the participant is reemployed by the employer before distribution is required to begin under this clause.

(B) EXCEPTION FOR CERTAIN FINANCED SECURITIES.—For purposes of this subsection, the account balance of a participant shall not include any employer securities acquired with the proceeds of the loan described in section 404(a)(9) until the close of the plan year in which such loan is repaid in full.

(C) LIMITED DISTRIBUTION PERIOD.—The plan provides that, unless the participant elects otherwise, the distribution of the participant's account balance will be in substantially equal periodic payments (not less frequently than annually) over a period not longer than the greater of—

(i) 5 years, or

(ii) in the case of a participant with an account balance in excess of $800,000, 5 years plus 1 additional year (but not more than 5 additional years) for each $160,000 or fraction thereof by which such balance exceeds $800,000.

(2) COST-OF-LIVING ADJUSTMENT.—The Secretary shall adjust the dollar amounts under paragraph (1)(C) at the same time and in the same manner as under section 415(d).

Amendments

• 2006, Pension Protection Act of 2006 (P.L. 109-280)

P.L. 109-280, §811, provides:

SEC. 811. PENSIONS AND INDIVIDUAL RETIREMENT ARRANGEMENT PROVISIONS OF ECONOMIC GROWTH AND TAX RELIEF RECONCILIATION ACT OF 2001 MADE PERMANENT.

Title IX of the Economic Growth and Tax Relief Reconciliation Act of 2001 [P.L. 107-16] shall not apply to the provisions of, and amendments made by, subtitles A through F of title VI [§§601-666]of such Act (relating to pension and individual retirement arrangement provisions).

• 2002, Job Creation and Worker Assistance Act of 2002 (P.L. 107-147)

P.L. 107-147, §411(j)(2)(A)-(B):

Amended Code Sec. 409(o)(1)(C)(ii) by striking "$500,000" both places it appears and inserting "$800,000" and by striking "$100,000" and inserting "$160,000". **Effective** as if included in the provision of P.L. 107-16 to which it relates [applies generally to years beginning after 12-31-2001.—CCH].

• 2001, Economic Growth and Tax Relief Reconciliation Act of 2001 (P.L. 107-16)

P.L. 107-16, §901(a)-(b), provides [but see P.L. 109-280, §811, above]:

SEC. 901. SUNSET OF PROVISIONS OF ACT.

(a) IN GENERAL.—All provisions of, and amendments made by, this Act shall not apply—

(1) to taxable, plan, or limitation years beginning after December 31, 2010, or

(2) in the case of title V, to estates of decedents dying, gifts made, or generation skipping transfers, after December 31, 2010.

(b) APPLICATION OF CERTAIN LAWS.—The Internal Revenue Code of 1986 and the Employee Retirement Income Security Act of 1974 shall be applied and administered to years, estates, gifts, and transfers described in subsection (a) as if the provisions and amendments described in subsection (a) had never been enacted.

• 1988, Technical and Miscellaneous Revenue Act of 1988 (P.L. 100-647)

P.L. 100-647, §1011B(i)(1):

Amended Code Sec. 409(o)(1)(A)(ii) by striking out "such year" and inserting in lieu thereof "distribution is required to begin under this clause". **Effective** as if included in the provision of P.L. 99-514 to which it relates.

P.L. 100-647, §1011B(i)(3):

Amended Code Sec. 409(o)(1)(A) by striking out "unless the participant otherwise elects" and inserting in lieu thereof "if the participant and, if applicable pursuant to section 401(a)(11) and 417, with the consent of the participant's spouse elects". **Effective** as if included in the provision of P.L. 99-514 to which it relates.

• 1986, Tax Reform Act of 1986 (P.L. 99-514)

P.L. 99-514, §1174(b)(1):

Amended Code Sec. 409 by redesignating subsection (o), as redesignated by Act Sec. 1854(a)(3)(A), as subsection (p) and by inserting after subsection (n) new subsection (o). **Effective** for distributions attributable to stock acquired after 12-31-86.

[Sec. 409(p)]

(p) PROHIBITED ALLOCATIONS OF SECURITIES IN AN S CORPORATION.—

(1) IN GENERAL.—An employee stock ownership plan holding employer securities consisting of stock in an S corporation shall provide that no portion of the assets of the plan attributable to (or allocable in lieu of) such employer securities may, during a nonallocation year, accrue (or be allocated directly or indirectly under any plan of the employer meeting the requirements of section 401(a)) for the benefit of any disqualified person.

(2) FAILURE TO MEET REQUIREMENTS.—

(A) IN GENERAL.—If a plan fails to meet the requirements of paragraph (1), the plan shall be treated as having distributed to any disqualified person the amount allocated to the account of such person in violation of paragraph (1) at the time of such allocation.

(B) CROSS REFERENCE.—

For excise tax relating to violations of paragraph (1) and ownership of synthetic equity, see section 4979A.

(3) NONALLOCATION YEAR.—For purposes of this subsection—

(A) IN GENERAL.—The term "nonallocation year" means any plan year of an employee stock ownership plan if, at any time during such plan year—

(i) such plan holds employer securities consisting of stock in an S corporation, and

(ii) disqualified persons own at least 50 percent of the number of shares of stock in the S corporation.

(B) ATTRIBUTION RULES.—For purposes of subparagraph (A)—

(i) IN GENERAL.—The rules of section 318(a) shall apply for purposes of determining ownership, except that—

(I) in applying paragraph (1) thereof, the members of an individual's family shall include members of the family described in paragraph (4)(D), and

(II) paragraph (4) thereof shall not apply.

(ii) DEEMED-OWNED SHARES.—Notwithstanding the employee trust exception in section 318(a)(2)(B)(i), an individual shall be treated as owning deemed-owned shares of the individual.

Solely for purposes of applying paragraph (5), this subparagraph shall be applied after the attribution rules of paragraph (5) have been applied.

(4) DISQUALIFIED PERSON.—For purposes of this subsection—

(A) IN GENERAL.—The term "disqualified person" means any person if—

(i) the aggregate number of deemed-owned shares of such person and the members of such person's family is at least 20 percent of the number of deemed-owned shares of stock in the S corporation, or

(ii) in the case of a person not described in clause (i), the number of deemed-owned shares of such person is at least 10 percent of the number of deemed-owned shares of stock in such corporation.

(B) TREATMENT OF FAMILY MEMBERS.—In the case of a disqualified person described in subparagraph (A)(i), any member of such person's family with deemed-owned shares shall be treated as a disqualified person if not otherwise treated as a disqualified person under subparagraph (A).

(C) DEEMED-OWNED SHARES.—

(i) IN GENERAL.—The term "deemed-owned shares" means, with respect to any person—

(I) the stock in the S corporation constituting employer securities of an employee stock ownership plan which is allocated to such person under the plan, and

(II) such person's share of the stock in such corporation which is held by such plan but which is not allocated under the plan to participants.

(ii) PERSON'S SHARE OF UNALLOCATED STOCK.—For purposes of clause (i)(II), a person's share of unallocated S corporation stock held by such plan is the amount of the unallocated stock which would be allocated to such person if the unallocated stock were allocated to all participants in the same proportions as the most recent stock allocation under the plan.

(D) MEMBER OF FAMILY.—For purposes of this paragraph, the term "member of the family" means, with respect to any individual—

(i) the spouse of the individual,

(ii) an ancestor or lineal descendant of the individual or the individual's spouse,

(iii) a brother or sister of the individual or the individual's spouse and any lineal descendant of the brother or sister, and

(iv) the spouse of any individual described in clause (ii) or (iii).

A spouse of an individual who is legally separated from such individual under a decree of divorce or separate maintenance shall not be treated as such individual's spouse for purposes of this subparagraph.

(5) TREATMENT OF SYNTHETIC EQUITY.—For purposes of paragraphs (3) and (4), in the case of a person who owns synthetic equity in the S corporation, except to the extent provided in regulations, the shares of stock in such corporation on which such synthetic equity is based shall be treated as outstanding stock in such corporation and deemed-owned shares of such person if such treatment of synthetic equity of 1 or more such persons results in—

(A) the treatment of any person as a disqualified person, or

(B) the treatment of any year as a nonallocation year.

For purposes of this paragraph, synthetic equity shall be treated as owned by a person in the same manner as stock is treated as owned by a person under the rules of paragraphs (2) and (3) of section 318(a). If, without regard to this paragraph, a person is treated as a disqualified person or a year is treated as a nonallocation year, this paragraph shall not be construed to result in the person or year not being so treated.

(6) DEFINITIONS.—For purposes of this subsection—

(A) EMPLOYEE STOCK OWNERSHIP PLAN.—The term "employee stock ownership plan" has the meaning given such term by section 4975(e)(7).

(B) EMPLOYER SECURITIES.—The term "employer security" has the meaning given such term by section 409(l).

(C) SYNTHETIC EQUITY.—The term "synthetic equity" means any stock option, warrant, restricted stock, deferred issuance stock right, or similar interest or right that gives the holder the right to acquire or receive stock of the S corporation in the future. Except to the extent provided in regulations, synthetic equity also includes a stock appreciation right, phantom stock unit, or similar right to a future cash payment based on the value of such stock or appreciation in such value.

(7) REGULATIONS AND GUIDANCE.—

(A) IN GENERAL.—The Secretary shall prescribe such regulations as may be necessary to carry out the purposes of this subsection.

(B) AVOIDANCE OR EVASION.—The Secretary may, by regulation or other guidance of general applicability, provide that a nonallocation year occurs in any case in which the principal purpose of the ownership structure of an S corporation constitutes an avoidance or evasion of this subsection.

Amendments

• 2006, Pension Protection Act of 2006 (P.L. 109-280)

P.L. 109-280, §811, provides:

SEC. 811. PENSIONS AND INDIVIDUAL RETIREMENT ARRANGEMENT PROVISIONS OF ECONOMIC GROWTH AND TAX RELIEF RECONCILIATION ACT OF 2001 MADE PERMANENT.

Title IX of the Economic Growth and Tax Relief Reconciliation Act of 2001 [P.L. 107-16] shall not apply to the provisions of, and amendments made by, subtitles A through F of title VI [§§601-666]of such Act (relating to pension and individual retirement arrangement provisions).

• 2001, Economic Growth and Tax Relief Reconciliation Act of 2001 (P.L. 107-16)

P.L. 107-16, §656(a):

Amended Code Sec. 409 by redesignating subsection (p) as subsection (q) and by inserting after subsection (o) a new subsection (p). **Effective**, generally, for plan years beginning after 12-31-2004. For exceptions, see Act Sec. 656(d)(2), below.

P.L. 107-16, §656(d)(2), provides:

(2) EXCEPTION FOR CERTAIN PLANS.—In the case of any—

(A) employee stock ownership plan established after March 14, 2001, or

(B) employee stock ownership plan established on or before such date if employer securities held by the plan consist of stock in a corporation with respect to which an election under section 1362(a) of the Internal Revenue Code of 1986 is not in effect on such date,

the amendments made by this section shall apply to plan years ending after March 14, 2001.

P.L. 107-16, §901(a)-(b), provides [but see P.L. 109-280, §811, above]:

SEC. 901. SUNSET OF PROVISIONS OF ACT.

(a) IN GENERAL.—All provisions of, and amendments made by, this Act shall not apply—

(1) to taxable, plan, or limitation years beginning after December 31, 2010, or

(2) in the case of title V, to estates of decedents dying, gifts made, or generation skipping transfers, after December 31, 2010.

(b) APPLICATION OF CERTAIN LAWS.—The Internal Revenue Code of 1986 and the Employee Retirement Income Security Act of 1974 shall be applied and administered to years, estates, gifts, and transfers described in subsection (a) as if the provisions and amendments described in subsection (a) had never been enacted.

[Sec. 409(q)]

(q) CROSS REFERENCES.—

(1) For requirements for allowance of employee plan credit, see section 48(n).

(2) For assessable penalties for failure to meet requirements of this section, or for failure to make contributions required with respect to the allowance of an employee plan credit or employee stock ownership credit, see section 6699.

(3) For requirements for allowance of an employee stock ownership credit, see section 41.

Amendments

• 2006, Pension Protection Act of 2006 (P.L. 109-280)

P.L. 109-280, §811, provides:

SEC. 811. PENSIONS AND INDIVIDUAL RETIREMENT ARRANGEMENT PROVISIONS OF ECONOMIC GROWTH AND TAX RELIEF RECONCILIATION ACT OF 2001 MADE PERMANENT.

Title IX of the Economic Growth and Tax Relief Reconciliation Act of 2001 [P.L. 107-16] shall not apply to the provisions of, and amendments made by, subtitles A through F of title VI [§§601-666]of such Act (relating to pension and individual retirement arrangement provisions).

• 2001, Economic Growth and Tax Relief Reconciliation Act of 2001 (P.L. 107-16)

P.L. 107-16, §656(a):

Amended Code Sec. 409 by redesignating subsection (p) as subsection (q). **Effective**, generally, for plan years beginning after 12-31-2004. For exceptions, see Act Sec. 656(d)(2) in the amendment notes following Code Sec. 409(p).

P.L. 107-16, §901(a)-(b), provides [but see P.L. 109-280, §811, above]:

SEC. 901. SUNSET OF PROVISIONS OF ACT.

(a) IN GENERAL.—All provisions of, and amendments made by, this Act shall not apply—

(1) to taxable, plan, or limitation years beginning after December 31, 2010, or

(2) in the case of title V, to estates of decedents dying, gifts made, or generation skipping transfers, after December 31, 2010.

(b) APPLICATION OF CERTAIN LAWS.—The Internal Revenue Code of 1986 and the Employee Retirement Income Security Act of 1974 shall be applied and administered to years, estates, gifts, and transfers described in subsection (a) as if the provisions and amendments described in subsection (a) had never been enacted.

• 1986, Tax Reform Act of 1986 (P.L. 99-514)

P.L. 99-514, §1174(b)(1):

Amended Code Sec. 409 by redesignating subsection (o), as redesignated by Act Sec. 1854(a)(3)(A), as subsection (p). **Effective** for distributions attributable to stock acquired after 12-31-86.

P.L. 99-514, §1854(a)(3)(A):

Amended Code Sec. 409 by redesignating subsection (n) as subsection (o). **Effective**, generally, for sales of securities after the date of the enactment of this Act. For a special rule, see Act Sec. 1854(a)(3)(C)(ii) in the Amendment Notes following Code Sec. 409(n). [Amended by P.L. 100-647, §1018(t)(4)(G).]

• 1984, Deficit Reduction Act of 1984 (P.L. 98-369)

P.L. 98-369, §474(r)(15)(A):

Amended Code Sec. 409 (as redesignated by Act Sec. 491) by striking out "44G" each place it appeared in subsection (n) and inserting in lieu thereof "41". **Effective** for tax years beginning after 12-31-83, and to carrybacks from such years.

• 1981, Economic Recovery Tax Act of 1981 (P.L. 97-34)

P.L. 97-34, §331(c)(1)(G):

Amended Code Sec. 409A(n)(2) by inserting "or employee stock ownership credit" after "employee plan credit". **Effective** for tax years ending after 12-31-82.

P.L. 97-34, §331(c)(1)(H):

Added Code Sec. 409A(n)(3). **Effective** for tax years ending after 12-31-82.

• 1980, Technical Corrections Act of 1979 (P.L. 96-222)

P.L. 96-222, §101(a)(7)(B):

Amended Sec. 141 of P.L. 95-600 by revising paragraph (g). Revised paragraph (g) read as follows:

"(g) EFFECTIVE DATES FOR TAX CREDIT EMPLOYEE STOCK OWNERSHIP PLANS.—

"(1) IN GENERAL.—Except as otherwise provided in this subsection and subsection (h), the amendments made by this section shall apply with respect to qualified investment for taxable years beginning after December 31, 1978.

"(2) ELECTION TO HAVE AMENDMENTS APPLY DURING 1978.—At the election of the taxpayer, paragraph (1) shall be applied by substituting `December 31, 1977' for `December 31, 1978'; except that in the case of a plan in existence before December 31, 1978, any such election shall not affect the required allocation of employer securities attributable to qualified investment for taxable years beginning before January 1, 1979. An election under the preceding sentence shall be made at such time and in such manner as the Secretary of the Treasury or his delegate shall prescribe. Such an election, once made, shall be irrevocable.

"(3) VOTING RIGHT PROVISIONS.—Section 409A(e) of the Internal Revenue Code of 1954 (as added by subsection (a)) shall apply to plans to which section 409A of such Code applies, beginning with the first day of such application.

"(4) RIGHT TO DEMAND EMPLOYER SECURITIES, ETC.—Paragraphs (1)(A) and (2) of section 409A(h) of the Internal Revenue Code of 1954 (as added by subsection (a)) shall apply to distributions after December 31, 1978, made by a plan to which section 409A of such Code applies.

"(5) SUBSECTION (f)(7).—The amendment made by subsection (f)(7) shall apply to years beginning after December 31, 1978.

P.L. 96-222, §101(a)(7)(D):

Amended Code Sec. 409A(m). **Effective** for tax years beginning after 12-31-78, but also see special election at Act Sec. 101(a)(7)(B), above. Prior to amendment, Code Sec. 409A(m) read as follows:

(m) CONTRIBUTIONS OF STOCK OF CONTROLLING CORPORATION.—If the stock of a corporation which controls another corporation or which controls a corporation controlled by such other corporation is contributed to an ESOP of the controlled corporation, then no gain or loss shall be recognized, because of that contribution, to the controlled corporation. For purposes of this subsection, the term "control" has the same meaning as that term has in section 368(c).

P.L. 96-222, §101(a)(7)(E):

Amended Code Sec. 409A(h)(2) by adding "or of section 4975(e)(7)". **Effective** with respect to qualified investment for tax years beginning after 12-31-78 but also see special election at Act Sec. 101(a)(7)(B), above.

P.L. 96-222, §101(a)(7)(F):

Amended Code Sec. 409A(d) by adding "(or allocated to a participant's account in connection with matched employer and employee contributions)". **Effective** with respect to qualified investment for tax years beginning after 12-31-78 but also see special election at Act Sec. 101(a)(7)(B), above.

P.L. 96-222, §101(a)(7)(I)(i):

Amended Code Sec. 409A(f)(1). For the **effective** date and special election, see Act Sec. 101(a)(7)(B), above. Prior to amendment, Code Sec. 409A(f)(1) read as follows:

(1) IN GENERAL.—A plan meets the requirements of this subsection for a plan year only if it is established on or before the due date for the filing of the employer's tax return for the taxable year (including any extensions of such date) in which or with which the plan year ends.

P.L. 96-222, §101(a)(7)(I)(ii):

Amended Code Sec. 409(f)(2) by adding at the end of the sentence "with respect to the plan". For the **effective** date and special election, see Act Sec. 101(a)(7)(B), above.

P.L. 96-222, §101(a)(7)(J)(i):

Amended Code Sec. 409A(l)(2)(B) by striking out "class of stock" and inserting "class of common stock". For the **effective** date and special election, see Act Sec. 101(a)(7)(B), above.

P.L. 96-222, §101(a)(7)(J)(ii):

Amended Code Sec. 409A(l)(3). For the **effective** date and special election, see Act Sec. 101(a)(7)(B), above. Prior to amendment, Code Sec. 409A(l)(3) read as follows:

(3) PREFERRED STOCK MAY BE ISSUED IN CERTAIN CASES.—Noncallable preferred stock shall be treated as meeting the requirements of paragraph (1) if such stock is convertible at any time into stock which meets the requirements of paragraph (1) and if such conversion is at a conversion price which (as of the date of the acquisition by the ESOP) is reasonable.

P.L. 96-222, §101(a)(7)(L)(i)(VI), (ii)(I) and (II), (iii)(V) and (v)(VI) and (VII):

Amended Code Sec. 409A(m) by striking out "an ESOP" each place it appeared and inserting "a tax credit employee stock ownership plan"; amended Code Sec. 409A(a) (other than in the subsection heading) and Code Sec. 409A(1)(3) by striking out "ESOP" each place it appeared and inserting "tax credit employee stock ownership plan"; amended Code Sec. 409A (as amended by §101(a)(7)(I) and clauses (i) and (ii)) by striking out "ESOP" each place it appeared and inserting "employee plan"; amended the subsection heading of Code Sec. 409A by striking out "ESOP" and inserting "TAX CREDIT EMPLOYEE STOCK OWNERSHIP PLAN"; and amended the section heading of Code Sec. 409A by striking out **"ESOPS"** and inserting **"TAX CREDIT EMPLOYEE STOCK OWNERSHIP PLANS"**. **Effective** for tax years beginning after 12-31-78.

• 1978, Revenue Act of 1978 (P.L. 95-600)

P.L. 95-600, §141(a):

Added Code Sec. 409A. **Effective** for qualified investment for tax years beginning after 12-31-78.

[Sec. 409—Repealed]

Amendments

• 1984, Deficit Reduction Act of 1984 (P.L. 98-369)

P.L. 98-369, §491(b):

Repealed Code Sec. 409. **Effective** for obligations issued after 12-31-83. See, also, §491(f)(5) following Code Sec. 26(b). Prior to repeal, Code Sec. 409 read as follows:

SEC. 409. RETIREMENT BONDS.

[Sec. 409(a)]

(a) RETIREMENT BOND.—For purposes of this section and section 219(a), the term "retirement bond" means a bond issued under chapter 31 of title 31, which by its terms, or by regulations prescribed by the Secretary under such chapter—

(1) provides for payment of interest, or investment yield, only on redemption;

(2) provides that no interest, or investment yield, is payable if the bond is redeemed within 12 months after the date of its issuance;

(3) provides that it ceases to bear interest, or provide investment yield on the earlier of—

(A) the date on which the individual in whose name it is purchased (hereinafter in this section referred to as the "registered owner") attains age $70\frac{1}{2}$; or

(B) 5 years after the date on which the registered owner dies, but not later than the date on which he would have attained the age $70\frac{1}{2}$ had he lived;

(4) provides that, except in the case of a rollover contribution described in subsection (b)(3)(C) or in section 402(a)(5), 402(a)(7), 403(a)(4), 403(b)(8), or 408(d)(3) the registered owner may not contribute on behalf of any individual for the purchase of such bonds in excess of $2,000 for any taxable year; and

(5) is not transferable.

Amendments

• 1983 (P.L. 97-452)

P.L. 97-452, §2(c)(1):

Amended Code Sec. 409(a) by striking out "the Second Liberty Bond Act, as amended" and "Act" and inserting "chapter 31 of title 31" and "chapter", respectively. **Effective** 1-12-83.

• 1981, Economic Recovery Tax Act of 1981 (P.L. 97-34)

P.L. 97-34, 311(g)(1)(D):

Amended Code Sec. 409(a)(4) by striking out "1,500" and inserting "$2,000". **Effective** for tax years beginning after 12-31-81.

• 1980, Technical Corrections Act of 1979 (P.L. 96-222)

P.L. 96-222, §101(a)(14)(B):

Amended Code Sec. 409(a)(4) by adding "402(a)(7)" after "section 402(a)(5),". **Effective** for distributions or transfers made after 12-31-77, in tax years beginning after such date.

• 1978, Revenue Act of 1978 (P.L. 95-600)

P.L. 95-600, §156(c)(3):

Amended Code Sec. 409(a)(4) by inserting "403(b)(8)" after "403(a)(4)". **Effective** for distributions or transfers made after 12-31-77, in tax years beginning after such date [**effective** date changed by P.L. 96-222, §101(a)(13)(A).—CCH].

P.L. 95-600, §157(e)(1)(B):

Amended Code Sec. 409(a)(4) by inserting "on behalf of any individual" after "may not contribute". **Effective** for tax years beginning after 12-31-78.

• 1976, Tax Reform Act of 1976 (P.L. 94-455)

P.L. 94-455, §1501(b)(6):

Amended Code Sec. 409(a)(4) by substituting "for any taxable year" for the phrase "in any taxable year". **Effective** for tax years beginning after 12-31-76.

P.L. 94-455, §1906(b)(13)(A):

Amended the 1954 Code by substituting "Secretary" for "Secretary or his delegate" each place it appeared. **Effective** 2-1-77.

[Sec. 409(b)]

(b) INCOME TAX TREATMENT OF BONDS.—

(1) IN GENERAL.—Except as otherwise provided in this subsection, on the redemption of a retirement bond the entire proceeds shall be included in the gross income of the taxpayer entitled to the proceeds on redemption. If the registered owner has not tendered it for redemption before the close of the taxable year in which he attains age $70\frac{1}{2}$ such individual shall include in his gross income for such taxable year the amount of proceeds he would have received if the bond had been redeemed at age $70\frac{1}{2}$. The provisions of section 72 (relating to annuities) and section 1271 (relating to treatment of amounts received on retirement or sale or exchange of debt instruments) shall not apply to a retirement bond.

(2) BASIS.—The basis of a retirement bond is zero.

(3) EXCEPTIONS.—

(A) REDEMPTION WITHIN 12 MONTHS.—If a retirement bond is redeemed within 12 months after the date of its issuance, the proceeds are excluded from gross income if no deduction is allowed under section 219 on account of the purchase of such bond. The preceding sentence shall not apply to the extent that the bond was purchased with a rollover contribution described in subparagraph (C) of this paragraph or in section 402(a)(5), 402(a)(7), 403(a)(4), 403(b)(8), 405(b)(3), or 408(d)(3).

(B) REDEMPTION AFTER AGE $70\frac{1}{2}$.—If a retirement bond is redeemed after the close of the taxable year in which the registered owner attains age $70\frac{1}{2}$ the proceeds from the redemption of the bond are excluded from the gross income of the registered owner to the extent that such proceeds were includible in his gross income for such taxable year.

(C) ROLLOVER INTO AN INDIVIDUAL RETIREMENT ACCOUNT OR ANNUITY OR A QUALIFIED PLAN.—If a retirement bond is redeemed at any time before the close of the taxable year in which the registered owner attains age $70\frac{1}{2}$ and the registered owner transfers the entire amount of the proceeds from the redemption of the bond to an individual retirement account described in section 408(a) or to an individual retirement annuity described in section 408(b) (other than an endowment contract) which is maintained for the benefit of the registered owner of the bond, or to an employees' trust described in section 401(a) which is exempt from tax under section 501(a), an annuity plan described in section 403(a), or an annuity contract described in section 403(b) for the benefit of the registered owner, on or before the 60th day after the day on which he received the proceeds of such redemption, then the proceeds shall be excluded from gross income and the transfer shall be treated as a rollover contribution described in section 408(d)(3). This subparagraph does not apply in the case of a transfer to such an employee's trust or such an annuity unless no part of the value of such proceeds is attributable to any source other than a qualified rollover contribution. For purposes of the preceding sentence, the term "qualified rollover contribution" means any rollover contribution of a qualified total distribution (as defined in section 402(a)(5)(E)(i)) which is from such an employee's trust or annuity plan (other than an annuity plan or a trust forming part of a plan under which the individual was an employee within the meaning of section 401(c)(1) at the time contributions were made on his behalf under such plan), and which did not qualify as a rollover contribution by reason of section 402(a)(7). This subparagraph does not apply in the case of a transfer to an annuity contract described in section 403(b) unless no part of the value of such proceeds is attributable to any source other than a rollover contribution from such an annuity contract. This subparagraph shall not apply to any retirement bond if such bond is acquired by the owner by reason of the death of another individual and the owner was not the surviving spouse of such other individual.

(D) PARTIAL ROLLOVERS PERMITTED.—Rules similar to the rules of section 408(d)(3)(C) shall apply for purposes of subparagraph (C).

Amendments

• 1984, Deficit Reduction Act of 1984 (P.L. 98-369)

P.L. 98-369, §42(a)(7):

Amended Code Sec. 409(b)(1) [before repeal by Act Sec. 491]by striking out "section 1232 (relating to bonds and other evidences of indebtedness)" and inserting in lieu thereof "section 1271 (relating to treatment of amounts received on retirement or sale or exchange of debt instruments)". **Effective** for tax years ending after 7-18-84.

P.L. 98-369, §522(d)(13):

Amended Code Sec. 409(b)(3)(C) [before repeal by Act Sec. 491]by striking out the second sentence and inserting in lieu thereof two new sentences. **Effective** for distributions made after 7-18-84, in tax years ending after such date. Prior to amendment, the second sentence of Code Sec. 409(b)(3)(C) read as follows:

This subparagraph does not apply in the case of a transfer to such an employees' trust or such an annuity plan unless no part of the value of such proceeds is attributable to any source other than a rollover contribution from such an employees' trust or annuity plan (other than an annuity plan or a trust forming part of a plan under which the individual was an employee within the meaning of section 401(c)(1) at the time contributions were made on his behalf under the plan).

• 1982, Tax Equity and Fiscal Responsibility Act of 1982 (P.L. 97-248)

P.L. 97-248, §243(b)(1)(B):

Amended Code Sec. 409(b)(3)(C) by adding a new last sentence to the paragraph. **Effective** with respect to individuals dying after 12-31-83.

P.L. 97-248, §335(a)(2):

Amended Code Sec. 409(b)(3) by adding new subparagraph (D). **Effective** for distributions made after 12-31-82, in tax years ending after such date.

• 1981, Economic Recovery Tax Act of 1981 (P.L. 97-34)

P.L. 97-34, §311(g)(3):

Amended Code Sec. 409(b)(3)(A) by adding at the end the following new sentence: " The preceding sentence shall not apply to the extent that the bond was purchased with a rollover contribution described in subparagraph (C) of this paragraph or in section 402(a)(5), 402(a)(7), 403(a)(4), 403(b)(8), 405(b)(3), or 408(d)(3).". **Effective** for tax years beginning after 12-31-74.

• 1980, Technical Corrections Act of 1979 (P.L. 96-222)

P.L. 96-222, §101(a)(13)(A):

Amended Act Sec. 156(d) of P.L. 95-600 to change the effective date of the amendment of Code Sec. 409(b)(3)(C) by Act Sec. 156(c)(2) of P.L. 95-600 from "distributions or transfers made after December 31, 1978, in taxable years beginning after that date" to "distributions or transfers made after December 31, 1977, in taxable years beginning after that date."

• 1978, Revenue Act of 1978 (P.L. 95-600)

P.L. 95-600, §156(c)(2):

Amended Code Sec. 409(b)(3)(C) by striking out "or an annuity plan described in section 403(a)" in the first sentence and by inserting in lieu thereof "an annuity plan described in section 403(a), or an annuity contract described in section 403(b)", and by adding a new last sentence. **Effective** for distributions or transfers made after 12-31-78, in tax years beginning after such date.

• 1976, Tax Reform Act of 1976 (P.L. 94-455)

P.L. 94-455, §1901(a)(60):

Amended Code Sec. 409(b)(3)(C) by substituting "section 408(d)(3)" for "section 403(d)(3)". **Effective** for tax years beginning after 12-31-76.

[Sec. 409(c)]

(c) ADDITIONAL TAX ON CERTAIN REDEMPTIONS BEFORE AGE 59½.—

(1) EARLY REDEMPTION OF BOND.—If a retirement bond is redeemed by the registered owner before he attains age 59½ his tax under this chapter for the taxable year in which the bond is redeemed shall be increased by an amount equal to 10 percent of the amount of the proceeds of the redemption includible in his gross income for the taxable year.

(2) DISABILITY CASES.—Paragraph (1) does not apply for any taxable year during which the retirement bond is redeemed if, for that taxable year, the registered owner is disabled within the meaning of section 72(m)(7).

(3) REDEMPTION WITHIN ONE YEAR.—Paragraph (1) does not apply if the registered owner tenders the bond for redemption within 12 months after the date of its issuance.

Amendments

• 1974, Employee Retirement Income Security Act of 1974 (P.L. 93-406)

P.L. 93-406, §2002(c):

Added Code Sec. 409. **Effective** for tax years beginning after 12-31-74.

[Sec. 409A]

SEC. 409A. INCLUSION IN GROSS INCOME OF DEFERRED COMPENSATION UNDER NONQUALIFIED DEFERRED COMPENSATION PLANS.

[Sec. 409A(a)]

(a) RULES RELATING TO CONSTRUCTIVE RECEIPT.—

(1) PLAN FAILURES.—

(A) GROSS INCOME INCLUSION.—

(i) IN GENERAL.—If at any time during a taxable year a nonqualified deferred compensation plan—

(I) fails to meet the requirements of paragraphs (2), (3), and (4), or

(II) is not operated in accordance with such requirements,

all compensation deferred under the plan for the taxable year and all preceding taxable years shall be includible in gross income for the taxable year to the extent not subject to a substantial risk of forfeiture and not previously included in gross income.

(ii) APPLICATION ONLY TO AFFECTED PARTICIPANTS.—Clause (i) shall only apply with respect to all compensation deferred under the plan for participants with respect to whom the failure relates.

(B) INTEREST AND ADDITIONAL TAX PAYABLE WITH RESPECT TO PREVIOUSLY DEFERRED COMPENSATION.—

(i) IN GENERAL.—If compensation is required to be included in gross income under subparagraph (A) for a taxable year, the tax imposed by this chapter for the taxable year shall be increased by the sum of—

(I) the amount of interest determined under clause (ii), and

(II) an amount equal to 20 percent of the compensation which is required to be included in gross income.

(ii) INTEREST.—For purposes of clause (i), the interest determined under this clause for any taxable year is the amount of interest at the underpayment rate plus 1 percentage point on the underpayments that would have occurred had the deferred compensation been includible in gross income for the taxable year in which first deferred or, if later, the first taxable year in which such deferred compensation is not subject to a substantial risk of forfeiture.

(2) DISTRIBUTIONS.—

(A) IN GENERAL.—The requirements of this paragraph are met if the plan provides that compensation deferred under the plan may not be distributed earlier than—

(i) separation from service as determined by the Secretary (except as provided in subparagraph (B)(i)),

(ii) the date the participant becomes disabled (within the meaning of subparagraph (C)),

(iii) death,

(iv) a specified time (or pursuant to a fixed schedule) specified under the plan at the date of the deferral of such compensation,

(v) to the extent provided by the Secretary, a change in the ownership or effective control of the corporation, or in the ownership of a substantial portion of the assets of the corporation, or

(vi) the occurrence of an unforeseeable emergency.

(B) SPECIAL RULES.—

(i) SPECIFIED EMPLOYEES.—In the case of any specified employee, the requirement of subparagraph (A)(i) is met only if distributions may not be made before the date which is 6 months after the date of separation from service (or, if earlier, the date of death of the employee). For purposes of the preceding sentence, a specified employee is a key employee (as defined in section 416(i) without regard to paragraph (5) thereof) of a corporation any stock in which is publicly traded on an established securities market or otherwise.

(ii) UNFORESEEABLE EMERGENCY.—For purposes of subparagraph (A)(vi)—

(I) IN GENERAL.—The term "unforeseeable emergency" means a severe financial hardship to the participant resulting from an illness or accident of the participant, the participant's spouse, or a dependent (as defined in section 152(a)) of the participant, loss of the participant's property due to casualty, or other similar extraordinary and unforeseeable circumstances arising as a result of events beyond the control of the participant.

(II) LIMITATION ON DISTRIBUTIONS.—The requirement of subparagraph (A)(vi) is met only if, as determined under regulations of the Secretary, the amounts distributed with respect to an emergency do not exceed the amounts necessary to satisfy such emergency plus amounts necessary to pay taxes reasonably anticipated as a result of the distribution, after taking into account the extent to which such hardship is or may be relieved through reimbursement or compensation by insurance or otherwise or by liquidation of the participant's assets (to the extent the liquidation of such assets would not itself cause severe financial hardship).

(C) DISABLED.—For purposes of subparagraph (A)(ii), a participant shall be considered disabled if the participant—

(i) is unable to engage in any substantial gainful activity by reason of any medically determinable physical or mental impairment which can be expected to result in death or can be expected to last for a continuous period of not less than 12 months, or

(ii) is, by reason of any medically determinable physical or mental impairment which can be expected to result in death or can be expected to last for a continuous period of not less than 12 months, receiving income replacement benefits for a period of not less than 3 months under an accident and health plan covering employees of the participant's employer.

(3) ACCELERATION OF BENEFITS.—The requirements of this paragraph are met if the plan does not permit the acceleration of the time or schedule of any payment under the plan, except as provided in regulations by the Secretary.

(4) ELECTIONS.—

(A) IN GENERAL.—The requirements of this paragraph are met if the requirements of subparagraphs (B) and (C) are met.

(B) INITIAL DEFERRAL DECISION.—

(i) IN GENERAL.—The requirements of this subparagraph are met if the plan provides that compensation for services performed during a taxable year may be deferred at the participant's election only if the election to defer such compensation is made not later than the close of the preceding taxable year or at such other time as provided in regulations.

(ii) FIRST YEAR OF ELIGIBILITY.—In the case of the first year in which a participant becomes eligible to participate in the plan, such election may be made with respect to services to be performed subsequent to the election within 30 days after the date the participant becomes eligible to participate in such plan.

(iii) PERFORMANCE-BASED COMPENSATION.—In the case of any performance-based compensation based on services performed over a period of at least 12 months, such election may be made no later than 6 months before the end of the period.

(C) CHANGES IN TIME AND FORM OF DISTRIBUTION.—The requirements of this subparagraph are met if, in the case of a plan which permits under a subsequent election a delay in a payment or a change in the form of payment—

(i) the plan requires that such election may not take effect until at least 12 months after the date on which the election is made,

(ii) in the case of an election related to a payment not described in clause (ii), (iii), or (vi) of paragraph (2)(A), the plan requires that the payment with respect to which such election is made be deferred for a period of not less than 5 years from the date such payment would otherwise have been made, and

(iii) the plan requires that any election related to a payment described in paragraph (2)(A)(iv) may not be made less than 12 months prior to the date of the first scheduled payment under such paragraph.

Amendments

• 2005, Gulf Opportunity Zone Act of 2005 (P.L. 109-135)

P.L. 109-135, §403(hh)(2):

Amended Code Sec. 409A(a)(4)(C)(ii) by striking "first" before "payment with respect to which". **Effective** as if included in the provision of the American Jobs Creation Act of 2004 (P.L. 108-357) to which it relates [**effective**, generally, for amounts deferred after 12-31-2004.—CCH].

[Sec. 409A(b)]

(b) RULES RELATING TO FUNDING.—

(1) OFFSHORE PROPERTY IN A TRUST.—In the case of assets set aside (directly or indirectly) in a trust (or other arrangement determined by the Secretary) for purposes of paying deferred compensation under a nonqualified deferred compensation plan, for purposes of section 83 such assets shall be treated as property transferred in connection with the performance of services whether or not such assets are available to satisfy claims of general creditors—

(A) at the time set aside if such assets (or such trust or other arrangement) are located outside of the United States, or

(B) at the time transferred if such assets (or such trust or other arrangement) are subsequently transferred outside of the United States.

This paragraph shall not apply to assets located in a foreign jurisdiction if substantially all of the services to which the nonqualified deferred compensation relates are performed in such jurisdiction.

(2) EMPLOYER'S FINANCIAL HEALTH.—In the case of compensation deferred under a nonqualified deferred compensation plan, there is a transfer of property within the meaning of section 83 with respect to such compensation as of the earlier of—

(A) the date on which the plan first provides that assets will become restricted to the provision of benefits under the plan in connection with a change in the employer's financial health, or

(B) the date on which assets are so restricted,

whether or not such assets are available to satisfy claims of general creditors.

(3) TREATMENT OF EMPLOYER'S DEFINED BENEFIT PLAN DURING RESTRICTED PERIOD.—

(A) IN GENERAL.—If—

(i) during any restricted period with respect to a single-employer defined benefit plan, assets are set aside or reserved (directly or indirectly) in a trust (or other arrangement as determined by the Secretary) or transferred to such a trust or other arrangement for purposes of paying deferred compensation of an applicable covered employee under a nonqualified deferred compensation plan of the plan sponsor or member of a controlled group which includes the plan sponsor, or

(ii) a nonqualified deferred compensation plan of the plan sponsor or member of a controlled group which includes the plan sponsor provides that assets will become restricted to the provision of benefits under the plan to an applicable covered employee in connection with such restricted period (or other similar financial measure determined by the Secretary) with respect to the defined benefit plan, or assets are so restricted,

such assets shall, for purposes of section 83, be treated as property transferred in connection with the performance of services whether or not such assets are available to satisfy claims of general creditors. Clause (i) shall not apply with respect to any assets which are so set aside before the restricted period with respect to the defined benefit plan.

(B) RESTRICTED PERIOD.—For purposes of this section, the term "restricted period" means, with respect to any plan described in subparagraph (A)—

(i) any period during which the plan is in at-risk status (as defined in section 430(i));

(ii) any period the plan sponsor is a debtor in a case under title 11, United States Code, or similar Federal or State law, and

(iii) the 12-month period beginning on the date which is 6 months before the termination date of the plan if, as of the termination date, the plan is not sufficient for benefit liabilities (within the meaning of section 4041 of the Employee Retirement Income Security Act of 1974).

(C) SPECIAL RULE FOR PAYMENT OF TAXES ON DEFERRED COMPENSATION INCLUDED IN INCOME.—If an employer provides directly or indirectly for the payment of any Federal, State, or local income taxes with respect to any compensation required to be included in gross income by reason of this paragraph—

(i) interest shall be imposed under subsection (a)(1)(B)(i)(I) on the amount of such payment in the same manner as if such payment was part of the deferred compensation to which it relates,

(ii) such payment shall be taken into account in determining the amount of the additional tax under subsection (a)(1)(B)(i)(II) in the same manner as if such payment was part of the deferred compensation to which it relates, and

(iii) no deduction shall be allowed under this title with respect to such payment.

(D) OTHER DEFINITIONS.—For purposes of this section—

(i) APPLICABLE COVERED EMPLOYEE.—The term "applicable covered employee" means any—

(I) covered employee of a plan sponsor,

(II) covered employee of a member of a controlled group which includes the plan sponsor, and

(III) former employee who was a covered employee at the time of termination of employment with the plan sponsor or a member of a controlled group which includes the plan sponsor.

(ii) COVERED EMPLOYEE.—The term "covered employee" means an individual described in section 162(m)(3) or an individual subject to the requirements of section 16(a) of the Securities Exchange Act of 1934.

(4) INCOME INCLUSION FOR OFFSHORE TRUSTS AND EMPLOYER'S FINANCIAL HEALTH.—For each taxable year that assets treated as transferred under this subsection remain set aside in a trust or other arrangement subject to paragraph (1), (2), or (3), any increase in value in, or earnings with respect to, such assets shall be treated as an additional transfer of property under this subsection (to the extent not previously included in income).

(5) INTEREST ON TAX LIABILITY PAYABLE WITH RESPECT TO TRANSFERRED PROPERTY.—

(A) IN GENERAL.—If amounts are required to be included in gross income by reason of paragraph (1), (2), or (3) for a taxable year, the tax imposed by this chapter for such taxable year shall be increased by the sum of—

(i) the amount of interest determined under subparagraph (B), and

(ii) an amount equal to 20 percent of the amounts required to be included in gross income.

(B) INTEREST.—For purposes of subparagraph (A), the interest determined under this subparagraph for any taxable year is the amount of interest at the underpayment rate plus 1 percentage point on the underpayments that would have occurred had the amounts so required to be included in gross income by paragraph (1), (2), or (3) been includible in gross income for the taxable year in which first deferred or, if later, the first taxable year in which such amounts are not subject to a substantial risk of forfeiture.

Amendments

• 2008, Worker, Retiree, and Employer Recovery Act of 2008 (P.L. 110-458)

P.L. 110-458, §101(e):

Amended Code Sec. 409A(b)(3)(A)(ii) by inserting "to an applicable covered employee" after "under the plan". **Effective** as if included in the provision of the 2006 Act to which the amendment relates [**effective** for transfers or other reservation of assets after 8-17-2006.—CCH].

• 2006, Pension Protection Act of 2006 (P.L. 109-280)

P.L. 109-280, §116(a):

Amended Code Sec. 409A(b) by redesignating paragraphs (3) and (4) as paragraphs (4) and (5), respectively, and by inserting after paragraph (2) a new paragraph (3). **Effective** for transfers or other reservation of assets after 8-17-2006.

P.L. 109-280, §116(b):

Amended Code Sec. 409A(b)(4)-(5), as redesignated by Act Sec. 116(a), by striking "paragraph (1) or (2)" each place it appears and inserting "paragraph (1), (2), or (3)". **Effective** for transfers or other reservation of assets after 8-17-2006.

• 2005, Gulf Opportunity Zone Act of 2005 (P.L. 109-135)

P.L. 109-135, §403(hh)(3)(A)-(B), provides:

(3)(A) Notwithstanding section 885(d)(1) of the American Jobs Creation Act of 2004, subsection (b) of section 409A of the Internal Revenue Code of 1986 shall take effect on January 1, 2005.

(B) Not later than 90 days after the date of the enactment of this Act, the Secretary of the Treasury shall issue guidance under which a nonqualified deferred compensation plan which is in violation of the requirements of section 409A(b) of such Code shall be treated as not having violated such requirements if such plan comes into conformance with such requirements during such limited period as the Secretary may specify in such guidance.

[Sec. 409A(c)]

(c) NO INFERENCE ON EARLIER INCOME INCLUSION OR REQUIREMENT OF LATER INCLUSION.—Nothing in this section shall be construed to prevent the inclusion of amounts in gross income under any other provision of this chapter or any other rule of law earlier than the time provided in this section. Any amount included in gross income under this section shall not be required to be included in gross income under any other provision of this chapter or any other rule of law later than the time provided in this section.

[Sec. 409A(d)]

(d) OTHER DEFINITIONS AND SPECIAL RULES.—For purposes of this section:

(1) NONQUALIFIED DEFERRED COMPENSATION PLAN.—The term "nonqualified deferred compensation plan" means any plan that provides for the deferral of compensation, other than—

(A) a qualified employer plan, and

(B) any bona fide vacation leave, sick leave, compensatory time, disability pay, or death benefit plan.

(2) QUALIFIED EMPLOYER PLAN.—The term "qualified employer plan" means—

(A) any plan, contract, pension, account, or trust described in subparagraph (A) or (B) of section 219(g)(5) (without regard to subparagraph (A)(iii)),

(B) any eligible deferred compensation plan (within the meaning of section 457(b)), and

(C) any plan described in section 415(m).

(3) PLAN INCLUDES ARRANGEMENTS, ETC.—The term "plan" includes any agreement or arrangement, including an agreement or arrangement that includes one person.

(4) SUBSTANTIAL RISK OF FORFEITURE.—The rights of a person to compensation are subject to a substantial risk of forfeiture if such person's rights to such compensation are conditioned upon the future performance of substantial services by any individual.

(5) TREATMENT OF EARNINGS.—References to deferred compensation shall be treated as including references to income (whether actual or notional) attributable to such compensation or such income.

(6) AGGREGATION RULES.—Except as provided by the Secretary, rules similar to the rules of subsections (b) and (c) of section 414 shall apply.

[Sec. 409A(e)]

(e) REGULATIONS.—The Secretary shall prescribe such regulations as may be necessary or appropriate to carry out the purposes of this section, including regulations—

(1) providing for the determination of amounts of deferral in the case of a nonqualified deferred compensation plan which is a defined benefit plan,

(2) relating to changes in the ownership and control of a corporation or assets of a corporation for purposes of subsection (a)(2)(A)(v),

(3) exempting arrangements from the application of subsection (b) if such arrangements will not result in an improper deferral of United States tax and will not result in assets being effectively beyond the reach of creditors,

(4) defining financial health for purposes of subsection (b)(2), and

(5) disregarding a substantial risk of forfeiture in cases where necessary to carry out the purposes of this section.

Amendments

• 2004, American Jobs Creation Act of 2004 (P.L. 108-357)

P.L. 108-357, §885(a):

Amended subpart A of part I of subchapter D of chapter 1 by adding at the end a new Code Sec. 409A. **Effective** generally for amounts deferred after 12-31-2004. For special rules, see Act Sec. 885(d)(2)-(3), 885(e), and 885(f), below.

P.L. 108-357, §885(d)(2)-(3), provides:

(2) SPECIAL RULES.—

(A) EARNINGS.—The amendments made by this section shall apply to earnings on deferred compensation only to the extent that such amendments apply to such compensation.

(B) MATERIAL MODIFICATIONS.—For purposes of this subsection, amounts deferred in taxable years beginning before January 1, 2005, shall be treated as amounts deferred in a taxable year beginning on or after such date if the plan under which the deferral is made is materially modified after October 3, 2004, unless such modification is pursuant to the guidance issued under subsection (f).

(3) EXCEPTION FOR NONELECTIVE DEFERRED COMPENSATION.—The amendments made by this section shall not apply to any nonelective deferred compensation to which section 457 of the Internal Revenue Code of 1986 does not apply by reason of section 457(e)(12) of such Code, but only if such compensation is provided under a nonqualified deferred compensation plan—

(A) which was in existence on May 1, 2004,

(B) which was providing nonelective deferred compensation described in such section 457(e)(12) on such date, and

(C) which is established or maintained by an organization incorporated on July 2, 1974.

If, after May 1, 2004, a plan described in the preceding sentence adopts a plan amendment which provides a material change in the classes of individuals eligible to participate in the plan, this paragraph shall not apply to any nonelective deferred compensation provided under the plan on or after the date of the adoption of the amendment.

P.L. 108-357, §885(e), provides:

(e) GUIDANCE RELATING TO CHANGE OF OWNERSHIP OR CONTROL.—Not later than 90 days after the date of the enactment of this Act, the Secretary of the Treasury shall issue guidance on what constitutes a change in ownership or effective control for purposes of section 409A of the Internal Revenue Code of 1986, as added by this section.

P.L. 108-357, §885(f), as amended by P.L. 109-135, §403(hh)(4), provides:

(f) GUIDANCE RELATING TO TERMINATION OF CERTAIN EXISTING ARRANGEMENTS.—Not later than 60 days after the date of the enactment of this Act, the Secretary of the Treasury shall issue guidance providing a limited period during which a nonqualified deferred compensation plan adopted before January 1, 2005, may, without violating the requirements of paragraphs (2), (3), and (4) of section 409A(a) of the Internal Revenue Code of 1986 (as added by this section), be amended—

(1) to provide that a participant may terminate participation in the plan, or cancel an outstanding deferral election with regard to amounts deferred after December 31, 2004, but only if amounts subject to the termination or cancellation are includible in income of the participant as earned (or, if later, when no longer subject to substantial risk of forfeiture), and

(2) to conform to the requirements of such section 409A with regard to amounts deferred after December 31, 2004.

Subpart B—Special Rules

[Sec. 410]

SEC. 410. MINIMUM PARTICIPATION STANDARDS

[Sec. 410(a)]

(a) PARTICIPATION.—

(1) MINIMUM AGE AND SERVICE CONDITIONS.—

(A) GENERAL RULE.—A trust shall not constitute a qualified trust under section 401(a) if the plan of which it is a part requires, as a condition of participation in the plan, that an employee complete a period of service with the employer or employers maintaining the plan extending beyond the later of the following dates—

(i) the date on which the employee attains the age of 21; or

(ii) the date on which he completes 1 year of service.

(B) SPECIAL RULES FOR CERTAIN PLANS.—

(i) In the case of any plan which provides that after not more than 2 years of service each participant has a right to 100 percent of his accrued benefit under the plan which is nonforfeitable (within the meaning of section 411) at the time such benefit accrues, clause (ii) of subparagraph (A) shall be applied by substituting "2 years of service" for "1 year of service".

(ii) In the case of any plan maintained exclusively for employees of an educational institution (as defined in section 170(b)(1)(A)(ii)) by an employer which is exempt from tax under section 501(a) which provides that each participant having at least 1 year of service has a right to 100 percent of his accrued benefit under the plan which is nonforfeitable (within the meaning of section 411) at the time such benefit accrues, clause (i) of subparagraph (A) shall be applied by substituting "26" for "21". This clause shall not apply to any plan to which clause (i) applies.

(2) MAXIMUM AGE CONDITIONS.—A trust shall not constitute a qualified trust under section 401(a) if the plan of which it is a part excludes from participation (on the basis of age) employees who have attained a specified age.

(3) DEFINITION OF YEAR OF SERVICE.—

(A) GENERAL RULE.—For purposes of this subsection, the term "year of service" means a 12-month period during which the employee has not less than 1,000 hours of service. For purposes of this paragraph, computation of any 12-month period shall be made with reference to the date on which the employee's employment commenced, except that, under regulations prescribed by the Secretary of Labor, such computation may be made by reference to the first day of a plan year in the case of an employee who does not complete 1,000 hours of service during the 12-month period beginning on the date his employment commenced.

(B) SEASONAL INDUSTRIES.—In the case of any seasonal industry where the customary period of employment is less than 1,000 hours during a calendar year, the term "year of service" shall be such period as may be determined under regulations prescribed by the Secretary of Labor.

(C) HOURS OF SERVICE.—For purposes of this subsection, the term "hour of service" means a time of service determined under regulations prescribed by the Secretary of Labor.

(D) MARITIME INDUSTRIES.—For purposes of this subsection, in the case of any maritime industry, 125 days of service shall be treated as 1,000 hours of service. The Secretary of Labor may prescribe regulations to carry out this subparagraph.

(4) TIME OF PARTICIPATION.—A plan shall be treated as not meeting the requirements of paragraph (1) unless it provides that any employee who has satisfied the minimum age and service requirements specified in such paragraph, and who is otherwise entitled to participate in the plan, commences participation in the plan no later than the earlier of—

(A) the first day of the first plan year beginning after the date on which such employee satisfied such requirements, or

(B) the date 6 months after the date on which he satisfied such requirements,

unless such employee was separated from the service before the date referred to in subparagraph (A) or (B), whichever is applicable.

(5) BREAKS IN SERVICE.—

(A) GENERAL RULE.—Except as otherwise provided in subparagraphs (B), (C), and (D), all years of service with the employer or employers maintaining the plan shall be taken into account in computing the period of service for purposes of paragraph (1).

(B) EMPLOYEES UNDER 2-YEAR 100 PERCENT VESTING.—In the case of any employee who has any 1-year break in service (as defined in section 411(a)(6)(A)) under a plan to which the service requirements of clause (i) of paragraph (1)(B) apply, if such employee has not satisfied such requirements, service before such break shall not be required to be taken into account.

(C) 1-YEAR BREAK IN SERVICE.—In computing an employee's period of service for purposes of paragraph (1) in the case of any participant who has any 1-year break in service (as defined in section 411(a)(6)(A)), service before such break shall not be required to be taken into account under the plan until he has completed a year of service (as defined in paragraph (3)) after his return.

(D) NONVESTED PARTICIPANTS.—

(i) IN GENERAL.—For purposes of paragraph (1), in the case of a nonvested participant, years of service with the employer or employers maintaining the plan before any period of consecutive 1-year breaks in service shall not be required to be taken into account in computing the period of service if the number of consecutive 1-year breaks in service within such period equals or exceeds the greater of—

(I) 5, or

(II) the aggregate number of years of service before such period.

(ii) YEARS OF SERVICE NOT TAKEN INTO ACCOUNT.—If any years of service are not required to be taken into account by reason of a period of breaks in service to which clause (i) applies, such years of service shall not be taken into account in applying clause (i) to a subsequent period of breaks in service.

(iii) NONVESTED PARTICIPANT DEFINED.—For purposes of clause (i), the term "nonvested participant" means a participant who does not have any nonforfeitable right under the plan to an accrued benefit derived from employer contributions.

(E) SPECIAL RULE FOR MATERNITY OR PATERNITY ABSENCES.—

(i) GENERAL RULE.—In the case of each individual who is absent from work for any period—

(I) by reason of the pregnancy of the individual,

(II) by reason of the birth of a child of the individual,

(III) by reason of the placement of a child with the individual in connection with the adoption of such child by such individual, or

(IV) for purposes of caring for such child for a period beginning immediately following such birth or placement,

the plan shall treat as hours of service, solely for purposes of determining under this paragraph whether a 1-year break in service (as defined in section 411(a)(6)(A)) has occurred, the hours described in clause (ii).

(ii) HOURS TREATED AS HOURS OF SERVICE.—The hours described in this clause are—

(I) the hours of service which otherwise would normally have been credited to such individual but for such absence, or

(II) in any case in which the plan is unable to determine the hours described in subclause (I), 8 hours of service per day of such absence,

except that the total number of hours treated as hours of service under this clause by reason of any such pregnancy or placement shall not exceed 501 hours.

(iii) YEAR TO WHICH HOURS ARE CREDITED.—The hours described in clause (ii) shall be treated as hours of service as provided in this subparagraph—

(I) only in the year in which the absence from work begins, if a participant would be prevented from incurring a 1-year break in service in such year solely because the period of absence is treated as hours of service as provided in clause (i); or

(II) in any other case, in the immediately following year.

(iv) YEAR DEFINED.—For purposes of this subparagraph, the term "year" means the period used in computations pursuant to paragraph (3).

(v) INFORMATION REQUIRED TO BE FILED.—A plan shall not fail to satisfy the requirements of this subparagraph solely because it provides that no credit will be given pursuant to this subparagraph unless the individual furnishes to the plan administrator such timely information as the plan may reasonably require to establish—

(I) that the absence from work is for reasons referred to in clause (i), and

(II) the number of days for which there was such an absence.

Amendments

• 1989, Omnibus Budget Reconciliation Act of 1989 (P.L. 101-239)

P.L. 101-239, §7841(d)(6):

Amended Code Sec. 410(a)(2) by striking the comma before the period. **Effective** 12-19-89.

• 1986, Tax Reform Act of 1986 (P.L. 99-514)

P.L. 99-514, §1113(c):

Amended Code Sec. 410(a)(1)(B) by striking out "3 years" each place it appears and inserting in lieu thereof "2 years". **Effective** for plan years beginning after 12-31-88. However, for special rules, see Act Sec. 1113(f)(2)-(4), below.

P.L. 99-514, §1113(d)(A):

Amended Code Sec. 410(a)(5)(B) by striking out "3-year" and inserting in lieu thereof "2-year" in the heading. **Effective** for plan years beginning after 12-31-88. However, for special rules, see Act Sec. 1113(f)(2)-(4), below.

P.L. 99-514, §1113(f)(2)-(4), as amended by P.L. 101-239, §7861(a)(3)-(4), provides:

(2) SPECIAL RULE FOR COLLECTIVE BARGAINING AGREEMENTS.—In the case of a plan maintained pursuant to 1 or more collective bargaining agreements between employee representatives and 1 or more employers ratified before March 1, 1986, the amendments made by this section shall not apply to employees covered by any such agreement in plan years beginning before the earlier of—

(A) the later of—

(i) January 1, 1989, or

(ii) the date on which the last of such collective bargaining agreements terminates (determined without regard to any extension thereof after February 28, 1986), or

(B) January 1, 1991.

(3) PARTICIPATION REQUIRED.—The amendments made by this section shall not apply to any employee who does not have 1 hour of service in any plan year to which the amendments made by this section apply.

(4) REPEAL OF CLASS YEAR VESTING.—If a plan amendment repealing class year vesting is adopted after October 22, 1986, such amendment shall not apply to any employee for the 1st plan year to which the amendments made by subsections (b) and (e)(2) apply (and any subsequent plan year) if—

(A) such plan amendment would reduce the nonforfeitable right of such employee for such year, and

(B) such employee has at least 1 hour of service before the adoption of such plan amendment and after the beginning of such 1st plan year.

• 1986, Omnibus Budget Reconciliation Act of 1986 (P.L. 99-509)

P.L. 99-509, §9203(a)(2):

Amended Code Sec. 410(a)(2) by striking out "unless—" and all that follows and inserting in lieu thereof a period. For the **effective** date, see Act Sec. 9204, below. Prior to amendment, Code Sec. 410(a)(2) read as follows:

(2) MAXIMUM AGE CONDITIONS.—A trust shall not constitute a qualified trust under section 401(a) if the plan of which it is a part excludes from participation (on the basis of age) employees who have attained a specified age, unless—

(A) the plan is a—

(i) defined benefit plan, or

(ii) target benefit plan (as defined under regulations prescribed by the Secretary), and

(B) such employees begin employment with the employer after they have attained a specified age which is not more than 5 years before the normal retirement age under the plan.

P.L. 99-509, §9204, provides:

SEC. 9204. EFFECTIVE DATE; REGULATIONS.

(a) APPLICABILITY TO EMPLOYEES WITH SERVICE AFTER 1988.—

(1) IN GENERAL.—The amendments made by sections 9201 and 9202 shall apply only with respect to plan years beginning on or after January 1, 1988, and only to employees who have 1 hour of service in any plan year to which such amendments apply.

(2) SPECIAL RULE FOR COLLECTIVELY BARGAINED PLANS.—In the case of a plan maintained pursuant to 1 or more collective bargaining agreements between employee representatives and 1 or more employers ratified before March 1, 1986, paragraph (1) shall be applied to benefits pursuant to, and individuals covered by, any such agreement by substituting

for "January 1, 1988" the date of the commencement of the first plan year beginning on or after the earlier of—

(A) the later of—

(i) January 1, 1988, or

(ii) the date on which the last of such collective bargaining agreements terminate (determined without regard to any extension thereof after February 28, 1986), or

(B) January 1, 1990.

(b) APPLICABILITY OF AMENDMENTS RELATING TO NORMAL RETIREMENT AGE.—The amendments made by section 9203 shall apply only with respect to plan years beginning on or after January 1, 1988, and only with respect to service performed on or after such date.

(c) PLAN AMENDMENTS.—If any amendment made by this subtitle requires an amendment to any plan, such plan amendment shall not be required to be made before the first plan year beginning on or after January 1, 1989, if—

(1) during the period after such amendment takes effect and before such first plan year, the plan is operated in accordance with the requirements of such amendment, and

(2) such plan amendment applies retroactively to the period after such amendment takes effect and such first plan year.

A pension plan shall not be treated as failing to provide definitely determinable benefits or contributions, or to be operated in accordance with the provisions of the plan, merely because it operates in accordance with this subsection.

(d) INTERAGENCY COORDINATION.—The regulations and rulings issued by the Secretary of Labor, the regulations and rulings issued by the Secretary of the Treasury, and the regulations and rulings issued by the Equal Employment Opportunity Commission pursuant to the amendments made by this subtitle shall each be consistent with the others. The Secretary of Labor, the Secretary of the Treasury, and the Equal Employment Opportunity Commission shall each consult with the others to the extent necessary to meet the requirements of the preceding sentence.

(e) FINAL REGULATIONS.—The Secretary of Labor, the Secretary of the Treasury, and the Equal Employment Opportunity Commission shall each issue before February 1, 1988, such final regulations as may be necessary to carry out the amendments made by this subtitle.

• 1984, Retirement Equity Act of 1984 (P.L. 98-397)

P.L. 98-397, §202(a)(1):

Amended Code Sec. 410(a)(1)(A)(i) by striking out "25" and inserting in lieu thereof "21". **Effective** for plan years beginning after 12-31-84. Special rules appear in the notes for P.L. 98-397 following Code Sec. 401(a).

P.L. 98-397, §202(a)(2):

Amended Code Sec. 410(a)(1)(B)(ii) by striking out "`30' for `25'" and inserting in lieu thereof "`26' for `21'". **Effective** for plan years beginning after 12-31-84. Special rules appear in the notes for P.L. 98-397 following Code Sec. 401(a).

P.L. 98-397, §202(d)(1):

Amended Code Sec. 410(a)(5)(D). **Effective** for plan years beginning after 12-31-84. Special rules appear in the notes for P.L. 98-397 following Code Secs. 401(a) and 411(a). Prior to amendment, Code Sec. 410(a)(5)(D) read as follows:

(D) Nonvested participants.—In the case of a participant who does not have any nonforfeitable right to an accrued benefit derived from employer contributions, years of service with the employer or employers maintaining the plan before a break in service shall not be required to be taken into account in computing the period of service for purposes of paragraph (1) if the number of consecutive 1-year breaks in service equals or exceeds the aggregate number of such years of service before such break. Such aggregate number of years of service before such break shall be deemed not to include any years of service not required to be taken into account under this subparagraph by reason of any prior break in service.

P.L. 98-397, §202(e)(1):

Added Code Sec. 410(a)(5)(E). **Effective** in the case of absences from work which begin on or after the first day of the first plan year to which the amendments made by P.L. 98-397 apply. Special rules appear in Act Sec. 303(a)(2)(3) and (b) following Code Sec. 411.

• 1976, Tax Reform Act of 1976 (P.L. 94-455)

P.L. 94-455, §1901(a)(61)(A):

Amended Code Sec. 410(a)(5)(C) and (D) by substituting "purposes of paragraph (1)" for "purposes of subsection (a)(1)". **Effective** for tax years beginning after 12-31-76.

P.L. 94-455, §1906(b)(13)(A):

Amended the 1954 Code by substituting "Secretary" for "Secretary or his delegate" each place it appeared. **Effective** 2-1-77.

[Sec. 410(b)]

(b) MINIMUM COVERAGE REQUIREMENTS.—

(1) IN GENERAL.—A trust shall not constitute a qualified trust under section 401(a) unless such trust is designated by the employer as part of a plan which meets 1 of the following requirements:

(A) The plan benefits at least 70 percent of employees who are not highly compensated employees.

(B) The plan benefits—

(i) a percentage of employees who are not highly compensated employees which is at least 70 percent of

(ii) the percentage of highly compensated employees benefiting under the plan.

(C) The plan meets the requirements of paragaph (2).

(2) AVERAGE BENEFIT PERCENTAGE TEST.—

(A) IN GENERAL.—A plan shall be treated as meeting the requirements of this paragraph if—

(i) the plan benefits such employees as qualify under a classification set up by the employer and found by the Secretary not to be discriminatory in favor of highly compensated employees, and

(ii) the average benefit percentage for employees who are not highly compensated employees is at least 70 percent of the average benefit percentage for highly compensated employees.

(B) AVERAGE BENEFIT PERCENTAGE.—For purposes of this paragraph, the term "average benefit percentage" means, with respect to any group, the average of the benefit percentages calculated separately with respect to each employee in such group (whether or not a participant in any plan).

(C) BENEFIT PERCENTAGE.—For purposes of this paragraph—

(i) IN GENERAL.—The term "benefit percentage" means the employer-provided contribution or benefit of an employee under all qualified plans maintained by the employer, expressed as a percentage of such employee's compensation (within the meaning of section 414(s)).

(ii) PERIOD FOR COMPUTING PERCENTAGE.—At the election of an employer, the benefit percentage for any plan year shall be computed on the basis of contributions or benefits for—

(I) such plan year, or

(II) any consecutive plan year period (not greater than 3 years) which ends with such plan year and which is specified in such election.

An election under this clause, once made, may be revoked or modified only with the consent of the Secretary.

(D) EMPLOYEES TAKEN INTO ACCOUNT.—For purposes of determining who is an employee for purposes of determining the average benefit percentage under subparagraph (B)—

(i) except as provided in clause (ii), paragraph (4)(A) shall not apply, or

(ii) if the employer elects, paragraph (4)(A) shall be applied by using the lowest age and service requirements of all qualified plans maintained by the employer.

(E) QUALIFIED PLAN.—For purposes of this paragraph, the term "qualified plan" means any plan which (without regard to this subsection) meets the requirements of section 401(a).

(3) EXCLUSION OF CERTAIN EMPLOYEES.—For purposes of this subsection, there shall be excluded from consideration—

(A) employees who are included in a unit of employees covered by an agreement which the Secretary of Labor finds to be a collective bargaining agreement between employee representatives and one or more employers, if there is evidence that retirement benefits were the subject of good faith bargaining between such employee representatives and such employer or employers,

(B) in the case of a trust established or maintained pursuant to an agreement which the Secretary of Labor finds to be a collective bargaining agreement between air pilots represented in accordance with title II of the Railway Labor Act and one or more employers, all employees not covered by such agreement, and

(C) employees who are nonresident aliens and who receive no earned income (within the meaning of section 911(d)(2)) from the employer which constitutes income from sources within the United States (within the meaning of section 861(a)(3)).

Subparagraph (A) shall not apply with respect to coverage of employees under a plan pursuant to an agreement under such subparagraph. For purposes of subparagraph (B), management pilots who are not represented in accordance with title II of the Railway Labor Act shall be treated as covered by a collective bargaining agreement described in such subparagraph if the management pilots manage the flight operations of air pilots who are so represented and the management pilots are, pursuant to the terms of the agreement, included in the group of employees benefitting under the trust described in such subparagraph. Subparagraph (B) shall not apply in the case of a plan which provides contributions or benefits for employees whose principal duties are not customarily performed aboard an aircraft in flight (other than management pilots described in the preceding sentence).

(4) EXCLUSION OF EMPLOYEES NOT MEETING AGE AND SERVICE REQUIREMENTS.—

(A) IN GENERAL.—If a plan—

(i) prescribes minimum age and service requirements as a condition of participation, and

(ii) excludes all employees not meeting such requirements from participation,

then such employees shall be excluded from consideration for purposes of this subsection.

(B) REQUIREMENTS MAY BE MET SEPARATELY WITH RESPECT TO EXCLUDED GROUP.—If employees not meeting the minimum age or service requirements of subsection (a)(1) (without regard to subparagraph (B) thereof) are covered under a plan of the employer which meets the requirements of paragraph (1) separately with respect to such employees, such employees may be excluded from consideration in determining whether any plan of the employer meets the requirements of paragraph (1).

(C) REQUIREMENTS NOT TREATED AS BEING MET BEFORE ENTRY DATE.—An employee shall not be treated as meeting the age and service requirements described in this paragraph until the first date on which, under the plan, any employee with the same age and service would be eligible to commence participation in the plan.

(5) LINE OF BUSINESS EXCEPTION.—

(A) IN GENERAL.—If, under section 414(r), an employer is treated as operating separate lines of business for a year, the employer may apply the requirements of this subsection for such year separately with respect to employees in each separate line of business.

(B) PLAN MUST BE NONDISCRIMINATORY.—Subparagraph (A) shall not apply with respect to any plan maintained by an employer unless such plan benefits such employees as qualify under a classification set up by the employer and found by the Secretary not to be discriminatory in favor of highly compensated employees.

(6) DEFINITIONS AND SPECIAL RULES.—For purposes of this subsection—

(A) HIGHLY COMPENSATED EMPLOYEE.—The term "highly compensated employee" has the meaning given such term by section 414(q).

(B) AGGREGATION RULES.—An employer may elect to designate—

(i) 2 or more trusts,

(ii) 1 or more trusts and 1 or more annuity plans, or

(iii) 2 or more annuity plans,

as part of 1 plan intended to qualify under section 401(a) to determine whether the requirements of this subsection are met with respect to such trusts or annuity plans. If an employer elects to treat any trusts or annuity plans as 1 plan under this subparagraph, such trusts or annuity plans shall be treated as 1 plan for purposes of section 401(a)(4).

(C) SPECIAL RULES FOR CERTAIN DISPOSITIONS OR ACQUISITIONS.—

(i) IN GENERAL.—If a person becomes, or ceases to be, a member of a group described in subsection (b), (c), (m), or (o) of section 414, then the requirements of this subsection shall be treated as having been met during the transition period with respect to any plan covering employees of such person or any other member of such group if—

(I) such requirements were met immediately before each such change, and

(II) the coverage under such plan is not significantly changed during the transition period (other than by reason of the change in members of a group) or such plan meets such other requirements as the Secretary may prescribe by regulation.

(ii) TRANSITION PERIOD.—For purposes of clause (i), the term "transition period" means the period—

(I) beginning on the date of the change in members of a group, and

(II) ending on the last day of the 1st plan year beginning after the date of such change.

(D) SPECIAL RULE FOR CERTAIN EMPLOYEE STOCK OWNERSHIP PLANS.—A trust which is part of a tax credit employee stock ownership plan which is the only plan of an employer intended to qualify under section 401(a) shall not be treated as not a qualified trust under section 401(a) solely because it fails to meet the requirements of this subsection if—

(i) such plan benefits 50 percent or more of all the employees who are eligible under a nondiscriminatory classification under the plan, and

(ii) the sum of the amounts allocated to each participant's account for the year does not exceed 2 percent of the compensation of that participant for the year.

(E) ELIGIBILITY TO CONTRIBUTE.—In the case of contributions which are subject to section 401(k) or 401(m), employees who are eligible to contribute (or elect to have contributions made on their behalf) shall be treated as benefiting under the plan (other than for purposes of paragraph (2)(A)(ii)).

(F) EMPLOYERS WITH ONLY HIGHLY COMPENSATED EMPLOYEES.—A plan maintained by an employer which has no employees other than highly compensated employees for any year shall be treated as meeting the requirements of this subsection for such year.

(G) REGULATIONS.—The Secretary shall prescribe such regulations as may be necessary or appropriate to carry out the purposes of this subsection.

Amendments

• 2006, Pension Protection Act of 2006 (P.L. 109-280)

P.L. 109-280, §402(h)(1):

Amended Code Sec. 410(b)(3) by striking the last sentence and inserting two new sentences in its place. **Effective** for years beginning before, on, or after 8-17-2006. Prior to being stricken, the last sentence of Code Sec. 410(b)(3) read as follows:

Subparagraph (B) shall not apply in the case of a plan which provides contributions or benefits for employees whose principal duties are not customarily performed aboard aircraft in flight.

• 1988, Technical and Miscellaneous Revenue Act of 1988 (P.L. 100-647)

P.L. 100-647, §1011(h)(1)(A)-(B):

Amended Code Sec. 410(b)(4)(B) by striking out "do not meet" and inserting in lieu thereof "not meeting" and by striking out "and" before "are covered". **Effective** as if included in the provision of P.L. 99-514 to which it relates.

P.L. 100-647, §1011(h)(2):

Amended Code Sec. 410(b)(6) by redesignating subparagraph (F) as subparagraph (G) and by adding after subparagraph (E) a new subparagraph (F). **Effective** as if included in the provision of P.L. 99-514 to which it relates.

P.L. 100-647, §1011(h)(11):

Amended Code Sec. 410(b)(4) by adding at the end thereof new subparagraph (C). **Effective** as if included in the provision of P.L. 99-514 to which it relates.

P.L. 100-647, §3021(a)(13)(B):

Amended Code Sec. 410(b)(6)(C)(i)(II) by inserting "or such plan meets such other requirements as the Secretary may prescribe by regulation" before the end period. **Effective** as if included in the amendments made by section 1151 of P.L. 99-514.

• 1986, Tax Reform Act of 1986 (P.L. 99-514)

P.L. 99-514, §1112(a):

Amended Code Sec. 410(b). **Effective** for plan years beginning after 12-31-88. However, for a special rule see Act

Sec. 1112(e)(2), below. Prior to amendment, Code Sec. 410(b) read as follows:

(b) ELIGIBILITY.—

(1) IN GENERAL.—A trust shall not constitute a qualified trust under section 401(a) unless the trust, or two or more trusts, or the trust or trusts and annuity plan or plans are designated by the employer as constituting parts of a plan intended to qualify under section 401(a) which benefits either—

(A) 70 percent or more of all employees, or 80 percent or more of all the employees who are eligible to benefit under the plan if 70 percent or more of all the employees are eligible to benefit under the plan, excluding in each case employees who have not satisfied the minimum age and service requirements, if any, prescribed by the plan as a condition of participation, or

(B) such employees as qualify under a classification set up by the employer and found by the Secretary not to be discriminatory in favor of employees who are officers, shareholders, or highly compensated.

(2) SPECIAL RULE FOR CERTAIN PLANS.—A trust which is part of a tax credit employees stock ownership plan which is the only plan of an employer intended to qualify under section 401(a) shall not be treated as not a qualified trust under section 401(a) solely because it fails to meet the requirements of paragraph (1) if—

(A) it benefits 50 percent or more of all the employees who are eligible under the plan (excluding employees who have not satisfied the minimum age and service requirements, if any, prescribed by the plan as a condition of participation), and

(B) the sum of the amounts allocated to each participant's account for the year does not exceed 2 percent of the compensation of that participant for the year.

(3) EXCLUSION OF CERTAIN EMPLOYEES.—For purposes of paragraphs (1) and (2), there shall be excluded from consideration—

(A) employees not included in the plan who are included in a unit of employees covered by an agreement which the Secretary of Labor finds to be a collective bargaining agreement between employee representatives and one or more employers, if there is evidence that retirement benefits were the subject of good faith bargaining between such employee representatives and such employer or employers,

(B) in the case of a trust established or maintained pursuant to an agreement which the Secretary of Labor finds to be a collective bargaining agreement between air pilots represented in accordance with title II of the Railway Labor Act and one or more employers, all employees not covered by such agreement, and

(C) employees who are nonresident aliens and who receive no earned income (within the meaning of section 911(d)(2)) from the employer which constitutes income from sources within the United States (within the meaning of section 861(a)(3)).

Subparagraph (B) shall not apply in the case of a plan which provides contributions or benefits for employees whose principal duties are not customarily performed aboard aircraft in flight.

P.L. 99-514, §1112(e)(2), provides:

(2) SPECIAL RULE FOR COLLECTIVE BARGAINING AGREEMENTS.—In the case of a plan maintained pursuant to 1 or more collective bargaining agreements between employee representatives and 1 or more employers ratified before March 1, 1986, the amendments made by this section shall not apply to employees covered by any such agreement in plan years beginning before the earlier of—

(A) the later of—

(i) January 1, 1989, or

(ii) the date on which the last of such collective bargaining agreement[s] terminates (determined without regard to any extension thereof after February 28, 1986), or

(B) January 1, 1991.

• 1981, Economic Recovery Tax Act of 1981 (P.L. 97-34)

P.L. 97-34, §111(b)(4):

Amended Code Sec. 410(b)(3)(C) by striking out "section 911(b)" and inserting in lieu thereof "section 911(d)(2)". **Effective** with respect to tax years beginning after 12-31-81.

• 1980, Miscellaneous Revenue Act of 1980 (P.L. 96-605)

P.L. 96-605, §225(a):

Amended Code Sec. 410(b) by: (1) redesignating paragraph (2) as paragraph (3); (2) striking out "paragraph (1)" in paragraph (3) (as so redesignated) and inserting in lieu thereof "paragraphs (1) and (2)"; and (3) inserting after paragraph (1) new paragraph (2). **Effective** with respect to plan years beginning after 12-31-80.

• 1976, Tax Reform Act of 1976 (P.L. 94-455)

P.L. 94-455, §1906(b)(13)(A):

Amended 1954 Code by substituting "Secretary" for "Secretary or his delegate" each place it appeared. **Effective** 2-1-77.

[Sec. 410(c)]

(c) APPLICATION OF PARTICIPATION STANDARDS TO CERTAIN PLANS.—

(1) The provisions of this section (other than paragraph (2) of this subsection) shall not apply to—

(A) a governmental plan (within the meaning of section 414(d)),

(B) a church plan (within the meaning of section 414(e)) with respect to which the election provided by subsection (d) of this section has not been made,

(C) a plan which has not at any time after September 2, 1974, provided for employer contributions, and

(D) a plan established and maintained by a society, order, or association described in section 501(c)(8) or (9) if no part of the contributions to or under such plan are made by employers of participants in such plan.

(2) A plan described in paragraph (1) shall be treated as meeting the requirements of this section for purposes of section 401(a), except that in the case of a plan described in subparagraph (B), (C), or (D) of paragraph (1), this paragraph shall apply only if such plan meets the requirements of section 401(a)(3) (as in effect on September 1, 1974).

Amendments

• 1997, Taxpayer Relief Act of 1997 (P.L. 105-34)

P.L. 105-34, §1505(a)(3):

Amended Code Sec. 410(c)(2). **Effective**, generally, for tax years beginning on or after 8-5-97. For a special rule, see Act Sec. 1505(d)(2), below. Prior to amendment, Code Sec. 410(c)(2) read as follows:

(2) A plan described in paragraph (1) shall be treated as meeting the requirements of this section, for purposes of section 401(a), if such plan meets the requirements of section 401(a)(3) as in effect on September 1, 1974.

P.L. 105-34, §1505(d)(2), as amended by P.L. 105-206, §6015(b), and further amended by P.L. 109-280, §861(a)(2), provides:

(2) TREATMENT FOR YEARS BEGINNING BEFORE DATE OF ENACTMENT.—A governmental plan (within the meaning of section 414(d) of the Internal Revenue Code of 1986) shall be treated as satisfying the requirements of sections 401(a)(3), 401(a)(4),

401(a)(26), 401(k), 401(m), 403(b)(1)(D) and (b)(12)(A)(i), and 410 of such Code for all taxable years beginning before the date of enactment of this Act.

• **1976, Tax Reform Act of 1976 (P.L. 94-455)**

P.L. 94-455, §1901(a)(61)(B):

Amended Code Sec. 410(c)(1)(C) by substituting "September 2, 1974," for "the date of the enactment of the Employee Retirement Income Security Act of 1974". **Effective** with respect to tax years beginning after 12-31-76.

P.L. 94-455, §1901(a)(61)(C):

Amended Code Sec. 410(c)(2) by substituting "September 1, 1974" for "the day before the date of the enactment of this section". **Effective** with respect to tax years beginning after 12-31-76.

[Sec. 410(d)]

(d) ELECTION BY CHURCH TO HAVE PARTICIPATION, VESTING, FUNDING, ETC., PROVISIONS APPLY.—

(1) IN GENERAL.—If the church or convention or association of churches which maintains any church plan makes an election under this subsection (in such form and manner as the Secretary may by regulations prescribe), then the provisions of this title relating to participation, vesting, funding, etc. (as in effect from time to time) shall apply to such church plan as if such provisions did not contain an exclusion for church plans.

(2) ELECTION IRREVOCABLE.—An election under this subsection with respect to any church plan shall be binding with respect to such plan, and, once made, shall be irrevocable.

Amendments

• **1976, Tax Reform Act of 1976 (P.L. 94-455)**

P.L. 94-455, §1906(b)(13)(A):

Amended 1954 Code by substituting "Secretary" for "Secretary or his delegate" each place it appeared. **Effective** 2-1-77.

• **1974, Employee Retirement Income Security Act of 1974 (P.L. 93-406)**

P.L. 93-406, §1011:

Added Code Sec. 410. For the **effective** date, see Act Sec. 1017, below.

P.L. 93-406, §1017, as amended by P.L. 94-12, §402, provides as follows:

"ACT SEC. 1017. EFFECTIVE DATES AND TRANSITIONAL RULES.

"(a) General Rule.—Except as otherwise provided in this section, the amendments made by this part shall apply for plan years beginning after the date of the enactment of this Act.

"(b) Existing Plans.—Except as otherwise provided in subsections (c) through (i), in the case of a plan in existence on January 1, 1974, the amendments made by this part shall apply for plan years beginning after December 31, 1975.

"(c) Existing Plans Under Collective Bargaining Agreements.—

"(1) Application of vesting rules to certain plan provisions.—

"(A) Waiver of application.—In the case of a plan maintained on January 1, 1974, pursuant to one or more agreements which the Secretary of Labor finds to be collective bargaining agreements between employee representatives and one or more employers, during the special temporary waiver period the plan shall not be treated as not meeting the requirements of section 411(b)(1) or (2) of the Internal Revenue Code of 1954 solely by reason of a supplementary or special plan provision (within the meaning of subparagraph (D)).

"(B) Special temporary waiver period.—For purposes of this paragraph, the term `special temporary waiver period' means plan years beginning after December 31, 1975, and before the earlier of—

"(i) the date on which the last of the collective bargaining agreements relating to the plan terminates (determined without regard to any extension thereof agreed to after the date of the enactment of this Act), or

"(ii) January 1, 1981.

For purposes of clause (i), any plan amendment made pursuant to a collective bargaining agreement relating to the plan which amends the plan solely to conform to any requirement contained in this Act shall not be treated as a termination of such collective bargaining agreement.

"(C) Determination by secretary of labor required.—Subparagraph (A) shall not apply unless the Secretary of Labor determines that the participation and vesting rules in effect on the date of the enactment of this Act are not less favorable to the employees, in the aggregate, than the rules provided under sections 410 and 411 of the Internal Revenue Code of 1954.

"(D) Supplementary or special plan provisions.—For purposes of this paragraph, the term `supplementary or special plan provision' means any plan provision which—

"(i) provides supplementary benefits, not in excess of one-third of the basic benefit, in the form of an annuity for the life of the participant, or

"(ii) provides that, under a contractual agreement based on medical evidence as to the effects of working in an adverse environment for an extended period of time, a participant having 25 years of service is to be treated as having 30 years of service.

"(2) Application of funding rules.—

"(A) In general.—In the case of a plan maintained on January 1, 1974, pursuant to one or more agreements which the Secretary of Labor finds to be collective bargaining agreements between employee representatives and one or more employers, section 412 of the Internal Revenue Code of 1954, and other amendments made by this part to the extent such amendments relate to such section 412, shall not apply during the special temporary waiver period (as defined in paragraph (1)(B)).

"(B) Waiver of underfunding.—In the case of a plan maintained on January 1, 1974, pursuant to one or more agreements which the Secretary of Labor finds to be collective bargaining agreements between employee representatives and one or more employers, if by reason of subparagraph (A) the requirements of section 401(a)(7) of the Internal Revenue Code of 1954 apply without regard to the amendment of such section 401(a)(7) by section 1016(a)(2)(C) of this Act, the plan shall not be treated as not meeting such requirements solely by reason of the application of the amendments made by sections 1011 and 1012 of this Act or related amendments made by this part.

"(C) Labor organization conventions.—In the case of a plan maintained by a labor organization, which is exempt from tax under section 501(c)(5) of the Internal Revenue Code of 1954, exclusively for the benefit of its employees and their beneficiaries, section 412 of such Code and other amendments made by this part to the extent such amendments relate to such section 412, shall be applied by substituting for the term `December 31, 1975' in subsection (b), the earlier of—

"(i) the date on which the second convention of such labor organization held after the date of the enactment [September 2, 1974]of this Act ends, or

"(ii) December 31, 1980,

But in no event shall a date earlier than the later of December 31, 1975, or the date determined under subparagraph (A) or (B) be substituted.

"(d) Existing Plans May Elect New Provisions.—In the case of a plan in existence on January 1, 1974, the provisions of the Internal Revenue Code of 1954 relating to participation, vesting, funding, and form of benefit (as in effect from time to time) shall apply in the case of the plan year (which begins after the date of the enactment of this Act but before the applicable effective date determined under subsection (b) or (c)) selected by the plan administrator and to all subsequent plan years, if the plan administrator elects (in such manner and at such time as the Secretary of the Treasury or his delegate shall by regulations prescribe) to have such provisions so apply. Any election made under this subsection, once made, shall be irrevocable.

"(e) Certain Definitions and Special Rules.—Section 414 of the Internal Revenue Code of 1954 (other than subsections (b) and (c) of such section 414), as added by section 1015(a) of this Act, shall take effect on the date of the enactment of this Act.

"(f) Transitional Rules With Respect to Breaks in Service.—

"(1) Participation.—In the case of a plan to which section 410 of the Internal Revenue Code of 1954 applies, if any plan amendment with respect to breaks in service (which amendment is made or becomes effective after January 1, 1974, and before the date on which such section 410 first becomes effective with respect to such plan) provides that any employee's participation in the plan would commence at any date later than the later of—

"(A) the date on which his participation would commence under the break in service rules of section 410(a)(5) of such Code, or

"(B) the date on which his participation would commence under the plan as in effect on January 1, 1974,

such plan shall not constitute a plan described in section 403(a) or 405(a) of such Code and a trust forming a part of such plan shall not constitute a qualified trust under section 401(a) of such Code.

"(2) Vesting.—In the case of a plan to which section 411 of the Internal Revenue Code of 1954 applies, if any plan amendment with respect to breaks in service (which amendment is made or becomes effective after January 1, 1974, and before the date on which such section 411 first becomes effective with respect to such plan) provides that the nonforfeitable benefit derived from employer contributions to which any employee would be entitled is less than the lesser of the nonforfeitable benefit derived from employer contributions to which he would be entitled under—

"(A) the break in service rules of section 411(a)(6) of such Code, or

"(B) the plan as in effect on January 1, 1974,

such plan shall not constitute a plan described in section 403(a) or 405(a) of such Code and a trust forming a part of such plan shall not constitute a qualified trust under section 401(a) of such Code. Subparagraph (B) shall not apply if the break in service rules under the plan would have been in violation of any law or rule of law in effect on January 1, 1974.

"(g) 3-Year Delay for Certain Provisions.—Subparagraphs (B) and (C) of section 404(a)(1) shall apply only in the case of plan years beginning on or after 3 years after the date of the enactment of this Act.

"(h)(1) Except as provided in paragraph (2), section 413 of the Internal Revenue Code of 1954 shall apply to plan years beginning after December 31, 1953.

"(2)(A) For plan years beginning before the applicable effective date of section 410 of such Code, the provisions of paragraphs (1) and (8) of subsection (b) of such section 413 shall be applied by substituting '401(a)(3)' for '410'.

"(B) For plan years beginning before the applicable effective date of section 411 of such Code, the provisions of subsection (b)(2) of such section 413 shall be applied by substituting '401(a)(7)' for '411(d)(3)'.

"(C)(i) The provisions of subsection (b)(4) of such section 413 shall not apply to plan years beginning before the applicable effective date of section 411 of such Code.

"(ii) The provisions of subsection (b)(5) (other than the second sentence thereof) of such section 413 shall not apply to plan years beginning before the applicable effective date of section 412 of such Code."

"(i) Contributions to H. R. 10 Plans.—Notwithstanding subsections (b) and (c)(2), in the case of a plan in existence on January 1, 1974, the amendment made by section 1013(c)(2) of this Act shall apply, with respect to a plan which provides contributions or benefits for employees some or all of whom are employees within the meaning of section 401(c)(1) of the Internal Revenue Code of 1954, for plan years beginning after December 31, 1974, but only if the employer (within the meaning of section 401(c)(4) of such Code) elects in such manner and at such time as the Secretary of the Treasury or his delegate shall by regulations prescribe, to have such amendment so apply. Any election made under this subsection, once made, shall be irrevocable."

[Sec. 411]

SEC. 411. MINIMUM VESTING STANDARDS.

[Sec. 411(a)]

(a) GENERAL RULE.—A trust shall not constitute a qualified trust under section 401(a) unless the plan of which such trust is a part provides that an employee's right to his normal retirement benefit is nonforfeitable upon the attainment of normal retirement age (as defined in paragraph (8)) and in addition satisfies the requirements of paragraphs (1), (2), and (11) of this subsection and the requirements of subsection (b)(3), and also satisfies, in the case of a defined benefit plan, the requirements of subsection (b)(1) and, in the case of a defined contribution plan, the requirements of subsection (b)(2).

(1) EMPLOYEE CONTRIBUTIONS.—A plan satisfies the requirements of this paragraph if an employee's rights in his accrued benefit derived from his own contributions are nonforfeitable.

(2) EMPLOYER CONTRIBUTIONS.—

(A) DEFINED BENEFIT PLANS.—

(i) IN GENERAL.—In the case of a defined benefit plan, a plan satisfies the requirements of this paragraph if it satisfies the requirements of clause (ii) or (iii).

(ii) 5-YEAR VESTING.—A plan satisfies the requirements of this clause if an employee who has completed at least 5 years of service has a nonforfeitable right to 100 percent of the employee's accrued benefit derived from employer contributions.

(iii) 3 TO 7 YEAR VESTING.—A plan satisfies the requirements of this clause if an employee has a nonforfeitable right to a percentage of the employee's accrued benefit derived from employer contributions determined under the following table:

Years of service:	*The nonforfeitable percentage is:*
3	20
4	40
5	60
6	80
7 or more	100 .

(B) DEFINED CONTRIBUTION PLANS.—

(i) IN GENERAL.—In the case of a defined contribution plan, a plan satisfies the requirements of this paragraph if it satisfies the requirements of clause (ii) or (iii).

(ii) 3-YEAR VESTING.—A plan satisfies the requirements of this clause if an employee who has completed at least 3 years of service has a nonforfeitable right to 100 percent of the employee's accrued benefit derived from employer contributions.

(iii) 2 TO 6 YEAR VESTING.—A plan satisfies the requirements of this clause if an employee has a nonforfeitable right to a percentage of the employee's accrued benefit derived from employer contributions determined under the following table:

Years of service:	*The nonforfeitable percentage is:*
2	20
3	40
4	60
5	80
6 or more	100 .

(3) CERTAIN PERMITTED FORFEITURES, SUSPENSIONS, ETC.—For purposes of this subsection—

(A) FORFEITURE ON ACCOUNT OF DEATH.—A right to an accrued benefit derived from employer contributions shall not be treated as forfeitable solely because the plan provides that it is not payable if the participant dies (except in the case of a survivor annuity which is payable as provided in section 401(a)(11)).

(B) SUSPENSION OF BENEFITS UPON REEMPLOYMENT OF RETIREE.—A right to an accrued benefit derived from employer contributions shall not be treated as forfeitable solely because the plan provides that the payment of benefits is suspended for such period as the employee is employed, subsequent to the commencement of payment of such benefits—

(i) in the case of a plan other than a multiemployer plan, by the employer who maintains the plan under which such benefits were being paid; and

(ii) in the case of a multiemployer plan, in the same industry, the same trade or craft, and the same geographic area covered by the plan as when such benefits commenced.

The Secretary of Labor shall prescribe such regulations as may be necessary to carry out the purposes of this subparagraph, including regulations with respect to the meaning of the term "employed".

(C) EFFECT OF RETROACTIVE PLAN AMENDMENTS.—A right to an accrued benefit derived from employer contributions shall not be treated as forfeitable solely because plan amendments may be given retroactive application as provided in section 412(d)(2).

(D) WITHDRAWAL OF MANDATORY CONTRIBUTIONS.—

(i) A right to an accrued benefit derived from employer contributions shall not be treated as forfeitable solely because the plan provides that, in the case of a participant who does not have a nonforfeitable right to at least 50 percent of his accrued benefit derived from employer contributions, such accrued benefit may be forfeited on account of the withdrawal by the participant of any amount attributable to the benefit derived from mandatory contributions (as defined in subsection (c)(2)(C)) made by such participant.

(ii) Clause (i) shall not apply to a plan unless the plan provides that any accrued benefit forfeited under a plan provision described in such clause shall be restored upon repayment by the participant of the full amount of the withdrawal described in such clause plus, in the case of a defined benefit plan, interest. Such interest shall be computed on such amount at the rate determined for purposes of subsection (c)(2)(C) on the date of such repayment (computed annually from the date of such withdrawal). The plan provision required under this clause may provide that such repayment must be made (I) in the case of a withdrawal on a account of separation from service, before the earlier of 5 years after the first date on which the participant is subsequently re-employed by the employer, or the close of the first period of 5 consecutive 1-year breaks in service commencing after the withdrawal; or (II) in the case of any other withdrawal, 5 years after the date of the withdrawal.

(iii) In the case of accrued benefits derived from employer contributions which accrued before September 2, 1974, a right to such accrued benefit derived from employer contributions shall not be treated as forfeitable solely because the plan provides that an amount of such accrued benefit may be forfeited on account of the withdrawal by the participant of an amount attributable to the benefit derived from mandatory contributions (as defined in subsection (c)(2)(C)) made by such participant before September 2, 1974 if such amount forfeited is proportional to such amount withdrawn. This clause shall not apply to any plan to which any mandatory contribution is made after September 2, 1974. The Secretary shall prescribe such regulations as may be necessary to carry out the purposes of this clause.

(iv) For purposes of this subparagraph, in the case of any class-year plan, a withdrawal of employee contributions shall be treated as a withdrawal of such contributions on a plan year by plan year basis in succeeding order of time.

(v) For nonforfeitability where the employee has a nonforfeitable right to at least 50 percent of his accrued benefit, see section 401(a)(19).

(E) CESSATION OF CONTRIBUTIONS UNDER A MULTIEMPLOYER PLAN.—A right to an accrued benefit derived from employer contributions under a multiemployer plan shall not be treated as forfeitable solely because the plan provides that benefits accrued as a result of service with the participant's employer before the employer had an obligation to contribute under the plan may not be payable if the employer ceases contributions to the multiemployer plan.

(F) REDUCTION AND SUSPENSION OF BENEFITS BY A MULTIEMPLOYER PLAN.—A participant's right to an accrued benefit derived from employer contributions under a multiemployer plan shall not be treated as forfeitable solely because—

(i) the plan is amended to reduce benefits under section 418D or under section 4281 of the Employee Retirement Income Security Act of 1974, or

(ii) benefit payments under the plan may be suspended under section 418E or under section 4281 of the Employee Retirement Income Security Act of 1974.

(G) TREATMENT OF MATCHING CONTRIBUTIONS FORFEITED BY REASON OF EXCESS DEFERRAL OR CONTRIBUTION OR PERMISSIBLE WITHDRAWAL.—A matching contribution (within the meaning of section 401(m)) shall not be treated as forfeitable merely because such contribution is forfeitable if the contribution to which the matching contribution relates is treated as an excess contribution under section 401(k)(8)(B), an excess deferral under section 402(g)(2)(A), a permissible withdrawal under section 414(w), or an excess aggregate contribution under section 401(m)(6)(B).

(4) SERVICE INCLUDED IN DETERMINATION OF NONFORFEITABLE PERCENTAGE.—In computing the period of service under the plan for purposes of determining the nonforfeitable percentage under paragraph (2), all of an employee's years of service with the employer or employers maintaining the plan shall be taken into account, except that the following may be disregarded:

(A) years of service before age 18,

(B) years of service during a period for which the employee declined to contribute to a plan requiring employee contributions;

(C) years of service with an employer during any period for which the employer did not maintain the plan or a predecessor plan (as defined under regulations prescribed by the Secretary);

(D) service not required to be taken into account under paragraph (6);

(E) years of service before January 1, 1971, unless the employee has had at least 3 years of service after December 31, 1970;

(F) years of service before the first plan year to which this section applies, if such service would have been disregarded under the rules of the plan with regard to breaks in service as in effect on the applicable date; and

(G) in the case of a multiemployer plan, years of service—

(i) with an employer after—

(I) a complete withdrawal of that employer from the plan (within the meaning of section 4203 of the Employee Retirement Income Security Act of 1974), or

(II) to the extent permitted in regulations prescribed by the Secretary, a partial withdrawal described in section 4205(b)(2)(A)(i) of such Act in conjunction with the decertification of the collective bargaining representative, and

(ii) with any employer under the plan after the termination date of the plan under section 4048 of such Act.

(5) YEAR OF SERVICE.—

(A) GENERAL RULE.—For purposes of this subsection, except as provided in subparagraph (C), the term "year of service" means a calendar year, plan year, or other 12-consecutive month period designated by the plan (and not prohibited under regulations prescribed by the Secretary of Labor) during which the participant has completed 1,000 hours of service.

(B) HOURS OF SERVICE.—For purposes of this subsection, the term "hours of service" has the meaning provided by section 410(a)(3)(C).

(C) SEASONAL INDUSTRIES.—In the case of any seasonal industry where the customary period of employment is less than 1,000 hours during a calendar year, the term "year of service" shall be such period as may be determined under regulations prescribed by the Secretary of Labor.

(D) MARITIME INDUSTRIES.—For purposes of this subsection, in the case of any maritime industry, 125 days of service shall be treated as 1,000 hours of service. The Secretary of Labor may prescribe regulations to carry out the purposes of this subparagraph.

(6) BREAKS IN SERVICE.—

(A) DEFINITION OF 1-YEAR BREAK IN SERVICE.—For purposes of this paragraph, the term "1-year break in service" means a calendar year, plan year, or other 12-consecutive-month period designated by the plan (and not prohibited under regulations prescribed by the Secretary of Labor) during which the participant has not completed more than 500 hours of service.

(B) 1 YEAR OF SERVICE AFTER 1-YEAR BREAK IN SERVICE.—For purposes of paragraph (4), in the case of any employee who has any 1-year break in service, years of service before such break shall not be required to be taken into account until he has completed a year of service after his return.

(C) 5 CONSECUTIVE 1-YEAR BREAKS IN SERVICE UNDER DEFINED CONTRIBUTION PLAN.—For purposes of paragraph (4), in the case of any participant in a defined contribution plan, or an insured defined benefit plan which satisfies the requirements of subsection (b)(1)(F), who has 5 consecutive 1-year breaks in service, years of service after such 5-year period shall not be required to be taken into account for purposes of determining the nonforfeitable percentage of his accrued benefit derived from employer contributions which accrued before such 5-year period.

(D) NONVESTED PARTICIPANTS.—

(i) IN GENERAL.—For purposes of paragraph (4), in the case of a nonvested participant, years of service with the employer or employers maintaining the plan before any period of consecutive 1-year breaks in service shall not be required to be taken into account if the number of consecutive 1-year breaks in service within such period equals or exceeds the greater of—

(I) 5, or

(II) the aggregate number of years of service before such period.

(ii) YEARS OF SERVICE NOT TAKEN INTO ACCOUNT.—If any years of service are not required to be taken into account by reason of a period of breaks in service to which clause (i) applies, such years of service shall not be taken into account in applying clause (i) to a subsequent period of breaks in service.

(iii) NONVESTED PARTICIPANT DEFINED.—For purposes of clause (i), the term "nonvested participant" means a participant who does not have any nonforfeitable right under the plan to an accrued benefit derived from employer contributions.

(E) SPECIAL RULE FOR MATERNITY OR PATERNITY ABSENCES.—

(i) GENERAL RULE.—In the case of each individual who is absent from work for any period—

(I) by reason of the pregnancy of the individual,

(II) by reason of the birth of a child of the individual,

(III) by reason of the placement of a child with the individual in connection with the adoption of such child by such individual, or

(IV) for purposes of caring for such child for a period beginning immediately following such birth or placement,

the plan shall treat as hours of service, solely for purposes of determining under this paragraph whether a 1-year break in service has occurred, the hours described in clause (ii).

(ii) HOURS TREATED AS HOURS OF SERVICE.—The hours described in this clause are—

(I) the hours of service which otherwise would normally have been credited to such individual but for such absence, or

(II) in any case in which the plan is unable to determine the hours described in subclause (I), 8 hours of service per day of absence,

except that the total number of hours treated as hours of service under this clause by reason of any such pregnancy or placement shall not exceed 501 hours.

(iii) YEAR TO WHICH HOURS ARE CREDITED.—The hours described in clause (ii) shall be treated as hours of service as provided in this subparagraph—

(I) only in the year in which the absence from work begins, if a participant would be prevented from incurring a 1-year break in service in such year solely because the period of absence is treated as hours of service as provided in clause (i); or

(II) in any other case, in the immediately following year.

(iv) YEAR DEFINED.—For purposes of this subparagraph, the term "year" means the period used in computations pursuant to paragraph (5).

(v) INFORMATION REQUIRED TO BE FILED.—A plan shall not fail to satisfy the requirements of this subparagraph solely because it provides that no credit will be given pursuant to this subparagraph unless the individual furnishes to the plan administrator such timely information as the plan may reasonably require to establish—

(I) that the absence from work is for reasons referred to in clause (i), and

(II) the number of days for which there was such an absence.

(7) ACCRUED BENEFIT.—

(A) IN GENERAL.—For purposes of this section, the term "accrued benefit" means—

(i) in the case of a defined benefit plan, the employee's accrued benefit determined under the plan and, except as provided in subsection (c)(3), expressed in the form of an annual benefit commencing at normal retirement age, or

(ii) in the case of a plan which is not a defined benefit plan, the balance of the employee's account.

(B) EFFECT OF CERTAIN DISTRIBUTIONS.—Notwithstanding paragraph (4), for purposes of determining the employee's accrued benefit under the plan, the plan may disregard service performed by the employee with respect to which he has received—

(i) a distribution of the present value of his entire nonforfeitable benefit if such distribution was in an amount (not more than the dollar limit under section 411 (a)(11)(A)) permitted under regulations prescribed by the Secretary, or

(ii) a distribution of the present value of his nonforfeitable benefit attributable to such service which he elected to receive.

Clause (i) of this subparagraph shall apply only if such distribution was made on termination of the employee's participation in the plan. Clause (ii) of this subparagraph shall apply only if such distribution was made on termination of the employee's participation in the plan or under such other circumstances as may be provided under regulations prescribed by the Secretary.

(C) REPAYMENT OF SUBPARAGRAPH (B) DISTRIBUTIONS.—For purposes of determining the employee's accrued benefit under a plan, the plan may not disregard service as provided in subparagraph (B) unless the plan provides an opportunity for the participant to repay the full amount of the distribution described in such subparagraph (B) with, in the case of a defined benefit plan, interest at the rate determined for purposes of subsection (c)(2)(C) and provides that upon such repayment the employee's accrued benefit shall be recomputed by taking into account service so disregarded. This subparagraph shall apply only in the case of a participant who—

(i) received such a distribution in any plan year to which this section applies, which distribution was less than the present value of his accrued benefit,

(ii) resumes employment covered under the plan, and

(iii) repays the full amount of such distribution with, in the case of a defined benefit plan, interest at the rate determined for purposes of subsection (c)(2)(C).

The plan provision required under this subparagraph may provide that such repayment must be made (I) in the case of a withdrawal on account of separation from service, before the earlier of 5 years after the first date on which the participant is subsequently re-employed by the employer, or the close of the first period of 5 consecutive 1-year breaks in service commencing after the withdrawal; or (II) in the case of any other withdrawal, 5 years after the date of the withdrawal.

(D) ACCRUED BENEFIT ATTRIBUTABLE TO EMPLOYEE CONTRIBUTIONS.—The accrued benefit of an employee shall not be less than the amount determined under subsection (c)(2)(B) with respect to the employee's accumulated contributions.

(8) NORMAL RETIREMENT AGE.—For purposes of this section, the term "normal retirement age" means the earlier of—

(A) the time a plan participant attains normal retirement age under the plan, or

(B) the later of—

(i) the time a plan participant attains age 65, or

(ii) the 5th anniversary of the time a plan participant commenced participation in the plan.

(9) NORMAL RETIREMENT BENEFIT.—For purposes of this section, the term "normal retirement benefit" means the greater of the early retirement benefit under the plan, or the benefit under the plan commencing at normal retirement age. The normal retirement benefit shall be determined without regard to—

(A) medical benefits, and

(B) disability benefits not in excess of the qualified disability benefit.

For purposes of this paragraph, a qualified disability benefit is a disability benefit provided by a plan which does not exceed the benefit which would be provided for the participant if he separated from the service at normal retirement age. For purposes of this paragraph, the early retirement benefit under a plan shall be determined without regard to any benefits commencing before benefits payable under title II of the Social Security Act become payable which—

(i) do not exceed such social security benefits, and

(ii) terminate when such social security benefits commence.

(10) CHANGES IN VESTING SCHEDULE.—

(A) GENERAL RULE.—A plan amendment changing any vesting schedule under the plan shall be treated as not satisfying the requirements of paragraph (2) if the nonforfeitable percentage of the accrued benefit derived from employer contributions (determined as of the later of the date such amendment is adopted, or the date such amendment becomes effective) of any employee who is a participant in the plan is less than such nonforfeitable percentage computed under the plan without regard to such amendment.

(B) ELECTION OF FORMER SCHEDULE.—A plan amendment changing any vesting schedule under the plan shall be treated as not satisfying the requirements of paragraph (2) unless each participant having not less than 3 years of service is permitted to elect, within a reasonable period after the adoption of such amendment, to have his nonforfeitable percentage computed under the plan without regard to such amendment.

(11) RESTRICTIONS ON CERTAIN MANDATORY DISTRIBUTIONS.—

(A) IN GENERAL.—If the present value of any nonforfeitable accrued benefit exceeds $5,000 a plan meets the requirements of this paragraph only if such plan provides that such benefit may not be immediately distributed without the consent of the participant.

(B) DETERMINATION OF PRESENT VALUE.—For purposes of subparagraph (A), the present value shall be calculated in accordance with section 417(e)(3).

(C) DIVIDEND DISTRIBUTIONS OF ESOPS ARRANGEMENT.—This paragraph shall not apply to any distribution of dividends to which section 404(k) applies.

(D) SPECIAL RULE FOR ROLLOVER CONTRIBUTIONS.—A plan shall not fail to meet the requirements of this paragraph if, under the terms of the plan, the present value of the nonforfeitable accrued benefit is determined without regard to that portion of such benefit which is attributable to rollover contributions (and earnings allocable thereto). For purposes of this subparagraph, the term "rollover contributions" means any rollover contribution under sections 402(c), 403(a)(4), 403(b)(8), 408(d)(3)(A)(ii), and 457(e)(16).

(12) [Stricken.]

(13) SPECIAL RULES FOR PLANS COMPUTING ACCRUED BENEFITS BY REFERENCE TO HYPOTHETICAL ACCOUNT BALANCE OR EQUIVALENT AMOUNTS.—

(A) IN GENERAL.—An applicable defined benefit plan shall not be treated as failing to meet—

(i) subject to subparagraph (B), the requirements of subsection (a)(2), or

(ii) the requirements of subsection (a)(11) or (c), or the requirements of section 417(e), with respect to accrued benefits derived from employer contributions,

solely because the present value of the accrued benefit (or any portion thereof) of any participant is, under the terms of the plan, equal to the amount expressed as the balance in the hypothetical account described in subparagraph (C) or as an accumulated percentage of the participant's final average compensation.

(B) 3-YEAR VESTING.—In the case of an applicable defined benefit plan, such plan shall be treated as meeting the requirements of subsection (a)(2) only if an employee who has completed at least 3 years of service has a nonforfeitable right to 100 percent of the employee's accrued benefit derived from employer contributions.

(C) APPLICABLE DEFINED BENEFIT PLAN AND RELATED RULES.—For purposes of this subsection—

(i) IN GENERAL.—The term "applicable defined benefit plan" means a defined benefit plan under which the accrued benefit (or any portion thereof) is calculated as the balance of a hypothetical account maintained for the participant or as an accumulated percentage of the participant's final average compensation.

(ii) REGULATIONS TO INCLUDE SIMILAR PLANS.—The Secretary shall issue regulations which include in the definition of an applicable defined benefit plan any defined benefit plan (or any portion of such a plan) which has an effect similar to an applicable defined benefit plan.

Amendments

• 2008, Worker, Retiree, and Employer Recovery Act of 2008 (P.L. 110-458)

P.L. 110-458, §101(d)(2)(D)(i):

Amended Code Sec. 411(a)(3)(C) by striking "section 412(c)(2)" and inserting "section 412(d)(2)". **Effective** as if included in the provision of the 2006 Act to which the amendment relates [**effective** for plan years beginning after 2007.—CCH].

P.L. 110-458, §107(b)(2)(A)-(C):

Amended Code Sec. 411(a)(13)(A) by striking "paragraph (2)" in clause (i) and inserting "subparagraph B", by striking clause (ii) and inserting a new clause (ii), and by striking "paragraph (3)" in the matter following clause (ii) and inserting "subparagraph (C)". **Effective** as if included in the provision of the 2006 Act to which the amendment relates [**effective** generally for distributions made after 8-17-2006.—CCH]. Prior to being stricken, Code Sec. 411(a)(13)(A)(ii) read as follows:

(ii) the requirements of subsection (c) or section 417(e) with respect to contributions other than employee contributions,

P.L. 110-458, §109(b)(2)(A)-(B):

Amended Code Sec. 411(a)(3)(G) by striking "an erroneous automatic contribution" and inserting "a permissible withdrawal", and by striking "ERRONEOUS AUTOMATIC CONTRIBUTION" in the heading and inserting "PERMISSIBLE WITHDRAWAL". **Effective** as if included in the provision of the 2006 Act to which the amendment relates [**effective** for plan years beginning after 12-31-2007.—CCH].

• 2006, Pension Protection Act of 2006 (P.L. 109-280)

P.L. 109-280, §114(b)(1):

Amended Code Sec. 411(a)(3)(C) by striking "section 412(c)(8)" and inserting "section 412(c)(2) [412(d)(2)]". **Effective** for plan years beginning after 2007 [**effective** date amended by P.L. 110-458, §101(d)(3).—CCH].

P.L. 109-280, §701(b)(2):

Amended Code Sec. 411(a) by adding at the end a new paragraph (13). **Effective** generally for distributions made after 8-17-2006. For special rules, see Act Sec. 701(d) and (e)(3)-(5), below.

P.L. 109-280, §701(d) [as amended by P.L. 110-458, §107(c)(1)], provides:

(d) NO INFERENCE.—Nothing in the amendments made by this section shall be construed to create an inference with respect to—

(1) the treatment of applicable defined benefit plans or conversions to applicable defined benefit plans under sections 204(b)(1)(H) of the Employee Retirement Income Security Act of 1974, 4(i)(1) of the Age Discrimination in Employment Act of 1967, and 411(b)(1)(H) of the Internal Revenue Code of 1986, as in effect before such amendments, or

(2) the determination of whether an applicable defined benefit plan fails to meet the requirements of sections 203(a)(2), 204(c), or 205(g) of the Employee Retirement Income Security Act of 1974 or sections 411(a)(2), 411(c), or 417(e) of such Code, as in effect before such amendments, solely because the present value of the accrued benefit (or any portion thereof) of any participant is, under the terms of the plan, equal to the amount expressed as the balance in a hypothetical account or as an accumulated percentage of the participant's final average compensation.

For purposes of this subsection, the term "applicable defined benefit plan" has the meaning given such term by section 203(f)(3) of the Employee Retirement Income Security Act of 1974 and section 411(a)(13)(C) of such Code, as in effect after such amendments.

P.L. 109-280, §701(e)(3)-(6) [as amended by P.L. 110-458, §107(c)(2)(A)-(D)], provides:

(3) VESTING AND INTEREST CREDIT REQUIREMENTS.—In the case of a plan in existence on June 29, 2005, the requirements of clause (i) of section 411(b)(5)(B) of the Internal Revenue Code of 1986, clause (i) of section 204(b)(5)(B) of the Employee Retirement Income Security Act of 1974, and clause (i) of section 4(i)(10)(B) of the Age Discrimination in Employment Act of 1967 (as added by this Act) and the requirements of 203(f)(2) of the Employee Retirement Income Security Act of 1974 and section 411(a)(13)(B) of the Internal Revenue Code of 1986 (as so added) shall, for purposes of applying the amendments made by subsections (a) and (b), apply to years beginning after December 31, 2007, unless the plan sponsor elects the application of such requirements for any period on or after June 29, 2005, and before the first year beginning after December 31, 2007.

(4) SPECIAL RULE FOR COLLECTIVELY BARGAINED PLANS.—In the case of a plan maintained pursuant to 1 or more collective bargaining agreements between employee representatives and 1 or more employers ratified on or before the earlier of the date of the enactment of this Act, the requirements described in paragraph (3) shall, for purposes of applying the amendments made by subsections (a) and (b), not apply to plan years beginning before—

(A) the later of—

(i) the date on which the last of such collective bargaining agreements terminates (determined without regard to any extension thereof on or after such date of enactment), or

(ii) January 1, 2008, or

(B) January 1, 2010.

(5) CONVERSIONS.—The requirements of clause (ii) of section 411(b)(5)(B) of the Internal Revenue Code of 1986, clause (ii) of section 204(b)(5)(B) of the Employee Retirement Income Security Act of 1974, and clause (ii) of section 4(i)(10)(B) of the Age Discrimination in Employment Act of 1967 (as added by this Act), shall apply to plan amendments adopted on or after, and taking effect on or after, June 29, 2005, except that the plan sponsor may elect to have such amendments apply to plan amendments adopted before, and taking effect on or after, such date.

(6) SPECIAL RULE FOR VESTING REQUIREMENTS.—The requirements of section 203(f)(2) of the Employee Retirement Income Security Act of 1974 and section 411(a)(13)(B) of the Internal Revenue Code of 1986 (as added by this Act)—

(A) shall not apply to a participant who does not have an hour of service after the effective date of such requirements (as otherwise determined under this subsection); and

(B) in the case of a plan other than a plan described in paragraph (3) or (4), shall apply to plan years ending on or after June 29, 2005.

P.L. 109-280, §702, provides:

SEC. 702. REGULATIONS RELATING TO MERGERS AND ACQUISITIONS.

The Secretary of the Treasury or his delegate shall, not later than 12 months after the date of the enactment of this Act, prescribe regulations for the application of the amendments made by, and the provisions of, this title in cases where the conversion of a plan to an applicable defined benefit plan is made with respect to a group of employees who become employees by reason of a merger, acquisition, or similar transaction.

P.L. 109-280, §811, provides:

SEC. 811. PENSIONS AND INDIVIDUAL RETIREMENT ARRANGEMENT PROVISIONS OF ECONOMIC GROWTH AND TAX RELIEF RECONCILIATION ACT OF 2001 MADE PERMANENT.

Title IX of the Economic Growth and Tax Relief Reconciliation Act of 2001 [P.L. 107-16] shall not apply to the provisions of, and amendments made by, subtitles A through F of title VI [§§601-666]of such Act (relating to pension and individual retirement arrangement provisions).

P.L. 109-280, §902(d)(2)(A):

Amended Code Sec. 411(a)(3)(G) by inserting "an erroneous automatic contribution under section 414(w)," after "402(g)(2)(A),". **Effective** for plan years beginning after 12-31-2007.

P.L. 109-280, §902(d)(2)(B):

Amended the heading of Code Sec. 411(a)(3)(G) by inserting "OR ERRONEOUS AUTOMATIC CONTRIBUTION" before the period. **Effective** for plan years beginning after 12-31-2007.

P.L. 109-280, §904(a)(1):

Amended Code Sec. 411(a)(2). For the **effective** date, see Act Sec. 904(c), below. Prior to amendment, Code Sec. 411(a)(2) read as follows:

(2) EMPLOYER CONTRIBUTIONS.—Except as provided in paragraph (12), a plan satisfies the requirements of this paragraph if it satisfies the requirements of subparagraph (A) or (B).

(A) 5-YEAR VESTING.—A plan satisfies the requirements of this subparagraph if an employee who has completed at least 5 years of service has a nonforfeitable right to 100 percent of the employee's accrued benefit derived from employer contributions.

(B) 3 TO 7 YEAR VESTING.—A plan satisfies the requirements of this subparagraph if an employee has a nonforfeitable right to a percentage of the employee's accrued benefit derived from employer contributions determined under the following table:

Years of service:	The nonforfeitable percentage is:
3	20
4	40
5	60
6	80
7 or more	100

P.L. 109-280, §904(a)(2):

Amended Code Sec. 411(a) by striking paragraph (12). For the **effective** date, see Act Sec. 904(c), below. Prior to being stricken, Code Sec. 411(a)(12) read as follows:

(12) FASTER VESTING FOR MATCHING CONTRIBUTIONS.—In the case of matching contributions (as defined in section 401(m)(4)(A)), paragraph (2) shall be applied—

(A) by substituting "3 years" for "5 years" in subparagraph (A), and

(B) by substituting the following table for the table contained in subparagraph (B):

Years of service:	The nonforfeitable percentage is:
2	20
3	40
4	60
5	80
6 or more	100.

P.L. 109-280, §904(c), provides:

(c) EFFECTIVE DATES.—

(1) IN GENERAL.—Except as provided in paragraphs (2) and (4), the amendments made by this section shall apply to contributions for plan years beginning after December 31, 2006.

(2) COLLECTIVE BARGAINING AGREEMENTS.—In the case of a plan maintained pursuant to one or more collective bargaining agreements between employee representatives and one or more employers ratified before the date of the enactment of this Act, the amendments made by this section shall not apply to contributions on behalf of employees covered by any such agreement for plan years beginning before the earlier of—

(A) the later of—

(i) the date on which the last of such collective bargaining agreements terminates (determined without regard to any extension thereof on or after such date of the enactment); or

(ii) January 1, 2007; or

(B) January 1, 2009.

(3) SERVICE REQUIRED.—With respect to any plan, the amendments made by this section shall not apply to any employee before the date that such employee has 1 hour of service under such plan in any plan year to which the amendments made by this section apply.

(4) SPECIAL RULE FOR STOCK OWNERSHIP PLANS.—Notwithstanding paragraph (1) or (2), in the case of an employee stock ownership plan (as defined in section 4975(e)(7) of the Internal Revenue Code of 1986) which had outstanding on September 26, 2005, a loan incurred for the purpose of acquiring qualifying employer securities (as defined in section 4975(e)(8) of such Code), the amendments made by this section shall not apply to any plan year beginning before the earlier of—

(A) the date on which the loan is fully repaid, or

(B) the date on which the loan was, as of September 26, 2005, scheduled to be fully repaid.

P.L. 109-280, §1102(a)(1)(B) and (3), provides:

(B) MODIFICATION OF REGULATIONS.—The Secretary of the Treasury shall modify the regulations under sections 402(f), 411(a)(11), and 417 of the Internal Revenue Code of 1986 by substituting "180 days" for "90 days" each place it appears in Treasury Regulations sections 1.402(f)-1, 1.411(a)-11(c), and 1.417(e)-1(b).

(3) EFFECTIVE DATE.—The amendments and modifications made or required by this subsection shall apply to years beginning after December 31, 2006.

P.L. 109-280, §1102(b), provides:

(b) NOTIFICATION OF RIGHT TO DEFER.—

(1) IN GENERAL.—The Secretary of the Treasury shall modify the regulations under section 411(a)(11) of the Internal Revenue Code of 1986 and under section 205 of the Employee Retirement Income Security Act of 1974 to provide that the description of a participant's right, if any, to defer receipt of a distribution shall also describe the consequences of failing to defer such receipt.

(2) EFFECTIVE DATE.—

(A) IN GENERAL.—The modifications required by paragraph (1) shall apply to years beginning after December 31, 2006.

(B) REASONABLE NOTICE.—A plan shall not be treated as failing to meet the requirements of section 411(a)(11) of such Code or section 205 of such Act with respect to any description of consequences described in paragraph (1) made within 90 days after the Secretary of the Treasury issues the modifications required by paragraph (1) if the plan administrator makes a reasonable attempt to comply with such requirements.

• 2004, Working Families Tax Relief Act of 2004 (P.L. 108-311)

P.L. 108-311, §408(a)(14):

Amended the table contained in Code Sec. 411(a)(12)(B) by striking the last line and inserting a new line. **Effective** 10-4-2004. Prior to being stricken, the last line of the table contained in Code Sec. 411(a)(12)(B) read as follows:

6 . . . . 100.

• 2001, Economic Growth and Tax Relief Reconciliation Act of 2001 (P.L. 107-16)

P.L. 107-16, §633(a)(1)-(2):

Amended Code Sec. 411(a) by striking "A plan" in paragraph (2) and inserting "Except as provided in paragraph (12), a plan"; and by adding at the end a new paragraph (12). **Effective** generally for contributions for plan years beginning after 12-31-2001. For special rules, see Act Sec. 633(c)(2)-(3), below.

P.L. 107-16, §633(c)(2)-(3), provides:

(2) COLLECTIVE BARGAINING AGREEMENTS.—In the case of a plan maintained pursuant to one or more collective bargaining agreements between employee representatives and one or more employers ratified by the date of the enactment of this Act, the amendments made by this section shall not apply to contributions on behalf of employees covered by any such agreement for plan years beginning before the earlier of—

(A) the later of—

(i) the date on which the last of such collective bargaining agreements terminates (determined without regard to any extension thereof on or after such date of the enactment); or

(ii) January 1, 2002; or

(B) January 1, 2006.

(3) SERVICE REQUIRED.—With respect to any plan, the amendments made by this section shall not apply to any employee before the date that such employee has 1 hour of service under such plan in any plan year to which the amendments made by this section apply.

P.L. 107-16, §648(a)(1):

Amended Code Sec. 411(a)(11) by adding at the end a new subparagraph (D). **Effective** for distributions after 12-31-2001.

P.L. 107-16, §901(a)-(b), provides [but see P.L. 109-280, §811, above]:

SEC. 901. SUNSET OF PROVISIONS OF ACT.

(a) IN GENERAL.—All provisions of, and amendments made by, this Act shall not apply—

(1) to taxable, plan, or limitation years beginning after December 31, 2010, or

(2) in the case of title V, to estates of decedents dying, gifts made, or generation skipping transfers, after December 31, 2010.

(b) APPLICATION OF CERTAIN LAWS.—The Internal Revenue Code of 1986 and the Employee Retirement Income Security Act of 1974 shall be applied and administered to years, estates, gifts, and transfers described in subsection (a) as if the provisions and amendments described in subsection (a) had never been enacted.

• 1997, Taxpayer Relief Act of 1997 (P.L. 105-34)

P.L. 105-34, §1071(a)(1):

Amended Code Sec. 411(a)(11)(A) by striking "$3,500" and inserting "$5,000". **Effective** for plan years beginning after 8-5-97.

P.L. 105-34, §1071(a)(2)(A):

Amended Code Sec. 411(a)(7)(B) by striking "$3,500" each place it appears (other than the heading) and inserting "the dollar limit under section 411(a)(11)(A)". **Effective** for plan years beginning after 8-5-97.

• 1996, Small Business Job Protection Act of 1996 (P.L. 104-188)

P.L. 104-188, §1442(a)(1)-(2):

Amended Code Sec. 411(a)(2) by striking "subparagraph (A), (B), or (C)" and inserting "subparagraph (A) or (B)", and by striking subparagraph (C). For the **effective** date, see Act Sec. 1442(c), below. Prior to being stricken, Code Sec. 411(a)(2)(C) read as follows:

(C) MULTIEMPLOYER PLANS.—A plan satisfies the requirements of this subparagraph if—

(i) the plan is a multiemployer plan (within the meaning of section 414(f), and

(ii) under the plan—

(I) an employee who is covered pursuant to a collective bargaining agreement described in section 414(f)(1)(B) and who has completed at least 10 years of service and has a nonforfeitable right to 100 percent of the employee's accrued benefit derived from employer contributions, and

(II) the requirements of subparagraph (A) or (B) are met with respect to employees not described in subclause (I).

P.L. 104-188, §1442(c), provides:

(c) EFFECTIVE DATE.—The amendments made by this section shall apply to plan years beginning on or after the earlier of—

(1) the later of—

(A) January 1, 1997, or

(B) the date on which the last of the collective bargaining agreements pursuant to which the plan is maintained terminates (determined without regard to any extension thereof after the date of the enactment of this Act), or

(2) January 1, 1999.

Such amendments shall not apply to any individual who does not have more than 1 hour of service under the plan on or after the 1st day of the 1st plan year to which such amendments apply.

• 1994, Uruguay Round Agreements Act (P.L. 103-465)

P.L. 103-465, §767(a)(1):

Amended Code Sec. 411(a)(11)(B). **Effective** for plan years and limitation years beginning after 12-31-94; except that an employer may elect to treat the amendments made by this section as being effective on or after 12-8-94. Prior to amendment, Code Sec. 411(a)(11)(B) read as follows:

(B) DETERMINATION OF PRESENT VALUE.—

(i) IN GENERAL.—For purposes of subparagraph (A), the present value shall be calculated—

(I) by using an interest rate no greater than the applicable interest rate if the vested accrued benefit (using such rate) is not in excess of $25,000, and

(II) by using an interest rate no greater than 120 percent of the applicable interest rate if the vested accrued benefit exceeds $25,000 (as determined under subclause (I)).

In no event shall the present value determined under subclause (II) be less than $25,000.

(ii) APPLICABLE INTEREST RATE.—For purposes of clause (i), the term "applicable interest rate" means the interest rate which would be used (as of the date of the distribution) by the Pension Benefit Guaranty Corporation for purposes of determining the present value of a lump sum distribution on plan termination.

P.L. 103-465, §767(d)(2), provides:

(2) NO REDUCTION IN ACCRUED BENEFITS.—A participant's accrued benefit shall not be considered to be reduced in violation of section 411(d)(6) or section 204(g) of the Employee Retirement Income Security Act of 1974 merely because (A) the benefit is determined in accordance with section 417(e)(3)(A) of such Code, as amended by this Act, or section 205(g)(3) of the Employee Retirement Income Security Act of 1974, as amended by this Act, or (B) the plan applies section 415(b)(2)(E) of such Code, as amended by this Act.

• 1989, Omnibus Budget Reconciliation Act of 1989 (P.L. 101-239)

P.L. 101-239, §7861(a)(5)(A):

Amended Code Sec. 411(a)(3) by adding at the end thereof a new subparagraph (G). **Effective** as if included in the provision of P.L. 99-514 to which it relates.

P.L. 101-239, §7861(a)(6)(A):

Amended Code Sec. 411(a)(4)(A). **Effective** as if included in the provision of P.L. 99-514 to which it relates. Prior to amendment, Code Sec. 411(a)(4)((A) read as follows:

(A) years of service before age 18, except that in the case of a plan which does not satisfy subparagraph (A) or (B) of paragraph (2), the plan may not disregard any such year of service during which the employee was a participant;

P.L. 101-239, §7871(b)(1):

Amended Code Sec. 411(a)(8)(B). **Effective** as if included in the amendments made by section 9203 of P.L. 99-509. Prior to amendment, Code Sec. 411(a)(8)(B) read as follows:

(B) the latest of—

(i) the time a plan participant attains age 65,

(ii) in the case of a plan participant who commences participation in the plan within 5 years before attaining normal retirement age under the plan, the 5th anniversary of the time the plan participant commences participation in the plan, or

(iii) in the case of a plan participant not described in clause (ii), the 10th anniversary of the time the plan participant commences participation in the plan.

P.L. 101-239, §7881(m)(1)(D):

Amended Code Sec. 411(a)(7) by adding at the end thereof a new subparagraph (D). **Effective** as if included in the provision of P.L. 100-203 to which it relates.

• 1988, Technical and Miscellaneous Revenue Act of 1988 (P.L. 100-647)

P.L. 100-647, §1018(t)(8)(B):

Amended Code Sec. 411(a)(11)(A) by striking out "vested" and inserting in lieu thereof "nonforfeitable". **Effective** as if included in the provision of P.L. 99-514 to which it relates.

• 1986, Tax Reform Act of 1986 (P.L. 99-514)

P.L. 99-514, §1113(a):

Amended Code Sec. 411(a)(2). **Effective** for plan years beginning after 12-31-88. However, for special rules, see Act Sec. 1113(f)(2)-(4), below. Prior to amendment, Code Sec. 411(a)(2) read as follows:

(2) EMPLOYER CONTRIBUTIONS.—A plan satisfies the requirements of this paragraph if it satisfies the requirements of subparagraph (A), (B), or (C).

(A) 10-YEAR VESTING.—A plan satisfies the requirements of this subparagraph if an employee who has at least 10 years of service has a nonforfeitable right to 100 percent of his accrued benefit derived from employer contributions.

(B) 5- TO 15-YEAR VESTING.—A plan satisfies the requirements of this subparagraph if an employee who has completed at least 5 years of service has a nonforfeitable right to a percentage of his accrued benefit derived from employer contributions which percentage is not less than the percentage determined under the following table:

Years of service:	Nonforfeitable percentage
5	25
6	30
7	35
8	40
9	45
10	50
11	60
12	70
13	80
14	90
15 or more	100

(C) RULE OF 45.—

(i) A plan satisfies the requirements of this subparagraph if an employee who is not separated from the service, who has completed at least 5 years of service, and with respect to whom the sum of his age and years of service equals or exceeds 45, has a nonforfeitable right to a percentage of his accrued benefit derived from employer contributions determined under the following table:

If years of service equal or exceed—	and sum of age and service equals or exceeds—	then the nonforfeitable percentage is—
5	45	50
6	47	60
7	49	70
8	51	80
9	53	90
10	55	100

(ii) Notwithstanding clause (i), a plan shall not be treated as satisfying the requirements of this subparagraph unless any employee who has completed at least 10 years of service has a nonforfeitable right to not less than 50 percent of his accrued benefit derived from employer contributions and to not less than an additional 10 percent for each additional year of service thereafter.

P.L. 99-514, §1113(d)(B):

Amended Code Sec. 411(a)(10)(B) by striking out "5 years" and inserting in lieu thereof "3 years". **Effective** for plan years beginning after 12-31-88. However, for special rules, see Act Sec. 1113(f)(2)-(4), below.

P.L. 99-514, §1113(f)(2)-(4), as amended by P.L. 101-239, §7861(a)(3)-(4), provides:

(2) SPECIAL RULE FOR COLLECTIVE BARGAINING AGREEMENTS.—In the case of a plan maintained pursuant to 1 or more collective bargaining agreements between employee representatives and 1 or more employers ratified before March 1, 1986, the amendments made by this section shall not apply to employees covered by any such agreement in plan years beginning before the earlier of—

(A) the later of—

(i) January 1, 1989, or

(ii) the date on which the last of such collective bargaining agreements terminates (determined without regard to any extension thereof after February 28, 1986), or

(B) January 1, 1991.

(3) PARTICIPATION REQUIRED.—The amendments made by this section shall not apply to any employee who does not have 1 hour of service in any plan year to which the amendments made by this section apply.

(4) REPEAL OF CLASS YEAR VESTING.—If a plan amendment repealing class year vesting is adopted after October 22, 1986, such amendment shall not apply to any employee for the 1st plan year to which the amendments made by subsections (b) and (e)(2) apply (and any subsequent plan year) if—

(A) such plan amendment would reduce the nonforfeitable right of such employee for such year, and

(B) such employee has at least 1 hour of service before the adoption of such plan amendment and after the beginning of such 1st plan year.

P.L. 99-514, §1139(a):

Amended Code Sec. 411(a)(11)(B). **Effective** for distributions in plan years beginning after 12-31-84, except that such amendments shall not apply to any distributions in plan years beginning after 12-31-84, and before 1-1-87, if such distributions were made in accordance with the requirements of the regulations issued under P.L. 98-397. However, for a special rule, see Act Sec. 1139(d)(2), below. Prior to amendment, Code Sec. 411(a)(11)(B) read as follows:

(B) DETERMINATION OF PRESENT VALUE.—For purposes of subparagraph (A), the present value shall be calculated by using an interest rate not greater than the interest rate which would be used (as of the date of the distribution) by the Pension Benefit Guaranty Corporation for purposes of determining the present value of a lump sum distribution on plan termination.

P.L. 99-514, §1139(d)(2), provides:

(2) REDUCTION IN ACCRUED BENEFITS.—

(A) IN GENERAL.—If a plan—

(i) adopts a plan amendment before the close of the first plan year beginning on or before January 1, 1989, which provides for the calculation of the present value of the accrued benefits in the manner provided by the amendments made by this section, and

(ii) the plan reduces the accrued benefits for any plan year to which such plan amendment applies in accordance with such plan amendment,

such reduction shall not be treated as a violation of section 411(d)(6) of the Internal Revenue Code of 1986 or section 204(g) of the Employee Retirement Income Security Act of 1974 (29 U.S.C. 1054(g)).

(B) SPECIAL RULE.—In the case of a plan maintained by a corporation incorporated on April 11, 1934, which is headquartered in Tarrant County, Texas—

(i) such plan may be amended to remove the option of an employee to receive a lump sum distribution (within the meaning of section 402(e)(5) of such Code) if such amendment—

(I) is adopted within 1 year of the date of the enactment of this Act, and

(II) is not effective until 2 years after the employees are notified of such amendment, and

(ii) the present value of any accrued benefit of such plan determined during the 3-year period beginning on the date of the enactment of this Act shall be determined under the applicable interest rate (within the meaning of section 411(a)(11)(B)(ii) of such Code, except that if such value (as so determined) exceeds $50,000, then the value of any excess over $50,000 shall be determined by using the interest rate specified in the plan as of August 16, 1986.

P.L. 99-514, §1898(a)(4)(A)(i):

Amended Code Sec. 411(a)(3)(D)(ii) by striking out the last sentence and inserting in lieu thereof a new sentence. **Effective** as if included in the provision of P.L. 98-397 to which it relates. Prior to amendment, the last sentence read as follows:

In the case of a defined contribution plan, the plan provision required under this clause may provide that such repayment must be made before the participant has any one-year break in service commencing after the withdrawal.

P.L. 99-514, §1898(a)(4)(A)(ii):

Amended Code Sec. 411(a)(7)(C) by striking out the last sentence and inserting in lieu thereof a new sentence. **Effective** as if included in the provisions of P.L. 98-397 to which it relates. Prior to amendment, the last sentence read as follows:

In the case of a defined contribution plan, the plan provision required under this subparagraph may provide that such repayment must be made before the participant has 5 consecutive 1-year breaks in service commencing after such withdrawal.

P.L. 99-514, §1898(d)(1)(A)(i):

Amended Code Sec. 411(a)(11)(A). **Effective** as if included in the provision of P.L. 98-397 to which it relates. Prior to amendment, Code Sec. 411(a)(11)(A) read as follows:

(A) IN GENERAL.—If the present value of any accrued benefit exceeds $3,500, such benefit shall not be treated as nonforfeitable if the plan provides that the present value of such benefit could be immediately distributed without the consent of the participant.

P.L. 99-514, §1898(d)(1)(A)(ii):

Amended 411(a) by striking out "paragraphs (1) and (2)" in the matter preceding paragraph (1) and inserting in lieu thereof "paragraphs (1), (2), and (11)". **Effective** as if included in the provision of P.L. 98-397 to which it relates.

P.L. 99-514, §1898(d)(2)(A):

Amended Code Sec. 411(a)(11) by adding at the end thereof new subparagraph (C). **Effective** as if included in the provision of P.L. 98-397 to which it relates.

• 1986, Omnibus Budget Reconciliation Act of 1986 (P.L. 99-509)

P.L. 99-509, §9203(b)(2):

Amended Code Sec. 411(a)(8)(B). For the **effective** date, see Act Sec. 9204, below. Prior to amendment, Code Sec. 411(a)(8)(B) read as follows:

(B) the later of—

(i) the time a plan participant attains age 65, or

(ii) the 10th anniversary of the time a plan participant commenced participation in the plan.

P.L. 99-509, §9202(b)(3):

Amended the first sentence of Code Sec. 411(a) by striking out "paragraph (2) of subsection (b), and" and all that follows through the end thereof and inserting in lieu thereof "subsection (b)(3), and also satisfies, in the case of a defined benefit plan, the requirements of subsection (b)(1) and, in the case of a defined contribution plan, the requirements of subsection (b)(2).". For the **effective** date, see Act Sec. 9204, below. Prior to amendment, the first sentence Code Sec. 411(a) read as follows:

A trust shall not constitute a qualified trust under section 401(a) unless the plan of which such trust is a part provides that an employee's right to his normal retirement benefit is nonforfeitable upon the attainment of normal retirement age (as defined in paragraph (8)) and in addition satisfies the requirements of paragraphs (1), (2), and (11) of this subsection and the requirements of paragraph (2) of subsection (b), and in the case of a defined benefit plan, also satisfies the requirements of paragraph (1) of subsection (b).

P.L. 99-509, §9204, provides:

SEC. 9204. EFFECTIVE DATE; REGULATIONS.

(a) APPLICABILITY TO EMPLOYEES WITH SERVICE AFTER 1988.—

(1) IN GENERAL.—The amendments made by sections 9201 and 9202 shall apply only with respect to plan years beginning on or after January 1, 1988, and only to employees who have 1 hour of service in any plan year to which such amendments apply.

(2) SPECIAL RULE FOR COLLECTIVELY BARGAINED PLANS.—In the case of a plan maintained pursuant to 1 or more collective bargaining agreements between employee representatives and 1 or more employers ratified before March 1, 1986, paragraph (1) shall be applied to benefits pursuant to, and individuals covered by, any such agreement by substituting for "January 1, 1988" the date of the commencement of the first plan year beginning on or after the earlier of—

(A) the later of—

(i) January 1, 1988, or

(ii) the date on which the last of such collective bargaining agreements terminate (determined without regard to any extension thereof after February 28, 1986), or

(B) January 1, 1990.

(b) APPLICABILITY OF AMENDMENTS RELATING TO NORMAL RETIREMENT AGE.—The amendments made by section 9203 shall apply only with respect to plan years beginning on or after January 1, 1988, and only with respect to service performed on or after such date.

(c) PLAN AMENDMENTS.—If any amendment made by this subtitle requires an amendment to any plan, such plan amendment shall not be required to be made before the first plan year beginning on or after January 1, 1989, if—

(1) during the period after such amendment takes effect and before such first plan year, the plan is operated in accordance with the requirements of such amendment, and

(2) such plan amendment applies retroactively to the period after such amendment takes effect and such first plan year.

A pension plan shall not be treated as failing to provide definitely determinable benefits or contributions, or to be operated in accordance with the provisions of the plan, merely because it operates in accordance with this subsection.

(d) INTERGENCY COORDINATION.—The regulations and rulings issued by the Secretary of Labor, the regulations and rulings issued by the Secretary of the Treasury, and the regulations and rulings issued by the Equal Employment Opportunity Commission pursuant to the amendments made by this subtitle shall each be consistent with the others. The Secretary of Labor, the Secretary of the Treasury, and the Equal Employment Opportunity Commission shall each consult with the others to the extent necessary to meet the requirements of the preceding sentence.

(e) FINAL REGULATIONS.—The Secretary of Labor, the Secretary of the Treasury, and the Equal Employment Opportunity Commission shall each issue before February 1, 1988, such final regulations as may be necessary to carry out the amendments made by this subtitle.

• 1984, Retirement Equity Act of 1984 (P.L. 98-397)

P.L. 98-397, §202(b)

Amended Code Sec. 411(a)(4)(A) by striking out "22" and inserting in lieu thereof "18". **Effective** in the case of participants who have at least 1 hour of service under the plan on or after the first day of the first plan year to which the amendments made by P.L. 98-397 apply. Special rules appear in the notes for P.L. 98-397 following Code Sec. 401(a) and in Act Sec. 303(a)(2)-(3), below.

P.L. 98-397, §202(c):

Amended Code Sec. 411(a)(6)(C) by striking out "1-YEAR BREAK IN SERVICE" in the subparagraph heading and inserting in lieu thereof "5 CONSECUTIVE 1-YEAR BREAKS IN SERVICE", by striking out "any 1-year break in service" and inserting in lieu thereof "5 consecutive 1-year breaks in service", and by striking out "such break" each place it appears and inserting in lieu thereof "such 5-year period". **Effective** for plan years beginning after 12-31-84. Special rules appear in the notes for P.L. 98-397 following Code Sec. 401(a).

P.L. 98-397, §202(d)(2):

Amended Code Sec. 411(a)(6)(D). **Effective** for plan years beginning after 12-31-84. Special rules appear in Act Sec. 303(a)(2)-(3), below, and in the notes for P.L. 98-397 following Code Sec. 401(a). Prior to amendment, Code Sec. 411(a)(6)(D) read as follows:

(D) NONVESTED PARTICIPANTS.—For purposes of paragraph (4), in the case of a participant who, under the plan, does not have any nonforfeitable right to an accrued benefit derived from employer contributions, years of service before any 1-year break in service shall not be required to be taken into account if the number of consecutive 1-year breaks in service equals or exceeds the aggregate number of such years of service prior to such break. Such aggregate number of years of service before such break shall be deemed not to include any years of service not required to be taken into account under this subparagraph by reason of any prior break in service.

P.L. 98-397, §202(e)(2):

Added Code Sec. 411(a)(6)(E). **Effective** in the case of absences from work which begin on or after the first day of the first plan year to which the amendments made by P.L. 98-397 apply. Special rules appear in Act Sec. 303(a)(2)-(3) and (b) below and in the notes for P.L. 98-397 following Code Sec. 401(a).

P.L. 98-397, §202(f):

Amended Code Sec. 411(a)(7)(C) by striking out "any one-year break in service" and inserting in lieu thereof "5 consecutive 1-year breaks in service". **Effective** for plan years beginning after 12-31-84. Special rules appear in the notes for P.L. 98-397 following Code Sec. 401(a).

P.L. 98-397, §205(a):

Amended Code Sec. 411(a) by adding at the end thereof new paragraph (11). **Effective** for plan years beginning after 12-31-84. Special rules appear in the notes for P.L. 98-397 following Code Sec. 401(a).

P.L. 98-397, §205(b):

Amended Code Sec. 411(a)(7)(B) by striking out "$1,750" and inserting in lieu thereof "$3,500". **Effective** for plan years beginning after 12-31-84. Special rules appear in the notes for P.L. 98-397 following Code Sec. 401(a).

P.L. 98-397, §303(a)(2)-(3), provides:

(2) BREAK IN SERVICE RULES.—If, as of the day before the first day of the first plan year to which the amendments made by this Act apply, section 202(a) or (b) or 203(b) of the Employee Retirement Income Security Act of 1974 or section 410(a) or 411(a) of the Internal Revenue Code of 1954 (as in effect on the day before the date of the enactment of this Act) would not require any service to be taken into account, nothing in the amendments made by subsections (c) and (d) of section 102 of this Act and subsections (c) and (d) of section 202 of this Act shall be construed as requiring such service to be taken into account under such section 202(a) or (b), 203(b), 410(a), or 411(a); as the case may be.

(3) MATERNITY OR PATERNITY LEAVE.—The amendments made by sections 102(e) and 202(e) shall apply in the case of absences from work which begin on or after the first day of the first plan year to which the amendments made by this Act apply.

P.L. 98-397, §303(b), provides:

(b) SPECIAL RULE FOR AMENDMENTS RELATING TO MATERNITY OR PATERNITY ABSENCES.—If a plan is administered in a manner which would meet the amendments made by sections 102(e) and 202(e) (relating to certain maternity or paternity absences not treated as breaks in service), such plan need not be amended to meet such requirements until the earlier of—

(1) the date on which such plan is first otherwise amended after the date of the enactment of this Act, or

(2) the beginning of the first plan year beginning after December 31, 1986.

• 1980, Multiemployer Pension Plan Amendments Act of 1980 (P.L. 96-364)

P.L. 96-364, §206:

Amended Code Sec. 411(a) by adding subparagraphs (E) and (F) to paragraph (3), by striking out "and" at the end of subparagraph (4)(E), by adding "; and" at the end of subparagraph (4)(F), and by adding new subparagraph (G) at the end of paragraph (4). **Effective** 9-26-80.

• 1976, Tax Reform Act of 1976 (P.L. 94-455)

P.L. 94-455, §1901(a)(62)(A):

Amended Code Sec. 411(a) by substituting "paragraph (8)" for "subsection (a)(8)". **Effective** for tax years beginning after 12-31-76.

P.L. 94-455, §1901(a)(62)(B):

Amended Code Sec. 411(a)(3)(D)(iii) by substituting "September 2, 1974" for "the date of the enactment of the Employee Retirement Income Security Act of 1974" and by substituting "September 2, 1974" for "the date of the enactment of such Act". **Effective** with respect to tax years beginning after 12-31-76.

P.L. 94-455, §1901(a)(62)(C):

Amended Code Sec. 411(a)(7)(C) by changing the heading of the subparagraph to read "SUBPARAGRAPH (B)" IN LIEU OF "SUBPARAGRAPH(b)". **E ffective** with respect to tax years beginning after 12-31-76.

P.L. 94-455, §1906(b)(13)(A):

Amended 1954 Code by substituting "Secretary" for "Secretary or his delegate" each place it appeared. **Effective** 2-1-77.

[Sec. 411(b)]

(b) ACCRUED BENEFIT REQUIREMENTS.—

(1) DEFINED BENEFIT PLANS.—

(A) 3-PERCENT METHOD.—A defined benefit plan satisfies the requirements of this paragraph if the accrued benefit to which each participant is entitled upon his separation from the service is not less than—

(i) 3 percent of the normal retirement benefit to which he would be entitled if he commenced participation at the earliest possible entry age under the plan and served continuously until the earlier of age 65 or the normal retirement age specified under the plan, multiplied by

(ii) the number of years (not in excess of 33⅓) of his participation in the plan.

In the case of a plan providing retirement benefits based on compensation during any period, the normal retirement benefit to which a participant would be entitled shall be determined as if he continued to earn annually the average rate of compensation which he earned during consecutive years of service, not in excess of 10, for which his compensation was the highest. For purposes of this subparagraph, social security benefits and all other relevant factors used to compute benefits shall be treated as remaining constant as of the current year for all years after such current year.

(B) 133 ⅓ PERCENT RULE.—A defined benefit plan satisfies the requirements of this paragraph for a particular plan year if under the plan the accrued benefit payable at the normal retirement age is equal to the normal retirement benefit and the annual rate at which any individual who is or could be a participant can accrue the retirement benefits payable at normal retirement age under the plan for any later plan year is not more than 133⅓ percent of the annual rate at which he can accrue benefits for any plan year beginning on or after such particular plan year and before such later plan year. For purposes of this subparagraph—

(i) any amendment to the plan which is in effect for the current year shall be treated as in effect for all other plan years;

(ii) any change in an accrual rate which does not apply to any individual who is or could be a participant in the current year shall be disregarded;

(iii) the fact that benefits under the plan may be payable to certain employees before normal retirement age shall be disregarded; and

(iv) social security benefits and all other relevant factors used to compute benefits shall be treated as remaining constant as of the current year for all years after the current year.

(C) FRACTIONAL RULE.—A defined benefit plan satisfies the requirements of this paragraph if the accrued benefit to which any participant is entitled upon his separation from the service is not less than a fraction of the annual benefit commencing at normal retirement age to which he would be entitled under the plan as in effect on the date of his separation if he continued to earn annually until normal retirement age the same rate of compensation upon which his normal retirement benefit would be computed under the plan, determined as if he had attained normal retirement age on the date on which any such determination is made (but taking into account no more than the 10 years of service immediately preceding his separation from service). Such fraction shall be a fraction, not exceeding 1, the numerator of which is the total number of his years of participation in the plan (as of the date of his separation from the service) and the denominator of which is the total number of years he would have participated in the plan if he separated from the service at the normal retirement age. For purposes of this subparagraph, social security benefits and all other relevant factors used to compute benefits shall be treated as remaining constant as of the current year for all years after such current year.

(D) ACCRUAL FOR SERVICE BEFORE EFFECTIVE DATE.—Subparagraphs (A), (B), and (C) shall not apply with respect to years of participation before the first plan year to which this section applies, but a defined benefit plan satisfies the requirements of this subparagraph with respect to such years of participation only if the accrued benefit of any participant with respect to such years of participation is not less than the greater of—

(i) his accrued benefit determined under the plan, as in effect from time to time prior to September 2, 1974, or

(ii) an accrued benefit which is not less than one-half of the accrued benefit to which such participant would have been entitled if subparagraph (A), (B), or (C) applied with respect to such years of participation.

(E) FIRST TWO YEARS OF SERVICE.—Notwithstanding subparagraphs (A), (B), and (C) of this paragraph, a plan shall not be treated as not satisfying the requirements of this paragraph solely because the accrual of benefits under the plan does not become effective until the employee has two continuous years of service. For purposes of this subparagraph, the term "years of service" has the meaning provided by section 410(a)(3)(A).

(F) CERTAIN INSURED DEFINED BENEFIT PLANS.—Notwithstanding subparagraphs (A), (B), and (C), a defined benefit plan satisfies the requirements of this paragraph if such plan—

(i) is funded exclusively by the purchase of insurance contracts, and

(ii) satisfies the requirements of subparagraphs (B) and (C) of section 412(e)(3) (relating to certain insurance contract plans),

but only if an employee's accrued benefit as of any applicable date is not less than the cash surrender value his insurance contracts would have on such applicable date if the requirements of subparagraphs (D), (E), and (F) of section 412(e)(3) were satisfied.

(G) ACCRUED BENEFIT MAY NOT DECREASE ON ACCOUNT OF INCREASING AGE OR SERVICE.—Notwithstanding the preceding subparagraphs, a defined benefit plan shall be treated as not satisfying the requirements of this paragraph if the participant's accrued benefit is reduced on account of any increase in his age or service. The preceding sentence shall not apply to benefits under the plan commencing before entitlement to benefits payable under title II of the Social Security Act which benefits under the plan—

(i) do not exceed such social security benefits, and

(ii) terminate when such social security benefits commence.

(H) CONTINUED ACCRUAL BEYOND NORMAL RETIREMENT AGE.—

(i) IN GENERAL.—Notwithstanding the preceding subparagraphs, a defined benefit plan shall be treated as not satisfying the requirements of this paragraph if, under the plan, an employee's benefit accrual is ceased, or the rate of an employee's benefit accrual is reduced, because of the attainment of any age.

(ii) CERTAIN LIMITATIONS PERMITTED.—A plan shall not be treated as failing to meet the requirements of this subparagraph solely because the plan imposes (without regard to age) a limitation on the amount of benefits that the plan provides or a limitation on the number of years of service or years of participation which are taken into account for purposes of determining benefit accrual under the plan.

(iii) ADJUSTMENTS UNDER PLAN FOR DELAYED RETIREMENT TAKEN INTO ACCOUNT.—In the case of any employee who, as of the end of any plan year under a defined benefit plan, has attained normal retirement age under such plan—

(I) if distribution of benefits under such plan with respect to such employee has commenced as of the end of such plan year, then any requirement of this subparagraph for continued accrual of benefits under such plan with respect to such employee during such plan year shall be treated as satisfied to the extent of the actuarial equivalent of in-service distribution of benefits, and

(II) if distribution of benefits under such plan with respect to such employee has not commenced as of the end of such year in accordance with section 401(a)(14)(C), and the payment of benefits under such plan with respect to such employee is not suspended during such plan year pursuant to subsection (a)(3)(B), then any requirement of this subparagraph for continued accrual of benefits under such plan with respect to such employee during such plan year shall be treated as satisfied to the extent of any adjustment in the benefit payable under the plan during such plan year attributable to the delay in the distribution of benefits after the attainment of normal retirement age.

The preceding provisions of this clause shall apply in accordance with regulations of the Secretary. Such regulations may provide for the application of the preceding provisions of this clause, in the case of any such employee, with respect to any period of time within a plan year.

(iv) DISREGARD OF SUBSIDIZED PORTION OF EARLY RETIREMENT BENEFIT.—A plan shall not be treated as failing to meet the requirements of clause (i) solely because the subsidized portion of any early retirement benefit is disregarded in determining benefit accruals.

(v) COORDINATION WITH OTHER REQUIREMENTS.—The Secretary shall provide by regulation for the coordination of the requirements of this subparagraph with the requirements of subsection (a), sections 404, 410, and 415, and the provisions of this subchapter precluding discrimination in favor of highly compensated employees.

(2) DEFINED CONTRIBUTION PLANS.—

(A) IN GENERAL.—A defined contribution plan satisfies the requirements of this paragraph if, under the plan, allocations to the employee's account are not ceased, and the rate at which amounts are allocated to the employee's account is not reduced, because of the attainment of any age.

(B) APPLICATION TO TARGET BENEFIT PLANS.—The Secretary shall provide by regulation for the application of the requirements of this paragraph to target benefit plans.

(C) COORDINATION WITH OTHER REQUIREMENTS.—The Secretary may provide by regulation for the coordination of the requirements of this paragraph with the requirements of subsection (a), sections 404, 410, and 415, and the provisions of this subchapter precluding discrimination in favor of highly compensated employees.

(3) SEPARATE ACCOUNTING REQUIRED IN CERTAIN CASES.—A plan satisfies the requirements of this paragraph if—

(A) in the case of a defined benefit plan, the plan requires separate accounting for the portion of each employee's accrued benefit derived from any voluntary employee contributions permitted under the plan; and

(B) in the case of any plan which is not a defined benefit plan, the plan requires separate accounting for each employee's accrued benefit.

(4) YEAR OF PARTICIPATION.—

(A) DEFINITION.—For purposes of determining an employee's accrued benefit, the term "year of participation" means a period of service (beginning at the earliest date on which the employee is a participant in the plan and which is included in a period of service required to be taken into account under section 410(a)(5) determined without regard to section 410(a)(5)(E)) as determined under regulations prescribed by the Secretary of Labor which provide for the calculation of such period on any reasonable and consistent basis.

(B) LESS THAN FULL TIME SERVICE.—For purposes of this paragraph, except as provided in subparagraph (C), in the case of any employee whose customary employment is less than full time, the calculation of such employee's service on any basis which provides less than a ratable portion of the accrued benefit to which he would be entitled under the plan if his customary employment were full time shall not be treated as made on a reasonable and consistent basis.

(C) LESS THAN 1,000 HOURS OF SERVICE DURING YEAR.—For purposes of this paragraph, in the case of any employee whose service is less than 1,000 hours during any calendar year, plan year or other 12-consecutive month period designated by the plan (and not prohibited under regulations prescribed by the Secretary of Labor) the calculation of his period of service shall not be treated as not made on a reasonable and consistent basis solely because such service is not taken into account.

(D) SEASONAL INDUSTRIES.—In the case of any seasonal industry where the customary period of employment is less than 1,000 hours during a calendar year, the term "year of participation" shall be such period as determined under regulations prescribed by the Secretary of Labor.

(E) MARITIME INDUSTRIES.—For purposes of this subsection, in the case of any maritime industry, 125 days of service shall be treated as a year of participation. The Secretary of Labor may prescribe regulations to carry out the purposes of this subparagraph.

(5) SPECIAL RULES RELATING TO AGE.—

(A) COMPARISON TO SIMILARLY SITUATED YOUNGER INDIVIDUAL.—

(i) IN GENERAL.—A plan shall not be treated as failing to meet the requirements of paragraph (1)(H)(i) if a participant's accrued benefit, as determined as of any date under the terms of the plan, would be equal to or greater than that of any similarly situated, younger individual who is or could be a participant.

(ii) SIMILARLY SITUATED.—For purposes of this subparagraph, a participant is similarly situated to any other individual if such participant is identical to such other individual in every respect (including period of service, compensation, position, date of hire, work history, and any other respect) except for age.

(iii) DISREGARD OF SUBSIDIZED EARLY RETIREMENT BENEFITS.—In determining the accrued benefit as of any date for purposes of this subparagraph, the subsidized portion of any early retirement benefit or retirement-type subsidy shall be disregarded.

(iv) ACCRUED BENEFIT.—For purposes of this subparagraph, the accrued benefit may, under the terms of the plan, be expressed as an annuity payable at normal retirement age, the balance of a hypothetical account, or the current value of the accumulated percentage of the employee's final average compensation.

(B) APPLICABLE DEFINED BENEFIT PLANS.—

(i) INTEREST CREDITS.—

(I) IN GENERAL.—An applicable defined benefit plan shall be treated as failing to meet the requirements of paragraph (1)(H) unless the terms of the plan provide that any interest credit (or an equivalent amount) for any plan year shall be at a rate which is not greater than a market rate of return. A plan shall not be treated as failing to meet the requirements of this subclause merely because the plan provides for a reasonable minimum guaranteed rate of return or for a rate of return that is equal to the greater of a fixed or variable rate of return.

(II) PRESERVATION OF CAPITAL.—An applicable defined benefit plan shall be treated as failing to meet the requirements of paragraph (1)(H) unless the plan provides that an interest credit (or equivalent amount) of less than zero shall in no event result in the account balance or similar amount being less than the aggregate amount of contributions credited to the account.

(III) MARKET RATE OF RETURN.—The Secretary of the Treasury may provide by regulation for rules governing the calculation of a market rate of return for purposes of subclause (I) and for permissible methods of crediting interest to the account (including fixed or variable interest rates) resulting in effective rates of return meeting the requirements of subclause (I).

(ii) SPECIAL RULE FOR PLAN CONVERSIONS.—If, after June 29, 2005, an applicable plan amendment is adopted, the plan shall be treated as failing to meet the requirements of paragraph (1)(H) unless the requirements of clause (iii) are met with respect to each individual who was a participant in the plan immediately before the adoption of the amendment.

(iii) RATE OF BENEFIT ACCRUAL.—Subject to clause (iv), the requirements of this clause are met with respect to any participant if the accrued benefit of the participant under the terms of the plan as in effect after the amendment is not less than the sum of—

(I) the participant's accrued benefit for years of service before the effective date of the amendment, determined under the terms of the plan as in effect before the amendment, plus

(II) the participant's accrued benefit for years of service after the effective date of the amendment, determined under the terms of the plan as in effect after the amendment.

(iv) SPECIAL RULES FOR EARLY RETIREMENT SUBSIDIES.—For purposes of clause (iii)(I), the plan shall credit the accumulation account or similar amount with the amount of any early retirement benefit or retirement-type subsidy for the plan year in which the participant retires if, as of such time, the participant has met the age, years of service, and other requirements under the plan for entitlement to such benefit or subsidy.

(v) APPLICABLE PLAN AMENDMENT.—For purposes of this subparagraph—

(I) IN GENERAL.—The term "applicable plan amendment" means an amendment to a defined benefit plan which has the effect of converting the plan to an applicable defined benefit plan.

(II) SPECIAL RULE FOR COORDINATED BENEFITS.—If the benefits of 2 or more defined benefit plans established or maintained by an employer are coordinated in such a manner as to have the effect of the adoption of an amendment described in subclause (I), the sponsor of the defined benefit plan or plans providing for such coordination shall be treated as having adopted such a plan amendment as of the date such coordination begins.

(III) MULTIPLE AMENDMENTS.—The Secretary shall issue regulations to prevent the avoidance of the purposes of this subparagraph through the use of 2 or more plan amendments rather than a single amendment.

(IV) APPLICABLE DEFINED BENEFIT PLAN.—For purposes of this subparagraph, the term "applicable defined benefit plan" has the meaning given such term by section 411(a)(13).

(vi) TERMINATION REQUIREMENTS.—An applicable defined benefit plan shall not be treated as meeting the requirements of clause (i) unless the plan provides that, upon the termination of the plan—

(I) if the interest credit rate (or an equivalent amount) under the plan is a variable rate, the rate of interest used to determine accrued benefits under the plan shall be equal to the average of the rates of interest used under the plan during the 5-year period ending on the termination date, and

(II) the interest rate and mortality table used to determine the amount of any benefit under the plan payable in the form of an annuity payable at normal retirement age shall be the rate and table specified under the plan for such purpose as of the termination date, except that if such interest rate is a variable rate, the interest rate shall be determined under the rules of subclause (I).

(C) CERTAIN OFFSETS PERMITTED.—A plan shall not be treated as failing to meet the requirements of paragraph (1)(H)(i) solely because the plan provides offsets against benefits under the plan to the extent such offsets are otherwise allowable in applying the requirements of section 401(a).

(D) PERMITTED DISPARITIES IN PLAN CONTRIBUTIONS OR BENEFITS.—A plan shall not be treated as failing to meet the requirements of paragraph (1)(H) solely because the plan provides a disparity in contributions or benefits with respect to which the requirements of section 401(l) are met.

(E) INDEXING PERMITTED.—

(i) IN GENERAL.—A plan shall not be treated as failing to meet the requirements of paragraph (1)(H) solely because the plan provides for indexing of accrued benefits under the plan.

(ii) PROTECTION AGAINST LOSS.—Except in the case of any benefit provided in the form of a variable annuity, clause (i) shall not apply with respect to any indexing which results in an accrued benefit less than the accrued benefit determined without regard to such indexing.

(iii) INDEXING.—For purposes of this subparagraph, the term 'indexing' means, in connection with an accrued benefit, the periodic adjustment of the accrued benefit by means of the application of a recognized investment index or methodology.

(F) EARLY RETIREMENT BENEFIT OR RETIREMENT-TYPE SUBSIDY.—For purposes of this paragraph, the terms "early retirement benefit" and "retirement-type subsidy" have the meaning given such terms in subsection (d)(6)(B)(i).

(G) BENEFIT ACCRUED TO DATE.—For purposes of this paragraph, any reference to the accrued benefit shall be a reference to such benefit accrued to date.

Amendments

• 2008, Worker, Retiree, and Employer Recovery Act of 2008 (P.L. 110-458)

P.L. 110-458, §107(b)(1)(A)-(B):

Amended Code Sec. 411(b)(5) by striking "clause" in subparagraph (A)(iii) and inserting "subparagraph", and by inserting "otherwise" before "allowable" in subparagraph (C). **Effective** as if included in the provision of the 2006 Act to which the amendment relates [**effective** generally for periods beginning on or after 6-29-2005.—CCH].

P.L. 110-458, §107(b)(3):

Amended Code Sec. 411(b)(5)(B)(i)(II). **Effective** as if included in the provision of the 2006 Act to which the amendment relates [**effective** generally for periods beginning on or after 6-29-2005.—CCH]. Prior to amendment, Code Sec. 411(b)(5)(B)(i)(II) read as follows:

(II) PRESERVATION OF CAPITAL.—An interest credit (or an equivalent amount) of less than zero shall in no event result in the account balance or similar amount being less than the aggregate amount of contributions credited to the account.

• 2006, Pension Protection Act of 2006 (P.L. 109-280)

P.L. 109-280, §114(b)(2)(A)-(B):

Amended Code Sec. 411(b)(1)(F) by striking "paragraphs (2) and (3) of section 412(i)" in clause (ii) and inserting "subparagraphs (B) and (C) of section 412(e)(3)", and by striking "paragraphs (4), (5), and (6) of section 412(i)" and inserting "subparagraphs (D), (E), and (F) of section 412(e)(3)". **Effective** for plan years beginning after 2007 [**effective** date amended by P.L. 110-458, §101(d)(3).—CCH].

P.L. 109-280, §701(b)(1):

Amended Code Sec. 411(b) by adding at the end a new paragraph (5). **Effective** generally for periods beginning on or after 6-29-2005. For special rules, see Act Sec. 701(d) in the amendment notes following Code Sec. 411(a), above, and see Act Sec. 701(e)(3)-(5), below.

P.L. 109-280, §701(e)(3)-(6) [as amended by P.L. 110-458, §107(c)(2)(A)-(D)], provides:

(3) VESTING AND INTEREST CREDIT REQUIREMENTS.—In the case of a plan in existence on June 29, 2005, the requirements of clause (i) of section 411(b)(5)(B) of the Internal Revenue Code of 1986, clause (i) of section 204(b)(5)(B) of the Employee Retirement Income Security Act of 1974, and clause (i) of section 4(i)(10)(B) of the Age Discrimination in Employment Act of 1967 (as added by this Act) and the requirements of 203(f)(2) of the Employee Retirement Income Security Act of 1974 and section 411(a)(13)(B) of the Internal Revenue Code of 1986 (as so added) shall, for purposes of applying the amendments made by subsections (a) and (b), apply to years beginning after December 31, 2007, unless the plan sponsor elects the application of such requirements for any period on or after June 29, 2005, and before the first year beginning after December 31, 2007.

(4) SPECIAL RULE FOR COLLECTIVELY BARGAINED PLANS.—In the case of a plan maintained pursuant to 1 or more collective bargaining agreements between employee representatives and 1 or more employers ratified on or before the earlier of the date of the enactment of this Act, the requirements described in paragraph (3) shall, for purposes of applying the amendments made by subsections (a) and (b), not apply to plan years beginning before—

(A) the later of—

(i) the date on which the last of such collective bargaining agreements terminates (determined without regard to any extension thereof on or after such date of enactment), or

(ii) January 1, 2008, or

(B) January 1, 2010.

(5) CONVERSIONS.—The requirements of clause (ii) of section 411(b)(5)(B) of the Internal Revenue Code of 1986, clause (ii) of section 204(b)(5)(B) of the Employee Retirement Income Security Act of 1974, and clause (ii) of section 4(i)(10)(B) of the Age Discrimination in Employment Act of 1967 (as added by this Act), shall apply to plan amendments adopted on or after, and taking effect on or after, June 29, 2005, except that the plan sponsor may elect to have such amendments apply to plan amendments adopted before, and taking effect on or after, such date.

(6) SPECIAL RULE FOR VESTING REQUIREMENTS.—The requirements of section 203(f)(2) of the Employee Retirement Income Security Act of 1974 and section 411(a)(13)(B) of the Internal Revenue Code of 1986 (as added by this Act)—

(A) shall not apply to a participant who does not have an hour of service after the effective date of such requirements (as otherwise determined under this subsection); and

(B) in the case of a plan other than a plan described in paragraph (3) or (4), shall apply to plan years ending on or after June 29, 2005.

P.L. 109-280, §702, provides:

SEC. 702. REGULATIONS RELATING TO MERGERS AND ACQUISITIONS.

The Secretary of the Treasury or his delegate shall, not later than 12 months after the date of the enactment of this Act, prescribe regulations for the application of the amendments made by, and the provisions of, this title in cases where the conversion of a plan to an applicable defined benefit plan is made with respect to a group of employees who become employees by reason of a merger, acquisition, or similar transaction.

• 1989, Omnibus Budget Reconciliation Act of 1989 (P.L. 101-239)

P.L. 101-239, §7871(a)(1):

Amended Code Sec. 411(b)(2) by striking subparagraph (B) and by redesignating subparagraphs (C) and (D) as subparagraphs (B) and (C), respectively. **Effective** as if included in the amendments made by section 9202 of P.L. 99-509. Prior to amendment, Code Sec. 411(b)(2)(B) read as follows:

(B) DISREGARD OF SUBSIDIZED PORTION OF EARLY RETIREMENT BENEFIT.—A plan shall not be treated as failing to meet the requirements of subparagraph (A) solely because the subsidized portion of any early retirement benefit is disregarded in determining benefit accruals.

P.L. 101-239, §7871(a)(2):

Amended Code Sec. 411(b)(2)(C), as redesignated by paragraph (1), by striking "subparagraph" and inserting "paragraph". **Effective** as if included in the amendments made by section 9202 of P.L. 99-509.

• 1986, Omnibus Budget Reconciliation Act of 1986 (P.L. 99-509)

P.L. 99-509, §9202(b)(1)(A)-(B):

Amended Code Sec. 411(b)(1) by striking out "General Rules.—" and inserting in lieu thereof " Defined Benefit Plans.—", and by adding at the end thereof new subparagraph (H). For the **effective** date, see Act Sec. 9204 following Code Sec. 411(a).

P.L. 99-509, §9202(b)(2)(A)-(B):

Amended Code Sec. 411(b) by redesignating paragraphs (2) and (3) as paragraphs (3) and (4), respectively, and by inserting after paragraph (1) new paragraph (2). For the **effective** date, see Act Sec. 9204 following Code Sec. 411(a).

• 1984, Retirement Equity Act of 1984 (P.L. 98-397)

P.L. 98-397, §202(e)(3):

Amended Code Sec. 411(b)(3)(A) by inserting ", determined without regard to section 410(a)(5)(E)" after "section 410(a)(5)". **Effective** in the case of absences from work which begin on or after the first day of the first plan year to which the amendments made by P.L. 98-397 apply. Special rules appear in the notes for P.L. 98-397 following Code Secs. 401(a) and 411(a).

• 1976, Tax Reform Act of 1976 (P.L. 94-455)

P.L. 94-455, §1901(a)(62)(D):

Amended Code Sec. 411(b)(1)(D)(i) by substituting "September 2, 1974" for "the date of the enactment of the Employee Retirement Income Security Act of 1974". **Effective** with respect to tax years beginning after 12-31-76.

[Sec. 411(c)]

(c) ALLOCATION OF ACCRUED BENEFITS BETWEEN EMPLOYER AND EMPLOYEE CONTRIBUTIONS.—

(1) ACCRUED BENEFIT DERIVED FROM EMPLOYER CONTRIBUTIONS.—For purposes of this section, an employee's accrued benefit derived from employer contributions as of any applicable date is the excess, if any, of the accrued benefit for such employee as of such applicable date over the accrued benefit derived from contributions made by such employee as of such date.

(2) ACCRUED BENEFIT DERIVED FROM EMPLOYEE CONTRIBUTIONS.—

(A) PLANS OTHER THAN DEFINED BENEFIT PLANS.—In the case of a plan other than a defined benefit plan, the accrued benefit derived from contributions made by an employee as of any applicable date is—

(i) except as provided in clause (ii), the balance of the employee's separate account consisting only of his contributions and the income, expenses, gains, and losses attributable thereto, or

(ii) if a separate account is not maintained with respect to an employee's contributions under such a plan, the amount which bears the same ratio to his total accrued benefit as the total amount of the employee's contributions (less withdrawals) bears to the sum of such contributions and the contributions made on his behalf by the employer (less withdrawals).

(B) DEFINED BENEFIT PLANS.—In the case of a defined benefit plan, the accrued benefit derived from contributions made by an employee as of any applicable date is the amount equal to the employee's accumulated contributions expressed as an annual benefit commencing at normal retirement age, using an interest rate which would be used under the plan under section 417(e)(3) (as of the determination date).

(C) DEFINITION OF ACCUMULATED CONTRIBUTIONS.—For purposes of this subsection, the term "accumulated contributions" means the total of—

(i) all mandatory contributions made by the employee,

(ii) interest (if any) under the plan to the end of the last plan year to which subsection (a)(2) does not apply (by reason of the applicable effective date), and

(iii) interest on the sum of the amounts determined under clauses (i) and (ii) compounded annually—

(I) at the rate of 120 percent of the Federal mid-term rate (as in effect under section 1274 for the 1st month of a plan year) for the period beginning with the 1st plan year to which subsection (a)(2) applies (by reason of the applicable effective date) and ending with the date on which the determination is being made, and

(II) at the interest rate which would be used under the plan under section 417(e)(3) (as of the determination date) for the period beginning with the determination date and ending on the date on which the employee attains normal retirement age.

For purposes of this subparagraph, the term "mandatory contributions" means amounts contributed to the plan by the employee which are required as a condition of employment, as a condition of participation in such plan, or as a condition of obtaining benefits under the plan attributable to employer contributions.

(D) ADJUSTMENTS.—The Secretary is authorized to adjust by regulation the conversion factor described in subparagraph (B) from time to time as he may deem necessary.

(3) ACTUARIAL ADJUSTMENT.—For purposes of this section, in the case of any defined benefit plan, if an employee's accrued benefit is to be determined as an amount other than an annual benefit commencing at normal retirement age, or if the accrued benefit derived from contributions made by an employee is to be determined with respect to a benefit other than an annual benefit in the form of a single life annuity (without ancillary benefits) commencing at normal retirement age, the employee's accrued benefit, or the accrued benefits derived from contributions made by an employee, as the case may be, shall be the actuarial equivalent of such benefit or amount determined under paragraph (1) or (2).

Amendments

• 1989, Omnibus Budget Reconciliation Act of 1989 (P.L. 101-239)

P.L. 101-239, §7881(m)(1)(A):

Amended Code Sec. 411(c)(2)(C)(iii). **Effective** as if included in the provision of P.L. 100-203 to which it relates. Prior to amendment, Code Sec. 411(c)(2)(C)(iii) read as follows:

(iii) interest on the sum of the amounts determined under clauses (i) and (ii) compounded annually at the rate of 120 percent of the Federal mid-term rate (as in effect under section 1274 for the 1st month of a plan year) from the beginning of the first plan year to which subsection (a)(2) applies (by reason of the applicable effective date) to the date upon which the employee would attain normal retirement age.

P.L. 101-239, §7881(m)(1)(B):

Amended Code Sec. 411(c)(2)(B). **Effective** as if included in the provision of P.L. 100-203 to which it relates. Prior to amendment, Code Sec. 411(c)(2)(B) read as follows:

(B) DEFINED BENEFIT PLANS.—

(i) IN GENERAL.—In the case of a defined benefit plan providing an annual benefit in the form of a single life annuity (without ancillary benefits) commencing at normal retirement age, the accrued benefit derived from contributions made by an employee as of any applicable date is the annual benefit equal to the employee's accumulated contributions multiplied by the appropriate conversion factor.

(ii) APPROPRIATE CONVERSION FACTOR.—For purposes of clause (i), the term "appropriate conversion factor" means the factor necessary to convert an amount equal to the accumulated contributions to a single life annuity (without ancillary benefits) commencing at normal retirement age and shall be 10 percent for a normal retirement age of 65 years. For other normal retirement ages the conversion factor shall be determined in accordance with regulations prescribed by the Secretary.

P.L. 101-239, §7881(m)(1)(C):

Amended Code Sec. 411(c)(2) by striking subparagraph (E). **Effective** as if included in the provision of P.L. 100-203 to which it relates. Prior to amendment, Code Sec. 411(c)(2)(E) read as follows:

(E) LIMITATION.—The accrued benefit derived from employee contributions shall not exceed the greater of—

(i) the employee's accrued benefit under the plan, or

(ii) the accrued benefit derived from employee contributions determined as though the amounts calculated under clauses (ii) and (iii) of subparagraph (C) were zero.

• 1987, Revenue Act of 1987 (P.L. 100-203)

P.L. 100-203, §9346(b)(1)-(2)(A)-(B):

Amended Code Sec. 411(c)(2) by striking out "5 percent per annum" in subparagraph (C)(iii) and inserting in lieu thereof "120 percent of the Federal mid-term rate (as in effect under section 1274 for the 1st month of a plan year)"; and in the first sentence of subparagraph (D), by striking ", the rate of interest described in clause (iii) of subparagraph (C), or both,"; and by striking the second sentence of subparagraph (D). **Effective**, generally, for plan years beginning after 12-31-87. However, for an exception, see Act Sec. 9346(c)(2), below. Prior to amendment, the second sentence read as follows:

The rate of interest shall bear the relationship to 5 percent which the Secretary determines to be comparable to the relationship which the long-term money rates and investment yields for the last period of 10 calendar years ending at least 12 months before the beginning of the plan year bear to the long-term money rates and investment yields for the

10-calendar year period 1964 through 1973. No such adjustment shall be effective for a plan year beginning before the expiration of 1 year after such adjustment is determined and published.

P.L. 100-203, §9346(c)(2), provides:

(2) PLAN AMENDMENTS NOT REQUIRED UNTIL JANUARY 1, 1989.—If any amendment made by this section requires an amendment to any plan, such plan amendment shall not be required to be made before the first plan year beginning on or after January 1, 1989, if—

(A) during the period after such amendments made by this section take effect and before such first plan year, the plan is operated in accordance with the requirements of such amendments or in accordance with an amendment prescribed by the Secretary of the Treasury and adopted by the plan, and

(B) such plan amendment applies retroactively to the period after such amendments take effect and such first plan year.

A plan shall not be treated as failing to provide definitely determinable benefits or contributions, or to be operated in accordance with the provisions of the plan, merely because it operates in accordance with this subsection.

• 1976, Tax Reform Act of 1976 (P.L. 94-455)

P.L. 94-455, §1906(b)(13)(A):

Amended 1954 Code by substituting "Secretary" for "Secretary or his delegate" each place it appeared. **Effective** 2-1-77.

[Sec. 411(d)]

(d) SPECIAL RULES.—

(1) COORDINATION WITH SECTION 401(a)(4).—A plan which satisfies the requirements of this section shall be treated as satisfying any vesting requirements resulting from the application of section 401(a)(4) unless—

(A) there has been a pattern of abuse under the plan (such as a dismissal of employees before their accrued benefits become nonforfeitable) tending to discriminate in favor of employees who are highly compensated employees (within the meaning of section 414(q)), or

(B) there have been, or there is reason to believe there will be, an accrual of benefits or forfeitures tending to discriminate in favor of employees who are highly compensated employees (within the meaning of section 414(q)).

(2) PROHIBITED DISCRIMINATION.—Subsection (a) shall not apply to benefits which may not be provided for designated employees in the event of early termination of the plan under provisions of the plan adopted pursuant to regulations prescribed by the Secretary to preclude the discrimination prohibited by section 401(a)(4).

(3) TERMINATION OR PARTIAL TERMINATION; DISCONTINUANCE OF CONTRIBUTIONS.—Notwithstanding the provisions of subsection (a), a trust shall not constitute a qualified trust under section 401(a) unless the plan of which such trust is a part provides that—

(A) upon its termination or partial termination, or

(B) in the case of a plan to which section 412 does not apply, upon complete discontinuance of contributions under the plan,

the rights of all affected employees to benefits accrued to the date of such termination, partial termination, or discontinuance, to the extent funded as of such date, or the amounts credited to the employees' accounts, are nonforfeitable. This paragraph shall not apply to benefits or contributions which, under provisions of the plan adopted pursuant to regulations prescribed by the Secretary to preclude the discrimination prohibited by section 401(a)(4), may not be used for designated employees in the event of early termination of the plan. For purposes of this paragraph, in the case of the complete discontinuance of contributions under a profit-sharing or stock bonus plan, such plan shall be treated as having terminated on the day on which the plan administrator notifies the Secretary (in accordance with regulations) of the discontinuance.

(4) [Repealed.]

(5) TREATMENT OF VOLUNTARY EMPLOYEE CONTRIBUTIONS.—In the case of a defined benefit plan which permits voluntary employee contributions, the portion of an employee's accrued benefit derived from such contributions shall be treated as an accrued benefit derived from employee contributions under a plan other than a defined benefit plan.

(6) ACCRUED BENEFIT NOT TO BE DECREASED BY AMENDMENT.—

(A) IN GENERAL.—A plan shall be treated as not satisfying the requirements of this section if the accrued benefit of a participant is decreased by an amendment of the plan, other than an amendment described in section 412(d)(2), or section 4281 of the Employee Retirement Income Security Act of 1974.

(B) TREATMENT OF CERTAIN PLAN AMENDMENTS.—For purposes of subparagraph (A), a plan amendment which has the effect of—

(i) eliminating or reducing an early retirement benefit or a retirement-type subsidy (as defined in regulations), or

(ii) eliminating an optional form of benefit,

with respect to benefits attributable to service before the amendment shall be treated as reducing accrued benefits. In the case of a retirement-type subsidy, the preceding sentence shall apply only with respect to a participant who satisfies (either before or after the amendment) the preamendment conditions for the subsidy. The Secretary shall by regulations provide that this subparagraph shall not apply to any plan amendment which reduces or eliminates benefits or subsidies which create significant burdens or complexities for the plan and plan participants, unless such amendment adversely affects the rights of any participant in a more than de minimis manner. The Secretary may by regulations provide that this subparagraph shall not apply to a plan amendment described in clause (ii) (other than a plan amendment having an effect described in clause (i)).

(C) SPECIAL RULE FOR ESOPS.—For purposes of this paragraph, any—

(i) tax credit employee stock ownership plan (as defined in section 409(a)), or

(ii) employee stock ownership plan (as defined in section 4975(e)(7)),

shall not be treated as failing to meet the requirements of this paragraph merely because it modifies distribution options in a nondiscriminatory manner.

(D) PLAN TRANSFERS.—

(i) IN GENERAL.—A defined contribution plan (in this subparagraph referred to as the "transferee plan") shall not be treated as failing to meet the requirements of this subsection merely because the transferee plan does not provide some or all of the forms of distribution previously available under another defined contribution plan (in this subparagraph referred to as the "transferor plan") to the extent that—

(I) the forms of distribution previously available under the transferor plan applied to the account of a participant or beneficiary under the transferor plan that was transferred from the transferor plan to the transferee plan pursuant to a direct transfer rather than pursuant to a distribution from the transferor plan,

(II) the terms of both the transferor plan and the transferee plan authorize the transfer described in subclause (I),

(III) the transfer described in subclause (I) was made pursuant to a voluntary election by the participant or beneficiary whose account was transferred to the transferee plan,

(IV) the election described in subclause (III) was made after the participant or beneficiary received a notice describing the consequences of making the election, and

(V) the transferee plan allows the participant or beneficiary described in subclause (III) to receive any distribution to which the participant or beneficiary is entitled under the transferee plan in the form of a single sum distribution.

(ii) SPECIAL RULE FOR MERGERS, ETC.—Clause (i) shall apply to plan mergers and other transactions having the effect of a direct transfer, including consolidations of benefits attributable to different employers within a multiple employer plan.

(E) ELIMINATION OF FORM OF DISTRIBUTION.—Except to the extent provided in regulations, a defined contribution plan shall not be treated as failing to meet the requirements of this section merely because of the elimination of a form of distribution previously available thereunder. This subparagraph shall not apply to the elimination of a form of distribution with respect to any participant unless—

(i) a single sum payment is available to such participant at the same time or times as the form of distribution being eliminated, and

(ii) such single sum payment is based on the same or greater portion of the participant's account as the form of distribution being eliminated.

Amendments

• 2008, Worker, Retiree, and Employer Recovery Act of 2008 (P.L. 110-458)

P.L. 110-458, §101(d)(2)(D)(ii):

Amended Code Sec. 411(d)(6)(A) by striking "section 412(e)(2)" and inserting "section 412(d)(2)". **Effective** as if included in the provision of the 2006 Act to which the amendment relates [**effective** for plan years beginning after 2007.—CCH].

• 2006, Pension Protection Act of 2006 (P.L. 109-280)

P.L. 109-280, §114(b)(3):

Amended Code Sec. 411(d)(6)(A) by striking "section 412(c)(8)" and inserting "section 412(e)(2) [412(d)(2)]". **Effective** for plan years beginning after 2007 [**effective** date amended by P.L. 110-458, §101(d)(3).—CCH].

P.L. 109-280, §811, provides:

SEC. 811. PENSIONS AND INDIVIDUAL RETIREMENT ARRANGEMENT PROVISIONS OF ECONOMIC GROWTH AND TAX RELIEF RECONCILIATION ACT OF 2001 MADE PERMANENT.

Title IX of the Economic Growth and Tax Relief Reconciliation Act of 2001 [P.L. 107-16] shall not apply to the provisions of, and amendments made by, subtitles A through F of title VI [§§601-666]of such Act (relating to pension and individual retirement arrangement provisions).

• 2001, Economic Growth and Tax Relief Reconciliation Act of 2001 (P.L. 107-16)

P.L. 107-16, §645(a)(1):

Amended Code Sec. 411(d)(6) by adding at the end new subparagraphs (D) and (E). **Effective** for years beginning after 12-31-2001.

P.L. 107-16, §645(b)(1):

Amended Code Sec. 411(d)(6)(B) by inserting after the second sentence a new sentence. **Effective** on 6-7-2001.

P.L. 107-16, §645(b)(3), provides:

(3) SECRETARY DIRECTED.—Not later than December 31, 2003, the Secretary of the Treasury is directed to issue regulations under section 411(d)(6) of the Internal Revenue Code of 1986 and section 204(g) of the Employee Retirement Income Security Act of 1974, including the regulations required by the amendment made by this subsection. Such regulations shall apply to plan years beginning after December 31, 2003, or such earlier date as is specified by the Secretary of the Treasury.

P.L. 107-16, §901(a)-(b), provides [but see P.L. 109-280, §811, above]:

SEC. 901. SUNSET OF PROVISIONS OF ACT.

(a) IN GENERAL.—All provisions of, and amendments made by, this Act shall not apply—

(1) to taxable, plan, or limitation years beginning after December 31, 2010, or

(2) in the case of title V, to estates of decedents dying, gifts made, or generation skipping transfers, after December 31, 2010.

(b) APPLICATION OF CERTAIN LAWS.—The Internal Revenue Code of 1986 and the Employee Retirement Income Security Act of 1974 shall be applied and administered to years, estates, gifts, and transfers described in subsection (a) as if the provisions and amendments described in subsection (a) had never been enacted.

• 1992, Unemployment Compensation Amendments of 1992 (P.L. 102-318)

P.L. 102-318, §521(b)(44):

Amended Code Sec. 411(d)(3) by adding at the end thereof a new sentence. **Effective** for distributions after 12-31-92.

• 1986, Tax Reform Act of 1986 (P.L. 99-514)

P.L. 99-514, §1113(b):

Repealed Code Sec. 411(d)(4), as amended by Act Sec. 1898(a)(1)(A). **Effective** for plan years beginning after 12-31-88. However, for special rules, see Act Sec. 1113(e)(2) and (3), reproduced under Code Sec. 411(a). Prior to repeal, Code Sec. 411(d)(4) read as follows:

(4) CLASS-YEAR PLANS.—

(A) IN GENERAL.—The requirements of subsection (a)(2) shall be treated as satisfied in the case of a class-year plan if such plan provides that 100 percent of each employee's right to or derived from the contributions of the employer on the employee's behalf with respect to any plan year is nonforfeitable not later than when such participant was performing services for the employer as of the close of each of 5 plan years (whether or not consecutive) after the plan year for which the contributions were made.

(B) 5-YEAR BREAK IN SERVICE.—For purposes of subparagraph (A) if—

(i) any contributions are made on behalf of a participant with respect to any plan year, and

(ii) before such participant meets the requirements of subparagraph (A), such participant was not performing services for the employer as of the close of each of any 5 consecutive plan years after such plan year,

then the plan may provide that the participant forfeits any right to or derived from the contributions made with respect to such plan year.

(C) CLASS-YEAR PLAN.—For purposes of this section, the term "class-year plan" means a profit-sharing, stock bonus, or money purchase plan which provides for the separate nonforfeitability of employees' rights to or derived from the contributions for each plan year.

P.L. 99-514, §1114(b)(10):

Amended Code Sec. 411(d)(1)(A) and (B) by striking out "officers, shareholders, or highly compensated" and inserting in lieu thereof "highly compensated employees (within the meaning of section 414(q))". **Effective** for plan years beginning after 12-31-88. However, for a special rule, see Act Sec. 1114(c)(4), below.

P.L. 99-514, §1114(c)(4), provides:

(4) SPECIAL RULE FOR DETERMINING HIGHLY COMPENSATED EMPLOYEES.—For purposes of sections 401(k) and 401(m) of the Internal Revenue Code of 1986, in the case of an employer incorporated on December 15, 1924, if more than 50 percent of its employees in the top-paid group (within the meaning of section 414(q)(4) of such Code) earn less than $25,000 (indexed at the same time and in the same manner as under section 415(d) of such Code), then the highly compensated employees shall include employees described in section 414(q)(1)(C) of such Code determined without regard to the level of compensation of such employees.

P.L. 99-514, §1898(a)(1)(A):

Amended Code Sec. 411(d)(4). **Effective** for contributions made for plan years beginning after the date of the enactment of this Act; except that, in the case of a plan described in Section 302(b) of P.L. 98-397, it shall not apply to any plan year to which the amendments made by such Act do not apply by reason of section 302(b). Prior to amendment, Code Sec. 411(d)(4) read as follows:

(4) CLASS YEAR PLANS.—The requirements of subsection (a) shall be deemed to be satisfied in the case of a class year plan if such plan provides that 100 percent of each employee's right to or derived from the contributions of the employer on his behalf with respect to any plan year are nonforfeitable not later than the end of the 5th plan year following the plan year for which such contributions were made. For purposes of this section, the term "class year plan" means a profit-sharing, stock bonus, or money purchase plan which provides for the separate nonforfeitability of employees' rights to or derived from the contributions for each plan year.

P.L. 99-514, §1898(f)(1)(A):

Amended Code Sec. 411(d)(6) by adding at the end thereof new subparagraph (C). **Effective** as if included in the provision of P.L. 98-397 to which it relates.

• 1984, Retirement Equity Act of 1984 (P.L. 98-397)

P.L. 98-397, §301(a)(1):

Amended Code Sec. 411(d)(6). **Effective** for plan amendments made after 7-30-84. For special rules, see Act Sec. 302(d)(2), below, and the notes for P.L. 98-397 following Code Sec. 401(a). Prior to amendment, Code Sec. 411(d)(6) read as follows:

(6) ACCRUED BENEFIT NOT TO BE DECREASED BY AMENDMENT.—A plan shall be treated as not satisfying the requirements of this section if the accrued benefit of a participant is decreased by an amendment of the plan, other than an amendment described in section 412(c)(8), or section 4281 of the Employee Retirement Income Security Act of 1974.

P.L. 98-397, §302(d)(2), provides:

(2) SPECIAL RULE FOR COLLECTIVE BARGAINING AGREEMENTS.—In the case of a plan maintained pursuant to 1 or more collective bargaining agreements entered into before January 1, 1985, which are—

(A) between employee representatives and 1 or more employers, and

(B) successor agreements to 1 or more collective bargaining agreements which terminate after July 30, 1984, and before January 1, 1985,

the amendments made by section 301 shall not apply to plan amendments adopted before April 1, 1985, pursuant to such successor agreements (without regard to any modification or reopening after December 31, 1984).

P.L. 98-369, §552, provides:

Sec. 552. Partial Termination for Certain Pension Plans.

For purposes of section 411(d)(3) of the Internal Revenue Code of 1954 (relating to minimum vesting standards in the case of partial terminations), a partial termination shall not be treated as occurring if—

(1) the partial termination is a result of a decline in plan participation which—

(A) occurs by reason of the completion of the Trans-Alaska Oil Pipeline construction project, and

(B) occurred after December 31, 1975, and before January 1, 1980, with respect to participants employed in Alaska,

(2) no discrimination prohibited by section 401(a)(4) of such Code occurred with respect to such partial termination, and

(3) the plan administrator establishes to the satisfaction of the Secretary of the Treasury or his delegate that the benefits of this section will not accrue to the employers under the plan.

• 1980, Multiemployer Pension Plan Amendments Act of 1980 (P.L. 96-364)

P.L. 96-364, §206(5):

Amended Code Sec. 411(d)(6) by substituting "section 412(c)(8), or section 4281 of the Employee Retirement Income Security Act of 1974" for "section 412(c)(8)". **Effective** 9-26-80.

• 1976, Tax Reform Act of 1976 (P.L. 94-455)

P.L. 94-455, §1906(b)(13)(A):

Amended 1954 Code by substituting "Secretary" for "Secretary or his delegate" each place it appeared. **Effective** 2-1-77.

[Sec. 411(e)]

(e) APPLICATION OF VESTING STANDARDS TO CERTAIN PLANS.—

(1) The provisions of this section (other than paragraph (2)) shall not apply to—

(A) A governmental plan (within the meaning of section 414(d)),

(B) a church plan (within the meaning of section 414(e)) with respect to which the election provided by section 410(d) has not been made,

(C) a plan which has not, at any time after September 2, 1974, provided for employer contributions, and

(D) a plan established and maintained by a society, order, or association described in section 501(c)(8) or (9), if no part of the contributions to or under such plan are made by employers of participants in such plan.

(2) A plan described in paragraph (1) shall be treated as meeting the requirements of this section, for purposes of section 401(a), if such plan meets the vesting requirements resulting from the application of sections 401(a)(4) and 401(a)(7) as in effect on September 1, 1974.

Amendments

• 1976, Tax Reform Act of 1976 (P.L. 94-455)

P.L. 94-455, §1901(a)(62)(D):

Amended Code Sec. 411(e)(1)(C) by substituting "September 2, 1974" for "the date of the enactment of the Employee Retirement Income Security Act of 1974". **Effective** with respect to tax years beginning after 12-31-76.

P.L. 94-455, §1901(a)(62)(E):

Amended Code Sec. 411(e)(2) by substituting "September 1, 1974" for "the date before the date of the enactment of the Employee Retirement Income Security Act of 1974". **Effective** with respect to tax years beginning after 12-31-76.

• 1974, Employee Retirement Income Security Act of 1974 (P.L. 93-406)

P.L. 93-406, §1012(a):

Added Code Sec. 411. For **effective** dates and transitional rules governing this section, see the historical note for §1017, P.L. 93-406, following the text of Code Sec. 410(d).

P.L. 93-406, §1012(c), provides:

(c) Variations From Certain Vesting and Accrued Benefits Requirements.—In the case of any plan maintained on January 1, 1974, if, not later than 2 years after the date of the enactment [September 2, 1974] of this Act, the plan administrator petitions the Secretary of Labor, the Secretary of Labor may prescribe an alternate method which shall be treated as satisfying the requirements of subsection (a)(2) of section 411 of the Internal Revenue Code of 1954, or of subsection (b)(1) (other than subparagraph (D) thereof) of such section 411, or of both such provisions for a period of not more than 4 years. The Secretary may prescribe such alternate method only when he finds that—

(1) the application of such requirements would increase the costs of the plan to such an extent that there would result a substantial risk to the voluntary continuation of the plan or a substantial curtailment of benefit levels or the levels of employees' compensation.

(2) the application of such requirements or discontinuance of the plan would be adverse to the interests of plan participants in the aggregate, and

(3) a waiver or extension of time granted under section 412(d) or (e) would be inadequate.

In the case of any plan with respect to which an alternate method has been prescribed under the preceding provisions of this subsection for a period of not more than 4 years, if, not later than 1 year before the expiration of such period, the plan administrator petitions the Secretary of Labor for an extension of such alternate method, and the Secretary makes the findings required by the preceding sentence, such alternate method may be extended for not more than 3 years.

[Sec. 412]

SEC. 412. MINIMUM FUNDING STANDARDS.

[Sec. 412(a)]

(a) REQUIREMENT TO MEET MINIMUM FUNDING STANDARD.—

(1) IN GENERAL.—A plan to which this section applies shall satisfy the minimum funding standard applicable to the plan for any plan year.

(2) MINIMUM FUNDING STANDARD.—For purposes of paragraph (1), a plan shall be treated as satisfying the minimum funding standard for a plan year if—

(A) in the case of a defined benefit plan which is not a multiemployer plan, the employer makes contributions to or under the plan for the plan year which, in the aggregate, are not less than the minimum required contribution determined under section 430 for the plan for the plan year,

(B) in the case of a money purchase plan which is not a multiemployer plan, the employer makes contributions to or under the plan for the plan year which are required under the terms of the plan, and

(C) in the case of a multiemployer plan, the employers make contributions to or under the plan for any plan year which, in the aggregate, are sufficient to ensure that the plan does not have an accumulated funding deficiency under section 431 as of the end of the plan year.

[Sec. 412(b)]

(b) LIABILITY FOR CONTRIBUTIONS.—

(1) IN GENERAL.—Except as provided in paragraph (2), the amount of any contribution required by this section (including any required installments under paragraphs (3) and (4) of

section 430(j)) shall be paid by the employer responsible for making contributions to or under the plan.

(2) JOINT AND SEVERAL LIABILITY WHERE EMPLOYER MEMBER OF CONTROLLED GROUP.—If the employer referred to in paragraph (1) is a member of a controlled group, each member of such group shall be jointly and severally liable for payment of such contributions.

Caution: Code Sec. 412(b)(3), below, was added by P.L. 109-280, §212(c). For sunset provision, see P.L. 109-280, §221(c), in the amendment notes.

(3) MULTIEMPLOYER PLANS IN CRITICAL STATUS.—Paragraph (1) shall not apply in the case of a multiemployer plan for any plan year in which the plan is in critical status pursuant to section 432. This paragraph shall only apply if the plan sponsor adopts a rehabilitation plan in accordance with section 432(e) and complies with such rehabilitation plan (and any modifications of the plan).

Amendments

• 2008, Worker, Retiree, and Employer Recovery Act of 2008 (P.L. 110-458)

P.L. 110-458, §102(b)(2)(H):

Amended Code Sec. 412(b)(3) by striking "the plan adopts" and inserting "the plan sponsor adopts". **Effective** as if included in the provision of the 2006 Act to which the amendment relates [**effective** generally with respect to plan years beginning after 2007.—CCH].

• 2006, Pension Protection Act of 2006 (P.L. 109-280)

P.L. 109-280, §206, provides:

SEC. 206. SPECIAL RULE FOR CERTAIN BENEFITS FUNDED UNDER AN AGREEMENT APPROVED BY THE PENSION BENEFIT GUARANTY CORPORATION.

In the case of a multiemployer plan that is a party to an agreement that was approved by the Pension Benefit Guaranty Corporation prior to June 30, 2005, and that—

(1) increases benefits, and

(2) provides for special withdrawal liability rules under section 4203(f) of the Employee Retirement Income Security Act of 1974 (29 U.S.C. 1383),

the amendments made by sections 201, 202, 211, and 212 of this Act shall not apply to the benefit increases under any plan amendment adopted prior to June 30, 2005, that are funded pursuant to such agreement if the plan is funded in compliance with such agreement (and any amendments thereto).

P.L. 109-280, §212(c):

Amended Code Sec. 412(b), as amended by this Act, by adding at the end a new paragraph (3). **Effective** generally with respect to plan years beginning after 2007. For special rules, see Act Sec. 212(e)(2)-(3), below.

P.L. 109-280, §212(e)(2)-(3) [as amended by P.L. 110-458, §102(b)(3)(C)], provides:

(2) SPECIAL RULE FOR CERTAIN NOTICES.—In any case in which a plan's actuary certifies that it is reasonably expected that a multiemployer plan will be in critical status under section 432(b)(3) of the Internal Revenue Code of 1986, as added by this section, with respect to the first plan year beginning after 2007, the notice required under subparagraph (D) of such section may be provided at any time after the date of enactment, so long as it is provided on or before the last date for providing the notice under such subparagraph.

(3) SPECIAL RULE FOR CERTAIN RESTORED BENEFITS.—In the case of a multiemployer plan—

(A) with respect to which benefits were reduced pursuant to a plan amendment adopted on or after January 1, 2002, and before June 30, 2005, and

(B) which, pursuant to the plan document, the trust agreement, or a formal written communication from the plan sponsor to participants provided before June 30, 2005, provided for the restoration of such benefits,

the amendments made by this section shall not apply to such benefit restorations to the extent that any restriction on the providing or accrual of such benefits would otherwise apply by reason of such amendments.

P.L. 109-280, §221(c), provides:

(c) SUNSET.—

(1) IN GENERAL.—Except as provided in this subsection, notwithstanding any other provision of this Act, the provisions of, and the amendments made by, sections 201(b), 202, and 212 shall not apply to plan years beginning after December 31, 2014.

(2) FUNDING IMPROVEMENT AND REHABILITATION PLANS.—If a plan is operating under a funding improvement or rehabilitation plan under section 305 of such Act or 432 of such Code for its last year beginning before January 1, 2015, such plan shall continue to operate under such funding improvement or rehabilitation plan during any period after December 31, 2014, such funding improvement or rehabilitation plan is in effect and all provisions of such Act or Code relating to the operation of such funding improvement or rehabilitation plan shall continue in effect during such period.

[Sec. 412(c)]

(c) VARIANCE FROM MINIMUM FUNDING STANDARDS.—

(1) WAIVER IN CASE OF BUSINESS HARDSHIP.—

(A) IN GENERAL.—If—

(i) an employer is (or in the case of a multiemployer plan, 10 percent or more of the number of employers contributing to or under the plan are) unable to satisfy the minimum funding standard for a plan year without temporary substantial business hardship (substantial business hardship in the case of a multiemployer plan), and

(ii) application of the standard would be adverse to the interests of plan participants in the aggregate,

the Secretary may, subject to subparagraph (C), waive the requirements of subsection (a) for such year with respect to all or any portion of the minimum funding standard. The Secretary shall not waive the minimum funding standard with respect to a plan for more than 3 of any 15 (5 of any 15 in the case of a multiemployer plan) consecutive plan years[.]

(B) EFFECTS OF WAIVER.—If a waiver is granted under subparagraph (A) for any plan year—

(i) in the case of a defined benefit plan which is not a multiemployer plan, the minimum required contribution under section 430 for the plan year shall be reduced by the amount of the waived funding deficiency and such amount shall be amortized as required under section 430(e), and

(ii) in the case of a multiemployer plan, the funding standard account shall be credited under section 431(b)(3)(C) with the amount of the waived funding deficiency and such amount shall be amortized as required under section 431(b)(2)(C).

(C) WAIVER OF AMORTIZED PORTION NOT ALLOWED.—The Secretary may not waive under subparagraph (A) any portion of the minimum funding standard under subsection (a) for a plan year which is attributable to any waived funding deficiency for any preceding plan year.

(2) DETERMINATION OF BUSINESS HARDSHIP.—For purposes of this subsection, the factors taken into account in determining temporary substantial business hardship (substantial business hardship in the case of a multiemployer plan) shall include (but shall not be limited to) whether or not—

(A) the employer is operating at an economic loss,

(B) there is substantial unemployment or underemployment in the trade or business and in the industry concerned,

(C) the sales and profits of the industry concerned are depressed or declining, and

(D) it is reasonable to expect that the plan will be continued only if the waiver is granted.

(3) WAIVED FUNDING DEFICIENCY.—For purposes of this section and part III of this subchapter, the term "waived funding deficiency" means the portion of the minimum funding standard under subsection (a) (determined without regard to the waiver) for a plan year waived by the Secretary and not satisfied by employer contributions.

(4) SECURITY FOR WAIVERS FOR SINGLE-EMPLOYER PLANS, CONSULTATIONS.—

(A) SECURITY MAY BE REQUIRED.—

(i) IN GENERAL.—Except as provided in subparagraph (C), the Secretary may require an employer maintaining a defined benefit plan which is a single-employer plan (within the meaning of section 4001(a)(15) of the Employee Retirement Income Security Act of 1974) to provide security to such plan as a condition for granting or modifying a waiver under paragraph (1).

(ii) SPECIAL RULES.—Any security provided under clause (i) may be perfected and enforced only by the Pension Benefit Guaranty Corporation, or at the direction of the Corporation, by a contributing sponsor (within the meaning of section 4001(a)(13) of the Employee Retirement Income Security Act of 1974), or a member of such sponsor's controlled group (within the meaning of section 4001(a)(14) of such Act).

(B) CONSULTATION WITH THE PENSION BENEFIT GUARANTY CORPORATION.—Except as provided in subparagraph (C), the Secretary shall, before granting or modifying a waiver under this subsection with respect to a plan described in subparagraph (A)(i)—

(i) provide the Pension Benefit Guaranty Corporation with—

(I) notice of the completed application for any waiver or modification, and

(II) an opportunity to comment on such application within 30 days after receipt of such notice, and

(ii) consider—

(I) any comments of the Corporation under clause (i)(II), and

(II) any views of any employee organization (within the meaning of section 3(4) of the Employee Retirement Income Security Act of 1974) representing participants in the plan which are submitted in writing to the Secretary in connection with such application.

Information provided to the Corporation under this subparagraph shall be considered tax return information and subject to the safeguarding and reporting requirements of section 6103(p).

(C) EXCEPTION FOR CERTAIN WAIVERS.—

(i) IN GENERAL.—The preceding provisions of this paragraph shall not apply to any plan with respect to which the sum of—

(I) the aggregate unpaid minimum required contributions (within the meaning of section 4971(c)(4)) for the plan year and all preceding plan years, and

(II) the present value of all waiver amortization installments determined for the plan year and succeeding plan years under section 430(e)(2),

is less than $1,000,000.

(ii) TREATMENT OF WAIVERS FOR WHICH APPLICATIONS ARE PENDING.—The amount described in clause (i)(I) shall include any increase in such amount which would result if all applications for waivers of the minimum funding standard under this subsection which are pending with respect to such plan were denied.

(5) SPECIAL RULES FOR SINGLE-EMPLOYER PLANS.—

(A) APPLICATION MUST BE SUBMITTED BEFORE DATE 2½ MONTHS AFTER CLOSE OF YEAR.—In the case of a defined benefit plan which is not a multiemployer plan, no waiver may be granted under this subsection with respect to any plan for any plan year unless an application therefor is submitted to the Secretary not later than the 15th day of the 3rd month beginning after the close of such plan year.

(B) SPECIAL RULE IF EMPLOYER IS MEMBER OF CONTROLLED GROUP.—In the case of a defined benefit plan which is not a multiemployer plan, if an employer is a member of a controlled group, the temporary substantial business hardship requirements of paragraph (1) shall be treated as met only if such requirements are met—

(i) with respect to such employer, and

(ii) with respect to the controlled group of which such employer is a member (determined by treating all members of such group as a single employer).

The Secretary may provide that an analysis of a trade or business or industry of a member need not be conducted if the Secretary determines such analysis is not necessary because the taking into account of such member would not significantly affect the determination under this paragraph.

(6) ADVANCE NOTICE.—

(A) IN GENERAL.—The Secretary shall, before granting a waiver under this subsection, require each applicant to provide evidence satisfactory to the Secretary that the applicant has provided notice of the filing of the application for such waiver to each affected party (as defined in section 4001(a)(21) of the Employee Retirement Income Security Act of 1974). Such notice shall include a description of the extent to which the plan is funded for benefits which are guaranteed under title IV of the Employee Retirement Income Security Act of 1974 and for benefit liabilities.

(B) CONSIDERATION OF RELEVANT INFORMATION.—The Secretary shall consider any relevant information provided by a person to whom notice was given under subparagraph (A).

(7) RESTRICTION ON PLAN AMENDMENTS.—

(A) IN GENERAL.—No amendment of a plan which increases the liabilities of the plan by reason of any increase in benefits, any change in the accrual of benefits, or any change in the rate at which benefits become nonforfeitable under the plan shall be adopted if a waiver under this subsection or an extension of time under section 431(d) is in effect with respect to the plan, or if a plan amendment described in subsection (d)(2) which reduces the accrued benefit of any participant has been made at any time in the preceding 12 months (24 months in the case of a multiemployer plan). If a plan is amended in violation of the preceding sentence, any such waiver, or extension of time, shall not apply to any plan year ending on or after the date on which such amendment is adopted.

(B) EXCEPTION.—Subparagraph (A) shall not apply to any plan amendment which—

(i) the Secretary determines to be reasonable and which provides for only de minimis increases in the liabilities of the plan,

(ii) only repeals an amendment described in subsection (d)(2), or

(iii) is required as a condition of qualification under part I of subchapter D, of chapter 1.

Amendments

• 2008, Worker, Retiree, and Employer Recovery Act of 2008 (P.L. 110-458)

P.L. 110-458, §101(a)(2)(A):

Amended Code Sec. 412(c)(1)(A)(i) by striking "the plan is" and inserting "the plan are". **Effective** as if included in the provision of the 2006 Act to which the amendment relates [**effective** for plan years beginning after 2007.—CCH].

P.L. 110-458, §101(a)(2)(B):

Amended Code Sec. 412(c)(7)(A) by inserting "which reduces the accrued benefit of any participant" after "subsection (d)(2)". **Effective** as if included in the provision of the 2006 Act to which the amendment relates [**effective** for plan years beginning after 2007.—CCH].

• 2006, Pension Protection Act of 2006 (P.L. 109-280)

P.L. 109-280, §201(b) [as amended by P.L. 110-458, §102(a)], provides:

(b) SHORTFALL FUNDING METHOD.—

(1) IN GENERAL.—A multiemployer plan meeting the criteria of paragraph (2) may adopt, use, or cease using, the shortfall funding method and such adoption, use, or cessation of use of such method, shall be deemed approved by the Secretary of the Treasury under section 302(d)(1) of the Employee Retirement Income Security Act of 1974 and section 412(d)(1) of the Internal Revenue Code of 1986.

(2) CRITERIA.—A multiemployer pension plan meets the criteria of this clause if—

(A) the plan has not adopted, or ceased using the shortfall funding method during the 5-year period ending on the day before the date the plan is to use the method under paragraph (1); and

(B) the plan is not operating under an amortization period extension under section 304(d) of such Act and did not operate under such an extension during such 5-year period.

(3) SHORTFALL FUNDING METHOD DEFINED.— For purposes of this subsection, the term "shortfall funding method" means the shortfall funding method described in Treasury Regulations section 1.412(c)(1)-2 (26 C.F.R. 1.412(c)(1)-2).

(4) BENEFIT RESTRICTIONS TO APPLY.—The benefit restrictions under section 302(c)(7) of such Act and section 412(c)(7) of such Code shall apply during any period a multiemployer plan is on the shortfall funding method pursuant to this subsection.

(5) USE OF SHORTFALL METHOD NOT TO PRECLUDE OTHER OPTIONS.—Nothing in this subsection shall be construed to affect a multiemployer plan's ability to adopt the shortfall funding method with the Secretary's permission under otherwise applicable regulations or to affect a multiemployer plan's right to change funding methods, with or without the Secretary's consent, as provided in applicable rules and regulations.

P.L. 109-280, §201(d), provides:

(d) EFFECTIVE DATE.—

(1) IN GENERAL.—The amendments made by this section shall apply to plan years beginning after 2007.

(2) SPECIAL RULE FOR CERTAIN AMORTIZATION EXTENSIONS.—If the Secretary of the Treasury grants an extension under

section 304 of the Employee Retirement Income Security Act of 1974 and section 412(e) of the Internal Revenue Code of 1986 with respect to any application filed with the Secretary of the Treasury on or before June 30, 2005, the extension (and any modification thereof) shall be applied and administered under the rules of such sections as in effect before the enactment of this Act, including the use of the rate of interest determined under section 6621(b) of such Code.

[Sec. 412(d)]

(d) MISCELLANEOUS RULES.—

(1) CHANGE IN METHOD OR YEAR.—If the funding method or a plan year for a plan is changed, the change shall take effect only if approved by the Secretary.

(2) CERTAIN RETROACTIVE PLAN AMENDMENTS.—For purposes of this section, any amendment applying to a plan year which—

(A) is adopted after the close of such plan year but no later than $2^1/_2$ months after the close of the plan year (or, in the case of a multiemployer plan, no later than 2 years after the close of such plan year),

(B) does not reduce the accrued benefit of any participant determined as of the beginning of the first plan year to which the amendment applies, and

(C) does not reduce the accrued benefit of any participant determined as of the time of adoption except to the extent required by the circumstances,

shall, at the election of the plan administrator, be deemed to have been made on the first day of such plan year. No amendment described in this paragraph which reduces the accrued benefits of any participant shall take effect unless the plan administrator files a notice with the Secretary notifying him of such amendment and the Secretary has approved such amendment, or within 90 days after the date on which such notice was filed, failed to disapprove such amendment. No amendment described in this subsection shall be approved by the Secretary unless the Secretary determines that such amendment is necessary because of a temporary substantial business hardship (as determined under subsection (c)(2)) or a substantial business hardship (as so determined) in the case of a multiemployer plan and that a waiver under subsection (c) (or, in the case of a multiemployer plan, any extension of the amortization period under section 431(d)) is unavailable or inadequate.

(3) CONTROLLED GROUP.—For purposes of this section, the term "controlled group" means any group treated as a single employer under subsection (b), (c), (m), or (o) of section 414.

Amendments

• 2008, Worker, Retiree, and Employer Recovery Act of 2008 (P.L. 110-458)

P.L. 110-458, §101(a)(2)(C):

Amended Code Sec. 412(d)(1) by striking ", the valuation date," after "If the funding method". **Effective** as if included in the provision of the 2006 Act to which the amendment relates [**effective** for plan years beginning after 2007.—CCH].

[Sec. 412(e)]

(e) PLANS TO WHICH SECTION APPLIES.—

(1) IN GENERAL.—Except as provided in paragraphs (2) and (4), this section applies to a plan if, for any plan year beginning on or after the effective date of this section for such plan under the Employee Retirement Income Security Act of 1974—

(A) such plan included a trust which qualified (or was determined by the Secretary to have qualified) under section 401(a), or

(B) such plan satisfied (or was determined by the Secretary to have satisfied) the requirements of section 403(a).

(2) EXCEPTIONS.—This section shall not apply to—

(A) any profit-sharing or stock bonus plan,

(B) any insurance contract plan described in paragraph (3),

(C) any governmental plan (within the meaning of section 414(d)),

(D) any church plan (within the meaning of section 414(e)) with respect to which the election provided by section 410(d) has not been made,

(E) any plan which has not, at any time after September 2, 1974, provided for employer contributions, or

(F) any plan established and maintained by a society, order, or association described in section 501(c)(8) or (9), if no part of the contributions to or under such plan are made by employers of participants in such plan.

No plan described in subparagraph (C), (D), or (F) shall be treated as a qualified plan for purposes of section 401(a) unless such plan meets the requirements of section 401(a)(7) as in effect on September 1, 1974.

(3) CERTAIN INSURANCE CONTRACT PLANS.—A plan is described in this paragraph if—

(A) the plan is funded exclusively by the purchase of individual insurance contracts,

(B) such contracts provide for level annual premium payments to be paid extending not later than the retirement age for each individual participating in the plan, and commencing with the date the individual became a participant in the plan (or, in the case of an increase in benefits, commencing at the time such increase becomes effective),

(C) benefits provided by the plan are equal to the benefits provided under each contract at normal retirement age under the plan and are guaranteed by an insurance carrier (licensed under the laws of a State to do business with the plan) to the extent premiums have been paid,

(D) premiums payable for the plan year, and all prior plan years, under such contracts have been paid before lapse or there is reinstatement of the policy,

(E) no rights under such contracts have been subject to a security interest at any time during the plan year, and

(F) no policy loans are outstanding at any time during the plan year.

A plan funded exclusively by the purchase of group insurance contracts which is determined under regulations prescribed by the Secretary to have the same characteristics as contracts described in the preceding sentence shall be treated as a plan described in this paragraph.

(4) CERTAIN TERMINATED MULTIEMPLOYER PLANS.—This section applies with respect to a terminated multiemployer plan to which section 4021 of the Employee Retirement Income Security Act of 1974 applies until the last day of the plan year in which the plan terminates (within the meaning of section 4041A(a)(2) of such Act).

Amendments

• 2006, Pension Protection Act of 2006 (P.L. 109-280)

P.L. 109-280, §111(a):

Amended Code Sec. 412. **Effective** for plan years beginning after 12-31-2007. Prior to amendment, Code Sec. 412 read as follows:

SEC. 412. MINIMUM FUNDING STANDARDS.

[Sec. 412(a)]

(a) GENERAL RULE.—Except as provided in subsection (h), this section applies to a plan if, for any plan year beginning on or after the effective date of this section for such plan—

(1) such plan included a trust which qualified (or was determined by the Secretary to have qualified) under section 401(a), or

(2) such plan satisfied (or was determined by the Secretary to have satisfied) the requirements of section 403(a).

A plan to which this section applies shall have satisfied the minimum funding standard for such plan for a plan year if as of the end of such plan year, the plan does not have an accumulated funding deficiency. For purposes of this section and section 4971, the term "accumulated funding deficiency" means for any plan the excess of the total charges to the funding standard account for all plan years (beginning with the first plan year to which this section applies) over the total credits to such account for such years or, if less, the excess of the total charges to the alternative minimum funding standard account for such plan years over the total credits to such account for such years. In any plan year in which a multiemployer plan is in reorganization, the accumulated funding deficiency of the plan shall be determined under section 418B.

Amendments

• 1984, Deficit Reduction Act of 1984 (P.L. 98-369)

P.L. 98-369, §491(d)(25):

Amended Code Sec. 412(a)(2) by striking out "or 405(a)". **Effective** for obligations issued after 12-31-83.

• 1980, Multiemployer Pension Plan Amendments Act of 1980 (P.L. 96-364)

P.L. 96-364, §208(c):

Amended Code Sec. 412(a) by adding the last sentence. **Effective** 9-26-80.

• 1976, Tax Reform Act of 1976 (P.L. 94-455)

P.L. 94-455, §1906(b)(13)(A):

Amended 1954 Code by substituting "Secretary" for "Secretary or his delegate" each place it appeared. **Effective** 2-1-77.

[Sec. 412(b)]

(b) FUNDING STANDARD ACCOUNT.—

(1) ACCOUNT REQUIRED.—Each plan to which this section applies shall establish and maintain a funding standard account. Such account shall be credited and charged solely as provided in this section.

(2) CHARGES TO ACCOUNT.—For a plan year, the funding standard account shall be charged with the sum of—

(A) the normal cost of the plan for the plan year,

(B) the amounts necessary to amortize in equal annual installments (until fully amortized)—

(i) in the case of a plan in existence on January 1, 1974, the unfunded past service liability under the plan on the first day of the first plan year to which this section applies, over a period of 40 plan years,

(ii) in the case of a plan which comes into existence after January 1, 1974, the unfunded past service liability under the plan on the first day of the first plan year to which this section applies, over a period of 30 plan years,

(iii) separately, with respect to each plan year, the net increase (if any) in unfunded past service liability under the plan arising from plan amendments adopted in such year, over a period of 30 plan years,

(iv) separately, with respect to each plan year, the net experience loss (if any) under the plan, over a period of 5 plan years (15 plan years in the case of a multiemployer plan), and

(v) separately, with respect to each plan year, the net loss (if any) resulting from changes in actuarial assumptions used under the plan, over a period of 10 plan years (30 plan years in the case of a multiemployer plan),

(C) the amount necessary to amortize each waived funding deficiency (within the meaning of subsection (d)(3)) for each prior plan year in equal annual installments (until fully amortized) over a period of 5 plan years (15 plan years in the case of a multiemployer plan),

(D) the amount necessary to amortize in equal annual installments (until fully amortized) over a period of 5 plan years any amount credited to the funding standard account under paragraph (3)(D), and

(E) the amount necessary to amortize in equal annual installments (until fully amortized) over a period of 20 years the contributions which would be required to be made under the plan but for the provisions of subsection (c)(7)(A)(i)(I).

For additional requirements in the case of plans other than multiemployer plans, see subsection (l).

(3) CREDITS TO ACCOUNT.—For a plan year, the funding standard account shall be credited with the sum of—

(A) the amount considered contributed by the employer to or under the plan for the plan year,

(B) the amount necessary to amortize in equal annual installments (until fully amortized)—

(i) separately, with respect to each plan year, the net decrease (if any) in unfunded past service liability under the plan arising from plan amendments adopted in such year, over a period of 30 plan years,

(ii) separately, with respect to each plan year, the net experience gain (if any) under the plan, over a period of 5 plan years (15 plan years in the case of a multiemployer plan), and

(iii) separately, with respect to each plan year, the net gain (if any) resulting from changes in actuarial assumptions used under the plan, over a period of 10 plan years (30 plan years in the case of a multiemployer plan),

(C) the amount of the waived funding deficiency (within the meaning of subsection (d)(3)) for the plan year, and

(D) in the case of a plan year for which the accumulated funding deficiency is determined under the funding standard account if such plan year follows a plan year for which such deficiency was determined under the alternative minimum funding standard, the excess (if any) of any debit balance in the funding standard account (determined without regard to this subparagraph) over any debit balance in the alternative minimum funding standard account.

(4) COMBINING AND OFFSETTING AMOUNTS TO BE AMORTIZED.—Under regulations prescribed by the Secretary, amounts required to be amortized under paragraph (2) or paragraph (3), as the case may be—

(A) may be combined into one amount under such paragraph to be amortized over a period determined on the basis of the remaining amortization period for all items entering into such combined amount, and

(B) may be offset against amounts required to be amortized under the other such paragraph, with the resulting amount to be amortized over a period determined on the basis of the remaining amortization periods for all items entering into whichever of the two amounts being offset is the greater.

(5) INTEREST.—

(A) IN GENERAL.—The funding standard account (and items therein) shall be charged or credited (as determined under regulations prescribed by the Secretary) with interest at the appropriate rate consistent with the rate or rates of interest used under the plan to determine costs.

(B) REQUIRED CHANGE OF INTEREST RATE.—For purposes of determining a plan's current liability and for purposes of determining a plan's required contribution under section 412(l) for any plan year—

(i) IN GENERAL.—If any rate of interest used under the plan to determine cost is not within the permissible range, the plan shall establish a new rate of interest within the permissible range.

(ii) PERMISSIBLE RANGE.—For purposes of this subparagraph—

(I) IN GENERAL.—Except as provided in subclause (II) or (III), the term "permissible range" means a rate of interest which is not more than 10 percent above, and not more than 10 percent below, the weighted average of the rates of interest on 30-year Treasury securities during the 4-year period ending on the last day before the beginning of the plan year.

(II) SPECIAL RULE FOR YEARS 2004, 2005, 2006, AND 2007.—In the case of plan years beginning after December 31, 2003, and before January 1, 2008, the term "permissible range" means a rate of interest which is not above, and not more than 10 percent below, the weighted average of the rates of interest on amounts invested conservatively in long-term investment grade corporate bonds during the 4-year period ending on the last day before the beginning of the plan year. Such rates shall be determined by the Secretary on the basis of 2 or more indices that are selected periodically by the Secretary and that are in the top 3 quality levels available. The Secretary shall make the permissible range, and the indices and methodology used to determine the average rate, publicly available.

(III) SECRETARIAL AUTHORITY.—If the Secretary finds that the lowest rate of interest permissible under subclause (I) or (II) is unreasonably high, the Secretary may prescribe a lower rate of interest, except that such rate may not be less than 80 percent of the average rate determined under such subclause.

(iii) ASSUMPTIONS.—Notwithstanding subsection (c)(3)(A)(i), the interest rate used under the plan shall be—

(I) determined without taking into account the experience of the plan and reasonable expectations, but

(II) consistent with the assumptions which reflect the purchase rates which would be used by insurance companies to satisfy the liabilities under the plan.

(6) CERTAIN AMORTIZATION CHARGES AND CREDITS.—In the case of a plan which, immediately before the date of the enactment of the Multiemployer Pension Plan Amendments Act of 1980, was a multiemployer plan (within the meaning of section 414(f) as in effect immediately before such date)—

(A) any amount described in paragraph (2)(B)(ii), (2)(B)(iii), or (3)(B)(i) of this subsection which arose in a plan year beginning before such date shall be amortized in equal annual installments (until fully amortized) over 40 plan years, beginning with the plan year in which the amount arose;

(B) any amount described in paragraph (2)(B)(iv) or (3)(B)(ii) of this subsection which arose in a plan year beginning before such date shall be amortized in equal annual installments (until fully amortized) over 20 plan years, beginning with the plan year in which the amount arose;

(C) any change in past service liability which arises during the period of 3 plan years beginning on or after such date, and results from a plan amendment adopted before such date, shall be amortized in equal annual installments (until fully amortized) over 40 plan years, beginning with the plan year in which the change arises; and

(D) any change in past service liability which arises during the period of 2 plan years beginning on or after such date, and results from the changing of a group of participants from one benefit level to another benefit level under a schedule of plan benefits which—

(i) was adopted before such date, and

(ii) was effective for any plan participant before the beginning of the first plan year beginning on or after such date,

shall be amortized in equal annual installments (until fully amortized) over 40 plan years, beginning with the plan year in which the change arises.

(7) SPECIAL RULES FOR MULTIEMPLOYER PLANS.—For purposes of this section—

(A) WITHDRAWAL LIABILITY.—Any amount received by a multiemployer plan in payment of all or part of an employer's withdrawal liability under part 1 of subtitle E of title IV of the Employee Retirement Income Security Act of 1974 shall be considered an amount contributed by the employer to or under the plan. The Secretary may prescribe by regulation additional charges and credits to a multiemployer plan's funding standard account to the extent necessary to prevent withdrawal liability payments from being unduly reflected as advance funding for plan liabilities.

(B) ADJUSTMENTS WHEN A MULTIEMPLOYER PLAN LEAVES REORGANIZATION.—If a multiemployer plan is not in reorganization in the plan year but was in reorganization in the immediately preceding plan year, any balance in the funding standard account at the close of such immediately preceding plan year—

(i) shall be eliminated by an offsetting credit or charge (as the case may be), but

(ii) shall be taken into account in subsequent plan years by being amortized in equal annual installments (until fully amortized) over 30 plan years.

The preceding sentence shall not apply to the extent of any accumulated funding deficiency under section 418B(a) as of the end of the last plan year that the plan was in reorganization.

(C) PLAN PAYMENTS TO SUPPLEMENTAL PROGRAM OR WITHDRAWAL LIABILITY PAYMENT FUND.—Any amount paid by a plan during a plan year to the Pension Benefit Guaranty Corporation pursuant to section 4222 of such Act or to a fund exempt under section 501(c)(22) pursuant to section 4223 of such Act shall reduce the amount of contributions considered received by the plan for the plan year.

(D) INTERIM WITHDRAWAL LIABILITY PAYMENTS.—Any amount paid by an employer pending a final determination of the employer's withdrawal liability under part 1 of subtitle E of title IV of such Act and subsequently refunded to the employer by the plan shall be charged to the funding standard account in accordance with regulations prescribed by the Secretary.

(E) For purposes of the full funding limitation under subsection (c)(7), unless otherwise provided by the plan, the accrued liability under a multiemployer plan shall not include benefits which are not nonforfeitable under the plan after the termination of the plan (taking into consideration section 411(d)(3)).

(F) ELECTION FOR DEFERRAL OF CHARGE FOR PORTION OF NET EXPERIENCE LOSS.—

(i) IN GENERAL.—With respect to the net experience loss of an eligible multiemployer plan for the first plan year beginning after December 31, 2001, the plan sponsor may elect to defer up to 80 percent of the amount otherwise required to be charged under paragraph (2)(B)(iv) for any plan year beginning after June 30, 2003, and before July 1, 2005, to any plan year selected by the plan from either of the 2 immediately succeeding plan years.

(ii) INTEREST.—For the plan year to which a charge is deferred pursuant to an election under clause (i), the funding standard account shall be charged with interest on the deferred charge for the period of deferral at the rate determined under subsection (d) for multiemployer plans.

(iii) RESTRICTIONS ON BENEFIT INCREASES.—No amendment which increases the liabilities of the plan by reason of any increase in benefits, any change in the accrual of benefits, or any change in the rate at which benefits become nonforfeitable under the plan shall be adopted during any period for which a charge is deferred pursuant to an election under clause (i), unless—

(I) the plan's enrolled actuary certifies (in such form and manner prescribed by the Secretary) that the amendment provides for an increase in annual contributions which will exceed the increase in annual charges to the funding standard account attributable to such amendment, or

(II) the amendment is required by a collective bargaining agreement which is in effect on the date of enactment of this subparagraph.

If a plan is amended during any such plan year in violation of the preceding sentence, any election under this paragraph shall not apply to any such plan year ending on or after the date on which such amendment is adopted.

(iv) ELIGIBLE MULTIEMPLOYER PLAN.—For purposes of this subparagraph, the term "eligible multiemployer plan" means a multiemployer plan—

(I) which had a net investment loss for the first plan year beginning after December 31, 2001, of at least 10 percent of the average fair market value of the plan assets during the plan year, and

(II) with respect to which the plan's enrolled actuary certifies (not taking into account the application of this subparagraph), on the basis of the acutuarial assumptions used for the last plan year ending before the date of the enactment of this subparagraph, that the plan is projected to have an accumulated funding deficiency (within the meaning of subsection (a)) for any plan year beginning after June 30, 2003, and before July 1, 2006.

For purposes of subclause (I), a plan's net investment loss shall be determined on the basis of the actual loss and not under any actuarial method used under subsection (c)(2).

(v) EXCEPTION TO TREATMENT OF ELIGIBLE MULTIEMPLOYER PLAN.—In no event shall a plan be treated as an eligible multiemployer plan under clause (iv) if—

(I) for any taxable year beginning during the 10-year period preceding the first plan year for which an election is made under clause (i), any employer required to contribute to the plan failed to timely pay any excise tax imposed under section 4971 with respect to the plan,

(II) for any plan year beginning after June 30, 1993, and before the first plan year for which an election is made under clause (i), the average contribution required to be made by all employers to the plan does not exceed 10 cents per hour or no employer is required to make contributions to the plan, or

(III) with respect to any of the plan years beginning after June 30, 1993, and before the first plan year for which an election is made under clause (i), a waiver was granted under section 412(d) or section 303 of the Employee Retirement Income Security Act of 1974 with respect to the plan or an extension of an amortization period was granted under subsection (e) or section 304 of such Act with respect to the plan.

(vi) ELECTION.—An election under this subparagraph shall be made at such time and in such manner as the Secretary may prescribe.

Amendments

• 2006, Pension Protection Act of 2006 (P.L. 109-280)

P.L. 109-280, §104 (as amended by P.L. 111-192, §202(b)), provides:

SEC. 104. SPECIAL RULES FOR MULTIPLE EMPLOYER PLANS OF CERTAIN COOPERATIVES.

(a) GENERAL RULE.—Except as provided in this section, if a plan in existence on July 26, 2005, was an eligible cooperative plan or an eligible charity plan for its plan year which includes such date, the amendments made by this subtitle and subtitle B shall not apply to plan years beginning before the earlier of—

(1) the first plan year for which the plan ceases to be an eligible cooperative plan or an eligible charity plan, or

(2) January 1, 2017.

(b) INTEREST RATE.—In applying section 302(b)(5)(B) of the Employee Retirement Income Security Act of 1974 and section 412(b)(5)(B) of the Internal Revenue Code of 1986 (as in effect before the amendments made by this subtitle and subtitle B) to an eligible cooperative plan or an eligible charity plan for plan years beginning after December 31, 2007, and before the first plan year to which such amendments apply, the third segment rate determined under section 303(h)(2)(C)(iii) of such Act and section 430(h)(2)(C)(iii) of such Code (as added by such amendments) shall be used in lieu of the interest rate otherwise used.

(c) ELIGIBLE COOPERATIVE PLAN DEFINED.—For purposes of this section, a plan shall be treated as an eligible cooperative plan for a plan year if the plan is maintained by more than 1 employer and at least 85 percent of the employers are—

(1) rural cooperatives (as defined in section 401(k)(7)(B) of such Code without regard to clause (iv) thereof), or

(2) organizations which are—

(A) cooperative organizations described in section 1381(a) of such Code which are more than 50-percent owned by agricultural producers or by cooperatives owned by agricultural producers, or

(B) more than 50-percent owned, or controlled by, one or more cooperative organizations described in subparagraph (A).

A plan shall also be treated as an eligible cooperative plan for any plan year for which it is described in section 210(a) of the Employee Retirement Income Security Act of 1974 and is maintained by a rural telephone cooperative association described in section 3(40)(B)(v) of such Act.

(d) ELIGIBLE CHARITY PLAN DEFINED.—For purposes of this section, a plan shall be treated as an eligible charity plan for a plan year if the plan is maintained by more than one employer (determined without regard to section 414(c) of the Internal Revenue Code) and 100 percent of the employers are described in section 501(c)(3) of such Code.

P.L. 109-280, §105, provides:

SEC. 105. TEMPORARY RELIEF FOR CERTAIN PBGC SETTLEMENT PLANS.

(a) GENERAL RULE.—Except as provided in this section, if a plan in existence on July 26, 2005, was a PBGC settlement plan as of such date, the amendments made by this subtitle and subtitle B shall not apply to plan years beginning before January 1, 2014.

(b) INTEREST RATE.—In applying section 302(b)(5)(B) of the Employee Retirement Income Security Act of 1974 and section 412(b)(5)(B) of the Internal Revenue Code of 1986 (as in effect before the amendments made by this subtitle and subtitle B), to a PBGC settlement plan for plan years beginning after December 31, 2007, and before January 1, 2014, the third segment rate determined under section 303(h)(2)(C)(iii) of such Act and section 430(h)(2)(C)(iii) of such Code (as added by such amendments) shall be used in lieu of the interest rate otherwise used.

(c) PBGC SETTLEMENT PLAN.—For purposes of this section, the term "PBGC settlement plan" means a defined benefit plan (other than a multiemployer plan) to which section 302 of such Act and section 412 of such Code apply and—

(1) which was sponsored by an employer which was in bankruptcy, giving rise to a claim by the Pension Benefit Guaranty Corporation of not greater than $150,000,000, and the sponsorship of which was assumed by another employer that was not a member of the same controlled group as the bankrupt sponsor and the claim of the Pension Benefit Guaranty Corporation was settled or withdrawn in connection with the assumption of the sponsorship, or

(2) which, by agreement with the Pension Benefit Guaranty Corporation, was spun off from a plan subsequently terminated by such Corporation under section 4042 of the Employee Retirement Income Security Act of 1974.

P.L. 109-280, §106(a)-(c), provides:

SEC. 106. SPECIAL RULES FOR PLANS OF CERTAIN GOVERNMENT CONTRACTORS.

(a) GENERAL RULE.—Except as provided in this section, if a plan is an eligible government contractor plan, this subtitle and subtitle B shall not apply to plan years beginning before the earliest of—

(1) the first plan year for which the plan ceases to be an eligible government contractor plan,

(2) the effective date of the Cost Accounting Standards Pension Harmonization Rule, or

(3) January 1, 2011.

(b) INTEREST RATE.—In applying section 302(b)(5)(B) of the Employee Retirement Income Security Act of 1974 and section 412(b)(5)(B) of the Internal Revenue Code of 1986 (as in effect before the amendments made by this subtitle and subtitle B) to an eligible government contractor plan for plan years beginning after December 31, 2007, and before the first plan year to which such amendments apply, the third segment rate determined under section 303(h)(2)(C)(iii) of such Act and section 430(h)(2)(C)(iii) of such Code (as added by such amendments) shall be used in lieu of the interest rate otherwise used.

(c) ELIGIBLE GOVERNMENT CONTRACTOR PLAN DEFINED.—For purposes of this section, a plan shall be treated as an eligible government contractor plan if it is maintained by a corporation or a member of the same affiliated group (as defined by section 1504(a) of the Internal Revenue Code of 1986), whose primary source of revenue is derived from business performed under contracts with the United States that are subject to the Federal Acquisition Regulations (Chapter 1 of Title 48, C.F.R.) and that are also subject to the Defense Federal Acquisition Regulation Supplement (Chapter 2 of Title 48, C.F.R.), and whose revenue derived from such business in the previous fiscal year exceeded $5,000,000,000, and whose pension plan costs that are assignable under those contracts are subject to sections 412 and 413 of the Cost Accounting Standards (48 C.F.R. 9904.412 and 9904.413).

P.L. 109-280, §301(b)(1)(A)-(B):

Amended Code Sec. 412(b)(5)(B)(ii)(II) by striking "2006" and inserting "2008", and by striking "AND 2005" in the heading and inserting ", 2005, 2006, AND 2007". **Effective** 8-17-2006.

• 2004, Pension Funding Equity Act of 2004 (P.L. 108-218)

P.L. 108-218, §101(b)(1)(A):

Amended Code Sec. 412(b)(5)(B)(ii) by redesignating subclause (II) as subclause (III) and by inserting after subclause (I) a new subclause (II). **Effective** for plan years beginning after 12-31-2003.

P.L. 108-218, §101(b)(1)(B)(i)-(ii):

Amended Code Sec. 412(b)(5)(B)(ii)(III), as redesignated by Act Sec. 101(b)(1)(A), by inserting "or (II)" after "subclause (I)" the first place it appears, and by striking "subclause (I)" the second place it appears and inserting "such subclause". **Effective** for plan years beginning after 12-31-2003.

P.L. 108-218, §101(b)(1)(C):

Amended Code Sec. 412(b)(5)(B)(ii)(I) by inserting "or (III)" after "subclause (II)". **Effective** for plan years beginning after 12-31-2003.

P.L. 108-218, §101(c)(1)-(2) [as amended by P.L. 109-280, §301(c), and P.L. 110-458, §103(a)], provides:

(c) PROVISIONS RELATING TO PLAN AMENDMENTS.—

(1) IN GENERAL.—If this subsection applies to any plan or annuity contract amendment—

(A) such plan or contract shall be treated as being operated in accordance with the terms of the plan or contract during the period described in paragraph (2)(B)(i), and

(B) except as provided by the Secretary of the Treasury, such plan shall not fail to meet the requirements of section 411(d)(6) of the Internal Revenue Code of 1986 and section 204(g) of the Employee Retirement Income Security Act of 1974 by reason of such amendment.

(2) AMENDMENTS TO WHICH SECTION APPLIES.—

(A) IN GENERAL.—This subsection shall apply to any amendment to any plan or annuity contract which is made—

(i) pursuant to any amendment made by this section, and

(ii) on or before the last day of the first plan year beginning on or after January 1, 2009.

(B) CONDITIONS.—This subsection shall not apply to any plan or annuity contract amendment unless—

(i) during the period beginning on the date the amendment described in subparagraph (A)(i) takes effect and ending on the date described in subparagraph (A)(ii) (or, if earlier, the date the plan or contract amendment is adopted), the plan or contract is operated as if such plan or contract amendment were in effect; and

(ii) such plan or contract amendment applies retroactively for such period.

P.L. 108-218, §104(b):

Amended Code Sec. 412(b)(7) by adding at the end a new subparagraph (F). **Effective** 4-10-2004.

• 1997, Taxpayer Relief Act of 1997 (P.L. 105-34)

P.L. 105-34, §1521(c)(1):

Amended Code Sec. 412(b)(2) by striking "and" at the end of subparagraph (C), by striking the period at the end of subparagraph (D) and inserting ", and", and by inserting after subparagraph (D) a new subparagraph (E). **Effective**, generally, for plan years beginning after 12-31-98. For a special rule, see Act Sec. 1521(d)(2)(A)-(B) below.

P.L. 105-34, §1521(d)(2)(A)-(B), provides:

(2) SPECIAL RULE FOR UNAMORTIZED BALANCES UNDER EXISTING LAW.—The unamortized balance (as of the close of the plan year preceding the plan's first year beginning in 1999) of any amortization base established under section 412(c)(7)(D)(iii) of such Code and section 302(c)(7)(D)(iii) of such Act (as repealed by subsection (c)(3)) for any plan year beginning before 1999 shall be amortized in equal annual installments (until fully amortized) over a period of years equal to the excess of—

(A) 20 years, over

(B) the number of years since the amortization base was established.

• 1989, Omnibus Budget Reconciliation Act of 1989 (P.L. 101-239)

P.L. 101-239, §7881(d)(1)(A):

Amended Code Sec. 412(b)(5)(B)(iii) by striking "for purposes of this section and for purposes of determining current liability," after "subsection (c)(3)(A)(i),". **Effective** as if included in the provision of P.L. 100-203 to which it relates.

• 1987, Revenue Act of 1987 (P.L. 100-203)

P.L. 100-203, §9303(a)(2):

Amended Code Sec. 412(b)(2) by adding at the end thereof a new sentence. **Effective** with respect to plan years beginning after 12-31-88. However, for a special rule for steel companies, see Act Sec. 9303(e)(3) in the amendment notes following Code Sec. 412(l).

P.L. 100-203, §9307(a)(1)(A):

Amended Code Sec. 412(b)(2)(B)(iv), (2)(C), and (3)(B)(ii) by striking out "15 plan years" and inserting in lieu thereof "5 plan years (15 plan years in the case of a multiemployer plan)". **Effective** for years beginning after 12-31-87. For exceptions, see Act Sec. 9307(f)(2), below [**effective** date amended by P.L. 101-239, §7881(d)(3).—CCH].

P.L. 100-203, §9307(a)(1)(B):

Amended Code Sec. 412(b)(2)(B)(v) and (3)(B)(iii) by striking out "30 plan years" and inserting in lieu thereof "10 plan years (30 plan years in the case of a multiemployer plan)". **Effective** for years beginning after 12-31-87. For exceptions, see Act Sec. 9307(f)(2), below [**effective** date amended by P.L. 101-239, §7881(d)(3).—CCH].

P.L. 100-203, §9307(e)(1):

Amended Code Sec. 412(b)(5). **Effective** for years beginning after 12-31-87. For exceptions, see Act Sec. 9307(f)(2), below [**effective** date amended by P.L. 101-239, §7881(d)(3).—CCH]. Prior to amendment, Code Sec. 412(b)(5) read as follows:

(5) INTEREST.—The funding standard account (and items therein) shall be charged or credited (as determined under regulations prescribed by the Secretary) with interest at the appropriate rate consistent with the rate or rates of interest used under the plan to determine costs.

P.L. 100-203, §9307(f)(2), as amended by P.L. 100-239, §7881(d)(3), provides:

(2) AMORTIZATION OF GAINS AND LOSSES.—Sections 412(b)(2)(B)(iv) and 412(b)(3)(B)(ii) of the Internal Revenue Code of 1986 and sections 302(b)(2)(B)(iv) and 302(b)(3)(B)(ii) of the Employee Retirement Income Security Act of 1974 (as amended by paragraphs (1)(A) and (2)(A) of subsection (a)) shall apply to gains and losses established in years beginning after December 31, 1987. For purposes of the preceding sentence, any gain or loss determined by a valuation occurring as of January 1, 1988, shall be treated as established in years beginning before 1988 or at the election of the employer, shall be amortized in accordance with Internal Revenue Service Notice 89-52.

• 1980, Multiemployer Pension Plan Amendments Act of 1980 (P.L. 96-364)

P.L. 96-364, §203(1):

Amended Code Secs. 412(b)(2)(B)(ii) and (iii) and 412(b)(3)(B)(i) by striking out "(40 plan years in the case of a multiemployer plan)" following "30 plan years", amended Code Secs. 412(b)(2)(B)(iv) and 412(b)(3)(B)(ii) by striking out "(20 plan years in the case of a multiemployer plan)" following "15 plan years". **Effective** 9-26-80.

P.L. 96-364, §203(2):

Added Code Sec. 412(b)(6) and (7).

• 1976, Tax Reform Act of 1976 (P.L. 94-455)

P.L. 94-455, §1906(b)(13)(A):

Amended 1954 Code by substituting "Secretary" for "Secretary or his delegate" each place it appeared. **Effective** 2-1-77.

[Sec. 412(c)]

(c) SPECIAL RULES.—

(1) DETERMINATIONS TO BE MADE UNDER FUNDING METHOD.—For purposes of this section, normal costs, accrued liability, past service liabilities, and experience gains and losses shall be determined under the funding method used to determine costs under the plan.

(2) VALUATION OF ASSETS.—

(A) IN GENERAL.—For purposes of this section, the value of the plan's assets shall be determined on the basis of any reasonable actuarial method of valuation which takes into account fair market value and which is permitted under regulations prescribed by the Secretary.

(B) ELECTION WITH RESPECT TO BONDS.—The value of a bond or other evidence of indebtedness which is not in default as to principal or interest may, at the election of the plan administrator, be determined on an amortized basis running from initial cost at purchase to par value at maturity or earliest call date. Any election under this subparagraph shall be made at such time and in such manner as the Secretary shall by regulations provide, shall apply to all such evidences of indebtedness, and may be revoked only with the consent of the Secretary. In the case of a plan other than a multiemployer plan, this subparagraph shall not apply, but the Secretary may by regulations provide that the value of any dedicated bond portfolio of such plan shall be determined by using the interest rate under subsection (b)(5).

(3) ACTUARIAL ASSUMPTIONS MUST BE REASONABLE.—For purposes of this section, all costs, liabilities, rates of interest, and other factors under the plan shall be determined on the basis of actuarial assumptions and methods—

(A) in the case of—

(i) a plan other than a multiemployer plan, each of which is reasonable (taking into account the experience of the plan and reasonable expectations) or which, in the aggregate, result in a total contribution equivalent to that which would be determined if each such assumption and method were reasonable, or

(ii) a multiemployer plan, which, in the aggregate, are reasonable (taking into account the experiences of the plan and reasonable expectations), and

(B) which, in combination, offer the actuary's best estimate of anticipated experience under the plan.

(4) TREATMENT OF CERTAIN CHANGES AS EXPERIENCE GAIN OR LOSS.—For purposes of this section, if—

(A) a change in benefits under the Social Security Act or in other retirement benefits created under Federal or State law, or

(B) a change in the definition of the term "wages" under section 3121, or a change in the amount of such wages taken into account under regulations prescribed for purposes of section 401(a)(5),

results in an increase or decrease in accrued liability under a plan, such increase or decrease shall be treated as an experience loss or gain.

(5) CHANGE IN FUNDING METHOD OR IN PLAN YEAR REQUIRES APPROVAL.—(A) IN GENERAL.—If the funding method for a plan is changed, the new funding method shall become the funding method used to determine costs and liabilities under the plan only if the change is approved by the Secretary. If the plan year for a plan is changed, the new plan year shall become the plan year for the plan only if the change is approved by the Secretary.

(B) APPROVAL REQUIRED FOR CERTAIN CHANGES IN ASSUMPTIONS BY CERTAIN SINGLE-EMPLOYER PLANS SUBJECT TO ADDITIONAL FUNDING REQUIREMENT.—

(i) IN GENERAL.—No actuarial assumption (other than the assumptions described in subsection (l)(7)(C) used to determine the current liability for a plan to which this subparagraph applies may be changed without the approval of the Secretary.

(ii) PLANS TO WHICH SUBPARAGRAPH APPLIES.—This subparagraph shall apply to a plan only if—

(I) the plan is a defined benefit plan (other than a multiemployer plan) to which title IV of the Employee Retirement Income Security Act of 1974 applies;

(II) the aggregate unfunded vested benefits as of the close of the preceding plan year (as determined under section 4006(a)(3)(E)(iii) of the Employee Retirement Income Security Act of 1974) of such plan and all other plans maintained by the contributing sponsors (as defined in section 4001(a)(13) of such Act) and members of such sponsors' controlled groups (as defined in section 4001(a)(14) of such Act) which are covered by title IV of such Act (disregarding plans with no unfunded vested benefits) exceed $50,000,000; and

(III) the change in assumptions (determined after taking into account any changes in interest rate and mortality table) results in a decrease in the unfunded current liability of the plan for the current plan year that exceeds $50,000,000, or that exceeds $5,000,000 and that is 5 percent or more of the current liability of the plan before such change.

(6) FULL FUNDING.—If, as of the close of a plan year, a plan would (without regard to this paragraph) have an accumulated funding deficiency (determined without regard to the alternative minimum funding standard account permitted under subsection (g)) in excess of the full funding limitation—

(A) the funding standard account shall be credited with the amount of such excess, and

(B) all amounts described in paragraphs (2)(B), (C), and (D) and (3)(B) of subsection (b) which are required to be amortized shall be considered fully amortized for purposes of such paragraphs.

(7) FULL-FUNDING LIMITATION.—

(A) IN GENERAL.—For purposes of paragraph (6), the term "full-funding limitation" means the excess (if any) of—

(i) the lesser of (I) in the case of plan years beginning before January 1, 2004, the applicable percentage of current liability (including the expected increase in current liability due to benefits accruing during the plan year), or (II) the accrued liability (including normal cost) under the plan (determined under the entry age normal funding method if such accrued liability cannot be directly calculated under the funding method used for the plan), over

(ii) the lesser of—

(I) the fair market value of the plan's assets, or

(II) the value of such assets determined under paragraph (2).

(B) CURRENT LIABILITY.—For purposes of subparagraph (D) and subclause (I) of subparagraph (A)(i), the term "current liability" has the meaning given such term by subsection (l)(7) (without regard to subparagraphs (C) and (D) thereof) and using the rate of interest used under subsection (b)(5)(B).

(C) SPECIAL RULE FOR PARAGRAPH (6)(B).—For purposes of paragraph (6)(B), subparagraph (A)(i) shall be applied without regard to subclause (I) thereof.

(D) REGULATORY AUTHORITY.—The Secretary may by regulations provide—

(i) for adjustments to the percentage contained in subparagraph (A)(i) to take into account the respective ages or lengths of service of the participants, and

(ii) alternative methods based on factors other than current liability for the determination of the amount taken into account under subparagraph (A)(i).

(E) MINIMUM AMOUNT.—

(i) IN GENERAL.—In no event shall the full-funding limitation determined under subparagraph (A) be less than the excess (if any) of—

(I) 90 percent of the current liability of the plan (including the expected increase in current liability due to benefits accruing during the plan year), over

(II) the value of the plan's assets determined under paragraph (2).

(ii) CURRENT LIABILITY; ASSETS.—For purposes of clause (i)—

(I) the term "current liability" has the meaning given such term by subsection (l)(7) (without regard to subparagraph (D) thereof), and

(II) assets shall not be reduced by any credit balance in the funding standard account.

(F) APPLICABLE PERCENTAGE.—For purposes of subparagraph (A)(i)(I), the applicable percentage shall be determined in accordance with the following table:

In the case of any plan year beginning in—	*The applicable percentage is—*
2002	165
2003	170 .

(8) CERTAIN RETROACTIVE PLAN AMENDMENTS.—For purposes of this section, any amendment applying to a plan year which—

(A) is adopted after the close of such plan year but no later than 2 and one-half months after the close of the plan year (or, in the case of a multiemployer plan, no later than 2 years after the close of such plan year),

(B) does not reduce the accrued benefit of any participant determined as of the beginning of the first plan year to which the amendment applies, and

(C) does not reduce the accrued benefit of any participant determined as of the time of adoption except to the extent required by the circumstances,

shall, at the election of the plan administrator, be deemed to have been made on the first day of such plan year. No amendment described in this paragraph which reduces the accrued benefits of any participant shall take effect unless the plan administrator files a notice with the Secretary of Labor notifying him of such amendment and the Secretary of Labor has approved such amendment, or within 90 days after the date on which such notice was filed, failed to disapprove such amendment. No amendment described in this subsection shall be approved by the Secretary of Labor unless he determines that such amendment is necessary because of a substantial business hardship (as determined under subsection (d)(2)) and that a waiver under subsection (d)(1) is unavailable or inadequate.

(9) ANNUAL VALUATION.—

(A) IN GENERAL.—For purposes of this section, a determination of experience gains and losses and a valuation of the plan's liability shall be made not less frequently than once every year, except that such determination shall be made more frequently to the extent required in particular cases under regulations prescribed by the Secretary.

(B) VALUATION DATE.—

(i) CURRENT YEAR.—Except as provided in clause (ii), the valuation referred to in subparagraph (A) shall be made as of a date within the plan year to which the valuation refers or within one month prior to the beginning of such year.

(ii) USE OF PRIOR YEAR VALUATION.—The valuation referred to in subparagraph (A) may be made as of a date within the plan year prior to the year to which the valuation refers if, as of such date, the value of the assets of the plan are not less than 100 percent of the plan's current liability (as defined in paragraph (7)(B)).

(iii) ADJUSTMENTS.—Information under clause (ii) shall, in accordance with regulations, be actuarially adjusted to reflect significant differences in participants.

(iv) LIMITATION.—A change in funding method to use a prior year valuation, as provided in clause (ii), may not be made unless as of the valuation date within the prior plan year, the value of the assets of the plan are not less than 125 percent of the plan's current liability (as defined in paragraph (7)(B)).

(10) TIME WHEN CERTAIN CONTRIBUTIONS DEEMED MADE.—For purposes of this section—

(A) DEFINED BENEFIT PLANS OTHER THAN MULTIEMPLOYER PLANS.—In the case of a defined benefit plan other than a multiemployer plan, any contributions for a plan year made by an employer during the period—

(i) beginning on the day after the last day of such plan year, and

(ii) ending on the day which is 8½ months after the close of the plan year,

shall be deemed to have been made on such last day.

(B) OTHER PLANS.—In the case of a plan not described in subparagraph (A), any contributions for a plan year made by an employer after the last day of such plan year, but not later than two and one-half months after such day, shall be deemed to have been made on such last day. For purposes of this subparagraph, such two and one-half month period may be extended for not more than six months under regulations prescribed by the Secretary.

(11) LIABILITY FOR CONTRIBUTIONS.—

(A) IN GENERAL.—Except as provided in subparagraph (B), the amount of any contribution required by this section and any required installments under subsection (m) shall be paid by the employer responsible for contributing to or under the plan the amount described in subsection (b)(3)(A).

(B) JOINT AND SEVERAL LIABILITY WHERE EMPLOYER MEMBER OF CONTROLLED GROUP.—

(i) IN GENERAL.—In the case of a plan other than a multiemployer plan, if the employer referred to in subparagraph (A) is a member of a controlled group, each member of such group shall be jointly and severally liable for payment of such contribution or required installment.

(ii) CONTROLLED GROUP.—For purposes of clause (i), the term "controlled group" means any group treated as a single employer under subsection (b), (c), (m), or (o) of section 414.

(12) ANTICIPATION OF BENEFIT INCREASES EFFECTIVE IN THE FUTURE.—In determining projected benefits, the funding method of a collectively bargained plan described in section 413(a) (other than a multiemployer plan) shall anticipate benefit increases scheduled to take effect during the term of the collective bargaining agreement applicable to the plan.

Amendments

• 2006, Pension Protection Act of 2006 (P.L. 109-280)

P.L. 109-280, §811, provides:

SEC. 811. PENSIONS AND INDIVIDUAL RETIREMENT ARRANGEMENT PROVISIONS OF ECONOMIC GROWTH AND TAX RELIEF RECONCILIATION ACT OF 2001 MADE PERMANENT.

Title IX of the Economic Growth and Tax Relief Reconciliation Act of 2001 [P.L. 107-16] shall not apply to the provisions of, and amendments made by, subtitles A through F of title VI [§§601-666]of such Act (relating to pension and individual retirement arrangement provisions).

• **2002, Job Creation and Worker Assistance Act of 2002 (P.L. 107-147)**

P.L. 107-147, §411(v)(1)(A)-(B):

Amended Code Sec. 412(c)(9)(B) by striking "125 percent" and inserting "100 percent" in clause (ii), and by adding at the end a new clause (iv). **Effective** as if included in the provision of P.L. 107-16 to which it relates [**effective** for plan years beginning after 12-31-2001.—CCH].

• **2001, Economic Growth and Tax Relief Reconciliation Act of 2001 (P.L. 107-16)**

P.L. 107-16, §651(a)(1)-(2):

Amended Code Sec. 412(c)(7) by striking "the applicable percentage" in subparagraph (A)(i)(I) and inserting "in the case of plan years beginning before January 1, 2004, the applicable percentage"; and by amending subparagraph (F). **Effective** for plan years beginning after 12-31-2001. Prior to amendment, Code Sec. 412(c)(7)(F) read as follows:

(F) APPLICABLE PERCENTAGE.—For purposes of subparagraph (A)(i)(I), the applicable percentage shall be determined in accordance with the following table:

In the case of any plan year beginning in—	*The applicable percentage is—*
1999 or 2000	155
2001 or 2002	160
2003 or 2004	165
2005 and succeeding years	170

P.L. 107-16, §661(a):

Amended Code Sec. 412(c)(9). **Effective** for plan years beginning after 12-31-2001. Prior to amendment, Code Sec. 412(c)(9) read as follows:

(9) ANNUAL VALUATION.—For purposes of this section a determination of experience gains and losses and a valuation of the plan's liability shall be made not less frequently than once every year, except that such determination shall be made more frequently to the extent required in particular cases under regulations prescribed by the Secretary.

P.L. 107-16, §901(a)-(b), provides [but see P.L. 109-280, §811, above]:

SEC. 901. SUNSET OF PROVISIONS OF ACT.

(a) IN GENERAL.—All provisions of, and amendments made by, this Act shall not apply—

(1) to taxable, plan, or limitation years beginning after December 31, 2010, or

(2) in the case of title V, to estates of decedents dying, gifts made, or generation skipping transfers, after December 31, 2010.

(b) APPLICATION OF CERTAIN LAWS.—The Internal Revenue Code of 1986 and the Employee Retirement Income Security Act of 1974 shall be applied and administered to years, estates, gifts, and transfers described in subsection (a) as if the provisions and amendments described in subsection (a) had never been enacted.

• **1997, Taxpayer Relief Act of 1997 (P.L. 105-34)**

P.L. 105-34, §1521(a)(A)[(1)]-(B)[(2)]:

Amended Code Sec. 412(c)(7) by striking "150 percent" in subparagraph (A)(i)(I) and inserting "the applicable percentage", and by adding at the end a new subparagraph (F). **Effective**, generally, for plan years beginning after 12-31-98. For a special rule, see Act Sec. 1521(d)(2)(A)-(B).

P.L. 105-34, §1521(c)(3)(A):

Amended Code Sec. 412(c)(7)(D) by adding "and" at the end of clause (i), by striking ", and" at the end of clause (ii) and inserting a period, and by striking clause (iii). **Effective**, generally, for plan years beginning after 12-31-98. For a special rule, see Act Sec. 1521(d)(2)(A)-(B). Prior to being stricken, Code Sec. 412(c)(7)(D)(iii) read as follows:

(iii) for the treatment under this section of contributions which would be required to be made under the plan but for the provisions of subparagraph (A)(i)(I).

P.L. 105-34, §1521(d)(2)(A)-(B), provides:

(2) SPECIAL RULE FOR UNAMORTIZED BALANCES UNDER EXISTING LAW.—The unamortized balance (as of the close of the plan year preceding the plan's first year beginning in 1999) of any amortization base established under section 412(c)(7)(D)(iii) of such Code and section 302(c)(7)(D)(iii) of such Act (as repealed by subsection (c)(3)) for any plan year beginning before 1999 shall be amortized in equal annual installments (until fully amortized) over a period of years equal to the excess of—

(A) 20 years, over

(B) the number of years since the amortization base was established.

• **1994, Uruguay Round Agreements Act (P.L. 103-465)**

P.L. 103-465, §751(a)(10)(A):

Amended Code Sec. 412(c)(7)(A)(i) by inserting "(including the expected increase in current liability due to benefits accruing during the plan year)" after "current liability". **Effective** for plan years beginning after 12-31-94.

P.L. 103-465, §751(a)(10)(B):

Amended Code Sec. 412(c)(7) by adding at the end a new subparagraph (E). **Effective** for plan years beginning after 12-31-94.

P.L. 103-465, §751(a)(10)(C):

Amended Code Sec. 412(c)(7)(B). **Effective** for plan years beginning after 12-31-94. Prior to amendment, Code Sec. 412(c)(7)(B) read as follows:

(B) CURRENT LIABILITY.—For purposes of subparagraphs (A) and (D), the term "current liability" has the meaning given such term by subsection (l)(7) (without regard to subparagraph (D) thereof).

P.L. 103-465, §752(a)(1)-(2):

Amended Code Sec. 412(c)(5) by striking "If the funding method" and inserting "(A) IN GENERAL.—If the funding method", and by adding at the end a new subparagraph (B). **Effective** for changes in assumptions for plan years beginning after 10-28-93. For a special rule, see Act Sec. 752(b)(2), below.

P.L. 103-465, §752(b)(2), provides:

(2) CERTAIN CHANGES CEASE TO BE EFFECTIVE.—In the case of changes in assumptions for plan years beginning after December 31, 1992, and on or before October 28, 1993, such changes shall cease to be effective for plan years beginning after December 31, 1994, if—

(A) such change would have required the approval of the Secretary of the Treasury had such amendment applied to such change, and

(B) such change is not so approved.

P.L. 103-465, §753(a):

Amended Code Sec. 412(c) by adding at the end a new paragraph (12). **Effective** for plan years beginning after 12-31-94, with respect to collective bargaining agreements in effect on or after 1-1-95.

• **1989, Omnibus Budget Reconciliation Act of 1989 (P.L. 101-239)**

P.L. 101-239, §7881(a)(6)(A)(i)-(ii):

Amended Code Sec. 412(c)(9) by striking "3 years" and inserting "year", and by striking "3-YEAR" in the heading and inserting "ANNUAL". **E ffective** as if included in the provision of P.L. 100-203 to which it relates.

P.L. 101-239, §7881(b)(1)(A)(i)-(ii):

Amended Code Sec. 412(c)(10)(A) by inserting "defined benefit" before "plan other", and by striking "PLANS" in the heading and inserting "DEFINED BENEFIT PLANS". **E ffective** as if included in the provision of P.L. 100-203 to which it relates.

P.L. 101-239, §7881(b)(2)(A)(i)-(ii):

Amended Code Sec. 412(c)(10)(B) by striking "multiemployer plan" and inserting "plan not described in subparagraph (A)", and by striking "MULTIEMPLOYER" in the heading and inserting "OTHER". **E ffective** as if included in the provision of P.L. 100-203 to which it relates.

• **1987, Revenue Act of 1987 (P.L. 100-203)**

P.L. 100-203, §9301(a):

Amended Code Sec. 412(c)(7). **Effective** for years beginning after 12-31-87. Prior to amendment, Code Sec. 412(c)(7) read as follows:

(7) FULL FUNDING LIMITATION.—For purposes of paragraph (6), the term "full funding limitation" means the excess (if any) of—

(A) the accrued liability (including normal cost) under the plan (determined under the entry age normal funding method if such accrued liability cannot be directly calculated under the funding method used for the plan), over

(B) the lesser of the fair market value of the plan's assets or the value of such assets determined under paragraph (2).

P.L. 100-203, §9303(d)(1):

Amended Code Sec. 412(c)(2)(B) by adding at the end thereof a new sentence. **Effective** for years beginning after 12-31-87.

P.L. 100-203, §9304(a)(1):

Amended Code Sec. 412(c)(10). **Effective** for plan years beginning after 12-31-87. Prior to amendment, Code Sec. 412(c)(10) read as follows:

(10) TIME WHEN CERTAIN CONTRIBUTIONS DEEMED MADE.—For purposes of this section any contributions for a plan year made by an employer after the last day of such plan year, but not later than two and one-half months after such day, shall be deemed to have been made on such last day. For purposes of this paragraph, such two and one-half month period may be extended for not more than six months under regulations prescribed by the Secretary.

P.L. 100-203, §9305(b)(1):

Amended Code Sec. 412(c) by adding at the end thereof a new paragraph (11). **Effective** for plan years beginning after 12-31-87.

P.L. 100-203, §9307(b)(1):

Amended Code Sec. 412(c)(3). **Effective** for years beginning after 12-31-87. Prior to amendment, Code Sec. 412(c)(3) read as follows:

(3) ACTUARIAL ASSUMPTIONS MUST BE REASONABLE.—For purposes of this section, all costs, liabilities, rates of interest, and other factors under the plan shall be determined on the basis of actuarial assumptions and methods which, in the aggregate, are reasonable (taking into account the experience of the plan and reasonable expectations) and which, in combination, offer the actuary's best estimate of anticipated experience under the plan.

• 1976, Tax Reform Act of 1976 (P.L. 94-455)

P.L. 94-455, §1906(b)(13)(A):

Amended 1954 Code by substituting "Secretary" for "Secretary or his delegate" each place it appeared. **Effective** 2-1-77.

[Sec. 412(d)]

(d) VARIANCE FROM MINIMUM FUNDING STANDARD.—

(1) WAIVER IN CASE OF BUSINESS HARDSHIP.—If an employer or in the case of a multiemployer plan, 10 percent or more of the number of employers contributing to or under the plan, are unable to satisfy the minimum funding standard for a plan year without temporary substantial business hardship (substantial business hardship in the case of a multiemployer plan) and if application of the standard would be adverse to the interests of plan participants in the aggregate, the Secretary may waive the requirements of subsection (a) for such year with respect to all or any portion of the minimum funding standard other than the portion thereof determined under subsection (b)(2)(C). The Secretary shall not waive the minimum funding standard with respect to a plan for more than 3 of any 15 (5 of any 15 in the case of a multiemployer plan) consecutive plan years. The interest rate used for purposes of computing the amortization charge described in subsection (b)(2)(C) for any plan year shall be—

(A) in the case of a plan other than a multiemployer plan, the greater of (i) 150 percent of the Federal mid-term rate (as in effect under section 1274 for the 1st month of such plan year), or (ii) the rate of interest used under the plan in determining costs (including adjustments under subsection (b)(5)(B)), and

(B) in the case of a multiemployer plan, the rate determined under section 6621(b).

(2) DETERMINATION OF BUSINESS HARDSHIP.—For purposes of this section, the factors taken into account in determining temporary substantial business hardship (substantial business hardship in the case of a multiemployer plan) shall include (but shall not be limited to) whether or not—

(A) the employer is operating at an economic loss,

(B) there is substantial unemployment or underemployment in the trade or business and in the industry concerned,

(C) the sales and profits of the industry concerned are depressed or declining, and

(D) it is reasonable to expect that the plan will be continued only if the waiver is granted.

(3) WAIVED FUNDING DEFICIENCY.—For purposes of this section, the term "waived funding deficiency" means the portion of the minimum funding standard (determined without regard to subsection (b)(3)(C)) for a plan year waived by the Secretary and not satisfied by employer contributions.

(4) APPLICATION MUST BE SUBMITTED BEFORE DATE 2 1/2 MONTHS AFTER CLOSE OF YEAR.—In the case of a plan other than a multiemployer plan, no waiver may be granted under this subsection with respect to any plan for any plan year unless an application therefor is submitted to the Secretary not later than the 15th day of the 3rd month beginning after the close of such plan year.

(5) SPECIAL RULE IF EMPLOYER IS MEMBER OF CONTROLLED GROUP.—

(A) IN GENERAL.—In the case of a plan other than a multiemployer plan, if an employer is a member of a controlled group, the temporary substantial business hardship requirements of paragraph (1) shall be treated as met only if such requirements are met—

(i) with respect to such employer, and

(ii) with respect to the controlled group of which such employer is a member (determined by treating all members of such group as a single employer).

The Secretary may provide that an analysis of a trade or business or industry of a member need not be conducted if the Secretary determines such analysis is not necessary because the taking into account of such member would not significantly affect the determination under this subsection.

(B) CONTROLLED GROUP.—For purposes of subparagraph (A), the term "controlled group" means any group treated as a single employer under subsection (b), (c), (m), or (o) of section 414.

Amendments

• 1989, Omnibus Budget Reconciliation Act of 1989 (P.L. 101-239)

P.L. 101-239, §7881(b)(6)(A)(ii):

Amended Code Sec. 412(d)(1)(A) by inserting "(including adjustments under subsection (b)(5)(B))" after "costs". **Effective** as if included in the provision of P.L. 100-203 to which it relates.

• 1987, Revenue Act of 1987 (P.L. 100-203)

P.L. 100-203, §9306(a)(1)(A):

Amended Code Sec. 412(d) by adding at the end thereof new paragraph (4). For the **effective** date, see Act Sec. 9306(f)(1)-(3), below.

P.L. 100-203, §9306(a)(1)(B)(i)-(ii):

Amended Code Sec. 412(d) by striking out "substantial business hardship" in paragraphs (1) and (2) and inserting in lieu thereof "temporary substantial business hardship (substantial business hardship in the case of a multiemployer plan)", and by striking out "SUBSTANTIAL" in the headings of paragraphs (1) and (2). For the **effective** date, see Act Sec. 9306(f)(1)-(3), below.

P.L. 100-203, §9306(a)(1)(C):

Amended Code Sec. 412(d) by adding at the end thereof new paragraph (5). For the **effective** date, see Act Sec. 9306(f)(1)-(3), below.

P.L. 100-203, §9306(b)(1):

Amended Code Sec. 412(d)(1) by striking out "more than 5 of any 15" and inserting in lieu thereof "more than 3 of any 15 (5 of any 15 in the case of a multiemployer plan)". For the **effective** date, see Act Sec. 9306(f)(1)-(3), below.

P.L. 100-203, §9306(c)(1)(A):

Amended Code Sec. 412(d)(1) by striking out the last sentence and inserting in lieu thereof a new sentence. For the **effective** date, see Act Sec. 9306(f)(1)-(3), below. Prior to amendment, the last sentence read as follows:

The interest rate used for purposes of computing the amortization charge described in section 412(b)(2)(C) for a variance granted under this subsection shall be the rate determined under section 6621(b).

P.L. 100-203, §9306(f)(1)-(3), as amended by P.L. 101-239, §7881(c)(3), provides as follows:

(f) EFFECTIVE DATES.—

(1) IN GENERAL.—Except as provided in this subsection, the amendments made by this section shall apply in the case of—

(A) any application submitted after December 17, 1987, and

(B) any waiver granted pursuant to such an application.

(2) SPECIAL RULE FOR APPLICATION REQUIREMENT.—

(A) IN GENERAL.—The amendment made by subsections (a)(1)(A) and (a)(2)(A) shall apply to plan years beginning after December 31, 1987.

(B) TRANSITIONAL RULE FOR YEARS BEGINNING IN 1988.—In the case of any plan year beginning during calendar 1988, section 412(d)(4) of the 1986 Code and section 303(d)(1) of ERISA (as added by subsection (a)(1)) shall be applied by substituting "6th month" for "3rd month".

(3) SUBSECTION (b).—The amendments made by subsection (b) shall apply to waivers for plan years beginning after December 31, 1987. For purposes of applying such amendments, the number of waivers which may be granted for plan years after December 31, 1987, shall be determined without regard to any waivers granted for plan years beginning before January 1, 1988.

• 1986, Consolidated Omnibus Budget Reconciliation Act of 1985 (P.L. 99-272)

P.L. 99-272, §11015(b)(2)(A):

Amended Code Sec. 412(d)(1) by adding the sentence at the end thereof. **Effective** as of 1-1-86, except that it shall not apply with respect to terminations for which—

(1) notices of intent to terminate were filed with the Pension Benefit Guaranty Corporation under section 4041 of the Employee Retirement Income Security Act of 1974 before such date, or

(2) proceedings were commenced under section 4042 of such Act before such date.

For transitional rules see Act Sec. 11019(b)-(c) in the amendment notes following Code Sec. 402(a).

• 1976, Tax Reform Act of 1976 (P.L. 94-455)

P.L. 94-455, §1906(b)(13)(A):

Amended 1954 Code by substituting "Secretary" for "Secretary or his delegate" each place it appeared. **Effective** 2-1-77.

[Sec. 412(e)]

(e) EXTENSION OF AMORTIZATION PERIODS.—The period of years required to amortize any unfunded liability (described in any clause of subsection (b)(2)(B)) of any plan may be extended by the Secretary of Labor for a period of time (not in excess of 10 years) if he determines that such extension would carry out the purposes of the Employee Retirement Income Security Act of 1974 and would provide adequate protection for participants under the plan and their beneficiaries and if he determines that the failure to permit such extension would—

(1) result in—

(A) a substantial risk to the voluntary continuation of the plan, or

(B) a substantial curtailment of pension benefit levels or employee compensation, and

(2) be adverse to the interests of plan participants in the aggregate.

In the case of a plan other than a multiemployer plan, the interest rate applicable for any plan year under any arrangement entered into by the Secretary in connection with an extension granted under this subsection shall be the greater of (A) 150 percent of the Federal mid-term rate (as in effect under section 1274 for the 1st month of such plan year), or (B) the rate of interest used under the plan in determining costs. In the case of a multiemployer plan, such rate shall be the rate determined under section 6621(b).

Amendments

• 2006, Pension Protection Act of 2006 (P.L. 109-280)

P.L. 109-280, §107 (as added by P.L. 111-192, §202(a)), provides:

SEC. 107. APPLICATION OF EXTENDED AMORTIZATION PERIODS TO PLANS WITH DELAYED EFFECTIVE DATE.

(a) IN GENERAL.—If the plan sponsor of a plan to which section 104, 105, or 106 of this Act applies elects to have this section apply for any eligible plan year (in this section referred to as an "election year"), section 302 of the Employee Retirement Income Security Act of 1974 and section 412 of the Internal Revenue Code of 1986 (as in effect before the amendments made by this subtitle and subtitle B) shall apply to such year in the manner described in subsection (b) or (c), whichever is specified in the election. All references in this section to "such Act" or "such Code" shall be to such Act or such Code as in effect before the amendments made by this subtitle and subtitle B.

(b) APPLICATION OF 2 AND 7 RULE.—In the case of an election year to which this subsection applies—

(1) 2-YEAR LOOKBACK FOR DETERMINING DEFICIT REDUCTION CONTRIBUTIONS FOR CERTAIN PLANS.—For purposes of applying section 302(d)(9) of such Act and section 412(l)(9) of such Code, the funded current liability percentage (as defined in subparagraph (C) thereof) for such plan for such plan year shall be such funded current liability percentage of such plan for the second plan year preceding the first election year of such plan.

(2) CALCULATION OF DEFICIT REDUCTION CONTRIBUTION.— For purposes of applying section 302(d) of such Act and section 412(l) of such Code to a plan to which such sections apply (after taking into account paragraph (1))—

(A) in the case of the increased unfunded new liability of the plan, the applicable percentage described in section 302(d)(4)(C) of such Act and section 412(l)(4)(C) of such Code shall be the third segment rate described in sections 104(b), 105(b), and 106(b) of this Act, and

(B) in the case of the excess of the unfunded new liability over the increased unfunded new liability, such applicable percentage shall be determined without regard to this section.

(c) APPLICATION OF 15-YEAR AMORTIZATION.—In the case of an election year to which this subsection applies, for purposes of applying section 302(d) of such Act and section 412(l) of such Code—

(1) in the case of the increased unfunded new liability of the plan, the applicable percentage described in section 302(d)(4)(C) of such Act and section 412(l)(4)(C) of such Code for any pre-effective date plan year beginning with or after the first election year shall be the ratio of—

(A) the annual installments payable in each year if the increased unfunded new liability for such plan year were amortized over 15 years, using an interest rate equal to the third segment rate described in sections 104(b), 105(b), and 106(b) of this Act, to

(B) the increased unfunded new liability for such plan year, and

(2) in the case of the excess of the unfunded new liability over the increased unfunded new liability, such applicable percentage shall be determined without regard to this section.

(d) ELECTION.—

(1) IN GENERAL.—The plan sponsor of a plan may elect to have this section apply to not more than 2 eligible plan years with respect to the plan, except that in the case of a plan to which section 106 of this Act applies, the plan sponsor may only elect to have this section apply to 1 eligible plan year.

(2) AMORTIZATION SCHEDULE.—Such election shall specify whether the rules under subsection (b) or (c) shall apply to an election year, except that if a plan sponsor elects to have this section apply to 2 eligible plan years, the plan sponsor must elect the same rule for both years.

(3) OTHER RULES.—Such election shall be made at such time, and in such form and manner, as shall be prescribed by the Secretary of the Treasury, and may be revoked only with the consent of the Secretary of the Treasury.

(e) DEFINITIONS.—For purposes of this section—

(1) ELIGIBLE PLAN YEAR.—For purposes of this subparagraph, the term "eligible plan year" means any plan year beginning in 2008, 2009, 2010, or 2011, except that a plan year beginning in 2008 shall only be treated as an eligible plan year if the due date for the payment of the minimum required contribution for such plan year occurs on or after the date of the enactment of this clause.

(2) PRE-EFFECTIVE DATE PLAN YEAR.—The term "pre-effective date plan year" means, with respect to a plan, any plan year prior to the first year in which the amendments made by this subtitle and subtitle B apply to the plan.

(3) INCREASED UNFUNDED NEW LIABILITY.—The term "increased unfunded new liability" means, with respect to a year, the excess (if any) of the unfunded new liability over the amount of unfunded new liability determined as if the value of the plan's assets determined under subsection 302(c)(2) of such Act and section 412(c)(2) of such Code equaled the product of the current liability of the plan for the year multiplied by the funded current liability percentage (as defined in section 302(d)(8)(B) of such Act and 412(l)(8)(B) of such Code) of the plan for the second plan year preceding the first election year of such plan.

(4) OTHER DEFINITIONS.—The terms "unfunded new liability" and "current liability" shall have the meanings set forth in section 302(d) of such Act and section 412(l) of such Code.

P.L. 109-280, §201(d)(2), provides:

(2) SPECIAL RULE FOR CERTAIN AMORTIZATION EXTENSIONS.—If the Secretary of the Treasury grants an extension under section 304 of the Employee Retirement Income Security Act of 1974 and section 412(e) of the Internal Revenue Code of 1986 with respect to any application filed with the Secretary of the Treasury on or before June 30, 2005, the extension (and any modification thereof) shall be applied and administered under the rules of such sections as in effect before the enactment of this Act, including the use of the rate of interest determined under section 6621(b) of such Code.

• 1987, Revenue Act of 1987 (P.L. 100-203)

P.L. 100-203, §9306(c)(1)(B):

Amended Code Sec. 412(e) by striking out the last sentence and inserting in lieu thereof a new sentence. For the **effective** date, see Act Sec. 9306(f)(1)-(3) in the amendment notes following Code Sec. 412(d). Prior to amendment, the last sentence read as follows:

The interest rate applicable under any arrangement entered into by the Secretary in connection with an extension granted under this subsection shall be the rate determined under section 6621(b).

• 1986, Consolidated Omnibus Budget Reconciliation Act of 1985 (P.L. 99-272)

P.L. 99-272, §11015(b)(2)(B):

Amended Code Sec. 412(e) by adding the last sentence to paragraph (2). **Effective** as of 1-1-86, except that it shall not apply with respect to terminations for which—

(1) notices of intent to terminate were filed with the Pension Benefit Guaranty Corporation under section 4041 of the Employee Retirement Income Security Act of 1974 before such date, or

(2) proceedings were commenced under section 4042 of such Act before such date.

For transitional rules see Act Sec. 11019(b)-(c) in the amendment notes following Code Sec. 402(a).

[Sec. 412(f)]

(f) REQUIREMENTS RELATING TO WAIVERS AND EXTENSIONS.—

(1) BENEFITS MAY NOT BE INCREASED DURING WAIVER OR EXTENSION PERIOD.—No amendment of the plan which increases the liabilities of the plan by reason of any increase in benefits, any change in the accrual of benefits, or any change in the rate at which benefits become nonforfeitable under the plan shall be adopted if a waiver under subsection (d)(1) or an extension of time under subsection (e) is in effect with respect to the plan, or if a plan amendment described in subsection (c)(8) has been made at any time in the preceding 12 months (24 months for multiemployer plans). If a plan is amended in violation of the preceding sentence, any such waiver or extension of time shall not apply to any plan year ending on or after the date on which such amendment is adopted.

(2) EXCEPTION.—Paragraph (1) shall not apply to any plan amendment which—

(A) the Secretary of Labor determines to be reasonable and which provides for only de minimis increases in the liabilities of the plan,

(B) only repeals an amendment described in subsection (c)(8), or

(C) is required as a condition of qualification under this part.

(3) SECURITY FOR WAIVERS AND EXTENSIONS; CONSULTATIONS.—

(A) SECURITY MAY BE REQUIRED.—

(i) IN GENERAL.—Except as provided in subparagraph (C), the Secretary may require an employer maintaining a defined benefit plan which is a single-employer plan (within the meaning of section 4001(a)(15) of the Employee Retirement Income Security Act of 1974) to provide security to such plan as a condition for granting or modifying a waiver under subsection (d) or an extension under subsection (e).

(ii) SPECIAL RULES.—Any security provided under clause (i) may be perfected and enforced only by the Pension Benefit Guaranty Corporation, or at the direction of the Corporation, by a contributing sponsor (within the meaning of section 4001(a)(13) of such Act), or a member of such sponsor's controlled group (within the meaning of section 4001(a)(14) of such Act).

(B) CONSULTATION WITH THE PENSION BENEFIT GUARANTY CORPORATION.—Except as provided in subparagraph (C), the Secretary shall, before granting or modifying a waiver under subsection (d) or an extension under subsection (e) with respect to a plan described in subparagraph (A)(i)—

(i) provide the Pension Benefit Guaranty Corporation with—

(I) notice of the completed application for any waiver, extension, or modification, and

(II) an opportunity to comment on such application within 30 days after receipt of such notice, and

(ii) consider—

(I) any comments of the Corporation under clause (i)(II), and

(II) any views of any employee organization (within the meaning of section 3(4) of the Employee Retirement Income Security Act of 1974) representing participants in the plan which are submitted in writing to the Secretary in connection with such application.

Information provided to the corporation under this subparagraph shall be considered tax return information and subject to the safeguarding and reporting requirements of section 6103(p).

(C) EXCEPTION FOR CERTAIN WAIVERS AND EXTENSIONS.

(i) IN GENERAL.—The preceding provisions of this paragraph shall not apply to any plan with respect to which the sum of—

(I) the outstanding balance of the accumulated funding deficiencies (within the meaning of subsection (a) and section 302(a) of such Act) of the plan,

(II) the outstanding balance of the amount of waived funding deficiencies of the plan waived under subsection (d) or section 303 of such Act, and

(III) the outstanding balance of the amount of decreases in the minimum funding standard allowed under subsection (e) or section 304 of such Act,

is less than $1,000,000.

(ii) ACCUMULATED FUNDING DEFICIENCIES.—For purposes of clause (i)(I), accumulated funding deficiencies shall include any increase in such amount which would result if all applications for waivers of the minimum funding standard under subsection (d) or section 303 of such Act and for extensions of the amortization period under subsection (e) or section 304 of such Act which are pending with respect to such plan were denied.

(4) ADDITIONAL REQUIREMENTS.—

(A) ADVANCE NOTICE.—The Secretary shall, before granting a waiver under subsection (d) or an extension under subsection (e), require each applicant to provide evidence satisfactory to the Secretary that the applicant has provided notice of the filing of the application for such waiver or extension to each employee organization representing employees covered by the affected plan, and each participant, beneficiary, and alternate payee (within the meaning of section 414(p)(8)). Such notice shall include a description of the extent to which the plan is funded for benefits which are guaranteed under title IV of such Act and for benefit liabilities.

(B) CONSIDERATION OF RELEVANT INFORMATION.—The Secretary shall consider any relevant information provided by a person to whom notice was given under subparagraph (A).

Amendments

• 1989, Omnibus Budget Reconciliation Act of 1989 (P.L. 101-239)

P.L. 101-239, §7881(c)(1):

Amended the last sentence of Code Sec. 412(f)(4)(A) by striking "the benefit liabilities" and inserting "for benefit liabilities". **Effective** as if included in the provision of P.L. 100-203 to which it relates.

• 1987, Revenue Act of 1987 (P.L. 100-203)

P.L. 100-203, §9306(d)(1):

Amended Code Sec. 412(f)(4)(A) by striking out "plan," and inserting in lieu thereof "plan, and each participant, beneficiary, and alternate payee (within the meaning of section 414(p)(8)). Such notice shall include a description of the extent to which the plan is funded for benefits which are guaranteed under title IV of such Act and the benefit liabilities.". **Effective** for applications submitted more than 90 days after the date of the enactment of this Act.

P.L. 100-203, §9306(e)(1):

Amended Code Sec. 412(f)(3)(C) by striking out "$2,000,000" and inserting in lieu thereof "$1,000,000". For the **effective** date, see Act Sec. 9306(f)(1)-(3) in the amendment notes following Code Sec. 412(d).

• 1986, Consolidated Omnibus Budget Reconciliation Act of 1985 (P.L. 99-272)

P.L. 99-272, §11015(a)(2)(B)(i) and (ii):

Amended Code Sec. 412(f) by striking out the heading thereof and inserting in lieu thereof "(f) Requirements Relating to Waivers and Extensions.—", and by striking out the heading of paragraph (1) thereof and inserting in lieu thereof "(1) Benefits may not be increased during waiver or extension period.—". **Effective** with respect to applications for waivers, extensions, and modifications filed on or after the date of the enactment of this Act. Prior to amendment, the headings for Code Sec. 412(f) and (f)(1) read as follows:

(f) BENEFITS MAY NOT BE INCREASED DURING WAIVER OR EXTENSION PERIOD.—

(1) IN GENERAL.—

P.L. 99-272, §11015(a)(2)(A):

Amended Code Sec. 412(f) by adding at the end thereof new paragraph (3). **Effective** with respect to applications for waivers, extensions, and modifications filed on or after the date of the enactment of this Act.

P.L. 99-272, §11015(c)(4):

Amended Code Sec. 412(f) by adding at the end thereof new paragraph (4). **Effective** with respect to applications for waivers, extensions, and modifications filed on or after the date of the enactment of this Act.

[Sec. 412(g)]

(g) ALTERNATIVE MINIMUM FUNDING STANDARD.—

(1) IN GENERAL.—A plan which uses a funding method that requires contributions in all years not less than those required under the entry age normal funding method may maintain an alternative minimum funding standard account for any plan year. Such account shall be credited and charged solely as provided in this subsection.

(2) CHARGES AND CREDITS TO ACCOUNT.—For a plan year the alternative minimum funding standard account shall be—

(A) charged with the sum of—

(i) the lesser of normal cost under the funding method used under the plan or normal cost determined under the unit credit method,

(ii) the excess, if any, of the present value of accrued benefits under the plan over the fair market value of the assets, and

(iii) an amount equal to the excess (if any) of credits to the alternative minimum standard account for all prior plan years over charges to such account for all such years, and

(B) credited with the amount considered contributed by the employer to or under the plan for the plan year.

(3) SPECIAL RULES.—The alternative minimum funding standard account (and items therein) shall be charged or credited with interest in the manner provided under subsection (b)(5) with respect to the funding standard account.

[Sec. 412(h)]

(h) EXCEPTIONS.—This section shall not apply to—

(1) any profit-sharing or stock bonus plan,

(2) any insurance contract plan described in subsection (i),

(3) any governmental plan (within the meaning of section 414(d)),

(4) any church plan (within the meaning of section 414(e)) with respect to which the election provided by section 410(d) has not been made,

(5) any plan which has not, at any time after September 2, 1974, provided for employer contributions, or

(6) any plan established and maintained by a society, order, or association described in section 501(c)(8) or (9), if no part of the contributions to or under such plan are made by employers of participants in such plan.

No plan described in paragraph (3), (4), or (6) shall be treated as a qualified plan for purposes of section 401(a) unless such plan meets the requirements of section 401(a)(7) as in effect on September 1, 1974.

Amendments

• 1976, Tax Reform Act of 1976 (P.L. 94-455)

P.L. 94-455, §1901(a)(63):

Amended Code Sec. 412(h) by substituting "September 1, 1974" for "the day before the date of the enactment of the Employee Retirement Income Security Act of 1974" and amended Code Sec. 412(h)(5) by substituting "September 2, 1974" for "the date of the enactment of the Employee Retirement Income Security Act of 1974". **Effective** with respect to tax years beginning after 12-31-76.

[Sec. 412(i)]

(i) CERTAIN INSURANCE CONTRACT PLANS.—A plan is described in this subsection if—

(1) the plan is funded exclusively by the purchase of individual insurance contracts,

(2) such contracts provide for level annual premium payments to be paid extending not later than the retirement age for each individual participating in the plan, and commencing with the date the individual became a participant in the plan (or, in the case of an increase in benefits, commencing at the time such increase becomes effective),

(3) benefits provided by the plan are equal to the benefits provided under each contract at normal retirement age under the plan and are guaranteed by an insurance carrier (licensed under the laws of a State to do business with the plan) to the extent premiums have been paid,

(4) premiums payable for the plan year, and all prior plan years, under such contracts have been paid before lapse or there is reinstatement of the policy,

(5) no rights under such contracts have been subject to a security interest at any time during the plan year, and

(6) no policy loans are outstanding at any time during the plan year.

A plan funded exclusively by the purchase of group insurance contracts which is determined under regulations prescribed by the Secretary to have the same characteristics as contracts described in the preceding sentence shall be treated as a plan described in this subsection.

Amendments

• 1976, Tax Reform Act of 1976 (P.L. 94-455)

P.L. 94-455, §1906(b)(13)(A):

Amended 1954 Code by substituting "Secretary" for "Secretary or his delegate" each place it appeared. **Effective** 2-1-77.

• 1974, Employee Retirement Income Security Act of 1974 (P.L. 93-406)

P.L. 93-406, §1013(a):

Added Code Sec. 412. For **effective** dates and transitional rules governing this section, see the historical note for §1017, P.L. 93-406, following the text of Code Sec. 410(d).

P.L. 93-406, §1013(d), provides:

(d) Alternative Amortization Method for Certain Multiemployer Plans.—

(1) General rule.—In the case of any multiemployer plan (as defined in section 414(f) of the Internal Revenue Code of 1954) to which section 412 of such Code applies, if—

(A) on January 1, 1974, the contributions under the plan were based on a percentage of pay,

(B) the actuarial assumptions with respect to pay are reasonably related to past and projected experience, and

(C) the rates of interest under the plan are determined on the basis of reasonable actuarial assumptions,

the plan may elect (in such manner and at such time as may be provided under regulations prescribed by the Secretary of the Treasury or his delegate) to fund the unfunded past service liability under the plan existing as of the date 12 months following the first date on which such section 412 first applies to the plan by charging the funding standard account with an equal annual percentage of the aggregate pay of all participants in the plan in lieu of the level dollar charges to such account required under clauses (i), (ii), and (iii) of section 412(b)(2)(B) of such Code and section 302(b)(2)(B)(i), (ii), and (iii) of this Act.

(2) Limitation.—In the case of a plan which makes an election under paragraph (1), the aggregate of the charges required under such paragraph for a plan year shall not be less than the interest on the unfunded past service liabilities described in clauses (i), (ii), and (iii) of section 412(b)(2)(B) of the Internal Revenue Code of 1954.

[Sec. 412(j)]

(j) CERTAIN TERMINATED MULTIEMPLOYER PLANS.—This section applies with respect to a terminated multiemployer plan to which section 4021 of the Employee Retirement Income Security Act of 1974 applies, until the last day of the plan year in which the plan terminates, within the meaning of section 4041A(a)(2) of that Act.

Amendments

• 1980, Multiemployer Pension Plan Amendments Act of 1980 (P.L. 96-364)

P.L. 96-364, §203(3):

Added Code Sec. 412(j). **Effective** 9-26-80.

[Sec. 412(k)]

(k) FINANCIAL ASSISTANCE.—Any amount of any financial assistance from the Pension Benefit Guaranty Corporation to any plan, and any repayment of such amount, shall be taken into account under this section in such manner as determined by the Secretary.

Amendments

• 1980, Multiemployer Pension Plan Amendments Act of 1980 (P.L. 96-364)

P.L. 96-364, §203(3):

Added Code Sec. 412(k). **Effective** 9-26-80.

[Sec. 412(l)]

(l) ADDITIONAL FUNDING REQUIREMENTS FOR PLANS WHICH ARE NOT MULTIEMPLOYER PLANS.—

(1) IN GENERAL.—In the case of a defined benefit plan (other than a multiemployer plan) to which this subsection applies under paragraph (9) for any plan year, the amount charged to the funding standard account for such plan year shall be increased by the sum of—

(A) the excess (if any) of—

(i) the deficit reduction contribution determined under paragraph (2) for such plan year, over

(ii) the sum of the charges for such plan year under subsection (b)(2), reduced by the sum of the credits for such plan year under subparagraph (B) of subsection (b)(3), plus

(B) the unpredictable contingent event amount (if any) for such plan year.

Such increase shall not exceed the amount which, after taking into account charges (other than the additional charge under this subsection) and credits under subsection (b), is necessary to increase the funded current liability percentage (taking into account the expected increase in current liability due to benefits accruing during the plan year) to 100 percent.

(2) DEFICIT REDUCTION CONTRIBUTION.—For purposes of paragraph (1), the deficit reduction contribution determined under this paragraph for any plan year is the sum of—

(A) the unfunded old liability amount,

(B) the unfunded new liability amount,

(C) the expected increase in current liability due to benefits accruing during the plan year, and

(D) the aggregate of the unfunded mortality increase amounts.

(3) UNFUNDED OLD LIABILITY AMOUNT.—For purposes of this subsection—

(A) IN GENERAL.—The unfunded old liability amount with respect to any plan for any plan year is the amount necessary to amortize the unfunded old liability under the plan in equal annual installments over a period of 18 plan years (beginning with the 1st plan year beginning after December 31, 1988).

(B) UNFUNDED OLD LIABILITY.—The term "unfunded old liability" means the unfunded current liability of the plan as of the beginning of the 1st plan year beginning after December 31, 1987 (determined without regard to any plan amendment increasing liabilities adopted after October 16, 1987).

(C) SPECIAL RULES FOR BENEFIT INCREASES UNDER EXISTING COLLECTIVE BARGAINING AGREEMENTS.—

(i) IN GENERAL.—In the case of a plan maintained pursuant to 1 or more collective bargaining agreements between employee representatives and the employer ratified before October 29, 1987, the unfunded old liability amount with respect to such plan for any plan year shall be increased by the amount necessary to amortize the unfunded existing benefit increase liability in equal annual installments over a period of 18 plan years beginning with—

(I) the plan year in which the benefit increase with respect to such liability occurs, or

(II) if the taxpayer elects, the 1st plan year beginning after December 31, 1988.

(ii) Unfunded existing benefit increase liabilities.—For purposes of clause (i), the unfunded existing benefit increase liability means, with respect to any benefit increase under the agreements described in clause (i) which takes effect during or after the 1st plan year beginning after December 31, 1987, the unfunded current liability determined—

(I) by taking into account only liabilities attributable to such benefit increase, and

(II) by reducing (but not below zero) the amount determined under paragraph (8)(A)(ii) by the current liability determined without regard to such benefit increase.

(iii) EXTENSIONS, MODIFICATIONS, ETC. NOT TAKEN INTO ACCOUNT.—For purposes of this subparagraph, any extension, amendment, or other modification of an agreement after October 28, 1987, shall not be taken into account.

(D) SPECIAL RULE FOR REQUIRED CHANGES IN ACTUARIAL ASSUMPTIONS.—

(i) IN GENERAL.—The unfunded old liability amount with respect to any plan for any plan year shall be increased by the amount necessary to amortize the amount of additional unfunded old liability under the plan in equal annual installments over a period of 12 plan years (beginning with the first plan year beginning after December 31, 1994).

(ii) ADDITIONAL UNFUNDED OLD LIABILITY.—For purposes of clause (i), the term "additional unfunded old liability" means the amount (if any) by which—

(I) the current liability of the plan as of the beginning of the first plan year beginning after December 31, 1994, valued using the assumptions required by paragraph (7)(C) as in effect for plan years beginning after December 31, 1994, exceeds

(II) the current liability of the plan as of the beginning of such first plan year, valued using the same assumptions used under subclause (I) (other than the assumptions required by paragraph (7)(C)), using the prior interest rate, and using such mortality assumptions as were used to determine current liability for the first plan year beginning after December 31, 1992.

(iii) PRIOR INTEREST RATE.—For purposes of clause (ii), the term "prior interest rate" means the rate of interest that is the same percentage of the weighted average under subsection (b)(5)(B)(ii)(I) for the first plan year beginning after December 31, 1994, as the rate of interest used by the plan to determine current liability for the first plan year beginning after December 31, 1992, is of the weighted average under subsection (b)(5)(B)(ii)(I) for such first plan year beginning after December 31, 1992.

(E) OPTIONAL RULE FOR ADDITIONAL UNFUNDED OLD LIABILITY.—

(i) IN GENERAL.—If an employer makes an election under clause (ii), the additional unfunded old liability for purposes of subparagraph (D) shall be the amount (if any) by which—

(I) the unfunded current liability of the plan as of the beginning of the first plan year beginning after December 31, 1994, valued using the assumptions required by paragraph (7)(C) as in effect for plan years beginning after December 31, 1994, exceeds

(II) the unamortized portion of the unfunded old liability under the plan as of the beginning of the first plan year beginning after December 31, 1994.

(ii) ELECTION.—

(I) An employer may irrevocably elect to apply the provisions of this subparagraph as of the beginning of the first plan year beginning after December 31, 1994.

(II) If an election is made under this clause, the increase under paragraph (1) for any plan year beginning after December 31, 1994, and before January 1, 2002, to which this subsection applies (without regard to this subclause) shall not be less than the increase that would be required under paragraph (1) if the provisions of this title as in effect for the last plan year beginning before January 1, 1995, had remained in effect.

(4) UNFUNDED NEW LIABILITY AMOUNT.—For purposes of this subsection—

(A) IN GENERAL.—The unfunded new liability amount with respect to any plan for any plan year is the applicable percentage of the unfunded new liability.

(B) UNFUNDED NEW LIABILITY.—The term "unfunded new liability" means the unfunded current liability of the plan for the plan year determined without regard to—

(i) the unamortized portion of the unfunded old liability, the unamortized portion of the additional unfunded old liability, the unamortized portion of each unfunded mortality increase, and the unamortized portion of the unfunded existing benefit increase liability, and

(ii) the liability with respect to any unpredictable contingent event benefits (without regard to whether the event has occurred).

(C) APPLICABLE PERCENTAGE.—The term "applicable percentage" means, with respect to any plan year, 30 percent, reduced by the product of—

(i) .40 multiplied by

(ii) the number of percentage points (if any) by which the funded current liability percentage exceeds 60 percent.

(5) UNPREDICTABLE CONTINGENT EVENT AMOUNT.—

(A) IN GENERAL.—The unpredictable contingent event amount with respect to a plan for any plan year is an amount equal to the greatest of—

(i) the applicable percentage of the product of—

(I) 100 percent, reduced (but not below zero) by the funded current liability percentage for the plan year, multiplied by

(II) the amount of unpredictable contingent event benefits paid during the plan year, including (except as provided by the Secretary) any payment for the purchase of an annuity contract for a participant or beneficiary with respect to such benefits,

(ii) the amount which would be determined for the plan year if the unpredictable contingent event benefit liabilites were amortized in equal annual installments over 7 plan years (beginning with the plan year in which such event occurs), or

(iii) the additional amount that would be determined under paragraph (4)(A) if the unpredictable contingent event benefit liabilities were included in unfunded new liability notwithstanding paragraph (4)(B)(ii).

(B) APPLICABLE PERCENTAGE.—

In the case of plan years beginning in:	*The applicable percentage is:*
1989 and 1990	5
1991	10
1992	15
1993	20
1994	30
1995	40
1996	50
1997	60
1998	70
1999	80
2000	90
2001 and thereafter	100

(C) PARAGRAPH NOT TO APPLY TO EXISTING BENEFITS.—This paragraph shall not apply to unpredictable contingent event benefits (and liabilities attributable thereto) for which the event occurred before the first plan year beginning after December 31, 1988.

(D) SPECIAL RULE FOR FIRST YEAR OF AMORTIZATION.—Unless the employer elects otherwise, the amount determined under subparagraph (A) for the plan year in which the event occurs shall be equal to 150 percent of the amount determined under subparagraph (A)(i). The amount under subparagraph (A)(ii) for subsequent plan years in the amortization period shall be adjusted in the manner provided by the Secretary to reflect the application of this subparagraph.

(E) LIMITATION.—The present value of the amounts described in subparagraph (A) with respect to any one event shall not exceed the unpredictable contingent event benefit liabilities attributable to that event.

(6) SPECIAL RULES FOR SMALL PLANS.—

(A) PLANS WITH 100 OR FEWER PARTICIPANTS.—This subsection shall not apply to any plan for any plan year if on each day during the preceding plan year such plan had no more than 100 participants.

(B) PLANS WITH MORE THAN 100 BUT NOT MORE THAN 150 PARTICIPANTS.—In the case of a plan to which subparagraph (A) does not apply and which on each day during the preceding plan year had no more than 150 participants, the amount of the increase under paragraph (1) for such plan year shall be equal to the product of—

(i) such increase determined without regard to this subparagraph, multiplied by

(ii) 2 percent for the highest number of participants in excess of 100 on any such day.

(C) AGGREGATION OF PLANS.—For purposes of this paragraph, all defined benefit plans maintained by the same employer (or any member of such employer's controlled group) shall be treated as 1 plan, but only employees of such employer or member shall be taken into account.

(7) CURRENT LIABILITY.—For purposes of this subsection—

(A) IN GENERAL.—The term "current liability" means all liabilities to employees and their beneficiaries under the plan.

(B) TREATMENT OF UNPREDICTABLE CONTINGENT EVENT BENEFITS.—

(i) IN GENERAL.—For purposes of subparagraph (A), any unpredictable contingent event benefit shall not be taken into account until the event on which the benefit is contingent occurs.

(ii) UNPREDICTABLE CONTINGENT EVENT BENEFIT.—The term "unpredictable contingent event benefit" means any benefit contingent on an event other than—

(I) age, service, compensation, death, or disability, or

(II) an event which is reasonably and reliably predictable (as determined by the Secretary).

(C) INTEREST RATE AND MORTALITY ASSUMPTIONS USED.—Effective for plan years beginning after December 31, 1994—

(i) INTEREST RATE.—

(I) IN GENERAL.—The rate of interest used to determine current liability under this subsection shall be the rate of interest used under subsection (b)(5), except that the highest rate in the permissible range under subparagraph (B)(ii) thereof shall not exceed the specified percentage under subclause (II) of the weighted average referred to in such subparagraph.

(II) SPECIFIED PERCENTAGE.—For purposes of subclause (I), the specified percentage shall be determined as follows:

In the case of plan years beginning in calendar year:	*The specified percentage is:*
1995	109
1996	108
1997	107
1998	106
1999 and thereafter	105

(III) SPECIAL RULE FOR 2002 AND 2003.—For a plan year beginning in 2002 or 2003, notwithstanding subclause (I), in the case that the rate of interest used under subsection (b)(5) exceeds the highest rate permitted under subclause (I), the rate of interest used to determine current liability under this subsection may exceed the rate of interest otherwise permitted under subclause (I); except that such rate of interest shall not exceed 120 percent of the weighted average referred to in subsection (b)(5)(B)(ii).

(IV) SPECIAL RULE FOR 2004, 2005, 2006, AND 2007.—For plan years beginning in 2004, 2005, 2006, or 2007, notwithstanding subclause (I), the rate of interest used to determine current liability under this subsection shall be the rate of interest under subsection (b)(5).

(ii) MORTALITY TABLES.—

(I) COMMISSIONER'S STANDARD TABLE.—In the case of plan years beginning before the first plan year to which the first tables prescribed under subclause (II) apply, the mortality table used in determining current liability under this subsection shall be the table prescribed by the Secretary which is based on the prevailing commissioners' standard table (described in section 807(d)(5)(A)) used to determine reserves for group annuity contracts issued on January 1, 1993.

(II) SECRETARIAL AUTHORITY.—The Secretary may by regulation prescribe for plan years beginning after December 31, 1999, mortality tables to be used in determining current liability under this subsection. Such tables shall be based upon the actual experience of pension plans and projected trends in such experience. In prescribing such tables, the Secretary shall take into account results of available independent studies of mortality of individuals covered by pension plans.

(III) PERIODIC REVIEW.—The Secretary shall periodically (at least every 5 years) review any tables in effect under this subsection and shall, to the extent the Secretary determines necessary, by regulation update the tables to reflect the actual experience of pension plans and projected trends in such experience.

(iii) SEPARATE MORTALITY TABLES FOR THE DISABLED.—Notwithstanding clause (ii)—

(I) IN GENERAL.—In the case of plan years beginning after December 31, 1995, the Secretary shall establish mortality tables which may be used (in lieu of the tables under clause (ii)) to determine current liability under this subsection for individuals who are entitled to benefits under the plan on account of disability. The Secretary shall establish separate tables for individuals whose disabilities occur in plan years beginning before January 1, 1995, and for individuals whose disabilities occur in plan years beginning on or after such date.

(II) SPECIAL RULE FOR DISABILITIES OCCURRING AFTER 1994.—In the case of disabilities occurring in plan years beginning after December 31, 1994, the tables under subclause (I) shall apply only with respect to individuals described in such subclause who are disabled within the meaning of title II of the Social Security Act and the regulations thereunder.

(III) PLAN YEARS BEGINNING IN 1995.—In the case of any plan year beginning in 1995, a plan may use its own mortality assumptions for individuals who are entitled to benefits under the plan on account of disability.

(D) CERTAIN SERVICE DISREGARDED.—

(i) IN GENERAL.—In the case of a participant to whom this subparagraph applies, only the applicable percentage of the years of service before such individual became a participant shall be taken into account in computing the current liability of the plan.

(ii) APPLICABLE PERCENTAGE.—For purposes of this subparagraph, the applicable percentage shall be determined as follows:

If the years of participation are:	*The applicable percentage is:*
1	20
2	40
3	60
4	80
5 or more	100

(iii) PARTICIPANTS TO WHOM SUBPARAGRAPH APPLIES.—This subparagraph shall apply to any participant who, at the time of becoming a participant—

(I) has not accrued any other benefit under any defined benefit plan (whether or not terminated) maintained by the employer or a member of the same controlled group of which the employer is a member,

(II) who first becomes a participant under the plan in a plan year beginning after December 31, 1987, and

(III) has years of service greater than the minimum years of service necessary for eligibility to participate in the plan.

(iv) ELECTION.—An employer may elect not to have this subparagraph apply. Such an election, once made, may be revoked only with the consent of the Secretary.

(8) OTHER DEFINITIONS.—For purposes of this subsection—

(A) UNFUNDED CURRENT LIABILITY.—The term "unfunded current liability" means, with respect to any plan year, the excess (if any) of—

(i) the current liability under the plan, over

(ii) value of the plan's assets determined under subsection (c)(2).

(B) FUNDED CURRENT LIABILITY PERCENTAGE.—The term "funded current liability percentage" means, with respect to any plan year, the percentage which—

(i) the amount determined under subparagraph (A)(ii), is of

(ii) the current liability under the plan.

(C) CONTROLLED GROUP.—The term "controlled group" means any group treated as a single employer under subsection (b), (c), (m), and (o) of section 414.

(D) ADJUSTMENTS TO PREVENT OMISSIONS AND DUPLICATIONS.—The Secretary shall provide such adjustments in the unfunded old liability amount, the unfunded new liability amount, the unpredictable contingent event amount, the current payment amount, and any other charges or credits under this section as are necessary to avoid duplication or omission of any factors in the determination of such amounts, charges, or credits.

(E) DEDUCTION FOR CREDIT BALANCES.—For purposes of this subsection, the amount determined under subparagraph (A)(ii) shall be reduced by any credit balance in the funding standard account. The Secretary may provide for such reduction for purposes of any other provision which references this subsection.

(9) APPLICABILITY OF SUBSECTION.—

(A) IN GENERAL.—Except as provided in paragraph (6)(A), this subsection shall apply to a plan for any plan year if its funded current liability percentage for such year is less than 90 percent.

(B) EXCEPTION FOR CERTAIN PLANS AT LEAST 80 PERCENT FUNDED.—Subparagraph (A) shall not apply to a plan for a plan year if—

(i) the funded current liability percentage for the plan year is at least 80 percent, and

(ii) such percentage for each of the 2 immediately preceding plan years (or each of the 2d and 3d immediately preceding plan years) is at least 90 percent.

(C) FUNDED CURRENT LIABILITY PERCENTAGE.—For purposes of subparagraphs (A) and (B), the term "funded current liability percentage" has the meaning given such term by paragraph (8)(B), except that such percentage shall be determined for any plan year—

(i) without regard to paragraph (8)(E), and

(ii) by using the rate of interest which is the highest rate allowable for the plan year under paragraph (7)(C).

(D) TRANSITION RULES.—For purposes of this paragraph:

(i) FUNDED PERCENTAGE FOR YEARS BEFORE 1995.—The funded current liability percentage for any plan year beginning before January 1, 1995, shall be treated as not less than 90 percent only if for such plan year the plan met one of the following requirements (as in effect for such year):

(I) The full-funding limitation under subsection (c)(7) for the plan was zero.

(II) The plan had no additional funding requirement under this subsection (or would have had no such requirement if its funded current liability percentage had been determined under subparagraph (C)).

(III) The plan's additional funding requirement under this subsection did not exceed the lesser of 0.5 percent of current liability or $5,000,000.

(ii) SPECIAL RULE FOR 1995 AND 1996.—For purposes of determining whether subparagraph (B) applies to any plan year beginning in 1995 or 1996, a plan shall be treated as meeting the requirements of subparagraph (B)(ii) if the plan met the requirements of clause (i) of this subparagraph for any two of the plan years beginning in 1992, 1993, and 1994 (whether or not consecutive).

(10) UNFUNDED MORTALITY INCREASE AMOUNT.—

(A) IN GENERAL.—The unfunded mortality increase amount with respect to each unfunded mortality increase is the amount necessary to amortize such increase in equal annual installments over a period of 10 plan years (beginning with the first plan year for which a plan uses any new mortality table issued under paragraph (7)(C)(ii)(II) or (III)).

(B) UNFUNDED MORTALITY INCREASE.—For purposes of subparagraph (A), the term "unfunded mortality increase" means an amount equal to the excess of—

(i) the current liability of the plan for the first plan year for which a plan uses any new mortality table issued under paragraph (7)(C)(ii)(II) or (III), over

(ii) the current liability of the plan for such plan year which would have been determined if the mortality table in effect for the preceding plan year had been used.

(11) PHASE-IN OF INCREASES IN FUNDING REQUIRED BY RETIREMENT PROTECTION ACT OF 1994.—

(A) IN GENERAL.—For any applicable plan year, at the election of the employer, the increase under paragraph (1) shall not exceed the greater of—

(i) the increase that would be required under paragraph (1) if the provisions of this title as in effect for plan years beginning before January 1, 1995, had remained in effect, or

(ii) the amount which, after taking into account charges (other than the additional charge under this subsection) and credits under subsection (b), is necessary to increase the funded current liability percentage (taking into account the expected increase in current liability due to benefits accruing during the plan year) for the applicable plan year to a percentage equal to the sum of the initial funded current liability percentage of the plan plus the applicable number of percentage points for such applicable plan year.

(B) APPLICABLE NUMBER OF PERCENTAGE POINTS.—

(i) INITIAL FUNDED CURRENT LIABILITY PERCENTAGE OF 75 PERCENT OR LESS.—Except as provided in clause (ii), for plans with an initial funded current liability percentage of 75 percent or less, the applicable number of percentage points for the applicable plan year is:

In the case of applicable plan years beginning in:	*The applicable number of percentage points is:*
1995	3
1996	6
1997	9
1998	12
1999	15
2000	19
2001	24

(ii) OTHER CASES.—In the case of a plan to which this clause applies, the applicable number of percentage points for any such applicable plan year is the sum of—

(I) 2 percentage points;

(II) the applicable number of percentage points (if any) under this clause for the preceding applicable plan year;

(III) the product of .10 multiplied by the excess (if any) of (a) 85 percentage points over (b) the sum of the initial funded current liability percentage and the number determined under subclause (II);

(IV) for applicable plan years beginning in 2000, 1 percentage point; and

(V) for applicable plan years beginning in 2001, 2 percentage points.

(iii) PLANS TO WHICH CLAUSE (ii) APPLIES.—

(I) IN GENERAL.—Clause (ii) shall apply to a plan for an applicable plan year if the initial funded current liability percentage of such plan is more than 75 percent.

(II) PLANS INITIALLY UNDER CLAUSE (i).—In the case of a plan which (but for this subclause) has an initial funded current liability percentage of 75 percent or less, clause (ii) (and not clause (i)) shall apply to such plan with respect to applicable plan years beginning after the first applicable plan year for which the sum of the initial funded current liability percentage and the applicable number of percentage points (determined under clause (i)) exceeds 75 percent. For purposes of applying clause (ii) to such a plan, the initial funded current liability percentage of such plan shall be treated as being the sum referred to in the preceding sentence.

(C) DEFINITIONS.—For purposes of this paragraph:

(i) The term "applicable plan year" means a plan year beginning after December 31, 1994, and before January 1, 2002.

(ii) The term "initial funded current liability percentage" means the funded current liability percentage as of the first day of the first plan year beginning after December 31, 1994.

(12) ELECTION FOR CERTAIN PLANS.—

(A) IN GENERAL.—In the case of a defined benefit plan established and maintained by an applicable employer, if this subsection did not apply to the plan for the plan year beginning in 2000 (determined without regard to paragraph (6)), then, at the election of the employer, the increased amount under paragraph (1) for any applicable plan year shall be the greater of—

(i) 20 percent of the increased amount under paragraph (1) determined without regard to this paragraph, or

(ii) the increased amount which would be determined under paragraph (1) if the deficit reduction contribution under paragraph (2) for the applicable plan year were determined without regard to subparagraphs (A), (B), and (D) of paragraph (2).

(B) RESTRICTIONS ON BENEFIT INCREASES.—No amendment which increases the liabilities of the plan by reason of any increase in benefits, any change in the accrual of benefits, or any change in the rate at which benefits become nonforfeitable under the plan shall be adopted during any applicable plan year, unless—

(i) the plan's enrolled actuary certifies (in such form and manner prescribed by the Secretary) that the amendment provides for an increase in annual contributions which will exceed the increase in annual charges to the funding standard account attributable to such amendment, or

(ii) the amendment is required by a collective bargaining agreement which is in effect on the date of enactment of this subparagraph.

If a plan is amended during any applicable plan year in violation of the preceding sentence, any election under this paragraph shall not apply to any applicable plan year ending on or after the date on which such amendment is adopted.

(C) APPLICABLE EMPLOYER.—For purposes of this paragraph, the term "applicable employer" means an employer which is—

(i) a commercial passenger airline,

(ii) primarily engaged in the production or manufacture of a steel mill product or the processing of iron ore pellets, or

(iii) an organization described in section 501(c)(5) and which established the plan to which this paragraph applies on June 30, 1955.

(D) APPLICABLE PLAN YEAR.—For purposes of this paragraph—

(i) IN GENERAL.—The term "applicable plan year" means any plan year beginning after December 27, 2003, and before December 28, 2005, for which the employer elects the application of this paragraph.

(ii) LIMITATION ON NUMBER OF YEARS WHICH MAY BE ELECTED.—An election may not be made under this paragraph with respect to more than 2 plan years.

(E) ELECTION.—An election under this paragraph shall be made at such time and in such manner as the Secretary may prescribe.

Amendments

• 2006, Pension Protection Act of 2006 (P.L. 109-280)

P.L. 109-280, §301(b)(2)(A)-(B):

Amended Code Sec. 412(l)(7)(C)(i)(IV) by striking "or 2005" and inserting ", 2005, 2006, or 2007", and by striking "AND 2005" in the heading and inserting ", 2005, 2006, AND 2007". **Effective** 8-17-2006.

• 2004, Pension Funding Equity Act of 2004 (P.L. 108-218)

P.L. 108-218, §101(b)(2):

Amended Code Sec. 412(l)(7)(C)(i) by adding at the end a new subclause (IV). **Effective** generally for plan years beginning after 12-31-2003. For special rules, see Act Sec. 101(d)(2), below, and Act Sec. 101(c)(1)-(2) in the amendment notes following Code Sec. 412(b).

P.L. 108-218, §101(d)(2), provides:

(2) LOOKBACK RULES.—For purposes of applying subsections (d)(9)(B)(ii) and (e)(1) of section 302 of the Employee Retirement Income Security Act of 1974 and subsections (l)(9)(B)(ii) and (m)(1) of section 412 of the Internal Revenue Code of 1986 to plan years beginning after December 31, 2003, the amendments made by this section may be applied as if such amendments had been in effect for all prior plan years. The Secretary of the Treasury may prescribe simplified assumptions which may be used in applying the amendments made by this section to such prior plan years.

P.L. 108-218, §102(b):

Amended Code Sec. 412(l) by adding at the end a new paragraph (12). **Effective** 4-10-2004.

P.L. 108-218, §102(c), provides:

(c) EFFECT OF ELECTION.—An election under section 302(d)(12) of the Employee Retirement Income Security Act of 1974 or section 412(l)(12) of the Internal Revenue Code of 1986 (as added by this section) with respect to a plan shall not invalidate any obligation (pursuant to a collective bargaining agreement in effect on the date of the election) to provide benefits, to change the accrual of benefits, or to change the rate at which benefits become nonforfeitable under the plan.

• 2002, Job Creation and Worker Assistance Act of 2002 (P.L. 107-147)

P.L. 107-147, §405(a)(1):

Amended Code Sec. 412(l)(7)(C)(i) by adding at the end a new subclause (III). **Effective** on 3-9-2002.

• 1994, Uruguay Round Agreements Act (P.L. 103-465)

P.L. 103-465, §751(a)(1)(A):

Amended Code Sec. 412(l)(1) by striking "which has an unfunded current liability" and inserting "to which this subsection applies under paragraph (9)". **Effective** for plan years beginning after 12-31-94.

P.L. 103-465, §751(a)(1)(B):

Amended Code Sec. 412(l) by adding at the end a new paragraph (9). **Effective** for plan years beginning after 12-31-94.

P.L. 103-465, §751(a)(2)(A):

Amended Code Sec. 412(l)(1)(A)(ii). **Effective** for plan years beginning after 12-31-94. Prior to amendment, Code Sec. 412(l)(1)(A)(ii) read as follows:

(ii) the sum of the charges for such plan year under subparagraphs (B) (other than clauses (iv) and (v) thereof), (C), and (D) of subsection (b)(2), reduced by the sum of the credits for such plan year under subparagraph (B)(i) of subsection (b)(3), plus

P.L. 103-465, §751(a)(2)(B):

Amended the last sentence of Code Sec. 412(l)(1). **Effective** for plan years beginning after 12-31-94. Prior to amendment, the last sentence of Code Sec. 412(l)(1) read as follows:

Such increase shall not exceed the amount necessary to increase the funded current liability percentage to 100 percent.

P.L. 103-465, §751(a)(3)(A)-(C):

Amended Code Sec. 412(l)(2) by striking "plus" at the end of subparagraph (A), by striking the period at the end of subparagraph (B) and inserting ", plus", and by adding at the end a new subparagraph (C). **Effective** for plan years beginning after 12-31-94.

P.L. 103-465, §751(a)(4)(A):

Amended Code Sec. 412(l)(3) by adding at the end new subparagraphs (D) and (E). **Effective** for plan years beginning after 12-31-94.

P.L. 103-465, §751(a)(4)(B):

Amended Code Sec. 412(l)(4)(B)(i) by inserting ", the unamortized portion of the additional unfunded old liability," after "old liability". **Effective** for plan years beginning after 12-31-94.

P.L. 103-465, §751(a)(5)(A)-(B):

Amended Code Sec. 412(l)(4)(C) by striking ".25" and inserting ".40" and by striking "35" and inserting "60". **Effective** for plan years beginning after 12-31-94.

P.L. 103-465, §751(a)(6)(A)(i)-(iv):

Amended Code Sec. 412(l)(5)(A) by striking "greater of" and inserting "greatest of" before clause (i), by striking "or" at the end of clause (i), by striking the period at the end of clause (ii) and inserting ", or", and by adding after clause (ii) a new clause (iii). **Effective** for plan years beginning after 12-31-94.

P.L. 103-465, §751(a)(6)(B):

Amended Code Sec. 412(l)(5) by adding at the end a new subparagraph (E). **Effective** for plan years beginning after 12-31-94.

P.L. 103-465, §751(a)(7)(A):

Amended Code Sec. 412(l)(7)(C). **Effective** for plan years beginning after 12-31-94. Prior to amendment, Code Sec. 412(l)(7)(C) read as follows:

(C) INTEREST RATES USED.—The rate of interest used to determine current liability shall be the rate of interest used under subsection (b)(5).

P.L. 103-465, §751(a)(7)(B)(i):

Amended Code Sec. 412(l)(2), as amended by Act Sec. 751(a)(3)(A)-(C), by striking "plus" at the end of subparagraph (B), by striking the period at the end of subparagraph (C) and inserting ", and", and by adding at the end a new subparagraph (D). **Effective** for plan years beginning after 12-31-94.

P.L. 103-465, §751(a)(7)(B)(ii):

Amended Code Sec. 412(l), as amended by Act Sec. 751(a)(1)(A)-(B), by adding at the end a new paragraph (10). **Effective** for plan years beginning after 12-31-94.

P.L. 103-465, §751(a)(7)(B)(iii):

Amended Code Sec. 412(l)(4)(B)(i), as amended by Act Sec. 751(a)(4)(B), by inserting "the unamortized portion of each unfunded mortality increase," after "additional unfunded old liability,". **Effective** for plan years beginning after 12-31-94.

P.L. 103-465, §751(a)(8):

Amended Code Sec. 412(l) by adding at the end a new paragraph (11). **Effective** for plan years beginning after 12-31-94.

P.L. 103-465, §769 [as amended by P.L. 105-34, §1508(a), P.L. 108-218, §201(a), and P.L. 109-280, §115(d)(1)], provides:

SEC. 769. SPECIAL FUNDING RULES FOR CERTAIN PLANS.

(a) FUNDING RULES NOT TO APPLY TO CERTAIN PLANS.—Any changes made by this Act to section 412 of the Internal Revenue Code of 1986 or to part 3 of subtitle B of title I of the Employee Retirement Income Security Act of 1974 shall not apply to—

(1) a plan which is, on the date of enactment of this Act, subject to a restoration payment schedule order issued by the Pension Benefit Guaranty Corporation that meets the requirements of section 1.412(c)(1)-3 of the Treasury Regulations, or

(2) a plan established by an affected air carrier (as defined under section 4001(a)(14)(C)(ii)(I) of such Act) and assumed by a new plan sponsor pursuant to the terms of a written agreement with the Pension Benefit Guaranty Corporation dated January 5, 1993, and approved by the United States Bankruptcy Court for the District of Delaware on December 30, 1992.

(b) CHANGE IN ACTUARIAL METHOD.—Any amortization installments for bases established under section 412(b) of the Internal Revenue Code of 1986 and section 302(b) of the Employee Retirement Income Security Act of 1974 for plan years beginning after December 31, 1987, and before January 1, 1993, by reason of nonelective changes under the frozen entry age actuarial cost method shall not be included in the calculation of offsets under section 412(l)(1)(A)(ii) of such Code and section 302(d)(1)(A)(ii) of such Act for the 1st 5 plan years beginning after December 31, 1994.

(c) TRANSITION RULES FOR CERTAIN PLANS.—

(1) IN GENERAL.—In the case of a plan that—

(A) was not required to pay a variable rate premium for the plan year beginning in 1996;

(B) has not, in any plan year beginning after 1995 and before 2009, merged with another plan (other than a plan sponsored by an employer that was in 1996 within the controlled group of the plan sponsor); and

(C) is sponsored by a company that is engaged primarily in the interurban or interstate passenger bus service,

except as provided in paragraph (3), the transition rules described in paragraph (2) shall apply for any plan year beginning after 1996 and before 2010.

(2) TRANSITION RULES.—The transition rules described in this paragraph are as follows:

(A) For purposes of section 412(l)(9)(A) of the Internal Revenue Code of 1986 and section 302(d)(9)(A) of the Employee Retirement Income Security Act of 1974—

(i) the funded current liability percentage for any plan year beginning after 1996 and before 2005 shall be treated as not less than 90 percent if for such plan year the funded current liability percentage is at least 85 percent, and

(ii) the funded current liability percentage for any plan year beginning after 2004 and before 2010 shall be treated as not less than 90 percent if for such plan year the funded current liability percentage satisfies the minimum percentage determined according to the following table:

In the case of a plan year beginning in:	*The minimum percentage is:*
2005	86 percent
2006	87 percent
2007	88 percent
2008	89 percent
2009 and thereafter	90 percent.

(B) Sections 412(c)(7)(E)(i)(I) of such Code and 302(c)(7)(E)(i)(I) of such Act shall be applied—

(i) by substituting "85 percent" for "90 percent" for plan years beginning after 1996 and before 2005, and

(ii) by substituting the minimum percentage specified in the table contained in subparagraph (A)(ii) for "90 percent" for plan years beginning after 2004 and before 2010.

(C) In the event the funded current liability percentage of a plan is less than 85 percent for any plan year beginning after 1996 and before 2005, except as provided in paragraph (3), the transition rules under subparagraphs (A) and (B) shall continue to apply to the plan if contributions for such a plan year are made to the plan in an amount equal to the lesser of—

(i) the amount necessary to result in a funded current liability percentage of 85 percent, or

(ii) the greater of—

(I) 2 percent of the plan's current liability as of the beginning of such plan year, or

(II) the amount necessary to result in a funded current liability percentage of 80 percent as of the end of such plan year.

For the plan year beginning in 2005 and for each of the 3 succeeding plan years, except as provided in paragraph (3), the transition rules under subparagraphs (A) and (B) shall continue to apply to the plan for such plan year only if contributions to the plan for such plan year equal at least the expected increase in current liability due to benefits accruing during such plan year.

(3) SPECIAL RULES.—In the case of plan years beginning in 2004, 2005, 2006, and 2007, the following transition rules shall apply in lieu of the transition rules described in paragraph (2):

(A) For purposes of section 412(l)(9)(A) of the Internal Revenue Code of 1986 and section 302(d)(9)(A) of the Employee Retirement Income Security Act of 1974, the funded current liability percentage for any plan year shall be treated as not less than 90 percent.

(B) For purposes of section 412(m) of the Internal Revenue Code of 1986 and section 302(e) of the Employee Retirement Income Security Act of 1974, the funded current liability percentage for any plan year shall be treated as not less than 100 percent.

(C) For purposes of determining unfunded vested benefits under section 4006(a)(3)(E)(iii) of the Employee Retirement Income Security Act of 1974, the mortality table shall be the mortality table used by the plan.

Act Sec. 769(c), as added by P.L. 105-34, §1508(a) is **effective** for plan years beginning after 12-31-96, and as amended by P.L. 108-218, §201(a), is **effective** for plan years beginning after 12-31-2003.

• 1989, Omnibus Budget Reconciliation Act of 1989 (P.L. 101-239)

P.L. 101-239, §7881(a)(1)(A):

Amended Code Sec. 412(l)(3)(C)(ii)(II) by inserting "(but not below zero)" after "reducing". **Effective** as if included in the provision of P.L. 100-203 to which it relates.

P.L. 101-239, §7881(a)(2)(A):

Amended Code Sec. 412(l)(4)(B)(i) by inserting "and the unamortized portion of the unfunded existing benefit increase liability" after "liability". **Effective** as if included in the provision of P.L. 100-203 to which it relates.

P.L. 101-239, §7881(a)(3)(A):

Amended Code Sec. 412(l)(5)(C) by striking "October 17, 1987" and inserting "the first plan year beginning after December 31, 1988". **Effective** as if included in the provision of P.L. 100-203 to which it relates.

P.L. 101-239, §7881:

Amended Code Sec. 412(l)(7)(D) by striking "and" at the end of clause (iii)(I), by striking the period at the end of clause (iii)(II) and inserting ", and", by adding at the end of clause (iii) a new subclause (III), and by adding at the end thereof a new clause (iv). **Effective** as if included in the provision of P.L. 100-203 to which it relates.

P.L. 101-239, §7881(a)(5)(A)(i)-(ii):

Amended Code Sec. 412(l)(8) by striking "reduced by any credit balance in the funding standard account" after "subsection (c)(2)" in subparagraph (A)(ii), and by adding at the end thereof a new subparagraph (E). **Effective** as if included in the provision of P.L. 100-203 to which it relates.

• 1988, Technical and Miscellaneous Revenue Act of 1988 (P.L. 100-647)

P.L. 100-647, §2005(a)(2)(A)(i)-(ii):

Amended Code Sec. 412(l)(3)(C) by striking out "October 17, 1987" in clause (i) and inserting in lieu thereof "October 29, 1987", and by striking out "October 16, 1987" in clause (iii) and inserting in lieu thereof "October 28, 1987". **Effec-**

tive as if included in the provision of P.L. 100-203 to which it relates.

P.L. 100-647, §2005(d)(1)(A)-(B):

Amended Code Sec. 412(l)(3)(C) by striking out "October 17, 1987" in clause (i) and inserting in lieu thereof "October 29, 1987", and by striking out "October 16, 1987" in clause (iii) and inserting in lieu thereof "October 28, 1987". **Effective** as if included in the provision of P.L. 100-203 to which it relates.

• 1987, Revenue Act of 1987 (P.L. 100-203)

P.L. 100-203, §9303(a)(1):

Amended Code Sec. 412 by adding at the end thereof new subsection (l). **Effective** with respect to plan years beginning after 12-31-88. However, for a special rule for steel companies, see Act Sec. 9303(e)(3), below.

P.L. 100-203, §9303(e)(3), as amended by P.L. 100-239, §7881(a)(7), provides as follows:

(3) SPECIAL RULE FOR STEEL COMPANIES.—

(A) IN GENERAL.—For any plan year beginning before January 1, 1994, any increase in the funding standard account under section 412(l) of the 1986 Code or section 302(d) of ERISA (as added by this section) with respect to any steel employee plan shall not exceed the sum of—

(i) the required percentage of the current liability under such plan, plus

(ii) the amount determined under subparagraph (C)(i) for such plan year.

(B) REQUIRED PERCENTAGE.—For purposes of subparagraph (A), the term "required percentage" means, with respect to any plan year, the excess (if any) of—

(i) the sum of—

(I) the funded current liability percentage as of the beginning of the 1st plan year beginning after December 31, 1988 (determined without regard to any plan amendment adopted after June 30, 1987), plus

(II) 1 percentage point for the plan year for which the determination under this paragraph is being made and for each prior plan year beginning after December 31, 1988, over

(ii) the funded current liability percentage as of the beginning of the plan year for which such determination is being made.

(C) SPECIAL RULES FOR CONTINGENT EVENTS.—In the case of any unpredictable contingent event benefit with respect to which the event on which such benefits are contingent occurs after December 17, 1987—

(i) AMORTIZATION AMOUNT.—For purposes of subparagraph (A)(ii), the amount determined under this clause for any plan year is the amount which would be determined if the unpredictable contingent event benefit liability were amortized in equal annual installments over 10 plan years (beginning with the plan year in which such event occurs).

(ii) BENEFIT AND CONTRIBUTIONS NOT TAKEN INTO ACCOUNT.—For purposes of subparagraph (B), in determining the funded current liability percentage for any plan year, there shall not be taken into account—

(I) the unpredictable contingent event benefit liability, or

(II) any amount contributed to the plan which is attributable to clause (i) (and any income allocable to such amount)

(D) STEEL EMPLOYEE PLAN.—For purposes of this paragraph, the term "steel employee plan" means any plan if—

(i) such plan is maintained by a steel company, and

(ii) substantially all of the employees covered by such plan are employees of such company.

(E) OTHER DEFINITIONS.—For purposes of this paragraph—

(i) STEEL COMPANY.—The term "steel company" means any corporation described in section 806(b) of the Steel Import Stabilization Act.

(ii) OTHER DEFINITIONS.—The terms "current liability", "funded current liability percentage", and "unpredictable contingent event benefit" have the meanings given such terms by section 412(l) of the 1986 Code (as added by this section).

(E)[(F)] SPECIAL RULE.—The provisions of this paragraph shall apply in the case of a company which was originally incorporated on April 25, 1927, in Michigan and reincorporated on June 3, 1968, in Delaware in the same manner as if such company were a steel company.

[Sec. 412(m)]

(m) QUARTERLY CONTRIBUTIONS REQUIRED.—

(1) IN GENERAL.—If a defined benefit plan (other than a multiemployer plan) which has a funded current liability percentage (as defined in subsection (l)(8)) for the preceding plan year of less than 100 percent fails to pay the full amount of a required installment for any plan year, then the rate of interest charged to the funding standard account under subsection (b)(5) with respect to the amount of the underpayment for the period of the underpayment shall be equal to the greater of—

(A) 175 percent of the Federal mid-term rate (as in effect under section 1274 for the 1st month of such plan year), or

(B) the rate of interest used under the plan in determining costs (including adjustments under subsection (b)(5)(B)).

(2) AMOUNT OF UNDERPAYMENT, PERIOD OF UNDERPAYMENT.—For purposes of paragraph (1)—

(A) AMOUNT.—The amount of the underpayment shall be the excess of—

(i) the required installment, over

(ii) the amount (if any) of the installment contributed to or under the plan on or before the due date for the installment.

(B) PERIOD OF UNDERPAYMENT.—The period for which interest is charged under this subsection with regard to any portion of the underpayment shall run from the due date for the installment to the date on which such portion is contributed to or under the plan (determined without regard to subsection (c)(10)).

(C) ORDER OF CREDITING CONTRIBUTIONS.—For purposes of subparagraph (A)(ii), contributions shall be credited against unpaid required installments in the order in which such installments are required to be paid.

(3) NUMBER OF REQUIRED INSTALLMENTS; DUE DATES.—For purposes of this subsection—

(A) PAYABLE IN 4 INSTALLMENTS.—There shall be 4 required installments for each plan year.

(B) TIME FOR PAYMENT OF INSTALLMENTS.—

In the case of the following required installments:	*The due date is:*
1st	April 15
2nd	July 15
3rd	October 15
4th	January 15 of the following year

(4) AMOUNT OF REQUIRED INSTALLMENT.—For purposes of this subsection—

(A) IN GENERAL.—The amount of any required installment shall be the applicable percentage of the required annual payment.

(B) REQUIRED ANNUAL PAYMENT.—For purposes of subparagraph (A), the term "required annual payment" means the lesser of—

(i) 90 percent of the amount required to be contributed to or under the plan by the employer for the plan year under section 412 (without regard to any waiver under subsection (d) thereof), or

(ii) 100 percent of the amount so required for the preceding plan year.

Clause (ii) shall not apply if the preceding plan year was not a year of 12 months.

(C) APPLICABLE PERCENTAGE.—For purposes of subparagraph (A), the applicable percentage shall be determined in accordance with the following table:

For plan years beginning in:	*The applicable percentage is:*
1989	6.25
1990	12.5
1991	18.75
1992 and thereafter	25.

(D) SPECIAL RULES FOR UNPREDICTABLE CONTINGENT EVENT BENEFITS.—In the case of a plan to which subsection (1) applies for any calendar year and which has any unpredictable contingent event benefit liabilities—

(i) LIABILITIES NOT TAKEN INTO ACCOUNT.—Such liabilities shall not be taken into account in computing the required annual payment under subparagraph (B).

(ii) INCREASE IN INSTALLMENTS.—Each required installment shall be increased by the greatest of—

(I) the unfunded percentage of the amount of benefits described in subsection (l)(5)(A)(i) paid during the 3-month period preceding the month in which the due date for such installment occurs,

(II) 25 percent of the amount determined under subsection (1)(5)(A)(ii) for the plan year, or

(III) 25 percent of the amount determined under subsection (l)(5)(A)(iii) for the plan year.

(iii) UNFUNDED PERCENTAGE.—For purposes of clause (ii)(I), the term "unfunded percentage" means the percentage determined under subsection (1)(5)(A)(i)(I) for the plan year.

(iv) LIMITATION ON INCREASE.—In no event shall the increases under clause (ii) exceed the amount necessary to increase the funded current liability percentage (within the meaning of subsection (l)(8)(B)) for the plan year to 100 percent.

(5) LIQUIDITY REQUIREMENT.—

(A) IN GENERAL.—A plan to which this paragraph applies shall be treated as failing to pay the full amount of any required installment to the extent that the value of the liquid assets paid in such installment is less than the liquidity shortfall (whether or not such liquidity shortfall exceeds the amount of such installment required to be paid but for this paragraph).

(B) PLANS TO WHICH PARAGRAPH APPLIES.—This paragraph shall apply to a defined benefit plan (other than a multiemployer plan or a plan described in subsection (l)(6)(A)) which—

(i) is required to pay installments under this subsection for a plan year, and

(ii) has a liquidity shortall for any quarter during such plan year.

(C) PERIOD OF UNDERPAYMENT.—For purposes of paragraph (1), any portion of an installment that is treated as not paid under subparagraph (A) shall continue to be treated as unpaid until the close of the quarter in which the due date for such installment occurs.

(D) LIMITATION ON INCREASE.—If the amount of any required installment is increased by reason of subparagraph (A), in no event shall such increase exceed the amount which, when added to prior installments for the plan year, is necessary to increase the funded current liability percentage (taking into account the expected increase in current liability due to benefits accruing during the plan year) to 100 percent.

(E) DEFINITIONS.—For purposes of this paragraph:

(i) LIQUIDITY SHORTFALL.—The term "liquidity shortfall" means, with respect to any required installment, an amount equal to the excess (as of the last day of the quarter for which such installment is made) of the base amount with respect to such quarter over the value (as of such last day) of the plan's liquid assets.

(ii) BASE AMOUNT.—

(I) IN GENERAL.—The term "base amount" means, with respect to any quarter, an amount equal to 3 times the sum of the adjusted disbursements from the plan for the 12 months ending on the last day of such quarter.

(II) SPECIAL RULE.—If the amount determined under subclause (I) exceeds an amount equal to 2 times the sum of the adjusted disbursements from the plan for the 36 months ending on the last day of the quarter and an enrolled actuary certifies to the satisfaction of the Secretary that such excess is the result of nonrecurring circumstances, the base amount with respect to such quarter shall be determined without regard to amounts related to those nonrecurring circumstances.

(iii) DISBURSEMENTS FROM THE PLAN.—The term "disbursements from the plan" means all disbursements from the trust, including purchase of annuities, payments of single sums and other benefits, and administrative expenses.

(iv) ADJUSTED DISBURSEMENTS.—The term "adjusted disbursements" means disbursements from the plan reduced by the product of—

(I) the plan's funded current liability percentage (as defined in subsection (l)(8)) for the plan year, and

(II) the sum of the purchases of annuities, payments of single sums, and such other disbursements as the Secretary shall provide in regulations.

(v) LIQUID ASSETS.—The term "liquid assets" means cash, marketable securities and such other assets as specified by the Secretary in regulations.

(vi) QUARTER.—The term "quarter" means, with respect to any required installment, the 3-month period preceding the month in which the due date for such installment occurs.

(F) REGULATIONS.—The Secretary may prescribe such regulations as are necessary to carry out this paragraph.

(6) FISCAL YEARS AND SHORT YEARS.—

(A) FISCAL YEARS.—In applying this subsection to a plan year beginning on any date other than January 1, there shall be substituted for the months specified in this subsection, the months which correspond thereto.

(B) SHORT PLAN YEAR.—This subsection shall be applied to plan years of less than 12 months in accordance with regulations prescribed by the Secretary.

(7) SPECIAL RULE FOR 2002.—In any case in which the interest rate used to determine current liability is determined under subsection (l)(7)(C)(i)(III), for purposes of applying paragraphs (1) and (4)(B)(ii) for plan years beginning in 2002, the current liability for the preceding plan year shall be redetermined using 120 percent as the specified percentage determined under subsection (l)(7)(C)(i)(II).

Amendments

• 2005, Gulf Opportunity Zone Act of 2005 (P.L. 109-135)

P.L. 109-135, §412(x)(1):

Amended Code Sec. 412(m)(4)(B)(i) by striking "subsection (c)" and inserting "subsection (d)". **Effective** 12-21-2005.

• 2004, Pension Funding Equity Act of 2004 (P.L. 108-218)

P.L. 108-218, §101(b)(3):

Amended Code Sec. 412(m)(7). **Effective** generally for plan years beginning after 12-31-2003. For a special rule, see Act Sec. 101(d)(2), below. See, also, P.L. 103-465, §769, as amended by P.L. 105-34 and P.L. 108-218, in the amendment notes for Code Sec. 412(l). Prior to amendment, Code Sec. 412(m)(7) read as follows:

(7) SPECIAL RULES FOR 2002 AND 2004.—In any case in which the interest rate used to determine current liability is determined under subsection (l)(7)(C)(i)(III)—

(A) 2002.—For purposes of applying paragraphs (1) and (4)(B)(ii) for plan years beginning in 2002, the current liability for the preceding plan year shall be redetermined using 120 percent as the specified percentage determined under subsection (l)(7)(C)(i)(II).

(B) 2004.—For purposes of applying paragraphs (1) and (4)(B)(ii) for plan years beginning in 2004, the current liability for the preceding plan year shall be redetermined using 105 percent as the specified percentage determined under subsection (l)(7)(C)(i)(II).

P.L. 108-218, §101(d)(2), provides:

(2) LOOKBACK RULES.—For purposes of applying subsections (d)(9)(B)(ii) and (e)(1) of section 302 of the Employee Retirement Income Security Act of 1974 and subsections (l)(9)(B)(ii) and (m)(1) of section 412 of the Internal Revenue Code of 1986 to plan years beginning after December 31, 2003, the amendments made by this section may be applied as if such amendments had been in effect for all prior plan years. The Secretary of the Treasury may prescribe simplified assumptions which may be used in applying the amendments made by this section to such prior plan years.

• 2002, Job Creation and Worker Assistance Act of 2002 (P.L. 107-147)

P.L. 107-147, §405(a)(2):

Amended Code Sec. 412(m) by adding at the end a new paragraph (7). **Effective** on 3-9-2002.

• 1997, Taxpayer Relief Act of 1997 (P.L. 105-34)

P.L. 105-34, §1604(b)(2)(A):

Amended Code Sec. 412(m)(5)(E)(ii)(II) by striking "clause (i)" and inserting "subclause (I)". **Effective** as if included in the section of P.L. 103-465 to which it relates [**effective** for plan years beginning after 12-31-94.—CCH].

• 1994, Uruguay Round Agreements Act (P.L. 103-465)

P.L. 103-465, §751(a)(6)(C)(i)-(iv):

Amended Code Sec. 412(m)(4)(D)(ii) by striking "greater of" and inserting "greatest of" before subclause (I), by striking "or" at the end of subclause (I), by striking the period at the end of subclause (II) and inserting ", or", and by adding after subclause (II) a new [sub]clause (III). **Effective** for plan years beginning after 12-31-94.

P.L. 103-465, §751(a)(9)(A):

Amended Code Sec. 412(m) by redesignating paragraph (5) as paragraph (6) and by inserting after paragraph (4) a new paragraph (5). **Effective** for plan years beginning after 12-31-94.

P.L. 103-465, §754(a)(1)-(2):

Amended Code Sec. 412(m)(1) by inserting "which has a funded current liability percentage (as defined in subsection (l)(8)) for the preceding plan year of less than 100 percent" before "fails", and by striking "any plan year" and inserting "the plan year". **Effective** for plan years beginning after 12-8-94.

• 1989, Omnibus Budget Reconciliation Act of 1989 (P.L. 101-239)

P.L. 101-239, §7881(b)(3)(A):

Amended Code Sec. 412(m)(1) by inserting "defined benefit" before "plan (other". **Effective** as if included in the provision of P.L. 100-203 to which it relates.

P.L. 101-239, §7881(b)(4)(A):

Amended Code Sec. 412(m)(4)(D). **Effective** as if included in the provision of P.L. 100-203 to which it relates. Prior to amendment, Code Sec. 412(m)(4)(D) read as follows:

(D) SPECIAL RULES FOR UNPREDICTABLE CONTINGENT EVENT BENEFITS.—In the case of a plan with any unpredictable contingent event benefit liabilities—

(i) such liabilities shall not be taken into account in computing the required annual payment under subparagraph (B), and

(ii) each required installment shall be increased by the greater of—

(I) the amount of benefits described in subsection (l)(5)(A)(i) paid during the 3-month period preceding the month in which the due date for such installment occurs, or

(II) 25 percent of the amount determined under subsection (l)(5)(A)(ii) for the plan year.

P.L. 101-239, §7881(b)(6)(A)(i):

Amended Code Sec. 412(m)(1)(B). **Effective** as if included in the provision of P.L. 100-203 to which it relates. Prior to amendment, Code Sec. 412(m)(1)(B) read as follows:

(B) the rate under subsection (b)(5).

• 1987, Revenue Act of 1987 (P.L. 100-203)

P.L. 100-203, §9304(b)(1):

Amended Code Sec. 412 by adding at the end thereof new subsection (m). **Effective** with respect to plan years beginning after 1988.

[Sec. 412(n)]

(n) IMPOSITION OF LIEN WHERE FAILURE TO MAKE REQUIRED CONTRIBUTIONS.—

(1) IN GENERAL.—In the case of a plan to which this section applies, if—

(A) any person fails to make a required installment under subsection (m) or any other payment required under this section before the due date for such installment or other payment, and

(B) the unpaid balance of such installment or other payment (including interest), when added to the aggregate unpaid balance of all preceding such installments or other payments for which payment was not made before the due date (including interest), exceeds $1,000,000,

then there shall be a lien in favor of the plan in the amount determined under paragraph (3) upon all property and rights to property, whether real or personal, belonging to such person and any other person who is a member of the same controlled group of which such person is a member.

(2) PLANS TO WHICH SUBSECTION APPLIES.—This subsection shall apply to a defined benefit plan (other than a multiemployer plan) for any plan year for which the funded current liability percentage (within the meaning of subsection (l)(8)(B)) of such plan is less than 100 percent. This subsection shall not apply to any plan to which section 4021 of the Employee Retirement Income Security Act of 1974 does not apply (as such section is in effect on the date of the enactment of the Retirement Protection Act of 1994).

(3) AMOUNT OF LIEN.—For purposes of paragraph (1), the amount of the lien shall be equal to the aggregate unpaid balance of required installments and other payments required under this section (including interest)—

(A) for plan years beginning after 1987, and

(B) for which payment has not been made before the due date.

(4) NOTICE OF FAILURE; LIEN.—

(A) NOTICE OF FAILURE.—A person committing a failure described in paragraph (1) shall notify the Pension Benefit Guaranty Corporation of such failure within 10 days of the due date for the required installment or other payment.

(B) PERIOD OF LIEN.—The lien imposed by paragraph (1) shall arise on the due date for the required installment or other payment and shall continue until the last day of the first plan year in which the plan ceases to be described in paragraph (1)(B). Such lien shall continue to run without regard to whether such plan continues to be described in paragraph (2) during the period referred to in the preceding sentence.

(C) CERTAIN RULES TO APPLY.—Any amount with respect to which a lien is imposed under paragraph (1) shall be treated as taxes due and owing the United States and rules similar to the rules of subsections (c), (d), and (e) of section 4068 of the Employee Retirement Income Security Act of 1974 shall apply with respect to a lien imposed by subsection (a) and the amount with respect to such lien.

(5) ENFORCEMENT.—Any lien created under paragraph (1) may be perfected and enforced only by the Pension Benefit Guaranty Corporation, or at the direction of the Pension Benefit Guaranty Corporation, by the contributing sponsor (or any member of the controlled group of the contributing sponsor).

(6) DEFINITIONS.—For purposes of this subsection—

(A) DUE DATE; REQUIRED INSTALLMENT.—The terms "due date" and "required installment" have the meanings given such terms by subsection (m), except that in the case of a payment other than a required installment, the due date shall be the date such payment is required to be made under this section.

(B) CONTROLLED GROUP.—The term "controlled group" means any group treated as a single employer under subsections (b), (c), (m), and (o) of section 414.

Amendments

• 1994, Uruguay Round Agreements Act (P.L. 103-465)

P.L. 103-465, §768(a)(1):

Amended Code Sec. 412(n)(2) by adding at the end a new sentence. **Effective** for installments and other payments required under Code Sec. 412 or under part 3 of subtitle B of P.L. 93-406 that become due on or after 12-8-94.

P.L. 103-465, §768(a)(2):

Amended Code Sec. 412(n)(3). **Effective** for installments and other payments required under Code Sec. 412 or under part 3 of subtitle B of P.L. 93-406 that become due on or after 12-8-94. Prior to amendment, Code Sec. 412(n)(3) read as follows:

(3) AMOUNT OF LIEN.—For purposes of paragraph (1), the amount of the lien shall be equal to the lesser of—

(A) the amount by which the unpaid balances described in paragraph (1)(B) (including interest) exceed $1,000,000, or

(B) the aggregate unpaid balance of required installments and other payments required under this section (including interest)—

(i) for plan years beginning after 1987, and

(ii) for which payment has not been made before the due date.

P.L. 103-465, §768(a)(3):

Amended Code Sec. 412(n)(4)(B) by striking "60th day following the" after "shall arise on". **Effective** for installments and other payments required under Code Sec. 412 or under part 3 of subtitle B of P.L. 93-406 that become due on or after 12-8-94.

• 1987, Revenue Act of 1987 (P.L. 100-203)

P.L. 100-203, §9304(e)(1):

Amended Code Sec. 412 by adding at the end thereof new subsection (n). **Effective** for plan years beginning after 12-31-87.

[Sec. 413]

SEC. 413. COLLECTIVELY BARGAINED PLANS, ETC.

[Sec. 413(a)]

(a) APPLICATION OF SUBSECTION (b).—Subsection (b) applies to—

(1) a plan maintained pursuant to an agreement which the Secretary of Labor finds to be a collective-bargaining agreement between employee representatives and one or more employers, and

(2) each trust which is a part of such plan.

[Sec. 413(b)]

(b) GENERAL RULE.—If this subsection applies to a plan, notwithstanding any other provision of this title—

(1) PARTICIPATION.—Section 410 shall be applied as if all employees of each of the employers who are parties to the collective-bargaining agreement and who are subject to the same benefit computation formula under the plan were employed by a single employer.

(2) DISCRIMINATION, ETC.—Sections 401(a)(4) and 411(d)(3) shall be applied as if all participants who are subject to the same benefit computation formula and who are employed by employers who are parties to the collective bargaining agreement were employed by a single employer.

(3) EXCLUSIVE BENEFIT.—For purposes of section 401(a), in determining whether the plan of an employer is for the exclusive benefit of his employees and their beneficiaries, all plan participants shall be considered to be his employees.

(4) VESTING.—Section 411 (other than subsection (d)(3)) shall be applied as if all employers who have been parties to the collective-bargaining agreement constituted a single employer, except that the application of any rules with respect to breaks in service shall be made under regulations prescribed by the Secretary of Labor.

(5) FUNDING.—The minimum funding standard provided by section 412 shall be determined as if all participants in the plan were employed by a single employer.

(6) LIABILITY FOR FUNDING TAX.—For a plan year the liability under section 4971 of each employer who is a party to the collective bargaining agreement shall be determined in a reasonable manner not inconsistent with regulations prescribed by the Secretary—

(A) first on the basis of their respective delinquencies in meeting required employer contributions under the plan, and

(B) then on the basis of their respective liabilities for contributions under the plan.

For purposes of this subsection and the last sentence of section 4971(a), an employer's withdrawal liability under part 1 of subtitle E of title IV of the Employee Retirement Income Security Act of 1974 shall not be treated as a liability for contributions under the plan.

(7) DEDUCTION LIMITATIONS.—Each applicable limitation provided by section 404(a) shall be determined as if all participants in the plan were employed by a single employer. The amounts contributed to or under the plan by each employer who is a party to the agreement, for the portion of his taxable year which is included within such a plan year, shall be considered not to exceed such a limitation if the anticipated employer contributions for such plan year (determined in a manner consistent with the manner in which actual employer contributions for such plan year are determined) do not exceed such limitation. If such anticipated contributions exceed such a limitation, the portion of each such employer's contributions which is not deductible under section 404 shall be determined in accordance with regulations prescribed by the Secretary.

(8) EMPLOYEES OF LABOR UNIONS.—For purposes of this subsection, employees of employee representatives shall be treated as employees of an employer described in subsection (a)(1) if such representatives meet the requirements of sections 401(a)(4) and 410 with respect to such employees.

(9) PLANS COVERING A PROFESSIONAL EMPLOYEE.—Notwithstanding subsection (a), in the case of a plan (and trust forming part thereof) which covers any professional employee, paragraph (1) shall be applied by substituting "section 410(a)" for "section 410", and paragraph (2) shall not apply.

Amendments

• 1988, Technical and Miscellaneous Revenue Act of 1988 (P.L. 100-647)

P.L. 100-647, §1011(h)(10):

Amended Code Sec. 413(b) by adding at the end thereof new paragraph (9). **Effective** as if included in the provision of P.L. 99-514 to which it relates.

• 1980, Multiemployer Pension Plan Amendments Act of 1980 (P.L. 96-364)

P.L. 96-364, §208(d):

Amended Code Sec. 413(b)(6) by adding the last sentence. **Effective** 9-26-80.

• 1976, Tax Reform Act of 1976 (P.L. 94-455)

P.L. 94-455, §1906(b)(13)(A):

Amended 1954 Code by substituting "Secretary" for "Secretary or his delegate" each place it appeared. **Effective** 2-1-77.

[Sec. 413(c)]

(c) PLANS MAINTAINED BY MORE THAN ONE EMPLOYER.—In the case of a plan maintained by more than one employer—

(1) PARTICIPATION.—Section 410(a) shall be applied as if all employees of each of the employers who maintain the plan were employed by a single employer.

(2) EXCLUSIVE BENEFIT.—For purposes of section 401(a), in determining whether the plan of an employer is for the exclusive benefit of his employees and their beneficiaries all plan participants shall be considered to be his employees.

(3) VESTING.—Section 411 shall be applied as if all employers who maintain the plan constituted a single employer, except that the application of any rules with respect to breaks in service shall be made under regulations prescribed by the Secretary of Labor.

(4) FUNDING.—

(A) IN GENERAL.—In the case of a plan established after December 31, 1988, each employer shall be treated as maintaining a separate plan for purposes of section 412 unless such plan uses a method for determining required contributions which provides that any employer contributes not less than the amount which would be required if such employer maintained a separate plan.

(B) OTHER PLANS.—In the case of a plan not described in subparagraph (A), the requirements of section 412 shall be determined as if all participants in the plan were employed by a single employer unless the plan administrator elects not later than the close of the first plan year of the plan beginning after the date of enactment of the Technical and Miscellaneous Revenue Act of 1988 to have the provisions of subparagraph (A) apply. An election under the preceding sentence shall take effect for the plan year in which made and, once made, may be revoked only with the consent of the Secretary.

(5) LIABILITY FOR FUNDING TAX.—For a plan year the liability under section 4971 of each employer who maintains the plan shall be determined in a reasonable manner not inconsistent with regulations prescribed by the Secretary—

(A) first on the basis of their respective delinquencies in meeting required employer contributions under the plan, and

(B) then on the basis of their respective liabilities for contributions under the plan.

(6) DEDUCTION LIMITATIONS.—

(A) IN GENERAL.—In the case of a plan established after December 31, 1988, each applicable limitation provided by section 404(a) shall be determined as if each employer were maintaining a separate plan.

(B) OTHER PLANS.—

(i) IN GENERAL.—In the case of a plan not described in subparagraph (A), each applicable limitation provided by section 404(a) shall be determined as if all participants in the plan were employed by a single employer, except that if an election is made under paragraph (4)(B), subparagraph (A) shall apply to such plan.

(ii) SPECIAL RULE.—If this subparagraph applies, the amounts contributed to or under the plan by each employer who maintains the plan (for the portion of the taxable year included within a plan year) shall be considered not to exceed any such limitation if the anticipated employer contributions for such plan year (determined in a reasonable manner not inconsistent with regulations prescribed by the Secretary) do not exceed such limitation. If such anticipated contributions exceed such a limitation, the portion of each such employer's contributions which is not deductible under section 404 shall be determined in accordance with regulations prescribed by the Secretary.

(7) ALLOCATIONS.—

(A) IN GENERAL.—Except as provided in subparagraph (B), allocations of amounts under paragraphs (4), (5), and (6) among the employers maintaining the plan shall not be inconsistent with regulations prescribed for this purpose by the Secretary.

(B) ASSETS AND LIABILITIES OF PLAN.—For purposes of applying paragraphs (4)(A) and (6)(A), the assets and liabilities of each plan shall be treated as the assets and liabilities which would be allocated to a plan maintained by the employer if the employer withdrew from the multiple employer plan.

Amendments

• 1990, Omnibus Budget Reconciliation Act of 1990 (P.L. 101-508)

P.L. 101-508, §11704(a)(4):

Amended Code Sec. 413(c)(7)(B) by striking "Asset" in the heading and inserting "Assets". **Effective** 11-5-90.

• 1988, Technical and Miscellaneous Revenue Act of 1988 (P.L. 100-647)

P.L. 100-647, §6058(a):

Amended Code Sec. 413(c)(4). **Effective** for plan years beginning after 11-10-88. Prior to amendment, Code Sec. 413(c)(4) read as follows:

(4) FUNDING.—The minimum funding standard provided by section 412 shall be determined as if all participants in the plan were employed by a single employer.

P.L. 100-647, §6058(b):

Amended Code Sec. 413(c)(6). **Effective** for plan years beginning after 11-10-88. Prior to amendment, Code Sec. 413(c)(6) read as follows:

(6) DEDUCTION LIMITATIONS.—Each applicable limitation provided by section 404(a) shall be determined as if all participants in the plan were employed by a single employer. The amounts contributed to or under the plan by each employer who maintains the plan, for the portion of this taxable year which is included within such a plan year, shall be considered not to exceed such a limitation if the anticipated employer contributions for such plan year (determined in a reasonable manner not inconsistent with regulations prescribed by the Secretary) do not exceed such limitation. If such anticipated contributions exceed such a limitation, the portion of each such employer's contributions which is not deductible under section 404 shall be determined in accordance with regulations prescribed by the Secretary.

P.L. 100-647, §6058(c):

Amended Code Sec. 413(c) by striking the last sentence and by inserting after paragraph (6) a new paragraph (7). **Effective** for plan years beginning after 11-10-88. Prior to amendment, the last sentence of Code Sec. 413(c) read as follows:

Allocations of amounts under paragraphs (4), (5), and (6), among the employers maintaining the plan, shall not be inconsistent with regulations prescribed for this purpose by the Secretary.

• 1976, Tax Reform Act of 1976 (P.L. 94-455)

P.L. 94-455, §1906(b)(13)(A):

Amended 1954 Code by substituting "Secretary" for "Secretary or his delegate" each place it appeared. **Effective** 2-1-77.

• 1974, Employee Retirement Income Security Act of 1974 (P.L. 93-406)

P.L. 93-406, §1014:

Added Code Sec. 413. For **effective** dates and transitional rules governing this section, see the historical note for §1017, P.L. 93-406, following the text of Code Sec. 410(d).

[Sec. 414]

SEC. 414. DEFINITIONS AND SPECIAL RULES.

[Sec. 414(a)]

(a) SERVICE FOR PREDECESSOR EMPLOYER.—For purposes of this part—

(1) in any case in which the employer maintains a plan of a predecessor employer, service for such predecessor shall be treated as service for the employer, and

(2) in any case in which the employer maintains a plan which is not the plan maintained by a predecessor employer, service for such predecessor shall, to the extent provided in regulations prescribed by the Secretary, be treated as service for the employer.

Amendments

• 1976, Tax Reform Act of 1976 (P.L. 94-455)

P.L. 94-455, §1906(b)(13)(A):

Amended 1954 Code by substituting "Secretary" for "Secretary or his delegate" each place it appeared. **Effective** 2-1-77.

[Sec. 414(b)]

(b) EMPLOYEES OF CONTROLLED GROUP OF CORPORATIONS.—For purposes of sections 401, 408(k), 408(p), 410, 411, 415, and 416, all employees of all corporations which are members of a controlled group of corporations (within the meaning of section 1563(a), determined without regard to section 1563(a)(4) and (e)(3)(C)) shall be treated as employed by a single employer. With respect to a plan adopted by more than one such corporation, the applicable limitations provided by section 404(a) shall be determined as if all such employers were a single employer, and allocated to each employer in accordance with regulations prescribed by the Secretary.

Amendments

• 1996, Small Business Job Protection Act of 1996 (P.L. 104-188)

P.L. 104-188, §1421(b)(9)(C):

Amended Code Sec. 414(b) by inserting "408(p)," after "408(k),". **Effective** for tax years beginning after 12-31-96.

• 1987, Revenue Act of 1987 (P.L. 100-203)

P.L. 100-203, §9305(c):

Amended Code Sec. 414(b) by striking out "the minimum funding standard of section 412, the tax imposed by section 4971, and" following "one such corporation" in the second sentence. **Effective** with respect to plan years beginning after 12-31-87.

• 1982, Tax Equity and Fiscal Responsibility Act of 1982 (P.L. 97-248)

P.L. 97-248, §240(c)(1):

Amended Code Sec. 414(b) by striking out "and 415" and inserting "415, and 416". **Effective** for years beginning after 12-31-83.

• 1978, Revenue Act of 1978 (P.L. 95-600)

P.L. 95-600, §152(d):

Amended Code Sec. 414(b) by inserting "408(k)," after "401,". **Effective** for tax years beginning after 12-31-78.

• 1976, Tax Reform Act of 1976 (P.L. 94-455)

P.L. 94-455, §1906(b)(13)(A):

Amended 1954 Code by substituting "Secretary" for "Secretary or his delegate" each place it appeared. **Effective** 2-1-77.

[Sec. 414(c)]

(c) EMPLOYEES OF PARTNERSHIPS, PROPRIETORSHIPS, ETC., WHICH ARE UNDER COMMON CONTROL.—For purposes of sections 401, 408(k), 408(p), 410, 411, 415, and 416, under regulations prescribed by the Secretary, all employees of trades or businesses (whether or not incorporated) which are under common control shall be treated as employed by a single employer. The regulations prescribed under this subsection shall be based on principles similar to the principles which apply in the case of subsection (b).

Amendments

• 1996, Small Business Job Protection Act of 1996 (P.L. 104-188)

P.L. 104-188, §1421(b)(9)(C):

Amended Code Sec. 414(c) by inserting "408(p)," after "408(k),". **Effective** for tax years beginning after 12-31-96.

• 1982, Tax Equity and Fiscal Responsibility Act of 1982 (P.L. 97-248)

P.L. 97-248, §240(c)(1):

Amended Code Sec. 414(c) by striking out "and 415" and inserting "415, and 416". **Effective** for years beginning after 12-31-83.

• 1978, Revenue Act of 1978 (P.L. 95-600)

P.L. 95-600, §152(d):

Amended Code Sec. 414(c) by inserting "408(k)," after "401,". **Effective** for tax years beginning after 12-31-78.

• 1976, Tax Reform Act of 1976 (P.L. 94-455)

P.L. 94-455, §1906(b)(13)(A):

Amended 1954 Code by substituting "Secretary" for "Secretary or his delegate" each place it appeared. **Effective** 2-1-77.

[Sec. 414(d)]

(d) GOVERNMENTAL PLAN.—For purposes of this part, the term "governmental plan" means a plan established and maintained for its employees by the Government of the United States, by the government of any State or political subdivision thereof, or by any agency or instrumentality of any of the foregoing. The term "governmental plan" also includes any plan to which the Railroad Retirement Act of 1935 or 1937 applies and which is financed by contributions required under that Act and any plan of an international organization which is exempt from taxation by reason of the International Organizations Immunities Act (59 Stat. 669). The term "governmental plan" includes a plan which is established and maintained by an Indian tribal government (as defined in section 7701(a)(40)), a subdivision of an Indian tribal government (determined in accordance with section 7871(d)), or an agency or instrumentality of either, and all of the participants of which are employees of such entity substantially all of whose services as such an employee are in the performance of essential governmental functions but not in the performance of commercial activities (whether or not an essential government function).

Amendments

• 2006, Pension Protection Act of 2006 (P.L. 109-280)

P.L. 109-280, §906(a)(1):

Amended Code Sec. 414(d) by adding at the end a new sentence. **Effective** for any year beginning on or after 8-17-2006.

P.L. 109-280, §1107, provides:

SEC. 1107. PROVISIONS RELATING TO PLAN AMENDMENTS.

(a) IN GENERAL.—If this section applies to any pension plan or contract amendment—

(1) such pension plan or contract shall be treated as being operated in accordance with the terms of the plan during the period described in subsection (b)(2)(A), and

(2) except as provided by the Secretary of the Treasury, such pension plan shall not fail to meet the requirements of section 411(d)(6) of the Internal Revenue Code of 1986 and section 204(g) of the Employee Retirement Income Security Act of 1974 by reason of such amendment.

(b) AMENDMENTS TO WHICH SECTION APPLIES.—

(1) IN GENERAL.—This section shall apply to any amendment to any pension plan or annuity contract which is made—

(A) pursuant to any amendment made by this Act or pursuant to any regulation issued by the Secretary of the Treasury or the Secretary of Labor under this Act, and

(B) on or before the last day of the first plan year beginning on or after January 1, 2009.

In the case of a governmental plan (as defined in section 414(d) of the Internal Revenue Code of 1986), this paragraph shall be applied by substituting "2011" for "2009".

(2) CONDITIONS.—This section shall not apply to any amendment unless—

(A) during the period—

(i) beginning on the date the legislative or regulatory amendment described in paragraph (1)(A) takes effect (or in the case of a plan or contract amendment not required by such legislative or regulatory amendment, the effective date specified by the plan), and

(ii) ending on the date described in paragraph (1)(B) (or, if earlier, the date the plan or contract amendment is adopted), the plan or contract is operated as if such plan or contract amendment were in effect; and

(B) such plan or contract amendment applies retroactively for such period.

• 2005, Katrina Emergency Tax Relief Act of 2005 (P.L. 109-73)

P.L. 109-73, §104 [repealed by P.L. 109-135, §201(b)(4)(A)], provides:

SEC. 104. PROVISIONS RELATING TO PLAN AMENDMENTS.

(a) IN GENERAL.—If this section applies to any amendment to any plan or annuity contract, such plan or contract shall be treated as being operated in accordance with the terms of the plan during the period described in subsection (b)(2)(A).

(b) AMENDMENTS TO WHICH SECTION APPLIES.—

(1) IN GENERAL.—This section shall apply to any amendment to any plan or annuity contract which is made—

(A) pursuant to any amendment made by this title, or pursuant to any regulation issued by the Secretary of the Treasury or the Secretary of Labor under this title, and

(B) on or before the last day of the first plan year beginning on or after January 1, 2007, or such later date as the Secretary of the Treasury may prescribe.

In the case of a governmental plan (as defined in section 414(d) of the Internal Revenue Code of 1986), subparagraph (B) shall be applied by substituting the date which is 2 years after the date otherwise applied under subparagraph (B).

(2) CONDITIONS.—This section shall not apply to any amendment unless—

(A) during the period—

(i) beginning on the date the legislative or regulatory amendment described in paragraph (1)(A) takes effect (or in the case of a plan or contract amendment not required by such legislative or regulatory amendment, the effective date specified by the plan), and

(ii) ending on the date described in paragraph (1)(B) (or, if earlier, the date the plan or contract amendment is adopted),

the plan or contract is operated as if such plan or contract amendment were in effect; and

(B) such plan or contract amendment applies retroactively for such period.

[Sec. 414(e)]

(e) CHURCH PLAN.—

(1) IN GENERAL.—For purposes of this part, the term "church plan" means a plan established and maintained (to the extent required in paragraph (2)(B)) for its employees (or their beneficiaries) by a church or by a convention or association of churches which is exempt from tax under section 501.

(2) CERTAIN PLANS EXCLUDED.—The term "church plan" does not include a plan—

(A) which is established and maintained primarily for the benefit of employees (or their beneficiaries) of such church or convention or association of churches who are employed in connection with one or more unrelated trades or businesses (within the meaning of section 513); or

(B) if less than substantially all of the individuals included in the plan are individuals described in paragraph (1) or (3)(B) (or their beneficiaries).

(3) DEFINITIONS AND OTHER PROVISIONS.—For purposes of this subsection—

(A) TREATMENT AS CHURCH PLAN.—A plan established and maintained for its employees (or their beneficiaries) by a church or by a convention or association of churches includes a plan maintained by an organization, whether a civil law corporation or otherwise, the principal purpose or function of which is the administration or funding of a plan or program for the provision of retirement benefits or welfare benefits, or both, for the employees of a church or a convention or association of churches, if such organization is controlled by or associated with a church or a convention or association of churches.

(B) EMPLOYEE DEFINED.—The term employee of a church or a convention or association of churches shall include—

(i) a duly ordained, commissioned, or licensed minister of a church in the exercise of his ministry, regardless of the source of his compensation;

(ii) an employee of an organization, whether a civil law corporation or otherwise, which is exempt from tax under section 501 and which is controlled by or associated with a church or a convention or association of churches; and

(iii) an individual described in subparagraph (E).

(C) CHURCH TREATED AS EMPLOYER.—A church or a convention or association of churches which is exempt from tax under section 501 shall be deemed the employer of any individual included as an employee under subparagraph (B).

(D) ASSOCIATION WITH CHURCH.—An organization, whether a civil law corporation or otherwise, is associated with a church or a convention or association of churches if it shares common religious bonds and convictions with that church or convention or association of churches.

(E) SPECIAL RULE IN CASE OF SEPARATION FROM PLAN.—If an employee who is included in a church plan separates from the service of a church or a convention or association of churches or an organization described in clause (ii) of paragraph (3)(B), the church plan shall not fail to meet the requirements of this subsection merely because the plan—

(i) retains the employee's accrued benefit or account for the payment of benefits to the employee or his beneficiaries pursuant to the terms of the plan; or

(ii) receives contributions on the employee's behalf after the employee's separation from such service, but only for a period of 5 years after such separation, unless the employee is disabled (within the meaning of the disability provisions of the church plan or, if there are no such provisions in the church plan, within the meaning of section 72(m)(7)) at the time of such separation from service.

(4) CORRECTION OF FAILURE TO MEET CHURCH PLAN REQUIREMENTS.—

(A) IN GENERAL.—If a plan established and maintained for its employees (or their beneficiaries) by a church or by a convention or association of churches which is exempt from tax under section 501 fails to meet one or more of the requirements of this subsection and corrects its failure to meet such requirements within the correction period, the plan shall be deemed to meet the requirements of this subsection for the year in which the correction was made and for all prior years.

(B) FAILURE TO CORRECT.—If a correction is not made within the correction period, the plan shall be deemed not to meet the requirements of this subsection beginning with the date on which the earliest failure to meet one or more of such requirements occurred.

(C) CORRECTION PERIOD DEFINED.—The term "correction period" means—

(i) the period ending 270 days after the date of mailing by the Secretary of a notice of default with respect to the plan's failure to meet one or more of the requirements of this subsection;

(ii) any period set by a court of competent jurisdiction after a final determination that the plan fails to meet such requirements, or, if the court does not specify such period, any reasonable period determined by the Secretary on the basis of all the facts and circumstances, but in any event not less than 270 days after the determination has become final; or

(iii) any additional period which the Secretary determines is reasonable or necessary for the correction of the default,

whichever has the latest ending date.

(5) SPECIAL RULES FOR CHAPLAINS AND SELF-EMPLOYED MINISTERS.—

(A) CERTAIN MINISTERS MAY PARTICIPATE.—For purposes of this part—

(i) IN GENERAL.—A duly ordained, commissioned, or licensed minister of a church is described in paragraph (3)(B) if, in connection with the exercise of their ministry, the minister—

(I) is a self-employed individual (within the meaning of section 401(c)(1)(B), or

(II) is employed by an organization other than an organization which is described in section 501(c)(3) and with respect to which the minister shares common religious bonds.

(ii) TREATMENT AS EMPLOYER AND EMPLOYEE.—For purposes of sections 403(b)(1)(A) and 404(a)(10), a minister described in clause (i)(I) shall be treated as employed by the minister's own employer which is an organization described in section 501(c)(3) and exempt from tax under section 501(a).

(B) SPECIAL RULES FOR APPLYING SECTION 403(b) TO SELF-EMPLOYED MINISTERS.—In the case of a minister described in subparagraph (A)(i)(I)—

(i) the minister's includible compensation under section 403(b)(3) shall be determined by reference to the minister's earned income (within the meaning of section 401(c)(2)) from such ministry rather than the amount of compensation which is received from an employer, and

(ii) the years (and portions of years) in which such minister was a self-employed individual (within the meaning of section 401(c)(1)(B)) with respect to such ministry shall be included for purposes of section 403(b)(4).

(C) EFFECT ON NON-DENOMINATIONAL PLANS.—If a duly ordained, commissioned, or licensed minister of a church in the exercise of his or her ministry participates in a church plan (within the meaning of this section) and in the exercise of such ministry is employed by an employer not otherwise participating in such church plan, then such employer may exclude such minister from being treated as an employee of such employer for purposes of applying sections 401(a)(3), 401(a)(4), and 401(a)(5), as in effect on September 1, 1974, and sections 401(a)(4), 401(a)(5), 401(a)(26), 401(k)(3), 401(m), 403(b)(1)(D) (including section 403(b)(12)), and 410 to any stock bonus, pension, profit-sharing, or annuity plan (including an annuity described in section 403(b) or a retirement income account described in section 403(b)(9)). The Secretary shall prescribe such regulations as may be necessary or appropriate to carry out the purpose of, and prevent the abuse of, this subparagraph.

(D) COMPENSATION TAKEN INTO ACCOUNT ONLY ONCE.—If any compensation is taken into account in determining the amount of any contributions made to, or benefits to be provided under, any church plan, such compensation shall not also be taken into account in determining the amount of any contributions made to, or benefits to be provided under, any other stock bonus, pension, profit-sharing, or annuity plan which is not a church plan.

(E) EXCLUSION.—In the case of a contribution to a church plan made on behalf of a minister described in subparagraph (A)(i)(II), such contribution shall not be included in the gross income of the minister to the extent that such contribution would not be so included if the minister was an employee of a church.

Amendments

• 1997, Taxpayer Relief Act of 1997 (P.L. 105-34)

P.L. 105-34, §1522(a)(1)-(2):

Amended Code Sec. 414(e)(5) by striking "not eligible to participate" in subparagraph (C) and inserting "not otherwise participating", and by adding at the end a new subparagraph (E). **Effective** for years beginning after 12-31-97.

P.L. 105-34, §1601(d)(6)(A):

Amended Code Sec. 414(e)(5)(A). **Effective** as if included in the provision of P.L. 104-188 to which it relates [**effective** for years beginning after 12-31-96.—CCH]. Prior to amendment, Code Sec. 414(e)(5)(A) read as follows:

(A) CERTAIN MINISTERS MAY PARTICIPATE.—For purposes of this part—

(i) IN GENERAL.—An employee of a church or a convention or association of churches shall include a duly ordained, commissioned, or licensed minister of a church who, in connection with the exercise of his or her ministry—

(I) is a self-employed individual (within the meaning of section 401(c)(1)(B)), or

(II) is employed by an organization other than an organization described in section 501(c)(3).

(ii) TREATMENT AS EMPLOYER AND EMPLOYEE.—

(I) SELF-EMPLOYED.—A minister described in clause (i)(I) shall be treated as his or her own employer which is an organization described in section 501(c)(3) and which is exempt from tax under section 501(a).

(II) OTHERS.—A minister described in clause (i)(II) shall be treated as employed by an organization described in section 501(c)(3) and exempt from tax under section 501(a).

• 1996, Small Business Job Protection Act of 1996 (P.L. 104-188)

P.L. 104-188, §1461(a):

Amended Code Sec. 414(e) by adding at the end a new paragraph (5). **Effective** for years beginning after 12-31-96.

• 1980, Multiemployer Pension Plan Act Amendments of 1980 (P.L. 96-364)

P.L. 96-364, §407(b):

Amended Code Sec. 414(e). **Effective** 1-1-74. Prior to amendment, Code Sec. 414(e) read as follows:

(e) CHURCH PLAN.—

(1) IN GENERAL.—For purposes of this part the term "church plan" means—

(A) a plan established and maintained for its employees by a church or by a convention or association of churches which is exempt from tax under section 501, or

(B) a plan described in paragraph (3).

(2) CERTAIN UNRELATED BUSINESS OR MULTIEMPLOYER PLANS.—The term "church plan" does not include a plan—

(A) which is established and maintained primarily for the benefit of employees (or their beneficiaries) of such church or convention or association of churches who are employed in connection with one or more unrelated trades or businesses (within the meaning of section 513), or

(B) which is a plan maintained by more than one employer, if one or more of the employers in the plan is not a church (or a convention or association of churches) which is exempt from tax under section 501.

(3) SPECIAL TEMPORARY RULE FOR CERTAIN CHURCH AGENCIES UNDER CHURCH PLAN.—

(A) Notwithstanding the provisions of paragraph (2)(B), a plan in existence on January 1, 1974, shall be treated as a church plan if it is established and maintained by a church or convention or association of churches and one or more agencies of such church (or convention or association) for the employees of such church (or convention or association) and the employees of one or more agencies of such church (or convention or association), and if such church (or convention or association) and each such agency is exempt from tax under section 501.

(B) Subparagraph (A) shall not apply to any plan maintained for employees of an agency with respect to which the plan was not maintained on January 1, 1974.

(C) Subparagraph (A) shall not apply with respect to any plan for any plan year beginning after December 31, 1982.

[Sec. 414(f)]

(f) MULTIEMPLOYER PLAN.—

(1) DEFINITION.—For purposes of this part, the term "multiemployer plan" means a plan—

(A) to which more than one employer is required to contribute,

(B) which is maintained pursuant to one or more collective bargaining agreements between one or more employee organizations and more than one employer, and

(C) which satisfies such other requirements as the Secretary of Labor may prescribe by regulation.

(2) CASES OF COMMON CONTROL.—For purposes of this subsection, all trades or businesses (whether or not incorporated) which are under common control within the meaning of subsection (c) are considered a single employer.

(3) CONTINUATION OF STATUS AFTER TERMINATION.—Notwithstanding paragraph (1), a plan is a multiemployer plan on and after its termination date under title IV of the Employee Retirement Income Security Act of 1974 if the plan was a multiemployer plan under this subsection for the plan year preceding its termination date.

(4) TRANSITIONAL RULE.—For any plan year which began before the date of the enactment of the Multiemployer Pension Plan Amendments Act of 1980, the term "multiemployer plan" means a plan described in this subsection as in effect immediately before that date.

(5) SPECIAL ELECTION.—Within one year after the date of the enactment of the Multiemployer Pension Plan Amendments Act of 1980, a multiemployer plan may irrevocably elect, pursuant to procedures established by the Pension Benefit Guaranty Corporation and subject to the provisions of section 4403(b) and (c) of the Employee Retirement Income Security Act of 1974, that the plan shall not be treated as a multiemployer plan for any purpose under such Act or this title, if for each of the last 3 plan years ending prior to the effective date of the Multiemployer Pension Plan Amendments Act of 1980—

(A) the plan was not a multiemployer plan because the plan was not a plan described in section 3(37)(A)(iii) of the Employee Retirement Income Security Act of 1974 and section 414(f)(1)(C) (as such provisions were in effect on the day before the date of the enactment of the Multiemployer Pension Plan Amendments Act of 1980); and

(B) the plan had been identified as a plan that was not a multiemployer plan in substantially all its filings with the Pension Benefit Guaranty Corporation, the Secretary of Labor and the Secretary.

(6) ELECTION WITH REGARD TO MULTIEMPLOYER STATUS.—

(A) Within 1 year after the enactment of the Pension Protection Act of 2006—

(i) An election under paragraph (5) may be revoked, pursuant to procedures prescribed by the Pension Benefit Guaranty Corporation, if, for each of the 3 plan years prior to the date of the enactment of that Act, the plan would have been a multiemployer plan but for the election under paragraph (5), and

(ii) a plan that meets the criteria in subparagraph (A) and (B) of paragraph (1) of this subsection or that is described in subparagraph (E) may, pursuant to procedures prescribed by the Pension Benefit Guaranty Corporation, elect to be a multiemployer plan, if—

(I) for each of the 3 plan years immediately preceding the first plan year for which the election under this paragraph is effective with respect to the plan, the plan has met those criteria or is so described,

(II) substantially all of the plan's employer contributions for each of those plan years were made or required to be made by organizations that were exempt from tax under section 501, and

(III) the plan was established prior to September 2, 1974.

(B) An election under this paragraph shall be effective for all purposes under this Act and under the Employee Retirement Income Security Act of 1974, starting with any plan year beginning on or after January 1, 1999, and ending before January 1, 2008, as designated by the plan in the election made under subparagraph (A)(ii).

(C) Once made, an election under this paragraph shall be irrevocable, except that a plan described in subparagraph (A)(ii) shall cease to be a multiemployer plan as of the plan year beginning immediately after the first plan year for which the majority of its employer contributions were made or required to be made by organizations that were not exempt from tax under section 501.

(D) The fact that a plan makes an election under subparagraph (A)(ii) does not imply that the plan was not a multiemployer plan prior to the date of the election or would not be a multiemployer plan without regard to the election.

(E) A plan is described in this subparagraph if it is a plan sponsored by an organization which is described in section 501(c)(5) and exempt from tax under section 501(a) and which was established in Chicago, Illinois, on August 12, 1881.

(F) MAINTENANCE UNDER COLLECTIVE BARGAINING AGREEMENT.—For purposes of this title and the Employee Retirement Income Security Act of 1974, a plan making an election under this paragraph shall be treated as maintained pursuant to a collective bargaining agreement if a collective bargaining agreement, expressly or otherwise, provides for or permits employer contributions to the plan by one or more employers that are signatory to such agreement, or participation in the plan by one or more employees of an employer that is signatory to such agreement, regardless of whether the plan was created, established, or maintained for such employees by virtue of another document that is not a collective bargaining agreement.

Amendments

• 2007, U.S. Troop Readiness, Veterans' Care, Katrina Recovery, and Iraq Accountability Appropriations Act, 2007 (P.L. 110-28)

P.L. 110-28, §6611(a)(2)(A)-(C):

Amended Code Sec. 414(f)(6), as amended by section 1106(b) of the Pension Protection Act of 2006 (P.L. 109-280), in subparagraph (A)(ii)(I), by striking "for each of the 3 plan years immediately before the date of enactment of the Pension Protection Act of 2006," and inserting "for each of the 3 plan years immediately preceding the first plan year for which the election under this paragraph is effective with respect to the plan,"; in subparagraph (B), by striking "starting with the first plan year ending after the date of the enactment of the Pension Protection Act of 2006" and inserting "starting with any plan year beginning on or after January 1, 1999, and ending before January 1, 2008, as designated by the plan in the election made under subparagraph (A)(ii)"; and by adding at the end a new subparagraph (F). **Effective** as if included in section 1106 of the Pension Protection Act of 2006 (P.L. 109-280) [**effective** 8-17-2006.—CCH].

P.L. 110-28, §6611(b)(2):

Amended Code Sec. 414(f)(6)(E), as amended by section 1106(b) of the Pension Protection Act of 2006 (P.L. 109-280), by striking "if it is a plan—" and all that follows and inserting "if it is a plan sponsored by an organization which is described in section 501(c)(5) and exempt from tax under section 501(a) and which was established in Chicago, Illinois, on August 12, 1881.". **Effective** as if included in section 1106 of the Pension Protection Act of 2006 (P.L. 109-280) [**effective** 8-17-2006.—CCH]. Prior to amendment, Code Sec. 414(f)(6)(E) read as follows:

(E) A plan is described in this subparagraph if it is a plan—

(i) that was established in Chicago, Illinois, on August 12, 1881; and

(ii) sponsored by an organization described in section 501(c)(5) and exempt from tax under section 501(a).

• 2006, Pension Protection Act of 2006 (P.L. 109-280)

P.L. 109-280, §1106(b):

Amended Code Sec. 414(f) by adding at the end a new paragraph (6). **Effective** 8-17-2006.

• 1980, Multiemployer Pension Plan Act Amendments of 1980 (P.L. 96-364)

P.L. 96-364, §207(a):

Amended Code Sec. 414(f). **Effective** 9-26-80. Prior to amendment, Code Sec. 414(f) read as follows:

"(f) MULTIEMPLOYER PLAN.—

"(1) IN GENERAL.—For purposes of this part, the term `multiemployer plan' means a plan—

"(A) to which more than one employer is required to contribute,

"(B) which is maintained pursuant to a collective-bargaining agreement between employee representatives and more than one employer,

"(C) under which the amount of contributions made under the plan for a plan year by each employer making such contributions is less than 50 percent of the aggregate amount of contributions made under the plan for that plan year by all employers making such contributions,

"(D) under which benefits are payable with respect to each participant without regard to the cessation of contributions by the employer who employed that participant except to the extent that such benefits accrued as a result of service with the employer before such employer was required to contribute to such plan, and

"(E) which satisfies such other requirements as the Secretary of Labor may by regulations prescribe.

"(2) SPECIAL RULES.—For purposes of this subsection—

"(A) If a plan is a multiemployer plan within the meaning of paragraph (1) for any plan year, subparagraph (C) of paragraph (1) shall be applied by substituting `75 percent' for `50 percent' for each subsequent plan year until the first plan year following a plan year in which the plan had one employer who made contributions of 75 percent or more of the aggregate amount of contributions made under the plan for that plan year by all employers making such contributions.

"(B) All corporations which are members of a controlled group of corporations (within the meaning of section 1563(a), determined without regard to section 1563(e)(3)(C)) shall be deemed to be one employer."

• 1976, Tax Reform Act of 1976 (P.L. 94-455)

P.L. 94-455, §1901(a)(64)(A):

Amended the heading of Code Sec. 414(f). **Effective** for tax years beginning after 12-31-76.

[Sec. 414(g)]

(g) PLAN ADMINISTRATOR.—For purposes of this part, the term "plan administrator" means—

(1) the person specifically so designated by the terms of the instrument under which the plan is operated;

(2) in the absence of a designation referred to in paragraph (1)—

(A) in the case of a plan maintained by a single employer, such employer,

(B) in the case of a plan maintained by two or more employers or jointly by one or more employers and one or more employee organizations, the association, committee, joint board of trustees, or other similar group of representatives of the parties who maintained the plan, or

(C) in any case to which subparagraph (A) or (B) does not apply, such other person as the Secretary may, by regulation, prescribe.

Amendments

• 1976, Tax Reform Act of 1976 (P.L. 94-455)

P.L. 94-455, §1906(b)(13)(A):

Amended 1954 Code by substituting "Secretary" for "Secretary or his delegate" each place it appeared. **Effective** 2-1-77.

[Sec. 414(h)]

(h) TAX TREATMENT OF CERTAIN CONTRIBUTIONS.—

(1) IN GENERAL.—Effective with respect to taxable years beginning after December 31, 1973, for purposes of this title, any amount contributed—

(A) to an employees' trust described in section 401(a), or

(B) under a plan described in section 403(a),

shall not be treated as having been made by the employer if it is designated as an employee contribution.

(2) DESIGNATION BY UNITS OF GOVERNMENT.—For purposes of paragraph (1), in the case of any plan established by the government of any State or political subdivision thereof, or by any agency or instrumentality of any of the foregoing, or a governmental plan described in the last sentence of section 414(d) (relating to plans of Indian tribal governments), where the contributions of employing units are designated as employee contributions but where any employing unit picks up the contributions, the contributions so picked up shall be treated as employer contributions.

Amendments

• 2006, Pension Protection Act of 2006 (P.L. 109-280)

P.L. 109-280, §906(b)(1)(C):

Amended Code Sec. 414(h)(2) by inserting "or a governmental plan described in the last sentence of section 414(d) (relating to plans of Indian tribal governments)," after "foregoing,". **Effective** for any year beginning on or after 8-17-2006.

• 1984, Deficit Reduction Act of 1984 (P.L. 98-369)

P.L. 98-369, §491(d)(26):

Amended Code Sec. 414(h)(1)(B) by striking out "or 405(a)". **Effective** for obligations issued after 12-31-83.

[Sec. 414(i)]

(i) DEFINED CONTRIBUTION PLAN.—For purposes of this part, the term "defined contribution plan" means a plan which provides for an individual account for each participant and for benefits based solely on the amount contributed to the participant's account, and any income, expenses, gains and losses, and any forfeitures of accounts of other participants which may be allocated to such participant's account.

[Sec. 414(j)]

(j) DEFINED BENEFIT PLAN.—For purposes of this part, the term "defined benefit plan" means any plan which is not a defined contribution plan.

[Sec. 414(k)]

(k) CERTAIN PLANS.—A defined benefit plan which provides a benefit derived from employer contributions which is based partly on the balance of the separate account of a participant shall—

(1) for purposes of section 410 (relating to minimum participation standards), be treated as a defined contribution plan,

(2) for purposes of sections 72(d) (relating to treatment of employee contributions as separate contract), 411(a)(7)(A) (relating to minimum vesting standards), 415 (relating to limita-

tions on benefits and contributions under qualified plans), and 401(m) (relating to nondiscrimination tests for matching requirements and employee contributions), be treated as consisting of a defined contribution plan to the extent benefits are based on the separate account of a participant and as a defined benefit plan with respect to the remaining portion of benefits under the plan, and

(3) for purposes of section 4975 (relating to tax on prohibited transactions), be treated as a defined benefit plan.

Amendments

• 1988, Technical and Miscellaneous Revenue Act of 1988 (P.L. 100-647)

P.L. 100-647, §1011A(b)(3):

Amended Code Sec. 414(k)(2) by inserting "72(d) (relating to treatment of employee contributions as separate contract)." before "411(a)(7)(A)". **Effective** as if included in the provision of P.L. 99-514 to which it relates.

• 1986, Tax Reform Act of 1986 (P.L. 99-514)

P.L. 99-514, §1117(c):

Amended Code Sec. 414(k)(2) by striking out "and 415 (relating to limitations on benefits and contributions under qualified plans)" and inserting in lieu thereof ", 415 (relating to limitations on benefits and contributions under qualified plans), and 401(m) (relating to nondiscrimination tests for matching requirements and employee contributions)". **Effective** for plan years beginning after 12-31-86. However, see Act Sec. 1117(d)(2) following Code Sec. 401.

[Sec. 414(l)]

(l) MERGER AND CONSOLIDATIONS OF PLANS OR TRANSFERS OF PLAN ASSETS.—

(1) IN GENERAL.—A trust which forms a part of a plan shall not constitute a qualified trust under section 401 and a plan shall be treated as not described in section 403(a) unless in the case of any merger or consolidation of the plan with, or in the case of any transfer of assets or liabilities of such plan to, any other trust plan after September 2, 1974, each participant in the plan would (if the plan then terminated) receive a benefit immediately after the merger, consolidation, or transfer which is equal to or greater than the benefit he would have been entitled to receive immediately before the merger, consolidation, or transfer (if the plan had then terminated). The preceding sentence does not apply to any multiemployer plan with respect to any transaction to the extent that participants either before or after the transaction are covered under a multiemployer plan to which Title IV of the Employee Retirement Income Security Act of 1974 applies.

(2) ALLOCATION OF ASSETS IN PLAN SPIN-OFFS, ETC.—

(A) IN GENERAL.—In the case of a plan spin-off of a defined benefit plan, a trust which forms part of—

(i) the original plan, or

(ii) any plan spun off from such plan, shall not constitute a qualified trust under this section unless the applicable percentage of excess assets are allocated to each of such plans.

(B) APPLICABLE PERCENTAGE.—For purposes of subparagraph (A), the term "applicable percentage" means, with respect to each of the plans described in clauses (i) and (ii) of subparagraph (A), the percentage determined by dividing—

(i) the excess (if any) of—

(I) the sum of the funding target and target normal cost determined under section 430, over

(II) the amount of the assets required to be allocated to the plan after the spin-off (without regard to this paragraph), by

(ii) the sum of the excess amounts determined separately under clause (i) for all such plans.

(C) EXCESS ASSETS.—For purposes of subparagraph (A), the term "excess assets" means an amount equal to the excess (if any) of—

(i) the fair market value of the assets of the original plan immediately before the spin-off, over

(ii) the amount of assets required to be allocated after the spin-off to all plans (determined without regard to this paragraph).

(D) CERTAIN SPUN-OFF PLANS NOT TAKEN INTO ACCOUNT.—

(i) IN GENERAL.—A plan involved in a spin-off which is described in clause (ii), (iii), or (iv) shall not be taken into account for purposes of this paragraph, except that the amount determined under subparagraph (C)(ii) shall be increased by the amount of assets allocated to such plan.

(ii) PLANS TRANSFERRED OUT OF CONTROLLED GROUPS.—A plan is described in this clause if, after such spin-off, such plan is maintained by an employer who is not a member of the same controlled group as the employer maintaining the original plan.

(iii) PLANS TRANSFERRED OUT OF MULTIPLE EMPLOYER PLANS.—A plan as described in this clause if, after the spin-off, any employer maintaining such plan (and any member of the same controlled group as such employer) does not maintain any other plan remaining after the spin-off which is also maintained by another employer (or member of the same controlled group as such other employer) which maintained the plan in existence before the spin-off.

(iv) TERMINATED PLANS.—A plan is described in this clause if, pursuant to the transaction involving the spin-off, the plan is terminated.

(v) CONTROLLED GROUP.—For purposes of this subparagraph, the term "controlled group" means any group treated as a single employer under subsection (b), (c), (m), or (o).

(E) PARAGRAPH NOT TO APPLY TO MULTIEMPLOYER PLANS.—This paragraph does not apply to any multiemployer plan with respect to any spin-off to the extent that participants either before or after the spin-off are covered under a multiemployer plan to which title IV of the Employee Retirement Income Security Act of 1974 applies.

(F) APPLICATION TO SIMILAR TRANSACTION.—Except as provided by the Secretary, rules similar to the rules of this paragraph shall apply to transactions similar to spin-offs.

(G) SPECIAL RULES FOR BRIDGE BANKS.—For purposes of this paragraph, in the case of a bridge depository institution established under section 11(i) of the Federal Deposit Insurance Act (12 U.S.C. 1821(i))—

(i) such bank shall be treated as a member of any controlled group which includes any insured bank (as defined in section 3(h) of such Act (12 U.S.C. 1813(h))—

(I) which maintains a defined benefit plan,

(II) which is closed by the appropriate bank regulatory authorities, and

(III) any asset and liabilities of which are received by the bridge depository institution, and

(ii) the requirements of this paragraph shall not be treated as met with respect to such plan unless during the 180-day period beginning on the date such insured bank is closed—

(I) the bridge depository institution has the right to require the plan to transfer (subject to the provisions of this paragraph) not more than 50 percent of the excess assets (as defined in subparagraph (C)) to a defined benefit plan maintained by the bridge depository institution with respect to participants or former participants (including retirees and beneficiaries) in the original plan employed by the bridge bank or formerly employed by the closed bank, and

(II) no other merger, spin-off, termination, or similar transaction involving the portion of the excess assets described in subclause (I) may occur without the prior written consent of the bridge depository institution.

Amendments

• 2008, Worker, Retiree, and Employer Recovery Act of 2008 (P.L. 110-458)

P.L. 110-458, §101(d)(2)(E):

Amended Code Sec. 414(l)(2)(B)(i)(I). **Effective** as if included in the provision of the 2006 Act to which the amendment relates [**effective** for plan years beginning after 2007.—CCH]. Prior to amendment, Code Sec. 414(l)(2)(B)(i)(I) read as follows:

(I) the amount determined under section 431(c)(6)(A)(i) in the case of a multiemployer plan (and the sum of the funding shortfall and target normal cost determined under section 430 in the case of any other plan), over

• 2008, Federal Housing Finance Regulatory Reform Act of 2008 (P.L. 110-289)

P.L. 110-289, §1604(b)(4):

Amended Code Sec. 414(l)(2)(G) by striking "bridge bank" and inserting "bridge depository institution". **Effective** 7-30-2008.

• 2006, Pension Protection Act of 2006 (P.L. 109-280)

P.L. 109-280, §114(c):

Amended Code Sec. 414(l)(2)(B)(i)(I). **Effective** for plan years beginning after 2007 [**effective** date amended by P.L. 110-458, §101(d)(3).—CCH]. Prior to amendment, Code Sec. 414(l)(2)(B)(i)(I) read as follows:

(I) the amount determined under section 412(c)(7)(A)(i) with respect to the plan, over

• 1988, Technical and Miscellaneous Revenue Act of 1988 (P.L. 100-647)

P.L. 100-647, §2005(c)(1):

Amended Code Sec. 414(l) by adding at the end thereof new paragraph (2). For the **effective** date, see Act Sec. 2005(c)(3), below.

P.L. 100-647, §2005(c)(2):

Amended Code Sec. 414(l) by striking out the heading "(l) MERGERS AND CONSOLIDATIONS OF PLANS OR TRANSFERS OF PLAN ASSETS.—" and inserting in lieu thereof "(l) MERGER AND CONSOLIDATIONS OF PLANS OR TRANSFERS OF PLAN ASSETS.—(1) IN GENERAL.—". For the **effective** date, see Act Sec. 2005(c)(3), below.

P.L. 100-647, §2005(c)(3), provides:

(3)(A) Except as provided in subparagraph (B), the amendments made by this subsection shall apply with respect to transactions occurring after July 26, 1988.

(B) The amendments made by this subsection shall not apply to any transaction occurring after July 26, 1988, if on or before such date the board of directors of the employer, approves such transaction or the employer took similar binding action.

P.L. 100-647, §6067(a):

Amended Code Sec. 414(l)(2) by adding at the end thereof new subparagraph (G). **Effective** with respect to transactions occurring after 7-26-88.

• 1984, Deficit Reduction Act of 1984 (P.L. 98-369)

P.L. 98-369, §491(d)(27):

Amended Code Sec. 414(l) by striking out "or 405". **Effective** for obligations issued after 12-31-83.

• 1980, Multiemployer Pension Plan Act Amendments of 1980 (P.L. 96-364)

P.L. 96-364, §208(a):

Amended Code Sec. 414(l) by substituting the last sentence therein for the following: "This paragraph shall apply in the case of a multiemployer plan only to the extent determined by the Pension Benefit Guaranty Corporation." **Effective** 9-26-80.

• 1976, Tax Reform Act of 1976 (P.L. 94-455)

P.L. 94-455, §1901(a)(64)(B):

Amended Code Sec. 414(l) by substituting "September 2, 1974" for "the date of the enactment of the Employee Retirement Income Security Act of 1974". **Effective** with respect to tax years beginning after 12-31-76.

• 1974, Employee Retirement Income Security Act of 1974 (P.L. 93-406)

P.L. 93-406, §1015:

Added Code Sec. 414. For **effective** dates and transitional rules governing this section, see the historical note for §1017, P. L. 93-406, following the text of Code Sec. 410(d).

[Sec. 414(m)]

(m) EMPLOYEES OF AN AFFILIATED SERVICE GROUP.—

(1) IN GENERAL.—For purposes of the employee benefit requirements listed in paragraph (4), except to the extent otherwise provided in regulations, all employees of the members of an affiliated service group shall be treated as employed by a single employer.

(2) AFFILIATED SERVICE GROUP.—For purposes of this subsection, the term "affiliated service group" means a group consisting of a service organization (hereinafter in this paragraph referred to as the "first organization") and one or more of the following:

(A) any service organization which—

(i) is a shareholder or partner in the first organization, and

(ii) regularly performs services for the first organization or is regularly associated with the first organization in performing services for third persons, and

(B) any other organization if—

(i) a significant portion of the business of such organization is the performance of services (for the first organization, for organizations described in subparagraph (A), or for both) of a type historically performed in such service field by employees, and

(ii) 10 percent or more of the interests in such organization is held by persons who are highly compensated employees (within the meaning of section 414(q)) of the first organization or an organization described in subparagraph (A).

(3) SERVICE ORGANIZATIONS.—For purposes of this subsection, the term "service organization" means an organization the principal business of which is the performance of services.

(4) EMPLOYEE BENEFIT REQUIREMENTS.—For purposes of this subsection, the employee benefit requirements listed in this paragraph are—

(A) paragraphs (3), (4), (7), (16), (17), and (26) of section 401(a), and

(B) sections 408(k), 408(p), 410, 411, 415, and 416.

(5) CERTAIN ORGANIZATIONS PERFORMING MANAGEMENT FUNCTIONS.—For purposes of this subsection, the term "affiliated service group" also includes a group consisting of—

(A) an organization the principal business of which is performing, on a regular and continuing basis, management functions for 1 organization (or for 1 organization and other organizations related to such 1 organization), and

(B) the organization (and related organizations) for which such functions are so performed by the organization described in subparagraph (A).

For purposes of this paragraph, the term "related organizations" has the same meaning as the term "related persons" when used in section 144(a)(3).

(6) OTHER DEFINITIONS.—For purposes of this subsection—

(A) ORGANIZATION DEFINED.—The term "organization" means a corporation, partnership, or other organization.

(B) OWNERSHIP.—In determining ownership, the principles of section 318(a) shall apply.

Amendments

• 1996, Small Business Job Protection Act of 1996 (P.L. 104-188)

P.L. 104-188, §1421(b)(9)(C):

Amended Code Sec. 414(m)(4)(B) by inserting "408(p)," after "408(k),". **Effective** for tax years beginning after 12-31-96.

• 1988, Technical and Miscellaneous Revenue Act of 1988 (P.L. 100-647)

P.L. 100-647, §1011(h)(5):

Amended Code Sec. 414(m)(4)(A) by striking out "and (16)" and inserting in lieu thereof "(16), (17), and (26)". **Effective** as if included in the provision of P.L. 99-514 to which it relates.

P.L. 100-647, §1011B(a)(16):

Amended Code Sec. 414(m)(4) by inserting "and" at the end of subparagraph (A), by striking out the comma at the end of subparagraph (B) and inserting in lieu thereof a period, and by striking out subparagraphs (C) and (D). **Effective** as if included in the provision of P.L. 99-514 to which it relates. Prior to amendment, Code Sec. 414(m)(4)(C) and (D) read as follows:

(C) section 105(h), and

(D) section 125.

• 1986, Tax Reform Act of 1986 (P.L. 99-514)

P.L. 99-514, §1114(b)(11):

Amended Code Sec. 414(m)(2)(B)(ii) by striking out "officers, highly compensated employees, or owners" and inserting in lieu thereof "highly compensated employees (within meaning of section 414(q))". **Effective** for years beginning after 12-31-88.

P.L. 99-514, §1301(j)(4):

Amended Code Sec. 414(m)(5) by striking out "section 103(b)(6)(C)" and inserting in lieu thereof "section 144(a)(3)". **Effective** for bonds issued after 8-15-86. However, for transitional rules, see Act Secs. 1312-1318 following Code Sec. 103.

• 1984, Deficit Reduction Act of 1984 (P.L. 98-369)

P.L. 98-369, §526(a)(1):

Amended Code Sec. 414(m)(6)(B) by striking out "section 267(c)" and inserting in lieu thereof "section 318(a)". **Effective** for tax years beginning after 12-31-84.

P.L. 98-369, §526(d)(2):

Struck out Code Sec. 414(m)(7). Prior to being stricken, it read as follows:

(7) PREVENTION OF AVOIDANCE.—The Secretary shall prescribe such regulations as may be necessary to prevent the avoidance with respect to service organizations, through the use of separate organizations, of any employee benefit requirement listed in paragraph (4). **Effective** 7-18-84.

• 1982, Tax Equity and Fiscal Responsibility Act of 1982 (P.L. 97-248)

P.L. 97-248, §240(c)(2):

Amended Code Sec. 414(m)(4)(B) by striking out "and 415" and inserting "415, and 416". **Effective** for years beginning after 12-31-83.

P.L. 97-248, §246(a):

Amended Code Sec. 414(m) by redesignating paragraphs (5) and (6) as (6) and (7) and inserting new paragraph (5). **Effective** for tax years beginning after 12-31-83.

• 1980, Miscellaneous Revenue Act of 1980 (P.L. 96-605)

P.L. 96-605, §201(a):

Amended Code Sec. 414 by adding a new subsection (m). **Effective** for plan years ending after 11-30-80. However, in the case of a plan in existence on 11-30-80, subsection (m) is applicable to plan years beginning after that date. P.L. 96-613, §5(a), also signed 12-28-80, made the identical change to Code Sec. 414.

[Sec. 414(n)]

(n) EMPLOYEE LEASING.—

(1) IN GENERAL.—For purposes of the requirements listed in paragraph (3), with respect to any person (hereinafter in this subsection referred to as the "recipient") for whom a leased employee performs services—

(A) the leased employee shall be treated as an employee of the recipient, but

(B) contributions or benefits provided by the leasing organization which are attributable to services performed for the recipient shall be treated as provided by the recipient.

(2) LEASED EMPLOYEE.—For purposes of paragraph (1), the term "leased employee" means any person who is not an employee of the recipient and who provides services to the recipient if—

(A) such services are provided pursuant to an agreement between the recipient and any other person (in this subsection referred to as the "leasing organization"),

(B) such person has performed such services for the recipient (or for the recipient and related persons) on a substantially full-time basis for a period of at least 1 year, and

(C) such services are performed under primary direction or control by the recipient.

(3) REQUIREMENTS.—For purposes of this subsection, the requirements listed in this paragraph are—

(A) paragraphs (3), (4), (7), (16), (17), and (26) of section 401(a),

(B) sections 408(k), 408(p), 410, 411, 415, and 416, and

(C) sections 79, 106, 117(d), 120, 125, 127, 129, 132, 137, 274(j), 505, and 4980B.

(4) TIME WHEN FIRST CONSIDERED AS EMPLOYEE.—

(A) IN GENERAL.—In the case of any leased employee, paragraph (1) shall apply only for purposes of determining whether the requirements listed in paragraph (3) are met for periods after the close of the period referred to in paragraph (2)(B).

(B) YEARS OF SERVICE.—In the case of a person who is an employee of the recipient (whether by reason of this subsection or otherwise), for purposes of the requirements listed in paragraph (3), years of service for the recipient shall be determined by taking into account any period for which such employee would have been a leased employee but for the requirements of paragraph (2)(B).

(5) SAFE HARBOR.—

(A) IN GENERAL.—In the case of requirements described in subparagraphs (A) and (B) of paragraph (3), this subsection shall not apply to any leased employee with respect to services performed for a recipient if—

(i) such employee is covered by a plan which is maintained by the leasing organization and meets the requirements of subparagraph (B), and

(ii) leased employee (determined without regard to this paragraph) do not constitute more than 20 percent of the recipient's nonhighly compensated work force.

(B) PLAN REQUIREMENTS.—A plan meets the requirements of this subparagraph if—

(i) such plan is a money purchase pension plan with a nonintegrated employer contribution rate for each participant of at least 10 percent of compensation,

(ii) such plan provides for full and immediate vesting, and

(iii) each employee of the leasing organization (other than employees who perform substantially all of their services for the leasing organization) immediately participates in such plan.

Clause (iii) shall not apply to any individual whose compensation from the leasing organization in each plan year during the 4-year period ending with the plan year is less than $1,000.

(C) DEFINITIONS.—For purposes of this paragraph—

(i) HIGHLY COMPENSATED EMPLOYEE.—The term "highly compensated employee" has the meaning given such term by section 414(q).

(ii) NONHIGHLY COMPENSATED WORK FORCE.—The term "nonhighly compensated work force" means the aggregate number of individuals (other than highly compensated employees)—

(I) who are employees of the recipient (without regard to this subsection) and have performed services for the recipient (or for the recipient and related persons) on a substantially full-time basis for a period of at least 1 year, or

(II) who are leased employees with respect to the recipient (determined without regard to this paragraph).

(iii) COMPENSATION.—The term "compensation" has the same meaning as when used in section 415; except that such term shall include—

(I) any employer contribution under a qualified cash or deferred arrangement to the extent not included in gross income under section 402(e)(3) or 402(h)(1)(B),

(II) any amount which the employee would have received in cash but for an election under a cafeteria plan (within the meaning of section 125), and

(III) any amount contributed to an annuity contract described in section 403(b) pursuant to a salary reduction agreement (within the meaning of section 3121(a)(5)(D)).

(6) OTHER RULES.—For purposes of this subsection—

(A) RELATED PERSONS.—The term "related persons" has the same meaning as when used in section 144(a)(3).

(B) EMPLOYEES OF ENTITIES UNDER COMMON CONTROL.—The rules of subsections (b), (c), (m), and (o) shall apply.

Amendments

• 1997, Taxpayer Relief Act of 1997 (P.L. 105-34)

P.L. 105-34, §1601(h)(2)(D)(i):

Amended Code Sec. 414(n)(3)(C) by inserting "137," after "132,". **Effective** as if included in the provision of P.L. 104-188 to which it relates [**effective** for tax years beginning after 12-31-96.—CCH].

• 1996, Small Business Job Protection Act of 1996 (P.L. 104-188)

P.L. 104-188, §1421(b)(9)(C):

Amended Code Sec. 414(n)(3)(B) by inserting "408(p)," after "408(k),". **Effective** for tax years beginning after 12-31-96.

P.L. 104-188, §1454(a):

Amended Code Sec. 414(n)(2)(C). **Effective** for years beginning after 12-31-96, but does not apply to any relationship determined under an IRS ruling issued before the date of the enactment of this Act pursuant to section 414(n)(2)(C) of the Internal Revenue Code of 1986 (as in effect on the day before such date) not to involve a leased employee. Prior to amendment, Code Sec. 414(n)(2)(C) read as follows:

(C) such services are of a type historically performed, in the business field of the recipient, by employees.

• 1992, Unemployment Compensation Amendments of 1992 (P.L. 102-318)

P.L. 102-318, §521(b)(20):

Amended Code Sec. 414(n)(5)(C)(iii)(I) by striking "section 402(a)(8)" and inserting "section 402(e)(3)". **Effective** for distributions after 12-31-92.

• 1990, Omnibus Budget Reconciliation Act of 1990 (P.L. 101-508)

P.L. 101-508, §11703(b)(1):

Amended Code Sec. 414(n)(2)(B) by striking "(6 months in the case of core health benefits)" after "at least 1 year". **Effective** as if included in the amendments made by section 1151 of P.L. 99-514.

• 1989 (P.L. 101-140)

P.L. 101-140, §203(a)(6)(A):

Amended Code Sec. 414(n)(3)(C) by striking "89," after "79,". **Effective** as if included in section 1151 of P.L. 99-514.

• 1989 (P.L. 101-136)

P.L. 101-136, §528, provides:

SEC. 528. No monies appropriated by this Act may be used to implement or enforce section 1151 of the Tax Reform Act of 1986 or the amendments made by such section.

• 1988, Technical and Miscellaneous Revenue Act of 1988 (P.L. 100-647)

P.L. 100-647, §1011(h)(5):

Amended Code Sec. 414(n)(3)(A) by striking out "and (16)" and inserting in lieu thereof "(16), (17), and (26)". **Effective** as if included in the provision of P.L. 99-514 to which it relates.

P.L. 100-647, §1011B(a)(19):

Amended Code Sec. 414(n)(3)(C) by striking out "132," and inserting in lieu thereof "132, 162(i)(2), 162(k),". **Effective** as if included in the provision of P.L. 99-514 to which it relates.

P.L. 100-647, §3011(b)(4), amended by P.L. 101-239, §7813(b)(1)-(2):

Amended Code Sec. 414(n)(3)(C), as amended by section 1011B(a), by striking out "162(i)(2), 162(k)," and by striking out "and 505" and inserting in lieu thereof "505, and 4980B". For the **effective** date, see Act Sec. 3011(d), below.

P.L. 100-647, §3011(d), provides:

(d) EFFECTIVE DATE.—The amendments made by this section shall apply to taxable years beginning after December 31, 1988, but shall not apply to any plan for any plan year to which section 162(k) of the Internal Revenue Code of 1986 (as in effect on the day before the date of the enactment of this Act) did not apply by reason of section 10001(e)(2) of the Consolidated Omnibus Budget Reconciliation Act of 1985.

• **1986, Tax Reform Act of 1986 (P.L. 99-514)**

P.L. 99-514, §1146(b)(2):

Amended Code Sec. 414(n)(1) by striking out "except to the extent otherwise provided in regulations," following "listed in paragraph (3)". **Effective** for tax years beginning after 12-31-83.

P.L. 99-514, §1151(i)(1):

Amended Code Sec. 414(n)(1) by striking out "pension requirements" and inserting in lieu thereof "requirements". For the **effective** date, as well as special rules and an exception, see Act Sec. 1151(k) following Code Sec. 89.

P.L. 99-514, §1151(i)(2):

Amended Code Sec. 414(n)(2)(B) by inserting "(6 months in the case of core health benefits)["] after "1 year". For the **effective** date, as well as special rules and an exception, see Act Sec. 1151(k) following Code Sec. 89.

P.L. 99-514, §1151(i)(3)(A)-(C):

Amended Code Sec. 414(n)(3) by striking out "PENSION REQUIREMENTS" and inserting in lieu thereof "REQUIREMENTS"; by striking out "pension requirements" and inserting in lieu thereof "requirements"; and by striking out "and" at the end of subparagraph (A), by striking out the period at the end of subparagraph (B) and inserting in lieu thereof ", and", and by adding at the end thereof new subparagraph (C). For the **effective** date, as well as special rules and an exception, see Act Sec. 1151(k) following Code Sec. 89.

P.L. 99-514, §1146(a)(2):

Amended Code Sec. 414(n)(4). **Effective** for tax years beginning after 12-31-83. Prior to amendment, Code Sec. 414(n)(4) read as follows:

(4) TIME WHEN LEASED EMPLOYEE IS FIRST CONSIDERED AS EMPLOYEE.—In the case of any leased employee, paragraph (1) shall apply only for purposes of determining whether the pension requirements listed in paragraph (3) are met for periods after the close of the 1-year period referred to in paragraph (2); except that years of service for the recipient shall be determined by taking into account the entire period for which the leased employee performed services for the recipient (or related persons).

P.L. 99-514, §1146(a)(1):

Amended Code Sec. 414(n)(5). **Effective** for services performed after 12-31-86. Prior to amendment, Code Sec. 414(n)(5) read as follows:

(5) SAFE HARBOR.—This subsection shall not apply to any leased employee if such employee is covered by a plan which is maintained by the leasing organization if, with respect to such employee, such plan—

(A) is a money purchase pension plan with a nonintegrated employer contribution rate of at least $7\frac{1}{2}$ percent, and

(B) provides for immediate participation and for full and immediate vesting.

P.L. 99-514, §1146(a)(3):

Amended Code Sec. 414(n)(6). **Effective** for tax years beginning after 12-31-83. Prior to amendment, Code Sec. 414(n)(6) read as follows:

(6) RELATED PERSONS.—For purposes of this subsection, the term "related persons" has the same meaning as when used in section 103(b)(6)(C).

P.L. 99-514, §1301(j)(4):

Amended Code Sec. 414(n)(6) by striking out "section 103(b)(6)(C)" and inserting in lieu thereof "section 144(a)(3)". **Effective** for bonds issued after 8-15-86. However, for transitional rules, see Act Secs. 1312-1318 following Code Sec. 103.

• **1984, Deficit Reduction Act of 1984 (P.L. 98-369)**

P.L. 98-369, §§526(b)(1), 713(i):

Amended Code Sec. 414(n)(2) by striking out "any person" in the material preceding subparagraph (A) and inserting in lieu thereof "any person who is not an employee of the recipient and". **Effective** for tax years beginning after 12-31-83.

• **1982, Tax Equity and Fiscal Responsibility Act of 1982 (P.L. 97-248)**

P.L. 97-248, §248(a):

Added new subsection (n). **Effective** for tax years beginning after 12-31-83.

[Sec. 414(o)]

(o) REGULATIONS.—The Secretary shall prescribe such regulations (which may provide rules in addition to the rules contained in subsections (m) and (n)) as may be necessary to prevent the avoidance of any employee benefit requirement listed in subsection (m)(4) or (n)(3) or any requirement under section 457 through the use of—

(1) separate organizations,

(2) employee leasing, or

(3) other arrangements.

The regulations prescribed under subsection (n) shall include provisions to minimize the recordkeeping requirements of subsection (n) in the case of an employer which has no top-heavy plans (within the meaning of section 416(g)) and which uses the services of persons (other than employees) for an insignificant percentage of the employer's total workload.

Amendments

• **1988, Technical and Miscellaneous Revenue Act of 1988 (P.L. 100-647)**

P.L. 100-647, §1011(e)(4):

Amended Code Sec. 414(o) by inserting "or any requirement under section 457" after "(n)(3)". **Effective** as if included in the provision of P.L. 99-514 to which it relates.

• **1986, Tax Reform Act of 1986 (P.L. 99-514)**

P.L. 99-514, §1146(b)(1):

Amended Code Sec. 414(o) by adding at the end thereof a new sentence. **Effective** for tax years beginning after 12-31-83. However, for special recordkeeping requirements, see Act Sec. 1146(c)(3), below.

P.L. 99-514, §1146(c)(3), provides:

(3) RECORDKEEPING REQUIREMENTS.—In the case of years beginning before the date of the enactment of this Act, the last sentence of section 414(o) shall be applied without regard to the requirement that an insignificant percentage of the workload be performed by persons other than employees.

• **1984, Deficit Reduction Act of 1984 (P.L. 98-369)**

P.L. 98-369, §526(d)(1):

Added Code Sec. 414(o). **Effective** 7-18-84.

[Sec. 414(p)]

(p) QUALIFIED DOMESTIC RELATIONS ORDER DEFINED.—For purposes of this subsection and section 401(a)(13)—

(1) IN GENERAL.—

(A) QUALIFIED DOMESTIC RELATIONS ORDER.—The term "qualified domestic relations order" means a domestic relations order—

(i) which creates or recognizes the existence of an alternate payee's right to, or assigns to an alternate payee the right to, receive all or a portion of the benefits payable with respect to a participant under a plan, and

(ii) with respect to which the requirements of paragraphs (2) and (3) are met.

(B) DOMESTIC RELATIONS ORDER.—The term "domestic relations order" means any judgment, decree, or order (including approval of a property settlement agreement) which—

(i) relates to the provision of child support, alimony payments, or marital property rights to a spouse, former spouse, child, or other dependent of a participant, and

(ii) is made pursuant to a State domestic relations law (including a community property law).

(2) ORDER MUST CLEARLY SPECIFY CERTAIN FACTS.—A domestic relations order meets the requirements of this paragraph only if such order clearly specifies—

(A) the name and the last known mailing address (if any) of the participant and the name and mailing address of each alternate payee covered by the order,

(B) the amount or percentage of the participant's benefits to be paid by the plan to each such alternate payee, or the manner in which such amount or percentage is to be determined,

(C) the number of payments or period to which such order applies, and

(D) each plan to which such order applies.

(3) ORDER MAY NOT ALTER AMOUNT, FORM, ETC., OF BENEFITS.—A domestic relations order meets the requirements of this paragraph only if such order—

(A) does not require a plan to provide any type or form of benefit, or any option, not otherwise provided under the plan,

(B) does not require the plan to provide increased benefits (determined on the basis of actuarial value), and

(C) does not require the payment of benefits to an alternate payee which are required to be paid to another alternate payee under another order previously determined to be a qualified domestic relations order.

(4) EXCEPTION FOR CERTAIN PAYMENTS MADE AFTER EARLIEST RETIREMENT AGE.—

(A) IN GENERAL.—A domestic relations order shall not be treated as failing to meet the requirements of subparagraph (A) of paragraph (3) solely because such order requires that payment of benefits be made to an alternate payee—

(i) in the case of any payment before a participant has separated from service, on or after the date on which the participant attains (or would have attained) the earliest retirement age,

(ii) as if the participant had retired on the date on which such payment is to begin under such order (but taking into account only the present value of the benefits actually accrued and not taking into account the present value of any employer subsidy for early retirement), and

(iii) in any form in which such benefits may be paid under the plan to the participant (other than in the form of a joint and survivor annuity with respect to the alternate payee and his or her subsequent spouse).

For purposes of clause (ii), the interest rate assumption used in determining the present value shall be the interest rate specified in the plan or, if no rate is specified, 5 percent.

(B) EARLIEST RETIREMENT AGE.—Purposes of this paragraph, the term "earliest retirement age" means the earlier of—

(i) the date on which the participant is entitled to a distribution under the plan, or

(ii) the later of—

(I) the date the participant attains age 50, or

(II) the earliest date on which the participant could begin receiving benefits under the plan if the participant separated from service.

(5) TREATMENT OF FORMER SPOUSE AS SURVIVING SPOUSE FOR PURPOSES OF DETERMINING SURVIVOR BENEFITS.—To the extent provided in any qualified domestic relations order—

(A) the former spouse of a participant shall be treated as a surviving spouse of such participant for purposes of sections 401(a)(11) and 417 (and any spouse of the participant shall not be treated as a spouse of the participant for such purposes), and

(B) if married for at least 1 year, the surviving former spouse shall be treated as meeting the requirements of section 417(d).

(6) PLAN PROCEDURES WITH RESPECT TO ORDERS.—

(A) NOTICE AND DETERMINATION BY ADMINISTRATOR.—In the case of any domestic relations order received by a plan—

(i) the plan administrator shall promptly notify the participant and each alternate payee of the receipt of such order and the plan's procedures for determining the qualified status of domestic relations orders, and

(ii) within a reasonable period after receipt of such order, the plan administrator shall determine whether such order is a qualified domestic relations order and notify the participant and each alternate payee of such determination.

(B) PLAN TO ESTABLISH REASONABLE PROCEDURES.—Each plan shall establish reasonable procedures to determine the qualified status of domestic relations orders and to administer distributions under such qualified orders.

(7) PROCEDURES FOR PERIOD DURING WHICH DETERMINATION IS BEING MADE.—

(A) IN GENERAL.—During any period in which the issue of whether a domestic relations order is a qualified domestic relations order is being determined (by the plan administrator, by a court of competent jurisdiction, or otherwise), the plan administrator shall separately account for the amounts (hereinafter in this paragraph referred to as the "segregated amounts") which would have been payable to the alternate payee during such period if the order had been determined to be a qualified domestic relations order.

(B) PAYMENT TO ALTERNATE PAYEE IF ORDER DETERMINED TO BE QUALIFIED DOMESTIC RELATIONS ORDER.—If within the 18-month period described in subparagraph (E) the order (or modification thereof) is determined to be a qualified domestic relations order, the plan administrator shall pay the segregated amounts (including any interest thereon) to the person or persons entitled thereto.

(C) PAYMENT TO PLAN PARTICIPANT IN CERTAIN CASES.—If within the 18-month period described in subparagraph (E)—

(i) it is determined that the order is not a qualified domestic relations order, or

(ii) the issue as to whether such order is a qualified domestic relations order is not resolved,

then the plan administrator shall pay the segregated amounts (including any interest thereon) to the person or persons who would have been entitled to such amounts if there had been no order.

(D) SUBSEQUENT DETERMINATION OR ORDER TO BE APPLIED PROSPECTIVELY ONLY.—Any determination that an order is a qualified domestic relations order which is made after the close of the 18-month period described in subparagraph (E) shall be applied prospectively only.

(E) DETERMINATION OF 18-MONTH PERIOD.—For purposes of this paragraph, the 18-month period described in this subparagraph is the 18-month period beginning with the date on which the first payment would be required to be made under the domestic relations order.

(8) ALTERNATE PAYEE DEFINED.—The term "alternate payee" means any spouse, former spouse, child or other dependent of a participant who is recognized by a domestic relations order as having a right to receive all, or a portion of, the benefits payable under a plan with respect to such participant.

(9) SUBSECTION NOT TO APPLY TO PLANS TO WHICH SECTION 401(a)(13) DOES NOT APPLY.—This subsection shall not apply to any plan to which section 401(a)(13) does not apply. For purposes of this title, except as provided in regulations, any distribution from an annuity contract under section 403(b) pursuant to a qualified domestic relations order shall be treated in the same manner as a distribution from a plan to which section 401(a)(13) applies.

(10) WAIVER OF CERTAIN DISTRIBUTION REQUIREMENTS.—With respect to the requirements of subsections (a) and (k) of section 401, section 403(b), section 409(d), and section 457(d), plan shall not be treated as failing to meet such requirements solely by reason of payments to an alternative payee pursuant to a qualified domestic relations order.

(11) APPLICATION OF RULES TO CERTAIN OTHER PLANS.—For purposes of this title, a distribution or payment from a governmental plan (as defined in subsection (d)) or a church plan (as described in subsection (e)) or an eligible deferred compensation plan (within the meaning of section 457(b)) shall be treated as made pursuant to a qualified domestic relations order if it is made pursuant to a domestic relations order which meets the requirement of clause (i) of paragraph (1)(A).

(12) TAX TREATMENT OF PAYMENTS FROM A SECTION 457 PLAN.—If a distribution or payment from an eligible deferred compensation plan described in section 457(b) is made pursuant to a qualified domestic relations order, rules similar to the rules of section 402(e)(1)(A) shall apply to such distribution or payment.

(13) CONSULTATION WITH THE SECRETARY.—In prescribing regulations under this subsection and section 401(a)(13), the Secretary of Labor shall consult with the Secretary.

Amendments

• 2006, Pension Protection Act of 2006 (P.L. 109-280)

P.L. 109-280, §811, provides:

SEC. 811. PENSIONS AND INDIVIDUAL RETIREMENT ARRANGEMENT PROVISIONS OF ECONOMIC GROWTH AND TAX RELIEF RECONCILIATION ACT OF 2001 MADE PERMANENT.

Title IX of the Economic Growth and Tax Relief Reconciliation Act of 2001 [P.L. 107-16] shall not apply to the provisions of, and amendments made by, subtitles A through F of title VI [§§601-666]of such Act (relating to pension and individual retirement arrangement provisions).

P.L. 109-280, §1001, provides:

SEC. 1001. REGULATIONS ON TIME AND ORDER OF ISSUANCE OF DOMESTIC RELATIONS ORDERS.

Not later than 1 year after the date of the enactment of this Act, the Secretary of Labor shall issue regulations under section 206(d)(3) of the Employee Retirement Security Act of 1974 and section 414(p) of the Internal Revenue Code of 1986 which clarify that—

(1) a domestic relations order otherwise meeting the requirements to be a qualified domestic relations order, including the requirements of section 206(d)(3)(D) of such Act and section 414(p)(3) of such Code, shall not fail to be treated as a qualified domestic relations order solely because—

(A) the order is issued after, or revises, another domestic relations order or qualified domestic relations order; or

(B) of the time at which it is issued; and

(2) any order described in paragraph (1) shall be subject to the same requirements and protections which apply to qualified domestic relations orders, including the provisions of section 206(d)(3)(H) of such Act and section 414(p)(7) of such Code.

• 2001, Economic Growth and Tax Relief Reconciliation Act of 2001 (P.L. 107-16)

P.L. 107-16, §635(a)(1)-(2):

Amended Code Sec. 414(p)(11) by inserting "or an eligible deferred compensation plan (within the meaning of section 457(b))" after "subsection (e))"; and by striking "GOVERNMENTAL AND CHURCH PLANS" in the heading and inserting "CERTAIN OTHER PLANS". **E ffective** for transfers, distributions, and payments made after 12-31-2001.

P.L. 107-16, §635(b):

Amended Code Sec. 414(p)(10) by striking "and section 409(d)" and inserting "section 409(d), and section 457(d)". **Effective** for transfers, distributions, and payments made after 12-31-2001.

P.L. 107-16, §635(c):

Amended Code Sec. 414(p) by redesignating paragraph (12) as paragraph (13) and inserting after paragraph (11) a new paragraph (12). **Effective** for transfers, distributions, and payments made after 12-31-2001.

P.L. 107-16, §901(a)-(b), provides [but see P.L. 109-280, §811, above]:

SEC. 901. SUNSET OF PROVISIONS OF ACT.

(a) IN GENERAL.—All provisions of, and amendments made by, this Act shall not apply—

(1) to taxable, plan, or limitation years beginning after December 31, 2010, or

(2) in the case of title V, to estates of decedents dying, gifts made, or generation skipping transfers, after December 31, 2010.

(b) APPLICATION OF CERTAIN LAWS.—The Internal Revenue Code of 1986 and the Employee Retirement Income Security Act of 1974 shall be applied and administered to years, estates, gifts, and transfers described in subsection (a) as if the provisions and amendments described in subsection (a) had never been enacted.

• 1989, Omnibus Budget Reconciliation Act of 1989 (P.L. 101-239)

P.L. 101-239, §7811(m)(5):

Amended Code Sec. 414(p)(10) by inserting "section" before "403(b)". **Effective** as if included in the provision of P.L. 100-647 to which it relates.

P.L. 101-239, §7841(a)(2):

Amended Code Sec. 414(p) by redesignating paragraph (11) as paragraph (12) and by inserting after paragraph (10) a new paragraph (11). **Effective** for transfers after 12-19-89 in tax years ending after such date.

• 1988, Technical and Miscellaneous Revenue Act of 1988 (P.L. 100-647)

P.L. 100-647, §1018(t)(8)(E)(i)–(ii):

Amended Code Sec. 414(p)(4)(B) by striking out "means earlier of" and inserting in lieu thereof "means the earlier of", and by striking out "in" each place it appears after "(i)" and "(ii)". **Effective** as if included in the provision of P.L. 99-514 to which it relates.

P.L. 100-647, §1018(t)(8)(F):

Amended Code Sec. 414(p)(10) by inserting", 403(b)," after "section 401". **Effective** as if included in the provision of P.L. 99-514 to which it relates.

P.L. 100-647, §1018(t)(8)(G):

Amended Code Sec. 414(p)(9) by adding at the end thereof a new sentence. **Effective** as if included in the provision of P.L. 99-514 to which it relates.

• 1986, Tax Reform Act of 1986 (P.L. 99-514)

P.L. 99-514, §1898(c)(7)(A)(ii):

Amended Code Sec. 414(p)(1)(B)(i) by striking out "to a spouse," and inserting in lieu thereof "to a spouse, former spouse,". **Effective** as if included in the provision of P.L. 98-397 to which it relates.

P.L. 99-514, §1899A(12):

Amended Code Sec. 414(p)(3)(B) by striking out the comma after "benefits". **Effective** 10-22-86.

P.L. 99-514, §1898(c)(7)(A)(vi)(I):

Amended Code Sec. 414(p)(4)(A) by striking out "In the case of any payment before a participant has separated from service, a" and inserting in lieu thereof "A", and by inserting "in the case of any payment before a participant has separated from service," before "on or" in clause (i). **Effective** as if included in the provision of P.L. 98-397 to which it relates.

P.L. 99-514, §1898(c)(7)(A)(vii):

Amended Code Sec. 414(p)(4)(B). **Effective** as if included in the provision of P.L. 98-397 to which it relates. Prior to amendment, Code Sec 414(p)(4)(B) read as follows:

(B) EARLIEST RETIREMENT AGE.—For purposes of this paragraph, the term "earliest retirement age" has the meaning given such term by section 417(f)(3), except that in the case of any defined contribution plan, the earliest retirement age shall be the date which is 10 years before the normal retirement age (within the meaning of section 411(a)(8)).

P.L. 99-514, §1898(c)(6)(A):

Amended Code Sec. 414(p)(5)(A) by striking out "sections 401(a)(11) and 417" and inserting in lieu thereof "sections 401(a)(11) and 417 (and any spouse of the participant shall not be treated as a spouse of the participant for such purposes)". **Effective** as if included in the provision of P.L. 98-397 to which it relates.

P.L. 99-514, §1898(c)(7)(A)(iv):

Amended Code Sec. 414(p)(5)(B) by striking out "the surviving spouse" and inserting in lieu thereof "the surviving former spouse". **Effective** as if included in the provision of P.L. 98-397 to which it relates.

P.L. 99-514, §1898(c)(7)(A)(iii):

Amended Code Sec. 414(p)(6)(A)(i) by striking out "any other alternate payee" and inserting in lieu thereof "each alternate payee". **Effective** as if included in the provision of P.L. 98-397 to which it relates.

P.L. 99-514, §1898(c)(2)(A)(i):

Amended Code Sec. 414(p)(7)(A) by striking out "shall segregate in a separate account in the plan or in an escrow account the amounts" and inserting in lieu thereof "shall separately account for the amounts (hereinafter in this paragraph referred to as the 'segregated amounts')". **Effective** as if included in the provision of P.L. 98-397 to which it relates.

P.L. 99-514, §1898(c)(2)(A)(ii)(I)-(II):

Amended Code Sec. 414(p)(7)(B) by striking out "18 months" and inserting in lieu thereof "the 18-month period described in subparagraph (E)", and by striking out "plus any interest" and inserting in lieu thereof "including any interest". **Effective** as if included in the provision of P.L. 98-397 to which it relates.

P.L. 99-514, §1898(c)(2)(A)(iii)(I)-(II):

Amended Code Sec. 414(p)(7)(C) by striking out "18 months" and inserting in lieu thereof "the 18-month period described in subparagraph (E)", and by striking out "plus any interest" and inserting in lieu thereof "including any interest". **Effective** as if included in the provision of P.L. 98-397 to which it relates.

P.L. 99-514, §1898(c)(2)(A)(iv):

Amended Code Sec. 414(p)(7)(D) by striking out "the 18-month period" and inserting in lieu thereof "the 18-month period described in subparagraph (E)". **Effective** as if included in the provision of P.L. 98-397 to which it relates.

P.L. 99-514, §1898(c)(2)(A)(v):

Amended Code Sec. 414(p)(7) by adding at the end thereof new subparagraph (E). **Effective** as if included in the provision of P.L. 98-397 to which it relates.

P.L. 99-514, §1898(c)(4)(A):

Amended Code Sec. 414(p) by redesignating paragraph (9) as paragraph (11) and by inserting after paragraph (8) new paragraph (9). **Effective** as if included in the provision of P.L. 98-397 to which it relates.

P.L. 99-514, §1898(c)(7)(A)(v):

Amended Code Sec. 414(p) by striking out the last sentence of paragraph (5) and by inserting after paragraph (9) new paragraph (10). **Effective** as if included in the provision of P.L. 98-397 to which it relates. Prior to amendment, the last sentence of paragraph (5) read as follows:

A plan shall not be treated as failing to meet the requirements of subsection (a) or (k) of section 401 which prohibit payment of benefits before termination of employment solely by reason of payments to an alternate payee pursuant to a qualified domestic relations order.

• 1984, Retirement Equity Act of 1984 (P.L. 98-397)

P.L. 98-397, §204(b):

Added Code Sec. 414(p). **Effective** 1-1-85, except that in the case of a domestic relations order entered before such date, the plan administrator—

(1) shall treat such order as a qualified domestic relations order if such administrator is paying benefits pursuant to such order on such date, and

(2) may treat any other such order entered before such date as a qualified domestic relations order even if such order does not meet the requirements of such amendments.

[Sec. 414(q)]

(q) HIGHLY COMPENSATED EMPLOYEE.—

(1) IN GENERAL.—The term "highly compensated employee" means any employee who—

(A) was a 5-percent owner at any time during the year or the preceding year, or

(B) for the preceding year—

(i) had compensation from the employer in excess of $80,000, and

(ii) if the employer elects the application of this clause for such preceding year, was in the top-paid group of employees for such preceding year.

The Secretary shall adjust the $80,000 amount under subparagraph (B) at the same time and in the same manner as under section 415(d), except that the base period shall be the calendar quarter ending September 30, 1996.

(2) 5-PERCENT OWNER.—An employee shall be treated as a 5-percent owner for any year if at any time during such year such employee was a 5-percent owner (as defined in section 416(i)(1)) of the employer.

(3) TOP-PAID GROUP.—An employee is in the top-paid group of employees for any year if such employee is in the group consisting of the top 20 percent of the employees when ranked on the basis of compensation paid during such year.

(4) COMPENSATION.—For purposes of this subsection, the term "compensation" has the meaning given such term by section 415(c)(3).

(5) EXCLUDED EMPLOYEES.—For purposes of subsection (r) and for purposes of determining the number of employees in the top-paid group, the following employees shall be excluded—

(A) employees who have not completed 6 months of service,

(B) employees who normally work less than 17½ hours per week,

(C) employees who normally work during not more than 6 months during any year,

(D) employees who have not attained age 21, and

(E) except to the extent provided in regulations, employees who are included in a unit of employees covered by an agreement which the Secretary of Labor finds to be a collective bargaining agreement between employee representatives and the employer.

Except as provided by the Secretary, the employer may elect to apply subparagraph (A), (B), (C), or (D) by substituting a shorter period of service, smaller number of hours or months, or lower age for the period of service, number of hours or months, or age (as the case may be) than that specified in such subparagraph.

(6) FORMER EMPLOYEES.—A former employee shall be treated as a highly compensated employee if—

(A) such employee was a highly compensated employee when such employee separated from service, or

(B) such employee was a highly compensated employee at any time after attaining age 55.

(7) COORDINATION WITH OTHER PROVISIONS.—Subsections (b), (c), (m), (n), and (o) shall be applied before the application of this subsection.

(8) SPECIAL RULE FOR NONRESIDENT ALIENS.—For purposes of this subsection and subsection (r), employees who are nonresident aliens and who receive no earned income (within the meaning of

section 911(d)(2)) from the employer which constitutes income from sources within the United States (within the meaning of section 861(a)(3)) shall not be treated as employees.

(9) CERTAIN EMPLOYEES NOT CONSIDERED HIGHLY COMPENSATED AND EXCLUDED EMPLOYEES UNDER PRE-ERISA RULES FOR CHURCH PLANS.—In the case of a church plan (as defined in subsection (e)), no employee shall be considered an officer, a person whose principal duties consist of supervising the work of other employees, or a highly compensated employee for any year unless such employee is a highly compensated employee under paragraph (1) for such year.

Amendments

• 2004, Working Families Tax Relief Act of 2004 (P.L. 108-311)

P.L. 108-311, §408(a)(15):

Amended Code Sec. 414(q)(7) by striking "section" and inserting "subsection". **Effective** 10-4-2004.

• 1997, Taxpayer Relief Act of 1997 (P.L. 105-34)

P.L. 105-34, §1601(d)(7):

Amended Code Sec. 414(q)(7) (as added by Act Sec. 1462 of P.L. 104-188) by redesignating it as paragraph (9). **Effective** as if included in the provision of P.L. 104-188 to which it relates [**effective** for tax years beginning after 12-31-96.—CCH].

• 1996, Small Business Job Protection Act of 1996 (P.L. 104-188)

P.L. 104-188, §1431(a):

Amended Code Sec. 414(q)(1). **Effective** for years beginning after 12-31-96, except that in determining whether an employee is a highly compensated employee for years beginning in 1997, this amendment shall be treated as having been in effect for years beginning in 1996. Prior to amendment, Code Sec. 414(q)(1) read as follows:

(1) IN GENERAL.—The term "highly compensated employee" means any employee who, during the year or the preceding year—

(A) was at any time a 5-percent owner,

(B) received compensation from the employer in excess of $75,000,

(C) received compensation from the employer in excess of $50,000 and was in the top-paid group of employees for such year, or

(D) was at any time an officer and received compensation greater than 50 percent of the amount in effect under section 415(b)(1)(A) for such year.

The Secretary shall adjust the $75,000 and $50,000 amounts under this paragraph at the same time and in the same manner as under section 415(d).

P.L. 104-188, §1431(b)(1):

Repealed Code Sec. 414(q)(6). **Effective** for years beginning after 12-31-96. Prior to repeal, Code Sec. 414(q)(6) read as follows:

(6) TREATMENT OF CERTAIN FAMILY MEMBERS.—

(A) IN GENERAL.—If any individual is a member of the family of a 5-percent owner or of a highly compensated employee in the group consisting of the 10 highly compensated employees paid the greatest compensation during the year, then—

(i) such individual shall not be considered a separate employee, and

(ii) any compensation paid to such individual (and any applicable contribution or benefit on behalf of such individual) shall be treated as if it were paid to (or on behalf of) the 5-percent owner or highly compensated employee.

(B) FAMILY.—For purposes of subparagraph (A), the term "family" means, with respect to any employee, such employee's spouse and lineal ascendants or descendants and the spouses of such lineal ascendants or descendants.

(C) RULES TO APPLY TO OTHER PROVISIONS.—

(i) IN GENERAL.—Except as provided in regulations and in clause (ii), the rules of subparagraph (A) shall be applied in determining the compensation of (or any contributions or benefits on behalf of) any employee for purposes of any section with respect to which a highly compensated employee is defined by reference to this subsection.

(ii) EXCEPTION FOR DETERMINING INTEGRATION LEVELS.—Clause (i) shall not apply in determining the portion of the compensation of a participant which is under the integration level for purposes of section 401(l).

P.L. 104-188, §1431(c)(1)(A):

Amended Code Sec. 414(q) by striking paragraphs (2), (5), and (12) and by redesignating paragraphs (3), (4), (7), (8), (9), (10), and (11) as paragraphs (2) through (8), respectively. **Effective** for years beginning after 12-31-96, except that in determining whether an employee is a highly compensated employee for years beginning in 1997, these amendments shall be treated as having been in effect for years beginning in 1996. Prior to amendment, Code Sec. 414(q)(2), (q)(5), and (q)(12) read as follows:

(2) SPECIAL RULE FOR CURRENT YEAR.—In the case of the year for which the relevant determination is being made, an employee not described in subparagraph (B), (C), or (D) of paragraph (1) for the preceding year (without regard to this paragraph) shall not be treated as described in subparagraph (B), (C), or (D) of paragraph (1) unless such employee is a member of the group consisting of the 100 employees paid the greatest compensation during the year for which such determination is being made.

* * *

(5) SPECIAL RULES FOR TREATMENT OF OFFICERS.—

(A) NOT MORE THAN 50 OFFICERS TAKEN INTO ACCOUNT.—For purposes of paragraph (1)(D), no more than 50 employees (or, if lesser, the greater of 3 employees or 10 percent of the employees) shall be treated as officers.

(B) AT LEAST 1 OFFICER TAKEN INTO ACCOUNT.—If for any year no officer of the employer is described in paragraph (1)(D), the highest paid officer of the employer for such year shall be treated as described in such paragraph.

* * *

(12) SIMPLIFIED METHOD FOR DETERMINING HIGHLY COMPENSATED EMPLOYEES.—

(A) IN GENERAL.—If an election by the employer under this paragraph applies to any year, in determining whether an employee is a highly compensated employee for such year—

(i) subparagraph (B) of paragraph (1) shall be applied by substituting "$50,000" for "$75,000", and

(ii) subparagraph (C) of paragraph (1) shall not apply.

(B) REQUIREMENT FOR ELECTION.—An election under this paragraph shall not apply to any year unless—

(i) at all times during such year, the employer maintained significant business activities (and employed employees) in at least 2 significantly separate geographic areas, and

(ii) the employer satisfies such other conditions as the Secretary may prescribe.

P.L. 104-188, §1431(c)(1)(E) (as amended by P.L. 105-206, §6018(c)):

Amended Code Sec. 414(q)(5), as redesignated by Act Sec. 1431(c)(1)(A), by striking "under paragraph (4) or the number of officers taken into account under paragraph (5)" after "top-paid group". **Effective** for years beginning after 12-31-96, except that in determining whether an employee is a highly compensated employee for years beginning in 1997, these amendments shall be treated as having been in effect for years beginning in 1996.

P.L. 104-188, §1434(b)(1):

Amended Code Sec. 414(q)(4), as redesignated by Act Sec. 1431. **Effective** for years beginning after 12-31-97. Prior to amendment, Code Sec. 414(q)(4) read as follows:

(4) COMPENSATION.—For purposes of this subsection—

(A) IN GENERAL.—The term "compensation" means compensation within the meaning of section 415(c)(3).

(B) CERTAIN PROVISIONS NOT TAKEN INTO ACCOUNT.—The determination under subparagraph (A) shall be made—

(i) without regard to sections 125, 402(e)(3), and 402(h)(1)(B), and

(ii) in the case of employer contributions made pursuant to a salary reduction agreement, without regard to section 403(b).

P.L. 104-188, §1462(a):

Amended Code Sec. 414(q), as amended by Act Sec. 1431(c)(1)(A), by adding at the end a new paragraph (7)[9]. **Effective** for years beginning after 12-31-96. See, also, Act Sec. 1462(b), below.

P.L. 104-188, §1462(b), provides:

(b) SAFE HARBOR AUTHORITY.—The Secretary of the Treasury may design nondiscrimination and coverage safe harbors for church plans.

• 1992, Unemployment Compensation Amendments of 1992 (P.L. 102-318)

P.L. 102-318, §521(b)(21):

Amemded Code Sec. 414(q)(7)(B)(i) by striking "402(a)(8)" and inserting "402(e)(3)". **Effective** for distributions after 12-31-92.

• 1988, Technical and Miscellaneous Revenue Act of 1988 (P.L. 100-647)

P.L. 100-647, §1011(d)(8):

Amended Code Sec. 414(q)(1)(D) by striking out "150 percent of the amount in effect under section 415(c)(1)(A)" and inserting in lieu thereof "50 percent of the amount in effect under section 415(b)(1)(A)". **Effective** as if included in the provision of P.L. 99-514 to which it relates.

P.L. 100-647, §1011(i)(1):

Amended Code Sec. 414(q)(1) by adding at the end thereof a new flush sentence. **Effective** as if included in the provision of P.L. 99-514 to which it relates.

P.L. 100-647, §1011(i)(2):

Amended Code Sec. 414(q)(6) by adding at the end thereof new subparagraph (C). **Effective** as if included in the provision of P.L. 99-514 to which it relates.

P.L. 100-647, §1011(i)(3)(A)(i)–(ii):

Amended Code Sec. 414(q)(8) by inserting "and" at the end of subparagraph (D), by striking ", and" at the end of subparagraph (E) and inserting in lieu thereof a period, and by striking out subparagraph (F), and by striking out "The" in the last sentence thereof and inserting in lieu thereof "Except as provided by the Secretary, the". **Effective** as if included in the provision of P.L. 99-514 to which it relates. Prior to amendment, Code Sec. 414(q)(8)(F) read as follows:

(F) employees who are nonresident aliens and who receive no earned income (within the meaning of section 911(d)(2)) from the employer which constitutes income from sources within the United States (within the meaning of section 861(a)(3)).

P.L. 100-647, §1011(i)(3)(B):

Amended Code Sec. 414(q) by adding at the end thereof new paragraph (11). **Effective** as if included in the provision of P.L. 99-514 to which it relates.

P.L. 100-647, §1011(i)(4)(A):

Amended Code Sec. 414(q)(8) by inserting "or the number of officers taken into account under paragraph (5)" after "paragraph (4)". **Effective** as if included in the provision of P.L. 99-514 to which it relates.

P.L. 100-647, §3021(b)(1):

Amended Code Sec. 414(q) by adding at the end thereof a new paragraph (12). **Effective** for years beginning after 12-31-86.

• 1986, Tax Reform Act of 1986 (P.L. 99-514)

P.L. 99-514, §1114(a):

Amended Code Sec. 414 by adding at the end thereof new subsection (q). **Effective** for years beginning after 12-31-86. For a special rule, see Act Sec. 1114(c)(4) following Code Sec. 401.

[Sec. 414(r)]

(r) SPECIAL RULES FOR SEPARATE LINE OF BUSINESS.—

(1) IN GENERAL.—For purposes of sections 129(d)(8) and 410(b), an employer shall be treated as operating separate lines of business during any year if the employer for bona fide business reasons operates separate lines of business.

(2) LINE OF BUSINESS MUST HAVE 50 EMPLOYEES, ETC.—A line of business shall not be treated as separate under paragraph (1) unless—

(A) such line of business has at least 50 employees who are not excluded under subsection (q)(5),

(B) the employer notifies the Secretary that such line of business is being treated as separate for purposes of paragraph (1), and

(C) such line of business meets guidelines prescribed by the Secretary or the employer receives a determination from the Secretary that such line of business may be treated as separate for purposes of paragraph (1).

(3) SAFE HARBOR RULE.—

(A) IN GENERAL.—The requirements of subparagraph (C) of paragraph (2) shall not apply to any line of business if the highly compensated employee percentage with respect to such line of business is—

(i) not less than one-half, and

(ii) not more than twice,

the percentage which highly compensated employees are of all employees of the employer. An employer shall be treated as meeting the requirements of clause (i) if at least 10 percent of all highly compensated employees of the employer perform services solely for such line of business.

(B) DETERMINATION MAY BE BASED ON PRECEDING YEAR.—The requirements of subparagraph (A) shall be treated as met with respect to any line of business if such requirements were met with respect to such line of business for the preceding year and if—

(i) no more than a de minimis number of employees were shifted to or from the line of business after the close of the preceding year, or

(ii) the employees shifted to or from the line of business after the close of the preceding year contained a substantially proportional number of highly compensated employees.

(4) HIGHLY COMPENSATED EMPLOYEE PERCENTAGE DEFINED.—For purposes of this subsection, the term "highly compensated employee percentage" means the percentage which highly compen-

sated employees performing services for the line of business are of all employees performing services for the line of business.

(5) ALLOCATION OF BENEFITS TO LINE OF BUSINESS.—For purposes of this subsection, benefits which are attributable to services provided to a line of business shall be treated as provided by such line of business.

(6) HEADQUARTERS PERSONNEL, ETC.—The Secretary shall prescribe rules providing for—

(A) the allocation of headquarters personnel among the lines of business of the employer, and

(B) the treatment of other employees providing services for more than 1 line of business of the employer or not in lines of business meeting the requirements of paragraph (2).

(7) SEPARATE OPERATING UNITS.—For purposes of this subsection, the term "separate line of business" includes an operating unit in a separate geographic area separately operated for a bona fide business reason.

(8) AFFILIATED SERVICE GROUPS.—This subsection shall not apply in the case of any affiliated service group (within the meaning of section 414(m)).

Amendments

• 1996, Small Business Job Protection Act of 1996 (P.L. 104-188)

P.L. 104-188, §1431(c)(1)(D):

Amended Code Sec. 414(r)(2)(A) by striking "subsection (q)(8)" and inserting "subsection (q)(5)". **Effective** for years beginning after 12-31-96, except that in determining whether an employee is a highly compensated employee for years beginning in 1997, this amendment shall be treated as having been in effect for years beginning in 1996.

• 1989 (P.L. 101-140)

P.L. 101-140, §203(a)(6)(B):

Amended Code Sec. 414(r)(1) by striking "sections 89 and" and inserting "section". **Effective** as if included in section 1151 of P.L. 99-514.

P.L. 101-140, §204(b)(1), provides:

(b) LINE OF BUSINESS TEST.—

(1) APPLICATION OF LINE OF BUSINESS TEST FOR PERIOD BEFORE GUIDELINES ISSUED.—In the case of any plan year beginning on or before the date the Secretary of the Treasury or his delegate issues guidelines and begins issuing determinations under section 414(r)(2)(C) of the Internal Revenue Code of 1986, an employer shall be treated as operating separate lines of business if the employer reasonably determines that it meets the requirements of section 414(r) (other than paragraph (2)(C) thereof) of such Code.

P.L. 101-140, §204(b)(2):

Amended Code Sec. 414(r)(1) by striking "section 410(b)" and inserting "sections 129(d)(8) and 410(b)". **Effective** for years beginning after 12-31-88.

• 1988, Technical and Miscellaneous Revenue Act of 1988 (P.L. 100-647)

P.L. 100-647, §3021(b)(2)(A):

Amended Code Sec. 414(r)(3). **Effective** for years beginning after 12-31-86. Prior to amendment, Code Sec. 414(r)(3) read as follows:

(3) SAFE HARBOR RULE.—The requirements of subparagraph (C) of paragraph (2) shall not apply to any line of business if the highly compensated employee percentage with respect to such line of business is—

(A) not less than one-half, and

(B) not more than twice,

the percentage which highly compensated employees are of all employees of the employer. An employer shall be treated as meeting the requirements of subparagraph (A) if at least 10 percent of all highly compensated employees of the employer perform services solely for such line of business.

• 1986, Tax Reform Act of 1986 (P.L. 99-514)

P.L. 99-514, §1115(a):

Amended Code Sec. 414 by adding at the end thereof a new subsection (r). **Effective** for years beginning after 12-31-86.

[Sec. 414(s)]

(s) COMPENSATION.—For purposes of any applicable provision—

(1) IN GENERAL.—Except as provided in this subsection, the term "compensation" has the meaning given such term by section 415(c)(3).

(2) EMPLOYER MAY ELECT NOT TO TREAT CERTAIN DEFERRALS AS COMPENSATION.—An employer may elect not to include as compensation any amount which is contributed by the employer pursuant to a salary reduction agreement and which is not includible in the gross income of an employee under section 125, 132(f)(4), 402(e)(3), 402(h) or 403(b).

(3) ALTERNATIVE DETERMINATION OF COMPENSATION.—The Secretary shall by regulation provide for alternative methods of determining compensation which may be used by an employer, except that such regulations shall provide that an employer may not use an alternative method if the use of such method discriminates in favor of highly compensated employees (within the meaning of subsection (q)).

(4) APPLICABLE PROVISION.—For purposes of this subsection, the term "applicable provision" means any provision which specifically refers to this subsection.

Amendments

• 2000, Community Renewal Tax Relief Act of 2000 (P.L. 106-554)

P.L. 106-554, §314(e)(2):

Amended Code Sec. 414(s)(2) by striking "section 125, 402(e)(3)" and inserting "section 125, 132(f)(4), 402(e)(3)". **Effective** as if included in the provision of P.L. 105-34 to which it relates [**effective** for tax years beginning after 12-31-97.—CCH].

• 1996, Small Business Job Protection Act of 1996 (P.L. 104-188)

P.L. 104-188, §1434(b)(2):

Amended Code Sec. 414(s)(2) by inserting "not" after "elect" in the text and heading thereof. **Effective** for years beginning after 12-31-97.

• 1992, Unemployment Compensation Amendments of 1992 (P.L. 102-318)

P.L. 102-318, §521(b)(22):

Amended Code Sec. 414(s)(2) by striking "402(a)(8)" and inserting "402(e)(3)". **Effective** for distributions after 12-31-92.

• 1988, Technical and Miscellaneous Revenue Act of 1988 (P.L. 100-647)

P.L. 100-647, §1011(j)(1):

Amended so much of Code Sec. 414(s) as precedes paragraph (2). **Effective** as if included in the provision of P.L. 99-514 to which it relates. Prior to amendment, so much of Code Sec. 414(s) as precedes paragraph (2) read as follows:

(s) COMPENSATION.—For purposes of this part—

(1) IN GENERAL.—The term "compensation" means compensation for service performed for an employer which (taking into account the provisions of this chapter) is currently includible in gross income.

P.L. 100-647, §1011(j)(2):

Amended Code Sec. 414(s) by striking out paragraph (2), by redesignating paragraphs (3) and (4) as paragraphs (2) and (3), respectively, and by adding at the end thereof new paragraph (4). **Effective** as if included in the provision of P.L. 99-514 to which it relates. Prior to amendment, Code Sec. 414(s)(2) read as follows:

(2) SELF-EMPLOYED INDIVIDUALS.—The Secretary shall prescribe regulations for the determination of the compensation of an employee who is a self-employed individual (within the meaning of section 401(c)(1)) which are based on the principles of paragraph (1).

• 1986, Tax Reform Act of 1986 (P.L. 99-514)

P.L. 99-514, §1115(a):

Amended Code Sec. 414 by adding at the end thereof a new subsection (s). **Effective** for years beginning after 12-31-86.

[Sec. 414(t)]

(t) APPLICATION OF CONTROLLED GROUP RULES TO CERTAIN EMPLOYEE BENEFITS.—

(1) IN GENERAL.—All employees who are treated as employed by a single employer under subsection (b), (c), or (m) shall be treated as employed by a single employer for purposes of an applicable section. The provisions of subsection (o) shall apply with respect to the requirements of an applicable section.

(2) APPLICABLE SECTION.—For purposes of this subsection, the term "applicable section" means section 79, 106, 117(d), 120, 125, 127, 129, 132, 137, 274(j), 505, or 4980B.

Amendments

• 1997, Taxpayer Relief Act of 1997 (P.L. 105-34)

P.L. 105-34, §1601(h)(2)(D)(ii):

Amended Code Sec. 414(t)(2) by inserting "137," after "132,". **Effective** as if included in the provision of P.L. 104-188 to which it relates [**effective** for tax years beginning after 12-31-96.—CCH].

• 1989 (P.L. 101-140)

P.L. 101-140, §203(a)(6)(C):

Amended Code Sec. 414(t)(2) by striking "89," after "79,". **Effective** as if included in section 1151 of P.L. 99-514.

• 1989 (P.L. 101-136)

P.L. 101-136, §528, provides:

SEC. 528. No monies appropriated by this Act may be used to implement or enforce section 1151 of the Tax Reform Act of 1986 or the amendments made by such section.

• 1988, Technical and Miscellaneous Revenue Act of 1988 (P.L. 100-647)

P.L. 100-647, §1011B(a)(17):

Amended Code Sec. 414(t)(2) by striking out "132," and inserting in lieu thereof "132, 162(i)(2), 162(k),". **Effective** as if included in the provision of P.L. 99-514 to which it relates.

P.L. 100-647, §1011B(a)(20):

Amended Code Sec. 414(t)(1) by striking out "of section 414" after "(m)" and "(o)". **Effective** as if included in the provision of P.L. 99-514 to which it relates.

P.L. 100-647, §3011(b)(5):

Amended Code Sec. 414(t)(2), as amended by section 1011B(a), by striking out "162(i)(2), 162(k)(2)[sic]," and by striking out "or 505" and inserting in lieu thereof "505, or 4980B". For the **effective** date, see Act Sec. 3011(d), below.

P.L. 100-647, §3011(d), provides:

(d) EFFECTIVE DATE.—The amendments made by this section shall apply to taxable years beginning after December 31, 1988, but shall not apply to any plan for any plan year to which section 162(k) of the Internal Revenue Code of 1986 (as in effect on the day before the date of the enactment of this Act) did not apply by reason of section 10001(e)(2) of the Consolidated Omnibus Budget Reconciliation Act of 1985.

• 1986, Tax Reform Act of 1986 (P.L. 99-514)

P.L. 99-514, §1151(e)(1):

Amended Code Sec. 414 by adding at the end thereof new subsection (t). For the **effective** date, as well as special rules and an exception, see Act Sec. 1151(k) following Code Sec. 89.

[Sec. 414(u)]

(u) SPECIAL RULES RELATING TO VETERANS' REEMPLOYMENT RIGHTS UNDER USERRA AND TO DIFFERENTIAL WAGE PAYMENTS TO MEMBERS ON ACTIVE DUTY.—

(1) TREATMENT OF CERTAIN CONTRIBUTIONS MADE PURSUANT TO VETERANS' REEMPLOYMENT RIGHTS.—If any contribution is made by an employer or an employee under an individual account plan with respect to an employee, or by an employee to a defined benefit plan that provides for employee contributions, and such contribution is required by reason of such employee's rights under chapter 43 of title 38, United States Code, resulting from qualified military service, then—

(A) such contribution shall not be subject to any otherwise applicable limitation contained in section 402(g), 402(h), 403(b), 404(a), 404(h), 408, 415, or 457, and shall not be taken into account in applying such limitations to other contributions or benefits under such plan or any other plan, with respect to the year in which the contribution is made,

(B) such contribution shall be subject to the limitations referred to in subparagraph (A) with respect to the year to which the contribution relates (in accordance with rules prescribed by the Secretary), and

(C) such plan shall not be treated as failing to meet the requirements of section 401(a)(4), 401(a)(26), 401(k)(3), 401(k)(11), 401(k)(12), 401(m), 403(b)(12), 408(k)(3), 408(k)(6), 408(p), 410(b), or 416 by reason of the making of (or the right to make) such contribution.

For purposes of the preceding sentence, any elective deferral or employee contribution made under paragraph (2) shall be treated as required by reason of the employee's rights under such chapter 43.

(2) REEMPLOYMENT RIGHTS UNDER USERRA WITH RESPECT TO ELECTIVE DEFERRALS.—

(A) IN GENERAL.—For purposes of this subchapter and section 457, if an employee is entitled to the benefits of chapter 43 of title 38, United States Code, with respect to any plan which provides for elective deferrals, the employer sponsoring the plan shall be treated as meeting the requirements of such chapter 43 with respect to such elective deferrals only if such employer—

(i) permits such employee to make additional elective deferrals under such plan (in the amount determined under subparagraph (B) or such lesser amount as is elected by the employee) during the period which begins on the date of the reemployment of such employee with such employer and has the same length as the lesser of—

(I) the product of 3 and the period of qualified military service which resulted in such rights, and

(II) 5 years, and

(ii) makes a matching contribution with respect to any additional elective deferral made pursuant to clause (i) which would have been required had such deferral actually been made during the period of such qualified military service.

(B) AMOUNT OF MAKEUP REQUIRED.—The amount determined under this subparagraph with respect to any plan is the maximum amount of the elective deferrals that the individual would have been permitted to make under the plan in accordance with the limitations referred to in paragraph (1)(A) during the period of qualified military service if the individual had continued to be employed by the employer during such period and received compensation as determined under paragraph (7). Proper adjustment shall be made to the amount determined under the preceding sentence for any elective deferrals actually made during the period of such qualified military service.

(C) ELECTIVE DEFERRAL.—For purposes of this paragraph, the term "elective deferral" has the meaning given such term by section 402(g)(3); except that such term shall include any deferral of compensation under an eligible deferred compensation plan (as defined in section 457(b)).

(D) AFTER-TAX EMPLOYEE CONTRIBUTIONS.—References in subparagraphs (A) and (B) to elective deferrals shall be treated as including references to employee contributions.

(3) CERTAIN RETROACTIVE ADJUSTMENTS NOT REQUIRED.—For purposes of this subchapter and subchapter E, no provision of chapter 43 of title 38, United States Code, shall be construed as requiring—

(A) any crediting of earnings to an employee with respect to any contribution before such contribution is actually made, or

(B) any allocation of any forfeiture with respect to the period of qualified military service.

(4) LOAN REPAYMENT SUSPENSIONS PERMITTED.—If any plan suspends the obligation to repay any loan made to an employee from such plan for any part of any period during which such employee is performing service in the uniformed services (as defined in chapter 43 of title 38, United States Code), whether or not qualified military service, such suspension shall not be taken into account for purposes of section 72(p), 401(a), or 4975(d)(1).

(5) QUALIFIED MILITARY SERVICE.—For purposes of this subsection, the term "qualified military service" means any service in the uniformed services (as defined in chapter 43 of title 38, United States Code) by any individual if such individual is entitled to reemployment rights under such chapter with respect to such service.

(6) INDIVIDUAL ACCOUNT PLAN.—For purposes of this subsection, the term "individual account plan" means any defined contribution plan (including any tax-sheltered annuity plan under section 403(b), any simplified employee pension under section 408(k), any qualified salary reduction arrangement under section 408(p), and any eligible deferred compensation plan (as defined in section 457(b)).

(7) COMPENSATION.—For purposes of sections 403(b)(3), 415(c)(3), and 457(e)(5), an employee who is in qualified military service shall be treated as receiving compensation from the employer during such period of qualified military service equal to—

(A) the compensation the employee would have received during such period if the employee were not in qualified military service, determined based on the rate of pay the employee would have received from the employer but for absence during the period of qualified military service, or

(B) if the compensation the employee would have received during such period was not reasonably certain, the employee's average compensation from the employer during the 12-month period immediately preceding the qualified military service (or, if shorter, the period of employment immediately preceding the qualified military service).

(8) USERRA REQUIREMENTS FOR QUALIFIED RETIREMENT PLANS.—For purposes of this subchapter and section 457, an employer sponsoring a retirement plan shall be treated as meeting the requirements of chapter 43 of title 38, United States Code, only if each of the following requirements is met:

(A) An individual reemployed under such chapter is treated with respect to such plan as not having incurred a break in service with the employer maintaining the plan by reason of such individual's period of qualified military service.

(B) Each period of qualified military service served by an individual is, upon reemployment under such chapter, deemed with respect to such plan to constitute service with the employer maintaining the plan for the purpose of determining the nonforfeitability of the individual's accrued benefits under such plan and for the purpose of determining the accrual of benefits under such plan.

(C) An individual reemployed under such chapter is entitled to accrued benefits that are contingent on the making of, or derived from, employee contributions or elective deferrals only to the extent the individual makes payment to the plan with respect to such contributions or deferrals. No such payment may exceed the amount the individual would have been permitted or required to contribute had the individual remained continuously employed by the employer throughout the period of qualified military service. Any payment to such plan shall be made during the period beginning with the date of reemployment and whose duration is 3 times the period of the qualified military service (but not greater than 5 years).

(9) TREATMENT IN THE CASE OF DEATH OR DISABILITY RESULTING FROM ACTIVE MILITARY SERVICE.—

(A) IN GENERAL.—For benefit accrual purposes, an employer sponsoring a retirement plan may treat an individual who dies or becomes disabled (as defined under the terms of the plan) while performing qualified military service with respect to the employer maintaining the plan as if the individual has resumed employment in accordance with the individual's reemployment rights under chapter 43 of title 38, United States Code, on the day preceding death or disability (as the case may be) and terminated employment on the actual date of death or disability. In the case of any such treatment, and subject to subparagraphs (B) and (C), any full or partial compliance by such plan with respect to the benefit accrual requirements of paragraph (8) with respect to such individual shall be treated for purposes of paragraph (1) as if such compliance were required under such chapter 43.

(B) NONDISCRIMINATION REQUIREMENT.—Subparagraph (A) shall apply only if all individuals performing qualified military service with respect to the employer maintaining the plan (as determined under subsections (b), (c), (m), and (o)) who die or became disabled as a result of performing qualified military service prior to reemployment by the employer are credited with service and benefits on reasonably equivalent terms.

(C) DETERMINATION OF BENEFITS.—The amount of employee contributions and the amount of elective deferrals of an individual treated as reemployed under subparagraph (A) for purposes of applying paragraph (8)(C) shall be determined on the basis of the individual's average actual employee contributions or elective deferrals for the lesser of—

(i) the 12-month period of service with the employer immediately prior to qualified military service, or

(ii) if service with the employer is less than such 12-month period, the actual length of continuous service with the employer.

(10) PLANS NOT SUBJECT TO TITLE 38.—This subsection shall not apply to any retirement plan to which chapter 43 of title 38, United States Code, does not apply.

(11) REFERENCES.—For purposes of this section, any reference to chapter 43 of title 38, United States Code, shall be treated as a reference to such chapter as in effect on December 12, 1994 (without regard to any subsequent amendment).

(12) TREATMENT OF DIFFERENTIAL WAGE PAYMENTS.—

(A) IN GENERAL.—Except as provided in this paragraph, for purposes of applying this title to a retirement plan to which this subsection applies—

(i) an individual receiving a differential wage payment shall be treated as an employee of the employer making the payment,

(ii) the differential wage payment shall be treated as compensation, and

(iii) the plan shall not be treated as failing to meet the requirements of any provision described in paragraph (1)(C) by reason of any contribution or benefit which is based on the differential wage payment.

(B) SPECIAL RULE FOR DISTRIBUTIONS.—

(i) IN GENERAL.—Notwithstanding subparagraph (A)(i), for purposes of section 401(k)(2)(B)(i)(I), 403(b)(7)(A)(ii), 403(b)(11)(A), or 457(d)(1)(A)(ii), an individual shall be treated as having been severed from employment during any period the individual is performing service in the uniformed services described in section 3401(h)(2)(A).

(ii) LIMITATION.—If an individual elects to receive a distribution by reason of clause (i), the plan shall provide that the individual may not make an elective deferral or employee contribution during the 6-month period beginning on the date of the distribution.

(C) NONDISCRIMINATION REQUIREMENT.—Subparagraph (A)(iii) shall apply only if all employees of an employer (as determined under subsections (b), (c), (m), and (o)) performing service in the uniformed services described in section 3401(h)(2)(A) are entitled to receive differential wage payments on reasonably equivalent terms and, if eligible to participate in a retirement plan maintained by the employer, to make contributions based on the payments on reasonably equivalent terms. For purposes of applying this subparagraph, the provisions of paragraphs (3), (4), and (5) of section 410(b) shall apply.

(D) DIFFERENTIAL WAGE PAYMENT.—For purposes of this paragraph, the term "differential wage payment" has the meaning given such term by section 3401(h)(2).

Amendments

• 2008, Heroes Earnings Assistance and Relief Tax Act of 2008 (P.L. 110-245)

P.L. 110-245, §104(b):

Amended Code Sec. 414(u) by redesignating paragraphs (9) and (10) as paragraphs (10) and (11), respectively, and by inserting after paragraph (8) a new paragraph (9). **Effective** generally with respect to deaths and disabilities occurring on or after 1-1-2007. For a special rule, see Act Sec. 104(d)(2), below.

P.L. 110-245, §104(d)(2), provides:

(2) PROVISIONS RELATING TO PLAN AMENDMENTS.—

(A) IN GENERAL.—If this subparagraph applies to any plan or contract amendment, such plan or contract shall be treated as being operated in accordance with the terms of the plan during the period described in subparagraph (B)(iii).

(B) AMENDMENTS TO WHICH SUBPARAGRAPH (A) APPLIES.—

(i) IN GENERAL.—Subparagraph (A) shall apply to any amendment to any plan or annuity contract which is made—

(I) pursuant to the amendments made by subsection (a) or pursuant to any regulation issued by the Secretary of the Treasury under subsection (a), and

(II) on or before the last day of the first plan year beginning on or after January 1, 2010.

In the case of a governmental plan (as defined in section 414(d) of the Internal Revenue Code of 1986), this clause shall be applied by substituting "2012" for "2010" in subclause (II).

(ii) CONDITIONS.—This paragraph shall not apply to any amendment unless—

(I) the plan or contract is operated as if such plan or contract amendment were in effect for the period described in clause (iii), and

(II) such plan or contract amendment applies retroactively for such period.

(iii) PERIOD DESCRIBED.—The period described in this clause is the period—

(I) beginning on the effective date specified by the plan, and

(II) ending on the date described in clause (i)(II) (or, if earlier, the date the plan or contract amendment is adopted).

P.L. 110-245, §105(b)(1)(A):

Amended Code Sec. 414(u), as amended by Act Sec. 103(b) [104(b)], by adding at the end a new paragraph (12). **Effective** for years beginning after 12-31-2008. For a special rule, see Act Sec. 105(c), below.

P.L. 110-245, §105(b)(1)(B):

Amended the heading for Code Sec. 414(u) by inserting "AND TO DIFFERENTIAL WAGE PAYMENTS TO MEMBERS ON ACTIVE DUTY" after " USERRA". **Effective** for years beginning after 12-31-2008. For a special rule, see Act Sec. 105(c), below.

P.L. 110-245, §105(c), provides:

(c) PROVISIONS RELATING TO PLAN AMENDMENTS.—

(1) IN GENERAL.—If this subsection applies to any plan or annuity contract amendment, such plan or contract shall be treated as being operated in accordance with the terms of the plan or contract during the period described in paragraph (2)(B)(i).

(2) AMENDMENTS TO WHICH SECTION [SUBSECTION] APPLIES.—

(A) IN GENERAL.—This subsection shall apply to any amendment to any plan or annuity contract which is made—

(i) pursuant to any amendment made by subsection (b)(1), and

(ii) on or before the last day of the first plan year beginning on or after January 1, 2010.

In the case of a governmental plan (as defined in section 414(d) of the Internal Revenue Code of 1986), this subparagraph shall be applied by substituting "2012" for "2010" in clause (ii).

(B) CONDITIONS.—This subsection shall not apply to any plan or annuity contract amendment unless—

(i) during the period beginning on the date the amendment described in subparagraph (A)(i) takes effect and ending on the date described in subparagraph (A)(ii) (or, if earlier, the date the plan or contract amendment is adopted), the plan or contract is operated as if such plan or contract amendment were in effect, and

(ii) such plan or contract amendment applies retroactively for such period.

• 1996, Small Business Job Protection Act of 1996 (P.L. 104-188)

P.L. 104-188, §1704(n)(1):

Amended Code Sec. 414 by adding at the end a new subsection (u). **Effective** as of 12-12-94.

[Sec. 414(v)]

(v) CATCH-UP CONTRIBUTIONS FOR INDIVIDUALS AGE 50 OR OVER.—

(1) IN GENERAL.—An applicable employer plan shall not be treated as failing to meet any requirement of this title solely because the plan permits an eligible participant to make additional elective deferrals in any plan year.

(2) LIMITATION ON AMOUNT OF ADDITIONAL DEFERRALS.—

(A) IN GENERAL.—A plan shall not permit additional elective deferrals under paragraph (1) for any year in an amount greater than the lesser of—

(i) the applicable dollar amount, or

(ii) the excess (if any) of—

(I) the participant's compensation (as defined in section 415(c)(3)) for the year, over

(II) any other elective deferrals of the participant for such year which are made without regard to this subsection.

(B) APPLICABLE DOLLAR AMOUNT.—For purposes of this paragraph—

(i) In the case of an applicable employer plan other than a plan described in section 401(k)(11) or 408(p), the applicable dollar amount shall be determined in accordance with the following table:

For taxable years beginning in:	The applicable dollar amount is:
2002	$1,000
2003	$2,000
2004	$3,000
2005	$4,000
2006 or thereafter	$5,000.

(ii) In the case of an applicable employer plan described in section 401(k)(11) or 408(p), the applicable dollar amount shall be determined in accordance with the following table:

For taxable years beginning in:	The applicable dollar amount is:
2002	$500
2003	$1,000
2004	$1,500
2005	$2,000
2006 or thereafter	$2,500.

(C) COST-OF-LIVING ADJUSTMENT.—In the case of a year beginning after December 31, 2006, the Secretary shall adjust annually the $5,000 amount in subparagraph (B)(i) and the $2,500 amount in subparagraph (B)(ii) for increases in the cost-of-living at the same time and in the same manner as adjustments under section 415(d); except that the base period taken into account shall be the calendar quarter beginning July 1, 2005, and any increase under this subparagraph which is not a multiple of $500 shall be rounded to the next lower multiple of $500.

(D) AGGREGATION OF PLANS.—For purposes of this paragraph, plans described in clauses (i), (ii), and (iv) of paragraph (6)(A) that are maintained by the same employer (as determined under subsection (b), (c), (m) or (o)) shall be treated as a single plan, and plans described in clause (iii) of paragraph (6)(A) that are maintained by the same employer shall be treated as a single plan.

(3) TREATMENT OF CONTRIBUTIONS.—In the case of any contribution to a plan under paragraph (1)—

(A) such contribution shall not, with respect to the year in which the contribution is made—

(i) be subject to any otherwise applicable limitation contained in section 401(a)(30), 402(h), 403(b), 408, 415(c), and 457(b)(2) (determined without regard to section 457(b)(3)), or

(ii) be taken into account in applying such limitations to other contributions or benefits under such plan or any other such plan, and

(B) except as provided in paragraph (4), such plan shall not be treated as failing to meet the requirements of section 401(a)(4), 401(k)(3), 401(k)(11), 403(b)(12), 408(k), 410(b), or 416 by reason of the making of (or the right to make) such contribution.

(4) APPLICATION OF NONDISCRIMINATION RULES.—

(A) IN GENERAL.—An applicable employer plan shall be treated as failing to meet the non-discrimination requirements under section 401(a)(4) with respect to benefits, rights, and features unless the plan allows all eligible participants to make the same election with respect to the additional elective deferrals under this subsection.

(B) AGGREGATION.—For purposes of subparagraph (A), all plans maintained by employers who are treated as a single employer under subsection (b), (c), (m), or (o) of section 414 shall be treated as 1 plan, except that a plan described in clause (i) of section 410(b)(6)(C) shall not be treated as a plan of the employer until the expiration of the transition period with respect to such plan (as determined under clause (ii) of such section).

(5) ELIGIBLE PARTICIPANT.—For purposes of this subsection, the term "eligible participant" means a participant in a plan—

(A) who would attain age 50 by the end of the taxable year,

(B) with respect to whom no other elective deferrals may (without regard to this subsection) be made to the plan for the plan (or other applicable) year by reason of the application of any limitation or other restriction described in paragraph (3) or comparable limitation or restriction contained in the terms of the plan.

(6) OTHER DEFINITIONS AND RULES.—For purposes of this subsection—

(A) APPLICABLE EMPLOYER PLAN.—The term "applicable employer plan" means—

(i) an employees' trust described in section 401(a) which is exempt from tax under section 501(a),

(ii) a plan under which amounts are contributed by an individual's employer for an annuity contract described in section 403(b),

(iii) an eligible deferred compensation plan under section 457 of an eligible employer described in section 457(e)(1)(A), and

(iv) an arrangement meeting the requirements of section 408(k) or (p).

(B) ELECTIVE DEFERRAL.—The term "elective deferral" has the meaning given such term by subsection (u)(2)(C).

(C) EXCEPTION FOR SECTION 457 PLANS.—This subsection shall not apply to a participant for any year for which a higher limitation applies to the participant under section 457(b)(3).

Amendments

• 2006, Pension Protection Act of 2006 (P.L. 109-280)

P.L. 109-280, §811, provides:

SEC. 811. PENSIONS AND INDIVIDUAL RETIREMENT ARRANGEMENT PROVISIONS OF ECONOMIC GROWTH AND TAX RELIEF RECONCILIATION ACT OF 2001 MADE PERMANENT.

Title IX of the Economic Growth and Tax Relief Reconciliation Act of 2001 [P.L. 107-16] shall not apply to the provisions of, and amendments made by, subtitles A through F of title VI [§§601-666]of such Act (relating to pension and individual retirement arrangement provisions).

• 2002, Job Creation and Worker Assistance Act of 2002 (P.L. 107-147)

P.L. 107-147, §411(o)(3):

Amended Code Sec. 414(v)(2) by adding at the end a new subparagraph (D). **Effective** as if included in the provision of P.L. 107-16 to which it relates [**effective** for tax years beginning after 12-31-2001.—CCH].

P.L. 107-147, §411(o)(4):

Amended Code Sec. 414(v)(3)(A)(i) by striking "section 402(g), 402(h), 403(b), 404(a), 404(h), 408(k), 408(p), 415, or 457" and inserting "section 401(a)(30), 402(h), 403(b), 408, 415(c), and 457(b)(2) (determined without regard to section 457(b)(3))". **Effective** as if included in the provision of P.L. 107-16 to which it relates [**effective** for tax years beginning after 12-31-2001.—CCH].

P.L. 107-147, §411(o)(5):

Amended Code Sec. 414(v)(3)(B) by striking "section 401(a)(4), 401(a)(26), 401(k)(3), 401(k)(11), 401(k)(12), 403(b)(12), 408(k), 408(p), 408B, 410(b), or 416" and inserting "section 401(a)(4), 401(k)(3), 401(k)(11), 403(b)(12), 408(k), 410(b), or 416". **Effective** as if included in the provision of P.L. 107-16 to which it relates [**effective** for tax years beginning after 12-31-2001.—CCH].

P.L. 107-147, §411(o)(6):

Amended Code Sec. 414(v)(4)(B) by inserting before the period at the end ", except that a plan described in clause (i) of section 410(b)(6)(C) shall not be treated as a plan of the employer until the expiration of the transition period with respect to such plan (as determined under clause (ii) of such section)". **Effective** as if included in the provision of P.L. 107-16 to which it relates [**effective** for tax years beginning after 12-31-2001.—CCH].

P.L. 107-147, §411(o)(7)(A)-(C):

Amended Code Sec. 414(v)(5) by striking ", with respect to any plan year," after "means," in the matter preceding subparagraph (A), by amending subparagraph (A), and by striking "plan year" and inserting "plan (or other applicable) year" in subparagraph (B). **Effective** as if included in the provision of P.L. 107-16 to which it relates [**effective** for tax years beginning after 12-31-2001.—CCH]. Prior to amendment, Code Sec. 414(v)(5)(A) read as follows:

(A) who has attained the age of 50 before the close of the plan year, and

P.L. 107-147, §411(o)(8):

Amended Code Sec. 414(v)(6)(C). **Effective** as if included in the provision of P.L. 107-16 to which it relates [**effective** for contributions in tax years beginning after 12-31-2001.—CCH]. Prior to amendment, Code Sec. 414(v)(6)(C) read as follows:

(C) EXCEPTION FOR SECTION 457 PLANS.—This subsection shall not apply to an applicable employer plan described in subparagraph (A)(iii) for any year to which section 457(b)(3) applies.

• 2001, Economic Growth and Tax Relief Reconciliation Act of 2001 (P.L. 107-16)

P.L. 107-16, §631(a):

Amended Code Sec. 414 by adding at the end a new subsection (v). **Effective** for contributions in tax years beginning after 12-31-2001.

P.L. 107-16, §901(a)-(b), provides [but see P.L. 109-280, §811, above]:

SEC. 901. SUNSET OF PROVISIONS OF ACT.

(a) IN GENERAL.—All provisions of, and amendments made by, this Act shall not apply—

(1) to taxable, plan, or limitation years beginning after December 31, 2010, or

(2) in the case of title V, to estates of decedents dying, gifts made, or generation skipping transfers, after December 31, 2010.

(b) APPLICATION OF CERTAIN LAWS.—The Internal Revenue Code of 1986 and the Employee Retirement Income Security Act of 1974 shall be applied and administered to years, estates, gifts, and transfers described in subsection (a) as if the provisions and amendments described in subsection (a) had never been enacted.

[Sec. 414(w)]

(w) SPECIAL RULES FOR CERTAIN WITHDRAWALS FROM ELIGIBLE AUTOMATIC CONTRIBUTION ARRANGEMENTS.—

(1) IN GENERAL.—If an eligible automatic contribution arrangement allows an employee to elect to make permissible withdrawals—

(A) the amount of any such withdrawal shall be includible in the gross income of the employee for the taxable year of the employee in which the distribution is made,

(B) no tax shall be imposed under section 72(t) with respect to the distribution, and

(C) the arrangement shall not be treated as violating any restriction on distributions under this title solely by reason of allowing the withdrawal.

In the case of any distribution to an employee by reason of an election under this paragraph, employer matching contributions shall be forfeited or subject to such other treatment as the Secretary may prescribe.

(2) PERMISSIBLE WITHDRAWAL.—For purposes of this subsection—

(A) IN GENERAL.—The term "permissible withdrawal" means any withdrawal from an eligible automatic contribution arrangement meeting the requirements of this paragraph which—

(i) is made pursuant to an election by an employee, and

(ii) consists of elective contributions described in paragraph (3)(B) (and earnings attributable thereto).

(B) TIME FOR MAKING ELECTION.—Subparagraph (A) shall not apply to an election by an employee unless the election is made no later than the date which is 90 days after the date of the first elective contribution with respect to the employee under the arrangement.

(C) AMOUNT OF DISTRIBUTION.—Subparagraph (A) shall not apply to any election by an employee unless the amount of any distribution by reason of the election is equal to the amount of elective contributions made with respect to the first payroll period to which the eligible automatic contribution arrangement applies to the employee and any succeeding payroll period beginning before the effective date of the election (and earnings attributable thereto).

(3) ELIGIBLE AUTOMATIC CONTRIBUTION ARRANGEMENT.—For purposes of this subsection, the term "eligible automatic contribution arrangement" means an arrangement under an applicable employer plan—

(A) under which a participant may elect to have the employer make payments as contributions under the plan on behalf of the participant, or to the participant directly in cash,

(B) under which the participant is treated as having elected to have the employer make such contributions in an amount equal to a uniform percentage of compensation provided under the plan until the participant specifically elects not to have such contributions made (or specifically elects to have such contributions made at a different percentage), and

(C) which meets the requirements of paragraph (4).

(4) NOTICE REQUIREMENTS.—

(A) IN GENERAL.—The administrator of a plan containing an arrangement described in paragraph (3) shall, within a reasonable period before each plan year, give to each employee to whom an arrangement described in paragraph (3) applies for such plan year notice of the employee's rights and obligations under the arrangement which—

(i) is sufficiently accurate and comprehensive to apprise the employee of such rights and obligations, and

(ii) is written in a manner calculated to be understood by the average employee to whom the arrangement applies.

(B) TIME AND FORM OF NOTICE.—A notice shall not be treated as meeting the requirements of subparagraph (A) with respect to an employee unless—

(i) the notice includes an explanation of the employee's right under the arrangement to elect not to have elective contributions made on the employee's behalf (or to elect to have such contributions made at a different percentage),

(ii) the employee has a reasonable period of time after receipt of the notice described in clause (i) and before the first elective contribution is made to make such election, and

(iii) the notice explains how contributions made under the arrangement will be invested in the absence of any investment election by the employee.

(5) APPLICABLE EMPLOYER PLAN.—For purposes of this subsection, the term "applicable employer plan" means—

(A) an employees' trust described in section 401(a) which is exempt from tax under section 501(a),

(B) a plan under which amounts are contributed by an individual's employer for an annuity contract described in section 403(b),

(C) an eligible deferred compensation plan described in section 457(b) which is maintained by an eligible employer described in section 457(e)(1)(A),

(D) a simplified employee pension the terms of which provide for a salary reduction arrangement described in section 408(k)(6), and

(E) a simple retirement account (as defined in section 408(p)).

(6) SPECIAL RULE.—A withdrawal described in paragraph (1) (subject to the limitation of paragraph (2)(C)) shall not be taken into account for purposes of section 401(k)(3) or for purposes of applying the limitation under section 402(g)(1).

Amendments

• 2008, Worker, Retiree, and Employer Recovery Act of 2008 (P.L. 110-458)

P.L. 110-458, §109(b)(5):

Amended Code Sec. 414(w)(5) by striking "and" at the end of subparagraph (B), by striking the period at the end of subparagraph (C) and inserting a comma, and by adding at the end new subparagraphs (D)-(E). **Effective** as if included in the provision of the 2006 Act to which the amendment relates [**effective** for plan years beginning after 12-31-2007.—CCH].

P.L. 110-458, §109(b)(4)(A)-(C):

Amended Code Sec. 414(w)(3) by inserting "and" after the comma at the end of subparagraph (B), by striking subparagraph (C), and redesignating subparagraph (D) as subparagraph (C). **Effective** as if included in the provision of the 2006 Act to which the amendment relates [**effective** for plan years beginning after 12-31-2007.—CCH]. Prior to being stricken, Code Sec. 414(w)(3)(C) read as follows:

(C) under which, in the absence of an investment election by the participant, contributions described in subparagraph (B) are invested in accordance with regulations prescribed by the Secretary of Labor under section 404(c)(5) of the Employee Retirement Income Security Act of 1974, and

P.L. 110-458, §109(b)(6):

Amended Code Sec. 414(w)(6) by inserting "or for purposes of applying the limitation under section 402(g)(1)" before the period at the end. **Effective** as if included in the provision of the 2006 Act to which the amendment relates [**effective** for plan years beginning after 12-31-2007.—CCH].

• 2006, Pension Protection Act of 2006 (P.L. 109-280)

P.L. 109-280, §902(d)(1):

Amended Code Sec. 414 by adding at the end a new subsection (w). **Effective** for plan years beginning after 12-31-2007.

[Sec. 414(x)]

(x) SPECIAL RULES FOR ELIGIBLE COMBINED DEFINED BENEFIT PLANS AND QUALIFIED CASH OR DEFERRED ARRANGEMENTS.—

(1) GENERAL RULE.—Except as provided in this subsection, the requirements of this title shall be applied to any defined benefit plan or applicable defined contribution plan which are part of an eligible combined plan in the same manner as if each such plan were not a part of the eligible combined plan. In the case of a termination of the defined benefit plan and the applicable defined contribution plan forming part of an eligible combined plan, the plan administrator shall terminate each such plan separately.

(2) ELIGIBLE COMBINED PLAN.—For purposes of this subsection—

(A) IN GENERAL.—The term "eligible combined plan" means a plan—

(i) which is maintained by an employer which, at the time the plan is established, is a small employer,

(ii) which consists of a defined benefit plan and an applicable defined contribution plan,

(iii) the assets of which are held in a single trust forming part of the plan and are clearly identified and allocated to the defined benefit plan and the applicable defined contribution plan to the extent necessary for the separate application of this title under paragraph (1), and

(iv) with respect to which the benefit, contribution, vesting, and nondiscrimination requirements of subparagraphs (B), (C), (D), (E), and (F) are met.

For purposes of this subparagraph, the term "small employer" has the meaning given such term by section 4980D(d)(2), except that such section shall be applied by substituting "500" for "50" each place it appears.

(B) BENEFIT REQUIREMENTS.—

(i) IN GENERAL.—The benefit requirements of this subparagraph are met with respect to the defined benefit plan forming part of the eligible combined plan if the accrued benefit of each participant derived from employer contributions, when expressed as an annual retirement benefit, is not less than the applicable percentage of the participant's final average pay. For purposes of this clause, final average pay shall be determined using the period of consecutive years (not exceeding 5) during which the participant had the greatest aggregate compensation from the employer.

(ii) APPLICABLE PERCENTAGE.—For purposes of clause (i), the applicable percentage is the lesser of—

(I) 1 percent multiplied by the number of years of service with the employer, or

(II) 20 percent.

(iii) SPECIAL RULE FOR APPLICABLE DEFINED BENEFIT PLANS.—If the defined benefit plan under clause (i) is an applicable defined benefit plan as defined in section 411(a)(13)(B) which meets the interest credit requirements of section 411(b)(5)(B)(i), the plan shall be treated as meeting the requirements of clause (i) with respect to any plan year if each participant receives a pay credit for the year which is not less than the percentage of compensation determined in accordance with the following table:

If the participant's age as of the beginning of the year is—	The percentage is—
30 or less	2
Over 30 but less than 40	4
40 or over but less than 50	6
50 or over	8.

(iv) YEARS OF SERVICE.—For purposes of this subparagraph, years of service shall be determined under the rules of paragraphs (4), (5), and (6) of section 411(a), except that the plan may not disregard any year of service because of a participant making, or failing to make, any elective deferral with respect to the qualified cash or deferred arrangement to which subparagraph (C) applies.

(C) CONTRIBUTION REQUIREMENTS.—

(i) IN GENERAL.—The contribution requirements of this subparagraph with respect to any applicable defined contribution plan forming part of an eligible combined plan are met if—

(I) the qualified cash or deferred arrangement included in such plan constitutes an automatic contribution arrangement, and

(II) the employer is required to make matching contributions on behalf of each employee eligible to participate in the arrangement in an amount equal to 50 percent of the elective contributions of the employee to the extent such elective contributions do not exceed 4 percent of compensation.

Rules similar to the rules of clauses (ii) and (iii) of section 401(k)(12)(B) shall apply for purposes of this clause.

(ii) NONELECTIVE CONTRIBUTIONS.—An applicable defined contribution plan shall not be treated as failing to meet the requirements of clause (i) because the employer makes nonelective contributions under the plan but such contributions shall not be taken into account in determining whether the requirements of clause (i)(II) are met.

(D) VESTING REQUIREMENTS.—The vesting requirements of this subparagraph are met if—

(i) in the case of a defined benefit plan forming part of an eligible combined plan an employee who has completed at least 3 years of service has a nonforfeitable right to 100 percent of the employee's accrued benefit under the plan derived from employer contributions, and

(ii) in the case of an applicable defined contribution plan forming part of [an] eligible combined plan—

(I) an employee has a nonforfeitable right to any matching contribution made under the qualified cash or deferred arrangement included in such plan by an employer with respect to any elective contribution, including matching contributions in excess of the contributions required under subparagraph (C)(i)(II), and

(II) an employee who has completed at least 3 years of service has a nonforfeitable right to 100 percent of the employee's accrued benefit derived under the arrangement from nonelective contributions of the employer.

For purposes of this subparagraph, the rules of section 411 shall apply to the extent not inconsistent with this subparagraph.

(E) UNIFORM PROVISION OF CONTRIBUTIONS AND BENEFITS.—In the case of a defined benefit plan or applicable defined contribution plan forming part of an eligible combined plan, the requirements of this subparagraph are met if all contributions and benefits under each such plan, and all rights and features under each such plan, must be provided uniformly to all participants.

(F) REQUIREMENTS MUST BE MET WITHOUT TAKING INTO ACCOUNT SOCIAL SECURITY AND SIMILAR CONTRIBUTIONS AND BENEFITS OR OTHER PLANS.—

(i) IN GENERAL.—The requirements of this subparagraph are met if the requirements of clauses (ii) and (iii) are met.

(ii) SOCIAL SECURITY AND SIMILAR CONTRIBUTIONS.—The requirements of this clause are met if—

(I) the requirements of subparagraphs (B) and (C) are met without regard to section 401(l), and

(II) the requirements of sections 401(a)(4) and 410(b) are met with respect to both the applicable defined contribution plan and defined benefit plan forming part of an eligible combined plan without regard to section 401(l).

(iii) OTHER PLANS AND ARRANGEMENTS.—The requirements of this clause are met if the applicable defined contribution plan and defined benefit plan forming part of an eligible combined plan meet the requirements of sections 401(a)(4) and 410(b) without being combined with any other plan.

(3) NONDISCRIMINATION REQUIREMENTS FOR QUALIFIED CASH OR DEFERRED ARRANGEMENT.—

(A) IN GENERAL.—A qualified cash or deferred arrangement which is included in an applicable defined contribution plan forming part of an eligible combined plan shall be treated as meeting the requirements of section 401(k)(3)(A)(ii) if the requirements of paragraph (2)(C) are met with respect to such arrangement.

(B) MATCHING CONTRIBUTIONS.—In applying section 401(m)(11) to any matching contribution with respect to a contribution to which paragraph (2)(C) applies, the contribution requirement of paragraph (2)(C) and the notice requirements of paragraph (5)(B) shall be substituted for the requirements otherwise applicable under clauses (i) and (ii) of section 401(m)(11)(A).

(4) SATISFACTION OF TOP-HEAVY RULES.—A defined benefit plan and applicable defined contribution plan forming part of an eligible combined plan for any plan year shall be treated as meeting the requirements of section 416 for the plan year.

(5) AUTOMATIC CONTRIBUTION ARRANGEMENT.—For purposes of this subsection—

(A) IN GENERAL.—A qualified cash or deferred arrangement shall be treated as an automatic contribution arrangement if the arrangement—

(i) provides that each employee eligible to participate in the arrangement is treated as having elected to have the employer make elective contributions in an amount equal to 4 percent of the employee's compensation unless the employee specifically elects not to have such contributions made or to have such contributions made at a different rate, and

(ii) meets the notice requirements under subparagraph (B).

(B) NOTICE REQUIREMENTS.—

(i) IN GENERAL.—The requirements of this subparagraph are met if the requirements of clauses (ii) and (iii) are met.

(ii) REASONABLE PERIOD TO MAKE ELECTION.—The requirements of this clause are met if each employee to whom subparagraph (A)(i) applies—

(I) receives a notice explaining the employee's right under the arrangement to elect not to have elective contributions made on the employee's behalf or to have the contributions made at a different rate, and

(II) has a reasonable period of time after receipt of such notice and before the first elective contribution is made to make such election.

(iii) ANNUAL NOTICE OF RIGHTS AND OBLIGATIONS.—The requirements of this clause are met if each employee eligible to participate in the arrangement is, within a reasonable period before any year, given notice of the employee's rights and obligations under the arrangement.

The requirements of clauses (i) and (ii) of section 401(k)(12)(D) shall be met with respect to the notices described in clauses (ii) and (iii) of this subparagraph.

(6) COORDINATION WITH OTHER REQUIREMENTS.—

(A) TREATMENT OF SEPARATE PLANS.—Section 414(k) shall not apply to an eligible combined plan.

(B) REPORTING.—An eligible combined plan shall be treated as a single plan for purposes of sections 6058 and 6059.

(7) APPLICABLE DEFINED CONTRIBUTION PLAN.—For purposes of this subsection—

(A) IN GENERAL.—The term "applicable defined contribution plan" means a defined contribution plan which includes a qualified cash or deferred arrangement.

(B) QUALIFIED CASH OR DEFERRED ARRANGEMENT.—The term "qualified cash or deferred arrangement" has the meaning given such term by section 401(k)(2).

Amendments

• 2008, Worker, Retiree, and Employer Recovery Act of 2008 (P.L. 110-458)

P.L. 110-458, §109(c)(1):

Amended Code Sec. 414(x)(1) by adding at the end a new sentence. **Effective** as if included in the provision of the 2006 Act to which the amendment relates [**effective** for plan years beginning after 12-31-2009.—CCH].

• 2006, Pension Protection Act of 2006 (P.L. 109-280)

P.L. 109-280, §903(a):

Amended Code Sec. 414, as amended by this Act, by adding at the end a new subsection (x). **Effective** for plan years beginning after 12-31-2009.

[Sec. 415]

SEC. 415. LIMITATIONS ON BENEFITS AND CONTRIBUTION UNDER QUALIFIED PLANS.

[Sec. 415(a)]

(a) GENERAL RULE.—

(1) TRUSTS.—A trust which is a part of a pension, profit-sharing, or stock bonus plan shall not constitute a qualified trust under section 401(a) if—

(A) in the case of a defined benefit plan, the plan provides for the payment of benefits with respect to a participant which exceed the limitation of subsection (b), or

(B) in the case of a defined contribution plan, contributions and other additions under the plan with respect to any participant for any taxable year exceed the limitation of subsection (c).

(2) SECTION APPLIES TO CERTAIN ANNUITIES AND ACCOUNTS.—In the case of—

(A) an employee annuity plan described in section 403(a),

(B) an annuity contract described in section 403(b), or

(C) a simplified employee pension described in section 408(k),

such a contract, plan, or pension shall not be considered to be described in section 403(a), 403(b), or 408(k), as the case may be, unless it satisfies the requirements of subparagraph (A) or subparagraph (B) of paragraph (1), whichever is appropriate, and has not been disqualified under subsection (g). In the case of an annuity contract described in section 403(b), the preceding sentence shall apply only to the portion of the annuity contract which exceeds the limitation of subsection (b) or the limitation of subsection (c), whichever is appropriate.

Amendments

• 2006, Pension Protection Act of 2006 (P.L. 109-280)

P.L. 109-280, §811, provides:

SEC. 811. PENSIONS AND INDIVIDUAL RETIREMENT ARRANGEMENT PROVISIONS OF ECONOMIC GROWTH AND TAX RELIEF RECONCILIATION ACT OF 2001 MADE PERMANENT.

Title IX of the Economic Growth and Tax Relief Reconciliation Act of 2001 [P.L. 107-16] shall not apply to the provisions of, and amendments made by, subtitles A through F of title VI [§§601-666]of such Act (relating to pension and individual retirement arrangement provisions).

• 2001, Economic Growth and Tax Relief Reconciliation Act of 2001 (P.L. 107-16)

P.L. 107-16, §632(a)(3)(C):

Amended Code Sec. 415(a)(2) by striking ", and the amount of the contribution for such portion shall reduce the exclusion allowance as provided in section 403(b)(2)" after "the limitation of subsection (c), whichever is appropriate". **Effective** for years beginning after 12-31-2001.

P.L. 107-16, §901(a)-(b), provides [but see P.L. 109-280, §811, above]:

SEC. 901. SUNSET OF PROVISIONS OF ACT.

(a) IN GENERAL.—All provisions of, and amendments made by, this Act shall not apply—

(1) to taxable, plan, or limitation years beginning after December 31, 2010, or

(2) in the case of title V, to estates of decedents dying, gifts made, or generation skipping transfers, after December 31, 2010.

(b) APPLICATION OF CERTAIN LAWS.—The Internal Revenue Code of 1986 and the Employee Retirement Income Security Act of 1974 shall be applied and administered to years, estates, gifts, and transfers described in subsection (a) as if the provisions and amendments described in subsection (a) had never been enacted.

• 1996, Small Business Job Protection Act of 1996 (P.L. 104-188)

P.L. 104-188, §1452(c)(1)(A)-(C):

Amended Code Sec. 415(a)(1) by adding "or" at the end of subparagraph (A), by striking ", or" at the end of subparagraph (B) and inserting a period, and by striking subparagraph (C). **Effective** for limitation years beginning after 12-31-99. Prior to being stricken, Code Sec. 415(a)(1)(C) read as follows:

(C) in any case in which an individual is a participant in both a defined benefit plan and a defined contribution plan maintained by the employer, the trust has been disqualified under subsection (g).

• 1984, Deficit Reduction Act of 1984 (P.L. 98-369)

P.L. 98-369, §491(d)(28):

Amended Code Sec. 415(a)(2) by striking out subparagraph (D), by striking out "or" at the end of subparagraph (C), by adding "or" at the end of subparagraph (B), and by striking out "405(a),". **Effective** for obligations issued after 12-31-83. Prior to being stricken, subparagraph (D) read as follows:

(D) a plan described in section 405(a),

• 1981, Economic Recovery Tax Act of 1981 (P.L. 97-34)

P.L. 97-34, §311(g)(4)(A):

Amended Code Sec. 415(a)(2). **Effective** for tax years beginning after 12-31-81. Prior to amendment, Code Sec. 415(a)(2) read as follows:

(2) SECTION APPLIES TO CERTAIN ANNUITIES AND ACCOUNTS.—Except as provided in paragraph (3), in the case of—

(A) an employee annuity plan described in section 403(a),

(B) an annuity contract described in section 403(b),

(C) an individual retirement account described in section 408(a),

(D) an individual retirement annuity described in section 408(b),

(E) a simplified employee pension,

(F) a plan described in section 405(a), or

(G) a retirement bond described in section 409,

such contract, annuity plan, account, annuity, plan, or bond shall not be considered to be described in section 403(a), 403(b), 405(a), 408(a), 408(b), 408(k), or 409, as the case may be, unless it satisfies the requirements of subparagraph (A) or subparagraph (B) of paragraph (1), whichever is appropriate, and has not been disqualified under subsection (g). In the case of an annuity contract described in section 403(b), the preceding sentence shall apply only to the portion of the annuity contract which exceeds the limitation of subsection (b) or the limitation of subsection (c), whichever is appropriate, and the amount of the contribution for such portion shall reduce the exclusion allowance as provided in section 403(b)(2).

P.L. 97-34, §311(h)(3):

Repealed Code Sec. 415(a)(3). **Effective** for tax years beginning after 12-31-81. Prior to repeal, Code Sec. 415(a)(3) read:

(3) ACCOUNTS, ETC., ESTABLISHED FOR NON-EMPLOYED SPOUSE.—Paragraph (2) shall not apply for any year to an account, annuity or bond described in section 408(a), 408(b), or 409, respectively, established for the benefit of the spouse of the individual contributing to such account, or for such annuity or bond, if a deduction is allowed under section 220 to such individual with respect to such contribution for such year.

• 1978, Revenue Act of 1978 (P.L. 95-600)

P.L. 95-600, §152(g)(1):

Amended Code Sec. 415(a)(2) by redesignating subparagraphs (E) and (F) as subparagraphs (F) and (G), and by inserting a new subparagraph (E). **Effective** for tax years beginning after 12-31-78.

P.L. 95-600, §152(g)(2):

Amended Code Sec. 415(a)(2) by inserting "408(k)," after "408(b),". **Effective** for tax years beginning after 12-31-78. (Caution: Congress apparently intended to amend Code Sec. 415(a)(2), although P.L. 95-600, §152(g)(2) by its language amends Code Sec. 415(b)(2).)

• **1976, Tax Reform Act of 1976 (P.L. 94-455)**

P.L. 94-455, § 1501(b)(3)(A):

Amended Code Sec. 415(a)(2) by substituting "Except as provided in paragraph (3), in the case" for "In the case". **Effective** for years beginning after 12-31-76.

P.L. 94-455, § 1501(b)(3)(B):

Added Code Sec. 415(a)(3). **Effective** for years beginning after 12-31-76.

• **1974, Employee Retirement Income Security Act of 1974 (P.L. 93-406)**

P.L. 93-406, § 2004(a)(2):

Added Code Sec. 415(a). **Effective**, generally, for years beginning after 1975. For special effective dates and transitional rules governing this section, see the special rule below and the historical note for § 1017, P.L. 93-406, following the text of Code Sec. 410(d).

P.L. 93-406, § 2004(d), provides:

(d) EFFECTIVE DATE.—

(1) GENERAL RULE.—The amendments made by this section shall apply to years beginning after December 31, 1975. The Secretary of the Treasury shall prescribe such regulations as may be necessary to carry out the provisions of this paragraph.

(2) TRANSITION RULE FOR DEFINED BENEFIT PLANS.—In the case of an individual who was an active participant in a defined benefit plan before October 3, 1973, if—

(A) the annual benefit (within the meaning of section 415(b)(2) of the Internal Revenue Code of 1954) payable to such participant on retirement does not exceed 100 percent of his annual rate of compensation on the earlier of (i) October 2, 1973, or (ii) the date on which he separated from the service of the employer,

(B) such annual benefit is no greater than the annual benefit which would have been payable to such participant on retirement if (i) all the terms and conditions of such plan in existence on such date had remained in existence until such retirement, and (ii) his compensation taken into account for any period after October 2, 1973, had not exceeded his annual rate of compensation on such date, and

(C) in the case of a participant who separated from the service of the employer prior to October 2, 1973, such annual benefit is no greater than his vested accrued benefit as of the date he separated from the service,

then such annual benefit shall be treated as not exceeding the limitation of subsection (b) of section 415 of the Internal Revenue Code of 1954.

[Sec. 415(b)]

(b) LIMITATION FOR DEFINED BENEFIT PLANS.—

(1) IN GENERAL.—Benefits with respect to a participant exceed the limitation of this subsection if, when expressed as an annual benefit (within the meaning of paragraph (2)), such annual benefit is greater than the lesser of—

(A) $160,000, or

(B) 100 percent of the participant's average compensation for his high 3 years.

(2) ANNUAL BENEFIT.—

(A) IN GENERAL.—For purposes of paragraph (1), the term "annual benefit" means a benefit payable annually in the form of a straight life annuity (with no ancillary benefits) under a plan to which employees do not contribute and under which no rollover contributions (as defined in sections 402(c), 403(a)(4), 403(b)(8), 408(d)(3), and 457(e)(16)) are made.

(B) ADJUSTMENT FOR CERTAIN OTHER FORMS OF BENEFIT.—If the benefit under the plan is payable in any form other than the form described in subparagraph (A), or if the employees contribute to the plan or make rollover contributions (as defined in sections 402(c), 403(a)(4), 403(b)(8), 408(d)(3), and 457(e)(16)), the determinations as to whether the limitation described in paragraph (1) has been satisfied shall be made, in accordance with regulations prescribed by the Secretary, by adjusting such benefit so that it is equivalent to the benefit described in subparagraph (A). For purposes of this subparagraph, any ancillary benefit which is not directly related to retirement income benefits shall not be taken into account; and that portion of any joint and survivor annuity which constitutes a qualified joint and survivor annuity (as defined in section 417) shall not be taken into account.

(C) ADJUSTMENT TO $160,000 LIMIT WHERE BENEFIT BEGINS BEFORE AGE 62.—If the retirement income benefit under the plan begins before age 62, the determination as to whether the $160,000 limitation set forth in paragraph (1)(A) has been satisfied shall be made, in accordance with regulations prescribed by the Secretary, by reducing the limitation of paragraph (1)(A) so that such limitation (as so reduced) equals an annual benefit (beginning when such retirement income benefit begins) which is equivalent to a $160,000 annual benefit beginning at age 62.

(D) ADJUSTMENT TO $160,000 LIMIT WHERE BENEFIT BEGINS AFTER AGE 65.—If the retirement income benefit under the plan begins after age 65, the determination as to whether the $160,000 limitation set forth in paragraph (1)(A) has been satisfied shall be made, in accordance with regulations prescribed by the Secretary, by increasing the limitation of paragraph (1)(A) so that such limitation (as so increased) equals an annual benefit (beginning when such retirement income benefit begins) which is equivalent to a $160,000 annual benefit beginning at age 65.

(E) LIMITATION ON CERTAIN ASSUMPTIONS.—

(i) For purposes of adjusting any limitation under subparagraph (C) and, except as provided in clause (ii), for purposes of adjusting any benefit under subparagraph (B), the interest rate assumption shall not be less than the greater of 5 percent or the rate specified in the plan.

(ii) For purposes of adjusting any benefit under subparagraph (B) for any form of benefit subject to section 417(e)(3), the interest rate assumption shall not be less than the greatest of—

(I) 5.5 percent,

(II) the rate that provides a benefit of not more than 105 percent of the benefit that would be provided if the applicable interest rate (as defined in section 417(e)(3)) were the interest rate assumption, or

(III) the rate specified under the plan.

(iii) For purposes of adjusting any limitation under subparagraph (D), the interest rate assumption shall not be greater than the lesser of 5 percent or the rate specified in the plan.

(iv) For purposes of this subsection, no adjustments under subsection (d)(1) shall be taken into account before the year for which such adjustment first takes effect.

(v) For purposes of adjusting any benefit or limitation under subparagraph (B), (C), or (D), the mortality table used shall be the applicable mortality table (within the meaning of section 417(e)(3)(B)).

(vi) In the case of a plan maintained by an eligible employer (as defined in section 408(p)(2)(C)(i)), clause (ii) shall be applied without regard to subclause (II) thereof.

(F) [Stricken.]

(G) SPECIAL LIMITATION FOR QUALIFIED POLICE OR FIREFIGHTERS.—In the case of a qualified participant, subparagraph (C) of this paragraph shall not apply.

(H) QUALIFIED PARTICIPANT DEFINED.—For purposes of subparagraph (G), the term "qualified participant" means a participant—

(i) in a defined benefit plan which is maintained by a State, Indian tribal government (as defined in section 7701(a)(4)), or any political subdivision thereof,

(ii) with respect to whom the period of service taken into account in determining the amount of the benefit under such defined benefit plan includes at least 15 years of service of the participant—

(I) as a full-time employee of any police department or fire department which is organized and operated by the State, Indian tribal government (as so defined), or any political subdivision maintaining such defined benefit plan to provide police protection, firefighting services, or emergency medical services for any area within the jurisdiction of such State, Indian tribal government (as so defined), or any political subdivision, or

(II) as a member of the Armed Forces of the United States.

(I) EXEMPTION FOR SURVIVOR AND DISABILITY BENEFITS PROVIDED UNDER GOVERNMENTAL PLANS.—Subparagraph (C) of this paragraph and paragraph (5) shall not apply to—

(i) income received from a governmental plan (as defined in section 414(d)) as a pension, annuity, or similar allowance as the result of the recipient becoming disabled by reason of personal injuries or sickness, or

(ii) amounts received from a governmental plan by the beneficiaries, survivors, or the estate of an employee as the result of the death of the employee.

(3) AVERAGE COMPENSATION FOR HIGH 3 YEARS.—For purposes of paragraph (1), a participant's high 3 years shall be the period of consecutive calendar years (not more than 3) during which the participant had the greatest aggregate compensation from the employer. In the case of an employee within the meaning of section 401(c)(1), the preceding sentence shall be applied by substituting for "compensation from the employer" the following: "the participant's earned income (within the meaning of section 401(c)(2) but determined without regard to any exclusion under section 911)".

(4) TOTAL ANNUAL BENEFITS NOT IN EXCESS OF $10,000.—Notwithstanding the preceding provisions of this subsection, the benefits payable with respect to a participant under any defined benefit plan shall be deemed not to exceed the limitation of this subsection if—

(A) the retirement benefits payable with respect to such participant under such plan and under all other defined benefit plans of the employer do not exceed $10,000 for the plan year, or for any prior plan year, and

(B) the employer has not at any time maintained a defined contribution plan in which the participant participated.

(5) REDUCTION FOR PARTICIPATION OR SERVICE OF LESS THAN 10 YEARS.—

(A) DOLLAR LIMITATION.—In the case of an employee who has less than 10 years of participation in a defined benefit plan, the limitation referred to in paragraph (1)(A) shall be the limitation determined under such paragraph (without regard to this paragraph) multiplied by a fraction—

(i) the numerator of which is the number of years (or part thereof) of participation in the defined benefit plan of the employer, and

(ii) the denominator of which is 10.

(B) COMPENSATION AND BENEFITS LIMITATIONS.—The provisions of subparagraph (A) shall apply to the limitations under paragraphs (1)(B) and (4), except that such subparagraph shall be applied with respect to years of service with an employer rather than years of participation in a plan.

(C) LIMITATION ON REDUCTION.—In no event shall subparagraph (A) or (B) reduce the limitations referred to in paragraphs (1) and (4) to an amount less than 1/10 of such limitation (determined without regard to this paragraph).

(D) APPLICATION TO CHANGES IN BENEFIT STRUCTURE.—To the extent provided in regulations, subparagraph (A) shall be applied separately with respect to each change in the benefit structure of a plan.

(6) COMPUTATION OF BENEFITS AND CONTRIBUTIONS.—The computation of—

(A) benefits under a defined contribution plan, for purposes of section 401(a)(4),

(B) contributions made on behalf of a participant in a defined benefit plan, for purposes of section 401(a)(4), and

(C) contributions and benefits provided for a participant in a plan described in section 414(k), for purposes of this section

shall not be made on a basis inconsistent with regulations prescribed by the Secretary.

(7) BENEFITS UNDER CERTAIN COLLECTIVELY BARGAINED PLANS.—For a year, the limitation referred to in paragraph (1)(B) shall not apply to benefits with respect to a participant under a defined benefit plan (other than a multiemployer plan)—

(A) which is maintained for such year pursuant to a collective bargaining agreement between employee representatives and one or more employers,

(B) which, at all times during such year, has at least 100 participants,

(C) under which benefits are determined solely by reference to length of service, the particular years during which service was rendered, age at retirement, and date of retirement,

(D) which provides that an employee who has at least 4 years of service has a nonforfeitable right to 100 percent of his accrued benefit derived from employer contributions, and

(E) which requires, as a condition of participation in the plan, that an employee complete a period of not more than 60 consecutive days of service with the employer or employers maintaining the plan.

This paragraph shall not apply to a participant whose compensation for any 3 years during the 10-year period immediately preceding the year in which he separates from service exceeded the average compensation for such 3 years of all participants in such plan. This paragraph shall not apply to a participant for any period for which he is a participant under another plan to which this section applies which is maintained by an employer maintaining this plan. For any year for which the paragraph applies to benefits with respect to a participant, paragraph (1)(A) and subsection (d)(1)(A) shall be applied with respect to such participant by substituting one-half the amount otherwise applicable for such year under paragraph (1)(A) for "$160,000".

(8) SOCIAL SECURITY RETIREMENT AGE DEFINED.—For purposes of this subsection, the term "social security retirement age" means the age used as the retirement age under section 216(l) of the Social Security Act, except that such section shall be applied—

(A) without regard to the age increase factor, and

(B) as if the early retirement age under section 216(l)(2) of such Act were 62.

(9) SPECIAL RULE FOR COMMERCIAL AIRLINE PILOTS.—

(A) IN GENERAL.—Except as provided in subparagraph (B), in the case of any participant who is a commercial airline pilot, if, as of the time of the participant's retirement, regulations prescribed by the Federal Aviation Administration require an individual to separate from service as a commercial airline pilot after attaining any age occurring on or after age 60 and before age 62, paragraph (2)(C) shall be applied by substituting such age for age 62.

(B) INDIVIDUALS WHO SEPARATE FROM SERVICE BEFORE AGE 60.—If a participant described in subparagraph (A) separates from service before age 60, the rules of paragraph (2)(C) shall apply.

(10) SPECIAL RULE FOR STATE, INDIAN TRIBAL, AND LOCAL GOVERNMENT PLANS.—

(A) LIMITATION TO EQUAL ACCRUED BENEFIT.—In the case of a plan maintained for its employees by any State or political subdivision thereof, or by any agency or instrumentality of the foregoing, or a governmental plan described in the last sentence of section 414(d) (relating to plans of Indian tribal governments), the limitation with respect to a qualified participant under this subsection shall not be less than the accrued benefit of the participant under the plan (determined without regard to any amendment of the plan made after October 14, 1987).

(B) QUALIFIED PARTICIPANT.—For purposes of this paragraph, the term "qualified participant" means a participant who first became a participant in the plan maintained by the employer before January 1, 1990.

(C) ELECTION.—(i) IN GENERAL.—This paragraph shall not apply to any plan unless each employer maintaining the plan elects before the close of the 1st plan year beginning after December 31, 1989, to have this subsection (other than paragraph (2)(G)) [applied].

(ii) REVOCATION OF ELECTION.—An election under clause (i) may be revoked not later than the last day of the third plan year beginning after the date of the enactment of this clause. The revocation shall apply to all plan years to which the election applied and to all subsequent plan years. Any amount paid by a plan in a taxable year ending after the revocation shall be includible in income in such taxable year under the rules of this chapter in effect for such taxable year, except that, for purposes of applying the limitations imposed by this section, any portion of such amount which is attributable to any taxable year during which the election was in effect shall be treated as received in such taxable year.

(11) SPECIAL LIMITATION RULE FOR GOVERNMENTAL AND MULTIEMPLOYER PLANS.—In the case of a governmental plan (as defined in section 414(d)) or a multiemployer plan (as defined in section 414(f)), subparagraph (B) of paragraph (1) shall not apply. Subparagraph (B) of paragraph (1) shall not apply to a plan maintained by an organization described in section 3121(w)(3)(A) except with respect to highly compensated benefits. For purposes of this paragraph, the term "highly compensated benefits" means any benefits accrued for an employee in any year on or after the first year in which such employee is a highly compensated employee (as defined in section 414(q)) of the organization described in section 3121(w)(3)(A). For purposes of applying paragraph (1)(B) to highly compensated benefits, all benefits of the employee otherwise taken into account (without regard to this paragraph) shall be taken into account.

Amendments

• 2008, Worker, Retiree, and Employer Recovery Act of 2008 (P.L. 110-458)

P.L. 110-458, §103(b)(2)(B)(i):

Amended Code Sec. 415(b)(2)(E)(v). **Effective** generally for years beginning after 12-31-2008. For an exception, see Act Sec. 103(b)(2)(B)(ii)(II), below. Prior to amendment, Code Sec. 415(b)(2)(E)(v) read as follows:

(v) For purposes of adjusting any benefit or limitation under subparagraph (B), (C), or (D), the mortality table used shall be the table prescribed by the Secretary. Such table shall be based on the prevailing commissioners' standard table (described in section 807(d)(5)(A)) used to determine reserves for group annuity contracts issued on the date the adjustment is being made (without regard to any other subparagraph of section 807(d)(5)).

P.L. 110-458, §103(b)(2)(B)(ii)(II), provides:

A plan sponsor may elect to have the amendment made by clause (i) apply to any year beginning after December 31, 2007, and before January 1, 2009, or to any portion of any such year.

P.L. 110-458, §122(a):

Amended Code Sec. 415(b)(2)(E) by adding at the end a new clause (vi). **Effective** for years beginning after 12-31-2008.

• 2006, Pension Protection Act of 2006 (P.L. 109-280)

P.L. 109-280, §303(a):

Amended Code Sec. 415(b)(2)(E)(ii). **Effective** for distributions made in years beginning after 12-31-2005. Prior to amendment, Code Sec. 415(b)(2)(E)(ii) read as follows:

(ii) For purposes of adjusting any benefit under subparagraph (B) for any form of benefit subject to section 417(e)(3), the applicable interest rate (as defined in section 417(e)(3)) shall be substituted for "5 percent" in clause (i), except that in the case of plan years beginning in 2004 or 2005, "5.5 percent" shall be substituted for "5 percent" in clause (i).

P.L. 109-280, §811, provides:

SEC. 811. PENSIONS AND INDIVIDUAL RETIREMENT ARRANGEMENT PROVISIONS OF ECONOMIC GROWTH AND TAX RELIEF RECONCILIATION ACT OF 2001 MADE PERMANENT.

Title IX of the Economic Growth and Tax Relief Reconciliation Act of 2001 [P.L. 107-16] shall not apply to the provisions of, and amendments made by, subtitles A through F of title VI [§§601-666]of such Act (relating to pension and individual retirement arrangement provisions).

P.L. 109-280, §832(a):

Amended Code Sec. 415(b)(3) by striking "both was an active participant in the plan and" following "during which the participant". **Effective** for years beginning after 12-31-2005.

P.L. 109-280, §867(a):

Amended Code Sec. 415(b)(11) by adding at the end three new sentences. **Effective** for years beginning after 12-31-2006.

P.L. 109-280, §906(b)(1)(A)(i)-(ii):

Amended Code Sec. 415(b)(2)(H) by striking "State or political subdivision" and inserting "State, Indian tribal government (as defined in section 7701(a)(40)), or any political subdivision" in clause (i); and by striking "State or political subdivision" each place it appears and inserting "State, Indian tribal government (as so defined), or any political subdivision" in clause (ii)(I). **Effective** for any year beginning on or after 8-17-2006.

P.L. 109-280, §906(b)(1)(B)(i):

Amended Code Sec. 415(b)(10)(A) by inserting "or a governmental plan described in the last sentence of section 414(d) (relating to plans of Indian tribal governments)," after "foregoing,". **Effective** for any year beginning on or after 8-17-2006.

P.L. 109-280, §906(b)(1)(B)(ii) [as amended by P.L. 110-458, §109(d)(1)]:

Amended the heading of Code Sec. 415(b)(10) by striking "SPECIAL RULE FOR STATE AND" and inserting "SPECIAL RULE FOR STATE, INDIAN TRIBAL, AND". **Effective** for any year beginning on or after 8-17-2006.

• 2004, Pension Funding Equity Act of 2004 (P.L. 108-218)

P.L. 108-218, §101(b)(4):

Amended Code Sec. 415(b)(2)(E)(ii) by inserting ", except that in the case of plan years beginning in 2004 or 2005, '5.5 percent' shall be substituted for '5 percent' in clause (i)" before the period at the end. **Effective** generally for plan years beginning after 12-31-2003. For a transition rule, see Act Sec. 101(d)(3), below.

P.L. 108-218, §101(d)(3), provides:

(3) TRANSITION RULE FOR SECTION 415 LIMITATION.—In the case of any participant or beneficiary receiving a distribution after December 31, 2003 and before January 1, 2005, the amount payable under any form of benefit subject to section 417(e)(3) of the Internal Revenue Code of 1986 and subject to adjustment under section 415(b)(2)(B) of such Code shall not, solely by reason of the amendment made by subsection (b)(4), be less than the amount that would have been so payable had the amount payable been determined using the applicable interest rate in effect as of the last day of the last plan year beginning before January 1, 2004.

• 2001, Economic Growth and Tax Relief Reconciliation Act of 2001 (P.L. 107-16)

P.L. 107-16, §611(a)(1)(A):

Amended Code Sec. 415(b)(1)(A) by striking "$90,000" and inserting "$160,000". **Effective** for years ending after 12-31-2001. For a special rule, see Act Sec. 611(i)(3), below.

P.L. 107-16, §611(a)(1)(B):

Amended Code Sec. 415(b)(2)(C) and (D) by striking "$90,000" in the headings and the text and inserting "$160,000". **Effective** for years ending after 12-31-2001. For a special rule, see Act Sec. 611(i)(3), below.

P.L. 107-16, §611(a)(1)(C):

Amended Code Sec. 415(b)(7) by striking "the greater of $68,212 or one-half the amount otherwise applicable for such year under paragraph (1)(A) for `$90,000'" and inserting "one-half the amount otherwise applicable for such year under paragraph (1)(A) for `$160,000'". **Effective** for years ending after 12-31-2001. For a special rule, see Act Sec. 611(i)(3), below.

P.L. 107-16, §611(a)(2):

Amended Code Sec. 415(b)(2)(C) by striking "the social security retirement age" each place it appears in the heading and text and inserting "age 62" and by striking the second sentence. **Effective** for years ending after 12-31-2001. For a special rule, see Act Sec. 611(i)(3), below. Prior to being stricken, the second sentence of Code Sec. 415(b)(2)(C) read as follows:

The reduction under this subparagraph shall be made in such manner as the Secretary may prescribe which is consistent with the reduction for old-age insurance benefits commencing before the social security retirement age under the Social Security Act.

P.L. 107-16, §611(a)(3):

Amended Code Sec. 415(b)(2)(D) by striking "the social security retirement age" each place it appears in the heading and text and inserting "age 65". **Effective** for years ending after 12-31-2001. For a special rule, see Act Sec. 611(i)(3), below.

P.L. 107-16, §611(a)(5)(A):

Amended Code Sec. 415(b)(2) by striking paragraph (F). **Effective** for years ending after 12-31-2001. For a special rule, see Act Sec. 611(i)(3), below. Prior to being stricken, Code Sec. 415(b)(2)(F) read as follows:

(F) PLANS MAINTAINED BY GOVERNMENTS AND TAX EXEMPT ORGANIZATIONS—In the case of a governmental plan (within the meaning of section 414(d)), a plan maintained by an organization (other than a governmental unit) exempt from tax under this subtitle, or a qualified merchant marine plan—

(i) subparagraph (C) shall be applied—

(I) by substituting "age 62" for "social security retirement age" each place it appears, and

(II) as if the last sentence thereof read as follows: "The reduction under this subparagraph shall not reduce the limitation of paragraph (1)(A) below (i) $75,000 if the benefit begins at or after age 55, or (ii) if the benefit begins before age 55, the equivalent of the $75,000 limitation for age 55.", and

(ii) subparagraph (D) shall be applied by substituting "age 65" for "social security retirement age" each place it appears.

For purposes of this subparagraph, the term "qualified merchant marine plan" means a plan in existence on January 1, 1986, the participants in which are merchant marine officers holding licenses issued by the Secretary of Transportation under title 46, United States Code.

P.L. 107-16, §611(a)(5)(B):

Amended Code Sec. 415(b)(9). **Effective** for years ending after 12-31-2001. For a special rule, see Act Sec. 611(i)(3), below. Prior to amendment, Code Sec. 415(b)(9) read as follows:

(9) SPECIAL RULE FOR COMMERCIAL AIRLINE PILOTS.—

(A) IN GENERAL.—Except as provided in subparagraph (B), in the case of any participant who is a commercial airline pilot—

(i) the rule of paragraph (2)(F)(i)(II) shall apply, and

(ii) if, as of the time of the participant's retirement, regulations prescribed by the Federal Aviation Administration require an individual to separate from service as a commercial airline pilot after attaining any age occurring on or after age 60 and before the social security retirement age, paragraph (2)(C) (after application of clause (i)) shall be applied by substituting such age for the social security retirement age.

(B) INDIVIDUALS WHO SEPARATE FROM SERVICE BEFORE AGE 60.—If a participant described in subparagraph (A) separates from service before age 60, the rules of paragraph (2)(F) shall apply.

P.L. 107-16, §611(a)(5)(C):

Amended Code Sec. 415(b)(10)(C)(i) by striking "applied without regard to paragraph (2)(F)" after "(other than paragraph (2)(G))". **Effective** for years ending after 12-31-2001. For a special rule, see Act Sec. 611(i)(3), below.

P.L. 107-16, §611(i)(3) (as added by P.L. 107-147, §411(j)(3)), provides:

(3) SPECIAL RULE.—In the case of [a] plan that, on June 7, 2001, incorporated by reference the limitation of section 415(b)(1)(A) of the Internal Revenue Code of 1986, section 411(d)(6) of such Code and section 204(g)(1) of the Employee Retirement Income Security Act of 1974 do not apply to a plan amendment that—

(A) is adopted on or before June 30, 2002,

(B) reduces benefits to the level that would have applied without regard to the amendments made by subsection (a) of this section, and

(C) is effective no earlier than the years described in paragraph (2).

P.L. 107-16, §641(e)(9):

Amended Code Sec. 415(b)(2)(A) and (B) by striking "and 408(d)(3)" and inserting "403(b)(8), 408(d)(3), and 457(e)(16)". **Effective**, generally, for distributions after 12-31-2001. For a special rule, see Act Sec. 641(f)(3) in the amendment notes following Code Sec. 457(e).

P.L. 107-16, §654(a)(1):

Amended Code Sec. 415(b)(11). **Effective** for years beginning after 12-31-2001. Prior to amendment, Code Sec. 415(b)(11) read as follows:

(11) SPECIAL LIMITATION RULE FOR GOVERNMENTAL PLANS.—In the case of a governmental plan (as defined in section 414(d)), subparagraph (B) of paragraph (1) shall not apply.

P.L. 107-16, §654(a)(2):

Amended Code Sec. 415(b)(7) by inserting "(other than a multiemployer plan)" after "defined benefit plan" in the matter preceding subparagraph (A). **Effective** for years beginning after 12-31-2001.

P.L. 107-16, §901(a)-(b), provides [but see P.L. 109-280, §811, above]:

SEC. 901. SUNSET OF PROVISIONS OF ACT.

(a) IN GENERAL.—All provisions of, and amendments made by, this Act shall not apply—

(1) to taxable, plan, or limitation years beginning after December 31, 2010, or

(2) in the case of title V, to estates of decedents dying, gifts made, or generation skipping transfers, after December 31, 2010.

(b) APPLICATION OF CERTAIN LAWS.—The Internal Revenue Code of 1986 and the Employee Retirement Income Security Act of 1974 shall be applied and administered to years, estates, gifts, and transfers described in subsection (a) as if the provisions and amendments described in subsection (a) had never been enacted.

• 1997, Taxpayer Relief Act of 1997 (P.L. 105-34)

P.L. 105-34, §1527(a):

Amended Code Sec. 415(b)(2)(G) by striking "participant—" and all that follows and inserting "participant, subparagraph (C) of this paragraph shall not apply." **Effective** for years beginning after 12-31-96. Prior to amendment, Code Sec. 415(b)(2)(G) read as follows:

(G) SPECIAL LIMITATION FOR QUALIFIED POLICE OR FIREFIGHTERS.—In the case of a qualified participant—

(i) subparagraph (C) shall not reduce the limitation of paragraph (1)(A) to an amount less than $50,000, and

(ii) the rules of subparagraph (F) shall apply.

The Secretary shall adjust the $50,000 amount in clause (i) at the same time and in the same manner as under section 415(d).

• **1996, Small Business Job Protection Act of 1996 (P.L. 104-188)**

P.L. 104-188, §1444(a):

Amended Code Sec. 415(b) by adding immediately after paragraph (10) a new paragraph (11). **Effective** for years beginning after 12-31-94. For a special rule, see Act Sec. 1444(e)(2), below.

P.L. 104-188, §1444(c):

Amended Code Sec. 415(b)(2) by adding at the end a new subparagraph (I). **Effective** for years beginning after 12-31-94. For a special rule, see Act Sec. 1444(e)(2), below.

P.L. 104-188, §1444(d)(1):

Amended Code Sec. 415(b)(10)(C) by adding at the end a new clause (ii). **Effective** with respect to revocations adopted after 8-20-96. For a special rule, see Act Sec. 1444(e)(2), below.

P.L. 104-188, §1444(d)(2):

Amended Code Sec. 415(b)(10)(C) is amended by striking "This" and inserting "(i) IN GENERAL.—This". **Effective** with respect to revocations adopted after 8-20-96. For a special rule, see Act Sec. 1444(e)(2), below.

P.L. 104-188, §1444(e)(2), provides:

(2) TREATMENT FOR YEARS BEGINNING BEFORE JANUARY 1, 1995.—Nothing in the amendments made by this section shall be construed to imply that a governmental plan (as defined in section 414(d) of the Internal Revenue Code of 1986) fails to satisfy the requirements of section 415 of such Code for any taxable year beginning before January 1, 1995.

P.L. 104-188, §1449(b)(1)-(2):

Amended Code Sec. 415(b)(2)(E) by striking "Except as provided in clause (ii), for purposes of adjusting any benefit or limitation under subparagraph (B) or (C)," in clause (i) and inserting "For purposes of adjusting any limitation under subparagraph (C) and, except as provided in clause (ii), for purposes of adjusting any benefit under subparagraph (B),", and by striking "For purposes of adjusting the benefit or limitation of any form of benefit subject to section 417(e)(3)," in clause (ii) and inserting "For purposes of adjusting any benefit under subparagraph (B) for any form of benefit subject to section 417(e)(3),". **Effective** as if included in the provision of section 767 of P.L. 103-465. For a transitional rule, see Act Sec. 1449(d), below.

P.L. 104-188, §1449(d), provides:

(d) TRANSITIONAL RULE.—In the case of a plan that was adopted and in effect before December 8, 1994, if—

(1) a plan amendment was adopted or made effective on or before the date of the enactment of this Act applying the amendments made by section 767 of the Uruguay Round Agreements Act, and

(2) within 1 year after the date of the enactment of this Act, a plan amendment is adopted which repeals the amendment referred to in paragraph (1), the amendment referred to in paragraph (1) shall not be taken into account in applying section 767(d)(3)(A) of the Uruguay Round Agreements Act, as amended by subsection (a).

P.L. 104-188, §1452(c)(2):

Amended Code Sec. 415(b)(5)(B) by striking "and subsection (e)" after "(4)". **Effective** for limitation years beginning after 12-31-99.

• **1994, Uruguay Round Agreements Act (P.L. 103-465)**

P.L. 103-465, §767(b)(1)-(3):

Amended Code Sec. 415(b)(2)(E) by redesignating clauses (ii) and (iii) as clauses (iii) and (iv), respectively, by striking clause (i) and inserting new clauses (i) and (ii), and by adding at the end a new clause (v). **Effective** for plan years and limitation years beginning after 12-31-94, except that an employer may elect to treat the amendments made by this section as being effective on or after 12-8-94. Prior to amendment, Code Sec. 415(b)(2)(E)(i) read as follows:

(i) For purposes of adjusting any benefit or limitation under subparagraph (B) or (C), the interest rate assumption shall not be less than the greater of 5 percent or the rate specified in the plan.

P.L. 103-465, §767(d)(3) (as amended by P.L. 104-188, §1449(a) and P.L. 105-34, §1604(b)(3)), provides:

(3) SECTION 415.—

(A) EXCEPTION.—A plan that was adopted and in effect before December 8, 1994, shall not be required to apply the amendments made by subsection (b) with respect to benefits accrued before the earlier of—

(i) the later of the date a plan amendment applying the amendments made by subsection (b) is adopted or made effective, or

(ii) the first day of the first limitation year beginning after December 31, 1999.

Determinations under section 415(b)(2)(E) of the Internal Revenue Code of 1986 before such earlier date shall be made with respect to such benefits on the basis of such section as in effect on December 7, 1994, and the provisions of the plan as in effect on December 7, 1994, but only if such provisions of the plan meet the requirements of such section (as so in effect).

(B) TIMING OF PLAN AMENDMENT.—A plan that operates in accordance with the amendments made by subsection (b) shall not be treated as failing to satisfy section 401(a) of the Internal Revenue Code of 1986 or as not being operated in accordance with the provisions of the plan until such date as the Secretary of the Treasury provides merely because the plan has not been amended to include the amendments made by subsection (b).

• **1992, Unemployment Compensation Amendments of 1992 (P.L. 102-318)**

P.L. 102-318, §521(b)(23):

Amended Code Sec. 415(b)(2)(A) by striking "sections 402(a)(5)" and inserting "sections 402(c)". **Effective** for distributions after 12-31-92.

P.L. 102-318, §521(b)(24):

Amended Code Sec. 415(b)(2)(B) by striking "sections 402(a)(5)" and inserting "sections 402(c)". **Effective** for distributions after 12-31-92.

• **1988, Technical and Miscellaneous Revenue Act of 1988 (P.L. 100-647)**

P.L. 100-647, §1011(d)(2):

Amended Code Sec. 415(b)(5)(D) by striking out "this paragraph" and inserting in lieu thereof "subparagraph (A)". **Effective** as if included in the provision of P.L. 99-514 to which it relates.

P.L. 100-647, §1011(d)(6):

Amended Code Sec. 415(b)(5)(B) by inserting "and subsection (e)" after "paragraphs (1)(B) and (4)". **Effective** as if included in the provision of P.L. 99-514 to which it relates.

P.L. 100-647, §6054(a):

Amended Code Sec. 415(b) by adding at the end thereof a new paragraph (10). **Effective**, generally, for years beginning after 12-31-82, except that Act Sec. 6054(b)(2) provides that Code Sec. 415(b)(10)(C) shall not apply to any year beginning before 1-1-90.

P.L. 100-647, §6059(a):

Amended Code Sec. 415(b)(2)(H)(ii) by striking out "20 years" and inserting in lieu thereof "15 years". **Effective** as if included in the amendments made by section 1106(b)(2) of P.L. 99-514.

• **1986, Tax Reform Act of 1986 (P.L. 99-514)**

P.L. 99-514, §1106(b)(1)(A)(i) and (ii):

Amended Code Sec. 415(b)(2)(C) and (D) by striking out "age 62" and "age 65" each place they appear and inserting in lieu thereof "the social security retirement age", and by striking out the last sentence of subparagraph (C) and inserting in lieu thereof a new sentence. For the **effective** date, see Act Sec. 1106(i) following Code Sec. 415(d). Prior to amendment, the last sentence of subparagraph (C) read as follows:

The reduction under this subparagraph shall not reduce the limitation of paragraph (1)(A) below—

(i) if the benefit begins at or after age 55, $75,000, or

(ii) if the benefit begins before age 55, the amount which is the equivalent of the $75,000 limitation for age 55.

P.L. 99-514, §1106(b)(i)(B):

Amended Code Sec. 415(b) by adding at the end thereof new paragraph (8). For the **effective** date, see Act Sec. 1106(i) following Code Sec. 415(d).

P.L. 99-514, §1106(b)(2):

Amended Code Sec 415(b)(2) by adding at the end thereof new subparagraphs (F)-(H). For the **effective** date, see Act Sec. 1106(i) following Code Sec. 415(d).

P.L. 99-514, §1106(b)(3):

Amended Code Sec. 415(b) by adding at the end thereof new paragraph (9). For the **effective** date, see Act Sec. 1106(i) following Code Sec. 415(d).

P.L. 99-514, §1106(f):

Amended Code Sec. 415(b)(5). For the **effective** date, see Act Sec. 1106(i) following Code Sec. 415(d). Prior to amendment, Code Sec. 415(b)(5) read as follows:

(5) REDUCTION FOR SERVICE LESS THAN 10 YEARS.—In the case of an employee who has less than 10 years of service with the employer, the limitation referred to in paragraph (1), and the limitation referred to in paragraph (4), shall be the limitation determined under such paragraph (without regard to this paragraph), multiplied by a fraction, the numerator of which is the number of years (or part thereof) of service with the employer and the denominator of which is 10.

P.L. 99-514, §1875(c)(9):

Amended Code Sec. 415(b)(2)(E)(iii) by striking out "adjusting any benefit or limitation under subparagraph (B), (C), or (D)" and inserting in lieu thereof "this subsection". **Effective** as if included in the provision of P.L. 98-369 to which it relates.

P.L. 99-514, §1898(b)(15)(C):

Amended Code Sec. 415(b)(2)(B) by striking out "as defined in section 401(a)(11)(G)(iii)" and inserting in lieu thereof "as defined in section 417". **Effective** as if included in the provision of P.L. 98-397 to which it relates.

• 1984, Deficit Reduction Act of 1984 (P.L. 98-369)

P.L. 98-369, §491(d)(29):

Amended Code Sec. 415(b)(2)(A) by striking out "408(d)(3), and 409(b)(3)(C)" and inserting in lieu thereof "and 408(d)(3)". **Effective** for obligations issued after 12-31-83.

P.L. 98-369, §491(d)(30):

Amended Code Sec. 415(b)(2)(B) by striking out "408(d)(3) and 409(b)(3)(C)" and inserting in lieu thereof "and 408(d)(3)". **Effective** for obligations issued after 12-31-83.

P.L. 98-369, §713(a)(1)(A):

Amended Code Sec. 415(b)(2)(C) by striking out the first sentence and inserting in lieu thereof a new sentence. **Effective** as if included in the provision of P.L. 97-248 to which it relates. Prior to amendment the first sentence of Code Sec. 415(b)(2)(C) read as follows:

If the retirement income benefit under the plan begins before age 62, the determination as to whether the $90,000 limitation set forth in paragraph (1)(A) has been satisfied shall be made, in accordance with regulations prescribed by the Secretary, by adjusting such benefit so that it is equivalent to such a benefit beginning at age 62.

P.L. 98-369, §713(a)(1)(B):

Amended Code Sec. 415(b)(2)(D). **Effective** as if included in the provision of P.L. 97-248 to which it relates. Prior to amendment, Code Sec. 415(b)(2)(D) read as follows:

(D) Adjustment to $90,000 Limitation Where Benefit Begins After Age 65.—If the retirement income benefit under the plan begins after age 65, the determination as to whether the $90,000 limitation set forth in paragraph (1)(A) has been satisfied shall be made, in accordance with regulations prescribed by the Secretary, by adjusting such benefit so that it is equivalent to such benefit beginning at age 65.

P.L. 98-369, §713(a)(1)(C)(i):

Amended Code Sec. 415(b)(2)(E)(i) and (iii) by striking out "any benefit" and inserting in lieu thereof "any benefit or limitation". **Effective** as if included in the provision of P.L. 97-248 to which it relates.

P.L. 98-369, §713(a)(1)(C)(ii):

Amended Code Sec. 415(b)(2)(E)(ii) by striking out "any benefit" and inserting in lieu thereof "any limitation". **Effective** as if included in the provision of P.L. 97-248 to which it relates.

• 1983, Technical Corrections Act of 1982 (P.L. 97-448)

P.L. 97-448, §306(a)(10):

Amended section 235(g)(5) of P.L. 97-248 by striking out "section 253" and inserting "section 242". For amended Act Sec. 235(g)(5), see the amendment note for P.L. 97-248, §235(e)(4), below.

• 1982, Tax Equity and Fiscal Responsibility Act of 1982 (P.L. 97-248)

P.L. 97-248, §235(a)(1):

Amended Code Sec. 415(b)(1)(A) by striking out "$75,000" and inserting "$90,000". For **effective** date and special rules, see P.L. 97-248, Act Sec. 235(g), below.

P.L. 97-248, §235(a)(3)(A):

Amended Code Sec. 415(b)(2)(C) by striking out "$75,000" each place it appeared and inserting "$90,000". For **effective** date and special rules, see P.L. 97-248, Act Sec. 235(g), below.

P.L. 97-248, §235(a)(3)(B):

Amended the last sentence of Code Sec. 415(b)(7) by striking out "by substituting `37,500' for `75,000'" and inserting in lieu thereof "by substituting the greater of $68,212 or one-half the amount otherwise applicable for such year under paragraph (1)(A) for `$90,000'". For **effective** date and special rules, see P.L. 97-248, Act Sec. 235(g), below.

P.L. 97-248, 235(e)(1):

Amended Code Sec. 415(b)(2)(C) by striking out "55" each place it appeared and inserting in lieu thereof "62". For **effective** date and special rules, see P.L. 97-248, Act Sec. 235(g), below.

P.L. 97-248, §235(e)(2):

Amended Code Sec. 415(b)(2)(C) by adding the new last sentence. For **effective** date and special rules, see P.L. 97-248, Act Sec. 235(g), below.

P.L. 97-248, §235(e)(3):

Amended Code Sec. 415(b)(2) by adding new subparagraph (D). For **effective** date and special rules, see P.L. 97-248, Act Sec. 235(g), below.

P.L. 97-248, §235(e)(4):

Amended Code Sec. 415(b)(2) by inserting new subparagraph (E). **Effective** as noted in Act Sec. 235(g), below.

P.L. 97-248, §235(g), as amended by P.L. 98-369, §713(a) and (f), provides:

(1) IN GENERAL.—

(A) NEW PLANS.—In the case of any plan which is not in existence on July 1, 1982, the amendments made by this section shall apply to years ending after July 1, 1982.

(B) EXISTING PLANS.—

(i) In the case of any plan which is in existence on July 1, 1982, the amendments made by this section shall apply to years beginning after December 31, 1982.

(ii) PLAN REQUIREMENTS.—A plan shall not be treated as failing to meet the requirements of section 401(a)(16) of the Internal Revenue Code of 1954 for any year beginning before January 1, 1984, merely because such plan provides for benefit or contribution limits which are in excess of the limitations under section 415 of such Code, as amended by this section. The preceding sentence shall not apply to any plan which provides such limits in excess of the limitation under section 415 of such Code before such amendments.

(2) AMENDMENTS RELATED TO COST-OF-LIVING ADJUSTMENTS.—

* * *

(3) TRANSITION RULE WHERE THE SUM OF DEFINED CONTRIBUTION AND DEFINED BENEFIT PLAN FRACTIONS EXCEEDS 1.0.—In the case of a plan which satisfied the requirements of section 415 of the Internal Revenue Code of 1954 for the last year beginning before January 1, 1983, the Secretary of the Treasury or his delegate shall prescribe regulations under which an

amount is subtracted from the numerator of the defined contribution plan fraction (not exceeding such numerator) so that the sum of the defined benefit plan fraction and the defined contribution plan fraction computed under section 415(e)(1) of the Internal Revenue Code of 1954 (as amended by the Tax Equity and Fiscal Responsibility Act of 1982) does not exceed 1.0 for such year. A similar rule shall apply with respect to the last plan year beginning before January 1, 1984, for purposes of applying section 416(h) of the Internal Revenue Code of 1954.

(4) RIGHT TO HIGHER ACCRUED DEFINED BENEFIT PRESERVED.—

(A) IN GENERAL.—In the case of an individual who is a participant before January 1, 1983, in a defined benefit plan which is in existence on July 1, 1982, and with respect to which the requirements of section 415 of such Code have been met for all years, if such individual's current accrued benefit under such plan exceeds the limitation of subsection (b) of section 415 of the Internal Revenue Code of 1954 (as amended by this section), then (in the case of such plan) for purposes of subsections (b) and (e) of such section, the limitation of such subsection (b) with respect to such individual shall be equal to such current accrued benefit.

(B) CURRENT ACCRUED BENEFIT DEFINED.—

(i) IN GENERAL.—For purposes of this paragraph, the term "current accrued benefit" means the individual's accrued benefit (at the close of the last year beginning before January 1, 1983) when expressed as an annual benefit (within the meaning of section 415(b)(2) of such Code as in effect before the amendments made by this Act). In the case of any plan described in the first sentence of paragraph (5), the preceding sentence shall be applied by substituting for "January 1, 1983" the applicable date determined under paragraph (5).

(ii) SPECIAL RULE.—For purposes of determining the amount of any individual's current accrued benefit—

(I) no change in the terms and conditions of the plan after July 1, 1982, and

(II) no cost-of-living adjustment occurring after July 1, 1982,

shall be taken into account. For purposes of subclause (I), any change in the terms and conditions of the plan pursuant to a collective bargaining agreement entered into before July 1, 1982, and ratified before September 3, 1982, shall be treated as a change made before July 1, 1982.

(5) SPECIAL RULE FOR COLLECTIVE BARGAINING AGREEMENTS.—In the case of a plan maintained on the date of the enactment of this Act pursuant to 1 or more collective bargaining agreements between employee representatives and 1 or more employers, the amendments made by this section and section 242 (relating to age 70½) shall not apply to years beginning before the earlier of—

(A) the date on which the last of the collective bargaining agreements relating to the plan terminates (determined without regard to any extension thereof agreed to after the date of the enactment of this Act), or

(B) January 1, 1986.

For purposes of subparagraph (A), any plan amendment made pursuant to a collective bargaining agreement relating to the plan which amends the plan solely to conform to any requirement added by this section and section 253 shall not be treated as a termination of such collective bargaining agreement.

• 1980, Technical Corrections Act of 1979 (P.L. 96-222)

P.L. 96-222, §101(a)(11)(A):

Amended Code Sec. 415(b)(7) by adding the third sentence. **Effective** for years beginning after 12-31-78.

P.L. 96-222, §101(a)(11)(B):

Amended Code Sec. 415(b)(7)(C). **Effective** for years beginning after 12-31-78. Prior to amendment, Code Sec. 415(b)(7)(C) read as follows:

(C) benefits under which are determined by multiplying a specified amount (which is the same amount for each participant) by the number of the participant's years of service,

• 1978, Revenue Act of 1978 (P.L. 95-600)

P.L. 95-600, §153(a):

Added Code Sec. 415(b)(7). **Effective** for years beginning after 12-31-78.

• 1976, Tax Reform Act of 1976 (P.L. 94-455)

P.L. 94-455, §1901(a)(65)(A):

Amended Code Sec. 415(b)(2)(A) by substituting "and 409(b)(3)(C))" for "and 409(b)(3)(C)". **Effective** with respect to tax years beginning after 12-31-76.

P.L. 94-455, §1901(a)(65)(B):

Amended Code Sec. 415(b)(2)(B) by substituting "(as defined in section 401(a)(11)(G)(iii))" for "(as defined in section 401(a)(11)(H)(iii))". **Effective** with respect to tax years beginning after 12-31-76.

P.L. 94-455, §1906(b)(13)(A):

Amended the 1954 Code by substituting "Secretary" for "Secretary or his delegate" each place it appeared. **Effective** 2-1-77.

• 1974, Employee Retirement Income Security Act of 1974 (P.L. 93-406)

P.L. 93-406, §2004(a)(2):

Added Code Sec. 415(b). **Effective**, generally, for years beginning after 1975. For special effective dates and transitional rules governing this section, see the footnote to Code Sec. 415(a) and the historical note for §1017, P.L. 93-406, following the text of Code Sec. 410(d).

[Sec. 415(c)]

(c) LIMITATION FOR DEFINED CONTRIBUTION PLANS.—

(1) IN GENERAL.—Contributions and other additions with respect to a participant exceed the limitation of this subsection if, when expressed as an annual addition (within the meaning of paragraph (2)) to the participant's account, such annual addition is greater than the lesser of—

(A) $40,000, or

(B) 100 percent of the participant's compensation.

(2) ANNUAL ADDITION.—For purposes of paragraph (1), the term "annual addition" means the sum for any year of—

(A) employer contributions,

(B) the employee contributions, and

(C) forfeitures.

For the purposes of this paragraph, employee contributions under subparagraph (B) are determined without regard to any rollover contributions (as defined in sections 402(c), 403(a)(4), 403(b)(8), 408(d)(3), and 457(e)(16)) without regard to employee contributions to a simplified employee pension which are excludable from gross income under section 408(k)(6). Subparagraph (B) of paragraph (1) shall not apply to any contribution for medical benefits (within the meaning of section 419A(f)(2)) after separation from service which is treated as an annual addition.

(3) PARTICIPANT'S COMPENSATION.—For purposes of paragraph (1)—

(A) IN GENERAL.—The term "participant's compensation" means the compensation of the participant from the employer for the year.

(B) SPECIAL RULE FOR SELF-EMPLOYED INDIVIDUALS.—In the case of an employee within the meaning of section 401(c)(1), subparagraph (A) shall be applied by substituting "the participant's earned income (within the meaning of section 401(c)(2) but determined without regard to any exclusion under section 911)" for "compensation of the participant from the employer".

(C) SPECIAL RULES FOR PERMANENT AND TOTAL DISABILITY.—In the case of a participant in any defined contribution plan—

(i) who is permanently and totally disabled (as defined in section 22(e)(3)),

(ii) who is not a highly compensated employee (within the meaning of section 414(q)), and

(iii) with respect to whom the employer elects, at such time and in such manner as the Secretary may prescribe, to have this subparagraph apply,

the term "participant's compensation" means the compensation the participant would have received for the year if the participant was paid at the rate of compensation paid immediately before becoming permanently and totally disabled. This subparagraph shall apply only if contributions made with respect to amounts treated as compensation under this subparagraph are nonforfeitable when made. If a defined contribution plan provides for the continuation of contributions on behalf of all participants described in clause (i) for a fixed or determinable period, this subparagraph shall be applied without regard to clauses (ii) and (iii).

(D) CERTAIN DEFERRALS INCLUDED.—The term "participant's compensation" shall include—

(i) any elective deferral (as defined in section 402(g)(3)), and

(ii) any amount which is contributed or deferred by the employer at the election of the employee and which is not includible in the gross income of the employee by reason of section 125, 132(f)(4), or 457.

(E) ANNUITY CONTRACTS.—In the case of an annuity contract described in section 403(b), the term "participant's compensation" means the participant's includible compensation determined under section 403(b)(3).

(4) [Stricken.]

(5) [Repealed.]

(6) SPECIAL RULE FOR EMPLOYEE STOCK OWNERSHIP PLANS.—If no more than one-third of the employer contributions to an employee stock ownership plan (as described in section 4975(e)(7)) for a year which are deductible under paragraph (9) of section 404(a) are allocated to highly compensated employees (within the meaning of section 414(q)), the limitations imposed by this section shall not apply to—

(A) forfeitures of employer securities (within the meaning of section 409) under such an employee stock ownership plan if such securities were acquired with the proceeds of a loan (as described in section 404(a)(9)(A)), or

(B) employer contributions to such an employee stock ownership plan which are deductible under section 404(a)(9)(B) and charged against the participant's account.

The amount of any qualified gratuitous transfer (as defined in section 664(g)(1)) allocated to a participant for any limitation year shall not exceed the limitations imposed by this section, but such amount shall not be taken into account in determining whether any other amount exceeds the limitations imposed by this section.

(7) SPECIAL RULES RELATING TO CHURCH PLANS.—

(A) ALTERNATIVE CONTRIBUTION LIMITATION.—

(i) IN GENERAL.—Notwithstanding any other provision of this subsection, at the election of a participant who is an employee of a church or a convention or association of churches, including an organization described in section 414(e)(3)(B)(ii), contributions and other additions for an annuity contract or retirement income account described in section 403(b) with respect to such participant, when expressed as an annual addition to such participant's account, shall be treated as not exceeding the limitation of paragraph (1) if such annual addition is not in excess of $10,000.

(ii) $40,000 AGGREGATE LIMITATION.—The total amount of additions with respect to any participant which may be taken into account for purposes of this subparagraph for all years may not exceed $40,000.

(B) NUMBER OF YEARS OF SERVICE FOR DULY ORDAINED, COMMISSIONED, OR LICENSED MINISTERS OR LAY EMPLOYEES.—For purposes of this paragraph—

(i) all years of service by—

(I) a duly ordained, commissioned, or licensed minister of a church, or

(II) a lay person,

as an employee of a church, a convention or association of churches, including an organization described in section 414(e)(3)(B)(ii), shall be considered as years of service for 1 employer, and

(ii) all amounts contributed for annuity contracts by each such church (or convention or association of churches) or such organization during such years for such minister or lay person shall be considered to have been contributed by 1 employer.

(C) FOREIGN MISSIONARIES.—In the case of any individual described in subparagraph (B) performing services outside the United States, contributions and other additions for an annuity contract or retirement income account described in section 403(b) with respect to such employee, when expressed as an annual addition to such employee's account, shall not be treated as exceeding the limitation of paragraph (1) if such annual addition is not in excess of $3,000. This subparagraph shall not apply with respect to any taxable year to any individual whose adjusted gross income for such taxable year (determined separately and without regard to community property laws) exceeds $17,000.

(D) ANNUAL ADDITION.—For purposes of this paragraph, the term "annual addition" has the meaning given such term by paragraph (2).

(E) CHURCH, CONVENTION OR ASSOCIATION OF CHURCHES.—For purposes of this paragraph, the terms "church" and "convention or association of churches" have the same meaning as when used in section 414(e).

Amendments

• 2006, Pension Protection Act of 2006 (P.L. 109-280)

P.L. 109-280, §811, provides:

SEC. 811. PENSIONS AND INDIVIDUAL RETIREMENT ARRANGEMENT PROVISIONS OF ECONOMIC GROWTH AND TAX RELIEF RECONCILIATION ACT OF 2001 MADE PERMANENT.

Title IX of the Economic Growth and Tax Relief Reconciliation Act of 2001 [P.L. 107-16] shall not apply to the provisions of, and amendments made by, subtitles A through F of title VI [§§601-666]of such Act (relating to pension and individual retirement arrangement provisions).

• 2005, Gulf Opportunity Zone Act of 2005 (P.L. 109-135)

P.L. 109-135, §407(b):

Amended Code Sec. 415(c)(7)(C) by striking "the greater of $3,000" and all that follows and inserting "$3,000. This subparagraph shall not apply with respect to any taxable year to any individual whose adjusted gross income for such taxable year (determined separately and without regard to community property laws) exceeds $17,000.". **Effective** as if included in the provision of the Economic Growth and Tax Relief Reconciliation Act of 2001 (P.L. 107-16) to which it relates [**effective** for tax years beginning after 12-31-2001.—CCH]. Prior to amendment, Code Sec. 415(c)(7)(C) read as follows:

(C) FOREIGN MISSIONARIES.—In the case of any individual described in subparagraph (B) performing services outside the United States, contributions and other additions for an annuity contract or retirement income account described in section 403(b) with respect to such employee, when expressed as an annual addition to such employee's account, shall not be treated as exceeding the limitation of paragraph (1) if such annual addition is not in excess of the greater of $3,000 or the employee's includible compensation determined under section 403(b)(3).

• 2004, Working Families Tax Relief Act of 2004 (P.L. 108-311)

P.L. 108-311, §408(a)(17):

Amended Code Sec. 415(c)(7)(C) by striking "subparagraph (D)" and inserting "subparagraph (B)". **Effective** 10-4-2004.

• 2002, Job Creation and Worker Assistance Act of 2002 (P.L. 107-147)

P.L. 107-147, §411(p)(4):

Amended Code Sec. 415(c)(7). **Effective** as if included in the provision of P.L. 107-16 to which it relates [**effective** for years beginning after 12-31-2001.—CCH]. Prior to amendment, Code Sec. 415(c)(7) read as follows:

(7) CERTAIN CONTRIBUTIONS BY CHURCH PLANS NOT TREATED AS EXCEEDING LIMIT.—

(A) IN GENERAL.—Notwithstanding any other provision of this subsection, at the election of a participant who is an employee of a church or a convention or association of churches, including an organization described in section 414(e)(3)(B)(ii), contributions and other additions for an annuity contract or retirement income account described in section 403(b) with respect to such participant, when expressed as an annual addition to such participant's account, shall be treated as not exceeding the limitation of paragraph (1) if such annual addition is not in excess of $10,000.

(B) $40,000 AGGREGATE LIMITATION.—The total amount of additions with respect to any participant which may be taken into account for purposes of this subparagraph for all years may not exceed $40,000.

(C) ANNUAL ADDITION.—For purposes of this paragraph, the term "annual addition" has the meaning given such term by paragraph (2).

• 2001, Economic Growth and Tax Relief Reconciliation Act of 2001 (P.L. 107-16)

P.L. 107-16, §611(b)(1):

Amended Code Sec. 415(c)(1)(A) by striking "$30,000" and inserting "$40,000". **Effective** for years beginning after 12-31-2001. For a special rule, see Act Sec. 611(i)(3), below.

P.L. 107-16, §611(i)(3) (as added by P.L. 107-147, §411(j)(3)), provides:

(3) SPECIAL RULE.—In the case of [a] plan that, on June 7, 2001, incorporated by reference the limitation of section 415(b)(1)(A) of the Internal Revenue Code of 1986, section 411(d)(6) of such Code and section 204(g)(1) of the Employee Retirement Income Security Act of 1974 do not apply to a plan amendment that—

(A) is adopted on or before June 30, 2002,

(B) reduces benefits to the level that would have applied without regard to the amendments made by subsection (a) of this section, and

(C) is effective no earlier than the years described in paragraph (2).

P.L. 107-16, §632(a)(1):

Amended Code Sec. 415(c)(1)(B) by striking "25 percent" and inserting "100 percent". **Effective** for years beginning after 12-31-2001.

P.L. 107-16, §632(a)(3)(D):

Amended Code Sec. 415(c)(3) by adding at the end a new subparagraph (E). **Effective** for years beginning after 12-31-2001.

P.L. 107-16, §632(a)(3)(E):

Amended Code Sec. 415(c) by striking paragraph (4). **Effective** for years beginning after 12-31-2001. Prior to being stricken, Code Sec. 415(c)(4) read as follows:

(4) SPECIAL ELECTION FOR SECTION 403(b) CONTRACTS PURCHASED BY EDUCATIONAL ORGANIZATIONS, HOSPITALS, HOME HEALTH SERVICE AGENCIES, AND CERTAIN CHURCHES, ETC.

(A) In the case of amounts contributed for an annuity contract described in section 403(b) for the year in which occurs a participant's separation from the service with an educational organization, a hospital, a home health service agency, a health and welfare service agency, or a church, convention or association of churches, or an organization described in section 414(e)(3)(B)(ii), at the election of the participant there is substituted for the amount specified in paragraph (1)(B) the amount of the exclusion allowance which would be determined under section 403(b)(2) (without regard to this section) for the participant's taxable year in which such separation occurs if the participant's years of service were computed only by taking into account his service for the employer (as determined for purposes of section 403(b)(2)) during the period of years (not exceeding ten) ending on the date of such separation.

(B) In the case of amounts contributed for an annuity contract described in section 403(b) for any year in the case of a participant who is an employee of an educational organization, a hospital, a home health service agency, a health and welfare service agency, or a church, convention or association of churches, or an organization described in section 414(e)(3)(B)(ii), at the election of the participant there is substituted for the amount specified in paragraph (1)(B) the least of—

(i) 25 percent of the participant's includible compensation (as defined in section 403(b)(3)) plus $4,000,

(ii) the amount of the exclusion allowance determined for the year under section 403(b)(2), or

(iii) $15,000.

(C) In the case of amounts contributed for an annuity contract described in section 403(b) for any year for a participant who is an employee of an educational organization, a hospital, a home health service agency, a health and welfare service agency, or a church, convention or association of churches, or an organization described in section 414(e)(3)(B)(ii), at the election of the participant the provisions of section 403(b)(2)(A) shall not apply.

(D)(i) The provisions of this paragraph apply only if the participant elects its application at the time and in the manner provided under regulations prescribed by the Secretary. Not more than one election may be made under subparagraph (A) by any participant. A participant who elects to have the provisions of subparagraph (A), (B), or (C) of this paragraph apply to him may not elect to have any other subparagraph of this paragraph apply to him. Any election made under this paragraph is irrevocable.

(ii) For purposes of this paragraph the term "educational organization" means an educational organization described in section 170(b)(1)(A)(ii).

(iii) For purposes of this paragraph the term "home health service agency" means an organization described in subsection 501(c)(3) which is exempt from tax under section 501(a) and which has been determined by the Secretary of Health, Education, and Welfare to be a home health agency (as defined in section 1861(o) of the Social Security Act).

(iv) For purposes of this paragraph, the terms "church" and "convention or association of churches" have the same meaning as when used in section 414(e).

P.L. 107-16, §632(a)(3)(F):

Amended Code Sec. 415(c)(7). **Effective** for years beginning after 12-31-2001. Prior to amendment, Code Sec. 415(c)(7) read as follows:

(7) CERTAIN CONTRIBUTIONS BY CHURCH PLANS NOT TREATED AS EXCEEDING LIMITS.—

(A) ALTERNATIVE EXCLUSION ALLOWANCE.—Any contribution or addition with respect to any participant, when expressed as an annual addition, which is allocable to the application of section 403(b)(2)(D) to such participant for such year, shall be treated as not exceeding the limitations of paragraph (1).

(B) CONTRIBUTIONS NOT IN EXCESS OF $40,000 ($10,000 PER YEAR).—

(i) IN GENERAL.—Notwithstanding any other provision of this subsection, at the election of a participant who is an employee of a church, a convention or association of churches, including an organization described in section 414(e)(3)(B)(ii), contributions and other additions for an annuity contract or retirement income account described in section 403(b) with respect to such participant, when expressed as an annual addition to such participant's account, shall be treated as not exceeding the limitation of paragraph (1) if such annual addition is not in excess of $10,000.

(ii) $40,000 AGGREGATE LIMITATION.—The total amount of additions with respect to any participant which may be taken into account for purposes of this subparagraph for all years may not exceed $40,000.

(iii) NO ELECTION IF PARAGRAPH (4)(A) ELECTION MADE.—No election may be made under this subparagraph for any year if an election is made under paragraph (4)(A) for such year.

(C) ANNUAL ADDITION.—For purposes of this paragraph, the term "annual addition" has the meaning given such term by paragraph (2).

P.L. 107-16, §641(e)(10):

Amended Code Sec. 415(c)(2) by striking "and 408(d)(3)" and inserting "408(d)(3), and 457(e)(16)". **Effective**, generally, for distributions after 12-31-2001. For a special rule, see Act Sec. 641(f)(3) in the amendment notes following Code Sec. 457(e).

P.L. 107-16, §901(a)-(b), provides [but see P.L. 109-280, §811, above]:

SEC. 901. SUNSET OF PROVISIONS OF ACT.

(a) IN GENERAL.—All provisions of, and amendments made by, this Act shall not apply—

(1) to taxable, plan, or limitation years beginning after December 31, 2010, or

(2) in the case of title V, to estates of decedents dying, gifts made, or generation skipping transfers, after December 31, 2010.

(b) APPLICATION OF CERTAIN LAWS.—The Internal Revenue Code of 1986 and the Employee Retirement Income Security Act of 1974 shall be applied and administered to years, estates, gifts, and transfers described in subsection (a) as if the provisions and amendments described in subsection (a) had never been enacted.

• 2000, Community Renewal Tax Relief Act of 2000 (P.L. 106-554)

P.L. 106-554, §314(e)(1):

Amended Code Sec. 415(c)(3)(D)(ii) by striking "section 125 or" and inserting "section 125, 132(f)(4), or". **Effective** as if included in the provision of P.L. 105-34 to which it relates [**effective** for tax years beginning after 12-31-97.—CCH].

• 1997, Taxpayer Relief Act of 1997 (P.L. 105-34)

P.L. 105-34, §1530(c)(3):

Amended Code Sec. 415(c)(6) by adding at the end thereof a new sentence. **Effective** for transfers made by trusts to, or for the use of, an employee stock ownership plan after 8-5-97.

• 1996, Small Business Job Protection Act of 1996 (P.L. 104-188)

P.L. 104-188, §1434(a):

Amended Code Sec. 415(c)(3) by adding at the end a new subparagraph (D). **Effective** for years beginning after 12-31-97.

P.L. 104-188, §1446(a):

Amended Code Sec. 415(c)(3)(C) by adding at the end a new sentence. **Effective** for years beginning after 12-31-96.

• 1994, Uruguay Round Agreements Act. (P.L. 103-465)

P.L. 103-465, §732(b)(2):

Amended Code Sec. 415(c)(1)(A) by striking "(or, if greater, 1/4 of the dollar limitation in effect under subsection (b)(1)(A))" after "$30,000". **Effective** for years beginning after 12-31-94.

• 1992, Unemployment Compensation Amendments of 1992 (P.L. 102-318)

P.L. 102-318, §521(b)(25):

Amended Code Sec. 415(c)(2) by striking "sections 402(a)(5)" and inserting "sections 402(c)". **Effective** for distributions after 12-31-92.

• 1989, Omnibus Budget Reconciliation Act of 1989 (P.L. 101-239)

P.L. 101-239, §7304(c)(1):

Amended Code Sec. 415(c)(6). **Effective** for years beginning after 7-12-89. Prior to amendment, Code Sec. 415(c)(6) read as follows:

(6) SPECIAL LIMITATION FOR EMPLOYEE STOCK OWNERSHIP PLAN.—

(A) In the case of an employee stock ownership plan (as defined in subparagraph (B)), under which no more than one-third of the employer contributions for a year are allocated to highly compensated employees (within the meaning of section 414(q)), the amount described in paragraph (1)(A) for a year with respect to any participant shall be equal to the sum of (i) the amount described in paragraph (1)(A) determined without regard to this paragraph and (ii) the lesser of the amount determined under clause (i) or the amount of employer securities contributed, or purchased with cash contributed, to the employee stock ownership plan.

(B) For purposes of this paragraph—

(i) the term "employee stock ownership plan" means an employee stock ownership plan (within the meaning of section 4975(e)(7)) or a tax credit employee stock ownership plan,

(ii) the term "employer securities" has the meaning given to such term by section 409,

(C) In the case of an employee stock ownership plan (as described in section 4975(e)(7)), under which no more than one-third of the employer contributions for a year which are deductible under paragraph (9) of section 404(a) are allocated to highly compensated employees (within the meaning of section 414(q)), the limitations imposed by this section shall not apply to—

(i) forfeitures of employer securities under an employee stock ownership plan (as described in section 4975(e)(7)) if such securities were acquired with the proceeds of a loan (as described in section 404(a)(9)(A)), or

(ii) employer contributions to such an employee stock ownership plan which are deductible under section 404(a)(9)(B) and charged against the participant's account.

• 1988, Technical and Miscellaneous Revenue Act of 1988 (P.L. 100-647)

P.L. 100-647, §1011(d)(7)(A)-(B):

Amended Code Sec. 415(c)(6)(A) by striking out "paragraph (c)(1)(A) (as adjusted for such year pursuant to subsection (d)(1))", and inserting in lieu thereof "paragraph (1)(A)"; and by striking out "paragraph (c)(1)(A) (as so adjusted)" and inserting in lieu thereof "paragraph (1)(A)". **Effective** as if included in the provision of P.L. 99-514 to which it relates.

• 1986, Tax Reform Act of 1986 (P.L. 99-514)

P.L. 99-514, §1106(a):

Amended Code Sec. 415(c)(1)(A). For the **effective** date, see Act Sec. 1106(i) following Code Sec. 415(d). Prior to amendment, Code Sec. 415(c)(1)(A) read as follows:

(A) $30,000, or

P.L. 99-514, §1106(b)(4):

Amended Code Sec. 415(c)(4)(A), (B), and (C) by inserting in each subparagraph "a health and welfare service agency," after "a home health service agency,". For the **effective** date, see Act Sec. 1106(i) following Code Sec. 415(d).

P.L. 99-514, §1106(e)(1):

Amended Code Sec. 415(c)(2)(B). For the **effective** date, see Act Sec. 1106(i) following Code Sec. 415(d). Prior to amendment, Code Sec. 415(c)(2)(B) read as follows:

(B) the lesser of—

(i) the amount of the employee contributions in excess of 6 percent of his compensation, or

(ii) one-half of the employee contributions, and

P.L. 99-514, §1106(e)(2):

Amended Code Sec. 415(c)(2) by adding at the end thereof a new sentence. For the **effective** date, see Act Sec. 1106(i) following Code Sec. 415(d).

P.L. 99-514, §1106(h), provides:

(h) PLANS MAY INCORPORATE SECTION 415 LIMITATIONS BY REFERENCE.—Notwithstanding any other provision of law, except as provided in regulations prescribed by the Secretary of the Treasury or his delegate, a plan may incorporate by reference the limitations under section 415 of the Internal Revenue Code of 1986.

P.L. 99-514, §1108(g)(5):

Amended Code Sec. 415(c)(2) by striking out "allowable as a deduction under section 219(a), and without regard to deductible employee contributions within the meaning of section 72(o)(5)" and inserting in lieu thereof "which are excludable from gross income under section 408(k)(6)". **Effective** for years beginning after 12-31-88.

P.L. 99-514, §1114(b)(12):

Amended Code Sec. 415(c)(3)(C)(ii) by striking out "an officer, owner, or highly compensated" and inserting in lieu thereof "a highly compensated employee (within the meaning of section 414(q))". **Effective** for years beginning after 12-31-88.

P.L. 99-514, §1174(d)(1):

Amended Code Sec. 415(c)(6)(A) by striking out "the group of employees consisting of officers, shareholders owning more than 10 percent of the employer's stock (determined under subparagraph (B)(iv)), or employees described in subparagraph (B)(iii)" and inserting in lieu thereof "highly compensated employees (within the meaning of section 414(q))". **Effective** for years beginning after 12-31-86.

P.L. 99-514, §1174(d)(2)(A):

Amended Code Sec. 415(c)(6)(B) by striking out clauses (iii) and (iv) thereof. **Effective** for years beginning after 12-31-86. Prior to amendment, Code Sec. 415(c)(6)(B)(iii) and (iv) read as follows:

(iii) an employee described in this clause is any participant whose compensation for a year exceeds an amount equal to twice the amount described in paragraph (c)(1)(A) for such year (as adjusted for such year pursuant to subsection (d)(1)), determined without regard to subparagraph (A) of this paragraph, and

(iv) an individual shall be considered to own more than 10 percent of the employer's stock if, without regard to stock held under the employee stock ownership plan, he owns (after application of section 1563(e)) more than 10 percent of the total combined voting power of all classes of stock entitled to vote or more than 10 percent of the total value of shares of all classes of stock.

P.L. 99-514, §1174(d)(2)(B):

Amended Code Sec. 415(c)(6)(C) by striking out "the group of employees consisting of officers, shareholders owning more than 10 percent of the employer's stock (determined under subparagraph (B)(iv)), or employees described in subparagraph (B)(iii)" and inserting in lieu thereof "highly compensated employees (within the meaning of section 414(q))". **Effective** for years beginning after 12-31-86.

P.L. 99-514, §1847(b)(4):

Amended Code Sec. 415(c)(3)(C)(i) by striking out "section 37(e)(3)" and inserting in lieu thereof "section 22(e)(3)". **Effective** as if included in the provision of P.L. 98-369 to which it relates.

P.L. 99-514, §1875(c)(11):

Amended Code Sec. 415(c)(3)(C) by striking out "a profit-sharing or stock bonus plan" and inserting in lieu thereof "any defined contribution plan". **Effective** as if included in the provision of P.L. 98-369 to which it relates.

• 1984, Deficit Reduction Act of 1984 (P.L. 98-369)

P.L. 98-369, §491(d)(31):

Amended Code Sec. 415(c)(2) by striking out "405(d)(3), 408(d)(3), and 409(b)(3)(C)" and inserting in lieu thereof "and 408(d)(3)". **Effective** for obligations issued after 12-31-83.

P.L. 98-369, §491(e)(6):

Amended Code Sec. 415(c)(6)(B)(ii) by striking out "section 409A" and inserting in lieu thereof "section 409". **Effective** 1-1-84.

P.L. 98-369, §713(d)(4)(B):

Amended Code Sec. 415(c)(6)(C) by striking out "paragraph (10) of section 404(a)" and inserting in lieu thereof "paragraph (9) of section 404(a)", by striking out "section 404(a)(10)(A)" and inserting in lieu thereof "section 404(a)(9)(A)", and by striking out "section 404(a)(10)(B)" and inserting in lieu thereof "section 404(a)(9)(B)". **Effective** as if included in the provision of P.L. 97-248 to which it relates.

P.L. 98-369, §713(d)(7)(A):

Amended Code Sec. 415(c) by striking out paragraph (7) and by redesignating paragraph (8) as paragraph (7). **Effective** as if included in the provision of P.L. 97-248 to which it relates. Prior to amendment, Code Sec. 415(c)(7) read as follows:

(7) Certain Level Premium Annuity Contracts Under Plans Benefiting Owner-Employees.—Paragraph (1)(B) shall not apply to a contribution described in section 401(e) which is made on behalf of a participant for a year to a plan which benefits an owner-employee (within the meaning of section 401(c)(3)), if—

(A) the annual addition determined under this section with respect to the participant for such year consists solely of such contribution, and

(B) the participant is not an active participant at any time during such year in a defined benefit plan maintained by the employer.

For purposes of this section and section 401(e), in the case of a plan which provides contributions or benefits for employees who are not owner-employees, such plan will not be treated as failing to satisfy section 401(a)(4) merely because contributions made on behalf of employees who are not owner-employees are not permitted to exceed the limitations of paragraph (1)(B).

P.L. 98-369, §713(k)(1):

Amended Code Sec. 415(c)(3)(C) by striking out "In the case of a participant" and inserting in lieu thereof "In the case of a participant in a profit-sharing or stock bonus plan". **Effective** as if included in the provision of P.L. 97-248 to which it relates.

P.L. 98-369, §713(k)(2):

Amended Code Sec. 415(c)(3)(C) by striking out the last sentence and inserting in lieu thereof a new sentence. **Effective** as if included in the provision of P.L. 97-248 to which it relates. Prior to amendment, the last sentence of Code Sec. 415(c)(3)(C) read as follows:

This subparagraph shall only apply if contributions made with respect to such participant are nonforfeitable when made.

• 1983, Social Security Amendments of 1983 (P.L. 98-21)

P.L. 98-21, §122(c)(5):

Amended Code Sec. 415(c)(3)(C)(i) by striking out "section 105(d)(4)" and inserting in place thereof "section 37(e)(3)". **Effective**, generally, for tax years beginning after 1983.

• 1982, Tax Equity and Fiscal Responsibility Act of 1982 (P.L. 97-248)

P.L. 97-248, §235(a)(2):

Amended Code Sec. 415(c)(1)(A) by striking out "$25,000" and inserting in lieu thereof "$30,000". For **effective** data and special rules, see P.L. 97-248, Act Sec. 235(g), in the amendment notes following Code Sec. 415(b).

P.L. 97-248, §238(d)(5):

Repealed Code Sec. 415(c)(5). **Effective** with respect to years beginning after 12-31-83. Prior to repeal, Code Sec. 415(c)(5) read as follows:

(5) APPLICATION WITH SECTION 404(e)(4).—In the case of a plan which provides contributions or benefits for employees some or all of whom are employees within the meaning of section 401(c)(1), the amount determined under paragraph (1)(B) with respect to any participant shall not be less than the amount deductible under section 404(e) with respect to any individual who is an employee within the meaning of section 401(c)(1).

P.L. 97-248, §251(c)(1):

Amended Code Sec. 415(c)(4) by striking out "or a home health service agency" wherever it appeared and inserting in lieu thereof "a home health service agency, or a church, convention or association of churches, or an organization described in section 414(e)(3)(B)(ii)"; by inserting "(as determined for purposes of section 403(b)(2))" after "service for the employer" in subparagraph (A); by adding clause (iv) at the end of subparagraph (D); and by striking out "AND HOME HEALTH SERVICE AGENCIES" in the heading and inserting in lieu thereof "HOME HEALTH SERVICE AGENCIES, AND CERTAIN CHURCHES, ETC." **E ffective** for years beginning after 12-31-81.

P.L. 97-248, §251(c)(2):

Amended Code Sec. 415(c) by adding new paragraph (8). **Effective** for years beginning after 12-31-81.

P.L. 97-248, §253(a):

Amended Code Sec. 415(c)(3). **Effective** for tax years beginning after 12-31-81. Prior to amendment, Code Sec. 415(c)(3) read:

(3) Participant's compensation.—For purposes of paragraph (1), the term "participant's compensation" means the compensation of the participant from the employer for the year. In the case of an employee within the meaning of section 401(c)(1), the preceding sentence shall be applied by substituting for "compensation of the participant from the employer" the following: "the participant's earned income (within the meaning of section 401(c)(2) but determined without regard to any exclusion under section 911)".

• 1981, Economic Recovery Tax Act of 1981 (P.L. 97-34)

P.L. 97-34, §311(g)(4)(B):

Amended Code Sec. 415(c)(2) by adding a new last sentence. **Effective** for tax years beginning after 12-31-81.

P.L. 97-34, §333(b)(1):

Added Code Sec. 415(c)(6)(C). **Effective** for tax years beginning after 12-31-81.

• 1980, Miscellaneous Revenue Act of 1980 (P.L. 96-605)

P.L. 96-605, §222(a):

Amended Code Sec. 415(c)(6)(A) by inserting ", or purchased with cash contributed," after "contributed". **Effective** with respect to years beginning after 12-31-80.

• 1980, Technical Corrections Act of 1979 (P.L. 96-222)

P.L. 96-222, §101(a)(7)(L)(i)(VII) and (iv)(I):

Amended Code Sec. 415(c)(6)(B)(i) by striking out "leveraged employee stock ownership plan" and inserting "employee stock ownership plan" and by striking out "an ESOP" and inserting "a tax credit employee stock ownership plan". **Effective** for tax years beginning after 12-31-78.

• 1978, Revenue Act of 1978 (P.L. 95-600)

P.L. 95-600, §141(f)(7):

Amended Code Sec. 415(c)(6)(B)(i) and (ii). **Effective** for years beginning after 12-31-78. Prior to amendment, Code Sec. 415(c)(6)(B)(i) and (ii) read as follows:

(B) For purposes of this paragraph—

(i) the term "employee stock ownership plan" means a plan which meets the requirements of section 4975(e)(7) or section 301(d) of the Tax Reduction Act of 1975,

(ii) the term "employer securities" means, in the case of an employee stock ownership plan within the meaning of section 4975(e)(7), qualifying employer securities within the meaning of section 4975(e)(8), but only if they are described in section 301(d)(9)(A) of the Tax Reduction Act of 1975, or, in the case of an employee stock ownership plan described in section 301(d)(2) of the Tax Reduction Act of 1975, employer securities within the meaning of section 301(d)(9)(A) of such Act,

• 1976, Tax Reform Act of 1976 (P.L. 94-455)

P.L. 94-455, §803(f)(1):

Added Code Sec. 415(c)(6). **Effective** for years beginning after 12-31-75.

P.L. 94-455, §1502(a)(1):

Added Code Sec. 415(c)(5). **Effective** for years beginning after 12-31-75.

P.L. 94-455, §1511(a):

Added Code Sec. 415(c)(7). **Effective** for years beginning after 12-31-75.

P.L. 94-455, §1901(b)(8)(D)(i):

Amended Code Sec. 415(c)(4)(A), (B), and (C) by substituting "educational organization" for "educational institution" each place it appeared. **Effective** with respect to tax years beginning after 12-31-76.

P.L. 94-455, §1901(b)(8)(D)(ii):

Amended Code Sec. 415(c)(4)(D)(ii). **Effective** with respect to tax years beginning after 12-31-76. Prior to amendment it read:

(ii) For purposes of this paragraph the term "educational institution" means an educational institution as defined in section 151(e)(4).

P.L. 94-455, §1901(b)(8)(D)(iii):

Amended Code Sec. 415(c)(4) by substituting in the paragraph's heading "educational organizations" for "educational institutions". **Effective** with respect to tax years beginning after 12-31-76.

P.L. 94-455, §1906(b)(13)(A):

Amended the 1954 Code by substituting "Secretary" for "Secretary or his delegate" each place it appeared. **Effective** 2-1-77.

• 1974, Employee Retirement Income Security Act of 1974 (P.L. 93-406)

P.L. 93-406, §2004(a)(2):

Added Code Sec. 415(c). **Effective**, generally, for years beginning after 1975. For special effective dates and transitional rules governing this section, see the footnote to Code Sec. 415(a) and the historical note for §1017, P.L. 93-406, following the text of Code Sec. 410(d).

[Sec. 415(d)]

(d) COST-OF-LIVING ADJUSTMENTS.—

(1) IN GENERAL.—The Secretary shall adjust annually—

(A) the $160,000 amount in subsection (b)(1)(A),

(B) in the case of a participant who separated from service, the amount taken into account under subsection (b)(1)(B), and

(C) the $40,000 amount in subsection (c)(1)(A),

for increases in the cost-of-living in accordance with regulations prescribed by the Secretary.

(2) METHOD.—The regulations prescribed under paragraph (1) shall provide for—

(A) an adjustment with respect to any calendar year based on the increase in the applicable index for the calendar quarter ending September 30 of the preceding calendar year over such index for the base period, and

(B) adjustment procedures which are similar to the procedures used to adjust benefit amounts under section 215(i)(2)(A) of the Social Security Act.

(3) BASE PERIOD.—For purpose of paragraph (2)—

(A) $160,000 AMOUNT.—The base period taken into account for purposes of paragraph (1)(A) is the calendar quarter beginning July 1, 2001.

(B) SEPARATIONS AFTER DECEMBER 31, 1994.—The base period taken into account for purposes of paragraph (1)(B) with respect to individuals separating from service with the employer after December 31, 1994, is the calendar quarter beginning July 1 of the calendar year preceding the calendar year in which such separation occurs.

(C) SEPARATIONS BEFORE JANUARY 1, 1995.—The base period taken into account for purposes of paragraph (1)(B) with respect to individuals separating from service with the employer before January 1, 1995, is the calendar quarter beginning October 1 of the calendar year preceding the calendar year in which such separation occurs.

(D) $40,000 AMOUNT.—The base period taken into account for purposes of paragraph (1)(C) is the calendar quarter beginning July 1, 2001.

(4) ROUNDING.—

(A) $160,000 AMOUNT.—Any increase under subparagraph (A) of paragraph (1) which is not a multiple of $5,000 shall be rounded to the next lowest multiple of $5,000. This subparagraph shall also apply for purposes of any provision of this title that provides for adjustments in accordance with the method contained in this subsection, except to the extent provided in such provision.

(B) $40,000 AMOUNT.—Any increase under subparagraph (C) of paragraph (1) which is not a multiple of $1,000 shall be rounded to the next lowest multiple of $1,000.

Amendments

• 2006, Pension Protection Act of 2006 (P.L. 109-280)

P.L. 109-280, §811, provides:

SEC. 811. PENSIONS AND INDIVIDUAL RETIREMENT ARRANGEMENT PROVISIONS OF ECONOMIC GROWTH AND TAX RELIEF RECONCILIATION ACT OF 2001 MADE PERMANENT.

Title IX of the Economic Growth and Tax Relief Reconciliation Act of 2001 [P.L. 107-16] shall not apply to the provisions of, and amendments made by, subtitles A through F of title VI [§§601-666]of such Act (relating to pension and individual retirement arrangement provisions).

• 2004, Working Families Tax Relief Act of 2004 (P.L. 108-311)

P.L. 108-311, §404(b)(2):

Amended Code Sec. 415(d)(4)(A) by adding at the end a new sentence. **Effective** as if included in the provision of the Economic Growth and Tax Relief Reconciliation Act of 2001 (P.L. 107-16) to which it relates [**effective** for years beginning after 12-31-2001.—CCH].

• 2001, Economic Growth and Tax Relief Reconciliation Act of 2001 (P.L. 107-16)

P.L. 107-16, §611(a)(4)(A)-(B):

Amended Code Sec. 415(d) by striking "$90,000" in paragraph (1)(A) and inserting "$160,000"; and in paragraph (3)(A) by striking "$90,000" in the heading and inserting "$160,000", and by striking "October 1, 1986" and inserting "July 1, 2001". **Effective** for years ending after 12-31-2001.

P.L. 107-16, §611(b)(2)(A)-(B):

Amended Code Sec. 415(d) by striking "$30,000" in paragraph (1)(C) and inserting "$40,000"; and in paragraph (3)(D) by striking "$30,000" in the heading and inserting "$40,000", and by striking "October 1, 1993" and inserting "July 1, 2001". **Effective** for years beginning after 12-31-2001. For a special rule, see Act Sec. 611(i)(3), below.

P.L. 107-16, §611(h):

Amended Code Sec. 415(d)(4). **Effective** for years beginning after 12-31-2001. For a special rule, see Act Sec. 611(i)(3), below. Prior to amendment, Code Sec. 415(d)(4) read as follows:

(4) ROUNDING.—Any increase under subparagraph (A) or (C) of paragraph (1) which is not a multiple of $5,000 shall be rounded to the next lowest multiple of $5,000.

P.L. 107-16, §611(i)(3) (as added by P.L. 107-147, §411(j)(3)), provides:

(3) SPECIAL RULE.—In the case of plan that, on June 7, 2001, incorporated by reference the limitation of section 415(b)(1)(A) of the Internal Revenue Code of 1986, section 411(d)(6) of such Code and section 204(g)(1) of the Employee Retirement Income Security Act of 1974 do not apply to a plan amendment that—

(A) is adopted on or before June 30, 2002,

(B) reduces benefits to the level that would have applied without regard to the amendments made by subsection (a) of this section, and

(C) is effective no earlier than the years described in paragraph (2).

P.L. 107-16, §901(a)-(b), provides [but see P.L. 109-280, §811, above]:

SEC. 901. SUNSET OF PROVISIONS OF ACT.

(a) IN GENERAL.—All provisions of, and amendments made by, this Act shall not apply—

(1) to taxable, plan, or limitation years beginning after December 31, 2010, or

(2) in the case of title V, to estates of decedents dying, gifts made, or generation skipping transfers, after December 31, 2010.

(b) APPLICATION OF CERTAIN LAWS.—The Internal Revenue Code of 1986 and the Employee Retirement Income Security Act of 1974 shall be applied and administered to years, estates, gifts, and transfers described in subsection (a) as if the provisions and amendments described in subsection (a) had never been enacted.

• 1994, Uruguay Round Agreements Act. (P.L. 103-465)

P.L. 103-465, §732(b)(1):

Amended Code Sec. 415(d). **Effective** for years beginning after 12-31-94. For a special rule, see Act Sec. 732(e)(2), below. Prior to amendment, Code Sec. 415(d) read as follows:

(d) COST-OF-LIVING ADJUSTMENTS.—

(1) IN GENERAL.—The Secretary shall adjust annually—

(A) the $90,000 amount in subsection (b)(1)(A), and

(B) in the case of a participant who is separated from service, the amount taken into account under subsection (b)(1)(B),

for increases in the cost of living in accordance with regulations prescribed by the Secretary. Such regulations shall provide for adjustment procedures which are similar to the procedures used to adjust primary insurance amounts ["benefit amounts", applicable to adjustments for years beginning after 1985] under section 215(i)(2)(A) of the Social Security Act.

(2) BASE PERIODS.—The base period taken into account—

(A) for purposes of subparagraph (A) of paragraph (1) is the calendar quarter beginning October 1, 1986 and

(B) for purposes of subparagraph (B) of paragraph (1) is the last calendar quarter of the calendar year before the calendar year in which the participant is separated from service.

(3) FREEZE ON ADJUSTMENT TO DEFINED CONTRIBUTION AND BENEFIT LIMITS.—The Secretary shall not make any adjustment under subparagraph (A) of paragraph (1) with respect to any year beginning after December 31, 1982, and before January 1, 1988.

P.L. 103-465, §732(e)(2), provides:

(2) ROUNDING NOT TO RESULT IN DECREASES.—The amendments made by this section providing for the rounding of indexed amounts shall not apply to any year to the extent the rounding would require the indexed amount to be reduced below the amount in effect for years beginning in 1994.

• 1986, Tax Reform Act of 1986 (P.L. 99-514)

P.L. 99-514, §1106(g)(1):

Amended Code Sec. 415(d)(1) by inserting "and" at the end of subparagraph (A), by striking out subparagraph (B), and by redesignating subparagraph (C) as subparagraph (B). For the **effective** date, see Act Sec. 1106(i) following Code Sec. 415(d). Prior to amendment, Code Sec. 415(d)(1)(B) read as follows:

(B) the $30,000 amount in subsection (c)(1)(A), and

P.L. 99-514, §1106(g)(2)(A)-(B):

Amended Code Sec. 415(d)(2) by striking out "subparagraphs (A) and (B)" and inserting in lieu thereof "subparagraph (A)", and by striking out "subparagraph (C)" and inserting in lieu thereof "subparagraph (B)". For the **effective** date, see Act Sec. 1106(i) following Code Sec. 415(d).

P.L. 99-514, §1106(g)(3):

Amended Code Sec. 415(d)(3) by striking out "subparagraph (A) or (B)" and inserting in lieu thereof "subparagraph (A)". For the **effective** date, see Act Sec 1106(i), below.

P.L. 99-514, §1106(i), as amended by P.L. 100-647, §1011(d)(5) and 6062(a), provides:

(i) EFFECTIVE DATES.—

(1) IN GENERAL.—Except as provided in this subsection, the amendments made by this section shall apply to years beginning after December 31, 1986.

(2) COLLECTIVE BARGAINING AGREEMENTS.—In the case of a plan in effect before March 1, 1986, pursuant to 1 or more collective bargaining agreements between employee representatives and 1 or more employers, the amendments made by this section (other than subsection (d)) shall not apply to contributions or benefits pursuant to such agreement in years beginning before October 1, 1991.

(3) RIGHT TO HIGHER ACCRUED DEFINED BENEFIT PRESERVED.—

(A) IN GENERAL.—In the case of an individual who is a participant (as of the 1st day of the 1st year to which the amendments made by this section apply) in a defined benefit plan which is in existence on May 6, 1986, and with respect to which the requirements of section 415 of the Internal Revenue Code of 1986 have been met for all plan years, if such individual's current accrued benefit under the plan exceeds the limitation of subsection (b) of section 415 of such Code (as amended by this section), then (in the case of such plan), for purposes of subsections (b) and (e) of such section, the limitation of such subsection (b)(1)(A) with respect to such individual shall be equal to such current accrued benefit.

(B) CURRENT ACCRUED BENEFIT DEFINED.—

(i) IN GENERAL.—For purposes of this paragraph, the term "current accrued benefit" means the individual's accrued benefit (at the close of the last year to which the amendments made by this section do not apply) when expressed as an annual benefit (within the meaning of section 415(b)(2) of such Code).

(ii) SPECIAL RULE.—For purposes of determining the amount of any individual's current accrued benefit—

(I) no change in the terms and conditions of the plan after May 5, 1986, and

(II) no cost-of-living adjustment occurring after May 5, 1986,

shall be taken into account. For purposes of subclause (I), any change in the terms and conditions of the plan pursuant to a collective bargaining agreement ratified before May 6, 1986, shall be treated as a change made before May 6, 1986.

(4) TRANSITION RULE WHERE THE SUM OF DEFINED CONTRIBUTION AND DEFINED BENEFIT PLAN FRACTIONS EXCEEDS 1.0.—In the case of a plan which satisfied the requirements of section 415 of the Internal Revenue Code of 1986 for its last year beginning before January 1, 1987, the Secretary of the Treasury or his delegate shall prescribe regulations under which an amount is subtracted from the numerator of the defined contribution plan fraction (not exceeding such numerator) so that the sum of the defined benefit plan fraction and the defined contribution plan fraction computed under section 415(e)(1) of such Code does not exceed 1.0 for such year (determined as if the amendments made by this section were in effect for such year).

(5) EFFECTIVE DATE FOR SUBSECTION (d).—

(A) IN GENERAL.—Except as provided in subparagraph (B), the amendment made by subsection (d) shall apply to benefits accruing in years beginning after December 31, 1988.

(B) COLLECTIVE BARGAINING AGREEMENTS.—In the case of a plan described in paragraph (2), the amendments made by subsection (d) shall apply to benefits accruing in years beginning on or after the earlier of—

(i) the later of—

(I) the date determined under paragraph (2)(A), or

(II) January 1, 1989, or

(ii) January 1, 1991.

(6) SPECIAL RULE FOR AMENDMENT MADE BY SUBSECTION (e).—The amendment made by subsection (e) shall not require the recomputation, for purposes of section 415(e) of the Internal Revenue Code of 1986, of the annual addition for any year beginning before 1987.

• 1984, Deficit Reduction Act of 1984 (P.L. 98-369)

P.L. 98-369, §15(a):

Amended Code Sec. 415(d)(3) by striking out "January 1, 1986" and by inserting in lieu thereof "January 1, 1988". **Effective** for tax years ending after 12-31-83.

P.L. 98-369, §15(b):

Amended Code Sec. 415(d)(2)(A) (as amended by Section 235(b)(2)(B) of P.L. 97-248) by striking out "October 1, 1984" and inserting in lieu thereof "October 1, 1986". **Effective** for tax years ending after 12-31-83.

• 1982, Tax Equity and Fiscal Responsibility Act of 1982 (P.L. 97-248)

P.L. 97-248, §235(b)(1):

Amended Code Sec. 415(d)(1) by striking out "primary insurance amounts" and inserting in lieu thereof "benefit amounts". **Effective** for adjustments for years beginning after 12-31-85. See also the amendment notes for P.L. 97-248, Act Sec. 235(g), following Code Sec. 415(b).

P.L. 97-248, §235(b)(2)(A):

Amended Code Sec. 415(d) by adding new subparagraph (3). **Effective** for adjustments for years beginning after 12-31-82. See also the amendment notes for P.L. 97-248, Act Sec. 235(g), following Code Sec. 415(b).

P.L. 97-248, §235(b)(2)(B):

Amended Code Sec. 415(d)(2) by striking out "1974" and inserting in lieu thereof "1984". **Effective** for adjustments for years beginning after 12-31-85. See also the amendment notes for P.L. 97-248, Act Sec. 235(g), following Code Sec. 415(b).

P.L. 97-248, §235(b)(3):

Amended Code Sec. 415(d)(1) by striking out "$75,000" in subparagraph (A) and inserting in lieu thereof "$90,000" and by striking out "$25,000" in subparagraph (B) and inserting in lieu thereof "$30,000". **Effective** for adjustments for years beginning after 12-31-82. See also the amendment notes for P.L. 97-248, Act Sec. 235(g), following Code Sec. 415(b).

• 1976, Tax Reform Act of 1976 (P.L. 94-455)

P.L. 94-455, §1906(b)(13)(A):

Amended 1954 Code by substituting "Secretary" for "Secretary or his delegate" each place it appeared. **Effective** 2-1-77.

• 1974, Employee Retirement Income Security Act of 1974 (P.L. 93-406)

P.L. 93-406, §2004(a)(2):

Added Code Sec. 415(d). **Effective**, generally, for years beginning after 1975. For special effective dates and transitional rules governing this section, see the footnote to Code Sec. 415(a) and the historical note for §1017, P.L. 93-406, following the text of Code Sec. 410(d).

[Sec. 415(e)—Repealed]

Amendments

• 1997, Taxpayer Relief Act of 1997 (P.L. 105-34)

P.L. 105-34, §1504(b), provides:

(b) REPEAL OF RULES IN SECTION 415(e).—The Secretary of the Treasury shall modify the regulations regarding the exclusion allowance under section 403(b)(2) of the Internal Revenue Code of 1986 to reflect the amendment made by section 1452(a) of the Small Business Job Protection Act of 1996. Such modification shall take effect for years beginning after December 31, 1999.

P.L. 105-34, §1530(c)(4)(A)-(B):

Amended Code Sec. 415(e) by redesignating paragraph (6) as paragraph (7), and by inserting after paragraph (5) a new paragraph (6). **Effective** for transfers made by trusts to, or for the use of, an employee stock ownership plan after 8-5-97.

• 1996, Small Business Job Protection Act of 1996 (P.L. 104-188)

P.L. 104-188, §1452(a):

Repealed Code Sec. 415(e). **Effective** for limitation years beginning after 12-31-99. Prior to repeal, Code Sec. 415(e) read as follows:

(e) LIMITATION IN CASE OF DEFINED BENEFIT PLAN AND DEFINED CONTRIBUTION PLAN FOR SAME EMPLOYEE.—

(1) IN GENERAL.—In any case in which an individual is a participant in both a defined benefit plan and a defined contribution plan maintained by the same employer, the sum of the defined benefit plan fraction and the defined contribution plan fraction for any year may not exceed 1.0.

(2) DEFINED BENEFIT PLAN FRACTION.—For purposes of this subsection, the defined benefit plan fraction for any year is a fraction—

(A) the numerator of which is the projected annual benefit of the participant under the plan (determined as of the close of the year), and

(B) the denominator of which is the lesser of—

(i) the product of 1.25, multiplied by the dollar limitation in effect under subsection (b)(1)(A) for such year, or

(ii) the product of—

(I) 1.4, multiplied by

(II) the amount which may be taken into account under subsection (b)(1)(B) with respect to such individual under the plan for such year.

(3) DEFINED CONTRIBUTION PLAN FRACTION.—For purposes of this subsection, the defined contribution plan fraction for any year is a fraction—

(A) the numerator of which is the sum of the annual additions to the participant's account as of the close of the year, and

(B) the denominator of which is the sum of the lesser of the following amounts determined for such year and for each prior year of service with the employer:

(i) the product of 1.25, multiplied by the dollar limitation in effect under subsection (c)(1)(A) for such year (determined without regard to subsection (c)(6)), or

(ii) the product of—

(I) 1.4, multiplied by—

(II) the amount which may be taken into account under subsection (c)(1)(B) (or subsection (c)(7), if applicable) with respect to such individual under such plan for such year.

(4) SPECIAL TRANSITION RULES FOR DEFINED CONTRIBUTION FRACTION.—In applying paragraph (3) with respect to years beginning before January 1, 1976—

(A) the aggregate amount taken into account under paragraph (3)(A) may not exceed the aggregate amount taken into account under paragraph (3)(B), and

(B) the amount taken into account under subsection (c)(2)(B)(i) for any year concerned is an amount equal to—

(i) the excess of the aggregate amount of employee contributions for all years beginning before January 1, 1976, during which the employee was an active participant of the plan, over 10 percent of the employee's aggregate compensation for all such years, multiplied by

(ii) a fraction the numerator of which is 1 and the denominator of which is the number of years beginning before January 1, 1976, during which the employee was an active participant in the plan.

Employee contributions made on or after October 2, 1973, shall be taken into account under subparagraph (B) of the preceding sentence only to the extent that the amount of such contributions does not exceed the maximum amount of contributions permissible under the plan as in effect on October 2, 1973.

(5) SPECIAL RULES FOR SECTIONS 403(b) AND 408.—For purposes of this section, any annuity contract described in section 403(b) (except in the case of a participant who has elected under subsection (c)(4)(D) to have the provisions of subsection (c)(4)(C) apply) for the benefit of a participant shall be treated as a defined contribution plan maintained by each employer with respect to which the participant has the control required under subsection (b) or (c) of section 414 (as modified by subsection (h)). For purposes of this section, any contribution by an employer to a simplified employee pension for an individual for a taxable year shall be treated as an employer contribution to a defined contribution plan for such individual for such year. In the case of any annuity contract described in section 403(b), the amount of the contribution disqualified by reason of subsection (g) shall reduce the exclusion allowance as provided in section 403(b)(2).

(6) SPECIAL TRANSITION RULE FOR DEFINED CONTRIBUTION FRACTION FOR YEARS ENDING AFTER DECEMBER 31, 1982.—

(A) IN GENERAL.—At the election of the plan administrator, in applying paragraph (3) with respect to any year ending after December 31, 1982, the amount taken into account under paragraph (3)(B) with respect to each participant for all years ending before January 1, 1983, shall be an amount equal to the product of—

(i) the amount determined under paragraph (3)(B) (as in effect for the year ending in 1982) for the year ending in 1982, multiplied by

(ii) the transition fraction.

(B) TRANSITION FRACTION.—The term "transition fraction" means a fraction—

(i) the numerator of which is the lesser of—

(I) $51,875, or

(II) 1.4, multiplied by 25 percent of the compensation of the participant for the year ending in 1981, and

(ii) the denominator of which is the lesser of—

(I) $41,500, or

(II) 25 percent of the compensation of the participant for the year ending in 1981.

(C) PLAN MUST HAVE BEEN IN EXISTENCE ON OR BEFORE JULY 1, 1982.—This paragraph shall apply only to plans which were in existence on or before July 1, 1982.

• 1984, Deficit Reduction Act of 1984 (P.L. 98-369)

P.L. 98-369, §713(a)(3):

Amended Code Sec. 415(e)(6) by adding at the end thereof a new subparagraph (C). **Effective** as if included in the provision of P.L. 97-248 to which it relates.

P.L. 98-369, §713(d)(7)(B):

Amended Code Sec. 415(e)(3)(B)(ii) by striking out "subsection (c)(7) or (8)" and inserting in lieu thereof "subsection (c)(7)". **Effective** as if included in the provision of P.L. 97-248 to which it relates.

• 1982, Tax Equity and Fiscal Responsibility Act of 1982 (P.L. 97-248)

P.L. 97-248, §235(c)(1):

Amended Code Sec. 415(e)(1) by striking out "1.4" and inserting in lieu thereof "1.0". For the **effective** date and special rules, see P.L. 97-248, Act Sec. 235(g), in the amendment notes for Code Sec. 415(b).

P.L. 97-248, §235(c)(2)(A):

Amended Code Sec. 415(e)(2)(B). For the **effective** date and special rules, see P.L. 97-248, Act Sec. 235(g), which follows Act Sec. 235(e)(4) in the amendment notes for Code Sec. 415(b). Prior to amendment, Code Sec. 415(e)(2)(B) read as follows:

(B) the denominator of which is the projected annual benefit of the participant under the plan (determined as of the close of the year) if the plan provided the maximum benefit allowable under subsection (b).

P.L. 97-248, §235(c)(2)(B):

Amended Code Sec. 415(e)(3)(B). For the **effective** date and special rules, see P.L. 97-248, Act Sec. 235(g), which follows Act Sec. 235(e)(4) in the amendment notes for Code Sec. 415(b). Prior to amendment, Code Sec. 415(e)(3)(B) read as follows:

(B) the denominator of which is the sum of the maximum amount of annual additions to such account which could have been made under subsection (c) for such year and for each prior year of service with the employer (determined without regard to paragraph (6) of such subsection).

P.L. 97-248, §235(d):

Amended Code Sec. 415(e) by adding a new paragraph (6) at the end thereof. For the **effective** date and special rules, see P.L. 97-248, Act Sec. 235(g), in the amendment notes for Code Sec. 415(b).

• 1981, Economic Recovery Tax Act of 1981 (P.L. 97-34)

P.L. 97-34, §311(g)(4)(C):

Amended Code Sec. 415(e)(5). **Effective** for tax years beginning after 12-31-81. Prior to amendment, Code Sec. 415 (e)(5) read as follows:

(5) SPECIAL RULES FOR SECTIONS 403(b) AND 408.—For purposes of this section, any annuity contract described in section 403(b) (except in the case of a participant who has elected under subsection (c)(4)(D) to have the provisions of subsection (c)(4)(C) apply), any individual retirement account described in section 408(a), any individual retirement annuity described in section 408(b), and any retirement bond described in section 409, for the benefit of a participant shall be treated as a defined contribution plan maintained by each employer with respect to which the participant has the control required under subsection (b) or (c) of section 414 (as modified by subsection (h)). For purposes of this section, any contribution by an employer to a simplified employee pension for an individual for a taxable year shall be treated as an employer contribution to a defined contribution plan for such individual for such year. In the case of any annuity contract described in section 403(b), the amount of the contribution disqualified by reason of subsection (g) shall reduce the exclusion allowance as provided in section 403(b)(2).

• 1980, Technical Corrections Act of 1979 (P.L. 96-222)

P.L. 96-222, §101(a)(10)(I):

Amended Code Sec. 415(e)(5) by striking out in the first sentence "any simplified employee pension" and by adding a new second sentence. **Effective** for years beginning after 4-1-80.

• 1978, Revenue Act of 1978 (P.L. 95-600)

P.L. 95-600, §152(g)(3):

Amended Code Sec. 415(e)(5) by inserting "any simplified employee pension," after "section 408(b)". **Effective** for tax years beginning after 12-31-78.

• 1976, Tax Reform Act of 1976 (P.L. 94-455)

P.L. 94-455, §803(b):

Amended Code Sec. 415(e)(5) by substituting "For purposes of this section," for "For purposes of this subsection,". **Effective** for years beginning after 12-31-75.

P.L. 94-455, §803(f):

Amended Code Sec. 415(e)(3)(B) by inserting "(determined without regard to paragraph (6) of such subsection)" after "employer". **Effective** for years beginning after 12-31-75.

• 1974, Employee Retirement Income Security Act of 1974 (P.L. 93-406)

P.L. 93-406, §2004(a)(2):

Added Code Sec. 415(e). **Effective**, generally, for years beginning after 1975. For special effective dates and transitional rules governing this section, see the footnote to Code Sec. 415(a) and the historical note for §1017, P.L. 93-406, following the text of Code Sec. 410(d).

P.L. 93-406, §2004(a)(3), provides:

(3) SPECIAL RULES FOR CERTAIN PLANS IN EFFECT ON DATE OF ENACTMENT [September 2, 1974].—In any case in which, on the date of enactment [September 2, 1974] of this Act, an individual is a participant in both a defined benefit plan and a defined contribution plan maintained by the same employer, and the sum of the defined benefit plan fraction and the defined contribution plan fraction for the year during

which such date occurs exceeds 1.4, the sum of such fractions may continue to exceed 1.4 if—

(A) the defined benefit plan fraction is not increased, by amendment of the plan or otherwise, after the date of enactment [September 2, 1974] of this Act, and

(B) no contributions are made under the defined contribution plan after such date.

A trust which is part of a pension, profit-sharing, or stock bonus plan described in the preceding sentence shall not be treated as not constituting a qualified trust under section 401(a) of the Internal Revenue Code of 1954 on account of the provisions of section 415(e) of such Code, as long as it is described in the preceding sentence of this subsection.

[Sec. 415(f)]

(f) COMBINING OF PLANS.—

(1) IN GENERAL.—For purposes of applying the limitations of subsections (b) and (c)—

(A) all defined benefit plans (whether or not terminated) of an employer are to be treated as one defined benefit plan, and

(B) all defined contribution plans (whether or not terminated) of an employer are to be treated as one defined contribution plan.

(2) EXCEPTION FOR MULTIEMPLOYER PLANS.—Notwithstanding paragraph (1) and subsection (g), a multiemployer plan (as defined in section 414(f)) shall not be combined or aggregated—

(A) with any other plan which is not a multiemployer plan for purposes of applying subsection (b)(1)(B) to such other plan, or

(B) with any other multiemployer plan for purposes of applying the limitations established in this section.

Amendments

• 2008, Worker, Retiree, and Employer Recovery Act of 2008 (P.L. 110-458)

P.L. 110-458, §108(g):

Amended Code Sec. 415(f) by striking paragraph (2) and by redesignating paragraph (3) as paragraph (2). **Effective** as if included in the provision of the 2006 Act to which the amendment relates [**effective** for years beginning after 12-31-2005.—CCH]. Prior to being stricken, Code Sec. 415(f)(2) read as follows:

(2) ANNUAL COMPENSATION TAKEN INTO ACCOUNT FOR DEFINED BENEFIT PLANS.—If the employer has more than one defined benefit plan—

(A) subsection (b)(1)(B) shall be applied separately with respect to each such plan, but

(B) in applying subsection (b)(1)(B) to the aggregate of such defined benefit plans for purposes of this subsection, the high 3 years of compensation taken into account shall be the period of consecutive calendar years (not more than 3) during which the individual had the greatest aggregate compensation from the employer.

• 2006, Pension Protection Act of 2006 (P.L. 109-280)

P.L. 109-280, §811, provides:

SEC. 811. PENSIONS AND INDIVIDUAL RETIREMENT ARRANGEMENT PROVISIONS OF ECONOMIC GROWTH AND TAX RELIEF RECONCILIATION ACT OF 2001 MADE PERMANENT.

Title IX of the Economic Growth and Tax Relief Reconciliation Act of 2001 [P.L. 107-16] shall not apply to the provisions of, and amendments made by, subtitles A through F of title VI [§§601-666]of such Act (relating to pension and individual retirement arrangement provisions).

• 2001, Economic Growth and Tax Relief Reconciliation Act of 2001 (P.L. 107-16)

P.L. 107-16, §654(b)(1):

Amended Code Sec. 415(f) by adding at the end a new paragraph (3). **Effective** for years beginning after 12-31-2001.

P.L. 107-16, §901(a)-(b), provides [but see P.L. 109-280, §811, above]:

SEC. 901. SUNSET OF PROVISIONS OF ACT.

(a) IN GENERAL.—All provisions of, and amendments made by, this Act shall not apply—

(1) to taxable, plan, or limitation years beginning after December 31, 2010, or

(2) in the case of title V, to estates of decedents dying, gifts made, or generation skipping transfers, after December 31, 2010.

(b) APPLICATION OF CERTAIN LAWS.—The Internal Revenue Code of 1986 and the Employee Retirement Income Security Act of 1974 shall be applied and administered to years, estates, gifts, and transfers described in subsection (a) as if the provisions and amendments described in subsection (a) had never been enacted.

• 1996, Small Business Job Protection Act of 1996 (P.L. 104-188)

P.L. 104-188, §1452(c)(3):

Amended Code Sec. 415(f)(1) by striking "subsections (b), (c), and (e)" and inserting "subsections (b) and (c)". **Effective** for limitation years beginning after 12-31-99.

[Sec. 415(g)]

(g) AGGREGATION OF PLANS.—Except as provided in subsection (f)(3), the Secretary, in applying the provisions of this section to benefits or contributions under more than one plan maintained by the same employer, and to any trusts, contracts, accounts, or bonds referred to in subsection (a)(2), with respect to which the participant has the control required under section 414(b) or (c), as modified by subsection (h), shall, under regulations prescribed by the Secretary, disqualify one or more trusts, plans, contracts, accounts, or bonds, or any combination thereof until such benefits or contributions do not exceed the limitations contained in this section. In addition to taking into account such other factors as may be necessary to carry out the purposes of subsection (f), the regulations prescribed under this paragraph shall provide that no plan which has been terminated shall be disqualified until all other trusts, plans, contracts, accounts, or bonds have been disqualified.

Amendments

• 2006, Pension Protection Act of 2006 (P.L. 109-280)

P.L. 109-280, §811, provides:

SEC. 811. PENSIONS AND INDIVIDUAL RETIREMENT ARRANGEMENT PROVISIONS OF ECONOMIC GROWTH AND TAX RELIEF RECONCILIATION ACT OF 2001 MADE PERMANENT.

Title IX of the Economic Growth and Tax Relief Reconciliation Act of 2001 [P.L. 107-16] shall not apply to the provisions of, and amendments made by, subtitles A through F of title VI [§§601-666]of such Act (relating to pension and individual retirement arrangement provisions).

• 2001, Economic Growth and Tax Relief Reconciliation Act of 2001 (P.L. 107-16)

P.L. 107-16, §632(b)(2)(B), provides:

(B) EXCLUSION ALLOWANCE.—Effective for limitation years beginning in 2000, in the case of any annuity contract described in section 403(b) of the Internal Revenue Code of 1986, the amount of the contribution disqualified by reason of section 415(g) of such Code shall reduce the exclusion allowance as provided in section 403(b)(2) of such Code.

P.L. 107-16, §654(b)(2):

Amended Code Sec. 415(g) by striking "The Secretary" and inserting "Except as provided in subsection (f)(3), the Secretary". **Effective** for years beginning after 12-31-2001.

P.L. 107-16, §901(a)-(b), provides [but see P.L. 109-280, §811, above]:

SEC. 901. SUNSET OF PROVISIONS OF ACT.

(a) IN GENERAL.—All provisions of, and amendments made by, this Act shall not apply—

(1) to taxable, plan, or limitation years beginning after December 31, 2010, or

(2) in the case of title V, to estates of decedents dying, gifts made, or generation skipping transfers, after December 31, 2010.

(b) APPLICATION OF CERTAIN LAWS.—The Internal Revenue Code of 1986 and the Employee Retirement Income Security Act of 1974 shall be applied and administered to years, estates, gifts, and transfers described in subsection (a) as if the provisions and amendments described in subsection (a) had never been enacted.

• 1996, Small Business Job Protection Act of 1996 (P.L. 104-188)

P.L. 104-188, §1452(c)(4):

Amended Code Sec. 415(g) by striking "subsections (e) and (f)" in the last sentence and inserting "subsection (f)". **Effective** for limitation years beginning after 12-31-99.

• 1976, Tax Reform Act of 1976 (P.L. 94-455)

P.L. 94-455, §1906(b)(13)(A):

Amended 1954 Code by substituting "Secretary" for "Secretary or his delegate" each place it appeared. **Effective** 2-1-77.

• 1974, Employee Retirement Income Security Act of 1974 (P.L. 93-406)

P.L. 93-406, §2004(a)(2):

Added Code Sec. 415(g). **Effective**, generally, for years beginning after 1975. For special effective dates and transitional rules governing this section, see the footnote to Code Sec. 415(a) and the historical note for §1017, P.L. 93-406, following the text of Code Sec. 410(d).

[Sec. 415(h)]

(h) 50 PERCENT CONTROL.—For purposes of applying subsections (b) and (c) of section 414 to this section, the phrase "more than 50 percent" shall be substituted for the phrase "at least 80 percent" each place it appears in section 1563(a)(1).

[Sec. 415(i)]

(i) RECORDS NOT AVAILABLE FOR PAST PERIODS.—Where for the period before January 1, 1976, or (if later) the first day of the first plan year of the plan, the records necessary for the application of this section are not available, the Secretary may by regulations prescribe alternative methods for determining the amounts to be taken into account for such period.

Amendments

• 1976, Tax Reform Act of 1976 (P.L. 94-455)

P.L. 94-455, §1906(b)(13)(A):

Amended 1954 Code by substituting "Secretary" for "Secretary or his delegate" each place it appeared. **Effective** 2-1-77.

• 1974, Employee Retirement Income Security Act of 1974 (P.L. 93-406)

P.L. 93-406, §2004(a)(2):

Added Code Sec. 415(i). **Effective**, generally, for years beginning after 1975. For special effective dates and transitional rules governing this section, see the footnote to Code Sec. 415(a) and the historical note for §1017, P.L. 93-406, following the text of Code Sec. 410(d).

[Sec. 415(j)]

(j) REGULATIONS; DEFINITION OF YEAR.—The Secretary shall prescribe such regulations as may be necessary to carry out the purposes of this section, including, but not limited to, regulations defining the term "year" for purposes of any provision of this section.

Amendments

• 1976, Tax Reform Act of 1976 (P.L. 94-455)

P.L. 94-455, §1906(b)(13)(A):

Amended 1954 Code by substituting "Secretary" for "Secretary or his delegate" each place it appeared. **Effective** 2-1-77.

• 1974, Employee Retirement Income Security Act of 1974 (P.L. 93-406)

P.L. 93-406, §2004(a)(2):

Added Code Sec. 415(j). **Effective**, generally, for years beginning after 1975. For special effective dates and transitional rules governing this section, see the footnote to Code Sec. 415(a) and the historical note for §1017, P.L. 93-406, following the text of Code Sec. 410(d).

[Sec. 415(k)]

(k) SPECIAL RULES.—

(1) DEFINED BENEFIT PLAN AND DEFINED CONTRIBUTION PLAN.—For purposes of this title, the term "defined contribution plan" or "defined benefit plan" means a defined contribution plan (within the meaning of section 414(i)) or a defined plan (within the meaning of section 414(j)), whichever applies, which is—

(A) a plan described in section 401(a) which includes a trust which is exempt from tax under section 501(a),

(B) an annuity plan described in section 403(a),

(C) an annuity contract described in section 403(b), or

(D) a simplified employee pension.

(2) CONTRIBUTIONS TO PROVIDE COST-OF-LIVING PROTECTION UNDER DEFINED BENEFIT PLANS.—

(A) IN GENERAL.—In the case of a defined benefit plan which maintains a qualified cost-of-living arrangement—

(i) any contribution made directly by an employee under such an arrangement shall not be treated as an annual addition for purposes of subsection (c), and

(ii) any benefit under such arrangement which is allocable to an employer contribution which was transferred from a defined contribution plan and to which the requirements of subsection (c) were applied shall, for purposes of subsection (b), be treated as a benefit derived from an employee contribution (and subsection (c) shall not again apply to such contribution by reason of such transfer).

(B) QUALIFIED COST-OF-LIVING ARRANGEMENT DEFINED.—For purposes of this paragraph, the term "qualified cost-of-living arrangement" means an arrangement under a defined benefit plan which—

(i) provides a cost-of-living adjustment to a benefit provided under such plan or a separate plan subject to the requirements of section 412, and

(ii) meets the requirements of subparagraphs (C), (D), (E), and (F) and such other requirements as the Secretary may prescribe.

(C) DETERMINATION OF AMOUNT OF BENEFIT.—An arrangement meets the requirement of this subparagraph only if the cost-of-living adjustment of participants is based—

(i) on increases in the cost-of-living after the annuity starting date, and

(ii) on average cost-of-living increases determined by reference to 1 or more indexes prescribed by the Secretary, except that the arrangement may provide that the increase for any year will not be less than 3 percent of the retirement benefit (determined without regard to such increase).

(D) ARRANGEMENT ELECTIVE; TIME FOR ELECTION.—An arrangement meets the requirements of this subparagraph only if it is elective, it is available under the same terms to all participants, and it provides that such election may at least be made in the year in which the participant—

(i) attains the earliest retirement age under the defined benefit plan (determined without regard to any requirement of separation from service), or

(ii) separates from service.

(E) NONDISCRIMINATION REQUIREMENTS.—An arrangement shall not meet the requirements of this subparagraph if the Secretary finds that a pattern of discrimination exists with respect to participation.

(F) SPECIAL RULES FOR KEY EMPLOYEES.—

(i) IN GENERAL.—An arrangement shall not meet the requirements of this paragraph if any key employee is eligible to participate.

(ii) KEY EMPLOYEE.—For purposes of this subparagraph, the term "key employee" has the meaning given such term by section 416(i)(1), except that in the case of a plan other than a top-heavy plan (within the meaning of section 416(g)), such term shall not include an individual who is a key employee solely by reason of section 416(i)(1)(A)(i).

(3) REPAYMENTS OF CASHOUTS UNDER GOVERNMENTAL PLANS.—In the case of any repayment of contributions (including interest thereon) to the governmental plan with respect to an amount previously refunded upon a forfeiture of service credit under the plan or under another governmental plan maintained by a State or local government employer within the same State, any such repayment shall not be taken into account for purposes of this section.

(4) SPECIAL RULES FOR SECTIONS 403(b) AND 408.—For purposes of this section, any annuity contract described in section 403(b) for the benefit of a participant shall be treated as a defined contribution plan maintained by each employer with respect to which the participant has the control required under subsection (b) or (c) of section 414 (as modified by subsection (h)). For purposes of this section, any contribution by an employer to a simplified employee pension plan for an individual for a taxable year shall be treated as an employer contribution to a defined contribution plan for such individual for such year.

Amendments

• 2006, Pension Protection Act of 2006 (P.L. 109-280)

P.L. 109-280, §811, provides:

SEC. 811. PENSIONS AND INDIVIDUAL RETIREMENT ARRANGEMENT PROVISIONS OF ECONOMIC GROWTH AND TAX RELIEF RECONCILIATION ACT OF 2001 MADE PERMANENT.

Title IX of the Economic Growth and Tax Relief Reconciliation Act of 2001 [P.L. 107-16] shall not apply to the provisions of, and amendments made by, subtitles A through F of title VI [§§601-666]of such Act (relating to pension and individual retirement arrangement provisions).

• 2001, Economic Growth and Tax Relief Reconciliation Act of 2001 (P.L. 107-16)

P.L. 107-16, §632(b)(1):

Amended Code Sec. 415(k) by adding at the end a new paragraph (4). **Effective** as noted in Act Sec. 632(b)(2)-(3), below.

P.L. 107-16, §632(b)(2)-(3), provides:

(2) EFFECTIVE DATE.—

(A) IN GENERAL.—The amendment made by paragraph (1) shall apply to limitation years beginning after December 31, 1999.

(B) EXCLUSION ALLOWANCE.—Effective for limitation years beginning in 2000, in the case of any annuity contract described in section 403(b) of the Internal Revenue Code of 1986, the amount of the contribution disqualified by reason of section 415(g) of such Code shall reduce the exclusion allowance as provided in section 403(b)(2) of such Code.

(3) ELECTION TO MODIFY SECTION 403(b) EXCLUSION ALLOWANCE TO CONFORM TO SECTION 415 MODIFICATION.—In the case of taxable years beginning after December 31, 1999, and before January 1, 2002, a plan may disregard the requirement in the regulations regarding the exclusion allowance under section 403(b)(2) of the Internal Revenue Code of 1986 that contributions to a defined benefit pension plan be treated as previously excluded amounts for purposes of the exclusion allowance.

P.L. 107-16, §901(a)-(b), provides [but see P.L. 109-280, §811, above]:

SEC. 901. SUNSET OF PROVISIONS OF ACT.

(a) IN GENERAL.—All provisions of, and amendments made by, this Act shall not apply—

(1) to taxable, plan, or limitation years beginning after December 31, 2010, or

(2) in the case of title V, to estates of decedents dying, gifts made, or generation skipping transfers, after December 31, 2010.

(b) APPLICATION OF CERTAIN LAWS.—The Internal Revenue Code of 1986 and the Employee Retirement Income Security Act of 1974 shall be applied and administered to years, estates, gifts, and transfers described in subsection (a) as if the provisions and amendments described in subsection (a) had never been enacted.

• 1997, Taxpayer Relief Act of 1997 (P.L. 105-34)

P.L. 105-34, §1526(b):

Amended Code Sec. 415(k) by adding at the end a new paragraph (3). **Effective**, generally, for permissive service credit contributions made in years beginning after 12-31-97. For a transition rule, see Act Sec. 1526(c)(2)(A)-(B), below.

P.L. 105-34, §1526(c)(2)(A)-(B), provides:

(2) TRANSITION RULE.—

(A) IN GENERAL.—In the case of an eligible participant in a governmental plan (within the meaning of section 414(d) of the Internal Revenue Code of 1986), the limitations of section 415(c)(1) of such Code shall not be applied to reduce the amount of permissive service credit which may be purchased to an amount less than the amount which was allowed to be purchased under the terms of the plan as in effect on the date of the enactment of this Act.

(B) ELIGIBLE PARTICIPANT.—For purposes of subparagraph (A), an eligible participant is an individual who first became a participant in the plan before the first plan year beginning after the last day of the calendar year in which the next regular session (following the date of the enactment of this Act) of the governing body with authority to amend the plan ends.

• 1996, Small Business Job Protection Act of 1996 (P.L. 104-188)

P.L. 104-188, §1452(c)(5):

Amended Code Sec. 415(k)(2)(A)(i). **Effective** for limitation years beginning after 12-31-99. Prior to amendment, Code Sec. 415(k)(2)(A)(i) read as follows:

(i) any contribution made directly by an employee under such arrangement—

(I) shall not be treated as an annual addition for purposes of subsection (c), but

(II) shall be so treated for purposes of subsection (e), and

P.L. 104-188, §1452(c)(6):

Amended Code Sec. 415(k)(2)(A)(ii) by striking "subsections (c) and (e)" and inserting "subsection (c)". **Effective** for limitation years beginning after 12-31-99.

P.L. 104-188, §1704(t)(75):

Amended Code Sec. 415(k)(1) by adding "or" at the end of subparagraph (C), by striking subparagraphs (D) and (E), and by redesignating subparagraph (F) as subparagraph (D). **Effective** 8-20-96. Prior to amendment, Code Sec. 415(k)(1)(D)-(E) read as follows:

(D) an individual retirement account described in section 408(a),

(E) an individual retirement annuity described in section 408(b), or

• 1988, Technical and Miscellaneous Revenue Act of 1988 (P.L. 100-647)

P.L. 100-647, §1011(d)(3)(A)-(B):

Amended Code Sec. 415(k)(2) by striking out "to the arrangement" in subparagraph (C)(ii) and inserting in lieu thereof "to such increase", and by striking out subparagraph (D) and inserting in lieu thereof new subparagraph (D). **Effective** as if included in the provision of P.L. 99-514 to which it relates. Prior to amendment, Code Sec. 415(k)(2)(D) read as follows:

(D) ARRANGEMENT ELECTIVE; TIME FOR ELECTION.—An arrangement meets the requirements of this subparagraph only if it is elective, it is available under the same terms to all participants, and it provides that such election may be made in—

(i) the year in which the participant—

(I) attains the earliest retirement age under the defined benefit plan (determined without regard to any requirement of separation from service), or

(II) separates from service, or

(ii) both such years.

P.L. 100-647, §1018(t)(8)(D):

Amended Act Sec. 1899A of P.L. 99-514 by striking out paragraph (13). **Effective** as if included in the provision of P.L. 99-514 to which it relates. Prior to being stricken, Act Sec. 1899A(13) stated:

(13) Subsection (k) of section 415 is amended to read as follows:

(k) DEFINITIONS OF DEFINED CONTRIBUTION PLAN AND DEFINED BENEFIT PLAN.—For purposes of this title, the term "defined contribution plan" or "defined benefit plan" means a defined contribution plan (within the meaning of section 414(i)) or a defined benefit plan (within the meaning of section 414(j)), whichever applies, which is—

(1) a plan described in section 401(a) which includes a trust which is exempt from tax under section 501(a),

(2) an annuity plan described in section 403(a),

(3) an annuity contract described in section 403(b),

(4) an individual retirement account described in section 408(a),

(5) an individual retirement annuity described in section 408(b), or

(6) a simplified employee pension.

• 1986, Tax Reform Act of 1986 (P.L. 99-514)

P.L. 99-514, §1106(c)(1):

Amended Code Sec. 415(k) by adding at the end thereof new paragraph (2). For the **effective** date, see Act Sec. 1106(i) following Code Sec. 415(d).

P.L. 99-514, §1899A(13):

Amended Code Sec. 415(k). **Effective** 10-22-86. Prior to amendment, Code Sec. 415(k) read as follows:

(k) SPECIAL RULES.—

(1) DEFINED BENEFIT PLAN AND DEFINED CONTRIBUTION PLAN.—For purposes of this title, the term "defined contribution plan" or "defined benefit plan" means a defined contribution plan (within the meaning of section 414(i)) or a defined benefit plan (within the meaning of section 414(j)), whichever applies, which is—

(A) a plan described in section 401(a) which includes a trust which is exempt from tax under section 501(a),

(B) an annuity plan described in section 403(a),

(C) an annuity contract described in section 403(b),

(D) an individual retirement account described in section 408(a),

(E) an individual retirement annuity described in section 408(b), or

(F) a simplified employee pension.

• 1984, Deficit Reduction Act of 1984 (P.L. 98-369)

P.L. 98-369, §491(d)(32):

Amended Code Sec. 415(k)(1) by striking out subparagraphs (C) and (H), by redesignating subparagraphs (D), (E), (F), and (G) as subparagraphs (C), (D), (E), and (F), respectively, by striking out ", or" at the end of subparagraph (F) (as so redesignated) and inserting in lieu thereof a period, and by adding "or" at the end of subparagraph (E) (as so redesignated). **Effective** for obligations issued after 12-31-83. Prior to amendment, Code Sec. 415(k)(1) read as follows:

(k) SPECIAL RULES.—

(1) DEFINED BENEFIT PLAN AND DEFINED CONTRIBUTION PLAN.—For purposes of this title the term "defined contribution plan" or "defined benefit plan" means a defined contribution plan (within the meaning of section 414(i)) or a defined benefit plan (within the meaning of section 414(j)), whichever applies, which is—

(A) a plan described in section 401(a) which includes a trust which is exempt from tax under section 501(a),

(B) an annuity plan described in section 403(a),

(C) a qualified bond purchase plan described in section 405(a),

(D) an annuity contract described in section 403(b),

(E) an individual retirement account described in section 408(a),

(F) an individual retirement annuity described in section 408(b),

(G) a simplified employee pension, or

(H) an individual retirement bond described in section 409.

• 1978, Revenue Act of 1978 (P.L. 95-600)

P.L. 95-600, §152(g)(4):

Amended Code Sec. 415(k)(1) by redesignating subparagraph (G) as subparagraph (H), by striking out "or" at the end of Code Sec. 415(k)(1)(F), and by inserting a new Code Sec. 415(k)(1)(G). **Effective** for tax years beginning after 12-31-78.

• 1974, Employee Retirement Income Security Act of 1974 (P.L. 93-406)

P.L. 93-406, §2004(a)(2):

Added Code Sec. 415(k). **Effective**, generally, for years beginning after 1975. For special effective dates and transitional rules governing this section, see the footnote to Code Sec. 415(a) and the historical note for §1017, P. L. 93-406, following the text of Code Sec. 410(d).

[Sec. 415(l)]

(l) TREATMENT OF CERTAIN MEDICAL BENEFITS.—

(1) IN GENERAL.—For purposes of this section, contributions allocated to any individual medical benefit account which is part of a pension or annuity plan shall be treated as an annual addition to a defined contribution plan for purposes of subsection (c). Subparagraph (B) of subsection (c)(1) shall not apply to any amount treated as an annual addition under the preceding sentence.

(2) INDIVIDUAL MEDICAL BENEFIT ACCOUNT.—For purposes of paragraph (1), the term "individual medical benefit account" means any separate account—

(A) which is established for a participant under a pension or annuity plan, and

(B) from which benefits described in section 401(h) are payable solely to such participant, his spouse, or his dependents.

Amendments

• 2005, Gulf Opportunity Zone Act of 2005 (P.L. 109-135)

P.L. 109-135, §412(y):

Amended Code Sec. 415(l)(1) by striking "individual medical account" and inserting "individual medical benefit account". **Effective** 12-21-2005.

• 1986, Tax Reform Act of 1986 (P.L. 99-514)

P.L. 99-514, §1852(h)(2):

Amended Code Sec. 415(l)(1) by adding at the end thereof a new sentence. **Effective** as if included in the provision of P.L. 98-369 to which it relates.

P.L. 99-514, §1852(h)(3):

Amended Code Sec. 415(l) by striking out "a defined benefit plan" each place it appears and inserting in lieu thereof "a pension or annuity plan". **Effective** as if included in the provision of P.L. 98-369 to which it relates.

• 1984, Deficit Reduction Act of 1984 (P.L. 98-369)

P.L. 98-369, §528(a):

Amended Code Sec. 415 by adding at the end thereof a new subsection (l). **Effective** for years beginning after 3-31-84.

[Sec. 415(m)]

(m) TREATMENT OF QUALIFIED GOVERNMENTAL EXCESS BENEFIT ARRANGEMENTS.—

(1) GOVERNMENTAL PLAN NOT AFFECTED.—In determining whether a governmental plan (as defined in section 414(d)) meets the requirements of this section, benefits provided under a qualified governmental excess benefit arrangement shall not be taken into account. Income accruing to a governmental plan (or to a trust that is maintained solely for the purpose of providing benefits under a qualified governmental excess benefit arrangement) in respect of a qualified governmental excess benefit arrangement shall constitute income derived from the exercise of an essential governmental function upon which such governmental plan (or trust) shall be exempt from tax under section 115.

(2) TAXATION OF PARTICIPANT.—For purposes of this chapter—

(A) the taxable year or years for which amounts in respect of a qualified governmental excess benefit arrangement are includible in gross income by a participant, and

(B) the treatment of such amounts when so includible by the participant,

shall be determined as if such qualified governmental excess benefit arrangement were treated as a plan for the deferral of compensation which is maintained by a corporation not exempt from tax under this chapter and which does not meet the requirements for qualification under section 401.

(3) QUALIFIED GOVERNMENTAL EXCESS BENEFIT ARRANGEMENT.—For purposes of this subsection, the term "qualified governmental excess benefit arrangement" means a portion of a governmental plan if—

(A) such portion is maintained solely for the purpose of providing to participants in the plan that part of the participant's annual benefit otherwise payable under the terms of the plan that exceeds the limitations on benefits imposed by this section,

(B) under such portion no election is provided at any time to the participant (directly or indirectly) to defer compensation, and

(C) benefits described in subparagraph (A) are not paid from a trust forming a part of such governmental plan unless such trust is maintained solely for the purpose of providing such benefits.

Amendments

• 1996, Small Business Job Protection Act of 1996 (P.L. 104-188)

P.L. 104-188, §1444(b)(1):

Amended Code Sec. 415 by adding at the end a new subsection (m). **Effective** for years beginning after 12-31-94. For a special rule, see Act Sec. 1444(e)(2), below.

P.L. 104-188, §1444(e)(2), provides:

(2) TREATMENT FOR YEARS BEGINNING BEFORE JANUARY 1, 1995.—Nothing in the amendments made by this section shall be construed to imply that a governmental plan (as defined in section 414(d) of the Internal Revenue Code of 1986) fails to satisfy the requirements of section 415 of such Code for any taxable year beginning before January 1, 1995.

[Sec. 415(n)]

(n) SPECIAL RULES RELATING TO PURCHASE OF PERMISSIVE SERVICE CREDIT.—

(1) IN GENERAL.—If a participant makes 1 or more contributions to a defined benefit governmental plan (within the meaning of section 414(d)) to purchase permissive service credit under such plan, then the requirements of this section shall be treated as met only if—

(A) the requirements of subsection (b) are met, determined by treating the accrued benefit derived from all such contributions as an annual benefit for purposes of subsection (b), or

(B) the requirements of subsection (c) are met, determined by treating all such contributions as annual additions for purposes of subsection (c).

(2) APPLICATION OF LIMIT.—For purposes of—

(A) applying paragraph (1)(A), the plan shall not fail to meet the reduced limit under subsection (b)(2)(C) solely by reason of this subsection, and

(B) applying pargraph (1)(B), the plan shall not fail to meet the percentage limitation under subsection (c)(1)(B) solely by reason of this subsection.

(3) PERMISSIVE SERVICE CREDIT.—For purposes of this subsection—

(A) IN GENERAL.—The term "permissive service credit" means service credit—

(i) recognized by the governmental plan for purposes of calculating a participant's benefit under the plan,

(ii) which such participant has not received under such governmental plan, and

(iii) which such participant may receive only by making a voluntary additional contribution, in an amount determined under such governmental plan, which does not exceed the amount necessary to fund the benefit attributable to such service credit.

Such term may include service credit for periods for which there is no performance of service, and, notwithstanding clause (ii), may include service credited in order to provide an increased benefit for service credit which a participant is receiving under the plan.

(B) LIMITATION ON NONQUALIFIED SERVICE CREDIT.—A plan shall fail to meet the requirements of this section if—

(i) more than 5 years of nonqualified service credit are taken into account for purposes of this subsection, or

(ii) any nonqualified service credit is taken into account under this subsection before the employee has at least 5 years of participation under the plan.

(C) NONQUALIFIED SERVICE CREDIT.—For purposes of subparagraph (B), the term "nonqualified service credit" means permissive service credit other than that allowed with respect to—

(i) service (including parental, medical, sabbatical, and similar leave) as an employee of the Government of the United States, any State or political subdivision thereof, or any agency or instrumentality of any of the foregoing (other than military service or service for credit which was obtained as a result of a repayment described in subsection (k)(3)),

(ii) service (including parental, medical, sabbatical, and similar leave) as an employee (other than as an employee described in clause (i)) of an educational organization described in section 170(b)(1)(A)(ii) which is a public, private, or sectarian school which provides elementary or secondary education (through grade 12), or a comparable level of education, as determined under the applicable law of the jurisdiction in which the service was performed,

(iii) service as an employee of an association of employees who are described in clause (i), or

(iv) military service (other than qualified military service under section 414(u)) recognized by such governmental plan.

In the case of service described in clause (i), (ii), or (iii), such service will be nonqualified service if recognition of such service would cause a participant to receive a retirement benefit for the same service under more than one plan.

(D) SPECIAL RULES FOR TRUSTEE-TO-TRUSTEE TRANSFERS.—In the case of a trustee-to-trustee transfer to which section 403(b)(13)(A) or 457(e)(17)(A) applies (without regard to whether the transfer is made between plans maintained by the same employer)—

(i) the limitations of subparagraph (B) shall not apply in determining whether the transfer is for the purchase of permissive service credit, and

(ii) the distribution rules applicable under this title to the defined benefit governmental plan to which any amounts are so transferred shall apply to such amounts and any benefits attributable to such amounts.

Amendments

• 2006, Pension Protection Act of 2006 (P.L. 109-280)

P.L. 109-280, §811, provides:

SEC. 811. PENSIONS AND INDIVIDUAL RETIREMENT ARRANGEMENT PROVISIONS OF ECONOMIC GROWTH AND TAX RELIEF RECONCILIATION ACT OF 2001 MADE PERMANENT.

Title IX of the Economic Growth and Tax Relief Reconciliation Act of 2001 [P.L. 107-16] shall not apply to the provisions of, and amendments made by, subtitles A through F of title VI [§§601-666]of such Act (relating to pension and individual retirement arrangement provisions).

P.L. 109-280, §821(a)(1)-(2):

Amended Code Sec. 415(n) by striking "an employee" and inserting "a participant" in paragraph (1), and by adding a new flush sentence at the end of paragraph (3)(A). **Effective** as if included in the amendments made by section 1526 of the Taxpayer Relief Act of 1997 (P.L. 105-34) [**effective** for permissive service credit contributions made in years beginning after 12-31-1997.—CCH].

P.L. 109-280, §821(b):

Amended Code Sec. 415(n)(3) by adding at the end a new subparagraph (D). **Effective** as if included in the amendments made by section 647 of the Economic Growth and Tax Relief Reconciliation Act of 2001 (P.L. 107-16) [**effective** for trustee-to-trustee transfers after 12-31-2001.—CCH].

P.L. 109-280, §821(c)(1)-(3):

Amended Code Sec. 415(n)(3) by striking "permissive service credit attributable to nonqualified service" each place it appears in subparagraph (B) and inserting "nonqualified service credit", by striking so much of subparagraph (C) as precedes clause (i) and inserting "(C) NONQUALIFIED SERVICE CREDIT.—For purposes of subparagraph (B), the term 'nonqualified service credit' means permissive service credit other than that allowed with respect to—", and by striking "elementary or secondary education (through grade 12), as determined under State law" in subparagraph (C)(ii) and inserting "elementary or secondary education (through grade 12), or a comparable level of education, as determined under the applicable law of the jurisdiction in which the service was performed". **Effective** as if included in the amendments made by section 1526 of the Taxpayer Relief Act of 1997 (P.L. 105-34) [**effective** for permissive service credit contributions made in years beginning after 12-31-1997.—CCH]. Prior to being stricken, so much of Code Sec. 415(n)(3)(C) as precedes clause (i) read as follows:

(C) NONQUALIFIED SERVICE.—For purposes of subparagraph (B), the term "nonqualified service" means service for which permissive service credit is allowed other than—

• 2005, Gulf Opportunity Zone Act of 2005 (P.L. 109-135)

P.L. 109-135, §412(z):

Amended the matter following Code Sec. 415(n)(3)(C)(iv) by striking "clauses" and inserting "clause". **Effective** 12-21-2005.

• 2001, Economic Growth and Tax Relief Reconciliation Act of 2001 (P.L. 107-16)

P.L. 107-16, §901(a)-(b), provides [but see P.L. 109-280, §811, above]:

SEC. 901. SUNSET OF PROVISIONS OF ACT.

(a) IN GENERAL.—All provisions of, and amendments made by, this Act shall not apply—

(1) to taxable, plan, or limitation years beginning after December 31, 2010, or

(2) in the case of title V, to estates of decedents dying, gifts made, or generation skipping transfers, after December 31, 2010.

(b) APPLICATION OF CERTAIN LAWS.—The Internal Revenue Code of 1986 and the Employee Retirement Income Security Act of 1974 shall be applied and administered to years, estates, gifts, and transfers described in subsection (a) as if the provisions and amendments described in subsection (a) had never been enacted.

• 1997, Taxpayer Relief Act of 1997 (P.L. 105-34)

P.L. 105-34, §1526(a):

Amended Code Sec. 415 by adding at the end a new subsection (n). **Effective**, generally, for permissive service credit contributions made in years beginning after 12-31-97. For a transition rule, see Act Sec. 1526(c)(2)(A)-(B), below.

P.L. 105-34, §1526(c)(2)(A)-(B), provides:

(2) TRANSITION RULE.—

(A) IN GENERAL.—In the case of an eligible participant in a governmental plan (within the meaning of section 414(d) of the Internal Revenue Code of 1986), the limitations of section 415(c)(1) of such Code shall not be applied to reduce the amount of permissive service credit which may be purchased to an amount less than the amount which was allowed to be purchased under the terms of the plan as in effect on the date of the enactment of this Act.

(B) ELIGIBLE PARTICIPANT.—For purposes of subparagraph (A), an eligible participant is an individual who first became a participant in the plan before the first plan year beginning after the last day of the calendar year in which the next regular session (following the date of the enactment of this Act) of the governing body with authority to amend the plan ends.

[Sec. 416]

SEC. 416. SPECIAL RULES FOR TOP-HEAVY PLANS.

[Sec. 416(a)]

(a) GENERAL RULE.—A trust shall not constitute a qualified trust under section 401(a) for any plan year if the plan of which it is a part is a top-heavy plan for such plan year unless such plan meets—

(1) the vesting requirements of subsection (b), and

(2) the minimum benefit requirements of subsection (c).

Amendments

• **1986, Tax Reform Act of 1986 (P.L. 99-514)**

P.L. 99-514, §1106(d)(3)(A):

Amended Code Sec. 416(a) by inserting "and" at the end of paragraph (1), by striking out ", and" at the end of paragraph (2) and inserting in lieu thereof a period, and by striking out paragraph (3). For the **effective** date, see Act Sec. 1106(i) following Code Sec. 415. Prior to amendment, Code Sec. 416(a)(3) read as follows:

(3) the limitation on compensation requirement of subsection (d).

[Sec. 416(b)]

(b) VESTING REQUIREMENTS.—

(1) IN GENERAL.—A plan satisfies the requirements of this subsection if it satisfies the requirements of either of the following subparagraphs:

(A) 3-YEAR VESTING.—A plan satisfies the requirements of this subparagraph if an employee who has completed at least 3 years of service with the employer or employers maintaining the plan has a nonforfeitable right to 100 percent of his accrued benefit derived from employer contributions.

(B) 6-YEAR GRADED VESTING.—A plan satisfies the requirements of this subparagraph if an employee has a nonforfeitable right to a percentage of his accrued benefit derived from employer contributions determined under the following table:

Years of service:	*The nonforfeitable percentage is:*
2	20
3	40
4	60
5	80
6 or more	100

(2) CERTAIN RULES MADE APPLICABLE.—Except to the extent inconsistent with the provisions of this subsection, the rules of section 411 shall apply for purposes of this subsection.

[Sec. 416(c)]

(c) PLAN MUST PROVIDE MINIMUM BENEFITS.—

(1) DEFINED BENEFIT PLANS.—

(A) IN GENERAL.—A defined benefit plan meets the requirements of this subsection if the accrued benefit derived from employer contributions of each participant who is a non-key employee, when expressed as an annual retirement benefit, is not less than the applicable percentage of the participant's average compensation for years in the testing period.

(B) APPLICABLE PERCENTAGE.—For purposes of subparagraph (A), the term "applicable percentage" means the lesser of—

(i) 2 percent multiplied by the number of years of service with the employer, or

(ii) 20 percent.

(C) YEARS OF SERVICE.—For purposes of this paragraph—

(i) IN GENERAL.—Except as provided in clause (ii) or (iii), years of service shall be determined under the rules of paragraphs (4), (5), and (6) of section 411(a).

(ii) EXCEPTION FOR YEARS DURING WHICH PLAN WAS NOT TOP-HEAVY.—A year of service with the employer shall not be taken into account under this paragraph if—

(I) the plan was not a top-heavy plan for any plan year ending during such year of service, or

(II) such year of service was completed in a plan year beginning before January 1, 1984.

(iii) EXCEPTION FOR PLAN UNDER WHICH NO KEY EMPLOYEE (OR FORMER KEY EMPLOYEE) BENEFITS FOR PLAN YEAR.—For purposes of determining an employee's years of service with the employer, any service with the employer shall be disregarded to the extent that such service occurs during a plan year when the plan benefits (within the meaning of section 410(b)) no key employee or former key employee.

(D) AVERAGE COMPENSATION FOR HIGH 5 YEARS.—For purposes of this paragraph—

(i) IN GENERAL.—A participant's testing period shall be the period of consecutive years (not exceeding 5) during which the participant had the greatest aggregate compensation from the employer.

(ii) YEAR MUST BE INCLUDED IN YEAR OF SERVICE.—The years taken into account under clause (i) shall be properly adjusted for years not included in a year of service.

(iii) CERTAIN YEARS NOT TAKEN INTO ACCOUNT.—Except to the extent provided in the plan, a year shall not be taken into account under clause (i) if—

(I) such year ends in a plan year beginning before January 1, 1984, or

(II) such year begins after the close of the last year in which the plan was a top-heavy plan.

(E) ANNUAL RETIREMENT BENEFIT.—For purposes of this paragraph, the term "annual retirement benefit" means a benefit payable annually in the form of a single life annuity (with no ancillary benefits) beginning at the normal retirement age under the plan.

(2) DEFINED CONTRIBUTION PLANS.—

(A) IN GENERAL.—A defined contribution plan meets the requirements of the subsection if the employer contribution for the year for each participant who is a non-key employee is not less than 3 percent of such participant's compensation (within the meaning of section 415). Employer matching contributions (as defined in section 401(m)(4)(A)) shall be taken into account for purposes of this subparagraph (and any reduction under this sentence shall not be taken into account in determining whether section 401(k)(4)(A) applies).

(B) SPECIAL RULE WHERE MAXIMUM CONTRIBUTION LESS THAN 3 PERCENT.—

(i) IN GENERAL.—The percentage referred to in subparagraph (A) for any year shall not exceed the percentage at which contributions are made (or required to be made) under the plan for the year for the key employee for whom such percentage is the highest for the year.

(ii) TREATMENT OF AGGREGATION GROUPS.—

(I) For purposes of this subparagraph, all defined contribution plans required to be included in an aggregation group under subsection (g)(2)(A)(i) shall be treated as one plan.

(II) This subparagraph shall not apply to any plan required to be included in an aggregation group if such plan enables a defined benefit plan required to be included in such group to meet the requirements of section 401(a)(4) or 410.

Amendments

• 2006, Pension Protection Act of 2006 (P.L. 109-280)

P.L. 109-280, §811, provides:

SEC. 811. PENSIONS AND INDIVIDUAL RETIREMENT ARRANGEMENT PROVISIONS OF ECONOMIC GROWTH AND TAX RELIEF RECONCILIATION ACT OF 2001 MADE PERMANENT.

Title IX of the Economic Growth and Tax Relief Reconciliation Act of 2001 [P.L. 107-16] shall not apply to the provisions of, and amendments made by, subtitles A through F of title VI [§§601-666]of such Act (relating to pension and individual retirement arrangement provisions).

• 2002, Job Creation and Worker Assistance Act of 2002 (P.L. 107-147)

P.L. 107-147, §411(k)(1):

Amended Code Sec. 416(c)(1)(C)(iii) by striking "EXCEPTION FOR FROZEN PLAN" and inserting "EXCEPTION FOR PLAN UNDER WHICH NO KEY EMPLOYEE (OR FORMER KEY EMPLOYEE) BENEFITS FOR PLAN YEAR". **E ffective** as if included in the provision of P.L. 107-16 to which it relates [**effective** for years beginning after 12-31-2001.—CCH].

• 2001, Economic Growth and Tax Relief Reconciliation Act of 2001 (P.L. 107-16)

P.L. 107-16, §613(b):

Amended Code Sec. 416(c)(2)(A) by adding at the end a new sentence. **Effective** for years beginning after 12-31-2001.

P.L. 107-16, §613(e)(A)-(B)[(1)-(2)]:

Amended Code Sec. 416(c)(1)(C) by striking "clause (ii)" in clause (i) and inserting "clause (ii) or (iii)"; and by adding at the end a new clause (iii). **Effective** for years beginning after 12-31-2001.

P.L. 107-16, §901(a)-(b), provides [but see P.L. 109-280, §811, above]:

SEC. 901. SUNSET OF PROVISIONS OF ACT.

(a) IN GENERAL.—All provisions of, and amendments made by, this Act shall not apply—

(1) to taxable, plan, or limitation years beginning after December 31, 2010, or

(2) in the case of title V, to estates of decedents dying, gifts made, or generation skipping transfers, after December 31, 2010.

(b) APPLICATION OF CERTAIN LAWS.—The Internal Revenue Code of 1986 and the Employee Retirement Income Security Act of 1974 shall be applied and administered to years, estates, gifts, and transfers described in subsection (a) as if the provisions and amendments described in subsection (a) had never been enacted.

• 1986, Tax Reform Act of 1986 (P.L. 99-514)

P.L. 99-514, §1106(d)(3)(B)(ii):

Amended Code Sec. 416(c)(2)(B) by striking out clause (ii) and by redesignating clause (iii) as clause (ii). For the **effective** date, see Act Sec. 1106(i) following Code Sec. 415. Prior to amendment, Code Sec. 416(c)(2)(B)(ii) read as follows:

(ii) DETERMINATION OF PERCENTAGE.—The determination referred to in clause (i) shall be determined for each key employee by dividing the contributions for such employee by so much of his total compensation for the year as does not exceed $200,000.

• 1984, Deficit Reduction Act of 1984 (P.L. 98-369)

P.L. 98-369, §524(c)(1):

Amended Code Sec. 416(c)(2) by striking out subparagraph (C). **Effective** for plan years beginning after 12-31-84. Prior to amendment, subparagraph (C) read as follows:

(C) Certain Amounts Not Taken Into Account.—For purposes of this paragraph, any employer contribution attributable to a salary reduction or similar arrangement shall not be taken into account.

P.L. 98-369, §524(e), provides:

(e) Qualification Requirements Modified if Regulations Not Issued.—

(1) In general.—If the Secretary of the Treasury or his delegate does not publish final regulations under section 416 of the Internal Revenue Code of 1954 (as in effect on the day before the date of the enactment of this Act) before January 1, 1985, the Secretary shall publish before such date plan amendment provisions which may be incorporated in a plan to meet the requirements of section 401(a)(10)(B)(ii) of such Code.

(2) Effect of Incorporation.—If a plan is amended to incorporate the plan amendment provisions described in paragraph (1), such plan shall be treated as meeting the requirements of section 401(a)(10)(B)(ii) of the Internal Revenue Code of 1954 during the period such amendment is in effect by not later than 6 months after the final regulations described in paragraph (1) are published.

(3) Failure by Secretary to Publish.—If the Secretary of the Treasury or his delegate does not publish plan amendment provisions described in paragraph (1), the plan shall be treated as meeting the requirements of section 401(a)(10)(B) of the Internal Revenue Code of 1954 if—

(A) such plan is amended to incorporate such requirements by reference, except that

(B) in the case of any optional requirement under section 416 of such Code, if such amendment does not specify the manner in which such requirement will be met, the employer shall be treated as having elected the requirement with respect to each employee which provides the maximum vested accrued benefit for such employee.

[Sec. 416(d)—Repealed]

• 1986, Tax Reform Act of 1986 (P.L. 99-514)

P.L. 99-514, §1106(d)(3)(B)(i):

Repealed Code Sec. 416(d). For the **effective** date, see Act Sec. 1106(i) following Code Sec. 415. Prior to amendment, Code Sec. 416(d) read as follows:

(d) NOT MORE THAN $200,000 IN ANNUAL COMPENSATION TAKEN INTO ACCOUNT.—

(1) IN GENERAL.—A plan meets the requirements of this subsection if the annual compensation of each employee taken into account under the plan does not exceed the first $200,000.

(2) COST-OF-LIVING ADJUSTMENTS.—The Secretary shall annually adjust the $200,000 amount contained in paragraph (1) of this subsection and in clause (ii) of subsection (c)(2)(B) at the same time and in the same manner as he adjusts the dollar amount contained in section 415(c)(1)(A).

• 1984, Deficit Reduction Act of 1984 (P.L. 98-369)

P.L. 98-369, §713(f)(5)(A):

Amended Code Sec. 416(d)(2) by striking out "in the same manner" and inserting in lieu thereof "at the same time and in the same manner". **Effective** as if included in the provision of P.L. 97-248 to which it relates.

[Sec. 416(e)]

(e) PLAN MUST MEET REQUIREMENTS WITHOUT TAKING INTO ACCOUNT SOCIAL SECURITY AND SIMILAR CONTRIBUTIONS AND BENEFITS.—A top-heavy plan shall not be treated as meeting the requirement of subsection (b) or (c) unless such plan meets such requirement without taking into account contributions or benefits under chapter 2 (relating to tax on self-employment income), chapter 21 (relating to Federal Insurance Contributions Act), title II of the Social Security Act, or any other Federal or State law.

[Sec. 416(f)]

(f) COORDINATION WHERE EMPLOYER HAS 2 OR MORE PLANS.—The Secretary shall prescribe such regulations as may be necessary or appropriate to carry out the purposes of this section where the employer has 2 or more plans including (but not limited to) regulations to prevent inappropriate omissions or required duplication of minimum benefits or contributions.

Amendments

• 1984, Deficit Reduction Act of 1984 (P.L. 98-369)

P.L. 98-369, §713(f)(6)(A):

Amended Code Sec. 416(f) by striking out "require" and inserting in lieu thereof "required". **Effective** as if included in the provision of P.L. 97-248 to which it relates.

[Sec. 416(g)]

(g) TOP-HEAVY PLAN DEFINED.—For purposes of this section—

(1) IN GENERAL.—

(A) PLANS NOT REQUIRED TO BE AGGREGATED.—Except as provided in subparagraph (B), the term "top-heavy plan" means, with respect to any plan year—

(i) any defined benefit plan if, as of the determination date, the present value of the cumulative accrued benefits under the plan for key employees exceeds 60 percent of the present value of the cumulative accrued benefits under the plan for all employees, and

(ii) any defined contribution plan if, as of the determination date, the aggregate of the accounts of key employees under the plan exceeds 60 percent of the aggregate of the accounts of all employees under such plan.

(B) AGGREGATED PLANS.—Each plan of an employer required to be included in an aggregation group shall be treated as a top-heavy plan if such group is a top-heavy group.

(2) AGGREGATION.—For purposes of this subsection—

(A) AGGREGATION GROUP.—

(i) REQUIRED AGGREGATION.—The term "aggregation group" means—

(I) each plan of the employer in which a key employee is a participant, and

(II) each other plan of the employer which enables any plan described in subclause (I) to meet the requirements of section 401(a)(4) or 410.

(ii) PERMISSIVE AGGREGATION.—The employer may treat any plan not required to be included in an aggregation group under clause (i) as being part of such group if such group would continue to meet the requirements of sections 401(a)(4) and 410 with such plan being taken into account.

(B) TOP-HEAVY GROUP.—The term "top-heavy group" means any aggregation group if—

(i) the sum (as of the determination date) of—

(I) the present value of the cumulative accrued benefits for key employees under all defined benefit plans included in such group, and

(II) the aggregate of the accounts of key employees under all defined contribution plans included in such group,

(ii) exceeds 60 percent of a similar sum determined for all employees.

(3) DISTRIBUTIONS DURING LAST YEAR BEFORE DETERMINATION DATE TAKEN INTO ACCOUNT.—

(A) IN GENERAL.—For purposes of determining—

(i) the present value of the cumulative accrued benefit for any employee, or

(ii) the amount of the account of any employee,

such present value or amount shall be increased by the aggregate distributions made with respect to such employee under the plan during the 1-year period ending on the determination date. The preceding sentence shall also apply to distributions under a terminated plan which if it had not been terminated would have been required to be included in an aggregation group.

(B) 5-YEAR PERIOD IN CASE OF IN-SERVICE DISTRIBUTION.—In the case of any distribution made for a reason other than severance from employment, death, or disability, subparagraph (A) shall be applied by substituting "5-year period" for "1-year period".

(4) OTHER SPECIAL RULES.—For purposes of this subsection—

(A) ROLLOVER CONTRIBUTIONS TO PLAN NOT TAKEN INTO ACCOUNT.—Except to the extent provided in regulations, any rollover contribution (or similar transfer) initiated by the employee and made after December 31, 1983, to a plan shall not be taken into account with respect to the transferee plan for purposes of determining whether such plan is a top-heavy plan (or whether any aggregation group which includes such plan is a top-heavy group).

(B) BENEFITS NOT TAKEN INTO ACCOUNT IF EMPLOYEE CEASES TO BE KEY EMPLOYEE.—If any individual is a non-key employee with respect to any plan for any plan year, but such individual was a key employee with respect to such plan for any prior plan year, any accrued benefit for such employee (and the account of such employee) shall not be taken into account.

(C) DETERMINATION DATE.—The term "determination date" means, with respect to any plan year—

(i) the last day of the preceding plan year, or

(ii) in the case of the first plan year of any plan, the last day of such plan year.

(D) YEARS.—To the extent provided in regulations, this section shall be applied on the basis of any year specified in such regulations in lieu of plan years.

(E) BENEFITS NOT TAKEN INTO ACCOUNT IF EMPLOYEE NOT EMPLOYED FOR LAST YEAR BEFORE DETERMINATION DATE.—If any individual has not performed services for the employer maintaining the plan at any time during the 1-year period ending on the determination date, any accrued benefit for such individual (and the account of such individual) shall not be taken into account.

(F) ACCRUED BENEFITS TREATED AS ACCRUING RATABLY.—The accrued benefit of any employee (other than a key employee) shall be determined—

(i) under the method which is used for accrual purposes for all plans of the employer, or

(ii) if there is no method described in clause (i), as if such benefit accrued not more rapidly than the slowest accrual rate permitted under section 411(b)(1)(C).

(G) SIMPLE RETIREMENT ACCOUNTS.—The term "top-heavy plan" shall not include a simple retirement account under section 408(p).

(H) CASH OR DEFERRED ARRANGEMENTS USING ALTERNATIVE METHODS OF MEETING NONDISCRIMINATION REQUIREMENTS.—The term "top-heavy plan" shall not include a plan which consists solely of—

(i) a cash or deferred arrangement which meets the requirements of section 401(k)(12) or 401(k)(13), and

(ii) matching contributions with respect to which the requirements of section 401(m)(11) or 401(m)(12) are met.

If, but for this subparagraph, a plan would be treated as a top-heavy plan because it is a member of an aggregation group which is a top-heavy group, contributions under the plan may be taken into account in determining whether any other plan in the group meets the requirements of subsection (c)(2).

Amendments

• 2006, Pension Protection Act of 2006 (P.L. 109-280)

P.L. 109-280, §811, provides:

SEC. 811. PENSIONS AND INDIVIDUAL RETIREMENT ARRANGEMENT PROVISIONS OF ECONOMIC GROWTH AND TAX RELIEF RECONCILIATION ACT OF 2001 MADE PERMANENT.

Title IX of the Economic Growth and Tax Relief Reconciliation Act of 2001 [P.L. 107-16] shall not apply to the provisions of, and amendments made by, subtitles A through F of title VI [§§601-666]of such Act (relating to pension and individual retirement arrangement provisions).

P.L. 109-280, §902(c)(1):

Amended Code Sec. 416(g)(4)(H)(i) by inserting "or 401(k)(13)" after "section 401(k)(12)". **Effective** for plan years beginning after 12-31-2007.

P.L. 109-280, §902(c)(2):

Amended Code Sec. 416(g)(4)(H)(ii) by inserting "or 401(m)(12)" after "section 401(m)(11)". **Effective** for plan years beginning after 12-31-2007.

• 2002, Job Creation and Worker Assistance Act of 2002 (P.L. 107-147)

P.L. 107-147, §411(k)(2):

Amended Code Sec. 416(g)(3)(B) by striking "separation from service" and inserting "severance from employment". **Effective** as if included in the provision of P.L. 107-16 to which it relates [**effective** for years beginning after 12-31-2001.—CCH].

• 2001, Economic Growth and Tax Relief Reconciliation Act of 2001 (P.L. 107-16)

P.L. 107-16, §613(c)(1):

Amended Code Sec. 416(g)(3). **Effective** for years beginning after 12-31-2001. Prior to amendment, Code Sec. 416(g)(3) read as follows:

(3) DISTRIBUTIONS DURING LAST 5 YEARS TAKEN INTO ACCOUNT.—For purposes of determining—

(A) the present value of the cumulative accrued benefit for any employee, or

(B) the amount of the account of any employee,

such present value or amount shall be increased by the aggregate distributions made with respect to such employee under the plan during the 5-year period ending on the determination date. The preceding sentence shall also apply to distributions under a terminated plan which if it had not been terminated would have been required to be included in an aggregation group.

P.L. 107-16, §613(c)(2)(A)-(B):

Amended Code Sec. 416(g)(4)(E) by striking "LAST 5 YEARS" in the heading and inserting "LAST YEAR BEFORE DETERMINATION DATE"; and by striking "5-year period" and inserting "1-year period". **Effective** for years beginning after 12-31-2001.

P.L. 107-16, §613(d):

Amended Code Sec. 416(g)(4) by adding at the end a new subparagraph (H). **Effective** for years beginning after 12-31-2001.

P.L. 107-16, §901(a)-(b), provides [but see P.L. 109-280, §811, above]:

SEC. 901. SUNSET OF PROVISIONS OF ACT.

(a) IN GENERAL.—All provisions of, and amendments made by, this Act shall not apply—

(1) to taxable, plan, or limitation years beginning after December 31, 2010, or

(2) in the case of title V, to estates of decedents dying, gifts made, or generation skipping transfers, after December 31, 2010.

(b) APPLICATION OF CERTAIN LAWS.—The Internal Revenue Code of 1986 and the Employee Retirement Income Security Act of 1974 shall be applied and administered to years, estates, gifts, and transfers described in subsection (a) as if the provisions and amendments described in subsection (a) had never been enacted.

• 1996, Small Business Job Protection Act of 1996 (P.L. 104-188)

P.L. 104-188, §1421(b)(7):

Amended Code Sec. 416(g)(4) by adding at the end a new subparagraph (G). **Effective** for tax years beginning after 12-31-96.

• 1986, Tax Reform Act of 1986 (P.L. 99-514)

P.L. 99-514, §1852(d)(2):

Amended Code Sec. 416(g)(4)(E). **Effective** as if included in the provision of P.L. 98-369 to which it relates. Prior to amendment, Code Sec. 416(g)(4)(E) read as follows:

(E) BENEFITS NOT TAKEN INTO ACCOUNT IF EMPLOYEE NOT EMPLOYED FOR LAST 5 YEARS.—If any individual has not received any compensation from any employer maintaining the plan (other than benefits under the plan) at any time during the 5-year period ending on the determination date, any accrued benefit for such individual (and the account of such individual) shall not be taken into account.

P.L. 99-514, §1118(a):

Amended Code Sec. 416(g)(4) by adding at the end thereof new subparagraph (F). **Effective** for plan years beginning after 12-31-86.

• 1984, Deficit Reduction Act of 1984 (P.L. 98-369)

P.L. 98-369, §524(b)(1):

Amended Code Sec. 416(g)(4) by adding new subparagraph (E). **Effective** for plan year beginning after 12-31-84.

P.L. 98-369, §713(f)(4):

Amended Code Sec. 416(g)(3) by adding at the end thereof a new sentence. **Effective** as if included in the provision of P.L. 97-248 to which it relates.

[Sec. 416(h)—Stricken]

Amendments

• 1996, Small Business Job Protection Act of 1996 (P.L. 104-188)

P.L. 104-188, §1452(c)(7):

Amended Code Sec. 416 by striking subsection (h). **Effective** for limitation years beginning after 12-31-99. Prior to being stricken, Code Sec. 416(h) read as follows:

(h) ADJUSTMENTS IN SECTION 415 LIMITS FOR TOP-HEAVY PLANS.—

(1) IN GENERAL.—In the case of any top-heavy plan, paragraphs (2)(B) and (3)(B) of section 415(e) shall be applied by substituting "1.0" for "1.25".

(2) EXCEPTION WHERE BENEFITS FOR KEY EMPLOYEES DO NOT EXCEED 90 PERCENT OF TOTAL BENEFITS AND ADDITIONAL CONTRIBUTIONS ARE MADE FOR NON-KEY EMPLOYEES.—Paragraph (1) shall not apply with respect to any top-heavy plan if the requirements of subparagraphs (A) and (B) of this paragraph are met with respect to such plan.

(A) MINIMUM BENEFIT REQUIREMENTS.—

(i) IN GENERAL.—The requirements of this subparagraph are met with respect to any top-heavy plan if such plan (and any plan required to be included in an aggregation group with such plan) meets the requirements of subsection (c) as modified by clause (ii).

(ii) MODIFICATIONS.—For purposes of clause (i)—

(I) paragraph (1)(B) of subsection (c) shall be applied by substituting "3 percent" for "2 percent", and by increasing (but not by more than 10 percentage points) 20 percent by 1 percentage point for each year for which such plan was taken into account under this subsection, and

(II) paragraph (2)(A) shall be applied by substituting "4 percent" for "3 percent".

(B) BENEFITS FOR KEY EMPLOYEES CANNOT EXCEED 90 PERCENT OF TOTAL BENEFITS.—A plan meets the requirements of this subparagraph if such plan would not be a top-heavy plan if "90 percent" were substituted for "60 percent" each place it appears in paragraphs (1)(A) and (2)(B) of subsection (g).

(3) TRANSITION RULE.—If, but for this paragraph, paragraph (1) would begin to apply with respect to any top-heavy plan, the application of paragraph (1) shall be suspended with respect to any individual so long as there are no—

(A) employer contributions, forfeitures, or voluntary nondeductible contributions allocated to such individual, or

(B) accruals for such individual under the defined benefit plan.

(4) COORDINATION WITH TRANSITIONAL RULE UNDER SECTION 415.—In the case of any top heavy plan to which paragraph (1) applies, section 415(e)(6)(B)(i) shall be applied by substituting "$41,500" for "$51,875".

[Sec. 416(i)]

(i) DEFINITIONS.—For purposes of this section—

(1) KEY EMPLOYEE.—

(A) IN GENERAL.—The term "key employee" means an employee who, at any time during the plan year, is—

(i) an officer of the employer having an annual compensation greater than $130,000,

(ii) a 5-percent owner of the employer, or

(iii) a 1-percent owner of the employer having an annual compensation from the employer of more than $150,000.

For purposes of clause (i), no more than 50 employees (or, if lesser, the greater of 3 or 10 percent of the employees) shall be treated as officers. In the case of plan years beginning after December 31, 2002, the $130,000 amount in clause (i) shall be adjusted at the same time and in the same manner as under section 415(d), except that the base period shall be the calendar quarter beginning July 1, 2001, and any increase under this sentence which is not a multiple of $5,000 shall be rounded to the next lower multiple of $5,000. Such term shall not include any officer or employee of an entity referred to in section 414(d) (relating to governmental plans). For purposes of determining the number of officers taken into account under clause (i), employees described in section 414(q)(5) shall be excluded.

(B) PERCENTAGE OWNERS.—

(i) 5-PERCENT OWNER.—For purposes of this paragraph, the term "5-percent owner" means—

(I) if the employer is a corporation, any person who owns (or is considered as owning within the meaning of section 318) more than 5 percent of the outstanding stock of the corporation or stock possessing more than 5 percent of the total combined voting power of all stock of the corporation, or

(II) if the employer is not a corporation, any person who owns more than 5 percent of the capital or profits interest in the employer.

(ii) 1-PERCENT OWNER.—For purposes of this paragraph, the term "1-percent owner" means any person who would be described in clause (i) if "1 percent" were substituted for "5 percent" each place it appears in clause (i).

(iii) CONSTRUCTIVE OWNERSHIP RULES.—For purposes of this subparagraph—

(I) subparagraph (C) of section 318(a)(2) shall be applied by substituting "5 percent" for "50 percent", and

(II) in the case of any employer which is not a corporation, ownership in such employer shall be determined in accordance with regulations prescribed by the Secretary which shall be based on principles similar to the principles of section 318 (as modified by subclause (I)).

(C) AGGREGATION RULES DO NOT APPLY FOR PURPOSES OF DETERMINING OWNERSHIP IN THE EMPLOYER.—The rules of subsections (b), (c), and (m) of section 414 shall not apply for purposes of determining ownership in the employer.

(D) COMPENSATION.—For purposes of this paragraph, the term "compensation" has the meaning given such term by section 414(q)(4).

(2) NON-KEY EMPLOYEE.—The term "non-key employee" means any employee who is not a key employee.

(3) SELF-EMPLOYED INDIVIDUALS.—In the case of a self-employed individual described in section 401(c)(1)—

(A) such individual shall be treated as an employee, and

(B) such individual's earned income (within the meaning of section 401(c)(2)) shall be treated as compensation.

(4) TREATMENT OF EMPLOYEES COVERED BY COLLECTIVE BARGAINING AGREEMENTS.—The requirements of subsections (b), (c), and (d) shall not apply with respect to any employee included in a unit of employees covered by an agreement which the Secretary of Labor finds to be a collective bargaining agreement between employee representatives and 1 or more employers if there is evidence that retirement benefits were the subject of good faith bargaining between such employee representatives and such employer or employers.

(5) TREATMENT OF BENEFICIARIES.—The terms "employee" and "key employee" include their beneficiaries.

(6) TREATMENT OF SIMPLIFIED EMPLOYEE PENSIONS.—

(A) TREATMENT AS DEFINED CONTRIBUTION PLANS.—A simplified employee pension shall be treated as a defined contribution plan.

(B) ELECTION TO HAVE DETERMINATIONS BASED ON EMPLOYER CONTRIBUTIONS.—In the case of a simplified employee pension, at the election of the employer, paragraphs (1)(A)(ii) and (2)(B) of subsection (g) shall be applied by taking into account aggregate employer contributions in lieu of the aggregate of the accounts of employees.

Amendments

• 2006, Pension Protection Act of 2006 (P.L. 109-280)

P.L. 109-280, §811, provides:

SEC. 811. PENSIONS AND INDIVIDUAL RETIREMENT ARRANGEMENT PROVISIONS OF ECONOMIC GROWTH AND TAX RELIEF RECONCILIATION ACT OF 2001 MADE PERMANENT.

Title IX of the Economic Growth and Tax Relief Reconciliation Act of 2001 [P.L. 107-16] shall not apply to the provisions of, and amendments made by, subtitles A through F of title VI [§§601-666]of such Act (relating to pension and individual retirement arrangement provisions).

• 2004, Working Families Tax Relief Act of 2004 (P.L. 108-311)

P.L. 108-311, §408(a)(16):

Amended Code Sec. 416(i)(1)(A) by striking "in the case of plan years" and inserting "In the case of plan years" in the matter following clause (iii). **Effective** 10-4-2004.

• 2001, Economic Growth and Tax Relief Reconciliation Act of 2001 (P.L. 107-16)

P.L. 107-16, §613(a)(1)(A)-(D):

Amended Code Sec. 416(i)(1)(A) by striking "or any of the 4 preceding plan years" in the matter preceding clause (i) following "during the plan year"; by striking clause (i) and inserting a new clause (i); by striking clause (ii) and redesignating clauses (iii) and (iv) as (ii) and (iii), respectively; and by striking the second sentence in the matter following clause (iii), as redesignated by Act Sec. 613(a)(1)(C), and inserting a new sentence. **Effective** for years beginning after 12-31-2001. Prior to amendment, Code Sec. 416(i)(1)(A) read as follows:

(A) IN GENERAL.—The term "key employee" means an employee who, at any time during the plan year or any of the 4 preceding plan years, is—

(i) an officer of the employer having an annual compensation greater than 50 percent of the amount in effect under section 415(b)(1)(A) for any such plan year,

(ii) 1 of the 10 employees having annual compensation from the employer of more than the limitation in effect under section 415(c)(1)(A) and owning (or considered as owning within the meaning of section 318) the largest interests in the employer,

(iii) a 5-percent owner of the employer, or

(iv) a 1-percent owner of the employer having an annual compensation from the employer of more than $150,000.

For purposes of clause (i), no more than 50 employees (or, if lesser, the greater of 3 or 10 percent of the employees) shall be treated as officers. For purposes of clause (ii), if 2 employees have the same interest in the employer, the employee having greater annual compensation from the employer shall be treated as having a larger interest. Such term shall not include any officer or employee of an entity referred to in section 414(d) (relating to governmental plans). For purposes of determining the number of officers taken into account under clause (i), employees described in section 414(q)(5) shall be excluded.

P.L. 107-16, §613(a)(2):

Amended Code Sec. 416(i)(1)(B)(iii) by striking "and subparagraph (A)(ii)" after "For purposes of this subparagraph". **Effective** for years beginning after 12-31-2001.

P.L. 107-16, §901(a)-(b), provides [but see P.L. 109-280, §811, above]:

SEC. 901. SUNSET OF PROVISIONS OF ACT.

(a) IN GENERAL.—All provisions of, and amendments made by, this Act shall not apply—

(1) to taxable, plan, or limitation years beginning after December 31, 2010, or

(2) in the case of title V, to estates of decedents dying, gifts made, or generation skipping transfers, after December 31, 2010.

(b) APPLICATION OF CERTAIN LAWS.—The Internal Revenue Code of 1986 and the Employee Retirement Income Security Act of 1974 shall be applied and administered to years, estates, gifts, and transfers described in subsection (a) as if the provisions and amendments described in subsection (a) had never been enacted.

• 1996, Small Business Job Protection Act of 1996 (P.L. 104-188)

P.L. 104-188, §1431(c)(1)(B):

Amended Code Sec. 416(i)(1)(D) by striking "section 414(q)(7)" and inserting "section 414(q)(4)". **Effective** for years beginning after 12-31-96, except that in determining whether an employee is a highly compensated employee for years beginning in 1997, the amendment shall be treated as having been in effect for years beginning in 1996.

P.L. 104-188, §1431(c)(1)(C):

Amended Code Sec. 416(i)(1)(A) by striking "section 414(q)(8)" and inserting "section 414(q)(5)". **Effective** for years beginning after 12-31-96, except that in determining whether an employee is a highly compensated employee for years beginning in 1997, the amendment shall be treated as having been in effect for years beginning in 1996.

• 1988, Technical and Miscellaneous Revenue Act of 1988 (P.L. 100-647)

P.L. 100-647, §1011(d)(8):

Amended Code Sec. 416(i)(1)(A)(i) by striking out "150 percent of the amount in effect under section 415(c)(1)(A)" and inserting in lieu thereof "50 percent of the amount in effect under section 415(b)(1)(A)". **Effective** as if included in the provision of P.L. 99-514 to which it relates.

P.L. 100-647, §1011(i)(4)(B):

Amended Code Sec. 416(i)(1)(A) by adding at the end thereof a new sentence. **Effective** as if included in the provision of P.L. 99-514 to which it relates.

P.L. 100-647, §1011(j)(3)(A):

Amended Code Sec. 416(i)(1) by adding at the end thereof new subparagraph (D). **Effective** for years beginning after 12-31-88.

• 1986, Tax Reform Act of 1986 (P.L. 99-514)

P.L. 99-514, §1852(d)(1):

Amended Code Sec. 416(i)(1)(A) by adding at the end thereof a new sentence. **Effective** as if included in the provision of P.L. 98-369 to which it relates.

• 1984, Deficit Reduction Act of 1984 (P.L. 98-369)

P.L. 98-369, §524(a)(1):

Amended Code Sec. 416(i)(1)(A)(i) by inserting "having an annual compensation greater than 150 percent of the amount in effect under section 415(c)(1)(A) for any such plan year" after "employer". **Effective** for plan years beginning after 1983.

P.L. 98-369, §713(f)(1)(A):

Amended Code Sec. 416(i)(1)(A) by striking out "any participant in an employer plan" and inserting in lieu thereof "an employee". **Effective** as if included in the provision of P.L. 97-248 to which it relates.

P.L. 98-369, §713(f)(1)(B):

Amended Code Sec. 416(i)(1)(A)(ii). **Effective** as if included in the provision of P.L. 97-248 to which it relates. Prior to amendment, Code Sec. 416(i)(1)(A)(ii) read as follows:

(ii) 1 of the 10 employees owning (or considered as owning within the meaning of section 318) the largest interests in the employer.

P.L. 98-369, §713(f)(1)(C):

Amended Code Sec. 416(i)(1)(A) by adding at the end thereof a new sentence. **Effective** as if included in the provision of P.L. 97-248 to which it relates.

P.L. 98-369, §713(f)(1)(D):

Amended Code Sec. 416(i)(1)(C) by striking out "DETERMINING 5-PERCENT OR 1-PERCENT OWNERS" in the subparagraph heading and inserting in lieu thereof "DETERMINING OWNERSHIP IN THE EMPLOYER". **E ffective** as if included in the provision of P.L. 97-248 to which it relates.

P.L. 98-369, §713(f)(6)(B):

Amended Code Sec. 416(i)(1)(B)(iii) by striking out "subparagraph (A)(ii)(II)" and inserting in lieu thereof "subparagraph (A)(ii)". **Effective** as if included in the provision of P.L. 97-248 to which it relates.

• 1982, Tax Equity and Fiscal Responsibility Act of 1982 (P.L. 97-248)

P.L. 97-248, §240(a):

Added Code Sec. 416. **Effective** for years beginning after 12-31-83.

[Sec. 417]

SEC. 417. DEFINITIONS AND SPECIAL RULES FOR PURPOSES OF MINIMUM SURVIVOR ANNUITY REQUIREMENTS.

[Sec. 417(a)]

(a) ELECTION TO WAIVE QUALIFIED JOINT AND SURVIVOR ANNUITY OR QUALIFIED PRERETIREMENT SURVIVOR ANNUITY.—

(1) IN GENERAL.—A plan meets the requirements of section 401(a)(11) only if—

(A) under the plan, each participant—

(i) may elect at any time during the applicable election period to waive the qualified joint and survivor annuity form of benefit or the qualified preretirement survivor annuity form of benefit (or both),

(ii) if the participant elects a waiver under clause (i), may elect the qualified optional survivor annuity at any time during the applicable election period, and

(iii) may revoke any such election at any time during the applicable election period, and

(B) the plan meets the requirements of paragraphs (2), (3), and (4) of this subsection.

(2) SPOUSE MUST CONSENT TO ELECTION.—Each plan shall provide that an election under paragraph (1)(A)(i) shall not take effect unless—

(A) (i) the spouse of the participant consents in writing to such election, (ii) such election designates a beneficiary (or a form of benefits) which may not be changed without spousal consent (or the consent of the spouse expressly permits designations by the participant without any requirement of further consent by the spouse), and (iii) the spouse's consent acknowledges the effect of such election and is witnessed by a plan representative or a notary public, or

(B) it is established to the satisfaction of a plan representative that the consent required under subparagraph (A) may not be obtained because there is no spouse, because the spouse cannot be located, or because of such other circumstances as the Secretary may by regulations prescribe.

Any consent by a spouse (or establishment that the consent of a spouse may not be obtained) under the preceding sentence shall be effective only with respect to such spouse.

(3) PLAN TO PROVIDE WRITTEN EXPLANATIONS.—

(A) EXPLANATION OF JOINT AND SURVIVOR ANNUITY.—Each plan shall provide to each participant, within a reasonable period of time before the annuity starting date (and consistent with such regulations as the Secretary may prescribe), a written explanation of—

(i) the terms and conditions of the qualified joint and survivor annuity and of the qualified optional survivor annuity,

(ii) the participant's right to make, and the effect of, an election under paragraph (1) to waive the joint and survivor annuity form of benefit,

(iii) the rights of the participant's spouse under paragraph (2), and

(iv) the right to make, and the effect of, a revocation of an election under paragraph (1).

(B) EXPLANATION OF QUALIFIED PRERETIREMENT SURVIVOR ANNUITY.—

(i) IN GENERAL.—Each plan shall provide to each participant, within the applicable period with respect to such participant (and consistent with such regulations as the Secretary may prescribe), a written explanation with respect to the qualified preretirement survivor annuity comparable to that required under subparagraph (A).

(ii) APPLICABLE PERIOD.—For purposes of clause (i), the term "applicable period" means, with respect to a participant, whichever of the following periods ends last:

(I) The period beginning with the first day of the plan year in which the participant attains age 32 and ending with the close of the plan year preceding the plan year in which the participant attains age 35.

(II) A reasonable period after the individual becomes a participant.

(III) A reasonable period ending after paragraph (5) ceases to apply to the participant.

(IV) A reasonable period ending after section 401(a)(11) applies to the participant.

In the case of a participant who separates from service before attaining age 35, the applicable period shall be a reasonable period after separation.

(4) REQUIREMENT OF SPOUSAL CONSENT FOR USING PLAN ASSETS AS SECURITY FOR LOANS.—Each plan shall provide that, if section 401(a)(11) applies to a participant when part or all of the participant's accrued benefit is to be used as security for a loan, no portion of the participant's accrued benefit may be used as security for such loan unless—

(A) the spouse of the participant (if any) consents in writing to such use during the 90-day period ending on the date on which the loan is to be so secured, and

(B) requirements comparable to the requirements of paragraph (2) are met with respect to such consent.

(5) SPECIAL RULES WHERE PLAN FULLY SUBSIDIZES COSTS.—

(A) IN GENERAL.—The requirements of this subsection shall not apply with respect to the qualified joint and survivor annuity form of benefit or the qualified preretirement survivor annuity form of benefit, as the case may be, if such benefit may not be waived (or another beneficiary selected) and if the plan fully subsidizes the costs of such benefit.

(B) DEFINITION.—For purposes of subparagraph (A), a plan fully subsidizes the costs of a benefit if under the plan the failure to waive such benefit by a participant would not result in a decrease in any plan benefits with respect to such participant and would not result in increased contributions from such participant.

(6) APPLICABLE ELECTION PERIOD DEFINED.—For purposes of this subsection, the term "applicable election period" means—

(A) in the case of an election to waive the qualified joint and survivor annuity form of benefit, the 180-day period ending on the annuity starting date, or

(B) in the case of an election to waive the qualified preretirement survivor annuity, the period which begins on the first day of the plan year in which the participant attains age 35 and ends on the date of the participant's death.

In the case of a participant who is separated from service, the applicable election period under subparagraph (B) with respect to benefits accrued before the date of such separation from service shall not begin later than such date.

(7) SPECIAL RULES RELATING TO TIME FOR WRITTEN EXPLANATION.—Notwithstanding any other provision of this subsection—

(A) EXPLANATION MAY BE PROVIDED AFTER ANNUITY STARTING DATE.—

(i) IN GENERAL.—A plan may provide the written explanation described in paragraph (3)(A) after the annuity starting date. In any case to which this subparagraph applies, the applicable election period under paragraph (6) shall not end before the 30th day after the date on which such explanation is provided.

(ii) REGULATORY AUTHORITY.—The Secretary may by regulations limit the application of clause (i), except that such regulations may not limit the period of time by which the annuity starting date precedes the provision of the written explanation other than by providing that the annuity starting date may not be earlier than termination of employment.

(B) WAIVER OF 30-DAY PERIOD.—A plan may permit a participant to elect (with any applicable spousal consent) to waive any requirement that the written explanation be provided at least 30 days before the annuity starting date (or to waive the 30-day requirement under subparagraph (A)) if the distribution commences more than 7 days after such explanation is provided.

Amendments

• 2006, Pension Protection Act of 2006 (P.L. 109-280)

P.L. 109-280, §1004(a)(1)(A)-(C):

Amended Code Sec. 417(a)(1)(A) by striking ", and" and inserting a comma in clause (i); by redesignating clause (ii) as clause (iii); and by inserting after clause (i) a new clause (ii). **Effective** generally for plan years beginning after 12-31-2007. For a special rule, see Act Sec. 1004(c)(2), below.

P.L. 109-280, §1004(a)(3):

Amended Code Sec. 417(a)(3)(A)(i) by inserting "and of the qualified optional survivor annuity" after "annuity". **Effective** generally for plan years beginning after 12-31-2007. For a special rule, see Act Sec. 1004(c)(2), below.

P.L. 109-280, §1004(c)(2), provides:

(2) SPECIAL RULE FOR COLLECTIVELY BARGAINED PLANS.—In the case of a plan maintained pursuant to 1 or more collective bargaining agreements between employee representatives and 1 or more employers ratified on or before the date of the enactment of this Act, the amendments made by this section shall not apply to plan years beginning before the earlier of—

(A) the later of—

(i) January 1, 2008, or

(ii) the date on which the last collective bargaining agreement related to the plan terminates (determined without regard to any extension thereof after the date of enactment of this Act), or

(B) January 1, 2009.

P.L. 109-280, §1102(a)(1)(A):

Amended Code Sec. 417(a)(6)(A) by striking "90-day" and inserting "180-day". **Effective** for years beginning after 12-31-2006.

P.L. 109-280, §1102(a)(1)(B) and (3), provides:

(B) MODIFICATION OF REGULATIONS.— The Secretary of the Treasury shall modify the regulations under sections 402(f), 411(a)(11), and 417 of the Internal Revenue Code of 1986 by substituting "180 days" for "90 days" each place it appears in Treasury Regulations sections 1.402(f)-1, 1.411(a)-11(c), and 1.417(e)-1(b).

(3) EFFECTIVE DATE.—The amendments and modifications made or required by this subsection shall apply to years beginning after December 31, 2006.

• **1996, Small Business Job Protection Act of 1996 (P.L. 104-188)**

P.L. 104-188, §1451(a):

Amended Code Sec. 417(a) by adding at the end a new paragraph (7). **Effective** for plan years beginning after 12-31-96.

• **1989, Omnibus Budget Reconciliation Act of 1989 (P.L. 101-239)**

P.L. 101-239, §7862(d)(1)(A):

Amended Code Sec. 417(a)(3)(B)(ii) by striking subclause (V) and inserting at the end thereof a new flush left sentence. **Effective** as if included in the provision of P.L. 99-514 to which it relates. Prior to amendment, Code Sec. 417(a)(3)(B)(ii)(V) read as follows:

(V) A reasonable period after separation from service in case of a participant who separates before attaining age 35.

• **1986, Tax Reform Act of 1986 (P.L. 99-514)**

P.L. 99-514, §1898(b)(4)(A)(i):

Amended Code Sec. 417(a)(1)(B) by striking out "paragraphs (2) and (3)" and inserting in lieu thereof "paragraphs (2), (3), and (4)". For the **effective** date, see Act Sec. 1898(b)(4)(C), below.

P.L. 99-514, §1898(D)(4)(A)(ii):

Amended Code Sec. 417(a) by redesignating paragraphs (4) and (5) as paragraphs (5) and (6), respectively, and by inserting after paragraph (3) new paragraph (4). For the **effective** date, see Act Sec. 1898(b)(4)(C), below.

P.L. 99-514, §1898(b)(4)(C), provides:

(C) EFFECTIVE DATES.—

(i) The amendments made by this paragraph shall apply with respect to loans made after August 18, 1985.

(ii) In the case of any loan which was made on or before August 18, 1985, and which is secured by a portion of the participant's accrued benefit, nothing in the amendments made by sections 103 and 203 of the Retirement Equity Act of 1984 shall prevent any distribution required by reason of a failure to comply with the terms of such loan.

(iii) For purposes of this subparagraph, any loan which is revised, extended, renewed, or renegotiated after August 18, 1985, shall be treated as made after August 18, 1985.

P.L. 99-514, §1898(b)(5)(A):

Amended Code Sec. 417(a)(3)(B). **Effective** as if included in the provision of P.L. 98-397 to which it relates. Prior to amendment, Code Sec. 417(a)(3)(B) read as follows:

(B) EXPLANATION OF QUALIFIED PRERETIREMENT SURVIVOR ANNUITY.—Each plan shall provide to each participant, within the period beginning with the first day of the plan year in which the participant attains age 32 and ending with the close of the plan year preceding the plan year in which the participant attains age 35 (and consistent with such regulations as the Secretary may prescribe), a written explanation with respect to the qualified preretirement survivor annuity comparable to that required under subparagraph (A).

P.L. 99-514, §1898(b)(6)(A):

Amended Code Sec. 417(a)(2)(A). **Effective** for plan years beginning after 10-22-86. Prior to amendment, Code Sec. 417(a)(2)(A) read as follows:

(A) the spouse of the participant consents in writing to such election, and the spouse's consent acknowledges the effect of such election and is witnessed by a plan representative or a notary public, or

P.L. 99-514, §1898(b)(11)(A):

Amended Code Sec. 417(a)(5)(A) (as redesignated by Act Sec. 1898(b)(4)(A)) by striking out "if the plan" and inserting in lieu thereof "if such benefit may not be waived (or another beneficiary selected) and if the plan". **Effective** as if included in the provision of P.L. 98-397 to which it relates.

P.L. 99-514, §1898(b)(15)(A):

Amended Code Sec. 417(a)(1) by striking out "section 401(a)(ii)" and inserting in lieu thereof "section 401(a)(11)". **Effective** as if included in the provision of P.L. 98-397 to which it relates.

[Sec. 417(b)]

(b) DEFINITION OF QUALIFIED JOINT AND SURVIVOR ANNUITY.—For purposes of this section and section 401(a)(11), the term "qualified joint and survivor annuity" means an annuity—

(1) for the life of the participant with a survivor annuity for the life of the spouse which is not less than 50 percent of (and is not greaterthan 100 percent of) the amount of the annuity which is payable during the joint lives of the participant and the spouse, and

(2) which is the actuarial equivalent of a single annuity for the life of the participant.

Such term also includes any annuity in a form having the effect of an annuity described in the preceding sentence.

[Sec. 417(c)]

(c) DEFINITION OF QUALIFIED PRERETIREMENT SURVIVOR ANNUITY.—For purposes of this section and section 401(a)(11)—

(1) IN GENERAL.—Except as provided in paragraph (2), the term "qualified preretirement survivor annuity" means a survivor annuity for the life of the surviving spouse of the participant if—

(A) the payments to the surviving spouse under such annuity are not less than the amounts which would be payable as a survivor annuity under the qualified joint and survivor annuity under the plan (or the actuarial equivalent thereof) if—

(i) in the case of a participant who dies after the date on which the participant attained the earliest retirement age, such participant had retired with an immediate qualified joint and survivor annuity on the day before the participant's date of death, or

(ii) in the case of a participant who dies on or before the date on which the participant would have attained the earliest retirement age, such participant had—

(I) separated from service on the date of death,

(II) survived to the earliest retirement age,

(III) retired with an immediate qualified joint and survivor annuity at the earliest retirement age, and

(IV) died on the day after the day on which such participant would have attained the earliest retirement age, and

(B) under the plan, the earliest period for which the surviving spouse may receive a payment under such annuity is not later than the month in which the participant would have attained the earliest retirement age under the plan.

In the case of an individual who separated from service before the date of such individual's death, subparagraph (A)(ii)(I) shall not apply.

(2) SPECIAL RULE FOR DEFINED CONTRIBUTION PLANS.—In the case of any defined contribution plan or participant described in clause (ii) or (iii) of section 401(a)(11)(B), the term "qualified preretirement survivor annuity" means an annuity for the life of the surviving spouse the actuarial equivalent of which is not less than 50 percent of the portion of the account balance of the participant (as of the date of death) to which the participant had a nonforfeitable right (within the meaning of section 411(a)).

(3) SECURITY INTERESTS TAKEN INTO ACCOUNT.—For purposes of paragraphs (1) and (2), any security interest held by the plan by reason of a loan outstanding to the participant shall be taken into account in determining the amount of the qualified preretirement survivor annuity.

Amendments

• 1986, Tax Reform Act of 1986 (P.L. 99-514)

P.L. 99-514, §1898(b)(1)(A):

Amended Code Sec. 417(c)(1) by adding at the end thereof a new sentence. **Effective** as if included in the provision of P.L. 98-397 to which it relates.

P.L. 99-514, §1898(b)(9)(A)(i):

Amended Code Sec. 417(c)(2) by striking out "the account balance of the participant as of the date of death" and inserting in lieu thereof "the portion of the account balance of the participant (as of the date of death) to which the participant had a nonforfeitable right (within the meaning of section 411(a))". **Effective** as if included in the provision of P.L. 98-397 to which it relates.

P.L. 99-514, §1898(b)(9)(A)(ii):

Amended Code Sec. 417(c) by adding at the end thereof new paragraph (3). **Effective** as if included in the provision of P.L. 98-397 to which it relates.

P.L. 99-514, §1898(b)(15)(B):

Amended Code Sec. 417(c)(1) by striking out "survivor annuity or the life of" in the matter preceding subparagraph (A) and inserting in lieu thereof "survivor annuity for the life of". **Effective** as if included in the provision of P.L. 98-397 to which it relates.

[Sec. 417(d)]

(d) SURVIVOR ANNUITIES NEED NOT BE PROVIDED IF PARTICIPANT AND SPOUSE MARRIED LESS THAN 1 YEAR.—

(1) IN GENERAL.—Except as provided in paragraph (2), a plan shall not be treated as failing to meet the requirements of section 401(a)(11) merely because the plan provides that a qualified joint and survivor annuity (or a qualified preretirement survivor annuity) will not be provided unless the participant and spouse had been married throughout the 1-year period ending on the earlier of—

(A) the participant's annuity starting date, or

(B) the date of the participant's death.

(2) TREATMENT OF CERTAIN MARRIAGES WITHIN 1 YEAR OF ANNUITY STARTING DATE FOR PURPOSES OF QUALIFIED JOINT AND SURVIVOR ANNUITIES.—For purposes of paragraph (1), if—

(A) a participant marries within 1 year before the annuity starting date, and

(B) the participant and the participant's spouse in such marriage have been married for at least a 1-year period ending on or before the date of the participant's death,

such participant and such spouse shall be treated as having been married throughout the 1-year period ending on the participant's annuity starting date.

[Sec. 417(e)]

(e) RESTRICTIONS ON CASH-OUTS.—

(1) PLAN MAY REQUIRE DISTRIBUTION IF PRESENT VALUE NOT IN EXCESS OF DOLLAR LIMIT.—A plan may provide that the present value of a qualified joint and survivor annuity or a qualified preretirement survivor annuity will be immediately distributed if such value does not exceed the amount that can be distributed without the participant's consent under section 411(a)(11). No distribution may be made under the preceding sentence after the annuity starting date unless the participant and the spouse of the participant (or where the participant has died, the surviving spouse) consents in writing to such distribution.

(2) PLAN MAY DISTRIBUTE BENEFIT IN EXCESS OF DOLLAR LIMIT ONLY WITH CONSENT.—If—

(A) the present value of the qualified joint and survivor annuity or the qualified preretirement survivor annuity exceeds the amount that can be distributed without the participant's consent under section 411(a)(11), and

(B) the participant and the spouse of the participant (or where the participant has died, the surviving spouse) consent in writing to the distribution,

the plan may immediately distribute the present value of such annuity.

(3) DETERMINATION OF PRESENT VALUE.—

(A) IN GENERAL.—For purposes of paragraphs (1) and (2), the present value shall not be less than the present value calculated by using the applicable mortality table and the applicable interest rate.

(B) APPLICABLE MORTALITY TABLE.—For purposes of subparagraph (A), the term "applicable mortality table" means a mortality table, modified as appropriate by the Secretary, based on the mortality table specified for the plan year under subparagraph (A) of section 430(h)(3) (without regard to subparagraph (C) or (D) of such section).

(C) APPLICABLE INTEREST RATE.—For purposes of subparagraph (A), the term "applicable interest rate" means the adjusted first, second, and third segment rates applied under rules similar to the rules of section 430(h)(2)(C) for the month before the date of the distribution or such other time as the Secretary may by regulations prescribe.

(D) APPLICABLE SEGMENT RATES.—For purposes of subparagraph (C), the adjusted first, second, and third segment rates are the first, second, and third segment rates which would be determined under section 430(h)(2)(C) if—

(i) section 430(h)(2)(D) were applied by substituting the average yields for the month described in subparagraph (C) for the average yields for the 24-month period described in such section,

(ii) section 430(h)(2)(G)(i)(II) were applied by substituting "section 417(e)(3)(A)(ii)(II)" for "section 412(b)(5)(B)(ii)(II)", and

(iii) the applicable percentage under section 430(h)(2)(G) were determined in accordance with the following table:

In the case of plan years beginning in:	The applicable percentage is:
2008	20 percent
2009	40 percent
2010	60 percent
2011	80 percent

Amendments

• 2008, Worker, Retiree, and Employer Recovery Act of 2008 (P.L. 110-458)

P.L. 110-458, §103(b)(2)(A):

Amended Code Sec. 417(e)(3)(D)(i) by striking "clause (ii)" and inserting "subparagraph (C)". **Effective** as if included in the provision of the 2006 Act to which the amendment relates [**effective** with respect to plan years beginning after 12-31-2007.—CCH].

• 2006, Pension Protection Act of 2006 (P.L. 109-280)

P.L. 109-280, §302(b):

Amended Code Sec. 417(e)(3). **Effective** with respect to plan years beginning after 12-31-2007. Prior to amendment, Code Sec. 417(e)(3) read as follows:

(3) DETERMINATION OF PRESENT VALUE.—

(A) IN GENERAL.—

(i) PRESENT VALUE.—Except as provided in subparagraph (B), for purposes of paragraphs (1) and (2), the present value shall not be less than the present value calculated by using the applicable mortality table and the applicable interest rate.

(ii) DEFINITIONS.—For purposes of clause (i)—

(I) APPLICABLE MORTALITY TABLE.—The term "applicable mortality table" means the table prescribed by the Secretary. Such table shall be based on the prevailing commissioners' standard table (described in section 807(d)(5)(A)) used to determine reserves for group annuity contracts issued on the date as of which present value is being determined (without regard to any other subparagraph of section 807(d)(5)).

(II) APPLICABLE INTEREST RATE.—The term "applicable interest rate" means the annual rate of interest on 30-year Treasury securities for the month before the date of distribution or such other time as the Secretary may by regulations prescribe.

(B) EXCEPTION.—In the case of a distribution from a plan that was adopted and in effect before the date of the enactment of the Retirement Protection Act of 1994, the present value of any distribution made before the earlier of—

(i) the later of the date a plan amendment applying subparagraph (A) is adopted or made effective, or

(ii) the first day of the first plan year beginning after December 31, 1999,

shall be calculated, for purposes of paragraphs (1) and (2), using the interest rate determined under the regulations of the Pension Benefit Guaranty Corporation for determining the present value of a lump sum distribution on plan termination that were in effect on September 1, 1993, and using the provisions of the plan as in effect on the day before such date of enactment; but only if such provisions of the plan met the requirements of section 417(e)(3) as in effect on the day before such date of enactment.

P.L. 109-280, §811, provides:

SEC. 811. PENSIONS AND INDIVIDUAL RETIREMENT ARRANGEMENT PROVISIONS OF ECONOMIC GROWTH AND TAX RELIEF RECONCILIATION ACT OF 2001 MADE PERMANENT.

Title IX of the Economic Growth and Tax Relief Reconciliation Act of 2001 [P.L. 107-16] shall not apply to the provisions of, and amendments made by, subtitles A through F of title VI [§§601-666]of such Act (relating to pension and individual retirement arrangement provisions).

• 2002, Job Creation and Worker Assistance Act of 2002 (P.L. 107-147)

P.L. 107-147, §411(r)(1)(A)-(B):

Amended Code Sec. 417(e) by striking "exceed the dollar limit under section 411(a)(11)(A)" and inserting "exceed the amount that can be distributed without the participant's consent under section 411(a)(11)" in paragraph (1), and by striking "exceeds the dollar limit under section 411(a)(11)(A)" and inserting "exceeds the amount that can be distributed without the participant's consent under section 411(a)(11)" in paragraph (2)(A). **Effective** as if included in the provision of P.L. 107-16 to which it relates [**effective** for distributions after 12-31-2001.—CCH].

• 2001, Economic Growth and Tax Relief Reconciliation Act of 2001 (P.L. 107-16)

P.L. 107-16, §901(a)-(b), provides [but see P.L. 109-280, §811, above]:

SEC. 901. SUNSET OF PROVISIONS OF ACT.

(a) IN GENERAL.—All provisions of, and amendments made by, this Act shall not apply—

(1) to taxable, plan, or limitation years beginning after December 31, 2010, or

(2) in the case of title V, to estates of decedents dying, gifts made, or generation skipping transfers, after December 31, 2010.

(b) APPLICATION OF CERTAIN LAWS.—The Internal Revenue Code of 1986 and the Employee Retirement Income Security Act of 1974 shall be applied and administered to years, estates, gifts, and transfers described in subsection (a) as if the provisions and amendments described in subsection (a) had never been enacted.

• 1997, Taxpayer Relief Act of 1997 (P.L. 105-34)

P.L. 105-34, §1071(a)(2)(A):

Amended Code Sec. 417(e)(1) and (2) by striking "$3,500" each place it appears (other than the headings) and inserting "the dollar limit under section 411(a)(11)(A)". **Effective** for plan years beginning after 8-5-97.

P.L. 105-34, §1071(a)(2)(B):

Amended Code Sec. 417(e)(1) and (2) by striking "$3,500" in the headings and inserting "DOLLAR LIMIT". **Effective** for plan years beginning after 8-5-97.

• 1994, Uruguay Round Agreements Act (P.L. 103-465)

P.L. 103-465, §767(a)(2):

Amended Code Sec. 417(e)(3). **Effective** for plan years and limitation years beginning after 12-31-94; except that an employer may elect to treat the amendments made by this section as being effective on or after 12-8-94. Prior to amendment, Code Sec. 417(e)(3) read as follows:

(3) DETERMINATION OF PRESENT VALUE.—

(A) IN GENERAL.—For purposes of paragraphs (1) and (2), the present value shall be calculated—

(i) by using an interest rate no greater than the applicable interest rate if the vested accrued benefit (using such rate) is not in excess of $25,000, and

(ii) by using an interest rate no greater than 120 percent of the applicable interest rate if the vested accrued benefit exceeds $25,000 (as determined under clause (i)).

In no event shall the present value determined under clause (ii) be less than $25,000.

(B) APPLICABLE INTEREST RATE.—For purposes of subparagraph (A), the term "applicable interest rate" means the interest rate which would be used (as of the date of the distribution) by the Pension Benefit Guaranty Corporation for purposes of determining the present value of a lump sum distribution on plan termination.

• 1988, Technical and Miscellaneous Revenue Act of 1988 (P.L. 100-647)

P.L. 100-647, §1018(u)(9):

Amended Code Sec. 417(e)(3)(A) by striking out "subclause (II)" and inserting in lieu thereof "clause (ii)". **Effective** as if included in the provision of P.L. 99-514 to which it relates.

• 1986, Tax Reform Act of 1986 (P.L. 99-514)

P.L. 99-514, §1139(b):

Amended Code Sec. 417(e)(3). For the **effective** date, as well as a special rule, see Act Sec. 1139(d), below. Prior to amendment, Code Sec. 417(e)(3) read as follows:

(3) Determination of Present Value.—For purposes of paragraphs (1) and (2), the present value of a qualified joint and survivor annuity or a qualified preretirement survivor annuity shall be determined as of the date of the distribution and by using an interest rate not greater than the interest rate which would be used (as of the date of the distribution) by the Pension Benefit Guaranty Corporation for purposes of determining the present value of a lump sum distribution on plan termination.

P.L. 99-514, §1139(d), as amended by P.L. 100-647, §1011A(k), provides:

(d) Effective Date.—

(1) In General.—The amendments made by this section shall apply to distributions in plan years beginning after December 31, 1984, except that such amendments shall not apply to any distributions in plan years beginning after December 31, 1984, and before January 1, 1987, if such distributions were made in accordance with the requirements of the regulations issued under the Retirement Equity Act of 1984.

(2) Reduction in Accrued Benefits.—

(A) In General.—If a plan—

(i) adopts a plan amendment before the close of the first plan year beginning on or after January 1, 1989, which provides for the calculation of the present value of the accrued benefits in the manner provided by the amendments made by this section, and

(ii) the plan reduces the accrued benefits for any plan year to which such plan amendment applies in accordance with such plan amendment,

such reduction shall not be treated as a violation of section 411(d)(6) of the Internal Revenue Code of 1986 or section 204(g) of the Employee Retirement Income Security Act of 1974 (29 U.S.C. 1054(g)).

(B) Special Rule.—In the case of a plan maintained by a corporation incorporated on April 11, 1934, which is headquartered in Tarrant County, Texas—

(i) such plan may be amended to remove the option of an employee to receive a lump sum distribution (within the meaning of section 402(e)(5) of such Code) if such amendment—

(I) is adopted within 1 year of the date of the enactment of this Act, and

(II) is not effective until 2 years after the employees are notified of such amendment, and

(ii) the present value of any vested accrued benefit of such plan determined during the 3-year period beginning on the date of the enactment of this Act shall be determined under the applicable interest rate (within the meaning of section 411(a)(11)(B)(ii) of such Code), except that if such value (as so determined) exceeds $50,000, then the value of any excess over $50,000 shall be determined by using the interest rate specified in the plan as of August 16, 1986.

[Sec. 417(f)]

(f) OTHER DEFINITIONS AND SPECIAL RULES.—For purposes of this section and section 401(a)(11)—

(1) VESTED PARTICIPANT.—The term "vested participant" means any participant who has a nonforfeitable right (within the meaning of section 411(a)) to any portion of such participant's accrued benefit.

(2) ANNUITY STARTING DATE.—

(A) IN GENERAL.—The term "annuity starting date" means—

(i) the first day of the first period for which an amount is payable as an annuity, or

(ii) in the case of a benefit not payable in the form of an annuity, the first day on which all events have occurred which entitle the participant to such benefit.

(B) SPECIAL RULE FOR DISABILITY BENEFITS.—For purposes of subparagraph (A), the first day of the first period for which a benefit is to be received by reason of disability shall be treated as the annuity starting date only if such benefit is not an auxiliary benefit.

(3) EARLIEST RETIREMENT AGE.—The term "earliest retirement age" means the earliest date on which, under the plan, the participant could elect to receive retirement benefits.

(4) PLAN MAY TAKE INTO ACCOUNT INCREASED COSTS.—A plan may take into account in any equitable manner (as determined by the Secretary) any increased costs resulting from providing a qualified joint or survivor annuity or a qualified preretirement survivor annuity.

(5) DISTRIBUTIONS BY REASON OF SECURITY INTERESTS.—If the use of any participant's accrued benefit (or any portion thereof) as security for a loan meets the requirements of subsection (a)(4), nothing in this section or section 411(a)(11) shall prevent any distribution required by reason of a failure to comply with the terms of such loan.

(6) REQUIREMENTS FOR CERTAIN SPOUSAL CONSENTS.—No consent of a spouse shall be effective for purposes of subsection (e)(1) or (e)(2) (as the case may be) unless requirements comparable to the requirements for spousal consent to an election under subsection (a)(1)(A) are met.

(7) CONSULTATION WITH THE SECRETARY OF LABOR.—In prescribing regulations under this section and section 401(a)(11), the Secretary shall consult with the Secretary of Labor.

Amendments

• 1986, Tax Reform Act of 1986 (P.L. 99-514)

P.L. 99-514, §1898(b)(4)(A)(iii):

Amended Code Sec. 417(f) by redesignating paragraph (5) as paragraph (6) and by inserting after paragraph (4) new paragraph (5). For the **effective** date, see Act Sec. 1898(b)(4)(C) in the amendment notes to Code Sec. 417(a).

P.L. 99-514, §1898(b)(8)(A):

Amended Code Sec. 417(f)(1) by striking out "the accrued benefit derived from employer contributions" and inserting in lieu thereof "such participant's accrued benefit". **Effective** for distributions after 10-22-86 [**effective** date amended by P.L. 101-239, §7862(d)(2).—CCH.]

P.L. 99-514, §1898(b)(10)(A):

Amended Code Sec. 417(f) (as amended by Act Sec. 1898(b)(4)) by redesignating paragraph (6) as paragraph (7) and by inserting after paragraph (5) new paragraph (6). **Effective** as if included in the provision of P.L. 98-397 to which it relates.

P.L. 99-514, §1898(b)(12)(A):

Amended Code Sec. 417(f)(2). **Effective** as if included in the provision of P.L. 98-397 to which it relates. Prior to amendment, Code Sec. 417(f)(2) read as follows:

(2) ANNUITY STARTING DATE.—The term "annuity starting date" means the first day of the first period for which an amount is received as an annuity (whether by reason of retirement or disability).

• 1984, Retirement Equity Act of 1984 (P.L. 98-397)

P.L. 98-397, §203(b):

Added Code Sec. 417. **Effective** only in the case of participants who have at least 1 hour of service under the plan on or after the date of enactment or have at least 1 hour of paid leave on or after such date. For special rules, see P.L. 98-397, §§302(b), 302(d)(2), 303(c)(2), 303(c)(3), 303(e) and 303(f) in the amendment notes for Code Sec. 401(a).

[Sec. 417(g)]

(g) DEFINITION OF QUALIFIED OPTIONAL SURVIVOR ANNUITY.—

(1) IN GENERAL.—For purposes of this section, the term "qualified optional survivor annuity" means an annuity—

(A) for the life of the participant with a survivor annuity for the life of the spouse which is equal to the applicable percentage of the amount of the annuity which is payable during the joint lives of the participant and the spouse, and

(B) which is the actuarial equivalent of a single annuity for the life of the participant.

Such term also includes any annuity in a form having the effect of an annuity described in the preceding sentence.

(2) APPLICABLE PERCENTAGE.—

(A) IN GENERAL.—For purposes of paragraph (1), if the survivor annuity percentage—

(i) is less than 75 percent, the applicable percentage is 75 percent, and

(ii) is greater than or equal to 75 percent, the applicable percentage is 50 percent.

(B) SURVIVOR ANNUITY PERCENTAGE.—For purposes of subparagraph (A), the term "survivor annuity percentage" means the percentage which the survivor annuity under the plan's qualified joint and survivor annuity bears to the annuity payable during the joint lives of the participant and the spouse.

Amendments

• 2006, Pension Protection Act of 2006 (P.L. 109-280)

P.L. 109-280, §1004(a)(2):

Amended Code Sec. 417 by adding at the end a new subsection (g). **Effective** generally for plan years beginning after 12-31-2007. For a special rule, see Act Sec. 1004(c)(2), below.

P.L. 109-280, §1004(c)(2), provides:

(2) SPECIAL RULE FOR COLLECTIVELY BARGAINED PLANS.—In the case of a plan maintained pursuant to 1 or more collective bargaining agreements between employee representatives and 1 or more employers ratified on or before the date of the enactment of this Act, the amendments made by this section shall not apply to plan years beginning before the earlier of—

(A) the later of—

(i) January 1, 2008, or

(ii) the date on which the last collective bargaining agreement related to the plan terminates (determined without regard to any extension thereof after the date of enactment of this Act), or

(B) January 1, 2009.

Subpart C—Special Rules for Multiemployer Plans

Sec. 418.	Reorganization status.
Sec. 418A.	Notice of reorganization and funding requirements.
Sec. 418B.	Minimum contribution requirement.
Sec. 418C.	Overburden credit against minimum contribution requirement.
Sec. 418D.	Adjustments in accrued benefits.
Sec. 418E.	Insolvent plans.

[Sec. 418]

SEC. 418. REORGANIZATION STATUS.

[Sec. 418(a)]

(a) GENERAL RULE.—A multiemployer plan is in reorganization for a plan year if the plan's reorganization index for that year is greater than zero.

[Sec. 418(b)]

(b) REORGANIZATION INDEX.—For purposes of this subpart—

(1) IN GENERAL.—A plan's reorganization index for any plan year is the excess of—

(A) the vested benefits charge for such year, over

(B) the net charge to the funding standard account for such year.

(2) NET CHARGE TO FUNDING STANDARD ACCOUNT.—The net charge to the funding standard account for any plan year is the excess (if any) of—

(A) the charges to the funding standard account for such year under section 412(b)(2), over

(B) the credits to the funding standard account under section 412(b)(3)(B).

(3) VESTED BENEFITS CHARGE.—The vested benefits charge for any plan year is the amount which would be necessary to amortize the plan's unfunded vested benefits as of the end of the base plan year in equal annual installments—

(A) over 10 years, to the extent such benefits are attribuable to persons in pay status, and

(B) over 25 years, to the extent such benefits are attributable to other participants.

(4) DETERMINATION OF VESTED BENEFITS CHARGE.—

(A) IN GENERAL.—The vested benefits charge for a plan year shall be based on an actuarial valuation of the plan as of the end of the base plan year, adjusted to reflect—

(i) any—

(I) decrease of 5 percent or more in the value of plan assets, or increase of 5 percent or more in the number of persons in pay status, during the period beginning on the first day of the plan year following the base plan year and ending on the adjustment date, or

(II) at the election of the plan sponsor, actuarial valuation of the plan as of the adjustment date or any later date not later than the last day of the plan year for which the determination is being made,

(ii) any change in benefits under the plan which is not otherwise taken into account under this subparagraph and which is pursuant to any amendment—

(I) adopted before the end of the plan year for which the determination is being made, and

(II) effective after the end of the base plan year and on or before the end of the plan year referred to in subclause (I), and

(iii) any other event (including an event described in subparagraph (B)(i)(I)) which, as determined in accordance with regulations prescribed by the Secretary, would substantially increase the plan's vested benefit charge.

(B) CERTAIN CHANGES IN BENEFIT LEVELS.—

(i) IN GENERAL.—In determining the vested benefits charge for a plan year following a plan year in which the plan was not in reorganization, any change in benefits which—

(I) results from the changing of a group of participants from one benefit level to another benefit level under a schedule of plan benefits as a result of changes in a collective bargaining agreement, or

(II) results from any other change in a collective bargaining agreement,

shall not be taken into account except to the extent provided in regulations prescribed by the Secretary.

(ii) PLAN IN REORGANIZATION.—Except as otherwise determined by the Secretary, in determining the vested benefits charge for any plan year following any plan year in which the plan was in reorganization, any change in benefits—

(I) described in clause (i)(I), or

(II) described in clause (i)(II) as determined under regulations prescribed by the Secretary,

shall, for purposes of subparagraph (A)(ii), be treated as a change in benefits pursuant to an amendment to a plan.

(5) BASE PLAN YEAR.—

(A) IN GENERAL.—The base plan year for any plan year is—

(i) if there is a relevant collective bargaining agreement, the last plan year ending at least 6 months before the relevant effective date, or

(ii) if there is no relevant collective bargaining agreement, the last plan year ending at least 12 months before the beginning of the plan year.

(B) RELEVANT COLLECTIVE BARGAINING AGREEMENT.—A relevant collective bargaining agreement is a collective bargaining agreement—

(i) which is in effect for at least 6 months during the plan year, and

(ii) which has not been in effect for more than 36 months as of the end of the plan year.

(C) RELEVANT EFFECTIVE DATE.—The relevant effective date is the earliest of the effective dates for the relevant collective bargaining agreements.

(D) ADJUSTMENT DATE.—The adjustment date is the date which is—

(i) 90 days before the relevant effective date, or

(ii) if there is no relevant effective date, 90 days before the beginning of the plan year.

(6) PERSON IN PAY STATUS.—The term "person in pay status" means—

(A) a participant or beneficiary on the last day of the base plan year who, at any time during such year, was paid an early, late, normal, or disability retirement benefit (or a death benefit related to a retirement benefit), and

(B) to the extent provided in regulations prescribed by the Secretary, any other person who is entitled to such a benefit under the plan.

(7) OTHER DEFINITIONS AND SPECIAL RULES.—

(A) UNFUNDED VESTED BENEFITS.—The term "unfunded vested benefits" means, in connection with a plan, an amount (determined in accordance with regulations prescribed by the Secretary) equal to—

(i) the value of vested benefits under the plan, less

(ii) the value of the assets of the plan.

(B) VESTED BENEFITS.—The term "vested benefits" means any nonforfeitable benefit (within the meaning of section 4001(a)(8) of the Employee Retirement Income Security Act of 1974).

(C) ALLOCATION OF ASSETS.—In determining the plan's unfunded vested benefits, plan assets shall first be allocated to the vested benefits attributable to persons in pay status.

(D) TREATMENT OF CERTAIN BENEFIT REDUCTIONS.—The vested benefits charge shall be determined without regard to reductions in accrued benefits under section 418D which are first effective in the plan year.

(E) WITHDRAWAL LIABILITY.—For purposes of this part, any outstanding claim for withdrawal liability shall not be considered a plan asset, except as otherwise provided in regulations prescribed by the Secretary.

[Sec. 418(c)]

(c) PROHIBITION OF NONANNUITY PAYMENTS.—Except as provided in regulations prescribed by the Pension Benefit Guaranty Corporation, while a plan is in reorganization a benefit with respect to a participant (other than a death benefit) which is attributable to employer contributions and which has a value of more than $1,750 may not be paid in a form other than an annuity which (by itself or in combination with social security, railroad retirement, or workers' compensation benefits) provides substantially level payments over the life of the participant.

[Sec. 418(d)]

(d) TERMINATED PLANS.—Any multiemployer plan which terminates under section 4041A(a)(2) of the Employee Retirement Income Security Act of 1974 shall not be considered in reorganization after the last day of the plan year in which the plan is treated as having terminated.

Amendments

• 1980, Multiemployer Pension Plan Amendments Act of 1980 (P.L. 96-364)

P.L. 96-364, §202(a):

Added Code Sec. 418. **Effective** with respect to each plan, on the first day of the first plan year begining on or after the earlier of—

(1) the date on which the last collective-bargaining agreement providing for employer contributions under the plan, which was in effect on the date of the enactment of this Act, expires, without regard to extensions agreed to after such date of enactment, or

(2) 3 years after September 26, 1980.

[Sec. 418A]

SEC. 418A. NOTICE OF REORGANIZATION AND FUNDING REQUIREMENTS.

[Sec. 418A(a)]

(a) NOTICE REQUIREMENT.—

(1) IN GENERAL.—If—

(A) a multiemployer plan is in reorganization for a plan year, and

(B) section 418B would require an increase in contributions for such plan year, the plan sponsor shall notify the persons described in paragraph (2) that the plan is in reorganization and that, if contributions to the plan are not increased, accrued benefits under the plan may be reduced or an excise tax may be imposed (or both such reduction and imposition may occur).

(2) PERSONS TO WHOM NOTICE IS TO BE GIVEN.—The persons described in this paragraph are—

(A) each employer who has an obligation to contribute under the plan (within the meaning of section 4212(a) of the Employee Retirement Income Security Act of 1974), and

(B) each employee organization which, for purposes of collective bargaining, represents plan participants employed by such an employer.

(3) OVERBURDEN CREDIT NOT TAKEN INTO ACCOUNT.—The determination under paragraph (1)(B) shall be made without regard to the overburden credit provided by section 418C.

[Sec. 418A(b)]

(b) ADDITIONAL REQUIREMENTS.—The Pension Benefit Guaranty Corporation may prescribe additional or alternative requirements for assuring, in the case of a plan with respect to which notice is required by subsection (a)(1), that the persons described in subsection (a)(2)—

(1) receive appropriate notice that the plan is in reorganization,

(2) are adequately informed of the implications of reorganization status, and

(3) have reasonable access to information relevant to the plan's reorganization status.

Amendments

• 1980, Multiemployer Pension Plan Amendments Act of 1980 (P.L. 96-364)

P.L. 96-364, §202(a):

Added Code Sec. 418A. **Effective** with respect to each plan, on the first day of the first plan year beginning on or after the earlier of—

(1) the date on which the last collective-bargaining agreement providing for employer contributions under the plan, which was in effect on the date of the enactment of this Act, expires, without regard to extensions agreed to after such date of enactment, or

(2) 3 years after September 26, 1980.

[Sec. 418B]

SEC. 418B. MINIMUM CONTRIBUTION REQUIREMENT.

[Sec. 418B(a)]

(a) ACCUMULATED FUNDING DEFICIENCY IN REORGANIZATION.—

(1) IN GENERAL.—For any plan year in which a multiemployer plan is in reorganization—

(A) the plan shall continue to maintain its funding standard account, and

(B) the plan's accumulated funding deficiency under section 412(a) for such plan year shall be equal to the excess (if any) of—

(i) the sum of the minimum contribution requirement for such plan year (taking into account any overburden credit under section 418C(a)) plus the plan's accumulated funding deficiency for the preceding plan year (determined under this section if the plan was in reorganization during such plan year or under section 412(a) if the plan was not in reorganization), over

(ii) amounts considered contributed by employers to or under the plan for the plan year (increased by any amount waived under subsection (f) for the plan year).

(2) TREATMENT OF WITHDRAWAL LIABILITY PAYMENTS.—For purposes of paragraph (1), withdrawal liability payments (whether or not received) which are due with respect to withdrawals before the end of the base plan year shall be considered amounts contributed by the employer to or under the plan if, as of the adjustment date, it was reasonable for the plan sponsor to anticipate that such payments would be made during the plan year.

[Sec. 418B(b)]

(b) MINIMUM CONTRIBUTION REQUIREMENT.—

(1) IN GENERAL.—Except as otherwise provided in this section for purposes of this subpart the minimum contribution requirement for a plan year in which a plan is in reorganization is an amount equal to the excess of—

(A) the sum of—

(i) the plan's vested benefits charge for the plan year; and

(ii) the increase in normal cost for the plan year determined under the entry age normal funding method which is attributable to plan amendments adopted while the plan was in reorganization, over

(B) the amount of the overburden credit (if any) determined under section 418C for the plan year.

(2) ADJUSTMENT FOR REDUCTIONS IN CONTRIBUTION BASE UNITS.—If the plan's current contribution base for the plan year is less than the plan's valuation contribution base for the plan year, the minimum contribution requirement for such plan year shall be equal to the product of the amount determined under paragraph (1) (after any adjustment required by this subpart other than this paragraph) multiplied by a fraction—

(A) the numerator of which is the plan's current contribution base for the plan year, and

(B) the denominator of which is the plan's valuation contribution base for the plan year.

(3) SPECIAL RULE WHERE CASH-FLOW AMOUNT EXCEEDS VESTED BENEFITS CHARGE.—

(A) IN GENERAL.—If the vested benefits charge for a plan year of a plan in reorganization is less than the plan's cash-flow amount for the plan year, the plan's minimum contribution requirement for the plan year is the amount determined under paragraph (1) (determined before the application of paragraph (2)) after substituting the term "cash-flow amount" for the term "vested benefits charge" in paragraph (1)(A).

(B) CASH-FLOW AMOUNT.—For purposes of subparagraph (A), a plan's cash-flow amount for a plan year is an amount equal to—

(i) the amount of the benefits payable under the plan for the base plan year, plus the amount of the plan's administrative expenses for the base plan year, reduced by

(ii) the value of the available plan assets for the base plan year determined under regulations prescribed by the Secretary,

adjusted in a manner consistent with section 418(b)(4).

[Sec. 418B(c)]

(c) CURRENT CONTRIBUTION BASE; VALUATION CONTRIBUTION BASE.—

(1) CURRENT CONTRIBUTION BASE.—For purposes of this subpart, a plan's current contribution base for a plan year is the number of contribution base units with respect to which contributions are required to be made under the plan for that plan year, determined in accordance with regulations prescribed by the Secretary.

(2) VALUATION CONTRIBUTION BASE.—

(A) IN GENERAL.—Except as provided in subparagraph (B), for purposes of this subpart a plan's valuation contribution base is the number of contribution base units for which contributions were received for the base plan year—

(i) adjusted to reflect declines in the contribution base which have occurred (or could reasonably be anticipated) as of the adjustment date for the plan year referred to in paragraph (1),

(ii) adjusted upward (in accordance with regulations prescribed by the Secretary) for any contribution base reduction in the base plan year caused by a strike or lockout or by unusual events, such as fire, earthquake, or severe weather conditions, and

(iii) adjusted (in accordance with regulations prescribed by the Secretary) for reductions in the contribution base resulting from transfers of liabilities.

(B) INSOLVENT PLANS.—For any plan year—

(i) in which the plan is insolvent (within the meaning of section 418E(b)(1)), and

(ii) beginning with the first plan year beginning after the expiration of all relevant collective bargaining agreements which were in effect in the plan year in which the plan became insolvent,

the plan's valuation contribution base is the greater of the number of contribution base units for which contributions were received for the first or second plan year preceding the first plan year in which the plan is insolvent, adjusted as provided in clause (ii) or (iii) of subparagraph (A).

(3) CONTRIBUTION BASE UNIT.—For purposes of this subpart, the term "contribution base unit" means a unit with respect to which an employer has an obligation to contribute under a multiemployer plan (as defined in regulations prescribed by the Secretary).

[Sec. 418B(d)]

(d) LIMITATION ON REQUIRED INCREASES IN RATE OF EMPLOYER CONTRIBUTIONS.—

(1) IN GENERAL.—Under regulations prescribed by the Secretary, the minimum contribution requirement applicable to any plan for any plan year which is determined under subsection (b) (without regard to subsection (b)(2)) shall not exceed an amount which is equal to the sum of—

(A) the greater of—

(i) the funding standard requirement for such plan year, or

(ii) 107 percent of—

(I) if the plan was not in reorganization in the preceding plan year, the funding standard requirement for such preceding plan year, or

(II) if the plan was in reorganization in the preceding plan year, the sum of the amount determined under this subparagraph for the preceding plan year and the amount (if any) determined under subparagraph (B) for the preceding plan year, plus

(B) if for the plan year a change in benefits is first required to be considered in computing the charges under section 412(b)(2)(A) or (B), the sum of—

(i) the increase in normal cost for a plan year determined under the entry age normal funding method due to increases in benefits described in section 418(b)(4)(A)(ii) (determined without regard to section 418(b)(4)(B)(ii)), and

(ii) the amount necessary to amortize in equal annual installments the increase in the value of vested benefits under the plan due to increases in benefits described in clause (i) over—

(I) 10 years, to the extent such increase in value is attributable to persons in pay status, or

(II) 25 years, to the extent such increase in value is attributable to other participants.

(2) FUNDING STANDARD REQUIREMENT.—For purposes of paragraph (1), the funding standard requirement for any plan year is an amount equal to the net charge to the funding standard account for such plan year (as defined in section 418(b)(2)).

(3) SPECIAL RULE FOR CERTAIN PLANS.—

(A) IN GENERAL.—In the case of a plan described in section 4216(b) of the Employee Retirement Income Security Act of 1974, if a plan amendment which increases benefits is adopted after January 1, 1980—

(i) paragraph (1) shall apply only if the plan is a plan described in subparagraph (B), and

(ii) the amount under paragraph (1) shall be determined without regard to subparagraph (1)(B).

(B) ELIGIBLE PLANS.—A plan is described in this subparagraph if—

(i) the rate of employer contributions under the plan for the first plan year beginning on or after the date on which an amendment increasing benefits is adopted, multiplied by the valuation contribution base for that plan year, equals or exceeds the sum of—

(I) the amount that would be necessary to amortize fully, in equal annual installments, by July 1, 1986, the unfunded vested benefits attributable to plan provisions in effect on July 1, 1977 (determined as of the last day of the base plan year); and

(II) the amount that would be necessary to amortize fully, in equal annual installments, over the period described in subparagraph (C), beginning with the first day of the first plan year beginning on or after the date on which the amendment is adopted, the unfunded vested benefits (determined as of the last day of the base plan year) attributable to each plan amendment after July 1, 1977; and

(ii) the rate of employer contributions for each subsequent plan year is not less than the lesser of—

(I) the rate which when multiplied by the valuation contribution base for that subsequent plan year produces the annual amount that would be necessary to complete the amortization schedule described in clause (i), or

(II) the rate for the plan year immediately preceding such subsequent plan year, plus 5 percent of such rate.

(C) PERIOD.—The period determined under this subparagraph is the lesser of—

(i) 12 years, or

(ii) a period equal in length to the average of the remaining expected lives of all persons receiving benefits under the plan.

(4) EXCEPTION IN CASE OF CERTAIN BENEFIT INCREASES.—Paragraph (1) shall not apply with respect to a plan, other than a plan described in paragraph (3), for the period of consecutive plan years in each of which the plan is in reorganization, beginning with a plan year in which occurs the earlier of the date of the adoption or the effective date of any amendment of the plan which increases benefits with respect to service performed before the plan year in which the adoption of the amendment occurred.

[Sec. 418B(e)]

(e) CERTAIN RETROACTIVE PLAN AMENDMENTS.—In determining the minimum contribution requirement with respect to a plan for a plan year under subsection (b), the vested benefits charge may be adjusted to reflect a plan amendment reducing benefits under section 412(c)(8).

[Sec. 418B(f)]

(f) WAIVER OF ACCUMULATED FUNDING DEFICIENCY.—

(1) IN GENERAL.—The Secretary may waive any accumulated funding deficiency under this section in accordance with the provisions of section 412(d)(1).

(2) TREATMENT OF WAIVER.—Any waiver under paragraph (1) shall not be treated as a waived funding deficiency (within the meaning of section 412(d)(3)).

[Sec. 418B(g)]

(g) ACTUARIAL ASSUMPTIONS MUST BE REASONABLE.—For purposes of making any determination under this subpart, the requirements of section 412(c)(3) shall apply.

Amendments

• 1980, Multiemployer Pension Plan Amendments Act of 1980 (P.L. 96-364)

P.L. 96-364, §202(a):

Added Code Sec. 418B. **Effective** with respect to each plan, on the first day of the first plan year beginning on or after the earlier of—

(1) the date on which the last collective-bargaining agreement providing for employer contributions under the plan, which was in effect on the date of the enactment of this Act, expires, without regard to extensions agreed to after such date of enactment, or

(2) 3 years after September 26, 1980.

[Sec. 418C]

SEC. 418C. OVERBURDEN CREDIT AGAINST MINIMUM CONTRIBUTION REQUIREMENT.

[Sec. 418C(a)]

(a) GENERAL RULE.—For purposes of determining the contribution under section 418B (before the application of section 418B(b)(2) or (d)), the plan sponsor of a plan which is overburdened for the plan year shall apply an overburden credit against the plan's minimum contribution requirement for the plan year (determined without regard to section 418B(b)(2) or (d) and without regard to this section.

[Sec. 418C(b)]

(b) DEFINITION OF OVERBURDENED PLAN.—A plan is overburdened for a plan year if—

(1) the average number of pay status participants under the plan in the base plan year exceeds the average of the number of active participants in the base plan year and the 2 plan years preceding the base plan year, and

(2) the rate of employer contributions under the plan equals or exceeds the greater of—

(A) such rate for the preceding plan year, or

(B) such rate for the plan year preceding the first year in which the plan is in reorganization.

[Sec. 418C(c)]

(c) AMOUNT OF OVERBURDEN CREDIT.—The amount of the overburden credit for a plan year is the product of—

(1) one-half of the average guaranteed benefit paid for the base plan year, and

(2) the overburden factor for the plan year.

The amount of the overburden credit for a plan year shall not exceed the amount of the minimum contribution requirement for such year (determined without regard to this section).

[Sec. 418C(d)]

(d) OVERBURDEN FACTOR.—For purposes of this section, the overburden factor of a plan for the plan year is an amount equal to—

(1) the average number of pay status participants for the base plan year, reduced by

(2) the average of the number of active participants for the base plan year and for each of the 2 plan years preceding the base plan year.

[Sec. 418C(e)]

(e) DEFINITIONS.—For purposes of this section—

(1) PAY STATUS PARTICIPANT.—The term "pay status participant" means, with respect to a plan, a participant receiving retirement benefits under the plan.

(2) NUMBER OF ACTIVE PARTICIPANTS.—The number of active participants for a plan year shall be the sum of—

(A) the number of active employees who are participants in the plan and on whose behalf contributions are required to be made during the plan year;

(B) the number of active employees who are not participants in the plan but who are in an employment unit covered by a collective bargaining agreement which requires the employees' employer to contribute to the plan unless service in such employment unit was never covered under the plan or a predecessor thereof, and

(C) the total number of active employees attributed to employers who made payment to the plan for the plan year of withdrawal liability pursuant to part 1 of subtitle E of title IV of the Employee Retirement Income Security Act of 1974, determined by dividing—

(i) the total amount of such payments, by

(ii) the amount equal to the total contributions received by the plan during the plan year divided by the average number of active employees who were participants in the plan during the plan year.

The Secretary shall by regulations provide alternative methods of determining active participants where (by reason of irregular employment, contributions on a unit basis, or otherwise) this paragraph does not yield a representative basis for determining the credit.

(3) AVERAGE NUMBER.—The term "average number" means, with respect to pay status participants for a plan year, a number equal to one-half the sum of—

(A) the number with respect to the plan as of the beginning of the plan year, and

(B) the number with respect to the plan as of the end of the plan year.

(4) AVERAGE GUARANTEED BENEFIT.—The average guaranteed benefit paid is 12 times the average monthly pension payment guaranteed under section 4022A(c)(1) of the Employee Retirement Income Security Act of 1974 determined under the provisions of the plan in effect at the beginning of the first plan year in which the plan is in reorganization and without regard to section 4022A(c)(2).

(5) FIRST YEAR IN REORGANIZATION.—The first year in which the plan is in reorganization is the first of a period of 1 or more consecutive plan years in which the plan has been in reorganization not taking into account any plan years the plan was in reorganization prior to any period of 3 or more consecutive plan years in which the plan was not in reorganization.

[Sec. 418C(f)]

(f) NO OVERBURDEN CREDIT IN CASE OF CERTAIN REDUCTIONS IN CONTRIBUTIONS.—

(1) IN GENERAL.—Notwithstanding any other provision of this section, a plan is not eligible for an overburden credit for a plan year if the Secretary finds that the plan's current contribution base for any plan year was reduced, without a corresponding reduction in the plan's unfunded vested benefits attributable to pay status participants, as a result of a change in an agreement providing for employer contributions under the plan.

(2) TREATMENT OF CERTAIN WITHDRAWALS.—For purposes of paragraph (1), a complete or partial withdrawal of an employer (within the meaning of part 1 of subtitle E of title IV of the Employee Retirement Income Security Act of 1974) does not impair a plan's eligibility for an overburden credit, unless the Secretary finds that a contribution base reduction described in paragraph (1) resulted from a transfer of liabilities to another plan in connection with the withdrawal.

[Sec. 418C(g)]

(g) MERGERS.—Notwithstanding any other provision of this section, if 2 or more multiemployer plans merge, the amount of the overburden credit which may be applied under this section with respect to the plan resulting from the merger for any of the 3 plan years ending after the effective date of the merger shall not exceed the sum of the used overburden credit for each of the merging plans for its last plan year ending before the effective date of the merger. For purposes of the preceding sentence, the used overburden credit is that portion of the credit which does not exceed the excess of the minimum contribution requirement determined without regard to any overburden credit under this section over the employer contributions required under the plan.

Amendments

• 1980, Multiemployer Pension Plan Amendments Act of 1980 (P.L. 96-364)

P.L. 96-364, §202(a):

Added Code Sec. 418C. **Effective** with respect to each plan, on the first day of the first plan year beginning on or after the earlier of—

(1) the date on which the last collective-bargaining agreement providing for employer contributions under the plan, which was in effect on the date of the enactment of this Act, expires, without regard to extensions agreed to after such date of enactment, or

(2) 3 years after September 26, 1980.

[Sec. 418D]

SEC. 418D. ADJUSTMENTS IN ACCRUED BENEFITS.

[Sec. 418D(a)]

(a) ADJUSTMENTS IN ACCRUED BENEFITS.—

(1) IN GENERAL.—Notwithstanding section 411, a multiemployer plan in reorganization may be amended, in accordance with this section, to reduce or eliminate accrued benefits attributable to employer contributions which, under section 4022A(b) of the Employee Retirement Income Security Act of 1974, are not eligible for the Pension Benefit Guaranty Corporation's guarantee. The preceding sentence shall only apply to accrued benefits under plan amendments (or plans) adopted after March 26, 1980, or under collective bargaining agreement entered into after March 26, 1980.

(2) ADJUSTMENT OF VESTED BENEFITS CHARGE.—In determining the minimum contribution requirement with respect to a plan for a plan year under section 418B(b), the vested benefits charge may be adjusted to reflect a plan amendment reducing benefits under this section or section 412(c)(8), but only if the amendment is adopted and effective no later than 2½ months after the end of the plan year, or within such extended period as the Secretary may prescribe by regulations under section 412(c)(10).

[Sec. 418D(b)]

(b) LIMITATION ON REDUCTION.—

(1) IN GENERAL.—Accrued benefits may not be reduced under this section unless—

(A) notice has been given, at least 6 months before the first day of the plan year in which the amendment reducing benefits is adopted, to—

(i) plan participants and beneficiaries,

(ii) each employer who has an obligation to contribute (within the meaning of section 4212(a) of the Employee Retirement Income Security Act of 1974) under the plan, and

(iii) each employee organization which, for purposes of collective bargaining, represents plan participants employed by such an employer,

that the plan is in reorganization and that, if contributions under the plan are not increased, accrued benefits under the plan will be reduced or an excise tax will be imposed on employers;

(B) in accordance with regulations prescribed by the Secretary—

(i) any category of accrued benefits is not reduced with respect to inactive participants to a greater extent proportionally than such category of accrued benefits is reduced with respect to active participants,

(ii) benefits attributable to employer contributions other than accrued benefits and the rate of future benefit accruals are reduced at least to an extent equal to the reduction in accrued benefits of inactive participants, and

(iii) in any case in which the accrued benefit of a participant or beneficiary is reduced by changing the benefit form or the requirements which the participant or beneficiary must satisfy to be entitled to the benefit, such reduction is not applicable to—

(I) any participant or beneficiary in pay status on the effective date of the amendment, or the beneficiary of such a participant, or

(II) any participant who has attained normal retirement age, or who is within 5 years of attaining normal retirement age, on the effective date of the amendment, or the beneficiary of any such participant; and

(C) the rate of employer contributions for the plan year in which the amendment becomes effective and for all succeeding plan years in which the plan is in reorganization equals or exceeds the greater of—

(i) the rate of employer contributions, calculated without regard to the amendment, for the plan year in which the amendment becomes effective, or

(ii) the rate of employer contributions for the plan year preceding the plan year in which the amendment becomes effective.

(2) INFORMATION REQUIRED TO BE INCLUDED IN NOTICE.—The plan sponsors shall include in any notice required to be sent to plan participants and beneficiaries under paragraph (1) information as to the rights and remedies of plan participants and beneficiaries as well as how to contact the Department of Labor for further information and assistance where appropriate.

[Sec. 418D(c)]

(c) NO RECOUPMENT.—A plan may not recoup a benefit payment which is in excess of the amount payable under the plan because of an amendment retroactively reducing accrued benefits under this section.

[Sec. 418D(d)]

(d) BENEFIT INCREASES UNDER MULTIEMPLOYER PLAN IN REORGANIZATION.—

(1) RESTORATION OF PREVIOUSLY REDUCED BENEFITS.—

(A) IN GENERAL.—A plan which has been amended to reduce accrued benefits under this section may be amended to increase or restore accrued benefits, or the rate of future benefit accruals, only if the plan is amended to restore levels of previously reduced accrued benefits of inactive participants and of participants who are within 5 years of attaining normal retirement age to at least the same extent as any such increase in accrued benefits or in the rate of future benefit accruals.

(B) BENEFIT INCREASES AND BENEFIT RESTORATIONS.—For purposes of this subsection, in the case of a plan which has been amended under this section to reduce accrued benefits—

(i) an increase in a benefit, or in the rate of future benefit accruals, shall be considered a benefit increase to the extent that the benefit, or the accrual rate, is thereby increased above the highest benefit level, or accrual rate, which was in effect under the terms of the plan before the effective date of the amendment reducing accrued benefits, and

(ii) an increase in a benefit, or in the rate of future benefit accruals, shall be considered a benefit restoration to the extent that the benefit, or the accrual rate, is not thereby increased above the highest benefit level, or accrual rate, which was in effect under the terms of the plan immediately before the effective date of the amendment reducing accrued benefits.

(2) UNIFORMITY IN BENEFIT RESTORATION.—If a plan is amended to partially restore previously reduced accrued benefit levels, or the rate of future benefit accruals, the benefits of inactive participants shall be restored in at least the same proportions as other accrued benefits which are restored.

(3) NO BENEFIT INCREASES IN YEAR OF BENEFIT REDUCTION.—No benefit increase under a plan may take effect in a plan year in which an amendment reducing accrued benefits under the plan, in accordance with this section, is adopted or first becomes effective.

(4) RETROACTIVE PAYMENTS.—A plan is not required to make retroactive benefit payments with respect to that portion of an accrued benefit which was reduced and subsequently restored under this section.

[Sec. 418D(e)]

(e) INACTIVE PARTICIPANT.—For purposes of this section, the term "inactive participant" means a person not in covered service under the plan who is in pay status under the plan or who has a nonforfeitable benefit under the plan.

[Sec. 418D(f)]

(f) REGULATIONS.—The Secretary may prescribe rules under which, notwithstanding any other provision of this section, accrued benefit reductions or benefit increases for different participant groups may be varied equitably to reflect variations in contribution rates and other relevant factors reflecting differences in negotiated levels of financial support for plan benefit obligations.

Amendments

• 1980, Multiemployer Pension Plan Amendments Act of 1980 (P.L. 96-364)

P.L. 96-364, §202(a):

Added Code Sec. 418D. **Effective** with respect to each plan, on the first day of the first plan year beginning on or after the earlier of—

(1) the date on which the last collective-bargaining agreement providing for employer contributions under the plan, which was in effect on the date of the enactment of this Act, expires, without regard to extensions agreed to after such date of enactment, or

(2) 3 years after September 26, 1980.

[Sec. 418E]

SEC. 418E. INSOLVENT PLANS.

[Sec. 418E(a)]

(a) SUSPENSION OF CERTAIN BENEFIT PAYMENTS.—Notwithstanding section 411, in any case in which benefit payments under an insolvent multiemployer plan exceed the resource benefit level, any such payments of benefits which are not basic benefits shall be suspended, in accordance with this section, to the extent necessary to reduce the sum of such payments and the payments of such basic benefits to the greater of the resource benefit level or the level of basic benefits, unless an alternative procedure is prescribed by the Pension Benefit Guaranty Corporation under section 4022A(g)(5) of the Employee Retirement Income Security Act of 1974.

[Sec. 418E(b)]

(b) DEFINITIONS.—For purposes of this section, for a plan year—

(1) INSOLVENCY.—A multiemployer plan is insolvent if the plan's available resources are not sufficient to pay benefits under the plan when due for the plan year, or if the plan is determined to be insolvent under subsection (d).

(2) RESOURCE BENEFIT LEVEL.—The term "resource benefit level" means the level of monthly benefits determined under subsections (c)(1) and (3) and (d)(3) to be the highest level which can be paid out of the plan's available resources.

(3) AVAILABLE RESOURCES.—The term "available resources" means the plan's cash, marketable assets, contributions, withdrawal liability payments, and earnings, less reasonable administrative expenses and amounts owed for such plan year to the Pension Benefit Guaranty Corporation under section 4261(b)(2) of the Employee Retirement Income Security Act of 1974.

(4) INSOLVENCY YEAR.—The term "insolvency year" means a plan year in which a plan is insolvent.

[Sec. 418E(c)]

(c) BENEFIT PAYMENTS UNDER INSOLVENT PLANS.—

(1) DETERMINATION OF RESOURCE BENEFIT LEVEL.—The plan sponsor of a plan in reorganization shall determine in writing the plan's resource benefit level for each insolvency year, based on the plan sponsor's reasonable projection of the plan's available resources and the benefits payable under the plan.

(2) UNIFORMITY OF THE BENEFIT SUSPENSION.—The suspension of benefit payments under this section shall, in accordance with regulations prescribed by the Secretary, apply in substantially uniform proportions to the benefits of all persons in pay status (within the meaning of section 418(b)(6)) under the plan, except that the Secretary may prescribe rules under which benefit

suspensions for different participant groups may be varied equitably to reflect variations in contribution rates and other relevant factors including differences in negotiated levels of financial support for plan benefit obligations.

(3) RESOURCE BENEFIT LEVEL BELOW LEVEL OF BASIC BENEFITS.—Notwithstanding paragraph (2), if a plan sponsor determines in writing a resource benefit level for a plan year which is below the level of basic benefits, the payment of all benefits other than basic benefits shall be suspended for that plan year.

(4) EXCESS RESOURCES.—

(A) IN GENERAL.—If, by the end of an insolvency year, the plan sponsor determines in writing that the plan's available resources in that insolvency year could have supported benefit payments above the resource benefit level for that insolvency year, the plan sponsor shall distribute the excess resources to the participants and beneficiaries who received benefit payments from the plan in that insolvency year, in accordance with regulations prescribed by the Secretary.

(B) EXCESS RESOURCES.—For purposes of this paragraph, the term "excess resources" means available resources above the amount necessary to support the resource benefit level, but no greater than the amount necessary to pay benefits for the plan year at the benefit levels under the plan.

(5) UNPAID BENEFITS.—If, by the end of an insolvency year, any benefit has not been paid at the resource benefit level, amounts up to the resource benefit level which were unpaid shall be distributed to the participants and beneficiaries, in accordance with regulations prescribed by the Secretary, to the extent possible taking into account the plan's total available resources in that insolvency year.

(6) RETROACTIVE PAYMENTS.—Except as provided in paragraph (4) or (5), a plan is not required to make retroactive benefit payments with respect to that portion of a benefit which was suspended under this section.

[Sec. 418E(d)]

(d) PLAN SPONSOR DETERMINATION.—

(1) TRIENNIAL TEST.—As of the end of the first plan year in which a plan is in reorganization, and at least every 3 plan years thereafter (unless the plan is no longer in reorganization), the plan sponsor shall compare the value of plan assets (determined in accordance with section 418B(b)(3)(B)(ii)) for that plan year with the total amount of benefit payments made under the plan for that plan year. Unless the plan sponsor determines that the value of plan assets exceeds 3 times the total amount of benefit payments, the plan sponsor shall determine whether the plan will be insolvent in any of the next 5 plan years. If the plan sponsor makes such a determination that the plan will be insolvent in any of the next 5 plan years, the plan sponsor shall make the comparison under this paragraph at least annually until the plan sponsor makes a determination that the plan will not be insolvent in any of the next 5 plan years.

(2) DETERMINATION OF INSOLVENCY.—If, at any time, the plan sponsor of a plan in reorganization reasonably determines, taking into account the plan's recent and anticipated financial experience, that the plan's available resources are not sufficient to pay benefits under the plan when due for the next plan year, the plan sponsor shall make such determination available to interested parties.

(3) DETERMINATION OF RESOURCE BENEFIT LEVEL.—The plan sponsor of a plan in reorganization shall determine in writing for each insolvency year the resource benefit level and the level of basic benefits no later than 3 months before the insolvency year.

Amendments

• 2006, Pension Protection Act of 2006 (P.L. 109-280)

P.L. 109-280, §213(a)(1)-(2):

Amended Code Sec. 418E(d)(1) by striking "3 plan years" the second place it appears and inserting "5 plan years"; and by adding at the end a new sentence. **Effective** with respect to the determinations made in plan years beginning after 2007.

[Sec. 418E(e)]

(e) NOTICE REQUIREMENTS.—

(1) IMPENDING INSOLVENCY.—If the plan sponsor of a plan in reorganization determines under subsection (d)(1) or (2) that the plan may become insolvent (within the meaning of subsection (b)(1)), the plan sponsor shall—

(A) notify the Secretary, the Pension Benefit Guaranty Corporation, the parties described in section 418A(a)(2), and the plan participants and beneficiaries of that determination, and

(B) inform the parties described in section 418A(a)(2) and the plan participants and beneficiaries that if insolvency occurs certain benefit payments will be suspended, but that basic benefits will continue to be paid.

(2) RESOURCE BENEFIT LEVEL.—No later than 2 months before the first day of each insolvency year, the plan sponsor of a plan in reorganization shall notify the Secretary, the Pension Benefit Guaranty Corporation, the parties described in section 418A(a)(2), and the plan participants and beneficiaries of the resource benefit level determined in writing for that insolvency year.

(3) POTENTIAL NEED FOR FINANCIAL ASSISTANCE.—In any case in which the plan sponsor anticipates that the resource benefit level for an insolvency year may not exceed the level of basic benefits, the plan sponsor shall notify the Pension Benefit Guaranty Corporation.

(4) REGULATIONS.—Notice required by this subsection shall be given in accordance with regulations prescribed by the Pension Benefit Guaranty Corporation, except that notice to the Secretary shall be given in accordance with regulations prescribed by the Secretary.

(5) CORPORATION MAY PRESCRIBE TIME.—The Pension Benefit Guaranty Corporation may prescribe a time other than the time prescribed by this section for the making of a determination or the filing of a notice under this section.

[Sec. 418E(f)]

(f) FINANCIAL ASSISTANCE.—

(1) PERMISSIVE APPLICATION.—If the plan sponsor of an insolvent plan for which the resource benefit level is above the level of basic benefits anticipates that, for any month in an insolvency year, the plan will not have funds sufficient to pay basic benefits, the plan sponsor may apply for financial assistance from the Pension Benefit Guaranty Corporation under section 4261 of the Employee Retirement Income Security Act of 1974.

(2) MANDATORY APPLICATION.—A plan sponsor who has determined a resource benefit level for an insolvency year which is below the level of basic benefits shall apply for financial assistance from the Pension Benefit Guaranty Corporation under section 4261 of the Employee Retirement Income Security Act of 1974.

[Sec. 418E(g)]

(g) FINANCIAL ASSISTANCE.—Any amount of any financial assistance from the Pension Benefit Guaranty Corporation to any plan, and any repayment of such amount, shall be taken into account under this subpart in such manner as determined by the Secretary.

Amendments

• 1980, Multiemployer Pension Plan Amendments Act of 1980, (P.L. 96-364)

P.L. 96-364, §202(a):

Added Code Sec. 418E. **Effective** with respect to each plan on the first day of the first plan year beginning on or after the earlier of—

(1) the date on which the last collective-bargaining agreement providing for employer contributions under the plan, which was in effect on the date of the enactment of this Act, expires, without regard to extensions agreed to after such date of enactment, or

(2) 3 years after September 26, 1980.

Subpart D—Treatment of Welfare Benefit Funds

[Sec. 419]

SEC. 419. TREATMENT OF FUNDED WELFARE BENEFIT PLANS.

[Sec. 419(a)]

(a) GENERAL RULE.—Contributions paid or accrued by an employer to a welfare benefit fund—

(1) shall not be deductible under this chapter, but

(2) if they would otherwise be deductible, shall (subject to the limitation of subsection (b)) be deductible under this section for the taxable year in which paid.

Amendments

• 1988, Technical and Miscellaneous Revenue Act of 1988 (P.L. 100-647)

P.L. 100-647, §1018(t)(2)(C):

Amended Code Sec. 419(a)(1) by striking out "subchapter" and inserting in lieu thereof "chapter". **Effective** as if included in the provision of P.L. 99-514 to which it relates.

• 1986, Tax Reform Act of 1986 (P.L. 99-514)

P.L. 99-514, §1851(b)(2)(C)(iv)(I) and (II):

Amended Code Sec. 419(a) by striking out "under section 162 or 212" and inserting in lieu thereof "under this subchapter", and by striking out "they satisfy the requirements of either of such sections" and inserting in lieu thereof "they would otherwise be deductible". **Effective** as if included in the provision of P.L. 98-369 to which it relates.

[Sec. 419(b)]

(b) LIMITATION.—The amount of the deduction allowable under subsection (a)(2) for any taxable year shall not exceed the welfare benefit fund's qualified cost for the taxable year.

[Sec. 419(c)]

(c) QUALIFIED COST.—For purposes of this section—

(1) IN GENERAL.—Except as otherwise provided in this subsection, the term "qualified cost" means, with respect to any taxable year, the sum of—

(A) the qualified direct cost for such taxable year, and

(B) subject to the limitation of section 419A(b), any addition to a qualified asset account for the taxable year.

(2) REDUCTION FOR FUNDS AFTER-TAX INCOME.—In the case of any welfare benefit fund, the qualified cost for any taxable year shall be reduced by such fund's after-tax income for such taxable year.

(3) QUALIFIED DIRECT COST.—

(A) IN GENERAL.—The term "qualified direct cost" means, with respect to any taxable year, the aggregate amount (including administrative expenses) which would have been allowable as a deduction to the employer with respect to the benefits provided during the taxable year, if—

(i) such benefits were provided directly by the employer, and

(ii) the employer used the cash receipts and disbursements method of accounting.

(B) TIME WHEN BENEFITS PROVIDED.—For purposes of subparagraph (A), a benefit shall be treated as provided when such benefit would be includible in the gross income of the employee if provided directly by the employer (or would be so includible but for any provision of this chapter excluding such benefit from gross income).

(C) 60-MONTH AMORTIZATION OF CHILD CARE FACILITIES.—

(i) IN GENERAL.—In determining qualified direct costs with respect to any child care facility for purposes of subparagraph (A), in lieu of depreciation the adjusted basis of such facility shall be allowable as a deduction ratably over a period of 60 months beginning with the month in which the facility is placed in service.

(ii) CHILD CARE FACILITY.—The term "child care facility" means any tangible property which qualifies under regulations prescribed by the Secretary as a child care center primarily for children of employees of the employer; except that such term shall not include any property—

(I) not of a character subject to depreciation; or

(II) located outside the United States.

(4) AFTER-TAX INCOME.—

(A) IN GENERAL.—The term "after-tax income" means, with respect to any taxable year, the gross income of the welfare benefit fund reduced by the sum of—

(i) the deductions allowed by this chapter which are directly connected with the production of such gross income, and

(ii) the tax imposed by this chapter on the fund for the taxable year.

(B) TREATMENT OF CERTAIN AMOUNTS.—In determining the gross income of any welfare benefit fund—

(i) contributions and other amounts received from employees shall be taken into account, but

(ii) contributions from the employer shall not be taken into account.

(5) ITEM ONLY TAKEN INTO ACCOUNT ONCE.—No item may be taken into account more than once in determining the qualified cost of any welfare benefit fund.

[Sec. 419(d)]

(d) CARRYOVER OF EXCESS CONTRIBUTIONS.—If—

(1) the amount of the contributions paid (or deemed paid under this subsection) by the employer during any taxable year to a welfare benefit fund, exceeds

(2) the limitation of subsection (b),

such excess shall be treated as an amount paid by the employer to such fund during the succeeding taxable year.

[Sec. 419(e)]

(e) WELFARE BENEFIT FUND.—For purposes of this section—

(1) IN GENERAL.—The term "welfare benefit fund" means any fund—

(A) which is part of a plan of an employer, and

(B) through which the employer provides welfare benefits to employees or their beneficiaries.

(2) WELFARE BENEFIT.—The term "welfare benefit" means any benefit other than a benefit with respect to which—

(A) section 83(h) applies,

(B) section 404 applies (determined without regard to section 404(b)(2)), or

(C) section 404A applies.

(3) FUND.—The term "fund" means—

(A) any organization described in paragraph (7), (9), (17), or (20) of section 501(c),

(B) any trust, corporation, or other organization not exempt from the tax imposed by this chapter, and

(C) to the extent provided in regulations, any account held for an employer by any person.

(4) TREATMENT OF AMOUNTS HELD PURSUANT TO CERTAIN INSURANCE CONTRACTS.—

(A) IN GENERAL.—Notwithstanding paragraph (3)(C), the term "fund" shall not include amounts held by an insurance company pursuant to an insurance contract if—

(i) such contract is a life insurance contract described in section 264(a)(1), or

(ii) such contract is a qualified nonguaranteed contract.

(B) QUALIFIED NONGUARANTEED CONTRACT.—

(i) IN GENERAL.—For purposes of this paragraph, the term "qualified nonguaranteed contract" means any insurance contract (including a reasonable premium stabilization reserve held thereunder) if—

(I) there is no guarantee of a renewal of such contract, and

(II) other than insurance protection, the only payments to which the employer or employees are entitled are experience rated refunds or policy dividends which are not guaranteed and which are determined by factors other than the amount of welfare benefits paid to (or on behalf of) the employees of the employer or their beneficiaries.

(ii) LIMITATION.—In the case of any qualified nonguaranteed contract, subparagraph (A) shall not apply unless the amount of any experience rated refund or policy dividend payable to an employer with respect to a policy year is treated by the employer as received or accrued in the taxable year in which the policy year ends.

Amendments

• 1987, Revenue Act of 1987 (P.L. 100-203)

P.L. 100-203, §10201(b)(4):

Amended Code Sec. 419(e)(2) by inserting "or" at the end of subparagraph (B), by striking out ", or" at the end of subparagraph (C), and inserting in lieu thereof a period, and by striking out subparagraph (D). **Effective** for tax years beginning after 12-31-87. However, for a special rule see Act Sec. 10201(c)(2) in the amendment notes following Code Sec. 81. Prior to amendment, Code Sec. 419(e)(2)(D) read as follows:

(D) an election under section 463 applies.

• 1986, Tax Reform Act of 1986 (P.L. 99-514)

P.L. 99-514, §1851(a)(8)(A):

Amended Code Sec. 419(e) by adding at the end thereof new paragraph (4). **Effective** as if included in the provision of P.L. 98-369 to which it relates. However, for a rule on the effective date of regulations, see Act Sec. 1851(a)(8)(B), below.

P.L. 99-514, §1851(a)(8)(B), provides:

(B) EFFECTIVE DATE OF REGULATIONS.—Except in the case of a reserve for post-retirement medical or life insurance benefits and any other arrangement between an insurance company and an employer under which the employer has a contractual right to a refund or dividend based solely on the experience of such employer, any account held for an employer by any person and defined as a fund in regulations issued pursuant to section 419(e)(3)(C) of the Internal Revenue Code of 1954 shall be considered a "fund" no earlier than 6 months following the date such regulations are published in final form.

[Sec. 419(f)]

(f) METHOD OF CONTRIBUTIONS, ETC., HAVING THE EFFECT OF A PLAN.—If—

(1) there is no plan, but

(2) there is a method or arrangement of employer contributions or benefits which has the effect of a plan,

this section shall apply as if there were a plan.

[Sec. 419(g)]

(g) EXTENSION TO PLANS FOR INDEPENDENT CONTRACTORS.—If any fund would be a welfare benefit fund (as modified by subsection (f)) but for the fact that there is no employee-employer relationship—

(1) this section shall apply as if there were such a relationship, and

(2) any reference in this section to the employer shall be treated as a reference to the person for whom services are provided, and any reference in this section to an employee shall be treated as a reference to the person providing the services.

Amendments

• 1986, Tax Reform Act of 1986 (P.L. 99-514)

P.L. 99-514, §1851(a)(1):

Amended Code Sec. 419(g)(1) by striking out "such a plan" and inserting in lieu thereof "such a relationship". **Effective** as if included in the provision of P.L. 98-369 to which it relates.

• 1984, Deficit Reduction Act of 1984 (P.L. 98-369)

P.L. 98-369, §511(a):

Added Code Sec. 419. **Effective** for contributions paid or accrued after 12-31-85, in tax years ending after such date. However, see Act Sec. 511(e)(2)-(5), below, for special rules and effective dates.

P.L. 98-369, §511(e)(2)-(7), as amended by P.L. 99-514, §1851(a), provides:

(2) Special Rule for Collective Bargaining Agreements.—In the case of plan maintained pursuant to 1 or more collective bargaining agreements—

(A) between employee representatives and 1 or more employers, and

(B) in effect on July 1, 1985 (or ratified on or before such date), the amendments made by this section shall not apply to years beginning before the date on which the last of the collective bargaining agreements relating to the plan terminates (determined without regard to any extension thereof agreed to after July 1, 1985).

(3) Special Rule for Paragraph (2).—For purposes of paragraph (2), any plan amendment made pursuant to a collective bargaining agreement relating to the plan which amends the plan solely to conform to any requirement added by this section shall not be treated as a termination of such collective bargaining agreement.

(4) Special Effective Date for Contributions of Facilities.—Notwithstanding paragraphs (1) and (2), the amendments made by this section shall apply in the case of—

(A) any contribution after June 22, 1984, of a facility to a welfare benefit fund, and

(B) any other contribution after June 22, 1984, to a welfare benefit fund to be used to acquire or improve a facility.

(5) Binding contract exceptions to paragraph (4).—Paragraph (4) shall not apply to any facility placed in service before January 1, 1987—

(A) which is acquired or improved by the fund (or contributed to the fund) pursuant to a binding contract in effect on June 22, 1984, and at all times thereafter, or

(B) the construction of which by or for the fund began before June 22, 1984.

(6) Amendments Related to Tax on Unrelated Business Income.—The amendments made by subsection (b) shall apply with respect to taxable years ending after December 31, 1985. For purposes of section 15 of the Internal Revenue Code of 1954, such amendments shall be treated as a change in the rate of a tax imposed by chapter 1 of such Code.

(7) Amendments Related to Excise Taxes on Certain Welfare Benefit Plans.—The amendments made by subsection (c) shall apply to benefits provided after December 31, 1985.

[Sec. 419A]

SEC. 419A. QUALIFIED ASSET ACCOUNT; LIMITATION ON ADDITIONS TO ACCOUNT.

[Sec. 419A(a)]

(a) GENERAL RULE.—For purposes of this subpart and section 512, the term "qualified asset account" means any account consisting of assets set aside to provide for the payment of—

(1) disability benefits,

(2) medical benefits,

(3) SUB or severance pay benefits, or

(4) life insurance benefits.

Amendments

• 1986, Tax Reform Act of 1986 (P.L. 99-514)

P.L. 99-514, §1851(a)(6)(B):

Amended Code Sec. 419A(a) by striking out "this subpart" and inserting in lieu thereof "this subpart and section 512". **Effective** as if included in the provision of P.L. 98-369 to which it relates.

[Sec. 419A(b)]

(b) LIMITATION ON ADDITIONS TO ACCOUNT.—No addition to any qualified asset account may be taken into account under section 419(c)(1)(B) to the extent such addition results in the amount in such account exceeding the account limit.

[Sec. 419A(c)]

(c) ACCOUNT LIMIT.—For purposes of this section—

(1) IN GENERAL.—Except as otherwise provided in this subsection, the account limit for any qualified asset account for any taxable year is the amount reasonably and actuarially necessary to fund—

(A) claims incurred but unpaid (as of the close of such taxable year) for benefits referred to in subsection (a), and

(B) administrative costs with respect to such claims.

(2) ADDITIONAL RESERVE FOR POST-RETIREMENT MEDICAL AND LIFE INSURANCE BENEFITS.—The account limit for any taxable year may include a reserve funded over the working lives of the covered employees and actuarially determined on a level basis (using assumptions that are reasonable in the aggregate) as necessary for—

(A) post-retirement medical benefits to be provided to covered employees (determined on the basis of current medical costs), or

(B) post-retirement life insurance benefits to be provided to covered employees.

(3) AMOUNT TAKEN INTO ACCOUNT FOR SUB OR SEVERANCE PAY BENEFITS.—

(A) IN GENERAL.—The account limit for any taxable year with respect to SUB or severance pay benefits is 75 percent of the average annual qualified direct costs for SUB or severance pay benefits for any 2 of the immediately preceding 7 taxable years (as selected by the fund).

(B) SPECIAL RULE FOR CERTAIN NEW PLANS.—In the case of any new plan for which SUB or severance pay benefits are not available to any key employee, the Secretary shall, by regulations, provide for an interim amount to be taken into account under paragraph (1).

(4) LIMITATION ON AMOUNTS TO BE TAKEN INTO ACCOUNT.—

(A) DISABILITY BENEFITS.—For purposes of paragraph (1), disability benefits payable to any individual shall not be taken into account to the extent such benefits are payable at an annual rate in excess of the lower of—

(i) 75 percent of such individual's average compensation for his high 3 years (within the meaning of section 415(b)(3)), or

(ii) the limitation in effect under section 415(b)(1)(A).

(B) LIMITATION ON SUB OR SEVERANCE PAY BENEFITS.—For purposes of paragraph (3), any SUB or severance pay benefit payable to any individual shall not be taken into account to the extent such benefit is payable at an annual rate in excess of 150 percent of the limitation in effect under section 415(c)(1)(A).

(5) SPECIAL LIMITATION WHERE NO ACTUARIAL CERTIFICATION.—

(A) IN GENERAL.—Unless there is an actuarial certification of the account limit determined under this subsection for any taxable year, the account limit for such taxable year shall not exceed the sum of the safe harbor limits for such taxable year.

(B) SAFE HARBOR LIMITS.—

(i) SHORT-TERM DISABILITY BENEFITS.—In the case of short-term disability benefits, the safe harbor limit for any taxable year is 17.5 percent of the qualified direct costs (other than insurance premiums) for the immediately preceding taxable year with respect to such benefits.

(ii) MEDICAL BENEFITS.—In the case of medical benefits, the safe harbor limit for any taxable year is 35 percent of the qualified direct costs (other than insurance premiums) for the immediately preceding taxable year with respect to medical benefits.

(iii) SUB OR SEVERANCE PAY BENEFITS.—In the case of SUB or severance pay benefits, the safe harbor limit for any taxable year is the amount determined under paragraph (3).

(iv) LONG-TERM DISABILITY OR LIFE INSURANCE BENEFITS.—In the case of any long-term disability benefit or life insurance benefit, the safe harbor limit for any taxable year shall be the amount prescribed by regulations.

(6) ADDITIONAL RESERVE FOR MEDICAL BENEFITS OF BONA FIDE ASSOCIATION PLANS.—

(A) IN GENERAL.—An applicable account limit for any taxable year may include a reserve in an amount not to exceed 35 percent of the sum of—

(i) the qualified direct costs, and

(ii) the change in claims incurred but unpaid,

for such taxable year with respect to medical benefits (other than post-retirement medical benefits).

(B) APPLICABLE ACCOUNT LIMIT.—For purposes of this subsection, the term "applicable account limit" means an account limit for a qualified asset account with respect to medical benefits provided through a plan maintained by a bona fide association (as defined in section 2791(d)(3) of the Public Health Service Act (42 U.S.C. 300gg-91(d)(3)).

Amendments

• 2006, Pension Protection Act of 2006 (P.L. 109-280)

P.L. 109-280, §843(a):

Amended Code Sec. 419A(c) by adding at the end a new paragraph (6). **Effective** for tax years beginning after 12-31-2006.

• 1996, Small Business Job Protection Act of 1996 (P.L. 104-188)

P.L. 104-188, §1704(t)(60):

Amended Code Sec. 419A(c)(3) by striking "SEVERENCE" in the heading and inserting "SEVERANCE". **E ffective** 8-20-96.

• 1986, Tax Reform Act of 1986 (P.L. 99-514)

P.L. 99-514, §1851(a)(5):

Amended Code Sec. 419A(c)(5)(A) by striking out "under paragraph (1)" and inserting in lieu thereof "under this subsection". **Effective** as if included in the provision of P.L. 98-369 to which it relates.

[Sec. 419A(d)]

(d) REQUIREMENT OF SEPARATE ACCOUNTS FOR POST-RETIREMENT MEDICAL OR LIFE INSURANCE BENEFITS PROVIDED TO KEY EMPLOYEES.—

(1) IN GENERAL.—In the case of any employee who is a key employee—

(A) a separate account shall be established for any medical benefits or life insurance benefits provided with respect to such employee after retirement, and

(B) medical benefits and life insurance benefits provided with respect to such employee after retirement may only be paid from such separate account.

The requirements of this paragraph shall apply to the first taxable year for which a reserve is taken into account under subsection (c)(2) and to all subsequent taxable years.

(2) COORDINATION WITH SECTION 415.—For purposes of section 415, any amount attributable to medical benefits allocated to an account established under paragraph (1) shall be treated as an annual addition to a defined contribution plan for purposes of section 415(c). Subparagraph (B) of section 415(c)(1) shall not apply to any amount treated as an annual addition under the preceding sentence.

(3) KEY EMPLOYEE.—For purposes of this section, the term "key employee" means any employee who, at any time during the plan year or any preceding plan year, is or was a key employee as defined in section 416(i).

Amendments

• 1986, Tax Reform Act of 1986 (P.L. 99-514)

P.L. 99-514, §1851(a)(2)(A)-(B):

Amended Code Sec. 419A(d)(2) by adding at the end thereof a new sentence. **Effective** as if included in P.L. 98-369 to which it relates.

P.L. 99-514, §1851(a)(2)(A)-(B):

Amended Code Sec. 419A(d)(1) by adding at the end thereof a new sentence. **Effective** as if included in P.L. 98-369 to which it relates.

[Sec. 419A(e)]

(e) SPECIAL LIMITATIONS ON RESERVES FOR MEDICAL BENEFITS OR LIFE INSURANCE BENEFITS PROVIDED TO RETIRED EMPLOYEES.—

(1) RESERVE MUST BE NONDISCRIMINATORY.—No reserve may be taken into account under subsection (c)(2) for post-retirement medical benefits or life insurance benefits to be provided to covered employees unless the plan meets the requirements of section 505(b) with respect to such benefits (whether or not such requirements apply to such plan). The preceding sentence shall not apply to any plan maintained pursuant to an agreement between employee representatives and 1 or more employers if the Secretary finds that such agreement is a collective bargaining agreement and the post-retirement medical benefits or life insurance benefits were the subject of good faith bargaining between such employee representatives and such employer or employers.

(2) LIMITATION ON AMOUNT OF LIFE INSURANCE BENEFITS.—Life insurance benefits shall not be taken into account under subsection (c)(2) to the extent the aggregate amount of such benefits to be provided with respect to the employee exceeds $50,000.

Amendments

• 1986, Tax Reform Act of 1986 (P.L. 99-514)

P.L. 99-514, §1851(a)(3)(A):

Amended Code Sec. 419A(e). **Effective** as if included in the provision of P.L. 98-369 to which it relates. Prior to amendment, Code Sec. 419A(e) read as follows:

(e) SPECIAL LIMITATIONS ON RESERVES FOR MEDICAL BENEFITS OR LIFE INSURANCE BENEFITS PROVIDED TO RETIRED EMPLOYEES.—

(1) BENEFITS MUST BE NONDISCRIMINATORY.—No reserve may be taken into account under subsection (c)(2) for post-retirement medical benefits or life insurance benefits to be provided to covered employees unless the plan meets the requirements of section 505(b)(1) with respect to such benefits.

(2) TAXABLE LIFE INSURANCE BENEFITS NOT TAKEN INTO ACCOUNT.—No life insurance benefit may be taken into account under subsection (c)(2) to the extent—

(A) such benefit is includible in gross income under section 79, or

(B) such benefit would be includible in gross income under section 101(b) (determined by substituting "$50,000" for "$5,000").

P.L. 99-514, §1851(a)(3)(B), as amended by P.L. 100-647, §1018(t)(2)(D), provides:

(B) Subsection (e) of section 419A, section 505, and section 4976(b)(1)(B) of the Internal Revenue Code of 1954 (as amended by subparagraph (A)) shall not apply to any group-term life insurance to the extent that the amendments made by section 223(a) of the Tax Reform Act of 1984 do not apply to such insurance by reason of paragraph (2) of section 223(d) of such Act.

[Sec. 419A(f)]

(f) DEFINITIONS AND OTHER SPECIAL RULES.—For purposes of this section—

(1) SUB OR SEVERANCE PAY BENEFIT.—The term "SUB or severance pay benefit" means—

(A) any supplemental unemployment compensation benefit (as defined in section 501(c)(17)(D)), and

(B) any severance pay benefit.

(2) MEDICAL BENEFIT.—The term "medical benefit" means a benefit which consists of the providing (directly or through insurance) of medical care (as defined in section 213(d)).

(3) LIFE INSURANCE BENEFIT.—The term "life insurance benefit" includes any other death benefit.

(4) VALUATION.—For purposes of this section, the amount of the qualified asset account shall be the value of the assets in such account (as determined under regulations).

(5) SPECIAL RULE FOR COLLECTIVE BARGAINED AND EMPLOYEE PAY-ALL PLANS.—No account limits shall apply in the case of any qualified asset account under a separate welfare benefit fund—

(A) under a collective bargaining agreement, or

(B) an employee pay-all plan under section 501(c)(9) if—

(i) such plan has at least 50 employees (determined without regard to subsection (h)(1)), and

(ii) no employee is entitled to a refund with respect to amounts in the fund, other than a refund based on the experience of the entire fund.

(6) EXCEPTION FOR 10-OR-MORE EMPLOYER PLANS.—

(A) IN GENERAL.—This subpart shall not apply in the case of any welfare benefit fund which is part of a 10 or more employer plan. The preceding sentence shall not apply to any plan which maintains experience-rating arrangements with respect to individual employers.

(B) 10 OR MORE EMPLOYER PLAN.—For purposes of subparagraph (A), the term "10 or more employer plan" means a plan—

(i) to which more than 1 employer contributes, and

(ii) to which no employer normally contributes more than 10 percent of the total contributions contributed under the plan by all employers.

(7) Adjustments for existing excess reserves.—

(A) Increase in account limit.—The account limit for any of the first 4 taxable years to which this section applies shall be increased by the applicable percentage of any existing excess reserves.

(B) Applicable percentage.—For purposes of subparagraph (A)—

In the case of:	The applicable percentage is:
The first taxable year to which this section applies	80
The second taxable year to which this section applies	60
The third taxable year to which this section applies	40
The fourth taxable year to which this section applies	20

(C) Existing excess reserve.—For purposes of computing the increase under subparagraph (A) for any taxable year, the term "existing excess reserve" means the excess (if any) of—

(i) the amount of assets set aside at the close of the first taxable year ending after July 18, 1984, for purposes described in subsection (a), over

(ii) the account limit determined under this section (without regard to this paragraph) for the taxable year for which such increase is being computed.

(D) Funds to which paragraph applies.—This paragraph shall apply only to a welfare benefit fund which, as of July 18, 1984, had assets set aside for purposes described in subsection (a).

Amendments

• 1988, Technical and Miscellaneous Revenue Act of 1988 (P.L. 100-647)

P.L. 100-647, §1018(t)(1)(C):

Amended Code Sec. 419A(f)(5) by striking out "accounts" and inserting in lieu thereof "account". **Effective** as if included in the provision of P.L. 99-514 to which it relates.

P.L. 100-647, §1018(t)(2):

Amended P.L. 99-514, §1851(a), by striking out paragraph (4) [see amendment note for P.L. 99-614, §1851(a)(4), below]. **Effective** as if included in the provision of P.L. 99-514 to which it relates.

• 1986, Tax Reform Act of 1986 (P.L. 99-514)

P.L. 99-514, §1851(a)(4):

Amended Code Sec. 419A(f)(5) by striking out "welfare benefit fund established under" and inserting in lieu thereof "wefare benefit fund maintained pursuant to". **Effective** as if included in the provision of P.L. 98-369 to which it relates.

P.L. 99-514, §1851(a)(7):

Amended Code Sec. 419A(f)(7) by striking out subparagraph (C) and inserting in lieu thereof new subparagraphs (C) and (D). **Effective** as if included in the provision of P.L. 98-369 to which it relates. Prior to amendment, Code Sec. 419A(f)(7)(C) read as follows:

(C) Existing excess reserve.—For purposes of this paragraph, the term "existing excess reserve" means the excess (if any) of—

(i) the amount of assets set aside for purposes described in subsection (a) as of the close of the first taxable year ending after the date of the enactment of the Tax Reform Act of 1984, over

(ii) the account limit which would have applied under this section to such taxable year if this section had applied to such taxable year.

P.L. 99-514, §1851(a)(13):

Amended Code Sec. 419A(f)(5). **Effective** as if included in the provision of P.L. 98-369 to which it relates. Prior to amendment, Code Sec. 419A(f)(5) read as follows:

(5) Higher limit in case of collectively bargained plans.—Not later than July 1, 1985, the Secretary shall by regulations provide for special account limits in the case of any qualified asset account under a welfare benefit fund established under a collective bargaining agreement.

[Sec. 419A(g)]

(g) Employer Taxed on Income of Welfare Benefit Fund in Certain Cases.—

(1) In general.—In the case of any welfare benefit fund which is not an organization described in paragraph (7), (9), (17), or (20) of section 501(c), the employer shall include in gross income for any taxable year an amount equal to such fund's deemed unrelated income for the fund's taxable year ending within the employer's taxable year.

(2) Deemed unrelated income.—For purposes of paragraph (1), the deemed unrelated income of any welfare benefit fund shall be the amount which would have been its unrelated business taxable income under section 512(a)(3) if such fund were an organization described in paragraph (7), (9), (17), or (20) of section 501(c).

(3) Coordination with section 419.—If any amount is included in the gross income of an employer for any taxable year under paragraph (1) with respect to any welfare benefit fund—

(A) the amount of the tax imposed by this chapter which is attributable to the amount so included shall be treated as a contribution paid to such welfare benefit fund on the last day of such taxable year, and

(B) the tax so attributable shall be treated as imposed on the fund for purposes of section 419(c)(4)(A).

Amendments

• 1986, Tax Reform Act of 1986 (P.L. 99-514)

P.L. 99-514, §1851(a)(9):

Amended Code Sec. 419A(g) by adding at the end thereof new paragraph (3). **Effective** as if included in the provision of P.L. 98-369 to which it relates.

[Sec. 419A(h)]

(h) AGGREGATION RULES.—For purposes of this subpart—

(1) AGGREGATION OF FUNDS.—

(A) MANDATORY AGGREGATION.—For purposes of subsections (c)(4), (d)(2), and (e)(2), all welfare benefit funds of an employer shall be treated as 1 fund.

(B) PERMISSIVE AGGREGATION FOR PURPOSES NOT SPECIFIED IN SUBPARAGRAPH (A).—For purposes of this section (other than the provisions specified in subparagraph (A)), at the election of the employer, 2 or more welfare benefit funds of such employer may (to the extent not inconsistent with the purposes of this subpart and section 512) be treated as 1 fund.

(2) TREATMENT OF RELATED EMPLOYERS.—Rules similar to the rules of subsections (b), (c), (m), and (n) of section 414 shall apply.

Amendments

• 1986, Tax Reform Act of 1986 (P.L. 99-514)

P.L. 99-514, §1851(a)(6)(A):

Amended Code Sec. 419A(h)(1). **Effective** as if included in the provision of P.L. 98-369 to which it relates. Prior to amendment, Code Sec. 419A(h)(1) read as follows:

(1) AGGREGATION OF FUNDS.—At the election of the employer, 2 or more welfare benefit funds of such employer may be treated as 1 fund.

[Sec. 419A(i)]

(i) REGULATIONS.—The Secretary shall prescribe such regulations as may be appropriate to carry out the purposes of this subpart. Such regulations may provide that the plan administrator of any welfare benefit fund which is part of a plan to which more than 1 employer contributes shall submit such information to the employers contributing to the fund as may be necessary to enable the employers to comply with the provisions of this section.

Amendments

• 1984, Deficit Reduction Act of 1984 (P.L. 98-369)

P.L. 98-369, §511(a):

Added Code Sec. 419A. **Effective** for contributions paid or accrued after 12-31-85, in tax years ending after such date. However, see Act Sec. 511(e)(2)-(5) under Code Sec. 419 for special rules and effective dates.

Subpart E—Treatment of Transfers to Retiree Health Accounts

Sec. 420. Transfers of excess pension assets to retiree health accounts.

[Sec. 420]

SEC. 420. TRANSFERS OF EXCESS PENSION ASSETS TO RETIREE HEALTH ACCOUNTS.

[Sec. 420(a)]

(a) GENERAL RULE.—If there is a qualified transfer of any excess pension assets of a defined benefit plan to a health benefits account which is part of such plan—

(1) a trust which is part of such plan shall not be treated as failing to meet the requirements of subsection (a) or (h) of section 401 solely by reason of such transfer (or any other action authorized under this section),

(2) no amount shall be includible in the gross income of the employer maintaining the plan solely by reason of such transfer,

(3) such transfer shall not be treated—

(A) as an employer reversion for purposes of section 4980, or

(B) as a prohibited transaction for purposes of section 4975, and

(4) the limitations of subsection (d) shall apply to such employer.

Amendments

• 2006, Pension Protection Act of 2006 (P.L. 109-280)

P.L. 109-280, §842(a)(1):

Amended Code Sec. 420(a) by striking "(other than a multiemployer plan)" following "of a defined benefit plan" in the material preceding paragraph (1). **Effective** for transfers made in tax years beginning after 12-31-2006.

[Sec. 420(b)]

(b) QUALIFIED TRANSFER.—For purposes of this section—

(1) IN GENERAL.—The term "qualified transfer" means a transfer—

(A) of excess pension assets of a defined benefit plan to a health benefits account which is part of such plan in a taxable year beginning after December 31, 1990,

(B) which does not contravene any other provision of law, and

(C) with respect to which the following requirements are met in connection with the plan—

(i) the use requirements of subsection (c)(1),

(ii) the vesting requirements of subsection (c)(2), and

(iii) the minimum cost requirements of subsection (c)(3).

(2) ONLY 1 TRANSFER PER YEAR.—

(A) IN GENERAL.—No more than 1 transfer with respect to any plan during a taxable year may be treated as a qualified transfer for purposes of this section.

(B) EXCEPTION.—A transfer described in paragraph (4) shall not be taken into account for purposes of subparagraph (A).

(3) LIMITATION ON AMOUNT TRANSFERRED.—The amount of excess pension assets which may be transferred in a qualified transfer shall not exceed the amount which is reasonably estimated to be the amount the employer maintaining the plan will pay (whether directly or through reimbursement) out of such account during the taxable year of the transfer for qualified current retiree health liabilities.

(4) SPECIAL RULE FOR 1990.—

(a) IN GENERAL.—Subject to the provisions of subsection (c), a transfer shall be treated as a qualified transfer if such transfer—

(i) is made after the close of the taxable year preceding the employer's first taxable year beginning after December 31, 1990, and before the earlier of—

(I) the due date (including extensions) for the filing of the return of tax for such preceding taxable year, or

(II) the date such return is filed, and

(ii) does not exceed the expenditures of the employer for qualified current retiree health liabilities for such preceding taxable year.

(B) DEDUCTION REDUCED.—The amount of the deductions otherwise allowable under this chapter to an employer for the taxable year preceding the employer's first taxable year beginning after December 31, 1990, shall be reduced by the amount of any qualified transfer to which this paragraph applies.

(C) COORDINATION WITH REDUCTION RULE.—Subsection (e)(1)(B) shall not apply to a transfer described in subparagraph (A).

(5) EXPIRATION.—No transfer made after December 31, 2013, shall be treated as a qualified transfer.

Amendments

• 2004, Pension Funding Equity Act of 2004 (P.L. 108-218)

P.L. 108-218, §204(a):

Amended Code Sec. 420(b)(5) by striking "December 31, 2005" and inserting "December 31, 2013". **Effective** 4-10-2004.

• 1999, Tax Relief Extension Act of 1999 (P.L. 106-170)

P.L. 106-170, §535(a)(1):

Amended Code Sec. 420(b)(5) by striking "in any taxable year beginning after December 31, 2000" and inserting "made after December 31, 2005". **Effective** for qualified transfers occurring after 12-17-99. For a transition rule, see Act Sec. 535(c)(2), below.

P.L. 106-170, §535(b)(2)(A):

Amended Code Sec. 420(b)(1)(C)(iii) by striking "benefits" and inserting "cost". **Effective** for qualified transfers occurring after 12-17-99. For a transition rule, see Act Sec. 535(c)(2), below.

P.L. 106-170, §535(c)(2), provides:

(2) TRANSITION RULE.—If the cost maintenance period for any qualified transfer after the date of the enactment of this Act includes any portion of a benefit maintenance period for any qualified transfer on or before such date, the amendments made by subsection (b) shall not apply to such portion of the cost maintenance period (and such portion shall be treated as a benefit maintenance period).

• 1994, Uruguay Round Agreements Act (P.L. 103-465)

P.L. 103-465, §731(a):

Amended Code Sec. 420(b)(5) by striking "1995" and inserting "2000". **Effective** for tax years beginning after 12-31-95.

P.L. 103-465, §731(c)(1):

Amended Code Sec. 420(b)(1)(C)(iii) by striking "cost" and inserting "benefits". **Effective** for qualified transfers occurring after 12-8-94.

[Sec. 420(c)]

(c) REQUIREMENTS OF PLANS TRANSFERRING ASSETS.—

(1) USE OF TRANSFERRED ASSETS.—

(A) IN GENERAL.—Any assets transferred to a health benefits account in a qualified transfer (and any income allocable thereto) shall be used only to pay qualified current retiree health liabilities (other than liabilities of key employees not taken into account under subsection (e)(1)(D)) for the taxable year of the transfer (whether directly or through reimbursement). In the case of a qualified future transfer or collectively bargained transfer to which subsection (f) applies, any assets so transferred may also be used to pay liabilities described in subsection (f)(2)(C).

(B) AMOUNTS NOT USED TO PAY FOR HEALTH BENEFITS.—

(i) IN GENERAL.—Any assets transferred to a health benefits account in a qualified transfer (and any income allocable thereto) which are not used as provided in subparagraph (A) shall be transferred out of the account to the transferor plan.

(ii) TAX TREATMENT OF AMOUNTS.—Any amount transferred out of an account under clause (i)—

(I) shall not be includible in the gross income of the employer for such taxable year, but

(II) shall be treated as an employer reversion for purposes of section 4980 (without regard to subsection (d) thereof).

(C) ORDERING RULE.—For purposes of this section, any amount paid out of a health benefits account shall be treated as paid first out of the assets and income described in subparagraph (A).

(2) REQUIREMENTS RELATING TO PENSION BENEFITS ACCRUING BEFORE TRANSFER.—

(A) IN GENERAL.—The requirements of this paragraph are met if the plan provides that the accrued pension benefits of any participant or beneficiary under the plan become nonforfeitable in the same manner which would be required if the plan had terminated immediately before the qualified transfer (or in the case of a participant who separated during the 1-year period ending on the date of the transfer, immediately before such separation).

(B) SPECIAL RULE FOR 1990.—In the case of a qualified transfer described in subsection (b)(4), the requirements of this paragraph are met with respect to any participant who separated from service during the taxable year to which such transfer relates by recomputing such participant's benefits as if subparagraph (A) had applied immediately before such separation.

(3) MINIMUM COST REQUIREMENTS.—

(A) IN GENERAL.—The requirements of this paragraph are met if each group health plan or arrangement under which applicable health benefits are provided provides that the applicable employer cost for each taxable year during the cost maintenance period shall not be less than the higher of the applicable employer costs for each of the 2 taxable years immediately preceding the taxable year of the qualified transfer or, in the case of a transfer which involves a plan maintained by an employer described in subsection (f)(2)(E)(i)(III), if the plan meets the requirements of subsection (f)(2)(D)(i)(II).

(B) APPLICABLE EMPLOYER COST.—For purposes of this paragraph, the term "applicable employer cost" means, with respect to any taxable year, the amount determined by dividing—

(i) the qualified current retiree health liabilities of the employer for such taxable year determined—

(I) without regard to any reduction under subsection (e)(1)(B), and

(II) in the case of a taxable year in which there was no qualified transfer, in the same manner as if there had been such a transfer at the end of the taxable year, by

(ii) the number of individuals to whom coverage for applicable health benefits was provided during such taxable year.

(C) ELECTION TO COMPUTE COST SEPARATELY.—An employer may elect to have this paragraph applied separately with respect to individuals eligible for benefits under title XVIII of the Social Security Act at any time during the taxable year and with respect to individuals not so eligible.

(D) COST MAINTENANCE PERIOD.—For purposes of this paragraph, the term "cost maintenance period" means the period of 5 taxable years beginning with the taxable year in which the qualified transfer occurs. If a taxable year is in two or more overlapping cost maintenance periods, this paragraph shall be applied by taking into account the highest applicable employer cost required to be provided under subparagraph (A) for such taxable year.

(E) REGULATIONS.—

(i) IN GENERAL.—The Secretary shall prescribe such regulations as may be necessary to prevent an employer who significantly reduces retiree health coverage during the cost maintenance period from being treated as satisfying the minimum cost requirement of this subsection.

(ii) INSIGNIFICANT COST REDUCTIONS PERMITTED.—

(I) IN GENERAL.—An eligible employer shall not be treated as failing to meet the requirements of this paragraph for any taxable year if, in lieu of any reduction of retiree health coverage permitted under the regulations prescribed under clause (i), the employer reduces applicable employer cost by an amount not in excess of the reduction in costs which would have occurred if the employer had made the maximum permissible reduction in retiree health coverage under such regulations. In applying such regulations to any subsequent taxable year, any reduction in applicable employer cost under this clause shall be treated as if it were an equivalent reduction in retiree health coverage.

(II) ELIGIBLE EMPLOYER.—For purposes of subclause (I), an employer shall be treated as an eligible employer for any taxable year if, for the preceding taxable year, the qualified current retiree health liabilities of the employer were at least 5 percent of the gross receipts of the employer. For purposes of this subclause, the rules of paragraphs (2), (3)(B), and (3)(C) of section 448(c) shall apply in determining the amount of an employer's gross receipts.

Amendments

• 2008, Worker, Retiree, and Employer Recovery Act of 2008 (P.L. 110-458)

P.L. 110-458, §108(i)(1):

Amended Code Sec. 420(c)(1)(A) by adding at the end a new sentence. **Effective** as if included in the provision of the 2006 Act to which the amendment relates [**effective** for transfers after 8-17-2006.—CCH].

• 2007, U.S. Troop Readiness, Veterans' Care, Katrina Recovery, and Iraq Accountability Appropriations Act, 2007 (P.L. 110-28)

P.L. 110-28, §6613(a):

Amended Code Sec. 420(c)(3)(A) by striking "transfer." and inserting "transfer or, in the case of a transfer which involves a plan maintained by an employer described in subsection (f)(2)(E)(i)(III), if the plan meets the requirements of subsection (f)(2)(D)(i)(II).". **Effective** for transfers after 5-25-2007.

• 2004, American Jobs Creation Act of 2004 (P.L. 108-357)

P.L. 108-357, §709(b)(1):

Amended Code Sec. 420(c)(3)(E) by adding at the end a new clause (ii). **Effective** for tax years ending after 10-22-2004.

P.L. 108-357, §709(b)(2):

Amended Code Sec. 420(c)(3)(E) by striking "The Secretary" and inserting "(i) IN GENERAL.—The Secretary". **Effective** for tax years ending after 10-22-2004.

• 1999, Tax Relief Extension Act of 1999 (P.L. 106-170)

P.L. 106-170, §535(b)(1):

Amended Code Sec. 420(c)(3). **Effective** for qualified transfers occurring after 12-17-99. For a transition rule, see Act Sec. 535(c)(2), below. Prior to amendment, Code Sec. 420(c)(3) read as follows:

(3) MAINTENANCE OF BENEFIT REQUIREMENTS.—

(A) IN GENERAL.—The requirements of this paragraph are met if each group health plan or arrangement under which applicable health benefits are provided provides that the applicable health benefits provided by the employer during each taxable year during the benefit maintenance period are substantially the same as the applicable health benefits provided by the employer during the taxable year immediately preceding the taxable year of the qualified transfer.

(B) ELECTION TO APPLY SEPARATELY.—An employer may elect to have this paragraph applied separately with respect to individuals eligible for benefits under title XVIII of the Social Security Act at any time during the taxable year and with respect to individuals not so eligible.

(C) BENEFIT MAINTENANCE PERIOD.—For purposes of this paragraph, the term "benefit maintenance period" means the period of 5 taxable years beginning with the taxable year in which the qualified transfer occurs. If a taxable year is in 2 or more benefit maintenance periods, this paragraph shall be applied by taking into account the highest level of benefits required to be provided under subparagraph (A) for such taxable year.

P.L. 106-170, §535(c)(2), provides:

(2) TRANSITION RULE.—If the cost maintenance period for any qualified transfer after the date of the enactment of this Act includes any portion of a benefit maintenance period for any qualified transfer on or before such date, the amendments made by subsection (b) shall not apply to such portion of the cost maintenance period (and such portion shall be treated as a benefit maintenance period).

• 1994, Uruguay Round Agreements Act (P.L. 103-465)

P.L. 103-465, §731(b):

Amended Code Sec. 420(c)(3). **Effective** for qualified transfers occurring after 12-8-94. Prior to amendment, Code Sec. 420(c)(3) read as follows:

(3) MINIMUM COST REQUIREMENTS.—

(A) IN GENERAL.—The requirements of this paragraph are met if each group health plan or arrangement under which applicable health benefits are provided provides that the applicable employer cost for each taxable year during the cost maintenance period shall not be less than the higher of the applicable employer costs for each of the 2 taxable years immediately preceding the taxable year of the qualified transfer.

(B) APPLICABLE EMPLOYER COST.—For purposes of this paragraph, the term "applicable employer cost" means, with respect to any taxable year, the amount determined by dividing—

(i) the qualified current retiree health liabilities of the employer for such taxable year determined—

(I) without regard to any reduction under subsection (e)(1)(B), and

(II) in the case of a taxable year in which there was no qualified transfer, in the same manner as if there had been such a transfer at the end of the taxable year, by

(ii) the number of individuals to whom coverage for applicable health benefits was provided during such taxable year.

(C) ELECTION TO COMPUTE COST SEPARATELY.—An employer may elect to have this paragraph applied separately with respect to individuals eligible for benefits under title XVIII of the Social Security Act at any time during the taxable year and with respect to individuals not so eligible.

(D) COST MAINTENANCE PERIOD.—For purposes of this paragraph, the term "cost maintenance period" means the period of 5 taxable years beginning with the taxable year in which the qualified transfer occurs. If a taxable year is in 2 or more overlapping cost maintenance periods, this paragraph shall be applied by taking into account the highest applicable employer cost required to be provided under subparagraph (A) for such taxable year.

[Sec. 420(d)]

(d) LIMITATIONS ON EMPLOYER.—For purposes of this title—

(1) DEDUCTION LIMITATIONS.—No deduction shall be allowed—

(A) for the transfer of any amount to a health benefits account in a qualified transfer (or any retransfer to the plan under subsection (c)(1)(B)),

(B) for qualified current retiree health liabilities paid out of the assets (and income) described in subsection (c)(1), or

(C) for any amounts to which subparagraph (B) does not apply and which are paid for qualified current retiree health liabilities for the taxable year to the extent such amounts are not greater than the excess (if any) of—

(i) the amount determined under subparagraph (A) (and income allocable thereto), over

(ii) the amount determined under subparagraph (B).

(2) NO CONTRIBUTIONS ALLOWED.—An employer may not contribute after December 31, 1990, any amount to a health benefits account or welfare benefit fund (as defined in section 419(e)(1)) with respect to qualified current retiree health liabilities for which transferred assets are required to be used under subsection (c)(1).

[Sec. 420(e)]

(e) DEFINITION AND SPECIAL RULES.—For purposes of this section—

(1) QUALIFIED CURRENT RETIREE HEALTH LIABILITIES.—For purposes of this section—

(A) IN GENERAL.—The term "qualified current retiree health liabilities" means, with respect to any taxable year, the aggregate amounts (including administrative expenses) which would have been allowable as a deduction to the employer for such taxable year with respect to applicable health benefits provided during such taxable year if—

(i) such benefits were provided directly by the employer, and

(ii) the employer used the cash receipts and disbursements method of accounting.

For purposes of the preceding sentence, the rule of section 419(c)(3)(B) shall apply.

(B) REDUCTIONS FOR AMOUNTS PREVIOUSLY SET ASIDE.—The amount determined under subparagraph (A) shall be reduced by the amount which bears the same ratio to such amount as—

(i) the value (as of the close of the plan year preceding the year of the qualified transfer) of the assets in all health benefits accounts or welfare benefit funds (as defined in section 419(e)(1)) set aside to pay for the qualified current retiree health liability, bears to

(ii) the present value of the qualified current retiree health liabilities for all plan years (determined without regard to this subparagraph).

(C) APPLICABLE HEALTH BENEFITS.—The term "applicable health benefits" means health benefits or coverage which are provided to—

(i) retired employees who, immediately before the qualified transfer, are entitled to receive such benefits upon retirement and who are entitled to pension benefits under the plan, and

(ii) their spouses and dependents.

(D) KEY EMPLOYEES EXCLUDED.—If an employee is a key employee (within the meaning of section 416(i)(1)) with respect to any plan year ending in a taxable year, such employee shall not be taken into account in computing qualified current retiree health liabilities for such taxable year or in calculating applicable employer cost under subsection (c)(3)(B).

(2) EXCESS PENSION ASSETS.—The term "excess pension assets" means the excess (if any) of—

(A) the lesser of—

(i) the fair market value of the plan's assets (reduced by the prefunding balance and funding standard carryover balance determined under section 430(f)), or

(ii) the value of plan assets as determined under section 430(g)(3) after reduction under section 430(f), over

(B) 125 percent of the sum of the funding target and the target normal cost determined under section 430 for such plan year.

(3) HEALTH BENEFITS ACCOUNT.—The term "health benefits account" means an account established and maintained under section 401(h).

(4) COORDINATION WITH SECTION 430 .—In the case of a qualified transfer, any assets so transferred shall not, for purposes of this section and section 430, be treated as assets in the plan.

(5) APPLICATION TO MULTIEMPLOYER PLANS.—In the case of a multiemployer plan, this section shall be applied to any such plan—

(A) by treating any reference in this section to an employer as a reference to all employers maintaining the plan (or, if appropriate, the plan sponsor), and

(B) in accordance with such modifications of this section (and the provisions of this title relating to this section) as the Secretary determines appropriate to reflect the fact the plan is not maintained by a single employer.

Amendments

• 2007, U.S. Troop Readiness, Veterans' Care, Katrina Recovery, and Iraq Accountability Appropriations Act, 2007 (P.L. 110-28)

P.L. 110-28, §6612(b):

Amended Code Sec. 420(e)(2)(B) by striking "funding shortfall" and inserting "funding target". **Effective** as if included in the provision of the Pension Protection Act of 2006 (P.L. 109-280) to which it relates [**effective** 8-17-2006.—CCH].

• 2006, Pension Protection Act of 2006 (P.L. 109-280)

P.L. 109-280, §114(d)(1):

Amended Code Sec. 420(e)(2). **Effective** for plan years beginning after 2007 [**effective** date amended by P.L. 110-458, §101(d)(3).—CCH]. Prior to amendment, Code Sec. 420(e)(2) read as follows:

(2) EXCESS PENSION ASSETS.—The term "excess pension assets" means the excess (if any) of—

(A) the amount determined under section 412(c)(7)(A)(ii), over

(B) the greater of—

(i) the amount determined under section 412(c)(7)(A)(i), or

(ii) 125 percent of current liability (as defined in section 412(c)(7)(B)).

The determination under this paragraph shall be made as of the most recent valuation date of the plan preceding the qualified transfer.

P.L. 109-280, §114(d)(2):

Amended Code Sec. 420(e)(4). **Effective** for plan years beginning after 2007 [**effective** date amended by P.L. 110-458, §101(d)(3).—CCH]. Prior to amendment, Code Sec. 420(e)(4) read as follows:

(4) COORDINATION WITH SECTION 412.—In the case of a qualified transfer to a health benefits account—

(A) any assets transferred in a plan year on or before the valuation date for such year (and any income allocable thereto) shall, for purposes of section 412, be treated as assets in the plan as of the valuation date for such year, and

(B) the plan shall be treated as having a net experience loss under section 412(b)(2)(B)(iv) in an amount equal to the amount of such transfer (reduced by any amounts transferred back to the pension plan under subsection (c)(1)(B)) and for which amortization charges begin for the first plan year after the plan year in which such transfer occurs, except that such section shall be applied to such amount by substituting "10 plan years" for "5 plan years".

P.L. 109-280, §842(a)(2):

Amended Code Sec. 420(e) by adding at the end a new paragraph (5). **Effective** for transfers made in tax years beginning after 12-31-2006.

• 1999, Tax Relief Extension Act of 1999 (P.L. 106-170)

P.L. 106-170, §535(b)(2)(B):

Amended Code Sec. 420(e)(1)(D) by striking "and shall not be subject to the minimum benefit requirements of subsection (c)(3)" and inserting "or in calculating applicable employer cost under subsection (c)(3)(B)". **Effective** for qualified transfers occurring after 12-17-99. For a transition rule, see Act Sec. 535(c)(2), below.

P.L. 106-170, §535(c)(2), provides:

(2) TRANSITION RULE.—If the cost maintenance period for any qualified transfer after the date of the enactment of this Act includes any portion of a benefit maintenance period for any qualified transfer on or before such date, the amendments made by subsection (b) shall not apply to such portion of the cost maintenance period (and such portion shall be treated as a benefit maintenance period).

• 1996, Small Business Job Protection Act of 1996 (P.L. 104-188)

P.L. 104-188, §1704(t)(32):

Amended Code Sec. 420(e)(1)(C) by striking "mean" and inserting "means". **Effective** 8-20-96.

• 1994, Uruguay Round Agreements Act (P.L. 103-465)

P.L. 103-465, §731(c)(2):

Amended Code Sec. 420(e)(1)(B). **Effective** for qualified transfers occurring after 12-8-94. Prior to amendment, Code Sec. 420(e)(1)(B) read as follows:

(B) REDUCTIONS FOR AMOUNTS PREVIOUSLY SET ASIDE.—The amount determined under subparagraph (A) shall be reduced by any amount previously contributed to a health benefits account or welfare benefit fund (as defined in section 419(e)(1)) to pay for the qualified current retiree health liabilities. The portion of any reserves remaining as of the close of December 31, 1990, shall be allocated on a pro rata basis to qualified current retiree health liabilities.

P.L. 103-465, §731(c)(3):

Amended Code Sec. 420(e)(1)(D) by striking "or in calculating applicable employer cost under subsection (c)(3)(B)" and inserting "and shall not be subject to the minimum benefit requirements of subsection (c)(3)". **Effective** for tax years beginning after 12-31-95.

• 1990, Omnibus Budget Reconciliation Act of 1990 (P.L. 101-508)

P.L. 101-508, §12011(a):

Amended part I of subchapter D of chapter 1 by adding a new subpart E (Code Sec. 420). **Effective**, generally, for transfers in tax years beginning after 12-31-90. For a special rule, see Act Sec. 12011(c)(2), below.

P.L. 101-508, §12011(c)(2), provides:

(2) WAIVER OF ESTIMATED TAX PENALTIES.—No addition to tax shall be made under section 6654 or section 6655 of the Internal Revenue Code of 1986 for the taxable year preceding the taxpayer's 1st taxable year beginning after December 31, 1990, with respect to any underpayment to the extent such underpayment was created or increased by reason of section 420(b)(4)(B) of such Code (as added by subsection (a)).

[Sec. 420(f)]

(f) QUALIFIED TRANSFERS TO COVER FUTURE RETIREE HEALTH COSTS AND COLLECTIVELY BARGAINED RETIREE HEALTH BENEFITS.—

(1) IN GENERAL.—An employer maintaining a defined benefit plan (other than a multiemployer plan) may, in lieu of a qualified transfer, elect for any taxable year to have the plan make—

(A) a qualified future transfer, or

(B) a collectively bargained transfer.

Except as provided in this subsection, a qualified future transfer and a collectively bargained transfer shall be treated for purposes of this title and the Employee Retirement Income Security Act of 1974 as if it were a qualified transfer.

(2) QUALIFIED FUTURE AND COLLECTIVELY BARGAINED TRANSFERS.—For purposes of this subsection—

(A) IN GENERAL.—The terms "qualified future transfer" and "collectively bargained transfer" mean a transfer which meets all of the requirements for a qualified transfer, except that—

(i) the determination of excess pension assets shall be made under subparagraph (B),

(ii) the limitation on the amount transferred shall be determined under subparagraph (C),

(iii) the minimum cost requirements of subsection (c)(3) shall be modified as provided under subparagraph (D), and

(iv) in the case of a collectively bargained transfer, the requirements of subparagraph (E) shall be met with respect to the transfer.

(B) EXCESS PENSION ASSETS.—

(i) IN GENERAL.—In determining excess pension assets for purposes of this subsection, subsection (e)(2) shall be applied by substituting "120 percent" for "125 percent".

(ii) REQUIREMENT TO MAINTAIN FUNDED STATUS.—If, as of any valuation date of any plan year in the transfer period, the amount determined under subsection (e)(2)(B) (after application of clause (i)) exceeds the amount determined under subsection (e)(2)(A), either—

(I) the employer maintaining the plan shall make contributions to the plan in an amount not less than the amount required to reduce such excess to zero as of such date, or

(II) there is transferred from the health benefits account to the plan an amount not less than the amount required to reduce such excess to zero as of such date.

(C) LIMITATION ON AMOUNT TRANSFERRED.—Notwithstanding subsection (b)(3), the amount of the excess pension assets which may be transferred—

(i) in the case of a qualified future transfer shall be equal to the sum of—

(I) if the transfer period includes the taxable year of the transfer, the amount determined under subsection (b)(3) for such taxable year, plus

(II) in the case of all other taxable years in the transfer period, the sum of the qualified current retiree health liabilities which the plan reasonably estimates, in accordance with guidance issued by the Secretary, will be incurred for each of such years, and

(ii) in the case of a collectively bargained transfer, shall not exceed the amount which is reasonably estimated, in accordance with the provisions of the collective bargaining agreement and generally accepted accounting principles, to be the amount the employer maintaining the plan will pay (whether directly or through reimbursement) out of such account during the collectively bargained cost maintenance period for collectively bargained retiree health liabilities.

(D) MINIMUM COST REQUIREMENTS.—

(i) IN GENERAL.—The requirements of subsection (c)(3) shall be treated as met if—

(I) in the case of a qualified future transfer, each group health plan or arrangement under which applicable health benefits are provided provides applicable health benefits during the period beginning with the first year of the transfer period and ending with the last day of the 4th year following the transfer period such that the annual average amount of the applicable employer cost during such period is not less than the applicable employer cost determined under subsection (c)(3)(A) with respect to the transfer, and

(II) in the case of a collectively bargained transfer, each collectively bargained group health plan under which collectively bargained health benefits are provided provides that the collectively bargained employer cost for each taxable year during the collectively bargained cost maintenance period shall not be less than the amount specified by the collective bargaining agreement.

(ii) ELECTION TO MAINTAIN BENEFITS FOR FUTURE TRANSFERS.—An employer may elect, in lieu of the requirements of clause (i)(I), to meet the requirements of subsection (c)(3) by meeting the requirements of such subsection (as in effect before the amendments made by section 535 of the Tax Relief Extension Act of 1999) for each of the years described in the period under clause (i)(I).

(iii) COLLECTIVELY BARGAINED EMPLOYER COST.—For purposes of this subparagraph, the term "collectively bargained employer cost" means the average cost per covered individual of providing collectively bargained retiree health benefits as determined in accordance with the applicable collective bargaining agreement. Such agreement may provide for an appropriate reduction in the collectively bargained employer cost to take into account any portion of the collectively bargained retiree health benefits that is provided or financed by a government program or other source.

(E) SPECIAL RULES FOR COLLECTIVELY BARGAINED TRANSFERS.—

(i) IN GENERAL.—A collectively bargained transfer shall only include a transfer which—

(I) is made in accordance with a collective bargaining agreement,

(II) before the transfer, the employer designates, in a written notice delivered to each employee organization that is a party to the collective bargaining agreement, as a collectively bargained transfer in accordance with this section, and

(III) involves a plan maintained by an employer which, in its taxable year ending in 2005, provided health benefits or coverage to retirees and their spouses and dependents under all of the benefit plans maintained by the employer, but only if the aggregate cost (including administrative expenses) of such benefits or coverage which would have been allowable as a deduction to the employer (if such benefits or coverage had been provided directly by the employer and the employer used the cash receipts and disbursements method of accounting) is at least 5 percent of the gross receipts of the employer (determined in accordance with the last sentence of subsection (c)(3)(E)(ii)(II)) for such taxable year, or a plan maintained by a successor to such employer.

(ii) USE OF ASSETS.—Any assets transferred to a health benefits account in a collectively bargained transfer (and any income allocable thereto) shall be used only to pay collectively bargained retiree health liabilities (other than liabilities of key employees not taken into account under paragraph (6)(B)(iii)) for the taxable year of the transfer or for any subsequent taxable year during the collectively bargained cost maintenance period (whether directly or through reimbursement).

(3) COORDINATION WITH OTHER TRANSFERS.—In applying subsection (b)(3) to any subsequent transfer during a taxable year in a transfer period or collectively bargained cost maintenance period, qualified current retiree health liabilities shall be reduced by any such liabilities taken into account with respect to the qualified future transfer or collectively bargained transfer to which such period relates.

(4) SPECIAL DEDUCTION RULES FOR COLLECTIVELY BARGAINED TRANSFERS.—In the case of a collectively bargained transfer—

(A) the limitation under subsection (d)(1)(C) shall not apply, and

(B) notwithstanding subsection (d)(2), an employer may contribute an amount to a health benefits account or welfare benefit fund (as defined in section 419(e)(1)) with respect to collectively bargained retiree health liabilities for which transferred assets are required to be used under subsection (c)(1)(B), and the deductibility of any such contribution shall be governed by the limits applicable to the deductibility of contributions to a welfare benefit fund under a collective bargaining agreement (as determined under section 419A(f)(5)(A)) without regard to whether such contributions are made to a health benefits account or welfare benefit fund and without regard to the provisions of section 404 or the other provisions of this section.

The Secretary shall provide rules to ensure that the application of this paragraph does not result in a deduction being allowed more than once for the same contribution or for 2 or more contributions or expenditures relating to the same collectively bargained retiree health liabilities.

(5) TRANSFER PERIOD.—For purposes of this subsection, the term "transfer period" means, with respect to any transfer, a period of consecutive taxable years (not less than 2) specified in the election under paragraph (1) which begins and ends during the 10-taxable-year period beginning with the taxable year of the transfer.

(6) TERMS RELATING TO COLLECTIVELY BARGAINED TRANSFERS.—For purposes of this subsection—

(A) COLLECTIVELY BARGAINED COST MAINTENANCE PERIOD.—The term "collectively bargained cost maintenance period" means, with respect to each covered retiree and his covered spouse and dependents, the shorter of—

(i) the remaining lifetime of such covered retiree and his covered spouse and dependents, or

(ii) the period of coverage provided by the collectively bargained health plan (determined as of the date of the collectively bargained transfer) with respect to such covered retiree and his covered spouse and dependents.

(B) COLLECTIVELY BARGAINED RETIREE HEALTH LIABILITIES.—

(i) IN GENERAL.—The term "collectively bargained retiree health liabilities" means the present value, as of the beginning of a taxable year and determined in accordance with the applicable collective bargaining agreement, of all collectively bargained health benefits (including administrative expenses) for such taxable year and all subsequent taxable years during the collectively bargained cost maintenance period.

(ii) REDUCTION FOR AMOUNTS PREVIOUSLY SET ASIDE.—The amount determined under clause (i) shall be reduced by the value (as of the close of the plan year preceding the year of the collectively bargained transfer) of the assets in all health benefits accounts or welfare benefit funds (as defined in section 419(e)(1)) set aside to pay for the collectively bargained retiree health liabilities.

(iii) KEY EMPLOYEES EXCLUDED.—If an employee is a key employee (within the meaning of section 416(I)[(i)](1)) with respect to any plan year ending in a taxable year, such employee shall not be taken into account in computing collectively bargained retiree health liabilities for such taxable year or in calculating collectively bargained employer cost under subsection (c)(3)(C).

(C) COLLECTIVELY BARGAINED HEALTH BENEFITS.—The term "collectively bargained health benefits" means health benefits or coverage which are provided to—

(i) retired employees who, immediately before the collectively bargained transfer, are entitled to receive such benefits upon retirement and who are entitled to pension benefits under the plan, and their spouses and dependents, and

(ii) if specified by the provisions of the collective bargaining agreement governing the collectively bargained transfer, active employees who, following their retirement, are entitled to receive such benefits and who are entitled to pension benefits under the plan, and their spouses and dependents.

(D) COLLECTIVELY BARGAINED HEALTH PLAN.—The term "collectively bargained health plan" means a group health plan or arrangement for retired employees and their spouses and dependents that is maintained pursuant to 1 or more collective bargaining agreements.

Amendments

• 2008, Worker, Retiree, and Employer Recovery Act of 2008 (P.L. 110-458)

P.L. 110-458, §108(i)(2):

Amended Code Sec. 420(f)(2)(D)(i)(I) by striking "such" before "the applicable". **Effective** as if included in the provision of the 2006 Act to which the amendment relates [**effective** for transfers after 8-17-2006.—CCH].

• 2007, U.S. Troop Readiness, Veterans' Care, Katrina Recovery, and Iraq Accountability Appropriations Act, 2007 (P.L. 110-28)

P.L. 110-28, §6612(a):

Amended Code Sec. 420(f)(2)(E)(i)(III) by striking "subsection (c)(2)(E)(ii)(II)" and inserting "subsection (c)(3)(E)(ii)(II)". **Effective** as if included in the provision of the Pension Protection Act of 2006 (P.L. 109-280) to which it relates [**effective** for transfers after 8-17-2006.—CCH].

• 2006, Pension Protection Act of 2006 (P.L. 109-280)

P.L. 109-280, §841(a):

Amended Code Sec. 420 by adding at the end a new subsection (f). **Effective** for transfers after 8-17-2006.

PART II—CERTAIN STOCK OPTIONS

[Sec. 421]

SEC. 421. GENERAL RULES.

[Sec. 421(a)]

(a) EFFECT OF QUALIFYING TRANSFER.—If a share of stock is transferred to an individual in a transfer in respect of which the requirements of section 422(a) or 423(a) are met—

(1) no income shall result at the time of the transfer of such share to the individual upon his exercise of the option with respect to such share;

(2) no deduction under section 162 (relating to trade or business expenses) shall be allowable at any time to the employer corporation, a parent or subsidiary corporation of such corporation, or a corporation issuing or assuming a stock option in a transaction to which section 424(a) applies, with respect to the share so transferred; and

(3) no amount other than the price paid under the option shall be considered as received by any of such corporations for the share so transferred.

Amendments

• 1990, Omnibus Budget Reconciliation Act of 1990 (P.L. 101-508)

P.L. 101-508, §11801(c)(9)(B)(i)(I)-(III):

Amended Code Sec. 421(a) by striking "422(a), 422A(a), 423(a), or 424(a)" and inserting "422(a) or 423(a)"; by striking in paragraph (1) "except as provided in section 422(c)(1)," preceding "no income"; and by striking in paragraph (2) "425(a)" and inserting "424(a)". **Effective** 11-5-90.

P.L. 101-508, §11821(b)(1)-(2), provides:

(b) SAVINGS PROVISION.—If—

(1) any provision amended or repealed by this part applied to—

(A) any transaction occurring before the date of the enactment of this Act,

(B) any property acquired before such date of enactment, or

(C) any item of income, loss, deduction, or credit taken into account before such date of enactment, and

(2) the treatment of such transaction, property, or item under such provision would (without regard to the amendments made by this part affect liability for tax for periods ending after such date of enactment,

nothing in the amendments made by this part shall be construed to affect the treatment of such transaction, property, or item for purposes of determining liability for tax for periods ending after such date of enactment.

• 1981, Economic Recovery Tax Act of 1981 (P.L. 97-34)

P.L. 97-34, §251(b)(1)(A):

Amended Code Sec. 421(a) by inserting "422A(a)," after "422(a),". For the **effective** date and transitional rules, see the historical comment for P.L. 97-34 following Code Sec. 422A(a).

[Sec. 421(b)]

(b) EFFECT OF DISQUALIFYING DISPOSITION.—If the transfer of a share of stock to an individual pursuant to his exercise of an option would otherwise meet the requirements of section 422(a) or 423(a) except that there is a failure to meet any of the holding period requirements of section 422(a)(1) or 423(a)(1), then any increase in the income of such individual or deduction from the income of his employer corporation for the taxable year in which such exercise occurred attributable to such disposition, shall be treated as an increase in income or a deduction from income in the taxable year of such individual or of such employer corporation in which such disposition occurred. No amount shall be required to be deducted and withheld under chapter 24 with respect to any increase in income attributable to a disposition described in the preceding sentence.

Amendments

• 2004, American Jobs Creation Act of 2004 (P.L. 108-357)

P.L. 108-357, §251(b):

Amended Code Sec. 421(b) by adding at the end a new sentence. **Effective** for stock acquired pursuant to options exercised after 10-22-2004.

• 1990, Omnibus Budget Reconciliation Act of 1990 (P.L. 101-508)

P.L. 101-508, §11801(c)(9)(B)(ii)(I)-(II):

Amended Code Sec. 421(b) by striking "422(a), 422A(a), 423(a), or 424(a)" and inserting "422(a) or 423(a)"; and by striking "422(a)(1), 422A(a)(1), 423(a)(1), or 424(a)(1)," and inserting "422(a)(1) or 423(a)(1),". **Effective** 11-5-90.

P.L. 101-508, §11821(b)(1)-(2), provides:

(b) SAVINGS PROVISION.—If—

(1) any provision amended or repealed by this part applied to—

(A) any transaction occurring before the date of the enactment of this Act,

(B) any property acquired before such date of enactment, or

(C) any item of income, loss, deduction, or credit taken into account before such date of enactment, and

(2) the treatment of such transaction, property, or item under such provision would (without regard to the amendments made by this part) affect liability for tax for periods ending after such date of enactment,

nothing in the amendments made by this part shall be construed to affect the treatment of such transaction, property, or item for purposes of determining liability for tax for periods ending after such date of enactment.

• 1981, Economic Recovery Tax Act of 1981 (P.L. 97-34)

P.L. 97-34, §251(b)(1)(A):

Amended Code Sec. 421(b) by inserting "422A(a)," after "422(a),". For the **effective** date and transitional rules, see the historical comment for P.L. 97-34 following Code Sec. 422A(a).

P.L. 97-34, §251(b)(1)(B):

Amended Code Sec. 421(b) by inserting "422A(a)(1)," after "section 422(a)(1),". For the **effective** date and transitional rules, see the historical comment for P.L. 97-34 following Code Sec. 422A(a).

[Sec. 421(c)]

(c) EXERCISE BY ESTATE.—

(1) IN GENERAL.—If an option to which this part applies is exercised after the death of the employee by the estate of the decedent, or by a person who acquired the right to exercise such option by bequest or inheritance or by reason of the death of the decedent, the provisions of subsection (a) shall apply to the same extent as if the option had been exercised by the decedent, except that—

(A) the holding period and employment requirements of sections 422(a) and 423(a) shall not apply, and

(B) any transfer by the estate of stock acquired shall be considered a disposition of such stock for purposes of section 423(c).

(2) DEDUCTION FOR ESTATE TAX.—If an amount is required to be included under section 423(c) in gross income of the estate of the deceased employee or of a person described in paragraph (1), there shall be allowed to the estate or such person a deduction with respect to the estate tax attributable to the inclusion in the taxable estate of the deceased employee of the net value for estate tax purposes of the option. For this purpose, the deduction shall be determined under section 691(c) as if the option acquired from the deceased employee were an item of gross income in respect of the decedent under section 691 and as if the amount includible in gross income under section 423(c) were an amount included in gross income under section 691 in respect of such item of gross income.

(3) BASIS OF SHARES ACQUIRED.—In the case of a share of stock acquired by the exercise of an option to which paragraph (1) applies—

(A) the basis of such share shall include so much of the basis of the option as is attributable to such share; except that the basis of such share shall be reduced by the excess (if any) of (i) the amount which would have been includible in gross income under section 423(c) if the employee had exercised the option on the date of this death and had held the share acquired pursuant to such exercise at the time of his death, over (ii) the amount which is includible in gross income under such section; and

(B) the last sentence of section 423(c) shall apply only to the extent that the amount includible in gross income under such section exceeds so much of the basis of the option as is attributable to such share.

Amendments

• 1990, Omnibus Budget Reconciliation Act of 1990 (P.L. 101-508)

P.L. 101-508, §11801(c)(9)(B)(iii)(I)-(V):

Amended Code Sec. 421(c) by striking in paragraph (1)(A) "422(a), 422A(a), 423(a), or 424(a)" and inserting "422(a) and 423(a)"; by striking in paragraph (1)(B) "sections 423(c) and 424(c)(1)" and inserting "section 423(c)"; by striking in paragraphs (2) and (3)(A) "422(c)(1), 423(c), or 424(c)(1)" each place it appears and inserting "423(c)"; by striking in paragraph (3)(B) "sections 422(c)(1), 423(c), and 424(c)(1)" and inserting "section 423(c)"; and by striking in paragraph (3)(B) "such sections" and inserting "such section". **Effective** 11-5-90.

P.L. 101-508, §11821(b)(1)-(2), provides:

(b) SAVINGS PROVISION.—If—

(1) any provision amended or repealed by this part applied to—

(A) any transaction occurring before the date of the enactment of this Act,

(B) any property acquired before such date of enactment, or

(C) any item of income, loss, deduction, or credit taken into account before such date of enactment, and

(2) the treatment of such transaction, property, or item under such provision would (without regard to the amendments made by this part affect liability for tax for periods ending after such date of enactment,

nothing in the amendments made by this part shall be construed to affect the treatment of such transaction, property, or item for purposes of determining liability for tax for periods ending after such date of enactment.

• 1981, Economic Recovery Tax Act of 1981 (P.L. 97-34)

P.L. 97-34, §251(b)(1)(A):

Amended Code Sec. 421(c)(1)(A) by inserting "422A(a)," after "422(a),". For the **effective** date and transitional rules, see the historical comment for P.L. 97-34 following Code Sec. 422A(a).

• 1964, Revenue Act of 1964 (P.L. 88-272)

P.L. 88-272, §221(a):

Amended Part II of subchapter D of chapter 1 (Code Sec. 421). **Effective** for tax years ending after 12-31-63. In the case of an option granted after 12-31-63, and before 1-1-65—

(A) paragraphs (1) and (2) of section 422(b) shall not apply, and

(B) paragraph (1) of section 425(h) shall not apply to any change in the terms of such option made before January 1, 1965, to permit such option to qualify under paragraphs (3), (4) and (5) of section 422(b).

Prior to amendment, Part II of subchapter D of chapter 1 read as follows:

"SEC. 421. EMPLOYEE STOCK OPTIONS.

"(a) Treatment of Restricted Stock Options.—If a share of stock is transferred to an individual pursuant to his exercise after 1949 of a restricted stock option, and no disposition of such share is made by him within 2 years from the date of the granting of the option nor within 6 months after the transfer of such share to him—

"(1) no income shall result at the time of the transfer of such share to the individual upon his exercise of the option with respect to such share;

"(2) no deduction under section 162 (relating to trade or business expenses) shall be allowable at any time to the employer corporation, a parent or subsidiary corporation of such corporation, or a corporation issuing or assuming a stock option in a transaction to which subsection (g) is applicable, with respect to the share so transferred; and

"(3) no amount other than the price paid under the option shall be considered as received by any of such corporations for the share so transferred.

This subsection and subsection (b) shall not apply unless (A) the individual, at the time he exercises the restricted stock option, is an employee of either the corporation granting such option, a parent or subsidiary corporation of such corporation, or a corporation or a parent or subsidiary of such corporation issuing or assuming a stock option in a transaction to which subsection (g) is applicable, or (B) the option is exercised by him within 3 months after the date he ceases to be an employee of such corporations. In applying paragraphs (2) and (3) of subsection (d) for purposes of the preceding sentence, there shall be substituted for the term `employer corporation' wherever it appears in such paragraphs the term `grantor corporation,' or the term `corporation issuing or assuming a stock option in a transaction to which subsection (g) is applicable,' as the case may be.

"(b) Special Rule Where Option Price Is Between 85 Percent and 95 Percent of Value of Stock.—If no disposition of a share of stock acquired by an individual on his exercise after 1949 of a restricted stock option is made by him within 2 years from the date of the granting of the option nor within 6 months after the transfer of such share to him, but, at the time the restricted stock option was granted, the option price (computed under subparagraph (d)(1)(A)) was less than 95 percent of the fair market value at such time of such share, then, in the event of any disposition of such share by him, or in the event of his death (whenever occurring) while owning such share, there shall be included as compensation (and not as gain upon the sale or exchange of a capital asset) in his gross income, for the taxable year in which falls the date of such disposition or for the taxable year closing with his death, whichever applies—

"(1) in the case of a share of stock acquired under an option qualifying under clause (i) of subparagraph (d)(1)(A), an amount equal to the amount (if any) by which the option price is exceeded by the lesser of—

"(A) the fair market value of the share at the time of such disposition or death, or

"(B) the fair market value of the share at the time the option was granted; or

"(2) in the case of stock acquired under an option qualifying under clause (ii) of subparagraph (d)(1)(A), an amount equal to the lesser of—

"(A) the excess of the fair market value of the share at the time of such disposition or death over the price paid under the option, or

"(B) the excess of the fair market value of the share at the time the option was granted over the option price (computed as if the option had been exercised at such time).

In the case of the disposition of such share by the individual, the basis of the share in his hands at the time of such disposition shall be increased by an amount equal to the amount so includible in his gross income.

"(c) Acquisition of New Stock.—If stock is received by an individual in a distribution to which section 305, 354, 355, 356, or 1036, or so much of section 1031 as relates to section 1036, applies and such distribution was made with respect to stock transferred to him upon his exercise of the option, such stock shall be considered as having been transferred to him on his exercise of such option. A similar rule shall be applied in the case of a series of such distributions.

"(d) Definitions.—For purposes of this section—

"(1) Restricted stock option.—The term `restricted stock option' means an option granted after February 26, 1945, to an individual, for any reason connected with his employment by a corporation, if granted by the employer corporation or its parent or subsidiary corporation, to purchase stock of any of such corporations, but only if—

"(A) at the time such option is granted—

"(i) the option price is at least 85 percent of the fair market value at such time of the stock subject to the option, or

"(ii) in the case of a variable price option, the option price (computed as if the option had been exercised when granted) is at least 85 percent of the fair market value of the stock at the time such option is granted; and

"(B) such option by its terms is not transferable by such individual otherwise than by will or the laws of descent and distribution, and is exercisable, during his lifetime, only by him; and

"(C) such individual, at the time the option is granted, does not own stock possessing more than 10 percent of the total combined voting power of all classes of stock of the employer corporation or of its parent or subsidiary corporation. This subparagraph shall not apply if at the time such option is granted the option price is at least 110 percent of the fair market value of the stock subject to the option and such option either by its terms is not exercisable after the expiration of 5 years from the date such option is granted or is exercised within one year after the date of enactment of this title. For purposes of this subparagraph—

"(i) such individual shall be considered as owning the stock owned, directly or indirectly, by or for his brothers and sisters (whether by the whole or half blood), spouse, ancestors, and lineal descendants; and

"(ii) stock owned, directly or indirectly, by or for a corporation, partnership, estate, or trust, shall be considered as being owned proportionately by or for its shareholders, partners, or beneficiaries; and

"(D) such option by its terms is not exercisable after the expiration of 10 years from the date such option is granted, if such option has been granted on or after June 22, 1954.

"(2) Parent corporation.—The term `parent corporation' means any corporation (other than the employer corporation) in an unbroken chain of corporations ending with the employer corporation if, at the time of the granting of the option, each of the corporations other than the employer corporation owns stock possessing 50 percent or more of the total combined voting power of all classes of stock in one of the other corporations in such chain.

"(3) Subsidiary corporation.—The term `subsidiary corporation' means any corporation (other than the employer corporation) in an unbroken chain of corporations beginning with the employer corporation if, at the time of the granting of the option, each of the corporations other than the last corporation in the unbroken chain owns stock possessing 50 percent or more of the total combined voting power of all classes of stock in one of the other corporations in such chain.

"(4) Disposition.—

"(A) General rule.—Except as provided in subparagraph (B), the term `disposition' includes a sale, exchange, gift, or a transfer of legal title, but does not include—

"(i) a transfer from a decedent to an estate or a transfer by bequest or inheritance;

"(ii) an exchange to which section 354, 355, 356, or 1036 (or so much of section 1031 as relates to section 1036) applies; or

"(iii) a mere pledge or hypothecation.

"(B) Joint tenancy.—The acquistion of a share of stock in the name of the employee and another jointly with the right of survivorship or a subsequent transfer of a share of stock into such joint ownership shall not be deemed a disposition, but a termination of such joint tenancy (except to the extent such employee acquires ownership of such stock) shall be treated as a disposition by him occurring at the time such joint tenancy is terminated.

"(5) Stockholder approval.—If the grant of an option is subject to approval by stockholders, the date of grant of the option shall be determined as if the option had not been subject to such approval.

"(6) Exercise by estate.—

"(A) In general.—If a restricted stock option is exercised subsequent to the death of the employee by the estate of the decedent, or by a person who acquired the right to exercise such option by bequest or inheritance or by reason of the death of the decedent, the provisions of this section shall apply to the same extent as if the option had been exercised by the decedent, except that—

"(i) the holding period and employment requirements of subsection (a) shall not apply, and

"(ii) any transfer by the estate of stock acquired shall be considered a disposition of such stock for purposes of subsection (b).

"(B) Deduction for estate tax.—If an amount is required to be included under subsection (b) in gross income of the estate of the deceased employee or of a person described in subparagraph (A), there shall be allowed to the estate or such person a deduction with respect to the estate tax attributable to the inclusion in the taxable estate of the deceased employee of the net value for estate tax purposes of the restricted stock option. For this purpose, the deduction shall be determined under section 691(c) as if the option acquired from the deceased employee were an item of gross income in respect of the decedent under section 691 and as if the amount includible in gross income under subsection (b) of this section were an amount included in gross income under section 691 in respect of such item of gross income.

"(C) Basis of shares acquired.—In the case of a share of stock acquired by the exercise of an option to which subparagraph (A) applies—

"(i) the basis of such share shall include so much of the basis of the option as is attributable to such share; except that the basis of such share shall be reduced by the excess (if any) of the amount, which would have been includible in gross income under subsection (b) if the employee had exercised the option and held such share at the time of his death, over the amount which is includible in gross income under subsection (b); and

"(ii) the last sentence of subsection (b) shall apply only to the extent that the amount includible in gross income under such subsection exceeds so much of the basis of the option as is attributable to such share.

"(7) Variable price option.—The term `variable price option' means an option under which the purchase price of the stock is fixed or determinable under a formula in which the only variable is the fair market value of the stock at any time during a period of 6 months which includes the time the option is exercised; except that in the case of options granted after September 30, 1958, such term does not include any such option in which such formula provides for determining such price by reference to the fair market value of the stock at any time before the option is exercised if such value may be greater than the average fair market value of the stock during the calendar month in which the option is exercised.

"(e) Modification, Extension, or Renewal of Option.—

"(1) Rules of application.—For purposes of subsection (d), if the terms of any option to purchase stock are modified, extended, or renewed, the following rules shall be applied with respect to transfers of stock made on the exercise of the option after the making of such modification, extension, or renewal—

"(A) such modification, extension, or renewal shall be considered as the granting of a new option,

"(B) the fair market value of such stock at the time of the granting of such option shall be considered as—

"(i) the fair market value of such stock on the date of the original granting of the option,

"(ii) the fair market value of such stock on the date of the making of such modification, extension, or renewal, or

"(iii) the fair market value of such stock at the time of the making of any intervening modification, extension, or renewal,

whichever is the highest.

Subparagraph (B) shall not apply if the aggregate of the monthly average fair market values of the stock subject to the option for the 12 consecutive calendar months before the date of the modification, extension, or renewal, divided by 12, is an amount less than 80 percent of the fair market value of such stock on the date of the original granting of the option or the date of the making of any intervening modification, extension, or renewal, whichever is the highest.

"(2) Definition of modification. — The term `modification' means any change in the terms of the option which gives the employee additional benefits under the option, but such term shall not include a change in the terms of the option—

"(A) attributable to the issuance or assumption of an option under subsection (g); or

"(B) to permit the option to qualify under subsection (d)(1)(B).

If an option is exercisable after the expiration of 10 years from the date such option is granted, subparagraph (B) shall not apply unless the terms of the option are also changed to make it not exercisable after the expiration of such period.

"(f) Effect of Disqualifying Disposition.—If a share of stock, acquired by an individual pursuant to his exercise of a restricted stock option, is disposed of by him within 2 years from the date of the granting of the option or within 6 months after the transfer of such share to him, then any increase in the income of such individual or deduction from the income of his employer corporation for the taxable year in which such exercise occurred attributable to such disposition, shall be treated as an increase in income or a deduction from income in the taxable year of such individual or of such employer corporation in which such disposition occurred.

"(g) Corporate Reorganizations, Liquidations, Etc.—For purposes of this section, the term `issuing or assuming a stock option in a transaction to which subsection (g) is applicable' means a substitution of a new option for the old option, or an assumption of the old option, by an employer corporation, or a parent or subsidiary of such corporation, by reason of a corporate merger, consolidation, acquisition of property or stock, separation, reorganization, or liquidation, if—

"(1) the excess of the aggregate fair market value of the shares subject to the option immediately after the substitution or assumption over the aggregate option price of such shares is not more than the excess of the aggregate fair market value of all shares subject to the option immediately before such substitution or assumption over the aggregate option price of such shares, and

"(2) the new option or the assumption of the old option does not give the employee additional benefits which he did not have under the old option.

For purposes of this subsection, the parent-subsidiary relationship shall be determined at the time of any such transaction under this subsection."

• 1958, Technical Amendments Act of 1958 (P.L.85-866)

P.L. 85-866, §25:

Added the last sentence in Sec. 421(a). **Effective** 1-1-54.

P.L. 85-866, §26:

Amended clause (ii) of paragraph (1)(A) and added paragraph (7). **Effective** 9-30-58. Prior to amendment, clause (ii) read:

"(ii) in case the purchase price of the stock under the option is fixed or determinable under a formula in which the only variable is the value of the stock at any time during a period of 6 months which includes the time the option is exercised, the option price (computed as if the option had been exercised when granted) is at least 85 percent of the value of the stock at the time such option is granted; and".

• 1958 (P.L. 85-320)

P.L. 85-320, §[1]:

Added subparagraph (C) to 1954 Code Sec. 421(d)(6). **Effective** for tax years ending after 12-31-56, but only in the case of employees dying after such date.

[Sec. 421(d)]

(d) CERTAIN SALES TO COMPLY WITH CONFLICT-OF-INTEREST REQUIREMENTS.—If—

(1) a share of stock is transferred to an eligible person (as defined in section 1043(b)(1)) pursuant to such person's exercise of an option to which this part applies, and

(2) such share is disposed of by such person pursuant to a certificate of divestiture (as defined in section 1043(b)(2)),

such disposition shall be treated as meeting the requirements of section 422(a)(1) or 423(a)(1), whichever is applicable.

Amendments

• 2004, American Jobs Creation Act of 2004 (P.L. 108-357)

P.L. 108-357, §905(a):

Amended Code Sec. 421 by adding at the end new subsection (d). **Effective** for sales after 10-22-2004.

[Sec. 422]

SEC. 422. INCENTIVE STOCK OPTIONS.

[Sec. 422(a)]

(a) IN GENERAL.—Section 421(a) shall apply with respect to the transfer of a share of stock to an individual pursuant to his exercise of an incentive stock option if—

(1) no disposition of such share is made by him within 2 years from the date of the granting of the option nor within 1 year after the transfer of such share to him, and

(2) at all times during the period beginning on the date of the granting of the option and ending on the day 3 months before the date of such exercise, such individual was an employee of either the corporation granting such option, a parent or subsidiary corporation of such corporation, or a corporation or a parent or subsidiary corporation of such corporation issuing or assuming a stock option in a transaction to which section 424(a) applies.

Amendments

• 1990, Omnibus Budget Reconciliation Act of 1990 (P.L. 101-508)

P.L. 101-508, §11801(c)(9)(A)(i):

Redesignated Code Sec. 422A as Code Sec. 422. **Effective** 11-5-90.

P.L. 101-508, §11801(c)(9)(C)(i):

Amended Code Sec. 422(a)(2) (as redesignated by Act Sec. 11801(c)(9)(A)) by striking "425(a)" and inserting "424(a)". **Effective** 11-5-90.

P.L. 101-508, §11821(b)(1)-(2), provides:

(b) SAVINGS PROVISION.—If—

(1) any provision amended or repealed by this part applied to—

(A) any transaction occurring before the date of the enactment of this Act,

(B) any property acquired before such date of enactment, or

(C) any item of income, loss, deduction, or credit taken into account before such date of enactment, and

(2) the treatment of such transaction, property, or item under such provision would (without regard to the amendments made by this part) affect liability for tax for periods ending after such date of enactment,

nothing in the amendments made by this part shall be construed to affect the treatment of such transaction, property, or item for purposes of determining liability for tax for periods ending after such date of enactment.

[Sec. 422(b)]

(b) INCENTIVE STOCK OPTION.—For purposes of this part, the term "incentive stock option" means an option granted to an individual for any reason connected with his employment by a corporation, if granted by the employer corporation or its parent or subsidiary corporation, to purchase stock of any of such corporations, but only if—

(1) the option is granted pursuant to a plan which includes the aggregate number of shares which may be issued under options and the employees (or class of employees) eligible to receive options, and which is approved by the stockholders of the granting corporation within 12 months before or after the date such plan is adopted;

(2) such option is granted within 10 years from the date such plan is adopted, or the date such plan is approved by the stockholders, whichever is earlier;

(3) such option by its terms is not exercisable after the expiration of 10 years from the date such option is granted;

(4) the option price is not less than the fair market value of the stock at the time such option is granted;

(5) such option by its terms is not transferable by such individual otherwise than by will or the laws of descent and distribution, and is exercisable, during his lifetime, only by him; and

(6) such individual, at the time the option is granted, does not own stock possessing more than 10 percent of the total combined voting power of all classes of stock of the employer corporation or of its parent or subsidiary corporation.

Such term shall not include any option if (as of the time the option is granted) the terms of such option provide that it will not be treated as an incentive stock option.

Amendments

• 1988, Technical and Miscellaneous Revenue Act of 1988 (P.L. 100-647)

P.L. 100-647, §1003(d)(1)(A):

Amended Code Sec. 422A(b) by adding at the end thereof a new sentence. **Effective** as if included in the provision of P.L. 99-514 to which it relates. For a special rule, see Act Sec. 1003(d)(1)(B), below.

P.L. 100-647, §1003(d)(1)(B), provides:

(B) In the case of an option granted after December 31, 1986, and on or before the date of the enactment of this Act, such option shall not be treated as an incentive stock option if the terms of such option are amended before the date 90 days after such date of enactment to provide that such option will not be treated as an incentive stock option.

P.L. 100-647, §1003(d)(2)(B):

Amended Code Sec. 422A(b) by adding "and" at the end of paragraph (5), by striking out "; and" at the end of paragraph (6) and inserting in lieu thereof a period, and by striking out paragraph (7). **Effective** as if included in the provision of P.L. 99-514 to which it relates. Prior to amendment, Code Sec. 422A(b)(7) read as follows:

(7) under the terms of the plan the aggregate fair market value (determined at the time the option is granted) of the stock with respect to which incentive stock options are exercisable for the 1st time by such individual during any calendar year (under all such plans of the individual's employer corporation and its parent and subsidiary corporations) shall not exceed $100,000.

• 1986, Tax Reform Act of 1986 (P.L. 99-514)

P.L. 99-514, §321(a):

Amended Code Sec. 422A(b)(6)-(8) by inserting "and" at the end of paragraph (6) and by striking out paragraphs (7) and (8) and inserting in lieu thereof paragraph (7). **Effective** for options granted after 12-31-86. Prior to amendment, Code Sec. 422A(b)(7) and (8) read as follows:

(7) such option by its terms is not exercisable while there is outstanding (within the meaning of subsection (c)(7)) any incentive stock option which was granted, before the granting of such option, to such individual to purchase stock in his employer corporation or in a corporation which (at the time of the granting of such option) is a parent or subsidiary corporation of the employer corporation, or in a predecessor corporation of any of such corporations, and

(8) in the case of an option granted after December 31, 1980, under the terms of the plan the aggregate fair market value (determined as of the time the option is granted) of the stock for which any employee may be granted incentive stock options in any calendar year (under all such plans of his employer corporation and its parent and subsidiary corporation) shall not exceed $100,000 plus any unused limit carryover to such year.

• 1983, Technical Corrections Act of 1982 (P.L. 97-448)

P.L. 97-448, §103(j)(1):

Amended Code Sec. 422A(b)(8) by striking out "granted options" and inserting in lieu thereof "granted incentive stock options". **Effective** as if included in the provision of P.L. 97-34 to which it relates.

[Sec. 422(c)]

(c) SPECIAL RULES.—

(1) GOOD FAITH EFFORTS TO VALUE STOCK.—If a share of stock is transferred pursuant to the exercise by an individual of an option which would fail to qualify as an incentive stock option under subsection (b) because there was a failure in an attempt, made in good faith, to meet the requirement of subsection (b)(4), the requirement of subsection (b)(4) shall be considered to have been met. To the extent provided in regulations by the Secretary, a similar rule shall apply for purposes of subsection (d).

(2) CERTAIN DISQUALIFYING DISPOSITIONS WHERE AMOUNT REALIZED IS LESS THAN VALUE AT EXERCISE.—If—

(A) an individual who has acquired a share of stock by the exercise of an incentive stock option makes a disposition of such share within either of the periods described in subsection (a)(1), and

(B) such disposition is a sale or exchange with respect to which a loss (if sustained) would be recognized to such individual,

then the amount which is includible in the gross income of such individual, and the amount which is deductible from the income of his employer corporation, as compensation attributable to the exercise of such option shall not exceed the excess (if any) of the amount realized on such sale or exchange over the adjusted basis of such share.

(3) CERTAIN TRANSFERS BY INSOLVENT INDIVIDUALS.—If an insolvent individual holds a share of stock acquired pursuant to his exercise of an incentive stock option, and if such share is transferred to a trustee, receiver, or any other similar fiduciary in any proceeding under title 11 or any other similar insolvency proceeding, neither such transfer, nor any other transfer of such share for the benefit of his creditors in such proceeding, shall constitute a disposition of such share for purposes of subsection (a)(1).

(4) PERMISSIBLE PROVISIONS.—An option which meets the requirements of subsection (b) shall be treated as an incentive stock option even if—

(A) the employee may pay for the stock with stock of the corporation granting the option,

(B) the employee has a right to receive property at the time of exercise of the option, or

(C) the option is subject to any condition not inconsistent with the provisions of subsection (b).

Subparagraph (B) shall apply to a transfer of property (other than cash) only if section 83 applies to the property so transferred.

(5) 10-PERCENT SHAREHOLDER RULE.—Subsection (b)(6) shall not apply if at the time such option is granted the option price is at least 110 percent of the fair market value of the stock subject to the option and such option by its terms is not exercisable after the expiration of 5 years from the date such option is granted.

(6) SPECIAL RULE WHEN DISABLED.—For purposes of subsection (a)(2), in the case of an employee who is disabled (within the meaning of section 22(e)(3)), the 3-month period of subsection (a)(2) shall be 1 year.

(7) FAIR MARKET VALUE.—For purposes of this section, the fair market value of stock shall be determined without regard to any restriction other than a restriction which, by its terms, will never lapse.

Amendments

• 1990, Omnibus Budget Reconciliation Act of 1990 (P.L. 101-508)

P.L. 101-508, §11801(c)(9)(C)(ii):

Amended Code Sec. 422(c) (as redesignated by Act Sec. 11801(c)(9)(A)) by striking paragraph (5) and by redesignating paragraphs (6), (7), and (8) as paragraphs (5), (6), and (7), respectively. **Effective** 11-5-90. Prior to repeal, Code Sec. 422(c)(5) read as follows:

(5) COORDINATION WITH SECTIONS 422 AND 424.—Sections 422 and 424 shall not apply to an incentive stock option.

P.L. 101-505,§11821(b)(1)-(2), provides:

(b) SAVINGS PROVISION.—If—

(1) any provision amended or repealed by this part applied to—

(A) any transaction occurring before the date of the enactment of this Act,

(B) any property acquired before such date of enactment, or

(C) any item of income, loss, deduction, or credit taken into account before such date of enactment, and

(2) the treatment of such transaction, property, or item under such provision would (without regard to the amendments made by this part) affect liability for tax for periods ending after such date of enactment,

nothing in the amendments made by this part shall be construed to affect the treatment of such transaction, property, or item for purposes of determining liability for tax for periods ending after such date of enactment.

• 1988, Technical and Miscellaneous Revenue Act of 1988 (P.L. 100-647)

P.L. 100-647, §1003(d)(2)(C):

Amended Code Sec. 422A(c)(1) by striking out "paragraph (7) of subsection (b)" and inserting in lieu thereof "subsection (d)". **Effective** as if included in the provision of P.L. 99-514 to which it relates.

• 1986, Tax Reform Act of 1986 (P.L. 99-514)

P.L. 99-514, §321(b)(1)(A)-(B):

Amended Code Sec. 422A(c)(4)-(10) by striking out paragraphs (4) and (7), and by redesignating paragraphs (5), (6), (8), (9), and (10) as paragraphs (4), (5), (6), (7), and (8), respectively. **Effective** for options granted after 12-31-86. Prior to amendment, Code Sec. 422A(c)(4) and (7) read as follows:

(4) CARRYOVER OF UNUSED LIMIT.—

(A) IN GENERAL.—If—

(i) $100,000 exceeds,

(ii) the aggregate fair market value (determined as of the time the option is granted) of the stock for which an employee was granted incentive stock options in any calendar year after 1980 (under all plans described in subsection (b) of his employer corporation and its parent and subsidiary corporations),

one-half of such excess shall be unused limit carryover to each of the 3 succeeding calendar years.

(B) AMOUNT CARRIED TO EACH YEAR.—The amount of the unused limit carryover from any calendar year which may be taken into account in any succeeding calendar year shall be the amount of such carryover reduced by the amount of such carryover which was used in prior calendar years.

(C) SPECIAL RULES.—For purposes of subparagraph (B)—

(i) the amount of options granted during any calendar year shall be treated as first using up the $100,000 limitation of subsection (b)(8), and

(ii) then shall be treated as using up unused limit carryovers to such year in the order of the calendar years in which the carryovers arose.

(7) OPTIONS OUTSTANDING.—For purposes of subsection (b)(7), any incentive stock option shall be treated as outstanding until such option is exercised in full or expires by reason of lapse of time.

P.L. 99-514, §321(b)(2):

Amended Code Sec. 422A(c)(1) by striking out "paragraph (8) of subsection (b) and paragraph (4) of this subsection" in the last sentence and inserting in lieu thereof "paragraph (7) of subsection (b)". **Effective** for options granted after 12-31-86.

P.L. 99-514, §1847(b)(5):

Amended Code Sec. 422A(c)(9) by striking out "section 37(e)(3)" and inserting in lieu thereof "section 22(e)(3)". **Effective** as if included in the provison of P.L. 98-369 to which it relates.

• 1984, Deficit Reduction Act of 1984 (P.L. 98-369)

P.L. 98-369, §555(a)(1):

Amended Code Sec. 422A(c) by adding paragraph (10). **Effective** for options granted after 3-20-84, except that such subsection shall not apply to any incentive stock option granted before 9-20-84, pursuant to a plan adopted or corporate action taken by the board of directors of the grantor corporation before 5-15-84.

P.L. 98-369, §2662(f)(1):

Amended Code Sec. 422A(c)(9) by striking out "section 105(d)(4)" and inserting in lieu thereof "section 37(e)(3)". **Effective** as if included in P.L. 98-21.

• 1983, Technical Corrections Act of 1982 (P.L. 97-448)

P.L. 97-448, §102(j)(2):

Amended Code Sec. 422A(c)(1) by adding a new sentence at the end thereof and by striking out the paragraph heading and inserting the paragraph heading. **Effective** as if included in the provision of P.L. 97-34 to which it relates. Prior to amendment, the paragraph heading for Code Sec. 422A(c)(1) read as follows:

"(1) EXERCISE OF OPTION WHEN PRICE IS LESS THAN VALUE OF STOCK.—"

P.L. 97-448, §102(j)(3):

Amended Code Sec. 422A(c)(2)(A) by striking out "the 2-year period" and inserting in lieu thereof "either of the periods". **Effective** as if included in the provision of P.L. 97-34 to which it relates.

P.L. 97-448, §102(j)(4):

Amended Code Sec. 422A(c)(4)(A)(ii) by striking out "granted options" and inserting in lieu thereof "granted incentive stock options". **Effective** as if included in the provision of P.L. 97-34 to which it relates.

• 1981, Economic Recovery Tax Act of 1981 (P.L. 97-34)

P.L. 97-34, §251(a):

Added Code Sec. 422A. For the **effective** dates and transitional rules see Act Sec. 251(c), below.

P.L. 97-34, §251(c), provides:

(c) EFFECTIVE DATES AND TRANSITIONAL RULES.—

(1) OPTIONS TO WHICH SECTION APPLIES.—

(A) IN GENERAL.—Except as provided in subparagraph (B), the amendments made by this section shall apply with respect to options granted on or after January 1, 1976, and exercised on or after January 1, 1981, or outstanding on such date.

(B) ELECTION AND DESIGNATION OF OPTIONS.—In the case of an option granted before January 1, 1981, the amendments made by this section shall apply only if the corporation granting such option elects (in the manner and at the time prescribed by the Secretary of the Treasury or his delegate) to have the amendments made by this section apply to such option. The aggregate fair market value (determined at the time the option is granted) of the stock for which any employee was granted options (under all plans of his employer corporation and its parent and subsidiary corporations) to which the amendments made by this section apply by reason of this subparagraph shall not exceed $50,000 per calendar year and shall not exceed $200,000 in the aggregate.

(2) CHANGES IN TERMS OF OPTIONS.—In the case of an option granted on or after January 1, 1976, and outstanding on the date of the enactment of this Act, paragraph (1) of section 425(h) of the Internal Revenue Code of 1954 shall not apply to any change in the terms of such option (or the terms of the plan under which granted, including shareholder approval) made within 1 year after such date of enactment to permit such option to qualify as an incentive stock option.

[Sec. 422(d)]

(d) $100,000 PER YEAR LIMITATION.—

(1) IN GENERAL.—To the extent that the aggregate fair market value of stock with respect to which incentive stock options (determined without regard to this subsection) are exercisable for the 1st time by any individual during any calendar year (under all plans of the individual's employer corporation and its parent and subsidiary corporations) exceeds $100,000, such options shall be treated as options which are not incentive stock options.

(2) ORDERING RULE.—Paragraph (1) shall be applied by taking options into account in the order in which they were granted.

(3) DETERMINATION OF FAIR MARKET VALUE.—For purposes of paragraph (1), the fair market value of any stock shall be determined as of the time the option with respect to such stock is granted.

Amendments

• 1988, Technical and Miscellaneous Revenue Act of 1988 (P.L. 100-647)

P.L. 100-647, §1003(d)(2)(A):

Amended Code Sec. 422A by adding at the end thereof new subsection (d). **Effective** as if included in the provision of P.L. 99-514 to which it relates.

[Sec. 422—Repealed]

Amendments

• 1990, Omnibus Budget Reconciliation Act of 1990 (P.L. 101-508)

P.L. 101-508, §11801(a)(20):

Repealed Code Sec. 422. **Effective** 11-5-90.

P.L. 101-508, §11821(b)(1)-(2), provides:

(b) SAVINGS PROVISION.—If—

(1) any provision amended or repealed by this part applied to—

(A) any transaction occurring before the date of the enactment of this Act,

(B) any property acquired before such date of enactment, or

(C) any item of income, loss, deduction, or credit taken into account before such date of enactment, and

(2) the treatment of such transaction, property, or item under such provision would (without regard to the amendments made by this part) affect liability for tax for periods ending after such date of enactment,

nothing in the amendments made by this part shall be construed to affect the treatment of such transaction, property, or item for purposes of determining liability for tax for periods ending after such date of enactment.

Prior to repeal, Code Sec. 422 read as follows:

SEC. 422. QUALIFIED STOCK OPTIONS.

[Sec. 422(a)]

(a) IN GENERAL.—Subject to the provisions of subsection (c)(1), section 421(a) shall apply with respect to the transfer of a share of stock to an individual pursuant to his exercise of a qualified stock option if—

(1) no disposition of such share is made by such individual within the 3-year period beginning on the day after the day of the transfer of such share, and

(2) at all times during the period beginning with the date of the granting of the option and ending on the day 3 months before the date of such exercise, such individual was an employee of either the corporation granting such option, a parent or subsidiary corporation of such corporation, or a corporation or a parent or subsidiary corporation of such corporation issuing or assuming a stock option in a transaction to which section 425(a) applies.

[Sec. 422(b)]

(b) QUALIFIED STOCK OPTION.—For purposes of this part, the term "qualified stock option" means an option granted to an individual after December 31, 1963 (other than a restricted stock option granted pursuant to a contract described in section 424(c)(3)(A)), and before May 21, 1976 (or, if it meets the requirements of subsection (c)(7), granted to an individual after May 20, 1976), for any reason connected with his employment by a corporation, if granted by the employer corporation or its parent or subsidiary corporation, to purchase stock of any of such corporations, but only if—

(1) the option is granted pursuant to a plan which includes the aggregate number of shares which may be issued under options, and the employees (or class of employees) eligible to receive options, and which is approved by the stockholders of the granting corporation within 12 months before or after the date such plan is adopted;

(2) such option is granted within 10 years from the date such plan is adopted, or the date such plan is approved by the stockholders, whichever is earlier;

(3) such option by its terms is not exercisable after the expiration of 5 years from the date such option is granted;

(4) except as provided in subsection (c)(1), the option price is not less than the fair market value of the stock at the time such option is granted;

(5) such option by its terms is not exercisable while there is outstanding (within the meaning of subsection (c)(2)) any qualified stock option (or restricted stock option) which was granted, before the granting of such option, to such individual to purchase stock in his employer corporation or in a corporation which (at the time of the granting of such option) is a parent or subsidiary corporation of the employer corporation, or in a predecessor corporation of any of such corporations;

(6) such option by its terms is not transferable by such individual otherwise than by will or the laws of descent and distribution, and is exercisable, during his lifetime, only by him; and

(7) such individual, immediately after such option is granted, does not own stock possessing more than 5 percent of the total combined voting power or value of all classes of stock of the employer corporation or of its parent or subsidiary corporation; except that if the equity capital of such corporation or corporations (determined at the time the option is granted) is less than $2,000,000, then, for purposes of applying the limitation of this paragraph, there shall be added to such 5 percent the percentage (not higher than 5 percent) which bears the same ratio to 5 percent as the difference between such equity capital and $2,000,000 bears to $1,000,000.

Amendments

• 1976, Tax Reform Act of 1976 (P.L. 94-455)

P.L. 94-455, §603(a):

Amended Code Sec. 422(b) by inserting "and before May 21, 1976 (or, if it meets the requirements of subsection (c)(7), granted to an individual after May 20, 1976)," after "section 424(c)(3)(A)),". **Effective** for tax years ending after 12-31-75.

[Sec. 422(c)]

(c) SPECIAL RULES.—

(1) EXERCISE OF OPTION WHEN PRICE IS LESS THAN VALUE OF STOCK.—If a share of stock is transferred pursuant to the exercise by an individual of an option which fails to qualify as a qualified stock option under subsection (b) because there was a failure in an attempt, made in good faith, to meet the requirement of subsection (b)(4), the requirement of subsection (b)(4) shall be considered to have been met, but there shall be included as compensation (and not as gain upon the sale or exchange of a capital asset) in his gross income for the taxable year in which such option is exercised, an amount equal to the lesser of—

(A) 150 percent of the difference between the option price and the fair market value of the share at the time the option was granted, or

(B) the difference between the option price and the fair market value of the share at the time of such exercise.

The basis of the share acquired shall be increased by an amount equal to the amount included in his gross income under this paragraph in the taxable year in which the exercise occurred.

(2) CERTAIN OPTIONS TREATED AS OUTSTANDING.—For purposes of subsection (b)(5)—

(A) any restricted stock option which is not terminated before January 1, 1965, and

(B) any qualified stock option granted after December 31, 1963,

shall be treated as outstanding until such option is exercised in full or expires by reason of the lapse of time. For purposes of the preceding sentence, a restricted stock option granted before January 1, 1964, shall not be treated as outstanding for any period before the first day on which (under the terms of such option) it may be exercised.

(3) OPTIONS GRANTED TO CERTAIN SHAREHOLDERS.—For purposes of subsection (b)(7)—

(A) the term "equity capital" means—

(i) in the case of one corporation, the sum of its money and other property (in an amount equal to the adjusted basis of such property for determining gain), less the amount of its indebtedness (other than indebtedness to shareholders), and

(ii) in the case of a group of corporations consisting of a parent and its subsidiary corporations, the sum of the equity capital of each of such corporations adjusted, under regulations prescribed by the Secretary, to eliminate the effect of intercorporate ownership and transactions among such corporations;

(B) the rules of section 425 (d) shall apply in determining the stock ownership of the individual; and

(C) stock which the individual may purchase under outstanding options shall be treated as stock owned by such individual.

If an individual is granted an option which permits him to purchase stock in excess of the limitation of subsection (b)(7) (determined by applying the rules of this paragraph), such option shall be treated as meeting the requirement of subsection (b)(7) to the extent that such individual could, if the option were fully exercised at the time of grant, purchase stock under such option without exceeding such limitation. The portion of such option which is treated as meeting the requirement of subsection (b)(7) shall be deemed to be that portion of the option which is first exercised.

(4) CERTAIN DISQUALIFYING DISPOSITIONS WHERE AMOUNT REALIZED IS LESS THAN VALUE AT EXERCISE.—If—

(A) an individual who has acquired a share of stock by the exercise of a qualified stock option makes a disposition of such share within the 3-year period described in subsection (a)(1), and

(B) such disposition is a sale or exchange with respect to which a loss (if sustained) would be recognized to such individual,

then the amount which is includible in the gross income of such individual, and the amount which is deductible from the income of his employer corporation, as compensation attributable to the exercise of such option shall not exceed the excess (if any) of the amount realized on such sale or exchange over the adjusted basis of such share.

(5) CERTAIN TRANSFERS BY INSOLVENT INDIVIDUALS.—If an insolvent individual holds a share of stock acquired pursuant to his exercise of a qualified stock option, and if such share is transferred to a trustee, receiver, or other similar fiduciary, in any proceeding under title 11 of the United States Code or any other similar insolvency proceeding, neither such transfer, nor any other transfer of such share for the benefit of his creditors in such proceeding, shall constitute a "disposition of such share" for purposes of subsection (a)(1).

(6) APPLICATION OF SUBSECTION (b)(5) WHERE OPTIONS ARE FOR STOCK OF SAME CLASS IN SAME CORPORATION.—The requirement of subsection (b)(5) shall be considered to have been met in the case of any option (referred to in this paragraph as "new option") granted to an individual if—

(A) the new option and all outstanding options referred to in subsection (b)(5) are to purchase stock of the same class in the same corporation, and

(B) the new option by its terms is not exercisable while there is outstanding (within the meaning of paragraph (2)) any qualified stock option (or restricted stock option) which was granted, before the granting of the new option, to such individual to purchase stock in such corporation at a price (determined as of the date of grant of the new option) higher than the option price of the new option.

(7) CERTAIN OPTIONS GRANTED AFTER MAY 20, 1976.—For purposes of subsection (b), an option granted after May 20, 1976, meets the requirements of this paragraph—

(A) if such option is granted to an individual pursuant to a written plan adopted before May 21, 1976, or

(B) if such option is a new option substituted, in a transaction to which section 425(a) applies, for an old option which was granted before May 21, 1976, or which met the requirements of subparagraph (A).

An option described in the preceding sentence shall be treated as ceasing to meet the requirements of this paragraph if it is not exercised before May 21, 1981.

Amendments

• 1980, Bankruptcy Tax Act of 1980. (P.L. 96-589)

P.L. 96-589, §6(i)(3):

Amended Code Sec. 422(c)(5) by striking out "under the Bankruptcy Act" and inserting in lieu thereof, "under title 11 of United States Code". **Effective** 10-1-79, but inapplicable to any proceeding under the Bankruptcy Act commenced before that date.

• 1976, Tax Reform Act of 1976 (P.L. 94-455)

P.L. 94-455, §603(b):

Added Code Sec. 422(c)(7). **Effective** for tax years ending after 12-31-75.

P.L. 94-455, §1906(b)(13)(A):

Amended the 1954 Code by substituting "Secretary" for "Secretary or his delegate" each place it appeared. **Effective** 2-1-77.

• 1964, Revenue Act of 1964 (P.L. 88-272)

P.L. 88-272, §221(a):

Added Code Sec. 422. Except as noted below, **effective** for tax years ending after 12-31-63.

In the case of an option granted after December 31, 1963, and before January 1, 1965—

(a) paragraphs (1) and (2) of section 422(b) shall not apply, and

(b) paragraph (1) of section 425(h) shall not apply to any change in the terms of such option made before January 1, 1965, to permit such option to qualify under paragraphs (3), (4) and (5) of section 422(b).

[Sec. 423]

SEC. 423. EMPLOYEE STOCK PURCHASE PLANS.

[Sec. 423(a)]

(a) GENERAL RULE.—Section 421(a) shall apply with respect to the transfer of a share of stock to an individual pursuant to his exercise of an option granted after December 31, 1963, under an employee stock purchase plan (as defined in subsection (b)) if—

(1) no disposition of such share is made by him within 2 years after the date of the granting of the option nor within 1 year after the transfer of such share to him; and

(2) at all times during the period beginning with the date of the granting of the option and ending on the day 3 months before the date of such exercise, he is an employee of the corporation granting such option, a parent or subsidiary corporation of such corporation, or a corporation or a parent or subsidiary corporation of such corporation issuing or assuming a stock option in a transaction to which section 424(a) applies.

Amendments

• 1990, Omnibus Budget Reconciliation Act of 1990 (P.L. 101-508)

P.L. 101-508, §11801(c)(9)(D)(i)-(ii):

Amended Code Sec. 423(a) by striking "(other than a restricted stock option granted pursuant to a plan described in section 424(c)(3)(B))" after "December 31, 1963"; and by striking "425(a)" and inserting "424(a)". **Effective** 11-5-90.

P.L. 101-508, §11821(b)(1)-(2), provides:

(b) SAVINGS PROVISION.—If—

(1) any provision amended or repealed by this part applied to—

(A) any transaction occurring before the date of the enactment of this Act,

(B) any property acquired before such date of enactment, or

(C) any item of income, loss, deduction, or credit taken into account before such date of enactment, and

(2) the treatment of such transaction, property, or item under such provision would (without regard to the amendments made by this part) affect liability for tax for periods ending after such date of enactment,

nothing in the amendments made by this part shall be construed to affect the treatment of such transaction, property, or item for purposes of determining liability for tax for periods ending after such date of enactment.

• 1984, Deficit Reduction Act of 1984 (P.L. 98-369)

P.L. 98-369, §1001(b)(5):

Amended Code Sec. 423(a)(1) by striking out "1 year" and inserting in lieu thereof "6 months". **Effective** for property acquired after 6-22-84, and before 1-1-88.

• 1976, Tax Reform Act of 1976 (P.L. 94-455)

P.L. 94-455, §1402(b)(1)(C):

Substituted "9 months" for "6 months" in Code Sec. 423(a). **Effective** for tax years beginning in 1977.

P.L. 94-455, §1402(b)(2):

Substituted "1 year" for "9 months" in Code Sec. 423(a). **Effective** for tax years beginning after 12-31-77.

[Sec. 423(b)]

(b) EMPLOYEE STOCK PURCHASE PLAN.—For purposes of this part, the term "employee stock purchase plan" means a plan which meets the following requirements:

(1) the plan provides that options are to be granted only to employees of the employer corporation or of its parent or subsidiary corporation to purchase stock in any such corporation;

(2) such plan is approved by the stockholders of the granting corporation within 12 months before or after the date such plan is adopted;

(3) under the terms of the plan, no employee can be granted an option if such employee, immediately after the option is granted, owns stock possessing 5 percent or more of the total combined voting power or value of all classes of stock of the employer corporation or of its parent or subsidiary corporation. For purposes of this paragraph, the rules of section 424(d) shall apply in determining the stock ownership of an individual, and stock which the employee may purchase under outstanding options shall be treated as stock owned by the employee;

(4) under the terms of the plan, options are to be granted to all employees of any corporation whose employees are granted any of such options by reason of their employment by such corporation, except that there may be excluded—

(A) employees who have been employed less than 2 years,

(B) employees whose customary employment is 20 hours or less per week,

(C) employees whose customary employment is for not more than 5 months in any calendar year, and

(D) highly compensated employees (within the meaning of section 414(q));

(5) under the terms of the plan, all employees granted such options shall have the same rights and privileges, except that the amount of stock which may be purchased by any employee under such option may bear a uniform relationship to the total compensation, or the basic or

regular rate of compensation, of employees, and the plan may provide that no employee may purchase more than a maximum amount of stock fixed under the plan;

(6) under the terms of the plan, the option price is not less than the lesser of—

(A) an amount equal to 85 percent of the fair market value of the stock at the time such option is granted, or

(B) an amount which under the terms of the option may not be less than 85 percent of the fair market value of the stock at the time such option is exercised;

(7) under the terms of the plan, such option cannot be exercised after the expiration of—

(A) 5 years from the date such option is granted if, under the terms of such plan, the option price is to be not less than 85 percent of the fair market value of such stock at the time of the exercise of the option, or

(B) 27 months from the date such option is granted, if the option price is not determinable in the manner described in subparagraph (A);

(8) under the terms of the plan, no employee may be granted an option which permits his rights to purchase stock under all such plans of his employer corporation and its parent and subsidiary corporations to accrue at a rate which exceeds $25,000 of fair market value of such stock (determined at the time such option is granted) for each calendar year in which such option is outstanding at any time. For purposes of this paragraph—

(A) the right to purchase stock under an option accrues when the option (or any portion thereof) first becomes exercisable during the calendar year;

(B) the right to purchase stock under an option accrues at the rate provided in the option, but in no case may such rate exceed $25,000 of fair market value of such stock (determined at the time such option is granted) for any one calendar year; and

(C) a right to purchase stock which has accrued under one option granted pursuant to the plan may not be carried over to any other option; and

(9) under the terms of the plan, such option is not transferable by such individual otherwise than by will or the laws of descent and distribution, and is exercisable, during his lifetime, only by him.

For purposes of paragraphs (3) to (9), inclusive, where additional terms are contained in an offering made under a plan, such additional terms shall, with respect to options exercised under such offering, be treated as a part of the terms of such plan.

Amendments

• 1990, Omnibus Budget Reconciliation Act of 1990 (P.L. 101-508)

P.L. 101-508, §11801(c)(9)(E):

Amended Code Sec. 423(b)(3) by striking "425(d)" and inserting "424(d)". **Effective** 11-5-90.

P.L. 101-508, §11821(b)(1)-(2), provides:

(b) SAVINGS PROVISION.—If—

(1) any provision amended or repealed by this part applied to—

(A) any transaction occurring before the date of the enactment of this Act,

(B) any property acquired before such date of enactment, or

(C) any item of income, loss, deduction, or credit taken into account before such date of enactment, and

(2) the treatment of such transaction, property, or item under such provision would (without regard to the amendments made by this part) affect liability for tax for periods ending after such date of enactment,

nothing in the amendments made by this part shall be construed to affect the treatment of such transaction, property, or item for purposes of determining liability for tax for periods ending after such date of enactment.

• 1986, Tax Reform Act of 1986 (P.L. 99-514)

P.L. 99-514, §1114(b)(13):

Amended Code Sec. 423(b)(4)(D) by striking out "officers, persons whose principal duties consist of supervising the work of other employees, or highly compensated employees" and inserting in lieu thereof "highly compensated employees (within the meaning of section 414(q))". **Effective**, generally, for years beginning after 12-31-86. However, for a special rule, see Act Sec. 1114(c)(4) below.

P.L. 99-514, §1114(c)(4) (repealed by P.L. 107-16, §663(a)), provided:

(4) SPECIAL RULE FOR DETERMINING HIGHLY COMPENSATED EMPLOYEES.—For purposes of sections 401(k) and 401(m) of the Internal Revenue Code of 1986, in the case of an employer incorporated on December 15, 1924, if more than 50 percent of its employees in the top-paid group (within the meaning of section 414(q)(4) of such Code) earn less than $25,000 (indexed at the same time and in the same manner as under section 415(d) of such Code), then the highly compensated employees shall include employees described in section 414(q)(1)(C) of such Code determined without regard to the level of compensation of such employees.

[Sec. 423(c)]

(c) SPECIAL RULE WHERE OPTION PRICE IS BETWEEN 85 PERCENT AND 100 PERCENT OF VALUE OF STOCK.—If the option price of a share of stock acquired by an individual pursuant to a transfer to which subsection (a) applies was less than 100 percent of the fair market value of such share at the time such option was granted, then, in the event of any disposition of such share by him which meets the holding period requirements of subsection (a), or in the event of his death (whenever occurring) while owning such share, there shall be included as compensation (and not as gain upon the sale or exchange of a capital asset) in his gross income, for the taxable year in which falls the date of such disposition or for the taxable year closing with his death, whichever applies, an amount equal to the lesser of—

(1) the excess of the fair market value of the share at the time of such disposition or death over the amount paid for the share under the option, or

(2) the excess of the fair market value of the share at the time the option was granted over the option price.

If the option price is not fixed or determinable at the time the option is granted, then for purposes of this subsection, the option price shall be determined as if the option were exercised at such time. In the case of the disposition of such share by the individual, the basis of the share in his hands at the time of such disposition shall be increased by an amount equal to the amount so includible in his gross income. No amount shall be required to be deducted and withheld under chapter 24 with respect to any amount treated as compensation under this subsection.

Amendments

• 2004, American Jobs Creation Act of 2004 (P.L. 108-357)

P.L. 108-357, §251(c):

Amended Code Sec. 423(c) by adding at the end a new sentence. **Effective** for stock acquired pursuant to options exercised after 10-22-2004.

• 1964, Revenue Act of 1964 (P.L. 88-272)

P.L. 88-272, §221(a):

Added Code Sec. 423. **Effective** for tax years ending after 12-31-63.

[Sec. 424]

SEC. 424. DEFINITIONS AND SPECIAL RULES.

[Sec. 424(a)]

(a) CORPORATE REORGANIZATIONS, LIQUIDATIONS, ETC.—For purposes of this part, the term "issuing or assuming a stock option in a transaction to which section 424(a) applies" means a substitution of a new option for the old option, or an assumption of the old option, by an employer corporation, or a parent or subsidiary of such corporation, by reason of a corporate merger, consolidation, acquisition of property or stock, separation, reorganization, or liquidation, if—

(1) the excess of the aggregate fair market value of the shares subject to the option immediately after the substitution or assumption over the aggregate option price of such shares is not more than the excess of the aggregate fair market value of all shares subject to the option immediately before such substitution or assumption over the aggregate option price of such shares, and

(2) the new option or the assumption of the old option does not give the employee additional benefits which he did not have under the old option.

For purposes of this subsection, the parent-subsidiary relationship shall be determined at the time of any such transaction under this subsection.

Amendments

• 1990, Omnibus Budget Reconciliation Act of 1990 (P.L. 101-508)

P.L. 101-508, §11801(c)(9)(A)(i):

Redesignated Code Sec. 425 as Code Sec. 424. **Effective** 11-5-90.

P.L. 101-508, §11801(c)(9)(F)(i):

Amended Code Sec. 424(a) (as redesignated by Act Sec. 11801(c)(9)(A)) by striking "425(a)" and inserting "424(a)". **Effective** 11-5-90.

P.L. 101-508, §11821(b)(1)-(2), provides:

(b) SAVINGS PROVISION.—If—

(1) any provision amended or repealed by this part applied to—

(A) any transaction occurring before the date of the enactment of this Act,

(B) any property acquired before such date of enactment, or

(C) any item of income, loss, deduction, or credit taken into account before such date of enactment, and

(2) the treatment of such transaction, property, or item under such provision would (without regard to the amendments made by this part) affect liability for tax for periods ending after such date of enactment,

nothing in the amendments made by this part shall be construed to affect the treatment of such transaction, property, or item for purposes of determining liability for tax for periods ending after such date of enactment.

[Sec. 424(b)]

(b) ACQUISITION OF NEW STOCK.—For purposes of this part, if stock is received by an individual in a distribution to which section 305, 354, 355, 356, or 1036 (or so much of section 1031 as relates to section 1036) applies, and such distribution was made with respect to stock transferred to him upon his exercise of the option, such stock shall be considered as having been transferred to him on his exercise of such option. A similar rule shall be applied in the case of a series of such distributions.

[Sec. 424(c)]

(c) DISPOSITION.—

(1) IN GENERAL.—Except as provided in paragraphs (2), (3), and (4), for purposes of this part, the term "disposition" includes a sale, exchange, gift, or a transfer of legal title, but does not include—

(A) a transfer from a decedent to an estate or a transfer by bequest or inheritance;

(B) an exchange to which section 354, 355, 356, or 1036 (or so much of section 1031 as relates to section 1036) applies; or

(C) a mere pledge or hypothecation.

(2) JOINT TENANCY.—The acquisition of a share of stock in the name of the employee and another jointly with the right of survivorship or a subsequent transfer of a share of stock into such joint ownership shall not be deemed a disposition, but a termination of such joint tenancy

(except to the extent such employee acquires ownership of such stock) shall be treated as a disposition by him occurring at the time such joint tenancy is terminated.

(3) SPECIAL RULE WHERE INCENTIVE STOCK IS ACQUIRED THROUGH USE OF OTHER STATUTORY OPTION STOCK.—

(A) NONRECOGNITION SECTIONS NOT TO APPLY.—If—

(i) there is a transfer of statutory option stock in connection with the exercise of any incentive stock option, and

(ii) the applicable holding period requirements (under section 422(a)(1) or 423(a)(1) are not met before such transfer,

then no section referred to in subparagraph (B) of paragraph (1) shall apply to such transfer.

(B) STATUTORY OPTION STOCK.—For purpose of subparagraph (A), the term "statutory option stock" means any stock acquired through the exercise of an incentive stock option or an option granted under an employee stock purchase plan.

(4) TRANSFERS BETWEEN SPOUSES OR INCIDENT TO DIVORCE.—In the case of any transfer described in subsection (a) of section 1041—

(A) such transfer shall not be treated as a disposition for purposes of this part, and

(B) the same tax treatment under this part with respect to the transferred property shall apply to the transferee as would have applied to the transferor.

Amendments

• 1996, Small Business Job Protection Act of 1996 (P.L. 104-188)

P.L. 104-188, §1702(h)(13):

Amended Code Sec. 424(c)(3)(B) by striking "a qualified stock option, an incentive stock option, an option granted under an employee stock purchase plan, or a restricted stock option" and inserting "an incentive stock option or an option granted under an employee stock purchase plan". **Effective** as if included in the provision of P.L. 101-508 to which it relates.

• 1990, Omnibus Budget Reconciliation Act of 1990 (P.L. 101-508)

P.L. 101-508, §11801(c)(9)(F)(ii):

Amended Code Sec. 424(c)(3)(A)(ii) (as redesignated by Act Sec. 11801(c)(9)(A)) by striking "422(a)(1), 422A(a)(1), 423(a)(1), or 424(a)(1)" and inserting "422(a)(1) or 423(a)(1)". **Effective** 11-5-90.

P.L. 101-508, §11821(b)(1)-(2), provides:

(b) SAVINGS PROVISION.—If—

(1) any provision amended or repealed by this part applied to—

(A) any transaction occurring before the date of the enactment of this Act,

(B) any property acquired before such date of enactment, or

(C) any item of income, loss, deduction, or credit taken into account before such date of enactment, and

(2) the treatment of such transaction, property, or item under such provision would (without regard to the amendments made by this part) affect liability for tax for periods ending after such date of enactment,

nothing in the amendments made by this part shall be construed to affect the treatment of such transaction, property, or item for purposes of determining liability for tax for periods ending after such date of enactment.

• 1988, Technical and Miscellaneous Revenue Act of 1988 (P.L. 100-647)

P.L. 100-647, §1018(l)(1):

Amended Code Sec. 425(c) by adding at the end thereof a new paragraph (4). **Effective** as if included in the provision of P.L. 99-514 to which it relates.

P.L. 100-647, §1018(l)(2):

Amended Code Sec. 425(c)(1) by striking out "paragraph (2) and (3)" and inserting in lieu thereof "paragraphs (2), (3), and (4)". **Effective** as if included in the provision of P.L. 99-514 to which it relates.

• 1983, Technical Corrections Act of 1982 (P.L. 97-448)

P.L. 97-448, §102(j)(6)(A):

Amended Code Sec. 425(c) by adding at the end thereof paragraph (3). **Effective** for transfers after 3-15-82.

P.L. 97-448, §102(j)(6)(B):

Amended Code Sec. 425(c)(1) by striking out "paragraph (2)" and inserting in lieu thereof "paragraphs (2) and (3)". **Effective** as if included in the provision of P.L. 97-34 to which it relates.

[Sec. 424(d)]

(d) ATTRIBUTION OF STOCK OWNERSHIP.—For purposes of this part, in applying the percentage limitations of sections 422(b)(6) and 423(b)(3)—

(1) the individual with respect to whom such limitation is being determined shall be considered as owning the stock owned, directly or indirectly, by or for his brothers and sisters (whether by the whole or half blood), spouse, ancestors, and lineal descendants; and

(2) stock owned, directly or indirectly, by or for a corporation, partnership, estate, or trust, shall be considered as being owned proportionately by or for its shareholders, partners, or beneficiaries.

Amendments

• 1990, Omnibus Budget Reconciliation Act of 1990 (P.L. 101-508)

P.L. 101-508, §11801(c)(9)(F)(iii):

Amended Code Sec. 424(d) (as redesignated by Act Sec. 11801(c)(9)(A)) by striking "422(b)(7), 422A(b)(6), 423(b)(3), and 424(b)(3)" and inserting "422(b)(6) and 423(b)(3)". **Effective** 11-5-90.

P.L. 101-508, §11821(b)(1)-(2), provides:

(b) SAVINGS PROVISION.—If—

(1) any provision amended or repealed by this part applied to—

(A) any transaction occurring before the date of the enactment of this Act,

(B) any property acquired before such date of enactment, or

(C) any item of income, loss, deduction, or credit taken into account before such date of enactment, and

(2) the treatment of such transaction, property, or item under such provision would (without regard to the amendments made by this part) affect liability for tax for periods ending after such date of enactment,

nothing in the amendments made by this part shall be construed to affect the treatment of such transaction, property, or item for purposes of determining liability for tax for periods ending after such date of enactment.

• 1981, Economic Recovery Tax Act of 1981 (P.L. 97-34)

P.L. 97-34, §251(b)(2):

Amended Code Sec. 425(d) by inserting "422A(b)(6)," after "422(b)(7),". For the **effective** date and transitional rules, see the historical comment for P.L. 97-34 following Code Sec. 422A(a).

[Sec. 424(e)]

(e) PARENT CORPORATION.—For purposes of this part, the term "parent corporation" means any corporation (other than the employer corporation) in an unbroken chain of corporations ending with the employer corporation if, at the time of the granting of the option, each of the corporations other than the employer corporation owns stock possessing 50 percent or more of the total combined voting power of all classes of stock in one of the other corporations in such chain.

[Sec. 424(f)]

(f) SUBSIDIARY CORPORATION.—For purposes of this part, the term "subsidiary corporation" means any corporation (other than the employer corporation) in an unbroken chain of corporations beginning with the employer corporation if, at the time of the granting of the option, each of the corporations other than the last corporation in the unbroken chain owns stock possessing 50 percent or more of the total combined voting power of all classes of stock in one of the other corporations in such chain.

[Sec. 424(g)]

(g) SPECIAL RULE FOR APPLYING SUBSECTIONS (e) AND (f).—In applying subsections (e) and (f) for purposes of section 422(a)(2) and 423(a)(2), there shall be substituted for the term "employer corporation" wherever it appears in subsections (e) and (f) the term "grantor corporation", or the term "corporation issuing or assuming a stock option in a transaction to which section 424(a) applies", as the case may be.

Amendments

• 1990, Omnibus Budget Reconciliation Act of 1990 (P.L. 101-508)

P.L. 101-508, §11801(c)(9)(F)(iv)(I)-(II):

Amended Code Sec. 424(g) (as redesignated by Act Sec. 11801(c)(9)(A)) by striking "422(a)(2), 422A(a)(2), 423(a)(2), and 424(a)(2)" and inserting "422(a)(2) and 423(a)(2)"; and by striking "425(a)" and inserting "424(a)". **Effective** 11-5-90.

P.L. 101-508, §11821(b)(1)-(2), provides:

(b) SAVINGS PROVISION.—If—

(1) any provision amended or repealed by this part applied to—

(A) any transaction occurring before the date of the enactment of this Act,

(B) any property acquired before such date of enactment, or

(C) any item of income, loss, deduction, or credit taken into account before such date of enactment, and

(2) the treatment of such transaction, property, or item under such provision would (without regard to the amendments made by this part) affect liability for tax for periods ending after such date of enactment,

nothing in the amendments made by this part shall be construed to affect the treatment of such transaction, property, or item for purposes of determining liability for tax for periods ending after such date of enactment.

P.L. 97-34, §251(b)(3):

Amended Code Sec. 425(g) by inserting "422A(a)(2)," after "422(a)(2),". For the **effective** date and transitional rules, see the historical comment for P.L. 97-34 following Code Sec. 422A(a).

[Sec. 424(h)]

(h) MODIFICATION, EXTENSION, OR RENEWAL OF OPTION.—

(1) IN GENERAL.—For purposes of this part, if the terms of any option to purchase stock are modified, extended, or renewed, such modification, extension, or renewal shall be considered as the granting of a new option.

(2) SPECIAL RULE FOR SECTION 423 OPTIONS.—In the case of the transfer of stock pursuant to the exercise of an option to which section 423 applies and which has been so modified, extended, or renewed, the fair market value of such stock at the time of the granting of the option shall be considered as whichever of the following is the highest—

(A) the fair market value of such stock on the date of the original granting of the option,

(B) the fair market value of such stock on the date of the making of such modification, extension, or renewal, or

(C) the fair market value of such stock at the time of the making of any intervening modification, extension, or renewal.

(3) DEFINITION OF MODIFICATION.—The term "modification" means any change in the terms of the option which gives the employee additional benefits under the option, but such term shall not include a change in the terms of the option—

(A) attributable to the issuance or assumption of an option under subsection (a);

(B) to permit the option to qualify under section 423(b)(9); or

(C) in the case of an option not immediately exercisable in full, to accelerate the time at which the option may be exercised.

Amendments

• 1990, Omnibus Budget Reconciliation Act of 1990 (P.L. 101-508)

P.L. 101-508, §11801(c)(9)(F)(v)(I)-(III):

Amended Code Sec. 424(h) (as redesignated by Act Sec. 11801(c)(9)(A)) by amending paragraph (2), by striking in paragraph (3)(B) "sections 422(b)(6), 423(b)(9), and 424(b)(2)" and inserting "section 423(b)(9)"; and by striking the sentence following paragraph (3)(C). **Effective** 11-5-90. Prior to amendment Code Sec. 424(h)(2) and the sentence following paragraph (3)(C) read as follows:

(2) SPECIAL RULES FOR SECTIONS 423 AND 424 OPTIONS.—

(A) In the case of the transfer of stock pursuant to the exercise of an option to which section 423 or 424 applies and which has been so modified, extended, or renewed, then, except as provided in subparagraph (B), the fair market value of such stock at the time of the granting of such option shall be considered as whichever of the following is the highest:

(i) the fair market value of such stock on the date of the original granting of the option,

(ii) the fair market value of such stock on the date of the making of such modification, extension, or renewal, or

(iii) the fair market value of such stock at the time of the making of any intervening modification, extension, or renewal.

(B) Subparagraph (A) shall not apply with respect to a modification, extension, or renewal of a restricted stock option before January 1, 1964 (or after December 31, 1963, if made pursuant to a binding written contract entered into before January 1, 1964), if the aggregate of the monthly average fair market values of the stock subject to the option for the 12 consecutive calendar months before the date of the modification, extension, or renewal, divided by 12, is an amount less than 80 percent of the fair market value of such stock on the date of the original granting of the option or the date of the making of any intervening modification, extension, or renewal, whichever is the highest.

(3) DEFINITION OF MODIFICATION.—* * *

* * *

If a restricted stock option is exercisable after the expiration of 10 years from the date such option is granted, subparagraph (B) shall not apply unless the terms of the option are also changed to make it not exercisable after the expiration of such period.

P.L. 101-508, §11821(b)(1)-(2), provides:

(b) SAVINGS PROVISION.—If—

(1) any provision amended or repealed by this part applied to—

(A) any transaction occurring before the date of the enactment of this Act,

(B) any property acquired before such date of enactment, or

(C) any item of income, loss, deduction, or credit taken into account before such date of enactment, and

(2) the treatment of such transaction, property, or item under such provision would (without regard to the amendments made by this part) affect liability for tax for periods ending after such date of enactment,

nothing in the amendments made by this part shall be construed to affect the treatment of such transaction, property, or item for purposes of determining liability for tax for periods ending after such date of enactment.

• 1984, Deficit Reduction Act of 1984 (P.L. 98-369)

P.L. 98-369, §555(b)[(c)]:

Amended Code Sec. 425(h)(3)(B) by striking out "422A(b)(5)," after "422(b)(6)". **Effective** with respect to modifications of options after 3-20-84.

• 1981, Economic Recovery Tax Act of 1981 (P.L. 97-34)

P.L. 97-34, §251(b)(4):

Amended Code Sec. 425(h)(3)(B) by inserting "422A(b)(5)," after "422(b)(6),". For the **effective** date and transitional rules, see the historical comment for P.L. 97-34 following Code Sec. 422A(a).

[Sec. 424(i)]

(i) STOCKHOLDER APPROVAL.—For purposes of this part, if the grant of an option is subject to approval by stockholders, the date of grant of the option shall be determined as if the option had not been subject to such approval.

[Sec. 424(j)]

(j) CROSS REFERENCES.—

For provisions requiring the reporting of certain acts with respect to a qualified stock option, an incentive stock option, options granted under employer stock purchase plans, or a restricted stock option, see section 6039.

Amendments

• 1983, Technical Corrections Act of 1982 (P.L. 97-448)

P.L. 97-448, §102(j)(5):

Amended Code Sec. 425(j) by inserting "an incentive stock option," after "qualified stock option,". **Effective** as if included in the provision of P.L. 97-34 to which it relates.

[Sec. 424—Repealed]

Amendments

• 1990, Omnibus Budget Reconciliation Act of 1990 (P.L. 101-508)

P.L. 101-508, §11801(a)(21):

Repealed Code Sec. 424. **Effective** 11-5-90.

P.L. 101-508, §11821(b)(1)-(2), provides:

(b) SAVINGS PROVISION.—If—

(1) any provision amended or repealed by this part applied to—

(A) any transaction occurring before the date of the enactment of this Act,

(B) any property acquired before such date of enactment, or

(C) any item of income, loss, deduction, or credit taken into account before such date of enactment, and

(2) the treatment of such transaction, property, or item under such provision would (without regard to the amendments made by this part) affect liability for tax for periods ending after such date of enactment,

nothing in the amendments made by this part shall be construed to affect the treatment of such transaction, property, or item for purposes of determining liability for tax for periods ending after such date of enactment.

Prior to repeal, Code Sec. 424 read as follows:

SEC. 424. RESTRICTED STOCK OPTIONS.

[Sec. 424(a)]

(a) IN GENERAL.—Section 421(a) shall apply with respect to the transfer of a share of stock to an individual pursuant to his exercise after 1949 of a restricted stock option, if—

(1) no disposition of such share is made by him within 2 years from the date of the granting of the option nor within

6 months [9 months for taxable years beginning in 1977; 1 year for taxable years beginning after December 31, 1977] after the transfer of such share to him, and

(2) at the time he exercises such option—

(A) he is an employee of either the corporation granting such option, a parent or subsidiary corporation of such corporation, or a corporation or a parent or subsidiary corporation of such corporation issuing or assuming a stock option in a transaction to which section 425(a) applies, or

(B) he ceased to be an employee of such corporations within the 3-month period preceding the time of exercise.

Amendments

• 1976, Tax Reform Act of 1976 (P.L. 94-455)

P.L. 94-455, §1402(b)(1)(C):

Substituted "9 months" for "6 months" in Code Sec. 424(a). **Effective** for tax years beginning in 1977.

P.L. 94-455, §1402(b)(2):

Substituted "1 year" for "9 months" in Code Sec. 424(a). **Effective** for tax years beginning after 12-31-77.

[Sec. 424(b)]

(b) RESTRICTED STOCK OPTION.—For purposes of this part, the term "restricted stock option" means an option granted after February 26, 1945, and before January 1, 1964 (or, if it meets the requirements of subsection (c)(3), an option granted after December 31, 1963), to an individual, for any reason connected with his employment by a corporation, if granted by the employer corporation or its parent or subsidiary corporation, to purchase stock of any of such corporations, but only if—

(1) at the time such option is granted—

(A) the option price is at least 85 percent of the fair market value at such time of the stock subject to the option, or

(B) in the case of a variable price option, the option price (computed as if the option had been exercised when granted) is at least 85 percent of the fair market value of the stock at the time such option is granted;

(2) such option by its terms is not transferable by such individual otherwise than by will or the laws of descent and distribution, and is exercisable, during his lifetime, only by him;

(3) such individual, at the time the option is granted, does not own stock possessing more than 10 percent of the total combined voting power of all classes of stock of the employer corporation or of its parent or subsidiary corporation. This paragraph shall not apply if at the time such option is granted the option price is at least 110 percent of the fair market value of the stock subject to the option, and such option either by its terms is not exercisable after the expiration of 5 years from the date such option is granted or is exercised within one year after August 16, 1954. For purposes of this paragraph, the provisions of section 425(d) shall apply in determining the stock ownership of an individual; and

(4) such option by its terms is not exercisable after the expiration of 10 years from the date such option is granted, if such option has been granted on or after June 22, 1954.

[Sec. 424(c)]

(c) SPECIAL RULES.—

(1) OPTIONS UNDER WHICH OPTION PRICE IS BETWEEN 85 PERCENT AND 95 PERCENT OF VALUE OF STOCK.—If no disposition of a share of stock acquired by an individual on his exercise after 1949 of a restricted stock option is made by him within 2 years from the date of the granting of the option nor within 1 year after the transfer of such share to him, but, at the time the restricted stock option was granted, the option price (computed under subsection (b)(1)) was less than 95 percent of the fair market value at such time of such share, then, in the event of any disposition of such share by him, or in the event of his death (whenever occurring) while owning such share, there shall be included as compensation (and not as gain upon the sale or exchange of a capital asset) in his gross income, for the taxable year in which falls the date of such disposition or for the taxable year closing with his death, whichever applies—

(A) in the case of a share of stock acquired under an option qualifying under subsection (b)(1)(A), an amount equal to the amount (if any) by which the option price is exceeded by the lesser of—

(i) the fair market value of the share at the time of such disposition or death, or

(ii) the fair market value of the share at the time the option was granted; or

(B) in the case of stock acquired under an option qualifying under subsection (b)(1)(B), an amount equal to the lesser of—

(i) the excess of the fair market value of the share at the time of such disposition or death over the price paid under the option, or

(ii) the excess of the fair market value of the share at the time the option was granted over the option price (computed as if the option had been exercised at such time).

In the case of a disposition of such share by the individual, the basis of the share in his hands at the time of such disposition shall be increased by an amount equal to the amount so includible in his gross income.

(2) VARIABLE PRICE OPTION.—For purposes of subsection (b)(1), the term "variable price option" means an option under which the purchase price of the stock is fixed or determinable under a formula in which the only variable is the fair market value of the stock at any time during a period of 1 year which includes the time the option is exercised; except that in the case of options granted after September 30, 1958, such term does not include any such option in which such formula provides for determining such price by reference to the fair market value of the stock at any time before the option is exercised if such value may be greater than the average fair market value of the stock during the calendar month in which the option is exercised.

(3) CERTAIN OPTIONS GRANTED AFTER DECEMBER 31, 1963.—For purposes of subsection (b), an option granted after December 31, 1963, meets the requirements of this paragraph if granted pursuant to—

(A) a binding written contract entered into before January 1, 1964, or

(B) a written plan adopted and approved before January 1, 1964, which (as of January 1, 1964, and as of the date of the granting of the option)—

(i) met the requirements of paragraphs (4) and (5) of section 423(b), or

(ii) was being administered in a way which did not discriminate in favor of officers, persons whose principal duties consist of supervising the work of other employees, or highly compensated employees.

An option described in the preceding sentence shall be treated as ceasing to meet the requirements of this paragraph if it is not exercised before May 21, 1981.

Amendments

• 1976, Tax Reform Act of 1976 (P.L. 94-455)

P.L. 94-455, §603(c):

Amended Code Sec. 424(c)(3) by adding at the end thereof the new sentence "An option described in the preceding sentence shall be treated as ceasing to meet the requirements of this paragraph if it is not exercised before May 21, 1981." **Effective** for tax years ending after 12-31-75.

P.L. 94-455, §1402(b)(1)(C):

Substituted "9 months" for "6 months" in Code Sec. 424(c)(1) and (2). **Effective** for tax years beginning in 1977.

P.L. 94-455, §1402(b)(2):

Substituted "1 year" for "9 months" in Code Sec. 424(c)(1) and (2). **Effective** for tax years beginning after 12-31-77.

• 1964, Revenue Act of 1964 (P.L. 88-272)

P.L. 88-272, §221(a):

Added Code Sec. 424. **Effective** for tax years ending after 12-31-63.

PART III—RULES RELATING TO MINIMUM FUNDING STANDARDS AND BENEFIT LIMITATIONS

Subpart A—Minimum Funding Standards for Pension Plans

[Sec. 430]

SEC. 430. MINIMUM FUNDING STANDARDS FOR SINGLE-EMPLOYER DEFINED BENEFIT PENSION PLANS.

[Sec. 430(a)]

(a) MINIMUM REQUIRED CONTRIBUTION.—For purposes of this section and section 412(a)(2)(A), except as provided in subsection (f), the term "minimum required contribution" means, with respect to any plan year of a defined benefit plan which is not a multiemployer plan—

(1) in any case in which the value of plan assets of the plan (as reduced under subsection (f)(4)(B)) is less than the funding target of the plan for the plan year, the sum of—

(A) the target normal cost of the plan for the plan year,

(B) the shortfall amortization charge (if any) for the plan for the plan year determined under subsection (c), and

(C) the waiver amortization charge (if any) for the plan for the plan year as determined under subsection (e);

(2) in any case in which the value of plan assets of the plan (as reduced under subsection (f)(4)(B)) equals or exceeds the funding target of the plan for the plan year, the target normal cost of the plan for the plan year reduced (but not below zero) by such excess.

[Sec. 430(b)]

(b) TARGET NORMAL COST.—For purposes of this section:

(1) IN GENERAL.—Except as provided in subsection (i)(2) with respect to plans in at-risk status, the term "target normal cost" means, for any plan year, the excess of—

(A) the sum of—

(i) the present value of all benefits which are expected to accrue or to be earned under the plan during the plan year, plus

(ii) the amount of plan-related expenses expected to be paid from plan assets during the plan year, over

(B) the amount of mandatory employee contributions expected to be made during the plan year.

(2) SPECIAL RULE FOR INCREASE IN COMPENSATION.—For purposes of this subsection, if any benefit attributable to services performed in a preceding plan year is increased by reason of any increase in compensation during the current plan year, the increase in such benefit shall be treated as having accrued during the current plan year.

Amendments

• 2008, Worker, Retiree, and Employer Recovery Act of 2008 (P.L. 110-458)

P.L. 110-458, § 101(b)(2)(A):

Amended Code Sec. 430(b). **Effective** generally for plan years beginning after 12-31-2008. For a special rule, Act Sec. 101(b)(3)(B), below. Prior to amendment, Code Sec. 430(b) read as follows:

(b) TARGET NORMAL COST.—For purposes of this section, except as provided in subsection (i)(2) with respect to plans in at-risk status, the term "target normal cost" means, for any plan year, the present value of all benefits which are expected to accrue or to be earned under the plan during the plan year. For purposes of this subsection, if any benefit attributable to services performed in a preceding plan year is increased by reason of any increase in compensation during the current plan year, the increase in such benefit shall be treated as having accrued during the current plan year.

P.L. 110-458, § 101(b)(3)(B), provides:

(B) ELECTION FOR EARLIER APPLICATION.—The amendments made by such paragraphs shall apply to a plan for the first plan year beginning after December 31, 2007, if the plan sponsor makes the election under this subparagraph. An election under this subparagraph shall be made at such time and in such manner as the Secretary of the Treasury or the Secretary's delegate may prescribe, and, once made, may be revoked only with the consent of the Secretary.

[Sec. 430(c)]

(c) SHORTFALL AMORTIZATION CHARGE.—

(1) IN GENERAL.—For purposes of this section, the shortfall amortization charge for a plan for any plan year is the aggregate total (not less than zero) of the shortfall amortization installments for such plan year with respect to any shortfall amortization base which has not been fully amortized under this subsection.

(2) SHORTFALL AMORTIZATION INSTALLMENT.—For purposes of paragraph (1)—

(A) DETERMINATION.—The shortfall amortization installments are the amounts necessary to amortize the shortfall amortization base of the plan for any plan year in level annual installments over the 7-plan-year period beginning with such plan year.

(B) SHORTFALL INSTALLMENT.—The shortfall amortization installment for any plan year in the 7-plan-year period under subparagraph (A) with respect to any shortfall amortization base is the annual installment determined under subparagraph (A) for that year for that base.

(C) SEGMENT RATES.—In determining any shortfall amortization installment under this paragraph, the plan sponsor shall use the segment rates determined under subparagraph (C) of subsection (h)(2), applied under rules similar to the rules of subparagraph (B) of subsection (h)(2).

(D) SPECIAL ELECTION FOR ELIGIBLE PLAN YEARS.—

(i) IN GENERAL.—If a plan sponsor elects to apply this subparagraph with respect to the shortfall amortization base of a plan for any eligible plan year (in this subparagraph and paragraph (7) referred to as an "election year"), then, notwithstanding subparagraphs (A) and (B)—

(I) the shortfall amortization installments with respect to such base shall be determined under clause (ii) or (iii), whichever is specified in the election, and

(II) the shortfall amortization installment for any plan year in the 9-plan-year period described in clause (ii) or the 15-plan-year period described in clause (iii), respectively, with respect to such shortfall amortization base is the annual installment determined under the applicable clause for that year for that base.

(ii) 2 PLUS 7 AMORTIZATION SCHEDULE.—The shortfall amortization installments determined under this clause are—

(I) in the case of the first 2 plan years in the 9-plan-year period beginning with the election year, interest on the shortfall amortization base of the plan for the election year (determined using the effective interest rate for the plan for the election year), and

(II) in the case of the last 7 plan years in such 9-plan-year period, the amounts necessary to amortize the remaining balance of the shortfall amortization base of the plan for the election year in level annual installments over such last 7 plan years (using the segment rates under subparagraph (C) for the election year).

(iii) 15-YEAR AMORTIZATION.—The shortfall amortization installments determined under this subparagraph are the amounts necessary to amortize the shortfall amortization base of the plan for the election year in level annual installments over the 15-plan-year period beginning with the election year (using the segment rates under subparagraph (C) for the election year).

(iv) ELECTION.—

(I) IN GENERAL.—The plan sponsor of a plan may elect to have this subparagraph apply to not more than 2 eligible plan years with respect to the plan, except that in the case of a plan described in section 106 of the Pension Protection Act of 2006, the plan sponsor may only elect to have this subparagraph apply to a plan year beginning in 2011.

(II) AMORTIZATION SCHEDULE.—Such election shall specify whether the amortization schedule under clause (ii) or (iii) shall apply to an election year, except that if a plan sponsor elects to have this subparagraph apply to 2 eligible plan years, the plan sponsor must elect the same schedule for both years.

(III) OTHER RULES.—Such election shall be made at such time, and in such form and manner, as shall be prescribed by the Secretary, and may be revoked only with the consent of the Secretary. The Secretary shall, before granting a revocation request, provide the Pension Benefit Guaranty Corporation an opportunity to comment on the conditions applicable to the treatment of any portion of the election year shortfall amortization base that remains unamortized as of the revocation date.

(v) ELIGIBLE PLAN YEAR.—For purposes of this subparagraph, the term "eligible plan year" means any plan year beginning in 2008, 2009, 2010, or 2011, except that a plan year shall only be treated as an eligible plan year if the due date under subsection (j)(1) for the payment of the minimum required contribution for such plan year occurs on or after the date of the enactment of this subparagraph.

(vi) REPORTING.—A plan sponsor of a plan who makes an election under clause (i) shall—

(I) give notice of the election to participants and beneficiaries of the plan, and

(II) inform the Pension Benefit Guaranty Corporation of such election in such form and manner as the Director of the Pension Benefit Guaranty Corporation may prescribe.

(vii) INCREASES IN REQUIRED INSTALLMENTS IN CERTAIN CASES.—For increases in required contributions in cases of excess compensation or extraordinary dividends or stock redemptions, see paragraph (7).

(3) SHORTFALL AMORTIZATION BASE.—For purposes of this section, the shortfall amortization base of a plan for a plan year is—

(A) the funding shortfall of such plan for such plan year, minus

(B) the present value (determined using the segment rates determined under subparagraph (C) of subsection (h)(2), applied under rules similar to the rules of subparagraph (B) of subsection (h)(2)) of the aggregate total of the shortfall amortization installments and waiver amortization installments which have been determined for such plan year and any succeeding plan year with respect to the shortfall amortization bases and waiver amortization bases of the plan for any plan year preceding such plan year.

(4) FUNDING SHORTFALL.—For purposes of this section, the funding shortfall of a plan for any plan year is the excess (if any) of—

(A) the funding target of the plan for the plan year, over

(B) the value of plan assets of the plan (as reduced under subsection (f)(4)(B)) for the plan year which are held by the plan on the valuation date.

(5) EXEMPTION FROM NEW SHORTFALL AMORTIZATION BASE.—

(A) IN GENERAL.—In any case in which the value of plan assets of the plan (as reduced under subsection (f)(4)(A)) is equal to or greater than the funding target of the plan for the plan year, the shortfall amortization base of the plan for such plan year shall be zero.

(B) TRANSITION RULE.—

(i) IN GENERAL.—Except as provided in clause (iii), in the case of plan years beginning after 2007 and before 2011, only the applicable percentage of the funding target shall be taken into account under paragraph (3)(A) in determining the funding shortfall for purposes of paragraph (3)(A) and subparagraph (A).

(ii) APPLICABLE PERCENTAGE.—For purposes of subparagraph (A), the applicable percentage shall be determined in accordance with the following table:

In the case of a plan year beginning in calendar year:	The applicable percentage is
2008	92
2009	94
2010	96 .

(iii) TRANSITION RELIEF NOT AVAILABLE FOR NEW OR DEFICIT REDUCTION PLANS.—Clause (i) shall not apply to a plan—

(I) which was not in effect for a plan year beginning in 2007, or

(II) which was in effect for a plan year beginning in 2007 and which was subject to section 412(l) (as in effect for plan years beginning in 2007) for such year, determined after the application of paragraphs (6) and (9) thereof.

(6) EARLY DEEMED AMORTIZATION UPON ATTAINMENT OF FUNDING TARGET.—In any case in which the funding shortfall of a plan for a plan year is zero, for purposes of determining the shortfall amortization charge for such plan year and succeeding plan years, the shortfall amortization bases for all preceding plan years (and all shortfall amortization installments determined with respect to such bases) shall be reduced to zero.

(7) INCREASES IN ALTERNATE REQUIRED INSTALLMENTS IN CASES OF EXCESS COMPENSATION OR EXTRAORDINARY DIVIDENDS OR STOCK REDEMPTIONS.—

(A) IN GENERAL.—If there is an installment acceleration amount with respect to a plan for any plan year in the restriction period with respect to an election year under paragraph (2)(D), then the shortfall amortization installment otherwise determined and payable under such paragraph for such plan year shall, subject to the limitation under subparagraph (B), be increased by such amount.

(B) TOTAL INSTALLMENTS LIMITED TO SHORTFALL BASE.—Subject to rules prescribed by the Secretary, if a shortfall amortization installment with respect to any shortfall amortization base for an election year is required to be increased for any plan year under subparagraph (A)—

(i) such increase shall not result in the amount of such installment exceeding the present value of such installment and all succeeding installments with respect to such base (determined without regard to such increase but after application of clause (ii)), and

(ii) subsequent shortfall amortization installments with respect to such base shall, in reverse order of the otherwise required installments, be reduced to the extent necessary to limit the present value of such subsequent shortfall amortization installments (after application of this paragraph) to the present value of the remaining unamortized shortfall amortization base.

(C) INSTALLMENT ACCELERATION AMOUNT.—For purposes of this paragraph—

(i) IN GENERAL.—The term "installment acceleration amount" means, with respect to any plan year in a restriction period with respect to an election year, the sum of—

(I) the aggregate amount of excess employee compensation determined under subparagraph (D) with respect to all employees for the plan year, plus

(II) the aggregate amount of extraordinary dividends and redemptions determined under subparagraph (E) for the plan year.

(ii) ANNUAL LIMITATION.—The installment acceleration amount for any plan year shall not exceed the excess (if any) of—

(I) the sum of the shortfall amortization installments for the plan year and all preceding plan years in the amortization period elected under paragraph (2)(D) with respect to the shortfall amortization base with respect to an election year, determined without regard to paragraph (2)(D) and this paragraph, over

(II) the sum of the shortfall amortization installments for such plan year and all such preceding plan years, determined after application of paragraph (2)(D) (and in the case of any preceding plan year, after application of this paragraph).

(iii) CARRYOVER OF EXCESS INSTALLMENT ACCELERATION AMOUNTS.—

(I) IN GENERAL.—If the installment acceleration amount for any plan year (determined without regard to clause (ii)) exceeds the limitation under clause (ii), then, subject to subclause (II), such excess shall be treated as an installment acceleration amount with respect to the succeeding plan year.

(II) CAP TO APPLY.—If any amount treated as an installment acceleration amount under subclause (I) or this subclause with respect [to] any succeeding plan year, when added to other installment acceleration amounts (determined without regard to clause (ii)) with respect to the plan year, exceeds the limitation under clause (ii), the portion of such amount representing such excess shall be treated as an installment acceleration amount with respect to the next succeeding plan year.

(III) LIMITATION ON YEARS TO WHICH AMOUNTS CARRIED FOR.—No amount shall be carried under subclause (I) or (II) to a plan year which begins after the first plan year following the last plan year in the restriction period (or after the second plan year following such last plan year in the case of an election year with respect to which 15-year amortization was elected under paragraph (2)(D)).

(IV) ORDERING RULES.—For purposes of applying subclause (II), installment acceleration amounts for the plan year (determined without regard to any carryover under this clause) shall be applied first against the limitation under clause (ii) and then carryovers to such plan year shall be applied against such limitation on a first-in, first-out basis.

(D) EXCESS EMPLOYEE COMPENSATION.—For purposes of this paragraph—

(i) IN GENERAL.—The term "excess employee compensation" means, with respect to any employee for any plan year, the excess (if any) of—

(I) the aggregate amount includible in income under this chapter for remuneration during the calendar year in which such plan year begins for services performed by the employee for the plan sponsor (whether or not performed during such calendar year), over

(II) $1,000,000.

(ii) AMOUNTS SET ASIDE FOR NONQUALIFIED DEFERRED COMPENSATION.—If during any calendar year assets are set aside or reserved (directly or indirectly) in a trust (or other arrangement as determined by the Secretary), or transferred to such a trust or other arrangement, by a plan sponsor for purposes of paying deferred compensation of an employee under a nonqualified deferred compensation plan (as defined in section 409A) of the plan sponsor, then, for purposes of clause (i), the amount of such assets shall be treated as remuneration of the employee includible in income for the calendar year unless such amount is otherwise includible in income for such year. An amount to which the preceding sentence applies shall not be taken into account under this paragraph for any subsequent calendar year.

(iii) ONLY REMUNERATION FOR CERTAIN POST-2009 SERVICES COUNTED.—Remuneration shall be taken into account under clause (i) only to the extent attributable to services performed by the employee for the plan sponsor after February 28, 2010.

(iv) EXCEPTION FOR CERTAIN EQUITY PAYMENTS.—

(I) IN GENERAL.—There shall not be taken into account under clause (i)(I) any amount includible in income with respect to the granting after February 28, 2010, of service recipient stock (within the meaning of section 409A) that, upon such grant, is subject to a substantial risk of forfeiture (as defined under section 83(c)(1)) for at least 5 years from the date of such grant.

(II) SECRETARIAL AUTHORITY.—The Secretary may by regulation provide for the application of this clause in the case of a person other than a corporation.

(v) OTHER EXCEPTIONS.—The following amounts includible in income shall not be taken into account under clause (i)(I):

(I) COMMISSIONS.—Any remuneration payable on a commission basis solely on account of income directly generated by the individual performance of the individual to whom such remuneration is payable.

(II) CERTAIN PAYMENTS UNDER EXISTING CONTRACTS.—Any remuneration consisting of nonqualified deferred compensation, restricted stock, stock options, or stock appreciation rights payable or granted under a written binding contract that was in effect on March 1, 2010, and which was not modified in any material respect before such remuneration is paid.

(vi) SELF-EMPLOYED INDIVIDUAL TREATED AS EMPLOYEE.—The term "employee" includes, with respect to a calendar year, a self-employed individual who is treated as an employee under section 401(c) for the taxable year ending during such calendar year, and the term "compensation" shall include earned income of such individual with respect to such self-employment.

(vii) INDEXING OF AMOUNT.—In the case of any calendar year beginning after 2010, the dollar amount under clause (i)(II) shall be increased by an amount equal to—

(I) such dollar amount, multiplied by

(II) the cost-of-living adjustment determined under section 1(f)(3) for the calendar year, determined by substituting "calendar year 2009" for "calendar year 1992" in subparagraph (B) thereof.

If the amount of any increase under clause (i) is not a multiple of $1,000, such increase shall be rounded to the next lowest multiple of $1,000.

(E) EXTRAORDINARY DIVIDENDS AND REDEMPTIONS.—

(i) IN GENERAL.—The amount determined under this subparagraph for any plan year is the excess (if any) of the sum of the dividends declared during the plan year by the plan sponsor plus the aggregate amount paid for the redemption of stock of the plan sponsor redeemed during the plan year over the greater of—

(I) the adjusted net income (within the meaning of section 4043 of the Employee Retirement Income Security Act of 1974) of the plan sponsor for the preceding plan year, determined without regard to any reduction by reason of interest, taxes, depreciation, or amortization, or

(II) in the case of a plan sponsor that determined and declared dividends in the same manner for at least 5 consecutive years immediately preceding such plan year, the aggregate amount of dividends determined and declared for such plan year using such manner.

(ii) ONLY CERTAIN POST-2009 DIVIDENDS AND REDEMPTIONS COUNTED.—For purposes of clause (i), there shall only be taken into account dividends declared, and redemptions occurring, after February 28, 2010.

(iii) EXCEPTION FOR INTRA-GROUP DIVIDENDS.—Dividends paid by one member of a controlled group (as defined in section 412(d)(3)) to another member of such group shall not be taken into account under clause (i).

(iv) EXCEPTION FOR CERTAIN REDEMPTIONS.—Redemptions that are made pursuant to a plan maintained with respect to employees, or that are made on account of the death, disability, or termination of employment of an employee or shareholder, shall not be taken into account under clause (i).

(v) EXCEPTION FOR CERTAIN PREFERRED STOCK.—

(I) IN GENERAL.—Dividends and redemptions with respect to applicable preferred stock shall not be taken into account under clause (i) to the extent that dividends accrue with respect to such stock at a specified rate in all events and without regard to the plan sponsor's income, and interest accrues on any unpaid dividends with respect to such stock.

(II) APPLICABLE PREFERRED STOCK.—For purposes of subclause (I), the term "applicable preferred stock" means preferred stock which was issued before March 1, 2010 (or which was issued after such date and is held by an employee benefit plan subject to the provisions of title I of [the] Employee Retirement Income Security Act of 1974).

(F) OTHER DEFINITIONS AND RULES.—For purposes of this paragraph—

(i) PLAN SPONSOR.—The term "plan sponsor" includes any member of the plan sponsor's controlled group (as defined in section 412(d)(3)).

(ii) RESTRICTION PERIOD.—The term "restriction period" means, with respect to any election year—

(I) except as provided in subclause (II), the 3-year period beginning with the election year (or, if later, the first plan year beginning after December 31, 2009), and

(II) if the plan sponsor elects 15-year amortization for the shortfall amortization base for the election year, the 5-year period beginning with the election year (or, if later, the first plan year beginning after December 31, 2009).

(iii) ELECTIONS FOR MULTIPLE PLANS.—If a plan sponsor makes elections under paragraph (2)(D) with respect to 2 or more plans, the Secretary shall provide rules for the application of this paragraph to such plans, including rules for the ratable allocation of any installment acceleration amount among such plans on the basis of each plan's relative reduction in the plan's shortfall amortization installment for the first plan year in the amortization period described in subparagraph (A) (determined without regard to this paragraph).

(iv) MERGERS AND ACQUISITIONS.—The Secretary shall prescribe rules for the application of paragraph (2)(D) and this paragraph in any case where there is a merger or acquisition involving a plan sponsor making the election under paragraph (2)(D).

Amendments

• 2010, Preservation of Access to Care for Medicare Beneficiaries and Pension Relief Act of 2010 (P.L. 111-192)

P.L. 111-192, §201(b)(1):

Amended Code Sec. 430(c)(2) by adding at the end a new subparagraph (D). **Effective** for plan years beginning after 12-31-2007.

P.L. 111-192, §201(b)(2):

Amended Code Sec. 430(c) by adding at the end a new paragraph (7). **Effective** for plan years beginning after 12-31-2007.

P.L. 111-192, §201(b)(3)(A):

Amended Code Sec. 430(c)(1) by striking "the shortfall amortization bases for such plan year and each of the 6 preceding plan years" and inserting "any shortfall amortization base which has not been fully amortized under this subsection". **Effective** for plan years beginning after 12-31-2007.

• 2008, Worker, Retiree, and Employer Recovery Act of 2008 (P.L. 110-458)

P.L. 110-458, §101(b)(2)(B):

Amended Code Sec. 430(c)(5)(B)(iii) by inserting "beginning" before "after 2008". **Effective** as if included in the provision of the 2006 Act to which the amendment relates [**effective** with respect to plan years beginning after 12-31-2007.—CCH].

P.L. 110-458, §101(b)(2)(C):

Amended Code Sec. 430(c)(5)(B)(iv)(II) by inserting "for such year" after "beginning in 2007)". **Effective** as if included in the provision of the 2006 Act to which the amendment relates [**effective** with respect to plan years beginning after 12-31-2007.—CCH].

P.L. 110-458, §202(b)(1)-(2):

Amended Code Sec. 430(c)(5)(B) by striking clause (iii) and redesignating clause (iv) as clause (iii); and by striking clause (i) and inserting a new clause (i). **Effective** as if included in Act Sec. 112 of the Pension Protection Act of 2006 (P.L. 109-280) [**effective** with respect to plan years beginning after 12-31-2007.—CCH]. Prior to being stricken, Code Sec. 430(c)(5)(B)(i) and (iii) read as follows:

(i) IN GENERAL.—Except as provided in clauses (iii) and (iv), in the case of plan years beginning after 2007 and before 2011, only the applicable percentage of the funding target shall be taken into account under paragraph (3)(A) in determining the funding shortfall for the plan year for purposes of subparagraph (A).

* * *

(iii) LIMITATION.—Clause (i) shall not apply with respect to any plan year beginning after 2008 unless the shortfall amortization base for each of the preceding years beginning after 2007 was zero (determined after application of this subparagraph).

• 2006, Pension Protection Act of 2006 (P.L. 109-280)

P.L. 109-280, §115(a)-(c), provides:

SEC. 115. MODIFICATION OF TRANSITION RULE TO PENSION FUNDING REQUIREMENTS.

(a) IN GENERAL.—In the case of a plan that—

(1) was not required to pay a variable rate premium for the plan year beginning in 1996,

(2) has not, in any plan year beginning after 1995, merged with another plan (other than a plan sponsored by an employer that was in 1996 within the controlled group of the plan sponsor); and

(3) is sponsored by a company that is engaged primarily in the interurban or interstate passenger bus service,

the rules described in subsection (b) shall apply for any plan year beginning after December 31, 2007.

(b) MODIFIED RULES.—The rules described in this subsection are as follows:

(1) For purposes of section 430(j)(3) of the Internal Revenue Code of 1986 and section 303(j)(3) of the Employee Retirement Income Security Act of 1974, the plan shall be treated as not having a funding shortfall for any plan year.

(2) For purposes of—

(A) determining unfunded vested benefits under section 4006(a)(3)(E)(iii) of such Act, and

(B) determining any present value or making any computation under section 412 of such Code or section 302 of such Act,

the mortality table shall be the mortality table used by the plan.

(3) Section 430(c)(5)(B) of such Code and section 303(c)(5)(B) of such Act (relating to phase-in of funding target for exemption from new shortfall amortization base) shall each be applied by substituting "2012" for "2011" therein and by substituting for the table therein the following:

In the case of a plan year beginning in calendar year:	The applicable percentage is:
2008	90 percent
2009	92 percent
2010	94 percent
2011	96 percent.

(c) DEFINITIONS.—Any term used in this section which is also used in section 430 of such Code or section 303 of such Act shall have the meaning provided such term in such section. If the same term has a different meaning in such Code and such Act, such term shall, for purposes of this section, have the meaning provided by such Code when applied with respect to such Code and the meaning provided by such Act when applied with respect to such Act.

[Sec. 430(d)]

(d) RULES RELATING TO FUNDING TARGET.—For purposes of this section—

(1) FUNDING TARGET.—Except as provided in subsection (i)(1) with respect to plans in at-risk status, the funding target of a plan for a plan year is the present value of all benefits accrued or earned under the plan as of the beginning of the plan year.

(2) FUNDING TARGET ATTAINMENT PERCENTAGE.—The "funding target attainment percentage" of a plan for a plan year is the ratio (expressed as a percentage) which—

(A) the value of plan assets for the plan year (as reduced under subsection (f)(4)(B)), bears to

(B) the funding target of the plan for the plan year (determined without regard to subsection (i)(1)).

[Sec. 430(e)]

(e) WAIVER AMORTIZATION CHARGE.—

(1) DETERMINATION OF WAIVER AMORTIZATION CHARGE.—The waiver amortization charge (if any) for a plan for any plan year is the aggregate total of the waiver amortization installments for such plan year with respect to the waiver amortization bases for each of the 5 preceding plan years.

(2) WAIVER AMORTIZATION INSTALLMENT.—For purposes of paragraph (1)—

(A) DETERMINATION.—The waiver amortization installments are the amounts necessary to amortize the waiver amortization base of the plan for any plan year in level annual installments over a period of 5 plan years beginning with the succeeding plan year.

(B) WAIVER INSTALLMENT.—The waiver amortization installment for any plan year in the 5-year period under subparagraph (A) with respect to any waiver amortization base is the annual installment determined under subparagraph (A) for that year for that base.

(3) INTEREST RATE.—In determining any waiver amortization installment under this subsection, the plan sponsor shall use the segment rates determined under subparagraph (C) of subsection (h)(2), applied under rules similar to the rules of subparagraph (B) of subsection (h)(2).

(4) WAIVER AMORTIZATION BASE.—The waiver amortization base of a plan for a plan year is the amount of the waived funding deficiency (if any) for such plan year under section 412(c).

(5) EARLY DEEMED AMORTIZATION UPON ATTAINMENT OF FUNDING TARGET.—In any case in which the funding shortfall of a plan for a plan year is zero, for purposes of determining the waiver amortization charge for such plan year and succeeding plan years, the waiver amortization bases for all preceding plan years (and all waiver amortization installments determined with respect to such bases) shall be reduced to zero.

[Sec. 430(f)]

(f) REDUCTION OF MINIMUM REQUIRED CONTRIBUTION BY PREFUNDING BALANCE AND FUNDING STANDARD CARRYOVER BALANCE.—

(1) ELECTION TO MAINTAIN BALANCES.—

(A) PREFUNDING BALANCE.—The plan sponsor of a defined benefit plan which is not a multiemployer plan may elect to maintain a prefunding balance.

(B) FUNDING STANDARD CARRYOVER BALANCE.—

(i) IN GENERAL.—In the case of a defined benefit plan (other than a multiemployer plan) described in clause (ii), the plan sponsor may elect to maintain a funding standard carryover balance, until such balance is reduced to zero.

(ii) PLANS MAINTAINING FUNDING STANDARD ACCOUNT IN 2007.—A plan is described in this clause if the plan—

(I) was in effect for a plan year beginning in 2007, and

(II) had a positive balance in the funding standard account under section 412(b) as in effect for such plan year and determined as of the end of such plan year.

(2) APPLICATION OF BALANCES.—A prefunding balance and a funding standard carryover balance maintained pursuant to this paragraph—

(A) shall be available for crediting against the minimum required contribution, pursuant to an election under paragraph (3),

(B) shall be applied as a reduction in the amount treated as the value of plan assets for purposes of this section, to the extent provided in paragraph (4), and

(C) may be reduced at any time, pursuant to an election under paragraph (5).

(3) ELECTION TO APPLY BALANCES AGAINST MINIMUM REQUIRED CONTRIBUTION.—

(A) IN GENERAL.—Except as provided in subparagraphs (B) and (C), in the case of any plan year in which the plan sponsor elects to credit against the minimum required contribution for the current plan year all or a portion of the prefunding balance or the funding standard carryover balance for the current plan year (not in excess of such minimum required contribution), the minimum required contribution for the plan year shall be reduced as of the first day of the plan year by the amount so credited by the plan sponsor. For purposes of the preceding sentence, the minimum required contribution shall be determined after taking into account any waiver under section 412(c).

(B) COORDINATION WITH FUNDING STANDARD CARRYOVER BALANCE.—To the extent that any plan has a funding standard carryover balance greater than zero, no amount of the prefunding balance of such plan may be credited under this paragraph in reducing the minimum required contribution.

(C) LIMITATION FOR UNDERFUNDED PLANS.—The preceding provisions of this paragraph shall not apply for any plan year if the ratio (expressed as a percentage) which—

(i) the value of plan assets for the preceding plan year (as reduced under paragraph (4)(C)), bears to

(ii) the funding target of the plan for the preceding plan year (determined without regard to subsection (i)(1)),

is less than 80 percent. In the case of plan years beginning in 2008, the ratio under this subparagraph may be determined using such methods of estimation as the Secretary may prescribe.

(D) SPECIAL RULE FOR CERTAIN YEARS OF PLANS MAINTAINED BY CHARITIES.—

(i) IN GENERAL.—For purposes of applying subparagraph (C) for plan years beginning after August 31, 2009, and before September 1, 2011, the ratio determined under such subparagraph for the preceding plan year of a plan shall be the greater of—

(I) such ratio, as determined without regard to this subsection, or

(II) the ratio for such plan for the plan year beginning after August 31, 2007 and before September 1, 2008, as determined under rules prescribed by the Secretary.

(ii) SPECIAL RULE.—In the case of a plan for which the valuation date is not the first day of the plan year—

(I) clause (i) shall apply to plan years beginning after December 31, 2007, and before January 1, 2010, and

(II) clause (i)(II) shall apply based on the last plan year beginning before September 1, 2007, as determined under rules prescribed by the Secretary.

(iii) LIMITATION TO CHARITIES.—This subparagraph shall not apply to any plan unless such plan is maintained exclusively by one or more organizations described in section 501(c)(3).

(4) EFFECT OF BALANCES ON AMOUNTS TREATED AS VALUE OF PLAN ASSETS.—In the case of any plan maintaining a prefunding balance or a funding standard carryover balance pursuant to this subsection, the amount treated as the value of plan assets shall be deemed to be such amount, reduced as provided in the following subparagraphs:

(A) APPLICABILITY OF SHORTFALL AMORTIZATION BASE.—For purposes of subsection (c)(5), the value of plan assets is deemed to be such amount, reduced by the amount of the prefunding balance, but only if an election under paragraph (3) applying any portion of the prefunding balance in reducing the minimum required contribution is in effect for the plan year.

(B) DETERMINATION OF EXCESS ASSETS, FUNDING SHORTFALL, AND FUNDING TARGET ATTAINMENT PERCENTAGE.—

(i) IN GENERAL.—For purposes of subsections (a), (c)(4)(B), and (d)(2)(A), the value of plan assets is deemed to be such amount, reduced by the amount of the prefunding balance and the funding standard carryover balance.

(ii) SPECIAL RULE FOR CERTAIN BINDING AGREEMENTS WITH PBGC.—For purposes of subsection (c)(4)(B), the value of plan assets shall not be deemed to be reduced for a plan year by the amount of the specified balance if, with respect to such balance, there is in effect for a plan year a binding written agreement with the Pension Benefit Guaranty Corporation which provides that such balance is not available to reduce the minimum required contribution for the plan year. For purposes of the preceding sentence, the term "specified balance" means the prefunding balance or the funding standard carryover balance, as the case may be.

(C) AVAILABILITY OF BALANCES IN PLAN YEAR FOR CREDITING AGAINST MINIMUM REQUIRED CONTRIBUTION.—For purposes of paragraph (3)(C)(i) of this subsection, the value of plan assets is deemed to be such amount, reduced by the amount of the prefunding balance.

(5) ELECTION TO REDUCE BALANCE PRIOR TO DETERMINATIONS OF VALUE OF PLAN ASSETS AND CREDITING AGAINST MINIMUM REQUIRED CONTRIBUTION.—

(A) IN GENERAL.—The plan sponsor may elect to reduce by any amount the balance of the prefunding balance and the funding standard carryover balance for any plan year (but not below zero). Such reduction shall be effective prior to any determination of the value of plan assets for such plan year under this section and application of the balance in reducing the minimum required contribution for such plan for such plan year pursuant to an election under paragraph (2).

(B) COORDINATION BETWEEN PREFUNDING BALANCE AND FUNDING STANDARD CARRYOVER BALANCE.—To the extent that any plan has a funding standard carryover balance greater than zero, no election may be made under subparagraph (A) with respect to the prefunding balance.

(6) PREFUNDING BALANCE.—

(A) IN GENERAL.—A prefunding balance maintained by a plan shall consist of a beginning balance of zero, increased and decreased to the extent provided in subparagraphs (B) and (C), and adjusted further as provided in paragraph (8).

(B) INCREASES.—

(i) IN GENERAL.—As of the first day of each plan year beginning after 2008, the prefunding balance of a plan shall be increased by the amount elected by the plan sponsor for the plan year. Such amount shall not exceed the excess (if any) of—

(I) the aggregate total of employer contributions to the plan for the preceding plan year, over—

(II) the minimum required contribution for such preceding plan year.

(ii) ADJUSTMENTS FOR INTEREST.—Any excess contributions under clause (i) shall be properly adjusted for interest accruing for the periods between the first day of the current plan year and the dates on which the excess contributions were made, determined by using the effective interest rate for the preceding plan year and by treating contributions as being first used to satisfy the minimum required contribution.

(iii) CERTAIN CONTRIBUTIONS NECESSARY TO AVOID BENEFIT LIMITATIONS DISREGARDED.—The excess described in clause (i) with respect to any preceding plan year shall be reduced (but not below zero) by the amount of contributions an employer would be required to make under subsection (b), (c), or (e) of section 436 to avoid a benefit limitation which would otherwise be imposed under such paragraph for the preceding plan year. Any contribution which may be taken into account in satisfying the requirements of more than 1 of such paragraphs shall be taken into account only once for purposes of this clause.

(C) DECREASES.—The prefunding balance of a plan shall be decreased (but not below zero) by—

(i) as of the first day of each plan year after 2008, the amount of such balance credited under paragraph (2) (if any) in reducing the minimum required contribution of the plan for the preceding plan year, and

(ii) as of the time specified in paragraph (5)(A), any reduction in such balance elected under paragraph (5).

(7) FUNDING STANDARD CARRYOVER BALANCE.—

(A) IN GENERAL.—A funding standard carryover balance maintained by a plan shall consist of a beginning balance determined under subparagraph (B), decreased to the extent provided in subparagraph (C), and adjusted further as provided in paragraph (8).

(B) BEGINNING BALANCE.—The beginning balance of the funding standard carryover balance shall be the positive balance described in paragraph (1)(B)(ii)(II).

(C) DECREASES.—The funding standard carryover balance of a plan shall be decreased (but not below zero) by—

(i) as of the first day of each plan year after 2008, the amount of such balance credited under paragraph (2) (if any) in reducing the minimum required contribution of the plan for the preceding plan year, and

(ii) as of the time specified in paragraph (5)(A), any reduction in such balance elected under paragraph (5).

(8) ADJUSTMENTS FOR INVESTMENT EXPERIENCE.—In determining the prefunding balance or the funding standard carryover balance of a plan as of the first day of the plan year, the plan sponsor shall, in accordance with regulations prescribed by the Secretary, adjust such balance to reflect the rate of return on plan assets for the preceding plan year. Notwithstanding subsection (g)(3), such rate of return shall be determined on the basis of fair market value and shall properly take into account, in accordance with such regulations, all contributions, distributions, and other plan payments made during such period.

(9) ELECTIONS.—Elections under this subsection shall be made at such times, and in such form and manner, as shall be prescribed in regulations of the Secretary.

Amendments

• 2010, Preservation of Access to Care for Medicare Beneficiaries and Pension Relief Act of 2010 (P.L. 111-192)

P.L. 111-192, §204(b):

Amended Code Sec. 430(f)(3) by adding at the end a new subparagraph (D). **Effective** generally for plan years beginning after 8-31-2009. For a special rule, see Act Sec. 204(c)(2), below.

P.L. 111-192, §204(c)(2), provides:

(2) SPECIAL RULE.—In the case of a plan for which the valuation date is not the first day of the plan year, the amendments made by this section shall apply to plan years beginning after December 31, 2008.

• 2008, Worker, Retiree, and Employer Recovery Act of 2008 (P.L. 110-458)

P.L. 110-458, §101(b)(2)(D)(i)-(v):

Amended Code Sec. 430(f) by striking "as of the first day of the plan year" the second place it appears in the first sentence of paragraph (3)(A) [following "credited by the plan sponsor"], by striking "paragraph (2)" in paragraph (4)(A) and inserting "paragraph (3)", by striking "paragraph (1), (2), or (4) of section 206(g)" in paragraph (6)(B)(iii) and inserting "subsection (b), (c), or (e) of section 436", by striking "the sum of" following "(but not below zero) by" in paragraph (6)(C), and by striking "of the Treasury" following "by the Secretary" in paragraph (8). **Effective** as if included in the provision of the 2006 Act to which the amendment relates [**effective** with respect to plan years beginning after 12-31-2007.—CCH].

[Sec. 430(g)]

(g) VALUATION OF PLAN ASSETS AND LIABILITIES.—

(1) TIMING OF DETERMINATIONS.—Except as otherwise provided under this subsection, all determinations under this section for a plan year shall be made as of the valuation date of the plan for such plan year.

(2) VALUATION DATE.—For purposes of this section—

(A) IN GENERAL.—Except as provided in subparagraph (B), the valuation date of a plan for any plan year shall be the first day of the plan year.

(B) EXCEPTION FOR SMALL PLANS.—If, on each day during the preceding plan year, a plan had 100 or fewer participants, the plan may designate any day during the plan year as its valuation date for such plan year and succeeding plan years. For purposes of this subparagraph, all defined benefit plans (other than multiemployer plans) maintained by the same employer (or any member of such employer's controlled group) shall be treated as 1 plan, but only participants with respect to such employer or member shall be taken into account.

(C) APPLICATION OF CERTAIN RULES IN DETERMINATION OF PLAN SIZE.—For purposes of this paragraph—

(i) PLANS NOT IN EXISTENCE IN PRECEDING YEAR.—In the case of the first plan year of any plan, subparagraph (B) shall apply to such plan by taking into account the number of participants that the plan is reasonably expected to have on days during such first plan year.

(ii) PREDECESSORS.—Any reference in subparagraph (B) to an employer shall include a reference to any predecessor of such employer.

(3) DETERMINATION OF VALUE OF PLAN ASSETS.—For purposes of this section—

(A) IN GENERAL.—Except as provided in subparagraph (B), the value of plan assets shall be the fair market value of the assets.

(B) AVERAGING ALLOWED.—A plan may determine the value of plan assets on the basis of the averaging of fair market values, but only if such method—

(i) is permitted under regulations prescribed by the Secretary,

(ii) does not provide for averaging of such values over more than the period beginning on the last day of the 25th month preceding the month in which the valuation date occurs and ending on the valuation date (or a similar period in the case of a valuation date which is not the 1st day of a month), and

(iii) does not result in a determination of the value of plan assets which, at any time, is lower than 90 percent or greater than 110 percent of the fair market value of such assets at such time.

Any such averaging shall be adjusted for contributions, distributions, and expected earnings (as determined by the plan's actuary on the basis of an assumed earnings rate specified by the actuary but not in excess of the third segment rate applicable under subsection (h)(2)(C)(iii)), as specified by the Secretary.

(4) ACCOUNTING FOR CONTRIBUTION RECEIPTS.—For purposes of determining the value of assets under paragraph (3)—

(A) PRIOR YEAR CONTRIBUTIONS.—If—

(i) an employer makes any contribution to the plan after the valuation date for the plan year in which the contribution is made, and

(ii) the contribution is for a preceding plan year,

the contribution shall be taken into account as an asset of the plan as of the valuation date, except that in the case of any plan year beginning after 2008, only the present value (determined as of the valuation date) of such contribution may be taken into account. For purposes of the preceding sentence, present value shall be determined using the effective interest rate for the preceding plan year to which the contribution is properly allocable.

(B) SPECIAL RULE FOR CURRENT YEAR CONTRIBUTIONS MADE BEFORE VALUATION DATE.—If any contributions for any plan year are made to or under the plan during the plan year but before the valuation date for the plan year, the assets of the plan as of the valuation date shall not include—

(i) such contributions, and

(ii) interest on such contributions for the period between the date of the contributions and the valuation date, determined by using the effective interest rate for the plan year.

Amendments

• 2008, Worker, Retiree, and Employer Recovery Act of 2008 (P.L. 110-458)

P.L. 110-458, §121(b):

Amended the last sentence of Code Sec. 430(g)(3)(B). **Effective** as if included in the provision of the 2006 Act to which the amendment relates [**effective** with respect to plan years beginning after 12-31-2007.—CCH]. Prior to amendment, the last sentence of Code Sec. 430(g)(3)(B) read as follows:

Any such averaging shall be adjusted for contributions and distributions (as provided by the Secretary).

[Sec. 430(h)]

(h) ACTUARIAL ASSUMPTIONS AND METHODS.—

(1) IN GENERAL.—Subject to this subsection, the determination of any present value or other computation under this section shall be made on the basis of actuarial assumptions and methods—

(A) each of which is reasonable (taking into account the experience of the plan and reasonable expectations), and

(B) which, in combination, offer the actuary's best estimate of anticipated experience under the plan.

(2) INTEREST RATES.—

(A) EFFECTIVE INTEREST RATE.—For purposes of this section, the term "effective interest rate" means, with respect to any plan for any plan year, the single rate of interest which, if used to determine the present value of the plan's accrued or earned benefits referred to in subsection (d)(1), would result in an amount equal to the funding target of the plan for such plan year.

(B) INTEREST RATES FOR DETERMINING FUNDING TARGET.—For purposes of determining the funding target and target normal cost of a plan for any plan year, the interest rate used in determining the present value of the benefits of the plan shall be—

(i) in the case of benefits reasonably determined to be payable during the 5-year period beginning on the first day of the plan year, the first segment rate with respect to the applicable month,

(ii) in the case of benefits reasonably determined to be payable during the 15-year period beginning at the end of the period described in clause (i), the second segment rate with respect to the applicable month, and

(iii) in the case of benefits reasonably determined to be payable after the period described in clause (ii), the third segment rate with respect to the applicable month.

(C) SEGMENT RATES.—For purposes of this paragraph—

(i) FIRST SEGMENT RATE.—The term "first segment rate" means, with respect to any month, the single rate of interest which shall be determined by the Secretary for such month on the basis of the corporate bond yield curve for such month, taking into account only that portion of such yield curve which is based on bonds maturing during the 5-year period commencing with such month.

(ii) SECOND SEGMENT RATE.—The term "second segment rate" means, with respect to any month, the single rate of interest which shall be determined by the Secretary for such month on the basis of the corporate bond yield curve for such month, taking into account only that portion of such yield curve which is based on bonds maturing during the 15-year period beginning at the end of the period described in clause (i).

(iii) THIRD SEGMENT RATE.—The term "third segment rate" means, with respect to any month, the single rate of interest which shall be determined by the Secretary for such month on the basis of the corporate bond yield curve for such month, taking into account only that portion of such yield curve which is based on bonds maturing during periods beginning after the period described in clause (ii).

(D) CORPORATE BOND YIELD CURVE.—For purposes of this paragraph—

(i) IN GENERAL.—The term "corporate bond yield curve" means, with respect to any month, a yield curve which is prescribed by the Secretary for such month and which reflects the average, for the 24-month period ending with the month preceding such month, of monthly yields on investment grade corporate bonds with varying maturities and that are in the top 3 quality levels available.

(ii) ELECTION TO USE YIELD CURVE.—Solely for purposes of determining the minimum required contribution under this section, the plan sponsor may, in lieu of the segment rates determined under subparagraph (C), elect to use interest rates under the corporate bond yield curve. For purposes of the preceding sentence such curve shall be determined without regard to the 24-month averaging described in clause (i). Such election, once made, may be revoked only with the consent of the Secretary.

(E) APPLICABLE MONTH.—For purposes of this paragraph, the term "applicable month" means, with respect to any plan for any plan year, the month which includes the valuation date of such plan for such plan year or, at the election of the plan sponsor, any of the 4 months which precede such month. Any election made under this subparagraph shall apply to the plan year for which the election is made and all succeeding plan years, unless the election is revoked with the consent of the Secretary.

(F) PUBLICATION REQUIREMENTS.—The Secretary shall publish for each month the corporate bond yield curve (and the corporate bond yield curve reflecting the modification described in section 417(e)(3)(D)(i) for such month) and each of the rates determined under subparagraph (C) for such month. The Secretary shall also publish a description of the methodology used to determine such yield curve and such rates which is sufficiently detailed to enable plans to make reasonable projections regarding the yield curve and such rates for future months based on the plan's projection of future interest rates.

(G) TRANSITION RULE.—

(i) IN GENERAL.—Notwithstanding the preceding provisions of this paragraph, for plan years beginning in 2008 or 2009, the first, second, or third segment rate for a plan with respect to any month shall be equal to the sum of—

(I) the product of such rate for such month determined without regard to this subparagraph, multiplied by the applicable percentage, and

(II) the product of the rate determined under the rules of section 412(b)(5)(B)(ii)(II) (as in effect for plan years beginning in 2007), multiplied by a percentage equal to 100 percent minus the applicable percentage.

(ii) APPLICABLE PERCENTAGE.—For purposes of clause (i), the applicable percentage is 33⅓ percent for plan years beginning in 2008 and 66⅔ percent for plan years beginning in 2009.

(iii) NEW PLANS INELIGIBLE.—Clause (i) shall not apply to any plan if the first plan year of the plan begins after December 31, 2007.

(iv) ELECTION.—The plan sponsor may elect not to have this subparagraph apply. Such election, once made, may be revoked only with the consent of the Secretary.

(3) MORTALITY TABLES.—

(A) IN GENERAL.—Except as provided in subparagraph (C) or (D), the Secretary shall by regulation prescribe mortality tables to be used in determining any present value or making any computation under this section. Such tables shall be based on the actual experience of pension plans and projected trends in such experience. In prescribing such tables, the Secretary shall take into account results of available independent studies of mortality of individuals covered by pension plans.

(B) PERIODIC REVISION.—The Secretary shall (at least every 10 years) make revisions in any table in effect under subparagraph (A) to reflect the actual experience of pension plans and projected trends in such experience.

(C) SUBSTITUTE MORTALITY TABLE.—

(i) IN GENERAL.—Upon request by the plan sponsor and approval by the Secretary, a mortality table which meets the requirements of clause (iii) shall be used in determining any present value or making any computation under this section during the period of consecutive plan years (not to exceed 10) specified in the request.

(ii) EARLY TERMINATION OF PERIOD.—Notwithstanding clause (i), a mortality table described in clause (i) shall cease to be in effect as of the earliest of—

(I) the date on which there is a significant change in the participants in the plan by reason of a plan spinoff or merger or otherwise, or

(II) the date on which the plan actuary determines that such table does not meet the requirements of clause (iii).

(iii) REQUIREMENTS.—A mortality table meets the requirements of this clause if—

(I) there is a sufficient number of plan participants, and the pension plans have been maintained for a sufficient period of time, to have credible information necessary for purposes of subclause (II), and

(II) such table reflects the actual experience of the pension plans maintained by the sponsor and projected trends in general mortality experience.

(iv) ALL PLANS IN CONTROLLED GROUP MUST USE SEPARATE TABLE.—Except as provided by the Secretary, a plan sponsor may not use a mortality table under this subparagraph for any plan maintained by the plan sponsor unless—

(I) a separate mortality table is established and used under this subparagraph for each other plan maintained by the plan sponsor and if the plan sponsor is a member of a controlled group, each member of the controlled group, and

(II) the requirements of clause (iii) are met separately with respect to the table so established for each such plan, determined by only taking into account the participants of such plan, the time such plan has been in existence, and the actual experience of such plan.

(v) DEADLINE FOR SUBMISSION AND DISPOSITION OF APPLICATION.—

(I) SUBMISSION.—The plan sponsor shall submit a mortality table to the Secretary for approval under this subparagraph at least 7 months before the 1st day of the period described in clause (i).

(II) DISPOSITION.—Any mortality table submitted to the Secretary for approval under this subparagraph shall be treated as in effect as of the 1st day of the period described in clause (i) unless the Secretary, during the 180-day period beginning on the date of such submission, disapproves of such table and provides the reasons that such table fails to meet the requirements of clause (iii). The 180-day period shall be extended upon mutual agreement of the Secretary and the plan sponsor.

(D) SEPARATE MORTALITY TABLES FOR THE DISABLED.—Notwithstanding subparagraph (A)—

(i) IN GENERAL.—The Secretary shall establish mortality tables which may be used (in lieu of the tables under subparagraph (A)) under this subsection for individuals who are entitled to benefits under the plan on account of disability. The Secretary shall establish separate tables for individuals whose disabilities occur in plan years beginning before January 1, 1995, and for individuals whose disabilities occur in plan years beginning on or after such date.

(ii) SPECIAL RULE FOR DISABILITIES OCCURRING AFTER 1994.—In the case of disabilities occurring in plan years beginning after December 31, 1994, the tables under clause (i) shall apply only with respect to individuals described in such subclause who are disabled within the meaning of title II of the Social Security Act and the regulations thereunder.

(iii) PERIODIC REVISION.—The Secretary shall (at least every 10 years) make revisions in any table in effect under clause (i) to reflect the actual experience of pension plans and projected trends in such experience.

(4) PROBABILITY OF BENEFIT PAYMENTS IN THE FORM OF LUMP SUMS OR OTHER OPTIONAL FORMS.—For purposes of determining any present value or making any computation under this section, there shall be taken into account—

(A) the probability that future benefit payments under the plan will be made in the form of optional forms of benefits provided under the plan (including lump sum distributions, determined on the basis of the plan's experience and other related assumptions), and

(B) any difference in the present value of such future benefit payments resulting from the use of actuarial assumptions, in determining benefit payments in any such optional form of benefits, which are different from those specified in this subsection.

(5) APPROVAL OF LARGE CHANGES IN ACTUARIAL ASSUMPTIONS.—

(A) IN GENERAL.—No actuarial assumption used to determine the funding target for a plan to which this paragraph applies may be changed without the approval of the Secretary.

(B) PLANS TO WHICH PARAGRAPH APPLIES.—This paragraph shall apply to a plan only if—

(i) the plan is a defined benefit plan (other than a multiemployer plan) to which title IV of the Employee Retirement Income Security Act of 1974 applies,

(ii) the aggregate unfunded vested benefits as of the close of the preceding plan year (as determined under section 4006(a)(3)(E)(iii) of the Employee Retirement Income Security Act of 1974) of such plan and all other plans maintained by the contributing sponsors (as defined in section 4001(a)(13) of such Act) and members of such sponsors' controlled groups (as defined in section 4001(a)(14) of such Act) which are covered by title IV (disregarding plans with no unfunded vested benefits) exceed $50,000,000, and

(iii) the change in assumptions (determined after taking into account any changes in interest rate and mortality table) results in a decrease in the funding shortfall of the plan for the current plan year that exceeds $50,000,000, or that exceeds $5,000,000 and that is 5 percent or more of the funding target of the plan before such change.

Amendments

• 2008, Worker, Retiree, and Employer Recovery Act of 2008 (P.L. 110-458)

P.L. 110-458, §101(b)(2)(E)(i)-(iv):

Amended Code Sec. 430(h)(2) by inserting "and target normal cost" after "funding target" in subparagraph (B), by striking "liabilities" and inserting "benefits" in subparagraph (B), by striking "section 417(e)(3)(D)(i)) for such month" and inserting "section 417(e)(3)(D)(i) for such month)" in subparagraph (F), and by striking "subparagraph (B)" and inserting "subparagraph (C)" in subparagraph (F). **Effective** as if included in the provision of the 2006 Act to which the amendment relates [**effective** with respect to plan years beginning after 12-31-2007.—CCH].

[Sec. 430(i)]

(i) SPECIAL RULES FOR AT-RISK PLANS.—

(1) FUNDING TARGET FOR PLANS IN AT-RISK STATUS.—

(A) IN GENERAL.—In the case of a plan which is in at-risk status for a plan year, the funding target of the plan for the plan year shall be equal to the sum of—

(i) the present value of all benefits accrued or earned under the plan as of the beginning of the plan year, as determined by using the additional actuarial assumptions described in subparagraph (B), and

(ii) in the case of a plan which also has been in at-risk status for at least 2 of the 4 preceding plan years, a loading factor determined under subparagraph (C).

(B) ADDITIONAL ACTUARIAL ASSUMPTIONS.—The actuarial assumptions described in this subparagraph are as follows:

(i) All employees who are not otherwise assumed to retire as of the valuation date but who will be eligible to elect benefits during the plan year and the 10 succeeding plan years shall be assumed to retire at the earliest retirement date under the plan but not before the end of the plan year for which the at-risk funding target and at-risk target normal cost are being determined.

(ii) All employees shall be assumed to elect the retirement benefit available under the plan at the assumed retirement age (determined after application of clause (i)) which would result in the highest present value of benefits.

(C) LOADING FACTOR.—The loading factor applied with respect to a plan under this paragraph for any plan year is the sum of—

(i) $700, times the number of participants in the plan, plus

(ii) 4 percent of the funding target (determined without regard to this paragraph) of the plan for the plan year.

(2) TARGET NORMAL COST OF AT-RISK PLANS.—In the case of a plan which is in at-risk status for a plan year, the target normal cost of the plan for such plan year shall be equal to the sum of—

(A) the excess of—

(i) the sum of—

(I) the present value of all benefits which are expected to accrue or to be earned under the plan during the plan year, determined using the additional actuarial assumptions described in paragraph (1)(B), plus

(II) the amount of plan-related expenses expected to be paid from plan assets during the plan year, over

(ii) the amount of mandatory employee contributions expected to be made during the plan year, plus

(B) in the case of a plan which also has been in at-risk status for at least 2 of the 4 preceding plan years, a loading factor equal to 4 percent of the amount determined under subsection (b)(1)(A)(i) with respect to the plan for the plan year.

(3) MINIMUM AMOUNT.—In no event shall—

(A) the at-risk funding target be less than the funding target, as determined without regard to this subsection, or

(B) the at-risk target normal cost be less than the target normal cost, as determined without regard to this subsection.

(4) DETERMINATION OF AT-RISK STATUS.—For purposes of this subsection—

(A) IN GENERAL.—A plan is in at-risk status for a plan year if—

(i) the funding target attainment percentage for the preceding plan year (determined under this section without regard to this subsection) is less than 80 percent, and

(ii) the funding target attainment percentage for the preceding plan year (determined under this section by using the additional actuarial assumptions described in paragraph (1)(B) in computing the funding target) is less than 70 percent.

(B) TRANSITION RULE.—In the case of plan years beginning in 2008, 2009, and 2010, subparagraph (A)(i) shall be applied by substituting the following percentages for "80 percent":

(i) 65 percent in the case of 2008.

(ii) 70 percent in the case of 2009.

(iii) 75 percent in the case of 2010.

In the case of plan years beginning in 2008, the funding target attainment percentage for the preceding plan year under subparagraph (A) may be determined using such methods of estimation as the Secretary may provide.

(C) SPECIAL RULE FOR EMPLOYEES OFFERED EARLY RETIREMENT IN 2006.—

(i) IN GENERAL.—For purposes of subparagraph (A)(ii), the additional actuarial assumptions described in paragraph (1)(B) shall not be taken into account with respect to any employee if—

(I) such employee is employed by a specified automobile manufacturer,

(II) such employee is offered a substantial amount of additional cash compensation, substantially enhanced retirement benefits under the plan, or materially reduced employment duties on the condition that by a specified date (not later than December 31, 2010) the employee retires (as defined under the terms of the plan),

(III) such offer is made during 2006 and pursuant to a bona fide retirement incentive program and requires, by the terms of the offer, that such offer can be accepted not later than a specified date (not later than December 31, 2006), and

(IV) such employee does not elect to accept such offer before the specified date on which the offer expires.

(ii) SPECIFIED AUTOMOBILE MANUFACTURER.—For purposes of clause (i), the term "specified automobile manufacturer" means—

(I) any manufacturer of automobiles, and

(II) any manufacturer of automobile parts which supplies such parts directly to a manufacturer of automobiles and which, after a transaction or series of transactions ending in 1999, ceased to be a member of a controlled group which included such manufacturer of automobiles.

(5) TRANSITION BETWEEN APPLICABLE FUNDING TARGETS AND BETWEEN APPLICABLE TARGET NORMAL COSTS.—

(A) IN GENERAL.—In any case in which a plan which is in at-risk status for a plan year has been in such status for a consecutive period of fewer than 5 plan years, the applicable amount of the funding target and of the target normal cost shall be, in lieu of the amount determined without regard to this paragraph, the sum of—

(i) the amount determined under this section without regard to this subsection, plus

(ii) the transition percentage for such plan year of the excess of the amount determined under this subsection (without regard to this paragraph) over the amount determined under this section without regard to this subsection.

(B) TRANSITION PERCENTAGE.—For purposes of subparagraph (A), the transition percentage shall be determined in accordance with the following table:

If the consecutive number of years (including the plan year) the plan is in at-risk status is—	The transition percentage is—
1	20
2	40
3	60
4	80 .

(C) YEARS BEFORE EFFECTIVE DATE.—For purposes of this paragraph, plan years beginning before 2008 shall not be taken into account.

(6) SMALL PLAN EXCEPTION.—If, on each day during the preceding plan year, a plan had 500 or fewer participants, the plan shall not be treated as in at-risk status for the plan year. For purposes of this paragraph, all defined benefit plans (other than multiemployer plans) maintained by the same employer (or any member of such employer's controlled group) shall be treated as 1 plan, but only participants with respect to such employer or member shall be taken into account and the rules of subsection (g)(2)(C) shall apply.

P.L. 110-458, §101(b)(3)(B), provides:

(B) ELECTION FOR EARLIER APPLICATION.—The amendments made by such paragraphs shall apply to a plan for the first plan year beginning after December 31, 2007, if the plan sponsor makes the election under this subparagraph. An election under this subparagraph shall be made at such time and in such manner as the Secretary of the Treasury or the Secretary's delegate may prescribe, and, once made, may be revoked only with the consent of the Secretary.

Amendments

• 2008, Worker, Retiree, and Employer Recovery Act of 2008 (P.L. 110-458)

P.L. 110-458, §101(b)(2)(F)(i):

Amended Code Sec. 430(i)(2) by striking subparagraph (A) and inserting a new subparagraph (A), by striking "the target normal cost (determined without regard to this paragraph) of the plan for the plan year" in subparagraph (B) and inserting "the amount determined under subsection (b)(1)(A)(i) with respect to the plan for the plan year". **Effective** generally for plan years beginning after 12-31-2008. For an exception, see Act Sec. 101(b)(3)(B), below. Prior to being stricken, Code Sec, 430(i)(2)(A) read as follows:

(A) the present value of all benefits which are expected to accrue or be earned under the plan during the plan year, determined using the additional actuarial assumptions described in paragraph (1)(B), plus

P.L. 110-458, § 101(b)(2)(F)(ii):

Amended Code Sec. 430(i) by striking "subparagraph (A)(ii)" in the last sentence of paragraph (4)(B) and inserting "subparagraph (A)". **Effective** as if included in the provision of the 2006 Act to which the amendment relates [**effective** with respect to plan years beginning after 12-31-2007.—CCH].

[Sec. 430(j)]

(j) PAYMENT OF MINIMUM REQUIRED CONTRIBUTIONS.—

(1) IN GENERAL.—For purposes of this section, the due date for any payment of any minimum required contribution for any plan year shall be $8\frac{1}{2}$ months after the close of the plan year.

(2) INTEREST.—Any payment required under paragraph (1) for a plan year that is made on a date other than the valuation date for such plan year shall be adjusted for interest accruing for the period between the valuation date and the payment date, at the effective rate of interest for the plan for such plan year.

(3) ACCELERATED QUARTERLY CONTRIBUTION SCHEDULE FOR UNDERFUNDED PLANS.—

(A) FAILURE TO TIMELY MAKE REQUIRED INSTALLMENT.—In any case in which the plan has a funding shortfall for the preceding plan year, the employer maintaining the plan shall make the required installments under this paragraph and if the employer fails to pay the full amount of a required installment for the plan year, then the amount of interest charged under paragraph (2) on the underpayment for the period of underpayment shall be determined by using a rate of interest equal to the rate otherwise used under paragraph (2) plus 5 percentage points. In the case of plan years beginning in 2008, the funding shortfall for the preceding plan year may be determined using such methods of estimation as the Secretary may provide.

(B) AMOUNT OF UNDERPAYMENT, PERIOD OF UNDERPAYMENT.—For purposes of subparagraph (A)—

(i) AMOUNT.—The amount of the underpayment shall be the excess of—

(I) the required installment, over

(II) the amount (if any) of the installment contributed to or under the plan on or before the due date for the installment.

(ii) PERIOD OF UNDERPAYMENT.—The period for which any interest is charged under this paragraph with respect to any portion of the underpayment shall run from the due date for the installment to the date on which such portion is contributed to or under the plan.

(iii) ORDER OF CREDITING CONTRIBUTIONS.—For purposes of clause (i)(II), contributions shall be credited against unpaid required installments in the order in which such installments are required to be paid.

(C) NUMBER OF REQUIRED INSTALLMENTS; DUE DATES.—For purposes of this paragraph—

(i) PAYABLE IN 4 INSTALLMENTS.—There shall be 4 required installments for each plan year.

(ii) TIME FOR PAYMENT OF INSTALLMENTS.—The due dates for required installments are set forth in the following table:

In the case of the following required installment:	The due date is:
1st	April 15
2nd	July 15
3rd	October 15
4th	January 15 of the following year.

(D) AMOUNT OF REQUIRED INSTALLMENT.—For purposes of this paragraph—

(i) IN GENERAL.—The amount of any required installment shall be 25 percent of the required annual payment.

(ii) REQUIRED ANNUAL PAYMENT.—For purposes of clause (i), the term "required annual payment" means the lesser of—

(I) 90 percent of the minimum required contribution (determined without regard to this subsection) to the plan for the plan year under this section, or

(II) 100 percent of the minimum required contribution (determined without regard to this subsection or to any waiver under section 412(c)) to the plan for the preceding plan year.

Subclause (II) shall not apply if the preceding plan year referred to in such clause was not a year of 12 months.

(E) FISCAL YEARS, SHORT YEARS, AND YEARS WITH ALTERNATE VALUATION DATE.—

(i) FISCAL YEARS.—In applying this paragraph to a plan year beginning on any date other than January 1, there shall be substituted for the months specified in this paragraph, the months which correspond thereto.

(ii) SHORT PLAN YEAR.—This subparagraph shall be applied to plan years of less than 12 months in accordance with regulations prescribed by the Secretary.

(iii) PLAN WITH ALTERNATE VALUATION DATE.—The Secretary shall prescribe regulations for the application of this paragraph in the case of a plan which has a valuation date other than the first day of the plan year.

(F) QUARTERLY CONTRIBUTIONS NOT TO INCLUDE CERTAIN INCREASED CONTRIBUTIONS.—Subparagraph (D) shall be applied without regard to any increase under subsection (c)(7).

(4) LIQUIDITY REQUIREMENT IN CONNECTION WITH QUARTERLY CONTRIBUTIONS.—

(A) IN GENERAL.—A plan to which this paragraph applies shall be treated as failing to pay the full amount of any required installment under paragraph (3) to the extent that the value of the liquid assets paid in such installment is less than the liquidity shortfall (whether or not such liquidity shortfall exceeds the amount of such installment required to be paid but for this paragraph).

(B) PLANS TO WHICH PARAGRAPH APPLIES.—This paragraph shall apply to a plan (other than a plan described in subsection (g)(2)(B)) which—

(i) is required to pay installments under paragraph (3) for a plan year, and

(ii) has a liquidity shortfall for any quarter during such plan year.

(C) PERIOD OF UNDERPAYMENT.—For purposes of paragraph (3)(A), any portion of an installment that is treated as not paid under subparagraph (A) shall continue to be treated as unpaid until the close of the quarter in which the due date for such installment occurs.

(D) LIMITATION ON INCREASE.—If the amount of any required installment is increased by reason of subparagraph (A), in no event shall such increase exceed the amount which, when added to prior installments for the plan year, is necessary to increase the funding target attainment percentage of the plan for the plan year (taking into account the expected increase in funding target due to benefits accruing or earned during the plan year) to 100 percent.

(E) DEFINITIONS.—For purposes of this paragraph—

(i) LIQUIDITY SHORTFALL.—The term "liquidity shortfall" means, with respect to any required installment, an amount equal to the excess (as of the last day of the quarter for which such installment is made) of—

(I) the base amount with respect to such quarter, over

(II) the value (as of such last day) of the plan's liquid assets.

(ii) BASE AMOUNT.—

(I) IN GENERAL.—The term "base amount" means, with respect to any quarter, an amount equal to 3 times the sum of the adjusted disbursements from the plan for the 12 months ending on the last day of such quarter.

(II) SPECIAL RULE.—If the amount determined under subclause (I) exceeds an amount equal to 2 times the sum of the adjusted disbursements from the plan for the 36 months ending on the last day of the quarter and an enrolled actuary certifies to the satisfaction of the Secretary that such excess is the result of nonrecurring circumstances, the base amount with respect to such quarter shall be determined without regard to amounts related to those nonrecurring circumstances.

(iii) DISBURSEMENTS FROM THE PLAN.—The term "disbursements from the plan" means all disbursements from the trust, including purchases of annuities, payments of single sums and other benefits, and administrative expenses.

(iv) ADJUSTED DISBURSEMENTS.—The term "adjusted disbursements" means disbursements from the plan reduced by the product of—

(I) the plan's funding target attainment percentage for the plan year, and

(II) the sum of the purchases of annuities, payments of single sums, and such other disbursements as the Secretary shall provide in regulations.

(v) LIQUID ASSETS.—The term "liquid assets" means cash, marketable securities, and such other assets as specified by the Secretary in regulations.

(vi) QUARTER.—The term "quarter" means, with respect to any required installment, the 3-month period preceding the month in which the due date for such installment occurs.

(F) REGULATIONS.—The Secretary may prescribe such regulations as are necessary to carry out this paragraph.

Amendments

• 2010, Preservation of Access to Care for Medicare Beneficiaries and Pension Relief Act of 2010 (P.L. 111-192)

P.L. 111-192, §201(b)(3)(B):

Amended Code Sec. 430(j)(3) by adding at the end a new subparagraph (F). **Effective** for plan years beginning after 12-31-2007.

• 2008, Worker, Retiree, and Employer Recovery Act of 2008 (P.L. 110-458)

P.L. 110-458, §101(b)(2)(G)(i)-iv):

Amended Code Sec. 430(j)(3) by adding a new sentence at the end of subparagraph (A), by striking "section 302(c)" in subparagraph (D)(ii)(II) and inserting "section 412(c)", by adding at the end of subparagraph (E) a new clause (iii), and by striking "AND SHORT YEARS" in the heading of subparagraph (E) and inserting ", SHORT YEARS, AND YEARS WITH ALTERNATE VALUATION DATE". **Effective** as if included in the provision of the 2006 Act to which the amendment relates [**effective** with respect to plan years beginning after 12-31-2007.—CCH].

[Sec. 430(k)]

(k) IMPOSITION OF LIEN WHERE FAILURE TO MAKE REQUIRED CONTRIBUTIONS.—

(1) IN GENERAL.—In the case of a plan to which this subsection applies (as provided under paragraph (2)), if—

(A) any person fails to make a contribution payment required by section 412 and this section before the due date for such payment, and

(B) the unpaid balance of such payment (including interest), when added to the aggregate unpaid balance of all preceding such payments for which payment was not made before the due date (including interest), exceeds $1,000,000,

then there shall be a lien in favor of the plan in the amount determined under paragraph (3) upon all property and rights to property, whether real or personal, belonging to such person and any other person who is a member of the same controlled group of which such person is a member.

(2) PLANS TO WHICH SUBSECTION APPLIES.—This subsection shall apply to a defined benefit plan (other than a multiemployer plan) covered under section 4021 of the Employee Retirement Income Security Act of 1974 for any plan year for which the funding target attainment percentage (as defined in subsection (d)(2)) of such plan is less than 100 percent.

(3) AMOUNT OF LIEN.—For purposes of paragraph (1), the amount of the lien shall be equal to the aggregate unpaid balance of contribution payments required under this section and section 412 for which payment has not been made before the due date.

(4) NOTICE OF FAILURE; LIEN.—

(A) NOTICE OF FAILURE.—A person committing a failure described in paragraph (1) shall notify the Pension Benefit Guaranty Corporation of such failure within 10 days of the due date for the required contribution payment.

(B) PERIOD OF LIEN.—The lien imposed by paragraph (1) shall arise on the due date for the required contribution payment and shall continue until the last day of the first plan year in which the plan ceases to be described in paragraph (1)(B). Such lien shall continue to run without regard to whether such plan continues to be described in paragraph (2) during the period referred to in the preceding sentence.

(C) CERTAIN RULES TO APPLY.—Any amount with respect to which a lien is imposed under paragraph (1) shall be treated as taxes due and owing the United States and rules similar to the rules of subsections (c), (d), and (e) of section 4068 of the Employee Retirement Income Security Act of 1974 shall apply with respect to a lien imposed by subsection (a) and the amount with respect to such lien.

(5) ENFORCEMENT.—Any lien created under paragraph (1) may be perfected and enforced only by the Pension Benefit Guaranty Corporation, or at the direction of the Pension Benefit Guaranty Corporation, by the contributing sponsor (or any member of the controlled group of the contributing sponsor).

(6) DEFINITIONS.—For purposes of this subsection—

(A) CONTRIBUTION PAYMENT.—The term "contribution payment" means, in connection with a plan, a contribution payment required to be made to the plan, including any required installment under paragraphs (3) and (4) of subsection (j).

(B) DUE DATE; REQUIRED INSTALLMENT.—The terms "due date" and "required installment" have the meanings given such terms by subsection (j).

(C) CONTROLLED GROUP.—The term "controlled group" means any group treated as a single employer under subsections (b), (c), (m), and (o) of section 414.

Amendments

• 2008, Worker, Retiree, and Employer Recovery Act of 2008 (P.L. 110-458)

P.L. 110-458, §101(b)(2)(H)(i)-(ii):

Amended Code Sec. 430(k) by inserting "(as provided under paragraph (2))" after "applies" in paragraph (1), and by striking ", except" and all that follows in paragraph (6)(B) and inserting a period. **Effective** as if included in the provision of the 2006 Act to which the amendment relates [**effective** with respect to plan years beginning after 12-31-2007.—CCH]. Prior to amendment, Code Sec. 430(k)(6)(B) read as follows:

(B) DUE DATE; REQUIRED INSTALLMENT.—The terms "due date" and "required installment" have the meanings given such terms by subsection (j), except that in the case of a payment other than a required installment, the due date shall be the date such payment is required to be made under section 430.

[Sec. 430(l)]

(l) QUALIFIED TRANSFERS TO HEALTH BENEFIT ACCOUNTS.—In the case of a qualified transfer (as defined in section 420), any assets so transferred shall not, for purposes of this section, be treated as assets in the plan.

Amendments

• 2006, Pension Protection Act of 2006 (P.L. 109-280)

P.L. 109-280, §112(a):

Amended subchapter D of chapter 1 by adding at the end a new part III (Code Sec. 430). **Effective** with respect to plan years beginning after 12-31-2007.

[Sec. 431]

SEC. 431. MINIMUM FUNDING STANDARDS FOR MULTIEMPLOYER PLANS.

[Sec. 431(a)]

(a) IN GENERAL.—For purposes of section 412, the accumulated funding deficiency of a multiemployer plan for any plan year is—

(1) except as provided in paragraph (2), the amount, determined as of the end of the plan year, equal to the excess (if any) of the total charges to the funding standard account of the plan for all plan years (beginning with the first plan year for which this part applies to the plan) over the total credits to such account for such years, and

(2) if the multiemployer plan is in reorganization for any plan year, the accumulated funding deficiency of the plan determined under section 4243 of the Employee Retirement Income Security Act of 1974.

[Sec. 431(b)]

(b) FUNDING STANDARD ACCOUNT.—

(1) ACCOUNT REQUIRED.—Each multiemployer plan to which this part applies shall establish and maintain a funding standard account. Such account shall be credited and charged solely as provided in this section.

(2) CHARGES TO ACCOUNT.—For a plan year, the funding standard account shall be charged with the sum of—

(A) the normal cost of the plan for the plan year,

(B) the amounts necessary to amortize in equal annual installments (until fully amortized)—

(i) in the case of a plan which comes into existence on or after January 1, 2008, the unfunded past service liability under the plan on the first day of the first plan year to which this section applies, over a period of 15 plan years,

(ii) separately, with respect to each plan year, the net increase (if any) in unfunded past service liability under the plan arising from plan amendments adopted in such year, over a period of 15 plan years,

(iii) separately, with respect to each plan year, the net experience loss (if any) under the plan, over a period of 15 plan years, and

(iv) separately, with respect to each plan year, the net loss (if any) resulting from changes in actuarial assumptions used under the plan, over a period of 15 plan years,

(C) the amount necessary to amortize each waived funding deficiency (within the meaning of section 412(c)(3)) for each prior plan year in equal annual installments (until fully amortized) over a period of 15 plan years,

(D) the amount necessary to amortize in equal annual installments (until fully amortized) over a period of 5 plan years any amount credited to the funding standard account under section 412(b)(3)(D) (as in effect on the day before the date of the enactment of the Pension Protection Act of 2006), and

(E) the amount necessary to amortize in equal annual installments (until fully amortized) over a period of 20 years the contributions which would be required to be made under the plan but for the provisions of section 412(c)(7)(A)(i)(I) (as in effect on the day before the date of the enactment of the Pension Protection Act of 2006).

(3) CREDITS TO ACCOUNT.—For a plan year, the funding standard account shall be credited with the sum of—

(A) the amount considered contributed by the employer to or under the plan for the plan year,

(B) the amount necessary to amortize in equal annual installments (until fully amortized)—

(i) separately, with respect to each plan year, the net decrease (if any) in unfunded past service liability under the plan arising from plan amendments adopted in such year, over a period of 15 plan years,

(ii) separately, with respect to each plan year, the net experience gain (if any) under the plan, over a period of 15 plan years, and

(iii) separately, with respect to each plan year, the net gain (if any) resulting from changes in actuarial assumptions used under the plan, over a period of 15 plan years,

(C) the amount of the waived funding deficiency (within the meaning of section 412(c)(3)) for the plan year, and

(D) in the case of a plan year for which the accumulated funding deficiency is determined under the funding standard account if such plan year follows a plan year for which such deficiency was determined under the alternative minimum funding standard under section 412(g) (as in effect on the day before the date of the enactment of the Pension Protection Act of 2006), the excess (if any) of any debit balance in the funding standard account (determined without regard to this subparagraph) over any debit balance in the alternative minimum funding standard account.

(4) SPECIAL RULE FOR AMOUNTS FIRST AMORTIZED IN PLAN YEARS BEFORE 2008.—In the case of any amount amortized under section 412(b) (as in effect on the day before the date of the enactment of the Pension Protection Act of 2006) over any period beginning with a plan year beginning before 2008 in lieu of the amortization described in paragraphs (2)(B) and (3)(B), such amount shall continue to be amortized under such section as so in effect.

(5) COMBINING AND OFFSETTING AMOUNTS TO BE AMORTIZED.—Under regulations prescribed by the Secretary, amounts required to be amortized under paragraph (2) or paragraph (3), as the case may be—

(A) may be combined into one amount under such paragraph to be amortized over a period determined on the basis of the remaining amortization period for all items entering into such combined amount, and

(B) may be offset against amounts required to be amortized under the other such paragraph, with the resulting amount to be amortized over a period determined on the basis of the remaining amortization periods for all items entering into whichever of the two amounts being offset is the greater.

(6) INTEREST.—The funding standard account (and items therein) shall be charged or credited (as determined under regulations prescribed by the Secretary of the Treasury) with interest at the appropriate rate consistent with the rate or rates of interest used under the plan to determine costs.

(7) SPECIAL RULES RELATING TO CHARGES AND CREDITS TO FUNDING STANDARD ACCOUNT.—For purposes of this part—

(A) WITHDRAWAL LIABILITY.—Any amount received by a multiemployer plan in payment of all or part of an employer's withdrawal liability under part 1 of subtitle E of title IV of the Employee Retirement Income Security Act of 1974 shall be considered an amount contributed by the employer to or under the plan. The Secretary may prescribe by regulation additional charges and credits to a multiemployer plan's funding standard account to the extent necessary to prevent withdrawal liability payments from being unduly reflected as advance funding for plan liabilities.

(B) ADJUSTMENTS WHEN A MULTIEMPLOYER PLAN LEAVES REORGANIZATION.—If a multiemployer plan is not in reorganization in the plan year but was in reorganization in the immediately preceding plan year, any balance in the funding standard account at the close of such immediately preceding plan year—

(i) shall be eliminated by an offsetting credit or charge (as the case may be), but

(ii) shall be taken into account in subsequent plan years by being amortized in equal annual installments (until fully amortized) over 30 plan years.

The preceding sentence shall not apply to the extent of any accumulated funding deficiency under section 4243(a) of such Act as of the end of the last plan year that the plan was in reorganization.

(C) PLAN PAYMENTS TO SUPPLEMENTAL PROGRAM OR WITHDRAWAL LIABILITY PAYMENT FUND.—Any amount paid by a plan during a plan year to the Pension Benefit Guaranty Corporation pursuant to section 4222 of such Act or to a fund exempt under section 501(c)(22) pursuant to section 4223 of such Act shall reduce the amount of contributions considered received by the plan for the plan year.

(D) INTERIM WITHDRAWAL LIABILITY PAYMENTS.—Any amount paid by an employer pending a final determination of the employer's withdrawal liability under part 1 of subtitle E of title IV of such Act and subsequently refunded to the employer by the plan shall be charged to the funding standard account in accordance with regulations prescribed by the Secretary.

(E) ELECTION FOR DEFERRAL OF CHARGE FOR PORTION OF NET EXPERIENCE LOSS.—If an election is in effect under section 412(b)(7)(F) (as in effect on the day before the date of the enactment of the Pension Protection Act of 2006) for any plan year, the funding standard account shall be charged in the plan year to which the portion of the net experience loss deferred by such election was deferred with the amount so deferred (and paragraph (2)(B)(iii) shall not apply to the amount so charged).

(F) FINANCIAL ASSISTANCE.—Any amount of any financial assistance from the Pension Benefit Guaranty Corporation to any plan, and any repayment of such amount, shall be taken into account under this section and section 412 in such manner as is determined by the Secretary.

(G) SHORT-TERM BENEFITS.—To the extent that any plan amendment increases the unfunded past service liability under the plan by reason of an increase in benefits which are not payable as a life annuity but are payable under the terms of the plan for a period that does not exceed 14 years from the effective date of the amendment, paragraph (2)(B)(ii) shall be applied separately with respect to such increase in unfunded past service liability by substituting the number of years of the period during which such benefits are payable for "15".

(8) SPECIAL RELIEF RULES.—Notwithstanding any other provision of this subsection—

(A) AMORTIZATION OF NET INVESTMENT LOSSES.—

(i) IN GENERAL.—A multiemployer plan with respect to which the solvency test under subparagraph (C) is met may treat the portion of any experience loss or gain attributable to net investment losses incurred in either or both of the first two plan years ending after August 31, 2008, as an item separate from other experience losses, to be amortized in equal annual installments (until fully amortized) over the period—

(I) beginning with the plan year in which such portion is first recognized in the actuarial value of assets, and

(II) ending with the last plan year in the 30-plan year period beginning with the plan year in which such net investment loss was incurred.

(ii) COORDINATION WITH EXTENSIONS.—If this subparagraph applies for any plan year—

(I) no extension of the amortization period under clause (i) shall be allowed under subsection (d), and

(II) if an extension was granted under subsection (d) for any plan year before the election to have this subparagraph apply to the plan year, such extension shall not result in such amortization period exceeding 30 years.

(iii) NET INVESTMENT LOSSES.—For purposes of this subparagraph—

(I) IN GENERAL.—Net investment losses shall be determined in the manner prescribed by the Secretary on the basis of the difference between actual and expected returns (including any difference attributable to any criminally fraudulent investment arrangement).

(II) CRIMINALLY FRAUDULENT INVESTMENT ARRANGEMENTS.—The determination as to whether an arrangement is a criminally fraudulent investment arrangement shall be made under rules substantially similar to the rules prescribed by the Secretary for purposes of section 165.

(B) EXPANDED SMOOTHING PERIOD.—

(i) IN GENERAL.—A multiemployer plan with respect to which the solvency test under subparagraph (C) is met may change its asset valuation method in a manner which—

(I) spreads the difference between expected and actual returns for either or both of the first 2 plan years ending after August 31, 2008, over a period of not more than 10 years,

(II) provides that for either or both of the first 2 plan years beginning after August 31, 2008, the value of plan assets at any time shall not be less than 80 percent or greater than 130 percent of the fair market value of such assets at such time, or

(III) makes both changes described in subclauses (I) and (II) to such method.

(ii) ASSET VALUATION METHODS.—If this subparagraph applies for any plan year—

(I) the Secretary shall not treat the asset valuation method of the plan as unreasonable solely because of the changes in such method described in clause (i), and

(II) such changes shall be deemed approved by the Secretary under section 302(d)(1) of the Employee Retirement Income Security Act of 1974 and section 412(d)(1).

(iii) AMORTIZATION OF REDUCTION IN UNFUNDED ACCRUED LIABILITY.—If this subparagraph and subparagraph (A) both apply for any plan year, the plan shall treat any reduction in unfunded accrued liability resulting from the application of this subparagraph as a separate experience amortization base, to be amortized in equal annual installments (until fully amortized) over a period of 30 plan years rather than the period such liability would otherwise be amortized over.

(C) SOLVENCY TEST.—The solvency test under this paragraph is met only if the plan actuary certifies that the plan is projected to have sufficient assets to timely pay expected benefits and anticipated expenditures over the amortization period, taking into account the changes in the funding standard account under this paragraph.

(D) RESTRICTION ON BENEFIT INCREASES.—If subparagraph (A) or (B) apply [sic] to a multiemployer plan for any plan year, then, in addition to any other applicable restrictions on benefit increases, a plan amendment increasing benefits may not go into effect during either of the 2 plan years immediately following such plan year unless—

(i) the plan actuary certifies that—

(I) any such increase is paid for out of additional contributions not allocated to the plan immediately before the application of this paragraph to the plan, and

(II) the plan's funded percentage and projected credit balances for such 2 plan years are reasonably expected to be at least as high as such percentage and balances would have been if the benefit increase had not been adopted, or

(ii) the amendment is required as a condition of qualification under part I of subchapter D or to comply with other applicable law.

(E) REPORTING.—A plan sponsor of a plan to which this paragraph applies shall—

(i) give notice of such application to participants and beneficiaries of the plan, and

(ii) inform the Pension Benefit Guaranty Corporation of such application in such form and manner as the Director of the Pension Benefit Guaranty Corporation may prescribe.

Amendments

• 2010, Preservation of Access to Care for Medicare Beneficiaries and Pension Relief Act of 2010 (P.L. 111-192)

P.L. 111-192, §211(a)(2):

Amended Code Sec. 431(b) by adding at the end a new paragraph (8). For the **effective** date, see Act Sec. 211(b)(1)-(2), below.

P.L. 111-192, §211(b)(1)-(2), provides:

(b) EFFECTIVE DATES.—

(1) IN GENERAL.—The amendments made by this section shall take effect as of the first day of the first plan year ending after August 31, 2008, except that any election a plan makes pursuant to this section that affects the plan's funding standard account for the first plan year beginning after August 31, 2008, shall be disregarded for purposes of applying the provisions of section 305 of the Employee Retirement Income Security Act of 1974 and section 432 of the Internal Revenue Code of 1986 to such plan year.

(2) RESTRICTIONS ON BENEFIT INCREASES.—Notwithstanding paragraph (1), the restrictions on plan amendments increasing benefits in sections 304(b)(8)(D) of such Act and 431(b)(8)(D) of such Code, as added by this section, shall take effect on the date of enactment of this Act.

[Sec. 431(c)]

(c) ADDITIONAL RULES.—

(1) DETERMINATIONS TO BE MADE UNDER FUNDING METHOD.—For purposes of this part, normal costs, accrued liability, past service liabilities, and experience gains and losses shall be determined under the funding method used to determine costs under the plan.

(2) VALUATION OF ASSETS.—

(A) IN GENERAL.—For purposes of this part, the value of the plan's assets shall be determined on the basis of any reasonable actuarial method of valuation which takes into account fair market value and which is permitted under regulations prescribed by the Secretary.

(B) ELECTION WITH RESPECT TO BONDS.—The value of a bond or other evidence of indebtedness which is not in default as to principal or interest may, at the election of the plan administrator, be determined on an amortized basis running from initial cost at purchase to par value at maturity or earliest call date. Any election under this subparagraph shall be made at such time and in such manner as the Secretary shall by regulations provide, shall apply to all such evidences of indebtedness, and may be revoked only with the consent of the Secretary.

(3) ACTUARIAL ASSUMPTIONS MUST BE REASONABLE.—For purposes of this section, all costs, liabilities, rates of interest, and other factors under the plan shall be determined on the basis of actuarial assumptions and methods—

(A) each of which is reasonable (taking into account the experience of the plan and reasonable expectations), and

(B) which, in combination, offer the actuary's best estimate of anticipated experience under the plan.

(4) TREATMENT OF CERTAIN CHANGES AS EXPERIENCE GAIN OR LOSS.—For purposes of this section, if—

(A) a change in benefits under the Social Security Act or in other retirement benefits created under Federal or State law, or

(B) a change in the definition of the term "wages" under section 3121, or a change in the amount of such wages taken into account under regulations prescribed for purposes of section 401(a)(5),

results in an increase or decrease in accrued liability under a plan, such increase or decrease shall be treated as an experience loss or gain.

(5) FULL FUNDING.—If, as of the close of a plan year, a plan would (without regard to this paragraph) have an accumulated funding deficiency in excess of the full funding limitation—

(A) the funding standard account shall be credited with the amount of such excess, and

(B) all amounts described in subparagraphs (B), (C), and (D) of subsection (b) (2) and subparagraph (B) of subsection (b)(3) which are required to be amortized shall be considered fully amortized for purposes of such subparagraphs.

(6) FULL-FUNDING LIMITATION.—

(A) IN GENERAL.—For purposes of paragraph (5), the term "full-funding limitation" means the excess (if any) of—

(i) the accrued liability (including normal cost) under the plan (determined under the entry age normal funding method if such accrued liability cannot be directly calculated under the funding method used for the plan), over

(ii) the lesser of—

(I) the fair market value of the plan's assets, or

(II) the value of such assets determined under paragraph (2).

(B) MINIMUM AMOUNT.—

(i) IN GENERAL.—In no event shall the full-funding limitation determined under subparagraph (A) be less than the excess (if any) of—

(I) 90 percent of the current liability of the plan (including the expected increase in current liability due to benefits accruing during the plan year), over

(II) the value of the plan's assets determined under paragraph (2).

(ii) ASSETS.—For purposes of clause (i), assets shall not be reduced by any credit balance in the funding standard account.

(C) FULL FUNDING LIMITATION.—For purposes of this paragraph, unless otherwise provided by the plan, the accrued liability under a multiemployer plan shall not include benefits which are not nonforfeitable under the plan after the termination of the plan (taking into consideration section 411(d)(3)).

(D) CURRENT LIABILITY.—For purposes of this paragraph—

(i) IN GENERAL.—The term "current liability" means all liabilities to employees and their beneficiaries under the plan.

(ii) TREATMENT OF UNPREDICTABLE CONTINGENT EVENT BENEFITS.—For purposes of clause (i), any benefit contingent on an event other than—

(I) age, service, compensation, death, or disability, or

(II) an event which is reasonably and reliably predictable (as determined by the Secretary),

shall not be taken into account until the event on which the benefit is contingent occurs.

(iii) INTEREST RATE USED.—The rate of interest used to determine current liability under this paragraph shall be the rate of interest determined under subparagraph (E).

(iv) MORTALITY TABLES.—

(I) COMMISSIONERS' STANDARD TABLE.—In the case of plan years beginning before the first plan year to which the first tables prescribed under subclause (II) apply, the mortality table used in determining current liability under this paragraph shall be the table prescribed by the Secretary which is based on the prevailing commissioners' standard table (described in section 807(d)(5)(A)) used to determine reserves for group annuity contracts issued on January 1, 1993.

(II) SECRETARIAL AUTHORITY.—The Secretary may by regulation prescribe for plan years beginning after December 31, 1999, mortality tables to be used in determining current liability under this subsection. Such tables shall be based upon the actual experience of pension plans and projected trends in such experience. In prescribing such tables, the Secretary shall take into account results of available independent studies of mortality of individuals covered by pension plans.

(v) SEPARATE MORTALITY TABLES FOR THE DISABLED.—Notwithstanding clause (iv)—

(I) IN GENERAL.—The Secretary shall establish mortality tables which may be used (in lieu of the tables under clause (iv)) to determine current liability under this subsection for individuals who are entitled to benefits under the plan on account of disability. The Secretary shall establish separate tables for individuals whose disabilities occur in plan years beginning before January 1, 1995, and for individuals whose disabilities occur in plan years beginning on or after such date.

(II) SPECIAL RULE FOR DISABILITIES OCCURRING AFTER 1994.—In the case of disabilities occurring in plan years beginning after December 31, 1994, the tables under subclause (I) shall apply only with respect to individuals described in such subclause who are disabled within the meaning of title II of the Social Security Act and the regulations thereunder.

(vi) PERIODIC REVIEW.—The Secretary shall periodically (at least every 5 years) review any tables in effect under this subparagraph and shall, to the extent such Secretary determines necessary, by regulation update the tables to reflect the actual experience of pension plans and projected trends in such experience.

(E) REQUIRED CHANGE OF INTEREST RATE.—For purposes of determining a plan's current liability for purposes of this paragraph—

(i) IN GENERAL.—If any rate of interest used under the plan under subsection (b)(6) to determine cost is not within the permissible range, the plan shall establish a new rate of interest within the permissible range.

(ii) PERMISSIBLE RANGE.—For purposes of this subparagraph—

(I) IN GENERAL.—Except as provided in subclause (II), the term "permissible range" means a rate of interest which is not more than 5 percent above, and not more than 10 percent below, the weighted average of the rates of interest on 30-year Treasury securities during the 4-year period ending on the last day before the beginning of the plan year.

(II) SECRETARIAL AUTHORITY.—If the Secretary finds that the lowest rate of interest permissible under subclause (I) is unreasonably high, the Secretary may prescribe a lower rate of interest, except that such rate may not be less than 80 percent of the average rate determined under such subclause.

(iii) ASSUMPTIONS.—Notwithstanding paragraph (3)(A), the interest rate used under the plan shall be—

(I) determined without taking into account the experience of the plan and reasonable expectations, but

(II) consistent with the assumptions which reflect the purchase rates which would be used by insurance companies to satisfy the liabilities under the plan.

(7) ANNUAL VALUATION.—

(A) IN GENERAL.—For purposes of this section, a determination of experience gains and losses and a valuation of the plan's liability shall be made not less frequently than once every year, except that such determination shall be made more frequently to the extent required in particular cases under regulations prescribed by the Secretary.

(B) VALUATION DATE.—

(i) CURRENT YEAR.—Except as provided in clause (ii), the valuation referred to in subparagraph (A) shall be made as of a date within the plan year to which the valuation refers or within one month prior to the beginning of such year.

(ii) USE OF PRIOR YEAR VALUATION.—The valuation referred to in subparagraph (A) may be made as of a date within the plan year prior to the year to which the valuation refers if, as of such date, the value of the assets of the plan are not less than 100 percent of the plan's current liability (as defined in paragraph (6)(D) without regard to clause (iv) thereof).

(iii) ADJUSTMENTS.—Information under clause (ii) shall, in accordance with regulations, be actuarially adjusted to reflect significant differences in participants.

(iv) LIMITATION.—A change in funding method to use a prior year valuation, as provided in clause (ii), may not be made unless as of the valuation date within the prior plan year, the value of the assets of the plan are not less than 125 percent of the plan's current liability (as defined in paragraph (6)(D) without regard to clause (iv) thereof).

(8) TIME WHEN CERTAIN CONTRIBUTIONS DEEMED MADE.—For purposes of this section, any contributions for a plan year made by an employer after the last day of such plan year, but not later than two and one-half months after such day, shall be deemed to have been made on such last day. For purposes of this subparagraph, such two and one-half month period may be extended for not more than six months under regulations prescribed by the Secretary.

[Sec. 431(d)]

(d) EXTENSION OF AMORTIZATION PERIODS FOR MULTIEMPLOYER PLANS.—

(1) AUTOMATIC EXTENSION UPON APPLICATION BY CERTAIN PLANS.—

(A) IN GENERAL.—If the plan sponsor of a multiemployer plan—

(i) submits to the Secretary an application for an extension of the period of years required to amortize any unfunded liability described in any clause of subsection (b)(2)(B) or described in subsection (b)(4), and

(ii) includes with the application a certification by the plan's actuary described in subparagraph (B), the Secretary shall extend the amortization period for the period of time (not in excess of 5 years) specified in the application. Such extension shall be in addition to any extension under paragraph (2).

(B) CRITERIA.—A certification with respect to a multiemployer plan is described in this subparagraph if the plan's actuary certifies that, based on reasonable assumptions—

(i) absent the extension under subparagraph (A), the plan would have an accumulated funding deficiency in the current plan year or any of the 9 succeeding plan years,

(ii) the plan sponsor has adopted a plan to improve the plan's funding status,

(iii) the plan is projected to have sufficient assets to timely pay expected benefits and anticipated expenditures over the amortization period as extended, and

(iv) the notice required under paragraph (3)(A) has been provided.

(C) TERMINATION.—The preceding provisions of this paragraph shall not apply with respect to any application submitted after December 31, 2014.

(2) ALTERNATIVE EXTENSION.—

(A) IN GENERAL.—If the plan sponsor of a multiemployer plan submits to the Secretary an application for an extension of the period of years required to amortize any unfunded liability described in any clause of subsection (b)(2)(B) or described in subsection (b)(4), the Secretary may extend the amortization period for a period of time (not in excess of 10 years reduced by the number of years of any extension under paragraph (1) with respect to such unfunded liability) if the Secretary makes the determination described in subparagraph (B). Such extension shall be in addition to any extension under paragraph (1).

(B) DETERMINATION.—The Secretary may grant an extension under subparagraph (A) if the Secretary determines that—

(i) such extension would carry out the purposes of this Act and would provide adequate protection for participants under the plan and their beneficiaries, and

(ii) the failure to permit such extension would—

(I) result in a substantial risk to the voluntary continuation of the plan, or a substantial curtailment of pension benefit levels or employee compensation, and

(II) be adverse to the interests of plan participants in the aggregate.

(C) ACTION BY SECRETARY.—The Secretary shall act upon any application for an extension under this paragraph within 180 days of the submission of such application. If the Secretary rejects the application for an extension under this paragraph, the Secretary shall provide notice to the plan detailing the specific reasons for the rejection, including references to the criteria set forth above.

(3) ADVANCE NOTICE.—

(A) IN GENERAL.—The Secretary shall, before granting an extension under this subsection, require each applicant to provide evidence satisfactory to such Secretary that the applicant has provided notice of the filing of the application for such extension to each affected party (as defined in section 4001(a)(21) of the Employee Retirement Income Security Act of 1974) with respect to the affected plan. Such notice shall include a description of the extent to which the plan is funded for benefits which are guaranteed under title IV of such Act and for benefit liabilities.

(B) CONSIDERATION OF RELEVANT INFORMATION.—The Secretary shall consider any relevant information provided by a person to whom notice was given under paragraph (1).

Amendments

• 2006, Pension Protection Act of 2006 (P.L. 109-280)

P.L. 109-280, §206, provides:

SEC. 206. SPECIAL RULE FOR CERTAIN BENEFITS FUNDED UNDER AN AGREEMENT APPROVED BY THE PENSION BENEFIT GUARANTY CORPORATION.

In the case of a multiemployer plan that is a party to an agreement that was approved by the Pension Benefit Guaranty Corporation prior to June 30, 2005, and that—

(1) increases benefits, and

(2) provides for special withdrawal liability rules under section 4203(f) of the Employee Retirement Income Security Act of 1974 (29 U.S.C. 1383),

the amendments made by sections 201, 202, 211, and 212 of this Act shall not apply to the benefit increases under any plan amendment adopted prior to June 30, 2005, that are funded pursuant to such agreement if the plan is funded in compliance with such agreement (and any amendments thereto).

P.L. 109-280, §211(a):

Amended subpart A of part III of subchapter D of chapter 1, as added by this Act, by inserting after Code Sec. 430 a new Code Sec. 431. **Effective** generally for plan years beginning after 2007. For a special rule, see Act Sec. 211(b)(2), below.

P.L. 109-280, §211(b)(2), provides:

(2) SPECIAL RULE FOR CERTAIN AMORTIZATION EXTENSIONS.—If the Secretary of the Treasury grants an extension under section 304 of the Employee Retirement Income Security Act of 1974 and section 412(e) of the Internal Revenue Code of 1986 with respect to any application filed with the Secretary of the Treasury on or before June 30, 2005, the extension (and any modification thereof) shall be applied and administered under the rules of such sections as in effect before the enactment of this Act, including the use of the rate of interest determined under section 6621(b) of such Code.

»»→ Caution: Code Sec. 432, below, was added by P.L. 109-280. For sunset provision, see P.L. 109-280, §221(c), in the amendment notes.

[Sec. 432]

SEC. 432. ADDITIONAL FUNDING RULES FOR MULTIEMPLOYER PLANS IN ENDANGERED STATUS OR CRITICAL STATUS.

[Sec. 432(a)]

(a) GENERAL RULE.—For purposes of this part, in the case of a multiemployer plan in effect on July 16, 2006 —

(1) if the plan is in endangered status—

(A) the plan sponsor shall adopt and implement a funding improvement plan in accordance with the requirements of subsection (c), and

(B) the requirements of subsection (d) shall apply during the funding plan adoption period and the funding improvement period, and

(2) if the plan is in critical status—

(A) the plan sponsor shall adopt and implement a rehabilitation plan in accordance with the requirements of subsection (e), and

(B) the requirements of subsection (f) shall apply during the rehabilitation plan adoption period and the rehabilitation period.

[Sec. 432(b)]

(b) DETERMINATION OF ENDANGERED AND CRITICAL STATUS.—For purposes of this section—

(1) ENDANGERED STATUS.—A multiemployer plan is in endangered status for a plan year if, as determined by the plan actuary under paragraph (3), the plan is not in critical status for the plan year and, as of the beginning of the plan year, either—

(A) the plan's funded percentage for such plan year is less than 80 percent, or

(B) the plan has an accumulated funding deficiency for such plan year, or is projected to have such an accumulated funding deficiency for any of the 6 succeeding plan years, taking into account any extension of amortization periods under section 431(d).

For purposes of this section, a plan shall be treated as in seriously endangered status for a plan year if the plan is described in both subparagraphs (A) and (B).

(2) CRITICAL STATUS.—A multiemployer plan is in critical status for a plan year if, as determined by the plan actuary under paragraph (3), the plan is described in 1 or more of the following subparagraphs as of the beginning of the plan year:

(A) A plan is described in this subparagraph if—

(i) the funded percentage of the plan is less than 65 percent, and

(ii) the sum of—

(I) the fair market value of plan assets, plus

(II) the present value of the reasonably anticipated employer contributions for the current plan year and each of the 6 succeeding plan years, assuming that the terms of all collective bargaining agreements pursuant to which the plan is maintained for the current plan year continue in effect for succeeding plan years,

is less than the present value of all nonforfeitable benefits projected to be payable under the plan during the current plan year and each of the 6 succeeding plan years (plus administrative expenses for such plan years).

(B) A plan is described in this subparagraph if—

(i) the plan has an accumulated funding deficiency for the current plan year, not taking into account any extension of amortization periods under section 431(d), or

(ii) the plan is projected to have an accumulated funding deficiency for any of the 3 succeeding plan years (4 succeeding plan years if the funded percentage of the plan is 65 percent or less), not taking into account any extension of amortization periods under section 431(d).

(C) A plan is described in this subparagraph if—

(i)(I) the plan's normal cost for the current plan year, plus interest (determined at the rate used for determining costs under the plan) for the current plan year on the amount of unfunded benefit liabilities under the plan as of the last date of the preceding plan year, exceeds

(II) the present value of the reasonably anticipated employer and employee contributions for the current plan year,

(ii) the present value, as of the beginning of the current plan year, of nonforfeitable benefits of inactive participants is greater than the present value of nonforfeitable benefits of active participants, and

(iii) the plan has an accumulated funding deficiency for the current plan year, or is projected to have such a deficiency for any of the 4 succeeding plan years, not taking into account any extension of amortization periods under section 431(d).

(D) A plan is described in this subparagraph if the sum of—

(i) the fair market value of plan assets, plus

(ii) the present value of the reasonably anticipated employer contributions for the current plan year and each of the 4 succeeding plan years, assuming that the terms of all collective bargaining agreements pursuant to which the plan is maintained for the current plan year continue in effect for succeeding plan years,

is less than the present value of all benefits projected to be payable under the plan during the current plan year and each of the 4 succeeding plan years (plus administrative expenses for such plan years).

(3) ANNUAL CERTIFICATION BY PLAN ACTUARY.—

(A) IN GENERAL.—Not later than the 90th day of each plan year of a multiemployer plan, the plan actuary shall certify to the Secretary and to the plan sponsor—

(i) whether or not the plan is in endangered status for such plan year and whether or not the plan is or will be in critical status for such plan year, and

(ii) in the case of a plan which is in a funding improvement or rehabilitation period, whether or not the plan is making the scheduled progress in meeting the requirements of its funding improvement or rehabilitation plan.

(B) ACTUARIAL PROJECTIONS OF ASSETS AND LIABILITIES.—

(i) IN GENERAL.—In making the determinations and projections under this subsection, the plan actuary shall make projections required for the current and succeeding plan years of the current value of the assets of the plan and the present value of all liabilities to participants and beneficiaries under the plan for the current plan year as of the beginning of such year. The actuary's projections shall be based on reasonable actuarial estimates, assumptions, and methods that, except as provided in clause (iii), offer the actuary's best estimate of anticipated experience under the plan. The projected present value of liabilities as of the beginning of such year shall be determined based on the most recent of either—

(I) the actuarial statement required under section 103(d) of the Employee Retirement Income Security Act of 1974 with respect to the most recently filed annual report, or

(II) the actuarial valuation for the preceding plan year.

(ii) DETERMINATIONS OF FUTURE CONTRIBUTIONS.—Any actuarial projection of plan assets shall assume—

(I) reasonably anticipated employer contributions for the current and succeeding plan years, assuming that the terms of the one or more collective bargaining agreements pursuant to which the plan is maintained for the current plan year continue in effect for succeeding plan years, or

(II) that employer contributions for the most recent plan year will continue indefinitely, but only if the plan actuary determines there have been no significant demographic changes that would make such assumption unreasonable.

(iii) PROJECTED INDUSTRY ACTIVITY.—Any projection of activity in the industry or industries covered by the plan, including future covered employment and contribution levels, shall be based on information provided by the plan sponsor, which shall act reasonably and in good faith.

(C) PENALTY FOR FAILURE TO SECURE TIMELY ACTUARIAL CERTIFICATION.—Any failure of the plan's actuary to certify the plan's status under this subsection by the date specified in subparagraph (A) shall be treated for purposes of section 502(c)(2) of the Employee Retirement Income Security Act of 1974 as a failure or refusal by the plan administrator to file the annual report required to be filed with the Secretary under section 101(b)(1) of such Act.

(D) NOTICE.—

(i) IN GENERAL.—In any case in which it is certified under subparagraph (A) that a multiemployer plan is or will be in endangered or critical status for a plan year, the plan sponsor shall, not later than 30 days after the date of the certification, provide notification of the endangered or critical status to the participants and beneficiaries, the bargaining parties, the Pension Benefit Guaranty Corporation, and the Secretary of Labor.

(ii) PLANS IN CRITICAL STATUS.—If it is certified under subparagraph (A) that a multiemployer plan is or will be in critical status, the plan sponsor shall include in the notice under clause (i) an explanation of the possibility that—

(I) adjustable benefits (as defined in subsection (e)(8)) may be reduced, and

(II) such reductions may apply to participants and beneficiaries whose benefit commencement date is on or after the date such notice is provided for the first plan year in which the plan is in critical status.

(iii) MODEL NOTICE.—The Secretary, in consultation with the Secretary of Labor shall prescribe a model notice that a multiemployer plan may use to satisfy the requirements under clause (ii).

Amendments

• 2008, Worker, Retiree, and Employer Recovery Act of 2008 (P.L. 110-458)

P.L. 110-458, §102(b)(2)(A):

Amended Code Sec. 432(b)(3)(C) by striking "section 101(b)(4)" and inserting "section 101(b)(1)". **Effective** as if included in the provision of the 2006 Act to which the amendment relates [**effective** generally with respect to plan years beginning after 2007.—CCH]

P.L. 110-458, §102(b)(2)(B):

Amended Code Sec. 432(b)(3)(D)(iii) by striking "The Secretary of Labor" and inserting "The Secretary, in consultation with the Secretary of Labor". **Effective** as if included in the provision of the 2006 Act to which the amendment relates [**effective** generally with respect to plan years beginning after 2007.—CCH]

P.L. 110-458, §204, provides:

SEC. 204. TEMPORARY DELAY OF DESIGNATION OF MULTIEMPLOYER PLANS AS IN ENDANGERED OR CRITICAL STATUS.

(a) IN GENERAL.—Notwithstanding the actuarial certification under section 305(b)(3) of the Employee Retirement Income Security Act of 1974 and section 432(b)(3) of the Internal Revenue Code of 1986, if a plan sponsor of a multiemployer plan elects the application of this section, then, for purposes of section 305 of such Act and section 432 of such Code—

(1) the status of the plan for its first plan year beginning during the period beginning on October 1, 2008, and ending on September 30, 2009, shall be the same as the status of such plan under such sections for the plan year preceding such plan year, and

(2) in the case of a plan which was in endangered or critical status for the preceding plan year described in paragraph (1), the plan shall not be required to update its plan or schedules under section 305(c)(6) of such Act and section 432(c)(6) of such Code, or section 305(e)(3)(B) of such Act and section 432(e)(3)(B) of such Code, whichever is applicable, until the plan year following the first plan year described in paragraph (1).

If section 305 of the Employee Retirement Income Security Act of 1974 and section 432 of the Internal Revenue Code of 1986 did not apply to the preceding plan year described in paragraph (1), the plan actuary shall make a certification of the status of the plan under section 305(b)(3) of such Act and section 432(b)(3) of such Code for the preceding plan year in the same manner as if such sections had applied to such preceding plan year.

(b) EXCEPTION FOR PLANS BECOMING CRITICAL DURING ELECTION.—If—

(1) an election was made under subsection (a) with respect to a multiemployer plan, and

(2) such plan has, without regard to such election, been certified by the plan actuary under section 305(b)(3) of such Act and section 432(b)(3) of such Code to be in critical status for the first plan year described in subsection (a)(1),

then such plan shall be treated as a plan in critical status for such plan year for purposes of applying section 4971(g)(1)(A) of such Code, section 302(b)(3) of such Act (without regard to the second sentence thereof), and section 412(b)(3) of such Code (without regard to the second sentence thereof).

(c) ELECTION AND NOTICE.—

(1) ELECTION.—An election under subsection (a) shall—

(A) be made at such time and in such manner as the Secretary of the Treasury or the Secretary's delegate may prescribe and, once made, may be revoked only with the consent of the Secretary, and

(B) if the election is made—

(i) before the date the annual certification is submitted to the Secretary or the Secretary's delegate under section 305(b)(3) of such Act and section 432(b)(3) of such Code, be included with such annual certification, and

(ii) after such date, be submitted to the Secretary or the Secretary's delegate not later than 30 days after the date of the election.

(2) NOTICE TO PARTICIPANTS.—

(A) IN GENERAL.—Notwithstanding section 305(b)(3)(D) of such Act and section 431(b)(3)(D) of such Code, if the plan is neither in endangered nor critical status by reason of an election made under subsection (a)—

(i) the plan sponsor of a multiemployer plan shall not be required to provide notice under such sections, and

(ii) the plan sponsor shall provide to the participants and beneficiaries, the bargaining parties, the Pension Benefit Guaranty Corporation, and the Secretary of Labor a notice of the election and such other information as the Secretary of the Treasury (in consultation with the Secretary of Labor) may require—

(I) if the election is made before the date the annual certification is submitted to the Secretary or the Secretary's delegate under section 305(b)(3) of such Act and section 432(b)(3) of such Code, not later than 30 days after the date of the certification, and

(II) if the election is made after such date, not later than 30 days after the date of the election.

(B) NOTICE OF ENDANGERED STATUS.—Notwithstanding section 305(b)(3)(D) of such Act and section 431(b)(3)(D) of such Code, if the plan is certified to be in critical status for any plan year but is in endangered status by reason of an election made under subsection (a), the notice provided under such sections shall be the notice which would have been provided if the plan had been certified to be in endangered status.

[Sec. 432(c)]

(c) FUNDING IMPROVEMENT PLAN MUST BE ADOPTED FOR MULTIEMPLOYER PLANS IN ENDANGERED STATUS.—

(1) IN GENERAL.—In any case in which a multiemployer plan is in endangered status for a plan year, the plan sponsor, in accordance with this subsection—

(A) shall adopt a funding improvement plan not later than 240 days following the required date for the actuarial certification of endangered status under subsection (b)(3)(A), and

(B) within 30 days after the adoption of the funding improvement plan—

(i) shall provide to the bargaining parties 1 or more schedules showing revised benefit structures, revised contribution structures, or both, which, if adopted, may reasonably be expected to enable the multiemployer plan to meet the applicable benchmarks in accordance with the funding improvement plan, including—

(I) one proposal for reductions in the amount of future benefit accruals necessary to achieve the applicable benchmarks, assuming no amendments increasing contributions under the plan (other than amendments increasing contributions necessary to achieve the applicable benchmarks after amendments have reduced future benefit accruals to the maximum extent permitted by law), and

(II) one proposal for increases in contributions under the plan necessary to achieve the applicable benchmarks, assuming no amendments reducing future benefit accruals under the plan, and

(ii) may, if the plan sponsor deems appropriate, prepare and provide the bargaining parties with additional information relating to contribution rates or benefit reductions, alternative schedules, or other information relevant to achieving the applicable benchmarks in accordance with the funding improvement plan.

For purposes of this section, the term "applicable benchmarks" means the requirements applicable to the multiemployer plan under paragraph (3) (as modified by paragraph (5)).

(2) EXCEPTION FOR YEARS AFTER PROCESS BEGINS.—Paragraph (1) shall not apply to a plan year if such year is in a funding plan adoption period or funding improvement period by reason of the plan being in endangered status for a preceding plan year. For purposes of this section, such preceding plan year shall be the initial determination year with respect to the funding improvement plan to which it relates.

(3) FUNDING IMPROVEMENT PLAN.—For purposes of this section—

(A) IN GENERAL.—A funding improvement plan is a plan which consists of the actions, including options or a range of options to be proposed to the bargaining parties, formulated to provide, based on reasonably anticipated experience and reasonable actuarial assumptions, for the attainment by the plan during the funding improvement period of the following requirements:

(i) INCREASE IN PLAN'S FUNDING PERCENTAGE.—The plan's funded percentage as of the close of the funding improvement period equals or exceeds a percentage equal to the sum of—

(I) such percentage as of the beginning of such period, plus

(II) 33 percent of the difference between 100 percent and the percentage under subclause (I).

(ii) AVOIDANCE OF ACCUMULATED FUNDING DEFICIENCIES.—No accumulated funding deficiency for any plan year during the funding improvement period (taking into account any extension of amortization periods under section 431(d)).

(B) SERIOUSLY ENDANGERED PLANS.—In the case of a plan in seriously endangered status, except as provided in paragraph (5), subparagraph (A)(i)(II) shall be applied by substituting "20 percent" for "33 percent".

(4) FUNDING IMPROVEMENT PERIOD.—For purposes of this section—

(A) IN GENERAL.—The funding improvement period for any funding improvement plan adopted pursuant to this subsection is the 10-year period beginning on the first day of the first plan year of the multiemployer plan beginning after the earlier of—

(i) the second anniversary of the date of the adoption of the funding improvement plan, or

(ii) the expiration of the collective bargaining agreements in effect on the due date for the actuarial certification of endangered status for the initial determination year under subsection (b)(3)(A) and covering, as of such due date, at least 75 percent of the active participants in such multiemployer plan.

(B) SERIOUSLY ENDANGERED PLANS.—In the case of a plan in seriously endangered status, except as provided in paragraph (5), subparagraph (A) shall be applied by substituting "15-year period" for "10-year period".

(C) COORDINATION WITH CHANGES IN STATUS.—

(i) PLANS NO LONGER IN ENDANGERED STATUS.—If the plan's actuary certifies under subsection (b)(3)(A) for a plan year in any funding plan adoption period or funding improvement period that the plan is no longer in endangered status and is not in critical status, the funding plan adoption period or funding improvement period, whichever is applicable, shall end as of the close of the preceding plan year.

(ii) PLANS IN CRITICAL STATUS.—If the plan's actuary certifies under subsection (b)(3)(A) for a plan year in any funding plan adoption period or funding improvement period that the plan is in critical status, the funding plan adoption period or funding improvement period, whichever is applicable, shall end as of the close of the plan year preceding the first plan year in the rehabilitation period with respect to such status.

(D) PLANS IN ENDANGERED STATUS AT END OF PERIOD.—If the plan's actuary certifies under subsection (b)(3)(A) for the first plan year following the close of the period described in subparagraph (A) that the plan is in endangered status, the provisions of this subsection and subsection (d) shall be applied as if such first plan year were an initial determination year, except that the plan may not be amended in a manner inconsistent with the funding improvement plan in effect for the preceding plan year until a new funding improvement plan is adopted.

(5) SPECIAL RULES FOR SERIOUSLY ENDANGERED PLANS MORE THAN 70 PERCENT FUNDED.—

(A) IN GENERAL.—If the funded percentage of a plan in seriously endangered status was more than 70 percent as of the beginning of the initial determination year—

(i) paragraphs (3)(B) and (4)(B) shall apply only if the plan's actuary certifies, within 30 days after the certification under subsection (b)(3)(A) for the initial determination year, that, based on the terms of the plan and the collective bargaining agreements in effect at the time of such certification, the plan is not projected to meet the requirements of paragraph (3)(A) (without regard to paragraphs (3)(B) and (4)(B)), and

(ii) if there is a certification under clause (i), the plan may, in formulating its funding improvement plan, only take into account the rules of paragraph (3)(B) and (4)(B) for plan years in the funding improvement period beginning on or before the date on which the last of the collective bargaining agreements described in paragraph (4)(A)(ii) expires.

(B) SPECIAL RULE AFTER EXPIRATION OF AGREEMENTS.—Notwithstanding subparagraph (A)(ii), if, for any plan year ending after the date described in subparagraph (A)(ii), the plan actuary certifies (at the time of the annual certification under subsection (b)(3)(A) for such plan year) that, based on the terms of the plan and collective bargaining agreements in effect at the time of that annual certification, the plan is not projected to be able to meet the requirements of paragraph (3)(A) (without regard to paragraphs (3)(B) and (4)(B)), paragraphs (3)(B) and (4)(B) shall continue to apply for such year.

(6) UPDATES TO FUNDING IMPROVEMENT PLAN AND SCHEDULES.—

(A) FUNDING IMPROVEMENT PLAN.—The plan sponsor shall annually update the funding improvement plan and shall file the update with the plan's annual report under section 104 of the Employee Retirement Income Security Act of 1974.

(B) SCHEDULES.—The plan sponsor shall annually update any schedule of contribution rates provided under this subsection to reflect the experience of the plan.

(C) DURATION OF SCHEDULE.—A schedule of contribution rates provided by the plan sponsor and relied upon by bargaining parties in negotiating a collective bargaining agreement shall remain in effect for the duration of that collective bargaining agreement.

(7) IMPOSITION OF DEFAULT SCHEDULE WHERE FAILURE TO ADOPT FUNDING IMPROVEMENT PLAN.—

(A) IN GENERAL.—If—

(i) a collective bargaining agreement providing for contributions under a multiemployer plan that was in effect at the time the plan entered endangered status expires, and

(ii) after receiving one or more schedules from the plan sponsor under paragraph (1)(B), the bargaining parties with respect to such agreement fail to adopt a contribution schedule with terms consistent with the funding improvement plan and a schedule from the plan sponsor,

the plan sponsor shall implement the schedule described in paragraph (1)(B)(i)(I) beginning on the date specified in subparagraph (B).

(B) DATE OF IMPLEMENTATION.—The date specified in this subparagraph is the date which is 180 days after the date on which the collective bargaining agreement described in subparagraph (A) expires.

(8) FUNDING PLAN ADOPTION PERIOD.—For purposes of this section, the term "funding plan adoption period" means the period beginning on the date of the certification under subsection (b)(3)(A) for the initial determination year and ending on the day before the first day of the funding improvement period.

Amendments

• 2008, Worker, Retiree, and Employer Recovery Act of 2008 (P.L. 110-458)

P.L. 110-458, §102(b)(2)(C)(i)-(ii):

Amended Code Sec. 432(c) in paragraph (3), by striking "section 304(d)" in subparagraph (A)(ii) and inserting "section 431(d)", and in paragraph (7) by striking "to agree on" and all that follows in subparagraph (A)(ii) and inserting "to adopt a contribution schedule with terms consistent with the funding improvement plan and a schedule from the plan sponsor,", and by striking subparagraph (B) and inserting a new subparagraph (B). **Effective** as if included in the provision of the 2006 Act to which the amendment relates [**effective** generally with respect to plan years beginning after 2007.—CCH]. Prior to amendment, Code Sec. 432(c)(7) read as follows:

(7) IMPOSITION OF DEFAULT SCHEDULE WHERE FAILURE TO ADOPT FUNDING IMPROVEMENT PLAN.—

(A) IN GENERAL.—If—

(i) a collective bargaining agreement providing for contributions under a multiemployer plan that was in effect at the time the plan entered endangered status expires, and

(ii) after receiving one or more schedules from the plan sponsor under paragraph (1)(B), the bargaining parties with respect to such agreement fail to agree on changes to contribution or benefit schedules necessary to meet the applicable benchmarks in accordance with the funding improvement plan,

the plan sponsor shall implement the schedule described in paragraph (1)(B)(i)(I) beginning on the date specified in subparagraph (B).

(B) DATE OF IMPLEMENTATION.—The date specified in this subparagraph is the earlier of the date—

(i) on which the Secretary certifies that the parties are at an impasse, or

(ii) which is 180 days after the date on which the collective bargaining agreement described in subparagraph (A) expires.

P.L. 110-458, § 205, provides:

SEC. 205. TEMPORARY EXTENSION OF THE FUNDING IMPROVEMENT AND REHABILITATION PERIODS FOR MULTIEMPLOYER PENSION PLANS IN CRITICAL AND ENDANGERED STATUS FOR 2008 OR 2009.

(a) IN GENERAL.—If the plan sponsor of a multiemployer plan which is in endangered or critical status for a plan year beginning in 2008 or 2009 (determined after application of section 204) elects the application of this section, then, for purposes of section 305 of the Employee Retirement Income Security Act of 1974 and section 432 of the Internal Revenue Code of 1986—

(1) except as provided in paragraph (2), the plan's funding improvement period or rehabilitation period, whichever is applicable, shall be 13 years rather than 10 years, and

(2) in the case of a plan in seriously endangered status, the plan's funding improvement period shall be 18 years rather than 15 years.

(b) DEFINITIONS AND SPECIAL RULES.—For purposes of this section—

(1) ELECTION.—An election under this section shall be made at such time, and in such manner and form, as (in consultation with the Secretary of Labor) the Secretary of the Treasury or the Secretary's delegate may prescribe.

(2) DEFINITIONS.—Any term which is used in this section which is also used in section 305 of the Employee Retirement Income Security Act of 1974 and section 432 of the Internal Revenue Code of 1986 shall have the same meaning as when used in such sections.

(c) EFFECTIVE DATE.—This section shall apply to plan years beginning after December 31, 2007.

[Sec. 432(d)]

(d) RULES FOR OPERATION OF PLAN DURING ADOPTION AND IMPROVEMENT PERIODS.—

(1) SPECIAL RULES FOR PLAN ADOPTION PERIOD.—During the funding plan adoption period—

(A) the plan sponsor may not accept a collective bargaining agreement or participation agreement with respect to the multiemployer plan that provides for—

(i) a reduction in the level of contributions for any participants,

(ii) a suspension of contributions with respect to any period of service, or

(iii) any new direct or indirect exclusion of younger or newly hired employees from plan participation,

(B) no amendment of the plan which increases the liabilities of the plan by reason of any increase in benefits, any change in the accrual of benefits, or any change in the rate at which benefits become nonforfeitable under the plan may be adopted unless the amendment is required as a condition of qualification under part I of subchapter D of chapter 1 of the Internal Revenue Code of 1986 or to comply with other applicable law, and

(C) in the case of a plan in seriously endangered status, the plan sponsor shall take all reasonable actions which are consistent with the terms of the plan and applicable law and which are expected, based on reasonable assumptions, to achieve—

(i) an increase in the plan's funded percentage, and

(ii) postponement of an accumulated funding deficiency for at least 1 additional plan year.

Actions under subparagraph (C) include applications for extensions of amortization periods under section 304(d), use of the shortfall funding method in making funding standard account computations, amendments to the plan's benefit structure, reductions in future benefit accruals, and other reasonable actions consistent with the terms of the plan and applicable law.

(2) COMPLIANCE WITH FUNDING IMPROVEMENT PLAN.—

(A) IN GENERAL.—A plan may not be amended after the date of the adoption of a funding improvement plan so as to be inconsistent with the funding improvement plan.

(B) NO REDUCTION IN CONTRIBUTIONS.—A plan sponsor may not during any funding improvement period accept a collective bargaining agreement or participation agreement with respect to the multiemployer plan that provides for—

(i) a reduction in the level of contributions for any participants,

(ii) a suspension of contributions with respect to any period of service, or

(iii) any new direct or indirect exclusion of younger or newly hired employees from plan participation.

(C) SPECIAL RULES FOR BENEFIT INCREASES.—A plan may not be amended after the date of the adoption of a funding improvement plan so as to increase benefits, including future benefit accruals, unless the plan actuary certifies that the benefit increase is consistent with the funding improvement plan and is paid for out of contributions not required by the funding improvement plan to meet the applicable benchmark in accordance with the schedule contemplated in the funding improvement plan.

[Sec. 432(e)]

(e) REHABILITATION PLAN MUST BE ADOPTED FOR MULTIEMPLOYER PLANS IN CRITICAL STATUS.—

(1) IN GENERAL.—In any case in which a multiemployer plan is in critical status for a plan year, the plan sponsor, in accordance with this subsection—

(A) shall adopt a rehabilitation plan not later than 240 days following the required date for the actuarial certification of critical status under subsection (b)(3)(A), and

(B) within 30 days after the adoption of the rehabilitation plan—

(i) shall provide to the bargaining parties 1 or more schedules showing revised benefit structures, revised contribution structures, or both, which, if adopted, may reasonably be expected to enable the multiemployer plan to emerge from critical status in accordance with the rehabilitation plan, and

(ii) may, if the plan sponsor deems appropriate, prepare and provide the bargaining parties with additional information relating to contribution rates or benefit reductions, alternative schedules, or other information relevant to emerging from critical status in accordance with the rehabilitation plan.

The schedule or schedules described in subparagraph (B)(i) shall reflect reductions in future benefit accruals and adjustable benefits, and increases in contributions, that the plan sponsor determines are reasonably necessary to emerge from critical status. One schedule shall be designated as the default schedule and such schedule shall assume that there are no increases in contributions under the plan other than the increases necessary to emerge from critical status after future benefit accruals and other benefits (other than benefits the reduction or elimination of which are not permitted under section 411(d)(6)) have been reduced to the maximum extent permitted by law.

(2) EXCEPTION FOR YEARS AFTER PROCESS BEGINS.—Paragraph (1) shall not apply to a plan year if such year is in a rehabilitation plan adoption period or rehabilitation period by reason of the plan being in critical status for a preceding plan year. For purposes of this section, such preceding plan year shall be the initial critical year with respect to the rehabilitation plan to which it relates.

(3) REHABILITATION PLAN.—For purposes of this section—

(A) IN GENERAL.—A rehabilitation plan is a plan which consists of—

(i) actions, including options or a range of options to be proposed to the bargaining parties, formulated, based on reasonably anticipated experience and reasonable actuarial assumptions, to enable the plan to cease to be in critical status by the end of the rehabilitation period and may include reductions in plan expenditures (including plan mergers and consolidations), reductions in future benefit accruals or increases in contributions, if agreed to by the bargaining parties, or any combination of such actions, or

(ii) if the plan sponsor determines that, based on reasonable actuarial assumptions and upon exhaustion of all reasonable measures, the plan can not reasonably be expected to emerge from critical status by the end of the rehabilitation period, reasonable measures to emerge from critical status at a later time or to forestall possible insolvency (within the meaning of section 4245 of the Employee Retirement Income Security Act of 1974).

A rehabilitation plan must provide annual standards for meeting the requirements of such rehabilitation plan. Such plan shall also include the schedules required to be provided under paragraph (1)(B)(i) and if clause (ii) applies, shall set forth the alternatives considered, explain why the plan is not reasonably expected to emerge from critical status by the end of the rehabilitation period, and specify when, if ever, the plan is expected to emerge from critical status in accordance with the rehabilitation plan.

(B) UPDATES TO REHABILITATION PLAN AND SCHEDULES.—

(i) REHABILITATION PLAN.—The plan sponsor shall annually update the rehabilitation plan and shall file the update with the plan's annual report under section 104 of the Employee Retirement Income Security Act of 1974.

(ii) SCHEDULES.—The plan sponsor shall annually update any schedule of contribution rates provided under this subsection to reflect the experience of the plan.

(iii) DURATION OF SCHEDULE.—A schedule of contribution rates provided by the plan sponsor and relied upon by bargaining parties in negotiating a collective bargaining agreement shall remain in effect for the duration of that collective bargaining agreement.

(C) IMPOSITION OF DEFAULT SCHEDULE WHERE FAILURE TO ADOPT REHABILITATION PLAN.—

(i) IN GENERAL.—If—

(I) a collective bargaining agreement providing for contributions under a multiemployer plan that was in effect at the time the plan entered critical status expires, and

(II) after receiving one or more schedules from the plan sponsor under paragraph (1)(B), the bargaining parties with respect to such agreement fail to adopt a to adopt a [sic] contribution schedule with terms consistent with the rehabilitation plan and a schedule from the plan sponsor under paragraph (1)(B)(i),

the plan sponsor shall implement the default schedule described in the last sentence of paragraph (1) beginning on the date specified in clause (ii).

(ii) DATE OF IMPLEMENTATION.—The date specified in this clause is the date which is 180 days after the date on which the collective bargaining agreement described in clause (i) expires.

(4) REHABILITATION PERIOD.—For purposes of this section—

(A) IN GENERAL.—The rehabilitation period for a plan in critical status is the 10-year period beginning on the first day of the first plan year of the multiemployer plan following the earlier of—

(i) the second anniversary of the date of the adoption of the rehabilitation plan, or

(ii) the expiration of the collective bargaining agreements in effect on the due date for the actuarial certification of critical status for the initial critical year under subsection (a)(1) and covering, as of such date at least 75 percent of the active participants in such multiemployer plan.

If a plan emerges from critical status as provided under subparagraph (B) before the end of such 10-year period, the rehabilitation period shall end with the plan year preceding the plan year for which the determination under subparagraph (B) is made.

(B) EMERGENCE.—A plan in critical status shall remain in such status until a plan year for which the plan actuary certifies, in accordance with subsection (b)(3)(A), that the plan is not projected to have an accumulated funding deficiency for the plan year or any of the 9 succeeding plan years, without regard to the use of the shortfall method but taking into account any extension of amortization periods under section 431(d).

(5) REHABILITATION PLAN ADOPTION PERIOD.—For purposes of this section, the term "rehabilitation plan adoption period" means the period beginning on the date of the certification under subsection (b)(3)(A) for the initial critical year and ending on the day before the first day of the rehabilitation period.

(6) LIMITATION ON REDUCTION IN RATES OF FUTURE ACCRUALS.—Any reduction in the rate of future accruals under the default schedule described in the last sentence of paragraph (1) shall not reduce the rate of future accruals below—

(A) a monthly benefit (payable as a single life annuity commencing at the participant's normal retirement age) equal to 1 percent of the contributions required to be made with respect to a participant, or the equivalent standard accrual rate for a participant or group of participants under the collective bargaining agreements in effect as of the first day of the initial critical year, or

(B) if lower, the accrual rate under the plan on such first day.

The equivalent standard accrual rate shall be determined by the plan sponsor based on the standard or average contribution base units which the plan sponsor determines to be representative for active participants and such other factors as the plan sponsor determines to be relevant. Nothing in this paragraph shall be construed as limiting the ability of the plan sponsor to prepare and provide the bargaining parties with alternative schedules to the default schedule that establish lower or higher accrual and contribution rates than the rates otherwise described in this paragraph.

(7) AUTOMATIC EMPLOYER SURCHARGE.—

(A) IMPOSITION OF SURCHARGE.—Each employer otherwise obligated to make a contribution for the initial critical year shall be obligated to pay to the plan for such year a surcharge equal to 5 percent of the contribution otherwise required under the applicable collective bargaining agreement (or other agreement pursuant to which the employer contributes). For each succeeding plan year in which the plan is in critical status for a consecutive period of years beginning with the initial critical year, the surcharge shall be 10 percent of the contribution otherwise so required.

(B) ENFORCEMENT OF SURCHARGE.—The surcharges under subparagraph (A) shall be due and payable on the same schedule as the contributions on which the surcharges are based. Any failure to make a surcharge payment shall be treated as a delinquent contribution under section 515 of the Employee Retirement Income Security Act of 1974 and shall be enforceable as such.

(C) SURCHARGE TO TERMINATE UPON COLLECTIVE BARGAINING AGREEMENT RENEGOTIATION.—The surcharge under this paragraph shall cease to be effective with respect to employees covered by a collective bargaining agreement (or other agreement pursuant to which the employer contributes), beginning on the effective date of a collective bargaining agreement (or other such agreement) that includes terms consistent with a schedule presented by the plan sponsor under paragraph (1)(B)(i), as modified under subparagraph (B) of paragraph (3).

(D) SURCHARGE NOT TO APPLY UNTIL EMPLOYER RECEIVES NOTICE.—The surcharge under this paragraph shall not apply to an employer until 30 days after the employer has been notified by the plan sponsor that the plan is in critical status and that the surcharge is in effect.

(E) SURCHARGE NOT TO GENERATE INCREASED BENEFIT ACCRUALS.—Notwithstanding any provision of a plan to the contrary, the amount of any surcharge under this paragraph shall not be the basis for any benefit accrual under the plan.

(8) BENEFIT ADJUSTMENTS.—

(A) ADJUSTABLE BENEFITS.—

(i) IN GENERAL.—Notwithstanding section 411(d)(6), the plan sponsor shall, subject to the notice requirement under subparagraph (C), make any reductions to adjustable benefits which the plan sponsor deems appropriate, based upon the outcome of collective bargaining over the schedule or schedules provided under paragraph (1)(B)(i).

(ii) EXCEPTION FOR RETIREES.—Except in the case of adjustable benefits described in clause (iv)(III), the plan sponsor of a plan in critical status shall not reduce adjustable benefits of any participant or beneficiary whose benefit commencement date is before the date on which the plan provides notice to the participant or beneficiary under subsection (b)(3)(D) for the initial critical year.

(iii) PLAN SPONSOR FLEXIBILITY.—The plan sponsor shall include in the schedules provided to the bargaining parties an allowance for funding the benefits of participants with respect to whom contributions are not currently required to be made, and shall reduce their benefits to the extent permitted under this title and considered appropriate by the plan sponsor based on the plan's then current overall funding status.

(iv) ADJUSTABLE BENEFIT DEFINED.—For purposes of this paragraph, the term "adjustable benefit" means—

(I) benefits, rights, and features under the plan, including post-retirement death benefits, 60-month guarantees, disability benefits not yet in pay status, and similar benefits,

(II) any early retirement benefit or retirement-type subsidy (within the meaning of section 411(d)(6)(B)(i)) and any benefit payment option (other than the qualified joint-and survivor annuity), and

(III) benefit increases that would not be eligible for a guarantee under section 4022A of the Employee Retirement Income Security Act of 1974 on the first day of initial critical year because the increases were adopted (or, if later, took effect) less than 60 months before such first day.

(B) NORMAL RETIREMENT BENEFITS PROTECTED.—Except as provided in subparagraph (A)(iv)(III), nothing in this paragraph shall be construed to permit a plan to reduce the level of a participant's accrued benefit payable at normal retirement age.

(C) NOTICE REQUIREMENTS.—

(i) IN GENERAL.—No reduction may be made to adjustable benefits under subparagraph (A) unless notice of such reduction has been given at least 30 days before the general effective date of such reduction for all participants and beneficiaries to—

(I) plan participants and beneficiaries,

(II) each employer who has an obligation to contribute (within the meaning of section 4212(a) of the Employee Retirement Income Security Act of 1974) under the plan, and

(III) each employee organization which, for purposes of collective bargaining, represents plan participants employed by such an employer.

(ii) CONTENT OF NOTICE.—The notice under clause (i) shall contain—

(I) sufficient information to enable participants and beneficiaries to understand the effect of any reduction on their benefits, including an estimate (on an annual or monthly basis) of any affected adjustable benefit that a participant or beneficiary would otherwise have been eligible for as of the general effective date described in clause (i), and

(II) information as to the rights and remedies of plan participants and beneficiaries as well as how to contact the Department of Labor for further information and assistance where appropriate.

(iii) FORM AND MANNER.—Any notice under clause (i)—

(I) shall be provided in a form and manner prescribed in regulations of the Secretary, in consultation with the Secretary of Labor,

(II) shall be written in a manner so as to be understood by the average plan participant, and

(III) may be provided in written, electronic, or other appropriate form to the extent such form is reasonably accessible to persons to whom the notice is required to be provided.

the [sic] Secretary shall in the regulations prescribed under subclause (I) establish a model notice that a plan sponsor may use to meet the requirements of this subparagraph.

(9) ADJUSTMENTS DISREGARDED IN WITHDRAWAL LIABILITY DETERMINATION.—

(A) BENEFIT REDUCTIONS.—Any benefit reductions under this subsection shall be disregarded in determining a plan's unfunded vested benefits for purposes of determining an employer's withdrawal liability under section 4201 of the Employee Retirement Income Security Act of 1974.

(B) SURCHARGES.—Any surcharges under paragraph (7) shall be disregarded in determining the allocation of unfunded vested benefits to an employer under section 4211 of such Act, except for purposes of determining the unfunded vested benefits attributable to an employer under section 4211(c)(4) of such Act or a comparable method approved under section 4211(c)(5) of such Act.

(C) SIMPLIFIED CALCULATIONS.—The Pension Benefit Guaranty Corporation shall prescribe simplified methods for the application of this paragraph in determining withdrawal liability.

Amendments

• 2008, Worker, Retiree, and Employer Recovery Act of 2008 (P.L. 110-458)

P.L. 110-458, §102(b)(2)(D)(i)-(v):

Amended Code Sec. 432(e) in paragraph (3)(C) by striking all that follows "to adopt a" in clause (i)(II) and inserting "to adopt a contribution schedule with terms consistent with the rehabilitation plan and a schedule from the plan sponsor under paragraph (1)(B)(i),", and by striking clause (ii) and inserting a new clause (ii), in paragraph (4) by striking "the date of" following "in effect on" in subparagraph (A)(ii), and by striking "and taking" in subparagraph (B) and inserting "but taking", in paragraph (6) by striking "paragraph (1)(B)(i)" and inserting "the last sentence of paragraph (1)", and by striking "established" and inserting "establish", in paragraph (8) by striking "section 204(g)" in subparagraph (A)(i) and inserting "section 411(d)(6)", by inserting "of the Employee Retirement Income Security Act of 1974" after "4212(a)" in subparagraph (C)(i)(II), by striking "the Secretary of Labor" in subparagraph (C)(iii)(I) and inserting "the Secretary, in consultation with the Secretary of Labor", and by striking "the [sic] Secretary of Labor" in the last sentence of subparagraph (C)(iii) and inserting "the Secretary", and in paragraph (9)(B) by striking "an employer's withdrawal liability" and inserting "the allocation of unfunded vested benefits to an employer". **Effective** as if included in the provision of the 2006 Act to which the amendment relates [**effective** generally with respect to plan years beginning after 2007.—CCH]. Prior to amendment, Code Sec. 432(e)(3)(C) read as follows:

(C) IMPOSITION OF DEFAULT SCHEDULE WHERE FAILURE TO ADOPT REHABILITATION PLAN.—

(i) IN GENERAL.—If—

(I) a collective bargaining agreement providing for contributions under a multiemployer plan that was in effect at the time the plan entered critical status expires, and

(II) after receiving one or more schedules from the plan sponsor under paragraph (1)(B), the bargaining parties with respect to such agreement fail to adopt a contribution or benefit schedules with terms consistent with the rehabilitation plan and the schedule from the plan sponsor under paragraph (1)(B)(i),

the plan sponsor shall implement the default schedule described in the last sentence of paragraph (1) beginning on the date specified in clause (ii).

(ii) DATE OF IMPLEMENTATION.—The date specified in this clause is the earlier of the date—

(I) on which the Secretary of Labor certifies that the parties are at an impasse, or

(II) which is 180 days after the date on which the collective bargaining agreement described in clause (i) expires.

[Sec. 432(f)]

(f) RULES FOR OPERATION OF PLAN DURING ADOPTION AND REHABILITATION PERIOD.—

(1) COMPLIANCE WITH REHABILITATION PLAN.—

(A) IN GENERAL.—A plan may not be amended after the date of the adoption of a rehabilitation plan under subsection (e) so as to be inconsistent with the rehabilitation plan.

(B) SPECIAL RULES FOR BENEFIT INCREASES.—A plan may not be amended after the date of the adoption of a rehabilitation plan under subsection (e) so as to increase benefits, including future benefit accruals, unless the plan actuary certifies that such increase is paid for out of additional contributions not contemplated by the rehabilitation plan, and, after taking into account the benefit increase, the multiemployer plan still is reasonably expected to emerge from critical status by the end of the rehabilitation period on the schedule contemplated in the rehabilitation plan.

(2) RESTRICTION ON LUMP SUMS AND SIMILAR BENEFITS.—

(A) IN GENERAL.—Effective on the date the notice of certification of the plan's critical status for the initial critical year under subsection (b)(3)(D) is sent, and notwithstanding section 411(d)(6), the plan shall not pay—

(i) any payment, in excess of the monthly amount paid under a single life annuity (plus any social security supplements described in the last sentence of section 411(a)(9)) to a participant or beneficiary whose annuity starting date (as defined in section 417(f)(2)) occurs after the date such notice is sent,

(ii) any payment for the purchase of an irrevocable commitment from an insurer to pay benefits, and

(iii) any other payment specified by the Secretary by regulations.

(B) EXCEPTION.—Subparagraph (A) shall not apply to a benefit which under section 411(a)(11) may be immediately distributed without the consent of the participant or to any makeup payment in the case of a retroactive annuity starting date or any similar payment of benefits owed with respect to a prior period.

(3) ADJUSTMENTS DISREGARDED IN WITHDRAWAL LIABILITY DETERMINATION.—Any benefit reductions under this subsection shall be disregarded in determining a plan's unfunded vested

benefits for purposes of determining an employer's withdrawal liability under section 4201 of the Employee Retirement Income Security Act of 1974.

(4) SPECIAL RULES FOR PLAN ADOPTION PERIOD.—During the rehabilitation plan adoption period—

(A) the plan sponsor may not accept a collective bargaining agreement or participation agreement with respect to the multiemployer plan that provides for—

(i) a reduction in the level of contributions for any participants,

(ii) a suspension of contributions with respect to any period of service, or

(iii) any new direct or indirect exclusion of younger or newly hired employees from plan participation, and

(B) no amendment of the plan which increases the liabilities of the plan by reason of any increase in benefits, any change in the accrual of benefits, or any change in the rate at which benefits become nonforfeitable under the plan may be adopted unless the amendment is required as a condition of qualification under part I of subchapter D of chapter 1 or to comply with other applicable law.

Amendments

• 2008, Worker, Retiree, and Employer Recovery Act of 2008 (P.L. 110-458)

P.L. 110-458, §102(b)(2)(E)(i)-(ii):

Amended Code Sec. 432(f)(2)(A)(i) by striking "section 411(b)(1)(A)" and inserting "section 411(a)(9)"; and by inserting at the end "to a participant or beneficiary whose annuity starting date (as defined in section 417(f)(2)) occurs after the date such notice is sent,". **Effective** as if included in the provision of the 2006 Act to which the amendment relates [**effective** generally with respect to plan years beginning after 2007.—CCH].

[Sec. 432(g)]

(g) EXPEDITED RESOLUTION OF PLAN SPONSOR DECISIONS.—If, within 60 days of the due date for adoption of a funding improvement plan under subsection (c) or a rehabilitation plan under subsection (e), the plan sponsor of a plan in endangered status or a plan in critical status has not agreed on a funding improvement plan or rehabilitation plan, then any member of the board or group that constitutes the plan sponsor may require that the plan sponsor enter into an expedited dispute resolution procedure for the development and adoption of a funding improvement plan or rehabilitation plan.

Amendments

• 2008, Worker, Retiree, and Employer Recovery Act of 2008 (P.L. 110-458)

P.L. 110-458, §102(b)(2)(F):

Amended Code Sec. 432(g) by inserting "under subsection (c)" after "funding improvement plan" the first place it appears. **Effective** as if included in the provision of the 2006 Act to which the amendment relates [**effective** generally with respect to plan years beginning after 2007.—CCH].

[Sec. 432(h)]

(h) NONBARGAINED PARTICIPATION.—

(1) BOTH BARGAINED AND NONBARGAINED EMPLOYEE-PARTICIPANTS.—In the case of an employer that contributes to a multiemployer plan with respect to both employees who are covered by one or more collective bargaining agreements and employees who are not so covered, if the plan is in endangered status or in critical status, benefits of and contributions for the nonbargained employees, including surcharges on those contributions, shall be determined as if those nonbargained employees were covered under the first to expire of the employer's collective bargaining agreements in effect when the plan entered endangered or critical status.

(2) NONBARGAINED EMPLOYEES ONLY.—In the case of an employer that contributes to a multiemployer plan only with respect to employees who are not covered by a collective bargaining agreement, this section shall be applied as if the employer were the bargaining party, and its participation agreement with the plan were a collective bargaining agreement with a term ending on the first day of the plan year beginning after the employer is provided the schedule or schedules described in subsections (c) and (e).

[Sec. 432(i)]

(i) DEFINITIONS; ACTUARIAL METHOD.—For purposes of this section—

(1) BARGAINING PARTY.—The term "bargaining party" means—

(A)(i) except as provided in clause (ii), an employer who has an obligation to contribute under the plan; or

(ii) in the case of a plan described under section 404(c), or a continuation of such a plan, the association of employers that is the employer settlor of the plan; and

(B) an employee organization which, for purposes of collective bargaining, represents plan participants employed by an employer who has an obligation to contribute under the plan.

(2) FUNDED PERCENTAGE.—The term "funded percentage" means the percentage equal to a fraction—

(A) the numerator of which is the value of the plan's assets, as determined under section 431(c)(2), and

(B) the denominator of which is the accrued liability of the plan, determined using actuarial assumptions described in section 431(c)(3).

(3) ACCUMULATED FUNDING DEFICIENCY.—The term "accumulated funding deficiency" has the meaning given such term in section 431(a).

(4) ACTIVE PARTICIPANT.—The term "active participant" means, in connection with a multiemployer plan, a participant who is in covered service under the plan.

(5) INACTIVE PARTICIPANT.—The term "inactive participant" means, in connection with a multiemployer plan, a participant, or the beneficiary or alternate payee of a participant, who—

(A) is not in covered service under the plan, and

(B) is in pay status under the plan or has a nonforfeitable right to benefits under the plan.

(6) PAY STATUS.—A person is in pay status under a multiemployer plan if—

(A) at any time during the current plan year, such person is a participant or beneficiary under the plan and is paid an early, late, normal, or disability retirement benefit under the plan (or a death benefit under the plan related to a retirement benefit), or

(B) to the extent provided in regulations of the Secretary, such person is entitled to such a benefit under the plan.

(7) OBLIGATION TO CONTRIBUTE.—The term "obligation to contribute" has the meaning given such term under section 4212(a) of the Employee Retirement Income Security Act of 1974.

(8) ACTUARIAL METHOD.—Notwithstanding any other provision of this section, the actuary's determinations with respect to a plan's normal cost, actuarial accrued liability, and improvements in a plan's funded percentage under this section shall be based upon the unit credit funding method (whether or not that method is used for the plan's actuarial valuation).

(9) PLAN SPONSOR.—For purposes of this section, section 431, and section 4971(g):

(A) IN GENERAL.—The term "plan sponsor" means, with respect to any multiemployer plan, the association, committee, joint board of trustees, or other similar group of representatives of the parties who establish or maintain the plan.

(B) SPECIAL RULE FOR SECTION 404(c) PLANS.—In the case of a plan described in section 404(c) (or a continuation of such plan), such term means the bargaining parties described in paragraph (1).

(10) BENEFIT COMMENCEMENT DATE.—The term "benefit commencement date" means the annuity starting date (or in the case of a retroactive annuity starting date, the date on which benefit payments begin).

Amendments

• 2008, Worker, Retiree, and Employer Recovery Act of 2008 (P.L. 110-458)

P.L. 110-458, §102(b)(2)(G)(i)-(ii):

Amended Code Sec. 432(i) by striking "section 412(a)" in paragraph (3) and inserting "section 431(a)", and by striking paragraph (9) and inserting a new paragraph (9). **Effective** as if included in the provision of the 2006 Act to which the amendment relates [**effective** generally with respect to plan years beginning after 2007.—CCH]. Prior to being stricken, Code Sec. 432(i)(9) read as follows:

(9) PLAN SPONSOR.—In the case of a plan described under section 404(c), or a continuation of such a plan, the term "plan sponsor" means the bargaining parties described under paragraph (1).

• 2006, Pension Protection Act of 2006 (P.L. 109-280)

P.L. 109-280, §206, provides:

SEC. 206. SPECIAL RULE FOR CERTAIN BENEFITS FUNDED UNDER AN AGREEMENT APPROVED BY THE PENSION BENEFIT GUARANTY CORPORATION.

In the case of a multiemployer plan that is a party to an agreement that was approved by the Pension Benefit Guaranty Corporation prior to June 30, 2005, and that—

(1) increases benefits, and

(2) provides for special withdrawal liability rules under section 4203(f) of the Employee Retirement Income Security Act of 1974 (29 U.S.C. 1383),

the amendments made by sections 201, 202, 211, and 212 of this Act shall not apply to the benefit increases under any plan amendment adopted prior to June 30, 2005, that are funded pursuant to such agreement if the plan is funded in compliance with such agreement (and any amendments thereto).

P.L. 109-280, §212(a):

Amended subpart A of part III of subchapter D of chapter 1, as amended by this Act, by inserting after Code Sec. 431 a new Code Sec. 432. **Effective** generally with respect to plan years beginning after 2007. For special rules, see Act Sec. 212(e)(2)-(3), below.

P.L. 109-280, §212(e)(2)-(3) [as amended by P.L. 110-458, §102(b)(3)(C)], provides:

(2) SPECIAL RULE FOR CERTAIN NOTICES.—In any case in which a plan's actuary certifies that it is reasonably expected that a multiemployer plan will be in critical status under section 432(b)(3) of the Internal Revenue Code of 1986, as added by this section, with respect to the first plan year beginning after 2007, the notice required under subparagraph (D) of such section may be provided at any time after the date of enactment, so long as it is provided on or before the last date for providing the notice under such subparagraph.

(3) SPECIAL RULE FOR CERTAIN RESTORED BENEFITS.—In the case of a multiemployer plan—

(A) with respect to which benefits were reduced pursuant to a plan amendment adopted on or after January 1, 2002, and before June 30, 2005, and

(B) which, pursuant to the plan document, the trust agreement, or a formal written communication from the plan sponsor to participants provided before June 30, 2005, provided for the restoration of such benefits,

the amendments made by this section shall not apply to such benefit restorations to the extent that any restriction on the providing or accrual of such benefits would otherwise apply by reason of such amendments.

P.L. 109-280, §221(c), provides:

(c) SUNSET.—

(1) IN GENERAL.—Except as provided in this subsection, notwithstanding any other provision of this Act, the provi-

sions of, and the amendments made by, sections 201(b), 202, and 212 shall not apply to plan years beginning after December 31, 2014.

(2) FUNDING IMPROVEMENT AND REHABILITATION PLANS.—If a plan is operating under a funding improvement or rehabilitation plan under section 305 of such Act or 432 of such Code for its last year beginning before January 1, 2015, such plan shall continue to operate under such funding improvement or rehabilitation plan during any period after December 31, 2014, such funding improvement or rehabilitation plan is in effect and all provisions of such Act or Code relating to the operation of such funding improvement or rehabilitation plan shall continue in effect during such period.

Subpart B—Benefit Limitations Under Single-Employer Plans

[Sec. 436]

SEC. 436. FUNDING-BASED LIMITS ON BENEFITS AND BENEFIT ACCRUALS UNDER SINGLE-EMPLOYER PLANS.

[Sec. 436(a)]

(a) GENERAL RULE.—For purposes of section 401(a)(29), a defined benefit plan which is a single-employer plan shall be treated as meeting the requirements of this section if the plan meets the requirements of subsections (b), (c), (d), and (e).

[Sec. 436(b)]

(b) FUNDING-BASED LIMITATION ON SHUTDOWN BENEFITS AND OTHER UNPREDICTABLE CONTINGENT EVENT BENEFITS UNDER SINGLE-EMPLOYER PLANS.—

(1) IN GENERAL.—If a participant of a defined benefit plan which is a single-employer plan is entitled to an unpredictable contingent event benefit payable with respect to any event occurring during any plan year, the plan shall provide that such benefit may not be provided if the adjusted funding target attainment percentage for such plan year—

(A) is less than 60 percent, or

(B) would be less than 60 percent taking into account such occurrence.

(2) EXEMPTION.—Paragraph (1) shall cease to apply with respect to any plan year, effective as of the first day of the plan year, upon payment by the plan sponsor of a contribution (in addition to any minimum required contribution under section 430) equal to—

(A) in the case of paragraph (1)(A), the amount of the increase in the funding target of the plan (under section 430) for the plan year attributable to the occurrence referred to in paragraph (1), and

(B) in the case of paragraph (1)(B), the amount sufficient to result in an adjusted funding target attainment percentage of 60 percent.

(3) UNPREDICTABLE CONTINGENT EVENT BENEFIT.—For purposes of this subsection, the term "unpredictable contingent event benefit" means any benefit payable solely by reason of—

(A) a plant shutdown (or similar event, as determined by the Secretary), or

(B) an event other than the attainment of any age, performance of any service, receipt or derivation of any compensation, or occurrence of death or disability.

Amendments

• 2008, Worker, Retiree, and Employer Recovery Act of 2008 (P.L. 110-458)

P.L. 110-458, §101(c)(2)(A)(i)-(ii):

Amended Code Sec. 436(b)(2) by striking "section 303" and inserting "section 430" in the matter preceding subparagraph (A), and by striking "a funding" and inserting "an adjusted funding" in subparagraph (B). **Effective** as if included in the provision of the 2006 Act to which the amendment relates [**effective** generally for plan years beginning after 12-31-2007.—CCH].

P.L. 110-458, §101(c)(2)(B)(i)-(ii):

Amended Code Sec. 436(b)(3) by inserting "BENEFIT" after "EVENT" in the heading, and by striking "any event" in subparagraph (B) and inserting "an event". **Effective** as if included in the provision of the 2006 Act to which the amendment relates [**effective** generally for plan years beginning after 12-31-2007.—CCH].

[Sec. 436(c)]

(c) LIMITATIONS ON PLAN AMENDMENTS INCREASING LIABILITY FOR BENEFITS.—

(1) IN GENERAL.—No amendment to a defined benefit plan which is a single-employer plan which has the effect of increasing liabilities of the plan by reason of increases in benefits, establishment of new benefits, changing the rate of benefit accrual, or changing the rate at which benefits become nonforfeitable may take effect during any plan year if the adjusted funding target attainment percentage for such plan year is—

(A) less than 80 percent, or

(B) would be less than 80 percent taking into account such amendment.

(2) EXEMPTION.—Paragraph (1) shall cease to apply with respect to any plan year, effective as of the first day of the plan year (or if later, the effective date of the amendment), upon payment by the plan sponsor of a contribution (in addition to any minimum required contribution under section 430) equal to—

(A) in the case of paragraph (1)(A), the amount of the increase in the funding target of the plan (under section 430) for the plan year attributable to the amendment, and

(B) in the case of paragraph (1)(B), the amount sufficient to result in an adjusted funding target attainment percentage of 80 percent.

(3) EXCEPTION FOR CERTAIN BENEFIT INCREASES.—Paragraph (1) shall not apply to any amendment which provides for an increase in benefits under a formula which is not based on a participant's compensation, but only if the rate of such increase is not in excess of the contemporaneous rate of increase in average wages of participants covered by the amendment.

[Sec. 436(d)]

(d) LIMITATIONS ON ACCELERATED BENEFIT DISTRIBUTIONS.—

(1) FUNDING PERCENTAGE LESS THAN 60 PERCENT.—A defined benefit plan which is a single-employer plan shall provide that, in any case in which the plan's adjusted funding target attainment percentage for a plan year is less than 60 percent, the plan may not pay any prohibited payment after the valuation date for the plan year.

(2) BANKRUPTCY.—A defined benefit plan which is a single-employer plan shall provide that, during any period in which the plan sponsor is a debtor in a case under title 11, United States Code, or similar Federal or State law, the plan may not pay any prohibited payment. The preceding sentence shall not apply on or after the date on which the enrolled actuary of the plan certifies that the adjusted funding target attainment percentage of such plan is not less than 100 percent.

(3) LIMITED PAYMENT IF PERCENTAGE AT LEAST 60 PERCENT BUT LESS THAN 80 PERCENT.—

(A) IN GENERAL.—A defined benefit plan which is a single-employer plan shall provide that, in any case in which the plan's adjusted funding target attainment percentage for a plan year is 60 percent or greater but less than 80 percent, the plan may not pay any prohibited payment after the valuation date for the plan year to the extent the amount of the payment exceeds the lesser of—

(i) 50 percent of the amount of the payment which could be made without regard to this section, or

(ii) the present value (determined under guidance prescribed by the Pension Benefit Guaranty Corporation, using the interest and mortality assumptions under section 417(e)) of the maximum guarantee with respect to the participant under section 4022 of the Employee Retirement Income Security Act of 1974.

(B) ONE-TIME APPLICATION.—

(i) IN GENERAL.—The plan shall also provide that only 1 prohibited payment meeting the requirements of subparagraph (A) may be made with respect to any participant during any period of consecutive plan years to which the limitations under either paragraph (1) or (2) or this paragraph applies.

(ii) TREATMENT OF BENEFICIARIES.—For purposes of this subparagraph, a participant and any beneficiary on his behalf (including an alternate payee, as defined in section 414(p)(8)) shall be treated as 1 participant. If the accrued benefit of a participant is allocated to such an alternate payee and 1 or more other persons, the amount under subparagraph (A) shall be allocated among such persons in the same manner as the accrued benefit is allocated unless the qualified domestic relations order (as defined in section 414(p)(1)(A)) provides otherwise.

(4) EXCEPTION.—This subsection shall not apply to any plan for any plan year if the terms of such plan (as in effect for the period beginning on September 1, 2005, and ending with such plan year) provide for no benefit accruals with respect to any participant during such period.

(5) PROHIBITED PAYMENT.—For purpose of this subsection, the term "prohibited payment" means—

(A) any payment, in excess of the monthly amount paid under a single life annuity (plus any social security supplements described in the last sentence of section 411(a)(9)), to a participant or beneficiary whose annuity starting date (as defined in section 417(f)(2)) occurs during any period a limitation under paragraph (1) or (2) is in effect,

(B) any payment for the purchase of an irrevocable commitment from an insurer to pay benefits, and

(C) any other payment specified by the Secretary by regulations.

Such term shall not include the payment of a benefit which under section 411(a)(11) may be immediately distributed without the consent of the participant.

Amendments

• 2008, Worker, Retiree, and Employer Recovery Act of 2008 (P.L. 110-458)

P.L. 110-458, §101(c)(2)(C):

Amended Code Sec. 436(d)(5) by adding at the end a new flush sentence. **Effective** as if included in the provision of the 2006 Act to which the amendment relates [**effective** generally for plan years beginning after 12-31-2007.—CCH].

[Sec. 436(e)]

(e) LIMITATION ON BENEFIT ACCRUALS FOR PLANS WITH SEVERE FUNDING SHORTFALLS.—

(1) IN GENERAL.—A defined benefit plan which is a single-employer plan shall provide that, in any case in which the plan's adjusted funding target attainment percentage for a plan year is less than 60 percent, benefit accruals under the plan shall cease as of the valuation date for the plan year.

(2) EXEMPTION.—Paragraph (1) shall cease to apply with respect to any plan year, effective as of the first day of the plan year, upon payment by the plan sponsor of a contribution (in addition to any minimum required contribution under section 430) equal to the amount sufficient to result in an adjusted funding target attainment percentage of 60 percent.

Amendments

• 2010, Preservation of Access to Care for Medicare Beneficiaries and Pension Relief Act of 2010 (P.L. 111-192)

P.L. 111-192, §203(b), provides:

(b) INTERACTION WITH WRERA RULE.—Section 203 of the Worker, Retiree, and Employer Recovery Act of 2008 shall apply to a plan for any plan year in lieu of the amendments made by this section applying to sections 206(g)(4) of the Employee Retirement Income Security Act of 1974 and 436(e) of the Internal Revenue Code of 1986 only to the extent that such section produces a higher adjusted funding target attainment percentage for such plan for such year.

• 2008, Worker, Retiree, and Employer Recovery Act of 2008 (P.L. 110-458)

P.L. 110-458, §203, provides:

SEC. 203. TEMPORARY MODIFICATION OF APPLICATION OF LIMITATION ON BENEFIT ACCRUALS.

In the case of the first plan year beginning during the period beginning on October 1, 2008, and ending on September 30, 2009, sections 206(g)(4)(A) of the Employee Retirement Income Security Act of 1974 (29 U.S.C. 1056(g)(4)(A)) and 436(e)(1) of the Internal Revenue Code of 1986 shall be applied by substituting the plan's adjusted funding target attainment percentage for the preceding plan year for such percentage for such plan year but only if the adjusted funding target attainment percentage for the preceding plan year is greater.

[Sec. 436(f)]

(f) RULES RELATING TO CONTRIBUTIONS REQUIRED TO AVOID BENEFIT LIMITATIONS.—

(1) SECURITY MAY BE PROVIDED.—

(A) IN GENERAL.—For purposes of this section, the adjusted funding target attainment percentage shall be determined by treating as an asset of the plan any security provided by a plan sponsor in a form meeting the requirements of subparagraph (B).

(B) FORM OF SECURITY.—The security required under subparagraph (A) shall consist of—

(i) a bond issued by a corporate surety company that is an acceptable surety for purposes of section 412 of the Employee Retirement Income Security Act of 1974,

(ii) cash, or United States obligations which mature in 3 years or less, held in escrow by a bank or similar financial institution, or

(iii) such other form of security as is satisfactory to the Secretary and the parties involved.

(C) ENFORCEMENT.—Any security provided under subparagraph (A) may be perfected and enforced at any time after the earlier of—

(i) the date on which the plan terminates,

(ii) if there is a failure to make a payment of the minimum required contribution for any plan year beginning after the security is provided, the due date for the payment under section 430(j), or

(iii) if the adjusted funding target attainment percentage is less than 60 percent for a consecutive period of 7 years, the valuation date for the last year in the period.

(D) RELEASE OF SECURITY.—The security shall be released (and any amounts thereunder shall be refunded together with any interest accrued thereon) at such time as the Secretary may prescribe in regulations, including regulations for partial releases of the security by reason of increases in the adjusted funding target attainment percentage.

(2) PREFUNDING BALANCE OR FUNDING STANDARD CARRYOVER BALANCE MAY NOT BE USED.—No prefunding balance or funding standard carryover balance under section 430(f) may be used under subsection (b), (c), or (e) to satisfy any payment an employer may make under any such subsection to avoid or terminate the application of any limitation under such subsection.

(3) DEEMED REDUCTION OF FUNDING BALANCES.—

(A) IN GENERAL.—Subject to subparagraph (C), in any case in which a benefit limitation under subsection (b), (c), (d), or (e) would (but for this subparagraph and determined without regard to subsection (b)(2), (c)(2), or (e)(2)) apply to such plan for the plan year, the plan sponsor of such plan shall be treated for purposes of this title as having made an election under section 430(f) to reduce the prefunding balance or funding standard carryover balance by such amount as is necessary for such benefit limitation to not apply to the plan for such plan year.

(B) EXCEPTION FOR INSUFFICIENT FUNDING BALANCES.—Subparagraph (A) shall not apply with respect to a benefit limitation for any plan year if the application of subparagraph (A) would not result in the benefit limitation not applying for such plan year.

(C) RESTRICTIONS OF CERTAIN RULES TO COLLECTIVELY BARGAINED PLANS.—With respect to any benefit limitation under subsection (b), (c), or (e), subparagraph (A) shall only apply in the case of a plan maintained pursuant to 1 or more collective bargaining agreements between employee representatives and 1 or more employers.

Amendments

• 2008, Worker, Retiree, and Employer Recovery Act of 2008 (P.L. 110-458)

P.L. 110-458, §101(c)(2)(D)(i)-(ii):

Amended Code Sec. 436(f) by inserting "adjusted" before "funding" in paragraph (1)(D), and by striking "prefunding balance under section 430(f) or funding standard carryover balance" in paragraph (2) and inserting "prefunding balance or funding standard carryover balance under section 430(f)". **Effective** as if included in the provision of the 2006 Act to which the amendment relates [**effective** generally for plan years beginning after 12-31-2007.—CCH].

[Sec. 436(g)]

(g) NEW PLANS.—Subsections (b), (c), and (e) shall not apply to a plan for the first 5 plan years of the plan. For purposes of this subsection, the reference in this subsection to a plan shall include a reference to any predecessor plan.

[Sec. 436(h)]

(h) PRESUMED UNDERFUNDING FOR PURPOSES OF BENEFIT LIMITATIONS.—

(1) PRESUMPTION OF CONTINUED UNDERFUNDING.—In any case in which a benefit limitation under subsection (b), (c), (d), or (e) has been applied to a plan with respect to the plan year preceding the current plan year, the adjusted funding target attainment percentage of the plan for the current plan year shall be presumed to be equal to the adjusted funding target attainment percentage of the plan for the preceding plan year until the enrolled actuary of the plan certifies the actual adjusted funding target attainment percentage of the plan for the current plan year.

(2) PRESUMPTION OF UNDERFUNDING AFTER 10TH MONTH.—In any case in which no certification of the adjusted funding target attainment percentage for the current plan year is made with respect to the plan before the first day of the 10th month of such year, for purposes of subsections (b), (c), (d), and (e), such first day shall be deemed, for purposes of such subsection, to be the valuation date of the plan for the current plan year and the plan's adjusted funding target attainment percentage shall be conclusively presumed to be less than 60 percent as of such first day.

(3) PRESUMPTION OF UNDERFUNDING AFTER 4TH MONTH FOR NEARLY UNDERFUNDED PLANS.—In any case in which—

(A) a benefit limitation under subsection (b), (c), (d), or (e) did not apply to a plan with respect to the plan year preceding the current plan year, but the adjusted funding target attainment percentage of the plan for such preceding plan year was not more than 10 percentage points greater than the percentage which would have caused such subsection to apply to the plan with respect to such preceding plan year, and

(B) as of the first day of the 4th month of the current plan year, the enrolled actuary of the plan has not certified the actual adjusted funding target attainment percentage of the plan for the current plan year,

until the enrolled actuary so certifies, such first day shall be deemed, for purposes of such subsection, to be the valuation date of the plan for the current plan year and the adjusted funding target attainment percentage of the plan as of such first day shall, for purposes of such subsection, be presumed to be equal.to 10 percentage points less than the adjusted funding target attainment percentage of the plan for such preceding plan year.

[Sec. 436(i)]

(i) TREATMENT OF PLAN AS OF CLOSE OF PROHIBITED OR CESSATION PERIOD.—For purposes of applying this title—

(1) OPERATION OF PLAN AFTER PERIOD.—Unless the plan provides otherwise, payments and accruals will resume effective as of the day following the close of the period for which any limitation of payment or accrual of benefits under subsection (d) or (e) applies.

(2) TREATMENT OF AFFECTED BENEFITS.—Nothing in this subsection shall be construed as affecting the plan's treatment of benefits which would have been paid or accrued but for this section.

[Sec. 436(j)]

(j) TERMS RELATING TO FUNDING TARGET ATTAINMENT PERCENTAGE.—For purposes of this section—

(1) IN GENERAL.—The term "funding target attainment percentage" has the same meaning given such term by section 430(d)(2).

(2) ADJUSTED FUNDING TARGET ATTAINMENT PERCENTAGE.—The term "adjusted funding target attainment percentage" means the funding target attainment percentage which is determined under paragraph (1) by increasing each of the amounts under subparagraphs (A) and (B) of section 430(d)(2) by the aggregate amount of purchases of annuities for employees other than highly compensated employees (as defined in section 414(q)) which were made by the plan during the preceding 2 plan years.

(3) APPLICATION TO PLANS WHICH ARE FULLY FUNDED WITHOUT REGARD TO REDUCTIONS FOR FUNDING BALANCES.—

(A) IN GENERAL.—In the case of a plan for any plan year, if the funding target attainment percentage is 100 percent or more (determined without regard to the reduction in the value of assets under section 430(f)(4)), the funding target attainment percentage for purposes of paragraphs (1) and (2) shall be determined without regard to such reduction.

(B) TRANSITION RULE.—Subparagraph (A) shall be applied to plan years beginning after 2007 and before 2011 by substituting for "100 percent" the applicable percentage determined in accordance with the following table:

In the case of a plan year beginning in calendar year:	The applicable percentage is
2008	92
2009	94
2010	96 .

(C) LIMITATION.—Subparagraph (B) shall not apply with respect to any plan year beginning after 2008 unless the funding target attainment percentage (determined without regard to the reduction in the value of assets under section 430(f)(4)) of the plan for each preceding plan year beginning after 2007 was not less than the applicable percentage with respect to such preceding plan year determined under subparagraph (B).

(3)[(4)] SPECIAL RULE FOR CERTAIN YEARS.—Solely for purposes of any applicable provision—

(A) IN GENERAL.—For plan years beginning on or after October 1, 2008, and before October 1, 2010, the adjusted funding target attainment percentage of a plan shall be the greater of—

(i) such percentage, as determined without regard to this paragraph, or

(ii) the adjusted funding target attainment percentage for such plan for the plan year beginning after October 1, 2007, and before October 1, 2008, as determined under rules prescribed by the Secretary.

(B) SPECIAL RULE.—In the case of a plan for which the valuation date is not the first day of the plan year—

(i) subparagraph (A) shall apply to plan years beginning after December 31, 2007, and before January 1, 2010, and

(ii) subparagraph (A)(ii) shall apply based on the last plan year beginning before November 1, 2007, as determined under rules prescribed by the Secretary.

(C) APPLICABLE PROVISION.—For purposes of this paragraph, the term "applicable provision" means—

(i) subsection (d), but only for purposes of applying such paragraph to a payment which, as determined under rules prescribed by the Secretary, is a payment under a social security leveling option which accelerates payments under the plan before, and reduces payments after, a participant starts receiving social security benefits in order to provide substantially similar aggregate payments both before and after such benefits are received, and

(ii) subsection (e).

Amendments

• 2010, Preservation of Access to Care for Medicare Beneficiaries and Pension Relief Act of 2010 (P.L. 111-192)

P.L. 111-192, §203(a)(2):

Amended Code Sec. 436(j) by adding at the end a new paragraph (3)[(4)]. **Effective** generally for plan years beginning on or after 10-1-2008. For a special rule, see Act Sec. 203(c)(2), below.

P.L. 111-192, §203(b), provides:

(b) INTERACTION WITH WRERA RULE.—Section 203 of the Worker, Retiree, and Employer Recovery Act of 2008 shall apply to a plan for any plan year in lieu of the amendments made by this section applying to sections 206(g)(4) of the Employee Retirement Income Security Act of 1974 and 436(e) of the Internal Revenue Code of 1986 only to the extent that such section produces a higher adjusted funding target attainment percentage for such plan for such year.

P.L. 111-192, §203(c)(2), provides:

(2) SPECIAL RULE.—In the case of a plan for which the valuation date is not the first day of the plan year, the amendments made by this section shall apply to plan years beginning after December 31, 2007.

• 2008, Worker, Retiree, and Employer Recovery Act of 2008 (P.L. 110-458)

P.L. 110-458, §101(c)(2)(E)(i)-(ii):

Amended Code Sec. 436(j)(3) in subparagraph (A) by striking "without regard to this paragraph and" following "(determined", by striking "section 430(f)(4)(A)" and inserting "section 430(f)(4)", and by striking "paragraph (1)" and inserting "paragraphs (1) and (2)", and in subparagraph (C) by striking "without regard to this paragraph" and inserting "without regard to the reduction in the value of assets under section 430(f)(4)", and by inserting "beginning" before "after" each place it appears. **Effective** as if included in the provision of the 2006 Act to which the amendment relates [**effective** generally for plan years beginning after 12-31-2007.—CCH].

[Sec. 436(k)]

(k) SECRETARIAL AUTHORITY FOR PLANS WITH ALTERNATE VALUATION DATE.—In the case of a plan which has designated a valuation date other than the first day of the plan year, the Secretary may prescribe rules for the application of this section which are necessary to reflect the alternate valuation date.

Amendments

• 2008, Worker, Retiree, and Employer Recovery Act of 2008 (P.L. 110-458)

P.L. 110-458, §101(c)(2)(F):

Amended Code Sec. 436 by redesignating subsection (k) as subsection (m) and by inserting after subsection (j) new subsections (k)-(l). **Effective** as if included in the provision of the 2006 Act to which the amendment relates [**effective** generally for plan years beginning after 12-31-2007.—CCH].

[Sec. 436(l)]

(l) SINGLE-EMPLOYER PLAN.—For purposes of this section, the term "single-employer plan" means a plan which is not a multiemployer plan.

Amendments

• 2008, Worker, Retiree, and Employer Recovery Act of 2008 (P.L. 110-458)

P.L. 110-458, §101(c)(2)(F):

Amended Code Sec. 436 by redesignating subsection (k) as subsection (m) and by inserting after subsection (j) new subsections (k)-(l). **Effective** as if included in the provision of the 2006 Act to which the amendment relates [**effective** generally for plan years beginning after 12-31-2007.—CCH].

[Sec. 436(m)]

(m) SPECIAL RULE FOR 2008.—For purposes of this section, in the case of plan years beginning in 2008, the funding target attainment percentage for the preceding plan year may be determined using such methods of estimation as the Secretary may provide.

Amendments

• 2008, Worker, Retiree, and Employer Recovery Act of 2008 (P.L. 110-458)

P.L. 110-458, §101(c)(2)(F):

Amended Code Sec. 436 by redesignating subsection (k) as subsection (m). **Effective** as if included in the provision of the 2006 Act to which the amendment relates [**effective** generally for plan years beginning after 12-31-2007.—CCH].

• 2006, Pension Protection Act of 2006 (P.L. 109-280)

P.L. 109-280, §113(a)(1)(B):

Amended part III of subchapter D of chapter 1 by adding at the end a new subpart B (Code Sec. 436). **Effective** generally for plan years beginning after 12-31-2007. For a special rule, see Act Sec. 113(b)(2), below.

P.L. 109-280, §113(b)(2) [as amended by P.L. 110-458], provides:

(2) COLLECTIVE BARGAINING EXCEPTION.—In the case of a plan maintained pursuant to 1 or more collective bargaining agreements between employee representatives and 1 or more employers ratified before January 1, 2008, the amendments made by this section shall not apply to plan years beginning before the earlier of—

(A) the later of—

(i) the date on which the last collective bargaining agreement relating to the plan terminates (determined without regard to any extension thereof agreed to after the date of the enactment of this Act), or

(ii) the first day of the first plan year to which the amendments made by this section would (but for this paragraph) apply, or

(B) January 1, 2010.

For purposes of subparagraph (A)(i), any plan amendment made pursuant to a collective bargaining agreement relating to the plan which amends the plan solely to conform to any requirement added by this section shall not be treated as a termination of such collective bargaining agreement.

Subchapter E—Accounting Periods and Methods of Accounting

PART I—ACCOUNTING PERIODS

[Sec. 441]

SEC. 441. PERIOD FOR COMPUTATION OF TAXABLE INCOME.

[Sec. 441(a)]

(a) COMPUTATION OF TAXABLE INCOME.—Taxable income shall be computed on the basis of the taxpayer's taxable year.

[Sec. 441(b)]

(b) TAXABLE YEAR.—For purposes of this subtitle, the term "taxable year" means—

(1) the taxpayer's annual accounting period, if it is a calendar year or a fiscal year;

(2) the calendar year, if subsection (g) applies;

(3) the period for which the return is made, if a return is made for a period of less than 12 months; or

(4) in the case of a DISC filing a return for a period of at least 12 months, the period determined under subsection (h).

Amendments

• 2007, Tax Technical Corrections Act of 2007 (P.L. 110-172)

P.L. 110-172, §11(g)(7)(A):

Amended Code Sec. 441(b)(4) by striking "FSC or" following "in the case of a". **Effective** 12-29-2007.

• 1984, Deficit Reduction Act of 1984 (P.L. 98-369)

P.L. 98-369, §803(a):

Amended Code Sec. 441(b) by striking out "or" at the end of paragraph (2), by striking out the period at the end of paragraph (3) and inserting in lieu thereof "; or", and by adding new paragraph (4). **Effective** for tax years beginning after 12-31-84 [**effective** date changed by P.L. 99-514, §1876(i)]. For special and transitional rules, see Act Sec. 805(a)(2)-(b) under the amendment notes for Code Sec. 924.

[Sec. 441(c)]

(c) ANNUAL ACCOUNTING PERIOD.—For purposes of this subtitle, the term "annual accounting period" means the annual period on the basis of which the taxpayer regularly computes his income in keeping his books.

[Sec. 441(d)]

(d) CALENDAR YEAR.—For purposes of this subtitle, the term "calendar year" means a period of 12 months ending on December 31.

[Sec. 441(e)]

(e) FISCAL YEAR.—For purposes of this subtitle, the term "fiscal year" means a period of 12 months ending on the last day of any month other than December. In the case of any taxpayer who has made the election provided by subsection (f), the term means the annual period (varying from 52 to 53 weeks) so elected.

[Sec. 441(f)]

(f) ELECTION OF YEAR CONSISTING OF 52-53 WEEKS.—

(1) GENERAL RULE.—A taxpayer who, in keeping his books, regularly computes his income on the basis of an annual period which varies from 52 to 53 weeks and ends always on the same day of the week and ends always—

(A) on whatever date such same day of the week last occurs in a calendar month, or

(B) on whatever date such same day of the week falls which is nearest to the last day of a calendar month,

may (in accordance with the regulations prescribed under paragraph (3)) elect to compute his taxable income for purposes of this subtitle on the basis of such annual period. This paragraph shall apply to taxable years ending after the date of the enactment of this title.

(2) SPECIAL RULES FOR 52-53-WEEK YEAR.—

(A) EFFECTIVE DATES.—In any case in which the effective date or the applicability of any provision of this title is expressed in terms of taxable years beginning, including, or ending with reference to a specified date which is the first or last day of a month, a taxable year described in paragraph (1) shall (except for purposes of the computation under section 15) be treated—

(i) as beginning with the first day of the calendar month beginning nearest to the first day of such taxable year, or

(ii) as ending with the last day of the calendar month ending nearest to the last day of such taxable year,

as the case may be.

(B) CHANGE IN ACCOUNTING PERIOD.—In the case of a change from or to a taxable year described in paragraph (1)—

(i) if such change results in a short period (within the meaning of section 443) of 359 days or more, or of less than 7 days, section 443(b) (relating to alternative tax computation) shall not apply;

(ii) if such change results in a short period of less than 7 days, such short period shall, for purposes of this subtitle, be added to and deemed a part of the following taxable year; and

(iii) if such change results in a short period to which subsection (b) of section 443 applies, the taxable income for such short period shall be placed on an annual basis for purposes of such subsection by multiplying the gross income for such short period (minus the deductions allowed by this chapter for the short period, but only the adjusted amount of the deductions for personal exemptions as described in section 443(c)) by 365, by dividing the result by the number of days in the short period, and the tax shall be the same part of the tax computed on the annual basis as the number of days in the short period is of 365 days.

(3) SPECIAL RULE FOR PARTNERSHIPS, S CORPORATIONS, AND PERSONAL SERVICE CORPORATIONS.—The Secretary may by regulation provide terms and conditions for the application of this subsection to a partnership, S corporation, or personal service corporation (within the meaning of section 441(i)(2)).

(4) REGULATIONS.—The Secretary shall prescribe such regulations as he deems necessary for the application of this subsection.

Amendments

• 1986, Tax Reform Act of 1986 (P.L. 99-514)

P.L. 99-514, §104(b)(6):

Amended Code Sec. 441(f)(2)(B)(iii) by striking out "and by adding the zero bracket amount,". **Effective** for tax years beginning after 12-31-86. Prior to amendment, Code Sec. 441(f)(2)(B)(iii) read as follows:

(iii) if such change results in a short period to which subsection (b) of section 443 applies, the taxable income for such short period shall be placed on an annual basis for purposes of such subsection by multiplying the gross income for such short period (minus the deductions allowed by this chapter for the short period, but only the adjusted amount of the deductions for personal exemptions as described in section 443(c)) by 365, by dividing the result by the number of days in the short period, and by adding the zero bracket amount, and the tax shall be the same part of the tax computed on the annual basis as the number of days in the short period is of 365 days.

P.L. 99-514, §806(d):

Amended Code Sec. 441(f)(3)-(4) by redesignating paragraph (3) as paragraph (4) and by inserting after paragraph (2) new paragraph (3). **Effective**, generally, for tax years beginning after 12-31-86. However, for a special rule, see Act Sec. 806(e)(2), as amended by P.L. 100-647, §1008(e)(7)-(8), below.

P.L. 99-514, §806(e)(2), as amended by P.L. 100-647, §1008(e)(7)-(8), provides:

(2) CHANGE IN ACCOUNTING PERIOD.—In the case of any partnership, S corporation, or personal service corporation required by the amendments made by this section to change its accounting period for the taxpayer's first taxable year beginning after December 31, 1986—

(A) such change shall be treated as initiated by the partnership, S corporation, or personal service corporation,

(B) such change shall be treated as having been made with the consent of the Secretary, and

(C) with respect to any partner or shareholder of an S corporation which is required to include the items from more than 1 taxable year of the partnership or S corporation in any 1 taxable year, income in excess of expenses of such partnership or corporation for the short taxable year required by such amendments shall be taken into account ratably in each of the first 4 taxable years beginning after December 31, 1986, unless such partner or shareholder elects to include all such income in the partner's or shareholder's taxable year with or within which the partnership's or S corporation's short taxable year ends.

Subparagraph (C) shall apply to a shareholder of an S corporation only if such corporation was an S corporation for a taxable year beginning in 1986.

• 1984, Deficit Reduction Act of 1984 (P.L. 98-369)

P.L. 98-369, §474(b)(2):

Amended Code Sec. 441(f)(2)(A) by striking out "21" and inserting in lieu thereof "15". **Effective** for tax years beginning after 12-31-83, and to carrybacks from such years.

• 1977, Tax Reduction and Simplification Act of 1977 (P.L. 95-30)

P.L. 95-30, §102(b)(5):

Amended clause (iii) of Code Sec. 441(f)(2)(B). **Effective** for tax years beginning after 12-31-76. Prior to amendment, clause (iii) of Code Sec. 441(f)(2)(B) read as follows:

"(iii) if such change results in a short period to which subsection (b) of section 443 applies, the taxable income for such short period shall be placed on an annual basis for purposes of such subsection by multiplying such income by 365 and dividing the result by the number of days in the short period, and the tax shall be the same part of the tax computed on the annual basis as the number of days in the short period is of 365 days."

• 1976, Tax Reform Act of 1976 (P.L. 94-455)

P.L. 94-455 §1906(b)(13)(A):

Amended 1954 Code by substituting "Secretary" for "Secretary or his delegate" each place it appeared. **Effective** 2-1-77.

• 1964, Revenue Act of 1964 (P.L. 88-272)

P.L. 88-272, §235(c)(3):

Amended Sec. 441(f)(2)(A) by inserting ", including," immediately following the words "taxable years beginning". **Effective** for tax years ending after 12-31-63.

[Sec. 441(g)]

(g) NO BOOKS KEPT; NO ACCOUNTING PERIOD.—Except as provided in section 443 (relating to returns for periods of less than 12 months), the taxpayer's taxable year shall be the calendar year if—

(1) the taxpayer keeps no books;

(2) the taxpayer does not have an annual accounting period; or

(3) the taxpayer has an annual accounting period, but such period does not qualify as a fiscal year.

[Sec. 441(h)]

(h) TAXABLE YEAR OF DISC'S.—

(1) IN GENERAL.—For purposes of this subtitle, the taxable year of any DISC shall be the taxable year of that shareholder (or group of shareholders with the same 12-month taxable year) who has the highest percentage of voting power.

(2) SPECIAL RULE WHERE MORE THAN ONE SHAREHOLDER (OR GROUP) HAS HIGHEST PERCENTAGE.—If 2 or more shareholders (or groups) have the highest percentage of voting power under paragraph (1), the taxable year of the DISC shall be the same 12-month period as that of any such shareholder (or group).

(3) SUBSEQUENT CHANGES OF OWNERSHIP.—The Secretary shall prescribe regulations under which paragraphs (1) and (2) shall apply to a change of ownership of a corporation after the taxable year of the corporation has been determined under paragraph (1) or (2) only if such change is a substantial change of ownership.

(4) VOTING POWER DETERMINED.—For purposes of this subsection, voting power shall be determined on the basis of total combined voting power of all classes of stock of the corporation entitled to vote.

Amendments

• 2007, Tax Technical Corrections Act of 2007 (P.L. 110-172)

P.L. 110-172, §11(g)(7)(B)(i)-(ii):

Amended Code Sec. 441(h) by striking "FSC or" each place it appears, and by striking "FSC'S AND" in the heading thereof. **Effective** 12-29-2007. Prior to amendment, Code Sec. 441(h) read as follows:

(h) TAXABLE YEAR OF FSC'S AND DISC'S.—

(1) IN GENERAL.—For purposes of this subtitle, the taxable year of any FSC or DISC shall be the taxable year of that shareholder (or group of shareholders with the same 12-month taxable year) who has the highest percentage of voting power.

(2) SPECIAL RULE WHERE MORE THAN ONE SHAREHOLDER (OR GROUP) HAS HIGHEST PERCENTAGE.—If 2 or more shareholders (or groups) have the highest percentage of voting power under paragraph (1), the taxable year of the FSC or DISC shall be the same 12-month period as that of any such shareholder (or group).

(3) SUBSEQUENT CHANGES OF OWNERSHIP.—The Secretary shall prescribe regulations under which paragraphs (1) and (2) shall apply to a change of ownership of a corporation after the taxable year of the corporation has been determined under paragraph (1) or (2) only if such change is a substantial change of ownership.

(4) VOTING POWER DETERMINED.—For purposes of this subsection, voting power shall be determined on the basis of total combined voting power of all classes of stock of the corporation entitled to vote.

• 1984, Deficit Reduction Act of 1984 (P.L. 98-369)

P.L. 98-369, §803(b):

Amended Code Sec. 441 by adding at the end thereof new paragraph (h). **Effective** for tax years beginning after 12-31-84 [**effective** date changed by P.L. 99-514, §1876(i)]. For special and transitional rules, see Act Sec. 805(a)(2)-(b) under the amendment notes for Code Sec. 924.

[Sec. 441(i)]

(i) TAXABLE YEAR OF PERSONAL SERVICE CORPORATIONS.—

(1) IN GENERAL.—For purposes of this subtitle, the taxable year of any personal service corporation shall be the calendar year unless the corporation establishes, to the satisfaction of the Secretary, a business purpose for having a different period for its taxable year. For purposes of this paragraph, any deferral of income to shareholders shall not be treated as a business purpose.

(2) PERSONAL SERVICE CORPORATION.—For purposes of this subsection, the term "personal service corporation" has the meaning given such term by section 269A(b)(1), except that section 269A(b)(2) shall be applied—

(A) by substituting "any" for "more than 10 percent", and

(B) by substituting "any" for "50 percent or more in value" in section 318(a)(2)(C).

A corporation shall not be treated as a personal service corporation unless more than 10 percent of the stock (by value) in such corporation is held by employee-owners (within the meaning of section 269A(b)(2), as modified by the preceding sentence). If a corporation is a member of an affiliated group filing a consolidated return, all members of such group shall be taken into account in determining whether such corporation is a personal service corporation.

Amendments

• 1988, Technical and Miscellaneous Revenue Act of 1988 (P.L. 100-647)

P.L. 100-647, §1008(e)(4):

Amended Code Sec. 441(i)(2) by adding at the end thereof the last two sentences. **Effective** as if included in the provision of P.L. 99-514 to which it relates.

• 1986, Tax Reform Act of 1986 (P.L. 99-514)

P.L. 99-514, §806(c)(1):

Amended Code Sec. 441 by adding new subsection 441(i). **Effective**, generally, for tax years beginning after 12-31-86. However, for a special rule, see Act Sec. 806(e)(2) in the amendment notes to Code Sec. 441(f), above.

[Sec. 442]

SEC. 442. CHANGE OF ANNUAL ACCOUNTING PERIOD.

If a taxpayer changes his annual accounting period, the new accounting period shall become the taxpayer's taxable year only if the change is approved by the Secretary. For purposes of this subtitle, if a taxpayer to whom section 441(g) applies adopts an annual accounting period (as defined in section 441(c)) other than a calendar year, the taxpayer shall be treated as having changed his annual accounting period.

Amendments

• 1976, Tax Reform Act of 1976 (P.L. 94-455)

P.L. 94-455, §1906(b)(13)(A):

Amended 1954 Code by substituting "Secretary" for "Secretary of his delegate" each place it appeared. **Effective** 2-1-77.

[Sec. 443]

SEC. 443. RETURNS FOR A PERIOD OF LESS THAN 12 MONTHS.

[Sec. 443(a)]

(a) RETURNS FOR SHORT PERIOD.—A return for a period of less than 12 months (referred to in this section as "short period") shall be made under any of the following circumstances:

(1) CHANGE OF ANNUAL ACCOUNTING PERIOD.—When the taxpayer, with the approval of the Secretary, changes his annual accounting period. In such a case, the return shall be made for the

short period beginning on the day after the close of the former taxable year and ending at the close of the day before the day designated as the first day of the new taxable year.

(2) TAXPAYER NOT IN EXISTENCE FOR ENTIRE TAXABLE YEAR.—When the taxpayer is in existence during only part of what would otherwise be his taxable year.

Amendments

• 1976, Tax Reform Act of 1976 (P.L. 94-455)

P.L. 94-455, §1204(c)(2):

Repealed Code Sec. 443(a)(3). **Effective** with respect to action taken under section 6851, 6861, or 6862 of the 1954 Code where the notice and demand takes place after 2-28-77 [**effective** date amended by P.L. 94-528, §2(a)]. Prior to repeal, Code Sec. 443(a)(3) read as follows:

(3) TERMINATION OF TAXABLE YEAR FOR JEOPARDY.—When the Secretary or his delegate terminates the taxpayer's taxable year under section 6851 (relating to tax in jeopardy).

P.L. 94-455, §1906(b)(13)(A):

Amended the 1954 Code by substituting "Secretary" for "Secretary or his delegate" each place it appeared. **Effective** 2-1-77.

[Sec. 443(b)]

(b) COMPUTATION OF TAX ON CHANGE OF ANNUAL ACCOUNTING PERIOD.—

(1) GENERAL RULE.—If a return is made under paragraph (1) of subsection (a), the taxable income for the short period shall be placed on an annual basis by multiplying the modified taxable income for such short period by 12, dividing the result by the number of months in the short period. The tax shall be the same part of the tax computed on the annual basis as the number of months in the short period is of 12 months.

(2) EXCEPTION.—

(A) COMPUTATION BASED ON 12-MONTH PERIOD.—If the taxpayer applies for the benefits of this paragraph and establishes the amount of his taxable income for the 12-month period described in subparagraph (B), computed as if that period were a taxable year and under the law applicable to that year, then the tax for the short period, computed under paragraph (1), shall be reduced to the greater of the following:

(i) an amount which bears the same ratio to the tax computed on the taxable income for the 12-month period as the modified taxable income computed on the basis of the short period bears to the modified taxable income for the 12-month period; or

(ii) the tax computed on the modified taxable income for the short period.

The taxpayer (other than a taxpayer to whom subparagraph (B) (ii) applies) shall compute the tax and file his return without the application of this paragraph.

(B) 12-MONTH PERIOD.—The 12-month period referred to in subparagraph (A) shall be—

(i) the period of 12 months beginning on the first day of the short period, or

(ii) the period of 12 months ending at the close of the last day of the short period, if at the end of the 12 months referred to in clause (i) the taxpayer is not in existence or (if a corporation) has theretofore disposed of substantially all of its assets.

(C) APPLICATION FOR BENEFITS.—Application for the benefits of this paragraph shall be made in such manner and at such time as the regulations prescribed under subparagraph (D) may require; except that the time so prescribed shall not be later than the time (including extensions) for filing the return for the first taxable year which ends on or after the day which is 12 months after the first day of the short period. Such application, in case the return was filed without regard to this paragraph, shall be considered a claim for credit or refund with respect to the amount by which the tax is reduced under this paragraph.

(D) REGULATIONS.—The Secretary shall prescribe such regulations as he deems necessary for the application of this paragraph.

(3) MODIFIED TAXABLE INCOME DEFINED.—For purposes of this subsection the term "modified taxable income" means, with respect to any period, the gross income for such period minus the deductions allowed by this chapter for such period (but, in the case of a short period, only the adjusted amount of the deductions for personal exemptions).

Amendments

• 1986, Tax Reform Act of 1986 (P.L. 99-514)

P.L. 99-514, §104(b)(7)(A):

Amended Code Sec. 443(b)(1) by striking out ", and adding the zero bracket amount". **Effective** for tax years beginning after 12-31-86. Prior to amendment, Code Sec. 443(b)(1) read as follows:

(1) GENERAL RULE.—If a return is made under paragraph (1) of subsection (a), the taxable income for the short period shall be placed on an annual basis by multiplying the modified taxable income for such short period by 12, dividing the result by the number of months in the short period, and adding the zero bracket amount. The tax shall be the same part of the tax computed on the annual basis as the number of months in the short period is of 12 months.

P.L. 99-514, §104(b)(7)(B):

Amended Code Sec. 443(b)(2)(A)(ii). **Effective** for tax years beginning after 12-31-86. Prior to amendment, Code Sec. 443(b)(2)(A)(ii) read as follows:

(ii) the tax computed on the sum of the modified taxable income for the short period plus the zero bracket amounts.

• 1978, Revenue Act of 1978 (P.L. 95-600)

P.L. 95-600, §703(o)(1):

Amended Code Sec. 443(b)(2)(A) by striking out "taxable income" the second and third places it appeared in clause (i) and inserting in lieu thereof "modified taxable income", and by amending clause (ii). **Effective** for tax years beginning after 12-31-76. Prior to amendment, Code Sec. 443(b)(2)(A)(ii) read as follows:

"(ii) the tax computed on the taxable income for the short period without placing the taxable income on an annual basis."

P.L. 95-600, §703(o)(2):

Amended Code Sec. 443(b)(1). **Effective** for tax years beginning after 12-31-76. Prior to amendment, Code Sec. 443(b)(1) read as follows:

"(1) GENERAL RULE.—If a return is made under paragraph (1) of subsection (a), the taxable income for the short period shall be placed on an annual basis by multiplying the gross income for such short period (minus the deductions allowed by this chapter for the short period, but only the adjusted amount of the deductions for personal exemptions) by 12, dividing the result by the number of months in the short period, and adding the zero bracket amount. The tax shall be the same part of the tax computed on the annual basis as the number of months in the short period is of 12 months."

P.L. 95-600, §703(o)(3):

Added Code Sec. 443(b)(3). **Effective** for tax years beginning after 12-31-76.

• 1977, Tax Reduction and Simplification Act of 1977 (P.L. 95-30)

P.L. 95-30, §102(b)(6):

Amended paragraph (1) of Code Sec. 443(b). **Effective** for tax years beginning after 12-31-76. Prior to amendment, paragraph (1) of Sec. 443(b) read as follows:

"(1) GENERAL RULE.—If a return is made under paragraph (1) of subsection (a), the taxable income for the short period shall be placed on an annual basis by multiplying such income by 12 and dividing the result by the number of months in the short period. The tax shall be the same part of the tax computed on the annual basis as the number of months in the short period is of 12 months."

• 1976, Tax Reform Act of 1976 (P.L. 94-455)

P.L. 94-455, §1906(b)(13)(A):

Amended 1954 Code by substituting "Secretary" for "Secretary or his delegate" each place it appeared. **Effective** 2-1-77.

[Sec. 443(c)]

(c) ADJUSTMENT IN DEDUCTION FOR PERSONAL EXEMPTION.—In the case of a taxpayer other than a corporation, if a return is made for a short period by reason of subsection (a)(1) and if the tax is not computed under subsection (b)(2), then the exemptions allowed as a deduction under section 151 (and any deduction in lieu thereof) shall be reduced to amounts which bear the same ratio to the full exemptions as the number of months in the short period bears to 12.

[Sec. 443(d)]

(d) ADJUSTMENT IN COMPUTING MINIMUM TAX AND TAX PREFERENCES.—If a return is made for a short period by reason of subsection (a)—

(1) the alternative minimum taxable income for the short period shall be placed on an annual basis by multiplying such amount by 12 and dividing the result by the number of months in the short period, and

(2) the amount computed under paragraph (1) of section 55(a) shall bear the same relation to the tax computed on the annual basis as the number of months in the short period bears to 12.

Amendments

• 1986, Tax Reform Act of 1986 (P.L. 99-514)

P.L. 99-514, §701(e)(3):

Amended Code Sec. 443(d). **Effective**, generally, for tax years beginning after 12-31-86. However, for special rules and exceptions, see Act Sec. 701(f)(2)-(7) following Code Sec. 56. Prior to amendment, Code Sec. 443(d) read as follows:

(d) ADJUSTMENT IN COMPUTING MINIMUM TAX FOR TAX PREFERENCES—If a return is made for a short period by reason of subsection (a), then—

(1) in the case of a taxpayer other than a corporation, the alternative minimum taxable income for the short period shall be placed on an annual basis by multiplying that amount by 12 and dividing the result by the number of months in the short period, and the amount computed under paragraph (1) of section 55(a) shall be the same part of the tax computed on the annual basis as the number of months in the short period is of 12 months; and

(2) the $10,000 amount specified in section 56 (relating to minimum tax for tax preferences), modified as provided by section 58, shall be reduced to the amount which bears the same ratio to such specified amount as the number of days in the short period bears to 365.

• 1980, Technical Corrections Act of 1979 (P.L. 96-222)

P.L. 96-222, §104(a)(4)(H)(iii):

Amended Code Sec. 443(d)(2) by deleting "in the case of a corporation," which preceded "the $10,000 amount". **Effective** for tax years beginning after 12-31-78.

• 1978, Revenue Act of 1978 (P.L. 95-600)

P.L. 95-600, §421(e)(2):

Amended Code Sec. 443(d). **Effective** for tax years beginning after 12-31-78. Prior to amendment, Code Sec. 443(d) read as follows:

"(d) ADJUSTMENT IN EXCLUSION FOR COMPUTING MINIMUM TAX FOR TAX PREFERENCES.—If a return is made for a short period by reason of subsection (a), then the $10,000 amount specified in section 56 (relating to minimum tax for tax preferences), modified as provided by section 58, shall be reduced to the amount which bears the same ratio to such specified amount as the number of days in the short period bears to 365."

• 1976, Tax Reform Act of 1976 (P.L. 94-455)

P.L. 94-455, §301(e):

Amended Code Sec. 443 by substituting "$10,000" for "$30,000". **Effective** for items of tax preference for tax years beginning after 12-31-75, except in the case of a taxpayer which is a financial institution to which section 585 or 593 of the 1954 Code applies, in which case **effective** for tax years beginning after 12-31-77.

P.L. 94-455, §301(f):

Provided that for purposes of Code Sec. 21 the amendments made by §301 shall not be treated as a change in a rate of tax.

• 1969, Tax Reform Act of 1969 (P.L. 91-172)

P.L. 91-172, §301(b)(6):

Added new subsection 443(d). **Effective** 1-1-70.

[Sec. 443(e)]

(e) CROSS REFERENCES.—

For inapplicability of subsection (b) in computing—

(1) Accumulated earnings tax, see section 536.

(2) Personal holding company tax, see section 546.

(3) The taxable income of a regulated investment company, see section 852(b)(2)(E).

(4) The taxable income of a real estate investment trust, see section 857(b)(2)(C).

For returns for a period of less than 12 months in the case of a debtor's election to terminate a taxable year, see section 1398(d)(2)(E).

Amendments

• 2004, American Jobs Creation Act of 2004 (P.L. 108-357)

P.L. 108-357, §413(c)(6):

Amended Code Sec. 443(e) by striking paragraph (3) and by redesignating paragraphs (4) and (5) as paragraphs (3) and (4), respectively. **Effective** for tax years of foreign corporations beginning after 12-31-2004, and for tax years of United States shareholders with or within which such tax years of foreign corporations end. Prior to being stricken, Code Sec. 443(e)(3) read as follows:

(3) Undistributed foreign personal holding company income, see section 557.

• 1983, Technical Corrections Act of 1982 (P.L. 97-448)

P.L. 97-448, §304(a):

Amended the last sentence of Code Sec. 443(e) by striking out "section 1398(d)(3)(E)" and inserting in lieu thereof "section 1398(d)(2)(E)". **Effective** as if included in the amendments made by §3 of P.L. 96-589.

• 1980, Bankruptcy Tax Act of 1980 (P.L. 96-589)

P.L. 96-589, §3(d):

Amended Code Sec. 443(e) by adding the last sentence. **Effective** for bankruptcy cases commencing on or after 3-25-81.

• 1976, Tax Reform Act of 1976 (P.L. 94-455)

P.L. 94-455, §1607(b)(1)(C):

Amended Code Sec. 443(e)(5) by substituting "857(b)(2)(C)" for "857(b)(2)(D)." **Effective** as indicated in Act Sec. 1608(c), below.

P.L. 94-455, §1608(c), provides:

(c) ALTERNATIVE TAX AND NET OPERATING LOSS.—The amendments made by sections 1606 and 1607 shall apply to taxable years ending after the date of the enactment of this Act, except that in the case of a taxpayer which has a net operating loss (as defined in section 172(c) of the Internal Revenue Code of 1954) for any taxable year ending after the date of enactment of this Act for which the provisions of part II of subchapter M of chapter I of subtitle A of such Code apply to such taxpayer, such loss shall not be a net operating loss carryback under section 172 of such Code to any taxable year ending on or before the date of enactment of this Act.

• 1969, Tax Reform Act of 1969 (P.L. 91-172)

P.L. 91-172, §301(b)(6):

Redesignated old subsection (d) as (e). **Effective** 1-1-70.

• 1960 (P.L. 86-779)

P.L. 86-779, §10(i):

Amended Code Sec. 443(d) by adding new paragraph (5). **Effective** 1-1-61.

[Sec. 444]

SEC. 444. ELECTION OF TAXABLE YEAR OTHER THAN REQUIRED TAXABLE YEAR.

[Sec. 444(a)]

(a) GENERAL RULE.—Except as otherwise provided in this section, a partnership, S corporation, or personal service corporation may elect to have a taxable year other than the required taxable year.

Amendments

• 1988, Technical and Miscellaneous Revenue Act of 1988 (P.L. 100-647)

P.L. 100-647, §2004(e)(1)(A):

Amended Code Sec. 444(a) by striking out "as provided in subsections (b) and (c)" and inserting in lieu thereof "as otherwise provided in this section". **Effective** as if included in the provision of P.L. 100-203 to which it relates.

[Sec. 444(b)]

(b) LIMITATIONS ON TAXABLE YEARS WHICH MAY BE ELECTED.—

(1) IN GENERAL.—Except as provided in paragraphs (2) and (3), an election may be made under subsection (a) only if the deferral period of the taxable year elected is not longer than 3 months.

(2) CHANGES IN TAXABLE YEAR.—Except as provided in paragraph (3), in the case of an entity changing a taxable year, an election may be made under subsection (a) only if the deferral period of the taxable year elected is not longer than the shorter of—

(A) 3 months, or

(B) the deferral period of the taxable year which is being changed.

(3) SPECIAL RULE FOR ENTITIES RETAINING 1986 TAXABLE YEARS.—In the case of an entity's 1st taxable year beginning after December 31, 1986, an entity may elect a taxable year under subsection (a) which is the same as the entity's last taxable year beginning in 1986.

(4) DEFERRAL PERIOD.—For purposes of this subsection, except as provided in regulations, the term "deferral period" means, with respect to any taxable year of the entity, the months between—

(A) the beginning of such year, and

(B) the close of the 1st required taxable year ending within such year.

Amendments

• 1988, Technical and Miscellaneous Revenue Act of 1988 (P.L. 100-647)

P.L. 100-647, §2004(e)(13):

Amended Code Sec. 444(b)(4) by striking out "the term" and inserting in lieu thereof "except as provided in regulations, the term". **Effective** as if included in the provision of P.L. 100-203 to which it relates.

[Sec. 444(c)]

(c) EFFECT OF ELECTION.—If an entity makes an election under subsection (a), then—

(1) in the case of a partnership or S corporation, such entity shall make the payments required by section 7519, and

(2) in the case of a personal service corporation, such corporation shall be subject to the deduction limitations of section 280H.

[Sec. 444(d)]

(d) ELECTIONS.—

(1) PERSON MAKING ELECTION.—An election under subsection (a) shall be made by the partnership, S corporation, or personal service corporation.

(2) PERIOD OF ELECTION.—

(A) IN GENERAL.—Any election under subsection (a) shall remain in effect until the partnership, S corporation, or personal service corporation changes its taxable year or otherwise terminates such election. Any change to a required taxable year may be made without the consent of the Secretary.

(B) NO FURTHER ELECTION.—If an election is terminated under subparagraph (A) or paragraph (3)(A), the partnership, S corporation, or personal service corporation may not make another election under subsection (a).

(3) TIERED STRUCTURES, ETC.—

(A) IN GENERAL.—Except as otherwise provided in this paragraph—

(i) no election may be under subsection (a) with respect to any entity which is part of a tiered structure, and

(ii) an election under subsection (a) with respect to any entity shall be terminated if such entity becomes part of a tiered structure.

(B) EXCEPTIONS FOR STRUCTURES CONSISTING OF CERTAIN ENTITIES WITH SAME TAXABLE YEAR.—Subparagraph (A) shall not apply to any tiered structure which consists only of partnerships or S corporations (or both) all of which have the same taxable year.

Amendments

• 1988, Technical and Miscellaneous Revenue Act of 1988 (P.L. 100-647)

P.L. 100-647, §2004(e)(1)(B):

Amended Code Sec. 444(d)(3). **Effective** as if included in the provision of P.L. 100-203 to which it relates. Prior to amendment, Code Sec. 444(d)(3) read as follows:

(3) TIERED STRUCTURES, ETC.—No election may be made under subsection (a) with respect to an entity which is part of a tiered structure other than a tiered structure comprised of 1 or more partnerships or S corporations all of which have the same taxable year.

P.L. 100-647, §2004(e)(1)(C):

Amended Code Sec. 444(d)(2)(B) by striking out "under subparagraph (A)" and inserting in lieu thereof "under subparagraph (A) or paragraph (3)(A)". **Effective** as if included in the provision of P.L. 100-203 to which it relates.

P.L. 100-647, §2004(e)(12):

Amended Code Sec. 444(d)(2)(A) by inserting "or otherwise terminates such election" before the period at the end of the first sentence thereof. **Effective** as if included in the provision of P.L. 100-203 to which it relates.

[Sec. 444(e)]

(e) REQUIRED TAXABLE YEAR.—For purposes of this section, the term "required taxable year" means the taxable year determined under section 706(b), 1378, or 441(i) without taking into account any taxable year which is allowable by reason of business purposes. Solely for purposes of the preceding sentence, sections 706(b), 1378, and 441(i) shall be treated as in effect for taxable years beginning before January 1, 1987.

[Sec. 444(f)]

(f) PERSONAL SERVICE CORPORATION.—For purposes of this section, the term "personal service corporation" has the meaning given to such term by section 441(i)(2).

Amendments

• 1988, Technical and Miscellaneous Revenue Act of 1988 (P.L. 100-647)

P.L. 100-647, §2004(e)(2)(A):

Amended Code Sec. 444 by redesignating subsection (f) as subsection (g) and inserting after subsection (e) a new subsection (f). **Effective** as if included in the provision of P.L. 100-203 to which it relates.

[Sec. 444(g)]

(g) REGULATIONS.—The Secretary shall prescribe such regulations as may be necessary to carry out the provisions of this section, including regulations to prevent the avoidance of subsection (b)(2)(B) or (d)(2)(B) through the change in form of an entity.

Amendments

• 1988, Technical and Miscellaneous Revenue Act of 1988 (P.L. 100-647)

P.L. 100-647, §2004(e)(2)(A):

Amended Code Sec. 444 by redesignating subsection (f) as subsection (g) and inserting after subsection (e) a new subsection (f). **Effective** as if included in the provision of P.L. 100-203 to which it relates.

• 1987, Revenue Act of 1987 (P.L. 100-203)

P.L. 100-203, §10206(a)(1):

Amended part I of subchapter E of Chapter 1 by adding at the end thereof new section 444. For the **effective** date, see Act Sec. 10206(d), below.

P.L. 100-203, §10206(d), as amended by P.L. 100-647, §2004(e)(11), provides:

(d) EFFECTIVE DATES.—

(1) IN GENERAL.—Except as provided in this subsection, the amendments made by this section shall apply to taxable years beginning after December 31, 1986.

(2) REQUIRED PAYMENTS.—The amendments made by subsection (b) shall apply to applicable election years beginning after December 31, 1986.

(3) ELECTIONS.—Any election under section 444 of the Internal Revenue Code of 1986 (as added by subsection (a)) for an entity's 1st taxable year beginning after December 31, 1986, shall not be required to be made before the 90th day after the date of the enactment of this Act.

(4) SPECIAL RULE FOR EXISTING ENTITIES ELECTING S CORPORATION STATUS.—If a C corporation (within the meaning of section 1361(a)(2)) of the Internal Revenue Code of 1986) with a taxable year other than the calendar year—

(A) made an election after September 18, 1986, and before January 1, 1988, under section 1362 of such Code to be treated as an S corporation, and

(B) elected to have the calendar year as the taxable year of the S corporation,

then section 444(b)(2)(B) of such Code shall be applied by taking into account the deferral period of the last taxable year of the C corporation rather than the deferral period of the taxable year being changed. The preceding sentence shall apply only in the case of an election under section 444 of such Code made for a taxable year beginning before 1989.

PART II—METHODS OF ACCOUNTING

Subpart A—Methods of Accounting in General

[Sec. 446]

SEC. 446. GENERAL RULE FOR METHODS OF ACCOUNTING.

[Sec. 446(a)]

(a) GENERAL RULE.—Taxable income shall be computed under the method of accounting on the basis of which the taxpayer regularly computes his income in keeping his books.

[Sec. 446(b)]

(b) EXCEPTIONS.—If no method of accounting has been regularly used by the taxpayer, or if the method used does not clearly reflect income, the computation of taxable income shall be made under such method as, in the opinion of the Secretary, does clearly reflect income.

Amendments

• 1976, Tax Reform Act of 1976 (P.L. 94-455)

P.L. 94-455, §1906(b)(13)(A):

Amended 1954 Code by substituting "Secretary" for "Secretary or his delegate" each place it appeared. **Effective** 2-1-77.

[Sec. 446(c)]

(c) PERMISSIBLE METHODS.—Subject to the provisions of subsections (a) and (b), a taxpayer may compute taxable income under any of the following methods of accounting—

(1) the cash receipts and disbursements method;

(2) an accrual method;

(3) any other method permitted by this chapter; or

(4) any combination of the foregoing methods permitted under regulations prescribed by the Secretary.

Amendments

• 1976, Tax Reform Act of 1976 (P.L. 94-455)

P.L. 94-455, §1906(b)(13)(A):

Amended 1954 Code by substituting "Secretary" for "Secretary or his delegate" each place it appeared. **Effective** 2-1-77.

[Sec. 446(d)]

(d) TAXPAYER ENGAGED IN MORE THAN ONE BUSINESS.—A taxpayer engaged in more than one trade or business may, in computing taxable income, use a different method of accounting for each trade or business.

[Sec. 446(e)]

(e) REQUIREMENT RESPECTING CHANGE OF ACCOUNTING METHOD.—Except as otherwise expressly provided in this chapter, a taxpayer who changes the method of accounting on the basis of which he regularly computes his income in keeping his books shall, before computing his taxable income under the new method, secure the consent of the Secretary.

Amendments

• 1976, Tax Reform Act of 1976 (P.L. 94-455)

P.L. 94-455, §1906(b)(13)(A):

Amended 1954 Code by substituting "Secretary" for "Secretary or his delegate" each place it appeared. **Effective** 2-1-77.

[Sec. 446(f)]

(f) FAILURE TO REQUEST CHANGE OF METHOD OF ACCOUNTING.—If the taxpayer does not file with the Secretary a request to change the method of accounting, the absence of the consent of the Secretary to a change in the method of accounting shall not be taken into account—

(1) to prevent the imposition of any penalty, or the addition of any amount to tax, under this title, or

(2) to diminish the amount of such penalty or addition to tax.

Amendments

• 1984, Deficit Reduction Act of 1984 (P.L. 98-369)

P.L. 98-369, §161(a):

Amended Code Sec. 446 by adding subsection (f). **Effective** for tax years beginning after 7-18-84.

[Sec. 447]

SEC. 447. METHOD OF ACCOUNTING FOR CORPORATIONS ENGAGED IN FARMING.

[Sec. 447(a)]

(a) GENERAL RULE.—Except as otherwise provided by law, the taxable income from farming of—

(1) a corporation engaged in the trade or business of farming, or

(2) a partnership engaged in the trade or business of farming, if a corporation is a partner in such partnership,

shall be computed on an accrual method of accounting. This section shall not apply to the trade or business of operating a nursery or sod farm or to the raising or harvesting of trees (other than fruit and nut trees).

Amendments

• 1986, Tax Reform Act of 1986 (P.L. 99-514)

P.L. 99-514, §803(b)(7)(B):

Amended Code Sec. 447(a) by striking out "and with the capitalization of preproductive period of expenses described in subsection (b)". **Effective**, generally, for costs incurred after 12-31-86, in tax years ending after such date. However, for special and transitional rules, see Act Sec. 803(d)(2)-(7) following Code Sec. 312. Prior to amendment, Code Sec. 447(a) read as follows:

(a) GENERAL RULE.—Except as otherwise provided by law, the taxable income from farming of—

(1) a corporation engaged in the trade or business of farming, or

(2) a partnership engaged in the trade or business of farming, if a corporation is a partner in such partnership,

shall be computed on an accrual method of accounting and with the capitalization of preproductive period expenses described in subsection (b). This section shall not apply to the trade or business of operating a nursery or sod farm or to the raising or harvesting of trees (other than fruit and nut trees).

• 1978, Revenue Act of 1978 (P.L. 95-600)

P.L. 95-600, §353(a):

Amended Code Sec. 447(a) by striking out "nursery" and inserting in lieu thereof "nursery or sod farm". **Effective** for tax years beginning after 12-31-76.

P.L. 95-600, §703(d):

Amended Code Sec. 447(a) by striking out "preproductive expenses" and inserting in lieu thereof "preproductive period expenses". **Effective** 10-4-76.

[Sec. 447(b)]

(b) PREPRODUCTIVE PERIOD EXPENSES.—

For rules requiring capitalization of certain preproductive period expenses, see section 263A.

Amendments

• 1988, Technical and Miscellaneous Revenue Act of 1988 (P.L. 100-647)

P.L. 100-647, §1008(b)(5)(A)-(B):

Amended Code Sec. 447(b) by striking out "of" before "expenses", and by striking out "Of" before "Expenses" in the heading thereof. **Effective** as if included in the provision of P.L. 99-514 to which it relates.

• 1986, Tax Reform Act of 1986 (P.L. 99-514)

P.L. 99-514, §803(b)(7)(A):

Amended Code Sec. 447(b). **Effective**, generally, for costs incurred after 12-31-86, in tax years ending after such date. However, for special and transitional rules, see Act Sec. 803(d)(2)-(7) following Code Sec. 312. Prior to amendment, Code Sec. 447(b) read as follows:

(b) PREPRODUCTIVE PERIOD EXPENSES.—

(1) IN GENERAL.—For purposes of this section, the term "preproductive period expenses" means any amount which is attributable to crops, animals, or any other property having a crop or yield during the preproductive period of such property.

(2) EXCEPTIONS.—Paragraph (1) shall not apply—

(A) to taxes and interest, and

(B) to any amount incurred on account of fire, storm, flood, or other casualty or on account of disease or drought.

(3) PREPRODUCTIVE PERIOD DEFINED.—For purposes of this subsection, the term "preproductive period" means—

(A) in the case of property having a useful life of more than 1 year which will have more than 1 crop or yield, the period before the disposition of the first such marketable crop or yield, or

(B) in the case of any other property, the period before such property is disposed of.

For purposes of this section, the use by the taxpayer in the trade or business of farming of any supply produced in such trade or business shall be treated as a disposition.

[Sec. 447(c)]

(c) EXCEPTION FOR CERTAIN CORPORATIONS.—For purposes of subsection (a), a corporation shall be treated as not being a corporation if it is—

(1) an S corporation, or

(2) a corporation the gross receipts of which meet the requirements of subsection (d).

Amendments

• 1987, Revenue Act of 1987 (P.L. 100-203)

P.L. 100-203, §10205(a):

Amended Code Sec. 447 by striking out subsections (c) and (e), by redesignating subsection (d) as subsection (e), and by inserting after subsection (b) new subsections (c) and (d). **Effective** for tax years beginning after 12-31-87. Prior to amendment Code Sec. 447(c) read as follows:

(c) EXCEPTION FOR SMALL BUSINESS AND FAMILY CORPORATIONS.—For purposes of subsection (a), a corporation shall be treated as not being a corporation if it is—

(1) an S corporation,

(2) a corporation of which at least 50 percent of the total combined voting power of all classes of stock entitled to vote, and at least 50 percent of the total number of shares of all other classes of stock of the corporation, are owned by members of the same family, or

(3) a corporation the gross receipts of which meet the requirements of subsection (e).

• 1982, Subchapter S Revision Act of 1982 (P.L. 97-354)

P.L. 97-354, §5(a)(28):

Amended Code Sec. 447(c)(1). **Effective** for tax years beginning after 12-31-82. Prior to amendment, it read as follows:

"(1) an electing small business corporation (within the meaning of section 1371(b)),"

[Sec. 447(d)]

(d) GROSS RECEIPTS REQUIREMENTS.—

(1) IN GENERAL.— A corporation meets the requirements of this subsection if, for each prior taxable year beginning after December 31, 1975, such corporation (and any predecessor corporation) did not have gross receipts exceeding $1,000,000. For purposes of the preceding sentence, all corporations which are members of the same controlled group of corporations (within the meaning of section 1563(a)) shall be treated as 1 corporation.

(2) SPECIAL RULES FOR FAMILY CORPORATIONS.—

(A) IN GENERAL.—In the case of a family corporation, paragraph (1) shall be applied—

(i) by substituting "December 31, 1985," for "December 31, 1975,"; and

(ii) by substituting "$25,000,000" for "$1,000,000".

(B) GROSS RECEIPTS TEST.—

(i) CONTROLLED GROUPS.—Notwithstanding the last sentence of paragraph (1), in the case of a family corporation—

(I) except as provided by the Secretary, only the applicable percentage of gross receipts of any other member of any controlled group of corporations of which such corporation is a member shall be taken into account, and

(II) under regulations, gross receipts of such corporation or of another member of such group shall not be taken into account by such corporation more than once.

(ii) PASS-THRU ENTITIES.—For purposes of paragraph (1), if a family corporation holds directly or indirectly any interest in a partnership, estate, trust or other pass-thru entity, such corporation shall take into account its proportionate share of the gross receipts of such entity.

(iii) APPLICABLE PERCENTAGE.—For purposes of clause (i), the term "applicable percentage" means the percentage equal to a fraction—

(I) the numerator of which is the fair market value of the stock of another corporation held directly or indirectly as of the close of the taxable year by the family corporation, and

(II) the denominator of which is the fair market value of all stock of such corporation as of such time.

For purposes of this clause, the term "stock" does not include stock described in section 1563(c)(1).

(C) FAMILY CORPORATION.—For purposes of this section, the term "family corporation" means—

(i) any corporation if at least 50 percent of the total combined voting power of all classes of stock entitled to vote, and at least 50 percent of all other classes of stock of the corporation, are owned by members of the same family, and

(ii) any corporation described in subsection (h).

Amendments

• 1987, Revenue Act of 1987 (P.L. 100-203)

P.L. 100-203, §10205(a):

Amended Code Sec. 447 by striking out subsections (c) and (e), by redesignating subsection (d) as subsection (e), and by inserting after subsection (b) new subsections (c) and (d). **Effective** for tax years beginning after 12-31-87.

[Sec. 447(e)]

(e) MEMBERS OF THE SAME FAMILY.—For purposes of subsection (d)—

(1) the members of the same family are an individual, such individual's brothers and sisters, the brothers and sisters of such individual's parents and grandparents, the ancestors and lineal descendants of any of the foregoing, a spouse of any of the foregoing, and the estate of any of the foregoing,

(2) stock owned, directly or indirectly, by or for a partnership or trust shall be treated as owned proportionately by its partners or beneficiaries, and

(3) if 50 percent or more in value of the stock in a corporation (hereinafter in this paragraph referred to as "first corporation") is owned, directly or through paragraph (2), by or for members

of the same family, such members shall be considered as owning each class of stock in a second corporation (or a wholly owned subsidiary of such second corporation) owned, directly or indirectly, by or for the first corporation, in that proportion which the value of the stock in the first corporation which such members so own bears to the value of all the stock in the first corporation.

For purposes of paragraph (1), individuals related by the half blood or by legal adoption shall be treated as if they were related by the whole blood.

Amendments

• 1987, Revenue Act of 1987 (P.L. 100-203)

P.L. 100-203, §10205(a):

Amended Code Sec. 447 by striking out subsections (c) and (e), by redesignating subsection (d) as subsection (e), and by inserting after subsection (b) new subsections (c) and (d). **Effective** for tax years beginning after 12-31-87. Prior to amendment Code Sec. 447(e) read as follows:

(e) CORPORATIONS HAVING GROSS RECEIPTS OF $1,000,000 OR LESS.—A corporation meets the requirements of this subsection if, for each prior taxable year beginning after December 31, 1975, such corporation (and any predecessor corporation) did not have gross receipts exceeding $1,000,000. For purposes of the preceding sentence, all corporations which are members of a controlled group of corporations (within the meaning of section 1563(a)) shall be treated as one corporation.

P.L. 100-203, §10205(c)(1):

Amended Code Sec. 447(e) (as redesignated by subsection (a)) by striking out "subsection (c)(2)" and inserting in lieu thereof "subsection (d)". **Effective** for tax years beginning after 12-31-87.

[Sec. 447(f)]

(f) COORDINATION WITH SECTION 481.—In the case of any taxpayer required by this section to change its method of accounting for any taxable year—

(1) such change shall be treated as having been made with the consent of the Secretary,

(2) for purposes of section 481(a)(2), such change shall be treated as a change not initiated by the taxpayer, and

(3) under regulations prescribed by the Secretary, the net amount of adjustments required by section 481(a) to be taken into account by the taxpayer in computing taxable income shall be taken into account in each of the 10 taxable years (or the remaining taxable years where there is a stated future life of less than 10 taxable years) beginning with the year of change.

Amendments

• 1978, Revenue Act of 1978 (P.L. 95-600)

P.L. 95-600, §701(l)(1)(B):

Amended Code Sec. 447(f)(3). **Effective** for tax years beginning after 1976. Prior to amendment, Code Sec. 447(f)(3) read as follows:

(3) under regulations prescribed by the Secretary, the net amount of adjustments required by section 481(a) to be taken into account by the taxpayer in computing taxable income shall (except as otherwise provided in such regulations) be taken into account in each of the 10 taxable years beginning with the year of change.

[Sec. 447(g)]

(g) CERTAIN ANNUAL ACCRUAL ACCOUNTING METHODS.—

(1) IN GENERAL.—Notwithstanding subsection (a) or section 263A, if—

(A) for its 10 taxable years ending with its first taxable year beginning after December 31, 1975, a corporation or qualified partnership used an annual accrual method of accounting with respect to its trade or business of farming,

(B) such corporation or qualified partnership raises crops which are harvested not less than 12 months after planting, and

(C) such corporation or qualified partnership has used such method of accounting for all taxable years intervening between its first taxable year beginning after December 31, 1975, and the taxable year,

such corporation or qualified partnership may continue to employ such method of accounting for the taxable year with respect to its qualified farming trade or business.

(2) ANNUAL ACCRUAL METHOD OF ACCOUNTING DEFINED.—For purposes of paragraph (1), the term "annual accrual method of accounting" means a method under which revenues, costs, and expenses are computed on an accrual method of accounting and the preproductive expenses incurred during the taxable year are charged to harvested crops or deducted in determining the taxable income for such years.

(3) CERTAIN NONRECOGNITION TRANSFERS.—For purposes of this subsection, if—

(A) a corporation acquired substantially all the assets of a qualified farming trade or business from another corporation in a transaction in which no gain or loss was recognized to the tranferor or transferee corporation, or

(B) a qualified partnership acquired substantially all the assets of a qualified farming trade or business from one of its partners in a transaction to which section 721 applies,

the transferee corporation or qualified partnership shall be deemed to have computed its taxable income on an annual accrual method of accounting during the period for which the transferor corporation or partnership computed its taxable income from such trade or business on an annual accrual method.

(4) QUALIFIED PARTNERSHIP DEFINED.—For purposes of this subsection—

(A) QUALIFIED PARTNERSHIP.—The term "qualified partnership" means a partnership which is engaged in a qualified farming trade or business and each of the partners of which is a corporation other than—

(i) an S corporation, or

(ii) a personal holding company (within the meaning of section 542(a)).

(B) QUALIFIED FARMING TRADE OR BUSINESS.—

(i) IN GENERAL.—The term "qualified farming trade or business" means the trade or business of farming—

(I) sugar cane,

(II) any plant with a preproductive period (as defined in section 263A(e)(3)) of 2 years or less, and

(III) any other plant (other than any citrus or almond tree) if an election by the corporation under this subparagraph is in effect.

In the case of a partnership and for purposes of paragraph (3)(A), subclauses (II) and (III) shall not apply.

(ii) EFFECT OF ELECTION.—For purposes of paragraphs (1) and (2) of section 263A(e), any election under this subparagraph shall be treated as if it were an election under subsection (d)(3) of section 263A.

(iii) ELECTION.—Unless the Secretary otherwise consents, an election under this subparagraph may be made only for the corporation's 1st taxable year which begins after December 31, 1986, and during which the corporation engages in a farming business. Any such election, once made, may be revoked only with the consent of the Secretary.

Amendments

• 1990, Omnibus Budget Reconciliation Act of 1990 (P.L. 101-508)

P.L. 101-508, §11702(b)(1):

Amended Code Sec. 447(g)(4)(B). **Effective** as if included in the provision of P.L. 100-647 to which it relates. Prior to amendment, subparagraph (B) read as follows:

(B) QUALIFIED FARMING TRADE OR BUSINESS.—The term "qualified farming trade or business" means the trade or business of farming sugar cane.

P.L. 101-508, §11702(b)(2):

Amended Code Sec. 447(g)(1)(A) by striking "qualified farming trade or business" and inserting "trade or business of farming". **Effective** as if included in the provision of P.L. 100-647 to which it relates.

• 1988, Technical and Miscellaneous Revenue Act of 1988 (P.L. 100-647)

P.L. 100-647, §1008(b)(6):

Amended Code Sec. 447(g)(1) by striking out "trade or business of farming" each place it appears and inserting in lieu thereof "qualified farming trade or business". **Effective** as if included in the provision of P.L. 99-514 to which it relates.

• 1986, Tax Reform Act of 1986 (P.L. 99-514)

P.L. 99-514, §803(b)(7)(C):

Amended Code Sec. 447(g)(1) by striking out "If" and inserting in lieu thereof "Notwithstanding subsection (a) or section 263A, if". **Effective**, generally, for costs incurred after 12-31-86, in tax years ending after such date. However, for special and transitional rules, see Act Sec. 803(d)(2)-(7) following Code Sec. 312. Prior to amendment, Code Sec. 447(g)(1) read as follows:

(1) IN GENERAL.—Notwithstanding subsection (a) or section 263A, if—

(A) for its 10 taxable years ending with its first taxable year beginning after December 31, 1975, a corporation or qualified partnership used an annual accrual method of accounting with respect to its trade or business of farming,

(B) such corporations or qualified partnership raises crops which are harvested not less than 12 months after planting, and

(C) such corporation or qualified partnership has used such method of accounting for all taxable years intervening between its first taxable year beginning after December 31, 1975, and the taxable year,

such corporation or qualified partnership may continue to employ such method of accounting for the taxable year with respect to its trade or business of farming.

• 1982, Subchapter S Revision Act of 1982 (P.L. 97-354)

P.L. 97-354, §5(a)(29):

Amended Code Sec. 447(g)(4)(A)(i). **Effective** for tax years beginning after 12-31-82. Prior to amendment, it read as follows:

"(i) an electing small business corporation (within the meaning of section 1371(b)), or"

• 1982, Tax Equity and Fiscal Responsibility Act of 1982 (P.L. 97-248)

P.L. 97-248, §230(a)(1):

Amended Code Sec. 447(g) by inserting "or qualified partnership" after "corporation" each place it appeared in paragraph (1). **Effective** for tax years beginning after 12-31-81.

P.L. 97-248, §230(a)(2):

Amended Code Sec. 447(g)(3). **Effective** for tax years beginning after 12-31-81. Prior to amendment, it read as follows:

"(3) Certain Reorganizations.—For purposes of this subsection, if a corporation acquired substantially all the assets of a farming trade or business from another corporation in a transaction in which no gain or loss was recognized to the transferor or transferee corporation, the transferee corporation shall be deemed to have computed its taxable income on an annual accrual method of accounting during the period for which the transferor corporation computed its taxable income from such trade or business on an annual accrual method."

P.L. 97-248, §230(a)(3):

Amended Code Sec. 447(g) by adding at the end thereof new paragraph (4). **Effective** for tax years beginning after 12-31-81.

• 1978, Revenue Act of 1978 (P.L. 95-600)

P.L. 95-600, §703(d):

Amended Code Sec. 447(g)(2) by striking out "reproductive expenses" and inserting in lieu thereof "preproductive period expenses". **Effective** 10-4-76.

• 1976, Tax Reform Act of 1976 (P.L. 94-455)

P.L. 94-455, §207(c)(1)(A), as amended by P.L. 95-30, §404:

Added Code Sec. 447. Originally **effective** for tax years beginning after 12-31-76, but P.L. 95-30, §404, made the following change in the effective date:

(2) EFFECTIVE DATES.—

(A) IN GENERAL.—Except as provided in subparagraph (B), the amendments made by paragraph (1) shall apply to taxable years beginning after December 31, 1976.

(B) SPECIAL RULE FOR CERTAIN CORPORATIONS.—In the case of a corporation engaged in the trade or business of farming and with respect to which—

(i) members of two families (within the meaning of paragraph (1) of section 447 (d) of the Internal Revenue Code of 1954, as added by paragraph (1)) owned, on October 4, 1976 (directly or through the application of such section 447 (d)), at least 65 percent of the total combined voting power of all classes of stock of such corporation entitled to vote, and at least 65 percent of the total number of shares of all other classes of stock of such corporation; or

(ii) members of three families (within the meaning of paragraph (1) of such section 447 (d)) owned, on October 4, 1976 (directly or through the application of such section 447 (d)), at least 50 percent of the total combined voting power of all classes of stock of such corporation entitled to vote, and at least 50 percent of the total number of shares of all other classes of stock of such corporation; and substantially all of the stock of such corporation which was not so owned (directly or through the application of such section 447 (d)), by members of such three families was owned, on October 4, 1976, directly—

(I) by employees of the corporation or members of the families (within the meaning of section 267(c)(4) of such Code) of such employees, or

(II) by a trust for the benefit of the employees of such corporation which is described in section 401(a) of such Code and which is exempt from taxation under section 501(a) of such Code,

the amendments made by paragraph (1) shall apply to taxable years beginning after December 31, 1977.

P.L. 94-455, §207(c)(3), provides:

(3) ELECTION TO CHANGE FROM STATIC VALUE METHOD TO ACCRUAL METHOD OF ACCOUNTING.—

(A) IN GENERAL.—If—

(i) a corporation has computed its taxable income on an annual accrual method of accounting together with a static value method of accounting for deferred costs of growing crops for the 10 taxable years ending with its first taxable year beginning after December 31, 1975,

(ii) such corporation raises crops which are harvested not less than 12 months after planting, and

(iii) such corporation elects, within one year after the date of the enactment of this Act and in such manner as the Secretary of the Treasury or his delegate prescribes, to change to the annual accrual method of accounting (within the meaning of section 447(g)(2) of the Internal Revenue Code of 1954) for taxable years beginning after December 31, 1976,

such change shall be treated as having been made with the consent of the Secretary of the Treasury, and, under regulations prescribed by the Secretary of the Treasury or his delegate, the net amount of the adjustments required by section 481(a) of the Internal Revenue Code of 1954 to be taken into account by the taxpayer in computing taxable income shall (except as otherwise provided in such regulations) be taken into account in each of the 10 taxable years beginning with the year of change.

(B) COORDINATION WITH SECTION 447 OF THE CODE.—A corporation which elects under subparagraph (A) to change to the annual accrual method of accounting shall, for purposes of section 447(g) of the Internal Revenue Code of 1954, be deemed to be a corporation which has computed its taxable income on an annual accrual method of accounting for its 10 taxable years ending with its first taxable year beginning after December 31, 1975.

(C) CERTAIN CORPORATE REORGANIZATIONS.—For purposes of this paragraph, if a corporation acquired substantially all the assets of a farming trade or business from another corporation in a transaction in which no gain or loss was recognized to the transferor or transferee corporation, the transferee corporation shall be deemed to have computed its taxable income on an annual accrual method of accounting together with a static value method of accounting for deferred costs of growing crops during the period for which the transferor corporation computed its taxable income from such trade or business on such accrual and static value method.

[Sec. 447(h)]

(h) EXCEPTION FOR CERTAIN CLOSELY HELD CORPORATIONS.—

(1) IN GENERAL.—A corporation is described in this subsection if, on October 4, 1976, and at all times thereafter—

(A) members of 2 families (within the meaning of subsection (e)(1)) have owned (directly or through the application of subsection (e)) at least 65 percent of the total combined voting power of all classes of stock of such corporation entitled to vote, and at least 65 percent of the total number of shares of all other classes of stock of such corporation; or

(B)(i) members of 3 families (within the meaning of subsection (e)(1)) have owned (directly or through the application of subsection (e)) at least 50 percent of the total combined voting power of all classes of stock of such corporation entitled to vote, and at least 50 percent of the total number of shares of all other classes of stock of such corporation; and

(ii) substantially all of the stock of such corporation which is not so owned (directly or through the application of subsection (e)) by members of such 3 families is owned directly—

(I) by employees of the corporation or members of their families (within the meaning of section 267(c)(4)), or

(II) by a trust for the benefit of the employees of such corporation which is described in section 401(a) and which is exempt from taxation under section 501(a).

(2) STOCK HELD BY EMPLOYEES, ETC.—For purposes of this subsection, stock which—

(A) is owned directly by employees of the corporation or members of their families (within the meaning of section 267(c)(4)) or by a trust described in paragraph (1)(B)(ii)(II), and

(B) was acquired on or after October 4, 1976, from the corporation or from a member of a family which, on October 4, 1976, was described in subparagraph (A) or (B)(i) of paragraph (1),

shall be treated as owned by a member of a family which, on October 4, 1976, was described in subparagraph (A) or (B)(i) of paragraph (1).

(3) CORPORATION MUST BE ENGAGED IN FARMING.—This subsection shall apply only in the case of a corporation which was, on October 4, 1976, and at all times thereafter, engaged in the trade or business of farming.

Amendments

• 1987, Revenue Act of 1987 (P.L. 100-203)

P.L. 100-203, §10205(c)(2)(A)-(C):

Amended Code Sec. 447(h)(1) by striking out "This section shall not apply to any corporation" and inserting in lieu thereof "A corporation is described in this subsection", by striking out "subsection (d)" each place it appears and inserting in lieu thereof "subsection (e)", and by striking out "subsection (d)(1)" each place it appears and inserting in lieu thereof "subsection (e)(1)". **Effective** for tax years beginning after 12-31-87.

• 1978, Revenue Act of 1978 (P.L. 95-600)

P.L. 95-600, §351(a):

Added Code Sec. 447(h). **Effective** for tax years beginning after 12-31-77.

[Sec. 447(i)]

(i) SUSPENSE ACCOUNT FOR FAMILY CORPORATIONS.—

(1) IN GENERAL.—If any family corporation is required by this section to change its method of accounting for any taxable year (hereinafter in this subsection referred to as the "year of the change"), notwithstanding subsection (f), such corporation shall establish a suspense account under this subsection in lieu of taking into account adjustments under section 481(a) with respect to amounts included in the suspense account.

(2) INITIAL OPENING BALANCE.—The initial opening balance of the account described in paragraph (1) shall be the lesser of—

(A) the net adjustments which would have been required to be taken into account under section 481 but for this subsection, or

(B) the amount of such net adjustments determined as of the beginning of the taxable year preceding the year of change.

If the amount referred to in subparagraph (A) exceeds the amount referred to in subparagraph (B), notwithstanding paragraph (1), such excess shall be included in gross income in the year of the change.

(3) INCLUSION WHERE CORPORATION CEASES TO BE A FAMILY CORPORATION.—

(A) IN GENERAL.—If the corporation ceases to be a family corporation during any taxable year, the amount in the suspense account (after taking into account prior reductions) shall be included in gross income for such taxable year.

(B) SPECIAL RULE FOR CERTAIN TRANSFERS.—For purposes of subparagraph (A), any transfer in a corporation after December 15, 1987, shall be treated as a transfer to a person whose ownership could not qualify such corporation as a family corporation unless it is a transfer—

(i) to a member of the family of the transferor, or

(ii) in the case of a corporation described in subsection (h), to a member of a family which on December 15, 1987, held stock in such corporation which qualified the corporation under subsection (h).

(4) SUBCHAPTER C TRANSACTIONS.—The application of this subsection with respect to a taxpayer which is a party to any transaction with respect to which there is nonrecognition of gain or loss to any party by reason of subchapter C shall be determined under regulations prescribed by the Secretary.

(5) TERMINATION.—

(A) IN GENERAL.—No suspense account may be established under this subsection by any corporation required by this section to change its method of accounting for any taxable year ending after June 8, 1997.

(B) PHASEOUT OF EXISTING SUSPENSE ACCOUNTS.—

(i) IN GENERAL.—Each suspense account under this subsection shall be reduced (but not below zero) for each taxable year beginning after June 8, 1997, by an amount equal to the lesser of—

(I) the applicable portion of such account, or

(II) 50 percent of the taxable income of the corporation for the taxable year, or, if the corporation has no taxable income for such year, the amount of any net operating loss (as defined in section 172(c)) for such taxable year.

For purposes of the preceding sentence, the amount of taxable income and net operating loss shall be determined without regard to this paragraph.

(ii) COORDINATION WITH OTHER REDUCTIONS.—The amount of the applicable portion for any taxable year shall be reduced (but not below zero) by the amount of any reduction required for such taxable year under any other provision of this subsection.

(iv) INCLUSION IN INCOME.—Any reduction in a suspense account under this paragraph shall be included in gross income for the taxable year of the reduction.

(C) APPLICABLE PORTION.—For purposes of subparagraph (B), the term "applicable portion" means, for any taxable year, the amount which would ratably reduce the amount in the account (after taking into account prior reductions) to zero over the period consisting of such taxable year and the remaining taxable years in such first 20 taxable years.

(D) AMOUNTS AFTER 20TH YEAR.—Any amount in the account as of the close of the 20th year referred to in subparagraph (C) shall be treated as the applicable portion for each succeeding year thereafter to the extent not reduced under this paragraph for any prior taxable year after such 20th year.

Amendments

• 1997, Taxpayer Relief Act of 1997 (P.L. 105-34)

P.L. 105-34, §1081(a):

Amended Code Sec. 447(i) by striking paragraphs (3) and (4), by redesignating paragraphs (5) and (6) as paragraphs (3) and (4), respectively, and by adding at the end a new paragraph (5). **Effective** for tax years ending after 6-8-97. Prior to being stricken, Code Sec. 447(i)(3)-(4) read as follows:

(3) REDUCTION IN ACCOUNT IF FARMING BUSINESS CONTRACTS.—If—

(A) the gross receipts of the corporation from the trade or business of farming for the year of the change or any subsequent taxable year, is less than

(B) such gross receipts for the taxpayer's last taxable year beginning before the year of the change (or for the most recent taxable year for which a reduction in the suspense account was made under this paragraph),

the amount in the suspense account (after taking into account prior reductions) shall be reduced by the percentage by which the amount described in subparagraph (A) is less than the amount described in subparagraph (B).

(4) INCOME INCLUSIONS.—Any reduction in the suspense account under paragraph (3) shall be included in gross income for the taxable year of the reduction.

• 1987, Revenue Act of 1987 (P.L. 100-203)

P.L. 100-203, §10205(b):

Amended Code Sec. 447 by adding at the end thereof new subsection (i). **Effective** for tax years beginning after 12-31-87.

[Sec. 448]

SEC. 448. LIMITATION ON USE OF CASH METHOD OF ACCOUNTING.

[Sec. 448(a)]

(a) GENERAL RULE.—Except as otherwise provided in this section, in the case of a—

(1) C corporation,

(2) partnership which has a C corporation as a partner, or

(3) tax shelter,

taxable income shall not be computed under the cash receipts and disbursements method of accounting.

[Sec. 448(b)]

(b) EXCEPTIONS.—

(1) FARMING BUSINESS.—Paragraphs (1) and (2) of subsection (a) shall not apply to any farming business.

(2) QUALIFIED PERSONAL SERVICE CORPORATIONS.—Paragraphs (1) and (2) of subsection (a) shall not apply to a qualified personal service corporation, and such a corporation shall be treated as an individual for purposes of determining whether paragraph (2) of subsection (a) applies to any partnership.

(3) ENTITIES WITH GROSS RECEIPTS OF NOT MORE THAN $5,000,000.—Paragraphs (1) and (2) of subsection (a) shall not apply to any corporation or partnership for any taxable year if, for all prior taxable years beginning after December 31, 1985, such entity (or any predecessor) met the $5,000,000 gross receipts test of subsection (c).

[Sec. 448(c)]

(c) $5,000,000 GROSS RECEIPTS TEST.—For purposes of this section—

(1) IN GENERAL.—A corporation or partnership meets the $5,000,000 gross receipts test of this subsection for any prior taxable year if the average annual gross receipts of such entity for the 3-taxable-year period ending with such prior taxable year does not exceed $5,000,000.

(2) AGGREGATION RULES.—All persons treated as a single employer under subsection (a) or (b) of section 52 or subsection (m) or (o) of section 414 shall be treated as one person for purposes of paragraph (1).

(3) SPECIAL RULES.—For purposes of this subsection—

(A) NOT IN EXISTENCE FOR ENTIRE 3-YEAR PERIOD.—If the entity was not in existence for the entire 3-year period referred to in paragraph (1), such paragraph shall be applied on the basis of the period during which such entity (or trade or business) was in existence.

(B) SHORT TAXABLE YEARS.—Gross receipts for any taxable year of less than 12 months shall be annualized by multiplying the gross receipts for the short period by 12 and dividing the result by the number of months in the short period.

(C) GROSS RECEIPTS.—Gross receipts for any taxable year shall be reduced by returns and allowances made during such year.

(D) TREATMENT OF PREDECESSORS.—Any reference in this subsection to an entity shall include a reference to any predecessor of such entity.

Amendments

• 1988, Technical and Miscellaneous Revenue Act of 1988 (P.L. 100-647)

P.L. 100-647, §1008(a)(9):

Amended Code Sec. 448(c)(3) by adding at the end thereof new subparagraph (D). **Effective** as if included in the provision of P.L. 99-514 to which it relates.

[Sec. 448(d)]

(d) DEFINITIONS AND SPECIAL RULES.—For purposes of this section—

(1) FARMING BUSINESS.—

(A) IN GENERAL.—The term "farming business" means the trade or business of farming (within the meaning of section 263A(e)(4)).

(B) TIMBER AND ORNAMENTAL TREES.—The term "farming business" includes the raising, harvesting, or growing of trees to which section 263A(c)(5) applies.

(2) QUALIFIED PERSONAL SERVICE CORPORATION.—The term "qualified personal service corporation" means any corporation—

(A) substantially all of the activities of which involve the performance of services in the fields of health, law, engineering, architecture, accounting, actuarial science, performing arts, or consulting, and

(B) substantially all of the stock of which (by value) is held directly (or indirectly through 1 or more partnerships, S corporations, or qualified personal service corporations not described in paragraph (2) or (3) of subsection (a)) by—

(i) employees performing services for such corporation in connection with the activities involving a field referred to in subparagraph (A),

(ii) retired employees who had performed such services for such corporation,

(iii) the estate of any individual described in clause (i) or (ii), or

(iv) any other person who acquired such stock by reason of the death of an individual described in clause (i) or (ii) (but only for the 2-year period beginning on the date of the death of such individual).

To the extent provided in regulations which shall be prescribed by the Secretary, indirect holdings through a trust shall be taken into account under subparagraph (B).

(3) TAX SHELTER DEFINED.—The term "tax shelter" has the meaning given such term by section 461(i)(3) (determined after application of paragraph (4) thereof). An S corporation shall not be treated as a tax shelter for purposes of this section merely by reason of being required to file a notice of exemption from registration with a State agency described in section 461(i)(3)(A), but only if there is a requirement applicable to all corporations offering securities for sale in the State that to be exempt from such registration the corporation must file such a notice.

(4) SPECIAL RULES FOR APPLICATION OF PARAGRAPH (2).—For purposes of paragraph (2)—

(A) community property laws shall be disregarded,

(B) stock held by a plan described in section 401(a) which is exempt from tax under section 501(a) shall be treated as held by an employee described in paragraph (2)(B)(i), and

(C) at the election of the common parent of an affiliated group (within the meaning of section 1504(a)), all members of such group may be treated as 1 taxpayer for purposes of paragraph (2)(B) if 90 percent or more of the activities of such group involve the performance of services in the same field described in paragraph (2)(A).

(5) SPECIAL RULE FOR CERTAIN SERVICES.—

(A) IN GENERAL.—In the case of any person using an accrual method of accounting with respect to amounts to be received for the performance of services by such person, such person shall not be required to accrue any portion of such amounts which (on the basis of such person's experience) will not be collected if—

(i) such services are in fields referred to in paragraph (2)(A), or

(ii) such person meets the gross receipts test of subsection (c) for all prior taxable years.

(B) EXCEPTION.—This paragraph shall not apply to any amount if interest is required to be paid on such amount or there is any penalty for failure to timely pay such amount.

(C) REGULATIONS.—The Secretary shall prescribe regulations to permit taxpayers to determine amounts referred to in subparagraph (A) using computations or formulas which, based on experience, accurately reflect the amount of income that will not be collected by such person. A taxpayer may adopt, or request consent of the Secretary to change to, a computation or formula that clearly reflects the taxpayer's experience. A request under the preceding sentence shall be approved if such computation or formula clearly reflects the taxpayer's experience.

(6) TREATMENT OF CERTAIN TRUSTS SUBJECT TO TAX ON UNRELATED BUSINESS INCOME.—For purposes of this section, a trust subject to tax under section 511(b) shall be treated as a C corporation with respect to its activities constituting an unrelated trade or business.

(7) COORDINATION WITH SECTION 481.—In the case of any taxpayer required by this section to change its method of accounting for any taxable year—

(A) such change shall be treated as initiated by the taxpayer,

(B) such change shall be treated as made with the consent of the Secretary, and

(C) the period for taking into account the adjustments under section 481 by reason of such change—

(i) except as provided in clause (ii), shall not exceed 4 years, and

(ii) in the case of a hospital, shall be 10 years.

(8) USE OF RELATED PARTIES, ETC.—The Secretary shall prescribe such regulations as may be necessary to prevent the use of related parties, pass-thru entities, or intermediaries to avoid the application of this section.

Amendments

• 2002, Job Creation and Worker Assistance Act of 2002 (P.L. 107-147)

P.L. 107-147, §403(a):

Amended Code Sec. 448(d)(5). **Effective**, generally, for tax years ending after 3-9-2002. For a special rule, see Act Sec. 403(b)(2), below. Prior to amendment, Code Sec. 448(d)(5) read as follows:

(5) SPECIAL RULE FOR SERVICES.—In the case of any person using an accrual method of accounting with respect to amounts to be received for the performance of services by such person, such person shall not be required to accrue any portion of such amounts which (on the basis of experience) will not be collected. This paragraph shall not apply to any amount if interest is required to be paid on such amount or there is any penalty for failure to timely pay such amount.

P.L. 107-147, §403(b)(2), provides:

(2) CHANGE IN METHOD OF ACCOUNTING.—In the case of any taxpayer required by the amendments made by this section to change its method of accounting for its first taxable year ending after the date of the enactment of this Act—

(A) such change shall be treated as initiated by the taxpayer,

(B) such change shall be treated as made with the consent of the Secretary of the Treasury, and

(C) the net amount of the adjustments required to be taken into account by the taxpayer under section 481 of the Internal Revenue Code of 1986 shall be taken into account over a period of 4 years (or if less, the number of taxable years that the taxpayer used the method permitted under section 448(d)(5) of such Code as in effect before the date of the enactment of this Act) beginning with such first taxable year.

• 1988, Technical and Miscellaneous Revenue Act of 1988 (P.L. 100-647)

P.L. 100-647, §1008(a)(1)(A):

Amended Code Sec. 448(d)(2)(B) by striking out "or indirectly" and inserting in lieu thereof "(or indirectly through 1 or more partnerships, S corporations, or qualified personal service corporations not described in paragraph (2) or (3) of subsection (a))". **Effective** as if included in the provision of P.L. 99-514 to which it relates.

P.L. 100-647, §1008(a)(1)(B):

Amended Code Sec. 448(d) by adding at the end thereof new paragraph (8). **Effective** as if included in the provision of P.L. 99-514 to which it relates.

P.L. 100-647, §1008(a)(2):

Amended Code Sec. 448(d)(4)(C) by striking out "all such members" and inserting in lieu thereof "such group". **Effective** as if included in the provision of P.L. 99-514 to which it relates.

P.L. 100-647, §1008(a)(7):

Amended Code Sec. 448(d)(3) by adding at the end thereof a new sentence. **Effective** as if included in the provision of P.L. 99-514 to which it relates.

P.L. 100-647, §1008(a)(8):

Amended Code Sec. 448(d)(4)(C) by striking out "substantially all of" and inserting in lieu thereof "90 percent or more of". **Effective** as if included in the provision of P.L. 99-514 to which it relates.

P.L. 100-647, §6032(a):

Amended Code Sec. 448(d)(2) by adding at the end thereof a new sentence. **Effective** for tax years beginning after 12-31-86.

• 1986, Tax Reform Act of 1986 (P.L. 99-514)

P.L. 99-514, §801(a):

Amended subpart A of part II of subchapter E of chapter 1 by adding at the end thereof new Code Sec. 448. **Effective**, generally, for tax years beginning after 12-31-86. However, see Act Sec. 801(d)(2)-(5), below.

P.L. 99-514, §801(d)(2)-(5), as amended by P.L. 100-647, §1008(a)(5)-(6), provides:

(2) ELECTION TO RETAIN CASH METHOD FOR CERTAIN TRANSACTIONS.—A taxpayer may elect not to have the amendments made by this section apply to any loan or lease, or any transaction with a related party (within meaning of section 267(b) of the Internal Revenue Code of 1954, as in effect before the enactment of this Act), entered into on or before September 25, 1985. Any election under the preceding sentence may be made separately with respect to each transaction.

(3) CERTAIN CONTRACTS.—The Amendments made by this section shall not apply to—

(A) contracts for the acquisition or transfer of real property, and

(B) contracts for services related to the acquisition or development of real property,

but only if such contracts were entered into before September 25, 1985, and the sole element of the contract which has not been performed as of September 25, 1985, is payment for such property or service.

(4) TREATMENT OF AFFILIATED GROUP PROVIDING ENGINEERING SERVICES.—Each member of an affiliated group of corporations (within the meaning of section 1504(a) of the Internal Revenue Code of 1986) shall be allowed to use the cash receipts and disbursements method of accounting for any trade or business of providing engineering services with respect to taxable years ending after December 31, 1986, if the common parent of such group—

(A) was incorporated in the State of Delaware in 1970,

(B) was the successor to a corporation that was incorporated in the State of Illinois in 1949, and

(C) used a method of accounting for long-term contracts of accounting for a substantial part of its income from the performance of engineering services.

(5) SPECIAL RULE FOR PARAGRAPHS (2) AND (3).—If any loan, lease, contract, or evidence of any transaction to which paragraph (2) or (3) applies is transferred after June 10, 1987, to a person other than a related party (within the meaning of paragraph (2)), paragraph (2) or (3) shall cease to apply on and after the date of such transfer.

Subpart B—Taxable Year for Which Items of Gross Income Included

[Sec. 451]

SEC. 451. GENERAL RULE FOR TAXABLE YEAR OF INCLUSION.

[Sec. 451(a)]

(a) GENERAL RULE.—The amount of any item of gross income shall be included in the gross income for the taxable year in which received by the taxpayer, unless, under the method of accounting used in computing taxable income, such amount is to be properly accounted for as of a different period.

[Sec. 451(b)]

(b) SPECIAL RULE IN CASE OF DEATH.—In the case of the death of a taxpayer whose taxable income is computed under an accrual method of accounting, any amount accrued only by reason of the death of the taxpayer shall not be included in computing taxable income for the period in which falls the date of the taxpayer's death.

[Sec. 451(c)]

(c) SPECIAL RULE FOR EMPLOYEE TIPS.—For purposes of subsection (a), tips included in a written statement furnished an employer by an employee pursuant to section 6053(a) shall be deemed to be received at the time the written statement including such tips is furnished to the employer.

Amendments

• 1965, Social Security Amendments of 1965 (P.L. 89-97)

P.L. 89-97, §313(b):

Added Sec. 451(c). **Effective** for tips received by employees after 1965.

[Sec. 451(d)]

(d) SPECIAL RULE FOR CROP INSURANCE PROCEEDS OR DISASTER PAYMENTS.—In the case of insurance proceeds received as a result of destruction or damage to crops, a taxpayer reporting on the cash receipts and disbursements method of accounting may elect to include such proceeds in income for the taxable year following the taxable year of destruction or damage, if he establishes that, under his practice, income from such crops would have been reported in a following taxable year. For purposes of the preceding sentence, payments received under the Agricultural Act of 1949, as amended, or title II of the Disaster Assistance Act of 1988, as a result of (1) destruction or damage to crops caused by drought, flood, or any other natural disaster, or (2) the inability to plant crops because of such a natural disaster shall be treated as insurance proceeds received as a result of destruction or damage to crops. An election under this subsection for any taxable year shall be made at such time and in such manner as the Secretary prescribes.

Amendments

• 1988, Technical and Miscellaneous Revenue Act of 1988 (P.L. 100-647)

P.L. 100-647, §6033(a):

Amended Code Sec. 451(d) by inserting "or title II of the Disaster Assistance Act of 1988," after "the Agricultural Act of 1949, as amended," in the second sentence. **Effective** for payments received before, on, or after 11-10-88.

• 1976, Tax Reform Act of 1976 (P.L. 94-455)

P.L. 94-455, §2102(a):

Amended Code Sec. 451(d) by adding a new sentence after the first sentence. **Effective** for payments received after 12-31-73, in tax years ending after such date.

P.L. 94-455, §2102(b):

Amended the heading for Code Sec. 451(d) by substituting "Proceeds or Disaster Payments" for "Proceeds". **Effective** for payments received after 12-31-73, in tax years ending after such date.

P.L. 94-455, §1906(b)(13)(A):

Amended the 1954 Code by substituting "Secretary" for "Secretary or his delegate" each place it appeared. **Effective** 2-1-77.

• 1969, Tax Reform Act of 1969 (P.L. 91-172)

P.L. 91-172, §215(a):

Added Code Sec. 451(d). **Effective** for tax years ending after 12-30-69 (date of enactment).

[Sec. 451(e)]

(e) SPECIAL RULE FOR PROCEEDS FROM LIVESTOCK SOLD ON ACCOUNT OF DROUGHT, FLOOD, OR OTHER WEATHER-RELATED CONDITIONS.—

(1) IN GENERAL.—In the case of income derived from the sale or exchange of livestock in excess of the number the taxpayer would sell if he followed his usual business practices, a taxpayer reporting on the cash receipts and disbursements method of accounting may elect to include such income for the taxable year following the taxable year in which such sale or exchange occurs if he establishes that, under his usual business practices, the sale or exchange would not have occurred in the taxable year in which it occurred if it were not for drought, flood, or other weather-related conditions, and that such conditions had resulted in the area being designated as eligible for assistance by the Federal Government.

(2) LIMITATION.—Paragraph (1) shall apply only to a taxpayer whose principal trade or business is farming (within the meaning of section 6420(c)(3)).

(3) SPECIAL ELECTION RULES.—If section 1033(e)(2) applies to a sale or exchange of livestock described in paragraph (1), the election under paragraph (1) shall be deemed valid if made during the replacement period described in such section.

Amendments

• 2004, American Jobs Creation Act of 2004 (P.L. 108-357)

P.L. 108-357, §311(c):

Amended Code Sec. 451(e) by adding at the end a new paragraph (3). **Effective** for any tax year with respect to which the due date (without regard to extensions) for the return is after 12-31-2002.

• 1997, Taxpayer Relief Act of 1997 (P.L. 105-34)

P.L. 105-34, §913(a)(1)-(2):

Amended Code Sec. 451(e) by striking "drought conditions, and that these drought conditions" in paragraph (1) and inserting "drought, flood, or other weather-related conditions, and that such conditions" and by inserting ", FLOOD, OR OTHER WEATHER-RELATED CONDITIONS" after "DROUGHT" in the heading. **Effective** for sales and exchanges after 12-31-96.

• 1988, Technical and Miscellaneous Revenue Act of 1988 (P.L. 100-647)

P.L. 100-647, §6030(a):

Amended Code Sec. 451(e)(1) by striking out "(other than livestock described in section 1231(b)(3))" after "exchange of livestock". **Effective** for sales or exchanges occurring after 12-31-87.

• 1976, Tax Reform Act of 1976 (P.L. 94-455)

P.L. 94-455, §2141(a):

Added Code Sec. 451(e). **Effective** for tax years beginning after 12-31-75.

[Sec. 451(f)]

(f) SPECIAL RULE FOR UTILITY SERVICES.—

(1) IN GENERAL.— In the case of a taxpayer the taxable income of which is computed under an accrual method of accounting, any income attributable to the sale or furnishing of utility services to customers shall be included in gross income not later than the taxable year in which such services are provided to such customers.

(2) DEFINITION AND SPECIAL RULE.—For purposes of this subsection—

(A) UTILITY SERVICES.—The term "utility services" includes—

(i) the providing of electrical energy, water, or sewage disposal,

(ii) the furnishing of gas or steam through a local distribution system,

(iii) telephone or other communication services, and

(iv) the transporting of gas or steam by pipeline.

(B) YEAR IN WHICH SERVICES PROVIDED.—The taxable year in which services are treated as provided to customers shall not, in any manner, be determined by reference to—

(i) the period in which the customers' meters are read, or

(ii) the period in which the taxpayer bills (or may bill) the customers for such service.

Amendments

• 1986, Tax Reform Act of 1986 (P.L. 99-514)

P.L. 99-514, §821(a):

Amended Code Sec. 451 by adding at the end thereof new subsection (f). **Effective**, generally, for tax years beginning after 12-31-86. For special rules, see Act Sec. 821(b)(2)-(3), below.

P.L. 99-514, §821(b)(2)-(3), as amended by P.L. 100-647, §1008(h), provides:

(2) CHANGE IN METHOD OF ACCOUNTING.—If a taxpayer is required by the Amendments made by this section to change its method of accounting for any taxable year—

(A) such change shall be treated as initiated by the taxpayer,

(B) such change shall be treated as having been made with the consent of the Secretary, and

(C) the adjustments under section 481 of the Internal Revenue Code of 1954 by reason of such change shall be taken into account ratably over a period no longer than the first 4 taxable years beginning after December 31, 1986.

(3) SPECIAL RULE FOR CERTAIN CYCLE BILLING.—If a taxpayer for any taxable year beginning before August 16, 1986, for purposes of chapter 1 of the Internal Revenue Code of 1986 took into account income from services described in section 451(f) of such Code (as added by subsection (a)) on the basis of the period in which the customers' meters were read, then such treatment for such year shall be deemed to be proper. The preceding sentence shall also apply to any taxable year beginning after August 16, 1986, and before January 1, 1987, if the taxpayer treated such income in the same manner for the taxable year preceding such taxable year.

[Sec. 451(g)]

(g) TREATMENT OF INTEREST ON FROZEN DEPOSITS IN CERTAIN FINANCIAL INSTITUTIONS.—

(1) IN GENERAL.—In the case of interest credited during any calendar year on a frozen deposit in a qualified financial institution, the amount of such interest includible in the gross income of a qualified individual shall not exceed the sum of—

(A) the net amount withdrawn by such individual from such deposit during such calendar year, and

(B) the amount of such deposit which is withdrawable as of the close of the taxable year (determined without regard to any penalty for premature withdrawals of a time deposit).

(2) INTEREST TESTED EACH YEAR.—Any interest not included in gross income by reason of paragraph (1) shall be treated as credited in the next calendar year.

(3) DEFERRAL OF INTEREST DEDUCTION.—No deduction shall be allowed to any qualified financial institution for interest not includible in gross income under paragraph (1) until such interest is includible in gross income.

(4) FROZEN DEPOSIT.—For purposes of this subsection, the term "frozen deposit" means any deposit if, as of the close of the calendar year, any portion of such deposit may not be withdrawn because of—

(A) the bankruptcy or insolvency of the qualified financial institution (or threat thereof), or

(B) any requirement imposed by the State in which such institution is located by reason of the bankruptcy or insolvency (or threat thereof) of 1 or more financial institutions in the State.

(5) OTHER DEFINITIONS.—For purposes of this subsection, the terms "qualified individual", "qualified financial institution", and "deposit" have the same respective meanings as when used in section 165(l).

Amendments

• 1988, Technical and Miscellaneous Revenue Act of 1988 (P.L. 100-647)

P.L. 100-647, §1009(d)(3):

Amended Code Sec. 451 by redesignating subsection (f), as added by P.L. 99-514, §905(b), as subsection (g). **Effective** as if included in the provision of P.L. 99-514 to which it relates.

P.L. 100-647, §1009(d)(4), provides:

(4) If on the date of the enactment of this Act (or at any time before the date 1 year after such date of enactment) credit or refund of any overpayment of tax attributable to amendments made by section 905 of the Reform Act or by this subsection (or the assessment of any underpayment of tax so attributable) is barred by any law or rule of law—

(A) credit or refund of any such overpayment may nevertheless be made if claim therefore is filed before the date 1 year after such date of enactment, and

(B) assessment of any such underpayment may nevertheless be made if made before the date 1 year after such date of enactment.

• 1986, Tax Reform Act of 1986 (P.L. 99-514)

P.L. 99-514, §905(b):

Amended Code Sec. 451 by adding at the end thereof new subsection (f)[(g)]. **Effective**, generally, for tax years beginning after 12-31-82. For special rules, see Act Sec. 905(c)(2), below.

P.L. 99-514, §905(c)(2), provides:

(2) SPECIAL RULES FOR SUBSECTION (b).—

(A) The amendment made by subsection (b) shall apply to taxable years beginning after December 31, 1982, and before January 1, 1987, only if the qualified individual elects to have such amendment apply for all such taxable years.

(B) In the case of interest attributable to the period beginning January 1, 1983, and ending December 31, 1987, the interest deduction of financial institutions shall be determined without regard to paragraph (3) of section 451(f) of the Internal Revenue Code of 1986 (as added by subsection (b)).

[Sec. 451(h)]

(h) SPECIAL RULE FOR CASH OPTIONS FOR RECEIPT OF QUALIFIED PRIZES.—

(1) IN GENERAL.—For purposes of this title, in the case of an individual on the cash receipts and disbursements method of accounting, a qualified prize option shall be disregarded in determining the taxable year for which any portion of the qualified prize is properly includible in gross income of the taxpayer.

(2) QUALIFIED PRIZE OPTION; QUALIFIED PRIZE.—For purposes of this subsection—

(A) IN GENERAL.—The term "qualified prize option" means an option which—

(i) entitles an individual to receive a single cash payment in lieu of receiving a qualified prize (or remaining portion thereof), and

(ii) is exercisable not later than 60 days after such individual becomes entitled to the qualified prize.

(B) QUALIFIED PRIZE.—The term "qualified prize" means any prize or award which—

(i) is awarded as a part of a contest, lottery, jackpot, game, or other similar arrangement,

(ii) does not relate to any past services performed by the recipient and does not require the recipient to perform any substantial future service, and

(iii) is payable over a period of at least 10 years.

(3) PARTNERSHIP, ETC.—The Secretary shall provide for the application of this subsection in the case of a partnership or other pass-through entity consisting entirely of individuals described in paragraph (1).

Amendments

• 1998, Tax and Trade Relief Extension Act of 1998 (P.L. 105-277)

P.L. 105-277, § 5301(a):

Amended Code Sec. 451 by adding at the end a new subsection (h). **Effective**, generally, for any prize to which a person first becomes entitled after 10-21-98. For a transition rule, see Act Sec. 5301(b)(2)(A)-(B), below.

P.L. 105-277, § 5301(b)(2)(A)-(B), provides:

(2) TRANSITION RULE.—The amendment made by this section shall apply to any prize to which a person first becomes entitled on or before the date of enactment of this Act, except that in determining whether an option is a qualified prize option as defined in section 451(h)(2)(A) of the Internal Revenue Code of 1986 (as added by such amendment)—

(A) clause (ii) of such section 451(h)(2)(A) shall not apply, and

(B) such option shall be treated as a qualified prize option if it is exercisable only during all or part of the 18-month period beginning on July 1, 1999.

[Sec. 451(i)]

(i) SPECIAL RULE FOR SALES OR DISPOSITIONS TO IMPLEMENT FEDERAL ENERGY REGULATORY COMMISSION OR STATE ELECTRIC RESTRUCTURING POLICY.—

(1) IN GENERAL.—In the case of any qualifying electric transmission transaction for which the taxpayer elects the application of this section, qualified gain from such transaction shall be recognized—

(A) in the taxable year which includes the date of such transaction to the extent the amount realized from such transaction exceeds—

(i) the cost of exempt utility property which is purchased by the taxpayer during the 4-year period beginning on such date, reduced (but not below zero) by

(ii) any portion of such cost previously taken into account under this subsection, and

(B) ratably over the 8-taxable year period beginning with the taxable year which includes the date of such transaction, in the case of any such gain not recognized under subparagraph (A).

(2) QUALIFIED GAIN.—For purposes of this subsection, the term "qualified gain" means, with respect to any qualifying electric transmission transaction in any taxable year—

(A) any ordinary income derived from such transaction which would be required to be recognized under section 1245 or 1250 for such taxable year (determined without regard to this subsection), and

(B) any income derived from such transaction in excess of the amount described in subparagraph (A) which is required to be included in gross income for such taxable year (determined without regard to this subsection).

(3) QUALIFYING ELECTRIC TRANSMISSION TRANSACTION.—For purposes of this subsection, the term "qualifying electric transmission transaction" means any sale or other disposition before January 1, 2008 (before January 1, 2010, in the case of a qualified electric utility), of—

(A) property used in the trade or business of providing electric transmission services, or

(B) any stock or partnership interest in a corporation or partnership, as the case may be, whose principal trade or business consists of providing electric transmission services,

but only if such sale or disposition is to an independent transmission company.

(4) INDEPENDENT TRANSMISSION COMPANY.—For purposes of this subsection, the term "independent transmission company" means—

(A) an independent transmission provider approved by the Federal Energy Regulatory Commission,

(B) a person—

(i) who the Federal Energy Regulatory Commission determines in its authorization of the transaction under section 203 of the Federal Power Act (16 U.S.C. 824b) or by declaratory order is not a market participant within the meaning of such Commission's rules applicable to independent transmission providers, and

(ii) whose transmission facilities to which the election under this subsection applies are under the operational control of a Federal Energy Regulatory Commission-approved independent transmission provider before the close of the period specified in such authorization, but not later than the date which is 4 years after the close of the taxable year in which the transaction occurs, or

(C) in the case of facilities subject to the jurisdiction of the Public Utility Commission of Texas—

(i) a person which is approved by that Commission as consistent with Texas State law regarding an independent transmission provider, or

(ii) a political subdivision or affiliate thereof whose transmission facilities are under the operational control of a person described in clause (i).

(5) EXEMPT UTILITY PROPERTY.—For purposes of this subsection:

(A) IN GENERAL.—The term "exempt utility property" means property used in the trade or business of—

(i) generating, transmitting, distributing, or selling electricity, or

(ii) producing, transmitting, distributing, or selling natural gas.

(B) NONRECOGNITION OF GAIN BY REASON OF ACQUISITION OF STOCK.—Acquisition of control of a corporation shall be taken into account under this subsection with respect to a qualifying electric transmission transaction only if the principal trade or business of such corporation is a trade or business referred to in subparagraph (A).

(C) EXCEPTION FOR PROPERTY LOCATED OUTSIDE THE UNITED STATES.—The term "exempt utility property" shall not include any property which is located outside the United States.

(6) QUALIFIED ELECTRIC UTILITY.—For purposes of this subsection, the term "qualified electric utility" means a person that, as of the date of the qualifying electric transmission transaction, is vertically integrated, in that it is both—

(A) a transmitting utility (as defined in section 3(23) of the Federal Power Act (16 U.S.C. 796(23))) with respect to the transmission facilities to which the election under this subsection applies, and

(B) an electric utility (as defined in section 3(22) of the Federal Power Act (16 U.S.C. 796(22))).

(7) SPECIAL RULE FOR CONSOLIDATED GROUPS.—In the case of a corporation which is a member of an affiliated group filing a consolidated return, any exempt utility property purchased by another member of such group shall be treated as purchased by such corporation for purposes of applying paragraph (1)(A).

(8) TIME FOR ASSESSMENT OF DEFICIENCIES.—If the taxpayer has made the election under paragraph (1) and any gain is recognized by such taxpayer as provided in paragraph (1)(B), then—

(A) the statutory period for the assessment of any deficiency, for any taxable year in which any part of the gain on the transaction is realized, attributable to such gain shall not expire prior to the expiration of 3 years from the date the Secretary is notified by the taxpayer (in such manner as the Secretary may by regulations prescribe) of the purchase of exempt utility property or of an intention not to purchase such property, and

(B) such deficiency may be assessed before the expiration of such 3-year period notwithstanding any law or rule of law which would otherwise prevent such assessment.

(9) PURCHASE.—For purposes of this subsection, the taxpayer shall be considered to have purchased any property if the unadjusted basis of such property is its cost within the meaning of section 1012.

(10) ELECTION.—An election under paragraph (1) shall be made at such time and in such manner as the Secretary may require and, once made, shall be irrevocable.

(11) NONAPPLICATION OF INSTALLMENT SALES TREATMENT.—Section 453 shall not apply to any qualifying electric transmission transaction with respect to which an election to apply this subsection is made.

Amendments

• 2008, Energy Improvement and Extension Act of 2008 (P.L. 110-343)

P.L. 110-343, Division B, §109(a)(1):

Amended Code Sec. 451(i)(3) by inserting "(before January 1, 2010, in the case of a qualified electric utility)" after "January 1, 2008". **Effective** for transactions after 12-31-2007.

P.L. 110-343, Division B, §109(a)(2):

Amended Code Sec. 451(i) by redesignating paragraphs (6) through (10) as paragraphs (7) through (11), respectively, and by inserting after paragraph (5) a new paragraph (6). **Effective** for transactions after 12-31-2007.

P.L. 110-343, Division B, §109(b):

Amended Code Sec. 451(i)(4)(B)(ii) by striking "December 31, 2007" and inserting "the date which is 4 years after the close of the taxable year in which the transaction occurs". **Effective** as if included in Act Sec. 909 of the American Jobs Creation Act of 2004 [**effective** for transactions occurring after 10-22-2004, in tax years ending after such date.—CCH].

P.L. 110-343, Division B, §109(c):

Amended Code Sec. 451(i)(5) by adding at the end a new subparagraph (C). **Effective** for transactions after 10-3-2008.

• 2005, Energy Tax Incentives Act of 2005 (P.L. 109-58)

P.L. 109-58, §1305(a):

Amended Code Sec. 451(i)(3) by striking "2007" and inserting "2008". **Effective** for transactions occurring after 8-8-2005.

P.L. 109-58, §1305(b):

Amended Code Sec. 451(i)(4)(B)(ii) by striking "the close of the period applicable under subsection (a)(2)(B) as extended under paragraph (2)" and inserting "December 31, 2007". **Effective** as if included in the amendments made by section 909 of P.L. 108-357 [**effective** for transactions occurring after 10-22-2004, in tax years ending after such date.—CCH].

• 2004, American Jobs Creation Act of 2004 (P.L. 108-357)

P.L. 108-357, §909(a):

Amended Code Sec. 451 by adding at the end a new subsection (i). **Effective** for transactions occurring after 10-22-2004, in tax years ending after such date.

[Sec. 453]

SEC. 453. INSTALLMENT METHOD.

[Sec. 453(a)]

(a) GENERAL RULE.—Except as otherwise provided in this section, income from an installment sale shall be taken into account for purposes of this title under the installment method.

Amendments

• 2000, Installment Tax Correction Act of 2000 (P.L. 106-573)

P.L. 106-573, §2(a):

Repealed section 536(a)(1) of the Ticket to Work and Work Incentives Improvement Act of 1999 (P.L. 106-170), which amended Code Sec. 453(a). **Effective** with respect to sales and other dispositions occurring on or after the date of the enactment of P.L. 106-170 [**effective** 12-17-99.—CCH]. Thus, the amendment made to Code Sec. 453(a) never took effect and Code Sec. 453(a) is restored as it read prior to amendment by P.L. 106-170. Prior to the amendment's being stricken, Code Sec. 453(a) read as follows:

(a) USE OF INSTALLMENT METHOD.—

(1) IN GENERAL.—Except as otherwise provided in this section, income from an installment sale shall be taken into account for purposes of this title under the installment method.

(2) ACCRUAL METHOD TAXPAYER.—The installment method shall not apply to income from an installment sale if such income would be reported under an accrual method of accounting without regard to this section. The preceding sentence shall not apply to a disposition described in subparagraph (A) or (B) of subsection (l)(2).

• 1999, Tax Relief Extension Act of 1999 (P.L. 106-170)

P.L. 106-170, §536(a)(1):

Amended Code Sec. 453(a). **Effective** for sales or other dispositions occurring on or after 12-17-99. Prior to amendment, Code Sec. 453(a) read as follows:

(a) GENERAL RULE.—Except as otherwise provided in this section, income from an installment sale shall be taken into account for purposes of this title under the installment method.

• 1980, Installment Sales Revision Act of 1980 (P.L. 96-471)

P.L. 96-471, §2(a):

Amended Code Sec. 453(a). **Effective** for dispositions made after 10-19-80, in tax years ending after that date. Prior to amendment, Code Sec. 453(a) provided:

(a) DEALERS IN PERSONAL PROPERTY.—

(1) IN GENERAL.—Under regulations prescribed by the Secretary, a person who regularly sells or otherwise disposes of personal property on the installment plan may return as income therefrom in any taxable year that proportion of the installment payments actually received in that year which the gross profit, realized or to be realized when payment is completed, bears to the total contract price.

(2) TOTAL CONTRACT PRICE.—For purposes of paragraph (1), the total contract price of all sales of personal property on the installment plan includes the amount of carrying charges or interest which is determined with respect to such sales and is added on the books of account of the seller to the established cash selling price of such property. This paragraph shall not apply with respect to sales of personal property under a revolving credit type plan or with respect to sales or other dispositions of property the income from which is, under subsection (b), returned on the basis and in the manner prescribed in paragraph (1).

• 1976, Tax Reform Act of 1976 (P.L. 94-455)

P.L. 94-455, §1906(b)(13)(A):

Amended 1954 Code by substituting "Secretary" for "Secretary or his delegate" each place it appeared. **Effective** 2-1-77.

• 1964 (P.L. 88-539)

P.L. 88-539, §3(a):

Amended Code Sec. 453(a). **Effective** for sales made in tax years beginning on or after 1-1-60. Prior to amendment, Sec. 453(a) read as follows:

(a) DEALERS IN PERSONAL PROPERTY.—Under regulations prescribed by the Secretary or his delegate, a person who regularly sells or otherwise disposes of personal property on the installment plan may return as income therefrom in any taxable year that proportion of the installment payments actually received in that year which the gross profit, realized or to be realized when payment is completed, bears to the total contract price.

[Sec. 453(b)]

(b) INSTALLMENT SALE DEFINED.—For purposes of this section—

(1) IN GENERAL.—The term "installment sale" means a disposition of property where at least 1 payment is to be received after the close of the taxable year in which the disposition occurs.

(2) EXCEPTIONS.—The term "installment sale" does not include—

(A) DEALER DISPOSITIONS.—Any dealer disposition (as defined in subsection (l)).

(B) INVENTORIES OF PERSONAL PROPERTY.—A disposition of personal property of a kind which is required to be included in the inventory of the taxpayer if on hand at the close of the taxable year.

Amendments

• 1987, Revenue Act of 1987 (P.L. 100-203)

P.L. 100-203, §10202(b)(1):

Amended Code Sec. 453(b(2)(A). For the **effective** date, see the amendment notes following Code Sec. 453C. Prior to amendment, Code Sec. 453(b)(2)(A) read as follows:

(A) DEALER DISPOSITION OF PERSONAL PROPERTY.—A disposition of personal property on the installment plan by a person who regularly sells or otherwise disposes of personal property on the installment plan.

• 1980, Installment Sales Revision Act of 1980 (P.L. 96-471)

P.L. 96-471, §2(a):

Amended Code Sec. 453(b). **Effective** for dispositions made after 10-19-80, in tax years ending after that date. Prior to amendment, Code Sec. 453(b) provided:

(b) SALES OF REALTY AND CASUAL SALES OF PERSONALTY.—

(1) GENERAL RULE.—Income from—

(A) a sale or other disposition of real property, or

(B) a casual sale or other casual disposition of personal property (other than property of a kind which would properly be included in the inventory of the taxpayer if on hand at the close of the taxable year) for a price exceeding $1,000, may (under regulations prescribed by the Secretary) be returned on the basis and in the manner prescribed in subsection (a).

(2) LIMITATION.—Paragraph (1) shall apply only if in the taxable year of the sale or other disposition—

(A) there are no payments, or

(B) the payments (exclusive of evidences of indebtedness of the purchaser) do not exceed 30 percent of the selling price.

(3) PURCHASER EVIDENCES OF INDEBTEDNESS PAYABLE ON DEMAND OR READILY TRADABLE.—In applying this subsection, a bond or other evidence of indebtedness which is payable on demand, or which is issued by a corporation or a government or political subdivision thereof (A) with interest coupons attached or in registered form (other than one in registered form which the taxpayer establishes will not be readily tradable in an established securities market), or (B) in any other form designed to render such bond or other evidence of indebtedness readily tradable in an established securities market, shall not be treated as an evidence of indebtedness of the purchaser.

P.L. 96-471, §6(a)(7), provides:

(7) SPECIAL RULE FOR APPLICATION OF FORMER SECTION 453 TO CERTAIN DISPOSITIONS.—In the case of any disposition made on or before the date of the enactment of this Act in any taxable yer ending after such date, the provisions of section 453(b) of the Internal Revenue Code of 1954, as in effect before such date, shall be applied with respect to such disposition without regard to—

(A) paragraph (2) of such section 453(b), and

(B) any requirement that more than 1 payment be received.

• 1976, Tax Reform Act of 1976 (P.L. 94-455)

P.L. 94-455, §1906(b)(13)(A):

Amended the 1954 Code by substituting "Secretary" for "Secretary or his delegate" each place it appeared. **Effective** 2-1-77.

P.L. 94-455, §1951(b)(7)(A):

Amended Code Sec. 453(b)(2). **Effective** for tax years beginning after 12-31-76, but see savings clause under §1951(b)(7)(B) below. Prior to amendment Code Sec. 453(b)(2) read as follows:

(2) LIMITATION.—Paragraph (1) shall apply—

(A) In the case of a sale or other disposition during a taxable year beginning after December 31, 1953 (whether or not such taxable year ends after the date of enactment of this title), only if in the taxable year of the sale or other disposition—

(i) there are no payments, or

(ii) the payments (exclusive of evidences of indebtedness of the purchaser) do not exceed 30 per cent of the selling price.

(B) In the case of a sale or other disposition during a taxable year beginning before January 1, 1954, only if the income was (by reason of section 44(b) of the Internal Revenue Code of 1939) returnable on the basis and in the manner prescribed in section 44(a) of such code.

P.L. 94-455, §1951(b)(7)(B), provides:

(B) SAVINGS PROVISION.—Notwithstanding subparagraph (A), in the case of installment payments received during taxable years beginning after December 31, 1976, on account of a sale or other disposition made during a taxable year beginning before January 1, 1954, subsection (b)(1) of section 453 (relating to sales of realty and casual sales of personalty) shall apply only if the income was (by reason of section 44(b) of the Internal Revenue Code of 1939) returnable on the basis and in the manner prescribed in section 44(a) of such Code.

• 1969, Tax Reform Act of 1969 (P.L. 91-172)

P.L. 91-172, §412(a):

Added paragraph (b)(3). **Effective** for sales or other dispositions occurring after 5-27-69, which are not made pursuant to a binding written contract entered into on or before such date.

[Sec. 453(c)]

(c) INSTALLMENT METHOD DEFINED.—For purposes of this section, the term "installment method" means a method under which the income recognized for any taxable year from a disposition is that proportion of the payments received in that year which the gross profit (realized or to be realized when payment is completed) bears to the total contract price.

Amendments

• 1980, Installment Sales Revision Act of 1980 (P.L. 96-471)

P.L. 96-471, §2(a):

Amended Code Sec. 453(c). **Effective** for dispositions made after 10-19-80, in tax years ending after that date. Prior to amendment, Code Sec. 453(c) provided:

"(c) CHANGE FROM ACCRUAL TO INSTALLMENT BASIS.—

"(1) GENERAL RULE.—If a taxpayer entitled to the benefits of subsection (a) elects for any taxable year to report his taxable income on the installment basis, then in computing his taxable income for such year (referred to in this subsection as `year of change') or for any subsequent year—

"(A) installment payments actually received during any such year on account of sales or other dispositions of property made in any taxable year before the year of change shall not be excluded; but

"(B) the tax imposed by this chapter for any taxable year (referred to in this subsection as `adjustment year') beginning after December 31, 1953, shall be reduced by the adjustment computed under paragraph (2).

"(2) ADJUSTMENT IN TAX FOR AMOUNTS PREVIOUSLY TAXED.—In determining the adjustment referred to in paragraph (1)(B), first determine, for each taxable year before the year of change, the amount which equals the lesser of—

"(A) the portion of the tax for such prior taxable year which is attributable to the gross profit which was included in gross income for such prior taxable year, and which by reason of paragraph (1)(A) is includible in gross income for the taxable year, or

"(B) the portion of the tax for the adjustment year which is attributable to the gross profit described in subparagraph (A).

The adjustment referred to in paragraph (1)(B) for the adjustment year is the sum of the amounts determined under the preceding sentence.

"(3) RULE FOR APPLYING PARAGRAPH (2).—For purposes of paragraph (2), the portion of the tax for a prior taxable year, or for the adjustment year, which is attributable to the gross profit described in such paragraph is that amount which bears the same ratio to the tax imposed by this chapter, other than by sections 55 and 56, for such taxable year (computed without regard to paragraph (2)) as the gross profit described in such paragraph bears to the gross income for such taxable year.

"(4) REVOCATION OF ELECTION.—An election under paragraph (1) to report taxable income on the installment basis may be revoked by filing a notice of revocation, in such manner as the Secretary prescribes by regulations, at any time before the expiration of 3 years following the date of the filing of the tax return for the year of change. If such notice of revocation is timely filed—

"(A) the provisions of paragraph (1) and subsection (a) shall not apply to the year of change or for any subsequent year;

"(B) the statutory period for the assessment of any deficiency for any taxable year ending before the filing of such notice, which is attributable to the revocation of the election to use the installment basis, shall not expire before the expiration of 2 years from the date of the filing of such notice, and such deficiency may be assessed before the expiration of such 2-year period notwithstanding the provisions of any law or rule of law which would otherwise prevent such assessment; and

"(C) if refund or credit of any overpayment, resulting from the revocation of the election to use the installment basis, for any taxable year ending before the date of the filing of the notice of revocation is prevented on the date of such filing, or within one year from such date, by the operation of any law or rule of law (other than section 7121 or 7122), refund or credit of such overpayment may nevertheless be made or allowed if claim therefor is filed within one year from such date. No interest shall be allowed on the refund or credit of such overpayment for any period prior to the date of the filing of the notice of revocation.

"(5) ELECTION AFTER REVOCATION.—If the taxpayer revokes under paragraph (4) an election under paragraph (1) to report taxable income on the installment basis, no election under paragraph (1) may be made, except with the consent of the Secretary, for any subsequent taxable year before the fifth taxable year following the year of change with respect to which such revocation is made."

• 1980, Technical Corrections Act of 1979 (P.L. 96-222)

P.L. 96-222, §104(a)(4)(H)(iv):

Amended Code Sec. 453(c)(3) by changing "section 56" to "sections 55 and 56". **Effective** 10-4-76.

• 1978, Revenue Act of 1978 (P.L. 95-600)

P.L. 95-600, §703(j)(3):

Amended Code Sec. 453(c)(3). **Effective** 10-4-76. Prior to amendment, Code Sec. 453(c)(3) read as follows:

"(3) RULE FOR APPLYING PARAGRAPH (2).—For purposes of paragraph (2), the portion of the tax for a prior taxable year, or for the adjustment year, which is attributable to the gross profit described in such paragraph is that amount which bears the same ratio to the tax imposed by this chapter (or by the corresponding provisions of prior revenue laws), other than by section 56, for such taxable year (computed without regard to paragraph (2)) as the gross profit described in such paragraph bears to the gross income for such taxable year. For purposes of the preceding sentence, the provisions of chapter 1 (other than of subchapter D, relating to excess profits tax, and of subchapter E, relating to self-employment income) of the Internal Revenue Code of 1939 shall be treated as the corresponding provisions of the Internal Revenue Code of 1954."

• 1976, Tax Reform Act of 1976 (P.L. 94-455)

P.L. 94-455, §1901(a)(66)(A):

Amended Code Sec. 453(c)(3) by substituting "corresponding provisions of the Internal Revenue Code of 1954" for "corresponding provisions of the Internal Revenue Code of 1939". **Effective** for tax years beginning after 12-31-76.

P.L. 94-455, §1906(b)(13)(A):

Amended the 1954 Code by substituting "Secretary" for "Secretary or his delegate" each place it appeared. **Effective** 2-1-77.

• 1969, Tax Reform Act of 1969 (P.L. 91-172)

P.L. 91-172, §301(b)(7):

Amended Sec. 453(c)(3) by inserting ", other than by section 56," immediately following the first parenthetical phrase. **Effective** 1-1-70.

P.L. 91-172, §916(a):

Added paragraphs (c)(4) and (5). For the **effective** date, see Act Sec. 916(b), below.

P.L. 91-172, §916(b), provides:

(b) Effective Date.—The amendment made by subsection (a) shall apply to an election made for any year of change (as defined in section 453(c)(1) of the Internal Revenue Code of 1954) ending on or after the date of the enactment of this Act, and shall also apply to any such year of change which ended before such date if the 3-year statutory period for assessment of any deficiency for such year has not expired on the date of the enactment of this Act.

[Sec. 453(d)]

(d) ELECTION OUT.—

(1) IN GENERAL.—Subsection (a) shall not apply to any disposition if the taxpayer elects to have subsection (a) not apply to such disposition.

(2) TIME AND MANNER FOR MAKING ELECTION.—Except as otherwise provided by regulations, an election under paragraph (1) with respect to a disposition may be made only on or before the due date prescribed by law (including extensions) for filing the taxpayer's return of the tax imposed by this chapter for the taxable year in which the disposition occurs. Such an election shall be made in the manner prescribed by regulations.

(3) ELECTION REVOCABLE ONLY WITH CONSENT.—An election under paragraph (1) with respect to any disposition may be revoked only with the consent of the Secretary.

Amendments

• 2000, Installment Tax Correction Act of 2000 (P.L. 106-573)

P.L. 106-573, §2(a):

Repealed section 536(a)(2) of the Ticket to Work and Work Incentives Improvement Act of 1999 (P.L. 106-170), which amended Code Sec. 453(d)(1) by striking "(a)" each place it appeared and inserting "(a)(1)". **Effective** with respect to sales and other dispositions occurring on or after the date of the enactment of P.L. 106-170 [**effective** 12-17-99.—CCH]. Thus, the amendment made to Code Sec. 453(d)(1) never took effect and Code Sec. 453(d)(1) is restored to read as it did prior to amendment by P.L. 106-170.

• 1999, Tax Relief Extension Act of 1999 (P.L. 106-170)

P.L. 106-170, §536(a)(2):

Amended Code Sec. 453(d)(1) by striking "(a)" and inserting "(a)(1)" each place it appeared. **Effective** for sales or other dispositions occurring on or after 12-17-99.

• 1980, Installment Sales Revision Act of 1980 (P.L. 96-471)

P.L. 96-471, §2(a):

Amended Code Sec. 453(d). **Effective** for dispositions after 10-19-80, in tax years ending after that date. Prior to amendment, Code Sec. 453(d) provided:

(d) GAIN OR LOSS ON DISPOSITION OF INSTALLMENT OBLIGATIONS.—

(1) GENERAL RULE.—If an installment obligation is satisfied at other than its face value or distributed, transmitted, sold, or otherwise disposed of, gain or loss shall result to the extent of the difference between the basis of the obligation and—

(A) the amount realized, in the case of satisfaction at other than face value of a sale or exchange, or

(B) the fair market value of the obligation at the time of distribution, transmission, or disposition, in the case of the distribution, transmission, or disposition otherwise than by sale or exchange.

Any gain or loss so resulting shall be considered as resulting from the sale or exchange of the property in respect of which the installment was received.

(2) BASIS OF OBLIGATION.—The basis of an installment obligation shall be the excess of the face value of the obligation over an amount equal to the income which would be returnable were the obligation satisfied in full.

(3) SPECIAL RULE FOR TRANSMISSION AT DEATH.—Except as provided in section 691 (relating to recipients of income in respect of decedents), this subsection shall not apply to the transmission of installment obligations at death.

(4) EFFECT OF DISTRIBUTION IN CERTAIN LIQUIDATIONS.—

(A) LIQUIDATIONS TO WHICH SECTION 332 APPLIES.—If—

(i) an installment obligation is distributed in a liquidation to which section 332 (relating to complete liquidations of subsidiaries) applies, and

(ii) the basis of such obligation in the hands of the distributee is determined under section 334(b)(1),

then no gain or loss with respect to the distribution of such obligation shall be recognized by the distributing corporation.

(B) LIQUIDATIONS TO WHICH SECTION 337 APPLIES.—If—

(i) an installment obligation is distributed by a corporation in the course of a liquidation, and

(ii) under section 337 (relating to gain or loss on sales or exchanges in connection with certain liquidations) no gain or loss would have been recognized to the corporation if the corporation had sold or exchanged such installment obligation on the day of such distribution,

then no gain or loss shall be recognized to such corporation by reason of such distribution. The preceding sentence shall not apply to the extent that under paragraph (1) gain to the distributing corporation would be considered as gain to which section 341(f), 617(d)(1), 1245(a), 1250(a), 1251(c), 1252(a), or 1254(a) applies. In the case of any installment obligation which would have met the requirements of clauses (i) and (ii) of the first sentence of this subparagraph but for section 337(f), gain shall be recognized to such corporation by reason of such distribution only to the extent gain would have been recognized under section 337(f) if such corporation had sold or exchanged such installment obligation on the day of such distribution.

(5) LIFE INSURANCE COMPANIES.—In the case of a disposition of an installment obligation by any person other than a life insurance company (as defined in section 801(a)) to such an insurance company or to a partnership of which such an insurance company is a partner, no provision of this subtitle providing for the nonrecognition of gain shall apply with respect to any gain resulting under paragraph (1). If a corporation which is a life insurance company for the taxable year was (for the preceding taxable year) a corporation which was not a life insurance company, such corporation shall, for purposes of this paragraph and paragraph (1), be treated as having transferred to a life insurance company, on the last day of the preceding taxable year, all installment obligations which it held on such last day. A partnership of which a life insurance company becomes a partner shall, for purposes of this paragraph and paragraph (1), be treated as having transferred to a life insurance company, on the last day of the preceding taxable year of such partnership, all installment obligations which it holds at the time such insurance company becomes a partner.

• 1980, Crude Oil Windfall Profit Tax Act of 1980 (P.L. 96-223)

P.L. 96-223, §403(b)(2)(B):

Amended Code Sec. 453(d)(4)(B) by adding the last sentence. **Effective** with respect to distributions and dispositions pursuant to plans of liquidation adopted after 12-31-81.

• 1976, Tax Reform Act of 1976 (P.L. 94-455)

P.L. 94-455, §205(c)(1)(E):

Amended Code Sec. 453(d)(4)(B) by substituting "1252(a), or 1254(a)" for "or 1252(a)". **Effective** for tax years ending after 12-31-75.

P.L. 94-455, §1901(a)(66)(B):

Amended Code Sec. 453(d)(4)(B) by substituting, "617(d)(1)" for "or section 617(d)(1)". **Effective** for tax years beginning after 12-31-76.

• 1969, Tax Reform Act of 1969 (P.L. 91-172)

P.L. 91-172, §211(b):

Amended Code Sec. 453(d)(4)(B) by striking out "or 1250(a)" and inserting "1250(a), 1251(c), or 1252(a)". **Effective** for tax years beginning after 12-31-69.

• 1966, Foreign Investors Tax Act of 1966 (P.L. 89-809)

P.L. 89-809, §202(c):

Amended Code Sec. 453(d)(4)(A). **Effective** for distributions made after 11-13-66, the date of enactment. Prior to amendment, Sec. 453(d)(4)(A) read as follows:

"(a) Liquidations to Which Section 332 Applies.—If—

"(i) an installment obligation is distributed by one corporation to another corporation in the course of a liquidation, and

"(ii) under section 332 (relating to complete liquidations of subsidiaries) no gain or loss with respect to the receipt of such obligation is recognized in the case of the recipient corporation.

"then no gain or loss with respect to the distribution of such obligation shall be recognized in the case of the distributing corporation. If the basis of the property of the liquidating corporation in the hands of the distributee is determined under section 334(b)(2) then the preceding sentence shall not apply to the extent that under paragraph (1) gain to the distributing corporation would be considered as gain to which section 341(f) or section 617(d)(1), 1245(a), or 1250(a) applies."

• 1966 (P.L. 89-570)

P.L. 89-570, §[1(b)]:

Amended Code Sec. 453(d)(4)(A) and (B) by substituting "section 617(d)(1), 1245(a)," for "section 1245(a)". **Effective** for tax years ending after 9-12-66, the date of enactment, but only in respect of expenditures paid or incurred after that date.

• 1964 (P.L. 88-484)

P.L. 88-484, §[1(b)]:

Amended Code Sec. 453(d)(4)(A) and (B) by inserting "section 341(f) or" immediately before "section 1245(a)". **Effective** for transactions after 8-22-64, in tax years ending after such date.

• 1964, Revenue Act of 1964 (P.L. 88-272)

P.L. 88-272, §231(b)(5):

Amended Code Sec. 453(d)(4) to add "or 1250(a)" in the last sentence of subparagraphs (A) and (B). **Effective** for dispositions after 12-31-63, in tax years ending after such date.

• 1962, Revenue Act of 1962 (P.L. 87-834)

P.L. 87-834, §13(f)(5):

Amended Code Sec. 453(d)(4)(A) and (B) by adding the last sentences. **Effective** for tax years beginning after 12-31-62.

• 1958, Technical Amendments Act of 1958 (P.L. 85-866)

P.L. 85-866, §27:

Added paragraph (5) to subsection (d). **Effective** for tax years ending after 12-31-57, but only as to such transfers or other dispositions of installment obligations occurring after such date.

[Sec. 453(e)]

(e) SECOND DISPOSITIONS BY RELATED PERSONS.—

(1) IN GENERAL.—If—

(A) Any person disposes of property to a related person (hereinafter in this subsection referred to as the "first disposition"), and

(B) before the person making the first disposition receives all payments with respect to such disposition, the related person disposes of the property (hereinafter in this subsection referred to as the "second disposition"),

then, for purposes of this section, the amount realized with respect to such second disposition shall be treated as received at the time of the second disposition by the person making the first disposition.

(2) 2-YEAR CUTOFF FOR PROPERTY OTHER THAN MARKETABLE SECURITIES.—

(A) IN GENERAL.—Except in the case of marketable securities, paragraph (1) shall apply only if the date of the second disposition is not more than 2 years after the date of the first disposition.

(B) SUBSTANTIAL DIMINISHING OF RISK OF OWNERSHIP.—The running of the 2-year period set forth in subparagraph (A) shall be suspended with respect to any property for any period during which the related person's risk of loss with respect to the property is substantially diminished by—

(i) the holding of a put with respect to such property (or similar property),

(ii) the holding by another person of a right to acquire the property, or

(iii) a short sale or any other transaction.

(3) LIMITATION ON AMOUNT TREATED AS RECEIVED.—The amount treated for any taxable year as received by the person making the first disposition by reason of paragraph (1) shall not exceed the excess of—

(A) the lesser of—

(i) the total amount realized with respect to any second disposition of the property occurring before the close of the taxable year, or

(ii) the total contract price for the first disposition, over

(B) the sum of—

(i) the aggregate amount of payments received with respect to the first disposition before the close of such year, plus

(ii) the aggregate amount treated as received with respect to the first disposition for prior taxable years by reason of this subsection.

(4) FAIR MARKET VALUE WHERE DISPOSITION IS NOT SALE OR EXCHANGE.—For purposes of this subsection, if the second disposition is not a sale or exchange, an amount equal to the fair market value of the property disposed of shall be substituted for the amount realized.

(5) LATER PAYMENTS TREATED AS RECEIPT OF TAX PAID AMOUNTS.—If paragraph (1) applies for any taxable year, payments received in subsequent taxable years by the person making the first disposition shall not be treated as the receipt of payments with respect to the first disposition to the extent that the aggregate of such payments does not exceed the amount treated as received by reason of paragraph (1).

(6) EXCEPTION FOR CERTAIN DISPOSITIONS.—For purposes of this subsection—

(A) REACQUISITIONS OF STOCK BY ISSUING CORPORATION NOT TREATED AS FIRST DISPOSITIONS.—Any sale or exchange of stock to the issuing corporation shall not be treated as a first disposition.

(B) INVOLUNTARY CONVERSIONS NOT TREATED AS SECOND DISPOSITIONS.—A compulsory or involuntary conversion (within the meaning of section 1033) and any transfer thereafter shall not be treated as a second disposition if the first disposition occurred before the threat or imminence of the conversion.

(C) DISPOSITIONS AFTER DEATH.—Any transfer after the earlier of—

(i) the death of the person making the first disposition, or

(ii) the death of the person acquiring the property in the first disposition,

and any transfer thereafter shall not be treated as a second disposition.

(7) EXCEPTION WHERE TAX AVOIDANCE NOT A PRINCIPAL PURPOSE.—This subsection shall not apply to a second disposition (and any transfer thereafter) if it is established to the satisfaction of the Secretary that neither the first disposition nor the second disposition had as one of its principal purposes the avoidance of Federal income tax.

(8) EXTENSION OF STATUTE OF LIMITATIONS.—The period for assessing a deficiency with respect to a first disposition (to the extent such deficiency is attributable to the application of this subsection) shall not expire before the day which is 2 years after the date on which the person making the first disposition furnishes (in such manner as the Secretary may by regulations prescribe) a notice that there was a second disposition of the property to which this subsection may have applied. Such deficiency may be assessed notwithstanding the provisions of any law or rule of law which would otherwise prevent such assessment.

Amendments

• 1980, Installment Sales Revision Act of 1980 (P.L. 96-471)

P.L. 96-471, §2(a):

Amended Code Sec. 453(e). **Effective** for first dispositions made after 5-14-80. Prior to amendment, Code Sec. 453(e) provided:

(e) CARRYING CHARGES NOT INCLUDED IN TOTAL CONTRACT PRICE.—If the carrying charges or interest with respect to sales of personal property, the income from which is returned under subsection (a)(1), is not included in the total contract price, payments received with respect to such sales shall be treated as applying first against such carrying charges or interest. This subsection shall not apply with respect to sales or other dispositions of property the income from which is, under subsection (b), returned on the basis and in the manner prescribed in subsection (a)(1).

• 1964 (P.L. 88-539)

P.L. 88-539, §3(b):

Amended Code Sec. 453(e). **Effective** for sales made during tax years beginning after 12-31-63. Prior to amendment, Sec. 453(e) read as follows:

(e) REVOLVING CREDIT TYPE PLANS.—For purposes of subsection (a), the term `installment plan' includes a revolving credit type plan which provides that the purchaser of personal property at retail may pay for such property in a series of periodic payments of an agreed portion of the amounts due the seller under the plan, except that such term does not include any such plan with respect to a purchaser who uses his account primarily as an ordinary charge account.

• **1964, Revenue Act of 1964 (P.L. 88-272)**

P.L. 88-272, §222(a):

Added subsection (e). **Effective** for sales made during tax years beginning after 12-31-63.

[Sec. 453(f)]

(f) DEFINITIONS AND SPECIAL RULES.—For purposes of this section—

(1) RELATED PERSON.—Except for purposes of subsections (g) and (h), the term "related person" means—

(A) a person whose stock would be attributed under section 318(a) (other than paragraph (4) thereof) to the person first disposing of the property, or

(B) a person who bears a relationship described in section 267(b) to the person first disposing of the property.

(2) MARKETABLE SECURITIES.—The term "marketable securities" means any security for which, as of the date of the disposition, there was a market on an established securities market or otherwise.

(3) PAYMENT.—Except as provided in paragraph (4), the term "payment" does not include the receipt of evidences of indebtedness of the person acquiring the property (whether or not payment of such indebtedness is guaranteed by another person).

(4) PURCHASER EVIDENCES OF INDEBTEDNESS PAYABLE ON DEMAND OR READILY TRADABLE.—Receipt of a bond or other evidence of indebtedness which—

(A) is payable on demand, or

(B) is readily tradable,

shall be treated as receipt of payment.

(5) READILY TRADABLE DEFINED.—For purposes of paragraph (4), the term "readily tradable" means a bond or other evidence of indebtedness which is issued—

(A) with interest coupons attached or in registered form (other than one in registered form which the taxpayer establishes will not be readily tradable in an established securities market), or

(B) in any other form designed to render such bond or other evidence of indebtedness readily tradable in an established securities market.

(6) LIKE-KIND EXCHANGES.—In the case of any exchange described in section 1031(b)—

(A) the total contract price shall be reduced to take into account the amount of any property permitted to be received in such exchange without recognition of gain,

(B) the gross profit from such exchange shall be reduced to take into account any amount not recognized by reason of section 1031(b), and

(C) the term "payment", when used in any provision of this section other than subsection (b)(1), shall not include any property permitted to be received in such exchange without recognition of gain.

Similar rules shall apply in the case of an exchange which is described in section 356(a) and is not treated as a dividend.

(7) DEPRECIABLE PROPERTY.—The term "depreciable property" means property of a character which (in the hands of the transferee) is subject to the allowance for depreciation provided in section 167.

(8) PAYMENTS TO BE RECEIVED DEFINED.—The term "payments to be received" includes—

(A) the aggregate amount of all payments which are not contingent as to amount, and

(B) the fair market value of any payments which are contingent as to amount.

Amendments

• **2004, American Jobs Creation Act of 2004 (P.L. 108-357)**

P.L. 108-357, §897(a):

Amended Code Sec. 453(f)(4)(B) by striking "is issued by a corporation or a government or political subdivision thereof and" following "(B)". **Effective** for sales occurring on or after 10-22-2004.

• **1988, Technical and Miscellaneous Revenue Act of 1988 (P.L. 100-647)**

P.L. 100-647, §1018(u)(25):

Amended Code Sec. 453(f)(1) by striking out "subsection (g)" and inserting in lieu thereof "subsections (g)". **Effective** as if included in the provision of P.L. 99-514 to which it relates.

P.L. 100-647, §1018(u)(26):

Amended Code Sec. 453(f)(8) by striking out "payment to be" and inserting in lieu thereof "payments to be". **Effective** as if included in the provision of P.L. 99-514 to which it relates.

• **1986, Tax Reform Act of 1986 (P.L. 99-514)**

P.L. 99-514, §642(a)(3):

Amended Code Sec. 453(f)(1). **Effective**, generally, for sales after 10-22-86, in the tax years ending after such date. For a transitional rule for binding contracts see Act Sec. 643(c)(2), below. Prior to amendment, Code Sec. 453(f)(1) read as follows:

(1) RELATED PERSON.—Except for purposes of subsections (g) and (h), the term "related person" means a person whose stock would be attributed under section 318(a) (other than

paragraph (4) thereof) to the person first disposing of the property.

P.L. 99-514, §642(b)(1):

Amended Code Sec. 453(f) by adding at the end thereof new subsection (8). **Effective**, generally, for sales after 10-22-86, in the tax years ending after such date. For a transitional rule for binding contracts see Act Sec. 643(c)(2), below.

P.L. 99-514, §643(c)(2), as amended by P.L. 100-647, §1006(i)(3), provides:

(2) TRANSITIONAL RULE FOR BINDING CONTRACTS.—The amendments made by this section shall not apply to sales made after August 14, 1986, which are made pursuant to a binding contract in effect on August 14, 1986, and at all times thereafter.

• 1983, Technical Corrections Act of 1982 (P.L. 97-448)

P.L. 97-448, §303:

Amended Code Sec. 453(f)(6)(C) by inserting ", when used in any provision of this section other than subsection (b)(1)," after "the term `payment'". **Effective** for dispositions made after 10-19-80, in tax years ending after such date.

• 1980, Installment Sales Revision Act of 1980 (P.L. 96-471)

P.L. 96-471, §2(a):

Added Code Sec. 453(f). **Effective** for dispositions made after 10-19-80, in tax years ending after that date.

[Sec. 453(g)]

(g) SALE OF DEPRECIABLE PROPERTY TO CONTROLLED ENTITY.—

(1) IN GENERAL.—In the case of an installment sale of depreciable property between related persons—

(A) subsection (a) shall not apply,

(B) for purposes of this title—

(i) except as provided in clause (ii), all payments to be received shall be treated as received in the year of the disposition, and

(ii) in the case of any payments which are contingent as to the amount but with respect to which the fair market value may not be reasonably ascertained, the basis shall be recovered ratably, and

(C) the purchaser may not increase the basis of any property acquired in such sale by any amount before the time such amount is includible in the gross income of the seller.

(2) EXCEPTION WHERE TAX AVOIDANCE NOT A PRINCIPAL PURPOSE.—Paragraph (1) shall not apply if it is established to the satisfaction of the Secretary that the disposition did not have as one of its principal purposes the avoidance of Federal income tax.

(3) RELATED PERSONS.—For purposes of this subsection, the term "related persons" has the meaning given to such term by section 1239(b), except that such term shall include 2 or more partnerships having a relationship to each other described in section 707(b)(1)(B).

Amendments

• 1988, Technical and Miscellaneous Revenue Act of 1988 (P.L. 100-647)

P.L. 100-647, §1006(i)(1):

Amended Code Sec. 453(g)(1) by striking out subparagraph (A)-(B) and inserting in lieu thereof new subparagraphs (A)-(C). **Effective** as if included in the provision of P.L. 99-514 to which it relates. Prior to amendment, Code Sec. 453(g)(1)(A)-(B) read as follows:

(A) subsection (a) shall not apply, and

(B) for purposes of this title—

(i) except as provided in clause (ii), all payments to be received shall be treated as received in the year of the disposition, and

(ii) in the case of any payments which are contingent as to amount but with respect to which the fair market value may not be reasonably ascertained—

(I) the basis shall be recovered ratably, and

(II) the purchaser may not increase the basis of any property acquired in such sale by any amount before such time as the seller includes such amount in income.

P.L. 100-647, §1006(i)(2)(A):

Amended Code Sec. 453(g) by adding at the end thereof new paragraph (3). **Effective** as if included in the provision of P.L. 99-514 to which it relates.

P.L. 100-647, §1006(i)(2)(B):

Amended Code Sec. 453(g)(1) by striking out "(within the meaning of section 1239(b))" after "persons". **Effective** as if included in the provision of P.L. 99-514 to which it relates.

• 1986, Tax Reform Act of 1986 (P.L. 99-514)

P.L. 99-514, §642(a)(1)(D):

Amended Code Sec. 453(g) by striking out "80-PERCENT OWNED" and inserting in lieu thereof "CONTROLLED" in the heading thereof. **Effective**, generally, for sales after 10-22-86, in tax years ending after such date. For a transitional rule for binding contracts see Act Sec. 643(c)(2), below.

P.L. 99-514, §642(b)(2):

Amended Code Sec. 453(g)(1). **Effective**, generally, for sales after 10-22-86, in tax years ending after such date. For a traditional rule for binding contracts see Act Sec. 643(c)(2), below. Prior to amendment, Code Sec. 453(g)(1) read as follows:

(1) IN GENERAL.—In the case of an installment sale of depreciable property between related persons within the meaning of section 1239(b), subsection (a) shall not apply, and, for purposes of this title, all payments to be received shall be deemed received in the year of the disposition.

P.L. 99-514, §643(c)(2), as amended by P.L. 100-647, §1006(i)(3), provides:

(2) TRANSITIONAL RULE FOR BINDING CONTRACTS.—The amendments made by this section shall not apply to sales made after August 14, 1986, which are made pursuant to a binding contract in effect on August 14, 1986, and at all times thereafter.

• 1984, Deficit Reduction Act of 1984 (P.L. 98-369)

P.L. 98-369, §421(b)(6)(C):

Amended Code Sec. 453(g) by striking out "SPOUSE OR" from the subsection (g) heading. **Effective** for transfers after 7-18-84, in tax years ending after such date. Special rules appear in Act Sec. 421(d)(2)-(4) following Code Sec. 1041. Prior to the amendment, the heading for subsection (g) read as follows:

(g) SALE OF DEPRECIABLE PROPERTY TO SPOUSE OR 80-PERCENT OWNED ENTITY.—

• 1980, Installment Sales Revision Act of 1980 (P.L. 96-471)

P.L. 96-471, §2(a):

Added Code Sec. 453(g). **Effective** for dispositions made after 10-19-80, in tax years ending after that date.

[Sec. 453(h)]

(h) USE OF INSTALLMENT METHOD BY SHAREHOLDERS IN CERTAIN LIQUIDATIONS.—

(1) RECEIPT OF OBLIGATIONS NOT TREATED AS RECEIPT OF PAYMENT.—

(A) IN GENERAL.—If, in a liquidation to which section 331 applies, the shareholder receives (in exchange for the shareholder's stock) an installment obligation acquired in respect of a sale or exchange by the corporation during the 12-month period beginning on the date a plan of complete liquidation is adopted and the liquidation is completed during such 12-month period, then, for purposes of this section, the receipt of payments under such obligation (but not the receipt of such obligation) by the shareholder shall be treated as the receipt of payment for the stock.

(B) OBLIGATIONS ATTRIBUTABLE TO SALE OF INVENTORY MUST RESULT FROM BULK SALE.—Subparagraph (A) shall not apply to an installment obligation acquired in respect of a sale or exchange of—

(i) stock in trade of the corporation,

(ii) other property of a kind which would properly be included in the inventory of the corporation if on hand at the close of the taxable year, and

(iii) property held by the corporation primarily for sale to customers in the ordinary course of its trade or business,

unless such sale or exchange is to 1 person in 1 transaction and involves substantially all of such property attributable to a trade or business of the corporation.

(C) SPECIAL RULE WHERE OBLIGOR AND SHAREHOLDER ARE RELATED PERSONS.—If the obligor of any installment obligation and the shareholder are married to each other or are related persons (within the meaning of section 1239(b)), to the extent such installment obligation is attributable to the disposition by the corporation of depreciable property—

(i) subparagraph (A) shall not apply to such obligation, and

(ii) for purposes of this title, all payments to be received by the shareholder shall be deemed received in the year the shareholder receives the obligation.

(D) COORDINATION WITH SUBSECTION (e)(1)(A).—For purposes of subsection (e)(1)(A), dispostion of property by the corporation shall be treated also as disposition of such property by the shareholder.

(E) SALES BY LIQUIDATING SUBSIDIARIES.—For purposes of subparagraph (A), in the case of controlling corporate shareholder (within the meaning of section 368(c)) of a selling corporation, an obligation acquired in respect of a sale or exchange by the selling corporation shall be treated as so acquired by such controlling corporate shareholder. The preceding sentence shall be applied successively to each controlling corporate shareholder above such controlling corporate shareholder.

(2) DISTRIBUTIONS RECEIVED IN MORE THAN 1 TAXABLE YEAR OF SHAREHOLDER.—If—

(A) paragraph (1) applies with respect to any installment obligation received by a shareholder from a corporation, and

(B) by reason of the liquidation such shareholder receives property in more than 1 taxable year,

then, on completion of the liquidation, basis previously allocated to property so received shall be reallocated for all such taxable years so that the shareholder's basis in the stock of the corporation is properly allocated among all property received by such shareholder in such liquidation.

Amendments

• 1988, Technical and Miscellaneous Revenue Act of 1988 (P.L. 100-647)

P.L. 100-647, §1006(e)(7)(A):

Amended Code Sec. 453(h)(1)(B) by striking out "to one person" and inserting in lieu thereof "to 1 person in 1 transaction". **Effective** as if included in the provision of P.L. 99-514 to which it relates.

P.L. 100-647, §1006(e)(7)(B):

Amended Code Sec. 453(h)(1)(E) by striking out "section 368(c)(1)" and inserting in lieu thereof "section 368(c)". **Effective** as if included in the provision of P.L. 99-514 to which it relates.

• 1986, Tax Reform Act of 1986 (P.L. 99-514)

P.L. 99-514, §631(e)(8)(A):

Amended Code Sec. 453(h)(1)(A)-(B). **Effective** for (1) any distribution in complete liquidation, and any sale or exchange made by a corporation after 7-31-86, unless such corporation is completely liquidated before 1-1-87, (2) any transaction described in section 338 of the Internal Revenue Code of 1986 for which the acquisition date occurs after 12-31-86, and (3) any distribution (not in complete liquidation) made after 12-31-86. Prior to amendment, Code Sec. 453(h)(1)(A)-(B) read as follows:

(A) IN GENERAL.—If, in connection with a liquidation to which section 337 applies, in a transaction to which section 331 applies the shareholder receives (in exchange for the shareholder's stock) an installment obligation acquired in respect of a sale or exchange by the corporation during the 12-month period set forth in section 337(a), then, for purposes of this section, the receipt of payments under such obligation (but not the receipt of such obligation) by the shareholder shall be treated as the receipt of payment for the stock.

(B) OBLIGATIONS ATTRIBUTABLE TO SALE OF INVENTORY MUST RESULT FROM BULK SALE.—Subparagraph (A) shall not apply to an installment obligation described in section 337(b)(1)(B) unless such obligation is also described in section 337(b)(2)(B).

P.L. 99-514, §631(e)(8)(B):

Amended Code Sec. 453(h)(1)(E). **Effective** for (1) any distribution in complete liquidation, and any sale or exchange made by a corporation after 7-31-86, unless such corporation is completely liquidated before 1-1-87, (2) any transaction described in section 338 of the Internal Revenue Code of 1986 for which the acquisition date occurs after 12-31-86, and (3) any distribution (not in complete liquidation) made after 12-31-86. Prior to amendment, Code Sec. 453(h)(1)(E) read as follows:

(E) SALES BY LIQUIDATING SUBSIDIARY.—For purposes of subparagraph (A), in any case to which section 337(c)(3) applies, an obligation acquired in respect of a sale or exchange by the selling corporation shall be treated as so acquired by the corporation distributing the obligation to the shareholder.

P.L. 99-514, §631(e)(8)(C):

Amended Code Sec. 453(h) by striking out "SECTION 337" and inserting in lieu thereof "CERTAIN" in the heading thereof. **Effective** for (1) any distribution in complete liquidation, and any sale or exchange made by a corporation after 7-31-86, unless such corporation is completely liquidated before 1-1-87, (2) any transaction described in section 338 of the Internal Revenue Code of 1986 for which the acquisition date occurs after 12-31-86, and (3) any distribution (not in complete liquidation) made after 12-31-86.

• 1984, Deficit Reduction Act of 1984 (P.L. 98-369)

P.L. 98-369, §421(b)(6)(B):

Amended Code Sec. 453(h)(1)(C) by striking out "the obligor of any installment obligation and the shareholder are related persons" and inserting in lieu thereof "the obligor of any installment obligation and the shareholder are married to each other or are related persons". **Effective** for transfers after 7-18-84, in tax years ending after such date. Special rules appear in Act Sec. 421(d)(2)-(4) following Code Sec. 1041.

• 1980, Installment Sales Revision Act of 1980 (P.L. 96-471)

P.L. 96-471, §2(a):

Added Code Sec. 453(h). **Effective** for distributions of installment obligations made after 3-31-80.

[Sec. 453(i)]

(i) RECOGNITION OF RECAPTURE INCOME IN YEAR OF DISPOSITION.—

(1) IN GENERAL.—In the case of any installment sale of property to which subsection (a) applies—

(A) notwithstanding subsection (a), any recapture income shall be recognized in the year of the disposition, and

(B) any gain in excess of the recapture income shall be taken into account under the installment method.

(2) RECAPTURE INCOME.—For purposes of paragraph (1), the term "recapture income" means, with respect to any installment sale, the aggregate amount which would be treated as ordinary income under section 1245 or 1250 (or so much of section 751 as relates to section 1245 or 1250) for the taxable year of the disposition if all payments to be received were received in the taxable year of disposition.

Amendments

• 2000, Installment Tax Correction Act of 2000 (P.L. 106-573)

P.L. 106-573, §2(a):

Repealed Act Sec. 536(a)(2) of the Ticket to Work and Work Incentives Improvement Act of 1999 (P.L. 106-170), which amended Code Sec. 453(i)(1) by striking "(a)" each place it appeared and inserting "(a)(1)". **Effective** with respect to sales and other dispositions occurring on or after the date of the enactment of P.L. 106-170 [**effective** 12-17-99.—CCH]. Thus, the amendment made to Code Sec. 453(i)(1) never took effect and Code Sec. 453(i)(1) is restored to read as it did prior to amendment by P.L. 106-170.

• 1999, Tax Relief Extension Act of 1999 (P.L. 106-170)

P.L. 106-170, §536(a)(2):

Amended Code Sec. 453(i)(1) by striking "(a)" and inserting "(a)(1)" each place it appeared. **Effective** for sales or other dispositions occurring on or after 12-17-99.

• 1986, Tax Reform Act of 1986 (P.L. 99-514)

P.L. 99-514, §1809(c):

Amended Code Sec. 453(i)(2) by striking out "section 1245 or 1250" and inserting in lieu thereof "section 1245 or 1250 (or so much of section 751 as relates to section 1245 or 1250)". **Effective** as if included in the provision of P.L. 98-369 to which such amendment relates.

• 1984, Deficit Reduction Act of 1984 (P.L. 98-369)

P.L. 98-369, §112(a):

Amended Code Sec. 453(i). **Effective** for dispositions made after 6-6-84. Special rules appear below. Prior to amendment, it read as follows:

(i) APPLICATION WITH SECTION 179.—

(1) IN GENERAL.—In the case of an installment sale of section 179 property, subsection (a) shall not apply, and for purposes of this title, all payments to be received shall be deemed received in the year of disposition.

(2) LIMITATION.—Paragraph (1) shall apply only to the extent of the amount allowed as a deduction under section 179 with respect to the section 179 property.

P.L. 98-369, §112(b)(2) and (3), provides:

(2) EXCEPTION.—The amendments made by this Section shall not apply with respect to any disposition conducted pursuant to a contract which was binding on March 22, 1984, and at all times thereafter.

(3) SPECIAL RULE FOR CERTAIN DISPOSITIONS BEFORE OCTOBER 1, 1984.—The amendments made by this section shall not apply to any disposition before October 1, 1984, of all or substantially all of the personal property of a cable television business pursuant to a written offer delivered by the seller on June 20, 1984, but only if the last payment under the installment contract is due no later than October 1, 1989.

• 1981, Economic Recovery Tax Act of 1981 (P.L. 97-34)

P.L. 97-34, §202(c):

Added Code Sec. 453(i). **Effective** for property placed in service after 12-31-80, in tax years ending after such date.

[Sec. 453(j)]

(j) REGULATIONS.—

(1) IN GENERAL.—The Secretary shall prescribe such regulations as may be necessary or appropriate to carry out the provisions of this section.

(2) SELLING PRICE NOT READILY ASCERTAINABLE.—The regulations prescribed under paragraph (1) shall include regulations providing for ratable basis recovery in transactions where the gross profit or the total contract price (or both) cannot be readily ascertained.

Amendments

• 1981, Economic Recovery Tax Act of 1981 (P.L. 97-34)

P.L. 97-34, §202(c):

Redesignated Code Sec. 453(i) as Code Sec. 453(j). **Effective** for property placed in service after 12-31-80, in tax years ending after such date.

• 1980, Installment Sales Revision Act of 1980 (P.L. 96-471)

P.L. 96-471, §2(a):

Added Code Sec. 453(i). **Effective** for dispositions made after 10-19-80, in tax years ending after that date.

[Sec. 453(k)]

(k) CURRENT INCLUSION IN CASE OF REVOLVING CREDIT PLANS, ETC.—In the case of—

(1) any disposition of personal property under a revolving credit plan, or

(2) any installment obligation arising out of a sale of—

(A) stock or securities which are traded on an established securities market, or

(B) to the extent provided in regulations, property (other than stock or securities) of a kind regularly traded on an established market,

subsection (a) shall not apply, and, for purposes of this title, all payments to be received shall be treated as received in the year of disposition. The Secretary may provide for the application of this subsection in whole or in part for transactions in which the rules of this subsection otherwise would be avoided through the use of related parties, pass-thru entities, or intermediaries.

Amendments

• 2000, Installment Tax Correction Act of 2000 (P.L. 106-573)

P.L. 106-573, §2(a):

Repealed Act Sec. 536(a)(2) of P.L. 106-170, which amended Code Sec. 453(k) by striking "(a)" and inserting "(a)(1)". Thus, the amendment made to Code Sec. 453(k) never took effect and Code Sec. 453(k) is restored. **Effective** with respect to sales and other dispositions occurring on or after the date of the enactment of such Act (P.L. 106-170) [**effective** 12-17-99.—CCH].

• 1999, Tax Relief Extension Act of 1999 (P.L. 106-170)

P.L. 106-170, §536(a)(2):

Amended Code Sec. 453(k) by striking "(a)" and inserting "(a)(1)". **Effective** for sales or other dispositions occurring on or after 12-17-99.

• 1988, Technical and Miscellaneous Revenue Act of 1988 (P.L. 100-647)

P.L. 100-647, §1008(g)(1):

Amended Code Sec. 453 by redesignating subsection (j) as subsection (k). **Effective** as if included in the provision of P.L. 99-514 to which it relates.

P.L. 100-647, §2004(d)(5):

Amended Code Sec. 453(k) by striking out "and section 453A" after "subsection (a)". **Effective** as if included in the provision of P.L. 100-203 to which it relates.

• 1986, Tax Reform Act of 1986 (P.L. 99-514)

P.L. 99-514, §812(a):

Amended Code Sec. 453 by adding at the end thereof new subsection (j)[(k)]. **Effective**, generally, for tax years beginning after 12-31-86. However, see Act Sec. 812(c)(2)-(6), below.

P.L. 99-514, §812(c)(2)-(6), as amended by P.L. 100-647, §1008(g)(3)-(6), provides:

(2) SALES OF STOCK, ETC.—Section 453(k)(2) of the Internal Revenue Code of 1986, as added by subsection (a), shall apply to sales after December 31, 1986, in taxable years ending after such date.

(3) CHANGE IN METHOD OF ACCOUNTING.—In the case of any taxpayer who made sales under a revolving credit plan and was on the installment method under section 453 or 453A of the Internal Revenue Code of 1986 for such taxpayer's last taxable year beginning before January 1, 1987, the amendments made by this section shall be treated as a change in method of accounting for its 1st taxable year beginning after December 31, 1986, and—

(A) such change shall be treated as initiated by the taxpayer,

(B) such change shall be treated as having been made with the consent of the Secretary,

(C) the period for taking into account adjustments under section 481 of such Code by reason of such change shall be equal to 4 years, and

(D) except as provided in paragraph (4), the amount taken into account in each of such 4 years shall be the applicable percentage (determined in accordance with the following table) of the net adjustment:

In the case of the:	The applicable percentage is:
1st taxable year	15
2nd taxable year	25
3rd taxable year	30
4th taxable year	30

If the taxpayer's last taxable year beginning before January 1, 1987, was the taxpayer's 1st taxable year in which sales were made under a revolving credit plan, all adjustments under section 481 of such Code shall be taken into account in the taxpayer's 1st taxable year beginning after December 31, 1986.

(4) ACCELERATION OF ADJUSTMENTS WHERE CONTRACTION IN AMOUNT OF INSTALLMENT OBLIGATIONS.—

(A) IN GENERAL.—If the percentage determined under subparagraph (B) for any taxable year in the adjustment period exceeds the percentage which would otherwise apply under paragraph (3)(D) for such taxable year (determined after the application of this paragraph for prior taxable years in the adjustment period)—

(i) the percentage determined under subparagraph (B) shall be substituted for the applicable percentage which would otherwise apply under paragraph (3)(D), and

(ii) any increase in the applicable percentage by reason of clause (i) shall be applied to reduce the applicable percentage determined under paragraph (3)(D) for subsequent taxable years in the adjustment period (beginning with the 1st of such subsequent taxable years).

(B) DETERMINATION OF PERCENTAGE.—For purposes of subparagraph (A), the percentage determined under this subparagraph for any taxable year in the adjustment period is the excess (if any) of—

(i) the percentage determined by dividing the aggregate contraction in revolving installment obligations by the aggregate face amount of such obligations outstanding as of the close of the taxpayer's last taxable year beginning before January 1, 1987, over

(ii) the sum of the applicable percentages under paragraph (3)(D) (as modified by this paragraph) for prior taxable years in the adjustment period.

(C) AGGREGATE CONTRACTION IN REVOLVING INSTALLMENT OBLIGATIONS.—For purposes of subparagraph (B), the aggregate contraction in revolving installment obigations is the amount by which—

(i) the aggregate face amount of the revolving installment obligations outstanding as of the close of the taxpayer's last taxable year beginning before January 1, 1987, exceeds

(ii) the aggregate face amount of the revolving installment obligations outstanding as of the close of the taxable year involved.

(D) REVOLVING INSTALLMENT OBLIGATIONS.—For purposes of this paragraph, the term "revolving installment obligations" means installment obligations arising under a revolving credit plan.

(E) TREATMENT OF CERTAIN OBLIGATIONS DISPOSED OF ON OR BEFORE OCTOBER 26, 1987.—For purposes of subparagraphs (B)(i) and (C)(i), in determining the aggregate face amount of revolving installment obligations outstanding as of the close of the taxpayer's last taxable year beginning before January 1, 1987, there shall not be taken into account any obligation—

(i) which was disposed of to an unrelated person on or before October 26, 1987, or

(ii) was disposed of to an unrelated person on or after such date pursuant to a binding written contract in effect on October 26, 1987, and at all times thereafter before such disposition.

For purposes of the preceding sentence the term "unrelated person" means any person who is not a related person (as defined in section 453(g) of the Internal Revenue Code of 1986).

(5) LIMITATION ON LOSSES FROM SALES OF OBLIGATIONS UNDER REVOLVING CREDIT PLANS.—If 1 or more obligations arising under a revolving credit plan and taken into account under paragraph (3) are disposed of during the adjustment period, then, notwithstanding any other provision of law—

(A) no losses from such dispositions shall be recognized, and

(B) the aggregate amount of the adjustment for taxable years in the adjustment period (in reverse order of time) shall be reduced by the amount of such losses.

(6) ADJUSTMENT PERIOD.—For purposes of paragraphs (4) and (5), the adjustment period is the 4-year period under paragraph (3).

[Sec. 453(l)]

(l) DEALER DISPOSITIONS.—For purposes of subsection (b)(2)(A)—

(1) IN GENERAL.—The term "dealer disposition" means any of the following dispositions:

(A) PERSONAL PROPERTY.—Any disposition of personal property by a person who regularly sells or otherwise disposes of personal property of the same type on the installment plan.

(B) REAL PROPERTY.—Any disposition of real property which is held by the taxpayer for sale to customers in the ordinary course of the taxpayer's trade or business.

(2) EXCEPTIONS.—The term "dealer disposition" does not include—

(A) FARM PROPERTY.—The disposition on the installment plan of any property used or produced in the trade or business of farming (within the meaning of section 2032A(e)(4) or (5)).

(B) TIMESHARES AND RESIDENTIAL LOTS.—

(i) IN GENERAL.—Any dispositions described in clause (ii) on the installment plan if the taxpayer elects to have paragraph (3) apply to any installment obligations which arise from such dispositions. An election under this paragraph shall not apply with respect to an installment obligation which is guaranteed by any person other than an individual.

(ii) DISPOSITIONS TO WHICH SUBPARAGRAPH APPLIES.—A disposition is described in this clause if it is a disposition in the ordinary course of the taxpayer's trade or business to an individual of—

(I) a timeshare right to use or a timeshare ownership interest in residential real property for not more than 6 weeks per year, or a right to use specified campgrounds for recreational purposes, or

(II) any residential lot, but only if the taxpayer (or any related person) is not to make any improvements with respect to such lot.

For purposes of subclause (I), a timeshare right to use (or timeshare ownership interest in) property held by the spouse, children, grandchildren, or parents of an individual shall be treated as held by such individual.

(C) CARRYING CHARGES OR INTEREST.—Any carrying charges or interest with respect to a disposition described in subparagraph (A) or (B) which are added on the books of account of the seller to the established cash selling price of the property shall be included in the total contract price of the property and, if such charges or interest are not so included, any payments received shall be treated as applying first against such carrying charges or interest.

(3) PAYMENT OF INTEREST ON TIMESHARES AND RESIDENTIAL LOTS.—

(A) IN GENERAL.—In the case of any installment obligation to which paragraph (2)(B) applies, the tax imposed by this chapter for any taxable year for which payment is received on such obligation shall be increased by the amount of interest determined in the manner provided under subparagraph (B).

(B) COMPUTATION OF INTEREST.—

(i) IN GENERAL.—The amount of interest referred to in subparagraph (A) for any taxable year shall be determined—

(I) on the amount of the tax for such taxable year which is attributable to the payments received during such taxable year on installment obligations to which this subsection applies,

(II) for the period beginning on the date of sale, and ending on the date such payment is received, and

(III) by using the applicable Federal rate under section 1274 (without regard to subsection (d)(2) thereof) in effect at the time of the sale compounded semiannually.

(ii) INTEREST NOT TAKEN INTO ACCOUNT.—For purposes of clause (i), the portion of any tax attributable to the receipt of any payment shall be determined without regard to any interest imposed under subparagraph (A).

(iii) TAXABLE YEAR OF SALE.—No interest shall be determined for any payment received in the taxable year of the disposition from which the installment obligation arises.

(C) TREATMENT AS INTEREST.—Any amount payable under this paragraph shall be taken into account in computing the amount of any deduction allowable to the taxpayer for interest paid or accrued during such taxable year.

Amendments

• 1988, Technical and Miscellaneous Revenue Act of 1988 (P.L. 100-647)

P.L. 100-647, §2004(d)(1):

Amended Code Sec. 453(l)(1)(A) by striking out "disposes of personal property" and inserting in lieu thereof "disposes of personal property of the same type". **Effective** as if included in the provision of P.L. 100-203 to which it relates.

• 1987, Revenue Act of 1987 (P.L. 100-203)

P.L. 100-203, §10202(b)(2):

Amended Code Sec. 453 by adding at the end thereof new subsection (l). For the **effective** date, see the amendment notes following Code Sec. 453C.

[Sec. 453A]

SEC. 453A. SPECIAL RULES FOR NONDEALERS.

[Sec. 453A(a)]

(a) GENERAL RULE.—In the case of an installment obligation to which this section applies—

(1) interest shall be paid on the deferred tax liability with respect to such obligation in the manner provided under subsection (c), and

(2) the pledging rules under subsection (d) shall apply.

[Sec. 453A(b)]

(b) INSTALLMENT OBLIGATIONS TO WHICH SECTION APPLIES.—

(1) IN GENERAL.—This section shall apply to any obligation which arises from the disposition of any property under the installment method, but only if the sales price of such property exceeds $150,000.

(2) SPECIAL RULE FOR INTEREST PAYMENTS.—For purposes of subsection (a)(1), this section shall apply to an obligation described in paragraph (1) arising during a taxable year only if—

(A) such obligation is outstanding as of the close of such taxable year, and

(B) the face amount of all such obligations held by the taxpayer which arose during, and are outstanding as of the close of, such taxable year exceeds $5,000,000.

Except as provided in regulations, all persons treated as a single employer under subsection (a) or (b) of section 52 shall be treated as one person for purposes of this paragraph and subsection (c)(4).

(3) EXCEPTION FOR PERSONAL USE AND FARM PROPERTY.—An installment obligation shall not be treated as described in paragraph (1) if it arises from the disposition—

(A) by an individual of personal use property (within the meaning of section 1275(b)(3)), or

(B) of any property used or produced in the trade or business of farming (within the meaning of section 2032A(e)(4) or (5)).

(4) SPECIAL RULE FOR TIMESHARES AND RESIDENTIAL LOTS.—An installment obligation shall not be treated as described in paragraph (1) if it arises from a disposition described in section 453(l)(2)(B), but the provisions of section 453(l)(3) (relating to interest payments on timeshares and residential lots) shall apply to such obligation.

(5) SALES PRICE.—For purposes of paragraph (1), all sales or exchanges which are part of the same transaction (or a series of related transactions) shall be treated as 1 sale or exchange.

Amendments

• 1989, Omnibus Budget Reconciliation Act of 1989 (P.L. 101-239)

P.L. 101-239, §7812(c)(2):

Amended Code Sec. 453A(b)(3), before the amendment by Act Sec. 7815(g), by striking "(5)." and inserting "(5))." **Effective** as if included in the provision of P.L. 100-647 to which it relates. See the amendment note for Act Sec. 7815(g).

P.L. 101-239, §7815(g):

Amended Code Sec. 453A(b)(3). **Effective** as if included in the provision of P.L. 100-647 to which it relates. Prior to amendment, Code Sec. 453(A)(b)(3) read as follows:

(3) EXCEPTION FOR FARM PROPERTY.—An installment obligation shall not be treated as described in paragraph (1) if it arises from the disposition of any property used or produced in the trade or business of farming (within the meaning of section 2032A(e)(4) or (5)).

P.L. 101-239, §7821(a)(1):

Amended Code Sec. 453A(b)(2)(B) by striking "all obligations of the taxpayer described in paragraph (1)" and inserting "all such obligations held by the taxpayer". **Effective** as if included in the provision of P.L. 100-203 to which it relates.

• 1988, Technical and Miscellaneous Revenue Act of 1988 (P.L. 100-647)

P.L. 100-647, §2004(d)(7):

Amended Code Sec. 453A(b)(2) by striking out "for purposes of this paragraph" and inserting in lieu thereof "for purposes of this paragraph and subsection (c)(4)". **Effective** as if included in the provision of P.L. 100-203 to which it relates.

P.L. 100-647, §2004(d)(8):

Amended Code Sec. 453A(b)(3). **Effective** as if included in the provision of P.L. 100-203 to which it relates. Prior to amendment, Code Sec. 453A(b)(3) read as follows:

(3) EXCEPTION FOR PERSONAL USE AND FARM PROPERTY.—An installment obligation shall not be treated as described in paragraph (1) if it arises from the dispostion—

(A) by an individual of personal use property (within the meaning of section 1275(b)(3)), or

(B) of any property used or produced in the trade or business of farming (within the meaning of section 2032A(e)(4) or (5)).

P.L. 100-647, §5076(a):

Amended Code Sec. 453A(b)(1). **Effective**, generally, for sales after 12-31-88. However, for a special rule, see Act Sec. 5076(c)(2), below. Prior to amendment, Code Sec. 453A(b)(1) read as follows:

(1) IN GENERAL.—This section shall apply to any obligation which arises from the disposition of real property under the installment method which is property used in the taxpayer's trade or business or property held for the production of rental income, but only if the sales price of such property exceeds $150,000.

P.L. 100-647, §5076(b)(1):

Amended Code Sec. 453A by striking out "OF REAL PROPERTY" in the heading after "NONDEALERS". **Effective**, generally, for sales after 12-31-88. However, for a special rule, see Act Sec. 5076(c)(2), below.

P.L. 100-647, §5076(c)(2), provides:

(c)(2) BINDING CONTRACT, ETC.—The amendments made by this section shall not apply to any sale on or before December 31, 1990, if—

(A) such sale is pursuant to a written binding contract in effect on October 21, 1988, and at all times thereafter before such sale,

(B) such sale is pursuant to a letter of intent in effect on October 21, 1988, or

(C) there is a board of directors or shareholder approval for such sale on or before October 21, 1988.

[Sec. 453A(c)]

(c) INTEREST ON DEFERRED TAX LIABILITY.—

(1) IN GENERAL.—If an obligation to which this section applies is outstanding as of the close of any taxable year, the tax imposed by this chapter for such taxable year shall be increased by the amount of interest determined in the manner provided under paragraph (2).

(2) COMPUTATION OF INTEREST.—For purposes of paragraph (1), the interest for any taxable year shall be an amount equal to the product of—

(A) the applicable percentage of the deferred tax liability with respect to such obligation, multiplied by

(B) the underpayment rate in effect under section 6621(a)(2) for the month with or within which the taxable year ends.

(3) DEFERRED TAX LIABILITY.—For purposes of this section, the term "deferred tax liability" means, with respect to any taxable year, the product of—

(A) the amount of gain with respect to an obligation which has not been recognized as of the close of such taxable year, multiplied by

(B) the maximum rate of tax in effect under section 1 or 11, whichever is appropriate, for such taxable year.

For purposes of applying the preceding sentence with respect to so much of the gain which, when recognized, will be treated as long-term capital gain, the maximum rate on net capital gain under section 1(h) or 1201 (whichever is appropriate) shall be taken into account.

(4) APPLICABLE PERCENTAGE.—For purposes of this subsection, the term "applicable percentage" means, with respect to obligations arising in any taxable year, the percentage determined by dividing—

(A) the portion of the aggregate face amount of such obligations outstanding as of the close of such taxable year in excess of $5,000,000, by

(B) the aggregate face amount of such obligations outstanding as of the close of such taxable year.

(5) TREATMENT AS INTEREST.—Any amount payable under this subsection shall be taken into account in computing the amount of any deduction allowable to the taxpayer for interest paid or accrued during the taxable year.

(6) REGULATIONS.—The Secretary shall prescribe such regulations as may be necessary to carry out the provisions of this subsection including regulations providing for the application of this subsection in the case of contingent payments, short taxable years, and pass-thru entities.

Amendments

• 1993, Omnibus Budget Reconciliation Act of 1993 (P.L. 103-66)

P.L. 103-66, §13201(b)(4):

Amended Code Sec. 453A(c)(3) by adding at the end thereof the new sentence. **Effective** for tax years beginning after 12-31-92.

• 1989, Omnibus Budget Reconciliation Act of 1989 (P.L. 101-239)

P.L. 101-239, §7821(a)(4)(B):

Amended Code Sec. 453A(c) by redesignating paragraph (5) as paragraph (6) and by inserting after paragraph (4) a new paragraph (5). **Effective** as if included in the provision of P.L. 100-203 to which it relates.

[Sec. 453A(d)]

(d) PLEDGES, ETC., OF INSTALLMENT OBLIGATIONS.—

(1) IN GENERAL.—For purposes of section 453, if any indebtedness (hereinafter in this subsection referred to as "secured indebtedness") is secured by an installment obligation to which this section applies, the net proceeds of the secured indebtedness shall be treated as a payment received on such installment obligation as of the later of—

(A) the time the indebtedness becomes secured indebtedness, or

(B) the time the proceeds of such indebtedness are received by the taxpayer.

(2) LIMITATION BASED ON TOTAL CONTRACT PRICE.—The amount treated as received under paragraph (1) by reason of any secured indebtedness shall not exceed the excess (if any) of—

(A) the total contract price, over

(B) any portion of the total contract price received under the contract before the later of the times referred to in subparagraph (A) or (B) of paragraph (1) (including amounts previously treated as received under paragraph (1) but not including amounts not taken into account by reason of paragraph (3)).

(3) LATER PAYMENTS TREATED AS RECEIPT OF TAX PAID AMOUNTS.—If any amount is treated as received under paragraph (1) with respect to any installment obligation, subsequent payments received on such obligation shall not be taken into account for purposes of section 453 to the extent that the aggregate of such subsequent payments does not exceed the aggregate amount treated as received under paragraph (1).

(4) SECURED INDEBTEDNESS.—For purposes of this subsection indebtedness is secured by an installment obligation to the extent that payment of principal or interest on such indebtedness is directly secured (under the terms of the indebtedness or any underlying arrangements) by any interest in such installment obligation. A payment shall be treated as directly secured by an interest in an installment obligation to the extent an arrangement allows the taxpayer to satisfy all or a portion of the indebtedness with the installment obligation.

Amendments

• 1999, Tax Relief Extension Act of 1999 (P.L. 106-170)

P.L. 106-170, §536(b):

Amended Code Sec. 453A(d)(4) by adding at the end a new sentence. **Effective** for sales or other dispositions occurring on or after 12-17-99.

• 1989, Omnibus Budget Reconciliation Act of 1989 (P.L. 101-239)

P.L. 101-239, §7821(a)(2):

Amended Code Sec. 453A(d)(2)(B) by striking "before such secured indebtedness was incurred" and inserting "before the later of the times referred to in subparagraph (A) or (B) of paragraph (1)". **Effective** as if included in the provision of P.L. 100-203 to which it relates.

P.L. 101-239, §7821(a)(3):

Amended Code Sec. 453A(d)(1)(B) by inserting "the time" before "the proceeds". **Effective** as if included in the provision of P.L. 100-203 to which it relates.

• 1988, Technical and Miscellaneous Revenue Act of 1988 (P.L. 100-647)

P.L. 100-647, §6031, provides:

SEC. 6031. CERTAIN REPLEDGES PERMITTED.

(a) GENERAL RULE.—Section 453A(d) of the 1986 Code (relating to pledges, etc., of installment obligations) shall not apply to any pledge after December 17, 1987, of an installment obligation to secure any indebtedness if such indebtedness is incurred to refinance indebtedness which was outstanding on December 17, 1987, and which was secured on such date and all times thereafter before such refinancing by a pledge of such installment obligation.

(b) LIMITATION.—Subsection (a) shall not apply to the extent that the principal amount of the indebtedness resulting from the refinancing exceeds the principal amount of the refinanced indebtedness immediately before the refinancing.

(c) CERTAIN REFINANCINGS PERMITTED.—For purposes of subsection (a), if—

(1) a refinancing is attributable to the calling of indebtedness by the creditor, and

(2) such refinancing is not with the creditor under the refinanced indebtedness or a person related to such creditor, such refinancing shall, to the extent the refinanced indebtedness qualifies under subsections (a) and (b), be treated as a continuation of such refinanced indebtedness.

• 1987, Revenue Act of 1987 (P.L. 100-203)

P.L. 100-203, §10202(c)[1]:

Amended Code Sec. 453A. For the **effective** date, see the amendment notes following Code Sec. 453C. Prior to amendment Code Sec. 453A read as follows:

Sec. 453A. INSTALLMENT METHOD FOR DEALERS IN PERSONAL PROPERTY.

[Sec. 453A(a)]

(a) GENERAL RULE.—

(1) IN GENERAL.—Under regulations prescribed by the Secretary, a person who regularly sells or otherwise disposes of personal property on the installment plan may return as income therefrom in any taxable year that proportion of the installment payments actually received in that year which the gross profit, realized or to be realized when payment is completed, bears to the total contract price.

(2) TOTAL CONTRACT PRICE.—For purposes of paragraph (1), the total contract price of all sales of personal property on the installment plan includes the amount of carrying charges or interest which is determined with respect to such sales and is added on the books of account of the seller to the established cash selling price of such property.

Amendments

• 1986, Tax Reform Act of 1986 (P.L. 99-514)

P.L. 99-514, §812(b)(1):

Amended Code Sec. 453A(a)(2) by striking out the last sentence thereof. **Effective**, generally, for tax years beginning after 12-31-86. However, see Act Sec. 812(c)(2) following Code Sec. 453. Prior to amendment, the sentence read as follows: This paragraph shall not apply with respect to sales of personal property under a revolving credit type plan.

• 1980, Installment Sales Revision Act of 1980 (P.L. 96-471)

P.L. 96-471, §2(a):

Added Code Sec. 453A(a). **Effective** for tax years ending after 10-19-80.

[Sec. 453A(b)]

(b) CARRYING CHARGES NOT INCLUDED IN TOTAL CONTRACT PRICE.—If the carrying charges or interest with respect to sales of personal property, the income from which is returned under subsection (a)(1), is not included in the total contract price, payments received with respect to such sales shall be treated as applying first against such carrying charges or interest.

Amendments

• **1980, Installment Sales Revision Act of 1980 (P.L. 96-471)**

P.L. 96-471, §2(a):

Added Code Sec. 453A(b). **Effective** for tax years ending after 10-19-80.

[Sec. 453A(c)]

(c) CROSS REFERENCE.—

For disallowance of use of installment method for certain obligations, see section 453(k).

Amendments

• **1988, Technical and Miscellaneous Revenue Act of 1988 (P.L. 100-647)**

P.L. 100-647, §1008(g)(2):

Amended Code Sec. 453A(c) by striking out "453(j)" and inserting in lieu thereof "453(k)". **Effective** as if included in the provision of P.L. 99-514 to which it relates.

• **1986, Tax Reform Act of 1986 (P.L. 99-514)**

P.L. 99-514, §812(b)(2):

Amended Code Sec. 453A by adding at the end thereof new subsection (c). **Effective**, generally, for tax years beginning after 12-31-86. However, see Act Sec. 812(c)(2) following Code Sec. 453.

[Sec. 453A(e)]

(e) REGULATIONS.—The Secretary shall prescribe such regulations as may be necessary to carry out the purposes of this section, including regulations—

(1) disallowing the use of the installment method in whole or in part for transactions in which the rules of this section otherwise would be avoided through the use of related persons, pass-thru entities, or intermediaries, and

(2) providing that the sale of an interest in a partnership or other pass-thru entity will be treated as a sale of the proportionate share of the assets of the partnership or other entity.

Amendments

• **1988, Technical and Miscellaneous Revenue Act of 1988 (P.L. 100-647)**

P.L. 100-647, §2004(d)(2):

Amended Code Sec. 453A by adding at the end thereof a new subsection (e). **Effective** as if included in the provision of P.L. 100-203 to which it relates.

P.L. 100-647, §6031, provides:

SEC. 6031. CERTAIN REPLEDGES PERMITTED.

(a) GENERAL RULE.—Section 453A(d) of the 1986 Code (relating to pledges, etc., of installment obligations) shall not apply to any pledge after December 17, 1987, of an installment obligation to secure any indebtedness if such indebtedness is incurred to refinance indebtedness which was outstanding on December 17, 1987, and which was secured on such date and all times thereafter before such refinancing by a pledge of such installment obligation.

(b) LIMITATION.—Subsection (a) shall not apply to the extent that the principal amount of the indebtedness resulting from the refinancing exceeds the principal amount of the refinanced indebtedness immediately before the refinancing.

(c) CERTAIN REFINANCINGS PERMITTED.—For purposes of subsection (a), if—

(1) a refinancing is attributable to the calling of indebtedness by the creditor, and

(2) such refinancing is not with the creditor under the refinanced indebtedness or a person related to such creditor, such refinancing shall, to the extent the refinanced indebtedness qualifies under subsections (a) and (b), be treated as a continuation of such refinanced indebtedness.

[Sec. 453B]

SEC. 453B. GAIN OR LOSS ON DISPOSITION OF INSTALLMENT OBLIGATIONS.

[Sec. 453B(a)]

(a) GENERAL RULE.—If an installment obligation is satisfied at other than its face value or distributed, transmitted, sold, or otherwise disposed of, gain or loss shall result to the extent of the difference between the basis of the obligation and—

(1) the amount realized, in the case of satisfaction at other than face value or a sale or exchange, or

(2) the fair market value of the obligation at the time of distribution, transmission, or disposition, in the case of the distribution, transmission, or disposition otherwise than by sale or exchange.

Any gain or loss so resulting shall be considered as resulting from the sale or exchange of the property in respect of which the installment obligation was received.

[Sec. 453B(b)]

(b) BASIS OF OBLIGATION.—The basis of an installment obligation shall be the excess of the face value of the obligation over an amount equal to the income which would be returnable were the obligation satisfied in full.

[Sec. 453B(c)]

(c) SPECIAL RULE FOR TRANSMISSION AT DEATH.—Except as provided in section 691 (relating to recipients of income in respect of decedents), this section shall not apply to the transmission of installment obligations at death.

[Sec. 453B(d)]

(d) EXCEPTION FOR DISTRIBUTIONS TO WHICH SECTION 337(a) APPLIES.—Subsection (a) shall not apply to any distribution to which section 337(a) applies.

Amendments

• 1990, Omnibus Budget Reconciliation Act of 1990 (P.L. 101-508)

P.L. 101-508, §11702(a)(2):

Amended Code Sec. 453B(d). **Effective** as if included in the provision of P.L. 100-647 to which it relates. Prior to amendment, subsection (d) read as follows:

(d) EFFECT OF DISTRIBUTION IN LIQUIDATIONS TO WHICH SECTION 332 APPLIES.—If—

(1) an installment obligation is distributed in a liquidation to which section 332 (relating to complete liquidations of subsidiaries) applies, and

(2) the basis of such obligation in the hands of the distributee is determined under section 334(b)(1),

then no gain or loss with respect to the distribution of such obligation shall be recognized by the distributing corporation.

• 1986, Tax Reform Act of 1986 (P.L. 99-514)

P.L. 99-514, §631(e)(9):

Amended Code Sec. 453B(d). **Effective** for (1) any distribution in complete liquidation, and any sale or exchange, made by a corporation after 7-31-86, unless such corporation is completely liquidated before 1-1-87, (2) any transaction described in section 338 of the Internal Revenue Code of 1986 for which the acquisition date occurs after 12-31-86, and (3) any distribution (not in complete liquidation) made after 12-31-86. Prior to amendment, Code Sec. 453B(d) read as follows:

(d) EFFECT OF DISTRIBUTION IN CERTAIN LIQUIDATIONS.—

(1) LIQUIDATIONS TO WHICH SECTION 332 APPLIES.—If—

(A) an installment obligation is distributed in a liquidation to which section 332 (relating to complete liquidations of subsidiaries) applies, and

(B) the basis of such obligation in the hands of the distributee is determined under section 334(b)(1),

then no gain or loss with respect to the distribution of such obligation shall be recognized by the distributing corporation.

(2) LIQUIDATIONS TO WHICH SECTION 337 APPLIES.—If—

(A) an installment obligation is distributed by a corporation in the course of a liquidation, and

(B) under section 337 (relating to gain or loss on sales or exchanges in connection with certain liquidations) no gain or loss would have been recognized to the corporation if the corporation had sold or exchanged such installment obligation on the day of such distribution,

then no gain or loss shall be recognized to such corporation by reason of such distribution. The preceding sentence shall not apply to the extent that under subsection (a) gain to the distributing corporation would be considered as gain to which section 341(f), 617(d)(1), 1245(a), 1250(a), 1252(a), 1254(a), or 1276(a) applies. In the case of any installment obligation which would have met the requirements of subparagraphs (A) and (B) of the first sentence of this paragraph but for section 337(f), gain shall be recognized to such corporation by reason of such distribution only to the extent gain would have been recognized under section 337(f) if such corporation had sold or exchanged such installment obligation on the date of such distribution.

• 1984, Deficit Reduction Act of 1984 (P.L. 98-369)

P.L. 98-369, §43(c)(2):

Amended Code Sec. 453B(d)(2) by striking out "or 1254(a)" and inserting in lieu thereof "1254(a), or 1276(a)". **Effective** for tax years ending after 7-18-84.

P.L. 98-369, §492(b)(3):

Amended Code Sec. 453B(d)(2) by striking out "1251(c)" from the second sentence. **Effective** for tax years beginning after 12-31-83.

• 1983, Technical Corrections Act of 1982 (P.L. 97-448)

P.L. 97-448, §302:

Amended Code Sec. 453B(d)(2) by striking out "to the extent that under paragraph (1)" and inserting in lieu thereof "to the extent that under subsection (a)". **Effective** for dispositions made after 10-19-80, in tax years ending after such date.

• 1980, Installment Sales Revision Act of 1980 (P.L. 96-471)

P.L. 96-471, §2(c)(3):

Amended Code Sec. 453B(d) by adding the last sentence. **Effective** as if included in the amendments made by §403(b) of P.L. 96-223.

[Sec. 453B(e)]

(e) LIFE INSURANCE COMPANIES.—

(1) IN GENERAL.—In the case of a disposition of an installment obligation by any person other than a life insurance company (as defined in section 816(a)) to such an insurance company or to a partnership of which such an insurance company is a partner, no provision of this subtitle providing for the nonrecognition of gain shall apply with respect to any gain resulting under subsection (a). If a corporation which is a life insurance company for the taxable year was (for the preceding taxable year) a corporation which was not a life insurance company, such corporation shall, for purposes of this subsection and subsection (a), be treated as having transferred to a life insurance company, on the last day of the preceding taxable year, all installment obligations which it held on such last day. A partnership of which a life insurance company becomes a partner shall, for purposes of this subsection and subsection (a), be treated as having transferred to a life insurance company, on the last day of the preceding taxable year of such partnership, all installment obligations which it holds at the time such insurance company becomes a partner.

(2) SPECIAL RULE WHERE LIFE INSURANCE COMPANY ELECTS TO TREAT INCOME AS NOT RELATED TO INSURANCE BUSINESS.—Paragraph (1) shall not apply to any transfer or deemed transfer of an installment obligation if the life insurance company elects (at such time and in such manner as the Secretary may by regulations prescribe) to determine its life insurance company taxable income—

(A) by returning the income on such installment obligation under the installment method prescribed in section 453, and

(B) as if such income were an item attributable to a noninsurance business (as defined in section 806(b)(3)).

Amendments

• 1986, Tax Reform Act of 1986 (P.L. 99-514)

P.L. 99-514, §1011(b)(1):

Amended Code Sec. 453B(e)(2)(B) by striking out "806(c)(3)" and inserting in lieu thereof "806(b)(3)". **Effective** for tax years beginning after 12-31-86.

• 1984, Deficit Reduction Act of 1984 (P.L. 98-369)

P.L. 98-369, §211(b)(6)(A), (B):

Amended Code Sec. 453B(e)(1) by striking out "section 801(a)" and inserting in lieu thereof "section 816(a)". **Effective** for tax years beginning after 12-31-83.

P.L. 98-369, §211(b)(6)(A), (B):

Amended Code Sec. 453B(e)(2). **Effective** for tax years beginning after 12-31-83. Prior to amendment, Code Sec. 453B(e)(2) read as follows:

(2) SPECIAL RULE WHERE LIFE INSURANCE COMPANY ELECTS TO TREAT INCOME AS INVESTMENT INCOME.—Paragraph (1) shall not apply to any transfer or deemed transfer of an installment obligation if the life insurance company elects (at such time and in such manner as the Secretary may by regulations prescribe) to determine its life insurance company taxable income—

(A) by returning the income on such installment obligation under the installment method prescribed in section 453, and

(B) if such income would not otherwise be returnable as an item referred to in section 804(b) or as long-term capital gain, as if the income on such obligations were income specified in section 804(b).

• 1980, Installment Sales Revision Act of 1980 (P.L. 96-471)

P.L. 96-471, §2(a):

Added Code Sec. 453B(e). **Effective** for dispositions made after 10-19-80, in tax years ending after that date.

[Sec. 453B(f)]

(f) OBLIGATION BECOMES UNENFORCEABLE.—For purposes of this section, if any installment obligation is canceled or otherwise becomes unenforceable—

(1) the obligation shall be treated as if it were disposed of in a transaction other than a sale or exchange, and

(2) if the obligor and obligee are related persons (within the meaning of section 453(f)(1)), the fair market value of the obligation shall be treated as not less than its face amount.

Amendments

• 1980, Installment Sales Revision Act of 1980 (P.L. 96-471)

P.L. 96-471, §2(a):

Added Code Sec. 453B(f). **Effective** for installment obligations becoming unenforceable after 10-19-80.

[Sec. 453B(g)]

(g) TRANSFERS BETWEEN SPOUSES OR INCIDENT TO DIVORCE.—In the case of any transfer described in subsection (a) of section 1041 (other than a transfer in trust)—

(1) subsection (a) of this section shall not apply, and

(2) the same tax treatment with respect to the transferred installment obligation shall apply to the transferee as would have applied to the transferor.

Amendments

• 1986, Tax Reform Act of 1986 (P.L. 99-514)

P.L. 99-514, §1842(c):

Amended Code Sec. 453B(g) by striking out "section 1041" and inserting in lieu thereof "section 1041 (other than a transfer in trust)". **Effective** as if included in the provision of P.L. 98-369 to which it relates.

• 1984, Deficit Reduction Act of 1984 (P.L. 98-369)

P.L. 98-369, §421(b)(3):

Amended Code Sec. 453B by adding at the end thereof new subsection (g). **Effective** for transfers after 7-18-84, in tax years ending after such date. For special elections, see Act Sec. 421(d)(2)-(4) under Code Sec. 1041.

[Sec. 453B(h)]

(h) CERTAIN LIQUIDATING DISTRIBUTIONS BY S CORPORATIONS.—If—

(1) an installment obligation is distributed by an S corporation in a complete liquidation, and

(2) receipt of the obligation is not treated as payment for the stock by reason of section 453(h)(1),

then, except for purposes of any tax imposed by subchapter S, no gain or loss with respect to the distribution of the obligation shall be recognized by the distributing corporation. Under regulations prescribed by the Secretary, the character of the gain or loss to the shareholder shall be determined in accordance with the principles of section 1366(b).

Amendments

• 1988, Technical and Miscellaneous Revenue Act of 1988 (P.L. 100-647)

P.L. 100-647, §1006(e)(22):

Amended Code Sec. 453B by adding at the end thereof new subsection (h). **Effective** as if included in the provision of P.L. 99-514 to which it relates.

[Sec. 453C—Repealed]

Amendments

• 1987, Revenue Act of 1987 (P.L. 100-203)

P.L. 100-203, §10202(a)(1):

Repealed Code Sec. 453C. For the **effective** date, see P.L. 100-203, §10202(e), as amended by P.L. 100-647, §2004(d)(4), in the amendment notes for Code Sec. 453C(e), below. Prior to repeal, Code Sec. 453C read as follows:

SEC. 453C. CERTAIN INDEBTEDNESS TREATED AS PAYMENT ON INSTALLMENT OBLIGATIONS.

[Sec. 453C(a)]

(a) GENERAL RULE.—For purposes of sections 453 and 453A, if a taxpayer has allocable installment indebtedness for any taxable year, such indebtedness—

(1) shall be allocated on a pro rata basis to any applicable installment obligation of the taxpayer which—

(A) arises in such taxable year, and

(B) is outstanding as of the close of such taxable year, and

(2) shall be treated as a payment received on such obligation as of the close of such taxable year.

[Sec. 453C(b)]

(b) ALLOCABLE INSTALLMENT INDEBTEDNESS.—For purposes of this section—

(1) IN GENERAL.—The term "allocable installment indebtedness" means, with respect to any taxable year, the excess (if any) of—

(A) the installment percentage of the taxpayer's average quarterly indebtedness for such taxable year, over

(B) the aggregate amount treated as allocable installment indebtedness with respect to applicable installment obligations which—

(i) are outstanding as of the close of such taxable year, but

(ii) did not arise during such taxable year.

(2) INSTALLMENT PERCENTAGE.—The term "installment percentage" means the percentage (not in excess of 100 percent) determined by dividing—

(A) the face amount of all applicable installment obligations of the taxpayer outstanding as of the close of the taxable year, by

(B) the sum of—

(i) the aggregate adjusted bases of all assets not described in clause (ii) held as of the close of the taxable year, and

(ii) the face amount of all installment obligations outstanding as of such time.

For purposes of subparagraph (B)(i), a taxpayer may elect to compute the aggregate adjusted bases of all assets using the deduction for depreciation which is used in computing earnings and profits under section 312(k).

(3) SPECIAL RULES FOR PERSONAL USE PROPERTY.—For purposes of this subsection—

(A) for purposes of paragraph (2)(B), there shall not be taken into account any personal use property (within the meaning of section 1275(b)(3)) held by an individual or any installment obligation arising from the sale of such property, and

(B) for purposes of computing the taxpayer's average quarterly indebtedness under paragraph (1)(A), there shall not be taken into account any indebtedness with respect to which substantially all of the property securing such indebtedness is property described in subparagraph (A).

(4) SPECIAL RULE FOR CASUAL SALES.—If the taxpayer has no applicable installment obligations described in subclause (I) or (II) of subsection (e)(1)(A)(i) outstanding as of the close of the taxable year, then the taxpayer's allocable installment indebtedness of such taxable year, shall be computed by using the taxpayer's indebtedness as of the close of such taxable year (determined by not taking into account any indebtedness described in paragraph (3)(B)) in lieu of the taxpayer's average quarterly indebtedness.

Amendments

• 1988, Technical and Miscellaneous Revenue Act of 1988 (P.L. 100-647)

P.L. 100-647, §1008(f)(1)(A)-(B):

Amended Code Sec. 453C(b)(4) by striking out "at any time during" and inserting in lieu thereof "as of the close of", and by striking out "as of the close of such taxable year in lieu" and inserting in lieu thereof "as of the close of such taxable year (determined by not taking into account any indebtedness described in paragraph (3)(B)) in lieu". **Effective** as if included in the provision of P.L. 99-514 to which it relates. However, see Act Sec. 1008(f)(9), below.

P.L. 100-647, §1008(f)(9), provides:

(9) For purposes of applying the amendments made by this subsection and the amendments made by section 10202 of the Revenue Act of 1987, the provisions of this subsection shall be treated as having been enacted immediately before the enactment of the Revenue Act of 1987.

[Sec. 453C(c)]

(c) TREATMENT OF SUBSEQUENT PAYMENTS.—

(1) PAYMENTS TREATED AS RECEIPT OF TAX PAID AMOUNTS.—If any amount is treated as received under subsection (a) (after application of subsection (d)(2)) with respect to any apllicable installment obligation, subsequent payments received on such obligation shall not be taken into account for purposes of sections 453 and 453A to the extent that the aggregate amount of such subsequent payments does not exceed the aggregate amount treated as received on such obligation under subsection (a).

(2) REDUCTION OF ALLOCABLE INSTALLMENT INDEBTEDNESS.—For purposes of applying subsection (b)(1)(B) for the taxable year in which any payment to which paragraph (1) of this subsection applies was received (and for any subsequent taxable year), the allocable installment indebtedness with respect to the applicable installment obligation shall be reduced (but not below zero) by the amount of such payment not taken into account by reason of paragraph (1).

[Sec. 453C(d)]

(d) LIMITATION BASED ON TOTAL CONTRACT PRICE.—

(1) IN GENERAL.—The amount treated as received under subsection (a) (after application of paragraph (2)) with respect to any applicable installment obligation for any taxable year shall not exceed the excess (if any) of—

(A) the total contract price, over

(B) any portion of the total contract price received under the contract before the close of such taxable year—

(i) including amounts so treated under subsection (a) for all preceding taxable years (after application of paragraph (2)), but

(ii) not including amounts not taken into account by reason of subsection (c).

(2) EXCESS ALLOCABLE INSTALLMENT INDEBTEDNESS.—If the allocable installment indebtedness for any taxable year exceeds the amount which may be allocated under paragraph (1) to applicable installment obligations arising in (and outstanding as of the close of) such taxable year, such excess shall—

(A) subject to the limitations of paragraph (1), be allocated to applicable installment obligations outstanding as of the close of such taxable year which arose in preceding taxable years, beginning with applicable installment obligations arising in the earliest preceding taxable year, and

(B) be treated as a payment under subsection (a)(2).

Amendments

• 1988, Technical and Miscellaneous Revenue Act of 1988 (P.L. 100-647)

P.L. 100-647, §1008(f)(2):

Amended so much of paragraph (2) of Code Sec. 453C(d) as precedes subparagraph (A). **Effective** as if included in the provision of P.L. 99-514 to which it relates. However, see Act Sec. 1008(f)(9) in the amendment notes following Code Sec. 453C(b). Prior to amendment, so much of paragraph (2) of Code Sec. 453C(d) as precedes subparagraph (A) read as follows:

(2) EXCESS ALLOCABLE INSTALLMENT INDEBTEDNESS.—If, after application of paragraph (1), the allocable installment indebtedness for any taxable year exceeds the amount which may be allocated to applicable installment obligations arising in (and outstanding as of the close of) such taxable year, such excess shall—

[Sec. 453C(e)]

(e) DEFINITIONS AND SPECIAL RULES.—For purposes of this section—

(1) APPLICABLE INSTALLMENT OBLIGATION.—

(A) IN GENERAL.—The term "applicable installment obligation" means any obligation—

(i) which arises from the dispostion—

(I) after February 28, 1986, of personal property under the installment method by a person who regularly sells or otherwise disposes of personal property of the same type on the installment plan,

(II) after February 28, 1986, of real property under the installment method which is held by the taxpayer for sale to customers in the ordinary course of the taxpayer's trade or business, or

(III) after August 16, 1986, of real property under the installment method which is property used in the taxpayer's trade or business or property held for the production of rental income, but only if the sales price of such property exceeds $150,000 (determined after application of the rule under the last sentence of section 1274(c)(3)(A)(ii)), and

(ii) which is held by the seller or a member of the same affiliated group (within the meaning of section 1504(a), but without regard to section 1504(b)) as the seller.

Such term also includes any obligation held by any person if the basis of such obligation in the hands of such person is determined (in whole or in part) by reference to the basis of such obligation in the hands of another person and such obligation was an applicable installment obligation in the hands of such other person.

(B) EXCEPTION FOR PERSONAL USE AND FARM PROPERTY.—The term "applicable installment obligation" shall not include any obligation which arises from the disposition—

(i) by an individual of personal use property (within the meaning of section 1275(b)(3)), or

(ii) of any property used or produced in the trade or business of farming (within the meaning of section 2032A(e)(4) or (5)).

(2) AGGREGATION RULES.—Except as provided in regulations, for purposes of this section, all persons treated as a single employer under section 52 shall be treated as 1 taxpayer. The Secretary shall prescribe regulations for the treatment under this section of transactions between such persons.

(3) AGGREGATION OF OBLIGATIONS.—The Secretary may by regulations provide that all (or any portion of) applicable installment obligations of a taxpayer may be treated as 1 obligation.

(4) EXCEPTION FOR SALES OF TIMESHARES AND RESIDENTIAL LOTS.—

(A) IN GENERAL.—If a taxpayer elects the application of this paragraph, this section shall not apply to any installment obligation which—

(i) arises from a sale in the ordinary course of the taxpayer's trade or business to an individual of—

(I) a timeshare right to use or a timeshare ownership interest in residential real property for not more than 6 weeks, or a right to use specified campgrounds for recreational purposes, or

(II) any residential lot but only if the taxpayer (or any related person) is not to make any improvements with respect to such lot, and

(ii) which is not guaranteed by any person other than an individual.

For purposes of clause (i)(I), a timeshare right to use (or timeshare ownership interest in) property held by the spouse, children, grandchildren, or parents of an individual shall be treated as held by such individual.

(B) INTEREST ON DEFERRED TAX.—If subparagraph (A) applies to any installment obligation, interest shall be paid on the portion of any tax for any taxable year (determined without regard to any deduction allowable for such interest) which is attributable to the receipt of payments on such obligation in such year (other than payments received in the taxable year of the sale). Such interest shall be computed for the period from the date of the sale to the date on which the payment is received using the applicable Federal rate under section 1274 (without regard to subsection (d)(2) thereof) in effect at the time of the sale, compounded semiannually.

(C) TIME FOR PAYMENT.—Any interest payable under this paragraph with respect to a payment shall be treated as an addition to tax for the taxable year in which the payment is received, except that the amount of such interest shall be taken into account in computing the amount of any deduction allowable to the taxpayer for interest paid or accrued during such taxable year.

(5) REGULATIONS.—The Secretary shall prescribe regulations as may be necessary to carry out the purposes of this section, including regulations—

(A) disallowing the use of the installment method in whole or in part for transactions in which the rules of this section otherwise would be avoided through the use of related parties, pass-through entities, or intermediaries,

(B) providing for the proper treatment of reserves (including consistent treatment with assets held in the reserves), and

(C) providing that subsection (b)(4) shall not apply where necessary to prevent the avoidance of the application of this section.

Amendments

• 1988, Technical and Miscellaneous Revenue Act of 1988 (P.L. 100-647)

P.L. 100-647, §1008(f)(3):

Amended Code Sec. 453C(e)(1)(A) by adding at the end thereof a new sentence. **Effective** as if included in the provision of P.L. 99-514 to which it relates. However, see Act Sec. 1008(f)(9) in the amendment notes following Code Sec. 453C(b).

P.L. 100-647, §1008(f)(4):

Amended Code Sec. 453C(e)(2) by striking out "For" and inserting in lieu thereof "Except as provided in regulations, for". **Effective** as if included in the provision of P.L. 99-514 to which it relates. However, see Act Sec. 1008(f)(9) in the amendment notes following Code Sec. 453C(b).

P.L. 100-647, §1008(f)(5):

Amended Code Sec. 453C(e)(4)(B) by striking out "or (3)" after "subsection (d)(2)". **Effective** as if included in the provision of P.L. 99-514 to which it relates. However, see Act Sec. 1008(f)(9) in the amendment notes following Code Sec. 453C(b).

• 1987, Revenue Act of 1987 (P.L. 100-203)

P.L. 100-203, §10202(e), as amended by P.L. 100-647, §2004(d)(4), provides:

(e) EFFECTIVE DATES.—

(1) IN GENERAL.—Except as provided in this subsection, the amendments made by this section shall apply to dispositions in taxable years beginning after December 31, 1987.

(2) SPECIAL RULES FOR DEALERS.—

(A) IN GENERAL.—In the case of dealer dispositions (within the meaning of section 453(l)(1) of the Internal Revenue Code of 1986 as added by this section), the amendments made by subsections (a) and (b) shall apply to installment obligations arising from dispositions after December 31, 1987.

(B) SPECIAL RULES FOR OBLIGATIONS ARISING FROM DEALER DISPOSITIONS AFTER FEBRUARY 28, 1986, AND BEFORE JANUARY 1, 1988.—

(i) IN GENERAL.—In the case of an applicable installment obligation arising from a disposition described in subclause (I) or (II) of section 453C(e)(1)(A)(i) of the Internal Revenue Code of 1986 (as in effect before the amendments made by this section) before January 1, 1988, the amendments made by subsections (a) and (b) shall apply to taxable years begnning after December 31, 1987.

(ii) CHANGE IN METHOD OF ACCOUNTING.—In the case of any taxpayer who is required by clause (i) to change its method of accounting for any taxable year with respect to obligations described in clause (i)—

(I) such change shall be treated as initiated by the taxpayer,

(II) such change shall be treated as made with the consent of the Secretary of the Treasury or his delegate, and

(III) the net amount of adjustments required by section 481 of the Internal Revenue Code of 1986 shall be taken into account over a period not longer than 4 taxable years.

(C) CERTAIN RULES MADE APPLICABLE.—For purposes of this paragraph, rules similar to the rules of paragraphs (4) and (5) of section 812(c) of the Tax Reform Act of 1986 (as added by the Technical and Miscellaneous Revenue Act of 1988) shall apply.

(3) SPECIAL RULE FOR NONDEALERS.—

(A) ELECTION.—A taxpayer may elect, at such time and in such manner as the Secretary of the Treasury or his delegate may prescribe, to have the amendments made by subsections (a) and (c) apply to taxable years ending after December 31, 1986, with respect to dispositions and pledges occurring after August 16, 1986.

(B) PLEDGING RULES.—Except as provided in subparagraph (A)—

(i) IN GENERAL.—Section 453A(d) of the Internal Revenue Code of 1986 shall apply to any installment obligation which is pledged to secure any secured indebtedness (within the meaning of section 453A(d)(4) of such Code) after December 17, 1987, in taxable years ending after such date.

(ii) COORDINATION WITH SECTION 453C.—For purposes of section 453C of such Code (as in effect before its repeal), the face amount of any obligation to which section 453A(d) of such Code applies shall be reduced by the amount treated as payments on such obligation under section 453A(d) of such Code and the amount of any indebtedness secured by it shall not be taken into account.

(C) CERTAIN DISPOSITIONS DEEMED MADE ON 1ST DAY OF TAXABLE YEAR.—If the taxpayer makes an election under subparagraph (A), in the case of the taxpayer's 1st taxable year ending after December 31, 1986—

(i) dispositions after August 16, 1986, and before the 1st day of such taxable year shall be treated as made on such 1st day, and

(ii) subsections (b)(2)(B) and (c)(4) of section 453A of such Code shall be applied separately with respect to such dispositions by substituting for "$5,000,000" the amount which bears the same ratio to $5,000,000 as the number of days after August 16, 1986, and before such 1st day bears to 365.

(4) MINIMUM TAX.—The amendment made by subsection (d) shall apply to dispositions in taxable years beginning after December 31, 1986.

(5) COORDINATION WITH TAX REFORM ACT OF 1986.—The amendments made by this section shall not apply to any installment obligation or to any taxpayer during any period to the extent the amendments made by section 811 of the Tax Reform Act of 1986 do not apply to such obligation or during such period.

• 1986, Tax Reform Act of 1986 (P.L. 99-514)

P.L. 99-514, §811(a):

Amended subpart B of part II if subchapter E of chapter 1 by adding at the end thereof Code Sec. 453C. **Effective**, generally, for tax years ending after 12-31-86, with respect to dispositions after 2-28-86. For exceptions see Act Sec. 811(c)(2)-(8), below.

P.L. 99-514, §811(c)(2)-(8), as amended by P.L. 100-647, §1008(f)(6)-(8), and P.L. 105-34, §1088, provides:

[*Caution: Act Sec. 811(c)(2), below, is repealed effective August 5, 1998.—CCH.*]

(2) EXCEPTION FOR CERTAIN SALES OF PROPERTY BY A MANUFACTURER TO A DEALER.—

(A) IN GENERAL.—The amendments made by this section shall not apply to any installment obligation arising from the disposition of tangible personal property by a manufacturer (or any affiliate) to a dealer if—

(i) the dealer is obligated to pay on such obligation only when the dealer resells (or rents) the property,

(ii) the manufacturer has the right to repurchase the property at a fixed (or ascertainable) price after no later than the 9-month period beginning with the date of the sale, and

(iii) such disposition is in a taxable year with respect to which the requirements of subparagraph (B) are met.

(B) RECEIVABLES MUST BE AT LEAST 50 PERCENT OF TOTAL SALES.—

(i) IN GENERAL.—The requirements of this subparagraph are met with respect to any taxable year if for such taxable year and the preceding taxable year the aggregate face amount of installment obligations described in subparagraph (A) is as least 50 percent of the total sales to dealers giving rise to such obligations.

(ii) TAXPAYER MUST FAIL FOR 2 CONSECUTIVE YEARS.—A taxpayer shall be treated as failing to meet the requirements of clause (i) only if the taxpayer fails to meet the 50-percent test for both the taxable year and the preceding taxable year.

(C) TRANSITION RULE.—An obligation issued before the date of the enactment of this Act shall be treated as described in subparagraph (A) if, whithin 60 days after such date, the taxpayer modifies the terms of such obligation to conform to the requirements of subparagraph (A).

(D) APPLICATION WITH OTHER OBLIGATIONS.—In applying section 453C of the Internal Revenue Code of 1986 to any installment obligations to which the amendments made by this section apply, obligations described in subparagraph (A) shall not be treated as applicable installment obligations (within the meaning of section 453C(e)(1) of such Code).

(E) OTHER REQUIREMENTS.—This paragraph shall apply only if the taxpayer meets the requirements of subparagraphs (A) and (B) for its first taxable year beginning after the date of the enactment of this Act.

(3) EXCEPTION FOR CERTAIN OBLIGATIONS.—In applying the amendments made by this section to any installment obligation of a corporation incorporated on January 13, 1928, the following indebtedness shall not be taken into account in determining the allocable installment indebtedness if such corporation under section 453C of the Internal Revenue Code of 1986 (as added by this section):

(A) 12⅝ percent subordinated debentures with a total face amount of $175,000,000 issued pursuant to a trust indenture dated as of September 1, 1985.

(B) A revolving credit term loan in the maximum amount of $130,000,000 made pursuant to a revolving credit and security agreement dated as of September 6, 1985, payable in various stages with final payment due on August 31, 1992.

This paragraph shall also apply to indebtedness which replaces indebtedness described in this paragraph if such indebtedness does not exceed the amount and maturity of the indebtedness it replaces.

(4) SPECIAL RULE FOR RESIDENTIAL CONDOMINIUM PROJECT.—For purposes of applying the amendments made by this section, the term applicble installment obligation (within the meaning of section 453C(e)(1) of the Internal Revenue Code of 1986) shall not include any obligation arising in connection with sales from a residential condominium project—

(A) for which a contract to purchase land for the project was entered into at least 5 years before the date of the enactment of this Act,

(B) with respect to which land for the project was purchased before September 26, 1985,

(C) with respect to which building permits for the project were obtained, and construction commenced, before September 26, 1985,

(D) in conjunction with which not less than 80 units of low-income housing are deeded to a tax-exempt organization designated by a local government, and

(E) with respect to which at least $1,000,000 of expenses were incurred before September 26, 1985.

(5) SPECIAL RULE FOR QUALIFIED BUYOUT.—The amendments made by this section shall apply for taxable years ending after December 31, 1991, to a corporation if—

(A) such corporation was incorporated on May 25, 1984, for the purpose of acquiring all of the stock of another corporation,

(B) such acquisition took place on October 23, 1984,

(C) in connection with such acquisition, the corporation incurred indebtedness of approximately $151,000,000, and

(D) substantially all of the stock of the corporation is owned directly or indirectly by employees of the corporation the stock of which was acquired on October 23, 1984.

(6) SPECIAL RULE FOR SALES OF REAL PROPERTY BY DEALERS.—In the case of installment obligations arising from the sale of real property in the ordinary course of the trade or business of the taxpayer, any gain attributable to allocable installment indebtedness allocated to any such installment obligations which arise (or are deemed to arise)—

(A) in the 1st taxable year of the taxpayer ending after December 31, 1986, shall be taken into account ratably over the 3 taxable years beginning with such 1st taxable year, and.

(B) in the 2nd taxable year of the taxpayer ending after December 31, 1986, shall be taken into account ratably over the 2 taxable years beginning with such 2nd taxable year.

(7) SPECIAL RULE FOR SALES OF PERSONAL PROPERTY BY DEALERS.—In the case of installment obligations arising from the

sale of personal property in the ordinary course of the trade or business of the taxpayer, solely for purposes of determining the time for payment of tax and interest payable with respect to such tax—

(A) any increase in tax imposed by chapter 1 of the Internal Revenue Code of 1986 for the 1st taxable year of the taxpayer ending after December 31, 1986, by reason of the amendments made by this section shall be treated as imposed ratably over the 3 taxable years beginning with such 1st taxable year, and

(B) any increase in tax imposed by such chapter 1 for the 2nd taxable year of the taxpayer ending after December 31, 1986, (determined without regard to subparagraph (A)) by reason of the amendments made by this section shall be treated as imposed ratably over the 2 taxable years beginning with such 2nd taxable year.

(8) TREATMENT OF CERTAIN INSTALLMENT OBLIGATIONS.—Notwithstanding the amendments made by subtitle B of title III, gain with respect to installment payments received pursuant to notes issued in accordance with a note agreement dated as of August 29, 1980, where—

(A) such note agreement was executed pursuant to an agreement of purchase and sale dated April 25, 1980,

(B) more than 1/2 of the installment payments of the aggregate principal of such notes have been received by August 29, 1986, and

(C) the last installment payment of the principal of such notes is due August 29, 1989,

shall be taxed at a rate of 28 percent.

(9) SPECIAL RULES.—For purposes of section 453C of the 1986 Code (as added by subsection (a))—

(A) REVOLVING CREDIT PLANS, ETC.—The term "applicable installment obligation" shall not include any obligation arising out of any disposition or sale described in paragraph (1) or (2) of section 453(k) of such Code (as added by section 812(a)).

(B) CERTAIN DISPOSITIONS DEEMED MADE ON FIRST DAY OF TAXABLE YEAR.—In the case of a taxpayer's 1st taxable year ending after December 31, 1986, dispositions after February 28, 1986, and before the 1st day of such taxable year shall be treated as made on such 1st day.

• 1997, Taxpayer Relief Act of 1997 (P.L. 105-34)

P.L. 105-34, §1088 (as amended by P.L. 105-206, §6010(p)), provides:

SEC. 1088. TREATMENT OF EXCEPTION FROM INSTALLMENT SALES RULES FOR SALES OF PROPERTY BY A MANUFACTURER TO A DEALER.

(a) IN GENERAL.—Paragraph (2) of section 811(c) of the Tax Reform Act of 1986 is hereby repealed.

(b) EFFECTIVE DATE.—

(1) IN GENERAL.—The amendment made by this section shall apply to taxable years beginning more than 1 year after the date of the enactment of this Act.

(2) COORDINATION WITH SECTION 481.—In the case of any taxpayer required by this section to change its method of accounting for any taxable year—

(A) such changes shall be treated as initiated by the taxpayer,

(B) such changes shall be treated as made with the consent of the Secretary of the Treasury, and

(C) the net amount of the adjustments required to be taken into account under section 481(a) of the Internal Revenue Code of 1986 shall be taken into account ratably over the 4 taxable year period beginning with the first taxable year beginning more than 1 year after the date of the enactment of this Act.

[Sec. 454]

SEC. 454. OBLIGATIONS ISSUED AT DISCOUNT.

[Sec. 454(a)]

(a) NON-INTEREST-BEARING OBLIGATIONS ISSUED AT A DISCOUNT.—If, in the case of a taxpayer owning any non-interest-bearing obligation issued at a discount and redeemable for fixed amounts increasing at stated intervals or owning an obligation described in paragraph (2) of subsection (c), the increase in the redemption price of such obligation occurring in the taxable year does not (under the method of accounting used in computing his taxable income) constitute income to him in such year, such taxpayer may, at his election made in his return for any taxable year, treat such increase as income received in such taxable year. If any such election is made with respect to any such obligation, it shall apply also to all such obligations owned by the taxpayer at the beginning of the first taxable year to which it applies and to all such obligations thereafter acquired by him and shall be binding for all subsequent taxable years, unless on application by the taxpayer the Secretary permits him, subject to such conditions as the Secretary deems necessary, to change to a different method. In the case of any such obligations owned by the taxpayer at the beginning of the first taxable year to which his election applies, the increase in the redemption price of such obligations occurring between the date of acquisition (or, in the case of an obligation described in paragraph (2) of subsection (c), the date of acquisition of the series E bond involved) and the first day of such taxable year shall also be treated as income received in such taxable year.

Amendments

• 1976, Tax Reform Act of 1976 (P.L. 94-455)

P.L. 94-455, §1906(b)(13)(A):

Amended 1954 Code by substituting "Secretary" for "Secretary or his delegate" each place it appeared. **Effective** 2-1-77.

[Sec. 454(b)]

(b) SHORT-TERM OBLIGATIONS ISSUED ON DISCOUNT BASIS.—In the case of any obligation—

(1) of the United States; or

(2) of a State, or a possession of the United States, or any political subdivision of any of the foregoing, or of the District of Columbia,

which is issued on a discount basis and payable without interest at a fixed maturity date not exceeding 1 year from the date of issue, the amount of discount at which such obligation is originally sold shall not be considered to accrue until the date on which such obligation is paid at maturity, sold, or otherwise disposed of.

Amendments

• 1976, Tax Reform Act of 1976 (P.L. 94-455)

P.L. 94-455, §1901(c)(2):

Amended Code Sec. 454(b)(2) by substituting "State" for "State, a Territory,". **Effective** for tax years beginning after 12-31-76.

[Sec. 454(c)]

(c) MATURED UNITED STATES SAVINGS BONDS.—In the case of a taxpayer who—

(1) holds a series E United States savings bond at the date of maturity, and

(2) pursuant to regulations prescribed under chapter 31 of title 31 (A) retains his investment in such series E bond in an obligation of the United States, other than a current income obligation, or (B) exchanges such series E bond for another nontransferable obligation of the United States in an exchange upon which gain or loss is not recognized because of section 1037 (or so much of section 1031 as relates to section 1037),

the increase in redemption value (to the extent not previously includible in gross income) in excess of the amount paid for such series E bond shall be includible in gross income in the taxable year in which the obligation is finally redeemed or in the taxable year of final maturity, whichever is earlier. This subsection shall not apply to a corporation, and shall not apply in the case of any taxable year for which the taxpayer's taxable income is computed under an accrual method of accounting or for which an election made by the taxpayer under subsection (a) applies.

Amendments

• 1983 (P.L. 97-452)

P.L. 97-452, §2(c)(2):

Amended Code Sec. 454(c)(2) by striking out "the Second Liberty Bond Act" and substituting "chapter 31 of title 31". **Effective** 1-12-83.

• 1959 (P.L. 86-346)

P.L. 86-346, §102:

Amended the heading and first sentence of Code Sec. 454(c). **Effective** 9-22-59. Prior to amendment, they read as follows:

"(c) Matured United States Savings Bonds.—In the case of a taxpayer who—

"(1) holds a series E United States savings bond at the date of maturity, and

"(2) pursuant to regulations prescribed under the Second Liberty Bond Act retains his investment in the maturity value of such series E bond in an obligation, other than a current income obligation, which matures not more than 10 years from the date of maturity of such series E bond,

the increase in redemption value (to the extent not previously includible in gross income) in excess of the amount paid for such series E bond shall be includible in gross income in the taxable year in which the obligation is finally redeemed or in the taxable year of final maturity, whichever is earlier."

[Sec. 455]

SEC. 455. PREPAID SUBSCRIPTION INCOME.

[Sec. 455(a)]

(a) YEAR IN WHICH INCLUDED.—Prepaid subscription income to which this section applies shall be included in gross income for the taxable years during which the liability described in subsection (d) (2) exists.

[Sec. 455(b)]

(b) WHERE TAXPAYER'S LIABILITY CEASES.—In the case of any prepaid subscription income to which this section applies—

(1) If the liability described in subsection (d) (2) ends, then so much of such income as was not includible in gross income under subsection (a) for preceding taxable years shall be included in gross income for the taxable year in which the liability ends.

(2) If the taxpayer dies or ceases to exist, then so much of such income as was not includible in gross income under subsection (a) for preceding taxable years shall be included in gross income for the taxable year in which such death, or such cessation of existence, occurs.

[Sec. 455(c)]

(c) PREPAID SUBSCRIPTION INCOME TO WHICH THIS SECTION APPLIES.—

(1) ELECTION OF BENEFITS.—This section shall apply to prepaid subscription income if and only if the taxpayer makes an election under this section with respect to the trade or business in connection with which such income is received. The election shall be made in such manner as the Secretary may by regulations prescribe. No election may be made with respect to a trade or business if in computing taxable income the cash receipts and disbursements method of accounting is used with respect to such trade or business.

(2) SCOPE OF ELECTION.—An election made under this section shall apply to all prepaid subscription income received in connection with the trade or business with respect to which the taxpayer has made the election; except that the taxpayer may, to the extent permitted under regulations prescribed by the Secretary, include in gross income for the taxable year of receipt the entire amount of any prepaid subscription income if the liability from which it arose is to end within 12 months after the date of receipt. An election made under this section shall not apply to any prepaid subscription income received before the first taxable year for which the election is made.

(3) WHEN ELECTION MAY BE MADE.—

(A) WITH CONSENT.—A taxpayer may, with the consent of the Secretary, make an election under this section at any time.

(B) WITHOUT CONSENT.—A taxpayer may, without the consent of the Secretary, make an election under this section for his first taxable year in which he receives prepaid subscription income in the trade or business. Such election shall be made not later than the time prescribed by law for filing the return for the taxable year (including extensions thereof) with respect to which such election is made.

(4) PERIOD TO WHICH ELECTION APPLIES.—An election under this section shall be effective for the taxable year with respect to which it is first made and for all subsequent taxable years, unless the taxpayer secures the consent of the Secretary to the revocation of such election. For purposes of this title, the computation of taxable income under an election made under this section shall be treated as a method of accounting.

Amendments

• 1976, Tax Reform Act of 1976 (P.L. 94-455)

P.L. 94-455, §1901(a)(67):

Amended Code Sec. 455(c)(3)(B) by substituting "for his first taxable year in which he receives prepaid subscription income in the trade or business" for "for his first taxable year (i) which begins after December 31, 1957, and (ii) in which he receives prepaid subscription income in the trade or business". **Effective** with respect to tax years beginning after 12-31-76.

P.L. 94-455, §1906(b)(13)(A):

Amended the 1954 Code by substituting "Secretary" for "Secretary or his delegate" each place it appeared. **Effective** 2-1-77.

[Sec. 455(d)]

(d) DEFINITIONS.—For purposes of this section—

(1) PREPAID SUBSCRIPTION INCOME.—The term "prepaid subscription income" means any amount (includible in gross income) which is received in connection with, and is directly attributable to, a liability which extends beyond the close of the taxable year in which such amount is received, and which is income from a subscription to a newspaper, magazine, or other periodical.

(2) LIABILITY.—The term "liability" means a liability to furnish or deliver a newspaper, magazine, or other periodical.

(3) RECEIPT OF PREPAID SUBSCRIPTION INCOME.—Prepaid subscription income shall be treated as received during the taxable year for which it is includible in gross income under section 451 (without regard to this section).

[Sec. 455(e)]

(e) DEFERRAL OF INCOME UNDER ESTABLISHED ACCOUNTING PROCEDURES.—Notwithstanding the provisions of this section, any taxpayer who has, for taxable years prior to the first taxable year to which this section applies, reported his income under an established and consistent method or practice of accounting for prepaid subscription income (to which this section would apply if an election were made) may continue to report his income for taxable years to which this title applies in accordance with such method or practice.

Amendments

• 1958, Technical Amendments Act of 1958 (P.L. 85-866)

P.L. 85-866, §28:

Added Sec. 455. **Effective** 1-1-58.

[Sec. 456]

SEC. 456. PREPAID DUES INCOME OF CERTAIN MEMBERSHIP ORGANIZATIONS.

[Sec. 456(a)]

(a) YEAR IN WHICH INCLUDED.—Prepaid dues income to which this section applies shall be included in gross income for the taxable years during which the liability described in subsection (e)(2) exists.

[Sec. 456(b)]

(b) WHERE TAXPAYER'S LIABILITY CEASES.—In the case of any prepaid dues income to which this section applies—

(1) If the liability described in subsection (e)(2) ends, then so much of such income as was not includible in gross income under subsection (a) for preceding taxable years shall be included in gross income for the taxable year in which the liability ends.

(2) If the taxpayer ceases to exist, then so much of such income as was not includible in gross income under subsection (a) for preceding taxable years shall be included in gross income for the taxable year in which such cessation of existence occurs.

[Sec. 456(c)]

(c) PREPAID DUES INCOME TO WHICH THIS SECTION APPLIES.—

(1) ELECTION OF BENEFITS.—This section shall apply to prepaid dues income if and only if the taxpayer makes an election under this section with respect to the trade or business in connection with which such income is received. The election shall be made in such manner as the Secretary may by regulations prescribe. No election may be made with respect to a trade or business if in computing taxable income the cash receipts and disbursements method of accounting is used with respect to such trade or business.

(2) SCOPE OF ELECTION.—An election made under this section shall apply to all prepaid dues income received in connection with the trade or business with respect to which the taxpayer has made the election; except that the taxpayer may, to the extent permitted under regulations prescribed by the Secretary, include in gross income for the taxable year of receipt the entire amount of any prepaid dues income if the liability from which it arose is to end within 12 months after the date of receipt. Except as provided in subsection (d), an election made under this section shall not apply to any prepaid dues income received before the first taxable year for which the election is made.

(3) WHEN ELECTION MAY BE MADE.—

(A) WITH CONSENT.—A taxpayer may, with the consent of the Secretary, make an election under this section at any time.

(B) WITHOUT CONSENT.—A taxpayer may, without the consent of the Secretary, make an election under this section for its first taxable year in which it receives prepaid dues income in the trade or business. Such election shall be made not later than the time prescribed by law for filing the return for the taxable year (including extensions thereof) with respect to which such election is made.

(4) PERIOD TO WHICH ELECTION APPLIES.—An election under this section shall be effective for the taxable year with respect to which it is first made and for all subsequent taxable years, unless the taxpayer secures the consent of the Secretary to the revocation of such election. For purposes of this title, the computation of taxable income under an election made under this section shall be treated as a method of accounting.

Amendments

• 1976, Tax Reform Act of 1976 (P.L. 94-455)

P.L. 94-455, §1901(a)(68):

Amended Code Sec. 456(c)(3)(B) by substituting "for its first taxable year" for "for its first taxable year (i) which begins after December 31, 1960, and (ii)". **Effective** with respect to tax years beginning after 12-31-76.

P.L. 94-455, §1906(b)(13)(A):

Amended the 1954 Code by substituting "Secretary" for "Secretary or his delegate" each place it appeared. **Effective** 2-1-77.

[Sec. 456(d)]

(d) TRANSITIONAL RULE.—

(1) AMOUNT INCLUDIBLE IN GROSS INCOME FOR ELECTION YEARS.—If a taxpayer makes an election under this section with respect to prepaid dues income, such taxpayer shall include in gross income, for each taxable year to which such election applies, not only that portion of prepaid dues income received in such year otherwise includible in gross income for such year under this section, but shall also include in gross income for such year an additional amount equal to the amount of prepaid dues income received in the 3 taxable years preceding the first taxable year to which such election applies which would have been included in gross income in the taxable year had the election been effective 3 years earlier.

(2) DEDUCTIONS OF AMOUNTS INCLUDED IN INCOME MORE THAN ONCE.—A taxpayer who makes an election with respect to prepaid dues income, and who includes in gross income for any taxable year to which the election applies an additional amount computed under paragraph (1), shall be permitted to deduct, for such taxable year and for each of the 4 succeeding taxable years, an amount equal to one-fifth of such additional amount, but only to the extent that such additional amount was also included in the taxpayer's gross income during any of the 3 taxable years preceding the first taxable year to which such election applies.

[Sec. 456(e)]

(e) DEFINITIONS.—For purposes of this section—

(1) PREPAID DUES INCOME.—The term "prepaid dues income" means any amount (includible in gross income) which is received by a membership organization in connection with, and is directly attributable to, a liability to render services or make available membership privileges over a period of time which extends beyond the close of the taxable year in which such amount is received.

(2) LIABILITY.—The term "liability" means a liability to render services or make available membership privileges over a period of time which does not exceed 36 months, which liability shall be deemed to exist ratably over the period of time that such services are required to be rendered, or that such membership privileges are required to be made available.

(3) MEMBERSHIP ORGANIZATION.—The term "membership organization" means a corporation, association, federation, or other organization—

(A) organized without capital stock of any kind, and

(B) no part of the net earnings of which is distributable to any member.

(4) RECEIPT OF PREPAID DUES INCOME.—Prepaid dues income shall be treated as received during the taxable year for which it is includible in gross income under section 451 (without regard to this section).

Amendments

• 1961 (P.L. 87-109)

P.L. 87-109, §1(a):

Added Code Sec. 456. **Effective** for tax years beginning after 1960.

[Sec. 457]

SEC. 457. DEFERRED COMPENSATION PLANS OF STATE AND LOCAL GOVERNMENTS AND TAX-EXEMPT ORGANIZATIONS.

[Sec. 457(a)]

(a) YEAR OF INCLUSION IN GROSS INCOME.—

(1) IN GENERAL.—Any amount of compensation deferred under an eligible deferred compensation plan, and any income attributable to the amounts so deferred, shall be includible in gross income only for the taxable year in which such compensation or other income—

(A) is paid to the participant or other beneficiary, in the case of a plan of an eligible employer described in subsection (e)(1)(A), and

(B) is paid or otherwise made available to the participant or other beneficiary, in the case of a plan of an eligible employer described in subsection (e)(1)(B).

(2) SPECIAL RULE FOR ROLLOVER AMOUNTS.—To the extent provided in section 72(t)(9), section 72(t) shall apply to any amount includible in gross income under this subsection.

(3) SPECIAL RULE FOR HEALTH AND LONG-TERM CARE INSURANCE.—In the case of a plan of an eligible employer described in subsection (e)(1)(A), to the extent provided in section 402(l), paragraph (1) shall not apply to amounts otherwise includible in gross income under this subsection.

Amendments

• 2006, Pension Protection Act of 2006 (P.L. 109-280)

P.L. 109-280, §811, provides:

SEC. 811. PENSIONS AND INDIVIDUAL RETIREMENT ARRANGEMENT PROVISIONS OF ECONOMIC GROWTH AND TAX RELIEF RECONCILIATION ACT OF 2001 MADE PERMANENT.

Title IX of the Economic Growth and Tax Relief Reconciliation Act of 2001 [P.L. 107-16] shall not apply to the provisions of, and amendments made by, subtitles A through F of title VI [§§601-666]of such Act (relating to pension and individual retirement arrangement provisions).

P.L. 109-280, §845(b)(3):

Amended Code Sec. 457(a) by adding at the end a new paragraph (3). **Effective** for distributions in tax years beginning after 12-31-2006.

• 2001, Economic Growth and Tax Relief Reconciliation Act of 2001 (P.L. 107-16)

P.L. 107-16, §649(b)(1):

Amended Code Sec. 457(a). **Effective** for distributions after 12-31-2001. Prior to amendment, Code Sec. 457(a) read as follows:

(a) YEAR OF INCLUSION IN GROSS INCOME.—In the case of a participant in an eligible deferred compensation plan, any amount of compensation deferred under the plan, and any income attributable to the amounts so deferred, shall be includible in gross income only for the taxable year in which such compensation or other income is paid or otherwise made available to the participant or other beneficiary.

P.L. 107-16, §901(a)-(b), provides [but see P.L. 109-280, §811, above]:

SEC. 901. SUNSET OF PROVISIONS OF ACT.

(a) IN GENERAL.—All provisions of, and amendments made by, this Act shall not apply—

(1) to taxable, plan, or limitation years beginning after December 31, 2010, or

(2) in the case of title V, to estates of decedents dying, gifts made, or generation skipping transfers, after December 31, 2010.

(b) APPLICATION OF CERTAIN LAWS.—The Internal Revenue Code of 1986 and the Employee Retirement Income Security Act of 1974 shall be applied and administered to years, estates, gifts, and transfers described in subsection (a) as if the provisions and amendments described in subsection (a) had never been enacted.

[Sec. 457(b)]

(b) ELIGIBLE DEFERRED COMPENSATION PLAN DEFINED.—For purposes of this section, the term "eligible deferred compensation plan" means a plan established and maintained by an eligible employer—

(1) in which only individuals who perform service for the employer may be participants,

(2) which provides that (except as provided in paragraph (3)) the maximum amount which may be deferred under the plan for the taxable year (other than rollover amounts) shall not exceed the lesser of—

(A) the applicable dollar amount, or

(B) 100 percent of the participant's includible compensation,

(3) which may provide that, for 1 or more of the participant's last 3 taxable years ending before he attains normal retirement age under the plan, the ceiling set forth in paragraph (2) shall be the lesser of—

(A) twice the dollar amount in effect under subsection (b)(2)(A), or

(B) the sum of—

(i) the plan ceiling established for purposes of paragraph (2) for the taxable year (determined without regard to this paragraph), plus

(ii) so much of the plan ceiling established for purposes of paragraph (2) for taxable years before the taxable year as has not previously been used under paragaraph (2) or this paragraph,

(4) which provides that compensation will be deferred for any calendar month only if an agreement providing for such deferral has been entered into before the beginning of such month,

(5) which meets the distribution requirements of subsection (d), and

(6) except as provided in subsection (g), which provides that—

(A) all amounts of compensation deferred under the plan,

(B) all property and rights purchased with such amounts, and

(C) all income attributable to such amounts, property, or rights,

shall remain (until made available to the participant or other beneficiary) solely the property and rights of the employer (without being restricted to the provision of benefits under the plan), subject only to the claims of the employer's general creditors.

A plan which is established and maintained by an employer which is described in subsection (e)(1)(A) and which is administered in a manner which is inconsistent with the requirements of any of the preceding paragraphs shall be treated as not meeting the requirements of such paragraph as of the 1st plan year beginning more than 180 days after the date of notification by the Secretary of the inconsistency unless the employer corrects the inconsistency before the 1st day of such plan year.

Amendments

• 2006, Pension Protection Act of 2006 (P.L. 109-280)

P.L. 109-280, §811, provides:

SEC. 811. PENSIONS AND INDIVIDUAL RETIREMENT ARRANGEMENT PROVISIONS OF ECONOMIC GROWTH AND TAX RELIEF RECONCILIATION ACT OF 2001 MADE PERMANENT.

Title IX of the Economic Growth and Tax Relief Reconciliation Act of 2001 [P.L. 107-16] shall not apply to the provisions of, and amendments made by, subtitles A through F of title VI [§§601-666]of such Act (relating to pension and individual retirement arrangement provisions).

• 2001, Economic Growth and Tax Relief Reconciliation Act of 2001 (P.L. 107-16)

P.L. 107-16, §611(e)(1)(A):

Amended Code Sec. 457(b)(2)(A) by striking "$7,500" and inserting "the applicable dollar amount". **Effective** for years beginning after 12-31-2001. For a special rule, see Act Sec. 611(i)(3), below.

P.L. 107-16, §611(e)(1)(B):

Amended Code Sec. 457(b)(3)(A) by striking "$15,000" and inserting "twice the dollar amount in effect under subsection (b)(2)(A)". **Effective** for years beginning after 12-31-2001. For a special rule, see Act Sec. 611(i)(3), below.

P.L. 107-16, §611(i)(3) (as added by P.L. 107-147, §411(j)(3)), provides:

(3) SPECIAL RULE.—In the case of a plan that, on June 7, 2001, incorporated by reference the limitation of section 415(b)(1)(A) of the Internal Revenue Code of 1986, section 411(d)(6) of such Code and section 204(g)(1) of the Employee Retirement Income Security Act of 1974 do not apply to a plan amendment that—

(A) is adopted on or before June 30, 2002,

(B) reduces benefits to the level that would have applied without regard to the amendments made by subsection (a) of this section, and

(C) is effective no earlier than the years described in paragraph (2).

P.L. 107-16, §632(c)(1):

Amended Code Sec. 457(b)(2)(B) by striking "33 1/3 percent" and inserting "100 percent". **Effective** for years beginning after 12-31-2001.

P.L. 107-16, §641(a)(1)(B):

Amended Code Sec. 457(b)(2) by inserting "(other than rollover amounts)" after "taxable year". **Effective**, generally, for distributions after 12-31-2001. For a special rule, see Act Sec. 641(f)(3), below.

P.L. 107-16, §641(f)(3), provides:

(3) SPECIAL RULE.—Notwithstanding any other provision of law, subsections (h)(3) and (h)(5) of section 1122 of the Tax Reform Act of 1986 shall not apply to any distribution from an eligible retirement plan (as defined in clause (iii) or (iv) of section 402(c)(8)(B) of the Internal Revenue Code of 1986) on behalf of an individual if there was a rollover to such plan on behalf of such individual which is permitted solely by reason of any amendment made by this section.

P.L. 107-16, §901(a)-(b), provides [but see P.L. 109-280, §811, above]:

SEC. 901. SUNSET OF PROVISIONS OF ACT.

(a) IN GENERAL.—All provisions of, and amendments made by, this Act shall not apply—

(1) to taxable, plan, or limitation years beginning after December 31, 2010, or

(2) in the case of title V, to estates of decedents dying, gifts made, or generation skipping transfers, after December 31, 2010.

(b) APPLICATION OF CERTAIN LAWS.—The Internal Revenue Code of 1986 and the Employee Retirement Income Security Act of 1974 shall be applied and administered to years, estates, gifts, and transfers described in subsection (a) as if the provisions and amendments described in subsection (a) had never been enacted.

• 1996, Small Business Job Protection Act of 1996 (P.L. 104-188)

P.L. 104-188, §1448(b):

Amended Code Sec. 457(b)(6) by inserting "except as provided in subsection (g)," before "which provides that". For the **effective** date, see Act Sec. 1448(c), below.

P.L. 104-188, §1448(c), provides:

(1) IN GENERAL.—Except as provided in paragraph (2), the amendments made by this section shall apply to assets and income described in section 457(b)(6) of the Internal Revenue Code of 1986 held by a plan on and after the date of the enactment of this Act.

(2) TRANSITION RULE.—In the case of a plan in existence on the date of the enactment of this Act, a trust need not be established by reason of the amendments made by this section before January 1, 1999.

[Sec. 457(c)]

(c) LIMITATION.—The maximum amount of the compensation of any one individual which may be deferred under subsection (a) during any taxable year shall not exceed the amount in effect under subsection (b)(2)(A) (as modified by any adjustment provided under subsection (b)(3)).

Amendments

• 2006, Pension Protection Act of 2006 (P.L. 109-280)

P.L. 109-280, §811, provides:

SEC. 811. PENSIONS AND INDIVIDUAL RETIREMENT ARRANGEMENT PROVISIONS OF ECONOMIC GROWTH AND TAX RELIEF RECONCILIATION ACT OF 2001 MADE PERMANENT.

Title IX of the Economic Growth and Tax Relief Reconciliation Act of 2001 [P.L. 107-16] shall not apply to the provisions of, and amendments made by, subtitles A through F of title VI [§§601-666]of such Act (relating to pension and individual retirement arrangement provisions).

• 2001, Economic Growth and Tax Relief Reconciliation Act of 2001 (P.L. 107-16)

P.L. 107-16, §611(d)(3)(B):

Amended Code Sec. 457(c)(2) by striking "402(g)(8)(A)(iii)" and inserting "402(g)(7)(A)(iii)". **Effective** for years beginning after 12-31-2001.

P.L. 107-16, §611(e)(1)(A):

Amended Code Sec. 457(c)(1) by striking "$7,500" and inserting "the applicable dollar amount". **Effective** for years beginning after 12-31-2001.

P.L. 107-16, §611(i)(3) (as added by P.L. 107-147, §411(j)(3)), provides:

(3) SPECIAL RULE.—In the case of plan that, on June 7, 2001, incorporated by reference the limitation of section 415(b)(1)(A) of the Internal Revenue Code of 1986, section 411(d)(6) of such Code and section 204(g)(1) of the Employee Retirement Income Security Act of 1974 do not apply to a plan amendment that—

(A) is adopted on or before June 30, 2002,

(B) reduces benefits to the level that would have applied without regard to the amendments made by subsection (a) of this section, and

(C) is effective no earlier than the years described in paragraph (2).

P.L. 107-16, §615(a):

Amended Code Sec. 457(c), as amended by Act Sec. 611. **Effective** for years beginning after 12-31-2001. Prior to amendment, Code Sec. 457(c), as amended by Act Sec. 611, read as follows:

(c) INDIVIDUALS WHO ARE PARTICIPANTS IN MORE THAN 1 PLAN.—

(1) IN GENERAL.—The maximum amount of the compensation of any one individual which may be deferred under subsection (a) during any taxable year shall not exceed the applicable dollar amount (as modified by any adjustment provided under subsection (b)(3)).

(2) COORDINATION WITH CERTAIN OTHER DEFERRALS.—In applying paragraph (1) of this subsection—

(A) any amount excluded from gross income under section 403(b) for the taxable year, and

(B) any amount—

(i) excluded from gross income under section 402(e)(3) or section 402(h)(1)(B) or (k) for the taxable year, or

(ii) with respect to which a deduction is allowable by reason of a contribution to an organization described in section 501(c)(18) for the taxable year,

shall be treated as an amount deferred under subsection (a). In applying section 402(g)(7)(A)(iii) or 403(b)(2)(A)(ii), an amount deferred under subsection (a) for any year of service shall be taken into account as if described in section 402(g)(3)(C) or 403(b)(2)(A)(ii), respectively. Subparagraph (B) shall not apply in the case of a participant in a rural cooperative plan (as defined in section 401(k)(7)).

P.L. 107-16, §901(a)-(b), provides [but see P.L. 109-280, §811, above]:

SEC. 901. SUNSET OF PROVISIONS OF ACT.

(a) IN GENERAL.—All provisions of, and amendments made by, this Act shall not apply—

(1) to taxable, plan, or limitation years beginning after December 31, 2010, or

(2) in the case of title V, to estates of decedents dying, gifts made, or generation skipping transfers, after December 31, 2010.

(b) APPLICATION OF CERTAIN LAWS.—The Internal Revenue Code of 1986 and the Employee Retirement Income Security Act of 1974 shall be applied and administered to years, estates, gifts, and transfers described in subsection (a) as if the provisions and amendments described in subsection (a) had never been enacted.

• 1996, Small Business Job Protection Act of 1996 (P.L. 104-188)

P.L. 104-188, §1421(b)(3)(C):

Amended Code Sec. 457(c)(2)(B)(i) by striking "section 402(h)(1)(B)" and inserting "section 402(h)(1)(B) or (k)". **Effective** for tax years beginning after 12-31-96.

• 1992, Unemployment Compensation Amendments of 1992 (P.L.102-318)

P.L. 102-318, §521(b)(26):

Amended Code Sec. 457(c)(2)(B)(i) by striking "section 402(a)(8)" and inserting "section 402(e)(3)". **Effective** for distributions after 12-31-92.

• 1988, Technical and Miscellaneous Revenue Act of 1988 (P.L. 100-647)

P.L. 100-647, §1011(e)(1):

Amended Code Sec. 457(c)(2) by striking out "and paragraphs (2) and (3) of subsection (b)" after "(1) of this subsection". **Effective** as if included in the provision of P.L. 99-514 to which it relates.

P.L. 100-647, §6071(c):

Amended Code Sec. 457(c)(2), as amended by section 1107 of P.L. 99-514, by striking out "rural electric cooperative plan" and inserting in lieu thereof "rural cooperative plan". **Effective** for tax years beginning after 11-10-88.

[Sec. 457(d)]

(d) DISTRIBUTION REQUIREMENTS.—

(1) IN GENERAL.—For purposes of subsection (b)(5), a plan meets the distribution requirements of this subsection if—

(A) under the plan amounts will not be made available to participants or beneficiaries earlier than—

(i) the calendar year in which the participant attains age $70^1/_2$,

(ii) when the participant has a severance from employment with the employer, or

(iii) when the participant is faced with an unforeseeable emergency (determined in the manner prescribed by the Secretary in regulations),

(B) the plan meets the minimum distribution requirements of paragraph (2), and

(C) in the case of a plan maintained by an employer described in subsection (e)(1)(A), the plan meets requirements similar to the requirements of section 401(a)(31).

Any amount transferred in a direct trustee-to-trustee transfer in accordance with section 401(a)(31) shall not be includible in gross income for the taxable year of transfer.

(2) MINIMUM DISTRIBUTION REQUIREMENTS.—A plan meets the minimum distribution requirements of this paragraph if such plan meets the requirements of section 401(a)(9).

(3) SPECIAL RULE FOR GOVERNMENT PLAN.—An eligible deferred compensation plan of an employer described in subsection (e)(1)(A) shall not be treated as failing to meet the requirements of this subsection solely by reason of making a distribution described in subsection (e)(9)(A).

Amendments

• 2006, Pension Protection Act of 2006 (P.L. 109-280)

P.L. 109-280, §811, provides:

SEC. 811. PENSIONS AND INDIVIDUAL RETIREMENT ARRANGEMENT PROVISIONS OF ECONOMIC GROWTH AND TAX RELIEF RECONCILIATION ACT OF 2001 MADE PERMANENT.

Title IX of the Economic Growth and Tax Relief Reconciliation Act of 2001 [P.L. 107-16] shall not apply to the provisions of, and amendments made by, subtitles A through F of title VI [§§601-666]of such Act (relating to pension and individual retirement arrangement provisions).

• 2005, Katrina Emergency Tax Relief Act of 2005 (P.L. 109-73)

P.L. 109-73, §101(f)(2) [repealed by P.L. 109-135, §201(b)(4)(A)], provides:

(2) QUALIFIED HURRICANE KATRINA DISTRIBUTIONS TREATED AS MEETING PLAN DISTRIBUTION REQUIREMENTS.—For purposes of such Code, a qualified Hurricane Katrina distribution shall be treated as meeting the requirements of sections 401(k)(2)(B)(i), 403(b)(7)(A)(ii), 403(b)(11), and 457(d)(1)(A) of such Code.

• 2001, Economic Growth and Tax Relief Reconciliation Act of 2001 (P.L. 107-16)

P.L. 107-16, §641(a)(1)(C):

Amended Code Sec. 457(d)(1) by striking "and" at the end of subparagraph (A), by striking the period at the end of subparagraph (B) and inserting ",and", and by inserting after subparagraph (B) a new subparagraph (C) and a new flush sentence. **Effective**, generally, for distributions after 12-31-2001. For a special rule, see Act Sec. 641(f)(3), below.

P.L. 107-16, §641(f)(3), provides:

(3) SPECIAL RULE.—Notwithstanding any other provision of law, subsections (h)(3) and (h)(5) of section 1122 of the Tax Reform Act of 1986 shall not apply to any distribution from an eligible retirement plan (as defined in clause (iii) or (iv) of section 402(c)(8)(B) of the Internal Revenue Code of 1986) on behalf of an individual if there was a rollover to such plan on behalf of such individual which is permitted solely by reason of any amendment made by this section.

P.L. 107-16, §646(a)(3):

Amended Code Sec. 457(d)(1)(A)(ii) by striking "is separated from service" and inserting "has a severance from employment". **Effective** for distributions after 12-31-2001.

P.L. 107-16, §649(a):

Amended Code Sec. 457(d)(2). **Effective** for distributions after 12-31-2001. Prior to amendment, Code Sec. 457(d)(2) read as follows:

(2) MINIMUM DISTRIBUTION REQUIREMENTS.—A plan meets the minimum distribution requirements of this paragraph if such plan meets the requirements of subparagraphs (A), (B), and (C):

(A) APPLICATION OF SECTION 401(a)(9).—A plan meets the requirements of this subparagraph if the plan meets the requirements of section 401(a)(9).

(B) ADDITIONAL DISTRIBUTION REQUIREMENTS.—A plan meets the requirements of this subparagraph if—

(i) in the case of a distribution beginning before the death of the participant, such distribution will be made in a form under which—

(I) the amounts payable with respect to the participant will be paid at times specified by the Secretary which are not later than the time determined under section 401(a)(9)(G) (relating to incidental death benefits), and

(II) any amount not distributed to the participant during his life will be distributed after the death of the participant at least as rapidly as under the method of distributions being used under subclause (I) as of the date of his death, or

(ii) in the case of a distribution which does not begin before the death of the participant, the entire amount payable with respect to the participant will be paid during a period not to exceed 15 years (or the life expectancy of the surviving spouse if such spouse is the beneficiary).

(C) NONINCREASING BENEFITS.—A plan meets the requirements of this subparagraph if any distribution payable over a period of more than 1 year can only be made in substantially nonincreasing amounts (paid not less frequently than annually).

P.L. 107-16, §649(b)(2)(B):

Amended Code Sec. 457(d) by adding at the end a new paragraph (3). **Effective** for distributions after 12-31-2001.

P.L. 107-16, §901(a)-(b), provides [but see P.L. 109-280, §811, above]:

SEC. 901. SUNSET OF PROVISIONS OF ACT.

(a) IN GENERAL.—All provisions of, and amendments made by, this Act shall not apply—

(1) to taxable, plan, or limitation years beginning after December 31, 2010, or

(2) in the case of title V, to estates of decedents dying, gifts made, or generation skipping transfers, after December 31, 2010.

(b) APPLICATION OF CERTAIN LAWS.—The Internal Revenue Code of 1986 and the Employee Retirement Income Security Act of 1974 shall be applied and administered to years, estates, gifts, and transfers described in subsection (a) as if the provisions and amendments described in subsection (a) had never been enacted.

• 1989, Omnibus Budget Reconciliation Act of 1989 (P.L. 101-239)

P.L. 101-239, §7811(g)(4):

Amended Code Sec. 457(d)(1)(A)(iii) by striking the period at the end and inserting ", and". **Effective** as if included in the provision of P.L. 100-647 to which it relates.

P.L. 101-239, §7811(g)(5):

Amended Code Sec. 457(d)(2)(B)(i)(I) by adding "and" at the end. **Effective** as if included in the provision of P.L. 100-647 to which it relates.

• 1988, Technical and Miscellaneous Revenue Act of 1988 (P.L. 100-647)

P.L. 100-647, §1011(e)(2):

Amended Code Sec. 457(d)(1)(A). **Effective** as if included in the provision of P.L. 99-514 to which it relates. Prior to amendment, Code Sec. 457(d)(1)(A) read as follows:

(A) the plan provides that amounts payable under the plan will be made available to participants or other beneficiaries not earlier than when the participant is separated from service with the employer or is faced with an unforeseeable emergency (determined in the manner prescribed by the Secretary by regulation), and

P.L. 100-647, §1011(e)(10):

Amended Code Sec. 457(d)(2)(B)(i)(I). **Effective** as if included in the provision of P.L. 99-514 to which it relates. Prior to amendment, Code Sec. 457(d)(2)(B)(i)(I) read as follows:

(I) at least 2/3 of the total amount payable with respect to the participant will be paid during the life expectancy of such participant (determined as of the commencement of the distribution), and

[Sec. 457(e)]

(e) OTHER DEFINITIONS AND SPECIAL RULES.—For purposes of this section—

(1) ELIGIBLE EMPLOYER.—The term "eligible employer" means—

(A) a State, political subdivision of a State, and any agency or instrumentality of a State or political subdivision of a State, and

(B) any other organization (other than a governmental unit) exempt from tax under this subtitle.

(2) PERFORMANCE OF SERVICE.—The performance of service includes performance of service as an independent contractor and the person (or governmental unit) for whom such services are performed shall be treated as the employer.

(3) PARTICIPANT.—The term "participant" means an individual who is eligible to defer compensation under the plan.

(4) BENEFICIARY.—The term "beneficiary" means a beneficiary of the participant, his estate, or any other person whose interest in the plan is derived from the participant.

(5) INCLUDIBLE COMPENSATION.—The term "includible compensation" has the meaning given to the term "participant's compensation" by section 415(c)(3).

(6) COMPENSATION TAKEN INTO ACCOUNT AT PRESENT VALUE.—Compensation shall be taken into account at its present value.

(7) COMMUNITY PROPERTY LAWS.—The amount of includible compensation shall be determined without regard to any community property laws.

(8) INCOME ATTRIBUTABLE.—Gains from the disposition of property shall be treated as income attributable to such property.

(9) BENEFITS OF TAX EXEMPT ORGANIZATION PLANS NOT TREATED AS MADE AVAILABLE BY REASON OF CERTAIN ELECTIONS, ETC.—In the case of an eligible deferred compensation plan of an employer described in subsection (e)(1)(B)—

(A) TOTAL AMOUNT PAYABLE IS DOLLAR LIMIT OR LESS.—The total amount payable to a participant under the plan shall not be treated as made available merely because the participant may elect to receive such amount (or the plan may distribute such amount without the participant's consent) if—

(i) the portion of such amount which is not attributable to rollover contributions (as defined in section 411(a)(11)(D)) does not exceed the dollar limit under section 411(a)(11)(A), and

(ii) such amount may be distributed only if—

(I) no amount has been deferred under the plan with respect to such participant during the 2-year period ending on the date of the distribution, and

(II) there has been no prior distribution under the plan to such participant to which this subparagraph applied.

A plan shall not be treated as failing to meet the distribution requirements of subsection (d) by reason of a distribution to which this subparagraph applies.

(B) ELECTION TO DEFER COMMENCEMENT OF DISTRIBUTIONS.—The total amount payable to a participant under the plan shall not be treated as made available merely because the participant may elect to defer commencement of distributions under the plan if—

(i) such election is made after amounts may be available under the plan in accordance with subsection (d)(1)(A) and before commencement of such distributions, and

(ii) the participant may make only 1 such election.

(10) TRANSFERS BETWEEN PLANS.—A participant shall not be required to include in gross income any portion of the entire amount payable to such participant solely by reason of the transfer of such portion from 1 eligible deferred compensation plan to another eligible deferred compensation plan.

(11) CERTAIN PLANS EXCLUDED.—

(A) IN GENERAL.—The following plans shall be treated as not providing for the deferral of compensation:

(i) Any bona fide vacation leave, sick leave, compensatory time, severance pay, disability pay, or death benefit plan.

(ii) Any plan paying solely length of service awards to bona fide volunteers (or their beneficiaries) on account of qualified services performed by such volunteers.

(B) SPECIAL RULES APPLICABLE TO LENGTH OF SERVICE AWARD PLANS.—

(i) BONA FIDE VOLUNTEER.—An individual shall be treated as a bona fide volunteer for purposes of subparagraph (A)(ii) if the only compensation received by such individual for performing qualified services is in the form of—

(I) reimbursement for (or a reasonable allowance for) reasonable expenses incurred in the performance of such services, or

(II) reasonable benefits (including length of service awards), and nominal fees for such services, customarily paid by eligible employers in connection with the performance of such services by volunteers.

(ii) LIMITATION ON ACCRUALS.—A plan shall not be treated as described in subparagraph (A)(ii) if the aggregate amount of length of service awards accruing with respect to any year of service for any bona fide volunteer exceeds $3,000.

(C) QUALIFIED SERVICES.—For purposes of this paragraph, the term "qualified services" means fire fighting and prevention services, emergency medical services, and ambulance services.

(D) CERTAIN VOLUNTARY EARLY RETIREMENT INCENTIVE PLANS.—

(i) IN GENERAL.—If an applicable voluntary early retirement incentive plan—

(I) makes payments or supplements as an early retirement benefit, a retirement-type subsidy, or a benefit described in the last sentence of section 411(a)(9), and

(II) such payments or supplements are made in coordination with a defined benefit plan which is described in section 401(a) and includes a trust exempt from tax under section 501(a) and which is maintained by an eligible employer described in paragraph (1)(A) or by an education association described in clause (ii)(II),

such applicable plan shall be treated for purposes of subparagraph (A)(i) as a bona fide severance pay plan with respect to such payments or supplements to the extent such payments or supplements could otherwise have been provided under such defined benefit plan (determined as if section 411 applied to such defined benefit plan).

(ii) APPLICABLE VOLUNTARY EARLY RETIREMENT INCENTIVE PLAN.—For purposes of this subparagraph, the term "applicable voluntary early retirement incentive plan" means a voluntary early retirement incentive plan maintained by—

(I) a local educational agency (as defined in section 9101 of the Elementary and Secondary Education Act of 1965 (20 U.S.C. 7801)), or

(II) an education association which principally represents employees of 1 or more agencies described in subclause (I) and which is described in section 501(c)(5) or (6) and exempt from tax under section 501(a).

(12) EXCEPTION FOR NONELECTIVE DEFERRED COMPENSATION OF NONEMPLOYEES.—

(A) IN GENERAL.—This section shall not apply to nonelective deferred compensation attributable to services not performed as an employee.

(B) NONELECTIVE DEFERRED COMPENSATION.—For purposes of subparagraph (A), deferred compensation shall be treated as nonelective only if all individuals (other than those who have not satisfied any applicable initial service requirement) with the same relationship to the payor are covered under the same plan with no individual variations or options under the plan.

(13) SPECIAL RULE FOR CHURCHES.—The term "eligible employer" shall not include a church (as defined in section 3121(w)(3)(A)) or qualified church-controlled organization (as defined in section 3121(w)(3)(B)).

(14) TREATMENT OF QUALIFIED GOVERNMENTAL EXCESS BENEFIT ARRANGEMENTS.—Subsections (b)(2) and (c)(1) shall not apply to any qualified governmental excess benefit arrangement (as defined in section 415(m)(3)), and benefits provided under such an arrangement shall not be taken into account in determining whether any other plan is an eligible deferred compensation plan.

(15) APPLICABLE DOLLAR AMOUNT.—

(A) IN GENERAL.—The applicable dollar amount shall be the amount determined in accordance with the following table:

For taxable years beginning in calendar year:	*The applicable dollar amount:*
2002	$11,000
2003	$12,000
2004	$13,000
2005	$14,000
2006 or thereafter	$15,000.

(B) COST-OF-LIVING ADJUSTMENTS.—In the case of taxable years beginning after December 31, 2006, the Secretary shall adjust the $15,000 amount under subparagraph (A) at the same time and in the same manner as under section 415(d), except that the base period shall be the calendar quarter beginning July 1, 2005, and any increase under this paragraph which is not a multiple of $500 shall be rounded to the next lowest multiple of $500.

(16) ROLLOVER AMOUNTS.—

(A) GENERAL RULE.—In the case of an eligible deferred compensation plan established and maintained by an employer described in subsection (e)(1)(A), if—

(i) any portion of the balance to the credit of an employee in such plan is paid to such employee in an eligible rollover distribution (within the meaning of section 402(c)(4)),

(ii) the employee transfers any portion of the property such employee receives in such distribution to an eligible retirement plan described in section 402(c)(8)(B), and

(iii) in the case of a distribution of property other than money, the amount so transferred consists of the property distributed,

then such distribution (to the extent so transferred) shall not be includible in gross income for the taxable year in which paid.

(B) CERTAIN RULES MADE APPLICABLE.—The rules of paragraphs (2) through (7), (9), and (11) of section 402(c) and section 402(f) shall apply for purposes of subparagraph (A).

(C) REPORTING.—Rollovers under this paragraph shall be reported to the Secretary in the same manner as rollovers from qualified retirement plans (as defined in section 4974(c)).

(17) TRUSTEE-TO-TRUSTEE TRANSFERS TO PURCHASE PERMISSIVE SERVICE CREDIT.—No amount shall be includible in gross income by reason of a direct trustee-to-trustee transfer to a defined benefit governmental plan (as defined in section 414(d)) if such transfer is—

(A) for the purchase of permissive service credit (as defined in section 415(n)(3)(A)) under such plan, or

(B) a repayment to which section 415 does not apply by reason of subsection (k)(3) thereof.

(18) COORDINATION WITH CATCH-UP CONTRIBUTIONS FOR INDIVIDUALS AGE 50 OR OLDER.—In the case of an individual who is an eligible participant (as defined by section 414(v)) and who is a participant in an eligible deferred compensation plan of an employer described in paragraph (1)(A), subsections (b)(3) and (c) shall be applied by substituting for the amount otherwise determined under the applicable subsection the greater of—

(A) the sum of—

(i) the plan ceiling established for purposes of subsection (b)(2) (without regard to subsection (b)(3)), plus

(ii) the applicable dollar amount for the taxable year determined under section 414(v)(2)(B)(i), or

(B) the amount determined under the applicable subsection (without regard to this paragraph).

Amendments

• 2006, Pension Protection Act of 2006 (P.L. 109-280)

P.L. 109-280, §811, provides:

SEC. 811. PENSIONS AND INDIVIDUAL RETIREMENT ARRANGEMENT PROVISIONS OF ECONOMIC GROWTH AND TAX RELIEF RECONCILIATION ACT OF 2001 MADE PERMANENT.

Title IX of the Economic Growth and Tax Relief Reconciliation Act of 2001 [P.L. 107-16] shall not apply to the provisions of, and amendments made by, subtitles A through F of title VI [§§601-666]of such Act (relating to pension and individual retirement arrangement provisions).

P.L. 109-280, §825, provides:

SEC. 825. ELIGIBILITY FOR PARTICIPATION IN RETIREMENT PLANS.

An individual shall not be precluded from participating in an eligible deferred compensation plan by reason of having received a distribution under section 457(e)(9) of the Internal Revenue Code of 1986, as in effect prior to the enactment of the Small Business Job Protection Act of 1996.

P.L. 109-280, §829(a)(4):

Amended Code Sec. 457(e)(16)(B) by striking "and (9)" and inserting ", (9), and (11)". **Effective** for distributions after 12-31-2006.

P.L. 109-280, §1104(a)(1):

Amended Code Sec. 457(e)(11) by adding at the end a new subparagraph (D). **Effective** generally for tax years ending after 8-17-2006. For a special rule, see Act Sec. 1104(d)(4), below.

P.L. 109-280, §1104(d)(4), provides:

(4) CONSTRUCTION.—Nothing in the amendments made by this section shall alter or affect the construction of the Internal Revenue Code of 1986, the Employee Retirement Income Security Act of 1974, or the Age Discrimination in Employment Act of 1967 as applied to any plan, arrangement, or conduct to which such amendments do not apply.

• 2002, Job Creation and Worker Assistance Act of 2002 (P.L. 107-147)

P.L. 107-147, §411(o)(9):

Amended Code Sec. 457(e) by adding at the end a new paragraph (18). **Effective** as if included in the provision of P.L. 107-16 to which it relates [**effective** for contributions in tax years beginning after 12-31-2001.—CCH].

P.L. 107-147, §411(p)(5):

Amended Code Sec. 457(e)(5). **Effective** as if included in the provision of P.L. 107-16 to which it relates [**effective** for years beginning after 12-31-2001.—CCH]. Prior to amendment, Code Sec. 457(e)(5) read as follows:

(5) INCLUDIBLE COMPENSATION.—The term "includible compensation" means compensation for service performed for the employer which (taking into account the provisions of this section and other provisions of this chapter) is currently includible in gross income.

• 2001, Economic Growth and Tax Relief Reconciliation Act of 2001 (P.L. 107-16)

P.L. 107-16, §611(e)(2):

Amended Code Sec. 457(e)(15). **Effective** for years beginning after 12-31-2001. For a special rule, see Act Sec. 611(i)(3), below. Prior to amendment, Code Sec. 457(e)(15) read as follows:

(15) COST-OF-LIVING ADJUSTMENT OF MAXIMUM DEFERRAL AMOUNT.—The Secretary shall adjust the $7,500 amount specified in subsections (b)(2) and (c)(1) at the same time and in the same manner as under section 415(d), except that the base period shall be the calendar quarter ending September 30, 1994, and any increase under this paragraph

which is not a multiple of $500 shall be rounded to the next lowest multiple of $500.

P.L. 107-16, §611(i)(3) (as added by P.L. 107-147, §411(j)(3)), provides:

(3) SPECIAL RULE.—In the case of plan that, on June 7, 2001, incorporated by reference the limitation of section 415(b)(1)(A) of the Internal Revenue Code of 1986, section 411(d)(6) of such Code and section 204(g)(1) of the Employee Retirement Income Security Act of 1974 do not apply to a plan amendment that—

(A) is adopted on or before June 30, 2002,

(B) reduces benefits to the level that would have applied without regard to the amendments made by subsection (a) of this section, and

(C) is effective no earlier than the years described in paragraph (2).

P.L. 107-16, §641(a)(1)(A):

Amended Code Sec. 457(e) by adding at the end a new paragraph (16). **Effective**, generally, for distributions after 12-31-2001. For a special rule, see Act Sec. 641(f)(3), below.

P.L. 107-16, §641(f)(3), provides:

(3) SPECIAL RULE.—Notwithstanding any other provision of law, subsections (h)(3) and (h)(5) of section 1122 of the Tax Reform Act of 1986 shall not apply to any distribution from an eligible retirement plan (as defined in clause (iii) or (iv) of section 402(c)(8)(B) of the Internal Revenue Code of 1986) on behalf of an individual if there was a rollover to such plan on behalf of such individual which is permitted solely by reason of any amendment made by this section.

P.L. 107-16, §647(b):

Amended Code Sec. 457(e), as amended by Act Sec. 641, by adding after paragraph (16) a new paragraph (17). **Effective** for trustee-to-trustee transfers after 12-31-2001.

P.L. 107-16, §648(b):

Amended Code Sec. 457(e)(9)(A)(i) by striking "such amount" and inserting "the portion of such amount which is not attributable to rollover contributions (as defined in section 411(a)(11)(D))". **Effective** for distributions after 12-31-2001.

P.L. 107-16, §649(b)(2)(A):

Amended so much of Code Sec. 457(e)(9) as precedes subparagraph (A). **Effective** for distributions after 12-31-2001. Prior to amendment, so much of Code Sec. 457(e)(9) as preceded subparagraph (A) read as follows:

(9) BENEFITS NOT TREATED AS MADE AVAILABLE BY REASON OF CERTAIN ELECTIONS, ETC.—

P.L. 107-16, §901(a)-(b), provides [but see P.L. 109-280, §811, above]:

SEC. 901. SUNSET OF PROVISIONS OF ACT.

(a) IN GENERAL.—All provisions of, and amendments made by, this Act shall not apply—

(1) to taxable, plan, or limitation years beginning after December 31, 2010, or

(2) in the case of title V, to estates of decedents dying, gifts made, or generation skipping transfers, after December 31, 2010.

(b) APPLICATION OF CERTAIN LAWS.—The Internal Revenue Code of 1986 and the Employee Retirement Income Security Act of 1974 shall be applied and administered to years, estates, gifts, and transfers described in subsection (a) as if the provisions and amendments described in subsection (a) had never been enacted.

• 1997, Taxpayer Relief Act of 1997 (P.L. 105-34)

P.L. 105-34, §1071(a)(2)(A):

Amended Code Sec. 457(e)(9) by striking "$3,500" each place it appears (other than the headings) and inserting "the dollar limit under section 411(a)(11)(A)". **Effective** for plan years beginning after 8-5-97.

P.L. 105-34, §1071(a)(2)(B):

Amended Code Sec. 457(e)(9)(A) by striking "$3,500" in the heading and inserting "DOLLAR LIMIT". **E ffective** for plan years beginning after 8-5-97.

• 1996, Small Business Job Protection Act of 1996 (P.L. 104-188)

P.L. 104-188, §1444(b)(2):

Amended Code Sec. 457(e) by adding at the end a new paragraph (14). **Effective** for years beginning after 12-31-94. For a special rule, see Act Sec. 1444(e)(2), below.

P.L. 104-188, §1444(e)(2), provides:

(2) TREATMENT FOR YEARS BEGINNING BEFORE JANUARY 1, 1995.—Nothing in the amendments made by this section shall be construed to imply that a governmental plan (as defined in section 414(d) of the Internal Revenue Code of 1986) fails to satisfy the requirements of section 415 of such Code for any taxable year beginning before January 1, 1995.

P.L. 104-188, §1447(a):

Amended Code Sec. 457(e)(9). **Effective** for tax years beginning after 12-31-96. Prior to amendment, Code Sec. 457(e)(9) read as follows:

(9) BENEFITS NOT TREATED AS MADE AVAILABLE BY REASON OF CERTAIN ELECTIONS.—If—

(A) the total amount payable to a participant under the plan does not exceed $3,500, and

(B) no additional amounts may be deferred under the plan with respect to the participant,

the amount payable to the participant under the plan shall not be treated as made available merely because such participant may elect to receive a lump sum payable after separation from service and within 60 days of the election.

P.L. 104-188, §1447(b):

Amended Code Sec. 457(e), as amended by Act Sec. 1444(b)(2), by adding at the end a new paragraph (15). **Effective** for tax years beginning after 12-31-96.

P.L. 104-188, §1458(a):

Amended Code Sec. 457(e)(11). **Effective** for accruals of length of service awards after 12-31-96. Prior to amendment, Code Sec. 457(e)(11) read as follows:

(11) CERTAIN PLANS EXCEPTED.—Any bona fide vacation leave, sick leave, compensatory time, severance pay, disability pay, or death benefit plan shall be treated as a plan not providing for the deferral of compensation.

• 1989, Omnibus Budget Reconciliation Act of 1989 (P.L. 101-239)

P.L. 101-239, §7816(j):

Amended Code Sec. 457(e)(13). **Effective** as if included in the provision of P.L. 100-647 to which it relates. Prior to amendment, Code Sec. 457(e)(13) read as follows:

(13) EXCEPTION FOR CHURCH PLANS.—The term "eligible deferred compensation plan" shall not include a plan maintained by a church for church employees. For purposes of this paragraph, the term "church" has the meaning given such term by section 3121(w)(3)(A), including a qualified church-controlled organization (as defined in section 3121(w)(3)(B).

• 1988, Technical and Miscellaneous Revenue Act of 1988 (P.L. 100-647)

P.L. 100-647, §1011(e)(9):

Amended Code Sec. 457(e)(9) by inserting "after separation from service and" before "within 60 days". **Effective** for years beginning after 12-31-88.

P.L. 100-647, §6064(a)(1):

Amended Code Sec. 457(e) by adding at the end thereof new paragraph (11). **Effective**, generally, for tax years beginning after 12-31-87. For an exception, see Act Sec. 6064(d)(2)-(3) in the amendment notes following Code Sec. 457(f).

P.L. 100-647, §6064(b)(1):

Amended Code Sec. 457(e), as amended by section 1107 of the Reform Act, by adding at the end thereof new paragraph (12). **Effective**, generally, for tax years beginning after 12-31-87. For an exception, see Act Sec. 6064(d)(2)-(3) in the amendment notes following Code Sec. 457(f).

P.L. 100-647, §6064(c):

Amended Code Sec. 457(e), as amended by section 1107 of the Reform Act, by adding at the end thereof new paragraph (13). **Effective**, generally, for tax years beginning after 12-31-87. For an exception, see Act Sec. 6064(d)(2)-(3) in the amendment notes following Code Sec. 457(f).

[Sec. 457(f)]

(f) TAX TREATMENT OF PARTICIPANTS WHERE PLAN OR ARRANGEMENT OF EMPLOYER IS NOT ELIGIBLE.—

(1) IN GENERAL.—In the case of a plan of an eligible employer providing for a deferral of compensation, if such plan is not an eligible deferred compensation plan, then—

(A) the compensation shall be included in the gross income of the participant or beneficiary for the 1st taxable year in which there is no substantial risk of forfeiture of the rights to such compensation, and

(B) the tax treatment of any amount made available under the plan to a participant or beneficiary shall be determined under section 72 (relating to annuities, etc.).

(2) EXCEPTIONS.—Paragraph (1) shall not apply to—

(A) a plan described in section 401(a) which includes a trust exempt from tax under section 501(a),

(B) an annuity plan or contract described in section 403,

(C) that portion of any plan which consists of a transfer of property described in section 83,

(D) that portion of any plan which consists of a trust to which section 402(b) applies,

(E) a qualified governmental excess benefit arrangement described in section 415(m), and

(F) that portion of any applicable employment retention plan described in paragraph (4) with respect to any participant.

(3) DEFINITIONS.—For purposes of this subsection—

(A) PLAN INCLUDES ARRANGEMENTS, ETC.—The term "plan" includes any agreement or arrangement.

(B) SUBSTANTIAL RISK OF FORFEITURE.—The rights of a person to compensation are subject to a substantial risk of forfeiture if such person's rights to such compensation are conditioned upon the future performance of substantial services by any individual.

(4) EMPLOYMENT RETENTION PLANS.—For purposes of paragraph (2)(F)—

(A) IN GENERAL.—The portion of an applicable employment retention plan described in this paragraph with respect to any participant is that portion of the plan which provides benefits payable to the participant not in excess of twice the applicable dollar limit determined under subsection (e)(15).

(B) OTHER RULES.—

(i) LIMITATION.—Paragraph (2)(F) shall only apply to the portion of the plan described in subparagraph (A) for years preceding the year in which such portion is paid or otherwise made available to the participant.

(ii) TREATMENT.—A plan shall not be treated for purposes of this title as providing for the deferral of compensation for any year with respect to the portion of the plan described in subparagraph (A).

(C) APPLICABLE EMPLOYMENT RETENTION PLAN.—The term "applicable employment retention plan" means an employment retention plan maintained by—

(i) a local educational agency (as defined in section 9101 of the Elementary and Secondary Education Act of 1965 (20 U.S.C. 7801), or

(ii) an education association which principally represents employees of 1 or more agencies described in clause (i) and which is described in section 501(c) (5) or (6) and exempt from taxation under section 501(a).

(D) EMPLOYMENT RETENTION PLAN.—The term "employment retention plan" means a plan to pay, upon termination of employment, compensation to an employee of a local educational agency or education association described in subparagraph (C) for purposes of—

(i) retaining the services of the employee, or

(ii) rewarding such employee for the employee's service with 1 or more such agencies or associations.

Amendments

• 2006, Pension Protection Act of 2006 (P.L. 109-280)

P.L. 109-280, §1104(b)(1):

Amended Code Sec. 457(f)(2) by striking "and" at the end of subparagraph (D), by striking the period at the end of subparagraph (E) and inserting ", and", and by adding at the end a new subparagraph (F). **Effective** for tax years ending after 8-17-2006. For a special rule, see Act Sec. 1104(d)(4), below.

P.L. 109-280, §1104(b)(2):

Amended Code Sec. 457(f) by adding at the end a new paragraph (4). **Effective** for tax years ending after 8-17-2006. For a special rule, see Act Sec. 1104(d)(4), below.

P.L. 109-280, §1104(d)(4), provides:

(4) CONSTRUCTION.—Nothing in the amendments made by this section shall alter or affect the construction of the Internal Revenue Code of 1986, the Employee Retirement Income Security Act of 1974, or the Age Discrimination in Employment Act of 1967 as applied to any plan, arrangement, or conduct to which such amendments do not apply.

• 1996, Small Business Job Protection Act of 1996 (P.L. 104-188)

P.L. 104-188, §1444(b)(3):

Amended Code Sec. 457(f)(2) by striking "and" at the end of subparagraph (C), by striking the period at the end of subparagraph (D) and inserting ", and", and by inserting immediately thereafter a new subparagraph (E). **Effective** for years beginning after 12-31-94. For a special rule, see Act Sec. 1444(e)(2) in the amendment notes following Code Sec. 457(e).

• 1986, Tax Reform Act of 1986 (P.L. 99-514)

P.L. 99-514, §1107(a):

Amended Code Sec. 457. **Effective**, generally, for tax years beginning after 12-31-88. However, see Act Sec. 1107(c)(2)-(5), below, for special rules. Prior to amendment, Code Sec. 457 read as follows:

SEC. 457. DEFERRED COMPENSATION PLANS WITH RESPECT TO SERVICE FOR STATE AND LOCAL GOVERNMENTS.

[Sec. 457(a)]

(a) YEAR OF INCLUSION IN GROSS INCOME.—In the case of a participant in an eligible State deferred compensation plan, any amount of compensation deferred under the plan, and any income attributable to the amounts so deferred, shall be includible in gross income only for the taxable year in which such compensation or other income is paid or otherwise made available to the participant or other beneficiary.

[Sec. 457(b)]

(b) ELIGIBLE STATE DEFERRED COMPENSATION PLAN DEFINED.—For purposes of this section, the term "eligible State deferred compensation plan" means a plan established and maintained by a State—

(1) in which only individuals who perform service for the State may be participants,

(2) which provides that (except as provided in paragraph (3)) the maximum that may be deferred under the plan for the taxable year shall not exceed the lesser of—

(A) $7,500, or

(B) 33¹/₃ percent of the participant's includible compensation,

(3) which may provide that, for 1 or more of the participant's last 3 taxable years ending before he attains normal retirement age under the plan, the ceiling set forth in paragraph (2) shall be the lesser of—

(A) $15,000, or

(B) the sum of—

(i) the plan ceiling established for purposes of paragraph (2) for the taxable year (determined without regard to this paragraph), plus

(ii) so much of the plan ceiling established for purposes of paragraph (2) for taxable years before the taxable year as has not theretofore been used under paragraph (2) or this paragraph,

(4) which provides that compensation will be deferred for any calendar month only if an agreement providing for such deferral has been entered into before the beginning of such month,

(5) which does not provide that amounts payable under the plan will be made available to participants or other beneficiaries earlier than when the participant is separated from service with the State or is faced with an unforeseeable emergency (determined in the manner prescribed by the Secretary by regulation), and

(6) which provides that—

(A) all amounts of compensation deferred under the plan,

(B) all property and rights purchased with such amounts, and

(C) all income attributable to such amounts, property, or rights,

shall remain (until made available to the participant or other beneficiary) solely the property and rights of the State (without being restricted to the provision of benefits under the plan) subject only to the claims of the State's general creditors.

A plan which is administered in a manner which is inconsistent with the requirements of any of the preceding paragraphs shall be treated as not meeting the requirements of such paragraph as of the first plan year beginning more than 180 days after the date of notification by the Secretary of the inconsistency unless the State corrects the inconsistency before the first day of such plan year.

[Sec. 457(c)]

(c) INDIVIDUALS WHO ARE PARTICIPANTS IN MORE THAN ONE PLAN.—

(1) IN GENERAL.—The maximum amount of the compensation of any one individual which may be deferred under subsection (a) during any taxable year shall not exceed $7,500 (as modified by any adjustment provided under subsection (b)(3)).

(2) COORDINATION WITH SECTION 403(b).—In applying paragraph (1) of this subsection and paragraphs (2) and (3) of subsection (b), an amount excluded during a taxable year under section 403(b) shall be treated as an amount deferred under subsection (a). In applying clause (ii) of section 403(b)(2)(A), an amount deferred under subsection (a) for any year of service shall be taken into account as if described in such clause.

[Sec. 457(d)]

(d) OTHER DEFINITIONS AND SPECIAL RULES.—For purposes of this section—

(1) STATE.—The term "State" means a State, a political subdivision of a State, and an agency or instrumentality of a State or political subdivision of a State.

(2) PERFORMANCE OF SERVICE.—The performance of service includes performance of service as an independent contractor.

(3) PARTICIPANT.—The term "participant" means an individual who is eligible to defer compensation under the plan.

(4) BENEFICIARY.—The term "beneficiary" means a beneficiary of the participant, his estate, or any other person whose interest in the plan is derived from the participant.

(5) INCLUDIBLE COMPENSATION.—The term "includible compensation" means compensation for service performed for the State which (taking into account the provisions of this section and section 403(b)) is currently in gross income.

(6) COMPENSATION TAKEN INTO ACCOUNT AT PRESENT VALUE.—Compensation shall be taken into account at its present value.

(7) COMMUNITY PROPERTY LAWS.—The amount of includible compensation shall be determined without regard to any community property laws.

(8) INCOME ATTRIBUTABLE.—Gains from the disposition of property shall be treated as income attributable to such property.

(9) SECTION TO APPLY TO RURAL ELECTRIC COOPERATIVES.—

(A) IN GENERAL.—This section shall apply with respect to any participant in a plan of a rural electric cooperative in the same manner and to the same extent as if such plan were a plan of a State.

(B) RURAL ELECTRIC COOPERATIVE DEFINED.—For purposes of subparagraph (A), the term "rural electric cooperative" means—

(i) any organization which is exempt from tax under section 501(a) and which is engaged primarily in providing electric service on a mutual or cooperative basis, and

(ii) any organization described in paragraph (4) or (6) of section 501(c) which is exempt from tax under section 501(a) and at least 80 percent of the members of which are organizations described in clause (i).

(10) CERTAIN PLANS EXCEPTED.—Any bona fide vacation leave, sick leave, compensatory time, severance pay, disability pay, or death benefit plan shall be treated as a plan not providing for the deferral of compensation.

(11) EXCEPTION FOR NONELECTIVE DEFERRED COMPENSATION OF NONEMPLOYEES.—

(A) IN GENERAL.—This section shall not apply to nonelective deferred compensation attributable to services not performed as an employee.

(B) NONELECTIVE DEFERRED COMPENSATION.—For purposes of subparagraph (a), deferred compensation shall be treated as nonelective only if all individuals (other than those who have not satisfied any applicable initial service requirement) with the same relationship to the payor are covered under the same plan with no individual variations or options under the plan.

Amendments

• 1988, Technical and Miscellaneous Revenue Act of 1988 (P.L. 100-647)

P.L. 100-647, §6064(a)(2):

Amended Code Sec. 457(d) (as in effect on the day before the enactment of the Tax Reform Act of 1986) by adding at the end thereof new paragraph (10). **Effective**, generally, for tax years beginning after 12-31-87. However, for an exception, see Act Sec. 6064(d)(2)-(3), below.

P.L. 100-647, §6064(b)(2):

Amended Code Sec. 457(d), as in effect on the day before the date of the enactment of the Tax Reform Act of 1986, by adding at the end thereof new paragraph (11). See amendment note for P.L. 99-514, §1107(a), following Code Sec. 457(f). **Effective**, generally, for tax years beginning after 12-31-87. However, for an exception, see Act Sec. 6064(d)(2)-(3), below.

P.L. 100-647, §6064(d)(2)-(3), provides:

(2) EXCEPTION FOR CERTAIN COLLECTIVELY BARGAINED PLANS.—

(A) IN GENERAL.—Section 457 of the 1986 Code (as in effect before and after the amendments made by section 1107 of the Reform Act) shall not apply to nonelective deferred compensation provided under a plan in existence on December 31, 1987, and maintained pursuant to a collective bargaining agreement.

(B) NONELECTIVE PLAN.—For purposes of this paragraph, a nonelective plan is a plan which covers a broad group of employees and under which the covered employees earn nonelective deferred compensation under a definite, fixed and uniform benefit formula.

(C) TERMINATION.—This paragraph shall cease to apply to a plan as of the effective date of the first material modification of the plan agreed to after December 31, 1987.

(3) TREATMENT OF CERTAIN NONELECTIVE DEFERRED COMPENSATION.—Section 457 of the 1986 Code shall not apply to amounts deferred under a nonelective deferred compensation plan maintained by an eligible employer described in section 457(e)(1)(A) of the 1986 Code (as in effect after the Reform Act)—

(A) if such amounts were deferred from periods before July 14, 1988, or

(B) if—

(i) such amounts are deferred from periods on or after such date pursuant to an agreement which—

(I) was in writing on such date, and

(II) on such date provides for a deferral for each taxable year covered by the agreement of a fixed amount or of an amount determined pursuant to a fixed formula, and

(ii) the individual with respect to whom the deferral is made was covered under such agreement on such date.

Subparagraph (B) shall not apply to any taxable year ending after the date on which any modification of the amount or formula described in subparagraph (B)(i)(II) agreed to in writing before January 1, 1989, is effective. The preceding sentence shall not apply to a modification agreed to in writing before January 1, 1989, which does not increase any benefit of a participant. Amounts described in the first sentence of this paragraph shall be taken into account for purposes of applying section 457 of the 1986 Code to other amounts deferred under any eligible deferred compensation plan.

(4) STUDY.—The Secretary of the Treasury or his delegate shall conduct a study on the tax treatment of deferred compensation paid by State and local governments and tax-exempt organizations (including deferred compensation paid to independent contractors). Not later than January 1, 1990, the Secretary shall submit to the Committee on Ways and Means of the House of Representatives and the Committee on Finance of the Senate a report on the study conducted under this paragraph together with such recommendations as he may deem advisable.

• 1980, Technical Corrections Act of 1979 (P.L. 96-222)

P.L. 96-222, §101(a)(4):

Amended Code Sec. 457(d)(9)(B). **Effective** as provided in P.L. 95-600, §131(c) below. Prior to amendment, Code Sec. 457(d)(9)(B) read as follows:

(B) RURAL ELECTRIC COOPERATIVE DEFINED.—For purposes of subparagraph (A), the term "rural electric cooperative" means—

(i) any organization described in section 501(c)(12) which is exempt from tax under secton 501(a) and which is engaged primarily in providing electric service, and

(ii) any organization described in section 501(c)(6) which is exempt from tax under section 501(a) and all the members of which are organizations described in clause (i).

[Sec. 457(e)]

(e) TAX TREATMENT OF PARTICIPANT WHERE PLAN OR ARRANGEMENT OF STATE IS NOT ELIGIBLE.—

(1) IN GENERAL.—In the case of a plan of a State providing for a deferral of compensation, if such plan is not an eligible State deferred compensation plan, then—

(A) the compensation shall be included in the gross income of the participant or beneficiary for the first taxable year in which there is no substantial risk of forfeiture of the rights to such compensation, and

(B) the tax treatment of any amount made available under the plan to a participant or beneficiary shall be determined under section 72 (relating to annuities, etc.).

(2) EXCEPTIONS.—Paragraph (1) shall not apply to—

(A) a plan described in section 401(a) which includes a trust exempt from a tax under section 501(a),

(B) an annuity plan or contract described in section 403,

(C) that portion of any plan which consists of a transfer of property described in section 83, and

(D) that portion of any plan which consists of a trust to which section 402(b) applies.

(3) DEFINITIONS.—For purposes of this subsection—

(A) PLAN INCLUDES ARRANGEMENTS, ETC.—The term "plan" includes any agreement or arrangement.

(B) SUBSTANTIAL RISK OR FORFEITURE.—The rights of a person to compensation are subject to a substantial risk of forfeiture if such person's rights to such compensation are conditioned upon the future performance of substantial services by any individual.

Amendments

• 1984, Deficit Reduction Act of 1984 (P.L. 98-369)

P.L. 98-369, §491(d)(33):

Amended Code Sec. 457(e)(2) by striking out subparagraph (C) and by redesignating subparagraphs (D) and (E) as subparagraphs (C) and (D), respectively. **Effective** for obligations issued after 12-31-83. Prior to amendment, subparagraph (C) read as follows:

(C) a qualified bond purchase plan described in section 405(a),

• 1978, Revenue Act of 1978 (P.L. 95-600)

P.L. 95-600, §131(a):

Added Code Sec. 457. **Effective** as set forth in P.L. 95-600, §131(c), below.

P.L. 95-600, §131(c), as amended by P.L. 97-248, §252 provides:

(c) EFFECTIVE DATE.—

(1) IN GENERAL.—The amendments made by this section shall apply to taxable years beginning after December 31, 1978.

(2) TRANSITIONAL RULES.—

(A) IN GENERAL.—In the case of any taxable year beginning after December 31, 1978, and before January 1, 1982—

(i) any amount of compensation deferred under a plan of a State providing for a deferral of compensation (other than a plan described in section 457(e)(2) of the Internal Revenue Code of 1954), and any income attributable to the amounts so deferred, shall be includible in gross income only for the taxable year in which such compensation or other income is paid or otherwise made available to the participant or other beneficiary, but

(ii) the maximum amount of the compensation of any one individual which may be excluded from gross income by reason of clause (i) and by reason of section 457(a) of such Code during any such taxable year shall not exceed the lesser of—

(I) $7,500, or

(II) 33⅓ percent of the participant's includible compensation.

(B) APPLICATION OF CATCH-UP PROVISIONS IN CERTAIN CASES.—If, in the case of any participant for any taxable year, all of the plans are eligible State deferred compensation plans, then clause (ii) of subparagraph (A) of this paragraph shall be applied with the modification provided by paragraph (3) of section 457(b) of such Code.

(C) APPLICATIONS OF CERTAIN COORDINATION PROVISIONS.—In applying clause (ii) of subparagraph (A) of this paragraph and section 403(b)(2)(A)(ii) of such Code, rules similar to the rules of section 457(c)(2) of such Code shall apply.

(D) MEANING OF TERMS.—Except as otherwise provided in this paragraph, terms used in this paragraph shall have the same meaning as when used in section 457 of such Code.

(3) DEFERRED COMPENSATION PLANS FOR STATE JUDGES.—

(A) IN GENERAL.—The amendments made by this section shall not apply to any qualified State judicial plan.

(B) QUALIFIED STATE JUDICIAL PLAN.—For purposes of subparagraph (A), the term "qualified State judicial plan" means any retirement plan of a State for the exclusive benefit of judges or their beneficiaries if—

(i) such plan has been continuously in existence since December 31, 1978,

(ii) under such plan, all judges eligible to benefit under the plan—

(I) are required to participate, and

(II) are required to contribute the same fixed percentage of their basic or regular rate of compensation as judge,

(iii) under such plan, no judge has an option as to contributions or benefits the exercise of which would affect the amount of includible compensation,

(iv) the retirement payments of a judge under the plan are a percentage of the compensation of judges of that State holding similar positions, and

(v) the plan during any year does not pay benefits with respect to any participant which exceed the limitations of section 415(b) of the Internal Revenue Code of 1954.

P.L. 99-514, §1107(c)(2)-(5), as amended by P.L. 100-647, §1011(e)(6)-(7), provides:

(2) TRANSFERS AND CASH-OUTS.—Paragraphs (9) and (10) of section 457(e) of the Internal Revenue Code of 1986 (as amended by this section) shall apply to taxable years beginning after December 31, 1986.

(3) APPLICATION TO TAX-EXEMPT ORGANIZATIONS.—

(A) IN GENERAL.—Except as provided in subparagraph (B), the application of section 457 of the Internal Revenue Code of 1986 by reason of the amendments made by this section to deferred compensation plans established and maintained by organizations exempt form [sic] tax shall apply to taxable years beginning after December 31, 1986.

(B) EXISTING DEFERRALS AND ARRANGEMENTS.—Section 457 of such Code shall not apply to amounts deferred under a plan described in subparagraph (A) which—

(i) were deferred from taxable years beginning before January 1, 1987, or

(ii) are deferred from taxable years beginning after December 31, 1986, pursuant to an agreement which—

(I) was in writing on August 16, 1986,

(II) on such date provides for a deferral for each taxable year covered by the agreement of a fixed amount or of an amount determined pursuant to a fixed formula.

Clause (ii) shall not apply to any taxable year ending after the date on which any modification to the amount or formula described in subclause (II) is effective. Amounts described in the first sentence shall be taken into account for applying section 457 to other amounts deferred under any deferred compensation plan. This subparagraph shall apply to individuals who were covered under the plan and agreement on August 16, 1986.

(4) DEFERRED COMPENSATION PLANS FOR STATE JUDGES.—The amendments made by this section shall not apply to any qualified State judicial plan (as defined in section 131(c)(3)(B) of the Revenue Act of 1978 as amended by section 252 of the Tax Equity and Fiscal Responsibility Act of 1982).

(5) SPECIAL RULE FOR CERTAIN DEFERRED COMPENSATION PLANS.—The amendments made by this section shall not apply—

(A) to employees on August 16, 1986, of a nonprofit corporation organized under the laws of the State of Alabama maintaining a deferred compensation plan with respect to which the Internal Revenue Service issued a ruling dated March 17, 1976, that the plan would not affect the tax-exempt status of the corporation, or

(B) to individuals eligible to participate on August 16, 1986, in a deferred compensation plan with respect to which a letter dated November 6, 1975, submitted the original plan to the Internal Revenue Service, an amendment was submitted on November 19, 1975, and the Internal Revenue Service responded with a letter dated December 24, 1975,

but only with respect to deferrals under such plan.

[Sec. 457(g)]

(g) GOVERNMENTAL PLANS MUST MAINTAIN SET-ASIDES FOR EXCLUSIVE BENEFIT OF PARTICIPANTS.—

(1) IN GENERAL.—A plan maintained by an eligible employer described in subsection (e)(1)(A) shall not be treated as an eligible deferred compensation plan unless all assets and income of the plan described in subsection (b)(6) are held in trust for the exclusive benefit of participants and their beneficiaries.

(2) TAXABILITY OF TRUSTS AND PARTICIPANTS.—For purposes of this title—

(A) a trust described in paragraph (1) shall be treated as an organization exempt from taxation under section 501(a), and

(B) notwithstanding any other provision of this title, amounts in the trust shall be includible in the gross income of participants and beneficiaries only to the extent, and at the time, provided in this section.

(3) CUSTODIAL ACCOUNTS AND CONTRACTS.—For purposes of this subsection, custodial accounts and contracts described in section 401(f) shall be treated as trusts under rules similar to the rules under section 401(f).

(4) DEATH BENEFITS UNDER USERRA-QUALIFIED ACTIVE MILITARY SERVICE.—A plan described in paragraph (1) shall not be treated as an eligible deferred compensation plan unless such plan meets the requirements of section 401(a)(37).

Amendments

• 2008, Heroes Earnings Assistance and Relief Tax Act of 2008 (P.L. 110-245)

P.L. 110-245, §104(c)(3):

Amended Code Sec. 457(g) by adding at the end a new paragraph (4). **Effective** generally with respect to deaths and disabilities occurring on or after 1-1-2007. For a special rule, see Act Sec. 104(d)(2), below.

P.L. 110-245, §104(d)(2), provides:

(2) PROVISIONS RELATING TO PLAN AMENDMENTS.—

(A) IN GENERAL.—If this subparagraph applies to any plan or contract amendment, such plan or contract shall be treated as being operated in accordance with the terms of the plan during the period described in subparagraph (B)(iii).

(B) AMENDMENTS TO WHICH SUBPARAGRAPH (A) APPLIES.—

(i) IN GENERAL.—Subparagraph (A) shall apply to any amendment to any plan or annuity contract which is made—

(I) pursuant to the amendments made by subsection (a) or pursuant to any regulation issued by the Secretary of the Treasury under subsection (a), and

(II) on or before the last day of the first plan year beginning on or after January 1, 2010.

In the case of a governmental plan (as defined in section 414(d) of the Internal Revenue Code of 1986), this clause shall be applied by substituting "2012" for "2010" in subclause (II).

(ii) CONDITIONS.—This paragraph shall not apply to any amendment unless—

(I) the plan or contract is operated as if such plan or contract amendment were in effect for the period described in clause (iii), and

(II) such plan or contract amendment applies retroactively for such period.

(iii) PERIOD DESCRIBED.—The period described in this clause is the period—

(I) beginning on the effective date specified by the plan, and

(II) ending on the date described in clause (i)(II) (or, if earlier, the date the plan or contract amendment is adopted).

• 1996, Small Business Job Protection Act of 1996 (P.L. 104-188)

P.L. 104-188, §1448(a):

Amended Code Sec. 457 by adding at the end a new subsection (g). For the **effective** date, see Act Sec. 1448(c) in the amendment notes following Code Sec. 457(b).

[Sec. 457A]

SEC. 457A. NONQUALIFIED DEFERRED COMPENSATION FROM CERTAIN TAX INDIFFERENT PARTIES.

[Sec. 457A(a)]

(a) IN GENERAL.—Any compensation which is deferred under a nonqualified deferred compensation plan of a nonqualified entity shall be includible in gross income when there is no substantial risk of forfeiture of the rights to such compensation.

[Sec. 457A(b)]

(b) NONQUALIFIED ENTITY.—For purposes of this section, the term "nonqualified entity" means—

(1) any foreign corporation unless substantially all of its income is—

(A) effectively connected with the conduct of a trade or business in the United States, or

(B) subject to a comprehensive foreign income tax, and

(2) any partnership unless substantially all of its income is allocated to persons other than—

(A) foreign persons with respect to whom such income is not subject to a comprehensive foreign income tax, and

(B) organizations which are exempt from tax under this title.

[Sec. 457A(c)]

(c) DETERMINABILITY OF AMOUNTS OF COMPENSATION.—

(1) IN GENERAL.—If the amount of any compensation is not determinable at the time that such compensation is otherwise includible in gross income under subsection (a)—

(A) such amount shall be so includible in gross income when determinable, and

(B) the tax imposed under this chapter for the taxable year in which such compensation is includible in gross income shall be increased by the sum of—

(i) the amount of interest determined under paragraph (2), and

(ii) an amount equal to 20 percent of the amount of such compensation.

(2) INTEREST.—For purposes of paragraph (1)(B)(i), the interest determined under this paragraph for any taxable year is the amount of interest at the underpayment rate under section 6621 plus 1 percentage point on the underpayments that would have occurred had the deferred compensation been includible in gross income for the taxable year in which first deferred or, if later, the first taxable year in which such deferred compensation is not subject to a substantial risk of forfeiture.

[Sec. 457A(d)]

(d) OTHER DEFINITIONS AND SPECIAL RULES.—For purposes of this section—

(1) SUBSTANTIAL RISK OF FORFEITURE.—

(A) IN GENERAL.—The rights of a person to compensation shall be treated as subject to a substantial risk of forfeiture only if such person's rights to such compensation are conditioned upon the future performance of substantial services by any individual.

(B) EXCEPTION FOR COMPENSATION BASED ON GAIN RECOGNIZED ON AN INVESTMENT ASSET.—

(i) IN GENERAL.—To the extent provided in regulations prescribed by the Secretary, if compensation is determined solely by reference to the amount of gain recognized on the disposition of an investment asset, such compensation shall be treated as subject to a substantial risk of forfeiture until the date of such disposition.

(ii) INVESTMENT ASSET.—For purposes of clause (i), the term "investment asset" means any single asset (other than an investment fund or similar entity)—

(I) acquired directly by an investment fund or similar entity,

(II) with respect to which such entity does not (nor does any person related to such entity) participate in the active management of such asset (or if such asset is an interest in an entity, in the active management of the activities of such entity), and

(III) substantially all of any gain on the disposition of which (other than such deferred compensation) is allocated to investors in such entity.

(iii) COORDINATION WITH SPECIAL RULE.—Paragraph (3)(B) shall not apply to any compensation to which clause (i) applies.

(2) COMPREHENSIVE FOREIGN INCOME TAX.—The term "comprehensive foreign income tax" means, with respect to any foreign person, the income tax of a foreign country if—

(A) such person is eligible for the benefits of a comprehensive income tax treaty between such foreign country and the United States, or

(B) such person demonstrates to the satisfaction of the Secretary that such foreign country has a comprehensive income tax.

(3) NONQUALIFIED DEFERRED COMPENSATION PLAN.—

(A) IN GENERAL.—The term "nonqualified deferred compensation plan" has the meaning given such term under section 409A(d), except that such term shall include any plan that provides a right to compensation based on the appreciation in value of a specified number of equity units of the service recipient.

(B) EXCEPTION.—Compensation shall not be treated as deferred for purposes of this section if the service provider receives payment of such compensation not later than 12 months after the end of the taxable year of the service recipient during which the right to the payment of such compensation is no longer subject to a substantial risk of forfeiture.

(4) EXCEPTION FOR CERTAIN COMPENSATION WITH RESPECT TO EFFECTIVELY CONNECTED INCOME.—In the case a foreign corporation with income which is taxable under section 882, this section shall not apply to compensation which, had such compensation had been paid in cash on the date that such compensation ceased to be subject to a substantial risk of forfeiture, would have been deductible by such foreign corporation against such income.

(5) APPLICATION OF RULES.—Rules similar to the rules of paragraphs (5) and (6) of section 409A(d) shall apply.

[Sec. 457A(e)]

(e) REGULATIONS.—The Secretary shall prescribe such regulations as may be necessary or appropriate to carry out the purposes of this section, including regulations disregarding a substantial risk of forfeiture in cases where necessary to carry out the purposes of this section.

Amendments

• 2008, Tax Extenders and Alternative Minimum Tax Relief Act of 2008 (P.L. 110-343)

P.L. 110-343, Division C, §801(a):

Amended subpart B of part II of subchapter E of chapter 1 by inserting after Code Sec. 457 a new Code Sec. 457A. **Effective** generally for amounts deferred which are attributable to services performed after 12-31-2008. For a special rule, see Act Sec. 801(d)(2)-(5), below.

P.L. 110-343, Division C, §801(d)(2)-(5), provides:

(2) APPLICATION TO EXISTING DEFERRALS.—In the case of any amount deferred to which the amendments made by this section do not apply solely by reason of the fact that the amount is attributable to services performed before January 1, 2009, to the extent such amount is not includible in gross income in a taxable year beginning before 2018, such amounts shall be includible in gross income in the later of—

(A) the last taxable year beginning before 2018, or

(B) the taxable year in which there is no substantial risk of forfeiture of the rights to such compensation (determined in the same manner as determined for purposes of section 457A of the Internal Revenue Code of 1986, as added by this section).

(3) ACCELERATED PAYMENTS.—No later than 120 days after the date of the enactment of this Act, the Secretary shall issue guidance providing a limited period of time during which a nonqualified deferred compensation arrangement attributable to services performed on or before December 31, 2008, may, without violating the requirements of section 409A(a) of the Internal Revenue Code of 1986, be amended to conform the date of distribution to the date the amounts are required to be included in income.

(4) CERTAIN BACK-TO-BACK ARRANGEMENTS.—If the taxpayer is also a service recipient and maintains one or more nonqualified deferred compensation arrangements for its service providers under which any amount is attributable to services performed on or before December 31, 2008, the guidance issued under paragraph (4)[(3)] shall permit such arrangements to be amended to conform the dates of distribution under such arrangement to the date amounts are required to be included in the income of such taxpayer under this subsection.

(5) ACCELERATED PAYMENT NOT TREATED AS MATERIAL MODIFICATION.—Any amendment to a nonqualified deferred compensation arrangement made pursuant to paragraph (4) or (5) [(3) or (4)] shall not be treated as a material modification of the arrangement for purposes of section 409A of the Internal Revenue Code of 1986.

[Sec. 458]

SEC. 458. MAGAZINES, PAPERBACKS, AND RECORDS RETURNED AFTER THE CLOSE OF THE TAXABLE YEAR.

[Sec. 458(a)]

(a) EXCLUSION FROM GROSS INCOME.—A taxpayer who is on an accrual method of accounting may elect not to include in the gross income for the taxable year the income attributable to the qualified sale of any magazine, paperback, or record which is returned to the taxpayer before the close of the merchandise return period.

[Sec. 458(b)]

(b) DEFINITIONS AND SPECIAL RULES.—For purposes of this section—

(1) MAGAZINE.—The term "magazine" includes any other periodical.

(2) PAPERBACK.—The term "paperback" means any book which has a flexible outer cover and the pages of which are affixed directly to such outer cover. Such term does not include a magazine.

(3) RECORD.—The term "record" means a disc, tape, or similar object on which musical, spoken, or other sounds are recorded.

(4) SEPARATE APPLICATION WITH RESPECT TO MAGAZINES, PAPERBACKS, AND RECORDS.—If a taxpayer makes qualified sales of more than one category of merchandise in connection with the same trade or business, this section shall be applied as if the qualified sales of each such category were made in connection with a separate trade or business. For purposes of the preceding sentence, magazines, paperbacks, and records shall each be treated as a separate category of merchandise.

(5) QUALIFIED SALE.—A sale of a magazine, paperback, or record is a qualified sale if—

(A) at the time of sale, the taxpayer has a legal obligation to adjust the sales price of such magazine, paperback, or record if it is not resold, and

(B) the sales price of such magazine, paperback, or record is adjusted by the taxpayer because of a failure to resell it.

(6) AMOUNT EXCLUDED.—The amount excluded under this section with respect to any qualified sale shall be the lesser of—

(A) the amount covered by the legal obligation described in paragraph (5)(A), or

(B) the amount of the adjustment agreed to by the taxpayer before the close of the merchandise return period.

(7) MERCHANDISE RETURN PERIOD.—

(A) Except as provided in subparagraph (B), the term "merchandise return period" means, with respect to any taxable year—

(i) in the case of magazines, the period of 2 months and 15 days first occurring after the close of taxable year, or

(ii) in the case of paperbacks and records, the period of 4 months and 15 days first occurring after the close of the taxable year.

(B) The taxpayer may select a shorter period than the applicable period set forth in subparagraph (A).

(C) Any change in the merchandise return period shall be treated as a change in the method of accounting.

(8) CERTAIN EVIDENCE MAY BE SUBSTITUTED FOR PHYSICAL RETURN OF MERCHANDISE.—Under regulations prescribed by the Secretary, the taxpayer may substitute, for the physical return of magazines, paperbacks, or records required by subsection (a), certification or other evidence that the magazine, paperback, or record has not been resold and will not be resold if such evidence—

(A) is in the possession of the taxpayer at the close of the merchandise return period, and

(B) is satisfactory to the Secretary.

(9) REPURCHASED BY THE TAXPAYER NOT TREATED AS RESALE.—A repurchase by the taxpayer shall be treated as an adjustment of the sales price rather than as a resale.

[Sec. 458(c)]

(c) QUALIFIED SALES TO WHICH SECTION APPLIES.—

(1) ELECTION OF BENEFITS.—This section shall apply to qualified sales of magazines, paperbacks, or records, as the case may be, if and only if the taxpayer makes an election under this section with respect to the trade or business in connection with which such sales are made. An election under this section may be made without the consent of the Secretary. The election shall be made in such manner as the Secretary may by regulations prescribe and shall be made for any taxable year not later than the time prescribed by law for filing the return for such taxable year (including extensions thereof).

(2) SCOPE OF ELECTION.—An election made under this section shall apply to all qualified sales of magazines, paperbacks, or records, as the case may be, made in connection with the trade or business with respect to which the taxpayer has made the election.

(3) PERIOD TO WHICH ELECTION APPLIES.—An election under this section shall be effective for the taxable year for which it is made and for all subsequent taxable years, unless the taxpayer secures the consent of the Secretary to the revocation of such election.

(4) TREATMENT AS METHOD OF ACCOUNTING.—Except to the extent inconsistent with the provisions of this section, for purposes of this subtitle, the computation of taxable income under an election made under this section shall be treated as a method of accounting.

[Sec. 458(d)]

(d) 5-YEAR SPREAD OF TRANSITIONAL ADJUSTMENTS FOR MAGAZINES.—In applying section 481(c) with respect to any election under this section which applies to magazines, the period for taking into account any decrease in taxable income resulting from the application of section 481(a)(2) shall be the taxable year for which the election is made and the 4 succeeding taxable years.

[Sec. 458(e)]

(e) SUSPENSE ACCOUNT FOR PAPERBACKS AND RECORDS.—

(1) IN GENERAL.—In the case of any election under this section which applies to paperbacks or records, in lieu of applying section 481, the taxpayer shall establish a suspense account for the trade or business for the taxable year for which the election is made.

(2) INITIAL OPENING BALANCE.—The opening balance of the account described in paragraph (1) for the first taxable year to which the election applies shall be the largest dollar amount of returned merchandise which would have been taken into account under this section for any of the 3 immediately preceding taxable years if this section had applied to such preceding 3 taxable years. This paragraph and paragraph (3) shall be applied by taking into account only amounts attributable to the trade or business for which such account is established.

(3) ADJUSTMENTS IN SUSPENSE ACCOUNT.—At the close of each taxable year the suspense account shall be—

(A) reduced the excess (if any) of—

(i) the opening balance of the suspense account for the taxable year, over

(ii) the amount excluded from gross income for the taxable year under subsection (a), or

(B) increased (but not in excess of the initial opening balance) by the excess (if any) of—

(i) the amount excluded from gross income for the taxable year under subsection (a), over

(ii) the opening balance of the account for the taxable year.

(4) GROSS INCOME ADJUSTMENTS.—

(A) REDUCTIONS EXCLUDED FROM GROSS INCOME.—In the case of any reduction under paragraph (3)(A) in the account for the taxable year, an amount equal to such reduction shall be excluded from gross income for such taxable year.

(B) INCREASES ADDED TO GROSS INCOME.—In the case of any increase under paragraph (3)(B) in the account for the taxable year, an amount equal to such increase shall be included in gross income for such taxable year.

If the initial opening balance exceeds the dollar amount of returned merchandise which would have been taken into account under subsection (a) for the taxable year preceding the first taxable year for which the election is effective if this section had applied to such preceding taxable year, then an amount equal to the amount of such excess shall be included in gross income for such first taxable year.

(5) SUBCHAPTER C TRANSACTIONS.—The application of this subsection with respect to a taxpayer which is a party to any transaction with respect to which there is nonrecognition of gain or loss to any party to the transaction by reason of subchapter C shall be determined under regulations prescribed by the Secretary.

Amendments

• 1978, Revenue Act of 1978 (P.L. 95-600)

P.L. 95-600, §372(a):

Added Code Sec. 458. **Effective** for tax years beginning after 9-30-79.

[Sec. 460]

SEC. 460. SPECIAL RULES FOR LONG-TERM CONTRACTS.

[Sec. 460(a)]

(a) REQUIREMENT THAT PERCENTAGE OF COMPLETION METHOD BE USED.—In the case of any long-term contract, the taxable income from such contract shall be determined under the percentage of completion method (as modified by subsection (b)).

Amendments

• 1989, Omnibus Budget Reconciliation Act of 1989 (P.L. 101-239)

P.L. 101-239, §7621(a):

Amended Code Sec. 460(a). **Effective** for contracts entered into on or after 7-11-89. For special rules, see Act Sec. 7621(d)(2)-(3), below. Prior to amendment, Code Sec. 460(a) read as follows:

(a) PERCENTAGE OF COMPLETION-CAPITALIZED COST METHOD.—

(1) IN GENERAL.—In the case of any long-term contract—

(A) 90 percent of the items with respect to such contract shall be taken into account under the percentage of completion method (as modified by subsection (b)), and

(B) 10 percent of the items with respect to such contract shall be taken into account under the taxpayer's normal method of accounting.

(2) 90 PERCENT LOOK-BACK METHOD TO APPLY.—Upon completion of any long-term contract (or, with respect to any amount properly taken into account after completion of the contract, when such amount is so properly taken into account), the taxpayer shall pay (or shall be entitled to receive) interest determined by applying the look-back method of subsection (b)(3) to 90 percent of the items with respect to the contract.

P.L. 101-239, §7621(d)(2)-(3), provides:

(2) BINDING BIDS.—The amendments made by this section shall not apply to any contract resulting from the acceptance of a bid made before July 11, 1989. The preceding sentence shall apply only if the bid could not have been revoked or altered at any time on or after July 11, 1989.

(3) SPECIAL RULE FOR CERTAIN SHIP CONTRACTS.—The amendments made by this section shall not apply in the case of a

qualified ship contract (as defined in section 10203(b)(2)(B) of the Revenue Act of 1987).

P.L. 101-239, §7811(e)(1):

Amended Code Sec. 460(a)(2), prior to amendment by Act Sec. 7621(a), by inserting "(or, with respect to any amount properly taken into account after completion of the contract, when such amount is so properly taken into account)" after "any long-term contract". **Effective** as if included in the provision of P.L. 100-647 to which it relates.

• 1988, Technical and Miscellaneous Revenue Act of 1988 (P.L. 100-647)

P.L. 100-647, §5041(a)(1)-(2):

Amended Code Sec. 460(a) by striking out "70 percent" each place it appears (including the heading of paragraph (2)) and inserting in lieu thereof "90 percent", and by striking out "30 percent" in paragraph (1)(B) and inserting in lieu thereof "10 percent". **Effective**, generally, for contracts entered into on or after 6-21-88. For special rules see Act Sec. 5041(e) below.

P.L. 100-647, §5041(e), as amended by P.L. 101-239, §7815(e)(3), provides:

(e) EFFECTIVE DATES.—

(1) SUBSECTIONS (a), (b), AND (c).—

(A) IN GENERAL.—Except as otherwise provided in this paragraph, the amendments made by subsections (a), (b), and (c) shall apply to contracts entered into on or after June 21, 1988.

(B) BINDING BIDS.—The amendments made by subsections (a), (b), and (c) shall not apply to any contract resulting from the acceptance of a bid made before June 21, 1988. The preceding sentence shall apply only if the bid could not have been revoked or altered at any time on or after June 21, 1988.

(C) SPECIAL RULE FOR CERTAIN SHIP CONTRACTS.—The amendments made by subsections (a) and (b) shall not apply in the case of a qualified ship contract (as defined in section 10203(b)(2)(B) of the Revenue Act of 1987).

(2) SUBSECTION (d).—The amendment made by subsection (d) shall apply as if included in the amendments made by section 804 of the Reform Act; except that such amendment shall not apply to any contract completed in a taxable year ending before the date of the enactment of this Act, if the due date (determined with regard to extensions) for the return for such year is before such date of enactment.

• 1987, Revenue Act of 1987 (P.L. 100-203)

P.L. 100-203, §10203(a)(1)-(2):

Amended Code Sec. 460(a) by striking out "40 percent" each place it appears in the text and heading thereof and inserting in lieu thereof "70 percent", and by striking out "60 percent" and inserting in lieu thereof "30 percent". For the **effective** date, see Act Sec. 10203(b), below.

P.L. 100-203, §10203(b), provides:

(b) EFFECTIVE DATES.—

(1) IN GENERAL.—Except as provided in paragraph (2), the amendments made by this section shall apply to contracts entered into after October 13, 1987.

(2) SPECIAL RULE FOR CERTAIN SHIP CONTRACTS.—

(A) IN GENERAL.—The amendments made by this section shall not apply in the case of a qualified ship contract.

(B) QUALIFIED SHIP CONTRACT.—For purposes of subparagraph (A), the term "qualified ship contract" means any contract for the construction in the United States of not more than 5 ships if—

(i) such ships will not be constructed (directly or indirectly) for the Federal Government, and

(ii) the taxpayer reasonably expects to complete such contract within 5 years of the contract commencement date (as defined in section 460(g) of the Internal Revenue Code of 1986).

P.L. 100-203, §10204 provides:

SEC. 10204. AMORTIZATION OF PAST SERVICE PENSION COSTS.

(a) IN GENERAL.—For purposes of sections 263A and 460 of the Internal Revenue Code of 1986, the allocable costs (within the meaning of section 263A(a)(2) or section 460(c) of such Code, whichever is applicable) with respect to any property shall include contributions paid to or under a pension or annuity plan whether or not such contributions represent past service costs.

(b) EFFECTIVE DATE.—

(1) IN GENERAL.—Except as provided in paragraph (2), subsection (a) shall apply to costs incurred after December 31, 1987, in taxable years ending after such date.

(2) SPECIAL RULE FOR INVENTORY PROPERTY.—In the case of any property which is inventory in the hands of the taxpayer—

(A) IN GENERAL.—Subsection (a) shall apply to taxable years beginning after December 31, 1987.

(B) CHANGE IN METHOD OF ACCOUNTING.—If the taxpayer is required by this section to change its method of accounting for any taxable year—

(i) such change shall be treated as initiated by the taxpayer,

(ii) such change shall be treated as made with the consent of the Secretary of the Treasury or his delegate, and

(iii) the net amount of adjustments required by section 481 of the Internal Revenue Code of 1986 shall be taken into account over a period not longer than 4 taxable years.

[Sec. 460(b)]

(b) PERCENTAGE OF COMPLETION METHOD.—

(1) REQUIREMENTS OF PERCENTAGE OF COMPLETION METHOD.—Except as provided in paragraph (3), in the case of any long-term contract with respect to which the percentage of completion method is used—

(A) the percentage of completion shall be determined by comparing costs allocated to the contract under subsection (c) and incurred before the close of the taxable year with the estimated total contract costs, and

(B) upon completion of the contract (or, with respect to any amount properly taken into account after completion of the contract, when such amount is so properly taken into account), the taxpayer shall pay (or shall be entitled to receive) interest computed under the look-back method of paragraph (2).

In the case of any long-term contract with respect to which the percentage of completion method is used, except for purposes of applying the look-back method of paragraph (2), any income under the contract (to the extent not previously includible in gross income) shall be included in gross income for the taxable year following the taxable year in which the contract was completed. For purposes of subtitle F (other than sections 6654 and 6655), any interest required to be paid by the taxpayer under subparagraph (B) shall be treated as an increase in the tax imposed by this chapter for the taxable year in which the contract is completed (or, in the case of interest payable with respect to any amount properly taken into account after completion of the contract, for the taxable year in which the amount is so properly taken into account).

(2) LOOK-BACK METHOD.—The interest computed under the look-back method of this paragraph shall be determined by—

(A) first allocating income under the contract among taxable years before the year in which the contract is completed on the basis of the actual contract price and costs instead of the estimated contract price and costs,

(B) second, determining (solely for purposes of computing such interest) the overpayment or underpayment of tax for each taxable year referred to in subparagraph (A) which would result solely from the application of subparagraph (A), and

(C) then using the adjusted overpayment rate (as defined in paragraph (7)), compounded daily, on the overpayment or underpayment determined under subparagraph (B).

For purposes of the preceding sentence, any amount properly taken into account after completion of the contract shall be taken into account by discounting (using the Federal mid-term rate determined under section 1274(d) as of the time is so properly taken into account) such amount to its value as of the completion of the contract. The taxpayer may elect with respect to any contract to have the preceding sentence not apply to such contract.

(3) SPECIAL RULES.—

(A) SIMPLIFIED METHOD OF COST ALLOCATION.—In the case of any long-term contract, the Secretary may prescribe a simplified procedure for allocation of costs to such contract in lieu of the method of allocation under subsection (c).

(B) LOOK-BACK METHOD NOT TO APPLY TO CERTAIN CONTRACTS.—Paragraph (1)(B) shall not apply to any contract—

(i) the gross price of which (as of the completion of the contract) does not exceed the lesser of—

(I) $1,000,000, or

(II) 1 percent of the average annual gross receipts of the taxpayer for the 3 taxable years preceding the taxable year in which the contract was completed, and

(ii) which is completed within 2 years of the contract commencement date.

For purposes of this subparagraph, rules similar to the rules of subsections (e)(2) and (f)(3) shall apply.

(4) SIMPLIFIED LOOK-BACK METHOD FOR PASS-THRU ENTITIES.—

(A) IN GENERAL.—In the case of a pass-thru entity—

(i) the look-back method of paragraph (2) shall be applied at the entity level,

(ii) in determining overpayments and underpayments for purposes of applying paragraph (2)(B)—

(I) any increase in the income under the contract for any taxable year by reason of the allocation under paragraph (2)(A) shall be treated as giving rise to an underpayment determined by applying the highest rate for such year to such increase, and

(II) any decrease in such income for any taxable year by reason of such allocation shall be treated as giving rise to an overpayment determined by applying the highest rate for such year to such decrease, and

(iii) any interest required to be paid by the taxpayer under paragraph (2) shall be paid by such entity (and any interest entitled to be received by the taxpayer under paragraph (2) shall be paid to such entity).

(B) EXCEPTIONS.—

(i) CLOSELY HELD PASS-THRU ENTITIES.—This paragraph shall not apply to any closely held pass-thru entity.

(ii) FOREIGN CONTRACTS.—This paragraph shall not apply to any contract unless substantially all of the income from such contract is from sources in the United States.

(C) OTHER DEFINITIONS.—For purposes of this paragraph—

(i) HIGHEST RATE.—The term "highest rate" means—

(I) the highest rate of tax specified in section 11, or

(II) if at all times during the year involved more than 50 percent of the interest in the entity are held by individuals directly or through 1 or more other pass-thru entities, the highest rate of tax specified in section 1.

(ii) PASS-THRU ENTITY.—The term "pass-thru entity" means any—

(I) partnership,

(II) S corporation, or

(III) trust.

(iii) CLOSELY HELD PASS-THRU ENTITY.—The term "closely held pass-thru entity" means any pass-thru entity if, at any time during any taxable year for which there is income under the contract, 50 percent or more (by value) of the beneficial interests in such entity are held (directly or indirectly) by or for 5 or fewer persons. For purposes of the preceding sentence, rules similar to the constructive ownership rules of section 1563(e) shall apply.

(5) ELECTION TO USE 10-PERCENT METHOD.—

(A) GENERAL RULE.—In the case of any long-term contract with respect to which an election under this paragraph is in effect, the 10-percent method shall apply in determining the taxable income from such contract.

(B) 10-PERCENT METHOD.—For purposes of this paragraph.—

(i) IN GENERAL.—The 10-percent method is the percentage of completion method, modified so that any item which would otherwise be taken into account in computing taxable income with respect to a contract for any taxable year before the 10-percent year is taken into account in the 10-percent year.

(ii) 10-PERCENT YEAR.—The term "10-percent year" means the 1st taxable year as of the close of which at least 10 percent of the estimated total contract costs have been incurred.

(C) ELECTION.—An election under this paragraph shall apply to all long-term contracts of the taxpayer which are entered into during the taxable year in which the election is made or any subsequent taxable year.

(D) COORDINATION WITH OTHER PROVISIONS.—

(i) SIMPLIFIED METHOD OF COST ALLOCATION.—This paragraph shall not apply to any taxpayer which uses a simplified procedure for allocation of costs under paragraph (3)(A).

(ii) LOOK-BACK METHOD.—The 10-percent method shall be taken into account for purposes of applying the look-back method of paragraph (2) to any taxpayer making an election under this paragraph.

(6) ELECTION TO HAVE LOOK-BACK METHOD NOT APPLY IN DE MINIMIS CASES.—

(A) AMOUNTS TAKEN INTO ACCOUNT AFTER COMPLETION OF CONTRACT.—Paragraph (1)(B) shall not apply with respect to any taxable year (beginning after the taxable year in which the contract is completed) if—

(i) the cumulative taxable income (or loss) under the contract as of the close of such taxable year, is within

(ii) 10 percent of the cumulative look-back taxable income (or loss) under the contract as of the close of the most recent taxable year to which paragraph (1)(B) applied (or would have applied but for subparagraph (B)).

(B) DE MINIMIS DISCREPANCIES.—Paragraph (1)(B) shall not apply in any case to which it would otherwise apply if—

(i) the cumulative taxable income (or loss) under the contract as of the close of each prior contract year, is within

(ii) 10 percent of the cumulative look-back income (or loss) under the contract as of the close of such prior contract year.

(C) DEFINITIONS.—For purposes of this paragraph—

(i) CONTRACT YEAR.—The term "contract year" means any taxable year for which income is taken into account under the contract.

(ii) LOOK-BACK INCOME OR LOSS.—The look-back income (or loss) is the amount which would be the taxable income (or loss) under the contract if the allocation method set forth in paragraph (2)(A) were used in determining taxable income.

(iii) DISCOUNTING NOT APPLICABLE.—The amounts taken into account after the completion of the contract shall be determined without regard to any discounting under the 2nd sentence of paragraph (2).

(D) CONTRACTS TO WHICH PARAGRAPH APPLIES.—This paragraph shall only apply if the taxpayer makes an election under this subparagraph. Unless revoked with the consent of the Secretary, such an election shall apply to all long-term contracts completed during the taxable year for which election is made or during any subsequent taxable year.

(7) ADJUSTED OVERPAYMENT RATE.—

(A) IN GENERAL.—The adjusted overpayment rate for any interest accrual period is the overpayment rate in effect under section 6621 for the calendar quarter in which such interest accrual period begins.

(B) INTEREST ACCRUAL PERIOD.—For purposes of subparagraph (A), the term "interest accrual period" means the period—

(i) beginning on the day after the return due date for any taxable year of the taxpayer, and

(ii) ending on the return due date for the following taxable year.

For purposes of the preceding sentence, the term "return due date" means the date prescribed for filing the return of the tax imposed by this chapter (determined without regard to extensions).

Amendments

• 1997, Taxpayer Relief Act of 1997 (P.L. 105-34)

P.L. 105-34, §1211(a):

Amended Code Sec. 460(b) by adding at the end a new paragraph (6). **Effective** for contracts completed in tax years ending after 8-5-97.

P.L. 105-34, §1211(b)(1):

Amended Code Sec. 460(b)(2)(C) by striking "the overpayment rate established by section 6621" and inserting "the adjusted overpayment rate (as defined in paragraph (7))". **Effective** for contracts completed in tax years ending after 8-5-97, and, for purposes of Code Sec. 167(g), to property placed in service after 9-13-95.

P.L. 105-34, §1211(b)(2):

Amended Code Sec. 460(b) by adding at the end a new paragraph (7). **Effective** for contracts completed in tax years ending after 8-5-97, and, for purposes of Code Sec. 167(g), to property placed in service after 9-13-95.

• 1996, Small Business Job Protection Act of 1996 (P.L. 104-188)

P.L. 104-188, §1704(t)(28):

Amended Code Sec. 460(b)(1) by striking "the look-back method of paragraph (3)" and inserting "the look-back method of paragraph (2)". **Effective** 8-20-96.

• 1989, Omnibus Budget Reconciliation Act of 1989 (P.L. 101-239)

P.L. 101-239, §7621(b):

Amended Code Sec. 460(b) by adding at the end thereof a new paragraph (5). **Effective** for contracts entered into on or after 7-11-89. For special rules, see Act Sec. 7621(d)(2)-(3) following Code Sec. 460(a).

P.L. 101-239, §7621(c)(1):

Amended Code Sec. 460(b) by striking paragraph (1) and by redesignating paragraphs (2) through (5) as paragraphs (1) through (4), respectively. **Effective** for contracts entered into on or after 7-11-89. For special rules, see Act Sec. 7621(d)(2)-(3) following Code Sec. 460(a). Prior to amendment, Code Sec. 460(b)(1) read as follows:

(1) SUBSECTION (a) NOT TO APPLY WHERE PERCENTAGE OF COMPLETION METHOD USED.—Subsection (a) shall not apply to any long-term contract with respect to which amounts includible in gross income are determined under the percentage of completion method.

P.L. 101-239, §7621(c)(2)(A)-(B):

Amended Code Sec. 460(b)(1), as redesignated by paragraph (1), by striking "paragraph (4)" and inserting "paragraph (3)", and by striking "paragraph (3)" and inserting "paragraph (2)". **Effective** for contracts entered into on or after 7-11-89. For special rules, see Act Sec. 7621(d)(2)-(3) following Code Sec. 460(a).

P.L. 101-239, §7621(c)(3):

Amended Code Sec. 460(b)(3), as redesignated by paragraph (1), by striking "Paragraph (2)(B) and subsection (a)(2)" and inserting "Paragraph (1)(B)". **Effective** for contracts entered into on or after 7-11-89. For special rules, see Act Sec. 7621(d)(2)-(3) following Code Sec. 460(a).

P.L. 101-239, §7621(c)(4)(A)-(C):

Amended Code Sec. 460(b)(4)(A), as redesignated by paragraph (1), by striking "paragraph (3)" each place it appears and inserting "paragraph (2)", by striking "paragraph (3)(B)", and inserting "paragraph (2)(B)", and by striking "paragraph (3)(A)" and inserting "paragraph (2)(A)". **Effective** for contracts entered into on or after 7-11-89. For special rules, see Act Sec. 7621(d)(2)-(3) following Code Sec. 460(a).

P.L. 101-239, §7811(e)(2)(A)-(B):

Amended Code Sec. 460(b)(2)(B) by striking "any amount received or accrued" and inserting "any amount properly taken into account", and by striking "is so received or accrued" and inserting "is so properly taken into account". **Effective** as if included in the provision of P.L. 100-647 to which it relates.

P.L. 101-239, §7811(e)(3)(A)-(B):

Amended Code Sec. 460(b)(3) by striking "any amount received or accrued" in the second sentence and inserting "any amount properly taken into account", and by striking "is so [such amount was] received or accrued" in the second sentence and inserting "is so properly taken into account". **Effective** as if included in the provision of P.L. 100-647 to which it relates.

P.L. 101-239, §7811(e)(4):

Amended Code Sec. 460(b)(2) by adding at the end thereof a new sentence. **Effective** as if included in the provision of P.L. 100-647 to which it relates.

P.L. 101-239, §7811(e)(6):

Amended Code Sec. 460(b)(2) by adding at the end thereof a new sentence. **Effective** as if included in the provision of P.L. 100-647 to which it relates.

• 1988, Technical and Miscellaneous Revenue Act of 1988 (P.L. 100-647)

P.L. 100-647, §1008(c)(1)(A)-(C):

Amended Code Sec. 460(b)(3) by striking out "subparagraph" and inserting in lieu thereof "paragraph", by striking out "paragraph (1)" each place it appears in subparagraph (B) and inserting in lieu thereof "subparagraph (A)", and by striking out "paragraph (1)" in subparagraph (C) and inserting in lieu thereof "subparagraph (B)". **Effective** as if included in the provision of P.L. 99-514 to which it relates.

P.L. 100-647, §1008(c)(2)(A):

Amended Code Sec. 460(b) by adding at the end thereof new paragraph (4). **Effective** as if included in the provision of P.L. 99-514 to which it relates.

P.L. 100-647, §1008(c)(2)(B):

Amended Code Sec. 460(b)(2) by striking out "In" and inserting in lieu thereof "Except as provided in paragraph (4), in". **Effective** as if included in the provision of P.L. 99-514 to which it relates.

P.L. 100-647, §1008(c)(4)(A):

Amended Code Sec. 460(b)(3) by adding at the end thereof two new sentences. **Effective** as if included in the provision of P.L. 99-514 to which it relates.

P.L. 100-647, §1008(c)(4)(B):

Amended Code Sec. 460(b)(2)(B) by striking out "completion of the contract" and inserting in lieu thereof "completion of the contract (or, with respect to any amount received or accrued after completion of the contract, when such amount is so received or accrued)". **Effective** as if included in the provision of P.L. 99-514 to which it relates.

P.L. 100-647, §5041(d):

Amended Code Sec. 460(b) by adding at the end thereof a new paragraph (5). **Effective**, generally, for contracts entered into on or after 6-21-88. For special rules see Act Sec. 5401(e) in the amendment notes following Code Sec. 460(a).

[Sec. 460(c)]

(c) ALLOCATION OF COSTS TO CONTRACT.—

(1) DIRECT AND CERTAIN INDIRECT COSTS.—In the case of a long-term contract, all costs (including research and experimental costs) which directly benefit, or are incurred by reason of, the long-term contract activities of the taxpayer shall be allocated to such contract in the same manner as costs are allocated to extended period long-term contracts under section 451 and the regulations thereunder.

(2) COSTS IDENTIFIED UNDER COST-PLUS AND CERTAIN FEDERAL CONTRACTS.—In the case of a cost-plus long-term contract or a Federal long-term contract, any cost not allocated to such contract under paragraph (1) shall be allocated to such contract if such cost is identified by the taxpayer

(or a related person), pursuant to the contract or Federal, State, or local law or regulation, as being attributable to such contract.

(3) ALLOCATION OF PRODUCTION PERIOD INTEREST TO CONTRACT.—

(A) IN GENERAL.—Except as provided in subparagraphs (B) and (C), in the case of a long-term contract, interest costs shall be allocated to the contract in the same manner as interest costs are allocated to property produced by the taxpayer under section 263A(f).

(B) PRODUCTION PERIOD.—In applying section 263A(f) for purposes of subparagraph (A), the production period shall be the period—

(i) beginning on the later of—

(I) the contract commencement date, or

(II) in the case of a taxpayer who uses an accrual method with respect to long-term contracts, the date by which at least 5 percent of the total estimated costs (including design and planning costs) under the contract have been incurred, and

(ii) ending on the contract completion date.

(C) APPLICATION OF DE MINIMIS RULE.—In applying section 263A(f) for purposes of subparagraph (A), paragraph (1)(B)(iii) of such section shall be applied on a contract-by-contract basis; except that, in the case of a taxpayer described in subparagraph (B)(i)(II) of this paragraph, paragraph (1)(B)(iii) of section 263A(f) shall be applied on a property-by-property basis.

(4) CERTAIN COSTS NOT INCLUDED.—This subsection shall not apply to any—

(A) independent research and development expenses,

(B) expenses for unsuccessful bids and proposals, and

(C) marketing, selling, and advertising expenses.

(5) INDEPENDENT RESEARCH AND DEVELOPMENT EXPENSES.—For purposes of paragraph (4), the term "independent research and development expenses" means any expenses incurred in the performance of research or development, except that such term shall not include—

(A) any expenses which are directly attributable to a long-term contract in existence when such expenses are incurred, or

(B) any expenses under an agreement to perform research or development.

(6) SPECIAL RULE FOR ALLOCATION OF BONUS DEPRECIATION WITH RESPECT TO CERTAIN PROPERTY.—

(A) IN GENERAL.—Solely for purposes of determining the percentage of completion under subsection (b)(1)(A), the cost of qualified property shall be taken into account as a cost allocated to the contract as if subsection (k) of section 168 had not been enacted.

(B) QUALIFIED PROPERTY.—For purposes of this paragraph, the term "qualified property" means property described in section 168(k)(2) which—

(i) has a recovery period of 7 years or less, and

(ii) is placed in service after December 31, 2009, and before January 1, 2011 (January 1, 2012, in the case of property described in section 168(k)(2)(B)).

Amendments

• 2010, Creating Small Business Jobs Act of 2010 (P.L. 111-240)

P.L. 111-240, §2023(a):

Amended Code Sec. 460(c) by adding at the end a new paragraph (6). **Effective** for property placed in service after 12-31-2009.

[Sec. 460(d)]

(d) FEDERAL LONG-TERM CONTRACT.—For purposes of this section—

(1) IN GENERAL.—The term "Federal long-term contract" means any long-term contract—

(A) to which the United States (or any agency or instrumentality thereof) is a party, or

(B) which is a subcontract under a contract described in subparagraph (A).

(2) SPECIAL RULES FOR CERTAIN TAXABLE ENTITIES.—For purposes of paragraph (1), the rules of section 168(h)(2)(D) (relating to certain taxable entities not treated as instrumentalities) shall apply.

[Sec. 460(e)]

(e) EXCEPTION FOR CERTAIN CONSTRUCTION CONTRACTS.—

(1) IN GENERAL.—Subsections (a), (b), and (c)(1) and (2) shall not apply to—

(A) any home construction contract, or

(B) any other construction contract entered into by a taxpayer—

(i) who estimates (at the time such contract is entered into) that such contract will be completed within the 2-year period beginning on the contract commencement date of such contract, and

(ii) whose average annual gross receipts for the 3 taxable years preceding the taxable year in which such contract is entered into do not exceed $10,000,000.

In the case of a home construction contract with respect to which the requirements of clauses (i) and (ii) of subparagraph (B) are not met, section 263A shall apply notwithstanding subsection (c)(4) thereof.

(2) DETERMINATION OF TAXPAYER'S GROSS RECEIPTS.—For purposes of paragraph (1), the gross receipts of—

(A) all trades or businesses (whether or not incorporated) which are under common control with the taxpayer (within the meaning of section 52(b)),

(B) all members of any controlled group of corporations of which the taxpayer is a member, and

(C) any predecessor of the taxpayer or a person described in subparagraph (A) or (B),

for the 3 taxable years of such persons preceding the taxable year in which the contract described in paragraph (1) is entered into shall be included in the gross receipts of the taxpayer for the period described in paragraph (1)(B). The Secretary shall prescribe regulations which provide attribution rules that take into account, in addition to the persons and entities described in the preceding sentence, taxpayers who engage in construction contracts through partnerships, joint ventures, and corporations.

(3) CONTROLLED GROUP OF CORPORATIONS.—For purposes of this subsection, the term "controlled group of corporations" has the meaning given to such term by section 1563(a), except that—

(A) "more than 50 percent" shall be substituted for "at least 80 percent" each place it appears in section 1563(a)(1), and

(B) the determination shall be made without regard to subsections (a)(4) and (e)(3)(C) of section 1563.

(4) CONSTRUCTION CONTRACT.—For purposes of this subsection, the term "construction contract" means any contract for the building, construction, reconstruction, or rehabilitation of, or the installation of any integral component to, or improvements of, real property.

(5) SPECIAL RULE FOR RESIDENTIAL CONSTRUCTION CONTRACTS WHICH ARE NOT HOME CONSTRUCTION CONTRACTS.—In the case of any residential construction contract which is not a home construction contract, subsection (a) (as in effect on the day before the date of the enactment of the Revenue Reconciliation Act of 1989) shall apply except that such subsection shall be applied—

(A) by substituting "70 percent" for "90 percent" each place it appears, and

(B) by substituting "30 percent" for "10 percent".

(6) DEFINITIONS RELATING TO RESIDENTIAL CONSTRUCTION CONTRACTS.—For purposes of this subsection—

(A) HOME CONSTRUCTION CONTRACT.—The term "home construction contract" means any construction contract if 80 percent of the estimated total contract costs (as of the close of the taxable year in which the contract was entered into) are reasonably expected to be attributable to activities referred to in paragraph (4) with respect to—

(i) dwelling units (as defined in section 168(e)(2)(A)(ii)) contained in buildings containing 4 or fewer dwelling units (as so defined), and

(ii) improvements to real property directly related to such dwelling units and located on the site of such dwelling units.

For purposes of clause (i), each townhouse or rowhouse shall be treated as a separate building.

(B) RESIDENTIAL CONSTRUCTION CONTRACT.—The term "residential construction contract" means any contract which would be described in subparagraph (A) if clause (i) of such subparagraph reads as follows:

"(i) dwelling units (as defined in section 168(e)(2)(A)(ii)), and"

Amendments

• 1996, Small Business Job Protection Act of 1996 (P.L. 104-188)

P.L. 104-188, §1702(h)(15):

Amended Code Sec. 460(e)(6)(B) by striking "section 167(k)" and inserting "section 168(e)(2)(A)(ii)". **Effective** as if included in the provision of P.L. 101-508 to which such amendment relates.

• 1990, Omnibus Budget Reconciliation Act of 1990 (P.L. 101-508)

P.L. 101-508, §11812(b)(8):

Amended Code Sec. 460(e)(6)(A)(i) by striking "section 167(k)" and inserting "section 168(e)(2)(A)(ii)". **Effective**, generally, for property placed in service after 11-5-90. However, for exceptions see Act Sec. 11812(c)(2)-(3) below.

P.L. 101-508, §11812(c)(2)-(3), provides:

(2) EXCEPTION.—The amendments made by this section shall not apply to any property to which section 168 of the Internal Revenue Code of 1986 does not apply by reason of subsection (f)(5) thereof.

(3) EXCEPTION FOR PREVIOUSLY GRANDFATHER [sic] EXPENDITURES.—The amendments made by this section shall not apply to rehabilitation expenditures described in section 252(f)(5) of the Tax Reform Act of 1986 (as added by section 1002(l)(31) of the Technical and Miscellaneous Revenue Act of 1988).

• 1989, Omnibus Budget Reconciliation Act of 1989 (P.L. 101-239)

P.L. 101-239, §7621(c)(5):

Amended so much of Code Sec. 460(e)(5) as precedes subparagraph (A). **Effective** for contracts entered into on or after 7-11-89. For special rules, see Act Sec. 7621(d)(2)-(3) following Code Sec. 460(a). Prior to amendment, so much of Code Sec. 460(e)(5) as preceded subparagraph (A) read as follows:

(5) SPECIAL RULE FOR RESIDENTIAL CONSTRUCTION CONTRACTS WHICH ARE NOT HOME CONSTRUCTION CONTRACTS.—In the case of

any residential construction contract which is not a home construction contract, subsection (a) shall be applied—

P.L. 101-239, §7811(e)(5):

Amended Code Sec.460(e)(2) by striking "and" at the end of subparagraph (A), by inserting "and" at the end of subparagraph (B), and by adding at the end thereof a new subparagraph (C). **Effective** as if included in the provision of P.L. 100-647 to which it relates.

P.L. 101-239, §7815(e)(1)(A)-(B):

Amended Code Sec. 460(e)(6)(A) by striking "the building, construction, reconstruction, or rehabilitation of" and inserting "activities referred to in paragraph (4) with respect to", and by amending clause (i). **Effective** as if included in the provision of P.L. 100-647 to which it relates. Prior to amendment, Code Sec. 460(e)(6)(A)(i) read as follows:

(i) dwelling units contained in buildings containing 4 or fewer dwelling units, and

• 1988, Technical and Miscellaneous Revenue Act of 1988 (P.L. 100-647)

P.L. 100-647, §5041(b)(1):

Amended Code Sec. 460(e)(1). **Effective**, generally, for contracts entered into on or after 6-21-88. For special rules see Act Sec. 5041(e) in the amendment notes following Code Sec. 460(a). Prior to amendment, Code Sec. 460(e)(1) read as follows:

(1) IN GENERAL.—Subsections (a), (b), and (c)(1) and (2) shall not apply to any construction contract entered into by a taxpayer—

(A) who estimates (at the time such contract is entered into) that such contract will be completed within the 2-year period beginning on the contract commencement date of such contract, and

(B) whose average annual gross receipts for the 3 taxable years preceding the taxable year in which such contract is entered into do not exceed $10,000,000.

P.L. 100-647, §5041(b)(2):

Amended Code Sec. 460(e) by adding at the end thereof a new paragraph (5). **Effective**, generally, for contracts entered into on or after 6-21-88. For special rules see Act Sec. 5041(e) in the amendment notes following Code Sec. 460(a).

P.L. 100-647, §5041(b)(3):

Amended Code Sec. 460(e) by adding at the end thereof a new paragraph (6). **Effective**, generally, for contracts entered into on or after 6-21-88. For special rules see Act Sec. 5041(e) in the amendment notes following Code Sec. 460(a).

[Sec. 460(f)]

(f) LONG-TERM CONTRACT.—For purposes of this section—

(1) IN GENERAL.—The term "long-term contract" means any contract for the manufacture, building, installation, or construction of property if such contract is not completed within the taxable year in which such contract is entered into.

(2) SPECIAL RULE FOR MANUFACTURING CONTRACTS.—A contract for the manufacture of property shall not be treated as a long-term contract unless such contract involves the manufacture of—

(A) any unique item of a type which is not normally included in the finished goods inventory of the taxpayer, or

(B) any item which normally requires more than 12 calendar months to complete (without regard to the period of the contract).

(3) AGGREGATION, ETC.—For purposes of this subsection, under regulations prescribed by the Secretary—

(A) 2 or more contracts which are interdependent (by reason of pricing or otherwise) may be treated as 1 contract, and

(B) a contract which is properly treated as an aggregation of separate contracts may be so treated.

[Sec. 460(g)]

(g) CONTRACT COMMENCEMENT DATE.—For purposes of this section, the term "contract commencement date" means, with respect to any contract, the first date on which any costs (other than bidding expenses or expenses incurred in connection with negotiating the contract) allocable to such contract are incurred.

Amendments

• 1986, Tax Reform Act of 1986 (P.L. 99-514)

P.L. 99-514, §804(a):

Amended subpart B of part II of subchapter E of chapter 1 by adding new Code section 460. **Effective**, generally, for any contract entered into after 2-28-86. However, see Act Sec. 804(d)(2), below, for special rules.

P.L. 99-514, §804(b), provides:

(b) CHANGE IN REGULATIONS.—The Secretary of the Treasury or his delegate shall modify the income tax regulations relating to accounting for long-term contracts to carry out the provisions of section 460 of the Internal Revenue Code of 1986 (as added by subsection (a)).

P.L. 99-514, §804(d)(2), as amended by P.L. 100-647, §1008(c)(3), provides:

(2) CLARIFICATION OF TREATMENT OF INDEPENDENT RESEARCH AND DEVELOPMENT EXPENSES.—

(A) IN GENERAL.—For periods before, on, or after the date of enactment of this Act—

(i) any independent research and development expenses taken into account in determining the total contract price shall not be severable from the contract, and

(ii) any independent research and development expenses shall not be treated as amounts chargeable to capital account.

(B) INDEPENDENT RESEARCH AND DEVELOPMENT EXPENSES.—For purposes of subparagraph (A), the term "independent research and development expense" has the meaning given to such term by section 460(c)(5) of the Internal Revenue Code of 1986, as added by this section.

[Sec. 460(h)]

(h) REGULATIONS.—The Secretary shall prescribe such regulations as may be necessary or appropriate to carry out the purposes of this section, including regulations to prevent the use of related parties, pass-thru entities, intermediaries, options or other similar arrangements to avoid the application of this section.

Amendments

• 1988, Technical and Miscellaneous Revenue Act of 1988 (P.L. 100-647)

P.L. 100-647, §5041(c):

Amended Code Sec. 460 by adding at the end thereof a new subsection (h). **Effective**, generally, for contracts entered into on or after 6-21-88. For special rules see Act Sec. 5051(e) in the amendment notes following Code Sec. 460(a).

Subpart C—Taxable Year for Which Deductions Taken

Sec. 461. General rule for taxable year of deduction.
Sec. 464. Limitations on deductions for certain farming [expenses].
Sec. 465. Deductions limited to amount at risk.
Sec. 467. Certain payments for use of property or services.
Sec. 468. Special rules for mining and solid waste reclamation and closing costs.
Sec. 468A. Special rules for nuclear decommissioning costs.
Sec. 468B. Special rules for designated settlement funds.
Sec. 469. Passive activity losses and credits limited.
Sec. 470. Limitation on deductions allocable to property used by governments or other tax-exempt entities.

[Sec. 461]

SEC. 461. GENERAL RULE FOR TAXABLE YEAR OF DEDUCTION.

[Sec. 461(a)]

(a) GENERAL RULE.—The amount of any deduction or credit allowed by this subtitle shall be taken for the taxable year which is the proper taxable year under the method of accounting used in computing taxable income.

[Sec. 461(b)]

(b) SPECIAL RULE IN CASE OF DEATH.—In the case of the death of a taxpayer whose taxable income is computed under an accrual method of accounting, any amount accrued as a deduction or credit only by reason of the death of the taxpayer shall not be allowed in computing taxable income for the period in which falls the date of the taxpayer's death.

[Sec. 461(c)]

(c) ACCRUAL OF REAL PROPERTY TAXES.—

(1) IN GENERAL.—If the taxable income is computed under an accrual method of accounting, then, at the election of the taxpayer, any real property tax which is related to a definite period of time shall be accrued ratably over that period.

(2) WHEN ELECTION MAY BE MADE.—

(A) WITHOUT CONSENT.—A taxpayer may, without the consent of the Secretary, make an election under this subsection for his first taxable year in which he incurs real property taxes. Such an election shall be made not later than the time prescribed by law for filing the return for such year (including extensions thereof).

(B) WITH CONSENT.—A taxpayer may, with the consent of the Secretary, make an election under this subsection at any time.

Amendments

• 1976, Tax Reform Act of 1976 (P.L. 94-455)

P.L. 94-455, §1901(a)(69):

Amended Sec. 461(c) by striking paragraph (2), redesignating paragraph (3) as paragraph (2), and substituting therein "his first taxable year in which he" for "his first taxable year which begins after December 31, 1953, and ends after the date of enactment of this title in which the taxpayer". **Effective** with respect to tax years beginning after 12-31-76. Prior to its deletion, Code Sec. 461(c)(2) read as follows:

(2) SPECIAL RULES.—Paragraph (1) shall not apply to any real property tax, to the extent that such tax was allowable as a deduction under the Internal Revenue Code of 1939 for a taxable year which began before January 1, 1954. In the case of any real property tax which would, but for this subsection, be allowable as a deduction for the first taxable year of the taxpayer which begins after December 31, 1953, then, to the extent that such tax is related to any period before the first day of such first taxable year, the tax shall be allowable as a deduction for such first taxable year.

P.L. 94-455, §1906(b)(13)(A):

Amended the 1954 Code by substituting "Secretary" for "Secretary or his delegate" each place it appeared. **Effective** 2-1-77.

[Sec. 461(d)]

(d) LIMITATION ON ACCELERATION OF ACCRUAL OF TAXES.—

(1) GENERAL RULE.—In the case of a taxpayer whose taxable income is computed under an accrual method of accounting, to the extent that the time for accruing taxes is earlier than it would be but for any action of any taxing jurisdiction taken after December 31, 1960, then, under regulations prescribed by the Secretary, such taxes shall be treated as accruing at the time they would have accrued but for such action by such taxing jurisdiction.

(2) LIMITATION.—Under regulations prescribed by the Secretary, paragraph (1) shall be inapplicable to any item of tax to the extent that its application would (but for this paragraph) prevent all persons (including successors in interest) from ever taking such item into account.

Amendments

• 1976, Tax Reform Act of 1976 (P.L. 94-455)

P.L. 94-455, §1906(b)(13)(A):

Amended 1954 Code by substituting "Secretary" for "Secretary or his delegate" each place it appeared. **Effective** 2-1-77.

• 1960 (P.L. 86-781)

P.L. 86-781, §6(a):

Amended Code Sec. 461 by adding a new subsection (d). **Effective** for tax years ending after 1960.

[Sec. 461(e)]

(e) DIVIDENDS OR INTEREST PAID ON CERTAIN DEPOSITS OR WITHDRAWABLE ACCOUNTS.—Except as provided in regulations prescribed by the Secretary, amounts paid to, or credited to the accounts of, depositors or holders of accounts as dividends or interest on their deposits or withdrawable accounts (if such amounts paid or credited are withdrawable on demand subject only to customary notice to withdraw) by a mutual savings bank not having capital stock represented by shares, a domestic building and loan association, or a cooperative bank shall not be allowed as a deduction for the taxable year to the extent such amounts are paid or credited for periods representing more than 12 months. Any such amount not allowed as a deduction as the result of the application of the preceding sentence shall be allowed as a deduction for such other taxable year as the Secretary determines to be consistent with the preceding sentence.

Amendments

• 1976, Tax Reform Act of 1976 (P.L. 94-455)

P.L. 94-455, §1906(b)(13)(A):

Amended 1954 Code by substituting "Secretary" for "Secretary or his delegate" each place it appeared. **Effective** 2-1-77.

• 1962 (P.L. 87-876)

P.L. 87-876, §2(a):

Amended Code Sec. 461 by adding subsection (e). **Effective** with respect to tax years ending after 12-31-62.

[Sec. 461(f)]

(f) CONTESTED LIABILITIES.—If—

(1) the taxpayer contests an asserted liability,

(2) the taxpayer transfers money or other property to provide for the satisfaction of the asserted liability,

(3) the contest with respect to the asserted liability exists after the time of the transfer, and

(4) but for the fact that the asserted liability is contested, a deduction would be allowed for the taxable year of the transfer (or for an earlier taxable year) determined after application of subsection (h),

then the deduction shall be allowed for the taxable year of the transfer. This subsection shall not apply in respect of the deduction for income, war profits, and excess profits taxes imposed by the authority of any foreign country or possession of the United States.

Amendments

• 1984, Deficit Reduction Act of 1984 (P.L. 98-369)

P.L. 98-369, §91(e):

Amended Code Sec. 461(f)(4) by inserting "determined after application of subsection (h)" after "taxable year)". **Effective** as noted in Act Sec. 91(g)-(i), following Code Sec. 461(h).

• 1964, Revenue Act of 1964 (P.L. 88-272)

P. L. 88-272, §223(a)(1):

Added Code Sec. 461(f). **Effective**, generally, for tax years beginning after 12-31-53 and ending after 8-16-54. For exceptions, see Act Sec. 223(c) and (d), below.

P. L. 88-272, §223(c)-(d), provides:

"(c) Election as to Transfers in Taxable Years Beginning Before January 1, 1964.—

"(1) The amendments made by subsection (a) shall not apply to any transfer of money or other property described in subsection (a) made in a taxable year beginning before January 1, 1964, if the taxpayer elects, in the manner provided by regulations prescribed by the Secretary of the Treasury or his delegate, to have this paragraph apply. Such an election—

"(A) must be made within one year after the date of the enactment of this Act,

"(B) may not be revoked after the expiration of such one-year period, and

"(C) shall apply to all transfers described in the first sentence of this paragraph (other than transfers described in paragraph (2)).

In the case of any transfer to which this paragraph applies, the deduction shall be allowed only for the taxable year in which the contest with respect to such transfer is settled.

"(2) Paragraph (1) shall not apply to any transfer if the assessment of any deficiency which would result from the application of the election in respect of such transfer is, on the date of the election under paragraph (1), prevented by the operation of any law or rule of law.

"(3) If the taxpayer makes an election under paragraph (1), and if, on the date of such election, the assessment of any deficiency which results from the application of the election in respect of any transfer is not prevented by the operation of any law or rule of law, the period within which assessment of such deficiency may be made shall not expire earlier than 2 years after the date of the enactment of this Act.

"(d) Certain Other Transfers in Taxable Years Beginning Before January 1, 1964.—The amendments made by subsection (a) shall not apply to any transfer of money or other property described in subsection (a) made in a taxable year beginning before January 1, 1964, if—

"(1) no deduction has been allowed in respect of such transfer for any taxable year before the taxable year in which the contest with respect to such transfer is settled, and

"(2) refund or credit of any overpayment which would result from the application of such amendments to such transfer is prevented by the operation of any law or rule of law.

In the case of any transfer to which this subsection applies, the deduction shall be allowed for the taxable year in which the contest with respect to such transfer is settled."

[Sec. 461(g)]

(g) PREPAID INTEREST.—

(1) IN GENERAL.—If the taxable income of the taxpayer is computed under the cash receipts and disbursements method of accounting, interest paid by the taxpayer which, under regulations prescribed by the Secretary, is properly allocable to any period—

(A) with respect to which the interest represents a charge for the use or forbearance of money, and

(B) which is after the close of the taxable year in which paid,

shall be charged to capital account and shall be treated as paid in the period to which so allocable.

(2) EXCEPTION.—This subsection shall not apply to points paid in respect of any indebtedness incurred in connection with the purchase or improvement of, and secured by, the principal residence of the taxpayer to the extent that, under regulations prescribed by the Secretary, such payment of points is an established business practice in the area in which such indebtedness is incurred, and the amount of such payment does not exceed the amount generally charged in such area.

Amendments

• 1976, Tax Reform Act of 1976 (P.L. 94-455)

P.L. 94-455, §208(a):

Added Code Sec. 461(g). For **effective** date, see Act Sec. 208(b), below.

P.L. 94-455, §208(b), provides:

(1) IN GENERAL.—Except as provided in paragraph (2), the amendment made by subsection (a) shall apply to amounts paid after December 31, 1975, in taxable years ending after such date.

(2) CERTAIN AMOUNTS PAID BEFORE 1977.—The amendment made by subsection (a) shall not apply to amounts paid before January 1, 1977, pursuant to a binding contract or written loan commitment which existed on September 16, 1975 (and at all times thereafter), and which required prepayment of such amounts by the taxpayer.

[Sec. 461(h)]

(h) CERTAIN LIABILITIES NOT INCURRED BEFORE ECONOMIC PERFORMANCE.—

(1) IN GENERAL.—For purposes of this title, in determining whether an amount has been incurred with respect to any item during any taxable year, the all events test shall not be treated as met any earlier than when economic performance with respect to such item occurs.

(2) TIME WHEN ECONOMIC PERFORMANCE OCCURS.—Except as provided in regulations prescribed by the Secretary, the time when economic performance occurs shall be determined under the following principles:

(A) SERVICES AND PROPERTY PROVIDED TO THE TAXPAYER.—If the liability of the taxpayer arises out of—

(i) the providing of services to the taxpayer by another person, economic performance occurs as such person provides such services,

(ii) the providing of property to the taxpayer by another person, economic performance occurs as the person provides such property, or

(iii) the use of property by the taxpayer, economic performance occurs as the taxpayer uses such property.

(B) SERVICES AND PROPERTY PROVIDED BY THE TAXPAYER.—If the liability of the taxpayer requires the taxpayer to provide property or services, economic performance occurs as the taxpayer provides such property or services.

(C) WORKERS COMPENSATION AND TORT LIABILITIES OF THE TAXPAYER.—If the liability of the taxpayer requires a payment to another person and—

(i) arises under any workers compensation act, or

(ii) arises out of any tort,

economic performance occurs as the payments to such person are made. Subparagraphs (A) and (B) shall not apply to any liability described in the preceding sentence.

(D) OTHER ITEMS.—In the case of any other liability of the taxpayer, economic performance occurs at the time determined under regulations prescribed by the Secretary.

(3) EXCEPTION FOR CERTAIN RECURRING ITEMS.—

(A) IN GENERAL.—Notwithstanding paragraph (1) an item shall be treated as incurred during any taxable year if—

(i) the all events test with respect to such item is met during such taxable year (determined without regard to paragraph (1)),

(ii) economic performance with respect to such item occurs within the shorter of—

(I) a reasonable period after the close of such taxable year, or

(II) $8\frac{1}{2}$ months after the close of such taxable year,

(iii) such item is recurring in nature and the taxpayer consistently treats items of such kind as incurred in the taxable year in which the requirements of clause (i) are met, and

(iv) either—

(I) such item is not a material item, or

(II) the accrual of such item in the taxable year in which the requirements of clause (i) are met results in a more proper match against income than accruing such item in the taxable year in which economic performance occurs.

(B) FINANCIAL STATEMENTS CONSIDERED UNDER SUBPARAGRAPH (A)(iv).—In making a determination under subparagraph (A)(iv), the treatment of such item on financial statements shall be taken into account.

(C) PARAGRAPH NOT TO APPLY TO WORKERS COMPENSATION AND TORT LIABILITIES.—This paragraph shall not apply to any item described in subparagraph (C) of paragraph (2).

(4) ALL EVENTS TEST.—For purposes of this subsection, the all events test is met with respect to any item if all events have occurred which determine the fact of liability and the amount of such liability can be determined with reasonable accuracy.

(5) SUBSECTION NOT TO APPLY TO CERTAIN ITEMS.—This subsection shall not apply to any item for which a deduction is allowable under a provision of this title which specifically provides for a deduction for a reserve for estimated expenses.

Amendments

• 1987, Revenue Act of 1987 (P.L. 100-203)

P.L. 100-203, §10201(b)(5):

Amended Code Sec. 461(h)(5). **Effective** for tax years beginning after 12-31-87. Prior to amendment, Code Sec. 461(h)(5) read as follows:

(5) SUBSECTION NOT TO APPLY TO CERTAIN CASES TO WHICH OTHER PROVISIONS OF THIS TITLE SPECIFICALLY APPLY.—This subsection shall not apply to any item to which any of the following provisions apply:

(A) Section 463 (relating to vacation pay).

(C)([B]) Any other provisions of this title which specifically provides for a deduction for a reserve for estimated expenses.

• 1986, Tax Reform Act of 1986 (P.L. 99-514)

P.L. 99-514, §805(c)(5):

Amended Code Sec. 461(h)(5) by striking out subparagraph (A) and by redesignating subparagraphs (B), (C), and (D) as subparagraphs (A), (B), and (C). **Effective**, generally, for tax years beginning after 12-31-86. However, see Act Sec. 805(d)(2) following Code Sec. 81 for special rules. Prior to amendment, Code Sec. 461(h)(5)(A) read as follows:

(A) Subsection (c) or (f) of section 166 (relating to reserves for bad debts).

P.L. 99-514, §823(b)(1):

Amended Code Sec. 461(h)(5) by striking out subparagraph (B) and by redesignating subparagraph (C) as subparagraph (B). **Effective**, generally, for tax years beginning after 12-31-86. However, see Act Sec. 823(c)(2) under the amendment notes for Code Sec. 466 for special rules. Prior to amendment, Code Sec. 461(h)(5)(C) read as follows:

(C) Section 466 (relating to discount coupons).

• 1984, Deficit Reduction Act of 1984 (P.L. 98-369)

P.L. 98-369, §91(a):

Amended Code Sec. 461 by adding subsection (h). **Effective** as noted in Act Sec. 91(g)-(i) below.

P.L. 98-369, 91(g)-(i), as amended by P.L. 99-514, §1807(a), provides:

(g) EFFECTIVE DATES.—

(1) IN GENERAL.—Except as provided in this subsection and subsections (h) and (i), the amendments made by this section shall apply to amounts with respect to which a deduction would be allowable under chapter 1 of the Internal Revenue Code of 1954 (determined without regard to such amendments) after—

(A) in the case of amounts to which section 461(h) of such Code (as added by such amendments) applies, the date of the enactment of this Act, and

(B) in the case of amounts to which section 461(i) of such Code (as so added) applies, after March 31, 1984.

(2) TAXPAYER MAY ELECT EARLIER APPLICATION.—

(A) IN GENERAL.—In the case of amounts described in paragraph (1)(A), a taxpayer may elect to have the amendments made by this section apply to amounts which—

(i) are incurred on or before the date of the enactment of this Act (determined without regard to such amendments), and

(ii) are incurred after the date of the enactment of this Act (determined with regard to such amendments).

The Secretary of the Treasury or his delegate may by regulations provide that (in lieu of an election under the preceding sentence) a taxpayer may (subject to such conditions as such regulations may provide) elect to have subsection (h) of section 461 of such Code apply to the taxpayer's entire taxable year in which occurs July 19, 1984.

(B) ELECTION TREATED AS CHANGE IN THE METHOD OF ACCOUNTING.—For purposes of section 481 of the Internal Revenue Code of 1954, if an election is made under subparagraph (A) with respect to any amount, the application of the amendments made by this section shall be treated as a change in method of accounting—

(i) initiated by the taxpayer,

(ii) made with the consent of the Secretary of the Treasury, and

(iii) with respect to which section 481 of such Code shall be applied by substituting a 3-year adjustment period for a 10-year adjustment period.

(3) SECTION 461(h) TO APPLY IN CERTAIN CASES.—Notwithstanding paragraph (1), section 461(h) of the Internal Revenue Code of 1954 (as added by this section) shall be treated as being in effect to the extent necessary to carry out any amendments made by this section which take effect before section 461(h).

(4) EFFECTIVE DATE FOR TREATMENT OF MINING AND SOLID WASTE RECLAMATION AND CLOSING COSTS.—Except as otherwise provided in subsection (h), the amendments made by subsection (b) shall take effect on the date of the enactment of this Act with respect to taxable years ending after such date.

(5) RULES FOR NUCLEAR DECOMMISSIONING COSTS.—The amendments made by subsections (c) and (f) shall take effect on the date of the enactment of this Act with respect to taxable years ending after such date.

(6) MODIFICATION OF NET OPERATING LOSS CARRYBACK PERIOD.—The amendments made by subsection (d) shall apply to losses for taxable years beginning after December 31, 1983.

(h) EXCEPTION FOR CERTAIN EXISTING ACTIVITIES AND CONTRACTS.—If—

(1) EXISTING ACCOUNTING PRACTICES.—If, on March 1, 1984, any taxpayer was regularly computing his deduction for mining reclamation activities under a current cost method of accounting (as determined by the Secretary of the Treasury or his delegate), the liability for reclamation activities—

(A) for land disturbed before the date of the enactment of this Act, or

(B) to which paragraph (2) applies,

shall be treated as having been incurred when the land was disturbed.

(2) FIXED PRICE SUPPLY CONTRACT.—

(A) IN GENERAL.—In the case of any fixed price supply contract entered into before March 1, 1984, the amendments made by subsection (b) shall not apply to any minerals extracted from such property which are sold pursuant to such contract.

(B) NO EXTENSION OR RENOGOTIATION.—Subparagraph (A) shall not apply—

(i) to any extension of any contract beyond the period such contract was in effect on March 1, 1984, or

(ii) to any renegotiation of, or other change in, the terms and conditions of such contract in effect on March 1, 1984.

(i) TRANSITIONAL RULE FOR ACCRUED VACATION PAY.—

(1) IN GENERAL.—In the case of any taxpayer—

(A) with respect to whom a deduction was allowable (other than under section 463 of the Internal Revenue Code of 1954) for vested accrued vacation pay for the last taxable year ending before the date of the enactment of this Act, and

(B) who elects the application of section 463 of such Code for the first taxable year ending after the date of the enactment of this Act,

then, for purposes of section 463(b) of such Code, the opening balance of the taxpayer with respect to any vested accrued vacation pay shall be determined under section 463(b)(1) of such Code.

(2) VESTED ACCRUED VACATION PAY.—For purposes of this subsection, the term "vested accrued vacation pay" means any amount allowable under section 162(a) of such Code with respect to vacation pay of employees of the taxpayer (determined without regard to section 463 of such Code).

[Sec. 461(i)]

(i) SPECIAL RULES FOR TAX SHELTERS.—

(1) RECURRING ITEM EXCEPTION NOT TO APPLY.—In the case of a tax shelter, economic performance shall be determined without regard to paragraph (3) of subsection (h).

(2) SPECIAL RULE FOR SPUDDING OF OIL OR GAS WELLS.—

(A) IN GENERAL.—In the case of a tax shelter, economic performance with respect to amounts paid during the taxable year for drilling an oil or gas well shall be treated as having occurred within a taxable year if drilling of the well commences before the close of the 90th day after the close of the taxable year.

(B) DEDUCTION LIMITED TO CASH BASIS.—

(i) TAX SHELTER PARTNERSHIPS.—In the case of a tax shelter which is a partnership, in applying section 704(d) to a deduction or loss for any taxable year attributable to an item which is deductible by reason of subparagraph (A), the term "cash basis" shall be substituted for the term "adjusted basis".

(ii) OTHER TAX SHELTERS.—Under regulations prescribed by the Secretary, in the case of a tax shelter other than a partnership, the aggregate amount of the deductions allowable by reason of subparagraph (A) for any taxable year shall be limited in a manner similar to the limitation under clause (i).

(C) CASH BASIS DEFINED.—For purposes of subparagraph (B), a partner's cash basis in a partnership shall be equal to the adjusted basis of such partner's interest in the partnership, determined without regard to—

(i) any liability of the partnership, and

(ii) any amount borrowed by the partner with respect to such partnership which—

(I) was arranged by the partnership or by any person who participated in the organization, sale, or management of the partnership (or any person related to such person within the meaning of section 465(b)(3)(C)), or

(II) was secured by any asset of the partnership.

(3) TAX SHELTER DEFINED.—For purposes of this subsection, the term "tax shelter" means—

(A) any enterprise (other than a C corporation) if at any time interests in such enterprise have been offered for sale in any offering required to be registered with any Federal or State agency having the authority to regulate the offering of securities for sale,

(B) any syndicate (within the meaning of section 1256(e)(3)(B)), and

(C) any tax shelter (as defined in section 6662(d)(2)(C)(ii)).

(4) SPECIAL RULES FOR FARMING.—In the case of the trade or business of farming (as defined in section 464(e)), in determining whether an entity is a tax shelter, the definition of farming syndicate in section 464(c) shall be substituted for subparagraphs (A) and (B) of paragraph (3).

(5) ECONOMIC PERFORMANCE.—For purposes of this subsection, the term "economic performance" has the meaning given such term by subsection (h).

Amendments

• 2005, Gulf Opportunity Zone Act of 2005 (P.L. 109-135)

P.L. 109-135, §412(aa):

Amended Code Sec. 461(i)(3)(C) by striking "section 6662(d)(2)(C)(iii)" and inserting "section 6662(d)(2)(C)(ii)". **Effective** 12-21-2005.

• 1996, Small Business Job Protection Act of 1996 (P.L. 104-188)

P.L. 104-188, §1704(t)(78):

Amended Code Sec. 461(i)(3)(C) by striking "section 6662(d)(2)(C)(ii)" and inserting "section 6662(d)(2)(C)(iii)". **Effective** 8-20-96.

• 1990, Omnibus Budget Reconciliation Act of 1990 (P.L. 101-508)

P.L. 101-508, §11704(a)(5):

Amended Code Sec. 461(i)(3)(C). **Effective** 11-5-90. Prior to amendment, subparagraph (C) read as follows:

(C) any tax shelter (within the meaning of section 6662(d)(2)(C)(ii)).

• 1989, Omnibus Budget Reconciliation Act of 1989 (P.L. 101-239)

P.L. 101-239, §7721(c)(10) (as amended by P.L. 104-188, §1704(t)(24)):

Amended Code Sec. 461(i)(3)(C) by striking "section 6661(b)(2)(C)(ii)" and inserting "section 6662(d)(2)(C)(ii)".

Effective for returns the due date for which (determined without regard to extensions) is after 12-31-89.

• 1988, Technical and Miscellaneous Revenue Act of 1988 (P.L. 100-647)

P.L. 100-647, §1008(a)(3):

Amended Code Sec. 461(i)(2). **Effective** as if included in the provision of P.L. 99-514 to which it relates. Prior to amendment, Code Sec. 461(i)(2) read as follows:

(2) SPECIAL RULE FOR SPUDDING OF OIL OR GAS WELLS.—In the case of a tax shelter, economic performance with respect to the act of drilling an oil or gas well shall be treated as having occurred within a taxable year if drilling of the well commences before the close of the 90th day after the close of the taxable year.

• 1986, Tax Reform Act of 1986 (P.L. 99-514)

P.L. 99-514, §801(b)(1):

Amended so much of Code Sec. 461(i) as precedes paragraph (3) thereof. **Effective**, generally, for tax years beginning after 12-31-86. However, see Act Sec. 801(d)(2)-(4), following Code Sec. 448, for special rules. Prior to amendment, Code Sec. 461(i)(1) and (2) read as follows:

(i) TAX SHELTERS MAY NOT DEDUCT ITEMS EARLIER THAN WHEN ECONOMIC PERFORMANCE OCCURS.—

(1) IN GENERAL.—In the case of a tax shelter computing taxable income under the cash receipts and disbursements method of accounting, such tax shelter shall not be allowed a deduction under this chapter with respect to any item any earlier than the time when such item would be treated as incurred under subsection (h) (determined without regard to paragraph (3) thereof).

(2) EXCEPTION (TO EXTENT OF CASH BASIS) WHEN ECONOMIC PERFORMANCE OCCURS ON OR BEFORE THE 90TH DAY AFTER THE CLOSE OF THE TAXABLE YEAR.—

(A) IN GENERAL.—Paragraph (1) shall not apply to any item if economic performance with respect to such item occurs before the close of the 90th day after the close of the taxable year.

(B) DEDUCTION LIMITED TO CASH BASIS.—

(i) TAX SHELTER PARTNERSHIPS.—In the case of a tax shelter which is a partnership, in applying section 704(d) to a deduction or loss for any taxable year attributable to an item which is deductible by reason of subparagraph (A), the term "cash basis" shall be substituted for the term "adjusted basis".

(ii) OTHER TAX SHELTERS.—Under regulations prescribed by the Secretary, in the case of a tax shelter other than a partnership, the aggregate amount of the deductions allowable by reason of subparagraph (A) for any taxable year shall be limited in a manner similar to the limitation under clause (i).

(C) CASH BASIS DEFINED.—For purposes of subparagraph (B), a partner's cash basis in a partnership shall be equal to the adjusted basis of such partner's interest in the partnership, determined without regard to—

(i) any liability of the partnership, and

(ii) any amount borrowed by the partner with respect to such partnership which—

(I) was arranged by the partnership or by any person who participated in the organization, sale, or management of the partnership (or any person related to such person within the meaning of section 168(e)(4)), or

(II) was secured by any assets of the partnership.

(D) SPECIAL CASH BASIS RULE FOR SPUDDING OF OIL OR GAS WELLS.—Solely for purposes of applying subparagraph (A), economic performance with respect to the act of drilling of an oil or gas well shall be treated as occurring when the drilling of the well is commenced.

P.L. 99-514, §801(b)(2):

Amended Code Sec. 461(i)(4). **Effective**, generally, for tax years beginning after 12-31-86. However, see Act Sec. 801(d)(2)-(4), following Code Sec. 448, for special rules. Prior to amendment, Code Sec. 461(i)(4) read as follows:

(4) SPECIAL RULES FOR FARMING.—In the case of the trade or business of farming (as defined in section 464(e))—

(A) any tax shelter described in paragraph (3)(C) shall be treated as a farming syndicate for purposes of section 464; except that this subparagraph shall not apply for purposes of determining the income of an individual meeting the requirements of section 464(c)(2),

(B) section 464 shall be applied before this subsection, and

(C) in determining whether an entity is a tax shelter, the definition of farming syndicate in section 464(c) shall be substituted for subparagraphs (A) and (B) of paragraph (3).

P.L. 99-514, §1807(a)(1)(A):

Amended Code Sec. 461(i)(2)(A) by striking out "within 90 days after the close of the taxable year" and inserting in lieu thereof "before the close of the 90th day after the close of the taxable year". **Effective** as if included in the provision of P.L. 98-369 to which it relates. Prior to amendment, Code Sec. 461(i)(2)(A) read as follows:

(A) IN GENERAL.—Paragraph (1) shall not apply to any item if economic performance with respect to such item occurs within 90 days after the close of the taxable year.

P.L. 99-514, §1807(a)(1)(B):

Amended Code Sec. 461(i) by striking out "WITHIN 90 DAYS" in the heading for paragraph (2) and inserting in lieu thereof "ON OR BEFORE THE 90 th DAY". **E ffective** as if included in the provision of P.L. 98-369 to which it relates. Prior to amendment, the heading for Code Sec. 461(i)(2) read as follows:

(2) EXCEPTION (TO EXTENT OF CASH BASIS) WHEN ECONOMIC PERFORMANCE OCCURS WITHIN 90 DAYS AFTER THE CLOSE OF THE TAXABLE YEAR.—

P.L. 99-514, §1807(a)(2):

Amended subparagraph (A) of Code Sec. 461(i)(4). **Effective** as if included in the provision of P.L. 98-369 to which it relates. Prior to amendment, Code Sec. 461(i)(4)(A) read as follows:

(A) section 464 shall be applied to any tax shelter described in paragraph (3)(C),

P.L. 99-514, §1807(a)(8), provides:

(8) TRANSITIONAL RULE FOR CERTAIN AMOUNTS.—For purposes of section 461(h) of the Internal Revenue Code of 1954, economic performance shall be treated as occurring on the date of a payment to an insurance company if—

(A) such payment was made before November 23, 1985, for indemnification against a tort liability relating to personal injury or death caused by inhalation or ingestion of dust from asbestos-containing insulation products,

(B) such insurance company is unrelated to taxpayer,

(C) such payment is not refundable, and

(D) the taxpayer is not engaged in the mining of asbestos nor is any member of any affiliated group which includes the taxpayer so engaged.

P.L. 99-514, §1807(c), provides:

(c) TRANSITION RULE.—A taxpayer shall be allowed to use the cash receipts and disbursements method of accounting for taxable years ending after January 1, 1982, if such taxpayer—

(1) is a partnership which was founded in 1936,

(2) has over 1,000 professional employees,

(3) used a long-term contract method of accounting for a substantial part of its income from the performance of architectural and engineering services, and

(4) is headquartered in Chicago, Illinois.

• 1984, Deficit Reduction Act of 1984 (P.L. 98-369)

P.L. 98-369, §91(a):

Amended Code Sec. 461 by adding subsections (h) and (i). **Effective** as noted in Act Sec. 91(g)-(i) following Code Sec. 461(h).

[Sec. 461(j)]

(j) LIMITATION ON EXCESS FARM LOSSES OF CERTAIN TAXPAYERS.—

(1) LIMITATION.—If a taxpayer other than a C corporation receives any applicable subsidy for any taxable year, any excess farm loss of the taxpayer for the taxable year shall not be allowed.

(2) DISALLOWED LOSS CARRIED TO NEXT TAXABLE YEAR.—Any loss which is disallowed under paragraph (1) shall be treated as a deduction of the taxpayer attributable to farming businesses in the next taxable year.

(3) APPLICABLE SUBSIDY.—For purposes of this subsection, the term "applicable subsidy" means—

(A) any direct or counter-cyclical payment under title I of the Food, Conservation, and Energy Act of 2008, or any payment elected to be received in lieu of any such payment, or

(B) any Commodity Credit Corporation loan.

(4) EXCESS FARM LOSS.—For purposes of this subsection—

(A) IN GENERAL.—The term "excess farm loss" means the excess of—

(i) the aggregate deductions of the taxpayer for the taxable year which are attributable to farming businesses of such taxpayer (determined without regard to whether or not such deductions are disallowed for such taxable year under paragraph (1)), over

(ii) the sum of—

(I) the aggregate gross income or gain of such taxpayer for the taxable year which is attributable to such farming businesses, plus

(II) the threshold amount for the taxable year.

(B) THRESHOLD AMOUNT.—

(i) IN GENERAL.—The term "threshold amount" means, with respect to any taxable year, the greater of—

(I) $300,000 ($150,000 in the case of married individuals filing separately), or

(II) the excess (if any) of the aggregate amounts described in subparagraph (A)(ii)(I) for the 5-consecutive taxable year period preceding the taxable year over the aggregate amounts described in subparagraph (A)(i) for such period.

(ii) SPECIAL RULES FOR DETERMINING AGGREGATE AMOUNTS.—For purposes of clause (i)(II)—

(I) notwithstanding the disregard in subparagraph (A)(i) of any disallowance under paragraph (1), in the case of any loss which is carried forward under paragraph (2) from any taxable year, such loss (or any portion thereof) shall be taken into account for the first taxable year in which a deduction for such loss (or portion) is not disallowed by reason of this subsection, and

(II) the Secretary shall prescribe rules for the computation of the aggregate amounts described in such clause in cases where the filing status of the taxpayer is not the same for the taxable year and each of the taxable years in the period described in such clause.

(C) FARMING BUSINESS.—

(i) IN GENERAL.—The term "farming business" has the meaning given such term in section 263A(e)(4).

(ii) CERTAIN TRADES AND BUSINESSES INCLUDED.—If, without regard to this clause, a taxpayer is engaged in a farming business with respect to any agricultural or horticultural commodity—

(I) the term "farming business" shall include any trade or business of the taxpayer of the processing of such commodity (without regard to whether the processing is incidental to the growing, raising, or harvesting of such commodity), and

(II) if the taxpayer is a member of a cooperative to which subchapter T applies, any trade or business of the cooperative described in subclause (I) shall be treated as the trade or business of the taxpayer.

(D) CERTAIN LOSSES DISREGARDED.—For purposes of subparagraph (A)(i), there shall not be taken into account any deduction for any loss arising by reason of fire, storm, or other casualty, or by reason of disease or drought, involving any farming business.

(5) APPLICATION OF SUBSECTION IN CASE OF PARTNERSHIPS AND S CORPORATIONS.—In the case of a partnership or S corporation—

(A) this subsection shall be applied at the partner or shareholder level, and

(B) each partner's or shareholder's proportionate share of the items of income, gain, or deduction of the partnership or S corporation for any taxable year from farming businesses attributable to the partnership or S corporation, and of any applicable subsidies received by the partnership or S corporation during the taxable year, shall be taken into account by the partner or shareholder in applying this subsection to the taxable year of such partner or shareholder with or within which the taxable year of the partnership or S corporation ends.

The Secretary may provide rules for the application of this paragraph to any other pass-thru entity to the extent necessary to carry out the provisions of this subsection.

(6) ADDITIONAL REPORTING.—The Secretary may prescribe such additional reporting requirements as the Secretary determines appropriate to carry out the purposes of this subsection.

(7) COORDINATION WITH SECTION 469.—This subsection shall be applied before the application of section 469.

Amendments

• 2008, Heartland, Habitat, Harvest, and Horticulture Act of 2008 (P.L. 110-246)

P.L. 110-246, §15351(a):

Amended Code Sec. 461 by adding at the end a new subsection (j). **Effective** for tax years beginning after 12-31-2009.

[Sec. 463—Repealed]

Amendments

• 1987, Revenue Act of 1987 (P.L. 100-203)

P.L. 100-203, §10201(a):

Repealed Code Sec. 463. For the **effective** date, see Act Sec. 10201(c), below. Prior to repeal, Code Sec. 463 read as follows:

SEC. 463. ACCRUAL OF VACATION PAY.

[Sec. 463(a)]

(a) ALLOWANCE OF DEDUCTION.—At the election of a taxpayer whose taxable income is computed under an accrual method of accounting, if the conditions of section 162(a) are otherwise satisfied, the deduction allowable under section 162(a) with respect to vacation pay shall be an amount equal to the sum of—

(1) a reasonable addition to an account representing the taxpayer's liability for vacation pay earned by employees before the close of the taxable year and paid during the taxable year or within 8½ months following the close of the taxable year; plus

(2) the amount (if any) of the reduction at the close of the taxable year in the suspense account provided in subsection (c)(2).

Such liability for vacation pay earned before the close of the taxable year shall include amounts which, because of contingencies, would not (but for this section) be deductible under section 162(a) as an accrued expense. All payments with respect to vacation pay shall be charged to such account.

Amendments

• 1986, Tax Reform Act of 1986 (P.L. 99-514)

P.L. 99-514, §1165(a):

Amended Code Sec. 463(a)(1) by striking out "and expected to be paid during the taxable year or within 12 months following the close of the taxable year" and inserting in lieu thereof "and paid during the taxable year or within 8½ months following the close of the taxable year". **Effective** for tax years beginning after 12-31-86. For a transitional rule, see Act Sec. 1851(b)(1), below.

P.L. 99-514, §1851(b)(1), provides:

(1) TRANSITIONAL RULE FOR CERTAIN TAXPAYERS WITH FULL VESTED VACATION PAY PLANS.—

(A) IN GENERAL.—In the case of any taxpayer—

(i) who maintained a fully vested vacation pay plan where payments are expected to be paid (or are in fact paid) within 1 year after the accrual of the vacation pay, and

(ii) who makes an election under section 463 of the Internal Revenue Code of 1954 for such taxpayer's 1st taxable year ending after the date of the enactment of the Tax Reform Act of 1984,

in lieu of establishing a suspense account under such section 463, such election shall be treated as a change in the taxpayer's method of accounting and the adjustments required as a result of such change shall be taken into account under section 481 of such Code.

(B) EXTENSION OF TIME FOR MAKING ELECTION.—In the case of any taxpayer who meets the requirements of subparagraph (A)(1), the time for making an election under section 463 of such Code for such taxpayer's 1st taxable year ending after the date of the enactment of the Tax Reform Act of 1984 shall not expire before the date 6 months after the date of the enactment of this Act.

• 1984, Deficit Reduction Act of 1984 (P.L. 98-369)

P.L. 98-369, §561(a):

Amended Code Sec. 463(a)(1) by striking out "and payable during" and inserting in lieu thereof "and expected to be paid during". **Effective** for tax years beginning after 3-31-84.

[Sec. 463(b)]

(b) OPENING BALANCE.—The opening balance of the account described in subsection (a)(1) for its first taxable year shall, under regulations prescribed by the Secretary, be—

(1) in the case of a taxpayer who maintained a predecessor account for vacation pay under section 97 of the Technical Amendments Act of 1958, as amended, for his last taxable year ending before January 1, 1973, and who makes an election under this section for his first taxable year ending after December 31, 1972, the larger of—

(A) the balance in such predecessor account at the close of such last taxable year, or

(B) the amount determined as if the taxpayer had maintained an account described in subsection (a)(1) for such last taxable year, or

(2) in the case of any taxpayer not described in paragraph (1), an amount equal to the largest closing balance the taxpayer would have had for any of the tapayer's 3 taxable years immediately preceding such first taxable year if the taxpayer had maintained such account throughout such 3 immediately preceding taxable years.

Amendments

• 1976, Tax Reform Act of 1976 (P.L. 94-455)

P.L. 94-455, §1906(b)(13)(A):

Amended 1954 Code by substituting "Secretary" for "Secretary or his delegate" each place it appeared. **Effective** 2-1-77.

[Sec. 463(c)]

(c) SUSPENSE ACCOUNT FOR DEFERRED DEDUCTION.—

(1) INITIAL SUSPENSE ACCOUNT.—The amount of the suspense account at the beginning of the first taxable year for which the taxpayer maintains under this section an account (described in subsection (a)(1)) shall be the amount of the opening balance described in subsection (b) minus the amount, if any, allowed as deductions for prior taxable years for vacation pay accrued but not paid at the close of the taxable year preceding such first taxable year.

(2) ADJUSTMENTS IN SUSPENSE ACCOUNT.—At the close of each taxable year the suspense account shall be—

(A) reduced by the excess, if any, of the amount in the suspense account at the beginning of the taxable year over the amount in the account described in subsection (a)(1) at the close of the taxable year (after making the additions and charges for such taxable year provided in subsection (a)), or

(B) increased (but not to an amount greater than the initial balance of the suspense account) by the excess, if any of the amount in the account described in subsection (a)(1) at the close of the taxable year (after making the additions and charges for such taxable year provided in subsection (a)) over the amount in the suspense account at the beginning of the taxable year.

Amendments

• 1976, Tax Reform Act of 1976 (P.L. 94-455)

P.L. 94-455, §1906(b)(13)(A):

Amended 1954 Code by substituting "Secretary" for "Secretary or his delegate" each place it appeared. **Effective** 2-1-77.

[Sec. 463(d)]

(d) ELECTION.—An election under this section shall be made at such time and in such manner as the Secretary may by regulations prescribe.

Amendments

• 1976, Tax Reform Act of 1976 (P.L. 94-455)

P.L. 94-455, §1906(b)(13)(A):

Amended 1954 Code by substituting "Secretary" for "Secretary or his delegate" each place it appeared. **Effective** 2-1-77.

[Sec. 463(e)]

(e) CHANGES IN ACCOUNTING METHOD.—

(1) ESTABLISHMENT OF ACCOUNT NOT CONSIDERED CHANGE.—The establishment of an account described in subsection (a)(1) shall not be considered a change in method of accounting for purposes of section 446(e) (relating to requirement respecting change of accounting method), and no ajustment shall be required under section 481 by reason of the establishment of such account.

(2) CERTAIN TAXPAYERS TREATED AS HAVING INITIATED CHANGE.—If the taxpayer treated vacation pay under section 97 of the Technical Amendments Act of 1958, as amended, for his last taxable year ending before January 1, 1973, and if such taxpayer fails to make an election under this section for his first taxable year ending after December 31, 1972, then, for purposes of section 481, such taxpayer shall be treated as having initiated a change in method of accounting with respect to vacation pay for his first taxable year ending after December 31, 1972.

Amendments

• 1975 (P.L. 93-625)

P.L. 93-625, §4(a):

Added Code Sec. 463. **Effective** for tax years beginning after 12-31-73, except as noted in Act Sec. 4(d)(2), below.

P.L. 93-625, §4(d)(2), provides:

"If the taxpayer maintained an account for vacation pay under section 97 of the Technical Amendments Act of 1958, as amended, for his last taxable year ending before January 1, 1973, the amendments made by this section shall apply to taxable years ending after December 31, 1972."

• 1987, Revenue Act of 1987 (P.L.100-203)

P.L. 100-203, §10201(c), provides:

(c) EFFECTIVE DATE.—

(1) IN GENERAL.—The amendments made by this section shall apply to taxable years beginning after December 31, 1987.

(2) CHANGE IN METHOD OF ACCOUNTING.—In the case of any taxpayer who elected to have section 463 of the Internal Revenue Code of 1986 apply for such taxpayer's last taxable year beginning before January 1, 1988, and who is required to change his method of accounting by reason of the amendments made by this section—

(A) such change shall be treated as initiated by the taxpayer,

(B) such change shall be treated as having been made with the consent of the Secretary, and

(C) the net amount of adjustments required by section 481 of such Code to be taken into account by the taxpayer—

(i) shall be reduced by the balance in the suspense account under section 463(c) of such Code as of the close of such last taxable year, and

(ii) shall be taken into account over the 4-taxable year period beginning with the taxable year following such last taxable year as follows:

In the case of the:	*The percentage taken into account is:*
1st year	25
2nd year	5
3rd year	35
4th year	35.

Notwithstanding subparagraph (C)(ii), if the period the adjustments are required to be taken into account under section 481 of such Code is less than 4 years, such adjustments shall be taken into account ratably over such shorter period.

[Sec. 464]

SEC. 464. LIMITATIONS ON DEDUCTIONS FOR CERTAIN FARMING [EXPENSES].

[Sec. 464(a)]

(a) GENERAL RULE.—In the case of any farming syndicate (as defined in subsection (c)), a deduction (otherwise allowable under this chapter) for amounts paid for feed, seed, fertilizer, or other similar farm supplies shall only be allowed for the taxable year in which such feed, seed, fertilizer, or other supplies are actually used or consumed, or, if later, for the taxable year for which allowable as a deduction (determined without regard to this section).

[Sec. 464(b)]

(b) CERTAIN POULTRY EXPENSES.—In the case of any farming syndicate (as defined in subsection (c))—

(1) the cost of poultry (including egg-laying hens and baby chicks) purchased for use in a trade or business (or both for use in a trade or business and for sale) shall be capitalized and deducted ratably over the lesser of 12 months or their useful life in the trade or business, and

(2) the cost of poultry purchased for sale shall be deducted for the taxable year in which the poultry is sold or otherwise disposed of.

[Sec. 464(c)]

(c) FARMING SYNDICATE DEFINED.—

(1) IN GENERAL.—For purposes of this section, the term "farming syndicate" means—

(A) a partnership or any other enterprise other than a corporation which is not an S corporation engaged in the trade or business of farming, if at any time interests in such partnership or enterprise have been offered for sale in any offering required to be registered with any Federal or State agency having authority to regulate the offering of securities for sale, or

(B) a partnership or any other enterprise other than a corporation which is not an S corporation engaged in the trade or business of farming, if more than 35 percent of the losses during any period are allocable to limited partners or limited entrepreneurs.

(2) HOLDINGS ATTRIBUTABLE TO ACTIVE MANAGEMENT.—For purposes of paragraph (1)(B), the following shall be treated as an interest which is not held by a limited partner or a limited entrepreneur:

(A) in the case of any individual who has actively participated (for a period of not less than 5 years) in the management of any trade or business of farming, any interest in a partnership or other enterprise which is attributable to such active participation,

(B) in the case of any individual whose principal residence is on a farm, any partnership or other enterprise engaged in the trade or business of farming such farm,

(C) in the case of any individual who is actively participating in the management of any trade or business of farming or who is an individual who is described in subparagraph (A) or (B), any participation in the further processing of livestock which was raised in such trade or business (or in the trade or business referred to in subparagraph (A) or (B)),

(D) in the case of an individual whose principal business activity involves active participation in the management of a trade or business of farming, any interest in any other trade or business of farming, and,

(E) any interest held by a member of the family (or a spouse of any such member) of a grandparent of an individual described in subparagraph (A), (B), (C), or (D) if the interest in the partnership or the enterprise is attributable to the active participation of the individual described in subparagraph (A), (B), (C), or (D).

For purposes of subparagraph (A), where one farm is substituted for or added to another farm, both farms shall be treated as one farm. For purposes of subparagraph (E), the term "family" has the meaning given to such term by section 267(c)(4).

[Sec. 464(d)]

(d) EXCEPTION.—Subsection (a) shall not apply to any amount paid for supplies which are on hand at the close of the taxable year on account of fire, storm, or other casualty, or on account of disease or drought.

[Sec. 464(e)]

(e) DEFINITIONS.—For purposes of this section—

(1) FARMING.—The term "farming" means the cultivation of land or the raising or harvesting of any agricultural or horticultural commodity including the raising, shearing, feeding, caring for, training, and management of animals. For purposes of the preceding sentence, trees (other than trees bearing fruit or nuts) shall not be treated as an agricultural or horticultural commodity.

(2) LIMITED ENTREPRENEUR.—The term "limited entrepreneur" means a person who—

(A) has an interest in an enterprise other than as a limited partner, and

(B) does not actively participate in the management of such enterprise.

[Sec. 464(f)]

(f) SUBSECTIONS (a) AND (b) TO APPLY TO CERTAIN PERSONS PREPAYING 50 PERCENT OR MORE OF CERTAIN FARMING EXPENSES.—

(1) IN GENERAL.—In the case of a taxpayer to whom this subsection applies, subsections (a) and (b) shall apply to the excess prepaid farm supplies of such taxpayer in the same manner as if such taxpayer were a farming syndicate.

(2) TAXPAYER TO WHOM SUBSECTION APPLIES.—This subsection applies to any taxpayer for any taxable year if such taxpayer—

(A) does not use an accrual method of accounting,

(B) has excess prepaid farm supplies for the taxable year, and

(C) is not a qualified farm-related taxpayer.

(3) QUALIFIED FARM-RELATED TAXPAYER.—

(A) IN GENERAL.—For purposes of this subsection, the term "qualifed farm-related taxpayer" means any farm-related taxpayer if—

(i)(I) the aggregate prepaid farm supplies for the 3 taxable years preceding the taxable year are less than 50 percent of,

(II) the aggregate deductible farming expenses (other than prepaid farm supplies) for such 3 taxable years, or

(ii) the taxpayer has excess prepaid farm supplies for the taxable year by reason of any change in business operation directly attributable to extraordinary circumstances.

(B) FARM-RELATED TAXPAYER.—For purposes of this paragraph, the term "farm-related taxpayer" means any taxpayer—

(i) whose principal residence (within the meaning of section 121) is on a farm,

(ii) who has a principal occupation of farming, or

(iii) who is a member of the family (within the meaning of subsection (c)(2)(E)) of a taxpayer described in clause (i) or (ii).

(4) DEFINITIONS.—For purposes of this subsection—

(A) EXCESS PREPAID FARM SUPPLIES.—The term "excess prepaid farm supplies" means the prepaid farm supplies for the taxable year to the extent the amount of such supplies exceeds 50 percent of the deductible farming expenses for the taxable year (other than prepaid farm supplies).

(B) PREPAID FARM SUPPLIES.—The term "prepaid farm supplies" means any amounts which are described in subsection (a) or (b) and would be allowable for a subsequent taxable year under the rules of subsections (a) and (b).

(C) DEDUCTIBLE FARMING EXPENSES.—The term "deductible farming expenses" means any amount allowable as a deduction under this chapter (including any amount allowable as a deduction for depreciation or amortization) which is properly allocable to the trade or business of farming.

Amendments

• 1997, Taxpayer Relief Act of 1997 (P.L. 105-34)

P.L. 105-34, §312(d)(1):

Amended Code Sec. 464(f)(3)(B)(i) by striking "section 1034" and inserting "section 121". For the **effective** date, see Act Sec. 312(d)[(e)], below.

P.L. 105-34, §312(d)[(e)], provides:

(d) EFFECTIVE DATE.—

(1) IN GENERAL.—The amendments made by this section shall apply to sales and exchanges after May 6, 1997.

(2) SALES BEFORE DATE OF ENACTMENT.—At the election of the taxpayer, the amendments made by this section shall not apply to any sale or exchange before the date of the enactment of this Act.

(3) CERTAIN SALES WITHIN 2 YEARS AFTER DATE OF ENACTMENT.—Section 121 of the Internal Revenue Code of 1986 (as amended by this section) shall be applied without regard to subsection (c)(2)(B) thereof in the case of any sale or exchange of property during the 2-year period beginning on the date of the enactment of this Act if the taxpayer held such property on the date of the enactment of this Act and fails to meet the ownership and use requirements of subsection (a) thereof with respect to such property.

(4) BINDING CONTRACTS.—At the election of the taxpayer, the amendments made by this section shall not apply to a sale or exchange after the date of the enactment of this Act, if—

(A) such sale or exchange is pursuant to a contract which was binding on such date, or

(B) without regard to such amendments, gain would not be recognized under section 1034 of the Internal Revenue Code of 1986 (as in effect on the day before the date of the enactment of this Act) on such sale or exchange by reason of a new residence acquired on or before such date or with respect to the acquisition of which by the taxpayer a binding contract was in effect on such date.

This paragraph shall not apply to any sale or exchange by an individual if the treatment provided by section 877(a)(1) of the Internal Revenue Code of 1986 applies to such individual.

• 1986, Tax Reform Act of 1986 (P.L. 99-514)

P.L. 99-514, §404(a):

Added subsection (f) to Code Sec. 464. **Effective** for amounts paid or incurred after 3-1-86, in tax years beginning after such date.

P.L. 99-514, §404(b)(1):

Amended Code Sec. 464 by striking out "IN CASE OF FARMING SYNDICATES" and inserting in lieu thereof "FOR CERTAIN FARMING [EXPENSES]" in the heading thereof. **Effective** for amounts paid or incurred after 3-1-86, in tax years beginning after such date.

P.L. 99-514, §803(b)(8):

Amended Code Sec. 464(d). **Effective**, generally, for costs incurred after 12-31-86, in tax years ending after such date. However, see Act Sec. 803(d)(2)-(7), following Code Sec. 263A, for special rules. Prior to amendment, Code Sec. 464(d) read as follows:

(d) EXCEPTIONS.—Subsection (a) shall not apply to—

(1) any amount paid for supplies which are on hand at the close of the taxable year on account of fire, storm, flood, or other casualty or on account of disease or drought, or

(2) any amount required to be charged to capital account under section 278.

• 1982, Subchapter S Revision Act of 1982 (P.L. 97-354)

P.L. 97-354, §5(a)(30):

Amended Code Sec. 464(c)(1) by striking out "an electing small business corporation (as defined in section 1371(b))" each place it appears and inserting in lieu thereof "an S corporation". **Effective** for tax years beginnning after 12-31-82.

• 1978, Revenue Act of 1978 (P.L. 95-600)

P.L. 95-600, §701(1)(3):

Amended Code Sec. 464(c) by striking out "(within the meaning of section 267(c)(4))" and inserting in lieu thereof "(or a spouse of any such member)" in subparagraph (E), and adding a new last sentence. **Effective** as provided in P.L. 94-455, §207(a)(1).

• 1976, Tax Reform Act of 1976 (P.L. 94-455)

P.L. 94-455, §207(a)(1):

Added Code Sec. 464. **Effective** for tax years beginning after 12-31-75, except as noted below in §207(a)(3)(B), below.

P.L. 94-455, §207(a)(3)(B), provides:

(B) TRANSITIONAL RULE.—In the case of a farming syndicate in existence on December 31, 1975, and for which there was no change of membership throughout its taxable year beginning in 1976, the amendments made by this subsection shall apply to taxable years beginning after December 31, 1976.

[Sec. 464(g)]

(g) TERMINATION.—Except as provided in subsection (f), subsections (a) and (b) shall not apply to any taxable year beginning after December 31, 1986.

Amendments

• 1988, Technical and Miscellaneous Revenue Act of 1988 (P.L. 100-647)

P.L. 100-647, §1008(a)(4):

Amended Code Sec. 464 by adding at the end thereof new subsection (g). **Effective** as if included in the provision of P.L. 99-514 to which it relates.

[Sec. 465]

SEC. 465. DEDUCTIONS LIMITED TO AMOUNT AT RISK.

[Sec. 465(a)]

(a) LIMITATION TO AMOUNT AT RISK.—

(1) IN GENERAL.—In the case of—

(A) an individual, and

(B) a C corporation with respect to which the stock ownership requirement of paragraph (2) of section 542(a) is met,

engaged in an activity to which this section applies, any loss from such activity for the taxable year shall be allowed only to the extent of the aggregate amount with respect to which the taxpayer is at risk (within the meaning of subsection (b)) for such activity at the close of the taxable year.

(2) DEDUCTION IN SUCCEEDING YEAR.—Any loss from an activity to which this section applies not allowed under this section for the taxable year shall be treated as a deduction allocable to such activity in the first succeeding taxable year.

(3) SPECIAL RULES FOR APPLYING PARAGRAPH (1)(B).—For purposes of paragraph (1)(B)—

(A) section 544(a)(2) shall be applied as if such section did not contain the phrase "or by or for his partner"; and

(B) sections 544(a)(4)(A) and 544(b)(1) shall be applied by substituting "the corporation meet the stock ownership requirements of section 542(a)(2)" for "the corporation a personal holding company".

Amendments

• 1984, Deficit Reduction Act of 1984 (P.L. 98-369)

P.L. 98-369, §721(x)(2):

Amended Code Sec. 465(a)(1)(B) by striking out "a corporation" and inserting in lieu thereof "a C corporation". **Effective** as if included in P.L. 97-354.

• 1982, Subchapter S Revision Act of 1982 (P.L. 97-354)

P.L. 97-354, §5(a)(31)(A):

Amended Code Sec. 465(a)(1) by adding "and" at the end of subparagraph (A), by striking out subparagraph (B), and by redesignating subparagraph (C) as subparagraph (B). **Effective** for tax years beginning after 12-31-82. Prior to being stricken, Code Sec. 465(a)(1)(B) read as follows:

"(B) an electing small business corporation (as defined in section 1371(b)), and"

P.L. 97-354, §5(a)(31)(B):

Amended Code Sec. 465(a)(3) by striking out "paragraph (1)(C)" and inserting in lieu thereof "paragraph (1)(B)", and by striking out "PARAGRAPH (1)(C)" in the paragraph heading and inserting in lieu thereof "PARAGRAPH (1)(B)". **E ffective** for tax years beginning after 12-31-82.

• 1980, Technical Corrections Act of 1979 (P.L. 96-222)

P.L. 96-222, §102(a)(1)(A)(i):

Amended Code Sec. 465(a)(1)(C) by striking out "(determined by reference to the rules contained in section 318 rather than under section 544)". **Effective** as set forth in P.L. 95-600, §204, below.

P.L. 96-222, §102(a)(1)(A)(ii):

Added Code Sec. 465(a)(3). **Effective** as set forth in P.L. 95-600, §204, below.

• 1978, Revenue Act of 1978 (P.L. 95-600)

P.L. 95-600, §201(c):

Amended the heading of Code Sec. 465. **Effective** for tax years beginning after 12-31-78. Prior to amendment, the heading read as follows:

SEC. 465. DEDUCTIONS LIMITED TO AMOUNT AT RISK IN CASE OF CERTAIN ACTIVITIES.

P.L. 95-600, §202:

Amended Code Sec. 465(a). **Effective** as set forth in P.L. 95-600, §204, below. Prior to amendment, Code Sec. 465(a) read as follows:

"(a) GENERAL RULE.—In the case of a taxpayer (other than a corporation which is neither an electing small business corporation (as defined in section 1371(b)) nor a personal holding company (as defined in section 542)) engaged in an activity to which this section applies, any loss from such activity for the taxable year shall be allowed only to the extent of the aggregate amount with respect to which the taxpayer is at risk (within the meaning of subsection (b)) for such activity at the close of the taxable year. Any loss from such activity not allowed under this section for the taxable year shall be treated as a deduction allocable to such activity in the first succeeding taxable year."

P.L. 95-600, §204, as amended by P.L. 96-222, §102(a)(1)(E), provides:

SEC. 204. EFFECTIVE DATES.

(a) IN GENERAL.—The amendments made by this subtitle shall apply to taxable years beginning after December 31, 1978.

(b) TRANSITIONAL RULES.

(1) RECAPTURE PROVISIONS.—If the amount for which the taxpayer is at risk in any activity as of the close of the taxpayer's last taxable year beginning before January 1, 1979, is less than zero, section 465(e)(1) of the Internal Revenue Code of 1954 (as added by section 203 of this Act) shall be applied with respect to such activity of the taxpayer by substituting such negative amount for zero.

(2) SPECIAL TRANSITIONAL RULES FOR LEASING ACTIVITIES.—

(A) RULE FOR LEASES.—In the case of any activity described in section 465(c)(1)(C) of such Code in which a corporation described in section 465(a)(1)(C) of such Code is engaged, the amendments made by this subtitle shall not apply with respect to—

(i) leases entered into before November 1, 1978, and

(ii) leases where the property was ordered by the lessor or lessee before November 1, 1978.

(B) HOLDING OF INTERESTS FOR PURPOSES OF SUBPARAGRAPH (A).—Subparagraph (A) shall apply only to taxpayers who held their interests in the property on October 31, 1978.

[Sec. 465(b)]

(b) AMOUNTS CONSIDERED AT RISK.—

(1) IN GENERAL.—For purposes of this section, a taxpayer shall be considered at risk for an activity with respect to amounts including—

(A) the amount of money and the adjusted basis of other property contributed by the taxpayer to the activity, and

(B) amounts borrowed with respect to such activity (as determined under paragraph (2)).

(2) BORROWED AMOUNTS.—For purposes of this section, a taxpayer shall be considered at risk with respect to amounts borrowed for use in an activity to the extent that he—

(A) is personally liable for the repayment of such amounts, or

(B) has pledged property, other than property used in such activity, as security for such borrowed amount (to the extent of the net fair market value of the taxpayer's interest in such property).

No property shall be taken into account as security if such property is directly or indirectly financed by indebtedness which is secured by property described in paragraph (1).

(3) CERTAIN BORROWED AMOUNTS EXCLUDED.—

(A) IN GENERAL.—Except to the extent provided in regulations, for purposes of paragraph (1)(B), amounts borrowed shall not be considered to be at risk with respect to an activity if such amounts are borrowed from any person who has an interest in such activity or from a related person to a person (other than the taxpayer) having such an interest.

(B) EXCEPTIONS.—

(i) INTEREST AS CREDITOR.—Subparagraph (A) shall not apply to an interest as a creditor in the activity.

(ii) INTEREST AS SHAREHOLDER WITH RESPECT TO AMOUNTS BORROWED BY CORPORATION.—In the case of amounts borrowed by a corporation from a shareholder, subparagraph (A) shall not apply to an interest as a shareholder.

(C) RELATED PERSON.—For purposes of this subsection, a person (herein after in this paragraph referred to as the "related person") is related to any person if—

(i) the related person bears a relationship to such person specified in section 267(b) or section 707(b)(1), or

(ii) the related person and such person are engaged in trades or business under common control (within the meaning of subsections (a) and (b) of section 52).

For purposes of clause (i), in applying section 267(b) or 707(b)(1), "10 percent" shall be substituted for "50 percent."

(4) EXCEPTION.—Notwithstanding any other provision of this section, a taxpayer shall not be considered at risk with respect to amounts protected against loss through nonrecourse financing, guarantees, stop loss agreements, or other similar arrangements.

(5) AMOUNTS AT RISK IN SUBSEQUENT YEARS.—If in any taxable year the taxpayer has a loss from an activity to which subsection (a) applies, the amount with respect to which a taxpayer is considered to be at risk (within the meaning of subsection (b)) in subsequent taxable years with respect to that activity shall be reduced by that portion of the loss which (after the application of subsection (a)) is allowable as a deduction.

(6) QUALIFIED NONRECOURSE FINANCING TREATED AS AMOUNT AT RISK.—For purposes of this section—

(A) IN GENERAL.—Notwithstanding any other provision of this subsection, in the case of an activity of holding real property, a taxpayer shall be considered at risk with respect to the taxpayer's share of any qualified nonrecourse financing which is secured by real property used in such activity.

(B) QUALIFIED NONRECOURSE FINANCING.—For purposes of this paragraph, the term "qualified nonrecourse financing" means any financing—

(i) which is borrowed by the taxpayer with respect to the activity of holding real property,

(ii) which is borrowed by the taxpayer from a qualified person or represents a loan from any Federal, State, or local government or instrumentality thereof, or is guaranteed by any Federal, State, or local government,

(iii) except to the extent provided in regulations, with respect to which no person is personally liable for repayment, and

(iv) which is not convertible debt.

(C) SPECIAL RULE FOR PARTNERSHIPS.—In the case of a partnership, a partner's share of any qualified nonrecourse financing of such partnership shall be determined on the basis of the partner's share of liabilities of such partnership incurred in connection with such financing (within the meaning of section 752).

(D) QUALIFIED PERSON DEFINED.—For purposes of this paragraph—

(i) IN GENERAL.—The term "qualified person" has the meaning given such term by section 49(a)(1)(D)(iv).

(ii) CERTAIN COMMERCIALLY REASONABLE FINANCING FROM RELATED PERSONS.—For purposes of clause (i), section 49(a)(1)(D)(iv) shall be applied without regard to subclause (I) thereof (relating to financing from related persons) if the financing from the related person is commercially reasonable and on substantially the same terms as loans involving unrelated persons.

(E) ACTIVITY OF HOLDING REAL PROPERTY.—For purposes of this paragraph—

(i) INCIDENTAL PERSONAL PROPERTY AND SERVICES.—The activity of holding real property includes the holding of personal property and the providing of services which are incidental to making real property available as living accommodations.

(ii) MINERAL PROPERTY.—The activity of holding real property shall not include the holding of mineral property.

Amendments

• 1990, Omnibus Budget Reconciliation Act of 1990 (P.L. 101-508)

P.L. 101-508, §11813(b)(15):

Amended Code Sec. 465(b)(6)(D) by striking "46(c)(8)(D)(iv)" each place it appears and inserting "49(a)(1)(D)(iv)". **Effective**, generally, for property placed in service after 12-31-90. However, for exceptions see Act Sec. 11813(c)(2) below.

P.L. 101-508, §11813(c)(2), provides:

(2) EXCEPTIONS.—The amendments made by this section shall not apply to—

(A) any transition property (as defined in section 49(e) of the Internal Revenue Code of 1986 (as in effect on the day before the date of the enactment of this Act),

(B) any property with respect to which qualified progress expenditures were previously taken into account under section 46(d) of such Code (as so in effect), and

(C) any property described in section 46(b)(2)(C) of such Code (as so in effect).

• 1986, Tax Reform Act of 1986 (P.L. 99-514)

P.L. 99-514, §201(d)(7)(A):

Amended Code Sec. 465(b)(3)(C). **Effective**, generally, for property placed in service after 12-31-86, in tax years ending after such date. However, see Act Sec. 203, 204 and 251(d) following Code Sec. 168. Prior to amendment, Code Sec. 465(b)(3)(C) read as follows:

(C) RELATED PERSON DEFINED.—For purposes of subparagraph (A), the term "related person" has the meaning given such term by section 168(e)(4).

P.L. 99-514, §503(b):

Amended Code Sec. 465(b) by adding subsection (6). **Effective**, generally, for losses incurred after 12-31-86, with respect to property placed in service by the taxpayer after 12-31-86. However, see Act Sec. 503(c)(2)-(3), below, for special rules.

P.L. 99-514, §503(c)(2)-(3), provides:

(2) SPECIAL RULE FOR LOSSES OF S CORPORATION, PARTNERSHIP, OR PASS-THRU ENTITY.—In the case of an interest in an S corporation, a partnership, or other pass-thru entity acquired after December 31, 1986, the amendments made by this section shall apply to losses after December 31, 1986, which are attributable to property placed in service by the S corporation, partnership, or pass-thru entity on, before, or after January 1, 1986.

(3) SPECIAL RULE FOR ATHLETIC STADIUM.—The amendments made by this section shall not apply to any losses incurred by a taxpayer with respect to the holding of a multi-use athletic stadium in Pittsburgh, Pennsylvania, which the taxpayer acquired in a sale for which a letter of understanding was entered into before April 16, 1986.

• 1984, Deficit Reduction Act of 1984 (P.L. 98-369)

P.L. 98-369, §432(c):

Amended Code Sec. 465(b)(3). **Effective** for tax years beginning after 12-31-83; except that any loss from an activity described in section 465(c)(7)(A) of the Internal Revenue Code of 1954 (as amended by this section) which (but for the amendments made by this section) would have been treated as a deduction for the taxpayer's first tax year beginning after 12-31-83, under section 465(a)(2) of such Code shall be allowed as a deduction for such first tax year notwithstanding such amendments. Prior to amendment, Code Sec. 465(b)(3) read as follows:

(3) Certain Borrowed Amounts Excluded.—For purposes of paragraph (1)(B), amounts borrowed shall not be considered to be at risk with respect to an activity if such amounts are borrowed from any person who—

(A) has an interest (other than an interest as a creditor) in such activity, or

(B) has a relationship to the taxpayer specified within any one of the paragraphs of section 267(b).

• 1980, Technical Corrections Act of 1979 (P.L. 96-222)

P.L. 96-222, §102(a)(1)(D)(iii):

Amended Code Sec. 465(b)(5) by striking out "to which this section applies" and inserting "to which subsection (a) applies". **Effective** for tax years beginning after 12-31-78.

[Sec. 465(c)]

(c) ACTIVITIES TO WHICH SECTION APPLIES.—

(1) TYPES OF ACTIVITIES.—This section applies to any taxpayer engaged in the activity of—

(A) holding, producing, or distributing motion picture films or video tapes,

(B) farming (as defined in section 464(e)),

(C) leasing any section 1245 property (as defined in section 1245(a)(3)),

(D) exploring for, or exploiting, oil and gas resources, or

(E) exploring for, or exploiting, geothermal deposits (as defined in section 613(e)(2))

as a trade or business or for the production of income.

(2) SEPARATE ACTIVITIES.—For purposes of this section—

(A) IN GENERAL.—Except as provided in subparagraph (B), a taxpayer's activity with respect to each—

(i) film or video tape,

(ii) section 1245 property which is leased or held for leasing,

(iii) farm,

(iv) oil and gas property (as defined under section 614), or

(v) geothermal property (as defined under section 614),

shall be treated as a separate activity.

(B) AGGREGATION RULES.—

(i) SPECIAL RULE FOR LEASES OF SECTION 1245 PROPERTY BY PARTNERSHIPS OR S CORPORATIONS.—In the case of any partnership or S corporation, all activities with respect to section 1245 properties which—

(I) are leased or held for lease, and

(II) are placed in service in any taxable year of the partnership or S corporation,

shall be treated as a single activity.

(ii) OTHER AGGREGATION RULES.—Rules similar to the rules of subparagraphs (B) and (C) of paragraph (3) shall apply for purposes of this paragraph.

(3) EXTENSION TO OTHER ACTIVITIES.—

(A) IN GENERAL.—In the case of taxable years beginning after December 31, 1978, this section also applies to each activity—

(i) engaged in by the taxpayer in carrying on a trade or business or for the production of income, and

(ii) which is not described in paragraph (1).

(B) AGGREGATION OF ACTIVITIES WHERE TAXPAYER ACTIVELY PARTICIPATES IN MANAGEMENT OF TRADE OR BUSINESS.—Except as provided in subparagraph (C), for purposes of this section, activities described in subparagraph (A) which constitute a trade or business shall be treated as one activity if—

(i) the taxpayer actively participates in the management of such trade or business, or

(ii) such trade or business is carried on by a partnership or an S corporation and 65 percent or more of the losses for the taxable year is allocable to persons who actively participate in the management of the trade or business.

(C) AGGREGATION OR SEPARATION OF ACTIVITIES UNDER REGULATIONS.—The Secretary shall prescribe regulations under which activities described in subparagraph (A) shall be aggregated or treated as separate activities.

(D) APPLICATION OF SUBSECTION (b)(3).—In the case of an activity described in subparagraph (A), subsection (b)(3) shall apply only to the extent provided in regulations prescribed by the Secretary.

(4) EXCLUSION FOR CERTAIN EQUIPMENT LEASING BY CLOSELY-HELD CORPORATIONS.—

(A) IN GENERAL.—In the case of a corporation described in subsection (a)(1)(B) actively engaged in equipment leasing—

(i) the activity of equipment leasing shall be treated as a separate activity, and

(ii) subsection (a) shall not apply to losses from such activity.

(B) 50-PERCENT GROSS RECEIPTS TEST.—For purposes of subparagraph (A), a corporation shall not be considered to be actively engaged in equipment leasing unless 50 percent or more of the gross receipts of the corporation for the taxable year is attributable, under regulations prescribed by the Secretary, to equipment leasing.

(C) COMPONENT MEMBERS OF CONTROLLED GROUP TREATED AS A SINGLE CORPORATION.—For purposes of subparagraph (A), the component members of a controlled group of corporations shall be treated as a single corporation.

(5) WAIVER OF CONTROLLED GROUP RULE WHERE THERE IS SUBSTANTIAL LEASING ACTIVITY.—

(A) IN GENERAL.—In the case of the component members of a qualified leasing group, paragraph (4) shall be applied—

(i) by substituting "80 percent" for "50 percent" in subparagraph (B) thereof, and

(ii) as if paragraph (4) did not include subparagraph (C) thereof.

(B) QUALIFIED LEASING GROUP.—For purposes of this paragraph, the term "qualified leasing group" means a controlled group of corporations which, for the taxable year and each of the 2 immediately preceding taxable years, satisfied each of the following 3 requirements:

(i) AT LEAST 3 EMPLOYEES.—During the entire year, the group had at least 3 fulltime employees substantially all of the services of whom were services directly related to the equipment leasing activity of the qualified leasing members.

(ii) AT LEAST 5 SEPARATE LEASING TRANSACTIONS.—During the year, the qualified leasing members in the aggregate entered into at least 5 separate equipment leasing transactions.

(iii) AT LEAST $1,000,000 EQUIPMENT LEASING RECEIPTS.—During the year, the qualified leasing members in the aggregate had at least $1,000,000 in gross receipts from equipment leasing.

The term "qualified leasing group" does not include any controlled group of corporations to which, without regard to this paragraph, paragraph (4) applies.

(C) QUALIFIED LEASING MEMBER.—For purposes of this paragraph, a corporation shall be treated as a qualified leasing member for the taxable year only if for each of the taxable years referred to in subparagraph (B)—

(i) it is a component member of the controlled group of corporations, and

(ii) it meets the requirements of paragraph (4)(B) (as modified by subparagraph (A)(i) of this paragraph).

(6) DEFINITIONS RELATING TO PARAGRAPHS (4) AND (5)—.For purposes of paragraphs (4) and (5)—

(A) EQUIPMENT LEASING.—The term "equipment leasing" means—

(i) the leasing of equipment which is section 1245 property, and

(ii) the purchasing, servicing, and selling of such equipment.

(B) LEASING OF MASTER SOUND RECORDINGS, ETC., EXCLUDED.—The term "equipment leasing" does not include the leasing of master sound recordings, and other similar contractual arrangements with respect to tangible or intangible assets associated with literary, artistic, or musical properties.

(C) CONTROLLED GROUP OF CORPORATIONS; COMPONENT MEMBER.—The terms "controlled group of corporations" and "component member" have the same meanings as when used in section 1563. The determination of the taxable years taken into account with respect to any controlled group of corporations shall be made in a manner consistent with the manner set forth in section 1563.

(7) EXCLUSION OF ACTIVE BUSINESSES OF QUALIFIED C CORPORATIONS.—

(A) IN GENERAL.—In the case of a taxpayer which is a qualified C corporation—

(i) each qualifying business carried on by such taxpayer shall be treated as a separate activity, and

(ii) subsection (a) shall not apply to losses from such business.

(B) QUALIFIED C CORPORATION.—For purposes of subparagraph (A), the term "qualified C corporation" means any corporation described in subparagraph (B) of subsection (a)(1) which is not—

(i) a personal holding company (as defined in section 542(a)), or

(ii) a personal service corporation (as defined in section 269A(b) but determined by substituting "5 percent" for "10 percent" in section 269A(b)(2)).

(C) QUALIFYING BUSINESS.—For purposes of this paragraph, the term "qualifying business" means any active business if—

(i) during the entire 12-month period ending on the last day of the taxable year, such corporation had at least 1 full-time employee substantially all the services of whom were in the active management of such business,

(ii) during the entire 12-month period ending on the last day of the taxable year, such corporation had at least 3 full-time, nonowner employees substantially all of the services of whom were services directly related to such business,

(iii) the amount of the deductions attributable to such business which are allowable to the taxpayer solely by reason of sections 162 and 404 for the taxable year exceeds 15 percent of the gross income from such business for such year, and

(iv) such business is not an excluded business.

(D) SPECIAL RULES FOR APPLICATION OF SUBPARAGRAPH(c).—

(i) PARTNERSHIPS IN WHICH TAXPAYER IS A QUALIFIED CORPORATE PARTNER.—In the case of an active business of a partnership, if—

(I) the taxpayer is a qualified corporate partner in the partnership, and

(II) during the entire 12-month period ending on the last day of the partnership's taxable year, there was at least 1 full-time employee of the partnership (or of a qualified corporate partner) substantially all the services of whom were in the active management of such business,

then the taxpayer's proportionate share (determined on the basis of its profits interest) of the activities of the partnership in such business shall be treated as activities of the taxpayer (and clause (i) of subparagraph (C) shall not apply in determining whether such business is a qualifying business of the taxpayer).

(ii) QUALIFIED CORPORATE PARTNER.—For purposes of clause (i), the term "qualified corporate partner" means any corporation if—

(I) such corporation is a general partner in the partnership,

(II) such corporation has an interest of 10 percent or more in the profits and losses of the partnership, and

(III) such corporation has contributed property to the partnership in an amount not less than the lesser of $500,000 or 10 percent of the net worth of the corporation.

For purposes of subclause (III), and contribution of property other than money shall be taken into account at its fair market value.

(iii) DEDUCTION FOR OWNER EMPLOYEE CONPENSATION NOT TAKEN INTO ACCOUNT.—For purposes of clause (iii) of subparagraph (C), there shall not be taken into account any deduction in respect of compensation for personal services rendered by any employee (other than a non-owner employee) of the taxpayer or any member of such employee's family (within the meaning of section 318(a)(1)).

(iv) SPECIAL RULE FOR BANKS.—For purposes of clause (iii) of subparagraph (C), in the case of a bank (as defined in section 581) or a financial institution to which section 591 applies—

(I) gross income shall be determined without regard to the exclusion of interest from gross income under section 103, and

(II) in addition to the deductions described in such clause, there shall also be taken into account the amount of the deductions which are allowable for amounts paid or credited to the accounts of depositors or holders of accounts as dividends or interest on their deposits or withdrawable accounts under section 163 or 591.

(v) SPECIAL RULE FOR LIFE INSURANCE COMPANIES.—

(I) IN GENERAL.—Clause (iii) of subparagraph (C) shall not apply to any insurance business of a qualified life insurance company.

(II) INSURANCE BUSINESS.—For purposes of subclause (I), the term "insurance business" means any business which is not a noninsurance business (within the meaning of section 806(b)(3)).

(III) QUALIFIED LIFE INSURANCE COMPANY.—For purposes of subclause (I), the term "qualified life insurance company" means any company which would be a life insurance company as defined in section 816 if unearned premiums were not taken into account under subsections (a)(2) and (c)(2) of section 816.

(E) DEFINITIONS.—For purposes of this paragraph—

(i) NON-OWNER EMPLOYEE.—The term "non-owner employee" means any employee who does not own, at any time during the taxable year, more than 5 percent in value of the outstanding stock of the taxpayer. For purposes of the preceding sentence, section 318 shall apply, except that "5 percent" shall be substituted for "50 percent" in section 318(a)(2)(C).

(ii) EXCLUDED BUSINESS.—The term "excluded business" means—

(I) equipment leasing (as defined in paragraph (6)), and

(II) any business involving the use, exploitation, sale, lease, or other disposition of master sound recordings, motion picture films, video tapes, or tangible or intangible assets associated with literary, artistic, musical, or similar properties.

(iii) SPECIAL RULES RELATING TO COMMUNICATIONS INDUSTRY, ETC.—

(I) BUSINESS NOT EXCLUDED WHERE TAXPAYER NOT COMPLETELY AT RISK.—A business involving the use, exploitation, sale, lease, or other disposition of property described in subclause (II) of clause (ii) shall not constitute an excluded business by reason of such subclause if the taxpayer is at risk with respect to all amounts paid or incurred (or chargeable to capital account) in such business.

(II) CERTAIN LICENSED BUSINESSES NOT EXCLUDED.—For purposes of subclause (II) of clause (ii), the provision of radio, television, cable television, or similar services pursuant to a license or franchise granted by the Federal Communications Commission or any other Federal, State, or local authority shall not constitute an excluded business by reason of such subclause.

(F) AFFILIATED GROUP TREATED AS 1 TAXPAYER.—For purposes of this paragraph—

(i) IN GENERAL.—Except as provided in subparagraph (G), the component members of an affiliated group of corporations shall be treated as a single taxpayer.

(ii) AFFILIATED GROUP OF CORPORATIONS.—The term "affiliated group of corporations" means an affiliated group (as defined in section 1504(a)) which files or is required to file consolidated income tax returns.

(iii) COMPONENT MEMBER.—The term "component member" means an includible corporation (as defined in section 1504) which is a member of the affiliated group.

(G) LOSS OF 1 MEMBER OF AFFILIATED GROUP MAY NOT OFFSET INCOME OF PERSONAL HOLDING COMPANY OR PERSONAL SERVICE CORPORATION.—Nothing in this paragraph shall permit any loss of a member of an affiliated group to be used as an offset against the income of any other member of such group which is a personal holding company (as defined in section 542(a)) or a personal service corporation (as defined in section 269A(b) but determined by substituting "5 percent" for "10 percent" in section 269A(b)(2)).

Amendments

• 2004, American Jobs Creation Act of 2004 (P.L. 108-357)

P.L. 108-357, §413(c)(7):

Amended Code Sec. 465(c)(7)(B) by adding "or" at the end of clause (i), by striking clause (ii), and by redesignating clause (iii) as clause (ii). **Effective** for tax years of foreign corporations beginning after 12-31-2004, and for tax years of United States shareholders with or within which such tax years of foreign corporations end. Prior to being stricken, Code Sec. 465(c)(7)(B)(ii) read as follows:

(ii) a foreign personal holding company (as defined in section 552(a)), or

• 1990, Omnibus Budget Reconciliation Act of 1990 (P.L. 101-508)

P.L. 101-508, §11815(b)(3):

Amended Code Sec. 465(c)(1)(E) by striking "section 613(e)(3)" and inserting "section 613(e)(2)". **Effective** 11-5-90.

P.L. 101-508, §11821(b), provides:

(b) SAVINGS PROVISIONS.—If—

(1) any provision amended or repealed by this part applied to—

(A) any transaction occurring before the date of the enactment of this Act,

(B) any property acquired before such date of enactment, or

(C) any item of income, loss, deduction, or credit taken into account before such date of enactment, and

(2) the treatment of such transaction, property, or item under such provision would (without regard to the amendments made by this part) affect liability for tax for periods ending after such date of enactment,

nothing in the amendments made by this part shall be construed to affect the treatment of such transaction, property, or item for purposes of determining liability for tax for periods ending after such date of enactment.

• 1986, Tax Reform Act of 1986 (P.L. 99-514)

P.L. 99-514, §503(a):

Amended Code Sec. 465(c)(3) by striking out subparagraph (D) and by redesignating subparagraph (E) as subparagraph (D). **Effective**, generally, for losses incurred after 12-31-86, with respect to property placed in service by the taxpayer after 12-31-86. However, for special rules see Act Sec. 503(c)(2) and (3) in the amendment notes for Code Sec. 465(b). Prior to amendment, Code Sec. 465(c)(3)(D) read as follows:

(D) EXCLUSION FOR REAL PROPERTY.—In the case of activities described in subparagraph (A), the holding of real property (other than mineral property) shall be treated as a separate activity, and subsection (a) shall not apply to losses from such activity. For purposes of the preceding sentence, personal property and services which are incidental to making real property available as living accommodations shall be treated as part of the activity of holding such real property.

P.L. 99-514, §1011(b)(1):

Amended Code Sec. 465 (c)(7)(D)(v) by striking out "section 806(b)(3)". **Effective** for tax years beginning after 12-31-86. However, see Act Sec. 1011(d), below.

P.L. 99-514, §1011(d), provides:

(d) TREATMENT OF CERTAIN DISCOUNT BONDS.—

(1) IN GENERAL.—Notwithstanding the amendments made by subtitle B of title III, any gain recognized by a qualified life insurance company on the redemption at maturity of any bond which was issued before July 19, 1985, shall be subject to tax at the rate of 28 percent.

(2) QUALIFIED LIFE INSURANCE COMPANY.—For purposes of paragraph (1), the term "qualified life insurance company" means any of the following companies: Aetna, Provident Life and Accident, Massachusetts Mutual, Mutual Benefit, Connecticut Mutual, Phoenix Mutual, John Hancock, New England Life, Pennsylvania Mutual, Transamerica, Northwestern, Provident Mutual, Prudential, Mutual of Omaha, and Metropolitan.

• 1984, Deficit Reduction Act of 1984 (P.L. 98-369)

P.L. 98-369, §432(a):

Amended Code Sec. 465(c) by adding at the end thereof new paragraph (7). **Effective** for tax years beginning after 12-31-83; except that any loss from an activity described in section 465(c)(7)(A) of the Internal Revenue Code of 1954 (as amended by this section) which (but for the amendments made by this section would) have been treated as a deduction for the taxpayer's first tax year beginning after 12-31-83, under section 465(a)(2) of such Code shall be allowed as a deduction for such first tax year notwithstanding such amendment.

P.L. 98-369, §432(b):

Amended Code Sec. 465(c)(2). **Effective** for tax years beginning after 12-31-83; except that any loss from an activity described in section 465(c)(7)(A) of the Internal Revenue Code of 1954 (as amended by this section) which (but for the amendments made by this section) would have been treated as a deduction for the taxpayer's first tax year beginning after 12-31-83, under section 465(a)(2) of such Code shall be allowed as a deduction for such first tax year notwithstanding such amendment. Prior to amendment, it read as follows:

(2) Separate Activities.—For purposes of this section, a taxpayer's activity with respect to each—

(A) film or video tape,

(B) section 1245 property which is leased or held for leasing,

(C) farm,

(D) oil and gas property (as defined under section 614), or

(E) geothermal property (as defined under section 614)

shall be treated as a separate activity. A partner's interest in a partnership or a shareholder's interest in an S corporation shall be treated as a single activity to the extent that the partnership or the S corporation is engaged in activities described in any subparagraph of this paragraph.

• 1982, Subchapter S Revision Act of 1982 (P.L. 97-354)

P.L. 97-354, §5(a)(31)(C):

Amended the last sentence of Code Sec. 465(c)(2) by striking out "an electing small business corporation" the first place it appears and inserting in lieu thereof "an S corporation", and by striking out "an electing small business corporation" the second place it appears and inserting in lieu thereof "the S corporation". **Effective** for tax years beginning after 12-31-82.

P.L. 97-354, §5(a)(31)(D):

Amended Code Sec. 465(c)(3)(B)(ii) by striking out "electing small business corporation (as defined in section 1371(b))" and inserting in lieu thereof "an S corporation". **Effective** for tax years beginning after 12-31-82.

P.L. 97-354, §5(a)(31)(E):

Amended Code Sec. 465(c)(4)(A) by striking out "subsection (a)(1)(C)" and inserting in lieu thereof "subsection (a)(1)(B)". **Effective** for tax years beginning after 12-31-82.

• 1980, Technical Corrections Act of 1979 (P.L. 96-222)

P.L. 96-222, §102(a)(1)(D)(i):

Amended Code Sec. 465(c) by adding paragraphs (4), (5) and (6). **Effective** as set forth in P.L. 95-600, §204. See historical comment on P.L. 95-600, §204, under Code Sec. 465(a).

P.L. 96-222, §102(a)(1)(D)(ii):

Amended Code Sec. 465(c)(3)(D). **Effective** as set forth in P.L. 95-600, §204. See historical comment on P.L. 95-600, §204, under Code Sec. 465(a). Prior to amendment, Code Sec. 465(c)(3)(D) read as follows:

(D) EXCLUSIONS.—

(i) REAL PROPERTY.—In the case of activities described in subparagraph (A), the holding of real property (other than mineral property) shall be treated as a separate activity, and subsection (a) shall not apply to losses from such activity. For purposes of the preceding sentence, personal property and services which are incidental to making real property available as living accommodations shall be treated as part of the activity of holding such real property.

(ii) EQUIPMENT LEASING BY CLOSELY-HELD CORPORATIONS.—

(I) In the case of a corporation described in subsection (a)(1)(C) actively engaged in leasing equipment which is section 1245 property, the activity of leasing such equipment shall be treated, for purposes of subsection (a), as a separate activity and subsection (a) shall not apply to losses from such activity.

(II) A corporation described in subsection (a)(1)(C) shall not be considered to be actively engaged in leasing such equipment unless 50 percent or more of the gross receipts of the corporation for the taxable year are attributable, under regulations prescribed by the Secretary, to leasing and selling such equipment.

(III) For purposes of this paragraph, the leasing of master sound recordings, and other similar contractual arrangements with respect to tangible or intangible assets associated with literary, artistic, or musical properties shall not be treated as leasing equipment which is section 1245 property.

(IV) in the case of a controlled group of corporations (within the meaning of section 1563(a)), this paragraph shall be applied by treating the controlled group as a single corporation.

• 1978, Energy Tax Act of 1978 (P.L. 95-618)

P.L. 95-618, §402(d)(1):

Deleted "or" at the end of subparagraph (C), added "or" at the end of subparagraph (D), and inserted subparagraph (E) in Code Sec. 465(c). For **effective** date, see historical comment for P.L. 95-618, §402(e), under Code Sec. 263(c).

P.L. 95-618, §402(d)(2):

Amended Code Sec. 465(c)(2) by deleting "or" at the end of subparagaph (C), adding "or" at the end of subparagraph (D), and by inserting subparagraph (E). For **effective** date, see historical comment for P.L. 95-618, §402(e), under Code Sec. 263(c).

• 1978, Revenue Act of 1978 (P.L. 95-600)

P.L. 95-600, §201(a):

Added subsection (3) to Code Sec. 465(c). **Effective** as set forth in P.L. 95-600, §204. See historical comment on P.L. 95-600, §204, under Code Sec. 465(a).

[Sec. 465(d)]

(d) DEFINITION OF LOSS.—For purposes of this section, the term "loss" means the excess of the deductions allowable under this chapter for the taxable year (determined without regard to the first sentence of subsection (a)) and allocable to an activity to which this section applies over the income received or accrued by the taxpayer during the taxable year from such activity (determined without regard to subsection (e)(1)(A)).

Amendments

• 1980, Technical Corrections Act of 1979 (P.L. 96-222)

P.L. 96-222, §102(a)(1)(B):

Amended Code Sec. 465(d) by inserting at the end of the paragraph "(determined without regard to subsection (e)(1)(A))". **Effective** for tax years beginning after 12-31-78.

• 1978, Revenue Act of 1978 (P.L. 95-600)

P.L. 95-600, §701(k)(2):

Amended Code Sec. 465(d) by striking out "(determined without regard to this section)" and inserting in lieu thereof "(determined without regard to the first sentence of subsection (a))". **Effective** 10-4-76.

• 1976, Tax Reform Act of 1976 (P.L. 94-455)

P.L. 94-455, §204(a), as amended by P.L. 95-600, §701(k)(1):

Added Code Sec. 465. For **effective** date provisions, see Act Sec. 204(c), below.

P.L. 94-455, §204(c), provides:

(1) IN GENERAL.—Except as provided in paragraphs (2) and (3), the amendments made by this section shall apply to losses attributable to amounts paid or incurred in taxable years beginning after December 31, 1975. For purposes of this subsection, any amount allowed or allowable for depreciation or amortization for any period shall be treated as an amount paid or incurred in such period.

(2) SPECIAL TRANSITIONAL RULES FOR MOVIES AND VIDEO TAPES.—

(A) IN GENERAL.—In the case of any activity described in section 465(c)(1)(A) of the Internal Revenue Code of 1954, the amendments made by this section shall not apply to—

(i) deductions for depreciation or amortization with respect to property the principal production of which began before September 11, 1975, and for the purchase of which there was on September 11, 1975, and at all times thereafter a binding contract, and

(ii) deductions attributable to producing or distributing property the principal production of which began before September 11, 1975.

(B) EXCEPTION FOR CERTAIN AGREEMENTS WHERE PRINCIPAL PHOTOGRAPHY BEGAN BEFORE 1976.—In the case of any activity described in section 465(c)(1)(A) of the Internal Revenue Code of 1954, the amendments made by this section shall not apply to deductions attributable to the producing of a film the principal photography of which began on or before December 31, 1975, if—

(i) on September 10, 1975, there was an agreement with the director or a principal motion picture star, or on or before September 10, 1975, there had been expended (or committed to the production) an amount not less than the lower of $100,000 or 10 percent of the estimated costs of producing the film, and

(ii) the production takes place in the United States.

Subparagraph (A) shall apply only to taxpayers who held their interests on September 10, 1975. Subparagraph (B) shall apply only to taxpayers who held their interests on December 31, 1975.

(3) SPECIAL TRANSITIONAL RULES FOR LEASING ACTIVITIES.—

(A) RULE FOR LEASES OTHER THAN OPERATING LEASES.—In the case of any activity described in section 465(c)(1)(C) of the Internal Revenue Code of 1954, the amendments made by this section shall not apply with respect to—

(i) leases entered into before January 1, 1976, and

(ii) leases where the property was ordered by the lessor or lessee before January 1, 1976.

(B) HOLDING OF INTERESTS FOR PURPOSES OF SUBPARAGRAPH (A).—Subparagraph (A) shall apply only to taxpayers who held their interests in the property on December 31, 1975.

(C) SPECIAL RULE FOR OPERATING LEASES.—In the case of a lease described in section 46(e)(3)(B) of the Internal Revenue Code of 1954—

(i) subparagraph (A) shall be applied by substituting "May 1, 1976" for "January 1, 1976" each place it appears therein, and

(ii) subparagraph (B) shall be applied by substituting "April 30, 1976" for "December 31, 1975".

[Sec. 465(e)]

(e) RECAPTURE OF LOSSES WHERE AMOUNT AT RISK IS LESS THAN ZERO.—

(1) IN GENERAL.—If zero exceeds the amount for which the taxpayer is at risk in any activity at the close of any taxable year—

(A) the taxpayer shall include in his gross income for such taxable year (as income from such activity) an amount equal to such excess, and

(B) an amount equal to the amount so included in gross income shall be treated as a deduction allocable to such activity for the first succeeding taxable year.

(2) LIMITATION.—The excess referred to in paragraph (1) shall not exceed—

(A) the aggregate amount of the reductions required by subsection (b)(5) with respect to the activity by reason of losses for all prior taxable years beginning after December 31, 1978, reduced by

(B) the amounts previously included in gross income with respect to such activity under this subsection.

Amendments

• 1980, Technical Corrections Act of 1979 (P.L. 96-222)

P.L. 96-222, §102(a)(1)(C):

Amended Code Sec. 465(e)(2)(A) by inserting "by reason of losses" after "with respect to the activity". **Effective** as set forth in P.L. 95-600, §204. See historical comment on P.L. 95-600, §204, under Code Sec. 465(a).

• 1978, Revenue Act of 1978 (P.L. 95-600)

P.L. 95-600, §203:

Added Code Sec. 465(e). **Effective** as set forth in P.L. 95-600, §204. See historical comment on P.L. 95-600, §204, under Code Sec. 465(a).

[Sec. 466—Repealed]

Amendments

• 1986, Tax Reform Act of 1986 (P.L. 99-514)

P.L. 99-514, §823(a):

Repealed Code Sec. 466. **Effective** for tax years beginning after 12-31-86. However, see Act Sec. 823(c)(2), below, for rules relating to changes in method of accounting.

P.L. 99-514, §823(c)(2), provides:

(2) CHANGE IN METHOD OF ACCOUNTING.—In the case of any taxpayer who elected to have section 466 of the Internal Revenue Code of 1954 apply for such taxpayer's last taxable year beginning before January 1, 1987, and is required to change its method of accounting by reason of the amendments made by this section for any taxable year—

(A) such change shall be treated as initiated by the taxpayer,

(B) such change shall be treated as having been made with the consent of the Secretary, and

(C) the net amount of adjustments required by section 481 of the Internal Revenue Code of 1986 to be taken into account by the taxpayer shall—

(i) be reduced by the balance in the supense account under section 466(e) of such Code as of the close of such last taxable year, and

(ii) be taken into account over a period not longer than 4 years.

Prior to repeal, Code Sec. 466 read as follows:

SEC. 466. QUALIFIED DISCOUNT COUPONS REDEEMED AFTER CLOSE OF TAXABLE YEAR.

[Sec. 466(a)]

(a) ALLOWANCE OF DEDUCTION.—At the election of a taxpayer whose taxable income is computed under an accrual method of accounting, the deduction allowable under this chapter for the redemption costs of qualified discount coupons shall be an amount equal to the sum of—

(1) such costs incurred by the taxpayer with respect to coupons—

(A) which were outstanding at the close of the taxable year, and

(B) which were received by the taxpayer before the close of the redemption period for the taxable year, plus

(2) such costs (other than costs properly taken into account under paragraph (1) for a prior taxable year) incurred by the taxpayer during the taxable year.

[Sec. 466(b)]

(b) QUALIFIED DISCOUNT COUPONS.—For purposes of this section—

(1) IN GENERAL.—The term "qualified discount coupon" means a discount coupon which—

(A) was issued by the taxpayer,

(B) is redeemable by the taxpayer, and

(C) allows a discount on the purchase price of merchandise or other tangible personal property.

(2) METHOD OF ISSUANCE NOT TAKEN INTO ACCOUNT.—The determination of whether or not a discount coupon is a qualified discount coupon shall be made without regard to whether the coupon was issued through a newspaper, magazine, or other publication, by mail, on the pack or in the pack of merchandise, or otherwise.

(3) DISCOUNT ON ITEM CANNOT EXCEED $5.—A coupon shall not be a qualified discount coupon if—

(A) the face amount of such coupon is more than $5, or

(B) such coupon may be used with other coupons to bring about a price discount of more than $5 with respect to any item.

(4) THERE MUST BE REDEMPTION CHAIN.—A coupon shall not be a qualified discount coupon if the issuer directly redeems such coupon from the person using the coupon to receive a price discount. For purposes of the preceding sentence, corporations which are members of the same controlled group of corporations (within the meaning of section 1563(a)) as the issuer shall be treated as the issuer.

(5) REDEEMABLE BY TAXPAYER.—A coupon is redeemable by the taxpayer if the terms of the coupon require the taxpayer to redeem the coupon when presented for redemption in accordance with its terms.

[Sec. 466(c)]

(c) REDEMPTION COSTS; REDEMPTION PERIOD.—For purposes of this section—

(1) REDEMPTION COSTS.—The term "redemption cost" means, with respect to any coupon—

(A) the lesser of—

(i) the amount of the discount provided by the terms of the coupon, or

(ii) the amount incurred by the taxpayer for paying such discount, plus

(B) the amount incurred by the taxpayer for a payment to the retailer (or other person redeeming the coupon from the person receiving the price discount), but only if the amount so payable is stated on the coupon.

(2) REDEMPTION PERIOD.—

(A) IN GENERAL.—Except as provided in subparagraph (B), the redemption period for any taxable year is the 6-month period immediately following the close of the taxable year.

(B) TAXPAYER MAY SELECT SHORTER PERIOD.—The taxpayer may select a redemption period which is shorter than 6 months.

(C) CHANGE IN REDEMPTION PERIOD.—Any change in the redemption period shall be treated as a change in the method of accounting.

[Sec. 466(d)]

(d) QUALIFIED DISCOUNT COUPONS TO WHICH SECTION APPLIES.—

(1) ELECTION OF BENEFITS.—This section shall apply to qualified discount coupons if and only if the taxpayer makes an election under this section with respect to the trade or business in connection with which such coupons are issued. An election under this section may be made without the consent of the Secretary. The election shall be made in such manner as the Secretary may by regulations prescribe and

shall be made for any taxable year not later than the time prescribed by law for filing the return for such taxable year (including extensions thereof).

(2) SCOPE OF ELECTION.—An election made under this section shall apply to all qualified discount coupons issued in connection with the trade or business with respect to which the taxpayer has made the election.

(3) PERIOD TO WHICH ELECTION APPLIES.—An election under this section shall apply to the taxable year for which it is made and for all subsequent taxable years, unless the taxpayer secures the consent of the Secretary to the revocation of such election.

(4) TREATMENT AS METHOD OF ACCOUNTING.—Except to the extent inconsistent with the provisions of this section, for purposes of this subtitle, the computation of taxable income under an election made under this section shall be treated as a method of accounting.

[Sec. 466(e)]

(e) SUSPENSE ACCOUNT.—

(1) IN GENERAL.—In the case of any election under this section which (but for this subsection) would result in a net decrease in taxable income under section 481(a)(2), in lieu of applying section 481, the taxpayer shall establish a suspense account for the trade or business for the taxable year for which the election is made.

(2) INITIAL OPENING BALANCE.—The initial opening balance of the account described in paragraph (1) for the first taxable year to which the election applies shall be the amount by which—

(A) the largest dollar amount which would have been taken into account under subsection (a)(1) for any of the 3 immediately preceding taxable years if this section had applied to such 3 preceding taxable years, exceeds

(B) the sum of the increases in income (and the decreases in deductions) which (but for this subsection) would result under section 481(a)(2) for such first taxable year.

This subsection shall be applied by taking into account only amounts attributable to the trade or business for which such account is established.

(3) ADJUSTMENTS IN SUSPENSE ACCOUNT.—At the close of each taxable year, the suspense account shall be—

(A) reduced by the excess (if any) of—

(i) the opening balance of the suspense account for the taxable year, over

(ii) the amount deducted for the taxable year under subsection (a)(1), or

(B) increased (but not in excess of the initial opening balance) by the excess (if any) of—

(i) the amount deducted for the taxable year under subsection (a)(1), over

(ii) the opening balance of the suspense account for the taxable year.

(4) INCOME ADJUSTMENTS.—

(A) REDUCTIONS ALLOWED AS DEDUCTION.—In the case of any reduction under paragraph (3)(A) in the account for the taxable year, an amount equal to such reduction shall be allowed as a deduction for such taxable year.

(B) INCREASES ADDED TO GROSS INCOME.—In the case of any increase under paragraph (3)(B) in the account for the taxable year, an amount equal to such increase shall be allowed in gross income for such taxable year.

If the amount described in paragraph (2)(A) exceeds the dollar amount which would have been taken into account under subsection (a)(1) for the taxable year preceding the first taxable year for which the election is effective if this section had applied to such preceding taxable year, then an amount equal to the amount of such excess shall be included in gross income for such first taxable year.

(5) SUBCHAPTER C TRANSACTIONS.—The application of this subsection with respect to a taxpayer which is a party to any transaction with respect to which there is nonrecognition of gain or loss to any party to the transaction by reason of subchapter C shall be determined under regulations prescribed by the Secretary.

Amendments

• 1980, Technical Corrections Act of 1979 (P.L. 96-222)

P.L. 96-222, §103(a)(16):

Amended Code Sec. 466(e)(2)(B) by striking out "first taxable years" and inserting "first taxable year". **Effective** as set forth in P.L. 95-600, §373(c) following former Code Sec. 466(f).

[Sec. 466(f)]

(f) 10-YEAR SPREAD OF ANY NET INCREASE IN TAXABLE INCOME UNDER SECTION 481(a)(2).—In the case of any election under this section which results in a net increase in taxable income under section 481(a)(2), under regulations prescribed by the Secretary, such net increase shall (except as otherwise provided in such regulations) be taken into account by the taxpayer in computing taxable income in each of the 10 taxable years beginning with the year for which the election is made.

Amendments

• 1978, Revenue Act of 1978 (P.L. 95-600)

P.L. 95-600, §373(a):

Added Code Sec. 466. **Effective** as set forth in P.L. 95-600, §373(c).

P.L. 95-600, §373(c), provides:

(C) EFFECTIVE DATE.—

(1) IN GENERAL.—The amendments made by subsections (a) and (b) shall apply to taxable years ending after December 31, 1978.

(2) APPLICATION TO CERTAIN PRIOR TAXABLE YEARS.—

(A) IN GENERAL.—If—

(i) the taxpayer makes an election under section 466 of the Internal Revenue Code of 1954 for his first taxable year ending after December 31, 1978, and

(ii) for a continuous period of 1 or more taxable years each of which ends on or before December 31, 1978, the taxpayer used the method of accounting with respect to any type of discount coupons which was reasonably similar to the method of accounting provided by section 1.451-4 of the Income Tax Regulations,

then the taxpayer may make an election under this paragraph to have the method of accounting which he used for such continuous period treated as a valid method of accounting with respect to each such type of discount coupons for such period for purposes of the Internal Revenue Code of 1954. A taxpayer may make an election under this paragraph with respect to only one such continuous period.

(B) CERTAIN AMOUNTS TO WHICH METHOD OF ACCOUNTING APPLIES.—An accounting method which the taxpayer used for the period described in subparagraph (A) may include—

(i) costs of the type permitted by section 1.451-4 of the Income Tax Regulations to be included in the estimated average cost of redeeming coupons, plus

(ii) any amount designated or referred to on the coupon payable by the taxpayer to the person who allowed the discount on a sale by such person to the user of the coupon.

(C) SUSPENSE ACCOUNT NOT REQUIRED IN CERTAIN CASES.—A taxpayer whose election under this paragraph applies to all types of discount coupons which he issued during the continuous period referred to in subparagraph (A)(ii) shall not be required to establish a suspense account under section 466(e) of the Internal Revenue Code of 1954.

(D) RULES RELATING TO ELECTION UNDER THIS SUBSECTION.—An election under this paragraph may be made only before the expiration of the period for making an election under section 466 of the Internal Revenue Code of 1954 for the taxpayer's first taxable year ending after December 31, 1978. An election under this paragraph shall be made in such a manner and form as the Secretary of the Treasury or his delegate may by regulations prescribe. For purposes of the Internal Revenue Code of 1954, such an election shall be treated as a method of accounting, except that the approval of the Secretary of the Treasury or his delegate to the making of the election may not be required.

[Sec. 467]

SEC. 467. CERTAIN PAYMENTS FOR THE USE OF PROPERTY OR SERVICES.

[Sec. 467(a)]

(a) ACCRUAL METHOD ON PRESENT VALUE BASIS.—In the case of the lessor or lessee under any section 467 rental agreement, there shall be taken into account for purposes of this title for any taxable year the sum of—

(1) the amount of the rent which accrues during such taxable year as determined under subsection (b), and

(2) interest for the year on the amounts which were taken into account under this subsection for prior taxable years and which are unpaid.

[Sec. 467(b)]

(b) ACCRUAL OF RENTAL PAYMENTS.—

(1) ALLOCATION FOLLOWS AGREEMENT.—Except as provided in paragraph (2), the determination of the amount of the rent under any section 467 rental agreement which accrues during any taxable year shall be made—

(A) by allocating rents in accordance with the agreement, and

(B) by taking into account any rent to be paid after the close of the period in an amount determined under regulations which shall be based on present value concepts.

(2) CONSTANT RENTAL ACCRUAL IN CASE OF CERTAIN TAX AVOIDANCE TRANSACTIONS, ETC.—In the case of any section 467 rental agreement to which this paragraph applies, the portion of the rent which accrues during any taxable year shall be that portion of the constant rental amount with respect to such agreement which is allocable to such taxable year.

(3) AGREEMENTS TO WHICH PARAGRAPH (2) APPLIES.—Paragraph (2) applies to any rental payment agreement if—

(A) such agreement is a disqualified leaseback or long-term agreement, or

(B) such agreement does not provide for the allocation referred to in paragraph (1)(A).

(4) DISQUALIFIED LEASEBACK OR LONG-TERM AGREEMENT.—For purposes of this subsection, the term "disqualified leaseback or long-term agreement" means any section 467 rental agreement if—

(A) such agreement is part of a leaseback transaction or such agreement is for a term in excess of 75 percent of the statutory recovery period for the property, and

(B) a principal purpose for providing increasing rents under the agreement is the avoidance of tax imposed by this subtitle.

(5) EXCEPTIONS TO DISQUALIFICATION IN CERTAIN CASES.—The Secretary shall prescribe regulations setting forth circumstances under which agreements will not be treated as disqualified leaseback or long-term agreements, including circumstances relating to—

(A) changes in amounts paid determined by reference to price indices,

(B) rents based on a fixed percentage of lessee receipts or similar amounts,

(C) reasonable rent holidays, or

(D) changes in amounts paid to unrelated 3rd parties.

Amendments

• 1986, Tax Reform Act of 1986 (P.L. 99-514)

P.L. 99-514, §1807(b)(2)(A):

Amended Code Sec. 467(b)(4)(A) by striking out "statutory recover period" and inserting in lieu thereof "statutory recovery period". **Effective** as if included in the provision of P.L. 98-369 to which it relates.

[Sec. 467(c)]

(c) RECAPTURE OF PRIOR UNDERSTATED INCLUSIONS UNDER LEASEBACK OR LONG-TERM AGREEMENTS.—

(1) IN GENERAL.—If—

(A) the lessor under any section 467 rental agreement disposes of any property subject to such agreement during the term of such agreement, and

(B) such agreement is a leaseback or long-term agreement to which paragraph (2) of subsection (b) did not apply,

the recapture amount shall be treated as ordinary income. Such gain shall be recognized notwithstanding any other provision of this subtitle.

(2) RECAPTURE AMOUNT.—For purposes of paragraph (1), the term "recapture amount" means the lesser of—

(A) the prior understated inclusions, or

(B) the excess of the amount realized (or in the case of a disposition other than a sale, exchange, or involuntary conversion, the fair market value of the property) over the adjusted basis of such property.

The amount determined under subparagraph (B) shall be reduced by the amount of any gain treated as ordinary income on the disposition under any other provision of this subtitle.

(3) PRIOR UNDERSTATED INCLUSIONS.—For purposes of this subsection, the term "prior understated inclusion" means the excess (if any) of—

(A) the amount which would have been taken into account by the lessor under subsection (a) for periods before the disposition if subsection (b)(2) had applied to the agreement, over

(B) the amount taken into account under subsection (a) by the lessor for periods before the disposition.

(4) LEASEBACK OR LONG-TERM AGREEMENT.—For purposes of this subsection, the term "leaseback or long-term agreement" means any agreement described in subsection (b)(4)(A).

(5) SPECIAL RULES.—Under regulations prescribed by the Secretary—

(A) exceptions similar to the exceptions applicable under section 1245 or 1250 (whichever is appropriate) shall apply for purposes of this subsection,

(B) any transferee in a disposition excepted by reason of subparagraph (A) who has a transferred basis in the property shall be treated in the same manner as the transferor, and

Caution: Code Sec. 467(c)(5)(C), below, is subject to the sunset provision of the Jobs and Growth Tax Relief Reconciliation Act of 2003 (P.L. 108-27), §303. Absent Congressional action, the changes made to this provision by P.L. 108-27, or that take effect as if included in P.L. 108-27, do not apply after December 31, 2010. For more information about the sunset provision, see page XXI of the Preface to this publication and P.L. 108-27, §303, in the amendment notes. See the amendments notes for a history of amendments to this section and the effective date of each change.

(C) for purposes of sections 170(e) and 751(c), amounts treated as ordinary income under this section shall be treated in the same manner as amounts treated as ordinary income under section 1245 or 1250.

Amendments

• 2003, Jobs and Growth Tax Relief Reconciliation Act of 2003 (P.L. 108-27)

P.L. 108-27, §302(e)(4)(B)(ii):

Amended Code Sec. 467(c)(5)(C) by striking ", 341(e)(12)", after "170(e)". For the **effective** date, see Act Sec. 302(f), as amended by P.L. 108-311, §402(a)(6), below.

P.L. 108-27, §302(f), as amended by P.L. 108-311, §402(a)(6), provides:

(f) EFFECTIVE DATE.—

(1) IN GENERAL.—Except as provided in paragraph (2), the amendments made by this section shall apply to taxable years beginning after December 31, 2002.

(2) PASS-THRU ENTITIES.—In the case of a pass-thru entity described in subparagraph (A), (B), (C), (D), (E), or (F) of section 1(h)(10) of the Internal Revenue Code of 1986, as amended by this Act, the amendments made by this section shall apply to taxable years ending after December 31, 2002; except that dividends received by such an entity on or before such date shall not be treated as qualified dividend income (as defined in section 1(h)(11)(B) of such Code, as added by this Act).

P.L. 108-27, §303, as amended by P.L. 109-222, §102, provides:

SEC. 303. SUNSET OF TITLE.

All provisions of, and amendments made by, this title shall not apply to taxable years beginning after December 31, 2010, and the Internal Revenue Code of 1986 shall be applied and administered to such years as if such provisions and amendments had never been enacted.

• 1986, Tax Reform Act of 1986 (P.L. 99-514)

P.L. 99-514, §511(d)[(c)](2)(A) (as amended by P.L. 100-647, §1005(c)(10)):

Amended Code Sec. 467(c)(5)[(C)] by striking out "163(d)," after "sections". **Effective** for tax years beginning after 12-31-86.

P.L. 99-514, §631(e)(10):

Amended Code Sec. 467(c)(5)[(C)] by striking out "453B(d)(2),". **Effective** for (1) any distribution in complete liquidation, and any sale or exchange, made by a corporation after 7-31-86, unless such corporation is completely liquidated before 1-1-87, (2) any transaction described in section 338 of the Internal Revenue Code of 1986 for which the acquisition date occurs after 12-31-86, and (3) any distribution (not in complete liquidation) made after 12-31-86. However, see Act Sec. 633(b)-(f) following Code Sec. 26.

P.L. 99-514, §1807(b)(2)(B):

Amended Code Sec. 467(c)(4) by striking out "subsection (b)(3)(A)" and inserting in lieu thereof "subsection (b)(4)(A)". **Effective** as if included in the provision of P.L. 98-369 to which it relates.

[Sec. 467(d)]

(d) SECTION 467 RENTAL AGREEMENTS.—

(1) IN GENERAL.—Except as otherwise provided in this subsection, the term "section 467 rental agreements" means any rental agreement for the use of tangible property under which—

(A) there is at least one amount allocable to the use of property during a calendar year which is to be paid after the close of the calendar year following the calendar year in which such use occurs, or

(B) there are increases in the amount to be paid as rent under the agreement.

(2) SECTION NOT TO APPLY TO AGREEMENTS INVOLVING PAYMENTS OF $250,000 OR LESS.—This section shall not apply to any amount to be paid for the use of property if the sum of the following amounts does not exceed $250,000—

(A) the aggregate amount of payments received as consideration for such use of property, and

(B) the aggregate value of any other consideration to be received for such use of property.

For purposes of the preceding sentence, rules similar to the rules of clauses (ii) and (iii) of section 1274(c)(4)(C) shall apply.

Amendments

• 1986, Tax Reform Act of 1986 (P.L. 99-514)

P.L. 99-514, §1807(b)(2)(C):

Amended Code Sec. 467(d)(2) by striking out "section 1274(c)(2)(C)" and inserting in lieu thereof "section 1274(c)(4)(C)". **Effective** as if included in the provision of P.L. 98-369 to which it relates.

[Sec. 467(e)]

(e) DEFINITIONS.—For purposes of this section—

(1) CONSTANT RENTAL AMOUNT.—The term "constant rental amount" means, with respect to any section 467 rental agreement, the amount which, if paid as of the close of each lease period under the agreement, would result in an aggregate present value equal to the present value of the aggregate payments required under the agreement.

(2) LEASEBACK TRANSACTION.—A transaction is a leaseback transaction if it involves a leaseback to any person who had an interest in such property at any time within 2 years before such leaseback (or to a related person).

(3) STATUTORY RECOVERY PERIOD.—

(A) IN GENERAL.—

In the case of:	The statutory recovery period is:
3-year property	3 years
5-year property	5 years
7-year property	7 years
10-year property	10 years
15-year and 20-year property	15 years
Residential rental property and nonresidential real property	19 years
Any railroad grading or tunnel bore	50 years .

(B) SPECIAL RULE FOR PROPERTY NOT DEPRECIABLE UNDER SECTION 168.—In the case of property to which section 168 does not apply, subparagraph (A) shall be applied as if section 168 applies to such property.

(4) DISCOUNT AND INTEREST RATE.—For purposes of computing present value and interest under subsection (a)(2), the rate used shall be equal to 110 percent of the applicable Federal rate determined under section 1274(d) (compounded semiannually) which is in effect at the time the agreement is entered into with respect to debt instruments having a maturity equal to the term of the agreement.

(5) RELATED PERSON.—The term "related person" has the meaning given to such term by section 465(b)(3)(C).

(6) CERTAIN OPTIONS OF LESSEE TO RENEW NOT TAKEN INTO ACCOUNT.—Except as provided in regulations prescribed by the Secretary, there shall not be taken into account in computing the term of any agreement for purposes of this section any extension which is solely at the option of the lessee.

Amendments

• 1988, Technical and Miscellaneous Revenue Act of 1988 (P.L. 100-647)

P.L. 100-647, §1002(i)(2)(H):

Amended Code Sec. 467(e)(3)(A) by adding at the end thereof a new item in the table. **Effective** as if included in the provision of P.L. 99-514 to which it relates.

• 1986, Tax Reform Act of 1986 (P.L. 99-514)

P.L. 99-514, §201(d)(8)(A):

Amended Code Sec. 467(e)(3), as amended by Act Sec. 1879(f)(1)(A) and (B). **Effective**, generally, for property placed in service after 12-31-86, in tax years ending after such date. However, see Act Secs. 203, 204 and 251(d) following Code Sec. 168 for special and transitional rules. Prior to amendment, Code Sec. 467(e)(3) read as follows:

(3) STATUTORY RECOVERY PERIOD.—

(A) IN GENERAL.—

In the case of property which is:	The statutory recovery period is:
3-year property	3 years
5-year property	5 years
10-year property	10 years
Low-income housing	15 years
15-year public utility property	15 years
19-year real property	19 years

(B) SPECIAL RULE FOR PROPERTY WHICH IS NOT RECOVERY PROPERTY.—In the case of any property which is not recovery property, subparagraph (A) shall be applied as if such property were recovery property.

P.L. 99-514, §201(d)(8)(B):

Amended Code Sec. 467(e)(5), as amended by Act Sec. 1807(b)(2)(D), by striking out "section 168(e)(4)(D)" and inserting in lieu thereof "section 465(b)(3)(C)". **Effective**, generally, for property placed in service after 12-31-86, in tax years ending after such date. However, see Act Secs. 203, 204 and 251(d) following Code Sec. 168 for special and transitional rules.

• 1986, Tax Reform Act of 1986 (P.L. 99-514)

P.L. 99-514, §1807(b)(2)(D):

Amended Code Sec. 467(e)(5) by striking out "section 168(d)(4)(D)" and inserting in lieu thereof "section 168(e)(4)(D)". **Effective** as if included in the provision of P.L. 98-369 to which it relates.

P.L. 99-514, §1879(f)(1)(A)-(B):

Amended the table contained in Code Sec. 467(e)(3)(A) by striking out "18-year real property" and inserting in lieu thereof "19-year real property", and by striking out "18 years" and inserting in lieu thereof "19 years". **Effective** as if included in the amendments made by P.L. 99-121, § 103.

[Sec. 467(f)]

(f) COMPARABLE RULES WHERE AGREEMENT FOR DECREASING PAYMENTS.—Under regulations prescribed by the Secretary, rules comparable to the rules of this section shall also apply in the case of any agreement where the amount paid under the agreement for the use of property decreases during the term of the agreement.

[Sec. 467(g)]

(g) COMPARABLE RULES FOR SERVICES.—Under regulations prescribed by the Secretary, rules comparable to the rules of subsection (a)(2) shall also apply in the case of payments for services which meet requirements comparable to the requirements of subsection (d). The preceding sentence shall not apply to any amount to which section 404 or 404A (or any other provision specified in regulations) applies.

Amendments

• 1986, Tax Reform Act of 1986 (P.L. 99-514)

P.L. 99-514, §1807(b)(1):

Amended Code Sec. 467(g) by adding at the end thereof a new sentence. **Effective** as if included in the provision of P.L. 98-369 to which it relates.

[Sec. 467(h)]

(h) REGULATIONS.—The Secretary shall prescribe such regulations as may be appropriate to carry out the purposes of this section, including regulations providing for the application of this section in the case of contingent payments.

Amendments

• 1984, Deficit Reduction Act of 1984 (P.L. 98-369)

P.L. 98-369, §92(a):

Added Code Sec. 467. **Effective** with respect to agreements entered into after 6-8-84. Special rules appear in Act Sec. 92(c)(2)-(3), below.

P.L. 98-369, §92(c)(2)-(3), provides:

(2) EXCEPTIONS.—The amendments made by this section shall not apply—

(A) to any agreement entered into pursuant to a written agreement which was binding on June 8, 1984, and at all times thereafter,

(B) subject to the provisions of paragraph (3), to any agreement to lease property if—

(i) there was in effect a firm plan, evidenced by a board of directors' resolution, memorandum of agreement, or letter of intent on March 15, 1984, to enter into such an agreement, and

(ii) construction of the property was commenced (but such property was not placed in service) on or before March 15, 1984, and

(C) to any agreement to lease property if—

(i) the lessee of such property adopted a firm plan to lease the property, evidenced by a resolution of the Finance Committee of the Board of Directors of such lessee, on February 10, 1984,

(ii) the sum of the present values of the rents payable by the lessee under the lease at the inception thereof equals at least $91,223,034, assuming (for purposes of this clause)—

(I) the annual discount rate is 12.6 percent,

(II) the initial payment of rent occurs 12 months after the commencement of the lease, and

(III) subsequent payments of rents occur on the anniversary date of the initial payment, and

(iii) during—

(I) the first 5 years of the lease, at least 9 percent of the rents payable by the lessee under the agreement are paid, and

(II) the second 5 years of the lease, at least 16.25 percent of the rents payable by the lessee under the agreement are paid.

Paragraph (3)(B)(ii)(II) shall apply for purposes of clauses (ii) and (iii) of subparagraph (C), as if, as of the beginning of the last stage, the separate agreements were treated as 1 single agreement relating to all property covered by the agreements, including any property placed in service before the property to which the agreement for the last stage relates. If the lessor under the agreement described in subparagraph (C) leases the property from another person, this exception shall also apply to any agreement between the lessor and such person which is integrally related to, and entered into at the same time as, such agreement, and which calls for comparable payments of rent over the primary term of the agreement.

(3) SCHEDULE OF DEEMED RENTAL PAYMENTS.—

(A) IN GENERAL.—In any case to which paragraph (2)(B) applies, for purposes of the Internal Revenue Code of 1954, the lessor shall be treated as having received or accrued (and the lessee shall be treated as having paid or incurred) rents equal to the greater of—

(i) the amount of rents actually paid under the agreement during the taxable year, or

(ii) the amount of rents determined in accordance with the schedule under subparagraph (B) for such taxable year.

(B) SCHEDULE.—

(i) IN GENERAL.—The schedule under this subparagraph is as follows:

Portion of lease term:	Cumulative percentage of total rent deemed paid:
1st 1/5>	10
2nd 1/5>	25
3rd 1/5>	45
4th 1/5>	70
Last 1/5>	100

(ii) OPERATING RULES.—For purposes of this schedule—

(I) the rent allocable to each taxable year within any portion of a lease term described in such schedule shall be a level pro rata amount properly allocable to such taxable year, and

(II) any agreement relating to property which is to be placed in service in 2 or more stages shall be treated as 2 or more separate agreements.

(C) PARAGRAPH NOT TO APPLY.—This paragraph shall not apply to any agreement if the sum of the present values of all payments under the agreement is greater than the sum of the present value of all the payments deemed to be paid or received under the schedule under subparagraph (B). For purposes of computing any present value under this subparagraph, the annual discount rate shall be equal to 12 percent, compounded semiannually.

[Sec. 468]

SEC. 468. SPECIAL RULES FOR MINING AND SOLID WASTE RECLAMATION AND CLOSING COSTS.

[Sec. 468(a)]

(a) ESTABLISHMENT OF RESERVES FOR RECLAMATION AND CLOSING COSTS.—

(1) ALLOWANCE OF DEDUCTION.—If a taxpayer elects the application of this section with respect to any mining or solid waste disposal property, the amount of any deduction for qualified reclamation or closing costs for any taxable year to which such election applies shall be equal to the current reclamation or closing costs allocable to—

(A) in the case of qualified reclamation costs, the portion of the reserve property which was disturbed during such taxable year, and

(B) in the case of qualified closing costs, the production from the reserve property during such taxable year.

(2) OPENING BALANCE AND ADJUSTMENTS TO RESERVE.—

(A) OPENING BALANCE.—The opening balance of any reserve for its first taxable year shall be zero.

(B) INCREASE FOR INTEREST.—A reserve shall be increased each taxable year by an amount equal to the amount of interest which would have been earned during such taxable year on the opening balance of such reserve for such taxable year if such interest were computed—

(i) at the Federal short-term rate or rates (determined under section 1274) in effect, and

(ii) by compounding semiannually.

(C) RESERVE TO BE CHARGED FOR AMOUNTS PAID.—Any amount paid by the taxpayer during any taxable year for qualified reclamation or closing costs allocable to portions of the reserve property for which the election under paragraph (1) was in effect shall be charged to the appropriate reserve as of the close of the taxable year.

(D) RESERVE INCREASED BY AMOUNT DEDUCTED.—A reserve shall be increased each taxable year by the amount allowable as a deduction under paragraph (1) for such taxable year which is allocable to such reserve.

(3) ALLOWANCE OF DEDUCTION FOR EXCESS AMOUNTS PAID.—There shall be allowed as a deduction for any taxable year the excess of—

(A) the amounts described in paragraph (2)(C) paid during such taxable year, over

(B) the closing balance of the reserve for such taxable year (determined without regard to paragraph (2)(C)).

(4) LIMITATION ON BALANCE AS OF THE CLOSE OF ANY TAXABLE YEAR.—

(A) RECLAMATION RESERVES.—In the case of any reserve for qualified reclamation costs, there shall be included in gross income for any taxable year an amount equal to the excess of—

(i) the closing balance of the reserve for such taxable year, over

(ii) the current reclamation costs of the taxpayer for all portions of the reserve property disturbed during any taxable year to which the election under paragraph (1) applies.

(B) CLOSING COSTS RESERVES.—In the case of any reserve for qualified closing costs, there shall be included in gross income for any taxable year an amount equal to the excess of—

(i) the closing balance of the reserve for such taxable year, over

(ii) the current closing cost of the taxpayer with respect to the reserve property, determined as if all production with respect to the reserve property for any taxable year to which the election under paragraph (1) applies had occurred in such taxable year.

(C) ORDER OF APPLICATION.—This paragraph shall be applied after all adjustments to the reserve have been made for the taxable year.

(5) INCOME INCLUSIONS ON COMPLETION OR DISPOSITION.—Proper inclusion in income shall be made upon—

(A) the revocation of an election under paragraph (1), or

(B) completion of the closing, or disposition of any portion, of a reserve property.

Amendments

• 1990, Omnibus Budget Reconciliation Act of 1990 (P.L. 101-508)

P.L. 101-508, §11802(c):

Amended Code Sec. 468(a)(2)(B). **Effective** 11-5-90. Prior to amendment, Code Sec. 468(a)(2)(B) read as follows:

(B) INCREASE FOR INTEREST.—

(i) IN GENERAL.—A reserve shall be increased each taxable year by an amount equal to the amount of interest which would be earned during such taxable year on the opening balance of such reserve for such taxable year if such interest were computed—

(I) at the Federal short-term rate or rates (determined under section 1274) in effect, and

(II) by compounding semiannually.

(ii) PHASE-IN OF INTEREST RATE.—In the case of taxable years ending before 1987, the rate determined under clause (i)(I) shall be equal to the following percentage of such rate (determined without regard to this clause):

In the case of taxable years ending in:	The percentage is:
1984	70
1986	85

P.L. 101-508, §11821(b), provides:

(b) SAVINGS PROVISION.—If—

(1) any provision amended or repealed by this part applied to—

(A) any transaction occurring before the date of the enactment of this Act,

(B) any property acquired before such date of enactment, or

(C) any item of income, loss, deduction, or credit taken into account before such date of enactment, and

(2) the treatment of such transaction, property, or item under such provision would (without regard to the amendments made by this part) affect liability for tax for periods ending after such date of enactment,

nothing in the amendments made by this part shall be construed to affect the treatment of such transaction, property, or item for purposes of determining liability for tax for periods ending after such date of enactment.

[Sec. 468(b)]

(b) ALLOCATION FOR PROPERTY WHERE ELECTION NOT IN EFFECT FOR ALL TAXABLE YEARS.—If the election under subsection (a)(1) is not in effect for 1 or more taxable years in which the reserved property is disturbed (or production occurs), items with respect to the reserve property shall be allocated to the reserve in such manner as the Secretary may prescribe by regulations.

[Sec. 468(c)]

(c) REVOCATION OF ELECTION; SEPARATE RESERVES.—

(1) REVOCATION OF ELECTION.—

(A) IN GENERAL.—The taxpayer may revoke an election under subsection (a)(1) with respect to any property. Such revocation, once made, shall be irrevocable.

(B) TIME AND MANNER OF REVOCATION.—Any revocation under subparagraph (A) shall be made at such time and in such manner as the Secretary may prescribe.

(2) SEPARATE RESERVES REQUIRED.—If a taxpayer makes an election under subsection (a)(1), the taxpayer shall establish with respect to the property for which the election was made—

(A) a separate reserve for qualified reclamation costs, and

(B) a separate reserve for qualified closing costs.

[Sec. 468(d)]

(d) DEFINITIONS AND SPECIAL RULES RELATING TO RECLAMATION AND CLOSING COSTS.—For purposes of this section—

(1) CURRENT RECLAMATION AND CLOSING COSTS.—

(A) CURRENT RECLAMATION COSTS.—The term "current reclamation costs" means the amount which the taxpayer would be required to pay for qualified reclamation costs if the reclamation activities were performed currently.

(B) CURRENT CLOSING COSTS.—

(i) IN GENERAL.—The term "current closing costs" means the amount which the taxpayer would be required to pay for qualified closing costs if the closing activities were performed currently.

(ii) COSTS COMPUTED ON UNIT-OF-PRODUCTION OR CAPACITY METHOD.—Estimated closing costs shall—

(I) in the case of the closing of any mine site, be computed on the unit-of-production method of accounting, and

(II) in the case of the closing of any solid waste disposal site, be computed on the unit-of-capacity method.

(2) QUALIFIED RECLAMATION OR CLOSING COSTS.—The term "qualified reclamation or closing costs" means any of the following expenses:

(A) MINING RECLAMATION AND CLOSING COSTS.—Any expenses incurred for any land reclamation or closing activity which is conducted in accordance with a reclamation plan (including an amendment or modification thereof)—

(i) which—

(I) is submitted pursuant to the provisions of section 511 or 528 of the Surface Mining Control and Reclamation Act of 1977 (as in effect on January 1, 1984), and

(II) is part of a surface mining and reclamation permit granted under the provisions of title V of such Act (as so in effect), or

(ii) which is submitted pursuant to any other Federal or State law which imposes surface mining reclamation and permit requirements substantially similar to the requirements imposed by title V of such Act (as so in effect).

(B) SOLID WASTE DISPOSAL AND CLOSING COSTS.—

(i) IN GENERAL.—Any expenses incurred for any land reclamation or closing activity in connection with any solid waste disposal site which is conducted in accordance with any permit issued pursuant to—

(I) any provision of the Solid Waste Disposal Act (as in effect on January 1, 1984) requiring such activity, or

(II) any other Federal, State, or local law which imposes requirements substantially similar to the requirements imposed by the Solid Waste Disposal Act (as so in effect).

(ii) EXCEPTION FOR CERTAIN HAZARDOUS WASTE SITES.—Clause (i) shall not apply to that portion of any property which is disturbed after the property is listed in the national contingency plan established under section 105 of the Comprehensive Environmental Response, Compensation, and Liability Act of 1980.

(3) PROPERTY.—The term "property" has the meaning given such term by section 614.

(4) RESERVE PROPERTY.—The term "reserve property" means any property with respect to which a reserve is established under subsection (a)(1).

Amendments

• 1986, Tax Reform Act of 1986 (P.L. 99-514)

P.L. 99-514, §1807(a)(3)(A), (C):

Amended Code Sec. 468(a)(2) by adding at the end thereof new subparagraph (D). **Effective** as if included in the provision of P.L. 98-369 to which it relates.

P.L. 99-514, §1807(a)(3)(A), (C):

Amended Code Sec. 468(a)(1) by striking out "this subsection" and inserting in lieu thereof "this section". **Effective** as if included in the provision of P.L. 98-369 to which it relates.

P.L. 99-514, §1899A(14):

Amended Code Sec. 468(d)(2)(B)(ii) by striking out "Comprehensive Environmental, Compensation, and Liability Act of 1980" and inserting in lieu thereof "Comprehensive Environmental Response, Compensation, and Liability Act of 1980". **Effective** 10-22-86.

• 1984, Deficit Reduction Act of 1984 (P.L. 98-369)

P.L. 98-369, §91(b)(1):

Added Code Sec. 468. **Effective** for amounts with respect to which a deduction would be allowable under chapter 1 of the Internal Revenue Code of 1954 (determined without regard to such amendments) after—

(A) in the case of amounts to which section 461(h) of such Code (as added by such amendments) applies, the date of the enactment of this Act, and

(B) in the case of amounts to which section 461(i) of such Code (as so added) applies, after 3-31-84.

P.L. 98-369, §91(g)(2) (as amended by P.L. 99-514, §1807(a)) and (h)-(i), provides:

(2) TAXPAYER MAY ELECT EARLIER APPLICATION.—

(A) IN GENERAL.—In the case of amounts described in paragraph (1)(A), a taxpayer may elect to have the amendments made by this section apply to amounts which—

(i) are incurred on or before the date of the enactment of this Act (determined without regard to such amendments), and

(ii) are incurred after the date of the enactment of this Act (determined with regard to such amendments).

The Secretary of the Treasury or his delegate may by regulations provide that (in lieu of an election under the preceding sentence) a taxpayer may (subject to such conditions as such regulations may provide) elect to have subsection (h) of section 461 of such Code apply to the taxpayer's entire taxable year in which occurs July 19, 1984.

(B) ELECTION TREATED AS CHANGE IN THE METHOD OF ACCOUNTING.—For purposes of section 481 of the Internal Revenue Code of 1954, if an election is made under subparagraph (A) with respect to any amount, the application of the amendments made by this section shall be treated as a change in method accounting—

(i) initiated by the taxpayer,

(ii) made with the consent of the Secretary of the Treasury, and

(iii) with respect to which section 481 of such Code shall be applied by substituting a 3-year adjustment period for a 10-year adjustment period.

(h) EXCEPTION FOR CERTAIN EXISTING ACTIVITIES AND CONTRACTS.—If—

(1) EXISITNG ACCOUNTING PRACTICES.—If, on March 1, 1984, any taxpayer was regularly computing his deduction for mining reclamation activities under a current cost method of accounting (as determined by the Secretary of the Treasury or his delegate), the liability for reclamation activities—

(A) for land disturbed before the date of the enactment of this Act, or

(B) to which paragraph (2) applies,

shall be treated as having been incurred when the land was disturbed.

(2) FIXED PRICE SUPPLY CONTRACT.—

(A) IN GENERAL.—In the case of any fixed price supply contract entered into before March 1, 1984, the amendments made by subsection (b) shall not apply to any minerals extracted from such property which are sold pursuant to such contract.

(B) NO EXTENSION OR RENEGOTIATION.—Subparagraph (A) shall not apply—

(i) to any extension of any contract beyond the period such contract was in effect on March 1, 1984, or

(ii) to any renegotiation of, or other change in, the terms and conditions of such contract in effect on March 1, 1984.

(i) TRANSITIONAL RULE FOR ACCRUED VACATION PAY.—

(1) IN GENERAL.—In the case of any taxpayer—

(A) with respect to whom a deduction was allowable (other than under section 463 of the Internal Revenue Code of 1954) for vested accrued vacation pay for the last taxable year ending before the date of the enactment of this Act, and

(B) who elects the application of section 463 of such Code for the first taxable year ending after the date of the enactment of this Act,

then, for purposes of section 463(b) of such Code, the opening balance of the taxpayer with respect to any vested accrued vacation pay shall be determined under section 463(b)(1) of such Code.

(2) VESTED ACCRUED VACATION PAY.—For purposes of this subsection, the term "vested accrued vacation pay" means any amount allowable under section 162(a) of such Code with respect to vacation pay of employees of the taxpayer (determined without regard to section 463 of such Code).

[Sec. 468A]

SEC. 468A. SPECIAL RULES FOR NUCLEAR DECOMMISSIONING COSTS.

[Sec. 468A(a)]

(a) IN GENERAL.—If the taxpayer elects the application of this section, there shall be allowed as a deduction for any taxable year the amount of payments made by the taxpayer to a Nuclear Decommissioning Reserve Fund (hereinafter referred to as the "Fund") during such taxable year.

[Sec. 468A(b)]

(b) LIMITATION ON AMOUNTS PAID INTO FUND.—The amount which a taxpayer may pay into the Fund for any taxable year shall not exceed the ruling amount applicable to such taxable year.

Amendments

• 2005, Energy Tax Incentives Act of 2005 (P.L. 109-58)

P.L. 109-58, §1310(a):

Amended Code Sec. 468A(b). **Effective** for tax years beginning after 12-31-2005. Prior to amendment, Code Sec. 468A(b) read as follows:

(b) LIMITATION ON AMOUNTS PAID INTO FUND.—The amount which a taxpayer may pay into the Fund for any taxable year shall not exceed the lesser of—

(1) the amount of nuclear decommissioning costs allocable to the Fund which is included in the taxpayer's cost of service for ratemaking purposes for such taxable year, or

(2) the ruling amount applicable to such taxable year.

[Sec. 468A(c)]

(c) INCOME AND DEDUCTIONS OF THE TAXPAYER.—

(1) INCLUSION OF AMOUNTS DISTRIBUTED.—There shall be includible in the gross income of the taxpayer for any taxable year—

(A) any amount distributed from the Fund during such taxable year, other than any amount distributed to pay costs described in subsection (e)(4)(B), and

(B) except to the extent provided in regulations, amounts properly includible in gross income in the case of any deemed distribution under subsection (e)(6), any termination under subsection (e)(7), or the disposition of any interest in the nuclear powerplant.

(2) DEDUCTION WHEN ECONOMIC PERFORMANCE OCCURS.—In addition to any deduction under subsection (a), there shall be allowable as a deduction for any taxable year the amount of the nuclear decommissioning costs with respect to which economic performance (within the meaning of section 461(h)(2)) occurs during such taxable year.

[Sec. 468A(d)]

(d) RULING AMOUNT.—For purposes of this section—

(1) REQUEST REQUIRED.—No deduction shall be allowed for any payment to the Fund unless the taxpayer requests, and receives, from the Secretary a schedule of ruling amounts. For purposes of the preceding sentence, the taxpayer shall request a schedule of ruling amounts upon each renewal of the operating license of the nuclear powerplant.

(2) RULING AMOUNT.—The term "ruling amount" means, with respect to any taxable year, the amount which the Secretary determines under paragraph (1) to be necessary to—

(A) fund the total nuclear decommissioning costs with respect to such power plant over the estimated useful life of such power plant, and

(B) prevent any excessive funding of such costs or the funding of such costs at a rate more rapid than level funding, taking into account such discount rates as the Secretary deems appropriate.

(3) REVIEW OF AMOUNT.—The Secretary shall at least once during the useful life of the nuclear powerplant (or, more frequently, upon the request of the taxpayer) review, and revise if necessary, the schedule of ruling amounts determined under paragraph (1).

Amendments

• 2005, Energy Tax Incentives Act of 2005 (P.L. 109-58)

P.L. 109-58, §1310(b)(2):

Amended Code Sec. 468A(d)(2)(A). **Effective** for tax years beginning after 12-31-2005. Prior to amendment, Code Sec. 468A(d)(2)(A) read as follows:

(A) fund that portion of the nuclear decommissioning costs of the taxpayer with respect to the nuclear powerplant which bears the same ratio to the total nuclear decommissioning costs with respect to such nuclear powerplant as the period for which the Fund is in effect bears to the estimated useful life of such nuclear powerplant, and

P.L. 109-58, §1310(c):

Amended Code Sec. 468A(d)(1) by adding at the end a new sentence. **Effective** for tax years beginning after 12-31-2005.

[Sec. 468A(e)]

(e) NUCLEAR DECOMMISSIONING RESERVE FUND.—

(1) IN GENERAL.—Each taxpayer who elects the application of this section shall establish a Nuclear Decommissioning Reserve Fund with respect to each nuclear powerplant to which such election applies.

(2) TAXATION OF FUND.—

(A) IN GENERAL.—There is hereby imposed on the gross income of the Fund for any taxable year a tax at the rate of 20 percent, except that—

(i) there shall not be included in the gross income of the Fund any payment to the Fund with respect to which a deduction is allowable under subsection (a), and

(ii) there shall be allowed as a deduction to the Fund any amount paid by the Fund which is described in paragraph (4)(B) (other than an amount paid to the taxpayer) and which would be deductible under this chapter for purposes of determining the taxable income of a corporation.

(B) TAX IN LIEU OF OTHER TAXATION.—The tax imposed by subparagraph (A) shall be in lieu of any other taxation under this subtitle of the income from assets in the Fund.

(C) FUND TREATED AS CORPORATION.—For purposes of subtitle F—

(i) the Fund shall be treated as if it were a corporation, and

(ii) any tax imposed by this paragraph shall be treated as a tax imposed by section 11.

(3) CONTRIBUTIONS TO FUND.—Except as provided in subsection (f), the Fund shall not accept any payments (or other amounts) other than payments with respect to which a deduction is allowable under subsection (a).

(4) USE OF FUND.—The Fund shall be used exclusively for—

(A) satisfying, in whole or in part, any liability of any person contributing to the Fund for the decommissioning of a nuclear powerplant (or unit thereof),

(B) to pay administrative costs (including taxes) and other incidental expenses of the Fund (including legal, accounting, actuarial, and trustee expenses) in connection with the operation of the Fund, and

(C) to the extent that a portion of the Fund is not currently needed for purposes described in subparagraph (A) or (B), making investments.

(5) PROHIBITIONS AGAINST SELF-DEALING.—Under regulations prescribed by the Secretary, for purposes of section 4951 (and so much of this title as relates to such section), the Fund shall be treated in the same manner as a trust described in section 501(c)(21).

(6) DISQUALIFICATION OF FUND.—In any case in which the Fund violates any provision of this section or section 4951, the Secretary may disqualify such Fund from the application of this section. In any case to which this paragraph applies, the Fund shall be treated as having distributed all of its funds on the date such determination takes effect.

(7) TERMINATION UPON COMPLETION.—Upon substantial completion of the nuclear decommissioning of the nuclear powerplant with respect to which a Fund relates, the taxpayer shall terminate such Fund.

Amendments

• 2005, Energy Tax Incentives Act of 2005 (P.L. 109-58)

P.L. 109-58, §1310(d):

Amended Code Sec. 468A(e)(3) by striking "The Fund" and inserting "Except as provided in subsection (f), the Fund". **Effective** for tax years beginning after 12-31-2005.

P.L. 109-58, §1310(e)(1)-(3):

Amended Code Sec. 468A(e)(2) by striking "rate set forth in subparagraph (B)" in subparagraph (A) and inserting "rate of 20 percent", by striking subparagraph (B), and by redesignating subparagraphs (C) and (D) as subparagraphs (B) and (C), respectively. **Effective** for tax years beginning after 12-31-2005. Prior to being stricken, Code Sec. 468A(e)(2)(B) read as follows:

(B) RATE OF TAX.—For purposes of subparagraph (A), the rate set forth in this subparagraph is—

(i) 22 percent in the case of taxable years beginning in calendar year 1994 or 1995, and

(ii) 20 percent in the case of taxable years beginning after December 31, 1995.

• 1992, Energy Policy Act of 1992 (P.L. 102-486)

P.L. 102-486, §1917(a):

Amended Code Sec. 468A(e)(4)(C) by striking "described in section 501(c)(21)(B)(ii)" after "making investments". **Effective** for tax years beginning after 12-31-92.

P.L. 102-486, §1917(b)(1)-(2) (as amended by P.L. 104-188, §1704(j)(6)):

Amended Code Sec. 468A(e)(2) by striking "at a rate equal to the highest rate of tax specified in section 11(b)" in subparagraph (A) and inserting "at the rate set forth in subparagraph (B)", and by redesignating subparagraphs (B) and (C) as subparagraphs (C) and (D), respectively, and by inserting after subparagraph (A) new subparagraph (B). **Effective** for tax years beginning after 12-31-93. Section 15 of the Internal Revenue Code of 1986 shall not apply to any change in rate resulting from the amendment made by subsection (b).

[Sec. 468A(f)]

(f) TRANSFERS INTO QUALIFIED FUNDS.—

(1) IN GENERAL.—Notwithstanding subsection (b), any taxpayer maintaining a Fund to which this section applies with respect to a nuclear power plant may transfer into such Fund not more than an amount equal to the present value of the portion of the total nuclear decommissioning costs with respect to such nuclear power plant previously excluded for such nuclear power plant under subsection (d)(2)(A) as in effect immediately before the date of the enactment of this subsection.

(2) DEDUCTION FOR AMOUNTS TRANSFERRED.—

(A) IN GENERAL.—Except as provided in subparagraph (C), the deduction allowed by subsection (a) for any transfer permitted by this subsection shall be allowed ratably over the remaining estimated useful life (within the meaning of subsection (d)(2)(A)) of the nuclear power plant beginning with the taxable year during which the transfer is made.

(B) DENIAL OF DEDUCTION FOR PREVIOUSLY DEDUCTED AMOUNTS.—No deduction shall be allowed for any transfer under this subsection of an amount for which a deduction was previously allowed to the taxpayer (or a predecessor) or a corresponding amount was not included in gross income of the taxpayer (or a predecessor). For purposes of the preceding sentence, a ratable portion of each transfer shall be treated as being from previously deducted or excluded amounts to the extent thereof.

(C) TRANSFERS OF QUALIFIED FUNDS.—If—

(i) any transfer permitted by this subsection is made to any Fund to which this section applies, and

(ii) such Fund is transferred thereafter,

any deduction under this subsection for taxable years ending after the date that such Fund is transferred shall be allowed to the transferor for the taxable year which includes such date.

(D) SPECIAL RULES.—

(i) GAIN OR LOSS NOT RECOGNIZED ON TRANSFERS TO FUND.—No gain or loss shall be recognized on any transfer described in paragraph (1).

(ii) TRANSFERS OF APPRECIATED PROPERTY TO FUND.—If appreciated property is transferred in a transfer described in paragraph (1), the amount of the deduction shall not exceed the adjusted basis of such property.

(3) NEW RULING AMOUNT REQUIRED.—Paragraph (1) shall not apply to any transfer unless the taxpayer requests from the Secretary a new schedule of ruling amounts in connection with such transfer.

(4) NO BASIS IN QUALIFIED FUNDS.—Notwithstanding any other provision of law, the taxpayer's basis in any Fund to which this section applies shall not be increased by reason of any transfer permitted by this subsection.

Amendments

• 2005, Energy Tax Incentives Act of 2005 (P.L. 109-58)

P.L. 109-58, §1310(b)(1):

Amended Code Sec. 468A by redesignating subsections (f) and (g) as subsections (g) and (h), respectively, and by inserting after subsection (e) a new subsection (f). **Effective** for tax years beginning after 12-31-2005.

[Sec. 468A(g)]

(g) NUCLEAR POWERPLANT.—For purpose of this section, the term "nuclear powerplant" includes any unit thereof.

Amendments

• 2005, Energy Tax Incentives Act of 2005 (P.L. 109-58)

P.L. 109-58, §1310(b)(1):

Amended Code Sec. 468A by redesignating subsection (f) as subsection (g). **Effective** for tax years beginning after 12-31-2005.

[Sec. 468A(h)]

(h) TIME WHEN PAYMENTS DEEMED MADE.—For purposes of this section, a taxpayer shall be deemed to have made a payment to the Fund on the last day of a taxable year if such payment is made on account of such taxable year and is made within 2½ months after the close of such taxable year.

Amendments

• 2005, Energy Tax Incentives Act of 2005 (P.L. 109-58)

P.L. 109-58, §1310(b)(1):

Amended Code Sec. 468A by redesignating subsection (g) as subsection (h). **Effective** for tax years beginning after 12-31-2005.

• 1986, Tax Reform Act of 1986 (P.L. 99-514)

P.L. 99-514, §1807(a)(4)(A)(i):

Amended Code Sec. 468A by adding at the end thereof new subsection (g). **Effective** as if included in the provision of P.L. 98-369 to which it relates. However, for a transitional rule, see Act Sec. 1807(a)(4)(A)(ii), below.

P.L. 99-514, §1807(a)(4)(A)(ii), provides:

(ii) TRANSITIONAL RULE.—To the extent provided in regulations prescribed by the Secretary of the Treasury or his delegate, subsection (g) of section 468A of the Internal Revenue Code of 1954 (as added by clause (i)) shall be applied with respect to any payment on account of a taxable year beginning before January 1, 1987, as if it did not contain the requirement that the payment be made within 2½ months after the close of the taxable year. Such regulations may provide that, to the extent such payment to the Fund is made more than 2½ months after the close of the taxable year, any adjustment to the tax attributable to such payment shall not affect the amount of interest payable with respect to periods before the payment is made. Such regulations may provide appropriate adjustments to the deduction allowed under such section 468A for any such taxable year to take into account the fact that the payment to the Fund is made more than 2½ months after the close of the taxable year.

P.L. 99-514, §1807(a)(4)(B):

Amended Code Sec. 468A(c)(1)(A) by striking out "subsection (e)(2)(B)" and inserting in lieu thereof "subsection (e)(4)(B)". **Effective** as if included in the provision of P.L. 98-369 to which it relates.

P.L. 99-514, §1807(a)(4)(C):

Amended Code Sec. 468A(e)(2). **Effective** as if included in the provision of P.L. 98-369 to which it relates. Prior to amendment, Code Sec. 468A(e)(2) read as follows:

(2) TAXATION OF FUND.—There is imposed on the gross income of the Fund for any taxable year a tax at a rate equal to the maximum rate in effect under section 11(b), except that—

(A) there shall not be included in the gross income of the Fund any payment to the Fund with respect to which a deduction is allowable under subsection (a), and

(B) there shall be allowed as a deduction any amount paid by the Fund described in paragraph (4)(B) (other than to the taxpayer).

P.L. 99-514, §1807(a)(4)(D):

Amended Code Sec. 468A(e)(4) by striking out "and" at the end of subparagraph (A), by striking out the period at the end of subparagraph (B) and inserting in lieu thereof, ", and", and by adding at the end thereof new subparagraph (C). **Effective** as if included in the provision of P.L. 98-369 to which it relates.

P.L. 99-514, §1807(a)(4)(E)(i):

Amended Code Sec. 468A(a) by striking out "this subsection" and inserting in lieu thereof "this section". **Effective** as if included in the provision of P.L. 98-369 to which it relates.

P.L. 99-514, §1807(a)(4)(E)(ii):

Amended Code Sec. 468A(d) by striking out "this subsection" in the material preceding paragraph (1) and inserting in lieu thereof "this section". **Effective** as if included in the provision of P.L. 98-369 to which it relates.

P.L. 99-514, §1807(a)(4)(E)(iii):

Amended Code Sec. 468A(e) by striking out "Trust Fund" in the subsection heading and inserting in lieu thereof "Reserve Fund". **Effective** as if included in the provision of P.L. 98-369 to which it relates.

P.L. 99-514, §1807(a)(4)(E)(vi)(I) and (II):

Amended Code Sec. 468A(e)(1) by striking out "this subsection" and inserting in lieu thereof "this section", and by striking out "Trust Fund" and inserting in lieu thereof "Reserve Fund". **Effective** as if included in the provision of P.L. 98-369 to which it relates.

P.L. 99-514, §1807(a)(4)(E)(v)(I) and (II):

Amended Code Sec. 468A(e)(6) by striking out "this subsection" each place it appears and inserting in lieu thereof "this section", and by striking out "this subparagraph" and inserting in lieu thereof "this paragraph". **Effective** as if included in the provision of P.L. 98-369 to which it relates.

P.L. 99-514, §1807(a)(4)(E)(vi):

Amended Code Sec. 468A(f) by striking out "The term" and inserting in lieu thereof "for purposes of this section, the term". **Effective** as if included in the provision of P.L. 98-369 to which it relates.

• 1984, Deficit Reduction Act of 1984 (P.L. 98-369)

P.L. 98-369, §91(c)(1):

Added Code Sec. 468A. **Effective** for amounts with respect to which a deduction would be allowable under chapter 1 of the Internal Revenue Code of 1954 (determined without regard to such amendments) after—

(A) in the case of amounts to which section 461(h) of such Code (as added by such amendments) applies, the date of the enactment of this Act, and

(B) in the case of amounts to which section 461(i) of such Code (as so added) applies, after 3-31-84. Special rules appear in the amendment notes following Code Sec. 468.

[Sec. 468B]

SEC. 468B. SPECIAL RULES FOR DESIGNATED SETTLEMENT FUNDS.

[Sec. 468B(a)]

(a) IN GENERAL.—For purposes of section 461(h), economic performance shall be deemed to occur as qualified payments are made by the taxpayer to a designated settlement fund.

[Sec. 468B(b)]

(b) TAXATION OF DESIGNATED SETTLEMENT FUND.—

(1) IN GENERAL.—There is imposed on the gross income of any designated settlement fund for any taxable year a tax at a rate equal to the maximum rate in effect for such taxable year under section 1(e).

(2) CERTAIN EXPENSES ALLOWED.—For purposes of paragraph (1), gross income for any taxable year shall be reduced by the amount of any administrative costs (including State and local taxes) and other incidental expenses of the designated settlement fund (including legal, accounting, and actuarial expenses)—

(A) which are incurred in connection with the operation of the fund, and

(B) which would be deductible under this chapter for purposes of determining the taxable income of a corporation.

No other deduction shall be allowed to the fund.

(3) TRANSFERS TO THE FUND.—In the case of any qualified payment made to the fund—

(A) the amount of such payment shall not be treated as income of the designated settlement fund,

(B) the basis of the fund in any property which constitutes a qualified payment shall be equal to the fair market value of such property at the time of payment, and

(C) the fund shall be treated as the owner of the property in the fund (and any earnings thereon).

(4) TAX IN LIEU OF OTHER TAXATION.—The tax imposed by paragraph (1) shall be in lieu of any other taxation under this subtitle of income from assets in the designated settlement fund.

(5) COORDINATION WITH SUBTITLE F.—For purposes of subtitle F—

(A) a designated settlement fund shall be treated as a corporation, and

(B) any tax imposed by this subsection shall be treated as a tax imposed by section 11.

Amendments

• 1988, Technical and Miscellaneous Revenue Act of 1988 (P.L. 100-647)

P.L. 100-647, §1018(f)(4)(A)-(B):

Amended Code Sec. 468B(b)(2) by striking out "the corporation," and inserting in lieu thereof "a corporation.", and by striking out "no other" and inserting in lieu thereof "No other". **Effective** as if included in the provision of P.L. 99-514 to which it relates.

[Sec. 468B(c)]

(c) DEDUCTIONS NOT ALLOWED FOR TRANSFER OF INSURANCE AMOUNTS.—No deduction shall be allowable for any qualified payment by the taxpayer of any amounts received from the settlement of any insurance claim to the extent such amounts are excluded from the gross income of the taxpayer.

[Sec. 468B(d)]

(d) DEFINITIONS.—For purposes of this section—

(1) QUALIFIED PAYMENT.—The term "qualified payment" means any money or property which is transferred to any designated settlement fund pursuant to a court order, other than—

(A) any amount which may be transferred from the fund to the taxpayer (or any related person), or

(B) the transfer of any stock or indebtedness of the taxpayer (or any related person).

(2) DESIGNATED SETTLEMENT FUND.—The term "designated settlement fund" means any fund—

(A) which is established pursuant to a court order and which extinguishes completely the taxpayer's tort liability with respect to claims described in subparagraph (D),

(B) with respect to which no amounts may be transferred other than in the form of qualified payments,

(C) which is administered by persons a majority of whom are independent of the taxpayer,

(D) which is established for the principal purpose of resolving and satisfying present and future claims against the taxpayer (or any related person or formerly related person) arising out of personal injury, death, or property damage,

(E) under the terms of which the taxpayer (or any related person) may not hold any beneficial interest in the income or corpus of the fund, and

(F) with respect to which an election is made under this section by the taxpayer.

An election under this section shall be made at such time and in such manner as the Secretary shall by regulation prescribe. Such an election, once made, may be revoked only with the consent of the Secretary.

(3) RELATED PERSON.—The term "related person" means a person related to the taxpayer within the meaning of section 267(b).

Amendments

• 1988, Technical and Miscellaneous Revenue Act of 1988 (P.L. 100-647)

P.L. 100-647, §1018(f)(2):

Amended Code Sec. 468B(d)(2)(A). **Effective** as if included in the provision of P.L. 99-514 to which it relates. Prior to amendment, Code Sec. 468B(d)(2)(A) read as follows:

(A) which is established pursuant to a court order,

P.L. 100-647, §1018(f)(1):

Amended Code Sec. 468B(d)(1)(A) and (2)(E) by striking out "the taxpayer" and inserting in lieu thereof "the taxpayer (or any related person)". **Effective** as if included in the provision of P.L. 99-514 to which it relates.

[Sec. 468B(e)]

(e) NONAPPLICABILITY OF SECTION.—This section (other than subsection (g)) shall not apply with respect to any liability of the taxpayer arising under any workers' compensation Act or any contested liability of the taxpayer within the meaning of section 461(f).

Amendments

• 1990, Omnibus Budget Reconciliation Act of 1990 (P.L. 101-508)

P.L. 101-508, §11702(e)(1):

Amended Code Sec. 468B(e) by striking "This section", and inserting "This section (other than subsection (g))". **Effective** as if included in the provision of P.L. 100-647 to which it relates.

[Sec. 468B(f)]

(f) OTHER FUNDS.—Except as provided in regulations, any payment in respect of a liability described in subsection (d)(2)(D) (and not described in subsection (e)) to a trust fund or escrow fund which is not a designated settlement fund shall not be treated as constituting economic performance.

Amendments

• 1986, Tax Reform Act of 1986 (P.L. 99-514)

P.L. 99-514, §1807(a)(7)(A):

Amended Subpart C of part II of subchapter E of chapter 1 by adding at the end thereof a new Code section 468B. **Effective** as if included in the provision of P.L. 98-369 to which it relates. For a special rule, see Act Sec. 1807(a)(7)(C), below.

P.L. 99-514, §1807(a)(7)(C), as amended by P.L. 100-647, §1018(f)(3) and (5)(B), provides:

(C) SPECIAL RULE FOR TAXPAYER IN BANKRUPTCY REORGANIZATION.—In the case of any settlement fund which is established for claimants against a corporation which filed a petition for reorganization under chapter 11 of title 11, United States Code, on August 26, 1982, and which filed with a United States district court a first amended and restated plan of reorganization before March 1, 1986—

(i) any portion of such fund which is established pursuant to a court order and with qualified payments, which meets the requirements of subparagraphs (C) and (D) of section 468B(d)(2) of the Internal Revenue Code of 1954 (as added by this paragraph), and with respect to which an election is made under subparagraph (F) thereof, shall be treated as a designated settlement fund for purposes of section 468B of such Code,

(ii) such corporation (or any successor thereof) shall be liable for the tax imposed by section 468B of such Code on such portion of the fund (and the fund shall not be liable for such tax), such tax shall be deductible by the corporation, and the rate of tax under section 468B of such Code for any taxable year shall be equal to 15 percent, and

(iii) any transaction by any portion of the fund not described in clause (i) shall be treated as a transaction made by the corporation.

[Sec. 468B(g)]

(g) CLARIFICATION OF TAXATION OF CERTAIN FUNDS.—

(1) IN GENERAL.—Except as provided in paragraph (2), nothing in any provision of law shall be construed as providing that an escrow account, settlement fund, or similar fund is not subject to current income tax. The Secretary shall prescribe regulations providing for the taxation of any such account or fund whether as a grantor trust or otherwise.

(2) EXEMPTION FROM TAX FOR CERTAIN SETTLEMENT FUNDS.—An escrow account, settlement fund, or similar fund shall be treated as beneficially owned by the United States and shall be exempt from taxation under this subtitle if—

(A) it is established pursuant to a consent decree entered by a judge of a United States District Court,

(B) it is created for the receipt of settlement payments as directed by a government entity for the sole purpose of resolving or satisfying one or more claims asserting liability under the Comprehensive Environmental Response, Compensation, and Liability Act of 1980,

(C) the authority and control over the expenditure of funds therein (including the expenditure of contributions thereto and any net earnings thereon) is with such government entity, and

(D) upon termination, any remaining funds will be disbursed to such government entity for use in accordance with applicable law.

For purposes of this paragraph, the term "government entity" means the United States, any State or political subdivision thereof, the District of Columbia, any possession of the United States, and any agency or instrumentality of any of the foregoing.

Amendments

• 2006, Tax Relief and Health Care Act of 2006 (P.L. 109-432)

P.L. 109-432, Division A, §409(a):

Amended Code Sec. 468B(g) by striking paragraph (3). **Effective** as if included in section 201 of the Tax Increase Prevention and Reconciliation Act of 2005 (P.L. 109-222) [**effective** for accounts and funds established after 5-17-2006.—CCH]. Prior to being stricken, Code Sec. 468B(g)(3) read as follows:

(3) TERMINATION.—Paragraph (2) shall not apply to accounts and funds established after December 31, 2010.

• 2006, Tax Increase Prevention and Reconciliation Act of 2005 (P.L. 109-222)

P.L. 109-222, §201(a):

Amended Code Sec. 468B(g). **Effective** for accounts and funds established after 5-17-2006. Prior to amendment, Code Sec. 468B(g) read as follows:

(g) CLARIFICATION OF TAXATION OF CERTAIN FUNDS.—Nothing in any provision of law shall be construed as providing that an escrow account, settlement fund, or similar fund is not subject to current income tax. The Secretary shall prescribe regulations providing for the taxation of any such account or fund whether as a grantor trust or otherwise.

• 1988, Technical and Miscellaneous Revenue Act of 1988 (P.L. 100-647)

P.L. 100-647, §1018(f)(5)(A):

Amended Code Sec. 468B by adding at the end thereof a new subsection (g). **Effective** as if included in the provision of P.L. 99-514 to which it relates.

[Sec. 469]

SEC. 469. PASSIVE ACTIVITY LOSSES AND CREDITS LIMITED.

[Sec. 469(a)]

(a) DISALLOWANCE.—

(1) IN GENERAL.—If for any taxable year the taxpayer is described in paragraph (2), neither—

(A) the passive activity loss, nor

(B) the passive activity credit,

for the taxable year shall be allowed.

(2) PERSONS DESCRIBED.—The following are described in this paragraph:

(A) any individual, estate, or trust,

(B) any closely held C corporation, and

(C) any personal service corporation.

[Sec. 469(b)]

(b) DISALLOWED LOSS OR CREDIT CARRIED TO NEXT YEAR.—Except as otherwise provided in this section, any loss or credit from an activity which is disallowed under subsection (a) shall be treated as a deduction or credit allocable to such activity in the next taxable year.

[Sec. 469(c)]

(c) PASSIVE ACTIVITY DEFINED.—For purposes of this section—

(1) IN GENERAL.—The term "passive activity" means any activity—

(A) which involves the conduct of any trade or business, and

(B) in which the taxpayer does not materially participate.

(2) PASSIVE ACTIVITY INCLUDES ANY RENTAL ACTIVITY.—Except as provided in paragraph (7), the term "passive activity" includes any rental activity.

(3) WORKING INTERESTS IN OIL AND GAS PROPERTY.—

(A) IN GENERAL.—The term "passive activity" shall not include any working interest in any oil or gas property which the taxpayer holds directly or through an entity which does not limit the liability of the taxpayer with respect to such interest.

(B) INCOME IN SUBSEQUENT YEARS.—If any taxpayer has any loss for any taxable year from a working interest in any oil or gas property which is treated as a loss which is not from a passive activity, then any net income from such property (or any property the basis of which is determined in whole or in part by reference to the basis of such property) for any succeeding taxable year shall be treated as income of the taxpayer which is not from a passive activity. If the preceding sentence applies to the net income from any property for any taxable year, any credits allowable under subpart B (other than section 27(a)) or D of part IV of subchapter A for such taxable year which are attributable to such property shall be treated as credits not from a passive activity to the extent the amount of such credits does not exceed the regular tax liability of the taxpayer for the taxable year which is allocable to such net income.

(4) MATERIAL PARTICIPATION NOT REQUIRED FOR PARAGRAPHS (2) AND (3).—Paragraphs (2) and (3) shall be applied without regard to whether or not the taxpayer materially participates in the activity.

(5) TRADE OR BUSINESS INCLUDES RESEARCH AND EXPERIMENTATION ACTIVITY.—For purposes of paragraph (1)(A), the term "trade or business" includes any activity involving research or experimentation (within the meaning of section 174).

(6) ACTIVITY IN CONNECTION WITH TRADE OR BUSINESS OR PRODUCTION OF INCOME.—To the extent provided in regulations, for purposes of paragraph (1)(A), the term "trade or business" includes—

(A) any activity in connection with a trade or business, or

(B) any activity with respect to which expenses are allowable as a deduction under section 212.

(7) SPECIAL RULES FOR TAXPAYERS IN REAL PROPERTY BUSINESS.—

(A) IN GENERAL.—If this paragraph applies to any taxpayer for a taxable year—

(i) paragraph (2) shall not apply to any rental real estate activity of such taxpayer for such taxable year, and

(ii) this section shall be applied as if each interest of the taxpayer in rental real estate were a separate activity.

Notwithstanding clause (ii), a taxpayer may elect to treat all interests in rental real estate as one activity. Nothing in the preceding provisions of this subparagraph shall be construed as affecting the determination of whether the taxpayer materially participates with respect to any interest in a limited partnership as a limited partner.

(B) TAXPAYERS TO WHOM PARAGRAPH APPLIES.—This paragraph shall apply to a taxpayer for a taxable year if—

(i) more than one-half of the personal services performed in trades or businesses by the taxpayer during such taxable year are performed in real property trades or businesses in which the taxpayer materially participates, and

(ii) such taxpayer performs more than 750 hours of services during the taxable year in real property trades or businesses in which the taxpayer materially participates.

In the case of a joint return, the requirements of the preceding sentence are satisfied if and only if either spouse separately satisfies such requirements. For purposes of the preceding sentence, activities in which a spouse materially participates shall be determined under subsection (h).

(C) REAL PROPERTY TRADE OR BUSINESS.—For purposes of this paragraph, the term "real property trade or business" means any real property development, redevelopment, construction, reconstruction, acquisition, conversion, rental, operation, management, leasing, or brokerage trade or business.

(D) SPECIAL RULES FOR SUBPARAGRAPH (B).—

(i) CLOSELY HELD C CORPORATIONS.—In the case of a closely held C corporation, the requirements of subparagraph (B) shall be treated as met for any taxable year if more than 50 percent of the gross receipts of such corporation for such taxable year are derived from real property trades or businesses in which the corporation materially participates.

(ii) PERSONAL SERVICES AS AN EMPLOYEE.—For purposes of subparagraph (B), personal services performed as an employee shall not be treated as performed in real property trades or businesses. The preceding sentence shall not apply if such employee is a 5-percent owner (as defined in section 416(i)(1)(B)) in the employer.

Amendments

• 1996, Small Business Job Protection Act of 1996 (P.L. 104-188)

P.L. 104-188, §1704(d)(1):

Amended Code Sec. 469(c)(3)(B) by adding at the end thereof a new sentence. **Effective** for tax years beginning after 12-31-86.

• 1993, Omnibus Budget Reconciliation Act of 1993 (P.L. 103-66)

P.L. 103-66, §13143(a):

Amended Code Sec. 469(c) by adding at the end thereof new paragraph (7). **Effective** for tax years beginning after 12-31-93.

P.L. 103-66, §13143(b)(1):

Amended Code Sec. 469(c)(2) by striking "The" and inserting "Except as provided in paragraph (7), the". **Effective** for tax years beginning after 12-31-93.

[Sec. 469(d)]

(d) PASSIVE ACTIVITY LOSS AND CREDIT DEFINED.—For purposes of this section—

(1) PASSIVE ACTIVITY LOSS.—The term "passive activity loss" means the amount (if any) by which—

(A) the aggregate losses from all passive activities for the taxable year, exceed

(B) the aggregate income from all passive activities for such year.

(2) PASSIVE ACTIVITY CREDIT.—The term "passive activity credit" means the amount (if any) by which—

(A) the sum of the credits from all passive activities allowable for the taxable year under—

(i) subpart D of part IV of subchapter A, or

(ii) subpart B (other than section 27(a)) of such part IV, exceeds

(B) the regular tax liability of the taxpayer for the taxable year allocable to all passive activities.

[Sec. 469(e)]

(e) SPECIAL RULES FOR DETERMINING INCOME OR LOSS FROM A PASSIVE ACTIVITY.—For purposes of this section—

(1) CERTAIN INCOME NOT TREATED AS INCOME FROM PASSIVE ACTIVITY.—In determining the income or loss from any activity—

(A) IN GENERAL.—There shall not be taken into account—

(i) any—

(I) gross income from interest, dividends, annuities, or royalties not derived in the ordinary course of a trade or business,

(II) expenses (other than interest) which are clearly and directly allocable to such gross income, and

(III) interest expense properly allocable to such gross income, and

(ii) gain or loss not derived in the ordinary course of a trade or business which is attributable to the disposition of property—

(I) producing income of a type described in clause (i), or

(II) held for investment.

For purposes of clause (ii), any interest in a passive activity shall not be treated as property held for investment.

(B) RETURN ON WORKING CAPITAL.—For purposes of subparagraph (A), any income, gain, or loss which is attributable to an investment of working capital shall be treated as not derived in the ordinary course of a trade or business.

(2) PASSIVE LOSSES OF CERTAIN CLOSELY HELD CORPORATIONS MAY OFFSET ACTIVE INCOME.—

(A) IN GENERAL.—If a closely held C corporation (other than a personal service corporation) has net active income for any taxable year, the passive activity loss of such taxpayer for such taxable year (determined without regard to this paragraph)—

(i) shall be allowable as a deduction against net active income, and

(ii) shall not be taken into account under subsection (a) to the extent so allowable as a deduction.

A similar rule shall apply in the case of any passive activity credit of the taxpayer.

(B) NET ACTIVE INCOME.—For purposes of this paragraph, the term "net active income" means the taxable income of the taxpayer for the taxable year determined without regard to—

(i) any income or loss from a passive activity, and

(ii) any item of gross income, expense, gain, or loss described in paragraph (1)(A).

(3) COMPENSATION FOR PERSONAL SERVICES.—Earned income (within the meaning of section 911(d)(2)(A)) shall not be taken into account in computing the income or loss from a passive activity for any taxable year.

(4) DIVIDENDS REDUCED BY DIVIDENDS RECEIVED DEDUCTION.—For purposes of paragraphs (1) and (2), income from dividends shall be reduced by the amount of any dividends received deduction under section 243, 244 or 245.

Amendments

• 1988, Technical and Miscellaneous Revenue Act of 1988 (P.L. 100-647)

P.L. 100-647, §1005(a)(1):

Amended Code Sec. 469(e)(1)(A)(ii) by inserting "not derived in the ordinary course of a trade or business which is" after "gain or loss". **Effective** as if included in the provision of P.L. 99-514 to which it relates.

P.L. 100-647, §1005(c)(13), provides:

(13) For purposes of applying the amendments made by this subsection and the amendments made by section 10102 of the Revenue Act of 1987, the provisions of this subsection shall be treated as having been enacted immediately before the enactment of the Revenue Act of 1987.

[Sec. 469(f)]

(f) TREATMENT OF FORMER PASSIVE ACTIVITIES.—For purposes of this section—

(1) IN GENERAL.—If an activity is a former passive activity for any taxable year—

(A) any unused deduction allocable to such activity under subsection (b) shall be offset against the income from such activity for the taxable year,

(B) any unused credit allocable to such activity under subsection (b) shall be offset against the regular tax liability (computed after the application of paragraph (1)) allocable to such activity for the taxable year, and

(C) any such deduction or credit remaining after the application of subparagraphs (A) and (B) shall continue to be treated as arising from a passive activity.

(2) CHANGE IN STATUS OF CLOSELY HELD C CORPORATION OR PERSONAL SERVICE CORPORATION.—If a taxpayer ceases for any taxable year to be a closely held C corporation or personal service corporation, this section shall continue to apply to losses and credits to which this section applied for any preceding taxable year in the same manner as if such taxpayer continued to be a closely held C corporation or personal service corporation, whichever is applicable.

(3) FORMER PASSIVE ACTIVITY.—The term "former passive activity" means any activity which, with respect to the taxpayer—

(A) is not a passive activity for the taxable year, but

(B) was a passive activity for any prior taxable year.

[Sec. 469(g)]

(g) DISPOSITIONS OF ENTIRE INTEREST IN PASSIVE ACTIVITY.—If during the taxable year a taxpayer disposes of his entire interest in any passive activity (or former passive activity), the following rules shall apply:

(1) FULLY TAXABLE TRANSACTION.—

(A) IN GENERAL.—If all gain or loss realized on such disposition is recognized, the excess of—

(i) any loss from such activity for such taxable year (determined after the application of subsection (b)), over

(ii) any net income or gain for such taxable year from all other passive activities (determined after the application of subsection (b)),

shall be treated as a loss which is not from a passive activity.

(B) SUBPARAGRAPH (A) NOT TO APPLY TO DISPOSITION INVOLVING RELATED PARTY.—If the taxpayer and the person acquiring the interest bear a relationship to each other described in section 267(b) or section 707(b)(1), then subparagraph (A) shall not apply to any loss of the taxpayer until the taxable year in which such interest is acquired (in a transaction described in subparagraph (A)) by another person who does not bear such a relationship to the taxpayer.

(C) INCOME FROM PRIOR YEARS.—To the extent provided in regulations, income or gain from the activity for preceding taxable years shall be taken into account under subparagraph (A)(ii) for the taxable year to the extent necessary to prevent the avoidance of this section.

(2) DISPOSITION BY DEATH.—If an interest in the activity is transferred by reason of the death of the taxpayer—

(A) paragraph (1)(A) shall apply to losses described in paragraph (1)(A) to the extent such losses are greater than the excess (if any) of—

(i) the basis of such property in the hands of the transferee, over

(ii) the adjusted basis of such property immediately before the death of the taxpayer, and

(B) any losses to the extent of the excess described in subparagraph (A) shall not be allowed as a deduction for any taxable year.

(3) INSTALLMENT SALE OF ENTIRE INTEREST.—In the case of an installment sale of an entire interest in an activity to which section 453 applies, paragraph (1) shall apply to the portion of such losses for each taxable year which bears the same ratio to all such losses as the gain recognized on such sale during such taxable year bears to the gross profit from such sale (realized or to be realized when payment is completed).

Amendments

• 1996, Small Business Job Protection Act of 1996 (P.L. 104-188)

P.L. 104-188, §1704(e)(1):

Amended Code Sec. 469(g)(1)(A). **Effective** for tax years beginning after 12-31-86. Prior to amendment, Code Sec. 469(g)(1)(A) read as follows:

(A) IN GENERAL.—If all gain or loss realized on such disposition is recognized, the excess of—

(i) the sum of—

(I) any loss from such activity for such taxable year (determined after application of subsection (b)), plus

(II) any loss realized on such disposition, over

(ii) net income or gain for such taxable year from all passive activities (determined without regard to losses described in clause (i)),

shall be treated as a loss which is not from a passive activity.

• 1988, Technical and Miscellaneous Revenue Act of 1988 (P.L. 100-647)

P.L. 100-647, §1005(a)(2)(A):

Amended Code Sec. 469(g)(1)(A). **Effective** as if included in the provision of P.L. 99-514 to which it relates. Prior to amendment, Code Sec. 469(g)(1)(A) read as follows:

(A) IN GENERAL.—If all gain or loss realized on such disposition is recognized, any loss from such activity which has not previously been allowed as a deduction (and in the case of a passive activity for the taxable year, any loss realized on such disposition) shall not be treated as a passive activity loss and shall be allowable as a deduction against income in the following order:

(i) Income or gain from the passive activity for the taxable year (including any gain recognized on the disposition).

(ii) Net income or gain for the taxable year from all passive activities.

(iii) Any other income or gain.

P.L. 100-647, §1005(a)(2)(B):

Amended Code Sec. 469(g)(1)(C). **Effective** as if included in the provision of P.L. 99-514 to which it relates. Prior to amendment, Code Sec. 469(g)(1)(C) read as follows:

(C) COORDINATION WITH SECTION 1211.—In the case of any loss realized on the disposition of an interest in a passive activity, section 1211 shall be applied before subparagraph (A) is applied.

P.L. 100-647, §1005(a)(3)(A)-(B):

Amended Code Sec. 469(g)(2)(A) by striking out "paragraph (1)" and inserting in lieu thereof "paragraph (1)(A)"; and by striking out "such losses" the first place it appears and inserting in lieu thereof "losses described in paragraph (1)(A)". **Effective** as if included in the provision of P.L. 99-514 to which it relates.

P.L. 100-647, §1005(a)(4)(A)-(B):

Amended Code Sec. 469(g)(3) by striking out "realized (or to be realized)" and inserting in lieu thereof "(realized or to be realized", and by inserting a closing parenthesis after "completed". **Effective** as if included in the provision of P.L. 99-514 to which it relates.

P.L. 100-647, §1005(c)(13), provides:

(13) For purposes of applying the amendments made by this subsection and the amendments made by section 10102 of the Revenue Act of 1987, the provisions of this subsection shall be treated as having been enacted immediately before the enactment of the Revenue Act of 1987.

[Sec. 469(h)]

(h) MATERIAL PARTICIPATION DEFINED.—For purposes of this section—

(1) IN GENERAL.—A taxpayer shall be treated as materially participating in an activity only if the taxpayer is involved in the operations of the activity on a basis which is—

(A) regular,

(B) continuous, and

(C) substantial.

(2) INTERESTS IN LIMITED PARTNERSHIPS.—Except as provided in regulations, no interest in a limited partnership as a limited partner shall be treated as an interest with respect to which a taxpayer materially participates.

(3) TREATMENT OF CERTAIN RETIRED INDIVIDUALS AND SURVIVING SPOUSES.—A taxpayer shall be treated as materially participating in any farming activity for a taxable year if paragraph (4) or (5) of section 2032A(b) would cause the requirements of section 2032A(b)(1)(C)(ii) to be met with respect to real property used in such activity if such taxpayer had died during the taxable year.

(4) CERTAIN CLOSELY HELD C CORPORATIONS AND PERSONAL SERVICE CORPORATIONS.—A closely held C corporation or personal service corporation shall be treated as materially participating in an activity only if—

(A) 1 or more shareholders holding stock representing more than 50 percent (by value) of the outstanding stock of such corporation materially participate in such activity, or

(B) in the case of a closely held C corporation (other than a personal service corporation), the requirements of section 465(c)(7)(C) (without regard to clause (iv)) are met with respect to such activity.

(5) PARTICIPATION BY SPOUSE.—In determining whether a taxpayer materially participates, the participation of the spouse of the taxpayer shall be taken into account.

Amendments

• 1988, Technical and Miscellaneous Revenue Act of 1988 (P.L. 100-647)

P.L. 100-647, §1005(a)(5):

Amended Code Sec. 469(h)(4) by inserting "only" before "if". **Effective** as if included in the provision of P.L. 99-514 to which it relates.

P.L. 100-647, §1005(c)(13), provides:

(13) For purposes of applying the amendments made by this subsection and the amendments made by section 10102 of the Revenue Act of 1987, the provisions of this subsection shall be treated as having been enacted immediately before the enactment of the Revenue Act of 1987.

[Sec. 469(i)]

(i) $25,000 OFFSET FOR RENTAL REAL ESTATE ACTIVITIES.—

(1) IN GENERAL.—In the case of any natural person, subsection (a) shall not apply to that portion of the passive activity loss or the deduction equivalent (within the meaning of subsection (j)(5)) of the passive activity credit for any taxable year which is attributable to all rental real estate activities with respect to which such individual actively participated in such taxable year (and if any portion of such loss or credit arose in another taxable year, in such other taxable year).

(2) DOLLAR LIMITATION.—The aggregate amount to which paragraph (1) applies for any taxable year shall not exceed $25,000.

(3) PHASE-OUT OF EXEMPTION.—

(A) IN GENERAL.—In the case of any taxpayer, the $25,000 amount under paragraph (2) shall be reduced (but not below zero) by 50 percent of the amount by which the adjusted gross income of the taxpayer for the taxable year exceeds $100,000.

(B) SPECIAL PHASE-OUT OF REHABILITATION CREDIT.—In the case of any portion of the passive activity credit for any taxable year which is attributable to the rehabilitation credit determined under section 47, subparagraph (A) shall be applied by substituting "$200,000" for "$100,000".

(C) EXCEPTION FOR COMMERCIAL REVITALIZATION DEDUCTION.—Subparagraph (A) shall not apply to any portion of the passive activity loss for any taxable year which is attributable to the commercial revitalization deduction under section 1400I.

(D) EXCEPTION FOR LOW-INCOME HOUSING CREDIT.—Subparagraph (A) shall not apply to any portion of the passive activity credit for any taxable year which is attributable to any credit determined under section 42.

(E) ORDERING RULES TO REFLECT EXCEPTIONS AND SEPARATE PHASE-OUTS.—If subparagraph (B), (C), or (D) applies for a taxable year, paragraph (1) shall be applied—

(i) first to the portion of the passive activity loss to which subparagraph (C) does not apply,

→ Caution: Code Sec. 469(i)(3)(E)(ii)-(iv), below, was amended by P.L. 107-147, effective as if included in P.L. 107-16, and is subject to the sunset provision of the Economic Growth and Tax Relief Reconciliation Act of 2001 (P.L. 107-16), §901. Absent Congressional action, the changes made to this provision by P.L. 107-16, or that take effect as if included in P.L. 107-16, do not apply after December 31, 2010. For more information about the sunset provision, see page XXI of the Preface to this publication and P.L. 107-16, §901, in the amendment notes. See the amendments notes for a history of amendments to this section and the effective date of each change.

(ii) second to the portion of such loss to which subparagraph (C) applies,

(iii) third to the portion of the passive activity credit to which subparagraph (B) or (D) does not apply,

(iv) fourth to the portion of such credit to which subparagraph (B) applies, and

(v) then to the portion of such credit to which subparagraph (D) applies.

(F) ADJUSTED GROSS INCOME.—For purposes of this paragraph, adjusted gross income shall be determined without regard to—

(i) any amount includible in gross income under section 86,

(ii) the amounts excludable from gross income under sections 135 and 137,

→ Caution: Code Sec. 469(i)(3)(F)(iii), below, is subject to the sunset provision of the Economic Growth and Tax Relief Reconciliation Act of 2001 (P.L. 107-16), §901. Absent Congressional action, the changes made to this provision by P.L. 107-16, or that take effect as if included in P.L. 107-16, do not apply after December 31, 2010. For more information about the sunset provision, see page XXI of the Preface to this publication and P.L. 107-16, §901, in the amendment notes. See the amendments notes for a history of amendments to this section and the effective date of each change.

(iii) the amounts allowable as a deduction under sections 199, 219, 221, and 222 and

(iv) any passive activity loss or any loss allowable by reason of subsection (c)(7).

(4) SPECIAL RULE FOR ESTATES.—

(A) IN GENERAL.—In the case of taxable years of an estate ending less than 2 years after the date of the death of the decedent, this subsection shall apply to all rental real estate activities with respect to which such decedent actively participated before his death.

(B) REDUCTION FOR SURVIVING SPOUSE'S EXEMPTION.—For purposes of subparagraph (A), the $25,000 amount under paragraph (2) shall be reduced by the amount of the exemption under paragraph (1) (without regard to paragraph (3)) allowable to the surviving spouse of the decedent for the taxable year ending with or within the taxable year of the estate.

(5) MARRIED INDIVIDUALS FILING SEPARATELY.—

(A) IN GENERAL.—Except as provided in subparagraph (B), in the case of any married individual filing a separate return, this subsection shall be applied by substituting—

(i) "$12,500" for "$25,000" each place it appears,

(ii) "$50,000" for "$100,000" in paragraph (3)(A), and

(iii) "$100,000" for "$200,000" in paragraph (3)(B).

(B) TAXPAYERS NOT LIVING APART.—This subsection shall not apply to a taxpayer who—

(i) is a married individual filing a separate return for any taxable year, and

(ii) does not live apart from his spouse at all times during such taxable year.

(6) ACTIVE PARTICIPATION.—

(A) IN GENERAL.—An individual shall not be treated as actively participating with respect to any interest in any rental real estate activity for any period if, at any time during such period, such interest (including any interest of the spouse of the individual) is less than 10 percent (by value) of all interests in such activity.

(B) NO PARTICIPATION REQUIREMENT FOR LOW-INCOME HOUSING, REHABILITATION CREDIT, OR COMMERCIAL REVITALIZATION DEDUCTION.—Paragraphs (1) and (4)(A) shall be applied without regard to the active participation requirement in the case of—

(i) any credit determined under section 42 for any taxable year,

(ii) any rehabilitation credit determined under section 47, or

(iii) any deduction under section 1400I (relating to commercial revitalization deduction).

(C) INTEREST AS A LIMITED PARTNER.—Except as provided in regulations, no interest as a limited partner in a limited partnership shall be treated as an interest with respect to which the taxpayer actively participates.

(D) PARTICIPATION BY SPOUSE.—In determining whether a taxpayer actively participates, the participation of the spouse of the taxpayer shall be taken into account.

Amendments

• 2004, American Jobs Creation Act of 2004 (P.L. 108-357)

P.L. 108-357, §102(d)(5):

Amended Code Sec. 469(i)(3)(F)(iii) by inserting "199," before"219,". **Effective** for tax years beginning after 12-31-2004.

• 2002, Job Creation and Worker Assistance Act of 2002 (P.L. 107-147)

P.L. 107-147, §412(a):

Amended Code Sec. 469(i)(3)(E) by striking clauses (ii)-(iv) and inserting new clauses (ii)-(iv). **Effective** as if included in the provision of P.L. 106-554 to which it relates [**effective** 12-21-2000.—CCH]. Prior to amendment, Code Sec. 469(i)(3)(E)(ii)-(iv) read as follows:

(ii) second to the portion of the passive activity credit to which subparagraph (B) or (D) does not apply,

(iii) third to the portion of such credit to which subparagraph (B) applies,

(iv) fourth to the portion of such loss to which subparagraph (C) applies, and

• 2001, Economic Growth and Tax Relief Reconciliation Act of 2001 (P.L. 107-16)

P.L. 107-16, §431(c)(3):

Amended Code Sec. 469(i)(3)(F)[(iii)] by striking "and 221" and inserting ", 221, and 222". **Effective** for payments made in tax years beginning after 12-31-2001.

P.L. 107-16, §901(a)-(b), provides:

SEC. 901. SUNSET OF PROVISIONS OF ACT.

(a) IN GENERAL.—All provisions of, and amendments made by, this Act shall not apply—

(1) to taxable, plan, or limitation years beginning after December 31, 2010, or

(2) in the case of title V, to estates of decedents dying, gifts made, or generation skipping transfers, after December 31, 2010.

(b) APPLICATION OF CERTAIN LAWS.—The Internal Revenue Code of 1986 and the Employee Retirement Income Security Act of 1974 shall be applied and administered to years, estates, gifts, and transfers described in subsection (a) as if the provisions and amendments described in subsection (a) had never been enacted.

• 2000, Community Renewal Tax Relief Act of 2000 (P.L. 106-554)

P.L. 106-554, §101(b)(1):

Amended Code Sec. 469(i)(3) by redesignating subparagraphs (C), (D), and (E) as subparagraphs (D), (E), and (F), respectively, and by inserting after subparagraph (B) a new subparagraph (C). **Effective** 12-21-2000.

P.L. 106-554, §101(b)(2):

Amended Code Sec. 469(i)(3)(E), as resdesignated by Act Sec. 101(b)(1)(A) [Act Sec. 101(b)(1)]. **Effective** 12-21-2000. Prior to amendment, Code Sec. 469(i)(3)(E) read as follows:

(E) ORDERING RULES TO REFLECT EXCEPTION AND SEPARATE PHASE-OUT.—If subparagraph (B) or (C) applies for any taxable year, paragraph (1) shall be applied—

(i) first to the passive activity loss,

(ii) second to the portion of the passive activity credit to which subparagraph (B) or (C) does not apply,

(iii) third to the portion of such credit to which subparagraph (B) applies, and

(iv) then to the portion of such credit to which subparagraph (C) applies.

P.L. 106-554, §101(b)(3)(A):

Amended Code Sec. 469(i)(6)(B) by striking "or" at the end of clause (i), by striking the period at the end of clause (ii) and inserting ", or", and by adding at the end a new clause (iii). **Effective** 12-21-2000.

P.L. 106-554, §101(b)(3)(B):

Amended the heading for Code Sec. 469(i)(6)(B) by striking "OR REHABILITATION CREDIT" and inserting ", REHABILITATION CREDIT, OR COMMERCIAL REVITALIZATION DEDUCTION". **E ffective** 12-21-2000.

• 1998, Tax and Trade Relief Extension Act of 1998 (P.L. 105-277)

P.L. 105-277, §4003(a)(2)(D):

Amended Code Sec. 469(i)(3)(E)(iii). **Effective** as if included in the provision of P.L. 105-34 to which it relates [generally **effective** for interest payments due and paid after 12-31-97, on any qualified education loan.—CCH]. Prior to amendment, Code Sec. 469(i)(3)(E)(iii) read as follows:

(iii) any amount allowable as a deduction under section 219, and

• 1996, Small Business Job Protection Act of 1996 (P.L. 104-188)

P.L. 104-188, §1807(c)(4):

Amended Code Sec. 469(i)(3)(E)(ii). **Effective** for tax years beginning after 12-31-96. Prior to amendment, Code Sec. 469(i)(3)(E)(ii) read as follows:

(ii) the amount excludable from gross income under section 135,

• 1993, Omnibus Budget Reconciliation Act of 1993 (P.L. 103-66)

P.L. 103-66, §13143(b)(2):

Amended Code Sec. 469(i)(3)(E)(iv) by inserting "or any loss allowable by reason of subsection (c)(7)" after "loss". **Effective** for tax years beginning after 12-31-93.

• **1990, Omnibus Budget Reconciliation Act of 1990 (P.L. 101-508)**

P.L. 101-508, §11813(b)(16)(A):

Amended Code Sec. 469(i) by striking "rehabilitation investment credit (within the meaning of section 48(o))" and inserting "rehabilitation credit determined under section 47" in paragraphs (3)(B) and (6)(B)(ii). **Effective**, generally, for property placed in service after 12-31-90. However, for exceptions, see Act Sec. 11813(c)(2), below.

P.L. 101-508, §11813(c)(2), provides:

(2) EXCEPTIONS.—The amendments made by this section shall not apply to—

(A) any transition property (as defined in section 49(e) of the Internal Revenue Code of 1986 (as in effect on the day before the date of the enactment of this Act),

(B) any property with respect to which qualified progress expenditures were previously taken into account under section 46(d) of such Code (as so in effect), and

(C) any property described in section 46(b)(2)(C) of such Code (as so in effect).

• **1989, Omnibus Budget Reconciliation Act of 1989 (P.L. 101-239)**

P.L. 101-239, §7109(a):

Amended Code Sec. 469(i)(3) by redesignating subparagraph (D) as subparagraph (E) and by striking out subparagraphs (B) and (C) and inserting new subparagraphs (B)-(D). For the **effective** date, see Act Sec. 7109(b)(1)-(2) below. Prior to amendment, Code Sec. 469(i)(3)(B)-(C) read as follows:

(B) SPECIAL PHASE-OUT OF LOW-INCOME HOUSING AND REHABILITATION CREDITS.—In the case of any portion of the passive activity credit for any taxable year which is attributable to any credit to which paragraph (6)(b) applies, subparagraph (A) shall be applied by substituting "$200,000" for "$100,000".

(C) ORDERING RULE TO REFLECT SEPARATE PHASE-OUTS.—If subparagraph (B) applies for any taxable year, paragraph (1) shall be applied—

(i) first to the passive activity loss,

(ii) second to the portion of the passive activity credit to which subparagraph (B) does not apply, and

(iii) then to the portion of such credit to which subparagraph (B) applies.

P.L. 101-239, §7109(b)(1)-(2), provides:

(b) EFFECTIVE DATE.—

(1) IN GENERAL.—Except as provided in paragraph (2), the amendments made by this section shall apply to property placed in service after December 31, 1989, in taxable years ending after such date.

(2) SPECIAL RULE WHERE INTEREST HELD IN PASS-THRU ENTITY.—In the case of a taxpayer who holds an indirect interest in property described in paragraph (1), the amendment made by this section shall apply only if such interest is acquired after December 31, 1989.

• **1988, Technical and Miscellaneous Revenue Act of 1988 (P.L. 100-647)**

P.L. 100-647, §1005(a)(6):

Amended Code Sec. 469(i)(1) by striking out "in the taxable year in which such portion of such loss or credit arose" and inserting in lieu thereof "in such taxable year (and if any portion of such loss or credit arose in another taxable year, in such other taxable year)". **Effective** as if included in the provision of P.L. 99-514 to which it relates.

P.L. 100-647, §1005(a)(7):

Amended Code Sec. 469(i)(6)(C) by striking out "No" and inserting in lieu thereof "Except as provided in regulations, no". **Effective** as if included in the provision of P.L. 99-514 to which it relates.

P.L. 100-647, §1005(c)(13), provides:

(13) For purposes of applying the amendments made by this subsection and the amendments made by section 10102 of the Revenue Act of 1987, the provisions of this subsection shall be treated as having been enacted immediately before the enactment of the Revenue Act of 1987.

P.L. 100-647, §6009(c)(3):

Amended Code Sec. 469(i)(3)(D) by redesignating clauses (ii) and (iii) as clauses (iii) and (iv), respectively, and by inserting after clause (i) new clause (ii). **Effective** for tax years beginning after 12-31-89.

[Sec. 469(j)]

(j) OTHER DEFINITIONS AND SPECIAL RULES.—For purposes of this section—

(1) CLOSELY HELD C CORPORATION.—The term "closely held C corporation" means any C corporation described in section 465(a)(1)(B).

(2) PERSONAL SERVICE CORPORATION.—The term "personal service corporation" has the meaning given such term by section 269A(b)(1), except that section 269A(b)(2) shall be applied—

(A) by substituting "any" for "more than 10 percent", and

(B) by substituting "any" for "50 percent or more in value" in section 318(a)(2)(C).

A corporation shall not be treated as a personal service corporation unless more than 10 percent of the stock (by value) in such corporation is held by employee-owners (within the meaning of section 269A(b)(2), as modified by the preceding sentence).

(3) REGULAR TAX LIABILITY.—The term "regular tax liability" has the meaning given such term by section 26(b).

(4) ALLOCATION OF PASSIVE ACTIVITY LOSS AND CREDIT.—The passive activity loss and the passive activity credit (and the $25,000 amount under subsection (i)) shall be allocated to activities, and within activities, on a pro rata basis in such manner as the Secretary may prescribe.

(5) DEDUCTION EQUIVALENT.—The deduction equivalent of credits from a passive activity for any taxable year is the amount which (if allowed as a deduction) would reduce the regular tax liability for such taxable year by an amount equal to such credits.

(6) SPECIAL RULE FOR GIFTS.—In the case of a disposition of any interest in a passive activity by gift—

(A) the basis of such interest immediately before the transfer shall be increased by the amount of any passive activity losses allocable to such interest with respect to which a deduction has not been allowed by reason of subsection (a), and

(B) such losses shall not be allowable as a deduction for any taxable year.

(7) QUALIFIED RESIDENCE INTEREST.—The passive activity loss of a taxpayer shall be computed without regard to qualified residence interest (within the meaning of section 163(h)(3)).

(8) RENTAL ACTIVITY.—The term "rental activity" means any activity where payments are principally for the use of tangible property.

(9) ELECTION TO INCREASE BASIS OF PROPERTY BY AMOUNT OF DISALLOWED CREDIT.—For purposes of determining gain or loss from a disposition of any property to which subsection (g)(1) applies, the transferor may elect to increase the basis of such property immediately before the transfer by an amount equal to the portion of any unused credit allowable under this chapter which reduced the basis of such property for the taxable year in which such credit arose. If the taxpayer elects the application of this paragraph, such portion of the passive activity credit of such taxpayer shall not be allowed for any taxable year.

(10) COORDINATION WITH SECTION 280A.—If a passive activity involves the use of a dwelling unit to which section 280A(c)(5) applies for any taxable year, any income, deduction, gain, or loss allocable to such use shall not be taken into account for purposes of this section for such taxable year.

(11) AGGREGATION OF MEMBERS OF AFFILIATED GROUPS.—Except as provided in regulations, all members of an affiliated group which files a consolidated return shall be treated as 1 corporation.

(12) SPECIAL RULE FOR DISTRIBUTIONS BY ESTATES OR TRUSTS.—If any interest in a passive activity is distributed by an estate or trust—

(A) the basis of such interest immediately before such distribution shall be increased by the amount of any passive activity losses allocable to such interest, and

(B) such losses shall not be allowable as a deduction for any taxable year.

Amendments

• 1988, Technical and Miscellaneous Revenue Act of 1988 (P.L. 100-647)

P.L. 100-647, §1005(a)(8):

Amended Code Sec. 469(j)(6)(A) by inserting "with respect to which a deduction has not been allowed by reason of subsection (a)" before ", and". **Effective** as if included in the provision of P.L. 99-514 to which it relates.

P.L. 100-647, §1005(a)(9):

Amended Code Sec. 469(j) by adding at the end thereof new paragraphs (10) and (11). **Effective** as if included in the provision of P.L. 99-514 to which it relates.

P.L. 100-647, §1005(a)(11):

Amended Code Sec. 469(j) by adding at the end thereof new paragraph 12. **Effective** as if included in the provision of P.L. 99-514 to which it relates.

P.L. 100-647, §1005(c)(13), provides:

(13) For purposes of applying the amendments made by this subsection and the amendments made by section 10102 of the Revenue Act of 1987, the provisions of this subsection shall be treated as having been enacted immediately before the enactment of the Revenue Act of 1987.

[Sec. 469(k)]

(k) SEPARATE APPLICATION OF SECTION IN CASE OF PUBLICLY TRADED PARTNERSHIPS.—

(1) IN GENERAL.—This section shall be applied separately with respect to items attributable to each publicly traded partnership (and subsection (i) shall not apply with respect to items attributable to any such partnership). The preceding sentence shall not apply to any credit determined under section 42, or any rehabilitation credit determined under section 47, attributable to a publicly traded partnership to the extent the amount of any such credits exceeds the regular tax liability attributable to income from such partnership.

(2) PUBLICLY TRADED PARTNERSHIP.—For purposes of this section, the term "publicly traded partnership" means any partnership if—

(A) interests in such partnership are traded on an established securities market, or

(B) interests in such partnership are readily tradable on a secondary market (or the substantial equivalent thereof).

(3) COORDINATION WITH SUBSECTION (g).—For purposes of subsection (g), a taxpayer shall not be treated as having disposed of his entire interest in an activity of a publicly traded partnership until he disposes of his entire interest in such partnership.

(4) APPLICATION TO REGULATED INVESTMENT COMPANIES.—For purposes of this section, a regulated investment company (as defined in section 851) holding an interest in a qualified publicly traded partnership (as defined in section 851(h)) shall be treated as a taxpayer described in subsection (a)(2) with respect to items attributable to such interest.

Amendments

• 2004, American Jobs Creation Act of 2004 (P.L. 108-357)

P.L. 108-357, §331(g):

Amended Code Sec. 469(k) by adding at the end a new paragraph (4). **Effective** for tax years beginning after 10-22-2004.

• 1990, Omnibus Budget Reconciliation Act of 1990 (P.L. 101-508)

P.L. 101-508, §11813(b)(16)(B):

Amended Code Sec. 469(k)(1) by striking "rehabilitation investment credit (within the meaning of section 48(o))" and inserting "rehabilitation credit determined under section 47". **Effective**, generally, for property placed in service after 12-31-90. However, for exceptions, see Act Sec. 11813(c)(2) in the amendment notes following Code Sec. 469(i).

• 1988, Technical and Miscellaneous Revenue Act of 1988 (P.L. 100-647)

P.L. 100-647, §2004:

Amended Code Sec. 469(k) by adding at the end thereof a new paragraph (3). **Effective** as if included in the provision of P.L. 100-203 to which it relates.

• 1987, Revenue Act of 1987 (P.L. 100-203)

P.L. 100-203, §10212(a):

Amended Code Sec. 469 by redesignating subsections (k) and (l) as subsections (l) and (m), respectively, and by inserting after subsection (j) new subsection (k). **Effective** as if included in the amendments made by Act Sec. 501 of P.L. 99-514.

[Sec. 469(l)]

(l) REGULATIONS.—The Secretary shall prescribe such regulations as may be necessary or appropriate to carry out provisions of this section, including regulations—

(1) which specify what constitutes an activity, material participation, or active participation for purposes of this section,

(2) which provide that certain items of gross income will not be taken into account in determining income or loss from any activity (and the treatment of expenses allocable to such income),

(3) requiring net income or gain from a limited partnership or other passive activity to be treated as not from a passive activity,

(4) which provide for the determination of the allocation of interest expense for purposes of this section, and

(5) which deal with changes in marital status and changes between joint returns and separate returns.

Amendments

• 1987, Revenue Act of 1987 (P.L. 100-203)

P.L. 100-203, §10212(a):

Amended Code Sec. 469 by redesignating subsections (k) and (l) as subsections (l) and (m), respectively, and by inserting after subsection (j) new subsection (k). **Effective** as if included in the amendments made by Act Sec. 501 of P.L. 99-514.

[Sec. 469(m)]

(m) PHASE-IN OF DISALLOWANCE OF LOSSES AND CREDITS FOR INTEREST HELD BEFORE DATE OF ENACTMENT.—

(1) IN GENERAL.—In the case of any passive activity loss or passive activity credit for any taxable year beginning in calendar years 1987 through 1990, subsection (a) shall not apply to the applicable percentage of that portion of such loss (or such credit) which is attributable to pre-enactment interests.

(2) APPLICABLE PERCENTAGE.—For purposes of this subsection, the applicable percentage shall be determined in accordance with the following table:

In the case of taxable years beginning in:	*The applicable percentage is:*
1987	65
1988	40
1989	20
1990	10

(3) PORTION OF LOSS OR CREDIT ATTRIBUTABLE TO PRE-ENACTMENT INTERESTS.—For purposes of this subsection—

(A) IN GENERAL.—The portion of the passive activity loss (or passive activity credit) for any taxable year which is attributable to pre-enactment interests is the lesser of—

(i) the amount of the passive activity loss (or passive activity credit) which is disallowed for the taxable year under subsection (a) (without regard to this subsection), or

(ii) the amount of the passive activity loss (or passive activity credit) which would be disallowed for the taxable year (without regard to this subsection and without regard to any amount allocable to an activity for the taxable year under subsection (b)) taking into account only pre-enactment interests.

(B) PRE-ENACTMENT INTEREST.—

(i) IN GENERAL.—The term "pre-enactment interest" means any interest in a passive activity held by a taxpayer on the date of the enactment of the Tax Reform Act of 1986, and at all times thereafter.

(ii) BINDING CONTRACT EXCEPTION.—For purposes of clause (i), any interest acquired after such date of enactment pursuant to a written binding contract in effect on such date, and at all times thereafter, shall be treated as held on such date.

(iii) INTEREST IN ACTIVITIES.—The term "pre-enactment interest" shall not include an interest in a passive activity unless such activity was being conducted on such date of enactment. The preceding sentence shall not apply to an activity commencing after such date if—

(I) the property used in such activity is acquired pursuant to a written binding contract in effect on August 16, 1986, and at all times thereafter, or

(II) construction of property used in such activity began on or before August 16, 1986.

Amendments

• 1990, Omnibus Budget Reconciliation Act of 1990 (P.L. 101-508)

P.L. 101-508, §11704(a)(6):

Amended Code Sec. 469(m)(3)(A) by striking "preenactment" and inserting "pre-enactment". **Effective** 11-5-90.

• 1988, Technical and Miscellaneous Revenue Act of 1988 (P.L. 100-647)

P.L. 100-647, §1005(a)(12):

Amended Code Sec. 469(m) by striking out all that precedes subparagraph (B) of paragraph (3) and inserting new material preceding subparagraph (B) of paragraph (3). **Effective** as if included in the provision of P.L. 99-514 to which it relates. Prior to amendment, the material preceding subparagraph (B) of paragraph (3) read as follows:

(m) PHASE-IN OF DISALLOWANCE OF LOSSES AND CREDITS FOR INTERESTS HELD BEFORE DATE OF ENACTMENT.—

(1) IN GENERAL.—In the case of any passive activity loss or credit for any taxable year beginning in calendar years 1987 through 1990 which—

(A) is attributable to a pre-enactment interest, but

(B) is not attributable to a carryforward to such taxable year of any loss or credit which was disallowed under this section for a preceding taxable year,

there shall be disallowed under subsection (a) only the applicable percentage of the amount which (but for this subsection) would have been disallowed under subsection (a) for such taxable year.

(2) APPLICABLE PERCENTAGE.—For purposes of this subsection, the applicable percentage shall be determined in accordance with the following table:

In the case of taxable years beginning in:	*The applicable percentage is:*
1987	35
1988	60
1989	80
1990	90

(3) PORTION OF LOSS OR CREDIT ATTRIBUTABLE TO PRE-ENACTMENT INTERESTS.—For purposes of this subsection—

(A) IN GENERAL.—The portion of the passive activity loss for any taxable year which is attributable to pre-enactment interests shall be equal to the lesser of—

(i) the passive activity loss for such taxable year, or

(ii) the passive activity loss for such taxable year determined by taking into account only pre-enactment interests.

For purposes of this subparagraph, the deduction equivalent (within the meaning of subsection (j)(5)) of a passive activity credit shall be taken into account.

P.L. 100-647, §1005(c)(13), provides:

(13) For purposes of applying the amendments made by this subsection and the amendments made by section 10102 of the Revenue Act of 1987, the provisions of this subsection shall be treated as having been enacted immediately before the enactment of the Revenue Act of 1987.

• 1987, Revenue Act of 1987 (P.L. 100-203)

P.L. 100-203, §10212(a):

Amended Code Sec. 469 by redesignating subsections (k) and (l) as subsections (l) and (m), respectively, and by inserting after subsection (j) new subsection (k). **Effective** as if included in the amendments made by Act Sec. 501 of P.L. 99-514.

• 1986, Tax Reform Act of 1986 (P.L. 99-514)

P.L. 99-514, §501(a):

Amended subpart C of part II of subchapter E of chapter 1 by adding at the end thereof new Code Sec. 469. **Effective**, generally, for tax years beginning after 12-31-86. For special rules, see Act Sec. 501(c)(2)-(3), below. For a transitional rule, see Act Sec. 502, below.

P.L. 99-514, §501(c)(2)-(3), as amended by P.L. 100-647, §§1005(a)(10) and 4003(b)(2), provides:

(2) SPECIAL RULE FOR CARRYOVERS.—The amendments made by this section shall not apply to any loss, deduction, or credit carried to a taxable year beginning after December 31, 1986, from a taxable year beginning before January 1, 1987.

(4)[(3)] INCOME FROM SALES OF PASSIVE ACTIVITIES IN TAXABLE YEARS BEGINNING BEFORE JANUARY 1, 1987.—If—

(A) gain is recognized in a taxable year beginning after December 31, 1986, from a sale or exchange of an interest in an activity in a taxable year beginning before January 1, 1987, and

(B) such gain would have been treated as gain from a passive activity had section 469 of the Internal Revenue Code of 1986 (as added by this section) been in effect for the taxable year in which the sale or exchange occurred and for all succeeding taxable years,

then such gain shall be treated as gain from a passive activity for purposes of such section.

P.L. 99-514, §502, as amended by P.L. 99-509, §8073(a), provides:

SEC. 502. TRANSITIONAL RULE FOR LOW-INCOME HOUSING.

(a) GENERAL RULE.—Any loss sustained by a qualified investor with respect to an interest in a qualified low-income housing project for any taxable year in the relief period shall not be treated as a loss from a passive activity for purposes of section 469 of the Internal Revenue Code of 1986.

(b) RELIEF PERIOD.—For purposes of subsection (a), the term "relief period" means the period beginning with the taxable year in which the investor made his initial investment in the qualified low-income housing project and ending with whichever of the following is the earliest—

(1) the 6th taxable year after the taxable year in which the investor made his initial investment,

(2) the 1st taxable year after the taxable year in which the investor is obligated to make his last investment, or

(3) the taxable year preceding the 1st taxable year for which such project ceased to be a qualified low-income housing project.

(c) QUALIFIED LOW-INCOME HOUSING PROJECT.—For purposes of this section, the term "qualified low-income housing project" means any project if—

(1) such project meets the requirements of clause (i), (ii), (iii), or (iv) of section 1250(a)(1)(B) as of the date placed in service and for each taxable year thereafter which begins after 1986 and for which a passive loss may be allowable with respect to such project,

(2) the operator certifies to the Secretary of the Treasury or his delegate that such project met the requirements of paragraph (1) on the date of the enactment of this Act (or, if later, when placed in service) and annually thereafter,

(3) such project is constructed or acquired pursuant to a binding written contract entered into on or before August 16, 1986, and

(4) such project is placed in service before January 1, 1989.

(d) QUALIFIED INVESTOR.—For purposes of this section—

(1) IN GENERAL.—The term "qualified investor" means any natural person who holds (directly or through 1 or more entities) an interest in a qualified low-income housing project,

(A) if—

(i) in the case of a project placed in service on or before August 16, 1986, such person held an interest in such project on August 16, 1986, and such person made his initial investment after December 31, 1983, or

(ii) in the case of a project placed in service after August 16, 1986, such person made his initial investment after December 31, 1983, and such person held an interest in such project on December 31, 1986.

(B) if such investor is required to make payments after December 31, 1986, of 50 percent or more of the total original obligated investment for such interest.

For purposes of subparagraph (A), a person shall be treated as holding an interest on August 16, 1986, or December 31, 1986, if on such date such person had a binding contract to acquire such interest.

(2) TREATMENT OF ESTATES.—The estate of a decedent shall succeed to the treatment under this section of the decedent but only with respect to the 1st 2 taxable years of such estate ending after the date of the decedent's death.

(3) SPECIAL RULE FOR CERTAIN PARTNERSHIPS.—In the case of any property which is held by a partnership—

(A) which placed such property in service on or after December 31, 1985, and before August 17, 1986, and continuously held such property through the close of the taxable year for which the determination is being made, and

(B) which was not treated as a new partnership or as terminated at any time on or after the date on which such property was placed in service and through the close of the taxable year for which the determination is being made,

paragraph (1)(A)(i) shall be applied by substituting "December 31, 1988" for "August 16, 1986" the 2nd place it appears.

(4) SPECIAL RULE FOR CERTAIN RURAL HOUSING.—In the case of any interest in a qualified low-income housing project which—

(A) is assisted under section 515 of the Housing Act of 1949 (relating to the Farmers' Home Administration Program), and

(B) is located in a town with a population of less than 10,000 and which is not part of a metropolitan statistical area,

paragraph (1)(B) shall be applied by substituting "35 percent" for "50 percent" and subsection (b)(1) shall be applied by substituting "5th taxable year" for "6th taxable year". The preceding sentence shall not apply to any interest unless, on December 31, 1986, at least one-half of the number of payments required with respect to such interest remain to be paid.

(e) SPECIAL RULES.—

(1) WHERE MORE THAN 1 BUILDING IN PROJECT.—If there is more than 1 building in any project, the determination of when such project is placed in service shall be based on when the 1st building in such project is placed in service.

(2) ONLY CASH AND OTHER PROPERTY TAKEN INTO ACCOUNT.—In determining the amount any person invests in (or is obligated to invest in) any interest, only cash and other property shall be taken into account.

(3) COORDINATION WITH CREDIT.—No low-income housing credit shall be determined under section 42 of the Internal Revenue Code of 1986 with respect to any project with respect to which any person has been allowed any benefit under this section.

[Sec. 470]

SEC. 470. LIMITATION ON DEDUCTIONS ALLOCABLE TO PROPERTY USED BY GOVERNMENTS OR OTHER TAX-EXEMPT ENTITIES.

[Sec. 470(a)]

(a) LIMITATION ON LOSSES.—Except as otherwise provided in this section, a tax-exempt use loss for any taxable year shall not be allowed.

[Sec. 470(b)]

(b) DISALLOWED LOSS CARRIED TO NEXT YEAR.—Any tax-exempt use loss with respect to any tax-exempt use property which is disallowed under subsection (a) for any taxable year shall be treated as a deduction with respect to such property in the next taxable year.

[Sec. 470(c)]

(c) DEFINITIONS.—For purposes of this section—

(1) TAX-EXEMPT USE LOSS.—The term "tax-exempt use loss" means, with respect to any taxable year, the amount (if any) by which—

(A) the sum of—

(i) the aggregate deductions (other than interest) directly allocable to a tax-exempt use property, plus

(ii) the aggregate deductions for interest properly allocable to such property, exceed

(B) the aggregate income from such property.

(2) TAX-EXEMPT USE PROPERTY.—

(A) IN GENERAL.—The term "tax-exempt use property" has the meaning given to such term by section 168(h), except that such section shall be applied—

(i) without regard to paragraphs (1)(C) and (3) thereof, and

(ii) as if section 197 intangible property (as defined in section 197), and property described in paragraph (1)(B) or (2) of section 167(f), were tangible property.

(B) EXCEPTION FOR PARTNERSHIPS.—Such term shall not include any property which would (but for this subparagraph) be tax-exempt use property solely by reason of section 168(h)(6).

(C) CROSS REFERENCE.—For treatment of partnerships as leases to which section 168(h) applies, see section 7701(e).

Amendments

• 2007, Tax Technical Corrections Act of 2007 (P.L. 110-172)

P.L. 110-172, §7(c)(1):

Amended Code Sec. 470(c)(2). **Effective** as if included in the provision of the American Jobs Creation Act of 2004 (P.L. 108-357) to which it relates [**effective** generally for leases entered into after 3-12-2004, and in the case of property treated as tax-exempt use property other than by reason of a lease, to property acquired after 3-12-2004. For an exception, see P.L. 108-357, §849(b), in the amendment notes for Code Sec. 470(g).—CCH]. Prior to amendment, Code Sec. 470(c)(2) read as follows:

(2) TAX-EXEMPT USE PROPERTY.—The term "tax-exempt use property" has the meaning given to such term by section 168(h), except that such section shall be applied—

(A) without regard to paragraphs (1)(C) and (3) thereof, and

(B) as if property described in—

(i) section 167(f)(1)(B),

(ii) section 167(f)(2), and

(iii) section 197 intangible,

were tangible property.

Such term shall not include property which would (but for this sentence) be tax-exempt use property solely by reason of section 168(h)(6) if any credit is allowable under section 42 or 47 with respect to such property.

[Sec. 470(d)]

(d) EXCEPTION FOR CERTAIN LEASES.—This section shall not apply to any lease of property which meets the requirements of all of the following paragraphs:

(1) AVAILABILITY OF FUNDS.—

(A) IN GENERAL.—A lease of property meets the requirements of this paragraph if (at all times during the lease term) not more than an allowable amount of funds are—

(i) subject to any arrangement referred to in subparagraph (B), or

(ii) set aside or expected to be set aside,

to or for the benefit of the lessor or any lender, or to or for the benefit of the lessee to satisfy the lessee's obligations or options under the lease. For purposes of clause (ii), funds shall be treated as set aside or expected to be set aside only if a reasonable person would conclude, based on the facts and circumstances, that such funds are set aside or expected to be set aside.

(B) ARRANGEMENTS.—The arrangements referred to in this subparagraph include a defeasance arrangement, a loan by the lessee to the lessor or any lender, a deposit arrangement, a letter of credit collateralized with cash or cash equivalents, a payment undertaking agreement, prepaid rent (within the meaning of the regulations under section 467), a sinking fund arrangement, a guaranteed investment contract, financial guaranty insurance, and any similar arrangement (whether or not such arrangement provides credit support).

(C) ALLOWABLE AMOUNT.—

(i) IN GENERAL.—Except as otherwise provided in this subparagraph, the term "allowable amount" means an amount equal to 20 percent of the lessor's adjusted basis in the property at the time the lease is entered into.

(ii) HIGHER AMOUNT PERMITTED IN CERTAIN CASES.—To the extent provided in regulations, a higher percentage shall be permitted under clause (i) where necessary because of the credit-worthiness of the lessee. In no event may such regulations permit a percentage of more than 50 percent.

(iii) OPTION TO PURCHASE.—If under the lease the lessee has the option to purchase the property for a fixed price or for other than the fair market value of the property (determined at the time of exercise), the allowable amount at the time such option may be exercised may not exceed 50 percent of the price at which such option may be exercised.

(iv) NO ALLOWABLE AMOUNT FOR CERTAIN ARRANGEMENTS.—The allowable amount shall be zero with respect to any arrangement which involves—

(I) a loan from the lessee to the lessor or a lender,

(II) any deposit received, letter of credit issued, or payment undertaking agreement entered into by a lender otherwise involved in the transaction, or

(III) in the case of a transaction which involves a lender, any credit support made available to the lessor in which any such lender does not have a claim that is senior to the lessor.

For purposes of subclause (I), the term "loan" shall not include any amount treated as a loan under section 467 with respect to a section 467 rental agreement.

(2) LESSOR MUST MAKE SUBSTANTIAL EQUITY INVESTMENT.—

(A) IN GENERAL.—A lease of property meets the requirements of this paragraph if—

(i) the lessor—

(I) has at the time the lease is entered into an unconditional at-risk equity investment (as determined by the Secretary) in the property of at least 20 percent of the lessor's adjusted basis in the property as of that time, and

(II) maintains such investment throughout the term of the lease, and

(ii) the fair market value of the property at the end of the lease term is reasonably expected to be equal to at least 20 percent of such basis.

(B) RISK OF LOSS.—For purposes of clause (ii), the fair market value at the end of the lease term shall be reduced to the extent that a person other than the lessor bears a risk of loss in the value of the property.

(C) PARAGRAPH NOT TO APPLY TO SHORT-TERM LEASES.—This paragraph shall not apply to any lease with a lease term of 5 years or less.

(3) LESSEE MAY NOT BEAR MORE THAN MINIMAL RISK OF LOSS.—

(A) IN GENERAL.—A lease of property meets the requirements of this paragraph if there is no arrangement under which the lessee bears—

(i) any portion of the loss that would occur if the fair market value of the leased property were 25 percent less than its reasonably expected fair market value at the time the lease is terminated, or

(ii) more than 50 percent of the loss that would occur if the fair market value of the leased property at the time the lease is terminated were zero.

(B) EXCEPTION.—The Secretary may by regulations provide that the requirements of this paragraph are not met where the lessee bears more than a minimal risk of loss.

(C) PARAGRAPH NOT TO APPLY TO SHORT-TERM LEASES.—This paragraph shall not apply to any lease with a lease term of 5 years or less.

(4) PROPERTY WITH MORE THAN 7-YEAR CLASS LIFE.—In the case of a lease—

(A) of property with a class life (as defined in section 168(i)(1)) of more than 7 years, other than fixed-wing aircraft and vessels, and

(B) under which the lessee has the option to purchase the property,

the lease meets the requirements of this paragraph only if the purchase price under the option equals the fair market value of the property (determined at the time of exercise).

Amendments

• 2007, Tax Technical Corrections Act of 2007 (P.L. 110-172)

P.L. 110-172, §7(c)(2):

Amended Code Sec. 470(d)(1)(A) by striking "(at any time during the lease term)" and inserting "(at all times during the lease term)". **Effective** as if included in the provision of the American Jobs Creation Act of 2004 (P.L. 108-357) to which it relates [**effective** generally for leases entered into after 3-12-2004, and in the case of property treated as tax-exempt use property other than by reason of a lease, to property acquired after 3-12-2004. For an exception, see P.L. 108-357, §849(b), in the amendment notes for Code Sec. 470(g).—CCH].

[Sec. 470(e)]

(e) SPECIAL RULES.—

(1) TREATMENT OF FORMER TAX-EXEMPT USE PROPERTY.—

(A) IN GENERAL.—In the case of any former tax-exempt use property—

(i) any deduction allowable under subsection (b) with respect to such property for any taxable year shall be allowed only to the extent of any net income (without regard to such deduction) from such property for such taxable year, and

(ii) any portion of such unused deduction remaining after application of clause (i) shall be treated as a deduction allowable under subsection (b) with respect to such property in the next taxable year.

(B) FORMER TAX-EXEMPT USE PROPERTY.—For purposes of this subsection, the term "former tax-exempt use property" means any property which—

(i) is not tax-exempt use property for the taxable year, but

(ii) was tax-exempt use property for any prior taxable year.

(2) DISPOSITION OF ENTIRE INTEREST IN PROPERTY.—If during the taxable year a taxpayer disposes of the taxpayer's entire interest in tax-exempt use property (or former tax-exempt use property), rules similar to the rules of section 469(g) shall apply for purposes of this section.

(3) COORDINATION WITH SECTION 469 .—This section shall be applied before the application of section 469.

(4) COORDINATION WITH SECTIONS 1031 AND 1033.—

(A) IN GENERAL.—Sections 1031(a) and 1033(a) shall not apply if—

(i) the exchanged or converted property is tax-exempt use property subject to a lease which was entered into before March 13, 2004, and which would not have met the requirements of subsection (d) had such requirements been in effect when the lease was entered into, or

(ii) the replacement property is tax-exempt use property subject to a lease which does not meet the requirements of subsection (d).

(B) ADJUSTED BASIS.—In the case of property acquired by the lessor in a transaction to which section 1031 or 1033 applies, the adjusted basis of such property for purposes of this section shall be equal to the lesser of—

(i) the fair market value of the property as of the beginning of the lease term, or

(ii) the amount which would be the lessor's adjusted basis if such sections did not apply to such transaction.

[Sec. 470(f)]

(f) OTHER DEFINITIONS.—For purposes of this section—

(1) RELATED PARTIES.—The terms "lessor", "lessee", and "lender" each include any related party (within the meaning of section 197(f)(9)(C)(i)).

(2) LEASE TERM.—The term "lease term" has the meaning given to such term by section 168(i)(3).

(3) LENDER.—The term "lender" means, with respect to any lease, a person that makes a loan to the lessor which is secured (or economically similar to being secured) by the lease or the leased property.

(4) LOAN.—The term "loan" includes any similar arrangement.

[Sec. 470(g)]

(g) REGULATIONS.—The Secretary shall prescribe such regulations as may be necessary or appropriate to carry out the purposes of this section, including regulations which—

(1) allow in appropriate cases the aggregation of property subject to the same lease, and

(2) provide for the determination of the allocation of interest expense for purposes of this section.

Amendments

• 2004, American Jobs Creation Act of 2004 (P.L. 108-357)

P.L. 108-357, §848(a):

Amended subpart C of part II of subchapter E of chapter 1 by adding at the end a new Code Sec. 470. **Effective** generally for leases entered into after 3-12-2004, and in the case of property treated as tax-exempt use property other than by reason of a lease, to property acquired after 3-12-2004 [effective date amended by P.L. 109-135, §403(ff)]. For an exception, see Act Sec. 849(b), below.

P.L. 108-357, §849(b), provides:

(b) EXCEPTION.—

(1) IN GENERAL.—The amendments made by this part shall not apply to qualified transportation property.

(2) QUALIFIED TRANSPORTATION PROPERTY.—For purposes of paragraph (1), the term "qualified transportation property" means domestic property subject to a lease with respect to which a formal application—

(A) was submitted for approval to the Federal Transit Administration (an agency of the Department of Transportation) after June 30, 2003, and before March 13, 2004,

(B) is approved by the Federal Transit Administration before January 1, 2006, and

(C) includes a description of such property and the value of such property.

(3) EXCHANGES AND CONVERSION OF TAX-EXEMPT USE PROPERTY.—Section 470(e)(4) of the Internal Revenue Code of 1986, as added by section 848, shall apply to property exchanged or converted after the date of the enactment of this Act [10-22-2004.—CCH].

(4) INTANGIBLES AND INDIAN TRIBAL GOVERNMENTS.—The amendments made subsections (b)(2), (b)(3), and (e) of section 847, and the treatment of property described in clauses (ii) and (iii) of section 470(c)(2)(B) of the Internal Revenue Code of 1986 (as added by section 848) as tangible property, shall apply to leases entered into after October 3, 2004.

Subpart D—Inventories

[Sec. 471]

SEC. 471. GENERAL RULE FOR INVENTORIES.

[Sec. 471(a)]

(a) GENERAL RULE.—Whenever in the opinion of the Secretary the use of inventories is necessary in order clearly to determine the income of any taxpayer, inventories shall be taken by such taxpayer on such basis as the Secretary may prescribe as conforming as nearly as may be to the best accounting practice in the trade or business and as most clearly reflecting the income.

[Sec. 471(b)]

(b) ESTIMATES OF INVENTORY SHRINKAGE PERMITTED.—A method of determining inventories shall not be treated as failing to clearly reflect income solely because it utilizes estimates of inventory shrinkage that are confirmed by a physical count only after the last day of the taxable year if—

(1) the taxpayer normally does a physical count of inventories at each location on a regular and consistent basis, and

(2) the taxpayer makes proper adjustments to such inventories and to its estimating methods to the extent such estimates are greater than or less than the actual shrinkage.

Amendments

• 1997, Taxpayer Relief Act of 1997 (P.L. 105-34)

P.L. 105-34, §961(a):

Amended Code Sec. 471 by redesignating subsection (b) as subsection (c) and by inserting after subsection (a) a new subsection (b). **Effective**, generally, for tax years ending after 8-5-97. For a special rule, see Act Sec. 961(b)(2)(A)-(C), below.

P.L. 105-34, §961(b)(2)(A)-(C), provides:

(2) COORDINATION WITH SECTION 481.—In the case of any taxpayer permitted by this section to change its method of accounting to a permissible method for any taxable year—

(A) such changes shall be treated as initiated by the taxpayer,

(B) such changes shall be treated as made with the consent of the Secretary of the Treasury, and

(C) the period for taking into account the adjustments under section 481 by reason of such change shall be 4 years.

[Sec. 471(c)]

(c) CROSS REFERENCE.—

For rules relating to capitalization of direct and indirect costs of property, see section 263A.

Amendments

• 1997, Taxpayer Relief Act of 1997 (P.L. 105-34)

P.L. 105-34, §961(a):

Amended Code Sec. 471 by redesignating subsection (b) as subsection (c). **Effective**, generally, for tax years ending 8-5-97. For a special rule, see Act Sec. 961(b)(2)(A)-(C) in the amendment notes following Code Sec. 471(b).

• 1986, Tax Reform Act of 1986 (P.L. 99-514)

P.L. 99-514, §803(b)(4)(A)-(B):

Amended Code Sec. 471 by striking out "Whenever" and inserting in lieu thereof "(a) GENERAL RULE.—Whenever", and by adding at the end thereof new subsection (b). **Effective** for costs incurred after 12-31-86, in tax years ending after such date. However, see special and transitional rules following Code Sec. 263A.

• 1976, Tax Reform Act of 1976 (P.L. 94-455)

P.L. 94-455, §1906(b)(13)(A):

Amended 1954 Code by substituting "Secretary" for "Secretary or his delegate" each place it appeared. **Effective** 2-1-77.

[Sec. 472]

SEC. 472. LAST-IN, FIRST-OUT INVENTORIES.

[Sec. 472(a)]

(a) AUTHORIZATION.—A taxpayer may use the method provided in subsection (b) (whether or not such method has been prescribed under section 471) in inventorying goods specified in an application to use such method filed at such time and in such manner as the Secretary may prescribe. The change to, and the use of, such method shall be in accordance with such regulations as the Secretary may prescribe as necessary in order that the use of such method may clearly reflect income.

Amendments

• 1976, Tax Reform Act of 1976 (P.L. 94-455)

P.L. 94-455, §1906(b)(13)(A):

Amended 1954 Code by substituting "Secretary" for "Secretary or his delegate" each place it appeared. **Effective** 2-1-77.

[Sec. 472(b)]

(b) METHOD APPLICABLE.—In inventorying goods specified in the application described in subsection (a), the taxpayer shall:

(1) Treat those remaining on hand at the close of the taxable year as being: First, those included in the opening inventory of the taxable year (in the order of acquisition) to the extent thereof; and second, those acquired in the taxable year;

(2) Inventory them at cost; and

(3) Treat those included in the opening inventory of the taxable year in which such method is first used as having been acquired at the same time and determine their cost by the average cost method.

[Sec. 472(c)]

(c) CONDITION.—Subsection (a) shall apply only if the taxpayer establishes to the satisfaction of the Secretary that the taxpayer has used no procedure other than that specified in paragraphs (1) and (3) of subsection (b) in inventorying such goods to ascertain the income, profit, or loss of the first taxable year for which the method described in subsection (b) is to be used, for the purpose of a report or statement covering such taxable year—

(1) to shareholders, partners, or other proprietors, or to beneficiaries, or

(2) for credit purposes.

Amendments

• 1976, Tax Reform Act of 1976 (P.L. 94-455)

P.L. 94-455, §1906(b)(13)(A):

Amended 1954 Code by substituting "Secretary" for "Secretary or his delegate" each place it appeared. **Effective** 2-1-77.

[Sec. 472(d)]

(d) 3-YEAR AVERAGING FOR INCREASES IN INVENTORY VALUE.—The beginning inventory for the first taxable year for which the method described in subsection (b) is used shall be valued at cost. Any change in the inventory amount resulting from the application of the preceding sentence shall be taken into account ratably in each of the 3 taxable years beginning with the first taxable year for which the method described in subsection (b) is first used.

Amendments

• 1981, Economic Recovery Tax Act of 1981 (P.L. 97-34)

P.L. 97-34, §236(a):

Amended Code Sec. 472(d). **Effective** for tax years beginning after 12-31-81. Prior to amendment, Code Sec. 472(d) read as follows:

(d) PRECEDING CLOSING INVENTORY.—In determining income for the taxable year preceding the taxable year for which the method described in subsection (b) is first used, the closing inventory of such preceding year of the goods specified in the application referred to in subsection (a) shall be at cost.

[Sec. 472(e)]

(e) SUBSEQUENT INVENTORIES.—If a taxpayer, having complied with subsection (a), uses the method described in subsection (b) for any taxable year, then such method shall be used in all subsequent taxable years unless—

(1) with the approval of the Secretary a change to a different method is authorized; or,

(2) the Secretary determines that the taxpayer has used for any such subsequent taxable year some procedure other than that specified in paragraph (1) of subsection (b) in inventorying the goods specified in the application to ascertain the income, profit, or loss of such subsequent taxable year for the purpose of a report or statement covering such taxable year (A) to shareholders, partners, or other proprietors, or beneficiaries, or (B) for credit purposes; and requires a change to a method different from that prescribed in subsection (b) beginning with such subsequent taxable year or any taxable year thereafter.

If paragraph (1) or (2) of this subsection applies, the change to, and the use of, the different method shall be in accordance with such regulations as the Secretary may prescribe as necessary in order that the use of such method may clearly reflect income.

[Sec. 472(f)]

(f) USE OF GOVERNMENT PRICE INDEXES IN PRICING INVENTORY.—The Secretary shall prescribe regulations permitting the use of suitable published governmental indexes in such manner and circumstances as determined by the Secretary for purposes of the method described in subsection (b).

Amendments

• 1981, Economic Recovery Tax Act of 1981 (P.L. 97-34)

P.L. 97-34, §235:

Amended Code Sec. 472 by adding at the end thereof new subsection (f). **Effective** 8-13-81.

• 1976, Tax Reform Act of 1976 (P.L. 94-455)

P.L. 94-455, §1906(b)(13)(A):

Amended 1954 Code by substituting "Secretary" for "Secretary or his delegate" each place it appeared. **Effective** 2-1-77.

P.L. 94-455, §1901(b)(36)(A):

Repealed Code Sec. 472(f). **Effective** for tax years beginning after 12-31-76. Prior to repeal, Code Sec. 472 read as follows:

"(f) Cross Reference.—

For provisions relating to involuntary liquidation and replacement of LIFO inventories, see section 1321."

[Sec. 472(g)]

(g) CONFORMITY RULES APPLIED ON CONTROLLED GROUP BASIS.—

(1) IN GENERAL.—Except as otherwise provided in regulations, all members of the same group of financially related corporations shall be treated as 1 taxpayer for purposes of subsections (c) and (e)(2).

(2) GROUP OF FINANCIALLY RELATED CORPORATIONS.—For purposes of paragraph (1), the term "group of financially related corporations" means—

(A) any affiliated group as defined in section 1504 determined by substituting "50 percent" for "80 percent" each place it appears in section 1504(a) and without regard to section 1504(b), and

(B) any other group of corporations which consolidate or combine for purposes of financial statements.

Amendments

• 1984, Deficit Reduction Act of 1984 (P.L. 98-369)

P.L. 98-369, §95(a):

Amended Code Sec. 472 by adding at the end thereof new subsection (g). **Effective** for tax years beginning after 7-18-84.

[Sec. 473]

SEC. 473. QUALIFIED LIQUIDATIONS OF LIFO INVENTORIES.

[Sec. 473(a)]

(a) GENERAL RULE.—If, for any liquidation year—

(1) there is a qualified liquidation of goods which the taxpayer inventories under the LIFO method, and

(2) the taxpayer elects to have the provisions of this section apply with respect to such liquidation.

then the gross income of the taxpayer for such taxable year shall be adjusted as provided in subsection (b).

[Sec. 473(b)]

(b) ADJUSTMENT FOR REPLACEMENTS.—If the liquidated goods are replaced (in whole or in part) during any replacement year and such replacement is reflected in the closing inventory for such year, then the gross income for the liquidation year shall be—

(1) decreased by an amount equal to the excess of—

(A) the aggregate replacement cost of the liquidated goods so replaced during such year, over

(B) the aggregate cost of such goods reflected in the opening inventory of the liquidation year, or

(2) increased by an amount equal to the excess of—

(A) the aggregate cost reflected in such opening inventory of the liquidated goods so replaced during such year, over

(B) such aggregate replacement cost.

[Sec. 473(c)]

(c) QUALIFIED LIQUIDATION DEFINED.—For purposes of this section—

(1) IN GENERAL.—The term "qualified liquidation" means—

(A) a decrease in the closing inventory of the liquidation year from the opening inventory of such year, but only if

(B) the taxpayer establishes to the satisfaction of the Secretary that such decrease is directly and primarily attributable to a qualified inventory interruption.

(2) QUALIFIED INVENTORY INTERRUPTION DEFINED.—

(A) IN GENERAL.—The term "qualified inventory interruption" means a regulation, request, or interruption described in subparagraph (B) but only to the extent provided in the notice published pursuant to subparagraph (B).

(B) DETERMINATION BY SECRETARY.—Whenever the Secretary, after consultation with the appropriate Federal officers, determines—

(i) that—

(I) any Department of Energy regulation or request with respect to energy supplies, or

(II) any embargo, international boycott, or other major foreign trade interruption,

has made difficult or impossible the replacement during the liquidation year of any class of goods for any class of taxpayers, and

(ii) that the application of this section to that class of goods and taxpayers is necessary to carry out the purposes of this section,

he shall publish a notice of such determinations in the Federal Register, together with the period to be affected by such notice.

[Sec. 473(d)]

(d) OTHER DEFINITIONS AND SPECIAL RULES.—For purposes of this section—

(1) LIQUIDATION YEAR.—The term "liquidation year" means the taxable year in which occurs the qualified liquidation to which this section applies.

(2) REPLACEMENT YEAR.—The term "replacement year" means any taxable year in the replacement period; except that such term shall not include any taxable year after the taxable year in which replacement of the liquidated goods is completed.

(3) REPLACEMENT PERIOD.—The term "replacement period" means the shorter of—

(A) the period of the 3 taxable years following the liquidation year, or

(B) the period specified by the Secretary in a notice published in the Federal Register with respect to that qualified inventory interruption.

Any period specified by the Secretary under subparagraph (B) may be modified by the Secretary in a subsequent notice published in the Federal Register.

(4) LIFO METHOD.—The term "LIFO method" means the method of inventorying goods described in section 472.

(5) ELECTION.—

(A) IN GENERAL.—An election under subsection (a) shall be made subject to such conditions, and in such manner and form and at such time, as the Secretary may prescribe by regulation.

(B) IRREVOCABLE ELECTION.—An election under this section shall be irrevocable and shall be binding for the liquidation year and for all determinations for prior and subsequent taxable years insofar as such determinations are affected by the adjustments under this section.

[Sec. 473(e)]

(e) REPLACEMENT; INVENTORY BASIS.—For purposes of this chapter—

(1) REPLACEMENTS.—If the closing inventory of the taxpayer for any replacement year reflects an increase over the opening inventory of such goods for such year, the goods reflecting such increase shall be considered, in the order of their acquisition, as having been acquired in replacement of the goods most recently liquidated (whether or not in a qualified liquidation) and not previously replaced.

(2) AMOUNT AT WHICH REPLACEMENT GOODS TAKEN INTO ACCOUNT.—In the case of any qualified liquidation, any goods considered under paragraph (1) as having been acquired in replacement of the goods liquidated in such liquidation shall be taken into purchases and included in the closing inventory of the taxpayer for the replacement year at the inventory cost basis of the goods replaced.

[Sec. 473(f)]

(f) SPECIAL RULES FOR APPLICATION OF ADJUSTMENTS.—

(1) PERIOD OF LIMITATIONS.—If—

(A) an adjustment is required under this section for any taxable year by reason of the replacement of liquidated goods during any replacement year, and

(B) the assessment of a deficiency, or the allowance of a credit or refund of an overpayment of tax attributable to such adjustment, for any taxable year, is otherwise prevented by the operation of any law or rule of law (other than section 7122, relating to compromises),

then such deficiency may be assessed, or credit or refund allowed, within the period prescribed for assessing a deficiency or allowing a credit or refund for the replacement year if a notice for deficiency is mailed, or claim for refund is filed, within such period.

(2) INTEREST.—Solely for purposes of determining interest on any overpayment or underpayment attributable to an adjustment made under this section, such overpayment or underpayment shall be treated as an overpayment or underpayment (as the case may be) for the replacement year.

[Sec. 473(g)]

(g) COORDINATION WITH SECTION 472.—The Secretary shall prescribe such regulations as may be necessary to coordinate the provisions of this section with the provisions of section 472.

Amendments

• 1980 Crude Oil Windfall Profit Tax Act of 1980 (P.L. 96-223)

P.L. 96-223, §403(a)(1):

Added Code Sec. 473. **Effective** for qualified liquidations (within the meaning of Code Sec. 473(c)) in tax years ending after 10-31-79.

[Sec. 474]

SEC. 474. SIMPLIFIED DOLLAR-VALUE LIFO METHOD FOR CERTAIN SMALL BUSINESSES.

[Sec. 474(a)]

(a) GENERAL RULE.—An eligible small business may elect to use the simplified dollar-value method of pricing inventories for purposes of the LIFO method.

[Sec. 474(b)]

(b) SIMPLIFIED DOLLAR-VALUE METHOD OF PRICING INVENTORIES.—For purposes of this section—

(1) IN GENERAL.—The simplified dollar-value method of pricing inventories is a dollar-value method of pricing inventories under which—

(A) the taxpayer maintains a separate inventory pool for items in each major category in the applicable Government price index, and

(B) the adjustment for each such separate pool is based on the change from the preceding taxable year in the component of such index for the major category.

(2) APPLICABLE GOVERNMENT PRICE INDEX.—The term "applicable Government price index" means—

(A) except as provided in subparagraph (B), the Producer Price Index published by the Bureau of Labor Statistics, or

(B) in the case of a retailer using the retail method, the Consumer Price Index published by the Bureau of Labor Statistics.

(3) MAJOR CATEGORY.—The term "major category" means—

(A) in the case of the Producer Price Index, any of the 2-digit standard industrial classifications in the Producer Prices Data Report, or

(B) in the case of the Consumer Price Index, any of the general expenditure categories in the Consumer Price Index Detailed Report.

[Sec. 474(c)]

(c) ELIGIBLE SMALL BUSINESS.—For purposes of this section, a taxpayer is an eligible small business for any taxable year if the average annual gross receipts of the taxpayer for the 3 preceding taxable years do not exceed $5,000,000. For purposes of the preceding sentence, rules similar to the rules of section 448(c)(3) shall apply.

[Sec. 474(d)]

(d) SPECIAL RULES.—For purposes of this section—

(1) CONTROLLED GROUPS.—

(A) IN GENERAL.—In the case of a taxpayer which is a member of a controlled group, all persons which are component members of such group shall be treated as 1 taxpayer for purposes of determining the gross receipts of the taxpayer.

(B) CONTROLLED GROUP DEFINED.—For purposes of subparagraph (A), persons shall be treated as being component members of a controlled group if such persons would be treated as a single employer under section 52.

(2) ELECTION.—

(A) IN GENERAL.—The election under this section may be made without the consent of the Secretary.

(B) PERIOD TO WHICH ELECTION APPLIES.—The election under this section shall apply—

(i) to the taxable year for which it is made, and

(ii) to all subsequent taxable years for which the taxpayer is an eligible small business,

unless the taxpayer secures the consent of the Secretary to the revocation of such election.

(3) LIFO METHOD.—The term "LIFO method" means the method provided by section 472(b).

(4) TRANSITIONAL RULES.—

(A) IN GENERAL.—In the case of a year of change under this section—

(i) the inventory pools shall—

(I) in the case of the 1st taxable year to which such an election applies, be established in accordance with the major categories in the applicable Government price index, or

(II) in the case of the 1st taxable year after such election ceases to apply, be established in the manner provided by regulations under section 472;

(ii) the aggregate dollar amount of the taxpayer's inventory as of the beginning of the year of change shall be the same as the aggregate dollar value as of the close of the taxable year preceding the year of change, and

(iii) the year of change shall be treated as a new base year in accordance with procedures provided by regulations under section 472.

(B) YEAR OF CHANGE.—For purposes of this paragraph, the year of change under this section is—

(i) the 1st taxable year to which an election under this section applies, or

(ii) in the case of a cessation of such an election, the 1st taxable year after such election ceases to apply.

Amendments

• **1986, Tax Reform Act of 1986 (P.L. 99-514)**

P.L. 99-514, §802(a):

Amended Code Sec. 474. **Effective** for tax years beginning after 12-31-86. However, see Act Sec. 803(c)(2) below.

P.L. 99-514, §802(a), provides:

(2) TREATMENT OF TAXPAYERS WHO MADE ELECTIONS UNDER EXISTING SECTION 474.—The amendments made by this section shall not apply to any taxpayer who made an election under section 474 of the Internal Revenue Code of 1954 (as in effect on the day before the date of the enactment of this Act) for any period during which such election is in effect. Notwithstanding any provision of such section 474 (as so in effect), an election under such section may be revoked without the consent of the Secretary.

Prior to amendment, Code Sec. 474 read as follows:

SEC. 474. ELECTION BY CERTAIN SMALL BUSINESSES TO USE ONE INVENTORY POOL.

[Sec. 474(a)]

(a) IN GENERAL.—A taxpayer which is an eligible small business and which uses the dollar-value method of pricing inventories under the method provided by section 472(b) may elect to use one inventory pool for any trade or business of such taxpayer.

Amendments

• **1981, Economic Recovery Tax Act of 1981 (P.L. 97-34)**

P.L. 97-34, §237(a):

Added Code Sec. 474(a). **Effective** for tax years beginning after 12-31-81.

[Sec. 474(b)]

(b) ELIGIBLE SMALL BUSINESS DEFINED.—For purposes of this section a taxpayer is an eligible small business for any taxable year if the average annual gross receipts of the taxpayer do not exceed $2,000,000 for the 3-taxable-year period ending with the taxable year.

Amendments

• **1981, Economic Recovery Tax Act of 1981 (P.L. 97-34)**

P.L. 97-34, §237(a):

Added Code Sec. 474(b). **Effective** for tax years beginning after 12-31-81.

[Sec. 474(c)]

(c) SPECIAL RULES.—For purposes of this section—

(1) CONTROLLED GROUPS.—

(A) IN GENERAL.—In the case of a taxpayer which is a member of a controlled group, all persons which are component members of such group at any time during the calendar year shall be treated as one taxpayer for such year for purposes of determining the gross receipts of the taxpayer.

(B) CONTROLLED GROUP DEFINED.—For purposes of subparagraph (A), persons shall be treated as being members of a controlled group if such persons would be treated as a single employer under the regulations prescribed under section 52(b).

(2) ELECTION.—

(A) IN GENERAL.—The election under this section may be made without the consent of the Secretary and shall be made at such time and in such manner as the Secretary may by regulations prescribe.

(B) PERIOD TO WHICH ELECTION APPLIES.—The election under this section shall apply—

(i) to the taxable year for which it is made, and

(ii) to all subsequent taxable years for which the taxpayer is an eligible small business,

unless the taxpayer secures the consent of the Secretary to the revocation of such election.

(3) TRANSITIONAL RULES.—In the case of a taxpayer who changes the number of inventory pools maintained by him in a taxable year by reason of an election (or cessation thereof) under this section—

(A) the inventory pools combined or separated shall be combined or separated in the manner provided by regulations under section 472;

(B) the aggregate dollar value of the taxpayer's inventory as of the beginning of the first taxable year—

(i) for which an election under this section is in effect, or

(ii) after such election ceases to apply,

shall be the same as the aggregate dollar value as of the close of the taxable year preceding the taxable year described in clause (i) or (ii) (as the case may be), and

(C) the first taxable year for which an election under this section is in effect or after such election ceases to apply (as the case may be) shall be treated as a new base year in accordance with procedures provided by regulations under section 472.

• 1981, Economic Recovery Tax Act of 1981 (P.L. 97-34)

P.L. 97-34, §237(a):

Added Code Sec. 474(c). **Effective** for tax years beginning after 12-31-81.

P.L. 97-34, §238, provides:

SEC. 238. STUDY OF ACCOUNTING METHODS FOR INVENTORY.

(a) STUDY.—The Secretary of the Treasury shall conduct a full and complete study of methods of tax accounting for inventory with a view toward the development of simplified methods. Such study shall include (but shall not be limited to) an examination of the last-in first-out method and the cash receipts and disbursements method.

(b) REPORT.—Not later than December 31, 1982, the Secretary of the Treasury shall submit to the Committee on Ways and Means of the House of Representatives and to the Committee on Finance of the Senate a report on the study conducted under subsection (a), together with such recommendations as he deems appropriate.

[Sec. 475]

SEC. 475. MARK TO MARKET ACCOUNTING METHOD FOR DEALERS IN SECURITIES.

[Sec. 475(a)]

(a) GENERAL RULE.—Notwithstanding any other provision of this subpart, the following rules shall apply to securities held by a dealer in securities:

(1) Any security which is inventory in the hands of the dealer shall be included in inventory at its fair market value.

(2) In the case of any security which is not inventory in the hands of the dealer and which is held at the close of any taxable year—

(A) the dealer shall recognize gain or loss as if such security were sold for its fair market value on the last business day of such taxable year, and

(B) any gain or loss shall be taken into account for such taxable year.

Proper adjustment shall be made in the amount of any gain or loss subsequently realized for gain or loss taken into account under the preceding sentence. The Secretary may provide by regulations for the application of this paragraph at times other than the times provided in this paragraph.

[Sec. 475(b)]

(b) EXCEPTIONS.—

(1) IN GENERAL.—Subsection (a) shall not apply to—

(A) any security held for investment,

(B) (i) any security described in subsection (c)(2)(C) which is acquired (including originated) by the taxpayer in the ordinary course of a trade or business of the taxpayer and which is not held for sale, and (ii) any obligation to acquire a security described in clause (i) if such obligation is entered into in the ordinary course of such trade or business and is not held for sale, and

(C) any security which is a hedge with respect to—

(i) a security to which subsection (a) does not apply, or

(ii) a position, right to income, or a liability which is not a security in the hands of the taxpayer.

To the extent provided in regulations, subparagraph (C) shall not apply to any security held by a person in its capacity as a dealer in securities.

(2) IDENTIFICATION REQUIRED.—A security shall not be treated as described in subparagraph (A), (B), or (C) of paragraph (1), as the case may be, unless such security is clearly identified in the dealer's records as being described in such subparagraph before the close of the day on which it was acquired, originated, or entered into (or such other time as the Secretary may by regulations prescribe).

(3) SECURITIES SUBSEQUENTLY NOT EXEMPT.—If a security ceases to be described in paragraph (1) at any time after it was identified as such under paragraph (2), subsection (a) shall apply to any changes in value of the security occurring after the cessation.

(4) SPECIAL RULE FOR PROPERTY HELD FOR INVESTMENT.—To the extent provided in regulations, subparagraph (A) of paragraph (1) shall not apply to any security described in subparagraph (D) or (E) of subsection (c)(2) which is held by a dealer in such securities.

[Sec. 475(c)]

(c) DEFINITIONS.—For purposes of this section—

(1) DEALER IN SECURITIES DEFINED.—The term "dealer in securities" means a taxpayer who—

(A) regularly purchases securities from or sells securities to customers in the ordinary course of a trade or business; or

(B) regularly offers to enter into, assume, offset, assign or otherwise terminate positions in securities with customers in the ordinary course of a trade or business.

(2) SECURITY DEFINED.—The term "security" means any—

(A) share of stock in a corporation;

(B) partnership or beneficial ownership interest in a widely held or publicly traded partnership or trust;

(C) note, bond, debenture, or other evidence of indebtedness;

(D) interest rate, currency, or equity notional principal contract;

(E) evidence of an interest in, or a derivative financial instrument in, any security described in subparagraph (A), (B), (C), or (D), or any currency, including any option, forward contract, short position, and any similar financial instrument in such a security or currency; and

(F) position which—

(i) is not a security described in subparagraph (A), (B), (C), (D), or (E),

(ii) is a hedge with respect to such a security, and

(iii) is clearly identified in the dealer's records as being described in this subparagraph before the close of the day on which it was acquired or entered into (or such other time as the Secretary may by regulations prescribe).

Subparagraph (E) shall not include any contract to which section 1256(a) applies.

(3) HEDGE.—The term "hedge" means any position which manages the dealer's risk of interest rate or price changes or currency fluctuations, including any position which is reasonably expected to become a hedge within 60 days after the acquisition of the position.

(4) SPECIAL RULES FOR CERTAIN RECEIVABLES.—

(A) IN GENERAL.—Paragraph (2)(C) shall not include any nonfinancial customer paper.

(B) NONFINANCIAL CUSTOMER PAPER.— For purposes of subparagraph (A), the term "nonfinancial customer paper" means any receivable which—

(i) is a note, bond, debenture, or other evidence of indebtedness;

(ii) arises out of the sale of nonfinancial goods or services by a person the principal activity of which is the selling or providing of nonfinancial goods or services; and

(iii) is held by such person (or a person who bears a relationship to such person described in section 267(b) or 707(b)) at all times since issue.

Amendments

• 1999, Tax Relief Extension Act of 1999 (P.L. 106-170)

P.L. 106-170, §532(b)(1):

Amended Code Sec. 475(c)(3) by striking "reduces" and inserting "manages". **Effective** for any instrument held, acquired, or entered into, any transaction entered into, and supplies held or acquired on or after 12-17-99.

• 1998, IRS Restructuring and Reform Act of 1998 (P.L. 105-206)

P.L. 105-206, §7003(a):

Amended Code Sec. 475(c) by adding at the end a new paragraph (4). **Effective**, generally, for tax years ending after 7-22-98. For a special rule, see Act Sec. 7003(c)(2)(A)-(C), below.

P.L. 105-206, §7003(c)(2)(A)-(C), provides:

(2) CHANGE IN METHOD OF ACCOUNTING.—In the case of any taxpayer required by the amendments made by this section to change its method of accounting for its first taxable year ending after the date of the enactment of this Act—

(A) such change shall be treated as initiated by the taxpayer;

(B) such change shall be treated as made with the consent of the Secretary of the Treasury; and

(C) the net amount of the adjustments required to be taken into account by the taxpayer under section 481 of the Internal Revenue Code of 1986 shall be taken into account ratably over the 4-taxable-year period beginning with such first taxable year.

[Sec. 475(d)]

(d) SPECIAL RULES.—For purposes of this section—

(1) COORDINATION WITH CERTAIN RULES.—The rules of sections 263(g), 263A, and 1256(a) shall not apply to securities to which subsection (a) applies, and section 1091 shall not apply (and section 1092 shall apply) to any loss recognized under subsection (a).

(2) IMPROPER IDENTIFICATION.—If a taxpayer—

(A) identifies any security under subsection (b)(2) as being described in subsection (b)(1) and such security is not so described, or

(B) fails under subsection (c)(2)(F)(iii) to identify any position which is described in subsection (c)(2)(F) (without regard to clause (iii) thereof) at the time such identification is required,

the provisions of subsection (a) shall apply to such security or position, except that any loss under this section prior to the disposition of the security or position shall be recognized only to the extent of gain previously recognized under this section (and not previously taken into account under this paragraph) with respect to such security or position.

(3) CHARACTER OF GAIN OR LOSS.—

(A) IN GENERAL.—Except as provided in subparagraph (B) or section 1236(b)—

(i) IN GENERAL.—Any gain or loss with respect to a security under subsection (a)(2) shall be treated as ordinary income or loss.

(ii) SPECIAL RULE FOR DISPOSITIONS.—If—

(I) gain or loss is recognized with respect to a security before the close of the taxable year, and

(II) subsection (a)(2) would have applied if the security were held as of the close of the taxable year,

such gain or loss shall be treated as ordinary income or loss.

(B) EXCEPTION.—Subparagraph (A) shall not apply to any gain or loss which is allocable to a period during which—

(i) the security is described in subsection (b)(1)(C) (without regard to subsection (b)(2)),

(ii) the security is held by a person other than in connection with its activities as a dealer in securities, or

(iii) the security is improperly identified (within the meaning of subparagraph (A) or (B) of paragraph (2)).

[Sec. 475(e)]

(e) ELECTION OF MARK TO MARKET FOR DEALERS IN COMMODITIES.—

(1) IN GENERAL.—In the case of a dealer in commodities who elects the application of this subsection, this section shall apply to commodities held by such dealer in the same manner as this section applies to securities held by a dealer in securities.

(2) COMMODITY.—For purposes of this subsection and subsection (f), the term "commodity" means—

(A) any commodity which is actively traded (within the meaning of section 1092(d)(1));

(B) any notional principal contract with respect to any commodity described in subparagraph (A);

(C) any evidence of an interest in, or a derivative instrument in, any commodity described in subparagraph (A) or (B), including any option, forward contract, futures contract, short position, and any similar instrument in such a commodity; and

(D) any position which—

(i) is not a commodity described in subparagraph (A), (B), or (C),

(ii) is a hedge with respect to such a commodity, and

(iii) is clearly identified in the taxpayer's records as being described in this subparagraph before the close of the day on which it was acquired or entered into (or such other time as the Secretary may by regulations prescribe).

(3) ELECTION.—An election under this subsection may be made without the consent of the Secretary. Such an election, once made, shall apply to the taxable year for which made and all subsequent taxable years unless revoked with the consent of the Secretary.

Amendments

• 1997, Taxpayer Relief Act of 1997 (P.L. 105-34)

P.L. 105-34, §1001(b):

Amended Code Sec. 475 by redesignating subsection (e) as subsection (g) and by inserting after subsection (d) a new subsection (e). For the **effective** date, see Act Sec. 1001(d)(4), below.

P.L. 105-34, §1001(d)(4), provides:

(4) ELECTION OF MARK TO MARKET BY SECURITIES TRADERS AND TRADERS AND DEALERS IN COMMIDITIES.—

(A) IN GENERAL.—The amendments made by subsection (b) shall apply to taxable years ending after the date of the enactment of this Act.

(B) 4-YEAR SPREAD OF ADJUSTMENTS.—In the case of a taxpayer who elects under subsection (e) or (f) of section 475 of the Internal Revenue Code of 1986 (as added by this section) to change its method of accounting for the taxable year which includes the date of the enactment of this Act—

(i) any identification required under such subsection with respect to securities and commodities held on the date of the enactment of this Act shall be treated as timely made if made on or before the 30th day after such date of enactment, and

(ii) the net amount of the adjustments required to be taken into account by the taxpayer under section 481 of such Code shall be taken into account ratably over the 4-taxable year period beginning with such first taxable year.

[Sec. 475(f)]

(f) ELECTION OF MARK TO MARKET FOR TRADERS IN SECURITIES OR COMMODITIES.—

(1) TRADERS IN SECURITIES.—

(A) IN GENERAL.—In the case of a person who is engaged in a trade or business as a trader in securities and who elects to have this paragraph apply to such trade or business—

(i) such person shall recognize gain or loss on any security held in connection with such trade or business at the close of any taxable year as if such security were sold for its fair market value on the last business day of such taxable year, and

(ii) any gain or loss shall be taken into account for such taxable year.

Proper adjustment shall be made in the amount of any gain or loss subsequently realized for gain or loss taken into account under the preceding sentence. The Secretary may provide by regulations for the application of this subparagraph at times other than the times provided in this subparagraph.

(B) EXCEPTION.—Subparagraph (A) shall not apply to any security—

(i) which is established to the satisfaction of the Secretary as having no connection to the activities of such person as a trader, and

(ii) which is clearly identified in such person's records as being described in clause (i) before the close of the day on which it was acquired, originated, or entered into (or such other time as the Secretary may by regulations prescribe).

If a security ceases to be described in clause (i) at any time after it was identified as such under clause (ii), subparagraph (A) shall apply to any changes in value of the security occurring after the cessation.

(C) COORDINATION WITH SECTION 1259.—Any security to which subparagraph (A) applies and which was acquired in the normal course of the taxpayer's activities as a trader in securities shall not be taken into account in applying section 1259 to any position to which subparagraph (A) does not apply.

(D) OTHER RULES TO APPLY.—Rules similar to the rules of subsections (b)(4) and (d) shall apply to securities held by a person in any trade or business with respect to which an election under this paragraph is in effect. Subsection (d)(3) shall not apply under the preceding sentence for purposes of applying sections 1402 and 7704.

(2) TRADERS IN COMMODITIES.—In the case of a person who is engaged in a trade or business as a trader in commodities and who elects to have this paragraph apply to such trade or business, paragraph (1) shall apply to commodities held by such trader in connection with such trade or business in the same manner as paragraph (1) applies to securities held by a trader in securities.

(3) ELECTION.—The elections under paragraphs (1) and (2) may be made separately for each trade or business and without the consent of the Secretary. Such an election, once made, shall apply to the taxable year for which made and all subsequent taxable years unless revoked with the consent of the Secretary.

Amendments

• 1998, IRS Restructuring and Reform Act of 1998 (P.L. 105-206)

P.L. 105-206, §6010(a)(3):

Amended Code Sec. 475(f)(1)(D) by adding at the end a new sentence. **Effective** as if included in the provision of P.L. 105-34 to which it relates [generally **effective** for tax years ending after 8-5-97.—CCH].

• 1997, Taxpayer Relief Act of 1997 (P.L. 105-34)

P.L. 105-34, §1001(b):

Amended Code Sec. 475 by redesignating subsection (e) as subsection (g) and by inserting after new subsection (e) a new subsection (f). For the **effective** date, see Act Sec. 1001(d)(4) in the amendment notes following Code Sec. 475(e).

[Sec. 475(g)]

(g) REGULATORY AUTHORITY.—The Secretary shall prescribe such regulations as may be necessary or appropriate to carry out the purposes of this section, including rules—

(1) to prevent the use of year-end transfers, related parties, or other arrangements to avoid the provisions of this section,

(2) to provide for the application of this section to any security which is a hedge which cannot be identified with a specific security, position, right to income, or liability, and

(3) to prevent the use by taxpayers of subsection (c)(4) to avoid the application of this section to a receivable that is inventory in the hands of the taxpayer (or a person who bears a relationship to the taxpayer described in section 267(b) or 707(b)).

Amendments

• 2002, Job Creation and Worker Assistance Act of 2002 (P.L. 107-147)

P.L. 107-147, §417(10):

Amended Code Sec. 475(g)(3) by striking "sections" and inserting "section". **Effective** 3-9-2002.

• 2000, Community Renewal Tax Relief Act of 2000 (P.L. 106-554)

P.L. 106-554, §319(4):

Amended Code Sec. 475(g)(3) by striking "267(b) of" and inserting "267(b) or". **Effective** 12-21-2000.

• 1998, IRS Restructuring and Reform Act of 1998 (P.L. 105-206)

P.L. 105-206, §7003(b):

Amended Code Sec. 475(g) by striking "and" at the end of paragraph (1), by striking the period at the end of paragraph (2) and inserting ", and", and by adding at the end a new paragraph (3). **Effective**, generally, for tax years ending after 7-22-98. For a special rule, see Act Sec. 7003(c)(2)(A)-(C), below.

P.L. 105-206, §7003(c)(2)(A)-(C), provides:

(2) CHANGE IN METHOD OF ACCOUNTING.—In the case of any taxpayer required by the amendments made by this section to change its method of accounting for its first taxable year ending after the date of the enactment of this Act—

(A) such change shall be treated as initiated by the taxpayer,

(B) such change shall be treated as made with the consent of the Secretary of the Treasury, and

(C) the net amount of the adjustments required to be taken into account by the taxpayer under section 481 of the Internal Revenue Code of 1986 shall be taken into account ratably over the 4-taxable year period beginning with such first taxable year.

• 1997, Taxpayer Relief Act of 1997 (P.L. 105-34)

P.L. 105-34, §1001(b):

Amended Code Sec. 475 by redesignating subsection (e) as subsection (g). For the **effective** date, see Act Sec. 1001(d)(4) in the amendment notes following Code Sec. 475(e).

• **1993, Omnibus Budget Reconciliation Act of 1993 (P.L. 103-66)**

P.L. 103-66, §13223(a):

Amended subpart D of part II of subchapter E of chapter 1 by adding at the end thereof new Code Sec. 475. **Effective**, generally, for all tax years ending on or after 12-31-93. For a special rule, see Act Sec. 13223(c)(2)-(3), below.

P.L. 103-66, §13223(c)(2)-(3), provides:

(2) CHANGE IN METHOD OF ACCOUNTING.—In the case of any taxpayer required by this section to change its method of accounting for any taxable year—

(A) such change shall be treated as initiated by the taxpayer.

(B) such change shall be treated as made with the consent of the Secretary, and

(C) except as provided in paragraph (3), the net amount of the adjustments required to be taken into account by the taxpayer under section 481 of the Internal Revenue Code of 1986 shall be taken into account ratably over the 5-taxable year period beginning with the first taxable year ending on or after December 31, 1993.

(3) SPECIAL RULE FOR FLOOR SPECIALISTS AND MARKET MAKERS.—

(A) IN GENERAL.—If—

(i) a taxpayer (or any predecessor) used the last-in first-out (LIFO) method of accounting with respect to any qualified securities for the 5-taxable year period ending with its last taxable year ending before December 31, 1993, and

(ii) any portion of the net amount described in paragraph (2)(C) is attributable to the use of such method of accounting, then paragraph (2)(C) shall be applied by taking such portion into account ratably over the 15-taxable year period beginning with the first taxable year ending on or after December 31, 1993.

(B) QUALIFIED SECURITY.—For purposes of this paragraph, the term "qualified security" means any security acquired—

(i) by a floor specialist (as defined in section 1236(d)(2) of the Internal Revenue Code of 1986) in connection with the specialist's duties as a specialist on an exchange, but only if the security is one in which the specialist is registered with the exchange, or

(ii) by a taxpayer who is a market maker in connection with the taxpayer's duties as a market marker, but only if—

(I) the security is included on the National Association of Security Dealers Automated Quotation System,

(II) the taxpayer is registered as a market maker in such security with the National Association of Security Dealers, and

(III) as of the last day of the taxable year preceding the taxpayer's first taxable year ending on or after December 31, 1993, the taxpayer (or any predecessor) has been actively and regularly engaged as a market maker in such security for the 2-year period ending on such date (or, if shorter, the period beginning 61 days after the security was listed in such quotation system and ending on such date).

PART III—ADJUSTMENTS

[Sec. 481]

SEC. 481. ADJUSTMENTS REQUIRED BY CHANGES IN METHOD OF ACCOUNTING.

[Sec. 481(a)]

(a) GENERAL RULE.—In computing the taxpayer's taxable income for any taxable year (referred to in this section as the "year of the change")—

(1) if such computation is under a method of accounting different from the method under which the taxpayer's taxable income for the preceding taxable year was computed, then

(2) there shall be taken into account those adjustments which are determined to be necessary solely by reason of the change in order to prevent amounts from being duplicated or omitted, except there shall not be taken into account any adjustment in respect of any taxable year to which this section does not apply unless the adjustment is attributable to a change in the method of accounting initiated by the taxpayer.

Amendments

• **1958, Technical Amendments Act of 1958 (P.L. 85-866)**

P.L. 85-866, §29(a):

Amended paragraph (2) of Sec. 481(a). **Effective** for any change in method of accounting where the year of the change is a tax year beginning after 12-31-53 and ending after 8-16-54. However, the amendment does not apply if before 9-2-58 the taxpayer applied for a change in method of accounting in the manner provided by regulations and the taxpayer and the Secretary or his delegate agreed to the terms and conditions for making the change. Prior to amendment, paragraph (2) read as follows:

"(2) there shall be taken into account those adjustments which are determined to be necessary solely by reason of the change in order to prevent amounts from being duplicated or omitted, except there shall not be taken into account any adjustment in respect of any taxable year to which this section does not apply."

[Sec. 481(b)]

(b) LIMITATION ON TAX WHERE ADJUSTMENTS ARE SUBSTANTIAL.—

(1) THREE YEAR ALLOCATION.—If—

(A) the method of accounting from which the change is made was used by the taxpayer in computing his taxable income for the 2 taxable years preceding the year of the change, and

(B) the increase in taxable income for the year of the change which results solely by reason of the adjustments required by subsection (a)(2) exceeds $3,000,

then the tax under this chapter attributable to such increase in taxable income shall not be greater than the aggregate increase in the taxes under this chapter (or under the corresponding provisions of prior revenue laws) which would result if one-third of such increase in taxable income were included in taxable income for the year of the change and one-third of such increase were included for each of the 2 preceding taxable years.

(2) ALLOCATION UNDER NEW METHOD OF ACCOUNTING.—If—

(A) the increase in taxable income for the year of the change which results solely by reason of the adjustments required by subsection (a)(2) exceeds $3,000, and

(B) the taxpayer establishes his taxable income (under the new method of accounting) for one or more taxable years consecutively preceding the taxable year of the change for which the taxpayer in computing taxable income used the method of accounting from which the change is made,

then the tax under this chapter attributable to such increase in taxable income shall not be greater than the net increase in the taxes under this chapter (or under the corresponding provisions of prior revenue laws) which would result if the adjustments required by subsection (a)(2) were allocated to the taxable year or years specified in subparagraph (B) to which they are properly allocable under the new method of accounting and the balance of the adjustments required by subsection (a) (2) was allocated to the taxable year of the change.

(3) SPECIAL RULES FOR COMPUTATIONS UNDER PARAGRAPHS (1) AND (2).—For purposes of this subsection—

(A) There shall be taken into account the increase or decrease in tax for any taxable year preceding the year of the change to which no adjustment is allocated under paragraph (1) or (2) but which is affected by a net operating loss (as defined in section 172) or by a capital loss carryback or carryover (as defined in section 1212), determined with reference to taxable years with respect to which adjustments under paragraph (1) or (2) are allocated.

(B) The increase or decrease in the tax for any taxable year for which an assessment of any deficiency, or a credit or refund of any overpayment, is prevented by any law or rule of law, shall be determined by reference to the tax previously determined (within the meaning of section 1314 (a)) for such year.

(C) In applying section 7807(b)(1), the provisions of chapter 1 (other than subchapter E, relating to self-employment income) and chapter 2 of the Internal Revenue Code of 1939 shall be treated as the corresponding provisions of the Internal Revenue Code of 1939 [1954].

Amendments

• 1976, Tax Reform Act of 1976 (P.L. 94-455)

P.L. 94-455, §1901(a)(70):

Amended Code Sec. 481(b). **Effective** for tax years beginning after 12-31-76. Prior to amendment Sec. 481(b) read as follows:

(b) LIMITATION ON TAX WHERE ADJUSTMENTS ARE SUBSTANTIAL.—

(1) THREE YEAR ALLOCATION.—If—

(A) the method of accounting from which the change is made was used by the taxpayer in computing his taxable income for the 2 taxable years preceding the year of the change, and

(B) the increase in taxable income for the year of the change which results solely by reason of the adjustments required by subsection (a) (2), other than the amount of such adjustments to which paragraph (4) or (5) applies, exceeds $3,000,

then the tax under this chapter attributable to such increase in taxable income shall not be greater than the aggregate increase in the taxes under this chapter (or under the corresponding provisions of prior revenue laws) which would result if one-third of such increase in taxable income were included in taxable income for the year of the change and one-third of such increase were included for each of the 2 preceding taxable years.

(2) ALLOCATION UNDER NEW METHOD OF ACCOUNTING.—If—

(A) the increase in taxable income for the year of the change which results solely by reason of the adjustments required by subsection (a) (2), other than the amount of such adjustments to which paragraph (4) or (5) applies, exceeds $3,000, and

(B) the taxpayer establishes his taxable income (under the new method of accounting) for one or more taxable years consecutively preceding the taxable year of the change for which the taxpayer in computing taxable income used the method of accounting from which the change is made,

then the tax under this chapter attributable to such increase in taxable income shall not be greater than the net increase in the taxes under this chapter (or under the corresponding provisions of prior revenue laws) which would result if the adjustments required by subsection (a) (2), other than the amount of such adjustments to which paragraph (4) or (5) applies, were allocated to the taxable year or years specified in subparagraph (B) to which they are properly allocable under the new method of accounting and the balance of the adjustments required by subsection (a) (2), other than the amount of such adjustments to which paragraph (4) or (5) applies, was allocated to the taxable year of the change.

(3) SPECIAL RULES FOR COMPUTATIONS UNDER PARAGRAPHS (1) AND (2).—For purposes of this subsection—

(A) There shall be taken into account the increase or decrease in tax for any taxable year preceding the year of the change to which no adjustment is allocated under paragraph (1) or (2) but which is affected by a net operating loss (as defined in section 172) or by a capital loss carryback or carryover (as defined in section 1212), determined with reference to taxable years with respect to which adjustments under paragraph (1) or (2) are allocated.

(B) The increase or decrease in the tax for any taxable year for which an assessment of any deficiency, or a credit or refund of any overpayment, is prevented by any law or rule of law, shall be determined by reference to the tax previously determined (within the meaning of section 1314 (a)) for such year.

(C) In applying section 7807(b)(1), the provisions of chapter 1 (other than subchapter E, relating to self-employment income) and chapter 2 of the Internal Revenue Code of 1939 shall be treated as the corresponding provisions of the Internal Revenue Code of 1939.

(4) SPECIAL RULE FOR PRE-1954 ADJUSTMENTS GENERALLY.—Except as provided in paragraphs (5) and (6)—

(A) AMOUNT OF ADJUSTMENTS TO WHICH PARAGRAPH APPLIES.—The net amount of the adjustments required by subsection (a), to the extent that such amount does not exceed the net amount of adjustments which would have been required if the change in method of accounting had been made in the first taxable year beginning after December 31, 1953, and ending after August 16, 1954, shall be taken into account by the taxpayer in computing taxable income in the manner provided in subparagraph (B), but only if such net amount of such adjustment would increase the taxable income of such taxpayer by more than $3,000.

(B) YEARS IN WHICH AMOUNTS ARE TO BE TAKEN INTO ACCOUNT.—One-tenth of the net amount of the adjustments described in subparagraph (A) shall (except as provided in subparagraph (C)) be taken into account in each of the 10 taxable years beginning with the year of the change. The amount to be taken into account for each taxable year in the 10-year period shall be taken into account whether or not for such year the assessment of tax is prevented by operation of any law or rule of law. If the year of the change was a taxable year ending before January 1, 1958, and if the taxpayer so elects (at such time and in such manner as the Secretary or his delegate shall by regulations prescribe), the

10-year period shall begin with the first taxable year which begins after December 31, 1957. If the taxpayer elects under the preceding sentence to begin the 10-year period with the first taxable year which begins after December 31, 1957, the 10-year period shall be reduced by the number of years, beginning with the year of the change, in respect of which assessment of tax is prevented by operation of any law or rule of law on the date of the enactment of the Technical Amendments Act of 1958.

(C) LIMITATION ON YEARS IN WHICH ADJUSTMENTS CAN BE TAKEN INTO ACCOUNT.—The net amount of any adjustments described in subparagraph (A), to the extent not taken into account in prior taxable years under subparagraph (B)—

(i) in the case of a taxpayer who is an individual, shall be taken into account in the taxable year in which he dies or ceases to engage in a trade or business,

(ii) in the case of a taxpayer who is a partner, his distributive share of such net amount shall be taken into account in the taxable year in which the partnership terminates, or in which the entire interest of such partner is transferred or liquidated, or

(iii) in the case of a taxpayer who is a corporation, shall be taken into account in the taxable year in which such corporation ceases to engage in a trade or business unless such net amount of such adjustment is required to be taken into account by the acquiring corporation under section 381(c)(21).

(D) TERMINATION OF APPLICATION OF PARAGRAPH.—The provisions of this paragraph shall not apply with respect to changes in methods of accounting made in taxable years beginning after December 31, 1963.

(5) SPECIAL RULE FOR PRE-1954 ADJUSTMENTS IN CASE OF CERTAIN DECEDENTS.—A change from the cash receipts and disbursements method to the accrual method in any case involving the use of inventories, made on or after August 16, 1954, and before January 1, 1958, for a taxable year to which this section applies, by the executor or administrator of a decedent's estate in the first return filed by such executor or administrator on behalf of the decedent, shall be given effect in determining taxable income (other than for the purpose of computing a net operating loss carryback to any prior taxable year of the decedent), and, if the net amount of any adjustments required by subsection (a) in respect of taxable years to which this section does not apply would increase the taxable income of the decedent by more than $3,000, then the tax attributable to such net adjustments shall not exceed an amount equal to the tax that would have been payable on the cash receipts and disbursements method for the years for which the executor or administrator filed returns on behalf of the decedent, computed for each such year as though a ratable portion of the taxable income for such year had been received in each of 10 taxable years beginning and ending on the same dates as the taxable year for which the tax is being computed.

(6) APPLICATION OF PARAGRAPH (4).—Paragraph (4) shall not apply with respect to any taxpayer, if the taxpayer elects to take the net amount of the adjustments described in paragraph (4) (A) into account in the manner provided by paragraph (1) or (2). An election to take the net amount of such adjustments into account in the manner provided by paragraph (1) or (2) may be made only if the taxpayer consents in writing to the assessment, within such period as may be agreed on with the Secretary or his delegate, of any deficiency for the year of the change, to the extent attributable to taking the net amount of the adjustments described in paragraph (4) (A) into account in the manner provided by paragraph (1) or (2), even though at the time of filing such consent the assessment of such deficiency would otherwise be prevented by the operation of any law or rule of law. An election under this paragraph shall be made at such time and in such manner as the Secretary or his delegate shall by regulations prescribe.

• 1969, Tax Reform Act of 1969 (P.L. 91-172)

P.L. 91-172, §512(f):

Amended Code Sec. 481(b)(3)(A) by adding "carryback or" after "capital loss". **Effective** for net capital losses sustained in tax years beginning after 12-31-69.

• 1958, Technical Amendments Act of 1958 (P.L. 85-866)

P.L. 85-866, §29(a):

Added paragraphs (4), (5), and (6) to subsec. (b). **Effective** for any change in method of accounting where the year of the change is a tax year beginning after 12-31-53 and ending after 8-16-54. However, the amendment does not apply if before 9-2-58 the taxpayer applied for a change in method of accounting in the manner provided by regulations and the taxpayer and the Secretary or his delegate agreed to the terms and conditions for making the change.

P.L. 85-866, §29(b)(1):

Amended Code Sec. 481(b) by inserting after "subsection (a)(2)" each place it appeared in paragraph (1) or (2) the following: ", other than the amount of such adjustments to which paragraph (4) or (5) applies,". **Effective** for any change in method of accounting where the year of the change is a tax year beginning after 12-31-53 and ending after 8-16-54, except that the amendments made by Sec. 29(b)(1) do not apply if before 9-2-58 the taxpayer applied for a change in method of accounting in the manner provided by regulations and the taxpayer and the Secretary or his delegate agreed to the terms and conditions for making the change.

P.L. 85-866, §29(b)(2):

Amended Code Sec. 481(b) by substituting "the aggregate increase in the taxes" for "the aggregate of the taxes" in paragraph (1). **Effective** for any change in method of accounting where the year of the change is a tax year beginning after 12-31-53 and ending after 8-16-54, except that the amendments made by Sec. 29(b)(1) do not apply if before 9-2-58 the taxpayer applied for a change in method of accounting in the manner provided by regulations and the taxpayer and the Secretary or his delegate agreed to the terms and conditions for making the change.

P.L. 85-866, §29(b)(3):

Amended Code Sec. 481(b) by substituting "which would result if one-third of such increase in taxable income" for "which would result if one-third of such increase" in paragraph (1). **Effective** for any change in method of accounting where the year of the change is a tax year beginning after 12-31-53 and ending after 8-16-54, except that the amendments made by Sec. 29(b)(1) do not apply if before 9-2-58 the taxpayer applied for a change in method of accounting in the manner provided by regulations and the taxpayer and the Secretary or his delegate agreed to the terms and conditions for making the change.

P.L. 85-866, §29(b)(4):

Amended Code Sec. 481(b) by inserting after "the net increase in the taxes under this chapter" in paragraph (2) the following words: "(or under the corresponding provisions of prior revenue laws)". **Effective** for any change in method of accounting where the year of the change is a tax year beginning after 12-31-53 and ending after 8-16-54, except that the amendments made by Sec. 29(b)(1) do not apply if before 9-2-58 the taxpayer applied for a change in method of accounting in the manner provided by regulations and the taxpayer and the Secretary or his delegate agreed to the terms and conditions for making the change.

P.L. 85-866, §29(b)(5):

Amended Code Sec. 481(b) by striking out "paragraph (2)" each place it appeared in paragraph (3)(A) and inserting in lieu thereof "paragraph (1) or (2)". **Effective** for any change in method of accounting where the year of the change is a tax year beginning after 12-31-53 and ending after 8-16-54, except that the amendments made by Sec. 29(b)(1) do not apply if before 9-2-58 the taxpayer applied for a change in method of accounting in the manner provided by regulations and the taxpayer and the Secretary or his delegate agreed to the terms and conditions for making the change.

[Sec. 481(c)]

(c) ADJUSTMENTS UNDER REGULATIONS.—In the case of any change described in subsection (a), the taxpayer may, in such manner and subject to such conditions as the Secretary may by regulations prescribe, take the adjustments required by subsection (a)(2) into account in computing the tax imposed by this chapter for the taxable year or years permitted under such regulations.

Amendments

• 1976, Tax Reform Act of 1976 (P.L. 94-455)

P.L. 94-455, §1906(b)(13)(A):

Amended 1954 Code by substituting "Secretary" for "Secretary or his delegate" each place it appeared. **Effective** 2-1-77.

[Sec. 481(d)—Repealed]

Amendments

• 1980, Installment Sales Revision Act of 1980 (P.L. 96-471)

P.L. 96-471, §2(b)(3):

Repealed Code Sec. 481(d). **Effective** for dispositions made after 10-19-80, in tax years ending after that date. Prior to repeal, Code Sec. 481(d) read as follows:

(d) EXCEPTION FOR CHANGE TO INSTALLMENT BASIS.—This section shall not apply to a change to which section 453 (relating to change to installment method) applies.

[Sec. 482]

SEC. 482. ALLOCATION OF INCOME AND DEDUCTIONS AMONG TAXPAYERS.

In any case of two or more organizations, trades, or businesses (whether or not incorporated, whether or not organized in the United States, and whether or not affiliated) owned or controlled directly or indirectly by the same interests, the Secretary may distribute, apportion, or allocate gross income, deductions, credits, or allowances between or among such organizations, trades, or businesses, if he determines that such distribution, apportionment, or allocation is necessary in order to prevent evasion of taxes or clearly to reflect the income of any of such organizations, trades, or businesses. In the case of any transfer (or license) of intangible property (within the meaning of section 936(h)(3)(B)), the income with respect to such transfer or license shall be commensurate with the income attributable to the intangible.

Amendments

• 1986, Tax Reform Act of 1986 (P.L. 99-514)

P.L. 99-514, §1231(e)(1):

Amended Code Sec. 482 by adding at the end thereof a new sentence. **Effective** for tax years beginning after 12-31-86. However, see Act Sec. 1231(g)(2)-(5), below.

P.L. 99-514, §1231(g)(2)-(5), as amended by P.L. 100-647, §1012(n), provides:

(2) SPECIAL RULE FOR TRANSFER OF INTANGIBLES.—

(A) IN GENERAL.—The amendments made by subsection (e) shall apply to taxable years beginning after December 31, 1986, but only with respect to transfers after November 16, 1985, or licenses granted after such date (or before such date with respect to property not in existence or owned by the taxpayer on such date). In the case of any transfer (or license) which is not to a foreign person, the preceding sentence shall be applied by substituting "August 16, 1986" for "November 16, 1985".

(B) SPECIAL RULE FOR SECTION 936.—For purposes of section 936(h)(5)(C) of the Internal Revenue Code of 1986 the amendments made by subsection (e) shall apply to taxable years beginning after December 31, 1986, without regard to when the transfer (or license), if any, was made.

(3) SUBSECTION (f).—The amendment made by subsection (f) shall apply to taxable years beginning after December 31, 1982.

(4) TRANSITIONAL RULE.—In the case of a corporation—

(A) with respect to which an election under section 936 of the Internal Revenue Code of 1986 (relating to possessions tax credit) is in effect,

(B) which produced an end-product form in Puerto Rico on or before September 3, 1982,

(C) which began manufacturing a component of such product in Puerto Rico in its taxable year beginning in 1983, and

(D) with respect to which a Puerto Rican tax exemption was granted on June 27, 1983, such corporation shall treat such component as a separate product for such taxable year for purposes of determining whether such corporation had a significant business presence in Puerto Rico with respect to such product and its income with respect to such product.

(5) TRANSITIONAL RULE FOR INCREASE IN GROSS INCOME TEST.—

(A) IN GENERAL.—If—

(i) a corporation fails to meet the requirements of subparagraph (B) of section 936(a)(2) of the Internal Revenue Code of 1986 (as amended by subsection (d)(1)) for any taxable year beginning in 1987 or 1988,

(ii) such corporation would have met the requirements of such subparagraph (B) if such subparagraph had been applied without regard to the amendment made by subsection (d)(1), and

(iii) 75 percent or more of the gross income of such corporation for such taxable year (or, in the case of a taxable year beginning in 1988, for the period consisting of such taxable year and the preceding taxable year) was derived from the active conduct of a trade or business within a possession of the United States, such corporation shall nevertheless be treated as meeting the requirements of such subparagraph (B) for such taxable year if it elects to reduce the amount of the qualified possession source investment income for the taxable year by the amount of the shortfall determined under subparagraph (B) of this paragraph.

(B) DETERMINATION OF SHORTFALL.—The shortfall determined under this subparagraph for any taxable year is an amount equal to the excess of—

(i) 75 percent of the gross income of the corporation for the 3-year period (or part thereof) referred to in section 936(a)(2)(A) of such Code, over

(ii) the amount of the gross income of such corporation for such period (or part thereof) which was derived from the active conduct of a trade or business within a possession of the United States.

(C) SPECIAL RULE.—Any income attributable to the investment of the amount not treated as qualified possession source investment income under subparagraph (A) shall not be treated as qualified possession source investment income for any taxable year.

• 1976, Tax Reform Act of 1976 (P.L. 94-455)

P.L. 94-455, §1906(b)(13)(A):

Amended 1954 Code by substituting "Secretary" for "Secretary or his delegate" each place it appeared. **Effective** 2-1-77.

[Sec. 483]

SEC. 483. INTEREST ON CERTAIN DEFERRED PAYMENTS.

[Sec. 483(a)]

(a) AMOUNT CONSTITUTING INTEREST.—For purposes of this title, in the case of any payment—

(1) under any contract for the sale or exchange of any property, and

(2) to which this section applies,

there shall be treated as interest that portion of the total unstated interest under such contract which, as determined in a manner consistent with the method of computing interest under section 1272(a), is properly allocable to such payment.

[Sec. 483(b)]

(b) TOTAL UNSTATED INTEREST.—For purposes of this section, the term "total unstated interest" means, with respect to a contract for the sale or exchange of property, an amount equal to the excess of—

(1) the sum of the payments to which this section applies which are due under the contract, over

(2) the sum of the present values of such payments and the present values of any interest payments due under the contract.

For purposes of the preceding sentence, the present value of a payment shall be determined under the rules of section 1274(b)(2) using a discount rate equal to the applicable Federal rate determined under section 1274(d).

Amendments

• 1985 (P.L. 99-121)

P.L. 99-121, §101(a)(2)(A):

Amended Code Sec. 483(b) by striking out "120 percent of" after "rate equal to" in the last sentence. **Effective** for sales and exchanges after 6-30-85, in tax years ending after such date. The amendment made by P.L. 98-612, §2, shall not apply to sales and exchanges after 6-30-85, in tax years ending after such date. A special rule appears following Code Sec. 483(g).

[Sec. 483(c)]

(c) PAYMENTS TO WHICH SUBSECTION (a) APPLIES.—

(1) IN GENERAL.—Except as provided in subsection (d), this section shall apply to any payment on account of the sale or exchange of property which constitutes part or all of the sales price and which is due more than 6 months after the date of such sale or exchange under a contract—

(A) under which some or all of the payments are due more than 1 year after the date of such sale or exchange, and

(B) under which there is total unstated interest.

(2) TREATMENT OF OTHER DEBT INSTRUMENTS.—For purposes of this section, a debt instrument of the purchaser which is given in consideration for the sale or exchange of property shall not be treated as a payment, and any payment due under such debt instrument shall be treated as due under the contract for the sale or exchange.

(3) DEBT INSTRUMENT DEFINED.—For purposes of this subsection, the term "debt instrument" has the meaning given such term by section 1275(a)(1).

Amendments

• 1985 (P.L. 99-121)

P.L. 99-121, §101(a)(2)(B):

Amended Code Sec. 483(c)(1)(B). **Effective** for sales and exchanges after 6-30-85, in tax years ending after such date. The amendment made by P.L. 98-612, §2, shall not apply to sales and exchanges after 6-30-85, in tax years ending after such date. A special rule appears following Code Sec. 483(g). Prior to amendment, Code Sec. 483(c)(1)(B) read as follows:

(B) under which, using a discount rate equal to 110 percent of the applicable Federal rate determined under section 1274(d), there is total unstated interest.

[Sec. 483(d)]

(d) EXCEPTIONS AND LIMITATIONS.—

(1) COORDINATION WITH ORIGINAL ISSUE DISCOUNT RULES.—This section shall not apply to any debt instrument for which an issue price is determined under section 1273(b) (other than paragraph (4) thereof) or section 1274.

(2) SALES PRICES OF $3,000 OR LESS.—This section shall not apply to any payment on account of the sale or exchange of property if it can be determined at the time of such sale or exchange that the sales price cannot exceed $3,000.

(3) CARRYING CHARGES.—In the case of the purchaser, the tax treatment of amounts paid on account of the sale or exchange of property shall be made without regard to this section if any such amounts are treated under section 163(b) as if they included interest.

(4) CERTAIN SALES OF PATENTS.—In the case of any transfer described in section 1235(a) (relating to sale or exchange of patents), this section shall not apply to any amount contingent on the productivity, use, or disposition of the property transferred.

Amendments

• 1986, Tax Reform Act of 1986 (P.L. 99-514)

P.L. 99-514, §1803(a)(14)(B):

Amended Code Sec. 483(d)(1) by striking out "any debt instrument to which section 1272 applies" and inserting in lieu thereof "any debt instrument for which an issue price is determined under section 1273(b) (other than paragraph (4) thereof) or section 1274". **Effective** as if included in the provision of P.L. 98-369 to which it relates.

P.L. 99-514, §1803(a)(9), provides:

(9) TREATMENT OF TRANSFERS OF LAND BETWEEN RELATED PARTIES.—In the case of any sale or exchange before July 1, 1985, to which section 483(f) of the Internal Revenue Code of 1954 (as in effect on the day before the date of the enactment of Public Law 99-121) applies, such section shall be treated as providing that the discount rate to be used for purposes of section 483(c)(1) of such Code shall be 6 percent, compounded semiannually.

[Sec. 483(e)]

(e) MAXIMUM RATE OF INTEREST ON CERTAIN TRANSFERS OF LAND BETWEEN RELATED PARTIES.—

(1) IN GENERAL.—In the case of any qualified sale, the discount rate used in determining the total unstated interest rate under subsection (b) shall not exceed 6 percent, compounded semiannually.

(2) QUALIFIED SALE.—For purposes of this subsection, the term "qualified sale" means any sale or exchange of land by an individual to a member of such individual's family (within the meaning of section 267(c)(4)).

(3) $500,000 LIMITATION.—Paragraph (1) shall not apply to any qualified sale between individuals made during any calendar year to the extent that the sales price for such sale (when added to the aggregate sale price for prior qualified sales between such individuals during the calendar year) exceeds $500,000.

(4) NONRESIDENT ALIEN INDIVIDUALS.—Paragraph (1) shall not apply to any sale or exchange if any party to such sale or exchange is a nonresident alien individual.

Amendments

• 1985 (P.L. 99-121)

P.L. 99-121, §102(c)(2):

Amended Code Sec. 483(e)(1), as redesignated by Act Sec. 102(c)(1), by striking out "7 percent" and inserting in lieu thereof "6 percent". **Effective** for sales and exchanges after 6-30-85, in tax years ending after such date. The amendment made by P.L. 98-612, §2, shall not apply to sales and exchanges after 6-30-85, in tax years ending after such date. A special rule appears following Code Sec. 483(g).

[Sec. 483(f)]

(f) REGULATIONS.—The Secretary shall prescribe such regulations as may be necessary or appropriate to carry out the purposes of this section including regulations providing for the application of this section in the case of—

(1) any contract for the sale or exchange of property under which the liability for, or the amount or due date of, a payment cannot be determined at the time of the sale or exchange, or

(2) any change in the liability for, or the amount or due date of, any payment (including interest) under a contract for the sale or exchange of property.

[Sec. 483(g)]

(g) CROSS REFERENCES.—

(1) For treatment of assumptions, see section 1274(c)(4).

(2) For special rules for certain transactions where stated principal amount does not exceed $2,800,000, see section 1274A.

(3) For special rules in the case of the borrower under certain loans for personal use, see section 1275(b).

Amendments

• 1985 (P.L. 99-121)

P.L. 99-121, §102(c)(1):

Amended Code Sec. 483 by striking out subsection (e) and by redesignating subsections (f), (g), and (h) as subsections (e), (f), and (g), respectively. **Effective** for sales and exchanges after 6-30-85, in tax years ending after such date. The amendment made by P.L. 98-612, §2, shall not apply to sales and exchanges after 6-30-85, in tax years ending after such date. A special rule appears below. Prior to amendment, Code Sec. 483(e) read as follows:

(e) INTEREST RATES IN CASE OF PRINCIPAL RESIDENCES OR FARM LANDS.—

(1) IN GENERAL.—In the case of any debt instrument arising from a sale or exchange to which this subsection applies, subsections (b) and (c)(1)(B) shall be applied by using, in lieu of the discount rates determined under such subsections, discount rates determined under subsections (b) and (c)(1), respectively of this section as it was in effect before the amendments made by the Tax Reform Act of 1984.

(2) SALES OR EXCHANGES TO WHICH SUBSECTION APPLIES.—This subsection shall apply—

(A) to any sale or exchange by an individual of his principal residence (within the meaning of section 1034), and

(B) to any sale or exchange by a person of land used by such person as a farm (within the meaning of section 6420(c)(2)).

(3) LIMITATION.—Paragraph (1) shall apply to any sale or exchange by an individual of his principal residence (*within the meaning of section 1034), only to the extent the purchase price of such residence does not exceed $250,000. For purposes of the preceding sentence, the purchase price of a residence shall be determined without regard to this section.

P.L. 99-121, §102(c)(3):

Amended Code Sec. 483(g), as redesignated by Act Sec. 102(c)(1). **Effective** for sales and exchanges after 6-30-85, in tax years ending after such date. The amendment made by P.L. 98-612, §2, shall not apply to sales and exchanges after 6-30-85, in tax years ending after such date. A special rule appears below. Prior to redesignation and amendment, Code Sec. 483(h), read as follows:

(h) CROSS REFERENCE.—

For special rules in the case of the borrower under certain loans for personal use, see section 1275(b).

P.L. 99-121, §104, provides:

SEC. 104. SPECIAL RULE FOR CERTAIN WORKOUTS.

(a) GENERAL RULE.—Sections 483 and 1274 of the Internal Revenue Code of 1954 shall not apply to the issuance or modification of any written indebtedness if—

(1) such issuance or modification is in connection with a workout of a specified MLC loan which (as of May 31, 1985) was substantially in arrears, and

(2) the aggregate principal amount of indebtedness resulting from such workout does not exceed the sum (as of the time of the workout) of the outstanding principal amount of the specified MCL loan and any arrearages on such loan.

(b) SPECIFIED MLC LOAN.—For purposes of subsection (a), the term "specified MLC loan" means any loan which, in a submission dated June 17, 1985, on behalf of the New York State Mortgage Loan Enforcement and Administration Corporation, had one of the following loan numbers: 001, 005, 007, 012, 025, 038, 041, 042, 043, 049, 053, 064, 068, 090, 141, 180, or 188.

• 1984, Deficit Reduction Act of 1984 (P.L. 98-369)

P.L. 98-369, §41(b):

Amended Code Sec. 483. **Effective,** generally, for sales or exchanges after 12-31-84, but not for any sale or exchange pursuant to a written contract that was binding on 3-1-84, and at all times thereafter before the sale or exchange. Prior to amendment, Code Sec. 483 read as follows:

SEC. 483. INTEREST ON CERTAIN DEFERRED PAYMENTS.

[Sec. 483(a)]

(a) AMOUNT CONSTITUTING INTEREST.—For purposes of this title, in the case of any contract for the sale or exchange of property there shall be treated as interest that part of a payment to which this section applies which bears the same ratio to the amount of such payment as the total unstated interest under such contract bears to the total of the payments to which this section applies which are due under such contract.

[Sec. 483(b)]

(b) TOTAL UNSTATED INTEREST.—For purposes of this section, the term "total unstated interest" means, with respect to a contract for the sale or exchange of property, an amount equal to the excess of—

(1) the sum of the payments to which this section applies which are due under the contract, over

(2) the sum of the present values of such payments and the present values of any interest payments due under the contract.

For purposes of paragraph (2), the present value of a payment shall be determined, as of the date of the sale or exchange, by discounting such payment at the rate, and in the manner, provided in regulations prescribed by the Secretary. Such regulations shall provide for discounting on the basis of 6-month brackets and shall provide that the present value of any interest payment due not more than 6 months after the date of the sale or exchange is an amount equal to 100 percent of such payment.

Amendments

• 1976, Tax Reform Act of 1976 (P.L. 94-455)

P.L. 94-455, §1906(b)(13)(A):

Amended 1954 Code by substituting "Secretary" for "Secretary or his delegate" each place it appeared. **Effective** 2-1-77.

[Sec. 483(c)]

(c) PAYMENTS TO WHICH SECTION APPLIES.—

(1) IN GENERAL.—Except as provided in subsection (f), this section shall apply to any payment on account of the sale or exchange of property which constitutes part or all of the sales price and which is due more than 6 months after the date of such sale or exchange under a contract—

(A) under which some or all of the payments are due more than one year after the date of such sale or exchange, and

(B) under which, using a rate provided by regulations prescribed by the Secretary for purposes of this subparagraph, there is total unstated interest.

Any rate prescribed for determining whether there is total unstated interest for purposes of subparagraph (B) shall be at least one percentage point lower than the rate prescribed for purposes of subsection (b)(2).

(2) TREATMENT OF EVIDENCE OF INDEBTEDNESS.—For purposes of this section, an evidence of indebtedness of the purchaser given in consideration for the sale or exchange of property shall not be considered a payment, and any payment due under such evidence of indebtedness shall be treated as due under the contract for the sale or exchange.

Amendments

• 1976, Tax Reform Act of 1976 (P.L. 94-455)

P.L. 94-455, §1906(b)(13)(A):

Amended 1954 Code by substituting "Secretary" for "Secretary or his delegate" each place it appeared. **Effective** 2-1-77.

• 1964, Revenue Act of 1964 (P.L. 88-272)

P.L. 88-272, §224(a):

Added Code Sec. 483(c). **Effective** for payments made after 12-31-63, on account of sales or exchanges of property occurring after 6-30-63, other than any sale or exchange made pursuant to a binding written contract (including in irrevocable written option) entered into before 7-1-63.

[Sec. 483(d)]

(d) PAYMENTS THAT ARE INDEFINITE AS TO TIME, LIABILITY, OR AMOUNT.—In the case of a contract for the sale or exchange of property under which the liability for, or the amount or due date of, any portion of a payment cannot be determined at the time of the sale or exchange, this section shall be separately applied to such portion as if it (and any amount of interest attributable to such portion) were the only payments due under the contract; and such determinations of liability, amount, and due date shall be made at the time payment of such portion is made.

[Sec. 483(e)]

(e) CHANGE IN TERMS OF CONTRACT.—If the liability for, or the amount or due date of, any payment (including interest) under a contract for the sale or exchange of property is changed, the "total unstated interest" under the contract shall be recomputed and allocated (with adjustment for prior interest (including unstated interest) payments) under regulations prescribed by the Secretary.

Amendments

• 1976, Tax Reform Act of 1976 (P.L. 94-455)

P.L. 94-455, §1906(b)(13)(A):

Amended 1954 Code by substituting "Secretary" for "Secretary or his delegate" each place it appeared. **Effective** 2-1-77.

• 1964, Revenue Act of 1964 (P.L. 88-272)

P.L. 88-272, §224(a):

Added Code Sec. 483(e). **Effective** for payments made after 12-31-63, on account of sales or exchanges of property occurring after 6-30-63, other than any sale or exchange made pursuant to a binding written contract (including an irrevocable written option) entered into before 7-1-63.

[Sec. 483(f)]

(f) EXCEPTIONS AND LIMITATIONS.—

(1) SALES PRICE OF $3,000 OR LESS.—This section shall not apply to any payment on account of the sale or exchange of property if it can be determined at the time of such sale or exchange that the sales price cannot exceed $3,000.

(2) CARRYING CHARGES.—In the case of the purchaser, the tax treatment of amounts paid on account of the sale or exchange of property shall be made without regard to this section if any such amounts are treated under section 163(b) as if they included interest.

(3) TREATMENT OF SELLER.—In the case of the seller, the tax treatment of any amounts received on account of the sale or exchange of property shall be made without regard to this section if all of the gain, if any, on such sale or exchange would be considered as ordinary income.

(4) SALES OR EXCHANGES OF PATENTS.—This section shall not apply to any payments made pursuant to a transfer described in section 1235(a) (relating to sale or exchange of patents).

(5) ANNUITIES.—This section shall not apply to any amount the liability for which depends in whole or in part on the life

expectancy of one or more individuals and which constitutes an amount received as an annuity to which section 72 applies.

Amendments

• 1976, Tax Reform Act of 1976 (P.L. 94-455)

P.L. 94-455, §1901(b)(3)(B):

Amended Code Sec. 483(f)(3). **Effective** for tax years beginning after 12-31-76. Prior to amendment Code Sec. 483(f)(3) read as follows:

(3) TREATMENT OF SELLER.—In the case of the seller, the tax treatment of any amounts received on account of the sale or exchange of property shall be made without regard to this section if no part of any gain on such sale or exchange would be considered as gain from the sale or exchange of a capital asset or property described in section 1231.

• 1964, Revenue Act of 1964 (P.L. 88-272)

P.L. 88-272, §224(a):

Added Code Sec. 483. **Effective** for payments made after 12-31-63, on account of sales or exchanges of property occurring after 6-30-63, other than any sale or exchange made pursuant to a binding written contract (including an irrevocable written option) entered into before 7-1-63.

[Sec. 483(g)]

(g) MAXIMUM RATE OF INTEREST ON CERTAIN TRANSFERS OF LAND BETWEEN RELATED PARTIES.—

(1) IN GENERAL.—In the case of any qualified sale, the maximum interest rate used in determining the total unstated interest rate under the regulations under subsection (b) shall not exceed 7 percent, compounded semiannually.

(2) QUALIFIED SALE.—For purposes of this subsection, the term "qualified sale" means any sale or exchange of land by an individual to a member of such individual's family (within the meaning of section 267(c)(4)).

(3) $500,000 LIMITATION.—Paragraph (1) shall not apply to any qualified sale between individuals made during any calendar year to the extent that the sales price for such sale (when added to the aggregate sales price for prior qualified sales between such individuals during the calendar year) exceeds $500,000.

(4) NONRESIDENT ALIEN INDIVIDUALS.—Paragraph (1) shall not apply to any sale or exchange if any party to such sale or exchange is a nonresident alien individual.

Amendments

• 1983, Technical Corrections Act of 1982 (P.L. 97-448)

P.L. 97-448, §101(g):

Amended Code Sec. 483(g)(4) by striking out "This section" and inserting in lieu thereof "Paragraph (1)". **Effective** as if included in the provision of P.L. 97-34 to which it relates.

• 1981, Economic Recovery Tax Act of 1981 (P.L. 97-34)

P.L. 97-34, §126(a):

Added Code Sec. 483(g). **Effective** for payments made after 6-30-81, pursuant to sales or exchanges after such date.

P.L. 98-369, §44(b)(2)-(4), as amended by P.L. 98-612, §2 (j) and P.L. 99-514, §1803(b), provide:

(2) Revision of Section 482 Regulations.—Not later than 180 days after the date of the enactment of this Act, the Secretary of the Treasury or his delegate shall modify the safe harbor interest rates applicable under the regulations prescribed under section 482 of the Internal Revenue Code of 1954 so that such rates are consistent with the rates applicable under section 483 of such Code by reason of the amendments made by section 41.

(3) Clarification of Interest Accrual; Fair Market Value Rule in Case of Potentially Abusive Situations.—

(A) In General.—

(i) Clarification of Interest Accrual.—In the case of any sale or exchange—

(I) after March 1, 1984 nothing in section 483 of the Internal Revenue Code of 1954 shall permit any interest to be deductible before the period to which such interest is properly allocable, or

(II) after June 8, 1984, notwithstanding section 483 of the Internal Revenue Code of 1954 or any other provision of law, no interest shall be deductible before the period to which such interest is properly allocable.

(ii) Fair Market Rule.—In the case of any sale or exchange after March 1, 1984, such section 483 shall be treated as including provisions similar to the provisions of section 1274(b)(3) of such Code (as added by section 41).

(B) Exception for Binding Contracts.—

(i) Subparagraph (A)(i)(I) shall not apply to any sale or exchange pursuant to a written contract which was binding on March 1, 1984, and at all times thereafter before the sale or exchange.

(ii) Subparagraph (A)(i)(II) shall not apply to any sale or exchange pursuant to a written contract which was binding on June 8, 1984, and at all times thereafter before the sale or exchange.

(C) Interest Accrual Rule Not to Apply Where Substantially Equal Annual Payments.—Clause (i) of subparagraph (A) shall not apply to any debt instrument with substantially equal annual payments.

(4) SPECIAL RULES FOR SALES AFTER DECEMBER 3, 1984, AND JULY 1, 1985.—

(A) IN GENERAL.—In the case of any sale or exchange after December 31, 1984, and July 1, 1985, of property other than new section 38 property—

(i) sections 483(c)(1)(B) and 1274(c)(3) of the Internal Revenue Code of 1954 shall be applied by substituting the testing rate determined under subparagraph (B) for 110 percent of the applicable Federal rate determined under section 1274(d) of such Code, and

(ii) sections 483(b) and 1274(b) of such Code shall be applied by substituting the imputation rate determined under subparagraph (C) for 120 percent of the applicable Federal rate determined under section 1274(d) of such Code.

(B) TESTING RATE.—For purposes of this paragraph—

(i) IN GENERAL.—The testing rate determined under this subparagraph is the sum of—

(I) 9 percent, plus

(II) if the borrowed amount exceeds $2,000,000, the excess determined under clause (ii) multiplied by a fraction the numerator of which is the borrowed amount to the extent it exceeds $2,000,000, and the denominator of which is the borrowed amount.

(ii) EXCESS.—For purposes of clause (i), the excess determined under this clause is the excess of 110 percent of the applicable Federal rate determined under section 1274(d) of such Code over 9 percent.

(C) IMPUTATION RATE.—For purposes of this paragraph—

(i) IN GENERAL.—The imputation rate determined under this subparagraph is the sum of—

(I) 10 percent, plus

(II) if the borrowed amount exceeds $2,000,000, the excess determined under clause (ii) multiplied by a fraction the numerator of which is the borrowed amount to the extent it exceeds $2,000,000, and the denominator of which is the borrowed amount.

(ii) EXCESS.—For purposes of clause (i), the excess determined under this clause is the excess of 120 percent of the applicable Federal rate determined under section 1274(d) of such Code over 10 percent.

(D) BORROWED AMOUNT.—For purposes of this paragraph, the term "borrowed amount" means the stated principal amount.

(E) AGGREGATION RULES.—For purposes of this paragraph—

(i) all sales or exchanges which are part of the same transaction (or a series of related transactions) shall be treated as one sale or exchange, and

(ii) all debt instruments arising from the same transaction (or a series of related transactions) shall be treated as one debt instrument.

(F) CASH METHOD OF ACCOUNTING.—In the case of any sale or exchange before July 1, 1985, of property (other than new section 38 property) used in the active business of farming and in which the borrowed amount does not exceed $2,000,000—

(i) section 1274 of the Internal Revenue Code of 1954 shall not apply, and

(ii) interest on the obligation issued in connection with such sale or exchange shall be taken into account by both buyer and seller on the cash receipts and disbursements method of accounting.

The Secretary of the Treasury or his delegate may by regulation prescribe rules to prevent the mismatching of interest income and interest deductions in connection with obligations on which interest is computed on the cash receipts and disbursements method of accounting.

(G) Clarification of Application of this Paragraph, Etc.—This paragraph and paragraphs (5), (6), and (7) shall apply only in the case of sales or exchanges to which section 1274 or 483 of the Internal Revenue Code of 1954 (as amended by section 41) applies.

(5) GENERAL RULE FOR ASSUMPTIONS OF LOANS.—Except as provided in paragraphs (6) and (7), if any person—

(A) assumes, in connection with the sale or exchange of property, any debt obligation, or

(B) acquires any property subject to any debt obligation,

sections 1274 and 483 of the Internal Revenue Code of 1954 shall apply to such debt obligation by reason of such assumption (or such acquisition).

(6) EXCEPTION FOR ASSUMPTIONS OF LOANS MADE ON OR BEFORE OCTOBER 15, 1984.—

(A) IN GENERAL.—If any person—

(i) assumes, in connection with the sale or exchange of property, any debt obligation described in subparagraph (B) and issued on or before October 15, 1984, or

(ii) acquires any property subject to any such debt obligation issued on or before October 15, 1984,

sections 1274 and 483 of the Internal Revenue Code of 1954 shall not be applied to such debt obligation by reason of such assumption (or such acquisition) unless the terms and conditions of such debt obligation are modified in connection with the assumption (or acquisition).

(B) OBLIGATIONS DESCRIBED IN THIS SUBPARAGRAPH.—A debt obligation is described in this subparagraph if such obligation—

(i) was issued on or before October 15, 1984, and

(ii) was assumed (or property was taken subject to such obligation) in connection with the sale or exchange of property (including a deemed sale under section 338(a)) the sales price of which is not greater than $100,000,000.

(C) REGULATIONS.—The Secretary shall prescribe such regulations as may be appropriate to effect the purpose of this paragraph and paragraph (5), including regulations relating to tax-exempt obligations, government subsidized loans, or other instruments.

(D) CERTAIN EXEMPT TRANSACTIONS.—The Secretary shall prescribe regulations under which any transaction shall be exempt from the application of this paragraph if such exemption is not likely to significantly reduce the tax liability of the purchaser by reason of the overstatement of the adjusted basis of the acquired asset.

(7) EXCEPTION FOR ASSUMPTIONS OF LOANS WITH RESPECT TO CERTAIN PROPERTY.—

(A) IN GENERAL.—If any person—

(i) assumes, in connection with the sale or exchange of property described in subparagraph (B), any debt obligation, or

(ii) acquires any such property subject to any such debt obligation,

sections 1274 and 483 of the Internal Revenue Code of 1954 shall not be applied to such debt obligation by reason of such assumption (or such acquisition) unless the terms and conditions of such debt obligation are modified in connection with the assumption (or acquisition).

(B) SALES OR EXCHANGES TO WHICH THIS PARAGRAPH APPLIES.—This paragraph shall apply to any of the following sales or exchanges:

(i) RESIDENCES.—Any sale or exchange of a residence by an individual, an estate, or a testamentary trust, but only if—

(I) either—

(aa) such residence on the date of such sale or exchange (or in the case of an estate or testamentary trust, on the date of death of the decedent) was the principal residence (within the meaning of section 1034) of the individual or decedent, or

(bb) during the 2-year period ending on such date, no substantial portion of such residence was of a character subject to an allowance under this title for depreciation (or amortization in lieu thereof) in the hands of such individual or decedent, and

(II) such residence was not at any time, in the hands of such individual, estate, testamentary trust, or decedent, described in section 1221(1) (relating to inventory, etc.).

(ii) FARMS.—Any sale or exchange by a qualified person of—

(I) real property which was used as a farm (within the meaning of section 6420(c)(2)) at all times during the 3-year period ending on the date of such sale or exchange, or

(II) tangible personal property which was used in the active conduct of the trade or business of farming on such farm and is sold in connection with the sale of such farm,

but only if such property is sold or exchanged for use in the active conduct of the trade or business of farming by the transferee of such property.

(iii) TRADES OR BUSINESSES.—

(I) IN GENERAL.—Any sale or exchange by a qualified person of any trade or business.

(II) APPLICATION WITH SUBPARAGRAPH (B).—This subparagraph shall not apply to any sale or exchange of any property described in subparagraph (B).

(III) NEW SECTION 38 PROPERTY.—This subparagraph shall not apply to the sale or exchange of any property which, in the hands of the transferee, is new section 38 property.

(iv) SALE OF BUSINESS REAL ESTATE.—Any sale or exchange of any real property used in an active trade or business by a person who would be a qualified person if he disposed of his entire interest.

This subparagraph shall not apply to any transaction described in the last sentence of paragraph (6)(B) (relating to transaction in excess of $100,000,000).

(C) DEFINITIONS.—For purposes of this paragraph—

(i) QUALIFIED PERSON DEFINED.—The term "qualified person" means—

(I) a person who—

(aa) is an individual, estate, or testamentary trust,

(bb) is a corporation which immediately prior to the date of the sale or exchange has 35 or fewer shareholders, or

(cc) is a partnership which immediately prior to the date of the sale or exchange has 35 or fewer partners,

(II) is a 10-percent owner of a farm or a trade or business,

(III) pursuant to a plan, disposes of—

(aa) an interest in a farm or farm property, or

(bb) his entire interest in a trade or business and all substantially similar trades or businesses, and

(IV) the ownership interest of whom may be readily established by reason of qualified allocations (of the type described in section 168(j)(9)(B), one class of stock, or the like).

(ii) 10-PERCENT OWNER DEFINED.—The term "10-percent owner" means a person having at least a 10-percent ownership interest, applying the attribution rules of section 318 (other than subsection (a)(4)).

(iii) TRADE OR BUSINESS DEFINED.—

(I) IN GENERAL.—The term "trade or business" means any trade or business, including any line of business, qualifying as an active trade or business within the meaning of section 355.

(II) RENTAL OF REAL PROPERTY.—For purposes of this clause, the holding of real property for rental shall not be treated as an active trade or business.

* * *

(j) Clarification That Prior Effective Date Rules Not Affected.—Nothing in the amendment made by section 41(a) shall affect the application of any effective date provision (including any transitional rule) for any provision which was a predecessor to any provision contained in part V of subchapter P of chapter 1 of the Internal Revenue Code of 1954 (as added by section 41).

Subchapter F—Exempt Organizations

PART I—GENERAL RULE

[Sec. 501]

SEC. 501. EXEMPTION FROM TAX ON CORPORATIONS, CERTAIN TRUSTS, ETC.

[Sec. 501(a)]

(a) EXEMPTION FROM TAXATION.—An organization described in subsection (c) or (d) or section 401(a) shall be exempt from taxation under this subtitle unless such exemption is denied under section 502 or 503.

Amendments

• 1969, Tax Reform Act of 1969 (P.L. 91-172)

P.L. 91-172, §101 (j)(3):

Amended Code Sec. 501(a) by substituting "section 502 or 503" for "section 502, 503, or 504." **Effective** for tax years beginning after 12-31-69.

[Sec. 501(b)]

(b) TAX ON UNRELATED BUSINESS INCOME AND CERTAIN OTHER ACTIVITIES.—An organization exempt from taxation under subsection (a) shall be subject to tax to the extent provided in parts II, III, and VI of this subchapter, but (notwithstanding parts II, III and VI of this subchapter) shall be considered an organization exempt from income taxes for the purpose of any law which refers to organizations exempt from income taxes.

Amendments

• 1975 (P.L. 93-625)

P.L. 93-625, §10(c):

Amended Code Sec. 501(b) by substituting "Parts II, III, and VI" for "Parts II and III". **Effective** for tax years beginning after 12-31-74.

• 1969, Tax Reform Act of 1969 (P.L. 91-172)

P.L. 91-172, §101(j)(4):

Amended Code Sec. 501(b). **Effective** 1-1-70. Prior to amendment, Code Sec. 501(b) read as follows:

"(b) Tax on Unrelated Business Income.—An organization exempt from taxation under subsection (a) shall be subject to tax to the extent provided in part II of this subchapter (relating to tax on unrelated income), but, notwithstanding part II, shall be considered an organization exempt from income taxes for the purpose of any law which refers to organizations exempt from income taxes."

[Sec. 501(c)]

(c) LIST OF EXEMPT ORGANIZATIONS.—The following organizations are referred to in subsection (a):

(1) Any corporation organized under Act of Congress which is an instrumentality of the United States but only if such corporation—

(A) is exempt from Federal income taxes—

(i) under such Act as amended and supplemented before July 18, 1984, or

(ii) under this title without regard to any provision of law which is not contained in this title and which is not contained in a revenue Act, or

(B) is described in subsection (l).

(2) Corporations organized for the exclusive purpose of holding title to property, collecting income therefrom, and turning over the entire amount thereof, less expenses, to an organization which itself is exempt under this section. Rules similar to the rules of subparagraph (G) of paragraph (25) shall apply for purposes of this paragraph.

(3) Corporations, and any community chest, fund, or foundation, organized and operated exclusively for religious, charitable, scientific, testing for public safety, literary, or educational purposes, or to foster national or international amateur sports competition (but only if no part of its activities involve the provision of athletic facilities or equipment), or for the prevention of cruelty to children or animals, no part of the net earnings of which inures to the benefit of any private shareholder or individual, no substantial part of the activities of which is carrying on propaganda, or otherwise attempting, to influence legislation (except as otherwise provided in subsection (h)), and which does not participate in, or intervene in (including the publishing or distributing of statements), any political campaign on behalf of (or in opposition to) any candidate for public office.

(4)(A) Civic leagues or organizations not organized for profit but operated exclusively for the promotion of social welfare, or local associations of employees, the membership of which is limited to the employees of a designated person or persons in a particular municipality, and the net earnings of which are devoted exclusively to charitable, educational, or recreational purposes.

(B) Subparagraph (A) shall not apply to an entity unless no part of the net earnings of such entity inures to the benefit of any private shareholder or individual.

(5) Labor, agricultural, or horticultural organizations.

(6) Business leagues, chambers of commerce, real-estate boards, boards of trade, or professional football leagues (whether or not administering a pension fund for football players), not organized for profit and no part of the net earnings of which inures to the benefit of any private shareholder or individual.

(7) Clubs organized for pleasure, recreation, and other nonprofitable purposes, substantially all of the activities of which are for such purposes and no part of the net earnings of which inures to the benefit of any private shareholder.

(8) Fraternal beneficiary societies, orders, or associations—

(A) operating under the lodge system or for the exclusive benefit of the members of a fraternity itself operating under the lodge system, and

(B) providing for the payment of life, sick, accident, or other benefits to the members of such society, order, or association or their dependents.

(9) Voluntary employees' beneficiary associations providing for the payment of life, sick, accident, or other benefits to the members of such association or their dependents or designated beneficiaries, if no part of the net earnings of such association inures (other than through such payments) to the benefit of any private shareholder or individual. For purposes of providing for the payment of sick and accident benefits to members of such an association and their dependents, the term "dependent" shall include any individual who is a child (as defined in section 152(f)(1)) of a member who as of the end of the calendar year has not attained age 27.

(10) Domestic fraternal societies, orders, or associations, operating under the lodge system—

(A) the net earnings of which are devoted exclusively to religious, charitable, scientific, literary, educational, and fraternal purposes, and

(B) which do not provide for the payment of life, sick, accident, or other benefits.

(11) Teachers' retirement fund associations of a purely local character, if—

(A) no part of their net earnings inures (other than through payment of retirement benefits) to the benefit of any private shareholder or individual, and

(B) the income consists solely of amounts received from public taxation, amounts received from assessments on the teaching salaries of members, and income in respect of investments.

(12)(A) Benevolent life insurance associations of a purely local character, mutual ditch or irrigation companies, mutual or cooperative telephone companies, or like organizations; but only if 85 percent or more of the income consists of amounts collected from members for the sole purpose of meeting losses and expenses.

(B) In the case of a mutual or cooperative telephone company subparagraph (A) shall be applied without taking into account any income received or accrued—

(i) from a nonmember telephone company for the performance of communication services which involve members of the mutual or cooperative telephone company,

(ii) from qualified pole rentals,

(iii) from the sale of display listings in a directory furnished to the members of the mutual or cooperative telephone company, or

(iv) from the prepayment of a loan under section 306A, 306B, or 311 of the Rural Electrification Act of 1936 (as in effect on January 1, 1987).

(C) In the case of a mutual or cooperative electric company, subparagraph (A) shall be applied without taking into account any income received or accrued—

(i) from qualified pole rentals, or

(ii) from any provision or sale of electric energy transmission services or ancillary services if such services are provided on a nondiscriminatory open access basis under an open access transmission tariff approved or accepted by FERC or under an independent transmission provider agreement approved or accepted by FERC (other than income received or accrued directly or indirectly from a member),

(iii) from the provision or sale of electric energy distribution services or ancillary services if such services are provided on a nondiscriminatory open access basis to distribute electric energy not owned by the mutual or electric cooperative company—

(I) to end-users who are served by distribution facilities not owned by such company or any of its members (other than income received or accrued directly or indirectly from a member), or

(II) generated by a generation facility not owned or leased by such company or any of its members and which is directly connected to distribution facilities owned by such company or any of its members (other than income received or accrued directly or indirectly from a member),

(iv) from any nuclear decommissioning transaction, or

(v) from any asset exchange or conversion transaction.

(D) For purposes of this paragraph, the term "qualified pole rental" means any rental of a pole (or other structure used to support wires) if such pole (or other structure)—

(i) is used by the telephone or electric company to support one or more wires which are used by such company in providing telephone or electric services to its members, and

(ii) is used pursuant to the rental to support one or more wires (in addition to the wires described in clause (i)) for use in connection with the transmission by wire of electricity or of telephone or other communications.

For purposes of the preceding sentence, the term "rental" includes any sale of the right to use the pole (or other structure).

(E) For purposes of subparagraph (C)(ii), the term "FERC" means the Federal Energy Regulatory Commission and references to such term shall be treated as including the Public Utility Commission of Texas with respect to any ERCOT utility (as defined in section 212(k)(2)(B) of the Federal Power Act (16 U.S.C. 824k(k)(2)(B))).

(F) For purposes of subparagraph (C)(iv), the term "nuclear decommissioning transaction" means—

(i) any transfer into a trust, fund, or instrument established to pay any nuclear decommissioning costs if the transfer is in connection with the transfer of the mutual or cooperative electric company's interest in a nuclear power plant or nuclear power plant unit,

(ii) any distribution from any trust, fund, or instrument established to pay any nuclear decommissioning costs, or

(iii) any earnings from any trust, fund, or instrument established to pay any nuclear decommissioning costs.

(G) For purposes of subparagraph (C)(v), the term "asset exchange or conversion transaction" means any voluntary exchange or involuntary conversion of any property related to generating, transmitting, distributing, or selling electric energy by a mutual or cooperative electric company, the gain from which qualifies for deferred recognition under section 1031 or 1033, but only if the replacement property acquired by such company pursuant to such section constitutes property which is used, or to be used, for—

(i) generating, transmitting, distributing, or selling electric energy, or

(ii) producing, transmitting, distributing, or selling natural gas.

(H)(i) In the case of a mutual or cooperative electric company described in this paragraph or an organization described in section 1381(a)(2)(C), income received or accrued from a load loss transaction shall be treated as an amount collected from members for the sole purpose of meeting losses and expenses.

(ii) For purposes of clause (i), the term "load loss transaction" means any wholesale or retail sale of electric energy (other than to members) to the extent that the aggregate sales during the recovery period do not exceed the load loss mitigation sales limit for such period.

(iii) For purposes of clause (ii), the load loss mitigation sales limit for the recovery period is the sum of the annual load losses for each year of such period.

(iv) For purposes of clause (iii), a mutual or cooperative electric company's annual load loss for each year of the recovery period is the amount (if any) by which—

(I) the megawatt hours of electric energy sold during such year to members of such electric company are less than

(II) the megawatt hours of electric energy sold during the base year to such members.

(v) For purposes of clause (iv)(II), the term "base year" means—

(I) the calendar year preceding the start-up year, or

(II) at the election of the mutual or cooperative electric company, the second or third calendar years preceding the start-up year.

(vi) For purposes of this subparagraph, the recovery period is the 7-year period beginning with the start-up year.

(vii) For purposes of this subparagraph, the start-up year is the first year that the mutual or cooperative electric company offers nondiscriminatory open access or the calendar year which includes the date of the enactment of this subparagraph, if later, at the election of such company.

(viii) A company shall not fail to be treated as a mutual or cooperative electric company for purposes of this paragraph or as a corporation operating on a cooperative basis for purposes of section 1381(a)(2)(C) by reason of the treatment under clause (i).

(ix) For purposes of subparagraph (A), in the case of a mutual or cooperative electric company, income received, or accrued, indirectly from a member shall be treated as an amount collected from members for the sole purpose of meeting losses and expenses.

(13) Cemetery companies owned and operated exclusively for the benefit of their members or which are not operated for profit; and any corporation chartered solely for the purpose of the disposal of bodies by burial or cremation which is not permitted by its charter to engage in any business not necessarily incident to that purpose and no part of the net earnings of which inures to the benefit of any private shareholder or individual.

(14)(A) Credit unions without capital stock organized and operated for mutual purposes and without profit.

(B) Corporations or associations without capital stock organized before September 1, 1957, and operated for mutual purposes and without profit for the purpose of providing reserve funds for, and insurance of shares or deposits in—

(i) domestic building and loan associations,

(ii) cooperative banks without capital stock organized and operated for mutual purposes and without profit,

(iii) mutual savings banks not having capital stock represented by shares, or

(iv) mutual savings banks described in section 591(b).

(C) Corporations or associations organized before September 1, 1957, and operated for mutual purposes and without profit for the purpose of providing reserve funds for associations or banks described in clause (i), (ii), or (iii) of subparagraph (B); but only if 85 percent or more of the income is attributable to providing such reserve funds and to investments. This subparagraph shall not apply to any corporation or association entitled to exemption under subparagraph (B).

(15)(A) Insurance companies (as defined in section 816(a)) other than life (including interinsurers and reciprocal underwriters) if—

(i)(I) the gross receipts for the taxable year do not exceed $600,000, and

(II) more than 50 percent of such gross receipts consist of premiums, or

(ii) in the case of a mutual insurance company—

(I) the gross receipts of which for the taxable year do not exceed $150,000, and

(II) more than 35 percent of such gross receipts consist of premiums.

Clause (ii) shall not apply to a company if any employee of the company, or a member of the employee's family (as defined in section 2032A(e)(2)), is an employee of another company exempt from taxation by reason of this paragraph (or would be so exempt but for this sentence).

(B) For purposes of subparagraph (A), in determining whether any company or association is described in subparagraph (A), such company or association shall be treated as receiving during the taxable year amounts described in subparagraph (A) which are received during such year by all other companies or associations which are members of the same controlled group as the insurance company or association for which the determination is being made.

(C) For purposes of subparagraph (B), the term "controlled group" has the meaning given such term by section 831(b)(2)(B)(ii), except that in applying section 831(b)(2)(B)(ii) for purposes of this subparagraph, subparagraphs (B) and (C) of section 1563(b)(2) shall be disregarded.

(16) Corporations organized by an association subject to part IV of this subchapter or members thereof, for the purpose of financing the ordinary crop operations of such members or other producers, and operated in conjunction with such association. Exemption shall not be denied any such corporation because it has capital stock, if the dividend rate of such stock is fixed at not to exceed the legal rate of interest in the State of incorporation or 8 percent per annum, whichever is greater, on the value of the consideration for which the stock was issued,

and if substantially all such stock (other than nonvoting preferred stock, the owners of which are not entitled or permitted to participate, directly or indirectly, in the profits of the corporation, on dissolution or otherwise, beyond the fixed dividends) is owned by such association, or members thereof; nor shall exemption be denied any such corporation because there is accumulated and maintained by it a reserve required by State law or a reasonable reserve for any necessary purpose.

(17)(A) A trust or trusts forming part of a plan providing for the payment of supplemental unemployment compensation benefits, if—

(i) under the plan, it is impossible, at any time prior to the satisfaction of all liabilities with respect to employees under the plan, for any part of the corpus or income to be (within the taxable year or thereafter) used for, or diverted to, any purpose other than the providing of supplemental unemployment compensation benefits,

(ii) such benefits are payable to employees under a classification which is set forth in the plan and which is found by the Secretary not to be discriminatory in favor of employees who are highly compensated employees (within the meaning of section 414(q)), and

(iii) such benefits do not discriminate in favor of employees who are highly compensated employees (within the meaning of section 414(q)). A plan shall not be considered discriminatory within the meaning of this clause merely because the benefits received under the plan bear a uniform relationship to the total compensation, or the basic or regular rate of compensation, of the employees covered by the plan.

(B) In determining whether a plan meets the requirements of subparagraph (A), any benefits provided under any other plan shall not be taken into consideration, except that a plan shall not be considered discriminatory—

(i) merely because the benefits under the plan which are first determined in a nondiscriminatory manner within the meaning of subparagraph (A) are then reduced by any sick, accident, or unemployment compensation benefits received under State or Federal law (or reduced by a portion of such benefits if determined in a nondiscriminatory manner), or

(ii) merely because the plan provides only for employees who are not eligible to receive sick, accident, or unemployment compensation benefits under State or Federal law the same benefits (or a portion of such benefits if determined in a nondiscriminatory manner) which such employees would receive under such laws if such employees were eligible for such benefits, or

(iii) merely because the plan provides only for employees who are not eligible under another plan (which meets the requirements of subparagraph (A)) of supplemental unemployment compensation benefits provided wholly by the employer the same benefits (or a portion of such benefits if determined in a nondiscriminatory manner) which such employees would receive under such other plan if such employees were eligible under such other plan, but only if the employees eligible under both plans would make a classification which would be nondiscriminatory within the meaning of subparagraph (A).

(C) A plan shall be considered to meet the requirements of subparagraph (A) during the whole of any year of the plan if on one day in each quarter it satisfies such requirements.

(D) The term "supplemental unemployment compensation benefits" means only—

(i) benefits which are paid to an employee because of his involuntary separation from the employment of the employer (whether or not such separation is temporary) resulting directly from a reduction in force, the discontinuance of a plant or operation, or other similar conditions, and

(ii) sick and accident benefits subordinate to the benefits described in clause (i).

(E) Exemption shall not be denied under subsection (a) to any organization entitled to such exemption as an association described in paragraph (9) of this subsection merely because such organization provides for the payment of supplemental unemployment benefits (as defined in subparagraph (D)(i)).

(18) A trust or trusts created before June 25, 1959, forming part of a plan providing for the payment of benefits under a pension plan funded only by contributions of employees, if—

(A) under the plan, it is impossible, at any time prior to the satisfaction of all liabilities with respect to employees under the plan, for any part of the corpus or income to be (within the taxable year or thereafter) used for, or diverted to, any purpose other than the providing of benefits under the plan,

(B) such benefits are payable to employees under a classification which is set forth in the plan and which is found by the Secretary not to be discriminatory in favor of employees who are highly compensated employees (within the meaning of section 414(q)),

(C) such benefits do not discriminate in favor of employees who are highly compensated employees (within the meaning of section 414(q)). A plan shall not be considered discriminatory within the meaning of this subparagraph merely because the benefits received under the plan bear a uniform relationship to the total compensation, or the basic or regular rate of compensation, of the employees covered by the plan, and

(D) in the case of a plan under which an employee may designate certain contributions as deductible—

(i) such contributions do not exceed the amount with respect to which a deduction is allowable under section 219(b)(3),

(ii) requirements similar to the requirements of section 401(k)(3)(A)(ii) are met with respect to such elective contributions,

(iii) such contributions are treated as elective deferrals for purposes of section 402(g), and

(iv) the requirements of section 401(a)(30) are met.

For purposes of subparagraph (D)(ii), rules similar to the rules of section 401(k)(8) shall apply. For purposes of section 4979, any excess contribution under clause (ii) shall be treated as an excess contribution under a cash or deferred arrangement.

(19) A post or organization of past or present members of the Armed Forces of the United States, or an auxiliary unit or society of, or a trust or foundation for, any such post or organization—

(A) organized in the United States or any of its possessions,

(B) at least 75 percent of the members of which are past or present members of the Armed Forces of the United States and substantially all of the other members of which are individuals who are cadets or are spouses, widows,, widowers, ancestors, or lineal descendants of past or present members of the Armed Forces of the United States or of cadets, and

(C) no part of the net earnings of which inures to the benefit of any private shareholder or individual.

(20) An organization or trust created or organized in the United States, the exclusive function of which is to form part of a qualified group legal services plan or plans, within the meaning of section 120. An organization or trust which receives contributions because of section 120(c)(5)(C) shall not be prevented from qualifying as an organization described in this paragraph merely because it provides legal services or indemnification against the cost of legal services unassociated with a qualified group legal services plan.

(21)(A) A trust or trusts established in writing, created or organized in the United States, and contributed to by any person (except an insurance company) if—

(i) the purpose of such trust or trusts is exclusively—

(I) to satisfy, in whole or in part, the liability of such person for, or with respect to, claims for compensation for disability or death due to pneumoconiosis under Black Lung Acts,

(II) to pay premiums for insurance exclusively covering such liability,

(III) to pay administrative and other incidental expenses of such trust in connection with the operation of the trust and the processing of claims against such person under Black Lung Acts, and

(IV) to pay accident or health benefits for retired miners and their spouses and dependents (including administrative and other incidental expenses of such trust in connection therewith) or premiums for insurance exclusively covering such benefits; and

(ii) no part of the assets of the trust may be used for, or diverted to, any purpose other than—

(I) the purposes described in clause (i),

(II) investment (but only to the extent that the trustee determines that a portion of the assets is not currently needed for the purposes described in clause (i)) in qualified investments, or

(III) payment into the Black Lung Disability Trust Fund established under section 9501, or into the general fund of the United States Treasury (other than in satisfaction of any tax or other civil or criminal liability of the person who established or contributed to the trust).

(B) No deduction shall be allowed under this chapter for any payment described in subparagraph (A)(i)(IV) from such trust.

(C) Payments described in subparagraph (A)(i)(IV) may be made from such trust during a taxable year only to the extent that the aggregate amount of such payments during such taxable year does not exceed the excess (if any), as of the close of the preceding taxable year, of—

(i) the fair market value of the assets of the trust, over

(ii) 110 percent of the present value of the liability described in subparagraph (A)(i)(I) of such person.

The determinations under the preceding sentence shall be made by an independent actuary using actuarial methods and assumptions (not inconsistent with the regulations prescribed under section 192(c)(1)(A)) each of which is reasonable and which are reasonable in the aggregate.

(D) For purposes of this paragraph:

(i) The term "Black Lung Acts" means part C of title IV of the Federal Mine Safety and Health Act of 1977, and any State law providing compensation for disability or death due to that pneumoconiosis.

(ii) The term "qualified investments" means—

(I) public debt securities of the United States,

(II) obligations of a State or local government which are not in default as to principal or interest, and

(III) time or demand deposits in a bank (as defined in section 581) or an insured credit union (within the meaning of section 101(7) of the Federal Credit Union Act, 12 U.S.C. 1752(7)) located in the United States.

(iii) The term "miner" has the same meaning as such term has when used in section 402(d) of the Black Lung Benefits Act (30 U.S.C. 902(d)).

(iv) The term "incidental expenses" includes legal, accounting, actuarial, and trustee expenses.

(22) A trust created or organized in the United States and established in writing by the plan sponsors of multiemployer plans if—

(A) the purpose of such trust is exclusively—

(i) to pay any amount described in section 4223(c) or (h) of the Employee Retirement Income Security Act of 1974, and

(ii) to pay reasonable and necessary administrative expenses in connection with the establishment and operation of the trust and the processing of claims against the trust,

(B) no part of the assets of the trust may be used for, or diverted to, any purpose other than—

(i) the purposes described in subparagraph (A), or

(ii) the investment in securities, obligations, or time or demand deposits described in clause (ii) of paragraph (21)(D),

(C) such trust meets the requirements of paragraphs (2), (3), and (4) of section 4223(b), 4223(h), or, if applicable, section 4223(c) of the Employee Retirement Income Security Act of 1974, and

(D) the trust instrument provides that, on dissolution of the trust, assets of the trust may not be paid other than to plans which have participated in the plan or, in the case of a trust established under section 4223(h) of such Act, to plans with respect to which employers have participated in the fund.

(23) Any association organized before 1880 more than 75 percent of the members of which are present or past members of the Armed Forces and a principal purpose of which is to provide insurance and other benefits to veterans or their dependents.

(24) A trust described in section 4049 of the Employee Retirement Income Security Act of 1974 (as in effect on the date of the enactment of the Single-Employer Pension Plan Amendments Act of 1986).

(25)(A) Any corporation or trust which—

(i) has no more than 35 shareholders or beneficiaries,

(ii) has only 1 class of stock or beneficial interest, and

(iii) is organized for the exclusive purposes of—

(I) acquiring real property and holding title to, and collecting income from, such property, and

(II) remitting the entire amount of income from such property (less expenses) to 1 or more organizations described in subparagraph (C) which are shareholders of such corporation or beneficiaries of such trust.

For purposes of clause (iii), the term "real property" shall not include any interest as a tenant in common (or similar interest) and shall not include any indirect interest.

(B) A corporation or trust shall be described in subparagraph (A) without regard to whether the corporation or trust is organized by 1 or more organizations described in subparagraph (C).

(C) An organization is described in this subparagraph if such organization is—

(i) a qualified pension, profit sharing, or stock bonus plan that meets the requirements of section 401(a),

(ii) a governmental plan (within the meaning of section 414(d)),

(iii) the United States, any State or political subdivision thereof, or any agency or instrumentality of any of the foregoing, or

(iv) any organization described in paragraph (3).

(D) A corporation or trust shall in no event be treated as described in subparagraph (A) unless such corporation or trust permits its shareholders or beneficiaries—

(i) to dismiss the corporation's or trust's investment adviser, following reasonable notice, upon a vote of the shareholders or beneficiaries holding a majority of interest in the corporation or trust, and

(ii) to terminate their interest in the corporation or trust by either, or both, of the following alternatives, as determined by the corporation or trust:

(I) by selling or exchanging their stock in the corporation or interest in the trust (subject to any Federal or State securities law) to any organization described in subparagraph (C) so long as the sale or exchange does not increase the number of shareholders or beneficiaries in such corporation or trust above 35, or

(II) by having their stock or interest redeemed by the corporation or trust after the shareholder or beneficiary has provided 90 days notice to such corporation or trust.

(E)(i) For purposes of this title—

(I) a corporation which is a qualified subsidiary shall not be treated as a separate corporation, and

(II) all assets, liabilities, and items of income, deduction, and credit of a qualified subsidiary shall be treated as assets, liabilities, and such items (as the case may be) of the corporation or trust described in subparagraph (A).

(ii) For purposes of this subparagraph, the term "qualified subsidiary" means any corporation if, at all times during the period such corporation was in existence, 100 percent of the stock of such corporation is held by the corporation or trust described in subparagraph (A).

(iii) For purposes of this subtitle, if any corporation which was a qualified subsidiary ceases to meet the requirements of clause (ii), such corporation shall be treated as a new corporation acquiring all of its assets (and assuming all of its liabilities) immediately before such cessation from the corporation or trust described in subparagraph (A) in exchange for its stock.

(F) For purposes of subparagraph (A), the term "real property" includes any personal property which is leased under, or in connection with, a lease of real property, but only if the rent attributable to such personal property (determined under the rules of section 856(d)(1)) for the taxable year does not exceed 15 percent of the total rent for the taxable year attributable to both the real and personal property leased under, or in connection with, such lease.

(G)(i) An organization shall not be treated as failing to be described in this paragraph merely by reason of the receipt of any otherwise disqualifying income which is incidentally derived from the holding of real property.

(ii) Clause (i) shall not apply if the amount of gross income described in such clause exceeds 10 percent of the organization's gross income for the taxable year unless the organization establishes to the satisfaction of the Secretary that the receipt of gross income described in clause (i) in excess of such limitation was inadvertent and reasonable steps are being taken to correct the circumstances giving rise to such income.

(26) Any membership organization if—

(A) such organization is established by a State exclusively to provide coverage for medical care (as defined in section 213(d)) on a not-for-profit basis to individuals described in subparagraph (B) through—

(i) insurance issued by the organization, or

(ii) a health maintenance organization under an arrangement with the organization,

(B) the only individuals receiving such coverage through the organization are individuals—

(i) who are residents of such State, and

(ii) who, by reason of the existence or history of a medical condition—

(I) are unable to acquire medical care coverage for such condition through insurance or from a health maintenance organization, or

(II) are able to acquire such coverage only at a rate which is substantially in excess of the rate for such coverage through the membership organization,

(C) the composition of the membership in such organization is specified by such State, and

(D) no part of the net earnings of the organization inures to the benefit of any private shareholder or individual.

A spouse and any qualifying child (as defined in section 24(c)) of an individual described in subparagraph (B) (without regard to this sentence) shall be treated as described in subparagraph (B).

(27)(A) Any membership organization if—

(i) such organization is established before June 1, 1996, by a State exclusively to reimburse its members for losses arising under workmen's compensation acts,

(ii) such State requires that the membership of such organization consist of—

(I) all persons who issue insurance covering workmen's compensation losses in such State, and

(II) all persons and governmental entities who self-insure against such losses, and

(iii) such organization operates as a non-profit organization by—

(I) returning surplus income to its members or workmen's compensation policyholders on a periodic basis, and

(II) reducing initial premiums in anticipation of investment income.

(B) Any organization (including a mutual insurance company) if—

(i) such organization is created by State law and is organized and operated under State law exclusively to—

(I) provide workmen's compensation insurance which is required by State law or with respect to which State law provides significant disincentives if such insurance is not purchased by an employer, and

(II) provide related coverage which is incidental to workmen's compensation insurance,

(ii) such organization must provide workmen's compensation insurance to any employer in the State (for employees in the State or temporarily assigned out-of-State) which seeks such insurance and meets other reasonable requirements relating thereto,

(iii) (I) the State makes a financial commitment with respect to such organization either by extending the full faith and credit of the State to the initial debt of such organization or by providing the initial operating capital of such organization, and (II) in the case of periods after the date of enactment of this subparagraph, the assets of such organization revert to the State upon dissolution or State law does not permit the dissolution of such organization, and

(iv) the majority of the board of directors or oversight body of such organization are appointed by the chief executive officer or other executive branch official of the State, by the State legislature, or by both.

(28) The National Railroad Retirement Investment Trust established under section 15(j) of the Railroad Retirement Act of 1974.

(29) CO-OP HEALTH INSURANCE ISSUERS.—

(A) IN GENERAL.—A qualified nonprofit health insurance issuer (within the meaning of section 1322 of the Patient Protection and Affordable Care Act) which has received a loan or grant under the CO-OP program under such section, but only with respect to periods for which the issuer is in compliance with the requirements of such section and any agreement with respect to the loan or grant.

(B) CONDITIONS FOR EXEMPTION.—Subparagraph (A) shall apply to an organization only if—

(i) the organization has given notice to the Secretary, in such manner as the Secretary may by regulations prescribe, that it is applying for recognition of its status under this paragraph,

(ii) except as provided in section 1322(c)(4) of the Patient Protection and Affordable Care Act, no part of the net earnings of which inures to the benefit of any private shareholder or individual,

(iii) no substantial part of the activities of which is carrying on propaganda, or otherwise attempting, to influence legislation, and

(iv) the organization does not participate in, or intervene in (including the publishing or distributing of statements), any political campaign on behalf of (or in opposition to) any candidate for public office.

Amendments

• 2010, Health Care and Education Reconciliation Act of 2010 (P.L. 111-152)

P.L. 111-152, §1004(d)(4):

Amended Code Sec. 501(c)(9) by adding at the end a new sentence. **Effective** 3-30-2010.

• 2010, Patient Protection and Affordable Care Act (P.L. 111-148)

P.L. 111-148, §1322(h)(1):

Amended Code Sec. 501(c) by adding at the end a new paragraph (29). **Effective** 3-23-2010.

• 2006, Fallen Firefighters Assistance Tax Clarification Act of 2006 (P.L. 109-445)

P.L. 109-445, §2(a), provides:

(a) IN GENERAL.—For purposes of the Internal Revenue Code of 1986, payments made on behalf of any firefighter who died as the result of the October 2006 Esperanza Incident fire in southern California to any family member of such firefighter by an organization described in paragraph (1) or (2) of section 509(a) of such Code shall be treated as related to the purpose or function constituting the basis for such organization's exemption under section 501 of such Code if such payments are made in good faith using a reasonable and objective formula which is consistently applied,

(b) APPLICATION.—Subsection (a) shall apply only to payments made on or after October 26, 2006, and before June 1, 2007.

• 2006, Pension Protection Act of 2006 (P.L. 109-280)

P.L. 109-280, §811, provides:

SEC. 811. PENSIONS AND INDIVIDUAL RETIREMENT ARRANGEMENT PROVISIONS OF ECONOMIC GROWTH AND TAX RELIEF RECONCILIATION ACT OF 2001 MADE PERMANENT.

Title IX of the Economic Growth and Tax Relief Reconciliation Act of 2001 [P.L. 107-16] shall not apply to the provisions of, and amendments made by, subtitles A through F of title VI [§§601-666]of such Act (relating to pension and individual retirement arrangement provisions).

P.L. 109-280, §862(a):

Amended so much of Code Sec. 501(c)(21)(C) as precedes the last sentence. **Effective** for tax years beginning after 12-31-2006. Prior to amendment, so much of Code Sec. 501(c)(21)(C) as precedes the last sentence read as follows:

(C) Payments described in subparagraph (A)(i)(IV) may be made from such trust during a taxable year only to the extent that the aggregate amount of such payments during such taxable year does not exceed the lesser of—

(i) the excess (if any) (as of the close of the preceding taxable year) of—

(I) the fair market value of the assets of the trust, over

(II) 110 percent of the present value of the liability described in subparagraph (A)(i)(I) of such person, or

(ii) the excess (if any) of—

(I) the sum of a similar excess determined as of the close of the last taxable year ending before the date of the enactment of this subparagraph plus earnings thereon as of the close of the taxable year preceding the taxable year involved, over

(II) the aggregate payments described in subparagraph (A)(i)(IV) made from the trust during all taxable years beginning after the date of the enactment of this subparagraph.

• 2005, Gulf Opportunity Zone Act of 2005 (P.L. 109-135)

P.L. 109-135, §412(bb)(1)-(2):

Amended Code Sec. 501(c)(12) by striking "subparagraph (C)(iii)" in subparagraph (F) and inserting "subparagraph (C)(iv)", and by striking "subparagraph (C)(iv)" in subparagraph (G) and inserting "subparagraph (C)(v)". **Effective** 12-21-2005.

P.L. 109-135, §412(cc):

Amended Code Sec. 501(c)(22)(B)(ii) by striking "clause (ii) of paragraph (21)(B)" and inserting "clause (ii) of paragraph (21)(D)". **Effective** 12-21-2005.

• 2005, Energy Tax Incentives Act of 2005 (P.L. 109-58)

P.L. 109-58, §1304(a):

Amended Code Sec. 501(c)(12)(C) by striking the last sentence. **Effective** 8-8-2005. Prior to being stricken, the last sentence of Code Sec. 501(c)(12)(C) read as follows:

Clauses (ii) through (v) shall not apply to taxable years beginning after December 31, 2006.

P.L. 109-58, §1304(b):

Amended Code Sec. 501(c)(12)(H) by striking clause (x). **Effective** 8-8-2005. Prior to being stricken, Code Sec. 501(c)(12)(H)(x) read as follows:

(x) This subparagraph shall not apply to taxable years beginning after December 31, 2006.

• 2004, American Jobs Creation Act of 2004 (P.L. 108-357)

P.L. 108-357, §319(a)(1):

Amended Code Sec. 501(c)(12)(C) by striking clause (ii) and adding at the end new clauses (ii)-(v) and a new flush sentence. **Effective** for tax years beginning after 10-22-2004. Prior to being striken, Code Sec 501(c)(12)(C)(ii) read as follows:

(ii) from the prepayment of a loan under section 306A, 306B, or 311 of the Rural Electrification Act of 1936 (as in effect on January 1, 1987).

P.L. 108-357, §319(a)(2):

Amended Code Sec. 501(c)(12) by adding at the end new subparagraphs (E)-(G). **Effective** for tax years beginning after 10-22-2004.

P.L. 108-357, §319(b):

Amended Code Sec. 501(c)(12), as amended by Act Sec. 319(a)(2), by adding after subparagraph (G) new subparagraph (H). **Effective** for tax years beginning after 10-22-2004.

• 2004, Pension Funding Equity Act of 2004 (P.L. 108-218)

P.L. 108-218, §206(a):

Amended Code Sec. 501(c)(15)(A). **Effective** generally for tax years beginning after 12-31-2003. For a transition rule, see Act Sec. 206(e)(2), below. Prior to amendment, Code Sec. 501(c)(15)(A) read as follows:

(A) Insurance companies or associations other than life (including interinsurers and reciprocal underwriters) if the net written premiums (or, if greater, direct written premiums) for the taxable year do not exceed $350,000.

P.L. 108-218, §206(b):

Amended Code Sec. 501(c)(15)(C) by inserting ", except that in applying section 831(b)(2)(B)(ii) for purposes of this subparagraph, subparagraphs (B) and (C) of section 1563(b)(2) shall be disregarded" before the period at the end. **Effective** generally for tax years beginning after 12-31-2003. For a transition rule, see Act Sec. 206(e)(2), below.

P.L. 108-218, §206(e)(2), provides:

(2) TRANSITION RULE FOR COMPANIES IN RECEIVERSHIP OR LIQUIDATION.—In the case of a company or association which—

(A) for the taxable year which includes April 1, 2004, meets the requirements of section 501(c)(15)(A) of the Internal Revenue Code of 1986, as in effect for the last taxable year beginning before January 1, 2004, and

(B) on April 1, 2004, is in a receivership, liquidation, or similar proceeding under the supervision of a State court,

the amendments made by this section shall apply to taxable years beginning after the earlier of the date such proceeding ends or December 31, 2007.

• 2003, Military Family Tax Relief Act of 2003 (P.L. 108-121)

P.L. 108-121, §105(a):

Amended Code Sec. 501(c)(19)(B) by striking "or widowers" and inserting ", widowers, ancestors, or lineal descendants". **Effective** for tax years beginning after 11-11-2003.

• 2002, Victims of Terrorism Tax Relief Act of 2001 (P.L. 107-134)

P.L. 107-134, §104, provides:

SEC. 104. PAYMENTS BY CHARITABLE ORGANIZATIONS TREATED AS EXEMPT PAYMENTS.

(a) IN GENERAL.—For purposes of the Internal Revenue Code of 1986—

(1) payments made by an organization described in section 501(c)(3) of such Code by reason of the death, injury, wounding, or illness of an individual incurred as the result of the terrorist attacks against the United States on September 11, 2001, or an attack involving anthrax occurring on or after September 11, 2001, and before January 1, 2002, shall be treated as related to the purpose or function constituting the basis for such organization's exemption under section 501 of such Code if such payments are made in good faith using a reasonable and objective formula which is consistently applied; and

(2) in the case of a private foundation (as defined in section 509 of such Code), any payment described in paragraph (1) shall not be treated as made to a disqualified person for purposes of section 4941 of such Code.

(b) EFFECTIVE DATE.—This section shall apply to payments made on or after September 11, 2001.

• 2001, Railroad Retirement and Survivors' Improvement Act of 2001 (P.L. 107-90)

P.L. 107-90, §202:

Amended Code Sec. 501(c) by adding at the end a new paragraph (28). **Effective** 12-21-2001.

• 2001, Economic Growth and Tax Relief Reconciliation Act of 2001 (P.L. 107-16)

P.L. 107-16, §611(d)(3)(C):

Amended Code Sec. 501(c)(18)(D)(iii) by striking "(other than paragraph (4) thereof)" after "section 402(g)". **Effective** for years beginning after 12-31-2001. For a special rule, see Act Sec. 611(i)(3), below.

P.L. 107-16, §611(i)(3) (as added by P.L. 107-147, §411(j)(3)), provides:

(3) SPECIAL RULE.—In the case of [a] plan that, on June 7, 2001, incorporated by reference the limitation of section 415(b)(1)(A) of the Internal Revenue Code of 1986, section 411(d)(6) of such Code and section 204(g)(1) of the Employee Retirement Income Security Act of 1974 do not apply to a plan amendment that—

(A) is adopted on or before June 30, 2002,

(B) reduces benefits to the level that would have applied without regard to the amendments made by subsection (a) of this section, and

(C) is effective no earlier than the years described in paragraph (2).

P.L. 107-16, §901(a)-(b), provides [but see P.L. 109-280, §811, above]:

SEC. 901. SUNSET OF PROVISIONS OF ACT.

(a) IN GENERAL.—All provisions of, and amendments made by, this Act shall not apply—

(1) to taxable, plan, or limitation years beginning after December 31, 2010, or

(2) in the case of title V, to estates of decedents dying, gifts made, or generation skipping transfers, after December 31, 2010.

(b) APPLICATION OF CERTAIN LAWS.—The Internal Revenue Code of 1986 and the Employee Retirement Income Security Act of 1974 shall be applied and administered to years, estates, gifts, and transfers described in subsection (a) as if the provisions and amendments described in subsection (a) had never been enacted.

• 1997, Taxpayer Relief Act of 1997 (P.L. 105-34)

P.L. 105-34, §101(c):

Amended Code Sec. 501(c)(26) by adding a flush sentence. **Effective** for tax years beginning after 12-31-97.

P.L. 105-34, §963(a):

Amended Code Sec. 501(c)(27) by adding at the end a new subparagraph (B). **Effective** for tax years beginning after 12-31-97.

P.L. 105-34, §963(b):

Amended Code Sec. 501(c)(27) by inserting "(A)" after "(27)", by redesignating subparagraphs (A), (B), and (C) as clauses (i), (ii), and (iii), respectively, and by redesignating clauses (i) and (ii) of subparagraphs (B) and (C) (before redesignation) as subclauses (I) and (II), respectively. **Effective** for tax years beginning after 12-31-97.

• 1996, Health Insurance Portability and Accountability Act of 1996 (P.L. 104-191)

P.L. 104-191, §341(a):

Amended Code Sec. 501(c) by adding at the end a new paragraph (26). **Effective** for tax years beginning after 12-31-96.

P.L. 104-191, §342(a):

Amended Code Sec. 501(c), as amended by Act Sec. 341, by adding at the end a new paragraph (27). **Effective** for tax years ending after 8-21-96.

• 1996, Small Business Job Protection Act of 1996 (P.L. 104-188)

P.L. 104-188, §1704(j)(5):

Amended Code Sec. 501(c)(21)(D)(ii)(III) by striking "section 101(6)" and inserting "section 101(7)" and by striking "1752(6)" and inserting "1752(7)". **Effective** 8-20-96.

• 1996, Taxpayer Bill of Rights 2 (P.L. 104-168)

P.L. 104-168, §1311(b)(1):

Amended Code Sec. 501(c)(4) by inserting "(A)" after "(4)" and by adding at the end a new subparagraph (B). For the **effective** date, see Act Sec. 1311(d)(3), below. For a special rule, see Act Sec. 1311(b)(2), below.

P.L. 104-168, §1311(b)(2), provides:

(2) SPECIAL RULE FOR CERTAIN COOPERATIVES.—In the case of an organization operating on a cooperative basis which, before the date of the enactment of this Act, was determined by the Secretary of the Treasury or his delegate, to be described in section 501(c)(4) of the Internal Revenue Code of 1986 and exempt from tax under section 501(a) of such Code, the allocation or return of net margins or capital to the members of such organization in accordance with its incorporating statute and bylaws shall not be treated for purposes of such Code as the inurement of the net earnings of such organization to the benefit of any private shareholder or individual. The preceding sentence shall apply only if such statute and bylaws are substantially as such statute and bylaws were in existence on the date of the enactment of this Act.

P.L. 104-168, §1311(b)(2), provides:

(3) APPLICATION OF PRIVATE INUREMENT RULE TO TAX-EXEMPT ORGANIZATIONS DESCRIBED IN SECTION 501(c)(4).—

(A) IN GENERAL.—The amendment made by subsection (b) shall apply to inurement occurring on or after September 14, 1995.

(B) BINDING CONTRACTS.—The amendment made by subsection (b) shall not apply to any inurement occurring before January 1, 1997, pursuant to a written contract which was binding on September 13, 1995, and at all times thereafter before such inurement occurred.

• 1993, Omnibus Budget Reconciliation Act of 1993 (P.L. 103-66)

P.L. 103-66, §13146(a):

Amended Code Sec. 501(c)(25) by adding at the end thereof a new subparagraph (G). **Effective** for tax years beginning on or after 1-1-94.

P.L. 103-66, §13146(b):

Amended Code Sec. 501(c)(2) by adding at the end thereof a new sentence. **Effective** for tax years beginning on or after 1-1-94.

• 1992, Energy Policy Act of 1992 (P.L. 102-486)

P.L. 102-486, §1940(a):

Amended Code Sec. 501(c)(21). **Effective** for tax years beginning after 12-31-91. Prior to amendment, Code Sec. 501(c)(21) read as follows:

(21) A trust or trusts established in writing, created or organized in the United States, and contributed to by any person (except an insurance company) if—

(A) the purpose of such trust or trusts is exclusively—

(i) to satisfy, in whole or in part, the liability of such person for, or with respect to, claims for compensation for disability or death due to pneumoconiosis under Black Lung Acts;

(ii) to pay premiums for insurance exclusively covering liability; and

(iii) to pay administrative and other incidental expenses of such trust (including legal, accounting, actuarial, and trustee expenses) in connection with the operation of the trust and the processing of claims against such person under Black Lung Acts; and

(B) no part of the assets of the trust may be used for, or diverted to, any purpose other than—

(i) the purposes described in subparagraph (A), or

(ii) investment (but only to the extent that the trustee determines that a portion of the assets is not currently needed for the purposes described in subparagraph (A)) in—

(I) public debt securities of the United States,

(II) obligations of a State or local government which are not in default as to principal or interest, or

(III) time or demand deposits in a bank (as defined in section 581) or an insured credit union (within the meaning of section 101(6) of the Federal Credit Union Act. 12 U.S.C. 1752(6)) located in the United States, or

(iii) payment into the Black Lung Disability Trust Fund established under section 9501, or into the general fund of the United States Treasury (other than in satisfaction of any tax or other civil or criminal liability of the person who established or contributed to the trust).

For purposes of this paragraph the term "Black Lung Acts" means part C of title IV of the Federal Mine Safety and Health Act of 1977, and any State law providing compensation for disability or death due to pneumoconiosis.

• 1988, Technical and Miscellaneous Revenue Act of 1988 (P.L. 100-647)

P.L. 100-647, §1011(c)(7)(D):

Amended Code Sec. 501(c)(18)(D) by striking out "and" at the end of clause (ii), by striking out the period at the end of clause (iii) and inserting in lieu thereof ", and", and by inserting after clause (iii) new clause (iv). For the **effective** date, see Act Sec. 1011(c)(7)(E), below.

P.L. 100-647, §1011(c)(7)(E), provides:

(E)(i) Except as provided in clause (ii), the amendments made by this paragraph shall apply to plan years beginning after December 31, 1987.

(ii) In the case of a plan described in section 1105(c)(2) of the Reform Act, the amendments made by this paragraph shall not apply to contributions made pursuant to an agreement described in such section for plan years beginning before the earlier of—

(I) the later of January 1, 1988, or the date on which the last of such agreements terminates (determined without regard to any extension thereof after February 28, 1986), or

(II) January 1, 1989.

P.L. 100-647, §1016(a)(1)(A):

Amended Code Sec. 501(c)(25)(A) by adding at the end thereof a new sentence. **Effective** for property acquired by the organization after 6-10-87, except that such amendment shall not apply to any property acquired after 6-10-87, pursuant to a binding written contract in effect on 6-10-87, and at all times thereafter before such acquisition.

P.L. 100-647, §1016(a)(2):

Amended Code Sec. 501(c)(25) by striking out so much of subparagraph (D) as precedes clause (i) and inserting in lieu thereof new material preceding clause (i). **Effective** as if included in the provision of P.L. 99-514 to which it relates. Prior to amendment, the material preceding clause (i) read as follows:

(D) A corporation or trust described in this paragraph must permit its shareholders or beneficiaries—

P.L. 100-647, §1016(a)(3)(A):

Amended Code Sec. 501(c)(25) by adding at the end thereof new subparagraph (E). **Effective** as if included in the provision of P.L. 99-514 to which it relates.

P.L. 100-647, §1016(a)(3)(B):

Amended Code Sec. 501(c)(25)(C) by inserting "or" at the end of clause (iii), by striking out ", or" at the end of clause (iv) and inserting in lieu thereof a period, and by striking out clause (v). **Effective** as if included in the provision of P.L. 99-514 to which it relates. Prior to amendment, Code Sec. 501(c)(25)(C)(v) read as follows:

(V) any organization described in this paragraph.

P.L. 100-647, §1016(a)(4):

Amended Code Sec. 501(c)(25) by adding at the end thereof a new subparagraph (F). **Effective** as if included in the provision of P.L. 99-514 to which it relates.

P.L. 100-647, §1018(u)(14):

Amended Code Sec. 501(c)(23) by striking out "any association" and inserting in lieu thereof "Any association". **Effective** as if included in the provision of P.L. 99-514 to which it relates.

P.L. 100-647, §1018(u)(15):

Amended Code Sec. 501(c)(1) by striking out "any corporation organized" and inserting in lieu thereof "Any corporation organized". **Effective** as if included in the provision of P.L. 99-514 to which it relates.

P.L. 100-647, §2003(a)(1):

Amended Code Sec. 501(c)(12)(B) by striking out "or" at the end of clause (ii), by striking out the period at the end of clause (iii), and inserting in lieu thereof ", or", and by adding at the end thereof new clause (iv). **Effective** for tax years ending after the date of the enactment of P.L. 99-509.

P.L. 100-647, §2003(a)(2):

Amended Code Sec. 501(c)(12)(C). **Effective** for tax years ending after the date of the enactment of P.L. 99-509. Prior to amendment, Code Sec. 501(c)(12)(C) read as follows:

(C) In the case of a mutual or cooperative electric company, subparagraph (A) shall be applied without taking into account any income received or accrued from qualified pole rentals.

P.L. 100-647, §6203, provides:

Subparagraph (A) of section 501(c)(12) of the 1986 Code shall be applied without taking into account any income attributable to the cancellation of any loan originally made or guaranteed by the United States (or any agency or instrumentality thereof) if such cancellation occurs after 1986 and before 1990.

• 1987, Revenue Act of 1987 (P.L. 100-203)

P.L. 100-203, §10711(a)(2):

Amended Code Sec. 501(c)(3) by striking out "on behalf of any candidate" and inserting in lieu thereof "on behalf of (or in opposition to) any candidate". **Effective** with respect to activities after 12-22-87.

• 1986, Tax Reform Act of 1986 (P.L. 99-514)

P.L. 99-514, §1024(b):

Amended Code Sec. 501(c)(15). **Effective** for tax years beginning after 12-31-86. However, for transitional rules, see Act Sec. 1024(d) in the amendment notes following Code Sec. 824. Prior to amendment, Code Sec. 501(c)(15) read as follows:

(15) Mutual insurance companies or associations other than life or marine (including interinsurers and reciprocal underwriters) if the gross amount received during the taxable year from the items described in section 822(b) (other than paragraph (1)(D) thereof) and premiums (including deposits and assessments) does not exceed $150,000.

P.L. 99-514, §1109(a):

Amended Code Sec. 501(c)(18) by striking out "and" at the end of subparagraph (B), by striking out the period at the end of subparagraph (C) and inserting in lieu thereof ", and", and by adding at the end thereof new subparagraph (D). **Effective** for tax years beginning after 12-31-86.

P.L. 99-514, §1114(b)(14):

Amended Code Sec. 501(c)(17)(A)(ii) and (iii) and (c)(18)(B) and (C) by striking out "officers, shareholders, person whose principal duties consist of supervising the work of other employees, or highly compensated employees" and inserting in lieu thereof "highly compensated employees (within the meaning of section 414(q))". **Effective** for tax years beginning after 12-31-86.

P.L. 99-514, §1302, provides:

SEC. 1302. TREATMENT OF SECTION 501(c)(3) BONDS.

Nothing in the treatment of section 501(c)(3) bonds as private activity bonds under the amendments made by this title shall be construed as indicating how section 501(c)(3) bonds will be treated in future legislation, and any change in future legislation applicable to private activity bonds shall apply to section 501(c)(3) bonds only if expressly provided in such legislation.

P.L. 99-514, §1603(a):

Amended Code Sec. 501(c) by adding at the end thereof new paragraph (25). **Effective** for tax years beginning after 12-31-86.

P.L. 99-514, §1879(k)(1)(A)-(C):

Amended Code Sec. 501(c)(14)(B) by striking out "or" at the end of clause (ii), by striking out the period at the end of clause (iii) and inserting in lieu thereof a comma and "or" and by inserting at the end thereof new clause (iv). **Effective** for tax years ending after 8-13-81.

P.L. 99-514, §1899A(15):

Amended Code Sec. 501(c)(1)(A)(i) by striking out "the date of the enactment of the Tax Reform Act of 1984" and inserting in lieu thereof "July 18, 1984". **Effective** 10-22-86.

• 1986, Consolidated Omnibus Budget Reconciliation Act of 1985 (P.L. 99-272)

P.L. 99-272, §11012(b):

Amended Code Sec. 501(c) by adding at the end thereof new paragraph (24). **Effective** as of 1-1-86, except that it shall not apply with respect to terminations for which—

(1) notices of intent to terminate were filed with the Pension Benefit Guaranty Corporation under section 4041 of the Employee Retirement Income Security Act of 1974 before such date, or

(2) proceedings were commenced under section 4042 of such Act before such date.

For transitional rules see Act Sec. 11019(b)-(c) in the amendment notes following Code Sec. 402(a).

• 1984, Deficit Reduction Act of 1984 (P.L. 98-369)

P.L. 98-369, §1079:

Amended Code Sec. 501(c)(1), as amended by Act Sec. 2813 by striking out subparagraph (A) thereof and inserting in lieu thereof new subparagraph (A). **Effective** 7-18-84. Prior to amendment, subparagraph (A) read as follows:

(A) is exempt from Federal income taxes under such Act, as amended and supplemented, or

P.L. 98-369, §2813(b)(2):

Amended Code Sec. 501(c)(1). **Effective** 10-1-79. Prior to amendment, Code Sec. 501(c)(1) read as follows:

(1) Corporations organized under Act of Congress, if such corporations are instrumentalities of the United States and if, under such Act, as amended and supplemented, such corporations are exempt from Federal income taxes.

• 1983, Technical Corrections Act of 1982 (P.L. 97-448)

P.L. 97-448, §306(b)(5):

Amended Code Sec. 501(c)(23) by striking out "25 percent" and inserting in lieu thereof "75 percent". **Effective** as if included in the provision of P.L. 97-248 to which it relates.

• 1982, Tax Equity and Fiscal Responsibility Act of 1982 (P.L. 97-248)

P.L. 97-248, §354(a):

Amended Code Sec. 501(c)(19) by striking out "war veterans" the first place it appears and inserting "past or present members of the Armed Forces of the United States" and by amending subparagraph (B). **Effective** for tax years beginning after 9-3-82. Prior to amendment, subparagraph (B) read as follows:

"(B) at least 75 percent of the members of which are war veterans and substantially all of the other members of which are individuals who are veterans (but not war veterans), or are cadets, or are spouses, widows, or widowers of war veterans of such individuals, and".

P.L. 97-248, §354(b):

Amended Code Sec. 501(c)(23) by adding the new paragraph. **Effective** for tax years beginning after 9-3-82.

• 1981, Black Lung Benefits Revenue Act of 1991 (P.L. 97-119)

P.L. 97-119, §103(c)(1):

Amended Code Sec. 501(c)(21)(B)(iii) by striking out "established under section 3 of the Black Lung Benefits Revenue Act of 1977" and inserting in lieu thereof "established under section 9501". **Effective** 1-1-82.

• 1980, Miscellaneous Revenue Act of 1980 (P.L. 96-605)

P.L. 96-605, §106(a):

Amended Code Sec. 501(c)(12) by striking out "(12)" and inserting in lieu thereof "(12)(A)"; by striking out the second sentence; and by adding at the end thereof new subparagraphs (B), (C) and (D). **Effective** for all tax years to which the Internal Revenue Code of 1954 applies.

• 1980, Multiemployer Pension Plan Amendments Act of 1980 (P.L. 96-364)

P.L. 96-364, §209(a):

Amended Code Sec. 501(c). **Effective** for tax years ending after 9-26-80, by adding at the end thereof paragraph (22).

• 1980, Technical Corrections Act of 1979 (P.L. 96-222)

P.L. 96-222, §108(b)(2)(B):

Amended Code Sec. 501(c)(21) by changing "Federal Coal Mine Health and Safety Act of 1969" to "Federal Mine Safety and Health Act of 1977". **Effective** for contributions, acts, and expenditures made after 1977, in and for tax years beginning after such date.

• 1978, Revenue Act of 1978 (P.L. 95-600)

P.L. 95-600, §703(b)(2):

Amended Code Sec. 501(c)(20) by striking out "section 501(c)(20)" and inserting in lieu thereof "this paragraph". **Effective** 10-4-76.

• 1978 (P.L. 95-345)

P.L. 95-345, §1(a):

Added the last sentence to paragraph 12. **Effective** for tax years beginning after 12-31-74.

• 1978, Black Lung Benefits Revenue Act of 1977 (P.L. 95-227)

P.L. 95-227, §4(a):

Added paragraph (21) to Code Sec. 501(c). **Effective** for contributions, acts, and expenditures made after 1977, in and for tax years beginning after such date. However, this effective date was contingent upon enactment of P.L. 95-239, on 3-1-78.

• 1976 (P.L. 94-568)

P.L. 94-568, §[1](a):

Amended Code Sec. 501(c)(7). **Effective** for tax years beginning after 10-20-76. Prior to amendment Code Sec. 501(c)(7) read as follows:

"(7) Clubs organized and operated exclusively for pleasure, recreation, and other nonprofitable purposes no part of the net earnings of which inures to the benefit of any private shareholders."

• 1976, Tax Reform Act of 1976 (P.L. 94-455)

P.L. 94-455, §1307(d):

Added "(except as otherwise provided in subsection (h))" to Code Sec. 501(c)(3). **Effective** for tax years beginning after 12-31-76.

P.L. 94-455, §1313(a):

Added "or to foster national or international amateur sports competition (but only if no part of its activities involve the provision of athletic facilities or equipment)" to Code Sec. 501(c)(3). **Effective** 10-5-76.

P.L. 94-455, §1906(b)(13)(A):

Amended 1954 Code by substituting "Secretary" for "Secretary or his delegate" each place it appeared. **Effective** 2-1-77.

P.L. 94-455, §2134(b):

Added Code Sec. 501(c)(20). **Effective** for tax years beginning after 12-31-76, and ending before 1-1-82.

P.L. 94-455, §1313(c), provides:

(c) An organization which (without regard to the amendments made by this section) is an organization described in section 170(c)(2)(B), 501(c)(3), 2055(a)(2), or 2522(a)(2) of the Internal Revenue Code of 1954 shall not be treated as an organization not so described as a result of the amendments made by this section.

• 1972 (P.L. 92-418)

P.L. 92-418, §1(a):

Added paragraph (19) to Code Sec. 501(c). **Effective** for tax years beginning after 12-31-69.

• 1968, Gun Control Act of 1968 (P.L. 91-168)

P.L. 91-618, §1:

Amended Code Sec. 501(c)(13) by substituting "for the purpose of the disposal of bodies by burial or cremation which is" for "for burial purposes as a cemetery corporation and". **Effective** for tax years ending after 12-31-70.

• 1969, Tax Reform Act of 1969 (P.L. 91-172)

P.L. 91-172, §101(j)(5):

Amended Code Sec. 501(c) by substituting "part IV" for "part III" in paragraph (16). **Effective** 1-1-70.

P.L. 91-172, §121(b)(5)(A):

Amended Code Sec. 501(c)(9), (10) and added paragraph (18). **Effective** 1-1-70. Prior to amendment Sec. 501(c)(9), (10) read as follows:

"(9) Voluntary employees' beneficiary associations providing for the payment of life, sick, accident, or other benefits to the members of such association or their dependents, if—

"(A) no part of their net earnings inures (other than through such payments) to the benefit of any private shareholder or individual, and

"(B) 85 percent or more of the income consists of amounts collected from members and amounts contributed to the association by the employer of the members for the sole purpose of making such payments and meeting expenses.

"(10) Voluntary employees' beneficiary associations providing for the payment of life, sick, accident, or other benefits to the members of such association or their dependents or their designated beneficiaries, if—

"(A) admission to membership in such association is limited to individuals who are officers or employees of the United States Government, and

"(B) no part of the net earnings of such association inures (other than through such payments) to the benefit of any private shareholder or individual."

• 1966 (P.L. 89-800)

P.L. 89-800, §6(a):

Amended Code Sec. 501(c)(6) by substituting "boards of trade, or professional football leagues (whether or not administering a pension fund for football players)" for "or boards of trade". **Effective** for tax years ending after 11-8-66.

• 1966 (P.L. 89-352)

P.L. 89-352, §[1]:

Amended Code Sec. 501(c)(14). **Effective** for tax years ending after 2-2-66. Prior to amendment, Sec. 501(c)(14) read as follows:

"(14) Credit unions without capital stock organized and operated for mutual purposes and without profit; and corporations or associations without capital stock organized before September 1, 1957, and operated for mutual purposes and without profit for the purpose of providing reserve funds for, and insurance of, shares or deposits in—

"(A) domestic building and loan associations,

"(B) cooperative banks without capital stock organized and operated for mutual purposes and without profit, or

"(C) mutual savings banks not having capital stock represented by shares."

• 1962, Revenue Act of 1962 (P.L. 87-834)

P.L. 87-834, §8:

Amended Code Sec. 501(c)(15) by substituting "$150,000" for "$75,000". **Effective** 1-1-68.

• 1960 (P.L. 86-667)

P.L. 86-667, §1:

Amended Code Sec. 501(c) by adding paragraph (17). **Effective** for tax years beginning after 12-31-59.

• 1960 (P.L. 86-428)

P.L. 86-428, §[1]:

Amended Code Sec. 501(c)(14) by striking out "1951" and by substituting "1957". **Effective** for tax years beginning after 12-31-59.

• 1956, Life Insurance Company Tax Act for 1955 (P.L. 429, 84th Cong.)

P.L. 429, 84th Cong., §5(2):

Amended Sec. 501(c)(15) by substituting for the words "interest, dividends, rents," the words "the items described in section 822(b) (other than paragraph (1)(D) thereof)". **Effective** for tax years beginning after 12-31-54.

[Sec. 501(d)]

(d) RELIGIOUS AND APOSTOLIC ORGANIZATIONS.—The following organizations are referred to in subsection (a): Religious or apostolic associations or corporations, if such associations or corporations have a common treasury or community treasury, even if such associations or corporations engage in business for the common benefit of the members, but only if the members thereof include (at the time of filing their returns) in their gross income their entire pro rata shares, whether distributed or not, of the taxable income of the association or corporation for such year. Any amount so included in the gross income of a member shall be treated as a dividend received.

[Sec. 501(e)]

(e) COOPERATIVE HOSPITAL SERVICE ORGANIZATIONS.—For purposes of this title, an organization shall be treated as an organization organized and operated exclusively for charitable purposes, if—

(1) such organization is organized and operated solely—

(A) to perform, on a centralized basis, one or more of the following services which, if performed on its own behalf by a hospital which is an organization described in subsection (c)(3) and exempt from taxation under subsection (a), would constitute activities in exercising or performing the purpose or function constituting the basis for its exemption: data processing, purchasing (including the purchasing of insurance on a group basis), warehousing, billing and collection (including the purchase of patron accounts receivable on a recourse basis), food, clinical, industrial engineering, laboratory, printing, communications, record center, and personnel (including selection, testing, training, and education of personnel) services; and

(B) to perform such services solely for two or more hospitals each of which is—

(i) an organization described in subsection (c)(3) which is exempt from taxation under subsection (a),

(ii) a constituent part of an organization described in subsection (c)(3) which is exempt from taxation under subsection (a) and which, if organized and operated as a separate entity, would constitute an organization described in subsection (c)(3), or

(iii) owned and operated by the United States, a State, the District of Columbia, or a possession of the United States, or a political subdivision or an agency or instrumentality of any of the foregoing;

(2) such organization is organized and operated on a cooperative basis and allocates or pays, within $8^1/2$ months after the close of its taxable year, all net earnings to patrons on the basis of services performed for them; and

(3) if such organization has capital stock, all of such stock outstanding is owned by its patrons.

For purposes of this title, any organization which, by reason of the preceding sentence, is an organization described in subsection (c)(3) and exempt from taxation under subsection (a), shall be treated as a hospital and as an organization referred to in section 170(b)(1)(A)(iii).

Amendments

• 1997, Taxpayer Relief Act of 1997 (P.L. 105-34)

P.L. 105-34, §974(a):

Amended Code Sec. 501(e)(1)(A) by inserting "(including the purchase of patron accounts receivable on a recourse basis)" after "billing and collection". **Effective** for tax years beginning after 12-31-96.

• 1988, Technical and Miscellaneous Revenue Act of 1988 (P.L. 100-647)

P.L. 100-647, §6202(a):

Amended Code Sec. 501(e)(1) by inserting "(including the purchasing of insurance on a group basis)" after "purchasing". **Effective** for purchases before, on, or after 11-10-88.

• 1976, Tax Reform Act of 1976 (P.L. 94-455)

P.L. 94-455, §1312(a):

Added "clinical" after "food" to Code Sec. 501(e)(1)(A). **Effective** for tax years ending after 12-31-76.

• 1969, Tax Reform Act of 1969 (P.L. 91-172)

P.L. 91-172, §101(j)(6):

Amended the last sentence in Code Sec. 501(e) by substituting "section 170(b)(1)(A)(iii)" for "section 503(b)(5)." **Effective** 1-1-70.

• 1968, Revenue and Expenditure Control Act of 1968 (P.L. 90-364)

P.L. 90-364, §109(a):

Added Code Sec. 501(e) and redesignated former Code Sec. 501(e) as Code Sec. 501(f). **Effective** for tax years ending after 6-28-68.

[Sec. 501(f)]

(f) COOPERATIVE SERVICE ORGANIZATIONS OF OPERATING EDUCATIONAL ORGANIZATIONS.—For purposes of this title, if an organization is—

(1) organized and operated solely to hold, commingle, and collectively invest and reinvest (including arranging for and supervising the performance by independent contractors of investment services related thereto) in stocks and securities, the moneys contributed thereto by each of the members of such organization, and to collect income therefrom and turn over the entire amount thereof, less expenses, to such members,

(2) organized and controlled by one or more such members, and

(3) comprised solely of members that are organizations described in clause (ii) or (iv) of section 170(b)(1)(A)—

(A) which are exempt from taxation under subsection (a), or

(B) the income of which is excluded from taxation under section 115(a),

then such organization shall be treated as an organization organized and operated exclusively for charitable purposes.

Amendments

• 1974 (P.L. 93-310)

P.L. 93-310, §3:

Redesignated former Code Sec. 501(f) as Code Sec. 501(g) and added new Code Sec. 501(f). **Effective** for tax years ending after 12-31-73.

[Sec. 501(g)]

(g) DEFINITION OF AGRICULTURAL.—For purposes of subsection (c)(5), the term "agricultural" includes the art or science of cultivating land, harvesting crops or aquatic resources, or raising livestock.

Amendments

• 1976, Tax Reform Act of 1976 (P.L. 94-455)

P.L. 94-455, §2113 (a):

Redesignated former Code Sec. 501(g) as Code Sec. 501(h) and added new Code Sec. 501(g). **Effective** for tax years ending after 12-31-75.

[Sec. 501(h)]

(h) EXPENDITURES BY PUBLIC CHARITIES TO INFLUENCE LEGISLATION.—

(1) GENERAL RULE.—In the case of an organization to which this subsection applies, exemption from taxation under subsection (a) shall be denied because a substantial part of the activities of such organization consists of carrying on propaganda, or otherwise attempting, to influence legislation, but only if such organization normally—

(A) makes lobbying expenditures in excess of the lobbying ceiling amount for such organization for each taxable year, or

(B) makes grass roots expenditures in excess of the grass roots ceiling amount for such organization for each taxable year.

(2) DEFINITIONS.—For purposes of this subsection—

(A) LOBBYING EXPENDITURES.—The term "lobbying expenditures" means expenditures for the purpose of influencing legislation (as defined in section 4911(d)).

(B) LOBBYING CEILING AMOUNT.—The lobbying ceiling amount for any organization for any taxable year is 150 percent of the lobbying nontaxable amount for such organization for such taxable year, determined under section 4911.

(C) GRASS ROOTS EXPENDITURES.—The term "grass roots expenditures" means expenditures for the purpose of influencing legislation (as defined in section 4911(d) without regard to paragraph (1)(B) thereof).

(D) GRASS ROOTS CEILING AMOUNT.—The grass roots ceiling amount for any organization for any taxable year is 150 percent of the grass roots nontaxable amount for such organization for such taxable year, determined under section 4911.

(3) ORGANIZATIONS TO WHICH THIS SUBSECTION APPLIES.—This subsection shall apply to any organization which has elected (in such manner and at such time as the Secretary may prescribe) to have the provisions of this subsection apply to such organization and which, for the taxable year which includes the date the election is made, is described in subsection (c)(3) and—

(A) is described in paragraph (4), and

(B) is not a disqualified organization under paragraph (5).

(4) ORGANIZATIONS PERMITTED TO ELECT TO HAVE THIS SUBSECTION APPLY.—An organization is described in this paragraph if it is described in—

(A) section 170(b)(1)(A)(ii) (relating to educational institutions),

(B) section 170(b)(1)(A)(iii) (relating to hospitals and medical research organizations),

(C) section 170(b)(1)(A)(iv) (relating to organizations supporting government schools),

(D) section 170(b)(1)(A)(vi) (relating to organizations publicly supported by charitable contributions),

(E) section 509(a)(2) (relating to organizations publicly supported by admissions, sales, etc.), or

(F) section 509(a)(3) (relating to organizations supporting certain types of public charities) except that for purposes of this subparagraph, section 509(a)(3) shall be applied without regard to the last sentence of section 509(a).

(5) DISQUALIFIED ORGANIZATIONS.—For purposes of paragraph (3) an organization is a disqualified organization if it is—

(A) described in section 170(b)(1)(A)(i) (relating to churches),

(B) an integrated auxiliary of a church or of a convention or association of churches, or

(C) a member of an affiliated group of organizations (within the meaning of section 4911(f)(2)) if one or more members of such group is described in subparagraph (A) or (B).

(6) YEARS FOR WHICH ELECTION IS EFFECTIVE.—An election by an organization under this subsection shall be effective for all taxable years of such organization which—

(A) end after the date the election is made, and

(B) begin before the date the election is revoked by such organization (under regulations prescribed by the Secretary).

(7) NO EFFECT ON CERTAIN ORGANIZATIONS.—With respect to any organization for a taxable year for which—

(A) such organization is a disqualified organization (within the meaning of paragraph (5)), or

(B) an election under this subsection is not in effect for such organization,

nothing in this subsection or in section 4911 shall be construed to affect the interpretation of the phrase, "no substantial part of the activities of which is carrying on propaganda, or otherwise attempting, to influence legislation," under subsection (c)(3).

(8) AFFILIATED ORGANIZATIONS.—

For rules regarding affiliated organizations, see section 4911(f).

Amendments

• 1976, Tax Reform Act of 1976 (P.L. 94-455)

P.L. 94-455, §1307(a):

Redesignated Code Sec. 501(h) as Code Sec. 501(i) and added new Code Sec. 501(h). **Effective** for tax years ending after 12-31-76.

[Sec. 501(i)]

(i) PROHIBITION OF DISCRIMINATION BY CERTAIN SOCIAL CLUBS.—Notwithstanding subsection (a), an organization which is described in subsection (c)(7) shall not be exempt from taxation under subsection (a) for any taxable year if, at any time during such taxable year, the charter, bylaws, or other governing instrument, of such organization or any written policy statement of such organization contains a provision which provides for discrimination against any person on the basis of race, color, or religion. The preceding sentence to the extent it relates to discrimination on the basis of religion shall not apply to—

(1) an auxiliary of a fraternal beneficiary society if such society—

(A) is described in subsection (c)(8) and exempt from tax under subsection (a), and

(B) limits its membership to the members of a particular religion, or

(2) a club which in good faith limits its membership to the members of a particular religion in order to further the teachings or principles of that religion, and not to exclude individuals of a particular race or color.

Amendments

• 1980 (P.L. 96-601)

P.L. 96-601, §3(a):

Amended Code Sec. 501(i) by adding a new last sentence. **Effective** for tax years beginning after 10-20-76.

• 1976 (P.L. 94-568)

P.L. 94-568, §2(a), as amended by P.L. 95-600, §703(g)(2):

Amended Code Sec. 501 by adding a new subsection (g) after the existing subsection (g) [redesignated as subsection (i) by P.L. 95-600, §703(g)(2)(B).—CCH]. **Effective** for tax years beginning after 10-20-76.

[Sec. 501(j)]

(j) SPECIAL RULES FOR CERTAIN AMATEUR SPORTS ORGANIZATIONS.—

(1) IN GENERAL.—In the case of a qualified amateur sports organization—

(A) the requirement of subsection (c)(3) that no part of its activites involve the provision of athletic facilities or equipment shall not apply, and

(B) such organization shall not fail to meet the requirements of subsection (c)(3) merely because its membership is local or regional in nature.

(2) QUALIFIED AMATEUR SPORTS ORGANIZATION DEFINED.—For purposes of this subsection, the term "qualified amateur sports organization" means any organization organized and operated exclusively to foster national or international amateur sports competition if such organization is also organized and operated primarily to conduct national or international competition in sports or to support and develop amateur athletes for national or international competition in sports.

Amendments

• 1982, Tax Equity and Fiscal Responsibility Act of 1982 (P.L. 97-248)

P.L. 97-248, §286(a):

Added subsection (j). **Effective** 10-5-76.

[Sec. 501(k)]

(k) TREATMENT OF CERTAIN ORGANIZATIONS PROVIDING CHILD CARE.—For purposes of subsection (c)(3) of this section and sections 170(c)(2), 2055(a)(2), and 2522(a)(2), the term "educational purposes" includes the providing of care of children away from their homes if—

(1) substantially all of the care provided by the organization is for purposes of enabling individuals to be gainfully employed, and

(2) the services provided by the organization are available to the general public.

Amendments

• 1984, Deficit Reduction Act of 1984 (P.L. 98-369)

P.L. 98-369, §1032(a):

Amended Code Sec. 501 by redesignating subsection (k) as subsection (l) and inserting after subsection (j) new subsection (k). **Effective** for tax years beginning after 7-18-84.

[Sec. 501(l)]

(l) GOVERNMENT CORPORATIONS EXEMPT UNDER SUBSECTION (c)(1).—For purposes of subsection (c)(1), the following organizations are described in this subsection:

(1) The Central Liquidity Facility established under title III of the Federal Credit Union Act (12 U.S.C. 1795 et seq.).

(2) The Resolution Trust Corporation established under section 21A of the Federal Home Loan Bank Act.

(3) The Resolution Funding Corporation established under section 21B of the Federal Home Loan Bank Act.

(4) The Patient-Centered Outcomes Research Institute established under section 1181(b) of the Social Security Act.

Amendments

• 2010, Patient Protection and Affordable Care Act (P.L. 111-148)

P.L. 111-148, §6301(f):

Amended Code Sec. 501(l) by adding at the end a new paragraph (4). **Effective** 3-23-2010.

• 1989, Financial Institutions Reform, Recovery, and Enforcement Act of 1989 (P.L. 101-73)

P.L. 101-73, §1402(a):

Amended Code Sec. 501(l). **Effective** 8-9-89. Prior to amendment, Code Sec. 501(l) read as follows:

(l) GOVERNMENT CORPORATIONS EXEMPT UNDER SUBSECTION (c)(1).—The organization described in this subsection is the Central Liquidity Facility established under title III of the Federal Credit Union Act (12 U.S.C. 1795 et seq.).

• 1984, Deficit Reduction Act of 1984 (P.L. 98-369)

P.L. 98-369, §2813(b)(1):

Amended Code Sec. 501, as amended by Act Sec. 1032(a), by redesignating subsection (l) as subsection (m) and by adding after subsection (k) new subsection (l). **Effective** 10-1-79.

[Sec. 501(m)]

(m) CERTAIN ORGANIZATIONS PROVIDING COMMERCIAL-TYPE INSURANCE NOT EXEMPT FROM TAX.—

(1) DENIAL OF TAX EXEMPTION WHERE PROVIDING COMMERCIAL-TYPE INSURANCE IS SUBSTANTIAL PART OF ACTIVITIES.—An organization described in paragraph (3) or (4) of subsection (c) shall be exempt from tax under subsection (a) only if no substantial part of its activities consists of providing commercial-type insurance.

(2) OTHER ORGANIZATIONS TAXED AS INSURANCE COMPANIES ON INSURANCE BUSINESS.—In the case of an organization described in paragraph (3) or (4) of subsection (c) which is exempt from tax under subsection (a) after the application of paragraph (1) of this subsection—

(A) the activity of providing commercial-type insurance shall be treated as an unrelated trade or business (as defined in section 513), and

(B) in lieu of the tax imposed by section 511 with respect to such activity, such organization shall be treated as an insurance company for purposes of applying subchapter L with respect to such activity.

(3) COMMERCIAL-TYPE INSURANCE.—For purposes of this subsection, the term "commercial-type insurance" shall not include—

(A) insurance provided at substantially below cost to a class of charitable recipients,

(B) incidental health insurance provided by a health maintenance organization of a kind customarily provided by such organizations,

(C) property or casualty insurance provided (directly or through an organization described in section 414(e)(3)(B)(ii)) by a church or convention or association of churches for such church or convention or association of churches,

(D) providing retirement or welfare benefits (or both) by a church or a convention or association of churches (directly or through an organization described in section 414(e)(3)(A) or 414(e)(3)(B)(ii)) for the employees (including employees described in section 414(e)(3)(B)) of such church or convention or association of churches or the beneficiaries of such employees, and

(E) charitable gift annuities.

(4) INSURANCE INCLUDES ANNUITIES.—For purposes of this subsection, the issuance of annuity contracts shall be treated as providing insurance.

(5) CHARITABLE GIFT ANNUITY.—For purposes of paragraph (3)(E), the term "charitable gift annuity" means an annuity if—

(A) a portion of the amount paid in connection with the issuance of the annuity is allowable as a deduction under section 170 or 2055, and

(B) the annuity is described in section 514(c)(5) (determined as if any amount paid in cash in connection with such issuance were property).

Amendments

• 1988, Technical and Miscellaneous Revenue Act of 1988 (P.L. 100-647)

P.L. 100-647, §1010(b)(4)(A):

Amended Code Sec. 501(m)(3) by striking out "and" at the end of subparagraph (C), by striking out the period at the end of subparagraph (D) and inserting in lieu thereof ", and" and by adding at the end thereof new subparagraph (E). **Effective** as if included in the provision of P.L. 99-514 to which it relates.

P.L. 100-647, §1010(b)(4)(B):

Amended Code Sec. 501(m) by adding at the end thereof new paragraph (5). **Effective** as if included in the provision of P.L. 99-514 to which it relates.

[Sec. 501(n)]

(n) CHARITABLE RISK POOLS.—

(1) IN GENERAL.—For purposes of this title—

(A) a qualified charitable risk pool shall be treated as an organization organized and operated exclusively for charitable purposes, and

(B) subsection (m) shall not apply to a qualified charitable risk pool.

(2) QUALIFIED CHARITABLE RISK POOL.—For purposes of this subsection, the term "qualified charitable risk pool" means any organization—

(A) which is organized and operated solely to pool insurable risks of its members (other than risks related to medical malpractice) and to provide information to its members with respect to loss control and risk management,

(B) which is comprised solely of members that are organizations described in subsection (c)(3) and exempt from tax under subsection (a), and

(C) which meets the organizational requirements of paragraph (3).

(3) ORGANIZATIONAL REQUIREMENTS.—An organization (hereinafter in this subsection referred to as the "risk pool") meets the organizational requirements of this paragraph if—

(A) such risk pool is organized as a nonprofit organization under State law provisions authorizing risk pooling arrangements for charitable organizations,

(B) such risk pool is exempt from any income tax imposed by the State (or will be so exempt after such pool qualifies as an organization exempt from tax under this title),

(C) such risk pool has obtained at least $1,000,000 in startup capital from nonmember charitable organizations,

(D) such risk pool is controlled by a board of directors elected by its members, and

(E) the organizational documents of such risk pool require that—

(i) each member of such pool shall at all times be an organization described in subsection (c)(3) and exempt from tax under subsection (a),

(ii) any member which receives a final determination that it no longer qualifies as an organization described in subsection (c)(3) shall immediately notify the pool of such determination and the effective date of such determination, and

(iii) each policy of insurance issued by the risk pool shall provide that such policy will not cover the insured with respect to events occurring after the date such final determination was issued to the insured.

An organization shall not cease to qualify as a qualified charitable risk pool solely by reason of the failure of any of its members to continue to be an organization described in subsection (c)(3) if, within a reasonable period of time after such pool is notified as required under subparagraph (E)(ii), such pool takes such action as may be reasonably necessary to remove such member from such pool.

(4) OTHER DEFINITIONS.—For purposes of this subsection—

(A) STARTUP CAPITAL.—The term "startup capital" means any capital contributed to, and any program-related investments (within the meaning of section 4944(c)) made in, the risk pool before such pool commences operations.

(B) NONMEMBER CHARITABLE ORGANIZATION.—The term "nonmember charitable organization" means any organization which is described in subsection (c)(3) and exempt from tax under subsection (a) and which is not a member of the risk pool and does not benefit (directly or indirectly) from the insurance coverage provided by the pool to its members.

Amendments

• 1998, IRS Restructuring and Reform Act of 1998 (P.L. 105-206)

P.L. 105-206, §6023(6):

Amended the last sentence of paragraph (3) of Code Sec. 501(n) by striking "subparagraph (C)(ii)" and inserting "subparagraph (E)(ii)". **Effective** 7-22-98.

• 1996, Small Business Job Protection Act of 1996 (P.L. 104-188)

P.L. 104-188, §1114(a):

Amended Code Sec. 501 by redesignating subsection (n) as subsection (o) and by inserting after subsection (m) a new subsection (n). **Effective** for tax years beginning after 8-20-96.

[Sec. 501(o)]

(o) TREATMENT OF HOSPITALS PARTICIPATING IN PROVIDER-SPONSORED ORGANIZATIONS.—An organization shall not fail to be treated as organized and operated exclusively for a charitable purpose for purposes of subsection (c)(3) solely because a hospital which is owned and operated by such organization participates in a provider-sponsored organization (as defined in section 1855(d) of the Social Security Act), whether or not the provider-sponsored organization is exempt from tax. For purposes of subsection (c)(3), any person with a material financial interest in such a provider-sponsored organization shall be treated as a private shareholder or individual with respect to the hospital.

Amendments

• 1998, IRS Restructuring and Reform Act of 1998 (P.L. 105-206)

P.L. 105-206, §6023(7):

Amended Code Sec. 501(o) by striking "section 1853(e)" and inserting "section 1855(d)". **Effective** 7-22-98.

• 1997, Balanced Budget Act of 1997 (P.L. 105-33)

P.L. 105-33, §4041(a):

Amended Code Sec. 501 by redesignating subsection (o) as subsection (p) and by inserting after subsection (n) a new subsection (o). **Effective** 8-5-97.

[Sec. 501(p)]

(p) SUSPENSION OF TAX-EXEMPT STATUS OF TERRORIST ORGANIZATIONS.—

(1) IN GENERAL.—The exemption from tax under subsection (a) with respect to any organization described in paragraph (2), and the eligibility of any organization described in paragraph (2)

to apply for recognition of exemption under subsection (a), shall be suspended during the period described in paragraph (3).

(2) TERRORIST ORGANIZATIONS.—An organization is described in this paragraph if such organization is designated or otherwise individually identified—

(A) under section 212(a)(3)(B)(vi)(II) or 219 of the Immigration and Nationality Act as a terrorist organization or foreign terrorist organization,

(B) in or pursuant to an Executive order which is related to terrorism and issued under the authority of the International Emergency Economic Powers Act or section 5 of the United Nations Participation Act of 1945 for the purpose of imposing on such organization an economic or other sanction, or

(C) in or pursuant to an Executive order issued under the authority of any Federal law if—

(i) the organization is designated or otherwise individually identified in or pursuant to such Executive order as supporting or engaging in terrorist activity (as defined in section 212(a)(3)(B) of the Immigration and Nationality Act) or supporting terrorism (as defined in section 140(d)(2) of the Foreign Relations Authorization Act, Fiscal Years 1988 and 1989); and

(ii) such Executive order refers to this subsection.

(3) PERIOD OF SUSPENSION.—With respect to any organization described in paragraph (2), the period of suspension—

(A) begins on the later of—

(i) the date of the first publication of a designation or identification described in paragraph (2) with respect to such organization, or

(ii) the date of the enactment of this subsection, and

(B) ends on the first date that all designations and identifications described in paragraph (2) with respect to such organization are rescinded pursuant to the law or Executive order under which such designation or identification was made.

(4) DENIAL OF DEDUCTION.—No deduction shall be allowed under any provision of this title, including sections 170, 545(b)(2), 556(b)(2), 642(c), 2055, 2106(a)(2), and 2522, with respect to any contribution to an organization described in paragraph (2) during the period described in paragraph (3).

(5) DENIAL OF ADMINISTRATIVE OR JUDICIAL CHALLENGE OF SUSPENSION OR DENIAL OF DEDUCTION.—Notwithstanding section 7428 or any other provision of law, no organization or other person may challenge a suspension under paragraph (1), a designation or identification described in paragraph (2), the period of suspension described in paragraph (3), or a denial of a deduction under paragraph (4) in any administrative or judicial proceeding relating to the Federal tax liability of such organization or other person.

(6) ERRONEOUS DESIGNATION.—

(A) IN GENERAL.—If—

(i) the tax exemption of any organization described in paragraph (2) is suspended under paragraph (1),

(ii) each designation and identification described in paragraph (2) which has been made with respect to such organization is determined to be erroneous pursuant to the law or Executive order under which such designation or identification was made, and

(iii) the erroneous designations and identifications result in an overpayment of income tax for any taxable year by such organization,

credit or refund (with interest) with respect to such overpayment shall be made.

(B) WAIVER OF LIMITATIONS.—If the credit or refund of any overpayment of tax described in subparagraph (A)(iii) is prevented at any time by the operation of any law or rule of law (including res judicata), such credit or refund may nevertheless be allowed or made if the claim therefor is filed before the close of the 1-year period beginning on the date of the last determination described in subparagraph (A)(ii).

(7) NOTICE OF SUSPENSIONS.—If the tax exemption of any organization is suspended under this subsection, the Internal Revenue Service shall update the listings of tax-exempt organizations and shall publish appropriate notice to taxpayers of such suspension and of the fact that contributions to such organization are not deductible during the period of such suspension.

Amendments

• 2003, Military Family Tax Relief Act of 2003 (P.L. 108-121)

P.L. 108-121, §108(a):

Amended Code Sec. 501 by redesignating subsection (p) as subsection (q) and by inserting after subsection (o) a new subsection (p). **Effective** for designations made before, on, or after 11-11-2003.

[Sec. 501(q)]

(q) SPECIAL RULES FOR CREDIT COUNSELING ORGANIZATIONS.—

(1) IN GENERAL.—An organization with respect to which the provision of credit counseling services is a substantial purpose shall not be exempt from tax under subsection (a) unless such organization is described in paragraph (3) or (4) of subsection (c) and such organization is organized and operated in accordance with the following requirements:

(A) The organization—

(i) provides credit counseling services tailored to the specific needs and circumstances of consumers,

(ii) makes no loans to debtors (other than loans with no fees or interest) and does not negotiate the making of loans on behalf of debtors,

(iii) provides services for the purpose of improving a consumer's credit record, credit history, or credit rating only to the extent that such services are incidental to providing credit counseling services, and

(iv) does not charge any separately stated fee for services for the purpose of improving any consumer's credit record, credit history, or credit rating.

(B) The organization does not refuse to provide credit counseling services to a consumer due to the inability of the consumer to pay, the ineligibility of the consumer for debt management plan enrollment, or the unwillingness of the consumer to enroll in a debt management plan.

(C) The organization establishes and implements a fee policy which—

(i) requires that any fees charged to a consumer for services are reasonable,

(ii) allows for the waiver of fees if the consumer is unable to pay, and

(iii) except to the extent allowed by State law, prohibits charging any fee based in whole or in part on a percentage of the consumer's debt, the consumer's payments to be made pursuant to a debt management plan, or the projected or actual savings to the consumer resulting from enrolling in a debt management plan.

(D) At all times the organization has a board of directors or other governing body—

(i) which is controlled by persons who represent the broad interests of the public, such as public officials acting in their capacities as such, persons having special knowledge or expertise in credit or financial education, and community leaders,

(ii) not more than 20 percent of the voting power of which is vested in persons who are employed by the organization or who will benefit financially, directly or indirectly, from the organization's activities (other than through the receipt of reasonable directors' fees or the repayment of consumer debt to creditors other than the credit counseling organization or its affiliates), and

(iii) not more than 49 percent of the voting power of which is vested in persons who are employed by the organization or who will benefit financially, directly or indirectly, from the organization's activities (other than through the receipt of reasonable directors' fees).

(E) The organization does not own more than 35 percent of—

(i) the total combined voting power of any corporation (other than a corporation which is an organization described in subsection (c)(3) and exempt from tax under subsection (a)) which is in the trade or business of lending money, repairing credit, or providing debt management plan services, payment processing, or similar services,

(ii) the profits interest of any partnership (other than a partnership which is an organization described in subsection (c)(3) and exempt from tax under subsection (a)) which is in the trade or business of lending money, repairing credit, or providing debt management plan services, payment processing, or similar services, and

(iii) the beneficial interest of any trust or estate (other than a trust which is an organization described in subsection (c)(3) and exempt from tax under subsection (a)) which is in the trade or business of lending money, repairing credit, or providing debt management plan services, payment processing, or similar services.

(F) The organization receives no amount for providing referrals to others for debt management plan services, and pays no amount to others for obtaining referrals of consumers.

(2) ADDITIONAL REQUIREMENTS FOR ORGANIZATIONS DESCRIBED IN SUBSECTION (c)(3).—

(A) IN GENERAL.—In addition to the requirements under paragraph (1), an organization with respect to which the provision of credit counseling services is a substantial purpose and which is described in paragraph (3) of subsection (c) shall not be exempt from tax under subsection (a) unless such organization is organized and operated in accordance with the following requirements:

(i) The organization does not solicit contributions from consumers during the initial counseling process or while the consumer is receiving services from the organization.

(ii) The aggregate revenues of the organization which are from payments of creditors of consumers of the organization and which are attributable to debt management plan services do not exceed the applicable percentage of the total revenues of the organization.

(B) APPLICABLE PERCENTAGE.—

(i) IN GENERAL.—For purposes of subparagraph (A)(ii), the applicable percentage is 50 percent.

(ii) TRANSITION RULE.—Notwithstanding clause (i), in the case of an organization with respect to which the provision of credit counseling services is a substantial purpose and which is described in paragraph (3) of subsection (c) and exempt from tax under subsection (a) on the date of the enactment of this subsection, the applicable percentage is—

(I) 80 percent for the first taxable year of such organization beginning after the date which is 1 year after the date of the enactment of this subsection, and

(II) 70 percent for the second such taxable year beginning after such date, and

(III) 60 percent for the third such taxable year beginning after such date.

(3) ADDITIONAL REQUIREMENT FOR ORGANIZATIONS DESCRIBED IN SUBSECTION (c)(4).—In addition to the requirements under paragraph (1), an organization with respect to which the provision of credit counseling services is a substantial purpose and which is described in paragraph (4) of subsection (c) shall not be exempt from tax under subsection (a) unless such organization notifies the Secretary, in such manner as the Secretary may by regulations prescribe, that it is applying for recognition as a credit counseling organization.

(4) CREDIT COUNSELING SERVICES; DEBT MANAGEMENT PLAN SERVICES.—For purposes of this subsection—

(A) CREDIT COUNSELING SERVICES.—The term "credit counseling services" means—

(i) the providing of educational information to the general public on budgeting, personal finance, financial literacy, saving and spending practices, and the sound use of consumer credit,

(ii) the assisting of individuals and families with financial problems by providing them with counseling, or

(iii) a combination of the activities described in clauses (i) and (ii).

(B) DEBT MANAGEMENT PLAN SERVICES.—The term "debt management plan services" means services related to the repayment, consolidation, or restructuring of a consumer's debt, and includes the negotiation with creditors of lower interest rates, the waiver or reduction of fees, and the marketing and processing of debt management plans.

Amendments

• 2006, Pension Protection Act of 2006 (P.L. 109-280)

P.L. 109-280, §1220(a):

Amended Code Sec. 501 by redesignating subsection (q) as subsection (r) and by inserting after subsection (p) a new subsection (q). **Effective** generally for tax years beginning after 8-17-2006. For a transition rule, see Act Sec. 1220(c)(2), below.

P.L. 109-280, §1220(c)(2), provides:

(2) TRANSITION RULE FOR EXISTING ORGANIZATIONS.—In the case of any organization described in paragraph (3) or (4) [of]section 501(c) of the Internal Revenue Code of 1986 and with respect to which the provision of credit counseling services is a substantial purpose on the date of the enactment of this Act, the amendments made by this section shall apply to taxable years beginning after the date which is 1 year after the date of the enactment of this Act.

[Sec. 501(r)]

(r) ADDITIONAL REQUIREMENTS FOR CERTAIN HOSPITALS.—

(1) IN GENERAL.—A hospital organization to which this subsection applies shall not be treated as described in subsection (c)(3) unless the organization—

(A) meets the community health needs assessment requirements described in paragraph (3),

(B) meets the financial assistance policy requirements described in paragraph (4),

(C) meets the requirements on charges described in paragraph (5), and

(D) meets the billing and collection requirement described in paragraph (6).

(2) HOSPITAL ORGANIZATIONS TO WHICH SUBSECTION APPLIES.—

(A) IN GENERAL.—This subsection shall apply to—

(i) an organization which operates a facility which is required by a State to be licensed, registered, or similarly recognized as a hospital, and

(ii) any other organization which the Secretary determines has the provision of hospital care as its principal function or purpose constituting the basis for its exemption under subsection (c)(3) (determined without regard to this subsection).

(B) ORGANIZATIONS WITH MORE THAN 1 HOSPITAL FACILITY.—If a hospital organization operates more than 1 hospital facility—

(i) the organization shall meet the requirements of this subsection separately with respect to each such facility, and

(ii) the organization shall not be treated as described in subsection (c)(3) with respect to any such facility for which such requirements are not separately met.

(3) COMMUNITY HEALTH NEEDS ASSESSMENTS.—

(A) IN GENERAL.—An organization meets the requirements of this paragraph with respect to any taxable year only if the organization—

(i) has conducted a community health needs assessment which meets the requirements of subparagraph (B) in such taxable year or in either of the 2 taxable years immediately preceding such taxable year, and

(ii) has adopted an implementation strategy to meet the community health needs identified through such assessment.

(B) COMMUNITY HEALTH NEEDS ASSESSMENT.—A community health needs assessment meets the requirements of this paragraph if such community health needs assessment—

(i) takes into account input from persons who represent the broad interests of the community served by the hospital facility, including those with special knowledge of or expertise in public health, and

(ii) is made widely available to the public.

(4) FINANCIAL ASSISTANCE POLICY.—An organization meets the requirements of this paragraph if the organization establishes the following policies:

(A) FINANCIAL ASSISTANCE POLICY.—A written financial assistance policy which includes—

(i) eligibility criteria for financial assistance, and whether such assistance includes free or discounted care,

(ii) the basis for calculating amounts charged to patients,

(iii) the method for applying for financial assistance,

(iv) in the case of an organization which does not have a separate billing and collections policy, the actions the organization may take in the event of non-payment, including collections action and reporting to credit agencies, and

(v) measures to widely publicize the policy within the community to be served by the organization.

(B) POLICY RELATING TO EMERGENCY MEDICAL CARE.—A written policy requiring the organization to provide, without discrimination, care for emergency medical conditions (within the meaning of section 1867 of the Social Security Act (42 U.S.C. 1395dd)) to individuals regardless of their eligibility under the financial assistance policy described in subparagraph (A).

(5) LIMITATION ON CHARGES.—An organization meets the requirements of this paragraph if the organization—

(A) limits amounts charged for emergency or other medically necessary care provided to individuals eligible for assistance under the financial assistance policy described in paragraph (4)(A) to not more than the amounts generally billed to individuals who have insurance covering such care, and

(B) prohibits the use of gross charges.

(6) BILLING AND COLLECTION REQUIREMENTS.—An organization meets the requirement of this paragraph only if the organization does not engage in extraordinary collection actions before the organization has made reasonable efforts to determine whether the individual is eligible for assistance under the financial assistance policy described in paragraph (4)(A).

(7) REGULATORY AUTHORITY.—The Secretary shall issue such regulations and guidance as may be necessary to carry out the provisions of this subsection, including guidance relating to what constitutes reasonable efforts to determine the eligibility of a patient under a financial assistance policy for purposes of paragraph (6).

Amendments

• 2010, Patient Protection and Affordable Care Act (P.L. 111-148)

P.L. 111-148, §9007(a):

Amended Code Sec. 501 by redesignating subsection (r) as subsection (s) and by inserting after subsection (q) a new subsection (r). **Effective** for tax years beginning after 3-23-2010. For a special rule, see Act Sec. 9007(f)(2), below.

P.L. 111-148, §9007(f)(2), provides:

(2) COMMUNITY HEALTH NEEDS ASSESSMENT.—The requirements of section 501(r)(3) of the Internal Revenue Code of 1986, as added by subsection (a), shall apply to taxable years beginning after the date which is 2 years after the date of the enactment of this Act.

P.L. 111-148, §10903(a):

Amended Code Sec. 501(r)(5)(A), as added by Act Sec. 9007, by striking "the lowest amounts charged" and inserting "the amounts generally billed". **Effective** for tax years beginning after 3-23-2010.

[Sec. 501(s)]

(s) CROSS REFERENCE.—

For nonexemption of Communist-controlled organizations, see section 11(b) of the Internal Security Act of 1950 (64 Stat. 997; 50 U. S. C. 790 (b)).

Amendments

• 2010, Patient Protection and Affordable Care Act (P.L. 111-148)

P.L. 111-148, §9007(a):

Amended Code Sec. 501 by redesignating subsection (r) as subsection (s). **Effective** for tax years beginning after 3-23-2010.

• 2006, Pension Protection Act of 2006 (P.L. 109-280)

P.L. 109-280, §1220(a):

Amended Code Sec. 501 by redesignating subsection (q) as subsection (r). **Effective** generally for tax years beginning after 8-17-2006. For a transition rule, see Act Sec. 1220(c)(2) in the amendment notes following Code Sec. 501(q).

• 2003, Military Family Tax Relief Act of 2003 (P.L. 108-121)

P.L. 108-121, §108(a):

Amended Code Sec. 501 by redesignating subsection (p) as subsection (q). **Effective** for designations made before, on, or after 11-11-2003.

• 1997, Balanced Budget Act of 1997 (P.L. 105-33)

P.L. 105-33, §4041(a):

Amended Code Sec. 501 by redesignating subsection (o) as subsection (p). **Effective** 8-5-97.

• 1996, Small Business Job Protection Act of 1996 (P.L. 104-188)

P.L. 104-188, §1114(a):

Amended Code Sec. 501 by redesignating subsection (n) as subsection (o). **Effective** for tax years beginning after 8-20-96.

• 1986, Tax Reform Act of 1986 (P.L. 99-514)

P.L. 99-514, §1012(a):

Amended Code Sec. 501 by redesignating subsection (m) as subsection (n). **Effective** for tax years beginning after 12-31-86. However, for special rules, see Act Sec. 1012(c)(2)-(4), below.

P.L. 99-514, §1012(c)(2)-(4), as amended by P.L. 100-647, §1010(b)(1)-(2), provides:

(2) STUDY OF FRATERNAL BENEFICIARY ASSOCIATIONS.—The Secretary of the Treasury or his delegate shall conduct a study of organizations described in section 501(c)(8) of the Internal Revenue Code of 1986 and which received gross annual insurance premiums in excess of $25,000,000 for the taxable years of such organizations which ended during 1984. Not later than January 1, 1988, the Secretary of the Treasury shall submit to the Committee on Ways and Means of the House of Representatives, the Committee on Finance of the Senate, and the Joint Committee on Taxation the results of such study, together with such recommendations as he determines to be appropriate. The Secretary of the Treasury shall have authority to require the furnishing of such information as may be necessary to carry out the purposes of this paragraph.

(3) SPECIAL RULES FOR EXISTING BLUE CROSS OR BLUE SHIELD ORGANIZATIONS.—

(A) IN GENERAL.—In the case of any existing Blue Cross or Blue Shield organization (as defined in section 833(c)(2) of the Internal Revenue Code of 1986 as added by this section)—

(i) no adjustment shall be made under section 481 (or any other provision) of such Code on account of a change in its method of accounting for its 1st taxable year beginning after December 31, 1986, and

(ii) for purposes of determining gain or loss, the adjusted basis of any asset held on the 1st day of such taxable year shall be treated as equal to its fair market value as of such day.

(B) TREATMENT OF CERTAIN DISTRIBUTIONS.—For purposes of section 833(b)(3)(B), the surplus of any organization as of the beginning of its 1st taxable year beginning after December 31, 1986, shall be increased by the amount of any distribution (other than to policyholders) made by such organization after August 16, 1986, and before the beginning of such taxable year.

(C) RESERVE WEAKENING AFTER AUGUST 16, 1986.—Any reserve weakening after August 16, 1986, by an existing Blue Cross or Blue Shield organization shall be treated as occurring in such organization's 1st taxable year beginning after December 31, 1986.

(4) OTHER SPECIAL RULES.—

(A) The amendments made by this section shall not apply with respect to that portion of the business of Mutual of America which is attributable to pension business.

(B) The amendments made by this section shall not apply to that portion of the business of the Teachers Insurance Annuity Association-College Retirement Equities Fund which is attributable to pension business.

(C) The amendments made by this section shall not apply to—

(i) the retirement fund of the YMCA,

(ii) the Missouri Hospital Plan,

(iii) administrative services performed by municipal leagues, and

(iv) dental benefit coverage provided by a Delta Dental Plans Association organization through contracts with independent professional service providers so long as the provision of such coverage is the principal activity of such organization.

(D) For purposes of this paragraph, the term "pension business" means the administration of any plan described in section 401(a) of the Internal Revenue Code of 1954 which includes a trust exempt from tax under section 501(a), any plan under which amounts are contributed by an individual's employer for an annuity contract described in section 403(b) of such Code, any individual retirement plan described in section 408 of such Code, and any eligible deferred compensation plan to which section 457(a) of such Code applies.

• 1984, Deficit Reduction Act of 1984 (P.L. 98-369)

P.L. 98-369, §1032(a):

Amended Code Sec. 501 by redesignating subsection (k) as subsection (l). **Effective** for tax years beginning after 7-18-84.

P.L. 98-369, §2813(b)(1):

Amended Code Sec. 501, as amended by Act Sec. 1032(a), by redesignating subsection (l) as subsection (m). **Effective** 10-1-79.

• 1982, Tax Equity and Fiscal Responsibility Act of 1982 (P.L. 97-248)

P.L. 97-248, §286(a):

Redesignated subsection (j) as subsection (k). **Effective** 10-5-76.

• 1976 (P.L. 94-568)

P.L. 94-568, §2(a):

Redesignated Code Sec. 501(i) as Code Sec. 501(j). **Effective** for tax years beginning after 10-20-76.

• 1976, Tax Reform Act of 1976 (P.L. 94-455)

P.L. 94-455, §§2113(a), 3701(a)(1):

Redesignated Code Sec. 501(g) as Code Sec. 501(h), further redesignated such section to be Code Sec. 501(i). **Effective** for tax years ending after 12-31-75.

P.L. 94-455, §1307(a):

Redesignated Code Sec. 501(h) as Code Sec. 501(i). **Effective** for tax years beginning after 12-31-76.

• 1974 (P.L. 93-310)

P.L. 93-310, §3:

Redesignated Sec. 501(f) as Sec. 501(g). **Effective** 6-8-74.

• 1968, Revenue and Expenditure Control Act of 1968 (P.L. 90-364)

P.L. 90-364, §109(a):

Redesignated Sec. 501(e) as Sec. 501(f). **Effective** 6-28-68.

[Sec. 502]

SEC. 502. FEEDER ORGANIZATIONS.

[Sec. 502(a)]

(a) GENERAL RULE.—An organization operated for the primary purpose of carrying on a trade or business for profit shall not be exempt from taxation under section 501 on the ground that all of its profits are payable to one or more organizations exempt from taxation under section 501.

[Sec. 502(b)]

(b) SPECIAL RULE.—For purposes of this section, the term "trade or business" shall not include—

(1) the deriving of rents which would be excluded under section 512(b)(3), if section 512 applied to the organization,

(2) any trade or business in which substantially all the work in carrying on such trade or business is performed for the organization without compensation, or

(3) any trade or business which is the selling of merchandise, substantially all of which has been received by the organization as gifts or contributions.

Amendments

• 1969, Tax Reform Act of 1969 (P.L. 91-172)

P.L. 91-172, §121(b)(7):

Amended Code Sec. 502. **Effective** 1-1-70. Prior to amendment, Code Sec. 502 read as follows:

SEC. 502. FEEDER ORGANIZATIONS.

An organization operated for the primary purpose of carrying on a trade or business for profit shall not be exempt under section 501 on the ground that all of its profits are payable to one or more organizations exempt under section 501 from taxation. For purposes of this section, the term "trade or business" shall not include the rental by an organization of its real property (including personal property leased with the real property).

[Sec. 503]

SEC. 503. REQUIREMENTS FOR EXEMPTION.

[Sec. 503(a)]

(a) DENIAL OF EXEMPTION TO ORGANIZATIONS ENGAGED IN PROHIBITED TRANSACTIONS.—

(1) GENERAL RULE.—

(A) An organization described in section 501(c)(17) shall not be exempt from taxation under section 501(a) if it has engaged in a prohibited transaction after December 31, 1959.

(B) An organization described in section 401(a) which is referred to in section 4975(g)(2) or (3) shall not be exempt from taxation under section 501(a) if it has engaged in a prohibited transaction after March 1, 1954.

(C) An organization described in section 501(c)(18) shall not be exempt from taxation under section 501(a) if it has engaged in a prohibited transaction after December 31, 1969.

(2) TAXABLE YEARS AFFECTED.—An organization described in section 501(c)(17) or (18) or paragraph (a)(1)(B) shall be denied exemption from taxation under section 501(a) by reason of paragraph (1) only for taxable years after the taxable year during which it is notified by the Secretary that it has engaged in a prohibited transaction, unless such organization entered into such prohibited transaction with the purpose of diverting corpus or income of the organization from its exempt purposes, and such transaction involved a substantial part of the corpus or income of such organization.

Amendments

• 1976, Tax Reform Act of 1976 (P.L. 94-455)

P.L. 94-455, §1906(b)(13)(A):

Amended 1954 Code by substituting "Secretary" for "Secretary or his delegate" each place it appeared. **Effective** 2-1-77.

• 1974, Employee Retirement Income Security Act of 1974 (P.L. 93-406)

P.L. 93-406, §2003(b)(1), (2), (3):

Amended Code Sec. 503(a) by deleting "or (18)" after "section 501(c)(17)" in subsection (a)(1)(A), by adding "which is referred to in section 4975(g)(2) or (3)" after "described in section 401(a)" in subsection (a)(1)(B) and by substituting "or paragraph (a)(1)(B)" for "or section 401(a)". **Effective** 1-1-75.

• 1969, Tax Reform Act of 1969 (P.L. 91-172)

P.L. 91-172, §101(j)(7):

Amended Code Sec. 503(a)(1). **Effective** 1-1-70. Prior to amendment, Code Sec. 503(a)(1) read as follows:

(1) GENERAL RULE.—

(A) An organization described in section 501(c)(3) which is subject to the provisions of this section shall not be exempt from taxation under section 501(a) if it has engaged in a prohibited transaction after July 1, 1950.

(B) An organization described in section 501(c)(17) which is subject to the provisions of this section shall not be exempt from taxation under section 501(a) if it has engaged in a prohibited transaction after December 31, 1959.

(C) An organization described in section 401(a) which is subject to the provisions of this section shall not be exempt from taxation under section 501(a) if it has engaged in a prohibited transaction after March 1, 1954.

P.L. 91-172, §101(j)(8):

Substituted "section 501(c)(17)" for "section 501(c)(3) or (17)" in Code Sec. 503(a)(2). **Effective** 1-1-70.

P.L. 91-172, §121(b)(6)(B):

Amended Code Sec. 503(a)(1) by adding paragraph (C) and by substituting "(c)(17)" for "(c)(17) or (18)". **Effective** 1-1-70.

• 1960 (P.L. 86-667)

P.L. 86-667, §2(a):

Amended Code Sec. 503(a)(1). **Effective** for tax years beginning after 12-31-59. Prior to amendment, Sec. 503(a)(1) read as follows:

(1) GENERAL RULE.—An organization described in section 501(c)(3) which is subject to the provisions of this section shall not be exempt from taxation under section 501(a) if it has engaged in a prohibited transaction after July 1, 1950; and an organization described in section 401(a) which is

subject to the provisions of this section shall not be exempt from taxation under section 501(a) if it has engaged in a prohibited transaction after March 1, 1954.

Amended Code Sec. 503(a)(2) by striking out "section 501(c)(3)" and inserting in lieu thereof "section 501(c)(3) or (17)". **Effective** for taxable years beginning after December 31, 1959.

[Sec. 503(b)]

(b) PROHIBITED TRANSACTIONS.—For purposes of this section, the term "prohibited transaction" means any transaction in which an organization subject to the provisions of this section—

(1) lends any part of its income or corpus, without the receipt of adequate security and a reasonable rate of interest, to;

(2) pays any compensation, in excess of a reasonable allowance for salaries or other compensation for personal services actually rendered, to;

(3) makes any part of its services available on a preferential basis to;

(4) makes any substantial purchase of securities or any other property, for more than adequate consideration in money or money's worth, from;

(5) sells any substantial part of its securities or other property, for less than an adequate consideration in money or money's worth, to; or

(6) engages in any other transaction which results in a substantial diversion of its income or corpus to;

the creator of such organization (if a trust); a person who has made a substantial contribution to such organization; a member of the family (as defined in section 267 (c) (4)) of an individual who is the creator of such trust or who has made a substantial contribution to such organization; or a corporation controlled by such creator or person through the ownership, directly or indirectly, of 50 percent or more of the total combined voting power of all classes of stock entitled to vote or 50 percent or more of the total value of shares of all classes of stock of the corporation.

Amendments

• 1969, Tax Reform Act of 1969 (P.L. 91-172)

P.L. 91-172, §101(j)(14):

Repealed former Code Sec. 503(b). **Effective** 1-1-70, and redesignated former Code Sec. 503(c) as Code Sec. 503(b). Prior to repeal Sec. 503(b) read as follows:

(b) ORGANIZATIONS TO WHICH SECTION APPLIES.—This section shall apply to any organization described in section 501(c)(3) or (17) or section 401(a) except—

(1) a religious organization (other than a trust);

(2) an educational organization which normally maintains a regular faculty and curriculum and normally has a regularly enrolled body of pupils or students in attendance at the place where its educational activities are regularly carried on;

(3) an organization which normally receives a substantial part of its support (exclusive of income received in the exercise or performance by such organization of its charitable, educational, or other purpose or function constituting the basis for its exemption under section 501 (a)) from the United States or any State or political subdivision thereof or from direct or indirect contributions from the general public;

(4) an organization which is operated, supervised, controlled, or principally supported by a religious organization (other than a trust) which is itself not subject to the provisions of this section; and

(5) an organization the principal purposes or functions of which are the providing of medical or hospital care or medical education or medical research or agricultural research.

• 1960 (P.L. 86-667)

P.L. 86-667, §2(b):

Substituted "section 501(c)(3) or (17)" for "section 501(c)(3)." **Effective** for tax years beginning after 12-31-59.

[Sec. 503(c)]

(c) FUTURE STATUS OF ORGANIZATIONS DENIED EXEMPTION.—Any organization described in section 501(c)(17) or (18) or subsection (a)(1)(B) which is denied exemption under section 501(a) by reason of subsection (a) of this section, with respect to any taxable year following the taxable year in which notice of denial of exemption was received, may, under regulations prescribed by the Secretary, file claim for exemption, and if the Secretary, pursuant to such regulations, is satisfied that such organization will not knowingly again engage in a prohibited transaction, such organization shall be exempt with respect to taxable years after the year in which such claim is filed.

Amendments

• 1976, Tax Reform Act of 1976 (P.L. 94-455)

P.L. 94-455, §1906(b)(13)(A):

Amended 1954 Code by substituting "Secretary" for "Secretary or his delegate" each place it appeared. **Effective** 2-1-77.

• 1974, Employee Retirement Income Security Act of 1974 (P.L. 93-406)

P.L. 93-406, §2003(b)(3):

Amended Code Sec. 503(c) by substituting "or subsection (a)(1)(B)" for "or section 401(a)". **Effective** 1-1-75.

• 1969, Tax Reform Act of 1969 (P.L. 91-172)

P.L. 91-172, §101(j)(9), (14):

Redesignated former Code Sec. 503(d) as Code Sec. 503(c) and substituted "section 501(c)(17)" for "section 501(c)(3) or (17)." **Effective** 1-1-70.

P.L. 91-172, §121(b)(6)(B):

Amended Code Sec. 503(c) by changing "(c)(17)" to "(c)(17) or (18)." **Effective** 1-1-70.

• 1960 (P.L. 86-667)

P.L. 86-667, §2(c):

Amended Code Sec. 503(d) by striking out "section 501(c)(3)" and inserting in lieu thereof "section 501(c)(3) or (17)". **Effective** for tax years beginning after 12-31-59.

[Sec. 503(d)—Repealed]

Amendments

• 1990, Omnibus Budget Reconciliation Act of 1990 (P.L. 101-508)

P.L. 101-508, §11801(a)(22):

Repealed Code Sec. 503(d). **Effective** on the date of the enactment of this Act. Prior to repeal, Code Sec. 503(d) read as follows:

(d) SPECIAL RULE FOR LOANS.—For purposes of the application of subsection (b)(1), in the case of a loan by a trust described in section 401(a), the following rules shall apply with respect to a loan made before March 1, 1954, which would constitute a prohibited transaction if made on or after March 1, 1954:

(1) If any part of the loan is repayable prior to December 31, 1955, the renewal of such part of the loan for a period not extending beyond December 31, 1955, on the same terms, shall not be considered a prohibited transaction.

(2) If the loan is repayable on demand, the continuation of the loan without the receipt of adequate security and a reasonable rate of interest beyond December 31, 1955, shall be considered a prohibited transaction.

P.L. 101-508, §11821(b), provides:

(b) SAVINGS PROVISION.—If—

(1) any provision amended or repealed by this part applied to—

(A) any transaction occurring before the date of the enactment of this Act,

(B) any property acquired before such date of enactment, or

(C) any item of income, loss, deduction, or credit taken into account before such date of enactment, and

(2) the treatment of such transaction, property, or item under such provision would (without regard to the amendments made by this part) affect liability for tax for periods ending after such date of enactment,

nothing in the amendments made by this part shall be construed to affect the treatment of such transaction, property, or item for purposes of determining liability for tax for periods ending after such date of enactment.

• 1969, Tax Reform Act of 1969 (P.L. 91-172)

P.L. 91-172, §101(j)(10), (14):

Redesignated former Code Sec. 503(g) to be Code Sec. 503(d) and substituted "subsection (b)(1)" for "subsection (c)(1)." **Effective** 1-1-70.

[Sec. 503(e)]

(e) SPECIAL RULES.—For purposes of subsection (b)(1), a bond, debenture, note, or certificate or other evidence of indebtedness (hereinafter in this subsection referred to as "obligation") shall not be treated as a loan made without the receipt of adequate security if—

(1) such obligation is acquired—

(A) on the market, either (i) at the price of the obligation prevailing on a national securities exchange which is registered with the Securities and Exchange Commission, or (ii) if the obligation is not traded on such a national securities exchange, at a price not less favorable to the trust than the offering price for the obligation as established by current bid and asked prices quoted by persons independent of the issuer;

(B) from an underwriter, at a price (i) not in excess of the public offering price for the obligation as set forth in a prospectus or offering circular filed with the Securities and Exchange Commission, and (ii) at which a substantial portion of the same issue is acquired by persons independent of the issuer; or

(C) directly from the issuer, at a price not less favorable to the trust than the price paid currently for a substantial portion of the same issue by persons independent of the issuer;

(2) immediately following acquisition of such obligation—

(A) not more than 25 percent of the aggregate amount of obligations issued in such issue and outstanding at the time of acquisition is held by the trust, and

(B) at least 50 percent of the aggregate amount referred to in subparagraph (A) is held by persons independent of the issuer; and

(3) immediately following acquisition of the obligation, not more than 25 percent of the assets of the trust is invested in obligations of persons described in subsection (b).

Amendments

• 1969, Tax Reform Act of 1969 (P.L. 91-172)

P.L. 91-172, §101(j)(11):

Repealed former Code Sec. 503(e) (see below) and redesignated former Code Sec. 503(h) as Code Sec. 503(e), substituted "subsection (b)" for "subsection (c)" in paragraph (3) and substituted the matter preceding paragraph (1) for the following:

"(h) SPECIAL RULES RELATING TO LENDING BY SECTION 401(a) AND SECTION 501(c)(17) TRUSTS TO CERTAIN PERSONS.—For purposes of subsection (c)(1), a bond, debenture, note, or certificate or other evidence of indebtedness (hereinafter in this subsection referred to as `obligation') acquired by a trust described in section 401(a) or section 501(c)(17) shall not be treated as a loan made without the receipt of adequate security if—"

P.L. 91-172, §101(j)(14):

Repealed former Code Sec. 503(e). **Effective** 1-1-70. Prior to repeal, Sec. 503(e) read as follows:

(e) DISALLOWANCE OF CERTAIN CHARITABLE, ETC., DEDUCTIONS.—No gift or bequest for religious, charitable, scientific, literary, or educational purposes (including the encouragement of art and the prevention of cruelty to children or animals), otherwise allowable as a deduction under section 170, 642(c), 545(b)(2), 2055, 2106(a)(2), or 2522, shall be allowed as a deduction if made to an organization described in section 501(c)(3) which, in the taxable year of the organization in which the gift or bequest is made, is not exempt under section 501(a) by reason of this section. With respect to any taxable year of the organization for which the organization is not exempt pursuant to subsection (a) by reason of having engaged in a prohibited transaction with the purpose of diverting the corpus or income of such organization from its exempt purposes and such transaction involved a substantial part of such corpus or income, and which taxable year is the same, or prior to the, taxable year of the organization in which such transaction occurred, such deduction shall be disallowed the donor only if such donor or (if such donor is an individual) any member of his family (as defined in section 267(c)(4)) was a party to such prohibited transaction.

• 1960 (P.L. 86-667)

P.L. 86-667, §2(d):

Amended Code Sec. 503(h) by (1) striking out "section 401(a)" in the heading and inserting in lieu thereof "section 401(a) and section 501(c)(17)", and (2) by striking out "section 401(a)" in such subsection and inserting in lieu thereof "section 401(a) or section 501(c)(17)". **Effective** for tax years beginning after 12-31-59.

• 1958, Technical Amendments Act of 1958 (P.L. 85-866)

P.L. 85-866, §30(a):

Added subsec. (h) to Code Sec. 503. **Effective** for tax years ending after 3-15-56 except that nothing in subsec. (h) shall be construed to make any transaction a prohibited transaction which, under announcements of the IRS made with respect to section 503(c)(1) of the Internal Revenue Code of 1954 before 9-2-58, would not constitute a prohibited transaction. In the case of any bond, debenture, note, or certificate or other evidence of indebtedness acquired before 9-2-58 by a trust described in section 401(a) of such Code which is held on such date, paragraphs (2) and (3) of section 503(h) of such Code shall be treated as satisfied if such requirements would have been satisfied if such obligation had been acquired on 9-2-58.

[Sec. 503(f)]

(f) LOANS WITH RESPECT TO WHICH EMPLOYERS ARE PROHIBITED FROM PLEDGING CERTAIN ASSETS.—Subsection (b)(1) shall not apply to a loan made by a trust described in section 401(a) to the employer (or to a renewal of such a loan or, if the loan is repayable upon demand, to a continuation of such a loan) if the loan bears a reasonable rate of interest, and if (in the case of a making or renewal)—

(1) the employer is prohibited (at the time of such making or renewal) by any law of the United States or regulation thereunder from directly or indirectly pledging, as security for such a loan, a particular class or classes of his assets the value of which (at such time) represents more than one-half of the value of all his assets;

(2) the making or renewal, as the case may be, is approved in writing as an investment which is consistent with the exempt purposes of the trust by a trustee who is independent of the employer, and no other such trustee had previously refused to give such written approval; and

(3) immediately following the making or renewal, as the case may be, the aggregate amount loaned by the trust to the employer, without the receipt of adequate security, does not exceed 25 percent of the value of all the assets of the trust.

For purposes of paragraph (2), the term "trustee" means, with respect to any trust for which there is more than one trustee who is independent of the employer, a majority of such independent trustees. For purposes of paragraph (3), the determination as to whether any amount loaned by the trust to the employer is loaned without the receipt of adequate security shall be made without regard to subsection (e).

Amendments

• 1969, Tax Reform Act of 1969 (P.L. 91-172)

P.L. 91-172, §101(j)(12):

Repealed Code Sec. 503(f) and redesignated former Code Sec. 503(i) as Code Sec. 503(f), substituted "Subsection (b)(1)" for "Subsection (c)(1)" in the language preceding paragraph (1), and substituted "subsection (e)" for "subsection (h)" in the last sentence. **Effective** 1-1-70.

P.L. 91-172, §101(j)(14):

Repealed former Code Sec. 503(f). **Effective** 1-1-70. Prior to repeal, Sec. 503(f) read as follows:

(f) DEFINITION.—For purposes of this section, the term "gift or bequest" means any gift, contribution, bequest, devise, legacy, or transfer.

• 1958, Technical Amendments Act of 1958 (P.L. 85-866)

P.L. 85-866, §30(b):

Added subsec. (i) to Code Sec. 503. **Effective** for tax years ending after 9-2-58, but only with respect to periods after such date.

[Sec. 503(g)—Repealed]

Amendments

• 1974, Employee Retirement Income Security Act of 1974 (P.L. 93-406)

P.L. 93-406, §2003(b)(5):

Repealed Code Sec. 503(g). **Effective** 1-1-75. Prior to repeal, Code Sec. 503(g) read as follows:

(g) TRUSTS BENEFITING CERTAIN OWNER-EMPLOYEES.—

(1) PROHIBITED TRANSACTIONS.—In the case of a trust described in section 401(a) which is part of a plan providing contributions or benefits for employees some or all of whom are owner-employees (as defined in section 401(c)(3)) who control (within the meaning of section 401(d)(9)(B)) the trade or business with respect to which the plan is established, the term "prohibited transaction" also means any transaction in which such trust, directly or indirectly—

(A) lends any part of the corpus or income of the trust to;

(B) pays any compensation for personal services rendered to the trust to;

(C) makes any part of its services available on a preferential basis to; or

(D) acquires for the trust any property from, or sells any property to;

any person described in subsection (b) or to any such owner-employee, a member of the family (as defined in section 267(c)(4)) of any such owner-employee, or a corporation controlled by any such owner-employee through the ownership, directly or indirectly, of 50 percent or more of the total combined voting power of all classes of stock entitled to vote or 50 percent or more of the total value of shares of all classes of stock of the corporation.

(2) SPECIAL RULE FOR LOANS.—For purposes of the application of paragraph (1)(A), the following rules shall apply with respect to a loan made before the date of the enactment of this subsection which would be a prohibited transaction if made in a taxable year beginning after December 31, 1962:

(A) If any part of the loan is repayable prior to December 31, 1965, the renewal of such part of the loan for a period not extending beyond December 31, 1965, on the same terms, shall not be considered a prohibited transaction.

(B) If the loan is repayable on demand, the continuation of the loan beyond December 31, 1965, shall be considered a prohibited transaction.

• 1969, Tax Reform Act of 1969 (P.L. 91-172)

P.L. 91-172, §101(j)(13), (14):

Redesignated former Code Sec. 503(j) to be Code Sec. 503(g), and substituted "subsection (b)" for "subsection (c)" in the language in paragraph (1) which follows subparagraph (D). **Effective** 1-1-70.

• 1962, Self-Employed Individuals Tax Retirement Act of 1962 (P.L. 87-792)

P.L. 87-792, §6:

Added subsection (j) to Code Sec. 503. **Effective** 1-1-63.

[Sec. 504]

SEC. 504. STATUS AFTER ORGANIZATION CEASES TO QUALIFY FOR EXEMPTION UNDER SECTION 501(c)(3) BECAUSE OF SUBSTANTIAL LOBBYING OR BECAUSE OF POLITICAL ACTIVITIES.

[Sec. 504(a)]

(a) GENERAL RULE.—An organization which—

(1) was exempt (or was determined by the Secretary to be exempt) from taxation under section 501(a) by reason of being an organization described in section 501(c)(3), and

(2) is not an organization described in section 501(c)(3)—

(A) by reason of carrying on propaganda, or otherwise attempting, to influence legislation, or

(B) by reason of participating in, or intervening in, any political campaign on behalf of (or in opposition to) any candidate for public office,

shall not at any time thereafter be treated as an organization described in section 501(c)(4).

Amendments

• 1987, Revenue Act of 1987 (P.L. 100-203)

P.L. 100-203, §10711(b)(2)(A):

Amended Code Sec. 504 by striking out "SUBSTANTIAL LOBBYING" and inserting in lieu thereof "SUBSTANTIAL LOBBYING OR BECAUSE OF POLITICAL ACTIVITIES" in the section heading. **Effective** for activities after the date of enactment of this Act.

P.L. 100-203, §10711(b)(1):

Amended Code Sec. 504(a)(2). **Effective** for activities after the date of enactment of this Act. Prior to amendment, Code Sec. 504(a)(2) read as follows:

(2) is not an organization described in section 501(c)(3) by reason of carrying on propaganda, or otherwise attempting, to influence legislation,

[Sec. 504(b)]

(b) REGULATIONS TO PREVENT AVOIDANCE.—The Secretary shall prescribe such regulations as may be necessary or appropriate to prevent the avoidance of subsection (a), including regulations relating to a direct or indirect transfer of all or part of the assets of an organization to an organization controlled (directly or indirectly) by the same person or persons who control the transferor organization.

[Sec. 504(c)]

(c) CHURCHES, ETC.—Subsection (a) shall not apply to any organization which is a disqualified organization within the meaning of section 501(h)(5) (relating to churches, etc.) for the taxable year immediately preceding the first taxable year for which such organization is described in paragraph (2) of subsection (a).

Amendments

• 1976, Tax Reform Act of 1976 (P.L. 94-455)

P.L. 94-455, §1307(a)(2):

Added Code Sec. 504. **Effective** 10-5-76.

P.L. 94-455, §1307(a)(3), provides:

(3) RULES OF INTERPRETATION.—It is the intent of Congress that enactment of this section is not to be regarded in any way as an approval or disapproval of the decision of the Court of Appeals for the Tenth Circuit in *Christian Echoes, National Ministry, Inc. v. United States,* 470 F2d 849 (1972), or of the reasoning in any of the opinions leading to that decision.

[Sec. 505]

SEC. 505. ADDITIONAL REQUIREMENTS FOR ORGANIZATIONS DESCRIBED IN PARAGRAPH (9), (17), OR (20) OF SECTION 501(c).

[Sec. 505(a)]

(a) CERTAIN REQUIREMENTS MUST BE MET IN THE CASE OF ORGANIZATIONS DESCRIBED IN PARAGRAPH (9) OR (20) OF SECTION 501(c).—

(1) VOLUNTARY EMPLOYEES' BENEFICIARY ASSOCIATIONS, ETC.—An organization described in paragraph (9) or (20) of subsection (c) of section 501 which is part of a plan shall not be exempt from tax under section 501(a) unless such plan meets the requirements of subsection (b) of this section.

(2) EXCEPTION FOR COLLECTIVE BARGAINING AGREEMENTS.—Paragraph (1) shall not apply to any organization which is part of a plan maintained pursuant to an agreement between employee representatives and 1 or more employers if the Secretary finds that such agreement is a collective bargaining agreement and that such plan was the subject of good faith bargaining between such employee representatives and such employer or employers.

Amendments

• 1989 (P.L. 101-140)

P.L. 101-140, §203(a)(2):

Provides that Code Sec. 505(a)(1) as amended by Section 1011B(a)(27)(C) of P.L. 100-647 shall be applied as if the amendment made by such section had not been enacted. **Effective** as if included in Act Sec. 1151 of P.L. 99-514. Code Sec. 505(b)(1) as amended by Act Sec. 1011(B)(a)(27)(C) of P.L. 100-647 read as follows:

(1) VOLUNTARY EMPLOYEES' BENEFICIARY ASSOCIATIONS, ETC.—An organization described in paragraph (9) or (20) of subsection (c) of section 501 which is part of a plan shall not be exempt from tax under section 501(a) unless such plan meets the requirements of subsection (b) of this section. This paragraph shall not apply to any organization by reason of a failure to meet the requirements of subsection (b) with respect to a benefit to which section 89 applies.

• 1988, Technical and Miscellaneous Revenue Act of 1988 (P.L. 100-647)

P.L. 100-647, §1011B(a)(27)(C):

Amended Code Sec. 505(a)(1) by adding at the end thereof a new subsection [sentence]. **Effective** as if included in the provision of P.L. 99-514 to which it relates.

• 1986, Tax Reform Act of 1986 (P.L. 99-514)

P.L. 99-514, §1851(c)(1):

Amended Code Sec. 505(a)(1) by striking out "of an employer". **Effective** as if included in the provision of P.L. 98-369 to which it relates.

P.L. 99-514, §1851(c)(4):

Amended Code Sec. 505(a)(2). **Effective** as if included in the provision of P.L. 98-369 to which it relates. Prior to amendment, Code Sec. 505(a)(2) read as follows:

(2) EXCEPTION FOR COLLECTIVE BARGAINING AGREEMENTS.—Paragraph (1) shall not apply to any organization which is part of a plan maintained pursuant to 1 or more collective bargaining agreements between 1 or more employee organizations and 1 or more employers.

[Sec. 505(b)]

(b) NONDISCRIMINATION REQUIREMENTS.—

(1) IN GENERAL.—Except as otherwise provided in this subsection, a plan meets the requirements of this subsection only if—

(A) each class of benefits under the plan is provided under a classification of employees which is set forth in the plan and which is found by the Secretary not to be discriminatory in favor of employees who are highly compensated individuals, and

(B) in the case of each class of benefits, such benefits do not discriminate in favor of employees who are highly compensated individuals.

A life insurance, disability, severance pay, or supplemental unemployment compensation benefit shall not be considered to fail to meet the requirements of subparagraph (B) merely because the benefits available bear a uniform relationship to the total compensation, or the basic or regular rate of compensation, of employees covered by the plan.

(2) EXCLUSION OF CERTAIN EMPLOYEES.—For purposes of paragraph (1), there may be excluded from consideration—

(A) employees who have not completed 3 years of service,

(B) employees who have not attained age 21,

(C) seasonal employees or less than half-time employees,

(D) employees not included in this plan who are included in a unit of employees covered by an agreement between employee representatives and 1 or more employers which the Secretary finds to be a collective bargaining agreement if the class of benefits involved was the subject of good faith bargaining between such employee representatives and such employer or employers, and

(E) employees who are nonresident aliens and who receive no earned income (within the meaning of section 911(d)(2)) from the employer which constitutes income from sources within the United States (within the meaning of section 861(a)(3)).

(3) APPLICATION OF SUBSECTION WHERE OTHER NONDISCRIMINATION RULES PROVIDED.—In the case of any benefit for which a provision of this chapter other than this subsection provides nondiscrimination rules, paragraph (1) shall not apply but the requirements of this subsection shall be met only if the nondiscrimination rules so provided are satisfied with respect to such benefit.

(4) AGGREGATION RULES.—At the election of the employer, 2 or more plans of such employer may be treated as 1 plan for purposes of this subsection.

(5) HIGHLY COMPENSATED INDIVIDUAL.—For purposes of this subsection, the determination as to whether an individual is a highly compensated individual shall be made under rules similar to the rules for determining whether an individual is a highly compensated employee (within the meaning of section 414(q)).

(6) COMPENSATION.—For purposes of this subsection, the term "compensation" has the meaning given such term by section 414(s).

(7) COMPENSATION LIMIT.—A plan shall not be treated as meeting the requirements of this subsection unless under the plan the annual compensation of each employee taken into account for any year does not exceed $200,000. The Secretary shall adjust the $200,000 amount at the same time, and by the same amount, as any adjustment under section 401(a)(17)(B). This paragraph shall not apply in determining whether the requirements of section 79(d) are met.

Amendments

• 2006, Pension Protection Act of 2006 (P.L. 109-280)

P.L. 109-280, §811, provides:

SEC. 811. PENSIONS AND INDIVIDUAL RETIREMENT ARRANGEMENT PROVISIONS OF ECONOMIC GROWTH AND TAX RELIEF RECONCILIATION ACT OF 2001 MADE PERMANENT.

Title IX of the Economic Growth and Tax Relief Reconciliation Act of 2001 [P.L. 107-16] shall not apply to the provisions of, and amendments made by, subtitles A through F of title VI [§§601-666]of such Act (relating to pension and individual retirement arrangement provisions).

• 2001, Economic Growth and Tax Relief Reconciliation Act of 2001 (P.L. 107-16)

P.L. 107-16, §611(c)(1):

Amended Code Sec. 505(b)(7) by striking "$150,000" each place it appears and inserting "$200,000". **Effective** for years beginning after 12-31-2001. For a special rule, see Act Sec. 611(i)(3), below.

P.L. 107-16, §611(i)(3) (as added by P.L. 107-147, §411(j)(3)), provides:

(3) SPECIAL RULE.—In the case of [a] plan that, on June 7, 2001, incorporated by reference the limitation of section 415(b)(1)(A) of the Internal Revenue Code of 1986, section

411(d)(6) of such Code and section 204(g)(1) of the Employee Retirement Income Security Act of 1974 do not apply to a plan amendment that—

(A) is adopted on or before June 30, 2002,

(B) reduces benefits to the level that would have applied without regard to the amendments made by subsection (a) of this section, and

(C) is effective no earlier than the years described in paragraph (2).

P.L. 107-16, §901(a)-(b), provides [but see P.L. 109-280, §811, above]:

SEC. 901. SUNSET OF PROVISIONS OF ACT.

(a) IN GENERAL.—All provisions of, and amendments made by, this Act shall not apply—

(1) to taxable, plan, or limitation years beginning after December 31, 2010, or

(2) in the case of title V, to estates of decedents dying, gifts made, or generation skipping transfers, after December 31, 2010.

(b) APPLICATION OF CERTAIN LAWS.—The Internal Revenue Code of 1986 and the Employee Retirement Income Security Act of 1974 shall be applied and administered to years, estates, gifts, and transfers described in subsection (a) as if the provisions and amendments described in subsection (a) had never been enacted.

• 1993, Omnibus Budget Reconciliation Act of 1993 (P.L. 103-66)

P.L. 103-66, §13212(c)(1)(A)-(B):

Amended Code Sec. 505(b)(7) by striking "$200,000" in the first sentence and inserting "$150,000", and by striking the second sentence and inserting a new sentence. **Effective**, generally, for benefits accruing in plan years beginning after 12-31-93. For special rules, see Act Sec. 13212(d)(2)-(3), below.

P.L. 103-66, §13212(c)(2):

Amended Code Sec. 505(b)(7) by striking "$200,000" preceding "Compensation" in the heading. **Effective**, generally, for benefits accruing in plan years beginning after 12-31-93. For special rules, see Act Sec. 13212(d)(2)-(3), below.

P.L. 103-66, §13212(d)(2)-(3), provides:

(2) COLLECTIVELY BARGAINED PLANS.—In the case of a plan maintained pursuant to 1 or more collective bargaining agreements between employee representatives and 1 or more employers ratified before the date of the enactment of this Act, the amendments made by this section shall not apply to contributions or benefits pursuant to such agreements for plan years beginning before the earlier of—

(A) the latest of—

(i) January 1, 1994,

(ii) the date on which the last of such collective bargaining agreements terminates (without regard to any extension, amendment, or modification of such agreements on or after such date of enactment), or

(iii) in the case of a plan maintained pursuant to collective bargaining under the Railway Labor Act, the date of execution of an extension or replacement of the last of such collective bargaining agreements in effect on such date of enactment, or

(B) January 1, 1997.

(3) TRANSITION RULE FOR STATE AND LOCAL PLANS.—

(A) IN GENERAL.—In the case of an eligible participant in a governmental plan (within the meaning of section 414(d) of the Internal Revenue Code of 1986), the dollar limitation under section 401(a)(17) of such Code shall not apply to the extent the amount of compensation which is allowed to be taken into account under the plan would be reduced below the amount which was allowed to be taken into account under the plan as in effect on July 1, 1993.

(B) ELIGIBLE PARTICIPANT.—For purposes of subparagraph (A), an eligible participant is an individual who first became a participant in the plan during a plan year beginning before the 1st plan year beginning after the earlier of—

(i) the plan year in which the plan is amended to reflect the amendments made by this section, or

(ii) December 31, 1995.

(C) PLAN MUST BE AMENDED TO INCORPORATE LIMITS.—This paragraph shall not apply to any eligible participant of a plan unless the plan is amended so that the plan incorporates by reference the dollar limitation under section 401(a)(17) of the Internal Revenue Code of 1986, effective with respect to noneligible participants for plan years beginning after December 31, 1995 (or earlier if the plan amendment so provides).

• 1989 (P.L. 101-140)

P.L. 101-140, §203(a)(1):

Provides that Code Sec. 505(b)(2) as amended by Section 1151(g)(6) of P.L. 99-514 shall be applied as if the amendment made by such section had not been enacted. **Effective** as if included in Act Sec. 1151 of P.L. 99-514.

P.L. 101-140, §203(a)(2):

Provides that Code Sec. 505(b)(2) as amended by Section 1011B(a)(31)(B)(i)-(ii) of P.L. 100-647 shall be applied as if the amendment made by such section had not been enacted. **Effective** as if included in Act Sec. 1151 of P.L. 99-514. Code Sec. 505(b)(2) as amended by Act Sec. 1151(g)(6) of P.L. 99-514 and Act Sec. 1011B(a)(31)(B)(i)-(ii) of P.L. 100-647 read as follows:

(2) EXCLUSION OF CERTAIN EMPLOYEES.—For purposes of paragraph (1), there shall be excluded from consideration employees who are excluded from consideration under section 89(h).

P.L. 101-140, §204(c):

Amended Code Sec. 505(b)(7) by adding at the end thereof a new sentence. **Effective** as if included in the amendments made by Act Sec. 1011B(a)(32) of P.L. 100-647.

• 1989 (P.L. 101-136)

P.L. 101-136, §528, provides:

SEC. 528. No monies appropriated by this Act may be used to implement or enforce section 1151 of the Tax Reform Act of 1986 or the amendments made by such section.

• 1988, Technical and Miscellaneous Revenue Act of 1988 (P.L. 100-647)

P.L. 100-647, §1011B(a)(31)(B)(i)-(ii):

Amended Code Sec. 505(b)(2) by striking out "may" the first place it appears and inserting in lieu thereof "shall", and by striking out "may be" the second place it appears and inserting in lieu thereof "are". **Effective** as if included in the provision of P.L. 99-514 to which it relates.

P.L. 100-647, §1011B(a)(32):

Amended Code Sec. 505(b) by adding at the end thereof a new paragraph (7). **Effective** as if included in the provision of P.L. 99-514 to which it relates.

• 1986, Tax Reform Act of 1986 (P.L. 99-514)

P.L. 99-514, §1114(b)(16):

Amended Code Sec. 505 by striking out paragraph (5) of subsection (b) and inserting in lieu thereof new paragraph (5). **Effective** for years beginning after 12-31-87. Prior to amendment, Code Sec. 505(b)(5) read as follows:

(5) HIGHLY COMPENSATED INDIVIDUAL.—For purposes of this subsection, the term "highly compensated individual" has the meaning given such term by section 105(h)(5). For purposes of the preceding sentence, section 105(g)(5) shall be applied by substituting "10 percent" for "25 percent".

P.L. 99-514, §1151(e)(2)(B):

Amended Code Sec. 505(b)(4). **Effective** for years beginning after the later of 12-31-87 or the earlier of (1) the date which is 3 months after the date on which the Secretary of the Treasury or his delegate issues such regulations as are necessary to carry out the provisions of section 89 of the Internal Revenue Code of 1986 (as added by this section), or (2) 12-31-88. For special rules, see Act Sec. 1151(k)(2)-(4), below. Prior to amendment, Code Sec. 505(b)(4) read as follows:

(4) AGGREGATION RULES.—For purposes of this subsection—

(A) AGGREGATION OF PLANS.—At the election of the employer, 2 or more plans of such employer may be treated as 1 plan.

(B) TREATMENT OF RELATED EMPLOYERS.—Rules similar to the rules of subsections (b), (c), (m), and (n) of section 414 shall apply. For purposes of the preceding sentence, section 414(n) shall be applied without regard to paragraph (5).

P.L. 99-514, § 1151(g)(6):

Amended Code Sec. 505(b)(2). **Effective** for years beginning after the later of 12-31-87 or the earlier of (1) the date which is 3 months after the date on which the Secretary of the Treasury or his delegate issues such regulations as are necessary to carry out the provisions of section 89 of the Internal Revenue Code of 1986 (as added by this section), or (2) 12-31-88. For special rules, see Act Sec. 1151(k)(2)-(4), below. Prior to amendment, Code Sec. 505(b)(2) read as follows:

(2) EXCLUSION OF CERTAIN EMPLOYEES.—For purposes of paragraph (1), there may be excluded from consideration—

(A) employees who have not completed 3 years of service,

(B) employees who have not attained age 21,

(C) seasonal employees or less than half-time employees,

(D) employees not included in this plan who are included in a unit of employees covered by an agreement between employee representatives and 1 or more employers which the Secretary finds to be a collective bargaining agreement if the class of benefits involved was the subject of good faith bargaining between such employee representatives and such employer or employers, and

(E) employees who are nonresident aliens and who receive no earned income (within the meaning of section 911(d)(2)) from the employer which constitutes income from sources within the United States (within the meaning of section 861(a)(3)).

P.L. 99-514, § 1151(j)(3):

Amended Code Sec. 505(b) by adding a new paragraph (6). **Effective** for years beginning after the later of 12-31-87 or the earlier of (1) the date which is 3 months after the date on which the Secretary of the Treasury or his delegate issues such regulations as are necessary to carry out the provisions of section 89 of the Internal Revenue Code of 1986 (as added by this section), or (2) 12-31-88. For special rules, see Act Sec. 1151(k)(2)-(4), below.

P.L. 99-514, § 1151(k)(2)-(4), provides:

(2) SPECIAL RULE FOR COLLECTIVE BARGAINING PLAN.—In the case of a plan maintained pursuant to 1 or more collective bargaining agreements between employee representatives and 1 or more employers ratified before March 1, 1986, the amendments made by this section shall not apply to employees covered by such an agreement in years beginning before the earlier of—

(A) the date on which the last of such collective bargaining agreements terminates (determined without regard to any extension thereof after February 28, 1986, or

(B) January 1, 1991.

A plan shall not be required to take into account employees to which the preceding sentence applies for purposes of applying section 89 of the Internal Revenue Code of 1986 (as added by this section) to employees to which the preceding sentence does not apply for any year preceding the year described in the preceding sentence.

(3) EXCEPTION FOR CERTAIN GROUP-TERM INSURANCE PLANS.—In the case of a plan described in section 223(d)(2) of the Tax Reform Act of 1984, such plan shall be treated as meeting the requirements of section 89 of the Internal Revenue Code of 1986 (as added by this section) with respect to individuals described in section 223(d)(2) of such Act. An employer may elect to disregard such individuals in applying section 89 of such Code (as so added) to other employees of the employer.

(4) SPECIAL RULE FOR CHURCH PLANS.—In the case of a church plan (within the meaning of section 414(e)(3) of the Internal Revenue Code of 1986) maintaining an insured accident and health plan, the amendments made by this section shall apply to years beginning after December 31, 1988.

P.L. 99-514, § 1851(c)(2):

Amended Code Sec. 505(b)(1) by striking out "as provided in paragraph (2)" and inserting in lieu thereof "as otherwise provided in this subsection". **Effective** as if included in the provision of P.L. 98-369 to which it relates.

P.L. 99-514, § 1851(c)(3):

Amended Code Sec. 505(b)(1)(B) by striking out "highly compensated employees" and inserting in lieu thereof "highly compensated individuals". **Effective** as if included in the provision of P.L. 98-369 to which it relates.

[Sec. 505(c)]

(c) REQUIREMENT THAT ORGANIZATION NOTIFY SECRETARY THAT IT IS APPLYING FOR TAX-EXEMPT STATUS.—

(1) IN GENERAL.—An organization shall not be treated as an organization described in paragraph (9), (17), or (20) of section 501(c)—

(A) unless it has given notice to the Secretary, in such manner as the Secretary may by regulations prescribe, that it is applying for recognition of such status, or

(B) for any period before the giving of such notice, if such notice is given after the time prescribed by the Secretary by regulations for giving notice under this subsection.

(2) SPECIAL RULE FOR EXISTING ORGANIZATIONS.—In the case of any organization in existence on July 18, 1984, the time for giving notice under paragraph (1) shall not expire before the date 1 year after such date of the enactment.

Amendments

• 1986, Tax Reform Act of 1986 (P.L. 99-514)

P.L. 99-514, § 1899A(16):

Amended Code Sec. 505(c)(2) by striking out "the date of the enactment of the Tax Reform Act of 1984" and inserting in lieu thereof "July 18, 1984". **Effective** 10-22-86.

• 1984, Deficit Reduction Act of 1984 (P.L. 98-369)

P.L. 98-369, § 513(a):

Added new Code Sec. 505. **Effective** for tax years beginning after 12-31-84.

P.L. 98-369, § 513(c)(2), provides:

(2) Treatment of Certain Benefits in Pay Status as of January 1, 1985.—For purposes of determining whether a plan meets the requirements of section 505(b) of the Internal Revenue Code of 1954 (as added by subsection (a)), there may (at the election of the employer) be excluded from consideration all disability or severance payments payable to individuals who are in pay status as of January 1, 1985. The preceding sentence shall not apply to any payment to the extent such payment is increased by any plan amendment adopted after June 22, 1984.

PART II—PRIVATE FOUNDATIONS

[Sec. 507]

SEC. 507. TERMINATION OF PRIVATE FOUNDATION STATUS.

[Sec. 507(a)]

(a) GENERAL RULE.—Except as provided in subsection (b), the status of any organization as a private foundation shall be terminated only if—

(1) such organization notifies the Secretary (at such time and in such manner as the Secretary may by regulations prescribe) of its intent to accomplish such termination, or

(2)(A) with respect to such organization, there have been either willful repeated acts (or failures to act), or a willful and flagrant act (or failure to act), giving rise to liability for tax under chapter 42, and

(B) the Secretary notifies such organization that, by reason of subparagraph (A), such organization is liable for the tax imposed by subsection (c),

and either such organization pays the tax imposed by subsection (c) (or any portion not abated under subsection (g)) or the entire amount of such tax is abated under subsection (g).

Amendments

• 1976, Tax Reform Act of 1976 (P.L. 94-455)

P.L. 94-455, §1906(b)(13)(A):

Amended 1954 Code by substituting "Secretary" for "Secretary or his delegate" each place it appeared. **Effective** 2-1-77.

[Sec. 507(b)]

(b) SPECIAL RULES.—

(1) TRANSFER TO, OR OPERATION AS, PUBLIC CHARITY.—The status as a private foundation of any organization, with respect to which there have not been either willful repeated acts (or failures to act) or a willful and flagrant act (or failure to act) giving rise to liability for tax under chapter 42, shall be terminated if—

(A) such organization distributes all of its net assets to one or more organizations described in section 170(b)(1)(A) (other than in clauses (vii) and (viii)) each of which has been in existence and so described for a continuous period of at least 60 calendar months immediately preceding such distribution, or

(B)(i) such organization meets the requirements of paragraph (1), (2), or (3) of section 509(a) by the end of the 12-month period beginning with its first taxable year which begins after December 31, 1969, or for a continuous period of 60 calendar months beginning with the first day of any taxable year which begins after December 31, 1969,

(ii) such organization notifies the Secretary (in such manner as the Secretary may by regulations prescribe) before the commencement of such 12-month or 60-month period (or before the 90th day after the day on which regulations first prescribed under this subsection become final) that it is terminating its private foundation status, and

(iii) such organization establishes to the satisfaction of the Secretary (in such manner as the Secretary may by regulations prescribe) immediately after the expiration of such 12-month or 60-month period that such organization has complied with clause (i).

If an organization gives notice under subparagraph (B)(ii) of the commencement of a 60-month period and such organization fails to meet the requirements of paragraph (1), (2), or (3) of section 509(a) for the entire 60-month period, this part and chapter 42 shall not apply to such organization for any taxable year within such 60-month period for which it does meet such requirements.

(2) TRANSFEREE FOUNDATIONS.—For purposes of this part, in the case of a transfer of assets of any private foundation to another private foundation pursuant to any liquidation, merger, redemption, recapitalization, or other adjustment, organization, or reorganization, the transferee foundation shall not be treated as a newly created organization.

Amendments

• 1976, Tax Reform Act of 1976 (P.L. 94-455)

P.L. 94-455, §1906(b)(13)(A):

Amended 1954 Code by substituting "Secretary" for "Secretary or his delegate" each place it appeared. **Effective** 2-1-77.

[Sec. 507(c)]

(c) IMPOSITION OF TAX.—There is hereby imposed on each organization which is referred to in subsection (a) a tax equal to the lower of—

(1) the amount which the private foundation substantiates by adequate records or other corroborating evidence as the aggregate tax benefit resulting from the section 501(c)(3) status of such foundation, or

(2) the value of the net assets of such foundation.

[Sec. 507(d)]

(d) AGGREGATE TAX BENEFIT.—

(1) IN GENERAL.—For purposes of subsection (c), the aggregate tax benefit resulting from the section 501(c)(3) status of any private foundation is the sum of—

(A) the aggregate increases in tax under chapters 1, 11, and 12 (or the corresponding provisions of prior law) which would have been imposed with respect to all substantial contributors to the foundation if deductions for all contributions made by such contributors to the foundation after February 28, 1913, had been disallowed, and

(B) the aggregate increases in tax under chapter 1 (or the corresponding provisions of prior law) which would have been imposed with respect to the income of the private foundation for taxable years beginning after December 31, 1912, if (i) it had not been exempt from tax under section 501(a) (or the corresponding provisions of prior law), and (ii) in the case of a trust, deductions under section 642(c) (or the corresponding provisions of prior law) had been limited to 20 percent of the taxable income of the trust (computed without the benefit of section 642(c) but with the benefit of section 170(b)(1)(A)), and

(C) interest on the increases in tax determined under subparagraphs (A) and (B) from the first date on which each such increase would have been due and payable to the date on which the organization ceases to be a private foundation.

(2) SUBSTANTIAL CONTRIBUTOR.—

(A) DEFINITION.—For purposes of paragraph (1), the term "substantial contributor" means any person who contributed or bequeathed an aggregate amount of more than $5,000 to the private foundation, if such amount is more than 2 percent of the total contributions and bequests received by the foundation before the close of the taxable year of the foundation in which the contribution or bequest is received by the foundation from such person. In the case of a trust, the term "substantial contributor" also means the creator of the trust.

(B) SPECIAL RULES.—For purposes of subparagraph (A)—

(i) each contribution or bequest shall be valued at fair market value on the date it was received,

(ii) in the case of a foundation which is in existence on October 9, 1969, all contributions and bequests received on or before such date shall be treated (except for purposes of clause (i)) as if received on such date,

(iii) an individual shall be treated as making all contributions and bequests made by his spouse, and

(iv) any person who is a substantial contributor on any date shall remain a substantial contributor for all subsequent periods.

(C) PERSON CEASES TO BE SUBSTANTIAL CONTRIBUTOR IN CERTAIN CASES.—

(i) IN GENERAL.—A person shall cease to be treated as a substantial contributor with respect to any private foundation as of the close of any taxable year of such foundation if—

(I) during the 10-year period ending at the close of such taxable year such person (and all related persons) have not made any contribution to such private foundation,

(II) at no time during such 10-year period was such person (or any related person) a foundation manager of such private foundation, and

(III) the aggregate contributions made by such person (and related persons) are determined by the Secretary to be insignificant when compared to the aggregate amount of contributions to such foundation by one other person.

For purposes of subclause (III), appreciation on contributions while held by the foundation shall be taken into account.

(ii) RELATED PERSON.—For purposes of clause (i), the term "related person" means, with respect to any person, any other person who would be a disqualified person (within the meaning of section 4946) by reason of his relationship to such person. In the case of a contributor which is a corporation, the term also includes any officer or director of such corporation.

(3) REGULATIONS.—For purposes of this section, the determination as to whether and to what extent there would have been any increase in tax shall be made in accordance with regulations prescribed by the Secretary.

Amendments

• 1984, Deficit Reduction Act of 1984 (P.L. 98-369)

P.L. 98-369, §313(a):

Amended Code Sec. 507(d)(2) by adding new subparagraph (C). **Effective** for tax years beginning after 12-31-84.

• 1977 (P.L. 95-170)

P.L. 95-170, §3, provides:

"In determining whether a person is a substantial contributor within the meaning of section 507(d)(2) of the Internal Revenue Code of 1954 for purposes of applying section 4941 of such Code (relating to taxes on self-dealing), contributions made before October 9, 1969, which—

"(1) were made on account of or in lieu of payments required under a lease in effect before such date, and

"(2) were coincident with or by reason of the reduction in the required payments under such lease, shall not be taken into account. For purposes of applying section 507(d)(2)(B)(iv) of such Code, the preceding sentence shall be treated as having taken effect on January 1, 1970."

• 1976, Tax Reform Act of 1976 (P.L. 94-455)

P.L. 94-455, §1906(b)(13)(A):

Amended 1954 Code by substituting "Secretary" for "Secretary or his delegate" each place it appeared. **Effective** 2-1-77.

[Sec. 507(e)]

(e) VALUE OF ASSETS.—For purposes of subsection (c), the value of the net assets shall be determined at whichever time such value is higher: (1) the first day on which action is taken by the organization which culminates in its ceasing to be a private foundation, or (2) the date on which it ceases to be a private foundation.

[Sec. 507(f)]

(f) LIABILITY IN CASE OF TRANSFERS OF ASSETS FROM PRIVATE FOUNDATION.—For purposes of determining liability for the tax imposed by subsection (c) in the case of assets transferred by the private foundation, such tax shall be deemed to have been imposed on the first day on which action is taken by the organization which culminates in its ceasing to be a private foundation.

[Sec. 507(g)]

(g) ABATEMENT OF TAXES.—The Secretary may abate the unpaid portion of the assessment of any tax imposed by subsection (c), or any liability in respect thereof, if—

(1) the private foundation distributes all of its net assets to one or more organizations described in section 170(b)(1)(A) (other than in clauses (vii) and (viii)) each of which has been in existence and so described for a continuous period of at least 60 calendar months, or

(2) following the notification prescribed in section 6104(c) to the appropriate State officer, such State officer within one year notifies the Secretary, in such manner as the Secretary may by regulations prescribe, that corrective action has been initiated pursuant to State law to insure that the assets of such private foundation are preserved for such charitable or other purposes specified in section 501(c)(3) as may be ordered or approved by a court of competent jurisdiction, and upon completion of the corrective action, the Secretary receives certification from the appropriate State officer that such action has resulted in such preservation of assets.

Amendments

• 1976, Tax Reform Act of 1976 (P.L. 94-455)

P.L. 94-455, §1906(b)(13)(A):

Amended 1954 Code by substituting "Secretary" for "Secretary or his delegate" each place it appeared. **Effective** 2-1-77.

• 1969, Tax Reform Act of 1969 (P.L. 91-172)

P.L. 91-172, §101(a):

Added Code Sec. 507. **Effective** 1-1-70.

[Sec. 508]

SEC. 508. SPECIAL RULES WITH RESPECT TO SECTION 501(c)(3) ORGANIZATIONS.

[Sec. 508(a)]

(a) NEW ORGANIZATIONS MUST NOTIFY SECRETARY THAT THEY ARE APPLYING FOR RECOGNITION OF SECTION 501(c)(3) STATUS.—Except as provided in subsection (c), an organization organized after October 9, 1969, shall not be treated as an organization described in section 501(c)(3)—

(1) unless it has given notice to the Secretary, in such manner as the Secretary may by regulations prescribe, that it is applying for recognition of such status, or

(2) for any period before the giving of such notice, if such notice is given after the time prescribed by the Secretary by regulations for giving notice under this subsection.

Amendments

• 1976, Tax Reform Act of 1976 (P.L. 94-455)

P.L. 94-455, §1901(a)(71)(A):

Amended Code Sec. 508(a) by deleting the last sentence, which read: "For purposes of paragraph (2), the time prescribed for giving notice under this subsection shall not expire before the 90th day after the day on which regulations first prescribed under this subsection become final.". **Effective** for tax years beginning after 12-31-76.

P.L. 94-455, §1906(b)(13)(A):

Amended 1954 Code by substituting "Secretary" for "Secretary or his delegate" each place it appeared. **Effective** 2-1-77.

[Sec. 508(b)]

(b) PRESUMPTION THAT ORGANIZATIONS ARE PRIVATE FOUNDATIONS.—Except as provided in subsection (c), any organization (including an organization in existence on October 9, 1969) which is described in section 501(c)(3) and which does not notify the Secretary, at such time and in such manner as the Secretary may by regulations prescribe, that it is not a private foundation shall be presumed to be a private foundation.

Amendments

• 1976, Tax Reform Act of 1976 (P.L. 94-455)

P.L. 94-455, §1901(a)(71)(A):

Amended Code Sec. 508(b) by deleting the last sentence, which read: "The time prescribed for giving notice under this subsection shall not expire before the 90th day after the day on which regulations first prescribed under this subsection become final." **Effective** for tax years beginning after 12-31-76.

P.L. 94-455, §1906(b)(13)(A):

Amended 1954 Code by substituting "Secretary" for "Secretary or his delegate" each place it appeared. **Effective** 2-1-77.

[Sec. 508(c)]

(c) EXCEPTIONS.—

(1) MANDATORY EXCEPTIONS.—Subsections (a) and (b) shall not apply to—

(A) churches, their integrated auxiliaries, and conventions or associations of churches, or

(B) any organization which is not a private foundation (as defined in section 509(a)) and the gross receipts of which in each taxable year are normally not more than $5,000.

(2) EXCEPTIONS BY REGULATIONS.—The Secretary may by regulations exempt (to the extent and subject to such conditions as may be prescribed in such regulations) from the provisions of subsection (a) or (b) or both—

(A) educational organizations described in section 170(b)(1)(A)(ii), and

(B) any other class of organizations with respect to which the Secretary determines that full compliance with the provisions of subsections (a) and (b) is not necessary to the efficient administration of the provisions of this title relating to private foundations.

Amendments

• 1976, Tax Reform Act of 1976 (P.L. 94-455)

P.L. 94-455, §1901(b)(8)(E):

Amended Code Sec. 508(c)(2)(A). **Effective** for tax years beginning after 12-31-76. Prior to amendment, Sec. 508(c)(2)(A) read as follows:

(A) educational organizations which normally maintain a regular faculty and curriculum and normally have a regularly enrolled body of pupils or students in attendance at the place where their educational activities are regularly carried on; and

P.L. 94-455, §1906(b)(13)(A):

Amended 1954 Code by substituting "Secretary" for "Secretary or his delegate" each place it appeared. **Effective** 2-1-77.

[Sec. 508(d)]

(d) DISALLOWANCE OF CERTAIN CHARITABLE, ETC., DEDUCTIONS.—

(1) GIFT OR BEQUEST TO ORGANIZATIONS SUBJECT TO SECTION 507(c) TAX.—No gift or bequest made to an organization upon which the tax provided by section 507(c) has been imposed shall be allowed as a deduction under section 170, 545(b)(2), 642(c), 2055, 2106(a)(2), or 2522, if such gift or bequest is made—

(A) by any person after notification is made under section 507(a), or

(B) by a substantial contributor (as defined in section 507(d)(2)) in his taxable year which includes the first day on which action is taken by such organization which culminates in the imposition of tax under section 507(c) and any subsequent taxable year.

(2) GIFT OR BEQUEST TO TAXABLE PRIVATE FOUNDATION, SECTION 4947 TRUST, ETC.—No gift or bequest made to an organization shall be allowed as a deduction under section 170, 545(b)(2), 642(c), 2055, 2106(a)(2), or 2522, if such gift or bequest is made—

(A) to a private foundation or a trust described in section 4947 in a taxable year for which it fails to meet the requirements of subsection (e) (determined without regard to subsection (e)(2)), or

(B) to any organization in a period for which it is not treated as an organization described in section 501(c)(3) by reason of subsection (a).

(3) EXCEPTION.—Paragraph (1) shall not apply if the entire amount of the unpaid portion of the tax imposed by section 507(c) is abated by the Secretary under section 507(g).

Amendments

• 2004, American Jobs Creation Act of 2004 (P.L. 108-357)

P.L. 108-357, §413(c)(30):

Amended Code Sec. 508(d) by striking "556(b)(2)," each place it occurs immediately preceding "642(c), 2055". **Effective** for tax years of foreign corporations beginning after 12-31-2004 and for tax years of United States shareholders with or within which such tax years of foreign corporations end.

• 1976, Tax Reform Act of 1976 (P.L. 94-455)

P.L. 94-455, §1901(a)(71)(C):

Substituted "(e)(2)" for "(e)(2)(B) and (C)". **Effective** for tax years beginning after 12-31-76.

P.L. 94-455, §1906(b)(13)(A):

Amended 1954 Code by substituting "Secretary" for "Secretary or his delegate" each place it appeared. **Effective** 2-1-77.

[Sec. 508(e)]

(e) GOVERNING INSTRUMENTS.—

(1) GENERAL RULE.—A private foundation shall not be exempt from taxation under section 501(a) unless its governing instrument includes provisions the effects of which are—

(A) to require its income for each taxable year to be distributed at such time and in such manner as not to subject the foundation to tax under section 4942, and

(B) to prohibit the foundation from engaging in any act of self-dealing (as defined in section 4941 (d)), from retaining any excess business holdings (as defined in section 4943(c)), from making any investments in such manner as to subject the foundation to tax under section 4944, and from making any taxable expenditures (as defined in section 4945(d)).

(2) SPECIAL RULES FOR EXISTING PRIVATE FOUNDATIONS.—In the case of any organization organized before January 1, 1970, paragraph (1) shall not apply—

(A) to any period after December 31, 1971, during the pendency of any judicial proceeding begun before January 1, 1972, by the private foundation which is necessary to reform, or to excuse such foundation from compliance with, its governing instrument or any other instrument in order to meet the requirements of paragraph (1), and

(B) to any period after the termination of any judicial proceeding described in subparagraph (A) during which its governing instrument or any other instrument does not permit it to meet the requirements of paragraph (1).

Amendments

• 1976, Tax Reform Act of 1976 (P.L. 94-455)

P.L. 94-455, §1901(a)(71)(B):

Amended Code Sec. 508(e)(2) by deleting former subparagraph (A) which read "to any taxable year beginning before January 1, 1972," and by redesignating former subparagraphs (B) and (C) as (A) and (B). **Effective** for tax years beginning after 12-31-76.

• 1969, Tax Reform Act of 1969 (P.L. 91-172)

P.L. 91-172, §101(a):

Added Code Sec. 508. **Effective** 1-1-70, except that Code Secs. 508(a), (b) and (c) are effective on 10-9-69.

P.L. 91-172, §101(1)(6), provides:

Sec. 508(e) shall not apply to require inclusion in governing instruments of any provisions inconsistent with subsection 101(l) of the Tax Reform Act of 1969.

[Sec. 508(f)]

(f) ADDITIONAL PROVISIONS RELATING TO SPONSORING ORGANIZATIONS.—A sponsoring organization (as defined in section 4966(d)(1)) shall give notice to the Secretary (in such manner as the Secretary may provide) whether such organization maintains or intends to maintain donor advised funds (as defined in section 4966(d)(2)) and the manner in which such organization plans to operate such funds.

Amendments

• 2006, Pension Protection Act of 2006 (P.L. 109-280)

P.L. 109-280, §1235(b)(1):

Amended Code Sec. 508 by adding at the end a new subsection (f). **Effective** for organizations applying for tax-exempt status after 8-17-2006.

[Sec. 509]

SEC. 509. PRIVATE FOUNDATION DEFINED.

[Sec. 509(a)]

(a) GENERAL RULE.—For purposes of this title, the term "private foundation" means a domestic or foreign organization described in section 501(c)(3) other than—

(1) an organization described in section 170(b)(1)(A) (other than in clauses (vii) and (viii));

(2) an organization which—

(A) normally receives more than one-third of its support in each taxable year from any combination of—

(i) gifts, grants, contributions, or membership fees, and

(ii) gross receipts from admissions, sales of merchandise, performance of services, or furnishing of facilities, in an activity which is not an unrelated trade or business (within the meaning of section 513), not including such receipts from any person, or from any bureau or similar agency of a governmental unit (as described in section 170(c)(1)), in any taxable year to the extent such receipts exceed the greater of $5,000 or 1 percent of the organization's support in such taxable year,

from persons other than disqualified persons (as defined in section 4946) with respect to the organization, from governmental units described in section 170(c)(1), or from organizations described in section 170(b)(1)(A) (other than in clauses (vii) and (viii)), and

(B) normally receives not more than one-third of its support in each taxable year from the sum of—

(i) gross investment income (as defined in subsection (e)) and

(ii) the excess (if any) of the amount of the unrelated business taxable income (as defined in section 512) over the amount of the tax imposed by section 511;

(3) an organization which—

(A) is organized, and at all times thereafter is operated, exclusively for the benefit of, to perform the functions of, or to carry out the purposes of one or more specified organizations described in paragraph (1) or (2),

(B) is—

(i) operated, supervised, or controlled by one or more organizations described in paragraph (1) or (2),

(ii) supervised or controlled in connection with one or more such organizations, or

(iii) operated in connection with one or more such organizations, and

(C) is not controlled directly or indirectly by one or more disqualified persons (as defined in section 4946) other than foundation managers and other than one or more organizations described in paragraph (1) or (2); and

(4) an organization which is organized and operated exclusively for testing for public safety.

For purposes of paragraph (3), an organization described in paragraph (2) shall be deemed to include an organization described in section 501(c)(4), (5), or (6) which would be described in paragraph (2) if it were an organization described in section 501(c)(3).

Amendments

• 2006, Pension Protection Act of 2006 (P.L. 109-280)

P.L. 109-280, §1241(a):

Amended Code Sec. 509(a)(3)(B). **Effective** 8-17-2006. Prior to amendment, Code Sec. 509(a)(3)(B) read as follows:

(B) is operated, supervised, or controlled by or in connection with one or more organizations, described in paragraph (1) or (2), and

• 1975 (P.L. 94-81)

P.L. 94-81, §3:

Amended Code Sec. 509(a)(2)(B). **Effective** for unrelated business taxable income derived from trades and businesses which are acquired by the organization after 6-30-75. Prior to amendment, it read as follows:

"(B) normally receives not more than one-third of its support in each taxable year from gross investment income (as defined in subsection (e));"

[Sec. 509(b)]

(b) CONTINUATION OF PRIVATE FOUNDATION STATUS.—For purposes of this title, if an organization is a private foundation (within the meaning of subsection (a)) on October 9, 1969, or becomes a private foundation on any subsequent date, such organization shall be treated as a private foundation for all periods after October 9, 1969, or after such subsequent date, unless its status as such is terminated under section 507.

[Sec. 509(c)]

(c) STATUS OF ORGANIZATION AFTER TERMINATION OF PRIVATE FOUNDATION STATUS.—For purposes of this part, an organization the status of which as a private foundation is terminated under section 507 shall (except as provided in section 507(b)(2)) be treated as an organization created on the day after the date of such termination.

[Sec. 509(d)]

(d) DEFINITION OF SUPPORT.—For purposes of this part and chapter 42, the term "support" includes (but is not limited to)—

(1) gifts, grants, contributions, or membership fees,

(2) gross receipts from admissions, sales of merchandise, performance of services, or furnishing of facilities in any activity which is not an unrelated trade or business (within the meaning of section 513),

(3) net income from unrelated business activities, whether or not such activities are carried on regularly as a trade or business,

(4) gross investment income (as defined in subsection (e)),

(5) tax revenues levied for the benefit of an organization and either paid to or expended on behalf of such organization, and

(6) the value of services or facilities (exclusive of services or facilities generally furnished to the public without charge) furnished by a governmental unit referred to in section 170(c)(1) to an organization without charge.

Such term does not include any gain from the sale or other disposition of property which would be considered as gain from the sale or exchange of a capital asset, or the value of exemption from any Federal, State, or local tax or any similar benefit.

[Sec. 509(e)]

(e) DEFINITION OF GROSS INVESTMENT INCOME.—For purposes of subsection (d), the term "gross investment income" means the gross amount of income from interest, dividends, payments with respect to securities loans (as defined in section 512(a)(5)), rents, and royalties, but not including any such income to the extent included in computing the tax imposed by section 511. Such term shall also include income from sources similar to those in the preceding sentence.

Amendments

• 2006, Pension Protection Act of 2006 (P.L. 109-280)

P.L. 109-280, §1221(a)(2):

Amended Code Sec. 509(e) by adding at the end a new sentence. **Effective** for tax years beginning after 8-17-2006.

• 1978 (P.L. 95-345)

P.L. 95-345, §2(a)(1):

Amended Code Sec. 509(e) by adding "payments with respect to securities loans (as defined in section 512(a)(5))," after "dividends". **Effective** with respect to (1) amounts received after 12-31-76 as payments with respect to securities loans (as defined in Code Sec. 512(a)(5)), and (2) transfers of securities under agreements described in Code Sec. 1058 occurring after such date.

• 1969, Tax Reform Act of 1969 (P.L. 91-172)

P.L. 91-172, §101(a):

Added Code Sec. 509. **Effective** 1-1-70.

P.L. 91-172, §101(1)(7), provides:

"In the case of any trust created under the terms of a will or a codicil to a will executed on or before March 30, 1924, by which the testator bequeathed all of the outstanding common stock of a corporation in trust, the income of which trust is to be used principally for the benefit of those from time to time employed by the corporation and their families, the trustees of which trust are elected or selected from among the employees of such corporation, and which trust does not own directly any stock in any other corporation, if the trust makes an irrevocable election under this paragraph within one year after the date of the enactment of this Act, such trust shall be treated as not being a private foundation for purposes of the Internal Revenue Code of 1954 but shall be treated for purposes of such Code as if it were not exempt from tax under section 501(a) for any taxable year, beginning after the date of the enactment of this Act and before the date (if any) on which such trust has complied with the requirements of section 507 for termination of the status of an organization as a private foundation."

[Sec. 509(f)]

(f) REQUIREMENTS FOR SUPPORTING ORGANIZATIONS.—

(1) TYPE III SUPPORTING ORGANIZATIONS.—For purposes of subsection (a)(3)(B)(iii), an organization shall not be considered to be operated in connection with any organization described in paragraph (1) or (2) of subsection (a) unless such organization meets the following requirements:

(A) RESPONSIVENESS.—For each taxable year beginning after the date of the enactment of this subsection, the organization provides to each supported organization such information as the Secretary may require to ensure that such organization is responsive to the needs or demands of the supported organization.

(B) FOREIGN SUPPORTED ORGANIZATIONS.—

(i) IN GENERAL.—The organization is not operated in connection with any supported organization that is not organized in the United States.

(ii) TRANSITION RULE FOR EXISTING ORGANIZATIONS.—If the organization is operated in connection with an organization that is not organized in the United States on the date of the enactment of this subsection, clause (i) shall not apply until the first day of the third taxable year of the organization beginning after the date of the enactment of this subsection.

(2) ORGANIZATIONS CONTROLLED BY DONORS.—

(A) IN GENERAL.—For purposes of subsection (a)(3)(B), an organization shall not be considered to be—

(i) operated, supervised, or controlled by any organization described in paragraph (1) or (2) of subsection (a), or

(ii) operated in connection with any organization described in paragraph (1) or (2) of subsection (a),

if such organization accepts any gift or contribution from any person described in subparagraph (B).

(B) PERSON DESCRIBED.—A person is described in this subparagraph if, with respect to a supported organization of an organization described in subparagraph (A), such person is—

(i) a person (other than an organization described in paragraph (1), (2), or (4) of section 509(a)) who directly or indirectly controls, either alone or together with persons described in clauses (ii) and (iii), the governing body of such supported organization,

(ii) a member of the family (determined under section 4958(f)(4)) of an individual described in clause (i), or

(iii) a 35-percent controlled entity (as defined in section 4958(f)(3) by substituting "persons described in clause (i) or (ii) of section 509(f)(2)(B)" for "persons described in subparagraph (A) or (B) of paragraph (1)" in subparagraph (A)(i) thereof).

(3) SUPPORTED ORGANIZATION.—For purposes of this subsection, the term "supported organization" means, with respect to an organization described in subsection (a)(3), an organization described in paragraph (1) or (2) of subsection (a)—

(A) for whose benefit the organization described in subsection (a)(3) is organized and operated, or

(B) with respect to which the organization performs the functions of, or carries out the purposes of.

Amendments

• 2006, Pension Protection Act of 2006 (P.L. 109-280)

P.L. 109-280, §1241(b):

Amended Code Sec. 509 by adding at the end a new subsection (f). **Effective** 8-17-2006.

P.L. 109-280, §1241(c)-(d) and (e)(2), provides:

(c) CHARITABLE TRUSTS WHICH ARE TYPE III SUPPORTING ORGANIZATIONS—For purposes of section 509(a)(3)(B)(iii) of the Internal Revenue Code of 1986, an organization which is a trust shall not be considered to be operated in connection with any organization described in paragraph (1) or (2) of section 509(a) of such Code solely because—

(1) it is a charitable trust under State law,

(2) the supported organization (as defined in section 509(f)(3) of such Code) is a beneficiary of such trust, and

(3) the supported organization (as so defined) has the power to enforce the trust and compel an accounting.

(d) PAYOUT REQUIREMENTS FOR TYPE III SUPPORTING ORGANIZATIONS.—

(1) IN GENERAL.—The Secretary of the Treasury shall promulgate new regulations under section 509 of the Internal Revenue Code of 1986 on payments required by type III supporting organizations which are not functionally integrated type III supporting organizations. Such regulations shall require such organizations to make distributions of a percentage of either income or assets to supported organizations (as defined in section 509(f)(3) of such Code) in order to ensure that a significant amount is paid to such organizations.

(2) TYPE III SUPPORTING ORGANIZATION; FUNCTIONALLY INTEGRATED TYPE III SUPPORTING ORGANIZATION.—For purposes of paragraph (1), the terms "type III supporting organization" and "functionally integrated type III supporting organization" have the meanings given such terms under subparagraphs (A) and (B) section 4943(f)(5) of the Internal Revenue Code of 1986 (as added by this Act), respectively.

(e) EFFECTIVE DATES.—

* * *

(2) CHARITABLE TRUSTS WHICH ARE TYPE III SUPPORTING ORGANIZATIONS—Subsection (c) shall take effect—

(A) in the case of trusts operated in connection with an organization described in paragraph (1) or (2) of section 509(a) of the Internal Revenue Code of 1986 on the date of the enactment of this Act, on the date that is one year after the date of the enactment of this Act, and

(B) in the case of any other trust, on the date of the enactment of this Act.

PART III—TAXATION OF BUSINESS INCOME OF CERTAIN EXEMPT ORGANIZATIONS

[Sec. 511]

SEC. 511. IMPOSITION OF TAX ON UNRELATED BUSINESS INCOME OF CHARITABLE, ETC., ORGANIZATIONS.

[Sec. 511(a)]

(a) CHARITABLE, ETC., ORGANIZATIONS TAXABLE AT CORPORATION RATES.—

(1) IMPOSITION OF TAX.—There is hereby imposed for each taxable year on the unrelated business taxable income (as defined in section 512) of every organization described in paragraph (2) a tax computed as provided in section 11. In making such computation for purposes of this section, the term "taxable income" as used in section 11 shall be read as "unrelated business taxable income".

(2) ORGANIZATIONS SUBJECT TO TAX.—

(A) ORGANIZATIONS DESCRIBED IN SECTIONS 401(a) AND 501(c).—The tax imposed by paragraph (1) shall apply in the case of any organization (other than a trust described in subsection (b) or an organization described in section 501(c)(1)) which is exempt, except as provided in this part or part II (relating to private foundations), from taxation under this subtitle by reason of section 501(a).

(B) STATE COLLEGES AND UNIVERSITIES.—The tax imposed by paragraph (1) shall apply in the case of any college or university which is an agency or instrumentality of any government or any political subdivision thereof, or which is owned or operated by a government or any political subdivision thereof, or by any agency or instrumentality of one or more governments or political subdivisions. Such tax shall also apply in the case of any corporation wholly owned by one or more such colleges or universities.

Amendments

• 2010, Patient Protection and Affordable Care Act (P.L. 111-148)

P.L. 111-148, §1341(c) (as amended by P.L. 111-148, §10104(c)), provides:

(c) APPLICABLE REINSURANCE ENTITY.—For purposes of this section—

(1) IN GENERAL.—The term "applicable reinsurance entity" means a not-for-profit organization—

(A) the purpose of which is to help stabilize premiums for coverage in the individual market in a State during the first 3 years of operation of an Exchange for such markets within the State when the risk of adverse selection related to new rating rules and market changes is greatest; and

(B) the duties of which shall be to carry out the reinsurance program under this section by coordinating the funding and operation of the risk-spreading mechanisms designed to implement the reinsurance program.

(2) STATE DISCRETION.—A State may have more than 1 applicable reinsurance entity to carry out the reinsurance program under this section within the State and 2 or more States may enter into agreements to provide for an applicable reinsurance entity to carry out such program in all such States.

(3) ENTITIES ARE TAX-EXEMPT.—An applicable reinsurance entity established under this section shall be exempt from taxation under chapter 1 of the Internal Revenue Code of 1986. The preceding sentence shall not apply to the tax imposed by section 511 such Code (relating to tax on unrelated business taxable income of an exempt organization).

• 1978, Revenue Act of 1978 (P.L. 95-600)

P.L. 95-600, §301(b)(5)(A):

Amended Code Sec. 511(a)(1) by striking out "a normal tax and a surtax" and inserting in lieu thereof "a tax". **Effective** for tax years beginning after 12-31-78.

P.L. 95-600, §301(b)(5)(B):

Amended Code Sec. 511(a)(2) by striking out "taxes" each place it appears and inserting in leiu thereof "tax". **Effective** for tax years beginning after 12-31-78.

• 1969, Tax Reform Act of 1969 (P.L. 91-172)

P.L. 91-172, §121(a)(1):

Amended Code Sec. 511(a)(2)(A). **Effective** 1-1-70. Prior to amendment, Sec. 511(a)(2)(A) read as follows:

"(A) Organizations described in section 501(c)(2), (3), (5), (6), (14)(B) or (C), and (17), and section 401(a).—The taxes imposed by paragraph (1) shall apply in the case of any organization (other than a church, a convention or association of churches, or a trust described in subsection (b)) which is exempt, except as provided in this part, from taxation under this subtitle by reason of section 401(a) or of paragraph (3), (5), (6), (14)(B) or (C), or (17) of section 501(c). Such taxes shall also apply in the case of a corporation described in section 501(c)(2) if the income is payable to an organization which, itself is subject to the taxes imposed by paragraph (1) or to a church or to a convention or association of churches."

• 1966 (P.L. 89-352)

P.L. 89-352, §2:

Amended Code Sec. 511(a)(2)(A) by inserting "(14)(B) or (C)," immediately after "(6)," in the heading and in the text. **Effective** for tax years beginning after 2-2-66.

• 1960 (P.L. 86-667)

P.L. 86-667, §3(a):

Amended Code Sec. 511(a)(2) by striking out "and (6)" in the heading of subparagraph (A) and inserting in lieu thereof "(6), and (17)", and by striking out "or (6)" in the first sentence of subparagraph (A) and inserting in lieu thereof "(6), or (17)". **Effective** for tax years beginning after 12-31-59.

[Sec. 511(b)]

(b) TAX ON CHARITABLE, ETC., TRUSTS.—

(1) IMPOSITION OF TAX.—There is hereby imposed for each taxable year on the unrelated business taxable income of every trust described in paragraph (2) a tax computed as provided in section 1(e). In making such computation for purposes of this section, the term "taxable income" as used in section 1 shall be read as "unrelated business taxable income" as defined in section 512.

(2) CHARITABLE, ETC., TRUSTS SUBJECT TO TAX.—The tax imposed by paragraph (1) shall apply in the case of any trust which is exempt, except as provided in this part or part II (relating to private foundations), from taxation under this subtitle by reason of section 501(a) and which, if it were not for such exemption, would be subject to subchapter J (sec. 641 and following, relating to estates, trusts, beneficiaries, and decedents).

Amendments

• 1977, Tax Reduction and Simplification Act of 1977 (P.L. 95-30)

P.L. 95-30, §101(d)(6):

Amended paragraph (1) of Code Sec. 511(b) by striking out "section 1(d)" and inserting in lieu thereof "section 1(e)". **Effective** for tax years beginning after 12-31-76.

• 1969, Tax Reform Act of 1969 (P.L. 91-172)

P.L. 91-172, §121(a)(2):

Amended Code Sec. 511(b)(2). **Effective** 1-1-70. Prior to amendment, Code Sec. 511(b)(2) read as follows:

"(2) Charitable, etc., trusts subject to tax.—The tax imposed by paragraph (1) shall apply in the case of any trust which is exempt, except as provided in this part, from taxation under this subtitle by reason of section 501(c)(3) or (17) or section 401(a) and which, if it were not for such exemption, would be subject to subchapter J (sec. 641 and following, relating to estates, trusts, beneficiaries, and decedents)."

P.L. 91-172, §803(d)(2):

Amended Code Sec. 511(b)(1) by substituting "section 1(d)" for "section 1" in the first sentence thereof. **Effective** for tax years beginning after 12-31-70.

• 1960 (P.L. 86-667)

P.L. 86-667, §3(b):

Amended Code Sec. 511(b) by striking out "section 501(c)(3)" in paragraph (2) and by inserting in lieu thereof "section 501(c)(3) or (17)". **Effective** for tax years beginning after 12-31-59.

[Sec. 511(c)]

(c) SPECIAL RULE FOR SECTION 501(c)(2) CORPORATIONS.—If a corporation described in section 501(c)(2)—

(1) pays any amount of its net income for a taxable year to an organization exempt from taxation under section 501(a) (or which would pay such an amount but for the fact that the expenses of collecting its income exceed its income), and

(2) such corporation and such organization file a consolidated return for the taxable year,

such corporation shall be treated, for purposes of the tax imposed by subsection (a), as being organized and operated for the same purposes as such organization, in addition to the purposes described in section 501(c)(2).

Amendments

• 1969, Tax Reform Act of 1969 (P.L. 91-172)

P.L. 91-172, §121(a)(3):

Amended Code Sec. 511(c). **Effective** 1-1-70. Prior to amendment Sec. 511(c) read as follows:

"(c) Effective Date.—The tax imposed by this section shall apply, in the case of a trust described in section 401(a), only for taxable years beginning after June 30, 1954."

[Sec. 511(d)—Stricken]

Amendments

• **1988, Technical and Miscellaneous Revenue Act of 1988 (P.L. 100-647)**

P.L. 100-647, §1007(g)(6):

Amended Code Sec. 511 by striking out subsection (d). **Effective** as if included in the provision of P.L. 99-514 to which it relates. Prior to amendment, Code Sec. 511(d) read as follows:

(d) TAX PREFERENCES.—

(1) ORGANIZATIONS TAXABLE AT CORPORATE RATES.—If an organization is subject to tax on unrelated business taxable income pursuant to subsection (a), the tax imposed by section 56 shall apply to such organizations with respect to items of tax preference which enter into the computation of unrelated business taxable income in the same manner as section 56 applies to corporations.

(2) ORGANIZATIONS TAXABLE AS TRUSTS.—If an organization is subject to tax on unrelated business taxable income pursuant to subsection (b), the taxes imposed by section 55 shall apply to such organization with respect to items of tax preference which enter into the computation of unrelated business taxable income.

• **1983, Technical Corrections Act of 1982 (P.L. 97-448)**

P.L. 97-448, §306(a)(1)(A):

Amended P.L. 97-248, §201 by redesignating the second subsection (c) as subsection (d).

• **1982, Tax Equity and Fiscal Responsibility Act of 1982 (P.L. 97-248)**

P.L. 97-248, §201(d)(5):

Amended Code Sec. 511(d)(2) by striking out "and section 56 (as the case may be)". **Effective** for tax years beginning after 12-31-82.

• **1978, Revenue Act of 1978 (P.L. 95-600)**

P.L. 95-600, §421(e)(3):

Amended Code Sec. 511(d). **Effective** for tax years beginning after 12-31-78. Prior to amendment, Code Sec. 511(d) read as follows:

(d) TAX PREFERENCES.—The tax imposed by section 56 shall apply to an organization subject to tax under this section with respect to items of tax preference which enter into the computation of unrelated business taxable income.

• **1969, Tax Reform Act of 1969 (P.L. 91-172)**

P.L. 91-172, §301(b)(8):

Added Code Sec. 511(d). **Effective** 1-1-70.

[Sec. 512]

SEC. 512. UNRELATED BUSINESS TAXABLE INCOME.

[Sec. 512(a)]

(a) DEFINITION.—For purposes of this title—

(1) GENERAL RULE.—Except as otherwise provided in this subsection, the term "unrelated business taxable income" means the gross income derived by any organization from any unrelated trade or business (as defined in section 513) regularly carried on by it, less the deductions allowed by this chapter which are directly connected with the carrying on of such trade or business, both computed with the modifications provided in subsection (b).

(2) SPECIAL RULE FOR FOREIGN ORGANIZATIONS.—In the case of an organization described in section 511 which is a foreign organization, the unrelated business taxable income shall be—

(A) its unrelated business taxable income which is derived from sources within the United States and which is not effectively connected with the conduct of a trade or business within the United States, plus

(B) its unrelated business taxable income which is effectively connected with the conduct of a trade or business within the United States.

(3) SPECIAL RULES APPLICABLE TO ORGANIZATIONS DESCRIBED IN PARAGRAPH (7), (9), (17), OR (20) OF SECTION 501(c).—

(A) GENERAL RULE.—In the case of an organization described in paragraph (7), (9), (17), or (20) of section 501(c), the term "unrelated business taxable income" means the gross income (excluding any exempt function income), less the deductions allowed by this chapter which are directly connected with the production of the gross income (excluding exempt function income), both computed with the modifications provided in paragraphs (6), (10), (11), and (12) of subsection (b). For purposes of the preceding sentence, the deductions provided by sections 243, 244, and 245 (relating to dividends received by corporations) shall be treated as not directly connected with the production of gross income.

(B) EXEMPT FUNCTION INCOME.—For purposes of subparagraph (A), the term "exempt function income" means the gross income from dues, fees, charges, or similar amounts paid by members of the organization as consideration for providing such members or their dependents or guests goods, facilities, or services in furtherance of the purposes constituting the basis for the exemption of the organization to which such income is paid. Such term also means all income (other than an amount equal to the gross income derived from any unrelated trade or business regularly carried on by such organization computed as if the organization were subject to paragraph (1)), which is set aside—

(i) for a purpose specified in section 170(c)(4), or

(ii) in the case of an organization described in paragraph (9), (17), or (20) of section 501(c), to provide for the payment of life, sick, accident, or other benefits,

including reasonable costs of administration directly connected with a purpose described in clause (i) or (ii). If during the taxable year, an amount which is attributable to income so set aside is used for a purpose other than that described in clause (i) or (ii), such amount shall be included, under subparagraph (A), in unrelated business taxable income for the taxable year.

(C) APPLICABILITY TO CERTAIN CORPORATIONS DESCRIBED IN SECTION 501(c)(2).—In the case of a corporation described in section 501(c)(2), the income of which is payable to an organization described in paragraph (7), (9), (17), or (20) of section 501(c), subparagraph (A) shall apply as if such corporation were the organization to which the income is payable. For purposes of the preceding sentence, such corporation shall be treated as having exempt function income for a taxable year only if it files a consolidated return with such organization for such year.

(D) NONRECOGNITION OF GAIN.—If property used directly in the performance of the exempt function of an organization described in paragraph (7), (9), (17), or (20) of section 501(c) is sold by such organization, and within a period beginning 1 year before the date of such sale, and ending 3 years after such date, other property is purchased and used by such organization directly in the performance of its exempt function, gain (if any) from such sale shall be recognized only to the extent that such organization's sales price of the old property exceeds the organization's cost of purchasing the other property. For purposes of this subparagraph, the destruction in whole or in part, theft, seizure, requisition, or condemnation of property, shall be treated as the sale of such property, and rules similar to the rules provided by subsections (b), (c), (e), and (j) of section 1034 (as in effect on the day before the date of the enactment of the Taxpayer Relief Act of 1997) shall apply.

(E) LIMITATION ON AMOUNT OF SETASIDE IN THE CASE OF ORGANIZATIONS DESCRIBED IN PARAGRAPH (9), (17), OR (20) OF SECTION 501(c).—

(i) IN GENERAL.—In the case of any organization described in paragraph (9), (17), or (20) of section 501(c), a set-aside for any purpose specified in clause (ii) of subparagraph (B) may be taken into account under subparagraph (B) only to the extent that such set-aside does not result in an amount of assets set aside for such purpose in excess of the account limit determined under section 419A (without regard to subsection (f)(6) thereof) for the taxable year (not taking into account any reserve described in section 419A(c)(2)(A) for post-retirement medical benefits).

(ii) TREATMENT OF EXISTING RESERVES FOR POST-RETIREMENT MEDICAL OR LIFE INSURANCE BENEFITS.—

(I) Clause (i) shall not apply to any income attributable to an existing reserve for post-retirement medical or life insurance benefits.

(II) For purposes of subclause (I), the term "reserve for post-retirement medical or life insurance benefits" means the greater of the amount of assets set aside for purposes of post-retirement medical or life insurance benefits to be provided to covered employees as of the close of the last plan year ending before the date of the enactment of the Tax Reform Act of 1984 or on July 18, 1984.

(III) All payments during plan years ending on or after the date of the enactment of the Tax Reform Act of 1984 of post-retirement medical benefits or life insurance benefits shall be charged against the reserve referred to in subclause (II). Except to the extent provided in regulations prescribed by the Secretary, all plans of an employer shall be treated as 1 plan for purposes of the preceding sentence.

(iii) TREATMENT OF TAX EXEMPT ORGANIZATIONS.—This subparagraph shall not apply to any organization if substantially all of the contributions to such organization are made by employers who were exempt from tax under this chapter throughout the 5-taxable year period ending with the taxable year in which the contributions are made.

(4) SPECIAL RULE APPLICABLE TO ORGANIZATIONS DESCRIBED IN SECTION 501(c)(19).—In the case of an organization described in section 501(c)(19), the term "unrelated business taxable income" does not include any amount attributable to payments for life, sick, accident, or health insurance with respect to members of such organizations or their dependents which is set aside for the purpose of providing for the payment of insurance benefits or for a purpose specified in section 170(c)(4). If an amount set aside under the preceding sentence is used during the taxable year for a purpose other than a purpose described in the preceding sentence, such amount shall be included, under paragraph (1), in unrelated business taxable income for the taxable year.

(5) DEFINITION OF PAYMENTS WITH RESPECT TO SECURITIES LOANS.—

(A) The term "payments with respect to securities loans" includes all amounts received in respect of a security (as defined in section 1236(c)) transferred by the owner to another person in a transaction to which section 1058 applies (whether or not title to the security remains in the name of the lender) including—

(i) amounts in respect of dividends, interest, or other distributions,

(ii) fees computed by reference to the period beginning with the transfer of securities by the owner and ending with the transfer of identical securities back to the transferor by the transferee and the fair market value of the security during such period,

(iii) income from collateral security for such loan, and

(iv) income from the investment of collateral security.

(B) Subparagraph (A) shall apply only with respect to securities transferred pursuant to an agreement between the transferor and the transferee which provides for—

(i) reasonable procedures to implement the obligation of the transferee to furnish to the transferor, for each business day during such period, collateral with a fair market value not less than the fair market value of the security at the close of business on the preceding business day,

(ii) termination of the loan by the transferor upon notice of not more than 5 business days, and

(iii) return to the transferor of securities identical to the transferred securities upon termination of the loan.

Amendments

• 1997, Taxpayer Relief Act of 1997 (P.L. 105-34)

P.L. 105-34, §312(d)(5):

Amended Code Sec. 512(a)(3)(D) by inserting "(as in effect on the day before the date of the enactment of the Taxpayer Relief Act of 1997)" after "1034". For the **effective** date, see Act Sec. 312(d)[(e)], below.

P.L. 105-34, §312(d)[(e)] (as amended by P.L. 105-206, §6005(e)(3)), provides:

(d) EFFECTIVE DATE.—

(1) IN GENERAL.—The amendments made by this section shall apply to sales and exchanges after May 6, 1997.

(2) SALES ON OR BEFORE DATE OF ENACTMENT.—At the election of the taxpayer, the amendments made by this section shall not apply to any sale or exchange on or before the date of the enactment of this Act.

(3) CERTAIN SALES WITHIN 2 YEARS AFTER DATE OF ENACTMENT.—Section 121 of the Internal Revenue Code of 1986 (as amended by this section) shall be applied without regard to subsection (c)(2)(B) thereof in the case of any sale or exchange of property during the 2-year period beginning on the date of the enactment of this Act if the taxpayer held such property on the date of the enactment of this Act and fails to meet the ownership and use requirements of subsection (a) thereof with respect to such property.

(4) BINDING CONTRACTS—At the election of the taxpayer, the amendments made by this section shall not apply to a sale or exchange after the date of the enactment of this Act, if—

(A) such sale or exchange is pursuant to a contract which was binding on such date, or

(B) without regard to such amendments gain would not be recognized under section 1034 of the Internal Revenue Code of 1986 (as in effect on the day before the date of the enactment of this Act) on such sale or exchange by reason of a new residence acquired on or before such date or with respect to the acquisition of which by the taxpayer a binding contract was in effect on such date.

This paragraph shall not apply to any sale or exchange by an individual if the treatment provided by section 877(a)(1) of the Internal Revenue Code of 1986 applies to such individual.

• 1988, Technical and Miscellaneous Revenue Act of 1988 (P.L. 100-647)

P.L. 100-647, §1018(t)(2)(B):

Amended Code Sec. 512(a)(3)(E)(ii)(II) by striking out "subclause (II)" and inserting in lieu thereof "subclause (I)", and by striking out the comma at the end thereof and inserting in lieu thereof a period. **Effective** as if included in the provision of P.L. 99-514 to which it relates.

• 1986, Tax Reform Act of 1986 (P.L. 99-514)

P.L. 99-514, §1851(a)(10)(A):

Amended Code Sec. 512(a)(3)(E)(i) by striking out "determined under section 419A(c)" and inserting in lieu thereof "determined under section 419A (without regard to subsection (f)(6) thereof)". **Effective** as if included in the provision of P.L. 98-369 to it relates.

P.L. 99-514, §1851(a)(10)(B):

Amended Code Sec. 512(a)(3)(E) by striking out clause (ii) and by redesignating clauses (iii) and (iv) as clauses (ii) and (iii), respectively. **Effective** as if included in the provision of P.L. 98-369 to it relates. Prior to amendment, Code Sec. 512(a)(3)(E)(ii) read as follows:

(ii) NO SET ASIDE FOR FACILITIES.—No set aside for assets used in the provision of benefits described in clause (ii) of subparagraph (B) shall be taken into account.

P.L. 99-514, §1851(a)(10)(C)(i) and (ii):

Amended Code Sec. 512(a)(3)(E)(ii) (as redesignated by Act Sec. 1851(a)(10)(B)) by striking out "a existing reserve" in subclause (I) and inserting in lieu thereof "an existing reserve", and by striking out subclause (II) and inserting in lieu thereof new subclause (II). **Effective** as if included in the provision of P.L. 98-369 to it relates. Prior to amendment, Code Sec. 512(a)(3)(E)(ii)(II) read as follows:

(II) For purposes of subclause (I), the term "existing reserve [f]or post-retirement medical or life insurance benefit" means the amount of assets set aside as of the close of the last plan year ending before the date of the enactment of the Tax Reform Act of 1984 for purposes of post-retirement medical benefits or life insurance benefits to be provided to covered employees.

P.L. 99-514, §1851(a)(10)(D):

Amended Code Sec. 512(a)(3)(E)(iii) (as redesignated by Act Sec. 1851(a)(10)(B)) by striking out "paragraph shall not" and inserting in lieu thereof "subparagraph shall not". **Effective** as if included in the provision of P.L. 98-369 to it relates.

• 1984, Deficit Reduction Act of 1984 (P.L. 98-369)

P.L. 98-369, §511(b)(1)(A):

Amended Code Sec. 512(a)(3) by striking out "section 501(c)(7) or (9)" each place it appeared (including in the paragraph heading) and inserting in lieu thereof "paragraph (7), (9), (17), or (20) of section 501(c)". **Effective**, generally, for contributions paid or accrued after 12-31-85, in tax years ending after such date. Special rules appear in Act Sec. 511(e)(2)-(5) following Code Sec. 419.

P.L. 98-369, §511(b)(1)(B):

Amended Code Sec. 512(a)(3)(B)(ii) by striking out "section 501(c)(9)" and inserting in lieu thereof "paragraph (9), (17), or (20) of section 501(c)". **Effective**, generally, for contributions paid or accrued after 12-31-85, in tax years ending after such date. Special rules appear in Act Sec. 511(e)(2)-(5) following Code Sec. 419.

P.L. 98-369, §511(b)(2):

Amended Code Sec. 512(a)(3) by adding at the end thereof new subparagraph (E). **Effective**, generally, for contributions paid or accrued after 12-31-85, in tax years ending after such date. Special rules appear in Act Sec. 511(e)(2)-(5) following Code Sec. 419.

• 1978 (P.L. 95-345)

P.L. 95-345, §2(b):

Amended Code Sec. 512(a) by adding paragraph (5). **Effective** with respect to (1) amounts received after 12-31-76, as payments with respect to securities loans (as defined in Code Sec. 512(a)(5)), and (2) transfers of securities under agreements described in Code Sec. 1058 occurring after such date.

• 1976 (P.L. 94-568)

P.L. 94-568, §[1](b):

Amended Code Sec. 512(a)(3)(A) by adding the second sentence. **Effective** for tax years beginning after 10-20-76.

• **1972 (P.L. 92-418)**

P.L. 92-418, §1(b):

Added paragraph (4) to Code Sec. 512(a). **Effective** for tax years beginning after 12-31-69.

• **1969, Tax Reform Act of 1969 (P.L. 91-172)**

P.L. 91-172, §121(b)(1):

Amended Code Sec. 512(a). **Effective** 1-1-70. Prior to amendment Sec. 512(a) read as follows:

"(a) Definition.—The term "unrelated business taxable income" means the gross income derived by any organization from any unrelated trade or business (as defined in section 513) regularly carried on by it, less the deductions allowed by this chapter which are directly connected with the carrying on of such trade or business, both computed with the exceptions, additions, and limitations provided in subsection (b). In the case of an organization described in section 511 which is a foreign organization, the unrelated business taxable income shall be its unrelated business taxable income which is effectively connected with the conduct of a trade or business within the United States."

• **1966, Foreign Investors Tax Act of 1966 (P.L. 89-809)**

P.L. 89-809, §104(g):

Amended the last sentence of Code Sec. 512(a). **Effective** 1-1-67. Prior to amendment, such last sentence read as follows:

"In the case of an organization described in section 511 which is a foreign organization, the unrelated business taxable income shall be its unrelated business taxable income derived from sources within the United States determined under subchapter N (sec. 861 and following, relating to tax based on income from sources within or without the United States)."

[Sec. 512(b)]

(b) MODIFICATIONS.—The modifications referred to in subsection (a) are the following:

(1) There shall be excluded all dividends, interest, payments with respect to securities loans (as defined in subsection (a)(5)), amounts received or accrued as consideration for entering into agreements to make loans, and annuities, and all deductions directly connected with such income.

(2) There shall be excluded all royalties (including overriding royalties) whether measured by production or by gross or taxable income from the property, and all deductions directly connected with such income.

(3) In the case of rents—

(A) Except as provided in subparagraph (B), there shall be excluded—

(i) all rents from real property (including property described in section 1245(a)(3)(C)), and

(ii) all rents from personal property (including for purposes of this paragraph as personal property any property described in section 1245(a)(3)(B)) leased with such real property, if the rents attributable to such personal property are an incidental amount of the total rents received or accrued under the lease, determined at the time the personal property is placed in service.

(B) Subparagraph (A) shall not apply—

(i) if more than 50 percent of the total rent received or accrued under the lease is attributable to personal property described in Subparagraph (A)(ii), or

(ii) if the determination of the amount of such rent depends in whole or in part on the income or profits derived by any person from the property leased (other than an amount based on a fixed percentage or percentages of receipts or sales).

(C) There shall be excluded all deductions directly connected with rents excluded under subparagraph (A).

(4) Notwithstanding paragraph (1), (2), (3), or (5), in the case of debt-financed property (as defined in section 514) there shall be included, as an item of gross income derived from an unrelated trade or business, the amount ascertained under section 514(a)(1), and there shall be allowed, as a deduction, the amount ascertained under section 514(a)(2).

(5) There shall be excluded all gains or losses from the sale, exchange, or other disposition of property other than—

(A) stock in trade or other property of a kind which would properly be includible in inventory if on hand at the close of the taxable year, or

(B) property held primarily for sale to customers in the ordinary course of the trade or business.

There shall also be excluded all gains or losses recognized, in connection with the organization's investment activities, from the lapse or termination of options to buy or sell securities (as defined in section 1236(c)) or real property and all gains or losses from the forfeiture of good-faith deposits (that are consistent with established business practice) for the purchase, sale, or lease of real property in connection with the organization's investment activities. This paragraph shall not apply with respect to the cutting of timber which is considered, on the application of section 631, as a sale or exchange of such timber.

(6) The net operating loss deduction provided in section 172 shall be allowed, except that—

(A) the net operating loss for any taxable year, the amount of the net operating loss carryback or carryover to any taxable year, and the net operating loss deduction for any taxable year shall be determined under section 172 without taking into account any amount of income or deduction which is excluded under this part in computing the unrelated business taxable income; and

(B) the terms "preceding taxable year" and "preceding taxable years" as used in section 172 shall not include any taxable year for which the organization was not subject to the provisions of this part.

(7) There shall be excluded all income derived from research for (A) the United States, or any of its agencies or instrumentalities, or (B) any State or political subdivision thereof; and there shall be excluded all deductions directly connected with such income.

(8) In the case of a college, university, or hospital, there shall be excluded all income derived from research performed for any person, and all deductions directly connected with such income.

(9) In the case of an organization operated primarily for purposes of carrying on fundamental research the results of which are freely available to the general public, there shall be excluded all income derived from research performed for any person, and all deductions directly connected with such income.

(10) In the case of any organization described in section 511(a), the deduction allowed by section 170 (relating to charitable etc. contributions and gifts) shall be allowed (whether or not directly connected with the carrying on of the trade or business), but shall not exceed 10 percent of the unrelated business taxable income computed without the benefit of this paragraph.

(11) In the case of any trust described in section 511(b), the deduction allowed by section 170 (relating to charitable etc. contributions and gifts) shall be allowed (whether or not directly connected with the carrying on of the trade or business), and for such purpose a distribution made by the trust to a beneficiary described in section 170 shall be considered as a gift or contribution. The deduction allowed by this paragraph shall be allowed with the limitations prescribed in section 170 (b) (1) (A) and (B) determined with reference to the unrelated business taxable income computed without the benefit of this paragraph (in lieu of with reference to adjusted gross income).

(12) Except for purposes of computing the net operating loss under section 172 and paragraph (6), there shall be allowed a specific deduction of $1,000. In the case of a diocese, province of a religious order, or a convention or association of churches, there shall also be allowed, with respect to each parish, individual church, district, or other local unit, a specific deduction equal to the lower of—

(A) $1,000, or

(B) the gross income derived from any unrelated trade or business regularly carried on by such local unit.

(13) SPECIAL RULES FOR CERTAIN AMOUNTS RECEIVED FROM CONTROLLED ENTITIES.—

(A) IN GENERAL.—If an organization (in this paragraph referred to as the "controlling organization") receives or accrues (directly or indirectly) a specified payment from another entity which it controls (in this paragraph referred to as the "controlled entity"), notwithstanding paragraphs (1), (2), and (3), the controlling organization shall include such payment as an item of gross income derived from an unrelated trade or business to the extent such payment reduces the net unrelated income of the controlled entity (or increases any net unrelated loss of the controlled entity). There shall be allowed all deductions of the controlling organization directly connected with amounts treated as derived from an unrelated trade or business under the preceding sentence.

(B) NET UNRELATED INCOME OR LOSS.—For purposes of this paragraph—

(i) NET UNRELATED INCOME.—The term "net unrelated income" means—

(I) in the case of a controlled entity which is not exempt from tax under section 501(a), the portion of such entity's taxable income which would be unrelated business taxable income if such entity were exempt from tax under section 501(a) and had the same exempt purposes as the controlling organization, or

(II) in the case of a controlled entity which is exempt from tax under section 501(a), the amount of the unrelated business taxable income of the controlled entity.

(ii) NET UNRELATED LOSS.—The term "net unrelated loss" means the net operating loss adjusted under rules similar to the rules of clause (i).

(C) SPECIFIED PAYMENT.—For purposes of this paragraph, the term "specified payment" means any interest, annuity, royalty, or rent.

(D) DEFINITION OF CONTROL.—For purposes of this paragraph—

(i) CONTROL.—The term "control" means—

(I) in the case of a corporation, ownership (by vote or value) of more than 50 percent of the stock in such corporation,

(II) in the case of a partnership, ownership of more than 50 percent of the profits interests or capital interests in such partnership, or

(III) in any other case, ownership of more than 50 percent of the beneficial interests in the entity.

(ii) CONSTRUCTIVE OWNERSHIP.—Section 318 (relating to constructive ownership of stock) shall apply for purposes of determining ownership of stock in a corporation.

Similar principles shall apply for purposes of determining ownership of interests in any other entity.

(E) PARAGRAPH TO APPLY ONLY TO CERTAIN EXCESS PAYMENTS.—

(i) IN GENERAL.—Subparagraph (A) shall apply only to the portion of a qualifying specified payment received or accrued by the controlling organization that exceeds the amount which would have been paid or accrued if such payment met the requirements prescribed under section 482.

(ii) ADDITION TO TAX FOR VALUATION MISSTATEMENTS.—The tax imposed by this chapter on the controlling organization shall be increased by an amount equal to 20 percent of the larger of—

(I) such excess determined without regard to any amendment or supplement to a return of tax, or

(II) such excess determined with regard to all such amendments and supplements.

(iii) QUALIFYING SPECIFIED PAYMENT.—The term "qualifying specified payment" means a specified payment which is made pursuant to—

(I) a binding written contract in effect on the date of the enactment of this subparagraph, or

(II) a contract which is a renewal, under substantially similar terms, of a contract described in subclause (I).

(iv) TERMINATION.—This subparagraph shall not apply to payments received or accrued after December 31, 2009.

(F) RELATED PERSONS.—The Secretary shall prescribe such rules as may be necessary or appropriate to prevent avoidance of the purposes of this paragraph through the use of related persons.

(14) [Repealed.]

(15) Except as provided in paragraph (4), in the case of a trade or business—

(A) which consists of providing services under license issued by a Federal regulatory agency,

(B) which is carried on by a religious order or by an educational organization described in section 170(b)(1)(A)(ii) maintained by such religious order, and which was so carried on before May 27, 1959, and

(C) less than 10 percent of the net income of which for each taxable year is used for activities which are not related to the purpose constituting the basis for the religious order's exemption,

there shall be excluded all gross income derived from such trade or business and all deductions directly connected with the carrying on of such trade or business, so long as it is established to the satisfaction of the Secretary that the rates or other charges for such services are competitive with rates or other charges charged for similar services by persons not exempt from taxation.

(16)(A) Notwithstanding paragraph (5)(B), there shall be excluded all gains or losses from the sale, exchange, or other disposition of any real property described in subparagraph (B) if—

(i) such property was acquired by the organization from—

(I) a financial institution described in section 581 or 591(a) which is in conservatorship or receivership, or

(II) the conservator or receiver of such an institution (or any government agency or corporation succeeding to the rights or interests of the conservator or receiver),

(ii) such property is designated by the organization within the 9-month period beginning on the date of its acquisition as property held for sale, except that not more than one-half (by value determined as of such date) of property acquired in a single transaction may be so designated,

(iii) such sale, exchange, or disposition occurs before the later of—

(I) the date which is 30 months after the date of the acquisition of such property, or

(II) the date specified by the Secretary in order to assure an orderly disposition of property held by persons described in subparagraph (A), and

(iv) while such property was held by the organization, the aggregate expenditures on improvements and development activities included in the basis of the property are (or were) not in excess of 20 percent of the net selling price of such property.

(B) Property is described in this subparagraph if it is real property which—

(i) was held by the financial institution at the time it entered into conservatorship or receivership, or

(ii) was foreclosure property (as defined in section 514(c)(9)(H)(v)) which secured indebtedness held by the financial institution at such time.

For purposes of this subparagraph, real property includes an interest in a mortgage.

(17) TREATMENT OF CERTAIN AMOUNTS DERIVED FROM FOREIGN CORPORATIONS.—

(A) IN GENERAL.—Notwithstanding paragraph (1), any amount included in gross income under section 951(a)(1)(A) shall be included as an item of gross income derived from an unrelated trade or business to the extent the amount so included is attributable to insurance income (as defined in section 953) which, if derived directly by the organization, would be treated as gross income from an unrelated trade or business. There shall be allowed all deductions directly connected with amounts included in gross income under the preceding sentence.

(B) EXCEPTION.—

(i) IN GENERAL.—Subparagraph (A) shall not apply to income attributable to a policy of insurance or reinsurance with respect to which the person (directly or indirectly) insured is—

(I) such organization,

(II) an affiliate of such organization which is exempt from tax under section 501(a), or

(III) a director or officer of, or an individual who (directly or indirectly) performs services for, such organization or affiliate but only if the insurance covers primarily risks associated with the performance of services in connection with such organization or affiliate.

(ii) AFFILIATE.—For purposes of this subparagraph—

(I) IN GENERAL.—The determination as to whether an entity is an affiliate of an organization shall be made under rules similar to the rules of section 168(h)(4)(B).

(II) SPECIAL RULE.—Two or more organizations (and any affiliates of such organizations) shall be treated as affiliates if such organizations are colleges or universities described in section 170(b)(1)(A)(ii) or organizations described in section 170(b)(1)(A)(iii) and participate in an insurance arrangement that provides for any profits from such arrangement to be returned to the policyholders in their capacity as such.

(C) REGULATIONS.—The Secretary shall prescribe such regulations as may be necessary or appropriate to carry out the purposes of this paragraph, including regulations for the application of this paragraph in the case of income paid through 1 or more entities or between 2 or more chains of entities.

(18) TREATMENT OF MUTUAL OR COOPERATIVE ELECTRIC COMPANIES.—In the case of a mutual or cooperative electric company described in section 501(c)(12), there shall be excluded income which is treated as member income under subparagraph (H) thereof.

(19) TREATMENT OF GAIN OR LOSS ON SALE OR EXCHANGE OF CERTAIN BROWNFIELD SITES.—

(A) IN GENERAL.—Notwithstanding paragraph (5)(B), there shall be excluded any gain or loss from the qualified sale, exchange, or other disposition of any qualifying brownfield property by an eligible taxpayer.

(B) ELIGIBLE TAXPAYER.—For purposes of this paragraph—

(i) IN GENERAL.—The term "eligible taxpayer" means, with respect to a property, any organization exempt from tax under section 501(a) which—

(I) acquires from an unrelated person a qualifying brownfield property, and

(II) pays or incurs eligible remediation expenditures with respect to such property in an amount which exceeds the greater of $550,000 or 12 percent of the fair market value of the property at the time such property was acquired by the eligible taxpayer, determined as if there was not a presence of a hazardous substance, pollutant, or contaminant on the property which is complicating the expansion, redevelopment, or reuse of the property.

(ii) EXCEPTION.—Such term shall not include any organization which is—

(I) potentially liable under section 107 of the Comprehensive Environmental Response, Compensation, and Liability Act of 1980 with respect to the qualifying brownfield property,

(II) affiliated with any other person which is so potentially liable through any direct or indirect familial relationship or any contractual, corporate, or financial relationship (other than a contractual, corporate, or financial relationship which is created by the instruments by which title to any qualifying brownfield property is conveyed or financed or by a contract of sale of goods or services), or

(III) the result of a reorganization of a business entity which was so potentially liable.

(C) QUALIFYING BROWNFIELD PROPERTY.—For purposes of this paragraph—

(i) IN GENERAL.—The term "qualifying brownfield property" means any real property which is certified, before the taxpayer incurs any eligible remediation expenditures (other than to obtain a Phase I environmental site assessment), by an appropriate State agency (within the meaning of section 198(c)(4)) in the State in which such property is located as a brownfield site within the meaning of section 101(39) of the Comprehensive Environmental Response, Compensation, and Liability Act of 1980 (as in effect on the date of the enactment of this paragraph).

(ii) REQUEST FOR CERTIFICATION.—Any request by an eligible taxpayer for a certification described in clause (i) shall include a sworn statement by the eligible taxpayer and supporting documentation of the presence of a hazardous substance, pollutant, or contaminant on the property which is complicating the expansion, redevelopment, or reuse of the property given the property's reasonably anticipated future land uses or capacity for uses of the property (including a Phase I environmental site assessment and, if applicable, evidence of the property's presence on a local, State, or Federal list of brownfields or contaminated property) and other environmental assessments prepared or obtained by the taxpayer.

(D) QUALIFIED SALE, EXCHANGE, OR OTHER DISPOSITION.—For purposes of this paragraph—

(i) IN GENERAL.—A sale, exchange, or other disposition of property shall be considered as qualified if—

(I) such property is transferred by the eligible taxpayer to an unrelated person, and

(II) within 1 year of such transfer the eligible taxpayer has received a certification from the Environmental Protection Agency or an appropriate State agency (within the meaning of section 198(c)(4)) in the State in which such property is located that, as a result of the eligible taxpayer's remediation actions, such property would not be treated as a qualifying brownfield property in the hands of the transferee.

For purposes of subclause (II), before issuing such certification, the Environmental Protection Agency or appropriate State agency shall respond to comments received pursuant to clause (ii)(V) in the same form and manner as required under section 117(b) of the Comprehensive Environmental Response, Compensation, and Liability Act of 1980 (as in effect on the date of the enactment of this paragraph).

(ii) REQUEST FOR CERTIFICATION.—Any request by an eligible taxpayer for a certification described in clause (i) shall be made not later than the date of the transfer and shall include a sworn statement by the eligible taxpayer certifying the following:

(I) Remedial actions which comply with all applicable or relevant and appropriate requirements (consistent with section 121(d) of the Comprehensive Environmental Response, Compensation, and Liability Act of 1980) have been substantially completed, such that there are no hazardous substances, pollutants, or contaminants which complicate the expansion, redevelopment, or reuse of the property given the property's reasonably anticipated future land uses or capacity for uses of the property.

(II) The reasonably anticipated future land uses or capacity for uses of the property are more economically productive or environmentally beneficial than the uses of the property in existence on the date of the certification described in subparagraph (C)(i). For purposes of the preceding sentence, use of property as a landfill or other hazardous waste facility shall not be considered more economically productive or environmentally beneficial.

(III) A remediation plan has been implemented to bring the property into compliance with all applicable local, State, and Federal environmental laws, regulations, and standards and to ensure that the remediation protects human health and the environment.

(IV) The remediation plan described in subclause (III), including any physical improvements required to remediate the property, is either complete or substantially complete, and, if substantially complete, sufficient monitoring, funding, institutional controls, and financial assurances have been put in place to ensure the complete remediation of the property in accordance with the remediation plan as soon as is reasonably practicable after the sale, exchange, or other disposition of such property.

(V) Public notice and the opportunity for comment on the request for certification was completed before the date of such request. Such notice and opportunity for comment shall be in the same form and manner as required for public participation required under section 117(a) of the Comprehensive Environmental Response, Compensation, and Liability Act of 1980 (as in effect on the date of the enactment of this paragraph). For purposes of this subclause, public notice shall include, at a minimum, publication in a major local newspaper of general circulation.

(iii) ATTACHMENT TO TAX RETURNS.—A copy of each of the requests for certification described in clause (ii) of subparagraph (C) and this subparagraph shall be included in the tax return of the eligible taxpayer (and, where applicable, of the qualifying partnership) for the taxable year during which the transfer occurs.

(iv) SUBSTANTIAL COMPLETION.—For purposes of this subparagraph, a remedial action is substantially complete when any necessary physical construction is complete, all immediate threats have been eliminated, and all long-term threats are under control.

(E) ELIGIBLE REMEDIATION EXPENDITURES.—For purposes of this paragraph—

(i) IN GENERAL.—The term "eligible remediation expenditures" means, with respect to any qualifying brownfield property, any amount paid or incurred by the eligible taxpayer to an unrelated third person to obtain a Phase I environmental site assessment of the property, and any amount so paid or incurred after the date of the certification described in subparagraph (C)(i) for goods and services necessary to obtain a certification described in subparagraph (D)(i) with respect to such property, including expenditures—

(I) to manage, remove, control, contain, abate, or otherwise remediate a hazardous substance, pollutant, or contaminant on the property,

(II) to obtain a Phase II environmental site assessment of the property, including any expenditure to monitor, sample, study, assess, or otherwise evaluate the release, threat of release, or presence of a hazardous substance, pollutant, or contaminant on the property,

(III) to obtain environmental regulatory certifications and approvals required to manage the remediation and monitoring of the hazardous substance, pollutant, or contaminant on the property, and

(IV) regardless of whether it is necessary to obtain a certification described in subparagraph (D)(i)(II), to obtain remediation cost-cap or stoploss coverage, reopener or regulatory action coverage, or similar coverage under environmental insurance policies, or financial guarantees required to manage such remediation and monitoring.

(ii) EXCEPTIONS.—Such term shall not include—

(I) any portion of the purchase price paid or incurred by the eligible taxpayer to acquire the qualifying brownfield property,

(II) environmental insurance costs paid or incurred to obtain legal defense coverage, owner/operator liability coverage, lender liability coverage, professional liability coverage, or similar types of coverage,

(III) any amount paid or incurred to the extent such amount is reimbursed, funded, or otherwise subsidized by grants provided by the United States, a State, or a political subdivision of a State for use in connection with the property, proceeds of an issue of State or local government obligations used to provide financing for the property the interest of which is exempt from tax under section 103, or subsidized financing provided (directly or indirectly) under a Federal, State, or local program provided in connection with the property, or

(IV) any expenditure paid or incurred before the date of the enactment of this paragraph.

For purposes of subclause (III), the Secretary may issue guidance regarding the treatment of government-provided funds for purposes of determining eligible remediation expenditures.

(F) DETERMINATION OF GAIN OR LOSS.—For purposes of this paragraph, the determination of gain or loss shall not include an amount treated as gain which is ordinary income with respect to section 1245 or section 1250 property, including amounts deducted as section 198 expenses which are subject to the recapture rules of section 198(e), if the taxpayer had deducted such amounts in the computation of its unrelated business taxable income.

(G) SPECIAL RULES FOR PARTNERSHIPS.—

(i) IN GENERAL.—In the case of an eligible taxpayer which is a partner of a qualifying partnership which acquires, remediates, and sells, exchanges, or otherwise disposes of a qualifying brownfield property, this paragraph shall apply to the eligible taxpayer's distributive share of the qualifying partnership's gain or loss from the sale, exchange, or other disposition of such property.

(ii) QUALIFYING PARTNERSHIP.—The term "qualifying partnership" means a partnership which—

(I) has a partnership agreement which satisfies the requirements of section 514(c)(9)(B)(vi) at all times beginning on the date of the first certification received by the partnership under subparagraph (C)(i),

(II) satisfies the requirements of subparagraphs (B)(i), (C), (D), and (E), if "qualified partnership" is substituted for "eligible taxpayer" each place it appears therein (except subparagraph (D)(iii)), and

(III) is not an organization which would be prevented from constituting an eligible taxpayer by reason of subparagraph (B)(ii).

(iii) REQUIREMENT THAT TAX-EXEMPT PARTNER BE A PARTNER SINCE FIRST CERTIFICATION.—This paragraph shall apply with respect to any eligible taxpayer which is a partner of a partnership which acquires, remediates, and sells, exchanges, or otherwise disposes of a qualifying brownfield property only if such eligible taxpayer was a partner of the qualifying partnership at all times beginning on the date of the first certification received by the partnership under subparagraph (C)(i) and ending on the date of the sale, exchange, or other disposition of the property by the partnership.

(iv) REGULATIONS.—The Secretary shall prescribe such regulations as are necessary to prevent abuse of the requirements of this subparagraph, including abuse through—

(I) the use of special allocations of gains or losses, or

(II) changes in ownership of partnership interests held by eligible taxpayers.

(H) SPECIAL RULES FOR MULTIPLE PROPERTIES.—

(i) IN GENERAL.—An eligible taxpayer or a qualifying partnership of which the eligible taxpayer is a partner may make a 1-time election to apply this paragraph to more than 1 qualifying brownfield property by averaging the eligible remediation expenditures for all such properties acquired during the election period. If the eligible taxpayer or qualifying partnership makes such an election, the election shall apply to all qualified sales, exchanges, or other dispositions of qualifying brownfield properties the acquisition and transfer of which occur during the period for which the election remains in effect.

(ii) ELECTION.—An election under clause (i) shall be made with the eligible taxpayer's or qualifying partnership's timely filed tax return (including extensions) for the first taxable year for which the taxpayer or qualifying partnership intends to have the election apply. An election under clause (i) is effective for the period—

(I) beginning on the date which is the first day of the taxable year of the return in which the election is included or a later day in such taxable year selected by the eligible taxpayer or qualifying partnership, and

(II) ending on the date which is the earliest of a date of revocation selected by the eligible taxpayer or qualifying partnership, the date which is 8 years after the date described in subclause (I), or, in the case of an election by a qualifying partnership of which the eligible taxpayer is a partner, the date of the termination of the qualifying partnership.

(iii) REVOCATION.—An eligible taxpayer or qualifying partnership may revoke an election under clause (i)(II) by filing a statement of revocation with a timely filed tax return (including extensions). A revocation is effective as of the first day of the taxable year of the return in which the revocation is included or a later day in such taxable year selected by the eligible taxpayer or qualifying partnership. Once an eligible taxpayer or qualifying partnership revokes the election, the eligible taxpayer or qualifying partnership is ineligible to make another election under clause (i) with respect to any qualifying brownfield property subject to the revoked election.

(I) RECAPTURE.—If an eligible taxpayer excludes gain or loss from a sale, exchange, or other disposition of property to which an election under subparagraph (H) applies, and such property fails to satisfy the requirements of this paragraph, the unrelated business taxable income of the eligible taxpayer for the taxable year in which such failure occurs shall be determined by including any previously excluded gain or loss from such sale, exchange, or other disposition allocable to such taxpayer, and interest shall be determined at the overpayment rate established under section 6621 on any resulting tax for the period beginning with the due date of the return for the taxable year during which such sale, exchange, or other disposition occurred, and ending on the date of payment of the tax.

(J) RELATED PERSONS.—For purposes of this paragraph, a person shall be treated as related to another person if—

(i) such person bears a relationship to such other person described in section 267(b) (determined without regard to paragraph (9) thereof), or section 707(b)(1), determined by substituting '25 percent' for '50 percent' each place it appears therein, and

(ii) in the case such other person is a nonprofit organization, if such person controls directly or indirectly more than 25 percent of the governing body of such organization.

(K) TERMINATION.—Except for purposes of determining the average eligible remediation expenditures for properties acquired during the election period under subparagraph (H), this paragraph shall not apply to any property acquired by the eligible taxpayer or qualifying partnership after December 31, 2009.

Amendments

• 2008, Tax Extenders and Alternative Minimum Tax Relief Act of 2008 (P.L. 110-343)

P.L. 110-343, Division C, §306(a):

Amended Code Sec. 512(b)(13)(E)(iv) by striking "December 31, 2007" and inserting "December 31, 2009". **Effective** for payments received or accrued after 12-31-2007.

• 2006, Pension Protection Act of 2006 (P.L. 109-280)

P.L. 109-280, §1205(a):

Amended Code Sec. 512(b)(13) by redesignating subparagraph (E) as subparagraph (F) and by inserting after subparagraph (D) a new subparagraph (E). **Effective** for payments received or accrued after 12-31-2005.

• 2005, Gulf Opportunity Zone Act of 2005 (P.L. 109-135)

P.L. 109-135, §412(dd):

Amended Code Sec. 512(b)(1) by striking "section 512(a)(5)" and inserting "subsection (a)(5)". **Effective** 12-21-2005.

P.L. 109-135, §412(ee)(1)(A)-(B):

Amended Code Sec. 512(b) by redesignating paragraph (18), as added by P.L. 108-357, §702, as paragraph (19), and by moving such paragraph to the end of such subsection. **Effective** 12-21-2005.

• 2004, American Jobs Creation Act of 2004 (P.L. 108-357)

P.L. 108-357, §319(c):

Amended Code Sec. 512(b) by adding at the end a new paragraph (18). **Effective** for tax years beginning after 10-22-2004.

P.L. 108-357, §702(a):

Amended Code Sec. 512(b) by adding at the end a new paragraph (18)[(19)]. **Effective** for any gain or loss on the sale, exchange, or other disposition of any property acquired by the taxpayer after 12-31-2004. For a special rule, see Act Sec. 702(c), below.

P.L. 108-357, §702(c), provides:

(c) SAVINGS CLAUSE.—Nothing in the amendments made by this section shall affect any duty, liability, or other requirement imposed under any other Federal or State law. Notwithstanding section 128(b) of the Comprehensive Environmental Response, Compensation, and Liability Act of 1980, a certification provided by the Environmental Protection Agency or an appropriate State agency (within the meaning of section 198(c)(4) of the Internal Revenue Code of 1986) shall not affect the liability of any person under section 107(a) of such Act.

• 1998, IRS Restructuring and Reform Act of 1998 (P.L. 105-206)

P.L. 105-206, §6010(j)(1):

Amended Code Sec. 512(b)(13)(A) by inserting "or accrues" after "receives". **Effective** as if included in the provision of P.L. 105-34 to which it relates [generally **effective** for tax years beginning after 8-5-97.—CCH].

P.L. 105-206, §6010(j)(2):

Amended Code Sec. 512(b)(13)(B)(i)(I) by striking "(as defined in section 513A(a)(5)(A))" after "purposes". **Effective** as if included in the provision of P.L. 105-34 to which it relates [generally **effective** for tax years beginning after 8-5-97.—CCH].

P.L. 105-206, §6023(8):

Amended the heading for Code Sec. 512(b)(17)(B)(ii)(II) by striking "RULE" and inserting "RULE". **E ffective** 7-22-98.

• 1997, Taxpayer Relief Act of 1997 (P.L. 105-34)

P.L. 105-34, §1041(a):

Amended Code Sec. 512(b)(13). **Effective**, generally, for tax years beginning after 8-5-97. For a special rule, see Act Sec. 1041(b)(2), below. Prior to amendment, Code Sec. 512(b)(13) read as follows:

(13) Notwithstanding paragraphs (1), (2), or (3), amounts of interest, annuities, royalties, and rents derived from any organization (in this paragraph called the "controlled organization") of which the organization deriving such amounts (in this paragraph called the "controlling organization") has control (as defined in section 368(c)) shall be included as an item of gross income (whether or not the activity from which such amounts are derived represents a trade or business or is regularly carried on) in an amount which bears the same ratio as—

(A)(i) in the case of a controlled organization which is not exempt from taxation under section 501(a), the excess of the amount of taxable income of the controlled organization over the amount of such organization's taxable income which if derived directly by the controlling organization would not be unrelated business taxable income, or

(ii) in the case of a controlled organization which is exempt from taxation under section 501(a), the amount of unrelated business taxable income of the controlled organization, bears to

(B) the taxable income of the controlled organization (determined in the case of a controlled organization to which subparagraph (A)(ii) applies as if it were not an organization exempt from taxation under section 501(a)), but not less than the amount determined in clause (i) or (ii), as the case may be, of subparagraph (A),

both amounts computed without regard to amounts paid directly or indirectly to the controlling organization. There shall be allowed all deductions directly connected with amounts included in gross income under the preceding sentence.

P.L. 105-34, §1041(b)(2) (as amended by P.L. 105-206, §6010(j)(3)), provides:

(2) BINDING CONTRACTS.—The amendments made by this section shall not apply to any amount received or accrued during the first 2 taxable years beginning on or after the date of the enactment of this Act if such amount is received or accrued pursuant to a written binding contract in effect on June 8, 1997, and at all times thereafter before such amount is received or accrued. The preceding sentence shall not apply to any amount which would (but for the exercise of an option to accelerate payment of such amount) be received or accrued after such 2 taxable years.

• 1996, Small Business Job Protection Act of 1996 (P.L. 104-188)

P.L. 104-188, §1603(a):

Amended Code Sec. 512(b) by adding at the end a new paragraph (17). **Effective** for amounts included in gross income in any tax year beginning after 12-31-95.

• 1993, Omnibus Budget Reconciliation Act of 1993 (P.L. 103-66)

P.L. 103-66, §13147(a):

Amended Code Sec. 512(b) by adding at the end thereof a new paragraph (16). **Effective** for property acquired on or after 1-1-94.

P.L. 103-66, §13148(a):

Amended Code Sec. 512(b)(1) by inserting "amounts received or accrued as consideration for entering into agreements to make loans," before "and annuities". **Effective** for amounts received on or after 1-1-94.

P.L. 103-66, §13148(b)(1)-(3):

Amended Code Sec. 512(b)(5) by striking "all gains on" and inserting "all gains or losses recognized, in connection with the organization's investment activities, from", by striking ", written by the organization in connection with its investment activities," after "options", and by inserting "or real property and all gains or losses from the forefeiture of good-faith deposits (that are consistent with established business practice) for the purchase, sale, or lease of real property in connection with the organization's investment activities" before the period. **Effective** for amounts received on or after 1-1-94.

• 1990, Omnibus Budget Reconciliation Act of 1990 (P.L. 101-508)

P.L. 101-508, §11801(a)(23):

Repealed Code Sec. 512(b)(14). **Effective** 11-5-90. Prior to repeal, Code Sec. 512(b)(14) read as follows:

(14) Except as provided in paragraph (4), in the case of a church, or convention or association of churches, for taxable years beginning before January 1, 1976, there shall be excluded all gross income derived from a trade or business

and all deductions directly connected with the carrying on of such trade or business if such trade or business was carried on by such organization or its predecessor before May 27, 1969.

P.L. 101-508, §11821(b), provides:

(b) SAVINGS PROVISION.—If—

(1) any provision amended or repealed by this part applied to—

(A) any transaction occurring before the date of the enactment of this Act,

(B) any property acquired before such date of enactment, or

(C) any item of income, loss, deduction, or credit taken into account before such date of enactment, and

(2) the treatment of such transaction, property, or item under such provision would (without regard to the amendments made by this part) affect liability for tax for periods ending after such date of enactment,

nothing in the amendments made by this part shall be construed to affect the treatment of such transaction, property, or item for purposes of determining liability for tax for periods ending after such date of enactment.

• 1983, Technical Corrections Act of 1982 (P.L. 97-448)

P.L. 97-448, §102(m)(3):

Amended Code Sec. 512(b)(10) by striking out "5 percent" and inserting in lieu thereof "10 percent". **Effective** as if included in the provision of P.L. 97-34 to which it relates.

• 1978 (P.L. 95-345)

P.L. 95-345, §2(a)(2):

Amended Code Sec. 512(b)(1) by adding "payments with respect to securities loans (as defined in section 512(a)(5))," after "interest". **Effective** with respect to (1) amounts received after 12-31-76, as payments with respect to securities loans (as defined in Code Sec. 512(a)(5)), and (2) transfers of securities under agreements described in Code Sec. 1058 occurring after such date.

• 1976, Tax Reform Act of 1976 (P.L. 94-455)

P.L. 94-455, §1951(b)(8)(A):

Repealed Code Secs. 512(b)(13) and (14) and redesignated former paragraphs (15), (16), and (17) as paragraphs (13), (14), and (15). **Effective** with respect to tax years beginning after 12-31-76. Prior to repeal, Code Secs. 512(b)(13) and (14) read as follows:

(13) In the case of a trust—

(A) created by virtue of the provisions of the will of an individual who died after August 16, 1954, and before January 1, 1957,

(B) which, by virtue of the provisions of such will, is a limited partner in a partnership created under the laws of a State (i) providing for the creation of limited partnerships, and (ii) under which a limited partner has no right to take part in the control of the business without becoming liable as a general partner,

(C) which, at no time before or during a taxable year of the partnership ending within or with the taxable year of the trust, was (or was liable as) a general partner in such partnership, and

(D) which is required to distribute all of its income (within the meaning of section 643(b)) currently exclusively for religious, charitable, scientific, literary, or educational purposes, and which is required to distribute all of the corpus exclusively for such purposes,

there shall be excluded its share (determined under subsection (c) without regard to this paragraph and paragraph (11)) of gross income of the partnership as such limited partner and of the partnership deductions directly connected with such income, but, if such share of gross income exceeds such share of deductions, only to the extent that the partnership makes distributions during its taxable year which are attributable to such gross income. For purposes of the preceding sentence (i) any distribution made after the close of a partnership taxable year and on or before the 15th day of the fourth calendar month after the close of such taxable year shall be treated as made on the last day of such taxable year, and (ii) distributions shall be treated as attributable first to gross income other than gross income described in the preceding sentence, and shall be properly adjusted (under regulations prescribed by the Secretary or his delegate) to the extent necessary to reflect capital contributions to the partnership made by the trust, income of the partnership exempt from tax under this title, and other items.

(14) In the case of an organization which is described in section 501(c)(5), there shall be excluded all income used to establish, maintain, or operate a retirement home, hospital, or other similar facility for the exclusive use and benefit of the aged and infirm members of such an organization, which is derived from agricultural pursuits conducted on ground contiguous to the retirement home, hospital, or similar facility and further provided that such income does not provide more than 75 percent of the cost of maintaining and operating the retirement home, hospital, or similar facility; and there shall be excluded all deductions directly connected with such income.

P.L. 94-455, §1951(b)(8)(B), provides:

(B) SAVINGS PROVISION.—Notwithstanding subparagraph (A), income received in a taxable year beginning after December 31, 1975, shall be excluded from gross income in determining unrelated business taxable income, if such income would have been excluded by paragraph (13) or (14) of section 512(b) if received in a taxable year beginning before such date. Any deductions directly connected with income excluded under the preceding sentence in determining unrelated business taxable income shall also be excluded for such purpose.

P.L. 94-455, §1901(b)(8)(F):

Amended Code Sec. 512(b)(15)(B), as redesignated by P.L. 94-455, §1951(b)(8)(A), by substituting "educational organization described in section 170(b)(1)(A)(ii)" for "educational institution (as defined in section 151(e)(4))". **Effective** with respect to tax years beginning after 12-31-76.

P.L. 94-455, §1906(b)(13)(A):

Amended 1954 Code by substituting "Secretary" for "Secretary or his delegate" each place it appeared. **Effective** 2-1-77.

• 1976 (P.L. 94-396)

P.L. 94-396, §1:

Amended Code Sec. 512(b)(5) by adding the second sentence. **Effective** for gains on options which lapse or are terminated after 1-1-76.

• 1969, Tax Reform Act of 1969 (P.L. 91-172)

P.L. 91-172, §121(b):

Amended Code Sec. 512(b) by changing so much as precedes paragraph (1), by changing paragraphs (3), (4) and (12), and by adding paragraphs (15)-(17). **Effective** 1-1-70. Prior to amendment so much of Sec. 512(b) as precedes paragraph (1) and paragraphs (3), (4) and (12) read as follows:

(b) Exceptions, Additions, and Limitations.—The exceptions, additions, and limitations applicable in determining unrelated business taxable income are the following:

* * *

(3) There shall be excluded all rents from real property (including personal property leased with the real property), and all deductions directly connected with such rents.

(4) Notwithstanding paragraph (3), in the case of a business lease (as defined in section 514) there shall be included, as an item of gross income derived from an unrelated trade or business, the amount ascertained under section 514(a)(1), and there shall be allowed, as a deduction the amount ascertained under section 514(a)(2).

* * *

(12) There shall be allowed a specific deduction of $1,000.

• 1964 (P.L. 88-380)

P.L. 88-380, §[1]:

Added paragraph (14) to Sec. 512(b). **Effective** for tax years beginning after December 31, 1963.

• 1959 (P.L. 85-367)

P.L. 85-367, §[1]:

Added paragraph (13) to Sec. 512(b). **Effective** for tax years of trust beginning after December 31, 1955.

[Sec. 512(c)]

(c) SPECIAL RULES FOR PARTNERSHIPS.—

(1) IN GENERAL.—If a trade or business regularly carried on by a partnership of which an organization is a member is an unrelated trade or business with respect to such organization, such organization in computing its unrelated business taxable income shall, subject to the exceptions, additions, and limitations contained in subsection (b), include its share (whether or not distributed) of the gross income of the partnership from such unrelated trade or business and its share of the partnership deductions directly connected with such gross income.

(2) SPECIAL RULE WHERE PARTNERSHIP YEAR IS DIFFERENT FROM ORGANIZATION'S YEAR.—If the taxable year of the organization is different from that of the partnership, the amounts to be included or deducted in computing the unrelated business taxable income under paragraph (1) shall be based upon the income and deductions of the partnership for any taxable year of the partnership ending within or with the taxable year of the organization.

Amendments

• 1993, Omnibus Budget Reconciliation Act of 1993 (P.L. 103-66)

P.L. 103-66, §13145(a)(1)-(3):

Amended Code Sec. 512(c) by striking paragraph (2), by redesignating paragraph (3) as paragraph (2), and by striking "paragraph (1) or (2)" in paragraph (2) (as so redesignated) and inserting "paragraph (1)". **Effective** for partnership years beginning on or after 1-1-94. Prior to amendment, Code Sec. 512(c)(2) read as follows:

(2) SPECIAL RULE FOR PUBLICLY TRADED PARTNERSHIPS.—Notwithstanding any other provision of this section—

(A) any organization's share (whether or not distributed) of the gross income of a publicly traded partnership (as defined in section 469(k)(2)) shall be treated as gross income derived from an unrelated trade or business, and

(B) such organization's share of the partnership deductions shall be allowed in computing unrelated business taxable income.

• 1987, Revenue Act of 1987 (P.L. 100-203)

P.L. 100-203, §10213(a):

Amended Code Sec. 512(c). **Effective** for partnership interests acquired after 12-17-87. Prior to amendment, Code Sec. 512(c) read as follows:

(c) SPECIAL RULES APPLICABLE TO PARTNERSHIPS.—If a trade or business regularly carried on by a partnership of which an organization is a member is an unrelated trade or business with respect to such organization, such organization in computing its unrelated business taxable income shall, subject to the exceptions, additions, and limitations contained in subsection (b), include its share (whether or not distributed) of the gross income of the partnership from such unrelated trade or business and its share of the partnership deductions directly connected with such gross income. If the taxable year of the organization is different from that of the partnership, the amounts to be so included or deducted in computing the unrelated business taxable income shall be based upon the income and deductions of the partnership for any taxable year of the partnership ending within or with the taxable year of the organization.

[Sec. 512(d)]

(d) TREATMENT OF DUES OF AGRICULTURAL OR HORTICULTURAL ORGANIZATIONS.—

(1) IN GENERAL.—If—

(A) an agricultural or horticultural organization described in section 501(c)(5) requires annual dues to be paid in order to be a member of such organization, and

(B) the amount of such required annual dues does not exceed $100,

in no event shall any portion of such dues be treated as derived by such organization from an unrelated trade or business by reason of any benefits or privileges to which members of such organization are entitled.

(2) INDEXATION OF $100 AMOUNT.—In the case of any taxable year beginning in a calendar year after 1995, the $100 amount in paragraph (1) shall be increased by an amount equal to—

(A) $100, multiplied by

(B) the cost-of-living adjustment determined under section 1(f)(3) for the calendar year in which the taxable year begins, by substituting "calendar year 1994" for "calendar year 1992" in subparagraph (B) thereof.

(3) DUES.—For purposes of this subsection, the term "dues" means any payment (whether or not designated as dues) which is required to be made in order to be recognized by the organization as a member of the organization.

Amendments

• 1996, Small Business Job Protection Act of 1996 (P.L. 104-188)

P.L. 104-188, §1115(a):

Amended Code Sec. 512 by adding at the end a new subsection (d). **Effective** for tax years beginning after 12-31-86. For a transitional rule, see Act Sec. 1115(b)(2)-(3), below.

P.L. 104-188, §1115(b)(2)-(3), provides:

(2) TRANSITIONAL RULE.—If—

(A) for purposes of applying part III of subchapter F of chapter 1 of the Internal Revenue Code of 1986 to any taxable year beginning before January 1, 1987, an agricultural or horticultural organization did not treat any portion of membership dues received by it as income derived in an unrelated trade or business, and

(B) such organization had a reasonable basis for not treating such dues as income derived in an unrelated trade or business,

then, for purposes of applying such part III to any such taxable year, in no event shall any portion of such dues be treated as derived in an unrelated trade or business.

(3) REASONABLE BASIS.—For purposes of paragraph (2), an organization shall be treated as having a reasonable basis for not treating membership dues as income derived in an unrelated trade or business if the taxpayer's treatment of such dues was in reasonable reliance on any of the following:

(A) Judicial precedent, published rulings, technical advice with respect to the organization, or a letter ruling to the organization.

(B) A past Internal Revenue Service audit of the organization in which there was no assessment attributable to the reclassification of membership dues for purposes of the tax on unrelated business income.

(C) Long-standing recognized practice of agricultural or horticultural organizations.

[Sec. 512(e)]

(e) SPECIAL RULES APPLICABLE TO S CORPORATIONS.—

(1) IN GENERAL.—If an organization described in section 1361(c)(2)(A)(vi) or 1361(c)(6) holds stock in an S corporation—

(A) such interest shall be treated as an interest in an unrelated trade or business; and

(B) notwithstanding any other provision of this part—

(i) all items of income, loss, or deduction taken into account under section 1366(a), and

(ii) any gain or loss on the disposition of the stock in the S corporation

shall be taken into account in computing the unrelated business taxable income of such organization.

(2) BASIS REDUCTION.—Except as provided in regulations, for purposes of paragraph (1), the basis of any stock acquired by purchase (as defined in section 1361(e)(1)(C)) shall be reduced by the amount of any dividends received by the organization with respect to the stock.

(3) EXCEPTION FOR ESOPS.—This subsection shall not apply to employer securities (within the meaning of section 409(l)) held by an employee stock ownership plan described in section 4975(e)(7).

Amendments

• 2004, American Jobs Creation Act of 2004 (P.L. 108-357)

P.L. 108-357, §233(d):

Amended Code Sec. 512(e)(1) by inserting "1361(c)(2)(A)(vi) or" before "1361(c)(6)". **Effective** 10-22-2004.

• 1997, Taxpayer Relief Act of 1997 (P.L. 105-34)

P.L. 105-34, §1523(a):

Amended Code Sec. 512(e) by adding at the end a new paragraph (3). **Effective** for tax years beginning after 12-31-97.

P.L. 105-34, §1601(c)(4)(A):

Amended Code Sec. 512(e)(2) by striking "within the meaning of section 1012" and inserting "as defined in section 1361(e)(1)(C)". **Effective** as if included in the provision of P.L. 104-188 to which it relates [**effective** for tax years beginning after 12-31-97.—CCH].

P.L. 105-34, §1601(c)(4)(D):

Amended Code Sec. 512(e)(1) by striking "section 1361(c)(7)" and inserting "section 1361(c)(6)". **Effective** as if included in the provision of P.L. 104-188 to which it relates [**effective** for tax years beginning after 12-31-97.—CCH].

• 1996, Small Business Job Protetion Act of 1996 (P.L. 104-188)

P.L. 104-188, §1316(c):

Amended Code Sec. 512 by adding at the end a new subsection (e). **Effective** for tax years beginning after 12-31-97.

[Sec. 513]

SEC. 513. UNRELATED TRADE OR BUSINESS.

[Sec. 513(a)]

(a) GENERAL RULE.—The term "unrelated trade or business" means, in the case of any organization subject to the tax imposed by section 511, any trade or business the conduct of which is not substantially related (aside from the need of such organization for income or funds or the use it makes of the profits derived) to the exercise or performance by such organization of its charitable, educational, or other purpose or function constituting the basis for its exemption under section 501 (or, in the case of an organization described in section 511(a)(2)(B), to the exercise or performance of any purpose or function described in section 501(c)(3)), except that such term does not include any trade or business—

(1) in which substantially all the work in carrying on such trade or business is performed for the organization without compensation; or

(2) which is carried on, in the case of an organization described in section 501(c)(3) or in the case of a college or university described in section 511(a)(2)(B), by the organization primarily for the convenience of its members, students, patients, officers, or employees, or, in the case of a local association of employees described in section 501(c)(4) organized before May 27, 1969, which is the selling by the organization of items of work-related clothes and equipment and items normally sold through vending machines, through food dispensing facilities, or by snack bars, for the convenience of its members at their usual places of employment; or

(3) which is the selling of merchandise, substantially all of which has been received by the organization as gifts or contributions.

Amendments

• 1969, Tax Reform Act of 1969 (P.L. 91-172)

P.L. 91-172, §121(b)(4):

Amended Code Sec. 513(a) by replacing "employees; or" with "employees, or, in the case of a local association of employees described in section 501(c)(4) organized before May 27, 1969, which is the selling by the organization of items of work-related clothes and equipment and items normally sold through vending machines, through food dispensing facilities, or by snack bars, for the convenience of its members at their usual places of employment; or". **Effective** 1-1-70.

• 1984, Deficit Reduction Act of 1984 (P.L. 98-369)

P.L. 98-369, §311 (as amended by P.L. 99-514, §1834), provides:

SEC. 311. THE CONDUCTING OF CERTAIN GAMES OF CHANCE NOT TREATED AS UNRELATED TRADE OR BUSINESS.

(a) GENERAL RULE.—For purposes of section 513 of the Internal Revenue Code of 1954 (defining unrelated trade or business), the term "unrelated trade or business" does not include any trade or business which consists of conducting any game of chance if—

(1) such game of chance is conducted by a nonprofit organization,

(2) the conducting of such game by such organization does not violate any State or local law, and

(3) as of October 5, 1983—

(A) there was a State law (originally enacted on April 22, 1977) in effect which permitted the conducting of such game of chance by such nonprofit organization, but

(B) the conducting of such game of chance by organizations which were not nonprofit organizations would have violated such law.

(b) EFFECTIVE DATE.—Subsection (a) shall apply to games of chance conducted after June 30, 1981, in taxable years ending after such date.

[Sec. 513(b)]

(b) SPECIAL RULE FOR TRUSTS.—The term "unrelated trade or business" means, in the case of—

(1) a trust computing its unrelated business taxable income under section 512 for purposes of section 681; or

(2) a trust described in section 401(a), or section 501(c)(17), which is exempt from tax under section 501(a);

any trade or business regularly carried on by such trust or by a partnership of which it is a member.

Amendments

• 1960 (P.L. 86-667)

P.L. 86-667, §4:

Amended Code Sec. 513(b)(2) by striking out "section 401(a)" and inserting in lieu thereof "section 401(a), or section 501(c)(17),". **Effective** for tax years beginning after 12-31-59.

[Sec. 513(c)]

(c) ADVERTISING, ETC., ACTIVITIES.—For purposes of this section, the term "trade or business" includes any activity which is carried on for the production of income from the sale of goods or the performance of services. For purposes of the preceding sentence, an activity does not lose identity as a trade or business merely because it is carried on within a larger aggregate of similar activities or within a larger complex of other endeavors which may, or may not, be related to the exempt purposes of the organization. Where an activity carried on for profit constitutes an unrelated trade or business, no part of such trade or business shall be excluded from such classification merely because it does not result in profit.

Amendments

• 1969, Tax Reform Act of 1969 (P.L. 91-172)

P.L. 91-172, §121(c):

Amended Code Sec. 513(c). **Effective** 1-1-70. Prior to amendment Sec. 513(c) read as follows:

"(c) Special Rule for Certain Publishing Businesses.—If a publishing business carried on by an organization during a taxable year beginning before January 1, 1953, is, without regard to this subsection, an unrelated trade or business, but before the beginning of the third succeeding taxable year the business is carried on by it (or by a successor who acquired such business in a liquidation which would have constituted a tax-free exchange under section 112(b)(6) of the Internal Revenue Code of 1939) in such manner that the conduct thereof is substantially related to the exercise or performance by such organization (or such successor) of its educational or other purpose or function described in section 501(c)(3), such publishing business shall not be considered, for the taxable year, as an unrelated trade or business."

[Sec. 513(d)]

(d) CERTAIN ACTIVITIES OF TRADE SHOWS, STATE FAIRS, ETC.—

(1) GENERAL RULE.—The term "unrelated trade or business" does not include qualified public entertainment activities of an organization described in paragraph (2)(C), or qualified convention and trade show activities of an organization described in paragraph (3)(C).

(2) QUALIFIED PUBLIC ENTERTAINMENT ACTIVITIES.—For purposes of this subsection—

(A) PUBLIC ENTERTAINMENT ACTIVITY.—The term "public entertainment activity" means any entertainment or recreational activity of a kind traditionally conducted at fairs or expositions promoting agricultural and educational purposes, including, but not limited to, any activity one of the purposes of which is to attract the public to fairs or expositions or to promote the breeding of animals or the development of products or equipment.

(B) QUALIFIED PUBLIC ENTERTAINMENT ACTIVITY.—The term "qualified public entertainment activity" means a public entertainment activity which is conducted by a qualifying organization described in subparagraph (C) in—

(i) conjunction with an international, national, State, regional, or local fair or exposition,

(ii) accordance with the provisions of State law which permit the activity to be operated or conducted solely by such an organization, or by an agency, instrumentality, or political subdivision of such State, or

(iii) accordance with the provisions of State law which permit such an organization to be granted a license to conduct not more than 20 days of such activity on payment to the State of a lower percentage of the revenue from such licensed activity than the State requires from organizations not described in section 501(c)(3), (4), or (5).

(C) QUALIFYING ORGANIZATION.—For purposes of this paragraph, the term "qualifying organization" means an organization which is described in section 501(c)(3), (4), or (5) which regularly conducts, as one of its substantial exempt purposes, an agricultural and educational fair or exposition.

(3) QUALIFIED CONVENTION AND TRADE SHOW ACTIVITIES.—

(A) CONVENTION AND TRADE SHOW ACTIVITY.—The term "convention and trade show activity" means any activity of a kind traditionally conducted at conventions, annual meetings, or trade shows, including, but not limited to, any activity one of the purposes of which is to attract persons in an industry generally (without regard to membership in the sponsoring organization) as well as members of the public to the show for the purpose of displaying industry products or to stimulate interest in, and demand for, industry products or services, or to educate persons engaged in the industry in the development of new products and services or new rules and regulations affecting the industry.

(B) QUALIFIED CONVENTION AND TRADE SHOW ACTIVITY.—The term "qualified convention and trade show activity" means a convention and trade show activity carried out by a qualifying organization described in subparagraph (C) in conjunction with an international, national, State, regional, or local convention, annual meeting, or show conducted by an organization described in subparagraph (C) if one of the purposes of such organization in sponsoring the activity is the promotion and stimulation of interest in, and demand for, the products and services of that industry in general or to educate persons in attendance regarding new developments or products and services related to the exempt activities of the organization, and the show is designed to achieve such purpose through the character of the exhibits and the extent of the industry products displayed.

(C) QUALIFYING ORGANIZATION.—For purposes of this paragraph, the term "qualifying organization" means an organization described in section 501(c)(3), (4), (5), or (6) which regularly conducts as one of its substantial exempt purposes a show which stimulates interest in, and demand for, the products of a particular industry or segment of such industry or which educates persons in attendance regarding new developments or products and services related to the exempt activities of the organizations.

(4) SUCH ACTIVITIES NOT TO AFFECT EXEMPT STATUS.—An organization described in section 501(c)(3), (4), or (5) shall not be considered as not entitled to the exemption allowed under section 501(a) solely because of qualified public entertainment activities conducted by it.

Amendments

• 1986, Tax Reform Act of 1986 (P.L. 99-514)

P.L. 99-514, §1602(a):

Amended Code Sec. 513(d)(3)(B) by inserting "or to educate persons in attendance regarding new developments or products and services related to the exempt activities of the organization" after "industry in general". **Effective** for activities in tax years beginning 10-22-86.

P.L. 99-514, §1602(b):

Amended Code Sec. 513(d)(3)(C) by striking out "501(c)(5) or (6)" and inserting in lieu thereof "501(c)(3), (4), (5), or (6)" and by inserting before the period at the end thereof "or which educates persons in attendance regarding new developments or products and services related to the exempt activities of the organization". **Effective** for activities in tax years beginning 10-22-86.

• 1976, Tax Reform Act of 1976 (P.L. 94-455)

P.L. 94-455, §1305(a):

Added Code Sec. 513(d). **Effective** as provided in Act Sec. 1305(b), below.

P.L. 94-455, §1305(b), provides:

(b) EFFECTIVE DATES.—The amendments made by subsection (a) apply to qualified public entertainment activities in taxable years beginning after December 31, 1962, and to qualified convention and trade show activities in taxable years beginning after the date of enactment of this Act.

[Sec. 513(e)]

(e) CERTAIN HOSPITAL SERVICES.—In the case of a hospital described in section 170(b)(1)(A)(iii), the term "unrelated trade or business" does not include the furnishing of one or more of the services described in section 501(e)(1)(A) to one or more hospitals described in section 170(b)(1)(A)(iii) if—

(1) such services are furnished solely to such hospitals which have facilities to serve not more than 100 inpatients;

(2) such services, if performed on its own behalf by the recipient hospital, would constitute activities in exercising or performing the purpose or function constituting the basis for its exemption; and

(3) such services are provided at a fee or cost which does not exceed the actual cost of providing such services, such cost including straight line depreciation and a reasonable amount for return on capital goods used to provide such services.

Amendments

• 1976, Tax Reform Act of 1976 (P.L. 94-455)

P.L. 94-455, §1311(a):

Added Code Sec. 513(e). **Effective** as provided in Act Sec. 1311(b), below.

P.L. 94-455, §1311(b), provides:

(b) EFFECTIVE DATE.—The amendment made by this section shall apply to all taxable years to which the Internal Revenue Code of 1954 applies.

[Sec. 513(f)]

(f) CERTAIN BINGO GAMES.—

(1) IN GENERAL.—The term "unrelated trade or business" does not include any trade or business which consists of conducting bingo games.

(2) BINGO GAME DEFINED.—For purposes of paragraph (1), the term "bingo game" means any game of bingo—

(A) of a type in which usually—

(i) the wagers are placed,

(ii) the winners are determined, and

(iii) the distribution of prizes or other property is made,

in the presence of all persons placing wagers in such game,

(B) the conducting of which is not an activity ordinarily carried out on a commercial basis, and

(C) the conducting of which does not violate any State or local law.

Amendments

• 1978 (P.L. 95-502)

P.L. 95-502, §301(a), (b):

Added Code Sec. 513(f). **Effective** for tax years beginning after 1969.

[Sec. 513(g)]

(g) CERTAIN POLE RENTALS.—In the case of a mutual or cooperative telephone or electric company, the term "unrelated trade or business" does not include engaging in qualified pole rentals (as defined in section 501(c)(12)(D)).

Amendments

• 1980, Miscellaneous Revenue Act of 1980 (P.L. 96-605)

P.L. 96-605, §106(b):

Amended Code Sec. 513 by adding subsection (g). **Effective** for tax years beginning after 12-31-69.

[Sec. 513(h)]

(h) CERTAIN DISTRIBUTIONS OF LOW COST ARTICLES WITHOUT OBLIGATION TO PURCHASE AND EXCHANGES AND RENTALS OF MEMBER LISTS.—

(1) IN GENERAL.—In the case of an organization which is described in section 501 and contributions to which are deductible under paragraph (2) or (3) of section 170(c), the term "unrelated trade or business" does not include—

(A) activities relating to the distribution of low cost articles if the distribution of such articles is incidental to the solicitation of charitable contributions, or

(B) any trade or business which consists of—

(i) exchanging with another such organization, names and addresses of donors to (or members of) such organization, or

(ii) renting such names and addresses to another such organization.

(2) LOW COST ARTICLE DEFINED.—For purposes of this subsection—

(A) IN GENERAL.—The term "low cost article" means any article which has a cost not in excess of $5 to the organization which distributes such item (or on whose behalf such item is distributed).

(B) AGGREGATION RULE.—If more than 1 item is distributed by or on behalf of an organization to a single distributee in any calendar year, the aggregate of the items so distributed in such calendar year to such distributee shall be treated as 1 article for purposes of subparagraph (A).

(C) INDEXATION OF $5 AMOUNT.—In the case of any taxable year beginning in a calendar year after 1987, the $5 amount in subparagraph (A) shall be increased by an amount equal to—

(i) $5, multiplied by

(ii) the cost-of-living adjustment determined under section 1(f)(3) for the calendar year in which the taxable year begins by substituting "calendar year 1987" for "calendar year 1992" in subparagraph (B) thereof.

(3) DISTRIBUTION WHICH IS INCIDENTAL TO THE SOLICITATION OF CHARITABLE CONTRIBUTIONS DESCRIBED.—For purposes of this subsection, any distribution of low cost articles by an organization shall be treated as a distribution incidental to the solicitation of charitable contributions only if—

(A) such distribution is not made at the request of the distributee,

(B) such distribution is made without the express consent of the distributee, and

(C) the articles so distributed are accompanied by—

(i) a request for a charitable contribution (as defined in section 170(c)) by the distributee to such organization, and

(ii) a statement that the distributee may retain the low cost article regardless of whether such distributee makes a charitable contribution to such organization.

Amendments

• 1993, Omnibus Budget Reconciliation Act of 1993 (P.L. 103-66)

P.L. 103-66, §13201(b)(3)(H):

Amended Code Sec. 513(h)(2)(C)(ii) by striking "1989" and inserting "1992". **Effective** for tax years beginning after 12-31-92.

• 1990, Omnibus Budget Reconciliation Act of 1990 (P.L. 101-508)

P.L. 101-508, §11101(d)(1)(G):

Amended Code Sec. 513(h)(2)(C)(ii) by inserting ", by substituting `calendar year 1987' for `calendar year 1989' in subparagraph (B) thereof" before the period at the end. **Effective** for tax years beginning after 12-31-90.

• 1986, Tax Reform Act of 1986 (P.L. 99-514)

P.L. 99-514, §1601(a):

Amended Code Sec. 513 by adding at the end thereof new subsection (h). **Effective** for distributions of low cost articles and exchanges and rentals of member lists after 10-22-86.

[Sec. 513(i)]

(i) TREATMENT OF CERTAIN SPONSORSHIP PAYMENTS.—

(1) IN GENERAL.—The term "unrelated trade or business" does not include the activity of soliciting and receiving qualified sponsorship payments.

(2) QUALIFIED SPONSORSHIP PAYMENTS.—For purposes of this subsection—

(A) IN GENERAL.—The term "qualified sponsorship payment" means any payment made by any person engaged in a trade or business with respect to which there is no arrangement or expectation that such person will receive any substantial return benefit other than the use or acknowledgement of the name or logo (or product lines) of such person's trade or business in connection with the activities of the organization that receives such payment. Such a use or acknowledgement does not include advertising such person's products or services (including messages containing qualitative or comparative language, price information, or other indications of savings or value, an endorsement, or an inducement to purchase, sell, or use such products or services).

(B) LIMITATIONS.—

(i) CONTINGENT PAYMENTS.—The term "qualified sponsorship payment" does not include any payment if the amount of such payment is contingent upon the level of attendance at one or more events, broadcast ratings, or other factors indicating the degree of public exposure to one or more events.

(ii) SAFE HARBOR DOES NOT APPLY TO PERIODICALS AND QUALIFIED CONVENTION AND TRADE SHOW ACTIVITIES.—The term "qualified sponsorship payment" does not include—

(I) any payment which entitles the payor to the use or acknowledgement of the name or logo (or product lines) of the payor's trade or business in regularly scheduled and printed material published by or on behalf of the payee organization that is not related to and primarily distributed in connection with a specific event conducted by the payee organization, or

(II) any payment made in connection with any qualified convention or trade show activity (as defined in subsection (d)(3)(B)).

(3) ALLOCATION OF PORTIONS OF SINGLE PAYMENT.—For purposes of this subsection, to the extent that a portion of a payment would (if made as a separate payment) be a qualified sponsorship payment, such portion of such payment and the other portion of such payment shall be treated as separate payments.

Amendments

• 1997, Taxpayer Relief Act of 1997 (P.L. 105-34)

P.L. 105-34, §965(a):

Amended Code Sec. 513 by adding at the end thereof a new subsection (i). **Effective** for payments solicited or received after 12-31-97.

[Sec. 513(j)]

(j) DEBT MANAGEMENT PLAN SERVICES.—The term "unrelated trade or business" includes the provision of debt management plan services (as defined in section 501(q)(4)(B)) by any organization other than an organization which meets the requirements of section 501(q).

Amendments

• 2006, Pension Protection Act of 2006 (P.L. 109-280)

P.L. 109-280, §1220(b):

Amended Code Sec. 513 by adding at the end a new subsection (j). **Effective** generally for tax years beginning after 8-17-2006. For a transition rule, see Act Sec. 1220(c)(2), below.

P.L. 109-280, §1220(c)(2), provides:

(2) TRANSITION RULE FOR EXISTING ORGANIZATIONS.—In the case of any organization described in paragraph (3) or (4) [of]section 501(c) of the Internal Revenue Code of 1986 and

with respect to which the provision of credit counseling services is a substantial purpose on the date of the enactment of this Act, the amendments made by this section shall apply to taxable years beginning after the date which is 1 year after the date of the enactment of this Act.

[Sec. 514]

SEC. 514. UNRELATED DEBT-FINANCED INCOME.

[Sec. 514(a)]

(a) UNRELATED DEBT-FINANCED INCOME AND DEDUCTIONS.—In computing under section 512 the unrelated business taxable income for any taxable year—

(1) PERCENTAGE OF INCOME TAKEN INTO ACCOUNT.—There shall be included with respect to each debt-financed property as an item of gross income derived from an unrelated trade or business an amount which is the same percentage (but not in excess of 100 percent) of the total gross income derived during the taxable year from or on account of such property as (A) the average acquisition indebtedness (as defined in subsection (c)(7)) for the taxable year with respect to the property is of (B) the average amount (determined under regulations prescribed by the Secretary) of the adjusted basis of such property during the period it is held by the organization during such taxable year.

(2) PERCENTAGE OF DEDUCTIONS TAKEN INTO ACCOUNT.—There shall be allowed as a deduction with respect to each debt-financed property an amount determined by applying (except as provided in the last sentence of this paragraph) the percentage derived under paragraph (1) to the sum determined under paragraph (3). The percentage derived under this paragraph shall not be applied with respect to the deduction of any capital loss resulting from the carryback or carryover of net capital losses under section 1212.

(3) DEDUCTIONS ALLOWABLE.—The sum referred to in paragraph (2) is the sum of the deductions under this chapter which are directly connected with the debt-financed property or the income therefrom, except that if the debt-financed property is of a character which is subject to the allowance for depreciation provided in section 167, the allowance shall be computed only by use of the straight-line method.

Amendments

• 1976, Tax Reform Act of 1976 (P.L. 94-455)

P.L. 94-455, §1906(b)(13)(A):

Amended 1954 Code by substituting "Secretary" for "Secretary or his delegate" each place it appeared. **Effective** 2-1-77.

• 1969, Tax Reform Act of 1969 (P.L. 91-172)

P.L. 91-172, §121(d)(1):

Amended Code Sec. 514(a). **Effective** 1-1-70. Prior to amendment, the title of Code Sec. 514 and Sec. 514(a) read as follows:

SEC. 514. BUSINESS LEASES.

(a) Business Lease Rents and Deductions.—In computing under section 512 the unrelated business taxable income for any taxable year—

(1) Percentage of rents taken into account.—There shall be included with respect to each business lease, as an item of gross income derived from an unrelated trade or business, an amount which is the same percentage (but not in excess of 100 percent) of the total rents derived during the taxable year under such lease as (A) the business lease indebtedness, at the close of the taxable year, with respect to the premises covered by such lease is of (B) the adjusted basis, at the close of the taxable year, of such premises.

(2) Percentage of deductions taken into account.—There shall be allowed with respect to each business lease, as a deduction to be taken into account in computing unrelated business taxable income, an amount determined by applying the percentage derived under paragraph (1) to the sum determined under paragraph (3).

(3) Deductions allowable.—The sum referred to in paragraph (2) is the sum of the following deductions allowable under this chapter:

(A) Taxes and other expenses paid or accrued during the taxable year on or with respect to the real property subject to the business lease.

(B) Interest paid or accrued during the taxable year on the business lease indebtedness.

(C) A reasonable allowance for exhaustion, wear and tear (including a reasonable allowance for obsolescence) of the real property subject to such lease.

Where only a portion of the real property is subject to the business lease, there shall be taken into account under subparagraphs (A), (B), and (C) only those amounts which are properly allocable to the premises covered by such lease.

[Sec. 514(b)]

(b) DEFINITION OF DEBT-FINANCED PROPERTY.—

(1) IN GENERAL.—For purposes of this section, the term "debt-financed property" means any property which is held to produce income and with respect to which there is an acquisition indebtedness (as defined in subsection (c)) at any time during the taxable year (or, if the property was disposed of during the taxable year, with respect to which there was an acquisition indebtedness at any time during the 12-month period ending with the date of such disposition), except that such term does not include—

(A)(i) any property substantially all the use of which is substantially related (aside from the need of the organization for income or funds) to the exercise or performance by such organization of its charitable, educational, or other purpose or function constituting the basis for its exemption under section 501 (or, in the case of an organization described in section 511(a)(2)(B), to the exercise or performance of any purpose or function designated in section 501(c)(3)), or (ii) any property to which clause (i) does not apply, to the extent that its use is so substantially related;

(B) except in the case of income excluded under section 512(b)(5), any property to the extent that the income from such property is taken into account in computing the gross income of any unrelated trade or business;

(C) any property to the extent that the income from such property is excluded by reason of the provisions of paragraph (7), (8), or (9) of section 512(b) in computing the gross income of any unrelated trade or business;

(D) any property to the extent that it is used in any trade or business described in paragraph (1), (2), or (3) of section 513(a); or

(E) any property the gain or loss from the sale, exchange, or other disposition of which would be excluded by reason of the provisions of section 512(b)(19) in computing the gross income of any unrelated trade or business.

For purposes of subparagraph (A), substantially all the use of a property shall be considered to be substantially related to the exercise or performance by an organization of its charitable, educational, or other purpose or function constituting the basis for its exemption under section 501 if such property is real property subject to a lease to a medical clinic entered into primarily for purposes which are substantially related (aside from the need of such organization for income or funds or the use it makes of the rents derived) to the exercise or performance by such organization of its charitable, educational, or other purpose or function constituting the basis for its exemption under section 501.

(2) SPECIAL RULE FOR RELATED USES.—For purposes of applying paragraphs (1)(A), (C), and (D), the use of any property by an exempt organization which is related to an organization shall be treated as use by such organization.

(3) SPECIAL RULES WHEN LAND IS ACQUIRED FOR EXEMPT USE WITHIN 10 YEARS.—

(A) NEIGHBORHOOD LAND.—If an organization acquires real property for the principal purpose of using the land (commencing within 10 years of the time of acquisition) in the manner described in paragraph (1)(A) and at the time of acquisition the property is in the neighborhood of other property owned by the organization which is used in such manner, the real property acquired for such future use shall not be treated as debt-financed property so long as the organization does not abandon its intent to so use the land within the 10-year period. The preceding sentence shall not apply for any period after the expiration of the 10-year period, and shall apply after the first 5 years of the 10-year period only if the organization establishes to the satisfaction of the Secretary that it is reasonably certain that the land will be used in the described manner before the expiration of the 10-year period.

(B) OTHER CASES.—If the first sentence of subparagraph (A) is inapplicable only because—

(i) the acquired land is not in the neighborhood referred to in subparagraph (A), or

(ii) the organization (for the period after the first 5 years of the 10-year period) is unable to establish to the satisfaction of the Secretary that it is reasonably certain that the land will be used in the manner described in paragraph (1)(A) before the expiration of the 10-year period,

but the land is converted to such use by the organization within the 10-year period, the real property (subject to the provisions of subparagraph (D)) shall not be treated as debt-financed property for any period before such conversion. For purposes of this subparagraph, land shall not be treated as used in the manner described in paragraph (1)(A) by reason of the use made of any structure which was on the land when acquired by the organization.

(C) LIMITATIONS.—Subparagraphs (A) and (B)—

(i) shall apply with respect to any structure on the land when acquired by the organization, or to the land occupied by the structure, only if (and so long as) the intended future use of the land in the manner described in paragraph (1)(A) requires that the structure be demolished or removed in order to use the land in such manner;

(ii) shall not apply to structures erected on the land after the acquisition of the land; and

(iii) shall not apply to property subject to a lease which is a business lease (as defined in this section immediately before the enactment of the Tax Reform Act of 1976).

(D) REFUND OF TAXES WHEN SUBPARAGRAPH(b) APPLIES.—If an organization for any taxable year has not used land in the manner to satisfy the actual use condition of subparagraph (B) before the time prescribed by law (including extensions thereof) for filing the return for such taxable year, the tax for such year shall be computed without regard to the application of subparagraph (B), but if and when such use condition is satisfied, the provisions of subparagraph (B) shall then be applied to such taxable year. If the actual use condition of subparagraph (B) is satisfied for any taxable year after such time for filing the return, and if credit or refund of any overpayment for the taxable year resulting from the satisfaction of such use condition is prevented at the close of the taxable year in which the use condition is satisfied, by the operation of any law or rule of law (other than chapter 74, relating to closing agreements and compromises), credit or refund of such overpayment may nevertheless be allowed or made if claim therefor is filed before the expiration of 1 year after the close of the taxable year in which the use condition is satisfied.

(E) SPECIAL RULE FOR CHURCHES.—In applying this paragraph to a church or convention or association of churches, in lieu of the 10-year period referred to in subparagraphs (A) and

(B) a 15-year period shall be applied, and subparagraphs (A) and (B)(ii) shall apply whether or not the acquired land meets the neighborhood test.

Amendments

• 2005, Gulf Opportunity Zone Act of 2005 (P.L. 109-135)

P.L. 109-135, §412(ee)(2):

Amended Code Sec. 514(b)(1)(E) by striking "section 512(b)(18)" and inserting "section 512(b)(19)". **Effective** 12-21-2005.

• 2004, American Jobs Creation Act of 2004 (P.L. 108-357)

P.L. 108-357, §702(b):

Amended Code Sec. 514(b)(1) by striking "or" at the end of subparagraph (C), by striking the period at the end of subparagraph (D) and inserting "; or", and by inserting after subparagraph (D) a new subparagraph (E). **Effective** for any gain or loss on the sale, exchange, or other disposition of any property acquired by the taxpayer after 12-31-2004. For a special rule, see Act Sec. 702(c), below.

P.L. 108-357, §702(c), provides:

(c) SAVINGS CLAUSE.—Nothing in the amendments made by this section shall affect any duty, liability, or other requirement imposed under any other Federal or State law. Notwithstanding section 128(b) of the Comprehensive Environmental Response, Compensation, and Liability Act of 1980, a certification provided by the Environmental Protection Agency or an appropriate State agency (within the meaning of section 198(c)(4) of the Internal Revenue Code of 1986) shall not affect the liability of any person under section 107(a) of such Act.

• 1976, Tax Reform Act of 1976 (P.L. 94-455)

P.L. 94-455, §1901(a)(72)(C):

Amended Code Sec. 514(b)(3)(C)(iii). **Effective** for tax years beginning after 12-31-76. Prior to amendment, Sec. 514(b)(3)(C)(iii) read as follows:

(iii) shall not apply to property subject to a lease which is a business lease (as defined in subsection (f)).

P.L. 94-455, §1906(b)(13)(A):

Amended 1954 Code by substituting "Secretary" for "Secretary or his delegate" each place it appeared. **Effective** 2-1-77.

• 1975 (P.L. 93-625)

P.L. 93-625, §7(b)(2):

Deleted the following from the end of Code Sec. 514(b)(3)(D): "Interest on any overpayment for a taxable year resulting from the application of subparagraph (B) after the actual use condition is satisfied shall be allowed and paid at the rate of 4 percent per annum in lieu of 6 percent per annum." **Effective** 7-1-75.

• 1969, Tax Reform Act of 1969 (P.L. 91-172)

P.L. 91-172, §121(d)(1):

Added Code Sec. 514(b). **Effective** 1-1-70.

[Sec. 514(c)]

(c) ACQUISITION INDEBTEDNESS.—

(1) GENERAL RULE.—For purposes of this section, the term "acquisition indebtedness" means, with respect to any debt-financed property, the unpaid amount of—

(A) the indebtedness incurred by the organization in acquiring or improving such property;

(B) the indebtedness incurred before the acquisition or improvement of such property if such indebtedness would not have been incurred but for such acquisition or improvement; and

(C) the indebtedness incurred after the acquisition or improvement of such property if such indebtedness would not have been incurred but for such acquisition or improvement and the incurrence of such indebtedness was reasonably foreseeable at the time of such acquisition or improvement.

(2) PROPERTY ACQUIRED SUBJECT TO MORTGAGE, ETC.—For purposes of this subsection—

(A) GENERAL RULE.—Where property (no matter how acquired) is acquired subject to a mortgage or other similar lien, the amount of the indebtedness secured by such mortgage or lien shall be considered as an indebtedness of the organization incurred in acquiring such property even though the organization did not assume or agree to pay such indebtedness.

(B) EXCEPTIONS.—Where property subject to a mortgage is acquired by an organization by bequest or devise, the indebtedness secured by the mortgage shall not be treated as acquisition indebtedness during a period of 10 years following the date of the acquisition. If an organization acquires property by gift subject to a mortgage which was placed on the property more than 5 years before the gift, which property was held by the donor more than 5 years before the gift, the indebtedness secured by such mortgage shall not be treated as acquisition indebtedness during a period of 10 years following the date of such gift. This subparagraph shall not apply if the organization, in order to acquire the equity in the property by bequest, devise, or gift, assumes and agrees to pay the indebtedness secured by the mortgage, or if the organization makes any payment for the equity in the property owned by the decedent or the donor.

(C) LIENS FOR TAXES OR ASSESSMENTS.—Where State law provides that—

(i) a lien for taxes, or

(ii) a lien for assessments,

made by a State or a political subdivision thereof attaches to property prior to the time when such taxes or assessments become due and payable, then such lien shall be treated as similar to a mortgage (within the meaning of subparagraph (A)) but only after such taxes or assessments become due and payable and the organization has had an opportunity to pay such taxes or assessments in accordance with State law.

(3) EXTENSION OF OBLIGATIONS.—For purposes of this section, an extension, renewal, or refinancing of an obligation evidencing a pre-existing indebtedness shall not be treated as the creation of a new indebtedness.

(4) INDEBTEDNESS INCURRED IN PERFORMING EXEMPT PURPOSE.—For purposes of this section, the term "acquisition indebtedness" does not include indebtedness the incurrence of which is inherent in the performance or exercise of the purpose or function constituting the basis of the organization's exemption, such as the indebtedness incurred by a credit union described in section 501(c)(14) in accepting deposits from its members.

(5) ANNUITIES.—For purposes of this section, the term "acquisition indebtedness" does not include an obligation to pay an annuity which—

(A) is the sole consideration (other than a mortgage to which paragraph (2)(B) applies) issued in exchange for property if, at the time of the exchange, the value of the annuity is less than 90 percent of the value of the property received in the exchange,

(B) is payable over the life of one individual in being at the time the annuity is issued, or over the lives of two individuals in being at such time, and

(C) is payable under a contract which—

(i) does not guarantee a minimum amount of payments or specify a maximum amount of payments, and

(ii) does not provide for any adjustment of the amount of the annuity payments by reference to the income received from the transferred property or any other property.

(6) CERTAIN FEDERAL FINANCING.—

(A) IN GENERAL.—For purposes of this section, the term "acquisition indebtedness" does not include—

(i) an obligation, to the extent that it is insured by the Federal Housing Administration, to finance the purchase, rehabilitation, or construction of housing for low and moderate income persons, or

(ii) indebtedness incurred by a small business investment company licensed after the date of the enactment of the American Jobs Creation Act of 2004 under the Small Business Investment Act of 1958 if such indebtedness is evidenced by a debenture—

(I) issued by such company under section 303(a) of such Act, and

(II) held or guaranteed by the Small Business Administration.

(B) LIMITATION.—Subparagraph (A)(ii) shall not apply with respect to any small business investment company during any period that—

(i) any organization which is exempt from tax under this title (other than a governmental unit) owns more than 25 percent of the capital or profits interest in such company, or

(ii) organizations which are exempt from tax under this title (including governmental units other than any agency or instrumentality of the United States) own, in the aggregate, 50 percent or more of the capital or profits interest in such company.

(7) AVERAGE ACQUISITION INDEBTEDNESS.—For purposes of this section, the term "average acquisition indebtedness" for any taxable year with respect to a debt-financed property means the average amount, determined under regulations prescribed by the Secretary, of the acquisition indebtedness during the period the property is held by the organization during the taxable year, except that for the purpose of computing the percentage of any gain or loss to be taken into account on a sale or other disposition of debt-financed property, such term means the highest amount of the acquisition indebtedness with respect to such property during the 12-month period ending with the date of the sale or other disposition.

(8) SECURITIES SUBJECT TO LOANS.—For purposes of this section—

(A) payments with respect to securities loans (as defined in section 512(a)(5)) shall be deemed to be derived from the securities loaned and not from collateral security or the investment of collateral security from such loans,

(B) any deductions which are directly connected with collateral security for such loan, or with the investment of collateral security, shall be deemed to be deductions which are directly connected with the securities loaned, and

(C) an obligation to return collateral security shall not be treated as acquisition indebtedness (as defined in paragraph (1)).

(9) REAL PROPERTY ACQUIRED BY A QUALIFIED ORGANIZATION.—

(A) IN GENERAL.—Except as provided in subparagraph (B), the term "acquisition indebtedness" does not, for purposes of this section, include indebtedness incurred by a qualified organization in acquiring or improving any real property. For purposes of this paragraph, an interest in a mortgage shall in no event be treated as real property.

(B) EXCEPTIONS.—The provisions of subparagraph (A) shall not apply in any case in which—

(i) the price for the acquisition or improvement is not a fixed amount determined as of the date of the acquisition or the completion of the improvement;

(ii) the amount of any indebtedness or any other amount payable with respect to such indebtedness, or the time for making any payment of any such amount, is dependent, in whole or in part, upon any revenue, income, or profits derived from such real property;

(iii) the real property is at any time after the acquisition leased by the qualified organization to the person selling such property to such organization or to any person who bears a relationship described in section 267(b) or 707(b) to such person;

(iv) the real property is acquired by a qualified trust from, or is at any time after the acquisition leased by such trust to, any person who—

(I) bears a relationship which is described in subparagraph (C), (E), or (G) of section 4975(e)(2) to any plan with respect to which such trust was formed, or

(II) bears a relationship which is described in subparagraph (F) or (H) of section 4975(e)(2) to any person described in subclause (I);

(v) any person described in clause (iii) or (iv) provides the qualified organization with financing in connection with the acquisition or improvement; or

(vi) the real property is held by a partnership unless the partnership meets the requirements of clauses (i) through (v) and unless—

(I) all of the partners of the partnership are qualified organizations,

(II) each allocation to a partner of the partnership which is a qualified organization is a qualified allocation (within the meaning of section 168(h)(6)), or

(III) such partnership meets the requirements of subparagraph (E).

For purposes of subclause (I) of clause (vi), an organization shall not be treated as a qualified organization if any income of such organization is unrelated business income.

(C) QUALIFIED ORGANIZATION.—For purposes of this paragraph, the term "qualified organization" means—

(i) an organization described in section 170(b)(1)(A)(ii) and its affiliated support organizations described in section 509(a)(3);

(ii) any trust which constitutes a qualified trust under section 401;

(iii) an organization described in section 501(c)(25); or

(iv) a retirement income account described in section 403(b)(9).

(D) OTHER PASS-THRU ENTITIES; TIERED ENTITIES.—Rules similar to the rules of subparagraph (B)(vi) shall also apply in the case of any pass-thru entity other than a partnership and in the case of tiered partnerships and other entities.

(E) CERTAIN ALLOCATIONS PERMITTED.—

(i) IN GENERAL.—A partnership meets the requirements of this subparagraph if—

(I) the allocation of items to any partner which is a qualified organization cannot result in such partner having a share of the overall partnership income for any taxable year greater than such partner's share of the overall partnership loss for the taxable year for which such partner's loss share will be the smallest, and

(II) each allocation with respect to the partnership has substantial economic effect within the meaning of section 704(b)(2).

For purposes of this clause, items allocated under section 704(c) shall not be taken into account.

(ii) SPECIAL RULES.—

(I) CHARGEBACKS.—Except as provided in regulations, a partnership may without violating the requirements of this subparagraph provide for chargebacks with respect to disproportionate losses previously allocated to qualified organizations and disproportionate income previously allocated to other partners. Any chargeback referred to in the preceding sentence shall not be at a ratio in excess of the ratio under which the loss or income (as the case may be) was allocated.

(II) PREFERRED RATES OF RETURN, ETC.—To the extent provided in regulations, a partnership may without violating the requirements of this subparagraph provide for reasonable preferred returns or reasonable guaranteed payments.

(iii) REGULATIONS.—The Secretary shall prescribe such regulations as may be necessary to carry out the purposes of this subparagraph, including regulations which may provide for exclusion or segregation of items.

(F) SPECIAL RULES FOR ORGANIZATIONS DESCRIBED IN SECTION 501(c)(25).—

(i) IN GENERAL.—In computing under section 512 the unrelated business taxable income of a disqualified holder of an interest in an organization described in section 501(c)(25), there shall be taken into account—

(I) as gross income derived from an unrelated trade or business, such holder's pro rata share of the items of income described in clause (ii)(I) of such organization, and

(II) as deductions allowable in computing unrelated business taxable income, such holder's pro rata share of the items of deduction described in clause (ii)(II) of such organization.

Such amounts shall be taken into account for the taxable year of the holder in which (or with which) the taxable year of such organization ends.

(ii) DESCRIPTION OF AMOUNTS.—For purposes of clause (i)—

(I) gross income is described in this clause to the extent such income would (but for this paragraph) be treated under subsection (a) as derived from an unrelated trade or business, and

(II) any deduction is described in this clause to the extent it would (but for this paragraph) be allowable under subsection (a)(2) in computing unrelated business taxable income.

(iii) DISQUALIFIED HOLDER.—For purposes of this subparagraph, the term "disqualified holder" means any shareholder (or beneficiary) which is not described in clause (i) or (II) of subparagraph (C).

(G) SPECIAL RULES FOR PURPOSES OF THE EXCEPTIONS.—Except as otherwise provided by regulations—

(i) SMALL LEASES DISREGARDED.—For purposes of clauses (iii) and (iv) of subparagraph (B), a lease to a person described in such clause (iii) or (iv) shall be disregarded if no more than 25 percent of the leasable floor space in a building (or complex of buildings) is covered by the lease and if the lease is on commercially reasonable terms.

(ii) COMMERCIALLY REASONABLE FINANCING.—Clause (v) of subparagraph (B) shall not apply if the financing is on commercially reasonable terms.

(H) QUALIFYING SALES BY FINANCIAL INSTITUTIONS.—

(i) IN GENERAL.—In the case of a qualifying sale by a financial institution, except as provided in regulations, clauses (i) and (ii) of subparagraph (B) shall not apply with respect to financing provided by such institution for such sale.

(ii) QUALIFYING SALE.—For purposes of this clause, there is a qualifying sale by a financial institution if—

(I) a qualified organization acquires property described in clause (iii) from a financial institution and any gain recognized by the financial institution with respect to the property is ordinary income,

(II) the stated principal amount of the financing provided by the financial institution does not exceed the amount of the outstanding indebtedness (including accrued but unpaid interest) of the financial institution with respect to the property described in clause (iii) immediately before the acquisition referred to in clause (iii) or (v), whichever is applicable, and

(III) the present value (determined as of the time of the sale and by using the applicable Federal rate determined under section 1274(d)) of the maximum amount payable pursuant to the financing that is determined by reference to the revenue, income, or profits derived from the property cannot exceed 30 percent of the total purchase price of the property (including the contingent payments).

(iii) PROPERTY TO WHICH SUBPARAGRAPH APPLIES.—Property is described in this clause if such property is foreclosure property, or is real property which—

(I) was acquired by the qualified organization from a financial institution which is in conservatorship or receivership, or from the conservator or receiver of such an institution, and

(II) was held by the financial institution at the time it entered into conservatorship or receivership.

(iv) FINANCIAL INSTITUTION.—For purposes of this subparagraph, the term "financial institution" means—

(I) any financial institution described in section 581 or 591(a),

(II) any other corporation which is a direct or indirect subsidiary of an institution referred to in subclause (I) but only if, by virtue of being affiliated with such institution, such other corporation is subject to supervision and examination by a Federal or State agency which regulates institutions referred to in subclause (I), and

(III) any person acting as a conservator or receiver of an entity referred to in subclause (I) or (II) (or any government agency or corporation succeeding to the rights or interest of such person).

(v) FORECLOSURE PROPERTY.—For purposes of this subparagraph, the term "foreclosure property" means any real property acquired by the financial institution as the result of having bid on such property at foreclosure, or by operation of an agreement or process of law, after there was a default (or a default was imminent) on indebtedness which such property secured.

Amendments

• 2006, Pension Protection Act of 2006 (P.L. 109-280)

P.L. 109-280, §866(a):

Amended Code Sec. 514(c)(9)(C) by striking "or" after clause (ii), by striking the period at the end of clause (iii) and inserting "; or", and by inserting after clause (iii) a new clause (iv). **Effective** for tax years beginning on or after 8-17-2006.

• 2004, American Jobs Creation Act of 2004 (P.L. 108-357)

P.L. 108-357, §247(a):

Amended Code Sec. 514(c)(6). **Effective** for indebtedness incurred after 10-22-2004 by a small business investment company licensed after 10-22-2004. Prior to amendment, Code Sec. 514(c)(6) read as follows:

(6) CERTAIN FEDERAL FINANCING.—For purposes of this section, the term "acquisition indebtedness" does not include an obligation, to the extent that it is insured by the Federal Housing Administration, to finance the purchase, rehabilitation, or construction of housing for low and moderate income persons.

• 1993, Omnibus Budget Reconciliation Act of 1993 (P.L. 103-66)

P.L. 103-66, §13144(a):

Amended Code Sec. 514(c)(9) by adding at the end thereof new subparagraphs (G) and (H). **Effective**, generally, for acquisitions on or after 1-1-94. For a special rule, see Act Sec. 13144(c)(2) below.

P.L. 103-66, §13144(b)(1)-(2):

Amended Code Sec. 514(c)(9) by adding at the end of subparagraph (A) a new sentence, and by striking the last sentence of subparagraph (B). **Effective**, generally, for acquisitions on or after 1-1-94. For a special rule, see Act Sec. 13144(c)(2) below. Prior to amendment, the last sentence of Code Sec. 514(c)(9)(B) read as follows:

For purposes of this paragraph, an interest in a mortgage shall in no event be treated as real property.

P.L. 103-66, §13144(c)(2), provides:

(2) SMALL LEASES.—The provisions of section 514(c)(9)(G)(i) of the Internal Revenue Code of 1986 shall, in addition to any leases to which the provisions apply by reason of paragraph (1), apply to leases entered into on or after January 1, 1994.

• 1989, Omnibus Budget Reconciliation Act of 1989 (P.L. 101-239)

P.L. 101-239, §7811(l):

Amended Code Sec. 514(c)(9) by redesignating subparagraph (E), as added by section 1016 of P.L. 100-647, as subparagraph (F). **Effective** as if included in the provision of P.L. 100-647 to which it relates.

• 1988, Technical and Miscellaneous Revenue Act of 1988 (P.L. 100-647)

P.L. 100-647, §1016(a)(5)(A):

Amended Code Sec. 514(c)(9) by adding at the end thereof new subparagraph (E)[F]. **Effective** with respect to interests in the organization acquired after 6-10-87, except that it shall not apply to any such interest acquired after 6-10-87, pursuant to a binding written contract in effect on 6-10-87, and at all times thereafter before such acquisition.

P.L. 100-647, §1016(a)(6):

Amended Code Sec. 514(c)(9)(B) by striking out "clause (vi)" in the last sentence and inserting in lieu thereof "this paragraph". **Effective** as if included in the provision of P.L. 99-514 to which it relates.

P.L. 100-647, §2004(h)(1):

Amended Code Sec. 514(c)(9)(E) by adding at the end thereof a new clause (iii). **Effective** as if included in the provision of P.L. 100-203 to which it relates.

P.L. 100-647, §2004(h)(2):

Amended Code Sec. 514(c)(9)(E)(i) by striking out subclause (I) and by redesignating subclauses (II) and (III) as subclauses (I) and (II), respectively. **Effective** as if included in the provision of P.L. 100-203 to which it relates. Prior to amendment, Code Sec. 514(c)(9)(E)(I) read as follows:

(I) the allocation of items to any partner other than a qualified organization cannot result in such partner having a share of the overall partnership loss for any taxable year greater than such partner's share of the overall partnership income for the taxable year for which such partner's income share will be the smallest,

• 1987, Revenue Act of 1987 (P.L. 100-203)

P.L. 100-203, §10214(a):

Amended Code Sec. 514(c)(9)(B)(vi). **Effective** for property acquired by the partnership after 10-13-87, and partnership interests acquired after 10-13-87, except that the amendments do not apply in the case of any property (or partnership interest) acquired pursuant to a written binding contract in effect on 10-13-87, and at all times thereafter before such property (or interest) is acquired. Prior to amendment, Code Sec. 514(c)(9)(B)(vi) read as follows:

(vi) the real property is held by a partnership (which does not fail to meet the requirements of clauses (i) through (v)), and—

(I) any partner of the partnership is not a qualified organization, and

(II) the principal purpose of any allocation to any partner of the partnership which is a qualified organization which is not a qualified allocation (within the meaning of section 168(h)(6)) is the avoidance of income tax.

P.L. 100-203, §10214(b):

Amended Code Sec. 514(c)(9) by adding at the end thereof new subparagraph (E). **Effective** for property acquired by the partnership after 10-13-87, and partnership interests acquired after 10-13-87, except that the amendments do not apply in the case of any property (or partnership interest) acquired pursuant to a written binding contract in effect on 10-13-87, and at all times thereafter before such property (or interest) is acquired.

• 1986, Tax Reform Act of 1986 (P.L. 99-514)

P.L. 99-514, §201(d)(9):

Amended Code Sec. 514(c)(9)(B)(vi)(II), as amended by Act Sec. 1878(e)(3), by striking out "section 168(j)(9)" and inserting in lieu thereof "section 168(h)(6)". **Effective**, generally, for property placed in service after 12-31-86, in tax years ending after such date. See also Act Secs. 203, 204 and 251(d) reproduced in amendment notes for Code Sec. 168.

P.L. 99-514, §1603(b)(1)-(3):

Amended Code Sec. 514(c)(9)(C) by striking out "or" at the end of clause (i), by placing the period following clause (ii) with "; or", and by inserting at the end thereof new clause (iii). **Effective** for tax years beginning after 12-31-86. For a transitional rule, see Act Sec. 1607, below.

P.L. 99-514, §1607, provides:

SEC. 1607. TRANSITION RULE FOR ACQUISITION INDEBTEDNESS WITH RESPECT TO CERTAIN LAND.

For purposes of applying section 514(c) of the Internal Revenue Code of 1986, with respect to a disposition during calendar year 1986 or calendar year 1987 of land acquired during calendar year 1984, the term "acquisition indebtedness" does not include indebtedness incurred in connection with bonds issued after January 1, 1984, and before July 19, 1984, on behalf of an organization which is a community college and which is described in section 511(a)(2)(B) of such Code.

P.L. 99-514, §1878(e)(1), as amended by P.L. 100-647, §1018(u)(13)(A):

Amended Code Sec. 514(c)(9)(B) as amended by Act Sec. 1878(e)(3) by striking out "would be unrelated business taxable income (determined without regard to this paragraph)" in the second to last sentence and inserting in lieu thereof "is unrelated business taxable income". **Effective** as if included in the provision of P.L. 98-369 to which it relates.

P.L. 99-514, §1878(e)(2):

Amended Code Sec. 514(c)(9)(C)(i) by striking out "section 509(a)" and inserting in lieu thereof "section 509(a)(3)". **Effective** as if included in the provision of P.L. 98-369 to which it relates.

P.L. 99-514, §1878(e)(3):

Amended Code Sec. 514(c)(9)(B)(vi) and the last sentence of Code Sec. 514(c)(9)(B). **Effective** as if included in the provision of P.L. 98-369 to which it relates. Prior to amendment, Code Sec. 514(c)(9)(B)(vi) and the last sentence of Code Sec. 514(c)(9)(B) read as follows:

(vi) the real property is held by a partnership unless the partnership meets the requirements of clauses (i) through (v) and unless—

(I) all of the partners of the partnership are qualified organizations, or

(II) each allocation to a partner of the partnership which is a qualified organization is a qualified allocation (within the meaning of section 168(j)(9)).

For purposes of clause (vi)(I), an organization shall not be treated as a qualified organization if any income of such organization would be unrelated business taxable income (determined without regard to this paragraph).

• 1984, Deficit Reduction Act of 1984 (P.L. 98-369)

P.L. 98-369, §174(b)(5)(B):

Amended Code Sec. 514(c)(9)(B)(iii) by striking out "section 267(b)" and inserting in lieu thereof "section 267(b) or 707(b)". **Effective** for transactions after 12-31-83, in tax years ending after such date.

P.L. 98-369, §1034(a):

Amended Code Sec. 514(c)(9). **Effective** for indebtedness incurred after 7-18-84. For special rules, see Act Sec. 1034(c)(2) and (3), below. Prior to amendment, Code Sec. 514(c)(9) read as follows:

(9) Real Property Acquired By Qualified Trust.—For purposes of this section—

(A) In general.—Except as provided in subparagraph (B), the term "acquisition indebtedness" does not include indebtedness incurred by a qualified trust in acquiring or improving any real property.

(B) Exceptions.—The provisions of subparagraph (A) shall not apply in any case in which—

(i) the acquisition price is not a fixed amount determined as of the date of acquisition;

(ii) the amount of any indebtedness or any other amount payable with respect to such indebtedness, or the time for making any payment of any such amount, is dependent, in whole or in part, upon any revenue, income, or profits derived from such real property;

(iii) the real property is at any time after the acquisition leased by the qualified trust to the person selling such property to such trust or to any person who bears a relationship described in section 267(b) to such person;

(iv) the real property is acquired from, or is at any time after the acquisition leased by the qualified trust to, any person who—

(I) bears a relationship which is described in section 4975(e)(2)(C), (E), or (G) to any plan with respect to which such trust was formed, or

(II) bears a relationship which is described in section 4975(e)(2)(F) or (H) to any person described in subclause (I); or

(v) any person described in clause (iii) or (iv) provides the qualified trust with nonrecourse financing in connection with such transaction and such debt—

(I) is subordinate to any other indebtedness on such property, or

(II) bears interest at a rate which is significantly less than the rate available from any person not described in clause (iii) or (iv) at the time such indebtedness is incurred.

(C) Qualified Trust.—For purposes of this paragraph, the term "qualified trust" means any trust which constitutes a qualified trust under section 401.

P.L. 98-369, §1034(c)(2)-(3), provides:

(2) Exception for Indebtedness On Certain Property Acquired Before January 1, 1985.—

(A) The amendment made by subsection (a) shall not apply to any indebtedness incurred before January 1, 1985, by a partnership described in subparagraph (B) if such indebtedness is incurred with respect to property acquired (directly or indirectly) by such partnership before such date.

(B) A partnership is described in this subparagraph if—

(i) before October 21, 1983, the partnership was organized, a request for exemption with respect to such partnership was filed with the Department of Labor, and a private placement memorandum stating the maximum number of units in the partnership that would be offered had been circulated,

(ii) the interest in the property to be acquired, directly or indirectly (including through acquiring an interest in another partnership) by such partnership was described in such private placement memorandum, and

(iii) the marketing of partnership interests in such partnership is completed not later than 2 years after the later of the date of enactment of this Act or the date of publication in the Federal Register of such exemption by the Department of Labor and the aggregate number of units in such partnership sold does not exceed the amount described in clause (i).

(3) Exception for Indebtedness on Certain Property Acquired Before January 1, 1986.—

(A) The amendment made by subsection (a) shall not apply to any indebtedness incurred before January 1, 1986, by a partnership described in subparagraph (B) if such indebtedness is incurred with respect to property acquired (directly or indirectly) by such partnership before such date.

(B) A partnership is described in this paragraph if—

(i) before March 6, 1984, the partnership was organized and publicly announced, the maximum amount of interests which would be sold in such partnership, and

(ii) the marketing of partnership interests in such partnership is completed not later than the 90th day after the date of the enactment of this Act and the aggregate amount of interests in such partnership sold does not exceed the maximum amount described in clause (i).

For purposes of clause (i), the maximum amount taken into account shall be the greatest of the amounts shown in the registration statement, prospectus, or partnership agreement.

(C) Binding Contracts.—For purposes of this paragraph, property shall be deemed to have been acquired before January 1, 1986, if such property is acquired pursuant to a written contract which, on January 1, 1986, and at all times thereafter, required the acquisition of such property and such property is placed in service not later than 6 months after the date such contract was entered into.

• 1980, Miscellaneous Revenue Act of 1980 (P.L. 96-605)

P.L. 96-605, §110(a):

Amended Code Sec. 514(c) by adding at the end thereof subsection (9). **Effective** with respect to tax years beginning after 12-31-80. However, this amendment shall not be considered a precedent with respect to extending such amendment (or similar rules) to any person.

• 1978 (P.L. 95-345)

P.L. 95-345, §2(c):

Amended Code Sec. 514(c) by adding paragraph (8). **Effective** with respect to amounts received after 12-31-76, as payments with respect to securities loans (as defined in Code Sec. 512(a)(5)), and transfers of securities under agreements described in Code Sec. 1058 occurring after such date.

• 1976, Tax Reform Act of 1976 (P.L. 94-455)

P.L. 94-455, §1901(a)(72)(A):

Amended Code Sec. 514(c)(1). **Effective** for tax years beginning after 12-31-76. Prior to amendment, Sec. 514(c)(1) read as follows:

(c) ACQUISITION INDEBTEDNESS.—

(1) GENERAL RULE.—For purposes of this section, the term "acquisition indebtedness" means, with respect to any debt-financed property, the unpaid amount of—

(A) the indebtedness incurred by the organization in acquiring or improving such property;

(B) the indebtedness incurred before the acquisition or improvement of such property if such indebtedness would not have been incurred but for such acquisition or improvement; and

(C) the indebtedness incurred after the acquisition or improvement of such property if such indebtedness would not have been incurred but for such acquisition or improvement and the incurrence of such indebtedness was reasonably foreseeable at the time of such acquisition or improvement, except that in the case of any taxable year beginning before January 1, 1972, any indebtedness incurred before June 28, 1966, shall not be taken into account. In the case of an organization (other than a church or convention or association of churches) such indebtedness incurred before June 28, 1966, shall be taken into account if such indebtedness constitutes business lease indebtedness (as defined in subsection (g)).

P.L. 94-455, §1308(a):

Added Code Sec. 514(c)(2)(C). **Effective** for tax years ending after 12-31-69.

P.L. 94-455, §1906(b)(13)(A):

Amended 1954 Code by substituting "Secretary" for "Secretary or his delegate" each place it appeared. **Effective** 2-1-77.

• 1969, Tax Reform Act of 1969 (P.L. 91-172)

P.L. 91-172, §121(d)(1):

Added Code Sec. 514(c). **Effective** 1-1-70.

[Sec. 514(d)]

(d) BASIS OF DEBT-FINANCED PROPERTY ACQUIRED IN CORPORATE LIQUIDATION.—For purposes of this subtitle, if the property was acquired in a complete or partial liquidation of a corporation in exchange for its stock, the basis of the property shall be the same as it would be in the hands of the transferor corporation, increased by the amount of gain recognized to the transferor corporation upon such distribution and by the amount of any gain to the organization which was included, on account of such distribution, in unrelated business taxable income under subsection (a).

Amendments

• 1969, Tax Reform Act of 1969 (P.L. 91-172)

P.L. 91-172, §121(d)(1):

Added Code Sec. 514(d). **Effective** 1-1-70.

[Sec. 514(e)]

(e) ALLOCATION RULES.—Where debt-financed property is held for purposes described in subsection (b)(1)(A), (B), (C), or (D) as well as for other purposes, proper allocation shall be made with respect to basis, indebtedness, and income and deductions. The allocations required by this section shall be made in accordance with regulations prescribed by the Secretary to the extent proper to carry out the purposes of this section.

Amendments

• 1976, Tax Reform Act of 1976 (P.L. 94-455)

P.L. 94-455, §1906(b)(13)(A):

Amended 1954 Code by substituting "Secretary" for "Secretary or his delegate" each place it appeared. **Effective** 2-1-77.

• 1969, Tax Reform Act of 1969 (P.L. 91-172)

P.L. 91-172, §121(d)(1):

Added Code Sec. 514(e). **Effective** 1-1-70.

[Sec. 514(f)]

(f) PERSONAL PROPERTY LEASED WITH REAL PROPERTY.—For purposes of this section, the term "real property" includes personal property of the lessor leased by it to a lessee of its real estate if the lease of such personal property is made under, or in connection with, the lease of such real estate.

Amendments

• 1976, Tax Reform Act of 1976 (P.L. 94-455)

P.L. 94-455, §1901(a)(72)(B):

Amended Code Sec. 514 by redesignating former subsection "(h)" as subsection "(f)". **Effective** for tax years beginning after 12-31-76.

P.L. 94-455, §1901(a)(72)(D):

Amended Code Sec. 514(f). **Effective** for tax years beginning after 12-31-76. Prior to amendment, Sec. 514(f) read as follows:

(f) Personal Property Leased With Real Property.—For purposes of this section, the term "real property" and the term "premises" include personal property of the lessor leased by it to a lessee of its real estate if the lease of such personal property is made under, or in connection with, the lease of such real estate.

• 1969, Tax Reform Act of 1969 (P.L. 91-172)

P.L. 91-172, §121(d)(1):

Amended Code Sec. 514 by redesignating former subsection "(d)" as subsection "(h)". **Effective** 1-1-70.

[Sec. 514(f)—Stricken]

Amendments

• 1976, Tax Reform Act of 1976 (P.L. 94-455)

P.L. 94-455, §1901(a)(72)(B):

Amended Code Sec. 514 by striking out subsection (f). **Effective** for tax years beginning after 12-31-76. Prior to being stricken, Sec. 514(f) read as follows:

(f) DEFINITION OF BUSINESS LEASE.

(1) GENERAL RULE.—For purposes of this section, the term "business lease" means a lease for a term of more than 5 years of real property by an organization (or by a partnership of which it is a member), if at the close of the lessor's taxable year there is a business lease indebtedness (as defined in subsection (g)) with respect to such property.

(2) SPECIAL RULES FOR APPLYING PARAGRAPH (1).—For purposes of paragraph (1)—

(A) In computing the term of a lease which contains an option for renewal or extension, the term of such lease shall be considered as including any period for which such option may be exercised; and the term of any lease made pursuant to an exercise of such option shall include the period during which the prior lease was in effect. If real property is acquired subject to a lease, the term of such lease shall be considered to begin on the date of such acquisition.

(B) If the property has been occupied by the same lessee for a total period of more than 5 years commencing not earlier than the date of acquisition of the property by the organization or trust (whether such occupancy is under one or more leases, renewals, extensions, or continuations thereof), the occupancy of such lessee shall be considered to be under a lease for a term of more than 5 years within the meaning of paragraph (1). However, subsection (a) shall apply in the case of a tenancy described in this subparagraph (and not within subparagraph (A)) only with respect to the sixth and succeeding years of occupancy by the same lessee. For purposes of this subparagraph, the term "same lessee" shall include any lessee of the property whose relationship with a lessee of the same property is such that losses in respect of sales or exchanges of property between the 2 lessees would be disallowed under section 267 (a).

(3) EXCEPTIONS.—

(A) No lease shall be considered a business lease if—

(i) such lease is entered into primarily for purposes which are substantially related (aside from the need of such organization for income or funds or the use it makes of the rents derived) to the exercise or performance by such organization of its charitable, educational, or other purpose or function constituting the basis for its exemption under section 501, or

(ii) the lease is of premises in a building primarily designed for occupancy, and occupied, by the organization.

(B) If a lease for more than 5 years to a tenant is for only a portion of the real property, and space in the real property is rented during the taxable year under a lease for not more than 5 years to any other tenant of the organization, leases of the real property for more than 5 years shall be considered as business leases during the taxable year only if—

(i) the rents derived from the real property during the taxable year under leases for more than 5 years (not including, as a lease for more than 5 years, an occupancy which is considered as such a lease by reason of paragraph (2) (B)) represent 50 percent or more of the total rents derived during the taxable year from the real property; or the area of the premises occupied under leases for more than 5 years (not including, as a lease for more than 5 years, an occupancy which is considered as such a lease by reason of paragraph (2) (B)) represents, at any time during the taxable year, 50 percent or more of the total area of the real property rented at such time; or

(ii) the rent derived from the real property during the taxable year from any tenant under a lease for more than 5 years (including as a lease for more than 5 years an occupancy which is considered as such a lease by reason of paragraph (2) (B)), or from a group of tenants (under such leases) who are either members of an affiliated group (as defined in section 1504) or partners, represents more than 10 percent of the total rents derived during the taxable year from such property; or the area of the premises occupied by any one such tenant, or by any such group of tenants, represents at any time during the taxable year more than 10 percent of the total area of the real property rented at such time.

In the application of clause (i), if during the last half of the term of a lease a new lease is made to take effect after the expiration of such lease, the unexpired portion of such lease on the date the second lease is made shall not be treated as a part of the term of the second lease.

• **1969, Tax Reform Act of 1969 (P.L. 91-172)**

P.L. 91-172, §121(d)(2)(A):

Amended Code Sec. 514 by redesignating former subsection "(b)" as subsection "(f)". **Effective** 1-1-70.

P.L. 91-172, §121(d)(2)(B):

Amended Code Sec. 514(f)(1) by substituting "subsection (g)" for "subsection (c)". **Effective** 1-1-70.

[Sec. 514(g)]

(g) REGULATIONS.—The Secretary shall prescribe such regulations as may be necessary or appropriate to carry out the purposes of this section, including regulations to prevent the circumvention of any provision of this section through the use of segregated asset accounts.

Amendments

• **1984, Deficit Reduction Act of 1984 (P.L. 98-369)**

P.L. 98-369, §1034(b):

Amended Code Sec. 514 by adding new subsection (g). **Effective** for indebtedness incurred after 7-18-84. Special rules appear following Code Sec. 514(c).

[Sec. 514(g)—Repealed]

Amendments

• **1976, Tax Reform Act of 1976 (P.L. 94-455)**

P.L. 94-455, §1901(a)(72)(B):

Repealed Code Sec. 514(g). **Effective** for tax years beginning after 12-31-76. Prior to repeal, Code Sec. 514(g) read as follows:

(g) BUSINESS LEASE INDEBTEDNESS.—

(1) GENERAL RULE.—The term "business lease indebtedness" means, with respect to any real property leased for a term of more than 5 years, the unpaid amount of—

(A) the indebtedness incurred by the lessor in acquiring or improving such property;

(B) the indebtedness incurred before the acquisition or improvement of such property if such indebtedness would not have been incurred but for such acquisition or improvement; and

(C) the indebtedness incurred after the acquisition or improvement of such property if such indebtedness would not have been incurred but for such acquisition or improvement and the incurrence of such indebtedness was reasonably foreseeable at the time of such acquisition or improvement.

(2) PROPERTY ACQUIRED SUBJECT TO MORTGAGE, ETC.—Where real property is acquired subject to a mortgage or other similar lien, the amount of the indebtedness secured by such mortgage or lien shall be considered (whether the acquisition was by gift, devise, or purchase) as an indebtedness of the lessor incurred in acquiring such property even though the lessor did not assume or agree to pay such indebtedness, except that where real property was acquired by gift, bequest, or devise before July 1, 1950, subject to a mortgage or other similar lien, the amount of such mortgage or other similar lien shall not be considered as an indebtedness of the lessor incurred in acquiring such property.

(3) CERTAIN PROPERTY ACQUIRED BY GIFT, ETC.—Where real property was acquired by gift, bequest, or devise before July 1, 1950, subject to a lease requiring improvements in such property on the happening of stated contingencies, indebtedness incurred in improving such property in accordance with the terms of such lease shall not be considered as an indebtedness for purposes of this subsection.

(4) CERTAIN CORPORATIONS DESCRIBED IN SECTION 501(c)(2).—In the case of a corporation described in section 501 (c) (2), all of the stock of which was acquired before July 1, 1950, by an organization described in paragraph (3), (5), or (6) of section 501 (c) (and more than one-third of such stock was acquired by such organization by gift or bequest), any indebtedness incurred by such corporation before July 1, 1950, and any indebtedness incurred by such corporation on or after such date in improving real property in accordance with the terms of a lease entered into before such date, shall not be considered as an indebtedness with respect to such corporation or such organization for purposes of this subsection.

(5) CERTAIN TRUSTS DESCRIBED IN SECTION 401(a).—In the case of a trust described in section 401(a), or in the case of a corporation described in section 501 (c) (2) all of the stock of which was acquired prior to March 1, 1954, by a trust described in section 401(a), any indebtedness incurred by such trust or such corporation before March 1, 1954, in connection with real property which is leased before March 1, 1954, and any indebtedness incurred by such trust or such corporation on or after such date necessary to carry out the terms of such lease, shall not be considered as an indebtedness with respect to such trust or such corporation for purposes of this subsection.

(6) BUSINESS LEASE ON PORTION OF PROPERTY.—In determining the amount of the business lease indebtedness where only a portion of the real property is subject to a business lease, proper allocation to the premises covered by such lease shall be made of the indebtedness incurred by the lessor with respect to the real property.

(7) SPECIAL RULE APPLICABLE TO TRUSTS DESCRIBED IN SECTION 401(a).—In the application of paragraph (1), if a trust described in section 401(a) forming part of a stock bonus, pension, or profit-sharing plan of an employer lends any money to another trust described in section 401(a) forming part of a stock bonus, pension, or profit-sharing plan of the same employer, such loan shall not be treated as an indebt-

edness of the borrowing trust, except to the extent that the loaning trust—

(A) incurs any indebtedness in order to make such loan;

(B) incurred indebtedness before the making of such loan which would not have been incurred but for the making of such loan; or

(C) incurred indebtedness after the making of such loan which would not have been incurred but for the making of such loan and which was reasonably foreseeable at the time of making such loan.

(8) TRUSTS DESCRIBED IN SECTION 501(c)(17).—

(A) In the case of a trust described in section 501(c)(17), or in the case of a corporation described in section 501(c)(2), all of the stock of which was acquired before January 1, 1960, by a trust described in section 501(c)(17), any indebtedness incurred by such trust or such corporation before January 1, 1960, in connection with real property which is leased before January 1, 1960, and any indebtedness incurred by such trust or such corporation on or after such date necessary to carry out the terms of such lease, shall not be considered as an indebtedness with respect to such trust or such corporation for purposes of this subsection.

(B) In the application of paragraph (1), if a trust described in section 501(c)(17) forming part of a supplemental unemployment compensation benefit plan lends any money to another trust described in section 501(c)(17) forming part of the same plan, such loan shall not be treated as an indebtedness of the borrowing trust, except to the extent that the loaning trust—

(i) incurs any indebtedness in order to make such loan,

(ii) incurred indebtedness before the making of such loan which would not have been incurred but for the making of such loan, or

(iii) incurred indebtedness after the making of such loan which would not have been incurred but for the making of such loan and which was reasonably foreseeable at the time of making such loan.

• 1969, Tax Reform Act of 1969 (P.L. 91-172)

P.L. 91-172, §121(d)(2)(A):

Amended Code Sec. 514 by redesignating former subsection "(c)" as subsection "(g)". **Effective** 1-1-70.

• 1960 (P.L. 86-667)

P.L. 86-667, §5:

Amended Code Sec. 514(c) by adding a new paragraph (8). **Effective** for tax years beginning after 12-31-59.

[Sec. 515]

SEC. 515. TAXES OF FOREIGN COUNTRIES AND POSSESSIONS OF THE UNITED STATES.

The amount of taxes imposed by foreign countries and possessions of the United States shall be allowed as a credit against the tax of an organization subject to the tax imposed by section 511 to the extent provided in section 901; and in the case of the tax imposed by section 511, the term "taxable income" as used in section 901 shall be read as "unrelated business taxable income".

PART IV—FARMERS' COOPERATIVES

[Sec. 521]

SEC. 521. EXEMPTION OF FARMERS' COOPERATIVES FROM TAX.

[Sec. 521(a)]

(a) EXEMPTION FROM TAX.—A farmers' cooperative organization described in subsection (b)(1) shall be exempt from taxation under this subtitle except as otherwise provided in part I of subchapter T (sec. 1381 and following). Notwithstanding part I of subchapter T (sec. 1381 and following), such an organization shall be considered an organization exempt from income taxes for purposes of any law which refers to organizations exempt from income taxes.

Amendments

• 1962, Revenue Act of 1962 (P.L. 87-834)

P.L. 87-834, §17(b):

Amended Code Sec. 521(a) by substituting "part I of subchapter T (sec. 1381 and following)" for "section 522" in both places that it appears. **Effective** for tax years beginning after 12-31-62.

[Sec. 521(b)]

(b) APPLICABLE RULES.—

(1) EXEMPT FARMERS' COOPERATIVES.—The farmers' cooperatives exempt from taxation to the extent provided in subsection (a) are farmers', fruit growers', or like associations organized and operated on a cooperative basis (A) for the purpose of marketing the products of members or other producers, and turning back to them the proceeds of sales, less the necessary marketing expenses, on the basis of either the quantity or the value of the products furnished by them, or (B) for the purpose of purchasing supplies and equipment for the use of members or other persons, and turning over such supplies and equipment to them at actual cost, plus necessary expenses.

(2) ORGANIZATIONS HAVING CAPITAL STOCK.—Exemption shall not be denied any such association because it has capital stock, if the dividend rate of such stock is fixed at not to exceed the legal rate of interest in the State of incorporation or 8 percent per annum, whichever is greater, on the value of the consideration for which the stock was issued, and if substantially all such stock (other than nonvoting preferred stock, the owners of which are not entitled or permitted to participate, directly or indirectly, in the profits of the association, upon dissolution or otherwise, beyond the fixed dividends) is owned by producers who market their products or purchase their supplies and equipment through the association.

(3) ORGANIZATIONS MAINTAINING RESERVE.—Exemption shall not be denied any such association because there is accumulated and maintained by it a reserve required by State law or a reasonable reserve for any necessary purpose.

(4) TRANSACTIONS WITH NONMEMBERS.—Exemption shall not be denied any such association which markets the products of nonmembers in an amount the value of which does not exceed the value of the products marketed for members, or which purchases supplies and equipment for nonmembers in an amount the value of which does not exceed the value of the supplies and equipment purchased for members, provided the value of the purchases made for persons who are neither members nor producers does not exceed 15 percent of the value of all its purchases.

(5) BUSINESS FOR THE UNITED STATES.—Business done for the United States or any of its agencies shall be disregarded in determining the right to exemption under this section.

(6) NETTING OF LOSSES.—Exemption shall not be denied any such association because such association computes its net earnings for purposes of determining any amount available for distribution to patrons in the manner described in paragraph (1) of section 1388(j).

(7) CROSS REFERENCE.—

For treatment of value-added processing involving animals, see section 1388(k).

Amendments

• 2004, American Jobs Creation Act of 2004 (P.L. 108-357)

P.L. 108-357, §316(b):

Amended Code Sec. 521(b) by adding at the end a new paragraph (7). **Effective** for tax years beginning after 10-22-2004.

• 1986, Consolidated Omnibus Budget Reconciliation Act of 1985 (P.L. 99-272)

P.L. 99-272, §13210(b):

Amended Code Sec. 521(b) by adding at the end thereof new paragraph (6). **Effective** for tax years beginning after 12-31-62.

P.L. 99-272, §13210(c)(3), provides:

(3) NO INFERENCE.—Nothing in the amendments made by this section shall be construed to infer that a change in law is intended as to whether any patronage earnings may or not be offset by nonpatronage losses, and any determination of such issue shall be made as if such amendments had not been enacted.

PART V—SHIPOWNERS' PROTECTION AND INDEMNITY ASSOCIATIONS

[Sec. 526]

SEC. 526. SHIPOWNERS' PROTECTION AND INDEMNITY ASSOCIATIONS.

There shall not be included in gross income the receipts of shipowners' mutual protection and indemnity associations not organized for profit, and no part of the net earnings of which inures to the benefit of any private shareholder; but such corporations shall be subject as other persons to the tax on their taxable income from interest, dividends, and rents.

PART VI—POLITICAL ORGANIZATIONS

[Sec. 527]

SEC. 527. POLITICAL ORGANIZATIONS.

[Sec. 527(a)]

(a) GENERAL RULE.—A political organization shall be subject to taxation under this subtitle only to the extent provided in this section. A political organization shall be considered an organization exempt from income taxes for the purpose of any law which refers to organizations exempt from income taxes.

[Sec. 527(b)]

(b) TAX IMPOSED.—

(1) IN GENERAL.—A tax is hereby imposed for each taxable year on the political organization taxable income of every political organization. Such tax shall be computed by multiplying the political organization taxable income by the highest rate of tax specified in section 11(b).

(2) ALTERNATIVE TAX IN CASE OF CAPITAL GAINS.—If for any taxable year any political organization has a net capital gain, then, in lieu of the tax imposed by paragraph (1), there is hereby imposed a tax (if such a tax is less than the tax imposed by paragraph (1)) which shall consist of the sum of—

(A) a partial tax, computed as provided by paragraph (1), on the political organization taxable income determined by reducing such income by the amount of such gain, and

(B) an amount determined as provided in section 1201(a) on such gain.

Amendments

• 1978, Revenue Act of 1978 (P.L. 95-600)

P.L. 95-600, §301(b)(6):

Amended Code Sec. 527(b)(1). **Effective** for tax years beginning after 12-31-78. Prior to amendment, Code Sec. 527(b)(1) read as follows:

"(1) IN GENERAL.—A tax is hereby imposed for each taxable year on the political organization taxable income of every political organization. Such tax shall consist of a normal tax and surtax computed as provided in section 11 as though the political organization were a corporation and as though the political organization taxable income were the taxable income referred to in section 11. For purposes of this subsection, the surtax exemption provided by section 11(d) shall not be allowed."

• 1976, Tax Reform Act of 1976 (P.L. 94-455)

P.L. 94-455, §1901(b)(33)(C):

Substituted "net capital gain" for "net section 1201 gain" in Sec. 527(b)(2). **Effective** for tax years beginning after 12-31-76.

[Sec. 527(c)]

(c) POLITICAL ORGANIZATION TAXABLE INCOME DEFINED.—

(1) TAXABLE INCOME DEFINED.—For purposes of this section, the political organization taxable income of any organization for any taxable year is an amount equal to the excess (if any) of—

(A) the gross income for the taxable year (excluding any exempt function income), over

(B) the deductions allowed by this chapter which are directly connected with the production of the gross income (excluding exempt function income), computed with the modifications provided in paragraph (2).

(2) MODIFICATIONS.—For purposes of this subsection—

(A) there shall be allowed a specific deduction of $100,

(B) no net operating loss deduction shall be allowed under section 172, and

(C) no deduction shall be allowed under part VIII of subchapter B (relating to special deductions for corporations).

(3) EXEMPT FUNCTION INCOME.—For purposes of this subsection, the term "exempt function income" means any amount received as—

(A) a contribution of money or other property,

(B) membership dues, a membership fee or assessment from a member of the political organization,

(C) proceeds from a political fundraising or entertainment event, or proceeds from the sale of political campaign materials, which are not received in the ordinary course of any trade or business, or

(D) proceeds from the conducting of any bingo game (as defined in section 513(f)(2)),

to the extent such amount is segregated for use only for the exempt function of the political organization.

Amendments

• 1978 (P.L. 95-502)

P.L. 95-502, §302(a):

Added subparagraph (c)(3)(D). **Effective** as indicated in Act Sec. §302(b), below.

P.L. 95-502, §302(b), provides:

"(b)(1) The amendment made by subsection (a) shall apply to taxable years beginning after December 31, 1974, except that notwithstanding any other provision of law to the contrary, no amounts held at October 21, 1978, by an organization described in section 527(e)(1) of the Internal Revenue Code of 1954 in escrow, in separate accounts for the payment of Federal taxes, or in any other fund which are proceeds described in section 527(c)(3)(D) of such Code may be used, directly or indirectly, to make a contribution or expenditure (as defined in section 301(e) and (f) of the Federal Election Campaign Act of 1971; 2 U.S.C. 431(f)) in connection with any election held before January 1, 1979.

(2) Such amounts as described in (1) above shall not be considered as security or collateral for any loan by any State or national bank or any other person or organization."

[Sec. 527(d)]

(d) CERTAIN USES NOT TREATED AS INCOME TO CANDIDATE.—For purposes of this title, if any political organization—

(1) contributes any amount to or for the use of any political organization which is treated as exempt from tax under subsection (a) of this section,

(2) contributes any amount to or for the use of any organization described in paragraph (1) or (2) of section 509(a) which is exempt from tax under section 501(a), or

(3) deposits any amount in the general fund of the Treasury or in the general fund of any State or local government,

such amount shall be treated as an amount not diverted for the personal use of the candidate or any other person. No deduction shall be allowed under this title for the contribution or deposit of any amount described in the preceding sentence.

[Sec. 527(e)]

(e) OTHER DEFINITIONS.—For purposes of this section—

(1) POLITICAL ORGANIZATION.—The term "political organization" means a party, committee, association, fund, or other organization (whether or not incorporated) organized and operated primarily for the purpose of directly or indirectly accepting contributions or making expenditures, or both, for an exempt function.

(2) EXEMPT FUNCTION.—The term "exempt function" means the function of influencing or attempting to influence the selection, nomination, election, or appointment of any individual to any Federal, State, or local public office or office in a political organization, or the election of

Presidential or Vice-Presidential electors, whether or not such individual or electors are selected, nominated, elected, or appointed. Such term includes the making of expenditures relating to an office described in the preceding sentence which, if incurred by the individual, would be allowable as a deduction under section 162(a).

(3) CONTRIBUTIONS.—The term "contributions" has the meaning given to such term by section 271(b)(2).

(4) EXPENDITURES.—The term "expenditures" has the meaning given to such term by section 271(b)(3).

(5) QUALIFIED STATE OR LOCAL POLITICAL ORGANIZATION.—

(A) IN GENERAL.—The term "qualified State or local political organization" means a political organization—

(i) all the exempt functions of which are solely for the purposes of influencing or attempting to influence the selection, nomination, election, or appointment of any individual to any State or local public office or office in a State or local political organization,

(ii) which is subject to State law that requires the organization to report (and it so reports)—

(I) information regarding each separate expenditure from and contribution to such organization, and

(II) information regarding the person who makes such contribution or receives such expenditure,

which would otherwise be required to be reported under this section, and

(iii) with respect to which the reports referred to in clause (ii) are

(I) made public by the agency with which such reports are filed, and

(II) made publicly available for inspection by the organization in the manner described in section 6104(d).

(B) CERTAIN STATE LAW DIFFERENCES DISREGARDED.—An organization shall not be treated as failing to meet the requirements of subparagraph (A)(ii) solely by reason of 1 or more of the following:

(i) The minimum amount of any expenditure or contribution required to be reported under State law is not more than $300 greater than the minimum amount required to be reported under subsection (j).

(ii) The State law does not require the organization to identify 1 or more of the following:

(I) The employer of any person who makes contributions to the organization.

(II) The occupation of any person who makes contributions to the organization.

(III) The employer of any person who receives expenditures from the organization.

(IV) The occupation of any person who receives expenditures from the organization.

(V) The purpose of any expenditure of the organization.

(VI) The date any contribution was made to the organization.

(VII) The date of any expenditure of the organization.

(C) DE MINIMIS ERRORS.—An organization shall not fail to be treated as a qualified State or local political organization solely because such organization makes de minimis errors in complying with the State reporting requirements and the public inspection requirements described in subparagraph (A) as long as the organization corrects such errors within a reasonable period after the organization becomes aware of such errors.

(D) PARTICIPATION OF FEDERAL CANDIDATE OR OFFICE HOLDER.—The term "qualified State or local political organization" shall not include any organization otherwise described in subparagraph (A) if a candidate for nomination or election to Federal elective public office or an individual who holds such office—

(i) controls or materially participates in the direction of the organization,

(ii) solicits contributions to the organization (unless the Secretary determines that such solicitations resulted in de minimis contributions and were made without the prior knowledge and consent, whether explicit or implicit, of the organization or its officers, directors, agents, or employees), or

(iii) directs, in whole or in part, disbursements by the organization.

Amendments

• 2002 (P.L. 107-276)

P.L. 107-276, §2(b):

Amended Code Sec. 527(e) by adding at the end a new paragraph (5). **Effective** as if included in the amendments made by P.L. 106-230 [**effective** for expenditures made and contributions received after 7-1-2000, except that such amendment is not **effective** for expenditures made, or contributions received, after such date pursuant to a contract entered into on or before such date.—CCH].

• 1988, Technical and Miscellaneous Revenue Act of 1988 (P.L. 100-647)

P.L. 100-647, §1001(b)(3)(B):

Amended Code Sec. 527(e)(2) by adding at the end thereof a new sentence. **Effective** as if included in the provision of P.L. 99-514 to which it relates.

[Sec. 527(f)]

(f) EXEMPT ORGANIZATION, WHICH IS NOT POLITICAL ORGANIZATION, MUST INCLUDE CERTAIN AMOUNTS IN GROSS INCOME.—

(1) IN GENERAL.—If an organization described in section 501(c) which is exempt from tax under section 501(a) expends any amount during the taxable year directly (or through another organization) for an exempt function (within the meaning of subsection (e)(2)), then, notwithstanding any other provision of law, there shall be included in the gross income of such organization for the taxable year, and shall be subject to tax under subsection (b) as if it constituted political organization taxable income, an amount equal to the lesser of—

(A) the net investment income of such organization for the taxable year, or

(B) the aggregate amount so expended during the taxable year for such an exempt function.

(2) NET INVESTMENT INCOME.—For purposes of this subsection, the term "net investment income" means the excess of—

(A) the gross amount of income from interest, dividends, rents, and royalties, plus the excess (if any) of gains from the sale or exchange of assets over the losses from the sale or exchange of assets, over

(B) the deductions allowed by this chapter which are directly connected with the production of the income referred to in subparagraph (A).

For purposes of the preceding sentence, there shall not be taken into account items taken into account for purposes of the tax imposed by section 511 (relating to tax on unrelated business income).

(3) CERTAIN SEPARATE SEGREGATED FUNDS.—For purposes of this subsection and subsection (e)(1), a separate segregated fund (within the meaning of section 610 of title 18 or of any similar State statute, or within the meaning of any State statute which permits the segregation of dues moneys for exempt functions (within the meaning of subsection (e)(2))) which is maintained by an organization described in section 501(c) which is exempt from tax under section 501(a) shall be treated as a separate organization.

[Sec. 527(g)]

(g) TREATMENT OF NEWSLETTER FUNDS.—

(1) IN GENERAL.—For purposes of this section, a fund established and maintained by an individual who holds, has been elected to, or is a candidate (within the meaning of paragraph (3)) for nomination or election to, any Federal, State, or local elective public office for use by such individual exclusively for the preparation and circulation of such individual's newsletter shall, except as provided in paragraph (2), be treated as if such fund constituted a political organization.

(2) ADDITIONAL MODIFICATIONS.—In the case of any fund described in paragraph (1)—

(A) the exempt function shall be only the preparation and circulation of the newsletter, and

(B) the specific deduction provided by subsection (c)(2)(A) shall not be allowed.

(3) CANDIDATE.—For purposes of paragraph (1), the term "candidate" means, with respect to any Federal, State, or local elective public office, an individual who—

(A) publicly announces that he is a candidate for nomination or election to such office, and

(B) meets the qualifications prescribed by law to hold such office.

Amendments

• 1986, Tax Reform Act of 1986 (P.L. 99-514)

P.L. 99-514, §112 (b)(1)(A)-(B):

Amended Code Sec. 527(g) by striking out "section 24(c)(2)" in paragraph (1) and inserting in lieu thereof "paragraph (3)", and by adding new paragraph (3). **Effective** for tax years beginning after 12-31-86.

• 1984, Deficit Reduction Act of 1984 (P.L. 98-369)

P.L. 98-369, §474(r)(16):

Amended Code Sec. 527(g)(1) by striking out "section 41(c)(2)" and inserting in lieu thereof "section 24(c)(2)". **Effective** for tax years beginning after 12-31-83, and to carrybacks from such years.

• 1975 (P.L. 93-625)

P.L. 93-625, §10(a):

Added Code Sec. 527. **Effective** for tax years beginning after 12-31-74.

[Sec. 527(h)]

(h) SPECIAL RULE FOR PRINCIPAL CAMPAIGN COMMITTEES.—

(1) IN GENERAL.—In the case of a political organization, which is a principal campaign committee, paragraph (1) of subsection (b) shall be applied by substituting "the appropriate rates" for "the highest rate".

(2) PRINCIPAL CAMPAIGN COMMITTEE DEFINED.—

(A) IN GENERAL.—For purposes of this subsection, the term "principal campaign committee" means the political committee designated by a candidate for Congress as his principal campaign committee for purposes of—

(i) section 302(e) of the Federal Election Campaign Act of 1971 (2 U.S.C. 432(e)), and

(ii) this subsection.

(B) DESIGNATION.—A candidate may have only 1 designation in effect under subparagraph (A)(ii) at any time and such designation—

(i) shall be made at such time and in such manner as the Secretary may prescribe by regulations, and

(ii) once made, may be revoked only with the consent of the Secretary.

Nothing in this subsection shall be construed to require any designation where there is only one political committee with respect to a candidate.

Amendments

• 1984, Deficit Reduction Act of 1984 (P.L. 98-369)

P.L. 98-369, §722(c):

Amended Code Sec. 527(h)(2)(B) by adding at the end thereof a new sentence. **Effective** for tax years beginning after 12-31-81.

• 1981, Economic Recovery Tax Act of 1981 (P.L. 97-34)

P.L. 97-34, §128(a):

Added Code Sec. 527(h). **Effective** for tax years beginning after 12-31-81.

[Sec. 527(i)]

(i) ORGANIZATIONS MUST NOTIFY SECRETARY THAT THEY ARE SECTION 527 ORGANIZATIONS.—

(1) IN GENERAL.—Except as provided in paragraph (5), an organization shall not be treated as an organization described in this section—

(A) unless it has given notice to the Secretary electronically that it is to be so treated, or

(B) if the notice is given after the time required under paragraph (2), the organization shall not be so treated for any period before such notice is given or, in the case of any material change in the information required under paragraph (3), for the period beginning on the date on which the material change occurs and ending on the date on which such notice is given.

(2) TIME TO GIVE NOTICE.—The notice required under paragraph (1) shall be transmitted not later than 24 hours after the date on which the organization is established or, in the case of any material change in the information required under paragraph (3), not later than 30 days after such material change.

(3) CONTENTS OF NOTICE.—The notice required under paragraph (1) shall include information regarding—

(A) the name and address of the organization (including any business address, if different) and its electronic mailing address,

(B) the purpose of the organization,

(C) the names and addresses of its officers, highly compensated employees, contact person, custodian of records, and members of its Board of Directors,

(D) the name and address of, and relationship to, any related entities (within the meaning of section 168(h)(4)),

(E) whether the organization intends to claim an exemption from the requirements of subsection (j) or section 6033, and

(F) such other information as the Secretary may require to carry out the internal revenue laws.

(4) EFFECT OF FAILURE.—In the case of an organization failing to meet the requirements of paragraph (1) for any period, the taxable income of such organization shall be computed by taking into account any exempt function income (and any deductions directly connected with the production of such income) or, in the case of a failure relating to a material change, by taking into account such income and deductions only during the period beginning on the date on which the material change occurs and ending on the date on which notice is given under this subsection. For purposes of the preceding sentence, the term "exempt function income" means any amount described in a subparagraph of subsection (c)(3), whether or not segregated for use for an exempt function.

(5) EXCEPTIONS.—This subsection shall not apply to any organization—

(A) to which this section applies solely by reason of subsection (f)(1),

(B) which reasonably anticipates that it will not have gross receipts of $25,000 or more for any taxable year, or

(C) which is a political committee of a State or local candidate or which is a State or local committee of a political party.

(6) COORDINATION WITH OTHER REQUIREMENTS.—This subsection shall not apply to any person required (without regard to this subsection) to report under the Federal Election Campaign Act of 1971 (2 U.S.C. 431 et seq.) as a political committee.

Amendments

• 2002 (P.L. 107-276)

P.L. 107-276, §1(a):

Amended Code Sec. 527(i)(5) by striking "or" at the end of subparagraph (A), by striking the period at the end of subparagraph (B) and inserting ", or", and by adding at the end a new subparagraph (C). **Effective** as if included in the amendments made by P.L. 106-230 [generally **effective** on 7-1-2000. For an exception, see P.L. 106-230, §1(d)(2), below.—CCH].

P.L. 107-276, §6(a):

Amended Code Sec. 527(i)(4) by adding at the end a new sentence. **Effective** for failures occurring on or after 11-2-2002.

P.L. 107-276, §6(c):

Amended Code Sec. 527(i)(1)(A) by striking ", electronically and in writing," and inserting "electronically". **Effective** as if included in the amendments made by P.L. 106-230 [generally **effective** on 7-1-2000. For an exception, see P.L. 106-230, §1(d)(2), below.—CCH].

P.L. 107-276, §6(f):

Amended Code Sec. 527(i)(3) by striking "and" at the end of subparagraph (D), by redesignating subparagraph (E) as subparagraph (F), and by inserting after subparagraph (D) a new subparagraph (E). **Effective** for reports and notices required to be filed more than 30 days after 11-2-2002.

P.L. 107-276, §6(g)(1):

Amended Code Sec. 527(i)(1)(B) by inserting "or, in the case of any material change in the information required under paragraph (3), for the period beginning on the date on which the material change occurs and ending on the date on which such notice is given" after "given". For the **effective** date, see Act Sec. 6(h)(6), below.

P.L. 107-276, §6(g)(2):

Amended Code Sec. 527(i)(2) by inserting "or, in the case of any material change in the information required under paragraph (3), not later than 30 days after such material change" after "established". For the **effective** date, see Act Sec. 6(h)(6), below.

P.L. 107-276, §6(g)(3):

Amended Code Sec. 527(i)(4) by inserting before the period at the end the following: "or, in the case of a failure relating to a material change, by taking into account such income and deductions only during the period beginning on the date on which the material change occurs and ending on the date on which notice is given under this subsection". For the **effective** date, see Act Sec. 6(h)(6), below.

P.L. 107-276, §6(h)(6), provides:

(6) SUBSECTION (g).—

(A) IN GENERAL.—The amendments made by subsection (g) shall apply to material changes on or after the date of the enactment of this Act.

(B) TRANSITION RULE.—In the case of a material change occurring during the 30-day period beginning on the date of the enactment of this Act, a notice under section 527(i) of the Internal Revenue Code of 1986 (as amended by this Act) shall not be required to be filed under such section before the later of—

(i) 30 days after the date of such material change, or

(ii) 45 days after the date of the enactment of this Act.

• 2000 (P.L. 106-230)

P.L. 106-230, §1(a):

Amended Code Sec. 527 by adding at the end new subsection (i). **Effective** 7-1-2000. For an exception, see Act Sec. 1(d)(2), below.

P.L. 106-230, §1(d)(2), provides:

(2) ORGANIZATIONS ALREADY IN EXISTENCE.—In the case of an organization established before the date of the enactment of this section, the time to file the notice under section 527(i)(2) of the Internal Revenue Code of 1986, as added by this section, shall be 30 days after the date of the enactment of this section.

[Sec. 527(j)]

(j) REQUIRED DISCLOSURE OF EXPENDITURES AND CONTRIBUTIONS.—

(1) PENALTY FOR FAILURE.—In the case of—

(A) a failure to make the required disclosures under paragraph (2) at the time and in the manner prescribed therefor, or

(B) a failure to include any of the information required to be shown by such disclosures or to show the correct information,

there shall be paid by the organization an amount equal to the rate of tax specified in subsection (b)(1) multiplied by the amount to which the failure relates. For purposes of subtitle F, the amount imposed by this paragraph shall be assessed and collected in the same manner as penalties imposed by section 6652(c).

(2) REQUIRED DISCLOSURE.—A political organization which accepts a contribution, or makes an expenditure, for an exempt function during any calendar year shall file with the Secretary either—

(A)(i) in the case of a calendar year in which a regularly scheduled election is held—

(I) quarterly reports, beginning with the first quarter of the calendar year in which a contribution is accepted or expenditure is made, which shall be filed not later than the fifteenth day after the last day of each calendar quarter, except that the report for the quarter ending on December 31 of such calendar year shall be filed not later than January 31 of the following calendar year,

(II) a pre-election report, which shall be filed not later than the twelfth day before (or posted by registered or certified mail not later than the fifteenth day before) any election with respect to which the organization makes a contribution or expenditure, and which shall be complete as of the twentieth day before the election, and

(III) a post-general election report, which shall be filed not later than the thirtieth day after the general election and which shall be complete as of the twentieth day after such general election, and

(ii) in the case of any other calendar year, a report covering the period beginning January 1 and ending June 30, which shall be filed no later than July 31 and a report covering the period beginning July 1 and ending December 31, which shall be filed no later than January 31 of the following calendar year, or

(B) monthly reports for the calendar year, beginning with the first month of the calendar year in which a contribution is accepted or expenditure is made, which shall be filed not later than the twentieth day after the last day of the month and shall be complete as if [of] the last day of the month, except that, in lieu of filing the reports otherwise due in November and December of any year in which a regularly scheduled general election is held, a pre-general election report shall be filed in accordance with subparagraph (A)(i)(II), a post-general election report shall be filed in accordance with subparagraph (A)(i)(III), and a year end report shall be filed not later than January 31 of the following calendar year.

(3) CONTENTS OF REPORT.—A report required under paragraph (2) shall contain the following information:

(A) The amount, date, and purpose of each expenditure made to a person if the aggregate amount of expenditures to such person during the calendar year equals or exceeds $500 and the name and address of the person (in the case of an individual, including the occupation and name of employer of such individual).

(B) The name and address (in the case of an individual, including the occupation and name of employer of such individual) of all contributors which contributed an aggregate amount of $200 or more to the organization during the calendar year and the amount and date of the contribution.

Any expenditure or contribution disclosed in a previous reporting period is not required to be included in the current reporting period.

(4) CONTRACTS TO SPEND OR CONTRIBUTE.—For purposes of this subsection, a person shall be treated as having made an expenditure or contribution if the person has contracted or is otherwise obligated to make the expenditure or contribution.

(5) COORDINATION WITH OTHER REQUIREMENTS.—This subsection shall not apply—

(A) to any person required (without regard to this subsection) to report under the Federal Election Campaign Act of 1971 (2 U.S.C. 431 et seq.) as a political committee,

(B) to any State or local committee of a political party or political committee of a State or local candidate,

(C) to any organization which is a qualified State or local political organization,

(D) to any organization which reasonably anticipates that it will not have gross receipts of $25,000 or more for any taxable year,

(E) to any organization to which this section applies solely by reason of subsection (f)(1), or

(F) with respect to any expenditure which is an independent expenditure (as defined in section 301 of such Act).

(6) ELECTION.—For purposes of this subsection, the term "election" means—

(A) a general, special, primary, or runoff election for a Federal office,

(B) a convention or caucus of a political party which has authority to nominate a candidate for Federal office,

(C) a primary election held for the selection of delegates to a national nominating convention of a political party, or

(D) a primary election held for the expression of a preference for the nomination of individuals for election to the office of President.

(7) ELECTRONIC FILING.—Any report required under paragraph (2) with respect to any calendar year shall be filed in electronic form if the organization has, or has reason to expect to have, contributions exceeding $50,000 or expenditures exceeding $50,000 in such calendar year.

Amendments

• 2002 (P.L. 107-276)

P.L. 107-276, §2(a):

Amended Code Sec. 527(j)(5) by redesignating subparagraphs (C), (D), and (E) as subparagraphs (D), (E), and (F), respectively, and by inserting after subparagraph (B) a new subparagraph (C). **Effective** as if included in the amendments made by P.L. 106-230 [applicable to expenditures made and contributions received after 7-1-2000, except that such amendment shall not apply to expenditures made, or contributions received, after such date pursuant to a contract entered into on or before such date.—CCH].

P.L. 107-276, §4, provides:

SEC. 4. NOTIFICATION OF INTERACTION OF REPORTING REQUIREMENTS.

(a) IN GENERAL.— The Secretary of the Treasury, in consultation with the Federal Election Commission, shall publicize—

(1) the effect of the amendments made by this Act, and

(2) the interaction of requirements to file a notification or report under section 527 of the Internal Revenue Code of 1986 and reports under the Federal Election Campaign Act of 1971.

(b) INFORMATION.— Information provided under subsection (a) shall be included in any appropriate form, instruction, notice, or other guidance issued to the public by the Secretary of the Treasury or the Federal Election Commission regarding reporting requirements of political organizations (as defined in section 527 of the Internal Revenue Code of 1986) or reporting requirements under the Federal Election Campaign Act of 1971.

P.L. 107-276, §6(b):

Amended Code Sec. 527(j)(1) by adding at the end a new sentence. **Effective** for failures occurring on or after 11-2-2002.

P.L. 107-276, §6(e)(1)(A)-(B):

Amended Code Sec. 527(j)(3) by inserting ", date, and purpose" after "The amount" in subparagraph (A), and by inserting "and date" after "the amount" in subparagraph (B). **Effective** for reports and notices required to be filed more than 30 days after 11-2-2002.

P.L. 107-276, §6(e)(2):

Amended Code Sec. 527(j) by adding at the end a new paragraph (7). **Effective** for reports required to be filed on or after 6-30-2003.

• 2000 (P.L. 106-230)

P.L. 106-230, §2(a):

Amended Code Sec. 527, as amended by Act Sec. 1(a), by adding at the end new subsection (j). **Effective** for expenditures made and contributions received after 7-1-2000, except that such amendment shall not apply to expenditures made, or contributions received, after such date pursuant to a contract entered into on or before such date.

[Sec. 527(k)]

(k) PUBLIC AVAILABILITY OF NOTICES AND REPORTS.—

(1) IN GENERAL.—The Secretary shall make any notice described in subsection (i)(1) or report described in subsection (j)(7) available for public inspection on the Internet not later than 48 hours after such notice or report has been filed (in addition to such public availability as may be made under section 6104(d)(7)).

(2) ACCESS.—The Secretary shall make the entire database of notices and reports which are made available to the public under paragraph (1) searchable by the following items (to the extent the items are required to be included in the notices and reports):

(A) Names, States, zip codes, custodians of records, directors, and general purposes of the organizations.

(B) Entities related to the organizations.

(C) Contributors to the organizations.

(D) Employers of such contributors.

(E) Recipients of expenditures by the organizations.

(F) Ranges of contributions and expenditures.

(G) Time periods of the notices and reports.

Such database shall be downloadable.

Amendments

• 2002 (P.L. 107-276)

P.L. 107-276, §6(e)(3):

Amended Code Sec. 527, as amended by Act Sec. 5(a), by redesignating subsection (k) as subsection (l) and by inserting after subsection (j) a new subsection (k). **Effective** for reports required to be filed on or after 6-30-2003.

[Sec. 527(l)]

(l) AUTHORITY TO WAIVE.—The Secretary may waive all or any portion of the—

(1) tax assessed on an organization by reason of the failure of the organization to comply with the requirements of subsection (i), or

(2) amount imposed under subsection (j) for a failure to comply with the requirements thereof,

on a showing that such failure was due to reasonable cause and not due to willful neglect.

Amendments

• 2002 (P.L. 107-276)

P.L. 107-276, §5(a):

Amended Code Sec. 527 by adding at the end a new subsection (k). **Effective** for any tax assessed or amount imposed after 6-30-2000.

P.L. 107-276, §6(e)(3):

Amended Code Sec. 527, as amended by Act Sec. 5(a), by redesignating subsection (k) as subsection (l). **Effective** for reports required to be filed on or after 6-30-2003.

PART VII—CERTAIN HOMEOWNERS ASSOCIATIONS

[Sec. 528]

SEC. 528. CERTAIN HOMEOWNERS ASSOCIATIONS.

[Sec. 528(a)]

(a) GENERAL RULE.—A homeowners association (as defined in subsection (c)) shall be subject to taxation under this subtitle only to the extent provided in this section. A homeowners association shall be considered an organization exempt from income taxes for the purpose of any law which refers to organizations exempt from income taxes.

[Sec. 528(b)]

(b) TAX IMPOSED.—A tax is hereby imposed for each taxable year on the homeowners association taxable income of every homeowners association. Such tax shall be equal to 30 percent of the homeowners association taxable income (32 percent of such income in the case of a timeshare association).

Amendments

• 1997, Taxpayer Relief Act of 1997 (P.L. 105-34)

P.L. 105-34, §966(d):

Amended Code Sec. 528(b) by inserting before the period "(32 percent of such income in the case of a timeshare association". **Effective** for tax years beginning after 12-31-96.

• 1980, Miscellaneous Revenue Act of 1980 (P.L. 96-605)

P.L. 96-605, §105(a):

Amended Code Sec. 528(b). **Effective** with respect to tax years beginning after 12-31-80. Prior to amendment, Code Sec. 528(b) read as follows:

"(b) TAX IMPOSED.—

"(1) IN GENERAL.—A tax is hereby imposed for each taxable year on the homeowners association taxable income of every homeowners association. Such tax shall be computed by multiplying the homeowners association taxable income by the highest rate of tax specified in section 11(b).

"(2) ALTERNATIVE TAX IN CASE OF CAPITAL GAINS.—If for any taxable year any homeowner association has a net capital gain, then in lieu of the tax imposed by paragraph (1), there is hereby imposed a tax (if such tax is less than the tax imposed by paragraph (1)) which shall consist of the sum of—

"(A) a partial tax, computed as provided by paragraph (1), on the homeowners association taxable income determined by reducing such income by the amount of such gain, and

"(B) an amount determined as provided in section 1201(a) on such gain.".

• 1978, Revenue Act of 1978 (P.L. 95-600)

P.L. 95-600, §301(b)(7):

Amended Code Sec. 528(b)(1). **Effective** for tax years beginning after 12-31-78. Prior to amendment, Code Sec. 528(b)(1) read as follows:

(1) IN GENERAL.—A tax is hereby imposed for each taxable year on the homeowners association taxable income of every homeowners association. Such tax shall consist of a normal tax and surtax computed as provided in section 11 as though the homeowners association were a corporation and as though the homeowners association taxable income were the taxable income referred to in section 11. For purposes of this subsection, the surtax exemption provided by section 11(d) shall not be allowed.

• 1978, Revenue Act of 1978 (P.L. 95-600)

P.L. 95-600, §403(c)(2):

Amended Code Sec. 528(b)(2)(B). **Effective** 11-6-78. Prior to amendment, Code Sec. 528(b)(2)(B) read as follows:

(B) a tax of 30 percent of such gain.

[Sec. 528(c)]

(c) HOMEOWNERS ASSOCIATION DEFINED.—For purposes of this section—

(1) HOMEOWNERS ASSOCIATION.—The term "homeowners association" means an organization which is a condominium management association, a residential real estate management association, or a timeshare association if—

(A) such organization is organized and operated to provide for the acquisition, construction, management, maintenance, and care of association property,

(B) 60 percent or more of the gross income of such organization for the taxable year consists solely of amounts received as membership dues, fees, or assessments from—

(i) owners of residential units in the case of a condominium management association,

(ii) owners of residences or residential lots in the case of a residential real estate management association, or

(iii) owners of timeshare rights to use, or timeshare ownership interests in, association property in the case of a timeshare association,

(C) 90 percent or more of the expenditures of the organization for the taxable year are expenditures for the acquisition, construction, management, maintenance, and care of association property and, in the case of a timeshare association, for activities provided to or on behalf of members of the association,

(D) no part of the net earnings of such organization inures (other than by acquiring, constructing, or providing management, maintenance, and care of association property, and other than by a rebate of excess membership dues, fees, or assessments) to the benefit of any private shareholder or individual, and

(E) such organization elects (at such time and in such manner as the Secretary by regulations prescribes) to have this section apply for the taxable year.

(2) CONDOMINIUM MANAGEMENT ASSOCIATION.—The term "condominium management association" means any organization meeting the requirement of subparagraph (A) of paragraph (1) with respect to a condominium project substantially all of the units of which are used by individuals for residences.

(3) RESIDENTIAL REAL ESTATE MANAGEMENT ASSOCIATION.—The term "residential real estate management association" means any organization meeting the requirements of subparagraph (A) of paragraph (1) with respect to a subdivision, development, or similar area substantially all the lots or buildings of which may only be used by individuals for residences.

(4) TIMESHARE ASSOCIATION.—The term "timeshare association" means any organization (other than a condominium management association) meeting the requirement of subparagraph

(A) of paragraph (1) if any member thereof holds a timeshare right to use, or a timeshare ownership interest in, real property constituting association property.

(5) ASSOCIATION PROPERTY.—The term "association property" means—

(A) property held by the organization,

(B) property commonly held by the members of the organization,

(C) property within the organization privately held by the members of the organization, and

(D) property owned by a governmental unit and used for the benefit of residents of such unit.

In the case of a timeshare association, such term includes property in which the timeshare association, or members of the association, have rights arising out of recorded easements, covenants, or other recorded instruments to use property related to the timeshare project.

Amendments

• 1997, Taxpayer Relief Act of 1997 (P.L. 105-34)

P.L. 105-34, §966(a)(1)(A):

Amended Code Sec. 528(c)(1) by striking "or a residential real estate management association" and inserting ", a residential real estate management association, or a timeshare association" in the material preceding subparagraph (A). **Effective** for tax years beginning after 12-31-96.

P.L. 105-34, §966(a)(1)(B):

Amended Code Sec. 528(c)(1)(B) by striking "or" at the end of clause (i), by striking the period at the end of clause (ii) and inserting ", or", and by adding at the end a new clause (iii). **Effective** for tax years beginning after 12-31-96.

P.L. 105-34, §966(a)(1)(C):

Amended Code Sec. 528(c)(1)(C) by inserting "and, in the case of a timeshare association, for activities provided to or on behalf of members of the association" before the comma at the end. **Effective** for tax years beginning after 12-31-96.

P.L. 105-34, §966(a)(2):

Amended Code Sec. 528(c) by redesignating paragraph (4) as paragraph (5) and by inserting after paragraph (3) a new paragraph (4). **Effective** for tax years beginning after 12-31-96.

P.L. 105-34, §966(c):

Amended Code Sec. 528(c)(5), as redesignated by Act Sec. 966(a)(2), by adding at the end a new flush sentence. **Effective** for tax years beginning after 12-31-96.

• 1978, Revenue Act of 1978 (P.L. 95-600)

P.L. 95-600, §701(n)(1):

Amended Code Sec. 528(c)(2) by striking out "as residences" and inserting in lieu thereof "by individuals for residences". **Effective** for tax years beginning after 12-31-73.

[Sec. 528(d)]

(d) HOMEOWNERS ASSOCIATION TAXABLE INCOME DEFINED.—

(1) TAXABLE INCOME DEFINED.—For purposes of this section, the homeowners association taxable income of any organization for any taxable year is an amount equal to the excess (if any) of—

(A) the gross income for the taxable year (excluding any exempt function income), over

(B) the deductions allowed by this chapter which are directly connected with the production of the gross income (excluding exempt function income), computed with the modifications provided in paragraph (2).

(2) MODIFICATIONS.—For purposes of this subsection—

(A) there shall be allowed a specific deduction of $100,

(B) no net operating loss deduction shall be allowed under section 172, and

(C) no deduction shall be allowed under part VIII of subchapter B (relating to special deductions for corporations).

(3) EXEMPT FUNCTION INCOME.—For purposes of this subsection, the term "exempt function income" means any amount received as membership dues, fees, or assessments from—

(A) owners of condominium housing units in the case of a condominium management association,

(B) owners of real property in the case of a residential real estate management association, or

(C) owners of timeshare rights to use, or timeshare ownership interests in, real property in the case of a timeshare association.

Amendments

• 1997, Taxpayer Relief Act of 1997 (P.L. 105-34)

P.L. 105-34, §966(b):

Amended Code Sec. 528(d)(3) by striking "or" at the end of subparagraph (A), by striking the period at the end of subparagraph (B) and inserting ", or", and by adding at the end a new subparagraph (C). **Effective** for tax years beginning after 12-31-96.

• 1976, Tax Reform Act of 1976 (P.L. 94-455)

P.L. 94-455, §2101(a):

Added Code Sec. 528. **Effective** for tax years beginning after 12-31-73.

PART VIII—HIGHER EDUCATION SAVINGS ENTITIES

[Sec. 529]

SEC. 529. QUALIFIED TUITION PROGRAMS.

[Sec. 529(a)]

(a) GENERAL RULE.—A qualified tuition program shall be exempt from taxation under this subtitle. Notwithstanding the preceding sentence, such program shall be subject to the taxes imposed by section 511 (relating to imposition of tax on unrelated business income of charitable organizations).

Amendments

• 2006, Pension Protection Act of 2006 (P.L. 109-280)

P.L. 109-280, §1304(a), provides:

(a) PERMANENT EXTENSION OF MODIFICATIONS.—Section 901 of the Economic Growth and Tax Relief Reconciliation Act of 2001 [P.L. 107-16] (relating to sunset provisions) shall not apply to section 402 of such Act (relating to modifications to qualified tuition programs).

• 2001, Economic Growth and Tax Relief Reconciliation Act of 2001 (P.L. 107-16)

P.L. 107-16, §402(a)(4)(A):

Amended Code Sec. 529 by striking "qualified State tuition" each place it appears and inserting "qualified tuition". **Effective** for tax years beginning after 12-31-2001.

P.L. 107-16, §402(a)(4)(D):

Amended the heading for Code Sec. 529 by striking "**STATE**" following "**QUALIFIED**". **Effective** for tax years beginning after 12-31-2001.

P.L. 107-16, §901(a)-(b), provides [but see P.L. 109-280, §1304(a), above]:

SEC. 901. SUNSET OF PROVISIONS OF ACT.

(a) IN GENERAL.—All provisions of, and amendments made by, this Act shall not apply—

(1) to taxable, plan, or limitation years beginning after December 31, 2010, or

(2) in the case of title V, to estates of decedents dying, gifts made, or generation skipping transfers, after December 31, 2010.

(b) APPLICATION OF CERTAIN LAWS.—The Internal Revenue Code of 1986 and the Employee Retirement Income Security Act of 1974 shall be applied and administered to years, estates, gifts, and transfers described in subsection (a) as if the provisions and amendments described in subsection (a) had never been enacted.

[Sec. 529(b)]

(b) QUALIFIED TUITION PROGRAM.—For purposes of this section—

(1) IN GENERAL.—The term "qualified tuition program" means a program established and maintained by a State or agency or instrumentality thereof or by 1 or more eligible educational institutions—

(A) under which a person—

(i) may purchase tuition credits or certificates on behalf of a designated beneficiary which entitle the beneficiary to the waiver or payment of qualified higher education expenses of the beneficiary, or

(ii) in the case of a program established and maintained by a State or agency or instrumentality thereof, may make contributions to an account which is established for the purpose of meeting the qualified higher education expenses of the designated beneficiary of the account, and

(B) which meets the other requirements of this subsection.

Except to the extent provided in regulations, a program established and maintained by 1 or more eligible educational institutions shall not be treated as a qualified tuition program unless such program provides that amounts are held in a qualified trust and such program has received a ruling or determination that such program meets the applicable requirements for a qualified tuition program. For purposes of the preceding sentence, the term "qualified trust" means a trust which is created or organized in the United States for the exclusive benefit of designated beneficiaries and with respect to which the requirements of paragraphs (2) and (5) of section 408(a) are met.

(2) CASH CONTRIBUTIONS.—A program shall not be treated as a qualified tuition program unless it provides that purchases or contributions may only be made in cash.

(3) SEPARATE ACCOUNTING.—A program shall not be treated as a qualified tuition program unless it provides separate accounting for each designated beneficiary.

(4) NO INVESTMENT DIRECTION.—A program shall not be treated as a qualified tuition program unless it provides that any contributor to, or designated beneficiary under, such program may not directly or indirectly direct the investment of any contributions to the program (or any earnings thereon).

(5) NO PLEDGING OF INTEREST AS SECURITY.—A program shall not be treated as a qualified tuition program if it allows any interest in the program or any portion thereof to be used as security for a loan.

(6) PROHIBITION ON EXCESS CONTRIBUTIONS.—A program shall not be treated as a qualified tuition program unless it provides adequate safeguards to prevent contributions on behalf of a designated beneficiary in excess of those necessary to provide for the qualified higher education expenses of the beneficiary.

Amendments

• 2006, Pension Protection Act of 2006 (P.L. 109-280)

P.L. 109-280, §1304(a), provides:

(a) PERMANENT EXTENSION OF MODIFICATIONS.—Section 901 of the Economic Growth and Tax Relief Reconciliation Act of 2001 [P.L. 107-16] (relating to sunset provisions) shall not apply to section 402 of such Act (relating to modifications to qualified tuition programs).

• 2001, Economic Growth and Tax Relief Reconciliation Act of 2001 (P.L. 107-16)

P.L. 107-16, §402(a)(1)(A)-(B):

Amended Code Sec. 529(b)(1) by inserting "or by 1 or more eligible educational institutions" after "maintained by a State or agency or instrumentality thereof" in the matter preceding subparagraph (A), and by adding at the end a new flush sentence. **Effective** for tax years beginning after 12-31-2001.

P.L. 107-16, §402(a)(2):

Amended Code Sec. 529(b)(1)(A)(ii) by inserting "in the case of a program established and maintained by a State or agency or instrumentality thereof," before "may make". **Effective** for tax years beginning after 12-31-2001.

P.L. 107-16, §402(a)(3)(A):

Amended Code Sec. 529 by striking paragraph (3) of subsection (b) and by redesignating paragraphs (4), (5), (6), and (7) of such subsection as paragraphs (3), (4), (5), and (6), respectively. **Effective** for tax years beginning after 12-31-2001. Prior to being stricken, Code Sec. 529(b)(3) read as follows:

(3) REFUNDS.—A program shall not be treated as a qualified State tuition program unless it imposes a more than de minimis penalty on any refund of earnings from the account which are not—

(A) used for qualified higher education expenses of the designated beneficiary,

(B) made on account of the death or disability of the designated beneficiary, or

(C) made on account of a scholarship (or allowance or payment described in section 135(d)(1)(B) or (C)) received by the designated beneficiary to the extent the amount of the refund does not exceed the amount of the scholarship, allowance, or payment.

P.L. 107-16, §402(a)(4)(A):

Amended Code Sec. 529 by striking "qualified State tuition" each place it appears and inserting "qualified tuition". **Effective** for tax years beginning after 12-31-2001.

P.L. 107-16, §402(a)(4)(C):

Amended the heading for Code Sec. 529(b) by striking "QUALIFIED STATE TUITION" and inserting "QUALIFIED TUITION". **E ffective** for tax years beginning after 12-31-2001.

P.L. 107-16, §901(a)-(b), provides [but see P.L. 109-280, §1304(a), above]:

SEC. 901. SUNSET OF PROVISIONS OF ACT.

(a) IN GENERAL.—All provisions of, and amendments made by, this Act shall not apply—

(1) to taxable, plan, or limitation years beginning after December 31, 2010, or

(2) in the case of title V, to estates of decedents dying, gifts made, or generation skipping transfers, after December 31, 2010.

(b) APPLICATION OF CERTAIN LAWS.—The Internal Revenue Code of 1986 and the Employee Retirement Income Security Act of 1974 shall be applied and administered to years, estates, gifts, and transfers described in subsection (a) as if the provisions and amendments described in subsection (a) had never been enacted.

• 1997, Taxpayer Relief Act of 1997 (P.L. 105-34)

P.L. 105-34, §211(b)(4):

Amended Code Sec. 529(b)(5) by inserting "directly or indirectly" after "may not". **Effective** 1-1-98.

[Sec. 529(c)]

(c) TAX TREATMENT OF DESIGNATED BENEFICIARIES AND CONTRIBUTORS.—

(1) IN GENERAL.—Except as otherwise provided in this subsection, no amount shall be includible in gross income of—

(A) a designated beneficiary under a qualified tuition program, or

(B) a contributor to such program on behalf of a designated beneficiary,

with respect to any distribution or earnings under such program.

(2) GIFT TAX TREATMENT OF CONTRIBUTIONS.—For purposes of chapters 12 and 13—

(A) IN GENERAL.—Any contribution to a qualified tuition program on behalf of any designated beneficiary—

(i) shall be treated as a completed gift to such beneficiary which is not a future interest in property, and

(ii) shall not be treated as a qualified transfer under section 2503(e).

(B) TREATMENT OF EXCESS CONTRIBUTIONS.—If the aggregate amount of contributions described in subparagraph (A) during the calendar year by a donor exceeds the limitation for such year under section 2503(b), such aggregate amount shall, at the election of the donor, be taken into account for purposes of such section ratably over the 5-year period beginning with such calendar year.

(3) DISTRIBUTIONS.—

(A) IN GENERAL.—Any distribution under a qualified tuition program shall be includible in the gross income of the distributee in the manner as provided under section 72 to the extent not excluded from gross income under any other provision of this chapter.

(B) DISTRIBUTIONS FOR QUALIFIED HIGHER EDUCATION EXPENSES.—For purposes of this paragraph—

(i) IN-KIND DISTRIBUTIONS.—No amount shall be includible in gross income under subparagraph (A) by reason of a distribution which consists of providing a benefit to the distributee which, if paid for by the distributee, would constitute payment of a qualified higher education expense.

(ii) CASH DISTRIBUTIONS.—In the case of distributions not described in clause (i), if—

(I) such distributions do not exceed the qualified higher education expenses (reduced by expenses described in clause (i)), no amount shall be includible in gross income, and

(II) in any other case, the amount otherwise includible in gross income shall be reduced by an amount which bears the same ratio to such amount as such expenses bear to such distributions.

(iii) EXCEPTION FOR INSTITUTIONAL PROGRAMS.—In the case of any taxable year beginning before January 1, 2004, clauses (i) and (ii) shall not apply with respect to any distribution during such taxable year under a qualified tuition program established and maintained by 1 or more eligible educational institutions.

(iv) TREATMENT AS DISTRIBUTIONS.—Any benefit furnished to a designated beneficiary under a qualified tuition program shall be treated as a distribution to the beneficiary for purposes of this paragraph.

(v) COORDINATION WITH HOPE AND LIFETIME LEARNING CREDITS.—The total amount of qualified higher education expenses with respect to an individual for the taxable year shall be reduced—

(I) as provided in section 25A(g)(2), and

(II) by the amount of such expenses which were taken into account in determining the credit allowed to the taxpayer or any other person under section 25A.

(vi) COORDINATION WITH COVERDELL EDUCATION SAVINGS ACCOUNTS.—If, with respect to an individual for any taxable year—

(I) the aggregate distributions to which clauses (i) and (ii) and section 530(d)(2)(A) apply, exceed

(II) the total amount of qualified higher education expenses otherwise taken into account under clauses (i) and (ii) (after the application of clause (v)) for such year,

the taxpayer shall allocate such expenses among such distributions for purposes of determining the amount of the exclusion under clauses (i) and (ii) and section 530(d)(2)(A).

(C) CHANGE IN BENEFICIARIES OR PROGRAMS.—

(i) ROLLOVERS.—Subparagraph (A) shall not apply to that portion of any distribution which, within 60 days of such distribution, is transferred—

(I) to another qualified tuition program for the benefit of the designated beneficiary, or

(II) to the credit of another designated beneficiary under a qualified tuition program who is a member of the family of the designated beneficiary with respect to which the distribution was made.

(ii) CHANGE IN DESIGNATED BENEFICIARIES.—Any change in the designated beneficiary of an interest in a qualified tuition program shall not be treated as a distribution for purposes of subparagraph (A) if the new beneficiary is a member of the family of the old beneficiary.

(iii) LIMITATION ON CERTAIN ROLLOVERS.—Clause (i)(I) shall not apply to any transfer if such transfer occurs within 12 months from the date of a previous transfer to any qualified tuition program for the benefit of the designated beneficiary.

(D) OPERATING RULES.—For purposes of applying section 72—

(i) to the extent provided by the Secretary, all qualified tuition programs of which an individual is a designated beneficiary shall be treated as one program,

(ii) except to the extent provided by the Secretary, all distributions during a taxable year shall be treated as one distribution, and

(iii) except to the extent provided by the Secretary, the value of the contract, income on the contract, and investment in the contract shall be computed as of the close of the calendar year in which the taxable year begins.

(4) ESTATE TAX TREATMENT.—

(A) IN GENERAL.—No amount shall be includible in the gross estate of any individual for purposes of chapter 11 by reason of an interest in a qualified tuition program.

(B) AMOUNTS INCLUDIBLE IN ESTATE OF DESIGNATED BENEFICIARY IN CERTAIN CASES.—Subparagraph (A) shall not apply to amounts distributed on account of the death of a beneficiary.

(C) AMOUNTS INCLUDIBLE IN ESTATE OF DONOR MAKING EXCESS CONTRIBUTIONS.—In the case of a donor who makes the election described in paragraph (2)(B) and who dies before the close of the 5-year period referred to in such paragraph, notwithstanding subparagraph (A), the gross estate of the donor shall include the portion of such contributions properly allocable to periods after the date of death of the donor.

(5) OTHER GIFT TAX RULES.—For purposes of chapters 12 and 13—

(A) TREATMENT OF DISTRIBUTIONS.—Except as provided in subparagraph (B), in no event shall a distribution from a qualified tuition program be treated as a taxable gift.

(B) TREATMENT OF DESIGNATION OF NEW BENEFICIARY.—The taxes imposed by chapters 12 and 13 shall apply to a transfer by reason of a change in the designated beneficiary under the program (or a rollover to the account of a new beneficiary) unless the new beneficiary is—

(i) assigned to the same generation as (or a higher generation than) the old beneficiary (determined in accordance with section 2651), and

(ii) a member of the family of the old beneficiary.

(6) ADDITIONAL TAX.—The tax imposed by section 530(d)(4) shall apply to any payment or distribution from a qualified tuition program in the same manner as such tax applies to a payment or distribution from an Coverdell education savings account. This paragraph shall not apply to any payment or distribution in any taxable year beginning before January 1, 2004, which is includible in gross income but used for qualified higher education expenses of the designated beneficiary.

Amendments

• 2006, Pension Protection Act of 2006 (P.L. 109-280)

P.L. 109-280, §1304(a), provides:

(a) PERMANENT EXTENSION OF MODIFICATIONS.—Section 901 of the Economic Growth and Tax Relief Reconciliation Act of 2001 [P.L. 107-16] (relating to sunset provisions) shall not apply to section 402 of such Act (relating to modifications to qualified tuition programs).

•2005, Gulf Opportunity Zone Act of 2005 (P.L. 109-135)

P.L. 109-135, §412(ee)(3):

Amended Code Sec. 529(c)(6) by striking "education individual retirement account" and inserting "Coverdell education savings account". **Effective** 12-21-2005.

• 2004, Working Families Tax Relief Act of 2004 (P.L. 108-311)

P.L. 108-311, §406(a):

Amended Code Sec. 529(c)(5)(B). **Effective** as if included in the provision of the Taxpayer Relief Act of 1997 (P.L. 105-34) to which it relates [**effective** for transfers (including designations of new beneficiaries) made after 8-5-97.—CCH]. Prior to amendment, Code Sec. 529(c)(5)(B) read as follows:

(B) TREATMENT OF DESIGNATION OF NEW BENEFICIARY.—The taxes imposed by chapters 12 and 13 shall apply to a transfer by reason of a change in the designated beneficiary under the program (or a rollover to the account of a new beneficiary) only if the new beneficiary is a generation below the generation of the old beneficiary (determined in accordance with section 2651).

• 2001 (P.L. 107-22)

P.L. 107-22, §1(b)(3)(C):

Amended the heading for Code Sec. 529(c)(3)(B)(vi) by striking "EDUCATION INDIVIDUAL RETIREMENT" and inserting "COVERDELL EDUCATION SAVINGS". **E ffective** 7-26-2001.

• 2001, Economic Growth and Tax Relief Reconciliation Act of 2001 (P.L. 107-16)

P.L. 107-16, §402(a)(3)(B):

Amended Code Sec. 529 by adding at the end of subsection (c) a new paragraph (6). **Effective** for tax years beginning after 12-31-2001.

P.L. 107-16, §402(a)(4)(A):

Amended Code Sec. 529 by striking "qualified State tuition" each place it appears and inserting "qualified tuition". **Effective** for tax years beginning after 12-31-2001.

P.L. 107-16, §402(b)(1):

Amended Code Sec. 529(c)(3)(B). **Effective** for tax years beginning after 12-31-2001. Prior to amendment, Code Sec. 529(c)(3)(B) read as follows:

(B) IN-KIND DISTRIBUTIONS.—Any benefit furnished to a designated beneficiary under a qualified State tuition program shall be treated as a distribution to the beneficiary.

P.L. 107-16, §402(c)(1)-(3):

Amended Code Sec. 529(c)(3)(C) by striking "transferred to the credit" in clause (i) and inserting "transferred—" and new subclauses (I) and (II), by adding at the end a new clause (iii), and by inserting "OR PROGRAMS" after "BENEFICIARIES" in the heading. **Effective** for tax years beginning after 12-31-2001.

P.L. 107-16, §402(g)(1)-(2):

Amended Code Sec. 529(c)(3)(D) by inserting "except to the extent provided by the Secretary," before "all distributions" in clause (ii), and by inserting "except to the extent provided by the Secretary," before "the value" in clause (iii). **Effective** for tax years beginning after 12-31-2001.

P.L. 107-16, §901(a)-(b), provides [but see P.L. 109-280, §1304(a), above]:

SEC. 901. SUNSET OF PROVISIONS OF ACT.

(a) IN GENERAL.—All provisions of, and amendments made by, this Act shall not apply—

(1) to taxable, plan, or limitation years beginning after December 31, 2010, or

(2) in the case of title V, to estates of decedents dying, gifts made, or generation skipping transfers, after December 31, 2010.

(b) APPLICATION OF CERTAIN LAWS.—The Internal Revenue Code of 1986 and the Employee Retirement Income Security Act of 1974 shall be applied and administered to years, estates, gifts, and transfers described in subsection (a) as if the provisions and amendments described in subsection (a) had never been enacted.

• 1998, IRS Restructuring and Reform Act of 1998 (P.L. 105-206)

P.L. 105-206, §6004(c)(2):

Amended Code Sec. 529(c)(3)(A) by striking "section 72(b)" and inserting "section 72". **Effective** as if included in the provision of P.L. 105-34 to which it relates [generally **effective** 1-1-98.—CCH].

• 1997, Taxpayer Relief Act of 1997 (P.L. 105-34)

P.L. 105-34, §211(b)(3)(A)(i):

Amended Code Sec. 529(c)(2). **Effective** for transfers (including designations of new beneficiaries) made after 8-5-97. Prior to amendment, Code Sec. 529(c)(2) read as follows:

(2) CONTRIBUTIONS.—In no event shall a contribution to a qualified State tuition program on behalf of a designated beneficiary be treated as a taxable gift for purposes of chapter 12.

P.L. 105-34, §211(b)(3)(A)(ii):

Amended Code Sec. 529(c)(5). **Effective** for transfers (including designations of new beneficiaries) made after 8-5-97. Prior to amendment, Code Sec. 529(c)(5) read as follows:

(5) SPECIAL RULE FOR APPLYING SECTION 2503(e).—For purposes of section 2503(e), the waiver (or payment to an educational institution) of qualified higher education expenses of a designated beneficiary under a qualified State tuition program shall be treated as a qualified transfer.

P.L. 105-34, §211(b)(3)(B):

Amended Code Sec. 529(c)(4). **Effective** for estates of decedents dying after 6-8-97. Prior to amendment, Code Sec. 529(c)(4) read as follows:

(4) ESTATE TAX INCLUSION.—The value of any interest in any qualified State tuition program which is attributable to contributions made by an individual to such program on behalf of any designated beneficiary shall be includible in the gross estate of the contributor for purposes of chapter 11.

P.L. 105-34, §211(d):

Amended Code Sec. 529(c)(3)(A) by striking "section 72" and inserting "section 72(b)". **Effective**, generally, 1-1-98. For a transitional rule, see Act Sec. 211(f)(6), below.

P.L. 105-34, §211(f)(6), provides:

(6) TRANSITION RULE FOR PRE-AUGUST 20, 1996 CONTRACTS.—In the case of any contract issued prior to August 20, 1996, section 529(c)(3)(C) of the Internal Revenue Code of 1986 shall be applied for taxable years ending after August 20, 1996, without regard to the requirement that a distribution be transferred to a member of the family or the requirement that a change in beneficiaries may be made only to a member of the family.

[Sec. 529(d)]

(d) REPORTS.—Each officer or employee having control of the qualified tuition program or their designee shall make such reports regarding such program to the Secretary and to designated beneficiaries with respect to contributions, distributions, and such other matters as the Secretary may require. The reports required by this subsection shall be filed at such time and in such manner and furnished to such individuals at such time and in such manner as may be required by the Secretary.

Amendments

• 2006, Pension Protection Act of 2006 (P.L. 109-280)

P.L. 109-280, §1304(a), provides:

(a) PERMANENT EXTENSION OF MODIFICATIONS.—Section 901 of the Economic Growth and Tax Relief Reconciliation Act of 2001 [P.L. 107-16] (relating to sunset provisions) shall not apply to section 402 of such Act (relating to modifications to qualified tuition programs).

• 2001, Economic Growth and Tax Relief Reconciliation Act of 2001 (P.L. 107-16)

P.L. 107-16, §402(a)(4)(A):

Amended Code Sec. 529 by striking "qualified State tuition" each place it appears and inserting "qualified tuition". **Effective** for tax years beginning after 12-31-2001.

P.L. 107-16, §901(a)-(b), provides [but see P.L. 109-280, §1304(a), above]:

SEC. 901. SUNSET OF PROVISIONS OF ACT.

(a) IN GENERAL.—All provisions of, and amendments made by, this Act shall not apply—

(1) to taxable, plan, or limitation years beginning after December 31, 2010, or

(2) in the case of title V, to estates of decedents dying, gifts made, or generation skipping transfers, after December 31, 2010.

(b) APPLICATION OF CERTAIN LAWS.—The Internal Revenue Code of 1986 and the Employee Retirement Income Security Act of 1974 shall be applied and administered to years, estates, gifts, and transfers described in subsection (a) as if the provisions and amendments described in subsection (a) had never been enacted.

• 1997, Taxpayer Relief Act of 1997 (P.L. 105-34)

P.L. 105-34, §211(e)(2)(A):

Amended Code Sec. 529(d). **Effective** 1-1-98. Prior to amendment, Code Sec. 529(d) read as follows:

(d) REPORTING REQUIREMENTS.—

(1) IN GENERAL.—If there is a distribution to any individual with respect to an interest in a qualified State tuition program during any calendar year, each officer or employee having control of the qualified State tuition program or their designee shall make such reports as the Secretary may require regarding such distribution to the Secretary and to the designated beneficiary or the individual to whom the distribution was made. Any such report shall include such information as the Secretary may prescribe.

(2) TIMING OF REPORTS.—Any report required by this subsection—

(A) shall be filed at such time and in such matter as the Secretary prescribes, and

(B) shall be furnished to individuals not later than January 31 of the calendar year following the calendar year to which such report relates.

[Sec. 529(e)]

(e) OTHER DEFINITIONS AND SPECIAL RULES.—For purposes of this section—

(1) DESIGNATED BENEFICIARY.—The term "designated beneficiary" means—

(A) the individual designated at the commencement of participation in the qualified tuition program as the beneficiary of amounts paid (or to be paid) to the program,

(B) in the case of a change in beneficiaries described in subsection (c)(3)(C), the individual who is the new beneficiary, and

(C) in the case of an interest in a qualified tuition program purchased by a State or local government (or agency or instrumentality thereof) or an organization described in section 501(c)(3) and exempt from taxation under section 501(a) as part of a scholarship program operated by such government or organization, the individual receiving such interest as a scholarship.

(2) MEMBER OF FAMILY.—The term "member of the family" means, with respect to any designated beneficiary—

(A) the spouse of such beneficiary;

(B) an individual who bears a relationship to such beneficiary which is described in subparagraphs (A) through (G) of section 152(d)(2);

(C) the spouse of any individual described in subparagraph (B); and

(D) any first cousin of such beneficiary.

(3) QUALIFIED HIGHER EDUCATION EXPENSES.—

(A) IN GENERAL.—The term "qualified higher education expenses" means—

(i) tuition, fees, books, supplies, and equipment required for the enrollment or attendance of a designated beneficiary at an eligible educational institution;

(ii) expenses for special needs services in the case of a special needs beneficiary which are incurred in connection with such enrollment or attendance[; and]

(iii) expenses paid or incurred in 2009 or 2010 for the purchase of any computer technology or equipment (as defined in section 170(e)(6)(F)(i)) or Internet access and related services, if such technology, equipment, or services are to be used by the beneficiary and the beneficiary's family during any of the years the beneficiary is enrolled at an eligible educational institution.

Clause (iii) shall not include expenses for computer software designed for sports, games, or hobbies unless the software is predominantly educational in nature.

(B) ROOM AND BOARD INCLUDED FOR STUDENTS WHO ARE AT LEAST HALF-TIME.—

(i) IN GENERAL.—In the case of an individual who is an eligible student (as defined in section 25A(b)(3)) for any academic period, such term shall also include reasonable costs for such period (as determined under the qualified tuition program) incurred by the designated beneficiary for room and board while attending such institution. For purposes of subsection (b)(6), a designated beneficiary shall be treated as meeting the requirements of this clause.

(ii) LIMITATION.—The amount treated as qualified higher education expenses by reason of clause (i) shall not exceed—

(I) the allowance (applicable to the student) for room and board included in the cost of attendance (as defined in section 472 of the Higher Education Act of 1965 (20 U.S.C. 1087ll), as in effect on the date of the enactment of the Economic Growth and Tax Relief Reconciliation Act of 2001) as determined by the eligible educational institution for such period, or

(II) if greater, the actual invoice amount the student residing in housing owned or operated by the eligible educational institution is charged by such institution for room and board costs for such period.

(4) APPLICATION OF SECTION 514.—An interest in a qualified tuition program shall not be treated as debt for purposes of section 514.

(5) ELIGIBLE EDUCATIONAL INSTITUTION.—The term "eligible educational institution" means an institution—

(A) which is described in section 481 of the Higher Education Act of 1965 (20 U.S.C. 1088), as in effect on the date of the enactment of this paragraph, and

(B) which is eligible to participate in a program under title IV of such Act.

Amendments

• 2009, American Recovery and Reinvestment Tax Act of 2009 (P.L. 111-5)

P.L. 111-5, §1005(a):

Amended Code Sec. 529(e)(3)(A) by striking "and" at the end of clause (i), by striking the period at the end of clause (ii), and by adding at the end a new clause (iii) and flush sentence. **Effective** for expenses paid or incurred after 12-31-2008.

• 2006, Pension Protection Act of 2006 (P.L. 109-280)

P.L. 109-280, §1304(a), provides:

(a) PERMANENT EXTENSION OF MODIFICATIONS.—Section 901 of the Economic Growth and Tax Relief Reconciliation Act of 2001 [P.L. 107-16] (relating to sunset provisions) shall not apply to section 402 of such Act (relating to modifications to qualified tuition programs).

• 2004, Working Families Tax Relief Act of 2004 (P.L. 108-311)

P.L. 108-311, §207(21):

Amended Code Sec. 529(e)(2)(B) by striking "paragraphs (1) through (8) of section 152(a)" and inserting "subparagraphs (A) through (G) of section 152(d)(2)". **Effective** for tax years beginning after 12-31-2004.

• 2002, Job Creation and Worker Assistance Act of 2002 (P.L. 107-147)

P.L. 107-147, §417(11):

Amended Code Sec. 529(e)(3)(B)(i) by striking "subsection (b)(7)" and inserting "subsection (b)(6)". **Effective** 3-9-2002.

• 2001, Economic Growth and Tax Relief Reconciliation Act of 2001 (P.L. 107-16)

P.L. 107-16, §402(a)(4)(A):

Amended Code Sec. 529 by striking "qualified State tuition" each place it appears and inserting "qualified tuition". **Effective** for tax years beginning after 12-31-2001.

P.L. 107-16, §402(d):

Amended Code Sec. 529(e)(2) by striking "and" at the end of subparagraph (B), by striking the period at the end of subparagraph (C) and by inserting "; and", and by adding at the end a new subparagraph (D). **Effective** for tax years beginning after 12-31-2001.

P.L. 107-16, §402(e):

Amended Code Sec. 529(e)(3)(B)(ii). **Effective** for tax years beginning after 12-31-2001. Prior to amendment, Code Sec. 529(e)(3)(B)(ii) read as follows:

(ii) LIMITATION.—The amount treated as qualified higher education expenses by reason of the preceding sentence shall not exceed the minimum amount (applicable to the student) included for room and board for such period in the cost of attendance (as defined in section 472 of the Higher Education Act of 1965, 20 U.S.C. 1087ll, as in effect on the date of the enactment of this paragraph) for the eligible educational institution for such period.

P.L. 107-16, §402(f):

Amended Code Sec. 529(e)(3)(A). **Effective** for tax years beginning after 12-31-2001. Prior to amendment, Code Sec. 529(e)(3)(A) read as follows:

(A) IN GENERAL.—The term "qualified higher education expenses" means tuition, fees, books, supplies, and equipment required for the enrollment or attendance of a designated beneficiary at an eligible educational institution.

P.L. 107-16, §901(a)-(b), provides [but see 109-280, §1304(a), above]:

SEC. 901. SUNSET OF PROVISIONS OF ACT.

(a) IN GENERAL.—All provisions of, and amendments made by, this Act shall not apply—

(1) to taxable, plan, or limitation years beginning after December 31, 2010, or

(2) in the case of title V, to estates of decedents dying, gifts made, or generation skipping transfers, after December 31, 2010.

(b) APPLICATION OF CERTAIN LAWS.—The Internal Revenue Code of 1986 and the Employee Retirement Income Security Act of 1974 shall be applied and administered to years, estates, gifts, and transfers described in subsection (a) as if the provisions and amendments described in subsection (a) had never been enacted.

• 2000, Community Renewal Tax Relief Act of 2000 (P.L. 106-554)

P.L. 106-554, §319(5):

Amended the heading for Code Sec. 529(e)(3)(B) by striking "UNDER GUARANTEED PLANS" after "STUDENTS". **Effective** 12-21-2000.

• 1998, IRS Restructuring and Reform Act of 1998 (P.L. 105-206)

P.L. 105-206, §6004(c)(3):

Amended Code Sec. 529(e)(2). **Effective** as if included in the provision of P.L. 105-34 to which it relates [generally **effective** 1-1-98.—CCH]. Prior to amendment, Code Sec. 529(e)(2) read as follows:

(2) MEMBER OF FAMILY.—The term "member of the family" means—

(A) an individual who bears a relationship to another individual which is a relationship described in paragraphs (1) through (8) of section 152(a), and

(B) the spouse of any individual described in subparagraph (A).

• 1997, Taxpayer Relief Act of 1997 (P.L. 105-34)

P.L. 105-34, §211(a):

Amended Code Sec. 529(e)(3). **Effective** as if included in the amendments made by Act Sec. 1806 of P.L. 104-188 [generally **effective** for tax years ending after 8-20-96.—CCH]. Prior to amendment, Code Sec. 529(e)(3) read as follows:

(3) QUALIFIED HIGHER EDUCATION EXPENSES.—The term "qualified higher education expenses" means tuition, fees, books, supplies, and equipment required for the enrollment or attendance of a designated beneficiary at an eligible educational institution (as defined in section 135(c)(3)).

P.L. 105-34, §211(b)(1):

Amended Code Sec. 529(e)(2). **Effective** 1-1-98. Prior to amendment, Code Sec. 529(e)(2) read as follows:

(2) MEMBER OF FAMILY.—The term "member of the family" has the same meaning given such term as section 2032A(e)(2).

P.L. 105-34, §211(b)(2):

Amended Code Sec. 529(e) by adding a new paragraph (5). **Effective** for distributions after 12-31-97, with respect to expenses paid after such date (in tax years ending after such date), for education furnished in academic periods beginning after such date. For a transitional rule, see Act Sec. 211(f)(6), below.

P.L. 105-34, §211(f)(6), provides:

(6) TRANSITION RULE FOR PRE-AUGUST 20, 1996 CONTRACTS.—In the case of any contract issued prior to August 20, 1996, section 529(c)(3)(C) of the Internal Revenue Code of 1986 shall be applied for taxable years ending after August 20, 1996, without regard to the requirement that a distribution be transferred to a member of the family or the requirement that a change in beneficiaries may be made only to a member of the family.

P.L. 105-34, §1601(h)(1)(A):

Amended Code Sec. 529(e)(1)(B) by striking "subsection (c)(2)(C)" and inserting "subsection (c)(3)(C)". **Effective** as if included in the provision of P.L. 104-188 to which it relates [generally **effective** for tax years ending after 8-20-96.—CCH].

P.L. 105-34, §1601(h)(1)(B):

Amended Code Sec. 529(e)(1)(C) by inserting "(or agency or instrumentality thereof)" after "local government". **Effective** as if included in the provision of P.L. 104-188 to which it relates [generally **effective** for tax years ending after 8-20-96.—CCH].

• 1996, Small Business Job Protection Act of 1996 (P.L. 104-188)

P.L. 104-188, §1806(a):

Amended subchapter F of chapter 1 by adding at the end a new part VIII (Code Sec. 529). **Effective** for tax years ending after 8-20-96. For a transitional rule, see Act Sec. 1806(c)(2), below.

P.L. 104-188, §1806(c)(2), as amended by P.L. 105-34, §1601(h)(1)(C), provides:

(2) TRANSITION RULE.—If—

(A) a State or agency or instrumentality thereof maintains, on the date of the enactment of this Act, a program under which persons may purchase tuition credits or certificates on behalf of, or make contributions for education expenses of, a designated beneficiary, and

(B) such program meets the requirements of a qualified State tuition program before the later of—

(i) the date which is 1 year after such date of enactment, or

(ii) the first day of the first calendar quarter after the close of the first regular session of the State legislature that begins after such date of enactment,

then such program (as in effect on August 20, 1996) shall be treated as a qualified State tuition program with respect to contributions (and earnings allocable thereto) pursuant to contracts entered into under such program before the first date on which such program meets such requirements (determined without regard to this paragraph) and the provisions of such program (as so in effect) shall apply in lieu of section 529(b) of the Internal Revenue Code of 1986 with respect to such contributions and earnings.

For purposes of subparagraph (B)(ii), if a State has a 2-year legislative session, each year of such session shall be deemed to be a separate regular session of the State legislature.

[Sec. 529(f)]

(f) REGULATIONS.—Notwithstanding any other provision of this section, the Secretary shall prescribe such regulations as may be necessary or appropriate to carry out the purposes of this section and to prevent abuse of such purposes, including regulations under chapters 11, 12, and 13 of this title.

Amendments

• 2006, Pension Protection Act of 2006 (P.L. 109-280)

P.L. 109-280, §1304(b):

Amended Code Sec. 529 by adding at the end a new subsection (f). **Effective** 8-17-2006.

[Sec. 530]

SEC. 530. COVERDELL EDUCATION SAVINGS ACCOUNTS.

[Sec. 530(a)]

(a) GENERAL RULE.—A Coverdell education savings account shall be exempt from taxation under this subtitle. Notwithstanding the preceding sentence, the Coverdell education savings account shall be subject to the taxes imposed by section 511 (relating to imposition of tax on unrelated business income of charitable organizations).

Amendments

• 2001 (P.L. 107-22)

P.L. 107-22, §1(a)(2)(A)-(B):

Amended Code Sec. 530(a) by striking "An education individual retirement account" and inserting "A Coverdell education savings account", and by striking "the education individual retirement account" and inserting "the Coverdell education savings account". **Effective** 7-26-2001.

P.L. 107-22, §1(a)(5):

Amended the heading for Code Sec. 530. **Effective** 7-26-2001. Prior to amendment, the heading for Code Sec. 530 read as follows:

SEC. 530. EDUCATION INDIVIDUAL RETIREMENT ACCOUNTS.

[Sec. 530(b)]

(b) DEFINITIONS AND SPECIAL RULES.—For purposes of this section—

»»→ Caution: Code Sec. 530(b)(1)-(2), below, is subject to the sunset provision of the Economic Growth and Tax Relief Reconciliation Act of 2001 (P.L. 107-16), §901. Absent Congressional action, the changes made to this provision by P.L. 107-16, or that take effect as if included in P.L. 107-16, do not apply after December 31, 2010. For more information about the sunset provision, see page XXI of the Preface to this publication and P.L. 107-16, §901, in the amendment notes. See the amendments notes for a history of amendments to this section and the effective date of each change.

(1) COVERDELL EDUCATION SAVINGS ACCOUNT.—The term "Coverdell education savings account" means a trust created or organized in the United States exclusively for the purpose of paying the qualified education expenses of an individual who is the designated beneficiary of the trust (and designated as a Coverdell education savings account at the time created or organized), but only if the written governing instrument creating the trust meets the following requirements:

(A) No contribution will be accepted—

(i) unless it is in cash,

(ii) after the date on which such beneficiary attains age 18, or

(iii) except in the case of rollover contributions, if such contribution would result in aggregate contributions for the taxable year exceeding $2,000.

(B) The trustee is a bank (as defined in section 408(n)) or another person who demonstrates to the satisfaction of the Secretary that the manner in which that person will administer the trust will be consistent with the requirements of this section or who has so demonstrated with respect to any individual retirement plan.

(C) No part of the trust assets will be invested in life insurance contracts.

(D) The assets of the trust shall not be commingled with other property except in a common trust fund or common investment fund.

(E) Except as provided in subsection (d)(7), any balance to the credit of the designated beneficiary on the date on which the beneficiary attains age 30 shall be distributed within 30 days after such date to the beneficiary or, if the beneficiary dies before attaining age 30, shall be distributed within 30 days after the date of death of such beneficiary.

The age limitations in subparagraphs (A)(ii) and (E), and paragraphs (5) and (6) of subsection (d), shall not apply to any designated beneficiary with special needs (as determined under regulations prescribed by the Secretary).

(2) QUALIFIED EDUCATION EXPENSES.—

(A) IN GENERAL.—The term "qualified education expenses" means—

(i) qualified higher education expenses (as defined in section 529(e)(3)), and

(ii) qualified elementary and secondary education expenses (as defined in paragraph (3)).

(B) QUALIFIED TUITION PROGRAMS.—Such term shall include any contribution to a qualified tuition program (as defined in section 529(b)) on behalf of the designated beneficiary (as defined in section 529(e)(1)); but there shall be no increase in the investment in the contract for purposes of applying section 72 by reason of any portion of such contribution which is not includible in gross income by reason of subsection (d)(2).

»»→ Caution: Code Sec. 530(b)(3)-(4), below, is subject to the sunset provision of the Economic Growth and Tax Relief Reconciliation Act of 2001 (P.L. 107-16), §901. Absent Congressional action, the changes made to this provision by P.L. 107-16, or that take effect as if included in P.L. 107-16, do not apply after December 31, 2010. For more information about the sunset provision, see page XXI of the Preface to this publication and P.L. 107-16, §901, in the amendment notes. See the amendments notes for a history of amendments to this section and the effective date of each change.

(3) QUALIFIED ELEMENTARY AND SECONDARY EDUCATION EXPENSES.—

(A) IN GENERAL.—The term "qualified elementary and secondary education expenses" means—

(i) expenses for tuition, fees, academic tutoring, special needs services in the case of a special needs beneficiary, books, supplies, and other equipment which are incurred in connection with the enrollment or attendance of the designated beneficiary of the trust as an elementary or secondary school student at a public, private, or religious school,

(ii) expenses for room and board, uniforms, transportation, and supplementary items and services (including extended day programs) which are required or provided by a public, private, or religious school in connection with such enrollment or attendance, and

(iii) expenses for the purchase of any computer technology or equipment (as defined in section 170(e)(6)(F)(i)) or Internet access and related services, if such technology, equipment, or services are to be used by the beneficiary and the beneficiary's family during any of the years the beneficiary is in school.

Clause (iii) shall not include expenses for computer software designed for sports, games, or hobbies unless the software is predominantly educational in nature.

(B) SCHOOL.—The term "school" means any school which provides elementary education or secondary education (kindergarten through grade 12), as determined under State law.

(4) TIME WHEN CONTRIBUTIONS DEEMED MADE.—An individual shall be deemed to have made a contribution to a Coverdell education savings account on the last day of the preceding taxable year if the contribution is made on account of such taxable year and is made not later than the time prescribed by law for filing the return for such taxable year (not including extensions thereof).

Amendments

• 2006, Pension Protection Act of 2006 (P.L. 109-280)

P.L. 109-280, §1304(a), provides:

(a) PERMANENT EXTENSION OF MODIFICATIONS.—Section 901 of the Economic Growth and Tax Relief Reconciliation Act of 2001 [P.L. 107-16] (relating to sunset provisions) shall not apply to section 402 of such Act (relating to modifications to qualified tuition programs).

• 2005, Gulf Opportunity Zone Act of 2005 (P.L. 109-135)

P.L. 109-135, §412(ff)(1):

Amended Code Sec. 530(b) by striking paragraph (3) and by redesignating paragraphs (4) and (5) as paragraphs (3) and (4), respectively. **Effective** 12-21-2005. Prior to being stricken, Code Sec. 530(b)(3) read as follows:

(3) ELIGIBLE EDUCATIONAL INSTITUTION.—The term "eligible educational institution" has the meaning given such term by section 529(e)(5).

P.L. 109-135, §412(ff)(2):

Amended Code Sec. 530(b)(2)(A)(ii) by striking "paragraph (4)" and inserting "paragraph (3)". **Effective** 12-21-2005.

• 2001 (P.L. 107-22)

P.L. 107-22, §1(a)(1):

Amended Code Sec. 530 by striking "an education individual retirement account" each place it appears and inserting "a Coverdell education savings account". **Effective** 7-26-2001.

P.L. 107-22, §1(a)(3)(A)-(B):

Amended Code Sec. 530(b)(1) by striking "education individual retirement account" and inserting "Coverdell education savings account", and by striking "EDUCATION INDIVIDUAL RETIREMENT ACCOUNT" in the heading and inserting "COVERDELL EDUCATION SAVINGS ACCOUNT". **E ffective** 7-26-2001.

• 2001, Economic Growth and Tax Relief Reconciliation Act of 2001 (P.L. 107-16)

P.L. 107-16, §401(a)(1):

Amended Code Sec. 530(b)(1)(A)(iii) by striking "$500" and inserting "$2,000". **Effective** for tax years beginning after 12-31-2001.

P.L. 107-16, §401(c)(1):

Amended Code Sec. 530(b)(2). **Effective** for tax years beginning after 12-31-2001. Prior to amendment, Code Sec. 530(b)(2) read as follows:

(2) QUALIFIED HIGHER EDUCATION EXPENSES.—

(A) IN GENERAL.—The term "qualified higher education expenses" has the meaning given such term by section 529(e)(3), reduced as provided in section 25A(g)(2).

(B) QUALIFIED STATE TUITION PROGRAMS.—Such term shall include amounts paid or incurred to purchase tuition credits or certificates, or to make contributions to an account, under a qualified State tuition program (as defined in section 529(b)) for the benefit of the beneficiary of the account.

P.L. 107-16, §401(c)(2):

Amended Code Sec. 530(b) by adding at the end a new paragraph (4). **Effective** for tax years beginning after 12-31-2001.

P.L. 107-16, §401(c)(3)(A):

Amended Code Sec. 530(b)(1) by striking "higher" after "qualified". **Effective** for tax years beginning after 12-31-2001.

P.L. 107-16, §401(d):

Amended Code Sec. 530(b)(1) by adding at the end a new flush sentence. **Effective** for tax years beginning after 12-31-2001.

P.L. 107-16, §401(f)(1):

Amended Code Sec. 530(b), as amended by Act Sec. 401(c)(2), by adding at the end a new paragraph (5). **Effective** for tax years beginning after 12-31-2001.

P.L. 107-16, §402(a)(4)(A):

Amended Code Sec. 530(b)(2)(B) by striking "qualified State tuition" and inserting "qualified tuition". **Effective** for tax years beginning after 12-31-2001.

P.L. 107-16, §402(a)(4)(C):

Amended the heading for Code Sec. 530(b)(2)(B) by striking "QUALIFIED STATE TUITION" and inserting "QUALIFIED TUITION". **E ffective** for tax years beginning after 12-31-2001.

P.L. 107-16, §901(a)-(b), provides [but see P.L. 109-280, §1304(a), above]:

SEC. 901. SUNSET OF PROVISIONS OF ACT.

(a) IN GENERAL.—All provisions of, and amendments made by, this Act shall not apply—

(1) to taxable, plan, or limitation years beginning after December 31, 2010, or

(2) in the case of title V, to estates of decedents dying, gifts made, or generation skipping transfers, after December 31, 2010.

(b) APPLICATION OF CERTAIN LAWS.—The Internal Revenue Code of 1986 and the Employee Retirement Income Security Act of 1974 shall be applied and administered to years, estates, gifts, and transfers described in subsection (a) as if the provisions and amendments described in subsection (a) had never been enacted.

• 1998, IRS Restructuring and Reform Act of 1998 (P.L. 105-206)

P.L. 105-206, §6004(d)(1):

Amended Code Sec. 530(b)(1) by inserting "an individual who is" before "the designated beneficiary" in the material preceding subparagraph (A). **Effective** as if included in the provision of P.L. 105-34 to which it relates [**effective** for tax years beginning after 12-31-97.—CCH].

P.L. 105-206, §6004(d)(2)(A):

Amended Code Sec. 530(b)(1)(E). **Effective** as if included in the provision of P.L. 105-34 to which it relates [**effective** for tax years beginning after 12-31-97.—CCH]. Prior to amendment, Code Sec. 530(b)(1)(E) read as follows:

(E) Upon the death of the designated beneficiary, any balance to the credit of the beneficiary shall be distributed within 30 days after the date of death to the estate of such beneficiary.

[Sec. 530(c)]

(c) REDUCTION IN PERMITTED CONTRIBUTIONS BASED ON ADJUSTED GROSS INCOME.—

Caution: Code Sec. 530(c)(1), below, is subject to the sunset provision of the Economic Growth and Tax Relief Reconciliation Act of 2001 (P.L. 107-16), §901. Absent Congressional action, the changes made to this provision by P.L. 107-16, or that take effect as if included in P.L. 107-16, do not apply after December 31, 2010. For more information about the sunset provision, see page XXI of the Preface to this publication and P.L. 107-16, §901, in the amendment notes. See the amendments notes for a history of amendments to this section and the effective date of each change.

(1) IN GENERAL.—In the case of a contributor who is an individual, the maximum amount the contributor could otherwise make to an account under this section shall be reduced by an amount which bears the same ratio to such maximum amount as—

(A) the excess of—

(i) the contributor's modified adjusted gross income for such taxable year, over

(ii) $95,000 ($190,000 in the case of a joint return), bears to

(B) $15,000 ($30,000 in the case of a joint return).

(2) MODIFIED ADJUSTED GROSS INCOME.—For purposes of paragraph (1), the term "modified adjusted gross income" means the adjusted gross income of the taxpayer for the taxable year increased by any amount excluded from gross income under section 911, 931, or 933.

Amendments

• 2001, Economic Growth and Tax Relief Reconciliation Act of 2001 (P.L. 107-16)

P.L. 107-16, §401(b)(1)-(2):

Amended Code Sec. 530(c)(1) by striking "$150,000" in subparagraph (A)(ii) and inserting "$190,000", and by striking "$10,000" in subparagraph (B) and inserting "$30,000". **Effective** for tax years beginning after 12-31-2001.

P.L. 107-16, §401(e):

Amended Code Sec. 530(c)(1) by striking "The maximum amount which a contributor" and inserting "In the case of a contributor who is an individual, the maximum amount the contributor". **Effective** for tax years beginning after 12-31-2001.

P.L. 107-16, §901(a)-(b), provides:

SEC. 901. SUNSET OF PROVISIONS OF ACT.

(a) IN GENERAL.—All provisions of, and amendments made by, this Act shall not apply—

(1) to taxable, plan, or limitation years beginning after December 31, 2010, or

(2) in the case of title V, to estates of decedents dying, gifts made, or generation skipping transfers, after December 31, 2010.

(b) APPLICATION OF CERTAIN LAWS.—The Internal Revenue Code of 1986 and the Employee Retirement Income Security Act of 1974 shall be applied and administered to years, estates, gifts, and transfers described in subsection (a) as if the provisions and amendments described in subsection (a) had never been enacted.

[Sec. 530(d)]

(d) TAX TREATMENT OF DISTRIBUTIONS.—

(1) IN GENERAL.—Any distribution shall be includible in the gross income of the distributee in the manner as provided in section 72.

Caution: Code Sec. 530(d)(2), below, was amended by P.L. 107-16 and P.L. 108-311, and is subject to the sunset provision of the Economic Growth and Tax Relief Reconciliation Act of 2001 (P.L. 107-16), §901. Absent Congressional action, the changes made to this provision by P.L. 107-16, or that take effect as if included in P.L. 107-16, do not apply after December 31, 2010. For more information about the sunset provision, see page XXI of the Preface to this publication and P.L. 107-16, §901, in the amendment notes. See the amendments notes for a history of amendments to this section and the effective date of each change.

(2) DISTRIBUTIONS FOR QUALIFIED EDUCATION EXPENSES.—

(A) IN GENERAL.—No amount shall be includible in gross income under paragraph (1) if the qualified education expenses of the designated beneficiary during the taxable year are not less than the aggregate distributions during the taxable year.

(B) DISTRIBUTIONS IN EXCESS OF EXPENSES.—If such aggregate distributions exceed such expenses during the taxable year, the amount otherwise includible in gross income under paragraph (1) shall be reduced by the amount which bears the same ratio to the amount which would be includible in gross income under paragraph (1) (without regard to this subparagraph) as the qualified education expenses bear to such aggregate distributions.

(C) COORDINATION WITH HOPE AND LIFETIME LEARNING CREDITS AND QUALIFIED TUITION PROGRAMS.—For purposes of subparagraph (A)—

(i) CREDIT COORDINATION.—The total amount of qualified education expenses with respect to an individual for the taxable year shall be reduced—

(I) as provided in section 25A(g)(2), and

(II) by the amount of such expenses which were taken into account in determining the credit allowed to the taxpayer or any other person under section 25A.

(ii) COORDINATION WITH QUALIFIED TUITION PROGRAMS.—If, with respect to an individual for any taxable year—

(I) the aggregate distributions during such year to which subparagraph (A) and section 529(c)(3)(B) apply, exceed

(II) the total amount of qualified education expenses (after the application of clause (i)) for such year,

the taxpayer shall allocate such expenses among such distributions for purposes of determining the amount of the exclusion under subparagraph (A) and section 529(c)(3)(B).

(D) DISALLOWANCE OF EXCLUDED AMOUNTS AS DEDUCTION, CREDIT, OR EXCLUSION.—No deduction, credit, or exclusion shall be allowed to the taxpayer under any other section of this chapter for any qualified education expenses to the extent taken into account in determining the amount of the exclusion under this paragraph.

(3) SPECIAL RULES FOR APPLYING ESTATE AND GIFT TAXES WITH RESPECT TO ACCOUNT.—Rules similar to the rules of paragraphs (2), (4), and (5) of section 529(c) shall apply for purposes of this section.

(4) ADDITIONAL TAX FOR DISTRIBUTIONS NOT USED FOR EDUCATIONAL EXPENSES.—

(A) IN GENERAL.—The tax imposed by this chapter for any taxable year on any taxpayer who receives a payment or distribution from a Coverdell education savings account which is includible in gross income shall be increased by 10 percent of the amount which is so includible.

(B) EXCEPTIONS.—Subparagraph (A) shall not apply if the payment or distribution is—

(i) made to a beneficiary (or to the estate of the designated beneficiary) on or after the death of the designated beneficiary,

(ii) attributable to the designated beneficiary's being disabled (within the meaning of section 72(m)(7)),

(iii) made on account of a scholarship, allowance, or payment described in section 25A(g)(2) received by the designated beneficiary to the extent the amount of the payment or distribution does not exceed the amount of the scholarship, allowance, or payment,

(iv) made on account of the attendance of the designated beneficiary at the United States Military Academy, the United States Naval Academy, the United States Air Force Academy, the United States Coast Guard Academy, or the United States Merchant Marine Academy, to the extent that the amount of the payment or distribution does not exceed the costs of advanced education (as defined by section 2005(e)(3) of title 10, United States Code, as in effect on the date of the enactment of this section) attributable to such attendance, or

→ Caution: Former Code Sec. 530(d)(4)(B)(iv), below, was redesignated as Code Sec. 530(d)(4)(B)(v) by P.L. 108-121, and amended by P.L. 107-147, effective as if included in P.L. 107-16, and is subject to the sunset provision of the Economic Growth and Tax Relief Reconciliation Act of 2001 (P.L. 107-16), §901. Absent Congressional action, the changes made to this provision by P.L. 107-16, or that take effect as if included in P.L. 107-16, do not apply after December 31, 2010. For more information about the sunset provision, see page XXI of the Preface to this publication and P.L. 107-16, §901, in the amendment notes. See the amendments notes for a history of amendments to this section and the effective date of each change.

(v) an amount which is includible in gross income solely by application of paragraph (2)(C)(i)(II) for the taxable year.

→ Caution: Code Sec. 530(d)(4)(C), below, is subject to the sunset provision of the Economic Growth and Tax Relief Reconciliation Act of 2001 (P.L. 107-16), §901. Absent Congressional action, the changes made to this provision by P.L. 107-16, or that take effect as if included in P.L. 107-16, do not apply after December 31, 2010. For more information about the sunset provision, see page XXI of the Preface to this publication and P.L. 107-16, §901, in the amendment notes. See the amendments notes for a history of amendments to this section and the effective date of each change.

(C) CONTRIBUTIONS RETURNED BEFORE CERTAIN DATE.—Subparagraph (A) shall not apply to the distribution of any contribution made during a taxable year on behalf of the designated beneficiary if—

(i) such distribution is made before the first day of the sixth month of the taxable year following the taxable year, and

(ii) such distribution is accompanied by the amount of net income attributable to such excess contribution.

Any net income described in clause (ii) shall be included in gross income for the taxable year in which such excess contribution was made.

(5) ROLLOVER CONTRIBUTIONS.—Paragraph (1) shall not apply to any amount paid or distributed from a Coverdell education savings account to the extent that the amount received is paid,

not later than the 60th day after the date of such payment or distribution, into another Coverdell education savings account for the benefit of the same beneficiary or a member of the family (within the meaning of section 529(e)(2)) of such beneficiary who has not attained age 30 as of such date. The preceding sentence shall not apply to any payment or distribution if it applied to any prior payment or distribution during the 12-month period ending on the date of the payment or distribution.

(6) CHANGE IN BENEFICIARY.—Any change in the beneficiary of a Coverdell education savings account shall not be treated as a distribution for purposes of paragraph (1) if the new beneficiary is a member of the family (as so defined) of the old beneficiary and has not attained age 30 as of the date of such change.

(7) SPECIAL RULES FOR DEATH AND DIVORCE.—Rules similar to the rules of paragraphs (7) and (8) of section 220(f) shall apply. In applying the preceding sentence, members of the family (as so defined) of the designated beneficiary shall be treated in the same manner as the spouse under such paragraph (8).

(8) DEEMED DISTRIBUTION ON REQUIRED DISTRIBUTION DATE.—In any case in which a distribution is required under subsection (b)(1)(E), any balance to the credit of a designated beneficiary as of the close of the 30-day period referred to in such subsection for making such distribution shall be deemed distributed at the close of such period.

(9) MILITARY DEATH GRATUITY.—

(A) IN GENERAL.—For purposes of this section, the term "rollover contribution" includes a contribution to a Coverdell education savings account made before the end of the 1-year period beginning on the date on which the contributor receives an amount under section 1477 of title 10, United States Code, or section 1967 of title 38 of such Code, with respect to a person, to the extent that such contribution does not exceed—

(i) the sum of the amounts received during such period by such contributor under such sections with respect to such person, reduced by

(ii) the amounts so received which were contributed to a Roth IRA under section 408A(e)(2) or to another Coverdell education savings account.

(B) ANNUAL LIMIT ON NUMBER OF ROLLOVERS NOT TO APPLY.—The last sentence of paragraph (5) shall not apply with respect to amounts treated as a rollover by the subparagraph (A).

(C) APPLICATION OF SECTION 72.—For purposes of applying section 72 in the case of a distribution which is includible in gross income under paragraph (1), the amount treated as a rollover by reason of subparagraph (A) shall be treated as [an] investment in the contract.

Amendments

• 2008, Heroes Earnings Assistance and Relief Tax Act of 2008 (P.L. 110-245)

P.L. 110-245, §109(c):

Amended Code Sec. 530(d) by adding at the end a new paragraph (9). **Effective** generally with respect to deaths from injuries occurring on or after 6-17-2008. For a special rule, see Act Sec. 109(d)(2), below.

P.L. 110-245, §109(d)(2), provides:

(2) APPLICATION OF AMENDMENTS TO DEATHS FROM INJURIES OCCURRING ON OR AFTER OCTOBER 7, 2001, AND BEFORE ENACTMENT.—The amendments made by this section shall apply to any contribution made pursuant to section 408A(e)(2) or 530(d)(5) [sic] of the Internal Revenue Code of 1986, as amended by this Act, with respect to amounts received under section 1477 of title 10, United States Code, or under section 1967 of title 38 of such Code, for deaths from injuries occurring on or after October 7, 2001, and before the date of the enactment of this Act [6-17-2008.—CCH] if such contribution is made not later than 1 year after the date of the enactment of this Act.

• 2004, Working Families Tax Relief Act of 2004 (P.L. 108-311)

P.L. 108-311, §404(a):

Amended Code Sec. 530(d)(2)(C)(i) by striking "higher" after "qualified". **Effective** as if included in the provision of the Economic Growth and Tax Relief Reconciliation Act of 2001 (P.L. 107-16) to which it relates [**effective** for tax years beginning after 12-31-2001.—CCH].

P.L. 108-311, §406(b):

Amended Code Sec. 530(d)(4)(B)(iii) by striking "account holder" and inserting "designated beneficiary". **Effective** as if included in the provision of the Taxpayer Relief Act of 1997 (P.L. 105-34) to which it relates [**effective** for tax years beginning after 12-31-97.—CCH].

• 2003, Military Family Tax Relief Act of 2003 (P.L. 108-121)

P.L. 108-121, §107(a):

Amended Code Sec. 530(d)(4)(B) by striking "or" at the end of clause (iii), by redesignating clause (iv) as clause (v), and by inserting after clause (iii) a new clause (iv). **Effective** for tax years beginning after 12-31-2002.

• 2002, Job Creation and Worker Assistance Act of 2002 (P.L. 107-147)

P.L. 107-147, §411(f):

Amended Code Sec. 530(d)(4)(B)(iv) by striking "because the taxpayer elected under paragraph (2)(C) to waive the application of paragraph (2)" and inserting "by application of paragraph (2)(C)(i)(II)". **Effective** as if included in the provision of P.L. 107-16 to which it relates [**effective** for tax years beginning after 12-31-2001.—CCH].

• 2001 (P.L. 107-22)

P.L. 107-22, §1(a)(1):

Amended Code Sec. 530 by striking "an education individual retirement account" each place it appears and inserting "a Coverdell education savings account". **Effective** 7-26-2001.

P.L. 107-22, §1(a)(4):

Amended Code Sec. 530(d)(5) by striking "education individual retirement account" and inserting "Coverdell education savings account". **Effective** 7-26-2001.

• 2001, Economic Growth and Tax Relief Reconciliation Act of 2001 (P.L. 107-16)

P.L. 107-16, §401(c)(3)(A):

Amended Code Sec. 530(d)(2) by striking "higher" after "qualified" each place it appears. **Effective** for tax years beginning after 12-31-2001.

P.L. 107-16, §401(c)(3)(B):

Amended the heading for Code Sec. 530(d)(2) by striking "HIGHER" after "QUALIFIED". **E ffective** for tax years beginning after 12-31-2001.

P.L. 107-16, §401(f)(2)(A)-(B):

Amended Code Sec. 530(d)(4)(C) by striking clause (i) and inserting a new clause (i), and by striking "DUE DATE OF RETURN" in the heading and inserting "CERTAIN DATE". **E ffective** for tax years beginning after 12-31-2001. Prior to being stricken, Code Sec. 530(d)(4)(C)(i) read as follows:

(i) such distribution is made on or before the day prescribed by law (including extensions of time) for filing the beneficiary's return of tax for the taxable year or, if the beneficiary is not required to file such a return, the 15th day of the 4th month of the taxable year following the taxable year; and

P.L. 107-16, §401(g)(1):

Amended Code Sec. 530(d)(2)(C). **Effective** for tax years beginning after 12-31-2001. Prior to amendment, Code Sec. 530(d)(2)(C) read as follows:

(C) ELECTION TO WAIVE EXCLUSION.—A taxpayer may elect to waive the application of this paragraph for any taxable year.

P.L. 107-16, §401(g)(2)(C)(i)-(ii):

Amended Code Sec. 530(d)(2)(D) by striking "or credit" and inserting ", credit, or exclusion", and by striking "CREDIT OR DEDUCTION" in the heading and inserting "DEDUCTION, CREDIT, OR EXCLUSION". **E ffective** for tax years beginning after 12-31-2001.

P.L. 107-16, §901(a)-(b), provides:

SEC. 901. SUNSET OF PROVISIONS OF ACT.

(a) IN GENERAL.—All provisions of, and amendments made by, this Act shall not apply—

(1) to taxable, plan, or limitation years beginning after December 31, 2010, or

(2) in the case of title V, to estates of decedents dying, gifts made, or generation skipping transfers, after December 31, 2010.

(b) APPLICATION OF CERTAIN LAWS.—The Internal Revenue Code of 1986 and the Employee Retirement Income Security Act of 1974 shall be applied and administered to years, estates, gifts, and transfers described in subsection (a) as if the provisions and amendments described in subsection (a) had never been enacted.

• 2000, Community Renewal Tax Relief Act of 2000 (P.L. 106-554)

P.L. 106-554, §319(6):

Amended Code Sec. 530(d)(4)(B)(iii) by striking "; or" at the end and inserting ", or". **Effective** 12-21-2000.

• 1998, IRS Restructuring and Reform Act of 1998 (P.L. 105-206)

P.L. 105-206, §6004(d)(2)(B):

Amended Code Sec. 530(d)(7) by inserting at the end a new sentence. **Effective** as if included in the provision of P.L. 105-34 to which it relates [**effective** for tax years beginning after 12-31-97.—CCH].

P.L. 105-206, §6004(d)(2)(C):

Amended Code Sec. 530(d) by adding at the end a new paragraph (8). **Effective** as if included in the provision of P.L. 105-34 to which it relates [**effective** for tax years beginning after 12-31-97.—CCH].

P.L. 105-206, §6004(d)(3)(A):

Amended Code Sec. 530(d)(1) by striking "section 72(b)" and inserting "section 72". **Effective** as if included in the provision of P.L. 105-34 to which it relates [**effective** for tax years beginning after 12-31-97.—CCH].

P.L. 105-206, §6004(d)(5):

Amended Code Sec. 530(d)(2) by adding at the end a new subparagraph (D). **Effective** as if included in the provision of P.L. 105-34 to which it relates [**effective** for tax years beginning after 12-31-97.—CCH].

P.L. 105-206, §6004(d)(6):

Amended Code Sec. 530(d)(4)(B) by striking "or" at the end of clause (ii), by striking the period at the end of clause (iii) and inserting "; or", and by adding at the end a new clause (iv). **Effective** as if included in the provision of P.L. 105-34 to which it relates [**effective** for tax years beginning after 12-31-97.—CCH].

P.L. 105-206, §6004(d)(7):

Amended so much of Code Sec. 530(d)(4)(C) as precedes clause (ii). **Effective** as if included in the provision of P.L. 105-34 to which it relates [**effective** for tax years beginning after 12-31-97.—CCH]. Prior to amendment, so much of Code Sec. 530(d)(4)(C) as preceded clause (ii) read as follows:

(C) EXCESS CONTRIBUTIONS RETURNED BEFORE DUE DATE OF RETURN.—Subparagraph (A) shall not apply to the distribution of any contribution made during a taxable year on behalf of a designated beneficiary to the extent that such contribution exceeds $500 if—

(i) such distribution is received on or before the day prescribed by law (including extensions of time) for filing such contributor's return for such taxable year, and

P.L. 105-206, §6004(d)(8)(A):

Amended Code Sec. 530(d)(5) by striking the first sentence and inserting a new sentence. **Effective** as if included in the provision of P.L. 105-34 to which it relates [**effective** for tax years beginning after 12-31-97.—CCH]. Prior to amendment, the first sentence of Code Sec. 530(d)(5) read as follows:

Paragraph (1) shall not apply to any amount paid or distributed from an education individual retirement account to the extent that the amount received is paid into another education individual retirement account for the benefit of the same beneficiary or a member of the family (within the meaning of section 529(e)(2)) of such beneficiary not later than the 60th day after the date of such payment or distribution.

P.L. 105-206, §6004(d)(8)(B):

Amended Code Sec. 530(d)(6) by inserting "and has not attained age 30 as of the date of such change" before the period. **Effective** as if included in the provision of P.L. 105-34 to which it relates [**effective** for tax years beginning after 12-31-97.—CCH].

[Sec. 530(e)]

(e) TAX TREATMENT OF ACCOUNTS.—Rules similar to the rules of paragraphs (2) and (4) of section 408(e) shall apply to any Coverdell education savings account.

Amendments

• 2001 (P.L. 107-22)

P.L. 107-22, §1(a)(4):

Amended Code Sec. 530(e) by striking "education individual retirement account" and inserting "Coverdell education savings account". **Effective** 7-26-2001.

[Sec. 530(f)]

(f) COMMUNITY PROPERTY LAWS.—This section shall be applied without regard to any community property laws.

[Sec. 530(g)]

(g) CUSTODIAL ACCOUNTS.—For purposes of this section, a custodial account shall be treated as a trust if the assets of such account are held by a bank (as defined in section 408(n)) or another person who demonstrates, to the satisfaction of the Secretary, that the manner in which he will administer the account will be consistent with the requirements of this section, and if the custodial account would, except for the fact that it is not a trust, constitute an account described in subsection (b)(1). For purposes of this title, in the case of a custodial account treated as a trust by reason of the preceding sentence, the custodian of such account shall be treated as the trustee thereof.

[Sec. 530(h)]

(h) REPORTS.—The trustee of a Coverdell education savings account shall make such reports regarding such account to the Secretary and to the beneficiary of the account with respect to contributions, distributions, and such other matters as the Secretary may require. The reports required by this subsection shall be filed at such time and in such manner and furnished to such individuals at such time and in such manner as may be required.

Amendments

• **2001 (P.L. 107-22)**

P.L. 107-22, §1(a)(1):

Amended Code Sec. 530 by striking "an education individual retirement account" each place it appears and inserting "a Coverdell education savings account". **Effective** 7-26-2001.

• **1997, Taxpayer Relief Act of 1997 (P.L. 105-34)**

P.L. 105-34, §213(a):

Amended part VIII of subchapter F of chapter 1 by adding at the end a new Code Sec. 530. **Effective** for tax years beginning after 12-31-97.

Subchapter G—Corporations Used to Avoid Income Tax on Shareholders

PART I—CORPORATIONS IMPROPERLY ACCUMULATING SURPLUS

»»→ Caution: Code Sec. 531, below, was amended by P.L. 107-16 and P.L. 108-27, and is subject to the sunset provisions of the Economic Growth and Tax Relief Reconciliation Act of 2001 (P.L. 107-16), §901 and the Jobs and Growth Tax Relief Reconciliation Act of 2003 (P.L. 108-27), §303. Absent Congressional action, the changes made to this provision by P.L. 107-16, and P.L. 108-27, or that take effect as if included in P.L. 107-16, and P.L. 108-27, do not apply after December 31, 2010. For more information about the sunset provisions, see page XXI of the Preface to this publication and P.L. 107-16, §901, and P.L. 108-27, §303, in the amendment notes. See the amendments notes for a history of amendments to this section and the effective date of each change.

[Sec. 531]

SEC. 531. IMPOSITION OF ACCUMULATED EARNINGS TAX.

In addition to other taxes imposed by this chapter, there is hereby imposed for each taxable year on the accumulated taxable income (as defined in section 535) of each corporation described in section 532, an accumulated earnings tax equal to 15 percent of the accumulated taxable income.

Amendments

• **2003, Jobs and Growth Tax Relief Reconciliation Act of 2003 (P.L. 108-27)**

P.L. 108-27, §302(e)(5):

Amended Code Sec. 531 by striking "equal to" and all that follows and inserting "equal to 15 percent of the accumulated taxable income.". For the **effective** date, see Act Sec. 302(f), as amended by P.L. 108-311, §402(a)(6), below. Prior to amendment, Code Sec. 531 read as follows:

SEC. 531. IMPOSITION OF ACCUMULATED EARNINGS TAX.

In addition to other taxes imposed by this chapter, there is hereby imposed for each taxable year on the accumulated taxable income (as defined in section 535) of each corporation described in section 532, an accumulated earnings tax equal to the product of the highest rate of tax under section 1(c) and the accumulated taxable income.

P.L. 108-27, §302(f), as amended by P.L. 108-311, §402(a)(6), provides:

(f) EFFECTIVE DATE.—

(1) IN GENERAL.—Except as provided in paragraph (2), the amendments made by this section shall apply to taxable years beginning after December 31, 2002.

(2) PASS-THRU ENTITIES.—In the case of a pass-thru entity described in subparagraph (A), (B), (C), (D), (E), or (F) of section 1(h)(10) of the Internal Revenue Code of 1986, as amended by this Act, the amendments made by this section shall apply to taxable years ending after December 31, 2002; except that dividends received by such an entity on or before such date shall not be treated as qualified dividend income (as defined in section 1(h)(11)(B) of such Code, as added by this Act).

P.L. 108-27, §303, as amended by P.L. 109-222, §102, provides:

SEC. 303. SUNSET OF TITLE.

All provisions of, and amendments made by, this title shall not apply to taxable years beginning after December 31, 2010, and the Internal Revenue Code of 1986 shall be applied and administered to such years as if such provisions and amendments had never been enacted.

• 2001, Economic Growth and Tax Relief Reconciliation Act of 2001 (P.L. 107-16)

P.L. 107-16, §101(c)(4):

Amended Code Sec. 531 by striking "equal to" and all that follows and inserting "equal to the product of the highest rate of tax under section 1(c) and the accumulated taxable income.". **Effective** for tax years beginning after 12-31-2000. Prior to amendment, Code Sec. 531 read as follows:

SEC. 531. IMPOSITION OF ACCUMULATED EARNINGS TAX.

In addition to other taxes imposed by this chapter, there is hereby imposed for each taxable year on the accumulated taxable income (as defined in section 535) of each corporation described in section 532, an accumulated earnings tax equal to 39.6 percent of the accumulated taxable income.

P.L. 107-16, §901(a)-(b), provides:

SEC. 901. SUNSET OF PROVISIONS OF ACT.

(a) IN GENERAL.—All provisions of, and amendments made by, this Act shall not apply—

(1) to taxable, plan, or limitation years beginning after December 31, 2010, or

(2) in the case of title V, to estates of decedents dying, gifts made, or generation skipping transfers, after December 31, 2010.

(b) APPLICATION OF CERTAIN LAWS.—The Internal Revenue Code of 1986 and the Employee Retirement Income Security Act of 1974 shall be applied and administered to years, estates, gifts, and transfers described in subsection (a) as if the provisions and amendments described in subsection (a) had never been enacted.

• 1993, Omnibus Budget Reconciliation Act of 1993 (P.L. 103-66)

P.L. 103-66, §13201(b)(1):

Amended Code Sec. 531 by striking "28 percent" and inserting "36 percent". **Effective** for tax years beginning after 12-31-92.

P.L. 103-66, §13202(b):

Amended Code Sec. 531 (as amended by Act Sec. 13201) by striking "36 percent" and inserting "39.6 percent". **Effective** for tax years beginning after 12-31-92.

• 1988, Technical and Miscellaneous Revenue Act of 1988 (P.L. 100-647)

P.L. 100-647, §1001(a)(2)(A):

Amended Code Sec. 531. **Effective** for tax years beginning after 12-31-87. It shall not be treated as a change in a rate of tax for purposes of section 15 of the 1986 Code. Prior to amendment, Code Sec. 531 read as follows:

SEC. 531. IMPOSITION OF ACCUMULATED EARNINGS TAX.

In addition to other taxes imposed by this chapter, there is hereby imposed for each taxable year on the accumulated taxable income (as defined in section 535) of every corporation described in section 532, an accumulated earnings tax equal to the sum of—

(1) $27^1/_2$ percent of the accumulated taxable income not in excess of $100,000, plus

(2) $38^1/_2$ percent of the accumulated taxable income in excess of $100,000.

[Sec. 532]

SEC. 532. CORPORATIONS SUBJECT TO ACCUMULATED EARNINGS TAX.

[Sec. 532(a)]

(a) GENERAL RULE.—The accumulated earnings tax imposed by section 531 shall apply to every corporation (other than those described in subsection (b)) formed or availed of for the purpose of avoiding the income tax with respect to its shareholders or the shareholders of any other corporation, by permitting earnings and profits to accumulate instead of being divided or distributed.

[Sec. 532(b)]

(b) EXCEPTIONS.—The accumulated earnings tax imposed by section 531 shall not apply to—

(1) a personal holding company (as defined in section 542),

(2) a corporation exempt from tax under subchapter F (section 501 and following), or

(3) a passive foreign investment company (as defined in section 1297).

Amendments

• 2005, Gulf Opportunity Zone Act of 2005 (P.L. 109-135)

P.L. 109-135, §403(n)(1):

Amended Code Sec. 532(b) by striking paragraph (2) and redesignating paragraphs (3) and (4) as paragraphs (2) and (3), respectively. **Effective** as if included in the provision of the American Jobs Creation Act of 2004 (P.L. 108-357) to which it relates [**effective** for tax years of foreign corporations beginning after 12-31-2004, and for tax years of United States shareholders with or within which such tax years of foreign corporations end.—CCH]. Prior to being stricken, Code Sec. 532(b)(2) read as follows:

(2) a foreign personal holding company (as defined in section 552),

• 1997, Taxpayer Relief Act of 1997 (P.L. 105-34)

P.L. 105-34, §1122(d)(1):

Amended Code Sec. 532(b)(4) by striking "section 1296" and inserting "section 1297". **Effective** for tax years of United States persons beginning after 12-31-97, and tax years of foreign corporations ending with or within such tax years of United States persons.

• 1986, Tax Reform Act of 1986 (P.L. 99-514)

P.L. 99-514, §1235(f)(1):

Amended Code Sec. 532(b)(2)-(4) by striking out "or" at the end of paragraph (2), by striking out the period at the end of paragraph (3) and inserting in lieu thereof ", or" and by adding at the end thereof a new paragraph (4). **Effective** for tax years of foreign corporations beginning after 12-31-86.

[Sec. 532(c)]

(c) APPLICATION DETERMINED WITHOUT REGARD TO NUMBER OF SHAREHOLDERS.—The application of this part to a corporation shall be determined without regard to the number of shareholders of such corporation.

Amendments

• 1984, Deficit Reduction Act of 1984 (P.L. 98-369)

P.L. 98-369, §58(a):

Amended Code Sec. 532 by adding new subsection (c). **Effective** for tax years beginning after 7-18-84.

[Sec. 533]

SEC. 533. EVIDENCE OF PURPOSE TO AVOID INCOME TAX.

[Sec. 533(a)]

(a) UNREASONABLE ACCUMULATION DETERMINATIVE OF PURPOSE.—For purposes of section 532, the fact that the earnings and profits of a corporation are permitted to accumulate beyond the reasonable needs of the business shall be determinative of the purpose to avoid the income tax with respect to shareholders, unless the corporation by the preponderance of the evidence shall prove to the contrary.

[Sec. 533(b)]

(b) HOLDING OR INVESTMENT COMPANY.—The fact that any corporation is a mere holding or investment company shall be prima facie evidence of the purpose to avoid the income tax with respect to shareholders.

[Sec. 534]

SEC. 534. BURDEN OF PROOF.

[Sec. 534(a)]

(a) GENERAL RULE.—In any proceeding before the Tax Court involving a notice of deficiency based in whole or in part on the allegation that all or any part of the earnings and profits have been permitted to accumulate beyond the reasonable needs of the business, the burden of proof with respect to such allegation shall—

(1) if notification has not been sent in accordance with subsection (b), be on the Secretary, or

(2) if the taxpayer has submitted the statement described in subsection (c), be on the Secretary with respect to the grounds set forth in such statement in accordance with the provisions of such subsection.

Amendments

• 1976, Tax Reform Act of 1976 (P.L. 94-455)

P.L. 94-455, §1906(b)(13)(A):

Amended 1954 Code by substituting "Secretary" for "Secretary or his delegate" each place it appeared. **Effective** 2-1-77.

[Sec. 534(b)]

(b) NOTIFICATION BY SECRETARY.—Before mailing the notice of deficiency referred to in subsection (a), the Secretary may send by certified mail or registered mail a notification informing the taxpayer that the proposed notice of deficiency includes an amount with respect to the accumulated earnings tax imposed by section 531.

Amendments

• 1976, Tax Reform Act of 1976 (P.L. 94-455)

P.L. 94-455, §1906(b)(13)(A):

Amended 1954 Code by substituting "Secretary" for "Secretary or his delegate" each place it appeared. **Effective** 2-1-77.

P.L. 94-455, §1901(a)(73)(A):

Amended Code Sec. 534(b) by striking out the last sentence, which read as follows: "In the case of a notice of deficiency to which subsection (e)(2) applies and which is mailed on or before the 30th day after the date of the enactment of this sentence, the notification referred to in the preceding sentence may be mailed at any time on or before such 30th day."

• 1958, Technical Amendments Act of 1958 (P.L. 85-866)

P.L. 85-866, §89(b):

Struck out, in the first sentence of Sec. 534(b), the phrase "registered mail" and substituted the phrase "certified mail or registered mail". **Effective** where mailing occurs after 9-3-58.

• 1955 (P.L. 367, 84th Cong.)

P.L. 367, 84th Cong., §5:

Amended subsection (b) by adding the last sentence. Approved 8-11-55, and **effective** in accordance with the provisions of subsection (e).

[Sec. 534(c)]

(c) STATEMENT BY TAXPAYER.—Within such time (but not less than 30 days) after the mailing of the notification described in subsection (b) as the Secretary may prescribe by regulations, the taxpayer may submit a statement of the grounds (together with facts sufficient to show the basis thereof) on which the taxpayer relies to establish that all or any part of the earnings and profits have not been permitted to accumulate beyond the reasonable needs of the business.

Amendments

• 1976, Tax Reform Act of 1976 (P.L. 94-455)

P.L. 94-455, §1906(b)(13)(A):

Amended 1954 Code by substituting "Secretary" for "Secretary or his delegate" each place it appeared. **Effective** 2-1-77.

[Sec. 534(d)]

(d) JEOPARDY ASSESSMENT.—If pursuant to section 6861 (a) a jeopardy assessment is made before the mailing of the notice of deficiency referred to in subsection (a), for purposes of this section such notice of deficiency shall, to the extent that it informs the taxpayer that such deficiency includes the accumulated earnings tax imposed by section 531, constitute the notification described in subsection (b), and in that event the statement described in subsection (c) may be included in the taxpayer's petition to the Tax Court.

[Sec. 534(e)—Repealed]

Amendments

• 1976, Tax Reform Act of 1976 (P.L. 94-455)

P.L. 94-455, §1901(a)(73)(B):

Repealed Code Sec. 534(e). **Effective** with respect to tax years beginning after 12-31-76. Prior to repeal, Code Sec. 534(e) read as follows:

(e) APPLICATION OF SECTION.

(1) Notwithstanding any other provision of law, this section shall apply with respect to taxable years to which this subchapter applies and (except as provided in paragraph (2)) to taxable years to which the corresponding provisions of prior revenue laws apply.

(2) In the case of a notice of deficiency for a taxable year to which this subchapter does not apply, this section shall apply only in the case of proceedings tried on the merits after the date of the enactment of this paragraph.

• 1955 (P.L. 367, 84th Cong.)

P.L. 367, 84th Cong., 1st Sess., §4:

Amended subsection (e). **Effective** 8-11-55. Prior to amendment, the subsection read as follows:

(e) EFFECTIVE DATE.—This section shall apply only with respect to a notice of deficiency for a taxable year to which this subchapter applies which is mailed more than 90 days after the date of enactment of this title.

[Sec. 535]

SEC. 535. ACCUMULATED TAXABLE INCOME.

[Sec. 535(a)]

(a) DEFINITION.—For purposes of this subtitle, the term "accumulated taxable income" means the taxable income, adjusted in the manner provided in subsection (b), minus the sum of the dividends paid deduction (as defined in section 561) and the accumulated earnings credit (as defined in subsection (c)).

[Sec. 535(b)]

(b) ADJUSTMENTS TO TAXABLE INCOME.—For purposes of subsection (a), taxable income shall be adjusted as follows:

(1) TAXES.—There shall be allowed as a deduction Federal income and excess profits taxes and income, war profits, and excess profits taxes of foreign countries and possessions of the United States (to the extent not allowable as a deduction under section 275(a)(4)), accrued during the taxable year or deemed to be paid by a domestic corporation under section 902(a) or 960(a)(1) for the taxable year, but not including the accumulated earnings tax imposed by section 531, the personal holding company tax imposed by section 541, or the taxes imposed by corresponding sections of a prior income tax law.

(2) CHARITABLE CONTRIBUTIONS.—The deduction for charitable contributions provided under section 170 shall be allowed without regard to section 170(b)(2).

(3) SPECIAL DEDUCTIONS DISALLOWED.—The special deductions for corporations provided in part VIII (except section 248) of subchapter B (section 241 and following, relating to the deduction for dividends received by corporations, etc.) shall not be allowed.

(4) NET OPERATING LOSS.—The net operating loss deduction provided in section 172 shall not be allowed.

(5) CAPITAL LOSSES.—

(A) IN GENERAL.—Except as provided in subparagraph (B), there shall be allowed as a deduction an amount equal to the net capital loss for the taxable year (determined without regard to paragraph (7)(A)).

(B) RECAPTURE OF PREVIOUS DEDUCTIONS FOR CAPITAL GAINS.—The aggregate amount allowable as a deduction under subparagraph (A) for any taxable year shall be reduced by the lesser of—

(i) the nonrecaptured capital gains deductions, or

(ii) the amount of the accumulated earnings and profits of the corporation as of the close of the preceding taxable year.

(C) NONRECAPTURED CAPITAL GAINS DEDUCTIONS.—For purposes of subparagraph (B), the term "nonrecaptured capital gains deductions" means the excess of—

(i) the aggregate amount allowable as a deduction under paragraph (6) for preceding taxable years beginning after July 18, 1984, over

(ii) the aggregate of the reductions under subparagraph (B) for preceding taxable years.

(6) NET CAPITAL GAINS.—

(A) IN GENERAL.—There shall be allowed as a deduction—

(i) the net capital gain for the taxable year (determined with the application of paragraph (7)), reduced by

(ii) the taxes attributable to such net capital gain.

(B) ATTRIBUTABLE TAXES.—For purposes of subparagraph (A), the taxes attributable to the net capital gain shall be an amount equal to the difference between—

(i) the taxes imposed by this subtitle (except the tax imposed by this part) for the taxable year, and

(ii) such taxes computed for such year without including in taxable income the net capital gain for the taxable year (determined without the application of paragraph (7)).

(7) CAPITAL LOSS CARRYOVERS.—

(A) UNLIMITED CARRYFORWARD.—The net capital loss for any taxable year shall be treated as a short-term capital loss in the next taxable year.

(B) SECTION 1212 INAPPLICABLE.—No allowance shall be made for the capital loss carryback or carryforward provided in section 1212.

(8) SPECIAL RULES FOR MERE HOLDING OR INVESTMENT COMPANIES.—In the case of a mere holding or investment company—

(A) CAPITAL LOSS DEDUCTION, ETC., NOT ALLOWED.—Paragraphs (5) and (7)(A) shall not apply.

(B) DEDUCTION FOR CERTAIN OFFSETS.—There shall be allowed as a deduction the net short-term capital gain for the taxable year to the extent such gain does not exceed the amount of any capital loss carryover to such taxable year under section 1212 (determined without regard to paragraph (7)(B)).

(C) EARNINGS AND PROFITS.—For purposes of subchapter C, the accumulated earnings and profits at any time shall not be less than they would be if this subsection had applied to the computation of earnings and profits for all taxable years beginning after July 18, 1984.

(9) SPECIAL RULE FOR CAPITAL GAINS AND LOSSES OF FOREIGN CORPORATIONS.—In the case of a foreign corporation, paragraph (6) shall be applied by taking into account only gains and losses which are effectively connected with the conduct of a trade or business within the United States and are not exempt from tax under treaty.

(10) CONTROLLED FOREIGN CORPORATIONS.—There shall be allowed as a deduction the amount of the corporation's income for the taxable year which is included in the gross income of a United States shareholder under section 951(a). In the case of any corporation the accumulated taxable income of which would (but for this sentence) be determined without allowance of any deductions, the deduction under this paragraph shall be allowed and shall be appropriately adjusted to take into account any deductions which reduced such inclusion.

Amendments

• 2005, Gulf Opportunity Zone Act of 2005 (P.L. 109-135)

P.L. 109-135, §403(n)(2):

Amended Code Sec. 535(b) by adding at the end a new paragraph (10). **Effective** as if included in the provision of the American Jobs Creation Act of 2004 (P.L. 108-357) to which it relates [**effective** for tax years of foreign corporations beginning after 12-31-2004, and for tax years of United States shareholders with or within which such tax years of foreign corporations end.—CCH].

• 1986, Tax Reform Act of 1986 (P.L. 99-514)

P.L. 99-514, §1225(a):

Amended Code Sec. 535(b) by adding at the end thereof new paragraph (9). **Effective** for gains and losses realized on or after 1-1-86 [**effective** date changed by P.L. 100-647, §1012(k)].

P.L. 99-514, §1899A(17):

Amended Code Sec. 535(b)(5)(C)(i) and Code Sec. 535(b)(8)(C) by striking out "the date of the enactment of the Tax Reform Act of 1984" and inserting in lieu thereof "July 18, 1984". **Effective** 10-22-86.

• 1984, Deficit Reduction Act of 1984 (P.L. 98-369)

P.L. 98-369, §58(b):

Amended Code Sec. 535(b) by striking out paragraphs (5), (6), and (7) and inserting in lieu thereof new paragraphs (5), (6), (7), and (8). **Effective** for tax years beginning after 7-18-84. Prior to amendment, paragraphs (5), (6), and (7) read as follows:

(5) Capital Losses.—There shall be allowed as deductions losses from sales or exchanges of capital assets during the taxable year which are disallowed as deductions under section 1211(a).

(6) Net Capital Gains.—There shall be allowed as a deduction the net capital gain for the taxable year (determined without regard to the capital loss carryback or carryover provided in section 1212) minus the taxes imposed by this subtitle attributable to such net capital gain. The taxes attributable to such net capital gain shall be an amount equal to the difference between—

(A) the taxes imposed by this subtitle (except the tax imposed by this part) for such year, and

(B) such taxes computed for such year without including in taxable income the net capital gain for the taxable year (determined with regard to the capital loss carryback or carryover provided in section 1212).

(7) Capital Loss.—No allowance shall be made for the capital loss carryback or carryover provided in section 1212.

• 1976, Tax Reform Act of 1976 (P.L. 94-455)

P.L. 94-455, §1033(b)(3):

Substituted "section 902(a) or 960(a)(1)" for "section 902(a)(1) or 960(a)(1)(C)" in Code Sec. 535(b)(1). **Effective** as provided by Act Sec. 1033(c), below.

P.L. 94-455, §1033(c), provides:

(c) EFFECTIVE DATES.—The amendments made by this section shall apply—

(1) in respect of any distribution received by a domestic corporation after December 31, 1977, and

(2) in respect of any distribution received by a domestic corporation before January 1, 1978, in a taxable year of such corporation beginning after December 31, 1975, but only to the extent that such distribution is made out of the accumulated profits of a foreign corporation for a taxable year (of such foreign corporation) beginning after December 31, 1975.

For purposes of paragraph (2), a distribution made by a foreign corporation out of its profits which are attributable to a distribution received from a foreign corporation to which section 902(b) of the Internal Revenue Code of 1954 applies shall be treated as made out of the accumulated profits of a foreign corporation for a taxable year beginning before January 1, 1976, to the extent that such distribution was paid out of the accumulated profits of such foreign corporation for a taxable year beginning before January 1, 1976.

P.L. 94-455, §1901(a)(74):

Amended Code Sec. 535(b)(1) by striking out "(other than the excess profits tax imposed by subchapter E of chapter 2 of the Internal Revenue Code of 1939 for taxable years beginning after December 31, 1940)" after "Federal income and excess profits taxes". **Effective** for tax years beginning after 12-31-76.

P.L. 94-455, §1901(b)(20)(A):

Amended Code Sec. 535(b) by striking out paragraph (8). **Effective** for tax years beginning after 12-31-76. Prior to repeal, Sec. 535(b)(8) read as follows:

(8) BANK AFFILIATES.—There shall be allowed the deduction described in section 601 (relating to bank affiliates).

P.L. 94-455, §1901(b)(32)(C):

Amended Code Sec. 535(b) by striking out paragraphs (9) and (10). **Effective** for tax years beginning after 12-31-76. Prior to repeal, paragraphs (9) and (10) read as follows:

(9) DISTRIBUTIONS OF DIVESTED STOCK.—There shall be allowed as a deduction the amount of any dividend distribution received of divested stock (as defined in subsection (e) of section 1111), minus the taxes imposed by this subtitle attributable to such receipt, but only if the stock with respect to which the distribution is made was owned by the distributee on September 6, 1961, or was owned by the distributee for at least 2 years prior to the date on which the antitrust order (as defined in subsection (d) of section 1111) was entered.

(10) SPECIAL ADJUSTMENT ON DISPOSITION OF ANTITRUST STOCK RECEIVED AS A DIVIDEND.—If—

(A) a corporation received antitrust stock (as defined in section 301(f)) in a distribution to which section 301 applied,

(B) the amount of the distribution determined under section 301(f)(2) exceeded the basis of the stock determined under section 301(f)(3), and

(C) paragraph (9) did not apply in respect of such distribution,

then proper adjustment shall be made, under regulations prescribed by the Secretary or his delegate, if such stock (or other property the basis of which is determined by reference to the basis of such stock) is sold or exchanged.

P.L. 94-455, §1901(b)(33)(D):

Amended Code Sec. 535(b)(6). **Effective** for tax years beginning after 12-31-76. Prior to amendment, Code Sec. 535(b)(6) read as follows:

(6) LONG-TERM CAPITAL GAINS.—There shall be allowed as a deduction the excess of the net long-term capital gain for the taxable year over the net short-term capital loss for such year (determined without regard to the capital loss carryback or carryover provided in section 1212) minus the taxes imposed by this subtitle attributable to such excess. The taxes attributable to such excess shall be an amount equal to the difference between—

(A) the taxes imposed by this subtitle (except the tax imposed by this part) for such year, and

(B) such taxes computed for such year without including in taxable income the excess of the net long-term capital gain for the taxable year over the net short-term capital loss for such year (determined with regard to the capital loss carryback or carryover provided in section 1212).

• 1969, Tax Reform Act of 1969 (P.L. 91-172)

P.L. 91-172, §512(f):

Amended Code Sec. 535(b)(6) by inserting "capital loss carryback or carryover" in lieu of "capital loss carryover" in the first sentence and in subparagraph (B). Amended Code Sec. 535(b)(7). **Effective** with respect to net capital losses sustained in tax years beginning after 12-31-69. Prior to amendment, Code Sec. 535(b)(7) read as follows:

(7) Capital loss carryover.—No allowance shall be made for the capital loss carryover provided in section 1212.

• 1964, Revenue Act of 1964 (P.L. 88-272)

P.L. 88-272, §207(b)(4):

Amended paragraph (b)(1) by inserting the words "section 275(a)(4)" in lieu of "section 164(b)(6)". **Effective** 1-1-64.

• 1962, Revenue Act of 1962 (P.L. 87-834)

P.L. 87-834, §9(d)(2):

Amended Code Sec. 535(b)(1) by inserting immediately after "year" in line 7 the following: "or deemed to be paid by a domestic corporation under section 902(a)(1) or 960(a)(1)(C) for the taxable year."

• 1962 (P.L. 87-403)

P.L. 87-403, §3(b):

Added paragraphs (9) and (10) to subsection (b). **Effective** for distributions made after 2-2-62.

• 1958, Technical Amendments Act of 1958 (P.L. 85-866)

P.L. 85-866, §31:

Amended Code Sec. 535(b)(2) by deleting the phrase "the limitation in" following the phrase "without regard to". Amended Code Sec. 535(b)(6)(B). **Effective** 1-1-54. Prior to amendment, Sec. 535(b)(6)(B) read:

"(B) such taxes computed for such year without including such excess in taxable income."

[Sec. 535(c)]

(c) ACCUMULATED EARNINGS CREDIT.—

(1) GENERAL RULE.—For purposes of subsection (a), in the case of a corporation other than a mere holding or investment company the accumulated earnings credit is (A) an amount equal to such part of the earnings and profits for the taxable year as are retained for the reasonable needs of the business, minus (B) the deduction allowed by subsection (b)(6). For purposes of this paragraph, the amount of the earnings and profits for the taxable year which are retained is the amount by which the earnings and profits for the taxable year exceed the dividends paid deduction (as defined in section 561) for such year.

(2) MINIMUM CREDIT.—

(A) IN GENERAL.—The credit allowable under paragraph (1) shall in no case be less than the amount by which $250,000 exceeds the accumulated earnings and profits of the corporation at the close of the preceding taxable year.

(B) CERTAIN SERVICE CORPORATIONS.—In the case of a corporation the principal function of which is the performance of services in the field of health, law, engineering, architecture, accounting, actuarial science, performing arts, or consulting, subparagraph (A) shall be applied by substituting "$150,000" for "$250,000".

(3) HOLDING AND INVESTMENT COMPANIES.—In the case of a corporation which is a mere holding or investment company, the accumulated earnings credit is the amount (if any) by which $250,000 exceeds the accumulated earnings and profits of the corporation at the close of the preceding taxable year.

(4) ACCUMULATED EARNINGS AND PROFITS.—For purposes of paragraphs (2) and (3), the accumulated earnings and profits at the close of the preceding taxable year shall be reduced by the dividends which under section 563(a) (relating to dividends paid after the close of the taxable year) are considered as paid during such taxable year.

(5) CROSS REFERENCE.—

For denial of credit provided in paragraph (2) or (3) where multiple corporations are formed to avoid tax, see section 1551, and for limitation on such credit in the case of certain controlled corporations, see section 1561.

Amendments

• 1990, Omnibus Budget Reconciliation Act of 1990 (P.L. 101-508)

P.L. 101-508, §11801(c)(18):

Amended Code Sec. 535(c)(5) by striking "sections 1561 and 1564" and inserting "section 1561". **Effective** 11-5-90.

P.L. 101-508, §11821(b), provides:

(b) SAVINGS PROVISION.—If—

(1) any provision amended or repealed by this part applied to—

(A) any transaction occurring before the date of the enactment of this Act,

(B) any property acquired before such date of enactment, or

(C) any item of income, loss, deduction, or credit taken into account before such date of enactment, and

(2) the treatment of such transaction, property, or item under such provision would (without regard to the amendments made by this part) affect liability for tax for periods ending after such date of enactment,

nothing in the amendments made by this part shall be construed to affect the treatment of such transaction, property, or item for purposes of determining liability for tax for periods ending after such date of enactment.

• 1981, Economic Recovery Tax Act of 1981 (P.L. 97-34)

P.L. 97-34, §232(a):

Amended Code Sec. 535(c)(2). **Effective** for tax years beginning after 12-31-81. Prior to amendment, Code Sec. 535(c)(2) read as follows:

(2) MINIMUM CREDIT.—The credit allowable under paragraph (1) shall in no case be less than the amount by which $150,000 exceeds the accumulated earnings and profits of the corporation at the close of the preceding taxable year.

P.L. 97-34, §232(b)(1):

Amended Code Sec. 535(c)(3) by striking out "$150,000" and inserting in lieu thereof "$250,000". **Effective** for tax years beginning after 12-31-81.

• 1975, Tax Reduction Act of 1975 (P.L. 94-12)

P.L. 94-12, §304(a):

Amended Sec. 535(c)(2) and (3) by substituting "$150,000" for "$100,000." **Effective** for tax years beginning after 12-31-74.

• 1969, Tax Reform Act of 1969 (P.L. 91-172)

P.L. 91-172, §401(b)(2)(C):

Amended subsection (c)(5) by adding ", and for limitation on such credit in the case of certain controlled corporations, see sections 1561 and 1564". **Effective** for tax years beginning after 12-31-69.

• 1958, Technical Amendments Act of 1958 (P.L. 85-866)

P.L. 85-866, §205(a):

Struck out "$60,000" where it appeared in paragraphs (2) and (3) of Sec. 535(c) and substituted "$100,000". **Effective** 1-1-58.

[Sec. 535(d)]

(d) INCOME DISTRIBUTED TO UNITED STATES-OWNED FOREIGN CORPORATION RETAINS UNITED STATES CONNECTION.—

(1) IN GENERAL.—For purposes of this part, if 10 percent or more of the earnings and profits of any foreign corporation for any taxable year—

(A) is derived from sources within the United States, or

(B) is effectively connected with the conduct of a trade or business within the United States,

any distribution out of such earnings and profits (and any interest payment) received (directly or through 1 or more other entities) by a United States-owned foreign corporation shall be treated as derived by such corporation from sources within the United States.

(2) UNITED STATES-OWNED FOREIGN CORPORATION.—The term "United States-owned foreign corporation" has the meaning given to such term by section 904(h)(6).

Amendments

• 2004, American Jobs Creation Act of 2004 (P.L. 108-357)

P.L. 108-357, §402(b)(1):

Amended Code Sec. 535(d)(2) by striking "section 904(g)(6)" and inserting "section 904(h)(6)". **Effective** for losses for tax years beginning after 12-31-2006.

• 1984, Deficit Reduction Act of 1984 (P.L. 98-369)

P.L. 98-369, §125(a):

Amended Code Sec. 535 by adding new subsection (d). **Effective** for distributions and interest payments received by a U.S.-owned foreign corporation (within the meaning of Code Sec. 535(d)) on or after 5-23-83, in tax years ending on or after such date. In the case of a U.S.-owned foreign corporation in existence on 5-23-83, the amendment applies to tax years beginning after 12-31-84.

[Sec. 536]

SEC. 536. INCOME NOT PLACED ON ANNUAL BASIS.

Section 443(b) (relating to computation of tax on change of annual accounting period) shall not apply in the computation of the accumulated earnings tax imposed by section 531.

[Sec. 537]

SEC. 537. REASONABLE NEEDS OF THE BUSINESS.

[Sec. 537(a)]

(a) GENERAL RULE.—For purposes of this part, the term "reasonable needs of the business" includes—

(1) the reasonably anticipated needs of the business,

(2) the section 303 redemption needs of the business, and

(3) the excess business holdings redemption needs of the business.

[Sec. 537(b)]

(b) SPECIAL RULES.—For purposes of subsection (a)—

(1) SECTION 303 REDEMPTION NEEDS.—The term "section 303 redemption needs" means, with respect to the taxable year of the corporation in which a shareholder of the corporation died or any taxable year thereafter, the amount needed (or reasonably anticipated to be needed) to make a redemption of stock included in the gross estate of the decedent (but not in excess of the maximum amount of stock to which section 303(a) may apply).

(2) EXCESS BUSINESS HOLDINGS REDEMPTION NEEDS.—The term "excess business holdings redemption needs" means the amount needed (or reasonably anticipated to be needed) to redeem from a private foundation stock which—

(A) such foundation held on May 26, 1969 (or which was received by such foundation pursuant to a will or irrevocable trust to which section 4943(c)(5) applies), and

(B) constituted excess business holdings on May 26, 1969, or would have constituted excess business holdings as of such date if there were taken into account (i) stock received pursuant to a will or trust described in subparagraph (A), and (ii) the reduction in the total outstanding stock of the corporation which would have resulted solely from the redemption of stock held by the private foundation.

(3) OBLIGATIONS INCURRED TO MAKE REDEMPTIONS.—In applying paragraphs (1) and (2), the discharge of any obligation incurred to make a redemption described in such paragraphs shall be treated as the making of such redemption.

(4) PRODUCT LIABILITY LOSS RESERVES.—The accumulation of reasonable amounts for the payment of reasonably anticipated product liability losses (as defined in section 172(f)), as determined under regulations prescribed by the Secretary, shall be treated as accumulated for the reasonably anticipated needs of the business.

(5) NO INFERENCE AS TO PRIOR TAXABLE YEARS.—The application of this part to any taxable year before the first taxable year specified in paragraph (1) shall be made without regard to the fact that distributions in redemption coming within the terms of such paragraphs were subsequently made.

Amendments

• 1996, Small Business Job Protection Act of 1996 (P.L. 104-188)

P.L. 104-188, §1704(t)(33):

Amended Code Sec. 537(b)(4) by striking "section 172(i)" and inserting "section 172(f)". **Effective** 8-20-96.

• 1978, Revenue Act of 1978 (P.L. 95-600)

P.L. 95-600, §371(c):

Amended Code Sec. 537(b) by redesignating Code Sec. 537(b)(4) as (b)(5) and adding a new subparagraph (b)(4). **Effective** for tax years beginning after 9-30-79.

• 1976, Tax Reform Act of 1976 (P.L. 94-455)

P.L. 94-455, §1901(a)(75)(A):

Amended Code Sec. 537(b)(2) by striking out ", with respect to taxable years of the corporation ending after May 26, 1969," after "means". **Effective** for tax years beginning after 12-31-76.

P.L. 94-455, §1901(a)(75)(B):

Amended Code Sec. 537(b)(4) by striking out "or (2)" after "(1)". **Effective** for tax years beginning after 12-31-76.

• 1969, Tax Reform Act of 1969 (P.L. 91-172)

P.L. 91-172, §906(a):

Amended Code Sec. 537. **Effective** for the tax imposed by Code Sec. 531 with respect to tax years ending after 5-26-69. Prior to amendment Code Sec. 537 read as follows:

Sec. 537. Reasonable Needs of the Business.—For purposes of this part, the term "reasonable needs of the business" includes the reasonably anticipated needs of the business.

PART II—PERSONAL HOLDING COMPANIES

»»→ Caution: Code Sec. 541, below, was amended by P.L. 107-16 and P.L. 108-27, and is subject to the sunset provisions of the Economic Growth and Tax Relief Reconciliation Act of 2001 (P.L. 107-16), §901, and the Jobs and Growth Tax Relief Reconciliation Act of 2003 (P.L. 108-27), §303. Absent Congressional action, the changes made to this provision by P.L. 107-16, and P.L. 108-27, or that take effect as if included in P.L. 107-16, and P.L. 108-27, do not apply after December 31, 2010. For more information about the sunset provisions, see page XXI of the Preface to this publication and P.L. 107-16, §901, and P.L. 108-27, §303, in the amendment notes. See the amendments notes for a history of amendments to this section and the effective date of each change.

[Sec. 541]

SEC. 541. IMPOSITION OF PERSONAL HOLDING COMPANY TAX.

In addition to other taxes imposed by this chapter, there is hereby imposed for each taxable year on the undistributed personal holding company income (as defined in section 545) of every personal holding company (as defined in section 542) a personal holding company tax equal to 15 percent of the undistributed personal holding company income.

Amendments

• 2003, Jobs and Growth Tax Relief Reconciliation Act of 2003 (P.L. 108-27)

P.L. 108-27, §302(e)(6):

Amended Code Sec. 541 by striking "equal to" and all that follows and inserting "equal to 15 percent of the undistributed personal holding company income.". For the **effective** date, see Act Sec. 302(f), as amended by P.L. 108-311, §402(a)(6), below. Prior to amendment, Code Sec. 541 read as follows:

SEC. 541. IMPOSITION OF PERSONAL HOLDING COMPANY TAX.

In addition to other taxes imposed by this chapter, there is hereby imposed for each taxable year on the undistributed personal holding company income (as defined in section 545) of every personal holding company (as defined in section 542) a personal holding company tax equal to the product of the highest rate of tax under section 1(c) and the undistributed personal holding company income.

P.L. 108-27, §302(f), as amended by P.L. 108-311, §402(a)(6), provides:

(f) EFFECTIVE DATE.—

(1) IN GENERAL.—Except as provided in paragraph (2), the amendments made by this section shall apply to taxable years beginning after December 31, 2002.

(2) PASS-THRU ENTITIES.—In the case of a pass-thru entity described in subparagraph (A), (B), (C), (D), (E), or (F) of section 1(h)(10) of the Internal Revenue Code of 1986, as amended by this Act, the amendments made by this section shall apply to taxable years ending after December 31, 2002; except that dividends received by such an entity on or before such date shall not be treated as qualified dividend income (as defined in section 1(h)(11)(B) of such Code, as added by this Act).

P.L. 108-27, §303, as amended by P.L. 109-222, §102, provides:

SEC. 303. SUNSET OF TITLE.

All provisions of, and amendments made by, this title shall not apply to taxable years beginning after December 31, 2010, and the Internal Revenue Code of 1986 shall be applied and administered to such years as if such provisions and amendments had never been enacted.

• 2001, Economic Growth and Tax Relief Reconciliation Act of 2001 (P.L. 107-16)

P.L. 107-16, §101(c)(5):

Amended Code Sec. 541 by striking "equal to" and all that follows and inserting "equal to the product of the highest rate of tax under section 1(c) and the undistributed personal holding company income." **Effective** for tax years beginning after 12-31-2000. Prior to amendment, Code Sec. 541 read as follows:

SEC. 541. IMPOSITION OF PERSONAL HOLDING COMPANY TAX.

In addition to other taxes imposed by this chapter, there is hereby imposed for each taxable year on the undistributed personal holding company income (as defined in section 545) of every personal holding company (as defined in section 542) a personal holding company tax equal to 39.6 percent of the undistributed personal holding company income.

P.L. 107-16, §901(a)-(b), provides:

SEC. 901. SUNSET OF PROVISIONS OF ACT.

(a) IN GENERAL.—All provisions of, and amendments made by, this Act shall not apply—

(1) to taxable, plan, or limitation years beginning after December 31, 2010, or

(2) in the case of title V, to estates of decedents dying, gifts made, or generation skipping transfers, after December 31, 2010.

(b) APPLICATION OF CERTAIN LAWS.—The Internal Revenue Code of 1986 and the Employee Retirement Income Security Act of 1974 shall be applied and administered to years, estates, gifts, and transfers described in subsection (a) as if the provisions and amendments described in subsection (a) had never been enacted.

• 1993, Omnibus Budget Reconciliation Act of 1993 (P.L. 103-66)

P.L. 103-66, §13201(b)(2):

Amended Code Sec. 541 by striking "28 percent" and inserting "36 percent". **Effective** for tax years beginning after 12-31-92.

P.L. 103-66, §13202(b):

Amended Code Sec. 541 (as amended by Act Sec. 13201) by striking "36 percent" and inserting "39.6 percent". **Effective** for tax years beginning after 12-31-92.

• 1990, Omnibus Budget Reconciliation Act of 1990 (P.L. 101-508)

P.L. 101-508, §11802(f)(1):

Amended Code Sec. 541 by striking "(38.5 percent in the case of tax years beginning in 1987)" after "28 percent". **Effective** 11-5-90.

P.L. 101-508, §11821(b), provides:

(b) SAVINGS PROVISION.—If—

(1) any provision amended or repealed by this part applied to—

(A) any transaction occurring before the date of the enactment of this Act,

(B) any property acquired before such date of enactment, or

(C) any item of income, loss, deduction, or credit taken into account before such date of enactment, and

(2) the treatment of such transaction, property, or item under such provision would (without regard to the amendments made by this part) effect liability for tax for periods ending after such date of enactment,

nothing in the amendments made by this part shall be construed to affect the treatment of such transaction, property, or item for purposes of determining liability for tax for periods ending after such date of enactment.

• 1986, Tax Reform Act of 1986 (P.L. 99-514)

P.L. 99-514, §104(b)(8):

Amended Code Sec. 541 by striking out "50 percent" and inserting in lieu thereof "28 percent (38.5 percent in the case of taxable years beginning in 1987". **Effective** for tax years beginning after 12-31-86.

• 1981, Economic Recovery Tax Act of 1981 (P.L. 97-34)

P.L. 97-34, §101(d)(2):

Amended Code Sec. 541 by striking out "70 percent" and inserting in lieu thereof "50 percent". **Effective** for tax years beginning after 12-31-81.

• 1964, Revenue Act of 1964 (P.L. 88-272)

P.L. 88-272, §225(a):

Amended Code Sec. 541. **Effective** with respect to tax years beginning after 12-31-63. Prior to amendment, Sec. 541 read as follows:

"In addition to other taxes imposed by this chapter, there is hereby imposed for each taxable year on the undistributed personal holding company income (as defined in section 545) of every personal holding company (as defined in section 542) a personal holding company tax equal to the sum of—

(1) 75 percent of the undistributed personal holding company income not in excess of $2,000, plus

(2) 85 percent of the undistributed personal holding company income in excess of $2,000."

[Sec. 542]

SEC. 542. DEFINITION OF PERSONAL HOLDING COMPANY.

[Sec. 542(a)]

(a) GENERAL RULE.—For purposes of this subtitle, the term "personal holding company" means any corporation (other than a corporation described in subsection (c)) if—

(1) ADJUSTED ORDINARY GROSS INCOME REQUIREMENT.—At least 60 percent of its adjusted ordinary gross income (as defined in section 543(b)(2)) for the taxable year is personal holding company income (as defined in section 543(a)), and

(2) STOCK OWNERSHIP REQUIREMENT.—At any time during the last half of the taxable year more than 50 percent in value of its outstanding stock is owned, directly or indirectly, by or for not more than 5 individuals. For purposes of this paragraph, an organization described in section 401(a), 501(c)(17), or 509(a) or a portion of a trust permanently set aside or to be used exclusively for the purposes described in section 642(c) or a corresponding provision of a prior income tax law shall be considered an individual.

Amendments

• 1978, Revenue Act of 1978 (P.L. 95-600)

P.L. 95-600, §701(o)(1), provides:

"(o) DEFINITION OF PERSONAL HOLDING COMPANY.—

(1) IN GENERAL.—The last sentence of section 542(a)(2) of the Internal Revenue Code of 1954 (relating to stock ownership requirement) shall not apply in the case of an organization or trust organized or created before July 1, 1950, if at all times on or after July 1, 1950, and before the close of the taxable year such organization or trust has owned all of the common stock and at least 80 percent of the total number of shares of all other classes of stock of the corporation.

(2) EFFECTIVE DATE.—The provisions of paragraph (1) shall apply with respect to taxable years beginning after December 31, 1976."

• 1976, Tax Reform Act of 1976 (P.L. 94-455)

P.L. 94-455, §1901(a)(76)(A):

Amended Code Sec. 542(a)(2) by striking out the last sentence, which read as follows: "The preceding sentence shall not apply in the case of an organization or trust organized or created before July 1, 1950, if at all times on or after July 1, 1950, and before the close of the taxable year such organization or trust has owned all of the common stock and at least 80 percent of the total number of shares of all other classes of stock of the corporation." **Effective** for tax years beginning after 12-31-76.

• 1969, Tax Reform Act of 1969 (P.L. 91-172)

P.L. 91-172, §101(j)(16):

Amended Code Sec. 542(a)(2). **Effective** for tax years beginning after 12-31-69. Prior to amendment by P.L. 91-172, Code Sec. 542(a)(2) read as follows:

"(2) Stock ownership requirement.—At any time during the last half of the taxable year more than 50 percent in value of its outstanding stock is owned, directly or indirectly, by or for not more than 5 individuals. For purposes of this paragraph, an organization described in section 503(b) or a portion of a trust permanently set aside or to be used exclusively for the purposes described in section 642(c) or a corresponding provision of a prior income tax law shall be considered an individual. The preceding sentence shall not apply in the case of an organization or trust organized or created before July 1, 1950, if at all times on or after July 1, 1950, and before the close of the taxable year such organization or trust has owned all of the common stock and at least 80 percent of the total number of shares of all other classes of stock of the corporation, but only if such organization or trust is not denied exemption under section 504 or an unlimited charitable deduction is not denied under section 681(c) and, for this purpose—

"(A) all income of the corporation which is available for distribution as dividends to its shareholders at the close of any taxable year shall be deemed to have been distributed at the close of such year (whether or not any portion of such income was in fact distributed); and

"(B) section 504(a)(1) and section 681(c)(1) shall also not apply to income attributable to property of a decedent dying before January 1, 1951, which was transferred during his lifetime to a trust or property that was transferred under his will to such trust."

• 1964, Revenue Act of 1964 (P.L. 88-272)

P.L. 88-272, §225(b):

Amended Code Sec. 542(a)(1). **Effective** with respect to tax years beginning after 12-31-63. Prior to amendment, Sec. 542(a)(1) read as follows:

"(1) Gross income requirement.—At least 80 percent of its gross income for the taxable year is personal holding company income as defined in section 543, and".

• 1955 (P.L. 385, 84th Cong.)

P.L. 385, 84th Cong., §3:

Amended Sec. 452[542](a)(2). **Effective** for tax years beginning after 12-31-54.

[Sec. 542(b)]

(b) CORPORATIONS FILING CONSOLIDATED RETURNS.—

(1) GENERAL RULE.—In the case of an affiliated group of corporations filing or required to file a consolidated return under section 1501 for any taxable year, the adjusted ordinary gross income requirement of subsection (a) (1) of this section shall, except as provided in paragraphs (2) and (3), be applied for such year with respect to the consolidated adjusted ordinary gross

income and the consolidated personal holding company income of the affiliated group. No member of such an affiliated group shall be considered to meet such adjusted ordinary gross income requirement unless the affiliated group meets such requirement.

(2) INELIGIBLE AFFILIATED GROUP.—Paragraph (1) shall not apply to an affiliated group of corporations if—

(A) any member of the affiliated group of corporations (including the common parent corporation) derived 10 percent or more of its adjusted ordinary gross income for the taxable year from sources outside the affiliated group, and

(B) 80 percent or more of the amount described in subparagraph (A) consists of personal holding company income (as defined in section 543).

For purposes of this paragraph, section 543 shall be applied as if the amount described in subparagraph (A) were the adjusted ordinary gross income of the corporation.

(3) EXCLUDED CORPORATIONS.—Paragraph (1) shall not apply to an affiliated group of corporations if any member of the affiliated group (including the common parent corporation) is a corporation excluded from the definition of personal holding company under subsection (c).

(4) CERTAIN DIVIDEND INCOME RECEIVED BY A COMMON PARENT.—In applying paragraph (2) (A) and (B), personal holding company income and adjusted ordinary gross income shall not include dividends received by a common parent corporation from another corporation if—

(A) the common parent corporation owns, directly or indirectly, more than 50 percent of the outstanding voting stock of such other corporation, and

(B) such other corporation is not a personal holding company for the taxable year in which the dividends are paid.

(5) CERTAIN DIVIDEND INCOME RECEIVED FROM A NONINCLUDIBLE LIFE INSURANCE COMPANY.—In the case of an affiliated group of corporations filing or required to file a consolidated return under section 1501 for any taxable year, there shall be excluded from consolidated personal holding company income and consolidated adjusted ordinary gross income for purposes of this part dividends received by a member of the affiliated group from a life insurance company taxable under section 801 that is not a member of the affiliated group solely by reason of the application of paragraph (2) of subsection (b) of section 1504.

Amendments

• 1984, Deficit Reduction Act of 1984 (P.L. 98-369)

P.L. 98-369, §211(b)(7):

Amended Code Sec. 542(b)(5) by striking out "section 802" and inserting in lieu thereof "section 801". **Effective** for tax years beginning after 12-31-83.

• 1976, Tax Reform Act of 1976 (P.L. 94-455)

P.L. 94-455, §1901(a)(76)(B):

Amended Code Sec. 542(b)(2) by deleting ", other than an affiliated group of railroad corporations the common parent of which would be eligible to file a consolidated return under section 141 of the Internal Revenue Code of 1939 prior to its amendment by the Revenue Act of 1942," after "corporations" and before "if—". **Effective** for tax years beginning after 12-31-76.

• 1974 (P.L. 93-480)

P.L. 93-480, §3:

Amended Code Sec. 542(b) by adding paragraph (5). **Effective** for tax years beginning after 1973.

• 1964, Revenue Act of 1964 (P.L. 88-272)

P.L. 88-272, §225(k)(1):

Amended Code Sec. 542(b) by striking out "gross income" each place it appeared and inserting in lieu thereof "adjusted ordinary gross income". **Effective** for tax years beginning after 12-31-63.

[Sec. 542(c)]

(c) EXCEPTIONS.—The term "personal holding company" as defined in subsection (a) does not include—

(1) a corporation exempt from tax under subchapter F (sec. 501 and following);

(2) a bank as defined in section 581, or a domestic building and loan association within the meaning of section 7701(a)(19);

(3) a life insurance company;

(4) a surety company;

(5) a foreign corporation,

(6) a lending or finance company if—

(A) 60 percent or more of its ordinary gross income (as defined in section 543(b)(1)) is derived directly from the active and regular conduct of a lending or finance business;

(B) the personal holding company income for the taxable year (computed without regard to income described in subsection (d)(3) and income derived directly from the active and regular conduct of a lending or finance business, and computed by including as personal holding company income the entire amount of the gross income from rents, royalties, produced film rents, and compensation for use of corporate property by shareholders) is not more than 20 percent of the ordinary gross income;

(C) the sum of the deductions which are directly allocable to the active and regular conduct of its lending or finance business equals or exceeds the sum of—

(i) 15 percent of so much of the ordinary gross income derived therefrom as does not exceed $500,000, plus

(ii) 5 percent of so much of the ordinary gross income derived therefrom as exceeds $500,000; and

(D) the loans to a person who is a shareholder in such company during the taxable year by or for whom 10 percent or more in value of its outstanding stock is owned directly or indirectly (including, in the case of an individual, stock owned by members of his family as defined in section 544(a)(2)), outstanding at any time during such year do not exceed $5,000 in principal amount;

(7) a small business investment company which is licensed by the Small Business Administration and operating under the Small Business Investment Act of 1958 (15 U.S.C. 661 and following) and which is actively engaged in the business of providing funds to small business concerns under that Act. This paragraph shall not apply if any shareholder of the small business investment company owns at any time during the taxable year directly or indirectly (including, in the case of an individual, ownership by the members of his family as defined in section 544(a)(2)) a 5 per centum or more proprietary interest in a small business concern to which funds are provided by the investment company or 5 per centum or more in value of the outstanding stock of such concern; and

(8) a corporation which is subject to the jurisdiction of the court in a title 11 or similar case (within the meaning of section 368(a)(3)(A)) unless a major purpose of instituting or continuing such case is the avoidance of the tax imposed by section 541.

Amendments

• 2004, American Jobs Creation Act of 2004 (P.L. 108-357)

P.L. 108-357, §413(b)(1)(A)-(D):

Amended Code Sec. 542(c) by striking paragraph (5) and inserting "(5) a foreign corporation,", by striking paragraphs (7) and (10) and redesignating paragraphs (8) and (9) as paragraphs (7) and (8), respectively, by inserting "and" at the end of paragraph (7) (as so redesignated), and by striking "; and" at the end of paragraph (8) (as so redesignated) and inserting a period. **Effective** for tax years of foreign corporations beginning after 12-31-2004 and for tax years of United States shareholders with or within which such tax years of foreign corporations end. Prior to being stricken, Code Sec. 542(c)(5), (7) and (10) read as follows:

(5) a foreign personal holding company as defined in section 552;

***

(7) a foreign corporation (other than a corporation which has income to which section 543(a)(7) applies for the taxable year), if all of its stock outstanding during the last half of the taxable year is owned by nonresident alien individuals, whether directly or indirectly through foreign estates, foreign trusts, foreign partnerships, or other foreign corporations;

***

(10) a passive foreign investment company (as defined in section 1297).

• 1997, Taxpayer Relief Act of 1997 (P.L. 105-34)

P.L. 105-34, §1122(d)(1):

Amended Code Sec. 542(c)(10) by striking "section 1296" and inserting "section 1297". **Effective** for tax years of United States persons beginning after 12-31-97, and tax years of foreign corporations ending with or within such tax years of United States persons.

• 1986, Tax Reform Act of 1986 (P.L. 99-514)

P.L. 99-514, §1235(f)(2):

Amended Code Sec. 542(c) by striking out "and" at the end of paragraph (8), by striking out the period at the end of paragraph (9) and inserting in lieu thereof "; and", and by adding at the end thereof new paragraph (10). **Effective** for tax years of foreign corporations beginning after 12-31-86.

• 1982, Tax Equity and Fiscal Responsibility Act of 1982 (P.L. 97-248)

P.L. 97-248, §293(a):

Amended Code Sec. 542(c)(6)(C)(ii) by striking out "but not $1,000,000". **Effective** for tax years beginning after 12-31-81.

• 1980, Bankruptcy Tax Act of 1980 (P.L. 96-589)

P.L. 96-589, §5(a):

Amended Code Sec. 542(c) by striking out the period at the end of paragraph (8) and inserting in lieu thereof "; and", and by inserting a new paragraph (9). **Effective** for bankruptcy cases commencing after 12-31-80 and to similar cases commenced after that date. Also, the amendment will apply to a bankruptcy or similar case commenced on or after 10-1-79 (but prior to 1-1-81) if the special **effective** date election is made. See the historical comment for P.L. 96-589 in the amendments for Code Sec. 108(e) for the details of the election.

• 1976, Tax Reform Act of 1976 (P.L. 94-455)

P.L. 94-455, §1901(a)(76)(C):

Amended Code Sec. 542(c)(2) by striking out "without regard to subparagraphs (D) and (E) thereof" after "section 7701(a)(19)". **Effective** for tax years beginning after 12-31-76.

P.L. 94-455, §1901(a)(76)(D):

Amended Code Sec. 542(c)(8) by inserting "(15 U.S.C. 661 and following)" after "Small Business Investment Act of 1958". **Effective** for tax years beginning after 12-31-76.

• 1966, Foreign Investors Tax Act of 1966 (P.L. 89-809)

P.L. 89-809, §104(h)(1):

Amended Code Sec. 542(c)(7). **Effective** 1-1-67. Prior to amendment, Sec. 542(c)(7) read as follows:

"(7) a foreign corporation if—

"(A) its gross income from sources within the United States for the period specified in section 861(a)(2)(B) is less than 50 percent of its total gross income from all sources, and

"(B) all of its stock outstanding during the last half of the taxable year is owned by nonresident alien individuals, whether directly or indirectly through other foreign corporations;"

• 1964, Revenue Act of 1964 (P.L. 88-272)

P.L. 88-272, §225(c)(1):

Amended Code Sec. 542(c)(2). **Effective** for tax years beginning after 10-16-62. Prior to amendment, Sec. 542(c)(2) read as follows: "(2) a bank as defined in section 581;"

P.L. 88-272, §225(c)(2):

Amended Code Sec. 542(c) by striking out paragraphs (6), (7), (8), and (9), by renumbering paragraphs (10) and (11) as paragraphs (7) and (8), and by adding a new paragraph (6). **Effective** for tax years beginning after 12-31-63. Prior to amendment, Sec. 542(c)(6), (7), (8), and (9) read as follows:

"(6) a licensed personal finance company under State supervision, 80 percent or more of the gross income of which is lawful interest received from loans made to individuals in accordance with the provisions of applicable State law if at least 60 percent of such gross income is lawful interest—

"(A) received from individuals each of whose indebtedness to such company did not at any time during the taxable year exceed in principal amount the limit prescribed for small loans by such law (or, if there is no such limit, $500), and

"(B) not payable in advance or compounded and computed only on unpaid balances, and if the loans to a person, who is a shareholder in such company during the taxable year by or for whom 10 percent or more in value of its outstanding stock is owned directly or indirectly (including, in the case of an individual, stock owned by the members of his family as defined in section 544(a)(2)), outstanding at any time during such year do not exceed $5,000 in principal amount;

"(7) a lending company, not otherwise excepted by this subsection, authorized to engage and actively and regularly engaged in the small loan business (consumer finance business) under one or more State statutes providing for the direct regulation of such business, 80 percent or more of the gross income of which consists of either or both of the following—

"(A) lawful interest, discount, or other authorized charges received from loans made to individuals in accordance with the provisions of applicable State law, and

"(B) lawful income received from domestic subsidiary corporations (of which stock possessing at least 80 percent of the voting power of all classes of stock and of which at least 80 percent of each class of the nonvoting stock is owned directly by such lending company), which are themselves excepted under the paragraph or paragraph (6), (8), or (9) of this subsection,

if at least 60 percent of the gross income is lawful interest, discount, or other authorized charges received from loans made in accordance with the provisions of such small loan (consumer finance) laws to individuals, each of whose indebtedness to such company did not at any time during the taxable year exceed in principal amount the limit prescribed for small loans by such law (or, if there is no such limit, $1,500), and if the deductions allowed to such company under section 162 (relating to trade or business expenses), other than for compensation for personal services rendered by shareholders (including members of the shareholder's family as described in section 544(a)(2)), constitute 15 percent or more of its gross income, and the loans to a person, who is a shareholder in such company during the taxable year by or for whom 10 percent or more in value of its outstanding stock is owned directly or indirectly (including, in the case of an individual, stock owned by the members of his family as defined in section 544(a)(2)), outstanding at any time during such year do not exceed $5,000 in principal amount;

"(8) a loan or investment corporation, a substantial part of the business of which consists of receiving funds not subject to check and evidenced by installment or fully paid certificates of indebtedness or investment, and making loans and discounts, and the loans to a person who is a shareholder in such corporation during such taxable year by or for whom 10 percent or more in value of its outstanding stock is owned directly or indirectly (including, in the case of an individual, stock owned by the members of his family as defined in section 544(a)(2)) outstanding at any time during such year do not exceed $5,000 in principal amount;

"(9) a finance company, actively and regularly engaged in the business of purchasing or discounting accounts or notes receivable or installment obligations, or making loans secured by any of the foregoing or by tangible personal property, at least 80 percent of the gross income of which is derived from such business in accordance with the provisions of applicable State law or does not constitute personal holding company income as defined in section 543, if 60 percent of the gross income is derived from one or more of the following classes of transactions—

"(A) purchasing or discounting accounts or notes receivable, or installment obligations evidenced or secured by contracts of conditional sale, chattel mortgages, or chattel lease agreements, arising out of the sale of goods or services in the course of the transferor's trade or business;

"(B) making loans, maturing in not more than 36 months, to, and for the business purposes of, persons engaged in trade or business, secured by—

"(i) accounts or notes receivable, or installment obligations, described in subparagraph (A);

"(ii) warehouse receipts, bills of lading, trust receipts, chattel mortgages, bailments, or factor's liens, covering or evidencing the borrower's inventories;

"(iii) a chattel mortgage on property used in the borrower's trade or business;

except loans to any single borrower which for more than 90 days in the taxable year of the company exceed 15 percent of the average funds employed by the company during such taxable year;

"(C) making loans, in accordance with the provisions of applicable State law, secured by chattel mortgages on tangible personal property, the original amount of each of which is not less than the limit referred to in, or prescribed by, paragraph (6)(A), and the aggregate principal amount of which owing by any one borrower to the company at any time during the taxable year of the company does not exceed $5,000; and

"(D) if 30 percent or more of the gross income of the company is derived from one or more of the classes of transactions described in subparagraphs (A), (B), and (C), purchasing, discounting, or lending upon the security of, installment obligations of individuals where the transferor or borrower acquired such obligations either in transactions of the classes described in subparagraphs (A) and (C) or as a result of loans made by such transferor or borrower in accordance with the provisions of subparagraphs (A) and (B) of paragraph (6) or of subparagraphs (A) and (B) of paragraph (7) of this subsection, if the funds so supplied at all times bear an agreed ratio to the unpaid balance of the assigned installment obligations, and documents evidencing such obligations are held by the company;

provided that the deductions allowable under section 162 (relating to trade or business expenses), other than compensation for personal services rendered by shareholder's (including members of the shareholder's family as described in section 544(a)(2)), constitute 15 percent or more of the gross income, and that loans to a person who is a shareholder in such company during such taxable year by or for whom 10 percent or more in value or its outstanding stock is owned directly or indirectly (including, in the case of an individual, stock owned by members of his family as defined in section 544(a)(2)), outstanding at any time during such year do not exceed $5,000 in principal amount;".

• 1962 (P.L. 87-768)

P.L. 87-768, §1:

Amended Code Sec. 542(c)(7). **Effective** 1-1-62. Prior to amendment, Sec. 542(c)(7) read as follows:

"(7) a lending company, not otherwise excepted by this subsection, authorized to engage in the small loan business under one or more State statutes providing for the direct regulation of such business, 80 percent or more of the gross income of which is lawful interest, discount or other authorized charges—

"(A) received from loans maturing in not more than 36 months made to individuals in accordance with the provisions of applicable State law, and

"(B) which do not, in the case of any individual loan, exceed in the aggregate an amount equal to simple interest at the rate of 3 percent per month not payable in advance and computed only on unpaid balances, if at least 60 percent of the gross income is lawful interest, discount or other authorized charges received from individuals each of whose indebtedness to such company did not at any time during the taxable year exceed in principal amount the limit prescribed for small loans by such law (or, if there is no such limit, $500), and if the deductions allowed to such company under section 162 (relating to trade or business expenses), other than for compensation for personal services rendered by shareholders (including members of the shareholder's family as described in section 544(a)(2)) constitute 15 percent or more of its gross income, and the loans to a person, who is a shareholder in such company during the taxable year by or for whom 10 percent or more in value of its outstanding stock is owned directly or indirectly (including, in the case of an individual, stock owned by the members of his family as defined in section 544(a)(2)), outstanding at any time during such year do not exceed $5,000 in principal amount;".

• 1959 (P.L. 86-376)

P.L. 86-376, §3(a):

Amended Code Sec. 542(c) by substituting a semicolon for the period at the end of paragraph (10) and by adding a new paragraph (11). **Effective** for tax years beginning after 12-31-58.

[Sec. 542(d)]

(d) SPECIAL RULES FOR APPLYING SUBSECTION (c)(6).—

(1) LENDING OR FINANCE BUSINESS DEFINED.—

(A) IN GENERAL.—Except as provided in subparagraph (B), for purposes of subsection (c)(6), the term "lending or finance business" means a business of—

(i) making loans,

(ii) purchasing or discounting accounts receivable, notes, or installment obligations,

(iii) rendering services or making facilities available in connection with activities described in clauses (i) and (ii) carried on by the corporation rendering services or making facilities available, or

(iv) rendering services or making facilities available to another corporation which is engaged in the lending or finance business (within the meaning of this paragraph), if such services or facilities are related to the lending or finance business (within such meaning) of such other corporation and such other corporation and the corporation rendering services or making facilities available are members of the same affiliated group (as defined in section 1504).

(B) EXCEPTIONS.—For purposes of subparagraph (A), the term "lending or finance business" does not include the business of—

(i) making loans, or purchasing or discounting accounts receivable, notes, or installment obligations, if (at the time of the loan, purchase, or discount) the remaining maturity exceeds 144 months; unless—

(I) the loans, notes, or installment obligations are evidenced or secured by contracts of conditional sale, chattel mortgages, or chattel lease agreements arising out of the sale of goods or services in the course of the borrower's or transferor's trade or business, or

(II) the loans, notes, or installment obligations are made or acquired by the taxpayer and meet the requirements of subparagraph (C), or

(ii) making loans evidenced by, or purchasing, certificates of indebtedness issued in a series, under a trust indenture, and in registered form or with interest coupons attached.

For purposes of clause (i), the remaining maturity shall be treated as including any period for which there may be a renewal or extension under the terms of an option exercisable by the borrower.

(C) INDEFINITE MATURITY CREDIT TRANSACTIONS.—For purposes of subparagraph (B)(i), a loan, note, or installment obligation meets the requirements of this subparagraph if it is made under an agreement—

(i) under which the creditor agrees to make loans or advances (not in excess of an agreed upon maximum amount) from time to time to or for the account of the debtor upon request, and

(ii) under which the debtor may repay the loan or advance in full or in installments.

(2) BUSINESS DEDUCTIONS.—For purposes of subsection (c)(6)(C), the deductions which may be taken into account shall include only—

(A) deductions which are allowable only by reason of section 162 or section 404, except there shall not be included any such deduction in respect of compensation for personal services rendered by shareholders (including members of the shareholder's family as described in section 544(a)(2)), and

(B) deductions allowable under section 167, and deductions allowable under section 164 for real property taxes, but in either case only to the extent that the property with respect to which such deductions are allowable is used directly in the active and regular conduct of the lending or finance business.

(3) INCOME RECEIVED FROM CERTAIN AFFILIATED CORPORATIONS.—For purposes of subsection (c)(6)(B), in the case of a lending or finance company which meets the requirements of subsection (c)(6)(A), there shall not be treated as personal holding company income the lawful income received from a corporation which meets the requirements of subsection (c)(6) and which is a member of the same affiliated group (as defined in section 1504) of which such company is a member.

Amendments

• 1982, Tax Equity and Fiscal Responsibility Act of 1982 (P.L. 97-248)

P.L. 97-248, §293(b):

Amended Code Sec. 542(d)(1)(B)(i). **Effective** for tax years beginning after 12-31-80. Prior to amendment, it read as follows:

"(i) Making loans, or purchasing or discounting accounts receivable, notes, or installment obligations, if (at the time of the loan, purchase, or discount) the remaining maturity exceeds 60 months, unless the loans, notes, or installment obligations are evidenced or secured by contracts of conditional sale, chattel mortgages, or chattel lease agreements arising out of the sale of goods or services in the course of the borrower's or transferor's trade or business, or"

P.L. 97-248, §293(c):

Amended Code Sec. 542(d)(1) by adding at the end thereof new subparagraph (C). **Effective** for tax years beginning after 12-31-80.

• 1964, Revenue Act of 1964 (P.L. 88-272)

P.L. 88-272, §225(c)(3):

Added Code Sec. 542(d). **Effective** with respect to tax years beginning after 12-31-63.

[Sec. 543]

SEC. 543. PERSONAL HOLDING COMPANY INCOME.

[Sec. 543(a)]

(a) GENERAL RULE.—For purposes of this subtitle, the term "personal holding company income" means the portion of the adjusted ordinary gross income which consists of:

(1) DIVIDENDS, ETC.—Dividends, interest, royalties (other than mineral, oil, or gas royalties or copyright royalties), and annuities. This paragraph shall not apply to—

(A) interest constituting rent (as defined in subsection (b)(3)),

(B) interest on amounts set aside in a reserve fund under chapter 533 or 535 of title 46, United States Code,

(C) active business computer software royalties (within the meaning of subsection (d)), and

(D) interest received by a broker or dealer (within the meaning of section 3(a)(4) or (5) of the Securities and Exchange Act of 1934) in connection with—

(i) any securities or money market instruments held as property described in section 1221(a)(1),

(ii) margin accounts, or

(iii) any financing for a customer secured by securities or money market instruments.

(2) RENTS.—The adjusted income from rents; except that such adjusted income shall not be included if—

(A) such adjusted income constitutes 50 percent or more of the adjusted ordinary gross income, and

(B) the sum of—

(i) the dividends paid during the taxable year (determined under section 562),

(ii) the dividends considered as paid on the last day of the taxable year under section 563(d) (as limited by the second sentence of section 563(b)), and

(iii) the consent dividends for the taxable year (determined under section 565),

equals or exceeds the amount, if any, by which the personal holding company income for the taxable year (computed without regard to this paragraph and paragraph (6), and computed by including as personal holding company income copyright royalties and the adjusted income from mineral, oil, and gas royalties) exceeds 10 percent of the ordinary gross income.

(3) MINERAL, OIL, AND GAS ROYALTIES.—The adjusted income from mineral, oil, and gas royalties; except that such adjusted income shall not be included if—

(A) such adjusted income constitutes 50 percent or more of the adjusted ordinary gross income,

(B) the personal holding company income for the taxable year (computed without regard to this paragraph, and computed by including as personal holding company income copyright royalties and the adjusted income from rents) is not more than 10 percent of the ordinary gross income, and

(C) the sum of the deductions which are allowable under section 162 (relating to trade or business expenses) other than—

(i) deductions for compensation for personal services rendered by the shareholders, and

(ii) deductions which are specifically allowable under sections other than section 162,

equals or exceeds 15 percent of the adjusted ordinary gross income.

(4) COPYRIGHT ROYALTIES.—Copyright royalties; except that copyright royalties shall not be included if—

(A) such royalties (exclusive of royalties received for the use of, or right to use, copyrights or interests in copyrights on works created in whole, or in part, by any shareholder) constitute 50 percent or more of the ordinary gross income,

(B) the personal holding company income for the taxable year computed—

(i) without regard to copyright royalties, other than royalties received for the use of, or right to use, copyrights or interests in copyrights in works created in whole, or in part, by any shareholder owning more than 10 percent of the total outstanding capital stock of the corporation,

(ii) without regard to dividends from any corporation in which the taxpayer owns at least 50 percent of all classes of stock entitled to vote and at least 50 percent of the total value of all classes of stock and which corporation meets the requirements of this subparagraph and subparagraphs (A) and (C), and

(iii) by including as personal holding company income the adjusted income from rents and the adjusted income from mineral, oil, and gas royalties,

is not more than 10 percent of the ordinary gross income, and

(C) the sum of the deductions which are properly allocable to such royalties and which are allowable under section 162, other than—

(i) deductions for compensation for personal services rendered by the shareholders,

(ii) deductions for royalties paid or accrued, and

(iii) deductions which are specifically allowable under sections other than section 162,

equals or exceeds 25 percent of the amount by which the ordinary gross income exceeds the sum of the royalties paid or accrued and the amounts allowable as deductions under section 167 (relating to depreciation) with respect to copyright royalties.

For purposes of this subsection, the term "copyright royalties" means compensation, however designated, for the use of, or the right to use, copyrights in works protected by copyright issued under title 17 of the United States Code and to which copyright protection is also extended by the laws of any country other than the United States of America by virtue of any international treaty, convention, or agreement, or interests in any such copyrighted works, and includes payments from any person for performing rights in any such copyrighted work and payments (other than produced film rents as defined in paragraph (5)(B)) received for the use of, or right to use, films. For purposes of this paragraph, the term "shareholder" shall include any person who owns stock within the meaning of section 544. This paragraph shall not apply to active business computer software royalties.

(5) PRODUCED FILM RENTS.—

(A) Produced film rents; except that such rents shall not be included if such rents constitute 50 percent or more of the ordinary gross income.

(B) For purposes of this section, the term "produced film rents" means payments received with respect to an interest in a film for the use of, or right to use, such film, but only to the extent that such interest was acquired before substantial completion of production of such film. In the case of a producer who actively participates in the production of the film, such term includes an interest in the proceeds or profits from the film, but only to the extent such interest is attributable to such active participation.

(6) USE OF CORPORATE PROPERTY BY SHAREHOLDER.—

(A) Amounts received as compensation (however designated and from whomever received) for the use of, or the right to use, tangible property of the corporation in any case where, at any time during the taxable year, 25 percent or more in value of the outstanding stock of the corporation is owned, directly or indirectly, by or for an individual entitled to the use of the property (whether such right is obtained directly from the corporation or by means of a sublease or other arrangement).

(B) Subparagraph (A) shall apply only to a corporation which has personal holding company income in excess of 10 percent of its ordinary gross income.

(C) For purposes of the limitation in subparagraph (B), personal holding company income shall be computed—

(i) without regard to subparagraph (A) or paragraph (2),

(ii) by excluding amounts received as compensation for the use of (or right to use) intangible property (other than mineral, oil, or gas royalties or copyright royalties) if a substantial part of the tangible property used in connection with such intangible property is owned by the corporation and all such tangible and intangible property is used in the active conduct of a trade or business by an individual or individuals described in subparagraph (A), and

(iii) by including copyright royalties and adjusted income from mineral, oil, and gas royalties.

(7) PERSONAL SERVICE CONTRACTS.—

(A) Amounts received under a contract under which the corporation is to furnish personal services; if some person other than the corporation has the right to designate (by name or by description) the individual who is to perform the services, or if the individual who is to perform the services is designated (by name or by description) in the contract; and

(B) amounts received from the sale or other disposition of such a contract.

This paragraph shall apply with respect to amounts received for services under a particular contract only if at some time during the taxable year 25 percent or more in value of the outstanding stock of the corporation is owned, directly or indirectly, by or for the individual who has performed, is to perform, or may be designated (by name or by description) as the one to perform, such services.

(8) ESTATES AND TRUSTS.—Amounts includible in computing the taxable income of the corporation under part I of subchapter J (sec. 641 and following, relating to estates, trusts, and beneficiaries).

Amendments

• 2006 (P.L. 109-304)

P.L. 109-304, §17(e)(3):

Amended Code Sec. 543(a)(1)(B) by striking "section 511 or 607 of the Merchant Marine Act, 1936 (46 U.S.C. App. 1161 or 1177)" and substituting "chapter 533 or 535 of title 46, United States Code". **Effective** 10-6-2006.

• 1999, Tax Relief Extension Act of 1999 (P.L. 106-170)

P.L. 106-170, §532(c)(2)(E):

Amended Code Sec. 543(a)(1)(D)(i) by striking "section 1221(1)" and inserting "section 1221(a)(1)". **Effective** for any instrument held, acquired, or entered into, any transaction entered into, and supplies held or acquired on or after 12-17-99.

• 1996, Small Business Job Protection Act of 1996 (P.L. 104-188)

P.L. 104-188, §1704(t)(6):

Amended Code Sec. 543(a)(2)(B)(ii) by striking "section 563(c)" and inserting "section 563(d)". **Effective** 8-20-96.

• 1988, Technical and Miscellaneous Revenue Act of 1988 (P.L. 100-647)

P.L. 100-647, §6279(a):

Amended Code Sec. 543(a)(1) by striking out "and" at the end of subparagraph (B), by striking out the period at the end of subparagraph (C) and inserting in lieu thereof ", and" and by adding at the end thereof new subparagraph (D). **Effective** for interest received after 11-10-88, in tax years ending after such date.

• 1986, Tax Reform Act of 1986 (P.L. 99-514)

P.L. 99-514, §645(a)(1)(A)-(C):

Amended Code Sec. 543(a)(1) by striking out "and" at the end of subparagraph (A), by striking out the period at the end of subparagraph (B) and inserting in lieu thereof ", and", and by adding at the end thereof new subparagraph (C). **Effective** for royalties received before, on, and after 12-31-86. See, however, special rules provided by Act Sec. 645(b)-(d) following Code Sec. 543(b).

P.L. 99-514, §645(a)(4)(A):

Amended Code Sec. 543(a)(4) by adding at the end thereof a new sentence. **Effective** for royalties received before, on, and after 12-31-86. See, however, special rules provided by Act Sec. 645(b)-(d) following Code Sec. 543(b).

P.L. 99-514, §1899A(18):

Amended Code Sec. 543(a)(1)(B) by striking out "46 U.S.C." and inserting in lieu thereof "46 U.S.C. App.". **Effective** 10-22-86.

• 1984, Deficit Reduction Act of 1984 (P.L. 98-369)

P.L. 98-369, §712(i)(3):

Amended Code Sec. 543(a)(1) by striking out subparagraph (C), by adding "and" at the end of subparagraph (A), and striking out ", and" at the end of subparagraph (B) and inserting in lieu thereof a period. **Effective** as if included in the provision of P.L. 97-248 to which it relates. Prior to amendment, Code Sec. 543(a)(1)(C) read as follows:

(C) dividends to which section 302(b)(4) would apply if the corporation were an individual.

• 1982, Tax Equity and Fiscal Responsibility Act of 1982 (P.L. 97-248)

P.L. 97-248, §222(e)(6)(A)(C):

Amended Code Sec. 543(a)(1) by striking out "and" at the end of subparagraph (A); by striking out the period at the end of subparagraph (B) and inserting in lieu thereof ", and"; and by adding at the end thereof new subparagraph (C). **Effective**, generally, to distributions after 8-31-82. But see amendment notes for Code Sec. 331(b), P.L. 97-248, for special rules.

• 1976, Copyrights Act (P.L. 94-553)

P.L. 94-553, §105(d):

Amended Code Sec. 543(a)(4) by striking "(other than by reason of section 2 or 6 thereof)" following "United States Code". **Effective** 10-19-76.

• 1976, Tax Reform Act of 1976 (P.L. 94-455)

P.L. 94-455, §211(a):

Added the last sentence to Code Sec. 543(a)(5)(B). **Effective** for tax years ending on or after 12-31-75.

P.L. 94-455, §1901(b)(32)(D):

Amended Code Sec. 543(a)(1)(A) by inserting "and" at the end thereof. **Effective** for tax years beginning after 12-31-76.

P.L. 94-455, §1901(b)(32)(D):

Amended Code Sec. 543(a)(1)(B). **Effective** for tax years beginning after 12-31-76. Prior to amendment, Sec. 543(a)(1)(B) read as follows:

(B) interest on amounts set aside in a reserve fund under section 511 or 607 of the Merchant Marine Act, 1936, and".

P.L. 94-455, §1901(b)(32)(D):

Struck out Code Sec. 543(a)(1)(C). **Effective** for tax years beginning after 12-31-76. Prior to repeal, Sec. 543(a)(1)(C) read as follows:

(C) a dividend distribution of divested stock (as defined in subsection (e) of section 1111), but only if the stock with respect to which the distribution is made was owned by the distributee on September 6, 1961, or was owned by the distributee for at least 2 years before the date on which the antitrust order (as defined in subsection (d) of section 1111) was entered.

P.L. 94-455, §2106(a):

Amended Code Sec. 543(a)(6). **Effective** for tax years beginning after 12-31-76. Prior to amendment, Sec. 543(a)(6) read as follows:

(6) USE OF CORPORATION PROPERTY BY SHAREHOLDER.—Amounts received as compensation (however designated and from whomsoever received) for the use of, or right to use, property of the corporation in any case where, at any time during the taxable year, 25 percent or more in value of the outstanding stock of the corporation is owned, directly or indirectly, by or for an individual entitled to the use of the property; whether such right is obtained directly from the corporation or by means of a sublease or other arrangement. This paragraph shall apply only to a corporation which has personal holding company income for the taxable year (computed without regard to this paragraph and paragraph (2), and computed by including as personal holding company income copyright royalties and the adjusted income from mineral, oil, and gas royalties) in excess of 10 percent of its ordinary gross income.

• 1966, Foreign Investors Tax Act of 1966 (P.L. 89-809)

P.L. 89-809, §206(b)(1):

Amended Code Sec. 543(a)(2) by striking out the last sentence thereof. **Effective** 11-13-66. Prior to deletion, such last sentence read as follows:

"For purposes of applying this paragraph, royalties received for the use of, or for the privilege of using, a patent, invention, model, or design (whether or not patented), secret formula or process, or any other similar property right shall be treated as rent, if such property right is also used by the corporation receiving such royalties in the manufacture or production of tangible personal property held for lease to customers, and if the amount (computed without regard to this sentence) constituting rent from such leases to customers meets the requirements of subparagraph (A)."

• 1964 (P.L. 88-484)

P.L. 88-484, §3:

Amended Code Sec. 543(a)(2) by adding the last sentence. **Effective** for tax years beginning after 12-31-63.

• 1964, Revenue Act of 1964 (P.L. 88-272)

P.L. 88-272, §225(d):

Amended Code Sec. 543(a). **Effective** with respect to tax years beginning after 12-31-63. Prior to amendment, Sec. 543(a) read as follows:

"(a) General Rule.—For purposes of this subtitle, the term `personal holding company income' means the portion of the gross income which consists of:

"(1) Dividends, etc.—Dividends, interest, royalties (other than mineral, oil, or gas royalties or copyright royalties), and annuities. This paragraph shall not apply to interest constituting rent as defined in paragraph (7) or to interest on amounts set aside in a reserve fund under section 511 or 607 of the Merchant Marine Act, 1936. This paragraph shall not apply to a dividend distribution of divested stock (as defined in subsection (e) of section 1111) but only if the stock with respect to which the distribution is made was owned by the distributee on September 6, 1961, or was owned by the distributee for at least 2 years prior to the date on which the antitrust order (as defined in subsection (d) of section 1111) was entered.

"(2) Stock and securities transactions.—Except in the case of regular dealers in stock or securities, gains from the sale or exchange of stock or securities.

"(3) Commodities transactions.—Gains from futures transactions in any commodity on or subject to the rules of a board of trade or commodity exchange. This paragraph shall not apply to gains by a producer, processor, merchant, or handler of the commodity which arise out of bona fide hedging transactions reasonably necessary to the conduct of its business in the manner in which such business is customarily and usually conducted by others.

"(4) Estates and trusts.—Amounts includible in computing the taxable income of the corporation under part I of subchapter J (sec. 641 and following, relating to estates, trusts, and beneficiaries); and gains from the sale or other disposition of any interest in an estate or trust.

"(5) Personal service contracts.—

"(A) Amounts received under a contract under which the corporation is to furnish personal services; if some person other than the corporation has the right to designate (by name or by description) the individual who is to perform the services, or if the individual who is to perform the services is designated (by name or by description) in the contract; and

"(B) amounts received from the sale or other disposition of such a contract.

This paragraph shall apply with respect to amounts received for services under a particular contract only if at some time during the taxable year 25 percent or more in value of the outstanding stock of the corporation is owned, directly or indirectly, by or for the individual who has performed, is to perform, or may be designated (by name or by description) as the one to perform, such services.

"(6) Use of corporation property by shareholder.—Amounts received as compensation (however designated and from whomsoever received) for the use of, or right to use, property of the corporation in any case where, at any time during the taxable year, 25 percent or more in value of the outstanding stock of the corporation is owned, directly or indirectly, by or for an individual entitled to the use of the property; whether such right is obtained directly from the corporation or by means of a sublease or other arrangement. This paragraph shall apply only to a corporation which has personal holding company income for the taxable year, computed without regard to this paragraph and paragraph (7), in excess of 10 percent of its gross income. For purposes of the preceding sentence, copyright royalties constitute personal holding company income.

"(7) Rents.—Rents, unless constituting 50 percent or more of the gross income. For purposes of this paragraph, the term `rents' means compensation, however designated, for the use of, or right to use, property, and the interest on debts owed to the corporation, to the extent such debts represent the price for which real property held primarily for sale to customers in the ordinary course of its trade or business was sold or exchanged by the corporation; but does not include amounts constituting personal holding company income under paragraph (6).

"(8) Mineral, oil, or gas royalties.—Mineral, oil, or gas royalties, unless—

"(A) such royalties constitute 50 percent or more of the gross income, and

"(B) the deductions allowable under section 162 (relating to trade or business expenses) other than compensation for personal services rendered by the shareholders, constitute 15 percent or more of the gross income.

"(9) Copyright royalties.—Copyright royalties, unless—

"(A) such royalties (exclusive of royalties received for the use of, or right to use, copyrights or interests in copyrights on works created in whole, or in part, by any shareholder) constitute 50 percent or more of the gross income,

"(B) the personal holding company income for the taxable year not taking into account—

"(i) copyright royalties, other than royalties received for the use of, or right to use, copyrights or interests in copyrights in works created in whole, or in part, by any shareholder owning more than 10 percent of the total outstanding capital stock of the corporation, and

"(ii) dividends from any corporation in which the taxpayer owns at least 50 percent of all classes of stock entitled to vote and at least 50 percent of the total value of all classes of stock and which corporation meets the requirements of this subparagraph and subparagraphs (A) and (C) is 10 percent or less of the gross income, and

"(C) the deductions allowable under section 162 (other than deductions for compensation for personal services rendered by the shareholders and other than deductions for royalties to shareholders) constitute 50 percent or more of the gross income.

For purposes of this subsection, the term `copyright royalties' means compensation, however designated, for the use of, or the right to use, copyrights in works protected by copyright issued under title 17 of the United States Code (other than by reason of section 2 or 6 thereof), and to which copyright protection is also extended by the laws of any country other than the United States of America by virtue of any international treaty, convention or agreement, or interests in any such copyrighted works, and includes payments from any person for performing rights in any such copyrighted work. For purposes of this paragraph the term `shareholder' shall include any person who owns stock within the meaning of section 544. This paragraph shall not apply to compensation which is rent within the meaning of paragraph (7), determined without regard to the requirement that rents constitute 50 percent or more of the gross income."

• 1962 (P.L. 87-403)

P.L. 87-403, §3(c):

Added the last sentence to paragraph (1) of subsection (a). **Effective** for distributions made after 2-2-62.

• 1960 (P.L. 86-435)

P.L. 86-435, §1(a):

Amended Code Sec. 543(a) by adding a new paragraph (9). **Effective** for tax years beginning after 12-31-59.

P.L. 86-435, §1(b)(1):

Amended Code Sec. 543(a)(1) by striking out "(other than mineral, oil, or gas royalties)" and inserting in lieu thereof "(other than mineral, oil or gas royalties or copyright loyalties)". **Effective** for tax years beginning after 12-31-59.

P.L. 86-435, §1(b)(2):

Amended Code Sec. 543(a)(6) by adding the last sentence. **Effective** for tax years beginning after 12-31-59.

[Sec. 543(b)]

(b) DEFINITIONS.—For purposes of this part—

(1) ORDINARY GROSS INCOME.—The term "ordinary gross income" means the gross income determined by excluding—

(A) all gains from the sale or other disposition of capital assets, and

(B) all gains (other than those referred to in subparagraph (A)) from the sale or other disposition of property described in section 1231(b).

(2) ADJUSTED ORDINARY GROSS INCOME.—The term "adjusted ordinary gross income" means the ordinary gross income adjusted as follows:

(A) RENTS.—From the gross income from rents (as defined in the second sentence of paragraph (3) of this subsection) subtract the amount allowable as deductions for—

(i) exhaustion, wear and tear, obsolescence, and amortization of property other than tangible personal property which is not customarily retained by any one lessee for more than three years,

(ii) property taxes,

(iii) interest, and

(iv) rent,

to the extent allocable, under regulations prescribed by the Secretary, to such gross income from rents. The amount subtracted under this subparagraph shall not exceed such gross income from rents.

(B) MINERAL ROYALTIES, ETC.—From the gross income from mineral, oil, and gas royalties described in paragraph (4), and from the gross income from working interests in an oil or gas well, subtract the amount allowable as deductions for—

(i) exhaustion, wear and tear, obsolescence, amortization, and depletion,

(ii) property and severance taxes,

(iii) interest, and

(iv) rent,

to the extent allocable, under regulations prescribed by the Secretary, to such gross income from royalties or such gross income from working interests in oil or gas wells. The amount subtracted under this subparagraph with respect to royalties shall not exceed the gross income from such royalties, and the amount subtracted under this subparagraph with respect to working interests shall not exceed the gross income from such working interests.

(C) INTEREST.—There shall be excluded—

(i) interest received on a direct obligation of the United States held for sale to customers in the ordinary course of trade or business by a regular dealer who is making a primary market in such obligations, and

(ii) interest on a condemnation award, a judgment, and a tax refund.

(D) CERTAIN EXCLUDED RENTS.—From the gross income consisting of compensation described in subparagraph (D) of paragraph (3) subtract the amount allowable as deductions for the items described in clauses (i), (ii), (iii), and (iv) of subparagraph (A) to the extent allocable, under regulations prescribed by the Secretary, to such gross income. The amount subtracted under this subparagraph shall not exceed such gross income.

(3) ADJUSTED INCOME FROM RENTS.—The term "adjusted income from rents" means the gross income from rents, reduced by the amount subtracted under paragraph (2)(A) of this subsection. For purposes of the preceding sentence, the term "rents" means compensation, however designated, for the use of, or right to use, property, and the interest on debts owed to the corporation, to the extent such debts represent the price for which real property held primarily for sale to customers in the ordinary course of its trade or business was sold or exchanged by the corporation; but such term does not include—

(A) amounts constituting personal holding company income under subsection (a)(6),

(B) copyright royalties (as defined in subsection (a)(4)),

(C) produced film rents (as defined in subsection (a)(5)(B)),

(D) compensation, however designated, for the use of, or the right to use, any tangible personal property manufactured or produced by the taxpayer, if during the taxable year the taxpayer is engaged in substantial manufacturing or production of tangible personal property of the same type, or

(E) active business computer software royalties (as defined in subsection (d)).

(4) ADJUSTED INCOME FROM MINERAL, OIL, AND GAS ROYALTIES.—The term "adjusted income from mineral, oil, and gas royalties" means the gross income from mineral, oil, and gas royalties (including production payments and overriding royalties), reduced by the amount subtracted under paragraph (2)(B) of this subsection in respect of such royalties.

Amendments

• 2004, American Jobs Creation Act of 2004 (P.L. 108-357)

P.L. 108-357, §413(c)(8):

Amended Code Sec. 543(b)(1) by inserting "and" at the end of subparagraph (A), by striking ", and" at the end of subparagraph (B) and inserting a period, and by striking subparagraph (C). **Effective** for tax years of foreign corporations beginning after 12-31-2004 and for tax years of United States shareholders with or within which such tax years of foreign corporations end. Prior to being stricken, Code Sec. 543(b)(1)(C) read as follows:

(C) in the case of a foreign corporation all of the outstanding stock of which during the last half of the taxable year is owned by nonresident alien individuals (whether directly or indirectly through foreign estates, foreign trusts, foreign partnerships, or other foreign corporations), all items of income which would, but for this subparagraph, constitute personal holding company income under any paragraph of subsection (a) other than paragraph (7) thereof.

• 1986, Tax Reform Act of 1986 (P.L. 99-514)

P.L. 99-514, §645(a)(4)(B)(i)-(iii):

Amended Code Sec. 543(b)(3) by striking out "or" at the end of subparagraph (C), by striking out the period at the end of subparagraph (D) and inserting in lieu thereof ", or", and by adding at the end thereof new subparagraph (E). **Effective** for royalties received before, on, and after 12-31-86. For special rules, see Act Sec. 645(b)-(d), below.

P.L. 99-514, §645(b)-(d), provides:

(b) SPECIAL RULES FOR BROKER-DEALERS.—In the case of a broker-dealer which is part of an affiliated group which files a consolidated Federal income tax return, the common parent of which was incorporated in Nevada on January 27, 1972, the personal holding company income (within the meaning of section 543 of the Internal Revenue Code of 1986) of such broker-dealer, shall not include any interest received after the date of the enactment of this Act with respect to—

(1) any securities or money market instruments held as inventory,

(2) margin accounts, or

(3) any financing for a customer secured by securities or money market instruments.

(c) SPECIAL RULE FOR ROYALTIES RECEIVED BY QUALIFIED TAXPAYER.—

(1) IN GENERAL.—Any qualified royalty received or accrued in taxable years beginning after December 31, 1981, by a qualified taxpayer shall be treated in the same manner as a royalty with respect to software is treated under the amendments made by this section.

(2) QUALIFIED TAXPAYER.—For purposes of this subsection, a qualified taxpayer is any taxpayer incorporated on September 7, 1978, which is engaged in the trade or business of manufacturing dolls and accessories.

(3) QUALIFIED ROYALTY.—For purposes of this subsection, the term "qualified royalty" means any royalty arising from an agreement entered into in 1982 which permits the licensee to manufacture and sell dolls and accessories.

(d) SPECIAL RULE FOR TREATMENT OF ACTIVE BUSINESS COMPUTER ROYALTIES FOR S CORPORATION PURPOSES.—In the case of a taxpayer which was incorporated on May 3, 1977, in California and which elected to be taxed as an S corporation for its taxable year ending on December 31, 1985, any active business computer royalties (within the meaning of section 543(d) of the Internal Revenue Code of 1986 as added by this Act) which are received by the taxpayer in taxable years beginning after December 31, 1984, shall not be treated as passive investment income (within the meaning of section 1362(d)(3)(D)) for purposes of subchapter S of chapter 1 of such Code.

• 1976, Tax Reform Act of 1976 (P.L. 94-455)

P.L. 94-455, §1906(b)(13)(A):

Amended 1954 Code by substituting "Secretary" for "Secretary or his delegate" each place it appeared. **Effective** 2-1-77.

• 1966, Foreign Investors Tax Act of 1966 (P.L. 89-809)

P. L. 89-809, §104(h)(2):

Amended Code Sec. 543(b)(1) by deleting "and" at the end of subparagraph (A), by substituting ", and" for the period at the end of subparagraph (B), and by adding new subparagraph (C).

P. L. 89-809, §206(a):

Amended Code Sec. 543(b)(3) by striking out "but does not include amounts constituting personal holding company income under subsection (a)(6), nor copyright royalties (as defined in subsection (a)(4)) nor produced film rents (as defined in subsection (a)(5)(B))." and inserting in lieu thereof the following: "but such term does not include—

"(A) amounts constituting personal holding company income under subsection (a)(6),

"(B) copyright royalties (as defined in subsection (a)(4)),

"(C) produced film rents (as defined in subsection (a)(5)(B)), or

"(D) compensation, however designated, for the use of, or the right to use, any tangible personal property manufactured or produced by the taxpayer, if during the taxable year the taxpayer is engaged in substantial manufacturing or production of tangible personal property of the same type."

Effective, generally, for tax years beginning after 11-13-66, the date of enactment. However, at the election of the taxpayer, the amendment is also effective for tax years beginning on or before 11-13-66 and ending after 12-31-65.

P.L. 89-809, §206(b)(2):

Amended Code Sec. 543(b)(2) by adding new subparagraph (D). **Effective**, generally, for tax years beginning after 11-13-66, the date of enactment. However, at the election of the taxpayer, the amendment is also effective for tax years beginning on or before 11-13-66 and ending after 12-31-65.

• 1964, Revenue Act of 1964 (P.L. 88-272)

P.L. 88-272, §225(d):

Amended Code Sec. 543(b). **Effective** with respect to tax years beginning after 12-31-63. Prior to amendment, Sec. 543(b) read as follows:

"(b) Limitation on Gross Income in Certain Transactions.—For purposes of this part—

"(1) gross income and personal holding company income determined with respect to transactions described in section 543(a)(2) (relating to gains from stock and security transactions) shall include only the excess of gains over losses from such transactions, and

"(2) gross income and personal holding company income determined with respect to transactions described in section 543(a)(3) (relating to gains from commodity transactions) shall include only the excess of gains over losses from such transactions."

[Sec. 543(c)]

(c) GROSS INCOME OF INSURANCE COMPANIES OTHER THAN LIFE INSURANCE COMPANY.—In the case of an insurance company other than a life insurance company, the term "gross income" as used in this part means the gross income, as defined in section 832(b)(1), increased by the amount of losses incurred, as defined in section 832(b)(5), and the amount of expenses incurred, as defined in section 832(b)(6), and decreased by the amount deductible under section 832(c)(7) (relating to tax-free interest).

Amendments

• 1988, Technical and Miscellaneous Revenue Act of 1988 (P.L. 100-647)

P.L. 100-647, §1010(f)(5)(A)-(B):

Amended Code Sec. 543(c) by striking out "or Mutual" in the heading and inserting in lieu thereof "Insurance Companies" and by striking out "life or mutual" in the text and inserting in lieu thereof "a life insurance company". **Effective** as if included in the provision of P.L. 99-514 to which it relates.

[Sec. 543(d)]

(d) ACTIVE BUSINESS COMPUTER SOFTWARE ROYALTIES.—

(1) IN GENERAL.—For purposes of this section, the term "active business computer software royalties" means any royalties—

(A) received by any corporation during the taxable year in connection with the licensing of computer software, and

(B) with respect to which the requirements of paragraphs (2), (3), (4), and (5) are met.

(2) ROYALTIES MUST BE RECEIVED BY CORPORATION ACTIVELY ENGAGED IN COMPUTER SOFTWARE BUSINESS.—The requirements of this paragraph are met if the royalties described in paragraph (1)—

(A) are received by a corporation engaged in the active conduct of the trade or business of developing, manufacturing, or producing computer software, and

(B) are attributable to computer software which—

(i) is developed, manufactured, or produced by such corporation (or its predecessor) in connection with the trade or business described in subparagraph (A), or

(ii) is directly related to such trade or business.

(3) ROYALTIES MUST CONSTITUTE AT LEAST 50 PERCENT OF INCOME.—The requirements of this paragraph are met if the royalties described in paragraph (1) constitute at least 50 percent of the ordinary gross income of the corporation for the taxable year.

(4) DEDUCTIONS UNDER SECTIONS 162 AND 174 RELATING TO ROYALTIES MUST EQUAL OR EXCEED 25 PERCENT OF ORDINARY GROSS INCOME.—

(A) IN GENERAL.—The requirements of this paragraph are met if—

(i) the sum of the deductions allowable to the corporation under sections 162, 174, and 195 for the taxable year which are properly allocable to the trade or business described in paragraph (2) equals or exceeds 25 percent of the ordinary gross income of such corporation for such taxable year, or

(ii) the average of such deductions for the 5-taxable year period ending with such taxable year equals or exceeds 25 percent of the average ordinary gross income of such corporation for such period.

If a corporation has not been in existence during the 5-taxable year period described in clause (ii), then the period of existence of such corporation shall be substituted for such 5-taxable year period.

(B) DEDUCTIONS ALLOWABLE UNDER SECTION 162.—For purposes of subparagraph (A), a deduction shall not be treated as allowable under section 162 if it is specifically allowable under another section.

(C) LIMITATION ON ALLOWABLE DEDUCTIONS.—For purposes of subparagraph (A), no deduction shall be taken into account with respect to compensation for personal services rendered by the 5 individual shareholders holding the largest percentage (by value) of the outstanding stock of the corporation. For purposes of the preceding sentence—

(i) individuals holding less than 5 percent (by value) of the stock of such corporation shall not be taken into account, and

(ii) stock deemed to be owned by a shareholder solely by attribution from a partner under section 544(a)(2) shall be disregarded.

(5) DIVIDENDS MUST EQUAL OR EXCEED EXCESS OF PERSONAL HOLDING COMPANY INCOME OVER 10 PERCENT OF ORDINARY GROSS INCOME.—

(A) IN GENERAL.—The requirements of this paragraph are met if the sum of—

(i) the dividends paid during the taxable year (determined under section 562),

(ii) the dividends considered as paid on the last day of the taxable year under section 563(d) (as limited by the second sentence of section 563(b)), and

(iii) the consent dividends for the taxable year (determined under section 565),

equals or exceeds the amount, if any, by which the personal holding company income for the taxable year exceeds 10 percent of the ordinary gross income of such corporation for such taxable year.

(B) COMPUTATION OF PERSONAL HOLDING COMPANY INCOME.—For purposes of this paragraph, personal holding company income shall be computed—

(i) without regard to amounts described in subsection (a)(1)(C),

(ii) without regard to interest income during any taxable year—

(I) which is in the 5-taxable year period beginning with the later of the 1st taxable year of the corporation or the 1st taxable year in which the corporation conducted the trade or business described in paragraph (2)(A), and

(II) during which the corporation meets the requirements of paragraphs (2), (3), and (4), and

(iii) by including adjusted income from rents and adjusted income from mineral, oil, and gas royalties (within the meaning of paragraphs (2) and (3) of subsection (a)).

(6) SPECIAL RULES FOR AFFILIATED GROUP MEMBERS.—

(A) IN GENERAL.—In any case in which—

(i) the taxpayer receives royalties in connection with the licensing of computer software, and

(ii) another corporation which is a member of the same affiliated group as the taxpayer meets the requirements of paragraphs (2), (3), (4), and (5) with respect to such computer software,

the taxpayer shall be treated as having met such requirements.

(B) AFFILIATED GROUP.—For purposes of this paragraph, the term "affiliated group" has the meaning given such term by section 1504(a).

Amendments

• 1998, IRS Restructuring and Reform Act of 1998 (P.L. 105-206)

P.L. 105-206, §6023(9):

Amended Code Sec. 543(d)(5)(A)(ii) by striking "section 563(c)" and inserting "section 563(d)". **Effective** 7-22-98.

• 1986, Tax Reform Act of 1986 (P.L. 99-514)

P.L. 99-514, §645(a)(2):

Amended Code Sec. 543 by adding at the end thereof new subsection (d). **Effective** for royalties received before, on, and after 12-31-86. See, however, special rules provided by Act Sec. 645(b)-(d) following Code Sec. 543(b).

• 1964, Revenue Act of 1964 (P.L. 88-272)

P.L. 88-272, §225(k)(2):

Repealed Sec. 543(d). **Effective** 1-1-64. Prior to repeal, Code Sec. 543(d) read as follows:

"(d) Special Adjustment on Disposition of Antitrust Stock Received as a Dividend.—If—

"(1) a corporation received antitrust stock (as defined in section 301(f)) in a distribution to which section 301 applied,

"(2) the amount of the distribution determined under section 301(f)(2) exceeded the basis of the stock determined under section 301(f)(3), and

"(3) such distribution was includible in personal holding company income under subsection (a)(1),

then proper adjustment shall be made, under regulations prescribed by the Secretary or his delegate, to amounts includible in personal holding company income under subsection (a)(2) with respect to such stock (or other property the basis of which is determined by reference to the basis of such stock)."

• 1962 (P.L. 87-403)

P.L. 87-403, §3(c):

Added subsection (d). **Effective** for distributions made after 2-2-62.

[Sec. 544]

SEC. 544. RULES FOR DETERMINING STOCK OWNERSHIP.

[Sec. 544(a)]

(a) CONSTRUCTIVE OWNERSHIP.—For purposes of determining whether a corporation is a personal holding company, insofar as such determination is based on stock ownership under section 542(a)(2), section 543(a)(7), section 543(a)(6) or section 543(a)(4)—

(1) STOCK NOT OWNED BY INDIVIDUAL.—Stock owned, directly or indirectly, by or for a corporation, partnership, estate, or trust shall be considered as being owned proportionately by its shareholders, partners, or beneficiaries.

(2) FAMILY AND PARTNERSHIP OWNERSHIP.—An individual shall be considered as owning the stock owned, directly or indirectly, by or for his family or by or for his partner. For purposes of this paragraph, the family of an individual includes only his brothers and sisters (whether by the whole or half blood), spouse, ancestors, and lineal descendants.

(3) OPTIONS.—If any person has an option to acquire stock, such stock shall be considered as owned by such person. For purposes of this paragraph, an option to acquire such an option, and each one of a series of such options, shall be considered as an option to acquire such stock.

(4) APPLICATION OF FAMILY-PARTNERSHIP AND OPTION RULES.—Paragraphs (2) and (3) shall be applied—

(A) for purposes of the stock ownership requirement provided in section 542(a)(2), if, but only if, the effect is to make the corporation a personal holding company;

(B) for purposes of section 543(a)(7) (relating to personal service contracts), of section 543(a)(6) (relating to the use of property by shareholders), or of section 543(a)(4) (relating to copyright royalties), if, but only if, the effect is to make the amounts therein referred to includible under such paragraph as personal holding company income.

(5) CONSTRUCTIVE OWNERSHIP AS ACTUAL OWNERSHIP.—Stock constructively owned by a person by reason of the application of paragraph (1) or (3) shall, for purposes of applying paragraph (1) or (2), be treated as actually owned by such person; but stock constructively owned by an individual by reason of the application of paragraph (2) shall not be treated as owned by him for purposes of again applying such paragraph in order to make another the constructive owner of such stock.

(6) OPTION RULE IN LIEU OF FAMILY AND PARTNERSHIP RULE.—If stock may be considered as owned by an individual under either paragraph (2) or (3) it shall be considered as owned by him under paragraph (3).

Amendments

• 1964, Revenue Act of 1964 (P.L. 88-272)

P.L. 88-272, §225(k)(3):

Amended Code Sec. 544(a) by striking out "section 543(a)(5)" each place it appeared and inserting in lieu thereof "section 543(a)(7)", and by striking out "section 543(a)(9)" each place it appeared and inserting in lieu thereof "section 543 (a)(4)". **Effective** for tax years beginning after 12-31-63.

• 1960 (P.L. 86-435)

P.L. 86-435, §1(c)(1):

Amended Code Sec. 544(a) by striking out "For purposes of determining whether a corporation is a personal holding company, insofar as such determination is based on stock ownership under section 542(a)(2), section 543(a)(5), or section 543(a)(6)" and inserting in lieu thereof "For purposes of determining whether a corporation is a personal holding company, insofar as such determination is based on stock ownership under section 542(a)(2), section 543(a)(5), section 543(a)(6) or section 543(a)(9)". **Effective** for tax years beginning after 12-31-59.

P.L. 86-435, §1(c)(2):

Amended subparagraph (B) of paragraph (4) of section 544(a). **Effective** for tax years beginning after 12-31-59. Prior to amendment, subparagraph (B) read as follows:

"(B) for purposes of section 543(a)(5) (relating to personal service contracts), or of section 543(a)(6) (relating to the use of property by shareholders), if, but only if, the effect is to make the amounts therein referred to includible under such paragraph as personal holding company income."

[Sec. 544(b)]

(b) CONVERTIBLE SECURITIES.—Outstanding securities convertible into stock (whether or not convertible during the taxable year) shall be considered as outstanding stock—

(1) for purposes of the stock ownership requirement provided in section 542(a)(2), but only if the effect of the inclusion of all such securities is to make the corporation a personal holding company;

(2) for purposes of section 543(a)(7) (relating to personal service contracts), but only if the effect of the inclusion of all such securities is to make the amounts therein referred to includible under such paragraph as personal holding company income;

(3) for purposes of section 543(a)(6) (relating to the use of property by shareholders), but only if the effect of the inclusion of all such securities is to make the amounts therein referred to includible under such paragraph as personal holding company income; and

(4) for purposes of section 543(a)(4) (relating to copyright royalties), but only if the effect of the inclusion of all such securities is to make the amounts therein referred to includible under such paragraph as personal holding company income.

The requirement in paragraphs (1), (2), (3), and (4) that all convertible securities must be included if any are to be included shall be subject to the exception that, where some of the outstanding securities are convertible only after a later date than in the case of others, the class having the earlier conversion date may be included although the others are not included, but no convertible securities shall be included unless all outstanding securities having a prior conversion date are also included.

Amendments

• 1964, Revenue Act of 1964 (P.L. 88-272)

P.L. 88-272, §225(k) (3):

Amended Code Sec. 544(b) by striking out "section 543(a)(5)" and inserting in lieu thereof "section 543(a)(7)", and by striking out "section 543(a)(9)" and inserting in lieu thereof "section 543(a)(4)". **Effective** for tax years beginning after 12-31-63.

• 1960 (P.L. 86-435)

P.L. 86-435, §1(d):

Amended Code Sec. 544(b) by striking out "and" appearing at the end of paragraph (2), by striking out the period at the end of paragraph (3) and substituting "; and ", by adding a new paragraph (4), and by striking out "paragraphs (1), (2), and (3)" in the last sentence and substituting "paragraphs (1), (2), (3), and (4)". **Effective** for tax years beginning after 12-31-59.

[Sec. 545]

SEC. 545. UNDISTRIBUTED PERSONAL HOLDING COMPANY INCOME.

[Sec. 545(a)]

(a) DEFINITION.—For purposes of this part, the term "undistributed personal holding company income" means the taxable income of a personal holding company adjusted in the manner provided in subsections (b), (c), and (d), minus the dividends paid deduction as defined in section 561. In the case of a personal holding company which is a foreign corporation, not more than 10 percent in value of the outstanding stock of which is owned (within the meaning of section 958(a)) during the last half of the taxable year by United States persons, the term "undistributed personal holding company income" means the amount determined by multiplying the undistributed personal holding company income (determined without regard to this sentence) by the percentage in value of its outstanding stock which is the greatest percentage in value of its outstanding stock so owned by United States persons on any one day during such period.

Amendments

• 1966, Foreign Investors Tax Act of 1966 (P.L. 89-809)

P. L. 89-809, §104(h)(3)(A):

Amended Code Sec. 545(a). **Effective** 1-1-67. Prior to amendment, Sec. 545(a) read as follows:

"(a) DEFINITION.—For purposes of this part, the term `undistributed personal holding company income' means the taxable income of a personal holding company adjusted in the manner provided in subsections (b) and (c), minus the dividends paid deduction as defined in section 561."

For amendments made by earlier Acts, see amendment note under Sec. 545(d).

[Sec. 545(b)]

(b) ADJUSTMENTS TO TAXABLE INCOME.—For the purposes of subsection (a), the taxable income shall be adjusted as follows:

(1) TAXES.—There shall be allowed as a deduction Federal income and excess profits taxes and income, war profits and excess profits taxes of foreign countries and possessions of the United States (to the extent not allowable as a deduction under section 275(a)(4)), accrued during the taxable year or deemed to be paid by a domestic corporation under section 902(a) or 960(a)(1) for the taxable year, but not including the accumulated earnings tax imposed by section 531, the personal holding company tax imposed by section 541, or the taxes imposed by corresponding sections of a prior income tax law.

(2) CHARITABLE CONTRIBUTIONS.—The deduction for charitable contributions provided under section 170 shall be allowed, but in computing such deduction the limitations in section 170(b)(1)(A), (B), (D), and (E) shall apply, and section 170(b)(2) and (d)(1) shall not apply. For purposes of this paragraph, the term "contribution base" when used in section 170(b)(1) means the taxable income computed with the adjustments (other than the 10-percent limitation) provided in section 170(b)(2) and (d)(1) and without deduction of the amount disallowed under paragraph (6) of this subsection.

(3) SPECIAL DEDUCTIONS DISALLOWED.—The special deductions for corporations provided in part VIII (except section 248) of subchapter B (section 241 and following, relating to the deduction for dividends received by corporations, etc.) shall not be allowed.

(4) NET OPERATING LOSS.—The net operating loss deduction provided in section 172 shall not be allowed, but there shall be allowed as a deduction the amount of the net operating loss (as defined in section 172(c)) for the preceding taxable year computed without the deductions provided in part VIII (except section 248) of subchapter B.

(5) NET CAPITAL GAINS.—There shall be allowed as a deduction the net capital gain for the taxable year, minus the taxes imposed by this subtitle attributable to such net capital gain. The taxes attributable to such net capital gain shall be an amount equal to the difference between—

(A) the taxes imposed by this subtitle (except the tax imposed by this part) for such year, and

(B) such taxes computed for such year without including such net capital gain in taxable income.

(6) EXPENSES AND DEPRECIATION APPLICABLE TO PROPERTY OF THE TAXPAYER.—The aggregate of the deductions allowed under section 162 (relating to trade or business expenses) and section 167 (relating to depreciation), which are allocable to the operation and maintenance of property owned or operated by the corporation, shall be allowed only in an amount equal to the rent or other compensation received for the use of, or the right to use, the property, unless it is established (under regulations prescribed by the Secretary) to the satisfaction of the Secretary—

(A) that the rent or other compensation received was the highest obtainable, or, if none was received, that none was obtainable;

(B) that the property was held in the course of a business carried on bona fide for profit; and

(C) either that there was reasonable expectation that the operation of the property would result in a profit, or that the property was necessary to the conduct of the business.

(7) SPECIAL RULE FOR CAPITAL GAINS AND LOSSES OF FOREIGN CORPORATIONS.—In the case of a foreign corporation, paragraph (5) shall be applied by taking into account only gains and losses which are effectively connected with the conduct of a trade or business within the United States and are not exempt from tax under treaty.

Amendments

• 2006, Pension Protection Act of 2006 (P.L. 109-280)

P.L. 109-280, §1206(b)(2):

Amended Code Sec. 545(b)(2) by striking "and (D)" and inserting "(D), and (E)". **Effective** for contributions made in tax years beginning after 12-31-2005.

• 1986, Tax Reform Act of 1986 (P.L. 99-514)

P.L. 99-514, §1225(b):

Amended Code Sec. 545(b) by adding at the end thereof new paragraph (7). **Effective** for gains and losses realized on or after 1-1-86 [**effective** date changed by P.L. 100-647, §1012(k)].

• 1983, Technical Corrections Act of 1982 (P.L. 97-448)

P.L. 97-448, §102(m)(2):

Amended Code Sec. 545(b)(2) by striking out "5-percent" and inserting in lieu thereof "10-percent". **Effective** as if included in the provision of P.L. 97-34 to which it relates.

• 1976, Tax Reform Act of 1976 (P.L. 94-455)

P.L. 94-455, §1033(b)(4):

Substituted "section 902(a) or 960(a)(1)" for "section 902(a)(1) or 960(a)(1)(C)" in Code Sec. 545(b)(1). For the **effective** date, see Act Sec. 1033(c), below.

P.L. 94-455, §1033(c), provides:

(c) EFFECTIVE DATES.—The amendments made by this section shall apply—

(1) in respect of any distribution received by a domestic corporation after December 31, 1977, and

(2) in respect of any distribution received by a domestic corporation before January 1, 1978, in a taxable year of such corporation beginning after December 31, 1975, but only to the extent that such distribution is made out of the accumulated profits of a foreign corporation for a taxable year (of such foreign corporation) beginning after December 31, 1975.

For purposes of paragraph (2), a distribution made by a foreign corporation out of its profits which are attributable to a distribution received from a foreign corporation to which section 902(b) of the Internal Revenue Code of 1954 applies shall be treated as made out of the accumulated profits of a foreign corporation for a taxable year beginning before January 1, 1976, to the extent that such distribution was paid out of the accumulated profits of such foreign corporation for a taxable year beginning before January 1, 1976.

P.L. 94-455, §1901(a)(77)(A):

Amended Code Sec. 545(b)(1). **Effective** for tax years beginning after 12-31-76. Prior to amendment, Sec. 545(b)(1) read as follows:

(1) TAXES.—There shall be allowed as a deduction Federal income and excess profits taxes (other than the excess profits tax imposed by subchapter E of chapter 2 of the Internal Revenue Code of 1939 for taxable years beginning after December 31, 1940) and income, war profits and excess profits taxes of foreign countries and possessions of the United States (to the extent not allowable as a deduction under section 275(a)(4)), accrued during the taxable year or deemed to be paid by a domestic corporation under section 902(a)(1) or 960(a)(1)(C) for the taxable year, but not including the accumulated earnings tax imposed by section 531, the personal holding company tax imposed by section 541, or the taxes imposed by corresponding sections of a prior income tax law. A taxpayer which, for each taxable year in which it was subject to the tax imposed by section 500 of the Internal Revenue Code of 1939, deducted Federal income and excess profits taxes when paid for the purpose of computing subchapter A net income under such Code, shall deduct taxes under this paragraph when paid, unless the taxpayer elects, in its return for a taxable year ending after June 30, 1954, to deduct the taxes described in this paragraph when accrued. Such an election shall be irrevocable and shall apply to the taxable year for which the election is made and to all subsequent taxable years.

P.L. 94-455, §1901(a)(77)(B):

Amended Code Sec. 545(b) by striking out paragraph (7). **Effective** for tax years beginning after 12-31-76. Prior to repeal, Sec. 545(b)(7) read as follows:

(7) PAYMENT OF INDEBTEDNESS INCURRED PRIOR TO JANUARY 1, 1934.—There shall be allowed as a deduction amounts used or irrevocably set aside to pay or to retire indebtedness of any kind incurred before January 1, 1934, if such amounts are reasonable with reference to the size and terms of such indebtedness.

P.L. 94-455, §1901(b)(20)(B)(i):

Amended Code Sec. 545(b) by striking out former paragraph (6) and by redesignating former paragraph (8) as paragraph (6). **Effective** for tax years beginning after 12-31-76. Prior to repeal, Sec. 545(b)(6) read as follows:

(6) BANK AFFILIATES.—There shall be allowed the deduction described in section 601 (relating to bank affiliates.

P.L. 94-455, §1901(b)(20)(B)(ii):

Substituted "paragraph (6)" for "paragraph (8)" in Code Sec. 545(b)(2). **Effective** for tax years beginning after 12-31-76.

P.L. 94-455, §1901(b)(32)(E):

Amended Code Sec. 545(b) by striking out paragraphs (10) and (11). **Effective** for tax years beginning after 12-31-76. Prior to repeal, paragraphs (10) and (11) read as follows:

(10) DISTRIBUTIONS OF DIVESTED STOCK.—There shall be allowed as a deduction the amount of any income attributable to the receipt of a distribution of divested stock (as defined in subsection (e) of section 1111), minus the taxes imposed by this subtitle attributable to such receipt, but only if the stock with respect to which the distribution is made was owned by the distributee on September 6, 1961, or was owned by the distributee for at least 2 years prior to the date on which the antitrust order (as defined in subsection (d) of section 1111) was entered.

(11) SPECIAL ADJUSTMENT ON DISPOSITION OF ANTITRUST STOCK RECEIVED AS A DIVIDEND.—If—

(A) a corporation received antitrust stock (as defined in section 301(f)) in a distribution to which section 301 applied,

(B) the amount of the distribution determined under section 301(f)(2) exceeded the basis of the stock determined under section 301(f)(3), and

(C) paragraph (10) did not apply in respect of such distribution, then proper adjustment shall be made, under regulations prescribed by the Secretary or his delegate, if such stock (or other property the basis of which is determined by reference to the basis of such stock) is sold or exchanged.

P.L. 94-455, §1901(b)(33)(D):

Amended Code Sec. 545(b)(5). **Effective** for tax years beginning after 12-31-76. Prior to amendment, Sec. 545(b)(5) read as follows:

(5) LONG-TERM CAPITAL GAINS.—There shall be allowed as a deduction the excess of the net long-term capital gain for the taxable year over the net short-term capital loss for such year, minus the taxes imposed by this subtitle attributable to such excess. The taxes attributable to such excess shall be an amount equal to the difference between—

(A) the taxes imposed by this subtitle (except the tax imposed by this part) for such year, and

(B) such taxes computed for such year without including such excess in taxable income.

P.L. 94-455, §1906(b)(13)(A):

Amended 1954 Code by substituting "Secretary" for "Secretary or his delegate" each place it appeared. **Effective** 2-1-77.

P.L. 94-455, §1951(b)(9)(A):

Repealed Code Sec. 545(b)(9). Prior to repeal, Sec. 545(b)(9) read as follows:

(9) AMOUNT OF A LIEN IN FAVOR OF THE UNITED STATES.—There shall be allowed as a deduction the amount, not to exceed the taxable income of the taxpayer, of any lien in favor of the United States (notice of which has been filed as provided in section 6323(f)) to which the taxpayer is subject at the close of the taxable year. The sum of the amounts deducted under this paragraph with respect to any lien shall, for the purposes of this section, be added to the taxable income of the taxpayer for the taxable year in which such lien is satisfied or released. Where an amount is added to the taxable income of a corporation by reason of the preceding sentence of this paragraph, the shareholders of the corporation may, pursuant to regulations prescribed by the Secretary or his delegate, elect to compute the income tax with respect to such dividends as are attributable to such amount as though they were received ratably over the period the lien was in effect.

P.L. 94-455, §1951(b)(9)(B), provides:

(B) SAVINGS PROVISION.—Notwithstanding subparagraph (A), if any amount was deducted under paragraph (9) of section 545(b) in a taxable year beginning before January 1, 1977, on account of a lien which is satisfied or released in a taxable year beginning on or after such date, the amount so deducted shall be included in income, for purposes of section 545, as provided in the second sentence of such paragraph. Shareholders of any corporation which has amounts included in its income by reason of the preceding sentence may elect to compute the income tax on dividends attributable to amounts so included as provided in the third sentence of such paragraph.

• 1969, Tax Reform Act of 1969 (P.L. 91-172)

P.L. 91-172, §201(a)(2)(B):

Amended Code Sec. 545(b)(2). **Effective** for tax years beginning after 12-31-69. Prior to amendment, Code Sec. 545(b)(2) read as follows:

"(2) Charitable contributions.—The deduction for charitable contributions provided under section 170 shall be allowed, but in computing such deduction the limitations in section 170(b)(1)(A) and (B) shall apply, and section 170(b)(2) and (5) shall not apply. For purposes of this paragraph, the term `adjusted gross income' when used in section 170(b)(1) means the taxable income computed with the adjustments (other than the 5-percent limitation) provided in the first sentence of section 170(b)(2) and (5) and without deduction of the amount disallowed under paragraph (8) of this subsection."

• 1966, Federal Tax Lien Act of 1966 (P.L. 89-719)

P.L. 89-719, §101(b):

Amended Code Sec. 545(b)(9) by substituting "section 6323(f)" for "section 6323(a)(1), (2), or (3)". **Effective**, generally, after 11-2-66. For exceptions see the amendment note for Code Sec. 6323.

For amendments made by earlier Acts, see amendment note under Sec. 545(d).

[Sec. 545(c)—Repealed]

Amendments

• 1990, Omnibus Budget Reconciliation Act of 1990 (P.L. 101-508)

P.L. 101-508, §11801(a)(24):

Repealed Code Sec. 545(c). **Effective** 11-5-90. Prior to repeal, Code Sec. 545(c) read as follows:

(c) SPECIAL ADJUSTMENT TO TAXABLE INCOME.—

(1) IN GENERAL.—Except as otherwise provided in this subsection, for purposes of subsection (a) there shall be allowed as a deduction amounts used, or amounts irrevocably set aside (to the extent reasonable with reference to the size and terms of the indebtedness), to pay or retire qualified indebtedness.

(2) CORPORATIONS TO WHICH APPLICABLE.—This subsection shall apply only with respect to a corporation—

(A) which for at least one of the two most recent taxable years ending before February 26, 1964, was not a personal holding company under section 542, but would have been a personal holding company under section 542 for such taxable year if the law applicable for the first taxable year beginning after December 31, 1963, had been applicable to such taxable year, or

(B) to the extent that it succeeds to the deduction referred to in paragraph (1) by reason of section 381(c)(15).

(3) QUALIFIED INDEBTEDNESS.—

(A) IN GENERAL.—Except as otherwise provided in this paragraph, for purposes of this subsection the term "qualified indebtedness" means—

(i) the outstanding indebtedness incurred by the taxpayer after December 31, 1933, and before January 1, 1964, and

(ii) the outstanding indebtedness incurred after December 31, 1963, for the purpose of making a payment or set-aside referred to in paragraph (1) in the same taxable year, but, in the case of such a payment or set-aside which is made on or after the first day of the first taxable year beginning after December 31, 1963, only to the extent the deduction otherwise allowed in paragraph (1) with respect to such payment or set-aside is treated as nondeductible by reason of the election provided in paragraph (4).

(B) EXCEPTION.—For purposes of subparagraph (A), qualified indebtedness does not include any amounts which were, at any time after December 31, 1963, and before the payment or set-aside, owed to a person who at such time owned (or was considered as owning within the meaning of section 318(a)) more than 10 percent in value of the taxpayer's outstanding stock.

(C) REDUCTION FOR AMOUNTS IRREVOCABLY SET ASIDE.—For purposes of subparagraph (A), the qualified indebtedness with respect to a contract shall be reduced by amounts irrevocably set aside before the taxable year to pay or retire such indebtedness; and no deduction shall be allowed under paragraph (1) for payments out of amounts so set aside.

(4) ELECTION NOT TO DEDUCT.—A taxpayer may elect, under regulations prescribed by the Secretary, to treat as nondeductible an amount otherwise deductible under paragraph (1); but only if the taxpayer files such election on or before the 15th day of the third month following the close of the taxable year with respect to which such election applies, designating therein the amounts which are to be treated as nondeductible and specifying the indebtedness (referred to in paragraph (3)(A)(ii)) incurred for the purpose of making the payment or set-aside.

(5) LIMITATIONS.—The deduction otherwise allowed by this subsection for the taxable year shall be reduced by the sum of—

(A) the amount, if any, by which—

(i) the deductions allowed for the taxable year and all preceding taxable years beginning after December 31, 1963, for exhaustion, wear and tear, obsolescence, amortization, or depletion (other than such deductions which are disallowed in computing undistributed personal holding company income under subsection (b)(6)), exceed

(ii) any reduction, by reason of this subparagraph, of the deductions otherwise allowed by this subsection for such preceding taxable years, and

(B) the amount, if any, by which—

(i) the deductions allowed under subsection (b)(5) in computing undistributed personal holding company income for the taxable year and all preceding taxable years beginning after December 31, 1963, exceed

(ii) any reduction, by reason of this subparagraph, of the deductions otherwise allowed by this subsection for such preceding taxable years.

(6) PRO-RATA REDUCTION IN CERTAIN CASES.—For purposes of paragraph (3)(A), if property (of a character which is subject to an allowance for exhaustion, wear and tear, obsolescence, amortization, or depletion) is disposed of after December 31, 1963, the total amounts of qualified indebtedness of the taxpayer shall be reduced pro-rata in the taxable year of such disposition by the amount, if any, by which—

(A) the adjusted basis of such property at the time of such disposition, exceeds

(B) the amount of qualified indebtedness which ceased to be qualified indebtedness with respect to the taxpayer by reason of the assumption of the indebtedness by the transferee.

P.L. 101-508, §11821(b), provides:

(b) SAVINGS PROVISION.—If—

(1) any provision amended or repealed by this part applied to—

(A) any transaction occurring before the date of the enactment of this Act,

(B) any property acquired before such date of enactment, or

(C) any item of income, loss, deduction, or credit taken into account before such date of enactment, and

(2) the treatment of such transaction, property, or item under such provision would (without regard to the amendments made by this part) affect liability for tax for periods ending after such date of enactment,

nothing in the amendments made by this part shall be construed to affect the treatment of such transaction, property, or item for purposes of determining liability for tax for periods ending after such date of enactment.

• 1976, Tax Reform Act of 1976 (P.L. 94-455)

P.L. 94-455, §1901(a)(77)(C):

Substituted "February 26, 1964" for "the date of enactment of this subsection" in Code Sec. 545(c)(2)(A). **Effective** for tax years beginning after 12-31-76.

P.L. 94-455, §1901(b)(20)(B)(iii):

Substituted "(b)(6)" for "(b)(8)" in Code Sec. 545(c)(5)(A)(i). **Effective** for tax years beginning after 12-31-76.

P.L. 94-455, §1906(b)(13)(A):

Amended 1954 Code by substituting "Secretary" for "Secretary or his delegate" each place it appeared. **Effective** 2-1-77.

[Sec. 545(c)]

(c) CERTAIN FOREIGN CORPORATIONS.—In the case of a foreign corporation all of the outstanding stock of which during the last half of the taxable year is owned by nonresident alien individuals (whether directly or indirectly through foreign estates, foreign trusts, foreign partnerships, or other foreign corporations), the taxable income for purposes of subsection (a) shall be the income which constitutes personal holding company income under section 543(a)(7), reduced by the deductions attributable to such income, and adjusted, with respect to such income, in the manner provided in subsection (b).

Amendments

• 1990, Omnibus Budget Reconciliation Act of 1990 (P.L. 101-508)

P.L. 101-508, §11801(c)(10)(B):

Amended Code Sec. 545 by redesignating subsection (d) as subsection (c). **Effective** 11-5-90.

P.L. 101-508, §11821(b), provides:

(b) SAVINGS PROVISION.—If—

(1) any provision amended or repealed by this part applied to—

(A) any transaction occurring before the date of the enactment of this Act,

(B) any property acquired before such date of enactment, or

(C) any item of income, loss, deduction, or credit taken into account before such date of enactment, and

(2) the treatment of such transaction, property, or item under such provision would (without regard to the amendments made by this part) affect liability for tax for periods ending after such date of enactment,

nothing in the amendments made by this part shall be construed to affect the treatment of such transaction, property, or item for purposes of determining liability for tax for periods ending after such date of enactment.

• 1966, Foreign Investors Tax Act of 1966 (P.L. 89-809)

P.L. 89-809, §104(h)(3)(B):

Added new Code Sec. 545(d).

• 1964, Revenue Act of 1964 (P.L. 88-272)

P.L. 88-272, §207(b)(5):

Amended the first sentence of paragraph (b)(1) by inserting "section 275(a)(4)" in lieu of "section 164(b)(6)". **Effective** 1-1-64.

P.L. 88-272, §209(c)(2):

Amended the first sentence of paragraph (2) by inserting "section 170(b)(2) and (5)" in lieu of "section 170(b)(2)". **Effective** 1-1-64.

P.L. 88-272, §225(i):

Amended Code Sec. 545(a) by striking out "subsection (b)" and inserting in lieu thereof "subsections (b) and (c)". Added subsection (c). **Effective** for tax years beginning after 12-31-63.

• 1962, Revenue Act of 1962 (P.L. 87-834)

P.L. 87-834, §9(d)(2):

Amended Code Sec. 545(b)(1) by inserting immediately after "year" in line 7: "or deemed to be paid by a domestic corporation under section 902(a)(1) or 960(a)(1)(C) for the taxable year."

• 1962 (P.L. 87-403)

P.L. 87-403, §3(d):

Added paragraphs (10) and (11) to subsection (b). **Effective** for distributions made after 2-2-62.

• 1958, Technical Amendments Act of 1958 (P.L. 85-866)

P.L. 85-866, §32(a):

Amended Code Sec. 545(b)(2). **Effective** 1-1-54. Prior to amendment, Code Sec. 545(b)(2) read:

"(2) Charitable contributions.—The deduction for charitable contributions provided under section 170 shall be allowed but with the limitations in section 170(b)(1)(A) and (B) (in lieu of the limitation in section 170(b)(2)). For purposes of this paragraph, the term `adjusted gross income' when used in section 170(b)(1) means the taxable income computed with the adjustments provided in section 170(b)(2) and without the deduction of the amount disallowed under paragraph (8) of this subsection."

P.L. 85-866, §32(b):

Amended Code Sec. 545(b)(4) by adding all the material after the words "taxable year". **Effective** with respect to adjustments under Code Sec. 545(b)(4) for tax years beginning after 12-31-57.

[Sec. 546]

SEC. 546. INCOME NOT PLACED ON ANNUAL BASIS.

Section 443(b)(relating to computation of tax on change of annual accounting period) shall not apply in the computation of the personal holding company tax imposed by section 541.

[Sec. 547]

SEC. 547. DEDUCTION FOR DEFICIENCY DIVIDENDS.

[Sec. 547(a)]

(a) GENERAL RULE.—If a determination (as defined in subsection (c)) with respect to a taxpayer establishes liability for personal holding company tax imposed by section 541 (or by a corresponding provision of a prior income tax law) for any taxable year, a deduction shall be allowed to the taxpayer for the amount of deficiency dividends (as defined in subsection (d)) for the purpose of determining the personal holding company tax for such year, but not for the purpose of determining interest, additional amounts, or assessable penalties computed with respect to such personal holding company tax.

[Sec. 547(b)]

(b) RULES FOR APPLICATION OF SECTION.—

(1) ALLOWANCE OF DEDUCTION.—The deficiency dividend deduction shall be allowed as of the date the claim for the deficiency dividend deduction is filed.

(2) CREDIT OR REFUND.—If the allowance of a deficiency dividend deduction results in an overpayment of personal holding company tax for any taxable year, credit or refund with respect to such overpayment shall be made as if on the date of the determination 2 years remained before the expiration of the period of limitation on the filing of claim for refund for the taxable year to which the overpayment relates. No interest shall be allowed on a credit or refund arising from the application of this section.

[Sec. 547(c)]

(c) DETERMINATION.—For purposes of this section, the term "determination" means—

(1) a decision by the Tax Court or a judgment, decree, or other order by any court of competent jurisdiction, which has become final;

(2) a closing agreement made under section 7121; or

(3) under regulations prescribed by the Secretary, an agreement signed by the Secretary and by, or on behalf of, the taxpayer relating to the liability of such taxpayer for personal holding company tax.

Amendments

• 1976, Tax Reform Act of 1976 (P.L. 94-455)

P.L. 94-455, §1906(b)(13)(A):

Amended 1954 Code by substituting "Secretary" for "Secretary or his delegate" each place it appeared. **Effective** 2-1-77.

[Sec. 547(d)]

(d) DEFICIENCY DIVIDENDS.—

(1) DEFINITION.—For purposes of this section, the term "deficiency dividends" means the amount of the dividends paid by the corporation on or after the date of the determination and before filing claim under subsection (e), which would have been includible in the computation of the deduction for dividends paid under section 561 for the taxable year with respect to which the liability for personal holding company tax exists, if distributed during such taxable year. No dividends shall be considered as deficiency dividends for purposes of subsection (a) unless distributed within 90 days after the determination.

(2) EFFECT ON DIVIDENDS PAID DEDUCTION.—

(A) FOR TAXABLE YEAR IN WHICH PAID.—Deficiency dividends paid in any taxable year (to the extent of the portion thereof taken into account under subsection (a) in determining personal holding company tax) shall not be included in the amount of dividends paid for such year for purposes of computing the dividends paid deduction for such year and succeeding years.

(B) FOR PRIOR TAXABLE YEAR.—Deficiency dividends paid in any taxable year (to the extent of the portion thereof taken into account under subsection (a) in determining personal holding company tax) shall not be allowed for purposes of section 563(b) in the computation of the dividends paid deduction for the taxable year preceding the taxable year in which paid.

[Sec. 547(e)]

(e) CLAIM REQUIRED.—No deficiency dividend deduction shall be allowed under subsection (a) unless (under regulations prescribed by the Secretary) claim therefor is filed within 120 days after the determination.

Amendments

• 1976, Tax Reform Act of 1976 (P.L. 94-455)

P.L. 94-455, §1906(b)(13)(A):

Amended 1954 Code by substituting "Secretary" for "Secretary or his delegate" each place it appeared. **Effective** 2-1-77.

[Sec. 547(f)]

(f) SUSPENSION OF STATUTE OF LIMITATIONS AND STAY OF COLLECTION.—

(1) SUSPENSION OF RUNNING OF STATUTE.—If the corporation files a claim, as provided in subsection (e), the running of the statute of limitations provided in section 6501 on the making of assessments, and the bringing of distraint or a proceeding in court for collection, in respect of the deficiency and all interest, additional amounts, or assessable penalties, shall be suspended for a period of 2 years after the date of the determination.

(2) STAY OF COLLECTION.—In the case of any deficiency with respect to the tax imposed by section 541 established by a determination under this section—

(A) the collection of the deficiency and all interest, additional amounts, and assessable penalties shall, except in cases of jeopardy, be stayed until the expiration of 120 days after the date of the determination, and

(B) if claim for deficiency dividend deduction is filed under subsection (e), the collection of such part of the deficiency as is not reduced by the deduction for deficiency dividends provided in subsection (a) shall be stayed until the date the claim is disallowed (in whole or in part), and if disallowed in part collection shall be made only with respect to the part disallowed.

No distraint or proceeding in court shall be begun for the collection of an amount the collection of which is stayed under subparagraph (A) or (B) during the period for which the collection of such amount is stayed.

[Sec. 547(g)]

(g) DEDUCTION DENIED IN CASE OF FRAUD, ETC.—No deficiency dividend deduction shall be allowed under subsection (a) if the determination contains a finding that any part of the deficiency is due to fraud with intent to evade tax, or to wilful failure to file an income tax return within the time prescribed by law or prescribed by the Secretary in pursuance of law.

Amendments

• 1976, Tax Reform Act of 1976 (P.L. 94-455)

P.L. 94-455, §1906(b)(13)(A):

Amended 1954 Code by substituting "Secretary" for "Secretary or his delegate" each place it appeared. **Effective** 2-1-77.

[Sec. 547(h)—Repealed]

Amendments

• 1976, Tax Reform Act of 1976 (P.L. 94-455)

P.L. 94-455, §1901(a)(78):

Repealed Code Sec. 547(h). **Effective** with respect to tax years beginning after 12-31-76. Prior to repeal, Code Sec. 547(h) read as follows:

(h) EFFECTIVE DATE.—Subsections (a) through (f), inclusive, shall apply only with respect to determinations made more than 90 days after the date of enactment of this title. If the taxable year with respect to which the deficiency is asserted began before January 1, 1954, the term "deficiency dividend" includes only amounts which would have been includible in the computation under the Internal Revenue Code of 1939 of the basic surtax credit for such taxable year. Subsection (g) shall apply only if the taxable year with respect to which the deficiency is asserted begins after December 31, 1953.

PART III—FOREIGN PERSONAL HOLDING COMPANIES—[Repealed]

[Sec. 551—Repealed]

Amendments

• 2004, American Jobs Creation Act of 2004 (P.L. 108-357)

P.L. 108-357, §413(a)(1):

Repealed part III of subchapter G of chapter 1 (Code Secs. 551-558). **Effective** for tax years of foreign corporations beginning after 12-31-2004, and for tax years of United States shareholders with or within which such tax years of foreign corporations end. Prior to repeal, Code Sec. 551 read as follows:

SEC. 551. FOREIGN PERSONAL HOLDING COMPANY INCOME TAXED TO UNITED STATES SHAREHOLDERS.

[Sec. 551(a)]

(a) GENERAL RULE.—The undistributed foreign personal holding company income of a foreign personal holding company shall be included in the gross income of the citizens or residents of the United States, domestic corporations, domestic partnerships, and estates or trusts (other than foreign estates or trusts), who are shareholders in such foreign personal holding company (hereinafter called "United States shareholders") in the manner and to the extent set forth in this part.

Amendments

• 1988, Technical and Miscellaneous Revenue Act of 1988 (P.L. 100-647)

P.L. 100-647, §1012(bb)(1)(B):

Amended Code Sec. 551(a) by striking out "(other than estates or trusts the gross income of which under this subtitle includes only income from sources within the United States)" and inserting in lieu thereof "(other than foreign estates or trusts)". **Effective** for tax years of foreign corporations beginning after 12-31-86.

[Sec. 551(b)]

(b) AMOUNT INCLUDED IN GROSS INCOME.—Each United States shareholder, who was a shareholder on the day in the taxable year of the company which was the last day on which a United States group (as defined in section 552(a)(2)) existed with respect to the company, shall include in his gross income, as a dividend, for the taxable year in which or with which the taxable year of the company ends, the amount he would have received as a dividend (determined as if any distribution in liquidation actually made in such taxable year had not been made) if on such last day there had been distributed by the company, and received by the shareholders, an amount which bears the same ratio to the undistributed foreign personal holding company income of the company for the taxable year as the portion of such taxable year up to and including such last day bears to the entire taxable year.

Amendments

• 1964, Revenue Act of 1964 (P.L. 88-272)

P.L. 88-272, §225(f)(4):

Amended Code Sec. 551(b) by striking out "received as a dividend" and inserting in lieu thereof "received as a dividend (determined as if any distribution in liquidation actually made in such taxable year had not been made)". **Effective** for distributions made in any tax year of the distributing corporation beginning after 12-31-63.

[Sec. 551(c)—Repealed]

Amendments

• 1976, Tax Reform Act of 1976 (P.L. 94-455)

P.L. 94-455, §1901(b)(1)(F)(i):

Repealed Code Sec. 551(c). **Effective** with respect to tax years beginning after 12-31-76. Prior to repeal, Code Sec. 551(c) read as follows:

(c) DEDUCTION FOR OBLIGATIONS OF UNITED STATES AND ITS INSTRUMENTALITIES.—Each United States shareholder shall take into account in determining his income tax his proportionate share of partially tax-exempt interest on obligations described in section 35 or 242 which is included in the gross income of the company otherwise than by the application of the provisions of section 555 (b) (relating to the inclusion in the gross income of a foreign personal holding company of its distributive share of the undistributed foreign personal holding company income of another foreign personal holding company in which it is a shareholder). If the foreign personal holding company elects under section 171 to amortize the premiums on such obligations, for purposes of the preceding sentence each United States shareholder's proportionate share of such interest received by the foreign personal holding company shall be his proportionate share of such interest (determined without regard to this sentence) reduced by so much of the deduction under section 171 as is attributable to such share.

[Sec. 551(c)]

(c) INFORMATION IN RETURN.—Every United States shareholder who is required under subsection (b) to include in his gross income any amount with respect to the undistributed foreign personal holding company income of a foreign personal holding company and who, on the last day on which a United States group existed with respect to the company, owned 5 percent or more in value of the outstanding stock of such company, shall set forth in his return in complete detail the gross income, deductions and credits, taxable income, foreign personal holding company income, and undistributed foreign personal holding company income of such company.

Amendments

• 1976, Tax Reform Act of 1976 (P.L. 94-455)

P.L. 94-455, §1901(b)(1)(F)(i):

Redesignated former Code Sec. 551(d) as Sec. 551(c). **Effective** for tax years beginning after 12-31-76.

P.L. 94-455, §1901(a)(79):

Amended Code Sec. 551(c) by inserting "income" after "company". **Effective** for tax years beginning after 12-31-76.

[Sec. 551(d)]

(d) EFFECT ON CAPITAL ACCOUNT OF FOREIGN PERSONAL HOLDING COMPANY.—An amount which bears the same ratio to the undistributed foreign personal holding company income of the foreign personal holding company for its taxable year as the portion of such taxable year up to and including the last day on which a United States group existed with respect to the company bears to the entire taxable year, shall, for the purpose of determining the effect of distributions in subsequent taxable years by the corporation, be considered as paid-in surplus or as a contribution to capital, and the accumulated earnings and profits as of the close of the taxable year shall be correspondingly reduced, if such amount or any portion thereof is required to be included as a dividend, directly or indirectly, in the gross income of United States shareholders.

Amendments

• 1976, Tax Reform Act of 1976 (P.L. 94-455)

P.L. 94-455, §1901(b)(1)(F)(i):

Redesignated former Code Sec. 551(e) as Sec. 551(d). **Effective** for tax years beginning after 12-31-76.

[Sec. 551(e)]

(e) BASIS OF STOCK IN HANDS OF SHAREHOLDERS.—The amount required to be included in the gross income of a United States shareholder under subsection (b) shall, for the purpose of adjusting the basis of his stock with respect to which the distribution would have been made (if it had been made), be treated as having been reinvested by the shareholder as a contribution to the capital of the corporation; but only to the extent to which such amount is included in his gross income in his return, increased or decreased by any adjustment of such amount in the last determination of the shareholder's tax liability, made before the expiration of 6 years after the date prescribed by law for filing the return.

Amendments

• 1976, Tax Reform Act of 1976 (P.L. 94-455)

P.L. 94-455, §1901(b)(1)(F)(i):

Redesignated former Code Sec. 551(f) as Sec. 551(e). **Effective** for tax years beginning after 12-31-76.

[Sec. 551(f)]

(f) STOCK HELD THROUGH FOREIGN ENTITY.—For purposes of this section, stock of a foreign personal holding company owned (directly or through the application of this subsection) by—

(1) a foreign partnership or an estate or trust which is a foreign estate or trust, or

(2) a foreign corporation which is not a foreign personal holding company, shall be considered as being owned proportionately by its partners, beneficiaries, or shareholders.

In any case to which the preceding sentence applies, the Secretary may by regulations provide that rules similar to the rules of section 1298(b)(5) shall apply, and provide for such other adjustments in the application of this subchapter as may be necessary to carry out the purposes of this subsection.

Amendments

• 1997, Taxpayer Relief Act of 1997 (P.L. 105-34)

P.L. 105-34, §1122(d)(2):

Amended Code Sec. 551(f) by striking "section 1297(b)(5)" and inserting "section 1298(b)(5)". **Effective** for tax years of United States persons beginning after 12-31-97, and tax years of foreign corporations ending with or within such tax years of United States persons.

• 1988, Technical and Miscellaneous Revenue Act of 1988 (P.L. 100-647)

P.L. 100-647, §1012(bb)(1)(A)(i)-(ii):

Amended Code Sec. 551(f) by amending paragraph (1), and by striking out the last sentence and inserting in lieu thereof a new sentence. **Effective** for tax years of foreign corporations beginning after 12-31-86. Prior to amendment, paragraph (1) and the last sentence read as follows:

(1) a partnership, estate, or trust which is not a United States shareholder or an estate or trust which is a foreign estate or trust, or

* * *

In any case to which the preceding sentence applies, the Secretary may by regulations provide for such adjustments in the application of this part as may be necessary to carry out the purposes of the preceding sentence.

• 1986, Tax Reform Act of 1986 (P.L. 99-514)

P.L. 99-514, §1810(h)(2):

Amended Code Sec. 551(f)(1) by striking out "United States shareholder" and inserting in lieu thereof "United States shareholder or an estate or trust which is a foreign estate or trust". **Effective** as if included in the provision of P.L. 98-369 to which it relates.

• 1984, Deficit Reduction Act of 1984 (P.L. 98-369)

P.L. 98-369, §132(b):

Amended Code Sec. 551 by redesignating subsection (f) as subsection (g) and inserting new subsection (f). **Effective** for tax years of a foreign corporation beginning after 12-31-83—after 1984 with respect to stock of such corporation which is held (directly or indirectly, within the meaning of section 554 of the Internal Revenue Code of 1954) by a trust created before 6-30-53, if—(I) none of the beneficiaries of such trust was a citizen or resident of the United States at the time of its creation or within 5 years thereafter, and (II) such trust does not, after 7-1-83, acquire (directly or indirectly) stock of any foreign personal holding company other than a company described in clause (ii) [see below].

P.L. 98-369, 132(d)(1)(B)(ii), provides:

(ii) Description of Company.—A company is described in this clause if—

(I) substantially all of the assets of such company are stock or assets previously held by such trust, or

(II) such company ceases to be a foreign personal holding company before January 1, 1985.

[Sec. 551(g)]

(g) COORDINATION WITH PASSIVE FOREIGN INVESTMENT COMPANY PROVISIONS.—If, but for this subsection, an amount would be included in the gross income of any person under subsection (a) and under section 1293 (relating to current taxation of income from certain passive foreign investment companies), such amount shall be included in the gross income of such person only under subsection (a).

Amendments

• 1986, Tax Reform Act of 1986 (P.L. 99-514)

P.L. 99-514, §1235(e):

Amended Code Sec. 551 by redesignating subsection (g) as subsection (h) and by inserting after subsection (f) new subsection (g). **Effective** for tax years of foreign corporations beginning after 12-31-86.

[Sec. 551(h)]

(h) CROSS REFERENCES.—

(1) For basis of stock or securities in a foreign personal holding company acquired from a decedent, see section 1014(b)(5).

(2) For period of limitation on assessment and collection without assessment, in case of failure to include in gross income the amount properly includible therein under subsection (b), see section 6501.

• 1986, Tax Reform Act of 1986 (P.L. 99-514)

P.L. 99-514, §1235(e):

Redesignated subsection (g) as subsection (h). **Effective** for tax years of foreign corporations beginning after 12-31-86.

• 1984, Deficit Reduction Act of 1984 (P.L. 98-369)

P.L. 98-369, §132(b):

Amended Code Sec. 551 by redesignating subsection (f) as subsection (g). **Effective**, generally, to tax years of a foreign corporation beginning after 12-31-84. However, see the special rule following Code Sec. 551(f).

• 1976, Tax Reform Act of 1976 (P.L. 94-455)

P.L. 94-455, §1901(b)(1)(F)(i):

Redesignated former Code Sec. 551(g) as Sec. 551(f). **Effective** for tax years beginning after 12-31-76.

P.L. 94-455, §1901(b)(12)(A):

Amended Code Sec. 551(f) by striking out paragraph (3). **Effective** with respect to tax years beginning after 12-31-76. Prior to repeal, Code Sec. 551(f)(3) read as follows:

(3) For treatment of gain on liquidation of certain foreign personal holding companies, see section 342.

[Sec. 552—Repealed]

Amendments

• 2004, American Jobs Creation Act of 2004 (P.L. 108-357)

P.L. 108-357, §413(a)(1):

Repealed part III of subchapter G of chapter 1 (Code Secs. 551-558). **Effective** for tax years of foreign corporations beginning after 12-31-2004, and for tax years of United States shareholders with or within which such tax years of foreign corporations end. Prior to repeal, Code Sec. 552 read as follows:

SEC. 552. DEFINITION OF FOREIGN PERSONAL HOLDING COMPANY.

[Sec. 552(a)]

(a) GENERAL RULE.—For purposes of this subtitle, the term "foreign personal holding company" means any foreign corporation if—

(1) GROSS INCOME REQUIREMENT.—At least 60 percent of its gross income (as defined in section 555(a)) for the taxable year is foreign personal holding company income as defined in section 553; but if the corporation is a foreign personal holding company with respect to any taxable year ending after August 26, 1937, then, for each subsequent taxable year, the minimum percentage shall be 50 percent in lieu of 60 percent, until a taxable year during the whole of which the stock ownership required by paragraph (2) does not exist, or until the expiration of three consecutive taxable years in each of which less than 50 percent of the gross income is foreign personal holding company income. For purposes of this paragraph, there shall be included in the gross income the amount includible therein as a dividend by reason of the application of section 555(c)(2); and

(2) STOCK OWNERSHIP REQUIREMENT.—At any time during the taxable year more than 50 percent of—

(A) the total combined voting power of all classes of stock of such corporation entitled to vote, or

(B) the total value of the stock of such corporation,

is owned (directly or indirectly) by or for not more than 5 individuals who are citizens or residents of the United States (hereinafter in this part referred to as the "United States group").

Amendments

• 1986, Tax Reform Act of 1986 (P.L. 99-514)

P.L. 99-514, §1222(b):

Amended Code Sec. 552(a)(2). **Effective** for tax years of foreign corporations beginning after 12-31-86; except that for purposes of applying Code Secs. 951(a)(1)(B) and 956, it shall take effect on 8-16-86. However, for transitional and special rules, see Act Sec. 1222(c)(2)-(3), below. Prior to amendment, Code Sec. 552(a)(2) read as follows:

(2) STOCK OWNERSHIP REQUIREMENT.—At any time during the taxable year more than 50 percent in value of its outstanding stock is owned, directly or indirectly, by or for not more than five individuals who are citizens or residents of the United States, hereinafter called "United States group".

P.L. 99-514, §1222(c)(2)-(3), provides:

(2) TRANSITIONAL RULE.—In the case of any corporation treated as a controlled foreign corporation by reason of the amendments made by this section, property acquired before August 16, 1986, shall not be taken into account under section 956(b) of the Internal Revenue Code of 1986.

(3) SPECIAL RULE FOR BENEFICIARY OF TRUST.—In the case of an individual—

(A) who is a beneficiary of a trust which was established on December 7, 1979, under the laws of a foreign jurisdiction, and

(B) who was not a citizen or resident of the United States on the date the trust was established.

amounts which are included in the gross income of such beneficiary under section 951(a) of the Internal Revenue Code of 1986 with respect to stock held by the trust (and treated as distributed to the trust) shall be treated as the first amounts which are distributed by the trust to such beneficiary and as amounts to which section 959(a) of such Code applies.

[Sec. 552(b)]

(b) EXCEPTIONS.—The term "foreign personal holding company" does not include—

(1) a corporation exempt from tax under subchapter F (sec. 501 and following); and

(2) a corporation organized and doing business under the banking and credit laws of a foreign country if it is established (annually or at other periodic intervals) to the satisfaction of the Secretary that such corporation is not formed or availed of for the purpose of evading or avoiding United States income taxes which would otherwise be imposed upon its shareholders. If the Secretary is satisfied that such corporation is not so formed or availed of, he shall issue to such corporation annually or at other periodic intervals a certification that the corporation is not a foreign personal holding company.

Each United States shareholder of a foreign corporation which would, except for the provisions of paragraph (2), be a foreign personal holding company, shall attach to and file with his income tax return for the taxable year a copy of the certification by the Secretary made pursuant to paragraph (2). Such copy shall be filed with the taxpayer's return for the taxable year if he has been a shareholder of such corporation for any part of such year.

Amendments

• 1976, Tax Reform Act of 1976 (P.L. 94-455)

P.L. 94-455, §1906(b)(13)(A):

Amended 1954 Code by substituting "Secretary" for "Secretary or his delegate" each place it appeared. **Effective** 2-1-77.

[Sec. 552(c)]

(c) LOOK-THRU FOR CERTAIN DIVIDENDS AND INTEREST.—

(1) IN GENERAL.—For purposes of this part, any related person dividend or interest shall be treated as foreign personal holding company income only to the extent such dividend or interest is attributable (determined under rules similar to the rules of subparagraphs (C) and (D) of section 904(d)(3)) to income of the related person which would be foreign personal holding company income.

(2) RELATED PERSON DIVIDEND OR INTEREST.—For purposes of paragraph (1), the term "related person dividend or interest" means any dividend or interest which—

(A) is described in subparagraph (A) of section 954(c)(3), and

(B) is received from a related person which is not a foreign personal holding company (determined without regard to this subsection).

For purposes of the preceding sentence, the term "related person" has the meaning given such term by section 954(d)(3) (determined by substituting "foreign personal holding company" for "controlled foreign corporation" each place it appears).

Amendments

• 1988, Technical and Miscellaneous Revenue Act of 1988 (P.L. 100-647)

P.L. 100-647, §1012(bb)(1)(C):

Amended Code Sec. 552(c). **Effective** for tax years of foreign corporations beginning after 12-31-86. Prior to amendment, Code Sec. 552(c) read as follows:

(c) CERTAIN DIVIDENDS AND INTEREST NOT TAKEN INTO ACCOUNT.—For purposes of subsection (a)(1) and section 553(a)(1), gross income and foreign personal holding company income shall not include any dividends and interest which—

(1) are described in subparagraph (A) of section 954(c)(4), and

(2) are received from a related person which is not a foreign personal holding company (determined without regard to this subsection).

For purposes of the preceding sentence, the term "related person" has the meaning given such term by section 954(d)(3) (determined by substituting "foreign personal holding company" for "controlled foreign corporation" each place it appears).

• 1986, Tax Reform Act of 1986 (P.L. 99-514)

P.L. 99-514, §1810(h)(1):

Amended Code Sec. 552(c) by adding at the end thereof a new sentence. **Effective** as if included in the provision of P.L. 98-369 to which it relates.

• 1984, Deficit Reduction Act of 1984 (P.L. 98-369)

P.L. 98-369, §132(c):

Added Code Sec. 552(c). **Effective** for tax years of foreign corporations beginning after 3-15-84.

[Sec. 553—Repealed]

Amendments

• 2004, American Jobs Creation Act of 2004 (P.L. 108-357)

P.L. 108-357, §413(a)(1):

Repealed part III of subchapter G of chapter 1 (Code Secs. 551-558). **Effective** for tax years of foreign corporations beginning after 12-31-2004, and for tax years of United States shareholders with or within which such tax years of foreign corporations end. Prior to repeal, Code Sec. 553 read as follows:

SEC. 553. FOREIGN PERSONAL HOLDING COMPANY INCOME.

[Sec. 553(a)]

(a) FOREIGN PERSONAL HOLDING COMPANY INCOME.—For purposes of this subtitle, the term "foreign personal holding company income" means that portion of the gross income, determined for purposes of section 552, which consists of:

(1) DIVIDENDS, ETC.—Dividends, interest, royalties, and annuities. This paragraph shall not apply to active business computer software royalties (as defined in section 543(d)).

(2) STOCK AND SECURITIES TRANSACTIONS.—Except in the case of regular dealers in stock or securities, gains from the sale or exchange of stock or securities.

(3) COMMODITIES TRANSACTIONS.—Gains from futures transactions in any commodity on or subject to the rules of a board of trade or commodity exchange. This paragraph shall not apply to gains by a producer, processor, merchant, or handler of the commodity which arise out of bona fide hedging transactions reasonably necessary to the conduct of its business in the manner in which such business is customarily and usually conducted by others.

(4) ESTATES AND TRUSTS.—Amounts includible in computing the taxable income of the corporation under part I of subchapter J (sec. 641 and following, relating to estates, trusts, and beneficiaries); and gains from the sale or other disposition of any interest in an estate or trust.

(5) PERSONAL SERVICE CONTRACTS.—

(A) Amounts received under a contract under which the corporation is to furnish personal services; if some person other than the corporation has the right to designate (by name or by description) the individual who is to perform the services, or if the individual who is to perform the services is designated (by name or by description) in the contract; and

(B) amounts received from the sale or other disposition of such a contract.

This paragraph shall apply with respect to amounts received for services under a particular contract only if at some time during the taxable year 25 percent or more in value of the outstanding stock of the corporation is owned, directly or indirectly, by or for the individual who has performed, is to perform, or may be designated (by name or by description) as the one to perform, such services.

(6) USE OF CORPORATION PROPERTY BY SHAREHOLDER.—Amounts received as compensation (however designated and from whomsoever received) for the use of, or right to use, property of the corporation in any case where, at any time during the taxable year, 25 percent or more in value of the outstanding stock of the corporation is owned, directly or indirectly, by or for an individual entitled to the use of the property; whether such right is obtained directly from the corporation or by means of a sublease or other arrangement. This paragraph shall apply only to a corporation which has foreign personal holding company income for the taxable year, computed without regard to this paragraph and paragraph (7), in excess of 10 percent of its gross income.

(7) RENTS.—Rents, unless constituting 50 percent or more of the gross income. For purposes of this paragraph, the term "rents" means compensation, however designated, for the use of, or right to use, property; but does not include amounts constituting foreign personal holding company income under paragraph (6).

Amendments

• 1986, Tax Reform Act of 1986 (P.L. 99-514)

P.L. 99-514, §645(a)(3):

Amended Code Sec. 553(a)(1) by adding at the end thereof a new sentence. **Effective** for royalties received before, on, and after 12-31-86.

• 1976, Tax Reform Act of 1976 (P.L. 94-455)

P.L. 94-455, §1901(b)(32)(F):

Amended Code Sec. 553(a)(1). **Effective** for tax years beginning after 12-31-76. Prior to amendment, Sec. 553(a)(1) read as follows:

(1) DIVIDENDS, ETC.—Dividends, interest, royalties, and annuities. This paragraph shall not apply to a dividend distribution of divested stock (as defined in subsection (e) of section 1111) but only if the stock with respect to which the distribution is made was owned by the distributee on September 6, 1961, or was owned by the distributee for at least 2 years before the date on which the antitrust order (as defined in subsection (d) of section 1111) was entered.

[Sec. 553(b)]

(b) LIMITATION ON GROSS INCOME IN CERTAIN TRANSACTIONS.—For purposes of this part—

(1) gross income and foreign personal holding company income determined with respect to transactions described in subsection (a)(2) (relating to gains from stock and security transactions) shall include only the excess of gains over losses from such transactions, and

(2) gross income and foreign personal holding company income determined with respect to transactions described in subsection (a)(3) (relating to gains from commodity transactions) shall include only the excess of gains over losses from such transactions.

Amendments

• 1964, Revenue Act of 1964 (P.L. 88-272)

P.L. 88-272, §225(e):

Amended Code Sec. 553. **Effective** with respect to tax years beginning after 12-31-63. Prior to amendment, Sec. 553 read as follows:

SEC. 553. FOREIGN PERSONAL HOLDING COMPANY INCOME.

For purposes of this subtitle, the term `foreign personal holding company income' means the portion of the gross income, determined for purposes of section 552, which consists of personal holding company income, as defined in section 543, except that all interest, whether or not treated as rent, and all royalties, whether or not mineral, oil, or gas royalties or copyright royalties, shall constitute `foreign personal holding company income'.

• 1960 (P.L. 86-435)

P.L. 86-435, §1(e):

Amended Code Sec. 553 by adding the phrase "or copyright royalties" immediately following the phrase "gas royalties". **Effective** for tax years beginning after 12-31-59.

[Sec. 554—Repealed]

Amendments

• 2004, American Jobs Creation Act of 2004 (P.L. 108-357)

P.L. 108-357, §413(a)(1):

Repealed part III of subchapter G of chapter 1 (Code Secs. 551-558). **Effective** for tax years of foreign corporations beginning after 12-31-2004, and for tax years of United States shareholders with or within which such tax years of foreign corporations end. Prior to repeal, Code Sec. 554 read as follows:

SEC. 554. STOCK OWNERSHIP.

[Sec. 554(a)]

(a) CONSTRUCTIVE OWNERSHIP.—For purposes of determining whether a corporation is a foreign personal holding company, insofar as such determination is based on stock ownership under section 552(a)(2), section 553(a)(5), or section 553(a)(6)—

(1) STOCK NOT OWNED BY INDIVIDUAL.—Stock owned, directly or indirectly, by or for a corporation, partnership, estate, or trust shall be considered as being owned proportionately by its shareholders, partners, or beneficiaries.

(2) FAMILY AND PARTNERSHIP OWNERSHIP.—An individual shall be considered as owning the stock owned, directly or indirectly, by or for his family or by or for his partner. For purposes of this paragraph, the family of an individual includes only his brothers and sisters (whether by the whole or half blood), spouse, ancestors, and lineal descendants.

(3) OPTIONS.—If any person has an option to acquire stock, such stock shall be considered as owned by such person. For purposes of this paragraph, an option to acquire such an option, and each one of a series of such options, shall be considered as an option to acquire such stock.

(4) APPLICATION OF FAMILY-PARTNERSHIP AND OPTION RULES.—Paragraphs (2) and (3) shall be applied—

(A) for purposes of the stock ownership requirement provided in section 552(a)(2), if, but only if, the effect is to make the corporation a foreign personal holding company;

(B) for purposes of section 553(a)(5) (relating to personal service contracts) or of section 553(a)(6) (relating to the use of property by shareholders), if, but only if, the effect is to make the amounts therein referred to includible under such paragraph as foreign personal holding company income.

(5) CONSTRUCTIVE OWNERSHIP AS ACTUAL OWNERSHIP.—Stock constructively owned by a person by reason of the application of paragraph (1) or (3) shall, for purposes of applying paragraph (1) or (2), be treated as actually owned by such person; but stock constructively owned by an individual by reason of the application of paragraph (2) shall not be treated as owned by him for purposes of again applying such paragraph in order to make another the constructive owner of such stock.

(6) OPTION RULE IN LIEU OF FAMILY AND PARTNERSHIP RULE.—If stock may be considered as owned by an individual under either paragraph (2) or (3) it shall be considered as owned by him under paragraph (3).

[Sec. 554(b)]

(b) CONVERTIBLE SECURITIES.—Outstanding securities convertible into stock (whether or not convertible during the taxable year) shall be considered as outstanding stock—

(1) for purposes of the stock ownership requirement provided in section 552(a)(2), but only if the effect of the inclusion of all such securities is to make the corporation a foreign personal holding company;

(2) for purposes of section 553(a)(5) (relating to personal service contracts), but only if the effect of the inclusion of all such securities is to make the amounts therein referred to includible under such paragraph as foreign personal holding company income; and

(3) for purposes of section 553(a)(6) (relating to the use of property by shareholders), but only if the effect of the inclusion of all such securities is to make the amounts therein referred to includible under such paragraph as foreign personal holding company income.

The requirement in paragraphs (1), (2), and (3) that all convertible securities must be included if any are to be included shall be subject to the exception that, where some of the outstanding securities are convertible only after a later date than in the case of others, the class having the earlier conversion date may be included although the others are not included, but no convertible securities shall be included unless all outstanding securities having a prior conversion date are also included.

[Sec. 554(c)]

(c) SPECIAL RULES FOR APPLICATION OF SUBSECTION (a)(2).—For purposes of the stock ownership requirement provided in section 552(a)(2)—

(1) stock owned by a nonresident alien individual (other than a foreign trust or foreign estate) shall not be considered by reason of so much of subsection (a)(2) as relates to attribution through family membership as owned by a citizen or by a resident alien individual who is not the spouse of the nonresident individual and who does not otherwise own stock in such corporation (determined after the application of subsection (a), other than attribution through family membership), and

(2) stock of a corporation owned by any foreign person shall not be considered by reason of so much of subsection (a)(2) as relates to attribution through partners as owned by a citizen or resident of the United States who does not otherwise own stock in such corporation (determined after application of subsection (a) and paragraph (1), other than attribution through partners).

Amendments

• 1984, Deficit Reduction Act of 1984 (P.L. 98-369)

P.L. 98-369, §132(a):

Amended Code Sec. 554 by adding at the end thereof new subsection (c). **Effective** for tax years of foreign corporations beginning after 12-31-83.

• 1964, Revenue Act of 1964 (P.L. 88-272)

P.L. 88-272, §225(e):

Amended Code Sec. 554. **Effective** with respect to tax years beginning after 12-31-63. Prior to amendment, Sec. 554 read as follows:

SEC. 554. STOCK OWNERSHIP.

For purposes of determining whether a foreign corporation is a foreign personal holding company, insofar as such determination is based on stock ownership, the rules provided in section 54 shall be applicable as if any reference in such section to a personal holding company was a reference to a foreign personal holding company and as if any reference in such section to a provision of part II (relating to personal holding companies) was a reference to the corresponding provision of this part.

[Sec. 555—Repealed]

Amendments

• 2004, American Jobs Creation Act of 2004 (P.L. 108-357)

P.L. 108-357, §413(a)(1):

Repealed part III of subchapter G of chapter 1 (Code Secs. 551-558). **Effective** for tax years of foreign corporations beginning after 12-31-2004, and for tax years of United States shareholders with or within which such tax years of foreign corporations end. Prior to repeal, Code Sec. 555 read as follows:

SEC. 555. GROSS INCOME OF FOREIGN PERSONAL HOLDING COMPANIES.

[Sec. 555(a)]

(a) GENERAL RULE.—For purposes of this part, the term "gross income" means, with respect to a foreign corporation, gross income computed (without regard to the provisions of subchapter N (and following)) as if the foreign corporation were a domestic corporation which is a personal holding company.

[Sec. 555(b)]

(b) ADDITIONS TO GROSS INCOME.—In the case of a foreign personal holding company (whether or not a United States group, as defined in , existed with respect to such company on the last day of its taxable year) which was a shareholder in another foreign personal holding company on the day in the taxable year of the second company which was the last day on which a United States group existed with respect to the second company, there shall be included, as a dividend, in the gross income of the first company, for the taxable year in which or with which the taxable year of the second company ends, the amount the first company would have received as a dividend if on such last day there had been distributed by the second company, and received by the shareholders, an amount which bears the same ratio to the undistributed foreign personal holding company income of the second company for its taxable year as the portion of such taxable year up to and including such last day bears to the entire taxable year.

[Sec. 555(c)]

(c) APPLICATION OF SUBSECTION (b).—The rule provided in subsection (b)—

(1) shall be applied in the case of a foreign personal holding company for the purpose of determining its undistributed foreign personal holding company income which, or a part of which, is to be included in the gross income of its shareholders, whether United States shareholders or other foreign personal holding companies;

(2) shall be applied in the case of every foreign corporation with respect to which a United States group exists on some day of its taxable year, for the purpose of determining whether such corporation meets the gross income requirements of section 552(a)(1).

[Sec. 556—Repealed]

Amendments

• 2004, American Jobs Creation Act of 2004 (P.L. 108-357)

P.L. 108-357, §413(a)(1):

Repealed part III of subchapter G of chapter 1 (Code Secs. 551-558). **Effective** for tax years of foreign corporations beginning after 12-31-2004, and for tax years of United States shareholders with or within which such tax years of foreign corporations end. Prior to repeal, Code Sec. 556 read as follows:

SEC. 556. UNDISTRIBUTED FOREIGN PERSONAL HOLDING COMPANY INCOME.

[Sec. 556(a)]

(a) DEFINITION.—For purposes of this part, the term "undistributed foreign personal holding company income" means the taxable income of a foreign personal holding company adjusted in the manner provided in subsection (b), minus the dividends paid deduction (as defined in section 561).

[Sec. 556(b)]

(b) ADJUSTMENTS TO TAXABLE INCOME.—For the purposes of subsection (a), the taxable income shall be adjusted as follows:

(1) TAXES.—There shall be allowed as a deduction Federal income and excess profits taxes and income, war profits, and excess profits taxes of foreign countries and possessions of the United States (to the extent not allowable as a deduction under section 275(a)(4)), accrued during the taxable year, but not including the accumulated earnings tax imposed by section 531, the personal holding company tax imposed by section 541, or the taxes imposed by corresponding sections of a prior income tax law.

(2) CHARITABLE CONTRIBUTIONS.—The deduction for charitable contributions provided under section 170 shall be allowed, but in computing such deduction the limitations in section 170(b)(1)(A), (B), and (D) shall apply, and section 170(b)(2) and (d)(1) shall not apply. For purposes of this paragraph, the term "contribution base" when used in section 170(b)(1) means the taxable income computed with the adjustments (other than the 10-percent limitation) provided in section 170(b)(2) and (d)(1) and without the deduction of the amounts disallowed under paragraphs (5) and (6) of this subsection or the inclusion in gross income of the amounts includible therein as dividends by reason of the application of the provisions of section 555(b) (relating to the inclusion in gross income of a foreign personal holding company of its distributive share of the undistributed foreign personal holding company income of another company in which it is a shareholder).

(3) SPECIAL DEDUCTIONS DISALLOWED.—The special deductions for corporations provided in part VIII (except section 248 of subchapter B (section 241 and following, relating to the deduction for dividends received by corporations, etc.) shall not be allowed.

(4) NET OPERATING LOSS.—The net operating loss deduction provided in section 172 shall not be allowed, but there shall be allowed as a deduction the amount of the net operating loss (as defined in section 172(c)) for the preceding taxable year computed without the deductions provided in part VIII (except section 248) of subchapter B.

(5) EXPENSES AND DEPRECIATION APPLICABLE TO PROPERTY OF THE TAXPAYER.—The aggregate of the deductions allowed under section 162 (relating to trade or business expenses) and section 167 (relating to depreciation) which are allocable to the operation and maintenance of property owned or operated by the company, shall be allowed only in an amount equal to the rent or other compensation received for the use of, or the right to use, the property, unless it is established (under regulations prescribed by the Secretary) to the satisfaction of the Secretary—

(A) that the rent or other compensation received was the highest obtainable, or, if none was received, that none was obtainable;

(B) that the property was held in the course of a business carried on bona fide for profit; and

(C) either that there was reasonable expectation that the operation of the property would result in a profit, or that the property was necessary to the conduct of the business.

(6) TAXES AND CONTRIBUTIONS TO PENSION TRUSTS.—The deductions provided in section 164(e) (relating to taxes of a shareholder paid by the corporation) and in section 404 (relating to pension, etc., trusts) shall not be allowed.

Amendments

• 1990, Omnibus Budget Reconciliation Act of 1990 (P.L. 101-508)

P.L. 101-508, §11802(d)(1):

Amended Code Sec. 556(b)(1) by striking the last two sentences. **Effective** 11-5-90. Prior to repeal, the last two sentences of Code Sec. 556(b)(1) read as follows:

A taxpayer which, for each taxable year in which it was subject to the provisions of supplement P of the Internal Revenue Code of 1939, deducted Federal income and excess profits taxes when paid for the purpose of computing undistributed supplement P net income under such code, shall deduct taxes under this paragraph when paid, unless the corporation elects, under regulations prescribed by the Secretary, after the date of enactment of this title to deduct the taxes described in this paragraph when accrued. Such election shall be irrevocable and shall apply to the taxable year for which the election is made and to all subsequent taxable years.

P.L. 101-508, §11802(d)(2), provides:

(2) The amendment made by paragraph (1) shall not apply to any corporation with respect to which an election under the second sentence of section 556(b)(1) of the Internal Revenue Code of 1986 (as in effect before the amendment made by paragraph (1)) is in effect unless such corporation elects to have such amendment apply and agrees to such adjustments as the Secretary of the Treasury or his delegate may require.

P.L. 101-508, §11821(b), provides:

(b) SAVINGS PROVISION.—If—

(1) any provision amended or repealed by this part applied to—

(A) any transaction occurring before the date of the enactment of this Act,

(B) any property acquired before such date of enactment, or

(C) any item of income, loss, deduction, or credit taken into account before such date of enactment, and

(2) the treatment of such transaction, property, or item under such provision would (without regard to the amendments made by this part) affect liability for tax for periods ending after such date of enactment,

nothing in the amendments made by this part shall be construed to affect the treatment of such transaction, property, or item for purposes of determining liability for tax for periods ending after such date of enactment.

• 1983, Technical Corrections Act of 1982 (P.L. 97-448)

P.L. 97-448, §102(m)(2):

Amended Code Sec. 556(b)(2) by striking out "5-percent" and inserting in lieu thereof "10-percent". **Effective** as if included in the provision of P.L. 97-34 to which it relates.

• 1976, Tax Reform Act of 1976 (P.L. 94-455)

P.L. 94-455, §1901(a)(80):

Amended Code Sec. 556(b)(1) by striking out "(other than the excess profits tax imposed by subchapter E of chapter 2 of the Internal Revenue Code of 1939 for taxable years beginning after December 1, 1940)" after "Federal income and excess profits tax". **Effective** for tax years beginning after 12-31-76.

P.L. 94-455, §1901(b)(32)(G):

Amended Code Sec. 556(b) by striking out paragraphs (7) and (8). **Effective** with respect to tax years beginning after 12-31-76. Prior to repeal, Code Sec. 556(b)(7) and (8) read as follows:

(7) DISTRIBUTIONS OF DIVESTED STOCK.—There shall be allowed as a deduction the amount of any income attributable to the receipt of a distribution of divested stock (as defined in subsection (e) of section 1111), minus the taxes imposed by this subtitle attributable to such receipt, but only if the stock with respect to which the distribution is made was owned by the distributee on September 6, 1961, or was owned by the distributee for at least 2 years prior to the date on which the antitrust order (as defined in subsection (d) of section 1111) was entered.

(8) SPECIAL ADJUSTMENT ON DISPOSITION OF ANTITRUST STOCK RECEIVED AS A DIVIDEND.—If—

(A) a corporation received antitrust stock (as defined in section 301(f)) in a distribution to which section 301 applied,

(B) the amount of the distribution determined under section 301(f)(2) exceeded the basis of the stock determined under section 301(f)(3), and

(C) paragraph (7) did not apply in respect of such distribution,

then proper adjustment shall be made, under regulations prescribed by the Secretary or his delegate, if such stock (or other property the basis of which is determined by reference to the basis of such stock) is sold or exchanged.

P.L. 94-455, §1906(b)(13)(A):

Amended 1954 Code by substituting "Secretary" for "Secretary or his delegate" each place it appeared. **Effective** 2-1-77.

• 1969, Tax Reform Act of 1969 (P.L. 91-172)

P.L. 91-172, §201(a)(2)(B):

Amended Code Sec. 556(b)(2). **Effective** for tax years beginning after 12-31-69. Prior to amendment, Code Sec. 556(b)(2) read as follows:

(2) Charitable contributions.—The deduction for charitable contributions provided under section 170 shall be allowed, but in computing such deduction the limitations in section 170(b)(1)(A) and (B) shall apply, and section 170(b)(2) and (5) shall not apply. For purposes of this paragraph, the term "adjusted gross income" when used in section 170(b)(1) means the taxable income computed with the adjustments (other than the 5-percent limitation) provided in the first sentence of section 170(b) (2) and (5) and without the deduction of the amounts disallowed under paragraphs (5) and (6) of this subsection or the inclusion in gross income of the amounts includible therein as dividends by reason of the application of the provisions of section 555(b) (relating to the inclusion in gross income of a foreign personal holding company of its distributive share of the undistributed foreign personal holding company income of another company in which it is a shareholder).

• 1964, Revenue Act of 1964 (P.L. 88-272)

P.L. 88-272, §207(b)(6):

Amended paragraph (1) of subsection (b) by inserting "section 275(a)(4)" in lieu of "section 164(b)(6)". **Effective** 1-1-64.

P.L. 88-272, §209(c)(2):

Amended paragraph (2) of subsection (b) by inserting "section 170(b)(2) and (5)" in lieu of "section 170(b)(2)". **Effective** 1-1-64.

• 1962 (P.L. 87-403)

P.L. 87-403, §3(e):

Added paragraphs (7) and (8) to subsection (b). **Effective** for distributions made after 2-2-62.

• 1958, Technical Amendments Act of 1958 (P.L. 85-866)

P.L. 85-866, §33(a):

Amended the first sentence of Code Sec. 556(b)(2), and the second sentence of Code Sec. 556(b)(2) by substituting the words "(other than the 5-percent limitation) provided in the first sentence of section 170(b)(2)" for the words "provided in section 170(b)(2)". Prior to amendment, the first sentence read:

The deduction for charitable contributions provided under section 170 shall be allowed, but with the limitation in section 170(b)(1)(A) and (B) (in lieu of the limitation in section 170(b)(2)).

P.L. 85-866, §33(b):

Amended Code Sec. 556(b)(3) by substituting the phrase "section 248" for the phrase "sections 242 and 248". **Effective** for tax years ending after 12-31-57.

P.L. 85-866, §33(c):

Amended Code Sec. 556(b)(4) by adding all the material following the phrase "preceding taxable year". **Effective** for adjustments under Code Sec. 556(b)(4) for tax years ending after 12-31-57.

[Sec. 557—Repealed]

Amendments

• 2004, American Jobs Creation Act of 2004 (P.L. 108-357)

P.L. 108-357, §413(a)(1):

Repealed part III of subchapter G of chapter 1 (Code Secs. 551-558). **Effective** for tax years of foreign corporations beginning after 12-31-2004 and for tax years of United States shareholders with or within which such tax years of foreign corporations end. Prior to repeal, Code Sec. 557 read as follows:

SEC. 557. INCOME NOT PLACED ON ANNUAL BASIS.

Section 443(b) (relating to computation of tax on change of annual accounting period) shall not apply in the computation of the undistributed foreign personal holding company income under section 556.

[Sec. 558—Repealed]

Amendments

• **2004, American Jobs Creation Act of 2004 (P.L. 108-357)**

P.L. 108-357, §413(a)(1):

Repealed part III of subchapter G of chapter 1 (Code Secs. 551-558). **Effective** for tax years of foreign corporations beginning after 12-31-2004 and for tax years of United States shareholders with or within which such tax years of foreign corporations end. Prior to repeal, Code Sec. 558 read as follows:

SEC. 558. RETURNS OF OFFICERS, DIRECTORS, AND SHAREHOLDERS OF FOREIGN PERSONAL HOLDING COMPANIES.

For provisions relating to returns of officers, directors, and shareholders of foreign personal holding companies, see section 6035.

• **1958, Technical Amendments Act of 1958 (P.L. 85-866)**

P.L. 85-866, §30(d):

Added Code Sec. 558. **Effective** 1-1-54.

PART IV—DEDUCTION FOR DIVIDENDS PAID

[Sec. 561]

SEC. 561. DEFINITION OF DEDUCTION FOR DIVIDENDS PAID.

[Sec. 561(a)]

(a) GENERAL RULE.—The deduction for dividends paid shall be the sum of—

(1) the dividends paid during the taxable year,

(2) the consent dividends for the taxable year (determined under section 565), and

(3) in the case of a personal holding company, the dividend carryover described in section 564.

[Sec. 561(b)]

(b) SPECIAL RULES APPLICABLE.—In determining the deduction for dividends paid, the rules provided in section 562 (relating to rules applicable in determining dividends eligible for dividends paid deduction) and section 563 (relating to dividends paid after the close of the taxable year) shall be applicable.

Amendments

• **1976, Tax Reform Act of 1976 (P.L. 94-455)**

P.L. 94-455, §1901(b)(32)(H):

Amended Code Sec. 561(b). **Effective** for tax years beginning after 12-31-76. Prior to amendment, Sec. 561(b) read as follows:

(b) SPECIAL RULES APPLICABLE.—

(1) In determining the deduction for dividends paid, the rules provided in section 562 (relating to rules applicable in determining dividends eligible for dividends paid deduction) and section 563 (relating to dividends paid after the close of the taxable year) shall be applicable.

(2) If a corporation received antitrust stock (as defined in section 301 (f)) in a distribution to which section 301 applied and such corporation distributes such stock (or other property the basis of which is determined by reference to the basis of such stock) to its shareholders, proper adjustment shall be made, under regulations prescribed by the Secretary or his delegate, to the amount of the deduction provided for in subsection (a).

• **1962 (P.L. 87-403)**

P.L. 87-403, §3(f):

Amended subsection (b). **Effective** for distributions made after 2-2-62. Prior to amendment, subsection (b) read as follows:

(b) Special Rules Applicable.—In determining the deduction for dividends paid, the rules provided in section 562 (relating to rules applicable in determining dividends eligible for dividends paid deduction) and section 563 (relating to dividends paid after the close of the taxable year) shall be applicable.

[Sec. 562]

SEC. 562. RULES APPLICABLE IN DETERMINING DIVIDENDS ELIGIBLE FOR DIVIDENDS PAID DEDUCTION.

[Sec. 562(a)]

(a) GENERAL RULE.—For purposes of this part, the term "dividend" shall, except as otherwise provided in this section, include only dividends described in section 316 (relating to definition of dividends for purposes of corporate distributions).

[Sec. 562(b)]

(b) DISTRIBUTIONS IN LIQUIDATION.—

(1) Except in the case of a personal holding company described in section 542—

(A) in the case of amounts distributed in liquidation, the part of such distribution which is properly chargeable to earnings and profits accumulated after February 28, 1913, shall be treated as a dividend for purposes of computing the dividends paid deduction, and

(B) in the case of a complete liquidation occurring within 24 months after the adoption of a plan of liquidation, any distribution within such period pursuant to such plan shall, to the extent of the earnings and profits (computed without regard to capital losses) of the corporation for the taxable year in which such distribution is made, be treated as a dividend for purposes of computing the dividends paid deduction.

For purposes of subparagraph (A), a liquidation includes a redemption of stock to which section 302 applies. Except to the extent provided in regulations, the preceding sentence shall not apply in the case of any mere holding or investment company which is not a regulated investment company.

(2) In the case of a complete liquidation of a personal holding company occurring within 24 months after the adoption of a plan of liquidation, the amount of any distribution within such period pursuant to such plan shall be treated as a dividend for purposes of computing the dividends paid deduction, to the extent that such amount is distributed to corporate distributees and represents such corporate distributees' allocable share of the undistributed personal holding company income for the taxable year of such distribution computed without regard to this paragraph and without regard to subparagraph (B) of section 316(b)(2).

Amendments

• 2004, American Jobs Creation Act of 2004 (P.L. 108-357)

P.L. 108-357, §413(c)(9):

Amended Code Sec. 562(b)(1) by striking "or a foreign personal holding company described in section 552" immediately following "section 542". **Effective** for tax years of foreign corporations beginning after 12-31-2004, and for tax years of United States shareholders with or within which such tax years of foreign corporations end.

• 1986, Tax Reform Act of 1986 (P.L. 99-514)

P.L. 99-514, §1804(d)(1):

Amended Code Sec. 562(b)(1) by adding at the end thereof a new sentence. **Effective** for distributions after 9-27-85.

• 1982, Tax Equity and Fiscal Responsibility Act of 1982 (P.L. 97-248)

P.L. 97-248, §222(e)(7):

Amended Code Sec. 562(b)(1) by adding a new sentence at the end thereof. **Effective**, generally, for distributions after 8-31-82. But see amendment notes for Code Sec. 331(b), P.L. 97-248, for special rules.

• 1964, Revenue Act of 1964 (P.L. 88-272)

P.L. 88-272, §225(f)(3):

Amended Code Sec. 562(b). **Effective** for distributions made in any tax year of the distributing corporation beginning after 12-31-63. Prior to amendment, Code Sec. 562(b) read as follows:

"(b) Distributions in Liquidation.—In the case of amounts distributed in liquidation, the part of such distribution which is properly chargeable to earnings and profits accumulated after February 28, 1913, shall be treated as a dividend for purposes of computing the dividends paid deduction. In the case of a complete liquidation occurring within 24 months after the adoption of a plan of liquidation, any distribution within such period pursuant to such plan shall, to the extent of the earnings and profits (computed without regard to capital losses) of the corporation for the taxable year in which such distribution is made, be treated as a dividend for purposes of computing the dividends paid deduction."

[Sec. 562(c)]

(c) PREFERENTIAL DIVIDENDS.—The amount of any distribution shall not be considered as a dividend for purposes of computing the dividends paid deduction, unless such distribution is pro rata, with no preference to any share of stock as compared with other shares of the same class, and with no preference to one class of stock as compared with another class except to the extent that the former is entitled (without reference to waivers of their rights by shareholders) to such preference. In the case of a distribution by a regulated investment company to a shareholder who made an initial investment of at least $10,000,000 in such company, such distribution shall not be treated as not being pro rata or as being preferential solely by reason of an increase in the distribution by reason of reductions in administrative expenses of the company.

Amendments

• 1986, Tax Reform Act of 1986 (P.L. 99-514)

P.L. 99-514, §657(a):

Amended Code Sec. 562(c) by adding at the end thereof a new sentence. **Effective** for distributions after 10-22-86.

[Sec. 562(d)]

(d) DISTRIBUTIONS BY A MEMBER OF AN AFFILIATED GROUP.—In the case where a corporation which is a member of an affiliated group of corporations filing or required to file a consolidated return for a taxable year is required to file a separate personal holding company schedule for such taxable year, a distribution by such corporation to another member of the affiliated group shall be considered as a dividend for purposes of computing the dividends paid deduction if such distribution would constitute a dividend under the other provisions of this section to a recipient which is not a member of an affiliated group.

[Sec. 562(e)]

(e) SPECIAL RULES FOR REAL ESTATE INVESTMENT TRUSTS.—In the case of a real estate investment trust, in determining the amount of dividends under section 316 for purposes of computing the dividends paid deduction, the earnings and profits of such trust for any taxable year beginning after December 31, 1980, shall be increased by the total amount of gain (if any) on the sale or exchange of real property by such trust during such taxable year.

Amendments

• 1983, Technical Corrections Act of 1982 (P.L. 97-448)

P.L. 97-448, §102(c)(2):

Added Code Sec. 562(e). **Effective** as if included in the provision of P.L. 97-34 to which it relates.

[Sec. 563]

SEC. 563. RULES RELATING TO DIVIDENDS PAID AFTER CLOSE OF TAXABLE YEAR.

[Sec. 563(a)]

(a) ACCUMULATED EARNINGS TAX.—In the determination of the dividends paid deduction for purposes of the accumulated earnings tax imposed by section 531, a dividend paid after the close of any taxable year and on or before the 15th day of the third month following the close of such taxable year shall be considered as paid during such taxable year.

[Sec. 563(b)]

(b) PERSONAL HOLDING COMPANY TAX.—In the determination of the dividends paid deduction for purposes of the personal holding company tax imposed by section 541, a dividend paid after the close of any taxable year and on or before the 15th day of the third month following the close of such taxable year shall, to the extent the taxpayer elects in its return for the taxable year, be considered as paid during such taxable year. The amount allowed as a dividend by reason of the application of this subsection with respect to any taxable year shall not exceed either—

(1) The undistributed personal holding company income of the corporation for the taxable year, computed without regard to this subsection, or

(2) 20 percent of the sum of the dividends paid during the taxable year, computed without regard to this subsection.

Amendments

• 1969, Tax Reform Act of 1969 (P.L. 91-172)

P.L. 91-172, §914(a):

Amended paragraph (b)(2) by inserting "20 percent" in lieu of "10 percent". **Effective** for tax years beginning after 12-31-69.

[Sec. 563(c)—Stricken]

Amendments

• 2004, American Jobs Creation Act of 2004 (P.L. 108-357)

P.L. 108-357, §413(c)(10)(A)-(C):

Amended Code Sec. 563 by striking subsection (c) and by redesignating subsection (d) as subsection (c). **Effective** for tax years of foreign corporations beginning after 12-31-2004, and for tax years of United States shareholders with or within which such tax years of foreign corporations end. Prior to being stricken, Code Sec. 563(c) read as follows:

(c) FOREIGN PERSONAL HOLDING COMPANY TAX.—

(1) IN GENERAL.—In the determination of the dividends paid deduction for purposes of part III, a dividend paid after the close of any taxable year and on or before the 15th day of the 3rd month following the close of such taxable year shall, to the extent the company designates such dividend as being taken into account under this subsection, be considered as paid during such taxable year. The amount allowed as a deduction by reason of the application of this subsection with respect to any taxable year shall not exceed the undistributed foreign personal holding company income of the corporation for the taxable year computed without regard to this subsection.

(2) SPECIAL RULES.—In the case of any distribution referred to in paragraph (1)—

(A) paragraph (1) shall apply only if such distribution is to the person who was the shareholder of record (as of the last day of the taxable year of the foreign personal holding company) with respect to the stock for which such distribution is made,

(B) the determination of the person required to include such distribution in gross income shall be made under the principles of section 551(f), and

(C) any person required to include such distribution in gross or distributable net income shall include such distribution in income for such person's taxable year in which the taxable year of the foreign personal holding company ends.

• 1989, Omnibus Budget Reconciliation Act of 1989 (P.L. 101-239)

P.L. 101-239, §7401(b)(1):

Amended Code Sec. 563 by redesignating subsection (c) as subsection (d) and by inserting after subsection (b) a new subsection (c). **Effective** for tax years of foreign corporations beginning after 7-10-89. For special rules, see Act Sec. 7401(d)(2), below.

P.L. 101-239, §7401(d)(2), provides:

(2) SPECIAL RULES.—If any foreign corporation is required by the amendments made by this section to change its taxable year for its first taxable year beginning after July 10, 1989—

(A) such change shall be treated as initiated by the taxpayer,

(B) such change shall be treated as having been made with the consent of the Secretary of the Treasury or his delegate, and

(C) if, by reason of such change, any United States person is required to include in gross income for 1 taxable year amounts attributable to 2 taxable years of such foreign corporation, the amount which would otherwise be required to be included in gross income for such 1 taxable year by reason of the short taxable year of the foreign corporation resulting from such change shall be included in gross income ratably over the 4-taxable-year period beginning with such 1 taxable year.

[Sec. 563(c)]

(c) DIVIDENDS CONSIDERED AS PAID ON LAST DAY OF TAXABLE YEAR.—For the purpose of applying section 562(a), with respect to distributions under subsection (a) or (b) of this section, a distribution made after the close of a taxable year and on or before the 15th day of the third month following the close of the taxable year shall be considered as made on the last day of such taxable year.

Amendments

• **2004, American Jobs Creation Act of 2004 (P.L. 108-357)**

P.L. 108-357, §413(c)(10)(A)-(C):

Amended Code Sec. 563 by striking subsection (c), by redesignating subsection (d) as subsection (c), and by striking "subsection (a), (b), or (c)" in subsection (c) (as so redesignated) and inserting "subsection (a) or (b)". **Effective** for tax years of foreign corporations beginning after 12-31-2004, and for tax years of United States shareholders with or within which such tax years of foreign corporations end.

• **1989, Omnibus Budget Reconciliation Act of 1989 (P.L. 101-239)**

P.L. 101-239, §7401(b)(1):

Amended Code Sec. 563 by redesignating subsection (c) as subsection (d) and by inserting after subsection (b) a new subsection (c). **Effective** for tax years of foreign corporations beginning after 7-10-89. For special rules, see Act Sec. 7401(d)(2), below.

P.L. 101-239, §7401(b)(2):

Amended Code Sec. 563(d), as redesignated by paragraph (1), by striking "subsection (a) or (b)" and inserting "subsection (a), (b), or (c)". **Effective** for tax years of foreign corporations beginning after 7-10-89. For special rules, see Act Sec. 7401(d)(2), below.

P.L. 101-239, §7401(d)(2), provides:

(2) SPECIAL RULES.—If any foreign corporation is required by the amendments made by this section to change its taxable year for its first taxable year beginning after July 10, 1989—

(A) such change shall be treated as initiated by the taxpayer,

(B) such change shall be treated as having been made with the consent of the Secretary of the Treasury or his delegate, and

(C) if, by reason of such change, any United States person is required to include in gross income for 1 taxable year amounts attributable to 2 taxable years of such foreign corporation, the amount which would otherwise be required to be included in gross income for such 1 taxable year by reason of the short taxable year of the foreign corporation resulting from such change shall be included in gross income ratably over the 4-taxable-year period beginning with such 1 taxable year.

[Sec. 564]

SEC. 564. DIVIDEND CARRYOVER.

[Sec. 564(a)]

(a) GENERAL RULE.—For purposes of computing the dividends paid deduction under section 561, in the case of a personal holding company the dividend carryover for any taxable year shall be the dividend carryover to such taxable year, computed as provided in subsection (b), from the two preceding taxable years.

[Sec. 564(b)]

(b) COMPUTATION OF DIVIDEND CARRYOVER.—The dividend carryover to the taxable year shall be determined as follows:

(1) For each of the 2 preceding taxable years there shall be determined the taxable income computed with the adjustments provided in section 545 (whether or not the taxpayer was a personal holding company for either of such preceding taxable years), and there shall also be determined for each such year the deduction for dividends paid during such year as provided in section 561 (but determined without regard to the dividend carryover to such year).

(2) There shall be determined for each such taxable year whether there is an excess of such taxable income over such deduction for dividends paid or an excess of such deduction for dividends paid over such taxable income, and the amount of each such excess.

(3) If there is an excess of such deductions for dividends paid over such taxable income for the first preceding taxable year, such excess shall be allowed as a dividend carryover to the taxable year.

(4) If there is an excess of such deduction for dividends paid over such taxable income for the second preceding taxable year, such excess shall be reduced by the amount determined in paragraph (5), and the remainder of such excess shall be allowed as a dividend carryover to the taxable year.

(5) The amount of the reduction specified in paragraph (4) shall be the amount of the excess of the taxable income, if any, for the first preceding taxable year over such deduction for dividends paid, if any, for the first preceding taxable year.

[Sec. 564(c)—Repealed]

Amendments

• **1976, Tax Reform Act of 1976 (P.L. 94-455)**

P.L. 94-455, §1901(a)(81):

Repealed Code Sec. 564(c). **Effective** with respect to tax years beginning after 12-31-76. Prior to repeal, Code Sec. 564(c) read as follows:

(c) DETERMINATION OF DIVIDEND CARRYOVER FROM TAXABLE YEARS TO WHICH THIS SUBTITLE DOES NOT APPLY.—In a case where the first or second preceding taxable year began before the taxpayer's first taxable year under this subtitle, the amount of the dividend carryover to taxable years to which this subtitle applies shall be determined under the provisions of the Internal Revenue Code of 1939.

[Sec. 565]

SEC. 565. CONSENT DIVIDENDS.

[Sec. 565(a)]

(a) GENERAL RULE.—If any person owns consent stock (as defined in subsection (f)(1)) in a corporation on the last day of the taxable year of such corporation, and such person agrees, in a consent filed with the return of such corporation in accordance with regulations prescribed by the Secretary, to treat as a dividend the amount specified in such consent, the amount so specified shall, except as provided in subsection (b), constitute a consent dividend for purposes of section 561 (relating to the deduction for dividends paid).

Amendments

• 1976, Tax Reform Act of 1976 (P.L. 94-455)

P.L. 94-455, §1906(b)(13)(A):

Amended 1954 Code by substituting "Secretary" for "Secretary or his delegate" each place it appeared. **Effective** 2-1-77.

[Sec. 565(b)]

(b) LIMITATIONS.—A consent dividend shall not include—

(1) an amount specified in a consent which, if distributed in money, would constitute, or be part of, a distribution which would be disqualified for purposes of the dividends paid deduction under section 562(c) (relating to preferential dividends), or

(2) an amount specified in a consent which would not constitute a dividend (as defined in section 316) if the total amounts specified in consents filed by the corporation had been distributed in money to shareholders on the last day of the taxable year of such corporation.

[Sec. 565(c)]

(c) EFFECT OF CONSENT.—The amount of a consent dividend shall be considered, for purposes of this title—

(1) as distributed in money by the corporation to the shareholder on the last day of the taxable year of the corporation, and

(2) as contributed to the capital of the corporation by the shareholder on such day.

[Sec. 565(d)]

(d) CONSENT DIVIDENDS AND OTHER DISTRIBUTIONS.—If a distribution by a corporation consists in part of money or other property, the entire amount specified in the consents and the amount of such money or other property shall be considered together for purposes of applying this title.

[Sec. 565(e)]

(e) NONRESIDENT ALIENS AND FOREIGN CORPORATIONS.—In the case of a consent dividend which, if paid in money would be subject to the provisions of section 1441 (relating to withholding of tax on nonresident aliens) or section 1442 (relating to withholding of tax on foreign corporations), this section shall not apply unless the consent is accompanied by money, or such other medium of payment as the Secretary may by regulations authorize, in an amount equal to the amount that would be required to be deducted and withheld under sections 1441 or 1442 if the consent dividend had been, on the last day of the taxable year of the corporation, paid to the shareholder in money as a dividend. The amount accompanying the consent shall be credited against the tax imposed by this subtitle on the shareholder.

Amendments

• 1976, Tax Reform Act of 1976 (P.L. 94-455)

P.L. 94-455, §1906(b)(13)(A):

Amended 1954 Code by substituting "Secretary" for "Secretary or his delegate" each place it appeared. **Effective** 2-1-77.

[Sec. 565(f)]

(f) DEFINITIONS.—

(1) CONSENT STOCK.—Consent stock, for purposes of this section, means the class or classes of stock entitled, after the payment of preferred dividends, to a share in the distribution (other than in complete or partial liquidation) within the taxable year of all the remaining earnings and profits, which share constitutes the same proportion of such distribution regardless of the amount of such distribution.

(2) PREFERRED DIVIDENDS.—Preferred dividends, for purposes of this section, means a distribution (other than in complete or partial liquidation), limited in amount, which must be made on any class of stock before a further distribution (other than in complete or partial liquidation) of earnings and profits may be made within the taxable year.

Subchapter H—Banking Institutions

PART I—RULES OF GENERAL APPLICATION TO BANKING INSTITUTIONS

[Sec. 581]

SEC. 581. DEFINITION OF BANK.

For purposes of sections 582 and 584, the term "bank" means a bank or trust company incorporated and doing business under the laws of the United States (including laws relating to the District of Columbia) or of any State, a substantial part of the business of which consists of receiving deposits and making loans and discounts, or of exercising fiduciary powers similar to those permitted to national banks under authority of the Comptroller of the Currency, and which is subject by law to supervision and examination by State, or Federal authority having supervision over banking institutions. Such term also means a domestic building and loan association.

Amendments

• 1976, Tax Reform Act of 1976 (P.L. 94-455)

P.L. 94-455, §1901(c)(5):

Substituted "or of any State" for ", of any State, or of any Territory" and struck out ", Territorial" in Code Sec. 581. **Effective** for tax years beginning after 12-31-76.

• 1962 (P.L. 87-722)

P.L. 87-722, §5:

Amended Sec. 581 by substituting "authority of the Comptroller of the Currency" for "section 11(k) of the Federal Reserve Act (38 Stat. 262; 12 U. S. C. 248(k))". **Effective** 9-28-62.

[Sec. 582]

SEC. 582. BAD DEBTS, LOSSES, AND GAINS WITH RESPECT TO SECURITIES HELD BY FINANCIAL INSTITUTIONS.

[Sec. 582(a)]

(a) SECURITIES.—Notwithstanding sections 165(g)(1) and 166(e), subsections (a) and (b) of section 166 (relating to allowance of deduction for bad debts) shall apply in the case of a bank to a debt which is evidenced by a security as defined in section 165(g)(2)(C).

Amendments

• 1988, Technical and Miscellaneous Revenue Act of 1988 (P.L. 100-647)

P.L. 100-647, §1008(d)(3):

Amended Code Sec. 582(a) by striking out "subsections (a), (b), and (c) of section 166" and inserting in lieu thereof "subsections (a) and (b) of section 166". **Effective** as if included in the provision of P.L. 99-514 to which it relates.

[Sec. 582(b)]

(b) WORTHLESS STOCK IN AFFILIATED BANK.—For purposes of section 165(g)(1), where the taxpayer is a bank and owns directly at least 80 percent of each class of stock of another bank, stock in such other bank shall not be treated as a capital asset.

[Sec. 582(c)]

(c) BOND, ETC., LOSSES AND GAINS OF FINANCIAL INSTITUTIONS.—

(1) GENERAL RULE.—For purposes of this subtitle, in the case of a financial institution referred to in paragraph (2), the sale or exchange of a bond, debenture, note, or certificate or other evidence of indebtedness shall not be considered a sale or exchange of a capital asset. For purposes of the preceding sentence, any regular or residual interest in a REMIC shall be treated as an evidence of indebtedness.

(2) FINANCIAL INSTITUTIONS TO WHICH PARAGRAPH (1) APPLIES.—

(A) IN GENERAL.—For purposes of paragraph (1), the financial institutions referred to in this paragraph are—

(i) any bank (and any corporation which would be a bank except for the fact it is a foreign corporation),

(ii) any financial institution referred to in section 591,

(iii) any small business investment company operating under the Small Business Investment Act of 1958, and

(iv) any business development corporation.

(B) BUSINESS DEVELOPMENT CORPORATION.—For purposes of subparagraph (A), the term "business development corporation" means a corporation which was created by or pursuant to an act of a State legislature for purposes of promoting, maintaining, and assisting the economy and industry within such State on a regional or statewide basis by making loans to be used in trades and businesses which would generally not be made by banks within such region or State in the ordinary course of their business (except on the basis of a partial participation), and which is operated primarily for such purposes.

(C) LIMITATIONS ON FOREIGN BANKS.—In the case of a foreign corporation referred to in subparagraph (A)(i), paragraph (1) shall only apply to gains and losses which are effectively connected with the conduct of a banking business in the United States.

Amendments

• 2008, Emergency Economic Stabilization Act of 2008 (P.L. 110-343)

P.L. 110-343, Division A, §301, provides:

SEC. 301. GAIN OR LOSS FROM SALE OR EXCHANGE OF CERTAIN PREFERRED STOCK.

(a) IN GENERAL.—For purposes of the Internal Revenue Code of 1986, gain or loss from the sale or exchange of any applicable preferred stock by any applicable financial institution shall be treated as ordinary income or loss.

(b) APPLICABLE PREFERRED STOCK.—For purposes of this section, the term "applicable preferred stock" means any stock—

(1) which is preferred stock in—

(A) the Federal National Mortgage Association, established pursuant to the Federal National Mortgage Association Charter Act (12 U.S.C. 1716 et seq.), or

(B) the Federal Home Loan Mortgage Corporation, established pursuant to the Federal Home Loan Mortgage Corporation Act (12 U.S.C. 1451 et seq.), and

(2) which—

(A) was held by the applicable financial institution on September 6, 2008, or

(B) was sold or exchanged by the applicable financial institution on or after January 1, 2008, and before September 7, 2008.

(c) APPLICABLE FINANCIAL INSTITUTION.—For purposes of this section:

(1) IN GENERAL.—Except as provided in paragraph (2), the term "applicable financial institution" means—

(A) a financial institution referred to in section 582(c)(2) of the Internal Revenue Code of 1986, or

(B) a depository institution holding company (as defined in section 3(w)(1) of the Federal Deposit Insurance Act (12 U.S.C. 1813(w)(1))).

(2) SPECIAL RULES FOR CERTAIN SALES.—In the case of—

(A) a sale or exchange described in subsection (b)(2)(B), an entity shall be treated as an applicable financial institution only if it was an entity described in subparagraph (A) or (B) of paragraph (1) at the time of the sale or exchange, and

(B) a sale or exchange after September 6, 2008, of preferred stock described in subsection (b)(2)(A), an entity shall be treated as an applicable financial institution only if it was an entity described in subparagraph (A) or (B) of paragraph (1) at all times during the period beginning on September 6, 2008, and ending on the date of the sale or exchange of the preferred stock.

(d) SPECIAL RULE FOR CERTAIN PROPERTY NOT HELD ON SEPTEMBER 6, 2008.—The Secretary of the Treasury or the Secretary's delegate may extend the application of this section to all or a portion of the gain or loss from a sale or exchange in any case where—

(1) an applicable financial institution sells or exchanges applicable preferred stock after September 6, 2008, which the applicable financial institution did not hold on such date, but the basis of which in the hands of the applicable financial institution at the time of the sale or exchange is the same as the basis in the hands of the person which held such stock on such date, or

(2) the applicable financial institution is a partner in a partnership which—

(A) held such stock on September 6, 2008, and later sold or exchanged such stock, or

(B) sold or exchanged such stock during the period described in subsection (b)(2)(B).

(e) REGULATORY AUTHORITY.—The Secretary of the Treasury or the Secretary's delegate may prescribe such guidance, rules, or regulations as are necessary to carry out the purposes of this section.

(f) EFFECTIVE DATE.—This section shall apply to sales or exchanges occurring after December 31, 2007, in taxable years ending after such date.

• 2004, American Jobs Creation Act of 2004 (P.L. 108-357)

P.L. 108-357, §835(b)(3):

Amended Code Sec. 582(c)(1) by striking ", and any regular interest in a FASIT," after "in a REMIC". For the **effective** date, see Act Sec. 835(c), below.

P.L. 108-357, §835(c), provides:

(c) EFFECTIVE DATE.—

(1) IN GENERAL.—Except as provided in paragraph (2), the amendments made by this section shall take effect on January 1, 2005.

(2) EXCEPTION FOR EXISTING FASITS.—Paragraph (1) shall not apply to any FASIT in existence on the date of the enactment of this Act [10-22-2004.—CCH] to the extent that regular interests issued by the FASIT before such date continue to remain outstanding in accordance with the original terms of issuance.

• 1996, Small Business Job Protection Act of 1996 (P.L. 104-188)

P.L. 104-188, §1621(b)(4):

Amended Code Sec. 582(c)(1) by inserting ", and any regular interest in a FASIT," after "REMIC". **Effective** 9-1-97.

• 1990, Omnibus Budget Reconciliation Act of 1990 (P.L. 101-508)

P.L. 101-508, §11801(a)(25):

Repealed paragraphs (2), (3) and (4) of Code Sec. 582(c). **Effective** 11-5-90. Prior to repeal, Code Sec. 582(c)(2), (3), and (4) read as follows:

(2) TRANSITIONAL RULE FOR BANKS.—In the case of a bank, if the net long-term capital gains of the taxable year from sales or exchanges of qualifying securities exceed the net short-term capital losses of the taxable year from such sales or exchanges, such excess shall be considered as gain from the sale of a capital asset held for more than 1 year to the extent it does not exceed the net gain on sales and exchanges described in paragraph (1).

(3) SPECIAL RULES.—For purposes of this subsection—

(A) The term "qualifying security" means a bond, debenture, note, or certificate or other evidence of indebtedness held by a bank on July 11, 1969.

(B) The amount treated as capital gain or loss from the sale or exchange of a qualifying security shall be determined by multiplying the amount of capital gain or loss from the sale or exchange of such security (determined without regard to this subsection) by a fraction, the numerator of which is the number of days before July 12, 1969, that such security was held by the bank, and the denominator of which is the number of days the security was held by the bank.

(4) TRANSITIONAL RULE FOR BANKS.—In the case of a corporation which would be a bank except for the fact that it is a foreign corporation, the net gain, if any, for the taxable year on sales and exchanges described in paragraph (1) shall be considered as gain from the sale or exchange of a capital asset to the extent such net gain does not exceed the portion of any capital loss carryover to such taxable year which is attributable to capital losses on sales or exchanges described in paragraph (1) for a taxable year beginning before July 12, 1969. For purposes of the preceding sentence, the portion of a net capital loss for a taxable year which is attributable to capital losses on sales or exchanges described in paragraph (1) is the amount of the net capital loss on such sales or exchanges for such taxable year (but not in excess of the net capital loss for such taxable year).

P.L. 101-508, §11801(c)(11)(A)-(B):

Amended Code Sec. 582(c) by striking in paragraph (1) "paragraph (5)" and inserting "paragraph (2)" and by redesignating paragraph (5) as paragraph (2). **Effective** 11-5-90.

P.L. 101-508, §11821(b), provides:

(b) SAVINGS PROVISION.—If—

(1) any provision amended or repealed by this part applied to—

(A) any transaction occurring before the date of the enactment of this Act,

(B) any property acquired before such date of enactment, or

(C) any item of income, loss, deduction, or credit taken into account before such date of enactment, and

(2) the treatment of such transaction, property, or item under such provision would (without regard to the amendments made by this part) affect liability for tax for periods ending after such date of enactment,

nothing in the amendments made by this part shall be construed to affect the treatment of such transaction, property, or item for purposes of determining liability for tax for periods ending after such date of enactment.

• 1986, Tax Reform Act of 1986 (P.L. 99-514)

P.L. 99-514, §671(b)(4):

Amended Code Sec. 582(c)(1) by adding at the end thereof a new sentence. **Effective** for tax years beginning after 12-31-86.

P.L. 99-514, §901(d)(3)(A):

Amended Code Sec. 582(c)(1) by striking out "a financial institution to which section 585, 586, or 593 applies" and inserting in lieu thereof "a financial institution referred to in paragraph (5)". **Effective** for tax years beginning after 12-31-86.

P.L. 99-514, §901(d)(3)(B):

Amended Code Sec. 582(c) by adding at the end thereof new paragraph (5). **Effective** for tax years beginning after 12-31-86.

• 1984, Deficit Reduction Act of 1984 (P.L. 98-369)

P.L. 98-369, §1001(b)(6):

Amended Code Sec. 582(c)(2) by striking out "1 year" each place it appeared and inserting in lieu thereof "6 months". **Effective** for property acquired after 6-22-84 and before 1-1-88.

• 1976, Tax Reform Act of 1976 (P.L. 94-455)

P.L. 94-455, §1402(b)(1)(G):

Amended Code Sec. 582(c)(2) by substituting "9 months" for "6 months". **Effective** with respect to tax years beginning in 1977.

P.L. 94-455, §1402(b)(2):

Amended Code Sec. 582(c)(2) by substituting "1 year" for "9 months". **Effective** with respect to tax years beginning after 12-31-77.

P.L. 94-455, §1044(a):

Added Code Sec. 582(c)(4). For the **effective** date, see Act Sec. 1044(b), below.

P.L. 94-455, §1044(b), provides:

(b) EFFECTIVE DATE.—

(1) The amendment made by subsection (a) shall apply with respect to taxable years beginning after July 11, 1969.

(2) If the refund or credit of any overpayment attributable to the application of the amendment made by subsection (a) to any taxable year is otherwise prevented by the operation of any law or rule of law (other than section 7122 of the Internal Revenue Code of 1954, relating to compromises) on the day which is one year after the date of the enactment of this Act, such credit or refund shall be nevertheless allowed or made if claim therefor is filed on or before such day.

• 1969, Tax Reform Act of 1969 (P.L. 91-172)

P.L. 91-172, §433(a):

Amended Code Sec. 582(c). **Effective**, generally, for tax years beginning after 7-11-69. However, see Act Sec. 433(d)(2) below. Prior to amendment, Code Sec. 582(c) read as follows:

(c) Bond, etc., Losses of Banks.—For purposes of this subtitle, in the case of a bank, if the losses of the taxable year from sales or exchanges of bonds, debentures, notes, or certificates, or other evidences of indebtedness, issued by any corporation (including one issued by a government or political subdivision thereof), exceed the gains of the taxable year from such sales or exchanges, no such sale or exchange shall be considered a sale or exchange of a capital asset.

P.L. 91-172, §433(d)(2), provides:

(d)(2) Election for small business investment companies and business development corporations.—Notwithstanding paragraph (1) [General effective date—CCH.], in the case of a financial institution described in section 586(a) of the Internal Revenue Code of 1954, the amendments made by this section shall not apply for its taxable years beginning after July 11, 1969, and before July 11, 1974, unless the taxpayer so elects at such time and in such manner as shall be prescribed by the Secretary of the Treasury or his delegate. Such election shall be irrevocable and shall apply to all such taxable years.

• 1958, Technical Amendments Act of 1958 (P.L. 85-866)

P.L. 85-866, §34:

Amended Code Sec. 582(c) by deleting the phrase "with interest coupons or in registered form," following the phrase "or political subdivision thereof,".

[Sec. 584]

SEC. 584. COMMON TRUST FUNDS.

[Sec. 584(a)]

(a) DEFINITIONS.—For purposes of this subtitle, the term "common trust fund" means a fund maintained by a bank—

(1) exclusively for the collective investment and reinvestment of moneys contributed thereto by the bank in its capacity—

(A) as a trustee, executor, administrator, or guardian, or

(B) as a custodian of accounts—

(i) which the Secretary determines are established pursuant to a State law which is substantially similar to the Uniform Gifts to Minors Act as published by the American Law Institute, and

(ii) with respect to which the bank establishes, to the satisfaction of the Secretary, that it has duties and responsibilities similar to duties and responsibilities of a trustee or guardian; and

(2) in conformity with the rules and regulations, prevailing from time to time, of the Board of Governors of the Federal Reserve System or the Comptroller of the Currency pertaining to the collective investment of trust funds by national banks.

For purposes of this subsection, two or more banks which are members of the same affiliated group (within the meaning of section 1504) shall be treated as one bank for the period of affiliation with respect to any fund of which any of the member banks is trustee or two or more of the member banks are co-trustees.

Amendments

• 1976, Tax Reform Act of 1976 (P.L. 94-455)

P.L. 94-455, §2138(a):

Amended Code Sec. 584(a)(1). **Effective** 10-4-76. Prior to amendment Sec. 584(a)(1) read as follows:

(1) exclusively for the collective investment and reinvestment of moneys contributed thereto by the bank in its capacity as a trustee, executor, administrator, or guardian; and

• 1976 (P.L. 94-414)

P.L. 94-414, §1:

Amended Code Sec. 584(a) by adding the last sentence. **Effective** for tax years beginning after 12-31-75.

• 1962 (P.L. 87-722)

P.L. 87-722, §4:

Amended Sec. 584(a)(2) by inserting "or Comptroller of the Currency" immediately after "the Board of Governors of the Federal Reserve System". **Effective** 9-28-62.

[Sec. 584(b)]

(b) TAXATION OF COMMON TRUST FUNDS.—A common trust fund shall not be subject to taxation under this chapter and for purposes of this chapter shall not be considered a corporation.

»»→ Caution: The flush sentence in Code Sec. 584(c), below, is subject to the sunset provision of the Jobs and Growth Tax Relief Reconciliation Act of 2003 (P.L. 108-27), §303. Absent Congressional action, the changes made to this provision by P.L. 108-27, or that take effect as if included in P.L. 108-27, do not apply after December 31, 2010. For more information about the sunset provision, see page XXI of the Preface to this publication and P.L. 108-27, §303, in the amendment notes. See the amendments notes for a history of amendments to this section and the effective date of each change.

[Sec. 584(c)]

(c) INCOME OF PARTICIPANTS IN FUND.—Each participant in the common trust fund in computing its taxable income shall include, whether or not distributed and whether or not distributable—

(1) as part of its gains and losses from sales or exchanges of capital assets held for not more than 1 year, its proportionate share of the gains and losses of the common trust fund from sales or exchanges of capital assets held for not more than 1 year,

(2) as part of its gains and losses from sales or exchanges of capital assets held for more than 1 year, its proportionate share of the gains and losses of the common trust fund from sales or exchanges of capital assets held for more than 1 year, and

(3) its proportionate share of the ordinary taxable income or the ordinary net loss of the common trust fund, computed as provided in subsection (d).

The proportionate share of each participant in the amount of dividends received by the common trust fund and to which section 1(h)(11) applies shall be considered for purposes of such paragraph as having been received by such participant.

Amendments

• 2003, Jobs and Growth Tax Relief Reconciliation Act of 2003 (P.L. 108-27)

P.L. 108-27, §302(e)(7):

Amended Code Sec. 584(c) by adding at the end a new flush sentence. For the **effective** date, see Act Sec. 302(f), as amended by P.L. 108-311, §402(a)(6), below.

P.L. 108-27, §302(f), as amended by P.L. 108-311, §402(a)(6), provides:

(f) EFFECTIVE DATE.—

(1) IN GENERAL.—Except as provided in paragraph (2), the amendments made by this section shall apply to taxable years beginning after December 31, 2002.

(2) PASS-THRU ENTITIES.—In the case of a pass-thru entity described in subparagraph (A), (B), (C), (D), (E), or (F) of section 1(h)(10) of the Internal Revenue Code of 1986, as amended by this Act, the amendments made by this section shall apply to taxable years ending after December 31, 2002; except that dividends received by such an entity on or before such date shall not be treated as qualified dividend income (as defined in section 1(h)(11)(B) of such Code, as added by this Act).

P.L. 108-27, §303, as amended by P.L. 109-222, §102, provides:

SEC. 303. SUNSET OF TITLE.

All provisions of, and amendments made by, this title shall not apply to taxable years beginning after December 31, 2010, and the Internal Revenue Code of 1986 shall be applied and administered to such years as if such provisions and amendments had never been enacted.

• 1986, Tax Reform Act of 1986 (P.L. 99-514)

P.L. 99-514, §612(b)(2)(A):

Amended Code Sec. 584(c). **Effective** for tax years beginning after 12-31-86. Prior to amendment, Code Sec. 584(c) read as follows:

(c) INCOME OR PARTICIPANTS IN FUND.—

(1) INCLUSIONS IN TAXABLE INCOME.—Each participant in the common trust fund in computing its taxable income shall include, whether or not distributed and whether or not distributable—

(A) as part of its gains and losses from sales or exchanges of capital assets held for not more than 6 months, its proportionate share of the gains and losses of the common trust fund from sales or exchanges of capital assets held for not more than 6 months;

(B) as part of its gains and losses from sales or exchanges of capital assets held for more than 6 months, its proportionate share of the gains and losses of the common trust fund from sales or exchanges of capital assets held for more than 6 months;

(C) its proportionate share of the ordinary taxable income or the ordinary net loss of the common trust fund, computed as provided in Subsection (d).

(2) DIVIDENDS OR INTEREST RECEIVED.—The proportionate share of each participant in the amount of dividends or interest received by the common trust fund and to which

section 116 or 128 applies shall be considered for purposes of such section as having been received by such participant.

P.L. 99-514, §612(b)(2)(B):

Amended Code Sec. 584(c), as amended by Act Sec. 612(b)(2)(A), by striking out "6 months" each place it appears and inserting in lieu thereof "1 year" if the amendments made by section 1001 of the Tax Reform Act of 1984 cease to apply, effective with respect to property to which such amendments do not apply. **Effective** for tax years beginning after 12-31-86.

• 1984, Deficit Reduction Act of 1984 (P.L. 98-369)

P.L. 98-369, §1001(b)(7):

Amended Code Sec. 584(c)(1)(A) and (B) by striking out "1 year" each place it appeared and inserting in lieu thereof "6 months". **Effective** for property acquired after 6-22-84 and before 1-1-88.

• 1983, Technical Corrections Act of 1982 (P.L. 97-448)

P.L. 97-448, §103(a)(2):

Amended Code Sec. 584(c)(2). **Effective** as if included in the provision of P.L. 97-34 to which it relates. Prior to amendment, Code Sec. 584(c)(2) read as follows:

(2) DIVIDENDS OR INTEREST RECEIVED.—The proportionate share of each participant in the amount of dividends or interest received by the common trust fund and to which section 116 applies shall be considered for purposes of such section as having been received by such participant.

• 1981, Economic Recovery Tax Act of 1981 (P.L. 97-34)

P.L. 97-34, §301(b)(3):

Amended Code Sec. 584(c)(2), as in effect for taxable years beginning in 1981, by inserting "or 128" after "section 116". **Effective** for tax years ending after 9-30-81.

P.L. 97-34, §301(b)(6)(A):

Amended Code Sec. 584(c)(2), as in effect for taxable years beginning after 12-31-81, by inserting "or interest" after "dividends" each place it appears in the caption or text. **Effective** for tax years beginning after 12-31-81.

• 1980, Crude Oil Windfall Profits Tax Act of 1980 (P.L. 96-223)

P.L. 96-223, §404(b)(3):

Amended Code Sec. 584(c)(2) by inserting "or interest" after "dividends" each place it appears in the caption and in the text. **Effective** for tax years beginning after 12-31-80 and before 1-1-83. (P.L. 97-34, Act Sec. 302(b)(1), amended Act. Sec. 404(c) of P.L. 96-223 by striking out "1983" and inserting "1982".)

• 1976, Tax Reform Act of 1976 (P.L. 94-455)

P.L. 94-455, §1402(b)(1):

Amended Code Sec. 584(c)(1)(A) and (B) by substituting "9 months" for "6 months". **Effective** for tax years beginning in 1977.

P.L. 94-455, §1402(b)(2):

Amended Code Sec. 584(c)(1)(A) and (B) by substituting "1 year" for "9 months". **Effective** with respect to tax years beginning after 12-31-77.

P.L. 94-455, §1901(b)(1)(G):

Amended Code Sec. 584(c)(2). **Effective** for tax years beginning after 12-31-76. Prior to amendment, Sec. 584(c)(2) read as follows:

(2) DIVIDENDS AND PARTIALLY TAX EXEMPT INTEREST.—The proportionate share of each participant in the amount of dividends to which section 116 applies, and in the amount of partially tax exempt interest on obligations described in section 35 or section 242, received by the common trust fund shall be considered for purposes of such sections as having been received by such participant. If the common trust fund elects under section 171 (relating to amortizable bond premium) to amortize the premium on such obligations, for purposes of the preceding sentence the proportionate share of the participant of such interest received by the common trust fund shall be his proportionate share of such interest (determined without regard to this sentence) reduced by so much of the deduction under section 171 as is attributable to such share.

• 1964, Revenue Act of 1964 (P.L. 88-272)

P.L. 88-272, §201(d)(5):

Amended Code Sec. 584(c)(2) by deleting "section 34 or". **Effective** with respect to dividends received after 12-31-64, in tax years ending after such date.

[Sec. 584(d)]

(d) COMPUTATION OF COMMON TRUST FUND INCOME.—The taxable income of a common trust fund shall be computed in the same manner and on the same basis as in the case of an individual, except that—

(1) there shall be segregated the gains and losses from sales or exchanges of capital assets;

(2) after excluding all items of gain and loss from sales or exchanges of capital assets, there shall be computed—

(A) an ordinary taxable income which shall consist of the excess of the gross income over deductions; or

(B) an ordinary net loss which shall consist of the excess of the deductions over the gross income; and

(3) the deduction provided by section 170 (relating to charitable, etc., contributions and gifts) shall not be allowed.

Amendments

• 1977, Tax Reduction and Simplification Act of 1977 (P.L. 95-30)

P.L. 95-30, §101(d)(7):

Amended Code Sec. 584(d) by inserting "and" at the end of paragraph (2), by striking out ";and" at the end of paragraph (3) and inserting in lieu thereof a period, and by striking out paragraph (4). **Effective** for tax years beginning after 12-31-76. Prior to amendment paragraph (4) of Sec. 584(d) read as follows:

(4) the standard deduction provided in section 141 shall not be allowed.

[Sec. 584(e)]

(e) ADMISSION AND WITHDRAWAL.—No gain or loss shall be realized by the common trust fund by the admission or withdrawal of a participant. The admission of a participant shall be treated with respect to the participant as the purchase of, or an exchange for, the participating interest. The withdrawal of any participating interest by a participant shall be treated as a sale or exchange of such interest by the participant.

[Sec. 584(f)]

(f) DIFFERENT TAXABLE YEARS OF COMMON TRUST FUND AND PARTICIPANT.—If the taxable year of the common trust fund is different from that of a participant, the inclusions with respect to the taxable income of the common trust fund, in computing the taxable income of the participant for its taxable year, shall be based upon the taxable income of the common trust fund for any taxable year of the common trust fund ending within or with the taxable year of the participant.

[Sec. 584(g)]

(g) NET OPERATING LOSS DEDUCTION.—The benefit of the deduction for net operating losses provided by section 172 shall not be allowed to a common trust fund, but shall be allowed to the participants in the common trust fund under regulations prescribed by the Secretary.

Amendments

• 1976, Tax Reform Act of 1976 (P.L. 94-455)

P.L. 94-455, §1906(b)(13)(A):

Amended 1954 Code by substituting "Secretary" for "Secretary or his delegate" each place it appeared. **Effective** 2-1-77.

[Sec. 584(h)]

(h) NONRECOGNITION TREATMENT FOR CERTAIN TRANSFERS TO REGULATED INVESTMENT COMPANIES.—

(1) IN GENERAL.—If—

(A) a common trust fund transfers substantially all of its assets to one or more regulated investment companies in exchange solely for stock in the company or companies to which such assets are so transferred, and

(B) such stock is distributed by such common trust fund to participants in such common trust fund in exchange solely for their interests in such common trust fund,

no gain or loss shall be recognized by such common trust fund by reason of such transfer or distribution, and no gain or loss shall be recognized by any participant in such common trust fund by reason of such exchange.

(2) BASIS RULES.—

(A) REGULATED INVESTMENT COMPANY.—The basis of any asset received by a regulated investment company in a transfer referred to in paragraph (1)(A) shall be the same as it would be in the hands of the common trust fund.

(B) PARTICIPANTS.—The basis of the stock which is received in an exchange referred to in paragraph (1)(B) shall be the same as that of the property exchanged. If stock in more than one regulated investment company is received in such exchange, the basis determined under the preceding sentence shall be allocated among the stock in each such company on the basis of respective fair market values.

(3) TREATMENT OF ASSUMPTIONS OF LIABILITY.—

(A) IN GENERAL.—In determining whether the transfer referred to in paragraph (1)(A) is in exchange solely for stock in one or more regulated investment companies, the assumption by any such company of a liability of the common trust fund shall be disregarded.

(B) SPECIAL RULE WHERE ASSUMED LIABILITIES EXCEED BASIS.—

(i) IN GENERAL.—If, in any transfer referred to in paragraph (1)(A), the assumed liabilities exceed the aggregate adjusted bases (in the hands of the common trust fund) of the assets transferred to the regulated investment company or companies—

(I) notwithstanding paragraph (1), gain shall be recognized to the common trust fund on such transfer in an amount equal to such excess,

(II) the basis of the assets received by the regulated investment company or companies in such transfer shall be increased by the amount so recognized, and

(III) any adjustment to the basis of a participant's interest in the common trust fund as a result of the gain so recognized shall be treated as occurring immediately before the exchange referred to in paragraph (1)(B).

If the transfer referred to in paragraph (1)(A) is to two or more regulated investment companies, the basis increase under subclause (II) shall be allocated among such companies on the basis of the respective fair market values of the assets received by each of such companies.

(ii) ASSUMED LIABILITIES.—For purposes of clause (i), the term "assumed liabilities" means any liability of the common trust fund assumed by any regulated investment company in connection with the transfer referred to in paragraph (1)(A).

(C) ASSUMPTION.—For purposes of this paragraph, in determining the amount of any liability assumed, the rules of section 357(d) shall apply.

(4) COMMON TRUST FUND MUST MEET DIVERSIFICATION RULES.—This subsection shall not apply to any common trust fund which would not meet the requirements of section 368(a)(2)(F)(ii) if it were a corporation. For purposes of the preceding sentence, Government securities shall not be treated as securities of an issuer in applying the 25-percent and 50-percent test and such securities shall not be excluded for purposes of determining total assets under clause (iv) of section 368(a)(2)(F).

Amendments

• 1999, Miscellaneous Trade and Technical Corrections Act of 1999 (P.L. 106-36)

P.L. 106-36, §3001(c)(1)(A)-(B):

Amended Code Sec. 584(h)(3) by striking ", and the fact that any property transferred by the common trust fund is subject to a liability," following "trust fund" in subparagraph (A), and by striking clause (ii) of subparagraph (B) and inserting new subclause (ii) and subparagraph (C). **Effective** for transfers after 10-18-98. Prior to being stricken, subclause (ii) read as follows:

(ii) ASSUMED LIABILITIES.—For purposes of clause (i), the term "assumed liabilities" means the aggregate of—

(I) any liability of the common trust fund assumed by any regulated investment company in connection with the transfer referred to in paragraph (1)(A), and

(II) any liability to which property so transferred is subject.

• 1996, Small Business Job Protection Act of 1996 (P.L. 104-188)

P.L. 104-188, §1805(a):

Amended Code Sec. 584 by redesignating subsection (h) as subsection (i) and by inserting after subsection (g) a new subsection (h). **Effective** for transfers after 12-31-95.

[Sec. 584(i)]

(i) TAXABLE YEAR OF COMMON TRUST FUND.—

For purposes of this subtitle, the taxable year of any common trust fund shall be the calendar year.

Amendments

• 1996, Small Business Job Protection Act of 1996 (P.L. 104-188)

P.L. 104-188, §1805(a):

Amended Code Sec. 584 by redesignating subsection (h) as subsection (i). **Effective** for transfers after 12-31-95.

• 1988, Technical and Miscellaneous Revenue Act of 1988 (P.L. 100-647)

P.L. 100-647, §1008(e)(5)(A):

Amended Code Sec. 584 by adding at the end thereof new subsection (h). For **effective** date, see Act Sec. 1008(e)(5)(B), below.

P.L. 100-647, §1008(e)(5)(B), provides:

(B) The amendment made by subparagraph (A) shall apply only to taxable years beginning after December 31, 1987. For purposes of section 806(e)(2) of the Reform Act—

(i) a participant in a common trust fund shall be treated in the same manner as a partner, and

(ii) subparagraph (C) thereof shall be applied by substituting "December 31, 1987" for "December 31, 1986," and as if it did not contain the election to include all income in the short taxable year.

[Sec. 585]

SEC. 585. RESERVES FOR LOSSES ON LOANS OF BANKS.

[Sec. 585(a)]

(a) RESERVE FOR BAD DEBTS.—

(1) IN GENERAL.—Except as provided in subsection (c), a bank shall be allowed a deduction for a reasonable addition to a reserve for bad debts. Such deduction shall be in lieu of any deduction under section 166(a).

(2) BANK.—For purposes of this section—

(A) IN GENERAL.—The term "bank" means any bank (as defined in section 581).

(B) BANKING BUSINESS OF UNITED STATES BRANCH OF FOREIGN CORPORATION.—The term "bank" also includes any corporation to which subparagraph (A) would apply except for the fact that it is a foreign corporation. In the case of any such foreign corporation, this section shall apply only with respect to loans outstanding the interest on which is effectively connected with the conduct of a banking business within the United States.

Amendments

• 1996, Small Business Job Protection Act of 1996 (P.L. 104-188)

P.L. 104-188, §1616(b)(6):

Amended Code Sec. 585(a)(2)(A) by striking "other than an organization to which section 595 applies" after "(as defined in section 581)". **Effective** for tax years beginning after 12-31-95.

[Sec. 585(b)]

(b) ADDITION TO RESERVES FOR BAD DEBTS.—

(1) GENERAL RULE.—For purposes of subsection (a), the reasonable addition to the reserve for bad debts of any financial institution to which this section applies shall be an amount determined by the taxpayer which shall not exceed the addition to the reserve for losses on loans determined under the experience method as provided in paragraph (2).

(2) EXPERIENCE METHOD.—The amount determined under this paragraph for a taxable year shall be the amount necessary to increase the balance of the reserve for losses on loans (at the close of the taxable year) to the greater of—

(A) the amount which bears the same ratio to loans outstanding at the close of the taxable year as (i) the total bad debts sustained during the taxable year and the 5 preceding taxable years (or, with the approval of the Secretary, a shorter period), adjusted for recoveries of bad debts during such period, bears to (ii) the sum of the loans outstanding at the close of such 6 or fewer taxable years, or

(B) the lower of—

(i) the balance of the reserve at the close of the base year, or

(ii) if the amount of loans outstanding at the close of the taxable year is less than the amount of loans outstanding at the close of the base year, the amount which bears the same ratio to loans outstanding at the close of the taxable year as the balance of the reserve at the close of the base year bears to the amount of loans outstanding at the close of the base year.

For purposes of this paragraph, the base year shall be the last taxable year before the most recent adoption of the experience method, except that for taxable years beginning after 1987 the base year shall be the last taxable year beginning before 1988.

(3) REGULATIONS; DEFINITION OF LOAN.—The Secretary shall define the term loan and prescribe such regulations as may be necessary to carry out the purposes of this section.

Amendments

• 1990, Omnibus Budget Reconciliation Act of 1990 (P.L. 101-508)

P.L. 101-508, § 11801(a)(26):

Repealed Code Sec. 585(b)(2). **Effective** 11-5-90. Prior to repeal, Code Sec. 585(b)(2) read as follows:

(2) PERCENTAGE METHOD.—The amount determined under this paragraph for a taxable year shall be the amount necessary to increase the balance of the reserve for losses on loans (at the close of the taxable year) to the allowable percentage of eligible loans outstanding at such time, except that—

(A) If the reserve for losses on loans at the close of the base year is less than the allowable percentage of eligible loans outstanding at such time, the amount determined under this paragraph with respect to the difference shall not exceed one-fifth of such difference.

(B) If the reserve for losses on loans at the close of the base year is not less than the allowable percentage of eligible loans outstanding at such time, the amount determined under this paragraph shall be the amount necessary to increase the balance of the reserve at the close of the taxable year to (i) the allowable percentage of eligible loans outstanding at such time, or (ii) the balance of the reserve at the close of the base year, whichever is greater, but if the amount of eligible loans outstanding at the close of the taxable year is less than the amount of such loans outstanding at the close of the base year, the amount determined under clause (ii) shall be the amount necessary to increase the balance of the reserve at the close of the taxable year to the amount which bears the same ratio to eligible loans outstanding at the close of the taxable year as the balance of the reserve at the close of the base year bears to the amount of eligible loans outstanding at the close of the base year.

For purposes of this paragraph, the term "allowable percentage" means 1.8 percent for taxable years beginning before 1976; 1.2 percent for taxable years beginning after 1975 but before 1982; 1.0 percent for taxable years beginning in 1982; and 0.6 percent for taxable years beginning after 1982. The amount determined under this paragraph shall not exceed 0.6 percent of eligible loans outstanding at the close of the taxable year or an amount sufficient to increase the reserve for losses on loans to 0.6 percent of eligible loans outstanding at the close of the taxable year, whichever is greater. For purposes of this paragraph, the term "base year" means: for taxable years beginning before 1976, the last taxable year beginning on or before July 11, 1969, for taxable years beginning after 1975 but before 1983, the last taxable year beginning before 1976, and for taxable years beginning after 1982, the last taxable year beginning before 1983; except that for purposes of subparagraph (A) such term means the last taxable year before the most recent adoption of the percentage method, if later.

P.L. 101-508, § 11801(c)(12)(C):

Amended Code Sec. 585(b)(1) by striking "shall not exceed" and all that follows down through the period at the end thereof and inserting "shall not exceed the addition to the reserve for losses on loans determined under the experience method as provided in paragraph (2)." **Effective** 11-5-90. Prior to amendment, Code Sec. 585(b)(1) read as follows:

(1) GENERAL RULE.—For purposes of subsection (a), the reasonable addition to the reserve for bad debts of any financial institution to which this section applies shall be an amount determined by the taxpayer which shall not exceed the greater of—

(A) for taxable years beginning before 1988 the addition to the reserve for losses on loans determined under the percentage method as provided in paragraph (2), or

(B) the addition to the reserve for losses on loans determined under the experience method as provided in paragraph (3).

P.L. 101-508, § 11801(c)(12)(D)-(E):

Amended Code Sec. 585(b) by redesignating paragraphs (3) and (4) as paragraphs (2) and (3), and amending paragraph (3) (as redesignated). **Effective** 11-5-90. Prior to redesignation and amendment, Code Sec. 585(b)(3) read as follows:

(3) REGULATIONS; DEFINITION OF ELIGIBLE LOAN, ETC.—The Secretary shall define the terms "loan" and "eligible loan" and prescribe such regulations as may be necessary to carry out the purposes of this section; except that the term "eligible loan" shall not include—

(A) a loan to a bank (as defined in section 581),

(B) a loan to a domestic branch of a foreign corporation to which subsection (a)(2) applies,

(C) a loan secured by a deposit (i) in the lending bank, or (ii) in an institution described in subparagraph (A) or (B) if the lending bank has control over withdrawal of such deposit,

(D) a loan to or guaranteed by the United States, a possession or instrumentality thereof, or a State or a political subdivision thereof,

(E) a loan evidenced by a security as defined in section 165(g)(2)(C),

(F) a loan of Federal funds, and

(G) commercial paper, including short-term promissory notes which may be purchased on the open market.

P.L. 101-508, § 11821(b), provides:

(b) SAVINGS PROVISION.—If—

(1) any provision amended or repealed by this part applied to—

(A) any transaction occurring before the date of the enactment of this Act,

(B) any property acquired before such date of enactment, or

(C) any item of income, loss, deduction, or credit taken into account before such date of enactment, and

(2) the treatment of such transaction, property, or item under such provision would (without regard to the amendments made by this part) affect liability for tax for periods ending after such date of enactment,

nothing in the amendments made by this part shall be construed to affect the treatment of such transaction, property, or item for purposes of determining liability for tax for periods ending after such date of enactment.

[Sec. 585(c)]

(c) SECTION NOT TO APPLY TO LARGE BANKS.—

(1) IN GENERAL.—In the case of a large bank, this section shall not apply (and no deduction shall be allowed under any other provision of this subtitle for any addition to a reserve for bad debts).

(2) LARGE BANKS.—For purposes of this subsection, a bank is a large bank if, for the taxable year (or for any preceding taxable year beginning after December 31, 1986)—

(A) the average adjusted bases of all assets of such bank exceeded $500,000,000, or

(B) such bank was a member of a parent-subsidiary controlled group and the average adjusted bases of all assets of such group exceeded $500,000,000.

(3) 4-YEAR SPREAD OF ADJUSTMENTS.—

(A) IN GENERAL.—Except as provided in paragraph (4), in the case of any bank which for its last taxable year before the disqualification year maintained a reserve for bad debts—

(i) the provisions of this subsection shall be treated as a change in the method of accounting of such bank for the disqualification year,

(ii) such change shall be treated as having been made with the consent of the Secretary, and

(iii) the net amount of adjustments required by section 481(a) to be taken into account by the taxpayer shall be taken into account in each of the 4 taxable years beginning with the disqualification year with—

(I) the amount taken into account for the 1st of such taxable years being the greater of 10 percent of such net amount or such higher percentage of such net amount as the taxpayer may elect, and

(II) the amount taken into account in each of the 3 succeeding taxable years being equal to the applicable fraction (determined in accordance with the following table for the taxable year involved) of the portion of such net amount not taken into account under subclause (I).

If the case of the—	*The applicable fraction is—*
1st succeeding year	2/9
2nd succeeding year	1/3
3rd succeeding year	4/9

(B) SUSPENSION OF RECAPTURE FOR TAXABLE YEAR FOR WHICH BANK IS FINANCIALLY TROUBLED.—

(i) IN GENERAL.—In the case of a bank which is a financially troubled bank for any taxable year—

(I) no adjustment shall be taken into account under subparagraph (A) for such taxable year, and

(II) such taxable year shall be disregarded in determining whether any other taxable year is a taxable year for which an adjustment is required to be taken into account under subparagraph (A) or the amount of such adjustment.

(ii) EXCEPTION FOR ELECTIVE RECAPTURE FOR 1ST YEAR.—Clause (i) shall not apply to the 1st taxable year referred to in subparagraph (A)(iii)(I) if the taxpayer elects a higher percentage in accordance with such subparagraph.

(iii) FINANCIALLY TROUBLED BANK.—For purposes of clause (i), the term "financially troubled bank" means any bank if, for the taxable year, the nonperforming loan percentage of such bank exceeds 75 percent.

(iv) NONPERFORMING LOAN PERCENTAGE.—For purposes of clause (iii), the term "nonperforming loan percentage" means the percentage determined by dividing—

(I) the sum of the outstanding balances of nonperforming loans of the bank as of the close of each quarter of the taxable year, by

(II) the sum of the amounts of equity of the bank as of the close of each such quarter.

In the case of a bank which is a member of a parent-subsidiary controlled group for the taxable year, the preceding sentence shall be applied with respect to such group.

(v) OTHER DEFINITIONS.—For purposes of this subparagraph—

(I) NONPERFORMING LOANS.—The term "nonperforming loan" means any loan which is considered to be nonperforming by the primary Federal regulatory agency with respect to the bank.

(II) EQUITY.—The term "equity" means the equity of the bank as determined for Federal regulatory purposes.

(C) COORDINATION WITH ESTIMATED TAX PAYMENTS.—For purposes of applying section 6655(e)(2)(A)(i) with respect to any installment, the determination under subparagraph (B) of whether an adjustment is required to be taken into account under subparagraph (A) shall be made as of the last day prescribed for payment of such installment.

(4) ELECTIVE CUT-OFF METHOD.—If a bank makes an election under this paragraph for the disqualification year—

(A) the provisions of this subsection shall not be treated as a change in the method of accounting of the taxpayer for purposes of section 481,

(B) the taxpayer shall continue to maintain its reserve for loans held by the bank as of the 1st day of the disqualification year and charge against such reserve any losses resulting from loans held by the bank as of such 1st day, and

(C) no deduction shall be allowed under this section (or any other provision of this subtitle) for any addition to such reserve for the disqualification year or any subsequent taxable year.

If the amount of the reserve referred to in subparagraph (B) as of the close of any taxable year exceeds the outstanding balance (as of such time) of the loans referred to in subparagraph (B), such excess shall be included in gross income for such taxable year.

(5) DEFINITIONS.—For purposes of this subsection—

(A) PARENT-SUBSIDIARY CONTROLLED GROUP.—The term "parent-subsidiary controlled group" means any controlled group of corporations described in section 1563(a)(1). In determining the average adjusted bases of assets held by such a group, interests held by one member of such group in another member of such group shall be disregarded.

(B) DISQUALIFICATION YEAR.—The term "disqualification year" means, with respect to any bank, the 1st taxable year beginning after December 31, 1986, for which such bank was a large bank if such bank maintained a reserve for bad debts for the preceding taxable year.

(C) ELECTION MADE BY EACH MEMBER.—In the case of a parent-subsidiary controlled group, any election under this section shall be made separately by each member of such group.

Amendments

• 1988, Technical and Miscellaneous Revenue Act of 1988 (P.L. 100-647)

P.L. 100-647, §1009(a)(2)(A):

Amended Code Sec. 585(c)(5) by adding at the end thereof new subparagraph (C). **Effective** as if included in the provision of P.L. 99-514 to which it relates.

P.L. 100-647, §1009(a)(2)(B):

Amended Code Sec. 585(c)(3)(A)(iii)(I) by striking out "or such greater amount as the taxpayer may designate" and inserting in lieu thereof "or such higher percentage of such net amount as the taxpayer may elect". **Effective** as if included in the provision of P.L. 99-514 to which it relates.

P.L. 100-647, §1009(a)(2)(C):

Amended Code Sec. 585(c)(3)(B)(ii) by striking out "designates an amount" and inserting in lieu thereof "elects a higher percentage". **Effective** as if included in the provision of P.L. 99-514 to which it relates.

P.L. 100-647, §1009(a)(3):

Amended Code Sec. 585(c)(4) by adding at the end thereof a new sentence. **Effective** as if included in the provision of P.L. 99-514 to which it relates.

• 1987, Revenue Act of 1987 (P.L. 100-203)

P.L. 100-203, §10301(b)(2):

Amended Code Sec. 585(c)(3)(C) by striking out "section 6655(d)(3)" and inserting in lieu thereof "section 6655(e)(2)(A)(i)". **Effective** for tax years beginning after 12-31-87.

• 1986, Tax Reform Act of 1986 (P.L. 99-514)

P.L. 99-514, §901(a)(1):

Amended Code Sec. 585(a). **Effective** for tax years beginning after 12-31-86. Prior to amendment, Code Sec. 585(a) read as follows:

(a) INSTITUTIONS TO WHICH SECTION APPLIES.—This section shall apply to the following financial institutions:

(1) any bank (as defined in section 581) other than an organization to which section 593 applies, and

(2) any corporation to which paragraph (1) would apply except for the fact that it is a foreign corporation, and in the case of any such foreign corporation this section shall apply only with respect to loans outstanding the interest on which is effectively connected with the conduct of a banking business within the United States.

P.L. 99-514, §901(a)(2):

Amended Code Sec. 585 by adding at the end thereof new subsection (c). **Effective** for tax years beginning after 12-31-86.

P.L. 99-514, §901(d)(1):

Amended Code Sec. 585(b)(1) by striking out "section 166(c)" and inserting in lieu thereof "subsection (a)". **Effective** for tax years beginning after 12-31-86.

• 1981, Economic Recovery Tax Act of 1981 (P.L. 97-34)

P.L. 97-34, §267(a)(1):

Amended the first sentence after subparagraph (B) of paragraph (2) of section 585(b) by striking out "but before 1982; and 0.6 percent for taxable years beginning after 1981" and inserting in lieu thereof "but before 1982; 1.0 percent for taxable years beginning in 1982; and 0.6 percent for taxable years beginning after 1982". **Effective** for tax years beginning after 1981.

P.L. 97-34, §267(a)(2):

Amended the last sentence of paragraph (2) of section 585(b) by striking out "but before 1982, the last taxable year beginning before 1976, and for taxable years beginning after 1981, the last taxable year beginning before 1982" and inserting in lieu thereof "but before 1983, the last taxable year beginning before 1976, and for taxable years beginning after 1982, the last taxable year beginning before 1983". **Effective** for tax years beginning after 1981.

• 1976, Tax Reform Act of 1976 (P.L. 94-455)

P.L. 94-455, §1906(b)(13)(A):

Amended 1954 Code by substituting "Secretary" for "Secretary or his delegate" each place it appeared. **Effective** 2-1-77.

• 1969, Tax Reform Act of 1969 (P.L. 91-172)

P.L. 91-172, §431(a):

Added Code Sec. 585. **Effective** for tax years beginning after 7-11-69.

[Sec. 586—Repealed]

Amendments

• **1986, Tax Reform Act of 1986 (P.L. 99-514)**

P.L. 99-514, §901(c):

Repealed Code Sec. 586. **Effective** for tax years beginning after 12-31-86. Prior to repeal, Code Sec. 586 read as follows:

SEC. 586. RESERVES FOR LOSSES ON LOANS OF SMALL BUSINESS INVESTMENT COMPANIES, ETC.

(a) INSTITUTIONS TO WHICH SECTION APPLIES.—This section shall apply to the following financial institutions:

(1) any small business investment company operating under the Small Business Investment Act of 1958, and

(2) any business development corporation.

For purposes of this section, the term "business development corporation" means a corporation which was created by or pursuant to an act of a State legislature for purposes of promoting, maintaining, and assisting the economy and industry within such State on a regional or statewide basis by making loans to be used in trades and businesses which would generally not be made by banks (as defined in section 581) within such region or State in the ordinary course of their business (except on the basis of a partial participation), and which is operated primarily for such purposes.

(b) ADDITION TO RESERVES FOR BAD DEBTS.—

(1) GENERAL RULE.—For purposes of section 166(c), except as provided in paragraph (2) the reasonable addition to the reserve for bad debts of any financial institution to which this section applies shall be an amount determined by the taxpayer which shall not exceed the amount necessary to increase the balance of the reserve for bad debts (at the close of the taxable year) to the greater of—

(A) the amount which bears the same ratio to loans outstanding at the close of the taxable year as (i) the total bad debts sustained during the taxable year and the 5 preceding taxable years (or, with the approval of the Secretary, a shorter period), adjusted for recoveries of bad debts during such period, bears to (ii) the sum of the loans outstanding at the close of such 6 or fewer taxable years, or

(B) the lower of—

(i) the balance of the reserve at the close of the base year, or

(ii) if the amount of loans outstanding at the close of the taxable year is less than the amount of loans outstanding at the close of the base year, the amount which bears the same ratio to loans outstanding at the close of the taxable year as the balance of the reserve at the close of the base year bears to the amount of loans outstanding at the close of the base year.

For purposes of this subparagraph, the term "base year" means the last taxable year beginning on or before July 11, 1969.

(2) NEW FINANCIAL INSTITUTIONS.—In the case of any taxable year beginning not more than 10 years after the day before the first day on which a financial institution (or any predecessor) was authorized to do business as a financial institution described in subsection (a), the reasonable addition to the reserve for bad debts of such financial institution shall not exceed the larger of the amount determined under paragraph (1) or the amount necessary to increase the balance of the reserve for bad debts at the close of the taxable year to the amount which bears the same ratio (as determined by the Secretary) to loans outstanding at the close of the taxable year as (i) the total bad debts sustained by all institutions described in the applicable paragraph of subsection (a) during the 6 preceding taxable years (adjusted for recoveries of bad debts during such period), bears to (ii) the sum of the loans by all such institutions outstanding at the close of such taxable years.

• **1976, Tax Reform Act of 1976 (P.L. 94-455)**

P.L. 94-455, §1906(b)(13)(A):

Amended 1954 Code by substituting "Secretary" for "Secretary or his delegate" each place it appeared. **Effective** 2-1-77.

• **1969, Tax Reform Act of 1969 (P.L. 91-172)**

P.L. 91-172, §431(a):

Added Code Sec. 586. **Effective** for tax years beginning after 7-11-69.

PART II—MUTUAL SAVINGS BANKS, ETC.

[Sec. 591]

SEC. 591. DEDUCTION FOR DIVIDENDS PAID ON DEPOSITS.

[Sec. 591(a)]

(a) IN GENERAL.—In the case of mutual savings banks, cooperative banks, domestic building and loan associations, and other savings institutions chartered and supervised as savings and loan or similar associations under Federal or State law, there shall be allowed as deductions in computing taxable income amounts paid to, or credited to the accounts of, depositors or holders of accounts as dividends or interest on their deposits or withdrawable accounts, if such amounts paid or credited are withdrawable on demand subject only to customary notice of intention to withdraw.

Amendments

• **1981, Economic Recovery Tax Act of 1981 (P.L. 97-34)**

P.L. 97-34, §245(a)(1):

Amended Code Sec. 591 by inserting "(a) IN GENERAL.—" before "In". **Effective** with respect to tax years ending after 8-13-81.

• **1962, Revenue Act of 1962 (P.L. 87-834)**

P.L. 87-834, §6:

Amended Code Sec. 591 by striking out "and domestic building and loan associations" and inserting in lieu thereof "domestic building and loan associations, and other savings institutions chartered and supervised as savings and loan or similar associations under Federal or State law"; and by inserting after "dividends" the words "or interest". **Effective** 10-17-62.

[Sec. 591(b)]

(b) MUTUAL SAVINGS BANK TO INCLUDE CERTAIN BANKS WITH CAPITAL STOCK.—For purposes of this part, the term "mutual savings bank" includes any bank—

(1) which has capital stock represented by shares, and

(2) which is subject to, and operates under, Federal or State laws relating to mutual savings bank.

Amendments

• 1981, Economic Recovery Tax Act of 1981 (P.L. 97-34)

P.L. 97-34, §245(a)(2):

Amended Code Sec. 591 by adding at the end thereof new subsection (b). **Effective** with respect to tax years ending after 8-13-81.

[Sec. 593]

SEC. 593. RESERVES FOR LOSSES ON LOANS.

[Sec. 593(a)]

(a) RESERVE FOR BAD DEBTS.—

(1) IN GENERAL.—Except as provided in paragraph (2), in the case of—

(A) any domestic building and loan association,

(B) any mutual savings bank, or

(C) any cooperative bank without capital stock organized and operated for mutual purposes and without profit,

there shall be allowed a deduction for a reasonable addition to a reserve for bad debts. Such deduction shall be in lieu of any deduction under section 166(a).

(2) ORGANIZATION MUST MEET 60-PERCENT ASSET TEST OF SECTION 7701(a)(19).—This section shall apply to an association or bank referred to in paragraph (1) only if it meets the requirements of section 7701(a)(19)(C).

Amendments

• 1986, Tax Reform Act of 1986 (P.L. 99-514)

P.L. 99-514, §901(b)(1):

Amended Code Sec. 593(a). **Effective** for tax years beginning after 12-31-86. Prior to amendment, Code Sec. 593(a) read as follows:

(a) ORGANIZATIONS TO WHICH SECTION APPLIES.—This section shall apply to any mutual savings bank, domestic building and loan association, or cooperative bank without capital stock organized and operated for mutual purposes and without profit.

• 1981, Economic Recovery Tax Act of 1981 (P.L. 97-34)

P.L. 97-34, §245(c)(1):

Amended Code Sec. 593(a) by striking out "not having capital stock represented by shares". **Effective** with respect to tax years ending after 8-13-81.

[Sec. 593(b)]

(b) ADDITION TO RESERVES FOR BAD DEBTS.—

(1) IN GENERAL.—For purposes of subsection (a), the reasonable addition for the taxable year to the reserve for bad debts of any taxpayer described in subsection (a) shall be an amount equal to the sum of—

(A) the amount determined to be a reasonable addition to the reserve for losses on nonqualifying loans, computed in the same manner as is provided with respect to additions to the reserves for losses on loans of banks under section 585(b)(2), plus

(B) the amount determined by the taxpayer to be a reasonable addition to the reserve for losses on qualifying real property loans, but such amount shall not exceed the amount determined under paragraph (2) or (3), whichever is the larger, but the amount determined under this subparagraph shall in no case be greater than the larger of—

(i) the amount determined under paragraph (3), or

(ii) the amount which, when added to the amount determined under subparagraph (A), equals the amount by which 12 percent of the total deposits or withdrawable accounts of depositors of the taxpayer at the close of such year exceeds the sum of its surplus, undivided profits, and reserves at the beginning of such year (taking into account any portion thereof attributable to the period before the first taxable year beginning after December 31, 1951).

(2) PERCENTAGE OF TAXABLE INCOME METHOD.—

(A) IN GENERAL.—Subject to subparagraphs (B) and (C), the amount determined under this paragraph for the taxable year shall be an amount equal to 8 percent of the taxable income for such year.

(B) REDUCTION FOR AMOUNTS REFERRED TO IN PARAGRAPH (1)(A).—The amount determined under subparagraph (A) shall be reduced (but not below 0) by the amount determined under paragraph (1)(A).

(C) OVERALL LIMITATION ON PARAGRAPH.—The amount determined under this paragraph shall not exceed the amount necessary to increase the balance at the close of the taxable year of the reserve for losses on qualifying real property loans to 6 percent of such loans outstanding at such time.

(D) COMPUTATION OF TAXABLE INCOME.—For purposes of this paragraph, taxable income shall be computed—

(i) by excluding from gross income any amount included therein by reason of subsection (e),

(ii) without regard to any deduction allowable for any addition to the reserve for bad debts,

(iii) by excluding from gross income an amount equal to the net gain for the taxable year arising from the sale or exchange of stock of a corporation or of obligations the interest on which is excludable from gross income under section 103,

(iv) by excluding from gross income dividends with respect to which a deduction is allowable by part VIII of subchapter B, reduced by an amount equal to 8 percent of the dividends received deduction (determined without regard to section 596) for the taxable year, and

(v) if there is a capital gain rate differential (as defined in section 904(b)(3)(D)) for the taxable year, by excluding from gross income the rate differential portion (within the meaning of section 904(b)(3)(E)) of the lesser of—

(I) the net long-term capital gain for the taxable year, or

(II) the net long-term capital gain for the taxable year from the sale or exchange of property other than property described in clause (iii).

(3) EXPERIENCE METHOD.—The amount determined under this paragraph for the taxable year shall be computed in the same manner as is provided with respect to additions to the reserves for losses on loans of banks under section 585(b)(2).

Amendments

• 1990, Omnibus Budget Reconciliation Act of 1990 (P.L. 101-508)

P.L. 101-508, §11801(c)(12)(F), as amended by P.L. 104-188, §1704(t)(51):

Amended Code Sec. 593(b)(1)(A) and (3) by striking "section 585(b)(3)" and inserting "section 585(b)(2)". **Effective** 11-5-90.

P.L. 101-508, §11821(b), provides:

(b) SAVINGS PROVISION.—If—

(1) any provision amended or repealed by this part applied to—

(A) any transaction occurring before the date of the enactment of this Act,

(B) any property acquired before such date of enactment, or

(C) any item of income, loss, deduction, or credit taken into account before such date of enactment, and

(2) the treatment of such transaction, property, or item under such provision would (without regard to the amendments made by this part) affect liability for tax for periods ending after such date of enactment,

nothing in the amendments made by this part shall be construed to affect the treatment of such transaction, property, or item for purposes of determining liability for tax for periods ending after such date of enactment.

• 1988, Technical and Miscellaneous Revenue Act of 1988 (P.L. 100-647)

P.L. 100-647, §1003(c)(3):

Amended Code Sec. 593(b)(2)(D) by striking out "and" at the end of clause (iii), by striking out the period at the end of clause (iv) and inserting in lieu thereof ", and", and by adding at the end thereof new clause (v). **Effective** as if included in the provision of P.L. 99-514 to which it relates.

• 1986, Tax Reform Act of 1986 (P.L. 99-514)

P.L. 99-514, §311(b)(2):

Amended Code Sec. 593(b)(2)(E), as in effect before the amendments made by title IX, by adding "and" at the end of clause (iii), by striking out clause (iv), and by redesignating clause (v) as clause (iv). **Effective** for tax years beginning after 12-31-86. However, see Act Sec. 311(d)(2) under the amendment notes to Code Sec. 631. Prior to amendment, clause (iv) read as follows:

(iv) by excluding from gross income an amount equal to the lesser of 18/46 of the net long-term capital gain for the taxable year of 18/46 of the net long-term capital gain for the taxable year from the sale or exchange of property other than property described in clause (iii), and

P.L. 99-514, §901(b)(2)(A)-(B):

Amended code Sec. 593(b)(2) by striking out subparagraphs (A), (B), and (C) and inserting new subparagraphs (A) and (B) in lieu thereof, and by redesignating subparagraphs (D) and (E) as subparagraphs (C) and (D), respectively. **Effective** for tax years beginning after 12-31-86. Prior to amendment, subparagraphs (A), (B), and (C) read as follows:

(A) IN GENERAL.—Subject to subparagraphs (B), (C), and (D), the amount determined under this paragraph for the taxable year shall be an amount equal to the applicable percentage of the taxable income for such year (determined under the following table):

For a taxable year beginning in—	*The applicable percentage under this paragraph shall be—*
1976	43 percent.
1977	42 percent.
1978	41 percent.
1979 or thereafter	40 percent.

(B) REDUCTION OF APPLICABLE PERCENTAGE IN CERTAIN CASES.—If, for the taxable year, the percentage of the assets of a taxpayer described in subsection (a), which are assets described in section 7701(a)(19)(C), is less than—

(i) 82 percent of the total assets in the case of a taxpayer other than a mutual savings bank which is not described in section 591(b), the applicable percentage for such year provided by subparagraph (A) shall be reduced by 3/4 of 1 percentage point for each 1 percentage point of such difference, or

(ii) 72 percent of the total assets in the case of a mutual savings bank which is not described in section 591(b), the applicable percentage for such year provided by subparagraph (A) shall be reduced by 1 1/2 percentage points for each 1 percentage point of such difference.

If, for the taxable year, the percentage of the assets of such taxpayer which are assets described in section 7701(a)(19)(C) is less than 60 percent (50 percent for a taxable year beginning before 1973 in the case of a mutual savings bank which is not described in section 591(b)), this paragraph shall not apply.

(C) REDUCTION FOR AMOUNTS REFERRED TO IN PARAGRAPH (1)(A)—The amount determined under subparagraph (A) shall be reduced by that portion of the amount referred to in paragraph (1)(A) for the taxable year (not in excess of 100 percent) which bears the same ratio to such amount as (i) 18 percent (28 percent in the case of mutual savings banks which are not described in section 591(b)) bears to (ii) the percentage of the assets of the taxpayer for such year which are not assets described in section 7701(a)(19(C).

P.L. 99-514, §901(b)(3):

Amended Code Sec. 593(b) by striking out paragraphs (3) and (5) and by redesignating paragraph (4) as paragraph (3). **Effective** for tax years beginning after 12-31-86. Prior to amendment, paragraphs (3) and (5) read as follows:

(3) PERCENTAGE METHOD.—The amount determined under this paragraph to be a reasonable addition to the reserve for losses on qualifying real property loans shall be computed in the same manner as is provided with respect to additions to the reserves for losses on loans of banks under section 585(b)(2), reduced by the amount referred to in paragraph (1)(A) for the taxable year.

(5) DETERMINATION OF RESERVE FOR PERCENTAGE METHOD.—For purposes of paragraph (3), the amount deemed to be the balance of the reserve for losses on loans at the beginning of the taxable year shall be the total of the balances at such time of the reserve for losses on nonqualifying loans, the reserve for losses on qualifying real property loans, and the supplemental reserve for the losses on loans.

P.L. 99-514, §901(d)(2)(A):

Amended Code Sec. 593(b)(1) by striking out "section 166(c)" and inserting in lieu thereof "subsection (a)". **Effective** for tax years beginning after 12-31-86.

P.L. 99-514, §901(d)(2)(B)(i)-(ii):

Amended Code Sec. 593(b)(1)(B) by striking out "paragraph (2), (3), or (4), whichever amount is largest" and inserting in lieu thereof "paragraph (2) or (3), whichever is the larger", and by striking out "paragraph (4)" in clause (i) and inserting in lieu thereof "paragraph (3)". **Effective** for tax years beginning after 12-31-86.

P.L. 99-514, §901(d)(2)(B)[C]:

Amended Code Sec. 593(b)(2)(D) (as redesignated by subsection (b)(2)) by striking out "the applicable percentage (determined under subparagraph (A) and (B))" and inserting in lieu thereof "8 percent". **Effective** for tax years beginning after 12-31-86.

• 1981, Economic Recovery Tax Act of 1981 (P.L. 97-34)

P.L. 97-34, §245(b)(1):

Amended Code Sec. 593(b)(2)(B) by inserting "which is not described in section 591(b)" after "mutual savings bank" each place it appeared. **Effective** with respect to tax years ending after 8-13-81.

P.L. 97-34, §245(b)(2):

Amended Code Sec. 593(b)(2)(C) by inserting "which are not described in section 591(b)" after "mutual savings banks". **Effective** with respect to tax years ending after 8-13-81.

• 1980, Technical Corrections Act of 1979 (P.L. 96-222)

P.L. 96-222, §104(a)(3)(C):

Amended Code Sec. 593(b)(2)(E)(iv) by changing "3/8" each place it appears to "18/46".

• 1976, Tax Reform Act of 1976 (P.L. 94-455)

P.L. 94-455, §1901(a)(84)(A):

Amended Code Sec. 593(b)(2)(A). **Effective** for tax years beginning after 12-31-76. Prior to amendment, Sec. 593(b)(2)(A) read as follows:

(A) IN GENERAL.—Subject to subparagraphs (B), (C), and (D), the amount determined under this paragraph for the taxable year shall be an amount equal to the applicable percentage of the taxable income for such year (determined under the following table):

For a taxable year beginning in—	*The applicable percentage under this paragraph shall be—*
1969	60 percent
1970	57 percent
1971	54 percent
1972	51 percent
1973	49 percent
1974	47 percent
1975	45 percent
1976	43 percent
1977	42 percent
1978	41 percent
1979 or thereafter	40 percent

P.L. 94-455, §1901(a)(84)(D):

Substituted "subsection (e)" for "subsection (f)" in Code Sec. 593(b)(2)(E)(i). **Effective** for tax years beginning after 12-31-76.

• 1969, Tax Reform Act of 1969 (P.L. 91-172)

P.L. 91-172, §432(a):

Amended Code Secs. 593(b)(1)(A), 593(b)(2), 593(b)(3), 593(b)(4) and 593(b)(5). **Effective** for tax years beginning after 7-11-69. Prior to amendment Code Secs. 593(b)(1)(A), 593(b)(2), 593(b)(3), 593(b)(4) and 593(b)(5) read as follows:

(b) Addition to Reserves for Bad Debts.—

(1) In General.—* * *

(A) the amount determined under section 166(c) to be a reasonable addition to the reserve for losses on nonqualifying loans, plus

* * *

(2) Percentage of taxable income method.—The amount determined under this paragraph for the taxable year shall be the excess of—

(A) an amount equal to 60 percent of the taxable income for such year, over

(B) the amount referred to in paragraph (1)(A) for such year,

but the amount determined under this paragraph shall not exceed the amount necessary to increase the balance (as of the close of the taxable year) of the reserve for losses on qualifying real property loans to 6 percent of such loans outstanding at such time. For purposes of this paragraph, taxable income shall be computed (i) by excluding from gross income any amount included therein by reason of subsection (f), and (ii) without regard to any deduction allowable for any addition to the reserve for bad debts.

(3) Percentage of real property loans method.—The amount determined under this paragraph for the taxable year shall be an amount equal to the amount necessary to increase balance (as of the close of the taxable year) of the reserve for losses on qualifying real property loans to an amount equal to—

(A) 3 percent of such loans outstanding at such time, plus

(B) in the case of a taxpayer which is a new company and which does not have capital stock with respect to which distributions of property (as defined in section 317(a)) are not allowable as a deduction under section 591, an amount equal to—

(i) 2 percent of so much of the amount of such loans outstanding at such time as does not exceed $4,000,000, reduced (but not below zero) by

(ii) the amount, if any, of the balance (as of the close of such taxable year) of the taxpayer's supplemental reserve for losses on loans.

For purposes of subparagraph (B), a taxpayer is a new company for any taxable year only if such taxable year begins not more than 10 years after the first day on which it (or any predecessor) was authorized to do business as an organization described in subsection (a).

(4) Experience method.—The amount determined under this paragraph for the taxable year shall be an amount equal to the amount determined under section 166 (c) (without regard to this subsection) to be a reasonable addition to the reserve for losses on qualifying real property loans.

(5) Limitation in case of certain domestic building and loan associations.—If the percentage of the assets of a domestic building and loan association which are not assets described in section 7701(a)(19)(D)(ii) exceeds 36 percent for the taxable year (as determined for purposes of section 7701(a)(19) for such year), the amount determined under paragraph (2), and the amount determined under paragraph (3), shall in each case be the amount (determined without regard to this paragraph but with regard to the limits contained in paragraphs (2), (3), and (1)(B)) reduced by the amount determined under the following table:

If the percentage exceeds—	but does not exceed—	the reduction shall be the following proportion of the amount so determined without regard to this paragraph—
36 percent	37 percent	1/12
37 percent	38 percent	1/6
38 percent	39 percent	1/4
39 percent	40 percent	1/3
40 percent	41 percent	5/12

[Sec. 593(c)]

(c) TREATMENT OF RESERVES FOR BAD DEBTS.—

(1) ESTABLISHMENT OF RESERVES.—Each taxpayer described in subsection (a) which uses the reserve method of accounting for bad debts shall establish and maintain a reserve for losses on qualifying real property loans, a reserve for losses on nonqualifying loans, and a supplemental reserve for losses on loans. For purposes of this title, such reserves shall be treated as reserves for bad debts, but no deduction shall be allowed for any addition to the supplemental reserve for losses on loans.

(2) CERTAIN PRE-1963 RESERVES.—Notwithstanding the second sentence of paragraph (1), any amount allocated pursuant to paragraph (5) (as in effect immediately before the enactment of the Tax Reform Act of 1976) during a taxable year beginning before January 1, 1977, to the reserve for losses on qualifying real property loans out of the surplus, undivided profits, and bad debt reserves (determined as of December 31, 1962) attributable to the period before the first taxable year beginning after December 31, 1951, shall not be treated as a reserve for bad debts for any purpose other than determining the amount referred to in subsection (b)(1)(B), and for such purpose such amount shall be treated as remaining in such reserve.

(3) CHARGING OF BAD DEBTS TO RESERVES.—Any debt becoming worthless or partially worthless in respect of a qualifying real property loan shall be charged to the reserve for losses on such loans, and any debt becoming worthless or partially worthless in respect of a nonqualifying loan shall be charged to the reserve for losses on nonqualifying loans; except that any such debt may, at the election of the taxpayer, be charged in whole or in part to the supplemental reserve for losses on loans.

Amendments

• 1976, Tax Reform Act of 1976 (P.L. 94-455)

P.L. 94-455, §1901(a)(84)(B):

Amended Code Sec. 593(c) by striking out paragraphs (2), (3), (4), and (5), by redesignating paragraph (6) as paragraph (3), and by adding paragraph (2). **Effective** for tax years beginning after 12-31-76. Prior to amendment, paragraphs (2), (3), (4), and (5) of Code Sec. 593(c) read as follows:

(2) ALLOCATION OF PRE-1963 RESERVES.—For purposes of this section, the pre-1963 reserves shall, as of the close of December 31, 1962, be allocated to, and constitute the opening balance of—

(A) the reserve for losses on nonqualifying loans,

(B) the reserve for losses on qualifying real property loans, and

(C) the supplemental reserve for losses on loans.

(3) METHOD OF ALLOCATION.—The allocation provided by paragraph (2) shall be made—

(A) first, to the reserve described in paragraph (2)(A), to the extent such reserve is not increased above the amount which would be a reasonable addition under section 166(c) for a period in which the nonqualifying loans increased from zero to the amount thereof outstanding at the close of December 31, 1962;

(B) second, to the reserve described in paragraph (2)(B), to the extent such reserve is not increased above the amount which would be determined under paragraph (3)(A) or (4) of subsection (b) (whichever such amount is the larger) for a period in which the qualifying real property loans increased from zero to the amount thereof outstanding at the close of December 31, 1962; and

(C) then to the supplemental reserve for losses on loans.

(4) PRE-1963 RESERVES DEFINED.—For purposes of this subsection, the term "pre-1963 reserves" means the net amount, determined as of the close of December 31, 1962 (after applying subsection (d)(1)), accumulated in the reserve for bad debts pursuant to section 166(c) (or the corresponding provisions of prior revenue laws) for taxable years beginning after December 31, 1951.

(5) CERTAIN PRE-1952 SURPLUS.—If after the application of paragraph (3), the opening balance of the reserve described in paragraph (3)(B) is less than the amount described in paragraph (3)(B), then, for purposes of this subsection, the term "pre-1963 reserves" includes so much of the surplus, undivided profits, and bad debt reserves (determined as of December 31, 1962) attributable to the period before the first taxable year beginning after December 31, 1951, as does not exceed the amount by which such opening balance is less than the amount described in paragraph (3)(B). For purposes of the preceding sentence, the surplus, undivided profits, and bad debt reserves attributable to the period before the first taxable year beginning after December 31, 1951, shall be reduced by the amount thereof which is attributable to interest which would have been excludable from gross income under section 22(b)(4) of the Internal Revenue Code of 1939 (relating to interest on governmental obligations) or the corresponding provisions of prior laws. Notwithstanding the second sentence of paragraph (1), any amount which, by reason of the application of the first sentence of this paragraph, is allocated to the reserve described in paragraph (2)(B) shall not be treated as a reserve for bad debts for any purpose other than determining the amount referred to in subsection (b)(1)(B), and for such purpose such amount shall be treated as remaining in such reserve.

[Sec. 593(d)]

(d) LOANS DEFINED.—For purposes of this section—

(1) QUALIFYING REAL PROPERTY LOANS.—The term "qualifying real property loan" means any loan secured by an interest in improved real property or secured by an interest in real property which is to be improved out of the proceeds of the loan, but such term does not include—

(A) any loan evidenced by a security (as defined in section 165(g)(2)(C));

(B) any loan, whether or not evidenced by a security (as defined in section 165(g)(2)(C)), the primary obligor on which is—

(i) a government or political subdivision or instrumentality thereof;

(ii) a bank (as defined in section 581); or

(iii) another member of the same affiliated group;

(C) any loan, to the extent secured by a deposit in or share of the taxpayer; or

(D) any loan which, within a 60-day period beginning in one taxable year of the creditor and ending in its next taxable year, is made or acquired and then repaid or disposed of, unless the transactions by which such loan was made or acquired and then repaid or disposed of are established to be for bona fide business purposes.

For purposes of subparagraph (B)(iii), the term "affiliated group" has the meaning assigned to such term by section 1504(a); except that (i) the phrase "more than 50 percent" shall be substituted for the phrase "at least 80 percent" each place it appears in section 1504(a), and (ii) all corporations shall be treated as includible corporations (without any exclusion under section 1504(b)).

(2) NONQUALIFYING LOANS.—The term "nonqualifying loan" means any loan which is not a qualifying real property loan.

(3) LOAN.—The term "loan" means debt, as the term "debt" is used in section 166.

(4) TREATMENT OF INTERESTS IN REMIC'S.—A regular or residual interest in a REMIC shall be treated as a qualifying real property loan; except that, if less than 95 percent of the assets of such REMIC are qualifying real property loans (determined as if the taxpayer held the assets of the REMIC), such interest shall be so treated only if the proportion which the assets of such REMIC consist of such loans. For purposes of determining whether any interest in a REMIC qualifies under the preceding sentence, any interest in another REMIC held by such REMIC shall be treated as a qualifying real property loan under principles similar to the principles of the preceding sentence, except that if such REMIC's are part of a tiered structure, they shall be treated as 1 REMIC for purposes of this paragraph.

Amendments

• 1988, Technical and Miscellaneous Revenue Act of 1988 (P.L. 100-647)

P.L. 100-647, §1006(t)(25)(B):

Amended Code Sec. 593(d)(4) by adding at the end thereof a new sentence. **Effective** as if included in the provision of P.L. 99-514 to which it relates.

• 1986, Tax Reform Act of 1986 (P.L. 99-514)

P.L. 99-514, §671(b)(2):

Amended Code Sec. 593(d) by adding at the end thereof new paragraph (4). **Effective** for tax years beginning after 12-31-86.

• 1976, Tax Reform Act of 1976 (P.L. 94-455)

P.L. 94-455, §1901(a)(84)(C):

Repealed Code Sec. 593(d). **Effective** with respect to tax years beginning after 12-31-76. Prior to repeal, Code Sec. 593(d) read as follows:

(d) TAXABLE YEARS BEGINNING IN 1962 AND ENDING IN 1963.—In the case of a taxable year beginning before January 1, 1963, and ending after December 31, 1962, of a taxpayer described in subsection (a) which uses the reserve method of accounting for bad debts, the taxable income shall be the sum of—

(1) that portion of the taxable income allocable to the part of the taxable year occurring before January 1, 1963, reduced by the amount of the deduction for an addition to a reserve for bad debts which would be allowable under section 166(c) (without regard to the amendments made by section 6 of the Revenue Act of 1962) if such part year constituted a taxable year, plus

(2) that portion of the taxable income allocable to the part of the taxable year occurring after December 31, 1962, reduced by the amount of the deduction for an addition to a reserve for bad debts which would be allowed under section 166(c) (taking into account the amendments made by section 6 of the Revenue Act of 1962) if such part year constituted a taxable year.

For purposes of the preceding sentence, the taxable income shall be determined without regard to any deduction under section 166(c), and the portion thereof allocable to each part year shall be determined on the basis of the ratio which the number of days in such part year bears to the number of days in the entire taxable year.

Redesignated former Code Sec. 593(e) as Sec. 593(d). Effective for taxable years beginning after December 31, 1976.

[Sec. 593(e)]

(e) DISTRIBUTIONS TO SHAREHOLDERS.—

(1) IN GENERAL.—For purposes of this chapter, any distribution of property (as defined in section 317(a)) by a taxpayer having a balance described in subsection (g)(2)(A)(ii) to a shareholder with respect to its stock, if such distribution is not allowable as a deduction under section 591, shall be treated as made—

(A) first out of its earnings and profits accumulated in taxable years beginning after December 31, 1951, (and, in the case of an S corporation, the accumulated adjustments account, as defined in section 1368(e)(1)) to the extent thereof,

(B) then out of the balance taken into account under subsection (g)(2)(A)(ii) (properly adjusted for amounts charged against such reserves for taxable years beginning after December 31, 1987),

(C) then out of the supplemental reserve for losses on loans, to the extent thereof,

(D) then out of such other accounts as may be proper.

This paragraph shall apply in the case of any distribution in redemption of stock or in partial or complete liquidation of a taxpayer having a balance described in subsection (g)(2)(A)(ii), except that any such distribution shall be treated as made first out of the amount referred to in subparagraph (B), second out of the amount referred to in subparagraph (C), third out of the amount referred to in subparagraph (A), and then out of such other accounts as may be proper. This paragraph shall not apply to any transaction to which section 381 applies, or to any distribution to the Federal Savings and Loan Insurance Corporation (or any successor thereof) or the Federal Deposit Insurance Corporation in redemption of an interest in a taxpayer having a balance described in subsection (g)(2)(A)(ii), if such interest was originally received by any such entity in exchange for assistance provided under a provision of law referred to in section 597(c). This paragraph shall not apply to any distribution of all of the stock of a bank (as defined in section 581) to another corporation if, immediately after the distribution, such bank and such other corporation are members of the same affiliated group (as defined in section 1504) and the provisions of section 5(e) of the Federal Deposit Insurance Act (as in effect on December 31, 1995) or similar provisions are in effect.

(2) AMOUNTS CHARGED TO RESERVE ACCOUNTS AND INCLUDED IN GROSS INCOME.—If any distribution is treated under paragraph (1) as having been made out of the reserves described in subparagraphs (B) and (C) of such paragraph, the amount charged against such reserve shall be the amount which, when reduced by the amount of tax imposed under this chapter and attributable to the inclusion of such amount in gross income, is equal to the amount of such distribution; and the amount so charged against such reserve shall be included in gross income of the taxpayer.

(3) SPECIAL RULES.—

(A) For purposes of paragraph (1)(B), additions to the reserve for losses on qualifying real property loans for the taxable year in which the distribution occurs shall be taken into account.

(B) For purposes of computing under this section the amount of a reasonable addition to the reserve for losses on qualifying real property loans for any taxable year, any amount charged during any year to such reserve pursuant to the provisions of paragraph (2) shall not be taken into account.

Amendments

• 1997, Taxpayer Relief Act of 1997 (P.L. 105-34)

P.L. 105-34, §1601(f)(5)(A):

Amended Code Sec. 593(e)(1)(A) by inserting "(and, in the case of an S corporation, the accumulated adjustments account, as defined in section 1368(e)(1))" after "1951,". **Effective** as if included in the provision of P.L. 104-188 to which it relates [**effective** for tax years beginning after 12-31-95.—CCH].

• 1996, Small Business Job Protection Act of 1996 (P.L. 104-188)

P.L. 104-188, §1616(b)(7)(A):

Amended the material preceding Code Sec. 593(e)(1)(A) by striking "by a domestic building and load association or an institution that is treated as a mutual savings bank under section 591(b)" and inserting "by a taxpayer having a balance described in subsection (g)(2)(A)(ii)". **Effective** for tax years beginning after 12-31-95.

P.L. 104-188, §1616(b)(7)(B):

Amended Code Sec. 593(e)(1)(B). For the **effective** date, see Act Sec. 1616(c)(2), below. Prior to amendment, Code Sec. 593(e)(1)(B) read as follows:

(B) then out of the reserve for losses on qualifying real property loans, to the extent additions to such reserve exceed the additions which would have been allowed under subsection (b)(3),

P.L. 104-188, §1616(c)(2), provides:

(2) SUBSECTION (b)(7)(B).—The amendments made by subsection (b)(7)(B) shall not apply to any distribution with respect to preferred stock if—

(A) such stock is outstanding at all times after October 31, 1995, and before the distribution, and

(B) such distribution is made before the date which is 1 year after the date of the enactment of this Act (or, in the case of stock which may be redeemed, if later, the date which is 30 days after the earliest date that such stock may be redeemed).

P.L. 104-188, §1616(b)(7)(C):

Amended the second sentence of Code Sec. 593(e)(1) by striking "the association or an institution that is treated as a mutual savings bank under section 591(b)" and inserting "a taxpayer having a balance described in subsection (g)(2)(A)(ii)". **Effective** for tax years beginning after 12-31-95.

P.L. 104-188, §1616(b)(7)(D):

Amended the third sentence of Code Sec. 593(e)(1) by striking "an association" and inserting "a taxpayer having a balance described in subsection (g)(2)(A)(ii)". **Effective** for tax years beginning after 12-31-95.

P.L. 104-188, §1616(b)(7)(E):

Amended Code Sec. 593(e)(1) by adding at the end a new sentence. **Effective** for tax years beginning after 12-31-95.

• 1989, Financial Institutions Reform, Recovery, and Enforcement Act of 1989 (P.L. 101-73)

P.L. 101-73, §1401(b)(3):

Amended the last sentence of Code Sec. 593(e)(1). **Effective** 8-9-89. Prior to amendment, the last sentence of Code Sec. 593(e)(1) read as follows:

This paragraph shall not apply to any transaction to which section 381 (relating to carryovers in certain corporate acquisitions) applies, or to any distribution to the Federal Savings and Loan Insurance Corporation in redemption of an interest in an association, if such interest was originally received by the Federal Savings and Loan Insurance Corporation in exchange for financial assistance pursuant to section 406(f) of the National Housing Act (12 U.S.C. sec. 1729(f)).

• **1986, Tax Reform Act of 1986 (P.L. 99-514)**

P.L. 99-514, §901(d)(2)(C)[D]:

Amended Code Sec. 593(e)(1)(B) by striking out "subsection (b)(4)" and inserting in lieu thereof "subsection (b)(3)". **Effective** for tax years beginning after 12-31-86.

• **1981, Economic Recovery Tax Act of 1981 (P.L. 97-34)**

P.L. 97-34, §243:

Amended Code Sec. 593(e)(1) by striking out "applies." in the last sentence thereof and substituting therefor "applies, or to any distribution to the Federal Savings and Loan Insurance Corporation in redemption of an interest in an association, if such interest was originally received by the Federal Savings and Loan Insurance Corporation in exchange for financial assistance pursuant to section 406(f) of the National Housing Act (12 U.S.C. sec. 1729(f))." **Effective** for any distribution made on or after 1-1-81.

P.L. 97-34, §245(c)(2):

Amended Code Sec. 593(e)(1) by inserting "or an institution that is treated as a mutual savings bank under section 591(b)" after "association" each place it appeared. **Effective** with respect to tax years ending after 8-13-81.

• **1976, Tax Reform Act of 1976 (P.L. 94-455)**

P.L. 94-455, §1901(a)(84)(C):

Redesignated former Code Sec. 593(f) as Sec. 593(e). **Effective** for tax years beginning after 12-31-76.

• **1969, Tax Reform Act of 1969 (P.L. 91-172)**

P.L. 91-172, §432(b):

Amended Code Sec. 593(f)(1) by adding the last sentence thereof. **Effective** for tax years beginning after 7-11-69.

• **1962, Revenue Act of 1962 (P.L. 87-834)**

P.L. 87-834, §6:

Amended Code Sec. 593. Also amended the table of sections for part II of subchapter H of chapter 1 by striking out after Sec. 593, "Additions to reserve for bad debts." and inserting in lieu thereof "Reserves for losses on loans." **Effective** for tax years ending after 12-31-62, except that Code Sec. 593(f) is effective for distributions after 12-31-62, in tax years ending after such date. Prior to the amendment Sec. 593 read as follows:

SEC. 593. ADDITIONS TO RESERVE FOR BAD DEBTS.

In the case of a mutual savings bank not having capital stock represented by shares, a domestic building and loan association, and a cooperative bank without capital stock organized and operated for mutual purposes and without profit, the reasonable addition to a reserve for bad debts under section 166(c) shall be determined with due regard to the amount of the taxpayer's surplus or bad debt reserves existing at the close of December 31, 1951. In the case of a taxpayer described in the preceding sentence, the reasonable addition to a reserve for bad debts for any taxable year shall in no case be less than the amount determined by the taxpayer as the reasonable addition for such year; except that the amount determined by the taxpayer under this sentence shall not be greater than the lesser of—

(1) the amount of its taxable income for the taxable year, computed without regard to this section, or

(2) the amount by which 12 percent of the total deposits or withdrawable accounts of its depositors at the close of such year exceeds the sum of its surplus, undivided profits, and reserves at the beginning of the taxable year.

[Sec. 593(f)]

(f) TERMINATION OF RESERVE METHOD.—Subsections (a), (b), (c), and (d) shall not apply to any taxable year beginning after December 31, 1995.

Amendments

• **1996, Small Business Job Protection Act of 1996 (P.L. 104-188)**

P.L. 104-188, §1616(a):

Amended Code Sec. 593 by adding at the end a new subsection (f). **Effective** for tax years beginning after 12-31-95.

[Sec. 593(g)]

(g) 6-YEAR SPREAD OF ADJUSTMENTS.—

(1) IN GENERAL.—In the case of any taxpayer who is required by reason of subsection (f) to change its method of computing reserves for bad debts—

(A) such change shall be treated as a change in a method of accounting,

(B) such change shall be treated as initiated by the taxpayer and as having been made with the consent of the Secretary, and

(C) the net amount of the adjustments required to be taken into account by the taxpayer under section 481(a)—

(i) shall be determined by taking into account only applicable excess reserves, and

(ii) as so determined, shall be taken into account ratably over the 6-taxable year period beginning with the first taxable year beginning after December 31, 1995.

(2) APPLICABLE EXCESS RESERVES.—

(A) IN GENERAL.—For purposes of paragraph (1), the term "applicable excess reserves" means the excess (if any) of—

(i) the balance of the reserves described in subsection (c)(1) (other than the supplemental reserve) as of the close of the taxpayer's last taxable year beginning before January 1, 1996, over

(ii) the lesser of—

(I) the balance of such reserves as of the close of the taxpayer's last taxable year beginning before January 1, 1988, or

(II) the balance of the reserves described in subclause (I), reduced in the same manner as under section 585(b)(2)(B)(ii) on the basis of the taxable years described in clause (i) and this clause.

(B) SPECIAL RULE FOR THRIFTS WHICH BECOME SMALL BANKS.—In the case of a bank (as defined in section 581) which was not a large bank (as defined in section 585(c)(2)) for its first taxable year beginning after December 31, 1995—

(i) the balance taken into account under subparagraph (A)(ii) shall not be less than the amount which would be the balance of such reserves as of the close of its last taxable year beginning before such date if the additions to such reserves for all taxable years had been determined under section 585(b)(2)(A), and

(ii) the opening balance of the reserve for bad debts as of the beginning of such first taxable year shall be the balance taken into account under subparagraph (A)(ii) (determined after the application of clause (i) of this subparagraph).

The preceding sentence shall not apply for purposes of paragraphs (5) and (6) or subsection (e)(1).

(3) RECAPTURE OF PRE-1988 RESERVES WHERE TAXPAYER CEASES TO BE BANK.—If, during any taxable year beginning after December 31, 1995, a taxpayer to which paragraph (1) applied is not a bank (as defined in section 581), paragraph (1) shall apply to the reserves described in paragraph (2)(A)(ii) and the supplemental reserve; except that such reserves shall be taken into account ratably over the 6-taxable year period beginning with such taxable year.

(4) SUSPENSION OF RECAPTURE IF RESIDENTIAL LOAN REQUIREMENT MET.—

(A) IN GENERAL.—In the case of a bank which meets the residential loan requirement of subparagraph (B) for the first taxable year beginning after December 31, 1995, or for the following taxable year—

(i) no adjustment shall be taken into account under paragraph (1) for such taxable year, and

(ii) such taxable year shall be disregarded in determining—

(I) whether any other taxable year is a taxable year for which an adjustment is required to be taken into account under paragraph (1), and

(II) the amount of such adjustment.

(B) RESIDENTIAL LOAN REQUIREMENT.—A taxpayer meets the residential loan requirement of this subparagraph for any taxable year if the principal amount of the residential loans made by the taxpayer during such year is not less than the base amount for such year.

(C) RESIDENTIAL LOAN.—For purposes of this paragraph, the term "residential loan" means any loan described in clause (v) of section 7701(a)(19)(C) but only if such loan is incurred in acquiring, constructing, or improving the property described in such clause.

(D) BASE AMOUNT.—For purposes of subparagraph (B), the base amount is the average of the principal amounts of the residential loans made by the taxpayer during the 6 most recent taxable years beginning on or before December 31, 1995. At the election of the taxpayer who made such loans during each of such 6 taxable years, the preceding sentence shall be applied without regard to the taxable year in which such principal amount was the highest and the taxable year in such principal amount was the lowest. Such an election may be made only for the first taxable year beginning after such date, and, if made for such taxable year, shall apply to the succeeding taxable year unless revoked with the consent of the Secretary.

(E) CONTROLLED GROUPS.—In the case of a taxpayer which is a member of any controlled group of corporations described in section 1563(a)(1), subparagraph (B) shall be applied with respect to such group.

(5) CONTINUED APPLICATION OF FRESH START UNDER SECTION 585 TRANSITIONAL RULES.—In the case of a taxpayer to which paragraph (1) applied and which was not a large bank (as defined in section 585(c)(2)) for its first taxable year beginning after December 31, 1995:

(A) IN GENERAL.—For purposes of determining the net amount of adjustments referred to in section 585(c)(3)(A)(iii), there shall be taken into account only the excess (if any) of the reserve for bad debts as of the close of the last taxable year before the disqualification year over the balance taken into account by such taxpayer under paragraph (2)(A)(ii) of this subsection.

(B) TREATMENT UNDER ELECTIVE CUT-OFF METHOD.—For purposes of applying section 585(c)(4)—

(i) the balance of the reserve taken into account under subparagraph (B) thereof shall be reduced by the balance taken into account by such taxpayer under paragraph (2)(A)(ii) of this subsection, and

(ii) no amount shall be includible in gross income by reason of such reduction.

(6) SUSPENDED RESERVE INCLUDED AS SECTION 381(c) ITEMS.—The balance taken into account by a taxpayer under paragraph (2)(A)(ii) of this subsection and the supplemental reserve shall be treated as items described in section 381(c).

(7) CONVERSIONS TO CREDIT UNIONS.—In the case of a taxpayer to which paragraph (1) applied which becomes a credit union described in section 501(c) and exempt from taxation under section 501(a)—

(A) any amount required to be included in the gross income of the credit union by reason of this subsection shall be treated as derived from an unrelated trade or business (as defined in section 513), and

(B) for purposes of paragraph (3), the credit union shall not be treated as if it were a bank.

(8) REGULATIONS.—The Secretary shall prescribe such regulations as may be necessary to carry out this subsection and subsection (e), including regulations providing for the application of such subsections in the case of acquisitions, mergers, spin-offs, and other reorganizations.

Amendments

• 1996, Small Business Job Protection Act of 1996 (P.L. 104-188)

P.L. 104-188, §1616(a):

Amended Code Sec. 593 by adding at the end new subsection (g). **Effective** for tax years beginning after 12-31-95.

[Sec. 594]

SEC. 594. ALTERNATIVE TAX FOR MUTUAL SAVINGS BANKS CONDUCTING LIFE INSURANCE BUSINESS.

[Sec. 594(a)]

(a) ALTERNATIVE TAX.—In the case of a mutual savings bank not having capital stock represented by shares, authorized under State law to engage in the business of issuing life insurance contracts, and which conducts a life insurance business in a separate department the accounts of which are maintained separately from the other accounts of the mutual savings bank, there shall be imposed in lieu of the taxes imposed by section 11 or section 1201(a), a tax consisting of the sum of the partial taxes determined under paragraphs (1) and (2):

(1) A partial tax computed on the taxable income determined without regard to any items of gross income or deductions properly allocable to the business of the life insurance department, at the rates and in the manner as if this section had not been enacted; and

(2) A partial tax computed on the income of the life insurance department determined without regard to any items of gross income or deductions not properly allocable to such department, at the rates and in the manner provided in subchapter L (sec. 801 and following) with respect to life insurance companies.

Amendments

• 1956, Life Insurance Company Tax Act for 1955 (P.L. 429, 84th Cong.)

P.L. 429, 84th Cong., §5(3):

Amended Sec. 594(a)(2) by substituting for the words "the taxable income (as defined in section 803)" the words "the income". **Effective** for tax years beginning after 12-31-54.

[Sec. 594(b)]

(b) LIMITATIONS OF SECTION.—Subsection (a) shall apply only if the life insurance department would, if it were treated as a separate corporation, qualify as a life insurance company under section 816.

Amendments

• 1984, Deficit Reduction Act of 1984 (P.L. 98-369)

P.L. 98-369, §211(b)(8):

Amended Code Sec. 594(b) by striking out "section 801" and inserting in lieu thereof "section 816". **Effective** for tax years beginning after 12-31-83.

[Sec. 595—Repealed]

Amendments

• 1996, Small Business Job Protection Act of 1996 (P.L. 104-188)

P.L. 104-188, §1616(b)(8):

Repealed Code Sec. 595. **Effective** for property acquired in tax years beginning after 12-31-95. Prior to repeal, Code Sec. 595 read as follows:

CODE SEC. 595. FORECLOSURE ON PROPERTY SECURING LOANS.

(a) NONRECOGNITION OF GAIN OR LOSS AS A RESULT OF FORECLOSURE.—In the case of a creditor which is an organization described in section 593(a), no gain or loss shall be recognized, and no debt shall be considered as becoming worthless or partially worthless, as the result of such organization having bid in at foreclosure, or having otherwise reduced to ownership or possession by agreement or process of law, any property which was security for the payment of any indebtedness.

(b) CHARACTER OF PROPERTY.—For purposes of sections 166 and 1221, any property acquired in a transaction with respect to which gain or loss to an organization was not recognized by reason of subsection (a) shall be considered as property having the same characteristics as the indebtedness for which such property was security. Any amount realized by such organization with respect to such property shall be treated for purposes of this chapter as a payment on account of such indebtedness, and any loss with respect thereto shall be treated as a bad debt to which the provisions of section 166 (relating to allowance of a deduction for bad debts) apply.

(c) BASIS.—The basis of any property to which subsection (a) applies shall be the basis of the indebtedness for which such property was secured (determined as of the date of the acquisition of such property), properly increased for costs of acquisition.

(d) REGULATORY AUTHORITY.—The Secretary shall prescribe such regulations as he may deem necessary to carry out the purposes of this section.

• 1976, Tax Reform Act of 1976 (P.L. 94-455)

P.L. 94-455, §1906(b)(13)(A):

Amended 1954 Code by substituting "Secretary" for "Secretary or his delegate" each place it appeared. **Effective** 2-1-77.

• 1962, Revenue Act of 1962 (P.L. 87-834)

P.L. 87-834, §6:

Amended part II of subchapter H of chapter 1 by adding at the end thereof a new Sec. 595. Also amended the table of sections for such part by inserting after Sec. 594 "Sec. 595. Foreclosure on property securing loans." **Effective** for transactions described in Sec. 595(a) occurring after 12-31-62, in tax years ending after such date.

[Sec. 596—Repealed]

Amendments

• 1996, Small Business Job Protection Act of 1996 (P.L. 104-188)

P.L. 104-188, §1616(b)(9):

Repealed Code Sec. 596. **Effective** for tax years beginning after 12-31-95. Prior to repeal, Code Sec. 596 read as follows:

CODE SEC. 596. LIMITATION ON DIVIDENDS RECEIVED DEDUCTION.

In the case of an organization to which section 593 applies and which computes additions to the reserve for losses on loans for the taxable year under section 593(b)(2), the total amount allowed under sections 243, 244, and 245 (determined without regard to this section) for the taxable year as a deduction with respect to dividends received shall be reduced by an amount equal to 8 percent of such total amount.

• 1986, Tax Reform Act of 1986 (P.L. 99-514)

P.L. 99-514, §901(d)(4)(D):

Amended Code Sec. 596 by striking out "an amount equal to" and all that follows down through the period at the end thereof and inserting in lieu thereof "an amount equal to 8 percent of such total amount.". **Effective** for tax years beginning after 12-31-86.

• 1969, Tax Reform Act of 1969 (P.L. 91-172)

P.L. 91-172, §434(a):

Added Code Sec. 596. **Effective** for tax years beginning after 7-11-69.

[Sec. 597]

SEC. 597. TREATMENT OF TRANSACTIONS IN WHICH FEDERAL FINANCIAL ASSISTANCE PROVIDED.

[Sec. 597(a)]

(a) GENERAL RULE.—The treatment for purposes of this chapter of any transaction in which Federal financial assistance is provided with respect to a bank or domestic building and loan association shall be determined under regulations prescribed by the Secretary.

[Sec. 597(b)]

(b) PRINCIPLES USED IN PRESCRIBING REGULATIONS.—

(1) TREATMENT OF TAXABLE ASSET ACQUISITIONS.—In the case of any acquisition of assets to which section 381(a) does not apply, the regulations prescribed under subsection (a) shall—

(A) provide that Federal financial assistance shall be properly taken into account by the institution from which the assets were acquired, and

(B) provide the proper method of allocating basis among the assets so acquired (including rights to receive Federal financial assistance).

(2) OTHER TRANSACTIONS.—In the case of any transaction not described in paragraph (1), the regulations prescribed under subsection (a) shall provide for the proper treatment of Federal financial assistance and appropriate adjustments to basis or other tax attributes in connection with such assistance.

(3) DENIAL OF DOUBLE BENEFIT.—No regulations prescribed under this section shall permit the utilization of any deduction (or other tax benefit) if such amount was in effect reimbursed by nontaxable Federal financial assistance.

Amendments

• 1989, Omnibus Budget Reconciliation Act of 1989 (P.L. 101-239)

P.L. 101-239, §7841(e)(1):

Amended Code Sec. 597(b)(2) by striking "to reflect such treatment" and inserting "in connection with such assistance". **Effective** as if included in the amendments made by section 1401 of P.L. 101-73.

[Sec. 597(c)]

(c) FEDERAL FINANCIAL ASSISTANCE.—For purposes of this section, the term "Federal financial assistance" means—

(1) any money or other property provided with respect to a domestic building and loan association by the Federal Savings and Loan Insurance Corporation or the Resolution Trust Corporation pursuant to section 406(f) of the National Housing Act or section 21A of the Federal Home Loan Bank Act (or under any other similar provision of law), and

(2) any money or other property provided with respect to a bank or domestic building and loan association by the Federal Deposit Insurance Corporation pursuant to section 11(f) or 13(c) of the Federal Deposit Insurance Act (or under any other similar provision of law),

regardless of whether any note or other instrument is issued in exchange therefor.

Amendments

• 1990, Omnibus Budget Reconciliation Act of 1990 (P.L. 101-508)

P.L. 101-508, §11704(a)(7):

Amended Code Sec. 597(c) by striking "The purposes of" and inserting "For purposes of". **Effective** 11-5-90.

[Sec. 597(d)]

(d) DOMESTIC BUILDING AND LOAN ASSOCIATION.—For purposes of this section, the term "domestic building and loan association" has the meaning given such term by section 7701(a)(19) without regard to subparagraph (C) thereof.

Amendments

• 1989, Financial Insitutions Reform, Recovery, and Enforcement Act of 1989 (P.L. 101-73)

P.L. 101-73, §1401(a)(3)(A):

Amended Code Sec. 597. For the **effective** date, see Act Sec. 1401(c)(3), below.

P.L. 101-73, §1401(c)(3), provides:

(3) SUBSECTION (a)(3).—

(A) IN GENERAL.—The amendments made by subsection (a)(3) shall apply to any amount received or accrued by the financial institution on or after May 10, 1989, except that such amendments shall not apply to transfers on or after such date pursuant to an acquisition to which the amendment made by subsection (a)(1) does not apply.

(B) INTERIM RULE.—In the case of any payment pursuant to a transaction on or after May 10, 1989, and before the date on which the Secretary of the Treasury (or his delegate) takes action in exercise of his regulatory authority under section 597 of the Internal Revenue Code of 1986 (as amended by subsection (a)(3)), the taxpayer may rely on the legislative history for the amendments made by subsection (a)(3) in determining the proper treatment of such payment.

Prior to amendment, Code Sec. 597 read as follows:

SEC. 597. FSLIC OR FDIC FINANCIAL ASSISTANCE.

[Sec. 597(a)]

(a) EXCLUSION FROM GROSS INCOME.—Gross income of a domestic building and loan association does not include any amount of money or other property received from the Federal Savings and Loan Insurance Corporation pursuant to section 406(f) of the National Housing Act (12 U.S.C. sec. 1729(f)), regardless of whether any note or other instrument is issued in exchange therefor. Gross income of a bank does not include any amount of money or other property received from the Federal Deposit Insurance Corporation pursuant to sections 13(c), 15(c)(1), and 15(c)(2) of the Federal Deposit Insurance Act (12 U.S.C. 1821(f) and 1823(c)(1) and (c)(2)), regardless of whether any note or other instrument is issued in exchange therefor.

Amendments

• 1988, Technical and Miscellaneous Revenue Act of 1988 (P.L. 100-647)

P.L. 100-647, §4012(b)(2)(A):

Amended Code Sec. 597(a) by adding at the end thereof a new sentence. For the **effective** date, see Act Sec. 4012(b)(2)(E), below.

P.L. 100-647, §4012(b)(2)(E), provides:

(E) The amendments made by this paragraph shall apply to any transfer—

(i) after the date of the enactment of this Act, and before January 1, 1990, unless such transfer is pursuant to an acquisition occurring on or before such date of enactment, and

(ii) after December 31, 1989, if such transfer is pursuant to an acquisition occurring after such date of enactment and before January 1, 1990.

• 1981, Economic Recovery Tax Act of 1981 (P.L. 97-34)

P.L. 97-34, §244(a):

Added Code Sec. 597(a). **Effective** for payments made on or after 1-1-81.

[Sec. 597(b)]

(b) NO REDUCTION IN BASIS OF ASSETS.—No reduction in the basis of assets of a domestic building and loan association or bank shall be made on account of money or other property received under the circumstances referred to in subsection (a).

Amendments

• 1988, Technical and Miscellaneous Revenue Act of 1988 (P.L. 100-647)

P.L. 100-647, §4012(b)(2)(C):

Amended Code Sec. 597(b) by inserting "or bank" after "association". For the **effective** date, see Act Sec. 4012(b)(2)(E), below.

P.L. 100-647, §4012(b)(2)(E), provides:

(E) The amendments made by this paragraph shall apply to any transfer—

(i) after the date of the enactment of this Act, and before January 1, 1990, unless such transfer is pursuant to an acquisition occurring on or before such date of enactment, and

(ii) after December 31, 1989, if such transfer is pursuant to an acquisition occurring after such date of enactment and before January 1, 1990.

• 1986, Tax Reform Act of 1986 (P.L. 99-514)

P.L. 99-514, §904(b)(1):

Repealed Code Sec. 597. For the **effective** date, see Act Sec. 904(c), below.

P.L. 99-514, §904(c), as amended by P.L. 100-647, §4012(a)(1)-(2) and repealed by P.L. 101-73, §1401(a)(3)(B) and §1401(b)(1), provides:

(c) EFFECTIVE DATES.—

(1) SUBSECTION (a).—The amendments made by subsection (a) shall apply to acquisitions after December 31, 1989, in taxable years ending after such date [repealed].

(2) SUBSECTION (b).—

(A) IN GENERAL.—The amendments made by subsection (b) shall apply to transfers after December 31, 1989, in taxable years ending after such date; except that such amendments shall not apply to transfers after such date pursuant to an acquisition to which the amendments made by subsection (a) do not apply [repealed].

(B) CLARIFICATION OF TREATMENT OF AMOUNTS EXCLUDED UNDER SECTION 597.—Section 265(a)(1) of the Internal Revenue Code of 1986 (as amended by this title) shall not deny any deduction by reason of such deduction being allocable to amounts excluded from gross income under section 597 of the Internal Revenue Code of 1954 (as in effect on the day before the date of the enactment of this Act) [repealed].

• 1981, Economic Recovery Tax Act of 1981 (P.L. 97-34)

P.L. 97-34, §244(a):

Added Code Sec. 597(b). **Effective** for payments made on or after 1-1-81.

[Sec. 597(c)]

(c) REDUCTION OF TAX ATTRIBUTES BY 50 PERCENT OF AMOUNTS EXCLUDABLE UNDER SUBSECTION (a).—

(1) IN GENERAL.—50 percent of any amount excludable under subsection (a) for any taxable year shall be applied to reduce the tax attributes of the taxpayer as provided in paragraph (2).

(2) TAX ATTRIBUTES REDUCED; ORDER OF REDUCTION.—The reduction referred to in paragraph (1) shall be made in the following tax attributes in the following order:

(A) NOL.—Any pre-assistance net operating loss for the taxable year.

(B) INTEREST.—The amount of any interest with respect to which a deduction is allowable for the taxable year.

(C) BUILT-IN PORTFOLIO LOSSES.—Recognized built-in portfolio losses for the taxable year.

(3) PRE-ASSISTANCE NET OPERATING LOSS.—For purposes of paragraph (2)(A)—

(A) IN GENERAL.—The pre-assistance net operating loss shall be determined in the same manner as a pre-change loss under section 382(d), except that—

(i) the applicable financial institution shall be treated as the old loss corporation, and

(ii) the determination date shall be substituted for the change date.

(B) ORDERING RULE.—The reduction under paragraph (2)(A) shall be made in the carryovers in the order in which carryovers are taken into account under this chapter for the taxable year.

(4) RECOGNIZED BUILT-IN PORTFOLIO LOSSES.—For purposes of paragraph (2)(C), recognized built-in portfolio losses shall be determined in the same manner as recognized built-in losses under section 382(h), except that—

(A) the only assets taken in to account shall be—

(i) the loan portfolio,

(ii) marketable securities (within the meaning of section 453(f)(2)), and

(iii) property described in section 595(a),

(B) the rules of clauses (i) and (ii) of paragraph (3)(A) shall apply,

(C) there shall be no limit on the number of years in the recognition period, and

(D) section 382(h) shall be applied without regard to paragraph (3)(B) thereof.

(5) DEFINITIONS AND SPECIAL RULES.—For purposes of this subsection—

(A) APPLICABLE FINANCIAL INSTITUTION.—The term "applicable financial institution" means the domestic building and loan association or bank the financial condition of which was determined by the Federal Savings and Loan Insurance Corporation or the Federal Deposit Insurance Corporation to require the financial assistance described in subsection (a).

(B) DETERMINATION DATE.—The term "determination date" means the date of the determination under subparagraph (A). Except as provided by the Secretary, any subsequent revision or modification of such determination shall be treated as made on the original determination date.

(C) TAXABLE ASSET ACQUISITIONS.—

(i) IN GENERAL.—In the case of any acquisition of the assets of any applicable financial institution to which section 381 does not apply—

(I) paragraph (1) shall not apply to any amounts excludable under subsection (a) which are payments made at the time of the acquisition to the person acquiring such assets, and

(II) rights to receive future payments excludable under subsection (a) in connection with the acquisition shall be treated as provided in clause (ii).

(ii) TREATMENT OF FUTURE PAYMENTS.—

(I) IN GENERAL.—Rights to receive future payments described in clause (i)(II) shall be treated as assets to which basis is allocated.

(II) RECOVERY OF BASIS.—Any basis allocated under subclause (I) shall be recovered in such manner as the Secretary may provide, but in no event shall the amount recovered for any taxable year beginning before the taxable year in which the rights expire exceed the aggregate payments received with respect to such rights for all taxable years reduced by the amount of basis recovered with respect to such rights in preceding taxable years.

(III) APPLICATION OF PARAGRAPH (1).—Paragraph (1) shall apply to payments described in subclause (I) in a taxable year only to the extent such payments exceed the amount of basis recovered in such taxable year.

(D) TREATMENT OF REPAYMENTS.—If a taxpayer repays an amount to which paragraph (1) applied in a preceding taxable year, there shall be allowed as a deduction for the taxable year of repayment an amount equal to the reduction in tax attributes under paragraph (1) attributable to the amount repaid.

(E) CARRYOVERS.—If 50 percent of the amount excludable under subsection (a) for any taxable year exceeds the amount of the tax attributes described in paragraph (2) for such taxable year, then, for purposes of this subsection, the amount excludable under subsection (a) for the succeeding taxable year shall be increased by an amount equal to twice the amount of such excess.

(F) REGULATIONS.—The Secretary shall prescribe such regulations as may be necessary to carry out the provisions of this subsection.

Amendments

• 1988, Technical and Miscellaneous Revenue Act of 1988 (P.L. 100-647)

P.L. 100-647, §4012(c)(1):

Amended Code Sec. 597 by adding at the end thereof a new subsection (c). For the **effective** date, see Act Sec. 4012(c)(3), below.

P.L. 100-647, §4012(c)(3), as amended by P.L. 101-73, §1401(b)(2), provides:

(3) EFFECTIVE DATE.—The amendments made by this subsection shall apply to any transfer—

(A) after December 31, 1988, and before January 1, 1990, unles such transfer is pursuant to an acquisition occurring before January 1, 1989, and

(B) after December 31, 1989, if such transfer is pursuant to an acquisition occurring after December 31, 1988, and before January 1, 1990.

In the case of any bank or any institution treated as a domestic building and loan association for purposes of section 597 of the 1986 Code by reason of the amendment made by subsection (b)(2)(B), the amendments made by this subsection shall also apply to any transfer before January 1, 1989, to which the amendments made by subsection (b)(2) apply.

[Sec. 597(d)]

(d) DOMESTIC BUILDING AND LOAN ASSOCIATION.—For purpoes of thi section, the term "domestic building and loan association" has the meaning given such term by section 7701(a)(19) without regard to subparagraph (C) thereof.

Amendments

• 1988, Technical and Miscellaneous Revenue Act of 1988 (P.L. 100-647)

P.L. 100-647, §4012(b)(2)(B):

Amended Code Sec. 597(b) [sic], as amended by subsection (c)(1), by adding at the end thereof a new subsection (d). For the **effective** date, see Act Sec. 4012(b)(2)(E), below.

P.L. 100-647, §4012(b)(2)(D)(i):

Amended Code Sec. 597 by inserting "OR FDIC" after "FSLIC" in the heading. For the **effective** date, see Act Sec. 4012(b)(2)(E), below.

P.L. 100-647, §4012(b)(2)(E), provides:

(E) The amendments made by this paragraph shall apply to any transfer—

(i) after the date of the enactment of this Act, and before January 1, 1990, unless such transfer is pursuant to an acquisition occurring on or before such date of enactment, and

(ii) after December 31, 1989, if such transfer is pursuant to an acquisition occurring after such date of enactment and before January 1, 1990.

P.L. 101-73, §1401(c)(7), provides:

(7) CLARIFICATION OF PRIOR LAW.—Any reference to the Federal Savings and Loan Insurance Corporation in section 597 of the Internal Revenue Code of 1986 (as in effect on the day before the date of the enactment of this Act) shall be treated as including a reference to the Resolution Trust Corporation and the FSLIC Resolution Fund.

Subchapter I—Natural Resources

PART I—DEDUCTIONS

[Sec. 611]

SEC. 611. ALLOWANCE OF DEDUCTION FOR DEPLETION.

[Sec. 611(a)]

(a) GENERAL RULE.—In the case of mines, oil and gas wells, other natural deposits, and timber, there shall be allowed as a deduction in computing taxable income a reasonable allowance for depletion and for depreciation of improvements, according to the peculiar conditions in each case; such reasonable allowance in all cases to be made under regulations prescribed by Secretary. For purposes of this part, the term "mines" includes deposits of waste or residue, the extraction of ores or minerals from which is treated as mining under section 613(c). In any case in which it is ascertained as a result of operations or of development work that the recoverable units are greater or less than the prior estimate thereof, then such prior estimate (but not the basis for depletion) shall be revised and the allowance under this section for subsequent taxable years shall be based on such revised estimate.

Amendments

• 1976, Tax Reform Act of 1976 (P.L. 94-455)

P.L. 94-455, §1906(b)(13)(A):

Amended 1954 Code by substituting "Secretary" for "Secretary or his delegate" each place it appeared. **Effective** 2-1-77.

[Sec. 611(b)]

(b) SPECIAL RULES.—

(1) LEASES.—In the case of a lease, the deduction under this section shall be equitably apportioned between the lessor and lessee.

(2) LIFE TENANT AND REMAINDERMAN.—In the case of property held by one person for life with remainder to another person, the deduction under this section shall be computed as if the life tenant were the absolute owner of the property and shall be allowed to the life tenant.

(3) PROPERTY HELD IN TRUST.—In the case of property held in trust, the deduction under this section shall be apportioned between the income beneficiaries and the trustee in accordance with the pertinent provisions of the instrument creating the trust, or, in the absence of such provisions, on the basis of the trust income allocable to each.

(4) PROPERTY HELD BY ESTATE.—In the case of an estate, the deduction under this section shall be apportioned between the estate and the heirs, legatees, and devisees on the basis of the income of the estate allocable to each.

Amendments

• 1958, Technical Amendments Act of 1958 (P.L. 85-866)

P.L. 85-866, §35:

Amended Code Sec. 611(b)(4) by substituting the word "devisees" for the word "devises". **Effective** 1-1-54.

[Sec. 611(c)]

(c) CROSS REFERENCE.—

For other rules applicable to depreciation of improvements, see section 167.

[Sec. 612]

SEC. 612. BASIS FOR COST DEPLETION.

Except as otherwise provided in this subchapter, the basis on which depletion is to be allowed in respect of any property shall be the adjusted basis provided in section 1011 for the purpose of determining the gain upon the sale or other disposition of such property.

[Sec. 613]

SEC. 613. PERCENTAGE DEPLETION.

[Sec. 613(a)]

(a) GENERAL RULE.—In the case of the mines, wells, and other natural deposits listed in subsection (b), the allowance for depletion under section 611 shall be the percentage, specified in subsection (b), of the gross income from the property excluding from such gross income an amount equal to any rents or royalties paid or incurred by the taxpayer in respect of the property. Such allowance shall not exceed 50 percent (100 percent in the case of oil and gas properties) of the taxpayer's taxable income from the property (computed without allowances for depletion and without the deduction under section 199). For purposes of the preceding sentence, the allowable deductions taken into account with respect to expenses of mining in computing the taxable income from the property shall be decreased by an amount equal to so much of any gain which (1) is treated under section 1245 (relating to gain from disposition of certain depreciable property) as ordinary income, and (2) is properly allocable to the property. In no case shall the allowance for depletion under section 611 be less than it would be if computed without reference to this section.

Amendments

• 2004, American Jobs Creation Act of 2004 (P.L. 108-357)

P.L. 108-357, §102(d)(6):

Amended Code Sec. 613(a) by inserting "and without the deduction under section 199" after "without allowances for depletion". **Effective** for tax years beginning after 12-31-2004.

• 1990, Omnibus Budget Reconciliation Act of 1990 (P.L. 101-508)

P.L. 101-508, §11522(a):

Amended Code Sec. 613(a) by inserting "(100 percent in the case of oil and gas properties)" after "50 percent" in the second sentence. **Effective** for tax years beginning after 12-31-90.

• 1976, Tax Reform Act of 1976 (P.L. 94-455)

P.L. 94-455, §1901(b)(3)(K):

Substituted "ordinary income" for "gain from the sale or exchange of property which is neither a capital asset nor property described in section 1231" in Code Sec. 613(a). **Effective** for tax years beginning after 12-31-76.

• 1962, Revenue Act of 1962 (P.L. 87-834)

P.L. 87-834, §13(e):

Amended Code Sec. 613(a) by adding a new third sentence. **Effective** for tax years beginning after 12-31-62.

[Sec. 613(b)]

(b) PERCENTAGE DEPLETION RATES.—The mines, wells, and other natural deposits, and the percentages, referred to in subsection (a) are as follows:

(1) 22 PERCENT—

(A) sulphur and uranium; and

(B) if from deposits in the United States—anorthosite, clay, laterite, and nephelite syenite (to the extent that alumina and aluminum compounds are extracted therefrom), asbestos, bauxite, celestite, chromite, corundum, fluorspar, graphite, ilmenite, kyanite, mica, olivine, quartz crystals (radio grade), rutile, block steatite talc, and zircon, and ores of the following metals: antimony, beryllium, bismuth, cadmium, cobalt, columbium, lead, lithium, manganese, mercury, molybdenum, nickel, platinum and platinum group metals, tantalum, thorium, tin, titanium, tungsten, vanadium, and zinc.

(2) 15 PERCENT—If from deposits in the United States—

(A) gold, silver, copper, and iron ore, and

(B) oil shale (except shale described in paragraph (5)).

(3) 14 PERCENT—

(A) metal mines (if paragraph (1)(B) or (2)(A) does not apply), rock asphalt, and vermiculite; and

(B) if paragraph (1)(B), (5), or (6)(B) does not apply, ball clay, bentonite, china clay, sagger clay, and clay used or sold for use for purposes dependent on its refractory properties.

(4) 10 PERCENT—asbestos (if paragraph (1)(B) does not apply), brucite, coal, lignite, perlite, sodium chloride, and wollastonite.

(5) 7 1/2 PERCENT—clay and shale used or sold for use in the manufacture of sewer pipe or brick, and clay, shale, and slate used or sold for use as sintered or burned lightweight aggregates.

(6) 5 PERCENT—

(A) gravel, peat, pumice, sand, scoria, shale (except shale described in paragraph (2)(B) or (5)), and stone (except stone described in paragraph (7));

(B) clay used, or sold for use, in the manufacture of drainage and roofing tile, flower pots, and kindred products; and

(C) if from brine wells—bromine, calcium chloride, and magnesium chloride.

(7) 14 PERCENT—all other minerals, including, but not limited to, aplite, barite, borax, calcium carbonates, diatomaceous earth, dolomite, feldspar, fullers earth, garnet, gilsonite, granite, limestone, magnesite, magnesium carbonates, marble, mollusk shells (including clam shells and oyster shells), phosphate rock, potash, quartzite, slate, soapstone, stone (used or sold for use by the mine owner or operator as dimension stone or ornamental stone), thenardite, tripoli, trona, and (if paragraph (1)(B) does not apply) bauxite, flake graphite, fluorspar, lepido-

lite, mica, spodumene, and talc (including pyrophyllite), except that, unless sold on bid in direct competition with a bona fide bid to sell a mineral listed in paragraph (3), the percentage shall be 5 percent for any such other mineral (other than slate to which paragraph (5) applies) when used, or sold for use, by the mine owner or operator as rip rap, ballast, road material, rubble, concrete aggregates, or for similar purposes. For purposes of this paragraph, the term "all other minerals" does not include—

(A) soil, sod, dirt, turf, water, or mosses;

(B) minerals from sea water, the air, or similar inexhaustible sources or

(C) oil and gas wells.

For the purposes of this subsection, minerals (other than sodium chloride) extracted from brines pumped from a saline perennial lake within the United States shall not be considered minerals from an inexhaustible source.

Amendments

• 1975, Tax Reduction Act of 1975 (P.L. 94-12)

P.L. 94-12, § 501(b)(2):

Amended Sec. 613(b) by deleting subparagraph (A) of paragraph (1) and redesignating subparagraphs (B) and (C) as subparagraphs (A) and (B) respectively; by substituting "(1)(B)" for "(1)(C)" each place it appeared in paragraphs (3), (4) and (7); and by amending the last sentence of paragraph (7) by adding new clause (C). **Effective** 1-1-75, and apply to tax years ending after 12-31-74.

• 1969, Tax Reform Act of 1969 (P.L. 91-172)

P.L. 91-172, § 501(a):

Amended Sec. 613(b). **Effective** for tax years beginning after 10-9-69. Prior to amendment, Sec. 613(b) read as follows:

(b) Percentage Depletion Rates.—The mines, wells, and other natural deposits, and the percentages, referred to in subsection (a) are as follows:

(1) 27½ percent—oil and gas wells.

(2) 23 percent—

(A) sulfur and uranium; and

(B) if from deposits in the United States—anorthosite, clay, laterite, and nephelite syenite (to the extent that alumina and aluminum compounds are extracted therefrom), asbestos, bauxite, celestite, chromite, corundum, fluorspar, graphite, ilmenite, kyanite, mica, olivine, quartz crystals (radio grade), rutile, block steatite talc, and zircon, and ores of the following metals: antimony, beryllium, bismuth, cadmium, cobalt, columbium, lead, lithium, manganese, mercury, nickel, platinum and platinum group metals, tantalum, thorium, tin, titanium, tungsten, vanadium, and zinc.

(3) 15 percent—

(A) metal mines (if paragraph (2) (B) does not apply), rock asphalt, and vermiculite; and

(B) if neither paragraph (2)(B), (5), or (6)(B) applies ball clay, bentonite, china clay, sagger clay, and clay used or sold for use for purposes dependent on its refractory properties.

(4) 10 percent—asbestos (if paragraph (2)(B) does not apply), brucite, coal, lignite, perlite, sodium chloride, and wollastonite.

(5) 7½ percent—clay and shale used or sold for use in the manufacture of sewer pipe or brick, and clay, shale, and slate used or sold for use as sintered or burned lightweight aggregates.

(6) 5 percent—

(A) gravel, peat, pumice, sand, scoria, shale (except shale described in paragraph (5)), and stone (except stone described in paragraph (7));

(B) clay used or sold for use, in the manufacture of drainage and roofing tile, flower pots, and kindred products; and

(C) if from brine wells—bromine, calcium chloride, and magnesium chloride.

(7) 15 percent—all other minerals (including, but not limited to, aplite, barite, borax, calcium carbonites, diatomaceous earth, dolomite, feldspar, fullers earth, garnet, gilsonite, granite, limestone, magnesite, magnesium carbonates, marble, mollusk shells (including clam shells and oyster shells), phosphate rock, potash, quartzite, slate, soapstone, stone (used or sold for use by the mine owner or operator as dimension stone or ornamental stone), thenardite, tripoli, trona, and (if paragraph (2)(B) does not apply) bauxite, flake graphite, fluorspar, lepidolite, mica, spodumene, and talc, including pyrophyllite), except that, unless sold on bid in direct competition with a bona fide bid to sell a mineral listed in paragraph (3), the percentage shall be 5 percent for any such other mineral (other than slate to which paragraph (5) applies) when used, or sold for use, by the mine owner or operator as rip rap, ballast, road material, rubble, concrete aggregates, or for similar purposes. For purposes of this paragraph, the term "all other minerals" does not include—

(A) soil, sod, dirt, turf, water, or mosses; or

(B) minerals from sea water, the air, or similar inexhaustible sources.

• 1966, Foreign Investors Tax Act of 1966 (P.L. 89-809)

P.L. 89-809, § 207(a):

Amended Code Sec. 613(b) by inserting "clay, laterite, and nephelite syenite" after "anothosite" in paragraph (2)(B) and by substituting "if neither paragraph (2)(B) nor (5)(B) applies" for "if paragraph (5)(B) does not apply" in paragraph (3)(B). **Effective** 11-13-66.

P.L. 89-809, § 208(a):

Amended Code Sec. 613(b) by striking out "mollusk shells (including clam shells and oyster shells)," in paragraph (5)(A) and inserting the phrase after "marble," in paragraph (6). **Effective** 11-13-66.

P.L. 89-809, § 209(a):

Amended Code Sec. 613(b) by renumbering paragraphs (5) and (6) as (6) and (7) and by adding a new paragraph (5); by substituting "if neither paragraph (2)(B), (5), or (6)(B) applies" for "if neither paragraph (2)(B) nor (5)(B) applies" in paragraph (3)(B); by substituting "shale (except shale described in paragraph (5)), and stone (except stone described in paragraph (7))" for "shale, and stone, except stone described in paragraph (6)" in renumbered paragraph (6); by striking out in renumbered paragraph (6)(B) "building or paving brick" and "sewer pipe,"; and by inserting "(other than slate to which paragraph (5) applies)" after "any such other mineral" in renumbered paragraph (7). **Effective** 11-13-66.

• 1964 (P.L. 88-571)

P.L. 88-571, § 6(a):

Amended Code Sec. 613(b) by deleting "beryl" in paragraphs 2(B) and (6) and by inserting "beryllium" after "antimony" in paragraph 2(B). **Effective** 1-1-64.

• 1960, Public Debt and Tax Rate Extension Act of 1960 (P.L. 86-564)

P.L. 86-564, § 302(a), (c):

Amended Code Sec. 613(b) as follows:

(1) Amended paragraph (3). Prior to amendment it read as follows:

"(3) 15 percent—ball clay, bentonite, china clay, sagger clay, metal mines (if paragraph (2)(B) does not apply), rock asphalt, and vermiculite."

(2) Amended paragraph (5). Prior to amendment it read as follows:

"(5) 5 percent—

"(A) brick and tile clay, gravel, mollusk shells (including clam shells and oyster shells), peat, pumice, sand, scoria, shale, and stone, except stone described in paragraph (6); and

"(B) if from brine wells—bromine, calcium chloride, and magnesium chloride."

(3) Amended paragraph (6) by striking out "refractory and fire clay," where it appeared following "calcium carbonates,".

P.L. 86-564, §302(c), as amended by P.L. 86-781, provides:

"(c) Effective Date.—

"(1) In general.—Except as provided in paragraph (2), the amendments made by subsections (a) and (b) shall be applicable only with respect to taxable years beginning after December 31, 1960.

"(2) Calcium carbonates, etc.—

"(A) Election for past years.—In the case of calcium carbonates or other minerals when used in making cement, if an election is made by the taxpayer under subparagraph (C)—

"(i) the amendments made by subsection (b) shall apply to taxable years with respect to which such election is effective, and

"(ii) provisions having the same effect as the amendments made by subsection (b) shall be deemed to be included in the Internal Revenue Code of 1939 and shall apply to taxable years with respect to which such election is effective in lieu of the corresponding provisions of such Code.

"(B) Years to which applicable.—An election made under subparagraph (C) to have the provisions of this paragraph apply shall be effective for all taxable years beginning before January 1, 1961, in respect of which—

"(i) the assessment of a deficiency.

"(ii) the refund or credit of an overpayment, or

"(iii) the commencement of a suit for recovery of a refund under section 7405 of the Internal Revenue Code of 1954,

is not prevented on the date of the enactment of this paragraph by the operation of any law or rule of law. Such election shall also be effective for any taxable year beginning before January 1, 1961, in respect of which an assessment of a deficiency has been made but not collected on or before the date of the enactment of this paragraph.

"(C) Time and manner of election.—An election to have the provisions of this paragraph apply shall be made by the taxpayer on or before the 60th day after the date of publication in the Federal Register of final regulations issued under authority of subparagraph (F), and shall be made in such form and manner as the Secretary of the Treasury or his delegate shall prescribe by regulations. Such election, if made, may not be revoked.

"(D) Statutes of limitation.—Notwithstanding any other law, the period within which an assessment of a deficiency attributable to the application of the amendments made by subsection (b) may be made with respect to any taxable year to which such amendments apply under an election made under subparagraph (C), and the period within which a claim for refund or credit of an overpayment attributable to the application of such amendments may be made with respect to any such taxable year, shall not expire prior to one year after the last day for making an election under subparagraph (C). An election by a taxpayer under subparagraph (C) shall be considered as a consent to the application of the provisions of this subparagraph.

"(E) Terms; applicability of other laws.—Except where otherwise distinctly expressed or manifestly intended, terms used in this paragraph shall have the same meaning as when used in the Internal Revenue Code of 1954 (or corresponding provisions of the Internal Revenue Code of 1939) and all provisions of law shall apply with respect to this paragraph as if this paragraph were a part of such Code (or corresponding provisions of the Internal Revenue Code of 1939).

"(F) Regulations.—The Secretary of the Treasury or his delegate shall prescribe such regulations as may be necessary to carry out the provisions of this paragraph."

[Sec. 613(c)]

(c) DEFINITION OF GROSS INCOME FROM PROPERTY.—For purposes of this section—

(1) GROSS INCOME FROM THE PROPERTY.—The term "gross income from the property" means, in the case of a property other than an oil or gas well and other than a geothermal deposit, the gross income from mining.

(2) MINING.—The term "mining" includes not merely the extraction of the ores or minerals from the ground but also the treatment processes considered as mining described in paragraph (4) (and the treatment processes necessary or incidental thereto), and so much of the transportation of ores or minerals (whether or not by common carrier) from the point of extraction from the ground to the plants or mills in which such treatment processes are applied thereto as is not in excess of 50 miles unless the Secretary finds that the physical and other requirements are such that the ore or mineral must be transported a greater distance to such plants or mills.

(3) EXTRACTION OF THE ORES OR MINERALS FROM THE GROUND.—The term "extraction of the ores or minerals from the ground" includes the extraction by mine owners or operators of ores or minerals from the waste or residue of prior mining. The preceding sentence shall not apply to any such extraction of the mineral or ore by a purchaser of such waste or residue or of the rights to extract ores or minerals therefrom.

(4) TREATMENT PROCESSES CONSIDERED AS MINING.—The following treatment processes where applied by the mine owner or operator shall be considered as mining to the extent they are applied to the ore or mineral in respect of which he is entitled to a deduction for depletion under section 611:

(A) In the case of coal—cleaning, breaking, sizing, dust allaying, treating to prevent freezing, and loading for shipment;

(B) in the case of sulfur recovered by the Frasch process—cleaning, pumping to vats, cooling, breaking, and loading for shipment;

(C) in the case of iron ore, bauxite, ball and sagger clay, rock asphalt, and ores or minerals which are customarily sold in the form of a crude mineral product—sorting, concentrating, sintering, and substantially equivalent processes to bring to shipping grade and form, and loading for shipment;

(D) in the case of lead, zinc, copper, gold, silver, uranium, or fluorspar ores, potash, and ores or minerals which are not customarily sold in the form of the crude mineral product—crushing, grinding, and beneficiation by concentration (gravity, flotation, amalgamation, electrostatic, or magnetic), cyanidation, leaching, crystallization, precipitation (but not including electrolytic deposition, roasting, thermal or electric smelting, or refining), or by substantially equivalent processes or combination of processes used in the separation or extraction of the product or products from the ore or the mineral or minerals from other material from the mine or other natural deposit;

(E) the pulverization of talc, the burning of magnesite, the sintering and nodulizing of phosphate rock, the decarbonation of trona, and the furnacing of quicksilver ores;

(F) in the case of calcium carbonates and other minerals when used in making cement—all processes (other than preheating of the kiln feed) applied prior to the introduction of the kiln feed into the kiln, but not including any subsequent process;

(G) in the case of clay to which paragraph (5) or (6)(B) of subsection (b) applies—crushing, grinding, and separating the mineral from waste, but not including any subsequent process;

(H) in the case of oil shale—extraction from the ground, crushing, loading into the retort, and retorting (including in situ retorting), but not hydrogenation, refining, or any other process subsequent to retorting; and

(I) any other treatment process provided for by regulations prescribed by the Secretary which, with respect to the particular ore or mineral, is not inconsistent with the preceding provisions of this paragraph.

(5) TREATMENT PROCESSES NOT CONSIDERED AS MINING.—Unless such processes are otherwise provided for in paragraph (4) (or are necessary or incidental to processes so provided for), the following processes shall not be considered as "mining": electrolytic deposition, roasting, calcining, thermal or electric smelting, refining, polishing, fine pulverization, blending with other materials, treatment effecting a chemical change, thermal action, and molding or shaping.

Amendments

• 2005, Gulf Opportunity Zone Act of 2005 (P.L. 109-135)

P.L. 109-135, §412(gg):

Amended Code Sec. 613(c)(4)(H) by inserting "(including in situ retorting)" after "and retorting". **Effective** 12-21-2005.

• 1978, Energy Tax Act of 1978 (P.L. 95-618)

P.L. 95-618, §403(a)(2)(A):

Amended Code Sec. 613(c) by inserting "and other than a geothermal deposit" after "oil or gas well". **Effective** 10-1-78, to apply to tax years ending on or after such date.

• 1974 (P.L. 93-499)

P.L. 93-499, §2:

Amended Code Sec. 613(c)(4)(E) by adding "the decarbonation of trona," after "phosphate rock,". **Effective** for tax years beginning after 12-31-70.

• 1969, Tax Reform Act of 1969 (P.L. 91-172)

P.L. 91-172, §502(a):

Amended Sec. 613(c)(4) by deleting "and" at the end of subparagraph (G), by redesignating old subparagraph (H) to be (I), and by adding new subparagraph (H). **Effective** for tax years beginning after 12-30-69.

• 1966, Foreign Investors Tax Act of 1966 (P.L. 89-809)

P.L. 89-809, §209(b):

Amended Code Sec. 613(c)(4)(G) by substituting "paragraph (5) or (6)(B)" for "paragraph (5)(B)". **Effective** 11-13-66.

• 1960, Public Debt and Tax Rate Extension Act of 1960 (P.L. 86-564)

P.L. 86-564, §302(b):

Amended Code Sec. 613(c) as follows:

(1) Amended paragraph (2). Prior to amendment, it read as follows:

"(2) Mining.—The term `mining' includes not merely the extraction of the ores or minerals from the ground but also the ordinary treatment processes normally applied by mine owners or operators in order to obtain the commercially marketable mineral product or products, and so much of the transportation of ores or minerals (whether or not by common carrier) from the point of extraction from the ground to the plants or mills in which the ordinary treatment processes are applied thereto as is not in excess of 50 miles unless the Secretary or his delegate finds that the physical and other requirements are such that the ore or mineral must be transported a greater distance to such plants or mills."

(2) Struck out paragraph (4) and added new paragraphs (4) and (5). Prior to being stricken, old paragraph (4) read as follows:

"(4) Ordinary treatment processes.—The term `ordinary treatment processes' includes the following:

"(A) In the case of coal—cleaning, breaking, sizing, dust allaying, treating to prevent freezing, and loading for shipment;

"(B) in the case of sulfur recovered by the Frasch process—pumping to vats, cooling, breaking, and loading for shipment;

"(C) in the case of iron ore, bauxite, ball and sagger clay, rock asphalt, and minerals which are customarily sold in the form of a crude mineral product—sorting, concentrating, and sintering to bring to shipping grade and form, and loading for shipment;

"(D) in the case of lead, zinc, copper, gold, silver, or fluorspar ores, potash, and ores which are not customarily sold in the form of the crude mineral product—crushing, grinding, and beneficiation by concentration (gravity, flotation, amalgamation, electrostatic, or magnetic), cyanidation, leaching, crystallization, precipitation (but not including as an ordinary treatment process electrolytic deposition, roasting, thermal or electric smelting, or refining), or by substantially equivalent processes or combination of processes used in the separation or extraction of the product or products from the ore, including the furnacing of quicksilver ores; and

"(E) the pulverization of talc, the burning of magnesite, and the sintering and nodulizing of phosphate rock."

For the **effective** date, see P.L. 86-564, §302(c), as amended by P.L. 86-781, in the amendments for Code Sec. 613(b).

[Sec. 613(d)]

(d) DENIAL OF PERCENTAGE DEPLETION IN CASE OF OIL AND GAS WELLS.—Except as provided in Section 613A, in the case of any oil or gas well, the allowance for depletion shall be computed without reference to this section.

Amendments

• 1975, Tax Reduction Act of 1975 (P.L. 94-12)

P.L. 94-12, §501(b)(1):

Amended Sec. 613(d). **Effective** 1-1-75, and applicable to tax years ending after 12-31-74. Prior to amendment, Sec. 613(d) read as follows:

(d) Application of Percentage Depletion Rates to Certain Taxable Years Ending in 1954.—

(1) General rule.—At the election of the taxpayer in respect of any property (within the meaning of the Internal Revenue Code of 1939), the percentage specified in subsection (b) in the case of any mine, well, or other natural deposit listed in such subsection shall apply to a taxable year ending after December 31, 1953, to which the Internal Revenue Code of 1939 applies.

(2) Method of computation.—The allowance for depletion, in respect of any property for which an election is made under paragraph (1) for any taxable year, shall be an amount equal to the sum of—

(A) that portion of a tentative allowance, computed under the Internal Revenue Code of 1939 without regard to paragraph (1) of this subsection, which the number of days in such taxable year before January 1, 1954, bears to the total number of days in such taxable year; plus

(B) that portion of a tentative allowance, computed under the Internal Revenue Code of 1939 (as modified solely by the application of paragraph (1) of this subsection), which the number of days in such taxable year after December 31, 1953, bears to the total number of days in such taxable year.

• 1958, Technical Amendments Act of 1958 (P.L. 85-866)

P.L. 85-866, §36:

Added Code Sec. 613(d). If refund or credit of any overpayment resulting from the application of Sec. 613(d) is prevented on 9-2-58, or within 6 months from such date, by the operation of any law or rule of law (other than 1939 Code Secs. 3760 and 3761 or 1954 Code Secs. 7121 and 7122), refund or credit of such overpayment may, nevertheless, be made or allowed if claim therefor is filed within 6 months from such date. No interest shall be paid on any overpayment resulting from the application of this amendment. **Effective** 1-1-54.

[Sec. 613(e)]

(e) PERCENTAGE DEPLETION FOR GEOTHERMAL DEPOSITS.—

(1) IN GENERAL.—In the case of geothermal deposits located in the United States or in a possession of the United States, for purposes of subsection (a)—

(A) such deposits shall be treated as listed in subsection (b), and

(B) 15 percent shall be deemed to be the percentage specified in subsection (b).

(2) GEOTHERMAL DEPOSIT DEFINED.—For purposes of paragraph (1), the term "geothermal deposit" means a geothermal reservoir consisting of natural heat which is stored in rocks or in an aqueous liquid or vapor (whether or not under pressure). Such a deposit shall in no case be treated as a gas well for purposes of this section or section 613A, and this section shall not apply to a geothermal deposit which is located outside the United States or its possessions.

(3) PERCENTAGE DEPLETION NOT TO INCLUDE LEASE BONUSES, ETC.—In the case of any geothermal deposit, the term "gross income from the property" shall, for purposes of this section, not include any amount described in section 613A(d)(5).

Amendments

• 1996, Small Business Job Protection Act of 1996 (P.L. 104-188)

P.L. 104-188, §1704(t)(34):

Amended Code Sec. 613(e)(1)(B) by striking the comma at the end thereof and inserting a period. **Effective** 8-20-96.

• 1990, Omnibus Budget Reconciliation Act of 1990 (P.L. 101-508)

P.L. 101-508, §11815(b)(1):

Amended Code Sec. 613(e) by striking paragraph (2), and by redesignating paragraphs (3) and (4) as paragraphs (2) and (3), respectively. **Effective** 11-5-90. Prior to amendment, paragraph (2) read as follows:

(2) APPLICABLE PERCENTAGE.—For purposes of paragraph (1)—

In the case of taxable years beginning in calendar year—	The applicable percentage is—
1978, 1979, or 1980	22
1981	20
1982	18
1983	16
1984 and thereafter	15

P.L. 101-508, §11815(b)(2):

Amended Code Sec. 613(e)(1)(B). **Effective** 11-5-90. Prior to amendment, subparagraph (B) read as follows:

(B) the applicable percentage (determined under the table contained in paragraph (2)) shall be deemed to be the percentage specified in subsection (b).

P.L. 101-508, §11821(b), provides:

(b) SAVINGS PROVISION.—If—

(1) any provision amended or repealed by this part applied to—

(A) any transaction occurring before the date of the enactment of this Act,

(B) any property acquired before such date of enactment, or

(C) any item of income, loss, deduction, or credit taken into account before such date of enactment, and

(2) the treatment of such transaction, property, or item under such provision would (without regard to the amendments made by this part) affect liability for tax for periods ending after such date of enactment,

nothing in the amendments made by this part shall be construed to affect the treatment of such transaction, property, or item for purposes of determining liability for tax for periods ending after such date of enactment.

• 1986, Tax Reform Act of 1986 (P.L. 99-514)

P.L. 99-514, §412(a)(2):

Amended Code Sec. 613(e) by adding at the end thereof new paragraph (4). **Effective** for amounts received or accrued after 8-16-86, in tax years ending after such date.

• 1978, Energy Tax Act of 1978 (P.L. 95-618)

P.L. 95-618, §403(a)(1):

Added Code Sec. 613(e). **Effective** 10-1-78, to apply to tax years ending on or after such date.

[Sec. 613A]

SEC. 613A. LIMITATIONS ON PERCENTAGE DEPLETION IN CASE OF OIL AND GAS WELLS.

[Sec. 613A(a)]

(a) GENERAL RULE.—Except as otherwise provided in this section, the allowance for depletion under section 611 with respect to any oil or gas well shall be computed without regard to section 613.

[Sec. 613A(b)]

(b) EXEMPTION FOR CERTAIN DOMESTIC GAS WELLS.—

(1) IN GENERAL.—The allowance for depletion under section 611 shall be computed in accordance with section 613 with respect to—

(A) regulated natural gas, and

(B) natural gas sold under a fixed contract,

and 22 percent shall be deemed to be specified in subsection (b) of section 613 for purposes of subsection (a) of that section.

(2) NATURAL GAS FROM GEOPRESSURED BRINE.—The allowance for depletion under section 611 shall be computed in accordance with section 613 with respect to any qualified natural gas from geopressured brine, and 10 percent shall be deemed to be specified in subsection (b) of section 613 for purposes of subsection (a) of such section.

(3) DEFINITIONS.—For purposes of this subsection—

(A) NATURAL GAS SOLD UNDER A FIXED CONTRACT.—The term "natural gas sold under a fixed contract" means domestic natural gas sold by the producer under a contract, in effect on February 1, 1975, and at all times thereafter before such sale, under which the price for such gas cannot be adjusted to reflect to any extent the increase in liabilities of the seller for tax under this chapter by reason of the repeal of percentage depletion for gas. Price increases after February 1, 1975, shall be presumed to take increases in tax liabilities into account unless the taxpayer demonstrates to the contrary by clear and convincing evidence.

(B) REGULATED NATURAL GAS.—The term "regulated natural gas" means domestic natural gas produced and sold by the producer, before July 1, 1976, subject to the jurisdiction of the Federal Power Commission, the price for which has not been adjusted to reflect to any extent the increase in liability of the seller for tax under this chapter by reason of the repeal of percentage depletion for gas. Price increases after February 1, 1975, shall be presumed to take increases in tax liabilities into account unless the taxpayer demonstrates the contrary by clear and convincing evidence.

(C) QUALIFIED NATURAL GAS FROM GEOPRESSURED BRINE.—The term "qualified natural gas from geopressured brine" means any natural gas—

(i) which is determined in accordance with section 503 of the Natural Gas Policy Act of 1978 to be produced from geopressured brine, and

(ii) which is produced from any well the drilling of which began after September 30, 1978, and before January 1, 1984.

Amendments

• 1978, Energy Tax Act of 1978 (P.L. 95-618)

P.L. 95-618, §403(a)(2)(B); §403(b)(1):

Amended Code Sec. 613A(b). **Effective** 10-1-78, to apply to tax years ending on or after such date. Prior to amendment, Code Sec. 613A(b) read as follows:

"(b) EXEMPTION FOR CERTAIN DOMESTIC GAS WELLS.—

(1) IN GENERAL.—The allowance for depletion under section 611 shall be computed in accordance with section 613 with respect to—

(A) regulated natural gas,

(B) natural gas sold under a fixed contract, and

(C) any geothermal deposit in the United States or in a possession of the United States which is determined to be a gas well,

and 22 percent shall be deemed to be specified in subsection (b) of section 613 for purposes of subsection (a) of that section.

(2) DEFINITIONS.—For purposes of this subsection—

(A) NATURAL GAS SOLD UNDER A FIXED CONTRACT.—The term "natural gas sold under a fixed contract" means domestic natural gas sold by the producer under a contract, in effect on February 1, 1975, and at all times thereafter before such sale, under which the price for such gas cannot be adjusted to reflect to any extent the increase in liabilities of the seller for tax under this chapter by reason of the repeal of percentage depletion for gas. Price increases after February 1, 1975, shall be presumed to take increases in tax liabilities into account unless the taxpayer demonstrates to the contrary by clear and convincing evidence.

(B) REGULATED NATURAL GAS.—The term "regulated natural gas" means domestic natural gas produced and sold by the producer, before July 1, 1976, subject to the jurisdiction of the Federal Power Commission, the price for which has not been adjusted to reflect to any extent the increase in liability of the seller for tax under this chapter by reason of the repeal of percentage depletion for gas. Price increases after February 1, 1975, shall be presumed to take increases in tax liabilities into account unless the taxpayer demonstrates the contrary by clear and convincing evidence."

• 1976, Tax Reform Act of 1976 (P.L. 94-455)

P.L. 94-455, §1901(a)(86)(A):

Amended Code Sec. 613A(b)(1)(C) by striking out "within the meaning of section 613(b)(1)(A)" after "well". **Effective** for tax years beginning after 12-31-76.

[Sec. 613A(c)]

(c) EXEMPTION FOR INDEPENDENT PRODUCERS AND ROYALTY OWNERS.—

(1) IN GENERAL.—Except as provided in subsection (d), the allowance for depletion under section 611 shall be computed in accordance with section 613 with respect to—

(A) so much of the taxpayer's average daily production of domestic crude oil as does not exceed the taxpayer's depletable oil quantity; and

(B) so much of the taxpayer's average daily production of domestic natural gas as does not exceed the taxpayer's depletable natural gas quantity;

and 15 percent shall be deemed to be specified in subsection (b) of section 613 for purposes of subsection (a) of that section.

(2) AVERAGE DAILY PRODUCTION.—For purposes of paragraph (1)—

(A) the taxpayer's average daily production of domestic crude oil or natural gas for any taxable year, shall be determined by dividing his aggregate production of domestic crude oil or natural gas, as the case may be, during the taxable year by the number of days in such taxable year, and

(B) in the case of a taxpayer holding a partial interest in the production from any property (including an interest held in a partnership) such taxpayer's production shall be considered to be that amount of such production determined by multiplying the total production of such property by the taxpayer's percentage participation in the revenues from such property.

(3) DEPLETABLE OIL QUANTITY.—

(A) IN GENERAL.—For purposes of paragraph (1), the taxpayer's depletable oil quantity shall be equal to—

(i) the tentative quantity determined under subparagraph (B), reduced (but not below zero) by

(ii) except in the case of a taxpayer making an election under paragraph (6)(B), the taxpayer's average daily marginal production for the taxable year.

(B) TENTATIVE QUANTITY.—For purposes of subparagraph (A), the tentative quantity is 1,000 barrels.

(4) DAILY DEPLETABLE NATURAL GAS QUANTITY.—For purposes of paragraph (1), the depletable natural gas quantity of any taxpayer for any taxable year shall be equal to 6,000 cubic feet multiplied by the number of barrels of the taxpayer's depletable oil quantity to which the taxpayer elects to have this paragraph apply. The taxpayer's depletable oil quantity for any taxable year shall be reduced by the number of barrels with respect to which an election under this paragraph applies. Such election shall be made at such time and in such manner as the Secretary shall by regulations prescribe.

(5) [Stricken.]

(6) OIL AND NATURAL GAS PRODUCED FROM MARGINAL PROPERTIES.—

(A) IN GENERAL.—Except as provided in subsection (d) and subparagraph (B), the allowance for depletion under section 611 shall be computed in accordance with section 613 with respect to—

(i) so much of the taxpayer's average daily marginal production of domestic crude oil as does not exceed the taxpayer's depletable oil quantity (determined without regard to paragraph (3)(A)(ii)), and

(ii) so much of the taxpayer's average daily marginal production of domestic natural gas as does not exceed the taxpayer's depletable natural gas quantity (determined without regard to paragraph (3)(A)(ii)),

and the applicable percentage shall be deemed to be specified in subsection (b) of section 613 for purposes of subsection (a) of that section.

(B) ELECTION TO HAVE PARAGRAPH APPLY TO PRO RATA PORTION OF MARGINAL PRODUCTION.—If the taxpayer elects to have this subparagraph apply for any taxable year, the rules of subparagraph (A) shall apply to the average daily marginal production of domestic crude oil or domestic natural gas of the taxpayer to which paragraph (1) would have applied without regard to this paragraph.

(C) APPLICABLE PERCENTAGE.—For purposes of subparagraph (A), the term "applicable percentage" means the percentage (not greater than 25 percent) equal to the sum of—

(i) 15 percent, plus

(ii) 1 percentage point for each whole dollar by which $20 exceeds the reference price for crude oil for the calendar year preceding the calendar year in which the taxable year begins.

For purposes of this paragraph, the term "reference price" means, with respect to any calendar year, the reference price determined for such calendar year under section 45K(d)(2)(C).

(D) MARGINAL PRODUCTION.—The term "marginal production" means domestic crude oil or domestic natural gas which is produced during any taxable year from a property which—

(i) is a stripper well property for the calendar year in which the taxable year begins, or

(ii) is a property substantially all of the production of which during such calendar year is heavy oil.

(E) STRIPPER WELL PROPERTY.—For purposes of this paragraph, the term "stripper well property" means, with respect to any calendar year, any property with respect to which the amount determined by dividing—

(i) the average daily production of domestic crude oil and domestic natural gas from producing wells on such property for such calendar year, by

(ii) the number of such wells, is 15 barrel equivalents or less.

(F) HEAVY OIL.—For purposes of this paragraph, the term "heavy oil" means domestic crude oil produced from any property if such crude oil had a weighted average gravity of 20 degrees API or less (corrected to 60 degrees Fahrenheit).

(G) AVERAGE DAILY MARGINAL PRODUCTION.—For purposes of this subsection—

(i) the taxpayer's average daily marginal production of domestic crude oil or natural gas for any taxable year shall be determined by dividing the taxpayer's aggregate marginal production of domestic crude oil or natural gas, as the case may be, during the taxable year by the number of days in such taxable year, and

(ii) in the case of a taxpayer holding a partial interest in the production from any property (including any interest held in any partnership), such taxpayer's production shall be considered to be that amount of such production determined by multiplying the total production of such property by the taxpayer's percentage participation in the revenues from such property.

(H) TEMPORARY SUSPENSION OF TAXABLE INCOME LIMIT WITH RESPECT TO MARGINAL PRODUCTION.—The second sentence of subsection (a) of section 613 shall not apply to so much of the allowance for depletion as is determined under subparagraph (A) for any taxable year—

(i) beginning after December 31, 1997, and before January 1, 2008, or

(ii) beginning after December 31, 2008, and before January 1, 2010.

(7) SPECIAL RULES.—

(A) PRODUCTION OF CRUDE OIL IN EXCESS OF DEPLETABLE OIL QUANTITY.—If the taxpayer's average daily production of domestic crude oil exceeds his depletable oil quantity, the allowance under paragraph (1)(A) with respect to oil produced during the taxable year from each property in the United States shall be that amount which bears the same ratio to the amount of depletion which would have been allowable under section 613(a) for all of the taxpayer's oil produced from such property during the taxable year (computed as if section 613 applied to all of such production at the rate specified in paragraph (1) or (6), as the case may be) as his depletable oil quantity bears to the aggregate number of barrels representing the average daily production of domestic crude oil of the taxpayer for such year.

(B) PRODUCTION OF NATURAL GAS IN EXCESS OF DEPLETABLE NATURAL GAS QUANTITY.—If the taxpayer's average daily production of domestic natural gas exceeds his depletable natural gas quantity, the allowance under paragraph (1)(B) with respect to natural gas produced during the taxable year from each property in the United States shall be that amount which bears the same ratio to the amount of depletion which would have been allowable under section 613(a) for all of the taxpayers natural gas produced from such property during the taxable year (computed as if section 613 applied to all of such production at the rate specified in paragraph (1) or (6), as the case may be) as the amount of his depletable natural gas quantity in cubic feet bears to the aggregate number of cubic feet representing the average daily production of domestic natural gas of the taxpayer for such year.

(C) TAXABLE INCOME FROM THE PROPERTY.—If both oil and gas are produced from the property during the taxable year, for purposes of subparagraphs (A) and (B) the taxable income from the property, in applying the taxable income limitation in section 613(a), shall be allocated between the oil production and the gas production in proportion to the gross income during the taxable year from each.

(D) PARTNERSHIPS.—In the case of a partnership, the depletion allowance shall be computed separately by the partners and not by the partnership. The partnership shall allocate to each partner his proportionate share of the adjusted basis of each partnership oil or gas property. The allocation is to be made as of the later of the date of acquisition of the oil or gas property by the partnership, or January 1, 1975. A partner's proportionate share of the adjusted basis of partnership property shall be determined in accordance with his interest in partnership capital or income and, in the case of property contributed to the partnership by a partner, section 704(c) (relating to contributed property) shall apply in determining such share. Each partner shall separately keep records of his share of the adjusted basis in each oil and gas property of the partnership, adjust such share of the adjusted basis for any depletion taken on such property, and use such adjusted basis each year in the computation of his cost depletion or in the computation of his gain or loss on the disposition of such property by the partnership. For purposes of section 732 (relating to basis of distributed property other than money), the partnership's adjusted basis in mineral property shall be an amount equal to the sum of the partners' adjusted bases in such property as determined under this paragraph.

(8) BUSINESSES UNDER COMMON CONTROL; MEMBERS OF THE SAME FAMILY.—

(A) COMPONENT MEMBERS OF CONTROLLED GROUP TREATED AS ONE TAXPAYER.—For purposes of this subsection, persons who are members of the same controlled group of corporations shall be treated as one taxpayer.

(B) AGGREGATION OF BUSINESS ENTITIES UNDER COMMON CONTROL.—If 50 percent or more of the beneficial interest in two or more corporations, trusts, or estates is owned by the same or related persons (taking into account only persons who own at least 5 percent of such beneficial interest), the tentative quantity determined under paragraph (3)(B) shall be allocated among all such entities in proportion to the respective production of domestic crude oil during the period in question by such entities.

(C) ALLOCATION AMONG MEMBERS OF THE SAME FAMILY.—In the case of individuals who are members of the same family, the tentative quantity determined under paragraph (3)(B) shall be allocated among such individuals in proportion to the respective production of domestic crude oil during the period in question by such individuals.

(D) DEFINITION AND SPECIAL RULES.—For purposes of this paragraph—

(i) the term "controlled group of corporations" has the meaning given to such term by section 1563(a), except that section 1563(b)(2) shall not apply and except that "more than 50 percent" shall be substituted for "at least 80 percent" each place it appears in section 1563(a),

(ii) a person is a related person to another person if such persons are members of the same controlled group of corporations or if the relationship between such persons would result in a disallowance of losses under section 267 or 707(b), except that for this purpose the family of an individual includes only his spouse and minor children,

(iii) the family of an individual includes only his spouse and minor children, and

(iv) each 6,000 cubic feet of domestic natural gas shall be treated as 1 barrel of domestic crude oil.

(9) SPECIAL RULE FOR FISCAL YEAR TAXPAYERS.—In applying this subsection to a taxable year which is not a calendar year, each portion of such taxable year which occurs during a single calendar year shall be treated as if it were a short taxable year.

(10) CERTAIN PRODUCTION NOT TAKEN INTO ACCOUNT.—In applying this subsection, there shall not be taken into account the production of natural gas with respect to which subsection (b) applies.

(11) SUBCHAPTER S CORPORATIONS.—

(A) COMPUTATION OF DEPLETION ALLOWANCE AT SHAREHOLDER LEVEL.—In the case of an S corporation, the allowance for depletion with respect to any oil or gas property shall be computed separately by each shareholder.

(B) ALLOCATION OF BASIS.—The S corporation shall allocate to each shareholder his pro rata share of the adjusted basis of the S corporation in each oil or gas property held by the S corporation. The allocation shall be made as of the later of the date of acquisition of the property by the S corporation, or the first day of the first taxable year of the S corporation to which the Subchapter S Revison Act of 1982 applies. Each shareholder shall separately keep records of his share of the adjusted basis in each oil and gas property of the S corporation, adjust such share of the adjusted basis for any depletion taken on such property, and use such adjusted basis each year in the computation of his cost depletion or in the computation of his gain or loss on the disposition of such property by the S corporation. In the case of any distribution of oil or gas property to its shareholders by the S corporation, the corporation's adjusted basis in the property shall be an amount equal to the sum of the shareholders' adjusted bases in such property, as determined under this subparagraph.

Amendments

• 2008, Energy Improvement and Extension Act of 2008 (P.L. 110-343)

P.L. 110-343, Division B, §210:

Amended Code Sec. 613A(c)(6)(H) by striking "for any taxable year" and all that follows and inserting "for any taxable year—" and new clauses (i)-(ii). **Effective** 10-3-2008. Prior to amendment, Code Sec. 613A(c)(6)(H) read as follows:

(H) TEMPORARY SUSPENSION OF TAXABLE INCOME LIMIT WITH RESPECT TO MARGINAL PRODUCTION.—The second sentence of subsection (a) of section 613 shall not apply to so much of the allowance for depletion as is determined under subparagraph (A) for any taxable year beginning after December 31, 1997, and before January 1, 2008.

• 2006, Tax Relief and Health Care Act of 2006 (P.L. 109-432)

P.L. 109-432, Division A, §118(a):

Amended Code Sec. 613A(c)(6)(H) by striking "2006" and inserting "2008". **Effective** for tax years beginning after 12-31-2005.

• 2005, Energy Tax Incentives Act of 2005 (P.L. 109-58)

P.L. 109-58, §1322(a)(3)(B):

Amended Code Sec. 613A(c)(6)(C) by striking "section 29(d)(2)(C)" and inserting "section 45K(d)(2)(C)". **Effective** for credits determined under the Internal Revenue Code of 1986 for tax years ending after 12-31-2005.

• 2004, Working Families Tax Relief Act of 2004 (P.L. 108-311)

P.L. 108-311, §314(a):

Amended Code Sec. 613A(c)(6)(H) by striking "January 1, 2004" and inserting "January 1, 2006". **Effective** for tax years beginning after 12-31-2003.

• 2002, Job Creation and Worker Assistance Act of 2002 (P.L. 107-147)

P.L. 107-147, §607(a):

Amended Code Sec. 613A(c)(6)(H) by striking "2002" and inserting "2004". **Effective** for tax years beginning after 12-31-2001.

• 1999, Tax Relief Extension Act of 1999 (P.L. 106-170)

P.L. 106-170, §504(a):

Amended Code Sec. 613A(c)(6)(H) by striking "January 1, 2000" and inserting "January 1, 2002". **Effective** for tax years beginning after 12-31-99.

• 1997, Taxpayer Relief Act of 1997 (P.L. 105-34)

P.L. 105-34, §972(a):

Amended Code Sec. 613A(c)(6) by adding at the end a new subparagraph (H). **Effective** for tax years beginning after 12-31-97.

• 1996, Small Business Job Protection Act of 1996 (P.L. 104-188)

P.L. 104-188, §1702(e)(2):

Amended Code Sec. 613A(c)(3)(A)(i) by striking "the table contained in" after "under". **Effective** as if included in the provision of P.L. 101-508 to which it relates.

• 1990, Omnibus Budget Reconciliation Act of 1990 (P.L. 101-508)

P.L. 101-508, §11521(a):

Amended Code Sec. 613A(c) by striking paragraphs (9) and (10) and by redesignating paragraphs (11), (12), and (13) as paragraphs (9), (10), and (11), respectively. **Effective** for transfers after 10-11-90. Prior to amendment, Code Sec. 613(A)(c)(9) and (10) read as follows:

(9) TRANSFER OF OIL OR GAS PROPERTY.—

(A) In the case of a transfer (including the subleasing of a lease) after December 31, 1974 of an interest (including an interest in a partnership or trust) in any proven oil or gas property, this subsection shall not apply to the transferee (or sublessee) with respect to production of crude oil or natural gas attributable to such interest, and such production shall not be taken into account for any computation by the transferee (or sublessee) under this subsection. A property shall be treated as a proven oil or gas property if at the time of the transfer the principal value of the property has been demonstrated by prospecting or exploration or discovery work.

(B) Subparagraph (A) shall not apply in the case of—

(i) a transfer of property at death,

(ii) the transfer in an exchange to which section 351 applies if following the exchange the tentative quantity determined under paragraph (3)(B) is allocated under paragraph (8) between the transferor and transferee,

(iii) a change of beneficiaries of a trust by reason of the death, birth, or adoption of any vested beneficiary if the transferee was a beneficiary of such trust or is a lineal descendant of the settlor or any other vested beneficiary of such trust, except in the case of any trust where any beneficiary of such trust is a member of the family (as defined in section 267(c)(4)) of a settlor who created inter vivos and testamentary trusts for members of the family and such settlor died within the last six days of the fifth month in 1970 and the law in the jurisdiction in which such trust was created requires all or a portion of the gross or net proceeds of any royalty or other interest in oil, gas, or other mineral representing any percentage depletion allowance to be allocated to the principal of the trust,

(iv) a transfer of property between corporations which are members of the same controlled group of corporations (as defined in paragraph (8)(D)(i)), or

(v) a transfer of property between business entities which are under common control (within the meaning of paragraph (8)(B)) or between related persons in the same family (within the meaning of paragraph (8)(C)), or

(vi) a transfer of property between a trust and related persons in the same family (within the meaning of paragraph (8)(C)) to the extent that the beneficiaries of that trust are and continue to be related persons in the family that transferred the property, and to the extent that the tentative oil quantity is allocated among the members of the family (within the meaning of paragraph (8)(C)).

Clause (iv) or (v) shall apply only so long as the tentative oil quantity determined under paragraph (3)(B) is allocated under paragraph (8) between the transferor and transferee.

(10) TRANSFERS BY INDIVIDUALS TO CORPORATIONS.—

(A) IN GENERAL.—Paragraph (9)(A) shall not apply to a transfer by an individual of qualified property to a qualified transferee corporation solely in exchange for stock in such corporation.

(B) 1,000-BARREL LIMIT FOR CORPORATION.—A tentative quantity shall be determined for the qualified transferee corporation under this subsection.

(C) TRANSFEROR'S TENTATIVE QUANTITY REDUCED.—

(i) IN GENERAL.—The tentative quantity for the transferor (and his family) for any period shall be reduced by the transferor's pro rata share of the corporation's depletable quantity for such period.

(ii) PRO RATA SHARE.—For purposes of clause (i), a transferor's pro rata share for any period shall be—

(I) in the case of production from property to which subparagraph (A) applies, that portion of the corporation's depletable quantity which is allocable to production from such property, and

(II) in the case of production from all other property, that portion of the corporation's depletable quantity which is allocable to the production from such property, multiplied by a fraction the numerator of which is the fair market value of the transferor's stock in the corporation, and the denominator of which is the fair market value of all stock in the corporation.

(iii) DEPLETABLE QUANTITY.—For purposes of this paragraph, a corporation's depletable quantity for any period is the lesser of—

(I) such corporation's tentative quantity for such period (determined under paragraphs (3) and (8)), or

(II) such corporation's average daily production for such period.

(D) QUALIFIED TRANSFEREE CORPORATION DEFINED.—For purposes of this paragraph, the term "qualified transferee corporation" means a corporation all of the outstanding stock of which has been issued to individuals soley in exchange for qualified property held by such individuals.

(E) QUALIFIED PROPERTY DEFINED.—For purposes of this paragraph, the term "qualified property" means oil or gas property with respect to which—

(i) there has been no prior transfer to which paragraph (9)(A) applied, and

(ii) the transferor has made an election to have this paragraph apply.

The term also includes cash (not to exceed $1,000 in the aggregate) which one or more individuals transfer to the corporation and, in the case of any property, also includes necessary production equipment for such property which is in place when the property is transferred.

(F) TRANSFEROR MUST RETAIN STOCK DURING LIFETIME.—If at any time during his lifetime any transferor disposes of stock in the corporation (other than to a member of his family), then the depletable quantity of the corporation (determined without regard to this subparagraph) shall be reduced (for all periods on or after the date of the disposition) by an amount which bears the same ratio to such quantity as the fair market value of the stock so disposed of bears to the aggregate fair market value of all stock of the corporation on such date of disposition.

(G) SPECIAL RULES RELATING TO FAMILY OF TRANSFEROR.—

(i) IN GENERAL.—For purposes of this paragraph—

(I) the issuance of stock to a member of the family of the transferor shall be treated as issuance of stock to the transferor, and

(II) during the lifetime of the transferor, stock transferred to a member of the family of the transferor shall be treated as held by the transferor.

If stock described in the preceding sentence ceases to be held by a member of the family of the transferor, the transferor shall be treated as having disposed of such stock at the time of such cessation.

(ii) FAMILY DEFINED.—For purposes of this paragraph, the members of the family of an individual include only his spouse and minor children.

(H) PROPERTY SUBJECT TO LIABILITIES.—For purposes of this paragraph, section 357 shall be applied as if—

(i) references to section 351 include references to subparagraph (A) of this paragraph, and

(ii) the reference in subsection (a)(1) of section 357 to the nonrecognition of gain includes a reference to the nonapplication of paragraph (9)(A) of this subsection.

(I) ELECTION.—A transferor may make an election under this paragraph only in such manner as the Secretary may by regulations prescribe and only on or before the due date (including extensions) for filing the return of the corporation of the taxes imposed by this chapter for the corporation's first taxable year ending after the date of the transfer (or, if later, after the date of the enactment of this paragraph).

(J) REGULATIONS.—The Secretary shall prescribe such regulations as may be necessary to carry out the purposes of this paragraph.

P.L. 101-508, §11521(b):

Amended Code Sec. 613A(c)(11), as redesignated by Act Sec. 11521(a), by striking subparagraphs (C) and (D). **Effective** for transfers after 10-11-90. Prior to amendment, Code Sec. 613A(c)(11)(C) and (D) read as follows:

(C) COORDINATION WITH TRANSFER RULE OF PARAGRAPH (9).—For purposes of paragraph (9)—

(i) an S corporation shall be treated as a partnership, and the shareholders of the S corporation shall be treated as partners, and

(ii) an election by a C corporation to become an S corporation shall be treated as a transfer of all its properties effective on the day on which such election first takes effect.

(D) COORDINATION WITH TRANSFER RULE OF PARAGRAPH (10).—For purposes of paragraphs (9) and (10), if an S corporation becomes a C corporation, each shareholder shall be treated as having transferred to such corporation his pro rata share of all the assets of the S corporation.

P.L. 101-508, §11522(b)(1):

Amended Code Sec. 613A(c)(7)(C) by striking "50-percent" and inserting "taxable income". **Effective** for tax years beginning after 12-31-90.

P.L. 101-508, §11523(a):

Amended Code Sec. 613A(c)(6). **Effective** for tax years beginning after 12-31-90. Prior to amendment, Code Sec. 613A(c)(6) read as follows:

(6) OIL AND NATURAL GAS RESULTING FROM SECONDARY OR TERTIARY PROCESSES.—

(A) IN GENERAL.—Except as provided in subsection (d), the allowance for depletion under section 611 shall be computed in accordance with section 613 with respect to—

(i) so much of the taxpayer's average daily secondary or tertiary production of domestic crude oil as does not exceed the taxpayer's depletable oil quantity (determined without regard to paragraph (3)(A)(ii)); and

(ii) so much of the taxpayer's average daily secondary or tertiary production of domestic natural gas as does not exceed the taxpayer's depletable natural gas quantity (determined without regard to paragraph (3)(A)(ii));

and 22 percent shall be deemed to be specified in subsection (b) of section 613 for purposes of subsection (a) of that section.

(B) AVERAGE DAILY SECONDARY OR TERTIARY PRODUCTION.—For purposes of this subsection—

(i) the taxpayer's average daily secondary or tertiary production of domestic crude oil or natural gas for any taxable year shall be determined by dividing his aggregate production of domestic crude oil or natural gas, as the case may be, resulting from secondary or tertiary processes during the taxable year by the number of days in such taxable year, and

(ii) in the case of a taxpayer holding a partial interest in the production from any property (including any interest held in any partnership) such taxpayer's production shall be considered to be that amount of such production determined by multiplying the total production of such property by the taxpayer's percentage participation in the revenues from such property.

(C) TERMINATION.—This paragraph shall not apply after December 31, 1983.

P.L. 101-508, §11523(b)(1)-(2):

Amended Code Sec. 613A(c)(3)(A) by striking clause (ii) and inserting new clause (ii), and by striking the last sentence. **Effective** for tax years beginning after 12-31-90. Prior to amendment, Code Sec. 613A(c)(3)(A)(ii) and the last sentence of Code Sec. 613A(c)(3)(A) read as follows:

(ii) the taxpayer's average daily secondary or tertiary production for the taxable year.

Clause (ii) shall not apply after December 31, 1983.

P.L. 101-508, §11815(a)(1)(A)-(C):

Amended Code Sec. 613A(c) by striking "the applicable percentage (determined in accordance with the table contained in paragraph (5))" in paragraph (1) and inserting "15 percent", by amending subparagraph (B) of paragraph (3), and by striking paragraphs (5) and (7)(E). **Effective** 11-5-90. Prior to amendment, Code Sec. 613A(c)(3)(B), (c)(5), and (c)(7)(E) read as follows.

(B) PHASE-OUT TABLE.—For purposes of subparagraph (A)—

In the case of production during the calendar year:	**The tentative quantity in barrels is:**
1975	2,000
1976	1,800
1977	1,600
1978	1,400
1979	1,200
1980 and thereafter	1,000

* * *

(5) APPLICABLE PERCENTAGE.—For purposes of paragraph (1)—

In the case of production during the calendar year:	The applicable percentage is:
1975	22
1976	22
1977	22
1978	22
1979	22
1980	22
1981	20
1982	18
1983	16
1984 and thereafter	15

* * *

(E) SECONDARY OR TERTIARY PRODUCTION.—If the taxpayer has production from secondary or tertiary recovery processes during the taxable year, this paragraph (under regulations prescribed by the Secretary) shall be applied separately with respect to such production. This subparagraph shall not apply after December 31, 1983.

P.L. 101-508, §11815(a)(2)(A):

Amended Code Sec. 613A(c)(7) by striking "specified in paragraph (5)" in subparagraphs (A) and (B) and inserting "specified in paragraph (1)". **Effective** 11-5-90.

P.L. 101-508, §11815(a)(2)(B):

Amended Code Sec. 613A(c) by striking "determined under the table contained in paragraph (3)(B)" each place it appears in paragraphs (8)(B), (8)(C), and (9) and inserting "determined under paragraph (3)(B)". **Effective** 11-5-90.

P.L. 101-508, §11821(b), provides:

(b) SAVINGS PROVISION.—If—

(1) any provision amended or repealed by this part applied to—

(A) any transaction occurring before the date of the enactment of this Act,

(B) any property acquired before such date of enactment, or

(C) any item of income, loss, deduction, or credit taken into account before such date of enactment, and

(2) the treatment of such transaction, property, or item under such provision would (without regard to the amendments made by this part) affect liability for tax for periods ending after such date of enactment,

nothing in the amendments made by this part shall be construed to affect the treatment of such transaction, property, or item for purposes of determining liability for tax for periods ending after such date of enactment.

• 1984, Deficit Reduction Act of 1984 (P.L. 98-369)

P.L. 98-369, §25(b)(1):

Amended Code Sec. 613A(c)(2) by striking out the last sentence. **Effective** 1-1-84. Prior to amendment, the last sentence of Code Sec. 613A(c)(2) read as follows:

In applying this paragraph, there shall not be taken into account any production of crude oil or natural gas resulting from secondary or tertiary processes (as defined in regulations prescribed by the Secretary).

P.L. 98-369, §25(b)(2):

Amended Code Sec. 613A(c)(3)(A) by adding a new sentence at the end thereof. **Effective** 1-1-84.

P.L. 98-369, §25(b)(3):

Amended Code Sec. 613A(c)(7)(E) by adding at the end thereof a new sentence. **Effective** 1-1-84.

P.L. 98-369, §25(b)(4):

Amended Code Sec. 613A(c)(9)(A) by striking out "paragraph (1)" and inserting in lieu thereof "this subsection". **Effective** 1-1-84.

P.L. 98-369, §71(b):

Amended Code Sec. 613A(c)(7)(D) by striking out "an agreement described in section 704(c)(2) (relating to effect of partnership agreement on contributed property), such share shall be determined by taking such agreement into account" from the fourth sentence and inserting in lieu thereof "property contributed to the partnership by a partner, section 704(c) (relating to contributed property) shall apply in determining such share". **Effective** with respect to property contributed to the partnership after 3-31-84, in tax years ending after such date.

• 1983, Technical Corrections Act of 1982 (P.L. 97-448)

P.L. 97-448, §202(d)(1):

Amended Code Sec. 613A(c)(10)(E) by inserting "and, in the case of any property, also includes necessary production equipment for such property which is in place when the property is transferred" before the period at the end thereof. **Effective** for transfers in tax years ending after 12-31-74, but only for purposes of applying Code Sec. 613A to periods after 12-31-79.

• 1982, Subchapter S Revision Act of 1982 (P.L. 97-354)

P.L. 97-354, §3(a):

Added Code Sec. 613A(c)(13). **Effective** for to tax years beginning after 12-31-82.

• 1980 (P.L. 96-603)

P.L. 96-603, §3(a):

Amended Code Sec. 613A(c) by redesignating paragraphs (10) and (11) as (11) and (12), respectively, and by adding a new paragraph 10. **Effective** for production from periods after 1979 from property transferred after 1974.

• 1976, Tax Reform Act of 1976 (P.L. 94-455)

P.L. 94-455, §1901(a)(86)(B):

Substituted "without" for "with" in Code Sec. 613A(c)(6)(A)(i). **Effective** for tax years beginning after 12-31-76.

P.L. 94-455, §1906(b)(13)(A):

Amended 1954 Code by substituting "Secretary" for "Secretary or his delegate" each place it appeared. **Effective** 2-1-77.

P.L. 94-455, §2115(c)(1):

Amended Code Sec. 613A(c)(7)(D). **Effective** 1-1-75, and applicable to tax years ending after 12-31-74. Prior to amendment, Sec. 613A(c)(7)(D) read as follows:

(D) PARTNERSHIPS.—In the case of a partnership, the depletion allowance in the case of oil and gas wells to which this subsection applies shall be computed separately by the partners and not by the partnership.

P.L. 94-455, §2115(b)(1) and (e):

Amended Code Sec. 613A(c)(9)(B). **Effective** 1-1-75, and applicable to tax years ending after 12-31-74. Prior to amendment, Sec. 613A(c)(9)(B) read as follows:

(B) Subparagraph (A) shall not apply in the case of—

(i) a transfer of property at death, or

(ii) the transfer in an exchange to which section 351 applies if following the exchange the tentative quantity determined under the table contained in paragraph (3)(B) is allocated under paragraph (8) between the transferor and transferee.

[Sec. 613A(d)]

(d) LIMITATIONS ON APPLICATION OF SUBSECTION (c).—

(1) LIMITATION BASED ON TAXABLE INCOME.—The deduction for the taxable year attributable to the application of subsection (c) shall not exceed 65 percent of the taxpayer's taxable income for the year computed without regard to—

(A) any depletion on production from an oil or gas property which is subject to the provisions of subsection (c),

(B) any deduction allowable under section 199,

(C) any net operating loss carryback to the taxable year under section 172,

(D) any capital loss carryback to the taxable year under section 1212, and

(E) in the case of a trust, any distributions to its beneficiary, except in the case of any trust where any beneficiary of such trust is a member of the family (as defined in section 267(c)(4)) of a settlor who created inter vivos and testamentary trusts for members of the family and such settlor died within the last six days of the fifth month in 1970, and the law in the jurisdiction in which such trust was created requires all or a portion of the gross or net proceeds of any royalty or other interest in oil, gas, or other mineral representing any percentage depletion allowance to be allocated to the principal of the trust.

If an amount is disallowed as a deduction for the taxable year by reason of application of the preceding sentence, the disallowed amount shall be treated as an amount allowable as a deduction under subsection (c) for the following taxable year, subject to the application of the preceding sentence to such taxable year. For purposes of basis adjustments and determining whether cost depletion exceeds percentage depletion with respect to the production from a property, any amount disallowed as a deduction on the application of this paragraph shall be allocated to the respective properties from which the oil or gas was produced in proportion to the percentage depletion otherwise allowable to such properties under subsection (c).

(2) RETAILERS EXCLUDED.—Subsection (c) shall not apply in the case of any taxpayer who directly, or through a related person, sells oil or natural gas (excluding bulk sales of such items to commercial or industrial users), or any product derived from oil or natural gas (excluding bulk sales of aviation fuels to the Department of Defense)—

(A) through any retail outlet operated by the taxpayer or a related person, or

(B) to any person—

(i) obligated under an agreement or contract with the taxpayer or a related person to use a trademark, trade name, or service mark or name owned by such taxpayer or a related person, in marketing or distributing oil or natural gas or any product derived from oil or natural gas, or

(ii) given authority, pursuant to an agreement or contract with the taxpayer or a related person, to occupy any retail outlet owned, leased, or in any way controlled by the taxpayer or a related person.

Notwithstanding the preceding sentence this paragraph shall not apply in any case where the combined gross receipts from the sale of such oil, natural gas, or any product derived therefrom, for the taxable year of all retail outlets taken into account for purposes of this paragraph do not exceed $5,000,000. For purposes of this paragraph, sales of oil, natural gas, or any product derived from oil or natural gas shall not include sales made of such items outside the United States, if no domestic production of the taxpayer or a related person is exported during the taxable year or the immediately preceding taxable year.

(3) RELATED PERSON.—For purposes of this subsection, a person is a related person with respect to the taxpayer if a significant ownership interest in either the taxpayer or such person is held by the other, or if a third person has a significant ownership interest in both the taxpayer and such person. For purposes of the preceding sentence, the term "significant ownership interest" means—

(A) with respect to any corporation, 5 percent or more in value of the outstanding stock of such corporation,

(B) with respect to a partnership, 5 percent or more interest in the profits or capital of such partnership, and

(C) with respect to an estate or trust, 5 percent or more of the beneficial interests in such estate or trust.

For purposes of determining a significant ownership interest, an interest owned by or for a corporation, partnership, trust, or estate shall be considered as owned directly both by itself and proportionately by its shareholders, partners, or beneficiaries, as the case may be.

(4) CERTAIN REFINERS EXCLUDED.—If the taxpayer or one or more related persons engages in the refining of crude oil, subsection (c) shall not apply to the taxpayer for a taxable year if the average daily refinery runs of the taxpayer and such persons for the taxable year exceed 75,000 barrels. For purposes of this paragraph, the average daily refinery runs for any taxable year shall be determined by dividing the aggregate refinery runs for the taxable year by the number of days in the taxable year.

(5) PERCENTAGE DEPLETION NOT ALLOWED FOR LEASE BONUSES, ETC.—In the case of any oil or gas property to which subsection (c) applies, for purposes of section 613, the term "gross income from the property" shall not include any lease bonus, advance royalty, or other amount payable without regard to production from property.

Amendments

• 2005, Gulf Opportunity Zone Act of 2005 (P.L. 109-135)

P.L. 109-135, §403(a)(18):

Amended Code Sec. 613A(d)(1) by redesignating subparagraphs (B), (C), and (D) as subparagraphs (C), (D), and (E), respectively, and by inserting after subparagraph (A) a new subparagraph (B). **Effective** as if included in the provision of the American Jobs Creation Act of 2004 (P.L. 108-357) to which it relates [**effective** for tax years beginning after 12-31-2004.—CCH].

• 2005, Energy Tax Incentives Act of 2005 (P.L. 109-58)

P.L. 109-58, §1328(a):

Amended Code Sec. 613A(d)(4). **Effective** for tax years ending after 8-8-2005. Prior to amendment, Code Sec. 613A(d)(4) read as follows:

(4) CERTAIN REFINERS EXCLUDED.—If the taxpayer or a related person engages in the refining of crude oil, subsection (c) shall not apply to such taxpayer if on any day during the taxable year the refinery runs of the taxpayer and such person exceed 50,000 barrels.

• 1986, Tax Reform Act of 1986 (P.L. 99-514)

P.L. 99-514, §104(b)(9):

Amended Code Sec. 613A(d)(1) by striking out "(reduced in the case of an individual by the zero bracket amount)" after "taxable income". **Effective** for tax years beginning after 12-31-86.

P.L. 99-514, §412(a)(1):

Amended Code Sec. 613A(d) by adding at the end thereof new paragraph (5). **Effective** for amounts received or accrued after 8-16-86, in tax years ending after such date.

• 1983, Technical Corrections Act of 1982 (P.L. 97-448)

P.L. 97-448, §202(d)(2):

Amended Code Sec. 613A(d)(2) by inserting "(excluding bulk sales of aviation fuels to the Department of Defense)" after "any product derived from oil or natural gas" the first place it appears. **Effective** for bulk sales after 9-18-82.

• 1977, Tax Reduction and Simplification Act of 1977 (P.L. 95-30)

P.L. 95-30, §102(b)(7):

Amended paragraph (1) of Code Sec. 613A(d) by inserting "(reduced in the case of an individual by the zero bracket amount)" after "the taxpayer's taxable income". **Effective** for tax years beginning after 12-31-76.

• 1976, Tax Reform Act of 1976 (P.L. 94-455)

P.L. 94-455, §2115(a):

Amended Code Sec. 613A(d)(2). **Effective** 1-1-75, and applicable to tax years ending after 12-31-74. Prior to amendment, Sec. 613A(d)(2) read as follows:

(2) RETAILERS EXCLUDED.—Subsection (c) shall not apply in the case of any taxpayer who directly, or through a related person, sells oil or natural gas, or any product derived from oil or natural gas—

(A) through any retail outlet operated by the taxpayer or a related person, or

(B) to any person—

(i) obligated under an agreement or contract with the taxpayer or a related person to use a trademark, trade name, or service mark or name owned by such taxpayer or related persons, in marketing or distributing oil or natural gas or any product derived from oil or natural gas, or

(ii) given authority, pursuant to an agreement or contract with the taxpayer or a related person, to occupy any retail outlet owned, leased, or in any way controlled by the taxpayer or a related person.

P.L. 94-455, §2115(b)(2)(A):

Amended Code Sec. 613A(d)(1)(A). **Effective** 1-1-75, and applicable to tax years ending after 12-31-74. Prior to amendment, Sec. 613A(d)(1)(A) read as follows:

(A) depletion with respect to production of oil and gas subject to the provisions of subsection (c).

P.L. 94-455, §2115(b)(2)(B):

Amended Code Sec. 613A(d)(1)(B) by striking out "and" at the end of the subparagraph. **Effective** 1-1-75, and applicable to tax years ending after 12-31-74.

P.L. 94-455, §2115(b)(2)(C):

Amended Code Sec. 613A(d)(1)(C) by striking out a period and adding "and," at the end of the subparagraph. **Effective** 1-1-75, and applicable to tax years ending after 12-31-74.

P.L. 94-455, §2115(b)(2)(D):

Added Code Sec. 613A(d)(1)(D). **Effective** 1-1-75, and applicable to tax years ending after 12-31-74.

P.L. 94-455, §2115(d):

Amended Code Sec. 613A(d)(3) by adding the last sentence. **Effective** 1-1-75, and applicable to tax years ending after 12-31-74.

[Sec. 613A(e)]

(e) DEFINITIONS.—For purposes of this section—

(1) CRUDE OIL.—The term "crude oil" includes a natural gas liquid recovered from a gas well in lease separators or field facilities.

(2) NATURAL GAS.—The term "natural gas" means any product (other than crude oil) of an oil or gas well if a deduction for depletion is allowable under section 611 with respect to such product.

(3) DOMESTIC.—The term "domestic" refers to production from an oil or gas well located in the United States or in a possession of the United States.

(4) BARREL.—The term "barrel" means 42 United States gallons.

Amendments

• 1975, Tax Reduction Act of 1975 (P.L. 94-12)

P.L. 94-12, §501(a):

Added Code Sec. 613A. **Effective** 1-1-75, and applicable to tax years ending after 12-31-74.

[Sec. 614]

SEC. 614. DEFINITION OF PROPERTY.

[Sec. 614(a)]

(a) GENERAL RULE.—For the purpose of computing the depletion allowance in the case of mines, wells, and other natural deposits, the term "property" means each separate interest owned by the taxpayer in each mineral deposit in each separate tract or parcel of land.

[Sec. 614(b)]

(b) SPECIAL RULES AS TO OPERATING MINERAL INTERESTS IN OIL AND GAS WELLS OR GEOTHERMAL DEPOSITS.—In the case of oil and gas wells or geothermal deposits—

(1) IN GENERAL.—Except as otherwise provided in this subsection—

(A) all of the taxpayer's operating mineral interests in a separate tract or parcel of land shall be combined and treated as one property, and

(B) the taxpayer may not combine an operating mineral interest in one tract or parcel of land with an operating mineral interest in another tract or parcel of land.

(2) ELECTION TO TREAT OPERATING MINERAL INTERESTS AS SEPARATE PROPERTIES.—If the taxpayer has more than one operating mineral interest in a single tract or parcel of land, he may elect to treat one or more of such operating mineral interests as separate properties. The taxpayer may not have more than one combination of operating mineral interests in a single tract or parcel of land. If the taxpayer makes the election provided in this paragraph with respect to any interest in a tract or parcel of land, each operating mineral interest which is discovered or acquired by the taxpayer in such tract or parcel of land after the taxable year for which the election is made shall be treated—

(A) if there is no combination of interests in such tract or parcel, as a separate property unless the taxpayer elects to combine it with another interest, or

(B) if there is a combination of interests in such tract or parcel, as part of such combination unless the taxpayer elects to treat it as a separate property.

(3) CERTAIN UNITIZATION OR POOLING ARRANGEMENTS.—

(A) IN GENERAL.—Under regulations prescribed by the Secretary, if one or more of the taxpayer's operating mineral interests participate, under a voluntary or compulsory unitization or pooling agreement, in a single cooperative or unit plan of operation, then for the period of such participation—

(i) they shall be treated for all purposes of this subtitle as one property, and

(ii) the application of paragraphs (1), (2), and (4) in respect of such interests shall be suspended.

(B) LIMITATION.—Subparagraph (A) shall apply to a voluntary agreement only if all the operating mineral interests covered by such agreement—

(i) are in the same deposit, or are in 2 or more deposits the joint development or production of which is logical from the standpoint of geology, convenience, economy, or conservation, and

(ii) are in tracts or parcels of land which are contiguous or in close proximity.

(C) SPECIAL RULE IN THE CASE OF ARRANGEMENTS ENTERED INTO IN TAXABLE YEARS BEGINNING BEFORE JANUARY 1, 1964.—If—

(i) two or more of the taxpayer's operating mineral interests participate under a voluntary or compulsory unitization or pooling agreement entered into in any taxable year beginning before January 1, 1964, in a single cooperative or unit plan of operation,

(ii) the taxpayer, for the last taxable year beginning before January 1, 1964, treated such interests as two or more separate properties, and

(iii) it is determined that such treatment was proper under the law applicable to such taxable year,

such taxpayer may continue to treat such interests in a consistent manner for the period of such participation.

(4) MANNER, TIME, AND SCOPE OF ELECTION.—

(A) MANNER AND TIME.—Any election provided in paragraph (2) shall be made for each operating mineral interest, in the manner prescribed by the Secretary by regulations, not later than the time prescribed by law for filing the return (including extensions thereof) for whichever of the following taxable years is the later: The first taxable year beginning after December 31, 1963, or the first taxable year in which any expenditure for development or operation in respect of such operating mineral interest is made by the taxpayer after the acquisition of such interest.

(B) SCOPE.—Any election under paragraph (2) shall be for all purposes of this subtitle and shall be binding on the taxpayer for all subsequent taxable years.

(5) TREATMENT OF CERTAIN PROPERTIES.—If, on the day preceding the first day of the first taxable year beginning after December 31, 1963, the taxpayer has any operating mineral interests which he treats under subsection (d) of this section (as in effect before the amendments made by the Revenue Act of 1964), such treatment shall be continued and shall be deemed to have been adopted pursuant to paragraphs (1) and (2) of this subsection (as amended by such Act).

Amendments

• 1978, Energy Tax Act of 1978 (P.L. 95-618)

P.L. 95-618, §403(a)(2)(C):

Amended Code Sec. 614(b) by inserting "Or Geothermal Deposits" after "Gas Wells" in the subsection heading, and by inserting "or geothermal deposits" after "gas wells" in the first sentence of Code Sec. 614(b). **Effective** 10-1-78, to apply to tax years ending on or after such date.

• 1976, Tax Reform Act of 1976 (P.L. 94-455)

P.L. 94-455, §1906(b)(13)(A):

Amended 1954 Code by substituting "Secretary" for "Secretary or his delegate" each place it appeared. **Effective** 2-1-77.

• 1964, Revenue Act of 1964 (P.L. 88-272)

P.L. 88-272, §226(a):

Amended Code Sec. 614(b). **Effective** for tax years beginning after 12-31-63. Prior to amendment, Code Sec. 614(b) read as follows:

"(b) Special Rule as to Operating Mineral Interests.—

"(1) Election to aggregate separate interests.—If a taxpayer owns two or more separate operating mineral interests which constitute part or all of an operating unit, he may elect (for all purposes of this subtitle)—

"(A) to form one aggregation of, and to treat as one property, any two or more of such interests; and

"(B) to treat as a separate property each such interest which he does not elect to include within the aggregation referred to in subparagraph (A).

"For purposes of the preceding sentence, separate operating mineral interests which constitute part or all of an operating unit may be aggregated whether or not they are included in a single tract or parcel of land and whether or not they are included in contiguous tracts or parcels. A taxpayer may not elect to form more than one aggregation of operating mineral interests within any one operating unit.

"(2) Manner and scope of election.—The election provided by paragraph (1) shall be made, for each operating mineral interest in accordance with regulations prescribed by the Secretary or his delegate, not later than the time prescribed by law for filing the return (including extensions thereof) for whichever of the following taxable years is the later: The first taxable year beginning after December 31, 1953, or the first taxable year in which any expenditure for exploration, development, or operation in respect of the separate operating mineral interest is made by the taxpayer after the acquisition of such interest. Such an election shall be binding upon the taxpayer for all subsequent taxable years, except that the Secretary or his delegate may consent to a different treatment of the interest with respect to which the election has been made.

"(3) Operating mineral interests defined.—For purposes of this subsection, the term `operating mineral interest' includes only an interest in respect of which the costs of production of the mineral are required to be taken into account by the taxpayer for purposes of computing the 50 percent limitation provided for in section 613, or would be so required if the mine, well, or other natural deposit were in the production stage.

"(4) Termination with respect to mines.—Except in the case of oil and gas wells—

"(A) an election made under the provisions of this subsection shall not apply with respect to any taxable year beginning after December 31, 1957, and

"(B) if a taxpayer makes an election under the provisions of subsection (c)(3)(B) for any operating mineral interest which constitutes part or all of an operating unit, an election made under the provisions of this subsection shall not apply with respect to any operating mineral interest which constitutes part or all of such operating unit for any taxable year for which the election under subsection (c)(3)(B) is effective."

P.L. 88-272, §226(c), provides:

"(c) Allocation of Basis in Certain Cases.—For purposes of the Internal Revenue Code of 1954—

"(1) Fair market value rule.—Except as provided in paragraph (2) [below], if a taxpayer has a section 614(b) aggregation, then the adjusted basis (as of the first day of the first taxable year beginning after December 31, 1963) of each property included in such aggregation shall be determined by multiplying the adjusted basis of the aggregation by a fraction—

"(A) the numerator of which is the fair market value of such property, and

"(B) the denominator of which is the fair market value of such aggregation.

"For purposes of this paragraph, the adjusted basis and the fair market value of the aggregation, and the fair market value of each property included therein, shall be determined as of the day preceding the first day of the first taxable year which begins after December 31, 1963.

"(2) Allocation of adjustments, etc.—If the taxpayer makes an election under this paragraph with respect to any section 614(b) aggregation, then the adjusted basis (as of the first day of the first taxable year beginning after December 31, 1963) of each property included in such aggregation shall be the adjusted basis of such property at the time it was first included in the aggregation by the taxpayer, adjusted for that portion of those adjustments to the basis of the aggregation which are reasonably attributable to such property. If, under the preceding sentence, the total of the adjusted bases of the interests included in the aggregation exceeds the adjusted basis of the aggregation (as of the day preceding the first day of the first taxable year which begins after December 31, 1963), the adjusted bases of the properties which include such interests shall be adjusted, under regulations prescribed by the Secretary of the Treasury or his delegate, so that the total of the adjusted bases of such interests equals the adjusted basis of the aggregation. An election under this paragraph shall be made at such time and in such manner as the Secretary of the Treasury or his delegate shall by regulations prescribe.

"(3) Definitions.—For purposes of this subsection—

"(A) Section 614(b) aggregation.—The term `section 614(b) aggregation' means any aggregation to which section 614(b)(1)(A) of the Internal Revenue Code of 1954 (as in effect before the amendments made by subsection (a) of this section) applied for the day preceding the first day of the first taxable year beginning after December 31, 1963.

"(B) Property.—The term `property' has the same meaning as is applicable, under section 614 of the Internal Revenue Code of 1954, to the taxpayer for the first taxable year beginning after December 31, 1963.

• 1958, Technical Amendments Act of 1958 (P.L. 85-866)

P.L. 85-866, §37(a):

Added paragraph (4) to Code Sec. 614(b). **Effective** 1-1-54.

[Sec. 614(c)]

(c) SPECIAL RULES AS TO OPERATING MINERAL INTERESTS IN MINES.—

(1) ELECTION TO AGGREGATE SEPARATE INTERESTS.—Except in the case of oil and gas wells and geothermal deposits, if a taxpayer owns two or more separate operating mineral interests which constitute part or all of an operating unit, he may elect (for all purposes of this subtitle)—

(A) to form an aggregation of, and to treat as one property, all such interests owned by him which comprise any one mine or any two or more mines; and

(B) to treat as a separate property each such interest which is not included within an aggregation referred to in subparagraph (A).

For purposes of this paragraph, separate operating mineral interests which constitute part or all of an operating unit may be aggregated whether or not they are included in a single tract or parcel of land and whether or not they are included in contiguous tracts or parcels. For purposes of this paragraph, a taxpayer may elect to form more than one aggregation of operating mineral interests within any one operating unit; but no aggregation may include any operating mineral interest which is a part of a mine without including all of the operating mineral interests which are a part of such mine in the first taxable year for which the election to aggregate is effective, and any operating mineral interest which thereafter becomes a part of such mine shall be included in such aggregation.

(2) ELECTION TO TREAT A SINGLE INTEREST AS MORE THAN ONE PROPERTY.—Except in the case of oil and gas wells and geothermal deposits, if a single tract or parcel of land contains a mineral deposit which is being extracted, or will be extracted, by means of two or more mines for which expenditures for development or operation have been made by the taxpayer, then the taxpayer may elect to allocate to such mines, under regulations prescribed by the Secretary, all of the tract or parcel of land and of the mineral deposit contained therein, and to treat as a separate property that portion of the tract or parcel of land and of the mineral deposit so allocated to each mine. A separate property formed pursuant to an election under this paragraph shall be treated as a separate property for all purposes of this subtitle (including this paragraph). A separate property so formed may, under regulations prescribed by the Secretary, be included as a part of an aggregation in accordance with paragraphs (1) and (3). The election provided by this paragraph may not be made with respect to any property which is a part of an aggregation formed by the taxpayer under paragraph (1) except with the consent of the Secretary.

(3) MANNER AND SCOPE OF ELECTION.—The elections provided by paragraphs (1) and (2) shall be made, in accordance with regulations prescribed by the Secretary, not later than the time prescribed for filing the return (including extensions thereof) for the first taxable year—

(A) in which, in the case of an election under paragraph (1), any expenditure for development or operation in respect of the separate operating mineral interest is made by the taxpayer after the acquisition of such interest, or

(B) in which, in the case of an election under paragraph (2), expenditures for development or operation of more than one mine in respect of a property are made by the taxpayer after the acquisition of the property.

An election made under paragraph (1) or (2) for a taxable year shall be binding upon the taxpayer for such year and all subsequent taxable years, except that the Secretary may consent to a different treatment of any interest with respect to which an election has been made.

Amendments

• 1978, Energy Tax Act of 1978 (P.L. 95-618)

P.L. 95-618, §403(a)(2)(D):

Amended Code Sec. 614(c) by striking out "oil and gas wells" each place it appears and inserting in lieu thereof "oil and gas wells and geothermal deposits". **Effective** 10-1-78, for tax years ending on or after such date.

• 1976, Tax Reform Act of 1976 (P.L. 94-455)

P.L. 94-455, §1901(a)(87)(A)(i):

Amended Code Sec. 614(c) by striking out paragraph (4). For the **effective** date, see Act Sec. 1901(a)(87)(A)(ii), below. Prior to repeal, Sec. 614(c)(4) read as follows:

(4) SPECIAL RULE AS TO DEDUCTIONS UNDER SECTION 615(a) PRIOR TO AGGREGATION.—

(A) IN GENERAL.—If an aggregation of operating mineral interests formed under paragraph (1) includes any interest or interests in respect of which exploration expenditures, paid or incurred after the acquisition of such interest or interests, were deducted by the taxpayer under section 615(a) for any taxable year all or any portion of which precedes the date on which such aggregation becomes effective, or the date on which such interest or interests become a part of such aggregation (as the case may be), then the tax imposed by this chapter for such taxable year shall be recomputed as provided in subparagraph (B). In the case of any taxable year beginning before January 1, 1958, this subparagraph shall apply to exploration expenditures deducted in respect of any interest or interests for such taxable year, only if such interest or interests constitute part or all of any operating unit with respect to which the taxpayer makes an election pursuant to paragraph (3)(B) which is applicable with respect to such taxable year.

(B) RECOMPUTATION OF TAX.—A recomputation of the tax imposed by this chapter shall be made for each taxable year described in subparagraph (A) for which exploration expenditures were deducted as though, for each such year, an election had been made to aggregate the separate operating mineral interest or interests with respect to which such exploration expenditures were deducted with those operating mineral interests included in the aggregation formed under paragraph (1) in respect of which any expenditure for exploration, development, or operation had been made by the taxpayer before or during the taxable year to which such election would apply. A recomputation of the tax imposed by this chapter (or by the corresponding provisions of the Internal Revenue Code of 1939) shall also be made for taxable years affected by the recomputation described in the preceding sentence. If the tax so recomputed for any taxable year or years, by reason of the application of this paragraph, exceeds the tax liability previously determined for such year or years, such excess shall be taken into account in the first taxable year to which the election to aggregate under paragraph (1) applies and succeeding taxable years as provided in subparagraph (C).

(C) INCREASE IN TAX.—The tax imposed by this chapter for the first taxable year to which the election to aggregate under paragraph (1) applies, and for each succeeding taxable year until the full amount of the excess described in subparagraph (B) has been taken into account, shall be increased by an amount equal to the quotient obtained by dividing such excess by the total number of taxable years described in subparagraph (A) in respect of which—

(i) exploration expenditures were deducted by the taxpayer under section 615(a), and

(ii) the recomputation of tax described in the first sentence of subparagraph (B) results in an increase in tax or a reduction of a net operating loss.

If the taxpayer dies or ceases to exist, then so much of the excess described in subparagraph (B) as was not taken into account under the preceding sentence for taxable years preceding such death, or such cessation of existence, shall be taken into account for the taxable year in which such death, or such cessation of existence, occurs.

(D) BASIS ADJUSTMENT.—If the tax liability of a taxpayer is increased by reason of the application of this paragraph, proper adjustments shall be made with respect to the basis of the aggregated property owned by such taxpayer, in accordance with regulations prescribed by the Secretary or his delegate, as though the tax liability of the taxpayer for the prior taxable year or years had been determined in accordance with the recomputation of tax described in subparagraph (B).

P.L. 94-455, §1901(a)(87)(A)(ii), provides:

(ii) The amendment made by clause (i) shall apply with respect to elections to form aggregations of operating mineral interests made under section 614(c)(1) of the Internal Revenue Code of 1954 for taxable years beginning after December 31, 1976.

P.L. 94-455, §1901(a)(87)(B):

Amended the third sentence of Code Sec. 614(c)(2). **Effective** for tax years beginning after 12-31-76. Prior to amendment, the third sentence of Sec. 614(c)(2) read as follows: "A separate property so formed may, under regulations prescribed by the Secretary or his delegate, be included as a part of an aggregation in accordance with paragraphs (1) and (3), but the provisions of paragraph (4) shall not apply with respect to such separate property."

P.L. 94-455, §1901(a)(87)(C):

Amended Code Sec. 614(c)(3). **Effective** for tax years beginning after 12-31-76. Prior to amendment, Sec. 614(c)(3) read as follows:

(3) MANNER AND SCOPE OF ELECTION.—

(A) IN GENERAL.—Except as provided in subparagraph (D), the election provided by paragraph (1) shall be made for each operating mineral interest, in accordance with regulations prescribed by the Secretary or his delegate, not later than the time prescribed by law for filing the return (including extensions thereof) for whichever of the following taxable years is the later: The first taxable year beginning after December 31, 1957, or the first taxable year in which any expenditure for development or operation in respect of the separate operating mineral interest is made by the taxpayer after the acquisition of such interest. Except as provided in subparagraph (D), the election provided by paragraph (2) shall be made for any property, in accordance with regulations prescribed by the Secretary or his delegate, not later than the time prescribed by law for filing the return (including extensions thereof) for whichever of the following taxable years is the later: The first taxable year beginning after December 31, 1957, or the first taxable year in which expenditures for development or operation of more than one mine in respect of the property are made by the taxpayer after the acquisition of the property. No election may be made pursuant to this subparagraph for any operating mineral interest which constitutes part or all of an operating unit if the taxpayer makes an election pursuant to subparagraph (B) with respect to any operating mineral interest which constitutes part or all of such operating unit.

(B) TAXABLE YEARS BEGINNING BEFORE JANUARY 1, 1958.—The election provided by paragraph (1) may, at the election of the taxpayer, be made for each operating mineral interest, in accordance with regulations prescribed by the Secretary or his delegate, within the time provided in subparagraph (D), for whichever of the following taxable years is the later (not including any taxable year in respect of which an assessment of deficiency is prevented on the date of the enactment of the Technical Amendments Act of 1958 by the operation of any law or rule of law): The first taxable year of the taxpayer which begins after December 31, 1953, and ends after August 16, 1954, or the first taxable year in which any expenditure for development or operation in respect of the separate operating mineral interest is made by the taxpayer after the acquisition of such interest. The election provided by paragraph (2) may, at the election of the taxpayer, be made for any property, in accordance with regulations prescribed by the Secretary or his delegate, within the time prescribed in subparagraph (D), for whichever of the following taxable years is the later (not including any taxable year in respect of which an assessment of deficiency is prevented on the date of the enactment of the Technical Amendments Act of 1958 by the operation of any law or rule of law): The first taxable year beginning after December 31, 1953, and ending after August 16, 1954, or the first taxable year in which expenditures for development or operation of more than one mine in respect of the property are made by the taxpayer after the acquisition of the property.

(C) EFFECT.—An election made under paragraph (1) or (2) shall be binding upon the taxpayer for all subsequent taxable years, except that the Secretary or his delegate may consent to a different treatment of any interest with respect to which an election has been made.

(D) ELECTION AFTER FINAL REGULATIONS.—Notwithstanding any other provision of this paragraph the time for making an election under paragraph (1) or (2) shall not expire prior to the first day of the first month which begins more than 90 days after the date of publication in the Federal Register of final regulations issued under the authority of this subsection.

(E) STATUTE OF LIMITATIONS.—If the taxpayer makes an election pursuant to subparagraph (B) and if assessment of any deficiency for any taxable year resulting from such election is prevented on the first day of the first month which begins more than 90 days after the date of publication in the Federal Register of final regulations issued under authority of this subsection, or at any time within one year after such day, by the operation of any law or rule of law, such assessment may, nevertheless, be made if made within one year after such day. An election by a taxpayer pursuant to subparagraph (B) shall be considered as a consent to the assessment pursuant to this subparagraph of any such deficiency. If refund or credit of any overpayment of income tax resulting from an election made pursuant to subparagraph (B) is prevented on such day, or at any time within one year after such day, by the operation of any law or rule of law, refund or credit of such overpayment may, nevertheless, be made or allowed if claim therefor is filed within one year after such day. This subparagraph shall not apply to any taxable year in respect of which an assessment of a deficiency, or a refund or credit of an overpayment, as the case may be, is prevented by the operation of any law or rule of law on the date of the enactment of the Technical Amendments Act of 1958.

P.L. 94-455, §1906(b)(13)(A):

Amended 1954 Code by substituting "Secretary" for "Secretary or his delegate" each place it appeared. **Effective** 2-1-77.

• 1964, Revenue Act of 1964 (P.L. 88-272)

P.L. 88-272, §226(b)(1), (2):

Amended the heading of Code Sec. 614(c). **Effective** 1-1-64. Prior to amendment, it read "1958 Special Rules as to Operating Mineral Interest in Mines."

Repealed Sec. 614(c)(5) which read as follows:

"(5) Operating Mineral Interests Defined.—For purposes of this subsection, the term "operating mineral interest" has the meaning as assigned to it by subsection (b)(3)."

• 1958, Technical Amendments Act of 1958 (P.L. 85-866)

P.L. 85-866, §37(b):

Amended Code Sec. 614 by adding new subsec. (c). **Effective** for tax years beginning after 12-31-57, except that, at the taxpayer's election, the amendment applies for tax years beginning after 12-31-53 and ending after 8-16-54.

[Sec. 614(d)]

(d) OPERATING MINERAL INTERESTS DEFINED.—For purposes of this section, the term "operating mineral interest" includes only an interest in respect of which the costs of production of the mineral are required to be taken into account by the taxpayer for purposes of computing the taxable income limitation provided for in section 613, or would be so required if the mine, well, or other natural deposit were in the production stage.

Amendments

• 1990, Omnibus Budget Reconciliation Act of 1990 (P.L. 101-508)

P.L. 101-508, §11522(b)(2):

Amended Code Sec. 614(d) by striking "50 percent" and inserting "taxable income". **Effective** for tax years beginning after 12-31-90.

• 1964, Revenue Act of 1964 (P.L. 88-272)

P.L. 88-272, §226(b)(3):

Amended Code Sec. 614(d). **Effective** for tax years beginning after 12-31-63. Prior to amendment, Code Sec. 614(d) read as follows:

"(d) 1939 Code Treatment With Respect to Operating Mineral Interests in Case of Oil and Gas Wells.—In the case of oil and gas wells, any taxpayer may treat any property (determined as if the Internal Revenue Code of 1939 continued to apply) as if subsections (a) and (b) had not been enacted. If any such treatment would constitute an aggregation under subsection (b), such treatment shall be taken into account in applying subsection (b) to other property of the taxpayer."

• 1958, Technical Amendments Act of 1958 (P.L. 85-866)

P.L. 85-866, §37(c):

Amended Code Sec. 614 by adding new subsec. (d). **Effective** for tax years beginning after 12-31-53 and ending after 8-16-54.

[Sec. 614(e)]

(e) SPECIAL RULE AS TO NONOPERATING MINERAL INTERESTS.—

(1) AGGREGATION OF SEPARATE INTERESTS.—If a taxpayer owns two or more separate nonoperating mineral interests in a single tract or parcel of land or in two or more adjacent tracts or parcels of land, the Secretary shall, on showing by the taxpayer that a principal purpose is not the avoidance of tax, permit the taxpayer to treat (for all purposes of this subtitle) all such mineral interests in each separate kind of mineral deposit as one property. If such permission is granted for any taxable year, the taxpayer shall treat such interests as one property for all subsequent taxable years unless the Secretary consents to a different treatment.

(2) NONOPERATING MINERAL INTERESTS DEFINED.—For purposes of this subsection, the term "nonoperating mineral interests" includes only interests which are not operating mineral interests.

Amendments

• 1976, Tax Reform Act of 1976 (P.L. 94-455)

P.L. 94-455, §1906(b)(13)(A):

Amended 1954 Code by substituting "Secretary" for "Secretary or his delegate" each place it appeared. **Effective** 2-1-77.

• 1964, Revenue Act of 1964 (P.L. 88-272)

P.L. 88-272, §226(b)(4):

Amended Code Sec. 614(e)(2). **Effective** for tax years beginning after 12-31-63. Prior to amendment, Code Sec. 614(e)(2) read as follows:

"(2) Nonoperating Mineral Interests Defined.—For purposes of this subsection, the term `nonoperating mineral interests' includes only interests which are not operating mineral interests within the meaning of subsection (b)(3)."

• 1958, Technical Amendments Act of 1958 (P.L. 85-866)

P.L. 85-866, §37(b):

Amended Code Sec. 614 by redesignating subsec. (c) as subsec. (e). **Effective** with respect to tax years beginning after 12-31-57, except that at the taxpayer's election, they apply to taxable years beginning after 12-31-53 and ending after 8-16-54.

P.L. 85-866, §37(d):

Amended the first sentence of redesignated subsec. (e). **Effective** with respect to tax years beginning after 12-31-57, except that at the taxpayer's election, they apply to taxable years beginning after 12-31-53 and ending after 8-16-54. Prior to amendment, such first sentence read:

"If a taxpayer owns two or more separate nonoperating mineral interests in a single tract or parcel of land, or in two or more contiguous tracts or parcels of land, the Secretary or his delegate may, on showing of undue hardship, permit the taxpayer to treat (for all purposes of this subtitle) all such mineral interests as one property."

[Sec. 616]

SEC. 616. DEVELOPMENT EXPENDITURES.

[Sec. 616(a)]

(a) IN GENERAL.—Except as provided in subsections (b) and (d), there shall be allowed as a deduction in computing taxable income all expenditures paid or incurred during the taxable year for the development of a mine or other natural deposit (other than an oil or gas well) if paid or incurred after the existence of ores or minerals in commercially marketable quantities has been disclosed. This section shall not apply to expenditures for the acquisition or improvement of property of a character which is subject to the allowance for depreciation provided in section 167, but allowances for depreciation shall be considered, for purposes of this section, as expenditures.

Amendments

• 1986, Tax Reform Act of 1986 (P.L. 99-514)

P.L. 99-514, §411(b)(2)(C)(i):

Amended Code Sec. 616(a) by striking out "subsection (b)" and inserting in lieu thereof "subsections (b) and (d)". **Effective**, generally, for costs paid or incurred after 12-31-86, in tax years ending after such date. For a transitional rule, see Act Sec. 411(c)(2), below.

P.L. 99-514, §411(c)(2), provides:

(2) TRANSITION RULE.—The amendments made by this section shall not apply with respect to intangible drilling and development costs incurred by United States companies pursuant to a minority interest in a license for Netherlands or United Kingdom North Sea development if such interest was acquired on or before December 31, 1985.

[Sec. 616(b)]

(b) ELECTION OF TAXPAYER.—At the election of the taxpayer, made in accordance with regulations prescribed by the Secretary, expenditures described in subsection (a) paid or incurred during the taxable year shall be treated as deferred expenses and shall be deductible on a ratable basis as the units of produced ores or minerals benefited by such expenditures are sold. In the case of such expenditures paid or incurred during the development stage of the mine or deposit, the election shall apply only with respect to the excess of such expenditures during the taxable year over the net receipts during the taxable year from the ores or minerals produced from such mine or deposit. The election under this subsection, if made, must be for the total amount of such expenditures, or the total amount of such excess, as the case may be, with respect to the mine or deposit, and shall be binding for such taxable year.

Amendments

• 1976, Tax Reform Act of 1976 (P.L. 94-455)

P.L. 94-455, §1906(b)(13)(A):

Amended 1954 Code by substituting "Secretary" for "Secretary or his delegate" each place it appeared. **Effective** 2-1-77.

[Sec. 616(c)]

(c) ADJUSTED BASIS OF MINE OR DEPOSIT.—The amount of expenditures which are treated under subsection (b) as deferred expenses shall be taken into account in computing the adjusted basis of the mine or deposit, except that such amount, and the adjustments to basis provided in section 1016(a)(9), shall be disregarded in determining the adjusted basis of the property for the purpose of computing a deduction for depletion under section 611.

[Sec. 616(d)]

(d) SPECIAL RULES FOR FOREIGN DEVELOPMENT.—In the case of any expenditures paid or incurred with respect to the development of a mine or other natural deposit (other than an oil, gas, or geothermal well) located outside the United States—

(1) subsections (a) and (b) shall not apply, and

(2) such expenditures shall—

(A) at the election of the taxpayer, be included in adjusted basis for purposes of computing the amount of any deduction allowable under section 611 (without regard to section 613), or

(B) if subparagraph (A) does not apply, be allowed as a deduction ratably over the 10-taxable year period beginning with the taxable year in which such expenditures were paid or incurred.

Amendments

• 1986, Tax Reform Act of 1986 (P.L. 99-514)

P.L. 99-514, §411(b)(2)(A):

Amended Code Sec. 616 by redesignating subsection (d) as subsection (e), and by adding at the end of subsection (c) new subsection (d). **Effective**, generally, for costs paid or incurred after 12-31-86, in tax years ending after such date. For a transitional rule, see Act Sec. 411(c)(2) following Code Sec. 616(a).

[Sec. 616(e)]

(e) CROSS REFERENCE.—

For election of 10-year amortization of expenditures allowable as a deduction under subsection (a), see section 59(e).

Amendments

• 1988, Technical and Miscellaneous Revenue Act of 1988 (P.L. 100-647)

P.L. 100-647, §1007(g)(7):

Amended Code Sec. 616(e) by striking out "section 58(i)" and inserting in lieu thereof "section 59(e)". **Effective** as if included in the provision of P.L. 99-514 to which it relates.

• 1986, Tax Reform Act of 1986 (P.L. 99-514)

P.L. 99-514, §411(b)(2)(A):

Redesignated subsection (d) as subsection (e). **Effective**, generally, for costs paid or incurred after 12-31-86, in tax years ending after such date. For a transitional rule, see Act Sec. 411(c)(2) following Code Sec. 616(a).

• 1982, Tax Equity and Fiscal Responsibility Act of 1982 (P.L. 97-248)

P.L. 97-248, §201(d)(9)(C):

Added subsection (d). **Effective** for tax years beginning after 12-31-82.

[Sec. 617]

SEC. 617. DEDUCTION AND RECAPTURE OF CERTAIN MINING EXPLORATION EXPENDITURES.

[Sec. 617(a)]

(a) ALLOWANCE OF DEDUCTION.—

(1) GENERAL RULE.—At the election of the taxpayer, expenditures paid or incurred during the taxable year for the purpose of ascertaining the existence, location, extent, or quality of any deposit of ore or other mineral, and paid or incurred before the beginning of the development stage of the mine, shall be allowed as a deduction in computing taxable income. This subsection shall apply only with respect to the amount of such expenditures which, but for this subsection, would not be allowable as a deduction for the taxable year. This subsection shall not apply to expenditures for the acquisition or improvement of property of a character which is subject to the allowance for depreciation provided in section 167, but allowances for depreciation shall be considered, for purposes of this subsection, as expenditures paid or incurred. In no case shall this subsection apply with respect to amounts paid or incurred for the purpose of ascertaining the existence, location, extent, or quality of any deposit of oil or gas or of any mineral with respect to which a deduction for percentage depletion is not allowable under section 613.

(2) ELECTIONS.—

(A) METHOD.—Any election under this subsection shall be made in such manner as the Secretary may by regulations prescribe.

(B) TIME AND SCOPE.—The election provided by paragraph (1) for the taxable year may be made at any time before the expiration of the period prescribed for making a claim for credit or refund of the tax imposed by this chapter for the taxable year. Such an election for the taxable year shall apply to all expenditures described in paragraph (1) paid or incurred by the taxpayer during the taxable year or during any subsequent taxable year. Such an election may not be revoked unless the Secretary consents to such revocation.

(C) DEFICIENCIES.—The statutory period for the assessment of any deficiency for any taxable year, to the extent such deficiency is attributable to an election or revocation of an election under this subsection, shall not expire before the last day of the 2-year period beginning on the day after the date on which such election or revocation of election is made; and such deficiency may be assessed at any time before the expiration of such 2-year period, notwithstanding any law or rule of law which would otherwise prevent such assessment.

Amendments

• 1976, Tax Reform Act of 1976 (P.L. 94-455)

P.L. 94-455, §1901(a)(89):

Substituted "may not be revoked unless" for "may not be revoked after the last day of the third month following the month in which the final regulations issued under the authority of this subsection are published in the Federal Register, unless" in Code Sec. 617(a)(2)(B). **Effective** for tax years beginning after 12-31-76.

P.L. 94-455, §1906(b)(13)(A):

Amended 1954 Code by substituting "Secretary" for "Secretary or his delegate" each place it appeared. **Effective** 2-1-77.

• 1969, Tax Reform Act of 1969 (P.L. 91-172)

P.L. 91-172, §504(b)(1) and (2):

Amended the heading of Sec. 617. Prior to amendment, the heading read: "Additional exploration expenditures in the case of domestic mining". Amended the first sentence of paragraph (a)(1) by deleting "in the United States or on the Outer Continental Shelf (within the meaning of section 2 of the Outer Continental Shelf Lands Act, as amended and supplemented; 43 U. S. C. 1331)" which appeared immediately following the words "deposit of ore or other mineral". **Effective** with respect to exploration expenditures paid or incurred after 12-31-69. With respect to an election under Sec. 615(e) for purposes of Sec. 617, the effective date provisions of Sec. 504(d)(2) of P.L. 91-172, below, apply.

P.L. 91-172, §504(d)(2), provides:

(d)(2) Presumption of election under section 617.—For purposes of section 617 of the Internal Revenue Code of 1954, an election under section 615(e) of such Code, which is effective with respect to exploration expenditures paid or incurred before January 1, 1970, shall be treated as an election under section 617(a) of such Code with respect to exploration expenditures paid or incurred after December 31, 1969. The preceding sentence shall not apply to any taxpayer who notifies the Secretary of the Treasury or his delegate (at such time and in such manner as the Secretary or his delegate prescribes by regulations) that he does not desire his election under section 615(e) to be so treated.

[Sec. 617(b)]

(b) RECAPTURE ON REACHING PRODUCING STAGE.—

(1) RECAPTURE.—If, in any taxable year, any mine with respect to which expenditures were deducted pursuant to subsection (a) reaches the producing stage, then—

(A) If the taxpayer so elects with respect to all such mines reaching the producing stage during the taxable year, he shall include in gross income for the taxable year an amount equal to the adjusted exploration expenditures with respect to such mines, and the amount so included in income shall be treated for purposes of this subtitle as expenditures which (i) are paid or incurred on the respective dates on which the mines reach the producing stage, and (ii) are properly chargeable to capital account.

(B) If subparagraph (A) does not apply with respect to any such mine, then the deduction for depletion under section 611 with respect to the property shall be disallowed until the amount of depletion which would be allowable but for this subparagraph equals the amount of the adjusted exploration expenditures with respect to such mine.

(2) ELECTIONS.—

(A) METHOD.—Any election under this subsection shall be made in such manner as the Secretary may by regulations prescribe.

(B) TIME AND SCOPE.—The election provided by paragraph (1) for any taxable year may be made or changed not later than the time prescribed by law for filing the return (including extensions thereof) for such taxable year.

[Sec. 617(c)]

(c) RECAPTURE IN CASE OF BONUS OR ROYALTY.—If an election has been made under subsection (a) with respect to expenditures relating to a mining property and the taxpayer receives or accrues a bonus or a royalty with respect to such property, then the deduction for depletion under section 611 with respect to the bonus or royalty shall be disallowed until the amount of depletion which would be allowable but for this subsection equals the amount of the adjusted exploration expenditures with respect to the property to which the bonus or royalty relates.

[Sec. 617(d)]

(d) GAIN FROM DISPOSITIONS OF CERTAIN MINING PROPERTY.—

(1) GENERAL RULE.—Except as otherwise provided in this subsection, if mining property is disposed of the lower of—

(A) the adjusted exploration expenditures with respect to such property, or

(B) the excess of—

(i) the amount realized (in the case of a sale, exchange, or involuntary conversion), or the fair market value (in the case of any other disposition), over

(ii) the adjusted basis of such property,

shall be treated as ordinary income. Such gain shall be recognized notwithstanding any other provision of this subtitle.

(2) DISPOSITION OF PORTION OF PROPERTY.—For purposes of paragraph (1)—

(A) In the case of the disposition of a portion of a mining property (other than an undivided interest), the entire amount of the adjusted exploration expenditures with respect to such property shall be treated as attributable to such portion to the extent of the amount of the gain to which paragraph (1) applies.

(B) In the case of the disposition of an undivided interest in a mining property (or a portion thereof), a proportionate part of the adjusted exploration expenditures with respect to such property shall be treated as attributable to such undivided interest to the extent of the amount of the gain to which paragraph (1) applies.

This paragraph shall not apply to any expenditure to the extent the taxpayer establishes to the satisfaction of the Secretary that such expenditure relates neither to the portion (or interest therein) disposed of nor to any mine, in the property held by the taxpayer before the disposition, which has reached the producing stage.

(3) EXCEPTIONS AND LIMITATIONS.—Paragraphs (1), (2), and (3) of section 1245(b) (relating to exceptions and limitations with respect to gain from disposition of certain depreciable property) shall apply in respect of this subsection in the same manner and with the same effect as if references in section 1245(b) to section 1245 or any provision thereof were references to this subsection or the corresponding provisions of this subsection and as if references to section 1245 property were references to mining property.

(4) APPLICATION OF SUBSECTION.—This subsection shall apply notwithstanding any other provision of this subtitle.

(5) COORDINATION WITH SECTION 1254.—This subsection shall not apply to any disposition to which section 1254 applies.

Amendments

• 1986, Tax Reform Act of 1986 (P.L. 99-514)

P.L. 99-514, §413(b):

Amended Code Sec. 617(d) by adding at the end thereof new paragraph (5). **Effective**, generally, for any disposition of property which is placed in service by the taxpayer after 12-31-86. For an exception for binding contracts, see Act Sec. 413(c)(2), below.

P.L. 99-514, §413(c)(2), provides:

(2) EXCEPTION FOR BINDING CONTRACTS.—The amendments made by this section shall not apply to any disposition of property placed in service after December 31, 1986, if such property was acquired pursuant to a written contract which was entered into before September 26, 1985, and which was binding at all times thereafter.

• 1976, Tax Reform Act of 1976 (P.L. 94-455)

P.L. 94-455, §1901(b)(3)(K):

Substituted "ordinary income" for "gain from the sale or exchange of property which is neither a capital asset nor property described in section 1231" in Code Sec. 617(d)(1)(B)(ii). **Effective** for tax years beginning after 12-31-76.

P.L. 94-455, §1906(b)(13)(A):

Amended 1954 Code by substituting "Secretary" for "Secretary or his delegate" each place it appeared. **Effective** 2-1-77.

[Sec. 617(e)]

(e) BASIS OF PROPERTY.—

(1) BASIS.—The basis of any property shall not be reduced by the amount of any depletion which would be allowable but for the application of this section.

(2) ADJUSTMENTS.—The Secretary shall prescribe such regulations as he may deem necessary to provide for adjustments to the basis of property to reflect gain recognized under subsection (d)(1).

Amendments

• 1976, Tax Reform Act of 1976 (P.L. 94-455)

P.L. 94-455, §1906(b)(13)(A):

Amended 1954 Code by substituting "Secretary" for "Secretary or his delegate" each place it appeared. **Effective** 2-1-77.

[Sec. 617(f)]

(f) DEFINITIONS.—For purposes of this section—

(1) ADJUSTED EXPLORATION EXPENDITURES.—The term "adjusted exploration expenditures" means, with respect to any property or mine—

(A) the amount of the expenditures allowed for the taxable year and all preceding taxable years as deductions under subsection (a) to the taxpayer or any other person which are properly chargeable to such property or mine and which (but for the election under subsection (a)) would be reflected in the adjusted basis of such property or mine, reduced by

(B) for the taxable year and for each preceding taxable year, the amount (if any) by which (i) the amount which would have been allowable for percentage depletion under section 613 but for the deduction of such expenditures, exceeds (ii) the amount allowable for depletion under section 611,

properly adjusted for any amounts included in gross income under subsection (b) or (c) and for any amounts of gain to which subsection (d) applied.

(2) MINING PROPERTY.—The term "mining property" means any property (within the meaning of section 614 after the application of subsections (c) and (e) thereof) with respect to which any expenditures allowed as a deduction under subsection (a)(1) are properly chargeable.

(3) DISPOSAL OF COAL OR DOMESTIC IRON ORE WITH A RETAINED ECONOMIC INTEREST.—A transaction which constitutes a disposal of coal or iron ore under section 631(c) shall be treated as a disposition. In such a case, the excess referred to in subsection (d)(1)(B) shall be treated as equal to the gain (if any) referred to in section 631(c).

[Sec. 617(g)]

(g) SPECIAL RULES RELATING TO PARTNERSHIP PROPERTY.—

(1) PROPERTY DISTRIBUTED TO PARTNER.—In the case of any property or mine received by the taxpayer in a distribution with respect to part or all of his interest in a partnership, the adjusted exploration expenditures with respect to such property or mine include the adjusted exploration expenditures (not otherwise included under subsection (f)(1)) with respect to such property or mine immediately prior to such distribution, but the adjusted exploration expenditures with respect to any such property or mine shall be reduced by the amount of gain to which section 751(b) applied realized by the partnership (as constituted after the distribution) on the distribution of such property or mine.

(2) PROPERTY RETAINED BY PARTNERSHIP.—In the case of any property or mine held by a partnership after a distribution to a partner to which section 751(b) applied, the adjusted exploration expenditures with respect to such property or mine shall, under regulations prescribed by the Secretary, be reduced by the amount of gain to which section 751(b) applied realized by such partner with respect to such distribution on account of such property or mine.

Amendments

• 1976, Tax Reform Act of 1976 (P.L. 94-455)

P.L. 94-455, §1906(b)(13)(A):

Amended 1954 Code by substituting "Secretary" for "Secretary or his delegate" each place it appeared. **Effective** 2-1-77.

[Sec. 617(h)]

(h) SPECIAL RULES FOR FOREIGN EXPLORATION.—In the case of any expenditures paid or incurred before the development stage for the purpose of ascertaining the existence, location, extent, or quality of any deposit of ore or other mineral (other than an oil, gas, or geothermal well) located outside the United States—

(1) subsection (a) shall not apply, and

(2) such expenditures shall—

(A) at the election of the taxpayer, be included in adjusted basis for purposes of computing the amount of any deduction allowable under section 611 (without regard to section 613), or

(B) if subparagraph (A) does not apply, be allowed as a deduction ratably over the 10-taxable year period beginning with the taxable year in which such expenditures were paid or incurred.

Amendments

• 1986, Tax Reform Act of 1986 (P.L. 99-514)

P.L. 99-514, §411(b)(2)(B):

Amended Code Sec. 617(h). **Effective**, generally, for costs paid or incurred after 12-31-86, in tax years ending after such date. For a transitional rule, see Act Sec. 411(c)(2), below. Prior to amendment, Code Sec. 617(h) read as follows:

(h) LIMITATION.—

(1) IN GENERAL.—Subsection (a) shall apply to any amount paid or incurred after December 31, 1969, with respect to any deposit of ore or other mineral located outside the United States, only to the extent that such amount, when added to the amounts which are or have been deducted under subsection (a) and subsection (a) of section 615 (as in effect before the enactment of the Tax Reform Act of 1976) or the corresponding provisions of prior law, does not exceed $400,000.

(2) AMOUNTS TAKEN INTO ACCOUNT.—For purposes of paragraph (1), there shall be taken into account amounts deducted and amounts treated as deferred expenses by—

(A) the taxpayer, and

(B) any individual or corporation who has transferred to the taxpayer any mineral property.

(3) APPLICATION OF PARAGRAPH (2)(B).—Paragraph (2)(B) shall apply with respect to all amounts deducted before the latest such transfer from the individual or corporation to the taxpayer. Paragraph (2)(B) shall apply only if—

(A) the taxpayer acquired any mineral property from the individual or corporation under circumstances which make paragraph (7), (8), (11), (15), (17), (20), or (22) of section 113(a) of the Internal Revenue Code of 1939 apply to such transfer; or

(B) the taxpayer acquired any mineral property from the individual or corporation under circumstances which make section 334(b), 338, 362(a) and (b), 372(a), 374(b)(1), 1051, or 1082 apply to such transfer.

P.L. 99-514, §411(c)(2), provides:

(2) TRANSITION RULE.—The amendments made by this section shall not apply with respect to intangible drilling and development costs incurred by United States companies pursuant to a minority interest in a license for Netherlands or United Kingdom North Sea development if such interest was acquired on or before December 31, 1985.

• 1982, Tax Equity and Fiscal Responsibility Act of 1982 (P.L. 97-248)

P.L. 97-248, §224(c)(8):

Amended Code Sec. 617(h)(3)(B) by inserting "338," after "334(b),". **Effective** for any target corporation (within the meaning of Code Sec. 338) with respect to which the acquisition date (within the meaning of such section) occurs after 8-31-82. For special rules, see amendment notes under Code Sec. 338.

• 1976, Tax Reform Act of 1976 (P.L. 94-455)

P.L. 94-455, §1901(b)(21)(C):

Substituted "and subsection (a) of section 615 (as in effect before the enactment of the Tax Reform Act of 1976" for "and section 615(a) and the amounts which are or have been treated as deferred expenses under section 615(b)" in Code Sec. 617(h)(1). **Effective** for tax years beginning after 12-31-76.

P.L. 94-455, §1901(b)(21)(D):

Amended Code Sec. 617(h)(3). **Effective** for tax years beginning after 12-31-76. Prior to amendment, Sec. 617(h)(3) read as follows:

(3) APPLICATION OF PARAGRAPH (2)(B).—Paragraph (2)(B) shall apply with respect to all amounts deducted and all amounts treated as deferred expenses which were paid or incurred before the latest such transfer from the individual or corporation to the taxpayer. Paragraph (2)(B) shall apply only if—

(A) the taxpayer acquired any mineral property from the individual or corporation under circumstances which make paragraph (7), (8), (11), (15), (17), (20), or (22) of section 113(a) of the Internal Revenue Code of 1939 apply to such transfer;

(B) the taxpayer would be entitled under section 381(c)(10) to deduct expenses deferred under section 615(b) had the distributor or transferor corporation elected to defer such expenses; or

(C) the taxpayer acquired any mineral property from the individual or corporation under circumstances which make section 334(b), 362(a) and (b), 372(a), 373(b)(1), 1051, or 1082 apply to such transfer.

• **1969, Tax Reform Act of 1969 (P.L. 91-172)**

P.L. 91-172, §504(b)(3):

Inserted subsection (h). **Effective** 1-1-70. Prior to amendment, subsection (h) read as follows: "(h) Cross reference.—For additional rules applicable for purposes of this section, see subsections (f) and (g) of section 615."

• **1966 (P.L.89-570)**

P.L. 89-570, [§1(a)]:

Added Code Sec. 617. **Effective** for tax years ending after 9-12-66, the date of enactment, but only in respect of expenditures paid or incurred after that date.

[Sec. 617(i)—Repealed]

Amendments

• **1990, Omnibus Budget Reconciliation Act of 1990 (P.L. 101-508)**

P.L. 101-508, §11801(a)(27):

Repealed Code Sec. 617(i). **Effective** 11-5-90. Prior to repeal, Code Sec. 617(i) read as follows:

(i) CERTAIN PRE-1970 EXPLORATION EXPENDITURES.—If—

(1) the taxpayer receives mineral property in a transaction as a result of which the basis of such property in the hands of the transferee is determined by reference to the basis in the hands of the transferor,

(2) an election made by the transferor under subsection (e) of section 615(e) (as in effect before the enactment of the Tax Reform Act of 1976) applied with respect to expenditures which were made by him and which were properly chargeable to such property, and

(3) the taxpayer has made or makes an election under subsection (a),

then in the application of this section with respect to the transferee, the amounts allowed as deductions under such section 615 to the transferor, which (but for the transferor's election) would be reflected in the adjusted basis of such property in the hands of the transferee, shall be treated as expenditures allowed as deductions under subsection (a) to the transferor.

P.L. 101-508, §11821(b), provides:

(b) SAVINGS PROVISION.—If—

(1) any provision amended or repealed by this part applied to—

(A) any transaction occurring before the date of the enactment of this Act,

(B) any property acquired before such date of enactment, or

(C) any item of income, loss, deduction, or credit taken into account before such date of enactment, and

(2) the treatment of such transaction, property, or item under such provision would (without regard to the amendments made by this part) affect liability for tax for periods ending after such date of enactment,

nothing in the amendments made by this part shall be construed to affect the treatment of such transaction, property, or item for purposes of determining liability for tax for periods ending after such date of enactment.

• **1976, Tax Reform Act of 1976 (P.L. 94-455)**

P.L. 94-455, §1901(b)(21)(E):

Added Code Sec. 617(i). **Effective** for tax years beginning after 12-31-76.

[Sec. 617(i)]

(i) CROSS REFERENCE.—

For election of 10-year amortization of expenditures allowable as a deduction under this section, see section 59(e).

Amendments

• **1990, Omnibus Budget Reconciliation Act of 1990 (P.L. 101-508)**

P.L. 101-508, §11801(c)(13):

Amended Code Sec. 617 by redesignating subsection (j) as subsection (i). **Effective** 11-5-90.

P.L. 101-508, §11821(b), provides:

(b) SAVINGS PROVISION.—If—

(1) any provision amended or repealed by this part applied to—

(A) any transaction occurring before the date of the enactment of this Act,

(B) any property acquired before such date of enactment, or

(C) any item of income, loss, deduction, or credit taken into account before such date of enactment, and

(2) the treatment of such transaction, property, or item under such provision would (without regard to the amendments made by this part) affect liability for tax for periods ending after such date of enactment,

nothing in the amendments made by this part shall be construed to affect the treatment of such transaction, property, or item for purposes of determining liability for tax for periods ending after such date of enactment.

• **1988, Technical and Miscellaneous Revenue Act of 1988 (P.L. 100-647)**

P.L. 100-647, §1007(g)(7):

Amended Code Sec. 617(j) by striking out "section 58(i)" and inserting in lieu thereof "section 59(e)". **Effective** as if included in the provision of P.L. 99-514 to which it relates.

• **1983, Technical Corrections Act of 1982 (P.L. 97-448)**

P.L. 97-448, §306(a)(1)(A):

Amended P.L. 97-248, §201 by redesignating the second subsection (c) as subsection (d).

• **1982, Tax Equity and Fiscal Responsibility Act of 1982 (P.L. 97-248)**

P.L. 97-248, §201(d)(9)(D):

Added subsection (j). **Effective** for to tax years beginning after 12-31-82.

PART II—EXCLUSIONS FROM GROSS INCOME—[Repealed]

[Sec. 621—Repealed]

Amendments

• 1990, Omnibus Budget Reconciliation Act of 1990 (P.L. 101-508)

P.L. 101-508, §11801(a)(28):

Repealed part II of subchapter I of chapter 1, including Code Sec. 621. **Effective** 11-5-90. Prior to repeal, Code Sec. 621 read as follows:

SEC. 621. PAYMENTS TO ENCOURAGE EXPLORATION, DEVELOPMENT, AND MINING FOR DEFENSE PURPOSES.

There shall not be included in gross income any amount paid to a taxpayer by the United States (or any agency or instrumentality thereof), whether by grant or loan, and whether or not repayable, for the encouragement of exploration, development, or mining of critical and strategic minerals or metals pursuant to or in connection with any undertaking approved by the United States (or any of its agencies or instrumentalities) and for which an accounting is made or required to be made to an appropriate governmental agency, or any forgiveness or discharge of any part of such amount. Any expenditures (other than expenditures made after the repayment of such grant or loan) attributable to such grant or loan shall not be deductible by the taxpayer as an expense nor increase the basis of the taxpayer's property either for determining gain or loss on sale, exchange, or other disposition or for computing depletion or depreciation, but on the repayment of any portion of any such grant or loan which has been expended in accordance with the terms thereof such deductions and such increase in basis shall to the extent of such repayment be allowed as if made at the time of such repayment.

P.L. 101-508, §11821(b), provides:

(b) SAVINGS PROVISION.—If—

(1) any provision amended or repealed by this part applied to—

(A) any transaction occurring before the date of the enactment of this Act,

(B) any property acquired before such date of enactment, or

(C) any item of income, loss, deduction, or credit taken into account before such date of enactment, and

(2) the treatment of such transaction, property, or item under such provision would (without regard to the amendments made by this part) affect liability for tax for periods ending after such date of enactment,

nothing in the amendments made by this part shall be construed to affect the treatment of such transaction, property, or item for purposes of determining liability for tax for periods ending after such date of enactment.

PART III—SALES AND EXCHANGES

[Sec. 631]

SEC. 631. GAIN OR LOSS IN THE CASE OF TIMBER, COAL, OR DOMESTIC IRON ORE.

[Sec. 631(a)]

(a) ELECTION TO CONSIDER CUTTING AS SALE OR EXCHANGE.—If the taxpayer so elects on his return for a taxable year, the cutting of timber (for sale or for use in the taxpayer's trade or business) during such year by the taxpayer who owns, or has a contract right to cut, such timber (providing he has owned such timber or has held such contract right for a period of more than 1 year) shall be considered as a sale or exchange of such timber cut during such year. If such election has been made, gain or loss to the taxpayer shall be recognized in an amount equal to the difference between the fair market value of such timber, and the adjusted basis for depletion of such timber in the hands of the taxpayer. Such fair market value shall be the fair market value as of the first day of the taxable year in which such timber is cut, and shall thereafter be considered as the cost of such cut timber to the taxpayer for all purposes for which such cost is a necessary factor. If a taxpayer makes an election under this subsection, such election shall apply with respect to all timber which is owned by the taxpayer or which the taxpayer has a contract right to cut and shall be binding on the taxpayer for the taxable year for which the election is made and for all subsequent years, unless the Secretary, on showing of undue hardship, permits the taxpayer to revoke his election; such revocation, however, shall preclude any further elections under this subsection except with the consent of the Secretary. For purposes of this subsection and subsection (b), the term "timber" includes evergreen trees which are more than 6 years old at the time severed from the roots and are sold for ornamental purposes.

Amendments

• 2004, American Jobs Creation Act of 2004 (P.L. 108-357)

P.L. 108-357, §102(c), provides:

(c) SPECIAL RULE RELATING TO ELECTION TO TREAT CUTTING OF TIMBER AS A SALE OR EXCHANGE.—Any election under section 631(a) of the Internal Revenue Code of 1986 made for a taxable year ending on or before the date of the enactment of this Act [10-22-2004.—CCH]may be revoked by the taxpayer for any taxable year ending after such date. For purposes of determining whether such taxpayer may make a further election under such section, such election (and any revocation under this section) shall not be taken into account.

• 1984, Deficit Reduction Act of 1984 (P.L. 98-369)

P.L. 98-369, §1001(c)(1):

Amended Code Sec. 631(a) by striking out "for a period of more than 1 year" in the first sentence of subsection (a) and inserting in lieu thereof "on the first day of such year and for a period of more than 6 months before such cutting". **Effective** for property acquired after 6-22-84 and before 1-1-88.

• 1976, Tax Reform Act of 1976 (P.L. 94-455)

P.L. 94-455, §1402(b)(1):

Amended Code Sec. 631(a) by substituting "9 months" for "6 months". **Effective** with respect to tax years beginning in 1977.

P.L. 94-455, §1402(b)(2):

Amended Code Sec. 631(a) by substituting "1 year" for "9 months". **Effective** with respect to tax years beginning after 12-31-77.

P.L. 94-455, §1402(b)(3):

Amended Code Sec. 631(a) by striking out "before the beginning of such year" in the second parenthetical phrase of this subsection. **Effective** for tax years beginning after 12-31-76.

P.L. 94-455, §1906(b)(13)(A):

Amended 1954 Code by substituting "Secretary" for "Secretary or his delegate" each place it appeared. **Effective** 2-1-77.

• 1964, Revenue Act of 1964 (P.L. 88-272)

P.L. 88-272, §227(b)(1):

Amended the heading of Code Sec. 631. Prior to amendment, the heading read: "SEC. 631. GAIN OR LOSS IN THE CASE OF TIMBER OR COAL." **Effective** 1-1-64.

[Sec. 631(b)]

(b) DISPOSAL OF TIMBER.—In the case of the disposal of timber held for more than 1 year before such disposal, by the owner thereof under any form or type of contract by virtue of which such owner either retains an economic interest in such timber or makes an outright sale of such timber, the difference between the amount realized from the disposal of such timber and the adjusted depletion basis thereof, shall be considered as though it were a gain or loss, as the case may be, on the sale of such timber. In determining the gross income, the adjusted gross income, or the taxable income of the lessee, the deductions allowable with respect to rents and royalties shall be determined without regard to the provisions of this subsection. In the case of disposal of timber with a retained economic interest, the date of disposal of such timber shall be deemed to be the date such timber is cut, but if payment is made to the owner under the contract before such timber is cut the owner may elect to treat the date of such payment as the date of disposal of such timber. For purposes of this subsection, the term "owner" means any person who owns an interest in such timber, including a sublessor and a holder of a contract to cut timber.

Amendments

• 2004, American Jobs Creation Act of 2004 (P.L. 108-357)

P.L. 108-357, §315(a):

Amended Code Sec. 631(b) by striking "retains an economic interest in such timber" and inserting "either retains an economic interest in such timber or makes an outright sale of such timber". **Effective** for sales after 12-31-2004.

P.L. 108-357, §315(b)(1):

Amended Code Sec. 631(b) by striking "The date of disposal" in the third sentence and inserting "In the case of disposal of timber with a retained economic interest, the date of disposal". **Effective** for sales after 12-31-2004.

P.L. 108-357, §315(b)(2):

Amended Code Sec. 631(b) by striking "WITH A RETAINED ECONOMIC INTEREST" after "DISPOSAL OF TIMBER" in the heading. **Effective** for sales after 12-31-2004.

• 1984, Deficit Reduction Act of 1984 (P.L. 98-369)

P.L. 98-369, §1001(c)(2):

Amended Code Sec. 631 by striking out "1 year" in subsection (b) and inserting in lieu thereof "6 months". **Effective** for property acquired after 6-22-84, and before 1-1-88.

• 1976, Tax Reform Act of 1976 (P.L. 94-455)

P.L. 94-455, §1402(b)(1):

Amended Code Sec. 631(b) by substituting "9 months" for "6 months". **Effective** with respect to tax years beginning in 1977.

P.L. 94-455, §1402(b)(2):

Amended Code Sec. 631(b) by substituting "1 year" for "9 months". **Effective** with respect to tax years beginning after 12-31-77.

[Sec. 631(c)]

(c) DISPOSAL OF COAL OR DOMESTIC IRON ORE WITH A RETAINED ECONOMIC INTEREST.—In the case of the disposal of coal (including lignite), or iron ore mined in the United States, held for more than 1 year before such disposal, by the owner thereof under any form of contract by virtue of which such owner retains an economic interest in such coal or iron ore, the difference between the amount realized from the disposal of such coal or iron ore and the adjusted depletion basis thereof plus the deductions disallowed for the taxable year under section 272 shall be considered as though it were a gain or loss, as the case may be, on the sale of such coal or iron ore. If for the taxable year of such gain or loss the maximum rate of tax imposed by this chapter on any net capital gain is less than such maximum rate for ordinary income, such owner shall not be entitled to the allowance for percentage depletion provided in section 613 with respect to such coal or iron ore. This subsection shall not apply to income realized by any owner as a co-adventurer, partner, or principal in the mining of such coal or iron ore, and the word "owner" means any person who owns an economic interest in coal or iron ore in place, including a sublessor. The date of disposal of such coal or iron ore shall be deemed to be the date such coal or iron ore is mined. In determining the gross income, the adjusted gross income, or the taxable income of the lessee, the deductions allowable with respect to rents and royalties shall be determined without regard to the provisions of this subsection. This subsection shall have no application, for purposes of applying subchapter G, relating to corporations used to avoid income tax on shareholders (including the determinations of the amount of the deductions under section 535(b)(6) or section 545(b)(5)). This subsection shall not apply to any disposal of iron ore or coal—

(1) to a person whose relationship to the person disposing of such iron ore or coal would result in the disallowance of losses under section 267 or 707(b), or

(2) to a person owned or controlled directly or indirectly by the same interests which own or control the person disposing of such iron ore or coal.

Amendments

• **1986, Tax Reform Act of 1986 (P.L. 99-514)**

P.L. 99-514, §311(b)(3):

Amended Code Sec. 631(c) by striking out "Such owner" and inserting in lieu thereof "If for the taxable year of such gain or loss the maximum rate of tax imposed by this chapter on any net capital gain is less than such maximum rate for ordinary income, such owner". **Effective** for tax years beginning after 12-31-86. However, for a transitional rule, see Act Sec. 311(d)(2), below.

P.L. 99-514, §311(d)(2), provides:

(2) REVOCATION OF ELECTIONS UNDER SECTION 631(a).—Any election under section 631(a) of the Internal Revenue Code of 1954 made (whether by a corporation or a person other than a corporation) for a taxable year beginning before January 1, 1987, may be revoked by the taxpayer for any taxable year ending after December 31, 1986. For purposes of determining whether the taxpayer may make a further election under such section, such election (and any revocation under this paragraph) shall not be taken into account.

• **1984, Deficit Reduction Act of 1984 (P.L. 98-369)**

P.L. 98-369, §178(a):

Amended the last sentence of Code Sec. 631(c) by inserting "or coal" after "iron ore" each place it appeared. **Effective** for dispositions after 9-30-85. See Act Sec. 178(b)(2), below, for special rules regarding fixed contracts.

P.L. 98-369, §178(b)(2), provides:

(2) Special Rule for Fixed Contracts.—

(A) In General.—The amendment made by subsection (a) shall not apply to any disposition of an interest in coal by a person to a related person if such coal is subsequently sold before January 1, 1990, by either such person—

(i) to a person who is not a related person with respect to either such person, and

(ii) pursuant to a qualified fixed contract.

(B) Allocation Where More Than 1 Contract.—If, for any taxable year, there is a disposition described in subparagraph (A) which is not specifically allocable to a qualified fixed contract or to a contract which is not a qualified fixed contract, such disposition shall be treated as first allocable to the qualified fixed contract.

(C) Qualified Fixed Contract Defined.—The term "qualified fixed contract" means any contract for the sale of coal which—

(i) was entered into before June 12, 1984,

(ii) is binding at all times thereafter, and

(iii) cannot be adjusted to reflect to any extent the increase in liabilities of the person disposing of the coal for tax under chapter 1 of the Internal Revenue Code of 1954 by reason of the amendment made by subsection (a).

(D) Related Person.—For purposes of this paragraph, the term "related person" means a person who bears a relationship to another person described in the last sentence of section 631(c).

P.L. 98-369, §1001(c)(2):

Amended Code Sec. 631 by striking out "1 year" in subsection (c) and inserting in lieu thereof "6 months". **Effective** for property acquired after 6-22-84, and before 1-1-88.

• **1976, Tax Reform Act of 1976 (P.L. 94-455)**

P.L. 94-455, §1402(b)(1):

Amended Code Sec. 631(c) by substituting "9 months" for "6 months". **Effective** with respect to tax years beginning in 1977.

P.L. 94-455, §1402(b)(2):

Amended Code Sec. 631(c) by substituting "1 year" for "9 months". **Effective** with respect to tax years beginning after 12-31-77.

• **1964, Revenue Act of 1964 (P.L. 88-272)**

P.L. 88-272, §227(a)(1):

Amended Code Sec. 631(c). **Effective** with respect to tax years beginning after 12-31-63. Prior to amendment, Code Sec. 631(c) read as follows:

"(c) Disposal of Coal With a Retained Economic Interest.—In the case of the disposal of coal (including lignite), held for more than 6 months before such disposal, by the owner thereof under any form of contract by virtue of which such owner retains an economic interest in such coal, the difference between the amount realized from the disposal of such coal and the adjusted depletion basis thereof plus the deductions disallowed for the taxable year under section 272 shall be considered as though it were a gain or loss, as the case may be, on the sale of such coal. Such owner shall not be entitled to the allowance for percentage depletion provided in section 613 with respect to such coal. This subsection shall not apply to income realized by any owner as a co-adventurer, partner, or principal in the mining of such coal, and the word 'owner' means any person who owns an economic interest in coal in place, including a sublessor. The date of disposal of such coal shall be deemed to be the date such coal is mined. In determining the gross income, the adjusted gross income, or the taxable income of the lessee, the deductions allowable with respect to rents and royalties shall be determined without regard to the provisions of this subsection. This subsection shall have no application, for purposes of applying subchapter G, relating to corporations used to avoid income tax on shareholders (including the determinations of the amount of the deductions under section 535(b)(6) or section 545(b)(5))."

[Sec. 632—Repealed]

Amendments

• **1976, Tax Reform Act of 1976 (P.L. 94-455)**

P.L. 94-455, §1901(a)(90):

Repealed Code Sec. 632. **Effective** for tax years beginning after 12-31-76. Prior to repeal, Code Sec. 632 read as follows:

SEC. 632. SALE OF OIL OR GAS PROPERTIES.

In the case of a bona fide sale of any oil or gas property, or any interest therein, where the principal value of the property has been demonstrated by prospecting or exploration or discovery work done by the taxpayer, the portion of the tax imposed by section 1 attributable to such sale shall not exceed 33 percent of the selling price of such property or interest.

P.L. 94-455, §1906(b)(13)(A):

Amended 1954 Code by substituting "Secretary" for "Secretary or his delegate" each place it appeared. **Effective** 2-1-77.

• **1969, Tax Reform Act of 1969 (P.L. 91-172)**

P.L. 91-172, §803(d)(4)(A) and (B):

Amended Code Sec. 632 by striking out "surtax" and inserting in lieu thereof "tax", and by striking out "30 percent" and inserting in lieu thereof "33 percent". **Effective** for tax years beginning after 12-31-70.

PART IV—MINERAL PRODUCTION PAYMENTS

[Sec. 636]

SEC. 636. INCOME TAX TREATMENT OF MINERAL PRODUCTION PAYMENTS.

[Sec. 636(a)]

(a) CARVED-OUT PRODUCTION PAYMENT.—A production payment carved out of mineral property shall be treated, for purposes of this subtitle, as if it were a mortgage loan on the property, and shall not qualify as an economic interest in the mineral property. In the case of a production payment carved out for exploration or development of a mineral property, the preceding sentence shall apply only if and to the extent gross income from the property (for purposes of section 613) would be realized, in the absence of the application of such sentence, by the person creating the production payment.

[Sec. 636(b)]

(b) RETAINED PRODUCTION PAYMENT ON SALE OF MINERAL PROPERTY.—A production payment retained on the sale of a mineral property shall be treated, for purposes of this subtitle, as if it were a purchase money mortgage loan and shall not qualify as an economic interest in the mineral property.

[Sec. 636(c)]

(c) RETAINED PRODUCTION PAYMENT ON LEASE OF MINERAL PROPERTY.—A production payment retained in a mineral property by the lessor in a leasing transaction shall be treated, for purposes of this subtitle, insofar as the lessee (or his successors in interest) is concerned, as if it were a bonus granted by the lessee to the lessor payable in installments. The treatment of the production payment in the hands of the lessor shall be determined without regard to the provisions of this subsection.

[Sec. 636(d)]

(d) DEFINITION.—As used in this section, the term "mineral property" has the meaning assigned to the term "property" in section 614(a).

[Sec. 636(e)]

(e) REGULATIONS.—The Secretary shall prescribe such regulations as may be necessary to carry out the purposes of this section.

Amendments

• 1969, Tax Reform Act of 1969 (P.L. 91-172)

P.L. 91-172, §503(a):

Added part IV of subchapter I of chapter 1 (Code Sec. 636). **Effective** as set out in Sec. 503(c)(1)-(3) of P.L. 91-172.

P.L. 91-172, §503(c), provides:

(c)(1) General Rule.—The amendments made by this section shall apply with respect to mineral production payments created on or after August 7, 1969, other than mineral production payments created before January 1, 1971, pursuant to a binding contract entered into before August 7, 1969.

(2) Election.—At the election of the taxpayer (made at such time and in such manner as the Secretary of the Treasury or his delegate prescribes by regulations), the amendments made by this section shall apply with respect to all mineral production payments which the taxpayer carved out of mineral properties after the beginning of his last taxable year ending before August 7, 1969. No interest shall be allowed on any refund or credit of any overpayment resulting from such election for any taxable year ending before August 7, 1969.

(3) Special rule.—With respect to a taxpayer who does not elect the treatment provided in paragraph (2) and who carves out one or more mineral production payments on or after August 7, 1969, during the taxable year which includes such date, the amendments made by this section shall apply to such production payments only to the extent the aggregate amount of such production payments exceeds the lessor of—

(A) the excess of—

(i) the aggregate amount of production payments carved out and sold by the taxpayer during the 12-month period immediately preceding his taxable year which includes August 7, 1969, over

(ii) the aggregate amount of production payments carved out before August 7, 1969, by the taxpayer during his taxable year which includes such date, or

(B) the amount necessary to increase the amount of the taxpayer's gross income, within the meaning of chapter 1 of subtitle A of the Internal Revenue Code of 1954, for the taxable year which includes August 7, 1969, to an amount equal to the amount of deductions (other than any deduction under section 172 of such Code) allowable for such year under such chapter.

The preceding sentence shall not apply for purposes of determining the amount of any deduction allowable under section 611 or the amount of foreign tax credit allowable under section 904 of such Code.

PART V—CONTINENTAL SHELF AREAS

[Sec. 638]

SEC. 638. CONTINENTAL SHELF AREAS.

For purposes of applying the provisions of this chapter (including sections 861(a)(3) and 862(a)(3) in the case of the performance of personal services) with respect to mines, oil and gas wells, and other natural deposits—

(1) the term "United States" when used in a geographical sense includes the seabed and subsoil of those submarine areas which are adjacent to the territorial waters of the United States and over which the United States has exclusive rights, in accordance with international law, with respect to the exploration and exploitation of natural resources; and

(2) the terms "foreign country" and "possession of the United States" when used in a geographical sense include the seabed and subsoil of those submarine areas which are adjacent to the territorial waters of the foreign country or such possession and over which the foreign country (or the United States in case of such possession) has exclusive rights, in accordance with international law, with respect to the exploration and exploitation of natural resources, but this paragraph shall apply in the case of a foreign country only if it exercises, directly or indirectly, taxing jurisdiction with respect to such exploration or exploitation.

No foreign country shall, by reason of the application of this section, be treated as a country contiguous to the United States.

Amendments

• 1969, Tax Reform Act of 1969 (P.L. 91-172)

P.L. 91-172, §505(a):

Added new Part V (Sec. 638) to subchapter I of chapter 1. **Effective** 12-31-69.

Subchapter J—Estates, Trusts, Beneficiaries, and Decedents

PART I—ESTATES, TRUSTS, AND BENEFICIARIES

Subpart A—General Rules for Taxation of Estates and Trusts

[Sec. 641]

SEC. 641. IMPOSITION OF TAX.

[Sec. 641(a)]

(a) APPLICATION OF TAX.—The tax imposed by section 1(e) shall apply to the taxable income of estates or of any kind of property held in trust, including—

(1) income accumulated in trust for the benefit of unborn or unascertained persons or persons with contingent interests, and income accumulated or held for future distribution under the terms of the will or trust;

(2) income which is to be distributed currently by the fiduciary to the beneficiaries, and income collected by a guardian of an infant which is to be held or distributed as the court may direct;

(3) income received by estates of deceased persons during the period of administration or settlement of the estate; and

(4) income which, in the discretion of the fiduciary, may be either distributed to the beneficiaries or accumulated.

Amendments

• 1977, Tax Reduction and Simplification Act of 1977 (P.L. 95-30)

P.L. 95-30, §101(d)(8):

Amended Code Sec. 641(a) by striking out "section 1(d)" and inserting in lieu thereof "section 1(e)". **Effective** for tax years beginning after 12-31-76.

• 1969, Tax Reform Act of 1969 (P.L. 91-172)

P.L. 91-172, §803(d)(3):

Amended Code Sec. 641(a) by striking out "The taxes imposed by this chapter on individuals" in the first sentence thereof and inserting "The tax imposed by section 1(d)" in lieu thereof. **Effective** for tax years beginning after 12-31-70.

[Sec. 641(b)]

(b) COMPUTATION AND PAYMENT.—The taxable income of an estate or trust shall be computed in the same manner as in the case of an individual, except as otherwise provided in this part. The tax shall be computed on such taxable income and shall be paid by the fiduciary. For purposes of this subsection, a foreign trust or foreign estate shall be treated as a nonresident alien individual who is not present in the United States at any time.

Amendments

• 1997, Taxpayer Relief Act of 1997 (P.L. 105-34)

P.L. 105-34, §1601(i)(3)(B):

Amended Code Sec. 641(b) by adding at the end a new sentence. **Effective** as if included in the provision of P.L. 104-88 to which it relates [generally **effective** for tax years beginning after 12-31-96.—CCH].

[Sec. 641(c)—Stricken]

Amendments

• 1998, IRS Restructuring and Reform Act of 1998 (P.L. 105-206)

P.L. 105-206, §6007(f)(2):

Amended Code Sec. 641 by striking subsection (c) and by redesignating subsection (d) as subsection (c). **Effective** as if included in the provision of P.L. 105-34 to which it relates [**effective** for sales or exchanges after 8-5-97.—CCH]. Prior to being stricken, Code Sec. 641(c) read as follows:

(c) EXCLUSION OF INCLUDIBLE GAIN FROM TAXABLE INCOME.—

(1) GENERAL RULE.—For purposes of this part, the taxable income of a trust does not include the amount of any includible gain as defined in section 644(b) reduced by any deductions properly allocable thereto.

(2) CROSS REFERENCE.—

For the taxation of any includible gain, see section 644.

• 1976, Tax Reform Act of 1976 (P.L. 94-455)

P.L. 94-455, §701(e)(2):

Added Code Sec. 641(c). **Effective** for transfers in trust made after 5-21-76.

[Sec. 641(c)]

(c) SPECIAL RULES FOR TAXATION OF ELECTING SMALL BUSINESS TRUSTS.—

(1) IN GENERAL.—For purposes of this chapter—

(A) the portion of any electing small business trust which consists of stock in 1 or more S corporations shall be treated as a separate trust, and

(B) the amount of the tax imposed by this chapter on such separate trust shall be determined with the modifications of paragraph (2).

(2) MODIFICATIONS.—For purposes of paragraph (1), the modifications of this paragraph are the following:

(A) Except as provided in section 1(h), the amount of the tax imposed by section 1(e) shall be determined by using the highest rate of tax set forth in section 1(e).

(B) The exemption amount under section 55(d) shall be zero.

(C) The only items of income, loss, deduction, or credit to be taken into account are the following:

(i) The items required to be taken into account under section 1366.

(ii) Any gain or loss from the disposition of stock in an S corporation.

(iii) To the extent provided in regulations, State or local income taxes or administrative expenses to the extent allocable to items described in clauses (i) and (ii).

(iv) Any interest expense paid or accrued on indebtedness incurred to acquire stock in an S corporation.

No deduction or credit shall be allowed for any amount not described in this paragraph, and no item described in this paragraph shall be apportioned to any beneficiary.

(D) No amount shall be allowed under paragraph (1) or (2) of section 1211(b).

(3) TREATMENT OF REMAINDER OF TRUST AND DISTRIBUTIONS.—For purposes of determining—

(A) the amount of the tax imposed by this chapter on the portion of any electing small business trust not treated as a separate trust under paragraph (1), and

(B) the distributable net income of the entire trust,

the items referred to in paragraph (2)(C) shall be excluded. Except as provided in the preceding sentence, this subsection shall not affect the taxation of any distribution from the trust.

(4) TREATMENT OF UNUSED DEDUCTIONS WHERE TERMINATION OF SEPARATE TRUST.—If a portion of an electing small business trust ceases to be treated as a separate trust under paragraph (1), any carryover or excess deduction of the separate trust which is referred to in section 642(h) shall be taken into account by the entire trust.

(5) ELECTING SMALL BUSINESS TRUST.—For purposes of this subsection, the term "electing small business trust" has the meaning given such term by section 1361(e)(1).

Amendments

• 2007, Small Business and Work Opportunity Tax Act of 2007 (P.L. 110-28)

P.L. 110-28, §8236(a):

Amended Code Sec. 641(c)(2)(C) by inserting after clause (iii) a new clause (iv). **Effective** for tax years beginning after 12-31-2006.

• 1998, IRS Restructuring and Reform Act of 1998 (P.L. 105-206)

P.L. 105-206, §6007(f)(2):

Amended Code Sec. 641 by striking subsection (c) and by redesignating subsection (d) as subsection (c). **Effective** as if included in the provision of P.L. 105-34 to which it relates [**effective** for sales or exchanges after 8-5-97.—CCH].

• 1996, Small Business Job Protection Act of 1996 (P.L. 104-188)

P.L. 104-188, §1302(d):

Amended Code Sec. 641 by adding at the end a new subsection (d). **Effective** for tax years beginning after 12-31-96.

[Sec. 642]

SEC. 642. SPECIAL RULES FOR CREDITS AND DEDUCTIONS.

[Sec. 642(a)]

(a) FOREIGN TAX CREDIT ALLOWED.—An estate or trust shall be allowed the credit against tax for taxes imposed by foreign countries and possessions of the United States, to the extent allowed by section 901, only in respect of so much of the taxes described in such section as is not properly allocable under such section to the beneficiaries.

Amendments

• 1986, Tax Reform Act of 1986 (P.L. 99-514)

P.L. 99-514, §112(b)(2):

Amended Code Sec. 642(a). **Effective** for tax years beginning after 12-31-86. Prior to amendment, Code Sec. 642(a) read as follows:

(A) CREDITS AGAINST TAX.—

(1) FOREIGN TAXES.—An estate or trust shall be allowed the credit against tax for taxes imposed by foreign countries and possessions of the United States, to the extent allowed by section 901, only in respect of so much of the taxes described in such section as is not properly allocable under such section to the beneficiaries.

(2) POLITICAL CONTRIBUTIONS.—An estate or trust shall not be allowed the credit against tax for political contributions provided by section 24.

• 1984, Deficit Reduction Act of 1984 (P.L. 98-369)

P.L. 98-369, §474(r)(17):

Amended Code Sec. 642(a)(2) by striking out "section 41" and inserting in lieu thereof "section 24". **Effective** for tax years beginning after 12-31-83, and to carrybacks from such years.

• 1976, Tax Reform Act of 1976 (P.L. 94-455)

P.L. 94-455, §1901(b)(1)(H)(i):

Struck out Code Sec. 642(a)(1) and redesignated paragraphs (2) and (3) to be paragraphs (1) and (2), respectively. **Effective** for tax years beginning after 12-31-76. Prior to repeal, Code Sec. 642(a)(1) read as follows:

(1) PARTIALLY TAX-EXEMPT INTEREST.—An estate or trust shall be allowed the credit against tax for partially tax-exempt interest provided by section 35 only in respect of so much of such interest as is not properly allocable to any beneficiary under section 652 or 662. If the estate or trust elects under section 171 to treat as amortizable the premium on bonds with respect to the interest on which the credit is allowable under section 35, such credit (whether allowable to the estate or trust or to the beneficiary) shall be reduced under section 171(a)(3).

• 1971, Revenue Act of 1971 (P.L. 92-178)

P.L. 92-178, §701(b):

Added paragraph (3) to Code Sec. 642(a). **Effective** for tax years ending after 12-31-71, but only with respect to political contributions, payment of which is made after such date.

• 1964, Revenue Act of 1964 (P.L. 88-272)

P.L. 88-272, §201(d)(6)(A):

Amends Code Sec. 642(a) by deleting paragraph (3). **Effective** with respect to dividends received after 12-31-64, in tax years ending after such date. Prior to deletion, Sec. 642(a)(3) read as follows:

"(3) Dividends received by individuals.—An estate or trust shall be allowed the credit against tax for dividends received provided by section 34 only in respect of so much of such dividends as is not properly allocable to any beneficiary under section 652 or 662. For purposes of determining the time of receipt of dividends under section 34 and section 116, the amount of dividends properly allocable to a beneficiary under section 652 or 662 shall be deemed to have been received by the beneficiary ratably on the same dates that the dividends were received by the estate or trust."

[Sec. 642(b)]

(b) DEDUCTION FOR PERSONAL EXEMPTION.—

(1) ESTATES.—An estate shall be allowed a deduction of $600.

(2) TRUSTS.—

(A) IN GENERAL.—Except as otherwise provided in this paragraph, a trust shall be allowed a deduction of $100.

(B) TRUSTS DISTRIBUTING INCOME CURRENTLY.—A trust which, under its governing instrument, is required to distribute all of its income currently shall be allowed a deduction of $300.

(C) DISABILITY TRUSTS.—

(i) IN GENERAL.—A qualified disability trust shall be allowed a deduction equal to the exemption amount under section 151(d), determined—

(I) by treating such trust as an individual described in section 151(d)(3)(C)(iii), and

(II) by applying section 67(e) (without the reference to section 642(b)) for purposes of determining the adjusted gross income of the trust.

(ii) QUALIFIED DISABILITY TRUST.—For purposes of clause (i), the term "qualified disability trust" means any trust if—

(I) such trust is a disability trust described in subsection (c)(2)(B)(iv) of section 1917 of the Social Security Act (42 U.S.C. 1396p), and

(II) all of the beneficiaries of the trust as of the close of the taxable year are determined by the Commissioner of Social Security to have been disabled (within the meaning of section 1614(a)(3) of the Social Security Act, 42 U.S.C. 1382c(a)(3)) for some portion of such year.

A trust shall not fail to meet the requirements of subclause (II) merely because the corpus of the trust may revert to a person who is not so disabled after the trust ceases to have any beneficiary who is so disabled.

(3) DEDUCTIONS IN LIEU OF PERSONAL EXEMPTION.—The deductions allowed by this subsection shall be in lieu of the deductions allowed under section 151 (relating to deduction for personal exemption).

Amendments

• 2002, Victims of Terrorism Tax Relief Act of 2001 (P.L. 107-134)

P.L. 107-134, §116(a):

Amended Code Sec. 642(b). **Effective** for tax years ending on or after 9-11-2001. Prior to amendment, Code Sec 642(b) read as follows:

(b) DEDUCTION FOR PERSONAL EXEMPTION.—An estate shall be allowed a deduction of $600. A trust which, under its governing instrument, is required to distribute all of its income currently shall be allowed a deduction of $300. All other trusts shall be allowed a deduction of $100. The deductions allowed by this subsection shall be in lieu of the deductions allowed under section 151 (relating to deduction for personal exemption).

[Sec. 642(c)]

(c) DEDUCTION FOR AMOUNTS PAID OR PERMANENTLY SET ASIDE FOR A CHARITABLE PURPOSE.—

(1) GENERAL RULE.—In the case of an estate or trust (other than a trust meeting the specifications of subpart B), there shall be allowed as a deduction in computing its taxable income (in lieu of the deduction allowed by section 170(a), relating to deduction for charitable, etc., contributions and gifts) any amount of the gross income, without limitation, which pursuant to the terms of the governing instrument is, during the taxable year, paid for a purpose specified in section 170(c) (determined without regard to section 170(c)(2)(A)). If a charitable contribution is paid after the close of such taxable year and on or before the last day of the year following the close of such taxable year, then the trustee or administrator may elect to treat such contribution as paid during such taxable year. The election shall be made at such time and in such manner as the Secretary prescribes by regulations.

(2) AMOUNTS PERMANENTLY SET ASIDE.—In the case of an estate, and in the case of a trust (other than a trust meeting the specifications of subpart B) required by the terms of its governing instrument to set aside amounts which was—

(A) created on or before October 9, 1969, if—

(i) an irrevocable remainder interest is transferred to or for the use of an organization described in section 170(c), or

(ii) the grantor is at all times after October 9, 1969, under a mental disability to change the terms of the trust; or

(B) established by a will executed on or before October 9, 1969, if—

(i) the testator dies before October 9, 1972, without having republished the will after October 9, 1969, by codicil or otherwise,

(ii) the testator at no time after October 9, 1969, had the right to change the portions of the will which pertain to the trust, or

(iii) the will is not republished by codicil or otherwise before October 9, 1972, and the testator is on such date and at all times thereafter under a mental disability to republish the will by codicil or otherwise,

there shall also be allowed as a deduction in computing its taxable income any amount of the gross income, without limitation, which pursuant to the terms of the governing instrument is, during the taxable year, permanently set aside for a purpose specified in section 170(c), or is to be used exclusively for religious, charitable, scientific, literary, or educational purposes, or for the prevention of cruelty to children or animals, or for the establishment, acquisition, maintenance, or operation of a public cemetery not operated for profit. In the case of a trust, the preceding sentence shall apply only to gross income earned with respect to amounts transferred to the trust before October 9, 1969, or transferred under a will to which subparagraph (B) applies.

(3) POOLED INCOME FUNDS.—In the case of a pooled income fund (as defined in paragraph (5)), there shall also be allowed as a deduction in computing its taxable income any amount of the gross income attributable to gain from the sale of a capital asset held for more than 1 year, without limitation, which pursuant to the terms of the governing instrument is, during the taxable year, permanently set aside for a purpose specified in section 170(c).

(4) ADJUSTMENTS.—To the extent that the amount otherwise allowable as a deduction under this subsection consists of gain described in section 1202(a), proper adjustment shall be made for any exclusion allowable to the estate or trust under section 1202. In the case of a trust, the deduction allowed by this subsection shall be subject to section 681 (relating to unrelated business income).

(5) DEFINITION OF POOLED INCOME FUND.—For purposes of paragraph (3), a pooled income fund is a trust—

(A) to which each donor transfers property, contributing an irrevocable remainder interest in such property to or for the use of an organization described in section 170(b)(1)(A) (other than in clauses (vii) or (viii)), and retaining an income interest for the life of one or more beneficiaries (living at the time of such transfer),

(B) in which the property transferred by each donor is commingled with property transferred by other donors who have made or make similar transfers,

(C) which cannot have investments in securities which are exempt from taxes imposed by this subtitle,

(D) which includes only amounts received from transfers which meet the requirements of this paragraph,

(E) which is maintained by the organization to which the remainder interest is contributed and of which no donor or beneficiary of an income interest is a trustee, and

(F) from which each beneficiary of an income interest receives income, for each year for which he is entitled to receive the income interest referred to in subparagraph (A), determined by the rate of return earned by the trust for such year.

For purposes of determining the amount of any charitable contribution allowable by reason of a transfer of property to a pooled fund, the value of the income interest shall be determined on the basis of the highest rate of return earned by the fund for any of the 3 taxable years immediately preceding the taxable year of the fund in which the transfer is made. In the case of funds in existence less than 3 taxable years preceding the taxable year of the fund in which a transfer is made, the rate of return shall be deemed to be 6 percent per annum, except that the Secretary may prescribe a different rate of return.

(6) TAXABLE PRIVATE FOUNDATIONS.—In the case of a private foundation which is not exempt from taxation under section 501(a) for the taxable year, the provisions of this subsection shall not apply and the provisions of section 170 shall apply.

Amendments

• 1993, Omnibus Budget Reconciliation Act of 1993 (P.L. 103-66)

P.L. 103-66, §13113(d)(2):

Amended Code Sec. 642(c)(4). **Effective** for stock issued after 8-10-93. Prior to amendment, Code Sec. 642(c)(4) read as follows:

(4) ADJUSTMENTS.—In the case of a trust, the deduction allowed by this subsection shall be subject to section 681 (relating to unrelated business income).

• 1986, Tax Reform Act of 1986 (P.L. 99-514)

P.L. 99-514, §301(b)(6)(A)-(B):

Amended Code Sec. 642(c)(4) by striking out the 1st sentence. **Effective** for tax years beginning after 12-31-86. Prior to amendment, the 1st sentence of Code Sec. 642(c)(4) read as follows:

To the extent that the amount otherwise allowable as a deduction under this subsection consists of gain from the sale or exchange of capital assets held for more than 6 months, proper adjustment shall be made for any deduction allowable to the estate or trust under section 1202 (relating to deduction for excess of capital gains over capital losses).

• 1984, Deficit Reduction Act of 1984 (P.L. 98-369)

P.L. 98-369, §1001(b)(8):

Amended Code Sec. 642(c)(3) and (4) by striking out "1 year" each place it appeared and inserting in lieu thereof "6 months". **Effective** for property acquired after 6-22-84, and before 1-1-88.

• 1976, Tax Reform Act of 1976 (P.L. 94-455)

P.L. 94-455, §1402(b)(1)(J):

§1402(b)(1)(J) substituted "9 months" for "6 months" in Code Sec. 642(c)(3) and (4). **Effective** for tax years beginning in 1977.

P.L. 94-455, §1402(b)(2):

Substituted "1 year" for "9 months" in Code Sec. 642(c)(3) and (4). **Effective** for tax years beginning after 1977.

P.L. 94-455, §1906(b)(13)(A):

Amended 1954 Code by substituting "Secretary" for "Secretary or his delegate" each place it appeared. **Effective** 2-1-77.

• 1969, Tax Reform Act of 1969 (P.L. 91-172)

P.L. 91-172, §201(b):

Amended Code Sec. 642(c). **Effective** with respect to amounts paid, permanently set aside, or to be used for a charitable purpose in tax years beginning after 12-31-69, except section 642(c)(5) of the Internal Revenue Code of 1954 (as added by subsection (b)) shall apply to transfers in trust made after 7-31-69. Prior to amendment, Code Sec. 642(c), read as follows:

"(c) Deduction for Amounts Paid or Permanently Set Aside for a Charitable Purpose.—In the case of an estate or trust (other than a trust meeting the specifications of subpart B) there shall be allowed as a deduction in computing its taxable income (in lieu of the deductions allowed by section 170(a), relating to deduction for charitable, etc., contributions and gifts) any amount of the gross income, without limitation, which pursuant to the terms of the governing instrument is, during the taxable year, paid or permanently set aside for a purpose specified in section 170(c), or is to be used exclusively for religious, charitable, scientific, literary, or educational purposes, or for the prevention of cruelty to children or animals, or for the establishment, acquisition, maintenance or operation of a public cemetery not operated for profit. For this purpose, to the extent that such amount consists of gain from the sale or exchange of capital assets held for more than 6 months, proper adjustment of the deduction otherwise allowable under this subsection shall be made for any deduction allowable to the estate or trust under section 1202 (relating to deduction for excess of capital gains over capital losses). In the case of a trust, the deduction allowed by this subsection shall be subject to section 681 (relating to unrelated business income and prohibited transactions)."

[Sec. 642(d)]

(d) NET OPERATING LOSS DEDUCTION.—The benefit of the deduction for net operating losses provided by section 172 shall be allowed to estates and trusts under regulations prescribed by the Secretary.

Amendments

• 1976, Tax Reform Act of 1976 (P.L. 94-455)

P.L. 94-455, §1906(b)(13)(A):

Amended 1954 Code by substituting "Secretary" for "Secretary or his delegate" each place it appeared. **Effective** 2-1-77.

[Sec. 642(e)]

(e) DEDUCTION FOR DEPRECIATION AND DEPLETION.—An estate or trust shall be allowed the deduction for depreciation and depletion only to the extent not allowable to beneficiaries under sections 167(d) and 611(b).

Amendments

• 1990, Omnibus Budget Reconciliation Act of 1990 (P.L. 101-508)

P.L. 101-508, §11812(b)(9):

Amended Code Sec. 642(e) by striking "167(h)" and inserting "167(d)". **Effective** for property placed in service after 11-5-90. For exceptions, see Act Sec. 11812(c)(2)-(3), below.

P.L. 101-508, §11812(c)(2)-(3), provides:

(2) EXCEPTION.—The amendments made by this section shall not apply to any property to which section 168 of the Internal Revenue Code of 1986 does not apply by reason of subsection (f)(5) thereof.

(3) EXCEPTION FOR PREVIOUSLY GRANDFATHER EXPENDITURES.—The amendments made by this section shall not apply to rehabilitation expenditures described in section 252(f)(5) of the Tax Reform Act of 1986 (as added by section 1002(l)(31) of the Technical and Miscellaneous Revenue Act of 1988).

• 1962, Revenue Act of 1962 (P.L. 87-834)

P.L. 87-834, §13(c)(2):

Amended Code Sec. 642(e) by substituting "167(h)" for "167(g)" in the last line. **Effective** for tax years beginning after 12-31-61, and ending after 10-16-62.

[Sec. 642(f)]

(f) AMORTIZATION DEDUCTIONS.—The benefit of the deductions for amortization provided by sections 169 and 197 shall be allowed to estates and trusts in the same manner as in the case of an individual. The allowable deduction shall be apportioned between the income beneficiaries and the fiduciary under regulations prescribed by the Secretary.

Amendments

• 1993, Omnibus Budget Reconciliation Act of 1993 (P.L. 103-66)

P.L. 103-66, §13261(f)(2):

Amended Code Sec. 642(f) by striking "section 169" and inserting "sections 169 and 197". **Effective**, generally, with respect to property acquired after 8-10-93. However, for exceptions, see Act Sec. 13261(g)(2)-(3) below.

P.L. 103-66, §13261(g)(2)-(3), provides:

(2) ELECTION TO HAVE AMENDMENTS APPLY TO PROPERTY ACQUIRED AFTER JULY 25, 1991.—

(A) IN GENERAL.—If an election under this paragraph applies to the taxpayer—

(i) the amendments made by this section shall apply to property acquired by the taxpayer after July 25, 1991,

(ii) subsection (c)(1)(A) of section 197 of the Internal Revenue Code of 1986 (as added by this section) (and so much of subsection (f)(9)(A) of such section 197 as precedes clause (i) thereof) shall be applied with respect to the taxpayer by treating July 25, 1991, as the date of the enactment of such section, and

(iii) in applying subsection (f)(9) of such section, with respect to any property acquired by the taxpayer on or before the date of the enactment of this Act, only holding or use on July 25, 1991, shall be taken into account.

(B) ELECTION.—An election under this paragraph shall be made at such time and in such manner as the Secretary of the Treasury or his delegate may prescribe. Such an election by any taxpayer, once made—

(i) may be revoked only with the consent of the Secretary, and

(ii) shall apply to the taxpayer making such election and any other taxpayer under common control with the taxpayer (within the meaning of subparagraphs (A) and (B) of section 41(f)(1) of such Code) at any time after August 2, 1993, and on or before the date on which such election is made.

(3) ELECTIVE BINDING CONTRACT EXCEPTION.—

(A) IN GENERAL.—The amendments made by this section shall not apply to any acquisition of property by the taxpayer if—

(i) such acquisition is pursuant to a written binding contract in effect on the date of the enactment of this Act and at all times thereafter before such acquisition,

(ii) an election under paragraph (2) does not apply to the taxpayer, and

(iii) the taxpayer makes an election under this paragraph with respect to such contract.

(B) ELECTION.—An election under this paragraph shall be made at such time and in such manner as the Secretary of the Treasury or his delegate shall prescribe. Such an election, once made—

(i) may be revoked only with the consent of the Secretary, and

(ii) shall apply to all property acquired pursuant to the contract with respect to which such election was made.

• 1990, Omnibus Budget Reconciliation Act of 1990 (P.L. 101-508)

P.L. 101-508, §11801(c)(6)(B):

Amended Code Sec. 642(f) by striking "sections 169, 184, 187, and 188" and inserting "section 169". **Effective** 11-5-90.

P.L. 101-508, §11821(b), provides:

(b) SAVINGS PROVISION.—If—

(1) any provision amended or repealed by this part applied to—

(A) any transaction occurring before the date of the enactment of this Act,

(B) any property acquired before such date of enactment, or

(C) any item of income, loss, deduction, or credit taken into account before such date of enactment, and

(2) the treatment of such transaction, property, or item under such provision would (without regard to the amendments made by this part) affect liability for tax for periods ending after such date of enactment,

nothing in the amendments made by this part shall be construed to affect the treatment of such transaction, property, or item for purposes of determining liability for tax for periods ending after such date of enactment.

• 1981, Economic Recovery Tax Act of 1981 (P.L. 97-34)

P.L. 97-34, §212(d)(2)(D):

Amended Code Sec. 642(f) by striking out "188, and 191" and inserting in lieu thereof "and 188". **Effective** for expenditures incurred after 12-31-81, in tax years ending after such date.

P.L. 97-34, §212(e)(2), as amended by P.L. 97-448, §102(f)(1), provides:

(2) TRANSITIONAL RULE.—The amendments made by this section shall not apply with respect to any rehabilitation of a building if—

(A) the physical work on such rehabilitation began before January 1, 1982, and

(b) such building does not meet the requirements of paragraph (1) of section 48(g) of the Internal Revenue Code of 1954 (as amended by this Act).

• 1976, Tax Reform Act of 1976 (P.L. 94-455)

P.L. 94-455, §1906(b)(13)(A):

Amended 1954 Code by substituting "Secretary" for "Secretary or his delegate" each place it appeared. **Effective** 2-1-77.

P.L. 94-455, §1951(c)(2)(B):

Struck out "168," after the word "sections". **Effective** for tax years beginning after 12-31-76.

P.L. 94-455, §2124(a)(3)(B):

Substituted "188, and 191" for "and 188". **Effective** for additions to capital account made after 6-14-76 and before 6-15-81.

• **1971, Revenue Act of 1971 (P.L. 92-178)**

P.L. 92-178, §303(c)(4):

Amended Code Sec. 642(f) by substituting "187, and 188" for "and 187" in the first sentence. **Effective** for tax years ending after 12-31-71.

• **1969, Tax Reform Act of 1969 (P.L. 91-172)**

P.L. 91-172, §704(b)(2):

Amended the heading and first sentence of Code Sec. 642(f). **Effective** for tax years ending after 12-31-68. Prior to amendment, the heading and first sentence read as follows:

(f) Amortization of Emergency or Grain Storage Facilities.—The benefit of the deductions for amortization of emergency and grain storage facilities provided by sections 168 and 169 shall be allowed to estates and trusts in the same manner as in the case of an individual.

[Sec. 642(g)]

(g) DISALLOWANCE OF DOUBLE DEDUCTIONS.—Amounts allowable under section 2053 or 2054 as a deduction in computing the taxable estate of a decedent shall not be allowed as a deduction (or as an offset against the sales price of property in determining gain or loss) in computing the taxable income of the estate or of any other person, unless there is filed, within the time and in the manner and form prescribed by the Secretary, a statement that the amounts have not been allowed as deductions under section 2053 or 2054 and a waiver of the right to have such amounts allowed at any time as deductions under section 2053 or 2054. Rules similar to the rules of the preceding sentence shall apply to amounts which may be taken into account under section 2621(a)(2) or 2622(b). This subsection shall not apply with respect to deductions allowed under part II (relating to income in respect of decedents).

Amendments

• **1996, Small Business Job Protection Act of 1996 (P.L. 104-188)**

P.L. 104-188, §1704(t)(8):

Amended Code Sec. 642(g) by striking "under 2621(a)(2)" and inserting "under section 2621(a)(2)". **Effective** 8-20-96.

• **1989, Omnibus Budget Reconciliation Act of 1989 (P.L. 101-239)**

P.L. 101-239, §7811(j)(3):

Amended Code Sec. 642(g) by inserting after the first sentence a new sentence. **Effective** as if included in the provision of P.L. 100-647 to which it relates.

• **1976, Tax Reform Act of 1976 (P.L. 94-455)**

P.L. 94-455, §1906(b)(13)(A):

Amended 1954 Code by substituting "Secretary" for "Secretary or his delegate" each place it appeared. **Effective** 2-1-77.

P.L. 94-455, §2009(d):

Added "(or as an offset against the sales price of property in determining gain or loss)" to Code Sec. 642(g). **Effective** for tax years ending after 10-4-76.

• **1966 (P.L. 89-621)**

P.L. 89-621, §2:

Amended Code Sec. 642(g) by inserting "or of any other person" immediately after "shall not be allowed as a deduction in computing the taxable income of the estate." **Effective** for tax years ending after 10-4-66, but only with respect to amounts paid or incurred, and losses sustained, after that date.

[Sec. 642(h)]

(h) UNUSED LOSS CARRYOVERS AND EXCESS DEDUCTIONS ON TERMINATION AVAILABLE TO BENEFICIARIES.—If on the termination of an estate or trust, the estate or trust has—

(1) a net operating loss carryover under section 172 or a capital loss carryover under section 1212, or

(2) for the last taxable year of the estate or trust deductions (other than the deductions allowed under subsections (b) or (c)) in excess of gross income for such year,

then such carryover or such excess shall be allowed as a deduction, in accordance with regulations prescribed by the Secretary, to the beneficiaries succeeding to the property of the estate or trust.

Amendments

• **1976, Tax Reform Act of 1976 (P.L. 94-455)**

P.L. 94-455, §1906(b)(13)(A):

Amended 1954 Code by substituting "Secretary" for "Secretary or his delegate" each place it appeared. **Effective** 2-1-77.

[Sec. 642(i)]

(i) CERTAIN DISTRIBUTIONS BY CEMETERY PERPETUAL CARE FUNDS.—In the case of a cemetery perpetual care fund which—

(1) was created pursuant to local law by a taxable cemetery corporation for the care and maintenance of cemetery property, and

(2) is treated for the taxable year as a trust for purposes of this subchapter,

any amount distributed by such fund for the care and maintenance of gravesites which have been purchased from the cemetery corporation before the beginning of the taxable year of the trust and with respect to which there is an obligation to furnish care and maintenance shall be considered to be a distribution solely for purposes of sections 651 and 661, but only to the extent that the aggregate amount so distributed during the taxable year does not exceed $5 multiplied by the aggregate number of such gravesites.

Amendments

• 1978, Revenue Act of 1978 (P.L. 95-600)

P.L. 95-600, §113(a)(2)(B):

Repealed Code Sec. 642(i) and redesignated Code Sec. 642(j) as Code Sec. 642(i). **Effective** for contributions the payment of which is made after 12-31-78, in tax years beginning after such date. Prior to repeal, Code Sec. 642(i) read as follows:

(i) POLITICAL CONTRIBUTIONS.—An estate or trust shall not be allowed the deduction for contributions to candidates for public office provided by section 218.

• 1976 (P.L. 94-528)

P.L. 94-528, §[(1)](a):

Added Code Sec. 642(j). **Effective** 10-1-77, and shall apply to amounts distributed during tax years ending after 12-31-63.

• 1971, Revenue Act of 1971 (P.L. 92-178)

P.L. 92-178, §702(b);

Added new Code Sec. 642(i) and redesignated former Code Sec. 642(i) as Code Sec. 642(j). **Effective** for tax years ending after 12-31-71, but only with respect to political contributions, payment of which is made after such date.

[Sec. 642(j)—Stricken]

Amendments

• 1986, Tax Reform Act of 1986 (P.L. 99-514)

P.L. 99-514, §612(b)(3):

Amended Code Sec. 642 by striking out subsection (j). **Effective** for tax years beginning after 12-31-86. Prior to amendment, Code Sec. 642(j) read as follows:

(j) CROSS REFERENCES.—

For special rule for determining the time of receipt of dividends by a beneficiary under section 652 or 662, see section 116(c)(3).

• 1978, Revenue Act of 1978 (P.L. 95-600)

P.L. 95-600, §113(b)(2)(B):

Redesignated Code Sec. 642(k) as Code Sec. 642(j). **Effective** for contributions the payment of which is made after 12-31-78, in tax years beginning after such date.

• 1977, Tax Reduction and Simplification Act of 1977 (P.L. 95-30)

P.L. 95-30, §101(d)(9):

Amended Code Sec. 642(k). **Effective** for tax years beginning after 12-31-76. Prior to amendment, Code Sec. 642(k) read as follows:

(k) CROSS REFERENCES.—

(1) For disallowance of standard deduction in case of estates and trusts, see section 142(b)(4).

(2) For special rule for determining the time of receipt of dividends by a beneficiary under section 652 or 662, see section 116(c)(3).

• 1976 (P.L. 94-528)

P.L. 94-528, §[(1)](a):

Redesignated former Code Sec. 642(j) as Code Sec. 642(k). **Effective** 10-1-77, and shall apply to amounts distributed during tax years ending after 12-31-63.

• 1971, Revenue Act of 1971 (P.L. 92-178)

P.L. 92-178, §702(b):

Redesignated former Code Sec. 642(i) as Code Sec. 642(j).

• 1964, Revenue Act of 1964 (P.L. 88-272)

P.L. 88-272, §201(d)(6)(B):

Amended Code Sec. 642(i) by designating the first sentence as paragraph (1) and by adding paragraph (2). **Effective** with respect to dividends received after 12-31-64, in tax years ending after such date.

[Sec. 643]

SEC. 643. DEFINITIONS APPLICABLE TO SUBPARTS A, B, C, AND D.

[Sec. 643(a)]

(a) DISTRIBUTABLE NET INCOME.—For purposes of this part, the term "distributable net income" means, with respect to any taxable year, the taxable income of the estate or trust computed with the following modifications—

(1) DEDUCTION FOR DISTRIBUTIONS.—No deduction shall be taken under sections 651 and 661 (relating to additional deductions).

(2) DEDUCTION FOR PERSONAL EXEMPTION.—No deduction shall be taken under section 642(b) (relating to deduction for personal exemptions).

(3) CAPITAL GAINS AND LOSSES.—Gains from the sale or exchange of capital assets shall be excluded to the extent that such gains are allocated to corpus and are not (A) paid, credited, or required to be distributed to any beneficiary during the taxable year, or (B) paid, permanently set aside, or to be used for the purposes specified in section 642(c). Losses from the sale or exchange of capital assets shall be excluded, except to the extent such losses are taken into account in determining the amount of gains from the sale or exchange of capital assets which are paid, credited, or required to be distributed to any beneficiary during the taxable year. The exclusion under section 1202 shall not be taken into account.

(4) EXTRAORDINARY DIVIDENDS AND TAXABLE STOCK DIVIDENDS.—For purposes only of subpart B (relating to trusts which distribute current income only), there shall be excluded those items of gross income constituting extraordinary dividends or taxable stock dividends which the fiduciary, acting in good faith, does not pay or credit to any beneficiary by reason of his determination that such dividends are allocable to corpus under the terms of the governing instrument and applicable local law.

(5) TAX-EXEMPT INTEREST.—There shall be included any tax-exempt interest to which section 103 applies, reduced by any amounts which would be deductible in respect of disbursements allocable to such interest but for the provisions of section 265 (relating to disallowance of certain deductions).

(6) INCOME OF FOREIGN TRUST.—In the case of a foreign trust—

(A) There shall be included the amounts of gross income from sources without the United States, reduced by any amounts which would be deductible in respect of disbursements allocable to such income but for the provisions of section 265(a)(1) (relating to disallowance of certain deductions).

(B) Gross income from sources within the United States shall be determined without regard to section 894 (relating to income exempt under treaty).

(C) Paragraph (3) shall not apply to a foreign trust. In the case of such a trust, there shall be included gains from the sale or exchange of capital assets, reduced by losses from such sales or exchanges to the extent such losses do not exceed gains from such sales or exchanges.

(7) ABUSIVE TRANSACTIONS.—The Secretary shall prescribe such regulations as may be necessary or appropriate to carry out the purposes of this part, including regulations to prevent avoidance of such purposes.

If the estate or trust is allowed a deduction under section 642(c), the amount of the modifications specified in paragraphs (5) and (6) shall be reduced to the extent that the amount of income which is paid, permanently set aside, or to be used for the purposes specified in section 642(c) is deemed to consist of items specified in those paragraphs. For this purpose, such amount shall (in the absence of specific provisions in the governing instrument) be deemed to consist of the same proportion of each class of items of income of the estate or trust as the total of each class bears to the total of all classes.

Amendments

• 1996, Small Business Job Protection Act of 1996 (P.L. 104-188)

P.L. 104-188, §1906(b):

Amended Code Sec. 643(a) by inserting after paragraph (6) a new paragraph (7). **Effective** 8-20-96.

• 1993, Omnibus Budget Reconciliation Act of 1993 (P.L. 103-66)

P.L. 103-66, §13113(d)(3):

Amended Code Sec. 643(a)(3) by adding at the end thereof a new sentence. **Effective** for stock issued after 8-10-93.

• 1989, Omnibus Budget Reconciliation Act of 1989 (P.L. 101-239)

P.L. 101-239, §7811(b)(1):

Amended Code Sec. 643(a)(6)(C) by striking "(i)" and by striking ", and (ii)" and all that follows and inserting a period. **Effective** as if included in the provision of P.L. 100-647 to which it relates. Prior to amendment, Code Sec. 643(a)(6)(C) read as follows:

(C) Paragraph (3) shall not apply to a foreign trust. In the case of such a trust, (i) there shall be included gains from the sale or exchange of capital assets, reduced by losses from such sales or exchanges to the extent such losses do not exceed gains from such sales or exchanges, and (ii) the deduction under section 1202 (relating to deduction for excess of capital gains over capital losses) [Code Sec. 1202 was repealed by P.L. 99-514.—CCH.] shall not be taken into account.

P.L. 101-239, §7811(b)(2):

Amended Code Sec. 643(a)(6) by striking subparagraph (D). **Effective** as if included in the provision of P.L. 100-647 to which it relates. Prior to amendment, Code Sec. 643(a)(6)(D) read as follows:

(D) Effective for distributions made in taxable years beginning after December 31, 1975, the undistributed net income of each foreign trust for each taxable year beginning on or before December 31, 1975, remaining undistributed at the close of the last taxable year beginning on or before December 31, 1975, shall be redetermined by taking into account the deduction allowed by section 1202.

P.L. 101-239, §7811(f)(1):

Amended Code Sec. 643(a)(6)(A) by striking "section 265(1)" and inserting "section 265(a)(1)". **Effective** as if included in the provision of P.L. 100-647 to which it relates.

• 1986, Tax Reform Act of 1986 (P.L. 99-514)

P.L. 99-514, §301(b)(7):

Amended Code Sec. 643(a)(3) by striking out the last sentence. **Effective** for tax years beginning after 12-31-86. Prior to amendment, the last sentence read as follows:

The deduction under section 1202 (relating to deduction for excess of capital gains over capital losses) shall not be taken into account.

P.L. 99-514, §612(b)(4):

Repealed Code Sec. 643(a)(7). **Effective** for tax years beginning after 12-31-86. Prior to repeal, Code Sec. 643(a)(7) read as follows:

(7) DIVIDENDS OR INTEREST.—There shall be included the amount of any dividends or interest excluded from gross income pursuant to section 116 (relating to partial exclusion of dividends) or section 128 (relating to certain interest).

• 1983, Technical Corrections Act of 1982 (P.L. 97-448)

P.L. 97-448, §103(a)(3):

Amended Code Sec. 643(a)(7). **Effective** as if included in the provision of P.L. 97-34 to which it relates. Prior to amendment, Code Sec. 643(a)(7) read as follows:

"(7) Dividends or interest.—There shall be included the amount of any dividends or interest excluded from gross income pursuant to section 116 (relating to partial exclusion of dividends or interest received) or section 128 (relating to interest on certain savings certificates)."

• 1981, Economic Recovery Tax Act of 1981 (P.L. 97-34)

P.L. 97-34, §301(b)(4):

Amended Code Sec. 643(a)(7), as in effect for tax years beginning in 1981, by inserting "or section 128 (relating to interest on certain savings certificates)" after "received)". **Effective** for tax years ending after 9-30-81.

P.L. 97-34, §301(b)(6)(B):

Amended Code Sec. 643(a)(7), as in effect for tax years beginning after 12-31-81, by inserting "or interest" after "dividends" each place it appears in the caption or test. **Effective** for tax years beginning after 12-31-81.

• 1980, Crude Oil Windfall Profit Tax Act of 1980 (P.L. 96-223)

P.L. 96-223, §404(b)(4):

Amended Code Sec. 643(a)(7) by inserting "or interest" after "dividends" each place it appeared in the caption and in the text. **Effective** for tax years beginning after 12-31-80 and before 1-1-83. (P.L. 97-34, Act Sec. 302(b)(1), amended Act Sec. 404(c) of the Crude Oil Windfall Profit Tax Act of 1980, P.L. 96-223, by striking out "1983" and inserting "1982".)

• 1976, Tax Reform Act of 1976 (P.L. 94-455)

P.L. 94-455, §1013(c)(1):

Amended Code Sec. 643(a)(6)(C) by striking out "foreign trust created by a United States person" and inserting in lieu thereof "foreign trust". **Effective** for tax years beginning after 12-31-75.

P.L. 94-455, §1013(c)(2):

Added Code Sec. 643(a)(6)(D). **Effective** for tax years beginning after 12-31-75.

• 1962, Revenue Act of 1962 (P.L. 87-834)

P.L. 87-834, §7:

Amended Code Sec. 643(a)(6) by adding subsections (B) and (C). **Effective** with respect to distributions made after 12-31-62. Prior to the amendment, Sec. 643(a)(6) read as follows:

(6) Foreign Income.—In the case of a foreign trust, there shall be included the amounts of gross income from sources without the United States, reduced by any amounts which would be deductible in respect of disbursements allocable to such income but for the provisions of section 265(1) (relating to disallowance of certain deductions).

[Sec. 643(b)]

(b) INCOME.—For purposes of this subpart and subparts B, C, and D, the term "income", when not preceded by the words "taxable", "distributable net", "undistributed net", or "gross", means the amount of income of the estate or trust for the taxable year determined under the terms of the governing instrument and applicable local law. Items of gross income constituting extraordinary dividends or taxable stock dividends which the fiduciary, acting in good faith, determines to be allocable to corpus under the terms of the governing instrument and applicable local law shall not be considered income.

[Sec. 643(c)]

(c) BENEFICIARY.—For purposes of this part, the term "beneficiary" includes heir, legatee, devisee.

[Sec. 643(d)]

(d) COORDINATION WITH BACK-UP WITHHOLDING.—Except to the extent otherwise provided in regulations, this subchapter shall be applied with respect to payments subject to withholding under section 3406—

(1) by allocating between the estate or trust and its beneficiaries any credit allowable under section 31(c) (on the basis of their respective shares of any such payment taken into account under this subchapter),

(2) by treating each beneficiary to whom such credit is allocated as if an amount equal to such credit has been paid to him by the estate or trust, and

(3) by allowing the estate or trust a deduction in an amount equal to the credit so allocated to beneficiaries.

Amendments

• 1984, Deficit Reduction Act of 1984 (P.L. 98-369)

P.L. 98-369, §722(h)(3):

Amended Code Sec. 643 by adding section (d). **Effective** as if included in the amendments made by P.L. 98-67.

• 1983, Interest and Dividend Tax Compliance Act of 1983 (P.L.98-67)

P.L. 98-67, §102(a):

Repealed Code Sec. 643(d) as though it had not been enacted. **Effective** as of the close of 6-30-83. Prior to repeal, Code Sec. 643(d) read as follows:

(d) COORDINATION WITH WITHHOLDING ON INTEREST AND DIVIDENDS.—Except to the extent otherwise provided in regulations, this subchapter shall be applied with respect to payments subject to withholding under subchapter B of chapter 24—

(1) by allocating between the estate or trust and its beneficiaries any credit allowable under section 31(b) (on the basis of their respective shares of interest, dividends, and patronage dividends taken into account under this subchapter),

(2) by treating each beneficiary to whom such credit is allocated as if an amount equal to such credit has been paid to him by the estate or trust, and

(3) by allowing the estate or trust a deduction in an amount equal to the credit so allocated to beneficiaries.

• 1982, Tax Equity and Fiscal Responsibility Act of 1982 (P.L. 97-248)

P.L. 97-248, §302(b)(1):

Amended Code Sec. 643 by inserting at the end thereof new subsection (d). **Effective** for interest, dividends, and patronage dividends paid or credited after 6-30-83, but see amendment notes for P.L. 97-248 following Code Sec. 3451 for special rules.

• 1976, Tax Reform Act of 1976 (P.L. 94-455)

P.L. 94-455, §1013(e)(2):

Repealed Code Sec. 643(d). **Effective** for tax years ending after 12-31-75, but only in the case of foreign trusts created after 5-21-74, and transfers of property to foreign trusts after 5-21-74. Prior to repeal, Code Sec. 643(d) read as follows:

(d) FOREIGN TRUSTS CREATED BY UNITED STATES PERSONS.—For purposes of this part, the term "foreign trust created by a United States person" means that portion of a foreign trust (as defined in section 7701(a)(31)) attributable to money or property transferred directly or indirectly by a United States person (as defined in section 7701(a)(30)), or under the will of a decedent who at the date of his death was a United States citizen or resident.

• 1962, Revenue Act of 1962 (P.L. 87-834)

P.L. 87-834, §7:

Added to Code Sec. 643 a new subsection (d). **Effective** for distributions made after 12-31-62.

[Sec. 643(e)]

(e) TREATMENT OF PROPERTY DISTRIBUTED IN KIND.—

(1) BASIS OF BENEFICIARY.—The basis of any property received by a beneficiary in a distribution from an estate or trust shall be—

(A) the adjusted basis of such property in the hands of the estate or trust immediately before the distribution, adjusted for

(B) any gain or loss recognized to the estate or trust on the distribution.

(2) AMOUNT OF DISTRIBUTION.—In the case of any distribution of property (other than cash), the amount taken into account under sections 661(a)(2) and 662(a)(2) shall be the lesser of—

(A) the basis of such property in the hands of the beneficiary (as determined under paragraph (1)), or

(B) the fair market value of such property.

(3) ELECTION TO RECOGNIZE GAIN.—

(A) IN GENERAL.—In the case of any distribution of property (other than cash) to which an election under this paragraph applies—

(i) paragraph (2) shall not apply,

(ii) gain or loss shall be recognized by the estate or trust in the same manner as if such property had been sold to the distributee at its fair market value, and

(iii) the amount taken into account under sections 661(a)(2) and 662(a)(2) shall be the fair market value of such property.

(B) ELECTION.—Any election under this paragraph shall apply to all distributions made by the estate or trust during a taxable year and shall be made on the return of such estate or trust for such taxable year.

Any such election, once made, may be revoked only with the consent of the Secretary.

(4) EXCEPTION FOR DISTRIBUTIONS DESCRIBED IN SECTION 663(a).—This subsection shall not apply to any distribution described in section 663(a).

Amendments

• 1986, Tax Reform Act of 1986 (P.L. 99-514)

P.L. 99-514, §1806(a):

Amended Code Sec. 643(e)(3)(B), as redesignated by Act Sec. 1806(c). **Effective** as if included in the provision of P.L. 98-369 to which it relates. Prior to amendment, Code Sec. 64(e)(3)(B) read as follows:

(B) ELECTION—Any election under this paragraph shall be made by the estate or trust on its return for the taxable year for which the distribution was made.

P.L. 99-514, §1806(c)(1) and (2):

Amended Code Sec. 643 by redesignating subsection (d)[e] as subsection (e), and by redesignating subsection (e)[f] as subsection (f). **Effective** as if included in the provision of P.L. 98-369 to which it relates.

• 1984, Deficit Reduction Act of 1984 (P.L. 98-369)

P.L. 98-369, §81(a):

Amended Code Sec. 643 by adding at the end thereof new subsection (d)[e]. **Effective** for distributions after 6-1-84, in tax years ending after such date. See Act Sec. 81(b)(2), below, for special rules for making elections.

P.L. 98-369, §81(b)(2), provides:

(2) Time for Making Election.—In the case of any distribution before the date of the enactment of this Act—

(A) the time for making an election under section 643(d)(3) of the Internal Revenue Code of 1954 (as added by this section) shall not expire before January 1, 1985, and

(B) the requirement that such election be made on the return of the estate or trust shall not apply.

[Sec. 643(f)]

(f) TREATMENT OF MULTIPLE TRUSTS.—For purposes of this subchapter, under regulations prescribed by the Secretary, 2 or more trusts shall be treated as 1 trust if—

(1) such trusts have substantially the same grantor or grantors and substantially the same primary beneficiary or beneficiaries, and

(2) a principal purpose of such trusts is the avoidance of the tax imposed by this chapter.

For purposes of the preceding sentence, a husband and wife shall be treated as 1 person.

Amendments

• 1988, Technical and Miscellaneous Revenue Act of 1988 (P.L. 100-647)

P.L. 100-647, §1018(e), provides:

(e) PROVISION RELATED TO SECTION 1806 OF THE REFORM ACT.—If—

(1) on a return for the 1st taxable year of the trusts involved beginning after March 1, 1984, 2 or more trusts were treated as a single trust for purposes of the tax imposed by chapter 1 of the Internal Revenue Code of 1954,

(2) such trusts would have been required to be so treated but for the amendment made by section 1806(b) of the Reform Act, and

(3) such trusts did not accumulate any income during such taxable year and did not make any accumulation distributions during such taxable year,

then, notwithstanding the amendment made by section 1806(b) of the Reform Act, such trusts shall be treated as one trust for purposes of such taxable year.

• 1986, Tax Reform Act of 1986 (P.L. 99-514)

P.L. 99-514, §1806(c)(1) and (2):

Redesignated subsection (e)[f] as subsection (f). **Effective** for tax years beginning after 3-1-84, except that, in the case of a trust which was irrevocable on 3-1-84, such amendment shall so apply only to that portion of the trust which is attributable to contributions to corpus after 3-1-84.

• 1984, Deficit Reduction Act of 1984 (P.L. 98-369)

P.L. 98-369, §82(a):

Amended Code Sec. 643 by adding at the end thereof new subsection (e)[f]. **Effective** for tax years beginning after 3-1-84, except that, in the case of a trust which was irrevocable on 3-1-84, such amendment shall so apply only to that portion of the trust which is attributable to contributions to corpus after 3-1-84 [**effective** date changed by P.L. 99-514, §1806(b)].

[Sec. 643(g)]

(g) CERTAIN PAYMENTS OF ESTIMATED TAX TREATED AS PAID BY BENEFICIARY.—

(1) IN GENERAL.—In the case of a trust—

(A) the trustee may elect to treat any portion of a payment of estimated tax made by such trust for any taxable year of the trust as a payment made by a beneficiary of such trust,

(B) any amount so treated shall be treated as paid or credited to the beneficiary on the last day of such taxable year, and

(C) for purposes of subtitle F, the amount so treated—

(i) shall not be treated as a payment of estimated tax made by the trust, but

(ii) shall be treated as a payment of estimated tax made by such beneficiary on January 15 following the taxable year.

(2) TIME FOR MAKING ELECTION.—An election under paragraph (1) shall be made on or before the 65th day after the close of the taxable year of the trust and in such manner as the Secretary may prescribe.

(3) EXTENSION TO LAST YEAR OF ESTATE.—In the case of a taxable year reasonably expected to be the last taxable year of an estate—

(A) any reference in this subsection to a trust shall be treated as including a reference to an estate, and

(B) the fiduciary of the estate shall be treated as the trustee.

Amendments

• 1988, Technical and Miscellaneous Revenue Act of 1988 (P.L. 100-647)

P.L. 100-647, §1014(d)(3)(A)-(B):

Amended Code Sec. 643(g) by striking out the last sentence of paragraph (1), and by amending paragraph (2). **Effective** as if included in the provision of P.L. 99-514 to which it relates. Prior to amendment, the last sentence of paragraph (1) and paragraph (2) read as follows:

The preceding sentence shall apply only to the extent the payments of estimated tax made by the trust for the taxable year exceed the tax imposed by this chapter shown on its return for the taxable year.

(2) TIME FOR MAKING ELECTION.—An election under paragraph (1) may be made—

(A) only on the trust's return of the tax imposed by this chapter for the taxable year, and

(B) only if such return is filed on or before the 65th day after the close of the taxable year.

P.L. 100-647, §1014(d)(4):

Amended Code Sec. 643(g) by adding at the end thereof a new paragraph (3). **Effective** as if included in the provision of P.L. 99-514 to which it relates.

• 1986, Tax Reform Act of 1986 (P.L. 99-514)

P.L. 99-514, §1404(b):

Amended Code Sec. 643 by adding at the end thereof new subsection (g). **Effective** for tax years beginning after 12-31-86.

[Sec. 643(h)]

(h) DISTRIBUTIONS BY CERTAIN FOREIGN TRUSTS THROUGH NOMINEES.—For purposes of this part, any amount paid to a United States person which is derived directly or indirectly from a foreign trust of which the payor is not the grantor shall be deemed in the year of payment to have been directly paid by the foreign trust to such United States person.

Amendments

• 1996, Small Business Job Protection Act of 1996 (P.L. 104-188)

P.L. 104-188, §1904(c)(1):

Amended Code Sec. 643 by adding at the end a new subsection (h). **Effective** 8-20-96. For special and transitional rules, see Act Sec. 1904(d)(2) and (e), below.

P.L. 104-188, §1904(d)(2) and (e), provides:

(2) EXCEPTION FOR CERTAIN TRUSTS.—The amendments made by this section shall not apply to any trust—

(A) which is treated as owned by the grantor under section 676 or 677 (other than subsection (a)(3) thereof) of the Internal Revenue Code of 1986, and

(B) which is in existence on September 19, 1995.

The preceding sentence shall not apply to the portion of any such trust attributable to any transfer to such trust after September 19, 1995.

(e) TRANSITIONAL RULE.—If—

(1) by reason of the amendments made by this section, any person other than a United States person ceases to be treated as the owner of a portion of a domestic trust, and

(2) before January 1, 1997, such trust becomes a foreign trust, or the assets of such trust are transferred to a foreign trust,

no tax shall be imposed by section 1491 of the Internal Revenue Code of 1986 by reason of such trust becoming a foreign trust or the assets of such trust being transferred to a foreign trust.

[Sec. 643(i)]

(i) LOANS FROM FOREIGN TRUSTS.—For purposes of subparts B, C, and D—

(1) GENERAL RULE.—Except as provided in regulations, if a foreign trust makes a loan of cash or marketable securities (or permits the use of any other trust property) directly or indirectly to or by—

(A) any grantor or beneficiary of such trust who is a United States person, or

(B) any United States person not described in subparagraph (A) who is related to such grantor or beneficiary,

the amount of such loan (or the fair market value of the use of such property) shall be treated as a distribution by such trust to such grantor or beneficiary (as the case may be).

(2) DEFINITIONS AND SPECIAL RULES.—For purposes of this subsection—

(A) CASH.—The term "cash" includes foreign currencies and cash equivalents.

(B) RELATED PERSON.—

(i) IN GENERAL.—A person is related to another person if the relationship between such persons would result in a disallowance of losses under section 267 or 707(b). In applying section 267 for purposes of the preceding sentence, section 267(c)(4) shall be applied as if the family of an individual includes the spouses of the members of the family.

(ii) ALLOCATION.—If any person described in paragraph (1)(B) is related to more than one person, the grantor or beneficiary to whom the treatment under this subsection applies shall be determined under regulations prescribed by the Secretary.

(C) EXCLUSION OF TAX-EXEMPTS.—The term "United States person" does not include any entity exempt from tax under this chapter.

(D) TRUST NOT TREATED AS SIMPLE TRUST.—Any trust which is treated under this subsection as making a distribution shall be treated as not described in section 651.

(E) EXCEPTION FOR COMPENSATED USE OF PROPERTY.—In the case of the use of any trust property other than a loan of cash or marketable securities, paragraph (1) shall not apply to the extent that the trust is paid the fair market value of such use within a reasonable period of time of such use.

(3) SUBSEQUENT TRANSACTIONS.—If any loan (or use of property) is taken into account under paragraph (1), any subsequent transaction between the trust and the original borrower regarding the principal of the loan (by way of complete or partial repayment, satisfaction, cancellation, discharge, or otherwise) or the return of such property shall be disregarded for purposes of this title.

Amendments

• 2010, Hiring Incentives to Restore Employment Act (P.L. 111-147)

P.L. 111-147, §533(a)(1)-(2):

Amended Code Sec. 643(i)(1) by striking "directly or indirectly to" and inserting "(or permits the use of any other trust property) directly or indirectly to or by", and by inserting "(or the fair market value of the use of such property)" after "the amount of such loan". **Effective** for loans made, and uses of property, after 3-18-2010.

P.L. 111-147, §533(b):

Amended Code Sec. 643(i)(2) by adding at the end a new subparagraph (E). **Effective** for loans made, and uses of property, after 3-18-2010.

P.L. 111-147, §533(d)(1)-(3):

Amended Code Sec. 643(i)(3) by inserting "(or use of property)" after "If any loan", by inserting "or the return of such property" before "shall be disregarded", and by striking "REGARDING LOAN PRINCIPAL" following "SUBSEQUENT TRANSACTIONS" in the heading thereof. **Effective** for loans made, and uses of property, after 3-18-2010.

• 1996, Small Business Job Protection Act of 1996 (P.L. 104-188)

P.L. 104-188, §1906(c)(1):

Amended Code Sec. 643 by adding at the end a new subsection (i). **Effective** for loans of cash or marketable securities made after 9-19-95.

[Sec. 644]

SEC. 644. TAXABLE YEAR OF TRUSTS.

[Sec. 644(a)]

(a) IN GENERAL.—For purposes of this subtitle, the taxable year of any trust shall be the calendar year.

[Sec. 644(b)]

(b) EXCEPTION FOR TRUSTS EXEMPT FROM TAX AND CHARITABLE TRUSTS.—Subsection (a) shall not apply to a trust exempt from taxation under section 501(a) or a trust described in section 4947(a)(1).

Amendments

• 1997, Taxpayer Relief Act of 1997 (P.L. 105-34)

P.L. 105-34, §507(b)(1):

Amended subpart A of part I of subchapter J of chapter 1 by striking Code Sec. 644 and by redesignating Code Sec. 645 as Code Sec. 644. **Effective** for sales or exchanges after 8-5-97.

• 1986, Tax Reform Act of 1986 (P.L. 99-514)

P.L. 99-514, §1403(a):

Amended subpart A of part I of subchapter J by adding at the end thereof new Code Sec. 645. **Effective** for tax years beginning after 12-31-86. However, for a transitional rule, see Act Sec. 1403(c)(2), below.

P.L. 99-514, §1403(c)(2), provides:

(2) TRANSITION RULE.—With respect to any trust beneficiary who is required to include in gross income amounts under sections 652(a) or 662(a) of the Internal Revenue Code of 1986 in the 1st taxable year of the beneficiary beginning after December 31, 1986, by reason of any short taxable year of the trust required by the amendments made by this section, such income shall be ratably included in the income of the trust beneficiary over the 4-taxable year period beginning with such taxable year.

[Sec. 644—Stricken]

Amendments

• 1997, Taxpayer Relief Act of 1997 (P.L. 105-34)

P.L. 105-34, §507(b)(1):

Amended subpart A of part I of subchapter J of chapter 1 by striking Code Sec. 644 and by redesignating Code Sec. 645 as Code Sec. 644. **Effective** for sales or exchanges after 8-5-97. Prior to being stricken, Code Sec. 644 read as follows:

SEC. 644. SPECIAL RULE FOR GAIN ON PROPERTY TRANSFERRED TO TRUST AT LESS THAN FAIR MARKET VALUE.

[Sec. 644(a)]

(a) IMPOSITION OF TAX.—

(1) IN GENERAL.—If—

(A) a trust (or another trust to which the property is distributed) sells or exchanges property at a gain not more than 2 years after the date of the initial transfer of the property in trust by the transferor, and

(B) the fair market value of such property at the time of the initial transfer in trust by the transferor exceeds the adjusted basis of such property immediately after such transfer,

there is hereby imposed a tax determined in accordance with paragraph (2) on the includible gain recognized on such sale or exchange.

(2) AMOUNT OF TAX.—The amount of the tax imposed by paragraph (1) on any includible gain recognized on the sale or exchange of any property shall be equal to the sum of—

(A) the excess of—

(i) the tax which would have been imposed under this chapter for the taxable year of the transferor in which the sale or exchange of such property occurs had the amount of the includible gain recognized on such sale or exchange, reduced by any deductions properly allocable to such gain, been included in the gross income of the transferor for such taxable year, over

(ii) the tax actually imposed under this chapter for such taxable year of the transferor, plus

(B) if such sale or exchange occurs in a taxable year of the transferor which begins after the beginning of the taxable year of the trust in which such sale or exchange occurs, an amount equal to the amount determined under subparagraph (A) multiplied by the underpayment rate established under section 6621.

The determination of tax under clause (i) of subparagraph (A) shall be made by not taking into account any carryback, and by not taking into account any loss deduction to the extent that such loss or deduction may be carried by the transferor to any other taxable year.

(3) TAXABLE YEAR FOR WHICH TAX IMPOSED.—The tax imposed by paragraph (1) shall be imposed for the taxable year of the trust which begins with or within the taxable year of the transferor in which the sale or exchange occurs.

(4) TAX TO BE IN ADDITION TO OTHER TAXES.—The tax imposed by this subsection for any taxable year of the trust shall be in addition to any other tax imposed by this chapter for such taxable year.

Amendments

• 1986, Tax Reform Act of 1986 (P.L. 99-514)

P.L. 99-514, §1511(c)(5):

Amended Code Sec. 644(a)(2)(B) by striking out "the annual rate established under section 6621" and inserting in lieu thereof "the underpayment rate established under section 6621". **Effective** for purposes of determining interest for periods after 12-31-86.

• 1978, Revenue Act of 1978 (P.L. 95-600)

P.L. 95-600, §701(p)(1)(A):

Amended Code Sec. 644(a) by striking out "gain realized" wherever it appeared and inserting in lieu thereof "gain recognized". **Effective** for transfers in trust made after 5-21-76.

P.L. 95-600, §701(p)(2):

Amended Code Sec. 644(a)(2) by adding the last sentence. **Effective** for transfers in trust made after 5-21-76.

[Sec. 644(b)]

(b) DEFINITION OF INCLUDIBLE GAIN.—For purposes of this section, the term "includible gain" means the lesser of—

(1) the gain recognized by the trust on the sale or exchange of any property, or

(2) the excess of the fair market value of such property at the time of the initial transfer in trust by the transferor over the adjusted basis of such property immediately after such transfer.

[Sec. 644(c)]

(c) CHARACTER OF INCLUDIBLE GAIN.—For purposes of subsection (a)—

(1) the character of the includible gain shall be determined as if the property had actually been sold or exchanged by the transferor, and any activities of the trust with respect to the sale or exchange of the property shall be deemed to be activities of the transferor, and

(2) the portion of the includible gain subject to the provisions of section 1245 and section 1250 shall be determined in accordance with regulations prescribed by the Secretary.

[Sec. 644(d)]

(d) SPECIAL RULES.—

(1) SHORT SALES.—If the trust sells the property referred to in subsection (a) in a short sale within the 2-year period referred to in such subsection, such 2-year period shall be extended to the date of the closing of such short sale.

(2) SUBSTITUTED BASIS PROPERTY.—For purposes of this section, in the case of any property held by the trust which has a basis determined in whole or in part by reference to the basis of any other property which was transferred to the trust—

(A) the initial transfer of such property in trust by the transferor shall be treated as having occurred on the date of the initial transfer in trust of such other property,

(B) subsections (a)(1)(B) and (b)(2) shall be applied by taking into account the fair market value and the adjusted basis of such other property, and

(C) the amount determined under subsection (b)(2) with respect to such other property shall be allocated (under regulations prescribed by the Secretary) among such other property and all properties held by the trust which have a basis determined in whole or in part by reference to the basis of such other property.

Amendments

• 1978, Revenue Act of 1978 (P.L. 95-600)

P.L. 95-600, §701(p)(1)(B):

Amended Code Sec. 644(d). **Effective** for transfers in trust made after 5-21-76. Prior to amendment, Code Sec. 644(d) read as follows:

(d) SPECIAL RULE FOR SHORT SALES.—If the trust sells the property referred to in subsection (a) in a short sale within the 2-year period referred to in such subsection, such 2-year period shall be extended to the date of the closing of such short sale.

[Sec. 644(e)]

(e) EXCEPTIONS.—Subsection (a) shall not apply to property—

(1) acquired by the trust from a decedent or which passed to a trust from a decedent (within the meaning of section 1014), or

(2) acquired by a pooled income fund (as defined in section 642(c)(5)), or

(3) acquired by a charitable remainder annuity trust (as defined in section 664(d)(1)) or a charitable remainder unitrust (as defined in sections 664(d)(2) and (3)), or

(4) if the sale or exchange of the property occurred after the death of the transferor.

[Sec. 644(f)]

(f) SPECIAL RULE FOR INSTALLMENT SALES.—If the trust reports income under section 453 on any sale or exchange to which subsection (a) applies, under regulations prescribed by the Secretary—

(1) subsection (a) (other than the 2-year requirement of paragraph (1)(A) thereof) shall be applied as if each installment were a separate sale or exchange of property to which such subsection applies, and

(2) the term "includible gain" shall not include any portion of an installment received by the trust after the death of the transferor.

Amendments

• 1980, Installment Sales Revision Act of 1980 (P.L. 96-471)

P.L. 96-471, §2(b)(4):

Amended Code Sec. 644(f) by striking out "elects to report income under section 453" and substituting "reports income under section 453". **Effective** for dispositions made after 10-19-80, in tax years ending after that year.

• 1978, Revenue Act of 1978 (P.L. 95-600)

P.L. 95-600, §701(p)(3):

Amended Code Sec. 644(f)(1) by striking out "subsection (a)" and inserting in lieu thereof "subsection (a) (other than the 2-year requirement of paragraph (1)(A) thereof)". **Effective** for transfers in trust made after 5-21-76.

• 1976, Tax Reform Act of 1976 (P.L. 94-455)

P.L. 94-455, §701(e):

Added Code Sec. 644. **Effective** for transfers in trust made after 5-21-76.

[Sec. 645]

SEC. 645. CERTAIN REVOCABLE TRUSTS TREATED AS PART OF ESTATE.

[Sec. 645(a)]

(a) GENERAL RULE.—For purposes of this subtitle, if both the executor (if any) of an estate and the trustee of a qualified revocable trust elect the treatment provided in this section, such trust shall be treated and taxed as part of such estate (and not as a separate trust) for all taxable years of the estate ending after the date of the decedent's death and before the applicable date.

[Sec. 645(b)]

(b) DEFINITIONS.—For purposes of subsection (a)—

(1) QUALIFIED REVOCABLE TRUST.—The term "qualified revocable trust" means any trust (or portion thereof) which was treated under section 676 as owned by the decedent of the estate referred to in subsection (a) by reason of a power in the grantor (determined without regard to section 672(e)).

(2) APPLICABLE DATE.—The term "applicable date" means—

(A) if no return of tax imposed by chapter 11 is required to be filed, the date which is 2 years after the date of the decedent's death, and

(B) if such a return is required to be filed, the date which is 6 months after the date of the final determination of the liability for tax imposed by chapter 11.

[Sec. 645(c)]

(c) ELECTION.—The election under subsection (a) shall be made not later than the time prescribed for filing the return of tax imposed by this chapter for the first taxable year of the estate (determined with regard to extensions) and, once made, shall be irrevocable.

Amendments

• 1998, IRS Restructuring and Reform Act of 1998 (P.L. 105-206)

P.L. 105-206, §6013(a)(1):

Redesignated Code Sec. 646 as Code Sec. 645. **Effective** as if included in the provision of P.L. 105-34 to which it relates [**effective** for estates of decedents dying after 8-5-97.—CCH].

• 1997, Taxpayer Relief Act of 1997 (P.L. 105-34)

P.L. 105-34, §1305(a):

Amended subpart A of part I of subchapter J by adding at the end a new Code Sec. 646. **Effective** with respect to estates of decedents dying after 8-5-97.

»»→ Caution: Code Sec. 646, below, is subject to the sunset provision of the Economic Growth and Tax Relief Reconciliation Act of 2001 (P.L. 107-16), §901. Absent Congressional action, the changes made to this provision by P.L. 107-16, or that take effect as if included in P.L. 107-16, do not apply after December 31, 2010. For more information about the sunset provision, see page XXI of the Preface to this publication and P.L. 107-16, §901, in the amendment notes. See the amendments notes for a history of amendments to this section and the effective date of each change.

[Sec. 646]

SEC. 646. TAX TREATMENT OF ELECTING ALASKA NATIVE SETTLEMENT TRUSTS.

[Sec. 646(a)]

(a) IN GENERAL.—If an election under this section is in effect with respect to any Settlement Trust, the provisions of this section shall apply in determining the income tax treatment of the Settlement Trust and its beneficiaries with respect to the Settlement Trust.

[Sec. 646(b)]

(b) TAXATION OF INCOME OF TRUST.—Except as provided in subsection (f)(1)(B)(ii)—

(1) IN GENERAL.—There is hereby imposed on the taxable income of an electing Settlement Trust, other than its net capital gain, a tax at the lowest rate specified in section 1(c).

(2) CAPITAL GAIN.—In the case of an electing Settlement Trust with a net capital gain for the taxable year, a tax is hereby imposed on such gain at the rate of tax which would apply to such gain if the taxpayer were subject to a tax on its other taxable income at only the lowest rate specified in section 1(c).

Any such tax shall be in lieu of the income tax otherwise imposed by this chapter on such income or gain.

[Sec. 646(c)]

(c) ONE-TIME ELECTION.—

(1) IN GENERAL.—A Settlement Trust may elect to have the provisions of this section apply to the trust and its beneficiaries.

(2) TIME AND METHOD OF ELECTION.—An election under paragraph (1) shall be made by the trustee of such trust—

(A) on or before the due date (including extensions) for filing the Settlement Trust's return of tax for the first taxable year of such trust ending after the date of the enactment of this section, and

(B) by attaching to such return of tax a statement specifically providing for such election.

(3) PERIOD ELECTION IN EFFECT.—Except as provided in subsection (f), an election under this subsection—

(A) shall apply to the first taxable year described in paragraph (2)(A) and all subsequent taxable years, and

(B) may not be revoked once it is made.

[Sec. 646(d)]

(d) CONTRIBUTIONS TO TRUST.—

(1) BENEFICIARIES OF ELECTING TRUST NOT TAXED ON CONTRIBUTIONS.—In the case of an electing Settlement Trust, no amount shall be includible in the gross income of a beneficiary of such trust by reason of a contribution to such trust.

(2) EARNINGS AND PROFITS.—The earnings and profits of the sponsoring Native Corporation shall not be reduced on account of any contribution to such Settlement Trust.

[Sec. 646(e)]

(e) TAX TREATMENT OF DISTRIBUTIONS TO BENEFICIARIES.—Amounts distributed by an electing Settlement Trust during any taxable year shall be considered as having the following characteristics in the hands of the recipient beneficiary:

(1) First, as amounts excludable from gross income for the taxable year to the extent of the taxable income of such trust for such taxable year (decreased by any income tax paid by the trust with respect to the income) plus any amount excluded from gross income of the trust under section 103.

(2) Second, as amounts excludable from gross income to the extent of the amount described in paragraph (1) for all taxable years for which an election is in effect under subsection (c) with respect to the trust, and not previously taken into account under paragraph (1).

(3) Third, as amounts distributed by the sponsoring Native Corporation with respect to its stock (within the meaning of section 301(a)) during such taxable year and taxable to the recipient beneficiary as amounts described in section 301(c)(1), to the extent of current or accumulated earnings and profits of the sponsoring Native Corporation as of the close of such taxable year after proper adjustment is made for all distributions made by the sponsoring Native Corporation during such taxable year.

(4) Fourth, as amounts distributed by the trust in excess of the distributable net income of such trust for such taxable year.

Amounts distributed to which paragraph (3) applies shall not be treated as a corporate distribution subject to section 311(b), and for purposes of determining the amount of a distribution for purposes of paragraph (3) and the basis to the recipients, section 643(e) and not section 301(b) or (d) shall apply.

[Sec. 646(f)]

(f) SPECIAL RULES WHERE TRANSFER RESTRICTIONS MODIFIED.—

(1) TRANSFER OF BENEFICIAL INTERESTS.—If, at any time, a beneficial interest in an electing Settlement Trust may be disposed of to a person in a manner which would not be permitted by section 7(h) of the Alaska Native Claims Settlement Act (43 U.S.C. 1606(h)) if such interest were Settlement Common Stock—

(A) no election may be made under subsection (c) with respect to such trust, and

(B) if such an election is in effect as of such time—

(i) such election shall cease to apply as of the first day of the taxable year in which such disposition is first permitted,

(ii) the provisions of this section shall not apply to such trust for such taxable year and all taxable years thereafter, and

(iii) the distributable net income of such trust shall be increased by the current or accumulated earnings and profits of the sponsoring Native Corporation as of the close of such taxable year after proper adjustment is made for all distributions made by the sponsoring Native Corporation during such taxable year.

In no event shall the increase under clause (iii) exceed the fair market value of the trust's assets as of the date the beneficial interest of the trust first becomes so disposable. The earnings and profits of the sponsoring Native Corporation shall be adjusted as of the last day of such taxable year by the amount of earnings and profits so included in the distributable net income of the trust.

(2) STOCK IN CORPORATION.—If—

(A) stock in the sponsoring Native Corporation may be disposed of to a person in a manner which would not be permitted by section 7(h) of the Alaska Native Claims Settlement Act (43 U.S.C. 1606(h)) if such stock were Settlement Common Stock, and

(B) at any time after such disposition of stock is first permitted, such corporation transfers assets to a Settlement Trust,

paragraph (1)(B) shall be applied to such trust on and after the date of the transfer in the same manner as if the trust permitted dispositions of beneficial interests in the trust in a manner not permitted by such section 7(h).

(3) CERTAIN DISTRIBUTIONS.—For purposes of this section, the surrender of an interest in a Native Corporation or an electing Settlement Trust in order to accomplish the whole or partial redemption of the interest of a shareholder or beneficiary in such corporation or trust, or to

accomplish the whole or partial liquidation of such corporation or trust, shall be deemed to be a transfer permitted by section 7(h) of the Alaska Native Claims Settlement Act.

[Sec. 646(g)]

(g) TAXABLE INCOME.—For purposes of this title, the taxable income of an electing Settlement Trust shall be determined under section 641(b) without regard to any deduction under section 651 or 661.

[Sec. 646(h)]

(h) DEFINITIONS.—For purposes of this section—

(1) ELECTING SETTLEMENT TRUST.—The term "electing Settlement Trust" means a Settlement Trust which has made the election, effective for a taxable year, described in subsection (c).

(2) NATIVE CORPORATION.—The term "Native Corporation" has the meaning given such term by section 3(m) of the Alaska Native Claims Settlement Act (43 U.S.C. 1602(m)).

(3) SETTLEMENT COMMON STOCK.—The term "Settlement Common Stock" has the meaning given such term by section 3(p) of the Alaska Native Claims Settlement Act (43 U.S.C. 1602(p)).

(4) SETTLEMENT TRUST.—The term "Settlement Trust" means a trust that constitutes a settlement trust under section 3(t) of the Alaska Native Claims Settlement Act (43 U.S.C. 1602(t)).

(5) SPONSORING NATIVE CORPORATION.—The term "sponsoring Native Corporation" means the Native Corporation which transfers assets to an electing Settlement Trust.

[Sec. 646(i)]

(i) SPECIAL LOSS DISALLOWANCE RULE.—Any loss that would otherwise be recognized by a shareholder upon a disposition of a share of stock of a sponsoring Native Corporation shall be reduced (but not below zero) by the per share loss adjustment factor. The per share loss adjustment factor shall be the aggregate of all contributions to all electing Settlement Trusts sponsored by such Native Corporation made on or after the first day each trust is treated as an electing Settlement Trust expressed on a per share basis and determined as of the day of each such contribution.

[Sec. 646(j)]

(j) CROSS REFERENCE.—

For information required with respect to electing Settlement Trusts and sponsoring Native Corporations, see section 6039H.

Amendments

• 2001, Economic Growth and Tax Relief Reconciliation Act of 2001 (P.L. 107-16)

P.L. 107-16, §671(a):

Amended subpart A of part I of subchapter J of chapter 1 by adding at the end a new Code Sec. 646. **Effective** for tax years ending after 6-7-2001, and to contributions made to electing Settlement Trusts for such year or any subsequent year.

P.L. 107-16, §901(a)-(b), provides:

SEC. 901. SUNSET OF PROVISIONS OF ACT.

(a) IN GENERAL.—All provisions of, and amendments made by, this Act shall not apply—

(1) to taxable, plan, or limitation years beginning after December 31, 2010, or

(2) in the case of title V, to estates of decedents dying, gifts made, or generation skipping transfers, after December 31, 2010.

(b) APPLICATION OF CERTAIN LAWS.—The Internal Revenue Code of 1986 and the Employee Retirement Income Security Act of 1974 shall be applied and administered to years, estates, gifts, and transfers described in subsection (a) as if the provisions and amendments described in subsection (a) had never been enacted.

Subpart B—Trusts Which Distribute Current Income Only

[Sec. 651]

SEC. 651. DEDUCTION FOR TRUSTS DISTRIBUTING CURRENT INCOME ONLY.

[Sec. 651(a)]

(a) DEDUCTION.—In the case of any trust the terms of which—

(1) provide that all of its income is required to be distributed currently, and

(2) do not provide that any amounts are to be paid, permanently set aside, or used for the purposes specified in section 642(c) (relating to deduction for charitable, etc., purposes),

there shall be allowed as a deduction in computing the taxable income of the trust the amount of the income for the taxable year which is required to be distributed currently. This section shall not apply in any taxable year in which the trust distributes amounts other than amounts of income described in paragraph (1).

[Sec. 651(b)]

(b) LIMITATION ON DEDUCTION.—If the amount of income required to be distributed currently exceeds the distributable net income of the trust for the taxable year, the deduction shall be limited to the amount of the distributable net income. For this purpose, the computation of distributable net income shall not include items of income which are not included in the gross income of the trust and the deductions allocable thereto.

[Sec. 652]

SEC. 652. INCLUSION OF AMOUNTS IN GROSS INCOME OF BENEFICIARIES OF TRUSTS DISTRIBUTING CURRENT INCOME ONLY.

[Sec. 652(a)]

(a) INCLUSION.—Subject to subsection (b), the amount of income for the taxable year required to be distributed currently by a trust described in section 651 shall be included in the gross income of the beneficiaries to whom the income is required to be distributed, whether distributed or not. If such amount exceeds the distributable net income, there shall be included in the gross income of each beneficiary an amount which bears the same ratio to distributable net income as the amount of income required to be distributed to such beneficiary bears to the amount of income required to be distributed to all beneficiaries.

[Sec. 652(b)]

(b) CHARACTER OF AMOUNTS.—The amounts specified in subsection (a) shall have the same character in the hands of the beneficiary as in the hands of the trust. For this purpose, the amounts shall be treated as consisting of the same proportion of each class of items entering into the computation of distributable net income of the trust as the total of each class bears to the total distributable net income of the trust, unless the terms of the trust specifically allocate different classes of income to different beneficiaries. In the application of the preceding sentence, the items of deduction entering into the computation of distributable net income shall be allocated among the items of distributable net income in accordance with regulations prescribed by the Secretary.

Amendments

• 1976, Tax Reform Act of 1976 (P.L. 94-455)

P.L. 94-455, §1906(b)(13)(A):

Amended 1954 Code by substituting "Secretary" for "Secretary or his delegate" each place it appeared. **Effective** 2-1-77.

[Sec. 652(c)]

(c) DIFFERENT TAXABLE YEARS.—If the taxable year of a beneficiary is different from that of the trust, the amount which the beneficiary is required to include in gross income in accordance with the provisions of this section shall be based upon the amount of income of the trust for any taxable year or years of the trust ending within or with his taxable year.

Subpart C—Estates and Trusts Which May Accumulate Income or Which Distribute Corpus

[Sec. 661]

SEC. 661. DEDUCTION FOR ESTATES AND TRUSTS ACCUMULATING INCOME OR DISTRIBUTING CORPUS.

[Sec. 661(a)]

(a) DEDUCTION.—In any taxable year there shall be allowed as a deduction in computing the taxable income of an estate or trust (other than a trust to which subpart B applies), the sum of—

(1) any amount of income for such taxable year required to be distributed currently (including any amount required to be distributed which may be paid out of income or corpus to the extent such amount is paid out of income for such taxable year); and

(2) any other amounts properly paid or credited or required to be distributed for such taxable year;

but such deduction shall not exceed the distributable net income of the estate or trust.

Amendments

• 1983, Interest and Dividend Tax Compliance Act of 1983 (P.L. 98-67)

P.L. 98-67, §102(a):

Repealed the amendment made by P.L. 97-248 (see below), as of the close of 6-30-83, as though such amendment had not been made.

• 1982, Tax Equity and Fiscal Responsibility Act of 1982 (P.L. 97-248)

P.L. 97-248, §302(b)(2):

Amended Code Sec. 661(a) by adding at the end thereof the following sentence: "For purposes of paragraph (1), the amount of distributable net income shall be computed without the deduction allowed by section 642(c)." **Effective** for interest, dividends and patronage dividends paid or credited after 6-30-83.

[Sec. 661(b)]

(b) CHARACTER OF AMOUNTS DISTRIBUTED.—The amount determined under subsection (a) shall be treated as consisting of the same proportion of each class of items entering into the computation of distributable net income of the estate or trust as the total of each class bears to the total distributable net income of the estate or trust in the absence of the allocation of different classes of income under the specific terms of the governing instrument. In the application of the preceding sentence, the items of deduction entering into the computation of distributable net income (including the deduction allowed under section 642(c)) shall be allocated among the items of distributable net income in accordance with regulations prescribed by the Secretary.

Amendments

• **1976, Tax Reform Act of 1976 (P.L. 94-455)**

P.L. 94-455, §1906(b)(13)(A):

Amended 1954 Code by substituting "Secretary" for "Secretary or his delegate" each place it appeared. **Effective** 2-1-77.

[Sec. 661(c)]

(c) LIMITATION ON DEDUCTION.—No deduction shall be allowed under subsection (a) in respect of any portion of the amount allowed as a deduction under that subsection (without regard to this subsection) which is treated under subsection (b) as consisting of any item of distributable net income which is not included in the gross income of the estate or trust.

[Sec. 662]

SEC. 662. INCLUSION OF AMOUNTS IN GROSS INCOME OF BENEFICIARIES OF ESTATES AND TRUSTS ACCUMULATING INCOME OR DISTRIBUTING CORPUS.

[Sec. 662(a)]

(a) INCLUSION.—Subject to subsection (b), there shall be included in the gross income of a beneficiary to whom an amount specified in section 661(a) is paid, credited, or required to be distributed (by an estate or trust described in section 661), the sum of the following amounts:

(1) AMOUNTS REQUIRED TO BE DISTRIBUTED CURRENTLY.—The amount of income for the taxable year required to be distributed currently to such beneficiary, whether distributed or not. If the amount of income required to be distributed currently to all beneficiaries exceeds the distributable net income (computed without the deduction allowed by section 642(c), relating to deduction for charitable, etc. purposes) of the estate or trust, then, in lieu of the amount provided in the preceding sentence, there shall be included in the gross income of the beneficiary an amount which bears the same ratio to distributable net income (as so computed) as the amount of income required to be distributed currently to such beneficiary bears to the amount required to be distributed currently to all beneficiaries. For purposes of this section, the phrase "the amount of income for the taxable year required to be distributed currently" includes any amount required to be paid out of income or corpus to the extent such amount is paid out of income for such taxable year.

(2) OTHER AMOUNTS DISTRIBUTED.—All other amounts properly paid, credited, or required to be distributed to such beneficiary for the taxable year. If the sum of—

(A) the amount of income for the taxable year required to be distributed currently to all beneficiaries, and

(B) all other amounts properly paid, credited, or required to be distributed to all beneficiaries

exceeds the distributable net income of the estate or trust, then, in lieu of the amount provided in the preceding sentence, there shall be included in the gross income of the beneficiary an amount which bears the same ratio to distributable net income (reduced by the amounts specified in (A)) as the other amounts properly paid, credited or required to be distributed to the beneficiary bear to the other amounts properly paid, credited, or required to be distributed to all beneficiaries.

[Sec. 662(b)]

(b) CHARACTER OF AMOUNTS.—The amounts determined under subsection (a) shall have the same character in the hands of the beneficiary as in the hands of the estate or trust. For this purpose, the amounts shall be treated as consisting of the same proportion of each class of items entering into the computation of distributable net income as the total of each class bears to the total distributable net income of the estate or trust unless the terms of the governing instrument specifically allocate different classes of income to different beneficiaries. In the application of the preceding sentence, the items of deduction entering into the computation of distributable net income (including the deduction allowed under section 642(c)) shall be allocated among the items of distributable net income in accordance with regulations prescribed by the Secretary. In the application of this subsection to the amount determined under paragraph (1) of subsection (a), distributable net income shall be computed without regard to any portion of the deduction under section 642(c) which is not attributable to income of the taxable year.

Amendments

• 1976, Tax Reform Act of 1976 (P.L. 94-455)

P.L. 94-455, §1906(b)(13)(A):

Amended 1954 Code by substituting "Secretary" for "Secretary or his delegate" each place it appeared. **Effective** 2-1-77.

[Sec. 662(c)]

(c) DIFFERENT TAXABLE YEARS.—If the taxable year of a beneficiary is different from that of the estate or trust, the amount to be included in the gross income of the beneficiary shall be based on the distributable net income of the estate or trust and the amounts properly paid, credited, or required to be distributed to the beneficiary during any taxable year or years of the estate or trust ending within or with his taxable year.

[Sec. 663]

SEC. 663. SPECIAL RULES APPLICABLE TO SECTIONS 661 AND 662.

[Sec. 663(a)]

(a) EXCLUSIONS.—There shall not be included as amounts falling within section 661(a) or 662(a)—

(1) GIFTS, BEQUESTS, ETC.—Any amount which, under the terms of the governing instrument, is properly paid or credited as a gift or bequest of a specific sum of money or of specific property and which is paid or credited all at once or in not more than 3 installments. For this purpose an amount which can be paid or credited only from the income of the estate or trust shall not be considered as a gift or bequest of a specific sum of money.

(2) CHARITABLE, ETC., DISTRIBUTIONS.—Any amount paid or permanently set aside or otherwise qualifying for the deduction provided in section 642(c) (computed without regard to sections 508(d), 681, and 4948(c)(4)).

(3) DENIAL OF DOUBLE DEDUCTION.—Any amount paid, credited, or distributed in the taxable year, if section 651 or section 661 applied to such amount for a preceding taxable year of an estate or trust because credited or required to be distributed in such preceding taxable year.

Amendments

• 1969, Tax Reform Act of 1969 (P.L. 91-172)

P.L. 91-172, §101(j)(17):

Amended Code Sec. 663(a)(2) by substituting "sections 508(d), 681, and 4948(c)(4)" for "section 681." **Effective** 1-1-70.

[Sec. 663(b)]

(b) DISTRIBUTIONS IN FIRST SIXTY-FIVE DAYS OF TAXABLE YEAR.—

(1) GENERAL RULE.—If within the first 65 days of any taxable year of an estate or a trust, an amount is properly paid or credited, such amount shall be considered paid or credited on the last day of the preceding taxable year.

(2) LIMITATION.—Paragraph (1) shall apply with respect to any taxable year of an estate or a trust only if the executor of such estate or the fiduciary of such trust (as the case may be) elects, in such manner and at such time as the Secretary prescribes by regulations, to have paragraph (1) apply for such taxable year.

Amendments

• 1997, Taxpayer Relief Act of 1997 (P.L. 105-34)

P.L. 105-34, §1306(a):

Amended Code Sec. 663(b) by inserting "an estate or" before "a trust" each place it appears. **Effective** for tax years beginning after 8-5-97.

P.L. 105-34, §1306(b):

Amended Code Sec. 663(b)(2) by striking "the fiduciary of such trust" and inserting "the executor of such estate or the fiduciary of such trust (as the case may be)". **Effective** for tax years beginning after 8-5-97.

• 1976, Tax Reform Act of 1976 (P.L. 94-455)

P.L. 94-455, §1906(b)(13)(A):

Amended 1954 Code by substituting "Secretary" for "Secretary or his delegate" each place it appeared. **Effective** 2-1-77.

• 1969, Tax Reform Act of 1969 (P.L. 91-172)

P.L. 91-172, §331(b):

Amended Code Sec. 663(b)(2). **Effective** for tax years beginning after 12-31-68. Prior to amendment, Code Sec. 663(b)(2) read as follows:

(2) Limitation.—This subsection shall apply only to a trust—

(A) which was in existence prior to January 1, 1954,

(B) which, under the terms of its governing instrument, may not distribute in any taxable year amounts in excess of the income of the preceding taxable year, and

(C) on behalf of which the fiduciary elects to have this subsection apply.

The election authorized by subparagraph (C) shall be made for the first taxable year to which this part is applicable in accordance with such regulations as the Secretary or his delegate shall prescribe and shall be made not later than the time prescribed by law for filing the return for such year (including extensions thereof). If such election is made with respect to a taxable year, this subsection shall apply to all amounts properly paid or credited within the first 65 days of all subsequent taxable years of such trust.

[Sec. 663(c)]

(c) SEPARATE SHARES TREATED AS SEPARATE ESTATES OR TRUSTS.—For the sole purpose of determining the amount of distributable net income in the application of sections 661 and 662, in the case of a single trust having more than one beneficiary, substantially separate and independent shares of different beneficiaries in the trust shall be treated as separate trusts. Rules similar to the rules of the preceding provisions of this subsection shall apply to treat substantially separate and independent shares of different beneficiaries in an estate having more than 1 beneficiary as separate estates. The existence of such substantially separate and independent shares and the manner of treatment as separate trusts or estates, including the application of subpart D, shall be determined in accordance with regulations prescribed by the Secretary.

Amendments

• 1997, Taxpayer Relief Act of 1997 (P.L. 105-34)

P.L. 105-34, §1307(a)(1)-(2):

Amended Code Sec. 663(c) by inserting before the last sentence a new sentence, and by inserting "or estates" after "trusts" in the last sentence. **Effective** for estates of decedents dying after 8-5-97.

P.L. 105-34, §1307(b):

Amended Code Sec. 663(c) by inserting "ESTATES OR" before "TRUSTS" in the subsection heading. **Effective** for estates of decedents dying after 8-5-97.

• 1976, Tax Reform Act of 1976 (P.L. 94-455)

P.L. 94-455, §1906(b)(13)(A):

Amended 1954 Code by substituting "Secretary" for "Secretary or his delegate" each place it appeared. **Effective** 2-1-77.

[Sec. 664]

SEC. 664. CHARITABLE REMAINDER TRUSTS.

[Sec. 664(a)]

(a) GENERAL RULE.—Notwithstanding any other provision of this subchapter, the provisions of this section shall, in accordance with regulations prescribed by the Secretary, apply in the case of a charitable remainder annuity trust and a charitable remainder unitrust.

Amendments

• 1976, Tax Reform Act of 1976 (P.L. 94-455)

P.L. 94-455, §1906(b)(13)(A):

Amended 1954 Code by substituting "Secretary" for "Secretary or his delegate" each place it appeared. **Effective** 2-1-77.

[Sec. 664(b)]

(b) CHARACTER OF DISTRIBUTIONS.—Amounts distributed by a charitable remainder annuity trust or by a charitable remainder unitrust shall be considered as having the following characteristics in the hands of a beneficiary to whom is paid the annuity described in subsection (d)(1)(A) or the payment described in subsection (d)(2)(A):

(1) First, as amounts of income (other than gains, and amounts treated as gains, from the sale or other disposition of capital assets) includible in gross income to the extent of such income of the trust for the year and such undistributed income of the trust for prior years;

(2) Second, as a capital gain to the extent of the capital gain of the trust for the year and the undistributed capital gain of the trust for prior years;

(3) Third, as other income to the extent of such income of the trust for the year and such undistributed income of the trust for prior years; and

(4) Fourth, as a distribution of trust corpus.

For purposes of this section, the trust shall determine the amount of its undistributed capital gain on a cumulative net basis.

[Sec. 664(c)]

(c) TAXATION OF TRUSTS.—

(1) INCOME TAX.—A charitable remainder annuity trust and a charitable remainder unitrust shall, for any taxable year, not be subject to any tax imposed by this subtitle.

(2) EXCISE TAX.—

(A) IN GENERAL.—In the case of a charitable remainder annuity trust or a charitable remainder unitrust which has unrelated business taxable income (within the meaning of section 512, determined as if part III of subchapter F applied to such trust) for a taxable year, there is hereby imposed on such trust or unitrust an excise tax equal to the amount of such unrelated business taxable income.

(B) CERTAIN RULES TO APPLY.—The tax imposed by subparagraph (A) shall be treated as imposed by chapter 42 for purposes of this title other than subchapter E of chapter 42.

(C) TAX COURT PROCEEDINGS.—For purposes of this paragraph, the references in section 6212(c)(1) to section 4940 shall be deemed to include references to this paragraph.

Amendments

• 2006, Tax Relief and Health Care Act of 2006 (P.L. 109-432)

P.L. 109-432, Division A, §424(a):

Amended Code Sec. 664(c). **Effective** for tax years beginning after 12-31-2006. Prior to amendment, Code Sec. 664(c) read as follows:

(c) EXEMPTION FROM INCOME TAXES.—A charitable remainder annuity trust and a charitable remainder unitrust shall, for any taxable year, not be subject to any tax imposed by this subtitle, unless such trust, for such year, has unrelated business taxable income (within the meaning of section 512, determined as if part III of subchapter F applied to such trust).

[Sec. 664(d)]

(d) DEFINITIONS.—

(1) CHARITABLE REMAINDER ANNUITY TRUST.—For purposes of this section, a charitable remainder annuity trust is a trust—

(A) from which a sum certain (which is not less than 5 percent nor more than 50 percent of the initial net fair market value of all property placed in trust) is to be paid, not less often than annually, to one or more persons (at least one of which is not an organization described in section 170(c) and, in the case of individuals, only to an individual who is living at the time of the creation of the trust) for a term of years (not in excess of 20 years) or for the life or lives of such individual or individuals,

(B) from which no amount other than the payments described in subparagraph (A) and other than qualified gratuitous transfers described in subparagraph (C) may be paid to or for the use of any person other than an organization described in section 170(c),

(C) following the termination of the payments described in subparagraph (A), the remainder interest in the trust is to be transferred to, or for the use of, an organization described in section 170(c) or is to be retained by the trust for such a use or, to the extent the remainder interest is in qualified employer securities (as defined in subsection (g)(4)), all or part of such securities are to be transferred to an employee stock ownership plan (as defined in section 4975(e)(7)) in a qualified gratuitous transfer (as defined by subsection (g)), and

(D) the value (determined under section 7520) of such remainder interest is at least 10 percent of the initial net fair market value of all property placed in the trust.

(2) CHARITABLE REMAINDER UNITRUST.—For purposes of this section, a charitable remainder unitrust is a trust—

(A) from which a fixed percentage (which is not less than 5 percent nor more than 50 percent) of the net fair market value of its assets, valued annually, is to be paid, not less often than annually, to one or more persons (at least one of which is not an organization described in section 170(c) and, in the case of individuals, only to an individual who is living at the time of the creation of the trust) for a term of years (not in excess of 20 years) or for the life or lives of such individual or individuals,

(B) from which no amount other than the payments described in subparagraph (A) and other than qualified gratuitous transfers described in subparagraph (C) may be paid to or for the use of any person other than an organization described in section 170(c),

(C) following the termination of the payments described in subparagraph (A), the remainder interest in the trust is to be transferred to, or for the use of, an organization described in section 170(c) or is to be retained by the trust for such a use or, to the extent the remainder interest is in qualified employer securities (as defined in subsection (g)(4)), all or part of such securities are to be transferred to an employee stock ownership plan (as defined in section 4975(e)(7)) in a qualified gratuitous transfer (as defined by subsection (g)), and

(D) with respect to each contribution of property to the trust, the value (determined under section 7520) of such remainder interest in such property is at least 10 percent of the net fair market value of such property as of the date such property is contributed to the trust.

(3) EXCEPTION.—Notwithstanding the provisions of paragraphs (2)(A) and (B), the trust instrument may provide that the trustee shall pay the income beneficiary for any year—

(A) the amount of the trust income, if such amount is less than the amount required to be distributed under paragraph (2)(A), and

(B) any amount of the trust income which is in excess of the amount required to be distributed under paragraph (2)(A), to the extent that (by reason of subparagraph (A)) the aggregate of the amounts paid in prior years was less than the aggregate of such required amounts.

(4) SEVERANCE OF CERTAIN ADDITIONAL CONTRIBUTIONS.—If—

(A) any contribution is made to a trust which before the contribution is a charitable remainder unitrust, and

(B) such contribution would (but for this paragraph) result in such trust ceasing to be a charitable unitrust by reason of paragraph (2)(D),

such contribution shall be treated as a transfer to a separate trust under regulations prescribed by the Secretary.

Amendments

• 2000, Community Renewal Tax Relief Act of 2000 (P.L. 106-554)

P.L. 106-554, §319(7):

Amended Code Sec. 664(d)(1)(C) and (2)(C) by striking the period after "subsection (g))". **Effective** on 12-21-2000.

• 1998, IRS Restructuring and Reform Act of 1998 (P.L. 105-206)

P.L. 105-206, §6010(r):

Amended Code Sec. 664(d)(1)(C) and (2)(C) by adding ", and" at the end. **Effective** as if included in the provision of P.L. 105-34 to which it relates [generally **effective** for transfers in trust after 7-28-97.—CCH].

• 1997, Taxpayer Relief Act of 1997 (P.L. 105-34)

P.L. 105-34, §1089(a)(1):

Amended Code Sec. 664(d)(1)(A) and (2)(A) by inserting "nor more than 50 percent" after "not less than 5 percent". **Effective**, generally, for transfers in trust after 6-18-97. For a special rule, see Act Sec. 1089(b)(6)(B), below.

P.L. 105-34, §1089(b)(1):

Amended Code Sec. 664(d)(1) by striking "and" at the end of subparagraph (B), by striking the period at the end of subparagraph (C), and by adding at the end a new subparagraph (D). **Effective**, generally, for transfers in trust after 7-28-97. For a special rule, see Act Sec. 1089(b)(6)(B), below.

P.L. 105-34, §1089(b)(2):

Amended Code Sec. 664(d)(2) by striking "and" at the end of subparagraph (B), by striking the period at the end of subparagraph (C), and by adding at the end a new subparagraph (D). **Effective**, generally, for transfers in trust after 7-28-97. For a special rule, see Act Sec. 1089(b)(6)(B), below.

P.L. 105-34, §1089(b)(4):

Amended Code Sec. 664(d) by adding at the end a new paragraph (4). **Effective**, generally, for transfers in trust after 7-28-97. For a special rule, see Act Sec. 1089(b)(6)(B), below.

P.L. 105-34, §1089(b)(6)(B), provides:

(B) SPECIAL RULE FOR CERTAIN DECEDENTS.—The amendments made by this subsection shall not apply to transfers in trust under the terms of a will (or other testamentary instrument) executed on or before July 28, 1997, if the decedent—

(i) dies before January 1, 1999, without having republished the will (or amended such instrument) by codicil or otherwise, or

(ii) was on July 28, 1997, under a mental disability to change the disposition of his property and did not regain his competence to dispose of such property before the date of his death.

P.L. 105-34, §1530(a):

Amended Code Sec. 664(d)(1)(C) and (2)(C) by striking the period at the end thereof and inserting "or, to the extent the remainder interest is in qualified employer securities (as defined in subsection (g)(4)), all or part of such securities are to be transferred to an employee stock ownership plan (as defined in section 4975(e)(7)) in a qualified gratuitous transfer (as defined by subsection (g))." **Effective** for transfers made by trusts to, or for the use of, an employee stock ownership plan after 8-5-97.

P.L. 105-34, §1530(c)(5):

Amended Code Sec. 664(d)(1)(B) and (2)(B) by inserting "and other than qualified gratuitous transfers described in subparagraph (C)" after "subparagraph (A)". **Effective** for transfers made by trusts to, or for the use of, an employee stock ownership plan after 8-5-97.

[Sec. 664(e)]

(e) VALUATION FOR PURPOSES OF CHARITABLE CONTRIBUTION.—For purposes of determining the amount of any charitable contribution, the remainder interest of a charitable remainder annuity trust or charitable remainder unitrust shall be computed on the basis that an amount equal to 5 percent of the net fair market value of its assets (or a greater amount, if required under the terms of the trust instrument) is to be distributed each year.

Amendments

• 1969, Tax Reform Act of 1969 (P.L. 91-172)

P.L. 91-172, §201(e)(1):

Added Code Sec. 664. **Effective** with respect to transfers in trust made after 7-31-69.

[Sec. 664(f)]

(f) CERTAIN CONTINGENCIES PERMITTED.—

(1) GENERAL RULE.—If a trust would, but for a qualified contingency, meet the requirements of paragraph (1)(A) or (2)(A) of subsection (d), such trust shall be treated as meeting such requirements.

(2) VALUE DETERMINED WITHOUT REGARD TO QUALIFIED CONTINGENCY.—For purposes of determining the amount of any charitable contribution (or the actuarial value of any interest), a qualified contingency shall not be taken into account.

(3) QUALIFIED CONTINGENCY.—For purposes of this subsection, the term "qualified contingency" means any provision of a trust which provides that, upon the happening of a contingency, the payments described in paragraph (1)(A) or (2)(A) of subsection (d) (as the case may be) will terminate not later than such payments would otherwise terminate under the trust.

Amendments

• 1984, Deficit Reduction Act of 1984 (P.L. 98-369)

P.L. 98-369, §1022(d):

Amended Code Sec. 664 by adding section (f). **Effective** for transfers after 12-31-78. See Act Sec. 1022(e)(3), below, for special rules regarding statute of limitations.

P.L. 98-369, §1022(e)(3), provides:

(3) Statute of Limitations.—

(A) In General.—If on the date of the enactment of this Act (or at any time before the date 1 year after such date of enactment), credit or refund of any overpayment of tax attributable to the amendments made by this section is barred by any law or rule of law, such credit or refund of such overpayment may nevertheless be made if claim therefor is filed before the date 1 year after the date of the enactment of this Act.

(B) No Interest Where Statute Closed on Date of Enactment.—In any case where the making of the credit or refund of the overpayment described in subparagraph (A) is barred on the date of the enactment of this Act, no interest shall be allowed with respect to such overpayment (or any related adjustment) for the period before the date 180 days after the date on which the Secretary of the Treasury (or his delegate) is notified that the reformation has occurred.

[Sec. 664(g)]

(g) QUALIFIED GRATUITOUS TRANSFER OF QUALIFIED EMPLOYER SECURITIES.—

(1) IN GENERAL.—For purposes of this section, the term "qualified gratuitous transfer" means a transfer of qualified employer securities to an employee stock ownership plan (as defined in section 4975(e)(7)) but only to the extent that—

(A) the securities transferred previously passed from a decedent dying before January 1, 1999, to a trust described in paragraph (1) or (2) of subsection (d),

(B) no deduction under section 404 is allowable with respect to such transfer,

(C) such plan contains the provisions required by paragraph (3),

(D) such plan treats such securities as being attributable to employer contributions but without regard to the limitations otherwise applicable to such contributions under section 404, and

(E) the employer whose employees are covered by the plan described in this paragraph files with the Secretary a verified written statement consenting to the application of sections 4978 and 4979A with respect to such employer.

(2) EXCEPTION.—The term "qualified gratuitous transfer" shall not include a transfer of qualified employer securities to an employee stock ownership plan unless—

(A) such plan was in existence on August 1, 1996,

(B) at the time of the transfer, the decedent and members of the decedent's family (within the meaning of section 2032A(e)(2)) own (directly or through the application of section 318(a)) no more than 10 percent of the value of the stock of the corporation referred to in paragraph (4), and

(C) immediately after the transfer, such plan owns (after the application of section 318(a)(4)) at least 60 percent of the value of the outstanding stock of the corporation.

(3) PLAN REQUIREMENTS.—A plan contains the provisions required by this paragraph if such plan provides that—

(A) the qualified employer securities so transferred are allocated to plan participants in a manner consistent with section 401(a)(4),

(B) plan participants are entitled to direct the plan as to the manner in which such securities which are entitled to vote and are allocated to the account of such participant are to be voted,

(C) an independent trustee votes the securities so transferred which are not allocated to plan participants,

(D) each participant who is entitled to a distribution from the plan has the rights described in subparagraphs (A) and (B) of section 409(h)(1),

(E) such securities are held in a suspense account under the plan to be allocated each year, up to the applicable limitation under paragraph (7) (determined on the basis of fair market value of securities when allocated to participants), after first allocating all other annual additions for the limitation year, up to the limitations under sections 415(c) and (e), and

(F) on termination of the plan, all securities so transferred which are not allocated to plan participants as of such termination are to be transferred to, or for the use of, an organization described in section 170(c).

For purposes of the preceding sentence, the term "independent trustee" means any trustee who is not a member of the family (within the meaning of section 2032A(e)(2)) of the decedent or a 5-percent shareholder. A plan shall not fail to be treated as meeting the requirements of section 401(a) by reason of meeting the requirements of this subsection.

(4) QUALIFIED EMPLOYER SECURITIES.—For purposes of this section, the term "qualified employer securities" means employer securities (as defined in section 409(l)) which are issued by a domestic corporation—

(A) which has no outstanding stock which is readily tradable on an established securities market, and

(B) which has only 1 class of stock.

(5) TREATMENT OF SECURITIES ALLOCATED BY EMPLOYEE STOCK OWNERSHIP PLAN TO PERSONS RELATED TO DECEDENT OR 5-PERCENT SHAREHOLDERS.—

(A) IN GENERAL.—If any portion of the assets of the plan attributable to securities acquired by the plan in a qualified gratuitous transfer are allocated to the account of—

(i) any person who is related to the decedent (within the meaning of section 267(b)) or a member of the decedent's family (within the meaning of section 2032A(e)(2)), or

(ii) any person who, at the time of such allocation or at any time during the 1-year period ending on the date of the acquisition of qualified employer securities by the plan, is a 5-percent shareholder of the employer maintaining the plan, the plan shall be treated as having distributed (at the time of such allocation) to such person or shareholder the amount so allocated.

(B) 5-PERCENT SHAREHOLDER.—For purposes of subparagraph (A), the term "5-percent shareholder" means any person who owns (directly or through the application of section 318(a)) more than 5 percent of the outstanding stock of the corporation which issued such qualified employer securities or of any corporation which is a member of the same controlled group of corporations (within the meaning of section 409(l)(4)) as such corporation. For purposes of the preceding sentence, section 318(a) shall be applied without regard to the exception in paragraph (2)(B)(i) thereof.

(C) CROSS REFERENCE.—

For excise tax on allocations described in subparagraph (A), see section 4979A.

(6) TAX ON FAILURE TO TRANSFER UNALLOCATED SECURITIES TO CHARITY ON TERMINATION OF PLAN.—If the requirements of paragraph (3)(F) are not met with respect to any securities, there is hereby imposed a tax on the employer maintaining the plan in an amount equal to the sum of—

(A) the amount of the increase in the tax which would be imposed by chapter 11 if such securities were not transferred as described in paragraph (1), and

(B) interest on such amount at the underpayment rate under section 6621 (and compounded daily) from the due date for filing the return of the tax imposed by chapter 11.

(7) APPLICABLE LIMITATION.—

(A) IN GENERAL.—For purposes of paragraph (3)(E), the applicable limitation under this paragraph with respect to a participant is an amount equal to the lesser of—

(i) $30,000, or

(ii) 25 percent of the participant's compensation (as defined in section 415(c)(3)).

(B) COST-OF-LIVING ADJUSTMENT.—The Secretary shall adjust annually the $30,000 amount under subparagraph (A)(i) at the same time and in the same manner as under section 415(d), except that the base period shall be the calendar quarter beginning October 1, 1993, and any increase under this subparagraph which is not a multiple of $5,000 shall be rounded to the next lowest multiple of $5,000.

Amendments

• 2006, Pension Protection Act of 2006 (P.L. 109-280)

P.L. 109-280, §811, provides:

SEC. 811. PENSIONS AND INDIVIDUAL RETIREMENT ARRANGEMENT PROVISIONS OF ECONOMIC GROWTH AND TAX RELIEF RECONCILIATION ACT OF 2001 MADE PERMANENT.

Title IX of the Economic Growth and Tax Relief Reconciliation Act of 2001 [P.L. 107-16] shall not apply to the provisions of, and amendments made by, subtitles A through F of title VI [§§601-666]of such Act (relating to pension and individual retirement arrangement provisions).

P.L. 109-280, §868(a):

Amended Code Sec. 664(g)(3)(E) by inserting "(determined on the basis of fair market value of securities when allocated to participants)" after "paragraph (7)". **Effective** 8-17-2006.

• 2001, Economic Growth and Tax Relief Reconciliation Act of 2001 (P.L. 107-16)

P.L. 107-16, §632(a)(3)(H)(i)-(ii):

Amended Code Sec. 664(g) in paragraph (3)(E) by striking "limitations under section 415(c)" and inserting "applicable limitation under paragraph (7)", and by adding at the end a new paragraph (7). **Effective** for years beginning after 12-31-2001.

P.L. 107-16, §901(a)-(b), provides [but see P.L. 109-280, §811, above]:

SEC. 901. SUNSET OF PROVISIONS OF ACT.

(a) IN GENERAL.—All provisions of, and amendments made by, this Act shall not apply—

(1) to taxable, plan, or limitation years beginning after December 31, 2010, or

(2) in the case of title V, to estates of decedents dying, gifts made, or generation skipping transfers, after December 31, 2010.

(b) APPLICATION OF CERTAIN LAWS.—The Internal Revenue Code of 1986 and the Employee Retirement Income Security Act of 1974 shall be applied and administered to years, estates, gifts, and transfers described in subsection (a) as if the provisions and amendments described in subsection (a) had never been enacted.

• 1997, Taxpayer Relief Act of 1997 (P.L. 105-34)

P.L. 105-34, §1530(b):

Amended Code Sec. 664 by adding at the end a new subsection (g). **Effective** for transfers made by trusts to, or for the use of, an employee stock ownership plan after 8-5-97.

Subpart D—Treatment of Excess Distributions by Trusts

[Sec. 665]

SEC. 665. DEFINITIONS APPLICABLE TO SUBPART D.

[Sec. 665(a)]

(a) UNDISTRIBUTED NET INCOME.—For purposes of this subpart, the term "undistributed net income" for any taxable year means the amount by which the distributable net income of the trust for such taxable year exceeds the sum of—

(1) the amounts for such taxable year specified in paragraphs (1) and (2) of section 661(a), and

(2) the amount of taxes imposed on the trust attributable to such distributable net income.

Amendments

• 1969, Tax Reform Act of 1969 (P.L. 91-172)

P.L. 91-172, §331(a):

Amended Code Sec. 665(a). **Effective** for tax years beginning after 12-31-68. Prior to amendment, Code Sec. 665(a) read as follows:

(a) Undistributed Net Income.—For purposes of this subpart, the term "undistributed net income" for any taxable year means the amount by which distributable net income of the trust for such taxable year exceeds the sum of—

(1) the amounts for such taxable year specified in paragraphs (1) and (2) of section 661(a); and

(2) the amount of taxes imposed on the trust.

[Sec. 665(b)]

(b) ACCUMULATION DISTRIBUTION.—For purposes of this subpart, except as provided in subsection (c), the term "accumulation distribution" means, for any taxable year of the trust, the amount by which—

(1) the amounts specified in paragraph (2) of section 661(a) for such taxable year, exceed

(2) distributable net income for such year reduced (but not below zero) by the amounts specified in paragraph (1) of section 661(a).

For purposes of section 667 (other than subsection (c) thereof, relating to multiple trusts), the amounts specified in paragraph (2) of section 661(a) shall not include amounts properly paid, credited, or required to be distributed to a beneficiary from a trust (other than a foreign trust) as income accumulated before the birth of such beneficiary or before such beneficiary attains the age of 21. If the amounts properly paid, credited, or required to be distributed by the trust for the taxable year do not exceed the income of the trust for such year, there shall be no accumulation distribution for such year.

Amendments

• 1997, Taxpayer Relief Act of 1997 (P.L. 105-34)

P.L. 105-34, §507(a)(2):

Amended Code Sec. 665(b) by inserting "except as provided in subsection (c)," after "subpart,". **Effective** for distributions in tax years beginning after 8-5-97.

• 1976, Tax Reform Act of 1976 (P.L. 94-455)

P.L. 94-455, §701(b):

Added the sentence "For purposes of section 667 (other than subsection (c) thereof, relating to multiple trusts), the amounts specified in paragraph (2) of section 661(a) shall not include amounts properly paid, credited, or required to be distributed to a beneficiary from a trust (other than a foreign trust) as income accumulated before the birth of such beneficiary or before such beneficiary attains the age of 21." **Effective** for distributions made in tax years beginning after 12-31-75.

P.L. 94-455, §701(c):

Added the sentence "If the amounts properly paid, credited, or required to be distributed by the trust for the taxable year do not exceed the income of the trust for such year, there shall be no accumulation distribution for such year." **Effective** for distributions made in tax years beginning after 12-31-75.

• 1969, Tax Reform Act of 1969 (P.L. 91-172)

P.L. 91-172, §331(a), (d)(2)(A):

Amended Code Sec. 665(b). **Effective**, generally, for tax years beginning after 12-31-68. However, see Act Sec. 331(d)(2)(A), below. Before amendment, Code Sec. 665(b) read as follows:

(b) Accumulation Distributions of Trusts Other Than Certain Foreign Trusts.—For purposes of this subpart, in the case of a trust (other than a foreign trust created by a United States person), the term "accumulation distribution" for any taxable year of the trust means the amount (if in excess of $2,000) by which the amounts specified in paragraph (2) of section 661(a) for such taxable year exceed distributable net income reduced by the amounts specified in paragraph (1) of section 661(a). For purposes of this subsection, the amount specified in paragraph (2) of section 661(a) shall be determined without regard to section 666 and shall not include—

(1) amounts paid, credited, or required to be distributed to a beneficiary as income accumulated before the birth of such beneficiary or before such beneficiary attains the age of 21;

(2) amounts properly paid or credited to a beneficiary to meet the emergency needs of such beneficiary;

(3) amounts properly paid or credited to a beneficiary upon such beneficiary's attaining a specified age or ages if—

(A) the total number of such distributions cannot exceed 4 with respect to such beneficiary,

(B) the period between each such distribution to such beneficiary is 4 years or more, and

(C) as of January 1, 1954, such distributions are required by the specific terms of the governing instrument; and

(4) amounts properly paid or credited to a beneficiary as a final distribution of the trust if such final distribution is made more than 9 years after the date of the last transfer to such trust.

P.L. 91-172, §331(d)(2)(A), provides:

(A) Amounts paid, credited, or required to be distributed by a trust (other than a foreign trust created by a United States person) on or before the last day of a taxable year of the trust beginning before January 1, 1974, shall not be deemed to be accumulation distributions to the extent that such amounts were accumulated by a trust in taxable years of such trust beginning before January 1, 1969, and would have been excepted from the definition of an accumulation distribution by reason of paragraphs (1), (2), (3), or (4) of section 665(b) of the Internal Revenue Code of 1954, as in effect on December 31, 1968, if they had been distributed on the last day of the last taxable year of the trust beginning before January 1, 1969.

• 1962, Revenue Act of 1962 (P.L. 87-834)

P.L. 87-834, §7:

Amended Code Sec. 665(b) by striking out "(b) Accumulation Distribution.—For purposes of this subpart," and inserting in lieu thereof the following: "(b) Accumulation Distributions of Trusts Other Than Certain Foreign Trusts.—For purposes of this subpart, in the case of a trust (other than a foreign trust created by a United States person),". **Effective** for distributions made after 12-31-62.

[Sec. 665(c)]

(c) EXCEPTION FOR ACCUMULATION DISTRIBUTIONS FROM CERTAIN DOMESTIC TRUSTS.—For purposes of this subpart—

(1) IN GENERAL.—In the case of a qualified trust, any distribution in any taxable year beginning after the date of the enactment of this subsection shall be computed without regard to any undistributed net income.

(2) QUALIFIED TRUST.—For purposes of this subsection, the term "qualified trust" means any trust other than—

(A) a foreign trust (or, except as provided in regulations, a domestic trust which at any time was a foreign trust), or

(B) a trust created before March 1, 1984, unless it is established that the trust would not be aggregated with other trusts under section 643(f) if such section applied to such trust.

Amendments

• 1997, Taxpayer Relief Act of 1997 (P.L. 105-34)

P.L. 105-34, §507(a)(1):

Amended Code Sec. 665 by inserting after subsection (b) a new subsection (c). **Effective** for distributions in tax years beginning after 8-5-97.

[Sec. 665(c)—Stricken]

Amendments

• 1996, Small Business Job Protection Act of 1996 (P.L. 104-188)

P.L. 104-188, §1904(c)(2):

Amended Code Sec. 665 by striking subsection (c). **Effective** 8-20-96. For special and transitional rules, see Act Sec. 1904(d)(2) and (e), below. Prior to being stricken, Code Sec. 665(c) read as follows:

(c) SPECIAL RULE APPLICABLE TO DISTRIBUTIONS BY CERTAIN FOREIGN TRUSTS.—For purposes of this subpart, any amount paid to a United States person which is from a payor who is not a United States person and which is derived directly or indirectly from a foreign trust created by a United States person shall be deemed in the year of payment to have been directly paid by the foreign trust.

P.L. 104-188, §1904(d)(2) and (e), provides:

(2) EXCEPTION FOR CERTAIN TRUSTS.—The amendments made by this section shall not apply to any trust—

(A) which is treated as owned by the grantor under section 676 or 677 (other than subsection (a)(3) thereof) of the Internal Revenue Code of 1986, and

(B) which is in existence on September 19, 1995.

The preceding sentence shall not apply to the portion of any such trust attributable to any transfer to such trust after September 19, 1995.

(e) TRANSITIONAL RULE.—If—

(1) by reason of the amendments made by this section, any person other than a United States person ceases to be treated as the owner of a portion of a domestic trust, and

(2) before January 1, 1997, such trust becomes a foreign trust, or the assets of such trust are transferred to a foreign trust,

no tax shall be imposed by section 1491 of the Internal Revenue Code of 1986 by reason of such trust becoming a foreign trust or the assets of such trust being transferred to a foreign trust.

• 1969, Tax Reform Act of 1969 (P.L. 91-172)

P.L. 91-172, §331(a):

Amended Code Sec. 665(c). **Effective** for tax years beginning after 12-31-68. Prior to amendment, Code Sec. 665(c) read as follows:

(c) Accumulation Distribution of Certain Foreign Trusts.—For purposes of this subpart, in the case of a foreign trust created by a United States person, the term "accumulation distribution" for any taxable year of the trust means the amount by which the amounts specified in paragraph (2) of section 661(a) for such taxable year exceed distributable net income, reduced by the amounts specified in paragraph (1) of section 661(a). For purposes of this subsection, the amount specified in paragraph (2) of section 661(a) shall be determined without regard to section 666. Any amount paid to a United States person which is from a payor who is not a United States person and which is derived directly or indirectly from a foreign trust created by a United States person shall be deemed in the year of payment to have been directly paid by the foreign trust.

• 1962, Revenue Tax of 1962 (P.L. 87-834)

P.L. 87-834, §7:

Redesignated old Code Sec. 665(c) as 665(d); redesignated Sec. 665(d) as Sec. 665(e), and added a new Sec. 665(c). **Effective** with respect to distributions made after 12-31-62.

[Sec. 665(d)]

(d) TAXES IMPOSED ON THE TRUST.—For purposes of this subpart—

(1) IN GENERAL.—The term "taxes imposed on the trust" means the amount of the taxes which are imposed for any taxable year of the trust under this chapter (without regard to this subpart or part IV of subchapter A) and which, under regulations prescribed by the Secretary, are properly allocable to the undistributed portions of distributable net income and gains in excess of losses from sales or exchanges of capital assets. The amount determined in the preceding sentence shall be reduced by any amount of such taxes deemed distributed under section 666(b) and (c) to any beneficiary.

(2) FOREIGN TRUSTS.—In the case of any foreign trust, the term "taxes imposed on the trust" includes the amount, reduced as provided in the last sentence of paragraph (1), of any income, war profits, and excess profits taxes imposed by any foreign country or possession of the United States on such foreign trust which, as determined under paragraph (1), are so properly allocable. Under rules or regulations prescribed by the Secretary, in the case of any foreign trust of which the settlor or another person would be treated as owner of any portion of the trust under subpart E but for section 672(f), the term "taxes imposed on the trust" includes the allocable amount of any income, war profits, and excess profits taxes imposed by any foreign country or possession of the United States on the settlor or such other person in respect of trust income.

Amendments

• 1997, Taxpayer Relief Act of 1997 (P.L. 105-34)

P.L. 105-34, §1604(g)(2):

Amended Code Sec. 665(d)(1) by striking "or 669(d) and (e)" before "to any beneficiary." in the last sentence. **Effective** 8-5-97.

• 1996, Small Business Job Protection Act of 1996 (P.L. 104-188)

P.L. 104-188, §1904(b)(1):

Amended Code Sec. 665(d)(2) by adding at the end a new sentence. **Effective** 8-20-96. For special and transitional rules, see Act Sec. 1904(d)(2) and (e), below.

P.L. 104-188, §1904(d)(2) and (e), provides:

(2) EXCEPTION FOR CERTAIN TRUSTS.—The amendments made by this section shall not apply to any trust—

(A) which is treated as owned by the grantor under section 676 or 677 (other than subsection (a)(3) thereof) of the Internal Revenue Code of 1986, and

(B) which is in existence on September 19, 1995.

The preceding sentence shall not apply to the portion of any such trust attributable to any transfer to such trust after September 19, 1995.

(e) TRANSITIONAL RULE.—If—

(1) by reason of the amendments made by this section, any person other than a United States person ceases to be treated as the owner of a portion of a domestic trust, and

(2) before January 1, 1997, such trust becomes a foreign trust, or the assets of such trust are transferred to a foreign trust,

no tax shall be imposed by section 1491 of the Internal Revenue Code of 1986 by reason of such trust becoming a foreign trust or the assets of such trust being transferred to a foreign trust.

• 1986, Tax Reform Act of 1986 (P.L. 99-514)

P.L. 99-514, §1847(b)(16):

Amended Code Sec. 665(d)(1) by striking out "subpart A of part IV" and inserting in lieu thereof "part IV". **Effective** as if included in the provision of P.L. 98-369 to which it relates.

• 1978, Revenue Act of 1978 (P.L. 95-600)

P.L. 95-600, §701(q)(1)(A):

Amended Code Sec. 665(d). **Effective** for distributions made in tax years beginning after 12-31-75. Prior to amendment, Code Sec. 665(d) read as follows:

(d) TAXES IMPOSED ON THE TRUST.—For purposes of this subpart, the term "taxes imposed on the trust" means the amount of the taxes which are imposed for any taxable year of the trust under this chapter (without regard to this subpart) and which, under regulations prescribed by the Secretary, are properly allocable to the undistributed portions of distributable net income and gains in excess of losses from sales or exchanges of capital assets. The amount determined in the preceding sentence shall be reduced by any amount of such taxes deemed distributed under section 666(b) and (c) or 669(d) and (e) to any beneficiary.

• 1976, Tax Reform Act of 1976 (P.L. 94-455)

P.L. 94-455, §1906(b)(13)(A):

Amended 1954 Code by substituting "Secretary" for "Secretary or his delegate" each place it appeared. **Effective** 2-1-77.

• 1969, Tax Reform Act of 1969 (P.L. 91-172)

P.L. 91-172, §331(a):

Amended Code Sec. 665(d). **Effective** for tax years beginning after 12-31-68. Prior to amendment, Code Sec. 665(d) read as follows:

(d) Taxes Imposed on the Trust.—For purposes of this subpart, the term "taxes imposed on the trust" means the amount of the taxes which are imposed for any taxable year on the trust under this chapter (without regard to this subpart) and which, under regulations prescribed by the Secretary or his delegate, are properly allocable to the undistributed portion of the distributable net income. The amount determined in the preceding sentence shall be reduced by any amount of such taxes allowed, under sections 667 and 668, as a credit to any beneficiary on account of any accumulation distribution determined for any taxable year.

• 1962, Revenue Act of 1962 (P.L. 87-834)

P.L. 87-834, §7:

Redesignated old Code Sec. 665(c) as Sec. 665(d). **Effective** with respect to distributions made after 12-31-62.

[Sec. 665(e)]

(e) PRECEDING TAXABLE YEAR.—For purposes of this subpart—

(1) In the case of a foreign trust created by a United States person, the term "preceding taxable year" does not include any taxable year of the trust to which this part does not apply.

(2) In the case of a preceding taxable year with respect to which a trust qualified, without regard to this subpart, under the provisions of subpart B, for purposes of the application of this subpart to such trust for such taxable year, such trust shall, in accordance with regulations prescribed by the Secretary, be treated as a trust to which subpart C applies.

Amendments

• 1990, Omnibus Budget Reconciliation Act of 1990 (P.L. 101-508)

P.L. 101-508, §11802(f)(2):

Amended Code Sec. 665(e). **Effective** 11-5-90. Prior to amendment, Code Sec. 665(e) read as follows:

(e) PRECEDING TAXABLE YEAR.—For purposes of this subpart—

(1) in the case of a trust (other than a foreign trust created by a United States person), the term "preceding taxable year" does not include any taxable year of the trust—

(A) which precedes by more than 5 years the taxable year of the trust in which an accumulation distribution is made, if it is made in a taxable year beginning before January 1, 1974, or

(B) which begins before January 1, 1969, in the case of an accumulation distribution made during a taxable year beginning after December 31, 1973, and

(2) in the case of a foreign trust created by a United States person, such term does not include any taxable year of the trust to which this part does not apply.

In the case of a preceding taxable year with respect to which a trust qualifies (without regard to this subpart) under the provisions of subpart B, for purposes of the application of this subpart to such trust for such taxable year, such trust shall, in accordance with regulations prescribed by the Secretary, be treated as a trust to which subpart C applies.

P.L. 101-508, §11821(b), provides:

(b) SAVINGS PROVISION.—If—

(1) any provision amended or repealed by this part applied to—

(A) any transaction occurring before the date of the enactment of this Act,

(B) any property acquired before such date of enactment, or

(C) any item of income, loss, deduction, or credit taken into account before such date of enactment, and

(2) the treatment of such transaction, property, or item under such provision would (without regard to the amendments made by this part) affect liability for tax for periods ending after such date of enactment,

nothing in the amendments made by this part shall be construed to affect the treatment of such transaction, property, or item for purposes of determining liability for tax for periods ending after such date of enactment.

• 1976, Tax Reform Act of 1976 (P.L. 94-455)

P.L. 94-455, §701(d)(2):

Struck out Code Sec. 665(e)(1)(C), added "or" at the end of subparagraph (A), and substituted ", and" at the end of subparagraph (B) for ", or". **Effective** for distributions made in tax years beginning after 12-31-75. Prior to repeal, Code Sec. 665(e)(1)(C) read as follows:

(C) which begins before January 1, 1969, in the case of a capital gain distribution made during a taxable year beginning after December 31, 1968, and

P.L. 94-455, §1906(b)(13)(A):

Amended 1954 Code to substitute "Secretary" for "Secretary or his delegate" each place it appeared. **Effective** 2-1-77.

• 1969, Tax Reform Act of 1969 (P.L. 91-172)

P.L. 91-172, §331(a):

Amended Code Sec. 665(e). **Effective** for tax years beginning after 12-31-68. Prior to amendment, Code Sec. 665(e) read as follows:

(e) Preceding Taxable Year.—For purposes of this subpart, the term "preceding taxable year" does not include any taxable year of the trust to which this part does not apply. In the case of a preceding taxable year with respect to which a trust qualifies (without regard to this subpart) under the provisions of subpart B, for purposes of the application of this subpart to such trust for such taxable year, such trust shall, in accordance with regulations prescribed by the Secretary of his delegate, be treated as a trust to which subpart C applies.

• 1962, Revenue Act of 1962 (P.L. 87-834)

P.L. 87-834, §7:

Redesignated old Code Sec. 665(d) as Sec. 665(e). **Effective** with respect to distributions made after 12-31-62.

[Sec. 665(f)—Repealed]

Amendments

• 1976, Tax Reform Act of 1976 (P.L. 94-455)

P.L. 94-455, §701(d)(3):

Repealed Code Sec. 665(f). **Effective** for distributions made in tax years beginning after 12-31-75. Prior to repeal, Code Sec. 665(f) read as follows:

(f) UNDISTRIBUTED CAPITAL GAIN.—For purposes of this subpart, the term "undistributed capital gain" means, for any taxable year of the trust beginning after December 31, 1968, the amount by which—

(1) gains in excess of losses from the sale or exchange of capital assets, to the extent that such gains are allocated to corpus and are not (A) paid, credited, or required to be distributed to any beneficiary during such taxable year, or (B) paid, permanently set aside, or used for the purposes specified in section 642(c), exceed

(2) the amount of taxes imposed on the trust attributable to such gains.

For purposes of paragraph (1), the deduction under section 1202 (relating to deduction for excess of capital gains over capital losses) shall not be taken into account.

• 1969, Tax Reform Act of 1969 (P.L. 91-172)

P.L. 91-172, §331(a):

Added Code Sec. 665(f). **Effective** for tax years ending after 12-31-68.

[Sec. 665(g)—Repealed]

Amendments

• 1976, Tax Reform Act of 1976 (P.L. 94-455)

P.L. 94-455, §701(d)(3):

Repealed Code Sec. 665(g). **Effective** for distributions made in tax years beginning after 12-31-75. Prior to repeal, Code Sec. 665(g) read as follows:

(g) CAPITAL GAIN DISTRIBUTION.—For purposes of this subpart, the term "capital gain distribution" for any taxable year of the trust means, to the extent of undistributed capital gain, that portion of—

(1) the excess of the amounts specified in paragraph (2) of section 661(a) for such taxable year over distributable net income for such year reduced (but not below zero) by the amounts specified in paragraph (1) of section 661(a), over

(2) the undistributed net income of the trust for all preceding taxable years.

• 1971, Revenue Act of 1971 (P.L. 92-178)

P.L. 92-178, §306(a):

Amended the third line of Code Sec. 665(g) by deleting "for such taxable year" which formerly appeared after "undistributed capital gain". **Effective** for tax years beginning after 12-31-68.

• 1969, Tax Reform Act of 1969 (P.L. 91-172)

P.L. 91-172, §331(a):

Added Code Sec. 665(g). **Effective** for tax years beginning after 12-31-68.

[Sec. 666]

SEC. 666. ACCUMULATION DISTRIBUTION ALLOCATED TO PRECEDING YEARS.

[Sec. 666(a)]

(a) AMOUNT ALLOCATED.—In the case of a trust which is subject to subpart C, the amount of the accumulation distribution of such trust for a taxable year shall be deemed to be an amount within the meaning of paragraph (2) of section 661(a) distributed on the last day of each of the preceding taxable years, commencing with the earliest of such years, to the extent that such amount exceeds the total of any undistributed net income for all earlier preceding taxable years. The amount deemed to be distributed in any such preceding taxable year under the preceding sentence shall not exceed the undistributed net income for such preceding taxable year. For purposes of this subsection, undistributed net income for each of such preceding taxable years shall be computed without regard to such accumulation distribution and without regard to any accumulation distribution determined for any succeeding taxable year.

Amendments

• 1969, Tax Reform Act of 1969 (P.L. 91-172)

P.L. 91-172, §331(a)(d)(2)(B):

Amended Code Sec. 666(a). **Effective**, generally, for tax years beginning after 12-31-68. As to first sentence, however, P.L. 91-172, §331(d)(2)(B) provides as follows:

(B) For taxable years of a trust beginning before January 1, 1970, the first sentence of section 666(a) of the Internal Revenue Code of 1954 (as amended by this section) shall not apply, and the amount of the accumulation distribution of the trust for such taxable years shall be deemed to be an amount within the meaning of paragraph (2) of section 661(a) distributed on the last day of each of the preceding taxable years to the extent that such amount exceeds the total of any undistributed net income for any taxable years intervening between the taxable year with respect of which the accumulation distribution is determined and such preceding taxable year.

Prior to amendment, Code Sec. 666(a) read as follows:

(a) Amount Allocated.—In the case of a trust (other than a foreign trust created by a United States person) which for a taxable year beginning after December 31, 1953, is subject to subpart C, the amount of the accumulation distribution of such trust for such taxable year shall be deemed to be an amount within the meaning of paragraph (2) of section 661(a) distributed on the last day of each of the 5 preceding taxable years to the extent that such amount exceeds the total of any undistributed net incomes for any taxable years intervening between the taxable year with respect to which the accumulation distribution is determined and such preceding taxable year. The amount deemed to be distributed in any such preceding taxable year under the preceding sentence shall not exceed the undistributed net income of such preceding taxable year. For purposes of this subsection, undistributed net income for each of such 5 preceding taxable years shall be computed without regard to such accumulation distribution and without regard to any accumulation distribution determined for any succeeding taxable year. In the case of a foreign trust created by a United

States person, this subsection shall apply to the preceding taxable years of the trust without regard to any provision of the preceding sentences which would (but for this sentence) limit its application to the 5 preceding taxable years.

• **1962, Revenue Act of 1962 (P.L. 87-834)**

P.L. 87-834, §7:

Amended Code Sec. 666(a) by inserting after trust in line 1 the following "(other than a foreign trust created by a United States person)"; and by inserting after the period in line 15 a new sentence. **Effective** with respect to distributions made after 12-31-62.

[Sec. 666(b)]

(b) TOTAL TAXES DEEMED DISTRIBUTED.—If any portion of an accumulation distribution for any taxable year is deemed under subsection (a) to be an amount within the meaning of paragraph (2) of section 661(a) distributed on the last day of any preceding taxable year, and such portion of such distribution is not less than the undistributed net income for such preceding taxable year, the trust shall be deemed to have distributed on the last day of such preceding taxable year an additional amount within the meaning of paragraph (2) of section 661(a). Such additional amount shall be equal to the taxes (other than the tax imposed by section 55) imposed on the trust for such preceding taxable year attributable to the undistributed net income. For purposes of this subsection, the undistributed net income and the taxes imposed on the trust for such preceding taxable year attributable to such undistributed net income shall be computed without regard to such accumulation distribution and without regard to any accumulation distribution determined for any succeeding taxable year.

Amendments

• **1978, Revenue Act of 1978 (P.L. 95-600)**

P.L. 95-600, §421(d):

Amended Code Sec. 666(b) by striking out "taxes" in the text and inserting in lieu thereof "taxes (other than the tax imposed by section 55)". **Effective** for tax years beginning after 12-31-78.

• **1969, Tax Reform Act of 1969 (P.L. 91-172)**

P.L. 91-172, §331(a):

Amended Code Sec. 666(b). **Effective** for tax years beginning after 12-31-68. Prior to amendment, Code Sec. 666(b) read as follows:

(b) Total Taxes Deemed Distributed.—If any portion of an accumulation distribution for any taxable year is deemed under subsection (a) to be an amount within the meaning of paragraph (2) of section 661(a) distributed on the last day of any preceding taxable year, and such portion of such accumulation distribution is not less than the undistributed net income for such preceding taxable year, the trust shall be deemed to have distributed on the last day of such preceding taxable year an additional amount within the meaning of paragraph (2) of section 661(a). Such additional amount shall be equal to the taxes imposed on the trust for such preceding taxable year. For purposes of this subsection, the undistributed net income and the taxes imposed on the trust for such preceding taxable year shall be computed without regard to such accumulation distribution and without regard to any accumulation distribution determined for any succeeding taxable year.

[Sec. 666(c)]

(c) PRO RATA PORTION OF TAXES DEEMED DISTRIBUTED.—If any portion of an accumulation distribution for any taxable year is deemed under subsection (a) to be an amount within the meaning of paragraph (2) of section 661(a) distributed on the last day of any preceding taxable year and such portion of the accumulation distribution is less than the undistributed net income for such preceding taxable year, the trust shall be deemed to have distributed on the last day of such preceding taxable year an additional amount within the meaning of paragraph (2) of section 661(a). Such additional amount shall be equal to the taxes (other than the tax imposed by section 55) imposed on the trust for such taxable year attributable to the undistributed net income multiplied by the ratio of the portion of the accumulation distribution to the undistributed net income of the trust for such year. For purposes of this subsection, the undistributed net income and the taxes imposed on the trust for such preceding taxable year attributable to such undistributed net income shall be computed without regard to the accumulation distribution and without regard to any accumulation distribution determined for any succeeding taxable year.

Amendments

• **1980, Technical Corrections Act of 1979 (P.L. 96-222)**

P.L. 96-222, §104(a)(4)(H)(vi):

Amended Code Sec. 666(c) by adding "(other than the tax imposed by section 55)" after "equal to the taxes". **Effective** for tax years beginning after 12-31-78.

• **1969, Tax Reform Act of 1969 (P.L. 91-172)**

P.L. 91-172, §331(a):

Amended Code Sec. 666(c). **Effective** for tax years beginning after 12-31-68. Prior to amendment, Code Sec. 666(c) read as follows:

(c) Pro Rata Portion of Taxes Deemed Distributed.—If any portion of an accumulation distribution for any taxable year is deemed under subsection (a) to be an amount within the meaning of paragraph (2) of section 661(a) distributed on the last day of any preceding taxable year and such portion of the accumulation distribution is less than the undistributed net income for such preceding taxable year, the trust shall be deemed to have distributed on the last day of such preceding taxable year an additional amount within the meaning of paragraph (2) of section 661(a). Such additional amount shall be equal to the taxes imposed on the trust for such taxable year multiplied by the ratio of the portion of the accumulation distribution to the undistributed net income of the trust for such year. For purposes of this subsection, the undistributed net income and the taxes imposed on the trust for such preceding taxable year shall be computed without regard to the accumulation distribution and without regard to any accumulation distribution determined for any succeeding taxable year.

[Sec. 666(d)]

(d) RULE WHEN INFORMATION IS NOT AVAILABLE.—If adequate records are not available to determine the proper application of this subpart to an amount distributed by a trust, such amount shall be deemed to be an accumulation distribution consisting of undistributed net income earned during the earliest preceding taxable year of the trust in which it can be established that the trust was in existence.

Amendments

• 1969, Tax Reform Act of 1969 (P.L. 91-172)

P.L. 91-172, §331(a):

Added Code Sec. 666(d). **Effective** for tax years beginning after 12-31-68.

[Sec. 666(e)]

(e) DENIAL OF REFUND TO TRUSTS AND BENEFICIARIES.—No refund or credit shall be allowed to a trust or a beneficiary of such trust for any preceding taxable year by reason of a distribution deemed to have been made by such trust in such year under this section.

Amendments

• 1976, Tax Reform Act of 1976 (P.L. 94-455)

P.L. 94-455, §701(a)(2):

Added Code Sec. 666(e). **Effective** for distributions made in tax years beginning after 12-31-75.

[Sec. 667]

SEC. 667. TREATMENT OF AMOUNTS DEEMED DISTRIBUTED BY TRUST IN PRECEDING YEARS.

[Sec. 667(a)]

(a) GENERAL RULE.—The total of the amounts which are treated under section 666 as having been distributed by a trust in a preceding taxable year shall be included in the income of a beneficiary of the trust when paid, credited, or required to be distributed to the extent that such total would have been included in the income of such beneficiary under section 662(a)(2) (and, with respect to any tax-exempt interest to which section 103 applies, under section 662(b)) if such total had been paid to such beneficiary on the last day of such preceding taxable year. The tax imposed by this subtitle on a beneficiary for a taxable year in which any such amount is included in his income shall be determined only as provided in this section and shall consist of the sum of—

(1) a partial tax computed on the taxable income reduced by an amount equal to the total of such amounts, at the rate and in the manner as if this section had not been enacted,

(2) a partial tax determined as provided in subsection (b) of this section, and

(3) in the case of a foreign trust, the interest charge determined as provided in section 668.

Amendments

• 1976, Tax Reform Act of 1976 (P.L. 94-455)

P.L. 94-455, §701(a)(1):

Amended Code Sec. 667(a). **Effective** for distributions made in tax years beginning after 12-31-75. Prior to amendment, Code Sec. 667(a) read as follows:

(a) DENIAL OF REFUND TO TRUSTS.—No refund or credit shall be allowed to a trust for any preceding taxable year by reason of a distribution deemed to have been made by such trust in such year under section 666 or 669.

P.L. 94-455, §1014(a):

Struck out "and" at the end of paragraph (1), substituted ", and" for the period at the end of paragraph (2), and added a new paragraph (3). **Effective** for tax years beginning after 12-31-76.

• 1969, Tax Reform Act of 1969 (P.L. 91-172)

P.L. 91-172, §331(a):

Divided Code Sec. 667 into subsections (a) and (b) and amended new Code Sec. 667(a). **Effective** for tax years beginning after 12-31-68. Prior to amendment, Code Sec. 667 read as follows:

Sec. 667. DENIAL OF REFUND TO TRUSTS.

The amount of taxes imposed on the trust under this chapter, which would not have been payable by the trust for any preceding taxable year had the trust in fact made distributions at the times and in the amounts deemed under section 666, shall not be refunded or credited to the trust, but shall be allowed as a credit under section 668(b) against the tax of the beneficiaries who are treated as having received the distributions. For purposes of the preceding sentence, the amount of taxes which may not be refunded or credited to the trust shall be an amount equal to the excess of (1) the taxes imposed on the trust for any preceding taxable year (computed without regard to the accumulation distribution for the taxable year) over (2) the amount of taxes for such preceding taxable year imposed on the undistributed portion of distributable net income of the trust for such preceding taxable year after the application of this subpart on account of the accumulation distribution determined for such taxable year.

[Sec. 667(b)]

(b) TAX ON DISTRIBUTION.—

(1) IN GENERAL.—The partial tax imposed by subsection (a)(2) shall be determined—

(A) by determining the number of preceding taxable years of the trust on the last day of which an amount is deemed under section 666(a) to have been distributed,

(B) by taking from the 5 taxable years immediately preceding the year of the accumulation distribution the 1 taxable year for which the beneficiary's taxable income was the highest and the 1 taxable year for which his taxable income was the lowest,

(C) by adding to the beneficiary's taxable income for each of the 3 taxable years remaining after the application of subparagraph (B) an amount determined by dividing the amount deemed distributed under section 666 and required to be included in income under subsection (a) by the number of preceding taxable years determined under subparagraph (A), and

(D) by determining the average increase in tax for the 3 taxable years referred to in subparagraph (C) resulting from the application of such subparagraph.

The partial tax imposed by subsection (a)(2) shall be the excess (if any) of the average increase in tax determined under subparagraph (D), multiplied by the number of preceding taxable years determined under subparagraph (A), over the amount of taxes (other than the amount of taxes described in section 665(d)(2)) deemed distributed to the beneficiary under sections 666(b) and (c).

(2) TREATMENT OF LOSS YEARS.—For purposes of paragraph (1), the taxable income of the beneficiary for any taxable year shall be deemed to be not less than zero.

(3) CERTAIN PRECEDING TAXABLE YEARS NOT TAKEN INTO ACCOUNT.—For purposes of paragraph (1), if the amount of the undistributed net income deemed distributed in any preceding taxable year of the trust is less than 25 percent of the amount of the accumulation distribution divided by the number of preceding taxable years to which the accumulation distribution is allocated under section 666(a), the number of preceding taxable years of the trust with respect to which an amount is deemed distributed to a beneficiary under section 666(a) shall be determined without regard to such year.

(4) EFFECT OF OTHER ACCUMULATION DISTRIBUTIONS.—In computing the partial tax under paragraph (1) for any beneficiary, the income of such beneficiary for each of his prior taxable years shall include amounts previously deemed distributed to such beneficiary in such year under section 666 as a result of prior accumulation distributions (whether from the same or another trust).

(5) MULTIPLE DISTRIBUTIONS IN THE SAME TAXABLE YEAR.—In the case of accumulation distributions made from more than one trust which are includible in the income of a beneficiary in the same taxable year, the distributions shall be deemed to have been made consecutively in whichever order the beneficiary shall determine.

(6) ADJUSTMENT IN PARTIAL TAX FOR ESTATE AND GENERATION-SKIPPING TRANSFER TAXES ATTRIBUTABLE TO PARTIAL TAX.—

(A) IN GENERAL.—The partial tax shall be reduced by an amount which is equal to the pre-death portion of the partial tax multiplied by a fraction—

(i) the numerator of which is that portion of the tax imposed by chapter 11 or 13, as the case may be, which is attributable (on a proportionate basis) to amounts included in the accumulation distribution, and

(ii) the denominator of which is the amount of the accumulation distribution which is subject to the tax imposed by chapter 11 or 13, as the case may be.

(B) PARTIAL TAX DETERMINED WITHOUT REGARD TO THIS PARAGRAPH.—For purposes of this paragraph, the term "partial tax" means the partial tax imposed by subsection (a)(2) determined under this subsection without regard to this paragraph.

(C) PRE-DEATH PORTION.—For purposes of this paragraph, the pre-death portion of the partial tax shall be an amount which bears the same ratio to the partial tax as the portion of the accumulation distribution which is attributable to the period before the date of the death of the decedent or the date of the generation-skipping transfer bears to the total accumulation distribution.

Amendments

• 1986, Tax Reform Act of 1986 (P.L. 99-514)

P.L. 99-514, §104(b)(10):

Amended Code Sec. 667(b)(2). **Effective** for tax years beginning after 12-31-86. Prior to amendment, Code Sec. 667(b)(2) read as follows:

(2) TREATMENT OF LOSS YEARS.—For purposes of paragraph (1), the taxable income of the beneficiary for any taxable year shall be deemed to be not less than—

(A) in the case of a beneficiary who is an individual, the zero bracket amount for such year, or

(B) in the case of a beneficiary who is a corporation, zero.

• 1978, Revenue Act of 1978 (P.L. 95-600)

P.L. 95-600, §701(q)(1)(C):

Amended Code Sec. 667(b)(1) by inserting "(other than the amount of taxes described in section 665(d)(2))" after "taxes". **Effective** for distributions made in tax years beginning after 12-31-75.

P.L. 95-600, §702(o)(1):

Added 667(b)(6). **Effective** for estates of decedents dying after 12-31-79 and for generation-skipping transfers (within the meaning Code Sec. 2611(a)) made after 6-11-76.

• 1977, Tax Reduction and Simplification Act of 1977 (P.L. 95-30)

P.L. 95-30, §102(b)(8):

Amended paragraph (2) of Code Sec. 667(b). **Effective** for tax years beginning after 12-31-76. Prior to amendment, paragraph (2) of Code Sec. 667(b) read as follows:

(2) TREATMENT OF LOSS YEARS.—For purposes of paragraph (1), the taxable income of the beneficiary for any taxable year shall be deemed not to be less than zero.

• 1976, Tax Reform Act of 1976 (P.L. 94-455)

P.L. 94-455, §701(a)(1):

Amended Code Sec. 667(b). **Effective** for distributions made in tax years beginning after 12-31-75. Prior to amendment, Code Sec. 667(b) read as follows:

(b) AUTHORIZATION OF CREDIT TO BENEFICIARY.—There shall be allowed as a credit (without interest) against the tax imposed by this subtitle on the beneficiary an amount equal to the amount of the taxes deemed distributed to such beneficiary by the trust under sections 666(b) and (c) and 669(d) and (e) during preceding taxable years of the trust on the last day of which the beneficiary was in being, reduced by the amount of the taxes deemed distributed to such beneficiary for such preceding taxable years to the extent that such taxes are taken into account under sections 668(b)(1) and 669(b) in determining the amount of the tax imposed by section 668.

• 1969, Tax Reform Act of 1969 (P.L. 91-172)

P.L. 91-172, §331(a):

Added Code Sec. 667(b). **Effective** for tax years beginning after 12-31-68.

[Sec. 667(c)]

(c) SPECIAL RULE FOR MULTIPLE TRUSTS.—

(1) IN GENERAL.—If, in the same prior taxable year of the beneficiary in which any part of the accumulation distribution from a trust (hereinafter in this paragraph referred to as "third trust") is deemed under section 666(a) to have been distributed to such beneficiary, some part of prior distributions by each of 2 or more other trusts is deemed under section 666(a) to have been distributed to such beneficiary, then subsections (b) and (c) of section 666 shall not apply with respect to such part of the accumulation distribution from such third trust.

(2) ACCUMULATION DISTRIBUTIONS FROM TRUST NOT TAKEN INTO ACCOUNT UNLESS THEY EQUAL OR EXCEED $1,000.—For purposes of paragraph (1), an accumulation distribution from a trust to a beneficiary shall be taken into account only if such distribution, when added to any prior accumulation distributions from such trust which are deemed under section 666(a) to have been distributed to such beneficiary for the same prior taxable year of the beneficiary, equals or exceeds $1,000.

Amendments

• 1976, Tax Reform Act of 1976 (P.L. 94-455)

P.L. 94-455, §701(a)(1):

Added Code Sec. 667(c). **Effective** for distributions made in tax years beginning after 12-31-75.

[Sec. 667(d)]

(d) SPECIAL RULES FOR FOREIGN TRUST.—

(1) FOREIGN TAX DEEMED PAID BY BENEFICIARY.—

(A) IN GENERAL.—In determining the increase in tax under subsection (b)(1)(D) for any computation year, the taxes described in section 665(d)(2) which are deemed distributed under section 666(b) or (c) and added under subsection (b)(1)(C) to the taxable income of the beneficiary for any computation year shall, except as provided in subparagraphs (B) and (C), be treated as a credit against the increase in tax for such computation year under subsection (b)(1)(D).

(B) DEDUCTION IN LIEU OF CREDIT.—If the beneficiary did not choose the benefits of subpart A of part III of subchapter N with respect to the computation year, the beneficiary may in lieu of treating the amounts described in subparagraph (A) (without regard to subparagraph (C)) as a credit may treat such amounts as a deduction in computing the beneficiary's taxable income under subsection (b)(1)(C) for the computation year.

(C) LIMITATION ON CREDIT; RETENTION OF CHARACTER.—

(i) LIMITATION ON CREDIT.—For purposes of determining under subparagraph (A) the amount treated as a credit for any computation year, the limitations under subpart A of part III of subchapter N shall be applied separately with respect to amounts added under subsection (b)(1)(C) to the taxable income of the beneficiary for such computation year. For purposes of computing the increase in tax under subsection (b)(1)(D) for any computation year for which the beneficiary did not choose the benefits of subpart A of part III of subchapter N, the beneficiary shall be treated as having chosen such benefits for such computation year.

(ii) RETENTION OF CHARACTER.—The items of income, deduction, and credit of the Trust shall retain their character (subject to the application of section 904(f)(5)) to the extent necessary to apply this paragraph.

(D) COMPUTATION YEAR.—For purposes of this paragraph, the term "computation year" means any of the three taxable years remaining after application of subsection (b)(1)(B).

Amendments

• 1978, Revenue Act of 1978 (P.L. 95-600)

P.L. 95-600, §701(q)(1)(B):

Amended Code Sec. 667 by adding subsection (d). **Effective** for distributions made in tax years beginning after 12-31-75.

[Sec. 667(e)]

(e) RETENTION OF CHARACTER OF AMOUNTS DISTRIBUTED FROM ACCUMULATION TRUST TO NONRESIDENT ALIENS AND FOREIGN CORPORATIONS.—In the case of a distribution from a trust to a nonresident alien individual or to a foreign corporation, the first sentence of subsection (a) shall be applied as if the reference to the determination of character under section 662(b) applied to all amounts instead of just to tax-exempt interest.

Amendments

• 1978, Revenue Act of 1978 (P.L. 95-600)

P.L. 95-600, §701(r)(1):

Amended Code Sec. 667 by adding subsection (e). **Effective** for distributions made in tax years beginning after 12-31-75.

[Sec. 668]

SEC. 668. INTEREST CHARGE ON ACCUMULATION DISTRIBUTIONS FROM FOREIGN TRUSTS.

[Sec. 668(a)]

(a) GENERAL RULE.—For purposes of the tax determined under section 667(a)—

(1) INTEREST DETERMINED USING UNDERPAYMENT RATES.—The interest charge determined under this section with respect to any distribution is the amount of interest which would be determined on the partial tax computed under section 667(b) for the period described in paragraph (2) using the rates and the method under section 6621 applicable to underpayments of tax.

(2) PERIOD.—For purposes of paragraph (1), the period described in this paragraph is the period which begins on the date which is the applicable number of years before the date of the distribution and which ends on the date of the distribution.

(3) APPLICABLE NUMBER OF YEARS.—For purposes of paragraph (2)—

(A) IN GENERAL.—The applicable number of years with respect to a distribution is the number determined by dividing—

(i) the sum of the products described in subparagraph (B) with respect to each undistributed income year, by

(ii) the aggregate undistributed net income.

The quotient determined under the preceding sentence shall be rounded under procedures prescribed by the Secretary.

(B) PRODUCT DESCRIBED.—For purposes of subparagraph (A), the product described in this subparagraph with respect to any undistributed income year is the product of—

(i) the undistributed net income for such year, and

(ii) the sum of the number of taxable years between such year and the taxable year of the distribution (counting in each case the undistributed income year but not counting the taxable year of the distribution).

(4) UNDISTRIBUTED INCOME YEAR.—For purposes of this subsection, the term "undistributed income year" means any prior taxable year of the trust for which there is undistributed net income, other than a taxable year during all of which the beneficiary receiving the distribution was not a citizen or resident of the United States.

(5) DETERMINATION OF UNDISTRIBUTED NET INCOME.—Notwithstanding section 666, for purposes of this subsection, an accumulation distribution from the trust shall be treated as reducing proportionately the undistributed net income for undistributed income years.

(6) PERIODS BEFORE 1996.—Interest for the portion of the period described in paragraph (2) which occurs before January 1, 1996, shall be determined—

(A) by using an interest rate of 6 percent, and

(B) without compounding until January 1, 1996.

Amendments

• 1996, Small Business Job Protection Act of 1996 (P.L. 104-188)

P.L. 104-188, §1906(a):

Amended Code Sec. 668(a). **Effective** for distributions after 8-20-96. Prior to amendment, Code Sec. 668(a) read as follows:

(a) GENERAL RULE.—For purposes of the tax determined under section 667(a), the interest charge is an amount equal to 6 percent of the partial tax computed under section 667(b) multiplied by a fraction—

(1) the numerator of which is the sum of the number of taxable years between each taxable year to which the distribution is allocated under section 666(a) and the taxable year of the distribution (counting in each case the taxable year to which the distribution is allocated but not counting the taxable year of the distribution), and

(2) the denominator of which is the number of taxable years to which the distribution is allocated under section 666(a).

• 1976, Tax Reform Act of 1976 (P.L. 94-455)

P.L. 94-455, §701(a)(3):

Repealed Code Sec. 668(a). **Effective** for distributions made in tax years beginning after 12-31-75. Prior to repeal, Code Sec. 668(a) read as follows:

(a) GENERAL RULE.—The total of the amounts which are treated under sections 666 and 669 as having been distributed by the trust in a preceding taxable year shall be included in the income of a beneficiary of the trust when paid, credited, or required to be distributed to the extent that such total would have been included in the income of such beneficiary under section 662(a)(2) and (b) if such total had been paid to such beneficiary on the last day of such preceding taxable year. The tax imposed by this subtitle on a beneficiary for a taxable year in which any such amount is included in his income shall be determined only as provided in this section and shall consist of the sum of—

(1) a partial tax computed on the taxable income reduced by an amount equal to the total of such amounts, at the rate and in the manner as if this section had not been enacted,

(2) a partial tax determined as provided in subsection (b) of this section, and

(3) in the case of a beneficiary of a trust which is not required to distribute all of its income currently, a partial tax determined as provided in section 669.

For purposes of this subpart, a trust shall not be considered to be a trust which is not required to distribute all of its income currently for any taxable year prior to the first taxable year in which income is accumulated.

P.L. 94-455, §1014(b):

Added a new Code Sec. 668(a). **Effective** for tax years beginning after 12-31-76.

• 1969, Tax Reform Act of 1969 (P.L. 91-172)

P.L. 91-172, §331(a):

Amended Code Sec. 668(a). **Effective** for tax years beginning after 12-31-68. Prior to amendment, Code Sec. 668(a) read as follows:

(a) Amounts Treated as Received in Prior Taxable Years.—The total of the amounts which are treated under section 666 as having been distributed by the trust in a preceding taxable year shall be included in the income of a beneficiary or beneficiaries of the trust when paid, credited, or required to be distributed to the extent that such total would have been included in the income of such beneficiary or beneficiaries under section 662(a)(2) and (b) if such total had been paid to such beneficiary or beneficiaries on the last day of such preceding taxable year. The portion of such total included under the preceding sentence in the income of any beneficiary shall be based upon the same ratio as determined under the second sentence of section 662(a)(2) for the taxable year in respect of which the accumulation distribution is determined, except that proper adjustment of such ratio shall be made, in accordance with regulations prescribed by the Secretary or his delegate, for amounts which fall within paragraphs (1) through (4) of section 665(b). The tax of the beneficiaries attributable to the amounts treated as having been received on the last day of such preceding taxable year of the trust shall not be greater than the aggregate of the taxes attributable to those amounts had they been included in the gross income of the beneficiaries on such day in accordance with section 662(a)(2) and (b). Except as provided in section 669, in the case of a foreign trust created by a United States person the preceding sentence shall not apply to any beneficiary who is a United States person.

• 1962, Revenue Act of 1962 (P.L. 87-834)

P.L. 87-834, §7:

Amended Code Sec. 668(a) by inserting after the period in line 18 a new sentence. **Effective** for distributions made after 12-31-62.

[Sec. 668(b)]

(b) LIMITATION.—The total amount of the interest charge shall not, when added to the total partial tax computed under section 667(b), exceed the amount of the accumulation distribution (other than the amount of tax deemed distributed by section 666(b) or (c)) in respect of which such partial tax was determined.

Amendments

• 1976, Tax Reform Act of 1976 (P.L. 94-455)

P.L. 94-455, §701(a)(3):

Repealed Code Sec. 668(a). **Effective** for distributions made in tax years beginning after 12-31-75. Prior to repeal, Code Sec. 668(b) read as follows:

(b) TAX ON DISTRIBUTION.—

(1) ALTERNATIVE METHODS.—Except as provided in paragraph (2), the partial tax imposed by subsection (a)(2) shall be the lesser of—

(A) the aggregate of the taxes attributable to the amounts deemed distributed under section 666 had they been included in the gross income of the beneficiary on the last day of each respective preceding taxable year, or

(B) the tax determined by multiplying, by the number of preceding taxable years of the trust, on the last day of which an amount is deemed under section 666(a) to have been distributed, the average of the increase in tax attributable to recomputing the beneficiary's gross income for each of the beneficiary's 3 taxable years immediately preceding the year of the accumulation distribution by adding to the income of each of such years an amount determined by dividing the amount deemed distributed under section 666 and required to be included in income under subsection (a) by such number of preceding taxable years of the trust,

less an amount equal to the amount of taxes deemed distributed to the beneficiary under sections 666(b) and (c).

(2) SPECIAL RULES.—

(A) If a beneficiary was not in existence on the last day of a preceding taxable year of the trust with respect to which a distribution is deemed made under section 666(a), the partial tax under either paragraph (1)(A) or (1)(B) shall be computed as if the beneficiary were in existence on the last day of such year on the basis that the beneficiary had no gross income (other than amounts deemed distributed to him under sections 666 and 669 by the same or other trusts) and no deductions for such year.

(B) The partial tax shall not be computed under the provisions of subparagraph (B) of paragraph (1) if, in the same prior taxable year of the beneficiary in which any part of the accumulation distribution is deemed under section 666(a) to have been distributed to such beneficiary, some part of prior accumulation distributions by each of two or more other trusts is deemed under section 666(a) to have been distributed to such beneficiary.

(C) If the partial tax is computed under paragraph (1)(B), and the amount of the undistributed net income deemed distributed in any preceding taxable year of the trust is less than 25 percent of the amount of the accumulation distribution divided by the number of preceding taxable years to which the accumulation distribution is allocated under section 666(a), the number of preceding taxable years of the trust with respect to which an amount is deemed distributed to a beneficiary under section 666(a) shall be determined without regard to such year.

(3) EFFECT OF OTHER ACCUMULATION DISTRIBUTIONS AND CAPITAL GAIN DISTRIBUTIONS.—In computing the partial tax under paragraph (1) for any beneficiary, the income of such beneficiary for each of his prior taxable years—

(A) shall include amounts previously deemed distributed to such beneficiary in such year under section 666 or 669 as a result of prior accumulation distributions or capital gain distributions (whether from the same or another trust), and

(B) shall not include amounts deemed distributed to such beneficiary in such year under section 669 as a result of a capital gain distribution from the same trust in the current year.

(4) MULTIPLE DISTRIBUTIONS IN THE SAME TAXABLE YEAR.—In the case of accumulation distributions made from more than one trust which are includible in the income of a beneficiary in the same taxable year, the distributions shall be deemed to have been made consecutively in whichever order the beneficiary shall determine.

(5) INFORMATION REQUIREMENTS WITH RESPECT TO BENEFICIARY.—

(A) Except as provided in subparagraph (B), the partial tax shall not be computed under the provisions of paragraph (1)(A) unless the beneficiary supplies such information with respect to his income, for each taxable year with which or in which ends a taxable year of the trust on the last day of which an amount is deemed distributed under section 666(a), as the Secretary or his delegate prescribes by regulations.

(B) If by reason of paragraph (2)(B) the provisions of paragraph (1)(B) do not apply, the determination of the amount of the beneficiary's income for a taxable year for which the beneficiary has not supplied the information required under subparagraph (A) shall be made by the Secretary or his delegate on the basis of information available to him.

P.L. 94-455, §1014(b):

Added a new Code Sec. 668(b). **Effective** for tax years beginning after 12-31-76.

• **1969, Tax Reform Act of 1969 (P.L. 91-172)**

P.L. 91-172, §331(a):

Amended Code Sec. 668(b). **Effective** for tax years beginning after 12-31-68. Prior to amendment, Code Sec. 668(b) read as follows:

(b) Credit for Taxes Paid by Trust.—The tax imposed on beneficiaries under this chapter shall be credited with a pro rata portion of the taxes imposed on the trust under this chapter for such preceding taxable year which would not have been payable by the trust for such preceding taxable year had the trust in fact made distributions to such beneficiaries at the times and in the amounts specified in section 666.

[Sec. 668(c)]

(c) INTEREST CHARGE NOT DEDUCTIBLE.—The interest charge determined under this section shall not be allowed as a deduction for purposes of any tax imposed by this title.

Amendments

• **1990, Omnibus Budget Reconciliation Act of 1990 (P.L. 101-508)**

P.L. 101-508, §11802(f)(3):

Amended Code Sec. 668(c). **Effective** 11-5-90. Prior to amendment, Code Sec. 668(c) read as follows:

(c) SPECIAL RULES.—

(1) INTEREST CHARGE NOT DEDUCTIBLE.—The interest charge determined under this section shall not be allowed as a deduction for purposes of any tax imposed by this title.

(2) TRANSITIONAL RULE.—For purposes of this section, undistributed net income existing in a trust as of January 1, 1977, shall be treated as allocated under section 666(a) to the first taxable year beginning after December 31, 1976.

P.L. 101-508, §11821(b), provides:

(b) SAVINGS PROVISION.—If—

(1) any provision amended or repealed by this part applied to—

(A) any transaction occurring before the date of the enactment of this Act,

(B) any property acquired before such date of enactment, or

(C) any item of income, loss, deduction, or credit taken into account before such date of enactment, and

(2) the treatment of such transaction, property, or item under such provision would (without regard to the amendments made by this part) affect liability for tax for periods ending after such date of enactment,

nothing in the amendments made by this part shall be construed to affect the treatment of such transaction, property, or item for purposes of determining liability for tax for periods ending after such date of enactment.

• **1976, Tax Reform Act of 1976 (P.L. 94-455)**

P.L. 94-455, §1014(b):

Added Code Sec. 668(c). **Effective** for tax years beginning after 12-31-75.

Subpart E—Grantors and Others Treated as Substantial Owners

[Sec. 671]

SEC. 671. TRUST INCOME, DEDUCTIONS, AND CREDITS ATTRIBUTABLE TO GRANTORS AND OTHERS AS SUBSTANTIAL OWNERS.

Where it is specified in this subpart that the grantor or another person shall be treated as the owner of any portion of a trust, there shall then be included in computing the taxable income and credits of the grantor or the other person those items of income, deductions, and credits against tax of the trust which are attributable to that portion of the trust to the extent that such items would be taken into account under this chapter in computing taxable income or credits against the tax of an individual. Any remaining portion of the trust shall be subject to subparts A through D. No items of a trust shall be included in computing the taxable income and credits of the grantor or of any other person solely on the grounds of his dominion and control over the trust under section 61 (relating to definition of gross income) or any other provision of this title, except as specified in this subpart.

[Sec. 672]

SEC. 672. DEFINITIONS AND RULES.

[Sec. 672(a)]

(a) ADVERSE PARTY.—For purposes of this subpart, the term "adverse party" means any person having a substantial beneficial interest in the trust which would be adversely affected by the exercise or nonexercise of the power which he possesses respecting the trust. A person having a general power of appointment over the trust property shall be deemed to have a beneficial interest in the trust.

[Sec. 672(b)]

(b) NONADVERSE PARTY.—For purposes of this subpart, the term "nonadverse party" means any person who is not an adverse party.

[Sec. 672(c)]

(c) RELATED OR SUBORDINATE PARTY.—For purposes of this subpart, the term "related or subordinate party" means any nonadverse party who is—

(1) the grantor's spouse if living with the grantor;

(2) any one of the following: The grantor's father, mother, issue, brother or sister; an employee of the grantor; a corporation or any employee of a corporation in which the stock holdings of the grantor and the trust are significant from the viewpoint of voting control; a subordinate employee of a corporation in which the grantor is an executive.

For purposes of subsection (f) and sections 674 and 675, a related or subordinate party shall be presumed to be subservient to the grantor in respect of the exercise or nonexercise of the powers conferred on him unless such party is shown not to be subservient by a preponderance of the evidence.

Amendments

• 1996, Small Business Job Protection Act of 1996 (P.L. 104-188)

P.L. 104-188, §1904(a)(2):

Amended Code Sec. 672(c) by inserting "subsection (f) and" before "sections 674". **Effective** 8-20-96. For special and transitional rules, see Act Sec. 1904(d)(2) and (e) in the amendment notes following Code Sec. 672(f).

[Sec. 672(d)]

(d) RULE WHERE POWER IS SUBJECT TO CONDITION PRECEDENT.—A person shall be considered to have a power described in this subpart even though the exercise of the power is subject to a precedent giving of notice or takes effect only on the expiration of a certain period after the exercise of the power.

[Sec. 672(e)]

(e) GRANTOR TREATED AS HOLDING ANY POWER OR INTEREST OF GRANTOR'S SPOUSE.—

(1) IN GENERAL.—For purposes of this subpart, a grantor shall be treated as holding any power or interest held by—

(A) any individual who was the spouse of the grantor at the time of the creation of such power or interest, or

(B) any individual who became the spouse of the grantor after the creation of such power or interest, but only with respect to periods after such individual became the spouse of the grantor.

(2) MARITAL STATUS.—For purposes of paragraph (1)(A), an individual legally separated from his spouse under a decree of divorce or of separate maintenance shall not be considered as married.

Amendments

• 1988, Technical and Miscellaneous Revenue Act of 1988 (P.L. 100-647)

P.L. 100-647, §1014(a)(1):

Amended Code Sec. 672(e). **Effective** as if included in the provision of P.L. 99-514 to which it relates. Prior to amendment, Code Sec. 672(e) read as follows:

(e) GRANTOR TREATED AS HOLDING ANY POWER OR INTEREST OF GRANTOR'S SPOUSE.—For purposes of this subpart, if a grantor's spouse is living with the grantor at the time of the creation of any power or interest held by such spouse, the grantor shall be treated as holding such power or interest.

• 1986, Tax Reform Act of 1986 (P.L. 99-514)

P.L. 99-514, §1401(a):

Amended Code Sec. 672 by adding at the end thereof new subsection (e). **Effective** with respect to transfers in trust made after 3-1-86.

[Sec. 672(f)]

(f) SUBPART NOT TO RESULT IN FOREIGN OWNERSHIP.—

(1) IN GENERAL.—Notwithstanding any other provision of this subpart, this subpart shall apply only to the extent such application results in an amount (if any) being currently taken into account (directly or through 1 or more entities) under this chapter in computing the income of a citizen or resident of the United States or a domestic corporation.

(2) EXCEPTIONS.—

(A) CERTAIN REVOCABLE AND IRREVOCABLE TRUSTS.—Paragraph (1) shall not apply to any portion of a trust if—

(i) the power to revest absolutely in the grantor title to the trust property to which such portion is attributable is exercisable solely by the grantor without the approval or consent of any other person or with the consent of a related or subordinate party who is subservient to the grantor, or

(ii) the only amounts distributable from such portion (whether income or corpus) during the lifetime of the grantor are amounts distributable to the grantor or the spouse of the grantor.

(B) COMPENSATORY TRUSTS.—Except as provided in regulations, paragraph (1) shall not apply to any portion of a trust distributions from which are taxable as compensation for services rendered.

(3) SPECIAL RULES.—Except as otherwise provided in regulations prescribed by the Secretary—

(A) a controlled foreign corporation (as defined in section 957) shall be treated as a domestic corporation for purposes of paragraph (1), and

(B) paragraph (1) shall not apply for purposes of applying section 1297.

(4) RECHARACTERIZATION OF PURPORTED GIFTS.—In the case of any transfer directly or indirectly from a partnership or foreign corporation which the transferee treats as a gift or bequest, the Secretary may recharacterize such transfer in such circumstances as the Secretary determines to be appropriate to prevent the avoidance of the purposes of this subsection.

(5) SPECIAL RULE WHERE GRANTOR IS FOREIGN PERSON.—If—

(A) but for this subsection, a foreign person would be treated as the owner of any portion of a trust, and

(B) such trust has a beneficiary who is a United States person,

such beneficiary shall be treated as the grantor of such portion to the extent such beneficiary has made (directly or indirectly) transfers of property (other than in a sale for full and adequate consideration) to such foreign person. For purposes of the preceding sentence, any gift shall not be taken into account to the extent such gift would be excluded from taxable gifts under section 2503(b).

(6) REGULATIONS.—The Secretary shall prescribe such regulations as may be necessary or appropriate to carry out the purposes of this subsection, including regulations providing that paragraph (1) shall not apply in appropriate cases.

Amendments

• 1998, IRS Restructuring and Reform Act of 1998 (P.L. 105-206)

P.L. 105-206, §6011(c)(1):

Amended Code Sec. 672(f)(3)(B) by striking "section 1296" and inserting "section 1297". **Effective** as if included in the provision of P.L. 105-34 to which it relates **[effective** for tax years of U.S. persons beginning after 12-31-97, and tax years of foreign corporations ending with or within such tax years of U.S. persons.—CCH].

• 1996, Small Business Job Protection Act of 1996 (P.L. 104-188)

P.L. 104-188, §1904(a)(1):

Amended Code Sec. 672(f). **Effective** 8-20-96. For special and transitional rules, see Act Sec. 1904(d)(2) and (e), below. Prior to amendment, Code Sec. 672(f) read as follows:

(f) SPECIAL RULE WHERE GRANTOR IS FOREIGN PERSON.—

(1) IN GENERAL.—If—

(A) but for this subsection, a foreign person would be treated as the owner of any portion of a trust, and

(B) such trust has a beneficiary who is a United States person,

such beneficiary shall be treated as the grantor of such portion to the extent such beneficiary has made transfers of property by gift (directly or indirectly) to such foreign person. For purposes of the preceding sentence, any gift shall not be taken into account to the extent such gift would be excluded from taxable gifts under section 2503(b).

(2) REGULATIONS.—The Secretary shall prescribe such regulations as may be necessary to carry out the purposes of this subsection.

P.L. 104-188, §1904(d)(2) and (e), provides:

(2) EXCEPTIONS FOR CERTAIN TRUSTS.—The amendments made by this section shall not apply to any trust—

(A) which is treated as owned by the grantor under section 676 or 677 (other than subsection (a)(3) thereof) of the Internal Revenue Code of 1986, and

(B) which is in existence on September 19, 1995.

The preceding sentence shall not apply to the portion of any such trust attributable to any transfer to such trust after September 19, 1995.

(e) TRANSITIONAL RULE.—If—

(1) by reason of the amendments made by this section, any person other than a United States person ceases to be treated as the owner of a portion of a domestic trust, and

(2) before January 1, 1997, such trust becomes a foreign trust, or the assets of such trust are transferred to a foreign trust,

no tax shall be imposed by section 1491 of the Internal Revenue Code of 1986 by reason of such trust becoming a foreign trust or the assets of such trust being transferred to a foreign trust.

• 1990, Omnibus Budget Reconciliation Act of 1990 (P.L. 101-508)

P.L. 101-508, §11343(a):

Amended Code Sec. 672 by adding at the end thereof a new subsection (f). **Effective** for any trust created after 11-5-90, and any portion of a trust created on or before such date which is attributable to amounts contributed to the trust after such date.

[Sec. 673]

SEC. 673. REVERSIONARY INTERESTS.

[Sec. 673(a)]

(a) GENERAL RULE.—The grantor shall be treated as the owner of any portion of a trust in which he has a reversionary interest in either the corpus or the income therefrom, if, as of the inception of that portion of the trust, the value of such interest exceeds 5 percent of the value of such portion.

[Sec. 673(b)]

(b) REVERSIONARY INTEREST TAKING EFFECT AT DEATH OF MINOR LINEAL DESCENDANT BENEFICIARY.—In the case of any beneficiary who—

(1) is a lineal descendant of the grantor, and

(2) holds all of the present interests in any portion of a trust,

the grantor shall not be treated under subsection (a) as the owner of such portion solely by reason of a reversionary interest in such portion which takes effect upon the death of such beneficiary before such beneficiary attains age 21.

[Sec. 673(c)]

(c) SPECIAL RULE FOR DETERMINING VALUE OF REVERSIONARY INTEREST.—For purposes of subsection (a), the value of the grantor's reversionary interest shall be determined by assuming the maximum exercise of discretion in favor of the grantor.

[Sec. 673(d)]

(d) POSTPONEMENT OF DATE SPECIFIED FOR REACQUISITION.—Any postponement of the date specified for the reacquisition of possession or enjoyment of the reversionary interest shall be treated as a new transfer in trust commencing with the date on which the postponement is effective and terminating with the date prescribed by the postponement. However, income for any period shall not be included in the income of the grantor by reason of the preceding sentence if such income would not be so includible in the absence of such postponement.

Amendments

• **1988, Technical and Miscellaneous Revenue Act of 1988 (P.L. 100-647)**

P.L. 100-647, §1014(b):

Amended Code Sec. 673 by adding at the end thereof new subsections (c) and (d). **Effective** as if included in the provision of P.L. 99-514 to which it relates.

• **1986, Tax Reform Act of 1986 (P.L. 99-514)**

P.L. 99-514, §1402(a):

Amended Code Sec. 673. **Effective**, generally, with respect to transfers in trust made after 3-1-86. However, see Act Sec. 1402(c)(2), below.

P.L. 99-514, §1402(c)(2), provides:

(2) TRANSFERS PURSUANT TO PROPERTY SETTLEMENT AGREEMENT.—The amendments made by this section shall not apply to any transfer in trust made after March 1, 1986, pursuant to a binding property settlement agreement entered into on or before March 1, 1986, which required the taxpayer to establish a grantor trust and for the transfer of a specified sum of money or property to the trust by the taxpayer. This paragraph shall apply only to the extent of the amount required to be transferred under the agreement described in the preceding sentence.

Reproduced below is the text of Code Sec. 673 prior to amendment by P.L. 99-514.

SEC. 673. REVERSIONARY INTERESTS.

[Sec. 673(a)]

(a) GENERAL RULE.—The grantor shall be treated as the owner of any portion of a trust in which he has a reversionary interest in either the corpus or the income therefrom if, as of the inception of that portion of the trust, the interest will or may reasonably be expected to take effect in possession or enjoyment within 10 years commencing with the date of the transfer of that portion of the trust.

[Sec. 673(b)—Repealed]

Amendments

• **1969, Tax Reform Act of 1969 (P.L. 91-172)**

P.L. 91-172, §201(c):

Repealed Code Sec. 673(b). **Effective** for transfers in trust made after 4-22-69. Prior to repeal, Code Sec. 673(b) read as follows:

(b) EXCEPTION WHERE INCOME IS PAYABLE TO CHARITABLE BENEFICIARIES.—Subsection (a) shall not apply to the extent that the income of a portion of a trust in which the grantor has a reversionary interest is, under the terms of the trust, irrevocably payable for a period of at least 2 years (commencing with the date of the transfer) to a designated beneficiary, which beneficiary is of a type described in section 170 (b)(1)(A)(i), (ii), or (iii).

[Sec. 673(c)]

(c) REVERSIONARY INTEREST TAKING EFFECT AT DEATH OF INCOME BENEFICIARY.—The grantor shall not be treated under subsection (a) as the owner of any portion of a trust where his reversionary interest in such portion is not to take effect in possession or enjoyment until the death of the person or persons to whom the income therefrom is payable.

[Sec. 673(d)]

(d) POSTPONEMENT OF DATE SPECIFIED FOR REACQUISITION.—Any postponement of the date specified for the reacquisition of possession or enjoyment of the reversionary interest shall be treated as a new transfer in trust commencing with the date on which the postponement is effected and terminating with the date prescribed by the postponement. However, income for any period shall not be included in the income of the grantor by reason of the preceding sentence if such income would not be so includible in the absence of such postponement.

[Sec. 674]

SEC. 674. POWER TO CONTROL BENEFICIAL ENJOYMENT.

[Sec. 674(a)]

(a) GENERAL RULE.—The grantor shall be treated as the owner of any portion of a trust in respect of which the beneficial enjoyment of the corpus or the income therefrom is subject to a power of disposition, exercisable by the grantor or a nonadverse party, or both, without the approval or consent of any adverse party.

[Sec. 674(b)]

(b) EXCEPTIONS FOR CERTAIN POWERS.—Subsection (a) shall not apply to the following powers regardless of by whom held:

(1) POWER TO APPLY INCOME TO SUPPORT OF A DEPENDENT.—A power described in section 677(b) to the extent that the grantor would not be subject to tax under that section.

(2) POWER AFFECTING BENEFICIAL ENJOYMENT ONLY AFTER OCCURRENCE OF EVENT.—A power, the exercise of which can only affect the beneficial enjoyment of the income for a period commencing after the occurrence of an event such that a grantor would not be treated as the owner under section 673 if the power were a reversionary interest; but the grantor may be treated as the owner after the occurrence of the event unless the power is relinquished.

(3) POWER EXERCISABLE ONLY BY WILL.—A power exercisable only by will, other than a power in the grantor to appoint by will the income of the trust where the income is accumulated for such disposition by the grantor or may be so accumulated in the discretion of the grantor or a nonadverse party, or both, without the approval or consent of any adverse party.

(4) POWER TO ALLOCATE AMONG CHARITABLE BENEFICIARIES.—A power to determine the beneficial enjoyment of the corpus or the income therefrom if the corpus or income is irrevocably

payable for a purpose specified in section 170(c) (relating to definition of charitable contributions) or to an employee stock ownership plan (as defined in section 4975(e)(7)) in a qualified gratuitous transfer (as defined in section 664(g)(1)).

(5) POWER TO DISTRIBUTE CORPUS.—A power to distribute corpus either—

(A) to or for a beneficiary or beneficiaries or to or for a class of beneficiaries (whether or not income beneficiaries) provided that the power is limited by a reasonably definite standard which is set forth in the trust instrument; or

(B) to or for any current income beneficiary, provided that the distribution of corpus must be chargeable against the proportionate share of corpus held in trust for the payment of income to the beneficiary as if the corpus constituted a separate trust.

A power does not fall within the powers described in this paragraph if any person has a power to add to the beneficiary or beneficiaries or to a class of beneficiaries designated to receive the income or corpus, except where such action is to provide for after-born or after-adopted children.

(6) POWER TO WITHHOLD INCOME TEMPORARILY.—A power to distribute or apply income to or for any current income beneficiary or to accumulate the income for him, provided that any accumulated income must ultimately be payable—

(A) to the beneficiary from whom distribution or application is withheld, to his estate, or to his appointees (or persons named as alternate takers in default of appointment) provided that such beneficiary possesses a power of appointment which does not exclude from the class of possible appointees any person other than the beneficiary, his estate, his creditors, or the creditors of his estate, or

(B) on termination of the trust, or in conjunction with a distribution of corpus which is augmented by such accumulated income, to the current income beneficiaries in shares which have been irrevocably specified in the trust instrument.

Accumulated income shall be considered so payable although it is provided that if any beneficiary does not survive a date of distribution which could reasonably have been expected to occur within the beneficiary's lifetime, the share of the deceased beneficiary is to be paid to his appointees or to one or more designated alternate takers (other than the grantor or the grantor's estate) whose shares have been irrevocably specified. A power does not fall within the powers described in this paragraph if any person has a power to add to the beneficiary or beneficiaries or to a class of beneficiaries designated to receive the income or corpus except where such action is to provide for after-born or after-adopted children.

(7) POWER TO WITHHOLD INCOME DURING DISABILITY OF A BENEFICIARY.—A power exercisable only during—

(A) the existence of a legal disability of any current income beneficiary, or

(B) the period during which any income beneficiary shall be under the age of 21 years,

to distribute or apply income to or for such beneficiary or to accumulate and add the income to corpus. A power does not fall within the powers described in this paragraph if any person has a power to add to the beneficiary or beneficiaries or to a class of beneficiaries designated to receive the income or corpus, except where such action is to provide for after-born or after-adopted children.

(8) POWER TO ALLOCATE BETWEEN CORPUS AND INCOME.—A power to allocate receipts and disbursements as between corpus and income, even though expressed in broad language.

Amendments

• 1997, Taxpayer Relief Act of 1997 (P.L. 105-34)

P.L. 105-34, §1530(c)(6):

Amended Code Sec. 674(b)(4) by inserting before the period "or to an employee stock ownership plan (as defined in section 4975(e)(7)) in a qualified gratuitous transfer (as defined in section 664(g)(1))". **Effective** for transfers made by trusts to, or for the use of, an employee stock ownership plan after 8-5-97.

• 1986, Tax Reform Act of 1986 (P.L. 99-514)

P.L. 99-514, §1402(b)(1)(A)-(C):

Amended Code Sec. 674(b)(2) by striking out "the expiration of a period" and inserting in lieu thereof "the occurrence of an event", by striking out "the expiration of the period" and inserting in lieu thereof "the occurrence of the event", and by striking out "EXPIRATION OF 10-YEAR PERIOD" in the heading thereof and inserting in lieu thereof "OCCURRENCE OF EVENT". **Effective**, generally, with respect to transfers in trust made after 3-1-86. However, see Act Sec. 1402(c)(2) following Code Sec. 673.

[Sec. 674(c)]

(c) EXCEPTION FOR CERTAIN POWERS OF INDEPENDENT TRUSTEES.—Subsection (a) shall not apply to a power solely exercisable (without the approval or consent of any other person) by a trustee or trustees, none of whom is the grantor, and no more than half of whom are related or subordinate parties who are subservient to the wishes of the grantor—

(1) to distribute, apportion, or accumulate income to or for a beneficiary or beneficiaries, or to, for, or within a class of beneficiaries; or

(2) to pay out corpus to or for a beneficiary or beneficiaries or to or for a class of beneficiaries (whether or not income beneficiaries).

A power does not fall within the powers described in this subsection if any person has a power to add to the beneficiary or beneficiaries or to a class of beneficiaries designated to receive the income or corpus, except where such action is to provide for after-born or after-adopted children. For periods during which an individual is the spouse of the grantor (within the meaning of section 672(e)(2)), any reference in this subsection to the grantor shall be treated as including a reference to such individual.

Amendments

• 1988, Technical and Miscellaneous Revenue Act of 1988 (P.L. 100-647)

P.L. 100-647, §1014(a)(3):

Amended Code Sec. 674(c) by adding at the end thereof a new sentence. **Effective** as if included in the provision of P.L. 99-514 to which it relates.

[Sec. 674(d)]

(d) POWER TO ALLOCATE INCOME IF LIMITED BY A STANDARD.—Subsection (a) shall not apply to a power solely exercisable (without the approval or consent of any other person) by a trustee or trustees, none of whom is the grantor or spouse living with the grantor, to distribute, apportion, or accumulate income to or for a beneficiary or beneficiaries, or to, for, or within a class of beneficiaries, whether or not the conditions of paragraph (6) or (7) of subsection (b) are satisfied, if such power is limited by a reasonably definite external standard which is set forth in the trust instrument. A power does not fall within the powers described in this subsection if any person has a power to add to the beneficiary or beneficiaries or to a class of beneficiaries designated to receive the income or corpus except where such action is to provide for after-born or after-adopted children.

[Sec. 675]

SEC. 675. ADMINISTRATIVE POWERS.

The grantor shall be treated as the owner of any portion of a trust in respect of which—

(1) POWER TO DEAL FOR LESS THAN ADEQUATE AND FULL CONSIDERATION.—A power exercisable by the grantor or a nonadverse party, or both, without the approval or consent of any adverse party enables the grantor or any person to purchase, exchange, or otherwise deal with or dispose of the corpus or the income therefrom for less than an adequate consideration in money or money's worth.

(2) POWER TO BORROW WITHOUT ADEQUATE INTEREST OR SECURITY.—A power exercisable by the grantor or a nonadverse party, or both, enables the grantor to borrow the corpus or income, directly or indirectly, without adequate interest or without adequate security except where a trustee (other than the grantor) is authorized under a general lending power to make loans to any person without regard to interest or security.

(3) BORROWING OF THE TRUST FUNDS.—The grantor has directly or indirectly borrowed the corpus or income and has not completely repaid the loan, including any interest, before the beginning of the taxable year. The preceding sentence shall not apply to a loan which provides for adequate interest and adequate security, if such loan is made by a trustee other than the grantor and other than a related or subordinate trustee subservient to the grantor. For periods during which an individual is the spouse of the grantor (within the meaning of section 672(e)(2)), any reference in this paragraph to the grantor shall be treated as including a reference to such individual.

(4) GENERAL POWERS OF ADMINISTRATION.—A power of administration is exercisable in a nonfiduciary capacity by any person without the approval or consent of any person in a fiduciary capacity. For purposes of this paragraph, the term "power of administration" means any one or more of the following powers: (A) a power to vote or direct the voting of stock or other securities of a corporation in which the holdings of the grantor and the trust are significant from the viewpoint of voting control; (B) a power to control the investment of the trust funds either by directing investments or reinvestments, or by vetoing proposed investments or reinvestments, to the extent that the trust funds consist of stocks or securities of corporations in which the holdings of the grantor and the trust are significant from the viewpoint of voting control; or (C) a power to reacquire the trust corpus by substituting other property of an equivalent value.

Amendments

• 1988, Technical and Miscellaneous Revenue Act of 1988 (P.L. 100-647)

P.L. 100-647, §1014(a)(2):

Amended Code Sec. 675(3) by adding at the end thereof a new sentence. **Effective** as if included in the provision of P.L. 99-514 to which it relates.

[Sec. 676]

SEC. 676. POWER TO REVOKE.

[Sec. 676(a)]

(a) GENERAL RULE.—The grantor shall be treated as the owner of any portion of a trust, whether or not he is treated as such owner under any other provision of this part, where at any time the power to revest in the grantor title to such portion is exercisable by the grantor or a nonadverse party, or both.

[Sec. 676(b)]

(b) POWER AFFECTING BENEFICIAL ENJOYMENT ONLY AFTER OCCURRENCE OF EVENT.—Subsection (a) shall not apply to a power the exercise of which can only affect the beneficial enjoyment of the income for a period commencing after the occurrence of an event such that a grantor would not be treated as the owner under section 673 if the power were a reversionary interest. But the grantor may be treated as the owner after the occurrence of such event unless the power is relinquished.

Amendments

• 1986, Tax Reform Act of 1986 (P.L. 99-514)

P.L. 99-514, §1402(b)(2)(A)-(C):

Amended Code Sec. 676(b) by striking out "the expiration of a period" and inserting in lieu thereof "the occurrence of an event", by striking out "the expiration of such period" and inserting in lieu thereof "the occurrence of such event", and by striking out "EXPIRATION OF 10-YEAR PERIOD" in the heading thereof and inserting in lieu thereof "OCCURRENCE OF EVENT". **Effective**, generally, with respect to transfers in trust made after 3-1-86. However, see Act Sec. 1402(c)(2) following Code Sec. 673.

[Sec. 677]

SEC. 677. INCOME FOR BENEFIT OF GRANTOR.

[Sec. 677(a)]

(a) GENERAL RULE.—The grantor shall be treated as the owner of any portion of a trust, whether or not he is treated as such owner under section 674, whose income without the approval or consent of any adverse party is, or, in the discretion of the grantor or a nonadverse party, or both, may be—

(1) distributed to the grantor or the grantor's spouse;

(2) held or accumulated for future distribution to the grantor or the grantor's spouse; or

(3) applied to the payment of premiums on policies of insurance on the life of the grantor or the grantor's spouse (except policies of insurance irrevocably payable for a purpose specified in section 170(c) (relating to definition of charitable contributions)).

This subsection shall not apply to a power the exercise of which can only affect the beneficial enjoyment of the income for a period commencing after the occurrence of an event such that the grantor would not be treated as the owner under section 673 if the power were a reversionary interest; but the grantor may be treated as the owner after the occurrence of the event unless the power is relinquished.

Amendments

• 1986, Tax Reform Act of 1986 (P.L. 99-514)

P.L. 99-514, §1402(b)(3)(A)-(B):

Amended Code Sec. 677(a) by striking out "the expiration of a period" and inserting in lieu thereof "the occurrence of an event", and by striking out "the expiration of the period" and inserting in lieu thereof "the occurrence of the event". **Effective**, generally, with respect to transfers in trust made after 3-1-86. However, see Act Sec. 1402(c)(2) following Code Sec. 673.

• 1969, Tax Reform Act of 1969 (P.L. 91-172)

P.L. 91-172, §332(a)(1):

Amended Code Sec. 677(a)(1), (2) and (3) by striking out "the grantor" each place where it appears and inserting in lieu thereof "the grantor or the grantor's spouse". **Effective** with respect to property transferred in trust after 10-9-69.

[Sec. 677(b)]

(b) OBLIGATIONS OF SUPPORT.—Income of a trust shall not be considered taxable to the grantor under subsection (a) or any other provision of this chapter merely because such income in the discretion of another person, the trustee, or the grantor acting as trustee or co-trustee, may be applied or distributed for the support or maintenance of a beneficiary (other than the grantor's spouse) whom the grantor is legally obligated to support or maintain, except to the extent that such income is so applied or distributed. In cases where the amounts so applied or distributed are paid out of corpus or out of other than income for the taxable year, such amounts shall be considered to be an amount paid or credited within the meaning of paragraph (2) of section 661(a) and shall be taxed to the grantor under section 662.

Amendments

• 1969, Tax Reform Act of 1969 (P.L. 91-172)

P.L. 91-172, §332(a)(2):

Amended Code Sec. 677(b) by striking out "beneficiary" and inserting in lieu thereof "beneficiary (other than the grantor's spouse)". **Effective** with respect to property transferred in trust after 10-9-69.

[Sec. 678]

SEC. 678. PERSON OTHER THAN GRANTOR TREATED AS SUBSTANTIAL OWNER.

[Sec. 678(a)]

(a) GENERAL RULE.—A person other than the grantor shall be treated as the owner of any portion of a trust with respect to which:

(1) such person has a power exercisable solely by himself to vest the corpus or the income therefrom in himself, or

(2) such person has previously partially released or otherwise modified such a power and after the release or modification retains such control as would, within the principles of sections 671 to 677, inclusive, subject a grantor of a trust to treatment as the owner thereof.

[Sec. 678(b)]

(b) EXCEPTION WHERE GRANTOR IS TAXABLE.—Subsection (a) shall not apply with respect to a power over income, as originally granted or thereafter modified, if the grantor of the trust or a transferor (to whom section 679 applies) is otherwise treated as the owner under the provisions of this subpart other than this section.

Amendments

• 1976, Tax Reform Act of 1976 (P.L. 94-455)

P.L. 94-455, §1013(b):

Amended Code Sec. 678(b). **Effective** for tax years ending after 12-31-75, but only in the case of (A) foreign trusts created after 5-21-74, and (B) transfers of property to foreign trusts after 5-21-74. Prior to amendment, Code Sec. 678(b) read as follows:

(b) EXCEPTION WHERE GRANTOR IS TAXABLE.—Subsection (a) shall not apply with respect to a power over income, as originally granted or thereafter modified, if the grantor of the trust is otherwise treated as the owner under sections 671 to 677, inclusive.

[Sec. 678(c)]

(c) OBLIGATIONS OF SUPPORT.—Subsection (a) shall not apply to a power which enables such person, in the capacity of trustee or co-trustee, merely to apply the income of the trust to the support or maintenance of a person whom the holder of the power is obligated to support or maintain except to the extent that such income is so applied. In cases where the amounts so applied or distributed are paid out of corpus or out of other than income of the taxable year, such amounts shall be considered to be an amount paid or credited within the meaning of paragraph (2) of section 661(a) and shall be taxed to the holder of the power under section 662.

[Sec. 678(d)]

(d) EFFECT OF RENUNCIATION OR DISCLAIMER.—Subsection (a) shall not apply with respect to a power which has been renounced or disclaimed within a reasonable time after the holder of the power first became aware of its existence.

[Sec. 678(e)]

(e) CROSS REFERENCE.—

For provision under which beneficiary of trust is treated as owner of the portion of the trust which consists of stock in an S corporation, see section 1361(d).

Amendments

• 2000, Community Renewal Tax Relief Act of 2000 (P.L. 106-554)

P.L. 106-554, §319(8)(A):

Amended Code Sec. 678(e) by striking "an electing small business corporation" and inserting "an S corporation". **Effective** on 12-21-2000.

• 1983, Technical Corrections Act of 1982 (P.L. 97-448)

P.L. 97-448, §102(i)(2):

Added Code Sec. 678(e). **Effective** as if included in the provision of P.L. 97-34 to which it relates.

[Sec. 679]

SEC. 679. FOREIGN TRUSTS HAVING ONE OR MORE UNITED STATES BENEFICIARIES.

[Sec. 679(a)]

(a) TRANSFEROR TREATED AS OWNER.—

(1) IN GENERAL.—A United States person who directly or indirectly transfers property to a foreign trust (other than a trust described in section 6048(a)(3)(B)(ii)) shall be treated as the owner for his taxable year of the portion of such trust attributable to such property if for such year there is a United States beneficiary of any portion of such trust.

(2) EXCEPTIONS.—Paragraph (1) shall not apply—

(A) TRANSFERS BY REASON OF DEATH.—To any transfer by reason of the death of the transferor.

(B) TRANSFERS AT FAIR MARKET VALUE.—To any transfer of property to a trust in exchange for consideration of at least the fair market value of the transferred property. For purposes of the preceding sentence, consideration other than cash shall be taken into account at its fair market value.

(3) CERTAIN OBLIGATIONS NOT TAKEN INTO ACCOUNT UNDER FAIR MARKET VALUE EXCEPTION.—

(A) IN GENERAL.—In determining whether paragraph (2)(B) applies to any transfer by a person described in clause (ii) or (iii) of subparagraph (C), there shall not be taken into account—

(i) except as provided in regulations, any obligation of a person described in subparagraph (C), and

(ii) to the extent provided in regulations, any obligation which is guaranteed by a person described in subparagraph (C).

(B) TREATMENT OF PRINCIPAL PAYMENTS ON OBLIGATION.—Principal payments by the trust on any obligation referred to in subparagraph (A) shall be taken into account on and after the date of the payment in determining the portion of the trust attributable to the property transferred.

(C) PERSONS DESCRIBED.—The persons described in this subparagraph are—

(i) the trust,

(ii) any grantor, owner, or beneficiary of the trust, and

(iii) any person who is related (within the meaning of section 643(i)(2)(B)) to any grantor, owner, or beneficiary of the trust.

(4) SPECIAL RULES APPLICABLE TO FOREIGN GRANTOR WHO LATER BECOMES A UNITED STATES PERSON.—

(A) IN GENERAL.—If a nonresident alien individual has a residency starting date within 5 years after directly or indirectly transferring property to a foreign trust, this section and section 6048 shall be applied as if such individual transferred to such trust on the residency starting date an amount equal to the portion of such trust attributable to the property transferred by such individual to such trust in such transfer.

(B) TREATMENT OF UNDISTRIBUTED INCOME.—For purposes of this section, undistributed net income for periods before such individual's residency starting date shall be taken into account in determining the portion of the trust which is attributable to property transferred by such individual to such trust but shall not otherwise be taken into account.

(C) RESIDENCY STARTING DATE.—For purposes of this paragraph, an individual's residency starting date is the residency starting date determined under section 7701(b)(2)(A).

(5) OUTBOUND TRUST MIGRATIONS.—If—

(A) an individual who is a citizen or resident of the United States transferred property to a trust which was not a foreign trust, and

(B) such trust becomes a foreign trust while such individual is alive,

then this section and section 6048 shall be applied as if such individual transferred to such trust on the date such trust becomes a foreign trust an amount equal to the portion of such trust attributable to the property previously transferred by such individual to such trust. A rule similar to the rule of paragraph (4)(B) shall apply for purposes of this paragraph.

Amendments

• 1997, Taxpayer Relief Act of 1997 (P.L. 105-34)

P.L. 105-34, §1601(i)(2):

Amended Code Sec. 679(a)(3)(C)(ii)-(iii) by inserting ", owner," after "grantor". **Effective** as if included in the provision of P.L. 104-188 to which it relates [**effective** for transfers of property after 2-6-95.—CCH].

• 1996, Small Business Job Protection Act of 1996 (P.L. 104-188)

P.L. 104-188, §1903(a)(1):

Amended Code Sec. 679(a)(2) by striking subparagraph (B) and inserting a new subparagraph (B). **Effective** for transfers of property after 2-6-95. Prior to amendment, Code Sec. 679(a)(2)(B) read as follows:

(B) TRANSFERS WHERE GAIN IS RECOGNIZED TO TRANSFEROR.—To any sale or exchange of the property at its fair market value in a transaction in which all of the gain to the transferor is realized at the time of the transfer and is recognized either at such time or is returned as provided in section 453.

P.L. 104-188, §1903(a)(2):

Amended Code Sec. 679(a) by adding at the end a new paragraph (3). **Effective** for transfers of property after 2-6-95.

P.L. 104-188, §1903(b) (as amended by P.L. 105-206, §6018(g)):

Amended Code Sec. 679(a)(1) by striking "section 404(a)(4) Or [sic] 404A" and inserting "section 6048(a)(3)(B)(ii)". **Effective** for transfers of property after 2-6-95.

P.L. 104-188, §1903(c):

Amended Code Sec. 679(a) by adding at the end new paragraphs (4) and (5). **Effective** for transfers of property after 2-6-95.

• 1980 (P.L. 96-603)

P.L. 96-603, §2(b):

Amended Code Sec. 679(a)(1) by adding "Or [sic] 404A" following the phrase "in section 404(a)(4)". **Effective** with respect to employer contributions or accruals for tax years beginning after 1979. However, see the historical comment for P.L. 96-603 under Code Sec. 404A(h) for details of elections permitting retroactive application of this amendment with respect to foreign subsidiaries and permitting allowance of prior deductions in case of certain funded branch plans.

[Sec. 679(b)]

(b) TRUSTS ACQUIRING UNITED STATES BENEFICIARIES.—If—

(1) subsection (a) applies to a trust for the transferor's taxable year, and

(2) subsection (a) would have applied to the trust for his immediately preceding taxable year but for the fact that for such preceding taxable year there was no United States beneficiary for any portion of the trust,

then, for purposes of this subtitle, the transferor shall be treated as having income for the taxable year (in addition to his other income for such year) equal to the undistributed net income (at the close of such immediately preceding taxable year) attributable to the portion of the trust referred to in subsection (a).

[Sec. 679(c)]

(c) TRUSTS TREATED AS HAVING A UNITED STATES BENEFICIARY.—

(1) IN GENERAL.—For purposes of this section, a trust shall be treated as having a United States beneficiary for the taxable year unless—

(A) under the terms of the trust, no part of the income or corpus of the trust may be paid or accumulated during the taxable year to or for the benefit of a United States person, and

(B) if the trust were terminated at any time during the taxable year, no part of the income or corpus of such trust could be paid to or for the benefit of a United States person.

For purposes of subparagraph (A), an amount shall be treated as accumulated for the benefit of a United States person even if the United States person's interest in the trust is contingent on a future event.

(2) ATTRIBUTION OF OWNERSHIP.—For purposes of paragraph (1), an amount shall be treated as paid or accumulated to or for the benefit of a United States person if such amount is paid to or accumulated for a foreign corporation, foreign partnership, or foreign trust or estate, and—

(A) in the case of a foreign corporation, such corporation is a controlled foreign corporation (as defined in section 957(a)),

(B) in the case of a foreign partnership, a United States person is a partner of such partnership, or

(C) in the case of a foreign trust or estate, such trust or estate has a United States beneficiary (within the meaning of paragraph (1)).

(3) CERTAIN UNITED STATES BENEFICIARIES DISREGARDED.—A beneficiary shall not be treated as a United States person in applying this section with respect to any transfer of property to foreign trust if such beneficiary first became a United States person more than 5 years after the date of such transfer.

(4) SPECIAL RULE IN CASE OF DISCRETION TO IDENTIFY BENEFICIARIES.—For purposes of paragraph (1)(A), if any person has the discretion (by authority given in the trust agreement, by power of appointment, or otherwise) of making a distribution from the trust to, or for the benefit of, any person, such trust shall be treated as having a beneficiary who is a United States person unless—

(A) the terms of the trust specifically identify the class of persons to whom such distributions may be made, and

(B) none of those persons are United States persons during the taxable year.

(5) CERTAIN AGREEMENTS AND UNDERSTANDINGS TREATED AS TERMS OF THE TRUST.—For purposes of paragraph (1)(A), if any United States person who directly or indirectly transfers property to the trust is directly or indirectly involved in any agreement or understanding (whether written, oral, or otherwise) that may result in the income or corpus of the trust being paid or accumulated to or for the benefit of a United States person, such agreement or understanding shall be treated as a term of the trust.

(6) UNCOMPENSATED USE OF TRUST PROPERTY TREATED AS A PAYMENT.—For purposes of this subsection, a loan of cash or marketable securities (or the use of any other trust property) directly or indirectly to or by any United States person (whether or not a beneficiary under the terms of the trust) shall be treated as paid or accumulated for the benefit of a United States person. The preceding sentence shall not apply to the extent that the United States person repays the loan at a market rate of interest (or pays the fair market value of the use of such property) within a reasonable period of time.

Amendments

• 2010, Hiring Incentives to Restore Employment Act (P.L. 111-147)

P.L. 111-147, §531(a):

Amended Code Sec. 679(c)(1) by adding at the end a new sentence. **Effective** 3-18-2010.

P.L. 111-147, §531(b):

Amended Code Sec. 679(c) by adding at the end a new paragraph (4). **Effective** 3-18-2010.

P.L. 111-147, §531(c):

Amended Code Sec. 679(c), as amended by Act Sec. 531(b), by adding at the end a new paragraph (5). **Effective** 3-18-2010.

P.L. 111-147, §533(c):

Amended Code Sec. 679(c), as amended by this Act, by adding at the end a new paragraph (6). **Effective** for loans made, and uses of property, after 3-18-2010.

• 1996, Small Business Job Protection Act of 1996 (P.L. 104-188)

P.L. 104-188, §1903(d):

Amended Code Sec. 679(c) by adding at the end a new paragraph (3). **Effective** for transfers of property after 2-6-95.

P.L. 104-188, §1903(e):

Amended Code Sec. 679(c)(2)(A). **Effective** for transfers of property after 2-6-95. Prior to amendment, Code Sec. 679(c)(2)(A) read as follows:

(A) in the case of a foreign corporation, more than 50 percent of the total combined voting power of all classes of stock entitled to vote of such corporation is owned (within the meaning of section 958(a)) or is considered to be owned (within the meaning of section 958(b)) by United States shareholders (as defined in section 951(b)),

• 1976, Tax Reform Act of 1976 (P.L. 94-455)

P.L. 94-455, §1013(a):

Added Code Sec. 679. **Effective** for tax years ending after 12-31-75, but only in the case of (A) foreign trusts created after 5-21-74, and (B) transfers of property to foreign trusts after 5-21-74.

[Sec. 679(d)]

(d) PRESUMPTION THAT FOREIGN TRUST HAS UNITED STATES BENEFICIARY.—If a United States person directly or indirectly transfers property to a foreign trust (other than a trust described in section 6048(a)(3)(B)(ii)), the Secretary may treat such trust as having a United States beneficiary for purposes of applying this section to such transfer unless such person—

(1) submits such information to the Secretary as the Secretary may require with respect to such transfer, and

(2) demonstrates to the satisfaction of the Secretary that such trust satisfies the requirements of subparagraphs (A) and (B) of subsection (c)(1).

Amendments

• 2010, Hiring Incentives to Restore Employment Act (P.L. 111-147)

P.L. 111-147, §532(a):

Amended Code Sec. 679 by redesignating subsection (d) as subsection (e) and inserting after subsection (c) a new subsection (d). **Effective** for transfers of property after 3-18-2010.

[Sec. 679(e)]

(e) REGULATIONS.—The Secretary shall prescribe such regulations as may be necessary or appropriate to carry out the purposes of this section.

Amendments

• 2010, Hiring Incentives to Restore Employment Act (P.L. 111-147)

P.L. 111-147, §532(a):

Amended Code Sec. 679 by redesignating subsection (d) as subsection (e). **Effective** for transfers of property after 3-18-2010.

• 1996, Small Business Job Protection Act of 1996 (P.L. 104-188)

P.L. 104-188, §1903(f):

Amended Code Sec. 679 by adding at the end a new subsection (d). **Effective** for transfers of property after 2-6-95.

Subpart F—Miscellaneous

[Sec. 681]

SEC. 681. LIMITATION ON CHARITABLE DEDUCTION.

[Sec. 681(a)]

(a) TRADE OR BUSINESS INCOME.—In computing the deduction allowable under section 642(c) to a trust, no amount otherwise allowable under section 642(c) as a deduction shall be allowed as a deduction with respect to income of the taxable year which is allocable to its unrelated business income for such year. For purposes of the preceding sentence, the term "unrelated business income" means an amount equal to the amount which, if such trust were exempt from tax under section 501(a) by reason of section 501(c)(3), would be computed as its unrelated business taxable income under section 512 (relating to income derived from certain business activities and from certain property acquired with borrowed funds).

Amendments

• 1969, Tax Reform Act of 1969 (P.L. 91-172)

P.L. 91-172, §121(d)(2):

Amended Code Sec. 681(a) by changing "certain leases" to "certain property acquired with borrowed funds." **Effective** 1-1-70.

[Sec. 681(b)]

(b) CROSS REFERENCE.—

For disallowance of certain charitable, etc., deductions otherwise allowable under section 642(c), see sections 508(d) and 4948(c)(4).

Amendments

• 1969, Tax Reform Act of 1969 (P.L. 91-172)

P.L. 91-172, § 101(j)(18)-(19):

Repealed Code Sec. 681(b) and redesignated former Code Sec. 681(d) as Code Sec. 681(b). **Effective** 1-1-70. Prior to repeal, Code Sec. 681(b) read as follows:

(b) OPERATIONS OF TRUSTS.—

(1) LIMITATION ON CHARITABLE, ETC., DEDUCTION.—The amount otherwise allowable under section 642(c) as a deduction shall not exceed 20 percent of the taxable income of the trust (computed without the benefit of section 642(c) but with the benefit of section 170(b)(1)(A)) if the trust has engaged in a prohibited transaction, as defined in paragraph (2).

(2) PROHIBITED TRANSACTIONS.—For purposes of this subsection, the term "prohibited transaction" means any transaction after July 1, 1950, in which any trust while holding income or corpus which has been permanently set aside or is to be used exclusively for charitable or other purposes described in section 642(c)—

(A) lends any part of such income or corpus, without receipt of adequate security and a reasonable rate of interest, to;

(B) pays any compensation from such income or corpus, in excess of a reasonable allowance for salaries or other compensation for personal services actually rendered, to;

(C) makes any part of its services available on a preferential basis to;

(D) uses such income or corpus to make any substantial purchase of securities or any other property, for more than an adequate consideration in money or money's worth, from;

(E) sells any substantial part of the securities or other property comprising such income or corpus, for less than an adequate consideration in money or money's worth, to; or

(F) engages in any other transaction which results in a substantial diversion of such income or corpus to;

the creator of such trust; any person who has made a substantial contribution to such trust; a member of a family (as defined in section 267(c)(4)) of an individual who is the creator of the trust or who has made a substantial contribution to the trust; or a corporation controlled by any such creator or person through the ownership, directly or indirectly, of 50 percent or more of the total combined voting power of all classes of stock entitled to vote or 50 percent or more of the total value of shares of all classes of stock of the corporation.

(3) TAXABLE YEARS AFFECTED.—The amount otherwise allowable under section 642(c) as a deduction shall be limited as provided in paragraph (1) only for taxable years after the taxable year during which the trust is notified by the Secretary that it has engaged in such transaction, unless such trust entered into such prohibited transaction with the purpose of diverting such corpus or income from the purposes described in section 642(c), and such transaction involved a substantial part of such corpus or income.

(4) FUTURE CHARITABLE, ETC., DEDUCTIONS OF TRUST DENIED DEDUCTION UNDER PARAGRAPH (3).—If the deduction of any trust under section 642(c) has been limited as provided in this subsection, such trust, with respect to any taxable year following the taxable year in which notice is received of limitation of deduction under section 642(c), may, under regulations prescribed by the Secretary or his delegate, file claim for the allowance of the unlimited deduction under section 642(c), and if the Secretary, pursuant to such regulations, is satisfied that such trust will not knowingly again engage in a prohibited transaction, the limitation provided in paragraph (1) shall not apply with respect to taxable years after the year in which such claim is filed.

(5) DISALLOWANCE OF CERTAIN CHARITABLE, ETC., DEDUCTIONS.—No gift or bequest for religious, charitable, scientific, literary, or educational purposes (including the encouragement of art and the prevention of cruelty to children or animals), otherwise allowable as a deduction under section 170, 545 (b) (2), 642 (c), 2055, 2106 (a) (2), or 2522, shall be allowed as a deduction if made in trust and, in the taxable year of the trust in which the gift or bequest is made, the deduction allowed the trust under section 642 (c) is limited by paragraph (1). With respect to any taxable year of a trust in which such deduction has been so limited by reason of entering into a prohibited transaction with the purpose of diverting such corpus or income from the purposes described in section 642(c), and such transaction involved a substantial part of such income or corpus, and which taxable year is the same, or before the, taxable year of the trust in which such prohibited transaction occurred, such deduction shall be disallowed the donor only if such donor or (if such donor is an individual) any member of his family (as defined in section 267(c) (4)) was a party to such prohibited transaction.

(6) DEFINITION.—For purposes of this subsection, the term "gift or bequest" means any gift, contribution, bequest, devise, or legacy, or any transfer without adequate consideration.

[Sec. 681(c)—Repealed]

Amendments

• 1969, Tax Reform Act of 1969 (P.L. 91-172)

P.L. 91-172, § 101(j)(18):

Repealed Code Sec. 681(c). **Effective** 1-1-70. Prior to repeal, Code Sec. 681(c) read as follows:

(c) ACCUMULATED INCOME.—If the amounts permanently set aside, or to be used exclusively for the charitable and other purposes described in section 642(c) during the taxable year or any prior taxable year and not actually paid out by the end of the taxable year—

(1) are unreasonable in amount or duration in order to carry out such purposes of the trust;

(2) are used to a substantial degree for purposes other than those prescribed in section 642(c); or

(3) are invested in such a manner as to jeopardize the interests of the religious, charitable, scientific, etc., beneficiaries,

the amount otherwise allowable under section 642(c) as a deduction shall be limited to the amount actually paid out during the taxable year and shall not exceed 20 percent of the taxable income of the trust (computed without the benefit of section 642(c) but with the benefit of section 170(b)(1)(A)). Paragraph (1) shall not apply to income attributable to property of a decedent dying before January 1, 1951, which is transferred under his will to a trust created by such will. Paragraph (1) shall not apply to income attributable to property transferred to a trust before January 1, 1951, by the creator of such trust, if such trust was irrevocable on such date and if such income is required to be accumulated pursuant to the mandatory terms (as in effect on such date and at all times thereafter) of the instrument creating such trust. In the case of a trust created by the will of a decedent dying on or after January 1, 1951, if income is required to be accumulated pursuant to the mandatory terms of the will creating the trust, paragraph (1) shall apply only to income accumulated during a taxable year of the trust beginning more than 21 years after the date of death of the last life in being designated in the trust instrument.

• 1968 (P.L. 90-630)

P.L. 90-630, § 6(b):

Amended Code Sec. 681(c) by adding the next to last sentence therein. **Effective** with respect to tax years beginning after 12-31-53, and ending after 8-16-54. For purposes of Section 162(g)(4) of the Internal Revenue Code of 1939, provisions having the same effect as the amendment shall be treated as included in such 1939 section, effective with respect to tax years beginning after 12-31-50.

[Sec. 682]

SEC. 682. INCOME OF AN ESTATE OR TRUST IN CASE OF DIVORCE, ETC.

[Sec. 682(a)]

(a) INCLUSION IN GROSS INCOME OF WIFE.—There shall be included in the gross income of a wife who is divorced or legally separated under a decree of divorce or of separate maintenance (or who is separated from her husband under a written separation agreement) the amount of the income of any trust which such wife is entitled to receive and which, except for this section, would be includible in the gross income of her husband, and such amount shall not, despite any other provision of this subtitle, be includible in the gross income of such husband. This subsection shall not apply to that part of any such income of the trust which the terms of the decree, written separation agreement, or trust instrument fix, in terms of an amount of money or a portion of such income, as a sum which is payable for the support of minor children of such husband. In case such income is less than the amount specified in the decree, agreement, or instrument, for the purpose of applying the preceding sentence, such income, to the extent of such sum payable for such support, shall be considered a payment for such support.

[Sec. 682(b)]

(b) WIFE CONSIDERED A BENEFICIARY.—For purposes of computing the taxable income of the estate or trust and the taxable income of a wife to whom subsection (a) applies, such wife shall be considered as the beneficiary specified in this part.

Amendments

• 1984, Deficit Reduction Act of 1984 (P.L. 98-369)

P.L. 98-369, §422(d)(2):

Amended Code Sec. 682(b) by striking out "or section 71" following "to whom subsection (a)" and by striking out the last sentence. **Effective** with respect to divorce or separation instruments (as defined in Code Sec. 71(b)(2), as amended by Act Sec. 422) executed after 12-31-84. The amendment also applies to any divorce or separation instrument (as so defined) executed before 1-1-85, but modified on or after such date if the modification expressly provides that the amendment made by this section shall also apply to such modification. Prior to amendment, the last sentence of Code Sec. 682(b) read as follows:

A periodic payment under section 71 to any portion of which this part applies shall be included in the gross income of the beneficiary in the taxable year in which under this part such portion is required to be included.

[Sec. 682(c)]

(c) CROSS REFERENCE.—

For definitions of "husband" and "wife", as used in this section, see section 7701(a)(17).

[Sec. 683]

SEC. 683. USE OF TRUST AS AN EXCHANGE FUND.

[Sec. 683(a)]

(a) GENERAL RULE.—Except as provided in subsection (b), if property is transferred to a trust in exchange for an interest in other trust property and if the trust would be an investment company (within the meaning of section 351) if it were a corporation, then gain shall be recognized to the transferor.

Amendments

• 1976, Tax Reform Act of 1976 (P.L. 94-455)

P.L. 94-455, §2131(e)(1):

Amended Code Sec. 683(a). **Effective** 4-8-76, in tax years ending on or after such date. Prior to amendment, Code Sec. 683(a) read as follows:

(a) GENERAL RULE.—This part shall apply only to taxable years beginning after December 31, 1953, and ending after the date of the enactment of this title.

[Sec. 683(b)]

(b) EXCEPTION FOR POOLED INCOME FUNDS.—Subsection (a) shall not apply to any transfer to a pooled income fund (within the meaning of section 642(c)(5)).

Amendments

• 1976, Tax Reform Act of 1976 (P.L. 94-455)

P.L. 94-455, §2131(e)(1):

Amended Code Sec. 683(b). **Effective** 4-8-76, in tax years ending on or after such date. Prior to amendment, Code Sec. 683(b) read as follows:

(b) EXCEPTIONS.—In the case of any beneficiary of an estate or trust—

(1) this part shall not apply to any amount paid, credited, or to be distributed by the estate or trust in any taxable year of such estate or trust to which this part does not apply, and

(2) the Internal Revenue Code of 1939 shall apply for purposes of determining the amount includible in the gross income of the beneficiary.

To the extent that any amount paid, credited, or to be distributed by an estate or trust in the first taxable year of such estate or trust to which this part applies would be treated, if the Internal Revenue Code of 1939 were applicable, as paid, credited, or to be distributed on the last day of the preceding taxable year, such amount shall not be taken into account for purposes of this part but shall be taken into account as provided in the Internal Revenue Code of 1939.

»»→ Caution: The heading for Code Sec. 684, below, is subject to the sunset provision of the Economic Growth and Tax Relief Reconciliation Act of 2001 (P.L. 107-16), §901. Absent Congressional action, the changes made to this provision by P.L. 107-16, or that take effect as if included in P.L. 107-16, do not apply after December 31, 2010. For more information about the sunset provision, see page XXI of the Preface to this publication and P.L. 107-16, §901, in the amendment notes. See the amendments notes for a history of amendments to this section and the effective date of each change.

[Sec. 684]

SEC. 684. RECOGNITION OF GAIN ON CERTAIN TRANSFERS TO CERTAIN FOREIGN TRUSTS AND ESTATES AND NONRESIDENT ALIENS.

»»→ Caution: Code Sec. 684(a), below, is subject to the sunset provision of the Economic Growth and Tax Relief Reconciliation Act of 2001 (P.L. 107-16), §901. Absent Congressional action, the changes made to this provision by P.L. 107-16, or that take effect as if included in P.L. 107-16, do not apply after December 31, 2010. For more information about the sunset provision, see page XXI of the Preface to this publication and P.L. 107-16, §901, in the amendment notes. See the amendments notes for a history of amendments to this section and the effective date of each change.

[Sec. 684(a)]

(a) IN GENERAL.—Except as provided in regulations, in the case of any transfer of property by a United States person to a foreign estate or trust or to a nonresident alien, for purposes of this subtitle, such transfer shall be treated as a sale or exchange for an amount equal to the fair market value of the property transferred, and the transferor shall recognize as gain the excess of—

(1) the fair market value of the property so transferred, over

(2) the adjusted basis (for purposes of determining gain) of such property in the hands of the transferor.

Amendments

• 2001, Economic Growth and Tax Relief Reconciliation Act of 2001 (P.L. 107-16)

P.L. 107-16, §542(e)(1)(A):

Amended Code Sec. 684(a) by inserting "or to a nonresident alien" after "or trust". **Effective** for transfers after 12-31-2009.

P.L. 107-16, §542(e)(1)(C):

Amended the section heading for Code Sec. 684 by inserting "**AND NONRESIDENT ALIENS**" after "**ESTATES**". **Effective** for transfers after 12-31-2009.

P.L. 107-16, §901(a)-(b), provides:

SEC. 901. SUNSET OF PROVISIONS OF ACT.

(a) IN GENERAL.—All provisions of, and amendments made by, this Act shall not apply—

(1) to taxable, plan, or limitation years beginning after December 31, 2010, or

(2) in the case of title V, to estates of decedents dying, gifts made, or generation skipping transfers, after December 31, 2010.

(b) APPLICATION OF CERTAIN LAWS.—The Internal Revenue Code of 1986 and the Employee Retirement Income Security Act of 1974 shall be applied and administered to years, estates, gifts, and transfers described in subsection (a) as if the provisions and amendments described in subsection (a) had never been enacted.

»»→ Caution: Code Sec. 684(b), below, is subject to the sunset provision of the Economic Growth and Tax Relief Reconciliation Act of 2001 (P.L. 107-16), §901. Absent Congressional action, the changes made to this provision by P.L. 107-16, or that take effect as if included in P.L. 107-16, do not apply after December 31, 2010. For more information about the sunset provision, see page XXI of the Preface to this publication and P.L. 107-16, §901, in the amendment notes. See the amendments notes for a history of amendments to this section and the effective date of each change.

[Sec. 684(b)]

(b) EXCEPTIONS.—

(1) TRANSFERS TO CERTAIN TRUSTS.—Subsection (a) shall not apply to a transfer to a trust by a United States person to the extent that any United States person is treated as the owner of such trust under section 671.

(2) LIFETIME TRANSFERS TO NONRESIDENT ALIENS.—Subsection (a) shall not apply to a lifetime transfer to a nonresident alien.

Amendments

• 2001, Economic Growth and Tax Relief Reconciliation Act of 2001 (P.L. 107-16)

P.L. 107-16, §542(e)(1)(B):

Amended Code Sec. 684(b). **Effective** for transfers after 12-31-2009. Prior to amendment, Code Sec. 684(b) read as follows:

(b) EXCEPTION.—Subsection (a) shall not apply to a transfer to a trust by a United States person to the extent that any person is treated as the owner of such trust under section 671.

P.L. 107-16, §901(a)-(b), provides:

SEC. 901. SUNSET OF PROVISIONS OF ACT.

(a) IN GENERAL.—All provisions of, and amendments made by, this Act shall not apply—

(1) to taxable, plan, or limitation years beginning after December 31, 2010, or

(2) in the case of title V, to estates of decedents dying, gifts made, or generation skipping transfers, after December 31, 2010.

(b) APPLICATION OF CERTAIN LAWS.—The Internal Revenue Code of 1986 and the Employee Retirement Income Security Act of 1974 shall be applied and administered to years, estates, gifts, and transfers described in subsection (a) as if the provisions and amendments described in subsection (a) had never been enacted.

[Sec. 684(c)]

(c) TREATMENT OF TRUSTS WHICH BECOME FOREIGN TRUSTS.—If a trust which is not a foreign trust becomes a foreign trust, such trust shall be treated for purposes of this section as having transferred, immediately before becoming a foreign trust, all of its assets to a foreign trust.

Amendments

• 1997, Taxpayer Relief Act of 1997 (P.L. 105-34)

P.L. 105-34, §1131(b):

Amended subpart F of part I of subchapter J of chapter 1 by adding at the end new section 684. **Effective** 8-5-97.

[Sec. 685]

SEC. 685. TREATMENT OF FUNERAL TRUSTS.

[Sec. 685(a)]

(a) IN GENERAL.—In the case of a qualified funeral trust—

(1) subparts B, C, D, and E shall not apply, and

(2) no deduction shall be allowed by section 642(b).

[Sec. 685(b)]

(b) QUALIFIED FUNERAL TRUST.—For purposes of this subsection, the term "qualified funeral trust" means any trust (other than a foreign trust) if—

(1) the trust arises as a result of a contract with a person engaged in the trade or business of providing funeral or burial services or property necessary to provide such services,

(2) the sole purpose of the trust is to hold, invest, and reinvest funds in the trust and to use such funds solely to make payments for such services or property for the benefit of the beneficiaries of the trust,

(3) the only beneficiaries of such trust are individuals with respect to whom such services or property are to be provided at their death under contracts described in paragraph (1),

(4) the only contributions to the trust are contributions by or for the benefit of such beneficiaries,

(5) the trustee elects the application of this subsection, and

(6) the trust would (but for the election described in paragraph (5)) be treated as owned under subpart E by the purchasers of the contracts described in paragraph (1).

A trust shall not fail to be treated as meeting the requirement of paragraph (6) by reason of the death of an individual but only during the 60-day period beginning on the date of such death.

Amendments

• 1998, IRS Restructuring and Reform Act of 1998 (P.L. 105-206)

P.L. 105-206, §6013(b)(1):

Amended Code Sec. 685(b) by adding at the end a new flush sentence. **Effective** as if included in the provision of P.L. 105-34 to which it relates [**effective** for tax years ending after 8-5-97.—CCH].

[Sec. 685(c)—Repealed]

Amendments

• 2008, Hubbard Act (P.L. 110-317)

P.L. 110-317, §9(a):

Repealed Code Sec. 685(c). **Effective** for tax years beginning after 8-29-2008. Prior to repeal, Code Sec. 685(c) read as follows:

(c) DOLLAR LIMITATION ON CONTRIBUTIONS.—

(1) IN GENERAL.—The term "qualified funeral trust" shall not include any trust which accepts aggregate contributions by or for the benefit of an individual in excess of $7,000.

(2) RELATED TRUSTS.—For purposes of paragraph (1), all trusts having trustees which are related persons shall be treated as 1 trust. For purposes of the preceding sentence, persons are related if—

(A) the relationship between such persons is described in section 267 or 707(b),

(B) such persons are treated as a single employer under subsection (a) or (b) of section 52, or

(C) the Secretary determines that treating such persons as related is necessary to prevent avoidance of the purposes of this section.

(3) INFLATION ADJUSTMENT.—In the case of any contract referred to in subsection (b)(1) which is entered into during any calendar year after 1998, the dollar amount referred to

[in] paragraph (1) shall be increased by an amount equal to—

(A) such dollar amount, multiplied by

(B) the cost-of-living adjustment determined under section 1(f)(3) for such calendar year, by substituting "calendar year 1997" for "calendar year 1992" in subparagraph (B) thereof.

If any dollar amount after being increased under the preceding sentence is not a multiple of $100, such dollar amount shall be rounded to the nearest multiple of $100.

[Sec. 685(c)]

(c) APPLICATION OF RATE SCHEDULE.—Section 1(e) shall be applied to each qualified funeral trust by treating each beneficiary's interest in each such trust as a separate trust.

Amendments

• 2008, Hubbard Act (P.L. 110-317)

P.L. 110-317, §9(b):

Redesignated subsection (d) of Code Sec. 685 as subsection (c). **Effective** for tax years beginning after 8-29-2008.

[Sec. 685(d)]

(d) TREATMENT OF AMOUNTS REFUNDED TO PURCHASER ON CANCELLATION.—No gain or loss shall be recognized to a purchaser of a contract described in subsection (b)(1) by reason of any payment from such trust to such purchaser by reason of cancellation of such contract. If any payment referred to in the preceding sentence consists of property other than money, the basis of such property in the hands of such purchaser shall be the same as the trust's basis in such property immediately before the payment.

Amendments

• 2008, Hubbard Act (P.L. 110-317)

P.L. 110-317, §9(b):

Redesignated subsection (e) of Code Sec. 685 as subsection (d). **Effective** for tax years beginning after 8-29-2008.

[Sec. 685(e)]

(e) SIMPLIFIED REPORTING.—The Secretary may prescribe rules for simplified reporting of all trusts having a single trustee and of trusts terminated during the year.

Amendments

• 2008, Hubbard Act (P.L. 110-317)

P.L. 110-317, §9(b):

Redesignated subsection (f) of Code Sec. 685 as subsection (e). **Effective** for tax years beginning after 8-29-2008.

• 1998, IRS Restructuring and Reform Act of 1998 (P.L. 105-206)

P.L. 105-206, §6013(b)(2):

Amended Code Sec. 685(f) by inserting before the period at the end "and of trusts terminated during the year". **Effective** as if included in the provision of P.L. 105-34 to which it relates [**effective** for tax years ending after 8-5-97.—CCH].

• 1997, Taxpayer Relief Act of 1997 (P.L. 105-34)

P.L. 105-34, §1309(a):

Amended subpart F of part I of subchapter J of chapter 1 by adding at the end a new Code Sec. 685. **Effective** for tax years ending after 8-5-97.

PART II—INCOME IN RESPECT OF DECEDENTS

[Sec. 691]

SEC. 691. RECIPIENTS OF INCOME IN RESPECT OF DECEDENTS.

[Sec. 691(a)]

(a) INCLUSION IN GROSS INCOME.—

(1) GENERAL RULE.—The amount of all items of gross income in respect of a decedent which are not properly includible in respect of the taxable period in which falls the date of his death or a prior period (including the amount of all items of gross income in respect of a prior decedent, if the right to receive such amount was acquired by reason of the death of the prior decedent or by bequest, devise, or inheritance from the prior decedent) shall be included in the gross income, for the taxable year when received, of:

(A) the estate of the decedent, if the right to receive the amount is acquired by the decedent's estate from the decedent;

(B) the person who, by reason of the death of the decedent, acquires the right to receive the amount, if the right to receive the amount is not acquired by the decedent's estate from the decedent; or

(C) the person who acquires from the decedent the right to receive the amount by bequest, devise, or inheritance, if the amount is received after a distribution by the decedent's estate of such right.

(2) INCOME IN CASE OF SALE, ETC.—If a right, described in paragraph (1), to receive an amount is transferred by the estate of the decedent or a person who received such right by reason of the death of the decedent or by bequest, devise, or inheritance from the decedent, there shall be included in the gross income of the estate or such person, as the case may be, for the taxable period in which the transfer occurs, the fair market value of such right at the time of such transfer plus the amount by which any consideration for the transfer exceeds such fair market value. For purposes of this paragraph, the term "transfer" includes sale, exchange, or other disposition, or the satisfaction of an installment obligation at other than face value, but does not include transmission at death to the estate of the decedent or a transfer to a person pursuant to the right of such person to receive such amount by reason of the death of the decedent or by bequest, devise, or inheritance from the decedent.

(3) CHARACTER OF INCOME DETERMINED BY REFERENCE TO DECEDENT.—The right, described in paragraph (1), to receive an amount shall be treated, in the hands of the estate of the decedent or any person who acquired such right by reason of the death of the decedent, or by bequest, devise, or inheritance from the decedent, as if it had been acquired by the estate or such person in the transaction in which the right to receive the income was originally derived and the amount includible in gross income under paragraph (1) or (2) shall be considered in the hands of the estate or such person to have the character which it would have had in the hands of the decedent if the decedent had lived and received such amount.

(4) INSTALLMENT OBLIGATIONS ACQUIRED FROM DECEDENT.—In the case of an installment obligation reportable by the decedent on the installment method under section 453, if such obligation is acquired by the decedent's estate from the decedent or by any person by reason of the death of the decedent or by bequest, devise, or inheritance from the decedent—

(A) an amount equal to the excess of the face amount of such obligation over the basis of the obligation in the hands of the decedent (determined under section 453B) shall, for the purpose of paragraph (1), be considered as an item of gross income in respect of the decedent; and

(B) such obligation shall, for purposes of paragraphs (2) and (3), be considered a right to receive an item of gross income in respect of the decedent, but the amount includible in gross income under paragraph (2) shall be reduced by an amount equal to the basis of the obligation in the hands of the decedent (determined under section 453B).

(5) OTHER RULES RELATING TO INSTALLMENT OBLIGATIONS.—

(A) IN GENERAL.—In the case of an installment obligation reportable by the decedent on the installment method under section 453, for purposes of paragraph (2)—

(i) the second sentence of paragraph (2) shall be applied by inserting "(other than the obligor)" after "or a transfer to a person",

(ii) any cancellation of such an obligation shall be treated as a transfer, and

(iii) any cancellation of such an obligation occurring at the death of the decedent shall be treated as a transfer by the estate of the decedent (or, if held by a person other than the decedent before the death of the decedent, by such person).

(B) FACE AMOUNT TREATED AS FAIR MARKET VALUE IN CERTAIN CASES.—In any case to which the first sentence of paragraph (2) applies by reason of subparagraph (A), if the decedent and the obligor were related persons (within the meaning of section 453(f)(1)), the fair market value of the installment obligation shall be treated as not less than its face amount.

(C) CANCELLATION INCLUDES BECOMING UNENFORCEABLE.—For purposes of subparagraph (A), an installment obligation which becomes unenforceable shall be treated as if it were canceled.

Amendments

• 1987, Revenue Act of 1987 (P.L. 100-203)

P.L. 100-203, §10202(c)(3):

Amended Code Sec. 691(a)(4)-(5) by striking out "or 453A" after "section 453" each place it appears. For the **effective** date, see Act Sec. 10202(e), as amended by P.L. 100-647, §2004(d)(4), below.

P.L. 100-203, §10202(e), as amended by P.L. 100-647, §2004(d)(4), provides:

(e) EFFECTIVE DATES.—

(1) IN GENERAL.—Except as provided in this subsection, the amendments made by this section shall apply to dispositions in taxable years beginning after December 31, 1987.

(2) SPECIAL RULES FOR DEALERS.—

(A) IN GENERAL.—In the case of dealer dispositions (within the meaning of section 453A of the Internal Revenue Code of 1986), the amendments made by subsections (a) and (b) shall apply to installment obligations arising from dispositions after December 31, 1987.

(B) SPECIAL RULES FOR OBLIGATIONS ARISING FROM DEALER DISPOSITIONS AFTER FEBRUARY 28, 1986, AND BEFORE JANUARY 1, 1988.—

(i) IN GENERAL.—In the case of an applicable installment obligation arising from a disposition described in subclause (I) and (II) of section 453C(e)(1)(A)(i) of the Internal Revenue Code of 1986 (as in effect before the amendments made by this section) before January 1, 1988, the amendments made by subsections (a) and (b) shall apply to taxable years beginning after December 31, 1987.

(ii) CHANGE IN METHOD OF ACCOUNTING.—In the case of any taxpayer who is required by clause (i) to change its method of accounting for any taxable year with respect to obligations described in clause (i)—

(I) such change shall be treated as initiated by the taxpayer,

(II) such change shall be treated as made with the consent of the Secretary of the Treasury or his delegate, and

(III) the net amount of adjustments required by section 481 of the Internal Revenue Code of 1986 shall be taken into account over a period not longer than 4 taxable years.

(C) CERTAIN RULES MADE APPLICABLE.—For purposes of this paragraph, rules similar to the rules of paragraphs (4) and (5) of section 812(c) of the Tax Reform Act of 1986 (as added by the Technical and Miscellaneous Revenue Act of 1988) shall apply.

(3) SPECIAL RULE FOR NONDEALERS.—

(A) ELECTION.—A taxpayer may elect, at such time and in such manner as the Secretary of the Treasury or his delegate may prescribe, to have the amendments made by subsections (a) and (c) apply to taxable years ending after December 31, 1986, with respect to dispositions and pledges occurring after August 16, 1986.

(B) PLEDGING RULES.—Except as provided in subparagraph (A)—

(i) IN GENERAL.—Section 453A(d) of the Internal Revenue Code of 1986 shall apply to any installment obligation which is pledged to secure any secured indebtedness (within the meaning of section 453A(d)(4) of such Code) after December 17, 1987, in taxable years ending after such date.

(ii) COORDINATION WITH SECTION 453C.—For purposes of section 453C of such Code (as in effect before its repeal), the face amount of any obligation to which section 453A(d) of such Code applies shall be reduced by the amount treated as payments on such obligation under section 453A(d) of such Code and the amount of any indebtedness secured by it shall not be taken into account.

(4) MINIMUM TAX.—The amendment made by subsection (d) shall apply to dispositions in taxable years beginning after December 31, 1986.

(5) COORDINATION WITH TAX REFORM ACT OF 1986.—The amendments made by this section shall not apply to any installment obligation or to any taxpayer during any period to the extent the amendments made by section 811 of the Tax Reform Act of 1986 do not apply to such obligation or during such period.

• 1980, Installment Sales Revision Act of 1980 (P.L. 96-471)

P.L. 96-471, §2(b)(5)(A):

Amended Code Sec. 691(a)(4) by striking out "received by a decedent on the sale or other disposition of property, the income from which was properly reportable by the decedent on the installment basis under section 453" and substituting "reportable by the decedent on the installment method under section 453 or 453A". **Effective** for dispositions made after 10-19-80, in tax years ending after that date.

P.L. 96-471, §2(b)(5)(B):

Amended Code Sec. 691(a)(4)(A) and (B) by striking out "453(d)" and substituting "453B". **Effective** for dispositions made after 10-19-80, in tax years ending after that date.

P.L. 96-471, §3:

Amended Code Sec. 691(a) by adding paragraph (5). **Effective** in the case of decedents dying after 10-19-80.

[Sec. 691(b)]

(b) ALLOWANCE OF DEDUCTIONS AND CREDIT.—The amount of any deduction specified in section 162, 163, 164, 212, or 611 (relating to deductions for expenses, interest, taxes, and depletion) or credit specified in section 27 (relating to foreign tax credit), in respect of a decedent which is not properly allowable to the decedent in respect of the taxable period in which falls the date of his death, or a prior period, shall be allowed:

(1) EXPENSES, INTEREST, AND TAXES.—In the case of a deduction specified in section 162, 163, 164, or 212 and a credit specified in section 27, in the taxable year when paid—

(A) to the estate of the decedent; except that

(B) if the estate of the decedent is not liable to discharge the obligation to which the deduction or credit relates, to the person who, by reason of the death of the decedent or by bequest, devise, or inheritance acquires, subject to such obligation, from the decedent an interest in property of the decedent.

(2) DEPLETION.—In the case of the deduction specified in section 611, to the person described in subsection (a) (1) (A), (B), or (C) who, in the manner described therein, receives the income to which the deduction relates, in the taxable year when such income is received.

Amendments

• 1984, Deficit Reduction Act of 1984 (P.L. 98-369)

P.L. 98-369, §474(r)(18):

Amended Code Sec. 691(b) by striking out "section 33" each place it appeared and inserting in lieu thereof "section 27". **Effective** for tax years beginning after 12-31-83, and to carrybacks from such years.

(c) DEDUCTION FOR ESTATE TAX.—

(1) ALLOWANCE OF DEDUCTION.—

(A) GENERAL RULE.—A person who includes an amount in gross income under subsection (a) shall be allowed, for the same taxable year, as a deduction an amount which bears the same ratio to the estate tax attributable to the net value for estate tax purposes of all the items described in subsection (a) (1) as the value for estate tax purposes of the items of gross income or portions thereof in respect of which such person included the amount in gross income (or the amount included in gross income, whichever is lower) bears to the value for estate tax purposes of all the items described in subsection (a) (1).

(B) ESTATES AND TRUSTS.—In the case of an estate or trust, the amount allowed as a deduction under subparagraph (A) shall be computed by excluding from the gross income of the estate or trust the portion (if any) of the items described in subsection (a) (1) which is properly paid, credited, or to be distributed to the beneficiaries during the taxable year.

(2) METHOD OF COMPUTING DEDUCTION.—For purposes of paragraph (1)—

(A) The term "estate tax" means the tax imposed on the estate of the decedent or any prior decedent under section 2001 or 2101, reduced by the credits against such tax.

(B) The net value for estate tax purposes of all the items described in subsection (a) (1) shall be the excess of the value for estate tax purposes of all the items described in subsection (a) (1) over the deductions from the gross estate in respect of claims which represent the deductions and credit described in subsection (b). Such net value shall be determined with respect to the provisions of section 421(c)(2), relating to the deduction for estate tax with respect to stock options to which part II of subchapter D applies.

(C) The estate tax attributable to such net value shall be an amount equal to the excess of the estate tax over the estate tax computed without including in the gross estate such net value.

(3) SPECIAL RULE FOR GENERATION-SKIPPING TRANSFERS.—In the case of any tax imposed by chapter 13 on a taxable termination or a direct skip occurring as a result of the death of the transferor, there shall be allowed a deduction (under principles similar to the principles of this subsection) for the portion of such tax attributable to items of gross income of the trust which were not properly includible in the gross income of the trust for periods before the date of such termination.

(4) COORDINATION WITH CAPITAL GAIN PROVISIONS.—For purposes of sections 1(h), 1201, 1202, and 1211, the amount taken into account with respect to any item described in subsection (a)(1) shall be reduced (but not below zero) by the amount of the deduction allowable under paragraph (1) of this subsection with respect to such item.

Amendments

• 2004, Working Families Tax Relief Act of 2004 (P.L. 108-311)

P.L. 108-311, §402(a)(4):

Amended Code Sec. 691(c)(4) by striking "of any gain" following "1211, the amount". **Effective** as if included in section 302 of the Jobs and Growth Tax Relief Reconciliation Act of 2003 (P.L. 108-27) [**effective** generally for tax years beginning after 12-31-2002.—CCH].

• 1997, Taxpayer Relief Act of 1997 (P.L. 105-34)

P.L. 105-34, §1073(b)(1):

Amended Code Sec. 691(c)(1) by striking subparagraph (C). **Effective** for estates of decedents dying after 12-31-96. Prior to being stricken, Code Sec. 691(c)(1)(C) read as follows:

(C) EXCESS RETIREMENT ACCUMULATION TAX.—For purposes of this subsection, no deduction shall be allowed for the portion of the estate tax attributable to the increase in such tax under section 4980A(d).

• 1996, Small Business Job Protection Act of 1996 (P.L. 104-188)

P.L. 104-188, §1401(b)(9):

Amended Code Sec. 691(c) by striking paragraph (5). **Effective**, generally, for tax years beginning after 12-31-99. For a special transitional rule, see Act Sec. 1401(c)(2) in the amendment notes following Code Sec. 402(d). Prior to being stricken, Code Sec. 691(c)(5) read as follows:

(5) COORDINATION WITH SECTION 402(d).—For purposes of section 402(d) (other than paragraph (1)(C) thereof), the total taxable amount of any lump sum distribution shall be reduced by the amount of the deduction allowable under paragraph (1) of this subsection which is attributable to the total taxable amount (determined without regard to this paragraph).

• 1993, Omnibus Budget Reconciliation Act of 1993 (P.L. 103-66)

P.L. 103-66, §13113(d)(4):

Amended Code Sec. 691(c)(4) by striking "1201, and 1211" and inserting "1201, 1202, and 1211". **Effective** for stock issued after 8-10-93.

• 1992, Unemployment Compensation Amendments of 1992 (P.L. 102-318)

P.L. 102-318, §521(b)(27), as amended by P.L. 104-188, §1704(t)(73):

Amended Code Sec. 691(c)(5) by striking "402(e)" in the text and heading and inserting "402(d)". **Effective** for distributions after 12-31-92.

• 1990, Omnibus Budget Reconciliation Act of 1990 (P.L. 101-508)

P.L. 101-508, §11101(d)(4):

Amended Code Sec. 691(c)(4) by striking "1(j)" and inserting "1(h)". **Effective** for tax years beginning after 12-31-90.

• 1989, Omnibus Budget Reconciliation Act of 1989 (P.L. 101-239)

P.L. 101-239, §7841(d)(3):

Amended Code Sec. 691(c)(5) by striking "paragraph (1)(D)" and inserting "paragraph (1)(C)". **Effective** 12-19-89.

• 1988, Technical and Miscellaneous Revenue Act of 1988 (P.L. 100-647)

P.L. 100-647, §1011A(g)(10):

Amended Code Sec. 691(c)(1) by adding at the end thereof new subparagraph (C). **Effective** as if included in the provision of P.L. 99-514 to which it relates.

• 1986, Tax Reform Act of 1986 (P.L. 99-514)

P.L. 99-514, §301(b)(8)(A)-(B):

Amended Code Sec. 691(c)(4) by striking out "1201, 1202, and 1211, and for purposes of section 57(a)(9)" and inserting in lieu thereof "1(j), 1201, and 1211", and by striking out "CAPITAL GAIN DEDUCTION, ETC.—" in the paragraph heading and inserting in lieu thereof "CAPITAL GAIN PROVISIONS.—". **Effective** for tax years beginning after 12-31-86.

P.L. 99-514, §1432(a)(3):

Amended Code Sec. 691(c)(3). **Effective**, generally, for any generation-skipping transfer (within the meaning of section 2611 of the Internal Revenue Code of 1986) made after 10-22-86. However, for special rules, see Act Sec. 1433(b)-(d), as amended by P.L. 100-647, §1014(h)(2)-(4), below. Prior to amendment, Code Sec. 691(c)(3) read as follows:

(3) SPECIAL RULE FOR GENERATION-SKIPPING TRANSFERS.—For purposes of this section—

(A) the tax imposed by section 2601 or any State inheritance tax described in section 2602(c)(5)(B) on any generation-skipping transfer shall be treated as a tax imposed by section 2001 on the estate of the deemed transferor (as defined in section 2612(a));

(B) any property transferred in such a transfer shall be treated as if it were included in the gross estate of the deemed transferor at the value of such property taken into account for purposes of the tax imposed by section 2601; and

(C) under regulations prescribed by the secretary, any item of gross income subject to the tax imposed under section 2601 shall be treated as income described in subsection (a) if such item is not properly includible in the gross income of the trust on or before the date of the generation-skipping transfer (within the meaning of section 2611(a)) and if such transfer occurs at or after the death of the deemed transferor (as so defined).

P.L. 99-514, §1433(b)-(d), as amended by P.L. 100-647, §1014(h)(2)-(4), provides:

(b) SPECIAL RULES.—

(1) TREATMENT OF CERTAIN INTER VIVOS TRANSFERS MADE AFTER SEPTEMBER 25, 1985.—For purposes of subsection (a) (and chapter 13 of the Internal Revenue Code of 1986 as amended by this part), any inter vivos transfer after September 25, 1985, and on or before the date of the enactment of this Act shall be treated as if it were made on the 1st day after the date of enactment of this Act.

(2) EXCEPTIONS.—The amendments made by this subtitle shall not apply to—

(A) any generation-skipping transfer under a trust which was irrevocable on September 25, 1985, but only to the extent that such transfer is not made out of corpus added to the trust after September 25, 1985 (or out of income attributable to corpus so added),

(B) any generation-skipping transfer under a will or recovable trust executed before the date of the enactment of this Act if the decedent dies before January 1, 1987, and

(C) any generation-skipping transfer—

(i) under a trust to the extent such trust consists of property included in the gross estate of a decedent (other than property transferred by the decedent during his life after the date of the enactment of this Act), or reinvestments thereof, or

(ii) which is a direct skip which occurs by reason of the death of any decedent;

but only if such decedent was, on the date of the enactment of this Act, under a mental disability to change the disposition of his property and did not regain his competence to dispose of such property before the date of his death.

(3) TREATMENT OF CERTAIN TRANSFERS TO GRANDCHILDREN.—

(A) IN GENERAL.—For purposes of chapter 13 of the Internal Revenue Code of 1986, the term "direct skip" shall not include any transfer before January 1, 1990, from a transferor to a grandchild of the transferor to the extent the aggregate transfers from such transferor to such grandchild do not exceed $2,000,000.

(B) TREATMENT OF TRANSFERS IN TRUST.—For purposes of subparagraph (A), a transfer in trust for the benefit of a grandchild shall be treated as a transfer to such grandchild if (and only if)—

(i) during the life of the grandchild, no portion of the corpus or income of the trust may be distributed to (or for the benefit of) any person other than such grandchild,

(ii) the assets of the trust will be includible in the gross estate of the grandchild if the grandchild dies before the trust is terminated, and

(iii) all of the income of the trust for periods after the grandchild has attained age 21 will be distributed to (or for the benefit of) such grandchild not less frequently than annually.

(C) COORDINATION WITH SECTION 2653(a) OF THE 1986 CODE.—In the case of any transfer which would be a generation-skipping transfer but for subparagraph (A), the rules of section 2653(a) of the Internal Revenue Code of 1986 shall apply as if such transfer were a generation-skipping transfer.

(D) COORDINATION WITH TAXABLE TERMINATIONS AND TAXABLE DISTRIBUTIONS.—For purposes of chapter 13 of the Internal Revenue Code of 1986, the terms "taxable termination" and "taxable distribution" shall not include any transfer which would be a direct skip but for subparagraph (A).

(4) DEFINITIONS.—Terms used in this section shall have the same respective meanings as when used in chapter 13 of the Internal Revenue Code of 1986; except that section 2612(c)(2) of such Code shall not apply in determining whether an individual is a grandchild of the transferor.

(c) REPEAL OF EXISTING TAX ON GENERATION-SKIPPING TRANSFERS.—

(1) IN GENERAL.—In the case of any tax imposed by chapter 13 of the Internal Revenue Code of 1954 (as in effect on the day before the date of the enactment of this Act), such tax (including interest, additions to tax, and additional amounts) shall not be assessed and if assessed, the assessment shall be abated, and if collected, shall be credited or refunded (with interest) as an overpayment.

(2) WAIVER OF STATUTE OF LIMITATIONS.—If on the date of the enactment of this Act (or at any time within 1 year after such date of enactment) refund or credit of any overpayment of tax resulting from the application of paragraph (1) is barred by any law or rule of law, refund or credit of such overpayment shall, nevertheless, be made or allowed if claim therefore is filed before the date 1 year after the date of the enactment of this Act.

(d) ELECTION FOR CERTAIN TRANSFERS BENEFITING GRANDCHILD.—

(1) IN GENERAL.—For purposes of chapter 13 of the Internal Revenue Code of 1986 (as amended by this Act) and subsection (b) of this section, any transfer in trust for the benefit of a grandchild of a transferor shall be treated as a direct skip to such grandchild if—

(A) the transfer occurs before the date of enactment of this Act,

(B) the transfer would be a direct skip to a grandchild except for the fact that the trust instrument provides that, if the grandchild dies before vesting of the interest transferred, the interest is transferred to the grandchild's heir (rather than the grandchild's estate), and

(C) an election under this subsection applies to such transfer.

Any transfer treated as a direct skip by reason of the preceding sentence shall be subject to Federal estate tax on the grandchild's death in the same manner as if the contingent gift over had been to the grandchild's estate. Unless the grandchild otherwise directs by will, the estate of such grandchild shall be entitled to recover from the person receiving the property on the death of the grandchild any increase in Federal estate tax on the estate of the grandchild by reason of the preceding sentence.

(2) ELECTION.—An election under paragraph (1) shall be made at such time and in such manner as the Secretary of the Treasury or his delegate may prescribe.

• 1981, Economic Recovery Tax Act of 1981 (P.L. 97-34)

P.L. 97-34, §403(a)(2)(C):

Amended Code Sec. 691(c)(3)(A) by striking out "section 2602(c)(5)(C)" and inserting "section 2602(c)(5)(B)". **Effective** for estates of decedents dying after 12-31-81.

• 1980, Crude Oil Windfall Profit Tax Act of 1980 (P.L. 96-223)

P.L. 96-223, §401(a), (b):

Repealed Code Sec. 691(c)(2)(A) and (C), as amended by P.L. 94-455, Act Sec. 2005(a)(4). **Effective** with respect to decedents dying after 12-31-76. However, see the amendment note for P.L. 96-223, §401(a), that follows Code Sec. 1014(d), for the text of Act Sec. 401(d) that authorizes the election of the carryover basis rules in the case of a decedent dying after 12-31-76 and before 11-7-78.

• 1980, Technical Corrections Act of 1979 (P.L. 96-222)

P.L. 96-222, §101(a)(8)(A):

Amended Code Sec. 691(c) by adding new paragraph (5). **Effective** with respect to the estates of decedents dying after 4-1-80.

• 1978, Revenue Act of 1978 (P.L. 95-600)

P.L. 95-600, §515(a):

Postponed application of Code Sec. 691(c)(2)(A) and (C), as amended by P.L. 94-455, §2005(a), from estates of decedents dying after 12-31-76, to 12-31-79.

P.L. 95-600, §702(b)(1), (2):

Added Code Sec. 691(c)(4). **Effective** for decedents dying after 11-6-78.

• 1976, Tax Reform Act of 1976 (P.L. 94-455)

P.L. 94-455, §1901(a)(91):

Struck out the last sentence of Code Sec. 691(c)(1)(B). **Effective** for tax years beginning after 12-31-76. Prior to repeal, the last sentence read as follows:

This subparagraph shall apply to the same taxable years, and to the same extent, as is provided in section 683.

P.L. 94-455, §2005(a)(4):

Amended Code Sec. 691(c)(2)(A) and (C). **Effective** for estates of decedents dying after 12-31-79 (effective date amended by P.L. 95-600, 515(a)). Prior to amendment, Code Sec. 691(c)(2)(A) and (C) read as follows:

(A) The term "estate tax" means Federal and State estate taxes (within the meaning of section 1023(f)(3)).

* * *

(C) The estate tax attributable to such net value shall be an amount which bears the same ratio to the estate tax as such net value bears to the value of the gross estate.

P.L. 94-455, §2006(b):

Added Code Sec. 691(c)(3). **Effective** as noted in Act Sec. 2006(c), below.

P.L. 94-455, §2006(c), as amended by P.L. 95-600, §702(n)(1), (n)(5)(B), provides:

(c) EFFECTIVE DATES.—

(1) IN GENERAL.—Except as provided in paragraph (2), the amendments made by this section shall apply to any generation-skipping transfer (within the meaning of section 2611(a) of the Internal Revenue Code of 1954) made after June 11, 1976.

(2) EXCEPTIONS.—The amendments made by this section shall not apply to any generation-skipping transfer—

(A) under a trust which was irrevocable on June 11, 1976, but only to the extent that the transfer is not made out of corpus added to the trust after June 11, 1976, or

(B) in the case of a decedent dying before January 1, 1982, pursuant to a will (or revocable trust) which was in existence on June 11, 1976, and was not amended at any time after that date in any respect which will result in the creation of, or increasing the amount of, any generation-skipping transfer.

For purposes of subparagraph (B), if the decedent on June 11, 1976, was under a mental disability to change the disposition of his property, the period set forth in such subparagraph shall not expire before the date which is 2 years after the date on which he first regains his competence to dispose of such property.

(3) TRUST EQUIVALENTS.—For purposes of paragraph (2), in the case of a trust equivalent within the meaning of subsection (d) of section 2611 of the Internal Revenue Code of 1954, the provisions of such subsection (d) shall apply.

• 1964, Revenue Act of 1964 (P.L. 88-272)

P.L. 88-272, §221(c)(2):

Amended the last sentence of Code Sec. 691(c)(2)(B). **Effective** for tax years ending after 12-31-63. Prior to amendment, the last sentence read as follows:

Such net value shall be determined with regard to the provisions of section 421(d)(6)(B), relating to the deduction for estate tax with respect to restricted stock options.

[Sec. 691(d)]

(d) AMOUNTS RECEIVED BY SURVIVING ANNUITANT UNDER JOINT AND SURVIVOR ANNUITY CONTRACT.—

(1) DEDUCTION FOR ESTATE TAX.—For purposes of computing the deduction under subsection (c) (1) (A), amounts received by a surviving annuitant—

(A) as an annuity under a joint and survivor annuity contract where the decedent annuitant died after December 31, 1953, and after the annuity starting date (as defined in section 72(c)(4)), and

(B) during the surviving annuitant's life expectancy period,

shall, to the extent included in gross income under section 72, be considered as amounts included in gross income under subsection (a).

(2) NET VALUE FOR ESTATE TAX PURPOSES.—In determining the net value for estate tax purposes under subsection (c) (2) (B) for purposes of this subsection, the value for estate tax purposes of the items described in paragraph (1) of this subsection shall be computed—

(A) by determining the excess of the value of the annuity at the date of the death of the deceased annuitant over the total amount excludable from the gross income of the surviving annuitant under section 72 during the surviving annuitant's life expectancy period, and

(B) by multiplying the figure so obtained by the ratio which the value of the annuity for estate tax purposes bears to the value of the annuity at the date of the death of the deceased.

(3) DEFINITIONS.—For purposes of this subsection—

(A) The term "life expectancy period" means the period beginning with the first day of the first period for which an amount is received by the surviving annuitant under the contract and ending with the close of the taxable year with or in which falls the termination of the life expectancy of the surviving annuitant. For purposes of this subparagraph, the life expectancy of the surviving annuitant shall be determined, as of the date of the death of the deceased annuitant, with reference to actuarial tables prescribed by the Secretary.

(B) The surviving annuitant's expected return under the contract shall be computed, as of the death of the deceased annuitant, with reference to actuarial tables prescribed by the Secretary.

Amendments

• 1976, Tax Reform Act of 1976 (P.L. 94-455)

P.L. 94-455, §1906(b)(13)(A):

Amended 1954 Code by substituting "Secretary" for "Secretary or his delegate" each place it appeared. **Effective** 2-1-77.

[Sec. 691(e)]

(e) CROSS REFERENCE.—

For application of this section to income in respect of a deceased partner, see section 753.

Amendments

• 1976, Tax Reform Act of 1976 (P.L. 94-455)

P.L. 94-455, §1951(b)(10)(A):

Repealed Code Sec. 691(e) and redesignated former Code Sec. 691(f) as Code Sec. 691(e). **Effective** for tax years beginning after 12-31-76. Prior to repeal, Code Sec. 691(e) read as follows:

(e) INSTALLMENT OBLIGATIONS TRANSMITTED AT DEATH WHEN PRIOR LAW APPLIED TO TRANSMISSION.—

(1) IN GENERAL.—Effective with respect to the first taxable year to which the election referred to in paragraph (2) applies and to each taxable year thereafter, subsection (a)(4) shall apply in the case of installment obligations in respect of which section 44(d) of the Internal Revenue Code of 1939 (or the corresponding provisions of prior law) did not apply by reason of the filing of the bond referred to in such section or provisions. Subsection (c) of this section shall not apply in respect of any amount included in gross income by reason of this paragraph.

(2) ELECTION.—Installment obligations referred to in paragraph (1) may, at the election of the taxpayer holding such obligations, be treated as obligations in respect of which subsection (a)(4) applies. An election under this subsection for any taxable year shall be made not later than the time prescribed by law (including extensions thereof) for filing the return for such taxable year. The election shall be made in such manner as the Secretary or his delegate may by regulations prescribe.

(3) RELEASE OF BOND.—The liability under any bond filed under section 44(d) of the Internal Revenue Code of 1939 (or the corresponding provisions or prior law) in respect of which an election under this subsection applies is hereby released with respect to taxable years to which such election applies.

P.L. 94-455, §1951(b)(10)(B), provides:

(B) SAVINGS PROVISION.—Notwithstanding subparagraph (A), any election made under section 691(e) to have subsection (a)(4) of such section apply in the case of an installment obligation shall continue to be effective with respect to taxable years beginning after December 31, 1976. Section 691(c) shall not apply in respect of any amount included in gross income by reason of the preceding sentence. The liability under bond filed under section 44(d) of the Internal Revenue Code of 1939 (or corresponding provisions of prior law) in respect of which such an election applies is hereby released with respect to taxable years to which such election applies.

• 1964 (P.L. 88-570)

P.L. 88-570, §[1]:

Renumbered Code Sec. 691(e) as Code Sec. 691(f) and added Code Sec. 691(e). **Effective**, generally, after 9-2-64. The provision, therefore, will apply with respect to payments received in any year with respect to which the time prescribed by law (including extensions of time) for the filing of the tax return for that year has not yet expired.

[Sec. 692]

SEC. 692. INCOME TAXES OF MEMBERS OF ARMED FORCES, ASTRONAUTS, AND VICTIMS OF CERTAIN TERRORIST ATTACKS ON DEATH.

[Sec. 692(a)]

(a) GENERAL RULE.—In the case of any individual who dies while in active service as a member of the Armed Forces of the United States, if such death occurred while serving in a combat zone (as determined under section 112) or as a result of wounds, disease, or injury incurred while so serving—

(1) any tax imposed by this subtitle shall not apply with respect to the taxable year in which falls the date of his death, or with respect to any prior taxable year ending on or after the first day he so served in a combat zone after June 24, 1950; and

(2) any tax under this subtitle and under the corresponding provisions of prior revenue laws for taxable years preceding those specified in paragraph (1) which is unpaid at the date of his death (including interest, additions to the tax, and additional amounts) shall not be assessed, and if assessed the assessment shall be abated, and if collected shall be credited or refunded as an overpayment.

Amendments

• 2003, Military Family Tax Relief Act of 2003 (P.L. 108-121)

P.L. 108-121, §110(a)(3)(A):

Amended the heading of Code Sec. 692 by inserting ", ASTRONAUTS," after "FORCES". **Effective** with respect to any astronaut whose death occurs after 12-31-2002.

• 2002, Victims of Terrorism Tax Relief Act of 2001 (P.L. 107-134)

P.L. 107-134, §101(c)(1):

Amended the heading of Code Sec. 692. **Effective** for tax years ending before, on, or after 9-11-2001. For a waiver of limitations, see Act Sec. 101(d)(2), below. Prior to amendment, the heading of Code Sec. 692 read as follows:

SEC. 692. INCOME TAXES OF MEMBERS OF ARMED FORCES ON DEATH.

P.L. 107-134, §101(d)(2), provides:

(2) WAIVER OF LIMITATIONS.—If refund or credit of any overpayment of tax resulting from the amendments made by this section is prevented at any time before the close of the 1-year period beginning on the date of the enactment of this Act by the operation of any law or rule of law (including res judicata), such refund or credit may nevertheless be made or allowed if claim therefor is filed before the close of such period.

• 1976, Tax Reform Act of 1976 (P.L. 94-455)

P.L. 94-455, §1901(a)(92):

Amended the heading to Code Sec. 692. **Effective** for tax years beginning after 12-31-76. Prior to amendment, the section heading read as follows:

SEC. 692. INCOME TAXES ON MEMBERS OF ARMED FORCES ON DEATH.

• 1975 (P.L. 93-597)

P.L. 93-597, §4(a):

Amended Code Sec. 692(a) by substituting at the beginning thereof "(a) General Rule.—In the case of any individual who dies" for "In the case of any individual who dies during an induction period (as defined in section 112(c)(5))". **Effective** with respect to tax years ending on or after 2-28-61. See, also, the historical comment for P.L. 93-597 following the text of Code Sec. 692(b), for a special provision on refunds or credits resulting from this amendment.

[Sec. 692(b)]

(b) INDIVIDUALS IN MISSING STATUS.—For purposes of this section, in the case of an individual who was in a missing status within the meaning of section 6013(f)(3)(A), the date of his death shall be treated as being not earlier than the date on which a determination of his death is made under section 556 of title 37 of the United States Code. Except in the case of the combat zone designated for purposes of the Vietnam conflict, the preceding sentence shall not cause subsection (a)(1) to apply for any taxable year beginning more than 2 years after the date designated under section 112 as the date of termination of combatant activities in a combat zone.

Amendments

• 1986, Tax Reform Act of 1986 (P.L. 99-514)

P.L. 99-514, §1708(a)(2):

Amended the last sentence of Code Sec. 692(b). **Effective** for tax years beginning after 12-31-82. Prior to amendment, the last sentence of Code Sec. 692(b) read as follows:

The preceding sentence shall not cause subsection (a)(1) to apply to any taxable year beginning—

(1) after December 31, 1982, in the case of service in the combat zone designated for purposes of the Vietnam conflict, or

(2) more than 2 years after the date designated under section 112 as the date of termination of combatant activities in that zone, in the case of any combat zone other than that referred to in paragraph (1).

• 1983, Technical Corrections Act of 1982 (P.L. 97-448)

P.L. 97-448, §307(b):

Amended Code Sec. 692(b)(1) by striking out "January 2, 1978" and inserting in lieu thereof "December 31, 1982". **Effective** 1-12-83.

• 1976 (P.L. 94-569)

P.L. 94-569, §2(c):

Amended the second sentence of Code Sec. 692(b). **Effective** with respect to months after the month following the month in which this Act is enacted. Prior to amendment, the second sentence of Code Sec. 692(b) read as follows:

The preceding sentence shall not cause subsection (a)(1) to apply for any taxable year beginning more than 2 years after—

(1) the date of the enactment of this subsection, in the case of service in the combat zone designated for purposes of the Vietnam conflict, or

(2) the date designated under section 112 as the date of termination of combatant activities in that zone, in the case of any combat zone other than that referred to in paragraph (1).

• 1975 (P.L. 93-597)

P.L. 93-597, §4(a):

Added Code Sec. 692(b). **Effective** with respect to tax years ending on or after 2-28-61.

P.L. 93-597, §4(c), provides:

(c) REFUNDS AND CREDITS RESULTING FROM SECTION 692 OF CODE.—If the refund or credit of any overpayment for any taxable year ending on or after February 28, 1961, resulting from the application of section 692 of the Internal Revenue Code of 1954 (as amended by subsection (a) of this section) is prevented at any time before the expiration of one year after the date of the enactment of this Act by the operation of any law or rule of law, but would not have been so prevented if claim for refund or credit therefor were made on the due date for the return for the taxable year of his death (or any later year), refund or credit of such overpayment may, nevertheless, be made or allowed if claim therefor is filed before the expiration of such one-year period.

[Sec. 692(c)]

(c) CERTAIN MILITARY OR CIVILIAN EMPLOYEES OF THE UNITED STATES DYING AS A RESULT OF INJURIES.—

(1) IN GENERAL.—In the case of any individual who dies while a military or civilian employee of the United States, if such death occurs as a result of wounds or injury which was incurred while the individual was a military or civilian employee of the United States and which was incurred in a terroristic or military action, any tax imposed by this subtitle shall not apply—

(A) with respect to the taxable year in which falls the date of his death, and

(B) with respect to any prior taxable year in the period beginning with the last taxable year ending before the taxable year in which the wounds or injury were incurred.

(2) TERRORISTIC OR MILITARY ACTION.—For purposes of paragraph (1), the term "terroristic or military action" means—

(A) any terroristic activity which a preponderance of the evidence indicates was directed against the United States or any of its allies, and

(B) any military action involving the Armed Forces of the United States and resulting from violence or aggression against the United States or any of its allies (or threat thereof).

For purposes of the preceding sentence, the term "military action" does not include training exercises.

(3) TREATMENT OF MULTINATIONAL FORCES.—For purposes of paragraph (2), any multinational force in which the United States is participating shall be treated as an ally of the United States.

Amendments

• 2002, Victims of Terrorism Tax Relief Act of 2001 (P.L. 107-134)

P.L. 107-134, §113(b)(1)-(2):

Amended Code Sec. 692(c) by striking "outside the United States" following "and which was incurred" in paragraph (1); and by striking "SUSTAINED OVERSEAS" before the period in the heading. **Effective** for tax years ending on or after 9-11-2001.

• 1999 (P.L. 106-21)

P.L. 106-21, §1(a)(3), (b) and (d)(1), provide:

SECTION 1. AVAILABILITY OF CERTAIN TAX BENEFITS FOR SERVICES AS PART OF OPERATION ALLIED FORCE.

(a) GENERAL RULE.—For purposes of the following provisions of the Internal Revenue Code of 1986, a qualified hazardous duty area shall be treated in the same manner as if it were a combat zone (as determined under section 112 of such Code):

* * *

(3) Section 692 (relating to income taxes of members of Armed Forces on death).

* * *

(b) QUALIFIED HAZARDOUS DUTY AREA.—For purposes of this section, the term "qualified hazardous duty area" means any area of the Federal Republic of Yugoslavia (Serbia/Montenegro), Albania, the Adriatic Sea, and the northern Ionian Sea (above the 39th parallel) during the period (which includes the date of the enactment of this Act) that any member of the Armed Forces of the United States is entitled to special pay under section 310 of title 37, United States Code (relating to special pay: duty subject to hostile fire or imminent danger) for services performed in such area.

* * *

(d) EFFECTIVE DATES.—

(1) IN GENERAL.—Except as provided in paragraph (2), this section shall take effect on March 24, 1999.

• 1996 (P.L. 104-117)

P.L. 104-117, §1(a)(3), (b) and (e)(1), provide:

SECTION 1. TREATMENT OF CERTAIN INDIVIDUALS PERFORMING SERVICES IN CERTAIN HAZARDOUS DUTY AREAS.

(a) GENERAL RULE.—For purposes of the following provisions of the Internal Revenue Code of 1986, a qualified hazardous duty area shall be treated in the same manner as if it were a combat zone (as determined under section 112 of such Code):

* * *

(3) Section 692 (relating to income taxes of members of Armed Forces on death).

* * *

(b) QUALIFIED HAZARDOUS DUTY AREA.—For purposes of this section, the term "qualified hazardous duty area" means Bosnia and Herzegovina, Croatia, or Macedonia, if as of the date of the enactment of this section any member of the Armed Forces of the United States is entitled to special pay under section 310 of title 37, United States Code (relating to special pay; duty subject to hostile fire or imminent danger) for services performed in such country. Such term includes any such country only during the period such entitlement is in effect. Solely for purposes of applying section 7508 of the Internal Revenue Code of 1986, in the case of an individual who is performing services as part of Operation Joint Endeavor outside the United States while deployed away from such individual's permanent duty station, the term "qualified hazardous duty area" includes, during the period for which such entitlement is in effect, any area in which such services are performed.

* * *

(e) EFFECTIVE DATE.—

(1) IN GENERAL.—Except as provided in paragraph (2), the provisions of and amendments made by this section shall take effect on November 21, 1995.

• 1984, Deficit Reduction Act of 1984 (P.L. 98-369)

P.L. 98-369, §722(g)(2):

Amended Code Sec. 692 [(c)](1) by striking out "as a result of wounds or injury incurred" and inserting in lieu thereof "as a result of wounds or injury which was incurred while the individual was a military or civilian employee of the United States and which was incurred". **Effective** as if included in the amendments made by section 1 of P.L. 98-259. See, also, the special rules of Act Sec. 722(g)(4)-(5)(B), below.

P.L. 98-369, §722(g)(3):

Amended Code Sec. 692(c)(2)(A). **Effective** as if included in the amendments made by section 1 of P.L. 98-259. See, also, the special rules of Act Sec. 722(g)(4)-(5)(B), below. Prior to amendment, Code Sec. 692(c)(2)(A) read as follows:

(A) any terroristic activity directed against the United States or any of its allies, and

P.L. 98-369, §722(g)(4) and (5)(B), provide:

(4) TREATMENT OF DIRECTOR GENERAL OF MULTINATIONAL FORCE IN SINAI.—For purposes of section 692(c) of the Internal Revenue Code of 1954, the Director General of the Multinational Force and Observers in the Sinai who died on February 15, 1984, shall be treated as if he were a civilian employee of the United States while he served as such Director General.

[(5)](B) STATUTE OF LIMITATIONS WAIVED.—Notwithstanding section 6511 of the Internal Revenue Code of 1954, the time for filing a claim for credit or refund of any overpayment of tax resulting from the amendments made by this subsection shall not expire before the date 1 year after the date of the enactment of this Act.

• 1984 (P.L. 98-259)

P.L. 98-259, §1(a):

Amended Code Sec. 692 by adding new subsection (c). **Effective** with respect to all tax years (whether beginning before, on, or after 4-10-84) of individuals dying after 11-17-78 [**effective** date changed by P.L. 98-369, §722(g)].

Notwithstanding Code Sec. 6511, the time for filing a claim for credit or refund of any overpayment of tax resulting from the amendment made by subsection (a) shall not expire before the date 1 year after April 10, 1984, of this Act.

[Sec. 692(d)]

(d) INDIVIDUALS DYING AS A RESULT OF CERTAIN ATTACKS.—

(1) IN GENERAL.—In the case of a specified terrorist victim, any tax imposed by this chapter shall not apply—

(A) with respect to the taxable year in which falls the date of death, and

(B) with respect to any prior taxable year in the period beginning with the last taxable year ending before the taxable year in which the wounds, injury, or illness referred to in paragraph (3) were incurred.

(2) $10,000 MINIMUM BENEFIT.—If, but for this paragraph, the amount of tax not imposed by paragraph (1) with respect to a specified terrorist victim is less than $10,000, then such victim shall be treated as having made a payment against the tax imposed by this chapter for such victim's last taxable year in an amount equal to the excess of $10,000 over the amount of tax not so imposed.

(3) TAXATION OF CERTAIN BENEFITS.—Subject to such rules as the Secretary may prescribe, paragraph (1) shall not apply to the amount of any tax imposed by this chapter which would be computed by only taking into account the items of income, gain, or other amounts attributable to—

(A) deferred compensation which would have been payable after death if the individual had died other than as a specified terrorist victim, or

(B) amounts payable in the taxable year which would not have been payable in such taxable year but for an action taken after September 11, 2001.

(4) SPECIFIED TERRORIST VICTIM.—For purposes of this subsection, the term "specified terrorist victim" means any decedent—

(A) who dies as a result of wounds or injury incurred as a result of the terrorist attacks against the United States on April 19, 1995, or September 11, 2001, or

(B) who dies as a result of illness incurred as a result of an attack involving anthrax occurring on or after September 11, 2001, and before January 1, 2002.

Such term shall not include any individual identified by the Attorney General to have been a participant or conspirator in any such attack or a representative of such an individual.

(5) RELIEF WITH RESPECT TO ASTRONAUTS.—The provisions of this subsection shall apply to any astronaut whose death occurs in the line of duty, except that paragraph (3)(B) shall be applied by using the date of the death of the astronaut rather than September 11, 2001.

Amendments

• 2003, Military Family Tax Relief Act of 2003 (P.L. 108-121)

P.L. 108-121, §110(a)(1):

Amended Code Sec. 692(d) by adding at the end a new paragraph (5). **Effective** with respect to any astronaut whose death occurs after 12-31-2002.

• 2002, Victims of Terrorism Tax Relief Act of 2001 (P.L. 107-134)

P.L. 107-134, §101(a):

Amended Code Sec. 692 by adding at the end a new subsection (d). **Effective** for tax years ending before, on, or after 9-11-2001. For a waiver of limitations, see Act Sec. 101(d)(2) in the amendment notes for Code Sec. 692(a).

Subchapter K—Partners and Partnerships

PART I—DETERMINATION OF TAX LIABILITY

[Sec. 701]

SEC. 701. PARTNERS, NOT PARTNERSHIP, SUBJECT TO TAX.

A partnership as such shall not be subject to the income tax imposed by this chapter. Persons carrying on business as partners shall be liable for income tax only in their separate or individual capacities.

[Sec. 702]

SEC. 702. INCOME AND CREDITS OF PARTNER.

[Sec. 702(a)]

(a) GENERAL RULE.—In determining his income tax, each partner shall take into account separately his distributive share of the partnership's—

(1) gains and losses from sales or exchanges of capital assets held for not more than 1 year,

(2) gains and losses from sales or exchanges of capital assets held for more than 1 year,

(3) gains and losses from sales or exchanges of property described in section 1231 (relating to certain property used in a trade or business and involuntary conversions),

(4) charitable contributions (as defined in section 170(c)),

»»→ Caution: Code Sec. 702(a)(5), below, is subject to the sunset provision of the Jobs and Growth Tax Relief Reconciliation Act of 2003 (P.L. 108-27), §303. Absent Congressional action, the changes made to this provision by P.L. 108-27, or that take effect as if included in P.L. 108-27, do not apply after December 31, 2010. For more information about the sunset provision, see page XXI of the Preface to this publication and P.L. 108-27, §303, in the amendment notes. See the amendments notes for a history of amendments to this section and the effective date of each change.

(5) dividends with respect to which section 1(h)(11) or part VIII of subchapter B applies,

(6) taxes, described in section 901, paid or accrued to foreign countries and to possessions of the United States,

(7) other items of income, gain, loss, deduction, or credit, to the extent provided by regulations prescribed by the Secretary, and

(8) taxable income or loss, exclusive of items requiring separate computation under other paragraphs of this subsection.

Amendments

• 2003, Jobs and Growth Tax Relief Reconciliation Act of 2003 (P.L. 108-27)

P.L. 108-27, §302(e)(8):

Amended Code Sec. 702(a)(5). For the **effective** date, see Act Sec. 302(f), as amended by P.L. 108-311, §402(a)(6), below. Prior to amendment, Code Sec. 702(a)(5) read as follows:

(5) dividends with respect to which there is a deduction under part VIII of subchapter B,

P.L. 108-27, §302(f), as amended by P.L. 108-311, §402(a)(6), provides:

(f) EFFECTIVE DATE.—

(1) IN GENERAL.—Except as provided in paragraph (2), the amendments made by this section shall apply to taxable years beginning after December 31, 2002.

(2) PASS-THRU ENTITIES.—In the case of a pass-thru entity described in subparagraph (A), (B), (C), (D), (E), or (F) of section 1(h)(10) of the Internal Revenue Code of 1986, as amended by this Act, the amendments made by this section shall apply to taxable years ending after December 31, 2002; except that dividends received by such an entity on or before such date shall not be treated as qualified dividend income (as defined in section 1(h)(11)(B) of such Code, as added by this Act).

P.L. 108-27, §303, as amended by P.L. 109-222, §102, provides:

SEC. 303. SUNSET OF TITLE.

All provisions of, and amendments made by, this title shall not apply to taxable years beginning after December 31, 2010, and the Internal Revenue Code of 1986 shall be applied and administered to such years as if such provisions and amendments had never been enacted.

• 1986, Tax Reform Act of 1986 (P.L. 99-514)

P.L. 99-514, §612(b)(5):

Amended Code Sec. 702(a)(5). **Effective** for tax years beginning after 12-31-86. Prior to amendment, Code Sec. 702(a)(5) read as follows:

(5) dividends or interest with respect to which there is an exclusion under section 116 or 128, or a deduction under part VIII of subchapter B,

• 1984, Deficit Reduction Act of 1984 (P.L. 98-369)

P.L. 98-369, §1001(b)(9):

Amended Code Sec. 702(a)(1) and (2) by striking out "1 year" each place it appeared and inserting in lieu thereof "6 months". **Effective** for property acquired after 6-22-84, and before 1-1-88.

• 1983, Technical Corrections Act of 1982 (P.L. 97-448)

P.L. 97-448, §103(a)(4):

Amended Code Sec. 702(a)(5). **Effective** as if included in the provision of P.L. 97-34 to which it relates. Prior to amendment, Code Sec. 702(a)(5) read as follows:

(5) dividends or interest with respect to which there is provided an exclusion under section 116 or 128, or a deduction under part VIII of subchapter B,

• 1981, Economic Recovery Tax Act of 1981 (P.L. 97-34)

P.L. 97-34, §301(b)(5):

Amended Code Sec. 702(a)(5), as in effect for tax years beginning in 1981, by inserting "or 128" after 116. **Effective** for tax years ending after 9-30-81.

P.L. 97-34, §301(b)(6)(C):

Amended Code Sec. 702(a)(5), as in effect for tax years beginning after 12-31-81, by inserting "or interest" after "dividends". **Effective** for tax years beginning after 12-31-81.

• 1980, Crude Oil Windfall Profit Tax Act of 1980 (P.L. 96-223)

P.L. 96-223, §404(b)(5):

Amended Code Sec. 702(a)(5) by inserting "or interest" after "dividends". **Effective** for tax years beginning after 12-31-80 and before 1-1-83. (P.L. 97-34, Act Sec. 302(b)(1), amended Act Sec. 404(c) (the effective date provision for §404(b)(5) of P.L. 96-223, by striking out "1983" and inserting "1982".)

• 1976, Tax Reform Act of 1976 (P.L. 94-455)

P.L. 94-455, §1402(b)(1):

Substituted "9 months" for "6 months" in paragraphs (1) and (2). **Effective** for tax years beginning in 1977.

P.L. 94-455, §1402(b)(2):

Substituted "1 year" for "9 months" in paragraphs (1) and (2). **Effective** for tax years beginning after 1977.

P.L. 94-455, §1901(b)(1)(I):

Repealed paragraph (7) and redesignated paragraphs (8) and (9) as (7) and (8), respectively. **Effective** for tax years beginning after 12-31-76. Prior to repeal, paragraph (7) read as follows:

(7) partially tax-exempt interest on obligations of the United States or on obligations of instrumentalities of the United States as described in section 35 or section 242 (but, if the partnership elects to amortize the premiums on bonds as provided in section 171, the amount received on such obligations shall be reduced by the reduction provided under section 171(a)(3)),

P.L. 94-455, §1906(b)(13)(A):

Amended 1954 Code by substituting "Secretary" for "Secretary or his delegate" each place it appeared. **Effective** 2-1-77.

• 1964, Revenue Act of 1964 (P.L. 88-272)

P.L. 88-272, §201(d)(7):

Amended Code Sec. 702(a)(5) by deleting "a credit under section 34;" and by deleting the comma following "section 116". **Effective** with respect to dividends received after 12-31-64, in tax years ending after such date.

[Sec. 702(b)]

(b) CHARACTER OF ITEMS CONSTITUTING DISTRIBUTIVE SHARE.—The character of any item of income, gain, loss, deduction, or credit included in a partner's distributive share under paragraphs (1) through (7) of subsection (a) shall be determined as if such item were realized directly from the source from which realized by the partnership, or incurred in the same manner as incurred by the partnership.

Amendments

• 1976, Tax Reform Act of 1976 (P.L. 94-455)

P.L. 94-455, §1901(b)(1)(I):

Substituted "paragraphs (1) through (7)" for "paragraphs (1) through (8)". **Effective** for tax years beginning after 12-31-76.

[Sec. 702(c)]

(c) GROSS INCOME OF A PARTNER.—In any case where it is necessary to determine the gross income of a partner for purposes of this title, such amount shall include his distributive share of the gross income of the partnership.

[Sec. 702(d)]

(d) CROSS REFERENCE.—

For rules relating to procedures for determining the tax treatment of partnership items see subchapter C of chapter 63 (section 6221 and following).

Amendments

• 1982, Tax Equity and Fiscal Responsibility Act of 1982 (P.L. 97-248)

P.L. 97-248, §402(c)(1):

Amended Code Sec. 702 by adding new subsection (d). **Effective** for partnership tax years beginning after 9-3-82, and shall apply to any partnership tax year ending after 9-3-82 if the partnership, each partner, and each indirect partner requests such application and the Secretary of the Treasury or his delegate consents to such application.

[Sec. 703]

SEC. 703. PARTNERSHIP COMPUTATIONS.

[Sec. 703(a)]

(a) INCOME AND DEDUCTIONS.—The taxable income of a partnership shall be computed in the same manner as in the case of an individual except that—

(1) the items described in section 702(a) shall be separately stated, and

(2) the following deductions shall not be allowed to the partnership:

(A) the deductions for personal exemptions provided in section 151,

(B) the deduction for taxes provided in section 164(a) with respect to taxes, described in section 901, paid or accrued to foreign countries and to possessions of the United States,

(C) the deduction for charitable contributions provided in section 170,

(D) the net operating loss deduction provided in section 172,

(E) the additional itemized deductions for individuals provided in part VII of subchapter B (sec. 211 and following), and

(F) the deduction for depletion under section 611 with respect to oil and gas wells.

Amendments

• 1977, Tax Reduction and Simplification Act of 1977 (P.L. 95-30)

P.L. 95-30, §101(d)(10):

Amended paragraph (2) of Code Sec. 703(a) by striking out subparagraph (A) and by redesignating subparagraphs (B) through (G) as subparagraphs (A) through (F). **Effective** for tax years beginning after 12-31-76. Prior to deletion, paragraph (2) of Code Sec. 703(a) read as follows:

(A) the standard deduction provided in section 141,

• 1976, Tax Reform Act of 1976 (P.L. 94-455)

P.L. 94-455, §2115(c)(2):

Substituted "wells" for "production subject to the provisions of section 613A(c)" in Code Sec. 703(a)(2)(G). **Effective** 1-1-75 and applicable to tax years ending after 12-31-74.

• 1975, Tax Reduction Act of 1975 (P.L. 94-12)

P.L. 94-12, §501(b)(3):

Amended Sec. 703(a)(2) by adding new subparagraph (G). **Effective** 1-1-75 and applies to tax years ending after 12-31-74.

[Sec. 703(b)]

(b) ELECTIONS OF THE PARTNERSHIP.—Any election affecting the computation of taxable income derived from a partnership shall be made by the partnership, except that any election under—

(1) subsection (b)(5) or (c)(3) of section 108 (relating to income from discharge of indebtedness),

(2) section 617 (relating to deduction and recapture of certain mining exploration expenditures), or

(3) section 901 (relating to taxes of foreign countries and possessions of the United States),

shall be made by each partner separately.

Amendments

• **1993, Omnibus Budget Reconciliation Act of 1993 (P.L. 103-66)**

P.L. 103-66, §13150(c)(9):

Amended Code Sec. 703(b)(1) by striking "subsection (b)(5)" and inserting "subsection (b)(5) or (c)(3)". **Effective** for discharges after 12-31-92, in tax years ending after such date.

• **1988, Technical and Miscellaneous Revenue Act of 1988 (P.L. 100-647)**

P.L. 100-647, §1008(i):

Amended Code Sec. 703(b)(1) by striking out "or (d)(4)" after "(b)(5)". **Effective** as if included in the provision of P.L. 99-514 to which it relates.

• **1986, Tax Reform Act of 1986 (P.L. 99-514)**

P.L. 99-514, §511(d)[c](2)(B):

Amended Code Sec. 703(b) by striking out paragraph (3) and by redesignating paragraphs (4) and (5) as paragraphs (3) and (4), respectively. **Effective** for tax years beginning after 12-31-86. Prior to amendment, Code Sec. 703(b)(3) read as follows:

(3) section 163(d) (relating to limitation of interest on investment indebtedness),

P.L. 99-514, §701(e)(4)(E):

Amended Code Sec. 703(b), as amended by title V, by striking out paragraph (1) and by redesignating paragraphs (2) through (4) as paragraphs (1) through (3), respectively. For the **effective** dates, see Act Sec. 701(f) under the amendment notes to Code Sec. 56. Prior to amendment, Code Sec. 703(b)(1) read as follows:

(1) section 57(c) (defining net lease),

• **1980, Bankruptcy Tax Act of 1980 (P.L. 96-589)**

P.L. 96-589, §2(e)(1):

Amended Code Sec. 703(b). For the **effective** date, see the historical comment for P.L. 96-589 under Code Sec. 1017(d). Prior to amendment, Code Sec. 703(b) read as follows:

(b) ELECTIONS OF THE PARTNERSHIP.—Any election affecting the computation of taxable income derived from a partnership shall be made by the partnership, except that the election under section 901, relating to taxes of foreign countries and possessions of the United States, and any election under section 617 (relating to deduction and recapture of certain mining exploration expenditures), under section 57(c) (relating to definition of net lease), or under section 163(d) (relating to limitation on interest on investment indebtedness), shall be made by each partner separately.

• **1976, Tax Reform Act of 1976 (P.L. 94-455)**

P.L. 94-455, §1901(b)(21):

Struck out "under section 615 (relating to pre-1970 exploration expenditures)," before "under section 617". **Effective** for tax years beginning after 12-31-76.

• **1971, Revenue Act of 1971 (P.L. 92-178)**

P.L. 92-178, §403(c):

Amended Code Sec. 703(b). **Effective** for tax years beginning after 12-31-69, in the case of Code Sec. 57(c) and to tax years beginning after 12-31-71, in the case of Code Sec. 163(d). Prior to amendment, Code Sec. 703(b) read as follows:

(b) Elections of the Partnership.—Any election affecting the computation of taxable income derived from a partnership shall be made by the partnership, except that the election under section 901, relating to taxes of foreign countries and possessions of the United States, and any election under section 615 (relating to pre-1970 exploration expenditures) or under section 617 (relating to deduction and recapture of certain mining exploration expenditures), shall be made by each partner separately.

• **1969, Tax Reform Act of 1969 (P.L. 91-172)**

P.L. 91-172, §504(c)(3):

Amended Sec. 703(b). **Effective** with respect to exploration expenditures paid or incurred after 12-31-69. Prior to amendment, Sec. 703 (b) read as follows:

(b) Elections of the Partnership.—Any election affecting the computation of taxable income derived from a partnership shall be made by the partnership, except that the election under section 901, relating to taxes of foreign countries and possessions of the United States, and any election under section 615 (relating to exploration expenditures) or under section 617 (relating to additional exploration expenditures in the case of domestic mining), shall be made by each partner separately.

• **1966 (P.L. 89-570)**

P.L. 89-570, §3(b):

Amended Code Sec. 703(b) by inserting "and any election under section 615 (relating to exploration expenditures) or under section 617 (relating to additional exploration expenditures in the case of domestic mining)," immediately after "United States,". **Effective** for tax years ending after 9-12-66, the date of enactment, but only in respect of expenditures paid or incurred after that date.

[Sec. 704]

SEC. 704. PARTNER'S DISTRIBUTIVE SHARE.

[Sec. 704(a)]

(a) EFFECT OF PARTNERSHIP AGREEMENT.—A partner's distributive share of income, gain, loss, deduction, or credit shall, except as otherwise provided in this chapter, be determined by the partnership agreement.

Amendments

• **1976, Tax Reform Act of 1976 (P.L. 94-455)**

P.L. 94-455, §213(c)(2):

Substituted "except as otherwise provided in this chapter" for "except as otherwise provided in this section" in Code Sec. 704(a). **Effective** for partnership tax years beginning after 12-31-75.

[Sec. 704(b)]

(b) DETERMINATION OF DISTRIBUTIVE SHARE.—A partner's distributive share of income, gain, loss, deduction, or credit (or item thereof) shall be determined in accordance with the partner's interest in the partnership (determined by taking into account all facts and circumstances), if—

(1) the partnership agreement does not provide as to the partner's distributive share of income, gain, loss, deduction, or credit (or item thereof), or

(2) the allocation to a partner under the agreement of income, gain, loss, deduction, or credit (or item thereof) does not have substantial economic effect.

Amendments

• 1976, Tax Reform Act of 1976 (P.L. 94-455)

P.L. 94-455, §213(d):

Amended Code Sec. 704(b). **Effective** in the case of partnership tax years beginning after 12-31-75. Prior to amendment, Code Sec. 704(b) read as follows:

(b) DISTRIBUTIVE SHARE DETERMINED BY INCOME OR LOSS RATIO.—A partner's distributive share of any item of income, gain, loss, deduction, or credit shall be determined in accordance with his distributive share of taxable income or loss of the partnership, as described in section 702(a)(9), for the taxable year, if—

(1) the partnership agreement does not provide as to the partner's distributive share of such item, or

(2) the principal purpose of any provision in the partnership agreement with respect to the partner's distributive share of such item is the avoidance or evasion of any tax imposed by this subtitle.

[Sec. 704(c)]

(c) CONTRIBUTED PROPERTY.—

(1) IN GENERAL.—Under regulations prescribed by the Secretary—

(A) income, gain, loss, and deduction with respect to property contributed to the partnership by a partner shall be shared among the partners so as to take account of the variation between the basis of the property to the partnership and its fair market value at the time of contribution,

(B) if any property so contributed is distributed (directly or indirectly) by the partnership (other than to the contributing partner) within 7 years of being contributed—

(i) the contributing partner shall be treated as recognizing gain or loss (as the case may be) from the sale of such property in an amount equal to the gain or loss which would have been allocated to such partner under subparagraph (A) by reason of the variation described in subparagraph (A) if the property had been sold at its fair market value at the time of the distribution,

(ii) the character of such gain or loss shall be determined by reference to the character of the gain or loss which would have resulted if such property had been sold by the partnership to the distributee, and

(iii) appropriate adjustments shall be made to the adjusted basis of the contributing partner's interest in the partnership and to the adjusted basis of the property distributed to reflect any gain or loss recognized under this subparagraph, and

(C) if any property so contributed has a built-in loss—

(i) such built-in loss shall be taken into account only in determining the amount of items allocated to the contributing partner, and

(ii) except as provided in regulations, in determining the amount of items allocated to other partners, the basis of the contributed property in the hands of the partnership shall be treated as being equal to its fair market value at the time of contribution.

For purposes of subparagraph (C), the term "built-in loss" means the excess of the adjusted basis of the property (determined without regard to subparagraph (C)(ii)) over its fair market value at the time of contribution.

(2) SPECIAL RULE FOR DISTRIBUTIONS WHERE GAIN OR LOSS WOULD NOT BE RECOGNIZED OUTSIDE PARTNERSHIPS.—Under regulations prescribed by the Secretary, if—

(A) property contributed by a partner (hereinafter referred to as the "contributing partner") is distributed by the partnership to another partner, and

(B) other property of a like kind (within the meaning of section 1031) is distributed by the partnership to the contributing partner not later than the earlier of—

(i) the 180th day after the date of the distribution described in subparagraph (A), or

(ii) the due date (determined with regard to extensions) for the contributing partner's return of the tax imposed by this chapter for the taxable year in which the distribution described in subparagraph (A) occurs,

then to the extent of the value of the property described in subparagraph (B), paragraph (1)(B) shall be applied as if the contributing partner had contributed to the partnership the property described in subparagraph (B).

(3) OTHER RULES.—Under regulations prescribed by the Secretary, rules similar to the rules of paragraph (1) shall apply to contributions by a partner (using the cash receipts and disbursements method of accounting) of accounts payable and other accrued but unpaid items. Any reference in paragraph (1) or (2) to the contributing partner shall be treated as including a reference to any successor of such partner.

Amendments

• 2004, American Jobs Creation Act of 2004 (P.L. 108-357)

P.L. 108-357, §833(a):

Amended Code Sec. 704(c)(1) by striking "and" at the end of subparagraph (A), by striking the period at the end of subparagraph (B) and inserting ", and", and by adding at the end a new subparagraph (C). **Effective** for contributions made after 10-22-2004.

• 1997, Taxpayer Relief Act of 1997 (P.L. 105-34)

P.L. 105-34, §1063(a):

Amended Code Sec. 704(c)(1)(B) by striking "5 years" and inserting "7 years". **Effective** for property contributed to a partnership after 6-8-97. For a special rule, see Act Sec. 1063(b)(2), below.

P.L. 105-34, §1063(b)(2), provides:

(2) BINDING CONTRACTS.—The amendment made by subsection (a) shall not apply to any property contributed pursuant to a written binding contract in effect on June 8, 1997, and at all times thereafter before such contribution if such contract provides for the contribution of a fixed amount of property.

• 1992, Energy Policy Act of 1992 (P.L. 102-486)

P.L. 102-486, §1937(b)(1):

Amended Code Sec. 704(c)(1)(B) by striking out "is distributed" in the material preceding clause (i) and inserting "is distributed (directly or indirectly)". **Effective** for distributions on or after 6-25-92.

• 1989, Omnibus Budget Reconciliation Act of 1989 (P.L. 101-239)

P.L. 101-239, §7642(a):

Amended Code Sec. 704(c). **Effective** in the case of property contributed to the partnership after 10-3-89, in tax years ending after such date. Prior to amendment, Code Sec. 704(c) read as follows:

(c) CONTRIBUTED PROPERTY.—Under regulations prescribed by the Secretary, income, gain, loss, and deduction with respect to property contributed to the partnership by a partner shall be shared among partners so as to take account of the variation between the basis of the property to the partnership and its fair market value at the time of contribution. Under regulations prescribed by the Secretary, rules similar to the rules of the preceding sentence shall apply to contributions by a partner (using the cash receipts and disbursements method of accounting) of accounts payable and other accrued but unpaid items.

• 1984, Deficit Reduction Act of 1984 (P.L. 98-369)

P.L. 98-369, §71(a):

Amended Code Sec. 704(c). **Effective** with respect to property contributed to the partnership after 3-31-84, in tax years ending after such date. Prior to amendment, Code Sec. 704(c) read as follows:

(c) Contributed Property.—

(1) General Rule.—In determining a partner's distributive share of items described in section 702(a), depreciation, depletion, or gain or loss with respect to property contributed to the partnership by a partner shall, except to the extent otherwise provided in paragraph (2) or (3), be allocated among the partners in the same manner as if such property had been purchased by the partnership.

(2) Effect of Partnership Agreement.—If the partnership agreement so provides, depreciation, depletion, or gain or loss with respect to property contributed to the partnership by a partner shall, under regulations prescribed by the Secretary, be shared among the partners so as to take account of the variation between the basis of the property to the partnership and its fair market value at the time of contribution.

(3) Undivided Interests.—If the partnership agreement does not provide otherwise, depreciation, depletion, or gain or loss with respect to undivided interests in property contributed to a partnership shall be determined as though such undivided interests had not been contributed to the partnership. This paragraph shall apply only if all the partners had undivided interests in such property prior to contribution and their interests in the capital and profits of the partnership correspond with such undivided interests.

• 1976, Tax Reform Act of 1976 (P.L. 94-455)

P.L. 94-455, §1906(b)(13)(A):

Amended 1954 Code by substituting "Secretary" for "Secretary or his delegate" each place it appeared. **Effective** 2-1-77.

[Sec. 704(d)]

(d) LIMITATION ON ALLOWANCE OF LOSSES.—A partner's distributive share of partnership loss (including capital loss) shall be allowed only to the extent of the adjusted basis of such partner's interest in the partnership at the end of the partnership year in which such loss occurred. Any excess of such loss over such basis shall be allowed as a deduction at the end of the partnership year in which such excess is repaid to the partnership.

Amendments

• 1978, Revenue Act of 1978 (P.L. 95-600)

P.L. 95-600, §§201(b)(1), 204(a):

Amended Code Sec. 704(d) by striking out the last two sentences. **Effective** for tax years beginning after 12-31-78. Prior to amendment, the last two sentences read as follows:

For purposes of this subsection, the adjusted basis of any partner's interest in the partnership shall not include any portion of any partnership liability with respect to which the partner has no personal liability. The preceding sentence shall not apply with respect to any activity to the extent that section 465 (relating to limiting deductions to amounts at risk in case of certain activities) applies, nor shall it apply to any partnership the principal activity of which is investing in real property (other than mineral property).

P.L. 95-600, §201(b)(2), provides:

(2) TRANSITIONAL RULE.—In the case of a loss which was not allowed for any taxable year by reason of the last 2 sentences of section 704(d) of the Internal Revenue Code of 1954 (as in effect before November 6, 1978), such loss shall be treated as a deduction (subject to section 465(a) of such Code) for the first taxable year beginning after December 31, 1978. Section 465(a) of such Code (as amended by this section) shall not apply with respect to partnership liabilities to which the last 2 sentences of section 704(d) of such Code (as in effect on November 5, 1978) did not apply because of the provisions of section 213(f)(2) of the Tax Reform Act of 1976.

• 1976, Tax Reform Act of 1976 (P.L. 94-455)

P.L. 94-455, §213(e):

Added the last two sentences to Code Sec. 704(d). **Effective** for liabilities incurred after 12-31-76.

[Sec. 704(e)]

(e) FAMILY PARTNERSHIPS.—

(1) RECOGNITION OF INTEREST CREATED BY PURCHASE OR GIFT.—A person shall be recognized as a partner for purposes of this subtitle if he owns a capital interest in a partnership in which capital is a material income-producing factor, whether or not such interest was derived by purchase or gift from any other person.

(2) DISTRIBUTIVE SHARE OF DONEE INCLUDIBLE IN GROSS INCOME.—In the case of any partnership interest created by gift, the distributive share of the donee under the partnership agreement shall be includible in his gross income, except to the extent that such share is determined without allowance of reasonable compensation for services rendered to the partnership by the donor, and except to the extent that the portion of such share attributable to donated capital is proportionately greater than the share of the donor attributable to the donor's capital. The distributive share

of a partner in the earnings of the partnership shall not be diminished because of absence due to military service.

(3) PURCHASE OF INTEREST BY MEMBER OF FAMILY.—For purposes of this section, an interest purchased by one member of a family from another shall be considered to be created by gift from the seller, and the fair market value of the purchased interest shall be considered to be donated capital. The "family" of any individual shall include only his spouse, ancestors, and lineal descendants, and any trusts for the primary benefit of such persons.

[Sec. 704(f)]

(f) CROSS REFERENCE.—

For rules in the case of the sale, exchange, liquidation, or reduction of a partner's interest, see section 706(c)(2).

Amendments

• 1976, Tax Reform Act of 1976 (P.L. 94-455)

P.L. 94-455, §213(c)(3)(A):

Added Code Sec. 704(f). **Effective** in the case of partnership tax years beginning after 12-31-75.

[Sec. 705]

SEC. 705. DETERMINATION OF BASIS OF PARTNER'S INTEREST.

[Sec. 705(a)]

(a) GENERAL RULE.—The adjusted basis of a partner's interest in a partnership shall, except as provided in subsection (b), be the basis of such interest determined under section 722 (relating to contributions to a partnership) or section 742 (relating to transfers of partnership interests)—

(1) increased by the sum of his distributive share for the taxable year and prior taxable years of—

(A) taxable income of the partnership as determined under section 703(a),

(B) income of the partnership exempt from tax under this title, and

(C) the excess of the deductions for depletion over the basis of the property subject to depletion;

(2) decreased (but not below zero) by distributions by the partnership as provided in section 733 and by the sum of his distributive share for the taxable year and prior taxable years of—

(A) losses of the partnership, and

(B) expenditures of the partnership not deductible in computing its taxable income and not properly chargeable to capital account; and

(3) decreased (but not below zero) by the amount of the partner's deduction for depletion for any partnership oil and gas property to the extent such deduction does not exceed the proportionate share of the adjusted basis of such property allocated to such partner under section 613A(c)(7)(D).

Amendments

• 1984, Deficit Reduction Act of 1984 (P.L. 98-369)

P.L. 98-369, §722(e)(1):

Amended Code Sec. 705(a)(3). **Effective** 1-1-75. Prior to amendment, it read as follows:

(3) decreased (but not below zero), by the amount of the partner's deduction for depletion under section 611 with respect to oil and gas wells.

• 1976, Tax Reform Act of 1976 (P.L. 94-455)

P.L. 94-455, §2115(c)(3):

Struck out "and" in paragraph (1)(C), substituted "; and" for the period at the end of paragraph (2)(B), and added paragraph (3). **Effective** on 1-1-75, and applicable to tax years ending after 12-31-74.

[Sec. 705(b)]

(b) ALTERNATIVE RULE.—The Secretary shall prescribe by regulations the circumstances under which the adjusted basis of a partner's interest in a partnership may be determined by reference to his proportionate share of the adjusted basis of partnership property upon a termination of the partnership.

Amendments

• 1976, Tax Reform Act of 1976 (P.L. 94-455)

P.L. 94-455, §1906(b)(13)(A):

Amended 1954 Code by substituting "Secretary" for "Secretary or his delegate" each place it appeared. **Effective** 2-1-77.

[Sec. 706]

SEC. 706. TAXABLE YEARS OF PARTNER AND PARTNERSHIP.

[Sec. 706(a)]

(a) YEAR IN WHICH PARTNERSHIP INCOME IS INCLUDIBLE.—In computing the taxable income of a partner for a taxable year, the inclusions required by section 702 and section 707(c) with respect to a partnership shall be based on the income, gain, loss, deduction, or credit of the partnership for any taxable year of the partnership ending within or with the taxable year of the partner.

[Sec. 706(b)]

(b) TAXABLE YEAR.—

(1) PARTNERSHIP'S TAXABLE YEAR.—

(A) PARTNERSHIP TREATED AS TAXPAYER.—The taxable year of a partnership shall be determined as though the partnership were a taxpayer.

(B) TAXABLE YEAR DETERMINED BY REFERENCE TO PARTNERS.—Except as provided in subparagraph (C), a partnership shall not have a taxable year other than—

(i) the majority interest taxable year (as defined in paragraph (4)),

(ii) if there is no taxable year described in clause (i), the taxable year of all the principal partners of the partnership, or

(iii) if there is no taxable year described in clause (i) or (ii), the calendar year unless the Secretary by regulations prescribes another period.

(C) BUSINESS PURPOSE.—A partnership may have a taxable year not described in subparagraph (B) if it establishes, to the satisfaction of the Secretary, a business purpose therefor. For purposes of this subparagraph, any deferral of income to partners shall not be treated as a business purpose.

(2) PARTNER'S TAXABLE YEAR.—A partner may not change to a taxable year other than that of a partnership in which he is a principal partner unless he establishes, to the satisfaction of the Secretary, a business purpose therefor.

(3) PRINCIPAL PARTNER.—For the purpose of this subsection, a principal partner is a partner having an interest of 5 percent or more in partnership profits or capital.

(4) MAJORITY INTEREST TAXABLE YEAR; LIMITATION ON REQUIRED CHANGES.—

(A) MAJORITY INTEREST TAXABLE YEAR DEFINED.—For purposes of paragraph (1)(B)(i)—

(i) IN GENERAL.—The term "majority interest taxable year" means the taxable year (if any) which, on each testing day, constituted the taxable year of 1 or more partners having (on such day) an aggregate interest in partnership profits and capital of more than 50 percent.

(ii) TESTING DAYS.—The testing days shall be—

(I) the 1st day of the partnership taxable year (determined without regard to clause (i)), or

(II) the days during such representative period as the Secretary may prescribe.

(B) FURTHER CHANGE NOT REQUIRED FOR 3 YEARS.—Except as provided in regulations necessary to prevent the avoidance of this section, if, by reason of paragraph (1)(B)(i), the taxable year of a partnership is changed, such partnership shall not be required to change to another taxable year for either of the 2 taxable years following the year of change.

(5) APPLICATION WITH OTHER SECTIONS.—Except as provided in regulations, for purposes of determining the taxable year to which a partnership is required to change by reason of this subsection, changes in taxable years of other persons required by this subsection, section 441(i), section 584(h), section 644, or section 1378(a) shall be taken into account.

Amendments

• 1997, Taxpayer Relief Act of 1997 (P.L. 105-34)

P.L. 105-34, §507(b)(2):

Amended Code Sec. 706(b)(5) by striking "section 645" and inserting "section 644". **Effective** for sales or exchanges after 8-5-97.

• 1988, Technical and Miscellaneous Revenue Act of 1988 (P.L. 100-647)

P.L. 100-647, §1008(e)(1)(A):

Amended Code Sec. 706(b)(1)(B)(i). **Effective** as if included in the provision of P.L. 99-514 to which it relates. Prior to amendment, Code Sec. 706(b)(1)(B)(i) read as follows:

(i) the taxable year of 1 or more of its partners who have an aggregate interest in partnership profits and capital of greater than 50 percent,

P.L. 100-647, §1008(e)(1)(B):

Amended Code Sec. 706(b)(4). **Effective** as if included in the provision of P.L. 99-514 to which it relates. Prior to amendment, Code Sec. 706(b)(4) read as follows:

(4) APPLICATION OF MAJORITY INTEREST RULE.—Clause (i) of paragraph (1)(B) shall not apply to any taxable year of a partnership unless the period which constitutes the taxable year of 1 or more of its partners who have an aggregate interest in partnership profits and capital of greater than 50 percent has been the same for—

(A) the 3-taxable year period of such partner or partners ending on or before the beginning of such taxable year of the partnership, or

(B) if the partnership has not been in existence during all of such 3-taxable year period, the taxable years of such partner or partners ending with or within the period of existence.

This paragraph shall apply without regard to whether the same partners or interests are taken into account in determining the 50 percent interest during any period.

P.L. 100-647, §1008(e)(2):

Amended Code Sec. 706(b)(1)(B)(iii) by striking out "or such other period as the Secretary may prescribe in regulations" and inserting in lieu thereof "unless the Secretary by regulations prescribes another period". **Effective** as if included in the provision of P.L. 99-514 to which it relates.

P.L. 100-647, §1008(e)(3):

Amended Code Sec. 706(b) by adding at the end thereof new paragraph (5). **Effective** as if included in the provision of P.L. 99-514 to which it relates.

• 1986, Tax Reform Act of 1986 (P.L. 99-514)

P.L. 99-514, §806(a)(1):

Amended Code Sec. 706(b)(1). **Effective**, generally, for tax years beginning after 12-31-86. However, see Act Sec. 806(e)(2), below. Prior to amendment, Code Sec. 706(b)(1) read as follows:

(1) PARTNERSHIP'S TAXABLE YEAR.—The taxable year of a partnership shall be determined as though the partnership were a taxpayer. A partnership may not change to, or adopt, a taxable year other than that of all its principal partners unless it establishes, to the satisfaction of the Secretary, a business purpose therefor.

P.L. 99-514, §806(a)(2):

Amended Code Sec. 706(b) by adding at the end thereof new paragraph (4). **Effective**, generally, for tax years beginning after 12-31-86. However, see Act Sec. 806(e)(2), below.

P.L. 99-514, §806(a)(3):

Amended Code Sec. 706(b) by striking out "Adoption of" before "Taxable Year" in the heading. **Effective**, generally, for tax years beginning after 12-31-86. However, see Act Sec. 806(e)(2), below.

P.L. 99-514, §806(e)(2)-(3), as amended by P.L. 100-647, §1008(e)(7)-(8) and (10), provides:

(2) CHANGE IN ACCOUNTING PERIOD.—In the case of any partnership, S corporation, or personal service corporation required by the amendments made by this section to change its accounting period for the taxpayer's first taxable year beginning after December 31, 1986—

(A) such change shall be treated as initiated by the partnership, S corporation, or personal service corporation,

(B) such change shall be treated as having been made with the consent of the Secretary, and

(C) with respect to any partner or shareholder of an S corporation which is required to include the items from more than 1 taxable year of the partnership or S corporation in any 1 taxable year, income in excess of expenses of such partnership or corporation for the short taxable year required by such amendments shall be taken into account ratably in each of the first 4 taxable years beginning after December 31, 1986, unless such partner or shareholder elects to include all such income in the partner's or shareholder's taxable year with or within which the partnership's or S corporation's short taxable year ends.

Subparagraph (C) shall apply to a shareholder of an S corporation only if such corporation was an S corporation for a taxable year beginning in 1986.

(3) BASIS, ETC. RULES.—

(A) BASIS RULE.—The adjusted basis of any partner's interest in a partnership or shareholder's stock in an S corporation shall be determined as if all of the income to be taken into account ratably in the 4 taxable years referred to in paragraph (2)(C) were included in gross income for the 1st of such taxable years.

(B) TREATMENT OF DISPOSITIONS.—If any interest in a partnership or stock in an S corporation is disposed of before the last taxable year in the spread period, all amounts which would be included in the gross income of the partner or shareholder for subsequent taxable years in the spread period under paragraph (2)(C) and attributable to the interest or stock disposed of shall be included in gross income for the taxable year in which the disposition occurs. For purposes of the preceding sentence, the term "spread period" means the period consisting of the 4 taxable years referred to in paragraph (2)(C).

• 1976, Tax Reform Act of 1976 (P.L. 94-455)

P.L. 94-455, §1906(b)(13)(A):

Amended 1954 Code by substituting "Secretary" for "Secretary or his delegate" each place it appeared. **Effective** 2-1-77.

[Sec. 706(c)]

(c) CLOSING OF PARTNERSHIP YEAR.—

(1) GENERAL RULE.—Except in the case of a termination of a partnership and except as provided in paragraph (2) of this subsection, the taxable year of a partnership shall not close as the result of the death of a partner, the entry of a new partner, the liquidation of a partner's interest in the partnership, or the sale or exchange of a partner's interest in the partnership.

(2) TREATMENT OF DISPOSITIONS.—

(A) DISPOSITION OF ENTIRE INTEREST.—The taxable year of a partnership shall close with respect to a partner whose entire interest in the partnership terminates (whether by reason of death, liquidation, or otherwise).

(B) DISPOSITION OF LESS THAN ENTIRE INTEREST.—The taxable year of a partnership shall not close (other than at the end of a partnership's taxable year as determined under subsection (b) (1)) with respect to a partner who sells or exchanges less than his entire interest in the partnership or with respect to a partner whose interest is reduced (whether by entry of a new partner, partial liquidation of a partner's interest, gift, or otherwise).

Amendments

• 1997, Taxpayer Relief Act of 1997 (P.L. 105-34)

P.L. 105-34, §1246(a):

Amended Code Sec. 706(c)(2)(A). **Effective** for partnership tax years beginning after 12-31-97. Prior to amendment, Code Sec. 706(c)(2)(A) read as follows:

(A) DISPOSITION OF ENTIRE INTEREST.—The taxable year of a partnership shall close—

(i) with respect to a partner who sells or exchanges his entire interest in a partnership, and

(ii) with respect to a partner whose interest is liquidated, except that the taxable year of a partnership with respect to a partner who dies shall not close prior to the end of the partnership's taxable year.

P.L. 105-34, §1246(b):

Amended the heading of Code Sec. 706(c)(2). **Effective** for partnership tax years beginning after 12-31-97. Prior to amendment, the paragraph heading for Code Sec. 706(c)(2) read as follows:

(2) PARTNER WHO RETIRES OR SELLS INTEREST IN PARTNERSHIP.—

• 1984, Deficit Reduction Act of 1984 (P.L. 98-369)

P.L. 98-369, §72(b):

Amended Code Sec. 706(c)(2) by striking out the last sentence of subparagraph (A). **Effective** for amounts attributable to periods after 3-31-84 (in the case of items described in Code Sec. 706(d)(2), as added by Act Sec. 72(a)). It applies to amounts paid or accrued by the other partnership after 3-31-84, in the case of items described in Code Sec. 706(d)(3), as added by Act Sec. 72(a). Prior to amendment, the last sentence of Code Sec. 706(c)(2) read as follows:

Such partner's distributive share of items described in section 702(a) for such year shall be determined, under regulations prescribed by the Secretary, for the period ending with such sale, exchange, or liquidation.

P.L. 98-369, §72(b):

Amended Code Sec. 706(c)(2)(B) by striking out ", but such partner's distributive share of items described in section 702(a) shall be determined by taking into account his varying interests in the partnership during the taxable year", at the end thereof. **Effective** for amounts attributable to periods after 3-31-84 (in the case of items described in Code Sec. 706(d)(2), as added by Act Sec. 72(a)). It applies to amounts paid or accrued by the other partnership after 3-31-84, in the case of items described in Code Sec. 706(d)(3), as added by Act Sec. 72(a).

• 1976, Tax Reform Act of 1976 (P.L. 94-455)

P.L. 94-455, §213(c)(1):

Added "(whether by entry of a new partner, partial liquidation of a partner's interest, gift, or otherwise)" to Code Sec. 706(c)(2)(B). **Effective** in the case of partnership tax years beginning after 12-31-75.

P.L. 94-455, §1906(b)(13)(A):

Amended 1954 Code by substituting "Secretary" for "Secretary or his delegate" each place it appeared. **Effective** 2-1-77.

[Sec. 706(d)]

(d) DETERMINATION OF DISTRIBUTIVE SHARE WHEN PARTNER'S INTEREST CHANGES.—

(1) IN GENERAL.—Except as provided in paragraphs (2) and (3), if during any taxable year of the partnership there is a change in any partner's interest in the partnership, each partner's distributive share of any item of income, gain, loss, deduction, or credit of the partnership for such taxable year shall be determined by the use of any method prescribed by the Secretary by regulations which takes into account the varying interests of the partners in the partnership during such taxable year.

(2) CERTAIN CASH BASIS ITEMS PRORATED OVER PERIOD TO WHICH ATTRIBUTABLE.—

(A) IN GENERAL.—If during any taxable year of the partnership there is a change in any partner's interest in the partnership, then (except to the extent provided in regulations) each partner's distributive share of any allocable cash basis item shall be determined—

(i) by assigning the appropriate portion of such item to each day in the period to which it is attributable, and

(ii) by allocating the portion assigned to any such day among the partners in proportion to their interests in the partnership at the close of such day.

(B) ALLOCABLE CASH BASIS ITEM.—For purposes of this paragraph, the term "allocable cash basis item" means any of the following items with respect to which the partnership uses the cash receipts and disbursements method of accounting:

(i) Interest.

(ii) Taxes.

(iii) Payments for services or for the use of property.

(iv) Any other item of a kind specified in regulations prescribed by the Secretary as being an item with respect to which the application of this paragraph is appropriate to avoid significant misstatements of the income of the partners.

(C) ITEMS ATTRIBUTABLE TO PERIODS NOT WITHIN TAXABLE YEAR.—If any portion of any allocable cash basis item is attributable to—

(i) any period before the beginning of the taxable year, such portion shall be assigned under subparagraph (A)(i) to the first day of the taxable year, or

(ii) any period after the close of the taxable year, such portion shall be assigned under subparagraph (A)(i) to the last day of the taxable year.

(D) TREATMENT OF DEDUCTIBLE ITEMS ATTRIBUTABLE TO PRIOR PERIODS.—If any portion of a deductible cash basis item is assigned under subparagraph (C)(i) to the first day of any taxable year—

(i) such portion shall be allocated among persons who are partners in the partnership during the period to which such portion is attributable in accordance with their varying interests in the partnership during such period, and

(ii) any amount allocated under clause (i) to a person who is not a partner in the partnership on such first day shall be capitalized by the partnership and treated in the manner provided for in section 755.

(3) ITEMS ATTRIBUTABLE TO INTEREST IN LOWER TIER PARTNERSHIP PRORATED OVER ENTIRE TAXABLE YEAR.—If—

(A) during any taxable year of the partnership there is a change in any partner's interest in the partnership (hereinafter in this paragraph referred to as the "upper tier partnership"), and

(B) such partnership is a partner in another partnership (hereinafter in this paragraph referred to as the "lower tier partnership"),

then (except to the extent provided in regulations) each partner's distributive share of any item of the upper tier partnership attributable to the lower tier partnership shall be determined by assigning the appropriate portion (determined by applying principles similar to the principles of subparagraphs (C) and (D) of paragraph (2)) of each such item to the appropriate days during which the upper tier partnership is a partner in the lower tier partnership and by allocating the portion assigned to any such day among the partners in proportion to their interests in the upper tier partnership at the close of such day.

(4) TAXABLE YEAR DETERMINED WITHOUT REGARD TO SUBSECTION (c)(2)(A).—For purposes of this subsection, the taxable year of a partnership shall be determined without regard to subsection (c)(2)(A).

Amendments

• 1986, Tax Reform Act of 1986 (P.L. 99-514)

P.L. 99-514, §1805(a)(1)(A):

Amended Code Sec. 706(d)(2)(A)(i) by striking out "each such item" and inserting in lieu thereof "such item". **Effective** as if included in the provision of P.L. 98-369 to which it relates.

P.L. 99-514, §1805(a)(1)(B):

Amended Code Sec. 706(d)(2)(B) by striking out "which are described in paragraph (1) and" after "following items". **Effective** as if included in the provision of P.L. 98-369 to which it relates.

P.L. 99-514, §1805(a)(2):

Amended Code Sec. 706(d)(2)(C)(i) by striking out "the first day of such taxable year" and inserting in lieu thereof "the first day of the taxable year". **Effective** as if included in the provision of P.L. 98-369 to which it relates.

• 1984, Deficit Reduction Act of 1984 (P.L. 98-369)

P.L. 98-369, §72(a):

Amended Code Sec. 706 by adding new subsection (d) at the end thereof. **Effective** for amounts attributable to periods after 3-31-84 (in the case of items described in Code Sec. 706(d)(2), as added by Act Sec. 72(a)). It applies to amounts paid or accrued by the other partnership after 3-31-84, in the case of items described in Code Sec. 706(d)(3), as added by Act Sec. 72(a).

[Sec. 707]

SEC. 707. TRANSACTIONS BETWEEN PARTNER AND PARTNERSHIP.

[Sec. 707(a)]

(a) PARTNER NOT ACTING IN CAPACITY AS PARTNER.—

(1) IN GENERAL.—If a partner engages in a transaction with a partnership other than in his capacity as a member of such partnership, the transaction shall, except as otherwise provided in this section, be considered as occurring between the partnership and one who is not a partner.

(2) TREATMENT OF PAYMENTS TO PARTNERS FOR PROPERTY OR SERVICES.—Under regulations prescribed by the Secretary—

(A) TREATMENT OF CERTAIN SERVICES AND TRANSFERS OF PROPERTY.—If—

(i) a partner performs services for a partnership or transfers property to a partnership,

(ii) there is a related direct or indirect allocation and distribution to such partner, and

(iii) the performance of such services (or such transfer) and the allocation and distribution, when viewed together, are properly characterized as a transaction occurring between the partnership and a partner acting other than in his capacity as a member of the partnership,

such allocation and distribution shall be treated as a transaction described in paragraph (1).

(B) TREATMENT OF CERTAIN PROPERTY TRANSFERS.—If—

(i) there is a direct or indirect transfer of money or other property by a partner to a partnership,

(ii) there is a related direct or indirect transfer of money or other property by the partnership to such partner (or another partner), and

(iii) the transfers described in clauses (i) and (ii), when viewed together, are properly characterized as a sale or exchange of property,

such transfers shall be treated either as a transaction described in paragraph (1) or as a transaction between 2 or more partners acting other than in their capacity as members of the partnership.

Amendments

• 1986, Tax Reform Act of 1986 (P.L. 99-514)

P.L. 99-514, §1805(b):

Amended Code Sec. 707(a)(2)(B)(iii) by striking out "sale of property" and inserting in lieu thereof "sale or exchange of property". **Effective** as if included in the provision of P.L. 98-369 to which it relates.

• 1984, Deficit Reduction Act of 1984 (P.L. 98-369)

P.L. 98-369, §73(a):

Amended Code Sec. 707(a). **Effective** as noted in Act Sec. 73(b), below. Prior to amendment, Code Sec. 707(a) read as follows:

(a) Partner Not Acting in Capacity as Partner.—If a partner engages in a transaction with a partnership other than in his capacity as a member of such partnership, the transaction shall, except as otherwise provided in this section, be considered as occurring between the partnership and one who is not a partner.

P.L. 98-369, §73(b), provides:

(b) Effective Date.—

(1) In General.—The amendment made by subsection (a) shall apply—

(A) in the case of arrangements described in section 707(a)(2)(A) of the Internal Revenue Code of 1954 (as amended by subsection (a)), to services performed or property transferred after February 29, 1984, and

(B) in the case of transfers described in section 707(a)(2)(B) of such Code (as so amended), to property transferred after March 31, 1984.

(2) Binding Contract Exception.—The amendment made by subsection (a) shall not apply to a transfer of property described in section 707(a)(2)(B)(i) if such transfer is pursuant to a binding contract in effect on March 31, 1984, and at all times thereafter before the transfer.

(3) Exception for Certain Transfers.—The amendment made by subsection (a) shall not apply to a transfer of property described in section 707(a)(2)(B)(i) that is made before December 31, 1984, if—

(A) such transfer was proposed in a written private offering memorandum circulated before February 28, 1984;

(B) the out-of-pocket costs incurred with respect to such offering exceeded $250,000 as of February 28, 1984;

(C) The encumbrances placed on such property in anticipation of such transfer all constitute obligations for which neither the partnership nor any partner is liable; and

(D) the transferor of such property is the sole general partner of the partnership.

[Sec. 707(b)]

(b) CERTAIN SALES OR EXCHANGES OF PROPERTY WITH RESPECT TO CONTROLLED PARTNERSHIPS.—

(1) LOSSES DISALLOWED.—No deduction shall be allowed in respect of losses from sales or exchanges of property (other than an interest in the partnership), directly or indirectly, between—

(A) a partnership and a person owning, directly or indirectly, more than 50 percent of the capital interest, or the profits interest, in such partnership, or

(B) two partnerships in which the same persons own, directly or indirectly, more than 50 percent of the capital interests or profits interests.

In the case of a subsequent sale or exchange by a transferee described in this paragraph, section 267(d) shall be applicable as if the loss were disallowed under section 267(a)(1). For purposes of section 267(a)(2), partnerships described in subparagraph (B) of this paragraph shall be treated as persons specified in section 267(b).

(2) GAINS TREATED AS ORDINARY INCOME.—In the case of a sale or exchange, directly or indirectly, of property, which, in the hands of the transferee, is property other than a capital asset as defined in section 1221—

(A) between a partnership and a person owning, directly or indirectly, more than 50 percent of the capital interest, or profits interest, in such partnership, or

(B) between two partnerships in which the same persons own, directly or indirectly, more than 50 percent of the capital interests or profits interests,

any gain recognized shall be considered as ordinary income.

(3) OWNERSHIP OF A CAPITAL OR PROFITS INTEREST.—For purposes of paragraphs (1) and (2) of this subsection, the ownership of a capital or profits interest in a partnership shall be determined in accordance with the rules for constructive ownership of stock provided in section 267(c) other than paragraph (3) of such section.

Amendments

• 1986, Tax Reform Act of 1986 (P.L. 99-514)

P.L. 99-514, §642(a):

Amended Code Sec. 707(b)(2) by striking out "80 percent" each place it appears and inserting in lieu thereof "50 percent". For the **effective** date, see Act Sec. 642(c), below.

P.L. 99-514, §642(c), as amended by P.L. 100-647, §1006(i)(3), provides:

(c) EFFECTIVE DATE.—

(1) IN GENERAL.—Except as provided in paragraph (2), the amendments made by this section shall apply to sales after the date of the enactment of this Act, in taxable years ending after such date.

(2) TRADITIONAL RULE FOR BINDING CONTRACTS.—The amendments made by this section shall not apply to sales made after August 14, 1986, which are made pursuant to a binding contract in effect on August 14, 1986, and at all times thereafter.

P.L. 99-514, §1812(c)(3)(A):

Amended Code Sec. 707(b)(1)(A) and (2)(A) by striking out "a partner" and inserting in lieu thereof "a person". **Effective** for sales or exchanges after 9-27-85.

P.L. 99-514, §1812(c)(3)(B):

Amended Code Sec. 707(b)(1) by adding at the end thereof a new sentence. **Effective** as if included in the provision of P.L. 98-369 to which it relates.

• 1976, Tax Reform Act of 1976 (P.L. 94-455)

P.L. 94-455, §1901(b)(3):

Substituted "ordinary income" for "gain from the sale or exchange of property other than a capital asset" in Code Sec. 707(b)(2). **Effective** for tax years beginning after 12-31-76.

[Sec. 707(c)]

(c) GUARANTEED PAYMENTS.—To the extent determined without regard to the income of the partnership, payments to a partner for services or the use of capital shall be considered as made to one who is not a member of the partnership, but only for the purposes of section 61(a) (relating to gross income) and, subject to section 263, for purposes of section 162(a) (relating to trade or business expenses).

Amendments

• 1976, Tax Reform Act of 1976 (P.L. 94-455)

P.L. 94-455, §213(b)(3):

Substituted ", subject to section 263, for purposes of section 162(a)" for "and section 162(a)" in Code Sec. 707(c). **Effective** in the case of partnership tax years beginning after 12-31-75.

[Sec. 708]

SEC. 708. CONTINUATION OF PARTNERSHIP.

[Sec. 708(a)]

(a) GENERAL RULE.—For purposes of this subchapter, an existing partnership shall be considered as continuing if it is not terminated.

[Sec. 708(b)]

(b) TERMINATION.—

(1) GENERAL RULE.—For purposes of subsection (a), a partnership shall be considered as terminated only if—

(A) no part of any business, financial operation, or venture of the partnership continues to be carried on by any of its partners in a partnership, or

(B) within a 12-month period there is a sale or exchange of 50 percent or more of the total interest in partnership capital and profits.

(2) SPECIAL RULES.—

(A) MERGER OR CONSOLIDATION.—In the case of the merger or consolidation of two or more partnerships, the resulting partnership shall, for purposes of this section, be considered the continuation of any merging or consolidating partnership whose members own an interest of more than 50 percent in the capital and profits of the resulting partnership.

(B) DIVISION OF A PARTNERSHIP.—In the case of a division of a partnership into two or more partnerships, the resulting partnerships (other than any resulting partnership the members of which had an interest of 50 percent or less in the capital and profits of the prior partnership) shall, for purposes of this section, be considered a continuation of the prior partnership.

[Sec. 709]

SEC. 709. TREATMENT OF ORGANIZATION AND SYNDICATION FEES.

[Sec. 709(a)]

(a) GENERAL RULE.—Except as provided in subsection (b), no deduction shall be allowed under this chapter to the partnership or to any partner for any amounts paid or incurred to organize a partnership or to promote the sale of (or to sell) an interest in such partnership.

[Sec. 709(b)]

(b) DEDUCTION OF ORGANIZATION FEES.—

(1) ALLOWANCE OF DEDUCTION.—If a partnership elects the application of this subsection (in accordance with regulations prescribed by the Secretary) with respect to any organizational expenses—

(A) the partnership shall be allowed a deduction for the taxable year in which the partnership begins business in an amount equal to the lesser of—

(i) the amount of organizational expenses with respect to the partnership, or

(ii) $5,000, reduced (but not below zero) by the amount by which such organizational expenses exceed $50,000, and

(B) the remainder of such organizational expenses shall be allowed as a deduction ratably over the 180-month period beginning with the month in which the partnership begins business.

(2) DISPOSITIONS BEFORE CLOSE OF AMORTIZATION PERIOD.—In any case in which a partnership is liquidated before the end of the period to which paragraph (1)(B) applies, any deferred expenses attributable to the partnership which were not allowed as a deduction by reason of this section may be deducted to the extent allowable under section 165.

(3) ORGANIZATIONAL EXPENSES DEFINED.—The organizational expenses to which paragraph (1) applies, are expenditures which—

(A) are incident to the creation of the partnership;

(B) are chargeable to capital account; and

(C) are of a character which, if expended incident to the creation of a partnership having an ascertainable life, would be amortized over such life.

Amendments

• 2005, Gulf Opportunity Zone Act of 2005 (P.L. 109-135)

P.L. 109-135, §403(ll):

Amended Code Sec. 709(b)(1) by striking "taxpayer" both places it appears and inserting "partnership". **Effective** as if included in the provision of the American Jobs Creation Act of 2004 (P.L. 108-357) to which it relates [**effective** for amounts paid or incurred after 10-22-2004.—CCH].

• 2004, American Jobs Creation Act of 2004 (P.L. 108-357)

P.L. 108-357, §902(c)(1):

Amended Code Sec. 709(b) by redesignating paragraph (2) as paragraph (3) and by amending paragraph (1) [and inserting a new paragraph (2)]. **Effective** for amounts paid or incurred after 10-22-2004. Prior to amendment, Code Sec. 709(b)(1) read as follows:

(1) DEDUCTION.—Amounts paid or incurred to organize a partnership may, at the election of the partnership (made in accordance with regulations prescribed by the Secretary), be treated as deferred expenses. Such deferred expenses shall be allowed as a deduction ratably over such period of not less than 60 months as may be selected by the partnership (beginning with the month in which the partnership begins business), or if the partnership is liquidated before the end of such 60-month period, such deferred expenses (to the extent not deducted under this section) may be deducted to the extent provided in section 165.

P.L. 108-357, §902(c)(2):

Amended Code Sec. 709(b) by striking "AMORTIZATION" and inserting "DEDUCTION" in the heading. **Effective** for amounts paid or incurred after 10-22-2004.

• 1976, Tax Reform Act of 1976 (P.L. 94-455)

P.L. 94-455, §213(b):

Added Code Sec. 709. **Effective** in the case of amounts paid or incurred in tax years beginning after 12-31-76.

PART II—CONTRIBUTIONS, DISTRIBUTIONS, AND TRANSFERS

Subpart A—Contributions to a Partnership

[Sec. 721]

SEC. 721. NONRECOGNITION OF GAIN OR LOSS ON CONTRIBUTION.

[Sec. 721(a)]

(a) GENERAL RULE.—No gain or loss shall be recognized to a partnership or to any of its partners in the case of a contribution of property to the partnership in exchange for an interest in the partnership.

Amendments

• 1976, Tax Reform Act of 1976 (P.L. 94-455)

P.L. 94-455, §2131(b):

Inserted subsection designation "(a)" before the provisions of former Code Sec. 721. For the **effective** date, see Act Sec. 2131(f)(3)-(5), below.

P.L. 94-455, §2131(f)(3)-(5), provides:

(3) Except as provided in paragraph (4), the amendments made by subsections (b) and (c) shall apply to transfers made after February 17, 1976, in taxable years ending after such date.

(4) The amendments made by subsections (b) and (c) shall not apply to transfers to a partnership made on or before the 90th day after the date of the enactment of this Act if—

(A) either—

(i) a ruling request with respect to such transfers was filed with the Internal Revenue Service before March 27, 1976, or

(ii) a registration statement with respect to such transfers was filed with the Securities and Exchange Commission before March 27, 1976,

(B) the securities transferred were deposited on or before the 60th day after the date of the enactment of this Act, and

(C) either—

(i) the aggregate value (determined as of the close of the 60th day referred to in subparagraph (B), or, if earlier, the close of the deposit period) of the securities so transferred does not exceed $100,000,000, or

(ii) the securities transferred were all on deposit on February 29, 1976, pursuant to a registration statement referred to in subparagraph (A)(ii).

(5) If no registration statement was required to be filed with the Securities and Exchange Commission with respect to the transfer of securities to any partnership, then paragraph (4) shall be applied to such transfers—

(A) as if paragraph (4) did not contain subparagraph (A)(ii) thereof, and

(B) by substituting "$25,000,000" for "$100,000,000" in subparagraph (C)(i) thereof.

[Sec. 721(b)]

(b) SPECIAL RULE.—Subsection (a) shall not apply to gain realized on a transfer of property to a partnership which would be treated as an investment company (within the meaning of section 351) if the partnership were incorporated.

Amendments

• 1976, Tax Reform Act of 1976 (P.L. 94-455)

P.L. 94-455, §2131(b):

Added Code Sec. 721(b). For **effective** date, see Act Sec. 2131(f)(3)-(5) under Code Sec. 721(a).

[Sec. 721(c)]

(c) REGULATIONS RELATING TO CERTAIN TRANSFERS TO PARTNERSHIPS.—The Secretary may provide by regulations that subsection (a) shall not apply to gain realized on the transfer of property to a partnership if such gain, when recognized, will be includible in the gross income of a person other than a United States person.

Amendments

• 1997, Taxpayer Relief Act of 1997 (P.L. 105-34)

P.L. 105-34, §1131(b)[(c)](3):

Amended Code Sec. 721 by adding at the end a new subsection (c). **Effective** 8-5-97.

[Sec. 721(d)]

(d) TRANSFERS OF INTANGIBLES.—

For regulatory authority to treat intangibles transferred to a partnership as sold, see section 367(d)(3).

Amendments

• 1997, Taxpayer Relief Act of 1997 (P.L. 105-34)

P.L. 105-34, §1131(b)[(c)](5)(B):

Amended Code Sec. 721 by adding at the end a new subsection (d). **Effective** 8-5-97.

[Sec. 722]

SEC. 722. BASIS OF CONTRIBUTING PARTNER'S INTEREST.

The basis of an interest in a partnership acquired by a contribution of property, including money, to the partnership shall be the amount of such money and the adjusted basis of such property to the contributing partner at the time of the contribution increased by the amount (if any) of gain recognized under section 721(b) to the contributing partner at such time.

Amendments

• 1984, Deficit Reduction Act of 1984 (P.L. 98-369)

P.L. 98-369, §722(f)(1):

Amended Code Sec. 722 by striking out "gain recognized" and inserting in lieu thereof "gain recognized under section 721(b)". **Effective** as if included in the amendments made by section 2131 of P.L. 94-455.

• 1976, Tax Reform Act of 1976 (P.L. 94-455)

P.L. 94-455, §2131(c):

Substituted "contribution increased by the amount (if any) of gain recognized to the contributing partner at such time." for "contribution." in Code Sec. 722. **Effective** as provided in Act Sec. 2131(f)(3)-(5), below.

P.L. 94-455, §2131(f)(3)-(5), provides:

(3) Except as provided in paragraph (4), the amendments made by subsections (b) and (c) shall apply to transfers made after February 17, 1976, in taxable years ending after such date.

(4) The amendments made by subsections (b) and (c) shall not apply to transfers to a partnership made on or before the 90th day after the date of the enactment of this Act if—

(A) either—

(i) a ruling request with respect to such transfers was filed with the Internal Revenue Service before March 27, 1976, or

(ii) a registration statement with respect to such transfers was filed with the Securities and Exchange Commission before March 27, 1976,

(B) the securities transferred were deposited on or before the 60th day after the date of the enactment of this Act, and

(C) either—

(i) the aggregate value (determined as of the close of the 60th day referred to in subparagraph (B), or, if earlier, the close of the deposit period) of the securities so transferred does not exceed $100,000,000, or

(ii) the securities transferred were all on deposit on February 29, 1976, pursuant to a registration statement referred to in subparagraph (A)(ii).

(5) If no registration statement was required to be filed with the Securities and Exchange Commission with respect to the transfer of securities to any partnership, then paragraph (4) shall be applied to such transfers—

(A) as if paragraph (4) did not contain subparagraph (A)(ii) thereof, and

(B) by substituting "$25,000,000" for "$100,000,000" in subparagraph (C)(i) thereof.

[Sec. 723]

SEC. 723. BASIS OF PROPERTY CONTRIBUTED TO PARTNERSHIP.

The basis of property contributed to a partnership by a partner shall be the adjusted basis of such property to the contributing partner at the time of the contribution increased by the amount (if any) of gain recognized under section 721(b) to the contributing partner at such time.

Amendments

• 1984, Deficit Reduction Act of 1984 (P.L. 98-369)

P.L. 98-369, §722(f)(1):

Amended Code Sec. 723 by striking out "gain recognized" and inserting in lieu thereof "gain recognized under section 721(b)". **Effective** as if included in the amendments made by section 2131 of P.L. 94-455.

• 1976, Tax Reform Act of 1976 (P.L. 94-455)

P.L. 94-455, §2131(c):

Substituted "contribution increased by the amount (if any) of gain recognized to the contributing partner at such time." for "contribution." in Code Sec. 723. **Effective** as noted in Act Sec. 2131(f)(3)-(5), below.

P.L. 94-455, §2131(f)(3)-(5), provides:

(3) Except as provided in paragraph (4), the amendments made by subsections (b) and (c) shall apply to transfers made after February 17, 1976, in taxable years ending after such date.

(4) The amendments made by subsections (b) and (c) shall not apply to transfers to a partnership made on or before the 90th day after the date of the enactment of this Act if—

(A) either—

(i) a ruling request with respect to such transfers was filed with the Internal Revenue Service before March 27, 1976, or

(ii) a registration statement with respect to such transfers was filed with the Securities and Exchange Commission before March 27, 1976,

(B) the securities transferred were deposited on or before the 60th day after the date of the enactment of this Act, and

(C) either—

(i) the aggregate value (determined as of the close of the 60th day referred to in subparagraph (B), or, if earlier, the close of the deposit period) of the securities so transferred does not exceed $100,000,000, or

(ii) the securities transferred were all on deposit on February 29, 1976, pursuant to a registration statement referred to in subparagraph (A)(ii).

(5) If no registration statement was required to be filed with the Securities and Exchange Commission with respect to the transfer of securities to any partnership, then paragraph (4) shall be applied to such transfers—

(A) as if paragraph (4) did not contain subparagraph (A)(ii) thereof, and

(B) by substituting "$25,000,000" for "$100,000,000" in subparagraph (C)(i) thereof.

[Sec. 724]

SEC. 724. CHARACTER OF GAIN OR LOSS ON CONTRIBUTED UNREALIZED RECEIVABLES, INVENTORY ITEMS, AND CAPITAL LOSS PROPERTY.

[Sec. 724(a)]

(a) CONTRIBUTIONS OF UNREALIZED RECEIVABLES.—In the case of any property which—

(1) was contributed to the partnership by a partner, and

(2) was an unrealized receivable in the hands of such partner immediately before such contribution,

any gain or loss recognized by the partnership on the disposition of such property shall be treated as ordinary income or ordinary loss, as the case may be.

[Sec. 724(b)]

(b) CONTRIBUTIONS OF INVENTORY ITEMS.—In the case of any property which—

(1) was contributed to the partnership by a partner, and

(2) was an inventory item in the hands of such partner immediately before such contribution,

any gain or loss recognized by the partnership on the disposition of such property during the 5-year period beginning on the date of such contribution shall be treated as ordinary income or ordinary loss, as the case may be.

[Sec. 724(c)]

(c) CONTRIBUTIONS OF CAPITAL LOSS PROPERTY.—In the case of any property which—

(1) was contributed by a partner to the partnership, and

(2) was a capital asset in the hands of such partner immediately before such contribution,

any loss recognized by the partnership on the disposition of such property during the 5-year period beginning on the date of such contribution shall be treated as a loss from the sale of a capital asset to the extent that, immediately before such contribution, the adjusted basis of such property in the hands of the partner exceeded the fair market value of such property.

[Sec. 724(d)]

(d) DEFINITIONS.—For purposes of this section—

(1) UNREALIZED RECEIVABLE.—The term "unrealized receivable" has the meaning given such term by section 751(c) (determined by treating any reference to the partnership as referring to the partner).

(2) INVENTORY ITEM.—The term "inventory item" has the meaning given such term by section 751(d) (determined by treating any reference to the partnership as referring to the partner and by applying section 1231 without regard to any holding period therein provided).

(3) SUBSTITUTED BASIS PROPERTY.—

(A) IN GENERAL.—If any property described in subsection (a), (b), or (c) is disposed of in a nonrecognition transaction, the tax treatment which applies to such property under such subsection shall also apply to any substituted basis property resulting from such transaction. A similar rule shall also apply in the case of a series of non-recognition transactions.

(B) EXCEPTION FOR STOCK IN C CORPORATION.—Subparagraph (A) shall not apply to any stock in a C corporation received in an exchange described in section 351.

Amendments

• 1997, Taxpayer Relief Act of 1997 (P.L. 105-34)

P.L. 105-34, §1062(b)(3):

Amended Code Sec. 724(d)(2) by striking "section 751(d)(2)" and inserting "section 751(d)". **Effective** for sales, exchanges, and distributions after 8-5-97. For a special rule, see Act Sec. 1062(c)(2), below.

P.L. 105-34, §1062(c)(2), provides:

(2) BINDING CONTRACTS.—The amendments made by this section shall not apply to any sale or exchange pursuant to a written binding contract in effect on June 8, 1997, and at all times thereafter before such sale or exchange.

• 1996, Small Business Job Protection Act of 1996 (P.L. 104-188)

P.L. 104-188, §1704(t)(63):

Amended Code Sec. 724(d)(3)(B) by striking "Subpara-graph" and inserting "Subparagraph". **Effective** 8-20-96.

• 1984, Deficit Reduction Act of 1984 (P.L. 98-369)

P.L. 98-369, §74(a):

Added Code Sec. 724 to subpart A of part II of subchapter K of chapter 1. **Effective** for property contributed to a partnership after 3-31-84, in tax years ending after such date.

Subpart B—Distributions by a Partnership

[Sec. 731]

SEC. 731. EXTENT OF RECOGNITION OF GAIN OR LOSS ON DISTRIBUTION.

[Sec. 731(a)]

(a) PARTNERS.—In the case of a distribution by a partnership to a partner—

(1) gain shall not be recognized to such partner, except to the extent that any money distributed exceeds the adjusted basis of such partner's interest in the partnership immediately before the distribution, and

(2) loss shall not be recognized to such partner, except that upon a distribution in liquidation of a partner's interest in a partnership where no property other than that described in subparagraph (A) or (B) is distributed to such partner, loss shall be recognized to the extent of the excess of the adjusted basis of such partner's interest in the partnership over the sum of—

(A) any money distributed, and

(B) the basis to the distributee, as determined under section 732, of any unrealized receivables (as defined in section 751(c)) and inventory (as defined in section 751(d)).

Any gain or loss recognized under this subsection shall be considered as gain or loss from the sale or exchange of the partnership interest of the distributee partner.

Amendments

• 1997, Taxpayer Relief Act of 1997 (P.L. 105-34)

P.L. 105-34, §1062(b)(3):

Amended Code Sec. 731(a)(2)(B) by striking "section 751(d)(2)" and inserting "section 751(d)". **Effective** for sales, exchanges, and distributions after 8-5-97. For a special rule, see Act Sec. 1062(c)(2), below.

P.L. 105-34, §1062(c)(2), provides:

(2) BINDING CONTRACTS.—The amendments made by this section shall not apply to any sale or exchange pursuant to a written binding contract in effect on June 8, 1997, and at all times thereafter before such sale or exchange.

[Sec. 731(b)]

(b) PARTNERSHIPS.—No gain or loss shall be recognized to a partnership on a distribution to a partner of property, including money.

[Sec. 731(c)]

(c) TREATMENT OF MARKETABLE SECURITIES.—

(1) IN GENERAL.—For purposes of subsection (a)(1) and section 737—

(A) the term "money" includes marketable securities, and

(B) such securities shall be taken into account at their fair market value as of the date of the distribution.

(2) MARKETABLE SECURITIES.—For purposes of this subsection:

(A) IN GENERAL.—The term "marketable securities" means financial instruments and foreign currencies which are, as of the date of the distribution, actively traded (within the meaning of section 1092(d)(1)).

(B) OTHER PROPERTY.—Such term includes—

(i) any interest in—

(I) a common trust fund, or

(II) a regulated investment company which is offering for sale or has outstanding any redeemable security (as defined in section 2(a)(32) of the Investment Company Act of 1940) of which it is the issuer,

(ii) any financial instrument which, pursuant to its terms or any other arrangement, is readily convertible into, or exchangeable for, money or marketable securities,

(iii) any financial instrument the value of which is determined substantially by reference to marketable securities,

(iv) except to the extent provided in regulations prescribed by the Secretary, any interest in a precious metal which, as of the date of the distribution, is actively traded (within the meaning of section 1092(d)(1)) unless such metal was produced, used, or held in the active conduct of a trade or business by the partnership,

(v) except as otherwise provided in regulations prescribed by the Secretary, interests in any entity if substantially all of the assets of such entity consist (directly or indirectly) of marketable securities, money, or both, and

(vi) to the extent provided in regulations prescribed by the Secretary, any interest in an entity not described in clause (v) but only to the extent of the value of such interest which is attributable to marketable securities, money, or both.

(C) FINANCIAL INSTRUMENT.—The term "financial instrument" includes stocks and other equity interests, evidences of indebtedness, options, forward or futures contracts, notional principal contracts, and derivatives.

(3) EXCEPTIONS.—

(A) IN GENERAL.—Paragraph (1) shall not apply to the distribution from a partnership of a marketable security to a partner if—

(i) the security was contributed to the partnership by such partner, except to the extent that the value of the distributed security is attributable to marketable securities or money contributed (directly or indirectly) to the entity to which the distributed security relates,

(ii) to the extent provided in regulations prescribed by the Secretary, the property was not a marketable security when acquired by such partnership, or

(iii) such partnership is an investment partnership and such partner is an eligible partner thereof.

(B) LIMITATION ON GAIN RECOGNIZED.—In the case of a distribution of marketable securities to a partner, the amount taken into account under paragraph (1) shall be reduced (but not below zero) by the excess (if any) of—

(i) such partner's distributive share of the net gain which would be recognized if all of the marketable securities of the same class and issuer as the distributed securities held by the partnership were sold (immediately before the transaction to which the distribution relates) by the partnership for fair market value, over

(ii) such partner's distributive share of the net gain which is attributable to the marketable securities of the same class and issuer as the distributed securities held by the partnership immediately after the transaction, determined by using the same fair market value as used under clause (i).

Under regulations prescribed by the Secretary, all marketable securities held by the partnership may be treated as marketable securities of the same class and issuer as the distributed securities.

(C) DEFINITIONS RELATING TO INVESTMENT PARTNERSHIPS.—For purposes of subparagraph (A)(iii):

(i) INVESTMENT PARTNERSHIP.—The term "investment partnership" means any partnership which has never been engaged in a trade or business and substantially all of the assets (by value) of which have always consisted of—

(I) money,

(II) stock in a corporation,

(III) notes, bonds, debentures, or other evidences of indebtedness,

(IV) interest rate, currency, or equity notional principal contracts,

(V) foreign currencies,

(VI) interests in or derivative financial instruments (including options, forward or futures contracts, short positions, and similar financial instruments) in any asset described in any other subclause of this clause or in any commodity traded on or subject to the rules of a board of trade or commodity exchange,

(VII) other assets specified in regulations prescribed by the Secretary, or

(VIII) any combination of the foregoing.

(ii) EXCEPTION FOR CERTAIN ACTIVITIES.—A partnership shall not be treated as engaged in a trade or business by reason of—

(I) any activity undertaken as an investor, trader, or dealer in any asset described in clause (i), or

(II) any other activity specified in regulations prescribed by the Secretary.

(iii) ELIGIBLE PARTNER.—

(I) IN GENERAL.—The term "eligible partner" means any partner who, before the date of the distribution, did not contribute to the partnership any property other than assets described in clause (i).

(II) EXCEPTION FOR CERTAIN NONRECOGNITION TRANSACTIONS.—The term "eligible partner" shall not include the transferor or transferee in a nonrecognition transaction involving a transfer of any portion of an interest in a partnership with respect to which the transferor was not an eligible partner.

(iv) LOOK-THRU OF PARTNERSHIP TIERS.—Except as otherwise provided in regulations prescribed by the Secretary—

(I) a partnership shall be treated as engaged in any trade or business engaged in by, and as holding (instead of a partnership interest) a proportionate share of the assets of, any other partnership in which the partnership holds a partnership interest, and

(II) a partner who contributes to a partnership an interest in another partnership shall be treated as contributing a proportionate share of the assets of the other partnership.

If the preceding sentence does not apply under such regulations with respect to any interest held by a partnership in another partnership, the interest in such other partnership shall be treated as if it were specified in a subclause of clause (i).

(4) BASIS OF SECURITIES DISTRIBUTED.—

(A) IN GENERAL.—The basis of marketable securities with respect to which gain is recognized by reason of this subsection shall be—

(i) their basis determined under section 732, increased by

(ii) the amount of such gain.

(B) ALLOCATION OF BASIS INCREASE.—Any increase in basis attributable to the gain described in subparagraph (A)(ii) shall be allocated to marketable securities in proportion to their respective amounts of unrealized appreciation before such increase.

(5) SUBSECTION DISREGARDED IN DETERMINING BASIS OF PARTNER'S INTEREST IN PARTNERSHIP AND OF BASIS OF PARTNERSHIP PROPERTY.—Sections 733 and 734 shall be applied as if no gain were recognized, and no adjustment were made to the basis of property, under this subsection.

(6) CHARACTER OF GAIN RECOGNIZED.—In the case of a distribution of a marketable security which is an unrealized receivable (as defined in section 751(c)) or an inventory item (as defined in section 751(d)), any gain recognized under this subsection shall be treated as ordinary income to the extent of any increase in the basis of such security attributable to the gain described in paragraph (4)(A)(ii).

(7) REGULATIONS.—The Secretary shall prescribe such regulations as may be necessary or appropriate to carry out the purposes of this subsection, including regulations to prevent the avoidance of such purposes.

Amendments

• **1997, Taxpayer Relief Act of 1997 (P.L. 105-34)**

P.L. 105-34, §1062(b)(3):

Amended Code Sec. 731(c)(6) by striking "section 751(d)(2)" and inserting "section 751(d)". **Effective** for sales, exchanges, and distributions after 8-5-97. For a special rule, see Act Sec. 1062(c)(2), below.

P.L. 105-34, §1062(c)(2), provides:

(2) BINDING CONTRACTS.—The amendments made by this section shall not apply to any sale or exchange pursuant to a written binding contract in effect on June 8, 1997, and at all times thereafter before such sale or exchange.

• **1994, Uruguay Round Agreements Act (P.L. 103-465)**

P.L. 103-465, §741(a):

Amended Code Sec. 731 by redesignating subsection (c) as subsection (d) and by inserting after subsection (b) a new subsection (c). **Effective** for distributions after 12-8-94. For special rules, see Act Sec. 741(c)(2)-(5), below.

P.L. 103-465, §741(c)(2)-(5), provides:

(2) CERTAIN DISTRIBUTIONS BEFORE JANUARY 1, 1995.—The amendments made by this section shall not apply to any marketable security distributed before January 1, 1995, by the partnership which held such security on July 27, 1994.

(3) DISTRIBUTIONS IN LIQUIDATION OF PARTNER'S INTEREST.—The amendments made by this section shall not apply to the distribution of a marketable security in liquidation of a partner's interest in a partnership if—

(A) such liquidation is pursuant to a written contract which was binding on July 15, 1994, and at all times thereafter before the distribution, and

(B) such contract provides for the purchase of such interest not later than a date certain for—

(i) a fixed value of marketable securities that are specified in the contract, or

(ii) other property.

The preceding sentence shall not apply if the partner has the right to elect that such distribution be made other than in marketable securities.

(4) DISTRIBUTIONS IN COMPLETE LIQUIDATION OF PUBLICLY TRADED PARTNERSHIPS.—

(A) IN GENERAL.—The amendments made by this section shall not apply to the distribution of a marketable security in a qualified partnership liquidation if—

(i) the marketable securities were received by the partnership in a nonrecognition transaction in exchange for substantially all of the assets of the partnership,

(ii) the marketable securities are distributed by the partnership within 90 days after their receipt by the partnership, and

(iii) the partnership is liquidated before the beginning of the 1st taxable year of the partnership beginning after December 31, 1997.

(B) QUALIFIED PARTNERSHIP LIQUIDATION.—For purposes of subparagraph (A), the term "qualified partnership liquidation" means—

(i) a complete liquidation of a publicly traded partnership (as defined in section 7704(b) of the Internal Revenue Code of 1986) which is an existing partnership (as defined in section 10211(c)(2) of the Revenue Act of 1987), and

(ii) a complete liquidation of a partnership which is related to a partnership described in clause (i) if such liquidation is related to a complete liquidation of the partnership described in clause (i).

(5) MARKETABLE SECURITIES.—For purposes of this subsection, the term "marketable securities" has the meaning given such term by section 731(c) of the Internal Revenue Code of 1986, as added by this section.

[Sec. 731(d)]

(d) EXCEPTIONS.—This section shall not apply to the extent otherwise provided by section 736 (relating to payments to a retiring partner or a deceased partner's successor in interest), section 751 (relating to unrealized receivables and inventory items), and section 737 (relating to recognition of precontribution gain in case of certain distributions).

Amendments

• **1994, Uruguay Round Agreements Act (P.L. 103-465)**

P.L. 103-465, §741(a):

Amended Code Sec. 731 by redesignating subsection (c) as subsection (d). **Effective** for distributions after 12-8-94. For special rules, see Act Sec. 741(c)(2)-(5) in the amendments following Code Sec. 731(c).

• **1992, Energy Policy Act of 1992 (P.L. 102-486)**

P.L. 102-486, §1937(b)(2)(A)-(B):

Amended Code Sec. 731(c) by striking "and section 751" and inserting ", section 751", and by inserting ", and section 737 (relating to recognition of precontribution gain in case of certain distributions)" before the period at the end thereof. **Effective** for distributions on or after 6-25-92.

[Sec. 732]

SEC. 732. BASIS OF DISTRIBUTED PROPERTY OTHER THAN MONEY.

[Sec. 732(a)]

(a) DISTRIBUTIONS OTHER THAN IN LIQUIDATION OF A PARTNER'S INTEREST.—

(1) GENERAL RULE.—The basis of property (other than money) distributed by a partnership to a partner other than in liquidation of the partner's interest shall, except as provided in paragraph (2), be its adjusted basis to the partnership immediately before such distribution.

(2) LIMITATION.—The basis to the distributee partner of property to which paragraph (1) is applicable shall not exceed the adjusted basis of such partner's interest in the partnership reduced by any money distributed in the same transaction.

[Sec. 732(b)]

(b) DISTRIBUTIONS IN LIQUIDATION.—The basis of property (other than money) distributed by a partnership to a partner in liquidation of the partner's interest shall be an amount equal to the adjusted basis of such partner's interest in the partnership reduced by any money distributed in the same transaction.

[Sec. 732(c)]

(c) ALLOCATION OF BASIS.—

(1) IN GENERAL.—The basis of distributed properties to which subsection (a)(2) or (b) is applicable shall be allocated—

(A)(i) first to any unrealized receivables (as defined in section 751(c)) and inventory items (as defined in section 751(d)) in an amount equal to the adjusted basis of each such property to the partnership, and

(ii) if the basis to be allocated is less than the sum of the adjusted bases of such properties to the partnership, then, to the extent any decrease is required in order to have the adjusted bases of such properties equal the basis to be allocated, in the manner provided in paragraph (3), and

(B) to the extent of any basis remaining after the allocation under subparagraph (A), to other distributed properties—

(i) first by assigning to each such other property such other property's adjusted basis to the partnership, and

(ii) then, to the extent any increase or decrease in basis is required in order to have the adjusted bases of such other distributed properties equal such remaining basis, in the manner provided in paragraph (2) or (3), whichever is appropriate.

(2) METHOD OF ALLOCATING INCREASE.—Any increase required under paragraph (1)(B) shall be allocated among the properties—

(A) first to properties with unrealized appreciation in proportion to their respective amounts of unrealized appreciation before such increase (but only to the extent of each property's unrealized appreciation), and

(B) then, to the extent such increase is not allocated under subparagraph (A), in proportion to their respective fair market values.

(3) METHOD OF ALLOCATING DECREASE.—Any decrease required under paragraph (1)(A) or (1)(B) shall be allocated—

(A) first to properties with unrealized depreciation in proportion to their respective amounts of unrealized depreciation before such decrease (but only to the extent of each property's unrealized depreciation), and

(B) then, to the extent such decrease is not allocated under subparagraph (A), in proportion to their respective adjusted bases (as adjusted under subparagraph (A)).

Amendments

• 1997, Taxpayer Relief Act of 1997 (P.L. 105-34)

P.L. 105-34, §1061(a):

Amended Code Sec. 732(c). **Effective** for distributions after 8-5-97. Prior to amendment, Code Sec. 732(c) read as follows:

(c) ALLOCATION OF BASIS.—The basis of distributed properties to which subsection (a)(2) or subsection (b) is applicable shall be allocated—

(1) first to any unrealized receivables (as defined in section 751(c)) and inventory items (as defined in section 751(d)(2)) in an amount equal to the adjusted basis of each such property to the partnership (or if the basis to be allocated is less than the sum of the adjusted bases of such properties to the partnership, in proportion to such bases), and

(2) to the extent of any remaining basis, to any other distributed properties in proportion to their adjusted bases to the partnership.

P.L. 105-34, §1062(b)(3):

Amended Code Sec. 732(c)(1)(A), as amended, by striking "section 751(d)(2)" and inserting "section 751(d)". **Effective**, generally, for sales, exchanges, and distributions after 8-5-97. For a special rule, see Act Sec. 1062(c)(2), below.

P.L. 105-34, §1062(c)(2), provides:

(2) BINDING CONTRACTS.—The amendments made by this section shall not apply to any sale or exchange pursuant to a written binding contract in effect on June 8, 1997, and at all times thereafter before such sale or exchange.

[Sec. 732(d)]

(d) SPECIAL PARTNERSHIP BASIS TO TRANSFEREE.—For purposes of subsections (a), (b), and (c), a partner who acquired all or part of his interest by a transfer with respect to which the election provided in section 754 is not in effect, and to whom a distribution of property (other than money) is made with respect to the transferred interest within 2 years after such transfer, may elect, under regulations prescribed by the Secretary, to treat as the adjusted partnership basis of such property the adjusted basis such property would have if the adjustment provided in section 743(b) were in effect with respect to the partnership property. The Secretary may by regulations require the application of this subsection in the case of a distribution to a transferee partner, whether or not made within 2 years after the transfer, if at the time of the transfer the fair market value of the partnership property (other than money) exceeded 110 percent of its adjusted basis to the partnership.

Amendments

• 1976, Tax Reform Act of 1976 (P.L. 94-455)

P.L. 94-455, §1906(b)(13)(A):

Amended 1954 Code by substituting "Secretary" for "Secretary or his delegate" each place it appeared. **Effective** 2-1-77.

[Sec. 732(e)]

(e) EXCEPTION.—This section shall not apply to the extent that a distribution is treated as a sale or exchange of property under section 751(b) (relating to unrealized receivables and inventory items).

[Sec. 732(f)]

(f) CORRESPONDING ADJUSTMENT TO BASIS OF ASSETS OF A DISTRIBUTED CORPORATION CONTROLLED BY A CORPORATE PARTNER.—

(1) IN GENERAL.—If—

(A) a corporation (hereafter in this subsection referred to as the "corporate partner") receives a distribution from a partnership of stock in another corporation (hereafter in this subsection referred to as the "distributed corporation"),

(B) the corporate partner has control of the distributed corporation immediately after the distribution or at any time thereafter, and

(C) the partnership's adjusted basis in such stock immediately before the distribution exceeded the corporate partner's adjusted basis in such stock immediately after the distribution,

then an amount equal to such excess shall be applied to reduce (in accordance with subsection (c)) the basis of property held by the distributed corporation at such time (or, if the corporate partner does not control the distributed corporation at such time, at the time the corporate partner first has such control).

(2) EXCEPTION FOR CERTAIN DISTRIBUTIONS BEFORE CONTROL ACQUIRED.—Paragraph (1) shall not apply to any distribution of stock in the distributed corporation if—

(A) the corporate partner does not have control of such corporation immediately after such distribution, and

(B) the corporate partner establishes to the satisfaction of the Secretary that such distribution was not part of a plan or arrangement to acquire control of the distributed corporation.

(3) LIMITATIONS ON BASIS REDUCTION.—

(A) IN GENERAL.—The amount of the reduction under paragraph (1) shall not exceed the amount by which the sum of the aggregate adjusted bases of the property and the amount of money of the distributed corporation exceeds the corporate partner's adjusted basis in the stock of the distributed corporation.

(B) REDUCTION NOT TO EXCEED ADJUSTED BASIS OF PROPERTY.—No reduction under paragraph (1) in the basis of any property shall exceed the adjusted basis of such property (determined without regard to such reduction).

(4) GAIN RECOGNITION WHERE REDUCTION LIMITED.—If the amount of any reduction under paragraph (1) (determined after the application of paragraph (3)(A)) exceeds the aggregate adjusted bases of the property of the distributed corporation—

(A) such excess shall be recognized by the corporate partner as long-term capital gain, and

(B) the corporate partner's adjusted basis in the stock of the distributed corporation shall be increased by such excess.

(5) CONTROL.—For purposes of this subsection, the term "control" means ownership of stock meeting the requirements of section 1504(a)(2).

(6) INDIRECT DISTRIBUTIONS.—For purposes of paragraph (1), if a corporation acquires (other than in a distribution from a partnership) stock the basis of which is determined (by reason of being distributed from a partnership) in whole or in part by reference to subsection (a)(2) or (b), the corporation shall be treated as receiving a distribution of such stock from a partnership.

(7) SPECIAL RULE FOR STOCK IN CONTROLLED CORPORATION.—If the property held by a distributed corporation is stock in a corporation which the distributed corporation controls, this subsection shall be applied to reduce the basis of the property of such controlled corporation. This subsection shall be reapplied to any property of any controlled corporation which is stock in a corporation which it controls.

(8) REGULATIONS.—The Secretary shall prescribe such regulations as may be necessary to carry out the purposes of this subsection, including regulations to avoid double counting and to prevent the abuse of such purposes.

Amendments

• 1999, Tax Relief Extension Act of 1999 (P.L. 106-170)

P.L. 106-170, §538(a):

Amended Code Sec. 732 by adding at the end a new subsection (f). **Effective** for distributions made after 7-14-99. For an exception, see Act Sec. 538(b)(2), below.

P.L. 106-170, §538(b)(2), provides:

(2) PARTNERSHIPS IN EXISTENCE ON JULY 14, 1999.—In the case of a corporation which is a partner in a partnership as of July 14, 1999, the amendment made by this section shall apply to any distribution made (or treated as made) to such partner from such partnership after June 30, 2001, except that this paragraph shall not apply to any distribution after the date of the enactment of this Act unless the partner makes an election to have this paragraph apply to such distribution on the partner's return of Federal income tax for the taxable year in which such distribution occurs.

[Sec. 733]

SEC. 733. BASIS OF DISTRIBUTEE PARTNER'S INTEREST.

In the case of a distribution by a partnership to a partner other than in liquidation of a partner's interest, the adjusted basis to such partner of his interest in the partnership shall be reduced (but not below zero) by—

(1) the amount of any money distributed to such partner, and

(2) the amount of the basis to such partner of distributed property other than money, as determined under section 732.

[Sec. 734]

SEC. 734. ADJUSTMENT TO BASIS OF UNDISTRIBUTED PARTNERSHIP PROPERTY WHERE SECTION 754 ELECTION OR SUBSTANTIAL BASIS REDUCTION.

[Sec. 734(a)]

(a) GENERAL RULE.—The basis of partnership property shall not be adjusted as the result of a distribution of property to a partner unless the election, provided in section 754 (relating to optional adjustment to basis of partnership property), is in effect with respect to such partnership or unless there is a substantial basis reduction with respect to such distribution.

Amendments

• 2005, Gulf Opportunity Zone Act of 2005 (P.L. 109-135)

P.L. 109-135, §403(bb)(1):

Amended Code Sec. 734(a) by inserting "with respect to such distribution" before the period at the end. **Effective** as if included in the provision of the American Jobs Creation Act of 2004 (P.L. 108-357) to which it relates [**effective** for distributions after 10-22-2004.—CCH].

• 2004, American Jobs Creation Act of 2004 (P.L. 108-357)

P.L. 108-357, §833(c)(1):

Amended Code Sec. 734(a) by inserting before the period "or unless there is a substantial basis reduction". **Effective** for distributions after 10-22-2004.

P.L. 108-357, §833(c)(5)(A):

Amended the heading for Code Sec. 734. **Effective** for distributions after 10-22-2004. Prior to amendment, the heading for Code Sec. 734 read as follows:

SEC. 734. OPTIONAL ADJUSTMENT TO BASIS OF UNDISTRIBUTED PARTNERSHIP PROPERTY.

[Sec. 734(b)]

(b) METHOD OF ADJUSTMENT.—In the case of a distribution of property to a partner by a partnership with respect to which the election provided in section 754 is in effect or with respect to which there is a substantial basis reduction, the partnership shall—

(1) increase the adjusted basis of partnership property by—

(A) the amount of any gain recognized to the distributee partner with respect to such distribution under section 731(a)(1), and

(B) in the case of distributed property to which section 732(a)(2) or (b) applies, the excess of the adjusted basis of the distributed property to the partnership immediately before the distribution (as adjusted by section 732(d)) over the basis of the distributed property to the distributee, as determined under section 732, or

(2) decrease the adjusted basis of partnership property by—

(A) the amount of any loss recognized to the distributee partner with respect to such distribution under section 731(a)(2), and

(B) in the case of distributed property to which section 732(b) applies, the excess of the basis of the distributed property to the distributee, as determined under section 732, over the adjusted basis of the distributed property to the partnership immediately before such distribution (as adjusted by section 732(d)).

Paragraph (1)(B) shall not apply to any distributed property which is an interest in another partnership with respect to which the election provided in section 754 is not in effect.

Amendments

• 2005, Gulf Opportunity Zone Act of 2005 (P.L. 109-135)

P.L. 109-135, §403(bb)(2):

Amended so much of Code Sec. 734(b) as precedes paragraph (1). **Effective** as if included in the provision of the American Jobs Creation Act of 2004 (P.L. 108-357) to which it relates [**effective** for distributions after 10-22-2004.—CCH]. Prior to amendment, so much of Code Sec. 734(b) as precedes paragraph (1) read as follows:

(b) METHOD OF ADJUSTMENT.—In the case of a distribution of property to a partner, a partnership, with respect to which the election provided in section 754 is in effect or unless there is a substantial basis reduction, shall—

• **2004, American Jobs Creation Act of 2004 (P.L. 108-357)**

P.L. 108-357, §833(c)(2):

Amended Code Sec. 734(b) by inserting "or unless there is a substantial basis reduction" after "section 754 is in effect". **Effective** for distributions after 10-22-2004.

• **1984, Deficit Reduction Act of 1984 (P.L. 98-369)**

P.L. 98-369, §78(a):

Amended Code Sec. 734(b) by adding at the end thereof a new sentence. **Effective** for distributions after 3-1-84, in tax years ending after such date.

[Sec. 734(c)]

(c) ALLOCATION OF BASIS.—The allocation of basis among partnership properties where subsection (b) is applicable shall be made in accordance with the rules provided in section 755.

[Sec. 734(d)]

(d) SUBSTANTIAL BASIS REDUCTION.—

(1) IN GENERAL.—For purposes of this section, there is a substantial basis reduction with respect to a distribution if the sum of the amounts described in subparagraphs (A) and (B) of subsection (b)(2) exceeds $250,000.

(2) REGULATIONS.—

For regulations to carry out this subsection, see section 743(d)(2).

Amendments

• **2004, American Jobs Creation Act of 2004 (P.L. 108-357)**

P.L. 108-357, §833(c)(3):

Amended Code Sec. 734 by adding at the end a new subsection (d). **Effective** for distributions after 10-22-2004.

[Sec. 734(e)]

(e) EXCEPTION FOR SECURITIZATION PARTNERSHIPS.—For purposes of this section, a securitization partnership (as defined in section 743(f)) shall not be treated as having a substantial basis reduction with respect to any distribution of property to a partner.

Amendments

• **2004, American Jobs Creation Act of 2004 (P.L. 108-357)**

P.L. 108-357, §833(c)(4):

Amended Code Sec. 734 by inserting after subsection (d) a new subsection (e). **Effective** for distributions after 10-22-2004.

[Sec. 735]

SEC. 735. CHARACTER OF GAIN OR LOSS ON DISPOSITION OF DISTRIBUTED PROPERTY.

[Sec. 735(a)]

(a) SALE OR EXCHANGE OF CERTAIN DISTRIBUTED PROPERTY.—

(1) UNREALIZED RECEIVABLES.—Gain or loss on the disposition by a distributee partner of unrealized receivables (as defined in section 751(c)) distributed by a partnership, shall be considered as ordinary income or as ordinary loss, as the case may be.

(2) INVENTORY ITEMS.—Gain or loss on the sale or exchange by a distributee partner of inventory items (as defined in section 751(d)) distributed by a partnership shall, if sold or exchanged within 5 years from the date of the distribution, be considered as ordinary income or as ordinary loss, as the case may be.

Amendments

• **1997, Taxpayer Relief Act of 1997 (P.L. 105-34)**

P.L. 105-34, §1062(b)(3):

Amended Code Sec. 735(a)(2) by striking "section 751(d)(2)" and inserting "section 751(d)". **Effective**, generally, for sales, exchanges, and distributions after 8-5-97. For a special rule, see Act Sec. 1062(c)(2), below.

P.L. 105-34, §1062(c)(2), provides:

(2) BINDING CONTRACTS.—The amendments made by this section shall not apply to any sale or exchange pursuant to a written binding contract in effect on June 8, 1997, and at all times thereafter before such sale or exchange.

• **1976, Tax Reform Act of 1976 (P.L. 94-455)**

P.L. 94-455, §1901(b)(2):

Substituted "as ordinary income or as ordinary loss, as the case may be" for "gain or loss from the sale or exchange of property other than a capital asset" in Code Sec. 735(a)(1) and (2). **Effective** for tax years beginning after 12-31-76.

[Sec. 735(b)]

(b) HOLDING PERIOD FOR DISTRIBUTED PROPERTY.—In determining the period for which a partner has held property received in a distribution from a partnership (other than for purposes of subsection (a)(2)), there shall be included the holding period of the partnership, as determined under section 1223, with respect to such property.

[Sec. 735(c)]

(c) SPECIAL RULES.—

(1) WAIVER OF HOLDING PERIODS CONTAINED IN SECTION 1231.—For purposes of this section, section 751(d) (defining inventory item) shall be applied without regard to any holding period in section 1231(b).

(2) SUBSTITUTED BASIS PROPERTY.—

(A) IN GENERAL.—If any property described in subsection (a) is disposed of in a nonrecognition transaction, the tax treatment which applies to such property under such subsection shall also apply to any substituted basis property resulting from such transaction. A similar rule shall also apply in the case of a series of nonrecognition transactions.

(B) EXCEPTION FOR STOCK IN C CORPORATION.—Subparagraph (A) shall not apply to any stock in a C corporation received in an exchange described in section 351.

Amendments

• 1997, Taxpayer Relief Act of 1997 (P.L. 105-34)

P.L. 105-34, §1062(b)(3):

Amended Code Sec. 735(c)(1) by striking "section 751(d)(2)" and inserting "section 751(d)". **Effective**, generally, for sales, exchanges, and distributions after 8-5-97. For a special rule, see Act Sec. 1062(c)(2), below.

P.L. 105-34, §1062(c)(2), provides:

(2) BINDING CONTRACTS.—The amendments made by this section shall not apply to any sale or exchange pursuant to a written binding contract in effect on June 8, 1997, and at all times thereafter before such sale or exchange.

• 1984, Deficit Reduction Act of 1984 (P.L. 98-369)

P.L. 98-369, §74(b):

Amended Code Sec. 735 by adding new subsection (c) at the end thereof. **Effective** for property distributed after 3-31-84, in tax years ending after such date.

[Sec. 736]

SEC. 736. PAYMENTS TO A RETIRING PARTNER OR A DECEASED PARTNER'S SUCCESSOR IN INTEREST.

[Sec. 736(a)]

(a) PAYMENTS CONSIDERED AS DISTRIBUTIVE SHARE OR GUARANTEED PAYMENT.—Payments made in liquidation of the interest of a retiring partner or a deceased partner shall, except as provided in subsection (b), be considered—

(1) as a distributive share to the recipient of partnership income if the amount thereof is determined with regard to the income of the partnership, or

(2) as a guaranteed payment described in section 707(c) if the amount thereof is determined without regard to the income of the partnership.

[Sec. 736(b)]

(b) PAYMENTS FOR INTEREST IN PARTNERSHIP.—

(1) GENERAL RULE.—Payments made in liquidation of the interest of a retiring partner or a deceased partner shall, to the extent such payments (other than payments described in paragraph (2)) are determined, under regulations prescribed by the Secretary, to be made in exchange for the interest of such partner in partnership property, be considered as a distribution by the partnership and not as a distributive share or guaranteed payment under subsection (a).

(2) SPECIAL RULES.—For purposes of this subsection, payments in exchange for an interest in partnership property shall not include amounts paid for—

(A) unrealized receivables of the partnership (as defined in section 751(c)), or

(B) good will of the partnership, except to the extent that the partnership agreement provides for a payment with respect to good will.

(3) LIMITATION ON APPLICATION OF PARAGRAPH (2).—Paragraph (2) shall apply only if—

(A) capital is not a material income-producing factor for the partnership, and

(B) the retiring or deceased partner was a general partner in the partnership.

Amendments

• 1993, Omnibus Budget Reconciliation Act of 1993 (P.L. 103-66)

P.L. 103-66, §13262(a):

Amended Code Sec. 736(b) by adding at the end thereof new paragraph (3). **Effective**, generally, in the case of partners retiring or dying on or after 1-5-93. However, for exceptions, see Act Sec. 13262(c)(2) below.

P.L. 103-66, §13262(c)(2), provides:

(2) BINDING CONTRACT EXCEPTION.—The amendments made by this section shall not apply to any partner retiring on or after January 5, 1993, if a written contract to purchase such partner's interest in the partnership was binding on January 4, 1993, and at all times thereafter before such purchase.

• 1976, Tax Reform Act of 1976 (P.L. 94-455)

P.L. 94-455, §1906(b)(13)(A):

Amended 1954 Code by substituting "Secretary" for "Secretary or his delegate" each place it appeared. **Effective** 2-1-77.

[Sec. 736(c)—Stricken]

Amendments

• **1993, Omnibus Budget Reconciliation Act of 1993 (P.L. 103-66)**

P.L. 103-66, §13262(b)(2)(B):

Amended Code Sec. 736 by striking subsection (c). **Effective**, generally, in the case of partners retiring or dying on or after 1-5-93. However, for exceptions, see Act Sec. 13262(c)(2) below. Prior to amendment, Code Sec. 736(c) read as follows:

(c) CROSS REFERENCE.—

For limitation on the tax attributable to certain gain connected with section 1248 stock, see section 751(e).

P.L. 103-66, §13262(c)(2), provides:

(2) BINDING CONTRACT EXCEPTION.—The amendments made by this section shall not apply to any partner retiring on or after January 5, 1993, if a written contract to purchase such partner's interest in the partnership was binding on January 4, 1993, and at all times thereafter before such purchase.

• **1978, Revenue Act of 1978 (P.L. 95-600)**

P.L. 95-600, §701(u)(13)(B), (C):

Added Code Sec. 736(c). **Effective** for transfers beginning after 10-9-75, and to sales, exchanges, and distributions taking place after such date.

[Sec. 737]

SEC. 737. RECOGNITION OF PRECONTRIBUTION GAIN IN CASE OF CERTAIN DISTRIBUTIONS TO CONTRIBUTING PARTNER.

[Sec. 737(a)]

(a) GENERAL RULE.—In the case of any distribution by a partnership to a partner, such partner shall be treated as recognizing gain in an amount equal to the lesser of—

(1) the excess (if any) of (A) the fair market value of property (other than money) received in the distribution over (B) the adjusted basis of such partner's interest in the partnership immediately before the distribution reduced (but not below zero) by the amount of money received in the distribution, or

(2) the net precontribution gain of the partner.

Gain recognized under the preceding sentence shall be in addition to any gain recognized under section 731. The character of such gain shall be determined by reference to the proportionate character of the net precontribution gain.

[Sec. 737(b)]

(b) NET PRECONTRIBUTION GAIN.—For purposes of this section, the term "net precontribution gain" means the net gain (if any) which would have been recognized by the distributee partner under section 704(c)(1)(B) if all property which—

(1) had been contributed to the partnership by the distributee partner within 7 years of the distribution, and

(2) is held by such partnership immediately before the distribution,

had been distributed by such partnership to another partner.

Amendments

• **1997, Taxpayer Relief Act of 1997 (P.L. 105-34)**

P.L. 105-34, §1063(a):

Amended Code Sec. 737(b)(1) by striking "5 years" and inserting "7 years". **Effective**, generally, for property contributed to a partnership after 6-8-97. For a special rule, see Act Sec. 1063(b)(2), below.

P.L. 105-34, §1063(b)(2), provides:

(2) BINDING CONTRACTS.—The amendment made by subsection (a) shall not apply to any property contributed pursuant to a written binding contract in effect on June 8, 1997, and at all times thereafter before such contribution if such contract provides for the contribution of a fixed amount of property.

[Sec. 737(c)]

(c) BASIS RULES.—

(1) PARTNER'S INTEREST.—The adjusted basis of a partner's interest in a partnership shall be increased by the amount of any gain recognized by such partner under subsection (a). For purposes of determining the basis of the distributed property (other than money), such increase shall be treated as occurring immediately before the distribution.

(2) PARTNERSHIP'S BASIS IN CONTRIBUTED PROPERTY.—Appropriate adjustments shall be made to the adjusted basis of the partnership in the contributed property referred to in subsection (b) to reflect gain recognized under subsection (a).

Amendments

• **1994, Uruguay Round Agreements Act (P.L. 103-465)**

P.L. 103-465, §741(b)(1):

Amended the last sentence of Code Sec. 737(c)(1). **Effective** for distributions after 12-8-94. For special rules, see Act Sec. 741(c)(2)-(5) in the amendment notes following Code Sec. 737(e). Prior to amendment, the last sentence of Code Sec. 737(c)(1) read as follows:

Except for purposes of determining the amount recognized under subsection (a), such increase shall be treated as occurring immediately before the distribution.

[Sec. 737(d)]

(d) EXCEPTIONS.—

(1) DISTRIBUTIONS OF PREVIOUSLY CONTRIBUTED PROPERTY.—If any portion of the property distributed consists of property which had been contributed by the distributee partner to the partnership, such property shall not be taken into account under subsection (a)(1) and shall not be taken into account in determining the amount of the net precontribution gain. If the property distributed consists of an interest in an entity, the preceding sentence shall not apply to the extent that

the value of such interest is attributable to property contributed to such entity after such interest had been contributed to the partnership.

(2) COORDINATION WITH SECTION 751.—This section shall not apply to the extent section 751(b) applies to such distribution.

Amendments

• 1992, Energy Policy Act of 1992 (P.L. 102-486)

P.L. 102-486, §1937(a) (as amended by P.L. 104-188, §1704(j)(8)):

Amended subpart B of part II of subchapter K of chapter 1 by adding at the end thereof new Code Sec. 737. **Effective** for distributions on or after 6-25-92.

[Sec. 737(e)]

(e) MARKETABLE SECURITIES TREATED AS MONEY.—For treatment of marketable securities as money for purposes of this section, see section 731(c).

Amendments

• 1994, Uruguay Round Agreements Act (P.L. 103-465)

P.L. 103-465, §741(b)(2):

Amended Code Sec. 737 by adding at the end a new subsection (e). **Effective** for distributions after 12-8-94. For special rules, see Act Sec. 741(c)(2)-(5), below.

P.L. 103-465, §741(c)(2)-(5), provides:

(2) CERTAIN DISTRIBUTIONS BEFORE JANUARY 1, 1995.—The amendments made by this section shall not apply to any marketable security distributed before January 1, 1995, by the partnership which held such security on July 27, 1994.

(3) DISTRIBUTIONS IN LIQUIDATION OF PARTNER'S INTEREST.—The amendments made by this section shall not apply to the distribution of marketable security in liquidation of a partner's interest in a partnership if—

(A) such liquidation is pursuant to a written contract which was binding on July 15, 1994, and at all times thereafter before the distribution, and

(B) such contract provides for the purchase of such interest not later than a date certain for—

(i) a fixed value of marketable securities that are specified in the contract, or

(ii) other property.

The preceding sentence shall not apply if the partner has the right to elect that such distribution be made other than in marketable securities.

(4) DISTRIBUTIONS IN COMPLETE LIQUIDATION OF PUBLICLY TRADED PARTNERSHIPS.—

(A) IN GENERAL.—The amendments made by this section shall not apply to the distribution of a marketable security in a qualified partnership liquidation if—

(i) the marketable securities were received by the partnership in a nonrecognition transaction in exchange for substantially all of the assets of the partnership,

(ii) the marketable securities are distributed by the partnership within 90 days after their receipt by the partnership, and

(iii) the partnership is liquidated before the beginning of the 1st taxable year of the partnership beginning after December 31, 1997.

(B) QUALIFIED PARTNERSHIP LIQUIDATION.—For purpose of subparagraph (A), the term "qualified partnership liquidation" means—

(i) a complete liquidation of a publicly traded partnership (as defined in section 7704(b) of the Internal Revenue Code of 1986) which is an existing partnership (as defined in section 10211(c)(2) of the Revenue Act of 1987), and

(ii) a complete liquidation of a partnership which is related to a partnership described in clause (i) if such liquidation is related to a complete liquidation of the partnership described in clause (i).

(5) MARKETABLE SECURITIES.—For purposes of this subsection, the term "marketable securities" has the meaning given such term by section 731(c) of the Internal Revenue Code of 1986, as added by this section.

Subpart C—Transfers of Interests in a Partnership

[Sec. 741]

SEC. 741. RECOGNITION AND CHARACTER OF GAIN OR LOSS ON SALE OR EXCHANGE.

In the case of a sale or exchange of an interest in a partnership, gain or loss shall be recognized to the transferor partner. Such gain or loss shall be considered as gain or loss from the sale or exchange of a capital asset, except as otherwise provided in section 751 (relating to unrealized receivables and inventory items).

Amendments

• 2002, Job Creation and Worker Assistance Act of 2002 (P.L. 107-147)

P.L. 107-147, §417(12):

Amended Code Sec. 741 by striking "which have appreciated substantially in value" following "inventory items". **Effective** 3-9-2002.

[Sec. 742]

SEC. 742. BASIS OF TRANSFEREE PARTNER'S INTEREST.

The basis of an interest in a partnership acquired other than by contribution shall be determined under part II of subchapter O (sec. 1011 and following).

[Sec. 743]

SEC. 743. SPECIAL RULES WHERE SECTION 754 ELECTION OR SUBSTANTIAL BUILT-IN LOSS.

[Sec. 743(a)]

(a) GENERAL RULE.—The basis of partnership property shall not be adjusted as the result of a transfer of an interest in a partnership by sale or exchange or on the death of a partner unless the election provided by section 754 (relating to optional adjustment to basis of partnership property) is in effect with respect to such partnership or unless the partnership has a substantial built-in loss immediately after such transfer.

Amendments

• 2004, American Jobs Creation Act of 2004 (P.L. 108-357)

P.L. 108-357, §833(b)(1):

Amended Code Sec. 743(a) by inserting before the period "or unless the partnership has a substantial built-in loss immediately after such transfer". **Effective** for transfers after 10-22-2004. For a transition rule, see Act Sec. 833(d)(2)(B), below.

P.L. 108-357, §833(b)(6)(A):

Amended the heading for Code Sec. 743. **Effective** for transfers after 10-22-2004. For a transition rule, see Act Sec. 833(d)(2)(B), below. Prior to amendment, the heading for Code Sec. 743 read as follows:

SEC. 743. OPTIONAL ADJUSTMENT TO BASIS OF PARTNERSHIP PROPERTY.

P.L. 108-357, §833(d)(2)(B), provides:

(B) TRANSITION RULE.—In the case of an electing investment partnership which is in existence on June 4, 2004, section 743(e)(6)(H) of the Internal Revenue Code of 1986, as added by this section, shall not apply to such partnership and section 743(e)(6)(I) of such Code, as so added, shall be applied by substituting "20 years" for "15 years".

[Sec. 743(b)]

(b) ADJUSTMENT TO BASIS OF PARTNERSHIP PROPERTY.—In the case of a transfer of an interest in a partnership by sale or exchange or upon the death of a partner, a partnership with respect to which the election provided in section 754 is in effect or which has a substantial built-in loss immediately after such transfer shall—

(1) increase the adjusted basis of the partnership property by the excess of the basis to the transferee partner of his interest in the partnership over his proportionate share of the adjusted basis of the partnership property, or

(2) decrease the adjusted basis of the partnership property by the excess of the transferee partner's proportionate share of the adjusted basis of the partnership property over the basis of his interest in the partnership.

Under regulations prescribed by the Secretary, such increase or decrease shall constitute an adjustment to the basis of partnership property with respect to the transferee partner only. A partner's proportionate share of the adjusted basis of partnership property shall be determined in accordance with his interest in partnership capital and, in the case of property contributed to the partnership by a partner, section 704(c) (relating to contributed property) shall apply in determining such share. In the case of an adjustment under this subsection to the basis of partnership property subject to depletion, any depletion allowable shall be determined separately for the transferee partner with respect to his interest in such property.

Amendments

• 2004, American Jobs Creation Act of 2004 (P.L. 108-357)

P.L. 108-357, §833(b)(2):

Amended Code Sec. 743(b) by inserting "or which has a substantial built-in loss immediately after such transfer" after "section 754 is in effect". **Effective** for transfers after 10-22-2004. For a transition rule, see Act Sec. 833(d)(2)(B), below.

P.L. 108-357, §833(d)(2)(B), provides:

(B) TRANSITION RULE.—In the case of an electing investment partnership which is in existence on June 4, 2004, section 743(e)(6)(H) of the Internal Revenue Code of 1986, as added by this section, shall not apply to such partnership and section 743(e)(6)(I) of such Code, as so added, shall be applied by substituting "20 years" for "15 years".

• 1984, Deficit Reduction Act of 1984 (P.L. 98-369)

P.L. 98-369, §71(b):

Amended the third sentence of Code Sec. 743(b) by striking out "an agreement described in section 704(c)(2) (relating to effect of partnership agreement on contributed property), such share shall be determined by taking such agreement into account" and inserting in lieu thereof "property contributed to the partnership by a partner, section 704(c) (relating to contributed property) shall apply in determining such share". **Effective** with respect to property contributed to the partnership after 3-31-84, in tax years ending after such date.

• 1976, Tax Reform Act of 1976 (P.L. 94-455)

P.L. 94-455, §1906(b)(13)(A):

Amended 1954 Code by substituting "Secretary" for "Secretary or his delegate" each place it appeared. **Effective** 2-1-77.

[Sec. 743(c)]

(c) ALLOCATION OF BASIS.—The allocation of basis among partnership properties where subsection (b) is applicable shall be made in accordance with the rules provided in section 755.

[Sec. 743(d)]

(d) SUBSTANTIAL BUILT-IN LOSS.—

(1) IN GENERAL.—For purposes of this section, a partnership has a substantial built-in loss with respect to a transfer of an interest in a partnership if the partnership's adjusted basis in the partnership property exceeds by more than $250,000 the fair market value of such property.

(2) REGULATIONS.—The Secretary shall prescribe such regulations as may be appropriate to carry out the purposes of paragraph (1) and section 734(d), including regulations aggregating related partnerships and disregarding property acquired by the partnership in an attempt to avoid such purposes.

Amendments

• 2004, American Jobs Creation Act of 2004 (P.L. 108-357)

P.L. 108-357, §833(b)(3):

Amended Code Sec. 743 by adding at the end a new subsection (d). **Effective** for transfers after 10-22-2004. For a transition rule, see Act Sec. 833(d)(2)(B), below.

P.L. 108-357, §833(d)(2)(B), provides:

(B) TRANSITION RULE.—In the case of an electing investment partnership which is in existence on June 4, 2004, section 743(e)(6)(H) of the Internal Revenue Code of 1986, as added by this section, shall not apply to such partnership and section 743(e)(6)(I) of such Code, as so added, shall be applied by substituting "20 years" for "15 years".

[Sec. 743(e)]

(e) ALTERNATIVE RULES FOR ELECTING INVESTMENT PARTNERSHIPS.—

(1) NO ADJUSTMENT OF PARTNERSHIP BASIS.—For purposes of this section, an electing investment partnership shall not be treated as having a substantial built-in loss with respect to any transfer occurring while the election under paragraph (6)(A) is in effect.

(2) LOSS DEFERRAL FOR TRANSFEREE PARTNER.—In the case of a transfer of an interest in an electing investment partnership, the transferee partner's distributive share of losses (without regard to gains) from the sale or exchange of partnership property shall not be allowed except to the extent that it is established that such losses exceed the loss (if any) recognized by the transferor (or any prior transferor to the extent not fully offset by a prior disallowance under this paragraph) on the transfer of the partnership interest.

(3) NO REDUCTION IN PARTNERSHIP BASIS.—Losses disallowed under paragraph (2) shall not decrease the transferee partner's basis in the partnership interest.

(4) EFFECT OF TERMINATION OF PARTNERSHIP.—This subsection shall be applied without regard to any termination of a partnership under section 708(b)(1)(B).

(5) CERTAIN BASIS REDUCTIONS TREATED AS LOSSES.—In the case of a transferee partner whose basis in property distributed by the partnership is reduced under section 732(a)(2), the amount of the loss recognized by the transferor on the transfer of the partnership interest which is taken into account under paragraph (2) shall be reduced by the amount of such basis reduction.

(6) ELECTING INVESTMENT PARTNERSHIP.—For purposes of this subsection, the term "electing investment partnership" means any partnership if—

(A) the partnership makes an election to have this subsection apply,

(B) the partnership would be an investment company under section 3(a)(1)(A) of the Investment Company Act of 1940 but for an exemption under paragraph (1) or (7) of section 3(c) of such Act,

(C) such partnership has never been engaged in a trade or business,

(D) substantially all of the assets of such partnership are held for investment,

(E) at least 95 percent of the assets contributed to such partnership consist of money,

(F) no assets contributed to such partnership had an adjusted basis in excess of fair market value at the time of contribution,

(G) all partnership interests of such partnership are issued by such partnership pursuant to a private offering before the date which is 24 months after the date of the first capital contribution to such partnership,

(H) the partnership agreement of such partnership has substantive restrictions on each partner's ability to cause a redemption of the partner's interest, and

(I) the partnership agreement of such partnership provides for a term that is not in excess of 15 years.

The election described in subparagraph (A), once made, shall be irrevocable except with the consent of the Secretary.

(7) REGULATIONS.—The Secretary shall prescribe such regulations as may be appropriate to carry out the purposes of this subsection, including regulations for applying this subsection to tiered partnerships.

Amendments

• 2004, American Jobs Creation Act of 2004 (P.L. 108-357)

P.L. 108-357, §833(b)(4)(A):

Amended Code Sec. 743 by adding after subsection (d) a new subsection (e). **Effective** for transfers after 10-22-2004. For a transition rule, see Act Sec. 833(d)(2)(B), below.

P.L. 108-357, §833(d)(2)(B), provides:

(B) TRANSITION RULE.—In the case of an electing investment partnership which is in existence on June 4, 2004, section 743(e)(6)(H) of the Internal Revenue Code of 1986, as added by this section, shall not apply to such partnership and section 743(e)(6)(I) of such Code, as so added, shall be applied by substituting "20 years" for "15 years".

[Sec. 743(f)]

(f) EXCEPTION FOR SECURITIZATION PARTNERSHIPS.—

(1) NO ADJUSTMENT OF PARTNERSHIP BASIS.—For purposes of this section, a securitization partnership shall not be treated as having a substantial built-in loss with respect to any transfer.

(2) SECURITIZATION PARTNERSHIP.—For purposes of paragraph (1), the term "securitization partnership" means any partnership the sole business activity of which is to issue securities which provide for a fixed principal (or similar) amount and which are primarily serviced by the cash flows of a discrete pool (either fixed or revolving) of receivables or other financial assets that by their terms convert into cash in a finite period, but only if the sponsor of the pool reasonably believes that the receivables and other financial assets comprising the pool are not acquired so as to be disposed of.

Amendments

• 2004, American Jobs Creation Act of 2004 (P.L. 108-357)

P.L. 108-357, §833(b)(5):

Amended Code Sec. 743 by adding after subsection (e) a new subsection (f). **Effective** for transfers after 10-22-2004. For a transition rule, see Act Sec. 833(d)(2)(B), below.

P.L. 108-357, §833(d)(2)(B), provides:

(B) TRANSITION RULE.—In the case of an electing investment partnership which is in existence on June 4, 2004, section 743(e)(6)(H) of the Internal Revenue Code of 1986, as added by this section, shall not apply to such partnership and section 743(e)(6)(I) of such Code, as so added, shall be applied by substituting "20 years" for "15 years".

Subpart D—Provisions Common to Other Subparts

[Sec. 751]

SEC. 751. UNREALIZED RECEIVABLES AND INVENTORY ITEMS.

[Sec. 751(a)]

(a) SALE OR EXCHANGE OF INTEREST IN PARTNERSHIP.—The amount of any money, or the fair market value of any property, received by a transferor partner in exchange for all or a part of his interest in the partnership attributable to—

(1) unrealized receivables of the partnership, or

(2) inventory items of the partnership,

shall be considered as an amount realized from the sale or exchange of property other than a capital asset.

Amendments

• 1997, Taxpayer Relief Act of 1997 (P.L. 105-34)

P.L. 105-34, §1062(a):

Amended Code Sec. 751(a)(2). **Effective**, generally, for sales, exchanges, and distributions after 8-5-97. For a special rule, see Act Sec. 1062(c)(2), below. Prior to amendment, Code Sec. 751(a)(2) read as follows:

(2) inventory items of the partnership which have appreciated substantially in value,

P.L. 105-34, §1062(c)(2), provides:

(2) BINDING CONTRACTS.—The amendments made by this section shall not apply to any sale or exchange pursuant to a written binding contract in effect on June 8, 1997, and at all times thereafter before such sale or exchange.

[Sec. 751(b)]

(b) CERTAIN DISTRIBUTIONS TREATED AS SALES OR EXCHANGES.—

(1) GENERAL RULE.—To the extent a partner receives in a distribution—

(A) partnership property which is—

(i) unrealized receivables, or

(ii) inventory items which have appreciated substantially in value,

in exchange for all or a part of his interest in other partnership property (including money), or

(B) partnership property (including money) other than property described in subparagraph (A)(i) or (ii) in exchange for all or a part of his interest in partnership property described in subparagraph (A)(i) or (ii),

such transactions shall, under regulations prescribed by the Secretary, be considered as a sale or exchange of such property between the distributee and the partnership (as constituted after the distribution).

(2) EXCEPTIONS.—Paragraph (1) shall not apply to—

(A) a distribution of property which the distributee contributed to the partnership, or

(B) payments, described in section 736(a), to a retiring partner or successor in interest of a deceased partner.

(3) SUBSTANTIAL APPRECIATION.—For purposes of paragraph (1)—

(A) IN GENERAL.—Inventory items of the partnership shall be considered to have appreciated substantially in value if their fair market value exceeds 120 percent of the adjusted basis to the partnership of such property.

(B) CERTAIN PROPERTY EXCLUDED.—For purposes of subparagraph (A), there shall be excluded any inventory property if a principal purpose for acquiring such property was to avoid the provisions of this subsection relating to inventory items.

Amendments

• 1997, Taxpayer Relief Act of 1997 (P.L. 105-34)

P.L. 105-34, §1062(b)(1)(A):

Amended Code Sec. 751(b)(1) by striking subparagraphs (A) and (B) and inserting new subparagraphs (A) and (B). **Effective**, generally, for sales, exchanges, and distributions after 8-5-97. For a special rule, see Act Sec. 1062(c)(2), below. Prior to being stricken, Code Sec. 751(b)(1)(A)-(B) read as follows:

(A) partnership property described in subsection (a)(1) or (2) in exchange for all or a part of his interest in other partnership property (including money), or

(B) partnership property (including money) other than property described in subsection (a) (1) or (2) in exchange for all or a part of his interest in partnership property described in subsection (a) (1) or (2),

P.L. 105-34, §1062(b)(1)(B):

Amended Code Sec. 751(b) by adding at the end a new paragraph (3). **Effective**, generally, for sales, exchanges, and distributions after 8-5-97. For a special rule, see Act Sec. 1062(c)(2), below.

P.L. 105-34, §1062(c)(2), provides:

(2) BINDING CONTRACTS.—The amendments made by this section shall not apply to any sale or exchange pursuant to a written binding contract in effect on June 8, 1997, and at all times thereafter before such sale or exchange.

• 1976, Tax Reform Act of 1976 (P.L. 94-455)

P.L. 94-455, §1906(b)(13)(A):

Amended 1954 Code by substituting "Secretary" for "Secretary or his delegate" each place it appeared. **Effective** 2-1-77.

[Sec. 751(c)]

(c) UNREALIZED RECEIVABLES.—For purposes of this subchapter, the term "unrealized receivables" includes, to the extent not previously includible in income under the method of accounting used by the partnership, any rights (contractual or otherwise) to payment for—

(1) goods delivered, or to be delivered, to the extent the proceeds therefrom would be treated as amounts received from the sale or exchange of property other than a capital asset, or

(2) services rendered, or to be rendered.

For purposes of this section and, sections 731, 732, and 741 (but not for purposes of section 736), such termalso includes mining property (as defined in section 617(f)(2)), stock in a DISC (as described in section 992(a)), section 1245 property (as defined in section 1245(a)(3)), stock in certain foreign corporations (as described in section 1248), section 1250 property (as defined in section 1250(c)), farm land (as defined in section 1252(a)), franchises, trademarks, or trade names (referred to in section 1253(a)), and an oil, gas, or geothermal property (described in section 1254) but only to the extent of the amount which would be treated as gain to which section 617(d)(1), 995(c), 1245(a), 1248(a), 1250(a), 1252(a), 1253(a) or 1254(a) would apply if (at the time of the transaction described in this section or section 731, 732, or 741, as the case may be) such property had been sold by the partnership at its fair market value. For purposes of this section and, sections 731, 732, and 741 (but not for purposes of section 736), such term also includes any market discount bond (as defined in section 1278) and any short-term obligation (as defined in section 1283) but only to the extent of the amount which would be treated as ordinary income if (at the time of the transaction described in this section or section 731, 732, or 741, as the case may be) such property had been sold by the partnership.

Amendments

• 1998, IRS Restructuring and Reform Act of 1998 (P.L. 105-206)

P.L. 105-206, §6010(m):

Amended Code Sec. 751(c) by striking "731" each place it appears and inserting "731, 732,". **Effective** as if included in the provision of P.L. 105-34 to which it relates [**effective** for distributions after 8-5-97.—CCH].

• 1993, Omnibus Budget Reconciliation Act of 1993 (P.L. 103-66)

P.L. 103-66, §13262(b)(1)(A)-(B):

Amended Code Sec. 751(c) by striking "sections 731, 736, and 741" each place they appear and inserting ", sections 731 and 741 (but not for purposes of section 736)", and by striking "section 731, 736, or 741" each place it appears and inserting "section 731 or 741". **Effective**, generally, in the case of partners retiring or dying on or after 1-5-93. However, for exceptions, see Act Sec. 13262(c)(2) below.

P.L. 103-66, §13262(c)(2), provides:

(2) BINDING CONTRACT EXCEPTION.—The amendments made by this section shall not apply to any partner retiring on or after January 5, 1993, if a written contract to purchase such partner's interest in the partnership was binding on January 4, 1993, and at at all times thereafter before such purchase.

• 1986, Tax Reform Act of 1986 (P.L. 99-514)

P.L. 99-514, §201(d)(10):

Amended Code Sec. 751(c) by striking out "section 1245 recovery property (as defined in section 1245(a)(5))," after "section 1245(a)(3)),". **Effective**, generally, for property placed in service after 12-31-86, in tax years ending after such date. However, for transitional rules see Act Secs. 203, 204, and 251(d) following Code Sec. 168.

P.L. 99-514, §1899A(19):

Amended Code Sec. 751(c) by striking out "section 617(f)(2), stock" and inserting in lieu thereof "section 617(f)(2)), stock". **Effective** 10-22-86.

• 1984, Deficit Reduction Act of 1984 (P.L. 98-369)

P.L. 98-369, §43(c):

Added the sentence at the end of Code Sec. 751(c). **Effective** for tax years ending after 7-18-84.

P.L. 98-369, §492(b)(4):

Amended the second sentence of Code Sec. 751(c) by striking out "farm recapture property (as defined in section 1251(e)(1)),", and by striking out "1251(c),". **Effective** for tax years beginning after 12-31-83.

• **1983, Technical Corrections Act of 1982 (P.L. 97-448)**

P.L. 97-448, §102(a)(6):

Amended the second sentence of Code Sec. 751(c) by inserting "section 1245 recovery property (as defined in section 1245(a)(5))," after "section 1245(a)(3)),". **Effective** as if included in the provision of P.L. 97-34 to which it relates.

• **1978, Energy Tax Act of 1978 (P.L. 95-618)**

P.L. 95-618, §402(c)(5):

Amended Code Sec. 751(c) by striking out "oil or gas property" and inserting in lieu thereof "oil, gas, or geothermal property". For **effective** date, see historical comment for P.L. 95-618, §402(e), under Code Sec. 263(c).

• **1976, Tax Reform Act of 1976 (P.L. 94-455)**

P.L. 94-455, §205(b):

Added "and an oil or gas property (described in section 1254)" and struck out "or 1252(a)" and inserted in its place "1252(a), or 1254(a)". **Effective** for tax years ending after 12-31-75.

P.L. 94-455, §1042(c):

Struck out "(as defined in section 1245(a)(3))," and inserted in its place "(as defined in section 1245(a)(3)), stock in certain foreign corporations (as described in section 1248)," and substituted "1245(a), 1248(a)" for "1245(a)". **Effective** for transfers beginning after 10-9-75, and to sales, exchanges, and distributions taking place after such date.

P.L. 94-455, §1101(d):

Substituted "(as defined in section 617(f)(2), stock in a DISC (as described in section 992(a))," for "(as defined in section 617(f)(2))," and struck out "617(d)(1), 1245(a)," and inserted in its place "617(d)(1), 995(c), 1245(a),". **Effective** for sales, exchanges, or other dispositions after 12-31-76 (as amended by P.L. 95-600, §701(u)(12)(A)), in tax years ending after such date.

P.L. 94-455, §1901(a)(93):

Substituted "1245(a), 1250(a)," for "1245(a), or 1250(a)". **Effective** for tax years beginning after 1976.

P.L. 94-455, §2110(a):

Added "franchises, trademarks, or trade names (referred to in section 1253(a))," and substituted "1252(a), 1253(a)" for "1252(a)". **Effective** for transactions described in section 731, 736, 741, or 751 of the Internal Revenue Code of 1954 which occur after 12-31-76, in tax years ending after that date.

• **1969, Tax Reform Act of 1969 (P.L. 91-172)**

P.L. 91-172, §211(b):

Amended Code Sec. 751(c) by striking out "and section 1250 property (as defined in section 1250(c))" and inserting in lieu thereof "section 1250 property (as defined in section 1250(c)), farm recapture property (as defined in section 1251(e)(1)), and farm land (as defined in section 1252(a))"; and by striking out "1250(a)" and inserting in lieu thereof "1250(a), 1251(c), or 1252(a)". **Effective** for tax years beginning after 12-31-69.

• **1966 (P.L. 89-570)**

P.L. 89-570, §[1(c)]:

Amended the last sentence of Code Sec. 751(c) by substituting "mining property (as defined in section 617(f)(2)), section 1245 property (as defined in section 1245(a)(3))," for "section 1245 property (as defined in section 1245(a)(3))" and by substituting "section 617(d)(1), 1245(a)," for "section 1245(a)". **Effective** for tax years ending after 9-12-66, the date of enactment, but only in respect of expenditures paid or incurred after that date.

• **1964, Revenue Act of 1964 (P.L. 88-272)**

P.L. 88-272, §231(b)(6):

Amended the last sentence of Code Sec. 751(c) by inserting "and section 1250 property (as defined in section 1250(c))" and by adding "or 1250(a)" following "1245(a)". **Effective** as to dispositions after 12-31-63, in tax years ending after such date.

• **1962, Revenue Act of 1962 (P.L. 87-834)**

P.L. 87-834, §13(f)(1):

Amended Code Sec. 751(c) by adding the last sentence. **Effective** for tax years beginning after 12-31-62.

[Sec. 751(d)]

(d) INVENTORY ITEMS.—For purposes of this subchapter, the term "inventory items" means—

(1) property of the partnership of the kind described in section 1221(a)(1),

(2) any other property of the partnership which, on sale or exchange by the partnership, would be considered property other than a capital asset and other than property described in section 1231, and

(3) any other property held by the partnership which, if held by the selling or distributee partner, would be considered property of the type described in paragraph (1) or (2).

Amendments

• **2004, American Jobs Creation Act of 2004 (P.L. 108-357)**

P.L. 108-357, §413(c)(11):

Amended Code Sec. 751(d) by adding "and" at the end of paragraph (2), by striking paragraph (3), by redesignating paragraph (4) as paragraph (3), and by striking "paragraph (1), (2), or (3)" in paragraph (3) (as so redesignated) and inserting "paragraph (1) or (2)". **Effective** for tax years of foreign corporations beginning after 12-31-2004, and for tax years of United States shareholders with or within which such tax years of foreign corporations end. Prior to being stricken, Code Sec. 751(d)(3) read as follows:

(3) any other property of the partnership which, if sold or exchanged by the partnership, would result in a gain taxable under subsection (a) of section 1246 (relating to gain on foreign investment company stock), and

• **1999, Tax Relief Extension Act of 1999 (P.L. 106-170)**

P.L. 106-170, §532(c)(2)(F):

Amended Code Sec. 751(d)(1) by striking "section 1221(1)" and inserting "section 1221(a)(1)". **Effective** for any instrument held, acquired, or entered into, any transaction entered into, and supplies held or acquired on or after 12-17-99.

• **1997, Taxpayer Relief Act of 1997 (P.L. 105-34)**

P.L. 105-34, §1062(b)(2):

Amended Code Sec. 751(d). **Effective**, generally, for sales, exchanges, and distributions after 8-5-97. For a special rule, see Act Sec. 1062(c)(2), below. Prior to amendment, Code Sec. 751(d) read as follows:

(d) INVENTORY ITEMS WHICH HAVE APPRECIATED SUBSTANTIALLY IN VALUE.—

(1) SUBSTANTIAL APPRECIATION.—

(A) IN GENERAL.—Inventory items of the partnership shall be considered to have appreciated substantially in value if their fair market value exceeds 120 percent of the adjusted basis to the partnership of such property.

(B) CERTAIN PROPERTY EXCLUDED.—For purposes of subparagraph (A), there shall be excluded any inventory property if a principal purpose for acquiring such property was to avoid the provisions of this section relating to inventory items.

(2) INVENTORY ITEMS.—For purposes of this subchapter the term "inventory items" means—

(A) property of the partnership of the kind described in section 1221(1),

(B) any other property of the partnership which, on sale or exchange by the partnership, would be considered property other than a capital asset and other than property described in section 1231,

(C) any other property of the partnership which, if sold or exchanged by the partnership, would result in a gain taxable under subsection (a) of section 1246 (relating to gain on foreign investment company stock), and

(D) any other property held by the partnership which, if held by the selling or distributee partner, would be considered property of the type described in subparagraph (A), (B), or (C).

P.L. 105-34, §1062(c)(2), provides:

(2) BINDING CONTRACTS.—The amendments made by this section shall not apply to any sale or exchange pursuant to a written binding contract in effect on June 8, 1997, and at all times thereafter before such sale or exchange.

• 1993, Omnibus Budget Reconciliation Act of 1993 (P.L. 103-66)

P.L. 103-66, §13206(e)(1):

Amended Code Sec. 751(d)(1). **Effective** for sales, exchanges, and distributions after 4-30-93. Prior to amendment, Code Sec. 751(d)(1) read as follows:

(1) SUBSTANTIAL APPRECIATION.—Inventory items of the partnership shall be considered to have appreciated substantially in value if their fair market value exceeds—

(A) 120 percent of the adjusted basis to the partnership of such property, and

(B) 10 percent of the fair market value of all partnership property, other than money.

• 1962, Revenue Act of 1962 (P.L. 87-834)

P.L. 87-834, §14(b)(2):

Amended Code Sec. 751(d)(2) by deleting "and" at the end of paragraph (B), and by amending paragraph (C) and adding paragraph (D). **Effective** for tax years beginning after 12-31-62. Prior to amendment, paragraph (C) read as follows:

"(C) any other property held by the partnership which, if held by the selling or distributee partner, would be considered property of the type described in subparagraph (A) or (B)."

[Sec. 751(e)]

(e) LIMITATION ON TAX ATTRIBUTABLE TO DEEMED SALES OF SECTION 1248 STOCK.—For purposes of applying this section and sections 731 and 741 to any amount resulting from the reference to section 1248(a) in the second sentence of subsection (c), in the case of an individual, the tax attributable to such amount shall be limited in the manner provided by subsection (b) of section 1248 (relating to gain from certain sales or exchanges of stock in certain foreign corporation).

Amendments

• 1993, Omnibus Budget Reconciliation Act of 1993 (P.L. 103-66)

P.L. 103-66, §13262(b)(2)(A):

Amended Code Sec. 751(e) by striking "sections 731, 736, and 741" and by inserting "sections 731 and 741". **Effective**, generally, in the case of partners retiring or dying on or after 1-5-93. However, for exceptions, see Act Sec. 13262(c)(2) below.

P.L. 103-66, §13262(c)(2), provides:

(2) BINDING CONTRACT EXCEPTION.—The amendments made by this section shall not apply to any partner retiring on or after January 5, 1993, if a written contract to purchase such partner's interest in the partnership was binding on January 4, 1993, and at all times thereafter before such purchase.

• 1978, Energy Tax Act of 1978 (P.L. 95-618)

P.L. 95-618, §701(u)(13)(A):

Added Code Sec. 751(e). **Effective** for transfers beginning after 10-9-75, and to sales, exchanges, and distributions taking place after such date.

[Sec. 751(f)]

(f) SPECIAL RULES IN THE CASE OF TIERED PARTNERSHIPS, ETC.—In determining whether property of a partnership is—

(1) an unrealized receivable, or

(2) an inventory item,

such partnership shall be treated as owning its proportionate share of the property of any other partnership in which it is a partner. Under regulations, rules similar to the rules of the preceding sentence shall also apply in the case of interests in trusts.

Amendments

• 1984, Deficit Reduction Act of 1984 (P.L. 98-369)

P.L. 98-369, §76(a):

Added Code Sec. 751(f). **Effective** for distributions, sales, and exchanges made after 3-31-84, in tax years ending after such date.

[Sec. 752]

SEC. 752. TREATMENT OF CERTAIN LIABILITIES.

[Sec. 752(a)]

(a) INCREASE IN PARTNER'S LIABILITIES.—Any increase in a partner's share of the liabilities of a partnership, or any increase in a partner's individual liabilities by reason of the assumption by such partner of partnership liabilities, shall be considered as a contribution of money by such partner to the partnership.

[Sec. 752(b)]

(b) DECREASE IN PARTNER'S LIABILITIES.—Any decrease in a partner's share of the liabilities of a partnership, or any decrease in a partner's individual liabilities by reason of the assumption by the partnership of such individual liabilities, shall be considered as a distribution of money to the partner by the partnership.

[Sec. 752(c)]

(c) LIABILITY TO WHICH PROPERTY IS SUBJECT.—For purposes of this section, a liability to which property is subject shall, to the extent of the fair market value of such property, be considered as a liability of the owner of the property.

[Sec. 752(d)]

(d) SALE OR EXCHANGE OF AN INTEREST.—In the case of a sale or exchange of an interest in a partnership, liabilities shall be treated in the same manner as liabilities in connection with the sale or exchange of property not associated with partnerships.

Amendments

• 1984, Deficit Reduction Act of 1984 (P.L. 98-369)

P.L. 98-369, §79, provides:

SEC. 79. OVERRULING OF RAPHAN CASE.

(a) GENERAL RULE.—Section 752 of the Internal Revenue Code of 1954 (and the regulations prescribed thereunder) shall be applied without regard to the result reached in the case of Raphan vs the United States, 3 Cl. Ct. 457 (1983).

(b) REGULATIONS.—In amending the regulations prescribed under section 752 of such Code to reflect subsection (a), the Secretary of the Treasury or his delegate shall prescribe regulations relating to liabilities, including the treatment of guarantees, assumptions, indemnity agreements, and similar arrangements.

[Sec. 753]

SEC. 753. PARTNER RECEIVING INCOME IN RESPECT OF DECEDENT.

The amount includible in the gross income of a successor in interest of a deceased partner under section 736(a) shall be considered income in respect of a decedent under section 691.

[Sec. 754]

SEC. 754. MANNER OF ELECTING OPTIONAL ADJUSTMENT TO BASIS OF PARTNERSHIP PROPERTY.

If a partnership files an election, in accordance with regulations prescribed by the Secretary, the basis of partnership property shall be adjusted, in the case of a distribution of property, in the manner provided in section 734 and, in the case of a transfer of a partnership interest, in the manner provided in section 743. Such an election shall apply with respect to all distributions of property by the partnership and to all transfers of interests in the partnership during the taxable year with respect to which such election was filed and all subsequent taxable years. Such election may be revoked by the partnership, subject to such limitations as may be provided by regulations prescribed by the Secretary.

Amendments

• 1976, Tax Reform Act of 1976 (P.L. 94-455)

P.L. 94-455, §1906(b)(13)(A):

Amended 1954 Code by substituting "Secretary" for "Secretary or his delegate" each place it appeared. **Effective** 2-1-77.

[Sec. 755]

SEC. 755. RULES FOR ALLOCATION OF BASIS.

[Sec. 755(a)]

(a) GENERAL RULE.—Any increase or decrease in the adjusted basis of partnership property under section 734(b) (relating to the optional adjustment to the basis of undistributed partnership property) or section 743(b) (relating to the optional adjustment to the basis of partnership property in the case of a transfer of an interest in a partnership) shall, except as provided in subsection (b), be allocated—

(1) in a manner which has the effect of reducing the difference between the fair market value and the adjusted basis of partnership properties, or

(2) in any other manner permitted by regulations prescribed by the Secretary.

Amendments

• 1976, Tax Reform Act of 1976 (P.L. 94-455)

P.L. 94-455, §1906(b)(13)(A):

Amended 1954 Code by substituting "Secretary" for "Secretary or his delegate" each place it appeared. **Effective** 2-1-77.

[Sec. 755(b)]

(b) SPECIAL RULE.—In applying the allocation rules provided in subsection (a), increases or decreases in the adjusted basis of partnership property arising from a distribution of, or a transfer of an interest attributable to, property consisting of—

(1) capital assets and property described in section 1231(b), or

(2) any other property of the partnership,

shall be allocated to partnership property of a like character except that the basis of any such partnership property shall not be reduced below zero. If, in the case of a distribution, the adjustment to basis of property described in paragraph (1) or (2) is prevented by the absence of such property or by insufficient adjusted basis for such property, such adjustment shall be applied to subsequently acquired property of a like character in accordance with regulations prescribed by the Secretary.

Amendments

• 1976, Tax Reform Act of 1976 (P.L. 94-455)

P.L. 94-455, §1906(b)(13)(A):

Amended 1954 Code by substituting "Secretary" for "Secretary or his delegate" each place it appeared. **Effective** 2-1-77.

[Sec. 755(c)]

(c) NO ALLOCATION OF BASIS DECREASE TO STOCK OF CORPORATE PARTNER.—In making an allocation under subsection (a) of any decrease in the adjusted basis of partnership property under section 734(b)—

(1) no allocation may be made to stock in a corporation (or any person related (within the meaning of sections 267(b) and 707(b)(1)) to such corporation) which is a partner in the partnership, and

(2) any amount not allocable to stock by reason of paragraph (1) shall be allocated under subsection (a) to other partnership property.

Gain shall be recognized to the partnership to the extent that the amount required to be allocated under paragraph (2) to other partnership property exceeds the aggregate adjusted basis of such other property immediately before the allocation required by paragraph (2).

Amendments

• 2004, American Jobs Creation Act of 2004 (P.L. 108-357)

P.L. 108-357, §834(a):

Amended Code Sec. 755 by adding at the end a new subsection (c). **Effective** for distributions after 10-22-2004.

PART III—DEFINITIONS

[Sec. 761]

SEC. 761. TERMS DEFINED.

(a) PARTNERSHIP.—For purposes of this subtitle, the term "partnership" includes a syndicate, group, pool, joint venture or other unincorporated organization through or by means of which any business, financial operation, or venture is carried on, and which is not, within the meaning of this title [subtitle], a corporation or a trust or estate. Under regulations the Secretary may, at the election of all the members of an unincorporated organization, exclude such organization from the application of all or part of this subchapter, if it is availed of—

(1) for investment purposes only and not for the active conduct of a business,

(2) for the joint production, extraction, or use of property, but not for the purpose of selling services or property produced or extracted, or

(3) by dealers in securities for a short period for the purpose of underwriting, selling, or distributing a particular issue of securities,

if the income of the members of the organization may be adequately determined without the computation of partnership taxable income.

Amendments

• 1980, Technical Corrections Act of 1979 (P.L. 96-222)

P.L. 96-222, §102(a)(2)(C):

Amended Code Sec. 761(a) by deleting at the end of paragraph (1) "or", by adding at the end of paragraph (2) "or", and by adding paragraph (3). **Effective** for tax years beginning after 12-31-78.

• 1976, Tax Reform Act of 1976 (P.L. 94-455)

P.L. 94-455, §1906(b)(13)(A):

Amended 1954 Code by substituting "Secretary" for "Secretary or his delegate" each place it appeared. **Effective** 2-1-77.

[Sec. 761(b)]

(b) PARTNER.—For purposes of this subtitle, the term "partner" means a member of a partnership.

[Sec. 761(c)]

(c) PARTNERSHIP AGREEMENT.—For purposes of this subchapter, a partnership agreement includes any modifications of the partnership agreement made prior to, or at, the time prescribed by law for the filing of the partnership return for the taxable year (not including extensions) which are agreed to by all the partners, or which are adopted in such other manner as may be provided by the partnership agreement.

[Sec. 761(d)]

(d) LIQUIDATION OF A PARTNER'S INTEREST.—For purposes of this subchapter, the term "liquidation of a partner's interest" means the termination of a partner's entire interest in a partnership by means of a distribution, or a series of distributions, to the partner by the partnership.

[Sec. 761(e)]

(e) DISTRIBUTIONS OF PARTNERSHIP INTERESTS TREATED AS EXCHANGES.—Except as otherwise provided in regulations, for purposes of—

(1) section 708 (relating to continuation of partnership),

(2) section 743 (relating to optional adjustment to basis of partnership property), and

(3) any other provision of this subchapter specified in regulations prescribed by the Secretary, any distribution of an interest in a partnership (not otherwise treated as an exchange) shall be treated as an exchange.

Amendments

• 1986, Tax Reform Act of 1986 (P.L. 99-514)

P.L. 99-514, §1805(c)(2)(A)-(C):

Amended Code Sec. 761(e) by striking out "For purposes of" and inserting in lieu thereof "Except as otherwise provided in regulations, for purposes of", by striking out "any distribution (not otherwise treated as an exchange)" and inserting in lieu thereof "any distribution of an interest in a partnership (not otherwise treated as an exchange)", and by striking out "Distributions" in the subsection heading and inserting in lieu thereof "Distributions of Partnership Interests". **Effective** as if included in the provision of P.L. 98-369 to which it relates.

• 1984, Deficit Reduction Act of 1984 (P.L. 98-369)

P.L. 98-369, §75(b):

Amended Code Sec. 761 by redesignating subsection (e) as subsection (f) and by inserting after subsection (d) the new subsection (e). **Effective** for distributions, sales and exchanges made after 3-31-84, in tax years ending after such date.

[Sec. 761(f)]

(f) QUALIFIED JOINT VENTURE.—

(1) IN GENERAL.—In the case of a qualified joint venture conducted by a husband and wife who file a joint return for the taxable year, for purposes of this title—

(A) such joint venture shall not be treated as a partnership,

(B) all items of income, gain, loss, deduction, and credit shall be divided between the spouses in accordance with their respective interests in the venture, and

(C) each spouse shall take into account such spouse's respective share of such items as if they were attributable to a trade or business conducted by such spouse as a sole proprietor.

(2) QUALIFIED JOINT VENTURE.—For purposes of paragraph (1), the term "qualified joint venture" means any joint venture involving the conduct of a trade or business if—

(A) the only members of such joint venture are a husband and wife,

(B) both spouses materially participate (within the meaning of section 469(h) without regard to paragraph (5) thereof) in such trade or business, and

(C) both spouses elect the application of this subsection.

Amendments

• 2007, Small Business and Work Opportunity Tax Act of 2007 (P.L. 110-28)

P.L. 110-28, §8215(a):

Amended Code Sec. 761 by redesignating subsection (f) as subsection (g) and by inserting after subsection (e) a new subsection (f). **Effective** for tax years beginning after 12-31-2006.

[Sec. 761(g)]

(g) CROSS REFERENCE.—

For rules in the case of the sale, exchange, liquidation, or reduction of a partner's interest, see sections 704(b) and 706(c)(2).

Amendments

• 2007, Small Business and Work Opportunity Tax Act of 2007 (P.L. 110-28)

P.L. 110-28, §8215(a):

Amended Code Sec. 761 by redesignating subsection (f) as subsection (g). **Effective** for tax years beginning after 12-31-2006.

• 1984, Deficit Reduction Act of 1984 (P.L. 98-369)

P.L. 98-369, §75(b):

Amended Code Sec. 761 by redesignating subsection (e) as subsection (f). **Effective** for distributions, sales and exchanges made after 3-31-84, in tax years ending after such date.

• 1976, Tax Reform Act of 1976 (P.L. 94-455)

P.L. 94-455, §213(c)(3)(B):

Added Code Sec. 761(e). **Effective** for partnership tax years beginning after 12-31-75.

PART IV—SPECIAL RULES FOR ELECTING LARGE PARTNERSHIPS

[Sec. 771]

SEC. 771. APPLICATION OF SUBCHAPTER TO ELECTING LARGE PARTNERSHIPS.

The preceding provisions of this subchapter to the extent inconsistent with the provisions of this part shall not apply to an electing large partnership and its partners.

Amendments

• 1997, Taxpayer Relief Act of 1997 (P.L. 105-34)

P.L. 105-34, §1221(a):

Amended subchapter K by adding at the end a new part IV (Code Secs. 771-777). **Effective** for partnership tax years beginning after 12-31-97.

[Sec. 772]

SEC. 772. SIMPLIFIED FLOW-THROUGH.

[Sec. 772(a)]

(a) GENERAL RULE.—In determining the income tax of a partner of an electing large partnership, such partner shall take into account separately such partner's distributive share of the partnership's—

(1) taxable income or loss from passive loss limitation activities,

(2) taxable income or loss from other activities,

(3) net capital gain (or net capital loss)—

(A) to the extent allocable to passive loss limitation activities, and

(B) to the extent allocable to other activities,

(4) tax-exempt interest,

(5) applicable net AMT adjustment separately computed for—

(A) passive loss limitation activities, and

(B) other activities,

(6) general credits,

(7) low-income housing credit determined under section 42,

(8) rehabilitation credit determined under section 47,

(9) foreign income taxes, and

(10) other items to the extent that the Secretary determines that the separate treatment of such items is appropriate.

Amendments

• 2005, Energy Tax Incentives Act of 2005 (P.L. 109-58)

P.L. 109-58, §1322(a)(3)(I):

Amended Code Sec. 772(a) by inserting "and" at the end of paragraph (9), by striking paragraph (10), and by redesignating paragraph (11) as paragraph (10). **Effective** for credits determined under the Internal Revenue Code of 1986 for tax years ending after 12-31-2005. Prior to being stricken, Code Sec. 772(a)(10) read as follows:

(10) the credit allowable under section 29, and

[Sec. 772(b)]

(b) SEPARATE COMPUTATIONS.—In determining the amounts required under subsection (a) to be separately taken into account by any partner, this section and section 773 shall be applied separately with respect to such partner by taking into account such partner's distributive share of the items of income, gain, loss, deduction, or credit of the partnership.

[Sec. 772(c)]

(c) TREATMENT AT PARTNER LEVEL.—

(1) IN GENERAL.—Except as provided in this subsection, rules similar to the rules of section 702(b) shall apply to any partner's distributive share of the amounts referred to in subsection (a).

(2) INCOME OR LOSS FROM PASSIVE LOSS LIMITATION ACTIVITIES.—For purposes of this chapter, any partner's distributive share of any income or loss described in subsection (a)(1) shall be treated as an item of income or loss (as the case may be) from the conduct of a trade or business which is a single passive activity (as defined in section 469). A similar rule shall apply to a partner's distributive share of amounts referred to in paragraphs (3)(A) and (5)(A) of subsection (a).

(3) INCOME OR LOSS FROM OTHER ACTIVITIES.—

(A) IN GENERAL.—For purposes of this chapter, any partner's distributive share of any income or loss described in subsection (a)(2) shall be treated as an item of income or expense (as the case may be) with respect to property held for investment.

(B) DEDUCTIONS FOR LOSS NOT SUBJECT TO SECTION 67.—The deduction under section 212 for any loss described in subparagraph (A) shall not be treated as a miscellaneous itemized deduction for purposes of section 67.

(4) TREATMENT OF NET CAPITAL GAIN OR LOSS.—For purposes of this chapter, any partner's distributive share of any gain or loss described in subsection (a)(3) shall be treated as a long-term capital gain or loss, as the case may be.

(5) MINIMUM TAX TREATMENT.—In determining the alternative minimum taxable income of any partner, such partner's distributive share of any applicable net AMT adjustment shall be taken into account in lieu of making the separate adjustments provided in sections 56, 57, and 58 with respect to the items of the partnership. Except as provided in regulations, the applicable net AMT adjustment shall be treated, for purposes of section 53, as an adjustment or item of tax preference not specified in section 53(d)(1)(B)(ii).

(6) GENERAL CREDITS.—A partner's distributive share of the amount referred to in paragraph (6) of subsection (a) shall be taken into account as a current year business credit.

[Sec. 772(d)]

(d) OPERATING RULES.—For purposes of this section—

(1) PASSIVE LOSS LIMITATION ACTIVITY.—The term "passive loss limitation activity" means—

(A) any activity which involves the conduct of a trade or business, and

(B) any rental activity.

For purposes of the preceding sentence, the term "trade or business" includes any activity treated as a trade or business under paragraph (5) or (6) of section 469(c).

(2) TAX-EXEMPT INTEREST.—The term "tax-exempt interest" means interest excludable from gross income under section 103.

(3) APPLICABLE NET AMT ADJUSTMENT.—

(A) IN GENERAL.—The applicable net AMT adjustment is—

(i) with respect to taxpayers other than corporations, the net adjustment determined by using the adjustments applicable to individuals, and

(ii) with respect to corporations, the net adjustment determined by using the adjustments applicable to corporations.

(B) NET ADJUSTMENT.—The term "net adjustment" means the net adjustment in the items attributable to passive loss activities or other activities (as the case may be) which would result if such items were determined with the adjustments of sections 56, 57, and 58.

(4) TREATMENT OF CERTAIN SEPARATELY STATED ITEMS.—

(A) EXCLUSION FOR CERTAIN PURPOSES.—In determining the amounts referred to in paragraphs (1) and (2) of subsection (a), any net capital gain or net capital loss (as the case may be), and any item referred to in subsection (a)(11), shall be excluded.

(B) ALLOCATION RULES.—The net capital gain shall be treated—

(i) as allocable to passive loss limitation activities to the extent the net capital gain does not exceed the net capital gain determined by only taking into account gains and losses from sales and exchanges of property used in connection with such activities, and

(ii) as allocable to other activities to the extent such gain exceeds the amount allocated under clause (i).

A similar rule shall apply for purposes of allocating any net capital loss.

(C) NET CAPITAL LOSS.—The term "net capital loss" means the excess of the losses from sales or exchanges of capital assets over the gains from sales or exchange of capital assets.

(5) GENERAL CREDITS.—The term "general credits" means any credit other than the low-income housing credit, the rehabilitation credit, and the foreign tax credit.

(6) FOREIGN INCOME TAXES.—The term "foreign income taxes" means taxes described in section 901 which are paid or accrued to foreign countries and to possessions of the United States.

Amendments

• 2005, Energy Tax Incentives Act of 2005 (P.L. 109-58)

P.L. 109-58, §1322(a)(3)(J):

Amended Code Sec. 772(d)(5) by striking "the foreign tax credit, and the credit allowable under section 29" and inserting "and the foreign tax credit". **Effective** for credits determined under the Internal Revenue Code of 1986 for tax years ending after 12-31-2005.

[Sec. 772(e)]

(e) SPECIAL RULE FOR UNRELATED BUSINESS TAX.—In the case of a partner which is an organization subject to tax under section 511, such partner's distributive share of any items shall be taken into account separately to the extent necessary to comply with the provisions of section 512(c)(1).

[Sec. 772(f)]

(f) SPECIAL RULES FOR APPLYING PASSIVE LOSS LIMITATIONS.—If any person holds an interest in an electing large partnership other than as a limited partner—

(1) paragraph (2) of subsection (c) shall not apply to such partner, and

(2) such partner's distributive share of the partnership items allocable to passive loss limitation activities shall be taken into account separately to the extent necessary to comply with the provisions of section 469.

The preceding sentence shall not apply to any items allocable to an interest held as a limited partner.

Amendments

• 1997, Taxpayer Relief Act of 1997 (P.L. 105-34)

P.L. 105-34, §1221(a):

Added Code Sec. 772. **Effective** for partnership tax years beginning after 12-31-97.

[Sec. 773]

SEC. 773. COMPUTATIONS AT PARTNERSHIP LEVEL.

[Sec. 773(a)]

(a) GENERAL RULE.—

(1) TAXABLE INCOME.—The taxable income of an electing large partnership shall be computed in the same manner as in the case of an individual except that—

(A) the items described in section 772(a) shall be separately stated, and

(B) the modifications of subsection (b) shall apply.

(2) ELECTIONS.—All elections affecting the computation of the taxable income of an electing large partnership or the computation of any credit of an electing large partnership shall be made by the partnership; except that the election under section 901, and any election under section 108, shall be made by each partner separately.

(3) LIMITATIONS, ETC.—

(A) IN GENERAL.—Except as provided in subparagraph (B), all limitations and other provisions affecting the computation of the taxable income of an electing large partnership or the computation of any credit of an electing large partnership shall be applied at the partnership level (and not at the partner level).

(B) CERTAIN LIMITATIONS APPLIED AT PARTNER LEVEL.—The following provisions shall be applied at the partner level (and not at the partnership level):

(i) Section 68 (relating to overall limitation on itemized deductions).

(ii) Sections 49 and 465 (relating to at risk limitations).

(iii) Section 469 (relating to limitation on passive activity losses and credits).

(iv) Any other provision specified in regulations.

(4) COORDINATION WITH OTHER PROVISIONS.—Paragraphs (2) and (3) shall apply notwithstanding any other provision of this chapter other than this part.

[Sec. 773(b)]

(b) MODIFICATIONS TO DETERMINATION OF TAXABLE INCOME.—In determining the taxable income of an electing large partnership—

(1) CERTAIN DEDUCTIONS NOT ALLOWED.—The following deductions shall not be allowed:

(A) The deduction for personal exemptions provided in section 151.

(B) The net operating loss deduction provided in section 172.

(C) The additional itemized deductions for individuals provided in part VII of subchapter B (other than section 212 thereof).

(2) CHARITABLE DEDUCTIONS.—In determining the amount allowable under section 170, the limitation of section 170(b)(2) shall apply.

(3) COORDINATION WITH SECTION 67.—In lieu of applying section 67, 70 percent of the amount of the miscellaneous itemized deductions shall be disallowed.

[Sec. 773(c)]

(c) SPECIAL RULES FOR INCOME FROM DISCHARGE OF INDEBTEDNESS.—If an electing large partnership has income from the discharge of any indebtedness—

(1) such income shall be excluded in determining the amounts referred to in section 772(a), and

(2) in determining the income tax of any partner of such partnership—

(A) such income shall be treated as an item required to be separately taken into account under section 772(a), and

(B) the provisions of section 108 shall be applied without regard to this part.

Amendments

• 1997, Taxpayer Relief Act of 1997 (P.L. 105-34)

P.L. 105-34, §1221(a):

Added Code Sec. 773. **Effective** for partnership tax years beginning after 12-31-97.

[Sec. 774]

SEC. 774. OTHER MODIFICATIONS.

[Sec. 774(a)]

(a) TREATMENT OF CERTAIN OPTIONAL ADJUSTMENTS, ETC.—In the case of an electing large partnership—

(1) computations under section 773 shall be made without regard to any adjustment under section 743(b) or 108(b), but

(2) a partner's distributive share of any amount referred to in section 772(a) shall be appropriately adjusted to take into account any adjustment under section 743(b) or 108(b) with respect to such partner.

[Sec. 774(b)]

(b) CREDIT RECAPTURE DETERMINED AT PARTNERSHIP LEVEL.—

(1) IN GENERAL.—In the case of an electing large partnership—

(A) any credit recapture shall be taken into account by the partnership, and

(B) the amount of such recapture shall be determined as if the credit with respect to which the recapture is made had been fully utilized to reduce tax.

(2) METHOD OF TAKING RECAPTURE INTO ACCOUNT.—An electing large partnership shall take into account a credit recapture by reducing the amount of the appropriate current year credit to the extent thereof, and if such recapture exceeds the amount of such current year credit, the partnership shall be liable to pay such excess.

(3) DISPOSITIONS NOT TO TRIGGER RECAPTURE.—No credit recapture shall be required by reason of any transfer of an interest in an electing large partnership.

(4) CREDIT RECAPTURE.—For purposes of this subsection, the term "credit recapture" means any increase in tax under section 42(j) or 50(a).

[Sec. 774(c)]

(c) PARTNERSHIP NOT TERMINATED BY REASON OF CHANGE IN OWNERSHIP.—Subparagraph (B) of section 708(b)(1) shall not apply to an electing large partnership.

[Sec. 774(d)]

(d) PARTNERSHIP ENTITLED TO CERTAIN CREDITS.—The following shall be allowed to an electing large partnership and shall not be taken into account by the partners of such partnership:

(1) The credit provided by section 34.

(2) Any credit or refund under section 852(b)(3)(D) or 857(b)(3)(D).

Amendments

• 1998, IRS Restructuring and Reform Act of 1998 (P.L. 105-206)

P.L. 105-206, §6012(c):

Amended Code Sec. 774(d)(2) by inserting before the period "or 857(b)(3)(D)". **Effective** as if included in the provision of P.L. 105-34 to which it relates [**effective** for partnership tax years beginning after 12-31-97.—CCH].

[Sec. 774(e)]

(e) TREATMENT OF REMIC RESIDUALS.—For purposes of applying section 860E(e)(6) to any electing large partnership—

(1) all interests in such partnership shall be treated as held by disqualified organizations,

(2) in lieu of applying subparagraph (C) of section 860E(e)(6), the amount subject to tax under section 860E(e)(6) shall be excluded from the gross income of such partnership, and

(3) subparagraph (D) of section 860E(e)(6) shall not apply.

[Sec. 774(f)]

(f) SPECIAL RULES FOR APPLYING CERTAIN INSTALLMENT SALE RULES.—In the case of an electing large partnership—

(1) the provisions of sections 453(l)(3) and 453A shall be applied at the partnership level, and

(2) in determining the amount of interest payable under such sections, such partnership shall be treated as subject to tax under this chapter at the highest rate of tax in effect under section 1 or 11.

Amendments

• 1997, Taxpayer Relief Act of 1997 (P.L. 105-34)

P.L. 105-34, §1221(a):

Added Code Sec. 774. **Effective** for partnership tax years beginning after 12-31-97.

[Sec. 775]

SEC. 775. ELECTING LARGE PARTNERSHIP DEFINED.

[Sec. 775(a)]

(a) GENERAL RULE.—For purposes of this part—

(1) IN GENERAL.—The term "electing large partnership" means, with respect to any partnership taxable year, any partnership if—

(A) the number of persons who were partners in such partnership in the preceding partnership taxable year equaled or exceeded 100, and

(B) such partnership elects the application of this part.

To the extent provided in regulations, a partnership shall cease to be treated as an electing large partnership for any partnership taxable year if in such taxable year fewer than 100 persons were partners in such partnership.

(2) ELECTION.—The election under this subsection shall apply to the taxable year for which made and all subsequent taxable years unless revoked with the consent of the Secretary.

[Sec. 775(b)]

(b) SPECIAL RULES FOR CERTAIN SERVICE PARTNERSHIPS.—

(1) CERTAIN PARTNERS NOT COUNTED.—For purposes of this section, the term "partner" does not include any individual performing substantial services in connection with the activities of the partnership and holding an interest in such partnership, or an individual who formerly performed substantial services in connection with such activities and who held an interest in such partnership at the time the individual performed such services.

(2) EXCLUSION.—For purposes of this part, an election under subsection (a) shall not be effective with respect to any partnership if substantially all the partners of such partnership—

(A) are individuals performing substantial services in connection with the activities of such partnership or are personal service corporations (as defined in section 269A(b)) the owner-employees (as defined in section 269A(b)) of which perform such substantial services,

(B) are retired partners who had performed such substantial services, or

(C) are spouses of partners who are performing (or had previously performed) such substantial services.

(3) SPECIAL RULE FOR LOWER TIER PARTNERSHIPS.—For purposes of this subsection, the activities of a partnership shall include the activities of any other partnership in which the partnership owns directly an interest in the capital and profits of at least 80 percent.

[Sec. 775(c)]

(c) EXCLUSION OF COMMODITY POOLS.—For purposes of this part, an election under subsection (a) shall not be effective with respect to any partnership the principal activity of which is the buying and selling of commodities (not described in section 1221(a)(1)), or options, futures, or forwards with respect to such commodities.

Amendments

• 1999, Tax Relief Extension Act of 1999 (P.L. 106-170)

P.L. 106-170, §532(c)(2)(G):

Amended Code Sec. 775(c) by striking "section 1221(1)" and inserting "section 1221(a)(1)". **Effective** for any instrument held, acquired, or entered into, any transaction entered into, and supplies held or acquired on or after 12-17-99.

[Sec. 775(d)]

(d) SECRETARY MAY RELY ON TREATMENT ON RETURN.—If, on the partnership return of any partnership, such partnership is treated as an electing large partnership, such treatment shall be binding on such partnership and all partners of such partnership but not on the Secretary.

Amendments

• 1997, Taxpayer Relief Act of 1997 (P.L. 105-34)

P.L. 105-34, §1221(a):

Added Code Sec. 775. **Effective** for partnership tax years beginning after 12-31-97.

[Sec. 776]

SEC. 776. SPECIAL RULES FOR PARTNERSHIPS HOLDING OIL AND GAS PROPERTIES.

[Sec. 776(a)]

(a) COMPUTATION OF PERCENTAGE DEPLETION.—In the case of an electing large partnership, except as provided in subsection (b)—

(1) the allowance for depletion under section 611 with respect to any partnership oil or gas property shall be computed at the partnership level without regard to any provision of section 613A requiring such allowance to be computed separately by each partner,

(2) such allowance shall be determined without regard to the provisions of section 613A(c) limiting the amount of production for which percentage depletion is allowable and without regard to paragraph (1) of section 613A(d), and

(3) paragraph (3) of section 705(a) shall not apply.

[Sec. 776(b)]

(b) TREATMENT OF CERTAIN PARTNERS.—

(1) IN GENERAL.—In the case of a disqualified person, the treatment under this chapter of such person's distributive share of any item of income, gain, loss, deduction, or credit attributable to any partnership oil or gas property shall be determined without regard to this part. Such person's distributive share of any such items shall be excluded for purposes of making determinations under sections 772 and 773.

(2) DISQUALIFIED PERSON.—For purposes of paragraph (1), the term "disqualified person" means, with respect to any partnership taxable year—

(A) any person referred to in paragraph (2) or (4) of section 613A(d) for such person's taxable year in which such partnership taxable year ends, and

(B) any other person if such person's average daily production of domestic crude oil and natural gas for such person's taxable year in which such partnership taxable year ends exceeds 500 barrels.

(3) AVERAGE DAILY PRODUCTION.—For purposes of paragraph (2), a person's average daily production of domestic crude oil and natural gas for any taxable year shall be computed as provided in section 613A(c)(2)—

(A) by taking into account all production of domestic crude oil and natural gas (including such person's proportionate share of any production of a partnership),

(B) by treating 6,000 cubic feet of natural gas as a barrel of crude oil, and

(C) by treating as 1 person all persons treated as 1 taxpayer under section 613A(c)(8) or among whom allocations are required under such section.

Amendments

• 1997, Taxpayer Relief Act of 1997 (P.L. 105-34)

P.L. 105-34, §1221(a):

Added Code Sec. 776. **Effective** for partnership tax years beginning after 12-31-97.

[Sec. 777]

SEC. 777. REGULATIONS.

The Secretary shall prescribe such regulations as may be appropriate to carry out the purposes of this part.

Amendments

• 1997, Taxpayer Relief Act of 1997 (P.L. 105-34)

P.L. 105-34, §1221(a):

Added Code Sec. 777. **Effective** for partnership tax years beginning after 12-31-97.

Subchapter L—Insurance Companies

PART I—LIFE INSURANCE COMPANIES

Subpart A—Tax Imposed

[Sec. 801]

SEC. 801. TAX IMPOSED.

[Sec. 801(a)]

(a) TAX IMPOSED.—

(1) IN GENERAL.—A tax is hereby imposed for each taxable year on the life insurance company taxable income of every life insurance company. Such tax shall consist of a tax computed as provided in section 11 as though the life insurance company taxable income were the taxable income referred to in section 11.

(2) ALTERNATIVE TAX IN CASE OF CAPITAL GAINS.—

(A) IN GENERAL.—If a life insurance company has a net capital gain for the taxable year, then (in lieu of the tax imposed by paragraph (1)), there is hereby imposed a tax (if such tax is less than the tax imposed by paragraph (1)).

(B) AMOUNT OF TAX.—The amount of the tax imposed by this paragraph shall be the sum of—

(i) a partial tax, computed as provided by paragraph (1), on the life insurance company taxable income reduced by the amount of the net capital gain, and

(ii) an amount determined as provided in section 1201(a) on such net capital gain.

(C) NET CAPITAL GAIN NOT TAKEN INTO ACCOUNT IN DETERMINING SMALL LIFE INSURANCE COMPANY DEDUCTION.—For purposes of subparagraph (B)(i), the amount allowable as a deduction under paragraph (2) of section 804 shall be determined by reducing the tentative LICTI by the amount of the net capital gain (determined without regard to items attributable to noninsurance businesses).

Amendments

• 1986, Tax Reform Act of 1986 (P.L. 99-514)

P.L. 99-514, §1011(b)(3)(A)-(B):

Amended Code Sec. 801(a)(2)(C) by striking out "the amounts allowable as deductions under paragraphs (2) and (3)" and inserting in lieu thereof "the amount allowable as a deduction under paragraph (2)", and by striking out "Special Life Insurance Company Deduction and" in the heading. **Effective** for tax years beginning after 12-31-86. Prior to amendment, the heading read as follows:

(C) NET CAPITAL GAIN NOT TAKEN INTO ACCOUNT IN DETERMINING SPECIAL LIFE INSURANCE COMPANY DEDUCTION AND SMALL LIFE INSURANCE COMPANY DEDUCTION.—

[Sec. 801(b)]

(b) LIFE INSURANCE COMPANY TAXABLE INCOME.—For purposes of this part, the term "life insurance company taxable income" means—

(1) life insurance gross income, reduced by

(2) life insurance deductions.

[Sec. 801(c)]

(c) TAXATION OF DISTRIBUTIONS FROM PRE-1984 POLICYHOLDERS SURPLUS ACCOUNT.—

For provision taxing distributions to shareholders from pre-1984 policyholders surplus account, see section 815.

Amendments

• 1984, Deficit Reduction Act of 1984 (P.L. 98-369)

P.L. 98-369, §211(a):

Amended Part I of subchapter L of chapter 1 by adding Code Sec. 801. **Effective** for tax years beginning after 12-31-83. For transitional and special rules, see Act Sec. 216(a)-(b)(2), below.

P.L. 98-369, §216(a)-(b)(2), as amended by P.L. 99-514, §1822(e), provides:

Sec. 216. Reserves Computed on New Basis; Fresh Start.

(a) Recomputation of Reserves.—

(1) In General.—As of the beginning of the first taxable year beginning after December 31, 1983, for purposes of subchapter L of the Internal Revenue Code of 1954 (other than section 816 thereof), the reserve for any contract shall be recomputed as if the amendments made by this subtitle had applied to such contract when it was issued.

(2) Premiums Earned.—For the first taxable year beginning after December 31, 1983, in determining "premiums earned on insurance contracts during the taxable year" as provided in section 832(b)(4) of the Internal Revenue Code of 1954, life insurance reserves which are included in unearned premiums on outstanding business at the end of the preceding taxable year shall be determined as provided in section 807 of the Internal Revenue Code of 1954, as amended by this subtitle, as though section 807 was applicable to such reserves in such preceding taxable year.

(3) Issuance Date for Group Contracts.—For purposes of this subsection, the issuance date of any group contract shall be determined under section 807(e)(2) of the Internal Revenue Code of 1954 (as added by this subtitle), except that if such issuance date cannot be determined, the issuance date shall be determined on the basis by the Secretary of the Treasury or his delegate for purposes of this subsection.

(b) Fresh Start.—

(1) In General.—Except as provided in paragraph (2), in the case of any insurance company, any change in the method of accounting (and any change in the method of computing reserves) between such company's first taxable year beginning after December 31, 1983, and the preceding taxable year which is required solely by the amendments made by this subtitle shall be treated as not being a change in the method of accounting (or change in the method of computing reserves) for purposes of the Internal Revenue Code of 1954. The preceding sentence shall apply for purposes of computing the earnings and profits of any insurance company for its 1st taxable year beginning in 1984. The preceding sentence shall be applied by substituting "1985" for "1984" in the case of an insurance company which is a member of a controlled group (as defined in section 806(d)(3)), the common parent of which is

(A) a company having its principal place of business in Alabama and incorporated in Delaware on November 29, 1979, or

(B) a company having its principal place of business in Houston, Texas, and incorporated in Delaware on June 9, 1947.

(2) Treatment of Adjustments from Years Before 1984.—

(A) Adjustments Attributable to Decreases in Reserves.—No adjustment under section 810(d) of the Internal Revenue Code of 1954 (as in effect on the day before the date of the enactment of this Act) attributable to any decrease in reserves as a result of a change in a taxable year beginning before 1984 shall be taken into account in any taxable year beginning after 1983.

(B) Adjustments Attributable to Increases in Reserves.—

(i) In General.—Any adjustment under section 810(d) of the Internal Revenue Code of 1954 (as so in effect) attributable to an increase in reserves as a result of a change in a taxable year beginning before 1984 shall be taken into account in taxable years beginning after 1983 to the extent that—

(I) the amount of the adjustments which would be taken into account under such section in taxable years beginning after 1983 without regard to this subparagraph, exceeds

(II) the amount of any fresh start adjustment attributable to contracts for which there was such an increase in reserves as a result of such change.

(ii) Fresh Start Adjustment.—For purposes of clause (i), the fresh start adjustment with respect to any contract is the excess (if any) of—

(I) the reserve attributable to such contract as of the close of the taxpayer's last taxable year beginning before January 1, 1984, over

(II) the reserve for such contract as of the beginning of the taxpayer's first taxable year beginning after 1983 as recomputed under subsection (a) of this section.

(C) Related Income Inclusions Not Taken Into Account to the Extent Deduction Disallowed Under Subparagraph (b).—No premium shall be included in income to the extent such premium is directly related to an increase in a reserve for which a deduction is disallowed by subparagraph (B).

[Sec. 801—Repealed]

Amendments

• 1984, Deficit Reduction Act of 1984 (P.L. 98-369)

P.L. 98-369, §211(a):

Amended Part I of Subchapter L of Chapter 1 by adding a new Part I (Code Secs. 801-818). For transitional and special rules, see Act Sec. 216(a)-(b)(2) in the amendments for Code Sec. 801. The table of contents for former Part I and former subpart A, and Code Sec. 801, as in effect prior to P.L. 98-369, read as follows:

PART I—LIFE INSURANCE COMPANIES

Subpart A. Definition; tax imposed.
Subpart B. Investment income.
Subpart C. Gain and loss from operations.
Subpart D. Distributions to shareholders.
Subpart E. Miscellaneous provisions.

Subpart A—Definition; Tax Imposed

Sec. 801. Definition of life insurance company.
Sec. 802. Tax imposed.

SEC. 801. DEFINITION OF LIFE INSURANCE COMPANY.

[Sec. 801(a)]

(a) LIFE INSURANCE COMPANY DEFINED.—For purposes of this subtitle, the term "life insurance company" means an insurance company which is engaged in the business of issuing life insurance and annuity contracts (either separately or combined with health and accident insurance), or noncancellable contracts of health and accident insurance, if—

(1) its life insurance reserves (as defined in subsection (b)), plus

(2) unearned premiums, and unpaid losses (whether or not ascertained), on noncancellable life, health, or accident policies not included in life insurance reserves,

comprise more than 50 percent of its total reserves (as defined in subsection (c)).

[Sec. 801(b)]

(b) LIFE INSURANCE RESERVES DEFINED.—

(1) IN GENERAL.—For purposes of this part, the term "life insurance reserves" means amounts—

(A) which are computed or estimated on the basis of recognized mortality or morbidity tables and assumed rates of interest, and

(B) which are set aside to mature or liquidate, either by payment or reinsurance, future unaccrued claims arising from life insurance, annuity, and noncancellable health and accident insurance contracts (including life insurance or annuity contracts combined with noncancellable health and accident insurance) involving, at the time with respect to which the reserve is computed, life, health, or accident contingencies.

(2) RESERVES MUST BE REQUIRED BY LAW.—Except—

(A) in the case of policies covering life, health, and accident insurance combined in one policy issued on the weekly premium payment plan, continuing for life and not subject to cancellation, and

(B) as provided in paragraph (3),

in addition to the requirements set forth in paragraph (1), life insurance reserves must be required by law.

(3) ASSESSMENT COMPANIES.—In the case of an assessment life insurance company or association, the term "life insurance reserves" includes—

(A) sums actually deposited by such company or association with State officers pursuant to law as guaranty or reserve funds, and

(B) any funds maintained, under the charter or articles of incorporation or association (or bylaws approved by a State insurance commissioner) of such company or association, exclusively for the payment of claims arising under certificates of membership or policies issued on the assessment plan and not subject to any other use.

For purposes of this part, the rate of interest assumed in calculating the reserves described in subparagraphs (A) and (B) shall be 3 percent.

(4) DEFICIENCY RESERVES EXCLUDED.—The term "life insurance reserves" does not include deficiency reserves. For purposes of this subsection and subsection (c), the deficiency reserve for any contract is that portion of the reserve for such contract equal to the amount (if any) by which—

(A) the present value of the future net premiums required for such contract, exceeds

(B) the present value of the future actual premiums and consideration charged for such contract.

(5) AMOUNT OF RESERVES.—For purposes of this subsection, subsection (a), and subsection (c), the amount of any reserve (or portion thereof) for any taxable year shall be the mean of such reserve (or portion thereof) at the beginning and end of the taxable year.

Amendments

• 1976, Tax Reform Act of 1976 (P.L. 94-455)

P.L. 94-455, §1901(c)(6):

Struck out "State or Territorial officers" and substituted in its place "State officers". **Effective** for tax years beginning after 12-31-76.

• 1969, Tax Reform Act of 1969 (P.L. 91-172)

P.L. 91-172, §121(b)(5)(B):

Amended Code Sec. 801(b)(2) by inserting "and" at the end of subparagraph (A), by striking out subparagraph (B), and by redesignating subparagraph (C) as (B). **Effective** 1-1-70. Prior to amendment, subparagraph (B) read as follows:

"(B) in the case of policies issued by an organization which meets the requirements of section 501(c)(9) other than the requirement of subparagraph (B) thereof, and"

[Sec. 801(c)]

(c) TOTAL RESERVES DEFINED.—For purposes of subsection (a), the term "total reserves" means—

(1) life insurance reserves,

(2) unearned premiums, and unpaid losses (whether or not ascertained), not included in life insurance reserves, and

(3) all other insurance reserves required by law.

The term "total reserves" does not include deficiency reserves (within the meaning of subsection (b)(4)).

[Sec. 801(d)]

(d) ADJUSTMENTS IN RESERVES FOR POLICY LOANS.—For purposes only of determining under subsection (a) whether or not an insurance company is a life insurance company, the life insurance reserves, and the total reserves, shall each be reduced by an amount equal to the mean of the aggregates, at the beginning and end of the taxable year, of the policy loans outstanding with respect to contracts for which life insurance reserves are maintained.

[Sec. 801(e)]

(e) GUARANTEED RENEWABLE CONTRACTS.—For purposes of this part, guaranteed renewable life, health, and accident insurance shall be treated in the same manner as noncancellable life, health, and accident insurance.

[Sec. 801(f)]

(f) BURIAL AND FUNERAL BENEFIT INSURANCE COMPANIES.—A burial or funeral benefit insurance company engaged directly in the manufacture of funeral supplies or the performance of funeral services shall not be taxable under this part but shall be taxable under section 821 or section 831.

[Sec. 801(g)]

(g) CONTRACTS WITH RESERVES BASED ON SEGREGATED ASSET ACCOUNTS.—

(1) DEFINITIONS.—

(A) ANNUITY CONTRACTS INCLUDE VARIABLE ANNUITY CONTRACTS.—For purposes of this part, an "annuity contract" includes a contract which provides for the payment of a variable annuity computed on the basis of recognized mortality tables and the investment experience of the company issuing the contract.

(B) CONTRACTS WITH RESERVES BASED ON A SEGREGATED ASSET ACCOUNT.—For purposes of this part, a "contract with reserves based on a segregated asset account" is a contract—

(i) which provides for the allocation of all or part of the amounts received under the contract to an account which, pursuant to State law or regulation, is segregated from the general asset accounts of the company,

(ii) which is described in any paragraph of section 805(d) (other than a life, health or accident, property, casualty, or liability insurance contract) or which provides for the payment of annuities, and

(iii) under which the amounts paid in, or the amount paid out, reflect the investment return and the market value of the segregated asset account.

If a contract ceases to reflect current investment return and current market value, such contract shall not be considered as meeting the requirements of clause (iii) after such cessation.

(2) LIFE INSURANCE RESERVES.—For purposes of subsection (b)(1)(A) of this section, the reflection of the investment return and the market value of the segregated asset account shall be considered an assumed rate of interest.

(3) SEPARATE ACCOUNTING.—For purposes of this part, a life insurance company which issues contracts with reserves based on segregated asset accounts shall separately account for the various income, exclusion, deduction, asset, reserve, and other liability items properly attributable to such segregated asset accounts. For such items as are not accounted for directly, separate accounting shall be made—

(A) in accordance with the method regularly employed by such company, if such method is reasonable, and

(B) in all other cases, in accordance with regulations prescribed by the Secretary.

(4) INVESTMENT YIELD.—

(A) IN GENERAL.—For purposes of this part, the policy and other contract liability requirements, and the life insurance company's share of investment yield, shall be separately computed—

(i) with respect to the items separately accounted for in accordance with paragraph (3), and

(ii) excluding the items taken into account under clause (i).

(B) CAPITAL GAINS AND LOSSES.—If, without regard to subparagraph (A), the net shortterm capital gain exceeds the net longterm capital loss, such excess shall be allocated between clauses (i) and (ii) of subparagraph (A) in proportion to the respective contributions to such excess of the items taken into account under each such clause.

(5) POLICY AND OTHER CONTRACT LIABILITY REQUIREMENTS.—For purposes of this part—

(A) with respect to life insurance reserves based on segregated asset accounts, the adjusted reserves rate and the current earnings rate for purposes of section 805(b), and the rate of interest assumed by the taxpayer for purposes of sections 805(c) and 809(a)(2), shall be a rate equal to the current earnings rate determined under section 805(b)(2) with respect to the items separately accounted for in accordance with paragraph (3) reduced by the percentage obtained by dividing—

(i) any amount retained with respect to such reserves by the life insurance company from gross investment income (as defined in section 804(b)) on segregated assets, to the extent such retained amount exceeds the deductions allowable under section 804(c) which are attributable to such reserves, by

(ii) the means of such reserves; and

(B) with respect to reserves based on segregated asset accounts other than life insurance reserves, an amount equal to the product of—

(i) the rate of interest assumed as defined in subparagraph (A), and

(ii) the means of such reserves,

shall be included as interest paid within the meaning of section 805(e)(1).

(6) INCREASES AND DECREASES IN RESERVES.—For purposes of subsections (a) and (b) of section 810, the sum of the items described in section 810(c) taken into account as of the close of the taxable year shall, under regulations prescribed by the Secretary, be adjusted—

(A) by subtracting therefrom an amount equal to the sum of the amounts added from time to time (for the taxable year) to the reserves separately accounted for in accordance with paragraph (3) by reason of appreciation in value of assets (whether or not the assets have been disposed of), and

(B) by adding thereto an amount equal to the sum of the amounts subtracted from time to time (for the taxable year) from such reserves by reason of depreciation in value of assets (whether or not the assets have been disposed of).

The deduction allowable for items described in paragraphs (1) and (7) of section 809(d) with respect to segregated asset accounts shall be reduced to the extent that the amount of such items is increased for the taxable year by appreciation (or increased to the extent that the amount of such items is decreased for the taxable year by depreciation) not reflected in adjustments under the preceding sentence.

(7) BASIS OF ASSETS HELD FOR QUALIFIED PENSION PLAN CONTRACTS.—In the case of contracts described in any paragraph of section 805(d), the basis of each asset in a segregated asset account shall (in addition to all other adjustments to basis) be—

(A) increased by the amount of any appreciation in value, and

(B) decreased by the amount of any depreciation in value,

to the extent that such appreciation and depreciation are from time to time reflected in the increases and decreases in reserves or other items in paragraph (6) with respect to such contracts.

(8) ADDITIONAL SEPARATE COMPUTATIONS.—Under regulations prescribed by the Secretary, such additional separate computations shall be made, with respect to the items separately accounted for in accordance with paragraph (3), as may be necessary to carry out the purposes of this subsection and this part.

Amendments

• 1978, Revenue Act of 1978 (P.L. 95-600)

P.L. 95-600, §703(j)(4):

Amended paragraphs (1)(B)(ii) and (7) of Code Sec. 801(g) by striking out "subparagraph (A), (B), (C), (D), or (E) of section 805(d)(1)" and inserting in lieu thereof "any paragraph of section 805(d)". **Effective** 10-4-76.

• 1976, Tax Reform Act of 1976 (P.L. 94-455)

P.L. 94-455, §1505(a)(1):

Amended Code Sec. 801(g)(1)(B)(ii). **Effective** for tax years beginning after 12-31-75. Prior to amendment, Code Sec. 801(g)(1)(B)(ii) read as follows:

(ii) which provides for the payment of annuities, and

P.L. 94-455, §1505(a)(2):

Struck out "amount paid as annuities," and inserted in its place "amount paid out," in Code Sec. 801(g)(1)(B)(iii). **Effective** for tax years beginning after 12-31-75.

P.L. 94-455, §1906(b)(13)(A):

Amended 1954 Code by substituting "Secretary" for "Secretary or his delegate" each place it appeared. **Effective** 2-1-77.

• 1974, Employee Retirement Security Act of 1974 (P.L. 93-406)

P.L. 93-406, §2002(g)(11):

Amended Code Sec. 801(g)(7) by substituting "(D), or (E)" for "or (D)". **Effective** 1-1-75.

• 1962 (P.L. 87-858)

P.L. 87-858, §3(a):

Amended Code Sec. 801(g). **Effective** 1-1-62. Prior to amendment, Sec. 801(g) read as follows:

(g) Variable Annuities.—

(1) In general.—For purposes of this part, an annuity contract includes a contract which provides for the payment of a variable annuity computed on the basis of recognized mortality tables and the investment experience of the company issuing the contract.

(2) Adjusted reserves rate; assumed rate.—For purposes of this part—

(A) the adjusted reserves rate for any taxable year with respect to annuity contracts described in paragraph (1), and

(B) the rate of interest assumed by the taxpayer for any taxable year in calculating the reserve on any such contract, shall be a rate equal to the current earnings rate determined under paragraph (3).

(3) Current earnings rate.—For purposes of this part, the current earnings rate for any taxable year with respect to annuity contracts described in paragraph (1) is the current earnings rate determined under section 805(b)(2) with respect to such contracts, reduced by the percentage obtained by dividing—

(A) the amount of the actuarial margin charge on all annuity contracts described in paragraph (1) issued by the taxpayer, by

(B) the mean of the reserves for such contracts.

(4) Increases and decreases in reserves.—For purposes of subsections (a) and (b) of section 810, the sum of the items described in section 810(c) taken into account, as of the close of the taxable year shall, under regulations prescribed by the Secretary or his delegate, be adjusted—

(A) by subtracting therefrom an amount equal to the sum of the amounts added from time to time (for the taxable year) to the reserves for annuity contracts described in paragraph (1) by reason of appreciation in value of assets (whether or not the assets have been disposed of), and

(B) by adding thereto an amount equal to the sum of the amounts subtracted from time to time (for the taxable year) from such reserves by reason of depreciation in value of assets (whether or not the assets have been disposed of).

(5) Companies issuing variable annuities and other contracts.—In the case of a life insurance company which issues both annuity contracts described in paragraph (1) and other contracts, under regulations prescribed by the Secretary or his delegate—

(A) the policy and other contract liability requirements shall be considered to be the sum of—

(i) the policy and other contract liability requirements computed by reference to the items which relate to annuity contracts described in paragraph (1), and

(ii) the policy and other contract liability requirements computed by excluding the items taken into account under clause (i); and

(B) such additional separate computations, with respect to such annuity contracts and such other contracts, shall be made as may be necessary to carry out the purposes of this subsection and this part.

(6) Termination.—Paragraphs (1), (2), (3), (4), and (5) shall not apply with respect to any taxable year beginning after December 31, 1962.

• 1959, Life Insurance Company Income Tax Act of 1959 (P.L. 86-69)

P.L. 86-69, §2:

Revised Part I of subchapter L of chapter 1 of the 1954 Code. **Effective**, generally, for tax years beginning after 1957. Prior text not reproduced.

[Sec. 802—Repealed]

• 1984, Deficit Reduction Act of 1984 (P.L. 98-369)

P.L. 98-369, §211(a):

Amended Part I of Subchapter L of Chapter 1 by adding a new Part I (Code Secs. 801-818). For transitional and special rules, see Act Sec. 216(a)-(b)(2) in the amendments for Code Sec. 801. Prior to amendment, Code Sec. 802 read as follows:

SEC. 802. TAX IMPOSED.

[Sec. 802(a)]

(a) TAX IMPOSED.—

(1) IN GENERAL.—A tax is hereby imposed for each taxable year on the life insurance company taxable income of every life insurance company. Such tax shall consist of a tax computed as provided in section 11 as though the life insurance company taxable income were the taxable income referred to in section 11.

(2) ALTERNATIVE TAX IN CASE OF CAPITAL GAINS.—If for any taxable year any life insurance company has a net capital gain, then, in lieu of the tax imposed by paragraph (1), there is hereby imposed a tax (if such tax is less than the tax imposed by such paragraph) which shall consist of the sum of—

(A) a partial tax, computed as provided by paragraph (1), on the life insurance company taxable income determined by reducing the taxable investment income, and the gain from operations, by the amount of such net capital gain, and

(B) an amount determined as provided in section 1201(a) on such net capital gain.

Amendments

• 1978, Revenue Act of 1978 (P.L. 95-600)

P.L. 95-600, §301(b)(8):

Amended Code Sec. 802(a)(1) by striking out "a normal tax and surtax" and inserting in lieu thereof "a tax". **Effective** for tax years beginning after 12-31-78.

• 1976, Tax Reform Act of 1976 (P.L. 94-455)

P.L. 94-455, §1901(a)(95):

Struck out "beginning after December 31, 1957," after "taxable year" in Code Sec. 802(a)(1), struck out "beginning after December 31, 1961," after "taxable year" in Code Sec. 802(a)(2), and repealed Code Sec. 802(a)(3). **Effective** with respect to tax years beginning after 12-31-76. Prior to repeal, Code Sec. 802(a)(3) read as follows:

(3) SPECIAL RULE FOR 1959 AND 1960.—If any amount is subtracted from the policyholders surplus account under section 815(c)(3) for a taxable year beginning in 1959 or 1960 on account of a distribution in 1959 or 1960 (not including any distribution treated under section 815(d)(2)(B) as made in 1959 or 1960), the tax imposed for such taxable year on the life insurance company taxable income shall be the amount determined under paragraph (1) reduced by the following percentage of the amount by which the tax imposed by paragraph (1) is (without regard to this paragraph) increased, on account of the amount so subtracted, by reason of section 802(b)(3)—

(A) in the case of a taxable year beginning in 1959, 66⅔ percent; and

(B) in the case of a taxable year beginning in 1960, 33⅓ percent.

The preceding sentence shall not apply with respect to any payment treated as a distribution under section 815(d)(3).

P.L. 94-455, § 1901(b)(33):

Substituted "any life insurance company has a net capital gain" for "the net long-term capital gain of any life insurance company exceeds the net short-term capital loss" in Code Sec. 802(a)(2), and struck out "such excess" each place it appeared and inserted in its place "net capital gain". **Effective** for tax years beginning after 12-31-76.

[Sec. 802(b)]

(b) LIFE INSURANCE COMPANY TAXABLE INCOME DEFINED.—For purposes of this part, the term "life insurance company taxable income" means the sum of—

(1) the taxable investment income (as defined in section 804) or, if smaller, the gain from operations (as defined in section 809),

(2) if the gain from operations exceeds the taxable investment income, an amount equal to 50 percent of such excess, plus

(3) the amount subtracted from the policyholders' surplus account for the taxable year, as determined under section 815.

Amendments

• 1982, Tax Equity and Fiscal Responsibility Act of 1982 (P.L. 97-248)

P.L. 97-248, § 268, provides:

SECTION 268. UNDERPAYMENTS OF ESTIMATED TAX FOR 1982.

No addition to the tax shall be made under section 6655 of the Internal Revenue Code of 1954 (relating to failure by corporation to pay estimated income tax) for any period before December 15, 1982, with respect to any underpayment of estimated tax by a taxpayer with respect to any tax imposed by section 802(a), to the extent that such underpayment was created or increased by any provisions of this subtitle.

• 1969, Tax Reform Act of 1969 (P.L. 91-172)

P.L. 91-172, § 511(c):

Amended Code Sec. 802(a)(2)(B). **Effective** as to tax years beginning after 12-31-69. Prior to amendment, Code Sec. 802(a)(2)(B) read as follows:

"(B) an amount equal to 25 percent of such excess."

• 1964, Revenue Act of 1964 (P.L. 88-272)

P.L. 88-272, § 235(c)(1):

Amended the second sentence of Code Sec. 802(a)(1). **Effective** with respect to tax years ending after 12-31-63. Prior to amendment, such sentence read as follows: "Such tax shall consist of—

"(A) a normal tax on such income computed at the rate provided by section 11(b), and

"(B) a surtax, on so much of such income as exceeds $25,000, computed at the rate provided by section 11(c)."

• 1962 (P.L. 87-858)

P.L. 87-858, § 3(b)(1):

Amended Code Sec. 802(a)(2). **Effective** 1-1-62. Prior to amendment, Code Sec. 802 (a)(2) read as follows:

"(2) Tax in case of capital gains.—If for any taxable year beginning after December 31, 1958, the net long-term capital gain of any life insurance company exceeds the net short-term capital loss, there is hereby imposed a tax equal to 25 percent of such excess."

• 1959, Life Insurance Company Income Tax Act of 1959 (P.L. 86-69)

P.L. 86-69, § 2:

Revised Part I of subchapter L of chapter 1 of the 1954 Code. **Effective**, generally, for tax years beginning after 1957. Prior text not reproduced.

Subpart B—Life Insurance Gross Income

[Sec. 803]

SEC. 803. LIFE INSURANCE GROSS INCOME.

[Sec. 803(a)]

(a) IN GENERAL.—For purposes of this part, the term "life insurance gross income" means the sum of the following amounts:

(1) PREMIUMS.—

(A) The gross amount of premiums and other consideration on insurance and annuity contracts, less

(B) return premiums, and premiums and other consideration arising out of indemnity reinsurance.

(2) DECREASES IN CERTAIN RESERVES.—Each net decrease in reserves which is required by section 807(a) to be taken into account under this paragraph.

(3) OTHER AMOUNTS.—All amounts not includible under paragraph (1) or (2) which under this subtitle are includible in gross income.

[Sec. 803(b)]

(b) SPECIAL RULES FOR PREMIUMS.—

(1) CERTAIN ITEMS INCLUDED.—For purposes of subsection (a)(1)(A), the term "gross amount of premiums and other consideration" includes—

(A) advance premiums,

(B) deposits,

(C) fees,

(D) assessments,

(E) consideration in respect of assuming liabilities under contracts not issued by the taxpayer, and

(F) the amount of policyholder dividends reimbursable to the taxpayer by a reinsurer in respect of reinsured policies,

on insurance and annuity contracts.

(2) POLICYHOLDER DIVIDENDS EXCLUDED FROM RETURN PREMIUMS.—For purposes of subsection (a)(1)(B)—

(A) IN GENERAL.—Except as provided in subparagraph (B), the term "return premiums" does not include any policyholder dividends.

(B) EXCEPTION FOR INDEMNITY REINSURANCE.—Subparagraph (A) shall not apply to amounts of premiums or other consideration returned to another life insurance company in respect of indemnity reinsurance.

Amendments

• 1984, Deficit Reduction Act of 1984 (P.L. 98-369)

P.L. 98-369, §211(a):

Amended Part I of subchapter L of chapter 1 by adding Code Sec. 803. For transitional and special rules, see Act Sec. 216(a)-(b)(2) in the amendments for Code Sec. 801.

Subpart C—Life Insurance Deductions

[Sec. 804]

SEC. 804. LIFE INSURANCE DEDUCTIONS.

For purposes of this part, the term "life insurance deductions" means—

(1) the general deductions provided in section 805, and

(2) the small life insurance company deduction (if any) determined under section 806(a).

Amendments

• 1986, Tax Reform Act of 1986 (P.L. 99-514)

P.L. 99-514, §1011(b)(2):

Amended Code Sec. 804 by adding "and" at the end of paragraph (1) and by striking out paragraphs (2) and (3) and inserting in lieu thereof new paragraph (2). **Effective** for tax years beginning after 12-31-86. Prior to amendment, Code Sec. 804(2) and (3) read as follows:

(2) the special life insurance company deduction determined under section 806(a), and

(3) the small life insurance company deduction (if any) determined under section 806(b).

• 1984, Deficit Reduction Act of 1984 (P.L. 98-369)

P.L. 98-369, §211(a):

Amended Part I of subchapter L of chapter 1 by adding Code Sec. 804. **Effective** for tax years beginning after 12-31-83. However, for transitional and special rules, see Act Sec. 216(a)-(b)(2) under the amendment notes for Code Sec. 801.

[Sec. 804—Repealed]

• 1984, Deficit Reduction Act of 1984 (P.L. 98-369)

P.L. 98-369, §211(a):

Amended Part I of Subchapter L of Chapter 1 by adding a new Part I (Code Secs. 801-818). For transitional and special rules, see Act Sec. 216(a)-(b)(2) in the amendments for Code Sec. 801. The table of contents for former subpart B and Code Sec. 804, as in effect prior to P.L. 98-369, read as follows:

Subpart B—Investment Income

Sec. 804. Taxable investment income.

Sec. 805. Policy and other contract liability requirements.

Sec. 806. Certain changes in reserves and assets.

SEC. 804. TAXABLE INVESTMENT INCOME.

[Sec. 804(a)]

(a) IN GENERAL.—

(1) EXCLUSION OF POLICYHOLDERS' SHARE OF INVESTMENT YIELD.—The policyholders' share of each and every item of investment yield (including taxexempt interest and dividends received) of any life insurance company shall not be included in taxable investment income. For purposes of the preceding sentence, the policyholders' share of any item shall be that percentage obtained by dividing the policy and other contract liability requirements by the investment yield; except that if the policy and other contract liability requirements exceed the investment yield, then the policyholders' share of any item shall be 100 percent.

(2) TAXABLE INVESTMENT INCOME DEFINED.—For purposes of this part, the taxable investment income for any taxable year shall be an amount (not less than zero) equal to the amount (if any) of the net capital gain plus the sum of the life insurance company's share of each and every item of investment yield (including taxexempt interest and dividends received), reduced by—

(A) the sum of—

(i) the life insurance company's share of interest which under section 103 is excluded from gross income, and

(ii) the deductions for dividends received provided by sections 243, 244, and 245 (as modified by paragraph (4)) computed with respect to the life insurance company's share of the dividends received; and

(B) the small business deduction provided by paragraph (3).

For purposes of the preceding sentence, the life insurance company's share of any item shall be that percentage which, when added to the percentage obtained under the second sentence of paragraph (1), equals 100 percent.

(3) SMALL BUSINESS DEDUCTION.—For purposes of this part, the small business deduction is an amount equal to 10 percent of the investment yield for the taxable year. The deduction under this paragraph shall not exceed $25,000.

(4) APPLICATION OF SECTION 246(b).—In applying section 246(b) (relating to limitation on aggregate amount of deductions for dividends received) for purposes of this subsection, the limit on the aggregate amount of the deductions allowed by sections 243(a)(1), 244(a), and 245 shall be 85 percent of the taxable investment income computed without regard to the deductions allowed by such sections.

Amendments

• 1976, Tax Reform Act of 1976 (P.L. 94-455)

P.L. 94-455, §1901(a)(96):

Struck out paragraph (6). **Effective** for tax years beginning after 12-31-76. Prior to repeal, Code Sec. 804(a)(6) read as follows:

(6) EXCEPTION.—If it is established in any case that the application of the definition of taxable investment income contained in paragraph (2) results in the imposition of tax on—

(A) any interest which under section 103 is excluded from gross income,

(B) any amount of interest which under section 242 (as modified by paragraph (3)) is allowable as a deduction, or

(C) any amount of dividends received which under sections 243, 244, and 245 (as modified by paragraph (5)) is allowable as a deduction,

adjustment shall be made to the extent necessary to prevent such imposition.

P.L. 94-455, §1901(b)(1)(J):

Struck out paragraph (3), redesignated paragraphs (4) and (5) as paragraphs (3) and (4), respectively, struck out "paragraph (5)" and inserted "paragraph (4)" in its place in subsection (2)(A)(ii), and substituted "paragraph (3)" for "paragraph (4)" in subsection (2)(B). **Effective** for tax years beginning after 12-31-76. Prior to repeal, Code Sec. 804(a)(3) read as follows:

(3) PARTIALLY TAX-EXEMPT INTEREST.—For purposes of this part, the deduction allowed by section 242 shall be an amount which bears the same ratio to the amount determined under such section without regard to this paragraph as (A) the normal tax rate for the taxable year prescribed by section 11, bears to (B) the sum of the normal tax rate and the surtax rate for the taxable year prescribed by section 11.

P.L. 94-455, §1901(b)(1)(K):

Struck out clause (2)(A)(ii), redesignated clause (iii) as clause (ii), and inserted "and" at the end of clause (i). **Effective** for tax years beginning after 12-31-76. Prior to repeal, Code Sec. 804(a)(2)(A)(ii) read as follows:

(ii) the deduction for partially tax-exempt interest provided by section 242 (as modified by paragraph (3)) computed with respect to the life insurance company's share of such interest, and

P.L. 94-455, §1901(b)(1)(M):

Substituted "tax-exempt interest" for "tax-exempt interest, partially tax-exempt interest," in paragraph (1) and substituted "tax-exempt interest" for "tax-exempt interest, partially tax-exempt interest," in paragraph (2). **Effective** for tax years beginning after 12-31-76.

P.L. 94-455, §1901(b)(33):

Struck out "by which the net long-term capital gain exceeds the net short-term capital loss" and inserted in its place "of the net capital gain" in paragraph (2). **Effective** for tax years beginning after 12-31-76.

[Sec. 804(b)]

(b) GROSS INVESTMENT INCOME.—For purposes of this part, the term "gross investment income" means the sum of the following:

(1) INTEREST, ETC.—The gross amount of income from—

(A) interest, dividends, rents, and royalties,

(B) the entering into of any lease, mortgage, or other instrument or agreement from which the life insurance company derives interest, rents, or royalties, and

(C) the alteration or termination of any instrument or agreement described in subparagraph (B).

(2) SHORTTERM CAPITAL GAIN.—The amount (if any) by which the net shortterm capital gain exceeds the net longterm capital loss.

(3) TRADE OR BUSINESS INCOME.—The gross income from any trade or business (other than an insurance business) carried on by the life insurance company, or by a partnership of which the life insurance company is a partner. In computing gross income under this paragraph, there shall be excluded any item described in paragraph (1).

Except as provided in paragraph (2), in computing gross investment income under this subsection, there shall be excluded any gain from the sale or exchange of a capital asset, and any gain considered as gain from the sale or exchange of a capital asset.

Amendments

• 1976, Tax Reform Act of 1976 (P.L. 94-455)

P.L. 94-455, §1901(a)(96):

Struck out "In the case of a taxable year beginning after December 31, 1958, the" and inserted "The" in its place in Code Sec. 804(b)(2). **Effective** for tax years beginning after 12-31-76.

[Sec. 804(c)]

(c) INVESTMENT YIELD DEFINED.—For purposes of this part, the term "investment yield" means the gross investment income less the following deductions—

(1) INVESTMENT EXPENSES.—Investment expenses for the taxable year. If any general expenses are in part assigned to or included in the investment expenses, the total deduction under this paragraph shall not exceed the sum of—

(A) one-fourth of one percent at the mean of the assets (as defined in section 805(b)(4)) held at the beginning and end of the taxable year,

(B) the amount of the mortgage service fees for the taxable year, plus

(C) whichever of the following is the greater:

(i) one-fourth of the amount by which the investment yield (computed without any deduction for investment expenses allowed by this paragraph) exceeds 3¾ percent of the mean of the assets (as defined in section 805(b)(4)) held at the beginning and end of the taxable year, reduced by the amount described in subparagraph (B), or

(ii) one-fourth of one percent of the mean of the value of mortgages held at the beginning and end of the taxable year for which there are no mortgage service fees for the taxable year.

(2) REAL ESTATE EXPENSES.—The amount of taxes (as provided in section 164), and other expenses, for the taxable year exclusively on or with respect to the real estate owned by the company. No deduction shall be allowed under this paragraph for any amount paid out for new buildings, or for permanent improvements or betterments made to increase the value of any property.

(3) DEPRECIATION.—The deduction allowed by section 167. The deduction under this paragraph and paragraph (2) on account of any real estate owned and occupied for insurance purposes in whole or in part by a life insurance company shall be limited to an amount which bears the same ratio to such deduction (computed without regard to this sentence) as the rental value of the space not so occupied bears to the rental value of the entire property.

(4) DEPLETION.—The deduction allowed by section 611 (relating to depletion).

(5) TRADE OR BUSINESS DEDUCTIONS.—The deductions allowed by this subtitle (without regard to this part) which are attributable to any trade or business (other than an insurance business) carried on by the life insurance company, or by a partnership of which the life insurance company is a partner; except that in computing the deduction under this paragraph—

(A) there shall be excluded losses—

(i) from (or considered as from) sales or exchanges of capital assets,

(ii) from sales or exchanges of property used in the trade or business (as defined in section 1231(b)), and

(iii) from the compulsory or involuntary conversion (as a result of destruction, in whole or in part, theft or seizure, or an exercise of the power of requisition or condemnation or the threat or imminence thereof) of property used in the trade or business (as so defined).

(B) Any item, to the extent attributable to the carrying on of the insurance business, shall not be taken into account.

(C) The deduction for net operating losses provided in section 172, and the special deductions for corporations provided in part VIII of subchapter B, shall not be allowed.

[Sec. 804(d)]

(d) CROSS REFERENCE.—For reduction of the $25,000 amount provided in subsection (a)(4) in the case of certain controlled corporations, see sections 1561 and 1564.

Amendments

• 1969, Tax Reform Act of 1969 (P.L. 91-172)

P.L. 91-172, §401(b)(2)(D):

Added subsection (d). **Effective** for tax years beginning after 12-31-69.

• 1964, Revenue Act of 1964 (P.L. 88-272)

P.L. 88-272, §214(b)(3):

Amended subsection (a)(5) by substituting "243(a)(1), 244(a)" in lieu of "243(a), 244".

• 1962 (P.L. 87-858)

P.L. 87-858, §3(b)(2):

Amended Code Sec. 804(a)(2) by deleting "equal to the sum" and inserting in lieu thereof "equal to the amount (if any) by which the net long-term capital gain exceeds the net short-term capital loss plus the sum".

• 1959, Life Insurance Company Income Tax Act of 1959 (P.L. 86-69)

P.L. 86-69, §2:

Revised Part I of subchapter L of chapter 1 of the 1954 Code. **Effective**, generally, for tax years beginning after 1957. Prior text not reproduced.

[Sec. 805]

SEC. 805. GENERAL DEDUCTIONS.

[Sec. 805(a)]

(a) GENERAL RULE.—For purposes of this part, there shall be allowed the following deductions:

(1) DEATH BENEFITS, ETC.—All claims and benefits accrued, and all losses incurred (whether or not ascertained), during the taxable year on insurance and annuity contracts.

(2) INCREASES IN CERTAIN RESERVES.—The net increase in reserves which is required by section 807(b) to be taken into account under this paragraph.

(3) POLICYHOLDER DIVIDENDS.—The deduction for policyholder dividends (determined under section 808(c)).

(4) DIVIDENDS RECEIVED BY COMPANY.—

(A) IN GENERAL.—The deductions provided by sections 243, 244, and 245 (as modified by subparagraph (B))—

(i) for 100 percent dividends received, and

(ii) for the life insurance company's share of the dividends (other than 100 percent dividends) received.

(B) APPLICATION OF SECTION 246(b).—In applying section 246(b) (relating to limitation on aggregate amount of deductions for dividends received) for purposes of subparagraph (A), the limit on the aggregate amount of the deductions allowed by sections 243(a)(1), 244(a), and 245 shall be the percentage determined under section 246(b)(3) of the life insurance company taxable income (and such limitation shall be applied as provided in section 246(b)(3)), computed without regard to—

(i) the small life insurance company deduction,

(ii) the operations loss deduction provided by section 810,

(iii) the deductions allowed by sections 243(a)(1), 244(a), and 245, and

(iv) any capital loss carryback to the taxable year under section 1212(a)(1),

but such limit shall not apply for any taxable year for which there is a loss from operations.

(C) 100 PERCENT DIVIDEND.—For purposes of subparagraph (A)—

(i) IN GENERAL.—Except as provided in clause (ii), the term "100 percent dividend" means any dividend if the percentage used for purposes of determining the deduction allowable under section 243, 244, or 245(b) is 100 percent.

(ii) TREATMENT OF DIVIDENDS FROM NONINSURANCE COMPANIES.—The term "100 percent dividend" does not include any distribution by a corporation which is not an insurance company to the extent such distribution is out of tax-exempt interest, or out of the increase for the taxable year in policy cash values (within the meaning of subparagraph (F)) of life insurance policies and annuity and endowment contracts to which section 264(f) applies, or out of dividends which are not 100 percent dividends (determined with the application of this clause as if it applies to distributions by all corporations including insurance companies).

(D) SPECIAL RULES FOR CERTAIN DIVIDENDS FROM INSURANCE COMPANIES.—

(i) IN GENERAL.—In the case of any 100 percent dividend paid to any life insurance company out of the earnings and profits for any taxable year beginning after December 31, 1983, of another life insurance company if—

(I) the paying company's share determined under section 812 for such taxable year, exceeds

(II) the receiving company's share determined under section 812 for its taxable year in which the dividend is received or accrued,

the deduction allowed under section 243, 244, or 245(b) (as the case may be) shall be reduced as provided in clause (ii).

(ii) AMOUNT OF REDUCTION.—The reduction under this clause for a dividend is an amount equal to—

(I) the portion of such dividend attributable to prorated amounts, multipled by

(II) the percentage obtained by subtracting the share described in subclause (II) of clause (i) from the share described in subclause (I) of such clause.

(iii) PRORATED AMOUNTS.—For purposes of this subparagraph, the term "prorated amounts" means tax-exempt interest, the increase for the taxable year in policy cash values (within the meaning of subparagraph (F)) of life insurance policies and annuity and endowment contracts to which section 264(f) applies, and dividends other than 100 percent dividends.

(iv) PORTION OF DIVIDEND ATTRIBUTABLE TO PRORATED AMOUNTS.—For purposes of this subparagraph, in determining the portion of any dividend attributable to prorated amounts—

(I) any dividend by the paying corporation shall be treated as paid first out of earnings and profits for taxable years beginning after December 31, 1983, attributable to prorated amounts (to the extent thereof), and

(II) by determining the portion of earnings and profits so attributable without any reduction for the tax imposed by this chapter.

(v) SUBPARAGRAPH TO APPLY TO DIVIDENDS FROM OTHER INSURANCE COMPANIES.—Rules similar to the rules of this subsection shall apply in the case of 100 percent dividends paid by an insurance company which is not a life insurance company.

(E) CERTAIN DIVIDENDS RECEIVED BY FOREIGN CORPORATIONS.—Subparagraph (A)(i) (and not subparagraph (A)(ii)) shall apply to any dividend received by a foreign corporation from a domestic corporation which would be a 100 percent dividend if section 1504(b)(3) did not apply for purposes of applying section 243(b)(2).

(F) INCREASE IN POLICY CASH VALUES.—For purposes of subparagraphs (C) and (D)—

(i) IN GENERAL.—The increase in the policy cash value for any taxable year with respect to policy or contract is the amount of the increase in the adjusted cash value during such taxable year determined without regard to—

(I) gross premiums paid during such taxable year, and

(II) distributions (other than amounts includible in the policyholder's gross income) during such taxable year to which section 72(e) applies.

(ii) ADJUSTED CASH VALUE.—For purposes of clause (i), the term "adjusted cash value" means the cash surrender value of the policy or contract increased by the sum of—

(I) commissions payable with respect to such policy or contract for the taxable year, and

(II) asset management fees, surrender charges, mortality and expense charges, and any other fees or charges specified in regulations prescribed by the Secretary which are imposed (or which would be imposed were the policy or contract canceled) with respect to such policy or contract for the taxable year.

(5) OPERATIONS LOSS DEDUCTION.—The operations loss deduction (determined under section 810).

(6) ASSUMPTION BY ANOTHER PERSON OF LIABILITIES UNDER INSURANCE, ETC., CONTRACTS.—The consideration (other than consideration arising out of indemnity reinsurance) in respect of the assumption by another person of liabilities under insurance and annuity contracts.

(7) REIMBURSABLE DIVIDENDS.—The amount of policyholder dividends which—

(A) are paid or accrued by another insurance company in respect of policies the taxpayer has reinsured, and

(B) are reimbursable by the taxpayer under the terms of the reinsurance contract.

(8) OTHER DEDUCTIONS.—Subject to the modifications provided by subsection (b), all other deductions allowed under this subtitle for purposes of computing taxable income.

Except as provided in paragraph (3), no amount shall be allowed as a deduction under this part in respect of policyholder dividends.

Amendments

• 1997, Taxpayer Relief Act of 1997 (P.L. 105-34)

P.L. 105-34, §1084(b)[(d)](1)(A):

Amended Code Sec. 805(a)(4)(C)(ii) by inserting ", or out of the increase for the taxable year in policy cash values (within the meaning of subparagraph (F)) of life insurance policies and annuity and endowment contracts to which section 264(f) applies," after "tax-exempt interest". For the **effective** dates, see Act Sec. 1084(d)[(f)], below.

P.L. 105-34, §1084(b)[(d)](1)(B):

Amended Code Sec. 805(a)(4)(D)(iii) by striking "and" and inserting ", the increase for the taxable year in policy cash values (within the meaning of subparagraph (F)) of life insurance policies and annuity and endowment contracts to which section 264(f) applies, and". For the **effective** dates, see Act Sec. 1084(d)[(f)], below.

P.L. 105-34, §1084(b)[(d)](1)(C):

Amended Code Sec. 805(a)(4) by adding at the end a new subparagraph (F). For the **effective** dates, see Act Sec. 1084(d)[(f)], below.

P.L. 105-34, §1084(d)[(f)], as amended by P.L. 105-206, §6010(o)(3)(B), provides:

(d)[(f)] EFFECTIVE DATE.—The amendments made by this section shall apply to contracts issued after June 8, 1997, in taxable years ending after such date. For purposes of the preceding sentence, any material increase in the death benefit or other material change in the contract shall be treated as a new contract except that, in the case of a master contract (within the meaning of section 264(f)(4)(E) of the Internal Revenue Code of 1986), the addition of covered lives shall be treated as a new contract only with respect to such additional covered lives. For purposes of this subsection, an increase in the death benefit under a policy or contract issued in connection with a lapse described in section 501(d)(2) of the Health Insurance Portability and Accountability Act of 1996 shall not be treated as a new contract.

• 1996, Small Business Job Protection Act of 1996 (P.L. 104-188)

P.L. 104-188, §1702(h)(3):

Amended Code Sec. 805(a)(4)(E) by striking "243(b)(5)" and inserting "243(b)(2)". **Effective** as if included in the provision of P.L. 101-508 to which it relates.

• 1987, Revenue Act of 1987 (P.L. 100-203)

P.L. 100-203, §10221(c)(2):

Amended Code Sec. 805(a)(4)(B) by striking out "shall be 80 percent of the life insurance company taxable income" and inserting in lieu thereof "shall be the percentage determined under section 246(b)(3) of the life insurance company taxable income (and such limitation shall be applied as provided in section 246(b)(3))". **Effective** for dividends received or accrued after 12-31-87, in tax years ending after that date.

• 1986, Tax Reform Act of 1986 (P.L. 99-514)

P.L. 99-514, §611(a)(5):

Amended Code Sec. 805(a)(4)(B) by striking out "85 percent" and inserting in lieu thereof "80 percent". **Effective** for dividends received or accrued after 12-31-86, in tax years ending after such date.

P.L. 99-514, §1011(b)(4):

Amended Code Sec. 805(a)(4)(B)(i) by striking out "the special life insurance company deduction and". **Effective** for tax years beginning after 12-31-86.

P.L. 99-514, §1821(p):

Amended Code Sec. 805(a)(4) by redesignating subparagraph (D) as subparagraph (E) and by striking out subparagraph (C) and inserting in lieu thereof new subparagraphs (C) and (D). **Effective** as if included in the provision of P.L. 98-369 to which it relates. Prior to amendment, Code Sec. 805(a)(4)(C) read as follows:

(C) 100 PERCENT DIVIDEND.—The purposes of subparagraph (A), the term "100 percent dividend" means any dividend if the percentage used for purposes of determining the deduction allowable under section 243 or 244 is 100 percent. Such term does not include any dividend to the extent it is a distribution out of tax-exempt interest or out of dividends which are not 100 percent dividends (determined with the application of this sentence).

[Sec. 805(b)]

(b) MODIFICATIONS.—The modifications referred to in subsection (a)(8) are as follows:

(1) INTEREST.—In applying section 163 (relating to deduction for interest), no deduction shall be allowed for interest in respect of items described in section 807(c).

(2) CHARITABLE, ETC., CONTRIBUTIONS AND GIFTS.—In applying section 170—

(A) the limit on the total deductions under such section provided by section 170(b)(2) shall be 10 percent of the life insurance company taxable income computed without regard to—

(i) the deduction provided by section 170,

(ii) the deductions provided by paragraphs (3) and (4) of subsection (a),

(iii) the small life insurance company deduction,

(iv) any operations loss carryback to the taxable year under section 810, and

(v) any capital loss carryback to the taxable year under section 1212(a)(1), and

(B) under regulations prescribed by the Secretary, a rule similar to the rule contained in section 170(d)(2)(B) (relating to special rule for net operating loss carryovers) shall be applied.

(3) AMORTIZABLE BOND PREMIUM.—

(A) IN GENERAL.—Section 171 shall not apply.

(B) CROSS REFERENCE.—

For rules relating to amortizable bond premium, see section 811(b).

(4) NET OPERATING LOSS DEDUCTION.—Except as provided by section 844, the deduction for net operating losses provided in section 172 shall not be allowed.

(5) DIVIDENDS RECEIVED DEDUCTION.—Except as provided in subsection (a)(4), the deductions for dividends received provided by sections 243, 244, and 245 shall not be allowed.

Amendments

• 1986, Tax Reform Act of 1986 (P.L. 99-514)

P.L. 99-514, §805(c)(6):

Amended Code Sec. 805(b) by striking out paragraph (2) and by redesignating paragraphs (3), (4), (5), and (6) as paragraphs (2), (3), (4), and (5), respectively. **Effective**, generally, for tax years beginning after 12-31-86. However, see Act Sec. 805(d)(2), below. Prior to amendment, paragraph (2) read as follows:

(2) BAD DEBTS.—Section 166(c) (relating to reserve for bad debts) shall not apply.

P.L. 99-514, §805(d)(2), provides:

(2) CHANGE IN METHOD OF ACCOUNTING.—In the case of any taxpayer who maintained a reserve for bad debts for such taxpayer's last taxable year beginning before January 1, 1987, and who is required by the amendments made by this section to change its method of accounting for any taxable year—

(A) such change shall be treated as initiated by the taxpayer,

(B) such change shall be treated as made with the consent of the Secretary, and

(C) the net amount of adjustments required by section 481 of the Internal Revenue Code of 1986 to be taken into account by the taxpayer shall—

(i) in the case of a taxpayer maintaining a reserve under section 166(f), be reduced by the balance in the suspense account under section 166(f)(4) of such Code as of the close of such last taxable year, and

(ii) be taken into account ratably in each of the first 4 taxable years beginning after December 31, 1986.

P.L. 99-514, §1011(b)(4):

Amended Code Sec. 805(b)(3)(A)(iii) (prior to its redesignation by Act Sec. 805(c)(6)) by striking out "the special life insurance company deduction and". **Effective** for tax years beginning after 12-31-86.

• 1984, Deficit Reduction Act of 1984 (P.L. 98-369)

P.L. 98-369, §211(a):

Amended Part I of subchapter L of chapter 1 by adding Code Sec. 805. **Effective** for tax years beginning after 12-31-83. However, for transitional and special rules, see Act Sec. 216(a)-(b)(2) under the amendment notes for Code Sec. 801.

[Sec. 805—Repealed]

• 1984, Deficit Reduction Act of 1984 (P.L. 98-369)

P.L. 98-369, §211(a):

Amended Part I of Subchapter L of Chapter 1 by adding a new Part I (Code Secs. 801-818). For transitional and special rules, see Act Sec. 216(a)-(b)(2) in the amendments for Code Sec. 801. Code Sec. 805, as in effect prior to P.L. 98-369, read as follows:

SEC. 805. POLICY AND OTHER CONTRACT LIABILITY REQUIREMENTS.

[Sec. 805(a)]

(a) IN GENERAL.—For purposes of this part, the term "policy and other contract liability requirements" means, for any taxable year, the sum of—

(1) the adjusted life insurance reserves, multiplied by the adjusted reserves rate,

(2) the mean of the pension plan reserves at the beginning and end of the taxable year, multiplied by the current earnings rate, and

(3) the interest paid.

[Sec. 805(b)]

(b) ADJUSTED RESERVES RATE AND EARNINGS RATES.—

(1) ADJUSTED RESERVES RATE.—For purposes of this part, the adjusted reserves rate for any taxable year is the average earnings rate or, if lower, the current earnings rate.

(2) CURRENT EARNINGS RATE.—For purposes ofthis part, the current earnings rate for any taxable year is the amount determined by dividing—

(A) the taxpayer's investment yield for such taxable year, by

(B) the mean of the taxpayer's assets at the beginning and end of the taxable year.

(3) AVERAGE EARNINGS RATE.—

(A) IN GENERAL.—For purposes of this part, the average earnings rate for any taxable year is the average of the current earnings rates for such taxable year and for each of the 4 taxable years immediately preceding such taxable year (excluding any of such 4 taxable years for which the taxpayer was not an insurance company).

(B) SPECIAL RULE.—For purposes of subparagraph (A), the current earnings rate for any taxable year of any company which, for such year, is an insurance company (but not a life insurance company) shall be determined as if this part applied to such company for such year.

(4) ASSETS.—For purposes of this part, the term "assets" means all assets of the company (including nonadmitted assets), other than real and personal property (excluding money) used by it in carrying on an insurance trade or business. For purposes of this paragraph, the amount attributable to—

(A) real property and stock shall be the fair market value thereof, and

(B) any other asset shall be the adjusted basis of such asset for purposes of determining gain on sale or other disposition.

Amendments

• 1976, Tax Reform Act of 1976 (P.L. 94-455)

P.L. 94-455, §1901(a)(97):

Amended Code Sec. 805(b)(3)(B). **Effective** for tax years beginning after 12-31-76. Prior to amendment, Code Sec. 805(b)(3)(B) read as follows:

(B) SPECIAL RULES.—For purposes of subparagraph (A)—

(i) the current earnings rate for any taxable year beginning before January 1, 1958, shall be determined as if this part (as in effect for 1958) and section 381(c)(22) applied to such taxable year, and

(ii) the current earnings rate for any taxable year of any company which, for such year, is an insurance company (but not a life insurance company) shall be determined as if this part applied to such company for such year.

Struck out "(determined without regard to fair market value on December 31, 1958)" after "basis" in Code Sec. 805(b)(4)(B). **Effective** for tax years beginning after 12-31-76.

[Sec. 805(c)]

(c) ADJUSTED LIFE INSURANCE RESERVES.—

(1) ADJUSTED LIFE INSURANCE RESERVES DEFINED.—For purposes of this part, the term "adjusted life insurance reserves" means—

(A) the mean of the life insurance reserves (as defined in section 801(b)), other than pension plan reserves or reserves on any qualified contract, at the beginning and end of the taxable year, multiplied by

(B) that percentage which equals 100 percent—

(i) increased by that percentage which is 10 times the average rate of interest assumed by the taxpayer in calculating such reserves, and

(ii) reduced by that percentage which is 10 times the adjusted reserves rate.

(B) 0.9 raised to the power of n where n is the number (positive or negative) determined by subtracting—

(i) 100 times the average rate of interest assumed by the taxpayer in calculating such reserves, from

(ii) 100 times the adjusted reserves rate.

(2) AVERAGE INTEREST RATE ASSUMED.—For purposes of this part, the average rate of interest assumed in calculating reserves shall be computed—

(A) by multiplying each assumed rate of interest by the means of the amounts of such reserves computed at that rate at the beginning and end of the taxable year, and

(B) by dividing (i) the sum of the products ascertained under subparagraph (A), by (ii) the mean of the total of such reserves at the beginning and end of the taxable year.

Amendments

• 1982, Tax Equity and Fiscal Responsibility Act of 1982 (P.L. 97-248)

P.L. 97-248, §261:

Amended Code Sec. 805(c)(1)(B). **Effective** for tax years beginning after 12-31-81, and before 1-1-84.

P.L. 97-248, §264(c)(1):

Amended Code Sec. 805(c)(1)(A) by adding "or reserves on any qualified contract" after "pension plan reserves". **Effective** for tax years beginning after 12-31-81.

[Sec. 805(d)]

(d) PENSION PLAN RESERVES.—For purposes of this part, the term "pension plan reserves" means that portion of the life insurance reserves which is allocable to contracts—

(1) purchased under contracts entered into with trusts which (as of the time the contracts were entered into) were deemed to be (A) trusts described in section 401(a) and exempt from tax under section 501(a), or (B) trusts exempt from tax under section 165 of the Internal Revenue Code of 1939 or the corresponding provisions of prior revenue laws;

(2) purchased under contracts entered into under plans which (as of the time the contracts were entered into) were deemed to be plans described in section 403(a), or plans meeting the requirements of paragraphs (3), (4), (5), and (6) of section 165(a) of the Internal Revenue Code of 1939;

(3) provided for employees of the life insurance company under a plan which, for the taxable year, meets the requirements of paragraphs (3), (4), (5), (6), (7), (8), (11), (12), (13), (14), (15), (16), (19), (20), and (22) of section 401(a);

(4) purchased to provide retirement annuities for its employees by an organization which (as of the time the contracts were purchased) was an organization described in section 501(c)(3) which was exempt from tax under section

501(a) or was an organization exempt from tax under section 101(6) of the Internal Revenue Code of 1939 or the corresponding provisions of prior revenue laws, or purchased to provide retirement annuities for employees described in section 403(b)(1)(A)(ii) by an employer which is a State, a political subdivision of a State, or an agency or instrumentality of any one or more of the foregoing;

(5) purchased under contracts entered into with trusts which (at the time the contracts were entered into) were individual retirement accounts described in section 408(a) or under contracts entered into with individual retirement annuities described in section 408(b); or

(6) purchased by—

(A) a governmental plan (within the meaning of section 414(d)), or

(B) the Government of the United States, the government of any State or political subdivision thereof, or by any agency or instrumentality of the foregoing, for use in satisfying an obligation of such government, political subdivision, or agency or instrumentality to provide a benefit under a plan described in subparagraph (A).

Amendments

• 1980, Technical Corrections Act of 1979 (P.L. 96-222)

P.L. 96-222, §101(a)(7)(B):

Amended Act Sec. 141 of P.L. 95-600 by revising paragraph (g). For the **effective** dates, see the amendment note at §101(a)(7)(B), P.L. 96-222, following the text of Code Sec. 409A(n).

• 1978, Revenue Act of 1978 (P.L. 95-600)

P.L. 95-600, §141(f)(9):

Amended Code Sec. 805(d)(3) by striking out "and (20)" and inserting in lieu thereof "(20), and (22)". **Effective** with respect to qualified investment for tax years beginning after 12-31-78.

P.L. 95-600, §155(a):

Amended Code Sec. 805(d) by striking out "or" at the end of paragraph (4), by striking out the period at the end of paragraph (5) and inserting in lieu thereof "; or", and adding paragraph (6). **Effective** for tax years beginning after 12-31-78.

• 1976, Tax Reform Act of 1976 (P.L. 94-455)

P.L. 94-455, §1901(a)(97):

Amended Code Sec. 805(d). **Effective** for tax years beginning after 12-31-76. Prior to amendment, Code Sec. 805(d) read as follows:

(d) PENSION PLAN RESERVES.—

(1) PENSION PLAN RESERVES DEFINED.—For purposes of this part, the term "pension plan reserves" means that portion of the life insurance reserves which is allocable to contracts—

(A) purchased under contracts entered into with trusts which (as of the time the contracts were entered into) were deemed to be (i) trusts described in section 401(a) and exempt from tax under section 501(a), or (ii) trusts exempt from tax under section 165 of the Internal Revenue Code of 1939 or the corresponding provisions of prior revenue laws;

(B) purchased under contracts entered into under plans which (as of the time the contracts were entered into) were deemed to be plans described in section 403(a), or plans meeting the requirements of section 165(a)(3), (4), (5), and (6) of the Internal Revenue Code of 1939;

(C) provided for employees of the life insurance company under a plan which, for the taxable year, meets the requirements of section 401(a)(3), (4), (5), (6), (7), (8), (11), (12), (13), (14), (15), (16), (19), and (20);

(D) purchased to provide retirement annuities for its employees by an organization which (as of the time the contracts were purchased) was an organization described in section 501(c)(3) which was exempt from tax under section 501(a) or was an organization exempt from tax under section 101(6) of the Internal Revenue Code of 1939 or the corresponding provisions of prior revenue laws, or purchased to provide retirement annuities for employees described in section 403(b)(1)(A)(ii) by an employer which is a State, a political subdivision of a State, or an agency or instrumentality of any one or more of the foregoing; or

(E) purchased under contracts entered into with trusts which (at the time the contracts were entered into) were individual retirement accounts described in section 408(a) or under contracts entered into with individual retirement annuities described in section 408(b).

(2) SPECIAL TRANSITIONAL RULE.—For purposes of this part, the amount taken into account as pension plan reserves shall be—

(A) in the case of a taxable year beginning after December 31, 1957, and before January 1, 1959, zero;

(B) in the case of a taxable year beginning after December 31, 1958, and before January 1, 1960, 33⅓ percent of the amount thereof (determined without regard to this paragraph);

(C) in the case of a taxable year beginning after December 31, 1959, and before January 1, 1961, 66⅔ percent of the amount thereof (determined without regard to this paragraph); and

(D) in the case of a taxable year beginning after December 31, 1960, 100 percent of the amount thereof.

• 1976 (P.L. 94-267)

P.L. 94-267, §1(c):

Amended Code Sec. 805(d)(1)(C) by striking out "and (19)" and inserting in lieu thereof "(19), and (20)". **Effective** for payments made to an employee on or after 7-4-74. For technical rules, see the historical note, relating to §1(d), P.L. 94-267, following the text of Code Sec. 402(a)(5).

• 1974, Employee Retirement Income Security Act of 1974 (P.L. 93-406)

P.L. 93-406, §§1016(a)(6), 2002(g)(9), 2004(c)(3):

Amended Code Sec. 805(d)(1) by deleting "or" at the end of subparagraph (C), by substituting "foregoing; or" for "foregoing," at the end of subparagraph (D) and by adding new subparagraph (E). Code Sec. 805(d)(1) was further amended by substituting "(8), (11), (12), (13), (14), (15), (16), and (19)"; for "and (8);".

• 1964 (P.L. 88-571)

P.L. 88-571, §5(a):

Amended Code Sec. 805(d)(1)(D) by deleting the period immediately after "laws" and by inserting a new clause. **Effective** 1-1-64.

• 1962, Self-Employed Individuals Tax Retirement Act of 1962 (P.L. 87-792)

P.L. 87-792, §7:

Amended Code Sec. 805(d)(1) by striking out in subparagraph (B) "meeting the requirements of section 401(a)(3), (4), (5), and (6), or" and inserting in lieu thereof "described in section 403(a), or plans meeting"; and by striking out in subparagraph (C) "and (6)" and inserting in lieu thereof "(6), (7), and (8)". **Effective** 1-1-63.

[Sec. 805(e)]

(e) INTEREST PAID.—For purposes of this part, the interest paid for any taxable year is the sum of—

(1) INTEREST ON INDEBTEDNESS.—All interest for the taxable year on indebtedness, except on indebtedness incurred or continued to purchase or carry obligations the interest on which is wholly exempt from taxation under this chapter.

(2) AMOUNTS IN THE NATURE OF INTEREST.—All amounts in the nature of interest, whether or not guaranteed, for the taxable year on insurance or annuity contracts (including contracts supplementary thereto) which do not involve, at the time of accrual, life, health, or accident contingencies.

(3) DISCOUNT ON PREPAID PREMIUMS.—All amounts accrued for the taxable year for discounts in the nature of interest, whether or not guaranteed, on premiums or other consideration paid in advance on insurance or annuity contracts.

(4) INTEREST ON CERTAIN SPECIAL CONTINGENCY RESERVES.—Interest for the taxable year on special contingency reserves under contracts of group term life insurance or group health and accident insurance which are established and maintained for the provision of insurance on retired lives, for premium stabilization, or for a combination thereof.

(5) QUALIFIED GUARANTEED INTEREST.—Qualified guaranteed interest (within the meaning of subsection (f)).

For purposes of this subpart, the interest paid for any taxable year shall not include any interest paid or accrued after December 31, 1981, by a ceding company (or its affiliates) to any person in connection with a reinsurance agreement (other than interest on account of delay in making periodic settlements of income and expense items under the terms of the agreement).

Amendments

• 1982, Tax Equity and Fiscal Responsibility Act of 1982 (P.L. 97-248)

P.L. 97-248, §257(a):

Amended Code Sec. 805(e) by adding the last sentence at the end. **Effective** for interest paid or accrued after 1981. For transitional rules, see Act Sec. 257(b) below.

P.L. 97-248, §257(b), provides:

(b) Special Transitional Rule Where at Least 20 Percent of the Liabilities Reinsured Are Paid in Cash, Etc.—The amendment made by subsection (a) shall not apply with respect to any interest paid or incurred by a ceding company to a person who is a member of the same affiliated group (within the meaning of section 1504 of the Internal Revenue Code of 1954) on indebtedness evidenced by a note—

(1) which was entered into after December 31, 1981, with respect to a reinsurance contract under the terms of which an amount not less than 20 percent of the amounts reinsured was paid in cash to the reinsurer on the effective date of such contract,

(2) at least 40 percent of the principal of which had been paid by the ceding company in cash as of July 1, 1982, and

(3) the remaining balance of which is paid in cash before January 1, 1983.

P.L. 97-248, §264(a):

Amended Code Sec. 805(e) by adding at the end thereof new paragraph (5). **Effective** for tax years beginning after 12-31-81. For an exception, see Act Sec. 264(d)(2) below.

P.L. 97-248, §264(d)(2), provides:

(2) Guarantees for less than 12 months.—

(A) Moneys held before August 14, 1982.—The requirements of subparagraph (A)(ii) or (B)(ii)(I) of section 805(f)(1) of the Internal Revenue Code of 1954 (as added by subsection (b)) shall not apply to any moneys held under any contract on August 13, 1982 (and any interest on such moneys after such date).

(B) Contracts entered into after August 13, 1982, and before January 1, 1983.—A contract entered into after August 13, 1982, and before January 1, 1983, shall be treated as meeting the requirements of subparagraph (A)(ii) or (B)(ii)(I) of such Code if it meets such requirements on the first contract anniversary date.

• 1969, Tax Reform Act of 1969 (P.L. 91-172)

P.L. 91-172, §907(a)(1):

Amended Code Sec. 805(e)(4). **Effective** for tax years beginning after 12-31-57. Prior to amendment it read as follows:

"(4) Interest on certain special contingency reserves.—Interest for the taxable year on special contingency reserves established pursuant to section 8(d) of the Federal Employees' Group Life Insurance Act of 1954 (5 U.S.C. §2097(d))."

• 1959, Life Insurance Company Income Tax Act of 1959 (P.L. 86-69)

P.L. 86-69, §2:

Revised Part I of subchapter L of chapter 1 of the 1954 Code. **Effective**, generally, for tax years beginning after 1957. Prior text not reproduced.

[Sec. 805(f)]

(f) QUALIFIED GUARANTEED INTEREST AND QUALIFIED CONTRACTS.—For purposes of this section—

(1) IN GENERAL.—The term "qualified guaranteed interest" means any amount in the nature of interest for the taxable year on qualified contracts, but only if such amount is determined pursuant to—

(A) a stated rate of interest which is guaranteed—

(i) before the beginning of the period for which the interest accrues, and

(ii) for a period of not less than 12 months (or for a period ending not earlier than the close of the taxable year in which the contract was issued), or

(B) a rate or rates of interest which—

(i) meet the requirements of clause (i) of subparagraph (A), and

(ii) is determined under a formula or other method the terms of which—

(I) during the period referred to in subparagraph (A)(ii) may not be changed by the taxpayer, and

(II) are independent of the experience of the taxpayer.

(2) QUALIFIED CONTRACT.—The term "qualified contract" means any annuity contract (other than any contract described in subsection (d)) which—

(A) involves (at the time the qualified interest is credited under the contract) life contingencies,

(B) provides no right under State law for the policyholder to participate in the divisible surplus of the taxpayer, and

(C) provides that the taxpayer may from time to time credit amounts in the nature of interest in excess of amounts computed on the basis of any rate or rates guaranteed in the contract at the time it was entered into.

(3) SPECIAL RULE FOR PARTICIPATING CONTRACTS.—

(A) IN GENERAL.—In the case of an annuity contract which is not a qualified contract solely because it fails to satisfy the requirements of subparagraph (B) of paragraph (2), such contract shall be treated as a qualified contract and the amount taken into account as qualified guaranteed interest with respect to such contract shall be equal to the sum of—

(i) the amount of interest which would be assumed in calculating reserves with respect to such contract under section 810(c) if such interest were not taken into account under subsection (e), plus

(ii) 92.5 percent of the excess of—

(I) the amount of qualified guaranteed interest (determined without regard to this paragraph and as if such contract were a qualified contract), over

(II) the amount determined under clause (i).

(B) INTEREST NOT OTHERWISE TAKEN INTO ACCOUNT.—No deduction shall be allowed under any other provision of this part for the 7.5 percent of the excess described in subparagraph (A)(ii) which is not treated as qualified guaranteed interest.

Amendments

• 1982, Tax Equity and Fiscal Responsibility Act of 1982 (P.L. 97-248)

P.L. 97-248, §264(b):

Amended Code Sec. 805 by adding at the end thereof new subsection (f). **Effective** for tax years beginning after 12-31-81 except as provided in the amendment notes for P.L. 97-248, Act Sec. 264(d)(2) following Code Sec. 805(e).

[Sec. 805(g)]

(g) SPECIAL LIMITATION FOR GROUP PENSION CONTRACTS.—The amount determined under paragraphs (2) and (3) of subsection (a) for policy and other contract liability requirements for group pension contracts shall not exceed the amount actually credited to the policyholders whether such crediting is through premium rate computations, reserve increases, excess interest, experience rate credits, policyholder dividends or otherwise. The Secretary shall prescribe such regulations as may be necessary to carry out the purposes of this subsection.

Amendments

• 1982, Tax Equity and Fiscal Responsibility Act of 1982 (P.L. 97-248)

P.L. 97-248, §260(b):

Amended Code Sec. 805 by adding subsection (g). **Effective** for tax years beginning after 12-31-82 and before 1-1-84. For a special rule, see Act Sec. 260(c) below.

P.L. 97-248, §260(c), provides:

(c) Prohibition Against Changing the Qualification Status of Life Insurance Companies.—For any taxable year ending before January 1, 1984, a taxpayer shall not be treated as other than a life insurance company (as defined in section 801(a) of such Code) because of the effect of amounts held under contracts which would be described in section 805(d) of the Internal Revenue Code of 1954 except for the fact that such contracts do not contain permanent annuity purchase rate guarantees.

[Sec. 806]

SEC. 806. SMALL LIFE INSURANCE COMPANY DEDUCTION.

[Sec. 806(a)]

(a) SMALL LIFE INSURANCE COMPANY DEDUCTION.—

(1) IN GENERAL.—For purposes of section 804, the small life insurance company deduction for any taxable year is 60 percent of so much of the tentative LICTI for such taxable year as does not exceed $3,000,000.

(2) PHASEOUT BETWEEN $3,000,000 AND $15,000,000.—The amount of the small life insurance company deduction determined under paragraph (1) for any taxable year shall be reduced (but not below zero) by 15 percent of so much of the tentative LICTI for such taxable year as exceeds $3,000,000.

(3) SMALL LIFE INSURANCE COMPANY DEDUCTION NOT ALLOWABLE TO COMPANY WITH ASSETS OF $500,000,000 OR MORE.—

(A) IN GENERAL.—The small life insurance company deduction shall not be allowed for any taxable year to any life insurance company which, at the close of such taxable year, has assets equal to or greater than $500,000,000.

(B) ASSETS.—For purposes of this paragraph, the term "assets" means all assets of the company.

(C) VALUATION OF ASSETS.—For purposes of this paragraph, the amount attributable to—

(i) real property and stock shall be the fair market value thereof, and

(ii) any other asset shall be the adjusted basis of such asset for purposes of determining gain on sale or other disposition.

(D) SPECIAL RULE FOR INTERESTS IN PARTNERSHIPS AND TRUSTS.—For purposes of this paragraph—

(i) an interest in a partnership or trust shall not be treated as an asset of the company, but

(ii) the company shall be treated as actually owning its proportionate share of the assets held by the partnership or trust (as the case may be).

[Sec. 806(b)]

(b) TENTATIVE LICTI.—For purposes of this part—

(1) IN GENERAL.—The term "tentative LICTI" means life insurance company taxable income determined without regard to the small life insurance company deduction.

(2) EXCLUSION OF ITEMS ATTRIBUTABLE TO NONINSURANCE BUSINESSES.—The amount of the tentative LICTI for any taxable year shall be determined without regard to all items attributable to noninsurance businesses.

(3) NONINSURANCE BUSINESS.—

(A) IN GENERAL.—The term "noninsurance business" means any activity which is not an insurance business.

(B) CERTAIN ACTIVITIES TREATED AS INSURANCE BUSINESSES.—For purposes of subparagraph (A), any activity which is not an insurance business shall be treated as an insurance business if—

(i) it is of a type traditionally carried on by life insurance companies for investment purposes, but only if the carrying on of such activity (other than in the case of real estate) does not constitute the active conduct of a trade or business, or

(ii) it involves the performance of administrative services in connection with plans providing life insurance, pension, or accident and health benefits.

(C) LIMITATION ON AMOUNT OF LOSS FROM NONINSURANCE BUSINESS WHICH MAY OFFSET INCOME FROM INSURANCE BUSINESS.—In computing the life insurance company taxable income of any life insurance company, any loss from a noninsurance business shall be limited under the principles of section 1503(c).

Amendments

• 1986, Tax Reform Act of 1986 (P.L. 99-514)

P.L. 99-514, §1011(b)(5):

Amended Code Sec. 806(b)(1), as redesignated by Act Sec. 1011(a), by striking out "without regard to—" and all that follows and inserting in lieu thereof "without regard to the small life insurance company deduction." **Effective** for tax years beginning after 12-31-86. Prior to amendment, Code Sec. (b)(1) read as follows:

(1) IN GENERAL.—The term "tentative LICTI" means life insurance company taxable income determined without regard to—

(A) the special life insurance company deduction, and

(B) the small life insurance company deduction.

[Sec. 806(c)]

(c) SPECIAL RULE FOR CONTROLLED GROUPS.—

(1) SMALL LIFE INSURANCE COMPANY DEDUCTION DETERMINED ON CONTROLLED GROUP BASIS.— For purposes of subsection (a)—

(A) all life insurance companies which are members of the same controlled group shall be treated as 1 life insurance company, and

(B) any small life insurance company deduction determined with respect to such group shall be allocated among the life insurance companies which are members of such group in proportion to their respective tentative LICTI's.

(2) NONLIFE INSURANCE MEMBERS INCLUDED FOR ASSET TEST.—For purposes of subsection (a)(3), all members of the same controlled group (whether or not life insurance companies) shall be treated as 1 company.

(3) CONTROLLED GROUP.—For purposes of this subsection, the term "controlled group" means any controlled group of corporations (as defined in section 1563(a)); except that subsections (a)(4) and (b)(2)(D) of section 1563 shall not apply.

(4) ADJUSTMENTS TO PREVENT EXCESS DETRIMENT OR BENEFIT.—Under regulations prescribed by the Secretary, proper adjustments shall be made in the application of this subsection to prevent any excess detriment or benefit (whether from year-to-year or otherwise) arising from the application of this subsection.

Amendments

• 1986, Tax Reform Act of 1986 (P.L. 99-514)

P.L. 99-514, §1011(a):

Amended Code Sec. 806 by striking out subsection (a) and by redesignating subsections (b), (c), and (d), as subsections (a), (b), and (c), respectively. **Effective** for tax years beginning after 12-31-86. Prior to amendment, Code Sec. 806(a) read as follows:

(a) SPECIAL LIFE INSURANCE COMPANY DEDUCTION.—For purposes of section 804, the special life insurance company for any taxable year is 20 percent of the excess of the tentative LICTI for such taxable year over the small life insurance company deduction (if any).

P.L. 99-514, §1011(b)(6)(A)-(C):

Amended Code Sec. 806(c)(1), as redesignated by Act Sec. 1011(a), by striking out "subsections (a) and (b)" and inserting in lieu thereof "subsection (a)", by striking out "any special life insurance company deduction and", and by striking out "Special Life Insurance Company Deduction and Small" in the heading and inserting in lieu thereof "Small". **Effective** for tax years beginning after 12-31-86.

P.L. 99-514, §1011(b)(7):

Amended by Code Sec. 806(c)(2), as redesignated by Act Sec. 1011(a), by striking out "subsection (b)(3)" and inserting in lieu thereof "subsection (a)(3)". **Effective** for tax years beginning after 12-31-86.

P.L. 99-514, §1011(b)(8):

Amended Code Sec. 806(c), as redesignated by Act Sec. 1011(a), by striking out paragraph (4) and by redesignating paragraph (5) as paragraph (4). **Effective** for tax years beginning after 12-31-86. Prior to amendment, Code Sec. 806(c)(4) read as follows:

(4) ELECTION WITH RESPECT TO LOSS FROM OPERATIONS OF MEMBERS OF GROUP.—

(A) IN GENERAL.—Any life insurance company which is a member of a controlled group may elect to have its loss from operations for any taxable year not taken into account for purposes of determining the amount of the special life insurance company deduction for the life insurance companies which are members of such group and which do not file a consolidated return with such life insurance company for the taxable year.

(B) LIMITATION ON AMOUNT OF LOSS WHICH MAY OFFSET NONLIFE INCOME.—In the case of that portion of any loss from operations for any taxable year of a life insurance company which (but for subparagraph (A)) would have reduced tentative LICTI of other life insurance companies for such taxable year—

(i) only 80 percent of such portion may be used to offset nonlife income, and

(ii) to the extent such portion is used to offset nonlife income, the loss shall be treated as used at a rate of $1 for each 80 cents of income so offset.

For purposes of the preceding sentence, any such portion shall be used before the remaining portion of the loss from the same year and shall be treated at first being offset against income which is not nonlife income.

(C) NONLIFE INCOME.—

(i) IN GENERAL.—The term "nonlife income" means the portion of the life insurance company's taxable income for which the special life insurance company deduction was not allowable and any income of a corporation not subject to tax under this part.

(ii) SPECIAL RULE FOR TAXABLE YEARS BEGINNING BEFORE JANUARY 1, 1984.—In the case of a taxable year beginning before January 1, 1984, all life insurance company taxable income shall be treated as nonlife income.

P.L. 99-514, §1011(b)(11)(A):

Amended Code Sec. 806 by striking out "SPECIAL DEDUCTIONS" in the section heading and inserting in lieu thereof "SMALL LIFE INSURANCE COMPANY DEDUCTION". **Effective** for tax years beginning after 12-31-86.

P.L. 99-514, §1011(d), as amended by P.L. 100-647, §1010(a)(2)-(3), provides as follows:

(d) TREATMENT OF CERTAIN MARKET DISCOUNT BONDS.—

(1) IN GENERAL.—Notwithstanding the amendments made by subtitle B of title III, any gain recognized by a qualified life insurance company on the redemption at maturity of any market discount bond (as defined in section 1278 of the Internal Revenue Code of 1986) which was issued before July 19, 1984, and acquired by such company on or before September 25, 1985, shall be subject to tax at the rate of 31.6 percent. The preceding sentence shall apply only if the tax determined under the preceding sentence is less than the tax which would otherwise by imposed.

(2) QUALIFIED LIFE INSURANCE COMPANY.—For purposes of paragraph (1), the term `qualified life insurance company' means any life insurance company subject to tax under part I of subchapter L of chapter 1 of the Internal Revenue Code of 1986.

• 1984, Deficit Reduction Act of 1984 (P.L. 98-369)

P.L. 98-369, §211(a):

Amended Part I of subchapter L of chapter 1 by adding Code Sec. 806. **Effective** for tax years beginning after 12-31-83. For transitional and special rules, see Act Sec. 216(a)-(b)(2) in the amendments for Code Sec. 801. For a special election and rules relating to Code Sec. 806, see Act Sec. 217(b), (c), (h), (j)-(m), below.

P.L. 98-369, §217(b), (c), provides as follows:

(b) Treatment of Elections Under Section 453B(e)(2).—If an election is made under section 453B(e)(2) before January 1, 1984, with respect to any installment obligation, any income from such obligation shall be treated as attributable to a noninsurance business (as defined in section 806(c)(3) of the Internal Revenue Code of 1954).

(c) Determination of Tentative LICTI Where Corporation Made Certain Acquisitions in 1980, 1981, 1982, and 1983.—If—

(1) a corporation domiciled or having its principal place of business in Alabama, Arkansas, Oklahoma, or Texas acquired the assets of 1 or more insurance companies after 1979 and before April 1, 1983, and

(2) the bases of such assets in the hands of the corporation were determined under section 334(b)(2) of the Internal Revenue Code of 1954 or such corporation made an election under section 338 of such Code with respect to such assets,

then the tentative LICTI of the corporation holding such assets for taxable years beginning after December 31, 1983, shall, for purposes of determining the amount of the special deductions under section 806 of such Code, be increased by the deduction allowable under chapter 1 of such Code for the amortization of the cost of insurance contracts acquired in such asset acquisition (and any portion of any operations loss deduction attributable to such amortization).

P.L. 98-369, §217(h), provides:

(h) Determination of Assets of Controlled Group for Purposes of Small Life Insurance Company Deduction for 1984.—

(1) In General.—For purposes of applying paragraph (2) of section 806(d) of the Internal Revenue Code of 1954 (relating to non-life insurance members included for asset test) for the first taxable year beginning after December 31, 1983, the members of the controlled group referred to in such paragraph shall be treated as including only those members of such group which are described in paragraph (2) of this subsection if—

(A) an election under section 1504(c)(2) of such Code is not in effect for the controlled group for such taxable year,

(B) during such taxable year, the controlled group does not include a member which is taxable under part I of subchapter L of chapter 1 of such Code and which became a member of such group after September 27, 1983, and

(C) the sum of the contributions to capital received by members of the controlled group which are taxable under such part I during such taxable year from the members of the controlled group which are not taxable under such part does not exceed the aggregate dividends paid during such taxable year by the members of such group which are taxable under such part I.

(2) Members of Group Taken Into Account.—For purposes of paragraph (1), the members of the controlled group which are described in this paragraph are—

(A) any financial institution to which section 585 or 593 of such Code applies,

(B) any lending or finance business (as defined by section 542(d)),

(C) any insurance company subject to tax imposed by subchapter L of chapter 1 of such Code, and

(D) any securities broker.

P.L. 98-369, §217(j)-(m), provides:

(j) Reduction in Equity Base for Mutual Successor of Fraternal Benefit Society.—In the case of any mutual life insurance company which—

(1) is the successor to a fraternal benefit society, and

(2) which assumed the surplus of such fraternal benefit society in 1950 or in March of 1961,

for purposes of section 809 of the Internal Revenue Code of 1954 (as amended by this subtitle), the equity base of such mutual life insurance company shall be reduced by the amount of the surplus so assumed plus earnings thereon, (i) for taxable years before 1984, at a 7 percent interest rate, and (ii) for taxable years 1984 and following, at the average mutual earnings rate for such year.

(k) Special Rule for Certain Debt-Financed Acquisition of Stock.—If—

(1) a life insurance company owns the stock of another corporation through a partnership of which it is a partner,

(2) the stock of the corporation was acquired on January 14, 1981, and

(3) such stock was acquired by debt financing,

then, for purposes of determining the special deductions under section 806 of the Internal Revenue Code of 1954 (as amended by this subtitle), the amount of tentative LICTI of such life insurance company shall be computed without taking into account any income, gain, loss, or deduction attributable to the ownership of such stock.

(l) Treatment of Losses from Certain Guaranteed Interest Contracts.—

(1) In General.—For purposes of determining the amount of the special deductions under section 806 of the Internal Revenue Code of 1954 (as amended by this subtitle), for any taxable year beginning before January 1, 1988, the amount of tentative LICTI of any qualified life insurance company shall be computed without taking into account any income, gain, loss, or deduction attributable to a qualified GIC.

(2) Qualified Life Insurance Company.—For purposes of this subsection, the term "qualified life insurance company" means any life insurance company if—

(A) the accrual of discount less amortization of premium for bonds and short-term investments (as shown in the first footnote to Exhibit 3 of its 1983 annual statement for life insurance companies approved by the National Association of Insurance Commissioners (but excluding separate accounts) filed in its state of domicile) exceeds $72,000,000 but does not exceed $73,000,000, and

(B) such life insurance company makes an election under this subsection on its return for its first taxable year beginning after December 31, 1983.

(3) Qualified GIC.—The term "qualified GIC" means any group contract—

(A) which is issued before January 1, 1984,

(B) which specifies the contract maturity or renewal date,

(C) under which funds deposited by the contract holder plus interest guaranteed at the inception of the contract for the term of the contract and net of any specified expenses are paid as directed by the contract holder, and

(D) which is a pension plan contract (as defined in section 818(a) of the Internal Revenue Code of 1954).

(4) Scope of Election.—An election under this subsection shall apply to all qualified GIC's of a qualified life insurance company. Any such election, once made, shall be irrevocable.

(5) Income on Underlying Assets Taken Into Account.—In determining the amount of any income attributable to a qualified GIC, income on any asset attributable to such contract (as determined in the manner provided by the Secretary of the Treasury or his delegate) shall be taken into account.

(6) Limitation on tax benefit. The amount of any reduction in tax for any taxable year by reason of this subsection for any qualified life insurance company (or controlled group within the meaning of section 806(d)(3) of the Internal Revenue Code of 1954) shall not exceed the applicable amount set forth in the following table:

In the case of taxable years beginning in	*The reduction may not exceed*
1984	$4,500,000
1985	$4,500,000
1986	$3,000,000
1987	$2,000,000

(m) Special Rule for Certain Interests in Oil and Gas Properties.—

(1) In General.—For purposes of section 806 of the Internal Revenue Code of 1954, the ownership by a qualified life insurance company of any undivided interest in operating mineral interests with respect to any oil or gas properties held on December 31, 1983, shall be treated as an insurance business.

(2) Qualified Life Insurance Company.—For purposes of paragraph (1), the term "qualified life insurance company" means a mutual life insurance company which—

(A) was originally incorporated in March of 1857, and

(B) has a cost to such company (as of December 31, 1983) in the operating mineral interests described in paragraph (1) in excess of $250,000,000.

[Sec. 806—Repealed]

• 1984, Deficit Reduction Act of 1984 (P.L. 98-369)

P.L. 98-369, §211(a):

Amended Part I of Subchapter L of Chapter 1 by adding a new Part I (Code Secs. 801-818). For transitional and special rules, see Act Sec. 216(a)-(b)(2) in the amendments for Code Sec. 801. Prior to amendment, Code Sec. 806 read as follows:

SEC. 806. CERTAIN CHANGES IN RESERVES AND ASSETS.

[Sec. 806(a)]

(a) ADJUSTMENTS TO MEANS FOR CERTAIN TRANSFERS OF LIABILITIES.—For purposes of this part, if, during the taxable year, there is a change in life insurance reserves attributable to the transfer between the taxpayer and another person of liabilities under contracts taken into account in computing such reserves, then, under regulations prescribed by the Secretary, the means of such reserves, and the mean of the assets, shall be appropriately adjusted, on a daily basis, to reflect the amounts involved in such transfer. This subsection shall not apply to reinsurance ceded to the taxpayer or to another person.

Amendments

• 1976, Tax Reform Act of 1976 (P.L. 94-455)

P.L. 94-455, §1906(b)(13)(A):

Amended 1954 Code by substituting "Secretary" for "Secretary or his delegate" each place it appeared. **Effective** 2-1-77.

[Sec. 806(b)]

(b) CHANGE OF BASIS IN COMPUTING RESERVES.—If the basis for determining the amount of any item referred to in section 810(c) as of the close of the taxable year differs from the basis for such determination as of the beginning of the taxable year, then for purposes of this subpart the amount of such item—

(1) as of the close of the taxable year shall be computed on the old basis, and

(2) as of the beginning of the next taxable year shall be computed on the new basis.

Amendments

• 1959, Life Insurance Company Income Tax Act of 1959 (P.L. 86-69)

P.L. 86-69, §2:

Revised Part I of subchapter L of chapter 1 of the 1954 Code. **Effective**, generally, for tax years beginning after 1957. Prior text not reproduced.

[Sec. 807]

SEC. 807. RULES FOR CERTAIN RESERVES.

[Sec. 807(a)]

(a) DECREASE TREATED AS GROSS INCOME.—If for any taxable year—

(1) the opening balance for the items described in subsection (c), exceeds

(2)(A) the closing balance for such items, reduced by

(B) the amount of the policyholders' share of tax-exempt interest and the amount of the policyholder's share of the increase for the taxable year in policy cash values (within the meaning of section 805(a)(4)(F)) of life insurance policies and annuity and endowment contracts to which section 264(f) applies,

such excess shall be included in gross income under section 803(a)(2).

Amendments

• 2004, Pension Funding Equity Act of 2004 (P.L. 108-218)

P.L. 108-218, §205(b)(1):

Amended Code Sec. 807(a)(2)(B) by striking "the sum of (i)" following "(B)" and by striking "plus (ii) any excess described in section 809(a)(2) for the taxable year," following "to which section 264(f) applies,". **Effective** for tax years beginning after 12-31-2004.

• 1997, Taxpayer Relief Act of 1997 (P.L. 105-34)

P.L. 105-34, §1084(b)[(d)](2)(A):

Amended Code Sec. 807(a)(2)(B) by striking "interest," and inserting "interest and the amount of the policyholder's share of the increase for the taxable year in policy cash values (within the meaning of section 805(a)(4)(F)) of life insurance policies and annuity and endowment contracts to which section 264(f) applies,". For the **effective** date, see Act Sec. 1084(d)[(f)], below.

P.L. 105-34, §1084(d)[(f)], as amended by P.L. 105-206, §6010(o)(3)(B), provides:

(d)[(f)] EFFECTIVE DATE.—The amendments made by this section shall apply to contracts issued after June 8, 1997, in taxable years ending after such date. For purposes of the preceding sentence, any material increase in the death benefit or other material change in the contract shall be treated as a new contract except that, in the case of a master contract (within the meaning of section 264(f)(4)(E) of the Internal Revenue Code of 1986), the addition of covered lives shall be treated as a new contract only with respect to such additional covered lives. For purposes of this subsection, an increase in the death benefit under a policy or contract issued in connection with a lapse described in section 501(d)(2) of the Health Insurance Portability and Accountability Act of 1996 shall not be treated as a new contract.

[Sec. 807(b)]

(b) INCREASE TREATED AS DEDUCTION.—If for any taxable year—

(1)(A) the closing balance for the items described in subsection (c), reduced by

(B) the amount of the policyholders' share of tax-exempt interest and the amount of the policyholder's share of the increase for the taxable year in policy cash values (within the meaning of section 805(a)(4)(F)) of life insurance policies and annuity and endowment contracts to which section 264(f) applies, exceeds

(2) the opening balance for such items,

such excess shall be taken into account as a deduction under section 805(a)(2).

Amendments

• 2004, Pension Funding Equity Act of 2004 (P.L. 108-218)

P.L. 108-218, §205(b)(1):

Amended Code Sec. 807(b)(1)(B) by striking "the sum of (i)" following "(B)" and by striking "plus (ii) any excess described in section 809(a)(2) for the taxable year," following "to which section 264(f) applies,". **Effective** for tax years beginning after 12-31-2004.

• 1997, Taxpayer Relief Act of 1997 (P.L. 105-34)

P.L. 105-34, §1084(b)[(d)](2)(B):

Amended Code Sec. 807(b)(1)(B) by striking "interest," and inserting "interest and the amount of the policyholder's share of the increase for the taxable year in policy cash values (within the meaning of section 805(a)(4)(F)) of life insurance policies and annuity and endowment contracts to which section 264(f) applies,". For the **effective** date, see Act Sec. 1084(d)[(f)], below.

P.L. 105-34, §1084(d)[(f)], as amended by P.L. 105-206, §6010(o)(3)(B), provides:

(d)[(f)] EFFECTIVE DATE.—The amendments made by this section shall apply to contracts issued after June 8, 1997, in taxable years ending after such date. For purposes of the preceding sentence, any material increase in the death benefit or other material change in the contract shall be treated as a new contract except that, in the case of a master contract (within the meaning of section 264(f)(4)(E) of the Internal

Revenue Code of 1986), the addition of covered lives shall be treated as a new contract only with respect to such additional covered lives. For purposes of this subsection, an increase in the death benefit under a policy or contract issued in connection with a lapse described in section 501(d)(2) of the Health Insurance Portability and Accountability Act of 1996 shall not be treated as a new contract.

[Sec. 807(c)]

(c) ITEMS TAKEN INTO ACCOUNT.—The items referred to in subsections (a) and (b) are as follows:

(1) The life insurance reserves (as defined in section 816(b)).

(2) The unearned premiums and unpaid losses included in total reserves under section 816(c)(2).

(3) The amounts (discounted at the appropriate rate of interest) necessary to satisfy the obligations under insurance and annuity contracts, but only if such obligations do not involve (at the time with respect to which the computation is made under this paragraph) life, accident, or health contingencies.

(4) Dividend accumulations, and other amounts, held at interest in connection with insurance and annuity contracts.

(5) Premiums received in advance, and liabilities for premium deposit funds.

(6) Reasonable special contingency reserves under contracts of group term life insurance or group accident and health insurance which are established and maintained for the provision of insurance on retired lives, for premium stabilization, or for a combination thereof.

For purposes of paragraph (3), the appropriate rate of interest for any obligation is whichever of the following rates is the highest as of the time such obligation first did not involve life, accident, or health contingencies: the applicable Federal interest rate under subsection (d)(2)(B)(i), the prevailing State assumed interest rate under subsection (d)(2)(B)(ii), or the rate of interest assumed by the company in determining the guaranteed benefit. In no case shall the amount determined under paragraph (3) for any contract be less than the net surrender value of such contract. For purposes of paragraph (2) and section 805(a)(1), the amount of the unpaid losses (other than losses on life insurance contracts) shall be the amount of the discounted unpaid losses as defined in section 846.

Amendments

• 1987, Revenue Act of 1987 (P.L. 100-203)

P.L. 100-203, §10241(b)(2)(A):

Amended Code Sec. 807(c) by striking out "the higher of" and all that follows in the third to the last sentence and inserting in lieu thereof "whichever of the following rates is the highest as of the time such obligation first did not involve life, accident, or health contingencies: the applicable Federal interest rate under subsection (d)(2)(B)(i), the prevailing State assumed interest rate under subsection (d)(2)(B)(ii), or the rate of interest assumed by the company in determining the guaranteed benefit." **Effective** for contracts issued in tax years beginning after 12-31-87. Prior to amendment, the third to last sentence of Code Sec. 807(c) read as follows:

For purposes of paragraph (3), the appropriate rate of interest for any obligation is the higher of the prevailing State assumed interest rate as of the time such obligation first did not involve life, accident, or health contingencies or the rate of interest assumed by the company (as of such time) in determining the guaranteed benefit.

• 1986, Tax Reform Act of 1986 (P.L. 99-514)

P.L. 99-514, §1023(b):

Amended Code Sec. 807(c) by adding at the end thereof a new sentence. **Effective**, generally, for tax years beginning after 12-31-86. However, see Act Sec. 1023(e)(2)-(4), below.

P.L. 99-514, §1023(e)(2)-(4), as amended by P.L. 100-647, §1010(e)(3), provides:

(2) TRANSITIONAL RULE.—For the first taxable year beginning after December 31, 1986—

(A) the unpaid losses and the expenses unpaid (as defined in paragraphs (5)(B) and (6) of section 832(b) of the Internal Revenue Code of 1986) at the end of the preceding taxable year, and

(B) the unpaid losses as defined in sections 807(c)(2) and 807(a)(1) of such Code at the end of the preceding taxable year,

shall be determined as if the amendments made by this section had applied to such unpaid losses and expenses unpaid in the preceding taxable year and by using the interest rate and loss payment patterns applicable to accident years ending with calendar year 1987. For subsequent taxable years, such amendments shall be applied with respect to such unpaid losses and expenses unpaid by using the interest rate and loss payment patterns applicable to accident years ending with calendar year 1987.

(3) FRESH START.—

(A) IN GENERAL.—Except as otherwise provided in this paragraph, any difference between—

(i) the amount determined to be the unpaid losses and expenses unpaid for the year preceding the 1st taxable year of an insurance company beginning after December 31, 1986, determined without regard to paragraph (2), and

(ii) such amount determined with regard to paragraph (2), shall not be taken into account for purposes of the Internal Revenue Code of 1986.

(B) RESERVE STRENGTHENING IN YEARS AFTER 1985.—Subparagraph (A) shall not apply to any reserve strengthening in a taxable year beginning in 1986, and such strengthening shall be treated as occurring in the taxpayer's 1st taxable year beginning after December 31, 1986.

(C) EFFECT ON EARNINGS AND PROFITS.—The earnings and profits of an insurance company, for its 1st taxable year beginning after December 31, 1986, shall be increased by the amount of the difference determined under subparagraph (A) with respect to such company.

(4) APPLICATION OF FRESH START TO COMPANIES WHICH BECOME SUBJECT TO SECTION 831(a) TAX IN LATER TAXABLE YEAR.—If—

(A) an insurance company was not subject to tax under section 831(a) of the Internal Revenue Code of 1986 for its 1st taxable year beginning after December 31, 1986, by reason of being—

(i) subject to tax under section 831(b) of such Code, or

(ii) described in section 501(c) of such Code and exempt from tax under section 501(a) of such Code, and

(B) such company becomes subject to tax under such section 831(a) for later taxable year,

paragraph (2) and subparagraphs (A) and (C) of paragraph (3) shall be applied by treating such later taxable year as its 1st taxable year beginning after December 31, 1986, and by treating the calendar year in which such later taxable year begins as 1987; and paragraph (3)(B) shall not apply.

P.L. 99-514, §1821(a):

Amended Code Sec. 807(c) by adding at the end thereof a new sentence. **Effective** as if included in the provision of P.L. 98-369 to which it relates.

[Sec. 807(d)]

(d) METHOD OF COMPUTING RESERVES FOR PURPOSES OF DETERMINING INCOME.—

(1) IN GENERAL.—For purposes of this part (other than section 816), the amount of the life insurance reserves for any contract shall be the greater of—

(A) the net surrender value of such contract, or

(B) the reserve determined under paragraph (2).

In no event shall the reserve determined under the preceding sentence for any contract as of any time exceed the amount which would be taken into account with respect to such contract as of such time in determining statutory reserves (as defined in paragraph (6)).

(2) AMOUNT OF RESERVE.—The amount of the reserve determined under this paragraph with respect to any contract shall be determined by using—

(A) the tax reserve method applicable to such contract,

(B) the greater of—

(i) the applicable Federal interest rate, or

(ii) the prevailing State assumed interest rate, and

(C) the prevailing commissioners' standard tables for mortality and morbidity adjusted as appropriate to reflect the risks (such as substandard risks) incurred under the contract which are not otherwise taken into account.

(3) TAX RESERVE METHOD.—For purposes of this subsection—

(A) IN GENERAL.—The term "tax reserve method" means—

(i) LIFE INSURANCE CONTRACTS.—The CRVM in the case of a contract covered by the CRVM.

(ii) ANNUITY CONTRACTS.—The CARVM in the case of a contract covered by the CARVM.

(iii) NONCANCELLABLE ACCIDENT AND HEALTH INSURANCE CONTRACTS.—In the case of any noncancellable accident and health insurance contract (other than a qualified long-term care insurance contract, as defined in section 7702B(b)), a 2-year full preliminary term method.

(iv) OTHER CONTRACTS.—In the case of any contract not described in clause (i), (ii), or (iii)—

(I) the reserve method prescribed by the National Association of Insurance Commissioners which covers such contract (as of the date of issuance), or

(II) if no reserve method has been prescribed by the National Association of Insurance Commissioners which covers such contract, a reserve method which is consistent with the reserve method required under clause (i), (ii), or (iii) or under subclause (I) of this clause as of the date of the issuance of such contract (whichever is most appropriate).

(B) DEFINITION OF CRVM AND CARVM.—For purposes of this paragraph—

(i) CRVM.—The term "CRVM" means the Commissioners' Reserve Valuation Method prescribed by the National Association of Insurance Commissioners which is in effect on the date of the issuance of the contract.

(ii) CARVM.—The term "CARVM" means the Commissioners' Annuities Reserve Valuation Method prescribed by the National Association of Insurance Commissioners which is in effect on the date of the issuance of the contract.

(C) NO ADDITIONAL RESERVE DEDUCTION ALLOWED FOR DEFICIENCY RESERVES.—Nothing in any reserve method described under this paragraph shall permit any increase in the reserve because the net premium (computed on the basis of assumptions required under this subsection) exceeds the actual premiums or other consideration charged for the benefit.

(4) APPLICABLE FEDERAL INTEREST RATE; PREVAILING STATE ASSUMED INTEREST RATE.—For purposes of this subsection—

(A) APPLICABLE FEDERAL INTEREST RATE.—

(i) IN GENERAL.—Except as provided in clause (ii), the term "applicable Federal interest rate" means the annual rate determined by the Secretary under section 846(c)(2) for the calendar year in which the contract was issued.

(ii) ELECTION TO RECOMPUTE FEDERAL INTEREST RATE EVERY 5 YEARS.—

(I) IN GENERAL.—In computing the amount of the reserve with respect to any contract to which an election under this clause applies for periods during any recomputation period, the applicable Federal interest rate shall be the annual rate determined by the Secretary under section 846(c)(2) for the 1st year of such period. No change in the applicable Federal interest rate shall be made under the preceding sentence unless such change would equal or exceed 1/2 of 1 percentage point.

(II) RECOMPUTATION PERIOD.—For purposes of subclause (I), the term "recomputation period" means, with respect to any contract, the 5 calendar year period beginning with the 5th calendar year beginning after the calendar year in which the contract was issued (and each subsequent 5 calendar year period).

(III) ELECTION.—An election under this clause shall apply to all contracts issued during the calendar year for which the election was made or during any subsequent calendar year unless such election is revoked with the consent of the Secretary.

(IV) SPREAD NOT AVAILABLE.—Subsection (f) shall not apply to any adjustment required under this clause.

(B) PREVAILING STATE ASSUMED INTEREST RATE.—

(i) IN GENERAL.—The "prevailing State assumed interest rate" means, with respect to any contract, the highest assumed interest rate permitted to be used in computing life insurance reserves for insurance contracts or annuity contracts (as the case may be) under the insurance laws of at least 26 States. For purposes of the preceding sentence, the effect of nonforfeiture laws of a State on interest rates for reserves shall not be taken into account.

(ii) WHEN RATE DETERMINED.—The prevailing State assumed interest rate with respect to any contract shall be determined as of the beginning of the calendar year in which the contract was issued.

(5) PREVAILING COMMISSIONERS' STANDARD TABLES.—For purposes of this subsection—

(A) IN GENERAL.—The term "prevailing commissioners' standard tables" means, with respect to any contract, the most recent commissioners' standard tables prescribed by the National Association of Insurance Commissioners which are permitted to be used in computing reserves for that type of contract under the insurance laws of at least 26 States when the contract was issued.

(B) INSURER MAY USE OLD TABLES FOR 3 YEARS WHEN TABLES CHANGE.—If the prevailing commissioners' standard tables as of the beginning of any calendar year (hereinafter in this subparagraph referred to as the "year of change") is different from the prevailing commissioners' standard tables as of the beginning of the preceding calendar year, the issuer may use the prevailing commissioners' standard tables as of the beginning of the preceding calendar year with respect to any contract issued after the change and before the close of the 3-year period beginning on the first day of the year of change.

(C) SPECIAL RULE FOR CONTRACTS FOR WHICH THERE ARE NO COMMISSIONERS' STANDARD TABLES.—If there are no commissioners' standard tables applicable to any contract when it is issued, the mortality and morbidity tables used for purposes of paragraph (2)(C) shall be determined under regulations prescribed by the Secretary. When the Secretary by regulation changes the table applicable to a type of contract, the new table shall be treated (for purposes of subparagraph (B) and for purposes of determining the issue dates of contracts for which it shall be used) as if it were a new prevailing commissioner's standard table adopted by the twenty-sixth State as of a date (no earlier than the date the regulation is issued) specified by the Secretary.

(D) SPECIAL RULE FOR CONTRACTS ISSUED BEFORE 1948.—If—

(i) a contract was issued before 1948, and

(ii) there were no commissioners' standard tables applicable to such contract when it was issued,

the mortality and morbidity tables used in computing statutory reserves for such contracts shall be used for purposes of paragraph (2)(C).

(E) SPECIAL RULE WHERE MORE THAN 1 TABLE OR OPTION APPLICABLE.—If, with respect to any category of risks, there are 2 or more tables (or options under 1 or more tables) which meet the requirements of subparagraph (A) (or, where applicable, subparagraph (B) or (C)), the table (and option thereunder) which generally yields the lowest reserves shall be used for purposes of paragraph (2)(C).

(6) STATUTORY RESERVES.—The term "statutory reserves" means the aggregate amount set forth in the annual statement with respect to items described in section 807(c). Such term shall not include any reserve attributable to a deferred and uncollected premium if the establishment of such reserve is not permitted under section 811(c).

Amendments

• 2004, Pension Funding Equity Act of 2004 (P.L. 108-218)

P.L. 108-218, §205(b)(2)(A):

Amended the last sentence of Code Sec. 807(d)(1) by striking "section 809(b)(4)(B)" and inserting "paragraph (6)". **Effective** for tax years beginning after 12-31-2004.

P.L. 108-218, §205(b)(2)(B):

Amended Code Sec. 807(d) by adding at the end a new paragraph (6). **Effective** for tax years beginning after 12-31-2004.

• 1996, Health Insurance Portability and Accountability Act of 1996 (P.L. 104-191)

P.L. 104-191, §321(b):

Amended Code Sec. 807(d)(3)(A)(iii) by inserting "(other than a qualified long-term care insurance contract, as defined in section 7702B(b))" after "insurance contract". **Effective** for contracts issued after 12-31-97. For special rules of the above amendment, see Act Sec. 321(f)(2)-(5) and (g), below.

P.L. 104-191, §321(f)(2)-(5) and (g), provides:

(2) CONTINUATION OF EXISTING POLICIES.—In the case of any contract issued before January 1, 1997, which met the long-term care insurance requirements of the State in which the contract was sitused at the time the contract was issued—

(A) such contract shall be treated for purposes of the Internal Revenue Code of 1986 as a qualified long-term care insurance contract (as defined in section 7702B(b) of such Code), and

(B) services provided under, or reimbursed by, such contract shall be treated for such purposes as qualified long-term care services (as defined in section 7702B(c) of such Code).

In the case of an individual who is covered on December 31, 1996, under a State long-term care plan (as defined in section 7702B(f)(2) of such Code), the terms of such plan on such date shall be treated for purposes of the preceding sentence as a contract issued on such date which met the long-term care insurance requirements of such State.

(3) EXCHANGES OF EXISTING POLICIES.—If, after the date of enactment of this Act and before January 1, 1998, a contract providing for long-term care insurance coverage is exchanged solely for a qualified long-term care insurance contract (as defined in section 7702B(b) of such Code), no gain or loss shall be recognized on the exchange. If, in addition to a qualified long-term care insurance contract, money or other property is received in the exchange, then any gain shall be recognized to the extent of the sum of the money and the fair market value of the other property received. For purposes of this paragraph, the cancellation of a contract providing for long-term care insurance coverage and reinvestment of the cancellation proceeds in a qualified long-term care insurance contract within 60 days thereafter shall be treated as an exchange.

(4) ISSUANCE OF CERTAIN RIDERS PERMITTED.—For purposes of applying sections 101(f), 7702, and 7702A of the Internal Revenue Code of 1986 to any contract—

(A) the issuance of a rider which is treated as a qualified long-term care insurance contract under section 7702B, and

(B) the addition of any provision required to conform any other long-term care rider to be so treated,

shall not be treated as a modification or material change of such contract.

(5) APPLICATION OF PER DIEM LIMITATION TO EXISTING CONTRACTS.—The amount of per diem payments made under a contract issued on or before July 31, 1996, with respect to an insured which are excludable from gross income by reason of section 7702B of the Internal Revenue Code of 1986 (as added by this section) shall not be reduced under subsection (d)(2)(B) thereof by reason of reimbursements received under a contract issued on or before such date. The preceding sentence shall cease to apply as of the date (after July 31, 1996) such contract is exchanged or there is any contract modification which results in an increase in the amount of such per diem payments or the amount of such reimbursements.

(g) LONG-TERM CARE STUDY REQUEST.—The Chairman of the Committee on Ways and Means of the House of Representatives and the Chairman of the Committee on Finance of the Senate shall jointly request the National Association of Insurance Commissioners, in consultation with representatives of the insurance industry and consumer organizations, to formulate, develop, and conduct a study to determine the marketing and other effects of per diem limits on certain types of long-term care policies. If the National Association of Insurance Commissioners agrees to the study request, the National Association of Insurance Commissioners shall report the results of its study to such committees not later than 2 years after accepting the request.

• 1996, Small Business Job Protection Act of 1996 (P.L. 104-188)

P.L. 104-188, §1704(t)(61):

Amended Code Sec. 807(d)(3)(B)(ii) by striking "Commissoners'" and inserting "Commissioners'". **Effective** 8-20-96.

• 1987, Revenue Act of 1987 (P.L. 100-203)

P.L. 100-203, §10241(a):

Amended Code Sec. 807(d)(2)(B). **Effective** for contracts issued in tax years beginning after 12-31-87. Prior to amendment, Code Sec. 807(d)(2)(B) read as follows:

(B) the prevailing State assumed interest rate, and

P.L. 100-203, §10241(b)(1):

Amended Code Sec. 807(d)(4). **Effective** for contracts issued in tax years beginning after 12-31-87. Prior to amendment, Code Sec. 807(d)(4) read as follows:

(4) PREVAILING STATE ASSUMED INTEREST RATE.—For purposes of this subsection—

(A) IN GENERAL.—The term "prevailing State assumed interest rate" means, with respect to any contract, the highest assumed interest rate permitted to be used in computing life insurance reserves for insurance contracts or annuity contracts (as the case may be) under the insurance laws of at least 26 States. For purposes of the preceding sentence, the effect of the nonforfeiture laws of a state on interest rates for reserves shall not be taken into account.

(B) WHEN RATE DETERMINED.—Except as provided in subparagraph (C), the prevailing State assumed rate with respect to any contract shall be determined as of the beginning of the calendar year in which the contract was issued.

(C) ELECTION FOR NONANNUITY CONTRACTS.—In the case of a contract other than an annuity contract, the issuer may elect (at such time and in such manner as the Secretary shall by regulations prescribe) to determine the prevailing State assumed rate as of the beginning of the calendar year preceding the calendar year in which the contract was issued.

(D) RATE FOR NONCANCELLABLE ACCIDENT AND HEALTH INSURANCE CONTRACTS.—If there is no prevailing State assumed interest rate applicable under subparagraph (A) to any noncancellable accident and health insurance contract when it is issued, the prevailing State assumed interest rate for such contract shall be the prevailing State assumed interest rate which would be determined under subparagraph (A) for a whole life insurance contract issued on the date on which the noncancellable accident and health insurance contract is issued.

• 1986, Tax Reform Act of 1986 (P.L. 99-514)

P.L. 99-514, §1821(s):

Amended Code Sec. 807(d)(5)(C) by adding at the end thereof a new sentence. **Effective** as if included in the provision of P.L. 98-369 to which it relates.

[Sec. 807(e)]

(e) SPECIAL RULES FOR COMPUTING RESERVES.—

(1) NET SURRENDER VALUE.—For purposes of this section—

(A) IN GENERAL.—The net surrender value of any contract shall be determined—

(i) with regard to any penalty or charge which would be imposed on surrender, but

(ii) without regard to any market value adjustment on surrender.

(B) SPECIAL RULE FOR PENSION PLAN CONTRACTS.—In the case of a pension plan contract, the balance in the policyholder's fund shall be treated as the net surrender value of such contract. For purposes of the preceding sentence, such balance shall be determined with regard to any penalty or forfeiture which would be imposed on surrender but without regard to any market value adjustment.

(2) ISSUANCE DATE IN CASE OF GROUP CONTRACTS.—For purposes of this section, in the case of a group contract, the date on which such contract is issued shall be the date as of which the master

plan is issued (or, with respect to a benefit guaranteed to a participant after such date, the date as of which such benefit is guaranteed).

(3) SUPPLEMENTAL BENEFITS.—

(A) QUALIFIED SUPPLEMENTAL BENEFITS TREATED SEPARATELY.—For purposes of this part, the amount of the life insurance reserve for any qualified supplemental benefit—

(i) shall be computed separately as though such benefit were under a separate contract, and

(ii) shall, except to the extent otherwise provided in regulations, be the reserve taken into account for purposes of the annual statement approved by the National Association of Insurance Commissioners.

(B) SUPPLEMENTAL BENEFITS WHICH ARE NOT QUALIFIED SUPPLEMENTAL BENEFITS.—In the case of any supplemental benefit described in subparagraph (D) which is not a qualified supplemental benefit, the amount of the reserve determined under paragraph (2) of subsection (d) shall, except to the extent othewise provided in regulations, be the reserve taken into account for purposes of the annual statement approved by the National Association of Insurance Commissioners.

(C) QUALIFIED SUPPLEMENTAL BENEFIT.—For purposes of this paragraph, the term "qualified supplemental benefit" means any supplemental benefit described in subparagraph (D) if—

(i) there is a separately identified premium or charge for such benefit, and

(ii) any net surrender value under the contract attributable to any other benefit is not available to fund such benefit.

(D) SUPPLEMENTAL BENEFITS.—For purposes of this paragraph, the supplemental benefits described in this subparagraph are any—

(i) guaranteed insurability,

(ii) accidental death or disability benefit,

(iii) convertibility,

(iv) disability waiver benefit, or

(v) other benefit prescribed by regulations,

which is supplemental to a contract for which there is a reserve described in subsection (c).

(4) CERTAIN CONTRACTS ISSUED BY FOREIGN BRANCHES OF DOMESTIC LIFE INSURANCE COMPANIES.—

(A) IN GENERAL.—In the case of any qualified foreign contract, the amount of the reserve shall be not less than the minimum reserve required by the laws, regulations, or administrative guidance of the regulatory authority of the foreign country referred to in subparagraph (B) (but not to exceed the net level reserves for such contract).

(B) QUALIFIED FOREIGN CONTRACT.—For purposes of subparagraph (A), the term "qualified foreign contract" means any contract issued by a foreign life insurance branch (which has its principal place of business in a foreign country) of a domestic life insurance company if—

(i) such contract is issued on the life or health of a resident of such country,

(ii) such domestic life insurance company was required by such foreign country (as of the time it began operations in such country) to operate in such country through a branch, and

(iii) such foreign country is not contiguous to the United States.

(5) TREATMENT OF SUBSTANDARD RISKS.—

(A) SEPARATE COMPUTATION.—Except to the extent provided in regulations, the amount of the life insurance reserve for any qualified substandard risk shall be computed separately under subsection (d)(1) from any other reserve under the contract.

(B) QUALIFIED SUBSTANDARD RISK.—For purposes of subparagraph (A), the term "qualified substandard risk" means any substandard risk if—

(i) the insurance company maintains a separate reserve for such risk,

(ii) there is a separately identified premium or charge for such risk,

(iii) the amount of the net surrender value under the contract is not increased or decreased by reason of such risk, and

(iv) the net surrender value under the contract is not regularly used to pay premium charges for such risk.

(C) LIMITATION ON AMOUNT OF LIFE INSURANCE RESERVE.—The amount of the life insurance reserve determined for any qualified substandard risk shall in no event exceed the sum of the separately identified premiums charged for such risk plus interest less mortality charges for such risk.

(D) LIMITATION ON AMOUNT OF CONTRACTS TO WHICH PARAGRAPH APPLIES.—The aggregate amount of insurance in force under contracts to which this paragraph applies shall not exceed 10 percent of the insurance in force (other than term insurance) under life insurance contracts of the company.

(6) SPECIAL RULES FOR CONTRACTS ISSUED BEFORE JANUARY 1, 1989, UNDER EXISTING PLANS OF INSURANCE, WITH TERM INSURANCE OR ANNUITY BENEFITS.—For purposes of this part—

(A) IN GENERAL.—In the case of a life insurance contract issued before January 1, 1989, under an existing plan of insurance, the life insurance reserve for any benefit to which this paragraph applies shall be computed separately under subsection (d)(1) from any other reserve under the contract.

(B) BENEFITS TO WHICH THIS PARAGRAPH APPLIES.—This paragraph applies to any term insurance or annuity benefit with respect to which the requirements of clauses (i) and (ii) of paragraph (3)(C) are met.

(C) EXISTING PLAN OF INSURANCE.—For purposes of this paragraph, the term "existing plan of insurance" means, with respect to any contract, any plan of insurance which was filed by the company using such contract in one or more States before January 1, 1984, and is on file in the appropriate State for such contract.

(7) SPECIAL RULES FOR TREATMENT OF CERTAIN NONLIFE RESERVES.—

(A) IN GENERAL.—The amount taken into account for purposes of subsections (a) and (b) as—

(i) the opening balance of the items referred to in subparagraph (C), and

(ii) the closing balance of such items,

shall be 80 percent of the amount which (without regard to this subparagraph) would have been taken into account as such opening or closing balance, as the case may be.

(B) TRANSITIONAL RULE.—

(i) IN GENERAL.—In the case of any taxable year beginning on or after September 30, 1990, and before September 30, 1996, there shall be included in the gross income of any life insurance company an amount equal to $3\frac{1}{3}$ percent of such company's closing balance of the items referred to in subparagraph (C) for its most recent taxable year beginning before September 30, 1990.

(ii) TERMINATION AS LIFE INSURANCE COMPANY.—Except as provided in section 381(c)(22), if, for any taxable year beginning on or before September 30, 1996, the taxpayer ceases to be a life insurance company, the aggregate inclusions which would have been made under clause (i) for such taxable year and subsequent taxable years but for such cessation shall be taken into account for the taxable year preceding such cessation year.

(C) DESCRIPTION OF ITEMS.—For purposes of this paragraph, the items referred to in this subparagraph are the items described in subsection (c) which consist of unearned premiums and premiums received in advance under insurance contracts not described in section 816(b)(1)(B).

Amendments

• 1990, Omnibus Budget Reconciliation Act of 1990 (P.L. 101-508)

P.L. 101-508, §11302(a):

Amended Code Sec. 807(e) by adding at the end thereof a new paragraph (7). **Effective** for tax years beginning on or after 9-30-90.

[Sec. 807(f)]

(f) ADJUSTMENT FOR CHANGE IN COMPUTING RESERVES.—

(1) 10-YEAR SPREAD.—

(A) IN GENERAL.—For purposes of this part, if the basis for determining any item referred to in subsection (c) as of the close of any taxable year differs from the basis for such determination as of the close of the preceding taxable year, then so much of the difference between—

(i) the amount of the item at the close of the taxable year, computed on the new basis, and

(ii) the amount of the item at the close of the taxable year, computed on the old basis,

as is attributable to contracts issued before the taxable year shall be taken into account under the method provided in subparagraph (B).

(B) METHOD.—The method provided in this subparagraph is as follows:

(i) if the amount determined under subparagraph (A)(i) exceeds the amount determined under subparagraph (A)(ii), $\frac{1}{10}$ of such excess shall be taken into account, for each of the succeeding 10 taxable years, as a deduction under section 805(a)(2); or

(ii) if the amount determined under subparagraph (A)(ii) exceeds the amount determined under subparagraph (A)(i), $\frac{1}{10}$ of such excess shall be included in gross income, for each of the 10 succeeding taxable years, under section 803(a)(2).

(2) TERMINATION AS LIFE INSURANCE COMPANY.—Except as provided in section 381(c)(22) (relating to carryovers in certain corporate readjustments), if for any taxable year the taxpayer is not a life insurance company, the balance of any adjustments under this subsection shall be taken into account for the preceding taxable year.

Amendments

• 1984, Deficit Reduction Act of 1984 (P.L. 98-369)

P.L. 98-369, §211(a):

Amended Part I of subchapter L of chapter 1 by adding Code Sec. 807. **Effective** for tax years beginning after 12-31-83. For transitional and special rules, see Act Sec. 216(a)-(b)(2) in the amendments for Code Sec. 801. For other special rules relating to Code Sec. 807, see Act Secs. 216(b)(3) and 217(f) and (n), below.

P.L. 98-369, §216(b)(3), as amended by P.L. 99-514, §1822, provides as follows:

(3) Reinsurance Transactions, and Reserve Strengthening, after September 27, 1983.—

(A) In General.—Paragraph (1) shall not apply (and section 807(f) of the Internal Revenue Code of 1954 as amended by this subtitle shall apply)—

(i) to any reserve transferred pursuant to—

(I) a reinsurance agreement entered into after September 27, 1983, and before January 1, 1984, or

(II) a modification of a reinsurance agreement made after September 27, 1983, and before January 1, 1984, and

(ii) to any reserve strengthening reported for Federal income tax purposes after September 27, 1983, for a taxable year ending before January 1, 1984.

Clause (ii) shall not apply to the computation of reserves on any contract issued if such computation employs the reserve practice used for purposes of the most recent annual statement filed before September 27, 1983, for the type of contract with respect to which such reserves are set up. For purposes of this subparagraph, if the reinsurer's taxable year is not a calendar year, the first day of the reinsurer's first taxable year beginning after December 31, 1983, shall be substituted for "January 1, 1984" each place it appears.

(B) Treatment of Reserve Attributable to Section 818(c) Election.—In the case of any reserve described in subparagraph (A), for purposes of section 807(f) of the Internal Revenue Code of 1954, any change in the treatment of any contract to which an election under section 818(c) of such Code (as in effect on the day before the date of the enactment of this Act) applied shall be treated as a change in the basis for determining the amount of any reserve.

(C) 10-Year Spread Inapplicable Where No 10-Year Spread Under Prior Law.—In the case of any item to which section 807(f) of such Code applies by reason of subparagraph (A) or (B), such item shall be taken into account for the first taxable year beginning after December 31, 1983 (in lieu of over the 10-year period otherwise provided in such section) unless the item would have been required to be taken into account over a period of 10 taxable years under section 810(d) of such Code (as in effect on the day before the date of the enactment of this Act).

(D) Disallowance of Special Life Insurance Company Deduction and Small Life Insurance Company Deduction.—Any amount included in income under section 807(f) of such Code by reason of subparagraph (A) or (B) (and any income attributable to expenses transferred in connection with the transfer of reserves described in subparagraph (A)) shall not be taken into account for purposes of determining the amount of special life insurance company deduction and the small life insurance company deduction.

(E) Disallowance of Deductions Under Section 809(d).—No deduction shall be allowed under paragraph (5) or (6) of section 809(d) of such Code (as in effect before the amendment made by this subtitle) with respect to any amount described in either such paragraph which is transferred in connection with the transfer of reserves described in subparagraph (A).

P.L. 98-369, §217(f), provides:

(f) Treatment of Certain Assessment Life Insurance Companies.—

(1) Morality and Morbidity Tables.—In the case of a contract issued by an assessment life insurance company, the mortality and morbidity tables used in computing statutory reserves for such contract shall be used for purposes of paragraph (2)(C) of section 807(d) of the Internal Revenue Code of 1954 (as amended by this subtitle) if such tables were—

(A) in use since 1965, and

(B) developed on the basis of the experience of assessment life insurance companies in the State in which such assessment life insurance company is domiciled.

(2) Treatment of Certain Mutual Assessment Life Insurance Companies.—In the case of any contract issued by a mutual assessment life insurance company which—

(A) has been in existence since 1965, and

(B) operates under chapter 13 or 14 of the Texas Insurance Code,

for purposes of part I of subchapter L of chapter 1 of the Internal Revenue Code of 1954, the amount of the life insurance reserves for such contract shall be equal to the amount taken into account with respect to such contract in determining statutory reserves.

(3) Statutory Reserves.—For purposes of this subsection, the term "statutory reserves" has the meaning given to such term by section 809(b)(4)(B) of such Code.

P.L. 98-369, §217(n), as amended by P.L. 99-514, §1823, provides:

(n) Special Rule for Companies Using Net Level Reserve Method for Noncancellable Accident and Health Insurance Contracts.—A company shall be treated as meeting the requirements of section 807(d)(3)(A)(iii) of the Internal Revenue Code of 1954, as amended by this Act, with respect to any directly-written noncancellable accident and health insurance contract (whether under existing or new plans of insurance) for any taxable year if—

(1) such company—

(A) was using the net level reserve method to compute at least 99 percent of its statutory reserves on such contracts as of December 31, 1982, and

(B) received more than half its total direct premiums in 1982 from directly-written noncancellable accident and health insurance.

(2) after December 31, 1983, and through such taxable year, such company has continuously used the net level reserve method for computing at least 99 percent of its tax and statutory reserves on such contracts, and

(3) for any such contract for which the company does not use the net level reserve method, such company uses the same method for computing tax reserves as such company uses for computing its statutory reserves.

[Sec. 808]

SEC. 808. POLICYHOLDER DIVIDENDS DEDUCTION.

[Sec. 808(a)]

(a) POLICYHOLDER DIVIDEND DEFINED.—For purposes of this part, the term "policyholder dividend" means any dividend or similar distribution to policyholders in their capacity as such.

[Sec. 808(b)]

(b) CERTAIN AMOUNTS INCLUDED.—For purposes of this part, the term "policyholder dividend" includes—

(1) any amount paid or credited (including as an increase in benefits) where the amount is not fixed in the contract but depends on the experience of the company or the discretion of the management,

(2) excess interest,

(3) premium adjustments, and

(4) experience-rated refunds.

[Sec. 808(c)]

(c) AMOUNT OF DEDUCTION.—The deduction for policyholder dividends for any taxable year shall be an amount equal to the policyholder dividends paid or accrued during the taxable year.

Amendments

• 2004, Pension Funding Equity Act of 2004 (P.L. 108-218)

P.L. 108-218, §205(b)(3):

Amended Code Sec. 808(c). **Effective** for tax years beginning after 12-31-2004. Prior to amendment, Code Sec. 808(c) read as follows:

(c) AMOUNT OF DEDUCTION.—

(1) IN GENERAL.—Except as limited by paragraph (2), the deduction for policyholder dividends for any taxable year shall be an amount equal to the policyholder dividends paid or accrued during the taxable year.

(2) REDUCTION IN CASE OF MUTUAL COMPANIES.—In the case of a mutual life insurance company, the deduction for policyholder dividends for any taxable year shall be reduced by the amount determined under section 809.

[Sec. 808(d)]

(d) DEFINITIONS.—For purposes of this section—

(1) EXCESS INTEREST.—The term "excess interest" means any amount in the nature of interest—

(A) paid or credited to a policyholder in his capacity as such, and

(B) in excess of interest determined at the prevailing State assumed rate for such contract.

(2) PREMIUM ADJUSTMENT.—The term "premium adjustment" means any reduction in the premium under an insurance or annuity contract which (but for the reduction) would have been required to be paid under the contract.

(3) EXPERIENCE-RATED REFUND.—The term "experience-rated refund" means any refund or credit based on the experience of the contract or group involved.

Amendments

• 1986, Tax Reform Act of 1986 (P.L. 99-514)

P.L. 99-514, §1821(b):

Amended Code Sec. 808(d)(1)(B). **Effective** as if included in the provision of P.L. 98-369 to which it relates. Prior to amendment, Code Sec. 808(d)(1)(B) read as follows:

(B) determined at a rate in excess of the prevailing State assumed interest rate for such contract.

[Sec. 808(e)]

(e) TREATMENT OF POLICYHOLDER DIVIDENDS.—For purposes of this part, any policyholder dividend which—

(1) increases the cash surrender value of the contract or other benefits payable under the contract, or

(2) reduces the premium otherwise required to be paid,

shall be treated as paid to the policyholder and returned by the policyholder to the company as a premium.

Amendments

• 1984, Deficit Reduction Act of 1984 (P.L. 98-369)

P.L. 98-369, §211(a):

Amended Part I of subchapter L of chapter 1 by adding Code Sec. 808. **Effective** for tax years beginning after 12-31-83. However, for transitional and special rules, see Act Sec. 216(a)-(b)(2) in the amendments for Code Sec. 801.

[Sec. 808(f)]

(f) COORDINATION OF 1984 FRESH-START ADJUSTMENT WITH ACCELERATION OF POLICYHOLDER DIVIDENDS DEDUCTION THROUGH CHANGE IN BUSINESS PRACTICE.—

(1) IN GENERAL.—The amount determined under paragraph (1) of subsection (c) for the year of change shall (before any reduction under paragraph (2) of subsection (c)) be reduced by so much of the accelerated policyholder dividends deduction for such year as does not exceed the 1984 fresh-start adjustment of policyholder dividends (to the extent such adjustment was not previously taken into account under this subsection).

(2) YEAR OF CHANGE.—For purposes of this subsection, the term "year of change" means the taxable year in which the change in business practices which results in the accelerated policyholder dividends deduction takes effect.

(3) ACCELERATED POLICYHOLDER DIVIDENDS DEDUCTION DEFINED.—For purposes of this subsection, the term "accelerated policyholder dividends deduction" means the amount which (but for

this subsection) would be determined for the taxable year under paragrapah (1) of subsection (c) but which would have been determined (under such paragraph) for a later taxable year under the business practices of the taxpayer as in effect at the close of the preceding taxable year.

(4) 1984 FRESH-START ADJUSTMENT FOR POLICYHOLDER DIVIDENDS.—For purposes of this subsection, the term "1984 fresh-start adjustment for policyholder dividends" means the amounts held as of December 31, 1983, by the taxpayer as reserves for dividends to policyholders under section 811(b) (as in effect on the day before the date of the enactment of the Tax Reform Act of 1984) other than for dividends which accrued before January 1, 1984. Such amounts shall be properly reduced to reflect the amount of previously nondeductible policyholder dividends (as determined under section 809(f) as in effect on the day before the date of the enactment of the Tax Reform Act of 1984).

(5) SEPARATE APPLICATION WITH RESPECT TO LINES OF BUSINESS.—This subsection shall be applied separately with respect to each line of business of the taxpayer.

(6) SUBSECTION NOT TO APPLY TO MERE CHANGE IN DIVIDEND AMOUNT.—This subsection shall not apply to a mere change in the amount of policyholder dividends.

(7) SUBSECTION NOT TO APPLY TO POLICIES ISSUED AFTER DECEMBER 31, 1983.—

(A) IN GENERAL.—This subsection shall not apply to any policyholder dividend paid or accrued with respect to a policy issued after December 31, 1983.

(B) EXCHANGES OF SUBSTANTIALLY SIMILAR POLICIES.—For purposes of subparagraph (A), any policy issued after December 31, 1983, in exchange for a substantially similar policy issued on or before such date shall be treated as issued before January 1, 1984. A similar rule shall apply in the case of a series of exchanges.

(8) SUBSECTION TO APPLY TO POLICIES PROVIDED UNDER EMPLOYEE BENEFIT PLANS.—This subsection shall not apply to any policyholder dividend paid or accrued with respect to a group policy issued in connection with a plan to provide welfare benefits to employees (within the meaning of section 419(e)(2)).

Amendments

• 1986, Tax Reform Act of 1986 (P.L. 99-514)

P.L. 99-514, §1821(c):

Amended Code Sec. 808 by adding at the end thereof new subsection (f). **Effective** as if included in the provision of P.L. 98-369 to which it relates.

[Sec. 809—Repealed]

Amendments

• 2004, Pension Funding Equity Act of 2004 (P.L. 108-218)

P.L. 108-218, §205(a):

Repealed Code Sec. 809. **Effective** for tax years beginning after 12-31-2004. Prior to repeal, Code Sec. 809 read as follows:

SEC. 809. REDUCTION IN CERTAIN DEDUCTIONS OF MUTUAL LIFE INSURANCE COMPANIES.

[Sec. 809(a)]

(a) GENERAL RULE.—

(1) POLICYHOLDER DIVIDENDS.—In the case of any mutual life insurance company, the amount of the deduction allowed under section 808 shall be reduced (but not below zero) by the differential earnings amount.

(2) REDUCTION IN RESERVE DEDUCTION IN CERTAIN CASES.—In the case of any mutual life insurance company, if the differential earnings amount exceeds the amount allowable as a deduction under section 808 for the taxable year (determined without regard to this section), such excess shall be taken into account under subsections (a) and (b) of section 807.

(3) DIFFERENTIAL EARNINGS AMOUNT.—For purposes of this section, the term "differential earnings amount" means, with respect to any taxable year, an amount equal to the product of—

(A) the life insurance company's average equity base for the taxable year, multiplied by

(B) the differential earnings rate for such taxable year.

[Sec. 809(b)]

(b) AVERAGE EQUITY BASE.—For purposes of this section—

(1) IN GENERAL.—The term "average equity base" means, with respect to any taxable year, the average of—

(A) the equity base determined as of the close of the taxable year, and

(B) the equity base determined as of the close of the preceding taxable year.

(2) EQUITY BASE.—The term "equity base" means an amount determined in the manner prescribed by regulations equal to—

(A) the surplus and capital,

(B) adjusted as provided in paragraphs (3), (4), (5), and (6) of this subsection.

No item shall be taken into account more than once in determining equity base.

(3) INCREASE FOR NONADMITTED FINANCIAL ASSETS.—

(A) IN GENERAL.—The amount of the surplus and capital shall be increased by the amount of the nonadmitted financial assets.

(B) NONADMITTED FINANCIAL ASSETS.—For purposes of subparagraph (A), the term "nonadmitted financial asset" means any nonadmitted asset of the company which is—

(i) a bond,

(ii) stock,

(iii) real estate,

(iv) a mortgage loan on real estate, or

(v) any other invested asset.

(4) INCREASE WHERE STATUTORY RESERVES EXCEED TAX RESERVES.—

(A) IN GENERAL.—If—

(i) the aggregate amount of statutory reserves, exceeds

(ii) the aggregate amount of tax reserves,

the amount of the surplus and capital shall be increased by the amount of such excess.

(B) DEFINITIONS.—For purposes of this paragraph—

(i) STATUTORY RESERVES.—The term "statutory reserves" means the aggregate amount set forth in the annual statement with respect to items described in section 807(c). Such term shall not include any reserve attributable to a deferred and uncollected premium if the establishment of such reserve is not permitted under section 811(c).

(ii) TAX RESERVES.—The term "tax reserves" means the aggregate of the items described in section 807(c) as determined for purposes of section 807.

(5) INCREASE BY AMOUNT OF CERTAIN OTHER RESERVES.—The amount of the surplus and capital shall be increased by the sum of—

(A) the amount of any mandatory securities valuation reserve,

(B) the amount of any deficiency reserve, and

(C) the amount of any voluntary reserve or similar liability not described in subparagraph (A) or (B).

(6) ADJUSTMENT FOR NEXT YEAR'S POLICYHOLDER DIVIDENDS.—The amount of the surplus and capital shall be increased by 50 percent of the amount of any provision for policyholder dividends (or other similar liability) payable in the following taxable year.

Amendments

• 1986, Tax Reform Act of 1986 (P.L. 99-514)

P.L. 99-514, §1821(d):

Amended Code Sec. 809(b)(2) by adding at the end thereof a new sentence. **Effective** as if included in the provision of P.L. 98-369 to which it relates. For a special rule, see Act Sec. 1821(q) following Code Sec. 809(f).

[Sec. 809(c)]

(c) DIFFERENTIAL EARNINGS RATE.—

(1) IN GENERAL.—For purposes of this section, the differential earnings rate for any taxable year is the excess of—

(A) the imputed earnings rate for the taxable year, over

(B) the average mutual earnings rate for the second calendar year preceding the calendar year in which the taxable year begins.

(2) TRANSITIONAL RULE.—The differential earnings rate—

(A) for any taxable year beginning in 1984, or

(B) for purposes of computing the amount of underpayment under section 6655 (including the application of section 6655(d)(3)) for any taxable year beginning in 1985,

shall be equal to 7.8 percent.

(3) COORDINATION WITH ESTIMATED TAX PAYMENTS.—For purposes of applying section 6655 with respect to any installment of estimated tax, the amount of tax shall be determined by using the lesser of—

(A) the differential earnings rate of the second tax year preceding the taxable year for which the installment is made, or

(B) the differential earnings rate for the taxable year for which the installment is made.

Amendments

• 1986, Tax Reform Act of 1986 (P.L. 99-514)

P.L. 99-514, §1821(g):

Amended Code Sec. 809(c) by adding at the end thereof new paragraph (3). **Effective** as if included in the provision of P.L. 98-369 to which it relates. For a special rule, see Act Sec. 1821(q) following Code Sec. 809(f).

[Sec. 809(d)]

(d) IMPUTED EARNINGS RATE.—

(1) IN GENERAL.—For purposes of this section, the imputed earnings rate for any taxable year is—

(A) 16.5 percent in the case of taxable years beginning in 1984, and

(B) in the case of taxable years beginning after 1984, an amount which bears the same ratio to 16.5 percent as the current stock earnings rate for the taxable year bears to the base period stock earnings rate.

(2) CURRENT STOCK EARNINGS RATE.—For purposes of this subsection, the term "current stock earnings rate" means, with respect to any taxable year, the average of the stock earnings rates determined under paragraph (4) for the 3 calendar years preceding the calendar year in which the taxable year begins.

(3) BASE PERIOD STOCK EARNINGS RATE.—For purposes of this subsection, the base period stock earnings rate is the average of the stock earnings rates determined under paragraph (4) for calendar years 1981, 1982, and 1983.

(4) STOCK EARNINGS RATE.—

(A) IN GENERAL.—For purposes of this subsection, the stock earnings rate for any calendar year is the numerical average of the earnings rates of the 50 largest stock companies.

(B) EARNINGS RATE.—For purposes of subparagraph (A), the earnings rate of any stock company is the percentage (determined by the Secretary) which—

(i) the statement gain or loss from operations for the calendar year of such company, is of

(ii) such company's average equity base for such year.

(C) 50 LARGEST STOCK COMPANIES.—For purposes of this paragraph, the term "50 largest stock companies" means a group (as determined by the Secretary) of stock life insurance companies which consists of the 50 largest domestic stock life insurance companies which are subject to tax under this part. The Secretary—

(i) shall, for purposes of determining the base period stock earnings rate, exclude from the group determined under the preceding sentence any company which had a negative equity base at any time during 1981, 1982, or 1983,

(ii) shall exclude from such group for any calendar year any company which has a negative equity base, and

(iii) may by regulations exclude any other company which otherwise would have been included in such group if the inclusion of the excluded company or companies would, by reason of the small equity base of such company, seriously distort the stock earnings rate.

The aggregate number of companies excluded by the Secretary under clause (iii) shall not exceed the excess of 2 over the number of companies excluded under clause (ii).

(D) TREATMENT OF AFFILIATED GROUPS.—For purposes of this paragraph, all stock life insurance companies which are members of the same affiliated group shall be treated as one stock life insurance company.

Amendments

• 1988, Technical and Miscellaneous Revenue Act of 1988 (P.L. 100-647)

P.L. 100-647, §1018(u)(47):

Amended Code Sec. 809(d)(4)(C) by striking out "the Secretary—" and inserting in lieu thereof "The Secretary—". **Effective** as if included in the provision of P.L. 99-514 to which it relates.

• 1986, Tax Reform Act of 1986 (P.L. 99-514)

P.L. 99-514, §1821(e)(1):

Amended Code Sec. 809(d)(4)(C). **Effective** as if included in the provision of P.L. 98-369 to which it relates. For a special rule, see Act Sec. 1821(q) following Code Sec. 809(f). Prior to amendment, Code Sec. 809(d)(4)(C) read as follows:

(C) 50 LARGEST STOCK COMPANIES.—For purposes of this paragraph, the term "50 largest stock companies" means a group (as determined by the Secretary) of stock life insurance companies which consists of the 50 largest stock life insurance companies which are subject to tax under this part. The Secretary may by regulations provide for exclusion from the group determined under the preceding sentence of any stock life insurance company if (i) the equity of such company is not great enough for such company to be 1 of the 50 largest stock life insurance companies if the determination were made on the basis of equity, and (ii) by reason of the small equity base of such company, it has an earnings rate which would seriously distort the stock earnings rate.

P.L. 99-514, §1821(e)(2)(A):

Amended Code Sec. 809(d)(4)(C) by striking out "largest stock life insurance companies" and inserting in lieu thereof "largest domestic stock life insurance companies". **Effective** as if included in the provision of P.L. 98-369 to which it relates. For a special rule, see Act Sec. 1821(q) following Code Sec. 809(f).

[Sec. 809(e)]

(e) AVERAGE MUTUAL EARNINGS RATE.—For purposes of this section, the average mutual earnings rate for any calendar year is the percentage (determined by the Secretary) which—

(1) the aggregate statement gain or loss from operations for such year of domestic mutual life insurance companies, is of

(2) their aggregate average equity bases for such year.

Amendments

• **1986, Tax Reform Act of 1986 (P.L. 99-514)**

P.L. 99-514, §1821(e)(2)(B):

Amended Code Sec. 809(e)(1) by striking out "mutual life insurance companies" and inserting in lieu thereof "domestic mutual life insurance companies". **Effective** as if included in the provision of P.L. 98-369 to which it relates. For a special rule, see Act Sec. 1821(q) following Code Sec. 809(f).

[Sec. 809(f)]

(f) RECOMPUTATION IN SUBSEQUENT YEAR.—

(1) INCLUSION IN INCOME WHERE RECOMPUTED AMOUNT GREATER.—In the case of any mutual life insurance company, if—

(A) the recomputed differential earnings amount for any taxable year, exceeds

(B) the differential earnings amount determined under this section for such taxable year,

such excess shall be included in life insurance gross income for the succeeding taxable year.

(2) DEDUCTION WHERE RECOMPUTED AMOUNT SMALLER.—In the case of any mutual life insurance company, if—

(A) the differential earnings amount determined under this section for any taxable year, exceeds

(B) the recomputed differential earnings amount for such taxable year,

such excess shall be allowed as a life insurance deduction for the succeeding taxable year.

(3) RECOMPUTED DIFFERENTIAL EARNINGS AMOUNT.—For purposes of this subsection, the term "recomputed differential earnings amount" means, with respect to any taxable year, the amount which would be the differential earnings amount for such taxable year if the average mutual earnings rate taken into account under subsection (c)(1)(B) were the average mutual earnings rate for the calendar year in which the taxable year begins.

(4) SPECIAL RULE WHERE COMPANY CEASES TO BE MUTUAL LIFE INSURANCE COMPANY.—Except as provided in section 381(c)(22), if—

(A) a life insurance company is a mutual life insurance company for any taxable year, but

(B) such life insurance company is not a mutual life insurance company for the succeeding taxable year,

any adjustment under paragraph (1) or (2) by reason of the recomputed differential earnings amount for the first of such taxable years shall be taken into account for the first of such taxable years.

(5) SUBSECTION NOT TO APPLY FOR PURPOSES OF ESTIMATED TAX.—Section 6655 shall be applied to any taxable year without regard to any adjustments under this subsection for such year.

Amendments

• **1986, Tax Reform Act of 1986 (P.L. 99-514)**

P.L. 99-514, §1821(h):

Amended Code Sec. 809(f) by adding at the end thereof new paragraph (5). **Effective** as if included in the provision of P.L. 98-369 to which it relates. For a special rule, see Act Sec. 1821(q), below.

P.L. 99-514, §1821(q), provides:

(q) SPECIAL RULE FOR APPLICATION OF HIGH SURPLUS MUTUAL RULES.—In the case of any mutual life insurance company—

(1) which was incorporated on February 23, 1888, and

(2) which acquired a stock subsidiary during 1982,

the amount of such company's excess equity base for purposes of section 809(i) of such Code shall, notwithstanding the last sentence of section 809(i)(2)(D), equal $175,000,000.

P.L. 99-514, §1821(r):

Amended Code Sec. 809(f)(3) by striking out "subsection (c)(2)" and inserting in lieu thereof "subsection (c)(1)(B)". **Effective** as if included in the provision of P.L. 98-369 to which it relates. For a special rule, see Act Sec. 1821(q), below.

[Sec. 809(g)]

(g) DEFINITIONS AND SPECIAL RULES.—For purposes of this section—

(1) STATEMENT GAIN OR LOSS FROM OPERATIONS.—The term "statement gain or loss from operations" means the net gain or loss from operations required to be set forth in the annual statement, determined without regard to Federal income taxes, and—

(A) determined by substituting for the amount shown for policyholder dividends the amount of deduction for policyholder dividends determined under section 808 (without regard to section 808(c)(2)),

(B) determined on the basis of the tax reserves rather than statutory reserves, and

(C) properly adjusted for realized capital gains and losses and other relevant items.

(2) OTHER TERMS.—Except as otherwise provided in this section, the terms used in this section shall have the same respective meanings as when used in the annual statement.

(3) DETERMINATIONS BASED ON AMOUNT SET FORTH IN ANNUAL STATEMENT.—Except as otherwise provided in this section or in regulations, all determinations under this section shall be made on the basis of the amounts required to be set forth on the annual statement.

(4) ANNUAL STATEMENT.—The term "annual statement" means the annual statement for life insurance companies approved by the National Association of Insurance Commissioners.

(5) REDUCTION IN EQUITY BASE FOR PORTION OF EQUITY ALLOCABLE TO LIFE INSURANCE BUSINESS IN NONCONTIGUOUS WESTERN HEMISPHERE COUNTRIES.—The equity base of any mutual life insurance company shall be reduced by an amount equal to the portion of the equity base attributable to the life insurance business multiplied by a fraction—

(A) the numerator of which is the portion of the tax reserves which is allocable to life insurance contracts issued on the life of residents of countries in the Western Hemisphere which are not contiguous to the United States, and

(B) the denominator of which is the amount of the tax reserves allocable to life insurance contracts.

The preceding sentence shall not apply unless the fraction determined under the preceding sentence exceeds $1/20$.

(6) SPECIAL RULE FOR CERTAIN CONTRACTS ISSUED BEFORE JANUARY 1, 1985.—In determining the amount of tax reserves of a subsidiary of a mutual insurance company for purposes of subsection (b)(4), section 811(d) shall not apply with respect to any life insurance contract issued before January 1, 1985, under a plan of life insurance in existence on July 1, 1983.

Amendments

• **1986, Tax Reform Act of 1986 (P.L. 99-514)**

P.L. 99-514, §1821(f):

Amended Code Sec. 809(g)(1) by striking out so much of such paragraph as precedes subparagraph (B) and inserting in lieu thereof the new material. **Effective** as if included in the provision of P.L. 98-369 to which it relates. For a special rule, see Act Sec. 1821(q) following Code Sec. 809(f). Prior to amendment, Code Sec. 809(g)(1) read as follows:

(1) STATEMENT GAIN OR LOSS FROM OPERATIONS.—The term "statement gain or loss from operations" means the net gain or loss from operations required to be set forth in the annual statement—

(A) determined with regard to policyholder dividends (as defined in section 808) but without regard to Federal income taxes,

(B) determined on the basis of the tax reserves rather than statutory reserves, and

(C) properly adjusted for realized capital gains and losses and other relevant items.

[Sec. 809(h)]

(h) TREATMENT OF STOCK COMPANIES OWNED BY MUTUAL LIFE INSURANCE COMPANIES.—

(1) TREATMENT AS MUTUAL LIFE INSURANCE COMPANIES FOR PURPOSES OF DETERMINING STOCK EARNINGS RATES AND MUTUAL EARNINGS RATES.—Solely for purposes of subsections (d) and (e), a stock life insurance company shall be treated as a mutual life insurance company if stock possessing—

(A) at least 80 percent of the total combined voting power of all classes of stock of such stock life insurance company entitled to vote, or

(B) at least 80 percent of the total value of shares of all classes of stock of such stock life insurance company, is owned at any time during the calendar year directly (or through the application of section 318) by one or more mutual life insurance companies.

(2) TREATMENT OF AFFILIATED GROUP WHICH INCLUDES MUTUAL PARENT AND STOCK SUBSIDARY.—In the case of an affiliated group of corporations which includes a common parent which is a mutual life insurance company and one or more stock life insurance companies, for purposes of determining the average equity base of such common parent (and the statement gain or loss from operations)—

(A) stock in such stock life insurance companies held by such common parent (and dividends on such stock) shall not be taken into account, and

(B) such common parent and such stock life insurance companies shall be treated as though they were one mutual life insurance company.

(3) ADJUSTMENT WHERE STOCK COMPANY NOT MEMBER OF AFFILIATED GROUP.—In the case of any stock life insurance company which is described in paragraph (1) but is not a member of an affiliated group described in paragraph (2), under regulations, proper adjustments shall be made in the average equity bases (and statement gains or losses from operations) of mutual life insurance companies owning stock in such company as may be necessary or appropriate to carry out the purposes of this section.

[Sec. 809(i)]

(i) TRANSITIONAL RULE FOR CERTAIN HIGH SURPLUS MUTUAL LIFE INSURANCE COMPANIES.—

(1) IN GENERAL.—For purposes of subsection (a)(3), the average equity base of a high surplus mutual life insurance company for any taxable year shall not include the applicable percentage of the excess equity base of such company for such taxable year.

(2) DEFINITIONS.—For purposes of this subsection—

(A) EXCESS EQUITY BASE.—The term "excess equity base" means the excess of—

(i) the average equity base of the company for the taxable year, over

(ii) the amount which would be its average equity base if its equity percentage equaled the following percentage:

For taxable years beginning in:	*The percentage is:*
1984	14.5
1985 or 1986	14
1987 or 1988	13.5

In no case shall the the excess equity base for any taxable year be greater than the excess equity base for the company's first taxable year beginning in 1984.

(B) APPLICABLE PERCENTAGE.—The term "applicable percentage" means the percentage determined in accordance with the following table:

For taxable years beginning in:	*The applicable percentage is:*
1984	100
1985	80
1986	60
1987	40
1988	20
1989 or thereafter	0

(C) HIGH SURPLUS MUTUAL LIFE INSURANCE COMPANY.—The term "high surplus mutual life insurance company" means any mutual life insurance company if, for the taxable year beginning in 1984, its equity percentage exceeded 14.5 percent.

(D) EQUITY PERCENTAGE.—The term "equity percentage" means, with respect to any mutual life insurance company, the percentage which—

(i) the average equity base of such company (determined under this section without regard to this subsection) for a taxable year bears to

(ii) the average of—

(I) the assets of such company as of the close of the preceding taxable year, and

(II) the assets of such company as of the close of the taxable year.

For purposes of the preceding sentence, the assets of a company shall include all assets taken into account under this section in determining its equity base (after applying the principles of subsection (h)).

Amendments

• 1984, Deficit Reduction Act of 1984 (P.L. 98-369)

P.L. 98-369, §211(a):

Amended Part I of subchapter L of chapter 1 by adding Code Sec. 809. **Effective** for tax years beginning after 12-31-83. However, for transitional and special rules, see Act Sec. 216(a)-(b)(2) in the amendments for Code Sec. 801. For special rules relating to Code Sec. 809, see Act Secs. 217(g) and 219, below.

P.L. 98-369, §217(g), provides:

(g) TREATMENT OF REINSURANCE AGREEMENTS REQUIRED BY NAIC.—Effective for taxable years beginning after December 31, 1981, and before January 1, 1984, subsections (c)(1)(F) and (d)(12) of section 809 of the Internal Revenue Code of 1954 (as in effect on the day before the date of the enactment of this Act) shall not apply to dividends to policyholders reimbursed to the taxpayer by a reinsurer in respect of accident and health policies reinsured under a reinsurance agreement entered into before June 30, 1955, pursuant to the direction of the National Association of Insurance Commissioners and approved by the State insurance commissioner of the taxpayer's State of domicile. For purposes of subchapter L of chapter 1 of such Code (as in effect on the day before the date of the enactment of this Act) any such dividends shall be treated as dividends of the reinsurer and not the taxpayer.

P.L. 98-369, §219, provides:

SEC. 219. CLARIFICATION OF AUTHORITY TO REQUIRE CERTAIN INFORMATION.

Nothing in any provision of law shall be construed to prevent the Secretary of the Treasury or his delegate from requiring (from time to time) life insurance companies to provide such data with respect to taxable years beginning before January 1, 1984, as may be necessary to carry out the provisions of section 809 of such Code (as added by this title).

[Sec. 809(j)]

(j) DIFFERENTIAL EARNINGS RATE TREATED AS ZERO FOR CERTAIN YEARS.—Notwithstanding subsection (c) or (f), the differential earnings rate shall be treated as zero for purposes of computing both the differential earnings amount and the recomputed differential earnings amount for a mutual life insurance company's taxable years beginning in 2001, 2002, or 2003.

Amendments

• 2002, Job Creation and Worker Assistance Act of 2002 (P.L. 107-147)

P.L. 107-147, §611(a):

Amended Code Sec. 809 by adding at the end a new subsection (j). **Effective** for tax years beginning after 12-31-2000.

[Sec. 809—Repealed]

• 1984, Deficit Reduction Act of 1984 (P.L. 98-369)

P.L. 98-369, §211(a):

Amended Part I of Subchapter L of Chapter 1 by adding a new Part I (Code Secs. 801-818). Prior to amendment, the table of contents for former subpart C and Code Sec. 809 read as follows:

Subpart C—Gain and Loss from Operations

Sec. 809. In general.

Sec. 810. Rules for certain reserves.

Sec. 811. Dividends to policyholders.

Sec. 812. Operations loss deduction.

SEC. 809. IN GENERAL.

[Sec. 809(a)]

(a) EXCLUSION OF SHARE OF INVESTMENT YIELD SET ASIDE FOR POLICYHOLDERS.—

(1) AMOUNT.—The share of each and every item of investment yield (including tax-exempt interest and dividends received) of any life insurance company set aside for policyholders shall not be included in gain or loss from operations. For purposes of the preceding sentence, the share of any item set aside for policyholders shall be that percentage obtained by dividing the required interest by the investment yield; except that if the required interest exceeds the investment yield, then the share of any item set aside for policyholders shall be 100 percent.

(2) REQUIRED INTEREST.—For purposes of this part, the required interest for any taxable year is the sum of the amount of qualified guaranteed interest (within the meaning of section 805(f)(1)) and the products obtained by multiplying—

(A) each rate of interest required, or assumed by the taxpayer, in calculating the reserves described in section 810(c), by

(B) the means of the amount of such reserves computed at that rate at the beginning and end of the taxable year.

For purposes of subparagraphs (A) and (B) reserves on qualified contracts (within the meaning of section 805(f)(2)) shall not be taken into account.

Amendments

• 1982, Tax Equity and Fiscal Responsibility Act of 1982 (P.L. 97-248)

P.L. 97-248, §264(c)(2):

Amended Code Sec. 809(a)(2) by inserting "the amount of qualified guaranteed interest (within the meaning of section 805(f)(1)) and" after "the sum of" and by adding a new sentence at the end thereof. **Effective** for tax years beginning after 12-31-81. But see amendment notes for P.L. 97-248, following former Code Sec. 805(e) for a special rule.

• 1976, Tax Reform Act of 1976 (P.L. 94-455)

P.L. 94-455, §1901(b)(1)(M):

Substituted "tax-exempt interest" for "tax-exempt interest, partially tax-exempt interest,". **Effective** for tax years beginning after 12-31-76.

[Sec. 809(b)]

(b) GAIN AND LOSS FROM OPERATIONS.—

(1) GAIN FROM OPERATIONS DEFINED.—For purposes of this part, the term "gain from operations" means the amount by which the sum of the following exceeds the deductions provided by subsection (d):

(A) the life insurance company's share of each and every item of investment yield (including tax-exempt interest and dividends received);

(B) the amount (if any) of the net capital gain; and

(C) the sum of the items referred to in subsection (c).

(2) LOSS FROM OPERATIONS DEFINED.—For purposes of this part, the term "loss from operations" means the amount by which the sum of the deductions provided by subsection (d) exceeds the sum of—

(A) the life insurance company's share of each and every item of investment yield (including tax-exempt interest and dividends received);

(B) the amount (if any) of the net capital gain; and

(C) the sum of the items referred to in subsection (c).

(3) LIFE INSURANCE COMPANY'S SHARE.—For purposes of this subpart, the life insurance company's share of any item shall be that percentage which, when added to the percentage obtained under the second sentence of subsection (a)(1), equals 100 percent.

Amendments

• 1976, Tax Reform Act of 1976 (P.L. 94-455)

P.L. 94-455, §1901(a)(98):

Struck out paragraph (4). **Effective** for tax years ending after 12-31-76. Prior to repeal, Code Sec. 809(b)(4) read as follows:

(4) EXCEPTION.—If it is established in any case that the application of the definition of gain from operations contained in paragraph (1) results in the imposition of tax on—

(A) any interest which under section 103 is excluded from gross income,

(B) any amount of interest which under section 242 (as modified by section 804(a)(3)) is allowable as a deduction, or

(C) any amount of dividends received which under sections 243, 244, and 245 (as modified by subsection (d)(8)(B)) is allowable as a deduction,

adjustment shall be made to the extent necessary to prevent such imposition.

P.L. 94-455, §1901(b)(1)(M):

Struck out "tax-exempt interest, partially tax-exempt interest," and inserted "tax-exempt interest" in its place in paragraphs (1)(A) and (2)(A). **Effective** for tax years beginning after 12-31-76.

P.L. 94-455, §1901(b)(33):

Substituted "of the net capital gain" for "by which the net long-term capital gain exceeds the net short-term capital loss" in paragraphs (1)(B) and (2)(B). **Effective** for tax years beginning after 12-31-76.

• 1962 (P.L. 87-858)

P.L. 87-858, §3(b)(3):

Amended Code Sec. 809(b)(1) and (2) by deleting "and" at the end of subparagraph (A) by redesignating subparagraph (B) as (C), and by inserting a new subparagraph (B). **Effective** 1-1-62.

[Sec. 809(c)]

(c) GROSS AMOUNT.—For purposes of subsections (b)(1) and (2), the following items shall be taken into account:

(1) PREMIUMS.—The gross amount of premiums and other consideration, including—

(A) advance premiums,

(B) deposits,

(C) fees,

(D) assessments,

(E) consideration in respect of assuming liabilities under contracts not issued by the taxpayer, and

(F) the amount of dividends to policyholders reimbursed to the taxpayer by a reinsurer in respect of reinsured policies,

on insurance and annuity contracts (including contracts supplementary thereto); less return premiums, and premiums and other consideration arising out of reinsurance ceded. Except in the case of amounts of premiums or other consideration returned to another life insurance company in respect of reinsurance ceded, amounts returned where the amount is not fixed in the contract but depends on the experience of the company or the discretion of the management shall not be included in return premiums.

(2) DECREASES IN CERTAIN RESERVES.—Each net decrease in reserves which is required by section 810 or 811(b)(2) to be taken into account for purposes of this paragraph.

(3) OTHER AMOUNTS.—All amounts, not included in computing investment yield and not includible under paragraph (1) or (2), which under this subtitle are includible in gross income.

Except as included in computing investment yield, there shall be excluded any gain from the sale or exchange of a capital asset, and any gain considered as gain from the sale or exchange of a capital asset.

Amendments

• 1982, Tax Equity and Fiscal Responsibility Act of 1982 (P.L. 97-248)

P.L. 97-248, §255(b)(2):

Amended the first sentence of Code Sec. 809(c)(1). **Effective** for tax years beginning after 12-31-81. See also amendment notes for P.L. 97-248 following repealed Code Sec. 820 for special rules. Prior to amendment, it read as follows:

(1) Premiums.—The gross amount of premiums and other consideration (including advance premiums, deposits, fees, assessments, and consideration in respect of assuming liabilities under contracts not issued by the taxpayer) on insurance and annuity contracts (including contracts supplementary thereto); less return premiums, and premiums and other consideration arising out of reinsurance ceded.

[Sec. 809(d)]

(d) DEDUCTIONS.—For purposes of subsections (b)(1) and (2), there shall be allowed the following deductions:

(1) DEATH BENEFITS, ETC.—All claims and benefits accrued, and all losses incurred (whether or not ascertained), during the taxable year on insurance and annuity contracts (including contracts supplementary thereto).

(2) INCREASES IN CERTAIN RESERVES.—The net increase in reserves which is required by section 810 to be taken into account for purposes of this paragraph.

(3) DIVIDENDS TO POLICYHOLDERS.—The deduction for dividends to policyholders (determined under section 811(b)), other than the deduction provided under paragraph (12).

(4) OPERATIONS LOSS DEDUCTION.—The operations loss deduction (determined under section 812).

(5) CERTAIN NONPARTICIPATING CONTRACTS.—An amount equal to 10 percent of the increase for the taxable year in the reserves for nonparticipating contracts or (if greater) an amount equal to 3 percent of the premiums for the taxable year (excluding that portion of the premiums which is allocable to annuity features) attributable to nonparticipating contracts (other than group contracts) which are issued or renewed for periods of 5 years or more. For purposes of this paragraph, the term "reserves for nonparticipating contracts" means such part of the life insurance reserves (excluding that portion of the reserves which is allocable to annuity features) as relates to nonparticipating contracts (other than group contracts). For purposes of this paragraph and paragraph (6), the term "premiums" means the net amount of the premiums and other consideration taken into account under subsection (c)(1). For purposes of this paragraph, the period for which any contract is issued or renewed includes the period for which such contract is guaranteed renewable.

(6) CERTAIN ACCIDENT AND HEALTH INSURANCE AND GROUP LIFE INSURANCE.—An amount equal to 2 percent of the premiums for the taxable year attributable to accident and health insurance contracts (other than those to which paragraph (5) applies) and group life insurance contracts. The deduction under this paragraph for the taxable year and all preceding taxable years shall not exceed an amount equal to 50 percent of the premiums for the taxable year attributable to such contracts.

(7) ASSUMPTION BY ANOTHER PERSON OF LIABILITIES UNDER INSURANCE, ETC., CONTRACTS.—The consideration (other than consideration arising out of reinsurance ceded) in respect of the assumption by another person of liabilities under insurance and annuity contracts (including contracts supplementary thereto).

(8) TAX-EXEMPT INTEREST, DIVIDENDS, ETC.—

(A) LIFE INSURANCE COMPANY'S SHARE.—Each of the following items:

(i) the life insurance company's share of interest which under section 103 is excluded from gross income, and

(ii) the deductions for dividends received provided by sections 243, 244, and 245 (as modified by subparagraph (B)) computed with respect to the life insurance company's share of the dividends received.

(B) APPLICATION OF SECTION 246(b).—In applying section 246(b) (relating to limitation on aggregate amount of deductions for dividends received) for purposes of subparagraph (A)(ii), the limit on the aggregate amount of the deductions allowed by sections 243(a)(1), 244(a), and 245 shall be 85 percent of the gain from operations computed without regard to—

(i) the deductions provided by paragraphs (3), (5), and (6) of this subsection,

(ii) the operations loss deduction provided by section 812, and

(iii) the deductions allowed by sections 243(a)(1), 244(a), and 245,

but such limit shall not apply for any taxable year for which there is a loss from operations.

(9) INVESTMENT EXPENSES, ETC.—Investment expenses to the extent not allowed as a deduction under section 804(c)(1) in computing investment yield, and the amount (if any) by which the sum of the deductions allowable under section 804(c) exceeds the gross investment income.

(10) SMALL BUSINESS DEDUCTION.—A small business deduction in an amount equal to the amount determined under section 804(a)(3).

(11) OTHER DEDUCTIONS.—Subject to the modifications provided by subsection (e), all other deductions allowed under this subtitle for purposes of computing taxable income to the extent not allowed as deductions in computing investment yield.

(12) DIVIDENDS REIMBURSED.—The deduction for the amount of dividends to policyholders reimbursed by the taxpayer to another insurance company in respect of policies the taxpayer has reinsured (determined under section 811(c)).

Except as provided in paragraph (3), no amount shall be allowed as a deduction under this subsection in respect of dividends to policyholders.

Amendments

• 1982, Tax Equity and Fiscal Responsibility Act of 1982 (P.L. 97-248)

P.L. 97-248, §255(b)(3)-(4):

Amended Code Sec. 809(d) by adding ", other than the deduction provided under paragraph (12)" before the period at the end of paragraph (3), and by adding new paragraph (12). **Effective** for tax years beginning after 12-31-81. Also see amendment notes for P.L. 97-248 under repealed Code Sec. 820 for special rules.

• 1976, Tax Reform Act of 1976 (P.L. 94-455)

P.L. 94-455, §1508:

Added the last sentence to paragraph (5). **Effective** for tax years beginning after 12-31-57.

P.L. 94-455, §1901(a)(98):

Struck out paragraph (11) and redesignated paragraph (12) as paragraph (11). **Effective** for tax years beginning after 12-31-76. Prior to repeal, Code Sec. 809(d)(11) read as follows:

(11) CERTAIN MUTUALIZATION DISTRIBUTIONS.—The amount of distributions to shareholders made in 1958, 1959, 1960, 1961, and 1962 in acquisition of stock pursuant to a plan of mutualization adopted before January 1, 1958.

P.L. 94-455, §1901(b)(1)(J)(iv):

Substituted "section 804(a)(3)" for "section 804(a)(4)" in paragraph (10). **Effective** for tax years beginning after 12-31-76.

P.L. 94-455, §1901(b)(1)(L)(i):

Struck out Code Sec. 809(d)(8)(A)(ii), redesignated clause (iii) as clause (ii), and inserted "and" at the end of clause (i). **Effective** for tax years beginning after 12-31-76. Prior to repeal, Code Sec. 809(d)(8)(A)(ii) read as follows:

(ii) the deduction for partially tax-exempt interest provided by section 242 (as modified by section 804(a)(3)) computed with respect to the life insurance company's share of such interest, and

P.L. 94-455, §1901(b)(1)(L)(ii):

Struck out "subparagraph (iii)" from paragraph (8)(B) and inserted in lieu thereof "subparagraph (A)(ii),". **Effective** for tax years beginning after 12-31-76.

• 1964, Revenue Act of 1964 (P.L. 88-272)

P.L. 88-272, §214(b)(4):

Amended subsection (d)(8)(B) by substituting "243(a)(1), 244(a)" in lieu of "243(a), 244". **Effective** 1-1-64.

P.L. 88-272, §228(a)(1):

Amended paragraph (11) of subsection (d) by inserting "1961, and 1962" in lieu of "and 1961". **Effective** for tax years beginning after 12-31-63.

• 1962 (P.L. 87-790)

P.L. 87-790, §3(a):

Amended Code Sec. 809(d)(6) by striking out "group life insurance contracts and group accident and health insurance contracts" and inserting in lieu thereof "accident and health insurance contracts (other than those to which paragraph (5) applies) and group life insurance contracts", and by striking out the heading and inserting in lieu thereof "(6) CERTAIN ACCIDENT AND HEALTH INSURANCE AND GROUP LIFE INSURANCE.—". **Effective** 1-1-63.

• 1961 (P.L. 87-59)

P.L. 87-59, §2:

Amended Code Sec. 809(d)(11) by striking out "in 1958 and 1959" and inserting in lieu thereof "in 1958, 1959, 1960, and 1961." **Effective** for tax years beginning after 12-31-59.

[Sec. 809(e)]

(e) MODIFICATIONS.—The modifications referred to in subsection (d)(11) are as follows:

(1) INTEREST.—In applying section 163 (relating to deduction for interest), no deduction shall be allowed for qualified guaranteed interest (within the meaning of section 805(f)(1)) or interest in respect of items described in section 810(c).

(2) BAD DEBTS.—Section 166(c) (relating to reserve for bad debts) shall not apply.

(3) CHARITABLE, ETC., CONTRIBUTIONS AND GIFTS.—In applying section 170—

(A) the limit on the total deductions under such section provided by section 170(b)(2) shall be 10 percent of the gain from operations computed without regard to—

(i) the deduction provided by section 170,

(ii) the deductions provided by paragraphs (3), (5), (6), and (8) of subsection (d), and

(iii) any operations loss carryback to the taxable year under section 812; and

(B) under regulations prescribed by the Secretary, a rule similar to the rule contained in section 170(d)(2)(B) shall be applied.

(4) AMORTIZABLE BOND PREMIUM.—Section 171 shall not apply.

(5) NET OPERATING LOSS DEDUCTION.—Except as provided by section 844, the deduction for net operating losses provided in section 172 shall not be allowed.

(6) DIVIDENDS RECEIVED.—The deductions for dividends received provided by sections 243, 244, and 245 shall not be allowed.

Amendments

• 1983, Technical Corrections Act of 1982 (P.L. 97-448)

P.L. 97-448, §102(m)(1):

Amended Code Sec. 809(e)(3)(A) by striking out "5 percent" and inserting in lieu thereof "10 percent". **Effective** as if included in the provision of P.L. 97-34 to which it relates.

• 1982, Tax Equity and Fiscal Responsibility Act of 1982 (P.L. 97-248)

P.L. 97-248, §264(c)(3):

Amended paragraph (1) of Code Sec. 809(e) by inserting "qualified guaranteed interest (within the meaning of section 805(f)(1)) or" after "allowed for". **Effective** for tax years beginning after 12-31-81. But see amendment notes for P.L. 97-248 following former Code Sec. 805(e) for a special rule.

• 1976, Tax Reform Act of 1976 (P.L. 94-455)

P.L. 94-455, §1901(a)(98):

Substituted "(d)(11)" for "(d)(12)" in the first line. **Effective** for tax years beginning after 12-31-76.

P.L. 94-455, §1901(b)(1)(N):

Struck out paragraph (6) and redesignated paragraph (7) as paragraph (6). **Effective** for tax years beginning after 12-31-76. Prior to repeal, Code Sec. 809(e)(6) read as follows:

(6) PARTIALLY TAX-EXEMPT INTEREST.—The deduction for partially tax-exempt interest provided by section 242 shall not be allowed.

P.L. 94-455, §1906(b)(13)(A):

Amended 1954 Code by substituting "Secretary" for "Secretary or his delegate" each place it appeared. **Effective** 2-1-77.

• 1969, Tax Reform Act of 1969 (P.L. 91-172)

P.L. 91-172, §201(a)(2)(C):

Amended Code Sec. 809(e)(3). **Effective** for tax years beginning after 12-31-69. Prior to amendment, Code Sec. 809(e)(3) read as follows:

(3) Charitable, etc., contributions and gifts.—On applying section 170—

(A) the limit on the total deductions under such section provided by the first sentence of section 170(b)(2) shall be 5 percent of the gain from operations computed without regard to—

(i) the deduction provided by section 170.

(ii) the deductions provided by paragraphs (3), (5), (6), and (8) of subsection (d), and

(iii) any operations loss carryback to the taxable year under section 812; and

(B) under regulations prescribed by the Secretary or his delegate, a rule similar to the rule contained in section 170(b)(3) shall be applied.

P.L. 91-172, §907(c)(2)(B):

Amended Code Sec. 809(e)(5) by changing "The" to "Except as provided by section 844, the". **Effective** for losses incurred in tax years beginning after 12-31-62, but does not affect any tax liability for any tax year beginning before 1-1-67.

[Sec. 809(f)]

(f) LIMITATION ON CERTAIN DEDUCTIONS.—

(1) IN GENERAL.—The amount of the deductions under paragraphs (3), (5), and (6) of subsection (d) shall not exceed $250,000 plus the amount (if any) by which—

(A) the gain from operations for the taxable year, computed without regard to such deductions, exceeds

(B) the taxable investment income for the taxable year.

(2) APPLICATION OF LIMITATION.—The limitation provided by paragraph (1) shall apply first to the amount of the deduction under subsection (d)(3), then to the amount of the deduction under subsection (d)(6), and finally to the amount of the deduction under subsection (d)(5).

(f) LIMITATION ON CERTAIN DEDUCTIONS.—

(1) IN GENERAL.—The amount of the deductions under paragraphs (3), (5), and (6) of subsection (d) shall not exceed the greater of—

(A) $1,000,000, plus the amount (if any) by which—

(i) the gain from operations for the taxable year (computed without regard to such deductions), exceeds

(ii) the taxable investment income for the taxable year, or

(B) if the taxpayer elects for any taxable year, the amount determined under paragraph (2).

(2) ALTERNATIVE LIMITATION.—The amount determined under this paragraph for any taxable year shall be equal to the sum of—

(A) that portion of the deduction under subsection (d)(3) which is allocable to any contract described in section 805(d), and

(B) an amount equal to the sum of—

(i) so much of the base amount as does not exceed $1,000,000, plus

(ii) in the case of—

(I) a mutual life insurance company, 77.5 percent of the base amount, or

(II) a stock life insurance company, 85 percent of the base amount.

(3) REDUCTION IN $1,000,000 AMOUNT FOR LARGE INSURERS.—If the sum of the deductions under paragraphs (3), (5), and (6) of subsection (d) exceeds $4,000,000, then each of the $1,000,000 amounts in paragraphs (1) and (2) shall be reduced (but not below zero) by the amount which bears the same ratio to $1,000,000 as—

(A) the amount of such excess bears to,

(B) $4,000,000.

(4) BASE AMOUNT.—For purposes of paragraph (2)(B), the term "base amount" means the excess of—

(A) the amount of the deductions under paragraphs (3) and (5) of subsection (d) for the taxable year, over

(B) the amount determined under paragraph (2)(A) for such taxable year.

(5) APPLICATION OF LIMITATION.—The limitation provided by paragraph (1) shall apply first to the amount of the deduction under subsection (d)(3), then to the amount of the deduction under subsection (d)(5), and finally to the amount of the deduction under subsection (d)(6).

Amendments

• 1982, Tax Equity and Fiscal Responsibility Act of 1982 (P.L. 97-248)

P.L. 97-248, §259(a):

Amended Code Sec. 809(f). Except as provided below in Act Sec. 263, this change is **effective** for tax years beginning after 12-31-81, and before 1-1-84.

P.L. 97-248, §263(b), provides:

(1) Certain interest and premiums.—

(A) In general.—In the case of any taxable year beginning before January 1, 1982, if a taxpayer, on his return of tax for such taxable year, treated—

(i) any amount described in subparagraph (B) as an amount which was not a dividend to policyholders (within the meaning of section 811 of the Internal Revenue Code of 1954), or

(ii) any amount described in subparagraph (C) as not described in section 809(c)(1),

then such amounts shall be so treated for purposes of the Internal Revenue Code of 1954.

(B) Certain interest.—An amount is described in this subparagraph if such amount is in the nature of interest accrued for the taxable year on an insurance or annuity contract pursuant to—

(i) an interest rate guaranteed or fixed before the period of payment of such amount begins, or

(ii) any other method (fixed before such period begins) the terms of which during the period are beyond the control and are independent of the experience of the company, whether or not the interest rate or other method was guaranteed or fixed for any specified period of time.

(C) Amounts not treated as premiums.—An amount is described in this subparagraph if such amount represents the difference between—

(i) the amount of premiums received or mortality charges made under rates fixed in advance of the premium or mortality charge due date, and

(ii) the maximum premium or mortality charge which could be charged under the terms of the insurance or annuity contract.

(D) No inference.—The provisions of this paragraph shall constitute no inference with respect to the treatment of any item in taxable years beginning after December 31, 1981.

(2) Consolidated returns.—The provisions of section 818(f) of such Code, as amended by section 262, shall apply to any taxable year beginning before January 1, 1982, if the taxpayer filed a consolidated return before July 1, 1982 for such taxable year under section 1501 of such Code which, on such date (determined without regard to any amended return filed after June 30, 1982), was consistent with the provisions of section 818(f) of such Code, as so amended. In the case of a taxable year beginning in 1981, the preceding sentence shall be applied by substituting "September 16" for "July 1" and "September 15" for "June 30".

(3) Taxable years where period of limitation has run.—This subsection shall not apply to any taxable year with respect to which the statute of limitations for filing a claim for credit or refund has expired under any provision of law or by operation of law.

• 1962 (P.L. 87-858)

P.L. 87-858,.§3(c):

Amended Code Sec. 809(f)(2) by substituting "(d)(3)" for "(d)(6)" in line 2, "(d)(6)" for "(d)(5)" in line 3, and "(d)(5)" for "(d)(3)" in line 4. **Effective** 1-1-62.

[Sec. 809(g)—Repealed]

Amendments

• 1976, Tax Reform Act of 1976 (P.L. 94-455)

P.L. 94-455, §1901(a)(98):

Repealed Code Sec. 809(g). **Effective** for tax years beginning after 12-31-76. Prior to repeal, Code Sec. 809(g) read as follows:

(g) LIMITATIONS ON DEDUCTION FOR CERTAIN MUTUALIZATION DISTRIBUTIONS.—

(1) DEDUCTION NOT TO REDUCE TAXABLE INVESTMENT INCOME.—The amount of the deduction under subsection (d)(11) shall not exceed the amount (if any) by which—

(A) the gain from operations for the taxable year, computed without regard to such deduction (but after the application of subsection (f)), exceeds

(B) the taxable investment income for the taxable year.

(2) DEDUCTION NOT TO REDUCE TAX BELOW 1957 LAW.—The deduction under subsection (d)(11) for the taxable year shall be allowed only to the extent that such deduction (after the application of all other deductions provided by subsection (d)) does not reduce the amount of tax imposed by section 802(a)(1) for such taxable year below the amount of tax which would have been imposed by section 802(a) as in effect for 1957, if this part, as in effect for 1957, applied for such taxable year.

(3) APPLICATION OF SECTION 815.—That portion of any distribution with respect to which a deduction is allowed under subsection (d)(11) shall not be treated as a distribution to shareholders for purposes of section 815; except that in the case of any distribution made in 1959, 1960, 1961, or 1962, such portion shall be treated as a distribution with respect to which a reduction is required under section 815(e)(2)(B).

• 1964, Revenue Act of 1964 (P.L. 88-272)

P.L. 88-272, §228(a)(2):

Amended Code Sec. 809(g)(3) by striking out "or 1961" and inserting in lieu thereof "1961, or 1962". **Effective** for tax years beginning after 12-31-63.

• 1961 (P.L. 87-59)

P.L. 87-59, §2:

Amended Code Sec. 809(g)(3) by striking out "in 1959" and inserting in lieu thereof "in 1959, 1960, or 1961." **Effective** for tax years beginning after 12-31-59.

• 1959, Life Insurance Company Income Tax Act of 1959 (P.L. 86-69)

P.L. 86-69, §2:

Revised Part I of subchapter L of chapter 1 of the 1954 Code. **Effective,** generally, for tax years beginning after 1957. Prior text not reproduced.

[Sec. 810]

SEC. 810. OPERATIONS LOSS DEDUCTION.

[Sec. 810(a)]

(a) DEDUCTION ALLOWED.—There shall be allowed as a deduction for the taxable year an amount equal to the aggregate of—

(1) the operations loss carryovers to such year, plus

(2) the operations loss carrybacks to such year.

For purposes of this part, the term "operations loss deduction" means the deduction allowed by this subsection.

[Sec. 810(b)]

(b) OPERATIONS LOSS CARRYBACKS AND CARRYOVERS.—

(1) YEARS TO WHICH LOSS MAY BE CARRIED.—The loss from operations for any taxable year (hereinafter in th13is section referred to as the "loss year") shall be—

(A) an operations loss carryback to each of the 3 taxable years preceding the loss year,

(B) an operations loss carryover to each of the 15 taxable years following the loss year, and

(C) if the life insurance company is a new company for the loss year, an operations loss carryover to each of the 3 taxable years following the 15 taxable years described in subparagraph (B).

(2) AMOUNT OF CARRYBACKS AND CARRYOVERS.—The entire amount of the loss from operations for any loss year shall be carried to the earliest of the taxable years to which (by reason of paragraph (1)) such loss may be carried. The portion of such loss which shall be carried to each of the other taxable years shall be the excess (if any) of the amount of such loss over the sum of the offsets (as defined in subsection (d)) for each of the prior taxable years to which such loss may be carried.

(3) ELECTION FOR OPERATIONS LOSS CARRYBACKS.—In the case of a loss from operations for any taxable year, the taxpayer may elect to relinquish the entire carryback period for such loss. Such election shall be made by the due date (including extensions of time) for filing the return for the taxable year of the loss from operations for which the election is to be in effect, and, once made for any taxable year, such election shall be irrevocable for that taxable year.

(4) CARRYBACK FOR 2008 OR 2009 LOSSES.—

(A) IN GENERAL.—In the case of an applicable loss from operations with respect to which the taxpayer has elected the application of this paragraph, paragraph (1)(A) shall be applied by substituting any whole number elected by the taxpayer which is more than 3 and less than 6 for "3".

(B) APPLICABLE LOSS FROM OPERATIONS.—For purposes of this paragraph, the term "applicable loss from operations" means the taxpayer's loss from operations for a taxable year ending after December 31, 2007, and beginning before January 1, 2010.

(C) ELECTION.—

(i) IN GENERAL.—Any election under this paragraph may be made only with respect to 1 taxable year.

(ii) PROCEDURE.—Any election under this paragraph shall be made in such manner as may be prescribed by the Secretary, and shall be made by the due date (including extension of time) for filing the return for the taxpayer's last taxable year beginning in 2009. Any such election, once made, shall be irrevocable.

(D) LIMITATION ON AMOUNT OF LOSS CARRYBACK TO 5TH PRECEDING TAXABLE YEAR.—

(i) IN GENERAL.—The amount of any loss from operations which may be carried back to the 5th taxable year preceding the taxable year of such loss under subparagraph (A) shall not exceed 50 percent of the taxpayer's taxable income (computed without regard to the loss from operations for the loss year or any taxable year thereafter) for such preceding taxable year.

(ii) CARRYBACKS AND CARRYOVERS TO OTHER TAXABLE YEARS.—Appropriate adjustments in the application of the second sentence of paragraph (2) shall be made to take into account the limitation of clause (i).

Amendments

• 2009, Worker, Homeownership, and Business Assistance Act of 2009 (P.L. 111-92)

P.L. 111-92, §13(c):

Amended Code Sec. 810(b) by adding at the end a new paragraph (4). **Effective** generally for losses for operations arising in tax years ending after 12-31-2007. For a transitional rule, Act Sec. 13(e)(4), below. For a an exception, see Act Sec. 13(f), below.

P.L. 111-92, §13(e)(4), provides:

(4) TRANSITIONAL RULE.—In the case of any net operating loss (or, in the case of a life insurance company, any loss from operations) for a taxable year ending before the date of the enactment of this Act—

(A) any election made under section 172(b)(3) or 810(b)(3) of the Internal Revenue Code of 1986 with respect to such loss may (notwithstanding such section) be revoked before the due date (including extension of time) for filing the return for the taxpayer's last taxable year beginning in 2009, and

(B) any application under section 6411(a) of such Code with respect to such loss shall be treated as timely filed if filed before such due date.

P.L. 111-92, §13(f), provides:

(f) EXCEPTION FOR TARP RECIPIENTS.—The amendments made by this section shall not apply to—

(1) any taxpayer if—

(A) the Federal Government acquired before the date of the enactment of this Act an equity interest in the taxpayer pursuant to the Emergency Economic Stabilization Act of 2008,

(B) the Federal Government acquired before such date of enactment any warrant (or other right) to acquire any equity interest with respect to the taxpayer pursuant to the Emergency Economic Stabilization Act of 2008, or

(C) such taxpayer receives after such date of enactment funds from the Federal Government in exchange for an interest described in subparagraph (A) or (B) pursuant to a program established under title I of division A of the Emergency Economic Stabilization Act of 2008 (unless such taxpayer is a financial institution (as defined in section 3 of such Act) and the funds are received pursuant to a program established by the Secretary of the Treasury for the stated purpose of increasing the availability of credit to small businesses using funding made available under such Act), or

(2) the Federal National Mortgage Association and the Federal Home Loan Mortgage Corporation, and

(3) any taxpayer which at any time in 2008 or 2009 was or is a member of the same affiliated group (as defined in section 1504 of the Internal Revenue Code of 1986, determined without regard to subsection (b) thereof) as a taxpayer described in paragraph (1) or (2).

[Sec. 810(c)]

(c) COMPUTATION OF LOSS FROM OPERATIONS.—For purposes of this section—

(1) IN GENERAL.—The term "loss from operations" means the excess of the life insurance deductions for any taxable year over the life insurance gross income for such taxable year.

(2) MODIFICATIONS.—For purposes of paragraph (1)—

(A) the operations loss deduction shall not be allowed, and

(B) the deductions allowed by sections 243 (relating to dividends received by corporations), 244 (relating to dividends received on certain preferred stock of public utilities), and 245 (relating to dividends received from certain foreign corporations) shall be computed without regard to section 246(b) as modified by section 805(a)(4).

[Sec. 810(d)]

(d) OFFSET DEFINED.—

(1) IN GENERAL.—For purposes of subsection (b)(2), the term "offset" means, with respect to any taxable year, an amount equal to that increase in the operations loss deduction for the taxable year which reduces the life insurance company taxable income (computed without regard to paragraphs (2) and (3) of section 804) for such year to zero.

(2) OPERATIONS LOSS DEDUCTION.—For purposes of paragraph (1), the operations loss deduction for any taxable year shall be computed without regard to the loss from operations for the loss year or for any taxable year thereafter.

[Sec. 810(e)]

(e) NEW COMPANY DEFINED.—For purposes of this part, a life insurance company is a new company for any taxable year only if such taxable year begins not more than 5 years after the first day on which it (or any predecessor, if section 381(c)(22) applies) was authorized to do business as an insurance company.

[Sec. 810(f)]

(f) APPLICATION OF SUBTITLES A AND F IN RESPECT OF OPERATION LOSSES.—Except as provided in section 805(b)(5), subtitles A and F shall apply in respect of operation loss carrybacks, operation loss carryovers, and the operations loss deduction under this part, in the same manner and to the same extent as such subtitles apply in respect of net operating loss carrybacks, net operating loss carryovers, and the net operating loss deduction.

[Sec. 810(g)]

(g) TRANSITIONAL RULE.—For purposes of this section and section 812 (as in effect before the enactment of the Life Insurance Tax Act of 1984), this section shall be treated as a continuation of such section 812.

Amendments

• 1984, Deficit Reduction Act of 1984 (P.L. 98-369)

P.L. 98-369, §211(a):

Amended Part I of subchapter L of chapter 1 by adding Code Sec. 810. **Effective** for tax years beginning after 12-31-83. For transitional and special rules, see Act Sec. 216(a)-(b)(2) in the amendments for Code Sec. 801.

[Sec. 810—Repealed]

• 1984, Deficit Reduction Act of 1984 (P.L. 98-369)

P.L. 98-369, §211(a):

Amended Part I of Subchapter L of Chapter 1 by adding a new Part I (Code Secs. 801-818). Prior to amendment, Code Sec. 810 read as follows:

SEC. 810. RULES FOR CERTAIN RESERVES.

[Sec. 810(a)]

(a) ADJUSTMENT FOR DECREASE.—If the sum of the items described in subsection (c) as of the beginning of the taxable year exceeds the sum of such items as of the close of the taxable year (reduced by the amount of investment yield not included in gain or loss from operations for the taxable year by reason of section 809(a)(1)), the excess shall be taken into account as a net decrease referred to in section 809(c)(2).

[Sec. 810(b)]

(b) ADJUSTMENT FOR INCREASE.—If the sum of the items described in subsection (c) as of the close of the taxable year (reduced by the amount of the investment yield not included in gain or loss from the operations for the taxable year by reason of section 809(a)(1)) exceeds the sum of such items as of the beginning of the taxable year, the excess shall be taken into account as a net increase referred to in section 809(d)(2).

[Sec. 810(c)]

(c) ITEMS TAKEN INTO ACCOUNT.—The items referred to in subsections (a) and (b) are as follows:

(1) The life insurance reserves (as defined in section 801(b)).

(2) The unearned premiums and unpaid losses included in total reserves under section 801(c)(2).

(3) The amounts (discounted at the rates of interest assumed by the company) necessary to satisfy the obligations under insurance or annuity contracts (including contracts supplementary thereto), but only if such obligations do not involve (at the time with respect to which the computation is made under this paragraph) life, health, or accident contingencies.

(4) Dividend accumulations, and other amounts, held at interest in connection with insurance or annuity contracts (including contracts supplementary thereto).

(5) Premiums received in advance, and liabilities for premium deposit funds.

(6) Special contingency reserves under contracts of group term life insurance or group health and accident insurance which are established and maintained for the provision of insurance on retired lives, for premium stabilization, or for a combination thereof.

In applying this subsection, the same item shall be counted only once.

Amendments

• 1969, Tax Reform Act of 1969 (P.L. 91-172)

P.L. 91-172, §907(a)(2):

Amended Code Sec. 810(c) by adding paragraph (6). **Effective** 1-1-58.

[Sec. 810(d)]

(d) ADJUSTMENT FOR CHANGE IN COMPUTING RESERVES.—

(1) IN GENERAL.—If the basis for determining any item referred to in subsection (c) as of the close of any taxable year differs from the basis for such determination as of the close of the preceding taxable year, then so much of the difference between—

(A) the amount of the item at the close of the taxable year, computed on the new basis, and

(B) the amount of the item at the close of the taxable year, computed on the old basis,

as is attributable to contracts issued before the taxable year shall be taken into account for purposes of this subpart as follows:

(i) if the amount determined under subparagraph (A) exceeds the amount determined under subparagraph (B), 1/10 of such excess shall be taken into account, for each of the succeeding 10 taxable years, as a net increase to which section 809(d)(2) applies; or

(ii) if the amount determined under subparagraph (B) exceeds the amount determined under subparagraph (A), 1/10 of such excess shall be taken into account for each of the 10 succeeding taxable years, as a net decrease to which section 809(c)(2) applies.

(2) TERMINATION AS LIFE INSURANCE COMPANY.—Except as provided in section 381(c)(22) (relating to carryovers in certain corporate readjustments), if for any taxable year the taxpayer is not a life insurance company, the balance of any adjustments under this paragraph shall be taken into account for the preceding taxable year.

(3) EFFECT OF PRELIMINARY TERM ELECTION.—An election under section 818(c) shall not be treated as a change in the basis for determining an item referred to in subsection (c) to which this subsection applies. If an election under section 818(c) applies for the taxable year, the amounts of the items referred to in subparagraphs (A) and (B) of paragraph (1) shall be determined without regard to such election. If such an election would apply in respect of such item for the taxable year but for the new basis, the amount of the item referred to in subparagraph (B) shall be determined on the basis which would have been applicable under section 818(c) if the election applied in respect of the item for the taxable year.

[Sec. 810(e)—Repealed]

Amendments

• 1969, Tax Reform Act of 1969 (P.L. 91-172)

P.L. 91-172, §121(b)(5)(B):

Amended Code Sec. 810 by deleting subsection (e). **Effective** for tax years beginning after 12-31-69. Prior to deletion, subsection (e) read as follows:

"(e) Certain Decreases in Reserves of Voluntary Employees' Beneficiary Associations.—

"(1) Decreases due to voluntary lapses of policies issued before January 1, 1958.—For purposes of subsections (a) and (b), in the case of a life insurance company which meets the requirements of section 501(c)(9) other than the requirement of subparagraph (B) thereof, there shall be taken into account only 11½ percent of any decrease in the life insurance reserve on any policy issued before January 1, 1958, which is attributable solely to the voluntary lapse of such policy on or after January 1, 1958. In applying the preceding sentence, the decrease in the reserve for any policy shall be determined by reference to the amount of such reserve as of the beginning of the taxable year, reduced by any amount allowable as a deduction under section 809(d)(1) in respect of such policy by reason of such lapse. This paragraph shall apply for any taxable year only if the taxpayer has made an election under paragraph (3) which is effective for such taxable year.

"(2) Disallowance of carryovers from pre-1958 losses from operations.—In the case of a life insurance company to which paragraph (1) applies for the taxable year, section 812(b)(1) shall not apply with respect to any loss from operations for any taxable year beginning before January 1, 1958.

"(3) Election.—Paragraph (1) shall apply to any taxpayer for any taxable year only if the taxpayer elects, not later than the time prescribed by law (including extensions thereof) for filing the return for such taxable year, to have such paragraph apply. Such election shall be made in such manner as the Secretary or his delegate shall prescribe by regulations. Such election shall be effective for the taxable year for which made and for all succeeding taxable years, and shall not be revoked except with the consent of the Secretary or his delegate."

• 1959, Life Insurance Company Income Tax Act of 1959 (P.L. 86-69)

P.L. 86-69, §2:

Revised Part I of subchapter L of chapter 1 of the 1954 Code. **Effective**, generally, for tax years beginning after 1957. Prior text not reproduced.

Subpart D—Accounting, Allocation, and Foreign Provisions

[Sec. 811]

SEC. 811. ACCOUNTING PROVISIONS.

[Sec. 811(a)]

(a) METHOD OF ACCOUNTING.—All computations entering into the determination of the taxes imposed by this part shall be made—

(1) under an accrual method of accounting, or

(2) to the extent permitted under regulations prescribed by the Secretary, under a combination of an accrual method of accounting with any other method permitted by this chapter (other than the cash receipts and disbursements method).

To the extent not inconsistent with the preceding sentence or any other provision of this part, all such computations shall be made in a manner consistent with the manner required for purposes of the annual statement approved by the National Association of Insurance Commissioners.

[Sec. 811(b)]

(b) AMORTIZATION OF PREMIUM AND ACCRUAL OF DISCOUNT.—

(1) IN GENERAL.—The appropriate items of income, deductions, and adjustments under this part shall be adjusted to reflect the appropriate amortization of premium and the appropriate accrual of discount attributable to the taxable year on bonds, notes, debentures, or other evidences of indebtedness held by a life insurance company. Such amortization and accrual shall be determined—

(A) in accordance with the method regularly employed by such company, if such method is reasonable, and

(B) in all other cases, in accordance with regulations prescribed by the Secretary.

(2) SPECIAL RULES.—

(A) AMORTIZATION OF BOND PREMIUM.—In the case of any bond (as defined in section 171(d)), the amount of bond premium, and the amortizable bond premium for the taxable year, shall be determined under section 171(b) as if the election set forth in section 171(c) had been made.

(B) CONVERTIBLE EVIDENCE OF INDEBTEDNESS.—In no case shall the amount of premium on a convertible evidence of indebtedness include any amount attributable to the conversion features of the evidence of indebtedness.

(3) EXCEPTION.—No accrual of discount shall be required under paragraph (1) on any bond (as defined in section 171(d)), except in the case of discount which is—

(A) interest to which section 103 applies, or

(B) original issue discount (as defined in section 1273).

Amendments

• 1984, Deficit Reduction Act of 1984 (P.L. 98-369)

P.L. 98-369, §42(a)(8):

Amended Code Sec. 811(b)(3), as amended by Act Sec. 211(a), by striking out "section 1232(b)" and inserting in lieu thereof "section 1273". **Effective** for tax years ending after 7-18-84.

[Sec. 811(c)]

(c) NO DOUBLE COUNTING.—Nothing in this part shall permit—

(1) a reserve to be established for any item unless the gross amount of premiums and other consideration attributable to such item are required to be included in life insurance gross income,

(2) the same item to be counted more than once for reserve purposes, or

(3) any item to be deducted (either directly or as an increase in reserves) more than once.

Amendments

• 1984, Deficit Reduction Act of 1984 (P.L. 98-369)

P.L. 98-369, §714(a):

Amended former Code Sec. 811(c) by striking out "conventional coinsurance contract" and inserting in lieu thereof "reinsurance contract". **Effective** as if included in the provision of P.L. 97-248 to which it relates.

[Sec. 811(d)]

(d) METHOD OF COMPUTING RESERVES ON CONTRACT WHERE INTEREST IS GUARANTEED BEYOND END OF TAXABLE YEAR.—For purposes of this part (other than section 816), amounts in the nature of interest to be paid or credited under any contract for any period which is computed at a rate which—

(1) exceeds the greater of the prevailing State assumed interest rate or applicable Federal interest rate in effect under section 807 for the contract for such period, and

(2) is guaranteed beyond the end of the taxable year on which the reserves are being computed,

shall be taken into account in computing the reserves with respect to such contract as if such interest were guaranteed only up to the end of the taxable year.

Amendments

• 1988, Technical and Miscellaneous Revenue Act of 1988 (P.L. 100-647)

P.L. 100-647, §2004(p)(1):

Amended Code Sec. 811(d)(1) by striking out the "prevailing State assumed interest rate for the contract" and inserting in lieu thereof "the greater of the prevailing State assumed interest rate or applicable Federal interest rate in effect under section 807 for the contract". **Effective** as if included in the provision of P.L. 100-203 to which it relates.

[Sec. 811(e)]

(e) SHORT TAXABLE YEARS.—If any return of a corporation made under this part is for a period of less than the entire calendar year (referred to in this subsection as "short period"), then section 443 shall not apply in respect to such period, but life insurance company taxable income shall be determined, under regulations prescribed by the Secretary, on an annual basis by a ratable daily projection of the appropriate figures for the short period.

Amendments

• 1984, Deficit Reduction Act of 1984 (P.L. 98-369)

P.L. 98-369, §211(a):

Amended Part I of subchapter L of chapter 1 by adding Code Sec. 811. **Effective** for tax years beginning after 12-31-83. For transitional and special rules, see Act Sec. 216(a)-(b)(2) under the amendment notes for Code Sec. 801.

[Sec. 811—Repealed]

Amendments

• 1984, Deficit Reduction Act of 1984 (P.L. 98-369)

P.L. 98-369, §211(a):

Amended Part I of Subchapter L of Chapter 1 by adding a new Part I (Code Secs. 801-818). For transitional and special rules, see Act Sec. 216(a)-(b)(2) in the amendments for Code Sec. 801. Prior to amendment, Code Sec. 811 read as follows:

SEC. 811. DIVIDENDS TO POLICYHOLDERS.

[Sec. 811(a)]

(a) DIVIDENDS TO POLICYHOLDERS DEFINED.—For purposes of this part, the term "dividends to policyholders" means dividends and similar distributions to policyholders in their capacity as such. Such term does not include interest paid (as defined in section 805(e)).

[Sec. 811(b)]

(b) AMOUNT OF DEDUCTION.—

(1) IN GENERAL.—Except as limited by section 809(f), the deduction for dividends to policyholders for any taxable year shall be an amount equal to the dividends to policyholders paid during the taxable year—

(A) increased by the excess of (i) the amounts held at the end of the taxable year as reserves for dividends to policyholders (as defined in subsection (a)) payable during the year following the taxable year, over (ii) such amounts held at the end of the preceding taxable year, or

(B) decreased by the excess of (i) such amounts held at the end of the preceding taxable year, over (ii) such amounts held at the end of the taxable year.

For purposes of subparagraphs (A) and (B), there shall be included as amounts held at the end of any taxable year amounts set aside, before the 16th day of the third month of the year following such taxable year (or, in the case of a mutual savings bank subject to the tax imposed by section 594, before the 16th day of the fourth month of the year following such taxable year), for payment during the year following such taxable year.

(2) CERTAIN AMOUNTS TO BE TREATED AS NET DECREASES.—If the amount determined under paragraph (1)(B) exceeds the dividends to policyholders paid during the taxable year, the amount of such excess shall be a net decrease referred to in section 809(c)(2).

[Sec. 811(c)]

(c) SPECIAL RULE FOR DIVIDENDS TO POLICYHOLDERS UNDER REINSURANCE CONTRACTS.—If, under the terms of a reinsurance contract, a life insurance company (hereinafter referred to as "the reinsurer") is obligated to reimburse another life insurance company (hereinafter referred to as "the reinsured") for dividends to policyholders on the policies reinsured, the amount of the deduction for dividends reimbursed shall, for purposes of section 809(d)(12), be equal to the amount of dividends to policyholders—

(1) which were paid by the reinsured, and

(2) with respect to which the reinsurer reimbursed the reinsured under the terms of such contract.

The amount determined under the preceding sentence shall be properly adjusted to reflect the adjustments under subsection (b)(1).

Amendments

• 1982, Tax Equity and Fiscal Responsibility Act of 1982 (P.L. 97-248)

P.L. 97-248, §255(b)(1):

Amended Code Sec. 811 by adding new subsection (c). **Effective** for tax years beginning after 12-31-81. For a special rule, see amendment notes for P.L. 97-248 under Code Sec. 820.

• 1959, Life Insurance Company Income Tax Act of 1959 (P.L. 86-69)

P.L. 86-69, §2:

Revised Part I of subchapter L of chapter 1 of the 1954 Code. **Effective**, generally, for tax years beginning after 1957. Prior text not reproduced.

[Sec. 812]

SEC. 812. DEFINITION OF COMPANY'S SHARE AND POLICYHOLDERS' SHARE.

[Sec. 812(a)]

(a) GENERAL RULE.—

(1) COMPANY'S SHARE.—For purposes of section 805(a)(4), the term "company's share" means, with respect to any taxable year, the percentage obtained by dividing—

(A) the company's share of the net investment income for the taxable year, by

(B) the net investment income for the taxable year.

(2) POLICYHOLDERS' SHARE.—For purposes of section 807, the term "policyholders' share" means, with respect to any taxable year, the excess of 100 percent over the percentage determined under paragraph (1).

[Sec. 812(b)]

(b) COMPANY'S SHARE OF NET INVESTMENT INCOME.—

(1) IN GENERAL.—For purposes of this section, the company's share of net investment income is the excess (if any) of—

(A) the net investment income for the taxable year, over

(B) the sum of—

(i) the policy interest, for the taxable year, plus

(ii) the gross investment income's proportionate share of policyholder dividends for the taxable year.

(2) POLICY INTEREST.—For purposes of this subsection, the term "policy interest" means—

(A) required interest (at the greater of the prevailing State assumed rate or the applicable Federal interest rate) on reserves under section 807(c) (other than paragraph (2) thereof),

(B) the deductible portion of excess interest,

(C) the deductible portion of any amount (whether or not a policyholder dividend), and not taken into account under subparagraph (A) or (B), credited to—

(i) a policyholder's fund under a pension plan contract for employees (other than retired employees), or

(ii) a deferred annuity contract before the annuity starting date, and

(D) interest on amounts left on deposit with the company.

In any case where neither the prevailing State assumed interest rate nor the applicable Federal rate is used, another appropriate rate shall be used for purposes of subparagraph (A).

(3) GROSS INVESTMENT INCOME'S PROPORTIONATE SHARE OF POLICYHOLDER DIVIDENDS.—For purposes of paragraph (1), the gross investment income's proportionate share of policyholder dividends is—

(A) the deduction for policyholders' dividends determined under section 808 for the taxable year, but not including—

(i) the deductible portion of excess interest,

(ii) the deductible portion of policyholder dividends on contracts referred to in clauses (i) and (ii) of paragraph (2)(C), and

(iii) the deductible portion of the premium and mortality charge adjustments with respect to contracts paying excess interest for such year,

multiplied by

(B) the fraction—

(i) the numerator of which is gross investment income for the taxable year (reduced by the policy interest for such year), and

(ii) the denominator of which is life insurance gross income reduced by the excess (if any) of the closing balance for the items described in section 807(c) over the opening balance for such items for the taxable year.

For purposes of subparagraph (B)(ii), life insurance gross income shall be determined by including tax-exempt interest and by applying section 807(a)(2)(B) as if it did not contain clause (i) thereof.

Amendments

• 2004, Pension Funding Equity Act of 2004 (P.L. 108-218)

P.L. 108-218, §205(b)(4):

Amended Code Sec. 812(b)(3)(A) by striking "sections 808 and 809" and inserting "section 808". **Effective** for tax years beginning after 12-31-2004.

• 1988, Technical and Miscellaneous Revenue Act of 1988 (P.L. 100-647)

P.L. 100-647, §2004(p)(2):

Amended Code Sec. 812(b)(2) by striking out the last sentence and inserting in lieu thereof a new sentence. **Effective** as if included in the provision of P.L. 100-203 to which it relates. Prior to amendment, the last sentence read as follows:

In any case where the prevailing State assumed rate is not used, another appropriate rate shall be treated as the prevailing State assumed rate for purposes of subparagraph (A).

• 1987, Revenue Act of 1987 (P.L. 100-203)

P.L. 100-203, §10241(b)(2)(B)(i)-(ii):

Amended Code Sec. 812(b)(2) by striking out "at the prevailing State assumed rate or, where such rate is not used, another appropriate rate" and inserting in lieu thereof "at the greater of the prevailing State assumed rate or the applicable Federal interest rate", and by adding at the end thereof a new sentence. **Effective** for contracts issued in tax years beginning after 12-31-87.

• 1986, Tax Reform Act of 1986 (P.L. 99-514)

P.L. 99-514, §1821(i)(1)(A)-(D):

Amended Code Sec. 812(b)(2) by striking out "the prevailing State assumed rate" in subparagraph (A) and inserting in lieu thereof "the prevailing State assumed rate or, where such rate is not used, another appropriate rate", by striking out "and" at the end of subparagraph (B), by striking out the period at the end of subparagraph (C) and inserting in lieu thereof ", and", and by adding at the end thereof new subparagraph (D). **Effective** as if included in the provision of P.L. 98-369 to which it relates.

P.L. 99-514, §1821(i)(2)(A)-(B):

Amended Code Sec. 812(b)(3)(B) by striking out "(including tax-exempt interest)" in clause (ii), and by adding at the end thereof a new sentence. **Effective** as if included in the provision of P.L. 98-369 to which it relates.

[Sec. 812(c)]

(c) NET INVESTMENT INCOME—For purposes of this section, the term "net investment income" means—

(1) except as provided in paragraph (2), 90 percent of gross investment income; or

(2) in the case of gross investment income attributable to assets held in segregated asset accounts under variable contracts, 95 percent of gross investment income.

Amendments

• 1986, Tax Reform Act of 1986 (P.L. 99-514)

P.L. 99-514, §1821(i)(3):

Amended Code Sec. 812(c). **Effective** as if included in the provision of P.L. 98-369 to which it relates. Prior to amendment, Code Sec. 812(c) read as follows:

(c) NET INVESTMENT INCOME—For purposes of this section, the term "net investment income" means 90 percent of gross investment income.

[Sec. 812(d)]

(d) GROSS INVESTMENT INCOME.—For purposes of this section, the term "gross investment income" means the sum of the following:

(1) INTEREST, ETC.—The gross amount of income from—

(A) interest (including tax-exempt interest), dividends, rents, and royalties,

(B) the entering into of any lease, mortgage, or other instrument or agreement from which the life insurance company derives interest, rents, or royalties,

(C) the alteration or termination of any instrument or agreement described in subparagraph (B), and

(D) the increase for any taxable year in the policy cash values (within the meaning of section 805(a)(4)(F)) of life insurance policies and annuity and endowment contracts to which section 264(f) applies.

(2) SHORT-TERM CAPITAL GAIN.—The amount (if any) by which the net short-term capital gain exceeds the net long-term capital loss.

(3) TRADE OR BUSINESS INCOME.—The gross income from any trade or business (other than an insurance business) carried on by the life insurance company, or by a partnership of which the life insurance company is a partner. In computing gross income under this paragraph, there shall be excluded any item described in paragraph (1).

Except as provided in paragraph (2), in computing gross investment income under this subsection, there shall be excluded any gain from the sale or exchange of a capital asset, and any gain considered as gain from the sale or exchange of a capital asset.

Amendments

• 1997, Taxpayer Relief Act of 1997 (P.L. 105-34)

P.L. 105-34, §1084(b)[(d)](3):

Amended Code Sec. 812(d)(1) by striking "and" at the end of subparagraph (B), by striking the period at the end of subparagraph (C) and inserting ", and", and by adding at the end a new subparagraph (D). For the **effective** date, see Act Sec. 1084(d)[(f)], below.

P.L. 105-34, §1084(d)[(f)], as amended by P.L. 105-206, §6010(o)(3)(B), provides:

(d)[(f)] EFFECTIVE DATE.—The amendments made by this section shall apply to contracts issued after June 8, 1997, in taxable years ending after such date. For purposes of the preceding sentence, any material increase in the death benefit or other material change in the contract shall be treated as a new contract except that, in the case of a master contract (within the meaning of section 264(f)(4)(E) of the Internal Revenue Code of 1986), the addition of covered lives shall be treated as a new contract only with respect to such additional covered lives. For purposes of this subsection, an increase in the death benefit under a policy or contract issued in connection with a lapse described in section 501(d)(2) of the Health Insurance Portability and Accountability Act of 1996 shall not be treated as a new contract.

[Sec. 812(e)]

(e) DIVIDENDS FROM CERTAIN SUBSIDIARIES NOT INCLUDED IN GROSS INVESTMENT INCOME.—

(1) IN GENERAL.—For purposes of this section, the term "gross investment income" shall not include any dividend received by the life insurance company which is a 100 percent dividend.

(2) 100 PERCENT DIVIDEND DEFINED.—

(A) IN GENERAL.—Except as provided in subparagraphs (B) and (C), the term "100 percent dividend" means any dividend if the percentage used for purposes of determining the deduction allowable under section 243, 244, or 245(b) is 100 percent.

(B) CERTAIN DIVIDENDS OUT OF TAX-EXEMPT INTEREST, ETC.—The term "100 percent dividend" does not include any distribution by a corporation to the extent such distribution is out of tax-exempt interest or out of dividends which are not 100 percent dividends (determined with the application of this subparagraph).

(C) CERTAIN DIVIDENDS RECEIVED BY FOREIGN CORPORATIONS.—The term "100 percent dividends" does not include any dividend described in section 805(a)(4)(E) (relating to certain dividends in the case of foreign corporations).

Amendments

• 1988, Technical and Miscellaneous Revenue Act of 1988 (P.L. 100-647)

P.L. 100-647, §1018(h)(1):

Amended Code Sec. 812(e). **Effective** as if included in the amendments made by section 211 of P.L. 98-369. Prior to amendment, Code Sec. 812(e) read as follows:

(e) DIVIDENDS FROM CERTAIN SUBSIDIARIES NOT INCLUDED IN GROSS INVESTMENT INCOME.—For purposes of this section, the term "gross investment income" shall not include any dividend received by the life insurance company which is a 100-percent dividend (as defined in section 805(a)(4)(C)). Such term also shall not include any dividend described in section 805(a)(4)(D) (relating to certain dividends in the case of foreign corporations).

[Sec. 812(f)]

(f) NO DOUBLE COUNTING.—Under regulations, proper adjustments shall be made in the application of this section to prevent an item from being counted more than once.

Amendments

• 1984, Deficit Reduction Act of 1984 (P.L. 98-369)

P.L. 98-369, §211(a):

Amended Part I of subchapter L of chapter 1 by adding Code Sec. 812. **Effective** for tax years beginning after 12-31-83. However, for transitional and special rules, see Act Sec. 216(a)-(b)(2) under the amendment notes for Code Sec. 801.

[Sec. 812(g)—Stricken]

Amendments

• 1996, Small Business Job Protection Act of 1996 (P.L. 104-188)

P.L. 104-188, §1602(b)(2):

Amended Code Sec. 812 by striking subsection (g). For the **effective** date, see Act Sec. 1602(c)(1)-(3), below. Prior to being stricken, Code Sec. 812(g) read as follows:

(g) TREATMENT OF INTEREST PARTIALLY TAX-EXEMPT UNDER SECTION 133.—For purposes of this section and subsections (a) and (b) of section 807, the terms "gross investment income" and "tax-exempt interest" shall not include any interest received with respect to a securities acquisition loan (as defined in section 133(b)). Such interest shall not be included in life insurance gross income for purposes of subsection (b)(3).

P.L. 104-188, §1602(c)(1)-(3), provides:

(c) EFFECTIVE DATE.—

(1) IN GENERAL.—The amendments made by this section shall apply to loans made after the date of the enactment of this Act.

(2) REFINANCINGS.—The amendments made by this section shall not apply to loans made after the date of the enactment of this Act to refinance securities acquisition loans (determined without regard to section 133(b)(1)(B) of the Internal Revenue Code of 1986, as in effect on the day before the date of the enactment of this Act) made on or before such date or to refinance loans described in this paragraph if—

(A) the refinancing loans meet the requirements of section 133 of such Code (as so in effect),

(B) immediately after the refinancing the principal amount of the loan resulting from the refinancing does not exceed the principal amount of the refinanced loan (immediately before the refinancing), and

(C) the term of such refinancing loan does not extend beyond the last day of the term of the original securities acquisition loan.

For purposes of this paragraph, the term "securities acquisition loan" includes a loan from a corporation to an employee stock ownership plan described in section 133(b)(3) of such Code (as so in effect).

(3) EXCEPTION.—Any loan made pursuant to a binding written contract in effect before June 10, 1996, and at all times thereafter before such loan is made, shall be treated for purposes of paragraphs (1) and (2) as a loan made on or before the date of the enactment of this Act.

• 1986, Tax Reform Act of 1986 (P.L. 99-514)

P.L. 99-514, §1821(i)(4):

Amended Code Sec. 812 by adding at the end thereof new subsection (g). **Effective** as if included in the provision of P.L. 98-369 to which it relates.

[Sec. 812—Repealed]

Amendments

• 1984, Deficit Reduction Act of 1984 (P.L. 98-369)

P.L. 98-369, §211(a):

Amended Part I of Subchapter L of Chapter 1 by adding a new Part I (Code Secs. 801-818). For transitional and special rules, see Act Sec. 216(a)-(b)(2) in the amendments for Code Sec. 801. Prior to amendment, Code Sec. 812 read as follows:

SEC. 812. OPERATIONS LOSS DEDUCTION.

[Sec. 812(a)]

(a) DEDUCTION ALLOWED.—There shall be allowed as a deduction for the taxable year an amount equal to the aggregate of—

(1) the operations loss carryovers to such year, plus

(2) the operations loss carrybacks to such year.

For purposes of this part, the term "operations loss deduction" means the deduction allowed by this subsection.

[Sec. 812(b)]

(b) OPERATIONS LOSS CARRYBACKS AND CARRYOVERS.—

(1) YEARS TO WHICH LOSS MAY BE CARRIED.—The loss from operations for any taxable year (hereinafter in this section referred to as the "loss year") shall be—

(A) an operations loss carryback to each of the 3 taxable years preceding the loss year,

(B) an operations loss carryover to each of the 5 taxable years following the loss year, and

(C) subject to subsection (e), if the life insurance company is a new company for the loss year, an operations loss carryover to each of the 3 taxable years following the 5 taxable years described in subparagraph (B).

In the case of an operations loss for any taxable year ending after December 31, 1975, this paragraph shall be applied by substituting "15 taxable years" for "5 taxable years".

(2) AMOUNT OF CARRYBACKS AND CARRYOVERS.—The entire amount of the loss from operations for any loss year shall be carried to the earliest of the taxable years to which (by reason of paragraph (1)) such loss may be carried. The portion of such loss which shall be carried to each of the other taxable years shall be the excess (if any) of the amount of such loss over the sum of the offsets (as defined in subsection (d)) for each of the prior taxable years to which such loss may be carried.

(3) ELECTION FOR OPERATIONS LOSS CARRYBACKS.—In the case of a loss from operations for any taxable year ending after December 31, 1975, the taxpayer may elect to relinquish the entire carryback period for such loss. Such election shall be made by the due date (including extensions of time) for filing the return for the taxable year of the loss from operations for which the election is to be in effect, and once made for any taxable year, such election shall be irrevocable for that taxable year.

Amendments

• 1981, Economic Recovery Tax Act of 1981 (P.L. 97-34)

P.L. 97-34, §207(b):

Amended Code Sec. 812(b)(1) by striking out "7" and inserting in lieu thereof "15". **Effective** for net operating losses in tax years ending after 12-31-75. However, P.L. 97-34, §209(c), as amended by P.L. 97-448, §102(d)(2), provides that the amendment shall not apply to any amount that, under the law in effect on 1-11-83, could not be carried to a tax year ending in 1981.

• 1976, Tax Reform Act of 1976 (P.L. 94-455)

P.L. 94-455, §806(d):

Added the last sentence to paragraph (1) and added paragraph (3). **Effective** for losses incurred in tax years ending after 12-31-75.

P.L. 94-455, §1901(a)(99):

Amended Code Sec. 812(b)(1). **Effective** for tax years beginning after 12-31-76. Prior to amendment, Code Sec. 812(b)(1) read as follows:

(1) YEARS TO WHICH LOSS MAY BE CARRIED.

(A) IN GENERAL.—The loss from operations for any taxable year (hereinafter in this section referred to as the "loss year") beginning after December 31, 1954, shall be—

(i) an operations loss carryback to each of the 3 taxable years preceding the loss year,

(ii) an operations loss carryover to each of the 5 taxable years following the loss year, and

(iii) subject to subsection (e), if the life insurance company is a new company for the loss year, an operations loss carryover to each of the 3 taxable years following the 5 taxable years described in clause (ii).

(B) SPECIAL TRANSITIONAL RULES FOR CARRYBACKS.—A loss from operations for any taxable year beginning before January 1, 1958, shall not be an operations loss carryback to any taxable year beginning before January 1, 1955. A loss from operations for any taxable year beginning after December 31, 1957, shall not be an operations loss carryback to any taxable year beginning before January 1, 1958.

(C) APPLICATION FOR YEARS PRIOR TO 1958.—For purposes of this section, this part (as in effect for 1958) and section 381(c)(22) shall be treated as applying to all taxable years beginning after December 31, 1954, and before January 1, 1958.

[Sec. 812(c)]

(c) COMPUTATION OF LOSS FROM OPERATIONS.—In computing the loss from operations for purposes of this section—

(1) The operations loss deduction shall not be allowed.

(2) The deductions allowed by sections 243 (relating to dividends received by corporations), 244 (relating to dividends received on certain preferred stock of public utilities), and 245 (relating to dividends received from certain foreign corporations) shall be computed without regard to section 246(b) as modified by section 809(d)(8)(B).

[Sec. 812(d)]

(d) OFFSET DEFINED.—

(1) IN GENERAL.—For purposes of subsection (b)(2), the term "offset" means, with respect to any taxable year, an amount equal to that increase in the operations loss deduction for the taxable year which reduces the life insurance company taxable income (computed without regard to section 802(b)(3)) for such year to zero.

(2) OPERATIONS LOSS DEDUCTION.—For purposes of paragraph (1), the operations loss deduction for any taxable year shall be computed without regard to the loss from operations for the loss year or for any taxable year thereafter.

[Sec. 812(e)]

(e) NEW COMPANY DEFINED.—For purposes of this part, a life insurance company is a new company for any taxable year only if such taxable year begins not more than 5 years after the first day on which it (or any predecessor, if section 381(c)(22) applies or would have applied if in effect) was authorized to do business as an insurance company.

Amendments

• 1964 (P.L. 88-571)

P.L. 88-571, §[1(a)]:

Amended Code Sec. 812(e). **Effective** for a loss from operations for taxable years beginning after 12-31-55; except that, in the case of a nonqualified corporation as defined in Sec. 812(e)(2)(B) as in effect before such amendment—

(1) a loss from operations for a taxable year beginning in 1956 shall not be an operating loss carryover to the years 1962 and 1963, and there shall be no reduction in the portion of such loss from operations which may be carried to 1964 by reason of an offset with respect to the year 1962 or 1963, and

(2) a loss from operations for a taxable year beginning in 1957 shall not be an operating loss carryover to the year 1963, and there shall be no reduction in the portion of such loss from operations which may be carried to 1964 and 1965 by reason of an offset with respect to the year 1963.

Prior to amendment, Sec. 812(e) read as follows:

"(e) Rules Relating to New Companies.—

"(1) New company defined.—For purposes of this part, a life insurance company is a new company for any taxable year only if such taxable year begins not more than 5 years after the first day on which it (or any predecessor, if section 381(c)(22) applies or would have applied if in effect) was authorized to do business as an insurance company.

"(2) Limitations on 8-year carryover.—

"(A) In general.—For purposes of subsection (b)(1)(A)(iii), a life insurance company shall not be treated as a new company for any loss year if at any time during such year it was a nonqualified corporation. If, at any time during any taxable year after the loss year, the life insurance company is a nonqualified corporation, subsection (b)(1)(A)(iii) shall cease to apply with respect to such loss for such taxable year and all subsequent taxable years.

"(B) Nonqualified corporation defined.—For purposes of subparagraph (A), the term `nonqualified corporation' means any corporation connected through stock ownership with any other corporation (except a corporation taxable under part II or part III of this subchapter), if either of such corporations possesses at least 50 percent of the voting power of all classes of stock of the other such corporation. For purposes of subparagraph (A), a corporation shall be treated as becoming a nonqualified corporation at any time at which it becomes a party to a reorganization (other than a reorganization which is not described in any subparagraph of section 368(a)(1) other than subparagraphs (E) and (F) thereof)."

• 1962 (P.L. 87-858)

P.L. 87-858, §3(d)(1):

Amended Code Sec. 812(e)(2)(B) by inserting after "with any other corporation" in the first sentence the following: "(except a corporation taxable under part II or part III of this subchapter)." **Effective** with respect to all tax years beginning after 12-31-54, except that in the case of a nonqualified corporation, as defined in Sec. 812(e)(2)(B) as in effect prior to this amendment, a loss from operations for a tax year beginning in 1955 shall not be an operating loss carryover to the year 1961, and there shall be no reduction in the portion of such operating loss which may be carried to 1962 or 1963 by reason of an offset with respect to the year 1961.

[Sec. 812(f)]

(f) APPLICATION OF SUBTITLE A AND SUBTITLE F.—Except as provided in section 809(e), subtitle A and subtitle F shall apply in respect of operations loss carrybacks, operations loss carryovers, and the operations loss deduction under this part in the same manner and to the same extent as such subtitles apply in respect of net operating loss carrybacks, net operating loss carryovers, and the net operating loss deduction.

Amendments

• 1959, Life Insurance Company Income Tax Act of 1959 (P.L. 86-69)

P.L. 86-69, §2:

Revised Part I of subchapter L of chapter 1 of the 1954 Code. **Effective**, generally, for tax years beginning after 1957. Prior text not reproduced.

[Sec. 813—Repealed]

Amendments

• 1987, Revenue Act of 1987 (P.L. 100-203)

P.L. 100-203, §10242(c)(1):

Repealed Code Sec. 813. **Effective** for tax years beginning after 12-31-87. Prior to repeal, Code Sec. 813 read as follows:

SEC. 813. FOREIGN LIFE INSURANCE COMPANIES.

[Sec. 813(a)]

(a) ADJUSTMENT WHERE SURPLUS HELD IN THE UNITED STATES IS LESS THAN SPECIFIED MINIMUM.—

(1) IN GENERAL.—In the case of any foreign company taxable under this part, if—

(A) the required surplus determined under paragraph (2), exceeds

(B) the surplus held in the United States,

then its income effectively connected with the conduct of an insurance business within the United States shall be increased by an amount determined by multiplying such excess by such company's current investment yield. The preceding sentence shall be applied before computing the amount of the small life insurance company deduction, and any increase under the preceding sentence shall be treated as gross investment income.

(2) REQUIRED SURPLUS.—For purposes of this subsection—

(A) IN GENERAL.—The term "required surplus" means the amount determined by multiplying the taxpayer's total insurance liabilities on United States business by a percentage for the taxable year determined and proclaimed by the Secretary under subparagraph (B).

(B) DETERMINATION OF PERCENTAGE.—The percentage determined and proclaimed by the Secretary under this subparagraph shall be based on such data with respect to domestic life insurance companies for the preceding taxable year as the Secretary considers representative. Such percentage shall be computed on the basis of a ratio the numerator of which is the excess of the assets over the total insurance liabilities, and the denominator of which is the total insurance liabilities.

(3) CURRENT INVESTMENT YIELD.—For purposes of this subsection—

(A) IN GENERAL.—The term "current investment yield" means the percent obtained by dividing—

(i) the net investment income on assets held in the United States, by

(ii) the mean of the assets held in the United States during the taxable year.

(B) DETERMINATIONS BASED ON AMOUNT SET FORTH IN THE ANNUAL STATEMENT.—Except as otherwise provided in regulations, determinations under subparagraph (A) shall be made on the basis of the amounts required to be set forth on the annual statement approved by the National Association of Insurance Commissioners.

(4) OTHER DEFINITIONS.—For purposes of this subsection—

(A) SURPLUS HELD IN THE UNITED STATES.—The surplus held in the United States is the excess of the assets (determined under section 806(a)(3)(C)) held in the United States over the total insurance liabilities on United States business.

(B) TOTAL INSURANCE LIABILITIES.—For purposes of this subsection, the term "total insurance liabilities" means the sum of the total reserves (as defined in section 816(c)) plus (to the extent not included in total reserves) the items referred to in paragraphs (3), (4), (5), and (6) of section 807(c).

(5) REDUCTION OF SECTION 881 TAXES.—In the case of any foreign company taxable under this part, there shall be determined—

(A) the amount which would be subject to taxes under section 881 if the amount taxable under such section were determined without regard to sections 103 and 894, and

(B) the amount of the increase provided by paragraph (1).

The tax under section 881 (determined without regard to this paragraph) shall be reduced (but not below zero) by an amount which is the same proportion of such tax as the amount referred to in subparagraph (B) is of the amount referred to in subparagraph (A); but such reduction in taxes shall not exceed the increase in taxes under this part by reason of the increase provided by paragraph (1).

Amendments

• 1988, Technical and Miscellaneous Revenue Act of 1988 (P.L. 100-647)

P.L. 100-647, §1010(a)(1):

Amended Code Sec. 813(a)(1) by striking out "the special life insurance company deduction and " before "the small life insurance company". **Effective** as if included in the provision of P.L. 99-514 to which it relates.

• 1986, Tax Reform Act of 1986 (P.L. 99-514)

P.L. 99-514, §1011(b)(9):

Amended Code Sec. 813(a)(4)(A) by striking out "section 806(b)(3)(C)" and inserting in lieu thereof "section 806(a)(3)(C)". **Effective** for tax years beginning after 12-31-86.

P.L. 99-514, §1821(j):

Amended Code Sec. 813(a)(1) by adding at the end thereof a new sentence. **Effective** as if included in the provision of P.L. 98-369 to which it relates.

[Sec. 813(b)]

(b) ADJUSTMENT TO LIMITATION ON DEDUCTION FOR POLICYHOLDER DIVIDENDS IN THE CASE OF FOREIGN MUTUAL LIFE INSURANCE COMPANIES.—For purposes of section 809, the equity base of any foreign mutual life insurance company as of the close of any taxable year shall be increased by the amount of any excess determined under paragraph (1) of subsection (a) with respect to such taxable year.

[Sec. 813(c)]

(c) CROSS REFERENCE.—

For taxation of foreign corporations carrying on life insurance business within the United States, see section 842.

Amendments

• 1984, Deficit Reduction Act of 1984 (P.L. 98-369)

P.L. 98-369, §211(a):

Amended Part I of subchapter L of chapter 1 by adding Code Sec. 813. **Effective** for tax years beginning after 12-31-83. However, for transitional and special rules, see Act Sec. 216(a)-(b)(2) under the amendment notes for Code Sec. 801.

[Sec. 814]

SEC. 814. CONTIGUOUS COUNTRY BRANCHES OF DOMESTIC LIFE INSURANCE COMPANIES.

[Sec. 814(a)]

(a) EXCLUSION OF ITEMS.—In the case of a domestic mutual insurance company which—

(1) is a life insurance company,

(2) has a contiguous country life insurance branch, and

(3) makes the election provided by subsection (g) with respect to such branch,

there shall be excluded from each item involved in the determination of life insurance company taxable income the items separately accounted for in accordance with subsection (c).

[Sec. 814(b)]

(b) CONTIGUOUS COUNTRY LIFE INSURANCE BRANCH.—For purposes of this section, the term contiguous country life insurance branch means a branch which—

(1) issues insurance contracts insuring risks in connection with the lives or health of residents of a country which is contiguous to the United States,

(2) has its principal place of business in such contiguous country, and

(3) would constitute a mutual life insurance company if such branch were a separate domestic insurance company.

For purposes of this section, the term "insurance contract" means any life, health, accident, or annuity contract or reinsurance contract or any contract relating thereto.

[Sec. 814(c)]

(c) SEPARATE ACCOUNTING REQUIRED.—Any taxpayer which makes the election provided by subsection (g) shall establish and maintain a separate account for the various income, exclusion, deduction, asset, reserve, liability, and surplus items properly attributable to the contracts described in subsection (b). Such separate accounting shall be made—

(1) in accordance with the method regularly employed by such company, if such method clearly reflects income derived from, and the other items attributable to, the contracts described in subsection (b), and

(2) in all other cases, in accordance with regulations prescribed by the Secretary.

[Sec. 814(d)]

(d) RECOGNITION OF GAIN ON ASSETS IN BRANCH ACCOUNT.—If the aggregate fair market value of all the invested assets and tangible property which are separately accounted for by the domestic life insurance company in the branch account established pursuant to subsection (c) exceeds the aggregate adjusted basis of such assets for purposes of determining gain, then the domestic life insurance company shall be treated as having sold all such assets on the first day of the first taxable year for which the election is in effect at their fair market value on such first day. Notwithstanding any other provison of this chapter, the net gain shall be recognized to the domestic life insurance company on the deemed sale described in the preceding sentence.

[Sec. 814(e)]

(e) TRANSACTIONS BETWEEN CONTIGUOUS COUNTRY BRANCH AND DOMESTIC LIFE INSURANCE COMPANY.—

(1) REIMBURSEMENT FOR HOME OFFICE SERVICES, ETC.—Any payment, transfer, reimbursement, credit, or allowance which is made from a separate account established pursuant to subsection (c) to one or more other accounts of a domestic life insurance company as reimbursement for costs incurred for or with respect to the insurance (or reinsurance) of risks accounted for in such separate account shall be taken into account by the domestic life insurance company in the same manner as if such payment, transfer, reimbursement, credit, or allowance had been received from a separate person.

(2) REPATRIATION OF INCOME.—

(A) IN GENERAL.—Except as provided in subparagraph (B), any amount directly or indirectly transferred or credited from a branch account established pursuant to subsection (c) to one or more other accounts of such company shall, unless such transfer or credit is a reimbursement to which paragraph (1) applies, be added to the income of the domestic life insurance company.

(B) LIMITATION.—The addition provided by subparagraph (A) for the taxable year with respect to any contiguous country life insurance branch shall not exceed the amount by which—

(i) the aggregate decrease in the tentative LICTI of the domestic life insurance company for the taxable year and for all prior taxable years resulting solely from the application of subsection (a) of this section with respect to such branch, exceeds

(ii) the amount of additions to tentative LICTI pursuant to subparagraph (A) with respect to such contiguous country branch for all prior taxable years.

(C) TRANSITIONAL RULE.—For purposes of this paragraph, in the case of a prior taxable year beginning before January 1, 1984, the term "tentative LICTI" means life insurance company taxable income determined under this part (as in effect for such year) without regard to this paragraph.

[Sec. 814(f)]

(f) OTHER RULES.—

(1) TREATMENT OF FOREIGN TAXES.—

(A) IN GENERAL.—No income, war profits, or excess profits taxes paid or accrued to any foreign country or possession of the United States which is attributable to income excluded under subsection (a) shall be taken into account for purposes of subpart A of part III of subchapter N (relating to foreign tax credit) or allowable as a deduction.

(B) TREATMENT OF REPATRIATED AMOUNTS.—For purposes of sections 78 and 902, where any amount is added to the life insurance company taxable income of the domestic life insurance company by reason of subsection (e)(2), the contiguous country life insurance branch shall be treated as a foreign corporation. Any amount so added shall be treated as a dividend paid by a foreign corporation, and the taxes paid to any foreign country or possession of the United States with respect to such amount shall be deemed to have been paid by such branch.

(2) UNITED STATES SOURCE INCOME ALLOCABLE TO CONTIGUOUS COUNTRY BRANCH.—For purposes of sections 881, 882, and 1442, each contiguous country life insurance branch shall be treated as a foreign corporation. Such sections shall be applied to each such branch in the same manner as if such sections contained the provisions of any treaty to which the United States and the contiguous country are parties, to the same extent such provisions would apply if such branch were incorporated in such contiguous country.

[Sec. 814(g)]

(g) ELECTION.—A taxpayer may make the election provided by this subsection with respect to any contiguous country for any taxable year. An election made under this subsection for any taxable year shall remain in effect for all subsequent taxable years, except that it may be revoked with the consent of the Secretary. The election provided by this subsection shall be made not later than the time prescribed by law for filing the return for the taxable year (including extensions thereof) with respect to which such election is made, and such election and any approved revocation thereof shall be made in the manner provided by the Secretary.

[Sec. 814(h)]

(h) SPECIAL RULE FOR DOMESTIC STOCK LIFE INSURANCE COMPANIES.—At the election of a domestic stock life insurance company which has a contiguous country life insurance branch described in subsection (b) (without regard to the mutual requirement in subsection (b)(3)), the assets of such branch may be transferred to a foreign corporation organized under the laws of the contiguous country without the application of section 367. Subsection (a) shall apply to the stock of such foreign corporation as if such domestic company were a mutual company and as if the stock were an item described in subsection (c). Subsection (e)(2) shall apply to amounts transferred or credited to such domestic company as if such domestic company and such foreign corporation constituted one domestic mutual life insurance company. The insurance contracts which may be transferred pursuant to this subsection shall include only those which are similar to the types of insurance contracts issued by a mutual life insurance company. Notwithstanding the first sentence of this subsection, if the aggregate fair market value of the invested assets and tangible property which are separately accounted for by the domestic life insurance company in the branch account exceeds the aggregate adjusted basis of such assets for purposes of determining gain, the domestic life insurance company shall be deemed to have sold all such assets on the first day of the taxable year for which the election under this subsection applies and the net gain shall be recognized to the domestic life insurance company on the deemed sale, but not in excess of the proportion of such net gain which equals the proportion which the aggregate fair market value of such assets which are transferred pursuant to this subsection is of the aggregate fair market value of all such assets.

Amendments

• 1997, Taxpayer Relief Act of 1997 (P.L. 105-34)

P.L. 105-34, §1131(c)[(d)](1):

Amended Code Sec. 814(h) by striking "or 1491" at the end of the first sentence. **Effective** 8-5-97.

• 1984, Deficit Reduction Act of 1984 (P.L. 98-369)

P.L. 98-369, §211(a):

Amended Part I of subchapter L of chapter 1 by adding Code Sec. 814. **Effective** for tax years beginning after 12-31-83. However, for transitional and special rules, see Act Sec. 216(a)-(b)(2) under the amendment notes for Code Sec. 801. For a special rule relating to Code Sec. 814, see Act Sec. 217(a), below.

P.L. 98-369, §217(a), provides:

Sec. 217. OTHER SPECIAL RULES.

(a) New Section 814 Treated as Continuation of Section 819A.—For purposes of section 814 of the Internal Revenue Code of 1954 (relating to contiguous country branches of domestic life insurance companies)—

(1) any election under section 819A of such Code (as in effect on the day before the date of the enactment of this Act) shall be treated as an election under such section 814, and

(2) any reference to a provision of such section 814 shall be treated as including a reference to the corresponding provision of such section 819A.

[Sec. 815]

SEC. 815. DISTRIBUTIONS TO SHAREHOLDERS FROM PRE-1984 POLICYHOLDERS SURPLUS ACCOUNT.

[Sec. 815(a)]

(a) GENERAL RULE.—In the case of a stock life insurance company which has an existing policyholders surplus account, the tax imposed by section 801 for any taxable year shall be the amount which would be imposed by such section for such year on the sum of—

(1) life insurance company taxable income for such year (but not less than zero), plus

(2) the amount of direct and indirect distributions during such year to shareholders from such account.

For purposes of the preceding sentence, the term "indirect distribution" shall not include any bona fide loan with arms-length terms and conditions.

Amendments

• 1986, Tax Reform Act of 1986 (P.L. 99-514)

P.L. 99-514, §1821(k)(2):

Amended Code Sec. 815(a) by adding at the end thereof a new sentence. **Effective** as if included in the provision of P.L. 98-369 to which it relates. However, for a special rule, see Act Sec. 1821(k)(3), below.

P.L. 99-514, §1821(k)(3), provides:

(3) In the case of any loan made before March 1, 1986 (other than a loan which is renegotiated, extended, renewed, or revised after February 28, 1986), which does not meet the requirements of the last sentence of section 815(a) of the Internal Revenue Code of 1954 (as added by paragraph (2)), the amount of the indirect distribution for purposes of such section 815(a) shall be the foregone interest on the loan (determined by using the lowest rate which would have met the arms-length requirements of such sentence for such a loan).

[Sec. 815(b)]

(b) ORDERING RULE.—For purposes of this section, any distribution to shareholders shall be treated as made—

(1) first out of the shareholders surplus account, to the extent thereof,

(2) then out of the policyholders surplus account, to the extent thereof, and

(3) finally, out of other accounts.

[Sec. 815(c)]

(c) SHAREHOLDERS SURPLUS ACCOUNT.—

(1) IN GENERAL.—Each stock life insurance company which has an existing policyholders surplus account shall continue its shareholders surplus account for purposes of this part.

(2) ADDITIONS TO ACCOUNT.—The amount added to the shareholders surplus account for any taxable year beginning after December 31, 1983, shall be the excess of—

(A) the sum of—

(i) the life insurance company's taxable income (but not below zero),

(ii) the small life insurance company deduction provided by section 806, and

(iii) the deductions for dividends received provided by sections 243, 244, and 245 (as modified by section 805(a)(4)) and the amount of interest excluded from gross income under section 103, over

(B) the taxes imposed for the taxable year by section 801 (determined without regard to this section).

If for any taxable year a tax is imposed by section 55, under regulations proper adjustments shall be made for such year and all subsequent taxable years in the amounts taken into account under subparagraphs (A) and (B) of this paragraph and subparagraph (B) of subsection (d)(3).

(3) SUBTRACTIONS FROM ACCOUNT.—There shall be subtracted from the shareholders surplus account for any taxable year the amount which is treated under this section as distributed out of such account.

Amendments

• 1988, Technical and Miscellaneous Revenue Act of 1988 (P.L. 100-647)

P.L. 100-647, §1010(j)(1):

Amended Code Sec. 815(c)(2) by adding at the end thereof a new sentence. **Effective** for tax years beginning after 12-31-86.

• 1986, Tax Reform Act of 1986 (P.L. 99-514)

P.L. 99-514, §1011(b)(10):

Amended Code Sec. 815(c)(2)(A)(ii) by striking out "special deductions" and inserting in lieu thereof "small life insurance company deduction." **Effective** for tax years beginning after 12-31-86.

[Sec. 815(d)]

(d) POLICYHOLDERS SURPLUS ACCOUNT.—

(1) IN GENERAL.—Each stock life insurance company which has an existing policyholders surplus account shall continue such account.

(2) NO ADDITIONS TO ACCOUNT.—No amount shall be added to the policyholders surplus account for any taxable year beginning after December 31, 1983.

(3) SUBTRACTIONS FROM ACCOUNT.—There shall be subtracted from the policyholders surplus account for any taxable year an amount equal to the sum of—

(A) the amount which (without regard to subparagraph (B)) is treated under this section as distributed out of the policyholders surplus account, and

(B) the amount by which the tax imposed for the taxable year by section 801 is increased by reason of this section.

[Sec. 815(e)]

(e) EXISTING POLICYHOLDERS SURPLUS ACCOUNT.—For purposes of this section, the term "existing policyholders surplus account" means any policyholders surplus account which has a balance as of the close of December 31, 1983.

[Sec. 815(f)]

(f) OTHER RULES APPLICABLE TO POLICYHOLDERS SURPLUS ACCOUNT CONTINUED.—Except to the extent inconsistent with the provisions of this part, the provisions of subsections (d), (e), (f), and (g) of section 815 (and of sections 819(b), 6501(c)(6), 6501(k), 6511(d)(6), 6601(d)(3), and 6611(f)(4)) as in effect before the enactment of the Tax Reform Act of 1984 are hereby made applicable in respect of any policyholders surplus account for which there was a balance as of December 31, 1983.

Amendments

• 1986, Tax Reform Act of 1986 (P.L. 99-514)

P.L. 99-514, §1821(k)(1):

Amended Code Sec. 815(f) by striking out "section[s]6501(c)(6)" and inserting in lieu thereof "sections 819(b), 6501(c)(6)". **Effective** as if included in the provision of P.L. 98-369 to which it relates. However, for a special rule, see Act Sec. 1821(k)(3) following Code Sec. 815(a).

• 1984, Deficit Reduction Act of 1984 (P.L. 98-369)

P.L. 98-369, §211(a):

Amended Part I of subchapter L of chapter 1 by adding Code Sec. 815. **Effective** for tax years beginning after 12-31-83. However, for transitional and special rules, see Act Sec. 216(a)-(b)(2) under the amendments for Code Sec. 801.

[Sec. 815(g)]

(g) SPECIAL RULES APPLICABLE DURING 2005 AND 2006.—In the case of any taxable year of a stock life insurance company beginning after December 31, 2004, and before January 1, 2007—

(1) the amount under subsection (a)(2) for such taxable year shall be treated as zero, and

(2) notwithstanding subsection (b), in determining any subtractions from an account under subsections (c)(3) and (d)(3), any distribution to shareholders during such taxable year shall be treated as made first out of the policyholders surplus account, then out of the shareholders surplus account, and finally out of other accounts.

Amendments

• 2004, American Jobs Creation Act of 2004 (P.L. 108-357)

P.L. 108-357, §705(a):

Amended Code Sec. 815 by adding at the end a new subsection (g). **Effective** for tax years beginning after 12-31-2004.

[Sec. 815—Repealed]

Amendments

• 1984, Deficit Reduction Act of 1984 (P.L. 98-369)

P.L. 98-369, §211(a):

Amended Part I of Subchapter L of Chapter 1 by adding a new Part I (Code Secs. 801-818). For transitional and special rules, see Act Sec. 216(a)-(b)(2) in the amendments for Code Sec. 801. Prior to amendment, the table of contents for former subpart D and Code Sec. 815 read as follows:

Subpart D—Distributions to Shareholders

Sec. 815. Distributions to shareholders.

SEC. 815. DISTRIBUTIONS TO SHAREHOLDERS.

[Sec. 815(a)]

(a) GENERAL RULE.—For purposes of this section and section 802(b)(3), any distribution to shareholders after December 31, 1958, shall be treated as made—

(1) first out of the shareholders surplus account, to the extent thereof,

(2) then out of the policyholders surplus account, to the extent thereof, and

(3) finally out of other accounts.

Amendments

• 1964 (P.L. 88-571)

P.L. 88-571, §4(a)(1):

Amended Code Sec. 815(a) by striking out the second and third sentences. **Effective** 1-1-64. Prior to deletion, these sentences read as follows:

"For purposes of this section, the term `distribution' includes any distribution in redemption of stock or in partial or complete liquidation of the corporation, but does not include any distribution made by the corporation in its stock or in rights to acquire its stock, and does not (except for purposes of paragraph (3) and subsection (e)(2)(B)) include any distribution in redemption of stock issued before 1958 which at all times on and after the date of issuance and on and before the date of redemption is limited as to dividends and is callable, at the option of the issuer, at a price not in excess of 105 percent of the sum of the issue price and the amount of any contribution to surplus made by the original purchaser at the time of his purchase. Further, for purposes of this section, the term `distribution' does not include any distribution before January 1, 1964, of the stock of a controlled corporation to which section 355 applies, if such controlled corporation is an insurance company subject to the tax imposed by section 831 and control has been acquired prior to January 1, 1963, in a transaction qualifying as a reorganization under section 368(a)(1)(B)."

• 1962 (P.L. 87-858)

P.L. 87-858, §3(e):

Amended Code Sec. 815(a) by adding the last sentence. **Effective** 1-1-62.

[Sec. 815(b)]

(b) SHAREHOLDERS SURPLUS ACCOUNT.—

(1) IN GENERAL.—Each stock life insurance company shall, for purposes of this part, establish and maintain a shareholders surplus account. The amount in such account on January 1, 1958, shall be zero.

(2) ADDITIONS TO ACCOUNT.—The amount added to the shareholders surplus account for any taxable year beginning after December 31, 1957, shall be the amount by which—

(A) the sum of—

(i) the life insurance company taxable income (computed without regard to section 802(b)(3)),

(ii) in the case of a taxable year beginning after December 31, 1958, the amount (if any) of the net capital gain, reduced (in the case of a taxable year beginning after December 31, 1961) by the amount referred to in clause (i),

(iii) the deductions for dividends received provided by sections 243, 244, and 245 (as modified by section 809(d)(8)(B)) and the amount of interest excluded from gross income under section 103, and

(iv) the small business deduction provided by section 809(d)(10), exceeds

(B) the taxes imposed for the taxable year by section 802(a), determined without regard to section 802(b)(3).

(3) SUBTRACTIONS FROM ACCOUNT.—

(A) IN GENERAL.—There shall be subtracted from the shareholders surplus account for any taxable year the amount which is treated under this section as distributed out of such account.

(B) DISTRIBUTIONS IN 1958.—There shall be subtracted from the shareholders surplus account (to the extent thereof) for any taxable year beginning in 1958 the amount of distributions to shareholders made during 1958.

Amendments

• 1976, Tax Reform Act of 1976 (P.L. 94-455)

P.L. 94-455, §1901(b)(1)(O):

Struck out "the deduction for partially tax-exempt interest provided by section 242 (as modified by section 804(a)(3))," and struck out the comma after "809(d)(8)(B))" in clause (iii). **Effective** for tax years beginning after 12-31-76.

P.L. 94-455, §1901(b)(33)(H):

Substituted "of the net capital gain" for "by which the net long-term capital gain exceeds the net short-term capital loss" in clause (ii). **Effective** for tax years beginning after 12-31-76.

• 1964 (P.L. 88-571)

P.L. 88-571, §2:

Amended Code Sec. 815(b)(2)(A)(ii) by inserting the following at the end thereof: "reduced (in the case of a taxable year beginning after December 31, 1961) by the amount referred to in clause (i),". **Effective** 9-2-64.

[Sec. 815(c)]

(c) POLICYHOLDERS SURPLUS ACCOUNT.—

(1) IN GENERAL.—Each stock life insurance company shall, for purposes of this part, establish and maintain a policyholders surplus account. The amount in such account on January 1, 1959, shall be zero.

(2) ADDITIONS TO ACCOUNT.—The amount added to the policyholders surplus account for any taxable year beginning after December 31, 1958, shall be the sum of—

(A) an amount equal to 50 percent of the amount by which the gain from operations exceeds the taxable investment income,

(B) the deduction for certain nonparticipating contracts provided by section 809(d)(5) (as limited by section 809(f)), and

(C) the deduction for accident and health insurance and group life insurance contracts provided by section 809(d)(6) (as limited by section 809(f)).

(3) SUBTRACTIONS FROM ACCOUNT.—There shall be subtracted from the policyholders surplus account for any taxable year an amount equal to the sum of—

(A) the amount which (without regard to subparagraph (B)) is treated under this section as distributed out of the policyholders surplus account, and

(B) the amount by which the tax imposed for the taxable year by section 802(a) is increased by reason of section 802(b)(3).

Amendments

• 1976, Tax Reform Act of 1976 (P.L. 94-455)

P.L. 94-455, §1901(b)(24):

Struck out "(determined without regard to section 802(a)(3))" after "the amount" in Code Sec. 815(c)(3)(B). **Effective** for tax years beginning after 12-31-76.

• 1962 (P.L. 87-858)

P.L. 87-858, §3(b)(4):

Amended Code Sec. 815(c)(3)(B) by substituting "802(a)" for "802(a)(1)." **Effective** 1-1-62.

• 1962 (P.L. 87-790)

P.L. 87-790, §3(b):

Amended Code Sec. 815(c)(2)(C) by striking out "group life and group accident and health insurance contracts" and inserting in lieu thereof "accident and health insurance and group life insurance contracts." **Effective** 1-1-63.

[Sec. 815(d)]

(d) SPECIAL RULES.—

(1) ELECTION TO TRANSFER AMOUNTS FROM POLICYHOLDERS SURPLUS ACCOUNT TO SHAREHOLDERS SURPLUS ACCOUNT.—

(A) IN GENERAL.—A taxpayer may elect for any taxable year for which it is a life insurance company to subtract from its policyholders surplus account any amount in such account as of the close of such taxable year. The amount so subtracted, less the amount of the tax imposed with respect to such amount by reason of section 802(b)(3), shall be added to the shareholders surplus account as of the beginning of the succeeding taxable year.

(B) MANNER AND EFFECT OF ELECTION.—The election provided by subparagraph (A) shall be made (in such manner and in such form as the Secretary may by regulations prescribe) after the close of the taxable year and not later than the time prescribed by law for filing the return (including extensions thereof) for the taxable year. Such an election, once made, may not be revoked.

(2) TERMINATION AS LIFE INSURANCE COMPANY.—

(A) EFFECT OF TERMINATION.—Except as provided in section 381(c)(22) (relating to carryovers in certain corporate readjustments), if—

(i) for any taxable year the taxpayer is not an insurance company, or

(ii) for any two successive taxable years the taxpayer is not a life insurance company,

then the amount taken into account under section 802(b)(3) for the last preceding taxable year for which it was a life insurance company shall be increased (after the application of subparagraph (B)) by the amount remaining in its policyholders surplus account at the close of such last preceding taxable year.

(B) EFFECT OF CERTAIN DISTRIBUTIONS.—If for any taxable year the taxpayer is an insurance company but not a life insurance company, then any distribution to shareholders during such taxable year shall be treated as made on the last day of the last preceding taxable year for which the taxpayer was a life insurance company.

(3) TREATMENT OF CERTAIN INDEBTEDNESS.—If—

(A) the taxpayer makes any payment in discharge of its indebtedness, and

(B) such indebtedness is attributable to a distribution by the taxpayer to its shareholders after February 9, 1959,

then the amount of such payment shall, for purposes of this section and section 802(b)(3), be treated as a distribution in cash to shareholders, but only to the extent that the distribution referred to in subparagraph (B) was treated as made out of accounts other than the shareholders and policyholders surplus accounts.

(4) LIMITATION ON AMOUNT IN POLICYHOLDERS SURPLUS ACCOUNT.—There shall be treated as a subtraction from the policyholders surplus account for a taxable year for which the taxpayer is a life insurance company the amount by which the policyholders surplus account (computed at the end of the taxable year without regard to this paragraph) exceeds whichever of the following is the greatest—

(A) 15 percent of life insurance reserves at the end of the taxable year,

(B) 25 percent of the amount by which the life insurance reserves at the end of the taxable year exceed the life insurance reserves at the end of 1958, or

(C) 50 percent of the net amount of the premiums and other consideration taken into account for the taxable year under section 809(c)(1).

The amount so treated as subtracted, less the amount of the tax imposed with respect to such amount by reason of section 802(b)(3), shall be added to the shareholders surplus account as of the beginning of the succeeding taxable year.

(5) REDUCTION OF POLICYHOLDERS SURPLUS ACCOUNT FOR CERTAIN UNUSED DEDUCTIONS.—If—

(A) an amount added to the policyholders surplus account for any taxable year increased (or created) a loss from operations for such year, and

(B) any portion of the increase (or amount created) in the loss from operations referred to in subparagraph (A) did not reduce the life insurance company taxable income for any taxable year to which such loss was carried,

the policyholders surplus account for the taxable year referred to in subparagraph (A) shall be reduced by the amount described in subparagraph (B).

(6) RESTORATION OF AMOUNTS DISTRIBUTED OUT OF POLICYHOLDERS SURPLUS ACCOUNT.—Notwithstanding any other provision of this subchapter, no amount shall be subtracted from a taxpayer's policyholders surplus account with respect to a distribution made during the last month of the taxable year which, without regard to this paragraph, would be treated in whole or in part as a distribution out of the policyholders surplus account, to the extent that amounts so distributed are returned to the taxpayer no later than the time prescribed by law (including extensions thereof) for filing the taxpayer's return for the taxable year in which the distribution was made. For purposes of this paragraph, amounts returned to a taxpayer with respect to a distribution shall be first applied to the return of amounts which, without regard to this paragraph, would have been treated as distributed out of the policyholders surplus account. This paragraph shall not apply if, at the time such distribution was made, the taxpayer intended to avail itself of the provisions of this paragraph by having its shareholders return all or a part of such distribution. Nothing in this paragraph shall affect the tax treatment of the receipt of the distribution by any shareholder, and the basis to a shareholder of his stock in the taxpayer shall not be increased by reason of amounts returned under this paragraph to the extent that a dividends received deduction or exclusion was allowable in respect of the distribution of such amount under any provision of this title.

Amendments

• 1976 (P.L. 94-331)

P.L. 94-331, §1:

Amended Code Sec. 815(d) by adding paragraph (6). **Effective** for tax years ending after 12-31-75.

• 1964 (P.L. 88-571)

P.L. 88-571, §3(a):

Amended Code Sec. 815(d) by adding paragraph (5). **Effective** with respect to amounts added to policyholders surplus accounts for tax years beginning after 12-31-58.

[Sec. 815(e)]

(e) SPECIAL RULE FOR CERTAIN MUTUALIZATIONS.—

(1) IN GENERAL.—For purposes of this section and section 802(b)(3), any distribution to shareholders after December 31, 1958, in acquisition of stock pursuant to a plan of mutualization shall be treated—

(A) first, as made out of paid-in capital and paid-in surplus, to the extent thereof,

(B) thereafter, as made in two allocable parts—

(i) one part of which is made out of the other accounts referred to in subsection (a)(3), and

(ii) the remainder of which is a distribution to which subsection (a) applies.

(2) SPECIAL RULES.—

(A) ALLOCATION RATIO.—The part referred to in paragraph (1)(B)(i) is the amount which bears the same ratio to the amount to which paragraph (1)(B) applies as—

(i) the excess (determined as of December 31, 1958, and adjusted to the beginning of the year of the distribution as provided in subparagraph (B)) of the assets over the total liabilities, bears to

(ii) the sum (determined as of the beginning of the year of the distribution) of the excess described in clause (i), the amount in the shareholders surplus account, plus the amount in the policyholders surplus account.

(B) ADJUSTMENT FOR CERTAIN DISTRIBUTIONS.—The excess described in subparagraph (A)(i) shall be reduced by the aggregate of the prior distributions which have been treated under subsection (a)(3) as made out of accounts other than the shareholders surplus account and the policyholders surplus account.

Amendments

• 1959, Life Insurance Company Income Tax Act of 1959 (P.L. 86-69)

P.L. 86-69, §2:

Revised Part I of subchapter L of chapter 1 of the 1954 Code. **Effective**, generally, for tax years beginning after 1957. Prior text not reproduced.

[Sec. 815(f)]

(f) DISTRIBUTION DEFINED.—For purposes of this section, the term "distribution" includes any distribution in redemption of stock or in partial or complete liquidation of the corporation, but does not include—

(1) any distribution made by the corporation in its stock or in rights to acquire its stock;

(2) except for purposes of subsection (a)(3) and subsection (e)(2)(B), any distribution in redemption of stock issued before 1958 which at all times on and after the date of issuance and on and before the date of redemption is limited as to dividends and is callable, at the option of the issuer, at a price not in excess of 105 percent of the sum of the issue price and the amount of any contribution to surplus made by the original purchaser at the time of his purchase;

(3) any distribution after December 31, 1963, of the stock of a controlled corporation to which section 355 applies, if such controlled corporation is an insurance company subject to the tax imposed by section 831 and if—

(A) control was acquired prior to January 1, 1958, or

(B) control has been acquired after December 31, 1957—

(i) in a transaction qualifying as a reorganization under section 368(a)(1)(B), if the distributing corporation has at all times since December 31, 1957, owned stock representing not less than 50 percent of the total combined voting power of all classes of stock entitled to vote, and not less than 50 percent of the value of all classes of stock, of the controlled corporation, or

(ii) solely in exchange for stock of the distributing corporation which stock is immediately exchanged by the controlled corporation in a transaction qualifying as a reorganization under section 368(a)(1)(A) or (C), if the controlled corporation has at all times since its organization been wholly owned by the distributing corporation and the distributing corporation has at all times since December 31, 1957, owned stock representing not less than 50 percent of the total combined voting power of all classes of stock entitled to vote, and not less than 50 percent of the value of all classes of stock, of the corporation the assets of which have been transferred to the controlled corporation in section 368(a)(1)(A) or (C) reorganization;

(4) any distribution after December 31, 1966, of the stock of a controlled corporation to which section 355 applies, if such distribution is made to a corporation which immediately after the distribution is in control (within the meaning of section 368(c)) of both the distributing corporation and such controlled corporation and if such controlled corporation is a life insurance company of which the distributing corporation has been in control at all times since December 31, 1957; or

(5) any distribution after December 31, 1968, of the stock of a controlled corporation to which section 355 applies, if such distribution is made to a corporation which immediately after the distribution is the owner of all of the stock of all classes of both the distributing corporation and such controlled corporation and if, immediately before the distribution, the distributing corporation had been the owner of all of the stock of all classes of such controlled corporation at all times since December 31, 1957.

Paragraphs (3), (4), and (5) shall not apply to that portion of the distribution of stock of the controlled corporation equal to the increase in the aggregate adjusted basis of such stock after December 31, 1957, except to the extent such increase results from an acquisition of stock in the controlled corporation in a transaction described in paragraph (3)(B). If any part of the increase in the aggregate adjusted basis of stock of the controlled corporation after December 31, 1957, results from the transfer (other than as part of a transaction described in paragraph (3)(B)) by the distributing corporation to the controlled corporation of property which has a fair market value in excess of its adjusted basis at the time of the transfer, paragraphs (3), (4), and (5) also shall not apply to that portion of the distribution equal to such excess.

Amendments

• 1969, Tax Reform Act of 1969 (P.L. 91-172)

P.L. 91-172, §907(b)(1):

Amended Code Sec. 815(f) by deleting "or" from the end of paragraph (3), by deleting the period from the end of paragraph (4) and adding therefor ";or", by adding a new paragraph (5), by changing "Neither paragraph (3) nor paragraph (4) shall apply" in the next to the last sentence to "Paragraphs (3), (4), and (5) shall not apply" and by changing "paragraphs (3) and (4)" in the last sentence to "paragraphs (3), (4), and (5)". **Effective** for tax years beginning after 12-31-68.

• 1967 (P.L. 90-225)

P.L. 90-225, §4(a):

Amended Code Sec. 815(f) by striking out "or" at the end of paragraph (2), by striking out the period at the end of paragraph (3) and inserting in lieu thereof "; or", and by inserting paragraph (4). **Effective** for tax years beginning after 12-31-66.

P.L. 90-225, §4(b):

Amended the next to last sentence of Code Sec. 815(f) by striking out "Paragraph (3) shall not" and inserting in lieu thereof "Neither paragraph (3) nor paragraph (4) shall", and by striking out "subparagraph (B) of such paragraph" and inserting in lieu thereof "paragraph (3)(B)". Also amended the last sentence of Code Sec. 815(f) by striking out "paragraph (3) also" and inserting in lieu thereof "paragraphs (3) and (4) also". **Effective** for tax years beginning after 12-31-66.

• 1964 (P.L. 88-571)

P.L. 88-571, §4(a)(2):

Amended Code Sec. 815 by adding subsection (f). **Effective** 1-1-64.

[Sec. 815(g)]

(g) CERTAIN DISTRIBUTIONS RELATED TO FORMER SUBSIDIARIES.—If subsection (f)(5) applied to the distribution by a life insurance company of the stock of a corporation which was a controlled corporation—

(1) any distribution by such corporation to its shareholders (after the date of the distribution of its stock by the life insurance company), and

(2) any disposition of the stock of such corporation by the distributee corporation,

shall, for purposes of this section, be treated as a distribution to its shareholders by such life insurance company, until the amounts so treated equal the amount of the distribution of such stock which by reason of subsection (f)(5) was not included as a distribution for purposes of this section.

Amendments

• 1969, Tax Reform Act of 1969 (P.L. 91-172)

P.L. 91-172, §907(b)(2):

Amended Code Sec. 815 by adding subsection (g). **Effective** for tax years beginning after 12-31-68.

Subpart E—Definitions and Special Rules

[Sec. 816]

SEC. 816. LIFE INSURANCE COMPANY DEFINED.

[Sec. 816(a)]

(a) LIFE INSURANCE COMPANY DEFINED.—For purposes of this subtitle, the term "life insurance company" means an insurance company which is engaged in the business of issuing life insurance and annuity contracts (either separately or combined with accident and health insurance), or noncancellable contracts of health and accident insurance, if—

(1) its life insurance reserves (as defined in subsection (b)), plus

(2) unearned premiums, and unpaid losses (whether or not ascertained), on noncancellable life, accident, or health policies not included in life insurance reserves,

comprise more than 50 percent of its total reserves (as defined in subsection (c)). For purposes of the preceding sentence, the term "insurance company" means any company more than half of the business of which during the taxable year is the issuing of insurance or annuity contracts or the reinsuring of risks underwritten by insurance companies.

[Sec. 816(b)]

(b) LIFE INSURANCE RESERVES DEFINED.—

(1) IN GENERAL.—For purposes of this part, the term "life insurance reserves" means amounts—

(A) which are computed or estimated on the basis of recognized mortality or morbidity tables and assumed rates of interest, and

(B) which are set aside to mature or liquidate, either by payment or reinsurance, future unaccrued claims arising from life insurance, annuity, and noncancellable accident and health insurance contracts (including life insurance or annuity contracts combined with noncancellable accident and health insurance) involving, at the time with respect to which the reserve is computed, life, accident, or health contingencies.

(2) RESERVES MUST BE REQUIRED BY LAW.—Except—

(A) in the case of policies covering life, accident, and health insurance combined in one policy issued on the weekly premium payment plan, continuing for life and not subject to cancellation, and

(B) as provided in paragraph (3),

in addition to the requirements set forth in paragraph (1), life insurance reserves must be required by law.

(3) ASSESSMENT COMPANIES.—In the case of an assessment life insurance company or association, the term "life insurance reserves" includes—

(A) sums actually deposited by such company or association with State officers pursuant to law as guaranty or reserve funds, and

(B) any funds maintained, under the charter or articles of incorporation or association (or bylaws approved by a State insurance commissioner) of such company or association, exclusively for the payment of claims arising under certificates of membership or policies issued on the assessment plan and not subject to any other use.

(4) AMOUNT OF RESERVES.—For purposes of this subsection, subsection (a), and subsection (c), the amount of any reserve (or portion thereof) for any taxable year shall be the mean of such reserve (or portion thereof) at the beginning and end of the taxable year.

[Sec. 816(c)]

(c) TOTAL RESERVES DEFINED.—For purposes of subsection (a), the term "total reserves" means—

(1) life insurance reserves,

(2) unearned premiums, and unpaid losses (whether or not ascertained), not included in life insurance reserves, and

(3) all other insurance reserves required by law.

[Sec. 816(d)]

(d) ADJUSTMENTS IN RESERVES FOR POLICY LOANS.—For purposes only of determining under subsection (a) whether or not an insurance company is a life insurance company, the life insurance reserves, and the total reserves, shall each be reduced by an amount equal to the mean of the aggregates, at the beginning and end of the taxable year, of the policy loans outstanding with respect to contracts for which life insurance reserves are maintained.

[Sec. 816(e)]

(e) GUARANTEED RENEWABLE CONTRACTS.—For purposes of this part, guaranteed renewable life, accident, and health insurance shall be treated in the same manner as noncancellable life, accident, and health insurance.

[Sec. 816(f)]

(f) AMOUNTS NOT INVOLVING LIFE, ACCIDENT, OR HEALTH CONTINGENCIES.—For purposes only of determining under subsection (a) whether or not an insurance company is a life insurance company, amounts set aside and held at interest to satisfy obligations under contracts which do not contain permanent guarantees with respect to life, accident, or health contingencies shall not be included in reserves described in paragraph (1) or (3) of subsection (c).

[Sec. 816(g)]

(g) BURIAL AND FUNERAL BENEFIT INSURANCE COMPANIES.—A burial or funeral benefit insurance company engaged directly in the manufacture of funeral supplies or the performance of funeral services shall not be taxable under this part but shall be taxable under section 831.

Amendments

• 1988, Technical and Miscellaneous Revenue Act of 1988 (P.L. 100-647)

P.L. 100-647, §1010(f)(6):

Amended Code Sec. 816(g) by striking out "section 821 or" before "section 831". **Effective** as if included in the provision of P.L. 99-514 to which it relates.

• 1984, Deficit Reduction Act of 1984 (P.L. 98-369)

P.L. 98-369, §211(a):

Amended Part I of subchapter L of chapter 1 by adding Code Sec. 816. **Effective** for tax years beginning after 12-31-83. However, for transitional and special rules, see Act Sec. 216(a)-(b)(2) under the amendment notes for Code Sec. 801 and Act Sec. 217(i), below.

P.L. 98-369, §217(i), as amended by P.L. 100-647, §1010(h)(1), provides:

(i) Special Election to Treat Individual Noncancellable Accident and Health Contracts as Cancellable.—

(1) In General.—A mutual life insurance company may elect to treat all individual noncancellable (or guaranteed renewable) accident and health insurance contracts as though they were cancellable for purposes of section 816 of subchapter L of chapter 1 of the Internal Revenue Code of 1954.

(2) Effect of Election on Subsidiaries of Electing Parent.—For purposes of determining the amount of the small life insurance company deduction of any controlled group which includes a mutual company which made an election under paragraph (1), the taxable income of such electing company shall be taken into account under section 806(b)(2) of the Internal Revenue Code of 1954 (relating to phaseout of small life insurance company deduction).

(3) Election.—An election under paragraph (1) shall apply to the company's first taxable year beginning after December 31, 1983, and all taxable years thereafter.

(4) Time and Manner.—An election under paragraph (1) shall be made—

(A) on the return of the taxpayer for its first taxable year beginning after December 31, 1983, and

(B) in such manner as the Secretary of the Treasury or his delegate may prescribe.

[Sec. 816(h)]

(h) TREATMENT OF DEFICIENCY RESERVES.—For purposes of this section and section 842(b)(2)(B)(i), the terms "life insurance reserves" and "total reserves" shall not include deficiency reserves.

Amendments

• 1988, Technical and Miscellaneous Revenue Act of 1988 (P.L. 100-647)

P.L. 100-647, §2004(q)(1):

Amended Code Sec. 816(h) by striking out "section 842(c)(1)(A)" and inserting in lieu thereof "section 842(b)(2)(B)(i)". **Effective** as if included in the provision of P.L. 100-203 to which it relates.

• 1987, Revenue Act of 1987 (P.L. 100-203)

P.L. 100-203, §10242(c)(2):

Amended Code Sec. 816(h) by striking out "section 813(a)(4)(B)" and inserting in lieu thereof "section 842(c)(1)(A)". **Effective** for tax years beginning after 12-31-87.

• 1986, Tax Reform Act of 1986 (P.L. 99-514)

P.L. 99-514, §1821(l):

Amended Code Sec. 816 by adding at the end thereof new subsection (h). **Effective** as if included in the provision of P.L. 98-369 to which it relates.

[Sec. 817]

SEC. 817. TREATMENT OF VARIABLE CONTRACTS.

[Sec. 817(a)]

(a) INCREASES AND DECREASES IN RESERVES.—For purposes of subsections (a) and (b) of section 807, the sum of the items described in section 807(c) taken into account as of the close of the taxable year with respect to any variable contract shall, under regulations prescribed by the Secretary, be adjusted—

(1) by subtracting therefrom an amount equal to the sum of the amounts added from time to time (for the taxable year) to the reserves separately accounted for in accordance with subsection (c) by reason of appreciation in value of assets (whether or not the assets have been disposed of), and

(2) by adding thereto an amount equal to the sum of the amounts subtracted from time to time (for the taxable year) from such reserves by reason of depreciation in value of assets (whether or not the assets have been disposed of).

The deduction allowable for items described in paragraphs (1) and (6) of section 805(a) with respect to variable contracts shall be reduced to the extent that the amount of such items is increased for the taxable year by appreciation (or increased to the extent that the amount of such items is decreased for the taxable year by depreciation) not reflected in adjustments under the preceding sentence.

[Sec. 817(b)]

(b) ADJUSTMENT TO BASIS OF ASSETS HELD IN SEGREGATED ASSET ACCOUNT.—In the case of variable contracts, the basis of each asset in a segregated asset account shall (in addition to all other adjustments to basis) be—

(1) increased by the amount of any appreciation in value, and

(2) decreased by the amount of any depreciation in value,

to the extent such appreciation and depreciation are from time to time reflected in the increases and decreases in reserves or other items referred to in subsection (a) with respect to such contracts.

[Sec. 817(c)]

(c) SEPARATE ACCOUNTING.—For purposes of this part, a life insurance company which issues variable contracts shall separately account for the various income, exclusion, deduction, asset, reserve, and other liability items properly attributable to such variable contracts. For such items as are not accounted for directly, separate accounting shall be made—

(1) in accordance with the method regularly employed by such company, if such method is reasonable, and

(2) in all other cases, in accordance with regulations prescribed by the Secretary.

Amendments

• 2004, Pension Funding Equity Act of 2004 (P.L. 108-218)

P.L. 108-218, § 205(b)(5):

Amended Code Sec. 817(c) by striking "(other than section 809)" following "For purposes of this part". **Effective** for tax years beginning after 12-31-2004.

[Sec. 817(d)]

(d) VARIABLE CONTRACT DEFINED.—For purposes of this part, the term "variable contract" means a contract—

(1) which provides for the allocation of all or part of the amounts received under the contract to an account which, pursuant to State law or regulation, is segregated from the general asset accounts of the company,

(2) which—

(A) provides for the payment of annuities,

(B) is a life insurance contract, or

(C) provides for funding of insurance on retired lives as described in section 807(c)(6), and

(3) under which—

(A) in the case of an annuity contract, the amounts paid in, or the amount paid out, reflect the investment return and the market value of the segregated asset account,

(B) in the case of a life insurance contract, the amount of the death benefit (or the period of coverage) is adjusted on the basis of the investment return and the market value of the segregated asset account, or

(C) in the case of funds held under a contract described in paragraph (2)(C), the amounts paid in, or the amounts paid out, reflect the investment return and the market value of the segregated asset account.

If a contract ceases to reflect current investment return and current market value, such contract shall not be considered as meeting the requirements of paragraph (3) after such cessation. Paragraph (3) shall be applied without regard to whether there is a guarantee, and obligations under such guarantee which exceed obligations under the contract without regard to such guarantee shall be accounted for as part of the company's general account.

Amendments

• 1996, Small Business Job Protection Act of 1996 (P.L. 104-188)

P.L. 104-188, § 1611(a)(1):

Amended Code Sec. 817(d)(2) by striking "or" at the end of subparagraph (A), striking "and" at the end of subparagraph (B) and inserting "or", and inserting after subparagraph (B) a new subparagraph (C). **Effective** for tax years beginning after 12-31-95.

P.L. 104-188, § 1611(a)(2):

Amended Code Sec. 817(d)(3) by striking "or" at the end of subparagraph (A), striking the period at the end of subparagraph (B) and inserting ", or", and inserting a new subparagraph (C). **Effective** for tax years beginning after 12-31-95.

• 1986, Tax Reform Act of 1986 (P.L. 99-514)

P.L. 99-514, § 1821(t)(1):

Amended Code Sec. 817(d) by adding at the end thereof a new sentence. **Effective** for contracts issued after 12-31-86, and to contracts issued before 1-1-87, if such contract was treated as a variable contract on the taxpayer's return.

[Sec. 817(e)]

(e) PENSION PLAN CONTRACTS TREATED AS PAYING ANNUITY.—A pension plan contract which is not a life, accident, or health, property, casualty, or liability insurance contract shall be treated as a contract which provides for the payments of annuities for purposes of subsection (d).

[Sec. 817(f)]

(f) OTHER SPECIAL RULES.—

(1) LIFE INSURANCE RESERVES.—For purposes of subsection (b)(1)(A) of section 816, the reflection of the investment return and the market value of the segregated asset account shall be considered an assumed rate of interest.

(2) ADDITIONAL SEPARATE COMPUTATIONS.—Under regulations prescribed by the Secretary, such additional separate computations shall be made, with respect to the items separately accounted for in accordance with subsection (c), as may be necessary to carry out the purposes of this section and this part.

[Sec. 817(g)]

(g) VARIABLE ANNUITY CONTRACTS TREATED AS ANNUITY CONTRACTS.—For purposes of this part, the term "annuity contract" includes a contract which provides for the payment of a variable annuity computed on the basis of—

(1) recognized mortality tables, and

(2)(A) the investment experience of a segregated asset account, or

(B) the company-wide investment experience of the company.

Paragraph (2)(B) shall not apply to any company which issues contracts which are not variable contracts.

[Sec. 817(h)]

(h) TREATMENT OF CERTAIN NONDIVERSIFIED CONTRACTS.—

(1) IN GENERAL.—For purposes of subchapter L, section 72 (relating to annuities), and section 7702(a) (relating to definition of life insurance contract), a variable contract (other than a pension plan contract) which is otherwise described in this section and which is based on a segregated asset account shall not be treated as an annuity, endowment, or life insurance contract for any period (and any subsequent period) for which the investments made by such account are not, in accordance with regulations prescribed by the Secretary, adequately diversified.

(2) SAFE HARBOR FOR DIVERSIFICATION.—A segregated asset account shall be treated as meeting the requirements of paragraph (1) for any quarter of a taxable year if as of the close of such quarter—

(A) it meets the requirements of section 851(b)(3), and

(B) no more than 55 percent of the value of the total assets of the account are assets described in section 851(b)(3)(A)(i).

(3) SPECIAL RULE FOR INVESTMENTS IN UNITED STATES OBLIGATIONS.—To the extent that any segregated asset account with respect to a variable life insurance contract is invested in securities issued by the United States Treasury, the investments made by such accounts shall be treated as adequately diversified for purposes of paragraph (1).

(4) LOOK-THROUGH IN CERTAIN CASES.—For purposes of this subsection, if all of the beneficial interests in a regulated investment company or in a trust are held by 1 or more—

(A) insurance companies (or affiliated companies) in their general account or in segregated asset accounts, or

(B) fund managers (or affiliated companies) in connection with the creation or management of the regulated investment company or trust,

the diversification requirements of paragraph (1) shall be applied by taking into account the assets held by such regulated investment company or trust.

(5) INDEPENDENT INVESTMENT ADVISORS PERMITTED.—Nothing in this subsection shall be construed as prohibiting the use of independent investment advisors.

(6) GOVERNMENT SECURITIES FUNDS.—In determining whether a segregated asset account is adequately diversified for purposes of paragraph (1), each United States Government agency or instrumentality shall be treated as a separate issuer.

Amendments

• 1997, Taxpayer Relief Act of 1997 (P.L. 105-34)

P.L. 105-34, §1271(b)(8)(A)-(B):

Amended Code Sec. 817(h)(2) by striking "851(b)(4)" in subparagraph (A) and inserting "851(b)(3)", and by striking "851(b)(4)(A)(i)" in subparagraph (B) and inserting "851(b)(3)(A)(i)". **Effective** for tax years beginning after 8-5-97.

• 1988, Technical and Miscellaneous Revenue Act of 1988 (P.L. 100-647)

P.L. 100-647, §6080(a):

Amended Code Sec. 817(h) by adding at the end thereof new paragraph (6). **Effective** for tax years beginning after 12-31-87.

• 1986, Tax Reform Act of 1986 (P.L. 99-514)

P.L. 99-514, §1821(m)(1):

Amended Code Sec. 817(h) by striking out paragraphs (3) and (4) and inserting in lieu thereof new paragraphs (3), (4), and (5). **Effective** as if included in the provision of P.L. 98-369 to which it relates. Prior to amendment, Code Sec. 817(h)(3) and (4) read as follows:

(3) SPECIAL RULE FOR VARIABLE LIFE INSURANCE CONTRACTS INVESTING IN UNITED STATES OBLIGATIONS.—In the case of a segregated asset account with respect to variable life insurance contracts, paragraph (1) shall not apply in the case of securities issued by the United States Treasury which are owned by a regulated investment company or by a trust all the beneficial interests in which are held by 1 or more

segregated asset accounts of the company issuing the contract.

(4) INDEPENDENT INVESTMENT ADVISORS PERMITTED.—Nothing in this subsection shall be construed as prohibiting the use of independent investment advisors.

P.L. 99-514, §1821(m)(2):

Amended Code Sec. 817(h)(1) by striking out the last sentence. **Effective** as if included in the provision of P.L. 98-369 to which it relates. Prior to amendment, the last sentence read as follows:

For purposes of this paragraph and paragraph (2), beneficial interests in a regulated investment company or in a trust shall not be treated as 1 investment if all of the beneficial interests in such company or trust are held by 1 or more segregated asset accounts of 1 or more insurance companies.

• 1984, Deficit Reduction Act of 1984 (P.L. 98-369)

P.L. 98-369, §211(a):

Amended Part I of subchapter L of chapter 1 by adding Code Sec. 817. **Effective** for tax years beginning after 12-31-83. However, for transitional and special rules, see Act Sec. 216(a)-(b)(2) under the amendments for Code Sec. 801.

[Sec. 817—Repealed]

Amendments

P.L. 98-369, §211(a):

Amended Part I of Subchapter L of Chapter 1 by adding a new Part I (Code Secs. 801-818). The table of contents for former subpart E and Code Sec. 817, as in effect prior to amendement by P.L. 98-369, read as follows:

Subpart E—Miscellaneous Provisions

Sec. 817. Rules relating to certain gains and losses.

Sec. 818. Accounting provisions.

Sec. 819. Foreign life insurance companies.

Sec. 819A. Contiguous country branches of domestic life insurance companies.

SEC. 817. RULES RELATING TO CERTAIN GAINS AND LOSSES.

[Sec. 817(a)]

(a) TREATMENT OF CAPITAL GAINS AND LOSSES, ETC.—In the case of a life insurance company—

(1) in applying section 1231(a), the term "property used in the trade or business" shall be treated as including only—

(A) property used in carrying on an insurance business, of a character which is subject to the allowance for depreciation provided in section 167, held for more than 1 year, and real property used in carrying on an insurance business, held for more than 1 year, which is not described in section 1231(b)(1)(A), (B), or (C), and

(B) property described in section 1231(b)(2), and

(2) in applying section 1221(2), the reference to property used in trade or business shall be treated as including only property used in carrying on an insurance business.

Amendments

• 1976, Tax Reform Act of 1976 (P.L. 94-455)

P.L. 94-455, §1402(b)(1):

Struck out "6 months" and inserted "9 months" each place it appeared in Code Sec. 817(a)(1)(A). **Effective** for tax years beginning in 1977.

P.L. 94-455, §1402(b)(2):

Struck out "9 months" and inserted "1 year" each place it appeared in Code Sec. 817(a)(1)(A). **Effective** for tax years beginning after 12-31-77.

[Sec. 817(b)]

(b) GAIN ON PROPERTY HELD ON DECEMBER 31, 1958 AND CERTAIN SUBSTITUTED PROPERTY ACQUIRED AFTER 1958.—

(1) PROPERTY HELD ON DECEMBER 31, 1958.—In the case of property held by the taxpayer on December 31, 1958, if—

(A) the fair market value of such property on such date exceeds the adjusted basis for determining gain as of such date, and

(B) the taxpayer has been a life insurance company at all times on and after December 31, 1958,

the gain on the sale or other disposition of such property shall be treated as an amount (not less than zero) equal to the amount by which the gain (determined without regard to this subsection) exceeds the difference between the fair market value on December 31, 1958, and the adjusted basis for determining gain as of such date.

(2) CERTAIN PROPERTY ACQUIRED AFTER DECEMBER 31, 1958.—In the case of property acquired after December 31, 1958, and having a substituted basis (within the meaning of section 1016(b))—

(A) for purposes of paragraph (1), such property shall be deemed held continuously by the taxpayer since the beginning of the holding period thereof, determined with reference to section 1223,

(B) the fair market value and adjusted basis referred to in paragraph (1) shall be that of that property for which the holding period taken into account includes December 31, 1958,

(C) paragraph (1) shall apply only if the property or properties the holding periods of which are taken into account were held only by life insurance companies after December 31, 1958, during the holding periods so taken into account,

(D) the difference between the fair market value and adjusted basis referred to in paragraph (1) shall be reduced (not less than zero) by the excess of (i) the gain that would have been recognized but for this subsection on all prior sales or dispositions after December 31, 1958, of properties referred to in subparagraph (C), over (ii) the gain that was recognized on such sales or other dispositions, and

(E) the basis of such property shall be determined as if the gain which would have been recognized but for this subsection were recognized gain.

(3) PROPERTY DEFINED.—For purposes of paragraphs (1) and (2), the term "property" does not include insurance and annuity contracts (and contracts supplementary thereto) and property described in paragraph (1) of section 1221.

[Sec. 817(c)—Repealed]

Amendments

• 1976, Tax Reform Act of 1976 (P.L. 94-455)

P.L. 94-455, §1901(a)(100):

Repealed Code Sec. 817(c). **Effective** for tax years beginning after 12-31-76. Prior to repeal, Code Sec. 817(c) read as follows:

(c) LIMITATION ON CAPITAL LOSS CARRYOVERS.—A net capital loss for any taxable year beginning before January 1, 1959, shall not be taken into account.

[Sec. 817(d)—Repealed]

Amendments

• 1976, Tax Reform Act of 1976 (P.L. 94-455)

P.L. 94-455, §1951(b)(11):

Repealed Code Sec. 817(d). **Effective** for tax years beginning after 12-31-76. Prior to repeal, Code Sec. 817(d) read as follows:

(d) GAIN ON TRANSACTIONS OCCURRING PRIOR TO JANUARY 1, 1959.—For purposes of this part, there shall be excluded any gain from the sale or exchange of a capital asset, and any gain considered as gain from the sale or exchange of a capital asset, resulting from sales or other dispositions of property prior to January 1, 1959. Any gain after December 31, 1958, resulting from the sale or other disposition of property prior to January 1, 1959, which, but for this sentence, would be taken into account under section 1231, shall not be taken into account under section 1231 for purposes of this part.

P.L. 94-455, §1951(b)(11), provides:

(B) SAVINGS PROVISION.—Notwithstanding subparagraph (A), any gain in a taxable year beginning after December 31, 1976, from any sale or other disposition of property prior to January 1, 1959, would be excluded or not taken into account for purposes of part 1 of subchapter L of chapter 1 if subsection (d) of section 817 of such Code were still in effect for such taxable year, such gain shall be excluded for purposes of such part.

[Sec. 817(e)—Repealed]

Amendments

• **1976, Tax Reform Act of 1976 (P.L. 94-455)**

P.L. 94-455, §1901(a)(100):

Repealed Code Sec. 817(e). **Effective** for tax years beginning after 12-31-76. Prior to repeal, Code Sec. 817(e) read as follows:

(e) CERTAIN REINSURANCE TRANSACTIONS IN 1958.—For purposes of this part, the reinsurance in a single transaction, or in a series of related transactions, occurring in 1958, by a life insurance company of all of its insurance contracts of a particular type, through the assumption by another company or companies of all liabilities under such contracts, shall be treated as a sale of a capital asset.

• **1959, Life Insurance Company Income Tax Act of 1959 (P.L. 86-69)**

P.L. 86-69, §2:

Revised Part I of subchapter L of chapter 1 of the 1954 Code. **Effective**, generally, for tax years beginning after 1957. Prior text not reproduced.

[Sec. 817A]

SEC. 817A. SPECIAL RULES FOR MODIFIED GUARANTEED CONTRACTS.

[Sec. 817A(a)]

(a) COMPUTATION OF RESERVES.—In the case of a modified guaranteed contract, clause (ii) of section 807(e)(1)(A) shall not apply.

[Sec. 817A(b)]

(b) SEGREGATED ASSETS UNDER MODIFIED GUARANTEED CONTRACTS MARKED TO MARKET.—

(1) IN GENERAL.—In the case of any life insurance company, for purposes of this subtitle—

(A) Any gain or loss with respect to a segregated asset shall be treated as ordinary income or loss, as the case may be.

(B) If any segregated asset is held by such company as of the close of any taxable year—

(i) such company shall recognize gain or loss as if such asset were sold for its fair market value on the last business day of such taxable year, and

(ii) any such gain or loss shall be taken into account for such taxable year.

Proper adjustment shall be made in the amount of any gain or loss subsequently realized for gain or loss taken into account under the preceding sentence. The Secretary may provide by regulations for the application of this subparagraph at times other than the times provided in this subparagraph.

(2) SEGREGATED ASSET.—For purposes of paragraph (1), the term "segregated asset" means any asset held as part of a segregated account referred to in subsection (d)(1) under a modified guaranteed contract.

[Sec. 817A(c)]

(c) SPECIAL RULE IN COMPUTING LIFE INSURANCE RESERVES.—For purposes of applying section 816(b)(1)(A) to any modified guaranteed contract, an assumed rate of interest shall include a rate of interest determined, from time to time, with reference to a market rate of interest.

[Sec. 817A(d)]

(d) MODIFIED GUARANTEED CONTRACT DEFINED.—For purposes of this section, the term "modified guaranteed contract" means a contract not described in section 817—

(1) all or part of the amounts received under which are allocated to an account which, pursuant to State law or regulation, is segregated from the general asset accounts of the company and is valued from time to time with reference to market values,

(2) which—

(A) provides for the payment of annuities,

(B) is a life insurance contract, or

(C) is a pension plan contract which is not a life, accident, or health, property, casualty, or liability contract,

(3) for which reserves are valued at market for annual statement purposes, and

(4) which provides for a net surrender value or a policyholder's fund (as defined in section 807(e)(1)).

If only a portion of a contract is not described in section 817, such portion shall be treated for purposes of this section as a separate contract.

[Sec. 817A(e)]

(e) REGULATIONS.—The Secretary may prescribe regulations—

(1) to provide for the treatment of market value adjustments under sections 72, 7702, 7702A, and 807(e)(1)(B),

(2) to determine the interest rates applicable under sections 807(c)(3), 807(d)(2)(B), and 812 with respect to a modified guaranteed contract annually, in a manner appropriate for modified guaranteed contracts and, to the extent appropriate for such a contract, to modify or waive the applicability of section 811(d),

(3) to provide rules to limit ordinary gain or loss treatment to assets constituting reserves for modified guaranteed contracts (and not other assets) of the company,

(4) to provide appropriate treatment of transfers of assets to and from the segregated account, and

(5) as may be necessary or appropriate to carry out the purposes of this section.

Amendments

• 1996, Small Business Job Protection Act of 1996 (P.L. 104-188)

P.L. 104-188, §1612(a):

Amended subpart E of part I of subchapter L of chapter 1 by adding a new Code Sec. 817A. For the **effective** date, see Act Sec. 1612(c)(1)-(3), below.

P.L. 104-188, §1612(c)(1)-(3), provides:

(c) EFFECTIVE DATE.—

(1) IN GENERAL.—The amendments made by this section shall apply to taxable years beginning after December 31, 1995.

(2) TREATMENT OF NET ADJUSTMENTS.—Except as provided in paragraph (3), in the case of any taxpayer required by the amendments made by this section to change its calculation of reserves to take into account market value adjustments and to mark segregated assets to market for any taxable year—

(A) such changes shall be treated as a change in method of accounting initiated by the taxpayer,

(B) such changes shall be treated as made with the consent of the Secretary, and

(C) the adjustments required by reason of section 481 of the Internal Revenue Code of 1986, shall be taken into account as ordinary income by the taxpayer for the taxpayer's first taxable year beginning after December 31, 1995.

(3) LIMITATION ON LOSS RECOGNITION AND ON DEDUCTION FOR RESERVE INCREASES.—

(A) LIMITATION ON LOSS RECOGNITION.—

(i) IN GENERAL.—The aggregate loss recognized by reason of the application of section 481 of the Internal Revenue Code of 1986 with respect to section 817A(b) of such Code (as added by this section) for the first taxable year of the taxpayer beginning after December 31, 1995, shall not exceed the amount included in the taxpayer's gross income for such year by reason of the excess (if any) of—

(I) the amount of life insurance reserves as of the close of the prior taxable year, over

(II) the amount of such reserves as of the beginning of such first taxable year,

to the extent such excess is attributable to subsection (a) of such section 817A. Notwithstanding the preceding sentence, the adjusted basis of each segregated asset shall be determined as if all such losses were recognized.

(ii) DISALLOWED LOSS ALLOWED OVER PERIOD.—The amount of the loss which is not allowed under clause (i) shall be allowed ratably over the period of 7 taxable years beginning with the taxpayer's first taxable year beginning after December 31, 1995.

(B) LIMITATION ON DEDUCTION FOR INCREASE IN RESERVES.—

(i) IN GENERAL.—The deduction allowed for the first taxable year of the taxpayer beginning after December 31, 1995, by reason of the application of section 481 of such Code with respect to section 817A(a) of such Code (as added by this section) shall not exceed the aggregate built-in gain recognized by reason of the application of such section 481 with respect to section 817A(b) of such Code (as added by this section) for such first taxable year.

(ii) DISALLOWED DEDUCTION ALLOWED OVER PERIOD.—The amount of the deduction which is disallowed under clause (i) shall be allowed ratably over the period of 7 taxable years beginning with the taxpayer's first taxable year beginning after December 31, 1995.

(iii) BUILT-IN GAIN.—For purposes of this subparagraph, the built-in gain on an asset is the amount equal to the excess of—

(I) the fair market value of the asset as of the beginning of the first taxable year of the taxpayer beginning after December 31, 1995, over

(II) the adjusted basis of such asset as of such time.

[Sec. 818]

SEC. 818. OTHER DEFINITIONS AND SPECIAL RULES.

[Sec. 818(a)]

(a) PENSION PLAN CONTRACTS.—For purposes of this part, the term "pension plan contract" means any contract—

(1) entered into with trusts which (as of the time the contracts were entered into) were deemed to be trusts described in section 401(a) and exempt from tax under section 501(a) (or trusts exempt from tax under section 165 of the Internal Revenue Code of 1939 or the corresponding provisions of prior revenue laws);

(2) entered into under plans which (as of the time the contracts were entered into) were deemed to be plans described in section 403(a), or plans meeting the requirements of paragraphs (3), (4), (5), and (6) of section 165(a) of the Internal Revenue Code of 1939;

(3) provided for employees of the life insurance company under a plan which, for the taxable year, meets the requirements of paragraphs (3), (4), (5), (6), (7), (8), (11), (12), (13), (14), (15), (16), (17), (19), (20), (22), (26), and (27) of section 401(a);

(4) purchased to provide retirement annuities for its employees by an organization which (as of the time the contracts were purchased) was an organization described in section 501(c)(3) which was exempt from tax under section 501(a) (or was an organization exempt from tax under section 101(6) of the Internal Revenue Code of 1939 or the corresponding provisions of prior revenue laws), or purchased to provide retirement annuities for employees described in section 403(b)(1)(A)(ii) by an employer which is a State, a political subdivision of a State, or an agency or instrumentality of any one or more of the foregoing;

(5) entered into with trusts which (at the time the contracts were entered into) were individual retirement accounts described in section 408(a) or under contracts entered into with individual retirement annuities described in section 408(b); or

(6) purchased by—

(A) a governmental plan (within the meaning of section 414(d)) or an eligible deferred compensation plan (within the meaning of section 457(b)), or

(B) the Government of the United States, the government of any State or political subdivision thereof, or by any agency or instrumentality of the foregoing, or any organization (other than a governmental unit) exempt from tax under this subtitle, for use in satisfying an obligation of such government, political subdivision, agency or instrumentality, or organization to provide a benefit under a plan described in subparagraph (A).

Amendments

• 1988, Technical and Miscellaneous Revenue Act of 1988 (P.L. 100-647)

P.L. 100-647, §1011(e)(5)(A)(i)-(iv):

Amended Code Sec. 818(a)(6) by striking out "State" before "eligible" in subparagraph (A), by inserting "or any organization (other than a governmental unit) exempt from tax under this subtitle," after "foregoing," in subparagraph (B), by striking out "or" before "agency" in subparagraph (B), and by inserting ", or organization" after "instrumentality" the second place it appears in subparagraph (B). **Effective** for contracts issued after 12-31-86.

• 1986, Tax Reform Act of 1986 (P.L. 99-514)

P.L. 99-514, §1106(d)(3)(C):

Amended Code Sec. 818(a)(3) by inserting "(17)," after "(16),". **Effective**, generally, for years beginning after 12-31-86. For special rules, see Act Sec. 1106(i)(2)-(6) in the amendments for Code Sec. 401.

P.L. 99-514, §1112(d)(4):

Amended Code Sec. 818(a)(3) by striking out "and (22)" and inserting in lieu thereof "(22), and (26)". **Effective**, generally, for plan years beginning after 12-31-88. However, for special rules, see Act Sec. 1112(e)(2)-(3), in the amendments for Code Sec. 401.

P.L. 99-514, §1136(b):

Amended Code Sec. 818(a)(3), as amended by this Act, by striking out "and (26)" and inserting in lieu thereof "(26), and (27)". **Effective** for years beginning after 12-31-85.

P.L. 99-514, §1821(n):

Amended Code Sec. 818(a)(6)(A). **Effective** as if included in the provision of P.L. 98-369 to which it relates. Prior to amendment, Code Sec. 818(a)(6)(A) read as follows:

(A) a governmental plan (within the meaning of section 414(d)), or

[Sec. 818(b)]

(b) TREATMENT OF CAPITAL GAINS AND LOSSES, ETC.—In the case of a life insurance company—

(1) in applying section 1231(a), the term "property used in the trade or business" shall be treated as including only—

(A) property used in carrying on an insurance business, of a character which is subject to the allowance for depreciation provided in section 167, held for more than 1 year, and real property used in carrying on an insurance business, held for more than 1 year, which is not described in section 1231(b)(1)(A), (B), or (C), and

(B) property described in section 1231(b)(2), and

(2) in applying section 1221(a)(2), the reference to property used in trade or business shall be treated as including only property used in carrying on an insurance business.

Amendments

• 1999, Tax Relief Extension Act of 1999 (P.L. 106-170)

P.L. 106-170, §532(c)(3):

Amended Code Sec. 818(b)(2) by striking "section 1221(2)" and inserting "section 1221(a)(2)". **Effective** for any instrument held, acquired, or entered into, any transaction entered into, and supplies held or acquired on or after 12-17-99.

[Sec. 818(c)]

(c) GAIN ON PROPERTY HELD ON DECEMBER 31, 1958 AND CERTAIN SUBSTITUTED PROPERTY ACQUIRED AFTER 1958.—

(1) PROPERTY HELD ON DECEMBER 31, 1958.—In the case of property held by the taxpayer on December 31, 1958, if—

(A) the fair market value of such property on such date exceeds the adjusted basis for determining gain as of such date, and

(B) the taxpayer has been a life insurance company at all times on and after December 31, 1958,

the gain on the sale or other disposition of such property shall be treated as an amount (not less than zero) equal to the amount by which the gain (determined without regard to this subsection) exceeds the difference between the fair market value on December 31, 1958, and the adjusted basis for determining gain as of such date.

(2) CERTAIN PROPERTY ACQUIRED AFTER DECEMBER 31, 1958.—In the case of property acquired after December 31, 1958, and having a substituted basis (within the meaning of section 1016(b))—

(A) for purposes of paragraph (1), such property shall be deemed held continuously by the taxpayer since the beginning of the holding period thereof, determined with reference to section 1223,

(B) the fair market value and adjusted basis referred to in paragraph (1) shall be that of that property for which the holding period taken into account includes December 31, 1958,

(C) paragraph (1) shall apply only if the property or properties the holding periods of which are taken into account were held only by life insurance companies after December 31, 1958, during the holding periods so taken into account,

(D) the difference between the fair market value and adjusted basis referred to in paragraph (1) shall be reduced (to not less than zero) by the excess of (i) the gain that would have been recognized but for this subsection on all prior sales or dispositions after December 31, 1958, of properties referred to in subparagraph (C), over (ii) the gain which was recognized on such sales or other dispositions, and

(E) the basis of such property shall be determined as if the gain which would have been recognized but for this subsection were recognized gain.

(3) PROPERTY DEFINED.—For purposes of paragraphs (1) and (2), the term "property" does not include insurance and annuity contracts and property described in paragraph (1) of section 1221(a).

Amendments

• 1999, Tax Relief Extension Act of 1999 (P.L. 106-170)

P.L. 106-170, §532(c)(1)(D):

Amended Code Sec. 818(c)(3) by striking "section 1221" and inserting "section 1221(a)". **Effective** for any instrument held, acquired, or entered into, any transaction entered into, and supplies held or acquired on or after 12-17-99.

[Sec. 818(d)]

(d) INSURANCE OR ANNUITY CONTRACT INCLUDES CONTRACTS SUPPLEMENTARY THERETO.—For purposes of this part, the term "insurance or annuity contract" includes any contract supplementary thereto.

[Sec. 818(e)]

(e) SPECIAL RULES FOR CONSOLIDATED RETURNS.—

(1) ITEMS OF COMPANIES OTHER THAN LIFE INSURANCE COMPANIES.—If an election under section 1504(c)(2) is in effect with respect to an affiliated group for the taxable year, all items of the members of such group which are not life insurance companies shall not be taken into account in determining the amount of the tentative LICTI of members of such group which are life insurance companies.

(2) DIVIDENDS WITHIN GROUP.—In the case of a life insurance company filing or required to file a consolidated return under section 1501 with respect to any affiliated group for any taxable year, any determination under this part with respect to any dividend paid by one member of such group to another member of such group shall be made as if such group was not filing a consolidated return.

Amendments

• 1986, Tax Reform Act of 1986 (P.L. 99-514)

P.L. 99-514, §1821(o):

Amended Code Sec. 818(e). **Effective** as if included in the provision of P.L. 98-369 to which it relates. Prior to amendment, Code Sec. 818(e) read as follows:

(e) SPECIAL RULE FOR CONSOLIDATED RETURNS.—If an election under section 1504(c)(2) is in effect with respect to an affiliated group for the taxable year, all items of the members of such group which are not life insurance companies shall not be taken into account in determining the amount of the tentative LICTI of members of such group which are life insurance companies.

[Sec. 818(f)]

(f) ALLOCATION OF CERTAIN ITEMS FOR PURPOSES OF FOREIGN TAX CREDIT, ETC.—

(1) IN GENERAL.—Under regulations, in applying sections 861, 862, and 863 to a life insurance company, the deduction for policyholder dividends (determined under section 808(c)), reserve adjustments under subsections (a) and (b) of section 807, and death benefits and other amounts described in section 805(a)(1) shall be treated as items which cannot definitely be allocated to an item or class of gross income.

(2) ELECTION OF ALTERNATIVE ALLOCATION.—

(A) IN GENERAL.—On or before September 15, 1985, any life insurance company may elect to treat items described in paragraph (1) as properly apportioned or allocated among items of gross income to the extent (and in the manner) prescribed in regulations.

(B) ELECTION IRREVOCABLE.—Any election under subparagraph (A), once made, may be revoked only with the consent of the Secretary.

(3) ITEMS DESCRIBED IN SECTION 807(c) TREATED AS NOT INTEREST FOR SOURCE RULES, ETC.—For purposes of part I of subchapter N, items described in any paragraph of section 807(c) shall be treated as amounts which are not interest.

Amendments

• 1988, Technical and Miscellaneous Revenue Act of 1988 (P.L. 100-647)

P.L. 100-647, §1010(k):

Amended Code Sec. 818(f) by adding at the end thereof new paragraph (3). **Effective** as if included in the provision of P.L. 99-514 to which it relates.

• 1984, Deficit Reduction Act of 1984 (P.L. 98-369)

P.L. 98-369, §211(a):

Amended Part I of subchapter L of chapter 1 by adding Code Sec. 818. **Effective** for tax years beginning after 12-31-83. However, for transitional and special rules, see Act Sec. 216(a)-(b)(2) under the amendments for Code Sec. 801 and Act Sec. 216(b)(4) and (c), below.

P.L. 98-369, §216(b)(4) and (c), as amended by P.L. 99-514, §1822, and P.L. 100-647, §1018(i), provide:

(b)(4) Elections Under Section 818(c) After September 27, 1983, Not to Take Effect.—

(A) In General.—Except as provided in subparagraph (B), any election after September 27, 1983, under Section 818(c) of the Internal Revenue Code of 1954 (as in effect on the day before the date of the enactment of this Act) shall not take effect.

(B) Exception for Certain Contracts Issued Under Plan of Insurance First Filed After March 1, 1982, and Before September 28, 1983.—Paragraph (3) and subparagraph (A) of this paragraph shall not apply to any election under such section 818(c) if more than 95 percent of the reserves computed in accordance with such election are attributable to risks under life insurance contracts issued by the taxpayer under a plan of insurance first filed after March 1, 1982, and before September 28, 1983.

(C) Section 818(c) Elections Made by Certain Acquired Companies.—

(i) In General.—If [sic] the case of any corporation—

(I) which made an election under such section 818(c) before September 28, 1983, and

(II) which was acquired in a qualified stock purchase (as defined in section 338(c) of the Internal Revenue Code of 1954) before December 31, 1983,

the fact that such corporation is treated as a new corporation under section 338 of such Code shall not result in the election described in subclause (I) not applying to such new corporation.

(ii) Time for Making Section 818(c) or 338 Election.—In the case of any corporation described in clause (i), the time for making an election under section 818(c) of such Code (with respect to the first taxable year of the corporation beginning in 1983 and ending after September 28, 1983), or making an election under section 338 of such Code with respect to the qualified stock purchase described in clause (i)(II), shall not expire before the close of the 60th day after the date of the enactment of the Tax Reform Act of 1986.

(iii) Statute of Limitations.—In the case of any such election under section 818(c) or 338 of such Code which would not have been timely made but for clause (ii), the period for assessing any deficiency attributable to such election (or for filing claim for credit or refund of any overpayment attributable to such election) shall not expire before the date 2 years after the date of the enactment of this Act.

(5) Recapture of Reinsurance After December 31, 1983.—If (A) insurance or annuity contracts in force on December 31, 1983, are subject to a conventional coinsurance agreement entered into after December 31, 1981, and before January 1, 1984, and (B) such contracts are recaptured by the reinsured in any taxable year beginning after December 31, 1983, then—

(i) if the amount of the reserves with respect to the recaptured contracts, computed at the date of recapture, that the reinsurer would have taken into account under section 810(c) of the Internal Revenue Code of 1954 (as in effect on the day before the date of the enactment of this Act) exceeds the amount of the reserves with respect to the recaptured contracts, computed at the date of recapture, taken into account by the reinsurer under section 807(c) of the Internal Revenue Code of 1954 (as amended by this subtitle), such excess (but not greater than the amount of such excess if computed on January 1, 1984) shall be taken into account by the reinsurer under the method described in section 807(f)(1)(B)(ii) of the Internal Revenue Code of 1954 (as amended by this subtitle) commencing with the taxable year of recapture, and

(ii) the amount, if any, taken into account by the reinsurer under clause (i) for purposes of part I of subchapter L of chapter 1 of the Internal Revenue Code of 1954 shall be taken into account by the reinsured under the method described in section 807(f)(1)(B)(i) of the Internal Revenue Code of 1954 (as amended by this subtitle) commencing with the taxable year of recapture. The excess described in clause (i) shall be reduced by any portion of such excess to which section 807(f) of the Internal Revenue Code of 1954 applies by reason of paragraph (3) of this subsection. For purposes of this paragraph, the term "reinsurer" refers to the taxpayer that held reserves with respect to the recaptured contracts as of the end of the taxable year preceding the first taxable year beginning after December 31, 1983, and the term "reinsured" refers to the taxpayer to which such reserves are ultimately transferred upon termination.

(c) Election Not to Have Reserves Recomputed.—

(1) In General.—If a qualified life insurance company makes an election under this paragraph—

(A) subsection (a) shall not apply to such company, and

(B) as of the beginning of the first taxable year beginning after December 31, 1983, and thereafter, the reserve for any contract issued before the first day of such taxable year by such company shall be the statutory reserve for such contract (within the meaning of section 809(b)(4)(B)(i) of the Internal Revenue Code of 1954).

(2) Election with Respect to Contracts Issued After 1983 and Before 1989.—

(A) In General.—If—

(i) a qualified life insurance company makes an election under paragraph (1), and

(ii) the tentative LICTI (within the meaning of section 806(c) of such Code) of such company for its first taxable year beginning after December 31, 1983, does not exceed $3,000,000 (determined with regard to this paragraph), such company may elect under this paragraph to have the reserve for any contract issued on or after the first day of such first taxable year and before January 1, 1989, be equal the greater of the statutory reserve for such contract (adjusted as provided in subparagraph (B)) or the net surrender value of such contract (as defined in section 807(e)(1) of the Internal Revenue Code of 1954).

(B) Adjustment to Reserves.—If this paragraph applies to any contract, the opening and closing statutory reserves for such contract shall be adjusted as provided under the principles of section 805(c)(1) of such Code (as in effect for taxable years beginning in 1982 and 1983), except that section 805(c)(1) (B)(ii) of such Code (as so in effect) shall be applied by substituting—

(i) the prevailing State assumed interest rate (within the meaning of section 807(c)(4) of such Code), for

(ii) the adjusted reserves rate.

(3) Qualified Life Insurance Company.—For purposes of this subsection, the term "qualified life insurance company" means any life insurance company which, as of December 31, 1983, had assets of less than $100,000,000 (determined in the same manner as under section 806(b)(3) of such Code).

(4) Special Rules for Controlled Groups.—For purposes of applying the dollar limitations of paragraphs (2) and (3), rules similar to the rules of section 806(d) of such Code shall apply.

(5) Elections.—Any election under paragraph (1) or (2)—

(A) shall be made at such time and in such manner as the Secretary of the Treasury may prescribe, and

(B) once made, shall be irrevocable.

• 1984, Deficit Reduction Act of 1984 (P.L. 98-369)

P.L. 98-369, §1001(b)(10):

Amended Code Sec. 818(b)(1)(A) by striking out "1 year" each place it appeared and inserting in lieu thereof "6 months". **Effective** for property acquired after 6-22-84 and before 1-1-88.

[Sec. 818(g)]

(g) QUALIFIED ACCELERATED DEATH BENEFIT RIDERS TREATED AS LIFE INSURANCE.—For purposes of this part—

(1) IN GENERAL.—Any reference to a life insurance contract shall be treated as including a reference to a qualified accelerated death benefit rider on such contract.

(2) QUALIFIED ACCELERATED DEATH BENEFIT RIDERS.—For purposes of this subsection, the term "qualified accelerated death benefit rider" means any rider on a life insurance contract if the only payments under the rider are payments meeting the requirements of section 101(g).

(3) EXCEPTION FOR LONG-TERM CARE RIDERS.—Paragraph (1) shall not apply to any rider which is treated as a long-term care insurance contract under section 7702B.

Amendments

• 1996, Health Insurance Portability and Accountability Act of 1996 (P.L. 104-191)

P.L. 104-191, §332(a):

Amended Code Sec. 818 by adding at the end a new subsection (g). **Effective** 1-1-97. For a special rule see Act Sec. 332(b)(2), below.

P.L. 104-191, §332(b)(2), provides:

(2) ISSUANCE OF RIDER NOT TREATED AS MATERIAL CHANGE.—For purposes of applying sections 101(f), 7702, and 7702A of the Internal Revenue Code of 1986 to any contract—

(A) the issuance of a qualified accelerated death benefit rider (as defined in section 818(g) of such Code (as added by this Act)), and

(B) the addition of any provision required to conform an accelerated death benefit rider to the requirements of such section 818(g),

shall not be treated as a modification or material change of such contract.

[Sec. 818—Repealed]

Amendments

• 1984, Deficit Reduction Act of 1984 (P.L. 98-369)

P.L. 98-369, §211(a):

Amended Part I of Subchapter L of Chapter 1 by adding a new Part I (Code Secs. 801-818). For transitional and special rules, see Act Sec. 216(a)-(b)(2) in the amendments for Code Sec. 801. Prior to amendment, Code Sec. 818 read as follows:

SEC. 818. ACCOUNTING PROVISIONS.

[Sec. 818(a)]

(a) METHOD OF ACCOUNTING.—All computations entering into the determination of the taxes imposed by this part shall be made—

(1) under an accrual method of accounting, or

(2) to the extent permitted under regulations prescribed by the Secretary, under a combination of an accrual method of accounting with any other method permitted by this chapter (other than the cash receipts and disbursements method).

Except as provided in the preceding sentence, all such computations shall be made in a manner consistent with the manner required for purposes of the annual statement approved by the National Association of Insurance Commissioners.

Amendments

• 1976, Tax Reform Act of 1976 (P.L. 94-455)

P.L. 94-455, §1906(b)(13)(A):

Amended 1954 Code by substituting "Secretary" for "Secretary or his delegate" each place it appeared. **Effective** 2-1-77.

[Sec. 818(b)]

(b) AMORTIZATION OF PREMIUM AND ACCRUAL OF DISCOUNT.—

(1) IN GENERAL.—The appropriate items of income, deductions, and adjustments under this part shall be adjusted to reflect the appropriate amortization of premium and the appropriate accrual of discount attributable to the taxable year on bonds, notes, debentures, or other evidences of indebtedness held by a life insurance company. Such amortization and accrual shall be determined—

(A) in accordance with the method regularly employed by such company, if such method is reasonable, and

(B) in all other cases, in accordance with regulations prescribed by the Secretary or his delegate.

(2) SPECIAL RULES.—

(A) AMORTIZATION OF BOND PREMIUM.—In the case of any bond (as defined in section 171(d)) acquired after December 31, 1957, the amount of bond premium, and the amortizable bond premium for the taxable year, shall be determined under section 171(b) as if the election set forth in section 171(c) had been made.

(B) CONVERTIBLE EVIDENCES OF INDEBTEDNESS.—In no case shall the amount of premium on a convertible evidence of indebtedness include any amount attributable to the conversion features of the evidence of indebtedness.

(3) EXCEPTION.—For taxable years beginning after December 31, 1962, no accrual of discount shall be required under paragraph (1) on any bond (as defined in section 171(d)), except in the case of discount which is—

(A) interest to which section 103 applies, or

(B) original issue discount (as defined in section 1232(b)).

For purposes of section 805(b)(3)(A), the current earnings rate for any taxable year beginning before January 1, 1963, shall be determined as if the preceding sentence applied to such taxable year.

Amendments

• 1964, Revenue Act of 1964 (P.L. 88-272)

P.L. 88-272, §228(b)(1):

Added Code Sec. 818(b)(3).

[Sec. 818(c)]

(c) LIFE INSURANCE RESERVES COMPUTED ON PRELIMINARY TERM BASIS.—For purposes of this part (other than section 801), at the election of the taxpayer the amount taken into account as life insurance reserves with respect to contracts for which such reserves are computed on a preliminary term basis may be determined on either of the following bases;

(1) EXACT REVALUATION.—As if the reserves for all such contracts had been computed on a net level premium basis (using the same mortality assumptions and interest rates for both the preliminary term basis and the net level premium basis).

(2) APPROXIMATE REVALUATION.—The amount computed without regard to this subsection—

(A) increased by $19 per $1,000 of insurance in force (other than term insurance) under such contracts, less 1.9 percent of reserves under such contracts, and

(B) increased by $5 per $1,000 of term insurance in force under such contracts which at the time of issuance cover a period of more than 15 years, less 0.5 percent of reserves under such contracts.

If the taxpayer makes an election under either paragraph (1) or (2) for any taxable year, the basis adopted shall be adhered to in making the computations under this part (other than section 801) for the taxable year and all subsequent taxable years unless a change in the basis of computing such reserves is approved by the Secretary, except that if, pursuant to an election made for a taxable year beginning in 1958 or in effect for a taxable year beginning in 1981, the basis adopted is the basis provided in paragraph (2), the taxpayer may adopt the basis provided by paragraph (1) for its first taxable year beginning after 1958 or 1981, whichever is applicable.

Amendments

• 1982, Tax Equity and Fiscal Responsibility Act of 1982 (P.L. 97-248)

P.L. 97-248, §267(a)(1):

Amended Code Sec. 818(c)(2)(A) by striking out "$21" and inserting in lieu thereof "$19", and by striking out "2.1 percent" and inserting in lieu thereof "1.9 percent". **Effective** for tax years beginning after 12-31-81, but only with respect to reserves established under contracts entered into after 3-31-82.

P.L. 97-248, §267(a)(2):

Amended Code Sec. 818(c) by inserting "or in effect for a taxable year beginning in 1981" after "1958" the first place it appears in the last sentence of subsection (c), and by inserting "or 1981, whichever is applicable" after "1958" the second place it appears. **Effective** for tax years beginning after 12-31-81, but only with respect to reserves established under contracts entered into after 3-31-82.

• 1976, Tax Reform Act of 1976 (P.L. 94-455)

P.L. 94-455, §1906(b)(13)(A):

Amended 1954 Code by substituting "Secretary" for "Secretary or his delegate" each place it appeared. **Effective** 2-1-77.

[Sec. 818(d)]

(d) SHORT TAXABLE YEARS.—If any return of a corporation made under this part is for a period of less than the entire calendar year (referred to in this subsection as "short period"), then section 443 shall not apply in respect to such period, but—

(1) the taxable investment income and the gain or loss from operations shall be determined, under regulations prescribed by the Secretary, on an annual basis by a ratable daily projection of the appropriate figures for the short period.

(2) that portion of the life insurance company taxable income described in paragraphs (1) and (2) of section 802(b) shall be determined on an annual basis by treating the amounts ascertained under paragraph (1) as the taxable investment income and the gain or loss from operations for the taxable year, and

(3) that portion of the life insurance company taxable income described in paragraphs (1) and (2) of section 802(b) for the short period shall be the amount which bears the same ratio to the amount ascertained under paragraph (2) as the number of days in the short period bears to the number of days in the entire calendar year.

Amendments

• 1976, Tax Reform Act of 1976 (P.L. 94-455)

P.L. 94-455, §1906(b)(13)(A):

Amended 1954 Code by substituting "Secretary" for "Secretary or his delegate" each place it appeared. **Effective** 2-1-77.

[Sec. 818(e)]

(e) DENIAL OF DOUBLE DEDUCTIONS.—Nothing in this part shall permit the same item to be deducted more than once under subpart B and once under subpart C.

Amendments

• 1976, Tax Reform Act of 1976 (P.L. 94-455)

P.L. 94-455, §1901(a)(101):

Repealed Code Sec. 818(e) and redesignated former Code Sec. 818(f) as Code Sec. 818(e). **Effective** for tax years beginning after 12-31-76. Prior to repeal, Code Sec. 818(e) read as follows:

(e) TRANSITIONAL RULE FOR CHANGES IN METHOD OF ACCOUNTING.—

(1) IN GENERAL.—If the method of accounting required to be used in computing the taxpayer's taxes under this part for the taxable year 1958 is different from the method used in computing its taxes under this part for 1957, then there shall be ascertained the net amount of those adjustments which are determined (as of the close of 1957) to be necessary solely by reason of the change to the method required by subsection (a) in order to prevent amounts from being duplicated or omitted. The amount of the taxpayer's tax for 1957 shall be recomputed (under the law applicable to 1957, modified as provided in paragraph (4)) taking into account an amount equal to 1/10 of the net amount of the adjustments determined under the preceding sentence. The amount of increase or decrease (as the case may be) referred to in paragraph (2) or (3) shall be the amount of the increase or decrease ascertained under the preceding sentence, multiplied by 10.

(2) TREATMENT OF DECREASE.—For purposes of subtitle F, if the recomputation under paragraph (1) results in a decrease, the amount thereof shall be a decrease in the tax imposed for 1957; except that for purposes of computing the period of limitation on the making of refunds or the allowance of credits with respect to such overpayment, the amount of such decrease shall be treated as an overpayment of tax for 1959. No interest shall be paid, for any period before March 16, 1960, on any overpayment of the tax imposed for 1957 which is attributable to such decrease.

(3) TREATMENT OF INCREASE.—

(A) IN GENERAL.—For purposes of subtitle F (other than section 6016 and 6655), if the recomputation under paragraph (1) results in an increase, the amount thereof shall be treated as a tax imposed by this subsection for 1959. Such tax shall be payable in 10 equal annual installments, beginning with March 15, 1960.

(B) SPECIAL RULES.—For purposes of subparagraph (A)—

(i) No interest shall be paid on any installment described in subparagraph (A) for any period before the time prescribed in such subparagraph for the payment of such installment.

(ii) Section 6152(c) (relating to proration of deficiencies to installments) shall apply.

(iii) In applying section 6502(a)(1) (relating to collection after assessment), the assessment of any installment described in subparagraph (A) shall be treated as made at the time prescribed by such subparagraph for the payment of such installment.

(iv) Except as provided in section 381(c)(22), if for any taxable year the taxpayer is not a life insurance company, the time for payment of any remaining installments described in subparagraph (A) shall be the date (determined without regard to any extension of time) for filing the return for such taxable year.

(4) MODIFICATIONS OF 1957 TAX COMPUTATION.—In recomputing the taxpayer's tax for 1957 for purposes of paragraph (1)—

(A) section 804(b) (as in effect for 1957) shall not apply with respect to any amount required to be taken into account by such paragraph, and

(B) the amount of the deduction allowed by section 805 (as in effect for 1957) shall not be reduced by reason of any amount required to be taken into account by such paragraph.

• 1959, Life Insurance Company Income Tax Act of 1959 (P.L. 86-69)

P.L. 86-69, §2:

Revised Part I of subchapter L of chapter 1 of the 1954 Code. **Effective**, generally, for tax years beginning after 1957. Prior text not reproduced.

[Sec. 818(f)]

(f) SPECIAL RULES FOR CONSOLIDATED RETURN COMPUTATIONS.—For purposes of this part, in the case of a life insurance company filing or required to file a consolidated return under section 1501 for a taxable year, the following rules shall apply:

(1) POLICYHOLDERS' SHARE OF INVESTMENT YIELD.—The computation of the policyholders' share of investment yield under subparts B and C (including all determinations and computations incident thereto) shall be made as if such company were not filing a consolidated return.

(2) LIFE INSURANCE COMPANY TAXABLE INCOME.—

(A) IN GENERAL.—The amount of the consolidated life insurance company taxable income under paragraphs (1) and (2) of section 802(b) shall be determined by taking into account the life insurance company taxable income (including any case where deductions exceed income) of each life insurance company which is a member of the group (as computed separately under such paragraphs).

(B) CERTAIN AMOUNTS COMPUTED SEPARATELY.—For purposes of subparagraph (A), the determination of a life insurance company's taxable investment income and gain or loss from operations (after applying the limitation provided by section 809(f)) shall be made without regard to the taxable investment income or gain or loss from operations of any other such company.

(3) CONSOLIDATED NET CAPITAL GAIN.—If there is a consolidated net capital gain, then the partial tax referred to in section 802(a)(2)(A) shall be computed on—

(A) the consolidated life insurance company taxable income, reduced (but not below the sum of the amounts determined under section 802(b)(3)) by

(B) the amount of such consolidated net capital gain.

Amendments

• 1982, Tax Equity and Fiscal Responsibility Act of 1982 (P.L. 97-248)

P.L. 97-248, §262:

Amended Code Sec. 818(f). **Effective** for tax years beginning after 12-31-81, and before 1-1-84. For special rules for certain transactions in tax years beginning before 1-1-82 see the amendment note for P.L. 97-248 following former Code Sec. 809(f). Also see special rules in the amendment notes for P.L. 97-248 following former Code Sec. 818(h). Prior to amendment, Code Sec. 818(f) read as follows:

(f) COMPUTATION ON CONSOLIDATED RETURNS OF POLICYHOLDERS' SHARE OF INVESTMENT YIELD.—For purposes of this part, in the case of a life insurance company filing or required to file a consolidated return under section 1501 for a taxable year, the computations of the policyholders' share of investment yield under subparts B and C (including all determinations and computations incident thereto) shall be made as if such company were not filing a consolidated return.

• 1976, Tax Reform Act of 1976 (P.L. 94-455)

P.L. 94-455, §1901(a)(101):

Redesignated former Code Sec. 818(g) as Code Sec. 818(f). **Effective** for tax years beginning after 12-31-76.

• 1971 (P.L. 91-688)

P.L. 91-688, §1(a):

Added Code Sec. 818(g). **Effective** with respect to tax years beginning after 12-31-57.

P.L. 91-688, §§2 and 3, provide:

"Sec. 2. (a) If—

"(1) any insurance company subject to taxation under section 802 of the Internal Revenue Code of 1954 filed a consolidated return under section 1501 of such Code for any taxable year beginning after December 31, 1957, and ending before March 13, 1969, and

"(2) not later than one year after the date of the enactment of this Act—

"(A) such company elects (in such manner as the Secretary of the Treasury or his delegate may prescribe) to have this section apply,

"(B) such company files consent to the application of this section of all companies which at any time during any taxable year beginning after December 31, 1957, and ending before March 13, 1969, were members of the same affiliated group as such company, and

"(C) such company (and each company referred to in subparagraph (B)) files a separate return for the first taxable year beginning after December 31, 1957, for which such company filed a consolidated return and for each taxable year thereafter ending before the date of the enactment of this Act,

then notwithstanding any law or rule of law the requirement of filing a consolidated return shall be replaced by a requirement of separate returns for each company referred to in paragraph (2)(C) for each taxable year to which paragraph (2)(C) applies with respect to such company. Paragraph (2)(C) shall not apply with respect to any company for any taxable year the allowance of a credit for which is barred on the date of the enactment of this Act by res judicata or through the operation of section 7121 or section 7122 of the Internal Revenue Code of 1954.

"(b) If the making or allowance of any refund or credit, or the assessment of any deficiency, of income tax for any taxable year to which subsection (a)(2)(C) applies is prevented before the expiration of 2 years after the date of the enactment of this Act by any law or rule of law (other than sections 7121 and 7122 of such Code and other than res judicata), such refund or credit may nevertheless be made or allowed, and such deficiency may nevertheless be assessed, at any time before the expiration of such 2-year period, but only to the extent that the overpayment or deficiency is attributable to an election made under this section. No interest shall be allowed on any credit or refund described in the preceding sentence, and no interest shall be assessed with respect to any deficiency described in the preceding sentence, for any period before the day which is one year after the date of the enactment of this Act.

"Sec. 3. (a) For purposes of applying section 1212(a) of the Internal Revenue Code of 1954 (as amended by section 512 of the Tax Reform Act of 1969) in the case of a corporation which makes an election under subsection (b), any net capital loss sustained in a taxable year beginning after December 31, 1969, may not be carried back to any taxable year beginning before January 1, 1970, for which it was subject to taxation under section 802 of such Code, if the carryback of such loss would result in an increase in such corporation's income tax liability for any such taxable year.

"(b) An election to have the provisions of subsection (a) apply shall be made by a corporation—

"(1) in such form and manner as the Secretary of the Treasury or his delegate may prescribe, and

"(2) not later than the time prescribed by law for filing a claim for credit or refund of overpayment of income tax for the first taxable year beginning after December 31, 1969, in which such corporation sustains a net capital loss.

"(c) The Secretary of the Treasury or his delegate shall prescribe such regulations as he determines necessary to carry out the purposes of this section."

[Sec. 818(g)]

(g) ALLOCATION IN CASE OF REINSURANCE AGREEMENT INVOLVING TAX AVOIDANCE OR EVASION.—In the case of 2 or more related persons (within the meaning of section 1239(b)) who are parties to a reinsurance agreement, the Secretary may—

(1) allocate between or among such persons income (whether investment income, premium, or otherwise), deductions, assets, reserves, credits, and other items related to such agreement, or

(2) recharacterize any such items,

if he determines that such allocation or recharacterization is necessary to reflect the proper source and character of the taxable income (or any item described in paragraph (1) relating to such taxable income) of each such person.

Amendments

• 1982, Tax Equity and Fiscal Responsibility Act of 1982 (P.L. 97-248)

P.L. 97-248, §258(a):

Amended Code Sec. 818 by adding new subsection (g). **Effective** for agreements entered into after 9-3-82.

[Sec. 818(h)]

(h) METHOD OF COMPUTING RESERVES ON CONTRACT WHERE INTEREST IS GUARANTEED BEYOND END OF TAXABLE YEAR.—For purposes of this part (other than section 801), interest payable under any contract which is computed at a rate which—

(1) is in excess of the lowest rates which are assumed under such contract for any period in calculating the reserves under section 810(c) for the contract under which such interest is payable, and

(2) is guaranteed beyond the end of the taxable year on which the reserves are being computed,

shall be taken into account in computing the reserves with respect to such contract as if such interest were guaranteed only up to the end of the taxable year.

Amendments

• 1982, Tax Equity and Fiscal Responsibility Act of 1982 (P.L. 97-248)

P.L. 97-248, §260(a):

Amended Code Sec. 818, as amended by Act Sec. 259[8](a), by adding new subsection (h). **Effective** for tax years beginning after 12-31-81, and before 1-1-84, except where there are reserves on contracts where interest is guaranteed for extended periods, in which case the rules are as follows:

(A) In general.—The amendment made by section 260(a) shall apply to reserves computed for taxable years beginning after December 31, 1981, and before January 1, 1984, with respect to guarantees made after July 1, 1982, and before January 1, 1984.

(B) Special rule relating to reserves.—If, for any taxable year beginning before January 1, 1982—

(i) a taxpayer increased reserves pursuant to section 810(c)(4) of the Internal Revenue Code of 1954 to reflect interest guaranteed beyond the end of such taxable year, and

(ii) the Federal income tax liability of such taxpayer for all taxable years would be the same if such liability was computed with or without regard to such reserves, then such reserves shall, as of the beginning of the first taxable year of the taxpayer beginning after December 31, 1981, be recomputed as if section 818(h) of such Code (as added by this Act) applied to such reserves. If this subparagraph applies to any taxpayer, subparagraph (A) shall be applied with respect to such taxpayer by striking out `after July 1, 1982, and'.

[Sec. 819—Repealed]

Amendments

• 1984, Deficit Reduction Act of 1984 (P.L. 98-369)

P.L. 98-369, §211(a):

Amended Part I of Subchapter L of Chapter 1 by adding a new Part I (Code Secs. 801-818). For transitional and special rules, see Act Sec. 216(a)-(b)(2) in the amendments for Code Sec. 801. Prior to amendment, Code Sec. 819 read as follows:

SEC. 819. FOREIGN LIFE INSURANCE COMPANIES.

[Sec. 819(a)]

(a) ADJUSTMENT WHERE SURPLUS HELD IN UNITED STATES IS LESS THAN SPECIFIED MINIMUM.—

(1) IN GENERAL.—In the case of any foreign corporation taxable under this part, if the minimum figure determined under paragraph (2) exceeds the surplus held in the United States, then—

(A) the amount of the policy and other contract liability requirements (determined under section 805 without regard to this subsection), and

(B) the amount of the required interest (determined under section 809(a)(2) without regard to this subsection),

shall each be reduced by an amount determined by multiplying such excess by the current earnings rate (as defined in section 805(b)(2)).

(2) DEFINITIONS.—For purposes of paragraph (1)—

(A) The minimum figure is the amount determined by multiplying the taxpayer's total insurance liabilities on United States business by a percentage for the taxable year to be determined and proclaimed by the Secretary.

The percentage determined and proclaimed by the Secretary under the preceding sentence shall be based on such data with respect to domestic life insurance companies for the preceding taxable year as the Secretary considers representative. Such percentage shall be computed on the basis of a ratio the numerator of which is the excess of the assets over the total insurance liabilities, and the denominator of which is the total insurance liabilities.

(B) The surplus held in the United States is the excess of the assets held in the United States over the total insurance liabilities on United States business.

For purposes of this paragraph and subsection (b), the term "total insurance liabilities" means the sum of the total reserves (as defined in section 801(c)) plus (to the extent not included in total reserves) the items referred to in paragraphs (3), (4), and (5) of section 810(c).

(3) REDUCTION OF SECTION 881 TAX.—In the case of any foreign corporation taxable under this part, there shall be determined—

(A) the amount which would be subject to tax under section 881 if the amount taxable under such section were determined without regard to sections 103 and 894, and

(B) the amount of the reduction provided by paragraph (1).

The tax under section 881 (determined without regard to this paragraph) shall be reduced (but not below zero) by an amount which is the same proportion of such tax as the amount referred to in subparagraph (B) is of the amount referred to in subparagraph (A); but such reduction in tax shall not exceed the increase in tax under this part by reason of the reduction provided by paragraph (1).

Amendments

• 1976, Tax Reform Act of 1976 (P.L. 94-455)

P.L. 94-455, §1901(a)(102):

Amended the first sentence of paragraph (2) and substituted "under the preceding sentence" for "under clause (ii)" in the second sentence of paragraph (2). **Effective** for tax years beginning after 12-31-76. Prior to amendment, the first sentence of paragraph (2) read as follows:

For purposes of paragraph (1)—

(A) The minimum figure is the amount determined by multiplying the taxpayer's total insurance liabilities on United States business by—

(i) in the case of a taxable year beginning before January 1, 1959, 9 percent, and

(ii) in the case of a taxable year beginning after December 31, 1958, a percentage for such year to be determined and proclaimed by the Secretary or his delegate.

P.L. 94-455, §1906(b)(13)(A):

Amended 1954 Code by substituting "Secretary" for "Secretary or his delegate" each place it appeared. **Effective** 2-1-77.

[Sec. 819(b)]

(b) DISTRIBUTIONS TO SHAREHOLDERS.—

(1) IN GENERAL.—In applying sections 802(b)(3) and 815 with respect to a foreign corporation, the amount of the distributions to shareholders shall be determined by multiplying the total amount of the distributions to shareholders (within the meaning of section 815) of the foreign corporation by whichever of the following percentages is selected by the taxpayer for the taxable year:

(A) the percentage which the minimum figure for the taxable year (determined under subsection (a)(2)(A)) is of the excess of the assets of the company over the total insurance liabilities; or

(B) the percentage which the total insurance liabilities on United States business for the taxable year is of the company's total insurance liabilities.

(2) DISTRIBUTIONS PURSUANT TO CERTAIN MUTUALIZATIONS.—In applying section 815(e) with respect to a foreign corporation—

(A) the paid-in capital and paid-in surplus referred to in section 815(e)(1)(A) of a foreign corporation is the portion of such capital and surplus determined by multiplying such capital and surplus by the percentage selected for the taxable year under paragraph (1); and

(B) the excess referred to in section 815(e)(2)(A)(i) (without the adjustment provided by section 815(e)(2)(B)) is whichever of the following is the greater:

(i) the minimum figure for 1958 determined under subsection (a)(2)(A) computed by using a percentage of 9 percent in lieu of the percentage determined and proclaimed by the Secretary, or

(ii) the surplus described in subsection (a)(2)(B) (determined as of December 31, 1958).

Amendments

• 1976, Tax Reform Act of 1976 (P.L. 94-455)

P.L. 94-455, §1901(a)(102):

Amended Code Sec. 819(b)(2)(B)(i). **Effective** for tax years beginning after 12-31-76. Prior to amendment, Code Sec. 819(b)(2)(B)(i) read as follows:

(i) the minimum figure for 1958 determined under subsection (a)(2)(A), or

[Sec. 819(c)]

(c) CROSS REFERENCE.—

For taxation of foreign corporations carrying on life insurance business within the United States, see section 842.

Amendments

• 1966, Foreign Investors Tax Act of 1966 (P.L. 89-809)

P.L. 89-809, §104(i)(3):

Amended Code Sec. 819 by striking out subsections (a) and (d) and redesignating subsections (b) and (c) as subsections (a) and (b); by substituting "In the case of any foreign corporation taxable under this part," for "In the case of any company described in subsection (a)" in redesignated subsection (a)(1); by substituting "subsection (b)" for "subsection (c)" in the last sentence of redesignated subsection (a)(2); by adding new paragraph (3) to redesignated subsection (a); by substituting "with respect to a foreign corporation" for "for purposes of subsection (a)" each place it appears in redesignated subsection (b); by substituting "foreign corporation" for "foreign life insurance company" each place it appears in redesignated subsection (b); by substituting "subsection (a)(2)(A)" for "subsection (b)(2)(A)" each place it appears in redesignated subsection (b); by substituting "subsection (a)(2)(B)" for "subsection (b)(2)(B)" in redesignated subsection (b)(2)(B)(ii); and by adding new Code Sec. 819(c). **Effective** 1-1-67.

• 1959, Life Insurance Company Income Tax Act of 1959 (P.L. 86-69)

P.L. 86-69, §2:

Revised Part I of subchapter L of chapter 1 of the 1954 Code. **Effective**, generally, for tax years beginning after 1957. Prior text not reproduced.

[Sec. 819A—Repealed]

Amendments

• 1984, Deficit Reduction Act of 1984 (P.L. 98-369)

P.L. 98-369, §211(a):

Amended Part I of Subchapter L of Chapter 1 by adding a new Part I (Code Secs. 801-818). For transitional and special rules, see Act Sec. 216(a)-(b)(2) in the amendments for Code Sec. 801. Prior to amendment, Code Sec. 819A read as follows:

SEC. 819A. CONTIGUOUS COUNTRY BRANCHES OF DOMESTIC LIFE INSURANCE COMPANIES.

[Sec. 819A(a)]

(a) EXCLUSION OF ITEMS.—In the case of a domestic mutual insurance company which—

(1) is a life insurance company,

(2) has a contiguous country life insurance branch, and

(3) makes the election provided by subsection (g) with respect to such branch,

there shall be excluded from each and every item involved in the determination of life insurance company taxable income the items separately accounted for in accordance with subsection (c).

[Sec. 819A(b)]

(b) CONTIGUOUS COUNTRY LIFE INSURANCE BRANCH.—For purposes of this section, the term "contiguous country life insurance branch" means a branch which—

(1) issues insurance contracts insuring risks in connection with the lives or health of residents of a country which is contiguous to the United States,

(2) has its principal place of business in such contiguous country, and

(3) would constitute a mutual life insurance company if such branch were a separate domestic insurance company.

For purposes of this section, the term "insurance contract" means any life, health, accident, or annuity contract or reinsurance contract or any contract relating thereto.

[Sec. 819A(c)]

(c) SEPARATE ACCOUNTING REQUIRED.—Any taxpayer which makes the election provided by subsection (g) shall establish and maintain a separate account for the various income, exclusion, deduction, asset, reserve, liability, and surplus items properly attributable to the contracts described in subsection (b). Such separate accounting shall be made—

(1) in accordance with the method regularly employed by such company, if such method clearly reflects income derived from, and the other items attributable to, the contracts described in subsection (b), and

(2) in all other cases, in accordance with regulations prescribed by the Secretary.

[Sec. 819A(d)]

(d) RECOGNITION OF GAIN ON ASSETS IN BRANCH ACCOUNT.—If the aggregate fair market value of all the invested assets and tangible property which are separately accounted for by the domestic life insurance company in the branch account established pursuant to subsection (c) exceeds the aggregate adjusted basis of such assets for purposes of determining gain, then the domestic life insurance company shall be treated as having sold all such assets on the first day of the first taxable year for which the election is in effect at their fair market value on such first day. Notwithstanding any other provision of this chapter, the net gain shall be recognized to the domestic life insurance company on the deemed sale described in the preceding sentence.

[Sec. 819A(e)]

(e) TRANSACTIONS BETWEEN CONTIGUOUS COUNTRY BRANCH AND DOMESTIC LIFE INSURANCE COMPANY.—

(1) REIMBURSEMENT FOR HOME OFFICE SERVICES, ETC.—Any payment, transfer, reimbursement, credit, or allowance which is made from a separate account established pursuant to subsection (c) to one or more other accounts of a domestic life insurance company as reimbursement for costs incurred for or with respect to the insurance (or reinsurance) of risks accounted for in such separate account shall be taken into account by the domestic life insurance company in the same manner as if such payment, transfer, reimbursement, credit, or allowance had been received from a separate person.

(2) REPATRIATION OF INCOME.—

(A) IN GENERAL.—Except as provided in subparagraph (B), any amount directly or indirectly transferred or credited from a branch account established pursuant to subsection (c) to one or more other accounts of such company shall, unless such transfer or credit is a reimbursement to which paragraph (1) applies, be added to the life insurance company taxable income of the domestic life insurance company (as computed without regard to this paragraph).

(B) LIMITATION.—The addition provided by subparagraph (A) for the taxable year with respect to any contiguous country life insurance branch shall not exceed the amount by which—

(i) the aggregate decrease in the life insurance company taxable income of the domestic life insurance company for the taxable year and for all prior taxable years resulting solely from the application of subsection (a) of this section with respect to such branch, exceeds

(ii) the amount of additions to life insurance company taxable income pursuant to subparagraph (A) with respect to such contiguous country branch for all prior taxable years.

[Sec. 819A(f)]

(f) OTHER RULES.—

(1) TREATMENT OF FOREIGN TAXES.—

(A) IN GENERAL.—No income, war profits, or excess profits taxes paid or accrued to any foreign country or possession of the United States which is attributable to income excluded under subsection (a) shall be taken into account for purposes of subpart A of part III of subchapter N (relating to foreign tax credit) or allowable as a deduction.

(B) TREATMENT OF REPATRIATED AMOUNTS.—For purposes of sections 78 and 902, where any amount is added to the life insurance company taxable income of the domestic life insurance company by reason of subsection (e)(2), the contiguous country life insurance branch shall be treated as a foreign corporation. Any amount so added shall be treated as a dividend paid by a foreign corporation, and the taxes paid to any foreign country or possession of the United States with respect to such amount shall be deemed to have been paid by such branch.

(2) UNITED STATES SOURCE INCOME ALLOCABLE TO CONTIGUOUS COUNTRY BRANCH.—For purposes of sections 881, 882 and 1442, each contiguous country life insurance branch shall be treated as a foreign corporation. Such sections shall be applied to each such branch in the same manner as if such sections contained the provisions of any treaty to which the United States and the contiguous country are parties, to the same extent such provisions would apply if such branch were incorporated in such contiguous country.

[Sec. 819A(g)]

(g) ELECTION.—A taxpayer may make the election provided by this subsection with respect to any contiguous country for any taxable year beginning after December 31, 1975. An election made under this subsection for any taxable year shall remain in effect for all subsequent taxable years, except that it may be revoked with the consent of the Secretary. The election provided by this subsection shall be made not later than the time prescribed by law for filing the return for the taxable year (including extensions thereof) with respect to which such election is made, and such election and any approved revocation thereof shall be made in the manner provided by the Secretary.

[Sec. 819A(h)]

(h) SPECIAL RULE FOR DOMESTIC STOCK LIFE INSURANCE COMPANIES.—At the election of a domestic stock life insurance company which has a contiguous country life insurance branch described in subsection (b) (without regard to the mutual requirement in subsection (b)(3)), the assets of such branch may be transferred to a foreign corporation organized under the laws of the contiguous country without the application of section 367 or 1491. Subsection (a) shall apply to the stock of such foreign corporation as if such domestic company were a mutual company and as if the stock were an item described in subsection (c). Subsection (e)(2) shall apply to amounts transferred or credited to such domestic company as if such domestic company and such foreign corporation constituted one domestic mutual life insurance company. The insurance contracts which may be transferred pursuant to this subsection shall include only those which are similar to the types of insurance contracts issued by a mutual life insurance company. Notwithstanding the first sentence of this subsection, if the aggregate fair market value of the invested assets and tangible property which are separately accounted for by the domestic life insurance company in the branch account exceeds the aggregate adjusted basis of such assets for purposes of determining gain, the domestic life insurance company shall be deemed to have sold all such assets on the first day of the taxable year for which the election under this subsection applies and the net gain shall be recognized to the domestic life insurance company on the deemed sale, but not in excess of the proportion of such net gain which equals the proportion which the aggregate fair market value of such assets which are transferred pursuant to this subsection is of the aggregate fair market value of all such assets.

Amendments

• 1976, Tax Reform Act of 1976 (P.L. 94-455)

P.L. 94-455, §1043(a):

Added Code Sec. 819A. **Effective** for tax years beginning after 12-31-75.

[Sec. 820—Repealed]

Amendments

• 1982, Tax Equity and Fiscal Responsibility Act of 1982 (P.L. 97-248)

P.L. 97-248, §255(a):

Repealed Code Sec. 820. **Effective** for tax years beginning after 12-31-81, except for certain rules applicable to taxable years beginning before 1-1-82, as follows:

(A) In general.—In the case of any taxable year beginning before January 1, 1982—

(i) any determination as to whether any contract met the requirements of subsection (b) of section 820 of the Internal Revenue Code of 1954 (as in effect before its repeal by this section) shall be made solely by reference to the terms of the contract, and

(ii) the treatment of such contract under subsection (c) of such section 820 shall be made in accordance with the regulations under such section which were in effect on December 31, 1981.

(B) Paragraph not to apply if fraud involved.—The provisions of subparagraph (A) shall not apply with respect to any deficiency which the Secretary of the Treasury or his delegate establishes was due to fraud with intent to evade tax.

Prior to repeal Code Sec. 820 read as follows:

SEC. 820. OPTIONAL TREATMENT OF POLICIES REINSURED UNDER MODIFIED COINSURANCE CONTRACTS.

(a) In General.—

(1) Treatment as reinsured under conventional coinsurance contract.—Under regulations prescribed by the Secretary, an insurance or annuity policy reinsured under a modified coinsurance contract (as defined in subsection (b)) shall be treated, for purposes of this part (other than for purposes of section 801), as if such policy were reinsured under a conventional coinsurance contract.

(2) Consent of reinsured and reinsurer.—Paragraph (1) shall apply to an insurance or annuity policy reinsured under a modified coinsurance contract only if the reinsured and reinsurer consent, in such manner as the Secretary shall prescribe by regulations—

(A) to the application of paragraph (1) to all insurance and annuity policies reinsured under such modified coinsurance contract, and

(B) to the application of the rules provided by subsection (c) and the rules prescribed under such subsection.

Such consent, once given, may not be rescinded except with the approval of the Secretary.

(b) Definition of Modified Coinsurance Contract.—For purposes of this section, the term `modified coinsurance contract' means an indemnity reinsurance contract under the terms of which—

(1) a life insurance company (hereinafter referred to as `the reinsurer') agrees to indemnify another life insurance company (hereinafter referred to as `the reinsured') against a risk assumed by the reinsured under the insurance or annuity policy reinsured,

(2) the reinsured retains ownership of the assets in relation to the reserve on the policy reinsured,

(3) all or part of the gross investment income derived from such assets is paid by the reinsured to the reinsurer as a part of the consideration for the reinsurance of such policy, and

(4) the reinsurer is obligated for expenses incurred, and for Federal income taxes imposed, in respect of such gross investment income.

(c) Special Rules.—Under regulations prescribed by the Secretary, in applying subsection (a)(1) with respect to any insurance or annuity policy the following rules shall (to the extent not improper under the terms of the modified coinsurance contract under which such policy is reinsured) be applied in respect of the amount of such policy reinsured:

(1) Premiums and gross investment income.—The premiums (to the extent allocable to the participation of the reinsurer therein) received for the policy reinsured shall be treated as received by the reinsurer and not by the reinsured. The gross investment income (to the extent allocable to the participation of the reinsurer therein) derived from the assets in relation to the reserve on the policy reinsured shall be treated as gross investment income of the reinsurer and not of the reinsured. The gross investment income so treated shall be considered as derived proportionately from each of the various sources of gross investment income of the reinsured.

(2) Capital gains and losses.—The gains and losses from sales and exchanges of capital assets, and gains and losses considered as gains and losses from sales and exchanges of capital assets, of the reinsured shall (to the extent of the participation therein by the reinsurer under the terms of the modified coinsurance contract) be treated as gains and losses from sales and exchanges of capital assets of the reinsurer and not of the reinsured.

(3) Reserves and assets.—The reserve on the policy reinsured shall be treated as a part of the reserves of the reinsurer and not of the reinsured, and the assets in relation to such reserve shall be treated as owned by the reinsurer and not by the reinsured.

(4) Expenses.—The expenses (to the extent reimbursable by the reinsurer) incurred with respect to the policy reinsured and with respect to the assets referred to in paragraph (3) shall be treated as incurred by the reinsurer and not by the reinsured.

(5) Dividends to policyholders.—The dividends to policyholders paid in respect of the policy reinsured shall be treated as paid by the reinsurer and not by the reinsured. For purposes of the preceding sentence, the amount of dividends to policyholders treated as paid by the reinsurer shall be the amount paid, in respect of the policy reinsured, by the reinsurer to the reinsured as reimbursement for dividends to policyholders paid by the reinsured. This paragraph shall apply also in respect of an insurance or annuity policy reinsured under a conventional coinsurance contract.

(6) Rules prescribed by the Secretary.—Such other rules as may be prescribed by the Secretary.

In applying the rules provided by paragraphs (1), (2), (3), (4), and (5) and the rules prescribed under paragraph (6), an item shall be taken into account as income only once under subpart B and only once under subpart C by both the reinsured and the reinsurer, and an item shall be allowed as a deduction only once under subpart B and only once under subpart C to both the reinsured and the reinsurer."

P.L. 97-248, §256, provides the following special accounting rules relating to repeal of Code Sec. 820:

(a) In General.—For purposes of subchapter L of chapter 1 of the Internal Revenue Code of 1954, the provisions of this section shall apply to any contract—

(1) which was in effect on December 31, 1981, and

(2) to which section 820(a)(1) of such Code (as in effect before its repeal by section 255(a)) applied.

(b) Treatment of Reserves and Assets.—Except as provided in subsections (c) and (d), the reserves on the contract described in subsection (a) and the assets in relation to such reserves shall—

(1) as of the beginning of taxable year 1982, be treated as the reserves and assets of the reinsurer (and not the reinsured), and

(2) as of the end of taxable year 1982, be treated as the reserves and assets of the reinsured (and not the reinsurer).

(c) Allocation of Certain Section 820(c) Items.—Any amount described in paragraphs (1), (2), (4), and (5) of section 820(c) of such Code (as so in effect) with respect to any contract described in subsection (a) shall, beginning with taxable year 1982, be taken into account by the reinsured and the reinsurer in the same manner as such amounts would be taken into account under a modified coinsurance contract to which section 820(a)(1) of such Code (as so in effect) does not apply.

(d) Amounts Treated as Returned Under the Contract.—

(1) In general.—For taxable year 1982—

(A) in the case of the reinsurer, there shall be allowed as a deduction for ordinary and necessary business expenses under section 809(d)(11) of such Code an amount equal to the termination amount (and such amount shall not otherwise be taken into account in determining gain or loss from operations under section 809 of such Code), and

(B) in the case of the reinsured, the gross amount under section 809(c)(3) of such Code shall be increased by the termination amount.

(2) Adjustment for reserves of reinsured.—For purposes of subsections (a) and (b) of section 810 of such Code, the amount taken into account as of the close of taxable year 1982 by the reinsured shall be reduced for such taxable year (but not for purposes of determining such amount at the beginning of the next succeeding taxable year) by the excess (if any) of—

(A) the reserves on the contract as of January 1, 1982 (determined under the reinsured's method of computing reserves for tax purposes), over

(B) the termination amount.

This paragraph shall not apply to any portion of any policies with respect to which the taxpayer is both the reinsured and the reinsurer under contracts to which this section applies.

(3) Termination amount.—For purposes of this subsection, the term "termination amount" means the amount under the contract which the reinsurer would have returned to the reinsured upon termination of the contract if the contract had been terminated as of January 1, 1982.

(4) Certain amounts not taken into account under section 809(d)(5).—Any amount treated as the reserves of the reinsured by reason of subsection (b)(2) shall not be taken into account under section 809(d)(5) of the Internal Revenue Code of 1954.

(e) 3-Year Installment Payment of Taxes Owed by Reinsurer Resulting From Repeal of Section 820.—

(1) In general.—That portion of any tax imposed under chapter 1 of such Code (reduced by the sum of the credits allowable under subpart A of part IV of such chapter) on a reinsurer for taxable year 1982 which is attributable to the excess (if any) of—

(A) any decrease in reserves for such taxable year by reason of subsection (b), over

(B) the amount allowable as a deduction for such taxable year by reason of subsection (d)(1)(A),

may, at the election of the reinsurer, be paid in 3 equal annual installments.

(2) Time for payments.—

(A) In general.—The 3 installments under paragraph (1) shall be paid on March 15 of 1983, 1984, and 1985.

(B) First installment may be made in 2 payments.—The reinsurer may elect to pay one-half of the installment due March 15, 1983, on June 15, 1983.

(3) Acceleration of payments.—If—

(A) an election is made under paragraph (1), and

(B) before the tax attributable to such excess is paid in full any installment under this section is not paid on or before the date fixed by this section for its payment,

then the extension of time for payment of tax provided in this subsection shall cease to apply, and any portion of the tax payable in installments shall be paid on notice and demand from the Secretary of the Treasury or his delegate.

(4) Proration of deficiency to installments.—If an election is made under paragraph (1) and a deficiency attributable to the excess has been assessed, the deficiency shall be prorated to such installments. The part of the deficiency so prorated to any installment the date for payment of which has not arrived shall be collected at the same time as, and as part of, such installment. The part of the deficiency so prorated to any intallment the date for payment of which has arrived shall be paid on notice and demand from the Secretary of the Treasury or his delegate. This paragraph shall not apply if the deficiency is due to negligence, to intentional disregard of rules and regulations, or to fraud with intent to evade tax.

(5) Bond may be required.—If an election is made under this section, section 6165 of the Internal Revenue Code of 1954 shall apply as though the Secretary of the Treasury or his delegate were extending the time for payment of the tax.

(6) Extension of period of limitations.—The running of any period of limitations for the collection of the tax with respect to which an election is made under paragraph (1) shall be suspended for the period during which there are any unpaid installments of such tax.

(7) Interest on installments.—Rules similar to the rules of section 6601(b)(2) of such Code (without regard to the last sentence thereof) shall apply with respect to any tax for which an election is made under paragraph (1).

(f) Special Rule Allowing Reinsured To Revoke an Election Under Section 820.—

(1) In general.—In any case in which—

(A) a taxpayer is the reinsured under any contract—

(i) which took effect in 1980 or 1981, and

(ii) with respect to which an election under section 820 of the Internal Revenue Code of 1954 was made,

(B) the taxpayer has a loss from operations or its gain from operations (determined without regard to any deduction under paragraphs (3), (5), and (6) of section 809(d) of such Code) for the taxable year in which such contract took effect does not exceed the taxpayer's taxable investment income for such taxable year,

(C) such contract was not a contract with a person who, during the taxable year in which such contract took effect, was a member of the same affiliated group (determined under section 1504 of such Code without regard to subsection (b)) of which the taxpayer is a member, and

(D) the taxpayer makes an election under this subsection within 6 months after the date of the enactment of this Act,

then the provisions of paragraph (2) shall apply.

(2) Rules which apply if this subsection applies.—In any case described in paragraph (1)—

(A) the taxpayer shall, for all taxable years, be treated as not having made an election under section 820 of such Code with respect to the contract described in paragraph (1), but

(B) all other parties to the contract shall be treated as having made such election with respect to such contract for all taxable years.

(g) Taxable Year 1982.—For purposes of this section, the term "taxable year 1982" means, with respect to any taxpayer, the first taxable year of the taxpayer beginning after December 31, 1981.

(h) Regulations.—The Secretary of the Treasury or his delegate shall prescribe such regulations as may be necessary or appropriate to carry out the purposes of this section.

• 1976, Tax Reform Act of 1976 (P.L. 94-455)

P.L. 94-455, §1901(a)(103):

Struck out paragraph (6), redesignated paragraph (7) as paragraph (6), and substituted "and (5) and the rules prescribed under paragraph (6)" for "(5), and (6) and the rules prescribed under paragraph (7)". **Effective** for tax years beginning after 12-31-76. Prior to repeal, Code Sec. 820(c)(6) read as follows:

(6) REIMBURSEMENT FOR 1957 FEDERAL INCOME TAX.—Any amount paid in 1958 or any subsequent year by the reinsurer to the reinsured as reimbursement for Federal income taxes imposed for a taxable year beginning in 1957 or any preceding taxable year shall not be taken into account by the reinsured as an item under section 809(c) or by the reinsurer as a deduction under section 809(d).

P.L. 94-455, §1906(b)(13)(A):

Amended 1954 Code by substituting "Secretary" for "Secretary or his delegate" each place it appeared. **Effective** 2-1-77.

• 1959, Life Insurance Company Income Tax Act of 1959 (P.L. 86-69)

P.L. 86-69, §2:

Revised Part I of subchapter L of chapter 1 of the 1954 Code. **Effective**, generally, for tax years beginning after 1957. Prior text not reproduced.

PART II—MUTUAL INSURANCE COMPANIES (OTHER THAN LIFE AND CERTAIN MARINE INSURANCE COMPANIES AND OTHER THAN FIRE OR FLOOD INSURANCE COMPANIES WHICH OPERATE ON BASIS OF PERPETUAL POLICIES OR PREMIUM DEPOSITS)—[Repealed]

[Sec. 821—Repealed]

Amendments

• 1986, Tax Reform Act of 1986 (P.L. 99-514)

P.L. 99-514, §1024(a)(1):

Repealed Code Sec. 821. **Effective** for tax years beginning after 12-31- 86. Prior to repeal, Code Sec. 821 read as follows:

SEC. 821. TAX ON MUTUAL INSURANCE COMPANIES TO WHICH PART II APPLIES.

[Sec. 821(a)]

(a) IMPOSITION OF TAX.—

(1) IN GENERAL.—A tax is hereby imposed for each taxable year on the mutual insurance company taxable income of every mutual insurance company (other than a life insurance company and other than a fire, flood, or marine insurance company subject to the tax imposed by section 831). Such tax shall be computed by multiplying the mutual insurance company taxable income by the rates provided in section 11(b).

(2) CAP ON TAX WHERE INCOME IS LESS THAN $12,000.—The tax imposed by paragraph (1) on so much of the mutual insurance company taxable income as does not exceed $12,000 shall not exceed 32 percent (30 percent for taxable years beginning after December 31, 1982) of the amount by which such income exceeds $6,000.

Amendments

• 1981, Economic Recovery Tax Act of 1981 (P.L. 97-34)

P.L. 97-34, §231(b)(1):

Amended Code Sec. 821(a)(2). **Effective** for tax years beginning after 12-31-78; except that for purposes of applying Code Sec. 821(a)(2), as amended by this subsection, to tax years beginning before 1-1-82, the percentage referred to in such section shall be deemed to be 34 percent. Prior to amendment, Code Sec. 821(a)(2) read as follows:

(2) CAP ON TAX WHERE INCOME IS LESS THAN $12,000.—The tax imposed by paragraph (1) shall not exceed 34 percent of the amount by which the mutual insurance company taxable income exceeds $6,000.

• 1978, Revenue Act of 1978 (P.L. 95-600)

P.L. 95-600, §301(b)(9)(A):

Amended Code Sec. 821(a). **Effective** for tax years beginning after 12-31-78. Prior to amendment, Code Sec. 821(a) read as follows:

(a) IMPOSITION OF TAX.—A tax is hereby imposed for each taxable year on the mutual insurance company taxable income of every mutual insurance company (other than a life insurance company and other than a fire, flood, or marine insurance company subject to the tax imposed by section 831). Such tax shall consist of—

(1) NORMAL TAX.—A normal tax equal to—

(A) in the case of a taxable year ending after December 31, 1978, 22 percent of the mutual insurance company taxable income, or 44 percent of the amount by which such taxable income exceeds $6,000, whichever is lesser, or

(B) in the case of a taxable year ending after December 31, 1974, and before January 1, 1979—

(i) 20 percent of so much of the mutual insurance company taxable income as does not exceed $25,000, plus

(ii) 22 percent of so much of the mutual insurance company taxable income as exceeds $25,000,

or 44 percent of the amount by which such taxable income exceeds $6,000, whichever is lesser; plus

(2) SURTAX.—A surtax on the mutual insurance company taxable income computed as provided in section 11(c) as though the mutual insurance company taxable income were the taxable income referred to in section 11(c)."

• 1977, Tax Reduction and Simplification Act of 1977 (P.L. 95-30)

P.L. 95-30, §201:

Substituted "December 31, 1978" for "December 31, 1977" in Code Sec. 821(a)(1)(A) and "January 1, 1979" for "January 1, 1978" in Code Sec. 821(a)(1)(B). **Effective** 5-23-77.

• 1976, Tax Reform Act of 1976 (P.L. 94-455)

P.L. 94-455, §901(b)(1):

Amended paragraph (1). **Effective** for tax years ending after 12-31-74. Prior to amendment, Code Sec. 821(a)(1) read as follows:

(1) Normal Tax.—A normal tax of 22 percent of the mutual insurance company taxable income, or 44 percent of the amount by which such taxable income exceeds $6,000, whichever is the lesser; plus

P.L. 94-455, §1901(a)(104):

Struck out "beginning after December 31, 1963," after "taxable year" in the first sentence of Code Sec. 821(a). **Effective** for tax years beginning after 12-31-76.

• 1964, Revenue Act of 1964 (P.L. 88-272)

P.L. 88-272, §123(a):

Amended subsection (a). **Effective** for tax years beginning after 12-31-63. Prior to amendment, subsection (a) read as follows:

(a) IMPOSITION OF TAX.—A tax is hereby imposed for each taxable year beginning after December 31, 1962, on the mutual insurance company taxable income of every mutual insurance company (other than a life insurance company and other than a fire, flood, or marine insurance company subject to the tax imposed by section 831). Such tax shall consist of—

(1) NORMAL TAX.—

(A) TAXABLE YEARS BEGINNING BEFORE JULY 1, 1964.—In the case of taxable years beginning before July 1, 1964, a normal tax of 30 percent of the mutual insurance company taxable income, or 60 percent of the amount by which such taxable income exceeds $6,000, whichever is the lesser;

(B) Taxable years beginning after June 30, 1964.—In the case of taxable years beginning after June 30, 1964, a normal tax of 25 percent of the mutual insurance company taxable income, or 50 percent of the amount by which such taxable income exceeds $6,000, whichever is the lesser; plus

(2) Surtax.—A surtax of 22 percent of the mutual insurance company taxable income (computed without regard to

the deduction provided in section 242 for partially tax-exempt interest) in excess of $25,000.

[Sec. 821(b)]

(b) MUTUAL INSURANCE COMPANY TAXABLE INCOME DEFINED.—For purposes of this part, the term "mutual insurance company taxable income" means, with respect to any taxable year, the amount by which—

(1) the sum of—

(A) the taxable investment income (as defined in section 822(a)(1)),

(B) the statutory underwriting income (as defined in section 823(a)(1)), and

(C) the amounts required by section 824(d) to be subtracted from the protection against loss account, exceeds

(2) the sum of—

(A) the investment loss (as defined in section 822(a)(2)),

(B) the statutory underwriting loss (as defined in section 823(a)(2)), and

(C) the unused loss deduction provided by section 825(a).

[Sec. 821(c)]

(c) ALTERNATIVE TAX FOR CERTAIN SMALL COMPANIES.—

(1) IMPOSITION OF TAX.—

(A) IN GENERAL.—There is hereby imposed for each taxable year on the income of every mutual insurance company to which this subsection applies a tax (which shall be in lieu of the tax imposed by subsection (a)). Such tax shall be computed by multiplying the taxable investment income by the rates provided in section 11(b).

(B) CAP WHERE INCOME IS LESS THAN $6,000.—The tax imposed by subparagraph (A) on so much of the taxable investment income as does not exceed $6,000 shall not exceed 32 percent (30 percent for taxable years beginning after December 31, 1982) of the amount by which such income exceeds $3,000.

(2) GROSS AMOUNT RECEIVED, OVER $150,000 BUT LESS THAN $250,000.—If the gross amount received during the taxable year from the items described in section 822(b) (other than paragraph (1)(D) thereof) and premiums (including deposits and assessments) is over $150,000 but less than $250,000, the tax imposed by paragraph (1) shall be reduced to an amount which bears the same proportion to the amount of the tax determined under paragraph (1) as the excess over $150,000 of such gross amount received bears to $100,000.

(3) COMPANIES TO WHICH SUBSECTION APPLIES.—

(A) IN GENERAL.—Except as provided in subparagraph (B), this subsection shall apply to every mutual insurance company (other than a life insurance company and other than a fire, flood, or marine insurance company subject to the tax imposed by section 831) which received during the taxable year from the items described in section 822(b) (other than paragraph (1)(D) thereof) and premiums (including deposits and assessments) a gross amount in excess of $150,000 but not in excess of $500,000.

(B) EXCEPTIONS.—This subsection shall not apply to a mutual insurance company for the taxable year if

(i) there is in effect an election by such company made under subsection (d) to be taxable under subsection (a); or

(ii) there is any amount in the protection against loss account at the beginning of the taxable year.

Amendments

• 1981, Economic Recovery Tax Act of 1981 (P.L. 97-34)

P.L. 97-34, §231(b)(2):

Amended Code Sec. 821(c)(1)(B). **Effective** for tax years beginning after 12-31-78; except that for purposes of applying Code Sec. 821(c)(1)(B) to tax years beginning before 1-1-82, the percentage referred to in such section shall be deemed to be 34 percent. Prior to amendment, Code Sec. 821(c)(1)(B) read as follows:

(B) CAP WHERE INCOME IS LESS THAN $6,000.—The tax imposed by subparagraph (A) shall not exceed 34 percent of the amount by which the taxable investment income exceeds $3,000.

• 1978, Revenue Act of 1978 (P.L. 95-600)

P.L. 95-600, §301(b)(9)(B):

Amended Code Sec. 821(c)(1). **Effective** for tax years beginning after 12-31-78. Prior to amendment, Code Sec. 821(c)(1) read as follows:

(1) IMPOSITION OF TAX.—There is hereby imposed for each taxable year on the income of each mutual insurance company to which this subsection applies a tax (which shall be in lieu of the tax imposed by subsection (a)) computed as follows:

(A) NORMAL TAX.—A normal tax equal to—

(i) in the case of a taxable year ending after December 31, 1978, 22 percent of the taxable investment income, or 44 percent of the amount by which such taxable income exceeds $3,000, whichever is lesser, or

(ii) in the case of a taxable year ending after December 31, 1974, and before January 1, 1979, 20 percent of so much of the taxable investment income as does not exceed $25,000, plus 22 percent of so much of the taxable investment income as exceeds $25,000, or 44 percent of the amount by which such taxable income exceeds $3,000, whichever is lesser; plus

(B) SURTAX.—A surtax on the taxable investment income computed as provided in section 11(c) as though the taxable investment income were the taxable income referred to in section 11(c).

• 1977, Tax Reduction and Simplification Act of 1977 (P.L. 95-30)

P.L. 95-30, §201:

Substituted "December 31, 1978" for "December 31, 1977" in Code Sec. 821(c)(1)(A)(i) and "January 1, 1979" for "January 1, 1978" in Code Sec. 821(c)(1)(A)(ii). **Effective** 5-23-77.

• 1976, Tax Reform Act of 1976 (P.L. 94-455)

P.L. 94-455, §901(b)(2):

Amended Code Sec. 821(c)(1)(A). **Effective** for tax years ending after 12-31-74. Prior to amendment, Code Sec. 821(c)(1)(A) read as follows:

(A) Normal Tax.—A normal tax of 22 percent of the taxable investment income, or 44 percent of the amount by which such taxable income exceeds $3,000, whichever is the lesser; plus

P.L. 94-455, §1901(a)(104):

Struck out "In the case of taxable years beginning after December 31, 1963, there is" and inserting "There is" in its place at the beginning of Code Sec. 821(c)(1). **Effective** for tax years begining after 12-31-76.

• 1964, Revenue Act of 1964 (P.L. 88-272)

P.L. 88-272, §123(a)(2):

Amended paragraph (c)(1). **Effective** with respect to tax years beginning after 12-31-63. Prior to amendment, paragraph (1) read as follows:

"(1) Imposition of tax.—In the case of taxable years beginning after December 31, 1962, there is hereby imposed for each taxable year on the income of each mutual insurance company to which this subsection applies a tax (which shall be in lieu of the tax imposed by subsection (a)) computed as follows:

"(A) Normal tax.—

"(i) Taxable years beginning before July 1, 1964.—In the case of taxable years beginning before July 1, 1964, a normal tax of 30 percent of the taxable investment income, or 60 percent of the amount by which such taxable income exceeds $3,000, whichever is the lesser;

"(ii) Taxable years beginning after June 30, 1964.—In the case of taxable years beginning after June 30, 1964, a normal tax of 25 percent of the taxable investment income, or 50 percent of the amount by which such taxable income exceeds $3,000, whichever is the lesser; plus

"(B) Surtax.—A surtax of 22 percent of the taxable investment income (computed without regard to the deduction provided in section 242 for partially tax-exempt interest) in excess of $25,000."

[Sec. 821(d)]

(d) ELECTION TO INCLUDE STATUTORY UNDERWRITING INCOME OR LOSS.—

(1) IN GENERAL.—Any mutual insurance company which is subject to the tax imposed by subsection (c) may elect, in such manner and at such time as the Secretary may by regulations prescribe, to be subject to the tax imposed by subsection (a).

(2) EFFECT OF ELECTION.—If an election is made under paragraph (1), the electing company shall be subject to the tax imposed by subsection (a) (and shall not be subject to the tax imposed by subsection (c)) for the first taxable year for which such election is made and for all taxable years thereafter unless the Secretary consents to a revocation of such election.

Amendments

• 1976, Tax Reform Act of 1976 (P.L. 94-455)

P.L. 94-455, §1906(b)(13)(A):

Amended 1954 Code by substituting "Secretary" for "Secretary or his delegate" each place it appeared. **Effective** 2-1-77.

[Sec. 821(e)]

(e) TAX APPLICABLE TO MEMBER OF GROUP FILING CONSOLIDATED RETURN.—Notwithstanding any other provision of this section, if a mutual insurance company to which this section applies joins in the filing of a consolidated return (or is required to so file), the applicable tax shall consist of a normal tax and a surtax computed as provided in section 11 as though the mutual insurance company taxable income of such company were the taxable income referred to in section 11.

Amendments

• 1976, Tax Reform Act of 1976 (P.L. 94-455)

P.L. 94-455, §1507(b)(1):

Redesignated former Code Sec. 821(e) as 821(f) and added a new Code Sec. 821(e). **Effective** for tax years beginning after 12-31-80.

P.L. 94-455, §1901(a)(104):

Repealed former Code Sec. 821(e) and redesignated former Code Sec. 821(f) as Code Sec. 821(e). **Effective** for tax years beginning after 12-31-76. Prior to repeal, Code Sec. 821(e) read as follows:

(e) SPECIAL TRANSITIONAL UNDERWRITING LOSS.

(1) COMPANIES TO WHICH SUBSECTION APPLIES.—This subsection shall apply to every mutual insurance company which has been subject to the tax imposed by this section (as in effect before the enactment of this subsection) for the 5 taxable years immediately preceding January 1, 1962, and has incurred an underwriting loss for each of such 5 taxable years.

(2) REDUCTION OF STATUTORY UNDERWRITING INCOME.—For purposes of this part, the statutory underwriting income of a company described in paragraph (1) for the taxable year shall be the statutory underwriting income for the taxable year (determined without regard to this subsection) reduced by the amount by which—

(A) the sum of the underwriting losses of such company for the 5 taxable years immediately preceding January 1, 1962, exceeds

(B) the total amount by which the company's statutory underwriting income was reduced by reason of this subsection for prior taxable years.

(3) UNDERWRITING LOSS DEFINED.—For purposes of this subsection, the term "underwriting loss" means statutory underwriting loss, computed without any deduction under section 824(a) and without any deduction under section 832(c)(11).

(4) YEARS TO WHICH SUBSECTION APPLIES.—This subsection shall apply with respect to any taxable year beginning after December 31, 1962, and before January 1, 1968, for which the taxpayer is subject to the tax imposed by subsection (a).

[Sec. 821(f)]

(f) CROSS REFERENCES.—

(1) For exemption from tax of certain mutual insurance companies, see section 501(c)(15).

(2) For alternative tax in case of capital gains, see section 1201(a).

(3) For taxation of foreign corporations carrying on an insurance business within the United States, see section 842.

Amendments

• 1976, Tax Reform Act of 1976 (P.L. 94-455)

P.L. 94-455, §1507(b)(1):

Redesignated former Code Sec. 821(e) as Code Sec. 821(f). **Effective** for tax years beginning after 12-31-80.

P.L. 94-455, §1901(a)(104):

Redesignated former Code Sec. 821(f) as Code Sec. 821(e). **Effective** for tax years beginning after 12-31-76.

• 1966, Foreign Investors Tax Act of 1966 (P.L. 89-809)

P.L. 89-809, §104(i)(4):

Amended Code Sec. 821 by striking out subsection (e), by redesignating subsections (f) and (g) as subsections (e) and (f), and by adding new subsection (f)(3). **Effective** 1-1-67. Prior to deletion, subsection (e) read as follows:

"(e) No United States Insurance Business.—Foreign mutual insurance companies (other than a life insurance company and other than a fire, flood, or marine insurance company subject to the tax imposed by section 831) not carrying on an insurance business within the United States shall not be subject to this part but shall be taxable as other foreign corporations."

• 1963, Tax Rate Extension Act of 1963 (P.L. 88-52)

P.L. 88-52, §2:

Amended Code Secs. 821(a)(1) and (c)(1)(A) by substituting "1964" for "1963" wherever it appeared.

• 1962, Revenue Act of 1962 (P.L. 87-834)

P.L. 87-834, §8:

Amended part II of subchapter L of chapter 1, including Code Sec. 821. **Effective** 1-1-63. Prior to amendment the table of contents for part II and Code Sec. 821 read as follows:

PART II—MUTUAL INSURANCE COMPANIES (OTHER THAN LIFE OR MARINE OR FIRE INSURANCE COMPANIES ISSUING PERPETUAL POLICIES)

Sec. 821. Tax on mutual insurance companies (other than life or marine or fire insurance companies issuing perpetual policies).

Sec. 822. Determination of mutual insurance company taxable income.

Sec. 823. Other definitions.

SEC. 821. TAX ON MUTUAL INSURANCE COMPANIES (OTHER THAN LIFE OR MARINE OR FIRE INSURANCE COMPANIES ISSUING PERPETUAL POLICIES).

(a) Imposition of Tax on Mutual Companies Other Than Interinsurers.—There shall be imposed for each taxable year on the income of every mutual insurance company (other than a life or a marine insurance company or a fire insurance company subject to the tax imposed by section 831 and other than an interinsurer or reciprocal underwriter) a tax computed under paragraph (1) or paragraph (2), whichever is the greater:

(1) If the mutual insurance company taxable income (computed without regard to the deduction provided in section 242 for partially tax-exempt interest) is over $3,000, a tax computed as follows:

(A) Normal tax.—

(i) Taxable years beginning before July 1, 1963.—In the case of taxable years beginning before July 1, 1963, a normal tax of 30 percent of the mutual insurance company taxable income, or 60 percent of the amount by which such taxable income exceeds $3,000, whichever is the lesser;

(ii) Taxable years beginning after June 30, 1963.—In the case of taxable years beginning after June 30, 1963, a normal tax of 25 percent of the mutual insurance company taxable income, or 50 percent of the amount by which such taxable income exceeds $3,000, whichever is the lesser; plus

(B) Surtax.—A surtax of 22 percent of the mutual insurance company taxable income (computed without regard to the deduction provided in section 242 for partially tax-exempt interest) in excess of $25,000.

(2) If for the taxable year the gross amount of income from the items described in section 822(b) (other than paragraph (1)(D) thereof) and net premiums, minus dividends to policyholders, minus the interest which under section 103 is excluded from gross income, exceeds $75,000, a tax equal to 1 percent of the amount so computed, or 2 percent of the excess of the amount so computed over $75,000, whichever is the lesser.

(b) Imposition of Tax on Interinsurers.—In the case of every mutual insurance company which is an interinsurer or reciprocal underwriter (other than a life or a marine insurance company or a fire insurance company (subject to the tax imposed by section 831), if the mutual insurance company taxable income (computed as provided in subsection (a)(1)) is over $50,000, there shall be imposed for each taxable year on the mutual insurance company taxable income a tax computed as follows:

(1) Normal tax.—

(A) Taxable years beginning before July 1, 1963.—In the case of taxable years beginning before July 1, 1963, a normal tax of 30 percent of the mutual insurance company taxable income, or 60 percent of the amount by which such taxable income exceeds $50,000, whichever is the lesser;

(B) Taxable years beginning after June 30, 1963.—In the case of a taxable year beginning after June 30, 1963, a normal tax of 25 percent of the mutual insurance company taxable income, or 50 percent of the amount by which such taxable income exceeds $50,000, whichever is the lesser; plus

(2) Surtax.—A surtax of 22 percent of the mutual insurance company taxable income (computed as provided in subsection (a)(1)) in excess of $25,000, or 33 percent of the amount by which such taxable income exceeds $50,000, whichever is the lesser.

(c) Gross Amount Received, Over $75,000 but Less Than $125,000.—If the gross amount received during the taxable year from the items described in section 822(b) (other than paragraph (1)(D) thereof) and premiums (including deposits and assessments) is over $75,000 but less than $125,000, the tax imposed by subsection (a) or subsection (b), whichever applies, shall be reduced to an amount which bears the same proportion to the amount of the tax determined under such subsection as the excess over $75,000 of such gross amount received bears to $50,000.

(d) No United States Insurance Business.—Foreign mutual insurance companies (other than a life or marine insurance company or a fire insurance company subject to the tax imposed by section 831) not carrying on an insurance business within the United States shall not be subject to this part but shall be taxable as other foreign corporations.

(e) Alternative Tax on Capital Gains.—

For alternative tax in case of capital gains, see section 1201(a).

Amendments

• 1962, Tax Rate Extension Act of 1962 (P.L. 87-508)

P.L. 87-508, §2:

Amended Code Secs. 821(a)(1)(A) and (b)(1) by substituting "1963" for "1962" wherever it appeared.

• 1961, Tax Rate Extension Act of 1961 (P.L. 87-72)

P.L. 87-72, §2:

Amended Code Secs. 821(a)(1)(A) and (b)(1) by substituting "1962" for "1961".

• 1960, Public Debt and Tax Rate Extension Act of 1960 (P.L. 86-564)

P.L. 86-564, §201:

Amended Code Secs. 821(a)(1)(A) and (b)(1) by striking "1960" wherever it appeared and by substituting "1961".

• 1959, Tax Rate Extension Act of 1959 (P.L. 86-75)

P.L. 86-75, §2:

Substituted "1960" for "1959" in Code Secs. 821(a)(1)(A) and (b)(1).

• 1958, Tax Rate Extension Act of 1958 (P.L. 85-475)

P.L. 85-475, §2:

Substituted "July 1, 1959" for "July 1, 1958" in Code Sec. 821(a)(1)(A), and substituted "June 30, 1959" for "June 30, 1958" in Code Sec. 821(a)(1)(A).

• 1957, Tax Rate Extension Act of 1957 (P.L. 85-12)

P.L. 85-12, §2:

Substituted "July 1, 1958" for "April 1, 1957" and "June 30, 1958" for "March 31, 1957" in Code Secs. 821(a)(1)(A) and (b)(1).

• 1956, Tax Rate Extension Act of 1956 (P.L. 458, 84th Cong.)

P.L. 458, 84th Cong., §2:

Substituted "1957" for "1956" wherever it appeared in Code Secs. 821(a)(1)(A) and (b)(1).

• 1956, Life Insurance Company Tax Act for 1955 (P.L. 429, 84th Cong.)

P.L. 429, 84th Cong., §3(a)(1):

Amended Code Secs. 821(a)(2) and (c) by substituting "the items described in section 822(b) (other than paragraph (1)(D) thereof)" for "interest, dividends, rents". **Effective** 1-1-55.

• 1955, Tax Rate Extension Act of 1955 (P.L. 18, 84th Cong.)

P.L. 18, 84th Cong., §2:

Substituted "1956" for "1955" in Code Secs. 821(a)(1)(A) and (b)(1).

[Sec. 823—Repealed]

Amendments

• 1986, Tax Reform Act of 1986 (P.L. 99-514)

P.L. 99-514, §1024(a)(1):

Repealed Code Sec. 823. **Effective** for tax years beginning after 12-31-86. Prior to repeal, Code Sec. 823 read as follows:

SEC. 823. DETERMINATION OF STATUTORY UNDERWRITING INCOME OR LOSS.

[Sec. 823(a)]

(a) IN GENERAL.—For purposes of this part—

(1) The term "statutory underwriting income" means the amount by which—

(A) the gross income which would be taken into account in computing taxable income under section 832 if the taxpayer were subject to the tax imposed by section 831, reduced by the gross investment income, exceeds

(B) the sum of (i) the deductions which would be taken into account in computing taxable income if the taxpayer were subject to the tax imposed by section 831, reduced by the deductions provided in section 822(c), plus (ii) the deductions provided in subsection (c) and section 824(a).

(2) The term "statutory underwriting loss" means the excess of the amount referred to in paragraph (1)(B) over the amount referred to in paragraph (1)(A).

[Sec. 823(b)]

(b) MODIFICATIONS.—In applying subsection (a)—

(1) NET OPERATING LOSS DEDUCTION.—Except as provided by section 844, the deduction for net operating losses provided in section 172 shall not be allowed.

(2) INTERINSURERS.—In the case of a mutual insurance company which is an interinsurer or reciprocal underwriter—

(A) there shall be allowed as a deduction the increase for the taxable year in savings credited to subscriber accounts, or

(B) there shall be included as an item of gross income the decrease for the taxable year in savings credited to subscriber accounts.

For purposes of the preceding sentence, the term "savings credited to subscriber accounts" means such portion of the surplus as is credited to the individual accounts of subscribers before the 16th day of the third month following the close of the taxable year, but only if the company would be obligated to pay such amount promptly to such subscriber if he terminated his contract at the close of the company's taxable year. For purposes of determining his taxable income, the subscriber shall treat any such savings credited to his account as a dividend paid or declared.

Amendments

• 1969, Tax Reform Act of 1969 (P.L. 91-172)

P.L. 91-172, §907(c)(2)(B):

Amended Code Sec. 823(b)(1) by changing "The" to "Except as provided by section 844, the". **Effective** for losses incurred in tax years beginning after 12-31-62, but does not affect any tax liability for any tax year beginning before 1-1-67.

[Sec. 823(c)]

(c) SPECIAL DEDUCTION FOR SMALL COMPANY HAVING GROSS AMOUNT OF LESS THAN $1,100,000.—

(1) IN GENERAL.—If the gross amount received during the taxable year by a taxpayer subject to the tax imposed by section 821(a) from the items described in section 822(b) (other than paragraph (1)(D) thereof) and premiums (including deposits and assessments) does not equal or exceed $1,100,000, then in determining the statutory underwriting income or loss for the taxable year there shall be allowed an additional deduction of $6,000; except that if such gross amount exceeds $500,000, such additional deduction shall be equal to 1 percent of the amount by which $1,100,000 exceeds such gross amount.

(2) LIMITATION.—The amount of the deduction allowed under paragraph (1) shall not exceed the statutory underwriting income for the taxable year, computed without regard to any deduction under this subsection or section 824(a).

Amendments

• 1962, Revenue Tax Act of 1962 (P.L. 87-834)

P.L. 87-834, §8:

Added new Code Sec. 823. **Effective** 1-1-63.

[Sec. 824—Repealed]

Amendments

• 1986, Tax Reform Act of 1986 (P.L. 99-514)

P.L. 99-514, §1024(a)(1):

Repealed Code Sec. 824. **Effective** for tax years beginning after 12-31-86. For a transitional rule, see Act Sec. 1024(d)(1), below.

P.L. 99-514, §1024(d)(1), as amended by P.L. 100-647, §1010(f)(8), provides:

(d) TRANSITIONAL RULES.—

(1) TREATMENT OF AMOUNTS IN PROTECTION AGAINST LOSS ACCOUNT.—In the case of any insurance company which had a protection against loss account for its last taxable year beginning before January 1, 1987, there shall be included in the gross income of such company for any taxable year beginning after December 31, 1986, the amount which would have been included in gross income for such taxable year under section 824 of the Internal Revenue Code of 1954 (as in effect on the day before the date of the enactment of this Act). For purposes of the preceding sentence, no addition to such account shall be made for any taxable year beginning after December 31, 1986. In the case of a company taxable under section 831(b) of the Internal Revenue Code of 1986 (as amended by subsection (a)), any amount included in gross income under this paragraph shall be treated as gross investment income.

Reproduced immediately below is the text of Code Sec. 824 prior to repeal by P.L. 99-514.

SEC. 824. ADJUSTMENTS TO PROVIDE PROTECTION AGAINST LOSSES.

[Sec. 824(a)]

(a) ALLOWANCE OF DEDUCTION.—

(1) IN GENERAL.—In determining the statutory underwriting income or loss for any taxable year there shall be allowed as a deduction the sum of—

(A) an amount equal to 1 percent of the losses incurred during the taxable year (as determined under section 832(b)(5)), plus

(B) an amount equal to 25 percent of the underwriting gain for the taxable year, plus

(C) if the concentrated windstorm, etc., premium percentage for the taxable year exceeds 40 percent, an amount determined by applying so much of such percentage as exceeds 40 percent to the underwriting gain for the taxable year.

For purposes of this paragraph, the term "underwriting gain" means statutory underwriting income, computed without any deduction under this subsection.

(2) SPECIAL RULE FOR COMPANIES HAVING CONCENTRATED WINDSTORM, ETC., RISKS.—For purposes of paragraph (1)(C), the term "concentrated windstorm, etc., premium percentage" means, with respect to any taxable year, the percentage obtained by dividing—

(A) the amount of the premiums earned on insurance contracts during the taxable year (as defined in section 832(b)(4)), to the extent attributable to insuring against losses arising, either in any one State or within 200 miles of any fixed point selected by the taxpayer, from windstorm, hail, flood, earthquake, or similar hazards, by

(B) the amount of the premiums earned on insurance contracts during the taxable year (as so defined).

[Sec. 824(b)]

(b) PROTECTION AGAINST LOSS ACCOUNT.—Each insurance company subject to the tax imposed by section 821(a) for any taxable year shall, for purposes of this part, establish and maintain a protection against loss account.

[Sec. 824(c)]

(c) ADDITIONS TO ACCOUNT.—There shall be added to the protection against loss account for each taxable year an amount equal to the amount allowable as a deduction for the taxable year under subsection (a)(1).

[Sec. 824(d)]

(d) SUBTRACTIONS.—

(1) ANNUAL SUBTRACTIONS.—After applying subsection (c), there shall be subtracted for the taxable year from the protection against loss account—

(A) first, an amount equal to the excess (if any) of the deduction allowed under subsection (a) for the taxable year over the underwriting gain (within the meaning of subsection (a)(1)) for the taxable year,

(B) then, the amount (if any) by which—

(i) the sum of the investment loss for such year and the statutory underwriting loss (reduced by the amount referred to in subparagraph (A)) for such year, exceeds

(ii) the sum of the statutory underwriting income for such taxable year and the taxable investment income for such taxable year,

(C) next (in the order in which the losses occurred), amounts equal to the unused loss carryovers to such year,

(D) next, any amount remaining which was added to the account for the fifth preceding taxable year, minus one-half of the amount remaining in the account for such taxable year which was added by reason of subsection (a)(1)(B), and

(E) finally, the amount by which the total amount in the account exceeds whichever of the following is the greater:

(i) 10 percent of premiums earned on insurance contracts during the taxable year (as defined in section 832(b)(4)) less dividends to policyholders (as defined in section 832(c)(11)), or

(ii) the total amount in the account at the close of the preceding taxable year.

(2) RULES FOR CEILING ON PROTECTION AGAINST LOSS ACCOUNT.—For purposes of paragraph (1)(E), the total amount in the account shall be determined—

(A) after the application of this section without regard to paragraph (1)(E), and

(B) without taking into consideration amounts remaining in the account which were added, with respect to all taxable years, by reason of subsection (a)(1)(C).

(3) PRIORITIES.—The amounts required to be subtracted from the protection against loss account—

(A) under subparagraphs (A), (B), and (C) of paragraph (1) shall be subtracted—

(i) first (on a first-in, first-out, basis) from amounts in the account with respect to the five preceding taxable years and the taxable year, and

(ii) then from amounts in the account with respect to earlier years,

(B) under subparagraph (E) of paragraph (1) shall be subtracted only from amounts in the account with respect to the taxable year, and

(C) under subparagraphs (A), (B), (C), and (E) of paragraph (1) shall, if the amount to be subtracted from the total amounts in the account with respect to any taxable year is less than such total, be subtracted from each of the amounts (referred to in subsection (a)(1)) in the account with respect to such year in the proportion which each bears to such total.

(4) TERMINATION OF TAXABILITY UNDER SECTION 821.—If the taxpayer is not subject to tax under section 821 for any taxable year, the entire amount in the account at the close of the preceding taxable year shall be subtracted from the account in such preceding taxable year.

(5) ELECTION TO SUBTRACT AMOUNT FROM ACCOUNT.—

(A) A taxpayer may elect for any taxable year for which it is subject to tax under section 821(a) to subtract from its protection against loss account any amount which, but for the application of this subparagraph, would be in such account as of the close of such taxable year.

(B) The election provided by subparagraph (A) for any taxable year shall be made (in such manner and in such form as the Secretary may by regulations prescribe) after the close of such taxable year and not later than the time prescribed by law for filing the return (including extensions thereof) for the taxable year following such taxable year. Such an election, once made, may not be revoked.

Amendments

• 1976, Tax Reform Act of 1976 (P.L. 94-455)

P.L. 94-455, §1906(b)(13)(A):

Amended 1954 Code by substituting "Secretary" for "Secretary or his delegate" each place it appeared. **Effective** 2-1-77.

• 1962, Revenue Act of 1962 (P.L. 87-834)

P.L. 87-834, §8:

Added new Code Sec. 824. **Effective** 1-1-63.

[Sec. 825—Repealed]

Amendments

• 1986, Tax Reform Act of 1986 (P.L. 99-514)

P.L. 99-514, §1024(a)(1):

Repealed Code Sec. 825. **Effective** for tax years beginning after 12-31-86. For a transitional rule, see Act Sec. 1024(d)(2), below.

P.L. 99-514, §1024(d)(2), provides:

(2) TRANSITIONAL RULE FOR UNUSED LOSS CARRYOVER UNDER SECTION 825.—Any unused loss carryover under section 825 of the Internal Revenue Code of 1954 (as in effect on the day before the date of the enactment of this Act) which—

(A) is from a taxable year beginning before January 1, 1987, and

(B) could have been carried under such section to a taxable year beginning after December 31, 1986, but for the repeal made by subsection (a)(1),

shall be included in the net operating loss deduction under section 832(c)(10) of such Code without regard to the limitations of section 844(b) of such Code.

Reproduced immediately below is the text of Code Sec. 825 prior to repeal by P.L. 99-514.

SEC. 825. UNUSED LOSS DEDUCTION.

[Sec. 825(a)]

(a) AMOUNT OF DEDUCTION.—For purposes of this part, the unused loss deduction for the taxable year shall be an amount equal to the unused loss carryovers or carrybacks to the taxable year.

[Sec. 825(b)]

(b) UNUSED LOSS DEFINED.—For purposes of this part, the term "unused loss" means, with respect to any taxable year, the amount (if any) by which—

(1) the sum of the statutory underwriting loss and the investment loss, exceeds

(2) the sum of—

(A) the taxable investment income,

(B) the statutory underwriting income, and

(C) the amounts required by section 824(d) to be subtracted from the protection against loss account.

[Sec. 825(c)]

(c) LOSS YEAR DEFINED.—For purposes of this part, the term "loss year" means, with respect to any company subject to the tax imposed by section 821(a), any taxable year in which the unused loss (as defined in subsection (b)) of such taxpayer is more than zero.

[Sec. 825(d)]

(d) YEARS TO WHICH CARRIED.—

(1) IN GENERAL.—The unused loss for any taxable year shall be—

(A) an unused loss carryback to each of the 3 taxable years preceding the loss year, and

(B) an unused loss carryover to each of the 5 taxable years following the loss year.

In the case of an unused loss for a taxable year ending after December 31, 1975, such unused loss shall be an unused loss carryover to each of the 15 taxable years following the loss year.

(2) ELECTION FOR UNUSED LOSS CARRYBACKS.—In the case of an unused loss for any taxable year ending after December 31, 1975, the taxpayer may elect to relinquish the entire carryback period for such loss. Such election shall be made by the due date (including extensions of time) for filing the return for the taxable year of the unused loss for which the election is to be in effect, and once made for any taxable year, such election shall be irrevocable for that taxable year.

Amendments

• 1981, Economic Recovery Tax Act of 1981 (P.L. 97-34)

P.L. 97-34, §207(b):

Amended Code Sec. 825(d)(1) by striking out "7" and inserting in lieu thereof "15". **Effective** for net operating losses in tax years ending after 12-31-75. However, P.L. 97-34, §207(c), as amended by P.L. 97-448, §102(d)(2), provides that the amendment shall not apply to any amount that, under the law in effect on 1-11-83, could not be carried to a tax year ending in 1981.

• 1976, Tax Reform Act of 1976 (P.L. 94-455)

P.L. 94-455, §806(d)(2):

Amended Code Sec. 825(d). **Effective** for losses incurred in tax years ending after 12-31-75. Prior to amendment, Code Sec. 825(d) read as follows:

(d) YEARS TO WHICH CARRIED.—The unused loss for any loss year shall be—

(1) an unused loss carryback to each of the 3 taxable years preceding the loss year, and

(2) an unused loss carryover to each of the 5 taxable years following the loss year.

[Sec. 825(e)]

(e) AMOUNT OF CARRYBACKS AND CARRYOVERS.—The entire amount of the unused loss for any loss year shall be carried to the earliest of the taxable years to which such loss may be carried. The portion of such loss which shall be carried to each of the other taxable years shall be the excess (if any) of the amount of such loss over the sum of the offsets (as defined in subsection (f)) for each of the prior taxable years to which such loss may be carried.

[Sec. 825(f)]

(f) OFFSET DEFINED.—For purposes of subsection (e), the term "offset" means with respect to any taxable year (hereinafter referred to as the "offset year")—

(1) in the case of an unused loss carryback from the loss year to the offset year, the mutual insurance company taxable income for the offset year; or

(2) in the case of an unused loss carryover from the loss year to the offset year, an amount equal to the sum of—

(A) the amount required to be subtracted from the protection against loss account under section 824(d)(1)(C) for the offset year, plus

(B) the mutual insurance company taxable income for the offset year.

For purposes of paragraphs (1) and (2)(B), the mutual insurance company taxable income for the offset year shall be determined without regard to any unused loss carryback or carryover from the loss year or any taxable year thereafter.

[Sec. 825(g)]

(g) LIMITATIONS.—For purposes of this part, an unused loss shall not be carried—

(1) except as provided by section 844, to or from any taxable year for which the insurance company is not subject to the tax imposed by section 821(a), nor

(2) except as provided by section 844, to any taxable year if, between the loss year and such taxable year, there is an intervening taxable year for which the insurance company was not subject to the tax imposed by section 821(a).

Amendments

• 1976, Tax Reform Act of 1976 (P.L. 94-455)

P.L. 94-455, §1901(a)(106):

Struck out paragraph (1) and redesignated paragraphs (2) and (3) as paragraphs (1) and (2), respectively. **Effective** with respect to tax years beginning after 12-31-76. Prior to repeal, Code Sec. 825(g)(1) read as follows:

(1) to or from any taxable year beginning before January 1, 1963,

• 1969, Tax Reform Act of 1969 (P.L. 91-172)

P.L. 91-172, §907(c)(2)(C):

Amended Code Sec. 825(g)(2) and (3) by adding "except as provided by section 844,". **Effective** with respect to losses incurred in tax years beginning after 12-31-62, but shall not affect any tax liability for any tax year beginning before 1-1-67.

• 1962, Revenue Act of 1962 (P.L. 87-834)

P.L. 87-834, §8:

Added new Code Sec. 825. **Effective** 1-1-63.

PART II—OTHER INSURANCE COMPANIES

[Sec. 831]

SEC. 831. TAX ON INSURANCE COMPANIES OTHER THAN LIFE INSURANCE COMPANIES.

[Sec. 831(a)]

(a) GENERAL RULE.—Taxes computed as provided in section 11 shall be imposed for each taxable year on the taxable income of every insurance company other than a life insurance company.

[Sec. 831(b)]

(b) ALTERNATIVE TAX FOR CERTAIN SMALL COMPANIES.—

(1) IN GENERAL.—In lieu of the tax otherwise applicable under subsection (a), there is hereby imposed for each taxable year on the income of every insurance company to which this subsection applies a tax computed by multiplying the taxable investment income of such company for such taxable year by the rates provided in section 11(b).

(2) COMPANIES TO WHICH THIS SUBSECTION APPLIES.—

(A) IN GENERAL.—This subsection shall apply to every insurance company other than life (including interinsurers and reciprocal underwriters) if—

(i) the net written premiums (or, if greater, direct written premiums) for the taxable year do not exceed $1,200,000, and

(ii) such company elects the application of this subsection for such taxable year.

The election under clause (ii) shall apply to the taxable year for which made and for all subsequent taxable years for which the requirements of clause (i) are met. Such an election, once made, may be revoked only with the consent of the Secretary.

(B) CONTROLLED GROUP RULES.—

(i) IN GENERAL.—For purposes of subparagraph (A), in determining whether any company is described in clause (i) of subparagraph (A), such company shall be treated as receiving during the taxable year amounts described in such clause (i) which are received during such year by all other companies which are members of the same controlled group as the insurance company for which the determination is being made.

(ii) CONTROLLED GROUP.—For purposes of clause (i), the term "controlled group" means any controlled group of corporations (as defined in section 1563(a)); except that—

(I) "more than 50 percent" shall be substituted for "at least 80 percent" each place it appears in section 1563(a), and

(II) subsections (a)(4) and (b)(2)(D) of section 1563 shall not apply.

(3) LIMITATION ON USE OF NET OPERATING LOSSES.—For purposes of this part, except as provided in section 844, a net operating loss (as defined in section 172) shall not be carried—

(A) to or from any taxable year for which the insurance company is not subject to the tax imposed by subsection (a), or

(B) to any taxable year if, between the taxable year from which such loss is being carried and such taxable year, there is an intervening taxable year for which the insurance company was not subject to the tax imposed by subsection (a).

Amendments

• 2004, Pension Funding Equity Act of 2004 (P.L. 108-218)

P.L. 108-218, §206(d):

Amended Code Sec. 831(b)(2)(A)(i) by striking "exceed $350,000 but" following "for the taxable year". **Effective** generally for tax years beginning after 12-31-2003. For a transition rule, see Act Sec. 206(e)(2), below.

P.L. 108-218, §206(e)(2), provides:

(2) TRANSITION RULE FOR COMPANIES IN RECEIVERSHIP OR LIQUIDATION.—In the case of a company or association which—

(A) for the taxable year which includes April 1, 2004, meets the requirements of section 501(c)(15)(A) of the Internal Revenue Code of 1986, as in effect for the last taxable year beginning before January 1, 2004, and

(B) on April 1, 2004, is in a receivership, liquidation, or similar proceeding under the supervision of a State court,

the amendments made by this section shall apply to taxable years beginning after the earlier of the date such proceeding ends or December 31, 2007.

• 1988, Technical and Miscellaneous Revenue Act of 1988 (P.L. 100-647)

P.L. 100-647, §1010(f)(1):

Amended Code Sec. 831(b)(2)(A) by adding at the end thereof a new sentence. **Effective** as if included in the provision of P.L. 99-514 to which it relates.

P.L. 100-647, §1010(f)(9):

Amended Code Sec. 831(b) by adding at the end thereof new paragraph (3). **Effective** as if included in the provision of P.L. 99-514 to which it relates.

[Sec. 831(c)]

(c) INSURANCE COMPANY DEFINED.—For purposes of this section, the term "insurance company" has the meaning given to such term by section 816(a)).

Amendments

• 2004, Pension Funding Equity Act of 2004 (P.L. 108-218)

P.L. 108-218, §206(c):

Amended Code Sec. 831 by redesignating subsection (c) as subsection (d) and by inserting after subsection (b) a new subsection (c). **Effective** generally for tax years beginning after 12-31-2003. For a transition rule, see Act Sec. 206(e)(2), below.

P.L. 108-218, §206(e)(2), provides:

(2) TRANSITION RULE FOR COMPANIES IN RECEIVERSHIP OR LIQUIDATION.—In the case of a company or association which—

(A) for the taxable year which includes April 1, 2004, meets the requirements of section 501(c)(15)(A) of the Internal Revenue Code of 1986, as in effect for the last taxable year beginning before January 1, 2004, and

(B) on April 1, 2004, is in a receivership, liquidation, or similar proceeding under the supervision of a State court,

the amendments made by this section shall apply to taxable years beginning after the earlier of the date such proceeding ends or December 31, 2007.

[Sec. 831(d)]

(d) CROSS REFERENCES.—

(1) For alternative tax in case of capital gains, see section 1201(a).

(2) For taxation of foreign corporations carrying on an insurance business within the United States, see section 842.

(3) For exemption from tax for certain insurance companies other than life, see section 501(c)(15).

Amendments

• 2004, Pension Funding Equity Act of 2004 (P.L. 108-218)

P.L. 108-218, §206(c):

Amended Code Sec. 831 by redesignating subsection (c) as subsection (d). **Effective** generally for tax years beginning after 12-31-2003. For a transition rule, see Act Sec. 206(e)(2), below.

P.L. 108-218, §206(e)(2), provides:

(2) TRANSITION RULE FOR COMPANIES IN RECEIVERSHIP OR LIQUIDATION.—In the case of a company or association which—

(A) for the taxable year which includes April 1, 2004, meets the requirements of section 501(c)(15)(A) of the Internal Revenue Code of 1986, as in effect for the last taxable year beginning before January 1, 2004, and

(B) on April 1, 2004, is in a receivership, liquidation, or similar proceeding under the supervision of a State court,

the amendments made by this section shall apply to taxable years beginning after the earlier of the date such proceeding ends or December 31, 2007.

• 1986, Tax Reform Act of 1986 (P.L. 99-514)

P.L. 99-514, §1024(a)(4):

Amended Code Sec. 831. **Effective** for tax years beginning after 12-31-86. Prior to amendment, Code Sec. 831 read as follows:

SEC. 831. TAX ON INSURANCE COMPANIES (OTHER THAN LIFE OR MUTUAL), MUTUAL MARINE INSURANCE COMPANIES, AND CERTAIN MUTUAL FIRE OR FLOOD INSURANCE COMPANIES.

[Sec. 831(a)]

(a) IMPOSITION OF TAX.—Taxes computed as provided in section 11 shall be imposed for each taxable year on the taxable income of—

(1) every insurance company (other than a life or mutual insurance company),

(2) every mutual marine insurance company, and

(3) every mutual fire or flood insurance company—

(A) exclusively issuing perpetual policies, or

(B) whose principal business is the issuance of policies for which the premium deposits are the same, regardless of the length of the term for which the policies are written, if the unabsorbed portion of such premium deposits not required for losses, expenses, or establishment of reserves is returned or credited to the policyholder on cancellation or expiration of the policy.

Amendments

• 1976, Tax Reform Act of 1976 (P.L. 94-455)

P.L. 94-455, §1901(a)(107):

Substituted "on the taxable income" for "or the taxable income" in Code Sec. 831(a). **Effective** for tax years beginning after 12-31-76.

• 1962, Revenue Act of 1962 (P.L. 87-834)

P.L. 87-834, §8:

Amended Code Sec. 831(a). **Effective** 1-1-63. Prior to the amendment Sec. 831(a) read as follows:

SEC. 831. TAX ON INSURANCE COMPANIES (OTHER THAN LIFE OR MUTUAL), MUTUAL MARINE INSURANCE COMPANIES, AND MUTUAL FIRE INSURANCE COMPANIES ISSUING PERPETUAL POLICIES.

(a) Imposition of Tax.—Taxes computed as provided in section 11 shall be imposed for each taxable year on the taxable income of every insurance company (other than a life or mutual insurance company), every mutual marine insurance company, and every mutual fire insurance company exclusively issuing either perpetual policies or policies for which the sole premium charged is a single deposit which (except for such deduction of underwriting costs as may be provided) is refundable on cancellation or expiration of the policy.

[Sec. 831(b)]

(b) ELECTION FOR MULTIPLE LINE COMPANY TO BE TAXED ON TOTAL INCOME.—

(1) IN GENERAL.—Any mutual insurance company engaged in writing marine, fire, and casualty insurance which for any 5-year period beginning after December 31, 1941, and ending before January 1, 1962, was subject to the tax imposed by section 831 (or the tax imposed by corresponding provisions of prior law) may elect, in such manner and at such time as the Secretary may by regulations prescribe, to be subject to the tax imposed by section 831, whether or not marine insurance is its predominant source of premium income.

(2) EFFECT OF ELECTION.—If an election is made under paragraph (1), the electing company shall (in lieu of being subject to the tax imposed by section 821) be subject to the tax imposed by this section for taxable years beginning after December 31, 1961. Such election shall not be revoked except with the consent of the Secretary.

Amendments

• 1976, Tax Reform Act of 1976 (P.L. 94-455)

P.L. 94-455, §1906(b)(13)(A):

Amended 1954 Code by substituting "Secretary" for "Secretary or his delegate" each place it appeared. **Effective** 2-1-77.

• 1966, Foreign Investors Tax Act of 1966 (P.L. 89-809)

P.L. 89-809, §104(i)(6):

Amended Code Sec. 831 by striking out subsection (b) and by redesignating subsection (c) as subsection (b). **Effective** 1-1-67. Prior to deletion, subsection (b) read as follows:

"(b) No United States Insurance Business.—Foreign insurance companies (other than a life or mutual insurance company), foreign mutual marine insurance companies, and foreign mutual fire insurance companies described in subsection (a), not carrying on an insurance business within the United States, shall not be subject to this part but shall be taxable as other foreign corporations."

• 1962, Revenue Act of 1962 (P.L. 87-834)

P.L. 87-834, §8:

Redesignated former Code Sec. 831(c) as Sec. 831(d), and added a new subsection (c). **Effective** 10-17-62.

[Sec. 831(c)]

(c) CROSS REFERENCES.—

(1) For alternative tax in case of capital gains, see section 1201(a).

(2) For taxation of foreign corporations carrying on an insurance business within the United States, see section 842.

Amendments

• 1966, Foreign Investors Tax Act of 1966 (P.L. 89-809)

P.L. 89-809, §104(i)(6):

Amended former Code Sec. 831(d). **Effective** 1-1-67. Prior to amendment, Code Sec. 831(d) read as follows:

(d) Alternative Tax on Capital Gains.—

For alternative tax in case of capital gains, see section 1201(a).

• 1962, Revenue Act of 1962 (P.L. 87-834)

P.L. 87-834, §8:

Redesignated former Code Sec. 831(c) as Code Sec. 831(d). **Effective** 10-17-62.

[Sec. 832]

SEC. 832. INSURANCE COMPANY TAXABLE INCOME.

[Sec. 832(a)]

(a) DEFINITION OF TAXABLE INCOME.—In the case of an insurance company subject to the tax imposed by section 831, the term "taxable income" means the gross income as defined in subsection (b)(1) less the deductions allowed by subsection (c).

[Sec. 832(b)]

(b) DEFINITIONS.—In the case of an insurance company subject to the tax imposed by section 831—

(1) GROSS INCOME.—The term "gross income" means the sum of—

(A) the combined gross amount earned during the taxable year, from investment income and from underwriting income as provided in this subsection, computed on the basis of the underwriting and investment exhibit of the annual statement approved by the National Association of Insurance Commissioners,

(B) gain during the taxable year from the sale or other disposition of property,

(C) all other items constituting gross income under subchapter B, except that, in the case of a mutual fire insurance company exclusively issuing perpetual policies, the amount of single deposit premiums paid to such company shall not be included in gross income,

(D) in the case of a mutual fire or flood insurance company whose principal business is the issuance of policies—

(i) for which the premium deposits are the same (regardless of the length of the term for which the policies are written), and

(ii) under which the unabsorbed portion of such premium deposits not required for losses, expenses, or establishment of reserves is returned or credited to the policyholder on cancellation or expiration of the policy,

an amount equal to 2 percent of the premiums earned on insurance contracts during the taxable year with respect to such policies after deduction of premium deposits returned or credited during the same taxable year, and

(E) in the case of a company which writes mortgage guaranty insurance, the amount required by subsection (e)(5) to be subtracted from the mortgage guaranty account.

(2) INVESTMENT INCOME.—The term "investment income" means the gross amount of income earned during the taxable year from interest, dividends, and rents, computed as follows: To all interest, dividends, and rents received during the taxable year, add interest, dividends, and rents due and accrued at the end of the taxable year, and deduct all interest, dividends, and rents due and accrued at the end of the preceding taxable year.

(3) UNDERWRITING INCOME.—The term "underwriting income" means the premiums earned on insurance contracts during the taxable year less losses incurred and expenses incurred.

(4) PREMIUMS EARNED.—The term "premiums earned on insurance contracts during the taxable year" means an amount computed as follows:

(A) From the amount of gross premiums written on insurance contracts during the taxable year, deduct return premiums and premiums paid for reinsurance.

(B) To the result so obtained, add 80 percent of the unearned premiums on outstanding business at the end of the preceding taxable year and deduct 80 percent of the unearned premiums on outstanding business at the end of the taxable year.

(C) To the result so obtained, in the case of a taxable year beginning after December 31, 1986, and before January 1, 1993, add an amount equal to 3⅓ percent of unearned premiums on outstanding business at the end of the most recent taxable year beginning before January 1, 1987.

For purposes of this subsection, unearned premiums shall include life insurance reserves, as defined in section 816(b) but determined as provided in section 807. For purposes of this subsection, unearned premiums of mutual fire or flood insurance companies described in paragraph (1)(D) means (with respect to the policies described in paragraph (1)(D)) the amount of unabsorbed premium deposits which the company would be obligated to return to its policyholders at the close of the taxable year if all of its policies were terminated at such time; and the determination of such amount shall be based on the schedule of unabsorbed premium deposit returns for each such company then in effect. Premiums paid by the subscriber of a mutual flood insurance company described in paragraph (1)(D) or issuing exclusively perpetual policies shall be treated, for purposes of computing the taxable income of such subscriber, in the same manner as premiums paid by a policyholder to a mutual fire insurance company described in subparagraph (C) or (D) of paragraph (1).

(5) LOSSES INCURRED.—

(A) IN GENERAL.—The term "losses incurred" means losses incurred during the taxable year on insurance contracts computed as follows:

(i) To losses paid during the taxable year, deduct salvage and reinsurance recovered during the taxable year.

(ii) To the result so obtained, add all unpaid losses on life insurance contracts plus all discounted unpaid losses (as defined in section 846) outstanding at the end of the taxable year and deduct all unpaid losses on life insurance contracts plus all discounted unpaid losses outstanding at the end of the preceding taxable year.

(iii) To the results so obtained, add estimated salvage and reinsurance recoverable as of the end of the preceding taxable year and deduct estimated salvage and reinsurance recoverable as of the end of the taxable year.

The amount of estimated salvage recoverable shall be determined on a discounted basis in accordance with procedures established by the Secretary.

(B) REDUCTION OF DEDUCTION.—The amount which would (but for this subparagraph) be taken into account under subparagraph (A) shall be reduced by an amount equal to 15 percent of the sum of—

(i) tax-exempt interest received or accrued during such taxable year,

(ii) the aggregate amount of deductions provided by sections 243, 244, and 245 for—

(I) dividends (other than 100 percent dividends) received during the taxable year, and

(II) 100 percent dividends received during the taxable year to the extent attributable (directly or indirectly) to prorated amounts, and

(iii) the increase for the taxable year in policy cash values (within the meaning of section 805(a)(4)(F)) of life insurance policies and annuity and endowment contracts to which section 264(f) applies.

In the case of a 100 percent dividend paid by an insurance company, the portion attributable to prorated amounts shall be determined under subparagraph (E)(ii).

(C) EXCEPTION FOR INVESTMENTS MADE BEFORE AUGUST 8, 1986.—

(i) IN GENERAL.—Except as provided in clause (ii), subparagraph (B) shall not apply to any dividend or interest received or accrued on any stock or obligation acquired before August 8, 1986.

(ii) SPECIAL RULE FOR 100 PERCENT DIVIDENDS.—For purposes of clause (i), the portion of any 100 percent dividend which is attributable to prorated amounts shall be treated as received with respect to stock acquired on the later of—

(I) the date the payor acquired the stock or obligation to which the prorated amounts are attributable, or

(II) the 1st day on which the payor and payee were members of the same affiliated group (as defined in section 243(b)(2)).

(D) DEFINITIONS.—For purposes of this paragraph—

(i) PRORATED AMOUNTS.—The term "prorated amounts" means tax-exempt interest and dividends with respect to which a deduction is allowable under section 243, 244, or 245 (other than 100 percent dividends).

(ii) 100 PERCENT DIVIDEND.—

(I) IN GENERAL.—The term "100 percent dividend" means any dividend if the percentage used for purposes of determining the deduction allowable under section 243, 244, or 245(b) is 100 percent.

(II) CERTAIN DIVIDENDS RECEIVED BY FOREIGN CORPORATIONS.—A dividend received by a foreign corporation from a domestic corporation which would be a 100 percent dividend if section 1504(b)(3) did not apply for purposes of applying section 243(b)(2) shall be treated as a 100 percent dividend.

(E) SPECIAL RULES FOR DIVIDENDS SUBJECT TO PRORATION AT SUBSIDIARY LEVEL.—

(i) IN GENERAL.—In the case of any 100 percent dividend paid to an insurance company to which this part applies by any insurance company, the amount of the decrease in the deductions of the payee company by reason of the portion of such dividend attributable to prorated amounts shall be reduced (but not below zero) by the amount of the decrease in the deductions (or increase in income) of the payor company attributable to the application of this section or section 805(a)(4)(A) to such amounts.

(ii) PORTION OF DIVIDEND ATTRIBUTABLE TO PRORATED AMOUNTS.—For purposes of this subparagraph, in determining the portion of any dividend attributable to prorated amounts—

(I) any dividend by the paying corporation shall be treated as paid first out of earnings and profits attributable to prorated amounts (to the extent thereof), and

(II) by determining the portion of earnings and profits so attributable without any reduction for tax imposed by this chapter.

(6) EXPENSES INCURRED.—The term "expenses incurred" means all expenses shown on the annual statement approved by the National Association of Insurance Commissioners, and shall be computed as follows: To all expenses paid during the taxable year, add expenses unpaid at the end of the taxable year and deduct expenses unpaid at the end of the preceding taxable year. For purposes of this subchapter, the term "expenses unpaid" shall not include any unpaid loss adjustment expenses shown on the annual statement, but such unpaid loss adjustment expenses shall be included in unpaid losses. For the purpose of computing the taxable income subject to the tax imposed by section 831, there shall be deducted from expenses incurred (as defined in this paragraph) all expenses incurred which are not allowed as deductions by subsection (c).

(7) SPECIAL RULES FOR APPLYING PARAGRAPH (4).—

(A) REDUCTION NOT TO APPLY TO LIFE INSURANCE RESERVES.—Subparagraph (B) of paragraph (4) shall be applied with respect to insurance contracts described in section 816(b)(1)(B) by substituting "100 percent" for "80 percent" each place it appears in such subparagraph (B), and subparagraph (C) of paragraph (4) shall be applied by not taking such contracts into account.

(B) SPECIAL TREATMENT OF PREMIUMS ATTRIBUTABLE TO INSURING CERTAIN SECURITIES.—In the case of premiums attributable to insurance against default in the payment of principal or interest on securities described in section 165(g)(2)(C) with maturities of more than 5 years—

(i) subparagraph (B) of paragraph (4) shall be applied by substituting "90 percent" for "80 percent" each place it appears, and

(ii) subparagraph (C) of paragraph (4) shall be applied by substituting "1⅔ percent" for "3⅓ percent".

(C) TERMINATION AS INSURANCE COMPANY TAXABLE UNDER SECTION 831(a).—Except as provided in section 381(c)(22) (relating to carryovers in certain corporate readjustments), if, for any taxable year beginning before January 1, 1993, the taxpayer ceases to be an insurance company taxable under section 831(a), the aggregate adjustments which would be made under paragraph (4)(C) for such taxable year and subsequent taxable years but for such cessation shall be made for the taxable year preceding such cessation year.

(D) TREATMENT OF COMPANIES WHICH BECOME TAXABLE UNDER SECTION 831(a).—

(i) EXCEPTION TO PHASE-IN FOR COMPANIES WHICH WERE NOT TAXABLE, ETC., BEFORE 1987.—Subparagraph (C) of paragraph (4) shall not apply to any insurance company which, for each taxable year beginning before January 1, 1987, was not subject to the tax imposed by section 821(a) or 831(a) (as in effect on the day before the date of the enactment of the Tax Reform Act of 1986) by reason of being—

(I) subject to tax under section 821(c) (as so in effect), or

(II) described in section 501(c) (as so in effect) and exempt from tax under section 501(a).

(ii) PHASE-IN BEGINNING AT LATER DATE FOR COMPANIES NOT 1ST TAXABLE UNDER SECTION 831(a) IN 1987.—In the case of an insurance company—

(I) which was not subject to the tax imposed by section 831(a) for its 1st taxable year beginning after December 31, 1986, by reason of being subject to tax under section 831(b), or described in section 501(c) and exempt from tax under section 501(a), and

(II) which, for any taxable year beginning before January 1, 1987, was subject to the tax imposed by section 821(a) or 831(a) (as in effect on the day before the date of the enactment of the Tax Reform Act of 1986),

subparagraph (C) of paragraph (4) shall apply beginning with the 1st taxable year beginning after December 31, 1986, for which such company is subject to the tax imposed by section 831(a) and shall be applied by substituting the last day of the preceding taxable year for "December 31, 1986" and the 1st day of the 7th succeeding taxable year for "January 1, 1993".

(E) TREATMENT OF CERTAIN RECIPROCAL INSURERS.—In the case of a reciprocal (within the meaning of section 835(a)) which reports (as required by State law) on its annual statement reserves on unearned premiums net of premium acquisition expenses—

(i) subparagraph (B) of paragraph (4) shall be applied by treating unearned premiums as including an amount equal to such expenses, and

(ii) appropriate adjustments shall be made under subparagraph (c) of paragraph (4) to reflect the amount by which—

(I) such reserves at the close of the most recent taxable year beginning before January 1, 1987, are greater or less than,

(II) 80 percent of the sum of the amount under subclause (I) plus such premium acquisition expenses.

(8) SPECIAL RULES FOR APPLYING PARAGRAPH (4) TO TITLE INSURANCE PREMIUMS.—

(A) IN GENERAL.—In the case of premiums attributable to title insurance—

(i) subparagraph (B) of paragraph (4) shall be applied by substituting "the discounted unearned premiums" for "80 percent of the unearned premiums" each place it appears, and

(ii) subparagraph (C) of paragraph (4) shall not apply.

(B) METHOD OF DISCOUNTING.—For purposes of subparagraph (A), the amount of the discounted unearned premiums as of the end of any taxable year shall be the present value of such premiums (as of such time and separately with respect to premiums received in each calendar year) determined by using—

(i) the amount of the undiscounted unearned premiums at such time,

(ii) the applicable interest rate, and

(iii) the applicable statutory premium recognition pattern.

(C) DETERMINATION OF APPLICABLE FACTORS.—In determining the amount of the discounted unearned premiums as of the end of any taxable year—

(i) UNDISCOUNTED UNEARNED PREMIUMS.—The term "undiscounted unearned premiums" means the unearned premiums shown in the yearly statement filed by the taxpayer for the year ending with or within such taxable year.

(ii) APPLICABLE INTEREST RATE.—The term "applicable interest rate" means the annual rate determined under 846(c)(2) for the calendar year in which the premiums are received.

(iii) APPLICABLE STATUTORY PREMIUM RECOGNITION PATTERN.—The term "applicable statutory premium recognition pattern" means the statutory premium recognition pattern—

(I) which is in effect for the calendar year in which the premiums are received, and

(II) which is based on the statutory premium recognition pattern which applies to premiums received by the taxpayer in such calendar year.

For purposes of the preceding sentence, premiums received during any calendar year shall be treated as received in the middle of such year.

Amendments

• 1997, Taxpayer Relief Act of 1997 (P.L. 105-34)

P.L. 105-34, §1084(b)[(d)](4):

Amended Code Sec. 832(b)(5)(B) by striking "and" at the end of clause (i), by striking the period at the end of clause (ii) and inserting ", and", and by adding at the end a new clause (iii). For the **effective** date, see Act Sec. 1084(d)[(f)], below.

P.L. 105-34, §1084(d)[(f)], as amended by P.L. 105-206, §6010(o)(3)(B), provides:

(d)[(f)] EFFECTIVE DATE.—The amendments made by this section shall apply to contracts issued after June 8, 1997, in taxable years ending after such date. For purposes of the preceding sentence, any material increase in the death benefit or other material change in the contract shall be treated as a new contract except that, in the case of a master contract (within the meaning of section 264(f)(4)(E) of the Internal Revenue Code of 1986), the addition of covered lives shall be treated as a new contract only with respect to such additional covered lives. For purposes of this subsection, an increase in the death benefit under a policy or contract issued in connection with a lapse described in section 501(d)(2) of the Health Insurance Portability and Accountability Act of 1996 shall not be treated as a new contract.

• 1996, Small Business Job Protection Act of 1996 (P.L. 104-188)

P.L. 104-188, §1702(h)(3):

Amended Code Sec. 832(b)(5)(C)(ii)(II) and (D)(ii)(II) by striking "243(b)(5)" and inserting "243(b)(2)". **Effective** as if included in the provision of P.L. 101-508 to which it relates.

• 1990, Omnibus Budget Reconciliation Act of 1990 (P.L. 101-508)

P.L. 101-508, §11303(a):

Amended Code Sec. 832(b)(4) by striking "section 807, pertaining" and all that follows down through the period at the end of the first sentence which follows subparagraph (C) and inserting "section 807." **Effective**, generally, for tax years beginning on or after 9-30-90. However, for special rules, see Act Sec. 11303(c)(2)-(3), below. Prior to amendment, Code Sec. 832(b)(4)(C) read as follows:

(C) To the result so obtained, in the case of a taxable year beginning after December 31, 1986, and before January 1, 1993, add an amount equal to $3^1/_3$ percent of unearned premiums on outstanding business at the end of the most recent taxable year beginning before January 1, 1987.

For purposes of this subsection, unearned premiums shall include life insurance reserves, as defined in section 816(b) but determined as provided in section 807, pertaining to the life, burial, or funeral insurance, or annuity business of an insurance company subject to the tax imposed by section 831 and not qualifying as a life insurance company under section 816. For purposes of this subsection, unearned premiums of mutual fire or flood insurance companies described in paragraph (1)(D) means (with respect to the policies described in paragraph (1)(D)) the amount of unabsorbed premium desposits which the company would be obligated to return to its policyholders at the close of the taxable year if all of its policies were terminated at such time; and the determination of such amount shall be based on the schedule of unabsorbed premium deposit returns for each such company then in effect. Premiums paid by the subscriber of a mutual flood insurance company described in paragraph (1)(D) or issuing exclusively perpetual policies shall be treated, for purposes of computing the taxable income of such subscriber, in the same manner as premiums paid by a policyholder to a mutual fire insurance company described in subparagraph (C) or (D) of paragraph (1).

P.L. 101-508, §11303(b)(1) (as amended by P.L. 104-188, §1704(t)(45)):

Amended Code Sec. 832(b)(7)(A) by striking "amounts included in unearned premiums under the 2nd sentence of each [such] paragraph" and inserting "insurance contracts described in section 816(b)(1)(B)." **Effective**, generally, for tax years beginning on or after 9-30-90. However, for special rules, see Act Sec. 11303(c)(2)-(3), below.

P.L. 101-508, §11303(b)(2):

Amended Code Sec. 832(b)(7)(A) by striking "such amounts into account" and inserting "such contracts into account". **Effective**, generally, for tax years beginning on or after 9-30-90. However, for special rules, see Act Sec. 11303(c)(2)-(3), below.

P.L. 101-508, §11303(c)(2)-(3), provides:

(2) AMENDMENTS TREATED AS CHANGE IN METHOD OF ACCOUNTING.—In the case of any taxpayer who is required by reason of the amendments made by this section to change his method of computing reserves—

(A) such change shall be treated as a change in a method of accounting,

(B) such change shall be treated as initiated by the taxpayer,

(C) such change shall be treated as having been made with the consent of the Secretary, and

(D) the net adjustments which are required by section 481 of the Internal Revenue Code of 1986 to be taken into account by the taxpayer shall be taken into account over a period not to exceed 4 taxable years beginning with the taxpayer's first taxable year beginning on or after September 30, 1990.

(3) COORDINATION WITH SECTION 832(b)(4)(C).—The amendments made by this section shall not affect the application of section 832(b)(4)(C) of the Internal Revenue Code of 1986.

P.L. 101-508, §11305(a):

Amended Code Sec. 832(b)(5)(A). **Effective**, generally, for tax years beginning after 12-31-89. However, for special rules, see Act Sec. 11305(c)(2)-(5), below. Prior to amendment, Code Sec. 832(b)(5)(A) read as follows:

(A) IN GENERAL.—The term "losses incurred" means losses incurred during the taxable year on insurance contracts computed as follows:

(i) To losses paid during the taxable year, add salvage and reinsurance recoverable outstanding at the end of the preceding taxable year and deduct salvage and reinsurance recoverable outstanding at the end of the taxable year.

(ii) To the result so obtained, add all unpaid losses on life insurance contracts plus all discounted unpaid losses (as defined in section 846) outstanding at the end of the taxable year and deduct unpaid losses on life insurance contracts plus all discounted unpaid losses outstanding at the end of the preceding taxable year.

P.L. 101-508, §11305(c)(2)-(5), provides:

(2) AMENDMENTS TREATED AS CHANGE IN METHOD OF ACCOUNTING.—

(A) IN GENERAL.—In the case of any taxpayer who is required by reason of the amendments made by this section to change his method of computing losses incurred—

(i) such change shall be treated as a change in a method of accounting,

(ii) such change shall be treated as initiated by the taxpayer, and

(iii) such change shall be treated as having been made with the consent of the Secretary.

(B) ADJUSTMENTS.—In applying section 481 of the Internal Revenue Code of 1986 with respect to the change referred to in subparagraph (A)—

(i) only 13 percent of the net amount of adjustments (otherwise required by such section 481 to be taken into account by the taxpayer) shall be taken into account, and

(ii) the portion of such net adjustments which is required to be taken into account by the taxpayer (after the application of clause (i)) shall be taken into account over a period not to exceed 4 taxable years beginning with the taxpayer's 1st taxable year beginning after December 31, 1989.

(3) TREATMENT OF COMPANIES WHICH TOOK INTO ACCOUNT SALVAGE RECOVERABLE.—In the case of any insurance company which took into account salvage recoverable in determining losses incurred for its last taxable year beginning before January 1, 1990, 87 percent of the discounted amount of estimated salvage recoverable as of the close of such last taxable year shall be allowed as a deduction ratably over its 1st 4 taxable years beginning after December 31, 1989.

(4) SPECIAL RULE FOR OVERESTIMATES.—If for any taxable year beginning after December 31, 1989—

(A) the amount of the section 481 adjustment which would have been required without regard to paragraph (2) and any discounting, exceeds

(B) the sum of the amount of salvage recovered taken into account under section 832(b)(5)(A)(i) for the taxable year and any preceding taxable year beginning after December 31, 1989, attributable to losses incurred with respect to any accident year beginning before 1990 and the undiscounted amount of estimated salvage recoverable as of the close of the taxable year on account of such losses,

87 percent of such excess (adjusted for discounting used in determining the amount of salvage recoverable as of the close of the last taxable year of the taxpayer beginning before January 1, 1990) shall be included in gross income for such taxable year.

(5) EFFECT ON EARNINGS AND PROFITS.—The earnings and profits of any insurance company for its 1st taxable year beginning after December 31, 1989, shall be increased by the amount of the section 481 adjustment which would have been required but for paragraph (2). For purposes of applying sections 56, 902, 952(c)(1), and 960 of the Internal Revenue Code of 1986, earnings and profits of a corporation shall be determined by applying the principles of paragraph (2)(B).

P.L. 101-508, §11307, provides:

No addition to tax shall be made under section 6655 of the Internal Revenue Code of 1986 for any period before March 16, 1991, with respect to any underpayment to the extent such underpayment was created or increased by any provision of this part.

• 1988, Technical and Miscellaneous Revenue Act of 1988 (P.L. 100-647)

P.L. 100-647, §1010(c)(1)(A):

Amended Code Sec. 832(b)(7)(C) by striking out "this part" and inserting in lieu thereof "section 831(a)". **Effective** as if included in the provision of P.L. 99-514 to which it relates. For a special rule, see Act Sec. 1010(d)(3), below.

P.L. 100-647, §1010(c)(1)(B):

Amended Code Sec. 832(b)(7)(C) by striking out "NON-LIFE INSURANCE COMPANY" in the subparagraph heading and inserting in lieu thereof "INSURANCE COMPANY TAXABLE UNDER SECTION 831(a)". **Effective** as if included in the provision of P.L. 99-514 to which it relates. For a special rule, see Act Sec. 1010(d)(3), below.

P.L. 100-647, §1010(c)(2):

Amended Code Sec. 832(b)(7) by adding at the end thereof new subparagraphs (D)-(E). **Effective** as if included in the provision of P.L. 99-514 to which it relates. For a special rule, see Act Sec. 1010(d)(3), below.

P.L. 100-647, §1010(d)(2):

Amended Code Sec. 832(b)(5)(B)(ii)(II) by inserting "(directly or indirectly)" after "attributable". **Effective** as if included in the provision of P.L. 99-514 to which it relates. For a special rule, see Act Sec. 1010(d)(3), below.

P.L. 100-647, §1010(d)(3), provides:

(3) For purposes of section 832(b)(5)(C)(i) of the 1986 Code, any stock or obligation acquired on or after August 8, 1986, by an insurance company subject to the tax imposed by section 831 of the 1986 Code (hereinafter in this paragraph referred to as the "acquiring company") from another insurance company so subject (hereinafter in this paragraph referred to as the "transferor company") shall be treated as acquired on the date on which such stock or obligation was acquired by the transferor company if—

(A) the transferor company acquired such stock or obligation before August 8, 1986, and

(B) at all times after the date on which such stock or obligation was acquired by the transferor company and before the date of the acquisition by the acquiring company, the transferor company and the acquiring company were members of the same affiliated group filing a consolidated return.

For purposes of the preceding sentence, the date on which the stock or obligation was acquired by the transferor company shall be determined with regard to any prior application of the preceding sentence. For purposes of this paragraph, if the acquiring corporation or transferor corporation was a party to a reorganization described in section 368(a)(1)(F) of the 1986 Code, any reference to such corporation shall include a reference to any predecessor thereof involved in such reorganization.

• 1986, Tax Reform Act of 1986 (P.L. 99-514)

P.L. 99-514, §1021(a):

Amended Code Sec. 832(b) by striking out subparagraph (B) in the first sentence of paragraph (4) and inserting in lieu thereof subparagraphs (B) and (C). **Effective** for tax years beginning after 12-31-86. However, for a special transitional rule, see Act Sec. 1021(c)(2), below. Prior to amendment, Code Sec. 832(b)(4)(B) read as follows:

(B) To the result so obtained, add unearned premiums on outstanding business at the end of the preceding taxable year and deduct unearned premiums on outstanding business at the end of the taxable year.

P.L. 99-514, §1021(b):

Amended Code Sec. 832(b) by adding at the end thereof new paragraphs (7) and (8). **Effective** for tax years beginning after 12-31-86. However, for a special transitional rule, see Act Sec. 1021(c)(2), below.

P.L. 99-514, §1021(c)(2), provides:

(2) SPECIAL TRANSITIONAL RULE FOR TITLE INSURANCE COMPANIES.—For the 1st taxable year beginning after December 31, 1986, in the case of premiums attributable to title insurance—

(A) IN GENERAL.—The unearned premiums at the end of the preceding taxable year as defined in paragraph (4) of section 832(b) shall be determined as if the amendments made by this section had applied to such unearned premiums in the preceding taxable year and by using the interest rate and premium recognition pattern applicable to years ending in calendar year 1987.

(B) FRESH START.—Except as provided in subparagraph (C), any difference between—

(i) the amount determined to be unearned premiums for the year preceding the first taxable year of a title insurance company beginning after December 31, 1986, determined without regard to subparagraph (A), and

(ii) such amount determined with regard to subparagraph (A),

shall not be taken into account for purposes of the Internal Revenue Code of 1986.

(C) EFFECT ON EARNINGS AND PROFITS.—The earnings and profits of any insurance company for its 1st taxable year beginning after December 31, 1986, shall be increased by the amount of the difference determined under subparagraph (A) with respect to such company.

P.L. 99-514, §1022(a):

Amended Code Sec. 832(b)(5). **Effective** for tax years beginning after 12-31-86. Prior to amendment, Code Sec. 832(b)(5) read as follows:

(5) LOSSES INCURRED.—The term "losses incurred" means losses incurred during the taxable year on insurance contracts, computed as follows:

(A) to losses paid during the taxable year, add salvage and reinsurance recoverable outstanding at the end of the preceding taxable year and deduct salvage and reinsurance recoverable outstanding at the end of the taxable year.

(B) to the result so obtained, add all unpaid losses outstanding at the end of the taxable year and deduct unpaid losses outstanding at the end of the preceding taxable year.

P.L. 99-514, §1023(a)(1):

Amended Code Sec. 832(b)(5)(A)(ii), as amended by Act Sec. 1022. **Effective**, generally, for tax years beginning after 12-31-86. However, see Act Sec. 1023(e)(2)-(3), below, for a transitional rule. Prior to amendment by Act Sec. 1023(a)(1) and as amended by Act Sec. 1022, Code Sec. 832(b)(5)(A)(ii) read as follows:

(ii) To the result so obtained, add all unpaid losses outstanding at the end of the taxable year and deduct unpaid losses outstanding at the end of the preceding taxable year.

P.L. 99-514, §1023(a)(2):

Amended Code Sec. 832(b)(6) by inserting after the first sentence:

For purposes of this subchapter, the term "expenses unpaid" shall not include any unpaid loss adjustment expenses shown on the annual statement, but such unpaid loss adjustment expenses shall be included in unpaid losses. **Effective**, generally, for tax years beginning after 12-31-86. However, see Act Sec. 1023(e)(2)-(3), below, for a transitional rule.

P.L. 99-514, §1023(e)(2)-(3), provides:

(2) TRANSITIONAL RULE.—For the first taxable year beginning after December 31, 1986—

(A) the unpaid losses and the expenses unpaid (as defined in paragraphs (5)(B) and (6) of section 832(b) of the Internal Revenue Code of 1986) at the end of the preceding taxable year, and

(B) the unpaid losses as defined in sections 807(c)(2) and 805(a)(1) of such Code at the end of the preceding taxable year,

shall be determined as if the amendments made by this section had applied to such unpaid losses and expenses unpaid in the preceding taxable year and by using the interest rate and loss payment patterns applicable to accident years ending with calendar year 1987. For subsequent taxable years, such amendments shall be applied with respect to such unpaid losses and expenses unpaid by using the interest rate and loss payment patterns applicable to accident years ending with calendar year 1987.

(3) FRESH START.—

(A) IN GENERAL.—Except as otherwise provided in this paragraph, any difference between—

(i) the amount determined to be the unpaid losses and expenses unpaid for the year preceding the 1st taxable year of an insurance company beginning after December 31, 1986, determined without regard to paragraph (2), and

(ii) such amount determined with regard to paragraph (2),

shall not be taken into account for purposes of the Internal Revenue Code of 1986.

(B) RESERVE STRENGTHENING IN YEARS AFTER 1985.—Subparagraph (A) shall not apply to any reserve strengthening in a taxable year beginning in 1986, and such strengthening shall be treated as occurring in the taxpayer's 1st taxable year beginning after December 31, 1986.

(C) EFFECT ON EARNINGS AND PROFITS.—The earnings and profits of any insurance company for its 1st taxable year beginning after December 31, 1986, shall be increased by the amount of the difference determined under subparagraph (A) with respect to such company.

P.L. 99-514, §1024(c)(1):

Amended Code Sec. 832(b)(1)(C) by striking out "a mutual fire insurance company described in section 831(a)(3)(A)" and inserting in lieu thereof "a mutual fire insurance company exclusively issuing perpetual policies". **Effective** for tax years beginning after 12-31-86.

P.L. 99-514, §1024(c)(2):

Amended Code Sec. 832(b)(1)(D). **Effective** for tax years beginning after 12-31-86. Prior to amendment, Code Sec. 832(b)(1)(D) read as follows:

(D) in the case of a mutual fire or flood insurance company described in section 831(a)(3)(B), an amount equal to 2 percent of the premiums earned on insurance contracts during the taxable year with respect to policies described in section 831(a)(3)(B) after deduction of premium deposits returned or credited during the same taxable year, and

P.L. 99-514, §1024(c)(3)(A)-(B):

Amended Code Sec. 832(b)(4) by striking out "section 831(a)(3)(B)" each place it appears and inserting in lieu thereof "paragraph (1)(D)", and by striking out the last sentence and inserting a new sentence. **Effective** for tax years beginning after 12-31-86. Prior to amendment, the last sentence of Code Sec. 832(b)(4) read as follows:

Premiums paid by the subscriber of a mutual flood insurance company referred to in paragraph (3) of section 831(a) shall be treated, for purposes of computing the taxable income of such subscriber, in the same manner as premiums paid by a policy holder to a mutual fire insurance company referred to in such paragraph (3).

• 1984, Deficit Reduction Act of 1984 (P.L. 98-369)

P.L. 98-369, §211(b)(9):

Amended Code Sec. 832(b)(4) by striking out "section 801(b)" and inserting in lieu thereof "section 816(b) but determined as provided in section 807" and by striking out "section 801" and inserting in lieu thereof "section 816". **Effective** for tax years beginning after 12-31-83.

• 1976, Tax Reform Act of 1976 (P.L. 94-455)

P.L. 94-455, §1901(a)(108):

Struck out "Convention" and inserted "Association" each place it appeared. **Effective** for tax years beginning after 12-31-76.

• 1968 (P.L. 90-240)

P.L. 90-240, §5(a):

Amended Code Sec. 832(b)(1) by striking out "and" at the end of subparagraph (C), by striking out the period at the end of subparagraph (D) and inserting in lieu thereof ", and", and by adding a new subparagraph (E). **Effective** for tax years beginning after 12-31-66.

• 1962, Revenue Act of 1962 (P.L. 87-834)

P.L. 87-834, §8:

Amended Code Sec. 832(b)(1) by striking out "and" at the end of subparagraph (B); by inserting after section 831(a) in subparagraph (C) the following: "(3)(A)"; by substituting "and" for the period at the end of subparagraph (C); and by adding at the end thereof a new subparagraph. Also amended Code Sec. 832(b)(4) by inserting after the period in line 13 two new sentences. **Effective** 1-1-63.

• 1956, Life Insurance Company Tax Act of 1955 (P.L. 429, 84th Cong.)

P.L. 429, 84th Cong., §3(b)(1):

Amended Code Sec. 832(b)(4) by substituting for the words "section 806", the words "section 801(b)". **Effective** 1-1-55.

[Sec. 832(c)]

(c) DEDUCTIONS ALLOWED.—In computing the taxable income of an insurance company subject to the tax imposed by section 831, there shall be allowed as deductions:

(1) all ordinary and necessary expenses incurred, as provided in section 162 (relating to trade or business expenses);

(2) all interest, as provided in section 163;

(3) taxes, as provided in section 164;

(4) losses incurred, as defined in subsection (b) (5) of this section;

(5) capital losses to the extent provided in subchapter P (sec. 1201 and following, relating to capital gains and losses) plus losses from capital assets sold or exchanged in order to obtain funds to meet abnormal insurance losses and to provide for the payment of dividends and similar distributions to policyholders. Capital assets shall be considered as sold or exchanged in order to obtain funds to meet abnormal insurance losses and to provide for the payment of dividends and similar distributions to policyholders to the extent that the gross receipts from their sale or exchange are not greater than the excess, if any, for the taxable year of the sum of dividends and similar distributions paid to policyholders in their capacity as such, losses paid, and expenses paid over the sum of the items described in section 834(b) (other than paragraph (1)(D) thereof) and net premiums received. In the application of section 1212 for purposes of this section, the net capital loss for the taxable year shall be the amount by which losses for such year

from sales or exchanges of capital assets exceeds the sum of the gains from such sales or exchanges and whichever of the following amounts is the lesser:

(A) the taxable income (computed without regard to gains or losses from sales or exchanges of capital assets, or

(B) losses from the sale or exchange of capital assets sold or exchanged to obtain funds to meet abnormal insurance losses and to provide for the payment of dividends and similar distributions to policyholders;

(6) debts in the nature of agency balances and bills receivable which become worthless within the taxable year;

(7) the amount of interest earned during the taxable year which under section 103 is excluded from gross income;

(8) the depreciation deduction allowed by section 167 and the deduction allowed by section 611 (relating to depletion);

(9) charitable, etc., contributions, as provided in section 170;

(10) deductions (other than those specified in this subsection) as provided in part VI of subchapter B (sec. 161 and following, relating to itemized deductions for individuals and corporations) and in part I of subchapter D (sec. 401 and following, relating to pension, profit-sharing, stock bonus plans, etc.);

(11) dividends and similar distributions paid or declared to policyholders in their capacity as such, except in the case of a mutual fire insurance company described in subsection (b)(1)(C). For purposes of the preceding sentence, the term "dividends and similar distributions" includes amounts returned or credited to policyholders on cancellation or expiration of policies described in subsection (b)(1)(D). For purposes of this paragraph, the term "paid or declared" shall be construed according to the method of accounting regularly employed in keeping the books of the insurance company;

(12) the special deductions allowed by part VIII of subchapter B (sec. 241 and following, relating to dividends received); and

(13) in the case of a company which writes mortgage guaranty insurance, the deduction allowed by subsection (e).

Amendments

• 1986, Tax Reform Act of 1986 (P.L. 99-514)

P.L. 99-514, §1024(c)(4):

Amended Code Sec. 832(c)(5) by striking out "section 822(b)" and inserting in lieu thereof "section 834(b)". **Effective** for tax years beginning after 12-31-86.

P.L. 99-514, §1024(c)(5)(A)-(B):

Amended Code Sec. 832(c)(11) by striking out "section 831(a)(3)(A)" and inserting in lieu thereof "subsection (b)(1)(C)", and by striking out "section 831(a)(3)(B)" and inserting in lieu thereof "subsection (b)(1)(D)". **Effective** for tax years beginning after 12-31-86.

• 1976, Tax Reform Act of 1976 (P.L. 94-455)

P.L. 94-455, §1901(b)(1)(T):

Struck out "or to the deductions provided in section 242 for partially tax-exempt interest" after "capital assets" in Code Sec. 832(c)(5)(A). **Effective** for tax years beginning after 12-31-76.

P.L. 94-455, §1901(b)(1)(U):

Struck out "partially tax-exempt interest and to" after "relating to" in Code Sec. 832(c)(12). **Effective** for tax years beginning after 12-31-76.

• 1968 (P.L. 90-240)

P.L. 90-240, §5(b):

Amended Code Sec. 832(c) by striking out "and" at the end of paragraph (11), by striking out the period at the end of paragraph (12) and inserting in lieu thereof "; and", and by adding new paragraph (13). **Effective** for tax years beginning after 12-31-66.

• 1964, Revenue Act of 1964 (P.L. 88-272)

P.L. 88-272, §228(c):

Amended Code Sec. 832(c)(10) by adding the words "and in part I of subchapter D (sec. 401 and following, relating to pension, profit-sharing, stock bonus plans, etc.)". **Effective** for tax years beginning after 12-31-53, and ending after 8-16-54.

• 1962, Revenue Act of 1962 (P.L. 87-834)

P.L. 87-834, §8:

Amended Code Sec. 832(c) by striking out paragraph (11) and inserting in lieu thereof a new paragraph (11). **Effective** 1-1-63. Prior to amendment paragraph (11) read as follows:

"(11) dividends and similar distributions paid or declared to policy-holders in their capacity as such, except in the case of the mutual fire insurance company described in section 831(a). For purposes of the preceding sentence, the term `paid or declared' shall be construed according to the method of accounting regularly employed in keeping the books of the insurance company; and"

• 1956, Life Insurance Company Tax Act of 1955 (P.L. 429, 84th Cong.)

P.L. 429, 84th Cong., §3(b)(2) and (3):

Amended Code Sec. 832(c)(5) by substituting for the words "interest, dividends, rents, and net premiums received. In the application of section 1211", the words "the items described in section 822(b) (other than paragraph (1)(D) thereof) and net premiums received. In the application of section 1212". Also amended Code Sec. 832 (c)(8) by adding the words which follow "section 167". **Effective** 1-1-55.

[Sec. 832(d)]

(d) DOUBLE DEDUCTIONS.—Nothing in this section shall permit the same item to be deducted more than once.

Amendments

• 1966, Foreign Investors Tax Act of 1966 (P.L. 89-809)

P.L. 89-809, §104(i)(7):

Repealed Code Sec. 832(d) and redesignated Code Sec. 832(e) as Sec. 832(d). **Effective** 1-1-67. Prior to repeal, Code Sec. 832(d) read as follows:

(d) Taxable Income of Foreign Insurance Companies Other Than Life or Mutual and Foreign Mutual Marine.—In the case of a foreign insurance company (other than a life or mutual insurance company), a foreign mutual marine insurance company, and a foreign mutual fire insurance company described in section 831(a), the taxable income shall be the taxable income from sources within the United States. In the case of a company to which the preceding sentence applies, the deductions allowed in this section shall be allowed to the extent provided in subpart B of part II of subchapter N (sec. 881 and following) in the case of a foreign corporation engaged in trade or business within the United States.

[Sec. 832(e)]

(e) SPECIAL DEDUCTION AND INCOME ACCOUNT.—In the case of taxable years beginning after December 31, 1966, of a company which writes mortgage guaranty insurance—

(1) ADDITIONAL DEDUCTION.—There shall be allowed as a deduction for the taxable year, if bonds are purchased as required by paragraph (2), the sum of—

(A) an amount representing the amount required by State law or regulation to be set aside in a reserve for mortgage guaranty insurance losses resulting from adverse economic cycles; and

(B) an amount representing the aggregate of amounts so set aside in such reserve for the 8 preceding taxable years to the extent such amounts were not deducted under this paragraph in such preceding taxable years,

except that the deduction allowable for the taxable year under this paragraph shall not exceed the taxable income for the taxable year computed without regard to this paragraph or to any carryback of a net operating loss. For purposes of this paragraph, the amount required by State law or regulation to be so set aside in any taxable year shall not exceed 50 percent of premiums earned on insurance contracts (as defined in subsection (b)(4)) with respect to mortgage guaranty insurance for such year. For purposes of this subsection all amounts shall be taken into account on a first-in-time basis. The computation and deduction under this section of losses incurred (including losses resulting from adverse economic cycles) shall not be affected by the provisions of this subsection. For purposes of this subsection the terms "preceding taxable years" and "preceding taxable year" shall not include taxable years which began before January 1, 1967.

(2) PURCHASE OF BONDS.—The deduction under paragraph (1) shall be allowed only to the extent that tax and loss bonds are purchased in an amount equal to the tax benefit attributable to such deduction, as determined under regulations prescribed by the Secretary, on or before the date that any taxes (determined without regard to this subsection) due for the taxable year for which the deduction is allowed are due to be paid. If a deduction would be allowed but for the fact that tax and loss bonds were not timely purchased, such deduction shall be allowed to the extent such purchases are made within a reasonable time, as determined by the Secretary, if all interest and penalties, computed as if this sentence did not apply, are paid.

(3) MORTGAGE GUARANTY ACCOUNT.—Each company which writes mortgage guaranty insurance shall, for purposes of this part, establish and maintain a mortgage guaranty account.

(4) ADDITIONS TO ACCOUNT.—There shall be added to the mortgage guaranty account for each taxable year an amount equal to the amount allowed as a deduction for the taxable year under paragraph (1).

(5) SUBTRACTIONS FROM ACCOUNT AND INCLUSION IN GROSS INCOME.—After applying paragraph (4), there shall be subtracted for the taxable year from the mortgage guaranty account and included in gross income—

(A) the amount (if any) remaining which was added to the account for the tenth preceding taxable year, and

(B) the excess (if any) of the aggregate amount in the mortgage guaranty account over the aggregate amount in the reserve referred to in paragraph (1)(A). For purposes of determining such excess, the aggregate amount in the mortgage guaranty account shall be determined after applying subparagraph (A), and the aggregate amount in the reserve referred to in paragraph (1)(A) shall be determined by disregarding any amounts remaining in such reserve added for taxable years beginning before January 1, 1967.

(C) an amount (if any) equal to the net operating loss for the taxable year computed without regard to this subparagraph, and

(D) any amount improperly subtracted from the account under subparagraph (A), (B) or (C) to the extent that tax and loss bonds were redeemed with respect to such amount.

If a company liquidates or otherwise terminates its mortgage guaranty insurance business and does not transfer or distribute such business in an acquisition of assets referred to in section 381(a), the entire amount remaining in such account shall be subtracted. Except in the case where a company transfers or distributes its mortgage guaranty insurance in an acquisition of assets, referred to in section 381(a), if the company is not subject to the tax imposed by section 831 for any taxable year, the entire amount in the account at the close of the preceding taxable year shall be subtracted from the account in such preceding taxable year.

(6) LEASE GUARANTY INSURANCE; INSURANCE OF STATE AND LOCAL OBLIGATIONS.—In the case of any taxable year beginning after December 31, 1970, the provisions of this subsection shall also apply in all respects to a company which writes lease guaranty insurance or insurance on obligations the interest on which is excludable from gross income under section 103. In applying this subsection to such a company, any reference to mortgage guaranty insurance contained in this section shall be deemed to be a reference also to lease guaranty insurance and to insurance on obligations the interest on which is excludable from gross income under section 103; and in the case of insurance on obligations the interest on which is excludable from gross income under section 103, the references in paragraph (1) to "losses resulting from adverse economic cycles" include losses from declining revenues related to such obligations (as well as losses resulting from adverse economic cycles), and the time specified in subparagraph (A) of paragraph (5) shall be the twentieth preceding taxable year.

Amendments

• 1988, Technical and Miscellaneous Revenue Act of 1988 (P.L. 100-647)

P.L. 100-647, §1010(c)(3):

Amended Code Sec. 832(e)(5) by striking out "and" at the end of subparagraph (A) and by striking out the period at the end of subparagraph (B) and inserting in lieu thereof a comma. **Effective** as if included in the provision of P.L. 99-514 to which it relates.

• 1982, Tax Equity and Fiscal Responsibility Act of 1982 (P.L. 97-248)

P.L. 97-248, §234(b)(2)(A):

Amended Code Sec. 832(e)(2) by striking out ", as if no election to make installment payments under section 6152 is made". **Effective** for tax years beginning after 12-31-82.

• 1976, Tax Reform Act of 1976 (P.L. 94-455)

P.L. 94-455, §1906(b)(13)(A):

Amended 1954 Code by substituting "Secretary" for "Secretary or his delegate" each place it appeared. **Effective** 2-1-77.

• 1974 (P.L. 93-483)

P.L. 93-483, §5:

Amended Code Sec. 832(e) by adding paragraph (6). **Effective** 10-26-74.

• 1968 (P.L. 90-240)

P.L. 90-240, §5(c):

Added Code Sec. 832(e). **Effective** for tax years beginning after 12-31-66, except that so much of Code Sec. 832(e)(2) as provides for payment of interest and penalties for failure to make a timely purchase of tax and loss bonds shall not apply with respect to any period during which such bonds are not available for purchase.

P.L. 90-240, §5(g), provides:

"(g)(1) In the case of taxable years beginning before 1967, a company shall treat additions to reserve, required by State law or regulations for mortgage guaranty insurance losses resulting from adverse economic cycles, as unearned premiums for purposes of section 832(b)(4) of the Internal Revenue Code of 1954, but the amount so treated as unearned premiums in a taxable year shall not exceed 50 percent of premiums earned on insurance contracts (as defined in section 832(b)(4) of such Code), determined without regard to amounts added to the reserve, with respect to mortgage guaranty insurance for such year. The amount of unearned premiums at the close of 1966 shall be determined without regard to the preceding sentence for the purpose of applying 832(b)(4) of such Code to 1967. Additions to such a reserve shall not be treated as unearned premiums for any taxable year beginning after 1966.

"(2) If a mortgage guaranty insurance company made additions to a reserve which were so treated as unearned premiums described in paragraph (1), such company, in taxable years beginning after 1966, shall include in gross income (in addition to the items specified in section 832(b)(1) of such Code) the sum of the following amounts until there is included in gross income an amount equal to the aggregate additions to the reserve described in paragraph (1) for taxable years beginning before 1967:

"(A) an amount (if any) equal to the excess of losses incurred (as defined in section 832(b)(5) of such Code) for the taxable year over 35 percent of premiums earned on insurance contracts during the taxable year (as defined in section 832(b)(4) of such Code), determined without regard to amounts added to the reserve referred to in paragraph (1), with respect to mortgage guaranty insurance,

"(B) the amount (if any) remaining which was added to the reserve for the tenth preceding taxable year, and

"(C) the excess (if any) of—

"(i) the aggregate of amounts so treated as unearned premiums for all taxable years beginning before 1967 less the total of the amounts included in gross income under this paragraph for prior taxable years and the amounts included in gross income under subparagraphs (A) and (B) for the taxable year, over

"(ii) the aggregate of the additions made for taxable years beginning before 1967 which remain in the reserve at the close of the taxable year.

Amounts shall be taken into account on a first-in-time basis. For purposes of section 832(e) of such Code and this paragraph, if part of the reserve is reduced under State law or regulation, such reduction shall first apply to the extent of amounts added to the reserve for taxable years beginning before 1967, and only then to amounts added thereafter.

"(3) The provisions of this subsection shall apply to taxable years beginning after December 31, 1956."

[Sec. 832(f)]

(f) INTERINSURERS.—In the case of a mutual insurance company which is an interinsurer or reciprocal underwriter—

(1) there shall be allowed as a deduction the increase for the taxable year in savings credited to subscriber accounts, or

(2) there shall be included as an item of gross income the decrease for the taxable year in savings credited to subscriber accounts.

For purposes of the preceding sentence, the term "savings credited to subscriber accounts" means such portion of the surplus as is credited to the individual accounts of subscribers before the 16th day of the 3rd month following the close of the taxable year, but only if the company would be obligated to pay such amount promptly to such subscriber if he terminated his contract at the close of the company's taxable year. For purposes of determining his taxable income, the subscriber shall treat any such savings credited to his account as a dividend paid or declared.

Amendments

• 1986, Tax Reform Act of 1986 (P.L. 99-514)

P.L. 99-514, §1024(c)(6):

Amended Code Sec. 832 by adding at the end thereof new subsection (f). **Effective** for tax years beginning after 12-31-86.

[Sec. 832(g)]

(g) DIVIDENDS WITHIN GROUP.—In the case of an insurance company subject to tax under section 831(a) filing or required to file a consolidated return under section 1501 with respect to any affiliated group for any taxable year, any determination under this part with respect to any dividend paid by one member of such group to another member of such group shall be made as if such group were not filing a consolidated return.

Amendments

• 1988, Technical and Miscellaneous Revenue Act of 1988 (P.L. 100-647)

P.L. 100-647, §1010(d)(1):

Amended Code Sec. 832 by adding at the end thereof new subsection (g). **Effective** as if included in the provision of P.L. 99-514 to which it relates.

[Sec. 833]

SEC. 833. TREATMENT OF BLUE CROSS AND BLUE SHIELD ORGANIZATIONS, ETC.

[Sec. 833(a)]

(a) GENERAL RULE.—In the case of any organization to which this section applies—

(1) TREATED AS STOCK COMPANY.—Such organization shall be taxable under this part in the same manner as if it were a stock insurance company.

(2) SPECIAL DEDUCTION ALLOWED.—The deduction determined under subsection (b) for any taxable year shall be allowed.

(3) REDUCTIONS IN UNEARNED PREMIUM RESERVES NOT TO APPLY.—Subparagraph (B) of paragraph (4) of section 832(b) shall be applied by substituting "100 percent" for "80 percent", and subparagraph (C) of such paragraph (4) shall not apply.

[Sec. 833(b)]

(b) AMOUNT OF DEDUCTION.—

(1) IN GENERAL.—Except as provided in paragraph (2), the deduction determined under this subsection for any taxable year is the excess (if any) of—

(A) 25 percent of the sum of—

(i) the claims incurred during the taxable year and liabilities incurred during the taxable year under cost-plus contracts, and

(ii) the expenses incurred during the taxable year in connection with the administration, adjustment, or settlement of claims or in connection with the administration of cost-plus contracts, over

(B) the adjusted surplus as of the beginning of the taxable year.

(2) LIMITATION.—The deduction determined under paragraph (1) for any taxable year shall not exceed taxable income for such taxable year (determined without regard to such deduction).

(3) ADJUSTED SURPLUS.—For purposes of this subsection—

(A) IN GENERAL.—The adjusted surplus as of the beginning of any taxable year is an amount equal to the adjusted surplus as of the beginning of the preceding taxable year—

(i) increased by the amount of any adjusted taxable income for such preceding taxable year, or

(ii) decreased by the amount of any adjusted net operating loss for such preceding taxable year.

(B) SPECIAL RULE.—The adjusted surplus as of the beginning of the organization's 1st taxable year beginning after December 31, 1986, shall be its surplus as of such time. For purposes of the preceding sentence and subsection (c)(3)(C), the term "surplus" means the excess of the total assets over the total liabilities as shown on the annual statement.

(C) ADJUSTED TAXABLE INCOME.—The term "adjusted taxable income" means taxable income determined—

(i) without regard to the deduction determined under this subsection,

(ii) without regard to any carryforward or carryback to such taxable year, and

(iii) by increasing gross income by an amount equal to the net exempt income for the taxable year.

(D) ADJUSTED NET OPERATING LOSS.—The term "adjusted net operating loss" means the net operating loss for any taxable year determined with the adjustments set forth in subparagraph (C).

(E) NET EXEMPT INCOME.—The term "net exempt income" means—

(i) any tax-exempt interest received or accrued during the taxable year, reduced by any amount (not otherwise deductible) which would have been allowable as a deduction for the taxable year if such interest were not tax-exempt, and

(ii) the aggregate amount allowed as a deduction for the taxable year under sections 243, 244, and 245.

The amount determined under clause (ii) shall be reduced by the amount of any decrease in deductions allowable for the taxable year by reason of section 832(b)(5)(B) to the extent such decrease is attributable to deductions under sections 243, 244, and 245.

(4) ONLY HEALTH-RELATED ITEMS TAKEN INTO ACCOUNT.—Any determination under this subsection shall be made by only taking into account items attributable to the health-related business of the taxpayer.

Amendments

• 1997, Taxpayer Relief Act of 1997 (P.L. 105-34)

P.L. 105-34, §1604(d)(2)(A)(i)-(ii):

Amended Code Sec. 833(b)(1)(A) by inserting before the comma at the end of clause (i) "and liabilities incurred during the taxable year under cost-plus contracts", and by inserting before the comma at the end of clause (ii) "or in connection with the administration of cost-plus contracts". **Effective** as if included in the amendments made by Act Sec. 1012 of P.L. 99-514 [generally **effective** for tax years beginning after 12-31-86.—CCH].

[Sec. 833(c)]

(c) ORGANIZATIONS TO WHICH SECTION APPLIES.—

(1) IN GENERAL.—This section shall apply to—

(A) any existing Blue Cross or Blue Shield organization, and

(B) any other organization meeting the requirements of paragraph (3).

(2) EXISTING BLUE CROSS OR BLUE SHIELD ORGANIZATION.—The term "existing Blue Cross or Blue Shield organization" means any Blue Cross or Blue Shield organization if—

(A) such organization was in existence on August 16, 1986,

(B) such organization is determined to be exempt from tax for its last taxable year beginning before January 1, 1987, and

(C) no material change has occurred in the operations of such organization or in its structure after August 16, 1986, and before the close of the taxable year.

To the extent permitted by the Secretary, any successor to an organization meeting the requirements of the preceding sentence, and any organization resulting from the merger or consolidation of organizations each of which met such requirements, shall be treated as an existing Blue Cross or Blue Shield organization.

(3) OTHER ORGANIZATIONS.—

(A) IN GENERAL.—An organization meets the requirements of this paragraph for any taxable year if—

(i) substantially all the activities of such organization involve the providing of health insurance,

(ii) at least 10 percent of the health insurance provided by such organization is provided to individuals and small groups (not taking into account any medicare supplemental coverage),

(iii) such organization provides continuous full-year open enrollment (including conversions) for individuals and small groups,

(iv) such organization's policies covering individuals provide full coverage of preexisting conditions of high-risk individuals without a price differential (with a reasonable waiting period), and coverage is provided without regard to age, income, or employment status of individuals under age 65,

(v) at least 35 percent of its premiums are determined on a community rated basis, and

(vi) no part of its net earnings inures to the benefit of any private shareholder or individual.

(B) SMALL GROUP DEFINED.—For purposes of subparagraph (A), the term "small group" means the lesser of—

(i) 15 individuals, or

(ii) the number of individuals required for a small group under applicable State law.

(C) SPECIAL RULE FOR DETERMINING ADJUSTED SURPLUS.—For purposes of subsection (b), the adjusted surplus of any organization meeting the requirements of this paragraph as of the beginning of the 1st taxable year for which it meets such requirements shall be its surplus as of such time.

(4) TREATMENT AS EXISTING BLUE CROSS OR BLUE SHIELD ORGANIZATION.—

(A) IN GENERAL.—Paragraph (2) shall be applied to an organization described in subparagraph (B) as if it were a Blue Cross or Blue Shield organization.

(B) APPLICABLE ORGANIZATION.—An organization is described in this subparagraph if it—

(i) is organized under, and governed by, State laws which are specifically and exclusively applicable to not-for-profit health insurance or health service type organizations, and

(ii) is not a Blue Cross or Blue Shield organization or health maintenance organization.

(5) NONAPPLICATION OF SECTION IN CASE OF LOW MEDICAL LOSS RATIO.—Notwithstanding the preceding paragraphs, this section shall not apply to any organization unless such organization's percentage of total premium revenue expended on reimbursement for clinical services provided to enrollees under its policies during such taxable year (as reported under section 2718 of the Public Health Service Act) is not less than 85 percent.

Amendments

• 2010, Patient Protection and Affordable Care Act (P.L. 111-148)

P.L. 111-148, §9016(a):

Amended Code Sec. 833(c) by adding at the end a new paragraph (5). **Effective** for tax years beginning after 12-31-2009.

• 1998, Tax and Trade Relief Extension Act of 1998 (P.L. 105-277)

P.L. 105-277, §4003(g), provides:

(g) PROVISION RELATED TO SECTION 1042 OF 1997 ACT.—Rules similar to the rules of section 1.1502-75(d)(5) of the Treasury Regulations shall apply with respect to any organization described in section 1042(b) of the 1997 Act.

• 1997, Taxpayer Relief Act of 1997 (P.L. 105-34)

P.L. 105-34, §1042 (referring to P.L. 99-514, §1012(c)(4)(A)-(B), below), provides:

SEC. 1042. TERMINATION OF CERTAIN EXCEPTIONS FROM RULES RELATING TO EXEMPT ORGANIZATIONS WHICH PROVIDE COMMERCIAL-TYPE INSURANCE.

(a) IN GENERAL.—Subparagraphs (A) and (B) of section 1012(c)(4) of the Tax Reform Act of 1986 shall not apply to any taxable year beginning after December 31, 1997.

(b) SPECIAL RULES.—In the case of an organization to which section 501(m) of the Internal Revenue Code of 1986 applies solely by reason of the amendment made by subsection (a)—

(1) no adjustment shall be made under section 481 (or any other provision) of such Code on account of a change in its method of accounting for its first taxable year beginning after December 31, 1997, and

(2) for purposes of determining gain or loss, the adjusted basis of any asset held on the 1st day of such taxable year shall be treated as equal to its fair market value as of such day.

(c) RESERVE WEAKENING AFTER JUNE 8, 1997.—Any reserve weakening after June 8, 1997, by an organization described in subsection (b) shall be treated as occurring in such organization's 1st taxable year beginning after December 31, 1997.

(d) REGULATIONS.—The Secretary of the Treasury or his delegate may prescribe rules for providing proper adjustments for organizations described in subsection (b) with respect to short taxable years which begin during 1998 by reason of section 843 of the Internal Revenue Code of 1986.

• 1996, Health Insurance Portability and Accountability Act of 1996 (P.L. 104-191)

P.L. 104-191, §351(a):

Amended Code Sec. 833(c) by adding at the end a new paragraph (4). **Effective** for tax years ending after 12-31-96.

• 1986, Tax Reform Act of 1986 (P.L. 99-514)

P.L. 99-514, §1012(b)(1):

Amended Part III of subchapter L of chapter 1 by adding at the end thereof new Code Sec. 833. For the **effective** date, as well as several special rules, see Act Sec. 1012(c), below.

P.L. 99-514, §1012(c), as amended by P.L. 100-647, §1010(b)(1)-(2), provides:

(c) EFFECTIVE DATE.—

(1) IN GENERAL.—The amendments made by this section shall apply to taxable years beginning after December 31, 1986.

(2) STUDY OF FRATERNAL BENEFICIARY ASSOCIATIONS.—The Secretary of the Treasury or his delegate shall conduct a study of organizations described in section 501(c)(8) of the Internal Revenue Code of 1986 and which received gross annual insurance premiums in excess of $25,000,000 for the taxable years of such organizations which ended during 1984. Not later than January 1, 1988, the Secretary of the Treasury shall submit to the Committee on Ways and Means of the House of Representatives, the Committee on Finance of the Senate, and the Joint Committee on Taxation the results of such study, together with such recommendations as he determines to be appropriate. The Secretary of the Treasury shall have authority to require the furnishing of such information as may be necessary to carry out the purposes of this paragraph.

(3) SPECIAL RULES FOR EXISTING BLUE CROSS OR BLUE SHIELD ORGANIZATIONS.—

(A) IN GENERAL.—In the case of any existing Blue Cross or Blue Shield organization (as defined in section 833(c)(2) of the Internal Revenue Code of 1986 as added by this section)—

(i) no adjustment shall be made under section 481 (or any other provision) of such Code on account of a change in its method of accounting for its 1st taxable year beginning after December 31, 1986, and

(ii) for purposes of determining gain or loss, the adjusted basis of any asset held on the 1st day of such taxable year shall be treated as equal to its fair market value as of such day.

(B) TREATMENT OF CERTAIN DISTRIBUTIONS.—For purposes of section 833(b)(3)(B), the surplus of any organization as of the beginning of its 1st taxable year beginning after December 31, 1986, shall be increased by the amount of any distribution (other than to policyholders) made by such organization after August 16, 1986, and before the beginning of such taxable year.

(C) RESERVE WEAKENING AFTER AUGUST 16, 1986.—Any reserve weakening after August 16, 1986, by an existing Blue Cross or Blue Shield organization shall be treated as occurring in such organization's 1st taxable year beginning after December 31, 1986.

(4) OTHER SPECIAL RULES.—

(A) The amendments made by this section shall not apply with respect to that portion of the business of Mutual of America which is attributable to pension business.

(B) The amendments made by this section shall not apply to that portion of the business of the Teachers Insurance Annuity Association-College Retirement Equities Fund which is attributable to pension business.

(C) The amendments made by this section shall not apply to—

(i) the retirement fund of the YMCA,

(ii) the Missouri Hospital Plan,

(iii) administrative services performed by municipal leagues, and

(iv) dental benefit coverage provided by a Delta Dental Plans Association through contracts with independent professional service providers so long as the provision of such coverage is the principal activity of such organization.

(D) For purposes of this paragraph, the term "pension business" means the administration of any plan described in section 401(a) of the Internal Revenue Code of 1954 which includes a trust exempt from tax under section 501(a), any plan under which amounts are contributed by an individual's employer for an annuity contract described in section 403(b) of such Code, any individual retirement plan described in section 408 of such Code, and any eligible deferred compensation plan to which section 457(a) of such Code applies.

[Sec. 834]

SEC. 834. DETERMINATION OF TAXABLE INVESTMENT INCOME.

[Sec. 834(a)]

(a) GENERAL RULE.—For purposes of section 831(b), the term "taxable investment income" means the gross investment income, minus the deductions provided in subsection (c).

Amendments

• 1986, Tax Reform Act of 1986 (P.L. 99-514)

P.L. 99-514, §1024(c)(7):

Amended Code Sec. 834(a), as redesignated by Sec. 1024(a). **Effective** for tax years beginning after 12-31-86. Prior to amendment, Code Sec. 834(a) read as follows:

(a) DEFINITIONS.—For purposes of this part—

(1) The term "taxable investment income" means the gross investment income, minus the deductions provided in subsection (c).

(2) The term "investment loss" means the amount by which the deductions provided in subsection (c) exceed the gross investment income.

• 1962, Revenue Act of 1962 (P.L. 87-834)

P.L. 87-834, §8:

Amended the heading of Code Sec. 822 and subsection (a). **Effective** 1-1-63. Prior to amendment, the heading and subsection (a) of Code Sec. 822 read as follows:

SEC. 822. DETERMINATION OF MUTUAL INSURANCE COMPANY TAXABLE INCOME.

(a) DEFINITIONS.—For purposes of section 821, the term "mutual insurance company taxable income" means the gross investment income minus the deductions provided in subsection (c).

[Sec. 834(b)]

(b) GROSS INVESTMENT INCOME.—For purposes of subsection (a), the term "gross investment income" means the sum of the following:

(1) The gross amount of income during the taxable year from—

(A) interest, dividends, rents, and royalties,

(B) the entering into of any lease, mortgage, or other instrument or agreement from which the insurance company derives interest, rents, or royalties,

(C) the alteration or termination of any instrument or agreement described in subparagraph (B), and

(D) gains from sales or exchanges of capital assets to the extent provided in subchapter P (sec. 1201 and following, relating to capital gains and losses).

(2) The gross income during the taxable year from any trade or business (other than an insurance business) carried on by the insurance company, or by a partnership of which the insurance company is a partner. In computing gross income under this paragraph, there shall be excluded any item described in paragraph (1).

Amendments

• 1956, Life Insurance Company Tax Act of 1955 (P.L. 429, 84th Cong.)

P.L. 429, 84th Cong., §3(a)(3):

Amended Code Sec. 822(b). **Effective** 1-1-55. Prior to amendment Sec. 822(b) read as follows:

(b) GROSS INVESTMENT INCOME.—For purposes of subsection (a), the term `gross investment income' means the gross amount of income during the taxable year from interest, dividends, rents, and gains from sales or exchanges of capital assets to the extent provided in subchapter P (sec. 1201 and following, relating to capital gains and losses).

[Sec. 834(c)]

(c) DEDUCTIONS.—In computing taxable investment income, the following deductions shall be allowed:

(1) TAX-FREE INTEREST.—The amount of interest which under section 103 is excluded for the taxable year from gross income.

(2) INVESTMENT EXPENSES.—Investment expenses paid or accrued during the taxable year. If any general expenses are in part assigned to or included in the investment expenses, the total deduction under this paragraph shall not exceed one-fourth of 1 percent of the mean of the book value of the invested assets held at the beginning and end of the taxable year plus one-fourth of the amount by which taxable investment income (computed without any deduction for investment expenses allowed by this paragraph, for tax-free interest allowed by paragraph (1), or for dividends received allowed by paragraph (7)), exceeds $3\frac{3}{4}$ percent of the book value of the mean of the invested assets held at the beginning and end of the taxable year.

(3) REAL ESTATE EXPENSES.—Taxes (as provided in section 164), and other expenses, paid or accrued during the taxable year exclusively on or with respect to the real estate owned by the company. No deduction shall be allowed under this paragraph for any amount paid out for new buildings, or for permanent improvements or betterments made to increase the value of any property.

(4) DEPRECIATION.—The depreciation deduction allowed by section 167.

(5) INTEREST PAID OR ACCRUED.—All interest paid or accrued within the taxable year on indebtedness, except on indebtedness incurred or continued to purchase or carry obligations the interest on which is wholly exempt from taxation under this subtitle.

(6) CAPITAL LOSSES.—Capital losses to the extent provided in subchapter P (sec. 1201 and following) plus losses from capital assets sold or exchanged in order to obtain funds to meet abnormal insurance losses and to provide for the payment of dividends and similar distributions to policyholders. Capital assets shall be considered as sold or exchanged in order to obtain funds to meet abnormal insurance losses and to provide for the payment of dividends and similar distributions to policyholders to the extent that the gross receipts from their sale or exchange are not greater than the excess, if any, for the taxable year of the sum of dividends and similar distributions paid to policyholders, losses paid, and expenses paid over the sum of the items described in subsection (b) (other than paragraph (1)(D) thereof) and net premiums received. In the application of section 1212 for purposes of this section, the net capital loss for the taxable year shall be the amount by which losses for such year from sales or exchanges of capital assets exceeds the sum of the gains from such sales or exchanges and whichever of the following amounts is the lesser:

(A) the taxable investment income (computed without regard to gains or losses from sales or exchanges of capital assets); or

(B) losses from the sale or exchange of capital assets sold or exchanged to obtain funds to meet abnormal insurance losses and to provide for the payment of dividends and similar distributions to policyholders.

(7) SPECIAL DEDUCTIONS.—The special deductions allowed by part VIII (except section 248) of subchapter B (sec. 241 and following, relating to dividends received). In applying section 246(b) (relating to limitation on aggregate amount of deductions for dividends received) for purposes of this paragraph, the reference in such section to "taxable income" shall be treated as a reference to "taxable investment income."

(8) TRADE OR BUSINESS DEDUCTIONS.—The deductions allowed by this subtitle (without regard to this part) which are attributable to any trade or business (other than an insurance business) carried on by the insurance company, or by a partnership of which the insurance company is a partner, except that for purposes of this paragraph—

(A) any item, to the extent attributable to the carrying on of the insurance business, shall not be taken into account, and

(B) the deduction for net operating losses provided in section 172 shall not be allowed.

(9) DEPLETION.—The deduction allowed by section 611 (relating to depletion).

Amendments

• 1976, Tax Reform Act of 1976 (P.L. 94-455)

P.L. 94-455, §1901(a)(105):

Struck out "(other than obligations of the United States issued after September 24, 1917, and originally subscribed for by the taxpayer)" after "obligations" in paragraph (5). **Effective** for tax years beginning after 12-31-76.

P.L. 94-455, §1901(b)(1)(P):

Struck out "partially tax-exempt interest and" after "paragraph (1), or for" in paragraph (2). **Effective** for tax years beginning after 12-31-76.

P.L. 94-455, §1901(b)(1)(Q):

Struck out "or to the deduction provided in section 242 for partially tax-exempt interest" in paragraph (6)(A). **Effective** for tax years beginning after 12-31-76.

P.L. 94-455, §1901(b)(1)(R):

Struck out "partially tax-exempt interest and to" after "(sec. 241 and following, relating to" in paragraph (7). **Effective** for tax years beginning after 12-31-76.

• 1962, Revenue Tax Act of 1962 (P.L. 87-834)

P.L. 87-834, §8:

Amended Code Sec. 822(c) by substituting "taxable investment income" for "mutual insurance company taxable income" in lines 1, 10, and 44, and by inserting in Sec. 822(c)(7) after the period in line 3 a new sentence. **Effective** 1-1-63.

• 1956, Life Insurance Company Tax Act of 1955 (P.L. 429, 84th Cong.)

P.L. 429, 84th Cong., §3(a)(4):

Amended Code Sec. 822(c)(3). **Effective** 1-1-63. Prior to amendment, Sec. 822(c)(3) read as follows:

"(3) REAL ESTATE EXPENSES.—Taxes and other expenses paid or accrued during the taxable year exclusively on or with respect to the real estate owned by the company, not including taxes assessed against local benefits of a kind tending to increase the value of the property assessed, and not including any amount paid out for new buildings, or for permanent improvements or betterments made to increase the value of any property. The deduction allowed by this paragraph shall be allowed in the case of taxes imposed on a shareholder of a company on his interest as shareholder, which are paid or accrued by the company without reimbursement from the shareholder, but in such cases no deduction shall be allowed the shareholder for the amount of such taxes."

P.L. 429, 84th Cong., §3(a)(5):

Amended Code Sec. 822(c)(6) by substituting for the words "the sum of interest, dividends, rents, and net premiums received. In the application of section 1211", the words "the sum of the items described in subsection (b) (other than paragraph (1)(D) thereof) and net premiums received. In the application of section 1212". **Effective** 1-1-63.

P.L. 429, 84th Cong., §3(a)(6):

Added to paragraph (c) subparagraphs (8) and (9). **Effective** 1-1-63.

[Sec. 834(d)]

(d) OTHER APPLICABLE RULES.—

(1) RENTAL VALUE OF REAL ESTATE.—The deduction under subsection (c)(3) or (4) on account of any real estate owned and occupied in whole or in part by a mutual insurance company subject to the tax imposed by section 831 shall be limited to an amount which bears the same ratio to

such deduction (computed without regard to this paragraph) as the rental value of the space not so occupied bears to the rental value of the entire property.

(2) AMORTIZATION OF PREMIUM AND ACCRUAL OF DISCOUNT.—The gross amount of income during the taxable year from interest and the deduction provided in subsection (c)(1) shall each be decreased to reflect the appropriate amortization of premium and increased to reflect the appropriate accrual of discount attributable to the taxable year on bonds, notes, debentures, or other evidences of indebtedness held by a mutual insurance company subject to the tax imposed by section 831. Such amortization and accrual shall be determined—

(A) in accordance with the method regularly employed by such company, if such method is reasonable, and

(B) in all other cases, in accordance with regulations prescribed by the Secretary.

No accrual of discount shall be required under this paragraph on any bond (as defined in section 171(d)) except in the case of discount which is original issue discount (as defined in section 1273).

(3) DOUBLE DEDUCTIONS.—Nothing in this part shall permit the same item to be deducted more than once.

Amendments

• 1986, Tax Reform Act of 1986 (P.L. 99-514)

P.L. 99-514, §1024(c)(8)(A)-(B):

Amended Code Sec. 834(d), as redesignated by Act Sec. 1024(a), by striking out "section 821" each place it appears and inserting in lieu thereof "section 831", and by inserting before the period at the end of the last sentence of paragraph (2) the following: "except in the case of discount which is original issue discount (as defined in section 1273)". **Effective** for tax years beginning after 12-31-86.

• 1976, Tax Reform Act of 1976 (P.L. 94-455)

P.L. 94-455, §1901(a)(105):

Struck out "For taxable years beginning after December 31, 1962, no accrual" and inserted in its place "No accrual" in the last sentence of Code Sec. 822(d)(2). **Effective** for tax years beginning after 12-31-76.

P.L. 94-455, §1901(b)(1)(S):

Substituted "and the deduction provided in subsection (c)(1)" for ", the deduction provided in subsection (c)(1), and the deduction allowed by section 242 (relating to partially tax-exempt interest)" in paragraph (2). **Effective** for tax years beginning after 12-31-76.

P.L. 94-455, §1906(b)(13)(A):

Amended 1954 Code by substituting "Secretary" for "Secretary or his delegate" each place it appeared. **Effective** 2-1-77.

• 1964, Revenue Act of 1964 (P.L. 88-272)

P.L. 88-272, §228(b)(2):

Amended Code Sec. 822(d)(2) by adding the last sentence thereof. **Effective** for tax years beginning after 12-31-62.

• 1956, Life Insurance Company Tax Act of 1955 (P.L. 429, 84th Cong.)

P.L. 429, 84th Cong., §3(a)(7):

Amended Code Sec. 822(d)(1) by substituting for "subsection (e)(3) or (4)", the words "subsection (c)(3) or (4)". **Effective** 1-1-55.

[Sec. 834(e)]

(e) DEFINITIONS.—For purposes of this part—

(1) NET PREMIUMS.—The term "net premiums" means gross premiums (including deposits and assessments) written or received on insurance contracts during the taxable year less return premiums and premiums paid or incurred for reinsurance. Amounts returned where the amount is not fixed in the insurance contract but depends on the experience of the company or the discretion of the management shall not be included in return premiums but shall be treated as dividends to policyholders under paragraph (2).

(2) DIVIDENDS TO POLICYHOLDERS.—The term "dividends to policyholders" means dividends and similar distributions paid or declared to policyholders. For purposes of the preceding sentence, the term "paid or declared" shall be construed according to the method regularly employed in keeping the books of the insurance company.

Amendments

• 1986, Tax Reform Act of 1986 (P.L. 99-514)

P.L. 99-514, §1024(a)(3):

Redesignated Code Sec. 822 as Code Sec. 834. **Effective** for tax years beginning after 12-31-86.

• 1966, Foreign Investors Tax Act of 1966 (P.L. 89-809)

P.L. 89-809, §104(i)(5):

Repealed Code Sec. 822(e) and redesignated former Code Sec. 823(f) as Code Sec. 822(e). **Effective** 1-1-67.

• 1962, Revenue Act of 1962 (P.L. 87-834)

P.L. 87-834, §8:

Redesignated Code Sec. 823 as Code Sec. 822(f) and struck out the word "other" in the heading. **Effective** 1-1-63.

P.L. 89-809, §104(i)(5):

Repealed former Code Sec. 822(e). **Effective** 1-1-67. Prior to repeal Code Sec. 822(e) read as follows:

(e) FOREIGN MUTUAL INSURANCE COMPANIES OTHER THAN LIFE OR MARINE.—In the case of a foreign mutual insurance company (other than a life or marine insurance company or a fire insurance company subject to the tax imposed by section 831), the taxable investment income shall be the taxable income from sources within the United States (computed without regard to the deductions allowed by subsection (c)(7)), and the gross amount of income from the items described in subsection (b) (other than paragraph (1)(D) thereof) and net premiums shall be the amount of such income from sources within the United States. In the case of a company to which the preceding sentence applies, the deductions allowed in this section shall be allowed to the extent provided in subpart B of part II of subchapter N (sec. 851 and following) in the case of a foreign corporation engaged in trade or business within the United States.

• 1962, Revenue Act of 1962 (P.L. 87-834)

P.L. 87-834, §8:

Amended Code Sec. 822(e) by substituting "taxable investment income" for "mutual insurance company taxable income" in line 4.

• 1956, Life Insurance Company Tax Act of 1955 (P.L. 429, 84th Cong.)

P.L. 429, 84th Cong., §3(a)(8):

Amended Code Sec. 822(e) by substituting for the words "interest, dividends, rents," the words "items described in subsection (b) (other than paragraph (1)(D) thereof)". **Effective** 1-1-55.

[Sec. 835]

SEC. 835. ELECTION BY RECIPROCAL.

[Sec. 835(a)]

(a) IN GENERAL.—Except as otherwise provided in this section, any mutual insurance company which is an interinsurer or reciprocal underwriter (hereinafter in this section referred to as a "reciprocal") subject to the taxes imposed by section 831(a) may, under regulations prescribed by the Secretary, elect to be subject to the limitation provided in subsection (b). Such election shall be effective for the taxable year for which made and for all succeeding taxable years, and shall not be revoked except with the consent of the Secretary.

Amendments

• 1988, Technical and Miscellaneous Revenue Act of 1988 (P.L. 100-647)

P.L. 100-647, §1010(f)(2):

Amended Code Sec. 835(a) by striking out "section 821(a)" and inserting in lieu thereof "section 831(a)". **Effective** as if included in the provision of P.L. 99-514 to which it relates.

• 1976, Tax Reform Act of 1976 (P.L. 94-455)

P.L. 94-455, §1906(b)(13)(A):

Amended 1954 Code by substituting "Secretary" for "Secretary or his delegate" each place it appeared. **Effective** 2-1-77.

[Sec. 835(b)]

(b) LIMITATION.—The deduction for amounts paid or incurred in the taxable year to the attorney-in-fact by a reciprocal making the election provided in subsection (a) shall be limited to, but in no case increased by, the deductions of the attorney-in-fact allocable, in accordance with regulations prescribed by the Secretary, to the income received by the attorney-in-fact from the reciprocal.

Amendments

• 1976, Tax Reform Act of 1976 (P.L. 94-455)

P.L. 94-455, §1906(b)(13)(A):

Amended 1954 Code by substituting "Secretary" for "Secretary or his delegate" each place it appeared. **Effective** 2-1-77.

[Sec. 835(c)]

(c) EXCEPTION.—An election may not be made by a reciprocal under subsection (a) unless the attorney-in-fact of such reciprocal—

(1) is subject to the tax imposed by section 11;

(2) consents in such manner as the Secretary shall prescribe by regulations to make available such information as may be required during the period in which the election provided in subsection (a) is in effect, under regulations prescibed by the Secretary;

(3) reports the income received from the reciprocal and the deductions allocable thereto under the same method of accounting under which the reciprocal reports deductions for amounts paid to the attorney-in-fact; and

(4) files its return on the calendar year basis.

Amendments

• 1978, Revenue Act of 1978 (P.L. 95-600)

P.L. 95-600, §301(b)(10):

Amended Code Sec. 826(c)(1) by striking out "(1) is subject to the taxes imposed by section 11(b) and (c);" and by inserting "(1) is subject to the tax imposed by section 11;". **Effective** for tax years beginning after 12-31-78.

• 1976, Tax Reform Act of 1976 (P.L. 94-455)

P.L. 94-455, §1906(b)(13)(A):

Amended 1954 Code by substituting "Secretary" for "Secretary or his delegate" each place it appeared. **Effective** 2-1-77.

[Sec. 835(d)]

(d) CREDIT.—Any reciprocal electing to be subject to the limitation provided in subsection (b) shall be credited with so much of the tax paid by the attorney-in-fact as is attributable, under regulations prescribed by the Secretary, to the income received by the attorney-in-fact from the reciprocal in such taxable year.

Amendments

• 1986, Tax Reform Act of 1986 (P.L. 99-514)

P.L. 99-514, §1024(c)(9)(A):

Amended Code Sec. 835, as redesignated by Act Sec. 1024(a), by striking out subsection (d) and by redesignating subsections (e), (f), (g), and (h) as subsections (d), (e), (f), and (g), respectively, and by amending subsection (e) (as so redesignated). **Effective** for tax years beginning after 12-31-86. Prior to amendment, Code Sec. 835(d) read as follows:

(d) SPECIAL RULE.—In applying section 824(d)(1)(D), any amount which was added to the protection against loss account by reason of an election under this section shall be treated as having been added by reason of section 824(a)(1)(A).

• 1976, Tax Reform Act of 1976 (P.L. 94-455)

P.L. 94-455, §1906(b)(13)(A):

Amended 1954 Code by substituting "Secretary" for "Secretary or his delegate" each place it appeared. **Effective** 2-1-77.

[Sec. 835(e)]

(e) BENEFITS OF GRADUATED RATES DENIED.—Any increase in the taxable income of a reciprocal attributable to the limits provided in subsection (b) shall be taxed at the highest rate of tax specified in section 11(b).

Amendments

• **1986, Tax Reform Act of 1986 (P.L. 99-514)**

P.L. 99-514, §1024(c)(9)(A):

Redesignated subsection (f) as subsection (e). **Effective** for tax years beginning after 12-31-86.

P.L. 99-514, §1024(c)(9)(B):

Amended Code Sec. 835(e), as so redesignated. **Effective** for tax years beginning after 12-31-86. Prior to amendment, Code Sec. 835(e), as so redesignated, read as follows:

(e) SURTAX EXEMPTION DENIED.—Any increase in taxable income of a reciprocal attributable to the limitation provided in subsection (b) shall be taxed without regard to the surtax exemption provided in section 821(a)(2).

[Sec. 835(f)]

(f) ADJUSTMENT FOR REFUND.—If for any taxable year an attorney-in-fact is allowed a credit or refund for taxes paid with respect to which credit or refund to the reciprocal resulted under subsection (d), the taxes of such reciprocal for such taxable year shall be properly adjusted under regulations prescribed by the Secretary.

Amendments

• **1988, Technical and Miscellaneous Revenue Act of 1988 (P.L. 100-647)**

P.L. 100-647, §1010(f)(3):

Amended Code Sec. 835(f) by striking out "subsection (e)" and inserting in lieu thereof "subsection (d)". **Effective** as if included in the provision of P.L. 99-514 to which it relates.

• **1986, Tax Reform Act of 1986 (P.L. 99-514)**

P.L. 99-514, §1024(c)(9)(A):

Redesignated subsection (g) as subsection (f). **Effective** for tax years beginning after 12-31-86.

• **1976, Tax Reform Act of 1976 (P.L. 94-455)**

P.L. 94-455, §1906(b)(13)(A):

Amended 1954 Code by substituting "Secretary" for "Secretary or his delegate" each place it appeared. **Effective** 2-1-77.

[Sec. 835(g)]

(g) TAXES OF ATTORNEY-IN-FACT UNAFFECTED.—Nothing in this section shall increase or decrease the taxes imposed by this chapter on the income of the attorney-in-fact.

Amendments

• **1986, Tax Reform Act of 1986 (P.L. 99-514)**

P.L. 99-514, §1024(a):

Redesignated Code Sec. 826 as Code Sec. 835. **Effective** for tax years beginning after 12-31-86.

P.L. 99-514, §1024(c)(9)(A):

Redesignated subsection (h) as subsection (g). **Effective** for tax years beginning after 12-31-86.

• **1962, Revenue Act of 1962 (P.L. 87-834)**

P.L. 87-834, §8:

Added new Code Sec. 826. **Effective** 1-1-63.

PART III—PROVISIONS OF GENERAL APPLICATION

[Sec. 841]

SEC. 841. CREDIT FOR FOREIGN TAXES.

The taxes imposed by foreign countries or possessions of the United States shall be allowed as a credit against the tax of a domestic insurance company subject to the tax imposed by section 801 or 831, to the extent provided in the case of a domestic corporation in section 901 (relating to foreign tax credit). For purposes of the preceding sentence (and for purposes of applying section 906 with respect to a foreign corporation subject to tax under this subchapter), the term "taxable income" as used in section 904 means—

(1) in the case of the tax imposed by section 801, the life insurance company taxable income (as defined in section 801(b)), and

(2) in the case of the tax imposed by section 831, the taxable income (as defined in section 832(a)).

Amendments

• 1986, Tax Reform Act of 1986 (P.L. 99-514)

P.L. 99-514, §1024(c)(10)(A)-(D):

Amended Code Sec. 841 by striking out "section 801, 821, or 831" and inserting in lieu thereof "section 801 or 831", by inserting "and" at the end of paragraph (1), by striking out paragraph (2), and by redesignating paragraph (3) as paragraph (2). **Effective** for tax years beginning after 12-31-86. Prior to amendment, Code Sec. 841(2) read as follows:

(2) in the case of the tax imposed by section 821(a), the mutual insurance company taxable income (as defined in section 821(b)); and in the case of the tax imposed by section 821(c), the taxable investment income (as defined in section 822(a)), and

• 1984, Deficit Reduction Act of 1984 (P.L. 98-369)

P.L. 98-369, §211(b)(10):

Amended Code Sec. 841 by striking out "section 802" each place it appeared and inserting in lieu thereof "section 801," and by striking out "section 802(b)" and inserting in lieu thereof "section 801(b)". **Effective** for tax years beginning after 12-31-83.

• 1966, Foreign Investors Tax Act of 1966 (P.L. 89-809)

P.L. 89-809, §104(i)(8):

Amended the second sentence of Code Sec. 841 by inserting after "sentence" the following: "(and for purposes of applying section 906 with respect to a foreign corporation subject to tax under this subchapter)". **Effective** 1-1-67.

• 1962, Revenue Act of 1962 (P.L. 87-834)

P.L. 87-834, §8:

Amended Code Sec. 841 by striking out "and" at the end of paragraph (1), by renumbering paragraph (2) as paragraph (3), and by inserting after paragraph (1) a new paragraph (2). **Effective** 1-1-63.

• 1959, Life Insurance Company Income Tax Act of 1959 (P.L. 86-69)

P.L. 86-69, §3(b):

Amended Code Sec. 841 by striking out "811," where it appeared following "802," and by amending Sec. 841(1). **Effective** for tax years beginning after 12-31-57. Prior to amendment, Sec. 841(1) read as follows:

"(1) in the case of the tax imposed by section 802 or 811, the net investment income (as defined in section 803 (c)),".

• 1956, Life Insurance Company Tax Act of 1955 (P.L. 429, 84th Cong.)

P.L. 429, 84th Cong., §5(4):

Amended the first sentence of Sec. 841 by inserting "811," after "802,". Also, amended Code Sec. 841(1) to read as reproduced in the amendment note for P.L. 86-69, above. Prior to the amendment such paragraph read as follows: "(1) in the case of the tax imposed by section 802, the taxable income (as defined in section 803(g)),". **Effective** 1-1-55.

[Sec. 842]

SEC. 842. FOREIGN COMPANIES CARRYING ON INSURANCE BUSINESS.

[Sec. 842(a)]

(a) TAXATION UNDER THIS SUBCHAPTER.—If a foreign company carrying on an insurance business within the United States would qualify under part I or II of this subchapter for the taxable year if (without regard to income not effectively connected with the conduct of any trade or business within the United States) it were a domestic corporation, such company shall be taxable under such part on its income effectively connected with its conduct of any trade or business within the United States. With respect to the remainder of its income which is from sources within the United States, such a foreign company shall be taxable as provided in section 881.

[Sec. 842(b)]

(b) MINIMUM EFFECTIVELY CONNECTED NET INVESTMENT INCOME.—

(1) IN GENERAL.—In the case of a foreign company taxable under part I or II of this subchapter for the taxable year, its net investment income for such year which is effectively connected with the conduct of an insurance business within the United States shall be not less than the product of—

(A) the required U.S. assets of such company, and

(B) the domestic investment yield applicable to such company for such year.

(2) REQUIRED U.S. ASSETS.—

(A) IN GENERAL.—For purposes of paragraph (1), the required U.S. assets of any foreign company for any taxable year is an amount equal to the product of—

(i) the mean of such foreign company's total insurance liabilities on United States business, and

(ii) the domestic asset/liability percentage applicable to such foreign company for such year.

(B) TOTAL INSURANCE LIABILITIES.—For purposes of this paragraph—

(i) COMPANIES TAXABLE UNDER PART I.—In the case of a company taxable under part I, the term "total insurance liabilities" means the sum of the total reserves (as defined in section 816(c)) plus (to the extent not included in total reserves) the items referred to in paragraphs (3), (4), (5), and (6) of section 807(c).

(ii) COMPANIES TAXABLE UNDER PART II.—In the case of a company taxable under part II, the term "total insurance liabilities" means the sum of unearned premiums and unpaid losses.

(C) DOMESTIC ASSET/LIABILITY PERCENTAGE.—The domestic asset/liability percentage applicable for purposes of subparagraph (A)(ii) to any foreign company for any taxable year is a percentage determined by the Secretary on the basis of a ratio—

(i) the numerator of which is the mean of the assets of domestic insurance companies taxable under the same part of this subchapter as such foreign company, and

(ii) the denominator of which is the mean of the total insurance liabilities of the same companies.

(3) DOMESTIC INVESTMENT YIELD.—The domestic investment yield applicable for purposes of paragraph (1)(B) to any foreign company for any taxable year is the percentage determined by the Secretary on the basis of a ratio—

(A) the numerator of which is the net investment income of domestic insurance companies taxable under the same part of this subchapter as such foreign company, and

(B) the denominator of which is the mean of the assets of the same companies.

(4) ELECTION TO USE WORLDWIDE YIELD.—

(A) IN GENERAL.—If the foreign company makes an election under this paragraph, such company's worldwide current investment yield shall be taken into account in lieu of the domestic investment yield for purposes of paragraph (1)(B).

(B) WORLDWIDE CURRENT INVESTMENT YIELD.—For purposes of subparagraph (A), the term "worldwide current investment yield" means the percentage obtained by dividing—

(i) the net investment income of the company from all sources, by

(ii) the mean of all assets of the company (whether or not held in the United States).

(C) ELECTION.—An election under this paragraph shall apply to the taxable year for which made and all subsequent taxable years unless revoked with the consent of the Secretary.

(5) NET INVESTMENT INCOME.—For purposes of this subsection, the term "net investment income" means—

(A) gross investment income (within the meaning of section 834(b)), reduced by

(B) expenses allocable to such income.

Amendments

• 1988, Technical and Miscellaneous Revenue Act of 1988 (P.L. 100-647)

P.L. 100-647, §2004(q)(2)(A):

Amended Code Sec. 842(b)(3)(B) by striking out "held for the production of such income" after "the same companies". **Effective** as if included in the provision of P.L. 100-203 to which it relates.

P.L. 100-647, §2004(q)(2)(B):

Amended Code Sec. 842(b)(4)(B) by striking out "held for the production of investment income" after "United States)". **Effective** as if included in the provision of P.L. 100-203 to which it relates.

[Sec. 842(c)]

(c) SPECIAL RULES FOR PURPOSES OF SUBSECTION (b).—

(1) COORDINATION WITH SMALL LIFE INSURANCE COMPANY DEDUCTION.—In the case of a foreign company taxable under part I, subsection (b) shall be applied before computing the small life insurance company deduction.

(2) REDUCTION IN SECTION 881 TAXES.—

(A) IN GENERAL.—The tax under section 881 (determined without regard to this paragraph) shall be reduced (but not below zero) by an amount which bears the same ratio to such tax as—

(i) the amount of the increase in effectively connected income of the company resulting from subsection (b), bears to

(ii) the amount which would be subject to tax under section 881 if the amount taxable under such section were determined without regard to sections 103 and 894.

(B) LIMITATION ON REDUCTION.—The reduction under subparagraph (A) shall not exceed the increase in taxes under part I or II (as the case may be) by reason of the increase in effectively connected income of the company resulting from subsection (b).

(3) DATA USED IN DETERMINING DOMESTIC ASSET/LIABILITY PERCENTAGES AND DOMESTIC INVESTMENT YIELDS.—Each domestic asset/liability percentage, and each domestic investment yield, for any taxable year shall be based on such representative data with respect to domestic insurance companies for the second preceding taxable year as the Secretary considers appropriate.

Amendments

• 2004, Pension Funding Equity Act of 2004 (P.L. 108-218)

P.L. 108-218, §205(b)(6):

Amended Code Sec. 842(c) by striking paragraph (3) and by redesignating paragraph (4) as paragraph (3). **Effective** for tax years beginning after 12-31-2004. Prior to being stricken, Code Sec. 842(c)(3) read as follows:

(3) ADJUSTMENT TO LIMITATION ON DEDUCTION FOR POLICYHOLDER DIVIDENDS IN THE CASE OF FOREIGN MUTUAL LIFE INSURANCE COMPANIES.—For purposes of section 809, the equity base of any foreign mutual life insurance company as of the close of any taxable year shall be increased by the excess of—

(A) the required U.S. assets of the company (determined under subsection (b)(2)), over

(B) the mean of the assets held in the United States during the taxable year.

• 1989, Omnibus Budget Reconciliation Act of 1989 (P.L. 101-239)

P.L. 101-239, §7821(d)(2):

Amended Code Sec. 842(c)(4) by striking "YEILDS" in the paragraph heading and inserting "YIELDS". **E ffective** as if included in the provision of P.L. 100-203 to which it relates.

[Sec. 842(d)]

(d) REGULATIONS.—The Secretary shall prescribe such regulations as may be necessary or appropriate to carry out the purposes of this section, including regulations—

(1) providing for the proper treatment of segregated asset accounts,

(2) providing for proper adjustments in succeeding taxable years where the company's actual net investment income for any taxable year which is effectively connected with the conduct of an insurance business within the United States exceeds the amount required under subsection (b)(1),

(3) providing for the proper treatment of investments in domestic subsidiaries, and

(4) which may provide that, in the case of companies taxable under part II of this subchapter, determinations under subsection (b) will be made separately for categories of such companies established in such regulations.

Amendments

• 1988, Technical and Miscellaneous Revenue Act of 1988 (P.L. 100-647)

P.L. 100-647, §2004(q)(3):

Amended Code Sec. 842(d) by striking out "and" at the end of paragraph (2) by striking out the period at the end of paragraph (3) and inserting in lieu thereof ", and", and by adding at the end thereof new paragraph (4). **Effective** as if included in the provision of P.L. 100-203 to which it relates.

• 1987, Revenue Act of 1987 (P.L. 100-203)

P.L. 100-203, §10242(a):

Amended Code Sec. 842. **Effective** for tax years beginning after 12-31-87. Prior to amendment, Code Sec. 842 read as follows:

SEC. 842. FOREIGN CORPORATIONS CARRYING ON INSURANCE BUSINESS.

If a foreign corporation carrying on an insurance business within the United States would qualify under part I or II of this subchapter for the taxable year if (without regard to income not effectively connected with the conduct of any trade or business within the United States) it were a domestic corporation, such corporation shall be taxable under such part on its income effectively connected with its conduct of any trade or business within the United States. With respect to the remainder of its income, which is from sources within the United States, such a foreign corporation shall be taxable as provided in section 881.

• 1986, Tax Reform Act of 1986 (P.L. 99-514)

P.L. 99-514, §1024(c)(11):

Amended Code Sec. 842 by striking out "part I, II or III" and inserting in lieu thereof "part I or II". **Effective** for tax years beginning after 12-31-86.

• 1966, Foreign Investors Tax Act of 1966 (P.L. 89-809)

P.L. 89-809, §104(i)(1):

Amended Code Sec. 842. **Effective** 1-1-67. Prior to amendment, Sec. 842 read as follows:

SEC. 842. COMPUTATION OF GROSS INCOME.

The gross income of insurance companies subject to the tax imposed by section 802 or 831 shall not be determined in the manner provided in part I of subchapter N (relating to determination of sources of income).

• 1959, Life Insurance Company Income Tax Act of 1959 (P.L. 86-69)

P.L. 86-69, §3(f)(1):

Amended Code Sec. 842 by striking out ", 811," where it appeared following "802". **Effective** for tax years beginning after 12-31-57.

• 1956, Life Insurance Company Tax Act of 1955 (P.L. 429, 84th Cong.)

P.L. 429, 84th Cong., §5(5):

Amended Code Sec. 842 by substituting for "802 or 831", the words and figures "802, 811, or 831". **Effective** 1-1-55.

[Sec. 843]

SEC. 843. ANNUAL ACCOUNTING PERIOD.

For purposes of this subtitle, the annual accounting period for each insurance company subject to a tax imposed by this subchapter shall be the calendar year. Under regulations prescribed by the Secretary, an insurance company which joins in the filing of a consolidated return (or is required to so file) may adopt the taxable year of the common parent corporation even though such year is not a calendar year.

Amendments

• 1976, Tax Reform Act of 1976 (P.L. 94-455)

P.L. 94-455, §1507(b)(2):

Added the second sentence to Code Sec. 843. **Effective** for tax years beginning after 12-31-80.

• 1956, Life Insurance Company Tax Act of 1955 (P.L. 429, 84th Cong.)

P.L. 429, 84th Cong., §4:

Added Code Sec. 843. **Effective** 1-1-55.

[Sec. 844]

SEC. 844. SPECIAL LOSS CARRYOVER RULES.

[Sec. 844(a)]

(a) GENERAL RULE.—If an insurance company—

(1) is subject to the tax imposed by part I or II of this subchapter for the taxable year, and

(2) was subject to the tax imposed by a different part of this subchapter for a prior taxable year,

then any operations loss carryover under section 810 (or the corresponding provisions of prior law) or net operating loss carryover under section 172 (as the case may be) arising in such prior taxable year shall be included in its operations loss deduction under section 810(a) or net operating loss deduction under section 832(c)(10), as the case may be.

Amendments

• 1989, Omnibus Budget Reconciliation Act of 1989 (P.L. 101-239)

P.L. 101-239, §7841(d)(16):

Amended Code Sec. 844(a)(2) by striking "for the taxable year" and inserting "for a prior taxable year". **Effective** on 12-19-89.

• 1986, Tax Reform Act of 1986 (P.L. 99-514)

P.L. 99-514, §1024(c)(12):

Amended Code Sec 844(a). **Effective** for tax years beginning after 12-31-86. However, for a transitional rule, see Act Sec. 1024(d)(2) following Code Sec. 825. Prior to amendment, Code Sec. 844(a) read as follows:

(a) GENERAL RULE.—If an insurance company—

(1) is subject to the tax imposed by part I, II, or III of this subchapter for the taxable year, and

(2) was subject to the tax imposed by a different part of this subchapter for a prior taxable year beginning after December 31, 1962,

then any operations loss carryover under section 810 (or the corresponding provisions of prior law), unused loss carryover under section 825, or net operating loss carryover under section 172, as the case may be, arising in such prior taxable year shall be included in its operations loss deduction under section 810(a), unused loss deduction under section 825(a), or net operating loss deduction under section 832(c)(10), as the case may be.

P.L. 99-514, §1899A(20):

Amended Code Sec. 844(a) by striking out "prior law),, unused loss" and inserting in lieu thereof "prior law), unused loss". **Effective** 10-22-86.

• 1984, Deficit Reduction Act of 1984 (P.L. 98-369)

P.L. 98-369, §211(b)(11)(A):

Amended Code Sec. 844(a) by striking out "section 812", and inserting in lieu thereof "section 810 (or the corresponding provisions of prior law),", and by striking out "section 812(a)" and inserting in lieu thereof "section 810(a)". **Effective** for tax years beginning after 12-31-83.

[Sec. 844(b)]

(b) LIMITATION.—The amount included under section 810(a) or 832(c)(10) (as the case may be) by reason of the application of subsection (a) shall not exceed the amount that would have constituted the loss carryover under such section if for all relevant taxable years the company had been subject to the tax imposed by the part referred to in subsection (a)(1) rather than the part referred to in subsection (a)(2). For purposes of applying the preceding sentence, section 810(b)(1)(C) (relating to additional years to which losses may be carried by new life insurance companies) shall not apply.

Amendments

• 1986, Tax Reform Act of 1986 (P.L. 99-514)

P.L. 99-514, §1024(c)(12):

Amended Code Sec. 844(b). **Effective** for tax years beginning after 12-31-86. However, for a transitional rule, see Act Sec. 1024(d)(2), the text of which can be found under the amendment notes for Code Sec. 825. Prior to amendment, Code Sec. 844(b) read as follows:

(b) LIMITATION.—The amount included under section 810(a), 825(a), or 832(c)(10), as the case may be, by reason of the application of subsection (a) shall not exceed the amount that would have constituted the loss carryover under such section if for all relevant taxable years such company had been subject to the tax imposed by the part referred to in subsection (a)(1) rather than the part referred to in subsection (a)(2). For purposes of applying the preceding sentence—

(1) in the case of a mutual insurance company which becomes a stock insurance company, an amount equal to 25 percent of the deduction under section 832(c)(11) (relating to dividends to policyholders) shall not be allowed, and

(2) section 810(b)(1)(C) (relating to additional years to which losses may be carried by new life insurance companies) shall not apply.

• 1984, Deficit Reduction Act of 1984 (P.L. 98-369)

P.L. 98-369, §211(b)(11)(B):

Amended Code Sec. 844(b) by striking out "section 812(a)" and inserting in lieu thereof "section 810(a)", and by striking out "section 812(b)(1)(C)" in paragraph (2) and inserting in lieu thereof "section 810(b)(1)(C)". **Effective** for tax years beginning after 12-31-83.

• 1976, Tax Reform Act of 1976 (P.L. 94-455)

P.L. 94-455, §1901(b)(25):

Substituted "section 812(b)(1)(C)" for section "812(b)(1)(A)(iii)" in Code Sec. 844(b)(2). **Effective** for tax years beginning after 12-31-76.

[Sec. 844(c)]

(c) REGULATIONS.—The Secretary shall prescribe such regulations as may be necessary to carry out the purposes of this section.

Amendments

• 1969, Tax Reform Act of 1969 (P.L. 91-172)

P.L. 91-172, §907(c)(1):

Added Code Sec. 844. **Effective** for losses incurred in tax years beginning after 12-31-62, but shall not affect any tax liability for any tax year beginning before 1-1-67.

[Sec. 845]

SEC. 845. CERTAIN REINSURANCE AGREEMENTS.

[Sec. 845(a)]

(a) ALLOCATION IN CASE OF REINSURANCE AGREEMENT INVOLVING TAX AVOIDANCE OR EVASION.—In the case of 2 or more related persons (within the meaning of section 482) who are parties to a reinsurance agreement (or where one of the parties to a reinsurance agreement is, with respect to any contract covered by the agreement, in effect an agent of another party to such agreement or a conduit between related persons), the Secretary may—

(1) allocate between or among such persons income (whether investment income, premium, or otherwise), deductions, assets, reserves, credits, and other items related to such agreement,

(2) recharacterize any such items, or

(3) make any other adjustment,

if he determines that such allocation, recharacterization, or adjustment is necessary to reflect the proper amount, source, or character of the taxable income (or any item described in paragraph (1) relating to such taxable income) of each such person.

Amendments

• 2004, American Jobs Creation Act of 2004 (P.L. 108-357)

P.L. 108-357, §803(a):

Amended Code Sec. 845(a) by striking "source and character" and inserting "amount, source, or character". **Effective** for any risk reinsured after 10-22-2004.

[Sec. 845(b)]

(b) REINSURANCE CONTRACT HAVING SIGNIFICANT TAX AVOIDANCE EFFECT.—If the Secretary determines that any reinsurance contract has a significant tax avoidance effect on any party to such contract, the Secretary may make proper adjustments with respect to such party to eliminate such tax avoidance effect (including treating such contract with respect to such party as terminated on December 31 of each year and reinstated on January 1 of the next year).

Amendments

• 1984, Deficit Reduction Act of 1984 (P.L. 98-369)

P.L. 98-369, §212(a):

Added Code Sec. 845. Code Sec. 845(a) is **effective** with respect to any risk reinsured on or after 9-27-83. Code Sec. 845(b) is **effective** with respect to risks reinsured after 12-31-84. See Act Sec. 217(e), below, for special rules.

P.L. 98-369, §217(e), provides:

(e) Treatment of Certain Companies Operating Both as Stock and Mutual Company.—If, during the 10-year period ending on December 31, 1983, a company has, as authorized by the law of the State in which the company is domiciled, been operating as a mutual life insurance company with shareholders, such company shall be treated as a stock life insurance company.

[Sec. 846]

SEC. 846. DISCOUNTED UNPAID LOSSES DEFINED.

[Sec. 846(a)]

(a) DISCOUNTED LOSSES DETERMINED.—

(1) SEPARATELY COMPUTED FOR EACH ACCIDENT YEAR.—The amount of the discounted unpaid losses as of the end of any taxable year shall be the sum of the discounted unpaid losses (as of such time) separately computed under this section with respect to unpaid losses in each line of business attributable to each accident year.

(2) METHOD OF DISCOUNTING.—The amount of the discounted unpaid losses as of the end of any taxable year attributable to any accident year shall be the present value of such losses (as of such time) determined by using—

(A) the amount of the undiscounted unpaid losses as of such time,

(B) the applicable interest rate, and

(C) the applicable loss payment pattern.

(3) LIMITATION ON AMOUNT OF DISCOUNTED LOSSES.—In no event shall the amount of the discounted unpaid losses with respect to any line of business attributable to any accident year exceed the aggregate amount of unpaid losses with respect to such line of business for such accident year included on the annual statement filed by the taxpayer for the year ending with or within the taxable year.

(4) DETERMINATION OF APPLICABLE FACTORS.—In determining the amount of the discounted unpaid losses attributable to any accident year—

(A) the applicable interest rate shall be the interest rate determined under subsection (c) for the calendar year with which such accident year ends, and

(B) the applicable loss payment pattern shall be the loss payment pattern determined under subsection (d) which is in effect for the calendar year with which such accident year ends.

[Sec. 846(b)]

(b) DETERMINATION OF UNDISCOUNTED UNPAID LOSSES.—For purposes of this section—

(1) IN GENERAL.—Except as otherwise provided in this subsection, the term "undiscounted unpaid losses" means the unpaid losses shown in the annual statement filed by the taxpayer for the year ending with or within the taxable year of the taxpayer.

(2) ADJUSTMENT IF LOSSES DISCOUNTED ON ANNUAL STATEMENT.—If—

(A) the amount of unpaid losses shown in the annual statement is determined on a discounted basis, and

(B) the extent to which the losses were discounted can be determined on the basis of information disclosed on or with the annual statement,

the amount of the unpaid losses shall be determined without regard to any reduction attributable to such discounting.

[Sec. 846(c)]

(c) RATE OF INTEREST.—

(1) IN GENERAL.—For purposes of this section, the rate of interest determined under this subsection shall be the annual rate determined by the Secretary under paragraph (2).

(2) DETERMINATION OF ANNUAL RATE.—

(A) IN GENERAL.—The annual rate determined by the Secretary under this paragraph for any calendar year shall be a rate equal to the average of the applicable Federal mid-term rates (as defined in section 1274(d) but based on annual compounding) effective as of the beginning of each of the calendar months in the test period.

(B) TEST PERIOD.—For purposes of subparagraph (A), the test period is the most recent 60-calendar-month period ending before the beginning of the calendar year for which the determination is made; except that there shall be excluded from the test period any month beginning before August 1, 1986.

[Sec. 846(d)]

(d) LOSS PAYMENT PATTERN.—

(1) IN GENERAL.—For each determination year, the Secretary shall determine a loss payment pattern for each line of business by reference to the historical loss payment pattern applicable to such line of business. Any loss payment pattern determined by the Secretary shall apply to the accident year ending with the determination year and to each of the 4 succeeding accident years.

(2) METHOD OF DETERMINATION.—Determinations under paragraph (1) for any determination year shall be made by the Secretary—

(A) by using the aggregate experience reported on the annual statements of insurance companies,

(B) on the basis of the most recent published aggregate data from such annual statements relating to loss payment patterns available on the 1st day of the determination year,

(C) as if all losses paid or treated as paid during any year are paid in the middle of such year, and

(D) in accordance with the computational rules prescribed in paragraph (3).

(3) COMPUTATIONAL RULES.—For purposes of this subsection—

(A) IN GENERAL.—Except as otherwise provided in this paragraph, the loss payment pattern for any line of business shall be based on the assumption that all losses are paid—

(i) during the accident year and the 3 calendar years following the accident year, or

(ii) in the case of any line of business reported in the schedule or schedules of the annual statement relating to auto liability, other liability, medical malpractice, workers' compensation, and multiple peril lines, during the accident year and the 10 calendar years following the accident year.

(B) TREATMENT OF CERTAIN LOSSES.—Except as otherwise provided in this paragraph—

(i) in the case of any line of business not described in subparagraph (A)(ii), losses paid after the 1st year following the accident year shall be treated as paid equally in the 2nd and 3rd year following the accident year, and

(ii) in the case of a line of business described in subparagraph (A)(ii), losses paid after the close of the period applicable under subparagraph (A)(ii) shall be treated as paid in the last year of such period.

(C) SPECIAL RULE FOR CERTAIN LONG-TAIL LINES.—In the case of any long-tail line of business—

(i) the period taken into account under subparagraph (A)(ii) shall be extended (but not by more than 5 years) to the extent required under clause (ii), and

(ii) the amount of losses which would have been treated as paid in the 10th year after the accident year shall be treated as paid in such 10th year and each subsequent year in an amount equal to the amount of the losses treated as paid in the 9th year after the accident year (or, if lesser, the portion of the unpaid losses not theretofore taken into account).

Notwithstanding clause (ii), to the extent such unpaid losses have not been treated as paid before the last year of the extension, they shall be treated as paid in such last year.

(D) LONG-TAIL LINE OF BUSINESS.—For purposes of subparagraph (C), the term "long-tail line of business" means any line of business described in subparagraph (A)(ii) if the amount of losses which (without regard to subparagraph (C)) would be treated as paid in the 10th year after the accident year exceeds the losses treated as paid in the 9th year after the accident year.

(E) SPECIAL RULE FOR INTERNATIONAL AND REINSURANCE LINES OF BUSINESS.—Except as otherwise provided by regulations, any determination made under subsection (a) with respect to unpaid losses relating to the international or reinsurance lines of business shall be made using, in lieu of the loss payment pattern applicable to the respective lines of business, a pattern determined by the Secretary under paragraphs (1) and (2) based on the combined losses for all lines of business described in subparagraph (A)(ii).

(F) ADJUSTMENTS IF LOSS EXPERIENCE INFORMATION AVAILABLE FOR LONGER PERIODS.—The Secretary shall make appropriate adjustments in the application of this paragraph if annual statement data with respect to payment of losses is available for longer periods after the accident year than the periods assumed under the rules of this paragraph.

(G) SPECIAL RULE FOR 9TH YEAR IF NEGATIVE OR ZERO.—If the amount of the losses treated as paid in the 9th year after the accident year is zero or a negative amount, subparagraphs (C)(ii) and (D) shall be applied by substituting the average of the losses treated as paid in the 7th, 8th, and 9th years after the accident year for the losses treated as paid in the 9th year after the accident year.

(4) DETERMINATION YEAR.—For purposes of this section, the term "determination year" means calendar year 1987 and each 5th calendar year thereafter.

[Sec. 846(e)]

(e) ELECTION TO USE COMPANY'S HISTORICAL PAYMENT PATTERN.—

(1) IN GENERAL.—The taxpayer may elect to apply subsection (a)(2)(C) with respect to all lines of business by using a loss payment pattern determined by reference to the taxpayer's loss payment pattern for the most recent calendar year for which an annual statement was filed before the beginning of the accident year. Any such determination shall be made with the application of the rules of paragraphs (2)(C) and (3) of subsection (d).

(2) ELECTION.—

(A) IN GENERAL.—An election under paragraph (1) shall be made separately with respect to each determination year under subsection (d).

(B) PERIOD FOR WHICH ELECTION IN EFFECT.—Unless revoked with the consent of the Secretary, an election under paragraph (1) with respect to any determination year shall apply to accident years ending with the determination year and to each of the 4 succeeding accident years.

(C) TIME FOR MAKING ELECTION.—An election under paragraph (1) with respect to any determination year shall be made on the taxpayer's return for the taxable year in which (or with which) the determination year ends.

(3) NO ELECTION FOR INTERNATIONAL OR REINSURANCE BUSINESS.—No election under this subsection shall apply to any international or reinsurance line of business.

(4) REGULATIONS.—The Secretary shall prescribe such regulations as may be necessary or appropriate to carry out the purposes of this subsection including—

(A) regulations providing that a taxpayer may not make an election under this subsection if such taxpayer does not have sufficient historical experience for the line of business to determine a loss payment pattern, and

(B) regulations to prevent the avoidance (through the use of separate corporations or otherwise) of the requirement of this subsection that an election under this subsection applies to all lines of business of the taxpayer.

[Sec. 846(f)]

(f) OTHER DEFINITIONS AND SPECIAL RULES.—For purposes of this section—

(1) ACCIDENT YEAR.—The term "accident year" means the calendar year in which the incident occurs which gives rise to the related unpaid loss.

(2) UNPAID LOSS ADJUSTMENT EXPENSES.—The term "unpaid losses" includes any unpaid loss adjustment expenses shown on the annual statement.

(3) ANNUAL STATEMENT.—The term "annual statement" means the annual statement approved by the National Association of Insurance Commissioners which the taxpayer is required to file with insurance regulatory authorities of a State.

(4) LINE OF BUSINESS.—The term "line of business" means a category for the reporting of loss payment patterns determined on the basis of the annual statement for fire and casualty insurance companies for the calendar year ending with or within the taxable year, except that the multiple peril lines shall be treated as a single line of business.

(5) MULTIPLE PERIL LINES.—The term "multiple peril lines" means the lines of business relating to farmowners multiple peril, homeowners multiple peril, commercial multiple peril, ocean marine, aircraft (all perils) and boiler and machinery.

(6) SPECIAL RULE FOR CERTAIN ACCIDENT AND HEALTH INSURANCE LINES OF BUSINESS.—Any determination under subsection (a) with respect to unpaid losses relating to accident and health insurance lines of businesses (other than credit disability insurance) shall be made—

(A) in the case of unpaid losses relating to disability income, by using the general rules prescribed under section 807(d) applicable to noncancellable accident and health insurance contracts and using a mortality or morbidity table reflecting the taxpayer's experience; except that—

(i) the prevailing State assumed interest rate shall be the rate in effect for the year in which the loss occurred rather than the year in which the contract was issued, and

(ii) the limitation of subsection (a)(3) shall apply in lieu of the limitation of the last sentence of section 807(d)(1), and

(B) in all other cases, by using an assumption (in lieu of a loss payment pattern) that unpaid losses are paid in the middle of the year following the accident year.

Amendments

• 1988, Technical and Miscellaneous Revenue Act of 1988 (P.L. 100-647)

P.L. 100-647, §1010(e)(1):

Amended Code Sec. 846(f)(6)(B) by striking out "paid during the year" and inserting in lieu thereof "paid in the middle of the year". **Effective** as if included in the provision of P.L. 99-514 to which it relates.

[Sec. 846(g)]

(g) REGULATIONS.—The Secretary shall prescribe such regulations as may be necessary or appropriate to carry out the purposes of this section, including—

(1) regulations providing proper treatment of allocated reinsurance, and

(2) regulations providing appropriate adjustments in the application of this section to a taxpayer having a taxable year which is not the calendar year.

Amendments

• 1990, Omnibus Budget Reconciliation Act of 1990 (P.L. 101-508)

P.L. 101-508, §11305(b):

Amended Code Sec. 846(g) by adding "and" at the end of paragraph (1), by striking paragraph (2), and by redesignating paragraph (3) as paragraph (2). **Effective**, generally, for tax years beginning after 12-31-89. However, for special rules, see Act Sec. 11305(c)(2)-(5) below. Prior to amendment, Code Sec. 846(g)(2) read as follows:

(2) regulations providing proper treatment of salvage and re-insurance recoverable attributable to unpaid losses, and

P.L. 101-508, §11305(c)(2)-(5), provides:

(2) AMENDMENTS TREATED AS CHANGE IN METHOD OF ACCOUNTING.—

(A) IN GENERAL.—In the case of any taxpayer who is required by reason of the amendments made by this section to change his method of computing losses incurred—

(i) such change shall be treated as a change in a method of accounting,

(ii) such change shall be treated as initiated by the taxpayer, and

(iii) such change shall be treated as having been made with the consent of the Secretary.

(B) ADJUSTMENTS.—In applying section 481 of the Internal Revenue Code of 1986 with respect to the change referred to in subparagraph (A)—

(i) only 13 percent of the net amount of adjustments (otherwise required by such section 481 to be taken into account by the taxpayer) shall be taken into account, and

(ii) the portion of such net adjustments which is required to be taken into account by the taxpayer (after the application of clause (i)) shall be taken into account over a period not to exceed 4 taxable years beginning with the taxpayer's 1st taxable year beginning after December 31, 1989.

(3) TREATMENT OF COMPANIES WHICH TOOK INTO ACCOUNT SALVAGE RECOVERABLE.—In the case of any insurance company which took into account salvage recoverable in determining losses incurred for its last taxable year beginning before January 1, 1990, 87 percent of the discounted amount of estimated salvage recoverable as of the close of such last taxable year shall be allowed as a deduction ratably over its 1st 4 taxable years beginning after December 31, 1989.

(4) SPECIAL RULE FOR OVERESTIMATES.—If for any taxable year beginning after December 31, 1989—

(A) the amount of the section 481 adjustment which would have been required without regard to paragraph (2) and any discounting, exceeds

(B) the sum of the amount of salvage recovered taken into account under section 832(b)(5)(A)(i) for the taxable year and any preceding taxable year beginning after December 31, 1989, attributable to losses incurred with respect to any accident year beginning before 1990 and the undiscounted amount of estimated salvage recoverable as of the close of the taxable year on account of such losses,

87 percent of such excess (adjusted for discounting used in determining the amount of salvage recoverable as of the close of the last taxable year of the taxpayer beginning before January 1, 1990) shall be included in gross income for such taxable year.

(5) EFFECT ON EARNINGS AND PROFITS.—The earnings and profits of any insurance company for its 1st taxable year beginning after December 31, 1989, shall be increased by the amount of the section 481 adjustment which would have been required but for paragraph (2). For purposes of applying sections 56, 902, 952(c)(1), and 960 of the Internal Revenue Code of 1986, earnings and profits of a corporation shall be determined by applying the principles of paragraph (2)(B).

• 1988, Technical and Miscellaneous Revenue Act of 1988 (P.L. 100-647)

P.L. 100-647, §1010(e)(2):

Amended Code Sec. 846(g) by striking out "and" at the end of paragraph (1), by striking out the period at the end of paragraph (2) and inserting in lieu thereof ", and", and by adding at the end thereof new paragraph (3). **Effective** as if included in the provision of P.L. 99-514 to which it relates.

• 1986, Tax Reform Act of 1986 (P.L. 99-514)

P.L. 99-514, §1023(c):

Amended part IV of subchapter L of chapter 1 by adding at the end thereof new Code Sec. 846. **Effective**, generally, for tax years beginning after 12-31-86. However, see Act Sec. 1023(e)(2)-(3), below.

P.L. 99-514, §1023(e)(2)-(3), provides:

(2) TRANSITIONAL RULE.—For the first taxable year beginning after December 31, 1986—

(A) the unpaid losses and the expenses unpaid (as defined in paragraphs (5)(B) and (6) of section 832(b) of the Internal Revenue Code of 1986) at the end of the preceding taxable year, and

(B) the unpaid losses as defined in sections 807(c)(2) and 805(a)(1) of such Code at the end of the preceding taxable year,

shall be determined as if the amendments made by this section had applied to such unpaid losses and expenses unpaid in the preceding taxable year and by using the interest rate and loss payment patterns applicable to accident years ending with calendar year 1987. For subsequent taxable years, such amendments shall be applied with respect to such unpaid losses and expenses unpaid by using the interest rate and loss payment patterns applicable to accident years ending with calendar year 1987.

(3) FRESH START.—

(A) IN GENERAL.—Except as otherwise provided in this paragraph, any difference between—

(i) the amount determined to be the unpaid losses and expenses unpaid for the year preceding the 1st taxable year of an insurance company beginning after December 31, 1986, determined without regard to paragraph (2), and

(ii) such amount determined with regard to paragraph (2), shall not be taken into account for purposes of the Internal Revenue Code of 1986.

(B) RESERVE STRENGTHENING IN YEARS AFTER 1985.—Subparagraph (A) shall not apply to any reserve strengthening in a taxable year beginning in 1986, and such strengthening shall be treated as occurring in the taxpayer's 1st taxable year beginning after December 31, 1986.

(C) EFFECT ON EARNINGS AND PROFITS.—The earnings and profits of any insurance company for its 1st taxable year beginning after December 31, 1986, shall be increased by the amount of the difference determined under subparagraph (A) with respect to such company.

[Sec. 847]

SEC. 847. SPECIAL ESTIMATED TAX PAYMENTS.

In the case of taxable years beginning after December 31, 1987, of an insurance company required to discount unpaid losses (as defined in section 846)—

(1) ADDITIONAL DEDUCTION.—There shall be allowed as a deduction for the taxable year, if special estimated tax payments are made as required by paragraph (2), an amount not to exceed the excess of—

(A) the amount of the undiscounted, unpaid losses (as defined in section 846(b)) attributable to losses incurred in taxable years beginning after December 31, 1986, over

(B) the amount of the related discounted, unpaid losses determined under section 846,

to the extent such amount was not deducted under this paragraph in a preceding taxable year. Section 6655 shall be applied to any taxable year without regard to the deduction allowed under the preceding sentence.

(2) SPECIAL ESTIMATED TAX PAYMENTS.—The deduction under paragraph (1) shall be allowed only to the extent that such deduction would result in a tax benefit for the taxable year for which such deduction is allowed or any carryback year and only to the extent that special estimated tax payments are made in an amount equal to the tax benefit attributable to such deduction on or before the due date (determined without regard to extensions) for filing the return for the taxable year for which the deduction is allowed. If a deduction would be allowed but for the fact that special estimated tax payments were not timely made, such deduction shall be allowed to the extent such payments are made within a reasonable time, as determined by the Secretary, if all interest and penalties, computed as if this sentence did not apply, are paid. If amounts are included in gross income under paragraph (5) or (6) for any taxable year and an additional tax is due for such year (or any other year) as a result of such inclusion, an amount of special estimated tax payments equal to such additional tax shall be applied against such additional tax. If, after any such payment is so applied, there is an adjustment reducing the amount of such additional tax, in lieu of any credit or refund for such reduction, a special estimated tax payment shall be treated as made in an amount equal to the amount otherwise allowable as a credit or refund. To the extent that a special estimated tax payment is not used to offset additional tax due for any of the first 15 taxable years beginning after the year for which the payment was made, such special estimated tax payment shall be treated as an estimated tax payment made under section 6655 for the 16th year after the year for which the payment was made.

(3) SPECIAL LOSS DISCOUNT ACCOUNT.—Each company which is allowed a deduction under paragraph (1) shall, for purposes of this part, establish and maintain a special loss discount account.

(4) ADDITIONS TO SPECIAL LOSS DISCOUNT ACCOUNT.—There shall be added to the special loss discount account for each taxable year an amount equal to the amount allowed as a deduction for the taxable year under paragraph (1).

(5) SUBTRACTIONS FROM SPECIAL LOSS DISCOUNT ACCOUNT AND INCLUSION IN GROSS INCOME.—After applying paragraph (4), there shall be subtracted for the taxable year from the special loss discount account and included in gross income:

(A) The excess (if any) of the amount in the special loss discount account with respect to losses incurred in each taxable year over the amount of the excess referred to in paragraph (1) with respect to losses incurred in that year, and

(B) Any amount improperly subtracted from the special loss discount account under subparagraph (A) to the extent special estimated tax payments were used with respect to such amount.

To the extent that any amount added to the special loss discount account is not subtracted from such account before the 15th year after the year for which the amount was so added, such amount shall be subtracted from such account for such 15th year and included in gross income for such 15th year.

(6) RULES IN THE CASE OF LIQUIDATION OR TERMINATION OF TAXPAYER'S INSURANCE BUSINESS.—

(A) IN GENERAL.—If a company liquidates or otherwise terminates its insurance business and does not transfer or distribute such business in an acquisition of assets referred to in section 381(a), the entire amount remaining in such special loss discount account shall be subtracted and included in gross income. Except in the case where a company transfers or distributes its insurance business in an acquisition of assets, referred to in section 381(a), if the company is not subject to the tax imposed by section 801 or section 831 for any taxable year, the entire amount in the account at the close of the preceding taxable year shall be subtracted from the account in such preceding taxable year and included in gross income.

(B) ELIMINATION OF BALANCE OF PAYMENTS.—In any case to which subparagraph (A) applies, any special estimated tax payment remaining after the credit attributable to the inclusion under subparagraph (A) shall be voided.

(7) MODIFICATION OF THE AMOUNT OF SPECIAL ESTIMATED TAX PAYMENTS IN THE EVENT OF SUBSEQUENT MARGINAL RATE REDUCTION OR INCREASE.—In the event of a reduction in any tax rate provided under section 11 for any tax year after the enactment of this section, the Secretary shall prescribe regulations providing for a reduction in the amount of any special estimated tax payments made for years before the effective date of such section 11 rate reductions. Such reduction in the amount of such payments shall reduce the amount of such payments to the amount that they would have been if the special deduction permitted under paragraph (1) had occurred during a year that the lower marginal rate under section 11 applied. Similar rules shall be applied in the event of a marginal rate increase.

(8) TAX BENEFIT DETERMINATION.—The tax benefit attributable to the deduction under paragraph (1) shall be determined under regulations prescribed by the Secretary, by taking into account tax benefits that would arise from the carryback of any net operating loss for the year, as well as current year tax benefits. Tax benefits for the current year and carryback years shall include those that would arise from the filing of a consolidated return with another insurance company required to determine discounted, unpaid losses under section 846 without regard to the limitations on consolidation contained in section 1503(c). The limitations on consolidation contained in section 1503(c) shall not apply to the deduction allowed under paragraph (1).

(9) EFFECT ON EARNINGS AND PROFITS.—In determining the earnings and profits—

(A) any special estimated tax payment made for any taxable year shall be treated as a payment of income tax imposed by this title for such taxable year, and

(B) any deduction or inclusion under this section shall not be taken into account.

Nothing in the preceding sentence shall be construed to affect the application of section 56(g) (relating to adjustments based on adjusted current earnings).

(10) REGULATIONS.—The Secretary shall prescribe such regulations as may be necessary or appropriate to carry out the purposes of this section, including regulations—

(A) providing for the separate application of this section with respect to each accident year,

(B) such adjustments in the application of this section as may be necessary to take into account the tax imposed by section 55, and

(C) providing for the application of this section in cases where the deduction allowed under paragraph (1) for any taxable year is less than the excess referred to in paragraph (1) for such year.

Amendments

• 1989, Omnibus Budget Reconciliation Act of 1989 (P.L. 101-239)

P.L. 101-239, §7816(n)(1)(A)-(B):

Amended Code Sec. 847(1) by striking "separate estimated tax" and inserting "special estimated tax", and by striking "after December 31, 1986" and inserting "in taxable years beginning after December 31, 1986". **Effective** as if included in the provision of P.L. 100-647 to which it relates.

P.L. 101-239, §7816(n)(2):

Amended the first sentence of Code Sec. 847(2). **Effective** as if included in the provision of P.L. 100-647 to which it relates. Prior to amendment, the first sentence of Code Sec. 847(2) read as follows:

The deduction under paragraph (1) shall be allowed only to the extent that special estimated tax payments are made in an amount equal to the tax benefit attributable to such deduction, on or before the date that any taxes (determined without regard to this section) for the taxable year for which the deduction is allowed are due to be paid.

P.L. 101-239, §7816(n)(3):

Amended Code Sec. 847(5) by adding at the end thereof a new sentence. **Effective** as if included in the provision of P.L. 100-647 to which it relates.

P.L. 101-239, §7816(n)(4):

Amended Code Sec. 847(9) by striking "and" at the end of subparagraph (A), by striking the period at the end of subparagraph (B) and inserting ", and", and by adding at the end thereof a new subparagraph (C). **Effective** as if included in the provision of P.L. 100-647 to which it relates.

P.L. 101-239, §7816(n)(5):

Amended Code Sec. 847, as amended by paragraph (4), by redesignating paragraph (9) as paragraph (10) and by inserting after paragraph (8) a new paragraph (9). **Effective** as if included in the provision of P.L. 100-647 to which it relates.

P.L. 101-239, §7816(n)(6):

Amended Code Sec. 847(8) by adding at the end thereof a new sentence. **Effective** as if included in the provision of P.L. 100-647 to which it relates.

• 1988, Technical and Miscellaneous Revenue Act of 1988 (P.L. 100-647)

P.L. 100-647, §6077(a):

Amended Part III of Subchapter L of Chapter 1 by adding at the end thereof a new Code Sec. 847. **Effective** for tax years beginning after 12-31-87.

[Sec. 848]

SEC. 848. CAPITALIZATION OF CERTAIN POLICY ACQUISITION EXPENSES.

[Sec. 848(a)]

(a) GENERAL RULE.—In the case of an insurance company—

(1) specified policy acquisition expenses for any taxable year shall be capitalized, and

(2) such expenses shall be allowed as a deduction ratably over the 120-month period beginning with the first month in the second half of such taxable year.

[Sec. 848(b)]

(b) 5-YEAR AMORTIZATION FOR FIRST $5,000,000 OF SPECIFIED POLICY ACQUISITION EXPENSES.—

(1) IN GENERAL.—Paragraph (2) of subsection (a) shall be applied with respect to so much of the specified policy acquisition expenses of an insurance company for any taxable year as does not exceed $5,000,000 by substituting "60-month" for "120-month".

(2) PHASE-OUT.—If the specified policy acquisition expenses of an insurance company exceed $10,000,000 for any taxable year, the $5,000,000 amount under paragraph (1) shall be reduced (but not below zero) by the amount of such excess.

(3) SPECIAL RULE FOR MEMBERS OF CONTROLLED GROUP.—In the case of any controlled group—

(A) all insurance companies which are members of such group shall be treated as 1 company for purposes of this subsection, and

(B) the amount to which paragraph (1) applies shall be allocated among such companies in such manner as the Secretary may prescribe.

For purposes of the preceding sentence, the term "controlled group" means any controlled group of corporations as defined in section 1563(a); except that subsections (a)(4) and (b)(2)(D) of section 1563 shall not apply, and subsection (b)(2)(C) of section 1563 shall not apply to the extent it excludes a foreign corporation to which section 842 applies.

(4) EXCEPTION FOR ACQUISITION EXPENSES ATTRIBUTABLE TO CERTAIN REINSURANCE CONTRACTS.—Paragraph (1) shall not apply to any specified policy acquisition expenses for any taxable year which are attributable to premiums or other consideration under any reinsurance contract.

[Sec. 848(c)]

(c) SPECIFIED POLICY ACQUISITION EXPENSES.—For purposes of this section—

(1) IN GENERAL.—The term "specified policy acquisition expenses" means, with respect to any taxable year, so much of the general deductions for such taxable year as does not exceed the sum of —

(A) 1.75 percent of the net premiums for such taxable year on specified insurance contracts which are annuity contracts,

(B) 2.05 percent of the net premiums for such taxable year on specified insurance contracts which are group life insurance contracts, and

(C) 7.7 percent of the net premiums for such taxable year on specified insurance contracts not described in subparagraph (A) or (B).

(2) GENERAL DEDUCTIONS.—The term "general deductions" means the deductions provided in part VI of subchapter B (sec. 161 and following, relating to itemized deductions) and in part I of subchapter D (sec. 401 and following, relating to pension, profit sharing, stock bonus plans, etc.).

[Sec. 848(d)]

(d) NET PREMIUMS.—For purposes of this section—

(1) IN GENERAL.—The term "net premiums" means, with respect to any category of specified insurance contracts set forth in subsection (c)(1), the excess (if any) of—

(A) the gross amount of premiums and other consideration on such contracts, over

(B) return premiums on such contracts and premiums and other consideration incurred for reinsurance of such contracts.

The rules of section 803(b) shall apply for purposes of the preceding sentence.

(2) AMOUNTS DETERMINED ON ACCRUAL BASIS.—In the case of an insurance company subject to tax under part II of this subchapter, all computations entering into determinations of net premiums for any taxable year shall be made in the manner required under section 811(a) for life insurance companies.

(3) TREATMENT OF CERTAIN POLICYHOLDER DIVIDENDS AND SIMILAR AMOUNTS.—Net premiums shall be determined without regard to section 808(e) and without regard to other similar amounts treated as paid to, and returned by, the policyholder.

(4) SPECIAL RULES FOR REINSURANCE.—

(A) Premiums and other consideration incurred for reinsurance shall be taken into account under paragraph (1)(B) only to the extent such premiums and other consideration are includible in the gross income of an insurance company taxable under this subchapter or are subject to tax under this chapter by reason of subpart F of part III of subchapter N.

(B) The Secretary shall prescribe such regulations as may be necessary to ensure that premiums and other consideration with respect to reinsurance are treated consistently by the ceding company and the reinsurer.

[Sec. 848(e)]

(e) CLASSIFICATION OF CONTRACTS.—For purposes of this section—

(1) SPECIFIED INSURANCE CONTRACT.—

(A) IN GENERAL.—Except as otherwise provided in this paragraph, the term "specified insurance contract" means any life insurance, annuity, or noncancellable accident and health insurance contract (or any combination thereof).

(B) EXCEPTIONS.—The term "specified insurance contract" shall not include—

(i) any pension plan contract (as defined in section 818(a)),

(ii) any flight insurance or similar contract,

(iii) any qualified foreign contract (as defined in section 807(e)(4) without regard to paragraph (5) of this subsection),

(iv) any contract which is an Archer MSA (as defined in section 220(d)), and

(v) any contract which is a health savings account (as defined in section 223(d)).

(2) GROUP LIFE INSURANCE CONTRACT.—The term "group life insurance contract" means any life insurance contract—

(A) which covers a group of individuals defined by reference to employment relationship, membership in an organization, or similar factor,

(B) the premiums for which are determined on a group basis, and

(C) the proceeds of which are payable to (or for the benefit of) persons other than the employer of the insured, an organization to which the insured belongs, or other similar person.

(3) TREATMENT OF ANNUITY CONTRACTS COMBINED WITH NONCANCELLABLE ACCIDENT AND HEALTH INSURANCE.—Any annuity contract combined with noncancellable accident and health insurance shall be treated as a noncancellable accident and health insurance contract and not as an annuity contract.

(4) TREATMENT OF GUARANTEED RENEWABLE CONTRACTS.—The rules of section 816(e) shall apply for purposes of this section.

(5) TREATMENT OF REINSURANCE CONTRACT.—A contract which reinsures another contract shall be treated in the same manner as the reinsured contract.

(6) TREATMENT OF CERTAIN QUALIFIED LONG-TERM CARE INSURANCE CONTRACT ARRANGEMENTS.—An annuity or life insurance contract which includes a qualified long-term care insurance contract as a part of or a rider on such annuity or life insurance contract shall be treated as a specified insurance contract not described in subparagraph (A) or (B) of subsection (c)(1).

Amendments

• 2006, Pension Protection Act of 2006 (P.L. 109-280)

P.L. 109-280, §844(e):

Amended Code Sec. 848(e) by adding at the end a new paragraph (6). **Effective** for specified policy acquisition expenses determined for tax years beginning after 12-31-2009.

• 2003, Medicare Prescription Drug, Improvement, and Modernization Act of 2003 (P.L. 108-173)

P.L. 108-173, §1201(h):

Amended Code Sec. 848(e)(1)(B) by striking "and" at the end of clause (iii), by striking the period at the end of clause (iv) and inserting ", and", and by adding at the end a new clause (v). **Effective** for tax years beginning after 12-31-2003.

• 2000, Community Renewal Tax Relief Act of 2000 (P.L. 106-554)

P.L. 106-554, §202(a)(5):

Amended Code Sec. 848(e)(1)(B)(iv) by striking "medical savings account" and inserting "Archer MSA". **Effective** 12-21-2000.

P.L. 106-554, §202(b)(10):

Amended Code Sec. 848(e)(1)(B)(iv) by striking "a Archer" and inserting "an Archer". **Effective** 12-21-2000.

• 1996, Health Insurance Portability and Accountability Act of 1996 (P.L. 104-191)

P.L. 104-191, §301(h):

Amended Code Sec. 848(e)(1)(B) by striking "and" at the end of clause (ii), by striking the period at the end of clause (iii) and inserting ", and", and by adding at the end a new clause (iv). **Effective** for tax years beginning after 12-31-96.

[Sec. 848(f)]

(f) SPECIAL RULE WHERE NEGATIVE NET PREMIUMS.—

(1) IN GENERAL.—If for any taxable year there is a negative capitalization amount with respect to any category of specified insurance contracts set forth in subsection (c)(1)—

(A) the amount otherwise required to be capitalized under this section for such taxable year with respect to any other category of specified insurance contracts shall be reduced (but not below zero) by such negative capitalization amount, and

(B) such negative capitalization amount (to the extent not taken into account under subparagraph (A))—

(i) shall reduce (but not below zero) the unamortized balance (as of the beginning of such taxable year) of the amounts previously capitalized under subsection (a) (beginning with the amount capitalized for the most recent taxable year), and

(ii) to the extent taken into account as such a reduction, shall be allowed as a deduction for such taxable year.

(2) NEGATIVE CAPITALIZATION AMOUNT.—For purposes of paragraph (1), the term "negative capitalization amount" means, with respect to any category of specified insurance contracts, the percentage (applicable under subsection (c)(1) to such category) of the amount (if any) by which—

(A) the amount determined under subparagraph (B) of subsection (d)(1) with respect to such category, exceeds

(B) the amount determined under subparagraph (A) of subsection (d)(1) with respect to such category.

[Sec. 848(g)]

(g) TREATMENT OF CERTAIN CEDING COMMISSIONS.—Nothing in any provision of law (other than this section or section 197) shall require the capitalization of any ceding commission incurred on or after September 30, 1990, under any contract which reinsures a specified insurance contract.

Amendments

• **1993, Omnibus Budget Reconciliation Act of 1993 (P.L. 103-66)**

P.L. 103-66, §13261(d):

Amended Code Sec. 848(g) by striking "this section" and inserting "this section or section 197". **Effective**, generally, with respect to property acquired after 8-10-93. For a special election, see Act Sec. 13261(g)(2) and (3), below.

P.L. 103-66, §13261(g)(2), provides:

(2) ELECTION TO HAVE AMENDMENTS APPLY TO PROPERTY ACQUIRED AFTER JULY 25, 1991.—

(A) IN GENERAL.—If an election under this paragraph applies to the taxpayer—

(i) the amendments made by this section shall apply to property acquired by the taxpayer after July 25, 1991,

(ii) subsection (c)(1)(A) of section 197 of the Internal Revenue Code of 1986 (as added by this section) (and so much of subsection (f)(9)(A) of such section 197 as precedes clause (i) thereof) shall be applied with respect to the taxpayer by treating July 25, 1991, as the date of the enactment of such section, and

(iii) in applying subsection (f)(9) of such section, with respect to any property acquired by the taxpayer on or before the date of the enactment of this Act, only holding or use on July 25, 1991, shall be taken into account.

(B) ELECTION.—An election under this paragraph shall be made at such time and in such manner as the Secretary of the Treasury or his delegate may prescribe. Such an election by any taxpayer, once made—

(i) may be revoked only with the consent of the Secretary, and

(ii) shall apply to the taxpayer making such election and any other taxpayer under common control with the taxpayer (within the meaning of subparagraphs (A) and (B) of section 41(f)(1) of such Code) at any time after August 2, 1993, and on or before the date on which such election is made.

(3) ELECTIVE BINDING CONTRACT EXCEPTION.—

(A) IN GENERAL.—The amendments made by this section shall not apply to any acquisition of property by the taxpayer if—

(i) such acquisition is pursuant to a written binding contract in effect on the date of the enactment of this Act and at all times thereafter before such acquisition,

(ii) an election under paragraph (2) does not apply to the taxpayer, and

(iii) the taxpayer makes an election under this paragraph with respect to such contract.

(B) ELECTION.—An election under this paragraph shall be made at such time and in such manner as the Secretary of the Treasury or his delegate shall prescribe. Such an election, once made—

(i) may be revoked only with the consent of the Secretary, and

(ii) shall apply to all property acquired pursuant to the contract with respect to which such election was made.

[Sec. 848(h)]

(h) SECRETARIAL AUTHORITY TO ADJUST CAPITALIZATION AMOUNTS.—

(1) IN GENERAL.—Except as provided in paragraph (2), the Secretary may provide that a type of insurance contract will be treated as a separate category for purposes of this section (and prescribe a percentage applicable to such category) if the Secretary determines that the deferral of acquisition expenses for such type of contract which would otherwise result under this section is substantially greater than the deferral of acquisition expenses which would have resulted if actual acquisition expenses (including indirect expenses) and the actual useful life for such type of contract had been used.

(2) ADJUSTMENT TO OTHER CONTRACTS.—If the Secretary exercises his authority with respect to any type of contract under paragraph (1), the Secretary shall adjust the percentage which would otherwise have applied under subsection (c)(1) to the category which includes such type of contract so that the exercise of such authority does not result in a decrease in the amount of revenue received under this chapter by reason of this section for any fiscal year.

[Sec. 848(i)]

(i) TREATMENT OF QUALIFIED FOREIGN CONTRACTS UNDER ADJUSTED CURRENT EARNINGS PREFERENCE.—For purposes of determining adjusted current earnings under section 56(g), acquisition expenses with respect to contracts described in clause (iii) of subsection (e)(1)(B) shall be capitalized and amortized in accordance with the treatment generally required under generally accepted accounting principles as if this subsection applied to such contracts for all taxable years.

[Sec. 848(j)]

(j) TRANSITIONAL RULE.—In the case of any taxable year which includes September 30, 1990, the amount taken into account as the net premiums (or negative capitalization amount) with respect to any category of specified insurance contracts shall be the amount which bears the same ratio to the amount which (but for this subsection) would be so taken into account as the number of days in such taxable year on or after September 30, 1990, bears to the total number of days in such taxable year.

Amendments

• 1990, Omnibus Budget Reconciliation Act of 1990 (P.L. 101-508)

P.L. 101-508, §11301(a):

Amended part III of subchapter L of chapter 1 by adding at the end thereof a new Code Sec. 848. **Effective** for tax years ending on or after 9-30-90. Any capitalization required by reason of such amendment shall not be treated as a change of method of accounting for purposes of the Internal Revenue Code of 1986.

Subchapter M—Regulated Investment Companies and Real Estate Investment Trusts

PART I—REGULATED INVESTMENT COMPANIES

[Sec. 851]

SEC. 851. DEFINITION OF REGULATED INVESTMENT COMPANY.

[Sec. 851(a)]

(a) GENERAL RULE.—For purposes of this subtitle, the term "regulated investment company" means any domestic corporation—

(1) which, at all times during the taxable year—

(A) is registered under the Investment Company Act of 1940, as amended (15 U.S.C. 80a-1 to 80b-2) as a management company or unit investment trust, or

(B) has in effect an election under such Act to be treated as a business development company, or

(2) which is a common trust fund or similar fund excluded by section 3(c)(3) of such Act (15 U.S.C. 80a-3(c)) from the definition of "investment company" and is not included in the definition of "common trust fund" by section 584(a).

Amendments

• 1988, Technical and Miscellaneous Revenue Act of 1988 (P.L. 100-647)

P.L. 100-647, §1006(m)(1):

Amended Code Sec. 851(a)(1). **Effective** as if included in the provision of P.L. 99-514 to which it relates. Prior to amendment, Code Sec. 851(a)(1) read as follows:

(1) which, at all times during the taxable year, is registered under the Investment Company Act of 1940, as amended (15 U.S.C. 80a-1 to 80b-2), as a management company, business development company, or unit investment trust, or

• 1986, Tax Reform Act of 1986 (P.L. 99-514)

P.L. 99-514, §652(a):

Amended Code Sec. 851(a)(1) by striking out "either as a management company or as a unit investment trust" and inserting in lieu thereof "as a management company, business development company, or unit investment trust". **Effective** for tax years beginning after 12-31-86.

• 1984, Deficit Reduction Act of 1984 (P.L. 98-369)

P.L. 98-369, §1071(a)(1):

Amended Code Sec. 851(a) by striking out "(other than a personal holding company as defined in section 542)" following "domestic corporation". **Effective** for tax years beginning after 12-31-82. See also Act Sec. 1071(a)(5)(B)-(D) in the amendment notes following Code Sec. 852(a) for special rules.

• 1976, Tax Reform Act of 1976 (P.L. 94-455)

P.L. 94-455, §1901(a)(109):

Struck out "54 Stat. 789;" before "15 U.S.C. 80a-1" in Code Sec. 851(a)(1). **Effective** for tax years beginning after 12-31-76.

[Sec. 851(b)]

(b) LIMITATIONS.—A corporation shall not be considered a regulated investment company for any taxable year unless—

(1) it files with its return for the taxable year an election to be a regulated investment company or has made such election for a previous taxable year;

(2) at least 90 percent of its gross income is derived from—

(A) dividends, interest, payments with respect to securities loans (as defined in section 512(a)(5)), and gains from the sale or other disposition of stock or securities (as defined in section 2(a)(36) of the Investment Company Act of 1940, as amended) or foreign currencies, or other income (including but not limited to gains from options, futures or forward contracts) derived with respect to its business of investing in such stock, securities, or currencies, and

(B) net income derived from an interest in a qualified publicly traded partnership (as defined in subsection (h)); and

(3) at the close of each quarter of the taxable year—

(A) at least 50 percent of the value of its total assets is represented by—

(i) cash and cash items (including receivables), Government securities and securities of other regulated investment companies, and

(ii) other securities for purposes of this calculation limited, except and to the extent provided in subsection (e), in respect of any one issuer to an amount not greater in value than 5 percent of the value of the total assets of the taxpayer and to not more than 10 percent of the outstanding voting securities of such issuer, and

(B) not more than 25 percent of the value of its total assets is invested in—

(i) the securities (other than Government securities or the securities of other regulated investment companies) of any one issuer,

(ii) the securities (other than the securities of other regulated investment companies) of two or more issuers which the taxpayer controls and which are determined, under regulations prescribed by the Secretary, to be engaged in the same or similar trades or businesses or related trades or businesses, or

(iii) the securities of one or more qualified publicly traded partnerships (as defined in subsection (h)).

For purposes of paragraph (2), there shall be treated as dividends amounts included in gross income under section 951(a)(1)(A)(i) or 1293(a) for the taxable year to the extent that, under section 959(a)(1) or 1293(c) (as the case may be), there is a distribution out of the earnings and profits of the taxable year which are attributable to the amounts so included. For purposes of paragraph (2), the Secretary may by regulation exclude from qualifying income foreign currency gains which are not directly related to the company's principal business of investing in stock or securities (or options and futures with respect to stock or securities). For purposes of paragraph (2), amounts excludable from gross income under section 103(a) shall be treated as included in gross income. Income derived from a partnership (other than a qualified publicly traded partnership as defined in subsection (h)) or trust shall be treated as described in paragraph (2) only to the extent such income is attributable to items of income of the partnership or trust (as the case may be) which would be described in paragraph (2) if realized by the regulated investment company in the same manner as realized by the partnership or trust.

Amendments

• 2004, American Jobs Creation Act of 2004 (P.L. 108-357)

P.L. 108-357, §331(a):

Amended Code Sec. 851(b)(2). **Effective** for tax years beginning after 10-22-2004. Prior to amendment, Code Sec. 851(b)(2) read as follows:

(2) at least 90 percent of its gross income is derived from dividends, interest, payments with respect to securities loans (as defined in section 512(a)(5)), and gains from the sale or other disposition of stock or securities (as defined in section 2(a)(36) of the Investment Company Act of 1940, as amended) or foreign currencies, or other income (including but not limited to gains from options, futures, or forward contracts) derived with respect to its business of investing in such stock, securities, or currencies; and

P.L. 108-357, §331(b):

Amended Code Sec. 851(b) by inserting "(other than a qualified publicly traded partnership as defined in subsection (h))" after "derived from a partnership" in the last sentence. **Effective** for tax years beginning after 10-22-2004.

P.L. 108-357, §331(f):

Amended Code Sec. 851(b)(3)(B). **Effective** for tax years beginning after 10-22-2004. Prior to amendment, Code Sec. 851(b)(3)(B) read as follows:

(B) not more than 25 percent of the value of its total assets is invested in the securities (other than Government securities or the securities of other regulated investment companies) of any one issuer, or of two or more issuers which the taxpayer controls and which are determined, under regulations prescribed by the Secretary, to be engaged in the same or similar trades or businesses or related trades or businesses.

• 1997, Taxpayer Relief Act of 1997 (P.L. 105-34)

P.L. 105-34, §1271(a):

Amended Code Sec. 851(b) by striking paragraph (3), by adding "and" at the end of paragraph (2), and by redesignating paragraph (4) as paragraph (3). **Effective** for tax years beginning after 8-5-97. Prior to amendment, Code Sec. 851(b)(3) read as follows:

(3) less than 30 percent of its gross income is derived from the sale or disposition of any of the following which was held for less than 3 months:

(A) stock or securities (as defined in section 2(a)(36) of the Investment Company Act of 1940, as amended),

(B) options, futures, or forward contracts (other than options, futures, or forward contracts on foreign currencies), or

(C) foreign currencies (or options, futures, or forward contracts on foreign currencies) but only if such currencies (or options, futures, or forward contracts) are not directly related to the company's principal business of investing in stock or securities (or options and futures with respect to stocks or securities), and

P.L. 105-34, §1271(b)(1)(A)-(B):

Amended the material following Code Sec. 851(b)(3) (as redesignated by Act Sec. 1271(a)) by striking out "paragraphs (2) and (3)" and inserting "paragraph (2)", and by striking out the last sentence. **Effective** for tax years beginning after 8-5-97. Prior to amendment, the last sentence of Code Sec. 851(b)(3) read as follows:

In the case of the taxable year in which a regulated investment company is completely liquidated, there shall not be taken into account under paragraph (3) any gain from the sale, exchange, or distribution of any property after the adoption of the plan of complete liquidation.

• 1988, Technical and Miscellaneous Revenue Act of 1988 (P.L. 100-647)

P.L. 100-647, §1006(n)(1):

Amended Code Sec. 851(b) by adding at the end thereof a new sentence. **Effective** as if included in the provision of P.L. 99-514 to which it relates.

P.L. 100-647, §1006(n)(2)(A):

Amended Code Sec. 851(b)(3). Except as provided in Act Sec. 1006(n)(2)(C), **effective** as if included in the provision of

P.L. 99-514 to which it relates. Prior to amendment, Code Sec. 851(b)(3) read as follows:

(3) less than 30 percent of its gross income is derived from the sale or other disposition of stock or securities held for less than 3 months; and

P.L. 100-647, §1006(n)(2)(C), provides:

(C) Subparagraph (C) of section 851(b)(3) of the 1986 Code (as amended by Act Sec. 1006(n)(2) subparagraph (A)), and the amendment made by [Act Sec. 1006(n)(2)] subparagraph (B), shall apply to taxable years beginning after the date of the enactment of this Act.

P.L. 100-647, §1006(n)(2)(B):

Amended Code Sec. 851(b) by striking out "which are not ancillary" in the material following paragraph (4), and inserting in lieu thereof "which are not directly related". **Effective** as if included in the provision of P.L. 99-514 to which it relates.

P.L. 100-647, §1006(n)(5):

Amended Code Sec. 851(b) by adding at the end thereof the following new sentence: "In the case of the taxable year in which a regulated investment company is completely liquidated, there shall not be taken into account under paragraph (3) any gain from the sale, exchange, or distribution of any property after the adoption of the plan of complete liquidation." **Effective** as if included in the provision of P.L. 99-514 to which it relates.

• 1986, Tax Reform Act of 1986 (P.L. 99-514)

P.L. 99-514, §653(b):

Amended Code Sec. 851(b)(2) by striking out the semicolon at the end thereof and inserting in lieu thereof "(as defined in section 2(a)(36) of the Investment Company Act of 1940, as amended) or foreign currencies, or other income (including but not limited to gains from options, futures, or forward contracts) derived with respect to its business of investing in such stock, securities, or currencies;". **Effective** for tax years beginning after 10-22-86.

P.L. 99-514, §653(c):

Amended Code Sec. 851(b) by inserting before the last sentence thereof the following new sentence: For purposes of paragraph (2), the Secretary may by regulation exclude from qualifying income foreign currency gains which are not ancillary to the company's principal business of investing in stock or securities (or options and futures with respect to stock or securities)." **Effective** for tax years beginning after 10-22-86.

P.L. 99-514, §1235(f)(3)(A)-(B):

Amended the second sentence of Code Sec. 851(b) by striking out "section 951(a)(1)(A)(i)" and inserting in lieu thereof "section 951(a)(1)(A)(i) or 1293(a)", and by striking out "section 959(a)(1)" and inserting in lieu thereof "section 959(a)(1) or 1293(c) (as the case may be)". **Effective** for tax years of foreign corporations beginning after 12-31-86.

• 1983, Surface Transportation Act of 1982 (P.L. 97-424)

P.L. 97-424, §547(b)(1):

Amended Code Sec. 851(b) by striking out "103(a)(1)" and inserting in lieu thereof "103(a)".

• 1978, Revenue Act of 1978 (P.L. 95-600)

P.L. 95-600, §701(s)(1):

Amended Code Sec. 851(b) by adding at the end thereof a new last sentence. **Effective** for tax years beginning after 12-31-75.

• 1978 (P.L. 95-345)

P.L. 95-345, §2(a)(3):

Amended Code Sec. 851(b)(2) by adding "payments with respect to securities loans (as defined in section 512(a)(5))," after "interest". **Effective** with respect to (1) amounts received after 12-31-76, as payments with respect to securities loans (as defined in Code Sec. 512(a)(5)), and (2) transfers of securities under agreements described in Code Sec. 1058 occurring after such date.

• 1976, Tax Reform Act of 1976 (P.L. 94-455)

P.L. 94-455, §1901(a)(109):

Struck out "which began after December 31, 1941" after "taxable year" in Code Sec. 851(b)(1). **Effective** for tax years beginning after 12-31-76.

P.L. 94-455, §1906(b)(13)(A):

Amended 1954 Code by substituting "Secretary" for "Secretary or his delegate" each place it appeared. **Effective** 2-1-77.

• 1975, Tax Reduction Act of 1975 (P.L. 94-12)

P.L. 94-12, §602(a)(2):

Amended Code Sec. 851(b) by adding the last sentence therein. **Effective** for tax years of foreign corporations beginning after 12-31-75, and for tax years of U. S. shareholders within which or with which such tax years of such foreign corporations end.

[Sec. 851(c)]

(c) RULES APPLICABLE TO SUBSECTION (b)(3).—For purposes of subsection (b)(3) and this subsection—

(1) In ascertaining the value of the taxpayer's investment in the securities of an issuer, for the purposes of subparagraph (B), there shall be included its proper proportion of the investment of any other corporation, a member of a controlled group, in the securities of such issuer, as determined under regulations prescribed by the Secretary.

(2) The term "controls" means the ownership in a corporation of 20 percent or more of the total combined voting power of all classes of stock entitled to vote.

(3) The term "controlled group" means one or more chains of corporations connected through stock ownership with the taxpayer if—

(A) 20 percent or more of the total combined voting power of all classes of stock entitled to vote of each of the corporations (except the taxpayer) is owned directly by one or more of the other corporations, and

(B) the taxpayer owns directly 20 percent or more of the total combined voting power of all classes of stock entitled to vote, of at least one of the other corporations.

(4) The term "value" means, with respect to securities (other than those of majority-owned subsidiaries) for which market quotations are readily available, the market value of such securities; and with respect to other securities and assets, fair value as determined in good faith by the board of directors, except that in the case of securities of majority-owned subsidiaries which are investment companies such fair value shall not exceed market value or asset value, whichever is higher.

(5) The term "outstanding voting securities of such issuer" shall include the equity securities of a qualified publicly traded partnership (as defined in subsection (h)).

(6) All other terms shall have the same meaning as when used in the Investment Company Act of 1940, as amended.

Amendments

• **2004, American Jobs Creation Act of 2004 (P.L. 108-357)**

P.L. 108-357, §331(c):

Amended Code Sec. 851(c) by redesignating paragraph (5) as paragraph (6) and inserting after paragraph (4) a new paragraph (5). **Effective** for tax years beginning after 10-22-2004.

• **1997, Taxpayer Relief Act of 1997 (P.L. 105-34)**

P.L. 105-34, §1271(b)(2):

Amended Code Sec. 851(c) by striking "subsection (b)(4)" each place it appears (including the heading) and inserting "subsection (b)(3)". **Effective** for tax years beginning after 8-5-97.

[Sec. 851(d)]

(d) DETERMINATION OF STATUS.—A corporation which meets the requirements of subsections (b)(3) and (c) at the close of any quarter shall not lose its status as a regulated investment company because of a discrepancy during a subsequent quarter between the value of its various investments and such requirements unless such discrepancy exists immediately after the acquisition of any security or other property and is wholly or partly the result of such acquisition. A corporation which does not meet such requirements at the close of any quarter by reason of a discrepancy existing immediately after the acquisition of any security or other property which is wholly or partly the result of such acquisition during such quarter shall not lose its status for such quarter as a regulated investment company if such discrepancy is eliminated within 30 days after the close of such quarter and in such cases it shall be considered to have met such requirements at the close of such quarter for purposes of applying the preceding sentence.

Amendments

• **1997, Taxpayer Relief Act of 1997 (P.L. 105-34)**

P.L. 105-34, §1271(b)(3):

Amended Code Sec. 851(d) by striking "subsections (b)(4)" and inserting "subsections (b)(3)". **Effective** for tax years beginning after 8-5-97.

[Sec. 851(e)]

(e) INVESTMENT COMPANIES FURNISHING CAPITAL TO DEVELOPMENT CORPORATIONS.—

(1) GENERAL RULE.—If the Securities and Exchange Commission determines, in accordance with regulations issued by it, and certifies to the Secretary not earlier than 60 days prior to the close of the taxable year of a management company or a business development company described in subsection (a)(1), that such investment company is principally engaged in the furnishing of capital to other corporations which are principally engaged in the development or exploitation of inventions, technological improvements, new processes, or products not previously generally available, such investment company may, in the computation of 50 percent of the value of its assets under subparagraph (A) of subsection (b)(3) for any quarter of such taxable year, include the value of any securities of an issuer, whether or not the investment company owns more than 10 percent of the outstanding voting securities of such issuer, the basis of which, when added to the basis of the investment company for securities of such issuer previously acquired, did not exceed 5 percent of the value of the total assets of the investment company at the time of the subsequent acquisition of securities. The preceding sentence shall not apply to the securities of an issuer if the investment company has continuously held any security of such issuer (or of any predecessor company of such issuer as determined under regulations prescribed by the Secretary) for 10 or more years preceding such quarter of such taxable year.

(2) LIMITATION.—The provisions of this subsection shall not apply at the close of any quarter of a taxable year to an investment company if at the close of such quarter more than 25 percent of the value of its total assets is represented by securities of issuers with respect to each of which the investment company holds more than 10 percent of the outstanding voting securities of such issuer and in respect of each of which or any predecessor thereof the investment company has continuously held any security for 10 or more years preceding such quarter unless the value of its total assets so represented is reduced to 25 percent or less within 30 days after the close of such quarter.

(3) DETERMINATION OF STATUS.—For purposes of this subsection, unless the Securities and Exchange Commission determines otherwise, a corporation shall be considered to be principally engaged in the development or exploitation of inventions, technological improvements, new processes, or products not previously generally available, for at least 10 years after the date of the first acquisition of any security in such corporation or any predecessor thereof by such investment company if at the date of such acquisition the corporation or its predecessor was principally so engaged, and an investment company shall be considered at any date to be furnishing capital to any company whose securities it holds if within 10 years prior to such date it has acquired any of such securities, or any securities surrendered in exchange therefor, from such other company or predecessor thereof. For purposes of the certification under this subsection, the Securities and Exchange Commission shall have authority to issue such rules, regulations and orders, and to conduct such investigations and hearings, either public or private, as it may deem appropriate.

(4) DEFINITIONS.—The terms used in this subsection shall have the same meaning as in subsections (b)(3) and (c) of this section.

Amendments

• 1997, Taxpayer Relief Act of 1997 (P.L. 105-34)

P.L. 105-34, §1271(b)(4):

Amended Code Sec. 851(e)(1) by striking "subsection (b)(4)" and inserting "subsection (b)(3)". **Effective** for tax years beginning after 8-5-97.

P.L. 105-34, §1271(b)(5):

Amended Code Sec. 851(e)(4) by striking "subsections (b)(4)" and inserting "subsections (b)(3)". **Effective** for tax years beginning after 8-5-97.

• 1988, Technical and Miscellaneous Revenue Act of 1988 (P.L. 100-647)

P.L. 100-647, §1006(m)(2):

Amended Code Sec. 851(e)(1) by striking out "a registered management company or registered business development company" and inserting in lieu thereof "a management company or a business development company described in subsection (a)(1)". **Effective** as if included in the provision of P.L. 99-514 to which it relates.

• 1986, Tax Reform Act of 1986 (P.L. 99-514)

P.L. 99-514, §652(b):

Amended Code Sec. 851(e)(i) by striking out "registered management company" and inserting in lieu thereof "registered management company or registered business development company". **Effective** for tax years beginning after 12-31-86.

• 1976, Tax Reform Act of 1976 (P.L. 94-455)

P.L. 94-455, §1906(b)(13)(A):

Amended 1954 Code by substituting "Secretary" for "Secretary or his delegate" each place it appeared. **Effective** 2-1-77.

[Sec. 851(f)]

(f) CERTAIN UNIT INVESTMENT TRUSTS.—For purposes of this title—

(1) A unit investment trust (as defined in the Investment Company Act of 1940)—

(A) which is registered under such Act and issues periodic payment plan certificates (as defined in such Act) in one or more series,

(B) substantially all of the assets of which, as to all such series, consist of (i) securities issued by a single management company (as defined in such Act) and securities acquired pursuant to subparagraph (C), or (ii) securities issued by a single other corporation, and

(C) which has no power to invest in any other securities except securities issued by a single other management company, when permitted by such Act or the rules and regulations of the Securities and Exchange Commission,

shall not be treated as a person.

(2) In the case of a unit investment trust described in paragraph (1)—

(A) each holder of an interest in such trust shall, to the extent of such interest, be treated as owning a proportionate share of the assets of such trust;

(B) the basis of the assets of such trust which are treated under subparagraph (A) as being owned by a holder of an interest in such trust shall be the same as the basis of his interest in such trust; and

(C) in determining the period for which the holder of an interest in such trust has held the assets of the trust which are treated under subparagraph (A) as being owned by him, there shall be included the period for which such holder has held his interest in such trust.

This subsection shall not apply in the case of a unit investment trust which is a segregated asset account under the insurance laws or regulations of a State.

Amendments

• 1969, Tax Reform Act of 1969 (P.L. 91-172)

P.L. 91-172, §908(a):

Added Code Sec. 851(f). **Effective** for tax years of unit investment trusts ending after 12-31-68, and to tax years of holders of interests in such trusts ending with or within such tax years of such trusts. The enactment of this section shall not be construed to result in the realization of gain or loss by any unit investment trust or by any holder of an interest in a unit investment trust.

• 1958, Technical Amendments Act of 1958 (P.L. 85-866)

P.L. 85-866, §38:

Amended Code Sec. 851(e) by substituting, in paragraph (1), the phrase "not earlier than 60 days" for the phrase "not less than 60 days", and by substituting, in paragraph (2), the word "issuer" for the word "issues" following the phrase "of the outstanding voting securities of such". **Effective** 1-1-54.

[Sec. 851(g)—Stricken]

Amendments

• 1997, Taxpayer Relief Act of 1997 (P.L. 105-34)

P.L. 105-34, §1271(b)(6):

Amended Code Sec. 851 by striking subsection (g) and redesignating subsection (h) as subsection (g). **Effective** for tax years beginning after 8-5-97. Prior to being stricken, Code Sec. 851(g) read as follows:

(g) TREATMENT OF CERTAIN HEDGING TRANSACTIONS.—

(1) IN GENERAL.—In the case of any designated hedge, for purposes of subsection (b)(3), increases (and decreases) during the period of the hedge in the value of positions which are part of such hedge shall be netted.

(2) DESIGNATED HEDGE.—For purposes of this subsection, there is a designated hedge where—

(A) the taxpayer's risk of loss with respect to any position in property is reduced by reason of—

(i) the taxpayer having an option to sell, being under a contractual obligation to sell, or having made (and not closed) a short sale of substantially identical property,

(ii) the taxpayer being the grantor of an option to buy substantially identical property, or

(iii) under regulations prescribed by the Secretary, the taxpayer holding 1 or more other positions, and

(B) the positions which are part of the hedge are clearly identified by the taxpayer in the manner prescribed by regulations.

• 1988, Technical and Miscellaneous Revenue Act of 1988 (P.L. 100-647)

P.L. 100-647, §1006(n)(4):

Amended Code Sec. 851(g)(2)(A)(i) by striking out "contractual option" and inserting in lieu thereof "contractual obligation". **Effective** as if included in the provision of P.L. 99-514 to which it relates.

• 1986, Tax Reform Act of 1986 (P.L. 99-514)

P.L. 99-514, §653(a):

Amended Code Sec. 851 by adding at the end thereof a new subsection (g). **Effective** for tax years beginning after 10-22-86.

[Sec. 851(g)]

(g) SPECIAL RULE FOR SERIES FUNDS.—

(1) IN GENERAL.—In the case of a regulated investment company (within the meaning of subsection (a)) having more than one fund, each fund of such regulated investment company shall be treated as a separate corporation for purposes of this title (except with respect to the definitional requirement of subsection (a)).

(2) FUND DEFINED.—For purposes of paragraph (1) the term "fund" means a segregated portfolio of assets, the beneficial interests in which are owned by the holders of a class or series of stock of the regulated investment company that is preferred over all other classes or series in respect of such portfolio of assets.

Amendments

• 1997, Taxpayer Relief Act of 1997 (P.L. 105-34)

P.L. 105-34, §1271(b)(6):

Amended Code Sec. 851 by redesignating subsection (h) as subsection (g). **Effective** for tax years beginning after 8-5-97.

P.L. 105-34, §1271(b)(7):

Amended Code Sec. 851(g) (as redesignated by Act Sec. 1271(b)(6)) by striking paragraph (3). **Effective** for tax years beginning after 8-5-97. Prior to amendment, Code Sec. 851(g)(3) read as follows:

(3) SPECIAL RULE FOR ABNORMAL REDEMPTIONS.—

(A) IN GENERAL.—Any fund treated as a separate corporation under paragraph (1) shall not be disqualified under subsection (b)(3) for any taxable year by reason of sales resulting from abnormal redemptions on any day and occurring before the close of the 5th business day after such day if—

(i) the sum of the percentages determined under subparagraph (B) for the abnormal redemptions on such day and for abnormal redemptions on prior days during such taxable year exceeds 30 percent; and

(ii) the regulated investment company of which such fund is a part would meet the requirements of subsection (b)(3) for such taxable year if all the funds which are part of such company were treated as a single company.

(B) ABNORMAL REDEMPTIONS.—For purposes of subparagraph (A), the term "abnormal redemptions" means redemptions occurring on any day if the net redemptions on such day exceed 1 percent of the fund's net asset value.

(C) DETERMINATION OF NET ASSET VALUE.—For purposes of this paragraph, net asset value for any day shall be determined as of the close of the preceding day.

(D) LIMITATION.—For purposes of subparagraph (A), any sale or other disposition of stock or securities held less than 3 months occurring during any day shall be deemed to result from abnormal redemptions until the cumulative proceeds from such sales or dispositions occurring during such day, plus the cumulative net positive cash flow of the fund for preceding business days (if any) following the day with abnormal redemptions, exceed the amount of net redemptions on the day with abnormal redemptions.

• 1988, Technical and Miscellaneous Revenue Act of 1988 (P.L. 100-647)

P.L. 100-647, §1006(o)(1):

Amended Code Sec. 851 by redesignating subsection (q) as subsection (h). **Effective** as if included in the provision of P.L. 99-514 to which it relates.

P.L. 100-647, §1006(o)(2):

Amended Code Sec. 851(h) (as redesignated) by adding at the end thereof new paragraph (3). **Effective** as if included in the provision of P.L. 99-514 to which it relates.

• 1986, Tax Reform Act of 1986 (P.L. 99-514)

P.L. 99-514, §654(a):

Amended Code Sec. 851 by adding at the end thereof new subsection (q)[(h)]. **Effective** for tax years beginning after 10-22-86. However, see Act Sec. 654(b)(2), below.

P.L. 99-514, §654(b)(2), provides:

(2) TREATMENT OF CERTAIN EXISTING SERIES FUNDS.—In the case of a regulated investment company which has more than one fund on the date of the enactment of this act, and has before such date been treated for Federal income tax purposes as a single corporation—

(A) the amendment made by subsection (a), and the resulting treatment of each fund as a separate corporation, shall not give rise to the realization or recognition of income or loss by such regulated investment company, its funds, or its shareholders, and

(B) the tax attributes of such regulated investment company shall be appropriately allocated among its funds.

[Sec. 851(h)]

(h) QUALIFIED PUBLICLY TRADED PARTNERSHIP.—For purposes of this section, the term "qualified publicly traded partnership" means a publicly traded partnership described in section 7704(b) other than a partnership which would satisfy the gross income requirements of section 7704(c)(2) if qualifying income included only income described in subsection (b)(2)(A).

Amendments

• 2004, American Jobs Creation Act of 2004 (P.L. 108-357)

P.L. 108-357, §331(d):

Amended Code Sec. 851 by adding at the end a new subsection (h). **Effective** for tax years beginning after 10-22-2004.

[Sec. 852]

SEC. 852. TAXATION OF REGULATED INVESTMENT COMPANIES AND THEIR SHAREHOLDERS.

[Sec. 852(a)]

(a) REQUIREMENTS APPLICABLE TO REGULATED INVESTMENT COMPANIES.—The provisions of this part (other than subsection (c) of this section) shall not be applicable to a regulated investment company for a taxable year unless—

(1) the deduction for dividends paid during the taxable year (as defined in section 561, but without regard to capital gain dividends) equals or exceeds the sum of—

(A) 90 percent of its investment company taxable income for the taxable year determined without regard to subsection (b)(2)(D); and

(B) 90 percent of the excess of (i) its interest income excludable from gross income under section 103(a) over (ii) its deductions disallowed under sections 265, 171(a)(2), and

(2) either—

(A) the provisions of this part applied to the investment company for all taxable years ending on or after November 8, 1983, or

(B) as of the close of the taxable year, the investment company has no earnings and profits accumulated in any taxable year to which the provisions of this part (or the corresponding provisions of prior law) did not apply to it.

The Secretary may waive the requirements of paragraph (1) for any taxable year if the regulated investment company establishes to the satisfaction of the Secretary that it was unable to meet such requirements by reason of distributions previously made to meet the requirements of section 4982.

Amendments

• 1988, Technical and Miscellaneous Revenue Act of 1988 (P.L. 100-647)

P.L. 100-647, §1006(l)(8):

Amended Code Sec. 852(a) by adding at the end thereof a new sentence. **Effective** as if included in the provision of P.L. 99-514 to which it relates.

• 1986, Tax Reform Act of 1986 (P.L. 99-514)

P.L. 99-514, §1878(j)(1):

Amended Code Sec. 852(a) by adding "and" at the end of paragraph (1), by striking out paragraph (2), and by redesignating paragraph (3) as paragraph (2). **Effective** as if included in the provision of P.L. 98-369 to which it relates. Prior to amendment, Code Sec. 852(a)(2) read as follows:

(2) the investment company complies for such year with regulations prescribed by the Secretary for the purpose of ascertaining the actual ownership of its outstanding stock and,

• 1984, Deficit Reduction Act of 1984 (P.L. 98-369)

P.L. 98-369, §1071(a)(3):

Amended Code Sec. 852(a) by striking out "and" at the end of paragraph (1), by striking out the period at the end of paragraph (2) and inserting in lieu thereof ", and", and by adding at the end thereof new paragraph (3). **Effective** for tax years beginning after 12-31-82. However, see Act Sec. 1071(a)(5)(B)-(D), below for special rules.

P.L. 98-369, §1071(a)(5)(B)-(D), provides:

(B) Investment Companies Which Were Regulated Investment Companies for Years Ending Before November 8, 1983.—In the case of any investment company to which the provisions of part I of subchapter M of chapter 1 of the Internal Revenue Code of 1954 applied for any taxable year ending before November 8, 1983, for purposes of section 852(a)(3)(B) of the Internal Revenue Code of 1954 (as amended by this subsection), no earnings and profits accumulated in any taxable year ending before January 1, 1984, shall be taken into account.

(C) Investment Companies Beginning Business in 1983.—In the case of an investment company which began business in 1983 (and was not a successor corporation), earning and profits accumulated during its first taxable year shall not be taken into account for purposes of section 852(a)(3)(B) of such Code (as so amended).

(D) Investment Companies Registering Before November 8, 1983.—In the case of any investment company—

(i) which, during the period after December 31, 1981, and before November 8, 1983—

(I) was engaged in the active conduct of a trade or business,

(II) sold substantially all of its operating assets, and

(III) registered under the Investment Company Act of 1940 as either a management company or a unit investment trust, and

(ii) to which the provisions of part I of subchapter M of chapter 1 of the Internal Revenue Code of 1954 applied for its first taxable year beginning after November 8, 1983,

for purposes of section 852(a)(3)(A) of such Code (as amended by paragraph (3)), the provisions of part I of subchapter M of chapter 1 of such Code shall be treated as applying to such investment company for its first taxable year ending after November 8, 1983. For purposes of the preceding sentence, all members of an affiliated group (as defined in section 1504(a) of such Code) filing a consolidated return shall be treated as 1 taxpayer.

• 1976, Tax Reform Act of 1976 (P.L. 94-455)

P.L. 94-455, §1901(b)(6):

Substituted "section 103(a)" for "section 103(a)(1)" in Code Sec. 852(a)(1)(B). **Effective** for tax years beginning after 12-31-76.

P.L. 94-455, §1906(b)(13)(A):

Amended 1954 Code by substituting "Secretary" for "Secretary or his delegate" each place it appeared. **Effective** 2-1-77.

P.L. 94-455, §2137(a):

Amended Code Sec. 852(a)(1). **Effective** for tax years beginning after 12-31-75. Prior to amendment, Code Sec. 852(a)(1) read as follows:

(1) the deduction for dividends paid during the taxable year (as defined in section 561, but without regard to capital gains dividends) equals or exceeds 90 percent of its investment company taxable income for the taxable year (determined without regard to subsection (b)(3)(D)), and

• 1960 (P.L. 86-779)

P.L. 86-779, §10(b):

Struck out "this subchapter" in Code Sec. 852(a), and substituted "this part". **Effective** 1-1-61.

• 1958, Technical Amendments Act of 1958 (P.L. 85-866)

P.L. 85-866, §101(a):

Amended Code Sec. 852(a) by adding "(other than subsection (c) of this section)" after the words "this subchapter" (now "this part"). **Effective** for tax years of regulated investment companies beginning on or after 3-1-58.

[Sec. 852(b)]

(b) METHOD OF TAXATION OF COMPANIES AND SHAREHOLDERS.—

(1) IMPOSITION OF TAX ON REGULATED INVESTMENT COMPANIES.—There is hereby imposed for each taxable year upon the investment company taxable income of every regulated investment company a tax computed as provided in section 11, as though the investment company taxable income were the taxable income referred to in section 11. In the case of a regulated investment company which is a personal holding company (as defined in section 542) or which fails to comply for the taxable year with regulations prescribed by the Secretary for the purpose of ascertaining the actual ownership of its stock, such tax shall be computed at the highest rate of tax specified in section 11(b).

(2) INVESTMENT COMPANY TAXABLE INCOME.—The investment company taxable income shall be the taxable income of the regulated investment company adjusted as follows:

(A) There shall be excluded the amount of the net capital gain, if any.

(B) The net operating loss deduction provided in section 172 shall not be allowed.

(C) The deductions for corporations provided in part VIII (except section 248) in subchapter B (section 241 and following, relating to the deduction for dividends received, etc.) shall not be allowed.

(D) The deduction for dividends paid (as defined in section 561) shall be allowed, but shall be computed without regard to capital gain dividends and exempt-interest dividends.

(E) The taxable income shall be computed without regard to section 443(b) (relating to computation of tax on change of annual accounting period).

(F) The taxable income shall be computed without regard to section 454(b) (relating to short-term obligations issued on a discount basis) if the company so elects in a manner prescribed by the Secretary.

(3) CAPITAL GAINS.—

(A) IMPOSITION OF TAX.—There is hereby imposed for each taxable year in the case of every regulated investment company a tax, determined as provided in section 1201(a), on the excess, if any, of the net capital gain over the deduction for dividends paid (as defined in section 561) determined with reference to capital gain dividends only.

(B) TREATMENT OF CAPITAL GAIN DIVIDENDS BY SHAREHOLDERS.—A capital gain dividend shall be treated by the shareholders as a gain from the sale or exchange of a capital asset held for more than 1 year.

(C) DEFINITION OF CAPITAL GAIN DIVIDEND.—For purposes of this part, a capital gain dividend is any dividend, or part thereof, which is designated by the company as a capital gain dividend in a written notice mailed to its shareholders not later than 60 days after the close of its taxable year. If the aggregate amount so designated with respect to a taxable year of the company (including capital gains dividends paid after the close of the taxable year described in section 855) is greater than the net capital gain of the taxable year, the portion of each distribution which shall be a capital gain dividend shall be only that proportion of the amounts so designated which such net capital gain bears to the aggregate amount so designated; except that, if there is an increase in the excess described in subparagraph (A) of this paragraph for such year which results from a determination (as defined in section 860(e)), such designation may be made with respect to such increase at any time before the expiration of 120 days after the date of such determination. For purposes of this subparagraph, the amount of the net capital gain for a taxable year (to which an election under section 4982(e)(4) does not apply) shall be determined without regard to any net capital loss or net long-term capital loss attributable to transactions after October 31 of such year, and any such net capital loss or net long-term capital loss shall be treated as arising on the 1st day of the next taxable year. To the extent provided in regulations, the preceding sentence shall apply also for purposes of computing the taxable income of the regulated investment company.

(D) TREATMENT BY SHAREHOLDERS OF UNDISTRIBUTED CAPITAL GAINS.—

(i) Every shareholder of a regulated investment company at the close of the company's taxable year shall include, in computing his long-term capital gains in his return for his taxable year in which the last day of the company's taxable year falls, such amount as the company shall designate in respect of such shares in a written notice mailed to its shareholders at any time prior to the expiration of 60 days after close of its taxable year, but the amount so includible by any shareholder shall not exceed that part of the amount subjected to tax in subparagraph (A) which he would have received if all of such amount had been distributed as capital gain dividends by the company to the holders of such shares at the close of its taxable year.

(ii) For purposes of this title, every such shareholder shall be deemed to have paid, for his taxable year under clause (i), the tax imposed by subparagraph (A) on the amounts required by this subparagraph to be included in respect of such shares in computing his long-term capital gains for that year; and such shareholder shall be allowed credit or refund, as the case may be, for the tax so deemed to have been paid by him.

(iii) The adjusted basis of such shares in the hands of the shareholder shall be increased, with respect to the amounts required by this subparagraph to be included in computing his long-term capital gains, by the difference between the amount of such includible gains and the tax deemed paid by such shareholder in respect of such shares under clause (ii).

(iv) In the event of such designation the tax imposed by subparagraph (A) shall be paid by the regulated investment company within 30 days after close of its taxable year.

(v) The earnings and profits of such regulated investment company, and the earnings and profits of any such shareholder which is a corporation, shall be appropriately adjusted in accordance with regulations prescribed by the Secretary.

(E) CERTAIN DISTRIBUTIONS.—In the case of a distribution to which section 897 does not apply by reason of the second sentence of section 897(h)(1), the amount of such distribution which would be included in computing long-term capital gains for the shareholder under subparagraph (B) or (D) (without regard to this subparagraph)—

(i) shall not be included in computing such shareholder's long-term capital gains, and

(ii) shall be included in such shareholder's gross income as a dividend from the regulated investment company.

(4) LOSS ON SALE OR EXCHANGE OF STOCK HELD 6 MONTHS OR LESS.—

(A) LOSS ATTRIBUTABLE TO CAPITAL GAIN DIVIDEND.—If—

(i) subparagraph (B) or (D) of paragraph (3) provides that any amount with respect to any share is to be treated as long-term capital gain, and

(ii) such share is held by the taxpayer for 6 months or less,

then any loss (to the extent not disallowed under subparagraph (B)) on the sale or exchange of such share shall, to the extent of the amount described in clause (i), be treated as a long-term capital loss.

(B) LOSS ATTRIBUTABLE TO EXEMPT-INTEREST DIVIDEND.—If—

(i) a shareholder of a regulated investment company receives an exempt-interest dividend with respect to any share, and

(ii) such share is held by the taxpayer for 6 months or less,

then any loss on the sale or exchange of such share shall, to the extent of the amount of such exempt-interest dividend, be disallowed.

(C) DETERMINATION OF HOLDING PERIODS.—For purposes of this paragraph, in determining the period for which the taxpayer has held any share of stock—

(i) the rules of paragraphs (3) and (4) of section 246(c) shall apply, and

(ii) there shall not be taken into account any day which is more than 6 months after the date on which such share becomes ex-dividend.

(D) LOSSES INCURRED UNDER A PERIODIC LIQUIDATION PLAN.—To the extent provided in regulations, subparagraphs (A) and (B) shall not apply to losses incurred on the sale or exchange of shares of stock in a regulated investment company pursuant to a plan which provides for the periodic liquidation of such shares.

(E) AUTHORITY TO SHORTEN REQUIRED HOLDING PERIOD.—In the case of a regulated investment company which regularly distributes at least 90 percent of its net tax-exempt interest, the Secretary may by regulations prescribe that subparagraph (B) (and subparagraph (C) to the extent it relates to subparagraph (B)) shall be applied on the basis of a holding period requirement shorter than 6 months; except that such shorter holding period requirement shall not be shorter than the greater of 31 days or the period between the regular distributions of exempt-interest dividends.

(5) EXEMPT-INTEREST DIVIDENDS.—If, at the close of each quarter of its taxable year, at least 50 percent of the value (as defined in section 851(c)(4)) of the total assets of the regulated investment company consists of obligations described in section 103(a), such company shall be qualified to pay exempt-interest dividends, as defined herein, to its shareholders.

(A) DEFINITION.—An exempt-interest dividend means any dividend or part thereof (other than a capital gain dividend) paid by a regulated investment company and designated by it as an exempt-interest dividend in a written notice mailed to its shareholders not later than 60 days after the close of its taxable year. If the aggregate amount so designated with respect to a taxable year of the company (including exempt-interest dividends paid after the close of the taxable year as described in section 855) is greater than the excess of—

(i) the amount of interest excludable from gross income under section 103(a), over

(ii) the amounts disallowed as deductions under sections 265 and 171(a)(2), the portion of such distribution which shall constitute an exempt-interest dividend shall be only that proportion of the amount so designated as the amount of such excess for such taxable year bears to the amount so designated.

(B) TREATMENT OF EXEMPT-INTEREST DIVIDENDS BY SHAREHOLDERS.—An exempt-interest dividend shall be treated by the shareholders for all purposes of this subtitle as an item of interest excludable from gross income under section 103(a). Such purposes include but are not limited to—

(i) the determination of gross income and taxable income,

(ii) the determination of distributable net income under subchapter J,

(iii) the allowance of, or calculation of the amount of, any credit or deduction, and

(iv) the determination of the basis in the hands of any shareholder of any share of stock of the company.

(6) SECTION 311(b) NOT TO APPLY TO CERTAIN DISTRIBUTIONS.—Section 311(b) shall not apply to any distribution by a regulated investment company to which this part applies, if such distribution is in redemption of its stock upon the demand of the shareholder.

(7) TIME CERTAIN DIVIDENDS TAKEN INTO ACCOUNT.—For purposes of this title, any dividend declared by a regulated investment company in October, November, or December of any calendar year and payable to shareholders of record on a specified date in such a month shall be deemed—

(A) to have been received by each shareholder on December 31 of such calendar year, and

(B) to have been paid by such company on December 31 of such calendar year (or, if earlier, as provided in section 855).

The preceding sentence shall apply only if such dividend is actually paid by the company during January of the following calendar year.

(8) SPECIAL RULE FOR TREATMENT OF CERTAIN FOREIGN CURRENCY LOSSES.—To the extent provided in regulations, the taxable income of a regulated investment company (other than a company to which an election under section 4982(e)(4) applies) shall be computed without regard to any net foreign currency loss attributable to transactions after October 31 of such year, and any such net foreign currency loss shall be treated as arising on the 1st day of the following taxable year.

(9) DIVIDENDS TREATED AS RECEIVED BY COMPANY ON EX-DIVIDEND DATE.—For purposes of this title, if a regulated investment company is the holder of record of any share of stock on the record date for any dividend payable with respect to such stock, such dividend shall be included in gross income by such company as of the later of—

(A) the date such share became ex-dividend with respect to such dividend, or

(B) the date such company acquired such share.

(10) SPECIAL RULE FOR CERTAIN LOSSES ON STOCK IN PASSIVE FOREIGN INVESTMENT COMPANY.—To the extent provided in regulations, the taxable income of a regulated investment company (other than a company to which an election under section 4982(e)(4) applies) shall be computed without regard to any net reduction in the value of any stock of a passive foreign investment company with respect to which an election under section 1296(k) is in effect occurring after October 31 of the taxable year, and any such reduction shall be treated as occurring on the first day of the following taxable year.

Amendments

• 2007, Tax Technical Corrections Act of 2007 (P.L. 110-172)

P.L. 110-172, §11(a)(17)(A):

Amended Code Sec. 852(b)(4)(C). **Effective** 12-29-2007. Prior to amendment, Code Sec. 852(b)(4)(C) read as follows:

(C) DETERMINATION OF HOLDING PERIODS.—For purposes of this paragraph, the rules of paragraphs (3) and (4) of section 246(c) shall apply in determining the period for which the taxpayer has held any share of stock; except that "6 months" shall be substituted for each number of days specified in subparagraph (B) of section 246(c)(3).

• 2006, Tax Increase Prevention and Reconciliation Act of 2005 (P.L. 109-222)

P.L. 109-222, §505(c)(1):

Amended Code Sec. 852(b)(3) by adding at the end a new subparagraph (E). **Effective** for tax years of qualified investment entities beginning after 12-31-2005, except that no amount shall be required to be withheld under Code Sec. 1441, 1442, or 1445 with respect to any distribution before 5-17-2006 if such amount was not otherwise required to be withheld under any such section as in effect before such amendments.

• 1997, Taxpayer Relief Act of 1997 (P.L. 105-34)

P.L. 105-34, §1122(c)(2):

Amended Code Sec. 852(b) by adding at the end thereof a new paragraph (10). **Effective** for tax years of United States persons beginning after 12-31-97, and to tax years of foreign corporations ending with or within such tax years of United States persons.

P.L. 105-34, §1254(b)(2):

Amended Code Sec. 852(b)(3)(D)(iii) by striking "by 65 percent" and all that follows and inserting "by the difference between the amount of such includible gains and the tax deemed paid by such shareholder in respect of such shares under clause (ii).". **Effective** for tax years beginning after 8-5-97. Prior to amendment, Code Sec. 852(b)(3)(D)(iii) read as follows:

(iii) The adjusted basis of such shares in the hands of the shareholder shall be increased, with respect to the amounts required by this subparagraph to be included in computing his long-term capital gains, by 65 percent of so much of such amounts as equals the amount subject to tax in accordance with section 1201(a).

• 1996, Small Business Job Protection Act of 1996 (P.L. 104-188)

P.L. 104-188, §1602(b)(3):

Amended Code Sec. 852(b)(5) by striking subparagraph (C). For the **effective** date, see Act Sec. 1602(c), below. Prior to being stricken, Code Sec. 852(b)(5)(C) read as follows:

(C) INTEREST ON CERTAIN LOANS USED TO ACQUIRE EMPLOYER SECURITIES.—For purposes of this section—

(i) 50 percent of the amount of any loan of the regulated investment company which qualifies as a securities acquisition loan (as defined in section 133) shall be treated as an obligation described in section 103(a), and

(ii) 50 percent of the interest received on such loan shall be treated as interest excludable from gross income under section 103.

P.L. 104-188, §1602(c), provides:

(c) EFFECTIVE DATE.—

(1) IN GENERAL.—The amendments made by this section shall apply to loans made after the date of the enactment of this Act.

(2) REFINANCINGS.—The amendments made by this section shall not apply to loans made after the date of the enactment of this Act to refinance securities acquisition loans (determined without regard to section 133(b)(1)(B) of the Internal Revenue Code of 1986, as in effect on the day before the date of the enactment of this Act) made on or before such date or to refinance loans described in this paragraph if—

(A) the refinancing loans meet the requirements of section 133 of such Code (as so in effect),

(B) immediately after the refinancing the principal amount of the loan resulting from the refinancing does not exceed the principal amount of the refinanced loan (immediately before the refinancing), and

(C) the term of such refinancing loan does not extend beyond the last day of the term of the original securities acquisition loan.

For purposes of this paragraph, the term "securities acquisition loan" includes a loan from a corporation to an employee stock ownership plan described in section 133(b)(3) of such Code (as so in effect).

(3) EXCEPTION.—Any loan made pursuant to a binding written contract in effect before June 10, 1996, and at all times thereafter before such loan is made, shall be treated for purposes of paragraphs (1) and (2) as a loan made on or before the date of the enactment of this Act.

• 1993, Omnibus Budget Reconciliation Act of 1993 (P.L. 103-66)

P.L. 103-66, §13221(c)(1):

Amended Code Sec. 852(b)(3)(D)(iii) by striking "66 percent" and inserting "65 percent". **Effective** for tax years beginning on or after 1-1-93.

• 1989, Omnibus Budget Reconciliation Act of 1989 (P.L. 101-239)

P.L. 101-239, §7204(c)(1):

Amended Code Sec. 852(b) by adding at the end thereof a new paragraph (9). **Effective** for dividends in cases where the stock becomes ex-dividend after 12-19-89.

• 1988, Technical and Miscellaneous Revenue Act of 1988 (P.L. 100-647)

P.L. 100-647, §1006(l)(1)(A):

Amended Code Sec. 852(b) by redesignating paragraph (6), as added by P.L. 99-514, §651(b)(1)(A), as paragraph (7). **Effective** as if included in the provision of P.L. 99-514 to which it relates.

P.L. 100-647, §1006(l)(4)(A)-(B):

Amended Code Sec. 852(b)(3)(C) by striking out "net capital loss" each place it appears in the 3rd sentence and inserting in lieu thereof "net capital loss or net long-term capital loss", and by striking out "regulated investment company taxable income" in the last sentence and inserting in lieu thereof "the taxable income of the regulated investment company". **Effective** as if included in the provision of P.L. 99-514 to which it relates.

P.L. 100-647, §1006(l)(7):

Amended Code Sec. 852(b) by adding at the end thereof new paragraph (8). **Effective** as if included in the provision of P.L. 99-514 to which it relates.

P.L. 100-647, §1006(l)(9)(A)-(D):

Amended Code Sec. 852(b)(7) (as redesignated by paragraph (1) by striking out "in December" and inserting in lieu thereof "in October, November, or December", by striking out "in such month" and inserting in lieu thereof "in such a month", by striking out "on such date" in subparagraphs (A) and (B) and inserting in lieu thereof "on December 31 of such calendar year", and by striking out "before February 1" and inserting in lieu thereof "during January". **Effective** as if included in the provision of P.L. 99-514 to which it relates.

P.L. 100-647, §1011B(h)(4):

Amended Code Sec. 852(b)(5)(C) by striking out "paragraph" and inserting in lieu thereof "section". **Effective** as if included in the provision of P.L. 99-514 to which it relates.

• 1986, Tax Reform Act of 1986 (P.L. 99-514)

P.L. 99-514, §311(b)(1):

Amended Code Sec. 852(b)(3)(D)(iii) by striking out "72 percent" and inserting in lieu thereof "66 percent". **Effective** for tax years beginning after 12-31-86.

P.L. 99-514, §631(e)(11):

Amended Code Sec. 852(b) by adding at the end thereof new paragraph (6). For the **effective** date, see the amendment notes under Code Sec. 26.

P.L. 99-514, §651(b)(1)(A):

Amended Code Sec. 852(b) by adding at the end thereof new paragraph (6)[7]. **Effective** for calendar years beginning after 12-31-86.

P.L. 99-514, §651(b)(3):

Amended Code Sec. 852(b)(3)(C) by adding at the end thereof two new sentences. **Effective** for calendar years beginning after 12-31-86.

P.L. 99-514, §655(a)(1):

Amended Code Sec. 852(b)(3) by striking out "45 days" each place it appears and inserting in lieu thereof "60 days". **Effective** for tax years beginning after 10-22-86.

P.L. 99-514, §655(a)(2):

Amended Code Sec. 852(b)(5)(A) by striking out "45 days" each place it appears and inserting in lieu thereof "60 days". **Effective** for tax years beginning after 10-22-86.

P.L. 99-514, §1173(b)(1)(B):

Amended Code Sec. 852(b)(5) by adding at the end thereof new subparagraph (C). **Effective** for loans used to acquire employer securities after 10-22-86, including loans used to refinance loans used to acquire employer securities before such date if such loans were used to acquire employer securities after 5-23-84.

P.L. 99-514, §1804(c)(1):

Amended Code Sec. 852(b)(4)(B)(ii) by striking out "for less than 31 days" and inserting in lieu thereof "for 6 months or less". **Effective** for stock with respect to which the taxpayer's holding period begins after 3-28-85.

P.L. 99-514, §1804(c)(2):

Amended Code Sec. 852(b)(4)(C). **Effective** for stock with respect to which the taxpayer's holding period begins after 3-28-85. Prior to amendment, Code Sec. 852(b)(4)(C) read as follows:

(C) DETERMINATION OF HOLDING PERIODS.—For purposes of this paragraph, the rules of paragraphs (3) and (4) of section 246(c) shall apply in determining the period for which the taxpayer held any share of stock; except that for the number of days specified in subparagraph (B) of section 246(c)(3) there shall be substituted—

(i) "6 months" for purposes of subparagraph (A), and

(ii) "30 days" for purposes of subparagraph (B).

P.L. 99-514, §1804(c)(3):

Amended Code Sec. 852(b)(4)(D) by striking out "subparagraph (A)" and inserting in lieu thereof "subparagraphs (A) and (B)". **Effective** for stock with respect to which the taxpayer's holding period begins after 3-28-85.

P.L. 99-514, §1804(c)(4):

Amended Code Sec. 852(b)(4) by adding at the end thereof new subparagraph (E). **Effective** for stock with respect to which the taxpayer's holding period begins after 3-28-85.

P.L. 99-514, §1804(c)(5):

Amended Code Sec. 852(b) by striking out "Less Than 31 Days" and inserting in lieu thereof "6 Months or Less" in the paragraph heading for paragraph (4). **Effective** for stock with respect to which the taxpayer's holding period begins after 3-28-85.

P.L. 99-514, §1878(j)(2):

Amended Code Sec. 852(b)(1) by striking out the last sentence and inserting in lieu thereof "In the case of a regulated investment company which is a personal holding company (as defined in section 542) or which fails to comply for the taxable year with regulations prescribed by the Secretary for such tax shall be computed at the highest rate of tax specified in section 11(b)." **Effective** as if included in the provision of P.L. 98-369 to which it relates. Prior to amendment, the last sentence read as follows:

In the case of a regulated investment company which is a personal holding company (as defined in section 542), that tax shall be computed at the highest rate of tax specified in section 11(b).

• 1984, Deficit Reduction Act of 1984 (P.L. 98-369)

P.L. 98-369, §55(a)(1):

Amended Code Sec. 852(b)(4)(A). **Effective** for losses incurred with respect to shares of stock and beneficial interests for which the taxpayer's holding period begins after 7-18-84. Prior to amendment, it read as follows:

(A) Loss Attributable to Capital Gain Dividend.—If—

(i) under subparagraph (B) or (D) of paragraph (3) a shareholder of a regulated investment company is required, with respect to any share, to treat any amount as a long-term capital gain, and

(ii) such share is held by the taxpayer for less than 31 days,

then any loss (to the extent not disallowed under subparagraph (B)) on the sale or exchange of such share shall, to the extent of the amount described in clause (i), be treated as a long-term capital loss.

P.L. 98-369, §55(a)(2):

Amended Code Sec. 852(b)(4)(C). **Effective** for losses incurred with respect to shares of stock and beneficial interests for which the taxpayer's holding period begins after 7-18-84. Prior to amendment, it read as follows:

(C) Determination of Holding Periods.—For purposes of this paragraph, the rules of section 246(c)(3) shall apply in determining whether any share of stock has been held for less than 31 days; except that "30 days" shall be substituted for the number of days specified in subparagraph (B) of section 246(C)(3).

P.L. 98-369, §55(a)(3):

Amended Code Sec. 852(b)(4) by adding new subparagraph (D). **Effective** for losses incurred with respect to shares of stock and beneficial interests for which the taxpayer's holding period begins after 7-18-84.

P.L. 98-369, §1001(b)(11):

Amended Code Sec. 852(b)(3)(B) by striking out "1 year" and inserting in lieu thereof "6 months". **Effective** for property acquired after 6-22-84 and before 1-1-88.

P.L. 98-369, §1071(a)(2):

Amended Code Sec. 852(b)(1) by adding at the end thereof a new sentence. **Effective** for tax years beginning after 12-31-82. However, see Act Sec. 1071(a)(5)(B)-(D), following Code Sec. 852(a) for special rules.

P.L. 98-369, §1071(b)(1):

Amended Code Sec. 852(b)(2) by adding at the end thereof new subparagraph (F). **Effective** for tax years beginning after 12-31-82. However, see Act Sec. 1071(a)(5)(B)-(D), following Code Sec. 852(a) for special rules.

• 1983, Surface Transportation Act of 1982 (P.L. 97-424)

P.L. 97-424, §547(b)(2):

Amended Code Sec. 852(b)(5) by striking out "103(a)(1)" each place it appeared and inserting in lieu thereof "103(a)". **Effective** 1-6-83.

• 1980, Technical Corrections Act of 1979 (P.L. 96-222)

P.L. 96-222, §104(a)(3)(B):

Amended Code Sec. 852(b)(3)(D)(iii) by changing "70 percent" to "72 percent".

• 1978, Revenue Act of 1978 (P.L. 95-600)

P.L. 95-600, §301(b)(11):

Amended Code Sec. 852(b)(1). **Effective** for tax years beginning after 12-31-78. Prior to amendment, Code Sec. 852(b)(1) read as follows:

"(1) IMPOSITION OF NORMAL TAX AND SURTAX ON REGULATED INVESTMENT COMPANIES.—There is hereby imposed for each taxable year upon the investment company taxable income of every regulated investment company a normal tax and surtax computed as provided in section 11, as though the investment company taxable income were the taxable income referred to in section 11."

P.L. 95-600, §362(c):

Amended Code Sec. 852(b)(3)(C) by adding after "aggregate amount so designated" the clause "; except that, if there is an increase in the excess described in subparagraph (A) of this paragraph for such year which results from a determination (as defined in section 860(e)), such designation may be made with respect to such increase at any time before the expiration of 120 days after the date of such determination". **Effective** with respect to determinations made after 11-6-78.

P.L. 95-600, §701(s)(2):

Amended Code Sec. 852(b)(4). **Effective** for tax years beginning after 12-31-75. Prior to amendment, Code Sec. 852(b)(4) read as follows:

"(4) LOSS ON SALE OR EXCHANGE OF STOCK HELD LESS THAN 31 DAYS.—If—

(A) under subparagraph (B) or (D) of paragraph (3) a shareholder of a regulated investment company is required, with respect to any share, to treat any amount as a long-term capital gain, and

(B) such share is held by the taxpayer for less than 31 days, then any loss on the sale or exchange of such share shall, to the extent of the amount described in subparagraph (A) of this paragraph, be treated as loss from the sale or exchange of a capital asset held for more than 1 year. For purposes of this paragraph, the rules of section 246(c)(3) shall apply in determining whether any share of stock has been held for less than 31 days; except that "30 days" shall be substituted for the number of days specified in subparagraph (B) of section 246(c)(3)."

• 1976, Tax Reform Act of 1976 (P.L. 94-455)

P.L. 94-455, §1402(b)(1):

Substituted "9 months" for "6 months" in paragraphs (3)(B) and (4)(B). **Effective** for tax years beginning in 1977.

P.L. 94-455, §1402(b)(2):

Substituted "1 year" for "9 months" in paragraphs (3)(B) and (4)(B). **Effective** for tax years beginning in 1977.

P.L. 94-455, §1901(a)(110):

Struck out the last sentence in paragraph (3)(C). **Effective** for tax years beginning after 12-31-76. Prior to repeal, the last sentence of Code Sec. 852(b)(3)(C) read as follows:

For purposes of subparagraph (A)(ii), the deduction for dividends paid shall, in the case of a taxable year beginning before January 1, 1975, first be made from the amount subject to the tax in accordance with section 1201(a)(1)(B), to the extent thereof, and then from the amount subject to tax in accordance with section 1201(a)(1)(A).

P.L. 94-455, §1901(a)(110)(B)(i):

Struck out "by 75 percent of so much of such amounts as equals the amount subject to tax in accordance with section 1201(a)(1)(A) and by 70 percent (72 percent in the case of a taxable year beginning after December 31, 1969, and before January 1, 1971) of so much of such amounts as equals the amount subject to tax in accordance with section 1201(a)(1)(B) or (2)" in paragraph (3)(D)(iii) and inserted in its place "by 70 percent of so much of such amounts as equals the amount subject to tax in accordance with section 1201(a)". **Effective** for tax years beginning after 12-31-76.

P.L. 94-455, §1901(a)(110)(B)(ii), provides:

(ii) The amendment made by clause (i) shall not be considered to affect the amount of any increase in the basis of stock under the provisions of section 852(b)(3)(D)(iii) of the Internal Revenue Code of 1954 which is based upon amounts subject to tax under section 1201 of such Code in taxable years beginning before January 1, 1975.

P.L. 94-455, §1901(b)(1)(V):

Struck out the last sentence in Code Sec. 852(b)(1). **Effective** for tax years beginning after 12-31-76. Prior to repeal, the last sentence of Code Sec. 852(b)(1) read as follows:

For purposes of computing the normal tax under section 11, the taxable income and the dividends paid deduction of such investment company for the taxable year (computed without regard to capital gains dividends) shall be reduced by the deduction provided by section 242 (relating to partially tax-exempt interest).

P.L. 94-455, §1901(b)(33)(I):

Substituted "the amount of the net capital gain, if any" for "the excess, if any, of the net long-term capital gain over the net short-term capital loss" in Code Sec. 852(b)(2)(A). **Effective** for tax years beginning after 12-31-76.

P.L. 94-455, §1901(b)(33)(J):

Amended Code Sec. 852(b)(3)(A). **Effective** for tax years beginning after 12-31-76. Prior to amendment, Code Sec. 852(b)(3)(A) read as follows:

(A) IMPOSITION OF TAX.—There is hereby imposed for each taxable year in the case of every regulated investment company a tax, determined as provided in section 1201(a), on the excess, if any, of the net long-term capital gain over the sum of—

(i) the net short-term capital loss, and

(ii) the deduction for dividends paid (as defined in section 561) determined with reference to capital gains dividends only.

P.L. 94-455, §2137(b):

Amended Code Sec. 852(b)(2)(D). **Effective** for tax years beginning after 12-31-75. Prior to amendment, Code Sec. 852(b)(2)(D) read as follows:

(D) The deduction for dividends paid (as defined in section 561) shall be allowed, but shall be computed without regard to capital gains dividends.

P.L. 94-455, §2137(c):

Added a new paragraph (5). **Effective** for tax years beginning after 12-31-75.

P.L. 94-455, §1906(b)(13)(A):

Amended 1954 Code by substituting "Secretary" for "Secretary or his delegate" each place it appeared. **Effective** 2-1-77.

• 1969, Tax Reform Act of 1969 (P.L. 91-172)

P.L. 91-172, §511(c):

Amended Code Sec. 852(b)(3)(A) by substituting "determined as provided in section 1201(a), on" for "of 25 percent of" in the first sentence, and added the last sentence of Code Sec. 852(b)(3)(C). **Effective** for tax years beginning after 12-31-69.

P.L. 91-172, §511(c):

Amended Code Sec. 852(b)(3)(D)(iii). **Effective** for tax years beginning after 12-31-69. Prior to amendment, Code Sec. 852(b)(3)(D)(iii) read as follows:

(iii) The adjusted basis of such shares in the hands of the shareholder shall be increased by 75 percent of the amounts required by this subparagraph to be included in computing his long-term capital gains.

• 1964, Revenue Act of 1964 (P.L. 88-272)

P.L. 88-272, §229(a):

Amended Code Sec. 852(b)(3)(C) by substituting "45 days" for "30 days" in the first sentence, and amended Code Sec. 852(b)(3)(D)(i) by substituting "45 days" for "30 days".

• 1960 (P.L. 86-779)

P.L. 86-779, §10(b):

Amended Code Sec. 852(b)(3)(C) by striking out "A capital gain divided means" and by substituting "For purposes of this part, a capital gain dividend is". **Effective** 1-1-61.

• 1958, Technical Amendments Act of 1958 (P.L. 85-866)

P.L. 85-866, §39:

Amended Code Sec. 852(b) by adding paragraph (4). **Effective** for tax years ending after 12-31-57 with respect to shares acquired after 12-31-57.

• 1956 (P.L. 700, 84th Cong.)

P.L. 700, 84th Cong., §2:

Added subparagraph (D) to Code Sec. 852(b)(3). **Effective** 1-1-57.

[Sec. 852(c)]

(c) EARNINGS AND PROFITS.—

(1) IN GENERAL.—The earnings and profits of a regulated investment company for any taxable year (but not its accumulated earnings and profits) shall not reduced by any amount which is not allowable as a deduction in computing its taxable income for such taxable year. For purposes of this subsection, the term "regulated investment company" includes a domestic corporation which is a regulated investment company determined without regard to the requirements of subsection (a).

(2) COORDINATION WITH TAX ON UNDISTRIBUTED INCOME.—For purposes of applying this chapter to distributions made by a regulated investment company with respect to any calendar year, the earnings and profits of such company shall be determined without regard to any net capital loss (or net foreign currency loss) attributable to transactions after October 31 of such year, without regard to any net reduction in the value of any stock of a passive foreign investment company with respect to which an election under section 1296(k) is in effect occurring after October 31 of such year, and with such other adjustments as the Secretary may by regulations prescribe. The preceding sentence shall apply—

(A) only to the extent that the amount distributed by the company with respect to the calendar year does not exceed the required distribution for such calendar year (as determined under section 4982 by substituting "100 percent" for each percentage set forth in section 4982(b)(1)), and

(B) except as provided in regulations, only if an election under section 4982(e)(4) is not in effect with respect to such company.

(3) DISTRIBUTIONS TO MEET REQUIREMENTS OF SUBSECTION (a)(2)(B).—Any distribution which is made in order to comply with the requirements of subsection (a)(2)(B)—

(A) shall be treated for purposes of this subsection and subsection (a)(2)(B) as made from earnings and profits which, but for the distribution, would result in a failure to meet such requirements (and allocated to such earnings on a first-in, first-out basis), and

(B) to the extent treated under subparagraph (A) as made from accumulated earnings and profits, shall not be treated as a distribution for purposes of subsection (b)(2)(D) and section 855.

Amendments

• 1999, Tax Relief Extension Act of 1999 (P.L. 106-170)

P.L. 106-170, §566(a)(1):

Amended Code Sec. 852(c) by adding at the end a new paragraph (3). **Effective** for distributions after 12-31-2000.

• 1997, Taxpayer Relief Act of 1997 (P.L. 105-34)

P.L. 105-34, §1122(c)(3):

Amended Code Sec. 852(c)[(2)] by inserting ", without regard to any net reduction in the value of any stock of a passive foreign investment company with respect to which an election under section 1296(k) is in effect occurring after October 31 of such year," after "October 31 of such year". **Effective** for tax years of United States persons beginning after 12-31-97, and to tax years of foreign corporations ending with or within such tax years of United States persons.

• 1988, Technical and Miscellaneous Revenue Act of 1988 (P.L. 100-647)

P.L. 100-647, §1006(l)(3):

Amended Code Sec. 852(c)(2). **Effective** as if included in the provision of P.L. 99-514 to which it relates. Prior to amendment, Code Sec. 852(c)(2) read as follows:

(2) COORDINATION WITH TAX ON UNDISTRIBUTED INCOME.—A regulated investment company shall be treated as having sufficient earnings and profits to treat as a dividend any distribution (other than in a redemption to which section 302(a) applies) which is treated as a dividend by such company. The preceding sentence shall not apply to the extent that the amount distributed during any calendar year by the company exceeds the required distribution for such calendar year (as determined under section 4982).

• 1986, Tax Reform Act of 1986 (P.L. 99-514)

P.L. 99-514, §651(b)(2):

Amended Code Sec. 852(c). **Effective** for calendar years beginning after 12-31-86. Prior to amendment, Code Sec. 852(c) read as follows:

(c) EARNINGS AND PROFITS.—The earnings and profits of a regulated investment company for any taxable year (but not its accumulated earnings and profits) shall not be reduced by any amount which is not allowable as a deduction in computing its taxable income for such taxable year. For purposes of this subsection, the term "regulated investment company" includes a domestic corporation which is a regulated investment company determined without regard to the requirements of subsection (a).

• 1958, Technical Amendments Act of 1958 (P.L. 85-866)

P.L. 85-866, §101(b):

Added the present last sentence of Code Sec. 852(c). **Effective** for tax years of regulated investment companies beginning on or after 3-1-58.

[Sec. 852(d)]

(d) DISTRIBUTIONS IN REDEMPTION OF INTERESTS IN UNIT INVESTMENT TRUSTS.—In the case of a unit investment trust—

(1) which is registered under the Investment Company Act of 1940 (15 U.S.C. 80a-1 and following) and issues periodic payment plan certificates (as defined in such Act), and

(2) substantially all of the assets of which consist of securities issued by a management company (as defined in such Act),

section 562(c) (relating to preferential dividends) shall not apply to a distribution by such trust to a holder of an interest in such trust in redemption of part or all of such interest, with respect to the capital gain net income of such trust attributable to such redemption.

Amendments

• 1976, Tax Reform Act of 1976 (P.L. 94-455)

P.L. 94-455, §1901(a)(110):

Added "(15 U.S.C. 80a-1 and following)" to paragraph (1). **Effective** for tax years beginning after 12-31-76.

P.L. 94-455, §1901(b)(33)(N):

Substituted "capital gain net income" for "net capital gain". **Effective** for tax years beginning after 12-31-76.

• 1964, Revenue Act of 1964 (P.L. 88-272)

P.L. 88-272, §229(b):

Added Code Sec. 852(d). **Effective** for tax years of regulated investment companies ending after 12-31-63.

[Sec. 852(e)]

(e) PROCEDURES SIMILAR TO DEFICIENCY DIVIDEND PROCEDURES MADE APPLICABLE.—

(1) IN GENERAL.—If—

(A) there is a determination that the provisions of this part do not apply to an investment company for any taxable year (hereinafter in this subsection referred to as the "non-RIC year"), and

(B) such investment company meets the distribution requirements of paragraph (2) with respect to the non-RIC year,

for purposes of applying subsection (a)(2) to subsequent taxable years, the provisions of this part shall be treated as applying to such investment company for the non-RIC year. If the determination under subparagraph (A) is solely as a result of the failure to meet the requirements of subsection (a)(2), the preceding sentence shall also apply for purposes of applying subsection (a)(2) to the non-RIC year and the amount referred to in paragraph (2)(A)(i) shall be the portion of the accumulated earnings and profits which resulted in such failure.

(2) DISTRIBUTION REQUIREMENTS.—

(A) IN GENERAL.—The distribution requirements of this paragraph are met with respect to any non-RIC year if, within the 90-day period beginning on the date of the determination (or within such longer period as the Secretary may permit), the investment company makes 1 or more qualified designated distributions and the amount of such distributions is not less than the excess of—

(i) the portion of the accumulated earnings and profits of the investment company (as of the date of the determination) which are attributable to the non-RIC year, over

(ii) any interest payable under paragraph (3).

(B) QUALIFIED DESIGNATED DISTRIBUTION.—For purposes of this paragraph, the term "qualified designated distribution" means any distribution made by the investment company if—

(i) section 301 applies to such distribution, and

(ii) such distribution is designated (at such time and in such manner as the Secretary shall by regulations prescribe) as being taken into account under this paragraph with respect to the non-RIC year.

(C) EFFECT ON DIVIDENDS PAID DEDUCTION.—Any qualified designated distribution shall not be included in the amount of dividends paid for purposes of computing the dividends paid deduction for any taxable year.

(3) INTEREST CHARGE.—

(A) IN GENERAL.—If paragraph (1) applies to any non-RIC year of an investment company, such investment company shall pay interest at the underpayment rate established under section 6621—

(i) on an amount equal to 50 percent of the amount referred to in paragraph (2)(A)(i),

(ii) for the period—

(I) which begins on the last day prescribed for payment of the tax imposed for the non-RIC year (determined without regard to extensions), and

(II) which ends on the date the determination is made.

(B) COORDINATION WITH SUBTITLE F.—Any interest payable under subparagraph (A) may be assessed and collected at any time during the period during which any tax imposed for the taxable year in which the determination is made may be assessed and collected.

(4) PROVISION NOT TO APPLY IN THE CASE OF FRAUD.—The provisions of this subsection shall not apply if the determination contains a finding that the failure to meet any requirement of this part was due to fraud with intent to evade tax.

(5) DETERMINATION.—For purposes of this subsection, the term "determination" has the meaning given to such term by section 860(e). Such term also includes a determination by the investment company filed with the Secretary that the provisions of this part do not apply to the investment company for a taxable year.

Amendments

• 1999, Tax Relief Extension Act of 1999 (P.L. 106-170)

P.L. 106-170, §566(c):

Amended Code Sec. 852(e)(1) by adding at the end a new sentence. **Effective** for distributions after 12-31-2000.

• 1988, Technical and Miscellaneous Revenue Act of 1988 (P.L. 100-647)

P.L. 100-647, §1006(l)(10):

Amended Code Sec. 852(e)(1) by striking out "subsection (a)(3)" and inserting in lieu thereof "subsection (a)(2)". **Effective** as if included in the provision of P.L. 99-514 to which it relates.

P.L. 100-647, §1018(p):

Amended Code Sec. 852(e)(1) by striking out "subsection (a)(3)" and inserting in lieu thereof "subsection (a)(2)". **Effective** as if included in the provision of P.L. 99-514 to which it relates.

• 1986, Tax Reform Act of 1986 (P.L. 99-514)

P.L. 99-514, §1511(c)(6):

Amended Code Sec. 852(e)(3)(A) by striking out "the annual rate established under section 6621" and inserting in lieu thereof "the underpayment rate established under section 6621". **Effective** for purposes of determining interest for periods after 12-31-86.

• 1984, Deficit Reduction Act of 1984 (P.L. 98-369)

P.L. 98-369, §1071(a)(4):

Amended Code Sec. 852 by adding new subsection (e). **Effective** for tax years beginning after 12-31-82. However, see Act Sec. 1071(a)(5)(B)-(D) following Code Sec. 852(a) for special rules.

[Sec. 852(f)]

(f) TREATMENT OF CERTAIN LOAD CHARGES.—

(1) IN GENERAL.—If—

(A) the taxpayer incurs a load charge in acquiring stock in a regulated investment company and, by reason of incurring such charge or making such acquisition, the taxpayer acquires a reinvestment right,

(B) such stock is disposed of before the 91st day after the date on which such stock was acquired, and

(C) the taxpayer subsequently acquires stock in such regulated investment company or in another regulated investment company and the otherwise applicable load charge is reduced by reason of the reinvestment right.

the load charge referred to in subparagraph (A) (to the extent it does not exceed the reduction referred to in subparagraph (C)) shall not be taken into account for purposes of determining the amount of gain or loss on the disposition referred to in subparagraph (B). To the extent such charge is not taken into account in determining the amount of such gain or loss, such charge shall be treated as incurred in connection with the acquisition referred to in subparagraph (C) (including for purposes of reapplying this paragraph).

(2) DEFINITIONS AND SPECIAL RULES.—For purposes of this subsection—

(A) LOAD CHARGE.—The term "load charge" means any sales or similar charge incurred by a person in acquiring stock of a regulated investment company. Such term does not include any charge incurred by reason of the reinvestment of a dividend.

(B) REINVESTMENT RIGHT.—The term "reinvestment right" means any right to acquire stock of 1 or more regulated investment companies without the payment of a load charge or with the payment of a reduced charge.

(C) NONRECOGNITION TRANSACTIONS.—If the taxpayer acquires stock in a regulated investment company from another person in a transaction in which gain or loss is not recognized, the taxpayer shall succeed to the treatment of such other person under this subsection.

Amendments

• 1989, Omnibus Budget Reconciliation Act of 1989 (P.L. 101-239)

P.L. 101-239, §7204(b)(1):

Amended Code Sec. 852 by adding at the end thereof a new subsection (f). **Effective** for charges incurred after 10-3-89, in tax years ending after such date.

[Sec. 853]

SEC. 853. FOREIGN TAX CREDIT ALLOWED TO SHAREHOLDERS.

[Sec. 853(a)]

(a) GENERAL RULE.—A regulated investment company—

(1) more than 50 percent of the value (as defined in section 851(c)(4)) of whose total assets at the close of the taxable year consists of stock or securities in foreign corporations, and

(2) which meets the requirements of section 852(a) for the taxable year,

may, for such taxable year, elect the application of this section with respect to income, war profits, and excess profits taxes described in section 901(b)(1), which are paid by the investment company during such taxable year to foreign countries and possessions of the United States.

[Sec. 853(b)]

(b) EFFECT OF ELECTION.—If the election provided in subsection (a) is effective for a taxable year—

(1) the regulated investment company—

(A) shall not, with respect to such taxable year, be allowed a deduction under section 164(a) or a credit under section 901 for taxes to which subsection (a) is applicable, and

(B) shall be allowed as an addition to the dividends paid deduction for such taxable year the amount of such taxes;

(2) each shareholder of such investment company shall—

(A) include in gross income and treat as paid by him his proportionate share of such taxes, and

(B) treat as gross income from sources within the respective foreign countries and possessions of the United States, for purposes of applying subpart A of part III of subchapter N, the sum of his proportionate share of such taxes and the portion of any dividend paid by such investment company which represents income derived from sources within foreign countries or possessions of the United States.

[Sec. 853(c)]

(c) NOTICE TO SHAREHOLDERS.—The amounts to be treated by the shareholder, for purposes of subsection (b) (2), as his proportionate share of—

(1) taxes paid to any foreign country or possession of the United States, and

(2) gross income derived from sources within any foreign country or possession of the United States,

shall not exceed the amounts so designated by the company in a written notice mailed to its shareholders not later than 60 days after the close of its taxable year.

Amendments

• 1998, IRS Restructuring and Reform Act of 1998 (P.L. 105-206)

P.L. 105-206, §6010(k)(2):

Amended Code Sec. 853(c) by striking the last sentence. **Effective** as if included in the provision of P.L. 105-34 to which it relates [**effective** for dividends paid or accrued after 9-4-97.—CCH]. Prior to being stricken, the last sentence of Code Sec. 853(c) read as follows:

Such notice shall also include the amount of such taxes which (without regard to the election under this section) would not be allowable as a credit under section 901(a) to the regulated investment company by reason of section 901(k).

• 1997, Taxpayer Relief Act of 1997 (P.L. 105-34)

P.L. 105-34, §1053(b):

Amended Code Sec. 853(c) by adding at the end a new sentence. **Effective** for dividends paid or accrued more than 30 days after 8-5-97.

• 1986, Tax Reform Act of 1986 (P.L. 99-514)

P.L. 99-514, §655(a)(3):

Amended Code Sec. 853(c) by striking out "45 days" each place it appears and inserting in lieu thereof "60 days". **Effective** for tax years beginning after 10-22-86.

• 1964, Revenue Act of 1964 (P.L. 88-272)

P.L. 88-272, §229(a):

Amended Code Sec. 853(c) by substituting "45 days" for "30 days". **Effective** 2-26-64.

[Sec. 853(d)]

(d) MANNER OF MAKING ELECTION AND NOTIFYING SHAREHOLDERS.—The election provided in subsection (a) and the notice to shareholders required by subsection (c) shall be made in such manner as the Secretary may prescribe by regulations.

Amendments

• 1976, Tax Reform Act of 1976 (P.L. 94-455)

P.L. 94-455, §1906(b)(13)(A):

Amended 1954 Code by substituting "Secretary" for "Secretary or his delegate" each place it appeared. **Effective** 2-1-77.

[Sec. 853(e)]

(e) TREATMENT OF CERTAIN TAXES NOT ALLOWED AS A CREDIT UNDER SECTION 901.—This section shall not apply to any tax with respect to which the regulated investment company is not allowed a credit under section 901 by reason of subsection (k) or (l) of such section.

Amendments

• 2005, Gulf Opportunity Zone Act of 2005 (P.L. 109-135)

P.L. 109-135, §403(aa)(1):

Amended Code Sec. 853(e). **Effective** as if included in the provision of the American Jobs Creation Act of 2004 (P.L. 108-357) to which it relates [**effective** for amounts paid or accrued more than 30 days after 10-22-2004.—CCH]. Prior to amendment, Code Sec. 853(e) read as follows:

(e) TREATMENT OF TAXES NOT ALLOWED AS A CREDIT UNDER SECTION 901(k).—This section shall not apply to any tax with respect to which the regulated investment company is not allowed a credit under section 901 by reason of section 901(k).

• 1998, IRS Restructuring and Reform Act of 1998 (P.L. 105-206)

P.L. 105-206, §6010(k)(1):

Amended Code Sec. 853 by redesignating subsection (e) as subsection (f) and by inserting after subsection (d) a new subsection (e). **Effective** as if included in the provision of P.L. 105-34 to which it relates [**effective** for dividends paid or accrued after 9-4-97.—CCH].

[Sec. 853(f)]

(f) CROSS REFERENCES.—

(1) For treatment by shareholders of taxes paid to foreign countries and possessions of the United States, see section 164(a) and section 901.

(2) For definition of foreign corporation, see section 7701(a)(5).

Amendments

• 1998, IRS Restructuring and Reform Act of 1998 (P.L. 105-206)

P.L. 105-206, §6010(k)(1):

Amended Code Sec. 853 by redesignating subsection (e) as subsection (f). **Effective** as if included in the provision of P.L. 105-34 to which it relates [**effective** for dividends paid or accrued after 9-4-97.—CCH].

[Sec. 853A]

SEC. 853A. CREDITS FROM TAX CREDIT BONDS ALLOWED TO SHAREHOLDERS.

[Sec. 853A(a)]

(a) GENERAL RULE.—A regulated investment company—

(1) which holds (directly or indirectly) one or more tax credit bonds on one or more applicable dates during the taxable year, and

(2) which meets the requirements of section 852(a) for the taxable year,

may elect the application of this section with respect to credits allowable to the investment company during such taxable year with respect to such bonds.

[Sec. 853A(b)]

(b) EFFECT OF ELECTION.—If the election provided in subsection (a) is in effect for any taxable year—

(1) the regulated investment company shall not be allowed any credits to which subsection (a) applies for such taxable year,

(2) the regulated investment company shall—

(A) include in gross income (as interest) for such taxable year an amount equal to the amount that such investment company would have included in gross income with respect to such credits if this section did not apply, and

(B) increase the amount of the dividends paid deduction for such taxable year by the amount of such income, and

(3) each shareholder of such investment company shall—

(A) include in gross income an amount equal to such shareholder's proportionate share of the interest income attributable to such credits, and

(B) be allowed the shareholder's proportionate share of such credits against the tax imposed by this chapter.

[Sec. 853A(c)]

(c) NOTICE TO SHAREHOLDERS.—For purposes of subsection (b)(3), the shareholder's proportionate share of—

(1) credits described in subsection (a), and

(2) gross income in respect of such credits, shall not exceed the amounts so designated by the regulated investment company in a written notice mailed to its shareholders not later than 60 days after the close of its taxable year.

[Sec. 853A(d)]

(d) MANNER OF MAKING ELECTION AND NOTIFYING SHAREHOLDERS.—The election provided in subsection (a) and the notice to shareholders required by subsection (c) shall be made in such manner as the Secretary may prescribe.

[Sec. 853A(e)]

(e) DEFINITIONS AND SPECIAL RULES.—

(1) DEFINITIONS.—For purposes of this subsection—

(A) TAX CREDIT BOND.—The term "tax credit bond" means—

(i) a qualified tax credit bond (as defined in section 54A(d)),

(ii) a build America bond (as defined in section 54AA(d)), and

(iii) any bond for which a credit is allowable under subpart H of part IV of subchapter A of this chapter.

(B) APPLICABLE DATE.—The term "applicable date" means—

(i) in the case of a qualified tax credit bond or a bond described in subparagraph (A)(iii), any credit allowance date (as defined in section 54A(e)(1)), and

(ii) in the case of a build America bond (as defined in section 54AA(d)), any interest payment date (as defined in section 54AA(e)).

(2) STRIPPED TAX CREDIT BONDS.—If the ownership of a tax credit bond is separated from the credit with respect to such bond, subsection (a) shall be applied by reference to the instruments evidencing the entitlement to the credit rather than the tax credit bond.

[Sec. 853A(f)]

(f) REGULATIONS, ETC.—The Secretary shall prescribe such regulations or other guidance as may be necessary or appropriate to carry out the purposes of this section, including methods for determining a shareholder's proportionate share of credits.

Amendments

• 2009, American Recovery and Reinvestment Tax Act of 2009 (P.L. 111-5)

P.L. 111-5, §1541(a):

Amended part I of subchapter M of chapter 1 by inserting after Code Sec. 853 a new Code Sec. 853A. **Effective** for tax years ending after 2-17-2009.

[Sec. 854]

SEC. 854. LIMITATIONS APPLICABLE TO DIVIDENDS RECEIVED FROM REGULATED INVESTMENT COMPANY.

»»→ Caution: Code Sec. 854(a), below, is subject to the sunset provision of the Jobs and Growth Tax Relief Reconciliation Act of 2003 (P.L. 108-27), §303. Absent Congressional action, the changes made to this provision by P.L. 108-27, or that take effect as if included in P.L. 108-27, do not apply after December 31, 2010. For more information about the sunset provision, see page XXI of the Preface to this publication and P.L. 108-27, §303, in the amendment notes. See the amendments notes for a history of amendments to this section and the effective date of each change.

[Sec. 854(a)]

(a) CAPITAL GAIN DIVIDEND.—For purposes of section 1(h)(11) (relating to maximum rate of tax on dividends) and section 243 (relating to deductions for dividends received by corporations), a capital gain dividend (as defined in section 852(b)(3)) received from a regulated investment company shall not be considered as a dividend.

Amendments

• 2003, Jobs and Growth Tax Relief Reconciliation Act of 2003 (P.L. 108-27)

P.L. 108-27, §302(c)(1):

Amended Code Sec. 854(a) by inserting "section 1(h)(11) (relating to maximum rate of tax on dividends) and" after "For purposes of". For the **effective** date, see Act Sec. 302(f), as amended by P.L. 108-311, §402(a)(6), below.

P.L. 108-27, §302(f), as amended by P.L. 108-311, §402(a)(6), provides:

(f) EFFECTIVE DATE.—

(1) IN GENERAL.—Except as provided in paragraph (2), the amendments made by this section shall apply to taxable years beginning after December 31, 2002.

(2) PASS-THRU ENTITIES.—In the case of a pass-thru entity described in subparagraph (A), (B), (C), (D), (E), or (F) of section 1(h)(10) of the Internal Revenue Code of 1986, as amended by this Act, the amendments made by this section shall apply to taxable years ending after December 31, 2002; except that dividends received by such an entity on or before such date shall not be treated as qualified dividend income (as defined in section 1(h)(11)(B) of such Code, as added by this Act).

P.L. 108-27, §303, as amended by P.L. 109-222, §102, provides:

SEC. 303. SUNSET OF TITLE.

All provisions of, and amendments made by, this title shall not apply to taxable years beginning after December

31, 2010, and the Internal Revenue Code of 1986 shall be applied and administered to such years as if such provisions and amendments had never been enacted.

• **1964, Revenue Act of 1964 (P.L. 88-272)**

P.L. 88-272, §201(d)(8):

Amended Code Sec. 854(a) by deleting "section 34(a) (relating to credit for dividends received by individuals)," and by deleting the comma preceding "and section 243". **Effective** with respect to dividends received after 12-31-64, in tax years ending after such date.

[Sec. 854(b)]

(b) OTHER DIVIDENDS.—

(1) AMOUNT TREATED AS DIVIDEND.—

(A) DEDUCTION UNDER SECTION 243.—In any case in which—

(i) a dividend is received from a regulated investment company (other than a dividend to which subsection (a) applies), and

(ii) such investment company meets the requirements of section 852(a) for the taxable year during which it paid such dividend,

then, in computing any deduction under section 243, there shall be taken into account only that portion of such dividend designated under this subparagraph by the regulated investment company and such dividend shall be treated as received from a corporation which is not a 20-percent owned corporation.

»»→ Caution: Code Sec. 854(b)(1)(B), below, was added by P.L. 108-27 and amended by P.L. 108-311, and is subject to the sunset provision of the Jobs and Growth Tax Relief Reconciliation Act of 2003 (P.L. 108-27), §303. Absent Congressional action, the changes made to this provision by P.L. 108-27, or that take effect as if included in P.L. 108-27, do not apply after December 31, 2010. For more information about the sunset provision, see page XXI of the Preface to this publication and P.L. 108-27, §303, in the amendment notes. See the amendments notes for a history of amendments to this section and the effective date of each change.

(B) MAXIMUM RATE UNDER SECTION 1(H).—

(i) IN GENERAL.—In any case in which—

(I) a dividend is received from a regulated investment company (other than a dividend to which subsection (a) applies),

(II) such investment company meets the requirements of section 852(a) for the taxable year during which it paid such dividend, and

(III) the qualified dividend income of such investment company for such taxable year is less than 95 percent of its gross income,

then, in computing qualified dividend income, there shall be taken into account only that portion of such dividend designated by the regulated investment company.

(ii) GROSS INCOME.—For purposes of clause (i), in the case of 1 or more sales or other dispositions of stock or securities, the term "gross income" includes only the excess of—

(I) the net short-term capital gain from such sales or dispositions, over

(II) the net long-term capital loss from such sales or dispositions.

»»→ Caution: Code Sec. 854(b)(1)(C), below, was redesignated and amended by P.L. 108-27 and further amended by P.L. 108-311, and is subject to the sunset provision of the Jobs and Growth Tax Relief Reconciliation Act of 2003 (P.L. 108-27), §303. Absent Congressional action, the changes made to this provision by P.L. 108-27, or that take effect as if included in P.L. 108-27, do not apply after December 31, 2010. For more information about the sunset provision, see page XXI of the Preface to this publication and P.L. 108-27, §303, in the amendment notes. See the amendments notes for a history of amendments to this section and the effective date of each change.

(C) LIMITATIONS.—

(i) SUBPARAGRAPH (A).—The aggregate amount which may be designated as dividends under subparagraph (A) shall not exceed the aggregate dividends received by the company for the taxable year.

(ii) SUBPARAGRAPH (B).—The aggregate amount which may be designated as qualified dividend income under subparagraph (B) shall not exceed the sum of—

(I) the qualified dividend income of the company for the taxable year, and

(II) the amount of any earnings and profits which were distributed by the company for such taxable year and accumulated in a taxable year with respect to which this part did not apply.

»»→ Caution: Code Sec. 854(b)(2), below, was amended by P.L. 108-27, and P.L. 108-311, and is subject to the sunset provision of the Jobs and Growth Tax Relief Reconciliation Act of 2003 (P.L. 108-27), §303. Absent Congressional action, the changes made to this provision by P.L. 108-27, or that take effect as if included in P.L. 108-27, do not apply after December 31, 2010. For more information about the sunset provision, see page XXI of the Preface to this publication and P.L. 108-27, §303, in the amendment notes. See the amendments notes for a history of amendments to this section and the effective date of each change.

(2) NOTICE TO SHAREHOLDERS.—The amount of any distribution by a regulated investment company which may be taken into account as qualified dividend income for purposes of section

1(h)(11) and as dividends for purposes of the deduction under section 243 shall not exceed the amount so designated by the company in a written notice to its shareholders mailed not later than 60 days after the close of its taxable year.

(3) AGGREGATE DIVIDENDS.—For purposes of this subsection—

(A) IN GENERAL.—In computing the amount of aggregate dividends received, there shall only be taken into account dividends received from domestic corporations.

(B) DIVIDENDS.—For purposes of subparagraph (A), the term "dividend" shall not include any distribution from—

(i) a corporation which, for the taxable year of the corporation in which the distribution is made, or for the next preceding taxable year of the corporation, is a corporation exempt from tax under section 501 (relating to certain charitable, etc., organizations) or section 521 (relating to farmers' cooperative associations), or

(ii) a real estate investment trust which, for the taxable year of the trust in which the dividend is paid, qualifies under part II of subchapter M (section 856 and following).

(C) LIMITATIONS ON DIVIDENDS FROM REGULATED INVESTMENT COMPANIES.—In determining the amount of any dividend for purposes of this paragraph, a dividend received from a regulated investment company shall be subject to the limitations prescribed in this section.

(4) SPECIAL RULE FOR COMPUTING DEDUCTION UNDER SECTION 243.—For purposes of subparagraph (A) of paragraph (1), an amount shall be treated as a dividend for the purpose of paragraph (1) only if a deduction would have been allowable under section 243 to the regulated investment company determined—

(A) as if section 243 applied to dividends received by a regulated investment company,

(B) after the application of section 246 (but without regard to subsection (b) thereof), and

(C) after the application of section 246A.

»»→ Caution: Code Sec. 854(b)(5), below, was added by P.L. 108-27 and amended by P.L. 108-311, and is subject to the sunset provision of the Jobs and Growth Tax Relief Reconciliation Act of 2003 (P.L. 108-27), §303. Absent Congressional action, the changes made to this provision by P.L. 108-27, or that take effect as if included in P.L. 108-27, do not apply after December 31, 2010. For more information about the sunset provision, see page XXI of the Preface to this publication and P.L. 108-27, §303, in the amendment notes. See the amendments notes for a history of amendments to this section and the effective date of each change.

(5) QUALIFIED DIVIDEND INCOME.—For purposes of this subsection, the term "qualified dividend income" has the meaning given such term by section 1(h)(11)(B).

Amendments

• 2004, Working Families Tax Relief Act of 2004 (P.L. 108-311)

P.L. 108-311, §402(a)(5)(A)(i):

Amended Code Sec. 854(b)(1)(B) by striking clauses (iii) and (iv). **Effective** as if included in section 302 of the Jobs and Growth Tax Relief Reconciliation Act of 2003 (P.L. 108-27) [**effective** for tax years ending after 12-31-2002.—CCH]. Prior to being stricken, Code Sec. 854(b)(1)(B)(iii) and (iv) read as follows:

(iii) DIVIDENDS FROM REAL ESTATE INVESTMENT TRUSTS.—For purposes of clause (i)—

(I) paragraph (3)(B)(ii) shall not apply, and

(II) in the case of a distribution from a trust described in such paragraph, the amount of such distribution which is a dividend shall be subject to the limitations under section 857(c).

(iv) DIVIDENDS FROM QUALIFIED FOREIGN CORPORATIONS.—For purposes of clause (i), dividends received from qualified foreign corporations (as defined in section 1(h)(11)) shall also be taken into account in computing aggregate dividends received.

P.L. 108-311, §402(a)(5)(A)(ii):

Amended Code Sec. 854(b)(1)(B)(i). **Effective** as if included in section 302 of the Jobs and Growth Tax Relief Reconciliation Act of 2003 (P.L. 108-27) [**effective** for tax years ending after 12-31-2002.—CCH]. Prior to amendment, Code Sec. 854(b)(1)(B)(i) read as follows:

(i) IN GENERAL.—If the aggregate dividends received by a regulated investment company during any taxable year are less than 95 percent of its gross income, then, in computing the maximum rate under section 1(h)(11), rules similar to the rules of subparagraph (A) shall apply.

P.L. 108-311, §402(a)(5)(B):

Amended Code Sec. 854(b)(1)(C). **Effective** as if included in section 302 of the Jobs and Growth Tax Relief Reconciliation Act of 2003 (P.L. 108-27) [**effective** for tax years ending after 12-31-2002.—CCH]. Prior to amendment, Code Sec. 854(b)(1)(C) read as follows:

(C) LIMITATION.—The aggregate amount which may be designated as dividends under subparagraph (A) or (B) shall not exceed the aggregate dividends received by the company for the taxable year.

P.L. 108-311, §402(a)(5)(C):

Amended Code Sec. 854(b)(2) by striking "as a dividend for purposes of the maximum rate under section 1(h)(11) and" and inserting "as qualified dividend income for purposes of section 1(h)(11) and as dividends for purposes of". **Effective** as if included in section 302 of the Jobs and Growth Tax Relief Reconciliation Act of 2003 (P.L. 108-27) [**effective** for tax years ending after 12-31-2002.—CCH]. For a special rule, see Act. Sec. 402(a)(5)(F), below.

P.L. 108-311, §402(a)(5)(D):

Amended Code Sec. 854(b)(5). **Effective** as if included in section 302 of the Jobs and Growth Tax Relief Reconciliation Act of 2003 (P.L. 108-27) [**effective** for tax years ending after 12-31-2002.—CCH]. Prior to amendment, Code Sec. 854(b)(5) read as follows:

(5) COORDINATION WITH SECTION 1(h)(11).—For purposes of paragraph (1)(B), an amount shall be treated as a dividend only if the amount is qualified dividend income (within the meaning of section 1(h)(11)(B)).

P.L. 108-311, §402(a)(5)(F), provides:

(F) With respect to any taxable year of a regulated investment company or real estate investment trust ending on or before November 30, 2003, the period for providing notice of the qualified dividend amount to shareholders under sections 854(b)(2) and 857(c)(2)(C) of the Internal Revenue Code of 1986, as amended by this section, shall not expire before the date on which the statement under section 6042(c) of such Code is required to be furnished with respect to the last calendar year beginning in such taxable year.

• 2003, Jobs and Growth Tax Relief Reconciliation Act of 2003 (P.L. 108-27)

P.L. 108-27, § 302(c)(2):

Amended Code Sec. 854(b)(1) by redesignating subparagraph (B) as subparagraph (C) and by inserting after subparagraph (A) a new subparagraph (B). For the **effective** date, see Act Sec. 302(f), as amended by P.L. 108-311, § 402(a)(6), below.

P.L. 108-27, § 302(c)(3):

Amended Code Sec. 854(b)(1)(C), as redesignating by Act Sec. 302(c)(2), by striking "subparagraph (A)" and inserting "subparagraph (A) or (B)". For the **effective** date, see Act Sec. 302(f), as amended by P.L. 108-311, § 402(a)(6), below.

P.L. 108-27, § 302(c)(4):

Amended Code Sec. 854(b)(2) by inserting "the maximum rate under section 1(h)(11) and" after "for purposes of". For the **effective** date, see Act Sec. 302(f), as amended by P.L. 108-311, § 402(a)(6), below.

P.L. 108-27, § 302(c)(5):

Amended Code Sec. 854(b) by adding at the end a new paragraph (5). For the **effective** date, see Act Sec. 302(f), as amended by P.L. 108-311, § 402(a)(6), below.

P.L. 108-27, § 302(f), as amended by P.L. 108-311, § 402(a)(6), provides:

(f) EFFECTIVE DATE.—

(1) IN GENERAL.—Except as provided in paragraph (2), the amendments made by this section shall apply to taxable years beginning after December 31, 2002.

(2) PASS-THRU ENTITIES.—In the case of a pass-thru entity described in subparagraph (A), (B), (C), (D), (E), or (F) of section 1(h)(10) of the Internal Revenue Code of 1986, as amended by this Act, the amendments made by this section shall apply to taxable years ending after December 31, 2002; except that dividends received by such an entity on or before such date shall not be treated as qualified dividend income (as defined in section 1(h)(11)(B) of such Code, as added by this Act).

P.L. 108-27, § 303, as amended by P.L. 109-222, § 102, provides:

SEC. 303. SUNSET OF TITLE.

All provisions of, and amendments made by, this title shall not apply to taxable years beginning after December 31, 2010, and the Internal Revenue Code of 1986 shall be applied and administered to such years as if such provisions and amendments had never been enacted.

• 1988, Technical and Miscellaneous Revenue Act of 1988 (P.L. 100-647)

P.L. 100-647, § 1006(b)(2):

Amended Code Sec. 854(b)(3). **Effective** as if included in the provision of P.L. 99-514 to which it relates. Prior to amendment, Code Sec. 854(b)(3) read as follows:

(3) DEFINITIONS.—For purposes of this subsection—

(A) In the case of 1 or more sales or other dispositions of stock and securities, the term "gross income" includes only the excess of—

(i) the net short-term capital gain from such sales or dispositions, over

(ii) the net long-term capital loss from such sales or dispositions.

(B)(i) The term "aggregate dividends received" includes only dividends received from domestic corporations.

(ii) For purposes of clause (i), the term "dividend" shall not include any distribution from—

(I) a corporation which, for the taxable year of the corporation in which the distribution is made, or for the next preceding taxable year of the corporation, is a corporation exempt from tax under section 501 (relating to certain charitable, etc., organizations) or section 521 (relating to farmers' cooperative associations), or

(II) a real estate investment trust which, for the taxable year of the trust in which the dividend is paid, qualifies under part II of subchapter M (section 856 and following).

(iii) In determining the amount of any dividend for purposes of this subparagraph, a dividend received from a regulated investment company shall be subject to the limitations prescribed in this section.

• 1987, Revenue Act of 1987 (P.L. 100-203)

P.L. 100-203, § 10221(d)(3):

Amended Code Sec. 854(b)(1)(A) by inserting "and such dividend shall be treated as received from a corporation which is not a 20-percent owned corporation" before the period at the end thereof. **Effective** for dividends received or accrued after 12-31-87, in tax years ending after such date.

• 1986, Tax Reform Act of 1986 (P.L. 99-514)

P.L. 99-514, § 612(b)(6)(A) and (B)(i)-(iv):

Amended Code Sec. 854(a) by striking out "section 116 (relating to an exclusion for dividends received by individuals), and" following "For purposes of" in subsection (a); and by striking out subparagraph (B) of paragraph (1) and redesignating subparagraph (C) as subparagraph (B), by striking out "or (B)" in subparagraph (B) (as so redesignated), by striking out "the exclusion under section 116 and" following "for purposes of" in paragraph (2), and by amending subparagraph (B) of paragraph (3). **Effective** for tax years beginning after 12-31-86. Prior to amendment, Code Sec. 854(b)(1)(B) read as follows:

(B) EXCLUSION UNDER SECTION 116.—If the aggregate dividends received by a regulated investment company during any taxable year are less than 95 percent of its gross income, then, in computing the exclusion under section 116, rules similar to the rules of subparagraph (A) shall apply.

Prior to amendment, Code Sec. 854(b)(3)(B) read as follows:

(B) The term "aggregate dividends received" includes only dividends received from domestic corporations other than dividends described in section 116(b) (relating to dividends excluded from gross income). In determining the amount of any dividend for purposes of this subparagraph, the rules provided in section 116(c) (relating to certain distributions) shall apply.

P.L. 99-514, § 655(a)(4):

Amended Code Sec. 854(b)(2) by striking out "45 days" each place it appears and inserting in lieu thereof "60 days". **Effective** for tax years beginning after 10-22-86.

• 1984, Deficit Reduction Act of 1984 (P.L. 98-369)

P.L. 98-369, § 16(a):

Amended Code Sec. 854(b) by repealing P.L. 97-34, Act Sec. 302(c)(4), which amended Code Sec. 854(b) to read as shown below. **Effective** as if § 302(c)(4) of P.L. 97-34 had not been enacted.

(b) Other Dividends and Taxable Interest.—

(1) Deduction Under Section 243.—In the case of a dividend received from a regulated investment company (other than a dividend to which subsection (a) applies)—

(A) if such investment company meets the requirements of section 852(a) for the taxable year during which it paid such dividend; and

(B) the aggregate dividends received by such company during such taxable year are less than 75 percent of its gross income,

then, in computing the deduction under section 243, there shall be taken into account only that portion of the dividend which bears the same ratio to the amount of such dividend as the aggregate dividends received by such company during such taxable year bear to its gross income for such taxable year.

(2) Exclusion under Sections 116 and 128.—For purposes of sections 116 and 128, in the case of any dividend (other than a dividend described in subsection (a)) received from a regulated investment company which meets the requirements of section 852 for the taxable year in which it paid the dividend—

(A) the entire amount of such dividend shall be treated as a dividend if the aggregate dividends received by such company during the taxable year equal or exceed 75 percent of its gross income,

(B) the entire amount of such dividend shall be treated as interest if the aggregate interest received by such company during the taxable year equals or exceeds 75 percent of its gross income, or

(C) if subparagraphs (A) and (B) do not apply, a portion of such dividend shall be treated as a dividend (and a portion of such dividend shall be treated as interest) based on the portion of the company's gross income which consists of aggregate dividends or aggregate interest, as the case may be. For purposes of the preceding sentence, gross income and aggregate interest received shall each be reduced by so much of the deduction allowable by section 163 for the taxable year as does not exceed aggregate interest received for the taxable year.

(3) Notice to Shareholders.—The amount of any distribution by a regulated investment company which may be taken into account as a dividend for purposes of the exclusion under section 116 and the deduction under section 243 or as interest for purposes of section 128 shall not exceed the amount so designated by the company in a written notice to its shareholders mailed not later than 45 days after the close of its taxable year.

(4) Definitions.—For purposes of this subsection—

(A) The term "gross income" does not include gain from the sale or other disposition of stock or securities.

(B) The term "aggregate dividends received" includes only dividends received from domestic corporations other than dividends described in section 116(b)(2) (relating to dividends excluded from gross income). In determining the amount of any dividend for purposes of this subparagraph, the rules provided in section 116(c)(2) (relating to certain distributions) shall apply.

(C) The term "aggregate interest received" includes only interest described in section 128(c)(1).

P.L. 98-369, §52(a):

Amended Code Sec. 854(b)(1). **Effective** for tax years of regulated investment companies beginning after 7-18-84. Prior to amendment Code Sec. 854(b)(1) read as follows:

(1) General Rule.—In the case of a dividend received from a regulated investment company (other than a dividend to which subsection (a) applies)—

(A) if such investment company meets the requirements of section 852(a) for the taxable year during which it paid such dividend; and

(B) the aggregate dividends received by such company during such taxable year are less than 75 percent of its gross income,

then, in computing the exclusion under section 116, and the deduction under section 243, there shall be taken into account only that portion of the dividend which bears the same ratio to the amount of such dividend as the aggregate dividends received by such company during such taxable year bear to its gross income for such taxable year.

P.L. 98-369, §52(b):

Amended Code Sec. 854(b) by adding paragraph (4). **Effective** for tax years of regulated investment companies beginning after 7-18-84.

P.L. 98-369, §52(c):

Amended Code Sec. 854(b)(3)(A). **Effective** for tax years of regulated investment companies beginning after 7-18-84. Prior to amendment, Act Sec. 854(b)(3)(A) read as follows:

(A) The term "gross income" does not include gain from the sale or other disposition of stock or securities.

• 1981, Economic Recovery Tax Act of 1981 (P.L. 97-34)

P.L. 97-34, §302(c)(4) (repealed by P.L. 98-369, §16(a)):

Amended Code Sec. 854(b). **Effective** for tax years beginning after 12-31-84. Prior to amendment, Code Sec. 854(b) read as follows:

(b) Other Dividends and Taxable Interest.—

(1) Deduction under section 243.—In the case of a dividend received from a regulated investment company (other than a dividend to which subsection (a) applies)—

(A) if such investment company meets the requirements of section 852(a) for the taxable year during which it paid such dividend; and

(B) the aggregate dividends received by such company during such taxable year are less than 75 percent of its gross income,

then, in computing the deduction under section 243, there shall be taken into account only that portion of the dividend which bears the same ratio to the amount of such dividend as the aggregate dividends received by such company during such taxable year bear to its gross income for such taxable year.

(2) Exclusion under section 116.—In the case of a dividend (other than a dividend described in subsection (a)) received from a regulated investment company—

(A) which meets the requirements of section 852(a) for the taxable year in which it paid the dividend,

(B) the aggregate interest received by which during the taxable year is less than 75 percent of its gross income, and

(C) the aggregate dividends received by which during the taxable year is less than 75 percent of its gross income,

then, in computing the exclusion under section 116, there shall be taken into account only that portion of the dividend which bears the same ratio to the amount of such dividend as the sum of the aggregate dividends received and aggregate interest received bears to gross income. For purposes of the preceding sentence, gross income and aggregate interest received shall each be reduced by so much of the deduction allowable by section 163 for the taxable year as does not exceed aggregate interest received for the taxable year.

(3) Notice to shareholders.—The amount of any distribution by a regulated investment company which may be taken into account as a dividend for purposes of the exclusion under section 116, and the deduction under section 243 shall not exceed the amount so designated by the company in a written notice to its shareholders mailed not later than 45 days after the close of its taxable year.

(4) Definitions.—For purposes of this subsection—

(A) The term "gross income" does not include gain from the sale or other disposition of stock or securities.

(B) The term "aggregate dividends received" includes only dividends received from domestic corporations other than dividends described in section 116(b)(2) (relating to dividends excluded from gross income). In determining the amount of any dividend for purposes of this subparagraph, the rules provided in section 116(c)(2) (relating to certain distributions) shall apply.

(C) The term "aggregate interest received" includes only interest described in section 116(c)(1).

• 1980, Crude Oil Windfall Profit Tax of 1980 (P.L. 96-223)

P.L. 96-223, §404(b)(6):

Amended Code Sec. 854(b). **Effective** for tax years beginning after 12-31-80 and before 1-1-83. (P.L. 97-34, §302(b)(1), amended Act Sec. 404(c) of the Crude Oil Windfall Profit Tax Act of 1980 by striking out "1983" and inserting "1982".)

• 1964, Revenue Act of 1964 (P.L. 88-272)

P.L. 88-272, §201(d)(9), (10):

Amended Code Sec. 854(b)(1) and (2) by deleting "the credit under section 34 (a)." and by deleting the comma following "section 116". **Effective** with respect to dividends received after 12-31-64, in tax years ending after such date.

P.L. 88-272, §229(a):

Amended Code Sec. 854(b)(2) by substituting "45 days" for "30 days". **Effective** 2-26-64.

[Sec. 855]

SEC. 855. DIVIDENDS PAID BY REGULATED INVESTMENT COMPANY AFTER CLOSE OF TAXABLE YEAR.

[Sec. 855(a)]

(a) General Rule.—For purposes of this chapter, if a regulated investment company—

(1) declares a dividend prior to the time prescribed by law for the filing of its return for a taxable year (including the period of any extension of time granted for filing such return), and

(2) distributes the amount of such dividend to shareholders in the 12-month period following the close of such taxable year and not later than the date of the first regular dividend payment made after such declaration,

the amount so declared and distributed shall, to the extent the company elects in such return in accordance with regulations prescribed by the Secretary, be considered as having been paid during such taxable year, except as provided in subsections (b), (c) and (d).

Amendments

• 1976, Tax Reform Act of 1976 (P.L. 94-455)

P.L. 94-455, §1906(b)(13)(A):

Amended 1954 Code by substituting "Secretary" for "Secretary or his delegate" each place it appeared. **Effective** 2-1-77.

[Sec. 855(b)]

(b) RECEIPT BY SHAREHOLDER.—Except as provided in section 852(b)(7), amounts to which subsection (a) is applicable shall be treated as received by the shareholder in the taxable year in which the distribution is made.

Amendments

• 1988, Technical and Miscellaneous Revenue Act of 1988 (P.L. 100-647)

P.L. 100-647, §1006(l)(1)(B):

Amended Code Sec. 855(b) by striking out "section 852(b)(6)" and inserting in lieu thereof "section 852(b)(7)". **Effective** as if included in the provision of P.L. 99-514 to which it relates.

• 1986, Tax Reform Act of 1986 (P.L. 99-514)

P.L. 99-514, §651(b)(1)(B):

Amended Code Sec. 855(b) by striking out "Amounts" and inserting in lieu thereof "Except as provided in section 852(b)(6), amounts". **Effective** for calendar years beginning after 12-31-86.

[Sec. 855(c)]

(c) NOTICE TO SHAREHOLDERS.—In the case of amounts to which subsection (a) is applicable, any notice to shareholders required under this part with respect to such amounts shall be made not later than 60 days after the close of the taxable year in which the distribution is made.

Amendments

• 1986, Tax Reform Act of 1986 (P.L. 99-514)

P.L. 99-514, §655(a)(5):

Amended Code Sec. 855(c) by striking out "45 days" each place it appears and inserting in lieu thereof "60 days". **Effective** for tax years beginning after 10-22-86.

• 1964, Revenue Act of 1964 (P.L. 88-272)

P.L. 88-272, §229(a):

Amended Code Sec. 855(c) by substituting "45 days" for "30 days". **Effective** 2-26-64.

• 1960 (P.L. 86-779)

P.L. 86-779, §10(b):

Struck out "this subchapter" in Code Sec. 855(c), and substituted "this part". **Effective** 1-1-61.

[Sec. 855(d)]

(d) FOREIGN TAX ELECTION.—If an investment company to which section 853 is applicable for the taxable year makes a distribution as provided in subsection (a) of this section, the shareholders shall consider the amounts described in section 853(b)(2) allocable to such distribution as paid or received, as the case may be, in the taxable year in which the distribution is made.

PART II—REAL ESTATE INVESTMENT TRUSTS

[Sec. 856]

SEC. 856. DEFINITION OF REAL ESTATE INVESTMENT TRUST.

[Sec. 856(a)]

(a) IN GENERAL.—For purposes of this title, the term "real estate investment trust" means a corporation, trust or association—

(1) which is managed by one or more trustees or directors;

(2) the beneficial ownership of which is evidenced by transferable shares, or by transferable certificates of beneficial interest;

(3) which (but for the provisions of this part) would be taxable as a domestic corporation;

(4) which is neither (A) a financial institution referred to in section 582(c)(2), nor (B) an insurance company to which subchapter L applies;

(5) the beneficial ownership of which is held by 100 or more persons;

(6) subject to the provisions of subsection (k), which is not closely held (as determined under subsection (h)); and

(7) which meets the requirements of subsection (c).

Amendments

• 1997, Taxpayer Relief Act of 1997 (P.L. 105-34)

P.L. 105-34, §1251(b)(2):

Amended Code Sec. 856(a)(6) by inserting "subject to the provisions of subsection (k)," before "which is not". **Effective** for tax years beginning after 8-5-97.

• 1996, Small Business Job Protection Act of 1996 (P.L. 104-188)

P.L. 104-188, §1704(t)(35):

Amended Code Sec. 856(a)(4) by striking "section 582(c)(5)" and inserting "section 582(c)(2)". **Effective** 8-20-96.

• 1986, Tax Reform Act of 1986 (P.L. 99-514)

P.L. 99-514, §661(a)(1):

Amended Code Sec. 856(a)(6). **Effective** for tax years beginning after 12-31-86. Prior to amendment, Code Sec. 856(a)(6) read as follows:

(6) which would not be a personal holding company (as defined in section 542) if all of its adjusted ordinary gross income (as defined in section 543(b)(2)) constituted personal holding company income (as defined in section 543); and

P.L. 99-514, §901(d)(4)(E):

Amended Code Sec. 856(a)(4) by striking out "to which section 585, 586, or 593 applies" and inserting in lieu thereof "referred to in section 582(c)(5)". **Effective** for tax years beginning after 12-31-86.

• 1976, Tax Reform Act of 1976 (P.L. 94-455)

P.L. 94-455, §1603(a):

Repealed paragraph (4). **Effective** as provided in §1608(d), below. Prior to repeal, Code Sec. 856(a)(4) read as follows:

(4) which does not hold any property (other than foreclosure property, as defined in subsection (3)) primarily for sale to customers in the ordinary course of its trade or business;

P.L. 94-455, §1604(f)(1):

Amended so much of Code Sec. 856(a) as precedes paragraph (3). **Effective** as provided in §1608(d), below. Prior to amendment, Code Sec. 856(a)(1) and (2) read as follows:

(a) IN GENERAL.—For purposes of this subtitle, the term "real estate investment trust" means an unincorporated trust or an unincorporated association—

(1) which is managed by one or more trustees;

(2) the beneficial ownership of which is evidenced by transferable shares, or by transferable certificates of beneficial interest;

P.L. 94-455, §1604(f)(2):

Added a new paragraph (4). **Effective** 10-4-76.

P.L. 94-455, §1608(d), provides:

(d) OTHER AMENDMENTS.—

(1) Except as provided in paragraphs (2) and (3), the amendments made by sections 1603, 1604, and 1605 shall apply to taxable years of real estate investment trusts beginning after the date of the enactment of this Act.

(2) If, as a result of a determination (as defined in section 859(c) of the Internal Revenue Code of 1954), occurring after the date of enactment of this Act, with respect to the real estate investment trust, such trust does not meet the requirement of section 856(a)(4) of the Internal Revenue Code of 1954 (as in effect before the amendment of such section by this Act) for any taxable year beginning on or before the date of the enactment of this Act, such trust may elect, within 60 days after such determination in the manner provided in regulations prescribed by the Secretary of the Treasury or his delegate, to have the provisions of section 1603 (other than paragraphs (1), (2), (3), and (4) of section 1603(c)) apply with respect to such taxable year. Where the provisions of section 1603 apply to a real estate investment trust with respect to any taxable year beginning on or before the date of the enactment of this Act—

(A) credit or refund of any overpayment of tax which results from the application of section 1603 to such taxable year shall be made as if on the date of the determination (as defined in section 859(c) of the Internal Revenue Code of 1954) 2 years remained before the expiration of the period of limitation prescribed by section 6511 of such Code on the filing of claim for refund for the taxable year to which the overpayment relates.

(B) the running of the statute of limitations provided in section 6501 of such Code on the making of assessments, and the bringing of distraint or a proceeding in court for collection, in respect of any deficiency (as defined in section 6211 of such Code) established by such a determination, and all interest, additions to tax, additional amounts, or assessable penalties in respect thereof, shall be suspended for a period of 2 years after the date of such determination, and

(C) the collection of any deficiency (as defined in section 6211 of such Code) established by such determination and all interest, additions to tax, additional amounts, and assessable penalties in respect thereof shall, except in cases of jeopardy, be stayed until the expiration of 60 days after the date of such determination.

No distraint or proceeding in court shall be begun for the collection of an amount the collection of which is stayed under subparagraph (C) during the period for which the collection of such amount is stayed.

(3) Section 856(g)(3) of the Internal Revenue Code of 1954, as added by section 1604 of this Act, shall not apply with respect to a termination of an election, filed by a taxpayer under section 856(c)(1) of such Code on or before the date of the enactment of this Act, unless the provisions of part II of subchapter M of chapter 1 of subtitle A of such Code apply to such taxpayer for a taxable year ending after the date of the enactment of this Act for which such election is in effect.

• 1975 (P.L. 93-625)

P.L. 93-625, §6(b):

Amended Code Sec. 856(a)(4) by adding "(other than foreclosure property, as defined in subsection (e))". For the **effective** date, see the historical comment for P.L. 93-625 following the text of Code Sec. 856(e).

• 1964, Revenue Act of 1964 (P.L. 88-272)

P.L. 88-272, §225(k)(4):

Amended Code Sec. 856(a)(6) by deleting "gross income" and inserting in lieu thereof "adjusted ordinary gross income (as defined in section 543(b)(2))". **Effective** for tax years beginning after 12-31-63.

[Sec. 856(b)]

(b) DETERMINATION OF STATUS.—The conditions described in paragraphs (1) to (4), inclusive, of subsection (a) must be met during the entire taxable year, and the condition described in paragraph (5) must exist during at least 335 days of a taxable year of 12 months, or during a proportionate part of a taxable year of less than 12 months.

[Sec. 856(c)]

(c) LIMITATIONS.—A corporation, trust, or association shall not be considered a real estate investment trust for any taxable year unless—

(1) it files with its return for the taxable year an election to be a real estate investment trust or has made such election for a previous taxable year, and such election has not been terminated or revoked under subsection (g):

(2) at least 95 percent (90 percent for taxable years beginning before January 1, 1980) of its gross income (excluding gross income from prohibited transactions) is derived from—

(A) dividends;

(B) interest;

(C) rents from real property;

(D) gain from the sale or other disposition of stock, securities, and real property (including interests in real property and interests in mortgages on real property) which is not property described in section 1221(a)(1);

(E) abatements and refunds of taxes on real property;

(F) income and gain derived from foreclosure property (as defined in subsection (e));

(G) amounts (other than amounts the determination of which depends in whole or in part on the income or profits of any person) received or accrued as consideration for entering into agreements (i) to make loans secured by mortgages on real property or on interests in real property or (ii) to purchase or lease real property (including interests in real property and interests in mortgages on real property);

(H) gain from the sale or other disposition of a real estate asset which is not a prohibited transaction solely by reason of section 857(b)(6); and

(I) mineral royalty income earned in the first taxable year beginning after the date of the enactment of this subparagraph from real property owned by a timber real estate investment trust and held, or once held, in connection with the trade or business of producing timber by such real estate investment trust;

(3) at least 75 percent of its gross income (excluding gross income from prohibited transactions) is derived from—

(A) rents from real property;

(B) interest on obligations secured by mortgages on real property or on interests in real property;

(C) gain from the sale or other disposition of real property (including interests in real property and interests in mortgages on real property) which is not property described in section 1221(a)(1);

(D) dividends or other distributions on, and gain (other than gain from prohibited transactions) from the sale or other disposition of, transferable shares (or transferable certificates of beneficial interest) in other real estate investment trusts which meet the requirements of this part;

(E) abatements and refunds of taxes on real property;

(F) income and gain derived from foreclosure property (as defined in subsection (e));

(G) amounts (other than amounts the determination of which depends in whole or in part on the income or profits of any person) received or accrued as consideration for entering into agreements (i) to make loans secured by mortgages on real property or on interests in real property or (ii) to purchase or lease real property (including interests in real property and interests in mortgages on real property);

(H) gain from the sale or other disposition of a real estate asset which is not a prohibited transaction solely by reason of section 857(b)(6); and

(I) qualified temporary investment income; and

(4) at the close of each quarter of the taxable year—

(A) at least 75 percent of the value of its total assets is represented by real estate assets, cash and cash items (including receivables), and Government securities; and

(B)(i) not more than 25 percent of the value of its total assets is represented by securities (other than those includible under subparagraph (A)),

(ii) not more than 25 percent of the value of its total assets is represented by securities of one or more taxable REIT subsidiaries,

(iii) except with respect to a taxable REIT subsidiary and securities includible under subparagraph (A)—

(I) not more than 5 percent of the value of its total assets is represented by securities of any one issuer,

(II) the trust does not hold securities possessing more than 10 percent of the total voting power of the outstanding securities of any one issuer, and

(III) the trust does not hold securities having a value of more than 10 percent of the total value of the outstanding securities of any one issuer.

A real estate investment trust which meets the requirements of this paragraph at the close of any quarter shall not lose its status as a real estate investment trust because of a discrepancy during a subsequent quarter between the value of its various investments and such requirements (including a discrepancy caused solely by the change in the foreign currency exchange rate used to value a foreign asset) unless such discrepancy exists immediately after the acquisition of any security or other property and is wholly or partly the result of such acquisition. A real estate investment trust which does not meet such requirements (including a discrepancy caused solely by the change in the foreign currency exchange rate used to value a foreign asset) at the close of any quarter by reason of a discrepancy existing immediately after the acquisition of any security or other property which is wholly or partly the result of such acquisition during such quarter shall not lose its status for such quarter as a real estate investment trust if such discrepancy is eliminated within 30 days after the close of such quarter and in such cases it shall be considered to have met such requirements at the close of such quarter for purposes of applying the preceding sentence.

(5) For purposes of this part—

(A) The term "value" means, with respect to securities for which market quotations are readily available, the market value of such securities; and with respect to other securities and assets, fair value as determined in good faith by the trustees, except that in the case of securities of real estate investment trusts such fair value shall not exceed market value or asset value, whichever is higher.

(B) The term "real estate assets" means real property (including interests in real property and interests in mortgages on real property) and shares (or transferable certificates of beneficial interest) in other real estate investment trusts which meet the requirements of this part. Such term also includes any property (not otherwise a real estate asset) attributable to the temporary investment of new capital, but only if such property is stock or a debt instrument, and only for the 1-year period beginning on the date the real estate trust receives such capital.

(C) The term "interests in real property" includes fee ownership and co-ownership of land or improvements thereon, leaseholds of land or improvements thereon, options to acquire land or improvements thereon, and options to acquire leaseholds of land or improvements thereon, but does not include mineral, oil, or gas royalty interests.

(D) QUALIFIED TEMPORARY INVESTMENT INCOME.—

(i) IN GENERAL.—The term "qualified temporary investment income" means any income which—

(I) is attributable to stock or a debt instrument (within the meaning of section 1275(a)(1)),

(II) is attributable to the temporary investment of new capital, and

(III) is received or accrued during the 1-year period beginning on the date on which the real estate investment trust receives such capital.

(ii) NEW CAPITAL.—The term "new capital" means any amount received by the real estate investment trust—

(I) in exchange for stock (or certificates of beneficial interests) in such trust (other than amounts received pursuant to a dividend reinvestment plan), or

(II) in a public offering of debt obligations of such trust which have maturities of at least 5 years.

(E) A regular or residual interest in a REMIC shall be treated as a real estate asset, and any amount includible in gross income with respect to such an interest shall be treated as interest on an obligation secured by a mortgage on real property; except that, if less than 95 percent of the assets of such REMIC are real estate assets (determined as if the real estate investment trust held such assets), such real estate investment trust shall be treated as holding directly (and as receiving directly) its proportionate share of the assets and income of the REMIC. For purposes of determining whether any interest in a REMIC qualifies under the preceding sentence, any interest held by such REMIC in another REMIC shall be treated as a real estate asset under principles similar to the principles of the preceding sentence, except that, if such REMIC's are part of a tiered structure, they shall be treated as one REMIC for purposes of this subparagraph.

(F) All other terms shall have the same meaning as when used in the Investment Company Act of 1940, as amended (15 U.S.C. 80a-1 and following).

(G) TREATMENT OF CERTAIN HEDGING INSTRUMENTS.—Except to the extent as determined by the Secretary—

(i) any income of a real estate investment trust from a hedging transaction (as defined in clause (ii) or (iii) of section 1221(b)(2)(A)) which is clearly identified pursuant to section 1221(a)(7), including gain from the sale or disposition of such a transaction, shall not constitute gross income under paragraphs (2) and (3) to the extent that the transaction hedges any indebtedness incurred or to be incurred by the trust to acquire or carry real estate assets, and

(ii) any income of a real estate investment trust from a transaction entered into by the trust primarily to manage risk of currency fluctuations with respect to any item of income or gain described in paragraph (2) or (3) (or any property which generates such income or gain), including gain from the termination of such a transaction, shall not constitute gross income under paragraphs (2) and (3), but only if such transaction is clearly identified as such before the close of the day on which it was acquired, originated, or entered into (or such other time as the Secretary may prescribe).

(H) TREATMENT OF TIMBER GAINS.—

(i) IN GENERAL.—Gain from the sale of real property described in paragraph (2)(D) and (3)(C) shall include gain which is—

(I) recognized by an election under section 631(a) from timber owned by the real estate investment trust, the cutting of which is provided by a taxable REIT subsidiary of the real estate investment trust;

(II) recognized under section 631(b); or

(III) income which would constitute gain under subclause (I) or (II) but for the failure to meet the 1-year holding period requirement.

(ii) SPECIAL RULES.—

(I) For purposes of this subtitle, cut timber, the gain from which is recognized by a real estate investment trust pursuant to an election under section 631(a) described in clause (i)(I) or so much of clause (i)(III) as relates to clause (i)(I), shall be deemed to be sold to the taxable REIT subsidiary of the real estate investment trust on the first day of the taxable year.

(II) For purposes of this subtitle, income described in this subparagraph shall not be treated as gain from the sale of property described in section 1221(a)(1).

(iii) TERMINATION.—This subparagraph shall not apply to dispositions after the termination date.

(I) TIMBER REAL ESTATE INVESTMENT TRUST.—The term "timber real estate investment trust" means a real estate investment trust in which more than 50 percent in value of its total assets consists of real property held in connection with the trade or business of producing timber.

(J) SECRETARIAL AUTHORITY TO EXCLUDE OTHER ITEMS OF INCOME.—To the extent necessary to carry out the purposes of this part, the Secretary is authorized to determine, solely for purposes of this part, whether any item of income or gain which—

(i) does not otherwise qualify under paragraph (2) or (3) may be considered as not constituting gross income for purposes of paragraphs (2) or (3), or

(ii) otherwise constitutes gross income not qualifying under paragraph (2) or (3) may be considered as gross income which qualifies under paragraph (2) or (3).

(K) CASH.—If the real estate investment trust or its qualified business unit (as defined in section 989) uses any foreign currency as its functional currency (as defined in section 985(b)), the term "cash" includes such foreign currency but only to the extent such foreign currency—

(i) is held for use in the normal course of the activities of the trust or qualified business unit which give rise to items of income or gain described in paragraph (2) or (3) of subsection (c) or are directly related to acquiring or holding assets described in subsection (c)(4), and

(ii) is not held in connection with an activity described in subsection (n)(4).

(6) A corporation, trust, or association which fails to meet the requirements of paragraph (2) or (3), or of both such paragraphs, for any taxable year shall nevertheless be considered to have satisfied the requirements of such paragraphs for such taxable year if—

(A) following the corporation, trust, or association's identification of the failure to meet the requirements of paragraph (2) or (3), or of both such paragraphs, for any taxable year, a description of each item of its gross income described in such paragraphs is set forth in a schedule for such taxable year filed in accordance with regulations prescribed by the Secretary, and

(B) the failure to meet the requirements of paragraph (2) or (3), or of both such paragraphs, is due to reasonable cause and not due to willful neglect.

(7) RULES OF APPLICATION FOR FAILURE TO SATISFY PARAGRAPH (4).—

(A) IN GENERAL.—A corporation, trust, or association that fails to meet the requirements of paragraph (4) (other than a failure to meet the requirements of paragraph (4)(B)(iii) which is described in subparagraph (B)(i) of this paragraph) for a particular quarter shall nevertheless be considered to have satisfied the requirements of such paragraph for such quarter if—

(i) following the corporation, trust, or association's identification of the failure to satisfy the requirements of such paragraph for a particular quarter, a description of each asset that causes the corporation, trust, or association to fail to satisfy the requirements of such paragraph at the close of such quarter of any taxable year is set forth in a schedule for such quarter filed in accordance with regulations prescribed by the Secretary,

(ii) the failure to meet the requirements of such paragraph for a particular quarter is due to reasonable cause and not due to willful neglect, and

(iii)(I) the corporation, trust, or association disposes of the assets set forth on the schedule specified in clause (i) within 6 months after the last day of the quarter in which the corporation, trust or association's identification of the failure to satisfy the requirements of such paragraph occurred or such other time period prescribed by the Secretary and in the manner prescribed by the Secretary, or

(II) the requirements of such paragraph are otherwise met within the time period specified in subclause (I).

(B) RULE FOR CERTAIN DE MINIMIS FAILURES.—A corporation, trust, or association that fails to meet the requirements of paragraph (4)(B)(iii) for a particular quarter shall nevertheless be considered to have satisfied the requirements of such paragraph for such quarter if—

(i) such failure is due to the ownership of assets the total value of which does not exceed the lesser of—

(I) 1 percent of the total value of the trust's assets at the end of the quarter for which such measurement is done, and

(II) $10,000,000, and

(ii)(I) the corporation, trust, or association, following the identification of such failure, disposes of assets in order to meet the requirements of such paragraph within 6 months after the last day of the quarter in which the corporation, trust or association's identification of the failure to satisfy the requirements of such paragraph occurred or such other time period prescribed by the Secretary and in the manner prescribed by the Secretary, or

(II) the requirements of such paragraph are otherwise met within the time period specified in subclause (I).

(C) TAX.—

(i) TAX IMPOSED.—If subparagraph (A) applies to a corporation, trust, or association for any taxable year, there is hereby imposed on such corporation, trust, or association a tax in an amount equal to the greater of—

(I) $50,000, or

(II) the amount determined (pursuant to regulations promulgated by the Secretary) by multiplying the net income generated by the assets described in the schedule specified in subparagraph (A)(i) for the period specified in clause (ii) by the highest rate of tax specified in section 11.

(ii) PERIOD.—For purposes of clause (i)(II), the period described in this clause is the period beginning on the first date that the failure to satisfy the requirements of such paragraph (4) occurs as a result of the ownership of such assets and ending on the earlier of the date on which the trust disposes of such assets or the end of the first quarter when there is no longer a failure to satisfy such paragraph (4).

(iii) ADMINISTRATIVE PROVISIONS.—For purposes of subtitle F, the taxes imposed by this subparagraph shall be treated as excise taxes with respect to which the deficiency procedures of such subtitle apply.

(8) TERMINATION DATE.—For purposes of this subsection, the term "termination date" means, with respect to any taxpayer, the last day of the taxpayer's first taxable year beginning after the date of the enactment of this paragraph and before the date that is 1 year after such date of enactment.

Amendments

• 2008, Housing Assistance Tax Act of 2008 (P.L. 110-289)

P.L. 110-289, §3031(b):

Amended Code Sec. 856(c)(5)(G). **Effective** for transactions entered into after 7-30-2008. Prior to amendment, Code Sec. 856(c)(5)(G) read as follows:

(G) TREATMENT OF CERTAIN HEDGING INSTRUMENTS.—Except to the extent provided by regulations, any income of a real estate investment trust from a hedging transaction (as defined in clause (ii) or (iii) of section 1221(b)(2)(A)) which is clearly identified pursuant to section 1221(a)(7), including gain from the sale or disposition of such a transaction, shall not constitute gross income under paragraph (2) to the extent that the transaction hedges any indebtedness incurred or to be incurred by the trust to acquire or carry real estate assets.

P.L. 110-289, §3031(c):

Amended Code Sec. 856(c)(5) by adding at the end a new subparagraph (J). **Effective** for tax years beginning after 7-30-2008.

P.L. 110-289, §3032(a):

Amended the first sentence in the matter following Code Sec. 856(c)(4)(B)(iii)(III) by inserting "(including a discrepancy caused solely by the change in the foreign currency exchange rate used to value a foreign asset)" after "such requirements". **Effective** for tax years beginning after 7-30-2008.

P.L. 110-289, §3032(b):

Amended Code Sec. 856(c)(5), as amended by Act Sec. 3031(c), by adding at the end a new subparagraph (K). **Effective** for tax years beginning after 7-30-2008.

P.L. 110-289, §3041(1)-(2):

Amended Code Sec. 856(c)(4)(B)(ii) by striking "20 percent" and inserting "25 percent", and by striking "REIT subsidiaries" and all that follows and inserting "REIT subsidiaries,". **Effective** for tax years beginning after 7-30-2008. Prior to amendment, Code Sec. 856(c)(4)(B)(ii) read as follows:

(ii) not more than 20 percent of the value of its total assets is represented by securities of one or more taxable REIT subsidiaries (in the case of a quarter which closes on or before the termination date, 25 percent in the case of a timber real estate investment trust), and

• 2008, Heartland, Habitat, Harvest, and Horticulture Act of 2008 (P.L. 110-246)

P.L. 110-246, §15312(a):

Amended Code Sec. 856(c)(5) by adding after subparagraph (G) a new subparagraph (H). **Effective** for dispositions in tax years beginning after 5-22-2008.

P.L. 110-246, §15312(b):

Amended Code Sec. 856(c) by adding at the end a new paragraph (8). **Effective** 5-22-2008.

P.L. 110-246, §15313(a):

Amended Code Sec. 856(c)(2) by striking "and" at the end of subparagraph (G), by inserting "and" at the end of subparagraph (H), and by adding after subparagraph (H) a new subparagraph (I). **Effective** for tax years beginning after 5-22-2008.

P.L. 110-246, §15313(b):

Amended Code Sec. 856(c)(5), as amended by this Act, by adding after subparagraph (H) a new subparagraph (I). **Effective** for tax years beginning after 5-22-2008.

P.L. 110-246, §15314(a):

Amended Code Sec. 856(c)(4)(B)(ii) by inserting "(in the case of a quarter which closes on or before the termination date, 25 percent in the case of a timber real estate investment trust)" after "REIT subsidiaries". **Effective** for tax years beginning after 5-22-2008.

• 2005, Gulf Opportunity Zone Act of 2005 (P.L. 109-135)

P.L. 109-135, §403(d)(1):

Amended Code Sec. 856(c)(7). **Effective** as if included in the provision of the American Jobs Creation Act of 2004 (P.L. 108-357) to which it relates [**effective** for tax years beginning after 12-31-2000.—CCH]. Prior to amendment, Code Sec. 856(c)(7) read as follows:

(7) RULES OF APPLICATION FOR FAILURE TO SATISFY PARAGRAPH (4).—

(A) DE MINIMIS FAILURE.—A corporation, trust, or association that fails to meet the requirements of paragraph (4)(B)(iii) for a particular quarter shall nevertheless be considered to have satisfied the requirements of such paragraph for such quarter if—

(i) such failure is due to the ownership of assets the total value of which does not exceed the lesser of—

(I) 1 percent of the total value of the trust's assets at the end of the quarter for which such measurement is done, and

(II) $10,000,000, and

(ii)(I) the corporation, trust, or association, following the identification of such failure, disposes of assets in order to meet the requirements of such paragraph within 6 months after the last day of the quarter in which the corporation, trust or association's identification of the failure to satisfy the requirements of such paragraph occurred or such other time period prescribed by the Secretary and in the manner prescribed by the Secretary, or

(II) the requirements of such paragraph are otherwise met within the time period specified in subclause (I).

(B) FAILURES EXCEEDING DE MINIMIS AMOUNT.—A corporation, trust, or association that fails to meet the requirements of paragraph (4) for a particular quarter shall nevertheless be considered to have satisfied the requirements of such paragraph for such quarter if—

(i) such failure involves the ownership of assets the total value of which exceeds the de minimis standard described in subparagraph (A)(i) at the end of the quarter for which such measurement is done,

(ii) following the corporation, trust, or association's identification of the failure to satisfy the requirements of such paragraph for a particular quarter, a description of each asset that causes the corporation, trust, or association to fail to satisfy the requirements of such paragraph at the close of such quarter of any taxable year is set forth in a schedule for such quarter filed in accordance with regulations prescribed by the Secretary,

(iii) the failure to meet the requirements of such paragraph for a particular quarter is due to reasonable cause and not due to willful neglect,

(iv) the corporation, trust, or association pays a tax computed under subparagraph (C), and

(v)(I) the corporation, trust, or association disposes of the assets set forth on the schedule specified in clause (ii) within 6 months after the last day of the quarter in which the corporation, trust or association's identification of the failure to satisfy the requirements of such paragraph occurred or such other time period prescribed by the Secretary and in the manner prescribed by the Secretary, or

(II) the requirements of such paragraph are otherwise met within the time period specified in subclause (I).

(C) TAX.—For purposes of subparagraph (B)(iv)—

(i) TAX IMPOSED.—If a corporation, trust, or association elects the application of this subparagraph, there is hereby imposed a tax on the failure described in subparagraph (B) of such corporation, trust, or association. Such tax shall be paid by the corporation, trust, or association.

(ii) TAX COMPUTED.—The amount of the tax imposed by clause (i) shall be the greater of—

(I) $50,000, or

(II) the amount determined (pursuant to regulations promulgated by the Secretary) by multiplying the net income generated by the assets described in the schedule specified in subparagraph (B)(ii) for the period specified in clause (iii) by the highest rate of tax specified in section 11.

(iii) PERIOD.—For purposes of clause (ii)(II), the period described in this clause is the period beginning on the first date that the failure to satisfy the requirements of such paragraph (4) occurs as a result of the ownership of such assets and ending on the earlier of the date on which the trust disposes of such assets or the end of the first quarter when there is no longer a failure to satisfy such paragraph (4).

(iv) ADMINISTRATIVE PROVISIONS.—For purposes of subtitle F, the taxes imposed by this subparagraph shall be treated as excise taxes with respect to which the deficiency procedures of such subtitle apply.

• 2004, American Jobs Creation Act of 2004 (P.L. 108-357)

P.L. 108-357, §243(a)(1):

Amended Code Sec. 856(c) by striking paragraph (7). **Effective** for tax years beginning after 12-31-2000. Prior to being stricken, Code Sec. 856(c)(7) read as follows:

(7) STRAIGHT DEBT SAFE HARBOR IN APPLYING PARAGRAPH (4).—Securities of an issuer which are straight debt (as defined in section 1361(c)(5) without regard to subparagraph (B)(iii) thereof) shall not be taken into account in applying paragraph (4)(B)(iii)(III) if—

(A) the issuer is an individual, or

(B) the only securities of such issuer which are held by the trust or a taxable REIT subsidiary of the trust are straight debt (as so defined), or

(C) the issuer is a partnership and the trust holds at least a 20 percent profits interest in the partnership.

P.L. 108-357, §243(d):

Amended Code Sec. 856(c)(5)(G). **Effective** for transactions entered into after 12-31-2004 [effective date amended by P.L. 109-135, §403(d)(4)]. Prior to amendment, Code Sec. 856(c)(5)(G) read as follows:

(G) TREATMENT OF CERTAIN HEDGING INSTRUMENTS.—Except to the extent provided by regulations, any—

(i) payment to a real estate investment trust under an interest rate swap or cap agreement, option, futures contract, forward rate agreement, or any similar financial instrument, entered into by the trust in a transaction to reduce the interest rate risks with respect to any indebtedness incurred or to be incurred by the trust to acquire or carry real estate assets, and

(ii) gain from the sale or other disposition of any such investment,

shall be treated as income qualifying under paragraph (2).

P.L. 108-357, §243(f)(1):

Amended Code Sec. 856(c) by inserting after paragraph (6) a new paragraph (7). **Effective** for failures with respect to which the requirements of subparagraph (A) or (B) of section 856(c)(7) of the Internal Revenue Code are satisfied after 10-22-2004 [effective date amended by P.L. 109-135, §403(d)(4)].

P.L. 108-357, §243(f)(2):

Amended Code Sec. 856(c)(6) by striking subparagraphs (A) and (B), by redesignating subparagraph (C) as subparagraph (B), and by inserting before subparagraph (B) (as so redesignated) a new subparagraph (A). **Effective** for for failures with respect to which the requirements of paragraph (6) of section 856(c) of the Internal Revenue Code are satisfied after 10-22-2004 [effective date amended by P.L. 109-135, §403(d)(4)]. Prior to amendment, Code Sec. 856(c)(6)(A)-(B) read as follows:

(A) the nature and amount of each item of its gross income described in such paragraphs is set forth in a schedule attached to its income tax return for such taxable year;

(B) the inclusion of any incorrect information in the schedule referred to in subparagraph (A) is not due to fraud with intent to evade tax; and

P.L. 108-357, §835(b)(4):

Amended Code Sec. 856(c)(5)(E) by striking the last sentence. For the **effective** date, see Act Sec. 835(c), below. Prior to amendment, the last sentence of Code Sec. 856(c)(5)(E) read as follows:

The principles of the preceding provisions of this subparagraph shall apply to regular interests in a FASIT.

P.L. 108-357, §835(c), provides:

(c) EFFECTIVE DATE.—

(1) IN GENERAL.—Except as provided in paragraph (2), the amendments made by this section shall take effect on January 1, 2005.

(2) EXCEPTION FOR EXISTING FASITS.—Paragraph (1) shall not apply to any FASIT in existence on the date of the enactment of this Act [10-22-2004.—CCH] to the extent that regular interests issued by the FASIT before such date continue to remain outstanding in accordance with the original terms of issuance.

• 2000, Community Renewal Tax Relief Act of 2000 (P.L. 106-554)

P.L. 106-554, §319(9):

Amended Code Sec. 856(c)(7) by striking "paragraph (4)(B)(ii)(III)" and inserting "paragraph (4)(B)(iii)(III)". **Effective** 12-21-2000.

• 1999, Tax Relief Extension Act of 1999 (P.L. 106-170)

P.L. 106-170, §532(c)(2)(H):

Amended Code Sec. 856(c)(2)(D) by striking "section 1221(1)" and inserting "section 1221(a)(1)". **Effective** for any instrument held, acquired, or entered into, any transaction entered into, and supplies held or acquired on or after 12-17-99.

P.L. 106-170, §532(c)(2)(I):

Amended Code Sec. 856(c)(3)(C) by striking "section 1221(1)" and inserting "section 1221(a)(1)". **Effective** for any instrument held, acquired, or entered into, any transaction entered into, and supplies held or acquired on or after 12-17-99.

P.L. 106-170, §541(a):

Amended Code Sec. 856(c)(4)(B). For the **effective** date, see Act Sec. 546, below. Prior to amendment, Code Sec. 856(c)(4)(B) read as follows:

(B) not more than 25 percent of the value of its total assets is represented by securities (other than those includible under subparagraph (A)) for purposes of this calculation limited in respect of any one issuer to an amount not greater in value than 5 percent of the value of the total assets of the trust and to not more than 10 percent of the outstanding voting securities of such issuer.

P.L. 106-170, §541(b):

Amended Code Sec. 856(c) by adding at the end a new paragraph (7). For the **effective** date, see Act Sec. 546, below.

P.L. 106-170, §546, provides:

SEC. 546. EFFECTIVE DATE.

(a) IN GENERAL.—The amendments made by this subpart shall apply to taxable years beginning after December 31, 2000.

(b) TRANSITIONAL RULES RELATED TO SECTION 541.—

(1) EXISTING ARRANGEMENTS.—

(A) IN GENERAL.—Except as otherwise provided in this paragraph, the amendment made by section 541 shall not apply to a real estate investment trust with respect to—

(i) securities of a corporation held directly or indirectly by such trust on July 12, 1999;

(ii) securities of a corporation held by an entity on July 12, 1999, if such trust acquires control of such entity pursuant to a written binding contract in effect on such date and at all times thereafter before such acquisition;

(iii) securities received by such trust (or a successor) in exchange for, or with respect to, securities described in clause (i) or (ii) in a transaction in which gain or loss is not recognized; and

(iv) securities acquired directly or indirectly by such trust as part of a reorganization (as defined in section 368(a)(1) of the Internal Revenue Code of 1986) with respect to such trust if such securities are described in clause (i), (ii), or (iii) with respect to any other real estate investment trust.

(B) NEW TRADE OR BUSINESS OR SUBSTANTIAL NEW ASSETS.—Subparagraph (A) shall cease to apply to securities of a corporation as of the first day after July 12, 1999, on which such corporation engages in a substantial new line of business, or acquires any substantial asset, other than—

(i) pursuant to a binding contract in effect on such date and at all times thereafter before the acquisition of such asset;

(ii) in a transaction in which gain or loss is not recognized by reason of section 1031 or 1033 of the Internal Revenue Code of 1986; or

(iii) in a reorganization (as so defined) with another corporation the securities of which are described in paragraph (1)(A) of this subsection.

(C) LIMITATION ON TRANSITION RULES.—Subparagraph (A) shall cease to apply to securities of a corporation held, acquired, or received, directly or indirectly, by a real estate investment trust as of the first day after July 12, 1999, on which such trust acquires any additional securities of such corporation other than—

(i) pursuant to a binding contract in effect on July 12, 1999, and at all times thereafter; or

(ii) in a reorganization (as so defined) with another corporation the securities of which are described in paragraph (1)(A) of this subsection.

(2) TAX-FREE CONVERSION.—If—

(A) at the time of an election for a corporation to become a taxable REIT subsidiary, the amendment made by section 541 does not apply to such corporation by reason of paragraph (1); and

(B) such election first takes effect before January 1, 2004, such election shall be treated as a reorganization qualifying under section 368(a)(1)(A) of such Code.

• 1997, Taxpayer Relief Act of 1997 (P.L. 105-34)

P.L. 105-34, §1255(a)(1)-(3):

Amended Code Sec. 856(c) by adding "and" at the end of paragraph (3), by striking paragraphs (4) and (8), and by redesignating paragraphs (5), (6), and (7) as paragraphs (4), (5), and (6), respectively. **Effective** for tax years beginning after 8-5-97. Prior to amendment, Code Sec. 856(c)(4) and (8) read as follows:

(4) less than 30 percent of its gross income is derived from the sale or other disposition of—

(A) stock or securities held for less than 1 year;

(B) property in a transaction which is a prohibited transaction; and

(C) real property (including interests in real property and interests in mortgages on real property) held for less than 4 years other than—

(i) property compulsorily or involuntarily converted within the meaning of section 1033, and

(ii) property which is foreclosure property within the definition of section 856(e); and

* * *

(8) TREATMENT OF LIQUIDATING GAINS.—In the case of the taxable year in which a real estate investment trust is completely liquidated, there shall not be taken into account under paragraph (4) any gain from the sale, exchange, or distribution of any property after the adoption of the plan of complete liquidation.

P.L. 105-34, §1255(b)(1):

Amended Code Sec. 856(c)(5)(G), as redesignated by Act Sec. 1255(a)(3), by striking "and such agreement shall be treated as a security for purposes of paragraph (4)(A)" after "paragraph (2)". **Effective** for tax years beginning after 8-5-97.

P.L. 105-34, §1258:

Amended Code Sec. 856(c)(5)(G), as redesignated by Act Sec. 1255. **Effective** for tax years beginning after 8-5-97. Prior to amendment, Code Sec. 856(c)(5)(G) read as follows:

(G) TREATMENT OF CERTAIN INTEREST RATE AGREEMENTS.—Except to the extent provided by regulations, any—

(i) payment to a real estate investment trust under a bona fide interest rate swap or cap agreement entered into by the real estate investment trust to hedge any variable rate indebtedness of such trust incurred or to be incurred to acquire or carry real estate assets, and

(ii) any gain from the sale or other disposition of such agreement,

shall be treated as income qualifying under paragraph (2).

• 1996, Small Business Job Protection Act of 1996 (P.L. 104-188)

P.L. 104-188, §1621(b)(5):

Amended Code Sec. 856(c)(6)(E) by adding at the end a new sentence. **Effective** 9-1-97.

• 1988, Technical and Miscellaneous Revenue Act of 1988 (P.L. 100-647)

P.L. 100-647, §1006(p)(1):

Amended Code Sec. 856(c)(6)(D)(i)(I) (as added by P.L. 99-514, §662) by striking out "debt instrument" and inserting in lieu thereof "debt instrument (within the meaning of section 1275(a)(1))". **Effective** as if included in the provision of P.L. 99-514 to which it relates.

P.L. 100-647, §1006(p)(3):

Amended Code Sec. 856(c) by adding at the end thereof new paragraph (8). **Effective** as if included in the provision of P.L. 99-514 to which it relates.

P.L. 100-647, §1006(p)(4)(A):

Amended Code Sec. 856(c)(6) by adding at the end thereof new subparagraph (G). **Effective** for tax years ending after 11-10-88.

P.L. 100-647, §1006(p)(5):

Amended Code Sec. 856(c)(6)(D)(ii)(I) by striking out "stock in" and inserting in lieu thereof "stock (or certificates of beneficial interests) in". **Effective** as if included in the provision of P.L. 99-514 to which it relates.

P.L. 100-647, §1006(t)(11):

Amended Code Sec. 856(c)(6) by redesignating the last subparagraph as subparagraph (F) and by striking out subparagraph (D)[(E)] (added by P.L. 99-514) and inserting in lieu thereof new subparagraph (E). **Effective** as if included in the provision of P.L. 99-514 to which it relates. Prior to amendment, Code Sec. 856(c)(6)(D)[(E)] read as follows:

(D)[(E)] A regular or residual interest in a REMIC shall be treated as an interest in real property, and any amount includible in gross income with respect to such an interest shall be treated as interest; except that, if less than 95 percent of the assets of such REMIC are interests in real property (determined as if the taxpayer held such assets), such interest shall be so treated only in the proportion which the assets of the REMIC consist of such interests.

• 1986, Tax Reform Act of 1986 (P.L. 99-514)

P.L. 99-514, §662(b)(1):

Amended Code Sec. 865(c)(3) by striking out "and" at the end of subparagraph (G), by adding "and" at the end of subparagraph (H), and by inserting after subparagraph (H) new subparagraph (I). **Effective** for tax years beginning after 12-31-86.

P.L. 99-514, §662(b)(2):

Amended Code Sec. 856(c)(6)(B) by adding at the end thereof a new sentence. **Effective** for tax years beginning after 12-31-86.

P.L. 99-514, §662(b)(3):

Amended Code Sec. 856(c)(6) by redesignating subparagraph (D) as subparagraph (E) and by inserting after suparagraph (C) new subparagraph (D). **Effective** for tax years beginning after 12-31-86.

P.L. 99-514, §671(b)(1):

Amended Code Sec. 856(c)(6) by redesignating subparagraph (D)[(E)]as subparagraph (E)[(F)] and by inserting after subparagraph (C)[(D)]new subparagraph (D)[(E)]. **Effective** for tax years beginning after 12-31-86.

• 1984, Deficit Reduction Act of 1984 (P.L. 98-369)

P.L. 98-369, §1001(b)(12):

Amended Code Sec. 856(c)(4)(A) by striking out "1 year" each place it appeared and inserting in lieu thereof "6 months". **Effective** for property acquired after 6-22-84, and before 1-1-88.

• 1978, Revenue Act of 1978 (P.L. 95-600)

P.L. 95-600, §363(a)(1), (2):

Amended both Code Sec. 856(c)(2) and 856(c)(3) by striking out the word "and" at the end of subparagraph (F), by inserting the word "and" at the end of subparagraph (G), and by addlng the new subparagraph (H). **Effective** for tax years ending after 11-6-78.

P.L. 95-600, §363(a)(3):

Amended Code Sec. 856(c)(4)(B). **Effective** for tax years ending after 11-6-78. Prior to amendment, Code Sec. 856(c)(4)(B) read as follows:

"(B) section 1221(1) property (other than foreclosure property); and"

P.L. 95-600, §701(t)(2):

Amended Code Sec. 856(c)(3)(D) by inserting "(other than gain from prohibited transactions)" after "and gain". **Effective** 10-4-76.

• 1976, Tax Reform Act of 1976 (P.L. 94-455)

P.L. 94-455, §1402(b)(1):

Amended subparagraph (4)(A) by substituting "9 months" for "6 months". **Effective** for tax years beginning after 1977.

P.L. 94-455, §1402(b)(2):

Substituted "1 year" for "9 months" in subparagraph (4)(A). **Effective** for tax years beginning after 1977.

P.L. 94-455, §1602(a):

Added a new paragraph (7). For the **effective** date, see Act Sec. 1608(b), below.

P.L. 94-455, §1603(c)(1):

Added the parenthetical phrase "(excluding gross income from prohibited transactions)" in the first line of paragraph (3). For the **effective** date, see Act Sec. 1608(d), reproduced in amendment notes to Code Sec. 856(a).

P.L. 94-455, §1603(c)(2):

Inserted "which is not property described in section 1221(1)" before the semicolon at the end of subparagraph (2)(D). For the **effective** date, see Act Sec. 1608(d), reproduced in amendment notes to Code Sec. 856(a).

P.L. 94-455, §1603(c)(1)(3):

Inserted "which is not property described in section 1221(1)" before the semicolon at the end of subparagraph (3)(C). For the **effective** date, see Act Sec. 1608(d), reproduced in amendment notes to Code Sec. 856(a).

P.L. 94-455, §1604(a):

Amended paragraph (2) by substituting "95 percent (90 percent for taxable years beginning before January 1, 1980) of its gross income (excluding gross income from prohibited transactions)" for "90 percent of its gross income". For the **effective** date, see Act Sec. 1608(d), reproduced in amendment notes to Code Sec. 856(a).

P.L. 94-455, §1604(c)(1):

Amended paragraphs (2) and (3) by striking out "and" after the semicolon at the end of subparagraph (E), by inserting "and" after the semicolon at the end of subparagraph (F), and by adding new subparagraph (G). For the **effective** date, see Act Sec. 1608(d), reproduced in amendment notes to Code Sec. 856(a).

P.L. 94-455, §1604(d):

Amended paragraph (4). **Effective** as provided in Act Sec. 1608(d), reproduced in amendment notes to Code Sec. 856(a). Prior to amendment, paragraphs (4) and (5) read as follows:

(4) less than 30 percent of its gross income is derived from the sale or other disposition of—

(A) stock or securities held for less than 6 months; and

(B) real property (including interests in real property) not compulsorily or involuntarily converted within the meaning of section 1033, held for less than 4 years; and

(5) at the close of each quarter of the taxable year—

(A) at least 75 percent of the value of its total assets is represented by real estate assets, cash and cash items (including receivables), and Government securities; and

(B) not more than 25 percent of the value of its total assets is represented by securities (other than those includible under subparagraph (A)) for purposes of this calculation limited in respect of any one issuer to an amount not greater in value than 5 percent of the value of the total assets of the trust and to not more than 10 percent of the outstanding voting securities of such issuer.

P.L. 94-455, §1604(e):

Amended subparagraph (6)(C). **Effective** as provided in Act Sec. 1608(d), reproduced in amendment notes to Code Sec. 856(a). Prior to amendment, subparagraph (6)(C) read as follows:

(C) The term "interests in real property" includes fee ownership and co-ownership of land or improvements thereon and leaseholds of land or improvements thereon, but does not include mineral, oil, or gas royalty interests.

P.L. 94-455, §1604(f)(3):

Substituted "A corporation, trust, or association" for "A trust or association" at the beginning in the first line of Code Sec. 856(c). For the **effective** date, see Act Sec. 1608(d), reproduced in amendment notes to Code Sec. 856(a).

P.L. 94-455, §1604(k)(2):

Inserted ", and such election has not been terminated or revoked under subsection (g);" in place of the semicolon at the end of paragraph (1). For the **effective** date, see Act Sec. 1608(d) reproduced in amendment notes to Code Sec. 856(a).

P.L. 94-455, §1608(b), provides:

(b) TRUST NOT DISQUALIFIED IN CERTAIN CASES WHERE INCOME TESTS NOT MET.—The amendment made by section 1602 shall apply to taxable years of real estate investment trusts beginning after the date of the enactment of this Act. In addition, the amendments made by section 1602 shall apply to a taxable year of a real estate investment trust beginning before the date of the enactment of this Act if, as the result of a determination (as defined in section 859(c) of the Internal Revenue Code of 1954) with respect to such trust occurring after the date of the enactment of this Act, such trust for such taxable years does not meet the requirements of section 856(c)(2) or section 856(c)(3), or of both such sections, of such Code as in effect for such taxable year. In any case, the amendment made by section 1602(a) requiring a schedule to be attached to the income tax return of certain real estate investment trusts shall apply only to taxable years of such trusts beginning after the date of the enactment of this Act. If the amendments made by section 1602 apply to a taxable year ending on or before the date of enactment of this Act, the reference to paragraph (2)(B) in section 857(b)(5) of such Code, as amended, shall be considered to be a reference to paragraph (2)(C) of section 857(b) of such Code, as in effect immediately before the enactment of this Act.

P.L. 94-455, §1901(a)(111):

Struck out "which began after December 31, 1960" in front of the semicolon at the end of paragraph (1), and inserted "(15 U.S.C. 80a-1 and following)" in subparagraph (6)(D). **Effective** for tax years beginning after 12-31-76.

• 1975 (P.L. 93-625)

P.L. 93-625, §6(d)(1):

Amended paragraphs (2) and (3) of Code Sec. 856(c) by striking out "and" at the end of subparagraphs (D) therein, by adding "and" at the end of subparagraphs (E), and by adding new subparagraphs (F). For **effective** date, see the historical comment for P.L. 93-625 following the text of Code Sec. 856(e).

[Sec. 856(d)]

(d) RENTS FROM REAL PROPERTY DEFINED.—

(1) AMOUNTS INCLUDED.—For purposes of paragraphs (2) and (3) of subsection (c), the term "rents from real property" includes (subject to paragraph (2))—

(A) rents from interests in real property,

(B) charges for services customarily furnished or rendered in connection with the rental of real property, whether or not such charges are separately stated, and

(C) rent attributable to personal property which is leased under, or in connection with, a lease of real property, but only if the rent attributable to such personal property for the taxable year does not exceed 15 percent of the total rent for the taxable year attributable to both the real and personal property leased under, or in connection with, such lease.

For purposes of subparagraph (C), with respect to each lease of real property, rent attributable to personal property for the taxable year is that amount which bears the same ratio to total rent for the taxable year as the average of the fair market values of the personal property at the beginning and at the end of the taxable year bears to the average of the aggregate fair market values of both the real property and the personal property at the beginning and at the end of such taxable year.

(2) AMOUNTS EXCLUDED.—For purposes of paragraphs (2) and (3) of subsection (c), the term "rents from real property" does not include—

(A) except as provided in paragraphs (4) and (6), any amount received or accrued, directly or indirectly, with respect to any real or personal property, if the determination of such amount depends in whole or in part on the income or profits derived by any person from such property (except that any amount so received or accrued shall not be excluded from the term "rents from real property" solely by reason of being based on a fixed percentage or percentages of receipts or sales);

(B) except as provided in paragraph (8), any amount received or accrued directly or indirectly from any person if the real estate investment trust owns, directly or indirectly—

(i) in the case of any person which is a corporation, stock of such person possessing 10 percent or more of the total combined voting power of all classes of stock entitled to vote, or 10 percent or more of the total value of shares of all classes of stock of such person; or

(ii) in the case of any person which is not a corporation, an interest of 10 percent or more in the assets or net profits of such person; and

(C) any impermissible tenant service income (as defined in paragraph (7)).

(3) INDEPENDENT CONTRACTOR DEFINED.—For purposes of this subsection and subsection (e), the term "independent contractor" means any person—

(A) who does not own, directly or indirectly, more than 35 percent of the shares, or certificates of beneficial interest, in the real estate investment trust; and

(B) if such person is a corporation, not more than 35 percent of the total combined voting power of whose stock (or 35 percent of the total shares of all classes of whose stock), or, if such person is not a corporation, not more than 35 percent of the interest in whose assets or net profits is owned, directly or indirectly, by one or more persons owning 35 percent or more of the shares or certificates of beneficial interest in the trust.

In the event that any class of stock of either the real estate investment trust or such person is regularly traded on an established securities market, only persons who own, directly or indirectly, more than 5 percent of such class of stock shall be taken into account as owning any of the stock of such class for purposes of applying the 35 percent limitation set forth in subparagraph (B) (but all of the outstanding stock of such class shall be considered outstanding in order to compute the denominator for purpose of determining the applicable percentage of ownership).

(4) SPECIAL RULE FOR CERTAIN CONTINGENT RENTS.—Where a real estate investment trust receives or accrues, with respect to real or personal property, any amount which would be excluded from the term "rents from real property" solely because the tenant of the real estate investment trust receives or accrues, directly or indirectly, from subtenants any amount the determination of which depends in whole or in part on the income or profits derived by any person from such property, only a proportionate part (determined pursuant to regulations prescribed by the Secretary) of the amount received or accrued by the real estate investment trust from that tenant will be excluded from the term "rents from real property".

(5) CONSTRUCTIVE OWNERSHIP OF STOCK.—For purposes of this subsection, the rules prescribed by section 318(a) for determining the ownership of stock shall apply in determining the ownership of stock, assets, or net profits of any person; except that—

(A) "10 percent" shall be substituted for "50 percent" in subparagraph (C) of paragraphs (2) and (3) of section 318(a), and

(B) section 318(a)(3)(A) shall be applied in the case of a partnership by taking into account only partners who own (directly or indirectly) 25 percent or more of the capital interest, or the profits interest, in the partnership.

(6) SPECIAL RULE FOR CERTAIN PROPERTY SUBLEASED BY TENANT OF REAL ESTATE INVESTMENT TRUSTS.—

(A) IN GENERAL.—If—

(i) a real estate investment trust receives or accrues, with respect to real or personal property, amounts from a tenant which derives substantially all of its income with respect to such property from the subleasing of substantially all of such property, and

(ii) a portion of the amount such tenant receives or accrues, directly or indirectly, from subtenants consists of qualified rents,

then the amounts which the trust receives or accrues from the tenant shall not be excluded from the term "rents from real property" by reason of being based on the income or profits of such tenant to the extent the amounts so received or accrued are attributable to qualified rents received or accrued by such tenant.

(B) QUALIFIED RENTS.—For purposes of subparagraph (A), the term "qualified rents" means any amount which would be treated as rents from real property if received by the real estate investment trust.

(7) IMPERMISSIBLE TENANT SERVICE INCOME.—For purposes of paragraph (2)(C)—

(A) IN GENERAL.—The term "impermissible tenant service income" means, with respect to any real or personal property, any amount received or accrued directly or indirectly by the real estate investment trust for—

(i) services furnished or rendered by the trust to the tenants of such property, or

(ii) managing or operating such property.

(B) DISQUALIFICATION OF ALL AMOUNTS WHERE MORE THAN DE MINIMIS AMOUNT.—If the amount described in subparagraph (A) with respect to a property for any taxable year exceeds 1 percent of all amounts received or accrued during such taxable year directly or indirectly by the real estate investment trust with respect to such property, the impermissible tenant service income of the trust with respect to the property shall include all such amounts.

(C) EXCEPTIONS.—For purposes of subparagraph (A)—

(i) services furnished or rendered, or management or operation provided, through an independent contractor from whom the trust itself does not derive or receive any income or through a taxable REIT subsidiary of such trust shall not be treated as furnished, rendered, or provided by the trust, and

(ii) there shall not be taken into account any amount which would be excluded from unrelated business taxable income under section 512(b)(3) if received by an organization described in section 511(a)(2).

(D) AMOUNT ATTRIBUTABLE TO IMPERMISSIBLE SERVICES.—For purposes of subparagraph (A), the amount treated as received for any service (or management or operation) shall not be less than 150 percent of the direct cost of the trust in furnishing or rendering the service (or providing the management or operation).

(E) COORDINATION WITH LIMITATIONS.—For purposes of paragraphs (2) and (3) of subsection (c), amounts described in subparagraph (A) shall be included in the gross income of the corporation, trust, or association.

(8) SPECIAL RULE FOR TAXABLE REIT SUBSIDIARIES.—For purposes of this subsection, amounts paid to a real estate investment trust by a taxable REIT subsidiary of such trust shall not be excluded from rents from real property by reason of paragraph (2)(B) if the requirements of either of the following subparagraphs are met:

(A) LIMITED RENTAL EXCEPTION.—

(i) IN GENERAL.—The requirements of this subparagraph are met with respect to any property if at least 90 percent of the leased space of the property is rented to persons other than taxable REIT subsidiaries of such trust and other than persons described in paragraph (2)(B).

(ii) RENTS MUST BE SUBSTANTIALLY COMPARABLE.—Clause (i) shall apply only to the extent that the amounts paid to the trust as rents from real property (as defined in paragraph (1) without regard to paragraph (2)(B)) from such property are substantially comparable to such rents paid by the other tenants of the trust's property for comparable space.

(iii) TIMES FOR TESTING RENT COMPARABILITY.—The substantial comparability requirement of clause (ii) shall be treated as met with respect to a lease to a taxable REIT subsidiary of the trust if such requirement is met under the terms of the lease—

(I) at the time such lease is entered into,

(II) at the time of each extension of the lease, including a failure to exercise a right to terminate, and

(III) at the time of any modification of the lease between the trust and the taxable REIT subsidiary if the rent under such lease is effectively increased pursuant to such modification.

With respect to subclause (III), if the taxable REIT subsidiary of the trust is a controlled taxable REIT subsidiary of the trust, the term "rents from real property" shall not in any event include rent under such lease to the extent of the increase in such rent on account of such modification.

(iv) CONTROLLED TAXABLE REIT SUBSIDIARY.—For purposes of clause (iii), the term "controlled taxable REIT subsidiary" means, with respect to any real estate investment trust, any taxable REIT subsidiary of such trust if such trust owns directly or indirectly—

(I) stock possessing more than 50 percent of the total voting power of the outstanding stock of such subsidiary, or

(II) stock having a value of more than 50 percent of the total value of the outstanding stock of such subsidiary.

(v) CONTINUING QUALIFICATION BASED ON THIRD PARTY ACTIONS.—If the requirements of clause (i) are met at a time referred to in clause (iii), such requirements shall continue to be treated as met so long as there is no increase in the space leased to any taxable REIT subsidiary of such trust or to any person described in paragraph (2)(B).

(vi) CORRECTION PERIOD.—If there is an increase referred to in clause (v) during any calendar quarter with respect to any property, the requirements of clause (iii) shall be treated as met during the quarter and the succeeding quarter if such requirements are met at the close of such succeeding quarter.

(B) EXCEPTION FOR CERTAIN LODGING FACILITIES AND HEALTH CARE PROPERTY.—The requirements of this subparagraph are met with respect to an interest in real property which is a qualified lodging facility (as defined in paragraph (9)(D)) or a qualified health care property (as defined in subsection (e)(6)(D)(i)) leased by the trust to a taxable REIT subsidiary of the trust if the property is operated on behalf of such subsidiary by a person who is an eligible independent contractor. For purposes of this section, a taxable REIT subsidiary is not considered to be operating or managing a qualified health care property or qualified lodging facility solely because it—

(i) directly or indirectly possesses a license, permit, or similar instrument enabling it to do so, or

(ii) employs individuals working at such facility or property located outside the United States, but only if an eligible independent contractor is responsible for the daily supervision and direction of such individuals on behalf of the taxable REIT subsidiary pursuant to a management agreement or similar service contract.

(9) ELIGIBLE INDEPENDENT CONTRACTOR.—For purposes of paragraph (8)(B)—

(A) IN GENERAL.—The term "eligible independent contractor" means, with respect to any qualified lodging facility or qualified health care property (as defined in subsection (e)(6)(D)(i)), any independent contractor if, at the time such contractor enters into a management agreement or other similar service contract with the taxable REIT subsidiary to operate such qualified lodging facility or qualified health care property, such contractor (or any related person) is actively engaged in the trade or business of operating qualified lodging facilities or qualified health care properties, respectively, for any person who is not a related person with respect to the real estate investment trust or the taxable REIT subsidiary.

(B) SPECIAL RULES.—Solely for purposes of this paragraph and paragraph (8)(B), a person shall not fail to be treated as an independent contractor with respect to any qualified lodging facility or qualified health care property (as so defined) by reason of the following:

(i) The taxable REIT subsidiary bears the expenses for the operation of such qualified lodging facility or qualified health care property pursuant to the management agreement or other similar service contract.

(ii) The taxable REIT subsidiary receives the revenues from the operation of such qualified lodging facility or qualified health care property, net of expenses for such operation and fees payable to the operator pursuant to such agreement or contract.

(iii) The real estate investment trust receives income from such person with respect to another property that is attributable to a lease of such other property to such person that was in effect as of the later of—

(I) January 1, 1999, or

(II) the earliest date that any taxable REIT subsidiary of such trust entered into a management agreement or other similar service contract with such person with respect to such qualified lodging facility or qualified health care property.

(C) RENEWALS, ETC., OF EXISTING LEASES.—For purposes of subparagraph (B)(iii)—

(i) a lease shall be treated as in effect on January 1, 1999, without regard to its renewal after such date, so long as such renewal is pursuant to the terms of such lease as in effect on whichever of the dates under subparagraph (B)(iii) is the latest, and

(ii) a lease of a property entered into after whichever of the dates under subparagraph (B)(iii) is the latest shall be treated as in effect on such date if—

(I) on such date, a lease of such property from the trust was in effect, and

(II) under the terms of the new lease, such trust receives a substantially similar or lesser benefit in comparison to the lease referred to in subclause (I).

(D) QUALIFIED LODGING FACILITY.—For purposes of this paragraph—

(i) IN GENERAL.—The term "qualified lodging facility" means any lodging facility unless wagering activities are conducted at or in connection with such facility by any person who is engaged in the business of accepting wagers and who is legally authorized to engage in such business at or in connection with such facility.

(ii) LODGING FACILITY.—The term "lodging facility" means a—

(I) hotel,

(II) motel, or

(III) other establishment more than one-half of the dwelling units in which are used on a transient basis.

(iii) CUSTOMARY AMENITIES AND FACILITIES.—The term "lodging facility" includes customary amenities and facilities operated as part of, or associated with, the lodging facility so long as such amenities and facilities are customary for other properties of a comparable size and class owned by other owners unrelated to such real estate investment trust.

(E) OPERATE INCLUDES MANAGE.—References in this paragraph to operating a property shall be treated as including a reference to managing the property.

(F) RELATED PERSON.—Persons shall be treated as related to each other if such persons are treated as a single employer under subsection (a) or (b) of section 52.

Amendments

• 2008, Housing Assistance Tax Act of 2008 (P.L. 110-289)

P.L. 110-289, §3061(a):

Amended Code Sec. 856(d)(8)(B). **Effective** for tax years beginning after 7-30-2008. Prior to amendment, Code Sec. 856(d)(8)(B) read as follows:

(B) EXCEPTION FOR CERTAIN LODGING FACILITIES.—The requirements of this subparagraph are met with respect to an interest in real property which is a qualified lodging facility leased by the trust to a taxable REIT subsidiary of the trust if the property is operated on behalf of such subsidiary by a person who is an eligible independent contractor.

P.L. 110-289, §3061(b):

Amended Code Sec. 856(d)(9)(A) and (B). **Effective** for tax years beginning after 7-30-2008. Prior to amendment, Code Sec. 856(d)(9)(A) and (B) read as follows:

(A) IN GENERAL.—The term "eligible independent contractor" means, with respect to any qualified lodging facility, any independent contractor if, at the time such contractor enters into a management agreement or other similar service contract with the taxable REIT subsidiary to operate the facility, such contractor (or any related person) is actively engaged in the trade or business of operating qualified lodging facilities for any person who is not a related person with respect to the real estate investment trust or the taxable REIT subsidiary.

(B) SPECIAL RULES.—Solely for purposes of this paragraph and paragraph (8)(B), a person shall not fail to be treated as an independent contractor with respect to any qualified lodging facility by reason of any of the following:

(i) The taxable REIT subsidiary bears the expenses for the operation of the facility pursuant to the management agreement or other similar service contract.

(ii) The taxable REIT subsidiary receives the revenues from the operation of such facility, net of expenses for such operation and fees payable to the operator pursuant to such agreement or contract.

(iii) The real estate investment trust receives income from such person with respect to another property that is attributable to a lease of such other property to such person that was in effect as of the later of—

(I) January 1, 1999, or

(II) the earliest date that any taxable REIT subsidiary of such trust entered into a management agreement or other similar service contract with such person with respect to such qualified lodging facility.

• 2007, Tax Technical Corrections Act of 2007 (P.L. 110-172)

P.L. 110-172, §9(b):

Amended Code Sec. 856(d)(9)(D)(ii). **Effective** as if included in the provision of the Tax Relief Extension Act of 1999 (P.L. 106-170) to which it relates [**effective** for tax years beginning after 12-31-2000.—CCH]. Prior to amendment, Code Sec. 856(d)(9)(D)(ii) read as follows:

(ii) LODGING FACILITY.—The term "lodging facility" means a hotel, motel, or other establishment more than one-half of the dwelling units in which are used on a transient basis.

• 2004, American Jobs Creation Act of 2004 (P.L. 108-357)

P.L. 108-357, §243(b):

Amended Code Sec. 856(d)(8)(A). **Effective** for tax years beginning after 12-31-2000. Prior to amendment, Code Sec. 856(d)(8)(A) read as follows:

(A) LIMITED RENTAL EXCEPTION.—The requirements of this subparagraph are met with respect to any property if at least 90 percent of the leased space of the property is rented to persons other than taxable REIT subsidiaries of such trust and other than persons described in section 856(d)(2)(B). The preceding sentence shall apply only to the extent that the amounts paid to the trust as rents from real property (as defined in paragraph (1) without regard to paragraph (2)(B)) from such property are substantially comparable to such rents made by the other tenants of the trust's property for comparable space.

• 1999, Tax Relief Extension Act of 1999 (P.L. 106-170)

P.L. 106-170, §542(a):

Amended Code Sec. 856(d)(7)(C)(i) by inserting "or through a taxable REIT subsidiary of such trust" after "income". **Effective** for tax years beginning after 12-31-2000.

P.L. 106-170, §542(b)(1):

Amended Code Sec. 856(d) by adding at the end new paragraphs (8) and (9). **Effective** for tax years beginning after 12-31-2000.

P.L. 106-170, §542(b)(2):

Amended Code Sec. 856(d)(2)(B) by inserting "except as provided in paragraph (8)," after "(B)". **Effective** for tax years beginning after 12-31-2000.

P.L. 106-170, §542(b)(3)(A)(i):

Amended Code Sec. 856(d)(1) by striking "adjusted bases" each place it appeared and inserting "fair market values". **Effective** for tax years beginning after 12-31-2000.

P.L. 106-170, §542(b)(3)(B)(i):

Amended Code Sec. 856(d)(2)(B)(i) by striking "number" and inserting "value". **Effective** for amounts received or accrued in tax years beginning after 12-31-2000, except for amounts paid pursuant to leases in effect on 7-12-99, or pursuant to a binding contract in effect on such date and at all times thereafter.

P.L. 106-170, §561(a):

Amended Code Sec. 856(d)(3) by adding at the end a flush sentence. **Effective** for tax years beginning after 12-31-2000.

• 1997, Taxpayer Relief Act of 1997 (P.L. 105-34)

P.L. 105-34, §1252(a):

Amended Code Sec. 856(d)(2) by striking subparagraph (C) and the last sentence and inserting a new subparagraph (C). **Effective** for tax years beginning after 8-5-97. Prior to amendment, Code Sec. 856(d)(2)(C) and the last sentence read as follows:

(C) any amount received or accrued, directly or indirectly, with respect to any real or personal property if the real estate investment trust furnishes or renders services to the tenants of such property, or manages or operates such property, other than through an independent contractor from whom the trust itself does not derive or receive any income.

Subparagraph (C) shall not apply with respect to any amount if such amount would be excluded from unrelated business taxable income under section 512(b)(3) if received by an organization described in section 511(a)(2).

P.L. 105-34, §1252(b):

Amended Code Sec. 856(d) by adding at the end a new paragraph (7). **Effective** for tax years beginning after 8-5-97.

P.L. 105-34, §1253:

Amended Code Sec. 856(d)(5) by striking "except that" and all that follows and inserting "except that—" and subparagraphs (A) and (B). **Effective** for tax years beginning after 8-5-97. Prior to amendment, Code Sec. 856(d)(5) read as follows:

(5) CONSTRUCTIVE OWNERSHIP OF STOCK.—For purposes of this subsection, the rules prescribed by section 318(a) for determining the ownership of stock shall apply in determining the ownership of stock, assets, or net profits of any person; except that "10 percent" shall be substituted for "50 percent" in subparagraph (C) of section 318(a)(2) and 318(a)(3).

• 1988, Technical and Miscellaneous Revenue Act of 1988 (P.L. 100-647)

P.L. 100-647, §1006(q)(1):

Amended Code Sec. 856(d)(6)(A). **Effective** as if included in the provision of P.L. 99-514 to which it relates. Prior to amendment, Code Sec. 856(d)(6)(A) read as follows:

(A) IN GENERAL.—If—

(i) a real estate investment trust receives or accrues, with respect to real or personal property, amounts from a tenant which derives substantially all of its income with respect to such property from the subleasing of substantially all of such property, and

(ii) such tenant receives or accrues, directly or indirectly, from subtenants only amounts which are qualified rents,

then the amounts that the trust receives or accrues from the tenant shall not be excluded from the term "rents from real property" solely by reason of being based on the income or profits of such tenant.

• 1986, Tax Reform Act of 1986 (P.L. 99-514)

P.L. 99-514, §663(a):

Amended Code Sec. 856(d)(2) by adding at the end thereof a new sentence. **Effective** for tax years beginning after 12-31-86.

P.L. 99-514, §663(b)(1):

Amended Code Sec. 856(d) by adding at the end thereof new paragraph (6). **Effective** for tax years beginning after 12-31-86.

P.L. 99-514, §663(b)(3):

Amended Code Sec. 856(d)(2)(A) by striking out "paragraph (4)" and inserting in lieu thereof "paragraphs (4) and (6)". **Effective** for tax years beginning after 12-31-86.

• 1976, Tax Reform Act of 1976 (P.L. 94-455)

P.L. 94-455, §1604(b):

Amended Code Sec. 856(d). **Effective** 10-4-76. Prior to amendment, Code Sec. 856(d) read as follows:

(d) RENTS FROM REAL PROPERTY DEFINED.—For purposes of paragraphs (2) and (3) of subsection (c), the term "rents from real property" includes rents from interests in real property but does not include—

(1) any amount received or accrued, directly or indirectly, with respect to any real property, if the determination of such amount depends in whole or in part on the income or profits derived by any person from such property (except that any amount so received or accrued shall not be excluded from the term "rents from real property" solely by reason of being based on a fixed percentage or percentages of receipts or sales);

(2) any amount received or accrued directly or indirectly from any person if the real estate investment trust owns, directly or indirectly—

(A) in the case of any person which is a corporation, stock of such person possessing 10 percent or more of the total combined voting power of all classes of stock entitled to vote, or 10 percent or more of the total number of shares of all classes of stock of such person; or

(B) in the case of any person which is not a corporation, an interest of 10 percent or more in the assets or net profits of such person; and

(3) any amount received or accrued, directly or indirectly, with respect to any real property, if the real estate investment trust furnishes or renders services to the tenants of such property, or manages or operates such property, other than through an independent contractor from whom the trust itself does not derive or receive any income. For purposes of this paragraph, the term "independent contractor" means—

(A) a person who does not own, directly or indirectly, more than 35 percent of the shares, or certificates of beneficial interest, in the real estate investment trust, or

(B) a person, if a corporation, not more than 35 percent of the total combined voting power of whose stock (or 35 percent of the total shares of all classes of whose stock), or, if not a corporation, not more than 35 percent of the interest in whose assets or net profits is owned, directly or indirectly, by one or more persons owning 35 percent or more of the shares or certificates of beneficial interest in the trust.

For purposes of paragraphs (2) and (3), the rules prescribed by section 318(a) for determining the ownership of stock shall apply in determining the ownership of stock, assets, or net profits of any person; except that "10 percent" shall be substituted for "50 percent" in subparagraph (C) of sections 318(a)(2) and 318(a)(3).

• 1964 (P.L. 88-554)

P.L. 88-554, §5(b)(4):

Amended Code Sec. 856(d) by substituting "sections 318(a)(2) and 318(a)(3)" for "section 318(a)(2)". **Effective** 8-31-64.

• 1960 (P.L. 86-779)

P.L. 86-779, §10(a):

Added Code Sec. 856. **Effective** for tax years of real estate investment trusts beginning after 1960.

[Sec. 856(e)]

(e) SPECIAL RULES FOR FORECLOSURE PROPERTY.—

(1) FORECLOSURE PROPERTY DEFINED.—For purposes of this part, the term "foreclosure property" means any real property (including interests in real property), and any personal property incident to such real property, acquired by the real estate investment trust as the result of such trust having bid in such property at foreclosure, or having otherwise reduced such property to ownership or possession by agreement or process of law, after there was default (or default was imminent) on a lease of such property or on an indebtedness which such property secured. Such term does not include property acquired by the real estate investment trust as a result of indebtedness arising from the sale or other disposition of property of the trust described in section 1221(a)(1) which was not originally acquired as foreclosure property.

(2) GRACE PERIOD.—Except as provided in paragraph (3), property shall cease to be foreclosure property with respect to the real estate investment trust as of the close of the 3d taxable year following the taxable year in which the trust acquired such property.

(3) EXTENSIONS.—If the real estate investment trust establishes to the satisfaction of the Secretary that an extension of the grace period is necessary for the orderly liquidation of the trust's interests in such property, the Secretary may grant one extension of the grace period for such property. Any such extension shall not extend the grace period beyond the close of the 3d taxable year following the last taxable year in the period under paragraph (2).

(4) TERMINATION OF GRACE PERIOD IN CERTAIN CASES.—Any foreclosure property shall cease to be such on the first day (occurring on or after the day on which the real estate investment trust acquired the property) on which—

(A) a lease is entered into with respect to such property which, by its terms, will give rise to income which is not described in subsection (c)(3) (other than subparagraph (F) of such subsection), or any amount is received or accrued, directly or indirectly, pursuant to a lease entered into on or after such day which is not described in such subsection,

(B) any construction takes place on such property (other than completion of a building, or completion of any other improvement, where more than 10 percent of the construction of such building or other improvement was completed before default became imminent), or

(C) if such day is more than 90 days after the day on which such property was acquired by the real estate investment trust and the property is used in a trade or business which is conducted by the trust (other than through an independent contractor (within the meaning of section (d)(3)) from whom the trust itself does not derive or receive any income).

For purposes of subparagraph (C), property shall not be treated as used in a trade or business by reason of any activities of the real estate investment trust with respect to such property to the extent that such activities would not result in amounts received or accrued, directly or indirectly, with respect to such property being treated as other than rents from real property.

(5) TAXPAYER MUST MAKE ELECTION.—Property shall be treated as foreclosure property for purposes of this part only if the real estate investment trust so elects (in the manner provided in regulations prescribed by the Secretary) on or before the due date (including any extensions of time) for filing its return of tax under this chapter for the taxable year in which such trust acquires such property. A real estate investment trust may revoke any such election for a taxable

year by filing the revocation (in the manner provided by the Secretary) on or before the due date (including any extension of time) for filing its return of tax under this chapter for the taxable year. If a trust revokes an election for any property, no election may be made by the trust under this paragraph with respect to the property for any subsequent taxable year.

(6) SPECIAL RULE FOR QUALIFIED HEALTH CARE PROPERTIES.—For purposes of this subsection—

(A) ACQUISITION AT EXPIRATION OF LEASE.—The term "foreclosure property" shall include any qualified health care property acquired by a real estate investment trust as the result of the termination of a lease of such property (other than a termination by reason of a default, or the imminence of a default, on the lease).

(B) GRACE PERIOD.—In the case of a qualified health care property which is foreclosure property solely by reason of subparagraph (A), in lieu of applying paragraphs (2) and (3)—

(i) the qualified health care property shall cease to be foreclosure property as of the close of the second tarable year after the taxable year in which such trust acquired such property, and

(ii) if the real estate investment trust establishes to the satisfaction of the Secretary that an extension of the grace period in clause (i) is necessary to the orderly leasing or liquidation of the trust's interest in such qualified health care property, the Secretary may grant one or more extensions of the grace period for such qualified health care property.

Any such extension shall not extend the grace period beyond the close of the 6th year after the taxable year in which such trust acquired such qualified health care property.

(C) INCOME FROM INDEPENDENT CONTRACTORS.—For purposes of applying paragraph (4)(C) with respect to qualified health care property which is foreclosure property by reason of subparagraph (A) or paragraph (1), income derived or received by the trust from an independent contractor shall be disregarded to the extent such income is attributable to—

(i) any lease of property in effect on the date the real estate investment trust acquired the qualified health care property (without regard to its renewal after such date so long as such renewal is pursuant to the terms of such lease as in effect on such date), or

(ii) any lease of property entered into after such date if—

(I) on such date, a lease of such property from the trust was in effect, and

(II) under the terms of the new lease, such trust receives a substantially similar or lesser benefit in comparison to the lease referred to in subclause (I).

(D) QUALIFIED HEALTH CARE PROPERTY.—

(i) IN GENERAL.—The term "qualified health care property" means any real property (including interests therein), and any personal property incident to such real property, which—

(I) is a health care facility, or

(II) is necessary or incidental to the use of a health care facility.

(ii) HEALTH CARE FACILITY.—For purposes of clause (i), the term "health care facility" means a hospital, nursing facility, assisted living facility, congregate care facility, qualified continuing care facility (as defined in section 7872(g)(4)), or other licensed facility which extends medical or nursing or ancillary services to patients and which, immediately before the termination, expiration, default, or breach of the lease of or mortgage secured by such facility, was operated by a provider of such services which was eligible for participation in the medicare program under title XVIII of the Social Security Act with respect to such facility.

Amendments

• 1999, Tax Relief Extension Act of 1999 (P.L. 106-170)

P.L. 106-170, §532(c)(2)(J):

Amended Code Sec. 856(e)(1) by striking "section 1221(1)" and inserting "section 1221(a)(1)". **Effective** for any instrument held, acquired, or entered into, any transaction entered into, and supplies held or acquired on or after 12-17-99.

P.L. 106-170, §551(a):

Amended Code Sec. 856(e) by adding at the end a new paragraph (6). **Effective** for tax years beginning after 12-31-2000.

• 1997, Taxpayer Relief Act of 1997 (P.L. 105-34)

P.L. 105-34, §1257(a)(1):

Amended Code Sec. 856(e)(2) by striking "on the date which is 2 years after the date the trust acquired such property" and inserting "as of the close of the 3d taxable year following the taxable year in which the trust acquired such property". **Effective** for tax years beginning after 8-5-97.

P.L. 105-34, §1257(a)(2)(A)-(B):

Amended Code Sec. 856(e)(3) by striking "or more extensions" and inserting "extension", and by striking the last sentence and inserting a new sentence. **Effective** for tax years beginning after 8-5-97. Prior to amendment, the last sentence of Code Sec. 856(e)(3) read as follows:

Any such extension shall not extend the grace period beyond the date which is 6 years after the date such trust acquired such property.

P.L. 105-34, §1257(b):

Amended Code Sec. 856(e)(5) by striking the last sentence and inserting two new sentences. **Effective** for tax years beginning after 8-5-97. Prior to amendment, the last sentence of Code Sec. 856(e)(5) read as follows:

Any such election shall be irrevocable.

P.L. 105-34, §1257(c):

Amended Code Sec. 856(e)(4) by adding at the end a new flush sentence. **Effective** for tax years beginning after 8-5-97.

• 1978, Revenue Act of 1978 (P.L. 95-600)

P.L. 95-600, §363(c):

Amended Code Sec. 856(e)(3). **Effective** for extensions granted after 11-6-78, with respect to periods beginning after 12-31-77. Prior to amendment, Code Sec. 856(e)(3) read as follows:

(3) EXTENSIONS.—If the real estate investment trust establishes to the satisfaction of the Secretary that an extension of the grace period is necessary for the orderly liquidation of the trust's interests in such property, the Secretary may extend the grace period for such property. Any such extension shall be for a period of not more than 1 year, and not more than 2 extensions shall be granted with respect to any property.

• 1976, Tax Reform Act of 1976 (P.L. 94-455)

P.L. 94-455, §1603(c)(4):

Added "Such term does not include property acquired by the real estate investment trust as a result of indebtedness arising from the sale or other disposition of property of the trust described in section 1221(1) which was not originally acquired as foreclosure property" at the end of paragraph (1). **Effective** 10-4-76.

P.L. 94-455, §1906(b)(13)(A):

Amended 1954 Code by substituting "Secretary" for "Secretary or his delegate" each place it appeared. **Effective** 2-1-77.

• 1975 (P.L. 93-635)

P.L. 93-625, §6(a):

Added Code Sec. 856(e). **Effective** with respect to foreclosure property acquired after 12-31-73. Notwithstanding the provisions of Code Sec. 856(e)(5) (as added by P.L. 93-625), any taxpayer required to make an election with respect to foreclosure property sooner than 90 days after the date of enactment (1-3-75) may make that election at any time before the 91st day after such date.

[Sec. 856(f)]

(f) INTEREST.—

(1) IN GENERAL.—For purposes of paragraphs (2)(B) and (3)(B) of subsection (c), the term "interest" does not include any amount received or accrued, directly or indirectly, if the determination of such amount depends in whole or in part on the income or profits of any person except that—

(A) any amount so received or accrued shall not be excluded from the term "interest" solely by reason of being based on a fixed percentage or percentages of receipts or sales, and

(B) where a real estate investment trust receives any amount which would be excluded from the term "interest" solely because the debtor of the real estate investment trust receives or accrues any amount the determination of which depends in whole or in part on the income or profits of any person, only a proportionate part (determined pursuant to regulations prescribed by the Secretary) of the amount received or accrued by the real estate investment trust from the debtor will be excluded from the term "interest".

(2) SPECIAL RULE.—If—

(A) a real estate investment trust receives or accrues with respect to an obligation secured by a mortgage on real property or an interest in real property amounts from a debtor which derives substantially all of its gross income with respect to such property (not taking into account any gain on any disposition) from the leasing of substantially all of its interests in such property to tenants, and

(B) a portion of the amount which such debtor receives or accrues, directly or indirectly, from tenants consists of qualified rents (as defined in subsection (d)(6)(B)),

then the amounts which the trust receives or accrues from such debtor shall not be excluded from the term "interest" by reason of being based on the income or profits of such debtor to the extent the amounts so received are attributable to qualified rents received or accrued by such debtor.

Amendments

• 1988, Technical and Miscellaneous Revenue Act of 1988 (P.L. 100-647)

P.L. 100-647, §1006(q)(2):

Amended Code Sec. 856(f). **Effective** as if included in the provision of P.L. 99-514 to which it relates. Prior to amendment, Code Sec. 856(f) read as follows:

(f) INTEREST.—

(1) IN GENERAL.—For purposes of paragraphs (2)(B) and (3)(B) of subsection (c), the term "interest" does not include any amount received or accrued, (directly or indirectly) if the determination of such amount depends (in whole or in part) on the income or profits of any person, except that—

(A) any amounts so received or accrued shall not be excluded from the term "interest" solely by reason of being based on a fixed percentage or percentages of receipts or sales, and

(B) any amount so received or accrued with respect to an obligation secured by a mortgage on real property or an interest in real property shall not be excluded from the term "interest" solely by reason of being based on the income or profits of the debtor from such property, if—

(i) the debtor derives substantially all of its gross income with respect to such property from the leasing of substantially all of its interests in such property to tenants, and

(ii) the amounts received or accrued directly or indirectly by the debtor from such tenants are only qualified rents (as defined in subsection (d)(6)(B)).

(2) SPECIAL RULE.—Where a real estate investment trust receives or accrues any amount which would be excluded from the term "interest" solely because the debtor of the real estate investment trust receives or accrues any amount the determination of which depends (in whole or in part) on the income or profits of any person, only a proportionate part (determined under regulations prescribed by the Secretary) of the amount received or accrued by the real estate investment trust shall be excluded from the term "interest".

• 1986, Tax Reform Act of 1986 (P.L. 99-514)

P.L. 99-514, §663(b)(2):

Amended Code Sec. 856(f). **Effective** for tax years beginning after 12-31-86. However, for a transitional rule, see Act Sec. 669(c), below. Prior to amendment, Code Sec. 856(f) read as follows:

(f) INTEREST.—For purposes of paragraphs (2)(B) and (3)(B) of subsection (c), the term "interest" does not include any amount received or accrued, directly or indirectly, if the determination of such amount depends in whole or in part on the income or profits of any person except that:

(1) any amount so received or accrued shall not be excluded from the term "interest" solely by reason of being based on a fixed percentage or percentages of receipts or sales, and

(2) where a real estate investment trust receives or accrues any amount which would be excluded from the term "interest" solely because the debtor of the real estate investment trust receives or accrues any amount the determination of which depends in whole or in part on the income or profits of any person, only a proportionate part (determined pursuant to regulations prescribed by the Secretary) of the amount received or accrued by the real estate investment trust from such debtor will be excluded from the term "interest".

The provisions of this subsection shall apply only with respect to amounts received or accrued pursuant to loans made after May 27, 1976. For purposes of the preceding sentence, a loan is considered to be made before May 28, 1976, if such loan is made pursuant to a binding commitment entered into before May 28, 1976.

P.L. 99-514, §669(c), provides:

(c) RETENTION OF EXISTING TRANSITIONAL RULE.—The amendment made by section 663(b)(2) shall not apply with respect to amounts received or accrued pursuant to loans made before May 28, 1976. For purposes of the preceding sentence, a loan is considered to be made before May 28, 1976, if such loan is made pursuant to a binding commitment entered into before may 28, 1976.

• 1976, Tax Reform Act of 1976 (P.L. 94-455)

P.L. 94-455, §1604(g):

Added Code Sec. 856(f). **Effective** 10-1-76.

[Sec. 856(g)]

(g) TERMINATION OF ELECTION.—

(1) FAILURE TO QUALIFY.—An election under subsection (c)(1) made by a corporation, trust, or association shall terminate if the corporation, trust, or association is not a real estate investment trust to which the provisions of this part apply for the taxable year with respect to which the election is made, or for any succeeding taxable year unless paragraph (5) applies. Such termination shall be effective for the taxable year for which the corporation, trust, or association is not a real estate investment trust to which the provisions of this part apply, and for all succeeding taxable years.

(2) REVOCATION.—An election under subsection (c)(1) made by a corporation, trust, or association may be revoked by it for any taxable year after the first taxable year for which the election is effective. A revocation under this paragraph shall be effective for the taxable year in which made and for all succeeding taxable years. Such revocation must be made on or before the 90th day after the first day of the first taxable year for which the revocation is to be effective. Such revocation shall be made in such manner as the Secretary shall prescribe by regulations.

(3) ELECTION AFTER TERMINATION OR REVOCATION.—Except as provided in paragraph (4), if a corporation, trust, or association has made an election under subsection (c)(1) and such election has been terminated or revoked under paragraph (1) or paragraph (2), such corporation, trust, or association (and any successor corporation, trust, or association) shall not be eligible to make an election under subsection (c)(1) for any taxable year prior to the fifth taxable year which begins after the first taxable year for which such termination or revocation is effective.

(4) EXCEPTION.—If the election of a corporation, trust, or association has been terminated under paragraph (1), paragraph (3) shall not apply if—

(A) the corporation, trust, or association does not willfully fail to file within the time prescribed by law an income tax return for the taxable year with respect to which the termination of the election under subsection (c)(1) occurs;

(B) the inclusion of any incorrect information in the return referred to in subparagraph (A) is not due to fraud with intent to evade tax; and

(C) the corporation, trust, or association establishes to the satisfaction of the Secretary that its failure to qualify as a real estate investment trust to which the provisions of this part apply is due to reasonable cause and not due to willful neglect.

(5) ENTITIES TO WHICH PARAGRAPH APPLIES.—This paragraph applies to a corporation, trust, or association—

(A) which is not a real estate investment trust to which the provisions of this part apply for the taxable year due to one or more failures to comply with one or more of the provisions of this part (other than paragraph (2), (3), or (4) of subsection (c)),

(B) such failures are due to reasonable cause and not due to willful neglect, and

(C) if such corporation, trust, or association pays (as prescribed by the Secretary in regulations and in the same manner as tax) a penalty of $50,000 for each failure to satisfy a provision of this part due to reasonable cause and not willful neglect.

Amendments

• 2005, Gulf Opportunity Zone Act of 2005 (P.L. 109-135)

P.L. 109-135, §412(hh):

Amended Code Sec. 856(g)(5)(A) by striking "subsection (c)(6) or (c)(7) of section 856" and inserting "paragraph (2), (3), or (4) of subsection (c)". **Effective** 12-21-2005.

• 2004, American Jobs Creation Act of 2004 (P.L. 108-357)

P.L. 108-357, §243(f)(3)(A):

Amended Code Sec. 856(g)(1) by inserting "unless paragraph (5) applies" before the period at the end of the first sentence. **Effective** for failures with respect to which the requirements of paragraph (5) of section 856(g) of the Internal Revenue Code of 1986 are satisfied after 10-22-2004 [effective date amended by P.L. 109-135, § 403(d)(4)].

P.L. 108-357, § 243(f)(3)(B):

Amended Code Sec. 856(g) by adding at the end a new paragraph (5). **Effective** for failures with respect to which the requirements of paragraph (5) of section 856(g) of the Internal Revenue Code of 1986 are satisfied after 10-22-2004 [effective date amended by P.L. 109-135, § 403(d)(4)].

• 1976, Tax Reform Act of 1976 (P.L. 94-455)

P.L. 94-455, § 1604(k)(1):

Added Code Sec. 856(g). **Effective** 10-4-76.

[Sec. 856(h)]

(h) CLOSELY HELD DETERMINATIONS.—

(1) SECTION 542(a)(2) APPLIED.—

(A) IN GENERAL.—For purposes of subsection (a)(6), a corporation, trust, or association is closely held if the stock ownership requirement of section 542(a)(2) is met.

(B) WAIVER OF PARTNERSHIP ATTRIBUTION, ETC.—For purposes of subparagraph (A)—

(i) paragraph (2) of section 544(a) shall be applied as if such paragraph did not contain the phrase "or by or for his partner", and

(ii) sections 544(a)(4)(A) and 544(b)(1) shall be applied by substituting "the entity meet the stock ownership requirement of section 542(a)(2)" for "the corporation a personal holding company".

(2) SUBSECTIONS (a)(5) AND (6) NOT TO APPLY TO 1ST YEAR.—Paragraphs (5) and (6) of subsection (a) shall not apply to the 1st taxable year for which an election is made under subsection (c)(1) by any corporation, trust, or association.

(3) TREATMENT OF TRUSTS DESCRIBED IN SECTION 401(a).—

(A) LOOK-THRU TREATMENT.—

(i) IN GENERAL.—Except as provided in clause (ii), in determining whether the stock ownership requirement of section 542(a)(2) is met for purposes of paragraph (1)(A), any stock held by a qualified trust shall be treated as held directly by its beneficiaries in proportion to their actuarial interest in such trust and shall not be treated as held by such trust.

(ii) CERTAIN RELATED TRUSTS NOT ELIGIBLE.—Clause (i) shall not apply to any qualified trust if one or more disqualified persons (as defined in section 4975(e)(2), without regard to subparagraphs (B) and (I) thereof) with respect to such qualified trust hold in the aggregate 5 percent or more in value of the interests in the real estate investment trust and such real estate investment trust has accumulated earnings and profits attributable to any period for which it did not qualify as a real estate investment trust.

(B) COORDINATION WITH PERSONAL HOLDING COMPANY RULES.—If any entity qualifies as a real estate investment trust for any taxable year by reason of subparagraph (A), such entity shall not be treated as a personal holding company for such taxable year for purposes of part II of subchapter G of this chapter.

(C) TREATMENT FOR PURPOSES OF UNRELATED BUSINESS TAX.—If any qualified trust holds more than 10 percent (by value) of the interests in any pension-held REIT at any time during a taxable year, the trust shall be treated as having for such taxable year gross income from an unrelated trade or business in an amount which bears the same ratio to the aggregate dividends paid (or treated as paid) by the REIT to the trust for the taxable year of the REIT with or within which the taxable year of the trust ends (the "REIT year") as—

(i) the gross income (less direct expenses related thereto) of the REIT for the REIT year from unrelated trades or businesses (determined as if the REIT were a qualified trust), bears to

(ii) the gross income (less direct expenses related thereto) of the REIT for the REIT year.

This subparagraph shall apply only if the ratio determined under the preceding sentence is at least 5 percent.

(D) PENSION-HELD REIT.—The purposes of subparagraph (C)—

(i) IN GENERAL.—A real estate investment trust is a pension-held REIT if such trust would not have qualified as a real estate investment trust but for the provisions of this paragraph and if such trust is predominantly held by qualified trusts.

(ii) PREDOMINANTLY HELD.—For purposes of clause (i), a real estate investment trust is predominantly held by qualified trusts if—

(I) at least 1 qualified trust holds more than 25 percent (by value) of the interests in such real estate investment trust, or

(II) 1 or more qualified trusts (each of whom own more than 10 percent by value of the interests in such real estate investment trust) hold in the aggregate more than 50 percent (by value) of the interests in such real estate investment trust.

(E) QUALIFIED TRUST.—For purposes of this paragraph, the term "qualified trust" means any trust described in section 401(a) and exempt from tax under section 501(a).

Amendments

• **1993, Omnibus Budget Reconciliation Act of 1993 (P.L. 103-66)**

P.L. 103-66, §13149(a):

Amended Code Sec. 856(h) by adding at the end thereof a new paragraph (3). **Effective** for tax years beginning after 12-31-93.

• **1986, Tax Reform Act of 1986 (P.L. 99-514)**

P.L. 99-514, §661(a)(2):

Amended Code Sec. 856 by adding at the end thereof new subsection (h). **Effective** for tax years beginning after 12-31-86.

[Sec. 856(i)]

(i) TREATMENT OF CERTAIN WHOLLY OWNED SUBSIDIARIES.—

(1) IN GENERAL.—For purposes of this title—

(A) a corporation which is a qualified REIT subsidiary shall not be treated as a separate corporation, and

(B) all assets, liabilities, and items of income, deduction, and credit of a qualified REIT subsidiary shall be treated as assets, liabilities, and such items (as the case may be) of the real estate investment trust.

(2) QUALIFIED REIT SUBSIDIARY.—For purposes of this subsection, the term "qualified REIT subsidiary" means any corporation if 100 percent of the stock of such corporation is held by the real estate investment trust. Such term shall not include a taxable REIT subsidiary.

(3) TREATMENT OF TERMINATION OF QUALIFIED SUBSIDIARY STATUS.—For purposes of this subtitle, if any corporation which was a qualified REIT subsidiary ceases to meet the requirements of paragraph (2), such corporation shall be treated as a new corporation acquiring all of its assets (and assuming all of its liabilities) immediately before such cessation from the real estate investment trust in exchange for its stock.

Amendments

• **1999, Tax Relief Extension Act of 1999 (P.L. 106-170)**

P.L. 106-170, §543(b):

Amended Code Sec. 856(i)(2) by adding at the end a new sentence. **Effective** for tax years beginning after 12-31-2000.

• **1997, Taxpayer Relief Act of 1997 (P.L. 105-34)**

P.L. 105-34, §1262:

Amended Code Sec. 856(i)(2) by striking "at all times during the period such corporation was in existence" before the period. **Effective** for tax years beginning after 8-5-97.

• **1986, Tax Reform Act of 1986 (P.L. 99-514)**

P.L. 99-514, §662(a):

Amended Code Sec. 856 by adding at the end thereof new subsection (i). **Effective** for tax years beginning after 12-31-86.

[Sec. 856(j)]

(j) TREATMENT OF SHARED APPRECIATION MORTGAGES.—

(1) IN GENERAL.—Solely for purposes of subsection (c) of this section and section 857(b)(6), any income derived from a shared appreciation provision shall be treated as gain recognized on the sale of the secured property.

(2) TREATMENT OF INCOME.—For purposes of applying subsection (c) of this section and section 857(b)(6) to any income described in paragraph (1)—

(A) the real estate investment trust shall be treated as holding the secured property for the period during which it held the shared appreciation provision (or, if shorter, for the period during which the secured property was held by the person holding such property), and

(B) the secured property shall be treated as property described in section 1221(a)(1) if it is so described in the hands of the person holding the secured property (or it would be so described if held by the real estate investment trust).

(3) COORDINATION WITH PROHIBITED TRANSACTIONS SAFE HARBOR.—For purposes of section 857(b)(6)(C)—

(A) the real estate investment trust shall be treated as having sold the secured property when it recognizes any income described in paragraph (1), and

(B) any expenditures made by any holder of the secured property shall be treated as made by the real estate investment trust.

(4) COORDINATION WITH 4-YEAR HOLDING PERIOD.—

(A) IN GENERAL.—For purposes of section 857(b)(6)(C), if a real estate investment trust is treated as having sold secured property under paragraph (3)(A), the trust shall be treated as having held such property for at least 4 years if—

(i) the secured property is sold or otherwise disposed of pursuant to a case under title 11 of the United States Code,

(ii) the seller is under the jurisdiction of the court in such case, and

(iii) the disposition is required by the court or is pursuant to a plan approved by the court.

(B) EXCEPTION.—Subparagraph (A) shall not apply if—

(i) the secured property was acquired by the seller with the intent to evict or foreclose, or

(ii) the trust knew or had reason to know that default on the obligation described in paragraph (5)(A) would occur.

(5) DEFINITIONS.—For purposes of this subsection—

(A) SHARED APPRECIATION PROVISION.—The term "shared appreciation provision" means any provision—

(i) which is in connection with an obligation which is held by the real estate investment trust and is secured by an interest in real property, and

(ii) which entitles the real estate investment trust to receive a specified portion of any gain realized on the sale or exchange of such real property (or of any gain which would be realized if the property were sold on a specified date) or appreciation in value as of any specified date.

(B) SECURED PROPERTY.—The term "secured property" means the real property referred to in subparagraph (A).

Amendments

• 1999, Tax Relief Extension Act of 1999 (P.L. 106-170)

P.L. 106-170, §532(c)(2)(K):

Amended Code Sec. 856(j)(2)(B) by striking "section 1221(1)" and inserting "section 1221(a)(1)". **Effective** for any instrument held, acquired, or entered into, any transaction entered into, and supplies held or acquired on or after 12-17-99.

• 1997, Taxpayer Relief Act of 1997 (P.L. 105-34)

P.L. 105-34, §1261(a):

Amended Code Sec. 856(j) by redesignating paragraph (4) as paragraph (5) and by inserting after paragraph (3) a new paragraph (4). **Effective** for tax years beginning after 8-5-97.

P.L. 105-34, §1261(b):

Amended Code Sec. 856(j)(5)(A)(ii) by inserting before the period "or appreciation in value as of any specified date". **Effective** for tax years beginning after 8-5-97.

• 1988, Technical and Miscellaneous Revenue Act of 1988 (P.L. 100-647)

P.L. 100-647, §1006(p)(2), provides:

(2) Notwithstanding section 669 of the Reform Act, the amendment made by section 662(c) of the Reform Act shall apply to taxable years beginning after December 31, 1986, but only in the case of obligations acquired after October 22, 1986.

• 1986, Tax Reform Act of 1986 (P.L. 99-514)

P.L. 99-514, §662(c):

Amended Code Sec. 856 by adding at the end thereof a new subsection (j). **Effective** for tax years beginning after 12-31-86, but only in the case of obligations acquired after 10-22-86.

[Sec. 856(k)]

(k) REQUIREMENT THAT ENTITY NOT BE CLOSELY HELD TREATED AS MET IN CERTAIN CASES.—A corporation, trust, or association—

(1) which for a taxable year meets the requirements of section 857(f)(1), and

(2) which does not know, or exercising reasonable diligence would not have known, whether the entity failed to meet the requirement of subsection (a)(6),

shall be treated as having met the requirement of subsection (a)(6) for the taxable year.

Amendments

• 1997, Taxpayer Relief Act of 1997 (P.L. 105-34)

P.L. 105-34, §1251(b)(1):

Amended Code Sec. 856 by adding at the end a new subsection (k). **Effective** for tax years beginning after 8-5-97.

[Sec. 856(l)]

(l) TAXABLE REIT SUBSIDIARY.—For purposes of this part—

(1) IN GENERAL.—The term "taxable REIT subsidiary" means, with respect to a real estate investment trust, a corporation (other than a real estate investment trust) if—

(A) such trust directly or indirectly owns stock in such corporation, and

(B) such trust and such corporation jointly elect that such corporation shall be treated as a taxable REIT subsidiary of such trust for purposes of this part.

Such an election, once made, shall be irrevocable unless both such trust and corporation consent to its revocation. Such election, and any revocation thereof, may be made without the consent of the Secretary.

(2) THIRTY-FIVE PERCENT OWNERSHIP IN ANOTHER TAXABLE REIT SUBSIDIARY.—The term "taxable REIT subsidiary" includes, with respect to any real estate investment trust, any corporation (other than a real estate investment trust) with respect to which a taxable REIT subsidiary of such trust owns directly or indirectly—

(A) securities possessing more than 35 percent of the total voting power of the outstanding securities of such corporation, or

(B) securities having a value of more than 35 percent of the total value of the outstanding securities of such corporation.

The preceding sentence shall not apply to a qualified REIT subsidiary (as defined in subsection (i)(2)). For purposes of subparagraph (B), securities described in subsection (m)(2)(A) shall not be taken into account.

(3) EXCEPTIONS.—The term "taxable REIT subsidiary" shall not include—

(A) any corporation which directly or indirectly operates or manages a lodging facility or a health care facility, and

(B) any corporation which directly or indirectly provides to any other person (under a franchise, license, or otherwise) rights to any brand name under which any lodging facility or health care facility is operated.

Subparagraph (B) shall not apply to rights provided to an eligible independent contractor to operate or manage a lodging facility or a health care facility if such rights are held by such corporation as a franchisee, licensee, or in a similar capacity and such lodging facility or health care facility is either owned by such corporation or is leased to such corporation from the real estate investment trust.

(4) DEFINITIONS.—For purposes of paragraph (3)—

(A) LODGING FACILITY.—The term "lodging facility" has the meaning given to such term by subsection (d)(9)(D)(ii).

(B) HEALTH CARE FACILITY.—The term "health care facility" has the meaning given to such term by subsection (e)(6)(D)(ii).

Amendments

• 2008, Housing Assistance Tax Act of 2008 (P.L. 110-289)

P.L. 110-289, §3061(c)(1)-(2):

Amended the last sentence of Code Sec. 856(l)(3) by inserting "or a health care facility" after "a lodging facility", and by inserting "or health care facility" after "such lodging facility". **Effective** for tax years beginning after 7-30-2008.

• 2007, Tax Technical Corrections Act of 2007 (P.L. 110-172)

P.L. 110-172, §11(a)(18):

Amended Code Sec. 856(l)(2) by striking the last sentence and inserting a new last sentence. **Effective** 12-29-2007. Prior to being stricken, the last sentence of Code Sec. 856(l)(2) read as follows:

The rule of section 856(c)(7) shall apply for purposes of subparagraph (B).

• 2000, Community Renewal Tax Relief Act of 2000 (P.L. 106-554)

P.L. 106-554, §319(10):

Amended Code Sec. 856(l)(4)(A) by striking "paragraph (9)(D)(ii)" and inserting "subsection (d)(9)(D)(ii)". **Effective** 12-21-2000.

• 1999, Tax Relief Extension Act of 1999 (P.L. 106-170)

P.L. 106-170, §543(a):

Amended Code Sec. 856 by adding at the end a new subsection (l). **Effective** for tax years beginning after 12-31-2000.

[Sec. 856(m)]

(m) SAFE HARBOR IN APPLYING SUBSECTION (c)(4).—

(1) IN GENERAL.—In applying subclause (III) of subsection (c)(4)(B)(iii), except as otherwise determined by the Secretary in regulations, the following shall not be considered securities held by the trust:

(A) Straight debt securities of an issuer which meet the requirements of paragraph (2).

(B) Any loan to an individual or an estate.

(C) Any section 467 rental agreement (as defined in section 467(d)), other than with a person described in subsection (d)(2)(B).

(D) Any obligation to pay rents from real property (as defined in subsection (d)(1)).

(E) Any security issued by a State or any political subdivision thereof, the District of Columbia, a foreign government or any political subdivision thereof, or the Commonwealth of Puerto Rico, but only if the determination of any payment received or accrued under such security does not depend in whole or in part on the profits of any entity not described in this subparagraph or payments on any obligation issued by such an entity,

(F) Any security issued by a real estate investment trust.

(G) Any other arrangement as determined by the Secretary.

(2) SPECIAL RULES RELATING TO STRAIGHT DEBT SECURITIES.—

(A) IN GENERAL.—For purposes of paragraph (1)(A), securities meet the requirements of this paragraph if such securities are straight debt, as defined in section 1361(c)(5) (without regard to subparagraph (B)(iii) thereof).

(B) SPECIAL RULES RELATING TO CERTAIN CONTINGENCIES.—For purposes of subparagraph (A), any interest or principal shall not be treated as failing to satisfy section 1361(c)(5)(B)(i) solely by reason of the fact that—

(i) the time of payment of such interest or principal is subject to a contingency, but only if—

(I) any such contingency does not have the effect of changing the effective yield to maturity, as determined under section 1272, other than a change in the annual yield to maturity which does not exceed the greater of 1/4 of 1 percent or 5 percent of the annual yield to maturity, or

(II) neither the aggregate issue price nor the aggregate face amount of the issuer's debt instruments held by the trust exceeds $1,000,000 and not more than 12 months of unaccrued interest can be required to be prepaid thereunder, or

(ii) the time or amount of payment is subject to a contingency upon a default or the exercise of a prepayment right by the issuer of the debt, but only if such contingency is consistent with customary commercial practice.

(C) SPECIAL RULES RELATING TO CORPORATE OR PARTNERSHIP ISSUERS.—In the case of an issuer which is a corporation or a partnership, securities that otherwise would be described in paragraph (1)(A) shall be considered not to be so described if the trust holding such securities and any of its controlled taxable REIT subsidiaries (as defined in subsection (d)(8)(A)(iv)) hold any securities of the issuer which—

(i) are not described in paragraph (1) (prior to the application of this subparagraph), and

(ii) have an aggregate value greater than 1 percent of the issuer's outstanding securities determined without regard to paragraph (3)(A)(i).

(3) LOOK-THROUGH RULE FOR PARTNERSHIP SECURITIES.—

(A) IN GENERAL.—For purposes of applying subclause (III) of subsection (c)(4)(B)(iii)—

(i) a trust's interest as a partner in a partnership (as defined in section 7701(a)(2)) shall not be considered a security, and

(ii) the trust shall be deemed to own its proportionate share of each of the assets of the partnership.

(B) DETERMINATION OF TRUST'S INTEREST IN PARTNERSHIP ASSETS.—For purposes of subparagraph (A), with respect to any taxable year beginning after the date of the enactment of this subparagraph—

(i) the trust's interest in the partnership assets shall be the trust's proportionate interest in any securities issued by the partnership (determined without regard to subparagraph (A)(i) and paragraph (4), but not including securities described in paragraph (1)), and

(ii) the value of any debt instrument shall be the adjusted issue price thereof, as defined in section 1272(a)(4).

(4) CERTAIN PARTNERSHIP DEBT INSTRUMENTS NOT TREATED AS A SECURITY.—For purposes of applying subclause (III) of subsection (c)(4)(B)(iii)—

(A) any debt instrument issued by a partnership and not described in paragraph (1) shall not be considered a security to the extent of the trust's interest as a partner in the partnership, and

(B) any debt instrument issued by a partnership and not described in paragraph (1) shall not be considered a security if at least 75 percent of the partnership's gross income (excluding gross income from prohibited transactions) is derived from sources referred to in subsection (c)(3).

(5) SECRETARIAL GUIDANCE.—The Secretary is authorized to provide guidance (including through the issuance of a written determination, as defined in section 6110(b)) that an arrangement shall not be considered a security held by the trust for purposes of applying subclause (III) of subsection (c)(4)(B)(iii) notwithstanding that such arrangement otherwise could be considered a security under subparagraph (F) of subsection (c)(5).

(6) TRANSITION RULE.—

(A) IN GENERAL.—Notwithstanding paragraph (2)(C), securities held by a trust shall not be considered securities held by the trust for purposes of subsection (c)(4)(B)(iii)(III) during any period beginning on or before October 22, 2004, if such securities—

(i) are held by such trust continuously during such period, and

(ii) would not be taken into account for purposes of such subsection by reason of paragraph (7)(C) of subsection (c) (as in effect on October 22, 2004) if the amendments made by section 243 of the American Jobs Creation Act of 2004 had never been enacted.

(B) RULE NOT TO APPLY TO SECURITIES HELD AFTER MATURITY DATE.—Subparagraph (A) shall not apply with respect to any security after the later of October 22, 2004, or the latest maturity date under the contract (as in effect on October 22, 2004) taking into account any renewal or extension permitted under the contract if such renewal or extension does not significantly modify any other terms of the contract.

(C) SUCCESSORS.—If the successor of a trust to which this paragraph applies acquires securities in a transaction to which section 381 applies, such trusts shall be treated as a single entity for purposes of determining the holding period of such securities under subparagraph (A).

Amendments

• 2005, Gulf Opportunity Zone Act of 2005 (P.L. 109-135)

P.L. 109-135, §403(d)(2):

Amended Code Sec. 856(m) by adding at the end a new paragraph (6). **Effective** as if included in the provision of the American Jobs Creation Act of 2004 (P.L. 108-357) to which it relates [**effective** for tax years beginning after 12-31-2000.—CCH].

• 2004, American Jobs Creation Act of 2004 (P.L. 108-357)

P.L. 108-357, §243(a)(2):

Amended Code Sec. 856 by adding at the end a new subsection (m). **Effective** for tax years beginning after 12-31-2000.

[Sec. 856(n)]

(n) RULES REGARDING FOREIGN CURRENCY TRANSACTIONS.—

(1) IN GENERAL.—For purposes of this part—

(A) passive foreign exchange gain for any taxable year shall not constitute gross income for purposes of subsection (c)(2), and

(B) real estate foreign exchange gain for any taxable year shall not constitute gross income for purposes of subsection (c)(3).

(2) REAL ESTATE FOREIGN EXCHANGE GAIN.—For purposes of this subsection, the term "real estate foreign exchange gain" means—

(A) foreign currency gain (as defined in section 988(b)(1)) which is attributable to—

(i) any item of income or gain described in subsection (c)(3),

(ii) the acquisition or ownership of obligations secured by mortgages on real property or on interests in real property (other than foreign currency gain attributable to any item of income or gain described in clause (i)), or

(iii) becoming or being the obligor under obligations secured by mortgages on real property or on interests in real property (other than foreign currency gain attributable to any item of income or gain described in clause (i)),

(B) section 987 gain attributable to a qualified business unit (as defined by section 989) of the real estate investment trust, but only if such qualified business unit meets the requirements under—

(i) subsection (c)(3) for the taxable year, and

(ii) subsection (c)(4)(A) at the close of each quarter that the real estate investment trust has directly or indirectly held the qualified business unit, and

(C) any other foreign currency gain as determined by the Secretary.

(3) PASSIVE FOREIGN EXCHANGE GAIN.—For purposes of this subsection, the term "passive foreign exchange gain" means—

(A) real estate foreign exchange gain,

(B) foreign currency gain (as defined in section 988(b)(1)) which is not described in subparagraph (A) and which is attributable to—

(i) any item of income or gain described in subsection (c)(2),

(ii) the acquisition or ownership of obligations (other than foreign currency gain attributable to any item of income or gain described in clause (i)), or

(iii) becoming or being the obligor under obligations (other than foreign currency gain attributable to any item of income or gain described in clause (i)), and

(C) any other foreign currency gain as determined by the Secretary.

(4) EXCEPTION FOR INCOME FROM SUBSTANTIAL AND REGULAR TRADING.—Notwithstanding this subsection or any other provision of this part, any section 988 gain derived by a corporation, trust, or association from dealing, or engaging in substantial and regular trading, in securities (as defined in section 475(c)(2)) shall constitute gross income which does not qualify under paragraph (2) or (3) of subsection (c). This paragraph shall not apply to income which does not constitute gross income by reason of subsection (c)(5)(G).

Amendments

• 2008, Housing Assistance Tax Act of 2008 (P.L. 110-289)

P.L. 110-289, §3031(a):

Amended Code Sec. 856 by adding at the end a new subsection (n). **Effective** for gains and items of income recognized after 7-30-2008.

[Sec. 857]

SEC. 857. TAXATION OF REAL ESTATE INVESTMENT TRUSTS AND THEIR BENEFICIARIES.

[Sec. 857(a)]

(a) REQUIREMENTS APPLICABLE TO REAL ESTATE INVESTMENT TRUSTS.—The provisions of this part (other than subsection (d) of this section and subsection (g) of section 856) shall not apply to a real estate investment trust for a taxable year unless—

(1) the deduction for dividends paid during the taxable year (as defined in section 561, but determined without regard to capital gains dividends) equals or exceeds—

(A) the sum of—

(i) 90 percent of the real estate investment trust taxable income for the taxable year (determined without regard to the deduction for dividends paid (as defined in section 561) and by excluding any net capital gain); and

(ii) 90 percent of the excess of the net income from foreclosure property over the tax imposed on such income by subsection (b)(4)(A); minus

(B) any excess noncash income (as determined under subsection (e));

(2) either—

(A) the provisions of this part apply to the real estate investment trust for all taxable years beginning after February 28, 1986, or

(B) as of the close of the taxable year, the real estate investment trust has no earnings and profits accumulated in any non-REIT year.

For purposes of the preceding sentence, the term "non-REIT year" means any taxable year to which the provisions of this part did not apply with respect to the entity.

The Secretary may waive the requirements of paragraph (1) for any taxable year if the real estate investment trust establishes to the satisfaction of the Secretary that it was unable to meet such requirements by reason of distributions previously made to meet the requirements of section 4981.

Amendments

• 1999, Tax Relief Extension Act of 1999 (P.L. 106-170)

P.L. 106-170, §556(a):

Amended Code Sec. 857(a)(1)(A)(i) and (ii) by striking "95 percent (90 percent for taxable years beginning before January 1, 1980)" and inserting "90 percent". **Effective** for tax years beginning after 12-31-2000.

• 1997, Taxpayer Relief Act of 1997 (P.L. 105-34)

P.L. 105-34, §1251(a)(1):

Amended Code Sec. 857(a) by striking paragraph (2) and by redesignating paragraph (3) as paragraph (2). **Effective** for tax years beginning after 8-5-97. Prior to amendment, Code Sec. 857(a)(2) read as follows:

(2) the real estate investment trust complies for such year with regulations prescribed by the Secretary for the purpose of ascertaining the actual ownership of the outstanding shares, or certificates of beneficial interest, of such trust and,

• 1988, Technical and Miscellaneous Revenue Act of 1988 (P.L. 100-647)

P.L. 100-647, §1006(s)(4):

Amended Code Sec. 857(a) by adding at the end thereof a new sentence. **Effective** as if included in the provision of P.L. 99-514 to which it relates.

• 1986, Tax Reform Act of 1986 (P.L. 99-514)

P.L. 99-514, §661(b):

Amended Code Sec. 857(a) by striking out "and" at the end of paragraph (1), by striking out the period at the end of paragraph (2) and inserting in lieu thereof ", and", and by adding at the end thereof new paragraph (3). **Effective** for tax years beginning after 12-31-86.

P.L. 99-514, §664(a):

Amended Code Sec. 857(a)(1)(B). **Effective** for tax years beginning after 12-31-86. Prior to amendment, Code Sec. 857(a)(1)(B) read as follows:

(B) the sum of—

(i) the amount of any penalty imposed on the real estate investment trust by section 6697 which is paid by such trust during the taxable year; and

(ii) the net loss derived from prohibited transactions, and

• 1976, Tax Reform Act of 1976 (P.L. 94-455)

P.L. 94-455, §1604(j):

Amended paragraph (1). **Effective** 10-4-76. Prior to amendment, paragraph (1) read as follows:

(1) the deduction for dividends paid during the taxable year (as defined in section 561, but determined without regard to capital gains dividends) equals or exceeds the sum of—

(A) 90 percent of the real estate investment trust taxable income for the taxable year (determined without regard to the deduction for dividends paid (as defined in section 561)); and

(B) 90 percent of the excess of (i) the net income from foreclosure property over (ii) the tax imposed on such income by subsection (b)(4)(A), and

P.L. 94-455, §1604(k)(2):

Added "and subsection (g) of section 856" after "subsection (d) of this section" in Code Sec. 857(a). **Effective** 10-4-76.

P.L. 94-455, §1906(b)(13)(A):

Amended 1954 Code by substituting "Secretary" for "Secretary or his delegate" each place it appeared. **Effective** 2-1-77.

• 1975 (P.L. 93-625)

P.L. 93-625, §6(d)(2):

Amended Code Sec. 857(a)(1). For **effective** date, see the historical comment for P.L. 93-625 following the text of Code Sec. 856(e). Prior to amendment, Code Sec. 857(a)(1) read as follows:

"(1) the deduction for dividends paid during the taxable year (as defined in section 561, but without regard to capital gains dividends) equal or exceeds 90 percent of its real estate investment trust taxable income for the taxable year (determined without regard to subsection (b)(2)(C)), and".

[Sec. 857(b)]

(b) METHOD OF TAXATION OF REAL ESTATE INVESTMENT TRUSTS AND HOLDERS OF SHARES OR CERTIFICATES OF BENEFICIAL INTEREST.—

(1) IMPOSITION OF TAX ON REAL ESTATE INVESTMENT TRUSTS.—There is hereby imposed for each taxable year on the real estate investment trust taxable income of every real estate investment trust a tax computed as provided in section 11, as though the real estate investment trust taxable income were the taxable income referred to in section 11.

(2) REAL ESTATE INVESTMENT TRUST TAXABLE INCOME.—For purposes of this part, the term "real estate investment trust taxable income" means the taxable income of the real estate investment trust, adjusted as follows:

(A) The deductions for corporations provided in part VIII (except section 248) of subchapter B (section 241 and following, relating to the deduction for dividends received, etc.) shall not be allowed.

(B) The deduction for dividends paid (as defined in section 561) shall be allowed, but shall be computed without regard to that portion of such deduction which is attributable to the amount excluded under subparagraph (D).

(C) The taxable income shall be computed without regard to section 443(b) (relating to computation of tax on change of annual accounting period).

(D) There shall be excluded an amount equal to the net income from foreclosure property.

(E) There shall be deducted an amount equal to the tax imposed by paragraphs (5) and (7) of this subsection, section 856(c)(7)(C), and section 856(g)(5) for the taxable year.

(F) There shall be excluded an amount equal to any net income derived from prohibited transactions.

(3) CAPITAL GAINS.—

(A) ALTERNATIVE TAX IN CASE OF CAPITAL GAINS.—If for any taxable year a real estate investment trust has a net capital gain, then, in lieu of the tax imposed by subsection (b)(1), there is hereby imposed a tax (if such tax is less than the tax imposed by such subsection) which shall consist of the sum of—

(i) a tax, computed as provided in subsection (b)(1), on the real estate investment trust taxable income (determined by excluding such net capital gain and by computing the deduction for dividends paid without regard to capital gains dividends), and

(ii) a tax determined at the rates provided in section 1201(a) on the excess of the net capital gain over the deduction for dividends paid (as defined in section 561) determined with reference to capital gains dividends only.

(B) TREATMENT OF CAPITAL GAIN DIVIDENDS BY SHAREHOLDERS.—A capital gain dividend shall be treated by the shareholders or holders of beneficial interests as a gain from the sale or exchange of a capital asset held for more than 1 year.

(C) DEFINITION OF CAPITAL GAIN DIVIDEND.—For purposes of this part, a capital gain dividend is any dividend, or part thereof, which is designated by the real estate investment trust as a capital gain dividend in a written notice mailed to its shareholders or holders of beneficial interests at any time before the expiration of 30 days after the close of its taxable year (or mailed to its shareholders or holders of beneficial interests with its annual report for the taxable year); except that, if there is an increase in the excess described in subparagraph (A)(ii) of this paragraph for such year which results from a determination (as defined in section 860(e)), such designation may be made with respect to such increase at any time before the expiration of 120 days after the date of such determination. If the aggregate amount so designated with respect to a taxable year of the trust (including capital gain dividends paid after the close of the taxable year described in section 858) is greater than the net capital gain of the taxable year, the portion of each distribution which shall be a capital gain dividend shall be only that proportion of the amount so designated which such net capital gain bears to the aggregate amount so designated. For purposes of this subparagraph, the amount of the net capital gain for any taxable year which is not a calendar year shall be determined without regard to any net capital loss attributable to transactions after December 31 of such year, and any such [net] capital loss shall be treated as arising on the 1st day of the next taxable year. To the extent provided in regulations, the preceding sentence shall apply also for purposes of computing the taxable income of the real estate investment trust.

(D) TREATMENT BY SHAREHOLDERS OF UNDISTRIBUTED CAPITAL GAINS.—

(i) Every shareholder of a real estate investment trust at the close of the trust's taxable year shall include, in computing his long-term capital gains in his return for his taxable year in which the last day of the trust's taxable year falls, such amount as the trust shall designate in respect of such shares in a written notice mailed to its shareholders at any time prior to the expiration of 60 days after the close of its taxable year (or mailed to its shareholders or holders of beneficial interests with its annual report for the taxable year), but the amount so includible by any shareholder shall not exceed that part of the amount subjected to tax in subparagraph (A)(ii) which he would have received if all of such amount had been distributed as capital gain dividends by the trust to the holders of such shares at the close of its taxable year.

(ii) For purposes of this title, every such shareholder shall be deemed to have paid, for his taxable year under clause (i), the tax imposed by subparagraph (A)(ii) on the amounts required by this subparagraph to be included in respect of such shares in computing his long-term capital gains for that year; and such shareholders shall be allowed credit or refund as the case may be, for the tax so deemed to have been paid by him.

(iii) The adjusted basis of such shares in the hands of the holder shall be increased with respect to the amounts required by this subparagraph to be included in computing his long-term capital gains, by the difference between the amount of such includible gains and the tax deemed paid by such shareholder in respect of such shares under clause (ii).

(iv) In the event of such designation, the tax imposed by subparagraph (A)(ii) shall be paid by the real estate investment trust within 30 days after the close of its taxable year.

(v) The earnings and profits of such real estate investment trust, and the earnings and profits of any such shareholder which is a corporation, shall be appropriately adjusted in accordance with regulations prescribed by the Secretary.

(vi) As used in this subparagraph, the terms "shares" and "shareholders" shall include beneficial interests and holders of beneficial interests, respectively.

(E) COORDINATION WITH NET OPERATING LOSS PROVISIONS.—For purposes of section 172, if a real estate investment trust pays capital gain dividends during any taxable year, the amount of the net capital gain for such taxable year (to the extent such gain does not exceed the amount of such capital gain dividends) shall be excluded in determining—

(i) the net operating loss for the taxable year, and

(ii) the amount of the net operating loss of any prior taxable year which may be carried through such taxable year under section 172(b)(2) to a succeeding taxable year.

(F) CERTAIN DISTRIBUTIONS.—In the case of a shareholder of a real estate investment trust to whom section 897 does not apply by reason of the second sentence of section 897(h)(1), the amount which would be included in computing long-term capital gains for such shareholder under subparagraph (B) or (D) (without regard to this subparagraph)—

(i) shall not be included in computing such shareholder's long-term capital gains, and

(ii) shall be included in such shareholder's gross income as a dividend from the real estate investment trust.

(4) INCOME FROM FORECLOSURE PROPERTY.—

(A) IMPOSITION OF TAX.—A tax is hereby imposed for each taxable year on the net income from foreclosure property of every real estate investment trust. Such tax shall be computed by multiplying the net income from foreclosure property by the highest rate of tax specified in section 11(b).

(B) NET INCOME FROM FORECLOSURE PROPERTY.—For purposes of this part, the term "net income from foreclosure property" means the excess of—

(i) gain (including any foreign currency gain, as defined in section 988(b)(1)) from the sale or other disposition of foreclosure property described in section 1221(a)(1) and the gross income for the taxable year derived from foreclosure property (as defined in section 856(e)), but only to the extent such gross income is not described in (or, in the case of foreign currency gain, not attributable to gross income described in) section 856(c)(3) other than subparagraph (F) thereof, over

(ii) the deductions allowed by this chapter which are directly connected with the production of the income referred to in clause (i).

(5) IMPOSITION OF TAX IN CASE OF FAILURE TO MEET CERTAIN REQUIREMENTS.—If section 856(c)(6) applies to a real estate investment trust for any taxable year, there is hereby imposed on such trust a tax in an amount equal to the greater of—

(A) the excess of—

(i) 95 percent of the gross income (excluding gross income from prohibited transactions) of the real estate investment trust, over

(ii) the amount of such gross income which is derived from sources referred to in section 856(c)(2); or

(B) the excess of—

(i) 75 percent of the gross income (excluding gross income from prohibited transactions) of the real estate investment trust, over

(ii) the amount of such gross income which is derived from sources referred to in section 856(c)(3),

multiplied by a fraction the numerator of which is the real estate investment trust taxable income for the taxable year (determined without regard to the deductions provided in paragraphs (2)(B) and (2)(E), without regard to any net operating loss deduction, and by excluding any net capital gain) and the denominator of which is the gross income for the taxable year (excluding gross income from prohibited transactions; gross income and gain from foreclosure property (as defined in section 856(e), but only to the extent such gross income and gain is not described in subparagraph (A), (B), (C), (D), (E), or (G) of section 856(c)(3)); long-term capital gain; and short-term capital gain to the extent of any short-term capital loss).

(6) INCOME FROM PROHIBITED TRANSACTIONS.—

(A) IMPOSITION OF TAX.—There is hereby imposed for each taxable year of every real estate investment trust a tax equal to 100 percent of the net income derived from prohibited transactions.

(B) DEFINITIONS.—For purposes of this part—

(i) the term "net income derived from prohibited transactions" means the excess of the gain (including any foreign currency gain, as defined in section 988(b)(1)) from prohibited transactions over the deductions (including any foreign currency loss, as defined in section 988(b)(2)) allowed by this chapter which are directly connected with prohibited transactions;

(ii) in determining the amount of the net income derived from prohibited transactions, there shall not be taken into account any item attributable to any prohibited transaction for which there was a loss; and

(iii) the term "prohibited transaction" means a sale or other disposition of property described in section 1221(a)(1) which is not foreclosure property.

(C) CERTAIN SALES NOT TO CONSTITUTE PROHIBITED TRANSACTIONS.—For purposes of this part, the term "prohibited transaction" does not include a sale of property which is a real estate asset (as defined in section 856(c)(5)(B)) and which is described in section 1221(a)(1) if—

(i) the trust has held the property for not less than 2 years;

(ii) aggregate expenditures made by the trust, or any partner of the trust, during the 2-year period preceding the date of sale which are includible in the basis of the property do not exceed 30 percent of the net selling price of the property;

(iii)(I) during the taxable year the trust does not make more than 7 sales of property (other than sales of foreclosure property or sales to which section 1033 applies), or (II) the aggregate adjusted bases (as determined for purposes of computing earnings and profits) of property (other than sales of foreclosure property or sales to which section 1033 applies) sold during the taxable year does not exceed 10 percent of the aggregate bases (as so determined) of all of the assets of the trust as of the beginning of the taxable year, or (III) the fair market value of property (other than sales of foreclosure property or sales to which section 1033 applies) sold during the taxable year does not exceed 10 percent of the fair market value of all of the assets of the trust as of the beginning of the taxable year;

(iv) in the case of property, which consists of land or improvements, not acquired through foreclosure (or deed in lieu of foreclosure), or lease termination, the trust has held the property for not less than 2 years for production of rental income; and

(v) if the requirement of clause (iii)(I) is not satisfied, substantially all of the marketing and development expenditures with respect to the property were made through an independent contractor (as defined in section 856(d)(3)) from whom the trust itself does not derive or receive any income.

(D) CERTAIN SALES NOT TO CONSTITUTE PROHIBITED TRANSACTIONS.—For purposes of this part, the term "prohibited transaction" does not include a sale of property which is a real estate asset (as defined in section 856(c)(5)(B)) and which is described in section 1221(a)(1) if—

(i) the trust held the property for not less than 2 years in connection with the trade or business of producing timber,

(ii) the aggregate expenditures made by the trust, or a partner of the trust, during the 2-year period preceding the date of sale which—

(I) are includible in the basis of the property (other than timberland acquisition expenditures), and

(II) are directly related to operation of the property for the production of timber or for the preservation of the property for use as timberland,

do not exceed 30 percent of the net selling price of the property,

(iii) the aggregate expenditures made by the trust, or a partner of the trust, during the 2-year period preceding the date of sale which—

(I) are includible in the basis of the property (other than timberland acquisition expenditures), and

(II) are not directly related to operation of the property for the production of timber, or for the preservation of the property for use as timberland,

do not exceed 5 percent of the net selling price of the property,

(iv)(I) during the taxable year the trust does not make more than 7 sales of property (other than sales of foreclosure property or sales to which section 1033 applies), or

(II) the aggregate adjusted bases (as determined for purposes of computing earnings and profits) of property (other than sales of foreclosure property or sales to which section 1033 applies) sold during the taxable year does not exceed 10 percent of the aggregate bases (as so determined) of all of the assets of the trust as of the beginning of the taxable year, or

(III) the fair market value of property (other than sales of foreclosure property or sales to which section 1033 applies) sold during the taxable year does not exceed 10 percent of the fair market value of all of the assets of the trust as of the beginning of the taxable year,

(v) in the case that the requirement of clause (iv)(I) is not satisfied, substantially all of the marketing expenditures with respect to the property were made through an independent contractor (as defined in section 856(d)(3)) from whom the trust itself does not derive or receive any income, or, in the case of a sale on or before the termination date, a taxable REIT subsidiary, and

(vi) the sales price of the property sold by the trust is not based in whole or in part on income or profits, including income or profits derived from the sale or operation of such property.

(E) SPECIAL RULES.—In applying subparagraphs (C) and (D) the following special rules apply:

(i) The holding period of property acquired through foreclosure (or deed in lieu of foreclosure), or termination of the lease, includes the period for which the trust held the loan which such property secured, or the lease of such property.

(ii) In the case of a property acquired through foreclosure (or deed in lieu of foreclosure), or termination of a lease, expenditures made by, or for the account of, the mortgagor or lessee after default became imminent will be regarded as made by the trust.

(iii) Expenditures (including expenditures regarded as made directly by the trust, or indirectly by any partner of the trust, under clause (ii)) will not be taken into account if they relate to foreclosure property and did not cause the property to lose its status as foreclosure property.

(iv) Expenditures will not be taken into account if they are made solely to comply with standards or requirements of any government or governmental authority having relevant jurisdiction, or if they are made to restore the property as a result of losses arising from fire, storm or other casualty.

(v) The term "expenditures" does not include advances on a loan made by the trust.

(vi) The sale of more than one property to one buyer as part of one transaction constitutes one sale.

(vii) The term "sale" does not include any transaction in which the net selling price is less than $10,000.

(F) SALES NOT MEETING REQUIREMENTS.—In determining whether or not any sale constitutes a "prohibited transaction" for purposes of subparagraph (A), the fact that such sale does not meet the requirements of subparagraph (C) or (D) shall not be taken into account; and such determination, in the case of a sale not meeting such requirements, shall be made as if subparagraphs (C), (D), and (E) had not been enacted.

(G) SALES OF PROPERTY THAT ARE NOT A PROHIBITED TRANSACTION.—In the case of a sale on or before the termination date, the sale of property which is not a prohibited transaction through the application of subparagraph (D) shall be considered property held for investment or for use in a trade or business and not property described in section 1221(a)(1) for all purposes of this subtitle. For purposes of the preceding sentence, the reference to subparagraph (D) shall be a reference to such subparagraph as in effect on the day before the enactment of the Housing Assistance Tax Act of 2008, as modified by subparagraph (G) as so in effect.

(H) TERMINATION DATE.—For purposes of this paragraph, the term "termination date" has the meaning given such term by section 856(c)(8).

(7) INCOME FROM REDETERMINED RENTS, REDETERMINED DEDUCTIONS, AND EXCESS INTEREST.—

(A) IMPOSITION OF TAX.—There is hereby imposed for each taxable year of the real estate investment trust a tax equal to 100 percent of redetermined rents, redetermined deductions, and excess interest.

(B) REDETERMINED RENTS.—

(i) IN GENERAL.—The term "redetermined rents" means rents from real property (as defined in section 856(d)) to the extent the amount of the rents would (but for subparagraph (E)) be reduced on distribution, apportionment, or allocation under section 482 to clearly reflect income as a result of services furnished or rendered by a taxable REIT subsidiary of the real estate investment trust to a tenant of such trust.

(ii) EXCEPTION FOR DE MINIMIS AMOUNTS.—Clause (i) shall not apply to amounts described in section 856(d)(7)(A) with respect to a property to the extent such amounts do not exceed the one percent threshold described in section 856(d)(7)(B) with respect to such property.

(iii) EXCEPTION FOR COMPARABLY PRICED SERVICES.—Clause (i) shall not apply to any service rendered by a taxable REIT subsidiary of a real estate investment trust to a tenant of such trust if—

(I) such subsidiary renders a significant amount of similar services to persons other than such trust and tenants of such trust who are unrelated (within the meaning of section 856(d)(8)(F)) to such subsidiary, trust, and tenants, but

(II) only to the extent the charge for such service so rendered is substantially comparable to the charge for the similar services rendered to persons referred to in subclause (I).

(iv) EXCEPTION FOR CERTAIN SEPARATELY CHARGED SERVICES.—Clause (i) shall not apply to any service rendered by a taxable REIT subsidiary of a real estate investment trust to a tenant of such trust if—

(I) the rents paid to the trust by tenants (leasing at least 25 percent of the net leasable space in the trust's property) who are not receiving such service from such subsidiary are substantially comparable to the rents paid by tenants leasing comparable space who are receiving such service from such subsidiary, and

(II) the charge for such service from such subsidiary is separately stated.

(v) EXCEPTION FOR CERTAIN SERVICES BASED ON SUBSIDIARY'S INCOME FROM THE SERVICES.—Clause (i) shall not apply to any service rendered by a taxable REIT subsidiary of a real estate investment trust to a tenant of such trust if the gross income of such subsidiary from such service is not less than 150 percent of such subsidiary's direct cost in furnishing or rendering the service.

(vi) EXCEPTIONS GRANTED BY SECRETARY.—The Secretary may waive the tax otherwise imposed by subparagraph (A) if the trust establishes to the satisfaction of the Secretary that rents charged to tenants were established on an arms' length basis even though a taxable REIT subsidiary of the trust provided services to such tenants.

(C) REDETERMINED DEDUCTIONS.—The term "redetermined deductions" means deductions (other than redetermined rents) of a taxable REIT subsidiary of a real estate investment trust to the extent the amount of such deductions would (but for subparagraph (E)) be decreased on distribution, apportionment, or allocation under section 482 to clearly reflect income as between such subsidiary and such trust.

(D) EXCESS INTEREST.—The term "excess interest" means any deductions for interest payments by a taxable REIT subsidiary of a real estate investment trust to such trust to the extent that the interest payments are in excess of a rate that is commercially reasonable.

(E) COORDINATION WITH SECTION 482.—The imposition of tax under subparagraph (A) shall be in lieu of any distribution, apportionment, or allocation under section 482.

(F) REGULATORY AUTHORITY.—The Secretary shall prescribe such regulations as may be necessary or appropriate to carry out the purposes of this paragraph. Until the Secretary prescribes such regulations, real estate investment trusts and their taxable REIT subsidiaries may base their allocations on any reasonable method.

(8) LOSS ON SALE OR EXCHANGE OF STOCK HELD 6 MONTHS OR LESS.—

(A) IN GENERAL.—If—

(i) subparagraph (B) or (D) of paragraph (3) provides that any amount with respect to any share or beneficial interest is to be treated as a long-term capital gain, and

(ii) the taxpayer has held such share or interest for 6 months or less,

then any loss on the sale or exchange of such share or interest shall, to the extent of the amount described in clause (i), be treated as a long-term capital loss.

(B) DETERMINATION OF HOLDING PERIODS.—For purposes of this paragraph, in determining the period for which the taxpayer has held any share of stock or beneficial interest—

(i) the rules of paragraphs (3) and (4) of section 246(c) shall apply, and

(ii) there shall not be taken into account any day which is more than 6 months after the date on which such share or interest becomes ex-dividend.

(C) EXCEPTION FOR LOSSES INCURRED UNDER PERIODIC LIQUIDATION PLANS.—To the extent provided in regulations, subparagraph (A) shall not apply to any loss incurred on the sale or exchange of shares of stock of, or beneficial interest in, a real estate investment trust pursuant to a plan which provides for the periodic liquidation of such shares or interests.

(9) TIME CERTAIN DIVIDENDS TAKEN INTO ACCOUNT.—For purposes of this title, any dividend declared by a real estate investment trust in October, November, or December of any calendar year and payable to shareholders of record on a specified date in such a month shall be deemed—

(A) to have been received by each shareholder on December 31 of such calendar year, and

(B) to have been paid by such trust on December 31 of such calendar year (or, if earlier, as provided in section 858).

The preceding sentence shall apply only if such dividend is actually paid by the company during January of the following calendar year.

Amendments

• 2008, Housing Assistance Tax Act of 2008 (P.L. 110-289)

P.L. 110-289, §3033(a):

Amended Code Sec. 857(b)(4)(B)(i). **Effective** for gains recognized after 7-30-2008. Prior to amendment, Code Sec. 857(b)(4)(B)(i) read as follows:

(i) gain from the sale or other disposition of foreclosure property described in section 1221(a)(1) and the gross income for the taxable year derived from foreclosure property (as defined in section 856(e)), but only to the extent such gross income is not described in subparagraph (A), (B), (C), (D), (E), or (G) of section 856(c)(3), over

P.L. 110-289, §3033(b):

Amended Code Sec. 857(b)(6)(B)(i). **Effective** for gains and deductions recognized after 7-30-2008. Prior to amendment, Code Sec. 857(b)(6)(B)(i) read as follows:

(i) the term "net income derived from prohibited transactions" means the excess of the gain from prohibited transactions over the deductions allowed by this chapter which are directly connected with prohibited transactions;

P.L. 110-289, §3051(a)(1)-(3):

Amended Code Sec. 857(b)(6) by striking "4 years" in subparagraphs (C)(i), (C)(iv), and (D)(i) and inserting "2 years", by striking "4-year period" in subparagraphs (C)(ii), (D)(ii), and (D)(iii) and inserting "2-year period", and by striking "real estate asset" and all that follows through "if" in the matter preceding clause (i) of subparagraphs (C) and (D), respectively, and inserting "real estate asset (as defined in section 856(c)(5)(B)) and which is described in section 1221(a)(1) if". **Effective** for sales made after 7-30-2008. Prior to amendment, the matter preceding clause (i) of Code Sec. 857(b)(6)(C) and (D) read as follows:

(C) CERTAIN SALES NOT TO CONSTITUTE PROHIBITED TRANSACTIONS.—For purposes of this part, the term "prohibited transaction" does not include a sale of property which is a real estate asset as defined in section 856(c)(5)(B) if—

* * *

(D) CERTAIN SALES NOT TO CONSTITUTE PROHIBITED TRANSACTIONS.—For purposes of this part, the term "prohibited transaction" does not include a sale of property which is a real estate asset (as defined in section 856(c)(5)(B)) if—

P.L. 110-289, §3051(b)(1)-(2):

Amended Code Sec. 857(b)(6) by striking subparagraph (G) and redesignating subparagraphs (H) and (I) as subparagraphs (G) and (H), respectively, and in subparagraph (G), as so redesignated, by adding at the end a new sentence. **Effective** for sales made after 7-30-2008. Prior to being stricken, Code Sec. 857(b)(6)(G) read as follows:

(G) SPECIAL RULES FOR SALES TO QUALIFIED ORGANIZATIONS.—

(i) IN GENERAL.—In the case of the sale of a real estate asset (as defined in section 856(c)(5)(B)) to a qualified organization (as defined in section 170(h)(3)) exclusively for conservation purposes (within the meaning of section 170(h)(1)(C)), subparagraph (D) shall be applied—

(I) by substituting "2 years" for "4 years" in clause (i), and

(II) by substituting "2-year period" for "4-year period" in clauses (ii) and (iii).

(ii) TERMINATION.—This subparagraph shall not apply to sales after the termination date.

P.L. 110-289, §3052(1)-(2):

Amended Code Sec. 857(b)(6) by striking the semicolon at the end of subparagraph (C)(iii) and inserting ", or (III) the fair market value of property (other than sales of foreclosure property or sales to which section 1033 applies) sold during the taxable year does not exceed 10 percent of the fair market value of all of the assets of the trust as of the beginning of the taxable year;", and by adding "or" at the end of subclause (II) of subparagraph (D)(iv) and by adding at the end of such subparagraph a new subclause (III). **Effective** for sales made after 7-30-2008.

• 2008, Heartland, Habitat, Harvest, and Horticulture Act of 2008 (P.L. 110-246)

P.L. 110-246, §15311(c):

Amended Code Sec. 857(b)(3)(A)(ii) by striking "rate" and inserting "rates". **Effective** for tax years ending after 5-22-2008.

P.L. 110-246, §15315(a):

Amended Code Sec. 857(b)(6) by adding at the end a new subparagraph (G). **Effective** for dispositions in tax years beginning after 5-22-2008.

P.L. 110-246, §15315(b):

Amended Code Sec. 857(b)(6)(D)(v) by inserting ", or, in the case of a sale on or before the termination date, a taxable REIT subsidiary" after "any income". **Effective** for dispositions in tax years beginning after 5-22-2008.

P.L. 110-246, §15315(c):

Amended Code Sec. 857(b)(6), as amended by Act Sec. 15315(a), by adding at the end a new subparagraph (H). **Effective** for dispositions in tax years beginning after 5-22-2008.

P.L. 110-246, §15315(d):

Amended Code Sec. 857(b)(6), as amended by Act Sec. 15315(a) and (c), by adding at the end a new subparagraph (I). **Effective** for dispositions in tax years beginning after 5-22-2008.

• 2007, Tax Technical Corrections Act of 2007 (P.L. 110-172)

P.L. 110-172, §11(a)(17)(B):

Amended Code Sec. 857(b)(8)(B). **Effective** 12-29-2007. Prior to amendment, Code Sec. 857(b)(8)(B) read as follows:

(B) DETERMINATION OF HOLDING PERIOD.—For purposes of this paragraph, the rules of paragraphs (3) and (4) of section 246(c) shall apply in determining the period for which the taxpayer has held any share of stock or beneficial interest; except that "6 months" shall be substituted for the number of days specified in subparagraph (B) of section 246(c)(3).

• 2005, Gulf Opportunity Zone Act of 2005 (P.L. 109-135)

P.L. 109-135, §403(d)(3):

Amended Code Sec. 857(b)(2)(E) by striking "section 856(c)(7)(B)(iii), and section 856(g)(1)." and inserting "section 856(c)(7)(C), and section 856(g)(5)". **Effective** as if included in the provision of the American Jobs Creation Act of 2004 (P.L. 108-357) to which it relates [**effective** for tax years beginning after 10-22-2004.—CCH].

P.L. 109-135, §412(ii)(1)-(2):

Amended Code Sec. 857(b)(6) by striking "subparagraph (C)" and inserting "subparagraphs (C) and (D)" in subparagraph (E); and in subparagraph (F) by striking "subparagraph (C) of this paragraph" and inserting "subparagraph (C) or (D)", and by striking "subparagraphs (C) and (D)" and inserting "subparagraphs (C), (D), and (E)". **Effective** 12-21-2005.

• 2004, American Jobs Creation Act of 2004 (P.L. 108-357)

P.L. 108-357, §243(c):

Amended Code Sec. 857(b)(7)(B) by striking clause (ii) and by redesignating clauses (iii), (iv), (v), (vi), and (vii) as clauses (ii), (iii), (iv), (v), and (vi), respectively. **Effective** for tax years beginning after 10-22-2004. Prior to being stricken, Code Sec. 857(b)(7)(B)(ii) read as follows:

(ii) EXCEPTION FOR CERTAIN AMOUNTS.—Clause (i) shall not apply to amounts received directly or indirectly by a real estate investment trust—

(I) for services furnished or rendered by a taxable REIT subsidiary that are described in paragraph (1)(B) of section 856(d), or

(II) from a taxable REIT subsidiary that are described in paragraph (7)(C)(ii) of such section.

P.L. 108-357, §243(e):

Amended Code Sec. 857(b)(5)(A)(i) by striking "90 percent" and inserting "95 percent". **Effective** for tax years beginning after 10-22-2004.

P.L. 108-357, §243(f)(4):

Amended Code Sec. 857(b)(2)(E) by striking "(7)" and inserting "(7) of this subsection, section 856(c)(7)(B)(iii), and section 856(g)(1). [sic]". **Effective** for tax years ending after 10-22-2004 [effective date amended by P.L. 109-135, §403(d)(4)].

P.L. 108-357, §321(a):

Amended Code Sec. 857(b)(6) by redesignating subparagraphs (D) and (E) as subparagraphs (E) and (F), respectively, and by inserting after subparagraph (C) a new subparagraph (D). **Effective** for tax years beginning after 10-22-2004.

P.L. 108-357, §418(b):

Amended Code Sec. 857(b)(3) by adding at the end a new subparagraph (F). For the **effective** date, see Act Sec. 418(c), below.

P.L. 108-357, §418(c), as amended by P.L. 109-135, §403(p)(2), provides:

(c) EFFECTIVE DATE.—The amendments made by this section shall apply to—

(1) any distribution by a real estate investment trust which is treated as a deduction for a taxable year of such trust beginning after the date of the enactment of this Act, and

(2) any distribution by a real estate investment trust made after such date which is treated as a deduction under section 860 for a taxable year of such trust beginning on or before such date.

• 2002, Job Creation and Worker Assistance Act of 2002 (P.L. 107-147)

P.L. 107-147, §413(a)(1)-(2):

Amended Code Sec. 857(b)(7) by striking "the amount of which" and inserting "to the extent the amount of the rents" in clause (i) of subparagraph (B), and by striking "if the amount" and inserting "to the extent the amount" in subparagraph (C). **Effective** as if included in section 545 of P.L. 106-170 [**effective** for tax years beginning after 12-31-2000.—CCH].

P.L. 107-147, §417(13):

Amended Code Sec. 857(b)(7)(B)(i) by striking "subsection 856(d)" and inserting "section 856(d)". **Effective** 3-9-2002.

• 2000, Community Renewal Tax Relief Act of 2000 (P.L. 106-554)

P.L. 106-554, §311(b):

Amended Code Sec. 857(b)(7)(B)(ii). **Effective** as if included in the provision of P.L. 106-170 to which it relates [**effective** for tax years beginning after 12-31-2000.—CCH]. Prior to amendment, Code Sec. 857(b)(7)(B)(ii) read as follows:

(ii) EXCEPTION FOR CERTAIN SERVICES.—Clause (i) shall not apply to amounts received directly or indirectly by a real estate investment trust for services described in paragraph (1)(B) or (7)(C)(i) of section 856(d).

• 1999, Tax Relief Extension Act of 1999 (P.L. 106-170)

P.L. 106-170, §532(c)(2)(L):

Amended Code Sec. 857(b)(4)(B)(i) by striking "section 1221(1)" and inserting "section 1221(a)(1)". **Effective** for any instrument held, acquired, or entered into, any transaction entered into, and supplies held or acquired on or after 12-17-99.

P.L. 106-170, §532(c)(2)(M):

Amended Code Sec. 857(b)(6)(B)(iii) by striking "section 1221(1)" and inserting "section 1221(a)(1)". **Effective** for any instrument held, acquired, or entered into, any transaction entered into, and supplies held or acquired on or after 12-17-99.

P.L. 106-170, §545(a):

Amended Code Sec. 857(b) by redesignating paragraphs (7) and (8) as paragraphs (8) and (9), respectively, and by inserting after paragraph (6) a new paragraph (7). **Effective** for tax years beginning after 12-31-2000.

P.L. 106-170, §545(b):

Amended Code Sec. 857(b)(2)(E) by striking "paragraph (5)" and inserting "paragraphs (5) and (7)". **Effective** for tax years beginning after 12-31-2000.

P.L. 106-170, §556(b):

Amended Code Sec. 857(b)(5)(A)(i) by striking "95 percent (90 percent in the case of taxable years beginning before January 1, 1980)" and inserting "90 percent". **Effective** for tax years beginning after 12-31-2000.

• 1997, Taxpayer Relief Act of 1997 (P.L. 105-34)

P.L. 105-34, §1254(a):

Amended Code Sec. 857(b)(3) by redesignating subparagraph (D) as subparagraph (E) and by inserting after subparagraph (C) a new subparagraph (D). **Effective** for tax years beginning after 8-5-97.

P.L. 105-34, §1254(b)(1):

Amended Code Sec. 857(b)(7)(A)(i) by striking "subparagraph (B)" and inserting "subparagraph (B) or (D)". **Effective** for tax years beginning after 8-5-97.

P.L. 105-34, §1255(b)(2):

Amended Code Sec. 857(b)(5) by striking "section 856(c)(7)" and inserting "section 856(c)(6)". **Effective** for tax years beginning after 8-5-97.

P.L. 105-34, §1255(b)(3):

Amended Code Sec. 857(b)(6)(C) by striking "section 856(c)(6)(B)" and inserting "section 856(c)(5)(B)". **Effective** for tax years beginning after 8-5-97.

P.L. 105-34, §1260:

Amended Code Sec. 857(b)(6)(C)(iii)(I)-(II) by striking "(other than foreclosure property)" and inserting "(other than sales of foreclosure property or sales to which section 1033 applies)". **Effective** for tax years beginning after 8-5-97.

• 1988, Technical and Miscellaneous Revenue Act of 1988 (P.L. 100-647)

P.L. 100-647, §1006(s)(2):

Amended Code Sec. 857(b)(3)(C) by striking out "real estate investment trust taxable income" in the last sentence and inserting in lieu thereof "the taxable income of the real estate investment trust". **Effective** as if included in the provision of P.L. 99-514 to which it relates.

P.L. 100-647, §1006(s)(5)(A)-(D):

Amended Code Sec. 857(b)(8) by striking out "in December" and inserting in lieu thereof "in October, November, or December", by striking out "in such month" and inserting in lieu thereof "in such a month", by striking out "on such date" in subparagraphs (A) and (B) and inserting in lieu thereof "on December 31 of such calendar year", and by striking out "before February 1" and inserting in lieu thereof "during January". **Effective** with respect to dividends declared in 1988 and subsequent calendar years.

P.L. 100-647, §1018(u)(28):

Amended Code Sec. 857(b)(3)(C) by striking out "such [net]capital loss such" in the second to last sentence and inserting in lieu thereof "such [net] capital loss shall". **Effective** as if included in the provision of P.L. 99-514 to which it relates.

• 1986, Tax Reform Act of 1986 (P.L. 99-514)

P.L. 99-514, §665(a)(1):

Amended Code Sec. 857(b)(3) by adding at the end thereof new subparagraph (D). **Effective** for tax years beginning after 12-31-86.

P.L. 99-514, §665(a)(2):

Amended Code Sec. 857(b)(3)(C) by striking out the last sentence. **Effective** for tax years beginning after 12-31-86. Prior to amendment, the last sentence of Code Sec. 857(b)(3)(C) read as follows:

For purposes of this subparagraph, the net capital gain shall be deemed not to exceed the real estate investment trust taxable income (determined without regard to the deduction for dividends paid (as defined in section 561) for the taxable year).

P.L. 99-514, §665(b)(1):

Amended Code Sec. 857(b)(3)(C) by striking out "the close of its taxable year" and inserting in lieu thereof "the close of its taxable year (or mailed to its shareholders or holders of beneficial interests with its annual report for the taxable year)". **Effective** for tax years beginning after 12-31-86.

P.L. 99-514, §666(a)(1):

Amended Code Sec. 857(b)(6)(C)(iii). **Effective** for tax years beginning after 12-31-86. Prior to amendment, Code Sec. 857(b)(6)(C)(iii) read as follows:

(iii) during the taxable year the trust does not make more than 5 sales of property (other than foreclosure property); and

P.L. 99-514, §666(a)(2):

Amended Code Sec. 857(b)(6)(C)(ii) by striking out "20 percent" and inserting in lieu thereof "30 percent". **Effective** for tax years beginning after 12-31-86.

P.L. 99-514, §666(a)(3):

Amended Code Sec. 857(b)(6)(C) by striking out "and" at the end of clause (iii), by striking out the period at the end of clause (iv) and inserting in lieu thereof "; and", and by inserting after clause (iv) new clause (v). **Effective** for tax years beginning after 12-31-86.

P.L. 99-514, §666(b)(1):

Amended Code Sec. 857(b)(6)(B)(ii). **Effective** for tax years beginning after 12-31-86. Prior to amendment, Code Sec. 857(b)(6)(B)(ii) read as follows:

(ii) the term "net loss derived from prohibited transactions" means the excess of the deductions allowed by this chapter which are directly connected with prohibited transactions over the gain from prohibited transactions; and

P.L. 99-514, §666(b)(2):

Amended Code Sec. 857(b)(2)(F) by striking out "and there shall be included an amount equal to any net loss derived from prohibited transactions" after "prohibited transactions". **Effective** for tax years beginning after 12-31-86.

P.L. 99-514, §668(b)(1)(A):

Amended Code Sec. 857(b) by adding at the end thereof new paragraph (8). **Effective** for calendar years beginning after 12-31-86.

P.L. 99-514, §668(b)(3):

Amended Code Sec. 857(b)(3)(C) by adding at the end thereof two new sentences. **Effective** for calendar years beginning after 12-31-86.

• 1984, Deficit Reduction Act of 1984 (P.L. 98-369)

P.L. 98-369, §55(b):

Amended Code Sec. 857(b)(7). **Effective** for losses incurred with respect to shares of stock and beneficial interests with respect to which the taxpayer's holding period begins after 7-18-84. Prior to amendment, Code Sec. 857(b)(7) read as follows:

(7) Loss on Sale or Exchange of Stock Held Less Than 31 Days.—If—

(A) under subparagraph (B) of paragraph (3) a shareholder of, or a holder of a beneficial interest in, a real estate investment trust is required, with respect to any share or beneficial interest, to treat any amount as a long-term capital gain, and

(B) such share or interest is held by the taxpayer for less than 31 days,

then any loss on the sale or exchange of such share or interest shall, to the extent of the amount described in subparagraph (A) of this paragraph, be treated as loss from the sale or exchange of a capital asset held for more than 1 year. For purposes of this paragraph, the rules of section 246(c)(3) shall apply in determining whether any share of stock or beneficial interest has been held for less than 31 days; except that "30 days" shall be substituted for the number of days specified in subparagraph (B) of section 246(c)(3).

P.L. 98-369, §1001(b)(13):

Amended Code Sec. 857(b)(3)(B) and (7) [as in effect before the amendment by §55(b)] by striking out "1 year" each place it appeared and inserting in lieu thereof "6 months". **Effective** for property acquired after 6-22-84, and before 1-1-88.

• 1980, Technical Corrections Act of 1979 (P.L. 96-222)

P.L. 96-222, §103(a)(1):

Amended Code Sec. 857(b)(4)(A). **Effective** for tax years beginning after 12-31-78. Prior to amendment, Code Sec. 857(b)(4)(A) read as follows:

(A) IMPOSITION OF TAX.—There is hereby imposed for each taxable year on the net income from foreclosure property of every real estate investment trust a tax determined by applying section 11 to such income as if such income constituted the taxable income of a corporation taxable under section 11. For purposes of the preceding sentence, the surtax exemption shall be zero.

• 1978, Revenue Act of 1978 (P.L. 95-600)

P.L. 95-600, §301(b)(12):

Amended Code Sec. 857(b)(1). **Effective** for tax years beginning after 12-31-78. Prior to amendment, Code Sec. 857(b)(1) read as follows:

(1) IMPOSITION OF NORMAL TAX AND SURTAX ON REAL ESTATE INVESTMENT TRUSTS.—There is hereby imposed for each taxable year on the real estate investment trust taxable income of every real estate investment trust a normal tax and surtax computed as provided in section 11, as though the real estate investment trust taxable income were the taxable income referred to in section 11.

P.L. 95-600, §362(d)(3):

Amended Code Sec. 857(b)(3)(C) by striking out "section 859(c)" and inserting in lieu thereof "section 860(e)". **Effective** for determinations after 11-6-78.

P.L. 95-600, §363(b):

Added Code Sec. 857(b)(6)(C), (D), and (E). **Effective** for contributions made after 1-31-76.

P.L. 95-600, §403(c)(3):

Amended Code Sec. 857(b)(3)(A)(ii) by striking out "a tax of 30 percent of" and inserting in lieu thereof "a tax determined at the rate provided in section 1201(a) on". **Effective** 11-7-78.

• 1976, Tax Reform Act of 1976 (P.L. 94-455)

P.L. 94-455, §1402(b)(1):

Amended subparagraphs (3)(B) and (5)(B) by substituting "9 months" for "6 months". **Effective** for taxable years beginning in 1977.

P.L. 94-455, §1402(b)(2):

Substituted "1 year" for "9 months" in subparagraphs (3)(B) and (5)(B). **Effective** for tax years beginning after 1977.

P.L. 94-455, §1601(c):

Inserted "; except that, if there is an increase in the excess described in subparagraph (A)(ii) of this paragraph for such year which results from a determination (as defined in section 859(c)), such designation may be made with respect to such increase at any time before the expiration of 120 days after the date of such determination" in front of the period in the first sentence of subparagraph (3)(C). For **effective** date, see Act Sec. 1608(a) below.

P.L. 94-455, §1602(b)(1):

Redesignated paragraph (5) as paragraph (7) and added a new paragraph (5). For **effective** date, see Act Sec. 1608(b), below.

P.L. 94-455, §1606(a):

Struck out subparagraph (2)(E) and redesignated subparagraph (F) as subparagraph (D). **Effective** as provided in Act Sec. 1608(c), below. Prior to repeal, Code Sec. 857(b)(2)(E) read as follows:

(E) The net operating loss deduction provided in section 172 shall not be allowed.

P.L. 94-455, §1602(b)(2):

Added a new subparagraph (2)(E). For **effective** date, see Act Sec. 1608(b), below.

P.L. 94-455, §1603(b):

Added a new paragraph (6). For **effective** date, see Act Sec. 1608(d), reproduced in amendment notes to Code Sec. 856(a).

P.L. 94-455, §1603(c)(5):

Added a new subparagraph (2)(F). For **effective** date, see Act Sec. 1608(d), reproduced in amendment notes to Code Sec. 856(a).

P.L. 94-455, §1604(c):

Substituted "(D), (E), or (G)" for "(D), or (E)" in subdivision (4)(B)(i). For **effective** date, see Act Sec. 1608(d), reproduced in amendment notes to Code Sec. 856(a).

P.L. 94-455, §1606(d):

Substituted "subparagraph (D)" for "subparagraph (F)" in paragraph (2). The **effective** date is provided in Act Sec. 1608(c), below.

P.L. 94-455, §1607(a):

Amended subparagraph (3)(A). **Effective** as noted in Act Sec. 1608(c), below. Prior to amendment, subparagraph (3)(A) read as follows:

(A) IMPOSITION OF TAX.—There is hereby imposed for each taxable year in the case of every real estate investment trust a tax, determined as provided in section 1201(a), on the excess, if any, of the net long-term capital gain over the sum of—

(i) the net short-term capital loss; and

(ii) the deduction for dividends paid (as defined in section 561) determined with reference to capital gains dividends only.

P.L. 94-455, §1607(b):

Deleted subparagraph (2)(A) and redesignated subparagraphs (B), (C), and (D) and subparagraphs (A), (B), (C), respectively. **Effective** as provided in Act Sec. 1608(c), below. Prior to repeal, Code Sec. 857(b)(2)(A) read as follows:

(A) There shall be excluded the excess, if any, of the net long-term capital gain over the net short-term capital loss.

P.L. 94-455, §1607(b):

Struck out "shall be computed without regard to capital gains dividends and" after "allowed, but" in subparagraph (2)(B). **Effective** as provided in Act Sec. 1608(c), below.

P.L. 94-455, §1607(b):

Inserted "For purposes of this subparagraph, the net capital gain shall be deemed not to exceed the real estate investment trust taxable income (determined without regard to the deduction for dividends paid (as defined in section 561) for the taxable year)." after "so designated." in subparagraph (3)(C). **Effective** as provided in Act Sec. 1608(c), below.

P.L. 94-455, §1608(a), provides:

(a) DEFICIENCY DIVIDEND PROCEDURES.—The amendments made by section 1601 shall apply with respect to determinations (as defined in section 859(c) of the Internal Revenue Code of 1954) occurring after the date of the enactment of this Act. If the amendments made by section 1601 apply to a taxable year ending on or before the date of enactment of this Act:

(1) the reference to section 857(b)(3)(A)(ii) in sections 857(b)(3)(C) and 859(b)(1)(B) of such Code, as amended, shall be considered to be a reference to section 857(b)(3)(A) of such Code, as in effect immediately before the enactment of this Act, and

(2) the reference to section 857(b)(2)(B) in section 859(a) of such Code, as amended, shall be considered to be a reference to section 857(b)(2)(C) of such Code, as in effect immediately before the enactment of this Act.

P.L. 94-455, §1608(b), provides:

(b) TRUST NOT DISQUALIFIED IN CERTAIN CASES WHERE INCOME TESTS NOT MET.—The amendment made by section 1602 shall apply to taxable years of real estate investment trusts beginning after the date of the enactment of this Act. In addition, the amendments made by section 1602 shall apply to a taxable year of a real estate investment trust beginning before the date of the enactment of this Act if, as the result of a determination (as defined in section 859(c) of the Internal Revenue Code of 1954) with respect to such trust occurring after the date of the enactment of this Act, such trust for such taxable years does not meet the requirements of section 856(c)(2) or section 856(c)(3), or of both such sections, of such Code as in effect for such taxable year. In any case, the amendment made by section 1602(a) requiring a schedule to be attached to the income tax return of certain real estate investment trusts shall apply only to taxable years of such trusts beginning after the date of the enactment of this Act. If the amendments made by section 1602 apply to a taxable year ending on or before the date of enactment of this Act, the reference to paragraph (2)(B) in section 857(b)(5) of such Code, as amended, shall be considered to be a reference to paragraph (2)(C) of section 857(b) of such Code, as in effect immediately before the enactment of this Act.

P.L. 94-455, §1608(c), provides:

(c) ALTERNATIVE TAX AND NET OPERATING LOSS.—The amendments made by sections 1606 and 1607 shall apply to taxable years ending after the date of the enactment of this Act, except that in the case of a taxpayer which has a net operating loss (as defined in section 172(c) of the Internal Revenue Code of 1954) for any taxable year ending after the date of enactment of this Act for which the provisions of part II of subchapter M of chapter I of subtitle A of such Code apply to such taxpayer, such loss shall not be a net operating loss carryback under section 172 of such Code to any taxable year ending on or before the date of enactment of this Act.

P.L. 94-455, §1901(a)(112):

Struck out the last sentence of subparagraph (3)(C). **Effective** for tax years beginning after 12-31-76. Prior to repeal, the last sentence of subparagraph (3)(C) read as follows:

For purposes of subparagraph (A)(ii), in the case of a taxable year beginning before January 1, 1975, the deduction for dividends paid shall first be made from the amount subject to tax in accordance with section 1201(a)(1)(B), to the extent thereof, and then from the amount subject to tax in accordance with section 1201(a)(1)(A).

P.L. 94-455, §1901(b)(1)(V):

Struck out the last sentence of paragraph (1). **Effective** for tax years beginning after 12-31-76. Prior to repeal, the last sentence of paragraph (1) read as follows:

For purposes of computing the normal tax under section 11, the taxable income and the dividends paid deduction of such real estate investment trust for the taxable year (computed without regard to capital gains dividends) shall be reduced by the deduction provided by section 242 (relating to partially tax-exempt interest).

P.L. 94-455, §1901(b)(33)(K):

Struck out "excess of the net long-term capital gain over the net short-term capital loss" each place it appeared and inserted in its place "net capital gain". **Effective** for tax years beginning after 12-31-76.

• 1975 (P.L. 93-625)

P.L. 93-625, §6(c):

Amended Code Sec. 857(b) by redesignating paragraph (4) as paragraph (5) and by adding a new paragraph (4). For the **effective** date, see the historical comment for P.L. 93-625 following the text of Code Sec. 856(e).

P.L. 93-625, §6(d)(3):

Amended Code Sec. 857(b) by adding subparagraph (F) to paragraph (2). For the **effective** date, see the historical comment for P.L. 93-625 following the text of Code Sec. 856(e).

P.L. 93-625, §6(d)(4):

Amended Code Sec. 857(b)(2)(C) by adding at the end thereof the following: "and shall be computed without regard to that portion of such deduction which is attributable to the amount excluded under subparagraph (F)." For the **effective** date, see the historical comment for P.L. 93-625 following the text of Code Sec. 856(e).

• 1969, Tax Reform Act of 1969 (P.L. 91-172)

P.L. 91-172, §511(c)(3):

Substituted ", determined as provided in section 1201(a), on" for "of 25 percent of" in Sec. 857(b)(3)(A) and added the last sentence of Sec. 857(b)(3)(C). **Effective** for tax years beginning after 12-31-69.

»»→ Caution: Code Sec. 857(c), below, was amended by P.L. 108-27 and P.L. 108-311, and is subject to the sunset provision of the Jobs and Growth Tax Relief Reconciliation Act of 2003 (P.L. 108-27), §303. Absent Congressional action, the changes made to this provision by P.L. 108-27, or that take effect as if included in P.L. 108-27, do not apply after December 31, 2010. For more information about the sunset provision, see page XXI of the Preface to this publication and P.L. 108-27, §303, in the amendment notes. See the amendments notes for a history of amendments to this section and the effective date of each change.

[Sec. 857(c)]

(c) RESTRICTIONS APPLICABLE TO DIVIDENDS RECEIVED FROM REAL ESTATE INVESTMENT TRUSTS.—

(1) SECTION 243.—For purposes of section 243 (relating to deductions for dividends received by corporations), a dividend received from a real estate investment trust which meets the requirements of this part shall not be considered a dividend.

(2) SECTION (1)(h)(11).—

(A) IN GENERAL.—In any case in which—

(i) a dividend is received from a real estate investment trust (other than a capital gain dividend), and

(ii) such trust meets the requirements of section 856(a) for the taxable year during which it paid such dividend,

then, in computing qualified dividend income, there shall be taken into account only that portion of such dividend designated by the real estate investment trust.

(B) LIMITATION.—The aggregate amount which may be designated as qualified dividend income under subparagraph (A) shall not exceed the sum of—

(i) the qualified dividend income of the trust for the taxable year,

(ii) the excess of—

(I) the sum of the real estate investment trust taxable income computed under section 857(b)(2) for the preceding taxable year and the income subject to tax by reason of the application of the regulations under section 337(d) for such preceding taxable year, over

(II) the sum of the taxes imposed on the trust for such preceding taxable year under section 857(b)(1) and by reason of the application of such regulations, and

(iii) the amount of any earnings and profits which were distributed by the trust for such taxable year and accumulated in a taxable year with respect to which this part did not apply.

(C) NOTICE TO SHAREHOLDERS.—The amount of any distribution by a real estate investment trust which may be taken into account as qualified dividend income shall not exceed the amount so designated by the trust in a written notice to its shareholders mailed not later than 60 days after the close of its taxable year.

(D) QUALIFIED DIVIDEND INCOME.—For purposes of this paragraph, the term "qualified dividend income" has the meaning given such term by section 1(h)(11)(B).

Amendments

• 2004, Working Families Tax Relief Act of 2004 (P.L. 108-311)

P.L. 108-311, §402(a)(5)(E):

Amended Code Sec. 857(c)(2). **Effective** as if included in section 302 of the Jobs and Growth Tax Relief Reconciliation Act of 2003 (P.L. 108-27) [**effective** for tax years ending after 12-31-2002.—CCH]. For a special rule, see Act Sec. 402(a)(5)(F), below. Prior to amendment, Code Sec. 857(c)(2) read as follows:

(2) SECTION 1(h)(11).—For purposes of section 1(h)(11) (relating to maximum rate of tax on dividends)—

(A) rules similar to the rules of subparagraphs (B) and (C) of section 854(b)(1) shall apply to dividends received from a real estate investment trust which meets the requirements of this part, and

(B) for purposes of such rules, such a trust shall be treated as receiving qualified dividend income during any taxable year in an amount equal to the sum of—

(i) the excess of real estate investment trust taxable income computed under section 857(b)(2) for the preceding taxable year over the tax payable by the trust under section 857(b)(1) for such preceding taxable year, and

(ii) the excess of the income subject to tax by reason of the application of the regulations under section 337(d) for the preceding taxable year over the tax payable by the trust on such income for such preceding taxable year.

P.L. 108-311, §402(a)(5)(F), provides:

(F) With respect to any taxable year of a regulated investment company or real estate investment trust ending on or before November 30, 2003, the period for providing notice of the qualified dividend amount to shareholders under sections 854(b)(2) and 857(c)(2)(C) of the Internal Revenue Code of 1986, as amended by this section, shall not expire before the date on which the statement under section 6042(c) of such Code is required to be furnished with respect to the last calendar year beginning in such taxable year.

• 2003, Jobs and Growth Tax Relief Reconciliation Act of 2003 (P.L. 108-27)

P.L. 108-27, §302(d):

Amended Code Sec. 857(c). For the **effective** date, see Act Sec. 302(f), as amended by P.L. 108-311, §402(a)(6), below. Prior to amendment, Code Sec. 857(c) read as follows:

(c) RESTRICTIONS APPLICABLE TO DIVIDENDS RECEIVED FROM REAL ESTATE INVESTMENT TRUSTS.—For purposes of section 243 (relating to deductions for dividends received by corporations), a dividend received from a real estate investment trust which meets the requirements of this part shall not be considered as a dividend.

P.L. 108-27, §302(f), as amended by P.L. 108-311, §402(a)(6), provides:

(f) EFFECTIVE DATE.—

(1) IN GENERAL.—Except as provided in paragraph (2), the amendments made by this section shall apply to taxable years beginning after December 31, 2002.

(2) PASS-THRU ENTITIES.—In the case of a pass-thru entity described in subparagraph (A), (B), (C), (D), (E), or (F) of section 1(h)(10) of the Internal Revenue Code of 1986, as amended by this Act, the amendments made by this section

shall apply to taxable years ending after December 31, 2002; except that dividends received by such an entity on or before such date shall not be treated as qualified dividend income (as defined in section 1(h)(11)(B) of such Code, as added by this Act).

P.L. 108-27, §303, as amended by P.L. 109-222, §102, provides:

SEC. 303. SUNSET OF TITLE.

All provisions of, and amendments made by, this title shall not apply to taxable years beginning after December 31, 2010, and the Internal Revenue Code of 1986 shall be applied and administered to such years as if such provisions and amendments had never been enacted.

• 1986, Tax Reform Act of 1986 (P.L. 99-514)

P.L. 99-514, §612(b)(7):

Amended Code Sec. 857(c) by striking out "section 116 (relating to an exclusion for dividends received by individuals), and" after "For purposes of". **Effective** for tax years beginning after 12-31-86.

• 1984, Deficit Reduction Act of 1984 (P.L. 98-369)

P.L. 98-369, §16(a):

Repealed P.L. 97-34, Act Sec. 302(c)(5). **Effective** as if P.L. 97-34, §302(c)(5), had not been enacted. Code Sec. 857(c), as amended by P.L. 97-34, §302(c)(5), read as follows:

(c) LIMITATIONS APPLICABLE TO DIVIDENDS RECEIVED FROM REAL ESTATE INVESTMENT TRUSTS.—

(1) IN GENERAL.—For purposes of section 116 (relating to an exclusion for dividends received by individuals) and section 243 (relating to deductions for dividends received by corporations), a dividend received from a real estate investment trust which meets the requirements of this part shall not be considered as a dividend.

(2) TREATMENT FOR SECTION 128.—In the case of a dividend (other than a capital gain dividend, as defined in subsection (b)(3)(C)) received from a real estate investment trust which meets the requirements of this part for the taxable year in which it paid the dividend—

(A) such dividend shall be treated as interest if the aggregate interest received by the real estate investment trust for the taxable year equals or exceeds 75 percent of its gross income, or

(B) if subparagraph (A) does not apply, the portion of such dividend which bears the same ratio to the amount of such dividend as the aggregate interest received bears to gross income shall be treated as interest.

(3) ADJUSTMENTS TO GROSS INCOME AND AGGREGATE INTEREST RECEIVED.—For purposes of paragraph (2)—

(A) gross income does not include the net capital gain,

(B) gross income and aggregate interest received shall each be reduced by so much of the deduction allowable by section 163 for the taxable year (other than for interest on mortgages on real property owned by the real estate investment trust) as does not exceed aggregate interest received by the taxable year, and

(C) gross income shall be reduced by the sum of the taxes imposed by paragraphs (4), (5), and (6) of section 857(b).

(4) AGGREGATE INTEREST RECEIVED.—For purposes of this subsection, the term "aggregate interest received" means only interest described in section 128(c)(1).

(5) NOTICE TO SHAREHOLDERS.—The amount of any distribution by a real estate investment trust which may be taken into account as interest for purposes of the exclusion under section 128 shall not exceed the amount so designated by the trust in a written notice to its shareholders mailed not later than 45 days after the close of its taxable year.

• 1981, Economic Recovery Tax Act of 1981 (P.L. 97-34)

P.L. 97-34, §302(c)(5) (repealed by P.L. 98-369, §16(a)):

Amended Code Sec. 857(c). **Effective** for tax years beginning after 12-31-84. Prior to amendment, Code Sec. 857(c) read as follows:

(c) LIMITATIONS APPLICABLE TO DIVIDENDS RECEIVED FROM REAL ESTATE INVESTMENT TRUSTS.—

(1) CAPITAL GAIN DIVIDEND.—For purposes of section 116 (relating to exclusion for dividends and interest received by individuals), a capital gain dividend (as defined in subsection (b)(3)(C)) received from a real estate investment trust shall not be considered a dividend.

(2) OTHER DIVIDENDS.—In the case of a dividend received from a real estate investment trust (other than a dividend described in paragraph (1)), if—

(A) the real estate investment trust meets the requirements of this part for the taxable year during which it paid the dividend, and

(B) the aggregate interest received by the real estate investment trust for the taxable year is less than 75 percent of its gross income,

then, in computing the exclusion under section 116, there shall be taken into account only that portion of the dividend which bears the same ratio to the amount of such dividend as aggregate interest received bears to gross income.

(3) ADJUSTMENTS TO GROSS INCOME AND AGGREGATE INTEREST RECEIVED.—For purposes of paragraph (2)—

(A) gross income does not include the net capital gain,

(B) gross income and aggregate interest received shall each be reduced by so much of the deduction allowable by section 163 for the taxable year (other than for interest on mortgages on real property owned by the real estate investment trust) as does not exceed aggregate interest received for the taxable year, and

(C) gross income shall be reduced by the sum of the taxes imposed by paragraphs (4), (5), and (6) of section 857(b).

(4) AGGREGATE INTEREST RECEIVED.—For purposes of this subsection, the term "aggregate interest received" means only interest described in section 116(c)(1).

(5) NOTICE TO SHAREHOLDERS.—The amount of any distribution by a real estate investment trust which may be taken into account as a dividend for purposes of the exclusion under section 116 shall not exceed the amount so designated by the trust in a written notice to its shareholders mailed not later than 45 days after the close of its taxable year.

(6) CROSS REFERENCE.—

For restriction on dividends received by a corporation, see section 243(c)(2).

• 1980, Crude Oil Windfall Profit Tax Act of 1980 (P.L. 96-223)

P.L. 96-223, §404(b)(8):

Amended Code Sec. 857(c). **Effective** for tax years beginning after 12-31-80 and before 1-1-83. (P.L. 97-34, §302(b)(1), amended Act Sec. 404(c) of P.L. 96-223 by striking out "1983" and inserting "1982".)

• 1964, Revenue Act of 1964 (P.L. 88-272)

P.L. 88-272, §201(d)(11):

Amended Code Sec. 857(c) by deleting "section 34(a) (relating to credit for dividends received by individuals)," and by deleting the comma preceding "and section 243". **Effective** for dividends received after 12-31-64, in tax years ending after such date.

[Sec. 857(d)]

(d) EARNINGS AND PROFITS.—

(1) IN GENERAL.—The earnings and profits of a real estate investment trust for any taxable year (but not its accumulated earnings) shall not be reduced by any amount which is not allowable in computing its taxable income for such taxable year. For purposes of this subsection, the term "real estate investment trust" includes a domestic corporation, trust, or association which is a real estate investment trust determined without regard to the requirements of subsection (a).

(2) COORDINATION WITH TAX ON UNDISTRIBUTED INCOME.—A real estate investment trust shall be treated as having sufficient earnings and profits to treat as a dividend any distribution (other

than in a redemption to which section 302(a) applies) which is treated as a dividend by such trust. The preceding sentence shall not apply to the extent that the amount distributed during any calendar year by the trust exceeds the required distribution for such calendar year (as determined under section 4981).

(3) DISTRIBUTIONS TO MEET REQUIREMENTS OF SUBSECTION (a)(2)(B).—Any distribution which is made in order to comply with the requirements of subsection (a)(2)(B)—

(A) shall be treated for purposes of this subsection and subsection (a)(2)(B) as made from earnings and profits which, but for the distribution, would result in a failure to meet such requirements (and allocated to such earnings on a first-in, first-out basis), and

(B) to the extent treated under subparagraph (A) as made from accumulated earnings and profits, shall not be treated as a distribution for purposes of subsection (b)(2)(B) and section 858.

Amendments

• 1999, Tax Relief Extension Act of 1999 (P.L. 106-170)

P.L. 106-170, §566(a)(2):

Amended Code Sec. 857(d)(3)(A). **Effective** for distributions after 12-31-2000. Prior to amendment, Code Sec. 857(d)(3)(A) read as follows:

(A) shall be treated for purposes of this subsection and subsection (a)(2)(B) as made from the earliest earnings and profits accumulated in any taxable year to which the provisions of this part did not apply rather than the most recently accumulated earnings and profits, and

P.L. 106-170, §566(b):

Amended Code Sec. 857(d)(3)(B) by inserting before the period "and section 858". **Effective** for distributions after 12-31-2000.

• 1998, IRS Restructuring and Reform Act of 1998 (P.L. 105-206)

P.L. 105-206, §6012(g):

Amended Code Sec. 857(d)(3)(A) by striking "earliest accumulated earnings and profits (other than earnings and profits to which subsection (a)(2)(A) applies)" and inserting "earliest earnings and profits accumulated in any taxable year to which the provisions of this part did not apply". **Effective** as if included in the provision of P.L. 105-34 to which it relates [**effective** for tax years beginning after 8-5-97.—CCH].

P.L. 105-206, §7002, provides:

SEC. 7002. TERMINATION OF EXCEPTION FOR CERTAIN REAL ESTATE INVESTMENT TRUSTS FROM THE TREATMENT OF STAPLED ENTITIES.

(a) IN GENERAL.—Notwithstanding paragraph (3) of section 136(c) of the Tax Reform Act of 1984 (relating to stapled stock; stapled entities), the REIT gross income provisions shall be applied by treating the activities and gross income of members of the stapled REIT group properly allocable to any nonqualified real property interest held by the exempt REIT or any stapled entity which is a member of such group (or treated under subsection (c) as held by such REIT or stapled entity) as the activities and gross income of the exempt REIT in the same manner as if the exempt REIT and such group were one entity.

(b) NONQUALIFIED REAL PROPERTY INTEREST.— For purposes of this section—

(1) IN GENERAL.—The term "nonqualified real property interest" means, with respect to any exempt REIT, any interest in real property acquired after March 26, 1998, by the exempt REIT or any stapled entity.

(2) EXCEPTION FOR BINDING CONTRACTS, ETC.—Such term shall not include any interest in real property acquired after March 26, 1998, by the exempt REIT or any stapled entity if—

(A) the acquisition is pursuant to a written agreement (including a put option, buy-sell agreement, and an agreement relating to a third party default) which was binding on such date and at all times thereafter on such REIT or stapled entity; or

(B) the acquisition is described on or before such date in a public announcement or in a filing with the Securities and Exchange Commission.

(3) IMPROVEMENTS AND LEASES.—

(A) IN GENERAL.—Except as otherwise provided in this paragraph, the term "nonqualified real property interest" shall not include—

(i) any improvement to land owned or leased by the exempt REIT or any member of the stapled REIT group; and

(ii) any repair to, or improvement of, any improvement owned or leased by the exempt REIT or any member of the stapled REIT group,

if such ownership or leasehold interest is a qualified real property interest.

(B) LEASES.—The term "nonqualified real property interest' shall not include—

(i) any lease of a qualified real property interest if such lease is not otherwise such an interest; or

(ii) any renewal of a lease which is a qualified real property interest,

but only if the rent on any lease referred to in clause (i) or any renewal referred to in clause (ii) does not exceed an arm's length rate.

(C) TERMINATION WHERE CHANGE IN USE.—

(i) IN GENERAL.—Subparagraph (A) shall not apply to any improvement placed in service after December 31, 1999, which is part of a change in the use of the property to which such improvement relates unless the cost of such improvement does not exceed 200 percent of—

(I) the cost of such property; or

(II) if such property is substituted basis property (as defined in section 7701(a)(42) of the Internal Revenue Code of 1986), the fair market value of the property at the time of acquisition.

(ii) BINDING CONTRACTS.—For purposes of clause (i), an improvement shall be treated as placed in service before January 1, 2000, if such improvement is placed in service before January 1, 2004, pursuant to a binding contract in effect on December 31, 1999, and at all times thereafter.

(4) EXCEPTION FOR PERMITTED TRANSFERS, ETC.—The term "nonqualified real property interest" shall not include any interest in real property acquired solely as a result of a direct or indirect contribution, distribution, or other transfer of such interest from the exempt REIT or any member of the stapled REIT group to such REIT or any such member, but only to the extent the aggregate of the interests of the exempt REIT and all stapled entities in such interest in real property (determined in accordance with subsection (c)(1)) is not increased by reason of the transfer.

(5) TREATMENT OF ENTITIES WHICH ARE NOT STAPLED, ETC. ON MARCH 26, 1998.—Notwithstanding any other provision of this section, all interests in real property held by an exempt REIT or any stapled entity with respect to such REIT (or treated under subsection (c) as held by such REIT or stapled entity) shall be treated as nonqualified real property interests unless—

(A) such stapled entity was a stapled entity with respect to such REIT as of March 26, 1998, and at all times thereafter; and

(B) as of March 26, 1998, and at all times thereafter, such REIT was a real estate investment trust.

(6) QUALIFIED REAL PROPERTY INTEREST.— The term "qualified real property interest" means any interest in real property other than a non-qualified real property interest.

(c) TREATMENT OF PROPERTY HELD BY 10-PERCENT SUBSIDIARIES.—For purposes of this section—

(1) IN GENERAL.—Any exempt REIT and any stapled entity shall be treated as holding their proportionate shares of each interest in real property held by any 10-percent subsidiary entity of the exempt REIT or stapled entity, as the case may be.

(2) PROPERTY HELD BY 10-PERCENT SUBSIDIARIES TREATED AS NONQUALIFIED.—

(A) IN GENERAL.—Except as provided in subparagraph (B), any interest in real property held by a 10-percent subsidiary entity of an exempt REIT or stapled entity shall be treated as a nonqualified real property interest.

(B) EXCEPTION FOR INTERESTS IN REAL PROPERTY HELD ON MARCH 26, 1998, ETC.—In the case of an entity which was a 10-percent subsidiary entity of an exempt REIT or stapled entity on March 26, 1998, and at all times thereafter, an interest in real property held by such subsidiary entity shall be treated as a qualified real property interest if such interest would be so treated if held or acquired directly by the exempt REIT or the stapled entity.

(3) REDUCTION IN QUALIFIED REAL PROPERTY INTEREST IF INCREASE IN OWNERSHIP OF SUBSIDIARY.—If, after March 26, 1998, an exempt REIT or stapled entity increases its ownership interest in a subsidiary entity to which paragraph (2)(B) applies above its ownership interest in such subsidiary entity as of such date, the additional portion of each interest in real property which is treated as held by the exempt REIT or stapled entity by reason of such increased ownership shall be treated as a nonqualified real property interest.

(4) SPECIAL RULES FOR DETERMINING OWNERSHIP.—For purposes of this subsection—

(A) percentage ownership of an entity shall be determined in accordance with subsection (e)(4);

(B) interests in the entity which are acquired by an exempt REIT or a member of the stapled REIT group in any acquisition described in an agreement, announcement, or filing described in subsection (b)(2) shall be treated as acquired on March 26, 1998; and

(C) except as provided in guidance prescribed by the Secretary, any change in proportionate ownership which is attributable solely to fluctuations in the relative fair market values of different classes of stock shall not be taken into account.

(5) TREATMENT OF 60-PERCENT PARTNERSHIPS.—

(A) IN GENERAL.—If, as of March 26, 1998—

(i) an exempt REIT or stapled entity held directly or indirectly at least 60 percent of the capital or profits interest in a partnership; and

(ii) 90 percent or more of the capital interests and 90 percent or more of the profits interests in such partnership (other than interests held directly or indirectly by the exempt REIT or stapled entity) are, or will be, redeemable or exchangeable for consideration the amount of which is determined by reference to the value of shares of stock in the exempt REIT or stapled entity (or both),

paragraph (3) shall not apply to such partnership, and such REIT or entity shall be treated for all purposes of this section as holding all of the capital and profits interests in such partnership.

(B) LIMITATION TO ONE PARTNERSHIP.—If, as of January 1, 1999, more than one partnership owned by any exempt REIT or stapled entity meets the requirements of subparagraph (A), only the largest such partnership on such date (determined by aggregate asset bases) shall be treated as meeting such requirements.

(C) MIRROR ENTITY.—For purposes of subparagraph (A), an interest in a partnership formed after March 26, 1998, shall be treated as held by an exempt REIT or stapled entity on March 26, 1998, if such partnership is formed to mirror the stapling of an exempt REIT and a stapled entity in connection with an acquisition agreed to or announced on or before March 26, 1998.

(d) TREATMENT OF PROPERTY SECURED BY MORTGAGE HELD BY EXEMPT REIT OR MEMBER OF STAPLED REIT GROUP.—

(1) IN GENERAL.—In the case of any nonqualified obligation held by an exempt REIT or any member of the stapled REIT group, the REIT gross income provisions shall be applied by treating the exempt REIT as having impermissible tenant service income equal to—

(A) the interest income from such obligation which is properly allocable to the property described in paragraph (2), and

(B) the income of any member of the stapled REIT group from services described in paragraph (2) with respect to such property. If the income referred to in subparagraph (A) or (B) is of a 10-percent subsidiary entity, only the portion of such income which is properly allocable to the exempt REIT's or the stapled entity's interest in the subsidiary entity shall be taken into account.

(2) NONQUALIFIED OBLIGATION.—Except as otherwise provided in this subsection, the term "nonqualified obligation" means any obligation secured by a mortgage on an interest in real property if the income of any member of the stapled REIT group for services furnished with respect to such property would be impermissible tenant service income were such property held by the exempt REIT and such services furnished by the exempt REIT.

(3) EXCEPTION FOR CERTAIN MARKET RATE OBLIGATIONS.—Such term shall not include any obligation—

(A) payments under which would be treated as interest if received by a REIT; and

(B) the rate of interest on which does not exceed an arm's length rate.

(4) EXCEPTION FOR EXISTING OBLIGATIONS.— Such term shall not include any obligation—

(A) which is secured on March 26, 1998, by an interest in real property; and

(B) which is held on such date by the exempt REIT or any entity which is a member of the stapled REIT group on such date and at all times thereafter,

but only so long as such obligation is secured by such interest, and the interest payable on such obligation is not changed to a rate which exceeds an arm's length rate unless such change is pursuant to the terms of the obligation in effect on March 26, 1998. The preceding sentence shall not cease to apply by reason of the refinancing of the obligation if (immediately after the refinancing) the principal amount of the obligation resulting from the refinancing does not exceed the principal amount of the refinanced obligation (immediately before the refinancing) and the interest payable on such refinanced obligation does not exceed an arm's length rate.

(5) TREATMENT OF ENTITIES WHICH ARE NOT STAPLED, ETC. ON MARCH 26, 1998.—A rule similar to the rule of subsection (b)(5) shall apply for purposes of this subsection.

(6) INCREASE IN AMOUNT OF NONQUALIFIED OBLIGATIONS IF INCREASE IN OWNERSHIP OF SUBSIDIARY.—A rule similar to the rule of subsection (c)(3) shall apply for purposes of this subsection.

(7) COORDINATION WITH SUBSECTION (a).— This subsection shall not apply to the portion of any interest in real property that the exempt REIT or stapled entity holds or is treated as holding under this section without regard to this subsection.

(e) DEFINITIONS.—For purposes of this section—

(1) REIT GROSS INCOME PROVISIONS.—The term "REIT gross income provisions" means—

(A) paragraphs (2), (3), and (6) of section 856(c) of the Internal Revenue Code of 1986; and

(B) section 857(b)(5) of such Code.

(2) EXEMPT REIT.—The term "exempt REIT" means a real estate investment trust to which section 269B of the Internal Revenue Code of 1986 does not apply by reason of paragraph (3) of section 136(c) of the Tax Reform Act of 1984.

(3) STAPLED REIT GROUP.—The term "stapled REIT group" means, with respect to an exempt REIT, the group consisting of—

(A) all entities which are stapled entities with respect to the exempt REIT; and

(B) all entities which are 10-percent subsidiary entities of the exempt REIT or any such stapled entity.

(4) 10-PERCENT SUBSIDIARY ENTITY.—

(A) IN GENERAL.—The term "10-percent subsidiary entity" means, with respect to any exempt REIT or stapled entity, any entity in which the exempt REIT or stapled entity (as the case may be) directly or indirectly holds at least a 10-percent interest.

(B) EXCEPTION FOR CERTAIN C CORPORATION SUBSIDIARIES OF REITS.—A corporation which would, but for this subparagraph, be treated as a 10-percent subsidiary of an exempt REIT shall not be so treated if such corporation is taxable under section 11 of the Internal Revenue Code of 1986.

(C) 10-PERCENT INTEREST.—The term "10-percent interest" means—

(i) in the case of an interest in a corporation, ownership of 10 percent (by vote or value) of the stock in such corporation;

(ii) in the case of an interest in a partnership, ownership of 10 percent of the capital or profits interest in the partnership; and

(iii) in any other case, ownership of 10 percent of the beneficial interests in the entity.

(5) OTHER DEFINITIONS.—Terms used in this section which are used in section 269B or section 856 of such Code shall have the respective meanings given such terms by such section.

(f) GUIDANCE.—The Secretary may prescribe such guidance as may be necessary or appropriate to carry out the purposes of this section, including guidance to prevent the avoidance of such purposes and to prevent the double counting of income.

(g) EFFECTIVE DATE.—This section shall apply to taxable years ending after March 26, 1998.

• 1997, Taxpayer Relief Act of 1997 (P.L. 105-34)

P.L. 105-34, §1256:

Amended Code Sec. 857(d) by adding at the end a new paragraph (3). **Effective** for tax years beginning after 8-5-97.

• 1986, Tax Reform Act of 1986 (P.L. 99-514)

P.L. 99-514, §668(b)(2):

Amended Code Sec. 857(d). **Effective** for calendar years beginning after 12-31-86. Prior to amendment, Code Sec. 857(d) read as follows:

(d) EARNINGS AND PROFITS.—The earnings and profits of a real estate investment trust for any taxable year (but not its accumulated earnings and profits) shall not be reduced by any amount which is not allowable as a deduction in computing its taxable income for such taxable year. For purposes of this subsection, the term "real estate investment trust" includes a domestic corporation, trust, or association which is a real estate investment trust determined without regard to the requirements of subsection (a).

• 1976, Tax Reform Act of 1976 (P.L. 94-455)

P.L. 94-455, §1604(f)(3):

Struck out "a domestic unincorporated trust" and inserted in its place "a domestic corporation, trust," in the second sentence of Code Sec. 857(d). **Effective** 10-4-76.

• 1960 (P.L. 86-779)

P.L. 86-779, §10(a):

Added Code Sec. 857. **Effective** for tax years of real estate investment trusts beginning after 1960.

[Sec. 857(e)]

(e) EXCESS NONCASH INCOME.—

(1) IN GENERAL.—For purposes of subsection (a)(1)(B), the term "excess noncash income" means the excess (if any) of—

(A) the amount determined under paragraph (2) for the taxable year, over

(B) 5 percent of the real estate investment trust taxable income for the taxable year determined without regard to the deduction for dividends paid (as defined in section 561) and by excluding any net capital gain.

(2) DETERMINATION OF AMOUNT.—The amount determined under this paragraph for the taxable year is the sum of—

(A) the amount (if any) by which—

(i) the amounts includible in gross income under section 467 (relating to certain payments for the use of property or services), exceed

(ii) the amounts which would have been includible in gross income without regard to such section,

(B) any income on the disposition of a real estate asset if—

(i) there is a determination (as defined in section 860(e)) that such income is not eligible for nonrecognition under section 1031, and

(ii) failure to meet the requirements of section 1031 was due to reasonable cause and not to willful neglect,

(C) the amount (if any) by which—

(i) the amounts includible in gross income with respect to instruments to which section 860E(a) or 1272 applies, exceed

(ii) the amount of money and the fair market value of other property received during the taxable year under such instruments, and

(D) amounts includible in income by reason of cancellation of indebtedness.

Amendments

• 1997, Taxpayer Relief Act of 1997 (P.L. 105-34)

P.L. 105-34, §1259(1)-(4):

Amended Code Sec. 857(e)(2) by striking subparagraph (B), by striking the period at the end of subparagraph (C) and inserting a comma, by redesignating subparagraph (C) as subparagraph (B), and by adding at the end new subparagraphs (C) and (D). **Effective** for tax years beginning after 8-5-97. Prior to amendment, Code Sec. 857(e)(2)(B) read as follows:

(B) in the case of a real estate investment trust using the cash receipts and disbursements method of accounting, the amount (if any) by which—

(i) the amounts includible in gross income with respect to instruments to which section 1274 (relating to certain debt instruments issued for property) applies, exceed

(ii) the amount of money and the fair market value of other property received during the taxable year under such instruments; plus

• 1988, Technical and Miscellaneous Revenue Act of 1988 (P.L. 100-647)

P.L. 100-647, §1006(r):

Amended Code Sec. 857(e)(2)(B)(i) by striking out "as original issue discount on instruments" and inserting "with respect to instruments". **Effective** as if included in the provision of P.L. 99-514 to which it relates.

• 1986, Tax Reform Act of 1986 (P.L. 99-514)

P.L. 99-514, §664(b):

Amended Code Sec. 857 by redesignating subsection (e) as subsection (f) and by inserting after subsection (d) new subsection (e). **Effective** for tax years beginning after 12-31-86.

[Sec. 857(f)]

(f) REAL ESTATE INVESTMENT TRUSTS TO ASCERTAIN OWNERSHIP.—

(1) IN GENERAL.—Each real estate investment trust shall each taxable year comply with regulations prescribed by the Secretary for the purposes of ascertaining the actual ownership of the outstanding shares, or certificates of beneficial interest, of such trust.

(2) FAILURE TO COMPLY.—

(A) IN GENERAL.—If a real estate investment trust fails to comply with the requirements of paragraph (1) for a taxable year, such trust shall pay (on notice and demand by the Secretary and in the same manner as tax) a penalty of $25,000.

(B) INTENTIONAL DISREGARD.—If any failure under paragraph (1) is due to intentional disregard of the requirement under paragraph (1), the penalty under subparagraph (A) shall be $50,000.

(C) FAILURE TO COMPLY AFTER NOTICE.—The Secretary may require a real estate investment trust to take such actions as the Secretary determines appropriate to ascertain actual ownership if the trust fails to meet the requirements of paragraph (1). If the trust fails to take such actions, the trust shall pay (on notice and demand by the Secretary and in the same manner as tax) an additional penalty equal to the penalty determined under subparagraph (A) or (B), whichever is applicable.

(D) REASONABLE CAUSE.—No penalty shall be imposed under this paragraph with respect to any failure if it is shown that such failure is due to reasonable cause and not to willful neglect.

Amendments

• 1997, Taxpayer Relief Act of 1997 (P.L. 105-34)

P.L. 105-34, §1251(a)(2):

Amended Code Sec. 857 by redesignating paragraph (f) as paragraph (g) and by inserting after subsection (e) a new subsection (f). **Effective** for tax years beginning after 8-5-97.

[Sec. 857(g)]

(g) CROSS REFERENCE.—

For provisions relating to excise tax based on certain real estate investment trust taxable income not distributed during the taxable year, see section 4981.

Amendments

• 1997, Taxpayer Relief Act of 1997 (P.L. 105-34)

P.L. 105-34, §1251(a)(2):

Amended Code Sec. 857 by redesignating paragraph (f) as paragraph (g). **Effective** for tax years beginning after 8-5-97.

• 1986, Tax Reform Act of 1986 (P.L. 99-514)

P.L. 99-514, §664(b):

Redesignated subsection (e) as subsection (f). **Effective** for tax years beginning after 12-31-86.

• 1976, Tax Reform Act of 1976 (P.L. 94-455)

P.L. 94-455, §1605(b):

Added Code Sec. 857(e). **Effective** 10-4-76.

[Sec. 858]

Sec. 858. DIVIDEND PAID BY REAL ESTATE INVESTMENT TRUST AFTER CLOSE OF TAXABLE YEAR.

[Sec. 858(a)]

(a) GENERAL RULE.—For purposes of this part, if a real estate investment trust—

(1) declares a dividend before the time prescribed by law for the filing of its return for a taxable year (including the period of any extension of time granted for filing such return), and

(2) distributes the amount of such dividend to shareholders or holders of beneficial interests in the 12-month period following the close of such taxable year and not later than the date of the first regular dividend payment made after such declaration,

the amount so declared and distributed shall, to the extent the trust elects in such return (and specifies in dollar amounts) in accordance with regulations prescribed by the Secretary, be considered as having been paid only during such taxable year, except as provided in subsections (b) and (c).

Amendments

• 1976, Tax Reform Act of 1976 (P.L. 94-455)

P.L. 94-455, §1604(h):

Added "(and specifies in dollar amounts)". **Effective** as provided in Act Sec. 1608(d), reproduced in amendment notes under Code Sec. 856(a).

P.L. 94-455, §1906(b)(13)(A):

Amended 1954 Code by substituting "Secretary" for "Secretary or his delegate" each place it appeared. **Effective** 2-1-77.

[Sec. 858(b)]

(b) RECEIPT BY SHAREHOLDER.—Except as provided in section 857(b)(8), amounts to which subsection (a) applies shall be treated as received by the shareholder or holder of a beneficial interest in the taxable year in which the distribution is made.

Amendments

• 1986, Tax Reform Act of 1986 (P.L. 99-514)

P.L. 99-514, §668(b)(1)(B):

Amended Code Sec. 858(b) by striking out "Amounts" and inserting in lieu thereof "Except as provided in section 857(b)(8), amounts". **Effective** for calendar years beginning after 12-31-86.

[Sec. 858(c)]

(c) NOTICE TO SHAREHOLDERS.—In the case of amounts to which subsection (a) applies, any notice to shareholders or holders of beneficial interests required under this part with respect to such amounts shall be made not later than 30 days after the close of the taxable year in which the distribution is made (or mailed to its shareholders or holders of beneficial interests with its annual report for the taxable year).

Amendments

• 1986, Tax Reform Act of 1986 (P.L. 99-514)

P.L. 99-514, §665(b)(2):

Amended Code Sec. 858(c) by striking out "distribution is made" and inserting in lieu thereof "distribution is made (or mailed to its shareholders or holders of beneficial interests with its annual report for the taxable year)". **Effective** for tax years beginning after 12-31-86.

• 1960 (P.L. 86-779)

P.L. 86-779, §10(a):

Added Code Sec. 858. **Effective** for tax years of real estate investment trusts beginning after 1960.

[Sec. 859]

SEC. 859. ADOPTION OF ANNUAL ACCOUNTING PERIOD.

[Sec. 859(a)]

(a) GENERAL RULE.—For purposes of this subtitle—

(1) a real estate investment trust shall not change to any accounting period other than the calendar year, and

(2) a corporation, trust, or association may not elect to be a real estate investment trust for any taxable year beginning after October 4, 1976, unless its accounting period is the calendar year.

Paragraph (2) shall not apply to a corporation, trust, or association which was considered to be a real estate investment trust for any taxable year beginning on or before October 4, 1976.

Amendments

• 1986, Tax Reform Act of 1986 (P.L. 99-514)

P.L. 99-514, §661(c)(2):

Amended Code Sec. 859 by striking out "For purposes of" and inserting in lieu thereof "(a) General Rule.—For purposes of". **Effective** for tax years beginning after 12-31-86.

• 1978, Revenue Act of 1978 (P.L. 95-600)

P.L. 95-600, §362(d)(6):

Struck out Code Sec. 859 and redesignated Code Sec. 860 as Code Sec. 859. **Effective** 11-7-78. Prior to amendment Code Sec. 859 read as follows:

SEC. 859. DEDUCTION FOR DEFICIENCY DIVIDENDS.

[Sec. 859(a)]

(a) GENERAL RULE.—If a determination (as defined in subsection (c)) with respect to a real estate investment trust results in any adjustment (as defined in subsection (b)(1)) for any taxable year, a deduction shall be allowed to such trust for the amount of deficiency dividends (as defined in subsection (d)) for purposes of determining the deduction for dividends paid (for purposes of section 857) for such year.

[Sec. 859(b)]

(b) RULES FOR APPLICATION OF SECTION.—

(1) ADJUSTMENT.—For purposes of this section, the term "adjustment" means—

(A) any increase in the sum of—

(i) the real estate investment trust taxable income of the real estate investment trust (determined without regard to the deduction for dividends paid (as defined in section 561) and by excluding any net capital gain), and

(ii) the excess of the net income from foreclosure property (as defined in section 857(b)(4)(B)) over the tax on such income imposed by section 857(b)(4)(A),

(B) any increase in the amount of the excess described in section 857(b)(3)(A)(ii) (relating to the excess of the net capital gain over the deduction for capital gains dividends paid), and

(C) any decrease in the deduction for dividends paid (as defined in section 561) determined without regard to capital gains dividends.

(2) INTEREST AND ADDITIONS TO TAX DETERMINED WITH RESPECT TO THE AMOUNT OF DEFICIENCY DIVIDEND DEDUCTION ALLOWED.—For purposes of determining interest, additions to tax, and additional amounts—

(A) the tax imposed by this chapter (after taking into account the deduction allowed by subsection (a)) on the real estate investment trust for the taxable year with respect to which the determination is made shall be deemed to be increased by an amount equal to the deduction allowed by subsection (a) with respect to such taxable year,

(B) the last date prescribed for payment of such increase in tax shall be deemed to have been the last date prescribed for the payment of tax (determined in the manner provided by section 6601(b)) for the taxable year with respect to which the determination is made, and

(C) such increase in tax shall be deemed to be paid as of the date the claim for the deficiency dividend deduction is filed.

(3) CREDIT OR REFUND.—If the allowance of a deficiency dividend deduction results in an overpayment of tax for any taxable year, credit or refund with respect to such overpayment shall be made as if on the date of the determination 2 years remained before the expiration of the period of limitations on the filing of claim for refund for the taxable year to which the overpayment relates.

Amendments

• 1978, Revenue Act of 1978 (P.L. 95-600)

P.L. 95-600, §701(t)(4):

Amended Code Sec. 859(b)(2)(B) by striking out "section 6601(c)" and inserting in lieu thereof "section 6601(b)". **Effective** 10-4-76.

[Sec. 859(c)]

(c) DETERMINATION.—For purposes of this section, the term "determination" means—

(1) a decision by the Tax Court, or a judgment, decree, or other order by any court of competent jurisdiction, which has become final;

(2) a closing agreement made under section 7121; or

(3) under regulations prescribed by the Secretary, an agreement signed by the Secretary and by, or on behalf of, the real estate investment trust relating to the liability of such trust for tax.

[Sec. 859(d)]

(d) DEFICIENCY DIVIDENDS.—

(1) DEFINITION.—For purposes of this section, the term "deficiency dividends" means a distribution of property made by the real estate investment trust on or after the date of the determination and before filing claim under subsec-

tion (e), which would have been includible in the computation of the deduction for dividends paid under section 561 for the taxable year with respect to which the liability for tax resulting from the determination exists, if distributed during such taxable year. No distribution of property shall be considered as deficiency dividends for purposes of subsection (a) unless distributed within 90 days after the determination, and unless a claim for a deficiency dividend deduction with respect to such distribution is filed pursuant to subsection (e).

(2) LIMITATIONS.—

(A) ORDINARY DIVIDENDS.—The amount of deficiency dividends (other than deficiency dividends qualifying as capital gain dividends) paid by a real estate investment trust for the taxable year with respect to which the liability for tax resulting from the determination exists shall not exceed the sum of—

(i) the excess of the amount of increase referred to in subparagraph (A) of subsection (b)(1) over the amount of any increase in the deduction for dividends paid (computed without regard to capital gain dividends) for such taxable year which results from such determination, and

(ii) the amount of decrease referred to in subparagraph (C) of subsection (b)(1).

(B) CAPITAL GAIN DIVIDENDS.—The amount of deficiency dividends qualifying as capital gain dividends paid by a real estate investment trust for the taxable year with respect to which the liability for tax resulting from the determination exists shall not exceed the amount by which (i) the increase referred to in subparagraph (B) of subsection (b)(1) exceeds (ii) the amount of any dividends paid during such taxable year which are designated as capital gain dividends after such determination.

(3) EFFECT ON DIVIDENDS PAID DEDUCTION.—

(A) FOR TAXABLE YEAR IN WHICH PAID.—Deficiency dividends paid in any taxable year shall not be included in the amount of dividends paid for such year for purposes of computing the dividends paid deduction for such year.

(B) FOR PRIOR TAXABLE YEAR.—Deficiency dividends paid in any taxable year shall not be allowed for purposes of section 858(a) in the computation of the dividends paid deduction for the taxable year preceding the taxable year in which paid.

[Sec. 859(e)]

(e) CLAIM REQUIRED.—No deficiency dividend deduction shall be allowed under subsection (a) unless (under regulations prescribed by the Secretary) claim therefor is filed within 120 days after the date of the determination.

[Sec. 859(f)]

(f) SUSPENSION OF STATUTE OF LIMITATIONS AND STAY OF COLLECTION.—

(1) SUSPENSION OF RUNNING OF STATUTE.—If the real estate investment trust files a claim as provided in subsection (e), the running of the statute of limitations provided in section 6501 on the making of assessments, and the bringing of distraint or a proceeding in court for collection, in respect of the deficiency established by a determination under this section, and all interest, additions to tax, additional amounts, or assessable penalties in respect thereof, shall be suspended for a period of 2 years after the date of the determination.

(2) STAY OF COLLECTION.—In the case of any deficiency established by a determination under this section—

(A) the collection of the deficiency, and all interest, additions to tax, additional amounts, and assessable penalties in respect thereof, shall, except in cases of jeopardy, be stayed until the expiration of 120 days after the date of the determination, and

(B) if claim for a deficiency dividend deduction is filed under subsection (e), the collection of such part of the deficiency as is not reduced by the deduction for deficiency dividends provided in subsection (a) shall be stayed until the date the claim is disallowed (in whole or in part), and if disallowed in part collection shall be made only with respect to the part disallowed.

No distraint or proceeding in court shall be begun for the collection of an amount the collection of which is stayed under subparagraph (A) or (B) during the period for which the collection of such amount is stayed.

[Sec. 859(g)]

(g) DEDUCTION DENIED IN CASE OF FRAUD.—No deficiency dividend deduction shall be allowed under subsection (a) if the determination contains a finding that any part of any deficiency attributable to an adjustment with respect to the taxable year is due to fraud with intent to evade tax or to willful failure to file an income tax return within the time prescribed by law or prescribed by the Secretary in pursuance of law.

[Sec. 859(h)]

(h) PENALTY.—For assessable penalty with respect to liability for tax of real estate investment trust which is allowed a deduction under subsection (a), see section 6697.

Amendments

• 1976, Tax Reform Act of 1976 (P.L. 94-455)

P.L. 94-455, §1601(a):

Added Code Sec. 859. **Effective** as provided in §1608(a), below.

P.L. 94-455, §1608(a), provides:

(a) DEFICIENCY DIVIDEND PROCEDURES.—The amendments made by section 1601 shall apply with respect to determinations (as defined in section 859(c) of the Internal Revenue Code of 1954) occurring after the date of the enactment of this Act. If the amendments made by section 1601 apply to a taxable year ending on or before the date of enactment of this Act:

(1) the reference to section 857(b)(3)(A)(ii) in sections 857(b)(3)(C) and 859(b)(1)(B) of such Code, as amended, shall be considered to be a reference to section 857(b)(3)(A) of such Code, as in effect immediately before the enactment of this Act, and

(2) the reference to section 857(b)(2)(B) in section 859(a) of such Code, as amended, shall be considered to be a reference to section 857(b)(2)(C) of such Code, as in effect immediately before the enactment of this Act.

• 1978, Revenue Act of 1978 (P.L. 95-600)

P.L. 95-600, §701(t)(1):

Amended Code Sec. 859 (as redesignated by P.L. 95-600). **Effective** 10-4-76. Prior to amendment, Code Sec. 859 read as follows:

"SEC. 860. ADOPTION OF ANNUAL ACCOUNTING PERIOD.

For purposes of this subtitle, a real estate investment trust shall not change to or adopt any annual accounting period other than the calendar year."

• 1976, Tax Reform Act of 1976 (P.L. 94-455)

P.L. 94-455, §1604(i):

Added Code Sec. 860. **Effective** as provided in §1608(d), reproduced in amendment notes under Code Sec. 856(a).

[Sec. 859(b)]

(b) CHANGE OF ACCOUNTING PERIOD WITHOUT APPROVAL.—Notwithstanding section 442, an entity which has not engaged in any active trade or business may change its accounting period to a calendar year without the approval of the Secretary if such change is in connection with an election under section 856(c).

Amendments

• 1986, Tax Reform Act of 1986 (P.L. 99-514)

P.L. 99-514, §661(c)(1):

Amended Code Sec. 859 by adding at the end thereof new subsection (b). **Effective** for tax years beginning after 12-31-86.

PART III—PROVISIONS WHICH APPLY TO BOTH REGULATED INVESTMENT COMPANIES AND REAL ESTATE INVESTMENT TRUSTS

[Sec. 860]

SEC. 860. DEDUCTION FOR DEFICIENCY DIVIDENDS.

[Sec. 860(a)]

(a) GENERAL RULE.—If a determination with respect to any qualified investment entity results in any adjustment for any taxable year, a deduction shall be allowed to such entity for the amount of deficiency dividends for purposes of determining the deduction for dividends paid (for purposes of section 852 or 857, whichever applies) for such year.

[Sec. 860(b)]

(b) QUALIFIED INVESTMENT ENTITY DEFINED.—For purposes of this section, the term "qualified investment entity" means—

(1) a regulated investment company, and

(2) a real estate investment trust.

[Sec. 860(c)]

(c) RULES FOR APPLICATION OF SECTION.—

(1) INTEREST AND ADDITIONS TO TAX DETERMINED WITH RESPECT TO THE AMOUNT OF DEFICIENCY DIVIDEND DEDUCTION ALLOWED.—For purposes of determining interest, additions to tax, and additional amounts—

(A) the tax imposed by this chapter (after taking into account the deduction allowed by subsection (a)) on the qualified investment entity for the taxable year with respect to which the determination is made shall be deemed to be increased by an amount equal to the deduction allowed by subsection (a) with respect to such taxable year,

(B) the last date prescribed for payment of such increase in tax shall be deemed to have been the last date prescribed for the payment of tax (determined in the manner provided by section 6601(b)) for the taxable year with respect to which the determination is made, and

(C) such increase in tax shall be deemed to be paid as of the date the claim for the deficiency dividend deduction is filed.

(2) CREDIT OR REFUND.—If the allowance of a deficiency dividend deduction results in an overpayment of tax for any taxable year, credit or refund with respect to such overpayment shall be made as if on the date of the determination 2 years remained before the expiration of the period of limitations on the filing of claim for refund for the taxable year to which the overpayment relates.

[Sec. 860(d)]

(d) ADJUSTMENT.—For purposes of this section—

(1) ADJUSTMENT IN THE CASE OF REGULATED INVESTMENT COMPANY.—In the case of any regulated investment company, the term "adjustment" means—

(A) any increase in the investment company taxable income of the regulated investment company (determined without regard to the deduction for dividends paid (as defined in section 561)),

(B) any increase in the amount of the excess described in section 852(b)(3)(A) (relating to the excess of the net capital gain over the deduction for capital gain dividends paid), and

(C) any decrease in the deduction for dividends paid (as defined in section 561) determined without regard to capital gains dividends.

(2) ADJUSTMENT IN THE CASE OF REAL ESTATE INVESTMENT TRUST.—In the case of any real estate investment trust, the term "adjustment" means—

(A) any increase in the sum of—

(i) the real estate investment trust taxable income of the real estate investment trust (determined without regard to the deduction for dividends paid (as defined in section 561) and by excluding any net capital gain), and

(ii) the excess of the net income from foreclosure property (as defined in section 857(b)(4)(B)) over the tax on such income imposed by section 857(b)(4)(A),

(B) any increase in the amount of the excess described in section 857(b)(3)(A)(ii) (relating to the excess of the net capital gain over the deduction for capital gains dividends paid), and

(C) any decrease in the deduction for dividends paid (as defined in section 561) determined without regard to capital gains dividends.

[Sec. 860(e)]

(e) DETERMINATION.—For purposes of this section, the term "determination" means—

(1) a decision by the Tax Court, or a judgment, decree, or other order by any court of competent jurisdiction, which has become final;

(2) a closing agreement made under section 7121;

(3) under regulations prescribed by the Secretary, an agreement signed by the Secretary and by, or on behalf of, the qualified investment entity relating to the liability of such entity for tax; or

(4) a statement by the taxpayer attached to its amendment or supplement to a return of tax for the relevant tax year.

Amendments

• 2004, American Jobs Creation Act of 2004 (P.L. 108-357)

P.L. 108-357, §243(f)(5):

Amended Code Sec. 860(e) by striking "or" at the end of paragraph (2), by striking the period at the end of paragraph (3) and inserting "; or", and by adding at the end a new paragraph (4). **Effective** for statements filed after 10-22-2004 [effective date amended by P.L. 109-135, §403(d)(4)].

[Sec. 860(f)]

(f) DEFICIENCY DIVIDENDS.—

(1) DEFINITION.—For purposes of this section, the term "deficiency dividends" means a distribution of property made by the qualified investment entity on or after the date of the determination and before filing claim under subsection (g), which would have been includible in the computation of the deduction for dividends paid under section 561 for the taxable year with respect to which the liability for tax resulting from the determination exists if distributed during such taxable year. No distribution of property shall be considered as deficiency dividends for purposes of subsection (a) unless distributed within 90 days after the determination, and unless a claim for a deficiency dividend deduction with respect to such distribution is filed pursuant to subsection (g).

(2) LIMITATIONS.—

(A) ORDINARY DIVIDENDS.—The amount of deficiency dividends (other than deficiency dividends qualifying as capital gain dividends) paid by a qualified investment entity for the taxable year with respect to which the liability for tax resulting from the determination exists shall not exceed the sum of—

(i) the excess of the amount of increase referred to in subparagraph (A) of paragraph (1) or (2) of subsection (d) (whichever applies) over the amount of any increase in the deduction for dividends paid (computed without regard to capital gain dividends) for such taxable year which results from such determination, and

(ii) the amount of decrease referred to in subparagraph (C) of paragraph (1) or (2) of subsection (d) (whichever applies).

(B) CAPITAL GAIN DIVIDENDS.—The amount of deficiency dividends qualifying as capital gain dividends paid by a qualified investment entity for the taxable year with respect to which the liability for tax resulting from the determination exists shall not exceed the amount by which (i) the increase referred to in subparagraph (B) of paragraph (1) or (2) of subsection (d) (whichever applies), exceeds (ii) the amount of any dividends paid during such taxable year which are designated as capital gain dividends after such determination.

(3) EFFECT ON DIVIDENDS PAID DEDUCTION.—

(A) FOR TAXABLE YEAR IN WHICH PAID.—Deficiency dividends paid in any taxable year shall not be included in the amount of dividends paid for such year for purposes of computing the dividends paid deduction for such year.

(B) FOR PRIOR TAXABLE YEAR.—Deficiency dividends paid in any taxable year shall not be allowed for purposes of section 855(a) or 858(a) in the computation of the dividends paid deduction for the taxable year preceding the taxable year in which paid.

Amendments

• 1980, Technical Corrections Act of 1979 (P.L. 96-222)

P.L. 96-222, §103(a)(11)(B):

Amended Code Sec. 860(f) by striking out "Efficiency" in the subsection heading and inserting "Deficiency". **Effective** with respect to determinations after 11-6-78.

P.L. 96-222, §103(a)(11)(C):

Amended Code Sec. 860(f)(2)(A)(i) by striking out "computed without regard" and inserting "(computed without regard". **Effective** with respect to determinations after 11-6-78.

[Sec. 860(g)]

(g) CLAIM REQUIRED.—No deficiency dividend deduction shall be allowed under subsection (a) unless (under regulations prescribed by the Secretary) claim therefor is filed within 120 days after the date of the determination.

[Sec. 860(h)]

(h) SUSPENSION OF STATUTE OF LIMITATIONS AND STAY OF COLLECTION.—

(1) SUSPENSION OF RUNNING OF STATUTE.—If the qualified investment entity files a claim as provided in subsection (g), the running of the statute of limitations provided in section 6501 on the making of assessments, and the bringing of distraint or a proceeding in court for collection, in respect of the deficiency established by a determination under this section, and all interest, additions to tax, additional amounts, or assessable penalties in respect thereof, shall be suspended for a period of 2 years after the date of the determination.

(2) STAY OF COLLECTION.—In the case of any deficiency established by a determination under this section—

(A) the collection of the deficiency, and all interest, additions to tax, additional amounts, and assessable penalties in respect thereof, shall, except in cases of jeopardy, be stayed until the expiration of 120 days after the date of the determination, and

(B) if claim for a deficiency dividend deduction is filed under subsection (g), the collection of such part of the deficiency as is not reduced by the deduction for deficiency dividends provided in subsection (a) shall be stayed until the date the claim is disallowed (in whole or in part), and if disallowed in part collection shall be made only with respect to the part disallowed.

No distraint or proceeding in court shall be begun for the collection of an amount the collection of which is stayed under subparagraph (A) or (B) during the period for which the collection of such amount is stayed.

[Sec. 860(i)]

(i) DEDUCTION DENIED IN CASE OF FRAUD.—No deficiency dividend deduction shall be allowed under subsection (a) if the determination contains a finding that any part of any deficiency attributable to an adjustment with respect to the taxable year is due to fraud with intent to evade tax or to willfull failure to file an income tax return within the time prescribed by law or prescribed by the Secretary in pursuance of law.

[Sec. 860(j)]

(j) PENALTY.—

For assessable penalty with respect to liability for tax of a regulated investment company which is allowed a deduction under subsection (a), see section 6697.

Amendments

• 1986, Tax Reform Act of 1986 (P.L. 99-514)

P.L. 99-514, §667(b)(1):

Amended Code Sec. 860(j) by striking out "qualified investment entity" and inserting in lieu thereof "regulated investment company". **Effective** for tax years beginning after 12-31-86.

• 1978, Revenue Act of 1978 (P.L. 95-600)

P.L. 95-600, §362(a):

Added a new Code Sec. 860. **Effective** with respect to determinations after 11-6-78.

PART IV—REAL ESTATE MORTGAGE INVESTMENT CONDUITS

[Sec. 860A]

SEC. 860A. TAXATION OF REMIC's.

[Sec. 860A(a)]

(a) GENERAL RULE.—Except as otherwise provided in this part, a REMIC shall not be subject to taxation under this subtitle (and shall not be treated as a corporation, partnership, or trust for purposes of this subtitle).

Amendments

• 1988, Technical and Miscellaneous Revenue Act of 1988 (P.L. 100-647)

P.L. 100-647, § 1006(t)(20):

Amended Code Sec. 860A(a) by striking out "this chapter" each place it appears and inserting in lieu thereof "this subtitle". **Effective** as if included in the provision of P.L. 99-514 to which it relates.

[Sec. 860A(b)]

(b) INCOME TAXABLE TO HOLDERS.—The income of any REMIC shall be taxable to the holders of interests in such REMIC as provided in this part.

Amendments

• 1986, Tax Reform Act of 1986 (P.L. 99-514)

P.L. 99-514, § 671(a):

Amended subchapter M of chapter 1 by adding new Code Sec. 860A. **Effective** 1-1-87 [**effective** date changed by P.L. 100-647, § 1006(w)(1)].

[Sec. 860B]

SEC. 860B. TAXATION OF HOLDERS OF REGULAR INTERESTS.

[Sec. 860B(a)]

(a) GENERAL RULE.—In determining the tax under this chapter of any holder of a regular interest in a REMIC, such interest (if not otherwise a debt instrument) shall be treated as a debt instrument.

[Sec. 860B(b)]

(b) HOLDERS MUST USE ACCRUAL METHOD.—The amounts includible in gross income with respect to any regular interest in a REMIC shall be determined under the accrual method of accounting.

[Sec. 860B(c)]

(c) PORTION OF GAIN TREATED AS ORDINARY INCOME.—Gain on the disposition of a regular interest shall be treated as ordinary income to the extent such gain does not exceed the excess (if any) of—

(1) the amount which would have been includible in the gross income of the taxpayer with respect to such interest if the yield on such interest were 110 percent of the applicable Federal rate (as defined in section 1274(d) without regard to paragraph (2) thereof) as of the beginning of the taxpayer's holding period, over

(2) the amount actually includible in gross income with respect to such interest by the taxpayer.

[Sec. 860B(d)]

(d) CROSS REFERENCE.—

For special rules in determining inclusion of original issue discount on regular interests, see section 1272(a)(6).

Amendments

• 1986, Tax Reform Act of 1986 (P.L. 99-514)

P.L. 99-514, § 671(a):

Amended subchapter M of chapter 1 by adding new Code Sec. 860B. **Effective** 1-1-87 [**effective** date changed by P.L. 100-647, § 1006(w)(1)].

[Sec. 860C]

SEC. 860C. TAXATION OF RESIDUAL INTERESTS.

[Sec. 860C(a)]

(a) PASS-THRU OF INCOME OR LOSS.—

(1) IN GENERAL.—In determining the tax under this chapter of any holder of a residual interest in a REMIC, such holder shall take into account his daily portion of the taxable income or net loss of such REMIC for each day during the taxable year on which such holder held such interest.

(2) DAILY PORTION.—The daily portion referred to in paragraph (1) shall be determined—

(A) by allocating to each day in any calendar quarter its ratable portion of the taxable income (or net loss) for such quarter, and

(B) by allocating the amounts so allocated to any day among the holders (on such day) of residual interests in proportion to their respective holdings on such day.

[Sec. 860C(b)]

(b) DETERMINATION OF TAXABLE INCOME OR NET LOSS.—For purposes of this section—

(1) TAXABLE INCOME.—The taxable income of a REMIC shall be determined under an accrual method of accounting and, except as provided in regulations, in the same manner as in the case of an individual, except that—

(A) regular interests in such REMIC (if not otherwise debt instruments) shall be treated as indebtedness of such REMIC,

(B) market discount on any market discount bond shall be included in gross income for the taxable years to which it is attributable as determined under the rules of section 1276(b)(2) (and sections 1276(a) and 1277 shall not apply),

(C) there shall not be taken into account any item of income, gain, loss, or deduction allocable to a prohibited transaction,

(D) the deductions referred to in section 703(a)(2) (other than any deduction under section 212) shall not be allowed, and

(E) the amount of the net income from foreclosure property (if any) shall be reduced by the amount of the tax imposed by section 860G(c).

(2) NET LOSS.—The net loss of any REMIC is the excess of—

(A) the deductions allowable in computing the taxable income of such REMIC, over

(B) its gross income.

Such amount shall be determined with the modifications set forth in paragraph (1).

Amendments

• 1988, Technical and Miscellaneous Revenue Act of 1988 (P.L. 100-647)

P.L. 100-647, §1006(t)(8)(C):

Amended Code Sec. 860C(b)(1) by striking out "and" at the end of subparagraph (C), by striking out the period at the end of subparagraph (D) and inserting in lieu thereof ", and", and by adding at the end thereof new subparagraph (E). **Effective** as if included in the provision of P.L. 99-514 to which it relates.

P.L. 100-647, §1006(t)(21):

Amended Code Sec. 860C(b)(1) by striking out "and in the same manner" and inserting in lieu thereof "and, except as provided in regulations, in the same manner". **Effective** as if included in the provision of P.L. 99-514 to which it relates.

[Sec. 860C(c)]

(c) DISTRIBUTIONS.—Any distribution by a REMIC—

(1) shall not be included in gross income to the extent it does not exceed the adjusted basis of the interest, and

(2) to the extent it exceeds the adjusted basis of the interest, shall be treated as gain from the sale or exchange of such interest.

[Sec. 860C(d)]

(d) BASIS RULES.—

(1) INCREASE IN BASIS.—The basis of any person's residual interest in a REMIC shall be increased by the amount of the taxable income of such REMIC taken into account under subsection (a) by such person with respect to such interest.

(2) DECREASES IN BASIS.—The basis of any person's residual interest in a REMIC shall be decreased (but not below zero) by the sum of the following amounts:

(A) any distributions to such person with respect to such interest, and

(B) any net loss of such REMIC taken into account under subsection (a) by such person with respect to such interest.

[Sec. 860C(e)]

(e) SPECIAL RULES.—

(1) AMOUNTS TREATED AS ORDINARY.—Any amount taken into account under subsection (a) by any holder of a residual interest in a REMIC shall be treated as ordinary income or ordinary loss, as the case may be.

(2) LIMITATION ON LOSSES.—

(A) IN GENERAL.—The amount of the net loss of any REMIC taken into account by a holder under subsection (a) with respect to any calendar quarter shall not exceed the adjusted basis of such holder's residual interest in such REMIC as of the close of such calendar quarter (determined without regard to the adjustment under subsection (d)(2)(B) for such calendar quarter).

(B) INDEFINITE CARRYFORWARD.—Any loss disallowed by reason of subparagraph (A) shall be treated as incurred by the REMIC in the succeeding calendar quarter with respect to such holder.

(3) CROSS REFERENCE.—

For special treatment of income in excess of daily accruals, see section 860E.

Amendments

• 1988, Technical and Miscellaneous Revenue Act of 1988 (P.L. 100-647)

P.L. 100-647, §1006(t)(1):

Amended Code Sec. 860C(e)(1). **Effective** as if included in the provision of P.L. 99-514 to which it relates. Prior to amendment, Code Sec. 860C(e)(1) read as follows:

(1) AMOUNTS TREATED AS ORDINARY INCOME.—Any amount included in the gross income of any holder of a residual interest in a REMIC by reason of subsection (a) shall be treated as ordinary income.

• 1986, Tax Reform Act of 1986 (P.L. 99-514)

P.L. 99-514, §671(a):

Amended subchapter M of chapter 1 by adding new Code Sec. 860C. **Effective** on 1-1-87 [**effective** date changed by P.L. 100-647, §1006(w)(1)].

[Sec. 860D]

SEC. 860D. REMIC DEFINED.

[Sec. 860D(a)]

(a) GENERAL RULE.—For purposes of this title, the terms "real estate mortgage investment conduit" and "REMIC" mean any entity—

(1) to which an election to be treated as a REMIC applies for the taxable year and all prior taxable years,

(2) all of the interests in which are regular interests or residual interests,

(3) which has 1 (and only 1) class of residual interests (and all distributions, if any, with respect to such interests are pro rata),

(4) as of the close of the 3rd month beginning after the startup day and at all times thereafter, substantially all of the assets of which consist of qualified mortgages and permitted investments,

(5) which has a taxable year which is a calendar year, and

(6) with respect to which there are reasonable arrangements designed to ensure that—

(A) residual interests in such entity are not held by disqualified organizations (as defined in section 860E(e)(5)), and

(B) information necessary for the application of section 860E(e) will be made available by the entity.

In the case of a qualified liquidation (as defined in section 860F(a)(4)(A)), paragraph (4) shall not apply during the liquidation period (as defined in section 860F(a)(4)(B)).

Amendments

• 1990, Omnibus Budget Reconciliation Act of 1990 (P.L. 101-508)

P.L. 101-508, §11704(a)(8):

Amended Code Sec. 860D(a) by inserting a closing parenthesis before the period in the last sentence at the end thereof. **Effective** 11-5-90.

• 1988, Technical and Miscellaneous Revenue Act of 1988 (P.L. 100-647)

P.L. 100-647, §1006(t)(2)(A)(i):

Amended Code Sec. 860D(a)(4) by striking out "4th month ending after" and inserting in lieu thereof "3rd month beginning after". **Effective** as if included in the provision of P.L. 99-514 to which it relates.

P.L. 100-647, §1006(t)(2)(A)(ii):

Amended Code Sec. 860D(a)(4) by striking out "and each quarter ending thereafter" and inserting in lieu thereof "and at all times thereafter". **Effective** 1-1-88.

P.L. 100-647, §1006(t)(16)(A):

Amended Code Sec. 860D(a) by striking out "and" at the end of paragraph (4), by striking out the period at the end of paragraph (5) and inserting in lieu thereof ", and", and by adding at the end thereof new paragraph (6). **Effective** as if included in the provision of P.L. 99-514 to which it relates.

P.L. 100-647, §1006(t)(16)(D)(i), provides:

(D)(i) The amendments made by subparagraph (A) shall apply in the case of any REMIC where the start-up day (as defined in section 860G(a)(9) of the 1986 Code, as in effect on the day before the date of the enactment of this Act) is after March 31, 1988; except that such amendments shall not apply in the case of a REMIC formed pursuant to a binding written contract in effect on such date.

P.L. 100-647, §1006(t)(19):

Amended Code Sec. 860D(a) by adding at the end thereof a new sentence. **Effective** as if included in the provision of P.L. 99-514 to which it relates.

[Sec. 860D(b)]

(b) ELECTION.—

(1) IN GENERAL.—An entity (otherwise meeting the requirements of subsection (a)) may elect to be treated as a REMIC for its 1st taxable year. Such an election shall be made on its return for such 1st taxable year. Except as provided in paragraph (2), such an election shall apply to the taxable year for which made and all subsequent taxable years.

(2) TERMINATION.—

(A) IN GENERAL.—If any entity ceases to be a REMIC at any time during the taxable year, such entity shall not be treated as a REMIC for such taxable year or any succeeding taxable year.

(B) INADVERTENT TERMINATIONS.—If—

(i) an entity ceases to be a REMIC,

(ii) the Secretary determines that such cessation was inadvertent,

(iii) no later than a reasonable time after the discovery of the event resulting in such cessation, steps are taken so that such entity is once more a REMIC, and

(iv) such entity, and each person holding an interest in such entity at any time during the period specified pursuant to this subsection, agrees to make such adjustments (consistent with the treatment of such entity as a REMIC or a C corporation) as may be required by the Secretary with respect to such period,

then, notwithstanding such terminating event, such entity shall be treated as continuing to be a REMIC (or such cessation shall be disregarded for purposes of subparagraph (A)) whichever the Secretary determines to be appropriate.

Amendments

• 1986, Tax Reform Act of 1986 (P.L. 99-514)

P.L. 99-514, §671(a):

Amended subchapter M of chapter 1 by adding new Code Sec. 860D. **Effective** 1-1-87 [**effective** date changed by P.L. 100-647, §1006(w)(1)].

[Sec. 860E]

SEC. 860E. TREATMENT OF INCOME IN EXCESS OF DAILY ACCRUALS ON RESIDUAL INTERESTS.

[Sec. 860E(a)]

(a) EXCESS INCLUSIONS MAY NOT BE OFFSET BY NET OPERATING LOSSES.—

(1) IN GENERAL.—The taxable income of any holder of a residual interest in a REMIC for any taxable year shall in no event be less than the excess inclusion for such taxable year.

(2) SPECIAL RULE FOR AFFILIATED GROUPS.—All members of an affiliated group filing a consolidated return shall be treated as 1 taxpayer for purposes of this subsection.

(3) COORDINATION WITH SECTION 172.—Any excess inclusion for any taxable year shall not be taken into account—

(A) in determining under section 172 the amount of any net operating loss for such taxable year, and

(B) in determining taxable income for such taxable year for purposes of the 2nd sentence of section 172(b)(2).

(4) COORDINATION WITH MINIMUM TAX.—For purposes of part VI of subchapter A of this chapter—

(A) the reference in section 55(b)(2) to taxable income shall be treated as a reference to taxable income determined without regard to this subsection,

(B) the alternative minimum taxable income of any holder of a residual interest in a REMIC for any taxable year shall in no event be less than the excess inclusion for such taxable year, and

(C) any excess inclusion shall be disregarded for purposes of computing the alternative tax net operating loss deduction.

Amendments

• 1996, Small Business Job Protection Act of 1996 (P.L. 104-188)

P.L. 104-188, §1616(b)(10)(A)-(D):

Amended Code Sec. 860E(a) by striking "Except as provided in paragraph (2), the" in paragraph (1) and inserting "The", by striking paragraphs (2) and (4) and redesignating paragraphs (3), (5), and (6) [paragraph (6) is added by Act Sec. 1704(h)(1)] as paragraphs (2), (3), and (4), respectively, by striking in paragraph (2) (as so redesignated) all that follows "subsection" and inserting a period, and by striking the last sentence of paragraph (4) (as redesignated). For the **effective** date, see Act Sec. 1616(c)(1) and (4), below. Prior to amendment, Code Sec. 860E(a)(2)-(4) read as follows:

(2) EXCEPTION FOR CERTAIN FINANCIAL INSTITUTIONS.—Paragraph (1) shall not apply to any organization to which section 593 applies. The Secretary may by regulations provide that the preceding sentence shall not apply where necessary or appropriate to prevent avoidance of tax imposed by this chapter.

(3) SPECIAL RULE FOR AFFILIATED GROUPS.—All members of an affiliated group filing a consolidated return shall be treated as 1 taxpayer for purposes of this subsection, except that paragraph (2) shall be applied separately with respect to each corporation which is a member of such group and to which section 593 applies.

(4) TREATMENT OF CERTAIN SUBSIDIARIES.—

(A) IN GENERAL.—For purposes of this subsection, a corporation to which section 593 applies and each qualified subsidiary of such corporation shall be treated as a single corporation to which section 593 applies.

(B) QUALIFIED SUBSIDIARY.—For purposes of this subsection, the term "qualified subsidiary" means any corporation—

(i) all the stock of which, and substantially all the indebtedness of which, is held directly by the corporation to which section 593 applies, and

(ii) which is organized and operated exclusively in connection with the organization and operation of 1 or more REMIC's.

P.L. 104-188, §1616(c)(1) and (4), provides:

(1) IN GENERAL.—Except as otherwise provided in this subsection, the amendments made by this section shall apply to taxable years beginning after December 31, 1995.

***

(4) SUBSECTION (b)(10).—The amendments made by subsection (b)(10) shall not apply to any residual interest held by a taxpayer if such interest has been held by such taxpayer at all times after October 31, 1995.

P.L. 104-188, §1704(h)(1):

Amended Code Sec. 860E(a) by adding at the end a new paragraph (6). **Effective** as if included in the amendments made by section 671 of P.L. 99-514, unless the taxpayer elects to apply it only to tax years beginning after 8-20-96.

• 1988, Technical and Miscellaneous Revenue Act of 1988 (P.L. 100-647)

P.L. 100-647, §1006(t)(15):

Amended Code Sec. 860E(a) by adding at the end thereof new paragraphs (3)-(4). **Effective** as if included in the provision of P.L. 99-514 to which it relates.

P.L. 100-647, §1006(t)(27):

Amended Code Sec. 860E(a) by adding at the end thereof new paragraph (5). **Effective** as if included in the provision of P.L. 99-514 to which it relates.

[Sec. 860E(b)]

(b) ORGANIZATIONS SUBJECT TO UNRELATED BUSINESS TAX.—If the holder of any residual interest in a REMIC is an organization subject to the tax imposed by section 511, the excess inclusion of such holder for any taxable year shall be treated as unrelated business taxable income of such holder for purposes of section 511.

[Sec. 860E(c)]

(c) EXCESS INCLUSION.—For purposes of this section—

(1) IN GENERAL.—The term "excess inclusion" means, with respect to any residual interest in a REMIC for any calendar quarter, the excess (if any) of—

(A) the amount taken into account with respect to such interest by the holder under section 860C(a), over

(B) the sum of the daily accruals with respect to such interest for days during such calendar quarter while held by such holder.

To the extent provided in regulations, if residual interests in a REMIC do not have significant value, the excess inclusions with respect to such interests shall be the amount determined under subparagraph (A) without regard to subparagraph (B).

(2) DETERMINATION OF DAILY ACCRUALS.—

(A) IN GENERAL.—For purposes of this subsection, the daily accrual with respect to any residual interest for any day in any calendar quarter shall be determined by allocating to each day in such quarter its ratable portion of the product of—

(i) the adjusted issue price of such interest at the beginning of such quarter, and

(ii) 120 percent of the long-term Federal rate (determined on the basis of compounding at the close of each calendar quarter and properly adjusted for the length of such quarter).

(B) ADJUSTED ISSUE PRICE.—For purposes of this paragraph, the adjusted issue price of any residual interest at the beginning of any calendar quarter is the issue price of the residual interest (adjusted for contributions)—

(i) increased by the amount of daily accruals for prior quarters, and

(ii) decreased (but not below zero) by any distribution made with respect to such interest before the beginning of such quarter.

(C) FEDERAL LONG-TERM RATE.—For purposes of this paragraph, the term "Federal long-term rate" means the Federal long-term rate which would have applied to the residual interest under section 1274(d) (determined without regard to paragraph (2) thereof) if it were a debt instrument.

Amendments

• 1988, Technical and Miscellaneous Revenue Act of 1988 (P.L. 100-647)

P.L. 100-647, §1006(t)(13):

Amended Code Sec. 860E(c)(2)(B) by striking out "issue price of residual interest" and inserting in lieu thereof "issue price of the residual interest". **Effective** as if included in the provision of P.L. 99-514 to which it relates.

P.L. 100-647, §1006(t)(17)(A)-(B):

Amended Code Sec. 860E(c)(2)(B) by inserting "(adjusted for contributions)" after "residual interest" the second place it appears, and by striking "decreased by" in clause (ii) and inserting in lieu thereof "decreased (but not below zero) by". **Effective** as if included in the provision of P.L. 99-514 to which it relates.

[Sec. 860E(d)]

(d) TREATMENT OF RESIDUAL INTERESTS HELD BY REAL ESTATE INVESTMENT TRUSTS.—If a residual interest in a REMIC is held by a real estate investment trust, under regulations prescribed by the Secretary—

(1) any excess of—

(A) the aggregate excess inclusions determined with respect to such interests, over

(B) the real estate investment trust taxable income (within the meaning of section 857(b)(2), excluding any net capital gain),

shall be allocated among the shareholders of such trust in proportion to the dividends received by such shareholders from trust, and

(2) any amount allocated to a shareholder under paragraph (1) shall be treated as an excess inclusion with respect to a residual interest held by such shareholder.

Rules similar to the rules of the preceding sentence shall apply also in the case of regulated investment companies, common trust funds, and organizations to which part I of subchapter T applies.

Amendments

• 1988, Technical and Miscellaneous Revenue Act of 1988 (P.L. 100-647)

P.L. 100-647, §1006(t)(23):

Amended Code Sec. 860E(d) by adding at the end thereof a new sentence. **Effective** as if included in the provision of P.L. 99-514 to which it relates.

• 1986, Tax Reform Act of 1986 (P.L. 99-514)

P.L. 99-514, §671(a):

Amended subchapter M of chapter 1 by adding new Code Sec. 860E. **Effective** 1-1-87 [**effective** date changed by P.L. 100-647, §1006(w)(1)].

[Sec. 860E(e)]

(e) TAX ON TRANSFERS OF RESIDUAL INTERESTS TO CERTAIN ORGANIZATIONS, ETC.—

(1) IN GENERAL.—A tax is hereby imposed on any transfer of a residual interest in a REMIC to a disqualified organization.

(2) AMOUNT OF TAX.—The amount of the tax imposed by paragraph (1) on any transfer of a residual interest shall be equal to the product of—

(A) the amount (determined under regulations) equal to the present value of the total anticipated excess inclusions with respect to such interest for periods after such transfer, multiplied by

(B) the highest rate of tax specified in section 11(b)(1).

(3) LIABILITY.—The tax imposed by paragraph (1) on any transfer shall be paid by the transferor; except that, where such transfer is through an agent for a disqualified organization, such tax shall be paid by such agent.

(4) TRANSFEREE FURNISHES AFFIDAVIT.—The person (otherwise liable for any tax imposed by paragraph (1)) shall be relieved of liability for the tax imposed by paragraph (1) with respect to any transfer if—

(A) the transferee furnishes to such person an affidavit that the transferee is not a disqualified organization, and

(B) as of the time of the transfer, such person does not have actual knowledge that such affidavit is false.

(5) DISQUALIFIED ORGANIZATION.—For purposes of this section, the term "disqualified organization" means—

(A) the United States, any State or political subdivision thereof, any foreign government, any international organization, or any agency or instrumentality of any of the foregoing,

(B) any organization (other than a cooperative described in section 521) which is exempt from tax imposed by this chapter unless such organization is subject to the tax imposed by section 511, and

(C) any organization described in section 1381(a)(2)(C).

For purposes of subparagraph (A), the rules of section 168(h)(2)(D) (relating to treatment of certain taxable instrumentalities) shall apply; except that, in the case of the Federal Home Loan Mortgage Corporation, clause (ii) of such section shall not apply.

(6) TREATMENT OF PASS-THRU ENTITIES.—

(A) IMPOSITION OF TAX.—If, at any time during any taxable year of a pass-thru entity, a disqualified organization is the record holder of an interest in such entity, there is hereby imposed on such entity for such taxable year a tax equal to the product of—

(i) the amount of excess inclusions for such taxable year allocable to the interest held by such disqualified organization, multiplied by

(ii) the highest rate of tax specified in section 11(b)(1).

(B) PASS-THRU ENTITY.—For purposes of this paragraph, the term "pass-thru entity" means—

(i) any regulated investment company, real estate investment trust, or common trust fund,

(ii) any partnership, trust, or estate, and

(iii) any organization to which part I of subchapter T applies.

Except as provided in regulations, a person holding an interest in a pass-thru entity as a nominee for another person shall, with respect to such interest, be treated as a pass-thru entity.

(C) TAX TO BE DEDUCTIBLE.—Any tax imposed by this paragraph with respect to any excess inclusion of any pass-thru entity for any taxable year shall, for purposes of this title (other than this subsection), be applied against (and operate to reduce) the amount included in gross income with respect to the residual interest involved.

(D) EXCEPTION WHERE HOLDER FURNISHES AFFIDAVIT.—No tax shall be imposed by subparagraph (A) with respect to any interest in a pass-thru entity for any period if—

(i) the record holder of such interest furnishes to such pass-thru entity an affidavit that such record holder is not a disqualified organization, and

(ii) during such period, the pass-thru entity does not have actual knowledge that such affidavit is false.

(7) WAIVER.—The Secretary may waive the tax imposed by paragraph (1) on any transfer if—

(A) within a reasonable time after discovery that the transfer was subject to tax under paragraph (1), steps are taken so that the interest is no longer held by the disqualified organization, and

(B) there is paid to the Secretary such amounts as the Secretary may require.

(8) ADMINISTRATIVE PROVISIONS.—For purposes of subtitle F, the taxes imposed by this subsection shall be treated as excise taxes with respect to which the deficiency procedures of such subtitle apply.

Amendments

• 1988, Technical and Miscellaneous Revenue Act of 1988 (P.L. 100-647)

P.L. 100-647, §1006(t)(16)(B):

Amended Code Sec. 860E by adding at the end thereof new subsection (e). For the **effective** date, see Act Sec. 1006(t)(16)(D)(ii)-(iv), below:

P.L. 100-647, §1006(t)(16)(D)(ii)-(iv), provides:

(ii) The amendments made by subparagraphs (B) and (C) (except to the extent they relate to paragraph (6) of section 860E(e) of the 1986 Code as added by such amendments) shall apply to transfers after March 31, 1988; except that such amendments shall not apply to any transfer pursuant to a binding written contract in effect on such date.

(iii) Except as provided in clause (iv), the amendments made by subparagraphs (B) and (C) (to the extent they relate to paragraph (6) of section 860E(e) of the 1986 Code as so added) shall apply to excess inclusions for periods after March 31, 1988 but only to the extent such inclusions are—

(I) allocable to an interest in a pass-thru entity acquired after March 31, 1988, or

(II) allocable to an interest in a pass-thru entity acquired on or before March 31, 1988, but attributable to a residual interest acquired by the pass-thru entity after March 31, 1988.

For purposes of the preceding sentence, any interest in a pass-thru entity (or residual interest) acquired after March 31, 1988, pursuant to a binding written contract in effect on such date shall be treated as acquired before such date.

(iv) In the case of any real estate investment trust, regulated investment company, common trust fund, or publicly traded partnership, no tax shall be imposed under section 860E(e)(6) of the 1986 Code (as added by the amendment made by subparagraph (B)) for any taxable year beginning before January 1, 1989.

[Sec. 860E(f)]

(f) TREATMENT OF VARIABLE INSURANCE CONTRACTS.—Except as provided in regulations, with respect to any variable contract (as defined in section 817), there shall be no adjustment in the reserve to the extent of any excess inclusion.

Amendments

• 1988, Technical and Miscellaneous Revenue Act of 1988 (P.L. 100-647)

P.L. 100-647, § 1006(t)(26):

Amended Code Sec. 860E by adding at the end thereof new subsection (f). **Effective** as if included in the provision of P.L. 99-514 to which it relates.

[Sec. 860F]

SEC. 860F. OTHER RULES.

[Sec. 860F(a)]

(a) 100 PERCENT TAX ON PROHIBITED TRANSACTIONS.—

(1) TAX IMPOSED.—There is hereby imposed for each taxable year of a REMIC a tax equal to 100 percent of the net income derived from prohibited transactions.

(2) PROHIBITED TRANSACTION.—For purposes of this part, the term "prohibited transaction" means—

(A) DISPOSITION OF QUALIFIED MORTGAGE.—The disposition of any qualified mortgage transferred to the REMIC other than a disposition pursuant to—

(i) the substitution of a qualified replacement mortgage for a qualified mortgage (or the repurchase in lieu of substitution of a defective obligation),

(ii) a disposition incident to the foreclosure, default, or imminent default of the mortgage,

(iii) the bankruptcy or insolvency of the REMIC, or

(iv) a qualified liquidation.

(B) INCOME FROM NONPERMITTED ASSETS.—The receipt of any income attributable to any asset which is neither a qualified mortgage nor a permitted investment.

(C) COMPENSATION FOR SERVICES.—The receipt by the REMIC of any amount representing a fee or other compensation for services.

(D) GAIN FROM DISPOSITION OF CASH FLOW INVESTMENTS.—Gain from the disposition of any cash flow investment other than pursuant to any qualified liquidation.

(3) DETERMINATION OF NET INCOME.—For purposes of paragraph (1), the term "net income derived from prohibited transactions" means the excess of the gross income from prohibited transactions over the deductions allowed by this chapter which are directly connected with such transactions; except that there shall not be taken into account any item attributable to any prohibited transaction for which there was a loss.

(4) QUALIFIED LIQUIDATION.—For purposes of this part—

(A) IN GENERAL.—The term "qualified liquidation" means a transaction in which—

(i) the REMIC adopts a plan of complete liquidation,

(ii) such REMIC sells all its assets (other than cash) within the liquidation period, and

(iii) all proceeds of the liquidation (plus the cash), less assets retained to meet claims, are credited or distributed to holders of regular or residual interests on or before the last day of the liquidation period.

(B) LIQUIDATION PERIOD.—The term "liquidation period" means the period—

(i) beginning on the date of the adoption of the plan of liquidation, and

(ii) ending at the close of the 90th day after such date.

(5) EXCEPTIONS.—Notwithstanding subparagraphs (A) and (D) of paragraph (2), the term "prohibited transaction" shall not include any disposition—

(A) required to prevent default on a regular interest where the threatened default resulted from a default on 1 or more qualified mortgages, or

(B) to facilitate a clean-up call (as defined in regulations).

Amendments

• 1996, Small Business Job Protection Act of 1996 (P.L. 104-188)

P.L. 104-188, §1704(t)(74):

Amended Code Sec. 860F(a)(5) by striking "paragraph (1)" and inserting "paragraph (2)". **Effective** 8-20-96.

• 1988, Technical and Miscellaneous Revenue Act of 1988 (P.L. 100-647)

P.L. 100-647, §1006(t)(3)(A):

Amended Code Sec. 860F(a)(2)(A)(i). **Effective** as if included in the provision of P.L. 99-514 to which it relates. Prior to amendment, Code Sec. 860F(a)(2)(A)(i) read as follows:

(i) the substitution of a qualified replacement mortgage for a qualified mortgage.

P.L. 100-647, §1006(t)(3)(B)(i):

Amended Code Sec. 860F(a)(2) by striking out the last sentence of subparagraph (A). **Effective** as if included in the provision of P.L. 99-514 to which it relates. Prior to amendment, the last sentence of Code Sec. 860F(a)(2)(A) read as follows:

Notwithstanding the preceding sentence, the term "prohibited transaction" shall not include any disposition required to prevent default on a regular interest where the threatened default resulted from a default on 1 or more qualified mortgages.

P.L. 100-647, §1006(t)(3)(B)(ii):

Amended Code Sec. 860F(a) by adding at the end thereof new paragraph (5). **Effective** as if included in the provision of P.L. 99-514 to which it relates.

P.L. 100-647, §1006(t)(3)(C):

Amended Code Sec. 860F(a)(2)(D) by striking out "described in subsection (b)" after "qualified liquidation". **Effective** as if included in the provision of P.L. 99-514 to which it relates.

P.L. 100-647, §1006(t)(22)(B):

Amended Code Sec. 860F(a)(2)(A)(iii) by striking out "real estate mortgage pool" and inserting in lieu thereof "REMIC". **Effective** as if included in the provision of P.L. 99-514 to which it relates.

P.L. 100-647, §1006(t)(22)(C):

Amended Code Sec. 860F(a)(2)(C) by striking out "real estate mortgage pool" and inserting in lieu thereof "REMIC". **Effective** as if included in the provision of P.L. 99-514 to which it relates.

[Sec. 860F(b)]

(b) TREATMENT OF TRANSFERS TO THE REMIC.—

(1) TREATMENT OF TRANSFEROR.—

(A) NONRECOGNITION GAIN OR LOSS.—No gain or loss shall be recognized to the transferor on the transfer of any property to a REMIC in exchange for regular or residual interests in such REMIC.

(B) ADJUSTED BASES OF INTERESTS.—The adjusted bases of the regular and residual interests received in a transfer described in subparagraph (A) shall be equal to the aggregate adjusted bases of the property transferred in such transfer. Such amount shall be allocated among such interests in proportion to their respective fair market values.

(C) TREATMENT OF NONRECOGNIZED GAIN.—If the issue price of any regular or residual interest exceeds its adjusted basis as determined under subparagraph (B), for periods during which such interest is held by the transferor (or by any other person whose basis is determined in whole or in part by reference to the basis of such interest in the hand of the transferor)—

(i) in the case of a regular interest, such excess shall be included in gross income (as determined under rules similar to rules of section 1276(b)), and

(ii) in the case of a residual interest, such excess shall be included in gross income ratably over the anticipated period during which the REMIC will be in existence.

(D) TREATMENT OF NONRECOGNIZED LOSS.—If the adjusted basis of any regular or residual interest received in a transfer described in subparagraph (A) exceeds its issue price, for periods during which such interest is held by the transferor (or by any other person whose basis is determined in whole or in part by reference to the basis of such interest in the hand of the transferor)—

(i) in the case of a regular interest, such excess shall be allowable as a deduction under rules similar to the rules of section 171, and

(ii) in the case of a residual interest, such excess shall be allowable as a deduction ratably over the anticipated period during which the REMIC will be in existence.

(2) BASIS TO REMIC.—The basis of any property received by a REMIC in a transfer described in paragraph (1)(A) shall be its fair market value immediately after such transfer.

Amendments

• 1988, Technical and Miscellaneous Revenue Act of 1988 (P.L. 100-647)

P.L. 100-647, §1006(t)(4):

Amended Code Sec. 860F(b)(1)(A) by striking out "the transfer of any property to a REMIC" and inserting in lieu thereof "the transfer of any property to a REMIC in exchange for regular or residual interests in such REMIC". **Effective** as if included in the provision of P.L. 99-514 to which it relates.

P.L. 100-647, § 1006(t)(14):

Amended Code Sec. 860F(b)(1)(D)(ii) by striking out "the real estate mortgage pool" and inserting in lieu thereof "the REMIC". (Note also the amendment paragraph for Act Sec. 106(t)(22)(E), below.) **Effective** as if included in the provision of P.L. 99-514 to which it relates.

P.L. 100-647, § 1006(t)(22)(D):

Amended Code Sec. 860F(b)(1)(C)(ii) by striking out "real estate mortgage pool" and inserting in lieu thereof "REMIC". **Effective** as if included in the provision of P.L. 99-514 to which it relates.

P.L. 100-647, § 1006(t)(22)(E):

Amended Code Sec. 860F(b)(1)(D)(ii) by striking out "real estate mortgage pool" and inserting in lieu thereof "REMIC". **Effective** as if included in the provision of P.L. 99-514 to which it relates.

[Sec. 860F(c)]

(c) DISTRIBUTIONS OF PROPERTY.—If a REMIC makes a distribution of property with respect to any regular or residual interest—

(1) notwithstanding any other provision of this subtitle, gain shall be recognized to such REMIC on the distribution in the same manner as if it had sold such property to the distributee at its fair market value, and

(2) the basis of the distributee in such property shall be its fair market value.

[Sec. 860F(d)]

(d) COORDINATION WITH WASH SALE RULES.—For purposes of section 1091—

(1) any residual interest in a REMIC shall be treated as a security, and

(2) in applying such section to any loss claimed to have been sustained on the sale or other disposition of a residual interest in a REMIC—

(A) except as provided in regulations, any residual interest in any REMIC and any interest in a taxable mortgage pool (as defined in section 7701(i)) comparable to a residual interest in a REMIC shall be treated as substantially identical stock or securities, and

(B) subsections (a) and (e) of such section shall be applied by substituting "6 months" for "30 days" each place it appears.

[Sec. 860F(e)]

(e) TREATMENT UNDER SUBTITLE F.—For purposes of subtitle F, a REMIC shall be treated as a partnership (and holders of residual interests in such REMIC shall be treated as partners). Any return required by reason of the preceding sentence shall include the amount of the daily accruals determined under section 860E(c). Such return shall be filed by the REMIC. The determination of who may sign such return shall be made without regard to the first sentence of this subsection.

Amendments

• 1988, Technical and Miscellaneous Revenue Act of 1988 (P.L. 100-647)

P.L. 100-647, § 1006(t)(18)(A):

Amended Code Sec. 860F(e) by adding at the end thereof two new sentences. For the **effective** date, see Act Sec. 1006(t)(18)(B), below.

P.L. 100-647, § 1006(t)(18)(B), provides:

(B) Unless the REMIC otherwise elects, the amendment made by subparagraph (A) shall not apply to any REMIC where the start-up day (as defined in section 860G(a)(9) of the 1986 Code as in effect on the day before the date of the enactment of this Act) is before the date of the enactment of this Act.

• 1986, Tax Reform Act of 1986 (P.L. 99-514)

P.L. 99-514, § 671(a):

Amended subchapter M of chapter 1 by adding new Code Sec. 860F. **Effective** 1-1-87 [**effective** date changed by P.L. 100-647, § 1006(w)(1)].

[Sec. 860G]

SEC. 860G. OTHER DEFINITIONS AND SPECIAL RULES.

[Sec. 860G(a)]

(a) DEFINITIONS.—For purposes of this part—

(1) REGULAR INTEREST.—The term "regular interest" means any interest in a REMIC which is issued on the startup day with fixed terms and which is designated as a regular interest if—

(A) such interest unconditionally entitles the holder to receive a specified principal amount (or other similar amount), and

(B) interest payments (or other similar amount), if any, with respect to such interest at or before maturity—

(i) are payable based on a fixed rate (or to the extent provided in regulations, at a variable rate), or

(ii) consist of a specified portion of the interest payments on qualified mortgages and such portion does not vary during the period such interest is outstanding.

The interest shall not fail to meet the requirements of subparagraph (A) merely because the timing (but not the amount) of the principal payments (or other similar amounts) may be contingent on the extent of prepayments on qualified mortgages and the amount of income from permitted investments. An interest shall not fail to qualify as a regular interest solely because the specified principal amount of the regular interest (or the amount of interest accrued on the regular interest) can be reduced as a result of the nonoccurrence of 1 or more contingent payments with respect to any reverse mortgage loan held by the REMIC if, on the startup day for the REMIC, the sponsor reasonably believes that all principal and interest due under the regular interest will be paid at or prior to the liquidation of the REMIC.

(2) RESIDUAL INTEREST.—The term "residual interest" means an interest in a REMIC which is issued on the startup day, which is not a regular interest, and which is designated as a residual interest.

(3) QUALIFIED MORTGAGE.—The term "qualified mortgage" means—

(A) any obligation (including any participation or certificate of beneficial ownership therein) which is principally secured by an interest in real property and which—

(i) is transferred to the REMIC on the startup day in exchange for regular or residual interests in the REMIC,

(ii) is purchased by the REMIC within the 3-month period beginning on the startup day if, except as provided in the regulations, such purchase is pursuant to a fixed price contract in effect on the startup day, or

(iii) represents an increase in the principal amount under the original terms of an obligation described in clause (i) or (ii) if such increase—

(I) is attributable to an advance made to the obligor pursuant to the original terms of a reverse mortgage loan or other obligation,

(II) occurs after the startup day, and

(III) is purchased by the REMIC pursuant to a fixed price contract in effect on the startup day.

(B) any qualified replacement mortgage, and

(C) any regular interest in another REMIC transferred to the REMIC on the startup day in exchange for regular or residual interests in the REMIC.

For purposes of subparagraph (A), any obligation secured by stock held by a person as a tenant-stockholder (as defined in section 216) in a cooperative housing corporation (as so defined) shall be treated as secured by an interest in real property. For purposes of subparagraph (A), any obligation originated by the United States or any State (or any political subdivision, agency, or instrumentality of the United States or any State) shall be treated as principally secured by an interest in real property if more than 50 percent of such obligations which are transferred to, or purchased by, the REMIC are principally secured by an interest in real property (determined without regard to this sentence).

(4) QUALIFIED REPLACEMENT MORTGAGE.—The term "qualified replacement mortgage" means any obligation—

(A) which would be a qualified mortgage if transferred on the startup day in exchange for regular or residual interests in the REMIC, and

(B) which is received for—

(i) another obligation within the 3-month period beginning on the startup day, or

(ii) a defective obligation within the 2-year period beginning on the startup day.

(5) PERMITTED INVESTMENTS.—The term "permitted investments" means any—

(A) cash flow investment,

(B) qualified reserve asset, or

(C) foreclosure property.

(6) CASH FLOW INVESTMENT.—The term "cash flow investment" means any investment of amounts received under qualified mortgages for a temporary period before distribution to holders of interests in the REMIC.

(7) QUALIFIED RESERVE ASSET.—

(A) IN GENERAL.—The term "qualified reserve asset" means any intangible property which is held for investment and as part of a qualified reserve fund.

(B) QUALIFIED RESERVE FUND.—For purposes of subparagraph (A), the term "qualified reserve fund" means any reasonably required reserve to—

(i) provide for full payment of expenses of the REMIC or amounts due on regular interests in the event of defaults on qualified mortgages or lower than expected returns on cash flow investments, or

(ii) provide a source of funds for the purchase of obligations described in clause (ii) or (iii) of paragraph (3)(A).

The aggregate fair market value of the assets held in any such reserve shall not exceed 50 percent of the aggregate fair market value of all of the assets of the REMIC on the startup day, and the amount of any such reserve shall be promptly and appropriately reduced to the extent the amount held in such reserve is no longer reasonably required for purposes specified in clause (i) or (ii) of this subparagraph.

(C) SPECIAL RULE.—A reserve shall not be treated as a qualified reserve for any taxable year (and all subsequent taxable years) if more than 30 percent of the gross income from the assets in such fund for the taxable year is derived from the sale or other disposition of property held for less than 3 months. For purposes of the preceding sentence, gain on the disposition of a qualified reserve asset shall not be taken into account if the disposition giving rise to such gain is required to prevent default on a regular interest where the threatened default resulted from a default on 1 or more qualified mortgages.

(8) FORECLOSURE PROPERTY.—The term "foreclosure property" means property—

(A) which would be foreclosure property under section 856(e) (without regard to paragraph (5) thereof) if acquired by a real estate investment trust, and

(B) which is acquired in connection with the default or imminent default of a qualified mortgage held by the REMIC.

Solely for purposes of section 860D(a), the determination of whether any property is foreclosure property shall be made without regard to section 856(e)(4).

(9) STARTUP DAY.—The term "startup day" means the day on which the REMIC issues all of its regular and residual interests. To the extent provided in regulations, all interests issued (and all transfers to the REMIC) during any period (not exceeding 10 days) permitted in such regulations shall be treated as occurring on the day during such period selected by the REMIC for purposes of this paragraph.

(10) ISSUE PRICE.—The issue price of any regular or residual interest in a REMIC shall be determined under section 1273(b) in the same manner as if such interest were a debt instrument; except that if the interest is issued for property, paragraph (3) of section 1273(b) shall apply whether or not the requirements of such paragraph are met.

Amendments

• 2005, Gulf Opportunity Zone Act of 2005 (P.L. 109-135)

P.L. 109-135, §403(cc)(1)-(2):

Amended Code Sec. 860G(a)(3) by striking "the obligation" and inserting "a reverse mortgage loan or other obligation" in subparagraph (A)(iii)(I), and by striking all that follows subparagraph (C) and inserting two new sentences. **Effective** as if included in the provision of the American Jobs Creation Act of 2004 (P.L. 108-357) to which it relates (**effective** 1-1-2005, generally.—CCH]. Prior to amendment, all that followed Code Sec. 860G(a)(3)(C) read as follows:

For purposes of subparagraph (A) any obligation secured by stock held by a person as a tenant-stockholder (as defined in section 216) in a cooperative housing corporation (as so defined) shall be treated as secured by an interest in real property, and any reverse mortgage loan (and each balance increase on such loan meeting the requirements of subparagraph (A)(iii)) shall be treated as an obligation secured by an interest in real property. For purposes of subparagraph (A), if more than 50 percent of the obligations transferred to, or purchased by, the REMIC are originated by the United States or any State (or any political subdivision, agency, or instrumentality of the United States or any State) and are principally secured by an interest in real property, then each obligation transferred to, or purchased by, the REMIC shall be treated as secured by an interest in real property.

• 2004, American Jobs Creation Act of 2004 (P.L. 108-357)

P.L. 108-357, §835(b)(5)(A):

Amended Code Sec. 860G(a)(1) by adding at the end a new sentence. For the **effective** date, see Act Sec. 835(c), below.

P.L. 108-357, §835(b)(5)(B):

Amended the last sentence of Code Sec. 860G(a)(3) by inserting ", and any reverse mortgage loan (and each balance increase on such loan meeting the requirements of subparagraph (A)(iii)) shall be treated as an obligation secured by an interest in real property" before the period at the end. For the **effective** date, see Act Sec. 835(c), below.

P.L. 108-357, §835(b)(6):

Amended Code Sec. 860G(a)(3) by adding "and" at the end of subparagraph (B), by striking ", and" at the end of subparagraph (C) and inserting a period, and by striking subparagraph (D). For the **effective** date, see Act Sec. 835(c), below. Prior to being stricken, Code Sec. 860G(a)(3)(D) read as follows:

(D) any regular interest in a FASIT which is transferred to, or purchased by, the REMIC as described in clauses (i) and (ii) of subparagraph (A) but only if 95 percent or more of the value of the assets of such FASIT is at all times attributable to obligations described in subparagraph (A) (without regard to such clauses).

P.L. 108-357, §835(b)(7):

Amended Code Sec. 860G(a)(3), as amended by paragraph (6)[(5)], by adding at the end a new sentence. For the **effective** date, see Act Sec. 835(c), below.

P.L. 108-357, §835(b)(8)(A):

Amended Code Sec. 860G(a)(3)(A) by striking "or" at the end of clause (i), by inserting "or" at the end of clause (ii), and by inserting after clause (ii) a new clause (iii). For the **effective** date, see Act Sec. 835(c), below.

P.L. 108-357, §835(b)(8)(B):

Amended Code Sec. 860G(a)(7)(B). For the **effective** date, see Act Sec. 835(c), below. Prior to amendment, Code Sec. 860G(a)(7)(B) read as follows:

(B) QUALIFIED RESERVE FUND.—For purposes of subparagraph (A), the term "qualified reserve fund" means any reasonably required reserve to provide for full payment of expenses of the REMIC or amounts due on regular interests in the event of defaults on qualified mortgages or lower than expected returns on cash-flow investments. The amount of any such reserve shall be promptly and appropriately reduced as payments of qualified mortgages are received.

P.L. 108-357, §835(c), provides:

(c) EFFECTIVE DATE.—

(1) IN GENERAL.—Except as provided in paragraph (2), the amendments made by this section shall take effect on January 1, 2005.

(2) EXCEPTION FOR EXISTING FASITS.—Paragraph (1) shall not apply to any FASIT in existence on the date of the enactment of this Act [10-22-2004.—CCH]to the extent that regular interests issued by the FASIT before such date continue to remain outstanding in accordance with the original terms of issuance.

• 1996, Small Business Job Protection Act of 1996 (P.L. 104-188)

P.L. 104-188, §1621(b)(6):

Amended Code Sec. 860G(a)(3) by striking "and" at the end of subparagraph (B), by striking the period at the end of subparagraph (C) and inserting ",and", and by inserting after subparagraph (C) a new subparagraph (D). **Effective** 9-1-97.

• 1990, Omnibus Budget Reconciliation Act of 1990 (P.L. 101-508)

P.L. 101-508, §11704(a)(9):

Amended Code Sec. 860G(a)(3)(A) by striking the comma after "secured". **Effective** 11-5-90.

• 1989, Omnibus Budget Reconciliation Act of 1989 (P.L. 101-239)

P.L. 101-239, §7811(c)(9):

Amended Code Sec. 860G(a)(3) by striking "this subparagraph" and inserting "subparagraph (A)". **Effective** as if included in the provision of P.L. 100-647 to which it relates.

• 1988, Technical and Miscellaneous Revenue Act of 1988 (P.L. 100-647)

P.L. 100-647, §1006(t)(5)(A):

Amended Code Sec. 860G(a)(1). The amendment shall not apply to any REMIC where the startup day (as defined in section 860G(a)(9) of the 1986 Code as in effect on the day before 11-10-88) is before 7-1-87. Prior to amendment, Code Sec. 860G(a)(1) read as follows:

(1) REGULAR INTEREST.—The term "regular interest" means an interest in a REMIC the terms of which are fixed on the startup day, and which—

(A) unconditionally entitles the holder to receive a specified principal amount (or other similar amount), and

(B) provides that interest payments (or other similar amounts), if any, at or before maturity are payable based on a fixed rate (or to the extent provided in regulations, at a variable rate).

An interest shall not fail to meet the requirements of subparagraph (A) merely because the timing (but not the amount) of the principal payments (or other similar amounts) may be contingent on the extent of prepayments on qualified mortgages and the amount of income from permitted investments.

P.L. 100-647, §1006(t)(5)(B):

Amended Code Sec. 860G(a)(2). The amendment shall not apply to any REMIC where the startup day (as defined in section 860G(a)(9) of the 1986 Code as in effect on the day before 11-10-88) is before 7-1-87. Prior to amendment, Code Sec. 860G(a)(2) read as follows:

(2) RESIDUAL INTEREST.—The term "residual interest" means an interest in a REMIC which is not a regular interest and is designated as a residual interest.

P.L. 100-647, §1006(t)(5)(C)(i)-(iii):

Amended Code Sec. 860G(a)(3) by striking out "on or before the startup day" in subparagraph (A)(i) and inserting in lieu thereof "on the startup day in exchange for regular or residual interests in the REMIC", by inserting "if, except as provided in regulations, such purchase is pursuant to a fixed price contract in effect on the startup day" before the comma at the end of subparagraph (A)(ii), and by striking out "on or before the startup day" in subparagraph (C) and inserting in lieu thereof "on the startup day in exchange for regular or residual interests in the REMIC". The amendment shall not apply to any REMIC where the startup day (as defined in section 860G(a)(9) of the 1986 Code as in effect on the day before 11-10-88) is before 7-1-87.

P.L. 100-647, §1006(t)(5)(D):

Amended Code Sec. 860G(a)(4)(A). The amendment shall not apply to any REMIC where the startup day (as defined in section 860G(a)(9) of the 1986 Code as in effect on the day before 11-10-88) is before 7-1-87. Prior to amendment, Code Sec. 860G(a)(4)(A) read as follows:

(A) which would be described in paragraph (3)(A) if it were transferred to the REMIC on or before the startup day, and

P.L. 100-647, §1006(t)(5)(E):

Amended Code Sec. 860G(a)(9). The amendment shall not apply to any REMIC where the startup day (as defined in section 860G(a)(9) of the 1986 Code as in effect on the day before 11-10-88) is before 7-1-87. Prior to amendment, Code Sec. 860G(a)(9) read as follows:

(9) STARTUP DAY.—The term "startup day" means any day selected by a REMIC which is on or before the 1st day on which interests in such REMIC are issued.

P.L. 100-647, §1006(t)(6)(A)-(B):

Amended Code Sec. 860G(a)(3) by striking out "directly or indirectly," in subparagraph (A), and by adding at the end thereof a new sentence. **Effective** as if included in the provision of P.L. 99-514 to which it relates.

P.L. 100-647, §1006(t)(7):

Amended Code Sec. 860G(a)(7)(B) by inserting "or lower than expected returns on cash flow investments" before the period at the end of the first sentence. **Effective** as if included in the provision of P.L. 99-514 to which it relates.

P.L. 100-647, §1006(t)(8)(A)(i)-(ii):

Amended Code Sec. 860G(a)(8) by striking out "section 856(e)" in subparagraph (A) and inserting in lieu thereof "section 856(e) (without regard to paragraph (5) thereof)", and by striking out the last sentence and inserting in lieu thereof a new sentence. **Effective** as if included in the provision of P.L. 99-514 to which it relates. Prior to amendment, the last sentence read as follows:

Property shall cease to be foreclosure property with respect to the REMIC on the date which is 1 year after the date such real estate mortgage pool acquired such property.

[Sec. 860G(b)]

(b) TREATMENT OF NONRESIDENT ALIENS AND FOREIGN CORPORATIONS.—If the holder of a residual interest in a REMIC is a nonresident alien individual or a foreign corporation, for purposes of sections 871(a), 881, 1441, and 1442—

(1) amounts includible in the gross income of such holder under this part shall be taken into account when paid or distributed (or when the interest is disposed of), and

(2) no exemption from the taxes imposed by such sections (and no reduction in the rates of such taxes) shall apply to any excess inclusion.

The Secretary may by regulations provide that such amounts shall be taken into account earlier than as provided in paragraph (1) where necessary or appropriate to prevent the avoidance of tax imposed by this chapter.

[Sec. 860G(c)]

(c) TAX ON INCOME FROM FORECLOSURE PROPERTY.—

(1) IN GENERAL.—A tax is hereby imposed for each taxable year on the net income from foreclosure property of each REMIC. Such tax shall be computed by multiplying the net income from foreclosure property by the highest rate of tax specified in section 11(b).

(2) NET INCOME FROM FORECLOSURE PROPERTY.—For purposes of this part, the term "net income from foreclosure property" means the amount which would be the REMIC's net income from foreclosure property under section 857(b)(4)(B) if the REMIC were a real estate investment trust.

Amendments

• 1988, Technical and Miscellaneous Revenue Act of 1988 (P.L. 100-647)

P.L. 100-647, §1006(t)(8)(B):

Amended Code Sec. 860G by redesignating subsection (c) as subsection (d) and by inserting after subsection (b) new subsection (c). **Effective** as if included in the provision of P.L. 99-514 to which it relates.

[Sec. 860G(d)]

(d) TAX ON CONTRIBUTIONS AFTER STARTUP DATE.—

(1) IN GENERAL.—Except as provided in paragraph (2), if any amount is contributed to a REMIC after the startup day, there is hereby imposed a tax for the taxable year of the REMIC in which the contribution is received equal to 100 percent of the amount of such contribution.

(2) EXCEPTIONS.—Paragraph (1) shall not apply to any contribution which is made in cash and is described in any of the following subparagraphs:

(A) Any contribution to facilitate a cleanup call (as defined in regulations) or a qualified liquidation.

(B) Any payment in the nature of a guarantee.

(C) Any contribution during the 3-month period beginning on the startup day.

(D) Any contribution to a qualified reserve fund by any holder of a residual interest in the REMIC.

(E) Any other contribution permitted in regulations.

Amendments

• **1988, Technical and Miscellaneous Revenue Act of 1988 (P.L. 100-647)**

P.L. 100-647, §1006(t)(9)(A):

Amended Code Sec. 860G (as amended by paragraph (8)) by redesignating subsection (d) as subsection (e) and by inserting after subsection (c) new subsection (d). For the **effective** date, see Act Sec. 1006(t)(9)(B), below.

P.L. 100-647, §1006(t)(9)(B), provides:

(B) The amendment made by subparagraph (A) shall not apply to any REMIC where the startup day (as defined in section 860G(a)(9) of the 1986 Code as in effect on the day before the date of the enactment of this Act) is before July 1, 1987.

[Sec. 860G(e)]

(e) REGULATIONS.—The Secretary shall prescribe such regulations as may be necessary or appropriate to carry out the purposes of this part, including regulations—

(1) to prevent unreasonable accumulations of assets in a REMIC,

(2) permitting determinations of the fair market value of property transferred to a REMIC and issue price of interests in a REMIC to be made earlier than otherwise provided,

(3) requiring reporting to holders of residual interests of such information as frequently as is necessary or appropriate to permit such holders to compute their taxable income accurately,

(4) providing appropriate rules for treatment of transfers of qualified replacement mortgages to the REMIC where the transferor holds any interest in the REMIC, and

(5) providing that a mortgage will be treated as a qualified replacement mortgage only if it is part of a bona fide replacement (and not part of a swap of mortgages).

Amendments

• **1988, Technical and Miscellaneous Revenue Act of 1988 (P.L. 100-647)**

P.L. 100-647, §1006(t)(9)(A):

Amended Code Sec. 860G by redesignating subsection (d) as subsection (e). For the **effective** date, see Act Sec. 1006(t)(9)(B), below.

P.L. 100-647, §1006(t)(9)(B), provides:

(B) The amendment made by subparagraph (A) shall not apply to any REMIC where the startup day (as defined in section 860G(a)(9) of the 1986 Code as in effect on the day before the date of the enactment of this Act) is before July 1, 1987.

P.L. 100-647, §1006(t)(10):

Amended Code Sec. 860G(e) (as redesignated by paragraph (9)) by striking out "and" at the end of paragraph (2), by striking out the period at the end of paragraph (3) and inserting in lieu thereof a comma, and by adding at the end thereof new paragraph (4)-(5). **Effective** as if included in the provision of P.L. 99-514 to which it relates.

• **1986, Tax Reform Act of 1986 (P.L. 99-514)**

P.L. 99-514, §671(a):

Amended subchapter M of chapter 1 by adding new Code Sec. 860(G). **Effective** 1-1-87. [**effective** date changed by P.L. 100-647, §1006(w)(1)].

PART V—FINANCIAL ASSET SECURITIZATION INVESTMENT TRUSTS—[Repealed]

[Sec. 860H—Repealed]

Amendments

• **2004, American Jobs Creation Act of 2004 (P.L. 108-357)**

P.L. 108-357, §835(a):

Repealed part V of subchapter M of chapter 1 (Code Secs. 860H-860L). For the **effective** date, see Act Sec. 835(c), below.

P.L. 108-357, §835(c), provides:

(c) EFFECTIVE DATE.—

(1) IN GENERAL.—Except as provided in paragraph (2), the amendments made by this section shall take effect on January 1, 2005.

(2) EXCEPTION FOR EXISTING FASITS.—Paragraph (1) shall not apply to any FASIT in existence on the date of the enactment of this Act [10-22-2004.—CCH.]to the extent that regular interests issued by the FASIT before such date continue to remain outstanding in accordance with the original terms of issuance.

Prior to repeal, Code Sec. 860H read as follows:

SEC. 860H. TAXATION OF A FASIT; OTHER GENERAL RULES.

[Sec. 860H(a)]

(a) TAXATION OF FASIT.—A FASIT as such shall not be subject to taxation under this subtitle (and shall not be treated as a trust, partnership, corporation, or taxable mortgage pool).

[Sec. 860H(b)]

(b) TAXATION OF HOLDER OF OWNERSHIP INTEREST.—In determining the taxable income of the holder of the ownership interest in a FASIT—

(1) all assets, liabilities, and items of income, gain, deduction, loss, and credit of a FASIT shall be treated as assets, liabilities, and such items (as the case may be) of such holder,

(2) the constant yield method (including the rules of section 1272(a)(6)) shall be applied under an accrual method of accounting in determining all interest, acquisition discount, original issue discount, and market discount and all pre-

mium deductions or adjustments with respect to each debt instrument of the FASIT,

(3) there shall not be taken into account any item of income, gain, or deduction allocable to a prohibited transaction, and

(4) interest accrued by the FASIT which is exempt from tax imposed by this subtitle shall, when taken into account by such holder, be treated as ordinary income.

[Sec. 860H(c)]

(c) TREATMENT OF REGULAR INTERESTS.—For purposes of this title—

(1) a regular interest in a FASIT, if not otherwise a debt instrument, shall be treated as a debt instrument,

(2) section 163(e)(5) shall not apply to such an interest, and

(3) amounts includible in gross income with respect to such an interest shall be determined under an accrual method of accounting.

Amendments

• 1996, Small Business Job Protection Act of 1996 (P.L. 104-188)

P.L. 104-188, §1621(a):

Amended subchapter M of chapter 1 by adding at the end a new part V (Code Secs. 860H-860L). **Effective** 9-1-97.

[Sec. 860I—Repealed]

Amendments

• 2004, American Jobs Creation Act of 2004 (P.L. 108-357)

P.L. 108-357, §835(a):

Repealed part V of subchapter M of chapter 1 (Code Secs. 860H-860L). For the **effective** date, see Act Sec. 835(c), below.

P.L. 108-357, §835(c), provides:

(c) EFFECTIVE DATE.—

(1) IN GENERAL.—Except as provided in paragraph (2), the amendments made by this section shall take effect on January 1, 2005.

(2) EXCEPTION FOR EXISTING FASITS.—Paragraph (1) shall not apply to any FASIT in existence on the date of the enactment of this Act [10-22-2004.—CCH]to the extent that regular interests issued by the FASIT before such date continue to remain outstanding in accordance with the original terms of issuance.

Prior to repeal, Code Sec. 860I read as follows:

SEC. 860I. GAIN RECOGNITION ON CONTRIBUTIONS TO A FASIT AND IN OTHER CASES.

[Sec. 860I(a)]

(a) TREATMENT OF PROPERTY ACQUIRED BY FASIT.—

(1) PROPERTY ACQUIRED FROM HOLDER OF OWNERSHIP INTEREST OR RELATED PERSON.—If property is sold or contributed to a FASIT by the holder of the ownership interest in such FASIT (or by a related person) gain (if any) shall be recognized to such holder (or person) in an amount equal to the excess (if any) of such property's value under subsection (d) on the date of such sale or contribution over its adjusted basis on such date.

(2) PROPERTY ACQUIRED OTHER THAN FROM HOLDER OF OWNERSHIP INTEREST OR RELATED PERSON.—Property which is acquired by a FASIT other than in a transaction to which paragraph (1) applies shall be treated—

(A) as having been acquired by the holder of the ownership interest in the FASIT for an amount equal to the FASIT's cost of acquiring such property, and

(B) as having been sold by such holder to the FASIT at its value under subsection (d) on such date.

[Sec. 860I(b)]

(b) GAIN RECOGNITION ON PROPERTY OUTSIDE FASIT WHICH SUPPORTS REGULAR INTERESTS.—If property held by the holder of the ownership interest in a FASIT (or by any person related to such holder) supports any regular interest in such FASIT—

(1) gain shall be recognized to such holder (or person) in the same manner as if such holder (or person) had sold such property at its value under subsection (d) on the earliest date such property supports such an interest, and

(2) such property shall be treated as held by such FASIT for purposes of this part.

[Sec. 860I(c)]

(c) DEFERRAL OF GAIN RECOGNITION.—The Secretary may prescribe regulations which—

(1) provide that gain otherwise recognized under subsection (a) or (b) shall not be recognized before the earliest date on which such property supports any regular interest in such FASIT or any indebtedness of the holder of the ownership interest (or of any person related to such holder), and

(2) provide such adjustments to the other provisions of this part to the extent appropriate in the context of the treatment provided under paragraph (1).

[Sec. 860I(d)]

(d) VALUATION.—For purposes of this section—

(1) IN GENERAL.—The value of any property under this subsection shall be—

(A) in the case of a debt instrument which is not traded on an established securities market, the sum of the present values of the reasonably expected payments under such instrument determined (in the manner provided by regulations prescribed by the Secretary)—

(i) as of the date of the event resulting in the gain recognition under this section, and

(ii) by using a discount rate equal to 120 percent of the applicable Federal rate (as defined in section 1274(d)), or such other discount rate specified in such regulations, compounded semiannually, and

(B) in the case of any other property, its fair market value.

(2) SPECIAL RULE FOR REVOLVING LOAN ACCOUNTS.—For purposes of paragraph (1)—

(A) each extension of credit (other than the accrual of interest) on a revolving loan account shall be treated as a separate debt instrument, and

(B) payments on such extensions of credit having substantially the same terms shall be applied to such extensions beginning with the earliest such extension.

[Sec. 860I(e)]

(e) SPECIAL RULES.—

(1) NONRECOGNITION RULES NOT TO APPLY.—Gain required to be recognized under this section shall be recognized notwithstanding any other provision of this subtitle.

(2) BASIS ADJUSTMENTS.—The basis of any property on which gain is recognized under this section shall be increased by the amount of gain so recognized.

Amendments

• 1996, Small Business Job Protection Act of 1996 (P.L. 104-188)

P.L. 104-188, §1621(a):

Amended subchapter M of chapter 1 by adding at the end a new Code Sec. 860I. **Effective** 9-1-97.

P.L. 104-188, §1621(e), provides:

(e) TREATMENT OF EXISTING SECURITIZATION ENTITIES.—

(1) IN GENERAL.—In the case of the holder of the ownership interest in a pre-effective date FASIT—

(A) gain shall not be recognized under section 860L(d)(2) of the Internal Revenue Code of 1986 on property deemed contributed to the FASIT, and

(B) gain shall not be recognized under section 860I of such Code on property contributed to such FASIT,

until such property (or portion thereof) ceases to be properly allocable to a pre-FASIT interest.

(2) ALLOCATION OF PROPERTY TO PRE-FASIT INTEREST.—For purposes of paragraph (1), property shall be allocated to a pre-FASIT interest in such manner as the Secretary of the Treasury may prescribe, except that all property in a FASIT shall be treated as properly allocable to pre-FASIT interests if the fair market value of all such property does not exceed 107 percent of the aggregate principal amount of all outstanding pre-FASIT interests.

(3) DEFINITIONS.—For purposes of this subsection—

(A) PRE-EFFECTIVE DATE FASIT.—The term "pre-effective date FASIT" means any FASIT if the entity (with respect to which the election under section 860L(a)(3) of such Code was made) is in existence on August 31, 1997.

(B) PRE-FASIT INTEREST.—The term "pre-FASIT interest" means any interest in the entity referred to in subparagraph (A) which was issued before the startup day (other than any interest held by the holder of the ownership interest in the FASIT).

[Sec. 860J—Repealed]

Amendments

• 2004, American Jobs Creation Act of 2004 (P.L. 108-357)

P.L. 108-357, §835(a):

Repealed part V of subchapter M of chapter 1 (Code Secs. 860H-860L). For the **effective** date, see Act Sec. 835(c), below.

P.L. 108-357, §835(c), provides:

(c) EFFECTIVE DATE.—

(1) IN GENERAL.—Except as provided in paragraph (2), the amendments made by this section shall take effect on January 1, 2005.

(2) EXCEPTION FOR EXISTING FASITS.—Paragraph (1) shall not apply to any FASIT in existence on the date of the enactment of this Act [10-22-2004.—CCH]to the extent that regular interests issued by the FASIT before such date continue to remain outstanding in accordance with the original terms of issuance.

Prior to repeal, Code Sec. 860J read as follows:

SEC. 860J. NON-FASIT LOSSES NOT TO OFFSET CERTAIN FASIT INCLUSIONS.

[Sec. 860J(a)]

(a) IN GENERAL.—The taxable income of the holder of the ownership interest or any high-yield interest in a FASIT for any taxable year shall in no event be less than the sum of—

(1) such holder's taxable income determined solely with respect to such interests (including gains and losses from sales and exchanges of such interests), and

(2) the excess inclusion (if any) under section 860E(a)(1) for such taxable year.

[Sec. 860J(b)]

(b) COORDINATION WITH SECTION 172.—Any increase in the taxable income of any holder of the ownership interest or a high-yield interest in a FASIT for any taxable year by reason of subsection (a) shall be disregarded—

(1) in determining under section 172 the amount of any net operating loss for such taxable year, and

(2) in determining taxable income for such taxable year for purposes of the second sentence of section 172(b)(2).

[Sec. 860J(c)]

(c) COORDINATION WITH MINIMUM TAX.—For purposes of part VI of subchapter A of this chapter—

(1) the reference in section 55(b)(2) to taxable income shall be treated as a reference to taxable income determined without regard to this section,

(2) the alternative minimum taxable income of any holder of the ownership interest or a high-yield interest in a FASIT for any taxable year shall in no event be less than such holder's taxable income determined solely with respect to such interests, and

(3) any increase in taxable income under this section shall be disregarded for purposes of computing the alternative tax net operating loss deduction.

[Sec. 860J(d)]

(d) AFFILIATED GROUPS.—All members of an affiliated group filing a consolidated return shall be treated as one taxpayer for purposes of this section.

Amendments

• 1996, Small Business Job Protection Act of 1996 (P.L. 104-188)

P.L. 104-188, §1621(a):

Amended subchapter M of chapter 1 by adding at the end a new Code Sec. 860J. **Effective** 9-1-97.

[Sec. 860K—Repealed]

Amendments

• 2004, American Jobs Creation Act of 2004 (P.L. 108-357)

P.L. 108-357, §835(a):

Repealed part V of subchapter M of chapter 1 (Code Secs. 860H-860L). For the **effective** date, see Act Sec. 835(c), below.

P.L. 108-357, §835(c), provides:

(c) EFFECTIVE DATE.—

(1) IN GENERAL.—Except as provided in paragraph (2), the amendments made by this section shall take effect on January 1, 2005.

(2) EXCEPTION FOR EXISTING FASITS.—Paragraph (1) shall not apply to any FASIT in existence on the date of the enactment of this Act [10-22-2004.—CCH]to the extent that regular interests issued by the FASIT before such date continue to remain outstanding in accordance with the original terms of issuance.

Prior to repeal, Code Sec. 860K read as follows:

SEC. 860K. TREATMENT OF TRANSFERS OF HIGH-YIELD INTERESTS TO DISQUALIFIED HOLDERS.

[Sec. 860K(a)]

(a) GENERAL RULE.—In the case of any high-yield interest which is held by a disqualified holder—

(1) the gross income of such holder shall not include any income (other than gain) attributable to such interest, and

(2) amounts not includible in the gross income of such holder by reason of paragraph (1) shall be included (at the time otherwise includible under paragraph (1)) in the gross income of the most recent holder of such interest which is not a disqualified holder.

[Sec. 860K(b)]

(b) EXCEPTIONS.—Rules similar to the rules of paragraphs (4) and (7) of section 860E(e) shall apply to the tax imposed by reason of the inclusion in gross income under subsection (a).

[Sec. 860K(c)]

(c) DISQUALIFIED HOLDER.—For purposes of this section, the term "disqualified holder" means any holder other than—

(1) an eligible corporation (as defined in section 860L(a)(2)), or

(2) a FASIT.

[Sec. 860K(d)]

(d) TREATMENT OF INTERESTS HELD BY SECURITIES DEALERS.—

(1) IN GENERAL.—Subsection (a) shall not apply to any high-yield interest held by a disqualified holder if such holder is a dealer in securities who acquired such interest exclusively for sale to customers in the ordinary course of business (and not for investment).

(2) CHANGE IN DEALER STATUS.—

(A) IN GENERAL.—In the case of a dealer in securities which is not an eligible corporation (as defined in section 860L(a)(2)), if—

(i) such dealer ceases to be a dealer in securities, or

(ii) such dealer commences holding the high-yield interest for investment,

there is hereby imposed (in addition to other taxes) an excise tax equal to the product of the highest rate of tax specified in section 11(b)(1) and the income of such dealer attributable to such interest for periods after the date of such cessation or commencement.

(B) HOLDING FOR 31 DAYS OR LESS.—For purposes of subparagraph (A)(ii), a dealer shall not be treated as holding an interest for investment before the thirty-second day after the date such dealer acquired such interest unless such interest is so held as part of a plan to avoid the purposes of this paragraph.

(C) ADMINISTRATIVE PROVISIONS.—The deficiency procedures of subtitle F shall apply to the tax imposed by this paragraph.

[Sec. 860K(e)]

(e) TREATMENT OF HIGH-YIELD INTERESTS IN PASS-THRU ENTITIES.—

(1) IN GENERAL.—If a pass-thru entity (as defined in section 860E(e)(6)) issues a debt or equity interest—

(A) which is supported by any regular interest in a FASIT, and

(B) which has an original yield to maturity which is greater than each of—

(i) the sum determined under clauses (i) and (ii) of section 163(i)(1)(B) with respect to such debt or equity interest, and

(ii) the yield to maturity to such entity on such regular interest (determined as of the date such entity acquired such interest),

there is hereby imposed on the pass-thru entity a tax (in addition to other taxes) equal to the product of the highest rate of tax specified in section 11(b)(1) and the income of the holder of such debt or equity interest which is properly attributable to such regular interest. For purposes of the preceding sentence, the yield to maturity of any equity interest shall be determined under regulations prescribed by the Secretary.

(2) EXCEPTION.—Paragraph (1) shall not apply to arrangements not having as a principal purpose the avoidance of the purposes of this subsection.

Amendments

• 1996, Small Business Job Protection Act of 1996 (P.L. 104-188)

P.L. 104-188, §1621(a):

Amended subchapter M of chapter 1 by adding at the end a new Code Sec. 860K. **Effective** 9-1-97.

[Sec. 860L—Repealed]

Amendments

• 2004, American Jobs Creation Act of 2004 (P.L. 108-357)

P.L. 108-357, §835(a):

Repealed part V of subchapter M of chapter 1 (Code Secs. 860H-860L). For the **effective** date, see Act Sec. 835(c), below.

P.L. 108-357, §835(c), provides:

(c) EFFECTIVE DATE.—

(1) IN GENERAL.—Except as provided in paragraph (2), the amendments made by this section shall take effect on January 1, 2005.

(2) EXCEPTION FOR EXISTING FASITS.—Paragraph (1) shall not apply to any FASIT in existence on the date of the enactment of this Act [10-22-2004.—CCH]to the extent that regular interests issued by the FASIT before such date continue to remain outstanding in accordance with the original terms of issuance.

Prior to repeal, Code Sec. 860L read as follows:

SEC. 860L. DEFINITIONS AND OTHER SPECIAL RULES.

[Sec. 860L(a)]

(a) FASIT.—

(1) IN GENERAL.—For purposes of this title, the terms "financial asset securitization investment trust" and "FASIT" mean any entity—

(A) for which an election to be treated as a FASIT applies for the taxable year,

(B) all of the interests in which are regular interests or the ownership interest,

(C) which has only one ownership interest and such ownership interest is held directly by an eligible corporation,

(D) as of the close of the third month beginning after the day of its formation and at all times thereafter, substantially all of the assets of which (including assets treated as held by the entity under section 860I(b)(2)) consist of permitted assets, and

(E) which is not described in section 851(a).

A rule similar to the rule of the last sentence of section 860D(a) shall apply for purposes of this paragraph.

(2) ELIGIBLE CORPORATION.—For purposes of paragraph (1)(C), the term "eligible corporation" means any domestic C corporation other than—

(A) a corporation which is exempt from, or is not subject to, tax under this chapter,

(B) an entity described in section 851(a) or 856(a),

(C) a REMIC, and

(D) an organization to which part I of subchapter T applies.

(3) ELECTION.—An entity (otherwise meeting the requirements of paragraph (1)) may elect to be treated as a FASIT. Except as provided in paragraph (5), such an election shall apply to the taxable year for which made and all subsequent taxable years unless revoked with the consent of the Secretary.

(4) TERMINATION.—If any entity ceases to be a FASIT at any time during the taxable year, such entity shall not be treated as a FASIT after the date of such cessation.

(5) INADVERTENT TERMINATIONS, ETC.—Rules similar to the rules of section 860D(b)(2)(B) shall apply to inadvertent failures to qualify or remain qualified as a FASIT.

(6) PERMITTED ASSETS NOT TREATED AS INTEREST IN FASIT.—Except as provided in regulations prescribed by the Secretary, any asset which is a permitted asset at the time acquired by a FASIT shall not be treated at any time as an interest in such FASIT.

[Sec. 860L(b)]

(b) INTERESTS IN FASIT.—For purposes of this part—

(1) REGULAR INTEREST.—

(A) IN GENERAL.—The term "regular interest" means any interest which is issued by a FASIT on or after the startup date with fixed terms and which is designated as a regular interest if—

(i) such interest unconditionally entitles the holder to receive a specified principal amount (or other similar amount),

(ii) interest payments (or other similar amounts), if any, with respect to such interest are determined based on a fixed rate, or, except as otherwise provided by the Secretary, at a variable rate permitted under section 860G(a)(1)(B)(i),

(iii) such interest does not have a stated maturity (including options to renew) greater than 30 years (or such longer period as may be permitted by regulations),

(iv) the issue price of such interest does not exceed 125 percent of its stated principal amount, and

(v) the yield to maturity on such interest is less than the sum determined under section 163(i)(1)(B) with respect to such interest.

An interest shall not fail to meet the requirements of clause (i) merely because the timing (but not the amount) of the principal payments (or other similar amounts) may be contingent on the extent that payments on debt instruments held by the FASIT are made in advance of anticipated payments and on the amount of income from permitted assets.

(B) HIGH-YIELD INTERESTS.—

(i) IN GENERAL.—The term "regular interest" includes any high-yield interest.

(ii) HIGH-YIELD INTEREST.—The term "high-yield interest" means any interest which would be described in subparagraph (A) but for—

(I) failing to meet the requirements of one or more of clauses (i), (iv), or (v) thereof, or

(II) failing to meet the requirement of clause (ii) thereof but only if interest payments (or other similar amounts), if any, with respect to such interest consist of a specified portion of the interest payments on permitted assets and such portion does not vary during the period such interest is outstanding.

(2) OWNERSHIP INTEREST.—The term "ownership interest" means the interest issued by a FASIT after the startup day which is designated as an ownership interest and which is not a regular interest.

Amendments

• 1997, Taxpayer Relief Act of 1997 (P.L. 105-34)

P.L. 105-34, §1601(f)(6)(A):

Amended Code Sec. 860L(b)(1)(A) by striking "after the startup date" in the text preceding clause (i) and inserting "on or after the startup date". **Effective** as if included in the provision of P.L. 104-188 to which it relates [**effective** 9-1-97.—CCH].

[Sec. 860L(c)]

(c) PERMITTED ASSETS.—For purposes of this part—

(1) IN GENERAL.—The term "permitted asset" means—

(A) cash or cash equivalents,

(B) any debt instrument (as defined in section 1275(a)(1)) under which interest payments (or other similar amounts), if any, at or before maturity meet the requirements applicable under clause (i) or (ii) of section 860G(a)(1)(B),

(C) foreclosure property,

(D) any asset—

(i) which is an interest rate or foreign currency notional principal contract, letter of credit, insurance, guarantee against payment defaults, or other similar instrument permitted by the Secretary, and

(ii) which is reasonably required to guarantee or hedge against the FASIT's risks associated with being the obligor on interests issued by the FASIT,

(E) contract rights to acquire debt instruments described in subparagraph (B) or assets described in subparagraph (D),

(F) any regular interest in another FASIT, and

(G) any regular interest in a REMIC.

(2) DEBT ISSUED BY HOLDER OF OWNERSHIP INTEREST NOT PERMITTED ASSET.—The term "permitted asset" shall not include any debt instrument issued by the holder of the ownership interest in the FASIT or by any person related to such holder or any direct or indirect interest in such a debt instrument. The preceding sentence shall not apply to cash equivalents and to any other investment specified in regulations prescribed by the Secretary.

(3) FORECLOSURE PROPERTY.—

(A) IN GENERAL.—The term "foreclosure property" means property—

(i) which would be foreclosure property under section 856(e) (determined without regard to paragraph (5) thereof) if such property were real property acquired by a real estate investment trust, and

(ii) which is acquired in connection with the default or imminent default of a debt instrument held by the FASIT unless the security interest in such property was created for the principal purpose of permitting the FASIT to invest in such property.

Solely for purposes of subsection (a)(1), the determination of whether any property is foreclosure property shall be made without regard to section 856(e)(4).

(B) AUTHORITY TO REDUCE GRACE PERIOD.—In the case of property other than real property and other than personal property incident to real property, the Secretary may by regulation reduce for purposes of subparagraph (A) the periods otherwise applicable under paragraphs (2) and (3) of section 856(e).

[Sec. 860L(d)]

(d) STARTUP DAY.—For purposes of this part—

(1) IN GENERAL.—The term "startup day" means the date designated in the election under subsection (a)(3) as the startup day of the FASIT. Such day shall be the beginning of the first taxable year of the FASIT.

(2) TREATMENT OF PROPERTY HELD ON STARTUP DAY.—All property held (or treated as held under section 860I(b)(2)) by an entity as of the startup day shall be treated as contributed to such entity on such day by the holder of the ownership interest in such entity.

Amendments

• 1997, Taxpayer Relief Act of 1997 (P.L. 105-34)

P.L. 105-34, §1601(f)(6)(B):

Amended Code Sec. 860L(d)(2) by striking "section 860I(c)(2)" and inserting "section 860I(b)(2)". **Effective** as if included in the provision of P.L. 104-188 to which it relates [**effective** 9-1-97.—CCH].

[Sec. 860L(e)]

(e) TAX ON PROHIBITED TRANSACTIONS.—

(1) IN GENERAL.—There is hereby imposed for each taxable year of a FASIT a tax equal to 100 percent of the net income derived from prohibited transactions. Such tax shall be paid by the holder of the ownership interest in the FASIT.

(2) PROHIBITED TRANSACTIONS.—For purposes of this part, the term "prohibited transaction" means—

(A) except as provided in paragraph (3), the receipt of any income derived from any asset that is not a permitted asset,

(B) except as provided in paragraph (3), the disposition of any permitted asset other than foreclosure property,

(C) the receipt of any income derived from any loan originated by the FASIT, and

(D) the receipt of any income representing a fee or other compensation for services (other than any fee received as compensation for a waiver, amendment, or consent under permitted assets (other than foreclosure property) held by the FASIT).

(3) EXCEPTION FOR INCOME FROM CERTAIN DISPOSITIONS.—

(A) IN GENERAL.—Paragraph (2)(B) shall not apply to a disposition which would not be a prohibited transaction (as defined in section 860F(a)(2)) by reason of—

(i) clause (ii), (iii), or (iv) of section 860F(a)(2)(A), or

(ii) section 860F(a)(5),

if the FASIT were treated as a REMIC and permitted assets (other than cash or cash equivalents) were treated as qualified mortgages.

(B) SUBSTITUTION OF DEBT INSTRUMENTS; REDUCTION OF OVER-COLLATERALIZATION.—Paragraph (2)(B) shall not apply to—

(i) the substitution of a debt instrument described in subsection (c)(1)(B) for another debt instrument which is a permitted asset, or

(ii) the distribution of a debt instrument contributed by the holder of the ownership interest to such holder in order to reduce over-collateralization of the FASIT,

but only if a principal purpose of acquiring the debt instrument which is disposed of was not the recognition of gain (or the reduction of a loss) as a result of an increase in the market value of the debt instrument after its acquisition by the FASIT.

(C) LIQUIDATION OF CLASS OF REGULAR INTERESTS.—Paragraph (2)(B) shall not apply to the complete liquidation of any class of regular interests.

(D) INCOME FROM DISPOSITIONS OF FORMER HEDGE ASSETS.—Paragraph (2)(A) shall not apply to income derived from the disposition of—

(i) an asset which was described in subsection (c)(1)(D) when first acquired by the FASIT but on the date of such disposition was no longer described in subsection (c)(1)(D)(ii), or

(ii) a contract right to acquire an asset described in clause (i).

(4) NET INCOME.—For purposes of this subsection, net income shall be determined in accordance with section 860F(a)(3).

Amendments

• 1997, Taxpayer Relief Act of 1997 (P.L. 105-34)

P.L. 105-34, §1601(f)(6)(C):

Amended Code Sec. 860L(e)(2)(B) by inserting "other than foreclosure property" after "any permitted asset". **Effective** as if included in the provision of P.L. 104-188 to which it relates [**effective** 9-1-97.—CCH].

P.L. 105-34, §1601(f)(6)(D):

Amended Code Sec. 860L(e)(3)(A) by striking "if the FASIT" and all that follows and inserting new flush text after clause (ii). **Effective** as if included in the provision of P.L. 104-188 to which it relates [**effective** 9-1-97.—CCH]. Prior to amendment, Code Sec. 860L(e)(3)(A) read as follows:

(A) IN GENERAL.—Paragraph (2)(B) shall not apply to a disposition which would not be a prohibited transaction (as defined in section 860F(a)(2)) by reason of—

(i) clause (ii), (iii), or (iv) of section 860F(a)(2)(A), or

(ii) section 860F(a)(5), if the FASIT were treated as a REMIC and debt instruments described in subsection (c)(1)(B) were treated as qualified mortgages.

P.L. 105-34, §1601(f)(6)(E)(i):

Amended Code Sec. 860L(e)(3) by adding at the end a new subparagraph (D). **Effective** as if included in the provision of P.L. 104-188 to which it relates [**effective** 9-1-97.—CCH].

P.L. 105-34, §1601(f)(6)(E)(ii):

Amended Code Sec. 860L(e)(2)(A) by inserting "except as provided in paragraph (3)," before "the receipt". **Effective** as if included in the provision of P.L. 104-188 to which it relates [**effective** 9-1-97.—CCH].

[Sec. 860L(f)]

(f) COORDINATION WITH OTHER PROVISIONS.—

(1) WASH SALES RULES.—Rules similar to the rules of section 860F(d) shall apply to the ownership interest in a FASIT.

(2) SECTION 475.—Except as provided by the Secretary by regulations, if any security which is sold or contributed to a FASIT by the holder of the ownership interest in such FASIT was required to be marked-to-market under section 475 by such holder, section 475 shall continue to apply to such security; except that in applying section 475 while such security is held by the FASIT, the fair market value of such security for purposes of section 475 shall not be less than its value under section 860I(d).

[Sec. 860L(g)]

RELATED PERSON.—

(g) For purposes of this part, a person (hereinafter in this subsection referred to as the "related person") is related to any person if—

(1) the related person bears a relationship to such person specified in section 267(b) or section 707(b)(1), or

(2) the related person and such person are engaged in trades or businesses under common control (within the meaning of subsections (a) and (b) of section 52).

For purposes of paragraph (1), in applying section 267(b) or 707(b)(1), "20 percent" shall be substituted for "50 percent".

[Sec. 860L(h)]

(h) REGULATIONS.—The Secretary shall prescribe such regulations as may be necessary or appropriate to carry out the purposes of this part, including regulations to prevent the abuse of the purposes of this part through transactions which are not primarily related to securitization of debt instruments by a FASIT.

Amendments

• 1996, Small Business Job Protection Act of 1996 (P.L. 104-188)

P.L. 104-188, §1621(a):

Amended subchapter M of chapter 1 by adding at the end a new Code Sec. 860L. **Effective** 9-1-97.

P.L. 104-188, §1621(e), provides:

(e) TREATMENT OF EXISTING SECURITIZATION ENTITIES.—

(1) IN GENERAL.—In the case of the holder of the ownership interest in a pre-effective date FASIT—

(A) gain shall not be recognized under section 860L(d)(2) of the Internal Revenue Code of 1986 on property deemed contributed to the FASIT, and

(B) gain shall not be recognized under section 860I of such Code on property contributed to such FASIT,

until such property (or portion thereof) ceases to be properly allocable to a pre-FASIT interest.

(2) ALLOCATION OF PROPERTY TO PRE-FASIT INTEREST.—For purposes of paragraph (1), property shall be allocated to a pre-FASIT interest in such manner as the Secretary of the Treasury may prescribe, except that all property in a FASIT shall be treated as properly allocable to pre-FASIT interests if the fair market value of all such property does not exceed 107 percent of the aggregate principal amount of all outstanding pre-FASIT interests.

(3) DEFINITIONS.—For purposes of this subsection—

(A) PRE-EFFECTIVE DATE FASIT.—The term "pre-effective date FASIT" means any FASIT if the entity (with respect to which the election under section 860L(a)(3) of such Code was made) is in existence on August 31, 1997.

(B) PRE-FASIT INTEREST.—The term "pre-FASIT interest" means any interest in the entity referred to in subparagraph (A) which was issued before the startup day (other than any interest held by the holder of the ownership interest in the FASIT).

TOPICAL INDEX

References are to Code Section numbers.

A

C

F

H

P

Q

R

S

U

Y

Public Laws Amending the Internal Revenue Code

Public Law No.	Popular Name	Enactment Date
517, 83rd Cong.	Revised Organic Act of the Virgin Islands	7-22-54
703, 83rd Cong.	Atomic Energy Act of 1954	8-30-54
729, 83rd Cong.		8-31-54
746, 83rd Cong.		8-31-54
761, 83rd Cong.	Social Security Amendments of 1954	9-1-54
767, 83rd Cong.		9-1-54
1, 84th Cong.		1-20-55
9, 84th Cong.		3-2-55
18, 84th Cong.	Tax Rate Extension Act of 1955	3-30-55
74, 84th Cong.		6-15-55
299, 84th Cong.		8-9-55
306, 84th Cong.		8-9-55
317, 84th Cong.		8-9-55
321, 84th Cong.		8-9-55
333, 84th Cong.		8-9-55
354, 84th Cong.		8-11-55
355, 84th Cong.		8-11-55
366, 84th Cong.		8-11-55
367, 84th Cong.		8-11-55
379, 84th Cong.		8-12-55
384, 84th Cong.		8-12-55
385, 84th Cong.		8-12-55
396, 84th Cong.		1-28-56
398, 84th Cong.		1-28-56
400, 84th Cong.		1-28-56
414, 84th Cong.		2-20-56
429, 84th Cong.	Life Insurance Company Tax Act for 1955	3-13-56
458, 84th Cong.	Tax Rate Extension Act of 1956	3-29-56
466, 84th Cong.		4-2-56
495, 84th Cong.		4-27-56
511, 84th Cong.	Bank Holding Company Act of 1956	5-9-56
545, 84th Cong.		5-29-56
627, 84th Cong.	Federal-Aid Highway Act of 1956	6-29-56
628, 84th Cong.		6-29-56
629, 84th Cong.		6-29-56
700, 84th Cong.		7-11-56
726, 84th Cong.	Mutual Security Act of 1956	7-18-56
728, 84th Cong.	Narcotic Control Act of 1956	7-18-56
784, 84th Cong.		7-24-56
796, 84th Cong.		7-25-56
880, 84th Cong.	Social Security Amendments of 1956	8-1-56
881, 84th Cong.	Servicemen's and Veterans' Survivor Benefits Act	8-1-56
896, 84th Cong.		8-1-56
1010, 84th Cong.		8-6-56
1011, 84th Cong.		8-6-56
1015, 84th Cong.		8-7-56
1022, 84th Cong.		8-7-56
85-12	Tax Rate Extension Act of 1957	3-29-57
85-56	Veterans' Benefits Act of 1957	6-17-57
85-74		6-29-57
85-165		8-26-57
85-235		8-30-57
85-239		8-30-57

Public Law No.	Popular Name	Enactment Date
85-320		2-11-58
85-321		2-11-58
85-323		2-11-58
85-345		3-17-58
85-367		4-7-58
85-380		4-16-58
85-475	Tax Rate Extension Act of 1958	6-30-58
85-517		7-11-58
85-840	Social Security Amendments of 1958	8-28-58
85-859	Excise Tax Technical Changes Act of 1958	9-2-58
85-866	Technical Amendments Act of 1958	9-2-58
85-866	Small Business Tax Revision Act of 1958	9-2-58
85-881		9-2-58
86-28		5-19-59
86-69	Life Insurance Company Income Tax Act of 1959	6-25-59
86-70	Alaska Omnibus Bill	6-25-59
86-75	Tax Rate Extension Act of 1959	6-30-59
86-141		8-7-59
86-168	Farm Credit Act of 1959	8-18-59
86-175		8-21-59
86-280		9-16-59
86-319		9-21-59
86-342	Federal-Aid Highway Act of 1959	9-21-59
86-344		9-21-59
86-346		9-22-59
86-368		9-22-59
86-376		9-23-59
86-413		4-8-60
86-416		4-8-60
86-418		4-8-60
86-422		4-8-60
86-428		4-22-60
86-429	Narcotics Manufacturing Act of 1960	4-22-60
86-435		4-22-60
86-437		4-22-60
86-440		4-22-60
86-459	Dealer Reserve Income Adjustment Act of 1960	5-13-60
86-470		5-14-60
86-478		6-1-60
86-496		6-8-60
86-564	Public Debt and Tax Rate Extension Act of 1960	6-30-60
86-592		7-6-60
86-594		7-6-60
86-624	Hawaii Omnibus Act	7-12-60
86-667		7-14-60
86-707	Overseas Differentials and Allowances Act	9-6-60
86-723	Foreign Service Act Amendments of 1960	9-8-60
86-778	Social Security Amendments of 1960	9-13-60
86-779		9-14-60
86-780		9-14-60
86-781		9-14-60
87-6	Temporary Extended Unemployment Compensation Act of 1961	3-24-61
87-15		3-31-61
87-29		5-4-61
87-59		6-27-61
87-61	Federal-Aid Highway Act of 1961	6-29-61
87-64	Social Security Amendments of 1961	6-30-61

Public Law No.	Popular Name	Enactment Date
87-72	Tax Rate Extension Act of 1961	6-30-61
87-109		7-26-61
87-256	Mutual Educational and Cultural Exchange Act of 1961	9-21-61
87-293	Peace Corps Act	9-22-61
87-321		9-26-61
87-370		10-4-61
87-397		10-5-61
87-403		2-2-62
87-426		3-31-62
87-456	Tariff Classification Act of 1962	5-24-62
87-508	Tax Rate Extension Act of 1962	6-28-62
87-535	Sugar Act Amendments of 1962	7-13-62
87-682		9-25-62
87-710		9-27-62
87-722		9-28-62
87-768		10-9-62
87-770		10-9-62
87-790		10-10-62
87-792	Self-Employed Individuals Tax Retirement Act of 1962	10-10-62
87-794	Trade Expansion Act of 1962	10-11-62
87-834	Revenue Act of 1962	10-16-62
87-858		10-23-62
87-863		10-23-62
87-870		10-23-62
87-876		10-24-62
88-4		4-2-63
88-9		4-10-63
88-31		5-29-63
88-36		6-4-63
88-52	Tax Rate Extension Act of 1963	6-29-63
88-133		10-5-63
88-173		11-7-63
88-272	Revenue Act of 1964	2-26-64
88-342		6-30-64
88-348	Excise Tax Rate Extension Act of 1964	6-30-64
88-380		7-17-64
88-426	Government Employees Salary Act of 1964	8-14-64
88-484		8-22-64
88-539		8-31-64
88-554		8-31-64
88-563	Interest Equalization Tax Act	9-2-64
88-570		9-2-64
88-571		9-2-64
88-650		10-13-64
88-653		10-13-64
89-44	Excise Tax Reduction Act of 1965	6-21-65
89-97	Social Security Amendments of 1965	7-30-65
89-212		9-29-65
89-243	Interest Equalization Tax Extension Act of 1965	10-9-65
89-331	Sugar Act Amendments of 1965	11-8-65
89-352		2-2-66
89-354		2-2-66
89-365		3-8-66
89-368	Tax Adjustment Act of 1966	3-15-66
89-384		4-8-66
89-389		4-14-66
89-493		7-5-66
89-523		8-1-66

Public Law No.	Popular Name	Enactment Date
89-570		9-12-66
89-621		10-4-66
89-699		10-30-66
87-700		10-30-66
89-713		11-2-66
89-719	Federal Tax Lien Act of 1966	11-2-66
89-721		11-2-66
89-722		11-2-66
89-739		11-2-66
89-793		11-8-66
89-800		11-8-66
89-809	Foreign Investors Tax Act of 1966	11-13-66
90-26		6-13-67
90-59	Interest Equalization Tax Extension Act of 1967	7-31-67
90-73		8-29-67
90-78		8-31-67
90-225		12-27-67
90-240		1-2-68
90-248	Social Security Amendments of 1967	1-2-68
90-285		4-12-68
90-346		6-18-68
90-364	Revenue and Expenditure Control Act of 1968	6-28-68
90-607		10-21-68
90-615		10-21-68
90-618	Gun Control Act of 1968	10-22-68
90-619		10-22-68
90-621		10-22-68
90-622		10-22-68
90-624		10-22-68
90-630		10-22-68
90-634	Renegotiation Amendments Act of 1968	10-24-68
91-36		6-30-69
91-50		8-2-69
91-53		8-7-69
91-65		8-25-69
91-128	Interest Equalization Tax Extension Act of 1969	11-26-69
91-172	Tax Reform Act of 1969	12-30-69
91-215		3-17-70
91-258	Airport and Airway Revenue Act of 1970	5-21-70
91-373	Employment Security Amendments of 1970	8-10-70
91-420		9-25-70
91-513		10-27-70
91-518	Rail Passenger Service Act of 1970	10-30-70
91-605	Federal-Aid Highway Act of 1970	12-31-70
91-606	Disaster Relief Act of 1970	12-31-70
91-614	Excise, Estate, and Gift Tax Adjustment Act of 1970	12-31-70
91-618		12-31-70
91-659		1-8-71
91-673		1-12-71
91-676		1-12-71
91-677		1-12-71
91-678		1-12-71
91-679		1-12-71
91-680		1-12-71
91-681		1-12-71
91-683		1-12-71
91-684		1-12-71
91-686		1-12-71

Public Law No.	Popular Name	Enactment Date
91-687		1-12-71
91-688		1-12-71
91-691		1-12-71
91-693		1-12-71
92-5		3-17-71
92-9	Interest Equalization Tax Extension Act of 1971	4-1-71
92-41		7-1-71
92-138	Sugar Act Amendments of 1971	10-14-71
92-178	Revenue Act of 1971	12-10-71
92-279		4-26-72
92-310		6-6-72
92-329		6-30-72
92-336		7-1-72
92-418		8-29-72
92-512	State and Local Fiscal Assistance Act of 1972	10-20-72
92-558		10-25-72
92-580		10-27-72
92-603	Social Security Amendments of 1972	10-30-72
92-606		10-31-72
93-17	Interest Equalization Tax Extension Act of 1973	4-10-73
93-53		7-1-73
93-66		7-9-73
93-69		7-10-73
93-233		12-31-73
93-288	Disaster Relief Act of 1974	5-22-74
93-310		6-8-74
93-368		8-7-74
93-406	Employee Retirement Income Security Act of 1974	9-2-74
93-443	Federal Election Campaign Act Amendments of 1974	10-15-74
93-445		10-16-74
93-480		10-26-74
93-482		10-26-74
93-483		10-26-74
93-490		10-26-74
93-499		10-29-74
93-597		1-2-75
93-625		1-3-75
94-12	Tax Reduction Act of 1975	3-29-75
94-45	Emergency Compensation and Special Unemployment Assistance Extension Act of 1975	6-30-75
94-81		8-9-75
94-92		8-9-75
94-93		8-9-75
94-164	Revenue Adjustment Act of 1975	12-23-75
94-202		1-2-76
94-253		3-31-76
94-267		4-15-76
94-273	Fiscal Year Adjustment Act	4-21-76
94-280		5-5-76
94-283	Federal Election Campaign Act Amendments of 1976	5-11-76
94-331		6-30-76
94-396		9-3-76
94-401		9-7-76
94-414		9-17-76
94-452	Bank Holding Company Tax Act of 1976	10-2-76
94-455	Tax Reform Act of 1976	10-4-76
94-514		10-15-76
94-528		10-17-76

Public Law No.	Popular Name	Enactment Date
94-529		10-17-76
94-530		10-17-76
94-547		10-18-76
94-553	Copyrights Act	10-19-76
94-563		10-19-76
94-566	Unemployment Compensation Amendments of 1976	10-20-76
94-568		10-20-76
94-569		10-20-76
95-19	Emergency Unemployment Compensation Act of 1977	4-12-77
95-30	Tax Reduction and Simplification Act of 1977	5-23-77
95-147		10-28-77
95-171		11-12-77
95-172		11-12-77
95-176		11-14-77
95-210		12-13-77
95-216		12-20-77
95-227	Black Lung Benefits Revenue Act of 1977	2-10-78
95-339	New York City Loan Guarantee Act of 1978	8-8-78
95-345		8-15-78
95-423		10-6-78
95-427		10-7-78
95-458		10-14-78
95-472		10-17-78
95-473		10-17-78
95-479	Veterans' Disability Compensation and Survivors' Benefits Act of 1978	10-18-78
95-488		10-20-78
95-502	Inland Waterways Revenue Act of 1978	10-21-78
95-599	Surface Transportation Assistance Act of 1978	11-6-78
95-600	Revenue Act of 1978	11-6-78
95-615	Tax Treatment Extension Act of 1978	11-8-78
95-618	Energy Tax Act of 1978	11-9-78
95-628		11-10-78
96-39	Trade Agreements Act of 1979	7-26-79
96-72	Export Administration Act of 1979	9-29-79
96-84		10-10-79
96-167		12-29-79
96-178		1-2-80
96-187	Federal Election Campaign Act Amendments of 1979	1-8-80
96-222	Technical Corrections Act of 1979	4-1-80
96-223	Crude Oil Windfall Profit Tax Act of 1980	4-2-80
96-249	Food Stamp Act Amendments of 1980	5-26-80
96-265	Social Security Disability Amendments of 1980	6-9-80
96-272	Adoption Assistance and Child Welfare Act of 1980	6-17-80
96-283	Deep Seabed Hard Mineral Resources Act	6-28-80
96-298		7-1-80
96-364	Multiemployer Pension Plan Amendments Act of 1980	9-26-80
96-417	Customs Courts Act of 1980	10-10-80
96-439		10-13-80
96-451	Recreational Boating Safety and Facilities Improvement Act of 1980	10-14-80
96-454	Household Goods Transportation Act of 1980	10-15-80
96-465	Foreign Service Act of 1980	10-17-80
96-471	Installment Sales Revision Act of 1980	10-19-80
96-499	Omnibus Reconciliation Act of 1980	12-5-80
96-510	Comprehensive Environmental Response, Compensation, and Liability Act of 1980	12-11-80
96-541		12-17-80

Public Law No.	Popular Name	Enactment Date
103-305	Federal Aviation Administration Authorization Act of 1994	8-23-94
103-322	Violent Crime Control and Law Enforcement Act of 1994	9-13-94
103-337	National Defense Authorizations Act for Fiscal Year 1995	10-5-94
103-387	Social Security Domestic Employment Reform Act of 1994	10-22-94
103-429		10-31-94
103-465	Uruguay Round Agreements Act	12-8-94
104-7	Self-Employed Health Insurance Act	4-11-95
104-88	ICC Termination Act of 1995	12-29-95
104-117		3-20-96
104-134	Debt Collection Improvement Act of 1996	4-26-96
104-168	Taxpayer Bill of Rights 2	7-30-96
104-188	Small Business Job Protection Act of 1996	8-20-96
104-191	Health Insurance Portability and Accountability Act of 1996	8-21-96
104-193	Personal Responsibility and Work Opportunity Reconciliation Act of 1996	8-22-96
104-201	National Defense Authorization Act for Fiscal Year 1997	9-23-96
104-208	Deposit Insurance Funds Act of 1996	9-30-96
104-264	Federal Aviation Reauthorization Act of 1996	10-9-96
104-303	Water Resources Development Act of 1996	10-12-96
104-316	General Accounting Office Act of 1996	10-19-96
105-2	Airport and Airway Trust Fund Tax Reinstatement Act of 1997	2-28-97
105-33	Balanced Budget Act of 1997	8-5-97
105-34	Taxpayer Relief Act of 1997	8-5-97
105-35	Taxpayer Browsing Protection Act	8-5-97
105-61	Treasury and General Government Appropriations Act, 1998	10-10-97
105-65	Departments of Veterans Affairs and Housing and Urban Development, and Independent Agencies Appropriations Act, 1998	10-27-97
105-78	Departments of Labor, Health and Human Services and Education, and Related Agencies Appropriations Act, 1998	11-13-97
105-102		11-20-97
105-115	Food and Drug Administration (FDA) Modernization Act of 1997	11-21-97
105-130	Surface Transportation Extension Act of 1997	12-1-97
105-178	Transportation Equity Act for the 21st Century	6-9-98
105-206	Internal Revenue Service Restructuring and Reform Act of 1998	7-22-98
105-261		10-17-98
105-277	Tax and Trade Relief Extension Act of 1998	10-21-98
105-277	Vaccine Injury Compensation Program Modification Act	10-21-98
105-306	Noncitizen Benefit Clarification and Other Technical Amendments Act of 1998	10-28-98
106-21		4-19-99
106-36	Miscellaneous Trade and Technical Corrections Act of 1999	6-25-99
106-78	Agriculture, Rural Development, Food and Drug Administration, and Related Agencies Appropriations Act, 2000	10-22-99
106-170	Tax Relief Extension Act of 1999	12-17-99
106-181	Wendell H. Ford Aviation Investment and Reform Act for the 21st Century	4-5-2000
106-200	Trade and Development Act of 2000	5-18-2000
106-230		7-1-2000
106-408	Wildlife and Sport Fish Restoration Programs Improvement Act of 2000	11-1-2000

Public Law No.	Popular Name	Enactment Date
106-476	Imported Cigarette Compliance Act of 2000	11-9-2000
106-519	FSC Repeal and Extraterritorial Income Exclusion Act of 2000	11-15-2000
106-554	Community Renewal Tax Relief Act of 2000	12-21-2000
106-573	Installment Tax Correction Act of 2000	12-28-2000
107-15	Fallen Hero Survivor Benefit Fairness Act of 2001	6-5-2001
107-16	Economic Growth and Tax Relief Reconciliation Act of 2001	6-7-2001
107-22		7-26-2001
107-71	Aviation and Transportation Security Act	11-19-2001
107-90	Railroad Retirement and Survivors' Improvement Act of 2001	12-21-2001
107-110	No Child Left Behind Act of 2001	1-8-2002
107-116	Departments of Labor, Health and Human Services, and Education, and Related Agencies Appropriations Act, 2002	1-10-2002
107-131		1-16-2002
107-134	Victims of Terrorism Tax Relief Act of 2001	1-23-2002
107-147	Job Creation and Worker Assistance Act of 2002	3-9-2002
107-181	Clergy Housing Allowance Clarification Act of 2002	5-20-2002
107-210	Trade Act of 2002	8-6-2002
107-217		8-21-2002
107-276		11-2-2002
107-296	Homeland Security Act of 2002	11-25-2002
107-330	Veterans Benefits Act of 2002	12-6-2002
108-27	Jobs and Growth Tax Relief Reconciliation Act of 2003	5-28-2003
108-88	Surface Transportation Extension Act of 2003	9-30-2003
108-89		10-1-2003
108-121	Military Family Tax Relief Act of 2003	11-11-2003
108-173	Medicare Prescription Drug, Improvement, and Modernization Act of 2003	12-8-2003
108-176	Vision 100—Century of Aviation Reauthorization Act	12-12-2003
108-178		12-15-2003
108-189		12-19-2003
108-202	Surface Transportation Extension Act of 2004	2-29-2004
108-203	Social Security Protection Act of 2004	3-2-2004
108-218	Pension Funding Equity Act of 2004	4-10-2004
108-224	Surface Transportation Extension Act of 2004, Part II	4-30-2004
108-263	Surface Transportation Extension Act of 2004, Part III	6-30-2004
108-280	Surface Transportation Extension Act of 2004, Part IV	7-30-2004
108-310	Surface Transportation Extension Act of 2004, Part V	9-30-2004
108-311	Working Families Tax Relief Act of 2004	10-4-2004
108-357	American Jobs Creation Act of 2004	10-22-2004
108-375	Ronald W. Reagan National Defense Authorization Act for Fiscal Year 2005	10-28-2004
108-429	Miscellaneous Trade and Technical Corrections Act of 2004	12-3-2004
108-493		12-23-2004
109-6		3-31-2005
109-7		4-15-2005
109-14	Surface Transportation Extension Act of 2005	5-31-2005
109-20	Surface Transportation Extension Act of 2005, Part II	7-1-2005
109-35	Surface Transportation Extension Act of 2005, Part III	7-20-2005
109-37	Surface Transportation Extension Act of 2005, Part IV	7-22-2005
109-40	Surface Transportation Extension Act of 2005, Part V	7-28-2005
109-42	Surface Transportation Extension Act of 2005, Part VI	7-30-2005
109-58	Energy Tax Incentives Act of 2005	8-8-2005
109-59	Safe, Accountable, Flexible, Efficient Transportation Equity Act: A Legacy for Users	8-10-2005
109-73	Katrina Emergency Tax Relief Act of 2005	9-23-2005

Public Law No.	Popular Name	Enactment Date
109-74	Sportfishing and Recreational Boating Safety Amendments Act of 2005	9-29-2005
109-135	Gulf Opportunity Zone Act of 2005	12-21-2005
109-151		12-30-2005
109-171	Deficit Reduction Act of 2005	2-8-2006
109-222	Tax Increase Prevention and Reconciliation Act of 2005	5-17-2006
109-227	Heroes Earned Retirement Opportunities Act	5-29-2006
109-241	Coast Guard and Maritime Transportation Act of 2006	7-11-2006
109-280	Pension Protection Act of 2006	8-17-2006
109-304		10-6-2006
109-432	Tax Relief and Health Care Act of 2006	12-20-2006
109-433		12-20-2006
110-28	U.S. Troop Readiness, Veterans' Care, Katrina Recovery, and Iraq Accountability Appropriations Act, 2007	5-25-2007
110-28	Small Business and Work Opportunity Tax Act of 2007	5-25-2007
110-92		9-29-2007
110-140	Energy Independence and Security Act of 2007	12-19-2007
110-142	Mortgage Forgiveness Debt Relief Act of 2007	12-20-2007
110-161	Department of Transportation Appropriations Act, 2008	12-26-2007
110-166	Tax Increase Prevention Act of 2007	12-26-2007
110-172	Tax Technical Corrections Act of 2007	12-29-2007
110-176		1-4-2008
110-177	Court Security Improvement Act of 2007	1-7-2008
110-185	Economic Stimulus Act of 2008	2-13-2008
110-190	Airport and Airway Extension Act of 2008	2-28-2008
110-233	Genetic Information Nondiscrimination Act of 2008	5-21-2008
110-244	SAFETEA-LU Technical Corrections Act of 2008	6-6-2008
110-245	Heroes Earnings Assistance and Relief Tax Act of 2008	6-17-2008
110-246	Food, Conservation, and Energy Act of 2008	5-22-2008
110-246	Heartland, Habitat, Harvest, and Horticulture Act of 2008	5-22-2008
110-253	Federal Aviation Administration Extension Act of 2008	6-30-2008
110-289	Housing Assistance Tax Act of 2008	7-30-2008
110-289	Federal Housing Finance Regulatory Reform Act of 2008	7-30-2008
110-317	Hubbard Act	8-29-2008
110-318		9-15-2008
110-328	SSI Extension for Elderly and Disabled Refugees Act	9-30-2008
110-330	Federal Aviation Administration Extension Act of 2008, Part II	9-30-2008
110-343	Emergency Economic Stabilization Act of 2008	10-3-2008
110-343	Energy Improvement and Extension Act of 2008	10-3-2008
110-343	Tax Extenders and Alternative Minimum Tax Relief Act of 2008	10-3-2008
110-343	Paul Wellstone and Pete Domenici Mental Health Parity and Addiction Equity Act of 2008	10-3-2008
110-343	Heartland Disaster Tax Relief Act of 2008	10-3-2008
110-351	Fostering Connections to Success and Increasing Adoptions Act of 2008	10-7-2008
110-381	Michelle's Law	10-9-2008
110-428	Inmate Tax Fraud Prevention Act of 2008	10-15-2008
110-458	Worker, Retiree, and Employer Recovery Act of 2008	12-23-2008
111-3	Children's Health Insurance Program Reauthorization Act of 2009	2-4-2009
111-5	American Recovery and Reinvestment Tax Act of 2009	2-17-2009
111-8	Omnibus Appropriations Act, 2009	3-11-2009
111-12	Federal Aviation Administration Extension Act of 2009	3-30-2009
111-46		8-7-2009
111-68		10-1-2009

Public Law No.	Popular Name	Enactment Date
111-69	Fiscal Year 2010 Federal Aviation Administration Extension Act	10-1-2009
111-88		10-30-2009
111-92	Worker, Homeownership, and Business Assistance Act of 2009	11-6-2009
111-116	Fiscal Year 2010 Federal Aviation Administration Extension Act, Part II	12-16-2009
111-144	Temporary Extension Act of 2010	3-2-2010
111-147	Hiring Incentives to Restore Employment Act	3-18-2010
111-148	Patient Protection and Affordable Care Act	3-23-2010
111-152	Health Care and Education Reconciliation Act of 2010	3-30-2010
111-153	Federal Aviation Administration Extension Act of 2010	3-31-2010
111-159	TRICARE Affirmation Act	4-26-2010
111-161	Airport and Airway Extension Act of 2010	4-30-2010
111-173		5-27-2010
111-192	Preservation of Access to Care for Medicare Beneficiaries and Pension Relief Act of 2010	6-25-2010
111-197	Airport and Airway Extension Act of 2010, Part II	7-2-2010
111-198	Homebuyer Assistance and Improvement Act of 2010	7-2-2010
111-203	Dodd-Frank Wall Street Reform and Consumer Protection Act	7-21-2010
111-216	Airline Safety and Federal Aviation Administration Extension Act of 2010	8-1-2010
111-226		8-10-2010
111-237	Firearms Excise Tax Improvement Act of 2010	8-16-2010
111-240	Creating Small Business Jobs Act of 2010	9-27-2010
111-249	Airport and Airway Extension Act of 2010, Part III	9-30-2010